WITHDRAWN

TWENTIETH-CENTURY
CHILDREN'S WRITERS

Twentieth-Century Writers of the English Language

Twentieth-Century Children's Writers

Twentieth-Century Crime and Mystery Writers

Twentieth-Century Science-Fiction Writers

Twentieth-Century Romance and Historical Writers

Twentieth-Century Western Writers

TWENTIETH-CENTURY CHILDREN'S WRITERS

THIRD EDITION

WITH A PREFACE BY
NAOMI LEWIS

EDITOR
TRACY CHEVALIER

CONSULTING EDITOR
D.L. KIRKPATRICK

St J

St James Press

Chicago and London

Lib. Sc.
ReF.
PN
1009
AI
T9
1989

©1989 by St. James Press

For information, write:
ST. JAMES PRESS
233 East Ontario Street
Chicago 60611, U.S.A.
            or
3 Percy Street
London W1P 9FA, England.

All rights reserved.

British Library Cataloguing in Publication Data
Twentieth-century children's writers. —3rd ed.
  1. Children's literature in English, 1900– critical studies
  I. Chevalier, Tracy, *1962–*
  820.9'9282

ISBN 0-912289-95-3

First edition published 1978;
second edition 1983; third edition 1989.

Phototypesetting by A.L. Publishing Services
Voysey House, Barley Mow Passage, London, W4 4PT.

CONTENTS

PREFACE

The writers listed in this book—more than 800 in all—are the main 20th-century contributors in English to one or other branch of an extraordinary literature. It probably has, in written form, no precedent in history. It is of its own kind, not a watered-down form of adult writing, but the link between the two is close. "It is not so much a question of taking up one's stand on the lower rungs of the literary ladder," wrote that notable practitioner Mrs. Molesworth in 1893, "as of standing on another ladder altogether—one which has its own steps, its higher and lower positions of excellence." These positions of excellence are almost always unpredictably filled, sometimes even by middle-aged adults who have never written in this particular field before: an Adams, a Ransome. Children on the whole do not write good children's fiction; they are better on poetry. One of the best novels ever written by a real pre-adolescent child is wasted on children: Daisy Ashford's *The Young Visiters*. Though the low periods of this literature (one lasted for years in the earlier part of this century) have brought the kind into low esteem, its high phases have an incalculable effect on both readers and writers. Thus, in the two decades or so between 1851 (*The King of the Golden River*) and 1871 (*At the Back of the North Wind* and *Through the Looking-Glass*), numbers of authors in adult fields were tempted into the genre of children's fantasy: among them Thackeray with *The Rose and the Ring*, Frances Browne with *Granny's Wonderful Chair* (1857), Kingsley with *The Water-Babies* (1863), the mathematician Dodgson (Carroll) with *Alice* (1865), Dickens with *A Holiday Romance* (1868), Jean Ingelow with *Mopsa the Fairy* (1869)—richness indeed. Several of these writers—adult novelists though they considered themselves (George MacDonald was one)—are remembered today by their children's books alone. Interestingly, it was a hundred years later, in the 1950's and 1960's, that the next such flowering occurred.

How old is a child? It seems a modern problem, but it exercised Mrs. Trimmer, writing on "Books *for Children* and Books *for Young Persons*," in 1802: "Formerly," she complained, "all were reckoned *Children*, till they had at least attained their *fourteenth year*. Now ... we have *Young Persons* of *five* or *six* years old." The question teases us still.

How to distinguish the child's book from the adult's?—and is the distinction important? These questions are best considered after a view of the scene. As a recognised part of publishing, English books for the pleasure (as well as the improvement) of the young go back to Newbery's mid-18th century: a piece of literary history admirably charted by Harvey Darton, M.F. Thwaite, and others. What chiefly concerns us here is the strange course of children's literature of our own century, a course at first casual, minor, and freakish, then (post-war) a phenomenon. Suddenly, since the 1950's, children's books have become a major field of publishing and of international exchange; and where a prestigious medium exists, the gifted come. They came indeed, and brought such books as *Smith* and *The Mouse and His Child* and *A Wizard of Earthsea* and *The Owl Service*: a golden age had begun.

But look back to the first half century, post-Lang, post-Barrie, post-Nesbit, and the scene is puzzling, ill-defined. The reaction against Victorian taste sets in, lasts long. Books about children or fairies or both (*Dream Days*, de la Mare's *Songs of Childhood*, *Martin Pippin in the Apple Orchard*, *The Crock of Gold*, *When We Were Very Young*) are published for, and widely read, by adults. As for books *intended* for children, they are thin stuff indeed when they come from the average hand. Holiday adventure yarns and such, they obey the time's unspoken codes for junior reading: no deaths, disasters, poverty; no great emotions, no stern moral lessons—none of those features that gave such force to 19th-century fiction. Certainly not an echo is heard of current happenings, in Jarrow or Spain or Germany. The boarding school tale still thrives, that inviting daydream world of the day-school reader; enclosed in its private laws, as in its mock-Gothic walls, it generates its own emotional heat. Who ever writes about day schools? Few non-fantasy writers from this time are still being read today. Noel Streatfeild, perhaps; but she had the wit to write of children involved not in holiday play but in work, some form of skill: tennis, ballet, skating. Ransome? His fictional young have an occupation, too, an expertise: water and boats could indeed *be* the main characters. Besides, his tales—a kind of daydream cherished through years as a foreign correspondent in revolutionary Russia—were not really aimed at the young. They were written for and from his own buried youthful self.

Yet cross the frontier of reasoned fact, cross the frontier of time—in other words move into fantasy, move into history—and the rules, taboos, and codes no longer hold. And so, in this period, and just at the edge of the new, we find some of the most potent imaginative works of modern children's literature: *The Hobbit*, *The Midnight Folk* and *The Box of Delights*, *The Sword in the Stone* and *Mistress Masham's Repose*, *A Traveller in Time*, *Henrietta's House*, *Poor Cecco*, the Narnia tales of C.S. Lewis with their sadism, religion, and death. Only a few years away are *Tom's Midnight Garden* and *The Borrowers* and *The Lord of the Rings*, and *Elidor* and *Earthfasts* and *The Dark Is Rising* and *The Mark of the Horse Lord* and that stunning modern classic myth *The Iron Man*. What a rich harvest! Violence, mystery, exile, death, terror, loyalties, love and loss—all go freely through the gates of history and fantasy.

But there is another doorway, used by the youngest children of all. They meet these wonders and strangenesses in nursery rhymes—the wildest, most enigmatic poetry likely to come their way for years, perhaps for always—and in the great traditional fairytales. Not to have known them early, in Bruno Bettelheim's view, is to be deprived for life.

Fantasy (like history) is a convenient word, but really needs some defining. In verse or fiction it covers many forms. (Science fiction is a separate terrain, but the two share a frontier, which both quite frequently cross.) It can touch the everyday world with the supernatural (as in books by Garner or Farmer, as in most ghost stories). It can call in the past to the present (as in *Tom's Midnight Garden*). It can offer a total world, such as Earthsea, Middle-earth, Moominland. It can re-interpret myth and legend, as in *The Book of Three* or *The Owl Service* (both Mabinogion-based), or in the countless Arthurian variants. It encompasses the wish-themes (*Five Children and It*), the mirror-versions of life played out by animals (*The Wind in the Willows*, *Mrs. Frisby and the Rats of Nimh*, *Watership Down*) or by *things* (Hans Andersen), and of course all the tales giving life to dolls and toys (*Miss Hickory*, *Poor Cecco*, *The Mouse and His Child*; see too my own *The Silent Playmate*, an anthology of doll stories). Fantasy takes in the great field of nonsense (not so much absence of sense as a wild variation)—the brilliant games with words. Carroll and Lear are the masters still; but *The Phantom Tollbooth* must be the best original *modern* book in the Carroll line. The point must also be made that many of the worst as well as the greatest written works belong to the genre of fantasy. Failure waits for those who refuse to see that magic too has its laws; that every wish has its price; that the mean wisher can't wish beyond his own mean range.

What might not have been foretold by yesterday's crystal-gazer is the increasingly powerful place of fantasy in "older" children's fiction, not only the other-world fantasy of Tolkien and Le Guin, but in the fiction of current life. With English authors especially—perhaps because English life tends to become inexplicit when looked at closely; perhaps because England today lacks extremes of poverty as well as extremes of climate and landscape— the temptation to draw on dreams or magic or shifts of time is hard to resist. I doubt if one leading writer for the young *has* entirely resisted it (again I stress the point, in older fiction): certainly not Garner, Mayne, Farmer, Townsend, Dickinson, Garfield, Lively, Paton Walsh, Cresswell, Peyton, Aiken, Pearce, Mark—a list by no means complete. (Sometimes, as in *Smith* or *The Jersey Shore*, the past is used as alternative: the resulting strangenesses almost bring these books into the genre.) Yes, fantasy is the major English achievement in the older-fictional field. It can be found at the highest level in American writing too: authors who come to mind are Le Guin, Alexander, Hoban, O'Brien, Curry, Babbitt, Snyder, L'Engle. Interestingly, the works of the first four, at any rate, seem not so much specifically American as rooted in the common source of European legend and literature. Where the American junior novelist scores is in writing at a high level on modern American children or adolescents in modern situations—no calling on dreams, dips into time or the supernatural; see, for example, the best works of Byars, Fox, the Cleavers. In recent years, however, English non-fantasy writing begins to advance in quality (Jan Mark, Gene Kemp), though a strong particular theme— school, child friendships, autism, solitude, fatness, animals in the human world (G.D. Griffiths's *Abandoned*), and the problems of dual cultures— seems best able to lift non-fantasy now and again into "positions of excellence" (Mrs. Molesworth's useful phrase again).

Historical fiction has its own turns of history. In the Victorian century every leading adult novelist produced at least one substantial work in the genre: Charles Reade's *The Cloister and the Hearth*, for instance, a major work by a not-quite-major writer. But by the earlier years of the present century the genre had largely slipped into being a kind of popular costume drama (in fact, as a form of housewife's reading, it flourishes still). Its novelists, more concerned with fiction than history, tended to keep to well-trodden fields: the picturesque view of the English Civil War (Cavaliers and Roundheads), the French Revolution (and the languid English aristocrat Pimpernel), the Napoleonic Wars (good battle stuff for the boys; good home romance for the girls); Bonnie Prince Charlie, Bonnie King Charles, occasional dips into the colourful medieval, the roistering Elizabethan. Attitudes were uncomplicated: "our" side was the prettier side of the two opposing teams: the King's, the Cavaliers'. And so the appearance in 1934 of Geoffrey Trease's *Bows Against the Barons*, which neatly reversed the usual values (good peasants, bad "nobles"), remains a landmark. Trease soon grew beyond this simplistic phase, valuable though it was at the time. He is writing still (try his gripping *The Red Towers of Granada*), the most widely ranging historical novelist in the calendar. But I have to say that national history does not travel well. The exceptions are the themes that go beyond frontier differences: how to escape from slavery or, even worse, Nazi extermination.

So it could be said that, in the post-war renaissance, the whole of history, much of it scarcely touched, lay open to fiction writers. Not only was a change in the old fixed attitudes now acceptable (the human and analytic rather than the easy old right and wrong), but there were many fields where, indeed, no fixed view was established. (Are we for Saxon or Norman?) Rosemary Sutcliff, throwing a brilliant personal light on the murk and mists of Ancient Britain, gave an equally fair view of Briton and Roman soldier. In a range of effective books, Treece, Trease, Harnett, Picard, Burton, Paton Walsh, Hodges, Willard, Leeson, Garfield, Carter, Ray, Crossley-Holland are among those who have notably extended a reading child's experience of the historied past.

More exact attention has gone to another subject: the novel which centres on the black/white or black/black story. Picture books for the very young mingle black, brown, white in their illustrations in the most carefully natural fashion. Illustration is an asset too in stories for the 6 to 9 age group (often very good on simple "ethnic" matters). Yes, pictures are more easily managed than words. (Did E.L. Konigsburg make her point in *Jennifer, Hecate, Macbeth, William McKinley, and Me, Elizabeth* with words or pictures?) The more successful British authors in the field—Robert Leeson, for instance, (best in his historical trilogy *'Maroon Boy, Bess,* and *The White Horse*), have often been white; but this is changing (see James Berry's *A Thief in the Village*). Oddly, English non-white women writers are few. Yet they have some major subjects to hand—the break with rigid ethnic ritual customs is an obvious one.

It is from the United States, where black/white history runs deep, that the fiction of quality, from black writers, comes at the current time. Among the most striking of these are Virginia Hamilton (a stunning writer and a Newbery winner), Rosa Guy (*The Friends*), and Mildred D. Taylor (also a Newbery winner with her *Roll of Thunder, Hear My Cry*). Effective contemporary books have come from non-black writers too. Louise Fitzhugh's *Nobody's Family Is Going to Change* is one. William H. Armstrong's haunting *Sounder*, set in the early century, should not be forgotten (avoid the film, though, which managed to botch every point that makes the story memorable), nor should Elizabeth Borton de Treviño's *I, Juan de Pareja*, about the black servant of Velasquez with his own gift for painting. A notable Australian book of the 1960's, Hesba Brinsmead's *Pastures of the Blue Crane*, which concerns the native colour question in Queensland, also has a place on this list.

For a more deeply rooted issue in English life we must turn to the one of "class." Does it still exist? Evidently, for publishers and librarians are known to pause doubtfully at this or that text, murmuring the unlucky verdict: "too middle-class." At the same time *Peter Pan*, the Pooh books by Milne, *The Wind in the Willows*, *The Secret Garden*, and the class-ridden *Railway Children* are readily passed through the turnstiles.

Class, in fact, is intrinsic to most English fiction: *how* it is used is the point. Thus, what shocked the readers of *Jane Eyre* (1847) was that the lead role and marital prize (battered though it might be) went to a *governess*! Even in the new century a servant remained a background figure in fiction: strict housekeeper, vulgar cook, illiterate kitchenmaid. Accepted attitudes can be as readily observed in E. Nesbit's works as anywhere. Beguiled as we are by her narrative voice, her verve and invention, we have to allow that her cooks and maids and errand boys are almost always comics, cardboard figures of fun; that her main child characters when they cannot go to expensive schools, go to no school at all; that her only poor-boy hero, the little waif Dickie Harding, turns out to owe his gentle manners to his being the lost heir to an ancient noble line. She was, to be sure (like Shakespeare), taking the easy path with plots, and these came readily to hand. But the fact that they *came* to hand makes the point. (*The Children of the House*, by Pearce and Fairfax-Lucy, a book which is based on fact, movingly shows what was also true, the close bond between "upper class" children and servants in a great house when both feared and suffered from the harsh hand of authority.) Of course, with hindsight, novelists today can effectively present the old feudal injustices that were finally broken only by World War II. Peyton does this notably well in her late-Edwardian *Flambards*. The subject is too large, elusive, and deeply ramified to be tidied up in a phrase. But to present life only in terms of council houses and supermarkets is to shut the child, mentally speaking, in a viewless if conventionally furnished cell.

It should be clear by now that what runs between children's and adults' books is not a straight line but one as winding as the Thames on a map. It changes with tides and seasons; often it cannot be seen at all. It vanishes under flood. But there *is* a line. We are aware of this when a children's author seems to grow restless, begins to write of older characters, older problems, then, in the next book, steps over and is gone, for the time at least, from children's reading. This happens today to a number of leading writers: Gardam, Lively, Hoban. (William Mayne, to date, is one of the few who seems able to absorb the pangs of human life into his books while staying on the side of children's literature. His most complex, probably greatest book, *The Jersey Shore*, should be studied in this light. But read it in the English edition, which does not tamper with the end.) Alan Garner has said: "Most of the people who read my books are adults, whatever their ages." You could also say that whatever a childlike child is reading is for that time a children's book. I have known a simple 9-year-old to read and reread *Plain Tales from the Hills*, rejecting the *Just-So Stories*. Ah, but what did the reader find in it? The little Brontës, who knew no children's fiction as we now understand the term, read dull political newspapers—and turned the statesmen and military leaders into figures of fairytale. The youthful mind is immensely adaptable, taking the lowest when it is there, but capable of any feat if required.

Most of the commentary here has been about middle and older fiction, for this is where change and invention chiefly lie. Younger and youngest books abound, of course, mainly in series. I mention them at this point to say that, even in a first-reader, brilliance is possible. Arnold Lobel's *Frog and Toad, Mouse Tales, Owl at Home* are continually lit with this, a short tale in the last of these outstandingly. It is called "Tearwater Tea." Others that must be admired include Marjorie Weinman Sharmat's Nate the Great books, about a cool detective, not more than 9 years old; these say all that a story needs in their terse allotment of words. But even without such bright occasions, the standard of books for the 4 to 6, 7 to 9-year-old reader is higher than it was when some of these series started. Though the approach is simple, the language clear, the subjects often belong to the larger world.

But indeed, the younger the book (or, rather, the reader, looker, or listener) the greater the impact; picture books which aim at the youngest of all have an importance which is hard to overstate. They meet the human mind at its most susceptible. They convey at once what often cannot be comfortably said in words (the "colour" instance has already been given). They are looked at often; their words are remembered long. This is not the place to discuss their staggering range, good or bad, of manner and technique (they enter this volume primarily through the artist's invention of text and theme), but their subjects *are* to the point. When a picture book shows (and hundreds continue to do just this) a "comic" view of a man with a whip standing over a cowering circus lion or tiger, or of that no less obscene spectacle of a rodeo, it is fixing an assumption that these things are approved, amusing, accepted fun.

This holds, of course, through the whole of children's reading. Anyone who has read that remarkable (adult) short story "The Lottery" by Shirley Jackson will know what is meant by the word assumption—an obstinate and unreasoned superstition, artificially kept alive, with dire results. Somewhere along the line we have dropped the assumption that religious non-conformists should be publicly burned, that women, non-whites, the handicapped, and the (white, Anglo-Saxon) labouring poor are incapable of education. But assumption persists through children's books (not least in fable) that wolves are bad and must be exterminated; that whaling and furtrapping are all right because they happen in clean adventure, and far away at that. A child who reads Roberts or Griffiths or a novel such as *Julie of the Wolves* is unlikely, in later life, to run a battery farm or work in an animal-vivisecting laboratory. Well, fairly unlikely. The trouble is that more children have seen or read *Jaws* than have ever come across the works mentioned above. Animal abuse—vivisection especially— is only just beginning to have a lead treatment in a handful of novels. Rather few, considering. Is it that publishers are nervous of taking the manuscripts? True, it's a difficult area for a writer, but it *can* be done well: witness Richard Adams's *The Plague Dogs*.

But literature is no more static than life. Even in the few years since the second edition of this volume there have been significant changes in the writing, publishing, and subjects, too, of books meant for the young. Some of these changes are pragmatic and commercial; some belong to the whole social movement of the times. Subjects? Almost none is out of bounds. Mental and physical handicaps, parental misdemeanours, birth, death, homosexuality, incest— does anything still remain? Even the very young are provided with careful books about having cancer, epilepsy, deafness, being adopted, avoiding friendly strangers.

These open themes are useful adjuncts to one of the main new publishing cults: the teen novel, in mass production at the present time. It is in origin mainly American; an inviting path has already been laid down by such experienced hands as Judy Blume, Paula Danziger, Barbara Wersba, Paul Zindel, and others. Britain has its own practitioners: Jean Ure is one. But there are indefinable differences: the tempo?, the food?, the lingo? Still, all these books face many of the same problems, and resolve them in much the same way. Now and then, under the crude and unprepossessing covers of the month's output of teenery, an excellent novel may lurk, Wersba's *The Dream Watcher*, say, or several short story collections. But whether or not the teen-tale *does* provide the long-sought bridge between child and adult reading is hard to say. Evidence suggests that the readers of these books are often younger than the characters within: say 12, or even less.

One new interest that has arisen from the young themselves is in war, particularly in World War II, far enough off to be legend, near enough for real detail. The main attraction is in the personal impact: air raid warnings, rationing, the presence perhaps of a "refugee," child or adult. Being an evacuee—a favourite topic—has provided by far the most successful of all the home-based war novels for the young, Michelle Magorian's multi-prizewinning *Goodnight, Mister Tom*, a book unusual for its Dickensian pace of storytelling and its unashamed emotional attack.

But Britain, though bombed, was not "occupied," and the background to the war is scarcely found in English junior fiction. It is hard to think of a single writer for the young who deals with the turbulent years between 1933 and 1939 when not all were indifferent to the spread of the fascist disease through Europe. (An essential book for the interested older child is Shiela Grant Duff's informing personal record of the time, *The Parting of the Ways*.) Many excellent books have come from countries which knew the taste of Nazidom, but the one outstanding war book for the young with an English setting, but also with some awareness of Europe, is Sylvia Sherry's haunting mystery *Dark River, Dark Mountain*—too long out of print.

Bestsellers? That's a separate story: and, today especially, one too often linked with the intensive work of the high-powered modern publicity machine. Not entirely, of course. But a *Watership Down*, which, against all odds, became in a short time an all-age classic as well as selling in millions, is in any decade an extremely rare phenomenon. Still, there *are* successes at any given time. The Ahlbergs, with their larky pictures, jokey texts, and endless happy invention, well deserve their current acclaim. Roald Dahl, whose conspiratorial rapport with urchin taste is backed by considerable narrative skill (and first-rate promotion), is also the bookseller's joy as well as a relished name with the under-nines. His calculated link with his reader has, though, a curious side-effect. The appeal of his *young* books stops dead at the age frontier. The publicity machine does have its curious triumphs, and the oddest of these recently must be the clever, sick, deliberately disgusting cartoon item *Fungus the Bogeyman* by Raymond Briggs. It goes, of course, into (mostly) unreluctant hands. What puzzles the young (and possibly later historians), though, is not the book itself but the fact that what should be a private find is approved and even imposed by adults.

Not all the writers of the postwar Golden Age have disappeared. Leon Garfield is still actively writing, at his own level; so is Peter Dickinson, though in strange new fantasy areas; Joan Aiken too. A new work from E.L. Konigsburg would be a pleasure. But the real phenomonon is William Mayne, each of whose new books would be enough to make any unknown first-timer's reputation. And no two of these cover the same ground. Recent works such as *All the King's Men* and *Drift* are as brilliant as anything in the long Mayne list—except perhaps *The Jersey Shore*.

Who are today's top writers? Jan Mark has not added any outstanding book in the past few years (though she is certainly capable of doing so). As I have already said, she is one of the few English children's writers who can crystallise a fiction of excellence out of ordinary, almost eventless daily life. *Handles* is the example I would choose. Two newer writers do stand out from the rest: Janni Howker and Berlie Doherty. Howker has an intense, extraordinary talent, but we have yet to see its range. Doherty has shown range (and considerable talent), but a single major book is still to come.

Looking for winners is a tempting game, but the whole range of recent "original" (uncommissioned, non-formula) fiction is also full of interest. 126 entrants have been added to the present edition; not all, by any means, are newcomers, but their work of the past few years marks the time with promise and vitality. Among them (to list only a few) are James Aldridge, Robin Klein, Cynthia Voigt, Janet Lunn, Jenny Nimmo (see her effective younger fantasy trilogy), Ann Pilling, Ouida Sebestyen, James Watson (author of an excellent book set in present-day Chile, *Talking in Whispers*), as well as the already mentioned Doherty, Howker, Magorian, and Berry. In the list too are a number of artist-authors— artists who invent their own themes, write their own texts (disaster too often lies here)—and do this well enough to cross the invisible frontier between the skills. Already in this volume are, of course, Sendak the master, Steig the unmatchable, Burningham, the late Charles Keeping. The new list includes the names of Tony Ross, Anthony Browne, and Chris Van Allsburg—witty, imaginative, and gifted, they well deserve their place.

A certain quiet happening should be noted: the unobtrusive admission or return of Enid Blyton to many library shelves. She has never, of course, been out of print or out of children's hands. Yes, she is middle- class. Yes, she is (though she may not have known it) racist and sexist. Yes, she is verbally null: the sliced white bread of reading. But she is accepted as the comfortable stepping-stone that leads the non-addicted reader on to Other Books. I suspect she may gain a certain something in translation, for she is much liked in various parts of Europe, though her magic does not seem to cross the Atlantic.

I have called this literature paradoxical, but paradox is also another view of fact. One such fact is that the greatest children's writers rarely care much for children—give or take the selected child or two. Their works, they claim, were not aimed at the young at all. (It is only frankly commercial writers who firmly state the reverse.) The truth is that the works of Grahame and Nesbit and Andersen and Stevenson are written *from* or out of a childhood source, their own; something of their childhood selves has persisted, undissolved, into adult life. Though some particular boy or girl may have prompted the start of certain books (*Alice*, *Peter Rabbit*, *The Wind in the Willows*), the real child lay in the author. The same holds for *A Child's Garden of Verses*, *The Ugly Duckling*, *The Treasure Seekers*, *Swallows and Amazons*, *The Hobbit*. Disbelievers should study biography.

What qualifies entry into this literature? Is it that there are juveniles in the cast? Yes—but a number of works (of the Crusoe and Verne kind certainly; and much science fiction) do well enough without. (What views on *Lord of the Flies* and *A High Wind in Jamaica*?) Is it that the events, however adult, should be seen throughout as from a child's view? This takes us nearer. (But then, does a laisser-passer go to *What Maisie Knew* or *The Go-Between*?) Technique, perhaps? But, at least in the teenage novel, time-sequence tricks, all-dialogue narrative, and streams-of-thought have become no novelty. On the grounds of style *Dream Days* and *The Water-Babies* have been dismissed by the pusillanimous (what then keeps them alive?). Perhaps it is best to say that the theme of a children's book need not be within a child's experience but within the range of a child's imagination. Well ... One other point, and not the least significant, is that in children's literature at its best a kind of justice prevails. Justice? That ill-used word means very much to a child, the sinner no less than the sinned against. "Children who are innocent love justice; but most people are wicked, and prefer mercy." So observed Chesterton; he had been listening to youthful comments on Maeterlinck's *Blue Bird*. Man of aphorisms though he was, I doubt if he ever said anything more penetrating.

—NAOMI LEWIS

READING LIST

The following list includes critical works dealing in whole or in part with English-language creative writing for children in the 20th century. Not listed here are bibliographies and checklists, biographical collections, and books intended primarily as guides for parents and/or teachers. Studies of individual writers are cited in the appropriate entries.

Adams, Bess Porter, *About Books and Children: Historical Survey of Children's Literature*. New York, Holt, 1953.

Anderson, William D., and Patrick Groff, *A New Look at Children's Literature*. Belmont, California, Wadsworth, 1972.

Andrews, Siri, editor, *The Hewins Lectures 1947–1962*. Boston, Horn Book, 1963.

Arbuthnot, May Hill, *Children and Books*. Chicago, Scott Foresman, 1947; 7th edition, with Zena Sutherland, 1986.

Avery, Gillian, *Childhood's Pattern: A Study of the Heroes and Heroines of Children's Fiction 1770–1950*. London, Hodder and Stoughton, 1975.

Bader, Barbara, *American Picturebooks from Noah's Ark to the Beast Within*. New York, Macmillan, and London, Collier Macmillan, 1976.

Bechtel, Louise Seaman, *Books in Search of Children: Speeches and Essays*, edited by Virginia Haviland. New York, Macmillan, 1969; London, Hamish Hamilton, 1970.

Blishen, Edward, editor, *The Thorny Paradise: Writers on Writing for Children*. London, Kestrel, 1975.

Blount, Margaret, *Animal Land: The Creatures of Children's Fiction*. London, Hutchinson, 1974; New York, Morrow, 1975.

Broderick, Dorothy M., *Image of the Black in Children's Fiction*. New York, Bowker, 1973.

Brown, Marcia, *Lotus Seeds: Children, Pictures, and Books*. New York, Scribner, 1982.

Butler, Francelia, and Richard Rotert, editors, *Reflections on Literature for Children*. Hamden, Connecticut, Library Professional Publications, 1984.

Butler, Francelia, and Richard Rotert, editors, *Triumphs of the Spirit in Children's Literature*. Hamden, Connecticut, Library Professional Publications, 1986.

Butts, Dennis, editor, *Good Writers for Young Readers: Critical Essays*. London, Hart Davis, 1977.

Cadogan, Mary, and Patricia Craig, *You're a Brick, Angela! A New Look at Girls' Fiction from 1839–1975*. London, Gollancz, 1976; revised edition, 1986.

Cameron, Eleanor, *The Green and Burning Tree: On the Writing and Enjoyment of Children's Books*. Boston, Little Brown, 1969.

Carlson, Ruth Kearney, *Emerging Humanity: Multi-Ethnic Literature for Children and Adolescents*. Dubuque, Iowa, Brown, 1972.

Carpenter, Humphrey, *Secret Gardens: The Golden Age of Children's Literature*. London, Allen and Unwin, 1985.

Cass, Joan E., *Literature and the Young Child*. London, Longman, 1967; revised edition, 1984.

Chambers, Aidan, editor, *Booktalk: Occasional Writing on Literature and Children*. London, Bodley Head, and New York, Harper, 1985.

Chambers, Aidan, *Introducing Books to Children*. London, Heinemann, 1973; revised edition, Boston, Horn Book, 1983.

Chambers, Aidan, *The Reluctant Reader*. Oxford, Pergamon Press, 1969.

Chambers, Nancy, editor, *The Signal Approach to Children's Books*. London, Kestrel, 1980; Metuchen, New Jersey, Scarecrow Press, 1981.

Cott, Jonathan, *Pipers at the Gates of Dawn: The Wisdom of Children's Literature*. New York, Random House, 1983; London, Viking, 1984.

Crouch, Marcus, and Alec Ellis, editors, *Chosen for Children: An Account of the Books Which Have Been Awarded the Library Association Carnegie Medal 1936–1975*. London, Library Association, 1977.

Crouch, Marcus, *The Nesbit Tradition: The Children's Novel in England 1945–1970*. London, Benn, 1972; Totowa, New Jersey, Rowman and Littlefield, 1973.

Crouch, Marcus, *Treasure Seekers and Borrowers: Children's Books in Britain 1900–1960*. London, Library Association, 1962.

Culpan, Norman, and Clifford Waite, editors, *Variety Is King: Aspects of Fiction for Children*. Oxford, School Library Association, 1977.

Darton, F.J. Harvey, *Children's Books in England: Five Centuries of Social Life*. Cambridge, University Press, 1932; 3rd edition, edited by Brian Alderson, London and New York, Cambridge University Press, 1982.

Dixon, Bob, *Catching Them Young: Sex, Race and Class in Children's Fiction* and *Political Ideas in Children's Fiction*. London, Pluto Press, 2 vols., 1977.

Donelson, Kenneth L., and Alleen Pace Nilsen, *Literature for Today's Young Adults*. Chicago, Scott Foresman, 1980.

Egoff, Sheila, G.T. Stubbs, and L.F. Ashley, editors, *Only Connect: Readings on Children's Literature*. Toronto and New York, Oxford University Press, 1969.

Egoff, Sheila, *The Republic of Childhood: A Critical Guide to Canadian Children's Literature in English*. Toronto, Oxford University Press, 1967.

Egoff, Sheila, *Thursday's Child: Trends and Patterns in Contemporary Children's Literature*. Chicago, American Library Association, 1981.

Egoff, Sheila, *Worlds Within: Children's Fantasy from the Middle Ages to Today*. Chicago, American Library Association, 1988.

Ellis, Alec, *A History of Children's Reading and Literature*. Oxford, Pergamon Press, 1968.

Ellis, Anne W., *The Family Story in the 1960's*. London, Bingley, 1970.

Eyre, Frank, *20th Century Children's Books*. London, Longman, 1952; Boston, Bentley, 1953; revised edition, as *British Children's Books in the Twentieth Century*, Longman, 1971; New York, Dutton, 1973.

Fenwick, Sara Innis, editor, *A Critical Approach to Children's Literature*. Chicago, University of Chicago Press, 1967.

Field, Elinor Whitney, *Horn Book Reflections on Children's Books and Reading: Selected from...Horn Book Magazine 1949–1966*. Boston, Horn Book, 1969.

Fisher, Margery, *The Bright Face of Danger: An Exploration of the Adventure Story*. London, Hodder and Stoughton, 1986.

Fisher, Margery, *Intent upon Reading: A Critical Appraisal of Modern Fiction for Children*. Leicester, Brockhampton Press, 1961; New York, Watts, 1962; revised edition, Brockhampton Press, 1964.

Fisher, Margery, *Who's Who in Children's Books: A Treasury of the Familiar Characters of Childhood*. London, Weidenfeld and Nicolson, and New York, Holt Rinehart, 1975.

Fox, Geoff, and others, editors, *Writers, Critics and Children: Articles from Children's Literature in Education*. New York, Agathon Press, and London, Heinemann, 1976.

Fraser, James H., editor, *Society and Children's Literature*. Boston, Godine, 1978.

Fryatt, Norma R., editor, *A Horn Book Sampler on Children's Books and Reading...1924–1948*. Boston, Horn Book, 1959.

Gilderdale, Betty, *A Sea Change: 145 Years of New Zealand Junior Fiction*. Auckland, Longman Paul, 1982.

Gillespie, Margaret C., *Literature for Children: History and Trends*. Dubuque, Iowa, Brown, 1970.

Glazer, Joan I., and Gurney Williams III, *Introduction to Children's Literature*. New York, McGraw Hill, 1979.

Gose, Elliott, *Mere Creatures: A Study of Modern Fantasy Tales for Children*. Toronto, University of Toronto Press, 1988.

Green, Roger Lancelyn, *Tellers of Tales*. Leicester, Ward, 1946: revised edition, 1953; revised edition, London, Ward, and New York, Watts, 1965; revised edition, London, Kaye and Ward, 1969.

Harrison, Barbara, and Gregory Maguire, editors, *Innocence and Experience: Essays and Conversations on Children's Literature*. New York, Lothrop, 1987.

Haviland, Virginia, editor, *Children and Literature: Views and Reviews*. Chicago, Scott Foresman, 1973; London, Bodley Head, 1974.

Haviland, Virginia, editor, *The Openhearted Audience: Ten Authors Talk about Writing for Children*. Washington, D.C., Library of Congress, 1980.

Hazard, Paul, *Books, Children, and Men*, translated by Marguerite Mitchell. Boston, Horn Book, 1944; 5th edition, 1983.

Hearne, Betsy, and Marilyn Kaye, editors, *Celebrating Children's Books: Essays on Children's Literature in Honor of Zena Sutherland*. New York, Lothrop, 1981.

Heins, Paul, editor, *Crosscurrents of Criticism: Horn Book Essays 1968–1977*. Boston, Horn Book, 1977.

Higgins, James E., *Beyond Words: Mystical Fancy in Children's Literature*. New York, Teachers College Press, 1970.

Hildick, Wallace, *Children and Fiction: A Critical Study in Depth of the Artistic and Psychological Factors Involved in Writing Fiction for and about Children*. London, Evans, 1970; New York, World, 1971; revised edition, Evans, 1974.

Hollindale, Peter, *Choosing Books for Children*. London, Elek, 1974.

Huck, Charlotte S., and Doris A. Young, *Children's Literature in the Elementary School*. New York, Holt Rinehart, 1961; 3rd edition, 1976.

Human (and Anti-Human) Values in Children's Books. New York, Council on Interracial Books for Children, 1976.

Hunt, Peter, *Children's Book Research in Britain*. Cardiff, University of Wales, 1977; revised edition, with Beth Humphries and Sarah Wilkinson, 1982.

Hunt, Peter, editor, *Further Approaches to Research in Children's Literature*. Cardiff, University of Wales, 1982.

Hürlimann, Bettina, *Picture-Book World*, edited and translated by Brian W. Alderson. London, Oxford University Press, 1968; Cleveland, World, 1969.

Hürlimann, Bettina, *Three Centuries of Children's Books in Europe*, edited and translated by Brian W. Alderson. London, Oxford University Press, 1967; Cleveland, World, 1968.

Inglis, Fred, *The Promise of Happiness: Value and Meaning in Children's Fiction*. London, Cambridge University Press, 1981; New York, Cambridge University Press, 1982.

Jan, Isabelle, *On Children's Literature*, edited by Catherine Storr. London, Allen Lane, 1973; New York, Schocken, 1974.

Jones, Anthony, and June Buttrey, *Children and Stories*. Oxford, Blackwell, 1970.

Karl, Jean, *From Childhood to Childhood: Children's Books and Their Creators*. New York, Day, 1970.

Kingman, Lee, editor, *Newbery and Caldecott Medal Books 1956–1965* and *1966–1975*. Boston, Horn Book, 2 vols., 1965–75.

Kingston, Carolyn T., *The Tragic Mode in Children's Literature*. New York, Teachers College Press, 1974.

Lanes, Selma G., *Down the Rabbit Hole: Adventures and Misadventures in the Realm of Children's Literature*. New York, Atheneum, 1971; revised edition, 1976.

Leeson, Robert, *Children's Books and Class Society: Past and Present*. London, Writers and Readers, 1977.

Leeson, Robert, *Reading and Righting: The Past, Present and Future of Fiction for the Young*. London, Collins, 1985.

L'Engle, Madeleine, *Trailing Clouds of Glory: Spiritual Values in Children's Books*. Philadelphia, Westminster Press, 1985.

Lenz, Millicent, and Ramona M. Mahood, editors, *Young Adult Literature: Background and Criticism*. Chicago, American Library

Association, 1980.

Lewis, Naomi, *Fantasy Books for Children*. London, National Book League, 1975; revised edition, 1977.

Lickteig, Mary J., *An Introduction to Children's Literature*. Columbus, Ohio, Merrill, 1975.

Lochhead, Marion, *The Renaissance of Wonder in Children's Literature*. Edinburgh, Canongate, 1977.

Luecke, Fritz J., editor, *Children's Books: Views and Values*. Middletown, Connecticut, Xerox, 1973.

Lukens, Rebecca J., *A Critical Handbook of Children's Literature*. Chicago, Scott Foresman, 1976; revised edition, 1982; 3rd edition, 1986.

Lystad, Mary, *From Dr. Mather to Dr. Seuss: 200 Years of American Books for Children*. Boston, Hall, 1980.

MacCann, Donnarae, and Gloria Woodard, editors, *The Black American in Books for Children: Readings in Racism* and *Cultural Conformity in Books for Children: Further Readings in Racism*. Metuchen, New Jersey, Scarecrow Press, 2 vols., 1972–77; revised edition, 1 vol., 1985.

MacCann, Donnarae, and Olga Richard, *The Child's First Books: A Critical Study of Pictures and Texts*. New York, Wilson, 1973.

Magaliff, Cecile, *The Junior Novel: Its Relationship to Adolescent Reading*. Port Washington, New York, Kennikat Press, 1964.

Marshall, Margaret R., *An Introduction to the World of Children's Books*. Aldershot, Hampshire, Gower, 1982; revised edition, 1988.

Mason, Bobbie Ann, *The Girl Sleuth: A Feminist Guide*. Old Westbury, New York, Feminist Press, 1975.

McCaslin, Nellie, editor, *Children and Drama: A Collection of Essays*. New York, McKay, 1975; revised edition, New York, Longman, 1981.

McCaslin, Nellie, *Theatre for Children in the United States: A History*. Norman, University of Oklahoma Press, 1971.

McCaslin, Nellie, editor, *Theatre for Young Audiences*. New York, Longman, 1978.

McVitty, Walter, *Innocence and Experience: Essays on Contemporary Australian Children's Writers*. Melbourne, Nelson, 1982.

Meek, Margaret, Aidan Warlow, and Griselda Barton, editors, *The Cool Web: The Pattern of Children's Reading*. London, Bodley Head, 1977; New York, Atheneum, 1978.

Meigs, Cornelia, and others, *A Critical History of Children's Literature*. New York, Macmillan, 1953; revised edition, Macmillan, and London, Collier Macmillan, 1969.

Miller, Bertha Mahony, and Elinor Whitney Field, editors, *Newbery Medal Books 1922–1955* and *Caldecott Medal Books 1938–1957*. Boston, Horn Book, 2 vols., 1955–57.

Moore, Anne Carroll, *My Roads to Childhood*. New York, Doubleday, 1939.

Niall, Brenda, and Frances O'Neill, *Australia Through the Looking-Glass: Children's Fiction 1830–1980*. Melbourne, Melbourne University Press, 1984.

Nodelman, Perry, *Words about Pictures: The Narrative of Children's Picture Books*. Athens, University of Georgia Press, 1988.

Pickard, P.M., *I Could a Tale Unfold: Violence, Horror, and Sensationalism in Books for Children*. London, Tavistock, and New York, Humanities Press, 1961.

Purves, Alan C., and Dianne L. Monson, *Experiencing Children's Literature*. Chicago, Scott Foresman, 1984.

Quigly, Isabel, *The Heirs of Tom Brown: The English School Story*. London, Chatto and Windus, 1982.

Racist and Sexist Images in Children's Books. London, Writers and Readers, 1975.

Ray, Sheila G., *Children's Fiction*. Leicester, Brockhampton Press, 1970; revised edition, 1972.

Rees, David, *The Marble in the Water: Essays on Contemporary Writers of Fiction for Children and Young People*. Boston, Horn Book, 1980.

Richards, Jeffrey, editor, *Imperialism and Juvenile Literature*. Manchester, Manchester University Press, 1989.

Ringer, J.B., *Young Emigrants: New Zealand Juvenile Fiction 1833–1919*. Hamilton, New Zealand, Thackeray Street, 1980.

Robinson, Evelyn Rose, editor, *Readings about Children's Literature*. New York, McKay, 1966.

Rosenblum, Robert, *The Romantic Child: From Runge to Sendak*. London, Thames and Hudson, 1989.

Rudman, Masha Kabakow, *Children's Literature: An Issues Approach*. Lexington, Massachusetts, Heath, 1976; revised edition, White Plains, New York, Longman, 1984.

Ryan, John S., editor, *Australian Fantasy and Folklore*. Armidale, New South Wales, University of New England Department of Continuing Education, 1981.

Sadker, Myra Pollack, and David Miller Sadker, *Now Upon a Time: A Contemporary View of Children's Literature*. New York, Harper, 1977.

Sale, Roger, *Fairy Tales and After: From Snow White to E.B. White*. Cambridge, Massachusetts, Harvard University Press, 1978.

Saltman, Judith, *Modern Canadian Children's Books*. Toronto, Oxford University Press, 1987.

Saxby, H.M., *A History of Australian Children's Literature 1841–1941* and *1941–1970*. Sydney, Wentworth, 2 vols., 1969–71.

Sexism in Children's Books. London, Writers and Readers, 1976.

Shavit, Zohar, *Poetics of Children's Literature*. Athens, University of Georgia Press, 1986.

Smith, Dora V., *Fifty Years of Children's Books 1910–1960: Trends, Backgrounds, Influences*. Champaign, Illinois, National Council of Teachers of English, 1963.

Smith, Irene, *A History of the Newbery and Caldecott Medals*. New York, Viking Press, 1957.

Smith, James Steel, *A Critical Approach to Children's Literature*. New York, McGraw Hill, 1967.

Smith, Lillian, *The Unreluctant Years: A Critical Approach to Children's Literature*. Chicago, American Library Association, 1953.

Sorfleet, John Robert, editor, *Canadian Children's Drama and Theatre*. Guelph, Ontario, Canadian Children's Press, 1978.

Sutherland, Zena, editor, *The Arbuthnot Lectures 1970–1979*. Chicago, American Library Association, 1980.

Sutherland, Zena, editor, *Children in Libraries*. Chicago, University of Chicago Press, 1981.

Thomison, Dennis, editor, *Readings about Adolescent Literature*. Metuchen, New Jersey, Scarecrow Press, 1970.

Thwaite, Mary F., *From Primer to Pleasure: An Introduction to the History of Children's Books in England*. London, Library Association, 1963; revised edition, as *From Primer to Pleasure in Reading*, Library Association, 1972; Boston, Horn Book, 1973.

Townsend, John Rowe, *A Sense of Story: Essays on Contemporary Writers for Children*. London, Longman, and Philadelphia, Lippincott, 1971; revised edition, as *A Sounding of Storytellers*, London, Kestrel, and New York, Lippincott, 1979.

Townsend, John Rowe, *Written for Children: An Outline of English Children's Literature*. London, J. Garnet Miller, 1965; New York, Lothrop, 1967; revised edition, London, Kestrel, 1974; Philadelphia, Lippincott, 1975; revised edition, London, Kestrel, and New York, Harper, 1983; revised edition, London, Penguin, 1987; New York, Harper, 1988.

Trease, Geoffrey, *Tales Out of School: A Survey of Children's Fiction*. London, Heinemann, 1949; revised edition, 1964.

Tucker, Nicholas, *The Child and the Book: A Psychological and Literary Exploration*. London, Cambridge University Press, 1981; New York, Cambridge University Press, 1982.

Tucker, Nicholas, editor, *Suitable for Children? Controversies in Children's Literature*. London, Chatto and Windus, and Berkeley, University of California Press, 1976.

Vandergrift, Kay E., *Child and Story: The Literary Connection*. New York, Neal Schuman, 1980.

Vandergrift, Kay E., *Children's Literature: Theory, Research and Teaching*. Littleton, Colorado, Libraries Unlimited, 1989.

Varlejs, Jana, editor, *Young Adult Literature in the Seventies: A Selection of Readings*. Metuchen, New Jersey, Scarecrow Press, 1982.

Viguers, Ruth Hill, *Margin for Surprise: About Books, Children, and Librarians*. Boston, Little Brown, 1964; London, Constable, 1966.

Waggoner, Diana, *The Hills of Faraway: A Guide to Fantasy*. New York, Atheneum, 1978.

White, Dorothy Mary Neal, *About Books for Children*. Wellington, New Zealand Council for Educational Research, 1946; New York, Oxford University Press, 1948.

White, Mary Lou, *Children's Literature: Criticism and Response*. Columbus, Ohio, Merrill, 1976.

Wilkin, Binnie Tate, *Survival Themes in Fiction for Children and Young People*. Metuchen, New Jersey, Scarecrow Press, 1978.

Wintle, Justin, and Emma Fisher, *The Pied Pipers: Interviews with the Influential Creators of Children's Literature*. New York and London, Paddington Press, 1975.

EDITOR'S NOTE

Twentieth-Century Children's Writers includes English-language authors of fiction, poetry, and drama for children and young people. The selection of entrants is based on the recommendations of the advisers listed on page xix.

The main part of the book covers writers most of whose work for children was published after 1900; the appendix is of some important representative writers of the 19th century.

The entry for each writer consists of a biography, a complete list of separately published books, and a signed critical essay. Living entrants were invited to make a comment on their books for children.

Original British and United States editions of all books have been listed; other editions are listed only if they are first editions. Illustrators of first editions of children's books have been listed. Under "publications for children" we have listed books that at some time since their publication have been considered children's books. Retelling of myths and traditional tales are listed in the "other" section.

We would like to thank the entrants and contributors for their patience and cooperation in helping us compile this book.

ADVISERS

Peggy Appiah
Gillian Avery
Dorothy Butler
Francelia Butler
Mary Cadogan
Margaret N. Coughlan
Marcus Crouch
Pat Donlon
Julia Eccleshare
Barbara Elleman
Sarah Ellis
Matyelok Gibbs
Betty Gilderdale
Roger Lancelyn Green
Virginia Haviland
Ethel L. Heins
Fiona Lafferty
Robert Leeson

Naomi Lewis
Donnarae MacCann
Anne Scott MacLeod
Nellie McCaslin
Irma McDonough Milnes
Marcie Muir
Lance Salway
Nancy J. Schmidt
Rosemary Stones
Jon C. Stott
Zena Sutherland
John Rowe Townsend
Geoffrey Trease
Kay E. Vandergrift
Kaye Webb
Kerry White
Lee Wyndham

CONTRIBUTORS

Lucien L. Agosta
Janice M. Alberghene
William D. Anderson
Janice Antczak
Marilyn F. Apseloff
Fran Ashdown
Gillian Avery
Janet E. Baker
Jan Bakker
Keith Barker
Ann Bartholomew
Juliana Bayfield
Anthea Bell
Valerie Bierman
Susan P. Bloom
Betty Boegehold
Bill Boyle
J.S. Bratton
Julia Briggs
Valerie Brinkley-Willsher
Angela Bull
Clyde Robert Bulla
Mary Mehlman Burns
Dorothy Butler
Francelia Butler
Dennis Butts
Mary Cadogan
Alasdair K.D. Campbell
Margaret Campbell
Humphrey Carpenter
Anne Carter
Charles Causley
Charity Chang
Mary Blount Christian

John Churcher
Berna C. Clark
Pamela Cleaver
Ilene L. Cooper
Mary Silva Cosgrave
Patricia Craig
Hilary S. Crew
Marcus Crouch
Mary Croxson
Norman Culpan
Alan Edwin Day
Rosanne Fraine Donahue
Pat Donlon
Jane Doonan
Brian Doyle
Robert Dunbar
Peter du Sautoy
Audrey Eaglen
Julia Eccleshare
Judith Elkin
Barbara Elleman
Anne W. Ellis
Sarah Ellis
A.W. England
Claire England
Fred Erisman
Ellen G. Fader
Adele M. Fasick
Martha J. Fick
Tom Fitzgibbon
Sheila Flanagan
Rachel Fordyce
Jack Forman
Geoff Fox

Christine Doyle Francis
Gillian Freeman
Maggie Freeman
Norma R. Fryatt
Marcia G. Fuchs
James Cross Giblin
Betty Gilderdale
Michael Glover
Jacqueline L. Gmuca
Cecilia Gordon
John Gough
Margaret Greaves
Roger Lancelyn Green
M. Jean Greenlaw
Patrick Groff
Irene Haas
Eric Hadley
Dennis Hall
Graham Hammond
Nancy C. Hammond
Karen Stang Hanley
Jane Anne Hannigan
Anne Harvey
Ann G. Hay
Renée Haynes
Betsy Hearne
Diana Hebley
Peggy Heeks
Ethel L. Heins
Paul Heins
Ravenna Helson
Sam H. Henderson
James E. Higgins
Mary Hoffman
Peter Hollindale
Karen Nelson Hoyle
Peter Hunt
Fred Inglis
Sylvia Patterson Iskander
Clara O. Jackson
David H. Jenkinson
Coleman A. Jennings
Deidre Johnson
Raymond E. Jones
Ursula M. Jones
Nels Juleus
Antony Kamm
Marilyn Kaye
Hugh T. Keenan
George Kelley
R. Gordon Kelly
Edward Kemp
Meena Khorana
Eric A. Kimmel
Lee Kingman
Carolyn T. Kingston
Gillian Klein
Fiona Lafferty
Selma G. Lanes
Robert Leeson
Millicent Lenz
Linda S. Levstik
Claudia Lewis
Naomi Lewis
Mary J. Lickteig
Myra Cohn Livingston

Rebecca J. Lukens
Alan M. Lynskey
Mary Lystad
Donnarae MacCann
Anne Scott MacLeod
Gertrud Mander
Gwen Marsh
Margaret R. Marshall
Bobbie Ann Mason
Margaret F. Maxwell
Jill P. May
David McCord
Christine McDonnell
Myles McDowell
Joan McGrath
Walter McVitty
Margaret Meek
Leonard R. Mendelsohn
Cathryn M. Mercier
Jean F. Mercier
Susan Meyers
Colin Mills
Joan Mills
Irma McDonough Milnes
Naomi Mitchison
Christian H. Moe
Francis J. Molson
Doris Langley Moore
Caroline Moorehead
Anita Moss
Elaine Moss
Marcie Muir
Heather Neill
Stephanie Nettell
Mary Nettlefold
Peter F. Neumeyer
Brenda Niall
Alleen Pace Nilsen
Vivien Noakes
Osayimwense Osa
Ruth Osler
Jill Paton Walsh
Lissa Paul
Kit Pearson
Pat Pflieger
Neil Philip
Robert Protherough
Eric Quayle
Suzanne Rahn
Sheila G. Ray
Mary Rayner
David Rees
James Reeves
Selma K. Richardson
Mae Durham Roger
Jim Roginski
Nancy Tillman Romalov
James Roose-Evans
Gerald J. Rubio
Mary Rubio
Jean Russell
Glenn Edward Sadler
Alison Sage
Lance Salway
Lucy Saunders
H.M. Saxby

Vivian J. Scheinmann
Nancy J. Schmidt
Mabel D. Segun
Nancy Shepherdson
Carolyn Shute
Dorothy D. Siles
Sanjay Sircar
M. Sarah Smedman
Karen Patricia Smith
John Robert Sorfleet
John D. Stahl
Kenneth J. Sterck
Madeleine B. Stern
Rosemary Stones
Jon C. Stott
Zena Sutherland
Jennifer Taylor
Gillian Thomas
Joyce Thomas
Ann Thwaite
Divna Todorovich
John Rowe Townsend
Geoffrey Trease
Felicity Trotman

Margaret M. Tye
Malcolm Usrey
Kay E. Vandergrift
Peter Vansittart
Margaret Walker
George Walsh
Aidan Warlow
Fiona Waters
Brigitte Weeks
Joyce Irene Whalley
Joy Whitby
Kerry White
Frank Whitehead
Winifred Whitehead
Angela Wigan
Martin Williams
Denise Murcko Wilms
Barbara Ker Wilson
Jacqueline Brown Woody
Jessica Yates
Linda Yeatman
Jane Yolen
Laura M. Zaidman

TWENTIETH-CENTURY
CHILDREN'S WRITERS

Chester Aaron
Chinua Achebe
Richard Adams
Arnold Adoff
John Agard
Allan Ahlberg
Joan Aiken
Ruth Ainsworth
Vivien Alcock
Sue Ann Alderson
James Aldridge
Lloyd Alexander
Mabel Esther Allen
Eric Allen
E.M. Almedingen
Joseph A. Altsheler
C.W. Anderson
Prudence Andrew
J.S. Andrews
Peggy Appiah
Edward Ardizzone
Laura Adams Armer
Ronda Armitage
Richard Armstrong
William H. Armstrong
Ruth Arthur
Honor Arundel
Meshack Asare
Frank Asch
Bernard Ashley
M.E. Atkinson
Richard Atwater
Esther Averill
Gillian Avery
Harold Avery
Avi
W.V. Awdry
Natalie Babbitt
Martha Bacon
R.L. Bacon
Enid Bagnold
Carolyn Sherwin Bailey
Betty Baker
Margaret J. Baker
Margaret Balderson
Lynne Reid Banks
Angela Banner
Helen Bannerman
Cicely Mary Barker
Kitty Barne
Anne Mainwaring Barrett
J.M. Barrie
Margaret Stuart Barry
L. Frank Baum
Nina Bawden
Nina Beachcroft
S.G. Hulme Beaman
John and Patricia Beatty
Harry Behn
Hilaire Belloc
Ludwig Bemelmans
Nathaniel Benchley
Rex Benedict
Elisabeth Beresford
Leila Berg
James Berry

Herbert Best
Alfred Bestall
Bettina
Margery Williams Bianco
Violet Bibby
Clare Bice
Val Biro
Claire Huchet Bishop
Donald Bisset
Ann Blades
Joan W. Blos
Judy Blume
Enid Blyton
N.M. Bodecker
Michael Bond
Nancy Bond
Ruskin Bond
Frank Bonham
Crosby Bonsall
Arna Bontemps
Lucy Boston
Helen Dore Boylston
Christianna Brand
John Branfield
Angela Brazil
Nancy Breary
Elinor M. Brent-Dyer
Sue Ellen Bridgers
K.M. Briggs
Raymond Briggs
Robert Bright
Carol Ryrie Brink
Hesba Brinsmead
Joyce Lankester Brisley
Bill Brittain
L. Leslie Brooke
Walter R. Brooks
Marc Brown
Marcia Brown
Margaret Wise Brown
Palmer Brown
Pamela Brown
Roy Brown
Anthony Browne
Dorita Fairlie Bruce
Mary Grant Bruce
Anthony Buckeridge
Angela Bull
Clyde Robert Bulla
Eve Bunting
Robert Burch
Thornton Waldo Burgess
Ben Lucien Burman
Frances Hodgson Burnett
Sheila Burnford
John Burningham
Hester Burton
Virginia Lee Burton
Oliver Butterworth
Betsy Byars
Eleanor Cameron
Joanna Cannan
Eric Carle
Natalie Savage Carlson
Bruce Carter
Peter Carter

Sylvia Cassedy
Arthur Catherall
Rebecca Caudill
Charles Causley
Betty Cavanna
Winifred Cawley
Mary Chalmers
Aidan Chambers
Jill Chaney
Nan Chauncy
Christine Chaundler
Alice Childress
Joseph E. Chipperfield
Charlotte Chorpenning
Arthur Bowie Chrisman
John Christopher
Richard Church
Marchette Chute
John Ciardi
Patricia Clapp
Ann Nolan Clark
Catherine Anthony Clark
Leonard Clark
Mavis Thorpe Clark
Pauline Clarke
Beverly Cleary
Vera and Bill Cleaver
Bruce Clements
Dorothy Clewes
Lucille Clifton
Eleanor Clymer
Elizabeth Coatsworth
Mary Cockett
Barbara Cohen
Babette Cole
James Lincoln Collier
Hila Colman
Padraic Colum
Ellen Conford
Gordon Cooper
Lettice Cooper
Susan Cooper
Scott Corbett
W.J. Corbett
Alexander Cordell
William Corlett
Robert Cormier
Joy Cowley
John Craig
Helen Cresswell
Samuel Rutherford Crockett
Richmal Crompton
Gillian Cross
Kevin Crossley-Holland
Primrose Cumming
John Cunliffe
Julia Cunningham
Jane Louise Curry
W. Towrie Cutt
Roald Dahl
Alice Dalgliesh
Ruth Dallas
Maureen Daly
David Scott Daniell
Paula Danziger
Marjorie Darke

James Daugherty
Edgar and Ingri Parin d'Aulaire
Andrew Davies
Peter Dawlish
C. Day Lewis
Marguerite de Angeli
J.O. de Graft-Hanson
Joan de Hamel
Olive Dehn
Meindert De Jong
Walter de la Mare
Tomie de Paola
Beatrice Schenk de Regniers
Anne de Roo
Anita Desai
Elizabeth Borton de Treviño
Farrukh Dhondy
Peter Dickinson
Eilís Dillon
Lynley Dodd
Berlie Doherty
Nance Donkin
John Donovan
Mary Alice Downie
Brian Doyle
V.H. Drummond
William Pène du Bois
Tessa Duder
Maurice Duggan
Jane Duncan
Lois Duncan
Norman Duncan
Eileen Dunlop
Mary Durack
Roger Duvoisin
Edward Eager
Walter D. Edmonds
Dorothy Edwards
Monica Edwards
Cyprian Ekwensi
E.M. Ellin
Buchi Emecheta
Sylvia Engdahl
Elizabeth Enright
Eleanor Estes
Marie Hall Ets
Hubert Evans
Norma Farber
Eleanor Farjeon
Walter Farley
Penelope Farmer
G.E. Farrow
Max Fatchen
Louise Fatio
Cliff Faulknor
Edward Fenton
Kathleen Fidler
Rachel Field
Anne Fine
Charles J. Finger
George Finkel
Winifred Finlay
Aileen Fisher
Dorothy Canfield Fisher
Nicholas Fisk
John D. Fitzgerald

Louise Fitzhugh
Marjorie Flack
Paul Fleischman
Sid Fleischman
James Flora
Dennis Foon
Esther Forbes
Michael Foreman
Antonia Forest
Paula Fox
Barbara C. Freeman
Bill Freeman
Don Freeman
Fiona French
Simon French
Jean Fritz
Rosalie K. Fry
Roy Fuller
Rose Fyleman
J.G. Fyson
Wanda Gág
Ruth Stiles Gannett
Joyce Gard
Jane Gardam
Leon Garfield
Alan Garner
Eve Garnett
Doris Gates
Maurice Gee
Jean Craighead George
Adèle Geras
May Gibbs
Fred Gipson
Rumer Godden
John Gordon
Elizabeth Goudge
Bob Graham
Eleanor Graham
Harry Graham
Lorenz Graham
Kenneth Grahame
Hardie Gramatky
Nicholas Stuart Gray
Margaret Greaves
Roger Lancelyn Green
Bette Greene
Constance C. Greene
Eloise Greenfield
Ted Greenwood
Grey Owl
Frederick Grice
Helen V. Griffith
G.D. Griffiths
Helen Griffiths
Johnny Gruelle
Rosa Guy
Berta and Elmer Hader
Roderick Haig-Brown
Ann Halam
J.B.S. Haldane
Kathleen Hale
Aylmer Hall
Lynn Hall
Virginia Hamilton
Joyce Hansen
Michael Hardcastle

Lee Harding
Cynthia Harnett
Aurand Harris
Christie Harris
Geraldine Harris
Mary K. Harris
Rosemary Harris
Erik Haugaard
Charles Boardman Hawes
John F. Hayes
Carolyn Haywood
Mairi Hedderwick
Florence Parry Heide
Robert A. Heinlein
Marguerite Henry
Nat Hentoff
Constance Heward
Anita Hewett
Florence Hightower
Jamake Highwater
E.W. Hildick
Douglas Hill
Lorna Hill
S.E. Hinton
Russell Hoban
C. Walter Hodges
Syd Hoff
Grace Hogarth
Isabelle Holland
Holling C. Holling
Felice Holman
H.M. Hoover
Jacynth Hope-Simpson
Charlotte Hough
James A. Houston
James Howe
Edith Howes
Janni Howker
Monica Hughes
Richard Hughes
Shirley Hughes
Ted Hughes
Katharine Hull and Pamela Whitlock
Irene Hunt
Mabel Leigh Hunt
Peter Hunt
Kristin Hunter
Mollie Hunter
Norman Hunter
Johanna Hurwitz
Pat Hutchins
Sulamith Ish-Kishor
Jesse Jackson
Will James
Randall Jarrell
Ann Jellicoe
W.E. Johns
Annabel and Edgar Johnson
Crockett Johnson
Diana Wynne Jones
June Jordan
Aaron Judah
Norton Juster
Virginia Kahl
Josephine Kamm
Elijah Kariuki

Welwyn Katz
Geraldine Kaye
Ezra Jack Keats
Charles Keeping
Harold Keith
Victor Kelleher
Steven Kellogg
Eric Kelly
Gene Kemp
Carol Kendall
Richard Kennedy
X.J. Kennedy
Tim Kennemore
Judith Kerr
M.E. Kerr
Barbara Kimenye
Clive King
Dick King-Smith
Lee Kingman
Rudyard Kipling
Jim Kjelgaard
Norma Klein
Robin Klein
Eric Knight
Frank Knight
E.L. Konigsburg
Phyllis Krasilovsky
Joanna Halpert Kraus
Robert Kraus
Ruth Krauss
Joseph Krumgold
Karla Kuskin
Elisabeth Kyle
Lois Lamplugh
Evelyn Sibley Lampman
Jane Langton
Jean Lee Latham
Eleanor Lattimore
Ann Lawrence
Louise Lawrence
Robert Lawson
Munro Leaf
Dennis Lee
Mildred Lee
Tanith Lee
Robert Leeson
Amy Le Feuvre
Ursula K. Le Guin
Madeleine L'Engle
Lois Lenski
Julius Lester
Betty Levin
Sonia Levitin
Myron Levoy
C.S. Lewis
Elizabeth Foreman Lewis
Hilda Lewis
Joan M. Lexau
Betty Jean Lifton
Kenneth Lillington
Norman Lindsay
David Line
Joan Lingard
Eric Linklater
Leo Lionni
William Lipkind

Joseph Wharton Lippincott
Robert Lipsyte
Jean Little
Penelope Lively
Myra Cohn Livingston
Anita Lobel
Arnold Lobel
Elsie Locke
Hugh Lofting
Maud Hart Lovelace
Lois Lowry
Janet Lunn
Patricia Lynch
Elinor Lyon
Caroline Macdonald
Jean MacGibbon
Ellen MacGregor
Elisabeth MacIntyre
Claire Mackay
Constance D'Arcy Mackay
Walter Macken
Patricia MacLachlan
Margaret MacPherson
Angus MacVicar
Michelle Magorian
Gregory Maguire
Margaret Mahy
Kevin Major
Rosemary Manning
Ruth Manning-Sanders
Bessie Marchant
Jan Mark
Markoosie
James Marshall
David Martin
J.P. Martin
Patricia Miles Martin
John Masefield
Sharon Bell Mathis
Christobel Mattingley
William Mayne
Norma Fox Mazer
Anne McCaffrey
Geraldine McCaughrean
Tom McCaughren
Robert McCloskey
David McCord
Phyllis McGinley
Roger McGough
Eloise Jarvis McGraw
Iona McGregor
David McKee
Patricia McKillip
Robin McKinley
Allan Campbell McLean
Janet McNeill
Stephen W. Meader
Florence Crannell Means
Cornelia Meigs
Mary Melwood
Eve Merriam
Jean Merrill
Laurence Meynell
Madge Miller
A.A. Milne
Else Minarik

Elyne Mitchell
Naomi Mitchison
F.N. Monjo
L.M. Montgomery
Rutherford Montgomery
Dorothea Moore
Diana Moorhead
Ursula Moray Williams
Walt Morey
Alison Morgan
Helen Morgan
Jean Morris
Farley Mowat
Dhan Gopal Mukerji
Robert Munsch
Jill Murphy
Shirley Rousseau Murphy
Walter Dean Myers
Bill Naughton
Phyllis Reynolds Naylor
Violet Needham
Jan Needle
E. Nesbit
Evaline Ness
Emily Cheney Neville
Robert Newman
Ruth Nichols
William Nicholson
Helen Nicoll
Jenny Nimmo
Joan Lowery Nixon
Lilith Norman
Sterling North
Andre Norton
Mary Norton
Flora Nwapa
Robert Nye
Graham Oakley
Robert C. O'Brien
Asenath Odaga
Scott O'Dell
Eileen O'Faolain
Mary O'Hara
Anezi Okoro
Pamela Oldfield
Alfred Ollivant
Zibby Oneal
Judith O'Neill
Doris Orgel
Edward Ormondroyd
Pat O'Shea
Jenny Overton
Gareth Owen
Elsie J. Oxenham
C. Everard Palmer
M. Pardoe
Peggy Parish
Ruth Park
Richard Parker
Anne Parrish
Mary Elwyn Patchett
Katherine Paterson
Jill Paton Walsh
Brian Patten
Gary Paulsen
Isabel Maud Peacocke

Philippa Pearce
Howard Pease
Richard Peck
Robert Newton Peck
Bill Peet
Lucy Fitch Perkins
Maud and Miska Petersham
Ann Petry
K.M. Peyton
Joan Phipson
Barbara Leonie Picard
Meredith Ann Pierce
Ann Pilling
Daniel Manus Pinkwater
Stephanie Plowman
Marguerite Poland
Madeleine A. Polland
Josephine Poole
Eleanor H. Porter
Gene Stratton Porter
Sheena Porter
Beatrix Potter
Rhoda Power
Chris Powling
Rosamond Praeger
Jack Prelutsky
Evadne Price
Susan Price
Willard Price
Alison Prince
John Pudney
Christine Pullein-Thompson
Diana Pullein-Thompson
Josephine Pullein-Thompson
Virginia Pye
Gwynedd Rae
Arthur Ransome
Ellen Raskin
Marjorie Kinnan Rawlings
Mary Ray
Mary Rayner
James Reaney
David Rees
Leslie Rees
James Reeves
Meta Mayne Reid
H.A. and Margret Rey
Alice Hegan Rice
Frank Richards
Laura E. Richards
Antonia Ridge
E.V. Rieu
Charles G.D. Roberts
Elizabeth Madox Roberts
Keith Robertson
Joan G. Robinson
Anne Rockwell
Mary Rodgers
James Roose-Evans
Michael Rosen
Diana Ross
Tony Ross
Dick Roughsey
Glen Rounds
Gillian Rubinstein
Philip Rush

Cynthia Rylant
Marilyn Sachs
Andrew Salkey
Pamela Sargent
Julia Sauer
Malcolm Saville
Ruth Sawyer
Vernon Scannell
Richard Scarry
Jack Schaefer
Ann Schlee
Miriam Schlein
Bill Scott
Ouida Sebestyen
Jenny Seed
Mabel D. Segun
George Selden
Maurice Sendak
Kate Seredy
Ian Serraillier
Ernest Thompson Seton
Dr. Seuss
David Severn
Helen Sewell
Monica Shannon
Marjorie Weinman Sharmat
Margery Sharp
Sylvia Sherry
Louisa R. Shotwell
Shel Silverstein
Isaac Bashevis Singer
William Sleator
Barbara Sleigh
Louis Slobodkin
Esphyr Slobodkina
Alfred Slote
C. Fox Smith
Dodie Smith
Doris Buchanan Smith
Emma Smith
Vian Smith
William Jay Smith
Barbara Claassen Smucker
Caroline Dale Snedeker
Zilpha Keatley Snyder
Donald J. Sobol
Barbara Softly
Virginia Sorensen
Ivan Southall
Elizabeth George Speare
Eleanor Spence
Armstrong Sperry
E.C. Spykman
Mary Q. Steele
William O. Steele
William Steig
John Steptoe
James Stevenson
A.C. Stewart
Mary Stolz
Phil Stong
Margaret Storey
Catherine Storr
Herbert Strang
Joyce Stranger
Noel Streatfeild

L.A.G. Strong
Elizabeth Stucley
Rodie Sudbery
Donald Suddaby
Rosemary Sutcliff
Eve Sutton
Robert Swindells
Ronald Syme
John Symonds
Geraldine Symons
Ethel Talbot
Booth Tarkington
Joan Tate
Mildred D. Taylor
Sydney Taylor
Theodore Taylor
William Taylor
Albert Payson Terhune
Colin Thiele
James Thurber
Ann Thwaite
Eve Titus
Barbara Euphan Todd
H.E. Todd
J.R.R. Tolkien
Ruth Tomalin
Mary Tourtel
John Rowe Townsend
Katharine Tozer
P.L. Travers
Mary Treadgold
Geoffrey Trease
Henry Treece
Alvin Tresselt
Meriol Trevor
Jan Truss
John R. Tunis
Brinton Turkle
Ethel Turner
Philip Turner
Yoshiko Uchida
Tomi Ungerer
Bertha Upton
Jean Ure
Alison Uttley
Chris Van Allsburg
Hilda Van Stockum
John Verney
Elizabeth Gray Vining
Judith Viorst
Elfrida Vipont
Cynthia Voigt
Bernard Waber
Martin Waddell
Jenny Wagner
Jan Wahl
David Walker
Stuart Walker
Dorothy Wall
Ian Wallace
Mildred Pitts Walter
Phyl Wardell
D.J. Watkins-Pitchford
Clyde Watson
James Watson
Jenifer Wayne

Jean Webster
Rosemary Weir
Ronald Welch
Rosemary Wells
Barbara Wersba
Joyce West
Robert Westall
Percy Westerman
Nadia Wheatley
E.B. White
Eliza Orne White
T.H. White
Phyllis A. Whitney
Leonard Wibberley
Ester Wier
Kate Douglas Wiggin
Laura Ingalls Wilder
Barbara Willard
Nancy Willard
Jay Williams
Vera B. Williams

Henry Williamson
Barbara Ker Wilson
Gina Wilson
Jacqueline Wilson
Maia Wojciechowska
David Wood
Kerry Wood
Lorna Wood
Valerie Worth
Kit Wright
Patricia Wrightson
Olwen Wymark
May Wynne
Tim Wynne-Jones
Taro Yashima
Elizabeth Yates
Laurence Yep
Jane Yolen
Paul Zindel
Gene Zion
Charlotte Zolotow

APPENDIX

Jacob Abbott
Louisa May Alcott
Thomas Bailey Aldrich
Horatio Alger
F. Anstey
R.M. Ballantyne
Lewis Carroll
Susan Coolidge
Palmer Cox
Mary Mapes Dodge
Evelyn Everett-Green
Juliana Horatia Ewing
F.W. Farrar
George Manville Fenn
Martha Finley
Lucretia P. Hale
Joel Chandler Harris
G.A. Henty
Thomas Hughes
Jean Ingelow

Richard Jefferies
Charles Kingsley
Andrew Lang
Edward Lear
George MacDonald
Frederick Marryat
L.T. Meade
Mary Louisa Molesworth
James Otis
Howard Pyle
Talbot Baines Reed
Anna Sewell
Margaret Sidney
Robert Louis Stevenson
Frank R. Stockton
Hesba Stretton
Mark Twain
Mrs. O.F. Walton
Susan Warner
Charlotte Yonge

FOREIGN-LANGUAGE WRITERS

Chingiz Aitmatov
Mitsumasa Anno
Marcel Aymé
Barbara Bartos-Höppner
Hans Baumann
Gunnel Beckman
Paul Berna

Paul Biegel
Lygia Bojunga-Nunes
Dick Bruna
Jean de Brunhoff
Laurent de Brunhoff
Père Castor
Kornei Chukovsky

Václav Ctvrtek

Elfie Donnelly

Maurice Druon

Willi Fährmann

Rudolf Frank

Vadim Frolov

Maria Gripe

René Guillot

Monica Gydal

Leif Hamre

Evert Hartman

Christoph Hein

Helme Heine

Ota Hofman

Anne Holm

Chihiro Iwasaki

Janosch

Tove Jansson

Runer Jonsson

Erich Kästner

Yuri Korinetz

James Krüss

Guus Kuijer

Chizuko Kuratomi

Selma Lagerlöf

Astrid Lindgren

An Rutgers van der Loeff

André Maurois

Jörg Müller and Jörg Steiner

Chiyoko Nakatani

Christine Nöstlinger

José Luis Olaizola

Gudrun Pausewang

Carlo Picchio

Otfried Preussler

Jan Prochazka

Alf Prøysen

Bjarne Reuter

Hans Peter Richter

Gianni Rodari

Antoine de Saint-Exupéry

Felix Salten

José María Sánchez-Silva

Irmelin Sandman Lilius

Rafik Schami

Mario Soldati

Angela Sommer-Bodenburg

Aimée Sommerfelt

Miguel Torga

Michel Tournier

Edith Unnerstad

Anne-Cath. Vestly

Gabrielle Vincent

Shigeo Watanabe

Alki Zei

Reiner Zimnik

AARON, Chester. American. Born in Butler, Pennsylvania, 9 May 1923. Educated at Butler High School, graduated 1941; University of California, Los Angeles, 1945–48, and Berkeley, 1954–56, B.A. 1956; San Francisco State University, 1974–77, M.A. 1977. Served in the United States Army Armored Infantry, 1943–45. Married Marguarite Kelly in 1954 (divorced 1973); one stepson. X-ray technician, Kaiser Permanente, San Francisco, 1957–58; chief X-ray technician, Alta Bates Hospital, Berkeley, 1958–71; technical writer, MKI Engineering, San Francisco, 1971–72. Assistant Professor, 1972–82, and since 1983 Professor of English, Saint Mary's College, Moraga, California. Recipient: Huntington Hartford Foundation fellowship, 1950, 1951; Chapelbrook Foundation grant, 1970; National Endowment for the Arts grant, 1976. Agent: Ellen Levine Literary Agency, 432 Park Avenue, Suite 1205, New York, New York 10016. Address: P.O. Box 388, Occidental, California 95465, U.S.A.

PUBLICATIONS FOR CHILDREN

Fiction

Better Than Laughter. New York, Harcourt Brace, 1972; London, Gollancz, 1973.
An American Ghost, illustrated by David Lemon. New York, Harcourt Brace, 1973; London, Gollancz, 1974.
Hello to Bodega. New York, Atheneum, 1975.
Spill. New York, Atheneum, 1977.
Catch Calico! New York, Dutton, 1979.
Gideon. New York, Lippincott, 1982.
Duchess. New York, Lippincott, 1982.
Out of Sight, Out of Mind. New York, Lippincott, 1985.
Lackawanna. New York, Lippincott, 1986.

PUBLICATIONS FOR ADULTS

Novel

About Us. New York, McGraw Hill, 1967.

Play

The Cowbank (produced Berkeley, California, 1955).

*

Chester Aaron comments:

I have always liked to read stories. That means, to me, a series of events connected by growing excitement and continuing pleasure. With characters I could not necessarily admire but respect, almost envy. E.M. Forster's rule—the urge to know what happens next, the breathless need to keep turning pages—is always hovering in my mind somewhere, when I write. This is true whether I write for adults or young adults. I respect passion in people, and so my characters are usually committed to a certain behavior passionately. I even try to develop a prose that is impassioned as it moves the story forward. My love for animals often interferes with my love for people, and I am always on the alert for stories that will include both animals and humans. I am concerned with characters and families in conflict: often with themselves but always with their societies.

*　　*　　*

Chester Aaron, who "likes to read stories," is himself an excellent storyteller, with good plots, action, continual points of tension, and a special rapport with his teenage or younger central characters. His expertise on whatever may be his theme of the moment—oil spillage, sheep dog training, rivers in flood—is a further fictional asset.

Aaron's books belong in kind to the sterling old adventure genre, though with more inner subtleties. They are also allied to the novel of ideas, and this is both a merit and the reverse. The problem is not so much the ideas themselves as their narrative presentation. In the best of Aaron's books—notably *An American Ghost*—narrative and polemic are totally fused. In *Out of Sight, Out of Mind,* highly readable though it is, they are not fused at all.

A quick survey of Aaron's books shows something of his range of theme and treatment. *Spill* has an increasingly topical subject: an oil spill and its effects on the seabirds and creatures and on their would-be rescuers. A collision of tankers off the coast of northern California results in devastating pollution, threatening both a noted bird sanctuary, where migrating birds are just due to arrive, and an offshore area of unique marine life. Deeply involved in the emergency are members of a family whose home already serves as an unofficial animal hospital. Judy (14) is totally dedicated to the cause. Her older brother Jeff has begun to taste the illicit pleasures of independence; but he is still concerned about his secret find—a rare giant sea anemone living in an offshore reef. Has it survived? Judy sets out to discover the answer.

In *Catch Calico!* a 14-year-old boy, alone with a sick grandfather in their holiday mountain cabin, has to take on the responsibility of dealing with a much-loved cat with rabies. A further shock to separate fact and dream is the unravelling of a mystery linking the boy's father, dead in battle, with his grandfather's tales of his own heroic war days, which really never existed at all. Marty, the main character in *Duchess,* is a New York delinquent and gang leader. As an alternative to custody he is sent to his uncle's remote sheep ranch in California. His plans of escape come to nothing (the uncle is no fool), but his surly interest is roused at last by watching the prowess of Princess, a border collie sheep dog. The real awakening comes when Marty finds and feeds a starving pup and is allowed to keep and train it. Duchess becomes a winner—so does Marty, both at school and on the farm. He has found where his future lies.

Gideon is a powerful and important book, the story of a 14-year-old boy in the Warsaw ghetto who is determined to be a survivor. His Aryan looks and reckless temperament are a help (he starts by slipping out to join smuggling gangs in the city) but the price will be almost intolerably high. He is to lose every member of his family and every close companion of his journey. He will know the sewers and the barbed wire whip; he will escape from the crammed and waterless cattle truck—and be recaptured; he will be made to undress the victims of the gas chambers: he is one of the very few survivors of the rising at Treblinka. Gideon has had to change his whole identity, even to himself. It is what he seeks to reclaim, his lost Jewishness especially, when he sets down the tale for his own descendants.

Out of Sight, Out of Mind, with its touch of the supernatural—or should it be supranormal?—differs again from the rest. Young teenage twins, with a worldwide reputation for their miraculous extrasensory powers (not only can they read thoughts, they can move distant vehicles), are orphaned when their mother and father are killed in a plane crash. The parents were on their way to speak at a major international conference on psychic phenomena; the text of their speech ("Extrasensory Perception: A Key to World Peace") survives, and the twins plan to travel to Berkeley to deliver it themselves. But a certain foreign government wishes to capture the gifted pair; the hunt is on, and they have the terrible problem of finding shelter without endangering their hosts. What's more, adolescence is daily weakening their childhood powers. A thriller indeed!—fast-paced and gripping: you gladly suspend disbelief. The weakness of the book is its message itself, which could be replaced without changing the structure at all.

Lackawanna, Aaron's most recent book, is less convincing. In the Depression years, around 1930 and 1931, a group of orphaned children turn themselves into a kind of family; they live by begging, street singing, whatever each day offers. When the youngest (Herbie, aged nine) disappears during one of their freight car-jumping expeditions, a cross-country search begins. Eventful, poignant (poverty, like other extremes, is an effective fictional motif), the book is a real adventure yarn for juniors—though adults might puzzle here and there over detail. Had Aaron in mind Brecht's poem "The Children's Crusade"?

All the best elements in Aaron's fiction meet in *An American Ghost.* Albie is a boy in pioneer Wisconsin of the 1850's. He loves his family and accepts their beliefs and values. Thus, in the brief prelude, when two ragged boys (Indians?, runaway slaves?) are casually shot dead by Albie's father and their neighbour Sam, it does not occur to him to question this, any more than he questioned the killing that same day of a cougar (panther, puma, "American ghost—the name depending on who might be cursing it"). But Albie chances to be alone at home when the nearby river floods and the little white house is sent racing down towards the Mississippi, among the debris of drowned animals and wrecked dwellings. A great tree halts its course, which allows a cougar to enter the house: a female, about to give birth to cubs. Gradually boy and beast become allies. The real danger comes from a passing boat of drunken thieves, their vessel stuffed with loot and a sad mass of dying animals. The thieves capture Albie: maybe he'll fetch a ransom. He escapes. Finally, when land is sighted, the cougar takes each cub in turn to safety, and returns for the boy. Albie and his family are reunited. But the end, though enigmatic, is startling, even brilliant. In a moment of truth Albie confronts in himself his family's rooted values. True, it is hardly likely that a boy on his own so long ago could resist for long the mores, codes, and conventions of an entire people—but some readers today may feel themselves to be in a different position.

However harsh its theme, every Aaron book has an unquenchable spark of optimism, a hopeful energy, always to be found in the central youthful characters. His novels may not reach the bestseller lists, but the best of them have a lasting quality, and do not date at all. This is true of *Gideon* and of *Spill*—and most of all of *An American Ghost,* which should never be allowed to go out of print.

—Naomi Lewis

ACHEBE, Chinua. Nigerian. Born Albert Chinualumogu in Ogidi, 16 November 1930. Educated at Government College, Umuahia, 1944–47; University College, Ibadan, 1948–53, B.A. (London) 1953. Married Christiana Okoli in 1961; two sons and two daughters. Talks producer, Lagos, 1954–57, controller, Enugu, 1958–61, and director, Lagos, 1961–66, Nigerian Broadcasting Corporation; chairman, Citadel Books Ltd., Enugu, 1967. Senior Research Fellow, 1967–73, Professor of English, 1973–81, and since 1984 Professor Emeritus, University of Nigeria, Nsukka. Visiting Professor, 1972–75, and Fulbright Professor, 1987–88, University of Massachusetts, Amherst; Visiting Professor, University of Connecticut, Storrs, 1975–76; Regents' Lecturer, University of California, Los Angeles, 1984. Founding editor, Heinemann African Writers series, 1962–72 and since 1970 director, Heinemann Educational Books (Nigeria) Ltd., and Nwankwo-Ifejika Ltd. (later Nwamife), publishers, Enugu; since 1971 editor, *Okike: An African Journal of New Writing,* Nsukka. Member, University of Lagos Council, 1966; chairman, Society of Nigerian Authors, 1966, and Association of Nigerian Authors, 1982–86; Pro-Chancellor and Chairman of Council, Anambra State University of Technology, Enugu, 1986–88. Since 1981 member of the Executive Committee, Commonwealth Arts Organisation, London; since 1983 member, International Social Prospects Academy, Geneva. Recipient: Margaret Wrong Memorial prize, 1959; Nigerian National trophy, 1960; Rockefeller fellowship, 1960; Unesco fellowship, 1963; Jock Campbell award (*New Statesman*), 1965; Commonwealth Poetry prize, 1973; Neil Gunn International fellowship, 1974; Nigerian National Merit award, 1979; Commonwealth Foundation award, 1983. Litt.D.: Dartmouth College, Hanover, New Hampshire, 1972; University of Southampton, 1975; University of Ife, 1978; University of Nigeria, 1981; University of Kent, Canterbury, 1982; University of Guelph, Ontario, 1984; Mount Allison University, Sackville, New Brunswick, 1984; Franklin Pierce College, Rindge, New Hampshire, 1985; D. Univ.: University of Stirling, 1975; LL.D.: University of Prince Edward Island, Charlottetown, 1976; D.H.L.: University of Massachusetts, 1977. Honorary Fellow, Modern Language Association (USA), 1975; member, Order of the Federal Republic of Nigeria, 1979; Honorary Member, American Academy, 1982; Fellow, Royal Society of Literature, 1983. Address: P.O. Box 53, University of Nigeria, Nsukka, Anambra State, Nigeria.

PUBLICATIONS FOR CHILDREN

Fiction

Chike and the River, illustrated by Prue Theobalds.   London and New York, Cambridge University Press, 1966.
How the Leopard Got His Claws, with John Iroaganachi, illustrated by Per Christiansen.   Enugu, Nwamife, 1972; New York, Third Press, 1973.
The Flute, illustrated by Tayo Adenaike.   Enugu, Fourth Dimension, 1977.
The Drum, illustrated by John Roper.   Enugu, Fourth Dimension, 1977.

PUBLICATIONS FOR ADULTS

Novels

Things Fall Apart.   London, Heinemann, 1958; New York, McDowell Obolensky, 1959.
No Longer at Ease.   London, Heinemann, 1960; New York, Obolensky, 1961.
Arrow of God.   London, Heinemann, 1964; New York, Day, 1967.
A Man of the People.   London, Heinemann, and New York, Day, 1966.
Anthills of the Savannah.   London, Heinemann, 1987; New York, Doubleday, 1988.

Short Stories

The Sacrificial Egg and Other Stories.   Onitsha, Etudo, 1962.
Girls at War.   London, Heinemann, and New York, Doubleday, 1972.

Verse

Beware, Soul-Brother and Other Poems.   Enugu, Nwankwo-Ifejika, 1971; revised edition, Enugu, Nwamife, and London, Heinemann, 1972.
Christmas in Biafra and Other Poems.   New York, Doubleday, 1973.

Other

Morning Yet on Creation Day: Essays.   London, Heinemann, and
  New York, Doubleday, 1975.
*In Person: Achebe, Awoonor, and Soyinka at the University of
  Washington.*   Seattle, University of Washington African Studies
  Program, 1975.
The Trouble with Nigeria.   Enugu, Fourth Dimension, 1983; Lon-
  don, Heinemann, 1984.
The World of the Ogbanje.   Enugu, Fourth Dimension, 1986.
Hopes and Impediments: Selected Essays 1965–1987.   London,
  Heinemann, 1988.
The University and the Leadership Factor in Nigerian Politics.
  Enugu, ABIC, 1988.

Editor, with Dubem Okafor, *Don't Let Him Die: An Anthology of
  Memorial Poems for Christopher Okigbo.*   Enugu, Fourth
  Dimension, 1978.
Editor, with C.L. Innes, *African Short Stories.*   London,
  Heinemann, 1985.

*

Bibliography: in *Africana Library Journal* (New York), Spring 1970.

Critical Studies: *The Novels of Chinua Achebe* by G.D. Killam,
London, Heinemann, and New York, Africana, 1969, revised edition,
as *The Writings of Chinua Achebe,* Heinemann, 1977; *Chinua
Achebe* by Arthur Ravenscroft, London, Longman, 1969, revised
edition, 1977; *Chinua Achebe* by David Carroll, New York, Twayne,
1970, revised edition, London, Macmillan, 1980; *Chinua Achebe et
la tragédie de l'histoire* by Thomas Melone, Paris, Présence
Africaine, 1973; *Chinua Achebe* by Kate Turkington, London,
Arnold, 1977; *Critical Perspectives on Chinua Achebe* edited by
Bernth Lindfors and C.L. Innes, London, Heinemann, and
Washington, D.C., Three Continents, 1978; *Achebe's World: The
Historical and Cultural Context of the Novels of Chinua Achebe* by
Robert M. Wren, Washington, D.C., Three Continents, 1980,
London, Longman, 1981; *The Four Novels of Chinua Achebe: A
Critical Study* by Benedict C. Njoku, Bern, Switzerland, Lang, 1984;
L'Oeuvre de Chinua Achebe by Denise Coussy, Paris, Présence
Africaine, 1985.

*   *   *

Chinua Achebe's fiction is well-known to secondary school
children in English-speaking Africa because some of his novels
written for adults are included in school syllabuses. But Achebe also
writes fiction especially for children that he hopes will entertain,
excite, educate, and retrieve "our valid culture," e.g., Nigerian and
Igbo culture (*New Culture 1,* 1979, no. 9).
  The hero of *Chike and the River* comes from Umuofia, the same
village depicted in *Things Fall Apart.* Like Achebe's novels for
adults, *Chike and the River* includes proverbs, folk tales, dialogue
appropriate to the status of the speakers, and cultural details that are
unobtrusively woven into the story. Chike goes to the city of Onitsha
to live with his uncle, and learns that Onitsha is different from
Umuofia, but not necessarily better. Chike wants to cross the Niger
River from Onitsha to Asaba in a ferry, but he has no money to pay
the fare. In his efforts to obtain money the hero learns that one must
not write dishonest letters to British pen pals, has an encounter with
a money doubler, narrowly escapes paying for a bicycle he accidentally damages, and washes cars. Although all ends well, Chike's ferry
trip nearly turns into a disaster when he misses the return ferry and
the lorry in which he is sleeping is stolen by cloth thieves. This
fast-moving adventure story emphasizes "good" values which are

both implicit in the action and explicitly stated in proverbs.
  Achebe's other children's books are Igbo folk tales from which he
has created adventure stories. Achebe aims to create fictional situations in which children can identify themselves. In *How the Leopard
Got His Claws,* written with John Iroaganachi, the explanatory tale
of the title is greatly elaborated to include the story of how dog
became man's "slave," why animals are no longer friends, and why
hunter is the enemy of all animals. The story includes praise songs,
folk tales, and a deer's song, which is a poem "The Lament of the
Deer" by the late Nigerian poet Christopher Okigbo.
  The Drum and *The Flute* are also written in Igbo as *Igba* and *Oja.*
The Drum is based on a widespread West African folk tale about
tortoise's magic drum which he uses to feed other animals during a
drought. Achebe has created a situation in which the drum is obtained
from spirits in the underworld after tortoise threatens to kill a spirit
boy who eats a fruit that tortoise lost. Tortoise's desire for power and
aristocratic privileges leads to the drum being broken when he
appoints elephant as his drumbeater. After the drum is repaired and
produces too little food to satisfy the animal's greed, tortoise returns
to the underworld and again tricks the spirits into giving him a drum.
But this time the drum produces whips, wasps, and bees, which
explains why animals have been running in all directions ever since.
The story is told in contemporary language, and includes songs,
"traditional" rituals, and ideophones, such as "Aja mbene, Mbe
mbene, aja mbene" for tortoise's footsteps. Stylistically *The Flute* is
a similar story. It is based on a widespread folk tale theme of a woman
who is jealous of gifts that her co-wife's son obtains from spirits with
a magic flute, so she sends her own ill-mannered son to obtain similar
gifts, but is rewarded with death in the form of leprosy, smallpox,
and yaws.
  Achebe's children's fiction is characterized by the same creative
imagination and writing skill as his fiction for adults. Although it is
based on Nigerian and Igbo cultural traditions, its universal themes
make it understandable to children throughout Africa.

—Nancy J. Schmidt

———

ADAMS, Richard (George). British. Born in Newbury,
Berkshire, 9 May 1920. Educated at Bradfield College, Berkshire;
Worcester College, Oxford, B.A. in modern history 1948, M.A.
1953. Served in the British Army, 1940–45. Married Barbara
Elizabeth Acland in 1949; two daughters. Worked in the Ministry of
Housing and Local Government, London, 1948–68; Assistant
Secretary, Department of the Environment, London, 1968–74.
Writer-in-residence, University of Florida, Gainesville, 1975, and
Hollins College, Virginia, 1976. President, Royal Society for the
Prevention of Cruelty to Animals, 1980–82 (resigned). Independent
Conservative candidate for Spelthorne, 1983. Recipient: Library
Association Carnegie Medal, 1972; *Guardian* award, 1973. Fellow,
Royal Society of Literature, 1975. Agent: David Higham Associates
Ltd., 5–8 Lower John Street, London WIR 4HA. Address: 26 Church
Street, Whitchurch, Hampshire, England.

PUBLICATIONS FOR CHILDREN

Fiction

Watership Down.   London, Rex Collings, 1972; New York, Mac-
  millan, 1974.
Shardik.   London, Allen Lane-Rex Collings, 1974; New York,
  Simon and Schuster, 1975.

The Plague Dogs, illustrated by A. Wainwright. London, Allen
  Lane-Rex Collings, 1977; New York, Knopf, 1978.
The Bureaucats, illustrated by Robin Jacques. London, Viking
  Kestrel, 1985.

Verse

The Tyger Voyage, illustrated by Nicola Bayley. London, Cape, and
  New York, Knopf, 1976.
The Ship's Cat, illustrated by Alan Aldridge. London, Cape, and
  New York, Knopf, 1977.

Other

Nature Through the Seasons, with Max Hooper, illustrated by David
  Goddard and Adrian Williams. London, Kestrel, and New York,
  Simon and Schuster, 1975.
Nature Day and Night, with Max Hooper, illustrated by David
  Goddard and Stephen Lee. London, Kestrel, and New York,
  Viking Press, 1978.
The Watership Down Film Picture Book. London, Allen Lane, and
  New York, Macmillan, 1978.
The Iron Wolf and Other Stories (folktales), illustrated by Yvonne
  Gilbert and Jennifer Campbell. London, Allen Lane, 1980; as
  The Unbroken Web, New York, Crown, 1980.

Editor, *Grimm's Fairy Tales,* illustrated by Pauline Ellison. Lon-
  don, Routledge, 1981.
Editor, *Richard Adams's Favourite Animal Stories,* illustrated by
  Beverley Butcher. London, Octopus, 1981.
Editor, *The Best of Ernest Thompson Seton.* London, Fontana,
  1982.

PUBLICATIONS FOR ADULTS

Novels

The Girl in a Swing. London, Allen Lane, and New York, Knopf,
  1980.
Maia. London, Viking, 1984; New York, Knopf, 1985.
Traveller. New York, Knopf, 1988; London, Hutchinson, 1989.

Verse

The Legend of Te Tuna. Los Angeles, Sylvester and Orphanos,
  1982; London, Sidgwick and Jackson, 1986.

Other

Voyage Through the Antarctic, with Ronald Lockley. London,
  Allen Lane, 1982; New York, Knopf, 1983.
A Nature Diary. London, Viking, 1985; New York, Viking, 1986.

Editor, *Occasional Poets: An Anthology.* London, Viking, 1986.

*

Richard Adams comments:
  I do not, myself, recognise a distinction between publications for
children and for adults. It has always seemed to me that there are
only books and readers, and I agree with C.S. Lewis's view that a
book which is not worth reading when you are sixty is not worth
reading when you are six. *Watership Down* has been marketed as a
novel for readers of any age, both in Great Britain and the U.S.A.,
as well as in other countries. *Shardik* also is read both by children

and adults. In my view, the distinction may do more harm than good
by deterring children from reading books which they would enjoy if
left to themselves but which they have been told are "for adults."

*   *   *

  Richard Adams's three main books for children are all rich fat
reads for any child (or adult) who likes *Jane Eyre* and wants to lurk
in a corner with a good book. These works demonstrate an expansive
imagination, producing in *Watership Down* and *Shardik* coherently
imagined alien worlds. Tragedy, danger, death, the dark things of life
are placed alongside the continual renewing quality of society itself,
producing a vital dynamism. All combine a strong dramatic narrative
with a rich appreciation of the complexities of society. The first two
works revolve around the necessity for society, the ways in which it
is created by a community, and the links between an individual and
his or her society and responsibilities. In the third, *The Plague Dogs,*
Adams is more concerned to show the ways in which different parts
of society touch and involve themselves with one another, and yet
remain essentially unchanged by this interaction.
  Watership Down, Adams's best-known book, is the absorbing
story of a small group of rabbits' quest to found a new warren. The
narrative forms three main parts: the quest by the rabbits leaving their
home warren inspired by a vision of destruction, the founding of a
new warren at Watership Down after many adventures, and the war
of revenge they become involved in with the warren Efrafra in their
search for does to keep their warren alive.
  Adams's rabbits are anthropomorphised in their abilities to adapt
and use imagination in approaching the problems and dangers that
this quest involves, and in their capacity to enjoy stories, as shown
by the tales of El-ahrairah, a rabbit hero who, like many folk heros,
is an ingenious, daring trickster. The sense of rabbit experience is
formed partly through the rabbits' representation of themselves, their
behaviour and responses, and partly by the perspective of a distanced
narrative. Within the bounds set by what is possible for rabbits to do,
Adams creates a rich, complex community, capable of recognition
of a spiritual dimension and of acting from emotional appreciation
of situations.
  The rabbit society that Adams depicts is relatively sophisticated,
with a hierarchy of Chief Rabbit, his officers the Owsla, and the
ordinary rabbits. Throughout the book Adams provides variations on
this simple structure. The Sandleford warren is an old-fashioned
society and represents the basic blueprint. Cowslip's warren illustrates the decadence that dependence and deception bring. This
warren survives on the food provided by a man who culls the rabbits
for profit—an unacknowledged relationship which is the source of
the warren's disease. Their survival instincts have decayed. They
have no Chief Rabbit and consider tales of El-ahrairah old-fashioned.
Their development of pictorial art and abstract poetry illustrates how
their increasing sophistication has made them artificial and unnatural. Efrafra, under the leadership of General Woundwort, represents a dictatorship based on war as indicated by the Chief Rabbit's
martial title. It is an oppressive society, overpopulated and
claustrophobic. Rabbits here have had their natural behaviour patterns and individuality destroyed in the pursuit of the security of the
warren. The does reabsorb their young, and discontent is violently
put down. General Woundwort's megolomania makes him pursue
and attempt to destroy the Watership Down warren when they have
managed, with great resource, to help rabbits escape his regime. This
episode provides a highly dramatic climax. The Watership Down
warren operates as a benevolent, semi-democratic dictatorship,
capable of change and responsive to experience. It is to some extent
an idealised rabbit society.
  Watership Down can be enjoyed on various levels, as a simple,
powerful narrative or as a political allegory. Children and adults will
relish both these elements, as well as the sensitive, accurate portrayal
of nature.

Shardik is a fantasy epic where human beings are the main actors, led on by the cult of the bear, the eponymous Shardik. This is a powerful, violent, dark novel, occasionally interrupted by somewhat excessive use of the epic simile, but rich in its appreciation of emotional complexity and the contingency inevitable between morality and religion. The coming of a real bear to be Shardik, the power of God, inspires the Ortelgans, considered barbaric outsiders in the Beklan empire, to rise up, take over the main city, and establish a fragile rule through Kelderek, the priest king. Kelderek is an everyman figure, a simple hunter before his peculiar relationship to the bear transforms him. However, the precarious rule of the Ortelgans is defeated by a rebellion, its collapse assured by Shardik's escape from the city. Kelderek, in his pursuit of the bear into the wildest and most primitive countries of the empire, descends from priest king to slave. During these travails, Kelderek discovers his own spiritual capacity and a final resolution of the spiritual with the social, as shown in the transformation of the cult of Shardik from an imperialistic war cult to a humanistic, child-orientated religion.

Children and adolescents have a sharp appreciation of injustice. *Shardik* does not allow simplistic assessments of injustice from man to man, or man to animal, but demonstrates human fallibility in pursuit of certainty and the inadequacy that this inevitably brings to light. In many ways this book will appeal to adolescent angst.

With *The Plague Dogs* Adams returns to 20th-century England. It is the story of two dogs who escape from an animal experimentation clinic, their survival in the fell land, and the human reaction to them. It is an anti-vivisection novel, but has much more resonance than such an easy description would imply. Adams presents the unresolvable dilemma of the recognition of animals as sensate members of creation and hence worthy of respect, and of their role as man's servants, dependent on their use for their existence. The narrative moves between the dogs' endeavours to become wild animals to survive, the efforts of the research establishment to evade responsibility for the by now sheep-killing dogs, the local people's attempts to destroy them, and the nationwide hue and cry raised by Digby Driver, an amoral gutter press journalist.

The irony used is at times heavyhanded and facetious—the animal research establishment is referred by its acronym, ARSE. Adams presents the human characters in a mannered, simplistic fashion to arouse the reader's indignation. Unfortunately the effect is occasionally facile. The most humane, sensitive writing in the book is reserved for the two dogs, and their experience of what, to them, is an unreal situation—trying to be wild dogs on the fells. One of the dogs, Snitter, has undergone brain surgery in an experiment attempting to divide the ability to discern between objective and subjective reality. Whether or not a dog is in fact capable of such thought is impossible to determine, but from Snitter's gradually increasing madness and expanding sense of all reality emerging from his own head comes some of Adams's finest writing.

The end of the novel is sentimental, and somewhat improbable. Adams makes use of Sir Philip Scott and Mr. Lockley as *dei ex machina*, resurrects Snitter's master from his hospital bed, and indicates some awakening of moral sympathy in Digby Driver.

As in Adams's other books, the basic story powerfully maintains the reader's attention. The straightforward injustice of the dogs' treatment will appeal to a child's sense of the inequity of the world, creating a passionate desire to see the dogs survive while recognising its improbability. *The Plague Dogs* acknowledges the complexities of the relationship between humans and animals, by presenting the brutality inherent in nature, and showing the varied, unresolved nature of human motivation.

—Lucy Saunders

———

ADOFF, Arnold. American. Born in New York City, 16 July 1935. Educated at City College of New York, B.A. 1956; Columbia University, New York, 1956–58; New School for Social Research, New York, 1965–67. Served in the New York National Guard. Married Virginia Hamilton, *q.v.,* in 1960; one daughter and one son. Teacher in public schools, New York, 1957–69. Since 1977 literary agent, Yellow Springs, Ohio. Visiting Professor, Queens College, Flushing, New York, 1986–87. Recipient: National Council of Teachers of English award, for poetry, 1988. Address: Box 293, Yellow Springs, Ohio 45387, U.S.A.

PUBLICATIONS FOR CHILDREN

Verse

Ma nda lA, illustrated by Emily McCully.   New York, Harper, 1971.
Black Is Brown Is Tan, illustrated by Emily McCully.   New York, Harper, 1973.
Make a Circle, Keep Us In: Poems for a Good Day, illustrated by Ronald Himler.   New York, Delacorte Press, 1975.
Big Sister Tells Me That I'm Black, illustrated by Lorenzo Lynch.   New York, Holt Rinehart, 1976.
Tornado!, illustrated by Ronald Himler.   New York, Delacorte Press, 1977.
Under the Early Morning Trees, illustrated by Ronald Himler.   New York, Dutton, 1978.
Where Wild Willy, illustrated by Emily McCully.   New York, Harper, 1978.
Eats, illustrated by Susan Russo.   New York, Lothrop, 1979.
I Am the Running Girl, illustrated by Ronald Himler.   New York, Harper, 1979.
Friend Dog, illustrated by Troy Howell.   New York, Lippincott, 1980.
Today We Are Brother and Sister, illustrated by Glo Coalson.   New York, Lothrop, 1981.
OUTside INside Poems, illustrated by John Steptoe.   New York, Lothrop, 1981.
Birds, illustrated by Troy Howell.   New York, Lippincott, 1982.
All the Colors of the Race, illustrated by John Steptoe.   New York, Lothrop, 1982.
The Cabbages Are Chasing the Rabbits, illustrated by Janet Stevens.   San Diego, Harcourt Brace, 1985.
Sports Pages, illustrated by Steven Kuzma.   New York, Lippincott, 1986.
Flamboyan, illustrated by Karen Barbour.   San Diego, Harcourt Brace, 1988.
Greens, illustrated by Betsy Lewin.   New York, Lothrop, 1988.

Other

Malcolm X, illustrated by John Wilson.   New York, Crowell, 1970.

Editor, *I Am the Darker Brother: An Anthology of Modern Poems by Negro Americans.*   New York, Macmillan, 1968.
Editor, *Black on Black: Commentaries by Negro Americans.*   New York, Macmillan, 1968.
Editor, *City in All Directions: An Anthology of Modern Poems,* illustrated by Donald Carrick.   New York, Macmillan, 1969.
Editor, *Black Out Loud: An Anthology of Modern Poems by Black Americans,* illustrated by Alvin Hollingsworth.   New York, Macmillan, 1970.
Editor, *Brothers and Sisters: Modern Stories by Black Americans.*   New York, Macmillan, 1970.
Editor, *It Is the Poem Singing into Your Eyes: An Anthology of New Young Poets.*   New York, Harper, 1971.

Editor, *The Poetry of Black America: An Anthology of the 20th Century.* New York, Harper, 1973.
Editor, *My Black Me: A Beginning Book of Black Poetry.* New York, Dutton, 1974.
Editor, *Celebrations: A New Anthology of Black American Poetry.* Chicago, Follett, 1977.

*   *   *

Arnold Adoff has distinguished himself as a poet, anthologist, and biographer. His poetry is notable for its pungent musical quality, best appreciated when read aloud. Unusual word, phrase, and sentence configurations, which may appear arbitrary on the page, take on a rhythmic logic when spoken. His poems range in tone and mood from the festive to the meditative, but a common element is a sense of gentle warmth. This warmth is most clearly evident in his affectionate family portraits. *Make a Circle, Keep Us In* follows one day in a family's life, with the family portrayed as a strong unit which nurtures and protects itself. *Black Is Brown Is Tan* describes the everyday experiences of an interracial family. It begins by focussing on the wide spectrum of colors apparent in family members: for mother,

> i am black
> i am a brown sugar gown
> a tasty tan and coffee pumpkin pie
> with dark brown eyes and almond ears
> and my face gets ginger red
> when i puff and yell you into bed

for father,

> i am white i am white
> i am light
> with pinks and tiny tans
> dark hair growing on my arms
> that darken in the summer sun
> brown eyes big yellow ears

and for the children,

> black is brown is tan
> is girl is boy
> is nose is face
> is all the colors
> of the race

For every hue there is an expression of delight, and the description of family life extends the focus beyond color to encompass a family's delight in each other.

Ma nda lA displays through colorful illustrations by Emily McCully an African family's activities, accompanied by Adoff's sing-song verse, a simple compilation of sounds which evoke a sense of celebration.

Adoff's sensitive and understated expressions of feelings are particularly evident in his poems which center on an individual child's thoughts. The young daughter of a black mother and white father explores her own sense of identity in *All the Colors of the Race,* a series of related poems. The poems contain a variety of emotions. The young girl expresses pride in her varied ancestry, and a sense of affiliation with all the colors, religions, and cultures which have contributed to create her unique self. There is humor in her perception of her racial make-up:

> At the meeting
>   they said they wanted to send
> one white
>   and one black kid to the celebration,
> to make it even and equal.
> So
> I said to just send me and it would still be
>   fair,
> and we could still
>   save one round-trip fare.
> Then they waited to see if I was smiling
> before they laughed,
>   and my motion lost because I forgot
>   I couldn't be a boy.

But there is also a melancholy tone in a description of a family outing as she shows her awareness of potential prejudice:

> We live the same: our way,
> and walk
>   the same;
> and talk,
>   no matter where we live
>   and go.
> And most people
> smile at us on sunny Ohio afternoons
>   in parks and restaurants.
> But
> while we talk and smile
> and eat
>   our way through
> Sundays, we keep a corner
>   of our eyes for
>   any
>   bad guys.

OUTside INside Poems is the introspective yet simply expressed going on outside himself with what he's actually feeling. In *Big Sister Tells Me That I'm Black* a small boy offers a rousing cheer for himself and all who are like him.

Eats celebrates one of life's more carnal pleasures; it's a lively ode to good food and the joys of eating. *The Cabbages Are Chasing the Rabbits* is an energetic romp in which cabbages turn the tables on the rabbits who have been nibbling on them, and the result is a wild and crazy pursuit. With lyrical blank verse, *Sports Pages* extolls the thrill of victory and the agony of defeat in 37 poems celebrating young athletes, while *Greens* is an exuberant collection that presents imaginative observations on things that are the color green, from grasshoppers to pea soup.

Adoff captures the spirit of a growing child in *Flamboyan*. Set on an island in Puerto Rico, this is a rhythmic melange of poetry and prose which describes the days and dreams of a young girl whose hair is the color of the Flamboyan tree blossoms.

As an anthologist, Adoff is noted especially for his thoughtfully selected collections of black poetry which center on uplifting themes of hope, survival, and triumph. *My Black Me: A Beginning Book of Black Poetry* contains poems accessible to younger children by such poets as Langston Hughes, Nikki Giovanni, and Lucille Clifton. *I Am the Darker Brother: An Anthology of Modern Poems by Negro Americans* is a collection of more complex and sophisticated poems suitable for older children. *Malcolm X* is a forthright account of major events in the life of the controversial black leader. While limited in scope, the biography nonetheless offers a solid, general overview of the man and his mission.

A constant factor in Arnold Adoff's work is the imaginative expression of faith in people and their spirit. Each work, in its own way, salutes the human condition and its ability to triumph.

—Marilyn Kaye

———

AGARD, John. British. Born in British Guiana (now Guyana). Emigrated to England in 1977. Has worked as an actor and a performer with a jazz group. Recipient: Casa de las Américas Poetry prize (Cuba), 1982; Children's Rights Workshop Other award, 1986. Address: c/o Hodder and Stoughton, 47 Bedford Square, London WC1B 3DP, England.

PUBLICATIONS FOR CHILDREN

Fiction

Letters for Lettie and Other Stories, illustrated by Errol Lloyd. London, Bodley Head, 1979.
Dig Away Two-Hole Tim, illustrated by Jennifer Northway. London, Bodley Head, 1981.

Verse

I Din Do Nuttin and Other Poems, illustrated by Susanna Gretz. London, Bodley Head, 1983.
Say It Again, Granny! Twenty Poems from Caribbean Proverbs, illustrated by Susanna Gretz. London, Bodley Head, 1986.
Lend Me Your Wings, illustrated by Adrienne Kennaway. London, Hodder and Stoughton, 1987.

PUBLICATIONS FOR ADULTS

Verse

Shoot Me with Flowers. Privately printed, 1973.
Man to Pan. Havana, Casa de las Américas, 1982.
Limbo Dancer in the Dark. Privately printed, 1983.
Mangoes and Bullets: Selected and New Poems 1972–84. London, Pluto, 1985.

*   *   *

Try the best with what you have right now
If you don't have horse, then ride cow.

It is in his poetry that John Agard makes his greatest contribution to children's literature. Like the best authors, he brings something unique to children's experience—a view of the world tempered by his own childhood in Guyana, a feeling for the rhythms and cadences of its language, and a sophisticated understanding of the advantages and limitations of several forms of English. That he can make the "standard" forms work superbly is evident from many of his poems for adults. For children, with whom he communicates more directly, the lyrical Guyanese forms serve his purposes to perfection.

Agard is not only a literary poet but also a performing poet and has a strong sense of his audience. When he writes for children, he seems to see them sitting at his feet. He is more interested in the ideas and words he is delivering to them than in the creation of complex fictional characters with whom his readers might engage. This can

be a weakness: his first book, *Letters for Lettie,* is anecdotal and Lettie herself has little real character except for a Pollyanna-like optimism—seldom disappointed by her experiences—and an insatiable propensity for writing letters to everyone in sight. Though the other characters are mostly one-dimensional, Lettie's parents are more fully realised, as creatures from that other, adult world, who are caring and supportive of their daughter. The physical surroundings of the village are clearly suggested, a feeling of the community builds up, and one is left with a sense of having entered a pleasant and ultimately convincingly evoked world, even if nothing very much happens there.

Dig Away Two-Hole Tim has much of the same quality: it is chiefly his love of holes that distinguishes Tim, but a whole world of family, friends, creatures, plants, and environment comes to life. Fewer words and more pictures—a wholly successful collaboration with artist Jennifer Northway—require Agard to use language with economy: essentially a poet's art, and the poetic rather than the narrative form is dominant.

In *Lend Me Your Wings,* Agard is clearly working in verse and the happy collaboration with prize-winning artist Adrienne Kennaway results in a delightful book. Sister Fish and Brother Bird swap fins for wings and explore the alluring environments each has seen only from afar. But after a few hazardous encounters in sky or river, they are both grateful to return quickly to their own environments.

In his two collections of "official" verse for children, Agard is in his element. He shares with a special few contemporary children's poets an understanding of children and the way they see the adult world—which is not at all how adults see it—that enables him to speak directly to them. This joyous gift of empathy is proclaimed in the title poem of *I Din Do Nuttin* and echoes throughout the book. Next, he adds his assimilation of the wisdom of the common people, embodied by Granny in *Say It Again, Granny!* and her aphorisms for every eventuality, around which he has built his verses. Finally, he flavours the mixture with characteristic *joi de vivre* and channels it all into two highly disciplined but wholly disarming collections of poems that children will grasp at once and return to with delight.

—Gillian Klein

———

AHLBERG, Allan. British. Born 5 June 1938. Educated at Sunderland College of Education, 1963–66. Married the illustrator Janet Ahlberg (née Hall) in 1969; one daughter. Has had various jobs, including postman, soldier, schoolteacher, grave digger, and plumber's mate. Recipient: Children's Rights Workshop Other award, 1980; *Parents* magazine Best Book for Babies award, 1985; Maschler award, 1986; Federation of Children's Book Groups award, 1987. Address: 20 Nether Hall Lane, Birstall, Leicestershire LE4 4DT, England.

PUBLICATIONS FOR CHILDREN

Fiction

Brick Street Boys (Here Are the Brick Street Boys, A Place to Play, Sam the Referee, Fred's Dream, The Great Marathon Football Match), illustrated by Janet Ahlberg. London, Collins, 5 vols., 1975–76.
Burglar Bill, illustrated by Janet Ahlberg. London, Heinemann, and New York, Greenwillow, 1977.
Jeremiah in the Dark Woods, illustrated by Janet Ahlberg. London, Kestrel, 1977; New York, Viking Press, 1978.

The Vanishment of Thomas Tull, illustrated by Janet Ahlberg. London, A. and C. Black, and New York, Scribner, 1977.

The One and Only Two Heads, illustrated by Janet Ahlberg. London, Collins, 1979.

Son of a Gun, illustrated by Janet Ahlberg. London, Heinemann, 1979.

The Little Worm Book, illustrated by Janet Ahlberg. London, Granada, 1979; New York, Viking Press, 1980.

Two Wheels, Two Heads, illustrated by Janet Ahlberg. London, Collins, 1979.

Funnybones, illustrated by Janet Ahlberg. London, Heinemann, and New York, Greenwillow, 1980.

The History of a Pair of Sinners, illustrated by John Lawrence. London, Granada, 1980.

The Baby's Catalogue, illustrated by Janet Ahlberg. London, Kestrel, and Boston, Little Brown, 1982.

Ten in a Bed, illustrated by André Amstutz. London, Granada, 1983.

The Cinderella Show, illustrated by Janet Ahlberg. London and New York, Viking Kestrel, 1986.

The Jolly Postman, illustrated by Janet Ahlberg. London, Heinemann, and Boston, Little Brown, 1986.

Woof!, illustrated by Fritz Wegner. London, Viking Kestrel, 1986.

The Clothes Horse and Other Stories, illustrated by Janet Ahlberg. London, Viking Kestrel, 1987; New York, Viking Kestrel, 1988.

Verse

Cops and Robbers, illustrated by Janet Ahlberg. London, Heinemann, and New York, Greenwillow, 1978.

Each Peach Pear Plum, illustrated by Janet Ahlberg. London, Kestrel, 1978; New York, Viking Press, 1979.

Peepo!, illustrated by Janet Ahlberg. London, Kestrel, 1981; as *Peek-a-Boo!,* New York, Viking Press, 1981.

Please, Mrs. Butler, illustrated by Fritz Wegner. London, Kestrel, 1983.

Daisychains (*That's My Baby!, Summer Snowmen, Which Witch?, Ready Teddy Go, Monster Munch, The Good Old Dolls, Rent-a-Robot, Clowning About, One True Santa*), illustrated by Janet Ahlberg and André Amstutz. London, Heinemann, 9 vols., 1983–85.

The Mighty Slide, illustrated by Charlotte Voake. London and New York, Viking Kestrel, 1988.

Other

The Old Joke Book, illustrated by Janet Ahlberg. London, Kestrel, 1976; New York, Viking Press, 1977.

Happy Families (readers; U.S. editions as *Wacky Families*):

  Mr. Biff the Boxer, illustrated by Janet Ahlberg. London, Kestrel, 1980; New York, Golden Press, 1982.

  Mrs. Plug the Plumber, illustrated by Joe Wright. London, Kestrel, 1980; New York, Golden Press, 1982.

  Mrs. Wobble the Waitress, illustrated by Janet Ahlberg. London, Kestrel, 1980; New York, Golden Press, 1982.

  Master Salt the Sailor's Son, illustrated by André Amstutz. London, Kestrel, 1980; New York, Golden Press, 1982.

  Miss Jump the Jockey, illustrated by André Amstutz. London, Kestrel, 1980.

  Mr. Cosmo the Conjuror, illustrated by Joe Wright. London, Kestrel, 1980.

  Miss Brick the Builder's Baby, illustrated by Colin McNaughton. London, Penguin, 1981; New York, Golden Press, 1982.

  Mr. Buzz the Beeman, illustrated by Faith Jaques. London, Penguin, 1981; New York, Golden Press, 1982.

  Mr. and Mrs. Hay the Horse, illustrated by Colin McNaughton. London, Penguin, 1981; New York, Golden Press, 1982.

  Mrs. Lather's Laundry, illustrated by André Amstutz. London, Penguin, 1981; New York, Golden Press, 1982.

  Master Money the Millionaire, illustrated by André Amstutz. London, Penguin, 1981.

  Mr. Tick the Teacher, illustrated by Faith Jaques. London, Penguin, 1981.

  Miss Dose the Doctors' Daughter, illustrated by Fritz Wegner. London, Viking Kestrel, 1988.

  Master Bun the Bakers' Boy, illustrated by Fritz Wegner. London, Viking Kestrel, 1988.

  Mrs. Jolly's Joke Shop, illustrated by Colin McNaughton. London, Viking Kestrel, 1988.

  Mr. Creep the Crook, illustrated by André Amstutz. London, Viking Kestrel, 1988.

The Ha Ha Bonk Book (joke book), illustrated by Janet Ahlberg. London, Kestrel, and New York, Penguin, 1982.

Help Your Child to Read (*Fast Frog, Silly Sheep, Double Ducks, Bad Bear, Poorly Pig, Rubber Rabbit, Hip-Hippo-Ray, King Kangaroo, Mister Wolf, Spider Spy, Tell-Tale Tiger, Travelling Moose*), illustrated by Eric Hill and André Amstutz. London, Granada, 12 vols., 1982–83.

Foldaways (*Circus, Families, Monsters, Zoo*), illustrated by Colin McNaughton. London, Granada, 4 vols., 1984.

Slot Books (*Yum Yum, Playmates*), illustrated by Janet Ahlberg. London, Viking Kestrel, 2 vols., 1984–85; New York, Viking Kestrel, 2 vols., 1985.

Red Nose Readers (*Help!, Big Bad Pig, Happy Worm, Fee Fi Fo Fum, Make a Face, So Can I, Jumping, Bear's Birthday, Me and My Friend, Shirley's Shops, Push the Dog, Crash! Bang! Wallop!, Blow Me Down!, Giant Days, Good Manners Gorilla, Look Out for the Seals!, One Two Flea! Tiny Tim, Tell Us a Story*), illustrated by Colin McNaughton. London, Walker, 18 vols., 1985–86; first 4 vols. published New York, Random House, 1985.

Starting School, illustrated by Janet Ahlberg. London and New York, Viking Kestrel, 1988.

*

Allan Ahlberg comments:

Janet and I make picture books for our own pleasure and to earn a living. I've had other jobs, but writing is the best so far I've come upon: I think I'll stick at it.

How we work: I write; Janet illustrates; together we design. We are book *makers* rather than author and illustrator. What matters to us is the *printed bound object:* the whole book, cover to cover.

*   *   *

"Once upon a time there were three bears, seven dwarfs, five gorillas, a frog prince, some sleeping beauties...." This is the opening of *Jeremiah in the Dark Woods.* The opening and the book as a whole are good examples of Allan Ahlberg's liking for the conventions of storytelling, conventions which children enjoy too. In *Jeremiah* fairytale stories, characters, and themes are played with but there is no sense of his patronising the child audience. He understands that audience too well to do that—understands its conservatism and its delight in rediscovering and wearing out the already well-worn. The *Ha Ha Bonk Book* and *The Old Joke Book* both show this understanding at work. The latter in both its format and characterisation celebrates the world of the comic and children's delight in the same jokes they have been telling for the last five thousand years.

But a sense of convention can go deeper than that and I hope I won't be misunderstood when I say that there is something wholesome and decent about all his books. They don't present a troubled world or set out to disturb. In *Burglar Bill* and *Cops and*

Robbers policemen wear nice blue uniforms, are a bit dim, and, without the slightest whiff of corruption, get their man after a chase *on foot.* The villains—striped jerseys and masks are *de rigeur*—are not too villainous and are quite capable of reform if, like Burglar Bill, they meet the right Burglar Betty to settle down with.

That sense of the virtues of domestic life shows itself to best effect in the series of readers Ahlberg has produced under the general title of *Happy Families.* If all junior readers were like these how many more children who *can* read, *would.* Again we have a world in which people like each other, share and help. "And a happy time was had by all" (the ending of *Mr. Biff*) might stand for all of them: no irony, no self-parody intended.

In *Peepo!* we find another celebration of the happy family. The organising presence of the familiar game all parents play with their children is reworked in book form—you peep through a hole in the page onto a series of domestic scenes. The scenes are overtly nostalgic—of Ahlberg's own childhood and growing up through the war—which leads me to suggest that as with all good writers for children his sense of what will appeal to them derives from a strong sense of his own childhood. There is too that familiar and absolutely uncomplicated sense of security: "He sees the landing mirror/ With its rainbow rim/ And a mother with a baby/ Just like him./ He sees the bedroom door/ The cot made ready/ His father kissing him goodnight/ His ball/ And his teddy."

—Eric Hadley

AIKEN, Joan (Delano). British. Born in Rye, Sussex, 4 September 1924; daughter of the writer Conrad Aiken; sister of the writer Jane Aiken Hodge. Educated at Wychwood School, Oxford, 1936–40. Married 1) Ronald George Brown in 1945 (died 1955), one son and one daughter; 2) Julius Goldstein in 1976. Worked for the BBC, 1942–43; information officer, then librarian, United Nations Information Centre, London, 1943–49; sub-editor and features editor, *Argosy,* London, 1955–60; copywriter, J. Walter Thompson, London, 1960–61. Recipient: *Guardian* award, 1969; Mystery Writers of America Edgar Allan Poe award, 1972. Agent: A.M. Heath, 40–42 William IV Street, London WC2N 4DD; or, Brandt and Brandt, 1501 Broadway, New York, New York 10036, U.S.A. Address: The Hermitage, East Street, Petworth, West Sussex GU28 0AB, England.

PUBLICATIONS FOR CHILDREN

Fiction

All You've Ever Wanted and Other Stories, illustrated by Pat Marriott. London, Cape, 1953.
More Than You Bargained For and Other Stories, illustrated by Pat Marriott. London, Cape, 1955; New York, Abelard Schuman, 1957.
The Kingdom and the Cave, illustrated by Dick Hart. London, Abelard Schuman, 1960; New York, Doubleday, 1974.
The Wolves of Willoughby Chase, illustrated by Pat Marriott. London, Cape, 1962; New York, Doubleday, 1963.
Black Hearts in Battersea, illustrated by Robin Jacques. New York, Doubleday, 1964; London, Cape, 1965.
Nightbirds on Nantucket, illustrated by Pat Marriott. London, Cape, and New York, Doubleday, 1966.
The Whispering Mountain. London, Cape, 1968; New York, Doubleday, 1969.
A Necklace of Raindrops and Other Stories, illustrated by Jan Pienkowski. London, Cape, and New York, Doubleday, 1968.
Armitage, Armitage, Fly Away Home, illustrated by Betty Fraser. New York, Doubleday, 1968.
A Small Pinch of Weather and Other Stories, illustrated by Pat Marriott. London, Cape, 1969.
Night Fall. London, Macmillan, 1969; New York, Holt Rinehart, 1971.
Smoke from Cromwell's Time and Other Stories. New York, Doubleday, 1970.
The Green Flash and Other Tales of Horror, Suspense, and Fantasy. New York, Holt Rinehart, 1971.
The Cuckoo Tree, illustrated by Pat Marriott. London, Cape, and New York, Doubleday, 1971.
All and More, illustrated by Pat Marriott. London, Cape, 1971.
A Harp of Fishbones and Other Stories, illustrated by Pat Marriott. London, Cape, 1972.
Arabel's Raven, illustrated by Quentin Blake. London, BBC Publications, 1972; New York, Doubleday, 1974.
The Escaped Black Mamba, illustrated by Quentin Blake. London, BBC Publications, 1973.
All But a Few. London, Penguin, 1974.
The Bread Bin, illustrated by Quentin Blake. London, BBC Publications, 1974.
Midnight Is a Place. London, Cape, and New York, Viking Press, 1974.
Not What You Expected: A Collection of Short Stories. New York, Doubleday, 1974.
Mortimer's Tie, illustrated by Quentin Blake. London, BBC Publications, 1976.
A Bundle of Nerves: Stories of Horror, Suspense, and Fantasy. London, Gollancz, 1976.
The Faithless Lollybird and Other Stories, illustrated by Pat Marriott. London, Cape, 1977; New York, Doubleday, 1978.
The Far Forests: Tales of Romance, Fantasy, and Suspense. New York, Viking Press, 1977.
Go Saddle the Sea, illustrated by Pat Marriott. New York, Doubleday, 1977; London, Cape, 1978.
Tale of a One-Way Street and Other Stories, illustrated by Jan Pienkowski. London, Cape, 1978; New York, Doubleday, 1979.
Mice and Mendelson, music by John Sebastian Brown, illustrated by Babette Cole. London, Cape, 1978.
Mortimer and the Sword Excalibur, illustrated by Quentin Blake. London, BBC Publications, 1979.
The Spiral Stair, illustrated by Quentin Blake. London, BBC Publications, 1979.
A Touch of Chill: Stories of Horror, Suspense, and Fantasy. London, Gollancz, 1979; New York, Delacorte Press, 1980.
Arabel and Mortimer (includes *Mortimer's Tie, The Spiral Stair, Mortimer and the Sword Excalibur*), illustrated by Quentin Blake. London, Cape, 1980; New York, Doubleday, 1981.
The Shadow Guests. London, Cape, and New York, Delacorte Press, 1980.
Mortimer's Portrait on Glass, illustrated by Quentin Blake. London, Hodder and Stoughton, 1981.
The Stolen Lake, illustrated by Pat Marriott. London, Cape, and New York, Delacorte Press, 1981.
The Mystery of Mr. Jones's Disappearing Taxi, illustrated by Quentin Blake. London, Hodder and Stoughton, 1982.
A Whisper in the Night: Stories of Horror, Suspense, and Fantasy. London, Gollancz, 1982; New York, Delacorte Press, 1984.
Mortimer's Cross, illustrated by Quentin Blake. London, Cape, 1983; New York, Harper, 1984.
Bridle the Wind, illustrated by Pat Marriott. London, Cape, and New York, Delacorte Press, 1983.
The Kitchen Warriors, illustrated by Jo Worth. London, BBC Publications, 1983.

Up the Chimney Down (stories), illustrated by Pat Marriott. London, Cape, and New York, Harper, 1984.

Fog Hounds, Wind Cat, Sea Mice. London, Macmillan, 1984.

Mortimer Says Nothing and Other Stories, illustrated by Quentin Blake. London, Cape, 1985; New York, Harper, 1987.

The Last Slice of Rainbow and Other Stories, illustrated by Margaret Walty. London, Cape, 1985; New York, Harper, 1988.

Dido and Pa, illustrated by Pat Marriott. London, Cape, and New York, Delacorte Press, 1986.

Past Eight O'Clock: Goodnight Stories, illustrated by Jan Pienkowski. London, Cape, 1986.

A Goose on Your Grave. London, Gollancz, 1987.

The Moon's Revenge, illustrated by Alan Lee. London, Cape, and New York, Knopf, 1987.

The Teeth of the Gale, illustrated by Pat Marriott. London, Cape, and New York, Harper, 1988.

The Erl King's Daughter, illustrated by Paul Warren. London, Heinemann, 1988.

Voices. London, Hippo, 1988.

Give Yourself a Fright: Thirteen Tales of the Supernatural. New York, Delacorte Press, 1989.

Plays

Winterthing, music by John Sebastian Brown, illustrated by Arvis Stewart (produced Albany, New York, 1977). New York, Holt Rinehart, 1972; included in *Winterthing, and The Mooncusser's Daughter,* 1973.

Winterthing, and The Mooncusser's Daughter, music by John Sebastian Brown. London, Cape, 1973; *The Mooncusser's Daughter* published separately, New York, Viking Press, 1974.

Street, music by John Sebastian Brown, illustrated by Arvis Stewart (produced London, 1977). New York, Viking Press, 1978.

Moon Mill (produced London, 1982).

Television Plays: *The Dark Streets of Kimballs Green,* 1976; *The Apple of Trouble,* 1977; *Midnight Is a Place* (serial), from her own story, 1977; *The Rose of Puddle Fratrum,* 1978; *Armitage, Armitage, Fly Away Home,* from her own story, 1978.

Verse

The Skin Spinners, illustrated by Ken Rinciari. New York, Viking Press, 1976.

Other

The Kingdom under the Sea and Other Stories (retellings), illustrated by Jan Pienkowski. London, Cape, 1971.

Translator, *The Angel Inn,* by Contessa de Ségur, illustrated by Pat Marriott. London, Cape, 1976; Owings Mills, Maryland, Stemmer House, 1978.

PUBLICATIONS FOR ADULTS

Novels

The Silence of Herondale. New York, Doubleday, 1964; London, Gollancz, 1965.

The Fortune Hunters. New York, Doubleday, 1965.

Trouble with Product X. London, Gollancz, 1966; as *Beware of the Banquet,* New York, Doubleday, 1966.

Hate Begins at Home. London, Gollancz, 1967; as *Dark Interval,* New York, Doubleday, 1967.

The Ribs of Death. London, Gollancz, 1967; as *The Crystal Crow,*

New York, Doubleday, 1968.

The Embroidered Sunset. London, Gollancz, and New York, Doubleday, 1970.

Died on a Rainy Sunday. London, Gollancz, and New York, Holt Rinehart, 1972.

The Butterfly Picnic. London, Gollancz, 1972; as *A Cluster of Separate Sparks,* New York, Doubleday, 1972.

Voices in an Empty House. London, Gollancz, and New York, Doubleday, 1975.

Castle Barebane. London, Gollancz, and New York, Viking Press, 1976.

Last Movement. London, Gollancz, and New York, Doubleday, 1977.

The Five-Minute Marriage. London, Gollancz, 1977; New York, Doubleday, 1978.

The Smile of the Stranger. London, Gollancz, and New York, Doubleday, 1978.

The Lightning Tree. London, Gollancz, 1980; as *The Weeping Ash,* New York, Doubleday, 1980.

The Young Lady from Paris. London, Gollancz, 1982; as *The Girl from Paris,* New York, Doubleday, 1982.

Foul Matter. London, Gollancz, and New York, Doubleday, 1983.

Mansfield Revisited. London, Gollancz, 1984; New York, Doubleday, 1985.

Deception. London, Gollancz, 1987; as *If I Were You,* New York, Doubleday, 1987.

Blackground. London, Gollancz, and New York, Doubleday, 1989.

Short Stories

The Windscreen Weepers and Other Tales of Horror and Suspense. London, Gollancz, 1969.

Other

The Way to Write for Children. London, Elm Tree, 1982; New York, St. Martin's Press, 1983.

*

Joan Aiken comments:

My books for children fall into three categories. Collections of short stories which may be described as fairytales—i.e., magical, fantastic, supernatural, though set mainly in the present day. Full-length books for a slightly older age-group, say 11–14. These contain no magic or supernatural elements, but are set mostly in an imaginary 19th century. Shorter stories for younger children of a semi-fantastic nature about talking or at least extra-intelligent animals—i.e., *Arabel's Raven, Mice and Mendelson.*

*   *   *

For sheer energy and exuberance, Joan Aiken has no rival among contemporary English children's writers except perhaps Leon Garfield. Her stories heap incident on incident, invention on invention, in a spendthrift way that only a writer with endless imaginative resources could afford. Her versatility is as notable as her vigour. Besides her numerous novels and collections of original short stories, her writing for children includes plays, verse, retold tales, and a translation.

If there is a main line running through her fiction, it is the loose sequence of deliberately unhistorical novels which began in 1962 with *The Wolves of Willoughby Chase.* The action of these novels takes place in a period of English history that never was. In most of them, it is the reign of King James III, who came to the throne in 1832 and remained there in spite of the machinations of those who support the Hanoverian Pretender ("Bring back, bring back, oh bring back my Georgie to me," they sing). In *The Wolves of Willoughby Chase* wolves, driven by severe continental winters to migrate to Britain through the recently opened Channel Tunnel, roam the bleak northern landscape in which stands the turreted stately home of Sir Willoughby Green. But even the wolves are no more fierce and predatory than the wicked governess, Miss Slighcarp, whose villainy is duly exposed in a thorough, satisfying denouement.

Black Hearts in Battersea is largely about Hanoverian conspiracies against Good King James. Among the characters encountered in this story are the eccentric Duke of Battersea; his heir, Lord Bakerloo; and the King himself, a little, dapper, elderly Scottish gentleman who remarks, "Och, well, noo, Battersea…how's your gude lady?" There is also the sharp-eyed, sharp-tongued cockney waif Dido Twite, who in turn reappears as the heroine of *Nightbirds on Nantucket*. In the latter book, a plan to assassinate the King by means of a long-distance cannon fired across the Atlantic from Nantucket Island is fortunately thwarted.

By the time of *The Cuckoo Tree*, James III has gone to his rest, to be succeeded by Richard IV. The Hanoverians are still busy, intending to dispose of Richard and all the great ones of the land by a dastardly deed at the Coronation, but they are foiled again when Dido Twite rides to the rescue on an elephant. In *The Stolen Lake* the resourceful Dido is in action again, dealing with the problems of New Cumbria, Britain's oldest ally in Roman America (where peasants speak Latin). This book adds unlegend to unhistory by reviving King Arthur and facing him with a fat, sinister, 1300-year-old Guinevere who has been loyally preserving herself for him.

The James III novels are rich in humour and incident: full of wild exaggeration, staggering improbability and riotous melodrama. Their intricate plots, energetic development, and prolific character creation, together with a strong tendency to caricature, suggest the influence of Dickens. Nevertheless, Aiken is very much her own woman, and doesn't follow trodden paths, even her own. Since the mid-1970's she has written several novels for children with a somewhat different flavour and subject matter. In *Midnight Is a Place* the scene is largely a Satanic northern town at the time of the Industrial Revolution. *Go Saddle the Sea* began a sequence of adventure novels set in an unusual historical context—that of Spain in the years of upheaval that followed the Napoleonic wars. In the first book, Felix Brooke, orphaned son of an English soldier and a high-born Spanish lady, is making his way across Spain in quest of his English relatives; in the second, *Bridle the Wind*, he rescues a youngster called Juan from dreadful dangers and makes the startling discovery that Juan is really Juana; the third book, *The Teeth of the Gale*, has the two of them, now 18, join in a mission with a romantic outcome.

Aiken's story collections must receive shorter shrift here than they deserve. *All You've Ever Wanted* and *More Than You Bargained For* preceded the novels but display the same strong line in humorous fantasy and lavish use of ideas. Most of the stories are set in a modern world in which magic is an everyday matter, casually taken for granted. 30 years on from this pair *Up the Chimney Down* appeared, showing undiminished powers of invention; in fact stories from any of these three books would be at home in any of the others. In between had come, among much else, two brilliant collaborations with the artist Jan Pienkowski: *A Necklace of Raindrops*, which is a group of eight modern fairy stories for younger children, and *The Kingdom under the Sea*, retellings of East European folktales.

Arabel's Raven is the first of several books about Arabel and her irrepressible pet raven Mortimer, who likes diamonds and slot-machines and potato crisps and whose vocabulary consists, appropriately, of the one word "Nevermore."

Among Aiken's plays, *The Mooncusser's Daughter* is especially notable. Set on "the seacoast of Bohemia," it draws upon Shakespeare's *The Tempest* and *The Winter's Tale*, and includes pastiches of several Shakespeare songs: "When Force Twelve Gale doth loudly blow," for instance, and "Come unto this rockbound coast," and "O Caliban, where are you roaming?" Parodying Shakespeare is perhaps the ultimate literary audacity, but Joan Aiken gets away with it. She can get away with anything.

—John Rowe Townsend

AINSWORTH, Ruth (Gallard). British. Born in Manchester, Lancashire, 16 October 1908. Educated at Ipswich High School; Froebel Training Centre, Leicester. Married Frank L. Gilbert in 1935; three sons. Script writer, *Listen with Mother* and *English for Schools* series, BBC, London. Address: Field End, Corbridge, Northumberland NE45 5JP, England.

PUBLICATIONS FOR CHILDREN

Fiction

Tales about Tony, illustrated by Cora E.M. Paterson.   London, Epworth Press, 1936.
Mr. Popcorn's Friends.   London, Epworth Press, 1938.
The Gingerbread House.   London, Epworth Press, 1938.
The Ragamuffins.   London, Epworth Press, 1939.
Richard's First Term.   London, Epworth Press, 1940.
Five and a Dog.   London, Epworth Press, 1949.
"Listen with Mother" Tales, illustrated by Astrid Walford.   London, Heinemann, 1951.
Rufty Tufty the Golliwog, illustrated by Dorothy Craigie.   London, Heinemann, 1952.
Rufty Tufty at the Seaside, illustrated by Dorothy Craigie.   London, Heinemann, 1954.
Charles Stories and Others, from "Listen with Mother," illustrated by Sheila Hawkins.   London, Heinemann, 1954.
More about Charles and Other Stories, from "Listen with Mother," illustrated by Sheila Hawkins.   London, Heinemann, 1954.
The Snow Bear, illustrated by Rosemary Trew.   London, Heinemann, 1956.
Rufty Tufty Goes Camping, illustrated by Dorothy Craigie.   London, Heinemann, 1956.
Rufty Tufty Runs Away, illustrated by Dorothy Craigie.   London, Heinemann, 1957.
Five "Listen with Mother" Tales about Charles, illustrated by Matvyn Wright.   London, Adprint, 1957.
Nine Drummers Drumming, illustrated by John Mackay.   London, Heinemann, 1958.
Rufty Tufty Flies High, illustrated by D.G. Valentine.   London, Heinemann, 1959.
Cherry Stones: A Book of Fairy Stories, illustrated by Pat Humphreys.   London, Heinemann, 1960.
Rufty Tufty's Island, illustrated by D.G. Valentine.   London, Heinemann, 1960.
Lucky Dip: A Selection of Stories and Verses, illustrated by Geraldine Spence.   London, Penguin, 1961.
Rufty Tufty and Hattie, illustrated by D.G. Valentine.   London, Heinemann, 1962.
Far-Away Children, illustrated by Felice Trentin.   London, Heinemann, 1963; New York, Roy, 1968.
The Ten Tales of Shellover, illustrated by Antony Maitland.   London, Deutsch, 1963; New York, Roy, 1968.
The Wolf Who Was Sorry, illustrated by Doritie Kettlewell.   London, Heinemann, 1964; New York, Roy, 1968.

Rufty Tufty Makes a House, illustrated by D.G. Valentine. London, Heinemann, 1965.

Daisy the Cow, illustrated by Sarah Garland. London, Hamish Hamilton, 1966.

Horse on Wheels, illustrated by Janet Duchesne. London, Hamish Hamilton, 1966.

Jack Frost, illustrated by Jane Paton. London, Heinemann, 1966.

Roly the Railway Mouse, illustrated by Leslie Atkinson. London, Heinemann, 1967; as *Roly the Railroad Mouse,* New York, Watts, 1969.

The Aeroplane Who Wanted to See the Sea. London, Bancroft, 1968.

Boris the Teddy Bear. London, Bancroft, 1968.

Dougal the Donkey. London, Bancroft, 1968.

More Tales of Shellover, illustrated by Antony Maitland. London, Deutsch, and New York, Roy, 1968.

Mungo the Monkey. London, Bancroft, 1968.

The Old Fashioned Car. London, Bancroft, 1968.

The Rabbit and His Shadow. London, Bancroft, 1968.

The Noah's Ark, illustrated by Elsie Wrigley. London, Lutterworth Press, 1969.

The Bicycle Wheel, illustrated by Shirley Hughes. London, Hamish Hamilton, 1969.

Look, Do and Listen, illustrated by Bernadette Watts. London, Heinemann, and New York, Watts, 1969.

The Phantom Cyclist and Other Stories, illustrated by Antony Maitland. London, Deutsch, 1971; Chicago, Follett, 1974.

The Phantom Fisherboy: Tales of Mystery and Magic, illustrated by Shirley Hughes. London, Deutsch, 1974.

Bedtime Book. Maidenhead, Berkshire, Purnell, 1974.

Three's Company, illustrated by Prudence Seward. Guildford, Surrey, Lutterworth Press, 1974.

The Bear Who Liked Hugging People and Other Stories, illustrated by Antony Maitland. London, Heinemann, 1976; New York, Crane Russak, 1978.

The Phantom Roundabout and Other Ghostly Tales, illustrated by Shirley Hughes. London, Deutsch, 1977; as *The Phantom Carousel,* Chicago, Follett, 1978.

Up the Airy Mountain: Stories of Magic, illustrated by Eileen Browne. London, Heinemann, 1977.

Mr. Jumble's Toy Shop, illustrated by Paul Wrigley. Guildford, Surrey, Lutterworth Press, 1978.

The Talking Rock, illustrated by Joanna Stubbs. London, Deutsch, 1979.

The Mysterious Baba and Her Magic Caravan: Two Stories, illustrated by Joan Hickson. London, Deutsch, 1980.

The Pirate Ship and Other Stories, illustrated by Shirley Hughes. London, Heinemann, 1980.

Mermaids' Tales, illustrated by Dandi Palmer. Guildford, Surrey, Lutterworth Press, 1980.

The Little Yellow Taxi and His Friends, illustrated by Gary Inwood. Guildford, Surrey, Lutterworth Press, 1982.

Plays

Three Little Mushrooms: Four Puppet Plays (includes *Here We Go round the Buttercups, Lob's Silver Spoon, Hide-and-Seek, Hay-Making*). London, Heinemann, 1955.

More Little Mushrooms: Four Puppet Plays (includes *Three Clever Mushrooms, Tick-Tock, Christmas Eve, The White Stranger*). London, Heinemann, 1955.

Verse

All Different, illustrated by Linda Bramley. London, Heinemann, 1947.

The Evening Listens. London, Heinemann, 1953.

Other

The Ruth Ainsworth Readers (*The Cottage by the Sea; Little Wife Goody; The Robber; The Wild Boy; A Comfort for Owl; Sugar and Spice; Fun, Fires and Friends; Black Bill; A Pill for Owl; Tortoise in Trouble; The Pirate Ship; Hob the Dwarf*). London, Heinemann, 12 vols., 1953–55.

Look Ahead Readers, with Ronald Ridout, illustrated by John Mackay. London, Heinemann, 8 vols., 1956–57.

Books for Me to Read, with Ronald Ridout:
  Red Books (*Jill and Peter; The House of Hay; Come and Play; A Name of My Own; The Duck That Ran Away; Tim's Hoop*), illustrated by Ingeborg Meyer-Rey. London, Bancroft, 6 vols., 1964.
  Blue Books (*At the Zoo; What Are They?; Colours; Silly Billy; A Pram and a Bicycle; Pony, Pony*), illustrated by Gwyneth Mamlock. London, Bancroft, 6 vols., 1965.
  Yellow Books (*David's Picture, Andrew's Engine, Hunt the Thimble, Something Alive, The Singing Grasshopper, A Little Black Lamb*), illustrated by Susan Bailey. London, Bancroft, 6 vols., 1967.
  Green Books (*Susan's House; What Can You Hear?; Tim's Kite; Flippy the Frog; Huff the Hedgehog; A House for a Mouse*), illustrated by William Robert Shaw. London, Bancroft, 6 vols., 1968.

The Look about You Books (*In Woods and Fields, Down the Lane, Beside the Sea, By Pond and Stream, In Your Garden, In the Park*), illustrated by Jennie Corbett. London, Heinemann, 6 vols., 1967–69.

The Ruth Ainsworth Book, illustrated by Shirley Hughes. London, Heinemann, and New York, Watts, 1970.

Dandy the Donkey (reader). London, Bancroft, 1971.

The Wild Wood (reader). London, Bancroft, 1971.

Fairy Gold: Favourite Fairy Tales Retold for the Very Young, illustrated by Barbara Hope Steinberg. London, Heinemann, 1972.

Editor, *Book of Colours and Sounds.* London, Purnell, 1968.

*

Ruth Ainsworth comments:

I had a quiet childhood by the sea in Suffolk. Many of my stories have a background of lonely beaches, sand dunes, marram grass and small prints of bare feet. Mermaids occur as well as shrimps and anemones.

My father died when I was a baby. I started writing as soon as I could use a pencil and published poems in periodicals in my teens. I won a Gold Medal for poetry.

I love reading, biography, letters, novels, and poetry. I specially enjoy Jane Austen and Ivy Compton-Burnett. I like walking, architecture, looking at paintings and listening to music. My chief joy is seeing my family and my friends informally and often. Life in this small Northumberland town suits me pretty well, though I still feel that Suffolk is my native home.

*   *   *

When reading is new to children, stories are inextricably linked with their play. The fantastic has its roots in the workaday and the domestic. Playthings, toys, animals are anthropomorphised as friends. Ruth Ainsworth's books reflect this special time. Her external world is that of nurseries, gardens, and play places. Novice readers (and listeners) learn to understand stories as a particular kind of imaginative activity—and also as statements about what the world could be like. It pays to be kind; disobedience usually brings disaster.

Her early work showed that she could engage her audience without patronising or trivialising. *"Listen with Mother" Tales* and *Charles Stories* had uncluttered plots and their origin as radio scripts made them—like all her work—perfect for reading aloud. The Rufty Tufty books, about "the happiest little golliwog in Golliwog Village," may now have been made unpalatable by a heightened social sensitivity, but were well-meaning at the time.

The 1960's showed a new vibrancy in the writing: *Roly the Railway Mouse* has an endearing central character, lively pace, and skilled use of background. In *The Noah's Ark* the pairs of creatures inside George's toy ark come to life when he is asleep. The important business of "let's pretend" that is the plot of early childhood is cleverly realised. The best-rounded of her works are the Shellover Tales. An affable tortoise spins stories for the animals in Mrs. Candy's garden. The sharing of stories is a recurrent activity in Ainsworth's books: a natural mode of depicting justice, retribution, good deserts, and commonsense.

The Phantom stories show increased stealth in dealing with the unfamiliar (even the frightening). Realistic adventure is handled more acutely than in earlier books in *Three's Company,* a matter-of-fact telling of the close friendship between two girls and a boy. A story such as *Mr. Jumble's Toy Shop* from the late 1970's encapsulates this author's attraction for the very young. The frightened and lonely are comforted. Predators (horrid children with names like Basil and Edwina) are kept at bay. Problems are shared and solved in bedtime-story length episodes under the benevolent paternalism of the proprietor.

Children are not disturbed, puzzled, or challenged by Ruth Ainsworth's books but some lessons about the sophisticated play that is reading are well taught. Most important, the magical thinking in the stories and the timeless camaraderie between children, animals, and toys are confirmed, extended, and supported by the grown-ups. She also knows well the important driving power of "that's just like me" (and of "what happens next?") when one is new to the game.

—Colin Mills

AKERS, Floyd. See **BAUM, L. Frank.**

ALCOCK, Vivien (Dolores). British. Born in Worthing, Sussex, 23 September 1924. Educated at Devizes High School, Wiltshire; Oxford School of Art, 1940–42. Served as an ambulance driver in the Auxiliary Territorial Service, 1942–46. Married Leon Garfield, *q.v.,* in 1948; one adopted daughter. Artist, Gestetner Ltd., London, 1947–53; secretary, Whittington Hospital, London, 1953–58. Agent: John Johnson Ltd., 45–47 Clerkenwell Green, London EC1R 0HT. Address: 59 Wood Lane, London N6 5UD, England.

PUBLICATIONS FOR CHILDREN

Fiction

The Haunting of Cassie Palmer.   London, Methuen, 1980; New York, Delacorte Press, 1982.
The Stonewalkers.   London, Methuen, 1981; New York, Delacorte Press, 1983.
The Sylvia Game.   London, Methuen, 1982; New York, Delacorte Press, 1984.
Travellers by Night.   London, Methuen, 1983; New York, Delacorte Press, 1985.
Ghostly Companions, illustrated by Jane Lydbury.   London, Methuen, 1984; New York, Delacorte Press, 1987.
The Cuckoo Sister.   London, Methuen, and New York, Delacorte Press, 1985.
Wait and See, illustrated by Jill Bennett.   London, Deutsch, 1986.
The Mysterious Mr. Ross.   London, Methuen, and New York, Delacorte Press, 1987.
The Monster Garden.   London, Methuen, and New York, Delacorte Press, 1988.
The Thing in the Woods, illustrated by Sally Holmes.   London, Hamish Hamilton, 1989.
The Trial of Anna Cotman.   London, Methuen, 1989.

*

Vivien Alcock comments:
   I write for children because, most of all, I enjoy telling stories. I like to write about strange happenings—ghosts or secrets or misunderstandings—in an everyday setting, in which nothing may be quite what it seems.

*   *   *

Vivien Alcock combines an interest in children's relationships with their families and friends with an appreciation of her readers' need for a good story. Her heroines are usually aged between 11 and 13, and her novels are likely to appeal to youngsters of that age and younger. Her writing often contains supernatural or fantasy elements, and can be both humorous and scary.

Cassie, heroine of *The Haunting of Cassie Palmer,* is a seventh child of a seventh child, the daughter of a medium who expects great things of her. But Cassie hates her mother's world, and to prove she is normal takes up her brother and sister's dare to summon a spirit in a cemetery. To her horror a ghost does rise, that of Deverill, dark and disfigured. Although exciting, this novel is an immature work. Yet it does introduce themes that recur in later novels: the parent-child relationship, friendship, and most importantly, the redeeming power of a child's pity and love, for it is the strength of Cassie's caring which sets Deverill free from the grave.

As a boy Deverill was attacked by a crowd whose "faces were hard as stone;" similarly in *The Stonewalkers* a horde of stone statues attacks Poppy and friends when they are lost on the moors. Poppy and another girl are imprisoned in an old mine, but escape when the statues kill each other. Poppy wonders why the statues "feel such anger and hate, but not pity or love." This question can apply to Poppy's mother as well, who thinks that after her husband died, "it was like I turned to stone." Her anger is born of fear and loss. But the adventure on the moors softens both Poppy and her mother and makes affection between them possible.

The Sylvia Game is a great step forward in Alcock's development as a writer, being altogether more polished and better written. Emily, convalescing at the seaside, spies on her artist father and in the process meets Oliver, who spins her a yarn about her looking exactly like his drowned sister Sylvia. Sylvia is actually an ancestor and the subject of a Renoir portrait, of which Emily's father has painted a copy...is he a forger? What is Oliver's father Sir Robert up to? Children's lies are developed into an imaginative and frightening game. By the end of the story Emily and Oliver have both come to terms with their fathers as human beings rather than the giants they once thought them.

Kate, daughter of a prosperous Hampstead lawyer and narrator of

The Cuckoo Sister, discovers that she had an older sister Emma who was snatched from her pram as a baby. Throughout her childhood she uses this as an excuse for difficult behaviour. When Kate is 11 a girl turns up on the doorstep, cheaply dressed and poorly spoken, identified in a note from her "mother" as being the stolen Emma. With great sensitivity and sympathy, and always careful to maintain tension, Alcock analyses the feelings of the two girls from very different backgrounds as they grow to accept their family situation. Love overcomes extreme jealousy: in a tear-jerking scene, Kate mumbles to her putative sister, "I don't care who you are. I want you to stay."

The Mysterious Mr. Ross tells how Felicity rescues a stranger from the sea, and her attempts with her friend Bony to establish his identity. Albert Ross is a charming yet elusive character, fabricated from his own and other people's imaginings. The reader is gripped, hoping for a romantic or supernatural explanation but, disappointingly, Mr Ross is never fully explained. Alcock tells the reader only what is morally important about him, that in return for kindness he brings good luck.

The Monster Garden fuses the careful child-parent-sibling study of the later novels with a more sophisticated version of the child rescuing the feared outsider through love, as in *The Haunting of Cassie Palmer.* It extends beyond that, showing how the person who feels love—a love that here matures from the one-sided maternal to mutual affection—becomes more understanding from the experience. Beneath its light-hearted surface *The Monster Garden* is Alcock's most developed and also her fiercest novel. Most children will read it simply as an absorbing story about a girl who grows an endearing monster from a "bit of goo" from her father's genetic engineering laboratory, concealing it from her family, revealing it only to her friends, and eventually setting it free in the sea.

Alcock's readers are well entertained. They may also be influenced by her passionate affirmation of the value of love and kindness, and, as they grow into their teens, be helped in forming more adult relationships with their parents.

—Maggie Freeman

ALDERSON, Sue Ann. American; Canadian Landed Immigrant. Born in New York City, 11 September 1940. Educated at Antioch College, Yellow Springs, Ohio, 1957–62, B.A. in literature 1962; Ohio State University, Columbus, 1962–64, M.A. in English 1964; University of California, Berkeley, 1964–67. Married Evan Alderson in 1965 (divorced 1986); one daughter and one son. Instructor, Simon Fraser University, 1967–71, and Capilano College, 1972–80, both Vancouver, British Columbia. Assistant Professor, 1980–84, and since 1984 Associate Professor of Creative Writing, University of British Columbia, Vancouver. Address: 4004 West 32nd Avenue, Vancouver, British Columbia V6S 1Z6, Canada.

PUBLICATIONS FOR CHILDREN

Fiction

Bonnie McSmithers You're Driving Me Dithers, illustrated by Fiona Garrick. Edmonton, Tree Frog Press, 1974.
Hurry Up, Bonnie!, illustrated by Fiona Garrick. Edmonton, Tree Frog Press, 1976.
The Adventures of Prince Paul, illustrated by Jane Walsack. Vancouver, Fforbez, 1977.
The Finding Princess, illustrated by Jane Walsack. Vancouver,

Fforbez, 1977.
Bonnie McSmithers Is at It Again!, illustrated by Fiona Garrick. Edmonton, Tree Frog Press, 1979.
Comet's Tale, illustrated by Georgia Pow Graham. Edmonton, Tree Frog Press, 1983.
The Not Impossible Summer, illustrated by C. Rother. Toronto, Irwin, 1983.
The Something in Thurlo Darby's House, illustrated by Deborah Drew-Brook-Cormack. Toronto, Ginn, 1984; Huddersfield, Yorkshire, Schofield and Sims, 1985.
Ida and the Wool Smugglers, illustrated by Ann Blades. Toronto, Groundwood, 1987; New York, McElderry, 1988.

PUBLICATIONS FOR ADULTS

Other

Editor, *Explorations 1,* by Betty Coombs and Lalie Harcourt. Don Mills, Ontario, Addison Wesley, 1986.
Editor, *Explorations 2,* by Betty Coombs. Don Mills, Ontario, Addison Wesley, 1987.

*

Sue Ann Alderson comments:
My first book, *Bonnie McSmithers You're Driving Me Dithers,* grew from a story I made for my young daughter, in which I tried to explore our relationship and resolve our discord. Desires to explore feelings and relationships, and to resolve discord, have continued to inform all of my writing. I would like my books to empower the children they come to, enlarging their view of their worlds (inner as well as outer) and providing what insights I can that may enable them better to resolve the discords they encounter. I have been fortunate to be able to travel through three childhoods: my own (in New York, with my younger sister and psychologist-parents), my daughter's, and my son's (both in Canada). All three journeys have included side-trips, not only to what-is, but also to what-could-be, and lots to look at—and write about—along the way!

*   *   *

Sue Ann Alderson is a versatile writer who works in several genres for a variety of ages. Common to all her stories, from picture book texts to novels, are recurring themes of the empowerment of children, the joys of animals and nature, the pleasures of cooperative projects, and the value of individuality and imagination.

Two of Alderson's early works for children, a pair of fairytale-like stories, *The Finding Princess* and *The Adventures of Prince Paul,* are basically apprentice works. Although somewhat derivative they do show Alderson's talent for shaping a story, her quirky humour, and her interest in the natural world.

Best known of her works is a trio of picture books featuring a small heroine named Bonnie McSmithers who exasperates her mother and delights her readers with her vagueness, tardiness, eccentricity, and irrepressible confidence and energy. The texts move along with bouncing rhythms and each has a refrain that makes it perfect for reading aloud. In *Bonnie McSmithers You're Driving Me Dithers, Hurry Up, Bonnie!,* and *Bonnie McSmithers Is at It Again!,* Alderson artfully captures the personality and viewpoint of the preschool child.

In two novels for older children, *Comet's Tale* and *The Not Impossible Summer,* Alderson deals, in a wider-ranging format, with the theme of a child's growing confidence. *Comet's Tale* is a madcap fantasy of a family that pulls together to help save a threatened animal shelter. With its cartoon-like pace and crowded cast it tends to collapse under the weight of its own wackiness and its final effect is somewhat diffuse. Much more focussed and effective is *The Not Impossible Summer*. In this story of a summer vacation on an island Alderson again deals with a strained mother-daughter relationship and its resolution sparked by an heroic act by the protagonist Jenny, who rescues a lost and injured boy. Alderson leavens the seriousness of the theme with a restrained use of mayhem as when Jenny smuggles a cow into the basement, and with touches of pawky humour as when we are privy to the heroic exploits of Jenny's daring and splendid alter-ego.

Another island story and the most accomplished of Alderson's works is *Ida and the Wool Smugglers*. Ida, middle child in a turn-of-the-century farming family, is frustrated by being told she is too small to take on the responsibilities she longs for. One day while delivering bread to a neighbouring family she surprises a pair of sheep smugglers and in an act of bravery herds a ewe and two lambs to safety. Based on the history of Salt Spring Island off the coast of British Columbia the story is spare, plausible, and has the rhythm and energy of the truly accomplished picture book.

—Sarah Ellis

ALDRIDGE, (Harold Edward) James. Australian. Born in White Hills, Victoria, 10 July 1918. Educated at Swan Hill High School; London School of Economics. Married Dina Mitchnik in 1942; two sons. Writer, Melbourne *Herald* and *Sun*, 1937–38, and London *Daily Sketch* and *Sunday Dispatch*, 1939; European and Middle East war correspondent, Australian Newspaper Service and North American Newspaper Alliance, 1939–44; Tehran correspondent, *Time* and *Life*, 1944. Recipient: Rhys Memorial prize, 1945; World Peace Council gold medal; International Organization of Journalists prize, 1967; Lenin Memorial Peace prize, 1972; Australian Children's Book Council Book of the Year award, 1985; *Guardian* award, 1987. Lives in London. Agent: Curtis Brown, 162–168 Regent Street, London W1R 5TA, England.

PUBLICATIONS FOR CHILDREN

Fiction

The Flying 19, illustrated by Raymond Briggs. London, Hamish Hamilton, 1966.
The Marvelous Mongolian. Boston, Little Brown, and London, Macmillan, 1974.
The Broken Saddle. London, MacRae, 1982; New York, Watts, 1983.
The True Story of Lilli Stubeck. South Yarra, Victoria, Hyland House, 1984; London, Penguin, 1986.
The True Story of Spit MacPhee. Ringwood, Victoria, Viking, and London, Viking Kestrel, 1986.

PUBLICATIONS FOR ADULTS

Novels

Signed with Their Honour. London, Joseph, and Boston, Little Brown, 1942.
The Sea Eagle. London, Joseph, and Boston, Little Brown, 1944.
Of Many Men. London, Joseph, and Boston, Little Brown, 1946.
The Diplomat. London, Lane, 1949; Boston, Little Brown, 1950.

The Hunter. London, Lane, 1950; Boston, Little Brown, 1951.
Heroes of the Empty View. London, Lane, and New York, Knopf, 1954.
I Wish He Would Not Die. London, Bodley Head, 1957; New York, Doubleday, 1958.
The Last Exile. London, Hamish Hamilton, and New York, Doubleday, 1961.
A Captive in the Land. London, Hamish Hamilton, 1962; New York, Doubleday, 1963.
The Statesman's Game. London, Hamish Hamilton, and New York Doubleday, 1966.
My Brother Tom. London, Hamish Hamilton, 1966; as *My Brother Tom: A Love Story*, Boston, Little Brown, 1967.
A Sporting Proposition. London, Joseph, and Boston, Little Brown, 1973; as *Ride a Wild Pony*, London, Penguin, 1976.
Mockery in Arms. London, Joseph, 1974; Boston, Little Brown, 1975.
The Untouchable Juli. London, Joseph, 1975; Boston, Little Brown, 1976.
One Last Glimpse. London, Joseph, and Boston, Little Brown, 1977.
Goodbye Un-America. London, Joseph, and Boston, Little Brown, 1979.

Short Stories

Gold and Sand. London, Bodley Head, 1960.

Plays

The 49th State (produced London, 1947).
One Last Glimpse (produced Prague, 1981).

Television Plays: scripts for *Robin Hood* series.

Other

Undersea Hunting for Inexperienced Englishmen. London, Allen and Unwin, 1955.
Living Egypt, photographs by Paul Strand. London, MacGibbon and Kee, and New York, Horizon Press, 1969.
Cairo: Biography of a City. Boston, Little Brown, 1969; London, Macmillan, 1970.

*   *   *

In his 45 years as a writer, with several of his 23 books bedecked with honours, James Aldridge has written three novels specifically for children—but not the three which ended up being filmed by Disney or awarded prestigious children's literary awards. These—*A Sporting Proposition*, filmed and better known as *Ride a Wild Pony*, *The True Story of Lilli Stubeck*, and *The True Story of Spit MacPhee*—are part of an adult five-book sequence set, Faulkner-like, in one small town on the Murray River, the reinvented scene of Aldridge's own Australian childhood, and each narrated by or referring to the Quayle family. As far as Aldridge is concerned, all are *about* children and young people but were not written *for* them.

The Flying 19, illustrated by Raymond Briggs, is a short fantasy for young children about a London bus that can fly. *The Marvelous Mongolian* is a touching tale about one of those untameable wild horses who were hunted to the point of extinction, his indomitable journey across Europe in the company of a tiny Shetland pony, and the friendship through letters developed by the boy and girl anxiously following his fate at either end. Horses are a recurrent Aldridge motif: *The Broken Saddle* is very much the story of his own relationship with one special pony as a boy, with the same fierce feeling for the wild country of Australia as in *Spit MacPhee.*

Throughout all his work, Aldridge's strength is his sweeping narrative power. His constant preoccupation with how the forces and events of the past mould the present is subservient to the narrative, and his style is always straight and direct. His appeal to younger readers is not, then, surprising. *Lilli Stubeck* is a novel for older teens, exploring the motives behind the strangely intense bond between a refined elderly lady living in the town's "big house" and a wild, gypsy-like girl. As much as anything else, it is the book's haunting conclusion, truthful but too downbeat for many young readers, that nudges it into an older bracket, because *Spit MacPhee,* which succeeds with a younger audience, shares its central theme—the right of everyone to be themselves—but sets it into a gripping adventure that culminates in a classically tense courtroom drama and a splendidly happy ending.

In both books the small-town atmosphere is brilliantly evoked: the streets, the weather, the river, and people, adults who have known each other since school, with the enduring complexities of their relationships now affecting their children. There are characters from and allusions to the other novels in the sequence, and it is perhaps only accidental that they too are not accepted into the teenage category. Both books also portray society as a battleground for forces that, though tied to one particular time, are fighting a timeless war: new Australian versus old English values, Catholic versus Protestant, uninhibited rawness versus gentility, love of a cause versus love of people, the barefoot primitive versus civilisation in polished boots.

Spit himself is an 11-year-old orphan, rough, tough, cynically wise yet innocent and vulnerable with youth, who draws from readers of all ages an exasperated devotion. He lives with his apparently mad grandfather on the banks of the Murray River, with which he comes to feel, Huck-like, a life-giving affinity; when his grandfather dies he must fight to defeat those suffocatingly good intentions that will feed, clothe, bless, and destroy him. This cross-tug of moral currents holds the older reader, but the book has the classic qualities of the finest children's literature: the universal appeal of an exciting tale, along with a stretching of imaginative horizons to catch sight of the joys and pains of other lives in other times, and through them to understand our own.

—Stephanie Nettell

ALEXANDER, Lloyd (Chudley). American. Born in Philadelphia, Pennsylvania, 30 January 1924. Educated at Upper Darby Senior High School, Pennsylvania, graduated 1940; West Chester State College, Pennsylvania, 1942; Lafayette College, Easton, Pennsylvania, 1943; the Sorbonne, Paris, 1946. Served in the United States Army Combat Intelligence and Counter-Intelligence corps, 1942–46: Staff Sergeant. Married Janine Denni in 1946; one stepdaughter. Cartoonist, layout artist, copywriter, and trade magazine editor, 1947–70. Author-in-residence, schools in Springfield, Pennsylvania, 1967–68, and Temple University, Philadelphia, 1970–74. Since 1970 director, Carpenter Lane Chamber Music Society, Philadelphia; since 1973 member of the Editorial Advisory Board, *Cricket* magazine, La Salle, Illinois. Recipient: Jewish Book Council Isaac Siegel Memorial award, 1959; American Library Association Newbery Medal, 1969; National Book award, 1971; Silver Pencil award (Netherlands), 1981; American Book award, 1982; Children's Book award (Austria), 1984; Golden Cat award (Sweden), 1984; Catholic Library Association Regina Medal, 1986; Children's Book award (Norway), 1987; Church and Synagogue Library Association Ott award, 1987. Agent: Brandt and Brandt, 1501 Broadway, New York, New York 10036. Address: 1005 Drexel Avenue, Drexel Hill, Pennsylvania 19026, U.S.A.

PUBLICATIONS FOR CHILDREN

Fiction

Time Cat: The Remarkable Journeys of Jason and Gareth, illustrated by Bill Sokol. New York, Holt Rinehart, 1963; as *Nine Lives,* London, Cassell, 1963.
Prydain series:
  The Book of Three. New York, Holt Rinehart, 1964; London, Heinemann, 1966.
  The Black Cauldron. New York, Holt Rinehart, 1965; London, Heinemann, 1967.
  The Castle of Llyr. New York, Holt Rinehart, 1966; London, Heinemann, 1968.
  Taran Wanderer. New York, Holt Rinehart, 1967; London, Fontana, 1979.
  The High King. New York, Holt Rinehart, 1968; London, Fontana, 1979.
Coll and His White Pig, illustrated by Evaline Ness. New York, Holt Rinehart, 1965.
The Truthful Harp, illustrated by Evaline Ness. New York, Holt Rinehart, 1967.
The Marvelous Misadventures of Sebastian. New York, Dutton, 1970.
The King's Fountain, illustrated by Ezra Jack Keats. New York, Dutton, 1971.
The Four Donkeys, illustrated by Lester Abrams. New York, Holt Rinehart, 1972; Kingswood, Surrey, World's Work, 1974.
The Cat Who Wished to Be a Man. New York, Dutton, 1973.
The Foundling and Other Tales of Prydain, illustrated by Margot Zemach. New York, Holt Rinehart, 1973.
The Wizard in the Tree, illustrated by Laszlo Kubinyi. New York, Dutton, 1975.
The Town Cats and Other Tales, illustrated by Laszlo Kubinyi. New York, Dutton, 1977.
The First Two Lives of Lukas-Kasha. New York, Dutton, 1978.
Westmark series:
  Westmark. New York, Dutton, 1981.
  The Kestrel. New York, Dutton, 1982.
  The Beggar Queen. New York, Dutton, 1984.
The Illyrian Adventure. New York, Dutton, 1986.
The El Dorado Adventure. New York, Dutton, 1987.
The Drackenberg Adventure. New York, Dutton, 1988.
The Jedera Adventure. New York, Dutton, 1989.

Other

Border Hawk: August Bondi, illustrated by Bernard Krigstein. New York, Farrar Straus, 1958.
The Flagship Hope: Aaron Lopez illustrated by Bernard Krigstein. Philadelphia, Jewish Publication Society, 1960.

PUBLICATIONS FOR ADULTS

Novel

And Let the Credit Go. New York, Crowell, 1955.

Other

My Five Tigers. New York, Crowell, and London, Cassell, 1956.

Janine Is French.   New York, Crowell, 1958; London, Cassell, 1960.

My Love Affair with Music.   New York, Crowell, 1960; London, Cassell, 1961.

Park Avenue Vet, with Louis J. Camuti.   New York, Holt Rinehart, and London, Deutsch, 1962.

Fifty Years in the Doghouse.   New York, Putnam, 1964; as *Send for Ryan!,* London, W. H. Allen, 1965.

Translator, *The Wall and Other Stories,* by Jean-Paul Sartre.   New York, New Directions, 1948; as *Intimacy and Other Stories,* London, Nevill, 1949.

Translator, *Nausea,* by Jean-Paul Sartre.   New York, New Directions, 1949; London, Hamish Hamilton, 1962; as *The Diary of Antoine Roquentin,* London, Lehmann, 1949.

Translator, *Selected Writings,* by Paul Eluard.   New York, New Directions, 1951; London, Routledge, 1952; as *Uninterrupted Poetry: Selected Writings,* New Directions, 1975.

Translator, *The Sea Rose,* by Paul Vialar.   London and New York, Nevill, 1952.

*

Bibliography: *Lloyd Alexander, Evangeline Walton Ensley, Kenneth Morris: A Primary and Secondary Bibliography* by Kenneth J. Zahorski, Boston, Hall, 1981.

Critical Studies: *A Tribute to Lloyd Alexander* by Myra Cohn Livingston, Philadelphia, Drexel Institute, 1976; *Lloyd Alexander: A Critical Biography* by James S. Jacobs, unpublished dissertation, University of Georgia, 1978.

Lloyd Alexander comments:

After writing some dozen years for adults, writing for young people was the most creative and liberating experience of my life. In books for young people I was able to express my own deepest feelings far more than I could ever do in writing for adults. Though most of my books have been in the form of fantasy, I believe that is merely one of the many ways to express attitudes about real human relationships and problems.

*   *   *

Although he first wrote and translated adult literature, Lloyd Alexander turned to children's literature in the early 1960's when he sensed a feeling of despair in adult fiction and began to believe that there was little future in writing it. Since the publication of his first children's book in 1958, Alexander has been recognized as an outstanding 20th-century American author of children's literature. Since he does not write in one genre alone he is difficult to categorize. His overall contribution to children's literature reflects the diversity to be found in the field today. His tone, choice of subjects, and writing style suggest that Alexander understands today's society, children, and their reading interests.

In researching *Time Cat,* his first children's novel, Alexander returned to the Welsh legends he had read as a youth. Unwilling to use the legends as backdrop for just part of *Time Cat,* Alexander determined to write a full-length fantasy series based on Celtic myth.

Alexander's *Prydain* series begins with the established body of legends, literary patterns, and character types found in the *Mabinogion,* but it becomes a modern fantasy series early on, centering on 20th-century problems. Written during the United States' involvement in Vietnam, the series sees Taran, the youthful protagonist, move from a lowly assistant pig keeper to the ruler of a newly formed kingdom, and in the process learn to savor home and seek harmony among all people rather than enjoy the victories of war. In the end he seeks peace for all and hopes to rule democratically by fostering better lives for the poorest as well as the richest. Designed with a youthful audience in mind, the books replace the *Mabinogion*'s emphasis on legendary adult personalities with new young heroes. The series is not a simple recounting of Celtic legend, but rather an extension of old myths in a modern retelling. Alexander's story contains heroes that the child reader can identify with, an active plot based on the typical pattern of the circular journey, and resolutions which fit the standards of contemporary children's literature.

Because the old rulers disappear at the end of the series and Taran begins his reign without the help of the supernatural, the story becomes more American than Celtic in its overall tone. American critics have credited Alexander with a believable series which is contemporary in its tone and compelling in its lively characterizations, well-defined fantasy world, and adventurous plots. However, British critics have looked upon the series with less regard. The stories have been unfavorably compared to the original *Mabinogion* and the books of Tolkien. While British critics attest to Alexander's skill as a writer, they disdain his "flippancy" and "pedestrian" adventures. Nevertheless, the books are favorites among children in several countries.

Alexander's second major contribution to children's literature is the *Westmark* series, a three-book set depicting the horrors of revolution and unrest, and the conflicts caused by corrupt leadership. These books are quite different in tone and setting from the *Prydain* series. Written with an older audience in mind, the *Westmark* series is not based upon any earlier legends, but the story has events and characters reminiscent of the French Revolution. The main protagonist is a young orphan who rises to power through his friendship with the young princess of the kingdom. When a democratic government is formed at the end the "hero" and his young princess must go into exile. In the series Alexander successfully combines sub-plots, writes realistic dialogue, and exposes the inhumanities that leaders inflict upon those they rule. He makes it clear that his is a story about the need for freedom and democracy.

Alexander's next series, the Vesper books, is much more lighthearted. It contains a great deal of action and seems to be designed with a different audience in mind. The plots are fast-moving, the characters seem rather one-dimensional, and the settings too exotic. The action centers on the deeds of an independent and highly intelligent young heroine. Set in a four-year span during the 1800's, the adventures begin in Philadelphia where Vesper, a wealthy orphan, and her male guardian Professor Brinton Garrett live. Vesper's inheritance triggers each adventure in one way or another, and she and Professor Garrett set forth to a distant land. The books are shorter in length and dominated by action rather than conversation. Because the episodes are narrated by Professor Garrett, the heroine appears to be always in control, always self-confident. The reader watches an adventuresome young woman interact with those around her without getting a sense of her changing attitudes. The situations encountered always involve injustices against a minority, with Vesper helping the minority gain respectability. Swashbuckling adventure stories, the Vesper books contain enough action in their plots and exoticism in their settings to appeal to the typical teenager who watches adventure films or reads today's popular fiction. However, the books' adventures imply that something is wrong with the early colonialism of the western world, that people have sometimes been forced to abandon their cultural heritages in underdeveloped countries. In all of Vesper's adventures justice restores the rights of the natives, suggesting that large, highly industrialized governments have no right to inflict their values on others. Once again Alexander is placing modern day concerns in historical situations.

Alexander's short fairytales contain moral lessons, much as La Fontaine's fables did. Stories such as those found in *The Town Cats and Other Tales* appeal to dual audiences—adults can see the satires while children can enjoy the adventures. These tales provide a link between the writings of earlier fairytale authors such as Hans Christian Andersen and Oscar Wilde and 20th-century political social fantasy.

The diversity in Alexander's style and in his intended audience suggests that he is a serious writer who tries to keep in touch with his audience while implanting cultural ideals and exploring moral values in his stories. His body of works show how modern storytelling can be accomplished using traditional literary patterns.

—Jill P. May

———

ALLAN, Mabel Esther. Has also written as Jean Estoril; Priscilla Hagon; Anne Pilgrim. British. Born in Wallasey, Cheshire, 11 February 1915. Educated at private schools. Served in the British Women's Land Army during World War II. Agent: John Farquharson Ltd., 162–168 Regent Street, London W1R 5TB; or, 250 West 57th Street, New York, New York 10107, U.S.A. Address: 11 Oldfield Way, Heswall, Wirral, Merseyside L60 6RQ, England.

PUBLICATIONS FOR CHILDREN

Fiction

The Glen Castle Mystery. London, Warne, 1948.
The Adventurous Summer, illustrated by Isabel Veevers. London, Museum Press, 1948.
The Wyndhams Went to Wales, illustrated by Beryl Thornborough. London, Sylvan Press, 1948.
Mullion, illustrated by R. Walter Hall. London, Hutchinson, 1949.
Cilia of Chiltern's Edge, illustrated by Betty Ladler. London, Museum Press, 1949.
Trouble at Melville Manor, illustrated by Isabel Veevers. London, Museum Press, 1949.
Holiday at Arnriggs. London, Warne, 1949.
Chiltern Adventure, illustrated by T.R. Freeman. London, Blackie, 1950.
Jimmy John's Journey. London, Dean, 1949.
Over the Sea to School, illustrated by W. Mackinlay. London, Blackie, 1950.
School under Snowdon. London, Hutchinson, 1950.
Everyday Island. London, Museum Press. 1950.
Seven in Switzerland, illustrated by Isabel Veever. London, Blackie, 1950.
The Exciting River, illustrated by Helen Jacobs. London, Nelson, 1951.
Clues to Connemara, illustrated by Philip. London, Blackie, 1952.
The Maclains of Glen Gillean. London, Hutchinson, 1952.
Return to Derrykereen. London, Ward Lock, 1952.
A School in Danger, illustrated by Eric Winter. London, Blackie, 1952.
The School on Cloud Ridge. London, Hutchinson, 1952.
The School on North Barrule. London, Museum Press, 1952.
The Secret Valley, illustrated by C. Instrell. Leeds, E.J. Arnold, 1953.
Room for the Cuckoo: The Story of a Farming Year. London, Dent, 1953.
Three Go to Switzerland, illustrated by Isabel Veevers. London, Blackie, 1953.
Lucia Comes to School. London, Hutchinson, 1953.
Strangers at Brongwerne. London, Museum Press, 1953.
Meric's Secret Cottage. London, Blackie, 1954.
Adventure Royal, illustrated by C.W. Bacon. London, Blackie, 1954.

Here We Go Round: A Career Story for Girls. London, Heinemann, 1954.
Margaret Finds a Future. London, Hutchinson, 1954.
New Schools for Old. London, Hutchinson, 1954.
The Summer at Town's End, illustrated by Iris Weller. London, Harrap, 1954.
Adventures in Switzerland. London, Pickering and Inglis, 1955.
The Mystery of Derrydane, illustrated by Vera Chadwick. Huddersfield, Yorkshire, Schofield and Sims, 1955.
Changes for the Challoners. London, Ward Lock, 1955.
Glenvara. London, Hutchinson, 1955; as *Summer of Decision,* New York, Abelard Schuman, 1957.
Judith Teachers. London, Lane, 1955.
Swiss School. London, Hutchinson, 1955.
Adventure in Mayo. London, Ward Lock, 1956.
Balconies and Blue Nets: The Story of a Holiday in Brittany, illustrated by Peggy Beetles. London, Harrap, 1956.
Lost Lorrenden, illustrated by Shirley Hughes. London, Blackie, 1956.
Strangers in Skye. London, Heinemann, 1956; New York, Criterion, 1958.
Two in the Western Isles. London, Hutchinson, 1956.
The Vine-Clad Hill, illustrated by T.R. Freeman. London, Lane, 1956; as *Swiss Holiday,* New York, Vanguard Press, 1957.
Flora at Kilroinn. London, Blackie, 1956.
The Amber House. London, Hutchinson, 1956.
Ann's Alpine Adventure. London, Hutchinson, 1956.
At School in Skye, illustrated by Constance Marshall. London, Blackie, 1957.
Black Forest Summer. London, Bodley Head, 1957; New York, Vanguard Press, 1959.
Sara Goes to Germany. London, Hutchinson, 1957.
Blue Dragon Days. London, Heinemann, 1958; as *Romance in Italy,* New York, Vanguard Press, 1962.
The Conch Shell, illustrated by T.R. Freeman. London, Blackie, 1958.
The House by the Marsh, illustrated by Sheila Rose. London, Dent, 1958.
Rachel Tandy. London, Hutchinson, 1958.
Amanda Goes to Italy. London, Hutchinson, 1959.
Catrin in Wales. London, Bodley Head, 1959; New York, Vanguard Press, 1961.
A Play to the Festival. London, Heinemann, 1959; as *On Stage, Flory,* New York, Watts, 1961.
Shadow over the Alps. London, Hutchinson, 1960.
A Summer in Brittany. London, Dent, 1960; as *Hilary's Summer on Her Own,* New York, Watts, 1961.
Tansy of Tring Street, illustrated by Sally Holliday. London, Heinemann, 1960.
Holiday of Endurance. London, Dent, 1961.
Bluegate Girl. London, Hutchinson, 1961.
Pendron under the Water, illustrated by T.R. Freeman. London, Harrap, 1961.
Home to the Island, illustrated by Geoffrey Whittam. London, Dent, 1962; New York, Vanguard Press, 1966.
Signpost to Switzerland. London, Heinemann, 1962; New York, Criterion, 1964.
The Ballet Family, illustrated by A.R. Whitear. London, Methuen, 1963; New York, Criterion, 1966.
Kate Comes to England. London, Heinemann, 1963.
New York for Nicola. New York, Vanguard Press, 1963; London, White Lion, 1977.
The Sign of the Unicorn: A Thriller for Young People, illustrated by Shirley Hughes. London, Dent, and New York, Criterion, 1963.
It Happened in Arles. London, Heinemann, 1964; as *Mystery in*

Arles, New York, Vanguard Press, 1964.
The Ballet Family Again, illustrated by A.R. Whitear. London, Methuen, 1964; as *The Dancing Garlands,* New York, Criterion, 1968.
Fiona on the Fourteenth Floor, illustrated by Shirley Hughes. London, Dent, 1964; as *Mystery on the Fourteenth Floor,* New York, Criterion, 1965.
A Summer at Sea, illustrated by Geoffrey Whittam. London, Dent, 1965; New York, Vanguard Press, 1967.
The Way over Windle, illustrated by Raymond Briggs. London, Methuen, 1966.
Skiing to Danger. London, Heinemann, 1966; as *Mystery of the Ski Slopes,* New York, Criterion, 1966.
In Pursuit of Clarinda, illustrated by Margaret Wetherbee. London, Dent, 1966.
It Started in Madeira. London, Heinemann, 1967; as *The Mystery Began in Madeira,* New York, Criterion, 1967.
Missing in Manhattan, illustrated by Margaret Wetherbee. London, Dent, 1967; as *Mystery in Manhattan,* New York, Vanguard Press, 1968.
The Wood Street Secret, illustrated by Shirley Hughes. London, Methuen, 1968; New York, Abelard Schuman, 1970.
The Kraymer Mystery. New York, Criterion, 1969; London, Abelard Schuman, 1973.
Climbing to Danger. London, Heinemann, 1969; as *Mystery in Wales,* New York, Vanguard Press, 1971.
Dangerous Inheritance. London, Heinemann, 1970.
The Wood Street Group, illustrated by Shirley Hughes. London, Methuen, 1970.
Christmas at Spindle Bottom, illustrated by Lynette Hemmant. London, Dent, 1970.
The Secret Dancer, illustrated by Juliet Mozley. London, Dent, 1971.
The May Day Mystery. New York, Criterion, 1971; London, Severn House, 1980.
The Wood Street Rivals, illustrated by Shirley Hughes. London, Methuen, 1971.
An Island in a Green Sea, illustrated by Charles Robinson. New York, Atheneum, 1972; London, Dent, 1973.
Behind the Blue Gates. London, Heinemann, 1972.
Time to Go Back. London, Abelard Schuman, 1972; New York, Criterion, 1974.
The Wood Street Helpers, illustrated by Shirley Hughes. London, Methuen, 1973.
A Formidable Enemy. London, Heinemann, 1973; Nashville, Nelson, 1975.
Mystery in Rome. New York, Vanguard Press, 1974; as *The Bells of Rome,* London, Heinemann, 1975.
Crow's Nest. London, Abelard Schuman, 1974.
A Chill in the Lane. Nashville, Nelson, 1974.
The Night Wind, illustrated by Charles Robinson. New York, Atheneum, 1974; London, Severn House, 1982.
Ship of Danger. London, Heinemann, and New York, Criterion, 1974.
The Secret Players, illustrated by James Russell. Leicester, Brockhampton Press, 1974.
Bridge of Friendship. London, Dent, 1975; New York, Dodd Mead, 1977.
Romansgrove, illustrated by Gail Owens. New York, Atheneum, 1975.
The Flash Children, illustrated by Gavin Rowe. Leicester, Brockhampton Press, and New York, Dodd Mead, 1975.
Away from Wood Street, illustrated by Shirley Hughes. London, Methuen, 1975.
Trouble in the Glen, illustrated by Jutta Ash. London, Abelard Schuman, 1976.

The Rising Tide. London, Heinemann, 1976; New York, Walker, 1978.
My Family's Not Forever. London, Abelard Schuman, 1977.
The View Beyond My Father. London, Abelard Schuman, 1977; New York, Dodd Mead, 1978.
The Pine Street Pageant, illustrated by Rosemary Chanter. London, Abelard Schuman, 1978.
Wood Street and Mary Ellen, illustrated by Lesley Smith. London, Methuen, 1979.
Tomorrow Is a Lovely Day. London, Abelard Schuman, 1979; as *A Lovely Tomorrow,* New York, Dodd Mead, 1980.
Pine Street Goes Camping, illustrated by Patricia Drew. London, Abelard Schuman, 1980.
The Mills Down Below. London, Abelard Schuman, 1980; New York, Dodd Mead, 1981.
Strangers in Wood Street, illustrated by Lesley Smith. London, Methuen, 1981.
The Horns of Danger. New York, Dodd Mead, 1981.
The Pine Street Problem, illustrated by Patricia Drew. London, Abelard Schuman, 1981.
A Strange Enchantment. London, Abelard Schuman, 1981; New York, Dodd Mead, 1982.
Goodbye to Pine Street, illustrated by Patricia Drew. London, Abelard Schuman, 1982.
Growing Up in Wood Street, illustrated by Lesley Smith. London, Methuen, 1982.
Alone at Pine Street, illustrated by Patricia Drew. London, Abelard Schuman, 1983.
The Crumble Lane Adventure, illustrated by Nola Edwards. London, Methuen, 1983.
A Dream of Hunger Moss. New York, Dodd Mead, 1983; London, Severn House, 1985.
Friends at Pine Street, illustrated by Patricia Drew. London, Abelard Schuman, 1984.
A Secret in Spindle Bottom, illustrated by David Leeming. London, Abelard Schuman, 1984.
Trouble in Crumble Lane, illustrated by Jane Bottomley. London, Methuen, 1984.
The Flash Children in Winter, illustrated by Doreen Caldwell. London, Hodder and Stoughton, 1985.
The Pride of Pine Street, illustrated by Patricia Drew. London, Blackie, 1985.
The Crumble Lane Captives, illustrated by Jane Bottomley. London, Methuen, 1986.
A Mystery in Spindle Bottom, illustrated by Patricia MacCarthy. London, Blackie, 1986.
The Road to Huntingland. London, Severn House, 1986.
The Crumble Lane Mystery, illustrated by Jane Bottomley. London, Methuen, 1987.
Up the Victorian Staircase: A London Mystery. London, Severn House, 1987.
First Term at Ash Grove, illustrated by Liz Roberts. London, Blackie, 1988.

Fiction as Jean Estoril

Ballet for Drina, illustrated by Eve Guthrie and M.P. Steedman Davies. London, Hodder and Stoughton, 1957; New York, Vanguard Press, 1958.
Drina's Dancing Year. London, Hodder and Stoughton, 1958.
Drina Dances in Exile. London, Hodder and Stoughton, 1959.
Drina Dances in Italy, illustrated by Eve Guthrie and M.P. Steedman Davies. London, Hodder and Stoughton, 1959; New York, Vanguard Press, 1962.
Drina Dances Again. London, Hodder and Stoughton, 1960.
Drina Dances in New York. London, Hodder and Stoughton, 1961.

Drina Dances in Paris. London, Hodder and Stoughton, 1962.
Drina Dances in Madeira. London, Hodder and Stoughton, 1963.
Drina Dances in Switzerland. London, Hodder and Stoughton, 1964.
Drina Goes on Tour. Leicester, Brockhampton Press, 1965.
We Danced in Bloomsbury Square. London, Heinemann, 1967; Chicago, Follett, 1970; as *The Ballet Twins,* London, Macdonald, 1989.

Fiction as Anne Pilgrim

The First Time I Saw Paris. New York and London, Abelard Schuman, 1961.
Clare Goes to Holland. New York and London, Abelard Schuman, 1962.
A Summer in Provence. New York and London, Abelard Schuman, 1963.
Strangers in New York. New York and London, Abelard Schuman, 1964.
Selina's New Family, illustrated by Graham Byfield. New York and London, Abelard Schuman, 1967.

Fiction as Priscilla Hagon

Cruising to Danger, illustrated by William Plummer. Cleveland, World, 1966; London, Harrap, 1968.
Dancing to Danger, illustrated by Susanne Suba. Cleveland, World, 1967.
Mystery at Saint-Hilaire, illustrated by William Plummer. Cleveland, World, 1968.
Mystery at the Villa Bianca, illustrated by William Plummer. New York, World, 1969.
The Mystery of the Secret Square, illustrated by Ray Abel. New York, World, 1970.

PUBLICATIONS FOR ADULTS

Novel

Murder at the Flood. London, Stanley Paul, 1957.

Verse

The Haunted Valley and Other Poems. Privately printed, 1981.

Other

To Be an Author: A Short Autobiography. Privately printed, 1982.
More About Being an Author. Privately printed, 1985.
The Background Came First: My Books and Places. Privately printed, 2 vols., 1988.

*

Manuscript Collection: University of Southern Mississippi, Hattiesburg.

Mabel Esther Allan comments:

I am a collector of old girls' books and I soon found that, with a few exceptions, most authors had left little personal record. That was why I wrote two autobiographies, *To Be an Author* and *More About Being an Author,* and had them printed privately. I felt it was time to set the record straight. I also brought my poems together in a privately printed booklet, for they tell a good deal about me, and where I was living, and writing, at different times.

I have had a long writing life. But, though I wrote many, I didn't publish a book until 1948. Until then, as well as writing all those unpublished novels and children's books, I sold short stories, articles, and, during the war, poetry. In so many years my work has often changed: I feel I have done a great deal more than create "dream worlds." In the middle years I did certainly write a number of books for older girls that had "romantic" endings. But they *were* largely written between certain dates, and even then, I was writing other books.

In the early years I wrote for rather younger readers, and some of the books were fairly original. *Holiday at Arnriggs,* for instance, was about a group of Yorkshire boys, and one girl, who tried to make the long and complicated North Skelton sword dance a perfect thing. All my school stories were far ahead of their time, as even the *Times Literary Supplement* admitted when they based a front page article on one of them. My schools were all progressive and often coeducational. I believed that young people had the right to run their own affairs. I believed in self-discipline, rather than in imposed discipline. And my views haven't changed.

In the early 1970's there was a very great change. I wrote *An Island in a Green Sea, Time to Go Back,* and a number of others that had an autobiographical basis. One of the pleasures of being older, or old, is that one can look back and form early experiences into stories. *The Mills Down Below* was different. In that book I wrote about women's rights. I wish I had done more books on that theme.

From now on it is possible that I will write only for younger readers. I seem to be obsessed with the poorer streeets of Liverpool and with the Lancashire towns and moors. Gone are the days when I only wanted to write about New York.

My early books are eagerly collected by adults of all ages. In a way it makes me feel dead already, but, unlike most authors who are collected, I can still speak for myself.

*   *   *

Mabel Esther Allan's long writing career cannot easily be summarized. Her books vary in theme, have no settled pattern and are directed at no one single age-group. In other words, she defies that peculiarly English trait of classifying and labelling authors into clearly defined categories. Only since the early 1960's can a developing theme be noticed, and even then it is not exclusively consistent. The book that marked this switch in emphasis, *The Sign of the Unicorn,* first appeared in 1963. The themes developed here—personal unhappiness, unsettling and disturbing changes in home environment, sometimes voluntary but more often forced by circumstances, homesickness for the old, apprehension and fear at the new, a gradual change in attitude, helped in most cases by meeting new friends, and the cumulative effect they have on a teenage heroine on the verge of womanhood—are all conspicuous in later books like *Dangerous Inheritance* and *A Formidable Enemy,* and many others, usually set either in Paris or New York.

More recently Allan has taken up the challenge presented by the inner cities in an honest attempt to relate literature to the lives of working-class children who might otherwise find books wholly reflecting middle-class mores in situations and surroundings completely alien to their own. The Wood Street Gang series, rumbustious and fast-moving episodes from life in Liverpool, is concerned not with ponies, hilltrekking in the Scottish Highlands, ballet, or summer holidays in Brittany, but with encounters with the police, the formation of a pop group and the antagonism it meets when it needs to practise, and the inevitable hostility with rival gangs. It provides a splendid example, if example were necessary, of Allan's vitality, exuberance, and versatility.

—Alan Edwin Day

ALLEN, Alex B.   See **HEIDE, Florence Parry.**

ALLEN, Betsy.   See **CAVANNA, Betty.**

ALLEN, Eric.   Pseudonym for Eric Allen Ballard; also wrote as Paul Dallas; Edwin Harrison. British.   Born in London, 25 February 1908. Married Janet Ballard.   Jazz promoter in the 1930's and founder of *Hot News* jazz magazine, London, 1932; freelance writer in the Middle East, 1946–48, South Africa, 1948–52, Spain, Morocco, and Italy, 1952–59, and London, from 1959. *Died 2 March 1968.*

PUBLICATIONS FOR CHILDREN

Fiction

How Many Miles to Cyprus, illustrated by Janet Allen Ballard. London, Methuen, 1955.
Pepe Moreno, illustrated by Hazel Cook.   London, Faber, 1955; New York, A.S. Barnes, 1960.
Pepe Moreno and the Roller Skates, illustrated by David Knight. London, Faber, 1958; New York, A.S. Barnes, 1959.
Pepe on the Run, illustrated by David Knight.   London, Faber, 1959; New York, A.S. Barnes, 1960.
Pepe Moreno and the Dilapidated Donkey, illustrated by David Knight.   London, Faber, 1960; New York, A.S. Barnes, 1961.
The Story of Lorenzo the Magnificent, illustrated by David Knight. London, Faber, 1961.
Pepe Moreno's Quixotic Adventure, illustrated by David Knight. London, Faber, 1963.
The Latchkey Children, illustrated by Charles Keeping.   London, Oxford University Press, 1963.
Smitty and the Plural of Cactus [*Egyptian Cat*], illustrated by Andrew Dodds.   London, Nelson, 2 vols., 1965–66.

Plays

Television Series: *Pepe Moreno,* 1958.

Other

The Incredible Adventures of Don Quixote: A Retelling, illustrated by David Knight.   London, Faber, 1958.

PUBLICATIONS FOR ADULTS

Novels

Into My Parlour (as Paul Dallas).   London, Methuen, 1940.
Prayer Is Better Than Sleep.   London, Wells Gardner, 1946.
Death on Delivery.   London, Hammond, 1958.
Perilous Passport.   London, Hammond, 1958; as *Passport to Murder,* London, Corgi, 1959.
The Man Who Chose Death.   London, Hammond, 1959.
Canaries Also Sing.   London, Hammond, 1960.

Novels as Edwin Harrison

Diamonds Can Be Trouble.   London, Amalgamated Press, 1958.
The Fatal Hour.   London, Amalgamated Press, 1958.
Killer's Playground.   London, Amalgamated Press, 1959.
Witness to Murder.   London, Amalgamated Press, 1959.

Short Stories

Eric Allen's Broadcast Stories.   London, Rich and Cowan, 1947.

Plays

Television Plays: *The Pen of My Aunt* series, 1959; *Front Page* series, 1961; *Brother for Joe* series, 1961; *Bad Company,* 1962; *The Young Troubadour,* 1963.

*   *   *

Eric Allen particularly deserves recognition for *The Latchkey Children,* a runner-up for the Carnegie Medal in 1963. This novel was applauded as a worthy addition to the limited number of stories for children of the calibre of *The Family from One End Street* by Eve Garnett and *Magnolia Buildings* by Elizabeth Stucley. *The Latchkey Children* is competently constructed with a convincing portrayal of everyday life and its problems combined with a satisfying element of adventure.

The author leaves at least two definite impressions with his readers: a strong sense of place and a vivid picture of the humdrum daily lives of the five children who are the central characters in the story. The impression of place is achieved by the writer choosing a London council estate for the background to his plot, a setting ensuring appeal to a wide readership. The detail of the lives of "the latchkey children" is most painstakingly done and wholly authentic. It is a realistic picture of children with mothers at work: chores have to be performed, often reluctantly; meals have to be produced; agreements have to be made to stay at home to deal with tradesmen; money is in short supply.

To this down-to-earth setting is added a plausible degree of excitement and adventure with gang forays, a dog incident, and *the* tree issue. These adventure elements are credible: a difficult feat to achieve. The author also appeals to children's interests with the introduction of a television personality and film crew into the plot. The four children, who consider themselves friends and not a gang, form a lively group in the reader's mind rather than clear-cut individuals, and the West Indian boy Duke who joins the group is portrayed as a sympathetic character. The adult characters in the story are described, however small their roles in the plot, with an acute understanding of human weaknesses.

Although *The Latchkey Children* is probably Allen's best-known novel for children, he also wrote fiction for the younger 8–10 age group. The Pepe Moreno books set in Spain, and the Smitty books about a lively schoolboy offer much needed material of a high standard for an age group less well provided for than its older counterparts. Eric Allen made a worthwhile contribution to children's fiction, and although less prolific than similar writers such as E. W. Hildick and A. Stephen Tring, he is another writer who appears to have made a serious attempt to cater for children's varying reading needs: a task only a small number of writers are willing to attempt.

—Anne W. Ellis

ALMEDINGEN, E.M. (Martha Edith von Almedingen).
British. Born in St. Petersburg, Russia, 12 July 1898; emigrated to
England in 1923; became British citizen, 1932. Educated privately,
and at Xenia Nobility College; Petrograd University, 1916–20. Lec-
turer in English and medieval history and literature, Petrograd
University, 1921–22; Lecturer in Russian history and literature,
Oxford University, 1951. Recipient: *Atlantic Review* prize, for
autobiography, 1941. Fellow, Royal Society of Literature, 1951.
Died 5 March 1971.

PUBLICATIONS FOR CHILDREN

Fiction

One Little Tree: A Christmas Card of a Finnish Landscape, il-
   lustrated by Denise Brown.   London, Parrish, 1963; New York,
   Norton, 1968.
The Knights of the Golden Table, illustrated by Charles Keeping.
   London, Bodley Head, 1963; Philadelphia, Lippincott, 1964.
The Treasure of Siegfried, illustrated by Charles Keeping.   London,
   Bodley Head, 1964; Philadelphia, Lippincott, 1965.
Little Katia, illustrated by Victor Ambrus.   London, Oxford Univer-
   sity Press, 1966; as *Katia,* New York, Farrar Straus, 1967.
Young Mark, illustrated by Victor Ambrus.   London, Oxford
   University Press, 1967; New York, Farrar Straus, 1968.
A Candle at Dusk, illustrated by Doreen Roberts.   London, Oxford
   University Press, and New York, Farrar Straus, 1969.
Fanny, illustrated by Ian Ribbons.   London, Oxford University
   Press, and New York, Farrar Straus, 1970.
Ellen.   New York, Farrar Straus, 1970; London, Oxford University
   Press, 1971.
Anna, illustrated by Robert Micklewright.   London, Oxford
   University Press, and New York, Farrar Straus, 1972.
The Crimson Oak, illustrated by Kate Mellor.   London, Methuen,
   1981; New York, Putnam, 1983.

Other

Russian Fairy Tales, illustrated by Hazel Cook.   London, Muller,
   1957; as *Russian Folk and Fairy Tales,* New York, Putnam, 1963.
The Young Pavlova, illustrated by Denise Brown.   London, Parrish,
   1960; New York, Roy, 1961.
The Young Leonardo da Vinci, illustrated by Azpelicueta.   London,
   Parrish, 1963; New York, Roy, 1966.
A Picture History of Russia, illustrated by Clarke Hutton.   London,
   Oxford University Press, and New York, Watts, 1964.
The Young Catherine the Great, illustrated by Denise Brown.   Lon-
   don, Parrish, 1965; New York, Roy, 1966.
The Retreat from Moscow, illustrated by Sheila Bewley.   London,
   Parrish, 1966; New York, Warne, 1968.
The Story of Gudrun, Based on the Third Part of the Epic of Gudrun,
   illustrated by Enrico Arno.   New York, Norton, 1967.
I Remember St. Petersburg, illustrated by John Sergeant.   London,
   Longman, 1969; as *My St. Petersburg: A Reminiscence of
   Childhood,* New York, Norton, 1970.
Rus into Muscovy: The History of Early Russia, illustrated by
   Michael Charlton.   London, Longman, 1971; as *Land of Mus-
   covy,* New York, Farrar Straus, 1972.

PUBLICATIONS FOR ADULTS

Novels

Young Catherine.   London, Constable, 1937; New York, Stokes,

1938.
The Lion of the North.   London, Constable, 1938.
She Married Pushkin.   London, Constable, 1939.
Frossia.   London, Lane, 1943; New York, Harcourt Brace, 1944;
   abridged edition, London, Bodley Head, 1961.
Dasha.   London, Lane, 1944; New York, Harcourt Brace, 1945.
The Inmost Heart.   London, Lane, 1949; as *The Golden Sequence,*
   Philadelphia, Westminster Press, 1949.
Flame on the Water.   London, Hutchinson, 1952.
The Rock.   London, Hutchinson, 1953.
Stand Fast, Beloved City.   London, Hutchinson, 1954.
Ground Corn.   London, Hutchinson, 1955.
Fair Haven.   London, Hutchinson, 1956.
Stephen's Light.   London, Hutchinson, 1956; New York, Holt
   Rinehart, 1969.
The Scarlet Goose.   London, Hutchinson, 1957; New York, Holt
   Rinehart, 1970.
The Little Stairway.   London, Hutchinson, 1960; as *The Winter in
   the Heart,* New York, Appleton Century Crofts, 1960.
Dark Splendour.   London, Hutchinson, 1961.
The Ladies of St. Hedwigs.   London, Hutchinson, 1965; New York,
   Vanguard Press, 1967.
Too Early Lilac.   London, Hutchinson, 1970; New York, Vanguard
   Press, 1974.

Play

Storm at Westminster.   London and New York, Oxford University
   Press, 1952.

Verse

Rus.   London and New York, Oxford University Press, 1939.
Poloniae Testamentum.   London, Lane, 1942.
Out of Seir.   London, Lane, 1943.
The Unnamed Stream and Other Poems.   London, Bodley Head,
   1965.

Other

The Catholic Church in Russia Today.   London, Burns Oates, and
   New York, Kenedy, 1923.
The English Pope, Adrian IV.   London, Heath Cranton, 1925.
Women under Fire: Six Months in the Red Army.   London, Hutchin-
   son, 1930.
St. Gregory the Great.   Dublin, Irish Messenger, 1930.
The Wanderer.   Dublin, Irish Messenger, 1930.
Clear Skies at Last.   Dublin, Irish Messenger, 1931.
Destiny.   Dublin, Irish Messenger, 1931.
God and the Soviet.   Dublin, Irish Messenger, 1931.
From Rome to Canterbury.   London, Faith Press, and Milwaukee,
   Morehouse, 1933.
The Pilgrimage of a Soul.   London, Faith Press, and Milwaukee,
   Morehouse, 1934.
Through Many Windows Opened by the Book of Common Prayer.
   London, Faith Press, and Milwaukee, Morehouse, 1935.
Tomorrow Will Come (autobiography).   London, Lane, and Boston,
   Little Brown, 1941.
Dom Bernard Clements: A Portrait.   London, Lane, 1945.
The Almond.   London, Lane, 1947.
Within the Harbour.   London, Lane, 1950.
Late Arrival (includes *The Almond* and *Within the Harbour*).
   Philadelphia, Westminster Press, 1952.
Life of Many Colours: The Story of Grandmother Ellen.   London,
   Hutchinson, 1958; as *A Very Far Country,* New York, Appleton
   Century Crofts, 1958.

So Dark a Stream: A Study of the Emperor Paul I of Russia, 1754–1801. London, Hutchinson, 1959.
The Batsford Colour Book of Kittens. London, Batsford, 1961; as *Kittens in Color,* New York, Viking Press, 1961.
Catherine, Empress of Russia. New York, Dodd Mead, 1961; as *Catherine the Great: A Portrait,* London, Hutchinson, 1963.
The Empress Alexandra, 1872–1918: A Study. London, Hutchinson, 1961.
The Emperor Alexander II: A Study. London, Bodley Head, 1962.
The Emperor Alexander I. London, Bodley Head, 1964; New York, Vanguard Press, 1966.
An Unbroken Unity: A Memoir of Grand Duchess Serge of Russia, 1864–1918. London, Bodley Head, 1964.
The Romanovs: Three Centuries of an Ill-Fated Dynasty. London, Bodley Head, and New York, Holt Rinehart, 1966.
Francis of Assisi: A Portrait. London, Bodley Head, 1967; as *St. Francis of Assisi: A Great Life in Brief,* New York, Knopf, 1967.
Charlemagne: A Study. London, Bodley Head, 1968.
Leonardo da Vinci: A Portrait. London, Bodley Head, 1969.

Translator, *The Lord's Passion,* by Hrabanus Magnentius. London, Mowbray, 1938.

*　　*　　*

E.M. Almedingen's connection with writing for children has a long history. It began when her great-aunt, Catherine A. Almedingen, started to translate American and English children's classics into Russian. Then Catherine wrote her autobiography, *The Story of a Little Girl.* Published in 1874, it won the approval of Chekhov and Tolstoy and of countless Russian children until the 1917 revolution. The real Katia lived from 1829 to December 16, 1893, and, besides writing for children, she founded one of the best children's monthlies in Russia, *Rodnik.*

The book *Little Katia* is a version of *The Story of a Little Girl* by her great-niece, E.M. Almedingen. Katia was born in Russia, but was not Russian by blood-line because her father was Austro-Bavarian and her mother Danish. After living in three separate and very different homes before the age of 13, Katia journeyed to Moscow to enter a strict upper school where she was to live for four years.

Upper-class Russian life is pictured during the reign of the Czars. Life on farms and large estates, winter and summer, provides a scintillating background of sunshine and shadow for the story of a temperamental young girl. Occasional passages show the deep chasms in the social structure of the country: "...when I was a little girl there was a gulf between people like my father and anyone engaged in trade....Trade meant buying and selling. Uncle Nicholas and all his neighbors certainly sold timber and cattle....So did my father....But, from the social sense, the difference stood for an unsurmountable barrier. I believe that *kouptzy* (merchants) were often far more wealthy than any of us, but bags of gold as such did not matter."

Young Mark tells of a Ukrainian boy of 18th-century Russia. Almedingen reconstructs his journey, mostly on foot, from his native village in the Ukraine to St. Petersburg, to see the Hetman, who, he hoped, would help him to attain his life's goal—to be a singer. It was a journey marked by formidable reverses, menace, and treachery. Almedingen has imparted the history in a way that makes a varicolored background for an unusual story, with special attention to local custom, food, and the characters met on the road and in the marketplaces. The circumstances of the peasants are shown in clear contrast to the richness of the nobility, but not in a propagandistic way. Such, one feels, was the way it was, at that time, in that place.

Many of Almedingen's books are based on episodes in her own family history. *Anna* tells of her great-grandmother, a rare person because she was educated—unlike most Russian girls even in the upper class—and excelled in languages. Again we have a picture, clear in its details, of the life in a wealthy Russian merchant's home, though unusual because marked by devotion to study and the collecting of rare books in which even the Czarina Catherine took an interest. Religion was an integral part of this life. When Anna made a momentous discovery about herself, she paid a visit to St. Praskova's, the church she preferred, and lighted a large wax candle in front of an icon, as a "Signature to the discovery."

A story for younger children, *One Little Tree,* tells of a more modern day, though, with its close-knit family and child-like faith, the story may seem old-fashioned to some children. But once having read it, one finds it hard to forget. Eight-year-old Arni in a small Finnish village finds, one year, that in order to keep his promise to his sister to get a fir tree for their Christmas he has to cross the recently closed border into Russian-held territory. What might have been a bitter ending is retrieved by a Russian soldier who is touched by Arni's bravery and faith. Arni's parents who face hunger rather than sell their children's few treasures are convincingly portrayed.

Almedingen's *A Picture History of Russia* covers the story of Russia from about 500 A.D. to the date of its publication, 1964. It is necessarily a sweeping view of Russian history, but main events are highlighted, and there are movement and interesting information on every page. Like most of the author's other, more personalized narratives, it stands as an excellent introduction to that vast and still mysterious country.

—Norma R. Fryatt

ALTSHELER, Joseph A(lexander). American. Born in Three Springs, Kentucky, 29 April 1862. Educated at Liberty College, Glasgow, Kentucky; Vanderbilt University, Nashville. Married Sarah Boles in 1888; one son. Journalist, Louisville *Evening Post,* 1885, and *Courier-Journal,* 1885–92; staff member, New York *World,* from 1892, and editor of the magazine edition of the *World. Died 5 June 1919.*

PUBLICATIONS FOR CHILDREN

Fiction

The Hidden Mine. New York, Tait, 1896.
The Rainbow of Gold. New York, Home Book Company, 1896.
A Soldier of Manhattan. New York, Appleton, 1897; London, Smith Elder, 1898.
The Sun of Saratoga. New York, Appleton, 1897.
A Herald of the West. New York, Appleton, 1898.
In Circling Camps. New York, Appleton, 1900.
In Hostile Red. New York, Doubleday, 1900.
The Last Rebel. Philadelphia, Lippincott, 1900.
The Wilderness Road. New York, Appleton, and London, Lawrence and Bullen, 1901.
My Captive. New York, Appleton, 1902.
Before the Dawn. New York, Doubleday, and London, Hutchinson, 1903.
Guthrie of the Times, illustrated by F.R. Gruger. New York, Doubleday, 1904; London, Hutchinson, 1905.
The Young Trailers: A Story of Early Kentucky. New York, Appleton, 1907; London, Hodder and Stoughton, 1926.
The Forest Runners. New York, Appleton, 1908.
The Free Rangers. New York, Appleton, 1909.
The Last of the Chiefs. New York, Appleton, 1909.
The Recovery. New York, Lovell, 1909.
The Riflemen of the Ohio. New York, Appleton, 1910.
The Horsemen of the Plains, illustrated by Charles Livingston Bull.

New York, Macmillan, 1910.
The Scouts of the Valley. New York, Appleton, 1911.
The Quest of the Four. New York, Appleton, 1911.
The Border Watch. New York, Appleton, 1912.
The Texan Star [*Scouts, Triumph*]. New York, Appleton, 3 vols., 1912–13.
Apache Gold. New York, Appleton, 1913.
The Guns of Bull Run. New York, Appleton, 1914.
The Guns of Shiloh. New York, Appleton, 1914.
The Scouts of Stonewall, illustrated by Charles Wrenn. New York, Appleton, 1914.
The Sword of Antietam, illustrated by Charles Wrenn. New York, Appleton, 1914.
The Forest of Swords, illustrated by Charles Wrenn. New York, Appleton, 1915.
The Guns of Europe, illustrated by Charles Wrenn. New York, Appleton, 1915.
The Hosts of the Air, illustrated by Charles Wrenn. New York, Appleton, 1915.
The Rock of Chickamauga, illustrated by Charles Wrenn. New York, Appleton, 1915.
The Star of Gettysburg, illustrated by Charles Wrenn. New York, Appleton, 1915.
The Keepers of the Trail, illustrated by D.C. Hutchinson. New York, Appleton, 1916.
The Hunters of the Hills, illustrated by D.C. Hutchinson. New York, Appleton, 1916.
The Shades of the Wilderness, illustrated by Charles Wrenn. New York, Appleton, 1916.
The Tree of Appomattox, illustrated by Charles Wrenn. New York, Appleton, 1916.
The Eyes of the Woods, illustrated by D.C. Hutchinson. New York, Appleton, 1917.
The Rulers of the Lakes, illustrated by Charles Wrenn. New York, Appleton, 1917.
The Shadow of the North, illustrated by Charles Wrenn. New York, Appleton, 1917.
The Great Sioux Trail, illustrated by Charles Wrenn. New York, Appleton, 1918; London, Hodder and Stoughton, 1926.
The Lost Hunters, illustrated by Charles Wrenn. New York, Appleton, 1918; London, Harrap, 1920.
The Masters of the Peaks, illustrated by Charles Wrenn. New York, Appleton, 1918.
The Lords of the Wilds, illustrated by Charles Wrenn. New York, Appleton, 1919.
The Sun of Quebec, illustrated by Charles Wrenn. New York, Appleton, 1919.

PUBLICATIONS FOR ADULTS

Novel

The Candidate. New York, Harper, 1905.

* * *

In 1918, Joseph A. Altsheler was voted the most popular boys' writer in America by a public libraries committee. Since Altsheler's death in 1919, his popularity has eroded to the point where most of his work is out-of-print and only larger libraries still include Altsheler in their collections. However, for the 25 years before 1919, Altsheler produced immensely popular juvenile series featuring young men placed in some of the most exciting historical events in American history: from the French and Indian War to the beginning of the First World War.

The best of the series is the Young Trailer series which deals with the settling of the Ohio Valley. The best single volume is *The Young Trailers: A Story of Early Kentucky* where the struggling settlers fight off the Indian menace and the traitors among them to survive. In addition, Altsheler presents a hunt for salt and a dinosaur burial ground.

Altsheler was fascinated by American history and sometimes overdid the historical facts in his books. For example, his Civil War series includes solid efforts like *The Guns of Bull Run* and *The Scouts of Stonewall,* but Altsheler could also write a plodding volume like *The Tree of Appomattox,* slowed to a crawl by the burden of historical facts.

Although Altsheler's westerns like *The Texan Star, Apache Gold,* and *The Texan Scouts* present rugged teenage heroes, the portrayal of the Indian often borders on racism by today's standards.

When Altsheler and his family were traveling in Europe during the summer of 1914, they were trapped in Germany as World War I engulfed the continent. Although they managed eventually to get back to the United States, the ordeal broke Altsheler's health. Some of the horror of his brush with World War I can be found in *The Forest of Swords* and *The Guns of Europe,* written with uncharacteristic grimness and brutality.

Although Altsheler's reputation continues to remain high, his work is hard to find, and the change in popular taste leaves him with a readership of middle-aged people who re-read the juvenile books they enjoyed when they were young.

—George Kelley

———

ANDERSON, C(larence) W(illiam). American. Born in Wahoo, Nebraska, 12 April 1891. Educated at Wahoo High School; Art Institute, Chicago, three years. Married Madalena Paltenghi. Freelance artist and illustrator. Judge for American Horse Shows Association. Member, Society of American Graphic Artists. *Died 26 March 1971.*

PUBLICATIONS FOR CHILDREN (illustrated by the author)

Fiction

Billy and Blaze. New York, Macmillan, 1936.
Blaze and the Gypsies. New York, Macmillan, 1937; London, Country Life, 1939.
Blaze and the Forest Fire. New York, Macmillan, 1938.
Salute. New York, Macmillan, 1940.
High Courage. New York, Macmillan, 1941.
Bobcat. New York, Macmillan, 1949.
Blaze Finds the Trail. New York, Macmillan, 1950.
A Pony for Linda. New York, Macmillan, 1951.
Linda and the Indians. New York, Macmillan, 1952.
The Crooked Colt. New York, Macmillan, 1954.
Blaze and Thunderbolt. New York, Macmillan, 1955.
The Horse of Hurricane Hill. New York, Macmillan, 1956; Leicester, Brockhampton Press, 1958.
Afraid to Ride. New York, Macmillan, 1957; Leicester, Brockhampton Press, 1959.
Pony for Three. New York, Macmillan, 1958.
Blaze and the Mountain Lion. New York, Macmillan, 1959.
A Filly for Joan. New York, Macmillan, 1960.
Lonesome Little Colt. New York, Macmillan, 1961.
Great Heart. New York, Macmillan, 1962.
Blaze and the Indian Cave. New York, Macmillan, and London, Collier Macmillan, 1964.
Another Man o' War. New York, Macmillan, 1966; London, Collier

Macmillan, 1967.

Blaze and the Lost Quarry. New York, Macmillan, and London, Collier Macmillan, 1966.

The Outlaw. New York, Macmillan, and London, Collier Macmillan, 1967.

Blaze and the Gray Spotted Pony. New York, Macmillan, and London, Collier Macmillan, 1968.

Blaze Shows the Way. New York, Macmillan, and London, Collier Macmillan, 1969.

Phantom, Son of the Gray Ghost. New York, Macmillan, and London, Collier Macmillan, 1969.

Blaze Finds Forgotten Roads. New York, Macmillan, and London, Collier Macmillan, 1970.

The Blind Connemara. New York, Macmillan, and London, Collier Macmillan, 1971.

The Rumble Seat Pony. New York, Macmillan, and London, Collier Macmillan, 1971.

Other

Twenty Gallant Horses. New York, Macmillan, 1965.

Editor, *C.W. Anderson's Favorite Horse Stories.* New York, Dutton, 1967.

PUBLICATIONS FOR ADULTS

Other

And So to Bed: Seventy-Six Drawings. New York, Loring and Mussey, 1935.

Black, Bay, and Chestnut: Profiles of Twenty Favorite Horses. New York, Macmillan, 1939.

Deep Through the Heart: Profiles of Twenty Valiant Horses. New York, Macmillan, 1940.

Thoroughbreds. New York, Macmillan, 1942.

Big Red. New York, Macmillan, 1943.

Heads Up, Heels Down: A Handbook of Horsemanship and Riding. New York, Macmillan, 1944.

A Touch of Greatness. New York, Macmillan, 1945.

Tomorrow's Champion. New York, Macmillan, 1946.

Sketchbook. New York, Macmillan, 1948.

All Thoroughbreds. New York, Harper, 1948.

Post Parade. New York, Harper, 1949.

Horses Are Folks. New York, Harper, 1950.

Horse Show. New York, Harper, 1951.

Turf and Bluegrass. New York, Harper, 1952.

The Smashers. New York, Harper, 1954.

Grey, Bay, and Chestnut. New York, Harper, 1955.

Colts and Champions. New York, Harper, 1956.

Accent on Youth. New York, Harper, 1958.

Bred to Run. New York, Harper, 1960.

Complete Book of Horses and Horsemanship. New York, Macmillan, and London, Collier Macmillan, 1963.

The Look of a Thoroughbred. New York, Harper, 1963.

The World of Horses. New York, Harper, 1965.

Before the Bugle. New York, Macmillan, 1968.

Horse of the Century: Man o' War. New York, Macmillan, 1970.

The Miracle of Greek Sculpture. New York, Dutton, 1970.

*

Manuscript Collections: Kerlan Collection, University of Minnesota, Minneapolis; University of Oregon Library, Eugene.

Illustrator: *Honey, The City Bear,* 1937, *Remus Goes to Town,* 1938, *Rumpus Rabbit,* 1939, and *Honey on a Raft,* 1941, all by Madalena Paltenghi; *A Pony Called Lightning* by Miriam Mason, 1948; *Midnight, Rodeo Champion,* 1951, and *A Horse Named Joe,* 1956, both by Robert Edward Gard.

*   *   *

All young readers who love horses know Billy and Blaze. If they remain devoted to horses, they come to know C.W. Anderson's books for older children. For these deal, too, with horses whether in fiction or non-fiction. Non-fiction writing gave Anderson a means of sharing his vast knowledge gained from experience and research, while his fiction for older readers provided stories about children who love horses and who learn about horse care, breeding, raising, training, and racing, this information generally imparted by a groom, trainer, or other older person.

Anderson thought of himself as an artist only, but the editor who discovered Anderson as artist and illustrator, Doris Patee, provoked and encouraged the early texts which Anderson wrote to accompany his illustrations in *Billy and Blaze, Blaze and the Gypsies,* and *Blaze and the Forest Fire.* From these brief stories concerning young Billy and his horse Blaze (each book is basically an adventure story about Blaze) grew Anderson's writing ability.

Anderson's own enthusiasm for things equestrian permeates all his books. His observations and thoughts about horses for the cowboy, huntsperson, or jockey are detailed as the trainer or groom, often Black, explains to the young boy or girl in the story what makes a good horse, a courageous horse, a fast horse, and so on, as well as what constitutes a good owner. These are elements that Anderson's illustrations alone cannot capture, and thus, his simple text is essential, and well-written. Perhaps the best among this second group of Anderson's books are *Salute, High Courage, The Horse of Hurricane Hill,* and *A Filly for Joan.* Each contains a sense of action, represented by words such as "shining," "brushing," "polishing," "cleaning," "rubbing," all perhaps routine to someone whose living is made grooming a horse, but exciting to the reader. Pictures of horses often fill the stable wall or the young owner's room. Long talks with the groom or trainer, that embodiment of Anderson as horse lover and authority, may conclude at chapter's end with the senior's apology for having become enthused and having talked too much. It may represent an apology to the reader, a device to end a chapter, but to the horse fan the clever conclusion leads quickly to the next chapter.

Most chapters in these books tend to cover a single element in breeding, care, or racing, or one episode in what becomes little more than a collected series of horse stories. Anderson applied the same technique to his non-fiction when he gathered individual stories to create the collections *Black, Bay, and Chestnut* and *Deep Through the Heart.* His best non-fiction efforts are *Complete Book of Horses and Horsemanship* and *Big Red,* the latter being the story of Man o' War, introduced by the "softly slurred Negro voice" of Man o' War's trainer and exercise boy. Anderson may be criticized in the future for his rendition of the Black American dialect, but his depiction is never derogatory; often it is the Black groom who is dearly loved by the children and respected for his knowledge as the story unfolds.

Anderson has few rivals within his chosen field of writing and illustration. He combined a magnificent talent for illustrating all kinds of horses with an ability to write clearly and to convey to all ages his love and knowledge of horses.

—Edward Kemp

ANDREW, Prudence (Hastings, née Petch). British. Born in London, 23 May 1924. Educated at St. Anne's College, Oxford, B.A. (honours) in history 1946. Married G.H.L. Andrew in 1946; two daughters. Worked in the personnel department, Joseph Lucas Ltd., Birmingham, 1944–45; staff member, Nuffield Institute of Colonial Affairs, Oxford, 1945–47; history teacher, St. Michael's Convent School, Monmouthshire, 1956–60. Address: c/o Heinemann Ltd. 81 Fulham Road, London SW3 6RB, England.

PUBLICATIONS FOR CHILDREN

Fiction

Ginger over the Wall, illustrated by Charles Mozley. London, Lutterworth Press, 1962.
Ginger and Batty Bill, illustrated by Charles Mozley. London, Lutterworth Press, 1963.
Ginger and Number 10, illustrated by Charles Mozley. London, Lutterworth Press, 1964.
The Christmas Card, illustrated by Mary Russon. London, Hamish Hamilton, 1966.
Ginger among the Pigeons, illustrated by Charles Mozley. London, Lutterworth Press, 1966.
Mr. Morgan's Marrow, illustrated by Janet Duchesne. London, Hamish Hamilton, 1967.
A New Creature. London, Hutchinson, and New York, Putnam, 1968.
Dog!, illustrated by Trevor Stubley. London, Hamish Hamilton, 1968; Nashville, Nelson, 1973.
A Man with Your Advantages. London, Hutchinson, 1970.
Mister O'Brien. London, Heinemann, 1972; Nashville, Nelson, 1973.
Una and Grubstreet. London, Heinemann, 1972; as *Una and the Heaven Baby,* Nashville, Nelson, 1975.
Rodge, Silvie, and Munch, illustrated by Jael Jordan. London, Heinemann, 1973.
Goodbye to the Rat. London, Heinemann, 1974.
The Heroic Deeds of Jason Jones, illustrated by Jael Jordan. London, Heinemann, 1975.
Where Are You Going To, My Pretty Maid? London, Heinemann, 1977.
Robinson Daniel Crusoe. London, Heinemann, 1978; as *Close Within My Own Circle,* New York, Elsevier Nelson, 1980.
The Other Side of the Park. London, Heinemann, 1984.

PUBLICATIONS FOR ADULTS

Novels

The Hooded Falcon. London, Hutchinson, 1960; New York, Putnam, 1961.
Ordeal by Silence: A Story of Medieval Times. London, Hutchinson, and New York, Putnam, 1961.
A Question of Choice. London, Hutchinson, and New York, Putnam, 1962.
The Earthworms. London, Hutchinson, 1963; as *The Constant Star,* New York, Putnam, 1964.
A Sparkle from the Coal. London, Hutchinson, 1964.
A New Creature. London, Hutchinson, and New York, Putnam, 1968.
A Man with Your Advantages. London, Hutchinson, 1970.

*   *   *

Prudence Andrew made a notable contribution to children's literature between 1962 and 1984, reflecting some of the key points in its development in Britain during that period.

In the 1960's her four books about Ginger and his gang attracted attention; she had updated the popular "William" figure and placed him in an urban setting which also portrayed the newly emergent multi-cultural society. Andrew was one of the first children's writers to include black characters as an integral part of the story, and although *Ginger and Number 10* was criticised for her descriptions of these characters, it also won praise for its clear condemnation of racial prejudice.

Mister O'Brien and *Una and Grubstreet* are both mainstream children's novels, published in the early 1970's when teachers and librarians were looking for stories about what were seen as young people's problems. Mister O'Brien, a colourfully dressed, one-legged man, is a figment of handicapped Christopher's imagination, who makes his appearance whenever Christopher has to decide between two courses of action. It is Mister O'Brien who is responsible for his friendship with Penny and for his consequent decision to accomplish the difficult feat of walking 10 miles in a sponsored charity walk. Motherless Una seeks comfort and support in conversations with Grubstreet, a small toy bear, who represents her more responsible, sensible self in their imaginary exchanges. Both Christopher and Una learn to come to terms with their respective circumstances, Christopher with his handicap, Una with her father's remarriage.

Both these books are concerned with the parent-child relationship but this theme is taken a stage further in her two latest books. *Robinson Daniel Crusoe* is about a teenager whose loneliness arises largely from the pressures put upon him by his father who is trying to compensate, through his gifted son, for his own lack of success. In the end Daniel commits suicide, sailing off down the Mersey— several of Andrew's books have a Liverpool setting—on a raft in imitation of his hero Robinson Crusoe. In *The Other Side of the Park* the central character is a girl; she too is moving towards independence after the unexplained death of her much-loved great-grandmother provides a reason for her to crystallise her attitudes towards her father's apparent greed for money and her mother's need for help. Here, the support of her sensible boyfriend brings about a happier solution.

Andrew also contributed to several publishers' series which were aimed at groups recognised as having special reading needs. *The Christmas Card* and *Dog!* are two of her books written for younger children who need a short, readable story with a few clearly defined characters, with which to practise their newly acquired reading skills. *Goodbye to the Rat* and *Where Are You Going To, My Pretty Maid?,* on the other hand, are short novels for teenagers, both of them about groups of young people leaving school without qualifications and trying to find their feet in the adult world.

Andrew writes well-constructed, entertaining stories about both boys and girls; although she tackles unusual themes and gives the reader an insight into the characters, there is plenty of action and humour to keep the story moving at a steady pace. From the point of view of style, *Robinson Daniel Crusoe* represents her most interesting work. The story is told by Daniel's younger brother, Jimmy, who, being a football-oriented extrovert, is a complete contrast to the serious and ultimately tragic Daniel; his account of events is interspersed with extracts from Daniel's diaries, which enable the reader to understand Daniel's inner feelings, while Jimmy's comments help to lighten the story.

Andrew's gifts for reproducing conversation, for accurate observation, and for creating plausible characters are apparent throughout her work, even when she is writing to a formula. In *Mr. Morgan's Marrow,* one of her books for younger children, the Welsh setting comes out clearly through the characters' names and their turns of speech. In the two short books for teenagers, she economises by giving each of the characters a rather stereotyped background, but nevertheless manages to achieve documentary realism and plausibility of character. She is good on relationships—between children and parents, between children and their friends. In *Mister O'Brien,* Christopher's overprotective mother and his newfound friend Penny both come clearly from the page. Marion, the encouraging and supportive friend of Jason Jones, is another minor character who lives on in the reader's mind. These very rounded supporting characters contribute to the humour that is an important feature of Andrew's work.

Equally important is the fact that her characters achieve success, however modest. Handicapped Christopher, buoyed up by his wish to help Penny and his admiration for Scott of the Antarctic, walks his 10 miles for charity, Una is left with her wish for a baby brother likely to be fulfilled, Jason Jones, weedy and unsuccessful, wins newspaper glory almost involuntarily. Through their experiences, Andrew's heroes and heroines develop and grow and, in doing so, provide a rewarding and enriching reading experience.

—Sheila G. Ray

————

ANDREWS, J(ames) S(ydney). Also writes as Jim Andrews. Irish. Born in Belfast, Northern Ireland, 14 December 1934. Educated at Rossall School, Fleetwood, Lancashire. Married Judith Ann McCartan in 1962; three daughters. Until 1988 director, Isaac Andrews and Sons, Belfast. Address: c/o David and Charles Publishers, Brunel House, Newton Abbot, Devon TQ12 4PU, England.

PUBLICATIONS FOR CHILDREN

Fiction

The Bell of Nendrum. London, Bodley Head, 1969; as *The Green Hill of Nendrum,* New York, Hawthorn, 1970.
The Man from the Sea. London, Bodley Head, 1970; New York, Dutton, 1971.
Cargo for a King. London, Bodley Head, 1972; New York, Dutton, 1973.

PUBLICATIONS FOR ADULTS as Jim Andrews

Other

Catamarans for Cruising. London, Hollis and Carter, 1974.
Simple Sailing. Kingswood, Surrey, World's Work, 1975.
Food for Arthritics, Based on Dr. Dong's Diet, with Judy Andrews. London, Faber, 1982.
Twelve Ships A-Sailing: Thirty-Five Years of Home-Water Cruising. Newton Abbot, Devon, David and Charles, 1986.

*   *   *

The novels of J.S. Andrews share a number of features: a fascination with sailing and the sea, an awareness of the savagery of Ulster's history, a central role for young male heroes. They belong to the genre usually designated "historical fiction," of the kind which favours colour, action, and confrontation rather than totally convincing characterization or stylistic subtlety. Placed beside the work of a Rosemary Sutcliff or a Leon Garfield they have an old-fashioned feel, particularly in their no-nonsense emphasis on simplified notions

of moral and physical courage. They have, however, the merit of strong storylines; and, even more interestingly, their depictions of earlier Irish conflicts provide many illuminating parallels with what in recent years we have come to call the Ulster "troubles." As Andrews says in a prefatory note to *The Bell of Nendrum,* "the story is one of life a thousand years ago—towards the end of the so-called 'Dark Ages'. And in seeing this, we hold up a mirror, which in some way reflects our own astonishing existence…"

The hero of *The Bell of Nendrum* is Nial Ross, a 15-year-old obsessed with sailing, especially around the islands in Strangford Lough. He finds himself, as the result of a time slip, drawn backwards to the 10th century, when a monastic settlement on the island of Mahee is being ravaged by the Vikings. His stay with the welcoming and bemused monks is a tranquil prelude to the violence of the attack with which the book ends, a violence that is graphically and horrifically described. It is, however, Nial's knowledge that such violence will still be widespread in his own far-off century that gives the story its special frisson. He himself is a serious, sensible youth, cleancut and resilient, the type of whom Henty would have been proud; he does, though, retain a rather stolid sense of his Ulster-Scottish origins and values.

For the setting of *The Man from the Sea* Andrews chooses Ireland of the Early Bronze Age and as his locality the coastal landscape of Donaghadee Sound at the outer end of Belfast Lough. Here the hardships of a small fishing community, aggravated by the disappearance of its men on a fishing expedition, are temporarily eased by the sudden arrival of the charismatic and quasi-mystical figure of Hadra. Hadra's journey to "Albin" (southwest Scotland) to find the lost fishermen constitutes the central chapters of the novel, a journey which will end in his own death but, simultaneously, in the return to life of others. The young hero, Euan, one of those accompanying Hadra, learns principally of the need to accept hardship and loss, developing an earnest stoicism in the process.

Ragnor MacHelli, the 17-year-old hero of *Cargo for a King,* is the most immediately likeable of Andrews's characters. Following his father's murder he decides to carry on his business as a trader plying the pirate-infested waters between his native Isle of Man and Ireland's east coast. The year is 1210 and in power in Ulster is the treacherous Hugh de Lacy, whose machinations have earlier displaced the highly-regarded Sir John de Courcy. Ragnor throws his weight behind Sir John and in the ensuing maritime confrontations manages to assist in his restoration, avenge his father's death, and meet and fall in love with Afrin, a former slave-girl. This last element of the book is treated with considerable good humour and the portrayal of the young people's growing sexual awareness provides a refreshing diversion from the cut-and-thrust of successive sea-battles.

The topographical and historical precision of Andrews's stories evinces his respect for his native province and its inhabitants, past and present. One senses, beneath the muscular prose and the occasional moments of overt moralizing, a deep concern for the destinies of those whom one of the characters in *Cargo for a King* describes as "a strange, mountainy people, with a hardness and closeness resembling the granite rocks of their land."

—Robert Dunbar

————

APPIAH, Peggy. British. Born in Filkins, Gloucestershire, 21 May 1921; daughter of the politician Sir Stafford Cripps. Educated at Norland Place and Queen's College, London; Maltman's Green, Buckinghamshire; Whitehall Secretarial College. Married Joe E. Appiah in 1953; one son and three daughters. Formerly research assistant, Ministry of Information, London; secretary, Racial Unity, London. From 1968 chairman of the Advisory Committee, Kumasi Children's Home. Agent: David Higham Associates Ltd., 5–8 Lower John Street, London WIR 4HA, England. Address: P.O. Box 829, Kumasi, Ashanti, Ghana.

PUBLICATIONS FOR CHILDREN

Fiction

The Children of Ananse, illustrated by Mora Dickson. London, Evans, 1968.
Gift of the Mmoatia, illustrated by Nii O. Quao. Tema, Ghana Publishing Corporation, 1972.
Ring of Gold, illustrated by Laszlo Acs. London, Deutsch, 1976.

Other

Ananse the Spider: Tales from an Ashanti Village, illustrated by Peggy Wilson. New York, Pantheon, 1966.
Tales of an Ashanti Father, illustrated by Mora Dickson. London, Deutsch, 1967; Boston, Beacon Press, 1989.
The Pineapple Child and Other Tales from Ashanti, illustrated by Mora Dickson. London, Deutsch, 1969.
The Lost Earring (reader), illustrated by J. Jarvis. London, Evans, 1971.
Yao and the Python (reader), illustrated by J. Jarvis. London, Evans, 1971.
Why There Are So Many Roads (folktales), illustrated by A.A. Teye. Lagos, African Universities Press, 1972.
Why the Hyena Does Not Care for Fish and Other Tales from the Ashanti Gold Weights, illustrated by Joanna Stubbs. London, Deutsch, 1977.

PUBLICATIONS FOR ADULTS

Novels

A Smell of Onions. London, Longman, 1971.
A Dirge Too Soon. Tema, Ghana Publishing Corporation, 1976.

Verse

Poems of Three Generations. Kumasi, Ghana, University of Science and Technology, 1978.

*

Peggy Appiah comments:

All the books I have so far published have been about Ashanti, where I live. The country is full of stories, and I find the atmosphere conducive to writing. Life in Africa has much of the unexpected, and people are closely involved in each other's lives. I have tried to project its liveliness and interest in my books and to give children in other parts of the world some idea of the life of those in Ghana. I have also tried to write for Ghanaian children about themselves, as in the past they have had to depend on books with foreign backgrounds. Most of the books are about village and forest life, animals and birds. I was brought up in the country, and it is there my main interests lie. Kwaku Ananse the Spider is the Brer Rabbit of Ghana: *Aesop's Fables* are so like the Spider stories that Ghanaian children read them as such. The wind in the willows is the same one that breathes through the palm fronds. It is this universality of children's lore that I try to promote through my writing, hoping it will help to promote mutual understanding in this troubled world.

*   *   *

Peggy Appiah, first English, then, through her marriage, Ashanti, is in a singularly good position to write stories in English about Ashanti. Other parts of Ghana barely appear, but then why should they? Ashanti itself has an old and complex culture and enough stories to last a few lifetimes. People who live sociably in family and village groups without television and newspapers are apt to be good storytellers, and when one lives among them one can't help picking up the story habit. Appiah has done just that for a double audience in two countries: her stories must be as acceptable in Ghana as they are in England. By now there are thousands of children out there speaking and reading English as their second language but probably finding most English children's books a bit boring and unintelligible—nothing they can connect with.

They must enjoy Appiah's books and so will British children who are at all interested in other countries. Her stories often have an element of folklorist fantasy, though *A Smell of Onions* (originally published for adults) is amusingly factual, a tangled tale of village life, very much as it is elsewhere and as it might be told. *Gift of the Mmoatia* in which two little girls, one Ghanaian, the other British, make friends and share joys and troubles, shows both Appiah's gifts and her limitations. In Ghana the wee folk of the deep forest are plausible, but the English fairies are booksy. This is surely because the author doesn't believe in them whereas she can at least suspend disbelief in the strange little Mmoatia who helped the children! Abena's reactions and puzzlements during her English visit are charmingly and beautifully observed, especially her astonishment at the long English evenings. Appiah is very happy with the children in her stories as also with the animals and insects, including Ananse, the important spider who comes into so many West Coast stories, and into her book *Tales of an Ashanti Father,* for people live close to them and would not find it strange to speak their language—nor I think would Peggy Appiah.

—Naomi Mitchison

———

ARDIZZONE, Edward (Jeffrey Irving). British. Born with French nationality in Haiphong, Ton Kin, French Indo-China (now Vietnam), 16 October 1900; moved to England, 1905; became British citizen, 1921. Educated at Clayesmore School, Iwerne Minster, Dorset, 1913–17; Westminster School of Art, London, 1922–27. Served in the Royal Artillery, 1939–40; official war artist, 1940–45. Married Catherine Anderson in 1929; one daughter and two sons. Clerk, Eastern Telegraph Company and other firms, London, 1920–26; instructor in graphic design, Camberwell School of Art, London, 1948–52; instructor in audio-visual aids, UNESCO, Southern India, 1952–53; visiting tutor in etching and lithography, Royal College of Art, London, 1953–60. Individual shows: Bloomsbury Gallery, 1930, Leger Gallery, 1931–36, Nicholson Gallery, 1939, Leicester Galleries, 1948, Mayor Gallery, 1962, Victoria and Albert Museum, 1973, New Grafton Gallery 1975, Illustrator's Art, 1982, and Hunter and Seale Gallery, 1986, all in London; Scottish Arts Council Gallery, Edinburgh, 1979; group shows: London Group, 1935, New English Group, 1936, Royal Society of Painters in Water Colours, 1954, and Royal Academy Summer Exhibition from 1964, all in London. Recipient (for illustration): Library Association Kate Greenaway Medal, 1957. Fellow, Society of Industrial Artists; Associate, 1962, and Member, 1970, Royal Academy; Honorary Associate, Royal College of Art; Royal Designer in Industry, Royal Society of Arts, 1974. C.B.E. (Commander, Order of the British Empire), 1971. *Died 8 November 1979.*

PUBLICATIONS FOR CHILDREN (illustrated by the author)

Fiction

Little Tim and the Brave Sea Captain. London and New York, Oxford University Press, 1936; revised edition, London, Oxford University Press, and New York, Walck, 1955.
Lucy Brown and Mr. Grimes. London and New York, Oxford University Press, 1937; revised edition, London, Bodley Head, 1970; New York, Walck, 1971.
Tim and Lucy Go to Sea. London and New York, Oxford University Press, 1938; revised edition, London, Oxford University Press, and New York, Walck, 1958.
Nicholas and the Fast-Moving Diesel. London, Eyre and Spottiswoode, 1947; New York, Walck, 1959.
Paul, The Hero of the Fire. London, Penguin, 1948; Boston, Houghton Mifflin, 1949; revised edition, London, Constable, 1962; New York, Walck, 1963.
Tim to the Rescue. London and New York, Oxford University Press, 1949.
Tim and Charlotte. London and New York, Oxford University Press, 1951.
Tim in Danger. London and New York, Oxford University Press, 1953.
Tim All Alone. London, Oxford University Press, 1956; New York, Walck, 1961.
Johnny the Clockmaker. London, Oxford University Press, and New York, Walck, 1960.
Tim's Friend Towser. London, Oxford University Press, and New York, Walck, 1962.
Peter the Wanderer. London, Oxford University Press, 1963; New York, Walck, 1964.
Diana and Her Rhinoceros. London, Bodley Head, and New York, Walck, 1964.
Sarah and Simon and No Red Paint. London, Constable, 1965; New York, Delacorte Press, 1966.
Tim and Ginger. London, Oxford University Press, and New York, Walck, 1965.
Tim to the Lighthouse. London, Oxford University Press, and New York, Walck, 1968.
Johnny's Bad Day. London, Bodley Head, 1970; as *The Wrong Side of the Bed,* New York, Doubleday, 1970.
Tim's Last Voyage. London, Bodley Head, 1972; New York, Walck, 1973.
Ship's Cook Ginger. London, Bodley Head, 1977; New York, Macmillan, 1978.

Other

Editor, *Ardizzone's Hans Andersen: Fourteen Classic Tales,* translated by Stephen Corrin. London, Deutsch, 1978; New York, Atheneum, 1979.
Editor, *Ardizzone's English Fairy Tales: Twelve Classic Tales.* London, Deutsch, 1980.

PUBLICATIONS FOR ADULTS

Other

Baggage to the Enemy. London, Murray, 1941.

The Young Ardizzone: An Autobiographical Fragment. London, Studio Vista, and New York, Macmillan, 1970.
Diary of a War Artist. London, Bodley Head, 1974.
Visiting Dieppe. London, Warren, 1981.
Indian Diary 1952–53. London, Bodley Head, 1984.

*

Bibliography: "Edward Ardizzone: A Preliminary Hand-List of His Illustrated Books, 1929–1970" by Brian Alderson, in *The Private Library* (Pinner, Middlesex), Spring 1972.

Critical Study: *Edward Ardizzone, Artist and Illustrator* by Gabriel White, London, Bodley Head, 1979, New York, Schocken, 1980; *Edward Ardizzone* (exhibition catalogue), Edinburgh, Scottish Arts Council, 1979; *My Father and Edward Ardizzone: A Lasting Friendship* by Edward Booth-Clibborn, London, Hardy, 1983.

Illustrator: *In a Glass Darkly* by Sheridan Le Fanu, 1929; *The Library* by George Crabbe, 1930; *The Mediterranean* edited by Paul Bloomfield, 1935; *Tom, Dick, and Harriet* by A. Neil Lyons, 1937; *Great Expectations,* 1939, *Bleak House,* 1955, *David Copperfield,* 1955, and *Short Stories,* 1971, all by Charles Dickens; *The Local,* 1939, *Back to the Local,* 1949, *Londoners,* 1951, and *Showmen and Suckers,* 1951, all by Maurice Gorham; *Mimff,* 1939, *Mimff in Charge,* 1949, *Mimff Takes Over,* 1954, and *Mimff-Robinson,* 1958, all by H.J. Kaeser; *My Uncle Silas,* 1939, and *Sugar for the Horse,* 1957, both by H.E. Bates; *The Battle of France* by André Maurois, 1940; *The Road to Bordeaux* by C. Denis Freeman and Douglas Cooper, 1940; *Peacock Pie,* 1946, *The Story of Joseph,* 1958, *The Story of Moses,* 1959, *The Story of Samuel,* 1960, and *Stories from the Bible,* 1961, all by Walter de la Mare; *The Poems of François Villon,* 1946; *Hey Nonny Yes* edited by Hallam Fordham, 1947; *The Pilgrim's Progress* by John Bunyan, 1947; *Three Brothers and a Lady* by Margaret Black, 1947; *The True and Pathetic History of Desbarollda the Waltzing Mouse,* 1947, and *The Land of Green Ginger,* 1966, both by Noel Langley; *Camberwell School of Arts and Crafts Jubilee,* 1948; *Charles Dickens Birthday Book* edited by Enid Dickens Hawksley, 1948; *The Otterbury Incident,* 1948, and *Christmas Eve,* 1954, both by C. Day Lewis; *Somebody's Rocking My Dreamboat* by Noel Langley and Hazel Pynegar, 1949; *The Tale of Ali Baba* translated by J.C. Mardrus and E. Powys, 1949; *The Comedies* by Shakespeare, 1951; *The Blackbird in the Lilac,* 1952, *Pigeons and Princesses,* 1956, *Prefabulous Animiles,* 1957, *The Wandering Moon,* 1957, *Exploits of Don Quixote, Retold,* 1959, *Titus in Trouble,* 1959, *Hurdy-Gurdy,* 1961, *Sailor Rumbelow and Britannia,* 1962, *Sailor Rumbelow and Other Stories,* 1962, *The Story of Jackie Thimble,* 1964, *Three Tall Tales,* 1964, *The Secret Shoemakers,* 1966, *Rhyming Will,* 1967, *The Angel and the Donkey,* 1969, *How the Moon Began,* 1971, *Complete Poems for Children,* 1973, *The Lion That Flew,* 1974, *More Prefabulous Animiles,* 1975, *Arcadian Ballads,* 1977, and *The James Reeves Story Book,* 1978, all by James Reeves; *The Modern Prometheus* by Zareh Nubar, 1952; *The Warden,* 1952, and *Barchester Towers,* 1953, both by Anthony Trollope; *The Fantastic Tale of the Plucky Sailor and the Postage Stamp* by Stephen Corrin, 1954; *The Newcomes,* 1954, and *Henry Esmond,* 1956, both by W.M. Thackeray; *The Little Bookroom,* 1955, *Jim at the Corner,* 1958, *Eleanor Farjeon's Book,* 1960, *Italian Peepshow,* 1960, *Mrs. Malone,* 1962, *Kaleidoscope,* 1963, and *The Old Nurse's Stocking-Basket,* 1965, all by Eleanor Farjeon; *The Minnow on the Say* by Philippa Pearce, 1955; *Pictures on the Pavement* by G.W. Stonier, 1955; *The Suburban Child* by James Kenward, 1955; *Sun Slower Sun Faster* by Meriol Trevor, 1955; *Marshmallow* by Clare Newberry, 1956; *Hunting with Mr. Jorrocks* by R.S. Surtees, edited by Lionel Gough, 1956; *St. Luke's Life of Christ* translated by J.B. Phillips, 1956; *A Stickful of Nonpareil* by

George Scurfield, 1956; *Ding Dong Bell* by Peter Young, 1957; *Lottie*, 1957, *Elfrida and the Pig*, 1959, and *The Stuffed Dog*, 1967, all by John Symonds; *The School in Our Village* by Joan M. Goldman, 1957; *Brief to Counsel*, 1958, *Know about English Law*, 1965, and *Learn about English Law*, 1974, all by Henry Cecil; *Pinky-Pye*, 1958, *The Witch Family*, 1960, *The Alley*, 1964, *Miranda the Great*, 1967, and *The Tunnel of Hugsy Goode*, 1972, all by Eleanor Estes; *Father Brown Stories* by G.K. Chesterton, 1959; *The Godstone and the Blackymor* by T.H. White, 1959; *Holiday Trench*, 1959, and *Kidnappers at Coombe*, 1960, both by Joan Ballantyne; *T he Nine Lives of Island Mackenzie* by Ursula Moray Williams, 1959; *Boyhoods of Great Composers* by Catherine Gough, 2 vols., 1960, 1963; *Merry England* by Cyril Ray, 1960; *The Penny Fiddle*, 1960, and *Ann at Highwood Hall*, 1964, both by Robert Graves; *The Rib of the Green Umbrella* by Naomi Mitchison, 1960; *The Adventures of Huckleberry Finn*, 1961, and *The Adventures of Tom Sawyer*, 1961, both by Mark Twain; *Down in the Cellar* by Nicholas Stuart Gray, 1961; *Folk Songs of England, Ireland, Scotland, and Wales* edited by William Cole, 1961; *The Island of Fish in the Trees*, 1962, *The Land of Right Up and Down*, 1964, and *Kali and the Golden Mirror*, 1967, all by Eva-Lis Wuorio; *J.M. Barrie's Peter Pan* by Eleanor Graham, 1962; *London since 1912* by John Hayes, 1962; *Naughty Children* edited by Christianna Brand, 1962, and *Nurse Matilda*, 1964, *Nurse Matilda Goes to Town*, 1967, and *Nurse Matilda Goes to Hospital*, 1974, all by Brand; *A Ring of Bells* by John Betjeman, 1962; *The Singing Cupboard*, 1962, and *Swanhilda-of-the-Swans*, 1964, both by Dana Faralla; *The Story of Let's Make an Opera!* by Eric Crozier, 1962; *Stig of the Dump* by Clive King, 1963; *Hello, Elephant*, 1964, and *The Muffletumps*, 1966, both by Jan Wahl; *The Thirty-Nine Steps* by John Buchan, 1964; *The Milldale Riot* by Freda P. Nichols, 1965; *Old Perisher* by Diana Ross, 1965; *Timothy's Song* by William J. Lederer, 1965; *The Truants and Other Poems* by John Walsh, 1965; *The Year Round* by Leonard Clark, 1965; *Daddy-Long-Legs* by Jean Webster, 1966; *The Little Girl and the Tiny Doll*, 1966, and *The Night Ride*, 1973, both by Aingelda Ardizzone; *The Dragon* by Archibald Marshall, 1966; *The Eleanor Farjeon Book: A Tribute*, 1966; *The Growing Summer* by Noel Streatfeild, 1966; *Long Ago When I Was Young* by E. Nesbit, 1966; *In Search of Elsie Piddock* by Denys Blakelock, 1967; *A Likely Place* by Paula Fox, 1967; *Travels with a Donkey in the Cevennes*, 1967, and *Home from Sea*, 1970, both by Robert Louis Stevenson; *Robinson Crusoe* by Daniel Defoe, 1968; *Upsidedown Willie*, 1968, *Special Branch Willie*, 1969, and *Fire-Brigade Willie*, 1970, all by Dorothy Clewes; *Do You Remember What Happened* by Jean Chapman, 1969; *A Riot of Quiet* by Virginia Sicotte, 1969; *Dick Whittington, Retold* by Kathleen Lines, 1970; *The Old Ballad of the Babes in the Wood*, 1972; *Rain, Rain Don't Go Away* by Shirley Morgan, 1972; *The Second-Best Children in the World* by Mary Lavin, 1972; *The Little Fire Engine*, 1973, *The Little Train*, 1973, *The Little Steam Roller*, 1974, and *The Little Horse Bus*, 1974, all by Graham Greene; *Ardizzone's Kilvert* edited by William Plomer, abridged by Elizabeth Divine, 1976; *A Child's Christmas in Wales* by Dylan Thomas, 1978; *Twelve Fairy Tales from the Collection of Joseph Jacobs*, 1986.

*   *   *

Edward Ardizzone's books have for over 50 years been loved by succeeding generations of children all over the world. One of the most attractive aspects of his work is its presentation of an idiosyncratic, and instantly recognizable, view of life, always affectionate and sympathetic without ever lapsing into sentimentality. This sympathetic vision springs from his readiness to enter into the texture of his characters' experience—a readiness exemplified in the precise observation of apparently casual detail which authenticates his draughtsmanship. The purity and directness of his vision and

insight reveal something childlike in his own nature.

His writing is similarly perceptive and authentic. The seagoing adventures of Tim, his most famous creation, have many elements of romance—storm, shipwreck, last-minute rescue. At the same time, however, they are full of the homely detail of shipboard life. Tim may be the hero, but he is not immune from sea sickness, and we see him peeling potatoes and scrubbing floors as well as detecting fires and saving the ship's cat. The narrative is always strong and economical; the illustrations, with their comic-strip captions, are never merely ornamental, and the writing always carries the story forward. This is clearly an important factor in the popularity of the tales.

But Ardizzone did not simply tell tales. His work is an unpretentious celebration of certain human qualities and moral values. Most children find it easy to identify with the heroes and heroines, who are all (especially the boys) characterised by self-reliance, courage, and fortitude in adversity. They are often lonely and far from home. Their plans and hopes are threatened, whether by natural disaster or by the scorn and bullying of hostile figures (such as the taunting schoolboys in *Johnny the Clockmaker*). But they have perseverance and self-confidence, and there are always allies as well as enemies. The hero triumphs through his own doggedness and through the loyalty and affection which bind him to his friends. After the wildest exploits he returns to the familiarity of home, and the young reader, having lived through perilous voyages, is left with a reassuring sense of warmth and companionship. It is as if we are told: Life starts at home and, after a journey of adventure, conflict, and reconciliation, ends there.

—James Reeves

———————

ARMER, Laura Adams. American. Born in Sacramento, California, 12 January 1874. Educated in public and private schools; California School of Design, San Francisco. Married Sidney Armer in 1902; one son. Recipient: American Library Association Newbery Medal, 1932. *Died 3 March 1963.*

PUBLICATIONS FOR CHILDREN

Fiction

Waterless Mountain, illustrated by the author and Sidney Armer. New York, Longman, 1931.
Dark Circle of Branches, illustrated by Sidney Armer. New York, Longman, 1933.
The Trader's Children, illustrated by the author and Sidney Armer. New York, Longman, 1938.
The Forest Pool, illustrated by the author. New York, Longman, 1938.
Farthest West, illustrated by Sidney Armer. New York, Longman, 1939.

Other

Cactus, illustrated by Sidney Armer. New York, Stokes, 1934.
In Navajo Land, photographs by the author and Sidney and Austin Armer. New York, McKay, 1962.

PUBLICATIONS FOR ADULTS

Novel

Southwest. New York, Longman, 1935.

Other

Sand-Painting of the Navaho Indians.   New York, Exposition of
   Indian Tribal Arts, 1931.

*   *   *

Laura Adams Armer was in her fifth decade before she produced
her most important works of art and literature. It was at this time of
her life that she visited the Navaho Reservation in northern Arizona.
Following her first visit, when she recorded the country and the
culture with her camera, she returned yearly to learn about Navaho
folklore and folkways.

In addition to her extensive work with the Navaho, Armer also
worked with the Hopi. She painted local scenes and illustrated myths
of both Navaho and Hopi life. Her film of a Navaho ceremonial,
Mountain Chant, was a remarkable all-Indian picture in the
aboriginal language. Another of Armer's important contributions to
art/anthropology was her rendition of a hundred sacred sand paintings for the House of Navaho Religion in Santa Fe, New Mexico.

A decade later, still a serious student of Indian peoples, Armer
wrote her first book, *Waterless Mountain,* the story of an eight-year-
old Navaho Indian boy of the 20th century who feels a vocation to
become a medicine man. This book, illustrated by Armer and her
artist-husband, won the Newbery Medal. Other distinguished books
followed, most of them for the older child. *The Forest Pool,* a story
of two children in a Mexican jungle, with illustrations by the author,
was designed for the younger child.

Armer's place in American literature derives from her authentic
and humanistic portrayal of Navaho life, within its own context and
within a larger American context. She treats the American Indian as
a sensitive and intelligent human being in a family hogan rather than
as a raving beast on horseback, a not uncommon stereotype of her
time. Her entire range of art—paintings, film, fiction—is complementary, a singular achievement of a caring white person. Her
novels were forerunners of later books on the American Indian and
their problems of reconciling native traditional, rural values with an
American secular, urban world.

Armer's books are beautifully and sensitively written. They are
not easy reading: some children will, of course, persevere, and high
school students, not only of literature but also of anthropology and
sociology, should be encouraged to read them. For Armer's
meticulous studies of Indian personality and culture are important
for an understanding of the human spirit.

—Mary Lystad

————

ARMITAGE, Ronda (Jacqueline, née Minnitt).   New Zealander.
Born in Kaikoura, 11 March 1943. Educated at St. Cuthbert's College, Auckland; University of Auckland, 1963, 1969; Massey
University, Palmerston North, 1965; Hamilton Teachers College,
Diploma of Teaching, 1963. Married the artist David Armitage in
1966; one son and one daughter. Infant teacher, Duvauchelles,
1964–66, and Auckland, 1968–69; supply teacher, London, 1966;
adviser on children's books, Dorothy Butler Ltd., booksellers, Auckland, 1970–71; moved to Britain, 1974; assistant librarian, Lewes
Priory Comprehensive School, Sussex, 1976–77; from 1978 member of the supply teaching staff, East Sussex County Council.
Currently project worker at a family centre. Recipient: New Zealand
Library Association Esther Glen award, 1978. Agent: André
Deutsch, Ltd., 105 Great Russell Street, London WC1B 3LJ. Address: Old Tiles Cottage, Church Lane, Hellingly, East Sussex BN27
4HA, England.

PUBLICATIONS FOR CHILDREN (illustrated by David Armitage)

Fiction

The Lighthouse Keeper's Lunch.   London, Deutsch, 1977.
The Trouble with Mr. Harris.   London, Deutsch, 1978.
Don't Forget Matilda.   London, Deutsch, 1979.
The Bossing of Josie.   London, Deutsch, 1980; as *The Birthday
   Spell,* London, Hippo, 1981.
Ice Creams for Rosie.   London, Deutsch, 1981.
One Moonlit Night.   London, Deutsch, 1983.
Grandma Goes Shopping.   London, Deutsch, 1984.
The Lighthouse Keeper's Catastrophe.   London, Deutsch, 1986.

Other

Drinking.   Hove, Sussex, Wayland, 1987.

*

Ronda Armitage comments:
   To me the fascination of creating a picture book lies in making
something that will work in several different ways. I need to enjoy
writing it, but, equally, the story needs to work in terms of the young
child's experience. Unlike books for older children, picture books
are for reading aloud, so the story must flow smoothly and each
sentence needs to be rhythmic. This form of writing is perhaps more
akin to poetry than to prose in the sense that each word has to play
its part—after all, there aren't very many of them. And then there is
that other vital ingredient—that other half—the illustrations. Ideally
these should complement the text, filling it out, adding those
essential details that, if included in the text, would make the story
too unwieldy for the young.

*   *   *

Ronda Armitage has the knack of being able to write simple and
enjoyable picture-book texts, which are illustrated with matching
ingenuous charm by her husband David. The essential quality of
these books is their child-centredness. In an era when so much in this
genre seems calculated to impress sophisticated adults, it is refreshing to encounter books which are so clearly intended for the young
child, and keep his interests in mind.

In each of Armitage's amusing stories a problem is posed and then
solved. In *The Lighthouse Keeper's Lunch* seagulls steal food from
the picnic basket which Mrs. Grinling daily sends off to her husband
along a high wire suspended between her mainland cottage and the
lighthouse on the rocks. Knowing how interested children are in
food, the author is careful to *specify* the contents each day, and the
joke is that every meal is a gourmet's delight—a banquet, indeed,
for solo diner—rather than mere sandwiches. Particularly droll is her
attempt to send her pet cat Hamish along the wire in another basket,
as a deterrent to the marauding gulls: "Sadly, flying did not agree
with Hamish. His fur stood on end when the basket swayed, his
whiskers drooped when he peered down at the wet, blue sea and he
felt much too sick even to notice the seagulls, let alone scare them
away from the lunch."

In an equally droll sequel *The Lighthouse Keeper's Catastrophe*
(itself a kind of pun, Hamish being the cause of the problem) a
nervous Mr. Grinling is forced to take a ride on the precarious high
wire himself in order to get to the lighthouse in stormy weather.

In *The Trouble with Mr. Harris* the problem is the impatient new
postmaster who seems unfriendly towards the people of Hogeton. A
little girl shows them that he is really a shy person, unused to slow
village ways—and the story ends, typically, with a tea party. Matilda,
the subject of *Don't Forget Matilda,* is a particularly engaging

character—a baby bear of ebullient personality in a family given to forgetting things, even her name!

Grandma Goes Shopping is a cumulative tale, curiously redolent of some of Pat Hutchins's work, with lots of repetition and an ending ("…and then she set off for home…through the forest…down the hill…into the pond…and got home in time for tea") reminiscent of *Rosie's Walk.*

Knowing that children appreciate detail, Armitage instinctively specifies such things as items of clothing, contents of shopping lists and picnic baskets, or the type of shops in a village. Although her stories are simple, her style is never simplistic. It is distinguished by fluid, literate sentences which, rather than condescend, happily include words like "brusque" or "irascible" when these are ones which best suit their context. Her stories, while being entertaining and child-centred, manage to enrich and delight both imagination and vocabulary.

—Walter McVitty

ARMSTRONG, Richard. Also wrote as Cam Renton. British. Born in Northumberland, 18 June 1903. Educated at Walbottle Primary School, 1908–16. Married in 1926; one son. Worked as an errand boy, labourer, greaser, and crane driver in steelworks, Tyneside, 1916–19; sailor and radio operator, Merchant Navy, 1920–37; typist, secretary, architect's assistant, and undertaker's labourer, 1937–54. Recipient: Library Association Carnegie Medal, 1949. *Died in 1986.*

PUBLICATIONS FOR CHILDREN

Fiction

The Mystery of Obadiah, illustrated by Marjorie Sankey. London, Dent, 1943.
Sabotage at the Forge, illustrated by L.P. Lupton. London, Dent, 1946.
Sea Change, illustrated by M. Leszczynski. London, Dent, 1948.
The Whinstone Drift, illustrated by Michael A. Charlton. London, Dent, 1951.
Wanderlust: Voyage of a Little White Monkey, illustrated by Frederick K. Crooke. London, Faber, 1952.
Danger Rock, illustrated by M. Leszczynski. London, Dent, 1955; as *Cold Hazard,* Boston, Houghton Mifflin, 1956.
The Lost Ship: A Caribbean Adventure, illustrated by Edward Osmond. London, Dent, 1956; New York, Day, 1958.
No Time for Tankers, illustrated by Reg Gray. London, Dent, 1958; New York, Day, 1959.
Another Six. Oxford, Blackwell, 1959.
The Lame Duck, illustrated by D.G. Valentine. London, Dent, 1959; as *Ship Afire!,* New York, Day, 1961.
Before the Wind. Oxford, Blackwell, 1959.
Horseshoe Reef, illustrated by D.G. Valentine. London, Dent, 1960; New York, Duell, 1961.
Out of the Shallows, illustrated by D.G. Valentine. London, Dent, 1961.
Trial Trip, illustrated by D.G. Valentine. London, Dent, 1962; New York, Criterion, 1963.
The Ship Stealers (as Cam Renton), illustrated by Val Biro. Penshurst, Kent, Friday Press, 1963.
Island Odyssey, illustrated by Andrew Dodds. London, Dent, 1963; as *Fight for Freedom: An Adventure of World War II,* New York, McKay, 1966.
Big-Head (as Cam Renton), illustrated by Val Biro. Penshurst, Kent, Friday Press, 1964.
The Big Sea, illustrated by Andrew Dodds. London, Dent, 1964; New York, McKay, 1965.
The Greenhorn, illustrated by Roger Payne. London, Nelson, 1965.
The Secret Sea, illustrated by Roger Payne. London, Dent, and New York, McKay, 1966.
The Mutineers, illustrated by Gareth Floyd. London, Dent, and New York, McKay, 1968.
The Albatross, illustrated by Graham Humphreys. London, Dent, and New York, McKay, 1970.

Other

A History of Seafaring:
 1. *The Early Mariners.* London, Benn, 1967; New York, Praeger, 1968.
 2. *The Discoverers.* London, Benn, 1968; New York, Praeger, 1969.
 3. *The Merchantmen.* London, Benn, and New York, Praeger, 1969.
Themselves Alone: The Story of Men in Empty Places. London, Benn, and Boston, Houghton Mifflin, 1972.
Powered Ships: The Beginnings. London, Benn, 1975.

Editor, *Treasure and Treasure Hunters.* London, Hamish Hamilton, and New York, David White, 1969.

PUBLICATIONS FOR ADULTS

Novels

The Northern Maid. London, Dent, 1947.
Passage Home. London, Dent, 1952.
Sailor's Luck. London, Dent, 1959.
Storm Path. London, Dent, 1964.

Other

Grace Darling, Maid and Myth. London, Dent, 1965.

*

Richard Armstrong commented:

(1978) My ambition was to be a school teacher, but poverty and the First World War denied me the necessary education, and when the dust settled I did the next best thing and became a writer. This accounts for the didactic element in my books. My aim has been to tell young people groping through the fantasies of adolescence (and anyone else who wants to know) what the real world looks like to me and perhaps a little something of what life is all about. But first I had to provide my family with a roof overhead and three squares a day, so the main body of my work is a compromise between what I wanted to say in it and what my publishers would accept and pay for. From time to time I chanced my arm and wrote a book regardless, but the end result was always another pile of rejection slips, an increase in my overdraft and a frosty letter from my bank manager. Consequently what is considered by competent commentators, unconnected with the publishing trade, to be my best work to date—a novel on faith and three books for boys—remains unpublished and up for grabs.

*   *   *

The best writers of adventure stories for young people have three particular things to offer: their own experience of action, a straightforward style full of vitality, and a positive attitude to life in general. These qualities are abundantly present in the work of Richard Armstrong. You could add a talent for exciting plots, but these seem to grow naturally from his own experience of action and men.

Some of his early books were about boys in heavy industry, notably *Sabotage at the Forge* and *The Whinstone Drift,* but most of his books concern the sea and ships. Everything he wrote is authentic, based on his knowledge of ships and the men who sail them—as exciting as real-life adventure. Early in his writing career it was Armstrong's avowed intention to teach young readers something of the crafts and skills of steel workers, miners, and seamen, but the effect is far from didactic; he made all the details so fascinating that one's understanding of them enhances the drama of his stories. One appreciates how much depends on a man's skill and judgment, with moral issues and conflicts of temperament contributing to the tension.

His style makes sensible use of colloquial speech; it is vigorous and descriptive. His strength lay in his complete knowledge of the scene: he was not painting for effect; he was telling it as it is and with a rare feeling for words and the rhythms of language. He credited his readers with intellect as well as feeling, but he was no mandarin writer.

Nor do his plots follow a formula. The plot line emerges from situation and character; no two are the same. Wreckers, salvage, whaling, war are only a few of his themes. Several books concern youths for whom a voyage full of natural hazards and human conflicts marks an important stage in growing up. There is often an older man, captain or mate perhaps, who wins the boy's respect. Such men are imaginative and humane; their senses and intuition are alert to the pulse of communal feeling on board ship and they never act without regard to this. They take life and death decisions without any illusions—men of ideals, but realists too.

Often the adventure is shared by two boys of contrasting temperaments, linked by friendship, as in *Horseshoe Reef* and *The Big Sea* (though these are otherwise quite different stories). Others concern the interplay of personalities in a group of young people trapped and held under pressure, as in *Danger Rock*; in *The Mutineers* where they are marooned by choice in what should have been an island paradise; in *The Albatross* where they steal a ketch and make off with treasure trove but cannot land anywhere because of the law—a tragic adventure which only one survives.

The 15 boys of *The Mutineers* are also fleeing the law. They are all 16 or 17, emigrating to Australia under a training scheme. Having taken over the ship at gunpoint for kicks, they escape the consequences by sailing away in one of the boats. Bo-bo Bolton has the know-how to sail and to find the island, but it is Chick Hinshelwood who emerges as the leader. He is a good organiser, but he imposes his authority brutally and soon shows his appetite for power. Stubby, who could have stood up to him at the beginning, refuses the responsibility of leadership. This is an awesome story of brutalized human beings in a "prison" of their own making.

This book bears striking similarities to William Golding's *Lord of the Flies.* Both books say something of deep interest about human nature and about fear and the lust for power. But their messages are quite different: Armstrong's is positive, Golding's pessimistic. The contrast highlights an essential ingredient in a book for young readers if it is to appeal to them. However sad or horrifying the story, there must be characters with inner strength to identify with. We leave Stubby, Bo-bo, and Jake wiser and stronger for their appalling experiences.

Sea stories used to be a distinct category of fiction and one of the most popular, its readers not confined to the young only. But, regrettably, this is no longer so. Richard Armstrong was undoubtedly one of the masters of the genre (writing for adults as well as young people) and served it well for 20 years. Gradually, though, times and tastes change; he sensed this and reflected these changes. There is nothing old-fashioned about the youths in his later novels. They are less naive, more of a problem to themselves than his early heroes. It is characteristic of Armstrong that he never ceased to respond to each younger generation as it came. This sensitive rapport with his fellow men is at the heart of all his work.

—Gwen Marsh

ARMSTRONG, William H(oward). American. Born in Lexington, Virginia, 14 September 1914. Educated at Augusta Military Academy, 1929–32; Hampden-Sydney College, Virginia, 1932–36, A.B. (cum laude) 1936 (Phi Beta Kappa); University of Virginia, Charlottesville, 1937–38. Married Martha Stonestreet Williams in 1943 (died 1953); two sons and one daughter. History teacher, Virginia Episcopal School, 1939–44, and Kent School, Connecticut, 1945–76. Recipient: National Association of School Administrators National School Bell award, 1963; American Library Association Newbery Medal, 1970. D. Litt.: Hampden-Sydney College, 1986. Address: Kimadee Hill, Kent, Connecticut 06757, U.S.A.

PUBLICATIONS FOR CHILDREN

Fiction

Sounder, illustrated by James Barkley. New York, Harper, 1969; London, Gollancz, 1971.
Sour Land, illustrated by David B. Armstrong. New York, Harper, 1971.
The MacLeod Place, illustrated by Eros Keith. New York, Coward McCann, 1972.
The Mills of God, illustrated by David B. Armstrong. New York, Doubleday, 1973.
Joanna's Miracle. Nashville, Broadman, 1977.
The Tale of Tawny and Dingo, illustrated by Charles Mikolaycak. New York, Harper, 1979.

Other

Barefoot in the Grass: The Story of Grandma Moses. New York, Doubleday, 1970.
Animal Tales, illustrated by Mirko Hanák. New York, Doubleday, 1970.
Hadassah: Esther, The Orphan Queen, illustrated by Barbara Byfield. New York, Doubleday, 1972.
My Animals, illustrated by Mirko Hanák. New York, Doubleday, 1974.
The Education of Abraham Lincoln, illustrated by William Plummer. New York, Coward McCann, 1974.

PUBLICATIONS FOR ADULTS

Other

Study Is Hard Work. New York, Harper, 1956.
Through Troubled Waters. New York, Harper, 1957.
Peoples of the Ancient World, with Joseph Ward Swain. New York, Harper, 1959.

87 Ways to Help Your Child in School. Great Neck, New York, Barron's, 1961.

Tools of Thinking. Woodbury, New York, Barron's, 1968.

Word Power in Five Easy Lessons. Woodbury, New York, Barron's, 1969.

Study Tapes. Woodbury, New York, Barron's, 1975.

Study Tips: How to Improve Your Study Habits and Improve Your Grades. Woodbury, New York, Barron's, 1976; revised edition, 1983; as *Study Tactics,* 1983.

*

Manuscript Collection: Kerlan Collection, University of Minnesota, Minneapolis.

*   *   *

William H. Armstrong was for over 30 years a high school history teacher. His perspective of the past, his interest in social change, and his deep concern for individuals are reflected in the fictional as well as the biographical books he writes. Armstrong has written about ancient times (*The MacLeod Place*) and about early American history (*The Education of Abraham Lincoln*), but the 20th century—its social values and institutions, its social problems—is particularly compelling to him. For *Sounder* Armstrong won the Newbery Medal and other awards; it was also the basis of an extraordinary movie, an excellent example of good literature being used by another medium sensitively and accurately.

Sounder, in particular among Armstrong's books, reflects two developments in mid-20th-century American literature for children: a willingness to look at the presence and consequences of racial and ethnic inequities in the society; and a willingness to look at adolescent development, at the growing up process, including the pleasures and pains that accompany transition from childhood to adulthood. *Sounder* is about the rural south of the turn of the century, a society caught up in a web of ignorance, prejudice, and great poverty. The major concern is with a black family—its alienation from society and its love for one another, its lack of opportunity and its determination, its despair and its hope. The father, a sharecropper, steals food for his hungry family and is imprisoned; the mother toils with determination and skill to provide for her children; the older son walks on for miles and miles to find an education. After his father's death, this boy-child assumes a larger role in the family while still attending to youthful needs for learning and for making sense of his universe. He overcomes major obstacles in a way that his father's white jailers and white landlords never overcome them.

Armstrong writes about complicated characters and cultures in a careful, deliberate style made all the more clear because of its simplicity and honesty. His stories are for high school children, but adults are welcome to read them, for they offer extraordinarily moving pictures of people and their changing places in the world.

—Mary Lystad

———

ARTHUR, Ruth (Mabel). British. Born in Glasgow, Scotland, 26 May 1905. Educated at St. Columbus School, Kilmacolm, Renfrewshire; Froebel Educational Institute, Roehampton, London, Froebel certificate 1926. Married Frederick N. Huggins in 1932; two sons and four daughters. Froebel kindergarten teacher, Laurel Bank School, Glasgow, 1927–30, and High School, Loughton, Essex, 1930–32. *Died 6 March 1979.*

PUBLICATIONS FOR CHILDREN

Fiction

Friendly Stories, illustrated by C.F. Christie. London, Harrap, 1932.

The Crooked Brownie [in Town, at the Seaside], illustrated by R.M. Turvey. London, Harrap, 3 vols., 1936–42.

Pumpkin Pie. London, Collins, 1938.

Cowslip Mollie. London, Hutchinson, 1949.

Carolina's Holiday and Other Stories, illustrated by Dodie Masterman. London, Harrap, 1957.

The Daisy Cow and Other Stories of the Channel Islands, illustrated by Lucien Lowen. London, Harrap, 1958.

Carolina's Golden Bird and Other Stories, illustrated by Lucien Lowen. London, Harrap, 1958.

A Cottage for Rosemary, illustrated by M. Whitaker. London, Harrap, 1960.

Carolina and Roberto, illustrated by Lucien Lowen. London, Harrap, 1961.

Dragon Summer, illustrated by Margery Gill. London, Hutchinson, 1962; New York, Atheneum, 1963.

Carolina and the Sea Horse, and Other Stories, illustrated by Lucien Lowen. London, Harrap, 1964.

My Daughter Nicola, illustrated by Fermin Rocker. New York, Atheneum, 1965; London, Gollancz, 1966.

A Candle in Her Room, illustrated by Margery Gill. London, Gollancz, and New York, Atheneum, 1966.

Requiem for a Princess, illustrated by Margery Gill. London, Gollancz, and New York, Atheneum, 1967.

Portrait of Margarita, illustrated by Margery Gill. London, Gollancz, and New York, Atheneum, 1968.

The Whistling Boy, illustrated by Margery Gill. London, Gollancz, and New York, Atheneum, 1969.

The Saracen Lamp, illustrated by Margery Gill. London, Gollancz, and New York, Atheneum, 1970.

The Little Dark Thorn, illustrated by Margery Gill. London, Gollancz, and New York, Atheneum, 1971.

The Autumn People, illustrated by Margery Gill. London, Gollancz, and New York, Atheneum, 1973; as *The Autumn Ghosts,* London, Target, 1976.

After Candlemas, illustrated by Margery Gill. London, Gollancz, and New York, Atheneum, 1974; as *Candlemas Mystery,* London, Target, 1976.

On the Wasteland, illustrated by Margery Gill. London, Gollancz, and New York, Atheneum, 1975.

An Old Magic, illustrated by Margery Gill. London, Gollancz, and New York, Atheneum, 1977.

Miss Ghost. London, Gollancz, and New York, Atheneum, 1979.

Other

Mother Goose Stories. London, Collins, 1938.

*

Ruth Arthur commented:

(1978) I write about the intricacies of human relationships and the difficulties of adolescence. In my stories I try to introduce children of 11 and 12 upwards to some of the universal problems of the grown-up world such as adoption, divorce, loneliness, delinquency.

*   *   *

"I am rather an odd person," confesses Elspeth, the heroine-narrator of Ruth Arthur's *Miss Ghost,* published posthumously. One might say the same about the others. Her heroines are all, if not odd, highly sensitive, unconventional, often unhappy. Arthur deals in human problems, especially those of adolescent girls. In less skillful hands her stories might have seemed too much alike. To her concern for the distressed or deprived child, however, the writer added great understanding of the human heart, a strong sense of place, and, above all, exceptional skill in story-telling. Very quietly, avoiding publicity, without subscribing to any contemporary theory and indeed going against the stream of the literary fashions of her day, she nevertheless made a place for herself among the very best of those writing for the older girl.

Each of Arthur's novels has a girl for the central character who also tells the story. Often the girl is by choice a loner, but in each the solution of her problem lies in involvement with others. Far from showing the child in isolation, the writer always shows the value of the community, whether of a family or a village. Adults play a significant role in each story. Sometimes, in the most successful novels, the action spans several generations. The books deal with social problems, like adoption, broken marriages and the re-marriage of parents, fostering and children in care, but they must be seen as psychological, not sociological novels. Their object is to show the heroine working out her own salvation by discovering herself and others.

Next to the heroine, the most important element in each book is the setting. It may be the Cumbrian mountains—*The Little Dark Thorn*—or Cornwall—*Requiem for a Princess*—or East Anglia—*The Whistling Boy*—or Wales—*A Candle in Her Room*; always the spirit of place exerts a powerful influence. With this concern for places is often associated a feeling for the past which may manifest itself in the supernatural. So Willow in *Requiem for a Princess,* working out her personal problem while staying in an ancient Cornish house, finds herself caught up in the tragedy of a Spanish girl shipwrecked in Elizabethan times. By a neat reversal of the conventional ghost story, *The Saracen Lamp* shows the Lady Melisande, a grass-widow of the Hundred Years War, taking comfort in the visits of Perdita, a ghost from the 20th century.

The reader's involvement in these stories is ensured by Arthur's own concern and by her passionate writing—perhaps one must at times say over-writing. They are stories which demand the closest co-operation from the reader; without this they may become what indeed they may superficially appear to be, "magazine fiction."

Arthur was at her best in two stories with similar settings—west Wales—and similar constructions. *A Candle in Her Room* spans three generations and shows, with great subtlety and delicacy, a conflict of good and evil forces. Three sisters go to live in Pembrokeshire. The eldest, Melissa, gives herself joyously to her new life. The youngest is tolerant and easy-going. The middle girl, Judith, is a malcontent who hates the new life. Her discontent is focussed by Dido, a wooden doll found in the house. Dido, one must assume, had belonged to a witch and she is impregnated with evil. In an accident Melissa is crippled, and Judith takes advantage of this to steal her lover and has a child by him. This girl, Dilys, grows up, hated by her mother and father and fostered by Melissa, until at the beginning of the Second World War she goes to Poland with her Polish lover. They disappear. Melissa lives on in the big house, alone. After the War she finds herself haunted by dreams of a child. This is Nina, Dilys's daughter, now an orphan living in a refugee camp somewhere in Europe. Her wish to find the child forces Melissa to conquer her disability; she goes to find her grand-niece and brings her home. Back in Wales Nina finds the wooden doll. Dido's instinct for evil is as strong as ever, but Nina, who has lived through war and its aftermath, is made of tougher stuff than her mother and grandmother. She destroys the doll. Good triumphs! This story, so melodramatic in this summary, is written with deep conviction. It is tightly knit, and the inter-relationship of characters and their commitment to the country in which they live give it great strength. On the right reader it can make a lasting impression.

An Old Magic has a comparable setting and pattern. Again the scene is Wales and the story links three generations. But the working-out is very different. The writing is atmospheric, but there is less sharpness in the delineation of character. One consequently feels

rather less concern for the fortunes of the principals.

Whether the theme is historical or the mechanics supernatural, the essential matter of each of Arthur's novels is self-discovery. Her attractive, wayward, sometimes wilful heroines are, each in her own way, learning to distinguish between reality and fantasy. Their problems and their solutions must strike a chord of recognition in many young readers.

—Marcus Crouch

———

ARUNDEL, Honor (Morfydd). British. Born in Llanarmon, Gwynedd, 15 August 1919. Educated at Hayes Court, Kent; Somerville College, Oxford, 1938–39. Married Alex McCrindle in 1952; three daughters and one stepdaughter. Worked as a typist, journalist, engineer, and film, radio and theatre critic. *Died 8 June 1973.*

PUBLICATIONS FOR CHILDREN

Fiction

Green Street, illustrated by Eileen Armitage.   London, Hamish Hamilton, 1966; New York, Hawthorn, 1970.
The High House, illustrated by Eileen Armitage.   London, Hamish Hamilton, 1966; New York, Meredith Press, 1968.
Emma's Island.   London, Hamish Hamilton, 1968; New York, Hawthorn, 1970.
The Two Sisters.   London, Heinemann, 1968; New York, Meredith Press, 1969.
The Amazing Mr. Prothero, illustrated by Jane Paton.   London, Hamish Hamilton, 1968; Nashville, Nelson, 1972.
The Longest Weekend.   London, Hamish Hamilton, 1969; New York, Nelson, 1970.
The Girl in the Opposite Bed.   London, Hamish Hamilton, 1970; New York, Nelson, 1971.
Emma in Love.   London, Hamish Hamilton, 1970; Nashville, Nelson, 1972.
The Terrible Temptation.   London, Hamish Hamilton, and New York, Nelson, 1971.
A Family Failing.   London, Hamish Hamilton, and Nashville, Nelson, 1972.
The Blanket Word.   London, Hamish Hamilton, and Nashville, Nelson, 1973; as *Love Is a Blanket Word,* New York, Scholastic, 1976.

PUBLICATIONS FOR ADULTS

Play

Radio Play: *The Home Game,* 1960.

Other

The Freedom of Art.   London, Lawrence and Wishart, 1965.

Editor, with Maurice Carpenter and Jack Lindsay, *New Lyrical Ballads.*   London, Editions Poetry, 1945.

*   *   *

In the late 1960's and early 1970's, books for adolescents or "new adults" were finding their bearings in the gap between "popular" fiction—chiefly magazine stories for girls—and novels that laid claim to the high seriousness of "literature." There was a potential readership of competent, wordly-wise, yet sensitive teenagers, again, mostly girls, who needed variety in their reading matter. They wanted books that took seriously their growing awareness of the complexities of emotions and events and which did not give them moral instruction but, instead, sympathetic understanding of the predicaments that come with new freedoms. In this mid-20th-century development in writing for the young, Honor Arundel's novels are something of a landmark. They can be linked, in theme and treatment, to the kinds of writing that the women's movement in publishing has brought into prominence. They also show many of the preoccupations and much of the feeling tone of the 1960's.

Arundel's response to the demand for "realistic" stories was to avoid the mawkishness of formula fiction while using some of its oldest scenes: sick beds, family failings, and amorous encounters. She explores the ambivalences and ambiguities of moral dilemmas, especially those that arise in near-adult personal relationships. She exploits, with sensibility and good sense, new pains and awarenesses. She links adolescence and early childhood, which it resembles (the stories all have young children too), the pains of parenthood and the loss of innocence (and virginity). The heroines and their consorts have their families whose goodness is crushing or whose dependability is uncertain, but all are recognisable. Somehow the girls must spring the family trap until they are released by self-knowledge and less self-absorbed loving and caring. The seriousness and depth of the author's motivations are balanced by a wise good humour that constantly treads through the inevitable dumps that attend adolescent egocentrism. A preponderance of older Scottish worthies is offset by a number of unconventional artists who are seen as hardworking and hungry. The young stand poised in the middle, tugged by loyalties and attractions, by ideals and the inevitable realism of having to earn a living.

The plots move at a brisk pace and are conspicuously circumstantial so as to pack in enough significant details of contemporary living. Foreign holidays with music festivals, Highland jaunts and long train journeys, unexpected lavish generosity—all can be accounted for by the providentiality of rich and generous friends. Yet the heroines experience the common hazards of their generation, with examinations and first love vying for attention, despair and delight alternating over a weekend. Eileen (*The Longest Weekend*) has most to cope with: too-understanding parents and a three-year-old daughter. Jan (*The Terrible Temptation*; *The Blanket Word*) longs for order, calm, detachment, but is shaken by family demand and uncertainty. Emma, the best-known, has a bumpy course with her artist aunt and gifted brother. All of them long to be petted and indulged as the teenage culture suggests they should be. They want to bend others to their will and the world to their desires. But they are saved by a core of inner strength that grows out of their very female resilience which enables them to resist the seduction of males whose ambitions do not include them, and still be able to come to understand the need for collaborative partnership.

It is now possible to see more clearly the social criticism in these novels and to appreciate a quite clean break in style with much writing for the young in the previous decade. The text on the page is "readerly" with its untagged dialogue and first-person narration which gives the teller full egotistical scope. Yet Honor Arundel's authorial ease is deceptive, as many imitators have discovered, and re-readings re-establish the regard in which these stories may still be held.

—Margaret Meek

ASARE, Meshack (Yaw). Ghanaian. Born in Nyankumasi, 18 September 1945. Educated at the University of Science and Technology, Kumasi; University of Wisconsin, Madison; School of Journalism and Television, Berkshire, England. Married Rose Tachie Menson in 1969; four children. Teacher in elementary school, Tema, 1966–68, and at Lincoln Community School, Accra, 1969–79. From 1979 art director and illustrator, Educational Press and Manufacturers, Accra. Recipient: National Book award (Ghana), 1980; Noma award, 1982. Address: c/o Educational Press and Manufacturers, P.O. Box 9184, Airport, Accra, Ghana.

PUBLICATIONS FOR CHILDREN (illustrated by the author)

Fiction

Tawia Goes to Sea.   Accra, Ghana Publishing, 1970.
I Am Kofi.   Accra, Ghana Publishing, 1972.
Mansa Helps at Home.   Accra, Ghana Publishing, 1972.
The Brassman's Secret.   Accra, Educational Press, 1981.
The Canoe's Story.   Accra, Three Brothers and Cousins, 1982.
Chipo and the Bird on the Hill: A Tale of Ancient Zimbabwe.   Harare, Zimbabwe Publishing House, 1984.
Cat in Search of a Friend.   Brooklyn, Kane Miller, 1986.

*

Illustrator: *Akousa in Brazil* by Alero and Cecile McHardy, 1970.

*   *   *

Meshack Asare is an imaginative storyteller and talented artist who skillfully weaves cultural traditions and daily realities of life into picture stories for African children.

Some of Asare's earliest stories are school books for younger children about commonplace daily activities in which the illustrations provide the African context. *I Am Kofi* focuses on a boy's household chores such as carrying water, sweeping the floor, and fanning a fire, while *Mansa Helps at Home* focuses on a girl's activities including cooking, washing clothes, and feeding a younger sibling.

Asare illustrates his recent picture story for younger children, *Cat in Search of a Friend,* in the distinctive style that he had developed over the last two decades. This story, based on oral tradition, tells how cat sought protection from many animals, including monkey, lion, elephant, and rhino, as well as man, only to find that she is capable of being her own master.

The Brassman's Secret received the Noma award for African writing, the only children's book to receive this honor. In this highly original story the boy hero helps his father make goldweights, a process depicted in both words and detailed illustrations. During a celebration the hero falls asleep and in his dream asks a goldweight to tell its secret. When it does so it reveals its historical significance and symbolism. The dream is both exciting and frightening, and teaches the hero the lesson "Learn from the past."

A similar blend of cultural history and contemporary reality is found in *Chipo and the Bird on the Hill,* a book about Zimbabwe. The story focuses on a girl who listens to tales of the past about Zimbabwe and wants to learn where the Great Bird of legend went. The heroine finds a young boy to take her to see the stone bird and in the process sees weaving and iron smelting, and witnesses ceremonies associated with Zimbabwe, activities that are imaginatively reconstructed in the story and illustrations. Like Asare's other books published in Africa, this one demonstrates that excellent illustrations in picture books do not need to be in color.

Tawia Goes to Sea and *The Canoe's Story* are about fishing in southern Ghana. *The Canoe's Story* is a first-person narrative by a Wawa tree about its life in the forest, its feelings of pride and pleasure about the way it was cut down, carved into a canoe and transported to the sea, and its response to a new life among its canoe neighbors and the men and boys who use it for work and give it the new name "Never leave me." The canoe likes its life at the sea coast because in the forest no one ever liked and cared for it as do the people at the coast, who help it travel with sails and a motor and bring it many offerings. The illustrations complement the text, providing the coastal setting of the action.

Tawia Goes to Sea is located more specifically in a fishing village near Accra. The hero is too young to go to sea, but he carefully observes the fishermen and their boats, and the women who collect fish to sell. Using knowledge acquired from these observations Tawia makes a toy canoe of coconuts and launches it in the sea, only to have it swamped by a wave. The fishermen think Tawia is clever and promise to take him with them, and Tawia goes home and dreams of riding out to sea.

Asare's picture stories skillfully incorporate the cultural content of specific African settings in a manner that makes them widespread in their appeal to African children regardless of their cultural background. Moreover, his original and effective style of illustration can be reproduced on equipment available in Africa, thus serving as a model for illustrators of African-published children's books.

—Nancy J. Schmidt

ASCH, Frank. American. Born in Somerville, New Jersey, 6 August 1946. Educated at Cooper Union, New York, B.A. 1968. Has worked as a Montessori school teacher and in children's theatre. Address: c/o Holiday House, 18 East 53rd Street, New York, New York 10022, U.S.A.

PUBLICATIONS FOR CHILDREN (illustrated by the author)

Fiction

George's Store. New York, McGraw Hill, 1969.
Linda. New York, McGraw Hill, 1969.
Elvira Everything. New York, Harper, 1970.
The Blue Balloon. New York, McGraw Hill, 1971.
Yellow, Yellow, illustrated by Mark Alan Stamaty. New York, McGraw Hill, 1971.
Rebecka. New York, Harper, 1971.
I Met a Penguin. New York, McGraw Hill, 1972.
In the Eye of the Teddy. New York, Harper, 1973.
Gia and the Hundred Dollars' Worth of Bubble Gum. New York, McGraw Hill, 1974.
Good Lemonade, illustrated by Marie Zimmerman. New York and London, Watts, 1976.
Monkey Face. New York, Parents' Magazine Press, 1977; revised edition as *Bread and Honey,* 1981.
MacGoose's Grocery, illustrated by James Marshall. New York, Dial Press, 1978; London, Kestrel, 1979.
Moon Bear. New York, Scribner, 1978.
Turtle Tale. New York, Dial Press, 1978.
Popcorn. New York, Parents' Magazine Press, 1979.
Running with Rachel, with Jan Asch, photographs by Jan Asch and Robert Michael Buslow. New York, Dial Press, 1979.
Sand Cake. New York, Parents' Magazine Press, 1979; London, Viking Kestrel, 1980.

The Last Puppy. Englewood Cliffs, New Jersey, Prentice Hall, 1980; London, Evans, 1981.
Starbaby. New York, Scribner, 1980.
Goodnight Horsey. Englewood Cliffs, New Jersey, Prentice Hall, 1981.
Just Like Daddy. Englewood Cliffs, New Jersey, Prentice Hall, 1981; London, Transworld, 1984.
Happy Birthday Moon. Englewood Cliffs, New Jersey, Prentice Hall, 1982; London, Hodder and Stoughton, 1984.
Milk and Cookies. New York, Parents' Magazine Press, 1982.
Moon Cake. Englewood Cliffs, New Jersey, Prentice Hall, 1983; London, Hodder and Stoughton, 1984.
Moongame. Englewood Cliffs, New Jersey, Prentice Hall, 1984; London, Hodder and Stoughton, 1985.
Pearl's Promise. New York, Delacorte Press, 1984.
Skyfire. Englewood Cliffs, New Jersey, Prentice Hall, 1984; London, Hodder and Stoughton, 1985.
Bear Shadow. Englewood Cliffs, New Jersey, Prentice Hall, 1985; London, Hodder and Stoughton, 1986.
Bear's Bargain. Englewood Cliffs, New Jersey, Prentice Hall, 1985; London, Hodder and Stoughton, 1986.
Goodbye House. Englewood Cliffs, New Jersey, Prentice Hall, 1986; London, Hodder and Stoughton, 1987.
I Can Blink. New York, Crown, 1986.
I Can Roar. New York, Crown, 1986.
Pearl's Pirates. New York, Delacorte Press, 1987.
Oats and Wild Apples. New York, Holiday House, 1988.
Journey to Terezor. New York, Holiday House, 1989.

Verse

City Sandwich. New York, Greenwillow, 1978.
Country Pie. New York, Greenwillow, 1979.

Other

Little Devil's ABC [1,2,3] (readers). New York, Scribner, 2 vols., 1979.

*   *   *

To Frank Asch childhood and literature are equivalents. Like the age group that supports his expansive output, the writings manifest an aspiring restlessness, abrupt changes of direction, and an acute, if brief, fascination with a variety of ventures. There are realms of revelation and worlds of concealment, areas of enchantment alongside oodles of the ordinary. Asch is distinguished for the brevity of his texts, but he has shown himself capable of composing novels as well.

One recent undertaking, *Oats and Wild Apples,* balances the delights of the familiar with those that dwell among the shadows. A playful calf is coaxed by a fawn to try those pleasures that lie beyond the pasture fence. Nudging frogs and feasting upon wild apples prove blissful ventures, but the dark side of the forest, particularly the predators ("terrible only if they catch you"), is the source of a discomfiting awareness. Besides, the familiarity of the farm provides a security which quite offsets the sameness that the child-spirit tries to go beyond. The anxious calf returns to his mother, whom the approaching darkness has driven into the barn where light and the farmer-supplied oats provide solace from the shadows.

Even Fawn, child of the forest, enjoys the oats and the rest of what to him is altogether unfamiliar. He is offered the opportunity to dwell forever with his newfound friend, but he has no chance to ponder the invitation, as Mother Deer summons him at the barn door, and the two disappear into the shadows which for them contain all the delights of the ordinary. Light and dark, sun and shade hold treasures for discovery, and the contrast itself underlies the appealing entities that emerge from each of the opposites. But their dominion must be supreme and separate. The subjects of their respective realms have, however, the right from time to time to move from one to the other. And it appears to be the restless heritage of the childlike to exercise this privilege with rash frequency. Security can be confining, novelty devastating; oats are tasty, wild apples exotic. The playful spirit, the childlike quest, finds allurement both in novelty and in sameness. With the courtship of one, however, comes the relinquishing of the other.

Yellow, Yellow, a tale in less than 100 words, features immediate importance, enchantment, and enhanced self-image endowed upon a young boy by nothing more than finding a bright yellow construction hat. Acquisition of object and attributes prove temporary, however. The young finder is soon confronted by the original owner. Shadowing despair is in turn countered by youthful ingenuity. The key components of delight, "yellow" and "hat" can be revived by nothing more than a pair of scissors and a few sheets of construction paper to provide an oversized cap with the appropriate colour. Treasures are discovered then lost, but inventive desire can often reclaim what seems to have vanished for good. Astute insight probes the basics of desire, among them shape, colour and texture—each every bit as important to fancy as utility. Asch's unqualified popularity must derive in part from his own capability to sense those shifting but all too real fundamentals of delight.

Wherever it is that fancy is bred, it is probably not a near neighbor of novelty. Novelty either fizzles or proves to have questionable consequences. The appetite for novelty, that questing for the unnecessary, underlay the fall of man, and it too is a theme Asch touches upon. Eden-like joys of an enclosed, seemingly self-sufficient world provoke their own dissolution. Lion (*I Met a Penguin*) lives on an ocean islet with numerous friends, animal and human. Each day provides an unchanging ritual of pleasurable forgetfulness. They play in the morning, fish each afternoon, and cook their catch in the evening in a large communal pot. Apparently everyone is content with the routine until a serpent figure remarks on lion's incapacity as a fisherman. All agree with the assessment, and the pensive lion sets out to sea in order to ponder the consensus. Intemperate weather drives lion from the tropical isle all the way to the South Pole. Here, however, he establishes another utopian existence with a penguin who quickly becomes the love of his life. Contentment is curtailed when he brings up the bothersome question about his capacity as an angler. Her reply assures lion that he is competent. But assurance cannot still the meditative mode. Lion sets out to sea to reflect and a storm banishes him from an Antarctic bower. He is driven back to the original idyllic spot, but is now permanently subjected to memories of paradise lost. The inability to endure without reflection taints the most ideal of circumstances. And it is in this moment of sad reflection that the reader takes leave of lion—the creature of loving capacity whose awareness separates him from the bliss he is so capable of creating.

Certainly the children's tale does not of itself undertake philosophical consideration. Still, Asch's narratives contain an irresistible lure for entertaining certain questions. Does childhood cease with the onset of contemplation? Could it be that meditation forfeits more than it redeems? Seated as they are in that magical glade presided over by an innocent audience of children, Asch's picture books play with notions that innocence and unbridled pleasure are incompatible with reflection. Is the story destroying the aura it is created to sustain? Perhaps such queries are as unnecessary as they are threatening. Asch's books are fun, to be sure, but throughout there are signs that the author is fully aware of the fragility of the world he addresses.

Such restless reflection is apparently a condition shared by the author-artist with both his audience and his character creations. Shadows loom ominously, and they do block the light—but besides concealing, they project new forms, new narratives, and with these emerging tales, new possibilities and renewed relationships. Such is the case with his full-length novel, *Pearl's Promise,* where imminent death at any moment confronts a hapless mouse—and the victim's plight is effectively sustained for almost half of the book without any damage to the child world. Ingenuity might have its ingenuous qualities after all. The mouse characters share something with the total realism of a book like *Running with Rachel* where photographs replace drawings, and the endeavours follow the development of a young girl's commitment to running. Here too the seeds of discipline and achievement rise out of the dark side. "I looked down at my shadow. It seemed alive to me."

There seems to be salvation in shadows. In the incessant variated restlessness of the world of Frank Asch, there is the snaring and taming of those innumerable intriguing moments one might think are destined to vanish into thin air. His effort to capture the poetry of the urban mode (*City Sandwich*) assures us that "the subway always gives you more than just a ride." The tracks are fixed, etched as they are in bedrock. The path pursued is hidden from the sun. The stops are preset, the direction only to and fro. But for the ever-responsive rider, novelty, even enlightenment, are in the offing. So prodigious an output on the part of any author is certain to make many of the same stops, some to places forever unburnished and uninviting. Sometimes there is discovery, sometimes unwanted repetition. But the celebration of the moment endures. In such expectancy the spirit rightly associated with childhood lives on.

—Leonard R. Mendelsohn

———————

ASHLEY, Bernard. British. Born in London, 2 April 1935. Educated at Roan School, Blackheath, London, and Sir Joseph Williamson's School, Rochester, Kent, 1947–53; Trent Park College of Education, 1955–57, Cert. Ed. 1957; Cambridge Institute of Education, 1970–71, Cambridge associate diploma in primary education 1971. Served in the Royal Air Force, 1953–55. Married Iris Holbrook in 1958; three sons. Teacher, Kent Education Committee, Gravesend, 1957–65, Hertfordshire Education Committee, Hertford Heath, 1965–71, and Hartley Junior School, Newham, London, 1971–76. Since 1977 headteacher, Charlton Manor Junior School, London. Recipient: Children's Rights Workshop Other award, 1976. Address: 128 Heathwood Gardens, London SE7 8ER, England.

PUBLICATIONS FOR CHILDREN

Fiction

The Trouble with Donovan Croft, illustrated by Fermin Rocker. London, Oxford University Press, 1974.
Terry on the Fence, illustrated by Charles Keeping. London, Oxford University Press, 1975; New York, Phillips, 1977.
All My Men. London, Oxford University Press, 1977; New York, Phillips, 1978.
A Kind of Wild Justice, illustrated by Charles Keeping. London, Oxford University Press, 1978; New York, Phillips, 1979.
Break in the Sun, illustrated by Charles Keeping. London, Oxford University Press, and New York, Phillips, 1980.
Dinner Ladies Don't Count, illustrated by Janet Duchesne. London, MacRae, 1981.
I'm Trying to Tell You, illustrated by Lyn Jones. London, Kestrel, 1981.

Dodgem. London, MacRae, 1981; New York, Watts, 1982.
Linda's Lie, illustrated by Janet Duchesne. London, MacRae, and New York, Watts, 1982.
High Pavement Blues. London, MacRae, and New York, Watts, 1983.
Your Guess Is as Good as Mine, illustrated by Steven Cain. London, MacRae, and New York, Watts, 1983.
A Bit of Give and Take, illustrated by Trevor Stubley. London, Hamish Hamilton, 1984.
Janey. London, MacRae, 1985.
Running Scared. London, MacRae, 1986.
Clipper Street Stories (Calling for Sam, Taller Than Before, Down and Out, The Royal Visit, All I Ever Ask..., Sally Cinderella), illustrated by Jane Cope. London, Orchard, 6 vols., 1987–89.
Bad Blood. London, MacRae, 1988.
The Country Boy (novelization of his own television series). London, MacRae, 1989.

Plays

The Old Woman Who Lived in a Cola Can, music by David Smith (produced on tour, 1988).

Television Plays: *Running Scared,* from his own story, 1986; *The Country Boy* series, 1989.

Other

Don't Run Away (reader), illustrated by Ray Whittaker. London, Allman, 1965.
Wall of Death (reader), illustrated by Ray Whittaker. London, Allman, 1966.
Space Shot (reader), illustrated by Laszlo Acs. London, Allman, 1967.
The Big Escape (reader), illustrated by James Hunt. London, Allman, 1967.
The Men and the Boats: Britain's Life-Boat Service. London, Allman, 1968.
Weather Men. London, Allman, 1970; revised edition, 1974.

*

Bernard Ashley comments:
    Each of my full-length stories tells of a child's attempt to cope with a crisis point in life, each crisis presenting a problem as serious at the time as any he will later have to face as an adult: Donovan Croft, a black boy seemingly rejected in an alien environment; Terry, caught up in a frightening world of juvenile crime; Paul, in *All My Men,* struggling to secure his place in a new and unfriendly school; Patsy, in *Break in the Sun,* coming to terms with an unhappy home; and Simon, in *Dodgem,* being forced to fill the role of the adult. Excitement, humour, and personal relationships are some of the ingredients, but conflict, both internal and external, is the meat of each story, as it is of life.

*   *   *

    Bernard Ashley is a prolific and highly successful writer for children. Particularly in his early works he draws heavily on extensive experience as a junior school teacher and headmaster, although critics have sometimes detected tension between primary school protagonists and events and attitudes more appropriate for older readers. Ashley has moved increasingly into the world of the teenage novel, with occasional books for younger readers like *Dinner Ladies Don't Count.*
    Ashley came to notice in 1974 with *The Trouble with Donovan Croft,* one of the earliest British books to give a central role to a black child. Donovan *has* a problem and *is* one; that is the "trouble." A West Indian boy, he becomes mute when separated from his parents to be fostered with a white family. The book contains convincing scenes of incipient racism at home, school, and the football match. The climax, when Donovan breaks silence to shout a warning to his friend Keith, seems slightly contrived, and it is never really clear why nobody—including his loving father—has explained that his mother's absence to nurse a sick relative is only temporary. The story's conventional happy ending has rarely been a feature of Ashley's later work.
    In 1978 he began a sequence of tough stories of contemporary life, combining features of the thriller with those of the "problem" novel. Children in these books—a grubby non-reader and a bed-wetter among them—lead secret, dangerous lives. Ronnie exists on the fringes of violent crime (*A Kind of Wild Justice*), Kevin has to guard the family's market stall against takeover (*High Pavement Blues*), and the title character in *Janey* serves as a lookout for thieves. Conventional parent-child relationships are frequently reversed. Simon struggles to care for his father who was paralysed in the car crash that killed his mother (*Dodgem*); Kevin protects his mother and tries to bring back his deserting father; Ritchie sets about getting the transplant that may save his father (*Bad Blood*). These boys and girls have to cope with problems largely ignored by adults and to reconcile the conflicting demands of different worlds: home and school, criminal and lawful, black and white. In some cases the characters are uprooted from a familiar to a strange school, as in *All My Men* or *Taller Than Before;* others are plunged into an exotic but alien setting: Patsy escaping with a bargeload of amateur actors in *Break in the Sun* or Simon being hidden in a travelling fair in *Dodgem.*
    Technically Ashley is an excellent, uncondescending storyteller. In the later books he cuts cinematically from scene to scene, descriptions are vivid and convincing, and his dialogue is racy and immediate (therefore already dating in places) and is used well to define character. Titles and themes are frequently symbolic but within the capacity of young readers: Simon describes himself as a dodgem, "bashed into from all angles;" the "bad blood" is heredity and fraternal antipathy as well as leukemia.
    Although the books for younger readers sometimes offer a neatly extractable moral, the lessons of most of the novels are more complex and ambiguous. Few characters are shown as straightforwardly good or bad or understand the whole truth of a situation. Some readers are unhappy that "authority" is not always sympathetically portrayed (like the social services in *Dodgem*), or about the sexual behaviour in several books. Without much contrivance, however, Ashley's central characters move painfully towards greater understandings of themselves and the world, usually through significant relationships with others. Paul learns from Lorraine (*All My Men*), Ronnie from the school bus driver and Margit the Pakistani girl, and Janey from the elderly Mrs. Woodcroft.
    Ashley's novels are not for passive readers. They demand that we interpret events, assess characters, and judge motives much as we do in real life. It is not surprising that they have proved so popular in schools.

—Robert Protherough

ATKINSON, M(ary) E(velyn). British. Born in Highgate, London, 20 June 1899. Educated privately and at Leeson House, Langton Matravers, Dorset. Served as a British Red Cross nurse during World Wars I and II. Married George Neuberg Frankau in 1951. *Died in 1974.*

PUBLICATIONS FOR CHILDREN

Fiction

August Adventure, illustrated by Harold Jones. London, Cape, 1936.
Mystery Manor, illustrated by Harold Jones. London, Lane, 1937.
The Compass Points North, illustrated by Harold Jones. London, Lane, 1938.
Smugglers' Gap, illustrated by Harold Jones. London, Lane, 1939.
Going Gangster. London, Lane, 1940.
Crusoe Island, illustrated by Harold Jones. London, Lane, 1941.
Challenge to Adventure, illustrated by Stuart Tresilian. London, Lane, 1942.
The Monster of Widgeon Weir, illustrated by Stuart Tresilian. London, Lane, 1943.
The Nest of the Scarecrow, illustrated by Stuart Tresilian. London, Lane, 1944.
Problem Party, illustrated by Stuart Tresilian. London, Lane, 1945.
Chimney Cottage, illustrated by Dorothy Craigie. London, Lane, 1947.
The House on the Moor, illustrated by Charlotte Hough. London, Lane, 1948.
The Thirteenth Adventure, illustrated by Charlotte Hough. London, Lane, 1949.
Steeple Folly, illustrated by Charlotte Hough. London, Lane, 1950.
Castaway Camp, illustrated by Charlotte Hough. London, Lane, 1951.
Hunter's Moon, illustrated by Charlotte Hough. London, Lane, 1952.
The Barnstormers, illustrated by Charlotte Hough. London, Lane, 1953.
Riders and Raids, illustrated by Sheila Rose. London, Lane, 1955.
Unexpected Adventure, illustrated by Sheila Rose. London, Lane, 1955.
Horseshoes and Handlebars, illustrated by Sheila Rose. London, Lane, 1958; New York, A.S. Barnes, 1959.
Where There's a Will, illustrated by Wendy Marchant. London, Nelson, 1961.

Other

Editor, with G.T. Atkinson, *A Book of Giants and Dwarfs.* London, Dent, 1929.

PUBLICATIONS FOR ADULTS

Plays

Here Lies Matilda. London, Deane, 1931.
Beginner's Luck. London, Deane, and Boston, Baker, 1932.
Patchwork. London, Deane, and Boston, Baker, 1933.
The Chimney Corner. London, Deane, and Boston, Baker, 1934.
The Day's Good Cause. London, Deane, and Boston, Baker, 1935.
Crab-Apple Harvest. London, Deane, and Boston, Baker, 1936.
Going Rustic. London, Deane, and Boston, Baker, 1936.
Little White Jumbo. London, Pinker, 1937.
Can the Leopard? London, Deane, and Boston, Baker, 1939.
The Lights Go Up. London, Deane, 1945.

*   *   *

M.E. Atkinson's claim to be remembered rests entirely on her long series of books about the Lockett children and their friends which appeared at regular intervals between 1936 and 1949. In her later years she wrote about another group of children (Fricka Hammond

and her cousins) and also a number of not particularly good pony stories for girls. Most of the Lockett books were illustrated by two very different, but both excellent, artists—Stuart Tresilian and Harold Jones. Harold Jones's very first work was for *August Adventure,* Atkinson's first novel, and his pictures give an outward distinction to many of the books, which is not entirely belied by the stories themselves.

Atkinson has had little critical attention. In their histories of children's fiction, neither Frank Eyre nor John Rowe Townsend mention her, and Geoffrey Trease merely brackets her with David Severn and Malcolm Saville as one of the three outstanding exponents of the holiday adventure theme, sub-Arthur Ransome. Certainly the books carry all the familiar and much derided hallmarks of the fiction of the period. The Locketts—Jane, Bill, and Oliver—are relentlessly middle-class, and their world accepts as entirely natural private schools, cooks, and even titled friends. Moreover their parents are in India, and, as their author herself puts it, "the Lockett children have a positive flair for finding themselves alone and independent." Their language is inevitably dated. Things are "perfectly beastly," "frightfully important," "frantically secret." The device of pretending that everything really happened, that the Lockett's adventures are all true (written by them with the help of a convenient Aunt Margaret) sometimes wears a little thin. There are frequent cross-references to other books in the series, and these are sometimes irritatingly self-congratulatory. It is with some reluctance that the reader realizes he feels rather similar feelings to those of Peter Richards, the referee in *Challenge to Adventure,* who "enjoyed each sentence, eager for the strange story to unravel as fast as it could yet determined to miss nothing." This book, in fact the most "inbred" of the lot—the Locketts have been challenged to prove that things really do happen to them—is actually one of the most attractive and appealing and can still offer enormous enjoyment to young readers.

These long expansive stories (*Crusoe Island,* for instance, runs to well over three hundred pages) are still appealing because, though the plots may be rather contrived and the continual emphasis on adventure may become a little tedious, Atkinson was so good at character. In a cast of dozens, hardly one is a stereotype. In many ways, she was ahead of her time. Peter Richards may think that Jane is "more like a boy than a girl." Her creator knows that there are many girls who are happy to wear their brother's old shorts and ride his old bike. Fenella, too, is not a "tomboy" but a particularly masterful individual. Her fight with Bill in *Going Gangster* lacks the self-consciousness of a contemporary writer tying in knots in order to be non-sexist. Fenella and Nina too (whose leading part is in *Problem Party*) illustrate Atkinson's excellent ability to write about "grey" characters—neither black nor white but human and convincing. She was also ahead of her time in the degree of realism she allowed herself. Writing about the provision of an earth box for the dogs in *Crusoe Island,* she says "the problem was not one about which one usually writes in the polite type of book." Reading these books again for the first time for 30 years, I was pleased to recognize that safe, lively world I enjoyed so much when I read them first as a child during the war.

—Ann Thwaite

———

ATWATER, Richard (Tupper). American. Born Frederick Mund Atwater in Chicago, Illinois, 20 December 1892. Educated at the University of Chicago, 1907–17, Associate in Arts 1909, B.A. (honors) in Greek 1910. Married Florence H. Carroll; two daughters. Taught at the University of Chicago; columnist, *Tribune, Evening*

Post (as "Riq"), and *Daily News,* all Chicago. *Died in 1938.*

PUBLICATIONS FOR CHILDREN

Fiction

Doris and the Trolls, illustrated by John Gee. Chicago, Rand McNally, 1931.
Mr. Popper's Penguins, completed by Florence Atwater, illustrated by Robert Lawson. Boston, Little Brown, 1938; London, Harrap, 1939.

PUBLICATIONS FOR ADULTS

Verse

Rickety Rimes of Riq. Chicago, Ballou, 1925.

Other

Translator, *Secret History of Procopius.* New York, Covici Friede, 1934.

*   *   *

Penguins are engaging creatures. With their black and white "tuxedos," dignified, upright demeanor, and short, Chaplinesque steps, they are especially amusing to children. And when the penguins are *Mr. Popper's Penguins* (alliteration, assonance, and a sing-song beat), they are very funny, indeed.

Mr. Popper is a mild house painter. We meet him on his way home from work, clumsy and bungling, "spattered with paint and calcimine," with "bits of wallpaper clinging to his hair and whiskers": Mr. Popper is "rather an untidy man." Much to the chagrin of his tidy and practical wife he is also absent-minded, and quite a dreamer. He likes to sit with his pipe and read about far-away places—especially the North and South Poles. In fact, he is quite an authority on the subject.

Mr. Popper is particularly fond of penguins. Describing to his wife a movie he has seen about the Drake Expedition to the Antarctic, Mr. Popper concludes:

> I think the nicest part of all is the penguins. No wonder all the men on that expedition had such a good time playing with them. They are the funniest birds in the world. They don't fly like other birds. They walk erect like little men. When they get tired of walking they just lie down on their stomachs and slide. It would be very nice to have one as a pet.

One evening, as Mr. Popper is reading a new book from the library, *Antarctic Adventures,* listening to a radio-broadcast of Admiral Drake—direct (with static) from the South Pole—he suddenly hears Drake say: "Hello, Mr. Popper, up there in Stillwater. Thanks for your nice letter about the pictures of our last expedition. Watch for an answer. But not by letter, Mr. Popper. Watch for a surprise. Signing off. Signing off."

The "surprise" arrives at 432 Proudfoot Avenue the next day. Inside the large package, marked UNPACK AT ONCE and KEEP COOL and punched with air holes, is a live *penguin!* "Ork! Ork!" it squeals. "Gook! Gook!" And his name is Captain Cook. The fun begins! As if one penguin weren't fun enough, another—Greta—soon arrives from the Aquarium in Mammoth City. Ten baby penguins soon follow. 432 Proudfoot Avenue becomes a penguin paradise as Mr. Popper transforms first the living room, then the basement into an Arctic adventureland.

But pragmatic demands of the real world intervene. Money. It

takes a lot of it to feed 12 hungry penguins. Mr. Popper's solution: train the penguins, build up an act, hit the Big Time. The story slides along from there on its stomach, through many adventures, until finally Mr. Popper is confronted with a serious dilemma: sign a movie contract and take the troupe to Hollywood (not a very wholesome place to bring up penguins), or let Admiral Drake take them on an expedition to the North Pole (where there are as yet no penguins). He makes his sad decision. What a surprise when Drake invites Mr. Popper to come too!

Atwater's *Mr. Popper's Penguins* (lovingly completed by Atwater's wife Florence after his death) has been a favorite with younger children for over 50 years, with its perfect interplay of wild hilarity and dead-pan seriousness, its smoothly sliding, adventure-filled plot, its charming and lovable characters (gaily depicted by illustrator Robert Lawson) and vivid detail; and its portrayal of an ordinary man—"just a house painter"—who has his happiest dreams come true.

—Marcia G. Fuchs

———

AVERILL, Esther (Holden). Has also written as John Domino. American. Born in Bridgeport, Connecticut, 24 July 1902. Educated at Vassar College, Poughkeepsie, New York, B.A. 1923; Brooklyn Museum Art School. Member of the editorial department, *Women's Wear Daily,* New York, 1923–25; freelance journalist, Paris, 1925–31; founding publisher, Domino Press, Paris, 1931–34, and New York 1935–38; worked in the children's section of the New York Public Library. Address: 30 Joralemon Street, Apartment 11-A, Brooklyn, New York 11201, U.S.A.

PUBLICATIONS FOR CHILDREN

Fiction (illustrated by the author)

Powder: The Story of a Colt, The Duchess, and a Circus, with Lila Stanley, illustrated by Feodor Rojankovsky. Paris, Domino Press, New York, Smith and Haas, and London, Faber, 1933.
Flash: The Story of a Horse, A Coach-Dog, and the Gypsies, illustrated by Feodor Rojankovsky. Paris, Domino Press, New York, Smith and Haas, and London, Faber, 1934.
Fable of a Proud Poppy (as John Domino), illustrated by Emile Lahner. Paris, Domino Press, 1934.
The Cat Club; or, The Life and Times of Jenny Linsky. New York, Harper, 1944.
The Adventures of Jack Ninepins. New York, Harper, 1944.
The School for Cats. New York, Harper, 1947.
Jenny's First Party. New York, Harper, 1948.
Jenny's Moonlight Adventure. New York, Harper, 1949.
When Jenny Lost Her Scarf. New York, Harper, 1951.
Jenny's Adopted Brothers. New York, Harper, 1952.
How the Brothers Joined the Cat Club. New York, Harper, 1953; Kingswood, Surrey, World's Work, 1959.
Jenny's Birthday Book. New York, Harper, 1954.
Jenny Goes to Sea. New York, Harper, 1957.
Jenny's Bedside Book. New York, Harper, 1959.
The Fire Cat. New York, Harper, 1960; Kingswood, Surrey, World's Work, 1961.
The Hotel Cat. New York, Harper, 1969.
Captains of the City Streets. New York, Harper, 1972.
Jenny and the Cat Club (The Cat Club, Jenny's First Party, When Jenny Lost Her Scarf, Jenny's Adopted Brothers, How the Brothers Joined the Cat Club). New York, Harper, 1973; London, Fontana, 1976.

Other

The Voyages of Jacques Cartier, illustrated by Feodor Rojankovsky. New York, Domino Press, 1937; revised edition, as *Cartier Sails the St. Lawrence,* New York, Harper, 1956.
King Philip: The Indian Chief, illustrated by Vera Belsky. New York, Harper, 1950.
Eyes on the World: The Story and Work of Jacques Callot. New York, Funk and Wagnalls, 1969.

Editor, with Lila Stanley, *Daniel Boone: Historic Adventures of an American Hunter among the Indians,* illustrated by Feodor Rojankovsky. Paris, Domino Press, and London, Faber, 1931; revised edition, New York, Harper, 1945.

Translator, *Tales of Poindi,* by Jean Mariotti, illustrated by Feodor Rojankovsky. New York, Domino Press, 1938.

*   *   *

Jenny Linsky is undoubtedly Esther Averill's most famous and enduring character. Over a dozen books for younger readers have been written about this shy, orphan cat with the engaging personality. Most of the stories are short enough to be read comfortably in one sitting and concern the various adventures of Jenny and her fellow members of the Cat Club.

Averill's descriptive prose is characterized by a light, delicate touch. With deft strokes of the pen she endows Jenny and her companions with distinct personalities which are in keeping with their physical appearance. Jenny's quiet courage is sympathetically and humorously portrayed in *Jenny's Moonlight Adventure.* Her agonizing decision to rescue a friend's prize possession is realistically explored as she wavers from a firm decision not to help, to shame that she hasn't the courage to act, and finally to the conviction that she must help her friend.

Averill's world is black and white—good deeds are rewarded, bad deeds are punished, and transgressors of the Cat Club rules are made to see the error of their ways. Moral overtones are evident throughout Averill's fiction. There is an emphasis, for example, on the praiseworthiness of facing up to one's problems, admitting guilt when one has done wrong, and treating one's fellows properly. Jenny's initial encounter with the Cat Club teaches her that shyness is a handicap which may be overcome. Likewise, fear of the unknown in *Jenny's Moonlight Adventure* is shown to be diminished by a direct stand against those fears.

The understated style of Averill's writing makes her books a delight to read. She uses words sparingly to provide a setting, describe the characters and get the story under way. Her sure sense of story is evident—even in *Jenny's Bedside Book,* which lacks any action at all, the story-within-a-story technique holds the reader's attention.

The humor of Averill's work is derived from her straightforward tongue-in-cheek descriptions and the exaggerated dignity which she invests in her animal characters. Relationships between the characters are almost always positive. The books are full of tenderness and warm, loving friendships; with their gaiety and charm they have made an important contribution to the genre of children's fantasy, confirmed by their continuing popularity.

—Fran Ashdown

———

AVERY, Gillian (Elise). British. Born in Reigate, Surrey, 30 September 1926. Educated at Dunottar School, Reigate. Married A.O.J. Cockshut in 1952; one daughter. Junior reporter, *Surrey Mirror,* Redhill, 1944–47; staff member, *Chambers Encyclopaedia,* London, 1947–50; assistant illustrations editor, Clarendon Press, Oxford, 1950–54. Chairman, Children's Books History Society, 1987–89. Recipient: *Guardian* award, 1972. Address: 32 Charlbury Road, Oxford OX2 6UU, England.

PUBLICATIONS FOR CHILDREN

Fiction

The Warden's Niece, illustrated by Dick Hart. London, Collins, 1957.
Trespassers at Charlcote, illustrated by Dick Hart. London, Collins, 1958.
James Without Thomas, illustrated by John Verney. London, Collins, 1959.
The Elephant War, illustrated by John Verney. London, Collins, 1960; New York, Holt Rinehart, 1971.
To Tame a Sister, illustrated by John Verney. London, Collins, 1961; Princeton, New Jersey, Van Nostrand, 1964.
The Greatest Gresham, illustrated by John Verney. London, Collins, 1962.
The Peacock House, illustrated by John Verney. London, Collins, 1963.
The Italian Spring, illustrated by John Verney. London, Collins, 1964; New York, Holt Rinehart, 1972.
Call of the Valley, illustrated by Laszlo Acs. London, Collins, 1966; New York, Holt Rinehart, 1968.
A Likely Lad, illustrated by Faith Jaques. London, Collins, and New York, Holt Rinehart, 1971.
Ellen's Birthday, illustrated by Krystyna Turska. London, Hamish Hamilton, 1971.
Ellen and the Queen, illustrated by Krystyna Turska. London, Hamish Hamilton, 1972; Nashville, Nelson, 1974.
Jemima and the Welsh Rabbit, illustrated by John Lawrence. London, Hamish Hamilton, 1972.
Freddie's Feet, illustrated by Krystyna Turska. London, Hamish Hamilton, 1976.
Huck and Her Time Machine. London, Collins, 1977.
Mouldy's Orphan, illustrated by Faith Jaques. London, Collins, 1978.
Sixpence!, illustrated by Antony Maitland. London, Collins, 1979.

Other

Victorian People in Life and Literature. London, Collins, and New York, Holt Rinehart, 1970.
The Echoing Green: Memories of Victorian and Regency Youth. London, Collins, and New York, Viking Press, 1974.
Book of the Strange and Odd, illustrated by Michael Jackson. London, Kestrel, 1975.

Editor, *A Flat Iron for a Farthing,* by Juliana Horatia Ewing. London, Faith Press, 1959.
Editor, *Jan of the Windmill,* by Juliana Horatia Ewing. London, Faith Press, 1960.
Editor, *The Sapphire Treasury of Stories for Boys and Girls.* London, Gollancz, 1960.
Editor, *In the Window Seat: A Selection of Victorian Stories,* illustrated by Susan Einzig. London, Oxford University Press, 1960; Princeton, New Jersey, Van Nostrand, 1965.
Editor, *Father Phim,* by Annie Keary. London, Faith Press, 1962.
Editor, *Unforgettable Journeys,* illustrated by John Verney.-

London, Gollancz, 1965.
Editor, *School Remembered,* illustrated by John Verney. London, Gollancz, 1967; New York, Funk and Wagnalls, 1968.
Editor, *A Great Emergency, and A Very Ill-Tempered Family,* by Juliana Horatia Ewing. London, Gollancz, 1967.
Editor, *The Gold of Fairnilee and Other Stories,* by Andrew Lang. London, Gollancz, 1967.
Editor, *Village Children,* by Charlotte Yonge. London, Gollancz, 1967.
Editor, *Banning and Blessing,* by Margaret Roberts. London, Gollancz, 1967.
Editor, *The Hole in the Wall and Other Stories,* illustrated by Doreen Roberts. London, Oxford University Press, 1968.
Editor, *Victoria-Bess and Others,* by Brenda, Mrs. Gatty, and Frances Hodgson Burnett. London, Gollancz, 1968; as *Victorian Doll Stories,* New York, Schocken, 1969.
Editor, *The Wallypug of Why,* by G.E. Farrow, illustrated by Harry Furniss. London, Gollancz, 1968.
Editor, *Froggy's Little Brother,* by Brenda. London, Gollancz, 1968.
Editor, *My New Home,* by Mary Louisa Molesworth, illustrated by L. Leslie Brooke. London, Gollancz, 1968.
Editor, *The Life and Adventures of Lady Anne* (anonymous), illustrated by F.D. Bedford. London, Gollancz, 1969.
Editor, *Stephanie's Children,* by Margaret Roberts. London, Gollancz, 1969.
Editor, *Anne's Terrible Good Nature and Other Stories for Children,* by E.V. Lucas. London, Gollancz, 1970.
Editor, *The Rival Kings,* by Annie Keary. London, Gollancz, 1970.
Editor, *Red Letter Days,* illustrated by Krystyna Turska. London, Hamish Hamilton, 1971.

PUBLICATIONS FOR ADULTS

Novels

The Lost Railway. London, Collins, 1980.
Onlookers. London, Collins, 1983.

Other

Mrs. Ewing. London, Bodley Head, 1961; New York, Walck, 1964.
Nineteenth Century Children: Heroes and Heroines in English Children's Stories 1780–1900, with Angela Bull. London, Hodder and Stoughton, 1965.
Childhood's Pattern: A Study of the Heroes and Heroines of Children's Fiction 1770–1950. London, Hodder and Stoughton, 1975.

*   *   *

For over two decades Gillian Avery has been producing extremely believable children's stories set in the late Victorian era. She has a sympathetic understanding of her chosen period which is evoked without sentimental inflation or a retrospective smoothness. She manages to express the past *as* the present by underlining its unevenness and normality. Stringent observation of character and manners, and a flair for humorous incident, enhance the realism of her stories.

Avery recalls that when she wrote her first book she seemed to know more about the feelings of the children of 1875 than the self-assured attitudes of young people in the 1950's. She felt that there was an affinity between her own pre-war generation with its "meek acceptance of the power of the adult world" and the Victorian child who had always been accustomed to authoritarian treatment. However, the objective of her fictional children—even the most

diffident—is usually to assert themselves in some particular way. This often involves a flouting of the restraining conventions of the time, with consequent conflict or social unease. Avery makes this type of embarrassment acutely credible to readers brought up in today's more liberal environment. She also makes the most of the humorous elements which occur in these situations—especially when they arise from confrontations between children and adults. Her stories, despite their serious moments, are really domestic or social comedies.

The Warden's Niece was Avery's first book and it is still one of the most popular. She started writing it one winter as "an escape from the weeping…skies and raw fogs" of Manchester, where she was then living; appropriately the book begins with an escape of a different kind. Maria runs away from her dispiriting boarding school to her uncle, the Warden of an Oxford college. Although she has shown no sign of academic distinction, she hopes one day to become a lecturer in Latin and Greek. Her uncle encourages this creditable ambition, arranging for Maria to have lessons with the Smith brothers—the lordly Thomas, reasonable Joshua, and outrageous James. Their eccentric temporary tutor gives the children opportunities to explore their surroundings, and Maria stumbles on a mystery concerning a 17th-century boy. She feels that he is linked with a scrawled message which she discovers on the wall of a stately home. Determination to complete this piece of original research gives Maria the courage to play truant and even to gatecrash the Bodleian. The Oxford setting and historical associations give the book a strong appeal. It has, apparently, sent people to Oxford. Avery thinks it reflects her own romantic yearnings: "As an adolescent I felt about the place as many of my contemporaries felt about Hollywood."

The Elephant War also has an Oxford background. Its heroine, Harriet Jessop, is more timid than Maria but equally convincing. The awesome Smith brothers appear once more. Harriet thinks that they typify the intellectual life of Oxford which seems excitingly attractive to her. She is recruited by a formidable aunt into a campaign to save one of the London Zoo's elephants from being sent to America—to "slavery" in Barnum's Circus. This "cause" draws Harriet into a series of farcical events, and she falls foul of the Smith family who ridicule her campaigning zeal; but unexpectedly James Smith suddenly becomes her infuriating and disruptive ally. (Avery is particularly perceptive when describing the irritation that a bumptious small boy or girl can arouse in a more sensitive older child.) The point is effectively made that enthusiasms can get out of control.

In *The Greatest Gresham* the primly brought up Julia and Henry Gresham are—like Harriet Jessop—deeply aware of their own inadequacies. These are highlighted by their relationship with the next door children. Richard and Kate Holt live in a scruffy and disordered home, but they have an independence which Julia and Henry long to emulate. The Greshams force themselves to perform difficult and embarrassing feats suggested by the Holts; this is supposed to broaden their minds. The story has an intriguingly furtive atmosphere. The children form a secret society, and the Greshams are constantly afraid that their parents will declare the Holts "undesirable" and end the association.

A desire for genteel respectability and social position plays a big part in *A Likely Lad.* It was inspired by the reminiscences of Avery's father-in-law about his Lancashire boyhood. Bookish Willy Overs is the likely lad; his self-made, shopkeeper father intends him to begin work at 13 in an insurance office. Mr. Overs sees this as the start of a successful career for his son, and also as a means of establishing the superiority of his branch of the family over that of his patronizing in-laws. Willy's apprehensive but persistent resistance to the scheme eventually persuades his father to allow him to continue his education. The atmosphere of a working-class home at the turn of the century is expressed through the effects of unvarying domestic routines on the children. For instance, on their mother's baking day Willy and his brother have to suffer banishment from the cosy kitchen/living room to the boredom of an immaculate but icy and toyless parlour.

In the stories the sense of another time is conveyed externally: there are frequent descriptions of cold, dark rooms and the rituals of lighting fires and candles; of plush table covers, knickerbocker suits, and merino dresses. The psychological tone of Avery's books, however, is modern, and lively enough to appeal to a wide range of present-day readers. Everything in the books is seen from the children's point of view. This was certainly not the case in stories which were written for real life Victorian children. The naughtiest of their heroines would never have found herself in the situation of the little girl in *Ellen and the Queen* who has an illicit peep at Queen Victoria's legs!

—Mary Cadogan

———————

AVERY, (Charles) Harold. British. Born in Redditch, Worcestershire, in 1867. Educated at Dunheved College, Launceton, Cornwall; Midland Collegiate School, Birmingham; New College, Eastbourne; and in Dresden. Served in the Worcestershire Regiment during World War I. Lived in Evesham, Worcestershire. *Died in 1943.*

PUBLICATIONS FOR CHILDREN

Fiction

The School's Honour and Other Stories. London, Sunday School Union, 1894.
The Orderly Officer. London, S.P.C.K., 1894.
An Old Boy's Yarns. London, Cassell, 1895.
A Boy All Over, illustrated by Walter Buckley. London, Sampson Low, 1896.
Frank's First Term; or, Making a Man of Him. London, Nelson, 1896.
Soldiers of the Queen; or, Jack Fenleigh's Luck. London, Nelson, 1897.
The Dormitory Flag. London, Nelson, 1898.
Stolen or Strayed. London, Nelson, 1898.
The Triple Alliance. London, Nelson, 1898.
Mobsley's Mohicans. London, Nelson, 1899.
Gunpowder Treason and Plot, and Other Stories for Boys, with Fred Whishaw and R.B. Townshend. London, Nelson, 1900.
Heads or Tails. London, Nelson, 1900.
A Toast-Fag and Other Stories. London, Nelson, 1900.
All Play and No Work, illustrated by Harold Copping. London, Partridge, 1901.
With Wellington to Waterloo, illustrated by J. Finnemore. London, Wells Gardner, 1901.
Sale's Sharpshooters. London, Nelson, 1902.
An Armchair Adventurer. London, Simpkin Marshall, 1903.
The House on the Moor. London, Nelson, 1903.
Manor Pool Island. London, Collins, 1903.
Highway Pirates. London, Nelson, 1904.
Out of the Running. London, Collins, 1904.
Under Padlock and Seal. London, Nelson, 1905.
Firelock and Steel. London, Nelson, 1906.
The Magic Beads. London, Nelson, 1906.
Play the Game! London, Nelson, 1906.
Captain Swing. London, Nelson, 1907.

Through the Wood, illustrated by John Hassall. London, Nelson, 1907.
True to His Nickname. London, Nelson, 1907.
The Enchanted Egg. London, Nelson, 1908.
The Little Robinson Crusoes; or, Ronald and Betty's Adventures on an Uninhabited Island, illustrated by Harry Rountree. London, Nelson, 1908.
The Wizard's Wand. London, Nelson, 1908.
In the Days of Danger. London, Nelson, 1909.
Off the Wicket. London, Nelson, 1910.
Not Cricket! London, Partridge, 1911.
The Forbidden Room. London, Nelson, 1911.
Head of the School. London, Partridge, 1912.
Talford's Last Term. London, Partridge, 1912.
The Chartered Company. London, Nelson, 1915.
Line Up! London, Collins, 1918.
Caught Out. London, Collins, 1919.
Jack and the Redskins. London, Nelson, 1920.
The Runaways, illustrated by Gordon Browne. London, Collins, 1920.
Schoolboy Pluck. London, Nisbet, 1921.
A Choice of Chums. London, Nelson, 1922.
The Prefects' Patrol. London, Nisbet, 1922.
Between Two Schools. London, Nelson, 1923.
A Fifth Form Mystery. London, Boy's Own Paper, 1923.
The Spoil-Sport, and Double Dummy. London, Nelson, 1923.
The Adventures of Woodeny and Other Stories, with Ethel Talbot and Ada Holman. London, Nelson, 1923.
Pocket Thunder and Other Stories, with others. London, Nelson, 1926.
A Sixth-Form Feud. London, Ward Lock, 1926.
Who Goes There?, illustrated by Roy. London, Nelson, 1927.
Won for the School, illustrated by Archibald Webb. London, Collins, 1927.
Any Port in a Storm and Other Stories, with others. London, Nelson, 1928.
Day Boy Colours, illustrated by J. Phillips Paterson. London, Nelson, 1928.
Cock-House of Claverhill. London, Collins, 1929.
A Term on Trial. London, Partridge, 1930.
The Cock-House Cup. London, Nelson, 1933.
A Close Finish and Other School Stories. London, Partridge, 1934.
The Marlcot Mystery. London, Ward Lock, 1935.
Chums at Charlhurst. London, Nelson, 1936.
Through Thick and Thin, illustrated by J. Phillips Paterson. London, Nelson, 1938.
The Side Line. London, Ward Lock, 1939.
The Girl at the Helm. London, Nelson, 1941.

Other

"Wrinkles" for Young Writers. London, Chilver, 1902.
No Surrender! The Story of Captain Scott's Journey to the South Pole, illustrated by Rowland Hilder. London, Nelson, 1933.

Editor, *Adventure Afloat,* by Lord Thomas Cochrane. London, Nelson, 1907.
Editor, *Adventures in the Rifle Brigade,* by Sir John Kincaid. London, Nelson, 1907.

PUBLICATIONS FOR ADULTS

Novels

A Week at the Sea. London, Stanley Paul, 1910.

Every Dog His Day.   London, Stanley Paul, 1911.
Thumbs Up.   London, Nisbet, 1925.

*   *   *

Harold Avery is best remembered for his boys' school stories written before the First World War, although he was extremely prolific and his long career continued well into 1930's. His central theme was an affirmation of all things British, and his great talent was for reflecting and reinforcing popular tastes. He helped to make boys' schools seem respectable and even enviable places. But just as "Keep the Home Fires Burning" was written for the benefit of those not actually at the Front, so we can wonder if his British schoolboy really existed except in the imagination of the general public. This kind of book, however, helped to create him.

Avery was willing to try his hand at any current style or interest. In *The Little Robinson Crusoes,* for example, or in his many adventure stories, desert islands are natural paradises, natives are like unpredictable, violent children, and the inevitable men of action have stiff upper lips and an iron code of honour. He even attempted in *The Wizard's Wand* the mixture of magic and real life which E. Nesbit had made so successful; but Avery lacked her imagination, and the book is full of stereotypes.

What he lacked in subtlety, however, he made up for in enthusiasm, and his school stories have a bouncing life of their own. One of the most representative, *Frank's First Term,* tells the story of Frank, a "normal" English boy. He is fatherless, consequently becoming his mother's darling, until a far-seeing bachelor uncle arranges for him to be sent to boarding school with the rather curious admonition "now boy, be a man." In order that he should be believable, Frank himself is not an instant hero. It is Merredith, a fellow new boy, who has the "clear grey eyes" which always distinguish one of Avery's superior English gentlemen. By faultless example, Merredith encourages Frank to "bite hard on the bullet"; and although Frank is homesick and bullied, he keeps his unhappiness a secret from his mother. Merredith also persuades Frank to give up the company of boys who are tempting him into bad ways (principally betting). Finally, the cads are punished and Frank proves himself by saving the school flag from desecration by town boys. He can now return home at the term's end in triumph, "a man, instead of a milksop."

The success of Avery's books is not undeserved. His ground rules are laid down from the outset and we can distinguish bounders from bricks without difficulty. The enjoyment comes from watching the plot unfold, and from the sense of being invited into the confidences of a select and privileged club. Our faith in the Englishman (tacitly always a gentleman) becomes unshakeable: "to sneak" is the cardinal sin of the schoolboy code. Boys are taught loyalty to their own kind, however unpleasant the individual concerned may be; the same treatment rarely extends to "the rougher classes." As for "the fairer sex," they receive extreme courtesy and consideration, a doubtful compensation for their exclusion from the golden circle of male comradeship. Avery sets no great store by talent or originality. A schoolboy (and a gentleman) needs to be loyal and obedient "and let who will be clever." He recounts with obvious approval how a brilliant boy gives up all hope of further education and career to support his family as a copy clerk. His sentimentality is unashamed. There are no complexities in his moral judgements and he has no fear that they may appear ridiculous. In his later writing, the conviction wavers. His attempts to instill cynicism and intrigue only reveal the two-dimensional nature of his characters, and even the schools in his stories seem often in decline. There is little of the assurance that made his earlier books so compelling.

Avery's influence does still linger on, and not only in boys' annuals. Despite his earnest truisms, there is something very powerful in his picture of a golden era when boys will be boys on their way to becoming gentlemen and schooldays are the happiest time of our lives.

—Alison Sage

————

AVI (Avi Wortis).   American.   Born in New York City, 23 December 1937.   Educated at Elisabeth Irwin High School, New York; University of Wisconsin, Madison, B.A. in history 1959, M.A. in drama 1962; Columbia University, New York, M.S. in library science 1964. Married 1) Joan Gabriner (divorced), two sons; 2) Coppélia Kahn, one son. Staff member, Lincoln Center Library of the Performing Arts Theatre Collection, New York, 1962–70, and Lambeth Public Library, London, 1968; Assistant Professor and humanities librarian, Trenton State College, New Jersey, 1970–86. Since 1986 full-time writer. Regular reviewer, *Library Journal* and *School Library Journal,* both New York, 1965–73. Recipient: New York Public Library grant, 1969; New Jersey Council on the Arts grant, 1974, 1976, 1978; Christopher award, 1981; O'Dell award, 1984. Agent: Dorothy Markinko, McIntosh and Otis, 310 Madison Avenue, New York, New York 10017. Address: 15 Sheldon Street, Providence, Rhode Island 02906, U.S.A.

PUBLICATIONS FOR CHILDREN

Fiction

Things That Sometimes Happen, illustrated by Jodi Robbin.   New York, Doubleday, 1970.
Snail Tale, illustrated by Tom Kindron.   New York, Pantheon, 1972; London, Hutchinson, 1973.
No More Magic.   New York, Pantheon, 1975.
Captain Grey.   New York, Pantheon, 1977.
Emily Upham's Revenge, illustrated by Paul O. Zelinsky.   New York, Pantheon, 1978.
Night Journeys.   New York, Pantheon, 1979.
Encounter at Easton.   New York, Pantheon, 1980.
The History of Helpless Harry, illustrated by Paul O. Zelinsky.   New York, Pantheon, 1980.
Man from the Sky, illustrated by David Wiesner.   New York, Knopf, 1980.
A Place Called Ugly.   New York, Pantheon, 1981.
Who Stole the Wizard of Oz?, illustrated by Derek James.   New York, Knopf, 1981.
Sometimes I Think I Hear My Name.   New York, Pantheon, 1982.
Shadrach's Crossing.   New York, Pantheon, 1983.
Devil's Race.   New York, Lippincott, 1984.
The Fighting Ground.   New York, Lippincott, 1984.
S.O.R. Losers.   New York, Bradbury Press, 1984.
Bright Shadow.   New York, Bradbury Press, 1985.
Wolf Rider.   New York, Bradbury Press, 1986.
Romeo and Juliet—Together (and Alive!)—at Last.   New York, Orchard, 1987.
Something Upstairs: A Tale of Ghosts.   New York, Orchard, 1988.

*

Avi comments:

I hold a strong belief that most young people are as emotionally complex as adults. Some, I dare say, are more complex. What they usually (but not always) lack is the full range of adult experiences. At the same time these young people are under the control of worlds structured and ruled by adults. For many adults the control of young people is their one source of power.

These ideas deeply affect my work. I try to write about complex issues—young people in an adult world—full of irony and contradiction, in a narrative style that relies heavily on suspense with a texture rich in emotion and imagery. I take a great deal of satisfaction in using popular forms—the adventure, the mystery, the thriller—so as to hold my reader with the sheer pleasure of a good story. At the same time I try to resolve my books with an ambiguity that compels engagement. In short, I want my readers to feel, to think, sometimes to laugh. But most of all I want them to enjoy a good read.

*   *   *

Avi has written that he experienced a difficult adolescence. Perhaps because of his own troubled childhood he writes with sensitivity about young characters who do not fit in, creating believable characters and dialogue, and usually humorous situations that comment upon the pains and pleasures of growing up.

His best works are historical novels, in which he creates a vivid sense of colonial America and captures the consciousness of young characters attempting to come of age. In *The Fighting Ground* Jonathan longs to leave his father's corn field, join a regiment, and fight the enemy. His dreams about war are romantic, heroic, and as he will painfully learn, unrealistic. Fighting the hated British can mean taking the lives of innocent women and children. The book portrays Jonathan's move from innocence to horrifying experience unsentimentally and sympathetically.

Some of Avi's best books examine the darker layers of imaginative experience. *Something Upstairs* is a ghost tale about Kenny, who time-travels to 18th-century Providence to change the fate of Caleb, a young slave murdered in the attic of Kenny's house. In *Wolf Rider* 15-year-old Andrew tries to track down a dangerous psychotic, but has trouble convincing the authorities, who think he is emotionally disturbed because of his mother's recent death. Eventually he encounters the psychotic, a respectable professor in his father's math department.

Avi delights in creating comic adventures and in deflating adult authority. In *The History of Helpless Harry* 11-year-old Horatio Stockton Edgeworth plans revenge on Miss Trowbridge, who is caring for him while his parents are away. The tale subverts authority figures and celebrates the power of language with deft wordplay and amusing uses of alliteration, as when Horatio meets Miss Trowbridge and is "polished and pickled, buffeted and bullied, scrubbed and scolded."

S.O.R. Losers asks readers to question conventional values. At South Orange River Middle School the members of the Special Seventh-Grade Soccer Team don't care if they lose. They had all tried to escape required team sports until the administration found them out and assigned a decidedly unathletic teacher as their optimistic and dutiful coach. All the cheerleading from Mr. Lester is to no avail; the team maintains a perfect record of losses. In the book's sequel, *Romeo and Juliet—Together (And Alive!)—at Last*, Ed learns to his astonishment that his friend Saltz is in love with Anabell, and tries to bring the two shy students together in a hastily adapted production of *Romeo and Juliet*.

Avi deserves credit for his sensitive and humorous portrayals of adolescent characters, his willingness to question received values, and his ability to recreate the ambience of historical periods.

—Anita Moss

AWDRY, W(ilbert) V(ere). British. Born in Ampfield, Hampshire, 15 June 1911. Educated at Dauntsey's, West Lavington, Wiltshire, 1923–29; St. Peter's College, Oxford, 1929–32, M.A. 1932; Wycliffe Hall, Oxford, 1932–33, diploma in theology 1933. Married Margaret Emily Wale in 1938; one son and two daughters.

Schoolmaster, St. George's School, Jerusalem, 1933–36; ordained Church of England deacon, 1936, and priest, 1937: Curate, Odiham, Winchester, Hampshire, 1936–38, West Lavington, 1938–40, and Kings Norton, Birmingham, 1940–46; Rector, Elsworth with Knapwell, Cambridgeshire, 1946–53; Rural Dean, Bourn, Cambridgeshire, 1950–53; Vicar, Emneth, Norfolk, 1953–65. Since 1965, licensed to officiate in the Diocese of Gloucester. Agent: Austen Smith, Kaye and Ward Ltd., c/o Heinemann Ltd., 81 Fulham Road, London SW3 6RB. Address: 30 Rodborough Avenue, Stroud, Gloucestershire GL5 3RS, England.

PUBLICATIONS FOR CHILDREN

Fiction

The Three Railway Engines.   Leicester, Ward, 1945.
Thomas, The Tank Engine.   Leicester, Ward, 1946.
James, The Red Engine, illustrated by C. Reginald Dalby. Leicester, Ward, 1948.
Tank Engine Thomas Again, illustrated by C. Reginald Dalby. Leicester, Ward, 1949.
Troublesome Engines, illustrated by C. Reginald Dalby.   Leicester, Ward, 1950.
Henry, The Green Engine, illustrated by C. Reginald Dalby. Leicester, Ward, 1951.
Toby, The Tram Engine, illustrated by C. Reginald Dalby. Leicester, Ward, 1952.
Gordon, The Big Engine, illustrated by C. Reginald Dalby. Leicester, Ward, 1953.
Edward, The Blue Engine, illustrated by C. Reginald Dalby. Leicester, Ward, 1954.
Four Little Engines, illustrated by C. Reginald Dalby.   London, Ward, 1955.
Percy, The Small Engine, illustrated by C. Reginald Dalby.   London, Ward, 1956.
The Eight Famous Engines, illustrated by John Kenney.   London, Ward, 1957.
Duck and the Diesel Engine, illustrated by John Kenney.   London, Ward, 1958.
Belinda the Beetle, illustrated by Ionicus.   Leicester, Brockhampton Press, 1958.
The Little Old Engine, illustrated by John Kenney.   London, Ward, 1959.
The Twin Engines, illustrated by John Kenney.   London, Ward, 1960.
Branch Line Engines, illustrated by John Kenney.   London, Ward, 1961.
Belinda Beats the Band, illustrated by John Kenney.   Leicester, Brockhampton Press, 1961.
Gallant Old Engine, illustrated by John Kenney.   London, Ward, 1962.
Stepney, The Bluebell Engine, illustrated by Gunvor and Peter Edwards.   London, Ward, 1963.
Mountain Engines, illustrated by Gunvor and Peter Edwards.   London, Ward, 1964.
Very Old Engines, illustrated by Gunvor and Peter Edwards.   London, Ward, 1965.
Main Line Engines, illustrated by Gunvor and Peter Edwards.   London, Ward, 1966.
Small Railway Engines, illustrated by Gunvor and Peter Edwards.   London, Kaye and Ward, 1967.
Enterprising Engines, illustrated by Gunvor and Peter Edwards.   London, Kaye and Ward, 1968.
Oliver, The Western Engine, illustrated by Gunvor and Peter Edwards.   London, Kaye and Ward, 1969.
Duke, The Lost Engine, illustrated by Gunvor and Peter Edwards.

London, Kaye and Ward, 1970.
Tramway Engines, illustrated by Gunvor and Peter Edwards. London, Kaye and Ward, 1972.
Thomas's Christmas Party, illustrated by Clive Spong. London, Kaye and Ward, 1984.
Thomas Comes to Breakfast, illustrated by Clive Spong. London, Kaye and Ward, 1985.

Other

Railway Map of the Island of Sodor, illustrated by C. Reginald Dalby. London, Ward, 1958; revised version, London, Kaye and Ward, 1971, 1988.
Surprise Packet, illustrated by Peter Edwards. London, Kaye and Ward, 1972.
The Island of Sodor: Its People, History, and Railways. London, Kaye and Ward, 1987.
Thomas' A.B.C. [*Counting Book*]. London, Heinemann, 2 vols., 1987.

PUBLICATIONS FOR ADULTS

Other

Our Child Begins to Pray. Leicester, Ward, 1951.
The Birmingham and Gloucester Railway, with Peter Long. Gloucester, Sutton, 1987.

Editor, *Industrial Archaeology in Gloucestershire.* Cheltenham, Gloucestershire Community Council, 1973; revised edition, Cheltenham, Gloucestershire Society for Industrial Archaeology, 1975.
Editor, with Chris Cook, *A Guide to the Steam Railways of Great Britain.* London, Pelham, 1979; revised edition, 1984.

*

W.V. Awdry comments:

My father was a country clergyman very knowledgeable about railways. I was brought up accordingly. Naturally, when my son fell ill at the age of three, I amused him by telling him stories about engines. The first book, *The Three Railway Engines,* resulted.

Its popularity led the publisher to ask for more. As the series grew so did the need for consistency between book and book. A localised background area became essential. Hence the "discovery" of the fictional Island of Sodor between Barrow-in-Furness and the Isle of Man. Sodor was mapped for private use by 1951, and a map was published in 1958 (a much improved version appearing in 1971).

The stories are all based on fact. Granted the fiction that steam engines have personality and can express it, all else is authentic. Each story is based on some "off beat" incident which has happened to some engine, somewhere, some time. Thus all have an authentic railwaylike explanation.

*   *   *

When W.V. Awdry's *The Three Railway Engines* appeared in 1945, privately owned steam trains still covered the country. Using the popular format of around 50 pages with an illustration opposite each page of text, the book like its 25 successors consists of three stories, loosely connected by theme. With the exception of the Fat Controller, the major protagonists in the Railway Series are types of transport, predominantly steam engines. About their colourful flanks and enormous expressive faces, the luckless passengers, for ever clearing the tracks or pushing the train, swarm like creatures from Lilliput. It often seems in the early books that these skilfully differen-

tiated characters, Gordon the boastful bully or Edward the querulous newcomer, are pupils in a public school for trains. If the recalcitrant trucks represent youths from the local village to be licked into shape by their natural leaders, then the coaches, for instance Thomas the Tank Engine's Clarabel, are treated more respectfully, like sisters being shown the school. The stories themselves frequently present little homilies (Awdry is after all a clergyman who once wrote a book on children's prayer) such as "more haste less speed," i.e. don't leave your coaches at the station the way Thomas did. Or "pride comes before a fall": the trains that boast of their hill climbing fail as surely as those who, like Daisy the Diesel Engine, claim a skill in confronting stray animals. Inevitably in a series of this length one encounters repetition; the track round the next bend is ever likely to be blocked by subsidence, and one headstrong train after another is hauled from pond, field, or quarry. Presiding over this endearing world and offering its two rewards—a new coat of paint and the benediction "You are a really useful engine"—is the Fat Director (appropriately after nationalisation, the Fat Controller). His squire-archical power over both engines and passengers seems as limitless as the "blue remembered hills" of C. Reginald Dalby's exquisite illustrations.

In the late 1950's with steam on the wane, and John Kenney as illustrator, significant changes overtook the Railway Series. Fairly early on Awdry appears to have conceived a fictional home for his creations. As life and railways in England changed so the need may have become more pressing. He settled on the "Island of Sodor." Maps show it artfully filling the Irish Sea between the Isle of Man and the Lancashire coast. On its more limited scale the author began constructing the details of his imaginary world with the same loving care that Tolkien brought to his. A rail link with the British mainland, mimicking the function of the Bifrost Bridge of Norse mythology, screens out diesel engines instead of frost giants. In *Enterprising Engines,* where Oliver escapes to Sodor with the aid of friendly signalmen, the diesels left behind in England are characterised as the nameless denizens of a totalitarian railway system. Yet other diesels, or dismissively "spamcans," co-existing uneasily with the Fat Controller's steam trains, appear to fill much the same role as immigrant workers in the Britain of that period. On Sodor we also find a new complementary railway ruled, fittingly enough, by the Thin Controller. It must be said that though the stories in which these new trains figure do not want for inventiveness—*Very Old Engines* for instance is a full dress historical novel in miniature—they are not wholly successful. Here engines with unappealing, even unpronounceable names such as Rheneas or Skarloey occasionally break into broad Scots dialect. Such impenetrability in the text is unhappily and inadvertently complemented by the more impressionistic pictures of Gunvor and Peter Edwards. Increasingly too Awdry came to use his stories to advertise steam preservation societies like the Tallylyn Railway. Sometimes one suspects even the intended readership to be railway buffs rather than children. Yet undoubtedly in the Railway Series Awdry found the right medium for his creativity. In the Belinda stories talking cars jar with the people and eccentricity oversteps the mark, but the best of the train books, and these are the earliest, put their author almost on a par with Beatrix Potter or A.A. Milne.

Today the series has become a veritable family industry. Stories are available in compendia, annuals, single tale picture books, pop-ups, sequels from Christopher Awdry, and in two simplified versions; one of these last, on boards and illustrated with stills from the television readings, has a charm of its own. No new version however surpasses the originals which to this day provide avid enjoyment for anyone over two. Nor should intending "visitors" to Sodor miss the poker-faced gazeteer of the island put together by Awdry and his brother George.

—John Churcher

BB. See **WATKINS-PITCHFORD, D.J.**

––––––––

BABBITT, Natalie (Zane, née Moore). American. Born in Dayton, Ohio, 28 July 1932. Educated at Laurel School for Girls, Cleveland, graduated 1950; Smith College, Northampton, Massachusetts, 1950–54, B.A. in art 1954. Married Samuel F. Babbitt in 1954; two sons and one daughter. Instructor in writing and illustrating for children, Kirkland College, Clinton, New York, 1969–78. Recipient: Christopher award, 1976; George G. Stone Center for Children's Books award, 1979. Address: 26 Benefit Street, Providence, Rhode Island 02904, U.S.A.

PUBLICATIONS FOR CHILDREN (illustrated by the author)

Fiction

The Search for Delicious.   New York, Farrar Straus, 1969; London, Chatto and Windus, 1975.
Kneeknock Rise.   New York, Farrar Straus, 1970.
The Something.   New York, Farrar Straus, 1970.
Goody Hall.   New York, Farrar Straus, 1971; London, Dent, 1984.
The Devil's Storybook.   New York, Farrar Straus, 1974; London, Chatto and Windus, 1976.
Tuck Everlasting.   New York, Farrar Straus, 1975; London, Chatto and Windus, 1977.
The Eyes of the Amaryllis.   New York, Farrar Straus, 1977; London, Chatto and Windus, 1978.
Herbert Rowbarge.   New York, Farrar Straus, 1982; London, Dent, 1984.
The Devil's Other Storybook.   New York, Farrar Straus, 1987.

Verse

Dick Foote and the Shark.   New York, Farrar Straus, 1967.
Phoebe's Revolt.   New York, Farrar Straus, 1968.

*

Illustrator: *The Forty-Ninth Magician* by Samuel F. Babbitt, 1966; *Small Poems,* 1972, *More Small Poems,* 1976, *Still More Small Poems,* 1978, *Curlicues,* 1980, *Small Poems Again,* 1986, and *All the Small Poems,* 1987, all by Valerie Worth.

Natalie Babbitt comments:

I am motivated first by a simple passion for the English language, and second by a fascination with the many faces a single reality assumes when viewed through the filter of any given individual's biases, experiences, expectations, and/or desires. Though I am categorized as a writer of fantasy, I have never written about the true fairyland as defined by Tolkien, but rather concern myself with the above mentioned filters which lend every reality an aspect of fantasy. My stories in the main concern human beings and the effects their own fantasies/filters have upon their own realities.

*   *   *

Natalie Babbitt has made a special place for herself in the world of children's literature. Her stories are highly individual, notable for their humor, which is never condescending, and for their unusual themes. The messages in Babbitt's fiction are not the lessons on personal morality so commonly carried by children's books; the

statements made in *Kneeknock Rise, Goody Hall,* and most memorably in *Tuck Everlasting* are philosophic and general, rather than moralistic and particular. They are comments on human ways, needs, and oddities as visible to children as to adults.

One can point to problems. Some instances of Babbitt's humor are almost certainly beyond the ken of her readers, assuming those readers are children and not reviewers. The gentle parodies of Shakespeare, for example—"Rumble, rumble, foil and fumble/Choir adjourn and children mumble," or "Where the sea bucks, there buck I"—are unlikely to mean much to anyone under 12 (or maybe 22). And Babbitt's child characters are sometimes dim in comparison with the adults in the stories: quite often they are not nearly central enough to the action to satisfy a youthful reader. Talk without action is sometimes a drawback; the long prelude to the action of *Goody Hall,* amusing as it is in its scene-setting dialogue, is static and adult. It would play well on a stage, as Shakespeare's comic dialogues play well while they also inform the audience, but whether a child reader will stay with it is another question.

But even when the inaccessible is subtracted from Babbitt's stories, there is much left that is original, funny, and thoughtful. *The Devil's Storybook* is full of lighthearted malice properly ascribed to the devil and his offspring; *Kneeknock Rise* is a kindly look at the pleasures of harmless drama in everyday life; *The Search for Delicious* makes an old point about the relativity of value in a new way.

Babbitt's masterpiece is unquestionably *Tuck Everlasting.* She has chosen for this story a theme no less profound than the meaning and place of death in the universe of living things, yet her handling of this weighty subject is so deft and so gentle that the theme never overwhelms the characters or their poignant, believable tale.

The comparison that comes to mind is with E.B. White's *Charlotte's Web.* Both are fantasies, but barely: just enough to carry forward their themes without becoming so abstract as to lose touch with their young audiences. They are earthbound fantasies, both dealing plainly with life and death, telling stories that are sad and true and funny, all at once. The passage in which Tuck tells Winnie why she must choose mortality over life everlasting is surely one of the most moving in children's literature. He makes it simple, not just because Winnie is 11 years old and could not understand a complex discussion of immortality, but because the matter is to Tuck a simple one: "Life. Moving, growing, changing, never the same two minutes together....Being part of the whole thing, that's the blessing."

Babbitt's work since *Tuck Everlasting* is characteristically varied. *The Eyes of the Amaryllis* adds a touch of fantasy to its basic themes of maturation and acceptance. The quality of writing will hold readers whose tastes run to something more than the average adolescent novel, but the balance between fantasy and realism, and the connection between theme and form is less sure than in *Tuck Everlasting. Herbert Rowbarge* is an off-beat novel which seems to have slipped quietly out of sight since its publication. The reasons are perhaps not hard to guess. Though typically original and subtle, the story asks its readers to remain interested in a protagonist who is an adult for much of the narrative—and none too sympathetic an adult, at that.

The Devil's Other Storybook, on the other hand, easily matches the felicities of the first collection. The stories are brief and amusing, written with an economical wit accessible to almost anyone over the age of eight. Babbitt is not a prolific writer, but she doesn't need to be. Her writing is invariably interesting, and her best work has already placed her firmly in the top rank of 20th-century children's writers.

—Anne Scott MacLeod

––––––––

BACON, Martha (Sherman). American. Born in Berkeley, California, 2 April 1917. Educated at Anna Head School, Berkeley; Miss Barry's Foreign School, Florence; Barrington School, Great Barrington, Massachusetts. Married 1) Philip Oliver-Smith, three children; 2) R.B. Ballinger in 1963, two stepchildren. Editorial assistant, *Atlantic Monthly,* Boston, 1954–56; feature editor, *Vogue,* New York, 1956–57, and *Harper's Bazaar,* New York, 1957–59; Lecturer in Creative Writing, University of Rhode Island, Kingston, 1960–63; Lecturer, later Assistant Professor of English, Rhode Island College, Providence, 1965–81. Recipient: Borestone Poetry award, 1957. *Died in 1981.*

PUBLICATIONS FOR CHILDREN

Fiction

Sophia Scrooby Preserved, illustrated by Donald Omar White. Boston, Little Brown, 1968; London, Gollancz, 1971.
The Third Road, illustrated by Robin Jacques. Boston, Little Brown, 1971.
In the Company of Clowns: A Commedia, illustrated by Richard Cuffari. Boston, Little Brown, 1973.
Moth Manor: A Gothic Tale, illustrated by Gail Burroughs. Boston, Little Brown, 1978.

PUBLICATIONS FOR ADULTS

Novels

A Star Called Wormwood. New York, Random House, 1948; London, Hodder and Stoughton, 1950.
A Masque of Exile. New York, Potter, 1962; London, Heinemann, 1963.

Verse

Lament for the Chieftains and Other Poems. New York, Coward McCann, 1942.
Things Visible and Invisible. New York, Coward McCann, 1947.

Other

Puritan Promenade (essays). Boston, Houghton Mifflin, 1964.

Translator, *The Child Across the River,* by Giulietta d'Alessandro. New York, McDowell Obolensky, 1958.

*

Manuscript Collection: State University of New York Library, Buffalo.

Martha Bacon commented:
(1978) I began to write for children fairly recently. I found that the ideas which I wished to express were best realized in a story addressed to children. I enjoy writing these books because they allow the fancy to roam freely while the form remains disciplinary and even somewhat restricted. Clarity is essential and I enjoy pursuing it.

* * *

Teacher, poet, and novelist, Martha Bacon used her knowledge of literary craftsmanship to fit diverse writing styles to the small but distinguished and varied contribution she made to literature for children. In her first book, *Sophia Scrooby Preserved,* set in the late 18th century, her heroine is the daughter of an African chieftain; taken as a slave, the child is brought up and educated by the Scrooby family, surpassing in elegance and virtuosity the daughter of the house. While she is captured by pirates, held in bondage by a voodoo queen, and has other high adventures, Sophia preserves the mincing decorum of the period. Even the chapter titles—"As the hart panteth on the mountain so does Pansy pant for the joys of knowledge, and so great is her desire, and so earnest her efforts that success crowns her endeavors and she decks her brows with bays"—are part of Bacon's amusing parody of the florid style of the period; while her plot is clearly concocted pen-in-cheek, it is nevertheless relentlessly vigorous.

The Third Road is a deft time-shaft fantasy in which three lively children from a California household are taken by a unicorn into the formal elegance of a 17th-century Spanish court. While the merger of fantasy and realism is believable, the book lacks the ebullience of its predecessor or the cohesion of its successor, *In the Company of Clowns.* The latter is in the picaresque tradition, an adventure tale set in Italy early in the 18th century, and recreates vividly the casual and flamboyant life of the strolling players who are followed by the protagonist, a 12-year-old orphan who is bored with life as a convent scullery boy. *Moth Manor* is a skillful blend of realism and fantasy, the story of a doll house and its lively family, whose adventures are hidden from the child who tries valiantly to keep her great-aunt from the giving the doll house away.

—Zena Sutherland

———

BACON, R(onald) L(eonard). New Zealander. Born in Melbourne, Australia, in 1924. Married; three children. Has worked as a teacher. Currently Principal, Favona Primary School, Auckland. Address: Unit 3, 16 Turama Road, Royal Oak, Auckland, New Zealand.

PUBLICATIONS FOR CHILDREN

Fiction

The Boy and the Taniwha, illustrated by Para Matchitt. Auckland and London, Collins, 1966.
Rua and the Sea People, illustrated by Para Matchitt. Auckland and London, Collins, 1968.
Again the Bugles Blow, illustrated by V.J. Livingston. Auckland and London, Collins, 1973.
Hemi Dances, illustrated by Sandra O'Callaghan. Auckland, Waiatarua, 1985.
Hotu-Puku, illustrated by Frank Bates. Auckland, Waiatarua, 1985.
Little Pukeko and the Tiki, illustrated by Frank Bates. Auckland, Waiatarua, 1985.
Maui and Kuri, illustrated by Frank Bates. Auckland, Waiatarua, 1985.
Ruru and the Green Fairies, illustrated by Frank Bates. Auckland, Waiatarua, 1985.
A Legend of Kiwi, illustrated by Steven Dickinson. Auckland, Waiatarua, 1987.

Other

The House of the People (Maori legend), illustrated by Robert F. Jahnke. Auckland, Collins, 1977.
Hatupatu and the Bird Woman (Maori legend), illustrated by Stanley J. Woods. Auckland, Collins, 1979.
The Fish of Our Fathers (Maori legend), illustrated by R.H.G. Jahnke. Auckland, Waiatarua, 1984.
Wind (reader), illustrated by Philippa Stitchbury. Auckland, Ashton, 1984.
Creation Stories, illustrated by R.H.G. Jahnke. Auckland, Shortland, 1984.
Maui Stories, illustrated by Cliff Whiting. Auckland, Shortland, 1984.
Maori Legends: Seven Stories, illustrated by Philippa Stitchbury. Auckland, Shortland, 1984.
The Home of the Winds (Maori legend), illustrated by R.H.G. Jahnke. Auckland, Waiatarua, 1985.
The Bay (reader), illustrated by Sandra Morris. Auckland, Ashton, 1986.
Jessie's Flower (reader), illustrated by Liz Dodson. Auckland, Shortland, 1986.
Codes and Messages. Auckland, Shortland, 1987.
Games and Their Past, illustrated by Ian McNee and Rachel Jones. Auckland, Shortland, 1987.
The Greatest (reader), illustrated by Bryan Pollard and Margaret McGrath. Auckland, Shortland, 1987.
Let's Make Music (reader), illustrated by Deirdre Gardiner. Auckland, Shortland, 1987.
Publishing a Book, photographs by Richard Redgrove. Auckland, Shortland, 1987.
Rainy Day Ideas!, with Carol Hosking, illustrated by Rachel Jones. Auckland, Shortland, 1987.
In My Bed (reader), illustrated by Sandra Morris. Auckland, Shortland, 1988.
In My Room (reader), illustrated by Glenda Jones. Auckland, Shortland, 1988.
Just Me (reader), illustrated by Kelvin Hawley. Auckland, Shortland, 1988.
Off to Work (reader), illustrated by Kelvin Hawley. Auckland, Shortland, 1988.
Our Dog Sam (reader), illustrated by Helen Funnell. Auckland, Shortland, 1988.
Save Our Earth (reader), illustrated by Rodney McRae. Auckland, Shortland, 1988.
The Scarecrow (reader), illustrated by Isabel Lowe. Auckland, Shortland, 1988.
Weaving, illustrated by Heidi Fegan. Auckland, Shortland, 1988.
Grandma's Bicycle (reader), illustrated by Philip Webb. Auckland, Shortland, 1988.

PUBLICATIONS FOR ADULTS

Novels

In the Sticks. Auckland, Collins, 1963.
Along the Road. Auckland and London, Collins, 1964.

Other

Auckland: Gateway to New Zealand, photographs by Gregory Riethmaier. Auckland and London, Collins, 1968.
Auckland: Town and Around, photographs by Gregory Riethmaier. Auckland and London, Collins, 1973.

*   *   *

Writing for R.L. Bacon developed as a by-product of his busy and demanding career as a rural teacher. His first novel, *In the Sticks,* written for an adult audience but of interest to older children, describes the vicissitudes, the heartbreaks, the fun, and the excitement of the teacher working in the backblocks.

His first two picture books for children are both illustrated by the Maori artist Para Matchitt. *The Boy and the Taniwha* describes the life of the little Maori boy Hemi. He lives with his grandmother according to the traditional customs before the coming of the Pakeha. The story tells of Hemi's growth in knowledge and in courage when he finds the taniwha and passes the test of manhood. The text is illustrated magnificently by the lively shapes and colours of Para Matchitt's drawings. Two later picture books continue the theme of Maori life.

Rua and the Sea People tells of another Maori boy, Rua, and his life by the sea. The climax to this tale is the arrival of Captain Cook's ship in 1769, "big, as the meeting house on the marae was big." Rua does not hold as much interest as Hemi, and Para Matchitt has used a great deal of abstraction in his illustrations. These are striking but children do not have for them the warm affection that they have for his earlier illustrations.

In *Again the Bugles Blow* there is a return to the verve of *The Boy and the Taniwha.* This short novel describes one of the great moments in those sad inter-racial conflicts of the mid-19th century, the Land Wars. The main character is another lad named Rua, a contemporary Maori boy who lives in the inner city. By some sort of time shift he finds himself in the Auckland of the early 1860's. Attached to the British military forces during their thrust into the Waikato, Rua sees the tragic waste of war. The climax of the story describes one of the most courageous moments of the Maori warriors. Encircled at Orakau, short of food and water, under bombardment by the Armstrong guns, the defenders fought to the end. Rua had crept into the pa. He observed the call to surrender and the famous reply, "We shall fight on for ever, and ever and ever."

More recently Bacon has made a major contribution to New Zealand writing for children by retelling some of the major stories of Maori mythology in a simple and direct style. *Creation Stories, Maui Stories,* and *Maori Legends: Seven Stories* contain tales that are the heritage of all New Zealanders both Maori and non-Maori, and are a very welcome addition to accessible indigenous material.

The House of the People, The Fish of Our Fathers, and *The Home of the Winds* are a trilogy of books based upon traditional Maori life. They describe the making of a meeting house, the construction of a war canoe, and the building and fortification of a village or "pa" on a site that needs to be defended. The books are meticulously researched and finely detailed. The illustrations, especially in the latter two books, beautifully demonstrate the elaborate carving and the dignity of the ritual.

Little Pukeko and the Tiki and *A Legend of Kiwi* are further examples of the excellence the author demonstrates when dealing with material of a traditional nature.

Hemi Dances brings us to the contemporary world of break-dancing but is skilfully based upon movement in the natural world.

Bacon writes a crisp, uncluttered narrative, whether it is of the tragic dilemma of a boy caught between two warring armies or in retelling tales of myth, legend, and folklore. As a sensitive interpreter he has brought spiritual and imaginative nourishment from Maori culture to share with a much wider audience.

—Tom Fitzgibbon

————

BAGNOLD, Enid (Algerine). British. Born in Rochester, Kent,

27 October 1889. Educated at Prior's Field, Godalming, Surrey, in Marburg, Germany, Lausanne, Switzerland, and at the Villa Leona, Paris; studied painting with Walter Sickert. Served as a driver with the French Army during World War I. Married Sir Roderick Jones in 1920 (died 1962); three sons and one daughter. Recipient: Arts Theatre prize, 1951; American Academy Award of Merit, 1956. C.B.E. (Commander, Order of the British Empire), 1976. *Died 31 March 1981.*

PUBLICATIONS FOR CHILDREN

Fiction

Alice and Thomas and Jane, illustrated by the author and Laurian Jones.   London, Heinemann, 1930; New York, Knopf, 1931.
National Velvet, illustrated by Laurian Jones.   London, Heinemann, and New York, Morrow, 1935.

Play

National Velvet, adaptation of her own novel (produced London, 1946).   Published in *Embassy Successes 2,* London, Sampson Low, 1946; published separately, New York, Dramatists Play Service, 1961.

PUBLICATIONS FOR ADULTS

Novels

The Happy Foreigner.   London, Heinemann, and New York, Century, 1920.
Serena Blandish; or, The Difficulty of Getting Married (as A Lady of Quality).   London, Heinemann, 1924; New York, Doran, 1925.
The Squire.   London, Heinemann, 1938; as *The Door of Life,* New York, Morrow, 1938.
The Loved and Envied.   London, Heinemann, and New York, Doubleday, 1951.
The Girl's Journey: Containing The Happy Foreigner and The Squire.   London, Heinemann, and New York, Doubleday, 1954.

Plays

Lottie Dundass (produced Santa Barbara, California, and Wimbledon, 1942; London, 1943).   London, Heinemann, 1941; included in *Two Plays,* 1951.
Poor Judas (produced Bradford, 1946; London, 1951).   Included in *Two Plays,* 1951.
Two Plays (includes *Lottie Dundass* and *Poor Judas*).   London, Heinemann, 1951; as *Theatre: Two Plays,* New York, Doubleday, 1951.
Gertie (produced New York, 1952; as *Little Idiot,* produced London, 1953).
The Chalk Garden (produced New York, 1955; London, 1956).   New York, Random House, and London, Heinemann, 1956.
The Last Joke (produced London, 1960).   Included in *Four Plays,* 1970.
The Chinese Prime Minister (produced New York, 1964; Cambridge and London, 1965).   New York, Random House, and London, French, 1964.
Call Me Jacky (produced Oxford, 1968).   Included in *Four Plays,* 1970; revised version, as *A Matter of Gravity* (produced Washington, D.C., 1975; New York, 1976), London, Heinemann, and New York, French 1978.

Four Plays (includes *The Chalk Garden, The Last Joke, The Chinese Prime Minister, Call Me Jacky*).   London, Heinemann, 1970; Boston, Little Brown, 1971.

Verse

The Sailing Ships and Other Poems.   London, Heinemann, 1918.
Poems.   Andoversford, Gloucestershire, Whittington Press, 1980.

Other

A Diary Without Dates.   London, Heinemann, and Boston, Luce, 1918.
Enid Bagnold's Autobiography: From 1889.   London, Heinemann, 1969; Boston, Little Brown, 1970.
Letters to Frank Harris and Other Friends, edited by R.P. Lister.   Andoversford, Gloucestershire, Whittington Press, 1980.

Translator, *Alexander of Asia,* by Princess Marthe Bibesco.   London, Heinemann, 1935.

*

Critical Study: *Enid Bagnold: The Authorized Biography* by Anne Sebba, London, Weidenfeld and Nicolson, 1986; New York, Taplinger, 1987.

*   *   *

Enid Bagnold was not really a children's writer. She was a playwright of considerable talent, creating forceful characters and plots with real human interest. It is ironic, therefore, that many people know her best for her "children's" story, written many years ago, *National Velvet,* the film of which gave the child Elizabeth Taylor her first starring role. For those who know the story only from the highly inaccurate film I can only urge them to read the book, which deserved far better treatment.

On the surface it is a "pony book." The Sussex butcher's family of five girls and a boy are all horse mad, but they have only the delivery-cart pony between them. The youngest girl, Velvet, a skinny straw-haired child with braces on her teeth, cuts out pictures of horses and daydreams about them. Her chance comes when she wins for a shilling in a raffle a rawboned piebald horse. She rides him in a local gymkhana and he smashes up the jumps except for the wall, over which he sails in great style. Their delivery-lad, an ex-jockey, suggests jokingly that the Piebald should enter the Grand National and Velvet takes him seriously. Since the horse will not jump for anyone else and she can pass for a boy, she trains him herself. She suffers appallingly from nerves, and though they win the race she faints and all is revealed.

It is in the inter-relation of the characters that the author's skill is displayed. The adult reader sees how the different personalities of the sisters are contrasted, the placidity of their outsize mother compared to her eccentric small son who keeps his spit in a bottle, and Velvet herself, horrified by the publicity, insisting she did it not for fame or fortune but for the horse himself, so that he could fulfil his own potential. *National Velvet* can satisfy on many levels.

—Ann G. Hay

———

BAILEY, Carolyn Sherwin.   American.   Born in Hoosick Falls, New York, 25 October 1875. Educated at Lansingburgh Academy;

Teachers College, Columbia University, New York, graduated 1896; Montessori School, Rome; New York School of Social Work. Married Eben Clayton Hill in 1936. Principal, Jefferson Avenue Kindergarten, Springfield, Massachusetts; taught in New York City public schools; social worker, Warren Goddard House, New York; editor, children's department, *Delineator* magazine, New York; from 1916, editor, *American Childhood* magazine, Springfield, Massachusetts. Recipient: American Library Association Newbery Medal, 1947. *Died 23 December 1961.*

PUBLICATIONS FOR CHILDREN

Fiction

Stories for Sunday Telling. Boston, Pilgrim Press, 1916.
Stories for Any Day. Boston, Pilgrim Press, 1917.
Stories for Every Holiday. New York, Abingdon Press, 1918.
Once Upon a Time Animal Stories. Springfield, Massachusetts, Bradley, 1918.
The Outdoor Story Book. Boston, Pilgrim Press, 1918.
Everyday Stories, illustrated by Frederick Knowles. Springfield, Massachusetts, Bradley, 1919.
Hero Stories, illustrated by Frederick Knowles. Springfield, Massachusetts, Bradley, 1919.
The Enchanted Bugle and Other Stories. Dansville, New York, Owen, 1920.
The Torch of Courage and Other Stories. Springfield, Massachusetts, Bradley, 1921.
Flint: The Story of a Trail, illustrated by Charles Lassell. Springfield, Massachusetts, Bradley, 1922.
Reading Time Stories. Chicago, Whitman, 1923.
Surprise Stories. Chicago, Whitman, 1923.
When Grandfather Was a Boy: Stories. Boston, Pilgrim Press, 1923.
Friendly Tales: A Community Story Book. Springfield, Massachusetts, Bradley, 1923.
Lincoln Time Stories. Chicago, Whitman, 1924.
The Wonderful Tree and Other Golden Day Stories, illustrated by Joseph Dash. Chicago, Whitman, 1925.
Little Men and Women Stories. Chicago, Whitman, 1926.
The Wonderful Window and Other Stories, illustrated by Katherine Wireman. Nashville, Cokesbury Press, 1926.
The Wonderful Days, illustrated by C.B. Fall. Chicago, Whitman, 1929.
Read Aloud Stories, illustrated by Hildegard Lupprian. Springfield, Massachusetts, Bradley, 1929.
Li'l' Hannibal. New York, Platt and Munk, 1938.
Country-Stop, illustrated by Grace Paull. New York, Viking Press, 1942; as *Wishing-Well House,* London, Muller, 1950.
Pioneer Art in America, illustrated by Grace Paull. New York, Viking Press, 1944.
The Little Rabbit Who Wanted Red Wings, illustrated by Dorothy Grider. New York, Platt and Munk, 1945.
Miss Hickory, illustrated by Ruth Chrisman Gannett. New York, Viking Press, 1946; London, Hodder and Stoughton, 1977.
Merry Christmas Book, illustrated by Eunice Young Smith. Chicago, Whitman, 1948.
Old Man Rabbit's Dinner Party, illustrated by Robinson. New York, Platt and Munk, 1949; revised edition, 1961.
Enchanted Village (includes play *Land of the Free*), illustrated by Eileen Evans. New York, Viking Press, 1950.
Finnegan II, His Nine Lives, illustrated by Kate Seredy. New York, Viking Press, 1953.
The Little Red Schoolhouse, illustrated by Dorothy Bayley Morse. New York, Viking Press, 1957.

Flickertail, illustrated by Garry Mackenzie. New York, Walck, 1962.

Plays

Plays for the Children's Hour. Springfield, Massachusetts, Bradley, 1931.
This Way to Animal Land, with Ditzy Baker. Akron, Ohio, Saalfield, 1936.

Verse

Stories and Rhymes for a Child, illustrated by Christine Wright. Springfield, Massachusetts, Bradley, 1909.
Songs of Happiness, music by Mary B. Ehrmann. Springfield, Massachusetts, Bradley, 1912.
A Christmas Party, illustrated by Cyndy Szekeres. New York, Pantheon, 1975.

Other

Mother Goose: Old Rhymes Reproduced in Connection with Their Veracious History, illustrated by Peter Newell. New York, Holt, 1905.
The Jingle Primer: A First Book in Reading Based on Mother Goose Rhymes and Folk Tales, with Clara L. Brown. New York, American Book Company, 1906.
Firelight Stories: Folk Tales Retold, illustrated by Diantha Horne. Springfield, Massachusetts, Bradley, 1907.
Boys' Make-at-Home Things, with Marian Elizabeth Bailey. New York, Stokes, 1912.
Girls' Make-at-Home Things. New York, Stokes, 1912.
The Children's Book of Games and Parties. Chicago, Donohue, 1913.
Every Child's Folk Songs and Games. Springfield, Massachusetts, Bradley, 1914.
Boys and Girls of Colonial Days, illustrated by Uldene Shriver. Chicago, Flanagan, 1917.
The Way of the Gate (reader), with others. New York, Macmillan, 1917.
What to Do for Uncle Sam: A First Book of Citizenship. Chicago, Flanagan, 1918.
Stories of Great Adventures, illustrated by Clara Burd. Springfield, Massachusetts, Bradley, 1919.
Folk Stories and Fables, illustrated by Frederick Nagler. Springfield, Massachusetts, Bradley, 1919.
Broad Stripes and Bright Stars: Stories of American History, illustrated by Power O'Malley. Springfield, Massachusetts, Bradley, 1919.
Wonder Stories: The Best Myths, illustrated by Clara Burd. Springfield, Massachusetts, Bradley, 1920; London, Batsford, 1924.
In- and Out-door Play Games, illustrated by Cobb Shinn. Chicago, Whitman, 1923.
All the Year Play Games, illustrated by Cobb Shinn. Chicago, Whitman, 1924.
Boys and Girls of Pioneer Days. Chicago, Flanagan, 1924.
Stories from an Indian Cave: The Cherokee Cave Builders, illustrated by Joseph Dash. Chicago, Whitman, 1924.
Boys and Girls of Discovery Days, illustrated by Dorothy Dulin. Chicago, Flanagan, 1931.
In Nature's Fairyland. Dansville, New York, Owen, 1927.
Untold History Stories, illustrated by Lillian Titus. Dansville, New York, Owen, 1927.
Forest, Field, and Stream Stories (reader), illustrated by Dorothy Dulin. Chicago, Flanagan, 1928.

Boys and Girls of Today. Chicago, Flanagan, 1928.
Boys and Girls of Modern Days, illustrated by Dorothy Dulin. Chicago, Flanagan, 1929.
Boy Heroes in Making America, illustrated by Lea Norris and Power O'Malley. Chicago, Flanagan, 1931.
Our Friends at the Zoo (reader), with Alice Hanthorn, illustrated by Ruth Hallock. Springfield, Massachusetts, McLoughlin, 1934.
Children of the Handcrafts, illustrated by Grace Paull. New York, Viking Press, 1935.
Tell Me a Birthday Story, illustrated by Margaret Ayer. New York, Stokes, 1935.
Tops and Whistles: True Stories of Early American Toys and Children, illustrated by Grace Paull. New York, Viking Press, 1937.
From Mocassins to Wings: Stories of Our Travel Ways, illustrated by Margaret Ayer. Springfield, Massachusetts, Bradley, 1938.
Garden, Orchard, and Meadow Stories (reader), illustrated by Dorothy Dulin. Chicago, Flanagan, 1939.
Homespun Playdays, illustrated by Grace Paull. New York, Viking Press, 1941.

Editor, with Clara M. Lewis, *For the Children's Hour,* illustrated by C. William Breck. Springfield, Massachusetts, Bradley, 1906.
Editor, *Stories Children Need.* Springfield, Massachusetts, Bradley, 1916.
Editor, *Tell Me Another Story.* Springfield, Massachusetts, Bradley, 1918.
Editor, *The Three Musketeers,* by Alexandre Dumas, illustrated by Harold Brett. Springfield, Massachusetts, Bradley, 1920.
Editor, *Lorna Doone,* by R.D. Blackmore. Springfield, Massachusetts, Bradley, 1921.
Editor, *Merry Tales for Children.* Springfield, Massachusetts, Bradley, 1921.
Editor, *Evangeline,* by Henry Wadsworth Longfellow. Springfield, Massachusetts, Bradley, 1922.
Editor, *In the Animal World.* Springfield, Massachusetts, Bradley, 1924.
Editor, *Stories Children Want,* illustrated by Jack Perkins. Springfield, Massachusetts, Bradley, 1931.
Editor, *Schoolroom Plays and Projects.* Springfield, Massachusetts, Bradley, 1932.

PUBLICATIONS FOR ADULTS

Other

Daily Program of Gift and Occupation Work, with Clara M. Lewis. Springfield, Massachusetts, Bradley, 1904.
For the Story-Teller: Story Telling and Stories to Tell. Springfield, Massachusetts, Bradley, 1913.
Montessori Children. New York, Holt, 1915.
Letting in the Gang. Privately printed, 1916.
Everyday Play for Children. Chicago, Donohue, 1916.

Editor, *Sketches along Life's Road,* by Elizabeth Harrison. Boston, Stratford, 1930.
Editor, *The Story-Telling Hour.* New York, Dodd Mead, and London, Harrap, 1934.

*   *   *

Although the total body of Carolyn Sherwin Bailey's creative work is considerable, those works with the most lasting value are her series on pioneer arts and crafts in America and her *Miss Hickory,* which won the Newbery Medal. Included in the pioneer arts and crafts series are *Children of the Handcrafts, Tops and Whistles, Homespun Playdays,* and *Pioneer Arts in America.* These works are the result of their author's genuine interest in the history and artifacts of a bygone era. *Pioneer Art in America* is representative of the series. Details in this work as, for example, the weathervane, a wax doll, a silver teapot, a sparking lamp, the jewels of Sandwich, a fiddlin fool, and others are all touched with elements of suspense and drama and a strong flavor of historical accuracy. Such stories could have been thinly skeletal and dully factual. Instead they are fully fleshed out, balanced, fluid, and historically appealing, enough so to continue to captivate and hold readers.

Miss Hickory, however, is Bailey's classic work. Although her talent is evident in her early works, close acquaintance with the total body of her writing indicates she experienced a gradual but steady genesis as a creative artist. Like Carlo Collodi, A.A. Milne, L. Frank Baum, E. Nesbit, and others, Bailey used the toy device as literary motif. Her toy doll, Miss Hickory, is by no means a stillborn plaything, for into her Bailey has breathed life that requires no resuscitation from readers. Although Miss Hickory is sometimes as hardheaded as the hickory nut which is, indeed, her head, she is no inert replica of any ordinary toy or real life personage.

Unlike some toys now famous in literature Miss Hickory does not interact, except by implication, with either her creator or with other creatures of the human world. Instead, Miss Hickory's ostensible ties are with animal friends and acquaintances imbued with human characteristics—Crow, Chipmunk, Squirrel, Hen-Pheasant, and Mr. T. Willard-Brown, a barnyard cat. In her relationships with these friends Miss Hickory is spunky, spirited, sharp-tongued, and seemingly inflexible, yet inwardly she is often vulnerable and insecure. She is, nonetheless, never a real loser. Despite numerous near-calamities, with hickory nut for head and applewood twig for body, Miss Hickory proves herself a survivor, even after being deprived of head and brain by Squirrel, for she miraculously becomes a living, blossoming, fruit-bearing branch of an old apple tree. Thus Bailey, in giving Miss Hickory a life after death, has added a new dimension to the use of the toy motif and has given to children and other readers a most satisfying instance of the creative ideal.

—Charity Chang

————

BAKER, Betty (Lou). American. Born in Bloomsburg, Pennsylvania, 20 June 1928. Educated at schools in Orange, New Jersey. Married Robert George Venturo in 1948 (divorced 1965); one son. Dental assistant, owner of gift shop, lecturer. Formerly editor, *Roundup* magazine. *Recipient: Western Heritage award, 1964, 1971; Western Writers of America Spur award, 1968. Died 6 November 1987.*

PUBLICATIONS FOR CHILDREN

Fiction

The Sun's Promise, illustrated by Juliette Palmer. New York, Abelard Schuman, 1962; London, Abelard Schuman, 1963.
Little Runner of the Longhouse, illustrated by Arnold Lobel. New York, Harper, and Kingswood, Surrey, World's Work, 1962.
Killer-of-Death, illustrated by John Kaufmann. New York, Harper, 1963.
The Shaman's Last Raid, illustrated by Leonard Shortall. New York, Harper, 1963; as *The Medicine Man's Last Stand,* New York, Scholastic, 1965.

The Treasure of the Padres, illustrated by Leonard Shortall. New York, Harper, 1964.

Walk the World's Rim. New York, Harper, 1965.

The Blood of the Brave. New York, Harper, 1966.

The Dunderhead War. New York, Harper, 1967.

Do Not Annoy the Indians, illustrated by Harold Goodwin. New York, Macmillan, and London, Collier Macmillan, 1968.

The Pig War, illustrated by Robert Lopshire. New York, Harper, 1969; Kingswood, Surrey, World's Work, 1971.

And One Was a Wooden Indian. New York, Macmillan, 1970.

A Stranger and Afraid. New York, Macmillan, and London, Collier Macmillan, 1972.

The Big Push, illustrated by Bonnie Johnson. New York, Coward McCann, 1972.

The Spirit Is Willing. New York, Macmillan, 1974.

Dupper, illustrated by Chuck Eckart. New York, Greenwillow, 1976.

Save Sirrushany! (Also Agotha, Princess Gwyn, and All the Fearsome Beasts), illustrated by Erick Ingraham. New York, Macmillan, 1978.

Partners, illustrated by Emily McCully. New York, Greenwillow, 1978.

All-by-Herself, illustrated by Catherine Stock. New York, Greenwillow, 1980.

Santa Rat, illustrated by Tom Huffman. New York, Greenwillow, 1980.

The Great Desert Race. New York, Macmillan, 1980.

Danby and George, illustrated by Adrianne Lobel. New York, Greenwillow, 1981.

Worthington Botts and the Steam Machine, illustrated by Sal Murdocca. New York, Macmillan, 1981.

Seven Spells to Farewell. New York, Macmillan, 1982.

The Turkey Girl, illustrated by Harold Berson. New York, Macmillan, 1983.

My Sister Says, illustrated by Tricia Taggart. New York, Macmillan, 1984.

The Night Spider Case. New York, Macmillan, 1984.

Other

Arizona. New York, Coward McCann, 1969.

At the Center of the World: Based on Papago and Pima Myths, illustrated by Murray Tinkelman. New York, Macmillan, 1973.

Three Fools and a Horse (Apache folktale), illustrated by Glen Rounds. New York, Macmillan, 1975; Kingswood, Surrey, World's Work, 1977.

Settlers and Strangers: Native Americans of the Desert Southwest and History as They Saw It. New York, Macmillan, 1977.

No Help at All (Mayan legend), illustrated by Emily McCully. New York, Greenwillow, 1978.

Latki and the Lightning Lizard (Indian folktale), illustrated by Donald Carrick. New York, Macmillan, 1979.

Rat Is Dead and Ant Is Sad (Pueblo folktale), illustrated by Mamoru Funai. New York, Harper, 1981.

And Me, Coyote! (Indian folktales), illustrated by Maria Horvath. New York, Macmillan, and London, Macmillan, 1982.

Editor, *Great Ghost Stories of the Old West.* New York, Four Winds Press, 1968.

*

Manuscript Collections: University of California Library, Los Angeles; Kerlan Collection, University of Minnesota, Minneapolis.

*   *   *

Betty Baker carved a niche for herself as a writer of historical fiction about the southwestern United States and Mexico and of stories dealing with American Indians of the southwest. Her fiction ranges from gentle, humorous tales such as that of a little Iroquois boy who loves maple sugar—this one written using a controlled vocabulary for beginning readers *(Little Runner of the Longhouse)*—to historical fiction for young adolescents. She is at her best with one of these, *Walk the World's Rim,* a tightly plotted, well characterized story of the friendship of a young Indian boy and Esteban, the negro slave who was one of the four survivors of the ill-fated expedition led by Cabeza de Vaca in the 16th century. A companion piece to *Walk the World's Rim* is *A Stranger and Afraid,* the story of a young plains Indian captured by the Pueblo Indians of the southwest, who sees the expedition of Coronado as an opportunity to escape from the Pueblo Indians and to return to his people when he is given to the Spaniards as their guide.

Although Baker's early fiction emphasized the American Indian, she also wrote some interesting historical fiction. In *The Dunderhead War* she pairs an unlikely duo of 17-year-old Quincy Heffendorf from Missouri and his methodical German uncle, Fritz. This fast-paced story of the Mexican War of 1846 tells of the dangers and adventures which befell the ill-trained, undisciplined Missouri Volunteers and Quincy and his uncle, who followed the Volunteers in a wagon train. *The Great Desert Race* is based on an actual automobile race that was run between Los Angeles, California, and Phoenix, Arizona, over questionable or non-existent roads each year from 1908 through 1914. But Baker is at her best with her sensitive and sympathetic novels dealing with the American Indian during the transition period in the southwest when the white man first entered the area. *Killer-of-Death* is the finest of these stories. It is a moving tale of an Apache boy who comes to manhood just as the first white settlers entered Arizona—and what the coming of these strangers meant to the Apache nation.

Demonstrating her considerable versatility, Baker wrote several gently humorous fantasies in the talking beast-sorcerer tradition; *Save Sirrushany!* is the best of these. The author's historical fiction, fantasy, legends, and easy books for younger readers fill a real need for well written literature on a number of themes for children and adolescent readers.

—Margaret F. Maxwell

———

BAKER, Margaret J(oyce). British. Born in Reading, Berkshire, 21 May 1918. Educated at Roland Houses School, London; King's College, University of London, 1936–37. Mobile canteen driver for the Church Army during World War II. Address: 1 Church Close, Old Cleeve, Minehead, Somerset TA24 6HW, England.

PUBLICATIONS FOR CHILDREN

Fiction

"Nonsense," Said the Tortoise, illustrated by Leo Bates. Leicester, Brockhampton Press, 1949; as *Homer the Tortoise,* New York, McGraw Hill, 1950.

Four Farthings and a Thimble, illustrated by Decie Merwin. New York, Longman, 1950; London, Lane, 1952.

A Castle and Sixpence, illustrated by Decie Merwin. New York, Longman, 1951; London, Lane, 1953.

Treasure Trove, illustrated by T.R. Freeman. Leicester, Brockhampton Press, 1952.

Benbow and the Angels, illustrated by Dorothy Lake Gregory. New York, Longman, 1952; London, Harrap, 1956.

The Family That Grew and Grew, illustrated by Nora S. Unwin. New York, McGraw Hill, 1952; London, Nelson, 1954.

Homer Sees the Queen, illustrated by Garry Mackenzie. New York, McGraw Hill, 1953; Leicester, Brockhampton Press, 1956.

The Young Magicians, illustrated by T.R. Freeman. Leicester, Brockhampton Press, 1954.

Lions in the Potting Shed, illustrated by Marcia Lane Foster. Leicester, Brockhampton Press, 1954; as *Lions in the Woodshed,* New York, McGraw Hill, 1955.

The Wonderful Wellington Boots, illustrated by T.R. Freeman. Leicester, Brockhampton Press, 1955.

Acorns and Aerials, illustrated by Marcia Lane Foster. Leicester, Brockhampton Press, 1956.

The Bright High Flyer, illustrated by T.R. Freeman. Leicester, Brockhampton Press, and New York, Longman, 1957.

Tip and Run, illustrated by T.R. Freeman. Leicester, Brockhampton Press, 1958.

Homer Goes to Stratford, illustrated by T.R. Freeman. Leicester, Brockhampton Press, and Englewood Cliffs, New Jersey, Prentice Hall, 1958.

The Magic Sea Shell, illustrated by Marjorie-Anne Watts. London, Harrap, 1959; New York, Holt Rinehart, 1960.

The Birds of Thimblepins, illustrated by Elizabeth Grant. London, Harrap, 1960.

Homer in Orbit, illustrated by T.R. Freeman. Leicester, Brockhampton Press, 1961.

Into the Castle, illustrated by T.R. Freeman. Leicester, Brockhampton Press, 1962.

The Cats of Honeytown, illustrated by Keith Money. London, Harrap, 1962.

Away Went Galloper, illustrated by Norman Thelwell. London, Methuen, 1962; Chicago, Encyclopaedia Britannica Press, 1964.

Castaway Christmas, illustrated by Richard Kennedy. London, Methuen, 1963; New York, Farrar Straus, 1964.

Cut Off from Crumpets, illustrated by Richard Kennedy. London, Methuen, 1964.

The Shoe Shop Bears, illustrated by C. Walter Hodges. London, Harrap, 1964; New York, Farrar Straus, 1965.

Homer Goes West, illustrated by T.R. Freeman. Leicester, Brockhampton Press, 1965.

Hannibal and the Bears, illustrated by C. Walter Hodges. London, Harrap, 1965; New York, Farrar Straus, 1966.

Porterhouse Major, illustrated by Shirley Hughes. London, Methuen, and Englewood Cliffs, New Jersey, Prentice Hall, 1967.

Bears Back in Business, illustrated by Daphne Rowles. London, Harrap, and New York, Farrar Straus, 1967.

Hi-Jinks Joins the Bears, illustrated by Leslie Wood. London, Harrap, 1968; New York, Farrar Straus, 1969.

Home from the Hill, illustrated by Richard Kennedy. London, Methuen, 1968; New York, Farrar Straus, 1969.

Teabag and the Bears, illustrated by Leslie Wood. London, Harrap, 1970.

Snails' Place, illustrated by Jan Brychta. London, Dent, 1970.

The Last Straw, illustrated by Doreen Roberts. London, Methuen, 1971.

Boots and the Ginger Bears, illustrated by Leslie Wood. London, Harrap, 1972.

The Sand Bird, illustrated by Gareth Floyd. London, Methuen, and Nashville, Nelson, 1973.

Prickets Way, illustrated by Gavin Rowe. London, Methuen, 1973.

Lock Stock and Barrel, illustrated by Gareth Floyd. London, Methuen, 1974.

Sand in Our Shoes, illustrated by Fermin Rocker. London, Methuen, 1976.

The Gift Horse, illustrated by Mary Russon. London, Hodder and Stoughton, 1982.

Catch as Catch Can, illustrated by Susan Edwards. London, Hodder and Stoughton, 1982.

Beware of the Gnomes, illustrated by Alicia Garcia de Lynam. London, Hodder and Stoughton, 1985.

The Waiting Room Doll, illustrated by Alicia Garcia de Lynam. London, Hodder and Stoughton, 1986.

Fresh Fields for Daisy, illustrated by Alicia Garcia de Lynam. London, Hodder and Stoughton, 1987.

Other

The Fighting Cocks (reader). London, Pitman, 1949.

Anna Sewell and Black Beauty, illustrated by Imre Hofbauer. London, Harrap, 1956; New York, Longman, 1957.

*

Margaret J. Baker comments:

I like my stories to be humorous and unalarming. I want the stories meant for younger children especially to leave them with a feeling of happiness and security. I want to help children to understand animals and to love them. I want them to understand each other and the older generations. I want them to value gentleness and not to confuse it with weakness. When writing I want to show what I find lovely or funny, wonderful and strange. I think children can comprehend anything so long as it is plainly put. Inside I believe a child's feelings are the same as those of an adult. The only difference is that an adult can express the feelings more easily. Maybe that's part of the job of writing children's books. The writer acts as the children's spokesman. For this reason the writer needs to be on their side and to write from inside the characters in the story.

*   *   *

The years between seven and 10 are important for establishing a firm tradition of reading once the technique has been mastered. Margaret J. Baker's books largely fall into this category, providing pleasant, relatively undemanding stories with warm family backgrounds, full of action and excitements of a domestic kind.

Writing over a period of 40 years, Baker has shown remarkable consistency. One of her most recent books *Fresh Fields for Daisy* differs very little in concept from an early book like *Lions in the Potting Shed* where magic invades everyday life and makes a potentially dull situation lively, if fraught with difficulties. Daisy is a shop window display model rescued from destruction when her shop is bulldozed to make way for a new development. Finally befriended by three children, she makes a new life for herself in the country acting as a scarecrow where she eventually proves her worth by saving the crops from a fire.

In other recent books there is the typical mixture of fantasy and domesticity in stories which are amusing and strong on entertainment. Apple Crumble in *Beware of the Gnomes* is a garden gnome determined to be restored to his place in the garden from which he has been evicted by the National Trust. He is finally successful thanks to the efforts of an army of gnomes from a garden center who come to his aid. *The Waiting Room Doll* is a fast-moving account of a doll's adventures after she is dropped by her small owner in a doctor's waiting room. The world is seen through the doll's eyes and, before she is restored to her little girl, Poppy "assists" at a mother and baby clinic and at a slimming session from where she is stolen for comfort by lonely, fat Jennet. The book has its more poignant moments but it is basically a fairly cosy story in which Baker writes with her usual attention to detail, creating a wide range of characters and happenings so that the young reader's interest is held throughout.

An earlier book, *Away Went Galloper*, is perhaps typical of Baker's fantasy output. The story of a rocking horse that takes two children on magic journeys is not far removed from the Nesbit tradition in which the mixing of magic and real life creates problems which the children have to overcome. Unlike Nesbit's, these are books which will not be deeply remembered long after reading but they offer an enjoyable, well-constructed read for seven to nine-year-olds.

It was a realistic rather than a fantasy story that was runner-up for the Carnegie Medal in 1963. *Castaway Christmas* tells of the Ridley family's adventures coping with floods, danger, and near disaster, with adults conspicuous by their absence. The Ridleys also appear in *Sand in Our Shoes* where they again encounter near disaster when two children are carried out to sea in a leaky boat, and *real* disaster when their caravan home burns down. The characters in these books for slightly older readers are well defined and the plot arises largely from characterisation: the children's natures and feelings determine the action. Full of excitement, they are strong family adventures which, in traditional fashion, all end happily.

If the real life stories are written for older readers, the series of books beginning with *The Shoe Shop Bears* appeals to the youngest. The books describe the adventures and encounters of a family of teddy bears when they escape from the shoe shop where they had been kept to amuse children trying on new shoes.

Some of Baker's fantasies present a problem in requiring the reading ability that might be expected of an eight-year-old but presenting themes (about talking dress shop models and rag dolls, for instance) that good readers of eight or nine may find too babyish to hold their interest. Baker does not entirely avoid dealing with difficulties and conflicts in her books (Letty in *Cut Off from Crumpets* is distressed by the separation of her parents; Kennet's and Rose's father in *Beware of the Gnomes* has died in the Falklands), but she never handles them didactically. Her touch is light and she always manages to write from the child's point of view, which accounts in large measure for her consistent appeal.

—Valerie Brinkley-Willsher

———

BALDERSON, Margaret. Australian. Born in Concord, New South Wales, in 1935. Educated at a high school in Sydney. Formerly librarian in Sydney and house mistress at a girls' school. Recipient: Australian Children's Book Council Book of the Year award, 1969. Address: c/o Oxford University Press, Box 2784Y, Melbourne, Victoria 3001, Australia.

PUBLICATIONS FOR CHILDREN

Fiction

When Jays Fly to Bárbmo, illustrated by Victor Ambrus.   London, Oxford University Press, 1968; New York, World, 1969.
A Dog Called George, illustrated by Nikki Jones.   London, Oxford University Press, 1975.
Blue and Gold Day, illustrated by Roger Haldane.   Sydney and London, Angus and Robertson, 1979.

*   *   *

When Margaret Balderson became a resident worker in Norway she experienced in a deeply personal way the innate rhythms of that land as expressed through its seasons. In particular, the Dark Time of the long Arctic winter became for her symbolic of an oppression

of spirit which evaporates with the miracle of each spring, when the "whole of the radiant world" lies humble "in an attitude of silent thanksgiving," and when young people "run around in circles, laughing crazily at the patterns left…in the deep glittering snow." *When Jays Fly to Bárbmo* is Balderson's response to a land and its people. It is the slow, lyrically measured story of Ingeborg, a heroine descended in spirit from the epics of the Norsemen. Her country is under threat of invasion—a threat that fills the strongly drawn adult characters with dread and foreboding. When the invasion comes it not only destroys the quiet tenor of life, but it causes Ingeborg to question her heredity and hence her identity. Only when she is thrust into personal isolation and destroys, advisedly, her father's home—the last of all that she held dear—and completes the long and demanding trek to her Lapp grandfather can she face her own Dark Time and emerge as a person with a new life ahead. So the Germans depart, summer comes once more and Ingeborg goes "home." The land and its people return to the pattern of the seasons.

The author's second book is set in Canberra, Australia, and again reflects her gift of reshaping emotional experience into satisfying literary expression. She owns an old, shaggy English sheep dog called George, the blue-eyed hero of *A Dog Called George* who causes his adopted master, 10-year-old Tony, to come to terms with his place in the family and in society. Above all, Tony learns that man and beast must each be himself for George was George, always "ready for him with a paw for the shaking and an ear for the scratching—happy to see him come—unconcerned to see him go…."

The text of *Blue and Gold Day* with Roger Haldane's flowing line drawings and his sensitively complementary paintings is a lyrical record of the shifting sensory perceptions and emotional exuberance of two girls and their dog on a pre-breakfast visit to the beach. Counterpointed against the mundanely realistic thought stream of the narrator and snippets of highly sisterly conversation are images of sea and sand, rock pools and shells, and an overgrown track winding up from the beach past the lake, with its black swans and pelicans.

Once again Balderson demonstrates her ability to evoke place: the towering black hulks of Norway's mountains; a long, flat, narrow strip of paddock on the eastern side of Canberra; and here, the stretch of beach and Banksia scrub along one of the multitude of Australian coastal resorts—where all summer long every day seems to be blue-and-gold, lit with the promise of a boat to hire and pancakes for breakfast.

—H.M. Saxby

———

BANKS, Lynne Reid. British. Born in London, 31 July 1929. Educated at schools in Canada; Queen's Secretarial School, London, 1945–46; Italia Centre Stage School, London, 1946; Royal Academy of Dramatic Art, London, 1947–49. Married Chaim Stephenson in 1965; three sons. Actress in British repertory companies, 1949–54; secretary to the writer Wolf Mankowitz, 1954; interviewer, reporter and scriptwriter, Independent Television News, London, 1955–62; English teacher, Kibbutz Yasur School and Na'aman High School, Israel, 1963–71. Recipient: Yorkshire Arts Association award, 1977. Agent: Watson Little Ltd., 26 Charing Cross Road, Suite 8, London WC2H 0DG, England.

PUBLICATIONS FOR CHILDREN

Fiction

One More River.   London, Vallentine Mitchell, and New York,

Simon and Schuster, 1973.
Sarah and After: The Matriarchs.   London, Bodley Head, and New York, Doubleday, 1975.
The Adventures of King Midas, illustrated by George Him.   London, Dent, 1976.
The Farthest-Away Mountain, illustrated by Victor Ambrus.   London, Abelard Schuman, 1976; New York, Doubleday, 1977.
My Darling Villain.   London, Bodley Head, and New York, Harper, 1977.
I, Houdini: The Autobiography of a Self-Educated Hamster, illustrated by Terry Riley.   London, Dent, 1978; New York, Doubleday, 1988.
The Indian in the Cupboard, illustrated by Robin Jacques.   London, Dent, 1980; New York, Doubleday, 1981.
The Writing on the Wall.   London, Chatto and Windus, 1981; New York, Harper, 1982.
Maura's Angel, illustrated by Robin Jacques.   London, Dent, 1984.
The Fairy Rebel, illustrated by William Geldart.   London, Dent, 1985; New York, Doubleday, 1988.
Return of the Indian, illustrated by William Geldart.   London, Dent, 1986; New York, Doubleday, 1987.
Melusine.   London, Hamish Hamilton, 1988.

PUBLICATIONS FOR ADULTS

Novels

The L-Shaped Room.   London, Chatto and Windus, 1960; New York, Simon and Schuster, 1961.
An End to Running.   London, Chatto and Windus, 1962; as *House of Hope,* New York, Simon and Schuster, 1962.
Children at the Gate.   London, Chatto and Windus, and New York, Simon and Schuster, 1968.
The Backward Shadow.   London, Chatto and Windus, and New York, Simon and Schuster, 1970.
Two Is Lonely.   London, Chatto and Windus, and New York, Simon and Schuster, 1974.
Dark Quartet: The Story of the Brontës.   London, Weidenfeld and Nicolson, 1976; New York, Delacorte Press, 1977.
Path to the Silent Country: Charlotte Brontë's Years of Fame.   London, Weidenfeld and Nicolson, 1977; New York, Delacorte Press, 1978.
Defy the Wilderness.   London, Chatto and Windus, 1981.
The Warning Bell.   London, Hamish Hamilton, 1984; New York, St. Martin's Press, 1987.
Casualties.   London, Hamish Hamilton, 1986; New York, St. Martin's Press, 1987.

Plays

It Never Rains (televised 1954; produced Keighley, Yorkshire, 1954).   London, Deane, 1954.
Miss Pringle Plays Portia, with Victor Maddern.   London, Deane, 1955.
The Killer Dies Twice.   London, Deane, 1956.
All in a Row.   London, Deane, and Boston, Baker, 1956.
The Unborn (produced London, 1962).
Already It's Tomorrow (televised 1962).   London, French, 1962.
The Gift (produced London, 1965).

Radio Plays: *The Stowaway,* 1967; *Lame Duck,* 1978; *Purely from Principle,* 1984.

Television Plays: *It Never Rains,* 1954; *Already It's Tomorrow,* 1962; *The Wednesday Caller,* 1963; *Last Word on Julie,* 1964; *The Eye of the Beholder* (*She* series), 1977.

Other

The Kibbutz: Some Personal Reflections (address).   London, Anglo-Israel Association, 1972.
Letters to My Israeli Sons: The Story of Jewish Survival.   London, W.H. Allen, 1979; New York, Watts, 1980.
Torn Country: An Oral History of the Israeli War of Independence.   New York, Watts, 1982.

*

Manuscript Collection: Boston University.

Theatrical Activities:
Actress: **Radio**—*Purely from Principle,* 1984.

*   *   *

Lynne Reid Banks has written books for various ages. Her youngest audience will be for *The Adventures of King Midas,* a brightly illustrated, amusing, and readable reworking of the Greek story of the golden touch into a mixture of legend and fairytale; and for *The Farthest-Away Mountain,* in which it is the daughter of the house who takes up the heroic quest, and the traditional fairytale material is given a twist that will please the young feminist reader. *The Fairy Rebel,* an entertaining story in which Tiki defies the tyrannical and sadistic Fairy Queen to satisfy a young couple's longing for a child, is aimed at a similar age group; but the Queen's revenge is unexpected, cruel, and frightening, and the tone at times seems almost too mature and sophisticated for the intended audience.

The Indian in the Cupboard is a delightfully imaginative story for readers of 10 and over. Omri's cupboard brings his plastic toys to life, and the subsequent adventures with his Indian and a friend's tearful cowboy are very funny. Omri quickly discovers that Little Bull has a mind of his own, and, small as he is, demands attention and consideration. In the sequel, *Return of the Indian,* Omri rashly agrees to furnish Little Bull with modern weapons to defeat his enemies, with dire results. Both these books provide a gripping and eventful story, but also invite the reader to think more deeply about the implications lying quietly behind the adventures. This is true also of *I, Houdini.* Houdini is a hamster with quirky individuality, a philosophical turn of mind, considerable fluency of narration, and a very good conceit of himself. His adventures as an inveterate escapologist are amusing and hair-raising, and include some penetrating observations on the follies of mankind as well as sensible information about the true nature and needs of hamsters. Another story for this age group is *Maura's Angel,* set in Northern Ireland, its central character an 11-year-old girl from a Catholic family. Her father is off with the Provos, her elder brother in the Maze, and her mother worn out with worry and the effort of maintaining her remaining children. The account of the family's plight is effectively presented, and Maura is a thoroughly credible and sympathetic character. But the conception of Maura's guardian angel is less successful, and there is little attempt to say more about the political and religious background than that the men are "playing at war like boys and never really knowin' what it means, how much pain it costs."

The remaining novels are for teenagers. Although there are lively scenes in both books, the two Jewish novels are disappointing. *Sarah and After* tells the story of four generations of great "matriarchs" of the Old Testament, but there are too many major characters, and the author's recreation of the lifestyle of a past era lacks conviction. *One More River* could also, with advantage, have focussed on fewer issues. Of particular interest is the account of Lesley's gradual absorption into kibbutz life in spite of her initial sulky resentment at being whisked off without warning from her comfortable Canadian home; and there is a sensitive account of the Six Day War, which is sympathetic to Israeli aspirations without forgetting their effect on the dispossessed Arabs.

The remaining books are about "modern" teenage problems. In *My Darling Villain* Kate's racy, idiomatic account of her tempestuous relationship with Mark is absorbing and often very funny. In spite of a melodramatic ending there is a compelling realism in the conflicts between Kate's middle-class "hang-ups" and Mark's forthright working-class background and lack of reverence for authority. The central interest of *The Writing on the Wall* is in Tracy's fluctuating attitude towards the truly villainous Kev and the question of how far she will allow him to go with her. Also of note are the perceptive accounts of Tracy's family relationships and of Connie, the punk who hates violence and has a basic fund of common sense. Once again there are some hilariously funny scenes, especially during the eventful trip to Holland which culminates in a lurid encounter with porn-merchants-cum-drug-smugglers. But it is to be feared that too many young readers will relish the book for the details of the Amsterdam adventures and ignore the moral ending condemning both porn and drugs.

Melusine combines modern realism—and a lurking sex-abuse problem—with an ancient legend of a girl who could transform herself into a serpent. It is set in a crumbling French château where Roger and his family are spending their holiday. Though the serpent theme never becomes wholly convincing, the sense of mystery, fear, and suspense are well sustained, and the establishment of characters and relationships shows all the author's customary skill and insight. Like all Banks's books for young readers *Melusine* is both compulsive reading and thought-provoking, even though it leaves a sense of too much left unsaid, of questions touched upon but not satisfactorily resolved.

Although it now has a slightly old-fashioned look, and a "mature" heroine of 27, *The L-Shaped Room* is still Banks's best-known book in schools as elsewhere: but as the specifically teenage novels become better known it may well be superseded in the popularity stakes, for private reading at least.

—Winifred Whitehead

BANNER, Angela. Pseudonym for Angela Mary Maddison. British. Born in Bombay, India, 14 May 1923. Educated at Ancaster Gate and House, Bexhill, Sussex, 1933–37. Married Lionel Parsons in 1941; two children. Address: The Ant and Bee Partnership, c/o Grindlays Bank, 13 St. James's Square, London SW1Y 4LF, England.

PUBLICATIONS FOR CHILDREN

Fiction

Ant and Bee: An Alphabetical Story for Tiny Tots, illustrated by Bryan Ward. Leicester, Ward, 1950; New York, Watts, 1963.
More Ant and Bee, illustrated by Bryan Ward. London, Ward, 1956; New York, Watts, 1960.
Mr. Fork and Curly Fork: A Time Story. London, Ward, 1956.
One, Two, Three with Ant and Bee: A Counting Story, illustrated by Bryan Ward. London, Ward, 1958; New York, Watts, 1963.
Around the World with Ant and Bee, illustrated by Bryan Ward. London, Ward, 1958; New York, Watts, 1960.
More and More Ant and Bee: Another Alphabetical Story, illustrated by Bryan Ward. London, Ward, 1961; New York, Watts, 1962.

Ant and Bee and the Rainbow: A Story about Colours, illustrated by Bryan Ward. London, Ward, and New York, Watts, 1962.
Ant and Bee and Kind Dog: An Alphabetical Story, illustrated by Bryan Ward. London, Ward, and New York, Watts, 1963.
Happy Birthday with Ant and Bee, illustrated by Bryan Ward. London, Ward, and New York, Watts, 1964.
Ant and Bee and the ABC, illustrated by Bryan Ward. London, Ward, and New York, Watts, 1966.
Ant and Bee Time, illustrated by the author. London, Kaye and Ward, and New York, Watts, 1969.
Ant and Bee and the Secret, illustrated by the author. London, Kaye and Ward, and New York, Watts, 1970.
Ant and Bee and the Doctor, illustrated by the author. London, Kaye and Ward, and New York, Watts, 1971.
The Ant and Bee Big Buy Bag, illustrated by the author. London, Kaye and Ward, 1971.
Ant and Bee Go Shopping, illustrated by the author. London, Kaye and Ward, and New York, Watts, 1972.
Kind Dog on Monday, illustrated by the author. London, Ant and Bee Partnership, 1972.
Kind Dog Up and Down the Hill, illustrated by the author. London, Ant and Bee Partnership, 1972.
Which Two Will Meet?, illustrated by the author. London, Ant and Bee Partnership, 1972.
Dear Father Christmas, illustrated by the author. London, Ant and Bee Partnership, 1984.

*

Angela Banner comments:
The best reading teacher for a child is another child.
My books are made for shared-reading between children. No child is too young to "read" a few words from memory and so contribute to a story telling.
Early "memory reading" leads to reading confidence: too often destroyed by educating adults.

*   *   *

Angela Banner is the author (and sometimes also the illustrator) of the enormously popular series about Ant and Bee. She says she chose an ant and a bee because she used to be afraid of insects and she hoped her children would be different. But, in fact, their insectness is merely incidental. Their smallness is nicely exploited, and Bee does a good deal of flying about, often with Ant on his back. But they are not insects in the way that Mr. Jackson is a toad or Samuel Whiskers a rat. And they are not trying to be. They are zany, one-dimensional characters with enormous appeal for children. They come in small, fat, colourful packets as tempting as a box of Smarties.

The text may be tedious stuff for reading-aloud parents but at least they have the consolation of some bizarre ideas and surrealistic conjunctions and the knowledge that the books are educational as well as entertaining. The books are designed to encourage reading (with key words from a limited vocabulary), counting, telling the time, knowing the colours. The least overtly educational is one of the most successful. *Happy Birthday with Ant and Bee* is supposed to make children aware of the order of the days of the week, but is in fact more of a juvenile guide to the proper conduct of a birthday party. *One, Two, Three with Ant and Bee* can be guaranteed to teach children not only how to count but how to write and read their numbers. As for the reading books, Banner once said she chooses the key words first, "like cooking ingredients." Some of the key words are definitely odd. If you meet a 4-year-old who knows a *yew*-tree and a tea-*urn* when he sees them, you can be sure he has *Ant and Bee* in his house.

The effect of the whole series is to assure a child that books are fun and small, friendly, familiar objects, not glossy beautiful things that need to be treated reverently. The series could be called vulgar, brash, unsubtle, limited, marred by over-emphatic punctuation. But the books combine that mixture of the rational and irrational, the strange and familiar which children delight in. They are lively, funny, inventive, and instructive, and undoubtedly successful.

—Ann Thwaite

BANNERMAN, Helen (Brodie Cowan, née Watson). British. Born in Edinburgh, Scotland, 25 February 1862; brought up in Madeira. Educated at home, and at Miss Olliphant's school; University of St. Andrews, Fife, L.L.A. (external degree) 1887. Married William Burney Bannerman in 1889 (died 1924); two daughters and two sons. Lived in India from 1889. *Died 13 October 1946.*

PUBLICATIONS FOR CHILDREN (original editions published anonymously; illustrated by the author)

Fiction

The Story of Little Black Sambo. London, Grant Richards, 1899; New York, Stokes, 1900.
The Story of Little Black Mingo. London, Nisbet, 1901; New York, Stokes, 1902.
The Story of Little Black Quibba. London, Nisbet, 1902; New York, Stokes, 1903.
Little Degchie-Head: An Awful Warning to Bad Babas. London, Nisbet, 1903; as *The Story of Little Kettle-Head,* New York, Stokes, 1904.
Pat and the Spider: The Biter Bit. London, Nisbet, 1904; New York, Stokes, 1905.
The Story of the Teasing Monkey. London, Nisbet, 1906; New York, Stokes, 1907.
The Story of Little Black Quasha. London, Nisbet, and New York, Stokes, 1908.
The Story of Little Black Bobtail. London, Nisbet, and New York, Stokes, 1909.
The Story of Sambo and the Twins. New York, Stokes, 1936; London, Nisbet, 1937.
The Story of Little White Squibba. London, Chatto and Windus, 1966.

*

Critical Studies: *Little Black Sambo: A Closer Look: A History of...The Story of Little Black Sambo and Its Popularity/Controversy in the United States* by Phyllis J. Yuill, New York, Racism and Sexism Resource Center, 1976; *Sambo Sahib: The Story of Little Black Sambo and Helen Bannerman* by Elizabeth Hay, Edinburgh, Harris, and New York, Barnes and Noble, 1981.

*   *   *

Helen Bannerman's *The Story of Little Black Sambo* was made up by an Englishwoman living in India in the 1890's to amuse her children. When it was published, embellished by its author's own rather crude coloured illustrations, it was an immediate success and has been continuously in print ever since. It is easy to see why so many generations of children have enjoyed having it read to them—it has even been called "one of the funniest books in existence." The language is simple; there is a picture to look at on almost every other page; and the story-line has the riveting simplicity of a folk-tale. Little Black Sambo, given a fine new Red Coat, Blue Trousers, Purple Shoes, and Green Umbrella, goes out for a walk in the Jungle where he meets four Tigers who, one after another, agree not to eat him in return for one of his pieces of finery. (The Purple Shoes have to be worn as ear-muffs, while the fourth Tiger can only manage to hold the Green Umbrella by tying a knot in his tail.) The Tigers meet and quarrel over which of them is now the grandest. In the end, in a climax which small children find tremendously funny, the Tigers chase each other round a tree so fast that they simply melt away, leaving nothing but a great big pool of melted butter. Sambo's father, Black Jumbo, takes this home with him, and with it his mother, Black Mumbo, makes an enormous feast of pancakes, of which Sambo eats no fewer than "a Hundred and Sixty-nine."

In its various successors there is a similar pattern of repetition-with-variation, culminating in a ludicrous and often innocently bloodthirsty denouement: in *Little Black Mingo* the Mugger swallows the "horrid cross old woman," Black Noggy, complete with a tin of kerosene and a box of matches, with explosive results; in *Little Black Quibba* the Elephant and the Snake engage in a fight in which the Elephant falls over a cliff and ties his trunk together with the Snake into such a tight knot that the Snake (whose rear end is curled round a tree) is pulled out "longer and longer and thinner and thinner" until it breaks "with a Snap! into three pieces."

Since the 1930's in the United States and from 1972 on in Great Britain there has been vociferous unease about the racism implicit in these stories. It is true that if one takes the naming of the characters, together with the garishly coloured clothes they are so proud of, there is evident a certain unwitting condescension towards the black human protagonists which passed unnoticed 80 years ago but which properly raises qualms in the uneasy multi-racial climate of today. In fairness to Bannerman it should be mentioned that much of the American hostility to *Little Black Sambo* related not to her own drawings but to their appallingly offensive vulgarisation by other illustrators in the 50-odd unauthorised versions published in the U.S. (Through the unfortunate action of an intermediary she had lost control of the copyright in 1899 in return for a flat payment of £5.) Moreover the caricature style of her own illustrations is applied just as much to the white personae in her now-forgotten volumes as to the black ones in her popular successes. On the whole the fault seems to lie less in Bannerman than in the diseased state of our own culture in which the word Sambo (in the 19th century a proper name) has for several decades now been used only as a term of abuse. It is doubtful whether a normal child in a normal household will take any harm from these books, the more so since the child reader's natural inclination, whatever his colour, is to identify wholeheartedly with the Little Black hero or heroine. Nevertheless the offence they might cause to some readers is real, so that the sensitive teacher will be aware of the need to use tact and caution in introducing them into the classroom.

—Frank Whitehead

BARKER, Cicely Mary. British. Born in Croydon, Surrey, 28 June 1895. Educated at home, and at Croydon School of Art. Freelance artist: designed and painted screens and stained glass for St. George's, Waddon, and other churches in Surrey. *Died 16 February 1973.*

PUBLICATIONS FOR CHILDREN (illustrated by the author)

Fiction

The Lord of the Rushie River. London, Blackie, 1938; New York, Hippocrene, 1977.
Groundsel and Necklaces. London, Blackie, 1946; as *The Fairy's Gift,* Blackie, and New York, Hippocrene, 1977.

Play

When Spring Came In at the Window, music by Olive Linnell. London, Blackie, 1942.

Verse

Flower Fairies of the Spring. London, Blackie, 1923; New York, Macmillan, 1927.
Flower Fairies of the Summer. London, Blackie, 1925; New York, Macmillan, 1927.
Flower Fairies of the Autumn. London, Blackie, 1926; New York, Macmillan, 1927.
The Book of Flower Fairies. London, Blackie, 1927.
Fairies of the Trees. London, Blackie, 1940; as *Flower Fairies of the Trees,* 1961; New York, Hippocrene, 1976.
Flower Fairies of the Garden. London, Blackie, 1944; New York, Hippocrene, 1976.
Flower Fairies of the Wayside. London, Blackie, 1948; New York, Hippocrene, 1976.
Flower Fairy Picture Book (selection). London, Blackie, 1955.
Flower Fairies of the Winter. London, Blackie, and New York, Bedrick, 1985.

Other

A Flower Fairy Alphabet. London, Blackie, 1934; New York, Hippocrene, 1978.
Lively Stories (readers; *The Little House; Do You Know?.; The Click-Clock Man; The Why Girl; Hutch, The Peg Doll*). London, Macmillan, and New York, St. Martin's Press, 5 vols., 1954–55.
Lively Numbers (readers; *The Little Man, The Little Boats, The Lazy Giant*). London, Macmillan, and New York, St. Martin's Press, 3 vols., 1960–62.
Lively Words (readers). London, Macmillan, and New York, St. Martin's Press, 2 vols., 1961–62.
The Sand, The Sea, and the Sun (textbook). Glasgow, Gibson, 1970.
An A.B.C. of Flower Fairies. London, Blackie, 1978; New York, Hippocrene, 1980.

Editor, *Old Rhymes for All Times.* London, Blackie, 1928; New York, Dodge, 1932.
Editor, *Rhymes New and Old.* London, Blackie, 1933; Poughkeepsie, New York, Artists and Writers Guild, 1935; as *A Little Book of Rhymes New and Old,* Blackie, 1937.
Editor, *A Little Book of Old Rhymes.* London, Blackie, 1936; New York, Hippocrene, 1977.
Editor, *The Rhyming Rainbow: Poems.* London, Blackie, and New York, Hippocrene, 1977.

                                    *

Illustrator: *Guardian Angel Birthday Cards,* 1923; *Beautiful Bible*

Pictures, 1932; *The Little Picture Hymn Book,* 1933; *He Leadeth Me* by Dorothy O. Barker, 1936; *The Flower Fairies Gardening Year,* 1983.

                        *   *   *

For more than two generations the Flower Fairy books by Cicely Mary Barker have enchanted and instructed children. Her meticulous and subtle illustrations are outstanding for their botanical accuracy and detail, but also for the imaginative representation of the essential personification of the plants—the sturdiness of the bugle, the joy of the early crocus, the wistful forget-me-not. She was greatly influenced by the Pre-Raphaelite movement in mood and atmosphere.

It is for the illustrations in her books that she is best remembered, but the verses and text in the stories are worth more than the cursory glance they are often dismissed with. Her writing could in no way be described as being of great literary merit, and some lines move in a jerky and forced manner. But the individual rhymes contain such a wealth of detail on herbal remedies, plant cultivation, and old folk customs that to read them is to step back 50 years into the provident countryside. Children are exhorted to wait until the conkers fall rather than damage the tree in *Flower Fairies of the Autumn; Self Heal* is acknowledged to be a famous herb of healing in old days in *Flower Fairies of the Wayside,* and in *Fairies of the Trees* there is the instructive verse:

> There are cones on the tall, tall Pine tree,
> With its needles sharp and green;
> Small seeds in the cones are hidden,
> And they ripen there unseen.

The appeal of the verses lies in their simplicity and sincerity—there is nothing coy or vulgar here and they are easy to assimilate by the youngest child, often forming a first and memorable introduction to a knowledge of trees and plants. They have the same ease and brightness as all nursery rhymes, and the same degree of uncomplicated "chattiness."

Barker was deeply religious, and this is apparent in her prose writing, especially *The Lord of the Rushie River,* a moral tale of faith overcoming adversity. A sailor left his little girl in the care of a Dame Dinnage, paying her to look after Susan and his house while he went to sea for one last time. No sooner had his ship sailed than Dame Dinnage showed her true colours and poor Susan was fed on the poorest scraps and watered milk, and her clothes grew ragged while the Dame's old stocking bulged with the money meant for Susan's care. The little girl's only friends were the swans, especially one who seemed to be the Lord of the Rushie River. The swans eventually rescued Susan from her trials and tribulations, her father returned and even Dame Dinnage returned the money, having had no pleasure in her ill-gotten gains. Susan is saved from being too good to be true by her faith in the swans and her gentle care of the huge birds, and even modern children could find something in this simple and uncomplicated tale. It stops short of sentimentality by the noble portrayal of the birds and also the striking but sympathetic illustrations.

Cicely Mary Barker has a remembered place in 20th-century children's literature, remembered by the countless children who grew up with her drawings and her images printed on the mind's eye, her sensitivity and joy in small things passed on in so unspoilt a manner.

—Fiona Waters

BARNE, Kitty (Marion Catherine Barne). British. Born in 1883. Educated at the Royal College of Music, London. Served in the Women's Voluntary Service during World War II. Married Eric Streatfeild. Recipient: Library Association Carnegie Medal, 1941. *Died in 1957.*

PUBLICATIONS FOR CHILDREN

Fiction

Tomorrow, illustrated by Ethel King-Martyn.   London, Hodder and Stoughton, 1912.
The Easter Holidays, illustrated by Joan Kiddell-Monroe.   London, Heinemann, 1935; as *Secret of the Sandhills,* New York, Dodd Mead, 1949; London, Nelson, 1955.
Young Adventurers, illustrated by Ruth Gervis.   London, Nelson, 1936.
She Shall Have Music, illustrated by Ruth Gervis.   London, Dent, 1938; New York, Dodd Mead, 1939.
Family Footlights, illustrated by Ruth Gervis.   London, Dent, and New York, Dodd Mead, 1939.
Visitors from London, illustrated by Ruth Gervis.   London, Dent, and New York, Dodd Mead, 1940.
May I Keep Dogs?, illustrated by Arnrid Johnston.   London, Hamish Hamilton, 1941; New York, Dodd Mead, 1942; as *Bracken My Dog,* London, Dent, 1949.
We'll Meet in England, illustrated by Steven Spurrier.   London, Hamish Hamilton, 1942; New York, Dodd Mead, 1943.
Three and a Pigeon, illustrated by Steven Spurrier.   London, Hamish Hamilton, and New York, Dodd Mead, 1944.
In the Same Boat, illustrated by Ruth Gervis.   London, Dent, and New York, Dodd Mead, 1945.
Musical Honours, illustrated by Ruth Gervis.   London, Dent, and New York, Dodd Mead, 1947.
Dusty's Windmill, illustrated by Marcia Lane Foster.   London, Dent, 1949; as *The Windmill Mystery,* New York, Dodd Mead, 1950.
Roly's Dogs, illustrated by Alice Molony.   London, Dent, 1950; as *Dog Stars,* New York, Dodd Mead, 1951.
Barbie, illustrated by Marcia Lane Foster.   London, Dent, 1952; Boston, Little Brown, 1969.
Admiral's Walk, illustrated by Mary Gurnat.   London, Dent, 1953.
Rosina Copper, The Mystery Mare, illustrated by Alfons Purtscher.   London, Evans, 1954; New York, Dutton, 1956.
Cousin Beatie Learns the Fiddle.   Oxford, Blackwell, 1955.
Tann's Boarders, illustrated by Jill Crockford.   London, Dent, 1955.
Rosina and Son, illustrated by Marcia Lane Foster.   London, Dent, 1956.

Plays

Tomorrow, with D.W. Wheeler.   London, Curwen, 1910.
Winds, with D.W. Wheeler, music by Kitty Barne, illustrated by Lucy Barne.   London, Curwen, 1912.
Timothy's Garden, verses by D.W. Wheeler, illustrated by Lucy Barne.   London, Curwen, 1912.
Celandine's Secret, verses by D.W. Wheeler, illustrated by J.M. Saunders.   London, Curwen, 1914.
Peter and the Clock.   London, Curwen, 1919.
Susie Pays a Visit.   London, Curwen, 1921.
The Amber Gate: A Pageant Play.   London, Curwen, 1925.
Philemon and Baucis.   London, Gowans and Gray, and Boston, Baker, 1926.
Madge: A Camp-Fire Play.   London, Novello, 1928.
Adventurers: A Pageant Play.   London, Deane, 1931; Boston,

Baker, 1936.
The Grand Party, adaptation of the novel *Holiday House,* by Catherine Sinclair, in *The Theatre Window: Plays for Schools,* edited by W.T. Cunningham.   London, Arnold, 1933.
Two More Mimes from Folk Songs: The Wraggle, Taggle Gipsies, O!; Robin-a-Thrush.   London, Curwen, 1936.
Two Mimes from Folk Songs: The Frog and the Mouse, The Flowers in the Valley.   London, Curwen, 1937.
They Made the Royal Arms.   London, Deane, and Boston, Baker, 1937.
Shilling Teas.   London, Deane, and Boston, Baker, 1938.
Days of Glory: A Pageant Play.   London, Deane, 1946.
The "Local Ass": A Documentary Pageant Play for Girl Guides.   London, Girl Guides' Association, 1947.
The Lost Birthday.   London, Curwen, n.d.

Other

The Amber Gate, illustrated by Ruth Gervis.   London and New York, Nelson, 1933.
Songs and Stories for Acting, illustrated by Ruth Gervis.   Glasgow, Brown and Ferguson, 1939.
Listening to the Orchestra.   London, Dent, 1941; revised edition, 1946; Indianapolis, Bobbs Merrill, 1946.
Here Come the Girl Guides.   London, Girl Guides' Association, 1947.
Elizabeth Fry: A Story Biography.   London, Penguin, 1950.
Introducing Handel [*Mozart, Schubert*], illustrated by Jill Crockford.   London, Dent, and New York, Roy, 3 vols., 1955–57.

PUBLICATIONS FOR ADULTS

Novels

Mother at Large.   London, Chapman and Hall, 1938.
While the Music Lasted.   London, Chapman and Hall, 1943.
Enter Two Musicians.   London, Chapman and Hall, 1944.
Duet for Sisters.   London, Chapman and Hall, 1947.
Vespa.   London, Chapman and Hall, 1950.
Music Perhaps.   London, Chapman and Hall, 1953.

*   *   *

Though she produced a good deal of earlier work, mainly plays and now forgotten, it was not until a few years before World War II that Kitty Barne began to explore a field of children's fiction in which she became something of a pioneer. She would probably have disclaimed a title with quite such aggressive connotations. She was, however, in her quiet way, a very serious and responsible writer. Her junior novels were intended to reflect the real world, in which young characters faced problems and struggled to solve them. She never favoured the child-insulated world in which adults appeared only as fringe characters, tolerated only when the plot demanded their entrance. At a period when most modern stories were frankly escapist, dealing with holiday adventures or improbable juvenile detection, Barne, while not making her books superficially too dissimilar, let in a much-needed draught of fresh air.

The outbreak of war in 1939 gave her inspiration and immediately enlarged opportunities. No one could any longer pretend that young readers could or should be protected from reality. In her Carnegie-winner, *Visitors from London,* she dealt with the impact of London evacuees upon a Sussex village. Later, another Cockney evacuee was a key character in *Three and a Pigeon,* another story of the home front which also involved the black market in farm produce. *In the*

Same Boat tells of a Polish girl's escape to Britain and her schooldays there with her new-found English friend. Perhaps most noteworthy of all these novels is *Musical Honours,* in which the father, a returned prisoner-of-war from the Far East, faces all the problems of readjustment, not least the renewal of relationships with his elder children who remember him and with the younger who do not. This was probably one of the earliest children's books in which a parent was depicted as a flesh-and-blood person with faults, not as a love-and-authority symbol.

Both in her thought and in her language, Kitty Barne preferred to stretch her young readers, to overrate rather than underrate their capacity. She was against what she called "patronising simplicity" and "brightness." Children, she declared, did not mind long words or ideas that were a little big for them. She found an exhilaration in writing for them, and this emotion was communicated in the warmth and enthusiasm of her style.

—Geoffrey Trease

BARRETT, Anne Mainwaring (née Gillett). British. Born in Southsea, Hampshire, 7 May 1911. Educated at Sherborne School for Girls, Dorset. Married 1) Hugh Myles Boxer in 1933 (divorced 1940); 2) William Kenyon Tufnell Barrett in 1941 (divorced 1960), one daughter. Worked with Children's Film Foundation, London, 1960–65. *Died in December 1987.*

PUBLICATIONS FOR CHILDREN

Fiction

Caterpillar Hall, illustrated by Catherine Cummins. London, Collins, 1950.
Stolen Summer, illustrated by John Robinson. London, Collins, 1951; New York, Dodd Mead, 1953.
The Dark Island. London, Collins, 1952.
The Journey of Johnny Rew, illustrated by Shirley Hughes. London, Collins, 1954; Indianapolis, Bobbs Merrill, 1955.
Sheila Burton, Dental Assistant. London, Bodley Head, 1956.
Songberd's Grove, illustrated by David Knight. London, Collins, and Indianapolis, Bobbs Merrill, 1957.
Midway, illustrated by Margery Gill. London, Collins, 1967; New York, Coward McCann, 1968.

Play

Screenplay: *Treasure in Malta,* 1963.

*   *   *

Anne Mainwaring Barrett was a writer of considerable power whose work, on the whole, has not been accorded the continuing praise which it merits. Her best-known books are *Songberd's Grove* and *Midway.* Her earlier books are highly imaginative but are somewhat marred by the many strands to their plots. The first four novels have very improbable themes, but are written with an almost dreamlike quality, and this style, while it makes for very enjoyable reading, also tends to date them. *Caterpillar Hall* is an adventure in time: Penelope turns the gold band of her umbrella to take her back many years, revealing the early lives of other characters. *Stolen Summer* describes the summer spent by Jenny and her mother in a beautiful country house; to young readers of today the passion of James and

Jenny for all things Nelsonian—to the point of making models of the ships at Trafalgar—is the most entertaining aspect. *The Dark Island* is set in Ireland, and concerns the discovery by two children of a man who has lost his memory; this turns into a kind of spy-thriller as it unfolds. *The Journey of Johnny Rew* traces the hero's search for his unknown father. This story is memorable for the many remarkable characters whom Johnny encounters—especially old Sam Brisle the hedger and the charming, trusting ladylike Miss Merrament.

Songberd's Grove is a story of the Teddyboy era. Martin, a boy of some spirit, comes to live with his parents in an old tumbledown flat; in the same house dwell many diverse characters including the leader of the local spivs—Lenny. This story is more factual, and the gradual unfolding of the various situations which bring cheer to all of them—including the discovery that the street has some architectural merit—is carefully done. The architect has that "rarely met aura of true authority" which reduces Lenny to size and provides a lesson for all bullies.

In *Midway*—Barrett's finest book—Mark is the middle child of five, and as the family grew it was evident that Mark is the least clever. Gradually his father has lost interest in him, and Mark is always trying to prove his usefulness. The boy has a vivid imagination, and he invents a glorious tiger whom he calls "Midway" and in whom he confides his troubles and fears, and with whom all things are possible. Mark distrusts his father's fellow scientist, and when this rival attempts to steal his father's work, it is Mark who saves the day, so at last his father gives him the place in his affections to which Mark aspires. This is a splendid piece of writing which may well help any child who feels out of things at school or at home.

—Berna C. Clark

BARRIE, (Sir) J(ames) M(atthew). British. Born in Kirriemuir, Forfarshire (now Angus), Scotland, 9 May 1860. Educated at Misses Adam School, Kirriemuir; Glasgow Academy, 1868–70; Forfar Academy, 1870–72; Dumfries Academy, 1873–78; University of Edinburgh, 1878–82, M.A. 1882. Married the actress Mary Ansell in 1894 (divorced 1909). Drama and book critic, Edinburgh *Courant,* 1879–82; leader writer, Nottingham *Journal,* 1883–84. Lived in London after 1885: journalist, contributing to the *St. James's Gazette* and *British Weekly,* 1885–90. President, Society of Authors, 1928–37, and Dramatists' Club, 1934–37. LL.D.: University of St. Andrews, 1898; University of Edinburgh, 1909; D.Litt.: Oxford University, 1926; Cambridge University, 1930. Rector, University of St. Andrews, 1919–22; Chancellor, University of Edinburgh, 1930–37. Created Baronet, 1913; Order of Merit, 1922. *Died 19 June 1937.*

PUBLICATIONS FOR CHILDREN

Fiction

The Boy Castaways of Black Lake Island. Privately printed, 1901.
The Little White Bird (for adults). London, Hodder and Stoughton, 1902; as *The Little White Bird; or, Adventures in Kensington Gardens,* New York, Scribner, 1902; revised material for children, as *Peter Pan in Kensington Gardens,* illustrated by Arthur Rackham, 1906.
Peter and Wendy, illustrated by F.D. Bedford. London, Hodder and Stoughton, and New York, Scribner, 1911; as *Peter Pan and Wendy,* London, Hodder and Stoughton, 1921.

Plays

Peter Pan; or, The Boy Who Would Not Grow Up (produced London, 1904; Washington, D.C., and New York, 1905; revised version, produced London, 1905). Included in *Plays,* 1928.
When Wendy Grew Up: An Afterthought (produced London, 1908). London, Nelson, 1957; New York, Dutton, 1958.

PUBLICATIONS FOR ADULTS

Novels

Better Dead. London, Swan Sonnenschein Lowrey, 1887; Chicago, Rand McNally, 1891.
When a Man's Single: A Tale of Literary Life. London, Hodder and Stoughton, 1888; New York, Lovell, 1892.
The Little Minister. London, Cassell, 3 vols., 1891; New York, Lovell, 1891.
Sentimental Tommy: The Story of His Boyhood. London, Cassell, and New York, Scribner, 1896.
Tommy and Grizel. London, Cassell, and New York, Scribner, 1900.
Farewell Miss Julie Logan: A Wintry Tale. London, Hodder and Stoughton, and New York, Scribner, 1932.

Short Stories

Two of Them. New York, Lovell, 1893.
A Tillyloss Scandal. New York, Lovell, 1893.

Plays

Bandolero, The Bandit (produced Dumfries, 1877).
Caught Napping. Privately printed, 1883.
Richard Savage, with H.B. Marriott Watson (produced London, 1890). Privately printed, 1891.
Ibsen's Ghost; or, Toole Up-to-Date (produced London, 1891). Privately printed, 1939; edited by Penelope Griffin, London, Woolf, 1975.
Walker, London (produced London, 1892). London and New York, French, 1907.
The Professor's Love Story (produced New York, 1892; London, 1894). Included in *Plays,* 1942.
Becky Sharp, adaptation of the novel *Vanity Fair* by W.M. Thackeray (produced London, 1893).
Jane Annie; or, The Good Conduct Prize, with Arthur Conan Doyle, music by Ernest Ford (produced London, 1893). London, Chappell, and New York, Novello Ewer, 1893.
The Little Minister, adaptation of his own novel (produced Washington, D.C., New York, and London, 1897; as *Little Mary,* produced London, 1903). Included in *Plays,* 1942.
A Platonic Friendship (produced London, 1898).
The Wedding Guest (produced London, 1900). London, Fortnightly Review, and New York, Scribner, 1900.
Quality Street (produced London, 1902; New York, 1903). London, Hodder and Stoughton, 1913; New York, Scribner, 1918.
The Admirable Crichton (produced London, 1902; New York, 1903). London, Hodder and Stoughton, 1914; New York, Scribner, 1918.
Pantaloon (produced London, 1905). Included in *Half Hours,* 1914.
Alice Sit-by-the-Fire (produced London and New York, 1905). London, Hodder and Stoughton, and New York, Scribner, 1919.
Josephine (produced London, 1906).
Punch (produced London, 1906).
What Every Woman Knows (produced London, Atlantic City, New Jersey, and New York, 1908). London, Hodder and Stoughton, and New York, Scribner, 1918.
Old Friends (produced London, 1910; New York, 1917). Included

in *Plays,* 1928.
A Slice of Life (produced London, 1910; New York, 1912).
The Twelve-Pound Look (produced London, 1910; New York, 1911). Included in *Half Hours,* 1914.
Rosalind (produced London, 1912; New York, 1915). Included in *Half Hours,* 1914.
The Dramatists Get What They Want (produced London, 1912; as *The Censor and the Dramatists,* produced New York, 1913).
The Will (produced London and New York, 1913). Included in *Half Hours,* 1914.
The Adored One: A Legend of the Old Bailey (produced London, 1913; as *The Legend of Leonora,* produced New York, 1914; shortened version, as *Seven Women,* produced London, 1917). *Seven Women* included in *Plays,* 1928.
Half an Hour (produced London and New York, 1913). Included in *Plays,* 1928.
Half Hours (includes *Pantaloon, The Twelve-Pound Look, Rosalind, The Will*). London, Hodder and Stoughton, and New York, Scribner, 1914.
Der Tag (produced London, 1914; as *Der Tag; or, The Tragic Man,* produced New York, 1914). London, Hodder and Stoughton, and New York, Scribner, 1914.
Rosy Rapture, The Pride of the Beauty Chorus, music by H. Darewski and Jerome Kern (produced London, 1915).
The Fatal Typist (produced London, 1915).
The New Word (produced London, 1915; New York, 1917). Included in *Echoes of the War,* 1918.
The Real Thing at Last (produced London, 1916).
Irene Vanbrugh's Pantomime (produced London, 1916).
Shakespeare's Legacy (produced London, 1916). Privately printed, 1916.
A Kiss for Cinderella (produced London and New York, 1916). London, Hodder and Stoughton, and New York, Scribner, 1920.
The Old Lady Shows Her Medals (produced London and New York, 1917). Included in *Echoes of the War,* 1918.
Reconstructing the Crime (produced London, 1917).
Dear Brutus (produced London, 1917; New York, 1918). London, Hodder and Stoughton, and New York, Scribner, 1922.
La Politesse (produced London, 1918).
A Well-Remembered Voice (produced London, 1918). Included in *Echoes of the War,* 1918.
Echoes of the War (includes *The Old Lady Shows Her Medals, The New Word, Barbara's Wedding, A Well-Remembered Voice*). London, Hodder and Stoughton, and New York, Scribner, 1918.
Barbara's Wedding (produced London, 1927; New York, 1931). Included in *Echoes of the War,* 1918.
The Truth about the Russian Dancers (ballet), music by Arnold Bax (produced London, 1920). New York, Dance Perspectives, 1962.
Mary Rose (produced London and New York, 1920). London, Hodder and Stoughton, and New York, Scribner, 1924.
Shall We Join the Ladies? (produced London, 1921; New York, 1925). Included in *Plays,* 1928.
Neil and Tintinnabulum. Privately printed, 1925.
Representative Plays (includes *Quality Street, The Admirable Crichton, What Every Woman Knows, Dear Brutus, The Twelve-Pound Look, The Old Lady Shows Her Medals*), edited by W.L. Phelps. New York, Scribner, 1926.
The Plays of J.M. Barrie (includes *Peter Pan, The Admirable Crichton, Alice Sit-by-the-Fire, What Every Woman Knows, A Kiss for Cinderella, Dear Brutus, Mary Rose, Pantaloon, Half an Hour, Seven Women, Old Friends, Rosalind, The Twelve-Pound Look, The New Word, A Well-Remembered Voice, Barbara's Wedding, The Old Lady Shows Her Medals, Shall We Join the Ladies?*). London, Hodder and Stoughton, 1928; New York, Scribner, 1929; augmented edition, edited by A.E. Wilson (includes *Walker, Lon-*

don; *The Professor's Love Story; The Little Minister; The Wedding Guest; The Boy David*), Hodder and Stoughton, 1942.
The Boy David (produced Edinburgh and London, 1936; New York, 1941).   London, Davies, and New York, Scribner, 1938.

Screenplays: *The Little Minister,* 1915; *The Real Thing at Last,* 1916; *As You Like It,* with Robert Cullen, 1936.

Verse

Scotland's Lament: A Poem on the Death of Robert Louis Stevenson. Privately printed, 1895.

Other

The New Amphion.   Edinburgh, David Douglas, 1886.
Auld Licht Idylls.   London, Hodder and Stoughton, 1888; New York, Cassell, 1891.
A Window in Thrums.   London, Hodder and Stoughton, 1889; New York, Waverly, 1891.
An Edinburgh Eleven: Pencil Portraits from College Life.   London, Office of the British Weekly, 1889; New York, Lovell, 1892.
My Lady Nicotine.   London, Hodder and Stoughton, 1890; New York, Cassell, 1891.
A Holiday in Bed and Other Sketches.   New York, New York Publishing Company, 1892.
A Lady's Shoe.   New York, Brentano's, 1893.
An Auld Licht Manse and Other Sketches.   New York, Knox, 1893.
Allahakbarries C.C. (on cricket).   Privately printed, 1893.
Margaret Ogilvy, by Her Son.   New York, Scribner, and London, Hodder and Stoughton, 1896.
The Allahakbarrie Book of Broadway Cricket for 1899.   Privately printed, 1899.
George Meredith 1909.   London, Constable, 1909; as *Neither Dorking nor the Abbey,* Chicago, Browne's Bookstore, 1910.
The Works (Kirriemuir Edition).   London, Hodder and Stoughton, 10 vols., 1913.
Charles Frohman: A Tribute.   Privately printed, 1915.
Who Was Sarah Findley? by Mark Twain, with a Suggested Solution of the Mystery.   Privately printed, 1917.
The Works of J.M. Barrie.   New York, Scribner, 10 vols., 1918.
Courage: The Rectorial Address Delivered at St. Andrews University, May 3rd 1922.   London, Hodder and Stoughton, and New York, Scribner, 1922.
The Ladies' Shakespeare (lecture).   Privately printed, 1925.
The Works (Peter Pan Edition).   New York, Scribner, 14 vols., 1929–31.
The Entrancing Life (address).   London, Hodder and Stoughton, and New York, Scribner, 1930.
The Greenwood Hat, Being a Memoir of James Anon 1885–1887. Privately printed, 1930; revised edition, London, Davies, and New York, Scribner, 1937.
M'Connachie and J.M.B.: Speeches.   London, Davies, 1938; New York, Scribner, 1939.
Letters of J.M. Barrie, edited by Viola Meynell.   London, Davies, 1942; New York, Scribner, 1947.
Plays and Stories, edited by Roger Lancelyn Green.   London, Dent, 1962.

*

Bibliography: *Sir James M. Barrie: A Bibliography* by B.D. Cutler, New York, Greenberg, 1931.

Manuscript Collections: Beinecke Library, Yale University, New Haven, Connecticut; Lilly Library, Indiana University, Bloomington.

Critical Studies (selection): *J.M. Barrie* by F.J. Harvey Darton, London, Nisbet, 1929; *The Story of J.M.B. (Sir James Barrie)* by Denis Mackail, London, Davies, and New York, Scribner, 1941; *Fifty Years of Peter Pan,* London, Davies, 1954, and *J.M. Barrie,* London, Bodley Head, 1960, New York, Walck, 1961, both by Roger Lancelyn Green; *J.M. Barrie: The Man Behind the Image* by Janet Dunbar, London, Collins, and Boston, Houghton Mifflin, 1970; *Sir James Barrie* by Harry M. Geduld, New York, Twayne, 1971; *J.M. Barrie and the Lost Boys* by Andrew Birkin, London, Constable, and New York, Potter, 1979; *The Case of Peter Pan, or, The Impossibility of Children's Fiction* by Jacqueline Rose, London, Macmillan, 1984; *J.M. Barrie* by Leonée Ormond, Edinburgh, Scottish Academic Press, 1987.

*   *   *

It is not always realised that—a few private oddities apart—J.M. Barrie produced only one work for the young. But that one, a major myth of the new century, was written in many forms over many years, before and after the actual stage production. Indeed, it is fair to say that no important work discussed in the present volume can have a more curious history than *Peter Pan,* "that terrible masterpiece," as Peter Davies (see below) once called it. Where for a start is its authentic form to be found? Though that first stage production was in 1904, the play had to wait several years for a definitive printed version. The "story," the full-length definitive narrative (the longest, best, most satisfying of all the versions) did not appear until 1911. Yet clues can be found in Barrie's quite early adult writings.

Certain facts in Barrie's life have so fundamental a part in the making of *Peter Pan* that they should be set out here. He was a small-town Lowlands Scot, one of a weaver's large family. When David, the mother's favourite child, was killed in a skating accident on the eve of his 14th birthday, James, then aged 6 and hitherto of little account, set himself to compensate for the loss. The obsessive relationship that grew between mother and son was to mark the whole of his life, as writer and as man. Another intense relationship began towards the end of the century, when the once penniless young journalist had, quite rapidly, become the rich and celebrated novelist and playwright. This was with Sylvia and Arthur Llewellyn Davies (she was the daughter of George du Maurier) and their several— eventually five—small sons. These boys, devoted childish listeners, were in an immediate sense the kindlers of *Peter Pan*—Jack, Peter, and Michael (as their names confirm) especially.

In print, the magic boy first appeared by name in Barrie's adult novel *The Little White Bird* (1902) a strange first-person narrative about a wealthy bachelor clubman's attachment to a little boy, David. Taking this boy for walks in Kensington Gardens, the narrator tells him of the elusive Peter Pan, who can be found in the Gardens at night, when the gates are closed. A little girl (not motherly Wendy but a sturdy likeable child called Maimie Mannering) bravely stays behind at dusk, though her brother runs away, and she becomes Peter's friend. Four years later these chapters were taken out and reprinted as a separate book called *Peter Pan in Kensington Gardens,* with pictures by Arthur Rackham: its verve and magical atmosphere make it well worth reading today. Told verbally this was the form first known to the Davies boys.

But the roots of the tale go very much further back. In *Margaret Ogilvy* (1896) Barrie recalled how his mother's childhood had ended at 8, when she had to become the family's housekeeper. "The horror of my boyhood was," he noted, "that I knew a time would come when I must also give up games, and how it was to be done, I saw not." More revealing still are his novels *Sentimental Tommy* and *Tommy and Grizel.* Tommy, a clever, feckless dreamer who—disastrously— can't face adult responsibilities, plans a work of fiction:

a reverie about a little boy who was lost. His parents find him in a wood singing joyfully to himself because he thinks he can now be a boy for ever; and he fears that if they catch him they will compel him to grow into a man, so he runs further from them into the wood and is running still, singing to himself because he is always to be a boy.

But Barrie, unlike Tommy, had a shrewd and positive streak, and the gift of turning fancy into fact. Only a writer of great assurance could have hoped for a theatrical production of *Peter Pan* with its extraordinary cast and sets and flying devices. Beerbohm Tree, who had first offer, thought it hopelessly unworkable, original to excess. But Charles Frohman was more adventurous, and the vastly successful opening productions, on both sides of the Atlantic, were his.

Like most of Barrie's work, *Peter Pan* has been adored and reviled for much the same qualities: what some perhaps call charm, others call sentimental and whimsical. Possibly neither group has taken into account Barrie's outstanding craftsmanship as a playwright, or of his easy gift for gripping a reader's interest on the printed page. The sentimental and whimsical were certainly part of his stock-in-trade, but they were not accidentally used; by the time he wrote *Peter Pan,* the hard glint in the sentimentalist's pale blue eyes becomes increasingly evident. (It is, indeed, a wonderfully *heartless* book—as Barrie was well aware: see the final line of the novel.) A touch of self-satire can possibly be observed even in the obsessional mother-theme. Wendy is given many good lines, in the novel particularly; note her watching the mermaids "combing out their hair in a lazy way that quite irritated her"; note her scornful feelings when Hook has her tied to the mast.

No words of mine can tell you how Wendy despised those pirates. To the boys there was at least some glamour in the pirate calling, but all that she saw was that the ship had not been scrubbed for years. There was not a port-hole on the grimy glass of which you might not have written with your finger "Dirty pig"; and she had already written it several times.

Yet her role holds the seeds of its own defeat. "You need not be sorry for Wendy," writes Barrie. "She was one of the kind that like to grow up. In the end she grew up of her own free will a day quicker than other girls." By ceasing to be a child, she rapidly loses Peter, Ariel of the child-world; she loses in every sense the power to fly. The Wendy portrait, begun with such simple charm (the name was the pet-name of William Ernest Henley's short-lived daughter) has clearly got out of hand, reflecting an unadmitted conflict in Barrie himself.

Peter Pan: landmark or signpost? The first far more than the second; it seems to have stunned imitation at any notable level. Pan-followers ran to coyness rather than wit; and this affects the work's reputation still. True, it did give an impetus to theatre for children; it can also be said that it brought into the open the growing cult of childhood and fairies in writings meant for adults. From Grahame's *The Golden Age* in the 1890's to Milne's *When We Were Very Young* in the 1920's, this cult took in work of de la Mare, Eleanor Farjeon (*Martin Pippin*), Rose Fyleman, Saki, James Stephens (*The Crock of Gold*)—and other prose and verse, now classed as children's reading, which were certainly published for adults in their day. With *Peter Pan* the process works in reverse. Both play and novel were (like *Alice*) specifically meant for the young, but are now (like *Alice*) of increasing interest to adults. *Peter Pan* mirrors its time; it mirrors, though more obliquely, its author's mind. As an instance: Barrie first made his name (and almost wrecked it in his home town) by using his local Scottish background for copy. In *Peter Pan* the Scot is hard to trace. But in fact it is the northern stranger's eye that finds such appeal in the Edwardian middle-class nursery; in the social mystique

of Kensington Gardens; in the *mores* of prep school and public school. Is not Hook himself, most enigmatic of pirates, abjuring "bad form" even in death, an old Etonian? James Hook…odd that the author should give him his own name. But nothing is really simple in this work. How to explain the dog-kennel father, say, so many years pre-Thurber?

The position of *Peter Pan* today is a curious one. It is at once known and not known. Like other invented myths (Crusoe, Gulliver) its persons and ideas have currency among many who have neither read nor seen what Barrie wrote. Those who *do* read (or listen) often meet it only through feeble brief retellings (there are, alas, a number of these in print). They are missing much; the full text abounds in richness. *Peter Pan* is the secure child's dream of danger, of wild distances, of freedom from adult rules—but always (as in Sendak's *Where the Wild Things Are*) from a safe home base. It incorporates the traditional boy's adventure yarn which had so much delighted Barrie himself when young; indeed, much of the pirate/redskin material can be seen as a brilliant take-off of the genre. Peter himself is the absolute leader and hero-figure, the animator of action. But the children are not only onlookers; they are *in* the event, as themselves. It incorporates magic; the children actually fly. All these elements are combined on an island which accommodates redskins, pirates, mermaids, wolves with the greatest ease. For the young, the whole thing is a feast which lasts the longer by the skill—the continual sleight-of-hand—with which it is served. A "terrible masterpiece," yes, but the most complex and original of all its author's works, and a mine for Barrie-explorers.

—Naomi Lewis

———

BARRY, Margaret Stuart (née Bell) British. Born in Darlington, County Durham, 7 December 1927. Educated at schools in Richmond, Yorkshire, and at teacher training college, Liverpool, diploma 1947. Married Pierce Barry in 1957; two daughters and one son. Teacher, Lindisfarne Convent Preparatory School, Essex, 1947–49, and Woolten College, 1950–52; art teacher, Huyton, Lancashire; teacher, Alder Hey Children's Hospital, 1957–58. Agent: Curtis Brown, 162–168 Regent Street, London W1R 5TB. Address: 5 Belvidere Road, Liverpool L8 3TF, England.

PUBLICATIONS FOR CHILDREN

Fiction

Boffy and the Teacher Eater [*Mumford Ghosts*], illustrated by George Adamson. London, Harrap, 2 vols., 1971–74.
Tommy Mac, illustrated by Dinah Dryhurst. London, Longman, 1972.
Woozy, illustrated by John Castle. London, Harrap, 1973.
The Woozies Go to School, illustrated by John Castle. London, Harrap, 1973.
The Woozies on Television, illustrated by John Castle. London, Harrap, 1974.
Tommy Mac Battles On, illustrated by Dinah Dryhurst. London, Kestrel, 1974.
Tommy Mac on Safari, illustrated by Rosemary Evans. London, Kestrel, 1975.
Simon and the Witch, illustrated by Linda Birch. London, Collins, 1976.
Woozy and the Weight Watchers, illustrated by Andrea Smith. London, Harrap, 1977.

The Woozies Go Visiting, illustrated by Andrea Smith. London, Harrap, 1977.
Woozies Hold a Frubarb Week, illustrated by Andrea Smith. London, Harrap, 1977.
The Monster in Woozy Garden, illustrated by Andrea Smith. London, Harrap, 1977.
The Return of the Witch, illustrated by Linda Birch. London, Collins, 1978.
Maggie Gumption [*Flies High*], illustrated by Gunvor Edwards. London, Hutchinson, 2 vols., 1979–81.
The Witch of Monopoly Manor, illustrated by Linda Birch. London, Collins, 1980.
The Witch on Holiday, illustrated by Linda Birch. London, Collins, 1983.
The Witch V.I.P., illustrated by Linda Birch. London, Collins, 1987.
Diz and the Big Fat Burglar, illustrated by Paula Lawford. London, Hamish Hamilton, 1987.
Simon and the Witch in School. London, Collins, 1987.
The Witch's Holiday Club. London, Collins, 1988.

Other

Bill Books (readers), illustrated by Gwen Fulton. London, Collins, 12 vols., 1973.

* * *

Margaret Stuart Barry's reputation as a writer has come to rest upon her *Witch* stories, which have reached a wider reading and viewing public through their television dramatisation at peak children's viewing time.

Her earlier work shows talent and versatility and stands the test of time. Tommy Mac is the imaginative boy who believes that, in his teeming urban community, "there are adventures all around…All you have to do is to *look* for them." The *Woozy* tales are undemanding, but they have a lightness of wit that communicates to children of six to nine. The *Maggie Gumption* collections are delightfully quirky stories about a doll living in the attic of a large house populated by endearing eccentrics such as her rival Pinky Dars and Captain Bombast.

The joke at the center of the hilarious *Witch* books about Simon and his demonic crony is the friendship of a young boy and an apparently harmless old lady. She causes havoc at his school and within his community at the expense, usually, of the beleaguered adults. The fun is wry, ironic, rumbustious, sometimes nihilistic, but never condescending. Readers enjoy the humor that springs from the incongruous: the dear old lady is an anarchist! In her treatment of the teachers, in her behaviour in school, there's an upturning of the natural order of things. An early and brilliant story, *Boffy and the Teacher Eater,* also exploited the essential conservatism of classroom life and routines. Barry is good at depicting the defusion of social pretension. Simon's local do-gooder, Lady Fox-Custard, is ripe for exploitation, as is Maggie Gumption's superior friend Lady Serena Sumptious and the once-grand Ponsonby-Smythe who "could even say 'Ssh' poshly." The new boy who arrives at Tommy Mac's inner-city primary in a Bentley gets off to a bad start too.

Barry's writing proves that she has a fine ear tuned to the linguistic fun of word play, invented names, and jokes. The satisfaction for the reader—especially those called "reluctant"—is in being implicated in narrative which has its roots in the extended jokes that are playground lore. The art extends beyond the comedienne's when Barry draws upon the felt-life of schools and family banter. The confederacy of childhood is also splendidly caught. Simon's schoolmates (including Sally-Who's-on-Book-Four) and Tommy's community, who gather on the bombsite with their sandwiches for the ritual of the gang fight, are ebullient children of the 1980's, multi-

cultural in the widest sense, not caricatured or sentimentalised.

—Colin Mills

———

BAUM, L(yman) Frank. Also wrote as Floyd Akers; Laura Bancroft; John Estes Cooke; Hugh Fitzgerald; Suzanne Metcalf; Schuyler Staunton; Edith Van Dyne. American. Born in Chittenango, New York, 15 May 1856. Educated at schools in Syracuse, New York, and Peekskill Military Academy, New York, 1868–69. Married Maud Gage in 1882; four sons. Reporter, New York *World,* 1873–75; founding editor, *New Era,* Bradford, Pennsylvania, 1876; poultry farmer with B.W. Baum and Son: editor, *Poultry Record,* Syracuse, and columnist ("Poultry Yard"), *New York Farmer and Dairyman,* 1880; actor (as George Brooks) with May Roberts and the Sterling Comedy Company, New York, 1881; owner (as Louis F. Baum), Baum's Opera House, Richburg, New York, 1881–82; toured with his own repertory company, 1882–83; salesman, Baum's Ever-Ready Castorine axle grease, 1883–88; owner, Baum's Bazaar general store, Aberdeen, Dakota Territory, 1888–90; editor, Aberdeen *Saturday Pioneer,* 1890–91; reporter, Chicago *Post,* 1891; buyer, Siegel Cooper and Company, Chicago, 1891; salesman, Pitkin and Brooks crockery firm, Chicago, 1891–97; founder, National Association of Window Trimmers, 1897, and founding editor and publisher, *Show Window* magazine, Chicago, 1897–1902; founding director, Oz Film Manufacturing Company, Los Angeles, 1914–15. *Died 6 May 1919.*

PUBLICATIONS FOR CHILDREN

Fiction

A New Wonderland, illustrated by Frank Berbeck. New York, Russell, 1900; as *The Surprising Adventures of the Magical Monarch of Mo,* Indianapolis, Bobbs Merrill, 1903.
The Wonderful Wizard of Oz, illustrated by W.W. Denslow. Chicago, Hill, 1900; as *The New Wizard of Oz,* Indianapolis, Bobbs Merrill, 1903; London, Hodder and Stoughton, 1906; edited by Michael Patrick Hearn, New York, Schocken, 1983.
Dot and Tot of Merryland, illustrated by W.W. Denslow. Chicago, Hill, 1901.
The Master Key: An Electrical Fairy Tale, illustrated by Fanny Cory. Indianapolis, Bowen Merrill, 1901; London, Stevens and Brown, 1902.
The Life and Adventures of Santa Claus, illustrated by Mary Cowles Clark. Indianapolis, Bowen Merrill, and London, Stevens and Brown, 1902.
The Enchanted Island of Yew, illustrated by Fanny Cory. Indianapolis, Bobbs Merrill, 1903.
The Marvelous Land of Oz, illustrated by John R. Neill. Chicago, Reilly and Britton, and London, Revell, 1904.
Queen Zixi of Ix, illustrated by Frederick Richardson. New York, Century, 1905; London, Hodder and Stoughton, 1906.
The Woggle-Bug Book, illustrated by Ike Morgan. Chicago, Reilly and Britton, 1905.
John Dough and the Cherub, illustrated by John R. Neill. Chicago, Reilly and Britton, 1906; London, Constable, 1974.
Annabel (as Suzanne Metcalf). Chicago, Reilly and Britton, 1906.
Sam Steele's Adventures on Land and Sea (as Hugh Fitzgerald). Chicago, Reilly and Britton, 1906; as *The Boy Fortune Hunters in Alaska* (as Floyd Akers), 1908.
Twinkle Tales (as Laura Bancroft; *Bandit Jim Crow, Mr. Woodchuck,*

Prairie-Dog Town, Prince Mud-Turtle, Sugar-Loaf Mountain, Twinkle's Enchantment), illustrated by Maginel Wright Enright. Chicago, Reilly and Britton, 6 vols., 1906; as *Twinkle and Chubbins*, 1911.

Ozma of Oz, illustrated by John R. Neill. Chicago, Reilly and Britton, 1907; as *Princess Ozma of Oz*, London, Hutchinson, 1942.

Sam Steele's Adventures in Panama (as Hugh Fitzgerald). Chicago, Reilly and Britton, 1907; as *The Boy Fortune Hunters in Panama* (as Floyd Akers), 1908.

Policeman Bluejay (as Laura Bancroft), illustrated by Maginel Wright Enright. Chicago, Reilly and Britton, 1907; as *Babes in Birdland*, 1911.

Dorothy and the Wizard in Oz, illustrated by John R. Neill. Chicago, Reilly and Britton, 1908.

The Boy Fortune Hunters in Egypt [*China, Yucatan, the South Seas*] (as Floyd Akers). Chicago, Reilly and Britton, 4 vols., 1908–11.

The Road to Oz, illustrated by John R. Neill. Chicago, Reilly and Britton, 1909.

The Emerald City of Oz, illustrated by John R. Neill. Chicago, Reilly and Britton, 1910.

The Sea Fairies, illustrated by John R. Neill. Chicago, Reilly and Britton, 1911.

The Daring Twins, illustrated by Pauline Batchelder. Chicago, Reilly and Britton, 1911.

Sky Island, illustrated by John R. Neill. Chicago, Reilly and Britton, 1912.

Phoebe Daring, illustrated by Joseph Pierre Nuyttens. Chicago, Reilly and Britton, 1912.

The Patchwork Girl of Oz, illustrated by John R. Neill. Chicago, Reilly and Britton, 1913.

The Little Wizard Series (*Jack Pumpkinhead and the Sawhorse, Little Dorothy and Toto, Ozma and the Little Wizard, The Cowardly Lion and the Hungry Tiger, The Scarecrow and the Tin Woodman, Tik-Tok and the Nome King*). Chicago, Reilly and Britton, 6 vols., 1913; as *Little Wizard Stories of Oz*, Reilly and Britton, 1914; London, Simpkin, 1939.

Tik-Tok of Oz, illustrated by John R. Neill. Chicago, Reilly and Britton, 1914.

The Scarecrow of Oz, illustrated by John R. Neill. Chicago, Reilly and Britton, 1915.

Rinkitink in Oz, illustrated by John R. Neill. Chicago, Reilly and Britton, 1916.

The Snuggle Tales (*Little Bun Rabbit, Once upon a Time, The Yellow Hen, The Magic Cloak, The Ginger-Bread Man, Jack Pumpkinhead*), illustrated by John R. Neill. Chicago, Reilly and Britton, 6 vols., 1916–17; as *Oz-Man Tales*, 6 vols., 1920.

The Lost Princess of Oz, illustrated by John R. Neill. Chicago, Reilly and Britton, 1917.

The Tin Woodman of Oz, illustrated by John R. Neill. Chicago, Reilly and Britton, 1918.

The Magic of Oz, illustrated by John R. Neill. Chicago, Reilly and Lee, 1919; London, Armada, 1974.

Glinda of Oz, illustrated by John R. Neill. Chicago, Reilly and Lee, 1920.

Jaglon and the Tiger Fairies, illustrated by Dale Ulrey. Chicago, Reilly and Lee, 1953.

A Kidnapped Santa Claus. Indianapolis, Bobbs Merrill, 1961.

The Purple Dragon and Other Fantasies, edited by David L. Greene, illustrated by Tim Kirk. Lakemont, Georgia, Fictioneer, 1976.

Fiction as Edith Van Dyne

Aunt Jane's Nieces [*Abroad, at Millville, at Work, in Society, and Uncle John, on Vacation, on the Ranch, Out West, in the Red Cross*]. Chicago, Reilly and Britton, 10 vols., 1906–15.

The Flying Girl [*and Her Chum*]. Chicago, Reilly and Britton, 2 vols., 1911–12.

Mary Louise [*in the Country, Solves a Mystery, and the Liberty Girls, Adopts a Soldier*]. Chicago, Reilly and Britton, 4 vols., and Reilly and Lee, 1 vol., 1916–19.

Plays

The Wizard of Oz, music by Paul Tietjens, lyrics by Baum, adaptation of the novel by Baum (produced Chicago, 1902; revised version, as *There Is Something New under the Sun*, produced New York, 1903).

The Woggle-Bug, music by Frederic Chapin, adaptation of the novel *The Marvelous Land of Oz* by Baum (produced Chicago, 1905).

The Tik-Tok Man of Oz, music by Louis F. Gottschalk, adaptation of the story *Ozma of Oz* by Baum (produced Los Angeles, 1913).

Verse

By the Candelabra's Glare, illustrated by W. W. Denslow. Privately printed, 1898.

Father Goose, His Book, illustrated by W. W. Denslow. Chicago, Hill, and London, Werner, 1899.

The Army Alphabet, illustrated by Harry Kennedy. Chicago, Hill, 1900.

The Navy Alphabet, illustrated by Harry Kennedy. Chicago, Hill, 1900.

The Songs of Father Goose, music by Alberta N. Hall, illustrated by W. W. Denslow. Chicago, Hill, 1900.

Father Goose's Year Book: Quaint Quacks and Feathery Shafts for Mature Children, illustrated by Walter Enright. Chicago, Reilly and Britton, 1907.

Other

Mother Goose in Prose, illustrated by Maxfield Parrish. Chicago, Way and Williams, 1897; London, Duckworth, 1899.

American Fairy Tales, illustrated by Ike Morgan and others. Chicago, Hill, 1901; London, Constable, 1978; augmented edition, Indianapolis, Bobbs Merrill, 1908.

L. Frank Baum's Juvenile Speaker (miscellany), illustrated by John R. Neill and others. Chicago, Reilly and Britton, 1910; as *Baum's Own Book for Children*, 1912.

Animal Fairy Tales. Chicago, International Wizard of Oz Club, 1969.

PUBLICATIONS FOR ADULTS

Novels

The Fate of a Crown (as Schuyler Staunton). Chicago, Reilly and Britton, and London, Revell, 1905.

Daughters of Destiny (as Schuyler Staunton). Chicago, Reilly and Britton, 1906.

Tamawaca Folks (as John Estes Cooke). Macatawa, Michigan, Macatawa Press, 1907.

The Last Egyptian (published anonymously). Philadelphia, Stern, and London, Sisley, 1908.

Plays

The Maid of Arran, music and lyrics by Baum, adaptation of the novel *A Princess of Thule* by William Black (also director: produced Syracuse and New York City, 1882).

Matches (produced Richburg, New York, 1882).

Kilmorne; or, O'Connor's Dream (produced Syracuse, 1888).
Stagecraft: The Adventures of a Strictly Moral Man, music by Louis F. Gottschalk (produced Santa Barbara, California, 1914).
The Uplift of Lucifer; or, Raising Hell, music by Louis F. Gottschalk (produced Santa Barbara, California, 1915). Edited by Manuel Weltman, privately printed, 1963.
The Uplifters' Minstrels, music by Byron Gay (produced Del Mar, California, 1916).
The Orpheus Road Company, music by Louis F. Gottschalk (produced Coronado Beach, California, 1917).

Screenplays: *The Fairylogue and Radio-Plays,* 1908; *The Patchwork Girl of Oz,* 1914; *The Magic Cloak of Oz,* 1914; *The Babes in the Wood,* 1914; *The Last Egyptian,* 1914; *The New Wizard of Oz,* 1915.

Verse

The High-Jinks of L. Frank Baum (songs for Uplifters). Chicago, Wizard Press, 1959.

Other

The Book of the Hamburgs: A Brief Treatise upon the Mating, Rearing, and Management of the Different Varieties of Hamburgs. Hartford, Connecticut, Stoddard, 1886.
The Art of Decorating Dry Goods Windows and Interiors. Chicago, Show Window Publishing Company, 1900.
Our Landlady (*Saturday Pioneer* columns). Mitchell, South Dakota Writers' Project, 1941.

*

Bibliography: in *The Annotated Wizard of Oz* edited by Michael Patrick Hearn, New York, Potter, 1973.

Manuscript Collection: Columbia University, New York.

Critical Studies: *The Wizard of Oz and Who He Was* edited by Russel Nye and Martin Gardner, East Lansing, Michigan State University Press, 1957; *To Please a Child: A Biography of L. Frank Baum, Royal Historian of Oz* by Frank Joslyn Baum and Russell P. MacFall, Chicago, Reilly and Lee, 1961; *Wonderful Wizard, Marvelous Land* by Raylyn Moore, Bowling Green, Ohio, Popular Press, 1974.

*   *   *

L. Frank Baum has virtually been forced upon scholars and critics by the enduring popularity of *The Wonderful Wizard of Oz.* One result has been the discovery of an unexpected high quality elsewhere in the works of a prolific and uneven writer. And Baum was the kind of writer whose virtues are best appreciated only as one freely admits his shortcomings and his failures. Not that Baum had not had his early partisans. Edward Wagenknecht contributed a study, *Utopia Americana,* by 1929, and James Thurber praised Baum in 1934. But other comments virtually dismissed him as a poor stylist and an unimaginative tale-spinner.

Baum was indeed a poor stylist, but the stilted vocabulary and sentence structure of his early work relaxed considerably by the end of his career. More to the point perhaps is the size of his output. The least of it deserves the neglect it has received. Indeed, it is difficult to believe that the man who wrote the delightful fantasy *Queen Zixi of Ix* also offered the contrived and turgid *Dorothy and the Wizard in Oz.* A further problem has been that Baum wrote series books, and the Oz series kept Oz a vivid and interesting place. But children's series books have traditionally been considered unworthy of any

critic's time.

When Baum was good he was very good. And sometimes he was mysteriously good. It is true that in the *Wizard,* the Scarecrow already has the brainpower he seeks from the Wizard, the Tin Woodman already shows the goodness of heart he wants, and the Cowardly Lion is naturally brave. They need only be made aware of their true qualities. And it is clear that Dorothy, after being whirled away from a harsh and lonely existence on the Kansas plains and dropped down into a land of colour and adventure, most wanted (and needed) to find a way home again. But otherwise the effect and meaning of the *Wizard* remain somewhat elusive. If self-reliance is really the message, what about the magic of the slippers? And the simple *accident* of the Wicked Witch's death?

The Marvelous Land of Oz seems more overt and more adult in its intended meaning: it burlesques the suffragette movement. There is some questionable plotting in the book—the six-chapter episode that introduces that memorable pedant, the "highly magnified" and "thoroughly educated" Wogglebug, is otherwise extrinsic and expendable. And in the end, a young girl (Ozma) who had been thought to be a young boy (Tip) is made ruler of Oz—a mysterious conclusion for a satire on feminism. Indeed, the criticism that Oz is a land populated by little men, hollow men, stuffed men, and humbugs ruled over by sweet little girls but where the real power belongs to a strong female figure (Glinda) seems answerable only if one assumes that Baum's tongue was planted firmly and deliberately in his cheek.

The Oz series does include several books in which contrived characters and meandering geography attempt to substitute for plot or even relevant incident. The sprightly *The Patchwork Girl of Oz* rescues the series with interesting characters, broad comedy, and a sustained quest. The stories continued with respectable contributions thereafter, but Baum did have a penchant for repeating himself. *Tik-Tok of Oz* is an amalgam of elements from *The Marvelous Land of Oz* and *Ozma of Oz;* the Frogman of *The Lost Princess of Oz* is another humbug magician.

Thurber pointed out that although Baum rejected "heartache" and "fear" in his "Introduction" to the *Wizard,* we may be thankful that he did not in his tale. Indeed, the Tin Woodman simply chops up some attacking wolves in Chapter XII. And in a true horror, Baum revealed that the Woodman, as an inept forester, gradually became metal because he scarred and chopped away his own limbs. In *The Tin Woodman of Oz* he discovers his own discarded limbs and severed head in his tinsmith's workrooms!

Queen Zixi of Ix is a beautifully paced, more traditional fairy tale of a magic cloak and three wishes which are consistently and sometimes humorously misused. It has been justly called Baum's best book. And *The Life and Adventures of Santa Claus* is an episodic and sustained pagan history of the Christmas figure. Baum's short stories are also uneven but the best of them are equally praiseworthy. Indeed, a collection that included "Jugger-jook" (Baum's Peter Rabbit variant), "A Kidnapped Santa Claus" (partly based on the longer version), "The King Who Changed His Mind," "The Runaway Shadows," "The Yellow Ryl," "A Box of Robbers," and "The Witchcraft of Mary-Marie" might well make a case for Baum as what he once said he hoped to be, an American Hans Christian Andersen. One tale, "Prince Mud-Turtle," is worth dwelling on as a comment on Baum's arbitrary treatment of magic. It is his version of "The Frog Prince," but whereas in the original a tenacious love turns ugliness into beauty, in Baum's story the transformation simply happens. Perhaps we should remind ourselves that magic, even the magic of love, is fine, but self-reliance and a realistic self-knowledge must precede the true gift of love.

A great loss in the Baum canon is represented by *Rinkitink in Oz.* As originally written, it was a beautifully conceived tale of young prince Inga who rescued his imprisoned parents and, symbolically, entered his own manhood. To bring it into the Oz series, Baum had Dorothy take over at the moment of Inga's triumph (another female dea ex machina), utterly (if implicitly) emasculating his hero. If the original manuscript of *Rinkitink* had survived, surely we would have another Baum story to place beside the *Wizard, Queen Zixi, Santa Claus,* and the best of the short tales.

—Martin Williams

BAWDEN, Nina (née Mabey). British. Born in London, 19 January 1925. Educated at Ilford County High School; Somerville College, Oxford, B.A. 1946, M.A. 1951; Salzburg Seminar in American Studies, 1960. Married 1) H.W. Bawden in 1946, two sons (one deceased); 2) the broadcast executive A.S. Kark in 1954, one daughter. Assistant, Town and Country Planning Association, 1946–47; Justice of the Peace for Surrey, 1968–76. Regular reviewer, *Daily Telegraph,* London. Member, P.E.N. Executive Committee, 1968–71; President, Society of Women Writers and Journalists. Recipient: *Guardian* award, 1976; *Yorkshire Post* award, 1976. Fellow, Royal Society of Literature, 1970. Address: 22 Noel Road, London N1 8HA, England.

PUBLICATIONS FOR CHILDREN

Fiction

Devil by the Sea (for adults). London, Collins, 1957; Philadelphia, Lippincott, 1959; abridged edition (for children), London, Gollancz, and Lippincott, 1976.
The Secret Passage. London, Gollancz, 1963; as *The House of Secrets,* Philadelphia, Lippincott, 1964.
On the Run. London, Gollancz, 1964; as *Three on the Run,* Philadelphia, Lippincott, 1965.
The White Horse Gang. London, Gollancz, and Philadelphia, Lippincott, 1966.
The Witch's Daughter, illustrated by Shirley Hughes. London, Gollancz, and Philadelphia, Lippincott, 1966.
A Handful of Thieves. London, Gollancz, and Philadelphia, Lippincott, 1967.
The Runaway Summer. London, Gollancz, and Philadelphia, Lippincott, 1969.
Squib, illustrated by Shirley Hughes. London, Gollancz, and Philadelphia, Lippincott, 1971.
Carrie's War. London, Gollancz, and Philadelphia, Lippincott, 1973.
The Peppermint Pig, illustrated by Alexy Pendle. London, Gollancz, and Philadelphia, Lippincott, 1975.
Rebel on a Rock. London, Gollancz, and Philadelphia, Lippincott, 1978.
The Robbers, illustrated by Charles Keeping. London, Gollancz, and New York, Lothrop, 1979.
Kept in the Dark. London, Gollancz, and New York, Lothrop, 1982.
The Finding. London, Gollancz, and New York, Lothrop, 1985.
Princess Alice, illustrated by Phillida Gili. London, Deutsch, 1985.
Keeping Henry, illustrated by Ian Newsham. London, Gollancz, 1988; as *Henry,* New York, Lothrop, 1988.
The Outside Child. London, Gollancz, 1989.

Other

William Tell, illustrated by Pascale Allamand. London, Cape, and New York, Lothrop, 1981.

St. Francis of Assisi, illustrated by Pascale Allamand. London, Cape, and New York, Lothrop, 1983.

PUBLICATIONS FOR ADULTS

Novels

Who Calls the Tune. London, Collins, 1953; as *Eyes of Green,* New York, Morrow, 1953.
The Odd Flamingo. London, Collins, 1954.
Change Here for Babylon. London, Collins, 1955.
The Solitary Child. London, Collins, 1956; New York, Lancer, 1966.
Just Like a Lady. London, Longman, 1960; as *Glass Slippers Always Pinch,* Philadelphia, Lippincott, 1960.
In Honour Bound. London, Longman, 1961.
Tortoise by Candlelight. London, Longman, and New York, Harper, 1963.
Under the Skin. London, Longman, and New York, Harper, 1964.
A Little Love, A Little Learning. London, Longman, 1965; New York, Harper, 1966.
A Woman of My Age. London, Longman, and New York, Harper, 1967.
The Grain of Truth. London, Longman, and New York, Harper, 1968.
The Birds on the Trees. London, Longman, and New York, Harper, 1970.
Anna Apparent. London, Longman, and New York, Harper, 1972.
George Beneath a Paper Moon. London, Allen Lane, and New York, Harper, 1974.
Afternoon of a Good Woman. London, Macmillan, 1976; New York, Harper, 1977.
Familiar Passions. London, Macmillan, and New York, Morrow, 1979.
Walking Naked. London, Macmillan, 1981; New York, St. Martin's Press, 1982.
The Ice House. London, Macmillan, and New York, St. Martin's Press, 1983.
Circles of Deceit. London, Macmillan, and New York, St. Martin's Press, 1987.

*

Nina Bawden comments:
I consider my books for children as important as my adult work, and in some ways more challenging.

* * *

Nina Bawden is one of the very few children's writers who will admit to making a conscious adjustment to writing for children. Perhaps because she also writes for adults she is singularly free from the temptation to write for adults in the guise of children's books. Plot summaries of Bawden's early work might seem like run-of-the-mill escapism. The jewel thieves in *The Witch's Daughter,* the children-catch-villains theme of *A Handful of Thieves,* the Prime Minister's son saved from political kidnapping in *On the Run,* are typical examples. But Bawden is a subtle writer, who plays her themes with a difference. In *The Witch's Daughter* one of the children is blind; the Prime Minister's son in *On the Run* comes not from Ruritania but modern Africa; another of Bawden's runaways is an illegal Pakistani immigrant. Bawden's characters may have improbable adventures, but they never think, feel, or say unchildlike or improbable things. Their preoccupations, their relationships with the adults around them, their faults as well as their innocence and courage are entirely realistic and believable. This is childhood seen with particular clarity. There is also a very distinctive tone to Bawden's sympathy—a particular tenderness for children having a rough time, and for not very likeable children. Mary in *The Runaway Summer* is a good example. Lonely and miserable because her parents are getting divorced, she is beastly to her kind aunt, and even steals, and yet we never lose sympathy with her.

It is this element in Bawden's work that flowers in *Squib,* the story of a grossly neglected child. There are brilliant insights in this book—especially the pathetic muddle of half-baked fears (of walking in the woods, of witches) which overlie the awful knowledge that Squib has been shackled in a laundry basket, and simply confuse the children about what is real and what is not, so that they hardly know if they are playing or rescuing a real victim. However there is also a good deal of the apparatus of adventure that had been so strong an element in Bawden's work so far—a burning tower, a disastrous raid on Squib's caravan, and so to a happy ending that involves bringing in the adults to get things right. The emotional tone of this uncomplicated complication sits rather uneasily with the real subject of *Squib*—the compassion and fear of a little girl, the courage of a little boy, and the suffering of Squib himself.

With the appearance of *Carrie's War* it became clear Squib had been a transitional book. Carrie and her brother are evacuees in a Welsh village with a narrow, bigoted shopkeeper and his kindly, browbeaten sister. They would be miserable without the friendship of other villagers, especially Hepzibah, who feeds them love, food, and stories. Once more the plot concerns the precarious hold on reality of an imaginative child. Convinced by Hepzibah's tales Carrie comes to believe that she has committed a dreadful crime, and she carries the load of grief and guilt with her into adult life. Only when she brings her own children back with her to the village can the truth emerge and all be made well again. In this book Bawden has dispensed with the drama of external situations—there are no crooks, no villains but Carrie's own guilty fears. In a notable shift of feeling, Carrie reaches a glimpse of sympathy and understanding even for the horrible tyrant Mr. Evans. The book is a portrait of a whole community of people, their oddities and their feuds, seen through the bemused and only half-comprehending eyes of childhood. In this profound and affectionate book one has a sense of Bawden putting out her full strength as a writer as never before, and finding a way of writing with full complexity and delicacy still within the reach of children.

In *The Peppermint Pig* which followed, the mature, subtle, and fundamentally sunny atmosphere of *Carrie's War* was brought to a peak of achievement. *The Peppermint Pig* is about the sojourn in a country village of an Edwardian family whose father has gone abroad to seek his fortune. But the true subject is the painful relationship of happiness, hope, and the inexorable passing of time. These themes are delicately explored in the relationship of the children to their changed circumstances, the absence of their father, and the growth, flourishing, and death of Johnny, the pet pig. All the while the book with consummate skill plays on the difference of scale in the life of children and adults, bringing the two perspectives into brilliant direct contrast only on the last page. *The Peppermint Pig* is a small masterpiece.

Since *The Peppermint Pig* Bawden has to some extent resumed her earlier style, though not without differences. In *Rebel on a Rock* Carrie and her family visit a foreign country (a thinly disguised Greece) in which a dictator is in power and a revolution is simmering. In *The Robbers* a little boy brought up with all the appurtenances of privilege makes friends with a boy deprived of all material wealth but rich in affection. Trying to help the poorer boy's family they get into trouble and the law takes a different view of them because of their different social class. In both these books there is a return to a simpler texture and characters of instant credibility having child-sized adventures. But unlike her earlier books is the seriousness of

the backgrounds—political revolution played against family loyalty, or the unfairness of justice—and the consequent large import of childish escapades. A sad implied comment is made on children's adventure stories; this is what would really happen if children intervened in revolutions, or tried to restore the family fortunes.

With *Kept in the Dark* Bawden returns to a subject explored earlier in *Devil by the Sea,* published originally for adults, and then republished for children in a changed climate of opinion. The subject is the helplessness of children if the adults around them are not both beneficent and competent. The children in *Kept in the Dark* are being looked after by grandparents who are themselves being preyed upon by a half-uncle who bullies and threatens with seeming impunity. The children's terror and confusion are strongly conveyed; locked in the child's viewpoint the book conveys only partly the nature of the villain's badness, and his adult victims' weakness.

The Finding neatly inverts the typical Bawden statement of relations between adults and children—which has gradually emerged as her quintessential theme. The fantasy of adults—the machinations of a lethally awful grandmother, and the scheming of incompetent crooks—gets Alex, an adopted foundling, into trouble. Only his sister's childish understanding of his inner world can provide the means to find him. Once again a thriller plot is combined with satisfying characterisation to provide Bawden's typical balance of readability and depth.

Keeping Henry is a new departure. It is not so much fiction as very lightly fictionalised recollection, in which the author appears as herself, in her own family, telling us the true story of Henry, the family's pet squirrel, which they kept on a Welsh farm where they spent part of the war. The story is told with perfect simplicity and clarity, and certainly has the shapeliness and accessibility of Bawden's true fiction. Additionally it is fascinating to see the origins in the author's childhood experience of the material of both *Carrie's War* and *The Peppermint Pig,* each of which is illuminated by *Keeping Henry,* and each of which in turn throws light on the later book. *The Outside Child* like *Keeping Henry* is based on an autobiographical recollection, this time one of considerable mystery and force. Jane is brought up by aunts while her father, a seaman, comes and goes on his ship. Visiting him she sees a picture of his other family, her secret brother and sister. Filled with love and yearning for them she is reduced to childish spying, abetted by her friend. At the heart of the story is the selfishness and silliness of an emotional adult; the ending can only be cautiously happy. Bawden can now command the gripping readability of her early work without resorting to anything but wholly credible psychological drama. Balancing the different views of children and adults, whose relations have been gradually emerging over her whole career as a central subject of her writing for both adults and children, she never unfairly prefers an adult view. Deeply ingrained in this story is the sense of what kind of moral benchmark it is for adults to have the care of children.

From *The Secret Passage* to *The Outside Child* there is a very large development and flowering of Bawden's talent; it can still be said of her that more than any other contemporary writer for the young she understands and respects the childhood of her readers as well as that of her characters.

—Jill Paton Walsh

—————

BAXTER, Valerie. See MEYNELL, Laurence.

—————

BEACHCROFT, Nina. British. Born in London, 10 November 1931; daughter of the writer T.O. Beachcroft. Educated at Wimbledon High School; St. Hilda's College, Oxford, 1950–53, B.A. (honours) in English 1953. Married Richard Gardner in 1954; two daughters. Sub-editor, *Argosy,* London, 1953–55, and *Radio Times,* London, 1955–57. Agent: David Higham Associates Ltd., 5–8 Lower John Street, London W1R 4HA. Address: The Cottage, Datchworth Green, Knebworth, Hertfordshire, England.

PUBLICATIONS FOR CHILDREN

Fiction

Well Met by Witchlight. London, Heinemann, 1972; New York, Atheneum, 1973.
Under the Enchanter. London, Heinemann, 1974.
Cold Christmas: A Ghost Story. London, Heinemann, 1974.
A Spell of Sleep. London, Heinemann, 1976.
A Visit to Folly Castle. London, Heinemann, 1977.
A Farthing for the Fair, illustrated by Anthony Colbert. London, Heinemann, 1978.
The Wishing People. London, Heinemann, 1980; New York, Dutton, 1982.
The Genie and Her Bottle. London, Heinemann, 1983.
Beyond World's End. London, Heinemann, 1985.

*

Nina Beachcroft comments:

I have written, on and off, for most of my life. I wrote short stories, of which a few were published, until I worked on a short story magazine, when reading too many soon killed the urge to write them. I wrote two long unpublished (and unpublishable) adult novels, and it was not until my first daughter was about eight that I thought of trying something for children. I wrote three before I eventually got *Well Met by Witchlight* accepted by Heinemann. In trying very hard to please children, I found I was pleasing myself. I enjoy writing fantasy; fairy tales have always appealed to me, as has the best kind of science fiction. It's the imaginative idea behind the story that gets me off the ground; after that, my concern is, I suppose, to work it out in some of its implications and to tell a fast-moving, exciting story, always with its feet in everyday reality even if its head is in the clouds.

*   *   *

With the exception of *A Farthing for the Fair,* an historical novel written for the Long Ago Children Series, Nina Beachcroft's stories are tales of enchantment that appeal mainly to 8- to 10-year-olds. The underlying pattern is of an unexpected encounter—in a wood, on holiday, in the house next door, through a broken fence—with a mysterious stranger through whom the children are put in danger from some lurking evil. A satisfactory outcome is, of course, assured. In *Well Met by Witchlight* a good witch helps to fill in while Granny is in hospital, comforting the anxious children, assisting them to defeat the evil witch and restoring Granny to health. As the latter returns, the good witch conveniently, but also calmly and reassuringly, retreats into a hibernation which may become death. In *Cold Christmas* the sad little ghost who is seeking to allay the evil that killed her also helps Josephine to make contact with other guests in the chilly Georgian house where her family is spending Christmas. But although in these books the children have a lively individuality, there remains a sense of contrivance, a lack of some inner logic in the intrusion of the supernatural element which prevents satisfactory suspension of disbelief. *Under the Enchanter* suffers less from this

problem; it is powerful enough to be convincing, as terrified Laura battles alone to save her brother from the enchanter's fatal spells, her parents being "useless and unnoticing," strangely obtuse and even hostile when she tries to tell them something is seriously wrong with him. In *A Spell of Sleep* it is the relentless. mean-spirited, petty malice reawakened from 800 years ago that causes untold misery and threatens to drive the Turners from their home before the children's persistence finally wins them the appropriate help. Here there is a strong element of reality in the quarrel between neighbours to help carry conviction. *A Visit to Folly Castle* brings a new danger: the attractive, imaginative, and lively Sandra, who longs for a friend and fascinates Emma with all her moods and strange alien powers, nevertheless nearly betrays Emma's young brother to her parents' sinister plots.

After so much fear lurking uneasily behind the normal façade of life, it is almost a relief to turn to *The Wishing People.* For although the wooden figures on Martha's weatherhouse have the gift of granting wishes which, in true folk tradition, rarely turn out as expected, the general tone of this book is happier, more optimistic. Mr. and Mrs. Tom, the wishing people, work together with the children towards an acceptance of their individual imperfections: there is a consequent sense of growth in self-awareness on all sides which includes an understanding that reality can actually be more satisfying than dreams. *The Genie and Her Bottle,* inspired by *The Arabian Nights,* also explores wish granting. It was an enterprising idea to have a female genie for a change, though Leila is no credit to her sex, being a bored, supercilious, spiteful, and capricious Arabian princess, with thoroughly evil intent. But the children to whom she appears are more conventional—a brother and sister who are neglected by their upwardly mobile nouveau riche parents—and in spite of some inventive and comic episodes this is one of the more ordinary and derivative stories. *Beyond World's End,* on the other hand, inspired this time by John Wyndham's *The Kraken Wakes,* uses its material more imaginatively. Both Chris and his friend Jane, who accompanies him in his encounter with the extraterrestrial beings, have an engaging complexity of character and motivation, and their adventures are finely integrated into a story that reflects the ambivalences and untidiness of real life as well as providing an exciting and compelling science fiction story line.

All these stories minister to the child's perception of the unpredictability of the world, and his uneasy sense that adults are often unaware of or indifferent to their children's fears, leaving them to struggle unaided—perhaps even actively hindering them in their fight against the unseen evil they sense around them. And in spite of the conventionality of some of the plots there is a lively interest in the variety of detail and situation, and in the author's keen depiction of the fluctuations within individual relationships.

—Winifred Whitehead

BEAMAN, S(ydney) G(eorge) Hulme. British. Born in Tottenham, London, in 1886. Educated at Heatherley Studio, London. Married Maud Mary Poltock; one son and one daughter. Actor; artist; toymaker from 1914; writer for BBC Radio, London. *Died 4 February 1932.*

PUBLICATIONS FOR CHILDREN (illustrated by the author)

Fiction

The Road to Toytown. London, Oxford University Press, 1925.

Jerry and Joe.   London, Oxford University Press, 1925.
Trouble in Toyland.   London, Oxford University Press, 1925.
The Wooden Knight.   London, Oxford University Press, 1925.
Out of the Ark Books (*Teddy's New Job, Wally the Kangaroo, Grunty the Pig, Jimmy the Baby Elephant, Ham and the Egg, Jenny the Giraffe*).   London and New York, Warne, 6 vols., 1927.
The Tale of the Magician.   London, Oxford University Press, 1928.
The Tales of the Inventor.   London, Oxford University Press, 1928.
The Tale of Captain Brass, The Pirate.   London, Oxford University Press, 1928.
Tales of Toytown.   London, Oxford University Press, 1928; as *Ernest the Policeman,* New York, Oxford University Press, 1930.
John Trusty.   London, Collins, 1929.
Wireless in Toytown.   London, Collins, 1930.
The Toytown Book.   London and New York, Warne, 1930.
The Toytown Mystery.   London, Collins, 1932.
The Mayor's Sea Voyage.   London, Collins, 1938.
Stories from Toytown.   London, Oxford University Press, 1938.
The Arkville Dragon.   London, Collins, 1938.
Dirty Work at the Dog and Whistle, illustrated by Ernest Noble.   London, Lapworth, 1942.
Tea for Two, illustrated by Ernest Noble.   London, Lapworth, 1942.
The Brave Deed of Ernest the Policeman, illustrated by Ernest Noble.   London, Lapworth, 1942; as *Ernest the Brave,* London, Oldbourne, 1958.
Pistols for Two, illustrated by Ernest Noble.   London, Lapworth, 1942.
Mr. Noah's Holiday, illustrated by Ernest Noble.   London, Lapworth, 1942.
The Adventures of Larry the Lamb (*Frightfulness in the Theatre Royal, Dreadful Doings in Ark Street, Golf (Toytown Rules), Mr. Growser Moves*), illustrated by Ernest Noble.   London, Lapworth, 4 vols., 1943; *Mr. Growser Moves* published as *Mr. Growser Moves House,* London, Oldbourne, 1962.
Larry the Lamb.   London, Collins, 1946.
The Extraordinary Affair of Ernest the Policeman, illustrated by Ernest Noble.   London, Lapworth, 1947.
A Portrait of the Mayor, illustrated by Ernest Noble.   London, Lapworth, 1947.
The Disgraceful Business at Mrs. Goose's, with Betty Hulme Beaman, illustrated by Kenneth Lovell.   London, Oldbourne, 1958.
The Enchanted Ark, with Betty Hulme Beaman, illustrated by Kenneth Lovell.   London, Oldbourne, 1958.
Toytown Goes West, with Betty Hulme Beaman, illustrated by Kenneth Lovell.   London, Oldbourne, 1958.
The Theatre Royal and Punch and Judy, with Betty Hulme Beaman, illustrated by Kenneth Lovell.   London, Oldbourne, 1958.
A Toytown Christmas Party, illustrated by Kenneth Lovell.   London, Oldbourne, 1961.
The Toytown Treasure, with Betty Hulme Beaman, illustrated by Kenneth Lovell.   London, Oldbourne, 1961.
Larry the Plumber, with Betty Hulme Beaman, illustrated by Betty Larom.   London, Oldbourne, 1961.
The Conversion of Mrs. Growser, illustrated by Betty Larom.   London, Oldbourne, 1961.
The Great Toytown War, illustrated by Betty Larom.   London, Oldbourne, 1961.
How the Radio Came to Toytown, illustrated by Kenneth Lovell.   London, Oldbourne, 1961.
The Showing Up of Larry the Lamb, illustrated by Kenneth Lovell.   London, Oldbourne, 1963.
The Toytown Pantomine, illustrated by H. Faithful.   London, Oldbourne, 1963.
The Book of Toytown and Larry the Lamb.   London, Harrap, 1979.

Plays

Radio Series: *Toytown,* 1929–32.

Other

Aladdin, Retold.   London, Lane, 1924; New York, McBride, 1925.
The Seven Voyages of Sinbad the Sailor, Retold.   London, Lane, and New York, McBride, 1926.

*

Illustrator: *The Strange Case of Dr. Jekyll and Mr. Hyde* by Robert Louis Stevenson, 1930.

*   *   *

S.G. Hulme Beaman was creator, writer, and illustrator of the magic land of Toytown and all its enchanting characters, including Larry the Lamb, Dennis the Dachshund, Mr. Growser, Ernest the Policeman, the Mayor, the Magician, the Inventor, Mrs. Goose, et al. After his first collection, *Tales of Toytown,* was published in 1928, it caught the eye of May E. Jenkin, better-known as "Elizabeth" of the popular BBC radio programme Children's Hour, who produced it on the air with great success, in 1929. The plays were extremely successful and Beaman was commissioned to write more, turning out 36 stories over the next three years, until his untimely death in 1932 at the age of 45. The stories were broadcast in Children's Hour many times over the next 30 years and were firm favourites with children of all ages. They also appeared in book form, later winning popularity with a new generation when they appeared in a TV series in 1972, when the characters also appeared in a new children's comic-paper, *Toytown.*

Beaman's illustrations were unique inasmuch as he first carved his characters from wood, arranged them in his home-made model theatre, lit them, and then drew the resulting lay-out, so that his creations always appeared to have a wooden, but three-dimensional look about them.

The Toytown stories came over far more successfully on radio than on the printed page (probably because, after all, the vast majority were specifically written to be heard) and were performed in Children's Hour flawlessly and with enormous good humour by a talented cast. Derek McCulloch ("Uncle Mac"), Head of Children's Hour, played the role of Larry the Lamb, as well as narrating the plays.

The central figures in the Toytown tales were usually the mischievous pair, Larry the Lamb and his German-accented friend Dennis the Dachshund, who were forever getting themselves into complicated scrapes and incurring the wrath of the pompous Mayor, the irritable Mr. Growser ("It's dis-graceful and it ought not to be allowed!") and the rural-voiced, deliberate Ernest the Policeman ("I can see some names and addresses must be taken down!"). The delightfully eccentric Magician and Inventor (whose spells and inventions were always going wrong and ending in disaster) were also well to the fore.

In his three-dozen stories and radio plays about Toytown, S.G. Hulme Beaman created a magical and gently amusing miniature world which will remain affectionately in the memories of at least three generations.

—Brian Doyle

BEATTY, John and Patricia. Americans. **BEATTY, John (Louis):** Born in Portland, Oregon, 24 January 1922. Educated at Reed College, Portland, B.A. 1943; Stanford University, California, M.A. 1947; University of Washington, Seattle, Ph.D. in history 1953. Served in the United States Army 1943–45: Silver Star, Purple Heart. Married Patricia Robbins (i.e., Patricia Beatty) in 1950; one daughter. Instructor, Reed College, 1947–49, University of Washington, 1950–52, and University of Delaware, Newark, 1952–53; Assistant Professor, 1953–59, Associate Professor, 1959–75, and Professor of History, 1975, University of California, Riverside. Recipient: American Philosophical Society grant, 1959. *Died 23 March 1975.* **BEATTY, Patricia (née Robbins).** Has also written as Jean Bartholomew: Born in Portland, Oregon, 26 August 1922. Educated at Reed College, Portland, B.A. in history and English 1944; University of Idaho, Moscow, 1947–50; University of Washington, Seattle, 1951. Married 1) John Beatty in 1950 (died 1975), one daughter; 2) Carl G. Uhr in 1977. English and history teacher, Coeur d'Alene High School, Idaho, 1947–50; librarian, E.I. du Pont Company, Wilmington, Delaware, 1952–53, and Riverside Public Library, California, 1953–57; Instructor in Creative Writing, University of California, Riverside, 1967–68, and Los Angeles, 1968–69. Recipient: Western Writers of America award, 1984, 1987; O'Dell award, 1988. Address: 5085 Rockledge Drive, Riverside, California 92506, U.S.A.

PUBLICATIONS FOR CHILDREN

Fiction

At the Seven Stars, illustrated by Douglas Gorsline. New York, Macmillan, 1963; London, Chatto and Windus, 1966.
Campion Towers. New York, Macmillan, 1965; London, Chatto and Windus, 1967.
A Donkey for the King, illustrated by Ann Siberell. New York, Macmillan, 1966.
The Royal Dirk, illustrated by Franz Altschuler. New York, Morrow, 1966.
The Queen's Wizard. New York, Macmillan, 1967.
Witch Dog, illustrated by Franz Altschuler. New York, Morrow, 1968.
Pirate Royal. New York, Macmillan, and London, Collier Macmillan, 1969.
King's Knight's Pawn. New York, Morrow, 1971.
Holdfast. New York, Morrow, 1972.
Master Rosalind. New York, Morrow, 1974.
Who Comes to King's Mountain? New York, Morrow, 1975.

Fiction by Patricia Beatty

Indian Canoe-Maker, illustrated by Barbara Beaudreau. Caldwell, Idaho, Caxton Press, 1960.
Bonanza Girl, illustrated by Liz Dauber. New York, Morrow, 1962.
The Nickel-Plated Beauty, illustrated by Liz Dauber. New York, Morrow, 1964.
Squaw Dog, illustrated by Franz Altschuler. New York, Morrow, 1965.
The Queen's Own Grove, illustrated by Liz Dauber. New York, Morrow, 1966.
The Lady from Black Hawk, illustrated by Robert Frankenberg. New York, McGraw Hill, 1967.
Me, California Perkins, illustrated by Liz Dauber. New York, Morrow, 1968.
Blue Stars Watching. New York, Morrow, 1969.
Station Four. Chicago, Science Research Associates, 1969.
Hail Columbia, illustrated by Liz Dauber. New York, Morrow, 1970.

The Sea Pair, illustrated by Franz Altschuler. New York, Morrow, 1970.
A Long Way to Whiskey Creek. New York, Morrow, 1971.
O the Red Rose Tree, illustrated by Liz Dauber. New York, Morrow, 1972.
The Bad Bell of San Salvador. New York, Morrow, 1973.
Red Rock over the River. New York, Morrow, 1973.
How Many Miles to Sundown. New York, Morrow, 1974.
Rufus, Red Rufus, illustrated by Ted Lewin. New York, Morrow, 1975.
By Crumbs, It's Mine! New York, Morrow, 1976.
Something to Shout About. New York, Morrow, 1976.
Billy Bedamned, Long Gone By. New York, Morrow, 1977.
I Want My Sunday, Stranger! New York, Morrow, 1977.
Just Some Weeds from the Wilderness. New York, Morrow, 1978.
Wait for Me, Watch for Me, Eula Bee. New York, Morrow, 1978.
Lacy Makes a Match. New York, Morrow, 1979.
The Staffordshire Terror. New York, Morrow, 1979.
That's One Ornery Orphan. New York, Morrow, 1980.
Lupita Mañana. New York, Morrow, 1981.
Eight Mules from Monterey. New York, Morrow, 1982.
Jonathan Down Under. New York, Morrow, 1982.
Melinda Takes a Hand. New York, Morrow, 1983.
Turn Homeward, Hannalee. New York, Morrow, 1984.
The Coach That Never Came. New York, Morrow, 1985.
Behave Yourself, Bethany Brant. New York, Morrow, 1986.
Charley Skedaddle. New York, Morrow, 1987.
Be Ever Hopeful, Hannalee. New York, Morrow, 1988.
Sarah and Me and the Lady from the Sea. New York, Morrow, 1989.

PUBLICATIONS FOR ADULTS

Novel by Patricia Beatty

The Englishman's Mistress (as Jean Bartholomew). New York, Dell, 1975.

Other by John Beatty

Warwick and Holland, Being the Lives of Robert and Henry Rich. Denver, Alan Swallow, 1965.

Editor, with Oliver A. Johnson, *Heritage of Western Civilization: Select Readings.* Englewood Cliffs, New Jersey, Prentice Hall, 1958.

*

Manuscript Collection: University of California, Riverside.

Patricia Beatty comments:
For the most part I write of the historical past for young readers—and not only because of a personal, loving interest in history. I sense a growing disinterest among people of the English-speaking world in what has gone on before. This seems particularly true of many university students who say openly, "history began yesterday." I try to make the English and American "pasts" come to life in order to convince the 9 to 14 age group that people of the past were real people with real personalities and real problems and not text-book, dry-as-a-bone beings, mummified by time and bloodless footnotes.

*   *   *

John and Patricia Beatty have been two of the more prolific

authors of historical fiction for children, collaborating on a series of historical novels set in the British Isles. One hallmark of their work together has been concern for the accuracy of historical detail. Their articles in such journals as *Horn Book* have provided interesting insights on the challenges the authors faced in rendering dialects and period language so that both historic accuracy and clarity are served. Impressive as their careful research and writing are, however, these jointly authored stories are not as interesting as Patricia Beatty's more recent work. The British novels tend to turn complex issues such as the English Civil War and the highland clearances into romantic, swashbuckling affairs. Even the award-winning *The Royal Dirk* lacks the sense of character and place that mark Patricia Beatty's novels with American settings. Alan McCrae's story might have been more powerful if he had stayed in the highlands and faced Lord Cumberland's wrath rather than spend so much of the book with a fencing master in London.

Secondary characters in the Beattys' British novels tend to drift in and out without making a strong impression. Jessie Cameron, the highwayman's wife in *The Royal Dirk,* appears so briefly that the impact of her death on Alan seems exaggerated. In contrast, the characters in Patricia Beatty's American books are more fully developed. When Granny Brant in *Charley Skedaddle* is missing for two days, Charley's search for her and his careful nursing grow from a longterm, well-developed relationship. Other characters, such as Mr. Ponder in *By Crumbs, It's Mine!,* also emerge as integral—and often humorous—parts of Patricia Beatty's stories.

One of the most interesting aspects of Patricia Beatty's recent work is the contrast between her lighter western and first-person novels and her American Civil War books. The lighter works feature liberated young women who face up to the rigors of frontier life and treacherous men. When her father succumbs to "get-rich-quick" disease, Damaris Boyd in *By Crumbs, Its Mine!,* rallies and turns potential tragedy into a money-making venture. In *How Many Miles to Sundown* the heroine treks through the Southwest searching for her absent father. In these and other stories set in the American West Patricia Beatty sets up situations in which young women have a plausible degree of freedom despite the restrictions of their historical era. *Hail Columbia* for instance is one of the first novels for young people that provides a sympathetic portrait of the suffrage movement. For this alone these books would be interesting. It is a delightful bonus that they also display a sense of humor about the conditions that have historically constrained women.

Some of Patricia Beatty's best work are her novels set in the American Civil War. *Charley Skedaddle* is probably the finest of these. Charley is an Irish boy living in New York City. Seeking a way to avenge his brother's death at Gettysburg, and to escape from a prospective brother-in-law he dislikes, Charley joins the Union forces as a drummer boy. At the Battle of the Wilderness, anticipation turns to panic when he sees his friends killed, and shoots his first rebel. Charley "skedaddles"—runs off—and is eventually taken in by an old "witch woman" in the Blue Ridge mountains. Living with Granny Brant, Charley learns the difference between real courage and the bravado that led to his soldiering. The story ends as Charley is forced to escape the retreating Confederates and leave the life he has built for himself in the little mountain community. His promise to return when the war ends closes the story. Beatty does a fine job here of describing the misery of the last years of the Civil War and contrasting it with the hard but satisfying life of the mountain people. While there is some of the same romanticizing of mountain folk here as of highlanders in *The Royal Dirk,* the images of war are more down-to-earth, and Charlie's behavior is more believable.

Since her husband John's death, Patricia Beatty has remained a prolific writer of historical fiction—one of the few who can handle so broad a range of periods and styles. Her work is a good introduction to the genre for readers new to historical fiction. She can also be depended upon as a careful author who tries to be true to both the

literary and historical qualities of her stories.

—Linda S. Levstik

———

BEHN, Harry. Also wrote as Giles Behn. American.   Born in Prescott, Arizona, 24 September 1898. Educated at Stanford University, California, 1918; Harvard University, Cambridge, Massachusetts, B.S. 1922. Married Alice Lawrence in 1925; one daughter and two sons. Scenario writer, Metro-Goldwyn-Mayer, Twentieth Century-Fox, and Universal studios, Hollywood, 1925–35; Professor of Creative Writing, University of Arizona, Tucson, 1938–47. Founding director, Phoenix Little Theatre, 1922–23; Vice President, Tucson Regional Plan, 1940–47; founding editor, *Arizona Quarterly,* Tucson, 1942–47; founder, University of Arizona Press, 1960. Recipient: George G. Stone Center for Children's Books award, 1965. *Died 6 September 1973.*

PUBLICATIONS FOR CHILDREN

Fiction

The Painted Cave, illustrated by the author.   New York, Harcourt
   Brace, 1957.
Timmy's Search, illustrated by Barbara Cooney.   Greenwich, Connecticut, Seabury Press, 1958.
The Two Uncles of Pablo, illustrated by Mel Silverman.   New York,
   Harcourt Brace, 1959; London, Macmillan, 1960.
Roderick, illustrated by Mel Silverman.   New York, Harcourt
   Brace, 1961.
The Faraway Lurs, illustrated by the author.   Cleveland, World,
   1963; as *The Distant Lurs,* London, Gollancz, 1965.
Omen of the Birds, illustrated by the author.   Cleveland, World,
   1964; London, Gollancz, 1965.

Verse (illustrated by the author)

The Little Hill: Poems and Pictures.   New York, Harcourt Brace,
   1949.
All Kinds of Time.   New York, Harcourt Brace, 1950.
Windy Morning: Poems and Pictures.   New York, Harcourt Brace,
   1953.
The House Beyond the Meadow.   New York, Pantheon, 1955.
The Wizard in the Well: Poems and Pictures.   New York, Harcourt
   Brace, 1956.
The Golden Hive: Poems and Pictures.   New York, Harcourt Brace,
   1966.
What a Beautiful Noise, illustrated by Harold Berson.   New York,
   World, 1970.
Crickets and Bullfrogs and Whispers of Thunder, edited by Lee
   Bennett Hopkins.   New York, Harcourt Brace, 1984.

Other

Translator, *Cricket Songs* [and *More Cricket Songs*]: *Japanese
   Haiku.*   New York, Harcourt Brace, 2 vols., 1964–71.

PUBLICATIONS FOR ADULTS

Plays

Screenplays: *The Big Parade,* 1925; *Proud Flesh,* with Agnes

Christine Johnson, 1925; *La Bohème,* with Ray Doyle, 1926; *The Crowd,* with King Vidor and John V.A. Weaver, 1928; *The Racket,* with Del Andrews, 1928; *Frozen River,* 1929; *The Sin Sister,* with Andrew Bennison, 1929; *Hell's Angels,* with Howard Estabrook, 1930.

Verse

Siesta.   Phoenix, Golden Bough Press, 1931.
The Grand Canyon (as Giles Behn).   Privately printed, 1935.
Sombra.   Copenhagen, Christreu, 1961.

Other

Chrysalis: Concerning Children and Poetry.   New York, Harcourt Brace, 1968.

Translator, *The Duino Elegies,* by Rainer Maria Rilke.   Mount Vernon, New York, Peter Pauper Press, 1957.
Translator, with Peter Beilenson, *Haiku Harvest.*   Mount Vernon, New York, Peter Pauper Press, 1962.

*

Manuscript Collections: Kerlan Collection, University of Minnesota, Minneapolis; University of Oregon Library, Eugene.

*   *   *

It is a fascinating and far-flung legacy which Harry Behn has left to the child-reader and to those interested in literature for children, characterized, perhaps, by his own words, "Innocence is hardly more than a willingness to wonder." How unusual it is to think of Behn as a man of innocence—born in Arizona when it was still a territory, educated at Harvard, and world-traveled! And yet it is the right phrase, for his willingness to wonder and wander, his enthusiasms and curiosity moved within a changing world which he persisted in viewing, most often, through the eyes of the innocent.

His books, ranging from the child's poetic voice of *Windy Morning* through stories and novels and further poetry as well as translation of haiku, carry a thread of transcendentalism; it is the Indian Earth-Mother, the gods of the Sun People, the god Aplu, the rising of the sun, the "almost imperceptible experience of wonder, removed from knowledge." "When a child," he wrote in *Chrysalis,* "sees his first butterfly and becomes himself a flying flower, such innocence has in it more reality than any however heroic whiz around the planet." So it was that the language of a bug, a chicken, a crow, a storm, rain, or train could spell-bind him into poem or prose-making.

Like Walter de la Mare, he found elves and wizards, fairies and magical beings of whom to write; like Robert Louis Stevenson he became the child speaking in "Swing Song" or "Pirates." Yet his was an American heritage, rooted in world history. *All Kinds of Time* clearly expressed that "Seconds are bugs/minutes are children/hours are people/days are postmen/weeks are Sunday School/months are/north/south/east/west/and in between/seasons are/wild flowers/tame flowers/golden leaves/and snow/years are/Santa Claus/centuries are/George/Washington/and forever is God." This, and the poems within his other books of poetry for children are those of an American child and his particular wonder: "Tell me, tell me everything!/What makes it Winter/And then Spring?" he asks through the child in "Curiosity." Yet, the series of questions of the poem end with his own continuing questions, "Tell me! or don't even grown-ups know?" This search, therefore, led him on; it was not unusual that because of his love for seasons and simplicity he should turn to the translation of Japanese haiku, that he should examine the life of a crow in *Roderick* or Dawn Boy, the Indian, in *The Painted*

Cave; that his mother's childhood in Denmark should inspire him to write *The Faraway Lurs* or that his questioning of the correlation between Etruscan and American civilization spun itself out in *Omen of the Birds.*

Poetry, he wrote, "must be presented with careful incompleteness of information." Incompletion thus sustains curiosity; information is not a *raison d'être* for the poet, and "willingness to wonder" is Harry Behn's unique contribution to children's literature.

—Myra Cohn Livingston

———

BELLOC, (Joseph) Hilaire (Pierre).   British.   Born in St. Cloud, near Paris, France, 27 July 1870; brother of the writer Marie Belloc Lowndes; became British citizen, 1902. Educated at the Oratory School, Edgbaston, Warwickshire; Balliol College, Oxford (Brackenbury History Scholar), 1892–95, B.A. (honours) in history 1895. Served in the 10th Battery of the 8th Regiment of Artillery of the French Army, 1891. Married Elodie Agnes Hogan in 1896 (died 1914); three sons and two daughters. Journalist: editor, with A.H. Pollen, *Paternoster Review,* 1890–91; literary editor, London *Morning Post,* 1906–09; editor, with Maurice Baring, *North Street Gazette,* 1910; founder, with G.K. and Cecil Chesterton, and editor, with others, *New Witness,* 1911–12; editor, *G.K.'s Weekly,* 1936–38; columnist ("A Wanderer's Notebook"), *Sunday Times,* 1938–53. Liberal Member of Parliament for South Salford, 1906–10. Head of the English Department, East London College. LL.D.: University of Glasgow, 1902. Knight Commander with Star, Order of St. Gregory the Great, 1934. *Died 16 July 1953.*

PUBLICATIONS FOR CHILDREN

Verse

The Bad Child's Book of Beasts: Verses, illustrated by Basil Blackwood.   Oxford, Alden Press, and New York, Dutton, 1896.
More Beasts (for Worse Children): Verses, illustrated by Basil Blackwood.   London and New York, Arnold, 1897.
A Moral Alphabet, illustrated by Basil Blackwood.   London, Arnold, 1899.
Cautionary Tales for Children: Designed for the Admonition of Children Between the Ages of Eight and Fourteen Years: Verses, illustrated by Basil Blackwood.   London, Nash, 1907; New York, Knopf, 1922.
New Cautionary Tales: Verses, illustrated by Nicolas Bentley.   London, Duckworth, 1930; New York, Harper, 1931.
Cautionary Verses: The Collected Humorous Poems of Hilaire Belloc.   London, Duckworth, 1939; New York, Knopf, 1941.
Selected Cautionary Verses.   London, Penguin, 1950.

Other

Economics for Helen.   Bristol, Arrowsmith, and New York, McBride, 1924; as *Economics for Young People,* London and New York, Putnam, 1925.

PUBLICATIONS FOR ADULTS

Novels

Emmanuel Burden, Merchant....   London, Methuen, and New

York, Scribner, 1904.

Mr. Clutterbuck's Election. London, Nash, 1908.

A Change in the Cabinet. London, Methuen, 1909.

Pongo and the Bull. London, Constable, 1910.

The Girondin. London, Nelson, 1911; New York, Doubleday, 1912.

The Green Overcoat. Bristol, Arrowsmith, and New York, McBride, 1912.

The Mercy of Allah. London, Chatto and Windus, and New York, Appleton, 1922.

Mr. Petre. Bristol, Arrowsmith, and New York, McBride, 1925.

The Emerald of Catherine the Great. Bristol, Arrowsmith, and New York, Harper, 1926.

The Haunted House. Bristol, Arrowsmith, 1927; New York, Harper, 1928.

But Soft—We Are Observed! Bristol, Arrowsmith, 1928; as *Shadowed!*, New York, Harper, 1929.

Belinda: A Tale of Affection in Youth and Age. London, Constable, 1928; New York, Harper, 1929.

The Missing Masterpiece. Bristol, Arrowsmith, and New York, Harper, 1929.

The Man Who Made Gold. Bristol, Arrowsmith, 1930; New York, Harper, 1931.

The Postmaster-General. Bristol, Arrowsmith, and Philadelphia, Lippincott, 1932.

The Hedge and the Horse. London, Cassell, 1936.

Short Story

Bona Mors. Horsham, Sussex, Naldrett, 1953.

Play

The Candour of Maturity (produced London, 1912).

Verse

Verses and Sonnets. London, Ward and Downey, 1896.

The Modern Traveller. London, Arnold, 1898; New York, Knopf, 1923.

Verses. London, Duckworth, 1910; New York, Gomme, 1916.

More Peers. London, Swift, 1911; New York, Knopf, 1924.

Sonnets and Verse. London, Duckworth, 1923; New York, McBride, 1924; revised edition, Duckworth, 1938, 1954; New York, Sheed and Ward, 1939; as *Collected Verse,* London, Penguin, 1958.

(Poems). London, Benn, 1925.

The Chanty of the Nona. London, Faber, 1928.

The Praise of Wine: An Heroic Poem. Privately printed, 1931.

Ladies and Gentlemen: For Adults Only and Mature at That. London, Duckworth, 1932.

Songs of the South Country. London, Duckworth, 1951.

The Verse of Hilaire Belloc, edited by W.N. Roughead. London, Nonesuch Press, 1954; as *Complete Verse,* London, Duckworth, 1970.

Other

Danton: A Study. London, Nisbet, and New York, Scribner, 1899.

Lambkin's Remains. Oxford, Simpkin, and New York, Mansfield, 1900.

Paris. London, Arnold, 1900; New York, Scribner, 1907.

Robespierre: A Study. London, Nisbet, and New York, Scribner, 1901.

The Path to Rome. London, George Allen, and New York, Longman, 1902.

The Aftermath; or, Gleanings from a Busy Life, Called upon the Outer Cover, for Purposes of Sale, Caliban's Guide to Letters. London, Duckworth, and New York, Dutton, 1903.

The Great Inquiry (Only Authorised Version) Faithfully Reported. London, Duckworth, 1903.

The Old Road. London, Constable, 1904; Philadelphia, Lippincott, 1911.

Avril, Being Essays on the Poetry of the French Renaissance. London, Duckworth, and New York, Dutton, 1904.

An Open Letter on the Decay of Faith. London, Burns Oates, 1906.

Esto Perpetua: Algerian Studies and Impressions. London, Duckworth, 1906; New York, McBride, 1925.

Sussex, Painted by Wilfrid Ball. London, A. and C. Black, 1906; revised edition, as *The County of Sussex,* London, Cassell, 1936.

Hills and the Sea. London, Methuen, and New York, Scribner, 1906.

The Historic Thames. London, Dent, and New York, Dutton, 1907.

The Eye-Witness (incidents in history). London, Nash, and New York, Kings Treasuries of Literature, 1908.

The Catholic Church and Historical Truth (lecture). Preston, Lancashire, W. Watson, 1908.

On Nothing and Kindred Subjects. London, Methuen, 1908; New York, Dutton, 1909.

An Examination of Socialism. London, Catholic Truth Society, 1908; as *The Alternative,* London, Distributist, 1947.

The Pyrenees. London, Methuen, 1909; New York, Knopf, 1923.

On Everything. London, Methuen, 1909; New York, Dutton, 1910.

Marie Antoinette. London, Methuen, and New York, Doubleday, 1909.

The Church and Socialism. London, Catholic Truth Society, 1910.

The Ferrer Case. London, Catholic Truth Society, 1910.

The International. Philadelphia, Dolphin, 1910.

On Anything. London, Constable, and New York, Dutton, 1910.

On Something. London, Methuen, 1910; New York, Dutton, 1911.

The Party System, with Cecil Chesterton. London, Swift, 1911.

Socialism and the Servile State (debate with J. Ramsay MacDonald). London, South West London Federation of the Independent Labour Party, 1911.

First and Last. London, Methuen, 1911; New York, Dutton, 1912.

The French Revolution. London, Williams and Norgate, and New York, Holt, 1911.

The Battle of Blenheim [Malplaquet, Waterloo, Tourcoing, Crécy, Poitiers]. London, Swift, 5 vols., 1911–12, London, Rees, 1 vol., 1913; *Blenheim* published Philadelphia, Lippincott, 1936; revised edition of *Waterloo,* Rees, 1915; revised edition, as *Six British Battles,* Bristol, Arrowsmith, 1931.

The Four Men: A Farrago. London, Nelson, and Indianapolis, Bobbs Merrill, 1912.

The River of London. London, Foulis, 1912; Boston, Phillip, n.d.

Warfare in England. London, Williams and Norgate, and New York, Holt, 1912.

The Servile State. London, Foulis, 1912; Boston, Phillip, 1913.

This and That and the Other. London, Methuen, and New York, Dodd Mead, 1912.

The Stane Street: A Monograph. London, Constable, and New York, Dutton, 1913.

The Hilaire Belloc Calendar: A Quotation from the Works of Hilaire Belloc for Everyday in the Year. London, Frank Palmer, 1913.

The Book of the Bayeux Tapestry, Presenting the Complete Work in a Series of Colour Facsimiles. London, Chatto and Windus, and New York, Putnam, 1914.

Anti-Catholic History: How It Is Written. London, Catholic Truth Society, 1914.

Three Essays. Portland, Maine, Mosher, 1914.

The History of England from the First Invasion by the Romans to the Accession of King George the Fifth (volume 11 only). New York,

Catholic Publications Society of America, and London, Sands, 1915.

A General Sketch of the European War: The First and Second Phase. London, Nelson, 2 vols., 1915–16; as *The Elements of the Great War,* New York, Hearst, 2 vols., 1915–16.

A Picked Company, Being a Selection from the Writings of Hilaire Belloc, edited by E.V. Lucas. London, Methuen, 1915.

High Lights of the French Revolution. New York, Century, 1915.

The Two Maps of Europe and Some Other Aspects of the Great War. London, C. Arthur Pearson, 1915.

Land and Water Map of the War and How to Use It. London, Land and Water, 1915.

At the Sign of the Lion and Other Essays. Portland, Maine, Mosher, 1916.

The Last Days of the French Monarchy. London, Chapman and Hall, 1916.

The Second Year of the War. London, Burrup Mathieson and Sprague, 1916.

The Free Press. London, Allen and Unwin, 1918.

Religion and Civil Liberty. London, Catholic Truth Society, 1918.

The House of Commons and Monarchy. London, Allen and Unwin, 1920; New York, Harcourt Brace, 1922.

The Catholic Church and the Principle of Private Property. London, Catholic Truth Society, 1920.

Europe and the Faith. London, Constable, and New York, Paulist Press, 1920.

Pascal's Provincial Letters. London, Catholic Truth Society, 1921.

Catholic Social Reform Versus Socialism. London, Catholic Truth Society, 1922.

The Jews. London, Constable, 1922; Boston, Houghton Mifflin, 1937.

The Contrast. Bristol, Arrowsmith, 1923; New York, McBride, 1924.

The Road. Manchester, British Reinforced Concrete Engineering Company, and New York, Harper, 1923.

On (essays). London, Methuen, and New York, Doran, 1923.

The Political Effort. London, True Temperance Association, 1924.

The Campaign of 1812 and the Retreat from Moscow. London, Nelson, 1924; as *Napoleon's Campaign of 1812 and the Retreat from Moscow,* New York, Harper, 1926.

The Cruise of the "Nona." London, Constable, and Boston, Houghton Mifflin, 1925.

England and the Faith. London, Catholic Truth Society, 1925.

A History of England. London, Methuen, and New York, Putnam, 4 vols., 1925–31.

Miniatures of French History. London, Nelson, 1925; New York, Harper, 1926.

Hilaire Belloc (essays). London, Harrap, 1926.

The Highway and Its Vehicles, edited by Geoffrey Holme. London, The Studio, 1926.

Short Talks with the Dead and Others. London, Cayme Press, and New York, Harper, 1926.

Mrs. Markham's New History of England, Being an Introduction for Young People to the Current History and Institutions of Our Times. London, Cayme Press, 1926.

A Companion to Mr. Wells's "Outline of History." London, Sheed and Ward, 1926; San Francisco, Ecclesiastical Supply Association, 1927.

Mr. Belloc Still Objects to Mr. Wells's "Outline of History." London, Sheed and Ward, 1926; San Francisco, Ecclesiastical Supply Association, 1927.

The Catholic Church and History. London, Burns Oates, and New York, Macmillan, 1926.

Selected Works. London, Library Press, 9 vols., 1927.

Towns of Destiny. New York, McBride, 1927; as *Many Cities,* London, Constable, 1928.

Oliver Cromwell. London, Benn, 1927.

James the Second. London, Faber, and Philadelphia, Lippincott, 1928.

How the Reformation Happened. London, Cape, and New York, Dodd Mead, 1928.

A Conversation with an Angel and Other Essays. London, Cape, 1928; New York, Harper, 1929.

Joan of Arc. London, Cassell, and Boston, Little Brown, 1929.

Survivals and New Arrivals. London, Sheed and Ward, and New York, Macmillan, 1929.

Richelieu. Philadelphia, Lippincott, 1929; London, Benn, 1930.

Wolsey. London, Cassell, and Philadelphia, Lippincott, 1930.

A Pamphlet, July 27th, 1930. Privately printed, 1930s; as *World Conflict,* London, Catholic Truth Society, 1951.

Cranmer. London, Cassell, 1931; as *Cranmer, Archbishop of Canterbury 1533–1556,* Philadelphia, Lippincott, 1931.

On Translation (lecture). Oxford, Clarendon Press, 1931.

Essays of a Catholic Layman in England. London, Sheed and Ward, 1931; as *Essays of a Catholic,* New York, Macmillan, 1931.

A Conversation with a Cat and Others (essays). London, Cassell, and New York, Harper, 1931.

How We Got the Bible. London, Catholic Truth Society, 1932.

Napoleon. London, Cassell, and Philadelphia, Lippincott, 1932.

The Question and the Answer. New York, Bruce, 1932; London, Longman, 1938.

The Tactics and Strategy of the Great Duke of Marlborough. Bristol, Arrowsmith, 1933.

William the Conqueror. London, Davies, 1933; New York, Appleton, 1934.

Becket. London, Catholic Truth Society, 1933.

Charles the First, King of England. London, Cassell, and Philadelphia, Lippincott, 1933.

Cromwell. London, Cassell, and Philadelphia, Lippincott, 1934.

A Shorter History of England. London, Harrap, and New York, Macmillan, 1934.

Milton. London, Cassell, and Philadelphia, Lippincott, 1935.

Hilaire Belloc (humorous writings), edited by E.V. Knox. London, Methuen, 1935.

An Essay on the Restoration of Property. London, Distribution League, 1936; as *The Restoration of Property,* New York, Sheed and Ward, 1936.

Selected Essays, edited by John Edward Dineen. Philadelphia, Lippincott, 1936.

The Battle Ground (on Syria). London, Cassell, and Philadelphia, Lippincott, 1936.

Characters of the Reformation. London and New York, Sheed and Ward, 1936.

The Crusade: The World's Debate. London, Cassell, 1937; as *The Crusades: The World's Debate,* Milwaukee, Bruce, 1937.

The Crisis of Our Civilization. London, Cassell, 1937; as *The Crisis of Civilization,* New York, Fordham University Press, 1937.

An Essay on the Nature of Contemporary England. London, Constable, and New York, Sheed and Ward, 1937.

The Issue. New York and London, Sheed and Ward, 1937.

The Great Heresies. London and New York, Sheed and Ward, 1938.

Monarchy: A Study of Louis XIV. London, Cassell, 1938; as *Louis XIV,* New York, Harper, 1938.

Stories, Essays, and Poems. London, Dent, 1938.

The Case of Dr. Coulton. London, Sheed and Ward, 1938.

Return to the Baltic. London, Constable, 1938.

Charles II: The Last Rally. New York, Harper, 1939; as *The Last Rally: A Story of Charles II,* London, Cassell, 1940.

The Test Is Poland. London, Weekly Review, 1939.

On Sailing the Sea: A Collection of the Seagoing Writings of Hilaire Belloc, edited by W.N. Roughead. London, Methuen, 1939; Fair

Lawn, New Jersey, Essential Books, 1951.
The Catholic and the War. London, Burns Oates, 1940.
On the Place of Gilbert Chesterton in English Letters. London and New York, Sheed and Ward, 1940.
The Silence of the Sea and Other Essays. New York, Sheed and Ward, 1940; London, Cassell, 1941.
Places. New York, Sheed and Ward, 1941; London, Cassell, 1942.
Elizabethan Commentary. London, Cassell, 1942; as *Elizabeth: Creature of Circumstance,* New York, Harper, 1942.
Selected Essays. London, Methuen, 1948.
Hilaire Belloc: An Anthology of His Prose and Verse, edited by W.N. Roughead. London, Hart Davis, and Philadelphia, Lippincott, 1951.
One Thing and Another: A Miscellany from His Uncollected Essays, edited by Patrick Cahill. London, Hollis and Carter, 1955.
Essays, edited by Anthony Forster. London, Methuen, 1955.
Selected Essays, edited by J.B. Morton. London, Penguin, 1958.
Letters from Hilaire Belloc, edited by Robert Speaight. London, Hollis and Carter, and New York, Macmillan, 1958.
Advice. London, Harvill Press, 1960.
Belloc: A Biographical Anthology, edited by Herbert Van Thal and Jane Soames Nickerson. London, Allen and Unwin, and New York, Knopf, 1970.
Hilaire Belloc's Prefaces, Written for Fellow Authors, edited by J.A. De Chantigny. Chicago, Loyola University Press, 1971.

Editor, *Extracts from the Diaries and Letters of Hubert Howard.* Oxford, Hart, 1899.
Editor, *The Footpath Way: An Anthology for Walkers.* London, Sidgwick and Jackson, 1911.
Editor, *Travel Notes on a Holiday Tour in France,* by James Murray Allison. Privately printed, 1931.

Translator, *The Romance of Tristan and Iseult,* by J. Bedier. London, George Allen, 1903; New York, Boni, 1930.
Translator, *The Principles of War,* by Marshal Foch. London, Chapman and Hall, 1918; New York, Holt, 1920.
Translator, *Precepts and Judgments,* by Marshal Foch. London, Chapman and Hall, 1919; New York, Holt, 1920.

*

Bibliography: *The English First Editions of Hilaire Belloc…*by Patrick Cahill, privately printed, 1953.

Critical Studies (selection): *Hilaire Belloc* by Renée Haynes, London, Longman, 1953; *Hilaire Belloc: A Memoir* by J.B. Morton, London, Hollis and Carter, and New York, Sheed and Ward, 1955; *The Young Hilaire Belloc* by Marie Belloc Lowndes, New York, Kenedy, 1956; *The Life of Hilaire Belloc* by Robert Speaight, London, Hollis and Carter, and New York, Farrar Straus, 1957; *Belloc the Man* by Eleanor and Reginald Jebb, Westminster, Maryland, Newman, 1957; *Hilaire Belloc: Edwardian Radical* by John P. McCarthy, Indianapolis, Liberty Press, 1978; *Hilaire Belloc* by Michael H. Markel, Boston, Twayne, 1982; *Hilaire Belloc* by A.N. Wilson, London, Hamish Hamilton, and New York Atheneum, 1984; *Sailing with Mr. Belloc* by Dermod MacCarthy, London, Collins, 1986.

*   *   *

There would be no place for Hilaire Belloc in a book of this kind were it not for the gift children have for annexing books designed for their elders. He was no children's writer, although it might be argued that in some important ways he remained an adolescent all his life. His passionate advocacy of improbable, and especially unpopular, theses, his gusto, his dislike of a pedantic adherence to logical processes, all hinted at a certain permanent immaturity at odds with his formidable scholarship.

Young people once liked—and may turn to them again—the "Chester-Belloc" novels, but Belloc's lasting appeal to children rests upon his group of mock cautionary tales in which he made genial fun of a literary convention which was dying, if not dead, in his own childhood. The moral tales in verse written by Elizabeth Turner and others in the early years of the 19th century were serious in intent, concerned with warning the young of the consequences of sin—or even mildly bad behavior. By the end of the century these naive rhymes invited laughter. Belloc adopted the themes, and often the meters, of these archaic poems and, giving them only a slightly different emphasis, made them not merely parody but a genuinely original comic creation. Belloc's *Cautionary Tales* are not an isolated example. Among contemporaries Harry Graham in his *Ruthless Rhymes for Heartless Homes* guyed the same conventions. What gives Belloc's work its rare quality is that he, unlike others playing the same frivolous game, was a real poet. He was one of the outstanding verse technicians of the age with an absolute mastery of his craft, and he was without rival in the brevity and symmetry of his epigrams. The same perfection of craftsmanship that he devoted to "serious" verse he brought to the absurd accounts of Matilda—who cried wolf once too often—and Augustus King, the chewer of string, and Jim, who let go of nurse's hand and was eaten by a lion. Similar qualities are found, perhaps even more characteristically, in the shorter rhymes of *The Bad Child's Book of Beasts* and its sequels.

Belloc's epigrams and sonnets, and the rumbustious verses scattered through the prose works, make regular appearances in anthologies of verse for children, doubtless to the poet's posthumous amusement.

—Marcus Crouch

———

BEMELMANS, Ludwig. American. Born in Meran, Austria (now Merano, Italy), 27 April 1898; emigrated to the United States, 1914; became citizen, 1918. Educated at schools in Regensburg and Rothenburg, Bavaria. Served in the United States Army during World War I. Married Madeline Freund in 1935; one daughter. Worked in hotels and restaurants, 1914–17 and 1919–24; owner, Hapsburg House Restaurant, New York, 1925–35; writer for *New Yorker;* also an artist: exhibitions in galleries in the U.S. and abroad. Recipient: American Library Association Caldecott Medal, 1954. *Died 1 October 1962.*

PUBLICATIONS FOR CHILDREN (illustrated by the author)

Fiction

Hansi. New York, Viking Press, 1934; London, Lovat Dickson, 1935.
The Golden Basket. New York, Viking Press, 1936.
The Castle Number Nine. New York, Viking Press, 1937.
Quito Express. New York, Viking Press, 1938.
Rosebud. New York, Random House, 1942.
A Tale of Two Glimps. New York, CBS, 1947.
The Happy Place. Boston, Little Brown, 1952.
The High World. New York, Harper, 1954; London, Hamish Hamilton, 1958.
Parsley. New York, Harper, 1955.

Verse

Madeline. New York, Simon and Schuster, 1939; London, Verschoyle, 1952.
Fifi. New York, Simon and Schuster, 1940.
Sunshine. New York, Simon and Schuster, 1950.
Madeline's Rescue. New York, Viking Press, and London, Verschoyle, 1953.
Madeline's Christmas in Texas. Dallas, Nieman Marcus, 1955.
Madeline and the Bad Hat. New York, Viking Press, 1956; London, Deutsch, 1958.
Madeline and the Gypsies. New York, Viking Press, and London, Deutsch, 1959.
Welcome Home! New York, Harper, 1960; London, Hamish Hamilton, 1961.
Madeline in London. New York, Viking Press, 1961; London, Deutsch, 1962.
Marina. New York, Harper, 1962.
Madeline's Christmas, completed by Madeline and Barbara Bemelmans. New York, Viking Kestrel, and London, Deutsch, 1985.

PUBLICATIONS FOR ADULTS

Novels

Now I Lay Me Down to Sleep. New York, Viking Press, 1943; London, Hamish Hamilton, 1944.
The Blue Danube. New York, Viking Press, 1945; London, Hamish Hamilton, 1946.
Dirty Eddie. New York, Viking Press, 1947; London, Hamish Hamilton, 1948.
The Eye of God. New York, Viking Press, 1947; as *The Snow Mountain,* London, Hamish Hamilton, 1950.
The Woman of My Life. New York, Viking Press, and London, Hamish Hamilton, 1957.
Are You Hungry, Are You Cold. Cleveland, World, 1960; London, Mayflower, 1965.
The Street Where the Heart Lies. Cleveland, World, 1963.

Short Stories

I Love You, I Love You, I Love You. New York, Viking Press, 1942; London, Hamish Hamilton, 1943.

Other

My War with the United States. New York, Viking Press, 1937; London, Gollancz, 1938.
Life Class. New York, Viking Press, 1938; London, Lane, 1939.
Small Beer (essays). New York, Viking Press, 1939; London, Lane, 1940.
At Your Service: The Way of Life in a Hotel. Evanston, Illinois, Row Peterson, 1941.
Hotel Splendide. New York, Viking Press, 1941; London, Hamish Hamilton, 1942.
The Donkey Inside. New York, Viking Press, 1941; London, Hamish Hamilton, 1947.
Hotel Bemelmans. New York, Viking Press, 1946; London, Hamish Hamilton, 1956.
The Best of Times: An Account of Europe Revisited. New York, Simon and Schuster, 1948; London, Cresset Press, 1949.
How to Travel Incognito. Boston, Little Brown, 1952.
Father, Dear Father (autobiography). New York, Viking Press, and London, Hamish Hamilton, 1953.
To the One I Love the Best. New York, Viking Press, 1955.

The World of Bemelmans. New York, Viking Press, and London, Hamish Hamilton, 1955.
My Life in Art. New York, Harper, and London, Deutsch, 1958.
How to Have Europe All to Yourself. New York, European Travel Commission, 1960.
Italian Holiday. Boston, Houghton Mifflin, 1961.
On Board Noah's Ark. New York, Viking Press, 1962.
La Bonne Table (writings and drawings), edited by Donald and Eleanor Friede. New York, Simon and Schuster, and London, Deutsch, 1964.
Tell Them It Was Wonderful: Selected Writings, edited by Madeline Bemelmans. New York, Viking, 1985.

Editor, *Holiday in France.* Boston, Houghton Mifflin, 1957; London, Deutsch, 1958.

*

Manuscript Collection: May Massee Collection, Emporia State University, Kansas.

Illustrator: *Noodle* by Munro Leaf, 1937; *Literary Life and the Hell with It* by Whit Burnett, 1939.

*   *   *

The reputation of Ludwig Bemelmans rests solidly on his five picture books about Madeline, that daring little girl who lived in Paris with 11 other little girls and Miss Clavel in a house "covered with vines." Most of the other Bemelmans books are out of print now—story and picture books that children never adopted as they adopted *Madeline. The High World,* however, is still in circulation, and both *Parsley* and *Hansi* are available on library reference shelves. First a word about these and two others, before we take a closer look at the *Madelines* with their casual, comical couplets, their appealing little girl, and the large bright watercolor settings.

The scenes and people Bemelmans knew as a child growing up in the Austrian Tyrol are reflected in the two illustrated storybooks, *The High World* and *Hansi.* Small escapades and rich local color fill the pages of *Hansi,* while an avalanche and daring rescue based on a real incident bring *The High World* to its climax. Both books keep the reader fully involved and could in themselves have established Bemelmans as an important writer. *Parsley* is a large picture book of the *Madeline* size, filled with beautiful Bemelmans paintings of the forest where the stag named Parsley lived. It evidently failed to equal the *Madeline* books in appeal, perhaps because it verges on sentimentality and an unacceptable anthropomorphism at the end.

Quito Express, illustrated in chalky cinnamon colors, is the satisfying story of little Ecuadorian Pedro, a baby who crawled onto an express train and was carried away for four days, well cared for by a kindly conductor.

It seems a pity that another of the early books, *The Golden Basket,* is no longer available. In this storybook two little girls explore Bruges with their father. And wonder of wonders, they encounter one day 12 uniformed little girls out walking two by two with their Madame Severine. The littlest girl, one Madeleine, skips and hops behind them all saying "Boo-boo-boo!" Which brings us to the famous Madeline of the well-known picture books.

The first book, *Madeline,* was an instant success. Quite apart from the appealing verses and pictures, it offered a heroine to love and hospital experience (a magnetic topic for young readers). The books that followed were true to the original characterization of the independent little Madeline and continued to blend playful, easy versification with the sweeping pictorial art of the cartoonist-painter.

Readers know that foreign cities will be laid out for them to inspect in detail in the Bemelmans illustrations, glowing in color and full of movement—just as the verses move along rapidly and happily through the story. The Bemelmans touch in these books is light and warm, comical and endearing. There is nothing else quite like it. *Madeline's Rescue* brought Bemelmans the Caldecott Medal for "the most distinguished American picture book."

—Claudia Lewis

————

BENCHLEY, Nathaniel (Goddard). American. Born in Newton, Massachusetts, 13 November 1915; son of the writer Robert Benchley. Educated at Phillips Exeter Academy, Exeter, New Hampshire, 1931–34; Harvard University, Cambridge, Massachusetts, 1934–38, S.B. 1938. Served in the United States Naval Reserve, 1941–45. Married Marjorie Bradford in 1939; two sons, including the writer Peter Benchley. City reporter, New York *Herald Tribune,* 1939–41; assistant entertainment editor, *Newsweek,* New York, 1946–47. Recipient: Western Writers of America Spur award, 1973. *Died 14 December 1981.*

PUBLICATIONS FOR CHILDREN

Fiction

Red Fox and His Canoe, illustrated by Arnold Lobel. New York, Harper, 1964; Kingswood, Surrey, World's Work, 1969.
Oscar Otter, illustrated by Arnold Lobel. New York, Harper, 1966; Kingswood, Surrey, World's Work, 1967.
The Strange Disappearance of Arthur Cluck, illustrated by Arnold Lobel. New York, Harper, 1967; Kingswood, Surrey, World's Work, 1968.
A Ghost Named Fred, illustrated by Ben Shecter. New York, Harper, 1968; Kingswood, Surrey, World's Work, 1969.
Sam the Minuteman, illustrated by Arnold Lobel. New York, Harper, 1969; Kingswood, Surrey, World's Work, 1976.
The Several Tricks of Edgar Dolphin, illustrated by Mamoru Funai. New York, Harper, and Kingswood, Surrey, World's Work, 1970.
The Flying Lesson of Gerald Pelican, illustrated by Mamoru Funai. New York, Harper, 1970.
Gone and Back. New York, Harper, 1970.
Feldman Fieldmouse, illustrated by Hilary Knight. New York, Harper, 1971; London, Abelard Schuman, 1975.
Small Wolf, illustrated by Joan Sandin. New York, Harper, 1972; Kingswood, Surrey, World's Work, 1973.
The Magic Sled, illustrated by Mel Furukawa. New York, Harper, 1972; as *The Magic Sledge,* London, Deutsch, 1974.
Only Earth and Sky Last Forever. New York, Harper, 1972.
The Deep Dives of Stanley Whale, illustrated by Mischa Richter. New York, Harper, 1973; Kingswood, Surrey, World's Work, 1976.
Bright Candles. New York, Harper, 1974; London, Deutsch, 1976.
Beyond the Mists. New York, Harper, 1975.
A Necessary End. New York, Harper, 1976; London, Deutsch, 1978.
Snorri and the Strangers, illustrated by Don Bolognese. New York, Harper, 1976; Kingswood, Surrey, World's Work, 1978.
George, The Drummer Boy, illustrated by Don Bolognese. New York, Harper, 1977; Kingswood, Surrey, World's Work, 1978.
Kilroy and the Gull, illustrated by John Schoenherr. New York, Harper, 1977; London, Abelard Schuman, 1979.
Running Owl, The Hunter, illustrated by Mamoru Funai. New

York, Harper, 1979.
Demo and the Dolphin, illustrated by Stephen Gammell. New York, Harper, 1981.
Snip, illustrated by Irene Trivas. New York, Doubleday, 1981.
Walter, The Homing Pigeon, illustrated by Whitney Darrow, Jr. New York, Harper, 1981.

Other

Sinbad the Sailor, illustrated by Tom O'Sullivan. New York, Random House, 1960; London, Muller, 1964.

PUBLICATIONS FOR ADULTS

Novels

Side Street. New York, Harcourt Brace, 1950.
One to Grow On. New York, McGraw Hill, 1958.
Sail a Crooked Ship. New York, McGraw Hill, 1960; London, Hutchinson, 1961.
The Off-Islanders. New York, McGraw Hill, 1961; London, Hutchinson, 1962; as *The Russians Are Coming, The Russians Are Coming,* New York, Popular Library, 1966.
Catch a Falling Spy. New York, McGraw Hill, and London, Hutchinson, 1963.
A Winter's Tale. New York, McGraw Hill, and London, Hutchinson, 1964.
The Visitors. New York, McGraw Hill, 1964; London, Hutchinson, 1965.
A Firm Word or Two. New York, McGraw Hill, 1965.
The Monument. New York, McGraw Hill, and London, Hutchinson, 1966.
Welcome to Xanadu. New York, Atheneum, and London, Hutchinson, 1968.
The Wake of Icarus. New York, Atheneum, 1969.
Lassiter's Folly. New York, Atheneum, 1971.
The Hunter's Moon. Boston, Little Brown, 1972.
Portrait of a Scoundrel. New York, Doubleday, 1979.
Sweet Anarchy. New York, Doubleday, 1979.
All over Again. New York, Doubleday, 1981.
Speakeasy. New York, Doubleday, 1982.

Plays

The Frogs of Spring, adaptation of his novel *Side Street* (produced New York, 1953). New York, French, 1954.

Screenplay: *The Great American Pastime,* 1956.

Other

Robert Benchley: A Biography. New York, McGraw Hill, 1955; London, Cassell, 1956.
Humphrey Bogart. Boston, Little Brown, and London, Hutchinson, 1975.

Editor, *The Benchley Roundup* (writings by Robert Benchley). New York, Harper, 1954; London, Cassell, 1956.

*

Manuscript Collection: Mugar Memorial Library, Boston University.

*   *   *

An author of books for adults who for the last 17 years of his life wrote for children as well, Nathaniel Benchley produced a range of fiction for young children to teenagers. Often reflecting an interest in history or nature, his stories characteristically introduce animal or child protagonists yearning to do grown-up deeds who undertake adventures that caution them to wait for adulthood or thrust them into its early stages.

The author's picture books for young readers commonly employ practicable, uncondescending vocabulary, a strong dash of fantasy and humor, colorful illustrations, and lively stories. Works such as *The Deep Dives of Stanley Whale* and *The Flying Lesson of Gerald Pelican* center on adventurous young creature-heroes of air or water who become wiser by surviving foolhardy experiences. Other works in this category offer accurate and instructive introductions to history with authentically detailed illustrations. *Sam the Minuteman* and *George, The Drummer Boy* respectively show two youths on opposite sides confronting the start of the American Revolution and war's ugly realities. In *Small Wolf* an Indian boy witnesses the white man's relentless invasion of Native Americans' land; and in *Snorri and the Strangers* a 10th-century Norse boy born in North America and his parents flee from hostile Indians to the parents' native Greenland.

Directed toward readers between eight and 12 are three delightfully fanciful books that best represent this group. *Kilroy and the Gull* involves a captured young acrobatic orca brought to an aquarium where, bored and frustrated by his attempts to communicate with humans, he tricks his captors into returning him to sea, where with the help of a friendly gull he eventually establishes communication with marineland scientists playing music on shore. The story intermixes valid research and a brisk narrative. In *Feldman Fieldmouse* a baby mouse becomes too lazy when adopted as a pet by a boy who can talk to mice, and is educated by his visiting city uncle to work for his food and risk life for dreams like dancing under the moon. This humorous gem of a story is warmly appealing. With a less direct but still affecting narrative, *Demo and the Dolphin* focuses on a talking dolphin in ancient Greece who carries on his back to Delphi a boy seeking advice from the oracle for a fisherman father afraid of the sea. During the trip the pair encounter dangers and time-caught subjects like Odysseus en route from Troy, and return home with the oracle's ambiguous advice and a better grasp of the mythical past. Drawing on children's attraction to child-creature communication, all the above tales imaginatively combine comedy, fantasy, and charming characterizations within the context of a good story.

Believing in the need for the teenage novel to bridge the gap between child and adult fiction, Benchley in the 1970's produced five historical novels for young adults. Set in the 19th century, the award-winning *Gone and Back* compellingly chronicles young Obed Taylor's growth toward maturity and slow recognition of his father as a born loser as his family treks west from Nantucket to the Oklahoma Land Rush without striking success. An authentic historical setting and a mature theme are well integrated with the boy's experiences. In *Only Earth and Sky Last Forever* a 19th-century Cheyenne boy named Dark Elk, seeing the humiliation suffered by Agency Indians and wanting to prove himself a warrior, joins Crazy Horse who leads forays against the white man and fights at Little Big Horn. Peopled with convincing historical as well as fictional characters, the superbly written story vividly portrays the Indians' last struggle for survival. *Bright Candles* tells a fast-paced and well-researched story highlighting the Danish resistance during the Nazi regime through the figure of an adolescent boy who joins the Underground. Based on the 11th-century sagas, *Beyond the Mists* centers on a Danish youth disenchanted with warring on murderous Viking raids who survives shipwreck as a merchant seaman to join up with Leif Eriksson on a journey to North America before returning home. The richly detailed story excitingly depicts the Viking world.

Plumbing his wartime navy experience, Benchley in *A Necessary End* writes a perceptive account of service aboard a World War II sub chaser in training and in Pacific combat. Characterizing all the above novels are strong story-telling, detailed research, and interesting characters.

Benchley once described an effective children's book as one that does not talk down to readers, offers humor and suspense, and, he added, "You need a 'page-turner.'" His overall canon admirably reflects these qualities. When Benchley died in 1981 he left a rich legacy indeed to children's fiction.

—Christian H. Moe

———

BENEDICT, Rex (Arthur). American. Born in Jet, Oklahoma, 27 June 1920. Educated at Jet High School, graduated 1938; Northwestern State University, Alva, Oklahoma, B.A. 1949; University of Oklahoma, Norman, 1949–50. Served in the United States Navy Air Corps, 1942–45, 1951–53: Lieutenant. Married Giusi Maria Usai in 1966. Orchestra director, Alva, 1938–41; orchestra manager, San Diego, 1945–46; film dubber, 1953–57, and film translator, 1957–60, Rome; publisher's reader, New York, 1960–65; printer, Corsair Press, New York; reviewer, *New York Times*, 1972–79. Address: Box 176, Jet, Oklahoma 73749, U.S.A.

PUBLICATIONS FOR CHILDREN

Fiction

Good Luck Arizona Man. New York, Pantheon, 1972; London, Hamish Hamilton, 1973.
Goodbye to the Purple Sage: The Last Great Ride of the Sheriff of Medicine Creek. New York, Pantheon, 1973; London, Hamish Hamilton, 1974.
Last Stand at Goodbye Gulch. New York, Pantheon, 1974; London, Hamish Hamilton, 1975.
The Ballad of Cactus Jack. New York, Pantheon, 1975; London, Hamish Hamilton, 1976.
Run for Your Sweet Life, illustrated by David Christiana. New York, Farrar Straus, 1986.

Verse

In the Green Grass Time. New York, Corsair Press, 1964.

Other

Oh...Brother Juniper, illustrated by Joan Berg. New York, Pantheon, 1963.

Translator, *One Moonless Night,* by Noële Lavaivre. New York, Braziller, 1964.
Translator, *The Polka Dot Twins,* by Augusto Lunel. New York, Braziller, 1964.

PUBLICATIONS FOR ADULTS

Verse

Moonwash. New York, Corsair Press, 1969.
Nights in the Gardens of Glebe. New York, Corsair Press, 1970.

Epitaph for a Lady. New York, Corsair Press, 1970.
Haloes for Heroes. New York, Corsair Press, 1971.

Translator, *The Prayers of Man,* edited by Alfonso Maria di Nola. New York, McDowell Obolensky, 1961.
Translator, *Amorous Tales from the Decameron.* New York, Fawcett, 1963.
Translator, *Those Cursed Tuscans,* by Curzio Malaparte. Athens, Ohio University Press, 1964.

*

Rex Benedict comments:
(1978) If there is one word that will catch the intent of my efforts in the novel for children, it is the word "mythical." In almost all my novels I have used the Old West as myth. Since facts of the west are so hopelessly lost in myth, I, instead of trying to disentangle them, confuse them even more in the hope of arriving at logic. There is no length to which one cannot go in writing about the west, so long as one is convincing. A professor in Canada is currently dramatizing for television one of the novels under the title *The Magic Lie.* I think, to judge by his title, he is on the right path. The treatment of the west is all a great, beautiful lie, but it is concealed by magic. In short, you don't even notice the prevarication. (I hope.)

*   *   *

At the beginning of *The Ballad of Cactus Jack* the leader of the once fearsome Pecos Gang finds himself in circumstances befitting mythical geriatrics. Still among the living, he is unwanted—dead or alive. It is a deplorable state, to be sure, for a man whose life has been devoted to spurring otherwise weary minds. He turns to preaching, a corollary trade, both devoted as they are to the proposition that the unaided spirit is often too weak to supply enough excitement to get through a week of ennui. Legendary vigilantes and purveyors of popular religion are both thriving upon a universal need for enthusiasm. However amusing the circumstance, it makes perfectly good sense that a desperado whose antics no longer chill the soul might try the pulpit. Here the hymns become ballads in praise of the backwoods minister, but ballads, as they are inclined to do, dwell on decline and imminent demise. Once again the sad truth will out. Cactus Jack is unwanted, dead or alive. Unwanted perhaps, but not unneeded. He has become a legend that induces a yawn, but the wearied reaction by no means implies that legends are any the less a necessity. It isn't only Cactus Jack who is threatened with premature rigor mortis, but a populace which thrilled to his exploits remains mired in a fatal malnourishment of the spirit.

Fortunately for us, Rex Benedict is able to retread if not resurrect Cactus Jack for those of us who have found his like and the whole landscape of the Wild West a personage and a domain crucial to our existence, but no longer viably transmitted through horse operas or dime novels. Even Benedict acknowledges that he was himself born a century too late to witness the actual phenomenon, and that aside from one writer, Zane Grey, and a single periodical, the spirit of the West was nowhere to be found. Scarce but imperative, the medium must be discovered which will dispense those qualities that the American West has furnished for much of Western civilization. That medium which Benedict supplies seemingly so effortlessly is a satiric blend that demonstrates a studied respect for the subject. Through five books the old western forms are very much at home in a world view that finds it painful to take almost anything seriously. Remarkably, Benedict's characters remain faithful to a world gone by and to the contemporary scene as well, much like Don Quixotes who are loyal to a world seemingly lost, yet who can patiently and efficiently explain its ways to incredulous contemporaries.

In league with the Spanish don, Cactus Jack refuses to acknowledge himself or his world as anachronisms. Adopting the grand old American entrepreneurship of P. T. Barnum, he offers a stupendous, if nonexistent, reward to anyone who might apprehend him. For big bucks lazy imaginations are quickly willing to step lively in forms to which they have become disinterested. They follow the scenario of Cactus Jack who finds it better to be shot in the back by a bounty-hunter than languish in glories past. For all the laughter that follows, *The Ballad of Cactus Jack* along with the rest of Benedict's fiction addresses some serious questions. What happens to a myth which is undead but which still feeds upon the lifeblood of a civilization? How is a legend reintroduced to a lethargic public?

Benedict and his heroes remain wisely attentive to both their own world and the largely incredulous bystanders and readers. It would be unfair and misleading to view his sagas simply as caricature, even if they do cater to a readership that delights in the security of polite ridicule. Not only is there ample savvy in the characters' insights into the human condition, as copiously demonstrated by the mixed-breed narrator of *Good Luck Arizona Man,* but such absurd situations as putting a price on one's own head serve to demonstrate the essential nature of the Western saga rather than flout its conventions.

Benedict depicts the elements comprising the western as games. Actually they are rituals. A game involves a situation where the participants begin as equals and end up unequal, while ritual is the exact opposite. Children's games like Cops and Robbers and Cowboys and Indians should be more properly termed rituals as all are equals in the scenario regardless of which side they stand on, or whether they capture and triumph or are snared and slain. All are equally credited with sustaining an ongoing spectacle. In *Goodbye to the Purple Sage* there is the frequently replayed scenario: "The sheriff had the Pecos Gang within fifty yards of the jail. They was just passin' the Hangin' Tree. That was when the wild shootin' celebration started." The capture never comes, and we are soon to sense that such elusiveness derives neither from the wiliness of the desperadoes nor the ineptitude of the sheriff (though clumsiness and incapacity are everywhere in evidence), but because the event is one of those quintessential rites of life. Even where everyone is a criminal, there inevitably emerges the ceremony in which the participants divide themselves into three groups, the pursuers, the pursued and the onlookers. Goodbye Gulch, the forbidden stretch of land on the other side of the river where degenerates run their own affairs according to their own liking, features one such observance undertaken by a group of ex-marshals, banished to this other side for forsaking the honor of their profession, and an equal number of pure-bred vigilantees. Each day the thugs break out of the jail, are chased by the marshals, are recaptured and returned to the jailhouse. Rest from the invigorating excitement is mutually enjoyed, the gunslingers reposing in their cells, the marshals keeping them company by slumbering on the other side of the bars—all awaiting the next day's break-out jamboree, featuring good fun with real bullets, each of which pierces one of the escapees' black hats.

It seems that there is not only honor among thieves, but a wholesome sense of ritual that unites people of all races and nationalities, all ages, and perhaps just as important, both sexes. Romance is not simply falling in love, but an enactment of aspects of the old Roman novella. The child's game proves to be no mere effort to play grown-up roles, but a crucially necessary rite of interaction. Such universal rituals lie behind the reason for the enduring interest in westerns, and certainly the venture is made all the more satisfying with the playful seriousness and knowing naivety of each of Benedict's sagas. They are always within the Wild West of old, and outside looking in with a chuckle at those absurdities which seem central to the expedition of life.

One of Benedict's subjects dwells not in the American West, but in central Italy. *Oh...Brother Juniper* features a monk who was a contemporary of St. Francis and St. Clare. Though an ocean and many lifestyles apart from the Wild West figures, Brother Juniper belongs to the same branch of the family of man as the stock characters of Benedict's westerns. Like the sheriff and the Pecos Gang, Brother Juniper takes the guiding principles of his profession with a literalness that is as comic as it is admirable. He gives away the order's silver bells to an impoverished woman, and when harshly rebuked by the general of the order is sorry only that he has been the cause of the hoarseness in his superior's voice. He does not mind being castigated; in fact, he rather likes it. The unassailable simplicity of his faith not only wins for him the admiration of St. Francis, but he is reputed to have driven the devil himself crazy through his unselfconscious display of piety.

The setting and intent of an Umbrian cloister and of a ramshackle sheriff's quarters in Goodbye Glutch could scarcely provide a greater contrast. But the commitment to ritual is as intense in one as in the other. Such rituals are not only a familiar landmark of Benedict's output, but they are probably at the heart of most literary ventures whether real or fictional, or whether intended for adults or for children. Benedict demonstrates that the bald revelation of the rite of life when pushed to its extremes is as delightful as it is serious.

—Leonard R. Mendelsohn

BERESFORD, Elisabeth. British. Born in Paris, France. Educated at St. Mary's Hall, Brighton; St. Catherines, Bramley; Ditchling Dame School, Sussex; Brighton and Hove High School. Served as a radio operator in the Women's Royal Naval Service during World War II. Married Max Robertson in 1949; one daughter and one son. Since 1948 freelance journalist. Lives in Alderney, Channel Islands. Agent: David Higham Associates Ltd., 5–8 Lower John Street, London WIR 4HA; or A.M. Heath, 79 St. Martin's Lane, London WC2N 4AA, England.

PUBLICATIONS FOR CHILDREN

Fiction

The Television Mystery. London, Parrish, 1957.
The Flying Doctor Mystery. London, Parrish, 1958.
Trouble at Tullington Castle. London, Parrish, 1958.
Cocky and the Missing Castle, illustrated by Jennifer Miles. London, Constable, 1959.
Gappy Goes West. London, Parrish, 1959.
The Tullington Film-Makers. London, Parrish, 1960.
Two Gold Dolphins, illustrated by Peggy Fortnum. London, Constable, 1961; Indianapolis, Bobbs Merrill, 1964.
Danger on the Old Pull 'n Push. London, Parrish, 1962.
Strange Hiding Place. London, Parrish, 1962.
Diana in Television. London, Collins, 1963.
The Missing Formula Mystery. London, Parrish, 1963.
The Mulberry Street Team, illustrated by Juliet Pannett. Penshurst, Kent, Friday Press, 1963.
Awkward Magic, illustrated by Judith Valpy. London, Hart Davis, 1964; as *The Magic World,* Indianapolis, Bobbs Merrill, 1965.
The Flying Doctor to the Rescue. London, Parrish, 1964.
Holiday for Slippy, illustrated by Pat Williams. Penshurst, Kent, Friday Press, 1964.
Game, Set, and Match. London, Parrish, 1965.
Knights of the Cardboard Castle, illustrated by C.R. Evans. London, Methuen, 1965.
Travelling Magic, illustrated by Judith Valpy. London, Hart Davis, 1965; as *The Vanishing Garden,* New York, Funk and Wagnalls, 1967.
The Hidden Mill, illustrated by Margery Gill. London, Benn, 1965; New York, Meredith Press, 1967.
Peter Climbs a Tree, illustrated by Margery Gill. London, Benn, 1966.
Fashion Girl. London, Collins, 1967.
The Black Mountain Mystery. London, Parrish, 1967.
Looking for a Friend, illustrated by Margery Gill. London, Benn, 1967.
The Island Bus, illustrated by Robert Hodgson. London, Methuen, 1968.
Sea-Green Magic, illustrated by Ann Tout. London, Hart Davis, 1968.
The Wombles, illustrated by Margaret Gordon. London, Benn, 1968; New York, Meredith Press, 1969.
David Goes Fishing, illustrated by Imre Hofbauer. London, Benn, 1969.
Gordon's Go-Kart, illustrated by Margery Gill. London, Benn, 1970.
Stephen and the Shaggy Dog, illustrated by Robert Hales. London, Methuen, 1970.
Vanishing Magic, illustrated by Ann Tout. London, Hart Davis, 1970.
The Wandering Wombles, illustrated by Oliver Chadwick. London, Benn, 1970.
Dangerous Magic, illustrated by Oliver Chadwick. London, Hart Davis, 1972.
The Invisible Womble and Other Stories, illustrated by Ivor Wood. London, Benn, 1973.
The Secret Railway, illustrated by James Hunt. London, Methuen, 1973.
The Wombles in Danger. London, Benn, 1973.
The Wombles at Work, illustrated by Margaret Gordon. London, Benn, 1973.
Invisible Magic, illustrated by Reg Gray. London, Hart Davis, 1974.
The Wombles Go to the Seaside. London, World Distributors, 1974.
The Wombles Gift Book, illustrated by Margaret Gordon. London, Benn, 1975.
The Snow Womble, illustrated by Margaret Gordon. London, Benn, 1975.
Snuffle to the Rescue, illustrated by Gunvor Edwards. London, Kestrel, 1975.
Tomsk and the Tired Tree, illustrated by Margaret Gordon. London, Benn, 1975.
Wellington and the Blue Balloon, illustrated by Margaret Gordon. London, Benn, 1975.
Orinoco Runs Away, illustrated by Margaret Gordon. London, Benn, 1975.
The Wombles Make a Clean Sweep, illustrated by Ivor Wood. London, Benn, 1975.
The Wombles to the Rescue, illustrated by Margaret Gordon. London, Benn, 1975.
The MacWomble's Pipe Band, illustrated by Margaret Gordon. London, Benn, 1976.
Madame Cholet's Picnic Party, illustrated by Margaret Gordon. London, Benn, 1976.
Bungo Knows Best, illustrated by Margaret Gordon. London, Benn, 1976.
Tobermory's Big Surprise, illustrated by Margaret Gordon. London, Benn, 1976.
The Wombles Go round the World, illustrated by Margaret Gordon. London, Benn, 1976.
The World of the Wombles, illustrated by Edgar Hodges. London, World Distributors, 1976.
Wombling Free, illustrated by Edgar Hodges. London, Benn, 1978.

Toby's Luck, illustrated by Doreen Caldwell.   London, Methuen, 1978.

Secret Magic, illustrated by Caroline Sharpe.   London, Hart Davis, 1978.

The Happy Ghost, illustrated by Joanna Carey.   London, Methuen, 1979.

The Treasure Hunters, illustrated by Joanna Carey.   London, Methuen, and New York, Elsevier Nelson, 1980.

Curious Magic, illustrated by Claire Upsdale-Jones.   London, Granada, and New York, Elsevier Nelson, 1980.

The Four of Us, illustrated by Trevor Stubley.   London, Hutchinson, 1981.

The Animals Nobody Wanted, illustrated by Joanna Carey.   London, Methuen, 1982.

The Tovers, illustrated by Geoffrey Beitz.   London, Methuen, 1982.

The Adventures of Poon, illustrated by Dinah Shedden.   London, Hutchinson, 1984.

The Mysterious Island, illustrated by Joanna Carey.   London, Methuen, 1984.

One of the Family, illustrated by Barrie Thorpe.   London, Hutchinson, 1985.

The Ghosts of Lupus Street School.   London, Methuen, 1986.

Strange Magic, illustrated by Cathy Wood.   London, Methuen, 1986.

Emily and the Haunted Castle, illustrated by Kate Rogers.   London, Hutchinson, 1987.

Once upon a Time Stories, illustrated by Alice Englander.   London, Methuen, 1987.

The Secret Room, illustrated by Michael Bragg.   London, Methuen, 1987.

The Armada Adventure.   London, Methuen, 1988.

The Island Railway, illustrated by Maggie Harrison.   London, Hamish Hamilton, 1988.

Rose.   London, Hutchinson, 1989.

Plays

The Wombles, adaptation of her own stories (produced London, 1974).

Screenplay: *The Wombles,* 1971.

Television Plays: 60 scripts for *The Wombles* series, from 1973.

Other

The Wombles Annual 1975–1978.   London, World Distributors, 4 vols., 1974–77.

Jack and the Magic Stove (folktale), illustrated by Rita van Bilsen.   London, Hutchinson, 1982.

PUBLICATIONS FOR ADULTS

Novels

Paradise Island.   London, Hale, 1963.

Escape to Happiness.   London, Hale, 1964; New York, Nordon, 1980.

Roses round the Door.   London, Hale, and New York, Paperback Library, 1965.

Island of Shadows.   London, Hale, 1966; New York, Dale, 1980.

Veronica.   London, Hale, 1967; New York, Nordon, 1980.

A Tropical Affair.   London, Hale, 1967; as *Tropical Affairs,* New York, Dell, 1978.

Saturday's Child.   London, Hale, 1968; as *Echoes of Love,* New York, Dell, 1979.

Love Remembered.   London, Hale, 1970; New York, Dale, 1978.

Love and the S.S. Beatrice.   London, Hale, 1972; as *Thunder of Her Heart,* New York, Dale, 1978.

Pandora.   London, Hale, 1974.

The Steadfast Lover.   London, Hale, 1980.

The Silver Chain.   London, Hale, 1980.

The Restless Heart.   New York, Valueback, 1982.

Flight to Happiness.   London, Hale, 1983.

A Passionate Adventure.   London, Hale, 1983.

Plays

Road to Albutal, with Nick Renton (produced Edinburgh, 1976).

The Best of Friends (produced in the Channel Islands, 1982).

Other

Move On, with Peter Spence.   London, BBC Publications, 1978.

*

Elisabeth Beresford comments:

The books are roughly in four categories: 1) straight adventure, 2) magic—children with very ordinary backgrounds, to whom quite extraordinary things happen, 3) The Wombles, who, it is hoped, will make children want to fight pollution and to think up ways of "making good use of bad rubbish" (Womble family motto). And will also make readers of all ages laugh!, and 4) romantic thrillers.

*   *   *

Elisabeth Beresford shares in some degree the dilemma of Conan Doyle. Doyle invented, in a lighter moment, an amateur detective, and Sherlock Holmes hung around his neck like a dead weight. Beresford invented the Wombles. She may not feel as bitterly about her success as Doyle did. There can be no doubt that, in writing these gently humorous tales, she is sharing with readers her own warm affection for these curious creatures. But, in achieving a runaway success with the Wombles, Beresford has distracted attention from her other, and not less important, writing.

She was an established writer long before she discovered her first Womble on Wimbledon Common. That she had not won high critical acclaim was due partly to the variety of her work—writers are expected to keep tidily to well-defined paths—partly to her readiness to accept the discipline of the "easy readers." A typical example of her stories with a contemporary "realistic" theme is *The Hidden Mill.* In this she takes an actual landscape, one of the decayed rivers of South London, and the derelict buildings on its banks. Three recognisable children from the back streets find that this grubby environment has a rich potential for adventure, dangerous games, and romance, all scaled down to real life. Even the happy ending is based on probability. The same unassuming professionalism underlies a later story, *The Island Railway,* in which a newcomer to the Channel Islands finds common cause with an islander in the revival of a disused railway. The problems and their resolution, the help and opposition of adults, are those of real life. There are no short cuts, no easy solutions, no extravagant successes. A small book is distinguished by quiet competence.

While writing this kind of story Beresford was engaged on more substantial fantasies in the E. Nesbit manner. *Dangerous Magic* is characteristic of these. A great struggle between the forces of good and evil takes place among familiar scenes in London with action mainly in a block of high-rise flats, and a great aerial battle is fought out above the Thames. Like many of the best fantasies it is a tale of high adventure told largely in comic terms. The unicorn which comes to life in a thunderstorm is firmly in the Nesbit tradition in its vanity, its colloquial speech, and its ultimate, if reluctant, heroism.

Among later fantasies *The Ghosts of Lupus Street School* stands out for its closeness to reality. The scene is a London school in the East End which is about to celebrate its centenary by being demolished. A small boy, conspicuously unacademic, is given the holiday task of writing up the school's history. In this he is helped, and sometimes hindered, by Violet, the very solid ghost of one of the original pupils. If there is a degree of didacticism inherent in the theme it is not allowed to come between the reader and his enjoyment of a lively and consistent story. It confirms Beresford's standing as a sound, conscientious writer who never quite realizes her potential, perhaps because she dissipates her creative energies on too many minor projects.

As for the Wombles, it is difficult to take a cold critical look at a legend. The original stories have been blurred by subsequent translation into other media, and the endearing characters are uncomfortably familiar as toys, puppets, and shambling pop singers. The literary Wombles belong to an ancient tradition, that of the moral tale. In their advocacy of old-fashioned virtues the Wombles are Victorian, but their insistence on conservation strikes a contemporary note. The invention in these stories lacks originality, as the writing lacks distinction, but the Wombles have acquired a life independent of the parent stories in which they first appeared. They seem destined for some kind of immortality.

—Marcus Crouch

BERG, Leila (Rita). British. Born in Salford, Lancashire, 12 November 1917. Educated at Manchester High School; London University. Married in 1940; one son and one daughter. Children's books editor, Methuen, publishers, London, 1958–60; editor, Salamander Books, Thomas Nelson, publishers, London, 1965; editor, Nippers and Little Nippers series, Macmillan Education Ltd., London, 1968–76. Co-founder, Bookspread (now Leila Berg's Bookspread), 1978. Recipient: Children's Book Circle Eleanor Farjeon award, 1974. Address: Alice's Cottage, Brook Street, Wivenhoe, near Colchester, Essex CO7 9DS, England.

PUBLICATIONS FOR CHILDREN

Fiction

Fourteen What-Do-You-Know Stories, illustrated by Stanley Jackson. London, Epworth Press, 1948; New York, Roy, 1949; as *How John Caught the Sea-Horse and Other Stories* and *The Penguin Who Couldn't Paddle and Other Stories,* London, Penguin, 2 vols., 1966–67.
The Adventures of Chunky, illustrated by George Downs. London, Oxford University Press, 1950.
The Nightingale and Other Stories, illustrated by Garry Mackenzie. London, Oxford University Press, 1951.
The Tired Train and Other Stories, illustrated by Jean Bailey. London, Parrish, 1952.
Little Pete Stories, illustrated by Henrietta Garland. London, Methuen, 1952; revised edition, London, Penguin, 1959.
Trust Chunky, illustrated by Peggy Fortnum. Leicester, Brockhampton Press, 1954.
Fire Engine by Mistake, illustrated by Val Biro. Leicester, Brockhampton Press, 1955.
The Story of the Little Car, illustrated by W.A. Sillince. London,

Epworth Press, 1955; as *The Little Car,* London, Methuen, 1972.
Lollipops: Stories and Poems, illustrated by Kathleen Dance. Leicester, Brockhampton Press, 1957.
Andy's Pit Pony, illustrated by Val Biro. Leicester, Brockhampton Press, 1958.
The Hidden Road, illustrated by B. Chapman. London, Hamish Hamilton, 1958.
A Box for Benny, illustrated by Jillian Willett. Leicester, Brockhampton Press, 1958; Indianapolis, Bobbs Merrill, 1961.
Three Men Went to Work, illustrated by Dorothy Clark. London, Methuen, 1960.
The Jolly Farm Book, illustrated by Lindy. London, Collins, 1960.
See How They Work, illustrated by Dorothy Clark. London, Methuen, 1962.
A Newt for Roddy, illustrated by Constance Marshall. London, Nelson, 1965.
My Dog Sunday, illustrated by Dick Hart. London, Hamish Hamilton, 1968.
A Day Out, illustrated by Ferelith Eccles Williams. London, Macmillan, 1968.
Finding a Key, illustrated by Jenny Williams. London, Macmillan, 1968.
Fish and Chips for Supper, illustrated by Richard Rose. London, Macmillan, 1968.
Jimmy's Story, illustrated by Richard Rose. London, Macmillan, 1968.
The Jumble Sale, illustrated by George Craig. London, Macmillan, 1968.
Lesley's Story, illustrated by George Craig. London, Macmillan, 1968.
Julie's Story, illustrated by Richard Rose. London, Macmillan, 1970.
Letters, illustrated by Ferelith Eccles Williams. London, Macmillan, 1970.
The Little Car Has a Day Out, illustrated by Leslie Wood. Leicester, Brockhampton Press, 1970.
Paul's Story, illustrated by Richard Rose. London, Macmillan, 1970.
Robert's Story, illustrated by Richard Rose. London, Macmillan, 1970.
Susan's Story, illustrated by Richard Rose. London, Macmillan, 1970.
Bouncing, illustrated by Margaret Belsky. London, Macmillan, 1971.
Doing the Pools, illustrated by Richard Rose. London, Macmillan, 1972.
The Doctor, illustrated by Val Biro. London, Macmillan, 1972.
Hospital Day, illustrated by Shirley Hughes. London, Macmillan, 1972.
Knitting, illustrated by George Him. London, Macmillan, 1972.
My Brother, illustrated by Linda Birch. London, Macmillan, 1972.
Put the Kettle On!, illustrated by John Dyke. London, Macmillan, 1972.
That Baby, illustrated by Margaret Belsky. London, Macmillan, 1972.
Tracy's Story, illustrated by Richard Rose. London, Macmillan, 1972.
Well, I Never!, illustrated by George Him. London, Macmillan, 1972.
A Band in School, illustrated by John Dyke. London, Macmillan, 1975.
Plenty of Room, illustrated by Joan Beales. London, Macmillan, 1975.
Grandad's Clock, illustrated by Joan Beales. London, Macmillan, 1976.
Snaps (Presents, The Birthday Races, Waiting for the Dark, Looking

for Elephants), photographs by John Walmsley. London, Macmillan, 4 vols., 1977.

Chatterbooks (*In a House I Know; A Tickle; The Hot, Hot Day; Our Walk*), photographs by John Walmsley. London, Methuen, 4 vols., 1981.

Time for One More (fiction and verse), illustrated by Gerald Rose. London, Methuen, 1986.

Steep Street series (*Rosie and Mister Brown, Loving Jonathan Jones, Call That a Hat!, Having Friends*), illustrated by Lisa Kopper. London, Methuen, 4 vols., 1987.

Other (English language adaptations)

Paint a Black Horse, illustrated by Beatrice Braun-Fock. London, Methuen, 1958.

Bamburu, Boy of Ghana. London, Methuen, 1958.

Noriko-San, Girl of Japan, illustrated by Anna Riwkin-Brick. London, Methuen, 1958.

Little Owl. London, Methuen, 1966.

Other

Folk Tales for Reading and Telling, illustrated by George Him. Leicester, Brockhampton Press, and Cleveland, World, 1966; as *Topsy Turvy Tales,* London, Methuen, 1984.

Small World (*Dogs, Bees, Worms, Blood and Plasters, Ducks, Rainbows, Cars, Vacuum Cleaners*), illustrated by Lisa Kopper. London, Methuen, 8 vols., 1983–85.

Tales for Telling, illustrated by Danuta Laskowska. London, Methuen, 1983.

Christmas, illustrated by Jane Bottomley and John Walmsley. Aylesbury, Buckinghamshire, Ginn, 1985.

Hanukka, illustrated by Jane Bottomley and John Walmsley. Aylesbury, Buckinghamshire, Ginn, 1985.

Editor, *Four Feet and Two, and Some with None: An Anthology of Verse,* illustrated by Shirley Burke and Marvin Bileck. London, Penguin, 1960.

Translator, with Ruth Baer, *Grown-Ups Don't Understand,* by Irmgard Keun, illustrated by Sylvia Stokeld. London, Parrish, 1955; as *The Bad Example,* New York, Harcourt Brace, 1955.

Translator, with Evelyn Ramsden, *The Singing Town,* by Thorbjørn Egner. London, Methuen, 1959.

PUBLICATIONS FOR ADULTS

Play

Raising Hell (produced Salisbury, 1972; London, 1973).

Other

Risinghill: Death of a Comprehensive School. London, Penguin, 1968.

Neill and Summerhill, photographs by John Walmsley. London, Penguin, 1969.

Children's Rights: Towards the Liberation of the Child, with others, edited by Julian Hall. London, Elek, and New York, Praeger, 1971.

The Train Back: A Search for Parents, with Pat Chapman. London, Allen Lane, 1972.

Look at Kids. London, Penguin, 1972.

Reading and Loving. London, Routledge, 1977.

*

Leila Berg comments:

I simply explore people and situations in a way that I feel is relevant to a child's experience, and that will hold a child through amusement, excitement, or a sense of wonder. This is how one writes for adults too—the only difference is relevance to a *child's* experience.

* * *

Leila Berg is a prolific writer for children and above all a story-teller whose wealth of experience of reading to children is very apparent in her writing. Her style is pruned of unnecessary detail, lively and colloquial, with events surely paced to reach a satisfying conclusion. She writes for the younger age range—stories to listen to or first stories to read for oneself. Her writing has now lost the occasional didacticism of her earlier work. It is based on her own experiences—her Salford Jewish childhood (*A Box for Benny*), her own children, the nursery she ran in her home and so forth. It has also been much shaped both by her desire to show children in literature as they really are—active, argumentative, thinking (e.g., *Little Pete Stories* or the recent *Steep Street* series)—and by her conviction of the need for a literature where the majority of children can read about themselves ("Nippers").

In Berg's supplementary readers for the "Nippers" series (which she also edits), her ideas about children's literature have found their fullest expression. The series has been attacked by teachers who object to the depiction of the realities of working-class life and by others who point to what they see as a stereotyped and patronising view of working people. Berg's books are not to be so lightly dismissed, however. She has an excellent ear, and these books are clear demonstrations of her skill in conveying with verve and wit the speech patterns and vocabulary of those considered till very recently to be "uncultured." Berg also brings to her urban working-class themes the traditional story patterns and repetitions of the teller of tales—in *Fish and Chips for Supper,* for example, we have the lively use of a cumulative tale.

It is not easy to assess Berg's contribution to children's literature. Her major innovations—dialogue true to the cadences of working-class speech and the presentation of positive working-class characters in their own environment—have had a major impact on children's book publishing and extended the range of possibilities open to other writers.

—Rosemary Stones

BERRY, James. British. Born in Fair Prospect, Jamaica, in 1925; moved to England in 1948. Overseas telegraphist, Post Office, London, 1951–77. Writer-in-residence, Vauxhall Manor School, London. Lives in Brighton, Sussex. Recipient: C. Day Lewis fellowship; Smarties prize, 1987. Address: c/o Hamish Hamilton, 27 Wrights Lane, London W8 5TZ, England.

PUBLICATIONS FOR CHILDREN

Fiction

A Thief in the Village and Other Stories. London, Hamish

Hamilton, 1987; New York, Orchard, 1988.

Verse

When I Dance. London, Hamish Hamilton, 1988.

PUBLICATIONS FOR ADULTS

Short Stories

The Girls and Yanga Marshall. London, Longman, 1987.

Verse

Fractured Circles. London, New Beacon, 1979.
Cut-Way Feelins, Loving, Lucy's Letters. Stafford, Strange Lime
    Fruit Stone, 1981.
Chain of Days. Oxford, Oxford University Press, 1985.

Other

Editor, *Bluefoot Traveller: An Anthology of Westindian Poets in
    Britain.* London, Limestone, 1976; revised edition, 1981.
Editor, *Dance to a Different Drum: Brixton Poetry Festival 1983:
    Poetry from a Community.* London, Brixton Festival, 1983.
Editor, *News for Babylon: The Chatto Book of Westindian-British
    Poetry.* London, Chatto and Windus, 1984.

*   *   *

James Berry's prize-winning collection of short stories, *A Thief in
the Village,* is a children's book of a particular kind, based on
recollection of childhood. The author grew up on a Caribbean island,
in a community of aching poverty, and his recall is extraordinary.
Certain aspects of the stories are uncompromisingly adult; they are
not overshaped by narrative design, and the language is used with
unlimited ambition and fluency. They have a clear-eyed, bleak
truthfulness that many adults flinch from deploying for children, and
in one or two of the stories Berry himself shows signs of arranging
the tale to make it more acceptable. The title story, for example, is
set into a frame in which a girl in school in England, encouraged by
an English teacher, writes down in Caribbean English a story from
home. This device is unsuccessful because it makes the story itself
seem to be in need of explanation, of which in fact it has no need.
And the happy endings—a girl gets a longed-for bike, and her mother
gets a man-friend; a boy accused of stealing a mouth organ is
vindicated; a child swept out to sea astride a swimming horse is
rescued—have an improbable quality, because the author himself has
undercut them by showing us so vividly a human context in which
the worst must often happen. These, however, are very minor
criticisms of a deeply poignant and masterly group of stories.
    "All Other Days Run into Sunday" is a microcosm of the whole
book. The sense of specialness which makes the day radiant to a
child: a wonderful scene in which the horses are washed in the sea,
the church-going for which everyone dresses up, and from which the
poorest skive off, even the food being better—all these things are
meticulously remembered, the *feel* of them is remembered and
accurately described, together with the authentic ring of the voices.
"Come, buoy," the ragged child tempts the protagonist on his way
to church, "Satan life much sweet sweet more than sainty sainty
life…" Delicately poised, the story contains both the viewpoint of
the child and that of the adult looking back. Terrified when asked the
way by white men in a car, taking them for "The Blackheart men"
who spirit away black children and tear out their hearts for medical
research, the narrator also thinks, "Nobody thinks how it looks like

inherited dread…"
    Throwing the lyrical beauties of the island into sharp relief are
stories of cruelty and despair. A mob of teenagers picks on a spastic
boy, and tries to take away and kill his pet mongoose. The boy's
offence is that of the man falsely accused of theft in the title story:
he is different. When the bullies set a dog on the mongoose, he
protects it with his own body. Adult help arrives, but although the
gang are all beaten and rebuked, they sneak off to plot a further
attempt to kill the mongoose and escape punishment. As sad as "Elias
and the Mongoose" is chilling is "Fanso and Granny Flo." Fanso's
father deserted his mother 13 years ago, before he was born. When
one day he comes calling Fanso is frantic to see more of him, and to
meet his half-brothers and sisters in the town. However, he is
defeated by the immovable bitterness of his mother and grandmother.
Gustus in the final story goes out into a hurricane to attempt to secure
his banana tree and save the crop. His distraught father finds him
badly injured. "Why you do this?" he asks. "I did wahn buy mi shoes,
Pappy…" Gustus says. Understanding too late, the father tears off
his own boots.
    This collection is more than the sum of its parts. Gradually a
portrait of poverty grows in the reader's mind. The adults are so hard
pressed, living on so slight a margin, that they have no time or
sympathy to spare for their children, and can give them only the bare
necessities. But the bicycles, the mouth organ, the pair of shoes that
the children long for are not material superfluities—materially they
could be done without—but spiritual necessities; they are what those
children need to grow.
    Before *A Thief in the Village* James Berry was published as a poet,
and with *When I Dance,* a collection of poems for children, he has
followed up both lines. The introduction to *When I Dance* pleads for
the poems to be read by white as well as black readers, in whatever
voice they can command, and justly points out that a refusal to read
black poetry perpetuates divisions in the body of shared literary
culture. In spite of this one must say the poems vary very widely,
both in their degree of deviation from standard English and in their
accessibility. It is the rhythm that gets lost when the reader stumbles,
and the rhythm is an important part of the force and flow of Berry's
style. His wonderful use of detail, and his tender human understanding for children battered but not yet beaten by adverse social
circumstance are still powerfully in evidence.

—Jill Paton Walsh

––––––––

BEST, (Oswald) Herbert. British. Born in Chester, Cheshire, 25
April 1894. Educated at King's School, Chester; Queens' College,
Cambridge, LL.B. 1914. Served in the Royal Engineers, 1914–19:
Lieutenant. Married the writer and illustrator Evangel Allena
Champlin (pseudonym: Erick Berry) in 1926 (died 1974). District
officer, British Colonial Civil Service, Nigeria, 1919–32. Lived in
the United States. Fellow, Royal Geographical Society. *Died in 1981.*

PUBLICATIONS FOR CHILDREN

Fiction

Garram the Hunter: A Boy of the Hill Tribes, illustrated by Erick
    Berry. New York, Doubleday, 1930; London, Lane, 1935.
Son of the Whiteman, illustrated by Erick Berry. New York,
    Doubleday, 1931.
Garram the Chief: The Story of the Hill Tribes, illustrated by Erick
    Berry. New York, Doubleday, 1932; London, Lane, 1935.

Flag of the Desert, illustrated by Erick Berry. New York, Viking Press, 1936; Oxford, Blackwell, 1937.

Tal of the Four Tribes, illustrated by Erick Berry. Oxford, Blackwell, and New York, Doubleday, 1938.

Gunsmith's Boy, illustrated by Erick Berry. Philadelphia, Winston, 1942; London, Newnes, 1944.

Young'un. New York, Macmillan, 1944; London, Cape, 1945.

Border Iron, illustrated by Erick Berry. New York, Viking Press, 1945; London, Newnes, 1946.

Watergate: A Story of the Irish on the Erie Canal, illustrated by Erick Berry. Philadelphia, Winston, 1951.

Not Without Danger: A Story of the Colony of Jamaica in Revolutionary Days, illustrated by Erick Berry. New York, Viking Press, 1951.

Ranger's Ransom, illustrated by Erick Berry. New York, Aladdin, 1953.

The Sea Warriors. New York, Macmillan, 1959.

Desmond's First Case, illustrated by Ezra Jack Keats. New York, Viking Press, 1961.

Bright Hunter of the Skies, illustrated by Bernarda Bryson. New York, Macmillan, 1961.

Carolina Gold. New York, Day, 1961.

Desmond the Dog Detective: The Case of the Lone Stranger, illustrated by Lilian Obligado. New York, Viking Press, 1962.

Desmond and the Peppermint Ghost: The Dog Detective's Third Case, illustrated by Lilian Obligado. New York, Viking Press, 1965.

Desmond and Dog Friday, illustrated by W.T. Mars. New York, Viking Press, 1968.

The Polynesian Triangle, with Erick Berry. New York, Funk and Wagnalls, 1968.

Other

Concertina Farm, with and illustrated by Erick Berry. London, Joseph, 1943.

The Long Portage: A Story of Ticonderoga and Lord Howe, illustrated by Erick Berry. New York, Viking Press, 1948; as *The Road to Ticonderoga; or, The Long Portage,* London, Penguin, 1954.

The Webfoot Warriors: The Story of UDT, the U.S. Navy's Underwear Demolition Team. New York, Day, 1962.

Parachute to Survival. New York, Day, 1964.

Men Who Changed the Map: A.D. 400 to 1914, with Erick Berry. New York, Funk and Wagnalls, 1968.

PUBLICATIONS FOR ADULTS

Novels

The Mystery of the Flaming Hut. London, Cassell, and New York, Harper, 1932.

The Skull Beneath the Eaves. London, Grayson, 1933.

Winds Whisper. London, Hurst and Blackett, 1937.

Low River. London, Hurst and Blackett, 1937.

The Twenty-Fifth Hour. London, Cape, and New York, Random House, 1940.

Whistle, Daughter, Whistle. New York, Macmillan, 1947.

The Columbus Cannon. New York, Viking Press, 1954.

Diane. New York, Morrow, 1954; London, Museum Press, 1955.

A Rumour of Drums. London, Cassell, 1962; New York, McKay, 1963.

Other

Writing for Children, with Erick Berry. New York, Viking Press, 1947; revised edition, Coral Gables, Florida, University of Miami Press, 1964.

*   *   *

Herbert Best was a prolific author who proved himself able to write successfully for a varied audience, from the youngsters who enjoy the adventures of Desmond the dog on up. By far his best-known and best-loved work is *Young'un,* the story of three adolescents whose mother has died in a fire and whose father, unable to face the tragedy and the losing struggle to maintain his ill-kept farm, deserts them and takes to the woods. But these youngsters are not pitiful waifs; they are proud, self-reliant, and brave, determined to hold the remains of their family together and to make a success of their failing farm. They face daunting difficulties, and the account of their struggles, the good moments and the bad, make a very special story. The hard work, the discomfort, the independence, and the warm neighbourliness were all a part of backwoods life at the end of the pioneer era, as they are even today. For all their quaint speech and customs, and their obvious lack of "book learning," they are not portrayed as bumpkins or yokels. They are highly skilled craftsmen and women, able to make or mend anything they need, dependent upon no repairman, social worker, or law enforcement officer. *Young'un* has about it a warm and enviable glow that no electric light can duplicate.

Unlike *Young'un,* most of Best's historical fiction was that of a journeyman writer. He selected a theme for its saleability, researched it meticulously, wrote, and then moved on to new fields, much in the spirit of the feature writer, as his *Writing for Children* plainly demonstrates. His output was workmanlike, and with the notable exception of *Young'un,* not too memorable. A fairly typical example of his historical fiction, *Bright Hunter of the Skies* is almost a manual of mediaeval falconry, given its setting in time by the presence of Holy Roman Emperor Frederick II, and made appealing by the addition of child-hero Jan. Similarly he drew upon the life lived in the Sahara for *Flag of the Desert,* of the Vikings for *The Sea Warriors,* etc.

His Desmond the Dog Detective series for younger readers is popular for its cute whimsicality, but unfortunately he emphasizes the undeniable charm and loveability of dogs and their boys chiefly by denigrating and excluding girls, and outmoded convention that modern children's literature can well do without. A true product of his times, Best exemplifies a benevolent but chauvinistic style unlikely to appeal to young readers of a more enlightened era.

—Joan McGrath

BESTALL, Alfred (Edmeades). British. Born in Mandalay, Burma, 14 December 1892. Educated at Rydal School, Colwyn Bay, Wales, 1904–11; Birmingham Central School of Art, 1911–13; Central School of Art, London, 1914, 1919–22. Served in the British Army, in Flanders, 1915–19. Freelance book and magazine illustrator: work appeared in *Punch, Tatler, Bystander, Passing Show,* and other periodicals. Wrote and illustrated Rupert serial for *Daily Express,* London, 1935–65. *Died 15 January 1986.*

PUBLICATIONS FOR CHILDREN (illustrated by the author)

Fiction

Boys and Girls Book (annual). London, Lane Publications, 4 vols., 1935–38.

Daily Express Rupert Annuals.   London, Daily Express, 41 vols., 1936–76 (and some episodes in later annuals).
Rupert Adventure Series.   London, Daily Express, 50 vols., 1948–63.
Adventure Books.   London, Oldbourne, 2 vols., n.d.
Rupert Colour Library.   Maidenhead, Berkshire, Purnell, 1976.

Other

Rupert: A Bear's Life, with George Perry.   London, Pavilion, 1985.

*

Bibliography: *The Rupert Index: A Bibliography of Rupert Bear* by W.O.G. Lofts and Derek J. Adley, privately printed, n.d.

Illustrator: *The Play's the Thing,* 1927, and *The Boy Next Door,* 1944, both by Enid Blyton; *A Book of Magic Rhymes* by Alfred Dunning, 1928; *Reading and Thinking* series, 7 vols., 1928–34; *Myths and Legends of Many Lands* by Evelyn Smith, 1930; *Tales from Many Lands* by D.V. Searle, 1930; *Kenilworth* by Sir Walter Scott; *The Pathfinder* by James Fenimore Cooper; *Thalaba the Destroyer* by Robert Southey; *The Black Tulip* and *The Three Musketeers* both by Alexandre Dumas, 1933; *The Disappearing Trick* by Agnes Frome, 1933; *The Spanish Gold-fish* by Dudley Glass, 1934; *New Times Reader 2,* 1934; *Mother Goose's Book of Nursery Rhymes,* 1936; *The Land of the Christmas Stocking* by Mabel Buchanan, 1936; *Salute to the Village* by Fay Inchfawn, 1943; *Countryside [Animal, Strange] Tales from "Blackwood,"* 3 vols., 1946–50; *Folk Tales of Wales* by Eirwen Jones, 1947; *A Sprite at School* by Constance M. White, 1947; *The Hive* by John Crompton, 1947.

*   *   *

See the essay on Mary Tourtel and Alfred Bestall.

———

BETTINA.   Pseudonym for Bettina Ehrlich, née Bauer.   British. Born in Vienna, Austria, 19 March 1903; emigrated to Britain, 1938; became citizen, 1947. Educated at Kunstgewerbeschule (school of applied arts), Vienna. Married the sculptor George Ehrlich in 1930 (died 1966). Freelance writer and artist. Recipient: Paris International Exhibition for Arts and Crafts medal, 1937. *Died 10 October 1985.*

PUBLICATIONS FOR CHILDREN (illustrated by the author)

Fiction

Poo-Tsee, The Water-Tortoise.   London, Chatto and Windus, 1943.
Cocolo.   London, Chatto and Windus, 1945; New York, Harper, 1948.
Carmello.   London, Chatto and Windus, 1945.
Cocolo Comes to America.   New York, Harper, 1949.
Cocolo's Home.   New York, Harper, 1950.
Castle in the Sand.   New York, Harper, 1951.
A Horse for the Island.   New York, Harper, 1952; London, Hamish Hamilton, 1953.
Piccolo.   New York, Harper, 1954.
Pantaloni.   New York, Harper, 1957; London, Oxford University Press, 1959.
Angelo and Rosaline.   London, Collins, 1957.
Trovato.   New York, Farrar Straus, 1959; London, Oxford Univer-

sity Press, 1960.
Paolo and Panetto.   London, Oxford University Press, 1960; New York, Watts, 1961.
For the Leg of a Chicken.   London, Collins, and New York, Watts, 1960.
Francesco and Francesca.   London, Oxford University Press, 1962.
Of Uncles and Aunts.   London, Oxford University Press, 1963; New York, Norton, 1964.
The Goat Boy.   London, Oxford University Press, 1965; New York, Norton, 1966.
Sardines and the Angel.   London, Oxford University Press, 1967.
Neretto.   London, Oxford University Press, 1969.
A Day in Venice.   London, Oxford University Press, 1973.

Other

Show Me Yours: A Little Paintbook.   London, Chatto and Windus, 1943.
Dolls.   London, Oxford University Press, 1962; New York, Farrar Straus, 1963.

*

Manuscript Collections: Kerlan Collection, University of Minnesota, Minneapolis; University of Oregon Library, Eugene.

Illustrator: *The Swans of Ballycastle* by Walter Hackett, 1954; *The Magic Christmas Tree* by Lee Kingman, 1956; *Piruwayu and the Rainbow* by Gilles Saint-Cérère, 1958; *Favorite Fairy Tales Told in England* by Virginia Haviland, 1959; *The Sorcerer's Apprentice and Other Stories* by John Hosier, 1960; *Tal and the Magic Barruget* by Eva-Lis Wuorio, 1965.

*   *   *

Bettina is best known for her picture books for five to nine-year-olds. The delicate charm of her watercolours is reminiscent of Ardizzone's and like his, her style is deceptively simple. As a young woman, she said she distrusted her spelling so much that she preferred to tell stories through pictures. Whether or not this is strictly true, her illustrations have the confidence and vigour of someone who habitually communicates visually. Their immediacy and movement carry the story from page to page so that the text can be relaxed and digressive—although nothing is mentioned that is not meticulously illustrated.

Bettina was born in Austria and spent much of her free time in Italy, although she lived in England from the outbreak of the Second World War until her death. The best of her books reflect her memories of pre-war Europe, where nothing more serious than a thunderstorm can trouble the innocent peace of a small community. Her simplicity is, however, not accidental, for she knew how to select the representative detail. The atmosphere she created in her little Italian cafés or Austrian pastures is vivid enough to support her quiet, understated stories. She had the ability—as in a fairy tale—to suspend belief, and, despite her foreign settings, we feel instantly at home. Statues, bronze angels, weathervanes, and the like have a life of their own, just as they would for children. A naiad or a nurse are both equally real.

Her best books have an element of magic. *Sardines and the Angel* tells how for the price of several ice creams the gentle Miss Higgins hears the story of Arturo, the little sardine seller. Arturo's family is too poor to afford ice creams, and one day, tempted beyond endurance, he spends some of the money from the sale of his father's fish on a strawberry cone. His father warns him that the bronze angel on the church spire knows about dishonest children, and, sure enough, the next time he gives way to temptation, there is the angel, standing in the café and demanding the largest ice cream cone. Arturo buys it for him, even though he knows he will be punished. Next day, a dreadful storm blows up when he is fishing with his father, but they are both saved when suddenly the angel appears and conjures up a favourable wind. After this, Arturo's parents believe in his strange friendship and they also allow him a weekly ice cream. Magic, moral, and reality are interwoven so well in this story that it is impossible to tell where one ends and the other begins. A similar effect is achieved in *The Goat Boy,* when Toni's goats are saved by a naiad; but this is less successful, largely because Toni himself is too passive in the story.

Bettina's careful attention to the concrete details of everyday life, even in her fantasy, has a child-like assurance, and her books are full of cheerful security, where the occasional cloud only serves to make the sunshine seem brighter.

—Alison Sage

BIANCO, Margery (Winifred) Williams. Prior to 1925 wrote as Margery Williams. British. Born in London, 22 July 1881. Educated privately and at schools in Philadelphia and Sharon Hill, Pennsylvania. Married Francisco Bianco; one son and one daughter, the illustrator Pamela Bianco. *Died 4 September 1944.*

PUBLICATIONS FOR CHILDREN

Fiction

The Velveteen Rabbit; or, How Toys Become Real, illustrated by William Nicholson. London, Heinemann, and New York, Doran, 1922.
The Little Wooden Doll, illustrated by Pamela Bianco. New York, Macmillan, 1925.
Poor Cecco: The Wonderful Story of a Wonderful Wooden Dog Who Was the Jolliest Toy in the House until He Went Out to Explore the World, illustrated by Arthur Rackham. London, Chatto and Windus, and New York, Doran, 1925.
The Apple Tree, illustrated by Boris Artzybasheff. New York, Doran, 1926.
The Adventures of Andy, illustrated by Leon Underwood. New York, Doran, 1927.
The Skin Horse, illustrated by Pamela Bianco. New York, Doran, 1927.
The Candlestick, illustrated by Ludovic Rodo. New York, Doubleday, 1929.
Other People's Houses. New York, Viking Press, 1930.
The House That Grew Smaller, illustrated by Rachel Field. New York, Macmillan, 1931.
A Street of Little Shops, illustrated by Grace Paull. New York, Doubleday, 1932; Kingswood, Surrey, World's Work, 1958.
The Hurdy-Gurdy Man, illustrated by Robert Lawson. New York, Oxford University Press, 1933; London, Oxford University Press, 1937.
The Good Friends, illustrated by Grace Paull. New York, Viking Press, 1934.
Winterbound, illustrated by Kate Seredy. New York, Viking Press, 1936.
Green Grows the Garden, illustrated by Grace Paull. New York,

Macmillan, 1936.
Franzi and Gizi, with Gisella Loeffler. New York, Messner, 1941.
Penny and the White Horse, illustrated by Marjory Collinson. New York, Messner, 1942.
Bright Morning, illustrated by Margaret Platt. New York, Viking Press, 1942; London, Collins, 1945.
Forward, Commandos!, illustrated by Rafaello Busoni. New York, Viking Press, 1944; London, Wells Gardner Darton, 1947.

Other

All about Pets, illustrated by Grace Gilkison. New York, Macmillan, 1930.
More about Animals, illustrated by Helen Torrey. New York, Macmillan, 1934.
Tales from a Finnish Tupa, with James Cloyd Bowman, illustrated by Laura Bannon. Chicago, Whitman, 1936; as *Tales from a Finnish Fireside,* London, Chatto and Windus, 1975.
Rufus the Fox: Adapted from the French of Samivel. New York, Harper, 1937.
The Five-and-a-Half Club (reader), with Mabel O'Donnell and Rona Munro, illustrated by Florence and Margaret Hoopes. Evanston, Illinois, Row Peterson, 1942; London, Nisbet, 1956.
Herbert's Zoo and Other Favorite Stories, with others, illustrated by Julian. New York, Simon and Schuster, 1949.
The New Five-and-a-Half Club (reader), with Mabel O'Donnell, illustrated by Margaret Ayer. Evanston, Illinois, Row Peterson, 1951.
Comprehension Cards. London, Nisbet, 24 vols., 1959.

Translator, *The African Saga,* by Blaise Cendrars. New York, Payson and Clarke, 1927.
Translator, *Little Black Stories for Little White Children,* by Blaise Cendrars, illustrated by Pierre Pinsard. New York, Payson and Clarke, 1929.
Translator, with Dagny Mortensen, *Sidsel Longskirt: A Girl of Norway,* by Hans Aanrud, illustrated by Ingri and Edgar Parin d'Aulaire. Philadelphia, Winston, 1935.
Translator, with Dagny Mortensen, *Solve Suntrap: A Boy of Norway,* by Hans Aanrud, illustrated by Ingri and Edgar Parin d'Aulaire. Philadelphia, Winston, 1935.

PUBLICATIONS FOR ADULTS

Novels

The Late Returning. London, Heinemann, and New York, Macmillan, 1902.
Spendthrift Summer. London, Heinemann, 1903.
The Price of Youth. London, Duckworth, and New York, Macmillan, 1904.
The Bar. London, Methuen, 1906.
The Thing in the Woods. London, Duckworth, 1913.

Play

Out of the Night: A Mystery Comedy, with Harold Hutchinson. London and New York, French, 1929.

Other

Paris. London, A. and C. Black, and New York, Macmillan, 1910.

Translator, *Four Cents an Acre: The Story of Louisiana under the*

French, by Georges Oudard.   New York, Brewer and Warren, 1931.

*   *   *

Some of the greatest books—among them *Alice, The Wind in the Willows,* and *The Hobbit*—have started life as private books. Conceived for the entertainment of individual children, they have only later, and then sometimes after processing, found a wider audience.

Margery Williams Bianco's *Poor Cecco* is of this company. It was made first for the author's daughter Pamela—genius out of genius; at 12 Pamela's drawings inspired Walter de la Mare to a set of charming "illustrative" verses, and she grew up to be equally distinguished as artist and writer. The Cecco of the title was a battered wooden dog, and the other characters were out of Pamela's toy-cupboard. They live in a necessarily closely knit community, form complicated relationships, and talk their own language. The modern reader who is privileged to look in on this private world is initially puzzled, but not for too long. *Poor Cecco* is one of the classic "toy" stories, deserving a place beside Rachel Field's *Hitty* and Rumer Godden's *Impunity Jane* among the very best of the genre.

Bianco knew, as all who enjoy the company of small children must, that toys are a very serious matter. There is plenty of laughter in *Poor Cecco,* but it is with, not at, the creatures whose destinies are worked out in these pages. The toys feel emotions rather like those of humans, but their actions are governed by certain physical limitations. They are animate but still made of wood, fabric, and stuffing.

They are nicely contrasted with the humans and the animals. There is a particularly convincing portrait of Murrum the cat, who comes nearest in this fundamentally kindly story to being the villain of the piece. The humans play a minor and passive role, apart from the postman who brings home Poor Cecco and his friends from their wanderings, tied together like a parcel and the postage duly paid with Poor Cecco's hard-earned pennies.

Unlike some improvised stories, *Poor Cecco* is tightly constructed. The plot is very compact, even if the entry of a major character—Jensina the Dutch doll—is delayed until well into the book; this is not a flaw so much as a calculated building-up to one of the crises of the narrative. Jensina is a splendid person, strongminded, resourceful, set against the home-bred dolls with their gossip and petty jealousies. The subtleties of characterisation are expressed always in dialogue rather than in description; each toy has his idiosyncracies of speech and his individual standpoint.

Bianco has always been well served by her illustrators. The first edition of *Poor Cecco* had seven colour-plates in Arthur Rackham's grandest manner, and a recent edition has drawings no less decorative and perhaps more penetrating by Antony Maitland. A lesser book, *The Hurdy-Gurdy Man,* was honoured with masterly designs by Robert Lawson. The book which comes nearest to *Poor Cecco—The Velveteen Rabbit*—is one of the very few illustrated by one of the greatest masters of this art, Sir William Nicholson.

The Velveteen Rabbit might be regarded as a trial run for *Poor Cecco.* It too is a story of toys and of the nursery magic which can give them a reality more sharp than that of the ordinary world. But here the writer lacks confidence, and her book is tentative and uncertain, full of the sententiousness into which many writers are prone to slip when the heat of inspiration cools. The moral, instead of being implicit in the narrative, has to be stated and underlined.

Bianco, although not prolific, ranged widely, with translations, educational readers, and a travel book about Paris. For most readers she remains, and rightly, a one-book woman. *Poor Cecco* contains the best of her: the tenderness, the sense of adventure and of fun, the sturdy common sense. As postscript to one of her innumerable letters to Bulka, which fill one memorable chapter, Tubby writes: "I love you more than Christmas and Easter and Fairyland." These are strong words, but they are rather what the reader feels about this uniquely

heart-warming book.

—Marcus Crouch

———

BIBBY, Violet (née Richardson).   British.   Born in Newport Pagnell, Buckinghamshire, 18 February 1908. Educated at Whitelands College, teaching diploma 1928; Central School of Art, London, 1928–30. Married Edmund Bibby in 1930; two sons. Teacher of English and arts and crafts, 1928–42, and part-time, 1942–69. Agent: Murray Pollinger, 4 Garrick Street, London WC2E 9BH. Address: 1 Cumberland Road, Angmering, Sussex BN16 4BG, England.

PUBLICATIONS FOR CHILDREN

Fiction

Saranne, illustrated by Hilary Abrahams.   London, Longman, 1969.
The Mirrored Shield, illustrated by Graham Humphreys.   London, Longman, 1970.
The Wildling, illustrated by Graham Humphreys.   London, Longman, 1971.
Many Waters.   London, Faber, 1974; as *Many Waters Cannot Quench Love,* New York, Morrow, 1975.
Tinner's Quest.   London, Faber, 1977.
The Phantom Horse, illustrated by Laszlo Acs.   London, Kaye and Ward, 1979.

*

Violet Bibby comments:

I have a strong feeling of "place," which has set off each book so far. My writing, I am told, is very "visual." I would have been a painter if I had not turned to writing seriously. I still paint evocative landscapes.

*   *   *

A craft or a lifestyle is the true hero of every one of Violet Bibby's books. *Saranne,* her first book, uses the world of canal narrowboats as a background for an adventure and mystery story. The way of life of canal folk is beautifully described; the characters, though simple, are vivid, and the plot is elaborate in a rather old-fashioned manner. The author's affection and enthusiasm for her subject shine through the book, and make a warm and pleasing result.

The Mirrored Shield treats in a similar manner of the craft of stonemason in the 15th century; *The Wildling* glass workers in the Sussex Weald in the early 17th century. All these books have a particular flavour; though carefully written, their plots and characters are rather mechanical; though lively, they lack the inner life which might make them transcend their function as the author's device to allow her to write about the life of their time and setting. However, Bibby is not a narrowly didactic writer, for she is able to infuse the details of her world and the minutiae of ancient crafts with the life and enthusiasm her characters never quite embody.

Many Waters might seem to be in the same mould. Once more there is an old and picturesque lifestyle—that of fen-dwellers in Cambridgeshire before the Dutchmen drained the marshes in the 1640's. But the character of Constancy, and her affection for a young Dutch engineer, are more successful, and more subtly drawn. The mysterious world of the wetlands is still the main subject, and, though the book is a little over-plotted, it is convincing and touching.

Tinner's Quest takes her largest canvas yet. With the intricate knowledge and talent for exposition which we by now expect of her, Bibby describes the life of Cornish tin miners and charts two generations of a mining family in their wanderings from Cornwall to America to Australia. Salan, the true central figure of the book, is Bibby's most interesting character. Speaking the old tongue, liking the old standing stones, with an instinctive feel for the lie of the lodes in the rock, he goes native when he gets to Australia, understanding and befriending the aborigines. The mystery of his crime, and the search for him by his wife and son make up the main movement of the book; the means by which an adit is cut to drain a flooded mine into the sea is a sub-plot as powerful as the main one. No one can make such matters as comprehensible and fascinating as Violet Bibby can; this is her best book.

—Jill Paton Walsh

BICE, Clare. Canadian. Born in Durham, Ontario, 24 January 1908. Educated at Aberdeen Public School, 1913–21, and Central Collegiate, 1921–26, both London, Ontario; University of Western Ontario, London, 1926–29, B.A. 1928; Art Students' League and Grand Central School of Art, both New York, 1930–31. Served in the Canadian Army, 1942–45: Corporal. Married Marion Agnes Reid in 1943; one son and one daughter. Curator, London Art Museum, Ontario, 1940–72. Teacher at Doon School of Art, and summer sessions at Queen's University, Kingston, Ontario, Mount Allison University, Sackville, New Brunswick, University of British Columbia, Vancouver, and University of Western Ontario. Painter: individual shows in Montreal, and London and Hamilton, Ontario; group shows: New York World's Fair, 1939; Canadian Army Exhibition, 1944; Canadian National Exhibition; Stratford Festival, Ontario. President, Canadian Art Museums Directors' Organization, 1966–68. Recipient: Canadian Government fellowship, 1952; Canada Arts Council senior fellowship, 1962, 1972; Centennial Medal, 1967. LL.D.: University of Western Ontario, 1962. Associate, 1938, Full Academician, 1964, and President, 1967–70, Royal Canadian Academy. Member, Order of Canada, 1973. *Died 18 May 1976.*

PUBLICATIONS FOR CHILDREN (illustrated by the author)

Fiction

Jory's Cove. New York, Macmillan, 1941.
Across Canada: Stories of Canadian Children. New York, Macmillan, 1949.
The Great Island. New York, Macmillan, 1954.
A Dog for Davie's Hill. Toronto, Macmillan, 1956.
Hurricane Treasure. Toronto, Macmillan, and New York, Viking Press, 1965.

*

Illustrator: *Animals, Plants, and Machines* by Lucy Sprague Mitchell and Margaret Wise Brown, 1944; *'T Aint Runnin' No More,* 1946, *The Bruce Beckons,* 1952, and *Silken Lines and Silver Hooks,* 1954, all by William Sherwood Fox; *Thunder in the Mountains* by Hilda Mary Hooke, 1947; *The Golden Pine Cone,* 1950, *The Sun Horse,* 1951, *The One-Winged Dragon,* 1955, *The Silver Man,* 1958, *The*

Diamond Feather, 1962, and *The Hunter and the Medicine Man,* 1966, all by Catherine Anthony Clark; *The Force Carries On* by T. Morris Longstreth, 1954; *At the Dark of the Moon* by Mabel Tinkiss Good, 1956; *The Great Canoe* by Adelaide Leitch, 1962; *Keen for Adventure* by William E. Corfield, 1967.

*   *   *

Clare Bice has received more attention as an artist known for fine landscapes and portraits than as a writer for children. The five juveniles which he wrote and illustrated vary in quality from the informative but uninspired *Across Canada: Stories of Canadian Children* to the exciting mystery and adventure stories which are set on the rugged eastern Canadian seacoast. These latter books, as well as the one set in the Scottish Highlands (*A Dog for Davie's Hill*), are successful both with children and from a literary point of view.

Bice's eye as a painter is both his strength and his undoing in *Across Canada.* The realistic illustrations give an appealing pastoral vision of Canadian provincial life, but the text itself is drab. The stories are more sketches of the landscapes he surveys—seacoasts, farms, prairies, mountains, forests and the Canadian north; there is little dramatic action or plot. At the center of each sketch is a child, ostensibly the subject of the piece, but description consists more of the superficial visual details noticed by the painter than of character analysis by the writer.

Mystery-adventure stories like *The Great Island* and *Hurricane Treasure* are more successful. In them, Bice creates a vivid setting, and he blends landscape with character and action more skillfully. One interesting technique in *The Great Island* is seen in his manipulations of time. We meet Angus, the boy protagonist, who takes us into three levels of time; his imagination turns backwards into the historical and mythic past of pirates and buried gold; his actual present consists of poverty and loneliness because his father must work in the big city to support them; and the future is secured because Angus's search for treasure leads to the community's obtaining a new fish-freezing plant which will furnish local employment for his father. Dramatic action is sustained throughout, and the skillful juxtapositioning of the past, present, and future gives depth to the story.

Hurricane Treasure is another mystery-adventure based on a treasure hunt. It features a haunted house which collapses in a storm, gothic-fashion, as well as Canadian Mounties on the trail of smugglers, but Bice treats this stock material realistically. One of the tensions in the story is between the local Nova Scotian villagers and the summer visitor-intruders towards whom the natives have ambivalent feelings. The conclusion, precipitated by the hurricane, furnishes a meager treasure of gold, but a greater treasure of understanding between people. When the air is cleared, blighted lives are restored, and everyone learns that appearances can deceive.

A Dog for Davie's Hill, set in the Scottish Highlands, is also successful in conveying a realistic sense of place. Basically a mystery story about sheep stealing, it is also a dog story, with a touching account of a boy and a dog's affection for each other. The book's character development gives it more depth.

Bice's strength as a writer is in conveying atmosphere and a sense of place and community. However, he also has commendable skill as a mystery-adventure story writer. His plots move quickly, and the humanitarian spirit which underlies his material rarely intrudes in the story.

—Mary Rubio

BIRO, Val (Balint Stephen Biro). British. Born in Budapest, Hungary, 6 October 1921. Educated at the Cistercian School, Budapest, graduated 1939; Central School of Arts and Crafts, London, 1939–42. Married 1) Vivien Woolley in 1945, one daughter; 2) Marie-Louise Ellaway in 1970, two stepchildren. Studio manager, Sylvan Press, London, 1944–46; production manager, C. and J. Temple, London, 1946–48; art director, John Lehmann, publishers, London, 1948–53; urban district councillor, 1966–70. Freelance artist and writer. Fellow, Chartered Society of Designers. Address: Bringe Cottage, Bosham, West Sussex PO18 8LQ, England.

PUBLICATIONS FOR CHILDREN (illustrated by the author)

Fiction

Bumpy's Holiday. London, Sylvan Press, 1943; New York, Transatlantic Arts, 1945.
Gumdrop: The Adventures of a Vintage Car. Leicester, Brockhampton Press, 1966; Chicago, Follett, 1967.
Gumdrop and the Farmer's Friend. Leicester, Brockhampton Press, 1967; Chicago, Follett, 1968.
Gumdrop on the Rally. Leicester, Brockhampton Press, 1968; Chicago, Follett, 1969.
Gumdrop on the Move. Leicester, Brockhampton Press, 1969; Chicago, Follett, 1970.
Gumdrop Goes to London. Leicester, Brockhampton Press, 1971.
Gumdrop Finds a Friend. Leicester, Brockhampton Press, 1973.
Gumdrop in Double Trouble. Leicester, Brockhampton Press, 1975.
Gumdrop and the Steamroller. London, Hodder and Stoughton, 1976; Chicago, Children's Press, 1977.
Gumdrop Posts a Letter. London, Hodder and Stoughton, 1976; Chicago, Children's Press, 1977; as *Gumdrop and the Birthday Surprise,* Milwaukee, Stevens, 1986.
Gumdrop on the Brighton Run. London, Hodder and Stoughton, 1976.
Gumdrop Has a Birthday. London, Hodder and Stoughton, 1977.
Gumdrop Gets His Wings. London, Hodder and Stoughton, 1979.
Gumdrop Finds a Ghost. London, Hodder and Stoughton, 1980.
Gumdrop and the Secret Switches. London, Hodder and Stoughton, 1981.
Gumdrop Makes a Start. London, Hodder and Stoughton, 1982.
Gumdrop and Horace. London, Hodder and Stoughton, 1982.
Gumdrop Races a Train. London, Hodder and Stoughton, 1982; Milwaukee, Stevens, 1986.
Gumdrop at Sea. London, Hodder and Stoughton, 1983.
Gumdrop at the Zoo. London, Hodder and Stoughton, 1983; Milwaukee, Stevens, 1985.
Gumdrop Gets a Lift. London, Hodder and Stoughton, 1983; Milwaukee, Stevens, 1986.
Gumdrop Goes to School. London, Hodder and Stoughton, 1983; Milwaukee, Stevens, 1986.
Gumdrop in a Hurry. London, Hodder and Stoughton, 1983; as *Gumdrop Beats the Clock,* Milwaukee, Stevens, 1986.
Gumdrop's Magic Journey. London, Hodder and Stoughton, 1984.
Gumdrop Goes Fishing. London, Hodder and Stoughton, 1984.
Gumdrop Has a Tummy Ache. London, Hodder and Stoughton, 1984.
Gumdrop Is the Best Car. London, Hodder and Stoughton, 1984; as *Gumdrop Is the Best,* Milwaukee, Stevens, 1985.
Gumdrop on the Farm. London, Hodder and Stoughton, 1984.
Gumdrop and the Monster. London, Hodder and Stoughton, 1985.
Gumdrop and the Farmyard Caper. Milwaukee, Stevens, 1985.
Gumdrop and the Great Sausage Caper. Milwaukee, Stevens, 1985.
Gumdrop Catches a Cold. Milwaukee, Stevens, 1985.
Gumdrop Floats Away. Milwaukee, Stevens, 1985.
Gumdrop to the Rescue. London, Hodder and Stoughton, 1986.
Gumdrop For Ever! London, Hodder and Stoughton, 1987.
Gumdrop and the Dinosaur. London, Hodder and Stoughton, 1988.
Gumdrop and the Pirates. London, Hodder and Stoughton, 1989.
Drango Dragon. Loughborough, Leicestershire, Ladybird, 1989.

Other

The Honest Thief: A Hungarian Folktale. Leicester, Brockhampton Press, 1972; New York, Holiday House, 1973.
Buster Is Lost! (reader). London, Macmillan, 1974.
A Dog and His Bone (reader). London, Macmillan, 1975.
Hungarian Folk-Tales. London, Oxford University Press, 1981; New York, Oxford University Press, 1982.
The Magic Doctor (retelling). London and New York, Oxford University Press, 1982.
Fables from Aesop (retelling). Aylesbury, Buckinghamshire, Ginn, and San Diego, Wright, 18 vols., 1983–88.
The Hobyahs (retelling). Oxford, Oxford University Press, 1985.
The Pied Piper of Hamelin (retelling). Oxford, Oxford University Press, and Morristown, New Jersey, Silver Burdett, 1985.
Tales from Hans Andersen. Aylesbury, Buckinghamshire, Ginn, and San Diego, Wright, 8 vols., 1985–89.
The Donkey That Sneezed (retelling). Oxford and New York, Oxford University Press, 1986.
Jack and the Beanstalk (retelling). Oxford, Oxford University Press, 1989.
Tobias and the Dragon: A Folk Tale from Hungary. London, Blackie, 1989.

*

Illustrator: *The Story of a Carrot* by Kate Barclay, 1944; *No Bombs at All,* 1944, and *Airman's Song Book,* 1945, both by Cyril H.W. Jackson; *Private Gallery* by P. Tabori, 1944; *Worlds Without End* by Denys Val Baker, 1945; *Escape from the Zoo,* 1945, *A Camel from the Desert,* 1947, and *The Penguin Goes Home,* 1951, all by Richard Parker; *Crusading Holiday* by Mary F. Moore, 1946; *England, The Mysterious Island* by P. Treves, 1948; *The Last Days of Pompeii* by Edward Bulwer-Lytton, 1948; *The Story of Joseph and Pharaoh* by Frances Dale, 1950; *Pilgrim's Progress* by John Bunyan, 1951; *Serena Blandish* by Enid Bagnold, 1951; *Zoo for Zanies* by Nicholas Husk, 1952; *The South African Twins,* 1953, and *The Australian Twins,* 1954, both by Daphne Rooke; *The Man Who Made Wine* by J.M. Scott, 1954; *David the Shepherd Boy* by Elizabeth Goudge, 1954; *Fit for a Bishop* by Stephen Bishop, 1955; *Fire Engine by Mistake,* 1955, *Andy's Pit Pony,* 1958, and *The Doctor,* 1972, all by Leila Berg; *The Casket and the Sword* by Norman Dale, 1956; *Tommy the Tugboat,* 1956, *Henry the Helicopter,* 1956, *Tommy Joins the Navy,* 1957, *Henry to the Rescue,* 1959, *Henry the Hero,* 1960, *Tommy's New Engine,* 1961, *Hovering with Henry,* 1961, *Henry in the News,* 1963, *Henry's Busy Winter,* 1964, *Tommy and the Lighthouse,* 1965, *Henry Joins the Police,* 1966, *Tommy and the Oil Rig,* 1967, *Henry and the Astronaut,* 1968, *Tommy and the Spanish Galleon,* 1969, *Henry and the Traction Engine,* 1970, *Tommy and the Yellow Submarine,* 1971, *Henry in the Mountains,* 1972, *Henry in Iceland,* 1973, *Ferryboat Tommy,* 1973, *Tommy in the Caribbean,* 1974, *Henry on Safari,* 1975, *Tommy and the Island,* 1977, and *Lizzie the Lifeboat,* 1985, all by Dora Thatcher; *To Arms for the Queen* by Eric Leyland, 1956; *Kettleby's Zoo* by Margaret Holden, 1957; *Andy and the Mascots,* 1957 [*the Water Crossing,* 1958, *the Sharpshooter,* 1959, *the Display Team,* 1959, *the Secret Papers,* 1961, *the Miniature War,* 1962, *the Royal Review,* 1963, *His Last Parade,*

1968], all by Reginald Taylor; *Hideaway Johnny* by David Scott Daniell, 1959; *The Story of Scotland* by Lawrence Stenhouse, 1961; *The Prisoner of Zenda* by Anthony Hope, 1961; *What a Lark,* 1961, and *Soap-Box Derby,* 1962, both by Rosemary Weir; *Man Makes Towns* by Kenneth Rudge, 1963; *The Ship Stealers,* 1963, and *Big-Head,* 1964, both by Cam Renton; *The Seas of Britain* by Peter Dawlish, 1963; *The Country Year* by Thurlow Craig, 1964; *Arabian Nights,* 1965; *The Wonderful Wizard of Oz,* 1965, and *The Marvelous Land of Oz,* 1967, both by L. Frank Baum; *The Sunday Telegraph Gardening Book* by Fred Whitsey, 1966; *Journal of My Service in India* by J. Corneille, 1966; *The Story of Fanny Burney* by Josephine Kamm, 1966; *The Field Bedside Book,* 1967; *The Ghost of June* by Rupert Croft-Cooke, 1968; *Kangaroo Tennis,* 1968, and *Benjie the Circus Dog,* 1969, both by Donald Bisset; *One Man's Happiness* by Lord Tweedsmuir, 1968; *Sally the Seal,* 1968, *James and Sally Again,* 1970, and *Mr. Bubbus and the Railway Smugglers,* 1976, all by Joan Drake; *Home Is the North* by Walt Morey, 1968; *Discovering Chesham* by Arnold Baines, 1968; *The Untravelled World* by Eric E. Shipton, 1969; *Picture Reference Book of the Georgians* by Boswell Taylor, 1969; *Garden Glory* by Ted Humphris, 1969; *The Terrible Trumpet* by William Wise, 1969; *Soldier Bear* by Geoffrey Morgan, 1970; *The Writ of Green Wax* by Edward Bohan, 1970; *Lovingly,* 1971, *Prayerfully,* 1972, and *Thankfully,* 1975, all by Helen Steiner Rice; *See, Hear and Speak* by Donald Sutherland, 1971; *American Wit and Wisdom* by James Dow, 1971; *The Cook Hostess' Book,* 1971, and *The Sherlock Holmes Cook Book,* 1976, both by Fanny Craddock; *The Good Food Guide,* 1971; *Making Friends with Music* by James Glennon, 1971; *The Jazz Band* by Helen Solomon, 1972; *Country Talk,* 1972, *More Country Talk,* 1973, *New Country Talk,* 1975, *New Country Talk Again,* 1977, *Country Talk Continued,* 1979, and *Latest Country Talk,* 1981, all by J.B.H. Peel; *Mr. Purpose* by Mimi Irving, 1972; *A Reading Book* by Leslie Alexander, 1972; *Tales of the Circus* by Jane MacMichael, 1972; *Victoria in the Wings,* 1972, *The Prince and the Quakeress,* 1976, *Epitaph for Three Women,* 1981, *The Sun in Splendour,* 1982, *The Red Rose of Anjou,* 1982, and other novels by Jean Plaidy; *Play the Best Courses* by Peter Allen, 1973; *Cubs with a Difference,* 1973, *Cubs Away,* 1974, *Cubs on Saturday,* 1976, and *Cubs Ahoy,* 1979, all by Stephen Andrews; *The Dinghy Stories* by Dawn Bowker, 1973; *Garry the Goblin* by Gladys Williams, 1973; *The Reporter* by Michael Pollard, 1973; *The Nose Knows,* 1974, *Dolls in Danger,* 1974, *The Case of the Condemned Cat,* 1975 [*Nervous Newsboy,* 1976, *Invisible Dog,* 1977, *Secret Scribbler,* 1978, *Phantom Frog,* 1979, *Treetop Treasure,* 1980], *The Menaced Midget,* 1975, *The Great Rabbit Robbery,* 1976, and *A Cat Called Amnesia,* 1977, all by E.W. Hildick; *Down the Kitchen Sink* by Beverley Nichols, 1974; *Faster Than Anything* by Peter John Stephens, 1974; *The Robert Carrier Cookery Course,* 1974; *The Sick Cow,* 1974, *George the Fire Engine,* 1976, *Changing of the Guard,* 1978, *The Very, Very Long Dog,* 1978, *The Roundabout Horse,* 1978, *Here Comes Wordman!,* 1979, *King of Beasts,* 1979, *The Big Sneeze,* 1980, *Jungle Silver,* 1981, *The Dial-a-Story Book,* 1981, *The Crawly Crawly Caterpillar,* 1981, *The Tiny Tiny Tadpole,* 1982, *The Scruffy Scruffy Dog,* 1983, *The Tiger Who Couldn't Be Bothered,* 1984, *The Clever Clever Cats,* 1985, *The Silly Silly Ghost,* 1987, *Bobby Brewster's Jigsaw Puzzle,* 1988, and *The Sleeping Policeman,* 1988, all by H.E. Todd; *Brer Rabbit and the Wonderful Tar-Baby,* 1975 [*Is Trapped,* 1975, *and the Alligator,* 1976, *Saves Brer Terrapin,* 1976], *Buttercup Day,* 1982, *Mike's Monkey,* 1982, *The Runaway Cow,* 1982, *Telltale Tommy,* 1982, *The Magic Mirror,* 1983, *The Forgotten Pets,* 1983, *Dame Topple's Buns,* 1983, and *The Three Wishes,* 1983, all by Enid Blyton; *Food and Drink from Your Garden,* and *The Rough Shoot,* both by Daniel Green, 1975; *Machines on the Farm* by John Denton, 1975; *Jim's Go-Kart* by Jeffrey Bevington, 1975; *The Best Games People Play* by Richard Sharp, 1976; *British Folk Customs* by Christina Hole, 1976; *Colibri Readers* edited by Dorothy Figueroa, 4 vols.,

1976–81; *Death to the Strangers!* by Philip Rush, 1977; *Catch the Plane!* by Delia Huddy, 1977; *On Target* by Ken Agar, 1977; *The Devil's Cut* by Clive King, 1978; *The Barley Sugar Ghosts* by Hazel Townson, 1978; *Out of an Egg* by Edward Ramsbottom and Joan Redmayne, 1978; *The Treasure of Dubarry Castle,* 1978, and *The Case of the Silver Lockets,* 1981, both by Lindsay Brown; *Yn Yr Ardd* by Edna Jenkins, 1978; *Sugar and Spice* edited by Giuseppi and Giuseppi, 1978; *Making the Most of It* by Theodora FitzGibbon, 1978; *The Daily Telegraph Cook's Book* by Bon Viveur, 1978; *A Bedside Cookbook* by Sheila Scotter, 1978; *The Sign of the Smiling Lion* by Peter J. Davies, 1979; *A Bucket of Nuts and a Herring Net* by John Jackson, 1979; *Worzel Gummidge* stories, 1979; *New Caribbean Readers* by Hilary Sherlock, 2 vols., 1980–81; *Surprise Bride,* 1980, and *The Big Fib,* 1984, both by Jean Chapman; *Shopping and Cooking in Europe* by Nicholas Courtney, 1980; *Where Are You Going,* 1980; *100 Bible Stories,* 1980, *100 New Testament Stories,* 1981, and *How Things Began* (3 vols.), 1986, all by Norman J. Bull; *Mr. Wolf and His Tail* by Ronald Deadman, 1981; *Dragon in the Drainpipe,* 1981, *Dragon in the Family,* 1985, and *Wishing Powder,* 1986, all by Maggie Prince; *The Virginian* by Owen Wister, 1981; *Bingo Bones and the Boggart,* 1982, and *Bingo Bones and the Funny Cube,* 1986, both by K.H. Roberts; *The Ivory Elephant's Orchard* by David Gamble, 1983; *The Wind in the Willows* by Kenneth Grahame, 1983; *Pulpit Cricket* by Fergus McKendrick, 1983; *Kokoleoko,* 1983, and *Mrs. Macaroni,* 1985, both by June Tillman; *Jack and the Robbers* by Jill Bennett, 1984; *Gluttony, Pride, and Lust* by Michael Geare and Michael Turner, 1984; *Dilbert* books by Kate Robertson, 4 vols., 1984; *The Brownies in Hospital,* 1984, *Air Day for the Brownies,* 1985, *The Brownies and the Fire,* 1985, *Brownies at the Zoo,* 1986, and *The Brownies and the Flood,* 1987, all by Pamela Sykes; *Computer Studies for You* by Stephen Doyle, 1985; *Time* by Paul Harding, 1985; *Talk It Over* by Sheila Lane, 1985; *Alice in Wonderland* by Lewis Carroll, 1986; *Bread,* 1986, *Mrs. Grindy's Shoes,* 1986, *Up in a Tree,* 1986, and *The Train Ride Story,* 1987, all by Joy Cowley; *Collected Tales from Aesop's Fables* (retelling), 1986, *The Hotchpotch Horse,* 1987, *A Kettle Full of Magic,* 1988, *The Odd Job Man and the Thousand Mile Boots,* 1988, and *Seasons,* 1989, all by Jean Kenward; *The Giant's Footsteps,* 1986, *The Missing Ring,* 1986, *The Mystery Voice,* 1986, and *Strangers in Town,* 1986, all by John Patience; *King Lear,* 1986, *Henry IV Part 1,* 1987, and *Much Ado About Nothing,* 1989, all by Shakespeare; *New Caribbean Readers* by Diane Browne, 1987; *Poor Rabbit,* and *Who Asked the Ants,* both by Pat Edwards, 1987; *The King's Jokes* by Margaret Mahy, 1987; *New Caribbean Readers* by Pamela Mordecai, 1987; *The Three Billy Goats Gruff* by Diana Perkins, 1987; *Clowns,* and *Races,* both by William Shepherd, 1987; *Crash, Bang, and Wallop* by Linda Allen, 1988; *I Dream* by Jill Eggleton, 1988.

Val Biro comments:

The joy of writing and illustrating the *Gumdrop* books derives partly from the fact that I own the real Gumdrop (a 1926 Austin 12-4) in which I often drive to schools where children can see the "original." As with other vintage car nuts, the old vehicle is my pride and joy, so it is very natural that I should go on writing about it, and feel enthusiastic in doing so. I also get a lot of pleasure in retelling some great stories from fable or folktale, be they from Aesop or from Hungary (my birthplace) in an accessible way for today's children. All the while, I write with a beady eye on the pictorial content, conscious of the luxury of being my own illustrator.

*   *   *

Val Biro has made his reputation by picture books for very young children, writing and illustrating them himself. The illustrations are as important as the text, if not more important, for this age group. His chief character is Gumdrop, a vintage car.

"He was a very old car, and his proper name was Austin Clifton Twelve-Four. But everybody called him Gumdrop. His owner, Mr. Oldcastle, was so lonely that he had to go to live with his daughter and sell his car, but he kept the old brass horn." A different incident, portrayed in large dramatic coloured pictures, follows on every page. Burglars steal Gumdrop and crash the car; various characters, including a gipsy family, secure interesting bits off the vehicle. The rest of the book is taken up with recovering everything, and ends up with a vintage car rally. The last page shows the cross-section of an Austin made in 1926. After that Gumdrop fills many books. He drives round London tangling with crooks, is involved with tractors and cranes, animals and people. A vehicle with real personality, he appeals to the young, who take an interest in cars at a very early age.

"There was a strange sight at the Red Lion one sunny morning in June. The vintage cars had come to start their big rally of the year. Never was there such a collection of fine old cars in the yard. Each had a Rally number fixed to it. Number 1 was an Alvis Duck-Back and Number 2 a Morris Bullnose. The model T Ford was Number 3....And then there was a blue car with a black hood and a brass horn. It was Number 9: an Austin Clifton Heavy Twelve-Four, vintage 1926, driven by Bill McArran. It was Gumdrop." So begins a typical story. This information occupies two pages of large well-spaced print because the vehicles themselves, their owners, and some young spectators, all with expressive faces, fill the entire background.

This particular rally involves a thief, a farmyard, a horse box, a pony club rally, a carnival procession, a crowd of pigs who have to be given a lift, a blazing hayrick, a fire engine, and an angry motor cycle. Gumdrop of course had lost his way, but he was awarded a brass starting handle as a special prize for solving the crime of the stolen prizes. The book ends on a good moral note. "Everyone cheered and all the cars sounded their horns. Gluurk-Gug and Bleep-Blip, Honk-Tonk and Tootle-Toot. Gumdrop was the happiest car in the rally because he had helped a lost little boy, a mayor in a procession, a farmer with ten little pigs...helped put out a fire and found the silver cups."

Gumdrop enjoys his 60th birthday complete with a breakdown adventure and lots of presents, including an old-fashioned AA brass badge presented to him by Lord Montagu at the Beaulieu Historic Motor Show, in *Gumdrop to the Rescue*. Vehicles showing the history of the motor car are drawn and named on the end papers inside the cover. Gumdrop himself is almost human, as in *Gumdrop For Ever!* when the "klaxon stopped bleeping as if it understood, 'though it must have been the wiring unshorting itself." His adventures keep up with the times. In a recent book, *Gumdrop and the Dinosaur*, he travels back in time 65 million years with the help of a computer. The names and lengths of the creatures line the end papers, all with friendly expressive faces which they keep all through the story.

—Margaret Campbell

———

BISHOP, Claire Huchet. French and American. Born in Europe; grew up in Brittany. Educated at the Collège Sévigné, Paris; University of London. Married Frank Bishop. Founding director, L'Heure Joyeuse children's library (the first in France), Paris, 1924–29; worked in the New York Public Library, 1932–36. Contributor to *Commonweal, Saturday Review*, and other periodicals. President,

International Council of Christians and Jews, 1975–77, and Jewish-Christian Fellowship of France, 1976–81. Recipient: Child Study Association of America award, 1953; Nicholas and Hedy International Brotherhood award, 1988. Address: 511 East 20th Street, New York, New York 10010, U.S.A.; or, 107 rue de Vaugirard, 75006 Paris, France.

PUBLICATIONS FOR CHILDREN

Fiction

The Five Chinese Brothers, illustrated by Kurt Wiese. New York, Coward McCann, 1938; London, Oxford University Press, 1939.
The Kings' Day, illustrated by Doris Spiegel. New York, Coward McCann, 1940.
The Ferryman, illustrated by Kurt Wiese. New York, Coward McCann, 1941; London, Faber, 1943.
The Man Who Lost His Head, illustrated by Robert McCloskey. New York, Viking Press, 1942.
Augustus, illustrated by Grace Paull. New York, Viking Press, 1945.
Pancakes-Paris, illustrated by Georges Schreiber. New York, Viking Press, 1947.
Blue Spring Farm. New York, Viking Press, 1948.
Bernard and His Dogs, illustrated by Maurice Brevannes. Boston, Houghton Mifflin, 1952.
Twenty and Ten, illustrated by William Pène du Bois. New York, Viking Press, 1952; London, Penguin, 1978.
All Alone, illustrated by Feodor Rojankovsky. New York, Viking Press, 1953.
The Big Loop, illustrated by Carles Fontseré. New York, Viking Press, 1955; London, Dent, 1958.
Toto's Triumph, illustrated by Claude Ponsot. New York, Viking Press, 1957; London, Dent, 1959.
A Present from Petros, illustrated by Dimitris Davis. New York, Viking Press, 1961.
Twenty-Two Bears, illustrated by Kurt Wiese. New York, Viking Press, 1964.
The Truffle Pig, illustrated by Kurt Wiese. New York, Coward McCann, 1971.
Georgette, illustrated by Ursula Landshoff. New York, Coward McCann, 1973.

Other

Christopher the Giant (on St. Christopher), illustrated by Berkeley Williams, Jr. Boston, Houghton Mifflin, 1950.
Martin de Porres, Hero, illustrated by Jean Charlot. Boston, Houghton Mifflin, 1954.
French Roundabout. New York, Dodd Mead, 1960; revised edition, 1966.
Lafayette: French-American Hero. Champaign, Illinois, Garrard, 1960.
Yeshu, Called Jesus, illustrated by Don Bolognese. New York, Farrar Straus, 1966; London, Constable, 1967.
Mozart: Music Magician, illustrated by Paul Frame. Champaign, Illinois, Garrard, 1968.
Here Is France. New York, Farrar Straus, 1969.
Johann Sebastian Bach: Music Giant, illustrated by Russell Hoover. Champaign, Illinois, Garrard, 1972.

Editor, *Happy Christmas: Tales for Boys and Girls,* illustrated by Ellen Raskin. New York, Stephen Daye Press, 1956.

PUBLICATIONS FOR ADULTS

Other

*French Children's Books for English-Speaking Children:
    A...Descriptive List...*   New York, Sheridan Square Press, 1938.
France Alive.   New York, McMullen, 1947.
All Things Common.   New York, Harper, 1950.
*How Catholics Look at Jews: Inquiries into Italian, French and
    Spanish Teaching Methods.*   New York, Paulist Press, 1974.

Editor, *Jesus and Israel,* by Jules Isaac, translated by Sally Gran.
    New York, Holt Rinehart, 1971.

*

Claire Huchet Bishop comments:
    My books for young people range from repeated patterns for the
four-year-old up to breathless adventures for the 12- to 13-year old.
Writing has always meant for me arduous work and rewarding
solace. Poetry was my first dedication which, somehow, evolved into
stories for children. Perhaps both kinds of writing have in common
a certain aptitude at intense dreamy feeling often typical of people
from French Brittany.

*   *   *

    Claire Huchet Bishop brings to American children a taste of
Europe—of different people and different customs. In her books one
can learn how truffles are found, what it was like to live in war-
deprived Paris, how it feels to herd sheep on a mountain by yourself.
Yet the author's interest is deeper than mere geographical or historical glimpses. She is discussing important and recurring problems in
a child's life.
    In *All Alone,* for example, a story designed for older children, a
young sheep herder must decide whether to save a new acquaintance
from death or abide by a strict village custom of having no dealings
with strangers. The peasant lad is faced with a choice between two
values—respect for his parents or regard for another human being.
It is a serious situation, including fear of punishment, and it is one
which could be the experience of any child in some form. Despite
his narrow training, the hero chooses the higher law of doing good
to his neighbor. Results show the wisdom of his act and encourage
a child reader to think for himself.
    Pancakes-Paris is still of interest, though it pictures the aftermath
of World War II. Its real topic is privation. Butter, milk, oranges, eggs,
and cocoa are familiar words to children, but in this story these
common foods are very scarce. So the custom of having delectable
crêpes before Lent is unknown to the younger children and just a
faint memory to the older ones. The disappearance of this tradition
is symbolic of a world from which beauty and gracious occasions
have been wiped away. It is a bleak scene of mud-colored dripping
plaster walls, made so by long periods of no heat, of water and onion
as a butter substitute, and of washing without soap. Against this dark
picture stands the staunch character of Charles, the oldest child, now
man of the family. It is his determination which makes it possible to
celebrate the holiday with pancakes as before the war, to bring a shaft
of light into the dreary monotony life has become. As in *All Alone*
the reader finds a hero who meets difficulties with spirit.
    Bishop writes books for very young children as well as the two
just discussed, designed for 8-to-12-year-olds. *The Truffle Pig,* like
Pancakes-Paris, takes place in France. Using words a child knows
well, the author creates a story full of country sounds and smells with
a lonely boy's love for a pig at its center: "It was tiny with a lovely
pink color. It looked very bright. Pierre liked it at once." Pierre
elegantly names his pet "Marcel" and the pig signifies his immediate

attachment for the boy with loud unmistakable grunts. Pierre's
loneliness dissolves. However, pigs usually go to market and Marcel
is no exception. In desperation, Pierre runs away with him. "Pierre
and Marcel made for the woods. The birds had gone to bed. The smell
of earth and plants filled the air. It was very quiet." What a nice
description of forest-feeling tucked beside the dark problem! But
while in the woods, Marcel displays a talent for finding truffles, and
this delicacy delivers the pig from market, Pierre from loneliness,
and Pierre's family from poverty.
    The Truffle Pig shows the author's versatility. She uses simple
words and a cadence and format suitable for younger children to
portray her vivid scenes and sensations. We do not begrudge the
and-they-lived-happily-ever-after ending. Like the other books, it
deals with a deep childhood problem—loneliness. Bishop has no
hesitation in bringing untrivial subjects to children but the writing is
appropriate for the audience.

—Carolyn T. Kingston

————

BISSET, Donald. British. Born in London, 30 August 1910.
Educated at the Warehousemen, Clerks and Drapers School, Ad-
dington, Surrey. Served in the Royal Artillery during World War II:
Lieutenant. Married Nancy Bisset in 1946 (divorced); one son.
Radio, television, and stage actor. Agent: (literary) A.M. Heath, 79
St. Martin's Lane, London WC2N 4AA; (theatre) Joseph and Wagg
Ltd., 78 New Bond Street, London W.1. Address: 33 Andrewes
House, Barbican, London EC2Y 8AB, England.

PUBLICATIONS FOR CHILDREN

Fiction

Anytime Stories, illustrated by the author.   London, Faber, 1954.
Sometime Stories, illustrated by the author.   London, Faber, 1957.
Next Time Stories, illustrated by the author.   London, Methuen,
    1959.
This Time Stories, illustrated by the author.   London, Methuen,
    1961.
Another Time Stories, illustrated by the author.   London, Methuen,
    1963.
Little Bear's Pony, illustrated by Shirley Hughes.   London, Benn,
    1966.
Hullo Lucy, illustrated by Gillian Kenny.   London, Benn, 1967.
Talks with a Tiger, illustrated by the author.   London, Methuen,
    1967.
Kangaroo Tennis, illustrated by Val Biro.   London, Benn, 1968.
Nothing, illustrated by the author.   London, Benn, 1969.
Upside Down Land.   Moscow, Progress Publishers, 1969.
Benjie the Circus Dog, illustrated by Val Biro.   London, Benn,
    1969.
Time and Again Stories, illustrated by the author.   London,
    Methuen, 1970.
Barcha the Tiger, illustrated by Derek Collard.   London, Benn,
    1971.
Tiger Wants More, illustrated by the author.   London, Methuen,
    1971.
Yak and the Sea Shell, illustrated by Lorraine Calaora.   London,
    Methuen, 1971.
Yak and the Painted Cave, illustrated by Lorraine Calaora.   London,
    Methuen, 1971.
Yak and the Buried Treasure, illustrated by Lorraine Calaora.

London, Methuen, 1972.
Yak and the Ice Cream, illustrated by Lorraine Calaora. London, Methuen, 1972.
Father Tingtang's Journey, illustrated by the author. London, Methuen, 1973.
Jenny Hopalong, illustrated by Derek Collard. London, Benn, 1973.
Yak Goes Home, illustrated by Lorraine Calaora. London, Methuen, 1973.
The Happy Horse, illustrated by David Sharpe. London, Benn, 1974.
The Adventures of Mandy Duck, illustrated by the author. London, Methuen, 1974.
Hazy Mountain, illustrated by Shirley Hughes. London, Kestrel, 1975.
"Oh Dear," Said the Tiger, illustrated by the author. London, Methuen, 1975.
Paws with Shapes, illustrated by Tony Hutchins. Maidenhead, Berkshire, Intercontinental Books, 1976.
Paws with Numbers, with Michael Morris, illustrated by Tony Hutchins. Maidenhead, Berkshire, Intercontinental Books, 1976.
The Lost Birthday, illustrated by the author. Moscow, Progress Publishers, 1976.
The Story of Smokey Horse, illustrated by the author. London, Methuen, 1977.
This Is Ridiculous, illustrated by the author. London, Beaver, 1977.
Journey to the Jungle. London, Beaver, 1977.
The Adventures of Yak, illustrated by the author. London, Methuen, 1978.
What Time Is It When It Isn't?, illustrated by the author. London, Methuen, 1980.
Johnny Here and There, illustrated by the author. London, Methuen, 1981.
The Hedgehog Who Rolled Uphill. London, Methuen, 1982.
The Joyous Adventures of Snakey Boo, illustrated by the author. London, Methuen, 1982.
Sleep Tight, Snakey Boo! London, Methuen, 1985.
Just a Moment! London, Methuen, 1987.

Plays

Television Series: *Yak,* 1971.

*

Donald Bisset comments:

All my books are modern fairy stories—animistic in concept—and, on the surface, nonsensical, but nevertheless they have meanings (varied).

*   *   *

Innocence is the essential quality of all Donald Bisset's work—a pure, shining, quite unselfconscious innocence that finds a delighted response in a small child's mind and has an extraordinary *cleansing* effect in an adult's. Of all the writers who protest that they write for only themselves, or the child within them, Bisset is one of the few I would believe. There is genuine simplicity, a total lack of contrivance or artifice or sophisticated humorous hindsight, in his style, plots (if plots there be—perhaps "sequence of events" is more accurate), characters, and dialogue. And yet at the same time there is a kind of artless art in the way he looks at words as if they were as new to him as to a four-year-old and follows them with wide-eyed logic to some daft conclusion; in the way he allows his fantasies to develop by the natural laws of free association; in the way he incorporates the very

page itself—the typesetting, his spiky little childlike drawings, the numbering—into the life of the story. The appeal is to the child of around four, five, six, who has learnt just enough of the rules of language, logic, real life, to appreciate seeing them bent, but who still remembers when they were mysterious and unexpected, who is still sufficiently immersed in the world of fairy stories and nursery rhymes to enjoy the comfortable recognition of their patterns, but who has gained enough intellectual distance from them to enjoy playing with and changing those familiar patterns.

The years—about 35—have scarcely changed Bisset. Perhaps the books tend more to be single units, but they still break up into separate chapter-stories, just a few pages long, bedtime reading at its most engaging. Characters zip in and out of different books: Tiger, who grows fat only on words and thrives on a special diet of stories featuring tigers; Komodo the dragon (sometimes papier-mâché) who breathes imaginary fire and dances imaginary polkas, sometimes very old and magical, fuelling a Thames steamboat; and various unnamed but somehow familiar Ducks, Beetles, and Snails. The sun, the moon, icebergs, puddles, clouds, rivers, flowers all have their roles to play, but so do quarrelling railway stations, words like Please and Sorry complaining of overwork, lost names whose letters become muddled, chapter headings themselves—yet the simple unaffected telling puts paid to hints of whimsy. The sheer effrontery of his little drawings that constantly interrupt the text, and the whole *joie de vivre* that lights up the gentle-hearted world of his imagination charm storyteller and small listener alike.

—Stephanie Nettell

———

BLADES, Ann (née Sager). Canadian. Born in Vancouver, British Columbia, 16 November 1947. Educated at Crofton House School, Vancouver; University of British Columbia, Vancouver, 1965–70, teaching certificate 1967; British Columbia Institute of Technology, 1972–74, registered nurse's qualification 1974. Married David Morrison in 1984 (second marriage); two sons. Elementary school teacher, Peace River North School District, Mile 18, British Columbia, 1967–68, Department of Indian Affairs and Northern Development, Taché, British Columbia, 1969, and Surrey School District, British Columbia, 1969–71; clerk, London, Ontario, 1972; registered nurse, Vancouver General Hospital, 1974–75, and Mt. St. Joseph Hospital, Vancouver, 1975–80. Artist: individual shows: Bau Xi Gallery, Vancouver, 1982, 1983, 1984, 1986; Bau Xi Gallery, Toronto, 1982, 1983. Recipient: Canadian Library Association award, 1972, and Howard-Gibbon Medal, for illustration, 1979; Canada Council grant, 1975, and prize, for illustration, 1979; Elizabeth Mrazik-Cleaver Canadian Picture Book award, 1986. Address: 2701 Crescent Drive, Surrey, British Columbia V4A 3J9, Canada.

PUBLICATIONS FOR CHILDREN (illustrated by the author)

Fiction

Mary of Mile 18. Montreal and Plattsburgh, New York, Tundra, 1971; London, Bodley Head, 1976.
A Boy of Taché. Montreal and Plattsburgh, New York, Tundra, 1973.
The Cottage at Crescent Beach. Toronto, Magook, 1977.

Other

By the Sea: An Alphabet Book. Toronto, Kids Can Press, 1985;

Cambridge, Cambridge University Press, 1987.

*

Illustrator: *Jacques the Woodcutter* by Michael Macklem, 1977; *A Salmon for Simon,* 1978, and *Pettranella,* 1980, both by Betty Waterton; *Six Darn Cows* by Margaret Laurence, 1979; *Anna's Pet* by Margaret Atwood and Joyce Barkhouse, 1980; *A Candle for Christmas* by Jean Speare, 1986; *Ida and the Wool Smugglers* by Sue Ann Alderson, 1987.

Ann Blades comments:

When I was 19, I went to teach in the two-room school at Mile 18, an isolated farming community in northern British Columbia. In early spring, wanting an activity to help pass the time and impressed by the apparent lack of relevant reading material for children in rural areas, I decided to write and illustrate a book for children. I began to work on *Mary of Mile 18,* using one of my pupils, Mary, and her family as the characters in the book. I finished writing and illustrating *Mary of Mile 18* the following year, while teaching in the two-room school at Taché, an Indian reserve in central British Columbia. The next year I wrote and illustrated *A Boy of Taché,* based on a true episode that occurred while I was teaching there.

Since 1976 I have worked primarily as an illustrator and painter, which I enjoy doing most. In 1982 I began selling paintings through the Bau Xi Gallery in Vancouver and Toronto.

*   *   *

Requirements for a textbook rarely provoke successful literary endeavours. But the paucity of school material meaningful to children in a schoolhouse tucked away in northern British Columbia became the touchstone of Ann Blades's invention. Her charges in a remote Mennonite community 18 miles off mile 73 of the Alaska Highway would comprehend little of the stoplights, sidewalks, and manicured parks which are veritable landmarks of conventional schoolbooks, but they would have intimate knowledge of the brilliant northern lights, and of isolation, solitude, and an almost overwhelming sense of sameness. And it was these familiar elements which inspired *Mary of Mile 18,* in which the lifestyle of Mary Fehr, bespectacled child within a closely knit family, emerges with simple poignancy. Mary hopes that something different will happen, and she believes the northern lights to be harbingers of promised novelty. Something does happen in the appearance of a pup which is half wolf. But pets are an unaffordable luxury, and the pup cannot be Mary's until he proves capable of contributing to the sustaining pattern of existence. *Mary of Mile 18* suggests that creative pedagogy does indeed border on art.

Blades's second book, *A Boy of Taché,* presents a more elaborate text and a more involved plot. It is also more self-consciously instructive with ecological concerns and observations on northern lifestyles arising from several asides. Za refuses to shoot a pregnant beaver, and it is observed that nowadays there is but an occasional eagle. The two companions pass by a nearby construction camp which is building a railway. But the learning is by no means intrusive. An intriguing theme unites change and continuity. The young Indian boy, Charlie, will now begin to hunt alone, since his beloved grandfather, whose life Charlie has saved, will be forced to retire. But the youthful hero will in fact become a hunter, and his dream of manhood differs little if at all from those of his ancestors.

In the past decade Blades's efforts have centered upon illustrating rather than writing. Her most recent book, *The Cottage at Crescent Beach,* provides a plausible surmise for this total commitment to the graphic arts. In this entrancing little book the picturesque quality of the words dominates any narrative stream. The intrigue of line, colour, and contrast are as apparent in the text as in the drawings.

The effect resembles more the presence at a picture gallery than that of sitting at the feet of a raconteur. This is not to say that the writing does not command willing attentiveness, but that the sights and styles of life in summer isolation have an appeal exclusive of any desire to learn what comes next. The lure of the moment makes the potential sameness of the hours into a delighted onslaught of experience of the present. Walks along the railroad track, swinging from trapeze trees, and shadows of maples outside a young girl's bedroom window convey enough suggestions of their own and thus do not require the support of a strong narrative line. To term her art work illustrations is to assume the subordination of pictures to text. Blades's involvement with both art and story suggests that her tales are as graphic as they are plot filled. Neither is servant to the other, as the present tense, that most mysterious of time frames, demands the service of pen and brush. The real plot of *The Cottage at Crescent Beach* is the sustained pleasure in a moment which is continually unfolding, even when arrested.

—Leonard R. Mendelsohn

———

BLOS, Joan W(insor). American. Born in New York City, 9 December 1928. Educated at Vassar College, Poughkeepsie, New York, B.A. 1950; City College of New York, M.A. in psychology 1957. Married Peter Blos, Jr., in 1953; one son (deceased) and one daughter. Research assistant, Jewish Board of Guardians, New York, 1949–50, and Yale University Child Study Center, New Haven, Connecticut, 1951–53; teacher assistant in psychology, City College of New York, 1950–51; associate editor in the Publications Division, 1959–66, and instructor in the Teacher Education Division, 1960–70, Bank Street College of Education, New York; research assistant and specialist in children's literature, Department of Psychiatry, 1970–72, and lecturer, School of Education, 1972–80, University of Michigan, Ann Arbor. Since 1980 writer and lecturer. Member of the Editorial Board, 1973–77, and U.S. editor, 1976–81, *Children's Literature in Education,* London. Recipient: American Book award, 1980; American Library Association Newbery Medal, 1980. Agent: Marilyn Marlow, Curtis Brown, 10 Astor Place, New York, New York 10003, U.S.A.

PUBLICATIONS FOR CHILDREN

Fiction

Joe Finds a Way, with Betty Miles, illustrated by Lee Ames. Syracuse, Singer, 1967.
"It's Spring," She Said, illustrated by Julie Maas. New York, Knopf, 1968.
Just Think!, with Betty Miles, illustrated by Pat Grant Porter. New York, Knopf, 1971.
A Gathering of Days: A New England Girl's Journal 1830–32. New York, Scribner, 1979.
Martin's Hats, illustrated by Marc Simont. New York, Morrow, 1984.
Brothers of the Heart: A Story of the Old Northwest 1837–38. New York, Scribner, 1985.
Old Henry, illustrated by Stephen Gammell. New York, Morrow, and London, Simon and Schuster, 1987.
The Grampa Days, illustrated by Emily Arnold McCully. New York, Simon and Schuster, 1989.
One Very Best Valentine's Day, illustrated by Emily Arnold McCully. New York, Simon and Schuster, 1989.

The Heroine of the Titanic.   New York, Morrow, 1989.
Lottie's Circus, illustrated by Irene Trivas.   New York, Morrow, 1989.

Other (readers; illustrated by Dan Dickas)

In the City.   New York, Macmillan, 1965.
People Read, with Betty Miles.   New York, Macmillan, 1965.

*

Manuscript Collection: Kerlan Collection, University of Minnesota, Minneapolis.

Joan W. Blos comments:

Words, for me, have always been important. It is said that I spoke at an early age and well before I entered school my father and mother were writing down the "poems" I spoke to them. "First in town it thunders and glitters," begins one surviving example. It rises to the question: "What will you do when the storm is out, and it is beginning to rain?" Observation and question continue to be the basis of what I write.

"Writing begins in caring," I say to the children when asked to speak in schools. By that I mean that writing begins with concern for the world, the events and the people therein. I believe that this world of ours matters and that our small lives count. Writing also means caring about the words which are set down on paper. It's a struggle for me and I wouldn't call it enjoyable. Once I told an interviewer that, although I don't like writing, I *love* having written. That's what keeps me going back—back to the pads and the pens and the pencils, the typewriter, and the wastebaskets (two!) which are under my desk. I think it's important for others to know that writing isn't something you do because you find it easy. Most of the time I'm grateful if I can do it at all. Beyond the caring for words, and one's world, writing has to do with caring for those for whom you write. I suppose that's why I write for children and am happy to hear from them. I like to think of my books, my works, as ways of saying things, to children, for whom I deeply care. However hard I find this work of writing, I would not, do not, want ever to give it up! I hope I get better and better at writing; I know that there is nothing that I would rather do.

*   *   *

Joan W. Blos's first novel for older children, *A Gathering of Days: A New England Girl's Journal 1830–32,* won numerous awards, among them the Newbery Medal and the American Book award. It is a well-crafted book of historical fiction with a protagonist, Catherine Hall, who is as vividly alive as any of her readers. Catherine's human qualities are revealed early as she wishes "that my hair were curly, as Matty's is, and our mother's." She delights in visiting the Shipmans, their nearest neighbors, but wishes that she could reciprocate with splendid dinners on special occasions (since her mother died years before the journal begins, that is not possible). Here is a real child, loving, usually obedient, but full of fun, too. Having taken great pride in assuming many of her mother's duties, Catherine resents her new stepmother who appears with little warning about halfway through the book, constantly referring to her as "she" or "her" in the journal. On the wedding day, Catherine writes, "On this day, in Boston, they married. I will not call her Mother." Her stepbrother, Daniel, later comes up with a compromise, "Mammann," as Catherine gradually adjusts. In contrast, she dearly loves her friend Cassie, whose death is a terrible blow. Eventually matters sort themselves out as Catherine comes to terms with herself and with those around her. She accepts both Cassie's death and her stepmother; as she prepares to set off on a trip at the end of the journal,

she has matured considerably from the girl who first began it.

Since *A Gathering of Days* Blos has created two imaginative picture books and another historical novel. In *Martin's Hats* an array of hats creates the impetus for young Martin's fantasies as he succeeds at one venture after another (cook, fireman, explorer, engineer, etc.). The adventures come to a satisfactory conclusion when he discovers the nightcap waiting for him on his bed. The second picture book, *Old Henry,* is written primarily in rhyming couplets on a timely theme, getting along with others despite differences, as Old Henry refuses to fix up his dilapidated house and rebuffs attempts by neighbors to help him and be friendly. The spirit of compromise eventually results in a potentially happy ending. Stephen Gammell's engaging colored pencil illustrations are a perfect accompaniment.

Blos's recent historical novel, *Brothers of the Heart: A Story of the Old Northwest 1837–38,* has a male protagonist. The tale, set in Michigan, is told through flashback using devices such as letters and journal and diary entries. These fictionalized accounts give the reader a strong sense of verisimilitude; the book rings true, for Blos has also captured the speech cadences and language of the period. Through friendships and relatives several of the characters are linked to Catherine Hall, from *A Gathering of Days,* so that readers can gain a sense of continuity.

The sharp characterization of the first historical fiction novel continues in *Brothers of the Heart* as Shem Perkins, born lame, attempts to make his own way after an unfortunate scene with his upset father. After running away from home, he receives gainful employment and is sent on a dangerous expedition which almost costs him his life but which ensures his maturity and builds his self-confidence, enabling him to return to his family and to the girl he will eventually marry. The reader also learns of another culture as Shem takes in the aged Ottowan Indian, Mary Goodhue, learning from her and tending to her until her death. Through her he discovers his own strengths and makes the realization that he and Mary's long-dead Indian husband were truly brothers of the heart.

The richness of the novel lies in the presentation of the growth of the Michigan region along with the development of characters and insight into the feelings of crippled Shem and the attitudes of others about him. The language, with its rhythms and lilt of earlier times, is remarkably spare, not replete with full-blown descriptions, yet giving the reader a strong sense of place and characterization. Blos has accomplished the fine feat of balancing history with universal human experience, uniting the book's past with the reader's present.

—Marilyn F. Apseloff

———

BLUME, Judy (née Sussman). American. Born in Elizabeth, New Jersey, 12 February 1938. Educated at New York University, B.S. in education 1960. Married 1) John M. Blume in 1959 (divorced), one daughter and one son; 2) Thomas A. Kitchens in 1976 (divorced); 3) George Cooper in 1987, one stepdaughter. Lives in New York City. Founder, Kids Fund. D.H.L.: Kean College, Union, New Jersey, 1987. Agent: Harold Ober Associates, 40 East 49th Street, New York, New York 10017, U.S.A.

PUBLICATIONS FOR CHILDREN

Fiction

The One in the Middle Is the Green Kangaroo, illustrated by Lois Axeman.   Chicago, Reilly and Lee, 1969.

Iggie's House. Englewood Cliffs, New Jersey, Bradbury Press, 1970; London, Heinemann, 1981.

Are You There, God? It's Me, Margaret. Englewood Cliffs, New Jersey, Bradbury Press, 1970; London, Gollancz, 1978.

Freckle Juice, illustrated by Sonia O. Lisker. New York, Four Winds Press, 1971; London, Heinemann, 1984.

Then Again, Maybe I Won't. Scarsdale, New York, Bradbury Press, 1971; London, Heinemann, 1979.

It's Not the End of the World. Scarsdale, New York, Bradbury Press, 1972; London, Heinemann, 1979.

Tales of a Fourth Grade Nothing, illustrated by Roy Doty. New York, Dutton, 1972; London, Bodley Head, 1979.

Otherwise Known as Sheila the Great. New York, Dutton, 1972; London, Bodley Head, 1979.

Deenie. Scarsdale, New York, Bradbury Press, 1973; London, Heinemann, 1980.

Blubber. Scarsdale, New York, Bradbury Press, 1974; London, Heinemann, 1980.

Forever. Scarsdale, New York, Bradbury Press, 1975; London, Gollancz, 1976.

Starring Sally J. Freedman as Herself. Scarsdale, New York, Bradbury Press, 1977; London, Heinemann, 1983.

Superfudge. New York, Dutton, and London, Bodley Head, 1980.

Tiger Eyes. Scarsdale, New York, Bradbury Press, 1981; London, Heinemann, 1982.

The Pain and the Great One, illustrated by Irene Trivas. New York, Bradbury Press, 1984; London, Heinemann, 1985.

Just as Long as We're Together. New York, Orchard, and London, Heinemann, 1987.

Other

The Judy Blume Diary: The Place to Put Your Own Feelings. New York, Dell, 1982.

PUBLICATIONS FOR ADULTS

Novels

Wifey. New York, Putnam, 1978; London, Macmillan, 1979.
Smart Women. New York, Putnam, 1983; London, Sphere, 1984.

Other

Letters to Judy: What Your Kids Wish They Could Tell You. New York, Putnam, and London, Heinemann, 1986.

*

Manuscript Collection: Kerlan Collection, University of Minnesota, Minneapolis.

Judy Blume comments:

Writing about young people comes naturally to me because I am blessed with almost total recall. Often young people will ask me how I know all their secrets. It's because I remember just about everything from age eight on, and many things that happened before that. I write sometimes from my own experiences, sometimes from my children's, and other times by imagining how I would feel and react if placed in a certain situation. I'm not sure where my ideas come from. And I don't like to think about that—it's too scary. I'm just grateful that when I finish one book there is usually a new idea waiting for me. I let each book evolve naturally. I find the first draft pure torture. Once that's finished I can relax, for it is the rewriting process that I really enjoy. I'm thankful for the thousands of letters I receive from my young fans each year. I owe my career to my readers!

* * *

Until the mid-1960's fiction for young people could be characterized for the most part by words such as predictable and simplistic; very little appeared that might disturb the reader unduly, and a tidy, happy ending was mandatory. Characters were often one-dimensional, and plots ranged from simple to silly. In 1967, however, a teen novel was published that forever destroyed the spoken and unspoken taboos defining junior fiction. S.E. Hinton's *The Outsiders,* a powerful story of class struggle in an Oklahoma high school, was iconoclastic in its gritty realism, its believable, doomed characters, and its uncompromising honesty. The book opened doors previously closed to teenage readers and in effect permitted a new generation of writers to tackle the real issues that concerned teenagers with honesty and realism.

It remained for another author to extend that frankness and realism into the world of literature for the younger adolescent, however. By 1970 Judy Blume had had two children's books published. The first, *The One in the Middle Is the Green Kangaroo,* was a pleasant but conventional picture book about second-grader Freddy Dissel, a middle child who feels ignored by parents and siblings until he becomes a hit in a school play. *Iggie's House* was a piece of junior fiction which dealt with the impact of a black family moving into a previously all-white suburban neighborhood. Reviewers were lukewarm about the book primarily because of the weakness of its characterizations, its predictable plot, and some dreadful dialogue. This reception made Blume decide to write a more honest novel about the early adolescent experience based on her vivid memories of what it was like to be an 11-year-old girl, and in the process to ignore publishing taboos and strictures. In 1970 that novel was published; subsequently *Are You There God? It's Me, Margaret* became one of the great success stories in children's publishing history.

This time critical response was anything but lukewarm; reviewers either loved *Are You There God?* or hated it. What was more important, however, was young readers' response to 11-year-old Margaret's wistful longings for religion, her period, breasts, and the first bra, all dished up with large dollops of the easy good humor that would become characteristic of many of Blume's later books. Preteen girls loved the book and wrote letters by the hundreds to tell Blume just how closely they identified with Margaret and shared a sense of cozy familiarity with her dilemmas. But it was only when the book appeared in paperback in 1974 that the hundreds of letters became thousands, all of them from readers who saw themselves and their lives reflected perfectly in the story.

Response to the book clearly reveals Blume's greatest gift as a writer for young people: her ability to share her own vividly remembered childhood experiences in ways that the reader can both understand and identify with easily and completely. At the same time Blume does not write down to her readers; she is uncompromising in the frankness of her topics and her refusal to be less than honest in her writing. As a result young people write to Blume as one 12-year-old did: "You are writing about me. I feel like you know all my secrets."

Her confidence in her success as a writer established with *Are You There God?,* Blume entered a highly prolific period. *Then Again, Maybe I Won't* is the story of 13-year-old Tony Miglione's attempts to cope with his upwardly mobile family as well as his burgeoning sexuality. The effects of divorce on a bewildered preteen girl is the subject of *It's Not the End of the World,* while *Deenie* is the story of a seventh-grader plagued by a mother who is determined that Deenie will become a model until the girl's diagnosis of scoliosis interferes with her plans. Children's cruelty toward one another is the subject of *Blubber,* a story of a fat girl, a born victim, who becomes the target of her entire class's ridicule and persecution with nearly disastrous results. In *Forever,* the joys and the disappointments of first love are shown through the story of Michael and Katherine; more importantly, however, the joys and disappointments of one's first sexual experiences are described clearly and explicitly, in a way that even preteens can understand. For this reason alone *Forever* has made Blume the most censored children's author in the United States for several years running.

Not all of Blume's books are of the "problem novel" type, however. Her *Tales of a Fourth Grade Nothing* and its sequel, *Superfudge,* are hilarious tales of the problems of dealing with a younger brother during "the terrible twos;" anyone, young or old, who has ever lived with two-year-olds will empathize with Peter's distress at the antics of his little brother Fudge. *Otherwise Known as Sheila the Great* is about a young girl who compensates for her insecurities by telling white lies to her friends and family; like *Tales of a Fourth Grade Nothing,* it is also a very funny story. Blume's most autobiographical novel, *Starring Sally J. Freedman as Herself,* has not been as popular as most of Blume's other books with either critics or young readers, but it is an accurate representation of the point of view of a child growing up in the wartime 1940's.

In 1981 the book that many critics felt was Blume's finest appeared. *Tiger Eyes* is the story of one family's struggle to overcome the shock and horror of a father's violent, unexpected death. Davey, the young protagonist, must not only deal with the loss of her parent but with her mother's inability to accept what has happened and the well meant if bumbling efforts of other relatives attempting to help. *Tiger Eyes* is notable for the strength of Blume's characterizations, often faulted by critics, and its complexities of plot and theme. Blume's latest novel, *Just as Long as We're Together,* is a return to the world of adolescent girls, much like an updated version of *Are You There God?*

In her 20 years as a writer Blume has achieved a pinnacle of success that few others ever have. She is the most widely read author of contemporary young people's fiction in the world, and her books have sold tens of millions of copies. She still receives up to 2000 letters a month from young readers; the most poignant of these have been collected in a book called *Letters to Judy.* Anyone who has any doubt about Blume's rapport with her readers might profitably look at this book.

Blume has achieved her success as a result of several factors. Her almost total recall of how it felt to be young makes her books speak directly to her readers. She is forthright and frank as no writer for young people had dared to before she appeared on the scene. At the same time her own sense of humor and her sense of what makes young readers laugh has softened some of her messages and made them palatable. Her books certainly have been controversial, but their acceptance by the young has been universal, and Blume has continued to breach old barriers and blaze new trails, an achievement of which few contemporary authors of books for any age group can boast.

—Audrey Eaglen

BLYTON, Enid (Mary). Also wrote as Mary Pollock. Born in East Dulwich, London, 11 August 1897. Educated at St. Christopher's School for Girls, Beckenham, Kent, 1907–15; Froebel Institute, Ipswich High School, 1916–18. Married 1) Hugh Pollock in 1924 (divorced 1942), two daughters; 2) Kenneth Darrell Waters in 1943 (died 1967). Taught at Bickley Park School, Kent, 1919;

nursery governess, Surbiton, Surrey, 1920–24. Columnist, "From My Window," 1923–27, "Letter to Children," 1927–29, and "Children's Page," 1929–45, *Teachers' World,* London; editor, *Sunny Stories* magazine, London, 1926–52, and *Enid Blyton Magazine,* London, 1953–59. Chairman of the Committee, Shaftesbury Society Children's Home, Beaconsfield, Buckinghamshire, 1954–67; Vice-President, Friends of the Cheyne Walk Centre, London, 1960–68. *Died 28 November 1968.*

PUBLICATIONS FOR CHILDREN

Fiction

The Enid Blyton Book of Fairies, illustrated by Horace J. Knowles. London, Newnes, 1924.
The Zoo Book. London, Newnes, 1924.
The Enid Blyton Book of Bunnies. London, Newnes, 1925.
The Book of Brownies, illustrated by Ernest Aris. London, Newnes, 1926; as *Brownie Tales,* London, Collins, 1964.
Tales Half Told. London, Nelson, 1926.
The Animal Book. London, Newnes, 1927.
Let's Pretend, illustrated by I. Bennington Angrave. London, Nelson, 1928.
Tarrydiddle Town. London, Nelson, 1929.
Cheerio! A Book for Boys and Girls. London, Birn, 1933.
Five [Fifteen, Twenty] Minute Tales. London, Methuen, 3 vols., 1933–40.
Letters from Bobs. Privately printed, 1933.
The Red Pixie Book, illustrated by Kathleen Nixon. London, Newnes, 1934.
Ten Minutes Tales: Twenty-Nine Varied Stories for Children. London, Methuen, 1934.
The Children's Garden. London, Newnes, 1935.
The Green Goblin Book. London, Newnes, 1935; shortened version, as *Feefo, Tuppeny, and Jinks,* London, Staples Press, 1951.
Hedgerow Tales, illustrated by V. Temple. London, Newnes, 1935.
The Famous Jimmy, illustrated by Benjamin Rabier. London, Muller, 1936; New York, Dutton, 1937.
The Yellow Fairy Book. London, Newnes, 1936.
Adventures of the Wishing Chair, illustrated by Hilda McGavin. London, Newnes, 1937.
The Adventures of Binkle and Flip, illustrated by Kathleen Nixon. London, Newnes, 1938.
Billy-Bob Tales, illustrated by May Smith. London, Methuen, 1938.
Mr. Galliano's Circus, illustrated by E.H. Davie. London, Newnes, 1938.
The Secret Island. Oxford, Blackwell, 1938.
Boys' and Girls' Circus Book, illustrated by Hilda McGavin. London, News Chronicle, 1939.
The Enchanted Wood, illustrated by Dorothy M. Wheeler. London, Newnes, 1939.
Hurrah for the Circus! Being Further Adventures of Mr. Galliano and His Famous Circus, illustrated by E.H. Davie. London, Newnes, 1939.
Naughty Amelia Jane! London, Newnes, 1939.
Boys' and Girls' Story Book. London, Newnes, 1940.
The Children of Cherry Tree Farm, illustrated by Harry Rountree. London, Country Life, 1940.
The Little Tree-House, Being the Adventures of Josie, Click, and Bun, illustrated by Dorothy M. Wheeler. London, Newnes, 1940; as *Josie, Click, and Bun and the Little Tree House,* 1951.
Mr. Meddle's Mischief, illustrated by Joyce Mercer and Rosalind M. Turvey. London, Newnes, 1940.
The Naughtiest Girl in the School. London, Newnes, 1940.

The Secret of Spiggy Holes. Oxford, Blackwell, 1940.

Tales of Betsy-May, illustrated by Joan Gale Thomas. London, Methuen, 1940.

The Treasure Hunters, illustrated by E. Wilson and Joyce Davies. London, Newnes, 1940.

The Adventures of Mr. Pink-Whistle. London, Newnes, 1941.

The Adventurous Four. London, Newnes, 1941.

Five O'Clock Tales. London, Methuen, 1941.

The Further Adventures of Josie, Click, and Bun, illustrated by Dorothy M. Wheeler. London, Newnes, 1941.

The Secret Mountain. Oxford, Blackwell, 1941.

The Twins at St. Clare's. London, Methuen, 1941.

The Children of Willow Farm, illustrated by Harry Rountree. London, Country Life, 1942.

Circus Days Again, illustrated by E.H. Davie. London, Newnes, 1942.

Happy Story Book. London, Hodder and Stoughton, 1942.

Enid Blyton's Little Books (Brer Rabbit, Bed-time Stories, Jolly Tales, Ho-Ho and Too Smart, Tales of the Toys, Happy Stories), illustrated by Alfred Kerr. London, Evans, 6 vols., 1942.

Five on a Treasure Island. London, Hodder and Stoughton, 1942; New York, Crowell, 1950.

Hello, Mr. Twiddle, illustrated by Hilda McGavin. London, Newnes, 1942.

I'll Tell You a Story, illustrated by Eileen A. Soper. London, Macmillan, 1942.

I'll Tell You Another Story. London, Macmillan, 1942.

John Jolly at Christmas Time [by the Sea, on the Farm, at the Circus]. London, Evans, 4 vols., 1942–45.

Mary Mouse and the Doll's House. Leicester, Brockhampton Press, 1942.

The Naughtiest Girl Again. London, Newnes, 1942.

The O'Sullivan Twins. London, Methuen, 1942.

Shadow, The Sheep-Dog. London, Newnes, 1942.

Six O'Clock Tales: Thirty-Three Short Stories for Children, illustrated by Dorothy M. Wheeler. London, Methuen, 1942.

More Adventures on Willow Farm. London, Country Life, 1943.

Bimbo and Topsy, illustrated by Lucy Gee. London, Newnes, 1943.

Dame Slap and Her School, illustrated by Dorothy M. Wheeler. London, Newnes, 1943.

Five Go Adventuring Again. London, Hodder and Stoughton, 1943; New York, Crowell, 1951.

The Magic Faraway Tree, illustrated by Dorothy M. Wheeler. London, Newnes, 1943.

Merry Story Book, illustrated by Eileen A. Soper. London, Hodder and Stoughton, 1943.

More Adventures of Mary Mouse. Leicester, Brockhampton Press, 1943.

The Mystery of the Burnt Cottage, illustrated by J. Abbey. London, Methuen, 1943; Los Angeles, McNaughton, 1946.

The Secret of Killimooin. Oxford, Blackwell, 1943.

Polly Piglet, illustrated by Eileen A. Soper. Leicester, Brockhampton Press, 1943.

Seven O'Clock Tales: Thirty Short Stories for Children. London, Methuen, 1943.

Summer Term at St. Clare's. London, Methuen, 1943.

The Toys Come to Life, illustrated by Eileen A. Soper. Leicester, Brockhampton Press, 1943.

At Appletree Farm. Leicester, Brockhampton Press, 1944.

Billy and Betty at the Seaside. Dundee, Valentine, 1944.

The Boy Next Door, illustrated by Alfred Bestall. London, Newnes, 1944.

The Dog That Went to Fairyland. Leicester, Brockhampton Press, 1944.

Claudine at St. Clare's. London, Methuen, 1944.

Come to the Circus, illustrated by Eileen A. Soper. Leicester, Brockhampton Press, 1944.

Eight O'Clock Tales, illustrated by Dorothy M. Wheeler. London, Methuen, 1944.

Five Run Away Together, illustrated by Eileen A. Soper. London, Hodder and Stoughton, 1944; Chicago, Reilly and Lee, 1960.

The Island of Adventure, illustrated by Stuart Tresilian. London, Macmillan, 1944; as *Mystery Island,* New York, Macmillan, 1945.

Jolly Little Jumbo. Leicester, Brockhampton Press, 1944.

Jolly Story Book, illustrated by Eileen A. Soper. London, Hodder and Stoughton, 1944.

Little Mary Mouse Again. Leicester, Brockhampton Press, 1944.

A Book of Naughty Children: The Mystery of the Disappearing Cat, illustrated by J. Abbey. London, Methuen, 1944; as *The Mystery of the Disappearing Cat,* Los Angeles, McNaughton, 1948.

Rainy Day Stories, illustrated by Nora S. Unwin. London, Evans, 1944.

The Second Form at St. Clare's, illustrated by W. Lindsay Cable. London, Methuen, 1944.

Tales of Toyland, illustrated by Hilda McGavin. London, Newnes, 1944.

The Three Golliwogs. London, Newnes, 1944.

The Blue Story Book, illustrated by Eileen A. Soper. London, Methuen, 1945.

The Brown Family, illustrated by E. and R. Buhler. London, News Chronicle, 1945.

The Caravan Family, illustrated by William Fyffe. London, Lutterworth Press, 1945.

The Conjuring Wizard and Other Stories, illustrated by Eileen A. Soper. London, Macmillan, 1945.

The Family at Red Roofs, illustrated by W. Spence. London, Lutterworth Press, 1945.

Fifth Formers at St. Clare's, illustrated by W. Lindsay Cable. London, Methuen, 1945.

Five Go to Smugglers' Top. London, Hodder and Stoughton, 1945; Chicago, Reilly and Lee, 1960.

Hallo, Little Mary Mouse, illustrated by Olive F. Openshaw. Leicester, Brockhampton Press, 1945.

Hollow Tree House, illustrated by Elizabeth Wall. London, Lutterworth Press, 1945.

The Mystery of the Secret Room. London, Methuen, 1945; Los Angeles, Parkwood Press, 1950.

The Naughtiest Girl Is a Monitor. London, Newnes, 1945.

Round the Clock Stories, illustrated by Nora S. Unwin. London, National Magazine Company, 1945.

The Runaway Kitten, illustrated by Eileen A. Soper. Leicester, Brockhampton Press, 1945.

Sunny Story Book. London, Hodder and Stoughton, 1945.

The Teddy Bear's Party, illustrated by Eileen A. Soper. Leicester, Brockhampton Press, 1945.

The Twins Go to Nursery-Rhyme Land, illustrated by Eileen A. Soper. Leicester, Brockhampton Press, 1945.

Amelia Jane Again. London, Newnes, 1946.

The Bad Little Monkey, illustrated by Eileen A. Soper. Leicester, Brockhampton Press, 1946.

The Castle of Adventure, illustrated by Stuart Tresilian. London, Macmillan, and New York, Macmillan, 1946.

The Children at Happy House, illustrated by Kathleen Gell. Oxford, Blackwell, 1946.

Chimney Corner Stories, illustrated by Pat Harrison. London, National Magazine Company, 1946.

First Term at Malory Towers. London, Methuen, 1946.

Five Go Off in a Caravan, illustrated by Eileen A. Soper. London, Hodder and Stoughton, 1946.

The Folk of the Faraway Tree, illustrated by Dorothy M. Wheeler. London, Newnes, 1946.

Gay Story Book, illustrated by Eileen A. Soper. London, Hodder and Stoughton, 1946.

Josie, Click, and Bun Again, illustrated by Dorothy M. Wheeler. London, Newnes, 1946.

The Little White Duck and Other Stories, illustrated by Eileen A. Soper. London, Macmillan, 1946.

Mary Mouse and Her Family, illustrated by Olive F. Openshaw. Leicester, Brockhampton Press, 1946.

The Mystery of the Spiteful Letters, illustrated by J. Abbey. London, Methuen, 1946.

The Put-em-Rights, illustrated by Elizabeth Wall. London, Lutterworth Press, 1946.

The Red Story Book. London, Methuen, 1946.

The Surprising Caravan, illustrated by Eileen A. Soper. Leicester, Brockhampton Press, 1946.

Tales of Green Hedges, illustrated by Gwen White. London, National Magazine Company, 1946.

The Train That Lost Its Way, illustrated by Eileen A. Soper. Leicester, Brockhampton Press, 1946.

The Adventurous Four Again, illustrated by Jessie Land. London, Newnes, 1947.

At Seaside Cottage, illustrated by Eileen A. Soper. Leicester, Brockhampton Press, 1947.

Five on Kirrin Island Again. London, Hodder and Stoughton, 1947.

The Green Story Book, illustrated by Eileen A. Soper. London, Methuen, 1947.

The Happy House Children Again, illustrated by Kathleen Gell. Oxford, Blackwell, 1947.

Here Comes Mary Mouse Again. Leicester, Brockhampton Press, 1947.

The House at the Corner, illustrated by Elsie Walker. London, Lutterworth Press, 1947.

Little Green Duck and Other Stories. Leicester, Brockhampton Press, 1947.

Lucky Story Book, illustrated by Eileen A. Soper. London, Hodder and Stoughton, 1947.

More about Josie, Click, and Bun, illustrated by Dorothy M. Wheeler. London, Newnes, 1947.

The Mystery of the Missing Necklace. London, Methuen, 1947.

Rambles with Uncle Nat, illustrated by Nora S. Unwin. London, National Magazine Company, 1947.

The "Saucy Jane" Family, illustrated by Kathleen Gell. London, Lutterworth Press, 1947.

A Second Book of Naughty Children: Twenty-Four Short Stories, illustrated by Kathleen Gell. London, Methuen, 1947.

The Second Form at Malory Towers. London, Methuen, 1947.

The Smith Family 1–3 (At Home, At the Zoo, At the Circus). Leeds, E.J. Arnold, 3 vols., 1947.

The Valley of Adventure, illustrated by Stuart Tresilian. London, Macmillan, and New York, Macmillan, 1947.

The Very Clever Rabbit. Leicester, Brockhampton Press, 1947.

The Adventures of Pip. London, Sampson Low, 1948.

The Boy with the Loaves and Fishes, illustrated by Elsie Walker. London, Lutterworth Press, 1948; New York, Roy, 1958 (?).

Come to the Circus, illustrated by Joyce M. Johnson (different book from the 1944 title). London, Newnes, 1948.

Bedtime Series. Leicester, Brockhampton Press, 2 vols., 1948.

Five Go Off to Camp. London, Hodder and Stoughton, 1948; as *Five on the Track of a Spook Train,* New York, Atheneum, 1972.

How Do You Do, Mary Mouse. Leicester, Brockhampton Press, 1948.

Just Time for a Story, illustrated by Grace Lodge. London, Macmillan, 1948; New York, St. Martin's Press, 1952.

Let's Have a Story, illustrated by George Bowe. London, Pitkin, 1948.

The Little Girl at Capernaum, illustrated by Elsie Walker. London,

Lutterworth Press, 1948; New York, Roy, 1958 (?).

Mister Icy-Cold. Oxford, Blackwell, 1948.

More Adventures of Pip. London, Sampson Low, 1948.

The Mystery of the Hidden House, illustrated by J. Abbey. London, Methuen, 1948.

Nature Tales. London, Johnston, 1948.

Now for a Story, illustrated by Frank Varty. Newcastle-upon-Tyne, Harold Hill, 1948.

The Red-Spotted Handkerchief and Other Stories, illustrated by Kathleen Gell. Leicester, Brockhampton Press, 1948.

The Sea of Adventure, illustrated by Stuart Tresilian. London, Macmillan, and New York, Macmillan, 1948.

The Secret of the Old Mill, illustrated by Eileen A. Soper. Leicester, Brockhampton Press, 1948.

Six Cousins at Mistletoe Farm, illustrated by Peter Beigel. London, Evans, 1948.

Tales after Tea. London, Laurie, 1948.

Tales of the Twins, illustrated by Eileen A. Soper. Leicester, Brockhampton Press, 1948.

They Ran Away Together, illustrated by Jeanne Farrar. Leicester, Brockhampton Press, 1948.

Third Year at Malory Towers, illustrated by Stanley Lloyd. London, Methuen, 1948.

We Want a Story, illustrated by George Bowe. London, Pitkin, 1948.

Bluebell [Daffodil, Poppy, Buttercup, Snowdrop, Marigold, Foxglove] Story Book. London, Gifford, 7 vols., 1949–55.

Bumpy and His Bus, illustrated by Dorothy M. Wheeler. London, Newnes, 1949.

A Cat in Fairyland and Other Stories. London, Pitkin, 1949.

The Circus Book. London, Latimer House, 1949.

The Dear Old Snow Man. Leicester, Brockhampton Press, 1949.

Don't Be Silly, Mr. Twiddle. London, Newnes, 1949.

The Enchanted Sea and Other Stories. London, Pitkin, 1949.

Good Morning Book, illustrated by Don and Ann Goring. London, National Magazine Company, 1949.

Five Get into Trouble, illustrated by Eileen A. Soper. London, Hodder and Stoughton, 1949; as *Five Caught in a Treacherous Plot,* New York, Atheneum, 1972.

Humpty Dumpty and Belinda. London, Collins, 1949.

Jinky's Joke and Other Stories, illustrated by Kathleen Gell. Leicester, Brockhampton Press, 1949.

Little Noddy Goes to Toyland, illustrated by Harmsen Van Beek. London, Sampson Low, 1949.

Mr. Tumpy and His Caravan, illustrated by Dorothy M. Wheeler. London, Sidgwick and Jackson, 1949; Los Angeles, McNaughton, 1951.

The Mountain of Adventure, illustrated by Stuart Tresilian. London, Macmillan, and New York, Macmillan, 1949.

The Mystery of the Pantomime Cat. London, Methuen, 1949.

Oh, What a Lovely Time. Leicester, Brockhampton Press, 1949.

The Rockingdown Mystery, illustrated by Gilbert Dunlop. London, Collins, 1949.

The Secret Seven, illustrated by George Brook. Leicester, Brockhampton Press, 1949; as *The Secret Seven and the Mystery of the Empty House,* Chicago, Children's Press, 1972.

A Story Party at Green Hedges, illustrated by Grace Lodge. London, Hodder and Stoughton, 1949.

The Strange Umbrella and Other Stories. London, Pitkin, 1949.

Tales after Supper. London, Laurie, 1949.

Those Dreadful Children, illustrated by Grace Lodge. London, Lutterworth Press, 1949.

Tiny Tales. Worcester, Littlebury, 1949.

The Upper Fourth at Malory Towers. London, Methuen, 1949.

Chuff the Chimney Sweep and Other Stories. London, Pitkin, 1950.

The Astonishing Ladder and Other Stories, illustrated by Eileen A.

Soper. London, Macmillan, 1950.

Five Fall into Adventure, illustrated by Eileen A. Soper. London, Hodder and Stoughton, 1950; New York, Atheneum, 1972.

Hurrah for Little Noddy, illustrated by Harmsen Van Beek. London, Sampson Low, 1950.

In the Fifth at Malory Towers, illustrated by Stanley Lloyd. London, Methuen, 1950.

The Magic Knitting Needles and Other Stories, illustrated by Eileen A. Soper. London, Macmillan, 1950.

Mister Meddle's Muddles, illustrated by Rosalind M. Turvey and Joyce Mercer. London, Newnes, 1950.

Mr. Pink-Whistle Interferes, illustrated by Dorothy M. Wheeler. London, Newnes, 1950.

The Mystery of the Invisible Thief, illustrated by Treyer Evans. London, Methuen, 1950.

The Pole Star Family, illustrated by Ruth Gervis. London, Lutterworth Press, 1950.

The Rilloby Fair Mystery, illustrated by Gilbert Dunlop. London, Collins, 1950.

Round the Year Stories. London, Coker, 1950.

Rubbalong Tales, illustrated by Norman Meredith. London, Macmillan, 1950.

The Seaside Family, illustrated by Ruth Gervis. London, Lutterworth Press, 1950.

Secret Seven Adventure, illustrated by George Brook. Leicester, Brockhampton Press, 1950; as *The Secret Seven and the Circus Adventure,* Chicago, Children's Press, 1972.

The Ship of Adventure, illustrated by Stuart Tresilian. London, Macmillan, and New York, Macmillan, 1950.

Six Cousins Again, illustrated by Maurice Tulloch. London, Evans, 1950.

Tales about Toys, illustrated by Jeanne Farrar. Leicester, Brockhampton Press, 1950.

The Three Naughty Children and Other Stories, illustrated by Eileen A. Soper. London, Macmillan, 1950.

Tricky the Goblin and Other Stories, illustrated by Eileen A. Soper. London, Macmillan, 1950.

We Do Love Mary Mouse. Leicester, Brockhampton Press, 1950.

Welcome Mary Mouse, illustrated by Olive F. Openshaw. Leicester, Brockhampton Press, 1950.

What an Adventure, illustrated by Eileen A. Soper. Leicester, Brockhampton Press, 1950.

The Wishing Chair Again. London, Newnes, 1950.

The Yellow Story Book, illustrated by Kathleen Gell. London, Methuen, 1950.

Boody the Great Goblin and Other Stories. London, Pitkin, 1951.

The "Queen Elizabeth" Family, illustrated by Ruth Gervis. London, Lutterworth Press, 1951.

Benny and the Princess and Other Stories. London, Pitkin, 1951.

The Big Noddy Book, illustrated by Harmsen Van Beek. London, Sampson Low, 1951 (and later volumes).

The Buttercup Farm Family, illustrated by Ruth Gervis. London, Lutterworth Press, 1951.

Down at the Farm. London, Sampson Low, 1951.

Father Christmas and Belinda. London, Collins, 1951.

Five on a Hike Together, illustrated by Eileen A. Soper. London, Hodder and Stoughton, 1951.

The Flying Goat and Other Stories. London, Pitkin, 1951.

Gay Street Book, illustrated by Grace Lodge. London, Latimer, 1951.

Hello Twins, illustrated by Molly Brett. Leicester, Brockhampton Press, 1951.

Here Comes Noddy Again, illustrated by Harmsen Van Beek. London, Sampson Low, 1951.

Hurrah for Mary Mouse. Leicester, Brockhampton Press, 1951.

Last Term at Malory Towers, illustrated by Stanley Lloyd. London,

Methuen, 1951.

Let's Go to the Circus. London, Odhams, 1951.

The Little Spinning House and Other Stories. London, Pitkin, 1951.

The Magic Snow-Bird and Other Stories. London, Pitkin, 1951.

The Mystery of the Vanished Prince, illustrated by Treyer Evans. London, Methuen, 1951.

Noddy and Big Ears Have a Picnic. London, Sampson Low, 1951.

Noddy and His Car, illustrated by Harmsen Van Beek. London, Sampson Low, 1951.

Noddy Has a Shock. London, Sampson Low, 1951.

Noddy Has More Adventures. London, Sampson Low, 1951.

Noddy Goes to the Seaside. London, Sampson Low, 1951.

Noddy Off to Rocking Horse Land. London, Sampson Low, 1951.

Noddy Painting Book. London, Sampson Low, 8 vols., 1951–57.

Noddy's House of Books. London, Sampson Low, 6 vols., 1951.

A Picnic Party with Enid Blyton, illustrated by Grace Lodge. London, Hodder and Stoughton, 1951.

Pippy and the Gnome and Other Stories. London, Pitkin, 1951.

A Prize for Mary Mouse. Leicester, Brockhampton Press, 1951.

The Proud Golliwog, illustrated by Molly Brett. Leicester, Brockhampton Press, 1951.

The Runaway Teddy Bear and Other Stories.. London, Pitkin, 1951.

The Six Bad Boys, illustrated by Mary Gernat. London, Lutterworth Press, 1951.

A Tale of Little Noddy. London, Sampson Low, 1951.

"Too-Wise" the Wonderful Wizard and Other Stories. London, Pitkin, 1951.

Up the Faraway Tree, illustrated by Dorothy M. Wheeler. London, Newnes, 1951.

Well Done, Secret Seven, illustrated by George Brook. Leicester, Brockhampton Press, 1951; as *The Secret Seven and the Tree House Adventure,* Chicago, Children's Press, 1972.

Bright Story Book, illustrated by Eileen A. Soper. Leicester, Brockhampton Press, 1952.

The Circus of Adventure, illustrated by Stuart Tresilian. London, Macmillan, 1952; New York, St. Martin's Press, 1953.

Come Along Twins, illustrated by Eileen A. Soper. Leicester, Brockhampton Press, 1952.

Five Have a Wonderful Time, illustrated by Eileen A. Soper. London, Hodder and Stoughton, 1952.

The Mad Teapot, illustrated by Molly Brett. Leicester, Brockhampton Press, 1952.

Mandy, Mops, and Cubby Find a House. London, Sampson Low, 1952.

Mandy, Mops, and Cubby Again. London, Sampson Low, 1952.

Mary Mouse and Her Bicycle, illustrated by Olive F. Openshaw. Leicester, Brockhampton Press, 1952.

Mr. Tumpy Plays a Trick on Saucepan. London, Sampson Low, 1952.

The Mystery of the Strange Bundle, illustrated by Treyer Evans. London, Methuen, 1952.

Noddy and Big Ears. London, Sampson Low, 1952.

Noddy and the Witch's Wand. London, Sampson Low, 1952.

Noddy's Colour Strip Book, illustrated by Harmsen Van Beek. London, Sampson Low, 1952.

Noddy Goes to School. London, Sampson Low, 1952.

Noddy's Ark of Books. London, Sampson Low, 5 vols., 1952.

Noddy's Car Gets a Squeak. London, Sampson Low, 1952.

Noddy's Penny Wheel Car. London, Sampson Low, 1952.

The Queer Mystery, illustrated by Norman Meredith. London, Staples Press, 1952.

The Rubadub Mystery, illustrated by Gilbert Dunlop. London, Collins, 1952.

Secret Seven on the Trail, illustrated by George Brook. Leicester, Brockhampton Press, 1952; as *The Secret Seven and the Railroad*

Mystery, Chicago, Children's Press, 1972.

The Very Big Secret, illustrated by Ruth Gervis.   London, Lutterworth Press, 1952.

Welcome Josie, Click, and Bun, illustrated by Dorothy M. Wheeler. London, Newnes, 1952.

Well Done, Noddy, illustrated by Harmsen Van Beek.   London, Sampson Low, 1952.

Clicky the Clockwork Clown, illustrated by Molly Brett.   Leicester, Brockhampton Press, 1953.

Five Go Down to the Sea, illustrated by Eileen A. Soper.   London, Hodder and Stoughton, 1953; Chicago, Reilly and Lee, 1961.

Go Ahead Secret Seven, illustrated by Bruno Kay.   Leicester, Brockhampton Press, 1953; as *The Secret Seven Get Their Man,* Chicago, Children's Press, 1972.

Gobo and Mr. Fierce.   London, Sampson Low, 1953.

Here Come the Twins, illustrated by Eileen A. Soper.   Leicester, Brockhampton Press, 1953.

Mandy Makes Cubby a Hat.   London, Sampson Low, 1953.

Mary Mouse and the Noah's Ark, illustrated by Olive F. Openshaw. Leicester, Brockhampton Press, 1953.

Mr. Tumpy in the Land of Wishes.   London, Sampson Low, 1953.

My Enid Blyton Story Book, illustrated by Willy Schermelé.   London, Juvenile Productions, 1953.

The Mystery of Holly Lane, illustrated by Treyer Evans.   London, Methuen, 1953.

New Noddy Colour Strip Book.   London, Sampson Low, 1953.

Noddy and the Cuckoo's Nest.   London, Sampson Low, 1953.

Noddy at the Seaside, illustrated by Harmsen Van Beek.   London, Sampson Low, 1953.

Noddy's Cut-Out Model Book.   London, Sampson Low, 1953.

Noddy Gets Captured.   London, Sampson Low, 1953.

Noddy Is Very Silly.   London, Sampson Low, 1953.

Noddy's Garage of Books, illustrated by Harmsen Van Beek.   London, Sampson Low, 5 vols., 1953.

The Secret of Moon Castle.   Oxford, Blackwell, 1953.

Snowball the Pony, illustrated by Iris Gillespie.   London, Lutterworth Press, 1953.

Visitors in the Night, illustrated by Molly Brett.   Leicester, Brockhampton Press, 1953.

Well Really Mr. Twiddle!, illustrated by Hilda McGavin.   London, Newnes, 1953.

Fun with the Twins, illustrated by Eileen A. Soper.   Leicester, Brockhampton Press, 1954.

Enid Blyton's Good Morning Book, illustrated by Willy Schermelé. London, Juvenile Productions, 1954.

Noddy Gets into Trouble.   London, Sampson Low, 1954.

What a Surprise!, illustrated by Molly Brett.   Leicester, Brockhampton Press, 1954.

The Adventure of the Secret Necklace, illustrated by Isabel Veevers. London, Lutterworth Press, 1954.

The Castle Without a Door and Other Stories.   London, Pitkin, 1954.

The Children at Green Meadows, illustrated by Grace Lodge.   London, Lutterworth Press, 1954.

Friendly Story Book, illustrated by Eileen A. Soper.   Leicester, Brockhampton Press, 1954.

Noddy Goes to the Fair.   London, Sampson Low, 1954.

Noddy Giant Painting Book.   London, Sampson Low, 1954.

Good Work, Secret Seven!, illustrated by Bruno Kay.   Leicester, Brockhampton Press, 1954; as *The Secret Seven and the Case of the Stolen Car,* Chicago, Children's Press, 1972.

Five Go to Mystery Moor.   London, Hodder and Stoughton, 1954; Chicago, Reilly and Lee, 1963.

How Funny You Are, Noddy.   London, Sampson Low, 1954.

Little Strip Picture Books.   London, Sampson Low, 1954 (and other volumes).

The Little Toy Farm and Other Stories.   London, Pitkin, 1954.

Mary Mouse to the Rescue.   Leicester, Brockhampton Press, 1954.

Merry Mister Meddle, illustrated by Rosalind M. Turvey and Joyce Mercer.   London, Newnes, 1954.

More about Amelia Jane, illustrated by Sylvia I. Venus.   London, Newnes, 1954.

The Mystery of Tally-Ho Cottage, illustrated by Treyer Evans.   London, Methuen, 1954.

Noddy and the Magic Rubber.   London, Sampson Low, 1954.

Noddy's Castle of Books, illustrated by Harmsen Van Beek.   London, Sampson Low, 5 vols., 1954.

Sooty, illustrated by Pierre Probst.   London, Collins, 1955.

Away Goes Sooty, illustrated by Pierre Probst.   London, Collins, 1955.

Benjy and the Others, illustrated by Kathleen Gell.   London, Latimer, 1955.

Bimbo and Blackie Go Camping, illustrated by Pierre Probst.   London, Collins, 1955.

Bobs, illustrated by Pierre Probst.   London, Collins, 1955.

Christmas with Scamp and Bimbo, illustrated by Pierre Probst. London, Collins, 1955.

Little Bedtime Books (The Cloud Kitten, The Doll That Fell Out of the Pram, Silly Sammy, The Surprising Broom, Amanda Going Away, The Balloon Pipe, The Golliwog and the Wireless, The Wizard Who Was Really a Nuisance).   London, Sampson Low, 8 vols., 1955–58.

Neddy the Little Donkey, illustrated by Romain Simon.   London, Collins, 1955.

Five Have Plenty of Fun.   London, Hodder and Stoughton, 1955.

Gobo in the Land of Dreams.   London, Sampson Low, 1955.

The Golliwog Grumbled, illustrated by Molly Brett.   Leicester, Brockhampton Press, 1955.

Holiday House, illustrated by Grace Lodge.   London, Evans, 1955.

The Laughing Kitten, illustrated by Paul Kaye.   London, Harvill Press, and New York, Roy, 1955.

Mandy, Mops, and Cubby and the Whitewash.   London, Sampson Low, 1955.

Mary Mouse in Nursery Rhyme Land.   Leicester, Brockhampton Press, 1955.

Mischief Again, photographs by Paul Kaye.   London, Harvill Press, and New York, Roy, 1955.

Mr. Pink-Whistle's Party, illustrated by Dorothy M. Wheeler.   London, Newnes, 1955.

Mr. Tumpy in the Land of Boys and Girls.   London, Sampson Low, 1955.

More Chimney Corner Stories, illustrated by Pat Harrison.   London, Latimer, 1955.

Noddy in Toyland.   London, Sampson Low, 1955.

Noddy Meets Father Christmas.   London, Sampson Low, 1955.

Ring o' Bells Mystery.   London, Collins, 1955.

The River of Adventure, illustrated by Stuart Tresilian.   London, Macmillan, and New York, St. Martin's Press, 1955.

Run-about's Holiday, illustrated by Lilian Chivers.   London, Lutterworth Press, 1955.

Secret Seven Win Through, illustrated by Bruno Kay.   Leicester, Brockhampton Press, 1955; as *The Secret Seven and the Hidden Cave Adventure,* Chicago, Children's Press, 1972.

Trouble for the Twins, illustrated by Eileen A. Soper.   Leicester, Brockhampton Press, 1955.

The Troublesome Three, illustrated by Leo.   London, Sampson Low, 1955.

You Funny Little Noddy!   London, Sampson Low, 1955.

Be Brave, Little Noddy!   London, Sampson Low, 1956.

Bom the Little Toy Drummer, illustrated by R. Paul-Höye. Leicester, Brockhampton Press, 1956.

The Clever Little Donkey, illustrated by Romain Simon.   London,

Collins, 1956.

Colin the Cow-Boy, illustrated by R. Caillé. London, Collins, 1956.

A Day with Mary Mouse, illustrated by Frederick White. Leicester, Brockhampton Press, 1956.

Animal Tales, illustrated by Romain Simon. London, Collins, 1956.

Noddy Play Day Painting Book. London, Sampson Low, 1956.

Five on a Secret Trail, illustrated by Eileen A. Soper. London, Hodder and Stoughton, 1956.

A Day with Noddy. London, Sampson Low, 1956.

Four in a Family, illustrated by Tom Kerr. London, Lutterworth Press, 1956.

The Mystery of the Missing Man, illustrated by Lilian Buchanan. London, Methuen, 1956.

Noddy and His Friends. London, Sampson Low, 1956.

Noddy and Tessie Bear. London, Sampson Low, 1956.

The Noddy Toy Station Books. London, Sampson Low, 5 vols., 1956.

The Rat-a-Tat Mystery, illustrated by Anyon Cook. London, Collins, 1956.

Scamp at School, illustrated by Pierre Probst. London, Collins, 1956.

Three Cheers Secret Seven, illustrated by Burgess Sharrocks. Leicester, Brockhampton Press, 1956; as *The Secret Seven and the Grim Secret,* Chicago, Children's Press, 1972.

Bom and His Magic Drumstick, illustrated by R. Paul-Höye. Leicester, Brockhampton Press, 1957.

Do Look Out, Noddy! London, Sampson Low, 1957.

Bom Painting Book. London, Dean, 1957.

Five Go to Billycock Hill, illustrated by Eileen A. Soper. London, Hodder and Stoughton, 1957.

Mary Mouse and the Garden Party, illustrated by Frederick White. Leicester, Brockhampton Press, 1957.

Mystery of the Strange Messages, illustrated by Lilian Buchanan. London, Methuen, 1957.

Noddy and the Bumpy Dog. London, Sampson Low, 1957.

Noddy's New Big Book. London, Sampson Low, 1957.

Secret Seven Mystery, illustrated by Burgess Sharrocks. Leicester, Brockhampton Press, 1957; as *The Secret Seven and the Missing Girl Mystery,* Chicago, Children's Press, 1972.

The Birthday Kitten, illustrated by Grace Lodge. London, Lutterworth Press, 1958.

Bom Goes Adventuring, illustrated by R. Paul-Höye. Leicester, Brockhampton Press, 1958.

Bom Goes to Ho Ho Village, illustrated by R. Paul Höye. Leicester, Brockhampton Press, 1958.

Bom Annual, illustrated by R. Paul-Höye and H.W. Felstead. London, Thames, 2 vols., 1958–59.

Clicky Gets into Trouble, illustrated by Molly Brett. Leicester, Brockhampton Press, 1958.

Five Get into a Fix, illustrated by Eileen A. Soper. London, Hodder and Stoughton, 1958.

Mary Mouse Goes to the Fair, illustrated by Frederick White. Leicester, Brockhampton Press, 1958.

Mr. Pink-Whistle's Big Book. London, Evans, 1958.

My Big-Ears Picture Book. London, Sampson Low, 1958.

My Noddy Picture Book. London, Sampson Low, 1958.

Noddy Has an Adventure. London, Sampson Low, 1958.

Puzzle for the Secret Seven, illustrated by Burgess Sharrocks. Leicester, Brockhampton Press, 1958; as *The Secret Seven and the Case of the Music Lover,* Chicago, Children's Press, 1972.

Rumble and Chuff, illustrated by David Walsh. London, Juvenile Productions, 2 vols., 1958.

You're a Good Friend, Noddy! London, Sampson Low, 1958.

The Noddy Shop Book. London, Sampson Low, 5 vols., 1958.

Bom and the Clown, illustrated by R. Paul-Höye. Leicester, Brock-

hampton Press, 1959.

Bom and the Rainbow, illustrated by R. Paul-Höye. Leicester, Brockhampton Press, 1959.

Hullo Bom and Wuffy Dog, illustrated by R. Paul-Höye. Leicester, Brockhampton Press, 1959.

Mary Mouse Has a Wonderful Idea, illustrated by Frederick White. Leicester, Brockhampton Press, 1959.

Noddy and the Bunkey. London, Sampson Low, 1959.

Noddy Goes to Sea. London, Sampson Low, 1959.

Noddy's Car Picture Book. London, Sampson Low, 1959.

Ragamuffin Mystery. London, Collins, 1959.

Secret Seven Fireworks, illustrated by Burgess Sharrocks. Leicester, Brockhampton Press, 1959; as *The Secret Seven and the Bonfire Mystery,* Chicago, Children's Press, 1972.

Adventure of the Strange Ruby, illustrated by Roger Payne. Leicester, Brockhampton Press, 1960.

Adventure Stories. London, Collins, 1960.

Bom Goes to Magic Town, illustrated by R. Paul-Höye. Leicester, Brockhampton Press, 1960.

Cheer Up, Little Noddy! London, Sampson Low, 1960.

Clicky and Tiptoe, illustrated by Molly Brett. Leicester, Brockhampton Press, 1960.

Five on Finniston Farm, illustrated by Eileen A. Soper. London, Hodder and Stoughton, 1960.

Good Old Secret Seven, illustrated by Burgess Sharrocks. Leicester, Brockhampton Press, 1960; as *The Secret Seven and the Old Fort Adventure,* Chicago, Children's Press, 1972.

Happy Day Stories, illustrated by Marcia Lane Foster. London, Evans, 1960.

Here Comes Bom, illustrated by R. Paul-Höye. Leicester, Brockhampton Press, 1960.

Mary Mouse Goes to Sea, illustrated by Frederick White. Leicester, Brockhampton Press, 1960.

Mystery Stories. London, Collins, 1960.

Noddy Goes to the Fair. London, Sampson Low, 1960.

Noddy's Tall Blue D[Green, Orange, Pink, Red, Yellow] Book. London, Sampson Low, 6 vols., 1960.

Will the Fiddle, illustrated by Grace Lodge. London, Instructive Arts, 1960.

Tales at Bedtime, illustrated by Hilda McGavin. London, Collins, 1961.

Bom at the Seaside, illustrated by R. Paul-Höye. Leicester, Brockhampton Press, 1961.

Bom Goes to the Circus, illustrated by R. Paul-Höye. Leicester, Brockhampton Press, 1961.

Five Go to Demon's Rocks, illustrated by Eileen A. Soper. London, Hodder and Stoughton, 1961.

Happy Holiday, Clicky, illustrated by Molly Brett. Leicester, Brockhampton Press, 1961.

Mary Mouse Goes Out for the Day, illustrated by Frederick White. Leicester, Brockhampton Press, 1961.

Mr. Plod and Little Noddy. London, Sampson Low, 1961.

The Mystery of Banshee Towers, illustrated by Lilian Buchanan. London, Methuen, 1961.

The Mystery That Never Was, illustrated by Gilbert Dunlop. London, Collins, 1961.

Noddy's Toyland Train Picture Book. London, Sampson Low, 1961.

Shock for the Secret Seven, illustrated by Burgess Sharrocks. Leicester, Brockhampton Press, 1961; as *The Secret Seven and the Case of the Dog Lover,* Chicago, Children's Press, 1972.

A Day at School with Noddy. London, Sampson Low, 1962.

Five Have a Mystery to Solve, illustrated by Eileen A. Soper. London, Hodder and Stoughton, 1962.

The Four Cousins, illustrated by Joan Thompson. London, Lutterworth Press, 1962.

Fun with Mary Mouse, illustrated by R. Paul-Höye. Leicester, Brockhampton Press, 1962.

Look Out Secret Seven, illustrated by Burgess Sharrocks. Leicester, Brockhampton Press, 1962; as *The Secret Seven and the Case of the Missing Medals,* Chicago, Children's Press, 1972.

Noddy and the Tootles. London, Sampson Low, 1962.

Stories for Monday [and *Tuesday*]. London, Oliphants, 2 vols., 1962.

The Boy Who Wanted a Dog, illustrated by Sally Michel. London, Lutterworth Press, 1963.

Five Are Together Again, illustrated by Eileen A. Soper. London, Hodder and Stoughton, 1963.

Fun for the Secret Seven, illustrated by Burgess Sharrocks. Leicester, Brockhampton Press, 1963; as *The Secret Seven and the Case of the Old Horse,* Chicago, Children's Press, 1972.

Sunshine Picture Story Book. Manchester, World Distributors, 1964 (and later volumes).

Happy Hours Story Book. London, Dean, 1964.

Mary Mouse and the Little Donkey, illustrated by R. Paul-Höye. Leicester, Brockhampton Press, 1964.

Noddy and the Aeroplane. London, Sampson Low, 1964.

Storybook for Fives to Sevens, illustrated by Dorothy Hall and Grace Shelton. London, Parrish, 1964.

Storytime Book. London, Dean, 1964.

Tell-a-Story Books. Manchester, World Distributors, 1964.

Trouble for the Twins. Leicester, Brockhampton Press, 1964.

The Boy Who Came Back, illustrated by Elsie Walker. London, Lutterworth Press, 1965.

Sunshine Book. London, Dean, 1965.

Treasure Box. London, Sampson Low, 1965.

The Man Who Stopped to Help, illustrated by Elsie Walker. London, Lutterworth Press, 1965.

Noddy and His Friends: A Nursery Picture Book. London, Sampson Low, 1965.

Noddy Treasure Box. London, Sampson Low, 1965.

The Fairy Folk Story Book. London, Collins, 1966.

Fireside Tales. London, Collins, 1966.

John and Mary series (*The Great Big Fish, How John Got His Ducklings, The Dog Who Would Go Digging, The Wheel That Ran Away, The Three Sailors, The Kitten That Disappeared, The Little Brown Bear, Tim Gets a Chance, Granny's Lovely Necklace*), illustrated by Fromont. Leicester, Brockhampton Press, 9 vols., 1966–68.

Pixie Tales. London, Collins, 1966.

Pixieland Story Book. London, Collins, 1966.

Stories for Bedtime. London, Dean, 1966.

Stories for You. London, Dean, 1966.

Holiday Annual [and *Magic, Pixie, Toy*] *Stories.* London, Low Marston, 4 vols., 1967.

Noddy and His Passengers. London, Sampson Low, 1967.

Noddy and the Magic Boots, Noddy's Funny Kite. London, Sampson Low, 1967.

Noddy and the Noah's Ark Adventure Picture Book. London, Sampson Low, 1967.

Noddy in Toyland Picture Book. London, Low Marston, 1967.

Noddy's Aeroplane Picture Book. London, Sampson Low, 1967.

The Playtime Story Book. Manchester, World Distributors, 4 vols., 1967.

Adventures on Willow Farm. London, Collins, 1968.

The Playtime Book. Manchester, World Distributors, 8 vols., 1968.

A Basket of Surprises, illustrated by Caroline Sharpe. London, Knight, 1970.

Fiction as Mary Pollock

Children of Kidillin. London, Newnes, 1940.

Three Boys and a Circus. London, Newnes, 1940.
Mischief at St. Rollo's. London, Newnes, 1943.
The Secret of Cliff Castle. London, Newnes, 1943.
The Adventures of Scamp. London, Newnes, 1943.
Smuggler Ben. London, Laurie, 1943.

Plays

A Book of Little Plays (includes *The Princess and the Swineherd, Sing a Song of Sixpence, Fairy Prisoners, Robin Hood, Peronel's Paint*). London, Nelson, 1926.

The Play's the Thing (includes *The Capture of the Robbers; Rag, Tag, and Bobtail; Rumpelstiltskin; The King's Jester; The Magic Apple; Merry Robin Hood; The King's Pocket Knife; In the Toyshop; The Cuckoo; The Rainbow Flowers; The Wishing-Glove; The Broken Statue*), music by Alec Rowley, illustrated by Alfred Bestall. London, Nelson, 1927; as *Plays for Older Children* and *Plays for Younger Children,* London, Newnes, 2 vols., 1940.

Six Enid Blyton Plays (includes *The Princess and the Enchanter, Robin Hood and the Butcher, The Enchanted Cap, A Visit to Nursery-Rhyme Land, The Squirrel's Secret, The Whistling Brownie*). London, Methuen, 1935.

How the Flowers Grow and Other Musical Plays (includes *The Fairy in the Box, The Magic Ball, The Toys at Night-Time, Who Stole the Crown?, Santa Claus Gets Busy*), music by Cecil Sharman. Exeter, Wheaton, 1939.

Cameo Plays, Book 4 (includes *The Making of a Rainbow, Poor Mr. Twiddle, The Three Wishes, The Donkey's Tail, Santa Claus Comes Down the Chimney, The Wind and the Sun, Brer Rabbit and Mr. Dog, The Little Green Imp*), edited by George H. Holroyd. Leeds, E.J. Arnold, 1939.

The Wishing Bean and Other Plays (includes *The Hole in the Sack, Spreading the News, The Queen's Garden, Sneezing Powder, The Land of Nursery Rhymes*). Oxford, Blackwell, 1939; as *Six Plays for Schools,* 1939.

Noddy in Toyland, music by Philip Green (produced London, 1954). London, Sampson Low, 1956.

Finding the Tickets. London, Evans, 1955.
Mr. Sly-One and Cats. London, Evans, 1955.
Mother's Meeting. London, Evans, 1955.
Who Will Hold the Giant? London, Evans, 1955.
The Famous Five, adaptation of her own stories (produced London, 1955).

Verse

Child Whispers. London, Saville, 1922.
Real Fairies. London, Saville, 1923.
Songs of Gladness, music by Alec Rowley. London, Saville, 1924.
Silver and Gold, illustrated by Lewis Baumer. London, Nelson, 1925; New York, Nelson, 1928.
The Enid Blyton Poetry Book: Ninety-Six Poems for the Twelve Months of the Year. London, Methuen, 1934.
Noddy Nursery Rhymes. London, Sampson Low, 1956.
Noddy's Own Nursery Rhymes. London, Sampson Low, 1958.

Other

Responsive Singing Games. London, Saville, 1923.
Reading Practice, 1–5, 8–9, 11. London, Nelson, 8 vols., 1925–26.
The Bird Book, illustrated by Roland Green. London, Newnes, 1926.
Aesop's Fables, Retold. London, Nelson, 1928.
Let's Pretend, illustrated by I. Bennington Angrave. London, Nelson, 1928.

Old English Stories, Retold. London, Nelson, 1928.
Pinkity's Pranks and Other Nature Fairy Tales, Retold. London, Nelson, 1928.
Tales of Brer Rabbit, Retold. London, Nelson, 1928.
Nature Lessons. London, Evans, 1929.
The Knights of the Round Table. London, Newnes, 1930.
Tales from the Arabian Nights. London, Newnes, 1930.
Tales of Ancient Greece. London, Newnes, 1930.
Tales of Robin Hood. London, Newnes, 1930.
Let's Read. London, Birn, 1933.
My First Reading Book. London, Birn, 1933.
Stories from World History (The Adventures of Odysseus, The Story of the Siege of Troy, Tales of the Ancient Greeks and Persians, Tales of the Romans). London, Evans, 4 vols., 1934.
Round the Year with Enid Blyton: Spring, Summer, Autumn, Winter. London, Evans, 4 vols., 1934.
The Old Thatch series (includes fiction; *The Talking Teapot and Other Tales; Hop, Skip and Jump; The Tale of Mr. Wumble; Brer Rabbit; The Adventures of Bobs; The Little Button-Elves; Animals at Home; Birds at Home; Brer Rabbit and His Friends; The Two Sillies and Other Stories; Round the Year Stories; A Book of Magic; The Watchman with 100 Eyes and Other Greek Tales; Children of Other Lands; A Visit to the Zoo; Tales of Old Thatch; Children of Other Days; King Arthur and His Knights; All about the Circus; Friends of the Countryside*). London, Johnston, 20 vols., 1934–39.
The Children's Garden. London, Newnes, 1935.
Heyo, Brer Rabbit! Tales of Brer Rabbit and His Friends, illustrated by Kathleen Nixon. London, Newnes, 1938.
Birds of Our Gardens, illustrated by Roland Green and Ernest Aris. London, Newnes, 1940.
The News Chronicle Boys' and Girls' Book. London, News Chronicle, 1940.
The Babar Story Book, from stories by Jean de Brunhoff. London, Methuen, 1941; shortened version, as *Tales of Babar,* 1942.
A Calendar for Children. London, Newnes, 1941.
Book of the Year, music by Alec Rowley, illustrated by Eileen A. Soper. London, Evans, 1941 (and later volumes).
Enid Blyton Readers, 1–7, 10–12. London, Macmillan, 10 vols., 1942–50.
The Further Adventures of Brer Rabbit, Being More Tales of Brer Rabbit and His Friends, illustrated by Ernest Aris. London, Newnes, 1942.
The Land of Far-Beyond, based on *Pilgrim's Progress* by John Bunyan. London, Methuen, 1942.
The Children's Life of Christ. London, Methuen, 1943.
The Christmas Book, illustrated by Treyer Evans. London, Macmillan, 1944.
Nature Lover's Book, illustrated by Donia Nachshen and Noel Hopking. London, Evans, 1944.
Tales from the Bible, illustrated by Eileen A. Soper. London, Methuen, 1944.
Nature Readers, 1–30. London, Macmillan, 30 vols., 1945–46.
The First Christmas, illustrated by Paul Henning. London, Methuen, 1945.
The Enid Blyton Holiday Book. London, Sampson Low, 1946 (and 11 later volumes).
Before I Go to Sleep: A Book of Bible Stories and Prayers for Children at Night. London, Latimer, 1947; Boston, Little Brown, 1953.
Enid Blyton's Treasury. London, Evans, 1947.
Jinky Nature Books. Leeds, E.J. Arnold, 4 vols., 1947.
Brer Rabbit and His Friends. London, Coker, 1948.
Brer Rabbit Book, illustrated by Grace Lodge. London, Latimer, 8 vols., 1948–58.
Let's Garden, illustrated by William McLaren. London, Latimer, 1948.

The Enid Blyton Nature Plates, with stories and notes, and reference book. London, Macmillan, 3 vols., 1949.
The Enid Blyton Bible Stories: Old Testament, with Bible pictures and reference book. London, Macmillan, 16 vols., 1949.
My Enid Blyton Bedside Book. London, Barker, 1949 (and 11 later volumes).
A Book of Magic. London, Macmillan, 1949.
My First Enid Blyton Book. London, Latimer, 1952 (and 2 later volumes).
The Enid Blyton Bible Stories: New Testament, with Bible pictures and reference book. London, Macmillan, 16 vols., 1952–53.
Animal Lover's Book. London, Evans, 1952.
Enid Blyton's Omnibus, illustrated by Jessie Land. London, Newnes, 1952.
My First Nature Book, illustrated by Eileen A. Soper. London, Macmillan, 1952 (and 2 later volumes).
Enid Blyton's Christmas Story, illustrated by Fritz Wegner. London, Hamish Hamilton, 1953.
The Story of Our Queen, illustrated by F.Stocks May. London, Muller, 1953.
Little Gift Books, illustrated by Pierre Probst. London, Hackett, 1954 (and later volumes).
Enid Blyton Magazine Annual. London, Evans, 1954 (and 3 later volumes).
The Greatest Book in the World, illustrated by Mabel Peacock. London, British and Foreign Bible Society, 1954.
Bible Stories from the Old [and *New*] *Testament,* illustrated by Grace Lodge. London, Lutterworth Press, 2 vols., 1955.
Favourite Book of Fables, from the Tales of La Fontaine, illustrated by Romain Simon. London, Collins, 1955.
What Shall I Be?, illustrated by Pierre Probst. London, Collins, 1955.
Playing at Home, with Sabine Schweitzer. London, Methuen, 1955.
Let's Have a Party, photographs by Paul Kaye. London, Harvill Press, 1956; New York, Roy, 1957 (?).
A Story Book of Jesus, illustrated by Elsie Walker. London, Macmillan, 1956.
New Testament Picture Books 1–2. London, Macmillan, 2 vols., 1957.
The School Companion, with others. London, New Educational Press, 1958.
A.B.C. with Noddy. London, Sampson Low, 1959.
Old Testament Picture Books. London, Macmillan, 1960.
Noddy's One, Two, Three Book. London, Sampson Low, 1961.
The Big Enid Blyton Book. London, Hamlyn, 1961.
Brer Rabbit Again, illustrated by Grace Lodge. London, Dean, 1963.
Tales of Brave Adventure, Retold. London, Dean, 1963.
Easy Reader. London, Collins, 1965 (and later volumes).
Brer Rabbit's a Rascal, illustrated by Grace Lodge. London, Dean, 1965.
Learn to Count [*Go Shopping, Read about Animals, Tell the Time*] *with Noddy.* London, Sampson Low, 4 vols., 1965.
Tales of Long Ago, Retold. London, Dean, 1965.
Enid Blyton's Bedtime Annual. Manchester, World Distributors, 1966 (and later volumes).
Enid Blyton's Playbook. London, Collins, 1966 (and later volumes).
Gift Book, illustrated by Willy Schermelé. London, Purnell, 1966.
Noddy Toyland ABC Picture Book. London, Sampson Low, 1967.

Editor, *Sunny Stories for Little Folks,* and *Sunny Stories 1937–52.* London, Newnes, 27 vols., 1926–52.
Editor, *Treasure Trove Readers.* Exeter, Wheaton, 4 vols., 1934.

Editor, *Nature Observation Pictures.* London, Warne, 4 vols., 1935.
Editor, *Birds of the Wayside and Woodland,* by Thomas A. Coward. London, Warne, 1936.
Editor, *The Children's Book of Prayers.* London, Muller, 1953.

PUBLICATIONS FOR ADULTS

Other

The Story of My Life. London, Pitman, 1952.

Editor, *The Teacher's Treasury.* London, Newnes, 2 vols., 1926.
Editor, *Modern Teaching: Practical Suggestions for Junior and Senior Schools.* London, Newnes, 6 vols., 1928.
Editor, *Modern Teaching in the Infant School.* London, Newnes, 4 vols., 1932.

*

Critical Studies: *Enid Blyton: A Biography* by Barbara Stoney, London, Hodder and Stoughton, 1974; *The Blyton Phenomenon: The Controversy Surrounding the World's Most Successful Children's Writer* by Sheila G. Ray, London, Deutsch, 1982; *The Enid Blyton Story* by Bob Mullan, London, Boxtree, 1987; *A Childhood at Green Hedges* by Imogen Smallwood, London, Methuen, 1989.

*　　*　　*

Although her work was first published in a magazine in 1917 and her first book, a 24-page pamphlet of verse, appeared in 1922, the stories which made Enid Blyton a household name with both adults and children did not begin to appear until the late 1930's, first in the weekly magazine *Enid Blyton's Sunny Stories,* and subsequently in book form.

Many adults recall with affection the two short fantasy series which begin respectively with *Adventures of the Wishing Chair* and *The Enchanted Wood.* The origins of both of these may be found in the Norse legends—the wishing chair having overtones of Frey's ship, and the faraway tree of Yggdrasill—but the strange lands which the children visit are far removed from the Norse tradition. They offer plenty of opportunity for slapstick humour and memorable non-human characters, and provide vivid images on which the more imaginative child can weave his own variations.

The Secret Seven and *The Famous Five* have been shown by many reading surveys to be the most widely read series. These provide exciting and undemanding reading material at an age when plenty of reading practice is important. They motivate children to want to read, and there is little which can be offered as an alternative with the same appeal. Blyton never paid any attention to the adult critic of children's literature, who in any case was not much in evidence until long after she was well-established, and she gave the children what she believed they wanted.

There are other series of mystery/adventure stories which are almost as well known and widely read. Blyton's stories in this genre appeal to children at an age when this type of story has the most appeal for them, at a time when links with their peer group are important and membership in a gang is most children's ideal. The exclusiveness of the Blyton characters may be criticised, but it is an accurate reflection of what children are like at this age. The *Adventure* books are more complex in both plot and characterisation than any of the others, and are therefore bought and praised by librarians and teachers who are selective in their purchase of Blyton books. There are two *Mystery* series: one of them features Fatty, "the master of disguises," and his friends in their attempts to outwit Mr. Goon

the policeman in solving mysteries; in the other the central character is the mysterious Barney with his unusual pet. Most memorable of the adventure stories are the five *Secret* books, in which Blyton made use of traditionally British popular literary motifs—the desert island, the kidnapped Ruritanian prince, and the secret Afro-Asian kingdom.

The circus life portrayed in the numerous circus stories was romanticised even for the 1940's, with the horse-drawn caravans and the lack of concern for the realities of compulsory education or regulations about children performing in public; but these stories again provide a setting for unusual characters, exciting adventures, and close contact with animals—early recognised by Blyton as a theme popular with children. Jimmy Brown's success with all kinds of animals in *Mr. Galliano's Circus* is a perfect wish-fulfilment story.

Most boys grow out of Blyton at the age of 10 or 11, but girls may go on reading her longer because of the existence of the school stories. Reading surveys carried out in the 1940's show that the school story was the most popular type of story among girls of 11–14. Blyton's first school stories were those about *The Naughtiest Girl,* set in a progressive, self-governing, coeducational school. Presumably designed so that they would not alienate the boy readers of *Sunny Stories,* in which they appeared as serials, they proved less popular than the later stories about *St. Clare's* and *Malory Towers.* These have worn remarkably well: the girls do not run into troubles of the trivial kind found in comparable stories, which would seem absurd to a schoolgirl of the 1980's, nor did Blyton rely on secret passages, lost heiresses, smugglers, or spies to add interest to the stories. The action arises out of the characters, and the simple psychology, showing why people behave as they do, may well stand the girl reader in good stead in later life; there is also some good slapstick comedy. Although the school story generally has never risen to great literary heights, Blyton's stories are good examples of the genre.

The nearest approach to "social realism" comes in *The Six Bad Boys,* the first edition of which included a preface of praise by Sir Basil Henriques, the well-known juvenile magistrate. This book reflected ideas prevalent in the post-war period: women were being encouraged to stay at home if they had school-age children, and the six boys who eventually come before the juvenile court are shown to have unsatisfactory homes and, particularly, unsatisfactory mothers. Although this may seem oversimplified and out of date in the liberated 1980's, there is still a lot of common sense to be found within the pages of this book.

Although Blyton published over 600 books, some of them (usually those in series) have made much more impact than others. Noddy is the character most frequently criticised by adults, but he probably makes most of his impression on children because of the colourful illustrations and the commercial "spinoffs" rather than because of his adventures.

Blyton has been criticised for her impoverished vocabulary, her undemanding style, her stereotyped characters, her incredible plots, her attitudes towards minority groups, her sexism, and her snobbishness. Although her books do tend to reflect middle-class attitudes of the 1930's and 1940's, these criticisms need to be examined carefully; to Blyton, plot was all important and where necessary she developed strong working-class characters such as Jack, whose skills enable the runaways to survive in *The Secret Island,* and Andy, the fisherman's boy, in *The Adventurous Four.*

The faults of plot, characterisation, and style for which she is criticised by adults contribute largely to her popularity with children. Readers are plunged straight into the plot, are told directly all they need to know and think about the characters, who tend to be all good or all bad, and are not held up by unfamiliar vocabulary or complex sentence structures. Simple and evocative words such as "horrid," "peculiar," and "exciting" tend to be overused. The stories are set in a world which does not exist but is familiar to every reader and the morality is simple and straightforward. Their simplicity makes them appeal to children of all abilities and so long as children are encouraged to move on to other books at the appropriate stage in their development, the reading of Blyton can help them to acquire vital reading skills through practice.

Blyton is perhaps the only children's writer who can be described as a household name. When the Cox Report on the teaching of English to 5–11-year-olds was published in 1988, 20 years after her death, the fact that her name was omitted from the list of 200 authors recommended for this age group attracted more media interest than any other feature of the report. The Secretary of State for Education was heard to say that she was a "good" author who didn't need publicity. Each year new editions of her books are published, while old stories and favourite characters appear in new guises. In the early 1980's, some additional titles written by a French author which took the Famous Five to more exotic locations were translated into English and published in paperback. In Germany, the story of Darrell Rivers of Malory Towers was continued, taking her into marriage and motherhood, but so far these have not been introduced to the British market.

Well over 300 Blyton titles were still in print at the end of the 1980's, including editions of the *Famous Five* stories linked to the popular television serialisation and modern adventure games, also based on the *Famous Five* series. Titles such as *The Wrecker's Tower Game* and *The Whispering Island Game* conjure up visions of those elements which helped to make their originator so popular.

Blyton has been the centre of passionate controversy since the 1950's; although the extent of her "banning" by parents, teachers, and librarians has probably been exaggerated, there are signs that in recent years her ability to encourage children to read has been recognised by adults concerned with children's reading. She was, above all, a skilled storyteller and many adults today must owe their pleasure in reading to this quality in her work.

—Sheila G. Ray

BODECKER, N(iels) M(ogens). Danish. Born in Copenhagen, Denmark, 13 January 1922; moved to the United States, 1952. Educated at the Technical Society School of Architecture, 1939–41, School of Applied Art, 1941–44, and School of Commerce, 1942–44, all Copenhagen. Served in the Royal Danish Artillery, 1945–47. Married Mary Ann Weld in 1952 (marriage dissolved 1959); three sons. Freelance writer and illustrator. Recipient: Society of Illustrators award, 1965; Christopher award, 1974, 1977. *Died 1 February 1988.*

PUBLICATIONS FOR CHILDREN (illustrated by the author)

Fiction

Miss Jaster's Garden. New York, Golden Press, 1971; London, Collins, 1973.
Good Night, Little A.B.C., with Robert Kraus. New York, Springfellow, 1972; London, Cape, 1974.
The Mushroom Center Disaster, illustrated by Erik Blegvad. New York, Atheneum, 1974.
The Lost String Quartet. New York, Atheneum, 1981.
Quimble Wood, illustrated by Branka Starr. New York, Atheneum, 1981.

Verse

It's Raining Said John Twaining: Danish Nursery Rhymes. New York, Atheneum, and London, Macmillan, 1973.
Let's Marry Said the Cherry and Other Nonsense Poems. New York, Atheneum, 1974; London, Faber, 1977.
Hurry, Hurry, Mary Dear! and Other Nonsense Poems. New York, Atheneum, 1976; London, Dent, 1979.
A Person from Britain Whose Head Was the Shape of a Mitten and Other Limericks. New York, Atheneum, and London, Dent, 1980.
Pigeon Cubes and Other Verse. New York, Atheneum, 1982.
Snowman Sniffles and Other Verse. New York, Atheneum, 1983; London, Faber, 1984.
Carrot Holes and Frisbee Trees, illustrated by Nina Winters. New York, Atheneum, 1983.

PUBLICATIONS FOR ADULTS

Verse

Digtervandring (Poets Ramble). Copenhagen, Forum, 1943.
Graa Fugle (Grey Birds). Copenhagen, Prior, 1946.

*

Illustrator: *Spillebog for Hus, Hjem, og Kro* (Book of Games for House, Home, and Inn) by Sigfred Pedersen, 1948; *Oh! What a Wonderful Wedding* by Virginia Rowans, 1953; *Half Magic,* 1954, *Knight's Castle,* 1956, *Magic by the Lake,* 1957, *The Time Garden,* 1958, *Magic or Not?,* 1959, *The Well-Wishers,* 1960, and *Seven-Day Magic,* 1962, all by Edward Eager; *The Bulls and the Bees* by Roger Eddy, 1956; *Cousins,* 1956, and *Beaux,* 1958, both by Evan Commager; *Songberd's Grove* by Anne Mainwaring Barrett, 1957; *Cadwallader: A Diversion* by Russell Lynes, 1959; *The S-Man,* by Mark Caine, 1960; *Sylvester, The Mouse with the Musical Ear* by Adelaide Holl, 1961; *David Copperfield* by Charles Dickens, 1962; *The Book of the Dance* by Agnes DeMille, 1963; *The Snake in the Carpool* by Miriam Schlein, 1963; *Lizzie's Twin* by Doris Adelberg, 1964; *Is There a Mouse in the House?* by Josephine Gibson, 1965; *Shoe Full of Shamrock* by Mary Francis Shura, 1965; *Good Night, Little One,* 1972, *Good Night, Richard Rabbit,* 1972, *The Night-Lite Calendar 1974* and *1975,* 1973–74, and *The Night-Lite Storybook,* 1975, all by Robert Kraus; *Mattie Fritts and the Flying Mushroom* by Michael Jennings, 1973; *A Little at a Time* by David A. Adler, 1977.

N.M. Bodecker commented:

(1978) My first collection of Danish verse, written when I was 19, came out in Copenhagen in 1943. Poetry was my first love, illustration came later, and writing for children later still. I changed language and country (though not nationality) at the age of 30, and for the next 20 years made my living as an illustrator, working on my English poetry after hours. When my first English book came out in New York, it may have looked as if an illustrator had suddenly turned writer. Actually the illustrator had been the writer in disguise. A troublesome disguise at times, for illustrating never gave me much pleasure. With *Let's Marry Said the Cherry* I finally picked up the thread I had dropped in Copenhagen 23 years earlier: writing and illustrating my own nonsense. Writing for children took me by surprise, I hadn't planned it, it just happened. The child in me would out.

I'm rather a late bloomer in many ways, and the closer I get to resemble an adult, the easier I find it to give the child in me free range: to sympathize with un-rung bells and boats tugging at their moorings, longing to perform according to their nature: to know that when the longing grows strong enough, the boat sails itself and the bell rings out unaided. Certainly, at night when I'm asleep, the piano in the garden room plays "Oranges and Lemons," or a little Schubert, perhaps.

*   *   *

Gifted with rare imagination and a wonderful sense of the absurd, N.M. Bodecker wrote both poetry and prose for children. His first English-language work, *Miss Jaster's Garden,* is a gentle tale of a very proper English maiden lady and her good friend Hedgie, and what happens when the flower seeds that Miss Jaster inadvertently drops on Hedgie's back grow and bloom. The simple story of Miss Jaster and her hedgehog friend scarcely prepares the reader for the remarkably imaginative miniature world of *The Mushroom Center Disaster,* a story which in its cozy British warmth and tender feeling for small living things (in this case, insects) is reminiscent of Grahame's *The Wind in the Willows,* but which in its exquisitely careful choice of words and in its poetic rhythm is Bodecker at his best. The story itself, a tale with ecological overtones of what happens when the remains of a picnic lunch are carelessly dropped on a tiny insect village, is slight, but the careful detail with which Bodecker describes the *modus vivendi* of the insects' miniature, and very humanly British, world is captivating.

In contrast to his earlier prose works, Bodecker's later whimsey, *The Lost String Quartet,* details the wacky and wonderful wanderings of the Daffodil String Quartet on their way to a concert in mid-January on the far side of the mountain, which ends with their performance, to considerable applause, of the Spring Quartet in E Minor for string beans, alpen horn, tirelin, and viola constrictor.

Bodecker made his greatest contribution to children's literature, however, with his nonsense verse for children, a growing corpus beginning with *It's Raining Said John Twaining.* This is a translation of Danish nursery rhymes done for Bodecker's three American-born sons; integrated with Bodecker's own illustrations, the poems have a tongue-twisting rhythm and logical illogic which cry to be read aloud. Here we find Miss Jaster reincarnated as Little Miss Price who rode with her mice over the ice, the three guinea pigs who went, like "Pussycat, Pussycat" of the old English nursery rhyme, to see the King, and a host of other zanies in the best nursery-rhyme tradition. The rhythms of traditional skipping rhymes and happily inspired word play animate Bodecker's poetry, which has justly been compared with that of Edward Lear, Ogden Nash, and Lewis Carroll. His further collections enlarged Bodecker's range of subject matter and cast of characters without exhausting his inspired nonsense.

—Margaret F. Maxwell

BOLTON, Evelyn.   See **BUNTING, Eve.**

BOND, (Thomas) Michael. British. Born in Newbury, Berkshire, 13 January 1926. Educated at Presentation College, Reading, 1934–40. Served in the Royal Air Force, 1943–44; Middlesex Regiment, British Army, 1944–47. Married 1) Brenda Mary Johnson in 1950 (divorced 1981), one daughter and one son; 2) Susan Marfrey Rogers in 1981. Cameraman, BBC Television, London, 1947–66. Director, Paddington and Company (Films) Ltd., London. Agent: Harvey Unna and Stephen Durbridge Ltd., 24–32 Pottery Lane, London W11 4LZ. Address: 22 Maida Avenue, London W2 1SR,

England.

PUBLICATIONS FOR CHILDREN

Fiction

A Bear Called Paddington, illustrated by Peggy Fortnum.   London, Collins, 1958; Boston, Houghton Mifflin, 1960.
More about Paddington, illustrated by Peggy Fortnum.   London, Collins, 1959; Boston, Houghton Mifflin, 1961.
Paddington Helps Out, illustrated by Peggy Fortnum.   London, Collins, 1960; Boston, Houghton Mifflin, 1961.
Paddington Abroad, illustrated by Peggy Fortnum.   London, Collins, 1961; Boston, Houghton Mifflin, 1972.
Paddington at Large, illustrated by Peggy Fortnum.   London, Collins, 1962; Boston, Houghton Mifflin, 1963.
Paddington Marches On, illustrated by Peggy Fortnum.   London, Collins, 1964; Boston, Houghton Mifflin, 1965.
Here Comes Thursday, illustrated by Daphne Rowles.   London, Harrap, 1966; New York, Lothrop, 1967.
Paddington at Work, illustrated by Peggy Fortnum.   London, Collins, 1966; Boston, Houghton Mifflin, 1967.
Paddington Goes to Town, illustrated by Peggy Fortnum.   London, Collins, and Boston, Houghton Mifflin, 1968.
Thursday Rides Again, illustrated by Beryl Sanders.   London, Harrap, 1968; New York, Lothrop, 1969.
Parsley's Good Deed, illustrated by Esor.   London, BBC Publications, 1969.
The Story of Parsley's Tail, illustrated by Esor.   London, BBC Publications, 1969.
Thursday Ahoy!, illustrated by Leslie Wood.   London, Harrap, 1969; New York, Lothrop, 1970.
Paddington Takes the Air, illustrated by Peggy Fortnum.   London, Collins, 1970; Boston, Houghton Mifflin, 1971.
Parsley's Last Stand.   London, BBC Publications, 1970.
Parsley's Problem Present.   London, BBC Publications, 1970.
Thursday in Paris, illustrated by Leslie Wood.   London, Harrap, 1971.
The Tales of Olga da Polga (Olga Makes a Wish, Olga's New Home, Olga Counts Her Blessings, Olga Makes Her Mark, Olga Takes a Bite, Olga's Second House, Olga Makes a Friend, Olga's Special Day), illustrated by Hans Helweg.   London, Penguin, 1971; New York, Macmillan, 1973.
Parsley the Lion, illustrated by Ivor Wood.   London, Collins, 1972.
Parsley Parade, illustrated by Ivor Wood.   London, Collins, 1972.
Paddington Bear, illustrated by Fred Banbery.   London, Collins, 1972; New York, Random House, 1973.
Paddington's Garden, illustrated by Fred Banbery.   London, Collins, 1972; New York, Random House, 1973.
The Day the Animals Went on Strike, illustrated by Jim Hodgson.   London, Studio Vista, 1972; New York, American Heritage Press, 1973.
Olga Meets Her Match, illustrated by Hans Helweg.   London, Longman, 1973; New York, Hastings House, 1975.
Paddington at the Circus, illustrated by Fred Banbery.   London, Collins, 1973; New York, Random House, 1974.
Paddington Goes Shopping, illustrated by Fred Banbery.   London, Collins, 1973; as *Paddington's Lucky Day,* New York, Random House, 1974.
Paddington on Top, illustrated by Peggy Fortnum.   London, Collins, 1974; Boston, Houghton Mifflin, 1975.
Paddington's Blue Peter Story Book, illustrated by Ivor Wood.   London, Collins, 1974; as *Paddington Takes to T.V.,* Boston, Houghton Mifflin, 1974.
Mr. Cram's Magic Bubbles, illustrated by Gioia Fiammenghi.

London, Penguin, 1975.

Windmill, illustrated by Tony Cattaneo. London, Studio Vista, 1975.

Paddington at the Seaside, illustrated by Fred Banbery. London, Collins, 1975; New York, Random House, 1978.

Paddington at the Tower, illustrated by Fred Banbery. London, Collins, 1975; New York, Random House, 1978.

Olga Carries On, illustrated by Hans Helweg. London, Kestrel, 1976; New York, Hastings House, 1977.

Paddington at the Station, illustrated by Barry Wilkinson. London, Collins, 1976.

Paddington Takes a Bath, illustrated by Barry Wilkinson. London, Collins, 1976.

Paddington Goes to the Sales, illustrated by Barry Wilkinson. London, Collins, 1976.

Paddington's New Room, illustrated by Barry Wilkinson. London, Collins, 1976.

Paddington Does It Himself. London, Collins, 1977.

Paddington Hits Out. London, Collins, 1977.

Paddington in the Kitchen. London, Collins, 1977.

Paddington's Birthday Party. London, Collins, 1977.

Paddington's Picture Book (collection), illustrated by Fred Banbery. London, Collins, 1978.

Paddington Takes the Test, illustrated by Peggy Fortnum. London, Collins, 1979; Boston, Houghton Mifflin, 1980.

J.D. Polson and the Liberty Head Dime, illustrated by Roger Wade Walker. London, Octopus, and New York, Mayflower, 1980.

Paddington in Touch. London, Collins, 1980.

Paddington and Aunt Lucy. London, Collins, 1980.

Paddington Weighs In. London, Collins, 1980.

Paddington at Home. London, Collins, 1980.

Paddington Goes Out. London, Collins, 1980.

J.D. Polson and the Dillogate Affair, illustrated by Roger Wade Walker. London, Hodder and Stoughton, 1981.

Paddington On Screen: A Second Blue Peter Storybook, illustrated by Barry Macey. London, Collins, 1981; Boston, Houghton Mifflin, 1982.

Olga Takes Charge, illustrated by Hans Helweg. London, Kestrel, 1982; New York, Dell, 1983.

J.D. Polson and the Great Unveiling, illustrated by Roger Wade Walker. London, Hodder and Stoughton, 1982.

The Caravan Puppets, illustrated by Vanessa Julian-Ottie. London, Collins, 1983.

Paddington's Storybook, illustrated by Peggy Fortnum. London, Collins, 1983; Boston, Houghton Mifflin, 1984.

Paddington on the River. London, Collins, 1983.

Paddington and the Knickerbocker Rainbow, illustrated by David McKee. London, Collins, 1984; New York, Putnam, 1985.

Paddington at the Zoo, illustrated by David McKee. London, Collins, 1984; New York, Putnam, 1985.

Paddington at the Fair, illustrated by David McKee. London, Collins, 1985; New York, Putnam, 1986.

Paddington's Painting Exhibition. London, Collins, 1985; as *Paddington's Art Exhibition,* New York, Putnam, 1986.

Paddington at the Palace. London, Collins, and New York, Putnam, 1986.

Paddington Minds the House. London, Collins, 1986; as *Paddington Cleans Up,* New York, Putnam, 1986.

Paddington Posts a Letter, with Karen Bond, illustrated by Toni Goffe. London, Hutchinson, 1986; as *Paddington Mails a Letter,* New York, Macmillan, 1986.

Paddington's Clock Book, with Karen Bond, illustrated by Toni Goffe. London, Hutchinson, and New York, Macmillan, 1986.

Paddington at the Airport, with Karen Bond, illustrated by Toni Goffe. London, Hutchinson, and New York, Macmillan, 1986.

On Four Wheels: Paddington's London, with Karen Bond, illustrated

by Toni Goffe. London, Hutchinson, 1986; as *Paddington's Wheel Book,* New York, Macmillan, 1986.

Oliver the Greedy Elephant, with Paul Parnes, illustrated by Jim Hodgson. London, Golden Books, 1986.

Paddington and the Marmalade Maze, illustrated by David McKee. London, Collins, 1987.

Paddington's Busy Day, illustrated by David McKee. London, Collins, 1987.

Paddington's Magical Christmas, illustrated by David McKee. London, Collins, 1988.

Paddington in the Kitchen. London, Collins, 1988.

Paddington Weighs In. London, Collins, 1988.

Paddington's Birthday Party. London, Collins, 1988.

Paddington in Touch. London, Collins, 1988.

Paddington Hits Out. London, Collins, 1988.

Paddington on the River. London, Collins, 1988.

Paddington and Aunt Lucy. London, Collins, 1988.

Plays

The Adventures of a Bear Called Paddington, with Alfred Bradley. London, French, 1974.

Paddington on Stage, with Alfred Bradley, illustrated by Peggy Fortnum. London, Collins, 1974; Boston, Houghton Mifflin, 1977.

Television Series: *The Herbs,* 1970; *The Adventures of Parsley* (puppet films).

Other

Herbs Annual. London, BBC Publications, 2 vols., 1969–70.

The Parsley Annual. London, BBC Publications, 2 vols., 1971–72.

How to Make Flying Things, photographs by Peter Kibble. London, Studio Vista, 1975.

Paddington's Loose-End Book: An ABC of Things to Do, illustrated by Ivor Wood. London, Collins, 1976.

Paddington's Party Book, illustrated by Ivor Wood. London, Collins, 1976.

The Great Big Paddington Book, illustrated by Ivor Wood. London, Collins, 1976; Cleveland, Collins World, 1977.

Fun and Games with Paddington, illustrated by Ivor Wood. London, Collins, 1977; Cleveland, Collins World, 1978.

Paddington's Pop-Up Book, illustrated by Ivor Wood. London, Collins, 1977.

Paddington's Colouring Books (*Paddington Carpenter* [*Conjuror, Cook, Golfer*]). London, Collins, 4 vols., 1977.

Paddington Pastime series (*Paddington's First* [*Word, Counting, Play*] *Book*), illustrated by Barry Wilkinson. London, Collins, 4 vols., 1977.

Paddington's Suitcase (includes *Paddington's Notebook* and *Paddington's Birthday Book*). London, Collins, 1983.

Editor, *Book of Bears* [*Mice*]. London, Purnell, 2 vols., 1971–72.

Translator, with Eve Barwell, *The Motormalgamation,* by H.G. Fischer-Tschop and Barbara von Johnson. London, Studio Vista, 1973.

PUBLICATIONS FOR ADULTS

Novels

Monsieur Pamplemousse. London, Hodder and Stoughton, 1984; New York, Beaufort, 1985.

Monsieur Pamplemousse and the Secret Mission. London, Hodder and Stoughton, 1984; New York, Beaufort, 1986.
Monsieur Pamplemousse on the Spot. London, Hodder and Stoughton, and New York, Beaufort, 1986.
Monsieur Pamplemousse Takes the Cure. London, Hodder and Stoughton, 1987; New York, Random House, 1988.
Monsieur Pamplemousse Aloft. London, Hodder and Stoughton, 1989.

Other

The Pleasures of Paris. London, Pavilion, 1987; New York, Potter, 1988.
The Life and Times of Paddington Bear, with Russell Ash. London, Pavilion, 1988.

*   *   *

It is almost impossible to think of Michael Bond without thinking of Paddington, so identified is he with his creation, one of the outstanding success stories of recent publishing. This success is due largely to the fact that Paddington is a bear. Teddies and other bears naturally appeal to children as symbolising love and security, and this one is certainly loved. His adventures, as children soon realise, are all certain to go wrong. Thus they have the pleasure of anticipation. Even very young children can become involved. In *Paddington Goes Shopping,* for instance, they can see in a few colourful pictures and brief texts what happens when Paddington is turned loose in a supermarket—he is buried under a load of groceries!

Bond's choice of a bear, although almost accidental, is very skilful. Paddington is not particularly bear-like: he behaves like a child and is generally regarded by the Browns as just another member of the family, albeit very accident-prone. By using a bear in this way, Bond has got the best of both worlds. He interests children who are fascinated by Paddington's propensity for disasters but he also attracts adults to whom the bear epitomises the well-meaning but bumbling adult whose behavior can be so amusing. Perhaps it is too much to say that Bond uses Paddington to illustrate human frailty and failings but undoubtedly he does pin-point many situations familiar to adults. By comparison, Olga da Polga can never match the general appeal of Paddington. She is definitely a guinea pig whose adventures are restricted to her natural surroundings; her relationship with humans is strictly traditional and lacks the supreme touch of fantasy which is the hallmark of the Paddington books where the animal is accepted as "human" throughout all the stories. Nobody looks askance at his going shopping or living as part of the Brown family and it is this dual aspect of Paddington (bear-appeal to children, human personification to adults) that makes Michael Bond's creation so outstanding.

—Margaret Walker

BOND, Nancy (Barbara). American. Born in Bethesda, Maryland, 8 January 1945. Educated at Concord-Carlisle Regional High School, Concord, Massachusetts, graduated 1962; Mount Holyoke College, South Hadley, Massachusetts, 1962–66, B.A. in English 1966; College of Librarianship Wales, Aberystwyth, Dyfed, 1971–72, diploma in librarianship 1972. Correspondent in the sales department, Houghton Mifflin, publishers, Boston, 1966–67; head of overseas sales publicity, Tutorial Books, Oxford University Press, London, 1967–68; assistant children's librarian, Lincoln Public Library, Massachusetts, 1969–71; head librarian, Levi Heywood Memorial Library, Gardner, Massachusetts, 1973–75; senior

secretary, Massachusetts Audubon Society, Lincoln, 1976–77. Since 1979 Instructor in Children's Literature, Simmons College, Boston; since 1980 salesperson, Barrow Book Store, Concord. Director, Mount Holyoke Alumnae *Quarterly,* 1979–82. Recipient: International Reading Association award, 1977; Welsh Arts Council Tir na n'Og award, 1977. Address: 109 The Valley Road, Concord, Massachusetts 01742, U.S.A.

PUBLICATIONS FOR CHILDREN

Fiction

A String in the Harp. New York, Atheneum, 1976.
The Best of Enemies. New York, Atheneum, 1978.
Country of Broken Stone. New York, Atheneum, 1980.
The Voyage Begun. New York, Atheneum, 1981.
A Place to Come Back To. New York, Macmillan, 1984.
Another Shore. New York, Macmillan, 1988.

*

Nancy Bond comments:
When I begin writing a book, I begin with an idea of what *may* happen and who some of the characters are who *may* be involved. The one thing I am sure of is where the book is set. Each of my stories is tied firmly to a geographical setting which then plays an important part in the development of the book. I believe that where a person lives, and what he or she knows, notices, and feels about it, has a great deal to do with who that person is—in order to know *who* you are you need to know *where* you are. My characters are much affected by their environments.

My first book, *A String in the Harp,* grew out of my experiences the year I spent living near Aberystwyth, Wales. In it, the American family notices and adjusts to the same things I did. *The Best of Enemies* and *A Place to Come Back To* are set in the town in Massachusetts where I grew up; the characters, while not modelled on specific individuals, are the kinds of people you could find living in Concord today. For *Country of Broken Stone* I wrote about a real part of England I have visited often and am fascinated by: the country around Hadrian's Wall. And in *The Voyage Begun* my setting is a small town on Cape Cod, on the Massachusetts coast, some time in the near future, while *Another Shore* takes place in Louisbourg, Nova Scotia, in 1744. With each of these I have the sense that the story could not have happened anywhere else, and the ideas I have now resting in the back of my mind for future books are all as securely fixed to definite places, even though their plots and characters are still somewhat vague.

*   *   *

Coping with life's changing patterns is ever constant, often difficult, and frequently, for children, especially traumatic. In her six novels to date Nancy Bond explores this nebulous theme through a variety of stories, each with different settings, individualized plots, and highly distinctive characters.

In *A String in the Harp* Bond uses the change theme as scaffolding around which she builds a strong, powerful story about a family's struggles to rebuild their lives after the mother dies in a car accident. David, the father, takes his children to Wales where they gradually learn, after many false starts and tattered feelings, to be a family again. This adjustment to a life without their mother, to each other as separate identities, and to a new and foreign place is skillfully molded into an intriguing and diverting story. Adding further dimension is a carefully threaded, gripping fantasy about the Welsh bard Taliesin's harp key, lost in the sixth century and returned, under strange and fantastical circumstances, by 12-year-old Peter. This harp key supplies a pivotal point in the family's coming together and is Bond's means of melding her story into a cohesive whole.

The Best of Enemies uses a similar theme but one handled much differently. Charlotte, who has enjoyed being the youngest child in a close, loving Massachusetts family, finds herself facing numerous changes: her mother has gone back to work, her sister has become involved with her own problems, one of her brothers has married, and her "special brother" is pursuing his own life, leaving her behind. Unwillingly she is drawn into a community scuffle, played out against the annual Patriot's Day festivity, but through this involvement Charlotte is able to face and accept the changing patterns of life. Once more Bond's theme becomes the structural beam while the plot is the brick work that holds it all together.

Set along Hadrian's Wall in England, *Country of Broken Stone* describes how Valerie and Edward's marriage forces adjustment on their newly combined families. Penelope, the protagonist, comfortable in the old, quiet, and organized life, finds the large, noisy group and her responsibilities as stepsister disquieting. Into this Bond introduces another troubling element—Ran, a local boy who arouses Penelope's curiosity and interest but whose upbringing, beliefs, and background are entirely alien to her own. Local legends with foreboding undertones, continued problems at Valerie's archaelogical dig, and a frightening brush fire highlight the suspense and broaden the impact of the family dynamics, eventually testing Penelope's feelings for her entire family and Ran as well.

The Voyage Begun again explores the theme of people's reaction to change, this time on several levels. 11-year-old Mickey, a rebellious, feisty girl, fights against change within herself as she comes to care first for a crotchety old boat builder and later for 16-year-old Paul who befriends her. Their struggle to help the old man after his home and boat are destroyed by vandals is set in a futuristic time on Cape Cod, when the world is quickly running out of energy, a crisis Bond uses to strengthen her theme as she subtly depicts the various characters reacting to their changing environment.

In *A Place to Come Back To* Bond returns to the characters and setting of *The Best of Enemies.* Charlotte, now 15, once more finds her inner world in turmoil as her interest in Oliver heightens and she finds she needs to make decisions she is not sure she is ready for.

Bond's latest novel, *Another Shore,* is set in the reconstructed village of Louisbourg, Nova Scotia. Once more using time travel as a vehicle Bond propels 18-year-old Lynn back to 1744. Time becomes the plot's antagonist as Lynn, unable to return to the 20th century, struggles to cope in an entirely different world.

All of these books are peopled with finely etched characters whose problems, sensitivities, joys, and successes are so succinctly defined that readers easily become involved in their lives. However, such definitive portrayals, plus the author's penchant for highly detailed descriptions, create exceptionally long books for the child reader and bring Bond her greatest criticism.

At the same time this length allows the author distinctively to place her story, thoroughly probe feelings, develop intricate, multi-levelled plots, and give a depth not often found in children's books. Although some paring could be accomplished without tempering the effect, the cross-generational friendship found in *The Best of Enemies* and *The Voyage Begun* and the mixing of people from different backgrounds in *A String in the Harp* and *Country of Broken Stone* are successful partly because of this slow and careful building. Readers who take the time will come away with echoes of well-turned phrases and vivid scenes and will have found rich, imaginative tales to long remember.

—Barbara Elleman

BOND, Ruskin. Indian. Born in Kasauli, Himachal, 19 May 1934. Educated at Bishop Cotton School, Simla, 1943–50. Freelance writer. Managing editor, *Imprint* magazine, Bombay, 1975–79. Recipient: Rhys Memorial prize for fiction, 1957. Address: Ivy Cottage, Landour, Mussoorie, Uttar Pradesh 248179, India.

PUBLICATIONS FOR CHILDREN

Fiction

The Hidden Pool, illustrated by Arup Das.   New Delhi, Children's Book Trust, 1966.
Grandfather's Private Zoo, illustrated by Mario Miranda.   Bombay, IBH, 1967.
Panther's Moon, illustrated by Tom Feelings.   New York, Random House, 1969.
The Last Tiger.   New Delhi, Government of India Publications, 1971.
Angry River, illustrated by Trevor Stubley.   London, Hamish Hamilton, 1972.
The Blue Umbrella, illustrated by Trevor Stubley.   London, Hamish Hamilton, 1974.
Night of the Leopard, illustrated by Eileen Green.   London, Hamish Hamilton, 1979.
Big Business, illustrated by Valerie Littlewood.   London, Hamish Hamilton, 1979.
The Cherry Tree, illustrated by Valerie Littlewood.   London, Hamish Hamilton, 1980.
The Road to the Bazaar (short stories), illustrated by Valerie Littlewood.   London, MacRae, 1980.
Flames in the Forest, illustrated by Valerie Littlewood.   London, MacRae, 1981.
The Adventures of Rusty, illustrated by Imtiaz Dharker.   New Delhi, Thomson Press, 1981.
Tigers Forever, illustrated by Valerie Littlewood.   London, MacRae, and New York, Watts, 1983.
Earthquake, illustrated by Valerie Littlewood.   London, MacRae, 1984.
Getting Granny's Glasses, illustrated by Barbara Walker.   London, MacRae, 1985.
Cricket for the Crocodile, illustrated by Barbara Walker.   London, MacRae, 1986.
The Adventures of Rama and Sita, illustrated by Valerie Littlewood.   London, MacRae, 1987.
The Eyes of the Eagle, illustrated by Valerie Littlewood.   London, MacRae, 1987.

Verse

To Live in Magic.   New Delhi, Thomson Press, 1983.

Other

The Wonderful World of Insects, Trees, and Wild Flowers, illustrated by Kamal Kishore.   Bombay, IBH, 1968.
Tales Told at Twilight (folktales), illustrated by Madhu Powle.   Bombay, IBH, 1970.
World of Trees, illustrated by Siddhartha Banerjee.   New Delhi, National Book Trust, 1974.
Who's Who at the Zoo, photographs by Raghu Rai.   New Delhi, National Book Trust, 1974.
Once upon a Monsoon Time (autobiography).   New Delhi, Orient Longman, 1974.
Man of Destiny: A Biography of Jawaharlal Nehru.   New Delhi, Orient, 1976.

A Garland of Memories (essays).   New Delhi, Mukul Prakashan, 1982.

Tales and Legends of India, illustrated by Sally Scott.   London, MacRae, and New York, Watts, 1982.

PUBLICATIONS FOR ADULTS

Novels

The Room on the Roof.   London, Deutsch, 1956; New York, Coward McCann, 1957.

An Axe for the Rani.   Delhi, Hind, 1972.

Love Is a Sad Song.   New Delhi, Orient, 1975.

A Flight of Pigeons.   Bombay, IBH, 1980.

The Young Vagrants.   Bombay, IBH, 1981.

Short Stories

The Neighbour's Wife and Other Stories.   Madras, Higginbothams, 1967.

My First Love and Other Stories.   Bombay, Pearl, 1968.

The Man-Eater of Manjari.   New Delhi, Sterling, 1974.

A Girl from Copenhagen.   New Delhi, India Paperbacks, 1977.

Ghosts of a Hill Station.   Bombay, IBH, 1983.

The Night Train at Deoli.   New Delhi, Penguin India, 1988.

Verse

It Isn't Time That's Passing: Poems 1970–1971.   Calcutta, Writers Workshop, 1972.

Lone Fox Dancing: Lyric Poems.   Calcutta, Writers Workshop, 1975.

Other

Strange Men, Strange Places.   Bombay, Pearl, 1969.

Beautiful Garhwal.   Dehra Dun, English Book Depot, 1988.

*

Ruskin Bond comments:

My early stories, written when I was in my 20's, were about my own childhood in India and some of the people I knew as I grew up. They were written for adults. Then, in my 30's, I began writing for children. By then, I probably had a better perspective on my own childhood and more insight into the lives of other Indian children. Although my father was British, I grew up as an Indian. There has been no division of loyalties; only a double inheritance.

My life, like Scheherazade's, has depended upon my ability to tell stories, and this has been the best and only way in which I have been able to make a living—and also choose the place of my abode, the foothills of the Himalayas. For over 25 years, ever since I was a boy out of school in Simla, I have been a teller of tales—short stories, tall stories, folk stories, true stories, unfinished stories....I am still a long way from Scheherazade's thousand and one tales, but then, I haven't the executioner's axe poised over me: only the rent to pay and books to buy and sometimes a chicken for myself and the family I share my life with....

*   *   *

The interplay between Ruskin Bond's personal experiences and their artistic expression in a variety of children's books allows him to weave his literary works into a harmonious pattern. From the material of his life Bond has fashioned two worlds: the secure and joyous world of the younger child, and the harsher reality faced by the adolescent.

In his autobiographical works like *Grandfather's Private Zoo* and "Uncle Ken" in *The Adventures of Rusty,* Bond recreates the happy years he spent with his grandparents in Dehra Dun, in the Himalayan foothills. Caring for his grandfather's menagerie of unusual housepets instilled in him a gentleness and respect for animals and nature that find expression in his writings. For instance, his non-fictional work, *Who's Who at the Zoo,* in addition to providing useful information and interesting anecdotes, also raises the reader's social consciousness to preserve wildlife; *To Live in Magic,* his collection of nature poems, presents a world where both man and nature are part of God's creation; and his fictional works like *Angry River* and *Flames in the Forest* portray the essential duality of nature. In the latter book the river that destroys becomes the symbol of life as young Romi and the animals flee to it from the burning jungle. A majority of the short stories in *The Road to the Bazaar* illustrate Bond's vision of childhood as a carefree age of mischief and fun, where the only worries are associated with cricket matches, beetle races, and parental anger at bad report cards. In this world there is a sense of security in friendship, and in the love and guidance of adults. This warmth permeates the timeless atmosphere of the Himalayan town where people know one another and children roam about without fear.

This safe world is shattered in both his autobiographical and fictional works as Bond portrays the loneliness and powerlessness of an only child who has lost his family. The adolescent's world is one of failure, economic pressures, drunken and abusive adults, and incompatible marriages. The dream of running away in *The Adventures of Rusty* and "The Great Train Journey" in *The Road to the Bazaar* becomes an essential coping device, as well as an heroic quest that leads to growth and a search for identity. Bond himself ran away as a teenager, an experience he fictionalizes in *The Room on the Roof,* in which Rusty, an Anglo-Indian youth who is without family, friends, or country, runs away from his insensitive guardian to find a place for himself in Indian society. Bond further explores his Anglo-Indian roots in *A Flight of Pigeons,* an historical novel set in the stormy period following the War of Independence, or Indian Mutiny, of 1857. Bond's ironic vision reveals that the mixed racial heritage of 14-year-old Ruth Labadoor and her mother first makes them victims of the holocaust, and then enables them to survive and communicate with their protectors. As the events move through the three worlds of the Europeans, Hindus, and Muslims the characters overcome racial, cultural, and political differences to form a common human bond. Although both *The Room on the Roof* and *A Flight of Pigeons* were originally intended for adults, they address typically adolescent concerns of identity, conflict with adult society, and teenage sexuality with seriousness and candour. Both novels fill a void in the children's literature of India where adolescent novels, far from exploring the inner person, are limited to mysteries and adventures, or novels of progress.

The several worlds of Bond are further unified by his style and treatment. Bond is a master storyteller who can take the leisurely setting of the Himalayan hill station, people it with lively characters, and still maintain the tension and drama of the story through a meticulously structured plot. His humorous treatment of the events and characters of this world at once endears them to us, as well as allows the author to distance himself from his personal experiences. Furthermore, recurrent images and metaphors—the shadow of the ancient tree on the house, the bougainvillea branch creeping through the open window, the bazaar as the life-giving principle, and the secret pond in the jungle as the microcosm of the world—which echo through his poetry, autobiographical pieces, and fiction lend depth and continuity to his writings.

—Meena Khorana

BONHAM, Frank. American. Born in Los Angeles, California, 25 February 1914. Attended Glendale College, California. Served in the United States Army, 1942–43. Married Gloria Bailey in 1938; three sons. Recipient: George G. Stone Center for Children's Books award, 1967. *Died 16 December 1988.*

PUBLICATIONS FOR CHILDREN

Fiction

Burma Rifles: A Story of Merrill's Marauders. New York, Crowell, 1960.
War Beneath the Sea. New York, Crowell, 1962.
Deepwater Challenge. New York, Crowell, 1963.
Honor Bound. New York, Crowell, 1963.
The Loud, Resounding Sea. New York, Crowell, 1963.
Speedway Contender. New York, Crowell, 1964.
Durango Street. New York, Dutton, 1965.
Mystery in Little Tokyo, illustrated by Kazue Mizumura. New York, Dutton, 1966.
The Mystery of the Red Tide, illustrated by Brinton Turkle. New York, Dutton, 1966.
The Ghost Front. New York, Dutton, 1968.
Mystery of the Fat Cat, illustrated by Alvin Smith. New York, Dutton, 1968.
The Nitty Gritty, illustrated by Alvin Smith. New York, Dutton, 1968.
The Vagabundos. New York, Dutton, 1969.
Viva Chicano. New York, Dutton, 1970.
Chief. New York, Dutton, 1971.
Cool Cat. New York, Dutton, 1971.
The Friends of the Loony Lake Monster. New York, Dutton, 1972.
Hey, Big Spender! New York, Dutton, 1972.
A Dream of Ghosts. New York, Dutton, 1973.
The Golden Bees of Tulami. New York, Dutton, 1974.
The Missing Persons League. New York, Dutton, 1976.
The Rascals from Haskell's Gym. New York, Dutton, 1977.
Devilhorn. New York, Dutton, 1978.
The Forever Formula. New York, Dutton, 1979.
Gimme an H, Gimme an E, Gimme an L, Gimme a P. New York, Scribner, 1980.
Premonitions. New York, Holt Rinehart, 1984.

PUBLICATIONS FOR ADULTS

Novels

Lost Stage Valley. New York, Simon and Schuster, 1948; Kingswood, Surrey, World's Work, 1950.
Bold Passage. New York, Simon and Schuster, 1950; London, Hodder and Stoughton, 1951.
Blood on the Land. New York, Ballantine, 1952; London, Muller, 1955.
Snaketrack. New York, Simon and Schuster, 1952.
The Outcast of Crooked River. London, Hodder and Stoughton, 1953.
Night Raid. New York, Ballantine, 1954.
The Feud at Spanish Ford. New York, Ballantine, 1954.
The Wild Breed. New York, Lion, 1955.
Rawhide Guns. New York, Popular Library, 1955.
Border Guns. London, Muller, 1956.
Defiance Mountain. New York, Popular Library, 1956; London, Consul, 1962.
Hardrock. New York, Ballantine, 1958; London, Muller, 1960.

Tough Country. New York, Dell, and London, Muller, 1958.
Last Stage West. New York, Dell, and London, Muller, 1959.
Sound of Gunfire. New York, Dell, 1959; London, Consul, 1960.
One for Sleep. New York, Fawcett, 1960; London, Muller, 1961.
The Skin Game. New York, Fawcett, 1962; London, Muller, 1963.
Trago.... New York, Dell, 1962.
By Her Own Hand. Derby, Connecticut, Monarch, 1963.
Cast a Long Shadow. New York, Simon and Schuster, 1964.
Logan's Choice. New York, Fawcett, 1964.
Break for the Border. New York, Berkley, 1980.
Fort Hogan. New York, Berkley, 1980.
The Eye of the Hunter. New York, Evans, 1989.

Plays

Television Series: *Wells Fargo, Restless Gun, Shotgun Slade,* and *Death Valley Days.*

*

Manuscript Collection: Kerlan Collection, University of Minnesota, Minneapolis.

*   *   *

Frank Bonham's novels for children are an adroitly controlled mix of cautionary tales, encouragement, and hope, spiced with earthy humor. In 1960 he published his first, *Burma Rifles,* based upon the exploits of Japanese-Americans who served with the Allies in World War II. He wrote for young people (age 10 and up) and stands as one of the most literate and effective authors of what is called realism. Most of Bonham's stories feature disadvantaged boys—blacks and Chicanos—who are forced to tackle outsized problems. *Durango Street* deals with the dilemma of Rufus Henry, a boy on parole trying to stay out of further trouble. This was praised by critics, and was followed by *Viva Chicano* and other singular successes in the same genre.

A skilled, inventive storyteller, Bonham had insights which could pierce a stone wall, but his most noticeable asset was compassion. His stories are therefore approved by teachers as "useful" in that they call attention to social ills. Fortunately, that discouraging epithet is ignored by readers who have discovered that Bonham's novels are, above all, outstanding entertainments.

In the mid-1970's Bonham enhanced his reputation and added to his audience with two definite departures. In these, he combines realism with unusual and convincing darts into fantasy. *The Golden Bees of Tulami* finds Cool Hankins, a black teenager, being leaned on by gangsters trying to force him to quit school and take up boxing for their profit. Cool meets a stranger from Africa, J.S. Kinsman, who arrives in Dogtown Ghetto with golden bees whose honey has a pacific effect on those who eat it. The miraculous substance is introduced with the hope of achieving world peace; greedy entrepreneurs, however, scotch the dream of the idealists. But Cool's relationship with Kinsman teaches the boy important lessons and he gains the courage to defy his would-be oppressors.

The Missing Persons League is suspenseful science fiction set in a bleak future when America is run by rigid bureaucrats; the world is dying of pollution, and individuals subsist on tasteless rations based on the number of people in each family. Again a young and spunky hero, Brian Foster, faces tough odds. His mother and sister have been missing for a year—a fact he keeps secret from the authorities for obvious reasons. While trying to find his missing relations, Brian also has to contend with a deadly enemy, Lt. Atticus, who suspects the truth, and is sure that the boy is breaking the law by growing forbidden food for himself and his father. The climax is a burst of excitement as Brian and the girl he loves learn the secret of their vanished kin and join them in a new world, just as icy Atticus is about to pounce.

It's safe to say that the stories of Bonham will continue to be read and enjoyed by those who appreciate the adventures of recognizable humans.

—Jean F. Mercier

————

BONSALL, Crosby (Newell).   Has also written as Crosby Newell. American.   Born on Long Island, New York, 2 January 1921. Studied at American School of Design, New York; New York University School of Architecture. Married to George Bonsall. Worked in advertising agencies. Lives in New Hampshire and New York City. Address: c/o Harper and Row, 10 East 53rd Street, New York, New York 10022, U.S.A.

PUBLICATIONS FOR CHILDREN

Fiction

Tell Me Some More, illustrated by Fritz Siebel.   New York, Harper, 1961; Kingswood, Surrey, World's Work, 1962.
Listen, Listen!, photographs by Ylla.   New York, Harper, and London, Hamish Hamilton, 1961.
Who's a Pest?, illustrated by the author.   New York, Harper, 1962; Kingswood, Surrey, World's Work, 1963.
Look Who's Talking, photographs by Ylla.   New York, Harper, 1962; London, Hamish Hamilton, 1963.
The Case of the Hungry Stranger, illustrated by the author.   New York, Harper, 1963; Kingswood, Surrey, World's Work, 1964.
What Spot?, illustrated by the author.   New York, Harper, and Kingswood, Surrey, World's Work, 1963.
It's Mine, illustrated by the author.   New York, Harper, 1964.
I'll Show You Cats, photographs by Ylla.   New York, Harper, 1964.
The Case of the Cat's Meow, illustrated by the author.   New York, Harper, 1965; Kingswood, Surrey, World's Work, 1966.
The Case of the Dumb Bells, illustrated by the author.   New York, Harper, 1966; Kingswood, Surrey, World's Work, 1967.
Here's Jellybean Reilly, photographs by Ylla.   New York, Harper, 1966.
Whose Eye Am I?, photographs by Ylla.   New York, Harper, 1968.
The Case of the Scaredy Cats, illustrated by the author.   New York, Harper, 1971; Kingswood, Surrey, World's Work, 1973.
The Day I Had to Play with My Sister, illustrated by the author.   New York, Harper, 1972; Kingswood, Surrey, World's Work, 1974.
Mine's the Best, illustrated by the author.   New York, Harper, 1973; Kingswood, Surrey, World's Work, 1974.
Piggle, illustrated by the author.   New York, Harper, 1973; Kingswood, Surrey, World's Work, 1974.
And I Mean It, Stanley, illustrated by the author.   New York, Harper, 1974; Kingswood, Surrey, World's Work, 1975.
Twelve Bells for Santa, illustrated by the author.   New York, Harper, 1977; Kingswood, Surrey, World's Work, 1979.
The Goodbye Summer.   New York, Greenwillow, 1979.
Who's Afraid of the Dark?   New York, Harper, 1980; Kingswood, Surrey, World's Work, 1981.
The Case of the Double Cross.   New York, Harper, 1980; Kingswood, Surrey, World's Work, 1981.
The Amazing the Incredible Super Dog.   New York, Harper, 1986.

Fiction as Crosby Newell

What Are You Looking At?, with George Bonsall.   New York, Treasure Books, 1954.
The Helpful Friends, with George Bonsall.   New York, Wonder Books, 1955.
The Surprise Party, illustrated by the author.   New York, Wonder Books, 1955.
Captain Kangaroo's Book, illustrated by Evan Jeffrey.   New York, Grosset and Dunlap, 1958.
Polar Bear Brothers, photographs by Ylla.   New York, Harper, 1960.
Kippy the Koala, photographs by George Leavens.   New York, Harper, 1960.
Hurry Up, Slowpoke, illustrated by the author.   New York, Grosset and Dunlap, 1961.

Other

Let Papa Sleep (reader), illustrated by Emily Reed.   New York, Grosset and Dunlap, 1963.

*

Illustrator: *The Really Truly Treasure Hunt,* 1954, and *The Big Joke,* 1955, both by George Bonsall; *August Explains* by Phil Ressner, 1963; *Go Away, Dog* by Joan L. Nodset, 1963; *Seesaw* by Joan Kahn, 1964; *Great Big Joke and Riddle Book* edited by Oscar Weigler, 1970.

*   *   *

For 25 years Crosby Bonsall has written almost exclusively within the *I Can Read* and *Early I Can Read* series of books. While not a school reading scheme, the beginning-to-read-series format is quite different from non-primer, non-series picture story books. Unfortunately authors of such series tend to be overlooked or undervalued. (Imagine if Dr. Seuss had never written anything except *Beginner Books,* or if Arnold Lobel had never written anything except the *Frog and Toad* books, or if Hoban had never written anything except *Frances* stories, and so on.)

Many of Bonsall's books are excellent readers and also impressive picture story books. The *Case* books are amusing stories of a motley assortment of children who investigate mysteries. Readers enjoy thinking through each of the mysteries and anticipating solutions from the clues in the pictures. In *The Case of the Hungry Stranger,* four boys search for the culprit who ate two blueberry pies. When it turns out that Marigold's dog has the guilty blue-stained mouth, Marigold is invited to share the third pie—outside(!) the boys' clubhouse, because a sign on the door says "No Girls Allowed."

Later, in *The Case of the Scaredy Cats,* Marigold and some other girls challenge the boys' pigheadedness with their slogan of "Girls Are As Good As Boys." Pigheadedness being what it is, the boys do not change, but this does not stop them sharing and playing with the girls, or vice versa. Beginning before the recent wave of feminism, some of Bonsall's writing contains gender stereotypes typical of its time. But this is less than might be imagined, and Bonsall has been quick to break down stereotype limitations in her later books.

Even her simplest stories transcend the extremely limited and repetitious vocabulary, letting the pictures and the setting carry almost the whole story. *Mine's the Best,* with its story of rivalry over balloons destroyed in the boastful competition to be "best" and the wholly satisfactory resolution of "Ours was the best," makes sense even without the words. The sense of voice character in boasting challenge and counter-challenge is very clear.

All of Bonsall's books rely on interaction between people, sometimes wordless or onesided, sometimes in full-scale verbal confrontation. *The Day I Had to Play with My Sister* presents a character (possibly a boy, or a girl in jeans) who does all the talking while trying in vain to teach the younger sister how to play hide and seek. *Who's Afraid of the Dark?* shows a young white boy who tells an older black girl that his dog Stella is afraid of the dark. But the accompanying illustrations reveal who really is afraid, and at the end, without words, show how this fear is overcome.

But Bonsall's most significant contribution to children's literature is in the wit and invention of her characters' verbal clashes. *Who's a Pest?* is outstanding, among Bonsall's other good books. Young Homer is plagued by his quadruplet sisters, Lolly, Molly, Polly, and Dolly—a formidable quartet for anyone: confident, self-sufficient, stereotyped girls, they would never want to play with Homer. Or is it that Homer, who disclaims having drawn moustaches on their four baby dolls, is plaguing them? Is Homer a pest? Everyone else seems to think so, even when he is only the victim of verbal circumstances. "What time is it now?" [asks a chipmunk]. "Two to two," said Homer. "Don't toot at me," said the chipmunk. "You're a pest!" This kind of word tangle snares Homer several times, hilariously, elaborately, like an Abbott and Costello vaudeville routine. At this level of readership there is nothing else like it. It is a little like Lewis Carroll for kindergarten!

Bonsall is usually her own illustrator. Her style is not the zany stereotyped grins and exuberance of Steven Kellogg, or the mannered nostalgia of Mercer Mayer, or the artistic streetwise cartoons of Maurice Sendak. Her characters are simple line drawings of robust little kids, a little like Charles Shultz's Charlie Brown mixed with a kewpie doll. They are immediately identifiable and appealing, and match the stories well.

So far Bonsall has written one novel, for older school-age children. In *The Goodbye Summer* Allie is a natural eccentric, an only child whose father was killed in Vietnam before she was born. Allie explains, "It's no fun having no father and sharing your mother with a bunch of boarders. I am half an orphan!" She also has a remarkable imagination that exaggerates truth beyond recognition. With great humour and narrative invention, Bonsall takes Allie (and her mother) through several domestic adventures, including a Fourth of July parade and a trip to the dump to get rid of the treasured detritus of her entire life. Eventually she realises that, no matter what she does, sooner or later everything says goodbye forever, but that this is balanced by the memories that are left—the lesson that her mother learned when she was widowed. This is a good lesson, very simply, naturally taught, with no didacticism. *The Goodbye Summer* stands comparison with Louis Fitzhugh's *Harriet the Spy,* Mary Rodgers's *Freaky Friday,* or some of Betsy Byars's novels, but with a lighter touch. It deserves to be much better known.

—John Gough

———————

BONTEMPS, Arna(ud Wendell). American. Born in Alexandria, Louisiana, 13 October 1902. Educated at San Fernando Academy, California, 1917–20; Pacific Union College, Angwin, California, A.B. 1923; University of Chicago, M.A. in library science 1943. Married Alberta Johnson in 1926; four daughters and two sons. Teacher, Harlem Academy, New York, Shiloh Academy, Chicago, and private schools in Huntsville, Alabama, 1924–38; worked for the Illinois Writers' Project of the Works Progress Administration in early 1940's; Professor of English and chief librarian, 1943–66, and writer-in-residence, 1971–73, Fisk University, Nashville; Visiting Professor, University of Illinois, Chicago Circle, 1966–68; Visiting Professor and curator of the James Weldon Johnson Collection at the Beinecke Library, Yale University, New Haven, Connecticut, 1969–71. Recipient: Pushkin prize, for poetry, 1926, 1927; *Crisis* prize, for poetry, 1927; *Opportunity* prize, for short story, 1932; Rosenwald fellowship, 1938, 1942; Guggenheim fellowship, 1949, 1954; Women's International League for Peace and Freedom Jane Addams award, 1956; Dow award, 1967. L.H.D.: Morgan State College, Baltimore, 1969; honorary degree: Berea College, Kentucky. *Died 4 June 1973.*

PUBLICATIONS FOR CHILDREN

Fiction

Popo and Fifina, Children of Haiti, with Langston Hughes, illustrated by E. Simms Campbell.   New York, Macmillan, 1932.
You Can't Pet a Possum, illustrated by Ilse Bischoff.   New York, Morrow, 1934.
Sad-Faced Boy, illustrated by Virginia Lee Burton.   Boston, Houghton Mifflin, 1937.
The Fast Sooner Hound, with Jack Conroy, illustrated by Virginia Lee Burton.   Boston, Houghton Mifflin, 1942.
Slappy Hooper, The Wonderful Sign Painter, with Jack Conroy, illustrated by Ursula Koering.   Boston, Houghton Mifflin, 1946.
Sam Patch, The High, Wide, and Handsome Jumper, with Jack Conroy, illustrated by Paul Brown.   Boston, Houghton Mifflin, 1951.
Chariot in the Sky, illustrated by Cyrus Baldridge.   Philadelphia, Winston, 1951.
Lonesome Boy, illustrated by Feliks Topolski.   Boston, Houghton Mifflin, 1955.
Mr. Kelso's Lion, illustrated by Len Ebert.   Philadelphia, Lippincott, 1970.

Other

We Have Tomorrow, photographs by Marian Palfi.   Boston, Houghton Mifflin, 1945.
Story of the Negro, illustrated by Raymond Lufkin.   New York, Knopf, 1948; revised edition, 1955.
George Washington Carver.   Evanston, Illinois, Row Peterson, 1950.
The Story of George Washington Carver, illustrated by Harper Johnson.   New York, Grosset and Dunlap, 1954.
Famous Negro Athletes.   New York, Dodd Mead, 1954.
Frederick Douglass: Slave, Fighter, Freeman, illustrated by Harper Johnson.   New York, Knopf, 1959.
Young Booker: Booker T. Washington's Early Days.   New York, Dodd Mead, 1972.

Editor, *Golden Slippers: An Anthology of Negro Poetry for Young Readers,* illustrated by Henrietta Sharon.   New York, Harper, 1941.

PUBLICATIONS FOR ADULTS

Novels

God Sends Sunday.   New York, Harcourt Brace, 1931.
Black Thunder.   New York, Macmillan, 1936.
Drums at Dusk.   New York, Macmillan, 1939; London, Harrap, 1940.

Short Stories

The Old South: A Summer Tragedy, and Other Stories of the Thirties.

New York, Dodd Mead, 1973.

Plays

When the Jack Hollers, with Langston Hughes (produced Cleveland, 1936).
St. Louis Woman, with Countée Cullen, music by Harold Arlen, lyrics by Johnny Mercer, adaptation of the novel *God Sends Sunday* by Bontemps (produced New York, 1946).
Free and Easy (produced Amsterdam, 1949).

Radio Script: *Jubilee,* with Langston Hughes, 1941.

Other plays: *Creole; Careless Love.*

Verse

Personals.   London, Breman, 1964.

Other

They Seek a City: A Study of Negro Migration, with Jack Conroy. New York, Doubleday, 1945; revised edition, as *Anyplace But Here,* New York, Hill and Wang, 1966.
American Missionary Association Archives in Fisk University Library.   Nashville, Fisk University, 1947.
100 Years of Negro Freedom.   New York, Dodd Mead, 1961.
Free at Last: The Life of Frederick Douglass.   New York, Dodd Mead, 1971.
Arna Bontemps-Langston Hughes Letters 1925–1967, edited by Charles H. Nichols.   New York, Dodd Mead, 1980.

Editor, *Father of the Blues: An Autobiography,* by W.C. Handy. New York, Macmillan, 1941.
Editor, with Langston Hughes, *The Poetry of the Negro 1746–1949: An Anthology.*   New York, Doubleday, 1949; revised edition, as *The Poetry of the Negro 1746–1970,* 1970.
Editor, with Langston Hughes, *The Book of Negro Folklore.*   New York, Dodd Mead, 1958.
Editor, *American Negro Poetry.*   New York, Hill and Wang, 1963; revised edition, 1974.
Editor, *Hold Fast to Dreams: Poems Old and New.*   Chicago, Follett, 1969.
Editor, *Great Slave Narratives.*   Boston, Beacon Press, 1969.
Editor, *The Harlem Renaissance Remembered: Essays.*   New York, Dodd Mead, 1972.

*

Bibliography: *James Weldon Johnson and Arna Wendell Bontemps: A Reference Guide* by Robert E. Fleming, Boston, Hall, 1978.

Manuscript Collections: Syracuse University Library, New York; Fisk University, Nashville; James Weldon Johnson Collection, Beinecke Library, Yale University, New Haven, Connecticut.

*   *   *

Arna Bontemps was a prolific, versatile writer whose books were trailblazers for the award-winning works of many of today's black writers—among them Virginia Hamilton, Ashley Bryan, Rosa Guy, Leo and Diane Dillon, and Gwendolyn Brooks. Bontemps's lasting legacy is his writing for children at a time when there were few books written by blacks for black children. His first was *Popo and Fifina,* written with Langston Hughes whom he met during the Harlem Renaissance in the 1920's. Popo and Fifina, ages eight and ten, are appealing, resourceful children of a Haitian family in a seacoast town. Their father is a fisherman who still finds time to make a red kite, their mother trains them in daily chores, their uncle introduces them to the art of wood designing. The setting is lush and tropical, sunny with mangoes and parrots, vibrant with sudden storms and the midnight music of drums in the forest.

Bontemps turned to Alabama for his next two stories. *You Can't Pet a Possum* is about eight-year-old Shine Boy and his pup Butch who get into trouble but are saved by Aunt Cindy, who finally agrees to let Butch join the family as long as he doesn't act as though he owned the house. "Do, I'm gonna take a stick and run him raggedy," threatens Aunt Cindy in the local vernacular. (Although he used it occasionally in his writing, Bontemps found the Negro dialect mostly offensive and demeaning.) The second story, *Sad-Faced Boy,* is about Slumber and his two brothers who hitchhike to Harlem to visit their uncle. The boys with harmonica, guitar, and drum form a successful band, and have adventures in the library and the subway, but come cold weather, thoughts of cotton and ripe persimmons soon send them back to their cabin in Alabama. *Sad-Faced Boy* was the first children's book in which Bontemps touched on the "lonesome boy" theme. He admitted that it was partly autobiographical in origin; as a boy he had looked in vain for lonesome boy stories.

Years later Bontemps explored this theme more fully in the haunting lyrical story *Lonesome Boy.* Bubber is so passionately devoted to his silver trumpet that he blows it loud, fast, and high everywhere he goes. His Grandpa warns him, "It ain't good to go traipsing around with a horn in your hand. You might get into devilment." Bubber grows up still playing his trumpet, all the way down to New Orleans where he plays to his heart's content until the eerie night he learns the meaning of his Grandpa's warning. The mystifying, opaque ending makes the story memorable and tantalizing.

The Fast Sooner Hound, co-written with Jack Conroy, is a lively humorous picture story about a long-legged, lop-eared hound who would "sooner run then eat." He wins a bet for his master by outrunning the Cannon Ball, the fastest train on wheels.

Bontemps's finest achievement is *Story of the Negro,* a book he wished he had had when he was in high school. It is a comprehensive, powerfully written history of the causes and consequences of slavery from the earliest times. The cruelty, suffering, and humiliations are heartbreaking; the struggles, survivals, and triumphs are extraordinary. The book demonstrates that from Aesop to Martin Luther King Jr., slaves and blacks have sought to arouse the conscience of the nation and the world.

—Mary Silva Cosgrave

———

BOSTON, Lucy (Maria, née Wood).   British.   Born in Southport, Lancashire, 10 December 1892.   Educated at Downs School, Seaford, Sussex; Somerville College, Oxford, 1914; trained in the Voluntary Aid Detachment, St. Thomas's Hospital, London. Served as a nurse in France during World War I. Married in 1917 (marriage dissolved 1935); one son. Recipient: Library Association Carnegie Medal, 1962. Address: The Manor, Hemingford Grey, Huntingdon PE18 9BN, England.

PUBLICATIONS FOR CHILDREN

Fiction

The Children of Green Knowe, illustrated by Peter Boston.

London, Faber, 1954; New York, Harcourt Brace, 1955.
The Chimneys of Green Knowe, illustrated by Peter Boston. Lon-
don, Faber, 1958; as *Treasure of Green Knowe,* New York,
Harcourt Brace, 1958.
The River at Green Knowe, illustrated by Peter Boston. London,
Faber, and New York, Harcourt Brace, 1959.
A Stranger at Green Knowe, illustrated by Peter Boston. London,
Faber, and New York, Harcourt Brace, 1961.
An Enemy at Green Knowe, illustrated by Peter Boston. London,
Faber, and New York, Harcourt Brace, 1964.
The Castle of Yew, illustrated by Margery Gill. London, Bodley
Head, and New York, Harcourt Brace, 1965.
The Sea-Egg, illustrated by Peter Boston. London, Faber, and New
York, Harcourt Brace, 1967.
The House That Grew, illustrated by Caroline Hemming. London,
Faber, 1969.
Nothing Said, illustrated by Peter Boston. London, Faber, and New
York, Harcourt Brace, 1971.
The Guardians of the House, illustrated by Peter Boston. London,
Bodley Head, 1974; New York, Atheneum, 1975.
The Fossil Snake, illustrated by Peter Boston. London, Bodley
Head, 1975; New York, Atheneum, 1976.
The Stones of Green Knowe, illustrated by Peter Boston. London,
Bodley Head, and New York, Atheneum, 1976.

PUBLICATIONS FOR ADULTS

Novels

Yew Hall. London, Faber, 1954.
Persephone. London, Collins, 1969; as *Strongholds,* New York,
Harcourt Brace, 1969.

Play

The Horned Man; or, Whom Will You Send to Fetch Her Away?
London, Faber, 1970.

Other

Memory in a House (autobiography). London, Bodley Head, 1973;
New York, Macmillan, 1974.
Perverse and Foolish: A Memoir of Childhood and Youth. London,
Bodley Head, and New York, Atheneum, 1979.

*

Critical Study: *Lucy Boston* by Jasper Rose, London, Bodley Head,
1965; New York, Walck, 1966.

*   *   *

Lucy Boston is one of the children's writers who, in the 1950's,
began decisively to redirect the course of juvenile fiction. Her earliest
books have an unusual delicacy and formality of structure: at a time
when predetermined adventure and pony stories were still proliferating, she infused a new seriousness and imaginative honesty into the
concept of writing for children.
The underlying theme of the Green Knowe series is continuity,
and this is pushed to an extreme in *The Stones of Green Knowe,* when
children from various centuries are brought together in a climactic
scene. 12th-century Roger is the first boy to live at the Norman
stronghold: "All [the] free reaches of the imagination were centred
for Roger in the new house that would stand to repel invaders, to
receive heroes, to outlast perils, to withstand in its living stone walls

the evils of witches and demons." The stories too are centred in the
house, and this economical device enables the author to deal effectively with time shifts and episodes of magic and danger. Everything
is contained within Green Knowe, which transmits its own validity.
Boston's "ghosts" are rendered in concrete terms, and the interaction between the past and the present (a common aspect of recent
fiction) gives an oblique fascination to the straightforward historical
events. In context the supernatural has a superrational basis; the
convergence of different times in moments of intensity or special
insight is an accepted convention. Boston has an unusual sensitivity,
nothing to do with whimsy or free-range airy-fairy effects: it is
simply expressed in an exquisite clarity of detail (down to the small
piece of quilt, "rose-coloured…with minute white sprays") and a
judicious use of fantastical motifs. She rarely goes too far: when she
does (in several episodes in *The River at Green Knowe,* for instance)
she steps back into her stride without fuss.
The River is the weakest of the Green Knowe stories; the children's
adventures are balanced awkwardly between the realistic and the
dreamlike, and the book lacks a satisfactory conclusion. Of the three
children, only Ping, the Chinese boy, reappears later in the series. In
A Stranger at Green Knowe he befriends an escaped gorilla and helps
it to hide in a bamboo thicket: this is the only one of the six books
that doesn't contain an element of magic. Instead, a number of
complex ideas of freedom and ethics and their violation are presented
in symbolical terms. It is entirely fitting that Ping, the displaced boy,
should be the hero of this story, not Tolly, great-grandson of the
owner of the house.
Tolly is the boy whose special responsiveness gives literal shape
to the sequence related by the old lady as she sews her patchwork
quilts. The romantic 17th-century children of Green Knowe, Toby,
Alexander, and Linnet, with their deer, squirrel, and superb horse
Feste, are the most elusive and ethereal of Boston's creations. The
historical characters in the second story (*The Chimneys of Green
Knowe*) have greater substance: blind Susan and her black companion Jacob are among the most entertaining and resourceful
children in fiction. Susan's disability simply makes her "special";
she isn't the least pathetic or repressed. Boston uses the deprivation
of one sense to exploit the others: "Everything that touched Susan
was something she couldn't see. But far from being afraid she wanted
to catch everything in the act of being real. She even put her finger
in the candle-flame to see what being burnt was like.…"
This is the most perfectly realized of the stories. The narrative
works on two levels on a realistic plane, and the historical evocations
are highly charged in a way that complements domestic accuracy. It
is an excellent blend of adventure and an exercise of the imagination.
Its effect, however, is less powerful than that of *An Enemy at Green
Knowe* (with its malevolent sorceress actually named Miss Melanie
D. Powers). Boston has most successfully eliminated all trace of fear
from her supernatural confrontations; but in *An Enemy* she acknowledges and examines the concepts of evil and destructiveness. The
other stories have a gentle aura of subtlety and precision; this bristles
with apprehension and generates a real sense of malignity.
Boston has written books for younger children: of these, *The
Sea-Egg* is the most original and persuasive. The basic motif, the one
impossible event that is right in poetic terms, is repeated later with
less conviction. The dryad of *Nothing Said,* the regenerated reptile
of *The Fossil Snake,* are presented in a context too slight to sustain
them. In *The Guardians of the House,* in the episode of the caves,
fantasy shades into fallacy. Boston's talent requires scope for extension of the central theme and elaboration of imagery.
Elizabeth Bowen commented on "the insufficiency of so-called
real life to the requirements of those who demand to be really alive."
The Green Knowe books help to close the gap in one direction: that
of belief in a tangible residue of the experience of past generations,
the overflow of one consciousness into another, the associative and
regenerative power of objects. Taken as a whole, the series is an

important contribution to children's literature.

—Patricia Craig

———

BOYLSTON, Helen Dore. American. Born in Portsmouth, New Hampshire, 4 April 1895. Educated at Portsmouth schools; Simmons College, Boston, one year; Massachusetts General Hospital, Boston, qualified nurse 1917. Served as an anesthesiologist with Harvard Unit at British Army Hospital, France, 1917–18: Captain. Head nurse and instructor in Anesthesia, Massachusetts General Hospital, 1918–21; Red Cross nurse, Albania and Poland, 1921–24; nurse, in private practice, New York, 1925–27; head nurse, Norwalk Hospital, Connecticut, in late 1940's. *Died 30 September 1984.*

PUBLICATIONS FOR CHILDREN

Fiction

Sue Barton, Student Nurse, illustrated by Forrest Orr.   Boston, Little
    Brown, 1936; London, Lane, 1939.
Sue Barton, Senior Nurse, illustrated by Forrest Orr.   Boston, Little
    Brown, 1937; London, Lane, 1940.
Sue Barton, Visiting Nurse, illustrated by Forrest Orr.   Boston,
    Little Brown, 1938; London, Lane, 1941.
Sue Barton, Rural Nurse, illustrated by Forrest Orr.   Boston, Little
    Brown, 1939; London, Lane, 1942.
Sue Barton, Superintendent of Nurses, illustrated by Forrest Orr.
    Boston, Little Brown, 1940; London, Lane, 1942.
Carol Goes Backstage, illustrated by Frederick Wallace.   Boston,
    Little Brown, 1941; as *Carol Goes on the Stage,* London, Lane,
    1943.
Carol Plays Summer Stock, illustrated by Major Felten.   Boston,
    Little Brown, 1942; as *Carol in Repertory,* London, Lane, 1944.
Carol on Broadway, illustrated by Major Felten.   Boston, Little
    Brown, 1944; as *Carol Comes to Broadway,* London, Lane, 1945.
Carol on Tour, illustrated by Major Felten.   Boston, Little Brown,
    1946; London, Lane, 1948.
Sue Barton, Neighborhood Nurse.   Boston, Little Brown, 1949;
    London, Lane, 1950.
Sue Barton, Staff Nurse.   Boston, Little Brown, 1952; London,
    Lane, 1953.

Jane Cobb Berry was uncredited co-author of *Sue Barton, Student Nurse, Neighborhood Nurse,* and *Staff Nurse,* and of the four Carol books.

Other

Clara Barton: Founder of the American Red Cross, illustrated by
    Paula Hutchinson.   New York, Random House, 1955.

PUBLICATIONS FOR ADULTS

Other

"Sister": The War Diary of a Nurse.   New York, Washburn, 1927.
Travels with Zenobia: Paris to Albania by Model T Ford, with Rose
    Wilder Lane, edited by William Holtz.   Columbia, University of
    Missouri Press, 1983.

*

Helen Dore Boylston commented:

(1978) Teenage girls about to decide how they propose to earn a living naturally lean toward the romantic. Nursing and acting have a romantic appeal, but young imaginations conjure up the most wildly inaccurate pictures of life in either profession. I am a nurse myself, and have loved it all my days. But nursing is quite, *quite* different from anything girls imagine. The same is true in regard to the theatre.   So, I proposed to give girls as *true* a picture as I was able. The nursing books were easy, naturally. As for the acting profession my neighbor and friend, Eva LeGallienne, is a very famous actress indeed. When I discussed my problem with her, she suggested that I spend an entire autumn and winter backstage in her theatre watching rehearsals, opening nights, and theatre life in general. I did so, and I also brought each completed manuscript to her for her criticisms and suggestions.

*   *   *

The series books created by the Stratemeyer syndicate were disavowed by educators and librarians, but Helen Dore Boylston offered to the adolescent girl two heroines who were acceptable— Sue Barton and Carol Page. These series were greeted by reviewers as either authoritative vocational stories about the nursing and theatre professions respectively or falsely glamorous. Later, the author was selected by the Landmark Series editor to write a biography of the founder of the American Red Cross, Clara Barton.

In seven volumes, Sue Barton progresses from a student nurse to various professional roles in her career. Plot is the strongest element in Boylston's technique, combining speed and suspense. Romance, mystery, and episodes of typhoid epidemic, hurricane, and pneumonia propel the momentum. Early in her student days, Sue meets Dr. Bill Barry to whom she becomes married five books and seven years later. A portion of each series book is devoted to reviewing earlier books and previewing the forthcoming book. The fifth book, *Sue Barton, Superintendent of Nurses,* was initially intended to conclude the series, as the couple is finally married and Sue announces a forthcoming child.

Character development is superficial, with changes in circumstances substituted for depth. Sue remains the calm and witty nurse, while Marianna merely changes from waif to sedate wife of an older man. Minor characters such as Tony, the Greek laundryman, and Veazie Ann Cooney, the New Hampshire housekeeper, offer local color through their stereotyped accents. Innumerable people have "twinkling eyes." Humor permeates the books with dialogue such as "superabundance of megalomania arising from excessive local prominence," and situations such as the dachshund sitting on Sue's wedding underwear and then becoming drunk.

Boston, New York City, and New Hampshire are settings drawn from the author's own background. Historical data is limited to the Henry Street Settlement in *Sue Barton, Visiting Nurse.* The authoritative aura created by the author is offset by clichés such as "I'm responsible for the kind of person she becomes," "Doctors should marry nurses," and "There ought always to be a baby in the house." However, there is strong support for the working woman. Sue's father advises, "Show the world what you can do before you settle down" and the nurse postpones marriage for professional experiences.

Although the Sue Barton series is a "period piece" with expressions such as "Zulu gone mad," New York described as "crawling with gangsters and Chinamen and murderers," and nursing procedures from the 1930's, the books remain in print in the United States and in Great Britain, and have been published in other languages.

As with the nurse series, the subject of each of the four Carol Page books is introduced in the title. A girl rises from high school debut to a small part in a New York play to apprenticeship with the summer theater, to Broadway and finally to a tour. Details in background are convincing and ample. As a contemporary reviewer stated, "a career story of this profession must not be rushed." Rightly referred to as a "second string heroine," Carol Page is currently an unknown character, and the books are out of print.

The biography of Clara Barton describes episodes in the nurse's life from age three to more than ninety, and is more substantial and readable than other juvenile biographies about her. The book suffers from superlatives in describing Barton as a faster runner, better pitcher, more politically knowledgeable and in general harder working than her contemporaries.

—Karen Nelson Hoyle

* * * * * * *

BRAND, (Mary) Christianna (née Milne). Also wrote as Mary Ann Ashe; Annabel Jones; Mary Roland; China Thompson. British. Born in Malaya, 17 December 1907; lived in India as a child. Educated at a Franciscan convent, Taunton, Somerset. Married Roland S. Lewis in 1939; one adopted daughter. Worked as governess, receptionist, dancer, model, salesperson, and secretary. *Died 11 March 1988.*

PUBLICATIONS FOR CHILDREN

Fiction

Danger Unlimited. New York, Dodd Mead, 1948; as *Welcome to Danger,* London, Foley House Press, 1950.
Nurse Matilda, illustrated by Edward Ardizzone. Leicester, Brockhampton Press, and New York, Dutton, 1964.
Nurse Matilda Goes to Town, illustrated by Edward Ardizzone. Leicester, Brockhampton Press, 1967; New York, Dutton, 1968.
Nurse Matilda Goes to Hospital, illustrated by Edward Ardizzone. London, Hodder and Stoughton, and New York, Dutton, 1974.

Other

Editor, *Naughty Children: An Anthology,* illustrated by Edward Ardizzone. London, Gollancz, 1962; New York, Dutton, 1963.

PUBLICATIONS FOR ADULTS

Novels

Death in High Heels. London, Lane, 1941; New York, Scribner, 1954.
Heads You Lose. London, Lane, 1941; New York, Dodd Mead, 1942.
Green for Danger. New York, Dodd Mead, 1944; London, Lane, 1945.
The Crooked Wreath. New York, Dodd Mead, 1946; as *Suddenly at His Residence,* London, Lane, 1947.
The Single Pilgrim (as Mary Roland). London, Sampson Low, and New York, Crowell, 1946.
Death of Jezebel. New York, Dodd Mead, 1948; London, Lane, 1949.
Cat and Mouse. London, Joseph, and New York, Knopf, 1950.
London Particular. London, Joseph, 1952; as *Fog of Doubt,* New York, Scribner, 1953.
Tour de Force. London, Joseph, and New York, Scribner, 1955.
The Three-Cornered Halo. London, Joseph, and New York, Scribner, 1957.

Starrbelow (as China Thompson). London, Hutchinson, and New York, Scribner, 1958.
Court of Foxes. London, Joseph, 1969; Northridge, California, Brooke House, 1977.
The Radiant Dove (as Annabel Jones). London, Joseph, 1974; New York, St. Martin's Press, 1975.
Alas, For Her That Met Me! (as Mary Ann Ashe). London, Star, 1976.
A Ring of Roses (as Mary Ann Ashe). London, Star, 1977.
The Honey Harlot. London, W.H. Allen, 1978.
The Rose in Darkness. London, Joseph, 1979.
The Brides of Aberdar. London, Joseph, 1982; New York, St. Martin's Press, 1983.
Crime on the Coast, and No Flowers by Request, with others. London, Gollancz, 1984.

Short Stories

What Dread Hand? London, Joseph, 1968.
Brand X. London, Joseph, 1974.
Buffet for Unwelcome Guests: The Best Short Stories of Christianna Brand, edited by Francis M. Nevins, Jr., and Martin H. Greenberg. Carbondale, Southern Illinois University Press, 1983.

Plays

Secret People (screenplay), with others, in *Making a Film,* edited by Lindsay Anderson. London, Allen and Unwin, and New York, Macmillan, 1952.

Screenplays: *Death in High Heels,* 1947; *The Mark of Cain,* with W.P. Lipscomb and Francis Cowdry, 1948; *Secret People,* with others, 1952.

Other

Heaven Knows Who. London, Joseph, and New York, Scribner, 1960.

*

Bibliography: "The Works of Christianna Brand" by Otto Penzler, in *Green for Danger,* San Diego, University of California Extension, 1978.

Christianna Brand commented:
(1978) I believe that children, in small families and the permissive age, have too few opportunities to be just mischievously naughty, and that they adore reading about children who *are.* The three "Nurse Matilda" books are about a huge family of children, and each chapter starts with a list of their misdeeds: "Tora was pouring treacle in to the Wellington boots. David was putting glue in the sandwiches," etc., each list ending, "And all the other children were doing simply dreadful things too." This has the children rolling about with laughter and mums write in to thank me for books they can bear to read over and over and over again. The theme is that Nurse Matilda is sent for—she is terribly ugly "with a nose like two potatoes"—and magics them all into goodness again, until they retrogress and she has to be sent for once more. It is an expansion of a story handed down through my family.

The anthology follows the same theme, being extracts from books about naughty children through the ages, from the Bible—where they ran out upon Elijah crying, "Go to, thou baldhead!" and were deservedly eaten up by two large bears—to the present day.

* * *

To the vast majority of English children today, nannies are creatures as mythical as dragons, but like dragons, they have their traditional habits and characteristics enshrined in children's literature. Christianna Brand's Nurse Matilda is a late but notable addition to the small, select band which includes Nana the dog and Mary Poppins.

Nurse Matilda, "the ugliest person you ever saw in your life" with "a nose like two potatoes," descends upon the enormous family of naughty Brown children to teach them the error of their ways. Her method is simple: when they are doing something naughty she bangs her magic stick, and they find themselves unable to stop, so that soon, of course, their naughtiness is no fun at all. As their manners improve she herself grows prettier, until when at last they are reformed characters (temporarily, at least), she leaves. "When my children don't want me, but do need me: then I must stay. When they no longer need me, but they do want me: then I have to go."

This is the pattern of all three books: *Nurse Matilda* is set in the Browns' home, *Nurse Matilda Goes to Town* takes the family to terrible Great-Aunt Adelaide's London house, *Nurse Matilda Goes to Hospital* lands them first in hospital and then by the sea—a seaside which has almost a surrealistic touch of Lewis Carroll about it. Each story contains an ingenious set-piece of naughtiness and culminates in a dream-like chase. These are humorous moral tales set in that Edwardian nursery world which will be most familiar to modern children from the works of E. Nesbit. Part of the appeal of the Brown children's naughtiness, one suspects, lies in the implicit presence of a fairly stern discipline in that nursery world, where you knew where you were and there was no question of you being mentally disturbed rather than plain naughty if you went pouring syrup into your siblings' Wellington boots.

The author tells us that the genesis of the books lies in a story told to the children of her own family, including her cousin Edward Ardizzone, whose illustrations complement the narrative perfectly. In Brand's version these three little *jeux d'esprit* have great style and verve, and perhaps show their oral origin in the success with which they can be read aloud. The story races along in an extravaganza of words, stopping every now and then for a little set-piece, a recital of the various awful things the children are up to, and ending in a chorus of: "And all the other children were doing simply dreadful things too." Very short, very funny, with not a word wasted, the three Nurse Matilda books surely deserve to rank as minor classics of writing for children.

—Anthea Bell

BRANFIELD, John (Charles). British. Born in Burrow Bridge, Somerset, 19 January 1931. Educated at Drax Grammar School, Yorkshire, 1943–50; Queens' College, Cambridge, 1950–53, M.A. in English 1956; University of Exeter, Devon, 1970–71, M.Ed. 1972. Married Kathleen Peplow in 1955; two daughters and two sons. English teacher, 1961–64, head of English, 1964–75, and sixth form tutor, 1975–81, Camborne Grammar School, later Camborne Comprehensive School, Cornwall. Recipient: English Speaking Union Page scholarship, 1974; Arts Council award, 1978. Agent: Hilary Rubinstein, A.P. Watt Ltd., 20 John Street, London WC1N 2DL. Address: Mingoose Villa, Mingoose, Mount Hawke, Truro, Cornwall.

PUBLICATIONS FOR CHILDREN

Fiction

Nancekuke.   London, Gollancz, 1972; as *The Poison Factory,* New York, Harper, 1972.
Sugar Mouse.   London, Gollancz, 1973; as *Why Me?,* New York, Harper, 1973.
The Scillies Trip.   London, Gollancz, 1975.
Castle Minalto; or, The Entertainment of Dr. Trevail.   London, Gollancz, 1979.
The Fox in Winter.   London, Gollancz, 1980; New York, Atheneum, 1982.
Brown Cow.   London, Gollancz, 1983.
Thin Ice.   London, Gollancz, 1983.
The Falklands Summer.   London, Gollancz, 1987.
The Day I Shot My Dad and Other Stories.   London, Gollancz, 1989.

Play

Television Play: *The Day I Shot My Dad,* 1976.

PUBLICATIONS FOR ADULTS

Novels

A Flag in the Map.   London, Eyre and Spottiswoode, 1960.
Look the Other Way.   London, Eyre and Spottiswoode, 1963.
In the Country.   London, Eyre and Spottiswoode, 1966.

*

Manuscript Collection: Kerlan Collection, University of Minnesota, Minneapolis.

John Branfield comments:
   Most of my books are about what I called in the preface to *Nancekuke* "real issues"; the right of the individual to protest, the difficulties of a young person learning to cope with a disability, the effects of experimenting with drugs, the problems of old age, and the mutual support that old and young can give to each other.   But I am not interested only in "problems," and I hope that I have written without didacticism. I value the traditional functions of the novel, the exploration of character and relationships, the evocation of place—usually Cornwall.

*   *   *

John Branfield's literary career has been unusual. He began in the 1960's with three adult novels, which were received with moderate enthusiasm but have not been kept in print. Then after a six-year gap he produced a successful teenage novel in 1972, rapidly followed by two others in the same purposeful vein. Since 1979 there have been five further novels, including one which departs entirely from his normal didactic approach and one which has an almost totally adult theme. Branfield is now generally thought of as a writer of challenging contemporary stories for older children. Of the seven novels which do in fact belong to that category, four at least have a common distinctive merit, yet differ quite sharply from each other.

Sugar Mouse, the second to be published, is perhaps the most original and the most likely to appeal to young teenagers, say ages 12 to 15. The 12-year-old heroine is a diabetic and her struggle to come to terms with her handicap is described with clinical realism alongside an interesting chain of events featuring ponies, dogs, and boyfriends. Sarah's stubborn folly and her violent quarrels with her family are at times hard to credit, as is her sudden conversion to good sense in the closing pages. Nevertheless, this is both an informative and a very readable story. *Nancekuke* is decidedly more sophisticated, offering some quite complex characters and a selection of social and personal issues for the reader to ponder. Attitudes towards military research, and the ramifications of investigative journalism are among the more prominent issues, and in each case Branfield strikes a pretty successful balance between making a case and showing that there are pros and cons in most situations. *The Fox in Winter* concentrates largely on a single issue, that of fair treatment for old people, and the author is more concerned to highlight the scandal of callousness than to present a balanced picture. This sort of approach is common enough in adult novels, but one may doubt the wisdom of confronting teenagers with such a harsh indictment when they lack the experience to put it in context. Nevertheless for those who can cope with the sombre theme, and some rather harrowing medical details, this novel has much to commend it, especially the portrayal of Tom Treloar, the indomitable old tyrant who eventually outwits his mercenary relations.

Of Branfield's five other novels for children, four are concerned with aspects of teenage deviation or self-discovery, and all of these are somewhat marred by too obvious didacticism, and also by thin story lines. Probably the most notable is *Thin Ice,* which is primarily concerned with problems of sexual orientation. The setting, as in *Brown Cow,* is a Yorkshire school and community in the immediate post-war period. Events are seen through the eyes of the school's reluctant head boy Andy Trewin, but the dominant character is the charismatic journalist Duncan Smith, whose homosexual activities lead to police intervention and a passionately described ordeal for Andy at the end of the book. Here again the author takes on the mantle of crusader for justice and makes few concessions to the needs of immature readers.

In complete contrast to his normal didacticism, Branfield's *Castle Minalto* belongs to the genre of gothic romance, and here he impresses as a most inventive and compulsive storyteller, capable of handling weird situations and larger-than-life characters. A return to this vein of writing might perhaps serve him well in the future.

—Alasdair K. D. Campbell

BRAZIL, Angela. British. Born in Preston, Lancashire, 30 November 1869. Educated at Manchester High School; Ellerslie College, Manchester; Heatherley Studio, London. Vice-President, 1920, and President, 1928, Coventry YWCA; Vice-President, Coventry Natural History and Scientific Society. *Died 13 March 1947.*

PUBLICATIONS FOR CHILDREN

Fiction

A Terrible Tomboy, illustrated by the author and Amy Brazil. London, Gay and Bird, 1904.
The Fortunes of Philippa. London, Blackie, 1906.
The Third Class at Miss Kaye's. London, Blackie, 1908.
The Nicest Girl in the School. London, Blackie, 1909; Boston, Caldwell, 1911.
Bosom Friends: A Seaside Story. London, Nelson, 1910.
The Manor House School, illustrated by F. Moorsom. London, Blackie, 1910; Boston, Caldwell, 1911.
A Fourth Form Friendship. London, Blackie, 1911.
The New Girl at St. Chad's. London, Blackie, 1911.
A Pair of Schoolgirls. London, Blackie, 1912.
The Leader of the Lower School. London, Blackie, 1913.
The Youngest Girl in the Fifth. London, Blackie, 1913.

The Girls of St. Cyprian's. London, Blackie, 1914.
The School by the Sea. London, Blackie, 1914.
The Jolliest Term on Record, illustrated by Balliol Salmon. London, Blackie, 1915.
For the Sake of the School. London, Blackie, 1915.
The Luckiest Girl in the School, illustrated by Balliol Salmon. London, Blackie, and New York, Stokes, 1916.
The Madcap of the School, illustrated by Balliol Salmon. London, Blackie, 1917; New York, Stokes, 1922.
The Slap-Bang Boys. London, Nelson, 1917.
A Patriotic Schoolgirl, illustrated by Balliol Salmon. London, Blackie, 1918.
For the School Colours, illustrated by Balliol Salmon. London, Blackie, 1918.
A Harum-Scarum Schoolgirl, illustrated by John Campbell. London, Blackie, 1919; New York, Stokes, 1920.
The Head Girl at The Gables, illustrated by Balliol Salmon. London, Blackie, 1919; New York, Stokes, 1920.
Two Little Scamps and a Puppy, illustrated by E. Blampied. London, Nelson, 1919.
A Gift from the Sea. London, Nelson, 1920.
A Popular Schoolgirl, illustrated by Balliol Salmon. London, Blackie, 1920; New York, Stokes, 1921.
The Princess of the School, illustrated by Frank Wiles. London, Blackie, 1920; New York, Stokes, 1921; as *A Princess at the School,* London, Armada, 1970.
Loyal to the School, illustrated by Treyer Evans. London, Blackie, 1921.
A Fortunate Term, illustrated by Treyer Evans. London, Blackie, 1921; as *Marjorie's Best Year,* New York, Stokes, 1923.
Monitress Merle, illustrated by Treyer Evans. London, Blackie, 1922.
The School in the South, illustrated by W. Smithson Broadhead. London, Blackie, 1922; as *The Jolliest School of All,* New York, Stokes, 1923.
The Khaki Boys and Other Stories. London, Nelson, 1923.
Schoolgirl Kitty, illustrated by W.E. Wightman. London, Blackie, 1923; New York, Stokes, 1924.
Captain Peggie, illustrated by W.E. Wightman. London, Blackie, and New York, Stokes, 1924.
Joan's Best Chum, illustrated by W.E. Wightman. London, Blackie, 1926; New York, Stokes, 1927.
Queen of the Dormitory and Other Stories, illustrated by P.B. Hickling. London, Cassell, 1926.
Ruth of St. Roman's, illustrated by F. Oldham. London, Blackie, 1927.
At School with Rachel, illustrated by W.E. Wightman. London, Blackie, 1928.
St. Catherine's College, illustrated by Frank Wiles. London, Blackie, 1929.
The Little Green School, illustrated by Frank Wiles. London, Blackie, 1931.
Nesta's New School, illustrated by J. Dewar Mills. London, Blackie, 1932; as *Amanda's New School,* London, Armada, 1970.
Jean's Golden Term. London, Blackie, 1934.
The School at The Turrets. London, Blackie, 1935.
An Exciting Term. London, Blackie, 1936.
Jill's Jolliest School. London, Blackie, 1937.
The School on the Cliff, illustrated by F.E. Hiley. London, Blackie, 1938.
The School on the Moor, illustrated by Henry Coller. London, Blackie, 1939.
The New School at Scawdale, illustrated by M. Mackinlay. London, Blackie, 1940.
Five Jolly Schoolgirls. London, Blackie, 1941.
The Mystery of the Moated Grange. London, Blackie, 1942.

The Secret of the Border Castle, illustrated by Charles Willis.   London, Blackie, 1943.

The School in the Forest, illustrated by J. Dewar Mills.   London, Blackie, 1944.

Three Terms at Uplands, illustrated by D.L. Mays.   London, Blackie, 1945.

The School on the Loch, illustrated by W. Lindsay Cable.   London, Blackie, 1946.

Plays

The Mischievous Brownie.   Edinburgh, Patterson, 1899.
The Fairy Gifts.   Edinburgh, Patterson, 1901.
Four Recitations.   Edinburgh, Patterson, 1903.
The Enchanted Fiddle.   Edinburgh, Patterson, 1903.
The Wishing Princess.   Edinburgh, Patterson, 1904.

Other

My Own Schooldays (autobiography).   London, Blackie, 1925.

*

Critical Study: *The Schoolgirl Ethic: The Life and Work of Angela Brazil* by Gillian Freeman, London, Allen Lane, 1976.

*   *   *

Angela Brazil pioneered the girls' school story in Great Britain and created a genre. Her name is synonymous with "jolly hockey sticks" fiction in spite of many excellent followers. Her first school story, *The Fortunes of Philippa,* was based on her mother's experiences of an English boarding school after early childhood in Rio de Janeiro, and contains a moving, psychologically accurate account of a nervous breakdown occasioned by a persecuting teacher. The book's success brought a commission from Blackie's, who remained her publishers until her death in 1947, although by that time her "works," as she called them, had deteriorated to a formula. The best are those written between 1911 (*The New Girl at St. Chad's* and *A Fourth Form Friendship*) and 1924 (*Captain Peggie*). There was a biography in 1926 (*My Own Schooldays*) which gives a carefully scissored and romanticized account.

Brazil's schooling was academically sound and emotionally disappointing. She longed for secret societies, boarding school, hockey, and amateur dramatics, and created them for her readers. Many girls, inspired by her books, became boarders, and found that real life in no way measured up to Brazil fiction. The books often have perfunctory plots with poor construction. It is the girls, the teaching staffs, and the intense relationships which give them life, and there is no doubt that Brazil really understood adolescent agonies. Passions, jealousies, resentments, and aims were charted with sympathy, as were the problems and responsibilities of headmistresses who appear in a wide range of personalities. Brazil believed in education for its own sake, free from the stress of examinations; loyalty to the family (particularly to mothers—fathers play virtually no part in her books); loyalty to England (*A Patriotic Schoolgirl* and *For the School Colours* are the best examples) and loyalty to *friends.* Aldred and Mabel in *A Fourth Form Friendship* suffer and enjoy the emotional intensity of a heterosexual liaison, and it must be stressed that Brazil was totally innocent of any underlying forces guiding her subconscious. It is interesting to note that in subsequent editions a kiss becomes a handshake, as behaviour patterns changed. In *Loyal to the School* a new principal *objected to seeing girls walking about the playground with their arms round each others waists or the display of any affections. She called such behaviour "early Victorian."*

Slang is an essential ingredient of the books and made the author unpopular with real headmistresses. Two High Mistresses of St. Paul's Girls' School (Miss Gray and Miss Strudwick) separately condemned her to two generations of pupils. Whether Brazil took the slang from schoolgirls (she claimed she did and rode the commuter train from Coventry to Leamington Spa to take it down from travelling pupils) or the schoolgirls from Brazil, it is difficult to decide. Some of it is incomprehensible—"it's a sneaking rag to prig their bikkies"—and some unlikely—"it's a blossomy idea, O Queen!" What is indisputable is that Brazil drew continuously on her own life, so that her biography can be charted from her work. A visit to a café, a gift of chocolates, hatred of a sister-in-law and adoration of a sick nephew (*A Patriotic Schoolgirl*) are all to be found in the seemingly inflexible format. *Schoolgirl Kitty* is built on personal relationships and events, Carrington is a surname she used as an alias for Brazil, and Lesbia Carrington in *For the School Colours* is based on herself.

—Gillian Freeman

———

BREARY, Nancy.   British.

PUBLICATIONS FOR CHILDREN

Fiction

Give a Form a Bad Name.   London, Newnes, 1943.
Two Thrilling Terms.   London, Blackie, 1943.
No Peace for the Prefects.   London, Newnes, 1944.
The Lower Fourth Excels Itself.   London, Newnes, 1945.
A School Divided.   London, Newnes, 1945.
This Time Next Term.   London, Blackie, 1945.
Junior Captain, illustrated by D.L. Mays.   London, Blackie, 1946.
The Snackboat Sails at Noon!, illustrated by Alfred Sindall.   London, Newnes, 1946.
The Impossible Prefect, illustrated by Leo Bates.   London, Blackie, 1947.
Juniors Will Be Juniors.   London, Newnes, 1947.
The Form That Liked to Be First, illustrated by W. Spence.   London, Blackie, 1948.
It Was Fun in the Fourth, illustrated by Joan Martin May.   London, Newnes, 1948.
Rachel Changes Schools, illustrated by D.L. Mays.   London, Blackie, 1948.
Mainly about the Fourth.   London, Newnes, 1949.
Five Sisters at Sedgewick, illustrated by W. Spence.   London, Blackie, 1950.
Dimity Drew's First Term.   London, Newnes, 1951.
The Reluctant Schoolgirl, illustrated by Louis Ward.   London, Blackie, 1951.
Hazel, Head Girl, illustrated by W. Spence.   London, Blackie, 1952.
At School with Petra, illustrated by Newton Whittaker.   London, Blackie, 1953.
Fourth Form Detectives, illustrated by Newton Whittaker.   London, Blackie, 1954.
The Rival Fourths, illustrated by Frank Haseler.   London, Blackie, 1955.
Study Number Six, illustrated by Betty Ladler.   London, Blackie, 1957.
The Mystery of the Motels, illustrated by Victor Bertoglio.   London,

Blackie, 1958.
So This Is School!, illustrated by Drake Brookshaw. London, Blackie, 1959.
The Amazing Friendship, illustrated by Drake Brookshaw. London, Blackie, 1960.
The Fourth Was Fun for Philippa, illustrated by Drake Brookshaw. London, Blackie, 1961.

*   *   *

Nancy Breary started to write school stories for girls in the 1940's and concentrated on producing separate stories rather than series: a more demanding task for the writer. Her school stories are notable for a lively style of writing, for idyllic settings, for plots heavily biased towards sometimes unlikely elements of mystery, and for characters who emerge victorious after many tribulations, inculcated with not necessarily desirable attitudes. Breary's conscientious effort to be up-to-date in approach is of transient value as topical references and current slang rapidly become out-of-date, but the verve, particularly of her earlier plots, ensured her popularity for a considerable number of years, although her books are now out of print.

Breary presents an almost fantasy world of boarding school, where schools with evocative names like Cordway House, Allerton Manor, or Highstanding are set in exquisitely perfect surroundings and peopled with schoolgirls whose exotic names include Zinnia, Nerissa, Tiffany, and Drusilla. In the tradition of Angela Brazil, Breary offers many of the standard school story themes (the start of term, a competition, a secret society, a drama activity, a run-away incident), but the special feature of her plots is the mystery element. It is a difficult feature to handle convincingly, and there is also the problem of such an element becoming too unrealistic. Breary handles the mystery theme with varying degrees of success: in *The Fourth Was Fun for Philippa* a slender mystery theme centres on a recluse author; *The Reluctant Schoolgirl* boasts a phantom; and *This Time Next Term* has the problem of a "tapper."

Characters constitute one of the most interesting areas of Breary's books. She brings out the differences in characters like Melanie, Elsa, and Philippa in *The Fourth Was Fun for Philippa,* has characters like Bridget in *This Time Next Term* pondering their feelings and reactions to certain situations, and has anti-school characters like Alison Anderson in *The Reluctant Schoolgirl* integrating and conforming eventually. Breary frequently introduces the device of a clash of personalities, with a satisfactory compromise inevitably reached by the protagonists.

The least attractive element in these school stories is the promotion of unacceptable attitudes, particularly to study and to social position: a weakness not confined to Breary alone, and perhaps a reflection of attitudes at the time her books were written.

To assess Nancy Breary's position as a writer of school stories is difficult, as she cannot be equated with the writers of established *series* of school stories for girls like Dorita Fairlie Bruce, Elsie Oxenham, Elinor M. Brent-Dyer and Enid Blyton. Nancy Breary is likely to be remembered for at least three reasons: for creating separate lively stories rather than repetitive series; for her capacity, not always successful, to bring the mystery element in the genre to a level never achieved before or since; and as the last of a host of now forgotten writers all strongly influenced by the writing of Angela Brazil.

—Anne W. Ellis

———

BRENT-DYER, Elinor M. Pseudonym for Gladys Eleanor May

Dyer. British. Born in South Shields, County Durham, 6 April 1894. Educated at St. Nicholas's school, South Shields and Westoe; City of Leeds Training College, 1915–17; Newcastle Conservatoire of Music. Teacher, 1912–15, at Baring Street School and other schools, South Shields, 1917–21, and at Western House School, Fareham, Hampshire, 1922–23; governess in Hereford, 1933–38; founding headmistress, Margaret Roper School, Hereford, 1938–48. *Died 20 September 1969.*

Publications for Children

Fiction

Gerry Goes to School, illustrated by Gordon Broe. Edinburgh, Chambers, 1922; Philadelphia, Lippincott, 1923.
A Head Girl's Difficulties, illustrated by Nina K. Brisley. Edinburgh, Chambers, 1923.
The Maids of La Rochelle, illustrated by Nina K. Brisley. Edinburgh, Chambers, 1924.
The School at the Chalet, illustrated by Nina K. Brisley. Edinburgh, Chambers, 1925.
Jo of the Chalet School, illustrated by Nina K. Brisley. Edinburgh, Chambers, 1926.
A Thrilling Term at Janeways, illustrated by F.M. Anderson. London, Nelson, 1927.
Seven Scamps Who Are Not All Boys, illustrated by Percy Tarrant. Edinburgh, Chambers, 1927.
The Princess of the Chalet School, illustrated by Nina K. Brisley. Edinburgh, Chambers, 1927.
The Head Girl of the Chalet School, illustrated by Nina K. Brisley. Edinburgh, Chambers, 1928.
Judy the Guide, illustrated by L.A. Govey. London, Nelson, 1928.
The New House Mistress. London, Nelson, 1928.
Heather Leaves School, illustrated by Percy Tarrant. Edinburgh, Chambers, 1929.
The Rivals of the Chalet School, illustrated by Nina K. Brisley. Edinburgh, Chambers, 1929.
Eustacia Goes to the Chalet School. Edinburgh, Chambers, 1930.
The School by the River. London, Burns Oates, 1930.
The Chalet School and Jo, illustrated by Nina K. Brisley. Edinburgh, Chambers, 1931.
The Feud in the Fifth Remove. London, Religious Tract Society, 1931.
Janie of La Rochelle. Edinburgh, Chambers, 1932.
The Little Marie-José. London, Burns Oates, 1932.
The Chalet Girls in Camp. Edinburgh, Chambers, 1932.
The Exploits of the Chalet Girls, illustrated by Nina K. Brisley. Edinburgh, Chambers, 1933.
The Chalet School and the Lintons, illustrated by Nina K. Brisley. Edinburgh, Chambers, 1934.
Carnation of the Upper Fourth. London, Religious Tract Society, 1934.
The New House at the Chalet School. Edinburgh, Chambers, 1935.
Jo Returns to the Chalet School, illustrated by Nina K. Brisley. Edinburgh, Chambers, 1936.
Monica Turns Up Trumps. London, Religious Tract Society, 1936.
Caroline the Second. London, Religious Tract Society, 1937.
The New Chalet School, illustrated by Nina K. Brisley. Edinburgh, Chambers, 1938; as *A United Chalet School,* London, Armada, 1988.
They Both Liked Dogs. London, Religious Tract Society, 1938.
The Chalet School in Exile. Edinburgh, Chambers, 1940.
The Chalet School Goes to It, illustrated by Nina K. Brisley. Edinburgh, Chambers, 1941; as *The Chalet School at War,* London, Armada, 1988.

The Highland Twins at the Chalet School.   Edinburgh, Chambers, 1942.
The Little Missus.   Edinburgh, Chambers, 1942.
Lavender Laughs in the Chalet School.   Edinburgh, Chambers, 1943.
Gay from China at the Chalet School.   Edinburgh, Chambers, 1944.
Jo to the Rescue.   Edinburgh, Chambers, 1945.
The Lost Staircase.   Edinburgh, Chambers, 1946.
Lorna at Wynyards.   London, Lutterworth Press, 1947.
Stepsisters for Lorna, illustrated by John Bruce.   London, Temple, 1948.
Three Go to the Chalet School.   Edinburgh, Chambers, 1949.
Peggy of the Chalet School.   Edinburgh, Chambers, 1950.
The Chalet School and the Island.   Edinburgh, Chambers, 1950.
Fardingdales.   London, Latimer, 1950.
The Chalet School and Rosalie.   Edinburgh, Chambers, 1951.
Carola Storms the Chalet School.   Edinburgh, Chambers, 1951.
Schoolgirls Abroad (*Verena Visits New Zealand, Bess on Her Own in Canada, A Quintette in Queensland, Sharlie's Kenya Diary*).   Edinburgh, Chambers, 4 vols., 1951.
The Chalet School in the Oberland.   Edinburgh, Chambers, 1952.
The Wrong Chalet School.   Edinburgh, Chambers, 1952.
Shocks for the Chalet School.   Edinburgh, Chambers, 1952.
Bride Leads the Chalet School.   Edinburgh, Chambers, 1953.
Changes for the Chalet School.   Edinburgh, Chambers, 1953.
Janie Steps In.   Edinburgh, Chambers, 1953.
The Susannah Adventure.   Edinburgh, Chambers, 1953.
Nesta Steps Out.   London, Oliphants, 1954.
Kennelmaid Nan.   London, Lutterworth Press, 1954.
Joey Goes to the Oberland.   Edinburgh, Chambers, 1954.
Chudleigh Hold.   Edinburgh, Chambers, 1954.
The Condor Crags Adventure.   Edinburgh, Chambers, 1954.
The Chalet School and Barbara.   Edinburgh, Chambers, 1954.
Beechy of the Harbour School.   London, Oliphants, 1955.
A Chalet Girl from Kenya.   Edinburgh, Chambers, 1955.
The Chalet School Does It Again.   Edinburgh, Chambers, 1955.
Tom Tackles the Chalet School.   Edinburgh, Chambers, 1955.
Top Secret.   Edinburgh, Chambers, 1955.
A Problem for the Chalet School.   Edinburgh, Chambers, 1956.
Leader in Spite of Herself.   London, Oliphants, 1956.
Mary-Lou of the Chalet School.   Edinburgh, Chambers, 1956.
A Genius at the Chalet School.   Edinburgh, Chambers, 1956; revised edition, London, Collins, 1969.
Excitements at the Chalet School.   Edinburgh, Chambers, 1957.
The New Mistress at the Chalet School.   Edinburgh, Chambers, 1957.
The Chalet School and Richenda.   Edinburgh, Chambers, 1958.
The Coming-of-Age of the Chalet School.   Edinburgh, Chambers, 1958.
Theodora and the Chalet School.   Edinburgh, Chambers, 1959.
Trials for the Chalet School.   Edinburgh, Chambers, 1959.
Joey & Co. in Tirol.   Edinburgh, Chambers, 1960.
Ruey Richardson—Chaletian.   Edinburgh, Chambers, 1960.
A Leader in the Chalet School.   Edinburgh, Chambers, 1961.
The Chalet School Wins the Trick.   Edinburgh, Chambers, 1961.
The Feud in the Chalet School.   Edinburgh, Chambers, 1962.
A Future Chalet School Girl.   Edinburgh, Chambers, 1962.
The School at Skelton Hall.   London, Parrish, 1962.
The Chalet School Reunion.   Edinburgh, Chambers, 1963.
The Chalet School Triplets.   Edinburgh, Chambers, 1963.
Trouble at Skelton Hall.   London, Parrish, 1963.
Jane and the Chalet School.   Edinburgh, Chambers, 1964.
Redheads at the Chalet School.   Edinburgh, Chambers, 1964.
Summer Term at the Chalet School.   Edinburgh, Chambers, 1965.
Adrienne and the Chalet School.   Edinburgh, Chambers, 1965.
Challenge for the Chalet School.   Edinburgh, Chambers, 1966.

Two Sams at the Chalet School.   Edinburgh, Chambers, 1967.
Althea Joins the Chalet School.   Edinburgh, Chambers, 1969.
Prefects of the Chalet School.   Edinburgh, Chambers, 1970.

Other

The Chalet Girls' Cook Book.   Edinburgh, Chambers, 1953.

Editor, *The Chalet Book for Girls 1–3.*   Edinburgh, Chambers, 3 vols., 1947–49.

PUBLICATIONS FOR ADULTS

Novel

Elizabeth the Gallant.   London, Butterworth, 1935.

Plays

My Lady Caprice (produced South Shields, County Durham, 1921).
Polly Danvers, Heiress (produced South Shields, County Durham, 1922).

*

Critical Study: *Behind the Chalet School* by Helen McClelland, Bognor Regis, Sussex, New Horizon, 1981.

*   *   *

From the early 1920's until her death in 1969 Elinor M. Brent-Dyer wrote almost 100 books for girls. These included historical and adventure stories, but it is for her 58 Chalet School books that this author is remembered. *The School at the Chalet* was published in 1925 and Brent-Dyer's international tri-lingual, non-denominational school in the "Austrian Tirol" soon caught the imagination of readers. It become so popular that a Chalet School Club was formed, attracting a large membership from many parts of the world.

The school, an intriguing amalgam of foreign glamour and British "grit," is founded by Madge Bettany, a young Englishwoman. Although inexperienced, Madge becomes the Chalet School's first headmistress, taking administrative, racial, and language complications in her stride: she is an unconventional principal, sometimes addressing one or other of her pupils as "honey" or "darling."

The school's family atmosphere is accentuated by the presence of Madge's sister, Joey, originally a junior pupil and later Head-Girl. In adult life Joey becomes prolific as a writer of girls' stories and as a breeder (she has eleven children). Despite the variety of pupils who come and go the vitality of the series rests largely on the character of Joey. As this lively and intrepid heroine grows older it is more difficult for the author to make her integral to the stories. However, even in the last book of the series—no. 58, published posthumously in 1970—Joey is still insisting that "if she lived to be a great-grandmother, she would be a Chalet girl to the end."

Initially the Chalet School's appeal owed a great deal to its location. Brent-Dyer ably conveys the charm of the school beside mist-swathed mountains and a lake "alive with dancing shadows." The books are sometimes over-lush. Gentians, marguerites, and alpen roses have a technicolour quality: floweriness spills over into descriptions of the girls in their flame-coloured ties, brown tunics, and shantung blouses. But this is counterbalanced by plenty of action. For instance, *The Princess of the Chalet School* includes—as well as a flowerstrewn masque, a garden party, and a wedding—two kidnapping attempts and an oversize thunderstorm which breaks every window in the valley and sets the school's playing fields on fire. The school buildings are saved from total destruction only by an equally violent hailstorm which opportunely covers everything with five inches of hail in as many minutes. Girls fall into icebound rivers or are stranded on exposed mountain sides: in the first five books alone Joey manages to save the lives of six girls and one dog.

The Chalet School survives after evacuation from the Nazis. It moves first to the Channel Islands, then to Wales and later to the Oberland. Brent-Dyer exploited several of the stock ingredients of girls' fiction including animals, babies, guiding, and country dance. A headmistress for many years, she understood the tastes of girls growing up between the wars, although by the late 1950's her books had become anachronistic.

—Mary Cadogan

BRIDGERS, Sue Ellen (née Hunsucker). American. Born in Greenville, North Carolina, 20 September 1942. Educated at East Carolina University, Greenville, 1960–63; Western Carolina University, Cullowhee, North Carolina, 1974–76, B.A. 1976. Married Ben Oshel Bridgers in 1963; two daughters and one son. Recipient: Christopher award, 1979; ALAN award, 1985. Agent: Elaine Markson Literary Agency, 44 Greenwich Avenue, New York, New York 10011. Address: P.O. Box 248, Sylva, North Carolina 28779, U.S.A.

PUBLICATIONS FOR CHILDREN

Fiction

Home Before Dark. New York, Knopf, 1976.
All Together Now. New York, Knopf, 1979.
Notes for Another Life. New York, Knopf, 1981.
Permanent Connections. New York, Harper, 1987.

PUBLICATIONS FOR ADULTS

Novel

Sara Will. New York, Harper, 1985.

*

Manuscript Collection: Hunter Library, Western Carolina University, Cullowhee, North Carolina.

Sue Ellen Bridgers comments:
The setting for my work is the American South. The characters springing from this rural environment are concerned with finding meaning in their lives through commonplace events. The changing seasons, the rituals of common experience, the rich legacies of their histories provide the backdrop for stories of these characters whom one might easily encounter on any small town street.

*   *   *

Sue Ellen Bridgers has established a solid reputation as a writer of moving realistic novels for young adults. Her young protagonists enact their emotional dramas in the context of family and neighbors, and are rooted in traditional southern life; home, land, church, and community remain abiding values to these rather unsophisticated but genuinely likeable people. Her young characters are usually sensitive, and her adults are rounded, caring, and sometimes flawed, not the persecuting and abusive authority figures who inhabit the pages

of so many young adult novels.

In her first three novels Bridgers centers her story on appealing adolescent girls who come to terms with their relationships to family and community members. In *Home Before Dark* 14-year-old Stella returns with her family to their rural North Carolina home after living for many years in Florida as migrant workers. After her mother's death and father's remarriage, Stella tries to live on her own in their old tenant house, but eventually recognizes that she still needs her family. In *All Together Now* 12-year-old Casey forms a friendship with Dwayne, a mentally retarded person who is initially fearful of girls until he learns to accept Casey. Later Casey's Uncle Taylor and grandmother intervene on behalf of Dwayne to keep him out of an institution. In *Notes for Another Life* 13-year-old Wren and 16-year-old Kevin experience intense fears about their father's mental illness and emotional trauma because of their mother's absence. Their strong and anchored grandmother gives them genuine love, but Kevin finally cannot sustain the emotional pressures in his life and attempts suicide. His family's unstinting love and a young minister's effective counseling help to heal Kevin, and bring him back into harmony with himself, the family, and the community.

In *Permanent Connections* Rob, in the throws of an identity crisis, finds comfort only in sex and drugs. When his rural North Carolina relative breaks his hip in an accident, Rob is sent to the family farm to help out. There he encounters a beautiful, talented but unhappy girl named Ellery. Resenting Ellery's accomplishments, Rob indulges in self-destructive bouts with alcohol and pot before realizing that his actions affect not only himself but also those closest to him. Bridgers presents an intensely realistic characterization of a narcissistic and spoiled adolescent who painfully learns to take responsibility for his own actions.

Bridgers writes honest and admirable fiction for young adults. With few novels to her credit, she has already earned a considerable reputation as a writer with exceptional narrative skill.

—Anita Moss

BRIGGS, K(atharine) M(ary). British. Born in London, 8 November 1898. Educated at Lansdowne House; Lady Margaret Hall, Oxford, M.A. 1923, Ph.D. 1952. Served in the Women's Auxiliary Air Force, 1941–45. Freelance writer. Headed an amateur theatrical touring company for 15 years. Visiting Professor, University of Pennsylvania, Philadelphia, 1970, and University of California, Berkeley, 1973. President, Folklore Society of London, 1967–70. D.Litt.: Oxford University, 1969. *Died 15 October 1980.*

PUBLICATIONS FOR CHILDREN

Fiction

The Legend of Maiden-Hair. London, Stockwell, 1915.
The Witches' Ride, illustrated by Winifred Briggs. Dunkeld, Perthshire, Capricornus, 1937.
The Prince, The Fox, and the Dragon, illustrated by Winifred Briggs. Dunkeld, Perthshire, Capricornus, 1938.
Hobberdy Dick. London, Eyre and Spottiswoode, 1955; New York, Greenwillow, 1977.
Kate Crackernuts. Oxford, Alden Press, 1963; revised edition, London, Kestrel, and New York, Greenwillow, 1979.

Plays

Stories Arranged for Mime (The Golden Goose; Whuppity Stories; Jesper, Who Herded Hares). Dunkeld, Perthshire, Capricornus,

3 vols., 1937.

Verse

Whispers: An Experiment in Lino Cuts, with Elspeth Briggs, il-
lustrated by the authors and Winifred Briggs. Dunkeld,
Perthshire, Capricornus, 1940.
The Twelve Days of Christmas, with others, illustrated by Winifred
Briggs. Dunkeld, Perthshire, Capricornus, 1952.

Other

Mime for Guides and Brownies. London, Girl Guides Association,
1955.
Abbey Lubbers, Banshees, and Boggarts: A Who's Who of Fairies,
illustrated by Yvonne Gilbert. London, Kestrel, and New York,
Pantheon, 1979.

PUBLICATIONS FOR ADULTS

Novels

The Lisles of Ellingham. Oxford, Alden Press, 1935.
The Castilians. Oxford, Alden Press, 1950.

Plays

The Garrulous Lady. London, Golden Vista Press, 1931.
The Peacemaker (produced Murthly, Perthshire, 1933). Dunkeld,
Perthshire, Capricornus, 1938.
The Fugitive. Dunkeld, Perthshire, Capricornus, 1938.
The Lady in the Dark. Dunkeld, Perthshire, Capricornus, 1949.

Other

A History of 75 Years. Privately printed, 1935.
*The Personnel of Fairyland: A Short Account of the Fairy People of
Great Britain for Those Who Tell Stories to Children.* Oxford,
Alden Press, 1953; Cambridge, Massachusetts, Bentley, 1954.
Dunkeld and Birman Guide. Oxford, Alden Press, 1956.
*The Anatomy of Puck: An Examination of Fairy Beliefs among
Shakespeare's Contemporaries and Successors.* London, Rout-
ledge, 1959; New York, Arno Press, 1977.
*Pale Hecate's Team: An Examination of the Beliefs on Witchcraft
and Magic among Shakespeare's Contemporaries and His Imme-
diate Successors.* London, Routledge, and New York,
Humanities Press, 1962.
The Fairies in Tradition and Literature. London, Routledge, 1967;
as *The Fairies in English Tradition and Literature,* Chicago,
University of Chicago Press, 1967.
*A Dictionary of British Folk-tales in the English Language:
Folk Narratives.* London, Routledge, 2 vols., 1970; as *Folk-
tales,* Bloomington, Indiana University Press, 2 vols., 1970.
Folk Legends. London, Routledge, and Bloomington, Indiana
University Press, 2 vols., 1971.
The Folklore of the Cotswolds. London, Batsford, and Totowa,
New Jersey, Rowman and Littlefield, 1974.
*A Dictionary of Fairies: Hobgoblins, Brownies, Bogies, and Other
Supernatural Creatures.* London, Allen Lane, 1976; as *An
Encyclopedia of Fairies,* New York, Pantheon, 1976.
A Sampler of British Folk-tales (selection from *A Dictionary of
British Folk-tales*). London, Routledge, 1977; as *British Folk-
tales,* New York, Pantheon, 1977.
The Vanishing People: A Study of Traditional Fairy Beliefs. Lon-
don, Batsford, and New York, Pantheon, 1978.
Nine Lives: Cats in Folklore. London, Routledge, and New York,

Pantheon, 1980.

Editor, with Ruth Lyndall Tongue, *Folktales of England.* London,
Routledge, and Chicago, University of Chicago Press, 1965.
Editor, *Somerset Folk-lore,* by Ruth Lyndall Tongue. London,
Folklore Society, 1965.
Editor, *The Last of the Astrologers: Mr. William Lilly's History of His
Life and Times from the Year 1602 to 1681.* London, Folklore
Society, 1974.

*

Critical Study: *Katharine Briggs: Story-Teller* by H. Ellis Davidson,
Cambridge, Lutterworth Press, 1986.

*   *   *

This is sadly not the place to try to assess the whole of K.M.
Briggs's work, which culminated in the enormous, definitive *A
Dictionary of British Folk-tales.* However, it was her long study of
folk-tales, and in particular the fairyfolk in all their manifestations,
which gave rise to her children's books, and her knowledge and
authority are evident in everything she wrote.

Neither *Hobberdy Dick* nor *Kate Crackernuts* are particularly easy
books for children. *Hobberdy Dick* is the more accessible of the
two—it is younger in tone, with a good deal of fun in it—but it
contains the death of a much-loved grandmother, besides
demonstrating the period convention that children obey their parents
automatically, however harsh the command, and presenting a
heroine who must endure slights, insults, and overwork with no real
hope of anything better (Anne's fortune does change—but only
through the intervention of Dick himself). *Kate Crackernuts* is set in
the Scottish Borders and Yorkshire, and most of the speech is in
dialect. Besides this, the glamour cast on Katherine, in which she
believes her head has been turned into that of a sheep, could be very
frightening for some children—and the carnal aspects of diabolism
are admitted in the passages to do with witchcraft.

For the persevering, though, both stories are immensely rewarding. Hobberdy Dick is a most endearing hobgoblin, and the reader
sympathises enormously with the problems, both practical and
spiritual, which he must solve through his characteristic domestic
loyalty. Kate Maxwell, one of the two Katherines in *Kate Crackernuts,* is a memorable heroine. Her bravery, determination, and love
for her step-sister, which take her twice into the fairy realms on behalf
of those weaker than she is (journeys which result in the saving of
two lives), are admirable and inspiring. Briggs set her two novels in
the 17th century, a time when people believed in witches and fairies
as a matter of course. Yet it is a period near enough our own to be
reasonably recognisable in its domestic detail: some of the rather
old-fashioned themes present in the stories, while absolutely appropriate for the period, also recall the Victorian children's novel.

Briggs started investigating folk-lore in the 1920's and 1930's, as
a reaction against the sentimental rubbish offered so frequently to
children. As one reads her work, one has the assurance that in all
things to do with the fairy kingdoms Briggs's knowledge is impeccable. This gives her books enormous strength: they are triumphant
examples of what good modern fairy stories should be. And for those
whose appetite is whetted and who want more, books like *Abbey
Lubbers, Banshees, and Boggarts* are most satisfying first reference
material. One can go on, too, to the many adult works, for K.M.
Briggs's fascination with Fairyland communicates itself to readers
young and old.

—Felicity Trotman

BRIGGS, Raymond (Redvers). British. Born in London, 18 January 1934. Educated at Rutlish School, Merton, Surrey; Wimbledon School of Art; Slade School of Fine Art, national diploma in design, 1953; University of London, diploma in fine art. Served in the British Army, 1953–55. Married Jean Taprell Clark in 1963 (died 1973). Since 1957 freelance illustrator and writer; since 1961 part-time lecturer in illustration, Brighton Polytechnic, Sussex. Recipient (for illustration): Library Association Kate Greenaway Medal, 1967, 1974; Boston *Globe-Horn Book* award, 1979; Victoria and Albert Museum Francis Williams prize, 1982; Children's Rights Workshop Other award, 1982; Broadcasting Press Guild award, for radio play, 1984. Address: Weston, Underhill Lane, Westmeston, Hassocks, Sussex BN6 8XG, England.

PUBLICATIONS FOR CHILDREN (illustrated by the author)

Fiction

Midnight Adventure. London, Hamish Hamilton, 1961.
The Strange House. London, Hamish Hamilton, 1961.
Sledges to the Rescue. London, Hamish Hamilton, 1963.
Jim and the Beanstalk. London, Hamish Hamilton, and New York, Coward McCann, 1970.
Father Christmas. London, Hamish Hamilton, and New York, Coward McCann, 1973.
Father Christmas Goes on Holiday. London, Hamish Hamilton, 1975.
Fungus the Bogeyman. London, Hamish Hamilton, 1977; New York, Random House, 1979.
The Snowman. London, Hamish Hamilton, and New York, Random House, 1978.
Gentleman Jim. London, Hamish Hamilton, 1980.
The Tin-Pot Foreign General and the Old Iron Woman. London, Hamish Hamilton, and Boston, Little Brown, 1984.
The Snowman (Building the Snowman, Dressing Up, Walking in the Air, The Party). London, Hamish Hamilton, and Boston, Little Brown, 4 vols., 1985.

Play

Gentleman Jim, adaptation of his own story (produced Nottingham, 1985).

Verse

Ring-a-Ring o' Roses. London, Hamish Hamilton, and New York, Coward McCann, 1962.

Other

Editor, *The White Land: A Picture Book of Traditional Rhymes and Verses.* London, Hamish Hamilton, and New York, Coward McCann, 1963.
Editor, *Fee Fi Fo Fum: A Picture Book of Nursery Rhymes.* London, Hamish Hamilton, and New York, Coward McCann, 1964.
Editor, *The Mother Goose Treasury.* London, Hamish Hamilton, and New York, Coward McCann, 1966.

PUBLICATIONS FOR ADULTS

Plays

When the Wind Blows, adaptation of his own book (broadcast 1983; produced Bristol and London, 1983; Washington, D.C., 1984).

London, French, 1983.

Screenplay: *When the Wind Blows,* 1987.

Radio Play: *When the Wind Blows,* 1983.

Other (illustrated by the author)

When the Wind Blows. London, Hamish Hamilton, and New York, Schocken, 1982.
Unlucky Wally. London, Hamish Hamilton, 1987.
Unlucky Wally Twenty Years On. London, Hamish Hamilton, 1989.

*

Illustrator: *The Wonderful Cornet* by Barbara Ker Wilson, 1958; *Peter and the Piskies* by Ruth Manning-Sanders, 1958, and *The Hamish Hamilton Book of Magical Beasts,* 1965, and *Festivals,* 1972, both edited by Manning-Sanders; *Peter's Busy Day* by A. Stephen Tring, 1959; *Look at Castles,* 1960, and *Look at Churches,* 1961, both by Alfred Duggan; *William's Wild Day Out* by Meriol Trevor, 1963; *The Hamish Hamilton Book of Myths and Legends* edited by Jacynth Hope-Simpson, 1964; *Whistling Rufus* by William Mayne, 1964, and *The Hamish Hamilton Book of Giants* edited by Mayne, 1968; *Stevie,* 1965, and *The Elephant and the Bad Baby,* 1969, both by Elfrida Vipont; *The Way over Windle* by Mabel Esther Allan, 1966; *The Flying 19* by James Aldridge, 1966; *The Christmas Book* edited by James Reeves, 1968, and *The Forbidden Forest* by Reeves, 1973; *Nuvolari and the Alfa Romeo,* 1968, and *Jimmy Murphy and the White Dusenberg,* 1968, both by Bruce Carter; *Lindbergh the Lone Flier,* 1968, and *Richthofen the Red Baron,* 1968, both by Nicholas Fisk; *Shackleton's Epic Voyage* by Michael Brown, 1969; *First Up Everest* by Showell Styles, 1969; *The Tale of Three Landlubbers* by Ian Serraillier, 1970; *The Fairy Tale Treasury* by Virginia Haviland, 1972; *All in a Day* by Mitsumasa Anno, 1986.

*   *   *

It is possible to tell stories only with pictures. In *The Snowman* Raymond Briggs has shown that he is capable of doing this with astonishing power. The appeal of the snowman is the appeal of the silent yet communicative toy—his melting is a small tragedy to the boy who has made him.

But Briggs's talent as a strip cartoonist is a talent with word as well as with image. He is obsessed with the world of the outsider. *Father Christmas,* working only on Christmas Eve, is not in the general run of jobs; *Fungus the Bogeyman,* with his alternative values, is hardly acceptable on the Surface; *Gentleman Jim,* the lavatory attendant, cannot "rise above" his underground toilet, try to be glamorous though he may; and it is this same Jim, retired, who, with his wife Hilda, tries to be an obedient and sensible citizen and build a fall-out shelter in *When the Wind Blows.* Brigg's most mature character by far is the child in *The Snowman.* The adults, in his great series of literary cartoon books, are inadequates, beaten by the system.

Being beaten by the system is no joke, but Briggs believes that most of us are, and that we could not survive unless we could see the funny side of our predicament. Being people, we communicate with words, and it is more often than not our command or lack of command of the *mot juste* for a given situation that decides whether we master it or it kicks us into the gutter.

Words are therefore the key to the greatness of Briggs's characters. Fungus has his own language which is very close to Surface language but just different enough to make us laugh at his approximations— Darkling (to his wife), Grape Nits (for breakfast); Gentleman Jim explores the obscurities of legal English, the purple passages of picaresque fiction, the glossy vocabulary of advertising, the contortions of bureaucratic jargon—all equally inaccessible to Jim who hasn't got his "Levels." But only in *When the Wind Blows* (the book in which the cradle rocks, the bough breaks—and civilization comes to an end) does Briggs admit that man, whatever his linguistic attainments, will always be a vulnerable pawn in the politicians' and bureaucrats' game.

In Britain the cartoon story with its bubble talk (a peculiarly difficult craft) has not had either the recognition or the following it has acquired in America or continental Europe. With the delectable *Father Christmas* Briggs began a revolution. With *When the Wind Blows,* a copy of which was given to every Member of Parliament by its publishers, he blew the field wide open.

—Elaine Moss

BRIGHT, Robert. Also wrote as Michael Douglas. American. Born in Sandwich, Massachusetts, 5 August 1902. Educated at Phillips Academy, Andover, Massachusetts; Princeton University, New Jersey, B.A. 1923. Married Katherine Bailey in 1931; one daughter and one son. Reporter, Baltimore *Sun,* 1925–26, and Paris *Times,* 1926–27; assistant to the President, Condé Nast Publications, New York, 1927–28; advertising manager, Revillon Frères, New York, 1928–36; instructor, Massachusetts Department of Education, Boston, 1948–51; lecturer, Emerson College, Boston, 1949; case worker, Department of Welfare, Taos, New Mexico, 1952; music and art critic, Santa Fe *New Mexican,* 1964–65. *Died 21 November 1988.*

PUBLICATIONS FOR CHILDREN (illustrated by the author)

Fiction

The Travels of Ching. New York, Scott, 1943; London, Collins, 1945.
Georgie. New York, Doubleday, 1944; London, Collins, 1945.
Me and the Bears. New York, Doubleday, 1951.
Hurrah for Freddie!, with Dorothy Brett. New York, Doubleday, 1953.
Miss Pattie. New York, Doubleday, 1954.
I Like Red. New York, Doubleday, 1955; Kingswood, Surrey, World's Work, 1964.
Georgie to the Rescue. New York, Doubleday, 1956; Kingswood, Surrey, World's Work, 1964.
The Friendly Bear. New York, Doubleday, 1957; Kingswood, Surrey, World's Work, 1967.
Georgie's Hallowe'en. New York, Doubleday, 1958; Kingswood, Surrey, World's Work, 1967.
My Red Umbrella. New York, Morrow, 1959.
Which Is Willy? New York, Doubleday, 1962; Kingswood, Surrey, World's Work, 1963.
Georgie and the Robbers. New York, Doubleday, 1963; Kingswood, Surrey, World's Work, 1964.
Georgie and the Magician. New York, Doubleday, 1966; Kingswood, Surrey, World's Work, 1967.
Gregory, The Noisiest and Strongest Boy in Grangers Grove. New York, Doubleday, 1969; Kingswood, Surrey, World's Work, 1970.
Georgie and the Noisy Ghost. New York, Doubleday, 1971; Kingswood, Surrey, World's Work, 1973.
Georgie Goes West. New York, Doubleday, 1973; Kingswood, Surrey, World's Work, 1975.
Georgie's Christmas Carol. New York, Doubleday, 1975;

Kingswood, Surrey, World's Work, 1978.
Georgie and the Buried Treasure. New York, Doubleday, 1979; Kingswood, Surrey, World's Work, 1981.
Georgie and the Baby Birds [*Ball of Yarn, Little Dog, Runaway Balloon*]. New York, Doubleday, 4 vols., 1983.

Verse

Round, Round World (as Michael Douglas). New York, Golden Press, 1960.
My Hopping Bunny. New York, Doubleday, 1960; Kingswood, Surrey, World's Work, 1967.

Other

Richard Brown and the Dragon. New York, Doubleday, 1952; Kingswood, Surrey, World's Work, 1964.

PUBLICATIONS FOR ADULTS

Novels

The Life and Death of Little Jo. New York, Doubleday, 1944; as *Little Jo,* London, Cresset Press, 1946.
The Intruders. New York, Doubleday, 1946; London, Cresset Press, 1948.
The Olivers: The Story of an Artist and His Family. New York, Doubleday, 1947.
The Spirit of the Chase. New York, Scribner, 1956; London, Cresset Press, 1957.

*

Robert Bright commented:

(1978) I intended to make a career as a novelist. But by the time I had published my third novel I realized that while I was gaining critical success I was not getting sufficient return to support a family. I had to be sensible, and so, sensibly, I turned to writing and illustrating picture books for children whose imagination commanded my respect and affection. What I have tried to do in my books is to present fantasy in the way of good stories with interesting characters and lots of humor and fun but with no silliness. So much of fantasy is apt to be silly, but good fantasy is logical and true. It teaches without straining, and above all, it does not abuse the confidence of the reader. I like to think therefore that those who have been brought up and are still being brought up in part with my books may always look back with pleasure at the imaginary worlds to which these stories introduced them.

*   *   *

The picture books of Robert Bright represent a curious divergence of opinion between the tastes of children and those of certain adult critics of children's literature. Bright's books continue to receive enthusiastic endorsements from young children, but he is seldom referred to in any serious discussion of children's literature, such as those written for teachers or librarians. While a note on his Georgie books is found in the American Library Association *Books for Elementary Schools* and *Children's Catalog,* Bright's work is generally dismissed out of hand by most compilers of selective bibliographies, even those exclusively of picture books.

Although Bright wrote this kind of book with several themes, what literary recognition he received comes almost entirely from his Georgie books. Their qualities help explain their attractiveness to children. These books are pleasant distortions of reality about a wise and brave but altogether gentle little ghost, named Georgie, who resides, unknown to them, with a rather docile and witless old couple. Bright recalled that the idea for Georgie stemmed from his own children badgering him to make up for them a ghost story. While they probably wanted a tale of dread and awe, it was to Bright's ultimate advantage as a publishable writer for the young that he decided against doing a genuine ghost story. Instead he chose a tongue-in-cheek treatment of the supernatural. This is the kind of book which fulfilled his ambition to enter into the child's world so as to invest it with stories that would have delighted him as a child. But one probable reason for lack of critical acclaim lies in his decision to illustrate his own books. While he did a generally good job of melding the pictures with the stories, his drawings are so utterly lacking in artistic merit that they have negatively influenced critics not perceptive to the obvious merits of plots and dialogue.

His illustrations aside, there is little doubt that Bright succeeded in his goal of delighting children. In each of his books about Georgie this smallish apparition heroically undertakes to set to rights some villainous action or unfortunate mishap. For example, in *Georgie and the Robbers* (to this point Georgie "never scared anybody, he was much too shy for that") Bright updated the well-known folk tale, "The Three Musicians." In this case Georgie and his animal playmates do scare away robbers hiding out in a barn and recover their loot. It is obvious here, and in other of his Georgie stories, that Bright took advantage of some of the motifs and traditions of folk literature that children enjoy hearing about. Among these motifs are the small person journeying away from home to a confrontation with a villain, followed by a showdown between good and evil and finally a rescue of the helpless. Bright's characters, as those in folk tales, are habitual in their behavior and unchanging in their motives. They are flat fictional personages whose behavior in stress situations is easily, and therefore happily, predictable by the child reader. Bright also borrowed from traditional literature his manner of talking directly to the reader, his highly melodramatic climaxes, his use of repetition and refrain for the sake of emphasis, and his choice of archaic settings. Other of Bright's books are reflections of the cumulative stories of folk literature. In *My Red Umbrella* and *I Like Red*, simple, repetitive, plotless structures, in which one thing or event in a sequence is much like that which it precedes and follows, Bright demonstrated again his dependence on folk literature.

—Patrick Groff

BRINK, Carol Ryrie. American. Born in Moscow, Idaho, 28 December 1895. Educated at Portland Academy, 1912–14; University of Idaho, Moscow, 1914–17; University of California, Berkeley, B.A. 1918. Married Raymond Woodard Brink in 1918 (died); one son and one daughter. Recipient: American Library Association Newbery Medal, 1936; University of Minnesota Kerlan award, 1978. D.Litt.: University of Idaho, 1965. *Died 15 August 1981.*

PUBLICATIONS FOR CHILDREN

Fiction

Anything Can Happen on the River!, illustrated by W. W. Berger. New York, Macmillan, 1934.
Caddie Woodlawn: A Frontier Story, illustrated by Kate Seredy. New York, Macmillan, 1935; London, Collier Macmillan, 1963.
Mademoiselle Misfortune, illustrated by Kate Seredy. New York, Macmillan, 1936.
Baby Island, illustrated by Helen Sewell. New York, Macmillan, 1937.

All over Town, illustrated by Dorothy Bayley. New York, Macmillan, 1939.
Lad with a Whistle, illustrated by Robert Ball. New York, Macmillan, 1941.
Magical Melons: More Stories about Caddie Woodlawn, illustrated by Marguerite Davis. New York, Macmillan, 1944.
Family Grandstand, illustrated by Jean McDonald Porter. New York, Viking Press, 1952.
The Highly Trained Dogs of Professor Petit, illustrated by Robert Henneberger. New York, Macmillan, 1953.
Family Sabbatical, illustrated by Susan Foster. New York, Viking Press, 1956.
The Pink Motel, illustrated by Sheila Greenwald. New York, Macmillan, 1959; London, Collier Macmillan, 1963.
Andy Buckram's Tin Men, illustrated by W.T. Mars. New York, Viking Press, 1966.
Winter Cottage, illustrated by Fermin Rocker. New York, Macmillan, 1968.
Two Are Better Than One, illustrated by Fermin Rocker. New York, Macmillan, and London, Collier Macmillan, 1968.
The Bad Times of Irma Baumlein, illustrated by Trina Schart Hyman. New York, Macmillan, and London, Collier Macmillan, 1972.
Louly, illustrated by Ingrid Fetz. New York, Macmillan, 1974.

Plays

The Cupboard Was Bare. Franklin, Ohio, Eldridge, 1928.
The Queen of the Dolls. Franklin, Ohio, Eldridge, 1928.
Caddie Woodlawn, adaptation of her own story (produced Minneapolis, 1957). New York, Macmillan, 1954.
Salute Mr. Washington, in *Plays* (Boston), March 1976.

Other

Narcissa Whitman: Pioneer to the Oregon Country, illustrated by Samuel Armstrong. Evanston, Illinois, Row Peterson, 1950.
Lafayette, illustrated by Dorothy Bayley Morse. Evanston, Illinois, Row Peterson, 1953.

Editor, *Best Short Stories for Children.* Evanston, Illinois, Row Peterson, 6 vols., 1936–41.

PUBLICATIONS FOR ADULTS as Carol Brink

Novels

Buffalo Coat. New York, Macmillan, 1944; London, Cassell, 1949.
Stopover. New York, Macmillan, 1951.
The Headland. New York, Macmillan, 1955; London, Gollancz, 1956.
Strangers in the Forest. New York, Macmillan, 1959.
Château St. Barnabé. New York, Macmillan, 1963.
Snow in the River. New York, Macmillan, 1964.
The Bellini Look. New York, Bantam, 1976.

Other

Harps in the Wind: The Story of the Singing Hutchinsons. New York, Macmillan, 1947.
The Twin Cities (on Minneapolis—St. Paul). New York, Macmillan, 1961.
Four Girls on a Homestead (reminiscences). Moscow, Idaho, Latah County Museum Society, 1978.

*

Manuscript Collections: Kerlan Collection, University of Minnesota, Minneapolis; University of Idaho Library, Moscow.

*   *   *

Carol Ryrie Brink's books indicate that she is equally at home in the past and the present. Her strength lies in presenting realistic family relationships and vivid personal portraits, made all the more interesting by her background knowledge of history. *Caddie Woodlawn* was reprinted more than 30 times during its first 30 years. Subtitled "A Frontier Story" it tells of 11-year-old Caddie's life with her family on a farm in Wisconsin. Although set at the time of the Civil War, the war plays no part in the story, for Brink has focused on the tense situation between the Indians and the white settlers. Caddie's long friendship with the Indians and their innate trust in her help to avert a threatened uprising and offer the reader an exciting and believable pioneer story. Brink must have been aware that books such as *Caddie Woodlawn* play an important part in the process of growing up, for in writing about the pioneer family and their way of life she reminds the reader that frontier life required qualities from children unheard of today. They took on real responsibilities as co-workers and shared equally in the family fortunes and failures.

Caddie Woodlawn was followed in 1944 by *Magical Melons* which gives further adventures of Caddie and her brothers but was never as popular as its predecessor. She wrote many other books, one of which, *Baby Island,* put forward the absurd and delightful situation of two girls shipwrecked with a lifeboat full of babies whom they cared for with love and ingenuity on a desert island. In her foreword Brink says she wrote this book for girls who love minding babies and couldn't find enough candidates. It is a delightful and amusing story lost to today's readers through the misfortunes of publishing. *Winter Cottage* tells of a city family feeling the hopelessness of the great depression. They leave the city for a winter in the country where their spirits are raised by the beauties of country living.

Whether writing of past or present, the strength of Brink's books lies in the carefully observed family relationships, which provide the basis for a wider circle as the child develops.

—Ann Bartholomew

———

BRINSMEAD, Hesba (Fay, née Hungerford). Australian. Born in Blue Mountains, New South Wales, 15 March 1922. Married Reginald Brinsmead in 1943; two sons. Educated through correspondence school, at high school in Wahroonga, and at Avondale College. Governess in Tasmania, two years; speech therapy teacher, western Victoria, 1945–48; kindergarten supervisor, Melbourne, two years; amateur actress, Box Hill City Drama Group, Melbourne, 1950–60. Since 1960 full-time writer. Recipient: Australian Children's Book Council Book of the Year award, 1965, 1972. Address: Weathertop, Shamara Road, Terranora, New South Wales 2485, Australia.

PUBLICATIONS FOR CHILDREN

Fiction

Pastures of the Blue Crane, illustrated by Annette Macarthur-Onslow. London, Oxford University Press, 1964; New York, Coward McCann, 1966.
Season of the Briar, illustrated by William Papas. London, Oxford

University Press, 1965; New York, Coward McCann, 1967.
Beat of the City, illustrated by William Papas. London, Oxford University Press, 1966; New York, Coward McCann, 1968.
A Sapphire for September, illustrated by Victor Ambrus. London, Oxford University Press, 1967.
Isle of the Sea Horse, illustrated by Peter Farmer. London, Oxford University Press, 1969.
Listen to the Wind, illustrated by Robert Micklewright. London, Oxford University Press, 1970.
Longtime Passing. Sydney and London, Angus and Robertson, 1971.
Who Calls from Afar?, illustrated by Ian Ribbons. London, Oxford University Press, 1971.
Echo in the Wilderness, illustrated by Graham Humphreys. London, Oxford University Press, 1972.
The Ballad of Benny Perhaps. Sydney, Cassell, 1977.
The Honey Forest, illustrated by Louise Hogan. Sydney, Hodder and Stoughton, 1978.
Once There Was a Swagman, illustrated by Noela Young. Melbourne and London, Oxford University Press, 1979.
Time for Tarquinia, illustrated by Bruce Riddell. Sydney and London, Hodder and Stoughton, 1981.
Longtime Dreaming. London, Angus and Robertson, 1982.
Christmas at Longtime. Sydney and London, Angus and Robertson, 1983.
The Sand Forest. Sydney, Angus and Robertson, 1985.
Someplace Beautiful, illustrated by Betina Ogden. Sydney, Hodder and Stoughton, 1986.
When You Come to the Ferry. Sydney, Hodder and Stoughton, 1988.

Other (readers)

Under the Silkwood, illustrated by Michael Payne. Sydney, Cassell, 1975.
The Wind Harp. Sydney, Cassell, 1977.
High Dive, and Free Is Lonely, illustrated by Craig Smith. Sydney and London, Hodder and Stoughton, 1979.

PUBLICATIONS FOR ADULTS

Other

I Will Not Say the Day Is Done. Chippendale, New South Wales, Alternative Publishing, 1983.

*

Manuscript Collection: National Library of Australia, Canberra.

Hesba Brinsmead comments:
At first I began writing for teenagers, as my younger son was about 12 and I could see that there was little for him to read that was within his life experience, yet at the same time compatible with his almost mature intelligence. Everything was too childish, or concerned itself with more living experience. I made my characters older, however, as young people are forward-looking, not wanting to dwell on the years they've passed but the things soon to come. Now, however, with grandchildren younger, yet quickly catching up, I'm more interested in writing in a way that people of 8 years and up might appreciate. I'm caught by noticing that quite young children play a part in all living, though mainly a passive role, a spectator role. So I wrote *Tarquinia,* about what I hoped was a timeless family, with timeless emotions and experiences—a family of ancient Etruscans. All ages are so transitory, so quickly merging. The main thing, I've

concluded, is to retain hope for the human race, and to keep this small flame burning.

                              *   *   *

Hesba Brinsmead's early novels have contemporary settings and modern, outgoing girls for heroines. In contrast, *Longtime Passing*, widely regarded as her best book, is the first of four books that draw on the author's own childhood on a remote farm. Brinsmead's particular talent is in the touch of magic she lends to her portrayal of people and places. Coincidence and chance keep the plots moving along, with the more improbable events tending to mar what are nominally realistic settings. Her joy of life is evident in all her books, although in some of the earlier novels, and in the more recent *The Sand Forest* and *Someplace Beautiful,* exuberance gives way to sweetness.

Ryl Mereweather, the heroine of the best of the early novels, *Pastures of the Blue Crane,* enjoys opportunities that would have astounded non-conforming literary forebears like *Little Women*'s Jo March. Ryl has wealth and independence but lacks "an island of peace." She finds this security in a run-down farm (once the family home) she is forced to share with her churlish (but with a heart of gold) grandfather. The crane of the title is a symbol of continuity, leaving its home each year but returning always to the same place. Ryl is the first of a series of heroines that have become something of a trademark for Brinsmead. She is goodlooking, impetuous, flamboyant, and energetic, a contrast to the more sombre and studious heroines in other Australian children's fiction of the 1960's and 1970's. The vitality of Brinsmead's characters was a welcome change from the usual emphasis on heroines negotiating "thorny paths," but as other critics have pointed out there is a cloying sameness about the string of characters with fanciful names that followed Ryl.

The Longtime books best show the author's talent for creating memorable characters and situations both poignant and humourous. Although set in the 1920's, the Longtime books are about pioneering life. The Truelance farm at Longtime, surrounded by forest, is only accessible by bullock team or on horseback. Edwin Truelance is an unlikely farmer, with a theology degree and a passion for music, and his wife Letty was a city girl. Somehow their apparent unsuitability fits them for a life in a place that had broken others, and they and their five children thrive despite isolation and hardship. The stories are told from the viewpoint of the youngest child, Teddy, who chaffs against the burdens of being "too little." *Longtime Passing* and *Longtime Dreaming* are full length novels, while *Once There Was a Swagman* and *Christmas at Longtime* are illustrated stories intended for younger children. Somewhat connected to this group of books is the short novel *The Honey Forest.* All are nostalgic—evoking and celebrating a lifestyle long gone from Australia. In the foreground is the theme of the importance of belonging to a place, and a concern for the environment apparent in Brinsmead's earlier novels.

Apart from *Time for Tarquinia* set in ancient Etruria, other recent books have contemporary settings. *The Sand Forest* is a return to the brash heroine and adventures of the earlier novels. Shipwrecks and lost treasure and two eccentric uncles make for a compelling, if unlikely, story. Clippie Nancarrow, a daredevil pilot from *Echo in the Wilderness* and *Who Calls from Afar?,* makes a reappearance in *The Sand Forest* to take part in a rescue mission and to provide a romantic interest. *Someplace Beautiful* is a whimsical novel about an attempt by children to save their local bookshop, and in *When You Come to the Ferry* two children and their grandmother have some unexpected adventures.

                                                    —Kerry White

                              ——————

BRISLEY, Joyce Lankester. British. Born in Bexhill, Sussex, 6 January 1896. Educated at a day school, Bexhill; Lambeth Art School, London. Freelance illustrator. *Died 20 September 1978.*

PUBLICATIONS FOR CHILDREN (illustrated by the author)

Fiction

Milly-Molly-Mandy Stories. London, Harrap, 1928; New York, McKay, 1976 (?).
More of Milly-Molly-Mandy. London, Harrap, 1929; New York, McKay, 1977.
Further Doings of Milly-Molly-Mandy. London, Harrap, and New York, McKay, 1932.
The Dawn Shops and Other Stories. London, Harrap, and New York, McKay, 1933.
Marigold in Godmother's House. London, Harrap, 1934.
Bunchy. London, Harrap, and New York, McKay, 1937.
The Adventures of Purl and Plain. London, Harrap, 1941.
Milly-Molly-Mandy Again. London, Harrap, 1948; New York, McKay, 1977.
Another Bunchy Book. London, Harrap, 1951.
Milly-Molly-Mandy & Co. London, Harrap, 1955; New York, McKay, 1977.
Milly-Molly-Mandy and Billy Blunt. London, Harrap, 1967; New York, McKay, 1977.
The Joyce Lankester Brisley Book, edited by Frank Waters. London, Harrap, 1981.

Plays

Three Little Milly-Molly-Mandy Plays (includes *Milly-Molly-Mandy Goes Errands* [*Keeps Shop, Meets Her Great Aunt*]). London, Harrap, 1938.

Verse

Lambs'-Tails and Suchlike: Verses and Sketches. London, Harrap, and New York, McKay, 1930.

Other

My Bible-Book. London, Harrap, 1940; New York, McKay, 1941.
Children of Bible Days. London, Harrap, 1970.

Editor, *The Wide, Wide World,* by Elizabeth Wetherell. London, University of London Press, 1950.

                              *

Illustrator: *Adventures of a Little Wooden Horse,* 1938, and *Pretenders' Island,* 1940, both by Ursula Moray Williams.

                              *   *   *

Most of Joyce Lankester Brisley's short stories concern the domestic events in the life of a small girl. Milly-Molly-Mandy "had a Father, and a Mother, and a Grandpa, and a Grandma, and an Uncle, and an Aunty; and they all lived together in a nice white cottage with a thatched roof."

In Milly-Molly-Mandy she created a likeable, believable little girl who is every child's better self, a child so cheerful, affectionate, and generous that she could very well seem too good to be true. It was no small achievement to bring this off so well, and to hit off so exactly the things which most please a child: the errands successfully run, the present for mother stitched in secret, the store-room transformed into a new bedroom all to herself, the railway carriage discovered in a field.

Her style is simple and exclamatory, designed for reading aloud, the vocabulary limited. There is little description but her own illustrations give a minimum of character to the various adults who might otherwise appear undifferentiated in their general twinkling benevolence.

Using the same basic setting of village life, in her stories about Bunchy Brisley crossed the boundary into fantasy. In a series of tales following one pattern, a lonely little girl who lives with her grandmother makes playmates for herself out of a pastry girl and cat, the figures on a scrap-work screen, the people in a pack of Happy Families cards and others. In her grandmother's absence these characters come to life and keep her company. These adventures are less convincing than the real doings of Milly-Molly-Mandy, but they have the same underlying warmth and affection for children.

Brisley's work now seems slightly dated and remote. There are an underlying condescension and sentimentality inherent, for example, in referring to a characters throughout as "little-friend-Susan." She wrote of a world without war or poverty or illness or anger, a world as warm and as welcoming, as comforting and as kindly as hot tea and toast beside the fire in winter, and if the country setting is romanticised, a land where every cottage is thatched and where mushrooms spring up in high summer, it is within its limitations none the worse for that, a place where everyone might like to have spent their childhood.

—Mary Rayner

———

BRITTAIN, Bill (William Brittain). American. Born in Rochester, New York, 16 December 1930. Educated at Spencerport High School, Spencerport, New York, graduated 1948; Colgate University, Hamilton, New York, 1948–50; Brockport State Teachers College (now State University College), New York, 1950–52, B.S. in education 1952; Hofstra University, Hempstead, New York, 1956–58, M.S. in education 1958. Married Virginia Connorton in 1954; one son and one daughter. Teacher, LeRoy Central Schools, New York, 1952–54, and in a public school, Lawrence, New York, 1954–60; teacher of English and reading, Lawrence Junior High School, New York, 1960–86. Address: 17 Wisteria Drive, Asheville, North Carolina 28804, U.S.A.

PUBLICATIONS FOR CHILDREN

Fiction

All the Money in the World, illustrated by Charles Robinson.   New York, Harper, 1979.
Devil's Donkey, illustrated by Andrew Glass.   New York, Harper, 1981.
The Wish Giver, illustrated by Andrew Glass.   New York, Harper, 1983.
Who Knew There'd Be Ghosts?, illustrated by Michele Chessare.   New York, Harper, 1985.
Dr. Dredd's Wagon of Wonders, illustrated by Andrew Glass.   New York, Harper, 1987.

The Fantastic Freshman.   New York, Harper, 1988.
My Buddy, The King.   New York, Harper, 1989.

PUBLICATIONS FOR ADULTS

Other

Survival Outdoors.   Derby, Connecticut, Monarch, 1977.

*

Manuscript Collection: American Heritage Center, University of Wyoming, Laramie.

Bill Brittain comments:
    I'm fascinated by the supernatural, particularly as it applies to wish fulfillment. My books reflect this fascination and deal with witchcraft, demons, haunted houses, and the like. I especially enjoy creating my "Coven Tree" series—*Devil's Donkey, The Wish Giver,* and *Dr. Dredd's Wagon of Wonders*—because the town of Coven Tree is an idealized form of the small village where I grew up.
    I don't try to teach lessons in my books. If the yarns send a shiver up some young spines and provide a laugh or two, I feel I've done my job well. I agree with the late Samuel Goldwyn: "If you want to send a message, use Western Union."

*   *   *

Although Bill Brittain is a prolific writer of mystery stories for adults, he is better known among young readers as the creator of weird and tantalizing characters. Brittain frequently flirts with a concept of evil cloaked in an often deceptively funny facade.

The Coven Tree stories—several books are set in this town—are moral tales based on the protagonists being driven by a strong wish or goal. In *The Wish Giver* three characters must each confront the results of their wishes and finally reverse the wish. Brittain's use of an evocative dark character to entice the protagonist into accepting great power reflects the theme revealed in *Faust* and other Mephistopheles tales. If human nature did not respond there would be no story. In *Devil's Donkey* Dan'l's challenge to beliefs in the power of an old witch leads to his enchantment as a donkey and the final encounter with Mr. Beel, the devil. *Dr. Dredd's Wagon of Wonders* pits evil Dr. Hugo Dredd against Calvin as both take up the challenge to bring rain to a drought-ridden town. Each of the Coven Tree stories is written in a smooth narrative mode with details that scare but do not terrorize, the language fostering moods of fear and revulsion but always balanced with a bit of humor and outrageousness.

The hilarious and exaggerated tickles the reader in Quentin's adventures in *All the Money in the World* when, after capturing Flan, a leprechaun, and wishing for all the money in the world, he discovers the consequences are a disaster. In *The Fantastic Freshman* Stanley is driven by one goal, to be a very important person. Given a tiny golden figurine enclosed in a blue glass pyramid and inscribed with the words "We will take good care of you," Stan takes the reader on a series of wildly improbable events all leading to the attainment of this goal. As in many of his other stories, the protagonist rethinks his goal and learns the heavy price one may have to pay for it.

Brittain offers the reader a chance both to be scared and to laugh as he draws characters and events that challenge the mind and fix firmly a concept of consequences to actions taken. He often uses an unusual or quirky approach to make a wish come true. Polly's temper and bad language is controlled by making her Jug-a-rum like a bull frog whenever she misspeaks. He has a wonderful way of unmasking people so that what appears to be beautiful and enviable is revealed as often ugly and undesirable.

—Jane Anne Hannigan

———

BRONSON, Lynn.   See **LAMPMAN, Evelyn Sibley.**

———

BROOKE, L(eonard) Leslie. British. Born in Birkenhead, Cheshire, 24 September 1862. Educated at Birkenhead School; Birkenhead Art School, 1880–82; St. John's Wood Art School, London, 1882–84; Royal Academy Art School, London (Armitage medal, 1888), 1884–88. Married his cousin Sybil Diana Brooke in 1894; two sons. Freelance artist and illustrator from 1888. *Died 1 May 1940.*

PUBLICATIONS FOR CHILDREN (illustrated by the author)

Verse

Johnny Crow's Garden.   London and New York, Warne, 1903.
Johnny Crow's Party.   London and New York, Warne, 1907.
Johnny Crow's New Garden.   London and New York, Warne, 1935.

*

Critical Study: *Leslie Brooke and Johnny Crow* by Henry Brooke, London, Warne, 1981; New York, Warne, 1982.

Illustrator: *Miriam's Ambition,* 1889, and *The Secret of the Old House,* 1890, both by Evelyn Everett-Green; *Thorndyke Manor* by Mary C. Rowsell, 1889; *The Light Princess and Other Fairy Stories* by George MacDonald, 1890; *Nurse Heatherdale's Story,* 1891, *The Girls and I,* 1892, *Mary,* 1893, *My New Home,* 1894, *The Carved Lions,* 1895, *Sheila's Mystery,* 1895, *The Oriel Window,* 1896, and *Miss Mouse and Her Boys,* 1897, all by Mary Louisa Molesworth; *Marian* by Annie E. Armstrong, 1892; *A Ring of Rubies* by L. T. Meade, 1892; *Bab* by Ismay Thorn, 1892; *Brownies and Rose-leaves,* 1892, and *Moonbeams and Brownies,* 1894, both by Roma White; *Penelope and Others* by Amy Walton, 1892; *A Hit and a Miss* by Eva Knatchbull Hugessen, 1893; *School in Fairyland* by E.H. Strain, 1896; *The Nursery Rhyme Book* edited by Andrew Lang, 1897; *Pippa Passes* by Robert Browning, 1898; *A Spring Song* by T. Nash, 1898; *Singing Time* by Arthur Somervell, 1899; *The Pelican Chorus and Other Verses,* 1899(?), *The Jumblies and Other Nonsense Verses,* 1900, and *Nonsense Songs,* 1900, all by Edward Lear; *Travels round Our Village* by Eleanor G. Hayden, 1901; *Barchester Towers* by Anthony Trollope, 1903; *The Story of the Three Little Pigs,* 1904; *Tom Thumb,* 1904; *Leslie Brooke's Children's Books 1–2,* 2 vols., 1904–05; *The Golden Goose,* 1905; *The Three Bears,* 1905; *The Golden Goose Book,* 1905; *The Book of Gilly* by Emily Lawless, 1906; *The House in the Wood and Other Old Fairy Stories,* 1909; *The Truth about Old King Cole* by George F. Hill, 1910; *The Tailor and the Crow,* 1911; *The Man in the Moon,* 1913; *Oranges and Lemons,* 1913; *A Nursery Rhyme Picture Book 1–2,* 2 vols., 1913–22; *Nursery Rhymes,* 1916; *Rhymes and Lullabies,* 1916; *Songs and Ditties,* 1916; *Tales and Jingles,* 1916; *Little Bo-Peep,* 1922; *This Little Pig Went to Market,* 1922; *Ring o' Roses,* 1922; *Mad Shepherds and Other Human Studies* by Lawrence P. Jacks, 1923; *A Roundabout Turn* by Robert H. Charles, 1930.

*   *   *

L. Leslie Brooke's stories have been described as "collector's pieces," but they are much more than this: they are perfect examples of the kind of writing which both parent and child can enjoy, each on his own level. The traditional tale—*The Three Little Pigs, The Three Bears, Tom Thumb, The Golden Goose*—are told directly and simply, with the repetition children love, and also with an ear for both the rhythms of English prose and its variety of sentence structure which lend a tough vitality to the stories even after much re-telling. The line drawings and colour illustrations are delightful, well integrated into the story, with a sly sense of humor which points up significant episodes. The morning after the abortive excursion to the turnip field, for instance, there is a picture of the wolf, waking up tardily at four o'clock, a partly eaten turnip still on the chair by his bed, and a picture on the wall of a wolf cooking fried back bacon, while on the next page the little pig is pictured already precariously climbing up the apple tree, his back legs dangling as he clutches the branch desperately with his front trotters. There is much fun for both alert adult and child in these stories and their accompanying illustrations, as also in the cunningly illustrated nursery rhymes of *Ring o' Roses.*

The gem of the collection is the *Johnny Crow* series, in which a dapper Johnny Crow creates a superb garden where he entertains a fascinating variety of farmyard and jungle animals. The pictures are again so detailed, so full of humour and so thoroughly integrated with the text that they enhance and expand the child's understanding particularly in those occasional wickedly satirical episodes which, as in Beatrix Potter's books, make no concessions to the myth that children cannot cope with words of more than two syllables.

> Then the Stork
> Gave a Philosophic Talk
> Till the Hippopotami
> Said: "Ask no further 'What am I?'"
> While the Elephant
> Said something quite irrelevant
> In Johnny Crow's Garden.

Here the long words roll off the adult's tongue in a manner very satisfying to the small child, for whom the accompanying illustrations make the joke explicit enough without any laboured explanations from a well-meaning parent or teacher. Most of the rhymes, of course, are much simpler than the ones just quoted; amusing, memorable verse which, together with the wealth of meaning in the drawings above them, makes the story-rite a pleasure for both parent and child, an excellent answer to the complaints of some parents that children's stories bore them stiff.

—Winifred Whitehead

———

BROOKS, Walter R(ollin). American. Born in Rome, New York, 9 January 1886. Educated at Rochester University, New York, 1904–06; New York Homeopathic Medical College, 1906–08. Married 1) Anne Shepard in 1909 (died); 2) Dorothy Collins in 1953. Associate editor, *Outlook,* New York, 1923–32; member of the editorial staff, *New Yorker,* 1933, and *Fiction Parade,* New York, 1933–37. *Died 17 August 1958.*

PUBLICATIONS FOR CHILDREN (illustrated by Kurt Wiese)

Fiction

To and Again, illustrated by Adolfo Best-Maugard.   New York,

Knopf, 1927; as *Freddy Goes to Florida,* 1949; as *Freddy's First Adventure,* London, Lane, 1949.
More To and Again. New York, Knopf, and London, George Allen, 1930; as *Freddy the Explorer,* London, Lane, 1949; as *Freddy Goes to the North Pole,* Knopf, 1951.
Freddy the Detective. New York, Knopf, 1932; London, Lane, 1950.
The Story of Freginald. New York, Knopf, 1936; as *Freddy and Freginald,* London, Lane, 1952.
The Clockwork Twin. New York, Knopf, 1937.
Wiggins for President. New York, Knopf, 1939; as *Freddy the Politician,* 1948.
Freddy's Cousin Weedly. New York, Knopf, 1940.
Freddy and the Ignormus. New York, Knopf, 1941.
Freddy and the Perilous Adventure. New York, Knopf, 1942.
Freddy and the Bean Home News. New York, Knopf, 1943.
Freddy and Mr. Camphor. New York, Knopf, 1944.
Freddy and the Popinjay. New York, Knopf, 1945.
Freddy the Pied Piper. New York, Knopf, 1946.
Freddy the Magician. New York, Knopf, 1947.
Jenny and the King of Smithia, illustrated by Decie Merwin. New York, Grosset and Dunlap, 1947.
Freddy Goes Camping. New York, Knopf, 1948.
Freddy Plays Football. New York, Knopf, 1949.
Freddy the Cowboy. New York, Knopf, 1950.
Freddy Rides Again. New York, Knopf, 1951.
Freddy the Pilot. New York, Knopf, 1952.
Freddy and the Space Ship. New York, Knopf, 1953.
Freddy and the Men from Mars. New York, Knopf, 1954.
Freddy and the Baseball Team from Mars. New York, Knopf, 1955.
Freddy and Simon the Dictator. New York, Knopf, 1956.
Freddy and the Flying Saucer Plans. New York, Knopf, 1957.
Freddy and the Dragon. New York, Knopf, 1958.
Henry's Dog Henry, illustrated by Aldren Watson. New York, Knopf, 1965.
Jimmy Takes Vanishing Lessons, illustrated by Don Bolognese. New York, Knopf, 1965.

Verse

The Collected Poems of Freddy the Pig. New York, Knopf, 1953.

PUBLICATIONS FOR ADULTS

Novel

Ernestine Takes Over. New York, Morrow, 1935; London, Jarrolds, 1937.

Other

New York: An Intimate Guide. New York, Knopf, 1931.

*   *   *

One of the most difficult juvenile genres to create is that of the anthropomorphic animal. Historically few of these characters have survived more than one generation, and deservedly so. One of the great American exceptions is Walter R. Brooks's Freddy the pig. This talking and thinking pig, jack of all trades and master of none, wore many hats, ranging from detective to magician to politician and beyond. For the child reader, events on Mr. Bean's farm are solely episodic, ranging from the hilarious to the darkly sinister, only slightly familiar to the present world. For the adult, the Bean farm, Freddy, and the other animals are boldly familiar archetypes of daily

events and people. A little of all the human traits can be found here through both the human and animal characters. Judging the series by contemporary children's literature standards, the books are beginning to date. The illustrations denote scenes, costumes, and vehicles no longer in use. Brooks's handling of stock character types, the American Indian for example, are now regarded as overtly stereotypical and thus harmful. Valid as these criticisms may be, the series should be considered in its proper scheme. Brooks indisputably raised the anthropomorphic genre to a higher level with Freddy when one stops to consider the 1950's output when the series was beginning. Freddy could not help but lessen library and bookseller's shelves of romantically portrayed doe-eyed kittens and puppies by being a real (human) animal with real feelings, ideas, and faults.

In the 1980's the U.S. publisher Alfred Knopf reissued the Freddy books in the hopes of capturing a new child audience. A failed attempt, it was stopped after eight books because sales did not live up to the publisher's expectations, despite wide reviewer notice and a well-designed publicity effort.

—Jim Roginski

———

BROWN, Marc (Tolon). American. Born in Erie, Pennsylvania, 25 November 1946. Educated at Cleveland Institute of Art, 1964–69, B.F.A. 1969. Married 1) Stephanie Marini in 1968 (divorced 1977), two sons; 2) Laurene Krasny in 1983, one daughter. Art director, WICU-TV, Erie, Pennsylvania, 1968–69; Assistant Professor of Art, Garland Junior College, Boston, 1969–76. Artist: numerous individual shows. Address: 562 Main Street, Hingham, Massachusetts 02043, U.S.A.

PUBLICATIONS FOR CHILDREN (illustrated by the author)

Fiction

Arthur's Nose. Boston, Little Brown, 1976.
Full House. Boston, Little Brown, 1977.
Lenny and Lola. New York, Dutton, 1978.
Moose and Goose. New York, Dutton, 1978.
Arthur's Eyes. Boston, Little Brown, 1979; London, Pepper Press, 1981.
The Cloud over Clarence. New York, Dutton, 1979.
Arthur's Valentine. Boston, Little Brown, 1980.
Pickle Things. New York, Parents' Magazine Press, 1980.
Witches Four. New York, Parents' Magazine Press, 1980; London, Hamish Hamilton, 1981.
The True Francine. Boston, Little Brown, 1981; London, Pepper Press, 1982.
Arthur Goes to Camp. Boston, Little Brown, 1982.
Arthur's Halloween. Boston, Little Brown, 1982.
Boat Book. New York, Golden Press, 1982.
Arthur's April Fool. Boston, Little Brown, and London, Pepper Press, 1983.
Arthur's Thanksgiving. Boston, Little Brown, 1983.
The Silly Tail Book. New York, Parents' Magazine Press, 1983.
Arthur's Christmas. Boston, Little Brown, 1984; London, Piccadilly Press, 1985.
The Bionic Bunny Show, with Laurene Krasny Brown. Boston, Little Brown, and London, Collins, 1984.
There's No Place like Home. New York, Parents' Magazine Press,

1984; London, Collins, 1986.
Arthur's Tooth.   Boston, Little Brown, 1985; London, Corgi, 1987.
Arthur's Teacher Trouble.   Boston, Little Brown, 1986; London, Piccadilly Press, 1987.
Arthur's Baby.   Boston, Little Brown, 1987.
D.W. Flips!   Boston, Little Brown, 1987; as *Roll Over D.W.,* London, Piccadilly Press, 1988.
D.W. All Wet.   Boston, Little Brown, 1988.
Arthur's Birthday.   Boston, Little Brown, 1989.

Other

One, Two, Three: An Animal Counting Book.   Boston, Little Brown, 1976.
Your First Garden Book.   Boston, Little Brown, 1981.
Boat Book.   New York, Golden Press, 1982.
Count to Ten.   New York, Golden Press, 1982.
Dinosaurs, Beware! A Safety Guide, with Stephen Krensky.   Boston, Little Brown, 1982; London, Collins, 1983.
Wings on Things.   New York, Random House, 1982.
Perfect Pigs: An Introduction to Manners, with Stephen Krensky.   Boston, Little Brown, 1983; London, Collins, 1984.
Spooky Riddles.   New York, Random House, 1983; London, Collins, 1984.
What Do You Call a Dumb Bunny? and Other Rabbit Riddles, Games, Jokes, and Cartoons.   Boston, Little Brown, and London, MacRae, 1983.
Dinosaurs Divorce: A Guide for Changing Families, with Laurene Krasny Brown.   Boston, Little Brown, 1986; London, Collins, 1987.
Visiting the Art Museum, with Laurene Krasny Brown.   New York, Dutton, 1986; as *Visiting an Exhibition,* London, Collins, 1986.
Dinosaurs Travel: A Guide for Families on the Go, with Laurene Krasny Brown.   Boston, Little Brown, 1988.
Baby Time, with Laurene Krasny Brown.   New York, Knopf, 1989.
The Family Read-Aloud Christmas Treasury, edited by Alice Low.   Boston, Little Brown, 1989.

Editor, *Finger Rhymes.*   New York, Dutton, 1980.
Editor, *Hand Rhymes.*   New York, Dutton, and London, Collins, 1985.
Editor, *Play Rhymes.*   New York, Dutton, 1987.
Editor, *Party Rhymes.*   New York, Dutton, 1988.
Editor, *One, Two, Buckle My Shoe.*   New York, Dutton, 1989.
Editor, *Can You Jump Like a Frog?*   New York, Dutton, 1989.

*

Illustrator: *What Makes the Sun Shine?* by Isaac Asimov, 1971; *The Dragon with a Thousand Wrinkles* by Mary Daem, 1971; *The Iron Lion* by Peter Dickinson, 1972; *I Found Them in the Yellow Pages,* 1973, and *There Goes Feathertop!,* 1979, both by Norma Farber; *The Little Green Thumb Window Garden* by Doug Morse, 1974; *Ride, Ride, Ride* by Marcia Wiesbauer, 1974; *The Four Corners of the Sky* by Ted Clymer, 1975; *Science Games* [*Puzzles, Tricks, Toys*] by Laurence White, 4 vols., 1975; *Super Sam and the Salad Garden* by Patty Wolcott, 1975; *How the Rabbit Stole the Moon* by Louise Moeri, 1977; *My Doctor Bag Book* by Kathleen Daly, 1977; *Little Owl* by Janwillem van de Wetering, 1978; *Why the Tides Ebb and Flow* by Joan Chase Bowden, 1979; *Rabbit's New Rug* by Judy Delton, 1979; *The Banza* by Diane Wolkstein, 1981; *What's So Funny, Ketu?,* 1981, and *Oh, Kojo! How Could You?,* 1984, both by Verna Aardema; *Swamp Monsters,* 1983, and *Go West, Swamp Monsters!,* 1985, both by Mary Blount Christian; *Little Witch's Big*

Night, 1984, and *Happy Birthday, Little Witch,* 1985, both by Deborah Hautzig; *Read-Aloud Rhymes for the Very Young* edited by Jack Prelutsky, 1986; *A World Full of Monsters* by John T. McQueen, 1986.

*   *   *

Learning and growing experiences are serious subjects for Marc Brown, but as his work so ably demonstrates, even serious subjects have their humorous aspects. In a body of work for children that ranges from discussions of gardening and museum visiting to the adventures of an anteater and his friends, Brown abandons neither his sense of purposefulness nor his sense of humor. A trained artist who was profoundly influenced by the interplay of pictures and text in Maurice Sendak's *Where the Wild Things Are,* he is also adept at using illustrations to give added dimension to his written text.

Brown is best known for the "Arthur Adventure" books, a series of picture books about a second-grade (and more recently, third-grade) anteater named Arthur, his friends, and his family. The honors garnered by these books from both children and adults testify to the various levels at which they may be enjoyed. Children easily identify with the likable Arthur; his family and schoolmates, from the obnoxious Francine to his little sister D.W., who wants to know whether she can have Arthur's room after the school bully pulverizes him, are equally recognizable to most elementary school children.

Thematically Brown demonstrates keen sensitivity to the problems and fears of his young audience. In *Arthur's Eyes, Arthur's Nose,* and *Arthur's Tooth,* the hero attempts to find acceptance when he is the only one of his friends to have an obvious physical difference. The stories emphasize self-acceptance as well as acceptance of others. Even more interesting are episodes in which Arthur finds himself in circumstances where there is a large discrepancy between how he knows he is supposed to feel about the situation, and the way he actually does feel. For instance, in *Arthur's Halloween,* Arthur's fears contrast with the excitement and confidence displayed by his friends and even his baby sister, to make the approach of the holiday a dreaded occasion. He is the envy of the class when the teacher selects him to direct the school play in *Arthur's Thanksgiving,* but is privately surprised by the burden of personal responsibility brought by this honor. *Arthur's Baby,* according to his mother and father, is going to be a wonderful addition to their household—but Arthur, like most children, has his doubts. Brown's consistent message, always delivered with sensitivity and humor, is that it is normal to feel apprehensive in these situations, and that they usually turn out well in the end.

The interplay between artwork and narrative in Brown's books makes them useful tools for encouraging children to develop the habit of noticing details as they read. Brown's gimmick of hiding his family's names in the illustrations can be used constructively as a stimulus for picking up other details. For instance, when Arthur worries about being the only first-grader who has not lost a tooth, Brown subtly inserts a picture of a student in a wheelchair, suggesting to the observant reader a more serious aspect of the problem of fitting in, without making a major issue of it. In the same book, Arthur's wild imaginings of what his trip to the dentist will be like are immediately followed by a more realistic but no less horrible depiction of the chaos in the child-filled waiting room; the observant reader will note the subtle irony. Thus Brown's texts and illustrations work together to promote a deeper understanding for the more sophisticated child, and to develop the invaluable skill of attention to detail in any child.

Brown has recently added stories about Arthur's sister D.W. to his repertoire. While generally appealing from a child's level, they do not have the depth of the best of the Arthur books. However, one recent work outside the Arthur series has received accolades from children and adults: *The Bionic Bunny Show,* a collaboration with

Brown's wife Laurene. Humor and instruction combine as the reader observes superhero Bionic Bunny (who has appeared in previous texts on Arthur's lunchbox) making an episode of his television show. The show itself proceeds in tandem with a backstage look at how the illusions of superpowers are produced. The book is interesting in its own right, and also useful for stimulating discussions about reality and fantasy with respect to television. In his insistence on attending to the serious concerns of elementary school-age children, as well as to the humor inherent in situations developing from those concerns, Marc Brown continues to create children's books which can be appreciated for their simplicity but enjoyed on more complex levels as well.

—Christine Doyle Francis

_____

BROWN, Marcia. American. Born in Rochester, New York, 13 July 1918. Educated at Woodstock College of Painting, New York, summers 1938–39; New York College for Teachers (now State University of New York), Albany, B.A. 1940; New School for Social Research, Art Students' League, and Columbia University, all New York. Drama teacher in high school, Cornwall, New York, 1940–43; library assistant, New York Public Library, 1943–48; teacher of puppetry, University of the West Indies, Kingston, Jamaica, 1953. Recipient: American Library Association Caldecott Medal, 1955, 1962, 1983. Address: c/o Scribner's, 866 Third Avenue, New York, New York 10022, U.S.A.

PUBLICATIONS FOR CHILDREN (illustrated by the author)

Fiction

The Little Carousel.   New York, Scribner, 1946.
Henry, Fisherman: A Story of the Virgin Islands.   New York, Scribner, 1949.
Skipper John's Cook.   New York, Scribner, 1951.
Felice.   New York, Scribner, 1958.
Taramindo!   New York, Scribner, 1960.
The Neighbors.   New York, Scribner, 1967.
How, Hippo!   New York, Scribner, 1969.
The Blue Jackal.   New York, Scribner, 1977.

Other

Stone Soup (retelling).   New York, Scribner, 1947.
Dick Whittington and His Cat (retelling).   New York, Scribner, 1950.
Puss in Boots (retelling).   New York, Scribner, 1952.
Cinderella (retelling).   New York, Scribner, 1954.
The Flying Carpet (retelling).   New York, Scribner, 1956.
Peter Piper's Alphabet.   New York, Scribner, 1959.
Once a Mouse (retelling).   New York, Scribner, 1961.
Backbone of the King (retelling).   New York, Scribner, 1966.
The Bun: A Tale from Russia.   New York, Harcourt Brace, 1972.
All Butterflies: An ABC.   New York, Scribner, 1974.
Listen to a Shape.   New York, Watts, 1979.

Touch Will Tell.   New York, Watts, 1979.
Walk with Your Eyes.   New York, Watts, 1979.
Shadow (retelling).   New York, Scribner, 1982.

PUBLICATIONS FOR ADULTS

Other

Lotus Seeds: Children, Pictures, and Books.   New York, Scribner, 1986.

*

Illustrator: *The Trail of Courage* by Virginia Watson, 1948; *The Steadfast Tin Soldier,* 1953, *The Wild Swans,* 1963, and *The Snow Queen,* 1972, all by Hans Christian Andersen; *Anansi* by Philip Sherlock, 1954; *The Three Billy Goats Gruff* by Peter C. Asbjoernsen and J.E. Moe, 1957; *Giselle* by Violette Verdy, 1970.

*   *   *

Although Marcia Brown is best known as an illustrator, she is also an author and the adapter of many traditional tales for children. Since she illustrates her own work and uses very different media and techniques to complement the essence of each text there is a special unity and sense of wholeness to her books. Brown's first picture book *The Little Carousel* is a realistic story which grew out of a scene she observed from her Greenwich Village apartment during her early years in New York City. Her experience as a storyteller for the New York Public Library also proved useful to her in capturing the sounds and the rhythms of a well-told tale in such works as *Stone Soup, Dick Whittington and His Cat,* and other tales adapted for picture-book audiences.

Brown's books represent different ways of making traditional literature accessible to young children. *Cinderella* retains the airy elegance and magical qualities of the original court drama in words as well as in illustrations. The language of the Indian fable *Once a Mouse* has the simple earthy strength of its character the hermit who "sat thinking about big and little" on both the opening and concluding pages.

Wherever Brown traveled she absorbed both visual and verbal images of the land and its traditions. Not only did her trip to Africa influence *Shadow,* but a visit to the Virgin Islands stimulated the creation of *Henry, Fisherman* and a stay in Hawaii led to her retelling of a Polynesian legend in *Backbone of the King,* her novel-length story of Pakaa and his son Ku.

In addition to her interpretations of folk literature, Brown has also written a number of concept books. *All Butterflies: An ABC* demonstrates her ability to use language sparsely, effectively, and in a way that can still delight children. Two words, in harmony with the illustration, make a statement or raise a question while introducing two letters of the alphabet. Thus: "All Zoo."

Brown has published three concept books illustrated with her own full-color photographs of nature, inviting young readers to observe their work and *Listen to a Shape, Walk with Your Eyes,* and know that *Touch Will Tell.* Poetic language serves as more than captions for the photographs as in "Looking can be/flying/with someone else's wings—/feeling/the beat of the rain/on the face/of a flower—/watching/a spider mending her web, torn by the rain."

—Kay E. Vandergrift

_____

BROWN, Margaret Wise. Also wrote as Timothy Hay; Golden MacDonald; Juniper Sage. American. Born in Brooklyn, New York, 23 May 1910. Educated at Chateau Brilliantmont, Lausanne, Switzerland, 1923–25; Dana Hall, Wellesley, Massachusetts, 1926–28; Hollins College, Virginia, 1928–32, B.A. in English 1932; Columbia University, New York, 1932; Bureau of Educational Experiments (now Bank Street College of Education), New York. Assistant to Lucy Sprague Mitchell, Bank Street Publications, New York, mid-1930's; editor, William R. Scott, publishers, New York, 1938–41. *Died 13 November 1952.*

PUBLICATIONS FOR CHILDREN

Fiction

When the Wind Blew, illustrated by Rosalie Slocum. New York, Harper, 1937.
Bumble Bugs and Elephants, illustrated by Clement Hurd. New York, Scott, 1938.
The Fish with the Deep Sea Smile, illustrated by Roberta Rauch. New York, Dutton, 1938.
The Little Fireman, illustrated by Esphyr Slobodkina. New York, Scott, 1938.
The Streamlined Pig, illustrated by Kurt Wiese. New York, Harper, 1938.
Little Pig's Picnic and Other Stories, illustrated by Walt Disney Studio. Boston, Heath, 1939; London, Collins, 1949.
Noisy Book, illustrated by Leonard Weisgard. New York, Scott, 1939.
Country Noisy Book, illustrated by Leonard Weisgard. New York, Scott, 1940.
Baby Animals, illustrated by Mary Cameron. New York, Random House, 1941.
The Polite Penguin, illustrated by H.A. Rey. New York, Harper, 1941.
The Poodle and the Sheep, illustrated by Leonard Weisgard. New York, Dutton, 1941.
The Seashore Noisy Book, illustrated by Leonard Weisgard. New York, Scott, 1941.
Don't Frighten the Lion!, illustrated by H.A. Rey. New York, Harper, 1942.
Indoor Noisy Book, illustrated by Leonard Weisgard. New York, Harper, 1942.
Night and Day, illustrated by Leonard Weisgard. New York, Harper, 1942.
The Runaway Bunny, illustrated by Clement Hurd. New York, Harper, 1942.
A Child's Good Night Book, illustrated by Jean Charlot. New York, Scott, 1943.
Little Chicken, illustrated by Leonard Weisgard. New York, Harper, 1943.
The Noisy Bird Book, illustrated by Leonard Weisgard and Audubon. New York, Scott, 1943.
SHHhhhh...bang: A Whispering Book, illustrated by Robert de Veyrac. New York, Harper, 1943.
The Big Fur Secret, illustrated by Robert de Veyrac. New York, Harper, 1944.
Black and White, illustrated by Charles Shaw. New York, Harper, 1944.
Horses (as Timothy Hay), illustrated by Dorothy Wagstaff. New York, Harper, 1944.
They All Saw It, photographs by Ylla. New York, Harper, 1944.
Willie's Walk to Grandmama, with Rockbridge Campbell, illustrated by Lucienne Bloch. New York, Scott, 1944.

The House of a Hundred Windows, illustrated by Robert de Veyrac. New York, Harper, 1945.
The Little Fisherman, illustrated by Dahlov Ipcar. New York, Scott, 1945.
Little Fur Family, illustrated by Garth Williams. New York, Harper, 1946.
The Man in the Manhole and the Fix-It Men (as Juniper Sage, with Edith Thacher Hurd), illustrated by Bill Ballantine. New York, Scott, 1946.
The Bad Little Duckhunter, illustrated by Clement Hurd. New York, Scott, 1947.
The Golden Egg Book, illustrated by Leonard Weisgard. New York, Simon and Schuster, 1947.
The First Story, illustrated by Marc Simont. New York, Harper, 1947.
Goodnight, Moon, illustrated by Clement Hurd. New York, Harper, 1947; Kingswood, Surrey, World's Work, 1975; pop-up edition, as *The Goodnight Moon Room,* New York, Harper, and London, Hardy, 1984.
The Sleepy Little Lion, photographs by Ylla. New York, Harper, 1947; London, Harvill Press, 1960.
The Winter Noisy Book, illustrated by Charles Shaw. New York, Harper, 1947.
Five Little Firemen, with Edith Thacher Hurd, illustrated by Tibor Gergely. New York, Simon and Schuster, 1948.
The Golden Sleepy Book, illustrated by Garth Williams. New York, Simon and Schuster, 1948.
The Little Farmer, illustrated by Esphyr Slobodkina. New York, Scott, 1948.
Wonderful Storybook, illustrated by J.P. Miller. New York, Simon and Schuster, 1948.
The Color Kittens, illustrated by Alice and Martin Provensen. New York, Simon and Schuster, 1949; London, Muller, 1951.
The Important Book, illustrated by Leonard Weisgard. New York, Harper, 1949.
The Little Cowboy, illustrated by Esphyr Slobodkina. New York, Scott, 1949.
My World, illustrated by Clement Hurd. New York, Harper, 1949.
A Pussycat's Christmas, illustrated by Helen Stone. New York, Crowell, 1949.
Two Little Miners, with Edith Thacher Hurd, illustrated by Richard Scarry. New York, Simon and Schuster, 1949.
Two Little Trains, illustrated by Jean Charlot. New York, Scott, 1949; Kingswood, Surrey, World's Work, 1960.
O, Said the Squirrel, photographs by Ylla. London, Harvill Press, 1950.
The Dream Book: First Comes the Dream, illustrated by Richard Floethe. New York, Random House, 1950.
The Little Fat Policeman, with Edith Thacher Hurd, illustrated by Alice and Martin Provensen. New York, Simon and Schuster, 1950.
The Peppermint Family, illustrated by Clement Hurd. New York, Harper, and London, Hamish Hamilton, 1950.
The Quiet Noisy Book, illustrated by Leonard Weisgard. New York, Harper, and London, Hamish Hamilton, 1950.
The Wonderful House, illustrated by J. P. Miller. New York, Simon and Schuster, and London, Muller, 1950; revised edition, Simon and Schuster, 1960.
Fox Eyes, illustrated by Jean Charlot. New York, Pantheon, 1951; London, Collins, 1979.
The Summer Noisy Book, illustrated by Leonard Weisgard. New York, Harper, 1951.
The Train to Timbuctoo, illustrated by Art Seiden. New York, Simon and Schuster, 1951; London, Muller, 1952.
Two Little Gardeners, with Edith Thacher Hurd, illustrated by Gertrude Elliott. New York, Simon and Schuster, 1951.

Christmas in the Barn, illustrated by Barbara Cooney.   New York, Crowell, 1952.

Dr. Squash, The Doll Doctor, illustrated by J.P. Miller.   New York, Simon and Schuster, 1952.

Mister Dog, The Dog Who Belonged to Himself, illustrated by Garth Williams.   New York, Simon and Schuster, 1952; London, Muller, 1954.

The Noon Balloon, illustrated by Leonard Weisgard.   New York, Harper, 1952.

Seven Little Postmen, with Edith Thacher Hurd, illustrated by Tibor Gergely.   New York, Simon and Schuster, 1952.

The Duck, photographs by Ylla.   New York, Harper, and London, Harvill Press, 1952.

The Golden Bunny and 17 Other Stories and Poems, illustrated by Leonard Weisgard.   New York, Simon and Schuster, 1953.

The Hidden House, illustrated by Aaron Fine.   New York, Holt, 1953.

The Sailor Dog, illustrated by Garth Williams.   New York, Simon and Schuster, 1953; London, Muller, 1954.

The Friendly Book, illustrated by Garth Williams.   New York, Simon and Schuster, 1954.

The Little Fir Tree, illustrated by Barbara Cooney.   New York, Crowell, 1954.

Little Indian, illustrated by Richard Scarry.   New York, Simon and Schuster, 1954; London, Golden Pleasure Books, 1964.

Wheel on the Chimney, illustrated by Tibor Gergely.   Philadelphia, Lippincott, 1954.

Willie's Adventures, illustrated by Crockett Johnson.   New York, Scott, 1954.

The Little Brass Band, illustrated by Clement Hurd.   New York, Harper, 1955.

Seven Stories about a Cat Named Sneakers, illustrated by Jean Charlot.   New York, Scott, 1955; as *Sneakers,* Reading, Massachusetts, Addison Wesley, 1979.

Young Kangaroo, illustrated by Symeon Shimin.   New York, Scott, 1955; Kingswood, Surrey, World's Work, 1959.

Big Red Barn, illustrated by Rosella Hartman.   New York, Scott, 1956.

David's Little Indian, illustrated by Remy Charlip.   New York, Scott, 1956.

Home for a Bunny, illustrated by Garth Williams.   New York, Simon and Schuster, 1956; London, Hamlyn, 1961.

Three Little Animals, illustrated by Garth Williams.   New York, Harper, 1956.

The Dead Bird, illustrated by Remy Charlip.   New York, Scott, 1958.

Four Fur Feet, illustrated by Remy Charlip.   New York, Scott, 1961.

On Christmas Eve, illustrated by Beni Montresor.   New York, Scott, 1961; London, Collins, 1963.

The Whispering Rabbit, illustrated by Garth Williams and Lilian Obligado.   New York, Golden Press, 1965.

The Steamroller, illustrated by Evaline Ness.   New York, Walker, 1974.

Once upon a Time in a Pigpen and Three Other Stories, illustrated by Ann Strugnell.   Reading, Massachusetts, Addison Wesley, 1980; London, Hutchinson, 1981.

Wonderful Storybook (selection), illustrated by J.P. Miller.   Racine, Wisconsin, Western, 1985.

Fiction as Golden MacDonald (illustrated by Leonard Weisgard)

Red Light, Green Light.   New York, Doubleday, 1944.
Little Lost Lamb.   New York, Doubleday, 1945.
Little Frightened Tiger.   New York, Doubleday, 1953.
Whistle for the Train.   New York, Doubleday, 1956.

Verse

Big Dog, Little Dog (as Golden MacDonald), illustrated by Leonard Weisgard.   New York, Doubleday, 1943.

The Little Island (as Golden MacDonald), illustrated by Leonard Weisgard.   New York, Doubleday, 1946.

Wait till the Moon Is Full, illustrated by Garth Williams.   New York, Harper, 1948.

The Dark Wood of the Golden Birds, illustrated by Leonard Weisgard.   New York, Harper, 1950.

A Child's Good Morning, illustrated by Jean Charlot.   New York, Scott, 1952.

Where Have You Been?, illustrated by Barbara Cooney.   New York, Crowell, 1952.

Sleepy ABC, illustrated by Esphyr Slobodkina.   New York, Lothrop, 1953.

Nibble Nibble, illustrated by Leonard Weisgard.   New York, Scott, 1959.

Other

The Children's Year (adapted from a work by Y. Lacôte), illustrated by Feodor Rojankovsky.   New York, Harper, 1937.

The Comical Tragedy or Tragical Comedy of Punch and Judy, illustrated by Leonard Weisgard.   New York, Scott, 1940.

The Fables of La Fontaine, illustrated by André Hellé.   New York, Harper, 1940.

Brer Rabbit: Stories from Uncle Remus, illustrated by A.B. Frost.   New York, Harper, 1941.

Animals, Plants, and Machines (reader), with Lucy Sprague Mitchell, illustrated by Clare Bice.   Boston, Heath, 1944.

Farm and City (reader), with Lucy Sprague Mitchell.   Boston, Heath, 1944.

Pussy Willow, illustrated by Leonard Weisgard.   New York, Simon and Schuster, 1952.

The Diggers, illustrated by Clement Hurd.   New York, Harper, and London, Hamish Hamilton, 1961.

*

Manuscript Collections: Westerly Public Library, Rhode Island; Kerlan Collection, University of Minnesota, Minneapolis.

*   *   *

Author of more than one hundred children's stories, Margaret Wise Brown pioneered by the late 1930's a new approach to writing for children in which a story goes beyond traditional narrative borders to focus directly on important aspects of a young child's world. She saw the latter consisting of such things as: a fascination with the world's colors and sights and smells which were so new to the child's senses; a concern with being lost and being found, good and bad, shy or lonely; and a delight in the recognizably nonsensical. Reflecting these interests, her books aimed at penetrating the child's reality.

The Noisy Books Series early exemplified the author's intent by appealing to the child's growing sensory awareness. In *Noisy Book* a dog named Muffin hears the noises a child would hear and has to guess the identity of one—a device employed in every book. Muffin listens to indoor sounds in *Indoor Noisy Book,* to rural sounds in *Country Noisy Book,* and to a quiet sound he can't recognize (until with the reader selects from such imaginative possibilities as fog drifting and birds dreaming) in *The Quiet Noisy Book.* The books use words and images in an imaginative and poetic manner to capture the child's attention.

New or familiar sights, the seasons, travel, and the child-feared night are subjects touched upon in stories like *The Noon Balloon, Wheel on the Chimney, Night and Day*, to mention a few. In the first a cat is airlifted over cities and natural topography. In *Wheel on the Chimney* a stork loses his family as they migrate south but rejoins them again in the spring as they return to their chimney nest. A lonely night cat and day cat visit in each other's worlds in *Night and Day*, and the latter stays with his companion after losing his fear of the night world. All three books persuasively accomplish the aim of their author.

A group of Brown's works center on a child's concerns with getting lost, being lonely or alone, and being loved and protected. The title character of *Young Kangaroo* leaves his mother's pouch only narrowly to escape being eaten by dingoes before gratefully returning to his mother's warm security. In *The Runaway Bunny* a rabbit is dissuaded from running away because his mother strongly reaffirms her love. *Little Chicken* deals with a chick who is left alone for the first time and returns home wiser for the experience. On a deeper plane, *The Little Island* tells of a kitten who learns that he, like an isolated island connected to one land under the sea, is a world of his own yet part of the world. These stories perceptively treat the child's innermost concerns.

Offering a valuable spectrum of the author's work is *The Fish with the Deep Sea Smile*, a collection of stories (including "Sneakers, That Rapscallion Cat") and poems demonstrating her sensitivity and skill as a poet as well as writer.

Margaret Wise Brown emerges as a major writer of children's literature. The rich legacy of work she has left us admirably testifies to her success in writing of the child's world.

—Christian H. Moe

BROWN, Palmer. American. Born in Chicago, Illinois, 10 May 1919. Educated at Swarthmore College, Pennsylvania, B.A. 1941; University of Pennsylvania, Philadelphia, M.A. Served in the United States Army Air Corps during World War II: Major. Address: 734 South Latches Lane, Merion, Pennsylvania 19066, U.S.A.

PUBLICATIONS FOR CHILDREN

Fiction

Beyond the Pawpaw Trees. New York, Harper, 1954; London, Methuen, 1956.
The Silver Nutmeg. New York, Harper, 1956; London, Methuen, 1957.
Cheerful. New York, Harper, 1957.
Something for Christmas. New York, Harper, 1958; London, Constable, 1960.
Hickory. New York, Harper, 1978.

*   *   *

Palmer Brown is a miniaturist. He brings to the tradition of animal and domestic fantasy a gift for creating small worlds where conflicts are played out against a background glowing with the colours of oriental carpets, butterfly wings, gypsy caravans, and the rosy pink of pawpaw jelly. He captures with particular intensity the childhood emotions of longing for travel and adventure, the joys of home and security, the excitement of a new friend and a new viewpoint, and the sadness of passage and change. In prose, verse, and pictures

Brown creates small stories of richness and gentle humour.

The two Anna Lavinia books, *Beyond the Pawpaw Trees* and *The Silver Nutmeg*, feature a heroine who journeys to other worlds, to an exotic desert beyond the point at which train tracks meet and to the land on the other side of a still dew-pond. The worlds beyond, like "Wonderland," are full of eating, of flying, of nonsense poetry and parody, of curious creatures, and of cliché and metaphor transformed into literal truth. And, like Alice, Anna Lavinia faces these oddities with courage, courtesy, and an earnest desire to make meaning out of confusion. The stories end with the return home of both Anna Lavinia and her rainbow-chasing father.

The shorter fable-like stories of mice, *Cheerful* and *Hickory*, are also stories of leaving home to confront the dangers and joys of the wide world. They share the gracefulness of the Anna Lavinia tales if not, perhaps, their rich variety. In *Hickory* Brown expands the visual element and much of the book's humour lies in details of the scratchy little drawings. There is also in this later book a sharper edge of sadness as Brown deals with the theme of death, and a sense of uncertainty as he leaves his characters not at home in the warmth of their families but *in medias res*, on a stage in their journey.

The genre of gentle, nature-based fantasy is one fraught with the pitfalls of whimsy and cuteness. Brown avoids all such traps as he creates well-crafted books of quiet wisdom and delight.

—Sarah Ellis

BROWN, Pamela (Beatrice). British. Born in Colchester, Essex, 31 December 1924. Educated at Colchester County High School, 1930–39; Brecon County School, 1939–41; Royal Academy of Dramatic Art, London, 1942–43. Married Donald Masters in 1949 (died 1962); two daughters. Producer, BBC Television, London, 1950–55, Scottish Television, Glasgow, 1956–57, and Granada Television, Manchester and London, 1958–62. *Died 26 January 1989.*

PUBLICATIONS FOR CHILDREN

Fiction

The Swish of the Curtain, illustrated by Newton Whittaker. London, Nelson, 1941; Philadelphia, Winston, 1943; revised edition, Leicester, Brockhampton Press, 1971; revised edition, Aylesbury, Buckinghamshire, Goodchild, 1984.
Maddy Alone, illustrated by Newton Whittaker. London, Nelson, 1945.
Golden Pavements, illustrated by Newton Whittaker. London, Nelson, 1947.
Blue Door Venture, illustrated by Newton Whittaker. London, Nelson, 1949.
To Be a Ballerina and Other Stories, illustrated by Marcia Lane Foster. London, Nelson, 1950.
Family Playbill, illustrated by Marcia Lane Foster. London, Nelson, 1951; as *Family Troupe*, New York, Harcourt Brace, 1953.
The Television Twins, illustrated by Marcia Lane Foster. London, Nelson, 1952.
Harlequin Corner, illustrated by Marcia Lane Foster. London, Nelson, 1953; New York, Meredith Press, 1969.
The Windmill Family, illustrated by Marcia Lane Foster. London, Nelson, 1954; New York, Crowell, 1955.
Louisa, illustrated by Sax. London, Nelson, 1955; New York,

Crowell, 1957.

Maddy Again, illustrated by Drake Brookshaw.   London, Nelson, 1956.

The Bridesmaids, illustrated by Peggy Beetles.   Leicester, Brockhampton Press, 1956; Philadelphia, McKay, 1957.

Showboat Summer, illustrated by Charles Paine.   Leicester, Brockhampton Press, 1957.

Back-stage Portrait, illustrated by Drake Brookshaw.   London, Nelson, 1957.

Understudy, illustrated by Drake Brookshaw.   London, Nelson, 1958.

First House, illustrated by Drake Brookshaw.   London, Nelson, 1959.

As Far as Singapore, illustrated by Peggy Beetles.   Leicester, Brockhampton Press, 1959.

The Other Side of the Street, illustrated by Nathan Mayer.   Leicester, Brockhampton Press, 1965; Chicago, Follett, 1967.

The Girl Who Ran Away, illustrated by Nathan Mayer.   Leicester, Brockhampton Press, 1968.

A Little Universe, illustrated by Faith Jaques.   Leicester, Brockhampton Press, 1970.

Summer Is a Festival.   Leicester, Brockhampton Press, 1972.

Looking after Libby.   Leicester, Brockhampton Press, 1974.

Every Day Is Market Day.   London, Hodder and Stoughton, 1977.

The Finishing School.   Aylesbury, Buckinghamshire, Goodchild, 1984.

Play

The Children of Camp Fortuna.   London, French, 1949.

*

Pamela Brown commented:

(1983) When I started writing I was still a child, and I wrote purely for my own enjoyment. On finding that it amused other children as well I continued to write for their diversion, and have done so ever since.

*   *   *

Pamela Brown wrote *The Swish of the Curtain* when she was still at school, and it has a freshness and liveliness of plot which surely reflect the youthfulness of the writer. Some of the reasons for its success may include the overriding commitment to acting and to the theatre which permeates much of Brown's work, the creation of a group of completely individual characters with whom readers can identify, and an action-packed and often highly entertaining plot.

For children interested in acting it is easy to see the appeal of a plot that consists of a series of drama-related activities: a drama competition, pantomime, open air production, and even a vividly recounted visit to Stratford-on-Avon. The seven children of the three families (Faynes, Halfords, and Darwins) are united in their theatrical ventures whatever the parental and adult opposition. The reader is fascinated by the diversity of character of the seven children involved, each of whom stands out as a definite individual. Some of the adult characters such as the children's friend the Bishop are affectionately portrayed, but others, particularly the children's archenemy Mrs. Potter-Smith, are presented with a degree of ruthlessness which a more mature writer might have diluted. It is a measure of the power and verve of this novel that a revised version was published in 1984. It has been fairly skilfully updated where necessary, although G.C.E. has already been superseded, the coinage was changed in 1971, and little maids belong to another era.

After the merited success of *The Swish of the Curtain,* Brown continued the series with *Maddy Alone, Golden Pavements, Maddy*

Again, and *Blue Door Venture.* The Maddy volumes are shorter than the rest of the series, but equally readable. Of the sequels, *Golden Pavements* is perhaps the most successful, and could rank as an excellent example of a career story with its account, now perhaps unfortunately dated, of life at drama school in London, the rigours of touring, the demands of repertory work, and the changing fortunes of the Darwins, Faynes, and Halfords before returning to Fenchester to form their own professional theatre company.

Brown continued over a period of almost 50 years to make a noteworthy contribution to fiction for children. Having trained for the stage herself, she frequently brought this interest to her novels whether the setting is historical or contemporary. *Family Playbill,* set in the Victorian period, is of particular interest with its account, through the eyes of Lexy Mannering, of the fluctuating fortunes of her actor-manager father, other members of the family, and the actors associated with them as they move from one grim town and seedy lodging to another to offer their repertoire to an often unresponsive audience.

Brown's last work was *The Finishing School,* a somewhat misleading title as it is an absorbing story of adjustment to life in Singapore during World War II. This story reflects the fears of the British in Singapore before Japanese occupation, the courage of a teenage girl Rosemary Langford in adapting to restricted prison camp life, and the inherent goodness of individuals faced with great crisis in their lives. The book portrays the contrast between the sheltered, affluent life of Rosemary's family before the Japanese occupation and the rigours of prison camp life. Strengths and weaknesses of character are painfully evident in the crisis situation.

Whatever her theme, Brown's strong points include the ability to tell an absorbing story, the skill to create convincing characters, an aptitude for highlighting the humour of differing situations and predicaments, and a realistic, perceptive, and unromanticised presentation. Brown used a formidable combination of factors to ensure her success over a long period.

—Anne W. Ellis

———

BROWN, Roy (Frederick).   British.   Born in Vancouver, British Columbia, Canada, 10 December 1921. Married Wendy Landman; two sons and two daughters. Primary school teacher, 1946–69; deputy head, Helen Allison School for autistic children, 1969–75. *Died 14 September 1982.*

PUBLICATIONS FOR CHILDREN

Fiction

A Saturday in Pudney, illustrated by James Hunt.   London, Abelard Schuman, 1966; New York, Macmillan, 1968.

The House on the Green, illustrated by Trevor Parkin.   Edinburgh, Oliver and Boyd, 1967.

Little Brown Mouse, illustrated by Constance Marshall.   London, University of London Press, 1967.

The Wonderful Weathercock, illustrated by Ferelith Eccles Williams.   London, University of London Press, 1967.

The Viaduct, illustrated by James Hunt.   London, Abelard Schuman, 1967; New York, Macmillan, 1968.

The Day of the Pigeons, illustrated by James Hunt.   London, Abelard Schuman, and New York, Macmillan, 1968.

The Saturday Man, illustrated by Trevor Ridley.   London, BBC

Publications, 1969.

The Wapping Warrior, illustrated by James Hunt. London, Chatto and Windus, 1969.

The River, illustrated by James Hunt. London, Abelard Schuman, 1970; as *Escape the River,* New York, Seabury Press, 1972.

The Thunder Pool, illustrated by Gareth Floyd. London, Abelard Schuman, 1971.

The Battle of Saint Street, illustrated by James Hunt. London, Abelard Schuman, and New York, Macmillan, 1971.

Flight of Sparrows. London, Abelard Schuman, 1972; New York, Macmillan, 1973.

Bolt Hole. London, Abelard Schuman, 1973; as *No Through Road,* New York, Seabury Press, 1974.

The White Sparrow. London, Abelard Schuman, 1974; New York, Seabury Press, 1975.

Shep the Second, illustrated by Clifford Bayly. London, Abelard Schuman, 1975.

The Siblings. London, Abelard Schuman, 1975; as *Find Debbie!,* New York, Seabury Press, 1976.

The Million Pound Mouse, illustrated by Joanna Stubbs. London, Abelard Schuman, 1975.

Chubb on the Trail, illustrated by Margaret Belsky. London, Abelard Schuman, 1976.

The Big Test, illustrated by James Hunt. London, Andersen Press, 1976.

The Cage. London, Abelard Schuman, and New York, Seabury Press, 1977.

A Nag Called Wednesday, illustrated by Jeroo Roy. London, Andersen Press, 1977.

Chubb to the Rescue, illustrated by Margaret Belsky. London, Abelard Schuman, 1977.

The Swing of the Gate. London, Andersen Press, and New York, Seabury Press, 1978.

Trojan Rides Again, illustrated by Ivan Hissey. London, Abelard Schuman, 1978.

Undercover Boy, illustrated by Pauline Carr. London, Andersen Press, 1978.

Cover Drive. London, Abelard Schuman, 1979.

Chips and the Crossword Gang, illustrated by Pauline Carr. London, Andersen Press, 1979.

Chubb Catches a Cold, illustrated by Margaret Belsky. London, Abelard Schuman, 1979.

Collision Course. London, Andersen Press, 1980; as *Suicide Course,* New York, Clarion, 1980.

Octopus. London, Andersen Press, 1981.

Chips and the River Rat, illustrated by Victoria Cooper. London, Andersen Press, 1981.

Chips and the Black Moth. London, Andersen Press, 1982.

Plays

Radio Plays: *News Extra!* series, 1973.

Other

A Book of Saints. London, Cassell, 1959.

The Children's Book of Old Testament Stories, illustrated by Hugh T. Marshall. London, Harrap, 1959.

The Children's Pinocchio, illustrated by Sheila Rose. London, Harrap, 1960.

The Children's Heidi, illustrated by Sheila Connelly. London, Harrap, 1963.

Port of Call, illustrated by Jack Trodd. London and New York, Abelard Schuman, 1965.

The Legend of Ulysses, illustrated by Mario Logli and Gabriele Santini. London, Hamlyn, 1965.

The Battle Against Fire, with William Stuart Thomson, illustrated by James Hunt. London, Abelard Schuman, 1966.

Reynard the Fox, illustrated by John Vernon Lord. London and New York, Abelard Schuman, 1969.

Runaway Guy (reader). London, Macmillan, 1980.

*   *   *

Among major children's writers of the 1970's Roy Brown was one particularly open to his times, in tune with their issues and concerns, and while the readability and human interest of his stories guarantee a wide readership the settings indicate a conscious desire to offer the non-academic urban child a means of identification. The years brought development in technique but not deviation from city backgrounds and characters at risk or disadvantage in modern society.

Brown first came to notice with *A Saturday in Pudney* which had an uncomplicated story line—the tracking down of a lost child and subsequent discovery of thieves—a large cast list of neighbourhood children (including two statutory girls, one West Indian), and a satisfying ending. *The Days of the Pigeons* used the twin search theme again, here the children's pursuit of the lost racing pigeons and the attempts of Mousy Lawson, on the run from an approved school, to contact his father, but this time plot structure and detailing moved forward in complexity. *The River* introduced three characters who recur with variations in later stories: the backward, disturbed child; the ex-Borstal bully; the boy who lets himself be led into crime through threats, promises, or his own inadequacies. We meet them in *Bolt Hole,* where Barry drifts into criminal associations because of the failure of other relationships, and in *Flight of Sparrows. The Siblings* centres on the disappearance of a psychotic 14-year old, but here we have moved up in the social scale to a block of flats, home of a local government official and his very desperate family.

One looks to Brown not for stylistic qualities nor for great originality but for good plots, authenticity of setting, and compassionate engagement with characters. Sympathy is shown to the petty criminal, the old and defenceless, the subnormal, who are seen as the victims of an unfeeling society: the settings with which readers grow familiar are London's river and waste grounds, its derelict houses, warehouses, and building sites. At first classified with Hildick, rather dismissively, as a "cement street" writer, Brown emerged as a key figure in the "relevant" children's fiction fashionable in the 1970's. Yet assessment of his contribution is difficult. The sentiment sometimes moves over into sentimentality: judgments like "Inside the big tough guy there's a wee laddie—maybe even a guid laddie—trying to get out" (*The Day of the Pigeons*) grate; the purple passages (see the last sequence of *The White Sparrow*) embarrass because they are out of key with the prevailing tone; characters are too often explained rather than revealed. The critical question is "If the themes weren't so topical would the literary merits be more suspect?" *The Siblings,* Brown's most powerful book, provides a partial answer. More than compensating for the weaknesses are the mastery of pace, the accessibility and humanity of the stories, and the enlargement of the reader's sympathies.

Later work consisted mainly of tough, fast-moving crime stories, such as *Cover Drive,* still with the characteristic Brown touches—the city settings, the interest in the outsider, the exploration of the father/son relationship—or the series of undemanding mysteries centred around Chips Regan, son of a policeman and, if anything, more astute than his father. Andersen Press, who publish the Chips series, have long been concerned to meet the demand for exciting but simple stories, and it would be churlish not to recognize the appeal of these predictable tales. One cannot, however, regard them as having marked an advance in Brown's development as a writer. Of the later books, the most typical—and most revealing of its author's preoccupation—is *Collision Course,* which charts the slow road to recovery of a disturbed and alienated young man, and the problems of the doctors and social workers who tried to help him.

—Peggy Heeks

————

BROWNE, Anthony (Edward Tudor). British. Born in Sheffield, Yorkshire, 11 September 1946. Educated at Whitcliffe Mount Grammar School, Cleckheaton, Yorkshire, 1957–63; Leeds College of Art, B.A. (honours) in graphic design 1967. Married Jane Franklin in 1980; one son and one daughter. Medical artist, Royal Infirmary, University of Manchester, 1968–70; designer, Gordon Fraser Greeting Cards, London, 1971–87. Recipient: Library Association Kate Greenaway Medal, 1983; Maschler award, 1983, 1988; Children's Literature prize (Germany), 1985. Address: The Chalk Garden, The Length, St.-Nicholas-at-Wade, Birchington, Kent CT7 0PJ, England.

PUBLICATIONS FOR CHILDREN (illustrated by the author)

Fiction

Through the Magic Mirror. London, Hamish Hamilton, and New York, Greenwillow, 1976.
A Walk in the Park. London, Hamish Hamilton, 1977.
Bear Hunt. London, Hamish Hamilton, 1979; New York, Atheneum, 1980.
Look What I've Got! London, MacRae, 1980; New York, Knopf, 1988.
Bear Goes to Town. London, Hamish Hamilton, 1982.
Gorilla. London, MacRae, 1983; New York, Knopf, 1985.
Willy the Wimp. London, MacRae, and New York, Knopf, 1984.
Willy the Champ. London, MacRae, and New York, Knopf, 1985.
Piggybook. London, MacRae, and New York, Knopf, 1986.
The Little Bear Book. London, Hamish Hamilton, 1988; New York, Doubleday, 1989.
I Like Books. London, MacRae, and New York, Knopf, 1989.
A Bear-y Tale. London, Hamish Hamilton, 1989.
The Tunnel. London, MacRae, 1989.

Other

Hansel and Gretel (retelling). London, MacRae, 1981; New York, Knopf, 1988.

*

Illustrator: *Knock, Knock! Who's There?* by Sally Grindley, 1985; *The Visitors Who Came to Stay,* 1985, and *Kirsty Knows Best,* 1987, both by Annalena McAfee; *Alice's Adventures in Wonderland* by Lewis Carroll, 1988.

Anthony Browne comments:

I have now produced a body of picture books which are unified by style and themes, and which offer a very particular view of the world of my characters. I try to make my books work on different levels—so what seems a very simple story, appreciated on one level—can also stimulate reflection upon the nature of society and its complex values. While my style is often concerned with the materiality of objects and figures, I assemble them then to refute the possibility of material reality—in this way revealing the interior states of the protagonists. I also try to make them funny!

*   *   *

Anthony Browne has made a major contribution to the development of the picture book, which is now no longer the prerogative of the very young. The "new" picture books for the not-so-young have a wide appeal. They have themes that are challenging and that formerly might well have been associated with adult experience, such as racial or sexual prejudice, conservation, satirical tilts at consumerism, fads and fashions, and the exploration of states of illness, divorce, and death. The picture book artists are equally uncompromising in their styles, which originate in adult art expression such as symbolism, expressionism, Northern European romanticism, and surrealism. Yet these picture books are nevertheless authentic "children's books."

Browne has produced a body of picture books that are unified by style and themes and that are entertaining, demanding, and provocative. The settings are generally domestic, and the stories are of survival strategies. His heroes and heroines, whether human or humanised animals, build bridges between social differences, deal with boredom, loneliness, and jealousy, compensate for spiritual neglect, overcome inappropriate dependency, and when possible, care for others. Browne eschews heavy-handed moral messages and radical transformations of circumstance; he shows the way things are, and how his protagonists respond. In so doing, Browne offers his readers models of good nature, generosity of spirit, pluck, and above all, resourcefulness.

Resourcefulness is the constant value that Browne celebrates. Toby in Browne's first picture book escapes the indifference of his parents with a bold step *Through the Magic Mirror,* which is a metaphor for the frontier between his internal and external worlds. Smudge and Charles are accompanied by a yob and a snob, but win for themselves a brief spell of perfect happiness in *A Walk in the Park.* *Look What I've Got!* tells the story of two boys, Jeremy and Sam. The former is blinded by his material advantages, while the latter has none; however, Sam is more than compensated by the power of his imagination to transform the world. Hannah in *Gorilla,* which won for Browne the first of his two Maschler awards, is encircled by goods and toys rather than the comfort of her father's arms and dreams up a gorilla to kiss. Browne's three picture books for the very young also affirm the value of resourcefulness. Bear, the eponymous hero, draws himself and his friends out of many dangers and difficulties, but his magic pencil is no wand. It has to be used constructively. The Piggots of *Piggybook,* and Willy, whether as wimp or champ, have all demonstrated their inner strengths by the time the boardcovers close upon their adventures. Resourcefulness manifests itself through the exercise of the imagination in all of Browne's characters, and the workings of the imagination are depicted rather than described.

Browne's prose style is flat and undecorated, his verbal texts brief, in contrast to his distinctive pictorial style and complex visual texts. When the two modes are brought together, the composite text is always capable of a wide range of interpretations. The pictures display the thoughts and conflicting emotions that lie behind the drama of events. These revelations of the inner and imaginative life of his characters greatly extend the perspectives Browne offers his reader-viewers.

The characteristics of his pictorial style are a fondness for surrealistic and fantastic imagery with symbolic functions, and a mode of depiction that, with its intense care to selected details and textures, gives the quality of non-photographic realism. Anthony Browne often makes free use of the images of the Belgian painter René Magritte, and occasionally reworks ideas on which the latter has based easel paintings. Examples may be found in *Through the Magic Mirror, A Walk in the Park,* and *Alice's Adventures in Wonderland.* The juxtapositions of ill-assorted objects and fantastic imagery with which Browne creates the surreal states of mind of his characters are a source of visual humour and surprise which keep children searching and turning the picture book pages. Browne's pictures contain a strong element of play.

Browne's rule for play is that any given object appearing out of context or odd in scale has a place in the internal logic of the visual narrative. The skills required for play are patience and close looking—close looking at the object itself, or noticing that same object in other illustrations and making the connection between the object's surface features and associated meanings. Browne can rely on his young beholders to know the rules of "hunt the page." Children like to examine pictures minutely, and objects that appear out of context will draw attention to themselves. His illustrations are rich with transtextual and intertextual allusions as well as occasional allusions to famous paintings. However, within the individual illustration, and the sum total of the turned pages in any particular picture book, all such references have a valid function in the sense of the world being pictured, and are not gratuitous details.

In the relationship between word and image the illustrations have many functions. As well as elaborating, specifying, and amplifying the verbal narrative, Browne's illustrations sometimes exemplify emotional moods at variance with the words. Always, what at first looks like a collision between the two narratives is no perverse accident, but an assertion of the contradictory nature of reality. Browne never hides the truth that social relationships are beset with risks and conflicting feelings, though he manages to make children laugh while conveying that truth.

Mention must be made of two collaborative works: *Hansel and Gretel* by the Brothers Grimm, and Lewis Carroll's *Alice's Adventures in Wonderland*. The former is arguably the most radical of Browne's interpretations, and the latter won the Kurt Maschler award in 1988. In his illustrations for *Hansel and Gretel*, Browne accepts that the folk tale is the expression of the psychic processes of the unconscious, and this one deals with the secret thoughts and fears that children experience when they are about five years old. His pictures display the nature of the emotions and give his readers a chance to recognise them. For this penetrating interpretation, which accords with a Freudian analysis of the tale, Browne employs a symbolic mode which includes sets of recurring images to represent the children's progression and independence, and regression and negative feelings about their mother, who shares the same facial features as those of the witch. Continuous close looking will raise questions about significant shapes, forms, patternings, and colours.

The Carroll collaboration shows Browne concentrating on the dream-vision of Alice's adventures, and using the devices of surrealism as a visual language to reflect Alice's unconscious. For many children who discover Wonderland by way of Browne the visual punnings and puzzles, the element of play, and the overt strangeness consciously experienced when reading the pictures may well have more allure than Carroll's text. Browne, here as in all his work, whether as author-illustrator or collaborator putting himself at the service of another's text, is an artist working for a large audience of all ages. At every level there is something to be enjoyed, considered, and discovered.

—Jane Doonan

BRUCE, Dorita Fairlie. British. Born in 1885. Lived in London for many years. *Died in September 1970.*

PUBLICATIONS FOR CHILDREN

Fiction

The Senior Prefect, illustrated by Wal Paget. London, Oxford University Press, 1920; as *Dimsie Goes to School,* 1933.
Dimsie Moves Up, illustrated by Wal Paget. London, Oxford University Press, 1921.
Dimsie Moves Up Again, illustrated by Gertrude D. Hammond. London, Oxford University Press, 1922.
Dimsie among the Prefects, illustrated by Gertrude D. Hammond. London, Oxford University Press, 1923.
The Girls of St. Bride's, illustrated by Henry Coller. London, Oxford University Press, 1923.
Dimsie Grows Up, illustrated by Henry Coller. London, Oxford University Press, 1924.
Dimsie, Head-Girl, illustrated by M.S. Reeve. London, Oxford University Press, 1925.
That Boarding School Girl, illustrated by Roy. London, Oxford University Press, 1925.
The New Girl and Nancy. London, Oxford University Press, 1926.
Nancy to the Rescue. London, Oxford University Press, 1927.
Dimsie Goes Back, illustrated by M.S. Reeve. London, Oxford University Press, 1927.
The New House-Captain, illustrated by M.S. Reeve. London, Oxford University Press, 1928.
The King's Curate. London, Murray, 1930.
The Best House in the School, illustrated by M.S. Reeve. London, Oxford University Press, 1930.
The Best Bat in the School. London, Oxford University Press, 1931.
The School on the Moor, illustrated by M.S. Reeve. London, Oxford University Press, 1931.
Captain of Springdale, illustrated by Henry Coller. London, Oxford University Press, 1932.
Mistress-Mariner. London, Murray, 1932.
Nancy at St. Bride's, illustrated by M.D. Johnston. London, Oxford University Press, 1933.
The New House at Springdale, illustrated by M.D. Johnston. London, Oxford University Press, 1934.
Nancy in the Sixth. London, Oxford University Press, 1935.
Dimsie Intervenes, illustrated by M.D. Johnston. London, Oxford University Press, 1937.
Nancy Returns to St. Bride's, illustrated by M.D. Johnston. London, Oxford University Press, 1938.
Prefects at Springdale, illustrated by M.D. Johnston. London, Oxford University Press, 1938.
Captain Anne, illustrated by M.D. Johnston. London, Oxford University Press, 1939.
The School in the Woods, illustrated by G.M. Anson. London, Oxford University Press, 1940.
Dimsie Carries On, illustrated by W. Bryce Hamilton. London, Oxford University Press, 1942.
Toby at Tibbs Cross, illustrated by Margaret Horder. London, Oxford University Press, 1943.
Nancy Calls the Tune, illustrated by Margaret Horder. London, Oxford University Press, 1944.
A Laverock Lilting, illustrated by Margaret Horder. London, Oxford University Press, 1945.
Wild Goose Quest. London, Lutterworth Press, 1945.
The Serendipity Shop, illustrated by Margaret Horder. London, Oxford University Press, 1947.
Triffeny, illustrated by Margaret Horder. London, Oxford University Press, 1950.
The Bees on Drumwhinnie, illustrated by Margaret Horder. London, Oxford University Press, 1952.
The Debatable Mound, illustrated by Patricia M. Lambe. London, Oxford University Press, 1953.
The Bartle Bequest, illustrated by Sylvia Green. London, Oxford University Press, 1955.
Sally Scatterbrain, illustrated by Betty Ladler. London, Blackie,

1956.
Sally Again, illustrated by Betty Ladler. London, Blackie, 1959.
Sally's Summer Term, illustrated by Joan Thompson. London, Blackie, 1961.
Dimsie Takes Charge (stories). Aylesbury, Buckinghamshire, Goodchild, 1985.

* * *

Between the first and second world wars Dorita Fairlie Bruce was an extremely popular writer for girls. Her most memorable books—the Dimsie, Nancy, and Springdale series—have school settings and clearly defined, likeable heroines with whom several generations of schoolgirl readers have identified. Bruce has sometimes been dismissed as merely an imitator of Angela Brazil, the creator of the 20th-century girls' school story. There *are* similarities in the intentional—and unconscious—humour of both authors, but Bruce's plots and characterizations have a subtlety and an uncontrived exuberance that are lacking in many of Brazil's stories.

Bruce's main characters grow up gradually during the course of a series: they progress from being naive but endearing juniors to responsible young adults. The well-ordered life of many girls' private schools is convincingly conveyed through descriptions of regular music practices and walks in crocodile, of girls discarding gymslips for silk dresses on special occasions, or standing around for hours on the boundary, fielding at cricket matches. School is shown as the world in microcosm; there is plenty of challenge—in rivalries between individuals and groups, or in the destructive influence of one girl over another. The author is at her best in describing friendships which are "fervent" but "healthy-minded." Strong aversion to excessively sentimental relationships is the keynote of many of Bruce's books. Prefects encourage sport as a potent corrective, while Dimsie and other juniors form an effective and long-lived "Anti-Soppist League" to put down "mushy" behaviour.

Bruce is less successful at manipulating the relationships in which her heroines become involved as adults. Most of them eventually marry, but schoolgirlish anti-soppism complicates the courting process: "Oh Peter....How can you say anything so horrible?," responds Dimsie when the man who she later marries first declares his love.

The authentic backgrounds of Bruce's stories partly derive from her own experiences as a boarding school pupil. She once wrote of her characters: "I go back to school with them...." Bruce was an officer in the Girls' Guildry and her fiction sometimes exploited this organization's character-building propensities.

She possessed a sense of scene and mood. The cosiness of a study tête-à-tête, for instance, is enhanced by its contrast with a winter gale raging outside over the sodden downs. Bruce was Scottish, and several of her books contain evocative descriptions of her country's lochs, islands, and hills. As well as schoolgirls' adventures she wrote several historical short stories and novels.

Bruce's books tended to dismiss intellectuals and progressives as cranks or useless day-dreamers. Through her straightforward schoolgirls she projected her ideals of practical Christianity (which she occasionally expressed as "helping lame dogs over stiles"), patriotism, and esprit de corps. It is a measure of her skill that she did so without obtrusively moralizing. Many adults today feel that her books constructively influenced their childhood and adolescence.

—Mary Cadogan

BRUCE, Mary Grant. Australian. Born in Sale, Victoria, in 1878. Educated at Sale local schools and in Gippsland district, Victoria. Writer and broadcaster for the Australian Imperial Forces during World War I. Married her cousin George E. Bruce in 1914 (died 1949); one son. Lived in England and Ireland, 1913–18 and 1927–39, and in England, 1954–58. From c.1900 children's page editor (as "Cinderella"), *Leader* magazine of Melbourne *Age;* briefly editor, *Woman's World* and *Woman;* broadcaster. Fellow, Royal Society of Literature. *Died 2 July 1958.*

PUBLICATIONS FOR CHILDREN

Fiction

A Little Bush Maid, illustrated by J. Macfarlane. Melbourne and London, Ward Lock, 1910.
Mates at Billabong, illustrated by J. Macfarlane. Melbourne and London, Ward Lock, 1911.
Timothy in Bushland, illustrated by J. Macfarlane. Melbourne and London, Ward Lock, 1912.
Glen Eyre, illustrated by J. Macfarlane. Melbourne and London, Ward Lock, 1912.
Norah of Billabong, illustrated by J. Macfarlane. Melbourne and London, Ward Lock, 1913.
Gray's Hollow, illustrated by Patric Dawson. Melbourne and London, Ward Lock, 1914.
From Billabong to London, illustrated by Fred Leist. Melbourne and London, Ward Lock, 1915.
Jim and Wally, illustrated by Bruno Salmon. Melbourne and London, Ward Lock, 1916.
'Possum, illustrated by J. Macfarlane. Melbourne and London, Ward Lock, 1917.
Dick, illustrated by J. Macfarlane. Melbourne and London, Ward Lock, 1918.
Captain Jim, illustrated by J. Macfarlane. Melbourne and London, Ward Lock, 1919.
Dick Lester of Kurrajong, illustrated by J. Macfarlane. Melbourne and London, Ward Lock, 1920.
Rossiter's Farm, illustrated by Esther Paterson. Melbourne, Whitcombe and Tombs, 1920.
Back to Billabong, illustrated by J. Macfarlane. Melbourne and London, Ward Lock, 1921.
The Cousin from Town, illustrated by Esther Paterson. Melbourne, Whitcombe and Tombs, 1922.
The Twins of Emu Plains, illustrated by Dewar Mills. Melbourne and London, Ward Lock, 1923.
Billabong's Daughter, illustrated by J. Macfarlane. Melbourne and London, Ward Lock, 1924.
The Houses of the Eagle, illustrated by Harold Copping. Melbourne and London, Ward Lock, 1925.
Hugh Stanford's Luck. Sydney, Cornstalk, 1925.
The Tower Rooms, illustrated by Dewar Mills. Melbourne and London, Ward Lock, 1926.
Robin, illustrated by Edgar A. Holloway. Sydney, Cornstalk, 1926; London, Angus and Robertson, 1938.
Billabong Adventurers, illustrated by J. Macfarlane. Melbourne and London, Ward Lock, 1927.
Anderson's Jo. Sydney, Cornstalk, 1927.
Golden Fiddles, illustrated by Dewar Mills. Melbourne and London, Ward Lock, 1928.
The Happy Traveller, illustrated by Laurie Taylor. Melbourne and London, Ward Lock, 1929.
Bill of Billabong, illustrated by A.A. Kent. Melbourne and London, Ward Lock, 1931.
Road to Adventure, illustrated by Laurie Taylor. Melbourne and

London, Ward Lock, 1932; New York, Minton Balch, 1933.
Billabong's Luck, illustrated by Laurie Taylor. Melbourne and London, Ward Lock, 1933.
"Seahawk," illustrated by J.F. Campbell. Melbourne and London, Ward Lock, 1934.
Wings above Billabong, illustrated by J.F. Campbell. Melbourne and London, Ward Lock, 1935.
Circus Ring, illustrated by J.F. Campbell. Melbourne and London, Ward Lock, 1936; New York, Putnam, 1937.
Billabong Gold, illustrated by J.F. Campbell. Melbourne and London, Ward Lock, 1937.
Told by Peter, illustrated by J.F. Campbell. Melbourne and London, Ward Lock, 1938.
Son of Billabong, illustrated by J.F. Campbell. Melbourne and London, Ward Lock, 1939.
Peter and Co., illustrated by J.F. Campbell. Melbourne and London, Ward Lock, 1940.
Karalta. Sydney and London, Angus and Robertson, 1941.
Billabong Riders. Melbourne and London, Ward Lock, 1942.

Other

The Stone Axe of Burkamukk: Aboriginal Legends Retold, illustrated by J. Macfarlane. Melbourne and London, Ward Lock, 1922.

PUBLICATIONS FOR ADULTS

Other

The Power Within: Four Broadcast Talks. Privately printed, 1941.

*

Critical Studies: *Seven Little Billabongs: The World of Ethel Turner and Mary Grant Bruce* by Brenda Niall, Melbourne, Melbourne University Press, 1979; *Billabong's Author: The Life of Mary Grant Bruce* by Alison Alexander, Sydney, Angus and Robertson, 1979; London, Angus and Robertson, 1980.

* * *

Mary Grant Bruce not only had a devoted following in her own country but many young English readers first learned about the hazards of the Australian bush, its strange bandicoots, wombats, kangaroos, and native bears, its exotic bell-birds and the laughing jackass, and other indigenous creatures, including the mythical Bunyip, through well-thumbed copies of her popular *Timothy in Bushland.* Others were introduced to aboriginal legends through *The Stone Axe of Burkamukk.* Most of her books were first published in England, but in the period between the first and second world wars many an Australian home gathered on its bookshelves, for family reading, a collection of the famous Billabong books, a series which began with *A Little Bush Maid* in 1910.

The Lintons of Billabong were a motherless family who lived on a prosperous station property in the north of Victoria, 17 miles from Cunjee, the nearest town. Billabong is a comfortably secure world in microcosm. Threat is usually external in the form of natural disaster—drought, flood, or bushfire—or of lawless creatures such as vagrant swagmen, cattle duffers, or gold thieves. The world outside only occasionally casts its shadow as when the Linton men are involved in World War I. But Billabong is always there, its wide shady verandahs, its long lagoon in which to swim, its creek for fishing which can dry up or run high, its scrub through which cattle roam, and its open paddocks across which to canter. Against this

background Norah Linton, the little bush maid, grows from childhood to womanhood; a fresh open country girl—stalwart yet feminine; resourceful yet lovingly dependent on her menfolk. Her older brother Jim, too, is proudly upright and dependable, and Norah is to marry his boisterous mate, Wally Meadows, who "laughed at life just as he laughed at Death, when it came near to touching him." Only when trouble threatens the Billabong folk does life become serious. This stable family group benignly ruled over by Mr. Linton embraces the homestead servants and the station hands. Brownie, ample, motherly, astutely aware that her cooking will hold the family together in any crisis and "regarded by the station as a species of stout angel in petticoats," and Murty O'Toole, the dry-mouthed Irish stockman, are closest to the family. But the arch-enemies Hogg the gardener and Lee Wing his Chinese help, along with Black Billy the stockboy, are all treated with the same respect as is meted to all visitors and to the many lame-dogs whom the Lintons befriend over the years.

The series reflects the social and economic climate of Australia which weathered both a world war and a depression. Gold is discovered on the property, and to meet expanding needs the Lintons turn to their own air transport in *Wings above Billabong.*

Mary Grant Bruce gives a good deal of explanatory background information, but because she is a first-class storyteller, she is able to regulate the pace of her narrative to her readers' interests. Her characters are made of stern stuff but are not unsentimental, perhaps predictable as well as being reliable. Their conflicts and alarms are always transitory and there is always a happy issue from any kind of adversity. Hence her plots are melodramatic rather than tragic. But her many books epitomised, even if they idealised, a recognisably outback Australian life-style of warm-hearted characters committed to the ideal of "mateship."

—H.M. Saxby

BUCKERIDGE, Anthony. British. Born in London, 20 June 1912. Educated at Seaford College, Sussex; University College, University of London. Served in the National Fire Service, 1939–45. Married 1) Sylvia Brown; 2) Eileen Selby; two sons and one daughter. Teacher, St. Lawrence College, Ramsgate, Kent, 1945–50; actor and broadcaster. Agent: John Goodchild L.R. Associates, 10 Mandeville Road, Aylesbury, Buckinghamshire HP21 8AA. Address: East Crink, Barcombe Mills, Lewes, Sussex BN8 5BL, England.

PUBLICATIONS FOR CHILDREN

Fiction

Jennings Goes to School. London, Collins, 1950.
Jennings Follows a Clue. London, Collins, 1951.
Jennings' Little Hut. London, Collins, 1951.
Jennings and Darbishire. London, Collins, 1952.
A Funny Thing Happened! London, Lutterworth Press, 1953.
Rex Milligan's Busy Term, illustrated by Mazure. London, Lutterworth Press, 1953.
Jennings' Diary. London, Collins, 1953.
According to Jennings. London, Collins, 1954.
Our Friend Jennings. London, Collins, 1955.
Rex Milligan Raises the Roof, illustrated by Mazure. London, Lutterworth Press, 1955.
Rex Milligan Holds Forth, illustrated by Mazure. London,

Lutterworth Press, 1955.
Thanks to Jennings.   London, Collins, 1957.
Take Jennings, For Instance, illustrated by Mays.   London, Collins, 1958.
Jennings, As Usual, illustrated by Mays.   London, Collins, 1959.
The Trouble with Jennings, illustrated by Mays.   London, Collins, 1960.
Just Like Jennings.   London, Collins, 1961.
Rex Milligan Reporting, illustrated by Mazure.   London, Lutterworth Press, 1961.
Leave It to Jennings, illustrated by Mays.   London, Collins, 1963.
Jennings, Of Course!, illustrated by Mays.   London, Collins, 1964.
Especially Jennings!, illustrated by Mays.   London, Collins, 1965.
A Bookful of Jennings.   London, Collins, 1966; revised edition, as *The Best of Jennings,* 1972.
Jennings Abounding, illustrated by Mays.   London, Collins, 1967.
Jennings in Particular, illustrated by Mays.   London, Collins, 1968.
Trust Jennings!, illustrated by Mays.   London, Collins, 1969.
The Jennings Report, illustrated by Mays.   London, Collins, 1970.
Typically Jennings!   London, Collins, 1971.
Speaking of Jennings.   London, Collins, 1973.
Jennings at Large.   London, Armada, 1977.

Plays

Draw the Line Somewhere (produced Ramsgate, Kent, 1948).
Happy Christmas, Jennings (produced Lewes, Sussex, 1969).
Jennings Abounding!, music by Hector Cortes and William Gomez (produced Lewes, Sussex, 1978).   London, French, 1980.
It Happened in Hamelin, music by Corin Buckeridge (produced Lewes, Sussex, 1980).
The Cardboard Conspiracy, music by Corin Buckeridge (produced Edinburgh, 1985).
Scaling the Cock (produced Chichester, 1986).

Radio Plays: *Jennings at School* series, 1948–74; *A Funny Thing Happened!*, 1963; *Liz*, 1974.

Television Series: *Rex Milligan*, 1954–55; *Jennings,* 1958, 1966.

Other

Editor, *Stories for Boys 1–2.*   London, Faber, 2 vols., 1957–65.
Editor, *In and Out of School: Stories.*   London, Faber, 1958.

*   *   *

Anthony Buckeridge's small schoolboy hero Jennings is something of a phenomenon. The series of books about him began to appear in the early 1950's, but Jennings and his bespectacled friend Darbishire, agelessly fixed at about 10 years old, are still popular, in spite of their attending the kind of establishment preparatory school unfamiliar to most of the readers of their adventures.

It may be, however, that the sheer artificiality of the enclosed boarding-school background contributes to the continued popularity of these stories. Farce flourishes in an atmosphere where strict rules of conduct are laid down, and broken. And Buckeridge struck a rich vein of schoolboy humour with Jennings, Darbishire, and their friends, tolerant Mr. Carter and choleric Mr. Wilkins, pompous headmaster Mr. Pemberton-Oakes, famous visiting Old Boy General Merridew, and the rest. It is a style of humour which has much in common with Richmal Crompton's William, with P.G. Wodehouse's school stories (and some of his later novels), with the howlers of Sellar and Yeatman's *1066 and All That* and Williams and Searle's *Down with Skool* books: witness the difficulties of Jennings and

Darbishire trying to converse with a friendly crew of French fishermen, Darbishire being unable to remember any French at all but "a passage which had caused him some trouble in class the previous day. So far as he had been able to judge, the translation was: *The gentleman who wears one green hat approaches himself all of a sudden.*"

The farcical situations of the books are neatly contrived, with Jennings inevitably getting caught in a web of his own mistaken but well-intentioned weaving. But what really counts is the back-chat among the boys themselves. Slang such as "wizard" and "supersonic," "bate" and "bish" may date, but Buckeridge's feelings for the way small boys talk and argue and amiably insult each other does not.

Moreover, the lasting popularity of the Jennings books is not just an interesting but a cheering phenomenon in the Britain of the 1980's, where there is growing anxiety about ordinary standards of literacy among schoolchildren, because to enjoy the wilful verbal misunderstandings and intentionally dreadful puns of Jennings and his friends, the reader undoubtedly needs to be literate himself, and to quite a high degree. To get the point of Jennings's malapropism when he tries to explain to the Head that a flippant verse in his textbook was "meant meteorologically" a child has to have some knowledge of the word "metaphorically." Altogether, it is good to see this very English type of humorous school story still enjoyed; educational methods and slang may change, but small boys and their healthy sense of comedy do not.

—Anthea Bell

———

BULL, Angela (Mary, née Leach). British. Born in Halifax, Yorkshire, 28 September 1936. Educated at Badminton School, Bristol, 1948–54; Edinburgh University (Mackenzie prize, 1959), 1955–59, M.A. (honours) in English 1959; St. Hugh's College, Oxford, 1959–61. Married Martin Wells Bull in 1962; one son and one daughter. English teacher, Casterton School, Kirkby Lonsdale, Westmorland, 1961–62; assistant, Medieval Manuscript Room, Bodleian Library, Oxford, 1962–63. Recipient: Children's Rights Workshop Other award, 1980. Agent: Murray Pollinger, 4 Garrick Street, London WC2E 9BH. Address: The Vicarage, Hall Bank Drive, Bingley, West Yorkshire BD16 4BZ, England.

PUBLICATIONS FOR CHILDREN

Fiction

The Friend with a Secret, illustrated by Lynton Lamb.   London, Collins, 1965; New York, Holt Rinehart, 1967.
Wayland's Keep, illustrated by Shirley Hughes.   London, Collins, 1966; New York, Holt Rinehart, 1967.
Child of Ebenezer.   London, Collins, 1974.
Treasure in the Fog, illustrated by Joanna Worth.   London, Collins, 1976.
Griselda.   London, Collins, 1977.
The Doll in the Wall, illustrated by Gareth Floyd.   London, Collins, 1978.
The Bicycle Parcel, illustrated by Jane Paton.   London, Hamish Hamilton, 1980.
The Accidental Twins, illustrated by Jill Bennett.   London, Faber,

1982.
A Hat for Emily, illustrated by Sue Dolman. London, Collins, 1986.
The Visitors, illustrated by Valerie Littlewood. London, Hamish Hamilton, 1986.
Green Gloves, illustrated by Thelma Lambert. London, Blackie, 1987.
A Wish at the Baby's Grave. London, Hippo, 1988.
Up the Attic Stairs. London, Virago, 1989.

Other

The Machine Breakers: The Story of the Luddites. London, Collins, 1980.
Anne Frank, illustrated by Stephen Gulbis. London, Hamish Hamilton, 1984.
Florence Nightingale, illustrated by Karen Heywood. London, Hamish Hamilton, 1985.
Marie Curie, illustrated by Edward Mortelmans. London, Hamish Hamilton, 1986.
Elizabeth Fry, illustrated by Edward Mortelmans. London, Hamish Hamilton, 1987.

PUBLICATIONS FOR ADULTS

Other

Nineteenth Century Children: Heroes and Heroines in English Children's Stories 1780–1900, with Gillian Avery. London, Hodder and Stoughton, 1965.
Noel Streatfeild: A Biography. London, Collins, 1984.

*

Angela Bull comments:

Because history sparks my imagination, nearly all my stories have a historical, or partly historical, background. My earliest stories were mainly Victorian. I spent two years researching Victorian children's books, and considerably longer building up a collection of them, so I had plenty of material to draw on. Social conditions were such that Victorian children did not have the independence necessary for active adventures. Their dramas tended to be inward, especially the drama of personal relationships; and this was the theme of most of my early books.

Moving from fiction to biography, I thought it was important to stress the ideas and ideals which motivated my subjects; and so, when I recently turned back to fiction, I found myself continuing to write about people and ideas, particularly in *Up the Attic Stairs,* which traces 80 years of the women's movement, as illustrated in the lives of four generations of provincial girls.

*   *   *

In the last 10 years Angela Bull has diversified her work in a way that could not easily have been foreseen in the 1960's and 1970's. Apart from non-fiction, her output at the present time comprises five longish, meticulously structured novels with fairly obvious moral or social implications; four short but still carefully plotted and purposeful stories for children in the middle age ranges; and three very simple, generously illustrated stories for the youngest group of readers. Eight of these 12 books are set wholly or partly in Victorian or Edwardian times, and all, with the exception of *The Bicycle Parcel* and possibly *The Doll in the Wall,* are much more likely to appeal to girls than to boys.

Not much need be said about the most junior group (*Green Gloves,*

The Bicycle Parcel, and *The Accidental Twins*). All are gentle mini-comedies with realistic modern backgrounds and, especially in *The Accidental Twins,* just a hint or two about personal behaviour. At a slightly more demanding level there is a ghost story with rather uncertain sidelights on racial prejudice (*A Wish at the Baby's Grave*); a Victorian foggy-night adventure, not very probable and slightly marred by an over-prominent moral lesson (*Treasure in the Fog*); a domestic episode from one of Queen Victoria's Scottish tours, this time totally convincing and rich in atmosphere, with its morality embedded in the action (*The Visitors*); and, somewhat broader in scope than the other three, a modern holiday adventure story, *The Doll in the Wall.* Within the limits of 112 pages Bull here contrives to set up and resolve a genuine mystery, involving nine or 10 distinct characters and providing quite digestible food for thought about the hazards of insensitive do-gooding.

Among the five full-length novels, the most recent, *Up the Attic Stairs,* stands very much apart from the others. Bull's approach here is quite openly didactic, her aims being to trace the development of feminist movements in the present century and encourage readers to think about the role of women in society. With its non-chronological method, rather stereotyped characters (with one or two exceptions), and constantly changing viewpoints this book certainly calls for a high level of concentration; those who do have the stamina to persist with it may gain something in the way of social awareness or empathy. By any yardstick it is more demanding than any of the others in this group, though all have quite complicated plots and large casts of characters. The two shortest, *Griselda* and *Wayland's Keep,* should certainly appeal to girls from a wide range of ages who have an interest in tracing their ancestors, since family trees are a major concern in both. In spite of its two heroines' traumatic ups and downs, *Griselda* is basically a heartwarming story of town and country, with a strong element of fairytale romance in the second half, rather reminiscent of Frances Hodgson Burnett. *Wayland's Keep* is more down-to-earth, and presents a sharp contrast between the squabbles and trivial anxieties of a modern family and the gradually revealed tragedy of their Victorian ancestors. Both are good stories of their kind, with the moralistic strain rarely obtruding too far, but in my opinion the two remaining novels with their greater range and depth of characters are the most notable of all. *The Friend with a Secret* recreates convincingly the divisions of society and the pervasive influence of religion in a Victorian seaport, but for child readers there is also an ingenious plot, a succession of dramatic incidents, and a memorable heroine in Olivia Lang, whose oppressive household provides a first glimpse of the Children of Ebenezer sect. In *Child of Ebenezer,* published nine years later, Bull seems to me to be at her very best. Here there is a political as well as a religious dimension as the Anglo-Irish conflict impinges on children and adults in three contrasting families. Sombre and even tragic elements are part of the pattern, but in the best Victorian tradition courage and loyalty have their reward in the end.

—Alasdair K.D. Campbell

———

BULLA, Clyde Robert. American. Born in King City, Missouri, 9 January 1914. Educated at Bray school, 1920–26; King City High School, 1926–27. Farmer until 1942; linotype operator and columnist, *Tri-County News,* King City, 1942–47. Recipient: George G. Stone Center for Children's Books award, 1968; Christopher award, 1972. Agent: Bill Berger Associates, 444 East 58th Street, New York, New York 10022. Address: 1230 Las Flores Drive, Los

Angeles, California 90041, U.S.A.

PUBLICATIONS FOR CHILDREN

Fiction

The Donkey Cart, illustrated by Lois Lenski. New York, Crowell, 1946.
Riding the Pony Express, illustrated by Grace Paull. New York, Crowell, 1948.
The Secret Valley, illustrated by Grace Paull. New York, Crowell, 1949.
Surprise for a Cowboy, illustrated by Grace Paull. New York, Crowell, 1950.
A Ranch for Danny, illustrated by Grace Paull. New York, Crowell, 1951.
Johnny Hong of Chinatown, illustrated by Dong Kingman. New York, Crowell, 1952.
Song of St. Francis, illustrated by Valenti Angelo. New York, Crowell, 1952.
Star of Wild Horse Canyon, illustrated by Grace Paull. New York, Crowell, 1953.
Eagle Feather, illustrated by Tom Two Arrows. New York, Crowell, 1953.
Squanto, Friend of the White Men, illustrated by Peter Burchard. New York, Crowell, 1954; as *Squanto, Friend of the Pilgrims,* New York, Crowell, 1969.
Down the Mississippi, illustrated by Peter Burchard. New York, Crowell, 1954.
White Sails to China, illustrated by Robert Henneberger. New York, Crowell, 1955.
The Poppy Seeds, illustrated by Jean Charlot. New York, Crowell, 1955.
John Billington, Friend of Squanto, illustrated by Peter Burchard. New York, Crowell, 1956.
The Sword in the Tree, illustrated by Paul Galdone. New York, Crowell, 1956.
Old Charlie, illustrated by Paul Galdone. New York, Crowell, 1957.
Ghost Town Treasure, illustrated by Don Freeman. New York, Crowell, 1957.
Pirate's Promise, illustrated by Peter Burchard. New York, Crowell, 1958.
The Valentine Cat, illustrated by Leonard Weisgard. New York, Crowell, 1959.
Three-Dollar Mule, illustrated by Paul Lantz. New York, Crowell, 1960.
The Sugar Pear Tree, illustrated by Taro Yashima. New York, Crowell, 1961.
Benito, illustrated by Valenti Angelo. New York, Crowell, 1961.
Viking Adventure, illustrated by Douglas Gorsline. New York, Crowell, 1963.
Indian Hill, illustrated by James Spanfeller. New York, Crowell, 1963.
White Bird, illustrated by Leonard Weisgard. New York, Crowell, 1966; London, Macdonald, 1969.
The Ghost of Windy Hill, illustrated by Don Bolognese. New York, Crowell, 1968.
Mika's Apple Tree: A Story of Finland, illustrated by Des Asmussen. New York, Crowell, 1968.
The Moon Singer, illustrated by Trina Schart Hyman. New York, Crowell, 1969.
New Boy in Dublin: A Story of Ireland, illustrated by Jo Polseno. New York, Crowell, 1969.
Pocahontas and the Strangers, illustrated by Peter Burchard. New York, Crowell, 1971.
Open the Door and See All the People, illustrated by Wendy Watson. New York, Crowell, 1972.
Dexter, illustrated by Glo Coalson. New York, Crowell, 1973.
The Wish at the Top, illustrated by Chris Conover. New York, Crowell, 1974.
Shoeshine Girl, illustrated by Leigh Grant. New York, Crowell, 1975.
Marco Moonlight, illustrated by Julia Noonan. New York, Crowell, 1976.
The Beast of Lor, illustrated by Ruth Sanderson. New York, Crowell, 1977.
Keep Running, Allen!, illustrated by Satomi Ichikawa. New York, Crowell, 1978.
Conquista!, with Michael Syson, illustrated by Ronald Himler. New York, Crowell, 1978.
Last Look, illustrated by Emily McCully. New York, Crowell, 1979.
Daniel's Duck, illustrated by Joan Sandin. New York, Harper, 1979.
The Stubborn Old Woman, illustrated by Anne Rockwell. New York, Crowell, 1980.
My Friend the Monster, illustrated by Michele Chessare. New York, Crowell, 1980.
A Lion to Guard Us, illustrated by Michele Chessare. New York, Crowell, 1981.
Almost a Hero, illustrated by Ben Stahl. New York, Dutton, 1981.
Poor Boy, Rich Boy, illustrated by Marcia Sewall. New York, Harper, 1982.
Dandelion Hill, illustrated by Bruce Degen. New York, Dutton, 1982.
Charlie's House, illustrated by Arthur Dorros. New York, Crowell, 1983.
The Cardboard Crown, illustrated by Michele Chessare. New York, Crowell, 1984.
The Chalk Box Kid, illustrated by Thomas B. Allen. New York, Random House, 1987.
Singing Sam, illustrated by Susan Magurn. New York, Random House, 1989.

Other

A Dog Named Penny (reader), illustrated by Kate Seredy. Boston, Ginn, 1955.
Stories of Favorite Operas, illustrated by Robert Galster. New York, Crowell, 1959.
A Tree Is a Plant, illustrated by Lois Lignell. New York, Crowell, 1960; London, A. and C. Black, 1962.
What Makes a Shadow?, illustrated by Adrienne Adams. New York, Crowell, 1962; London, A. and C. Black, 1965.
The Ring and the Fire: Stories from Wagner's Niebelung Operas, illustrated by Clare and John Ross. New York, Crowell, 1962.
St. Valentine's Day, illustrated by Valenti Angelo. New York, Crowell, 1965.
More Stories of Favorite Operas, illustrated by Joseph Low. New York, Crowell, 1965.
Lincoln's Birthday, illustrated by Ernest Crichlow. New York, Crowell, 1966.
Washington's Birthday, illustrated by Don Bolognese. New York, Crowell, 1967.
Flowerpot Gardens, illustrated by Henry Evans. New York, Crowell, 1967.
Stories of Gilbert and Sullivan Operas, illustrated by James and Ruth McCrea. New York, Crowell, 1968.
Jonah and the Great Fish, illustrated by Helga Aichinger. New York, Crowell, 1970.

Joseph the Dreamer, illustrated by Gordon Laite. New York, Crowell, 1971.
A Grain of Wheat: A Writer Begins. Boston, Godine, 1985.

Translator, *Noah and the Rainbow,* by Max Bollinger, illustrated by Helga Aichinger. New York, Crowell, 1972.

PUBLICATIONS FOR ADULTS

Novel

These Bright Young Dreams. Philadelphia, Penn, 1941.

*

Manuscript Collections: Kerlan Collection, University of Minnesota, Minneapolis; University of Oregon Library, Eugene; de Grummond Collection, University of Southern Mississippi, Hattiesburg.

Music: incidental music for plays—*The Bean-Pickers,* 1952, *A Change of Heart,* 1952, and *Strangers in a Strange Land,* 1952, all by Lois Lenski; songs—*We Are Thy Children,* 1952, *Songs of Mr. Small,* 1954, *Songs of the City,* 1956, *Up to Six,* 1956, *At Our House,* 1959, and *When I Grow Up,* 1960, all by Lois Lenski.

Clyde Robert Bulla comments:

When I was a boy I made up my own stories. Some were high adventure, with buried treasure, perilous journeys, and hair-breadth escapes. Some were quiet, about everyday people like those I knew. Others were about the mysteries of life—things that puzzled and haunted me and left me with a sense of wonder. These are the stories I began to write a long time afterward and the stories I am writing now.

*   *   *

Clyde Robert Bulla attracts young people to his books by building his plots quickly and believably, using simple language without condescension. He skillfully interweaves the plot with a sense of good and evil, right and wrong. The story of *White Bird* is contingent upon love as known and interpreted by the foundling boy and by the seemingly stern farmer who raises him. Plot develops from their relationship.

In *The Moon Singer* complex ideas are described in simple language. The peasant boy sings because he must, and sings especially well when the moon is full. His need to sing might be a microcosm of the need of any artist, the inner drive to create in spite of, rather than because of, society. There is the gentle yet persuasive suggestion that this is more than just a medieval tale of a boy who felt compelled to sing.

Shoeshine Girl is the story of stubborn and defiant 10-year-old Sarah Ida who must have money in her pocket and goes to work for Al, the shoeshine man. Bulla retains his direct style, and Sarah Ida's growth toward self-acceptance and a concern for other people is believable and sound.

The Stubborn Old Woman evokes the folktale tradition. She refuses to leave her endangered cliff farm or to show any sympathy for the orphan girl who determinedly seeks the old woman's guardianship for herself and her eight siblings. The happy solution to both problems and the cadence of language give texture to the tale.

Charlie in *Charlie's House* runs away from his peasant family, hoping to find a better life in London. He is caught, sold into white slavery, and sent to America as an indentured servant. His first master loses Charlie's bond in a card game with a cousin, a cruel man.

Charlie's pluck and determination help him in his new life, even in his attempt to escape. Bulla recreates life in the early 19th century with a clear sense of time and place. Charlie emerges as a credible boy whose life and adventures are well placed and blend well with the background Bulla provides.

Gregory is *The Chalk Box Kid.* When his father loses his job the family must move and Gregory has to share his room with Uncle Max, an unlikable man. He has no place of his own, but finds his escape in an abandoned building where he creates a fanciful chalk garden on the walls, the start of a possible resolution of his problems. At school, where his imagination and artistic ability are recognized and appreciated, Gregory finds that life need not be so grim. The teachers' compassionate interest and the friendliness of the students bolster his spirit. The sensitive picture of a struggling blue-collar family lends credence to the story. Bulla blends fantasy and reality smoothly and effectively, and provides a moving experience for the reader.

Whether Bulla is retelling stories of the opera or the Old Testament, or writing historical fiction or stories that reflect different cultures or inner conflict, there is a satisfying consistency in his treatment of each theme. His more than 60 books reveal integrity and respect for his audience.

—Mae Durham Roger

———

BUNTING, A.E. See **BUNTING, Eve.**

———

BUNTING, (Anne) Eve(lyn, née Bolton). Also writes as Evelyn Bolton; A.E. Bunting. American. Born in Maghera, County Londonderry, Northern Ireland, 19 December 1928; emigrated to the United States, 1958; became citizen, 1967. Educated at Methodist College, Belfast, 1936–45; Queen's University, Belfast, 1945–47. Married Edward Bunting in 1951; one daughter and two sons. Recipient: Society of Children's Book Writers Golden Kite award, 1976. Address: 1512 Rose Villa Street, Pasadena, California 91106, U.S.A.

PUBLICATIONS FOR CHILDREN

Fiction

A Gift for Lonny, illustrated by Robert Quackenbush. Lexington, Massachusetts, Ginn, 1973.
Box, Fox, Ox, and the Peacock, illustrated by Leslie Morrill. Lexington, Massachusetts, Ginn, 1974.
The Wild One, illustrated by Leo Summers. New York, Scholastic, 1974.
We Need a Bigger Zoo!, illustrated by Bob Barner. Lexington, Massachusetts, Ginn, 1974.
The Once-a-Year Day, illustrated by W.T. Mars. Chicago, Children's Press, 1974.
Barney the Beard, illustrated by Imero Gobbato. New York, Parents' Magazine Press, 1975; London, Warne, 1978.
The Dinosaur Machines (*The Day of the Dinosaurs, Death of a Dinosaur, The Dinosaur Trap, Escape from Tyrannosaurus*), illustrated by Judith Leo. St. Paul, Minnesota, EMC, 4 vols., 1975.

No Such Things...? (The Creature of Cranberry Cove, The Demon, The Ghost, The Tongue of the Ocean), illustrated by Scott Earle. St. Paul, Minnesota, EMC, 4 vols., 1976.

Josefina Finds the Prince, illustrated by Jan Palmer.   Champaign, Illinois, Garrard, 1976.

Blacksmith at Blueridge, photographs by Peter Fine.   New York, Scholastic, 1976.

Skateboard Saturday, photographs by Richard Hutchings.   New York, Scholastic, 1976.

One More Flight, illustrated by Diane de Groat.   New York and London, Warne, 1976.

Skateboard Four, illustrated by Phil Kantz.   Chicago, Whitman, 1976.

Winter's Coming, illustrated by Howard Knotts.   New York, Harcourt Brace, 1977.

The Big Cheese, illustrated by Sal Murdocca.   New York, Macmillan, 1977; London, Macmillan, 1980.

Cop Camp, photographs by Richard Hutchings.   New York, Scholastic, 1977.

Ghost of Summer.   New York, Warne, 1977.

Creative Science Fiction (Day of the Earthlings, The Followers, The Island of One, The Mirror Planet, The Robot People, The Space People, The Undersea People, the Mask), illustrated by Don Hendricks.   Mankato, Minnesota, Creative Education, 8 vols., 1978.

Creative Romance (Fifteen; For Always; The Girl in the Painting; Just Like Everyone Else; Nobody Knows But Me; Oh, Rick; A Part of the Dream; Survival Camp!; Two Different Girls; Maggie the Freak), illustrated by Robert Gadbois.   Mankato, Minnesota, Creative Education, 10 vols., 1978.

The Big Find, photographs by Richard Hutchings.   Mankato, Minnesota, Creative Education, 1978.

Magic and the Night River, illustrated by Allen Say.   New York, Harper, 1978.

Going Against Cool Calvin, illustrated by Don Brautigan.   New York, Scholastic, 1978.

The Haunting of Kildoran Abbey.   New York, Warne, 1978; London, Warne, 1979.

The Big, Red Barn, illustrated by Howard Knotts.   New York, Harcourt Brace, 1979.

The Cloverdale Switch.   New York, Lippincott, 1979.

Yesterday's Island, illustrated by Stephen Gammell.   New York, Warne, 1979.

Mr. Pride's Umbrella, illustrated by Maggie Ling.   London, Warne, 1980.

The Robot Birthday, illustrated by Marie DeJohn.   New York, Dutton, 1980.

Demetrius and the Golden Goblet, illustrated by Michael Hague.   New York, Harcourt Brace, 1980.

Terrible Things, illustrated by Stephen Gammell.   New York, Harper, 1980.

St. Patrick's Day in the Morning, illustrated by Jan Brett.   Boston, Houghton Mifflin, 1980.

Blackbird Singing, illustrated by Stephen Gammell.   New York, Macmillan, 1980.

The Empty Window, illustrated by Judy Clifford.   New York, Warne, 1980.

The Skate Patrol [Rides Again, and the Mystery Writer], illustrated by Don Madden.   Chicago, Whitman, 3 vols., 1980–82.

Goose Dinner, illustrated by Howard Knotts.   New York, Harcourt Brace, 1981.

The Waiting Game.   New York, Lippincott, 1981.

The Spook Birds, illustrated by Blanche Sims.   Chicago, Whitman, 1981.

The Happy Funeral, illustrated by Vo-Dinh Mai.   New York, Harper, 1982.

The Ghosts of Departure Point.   New York, Lippincott, 1982.

The Traveling Men of Ballycoo, illustrated by Kaethe Zemach.   New York, Harcourt Brace, 1983.

The Valentine Bears, illustrated by Jan Brett.   New York, Clarion, 1983.

Karen Kepplewhite Is the World's Best Kisser.   New York, Clarion, 1983.

Clancy's Coat, illustrated by Lorinda Bryan Cauley.   New York, Warne, 1984.

The Ghost Behind Me.   New York, Archway, 1984.

If I Asked You, Would You Stay?   New York, Lippincott, 1984.

Jane Martin, Dog Detective, illustrated by Amy Schwartz.   New York, Harcourt Brace, 1984.

The Man Who Could Call Down Owls, illustrated by Charles Mikolaycak.   New York, Macmillan, 1984.

Monkey in the Middle, illustrated by Lynn Munsinger.   New York, Harcourt Brace, 1984.

Someone Is Hiding on Alcatraz Island.   New York, Clarion, 1984; London, Fontana, 1986.

Strange Things Happen in the Woods.   New York, Archway, 1984.

Surrogate Sister.   New York, Lippincott, 1984; London, Hodder and Stoughton, 1985; as *Mother, How Could You*, New York, Simon and Schuster, 1986.

Face at the Edge of the World.   New York, Clarion, 1985; London, Fontana, 1987.

The Haunting of Safekeep.   New York, Lippincott, 1985.

Janet Hamm Needs a Date for the Dance.   New York, Clarion, 1986.

The Mother's Day Mice, illustrated by Jan Brett.   New York, Clarion, 1986.

Sixth-Grade Sleepover.   San Diego, Harcourt Brace, 1986.

Ghost's Hour, Spook's Hour, illustrated by Donald Carrick.   New York, Clarion, 1987.

Will You Be My Posslq?   San Diego, Harcourt Brace, 1987.

Happy Birthday, Dear Duck, illustrated by Jan Brett.   New York, Clarion, 1988.

How Many Days to America?, illustrated by Beth Peck.   New York, Clarion, 1988.

Is Anybody There?   New York, Lippincott, 1988.

A Sudden Silence.   San Diego, Harcourt Brace, 1988.

The Ghost Children.   New York, Clarion, 1989.

The Wednesday Surprise, illustrated by Donald Carrick.   New York, Clarion, 1989.

Fiction as Evelyn Bolton (illustrated by John Keely)

Stable of Fear.   Mankato, Minnesota, Creative Education, 1974.

Lady's Girl.   Mankato, Minnesota, Creative Education, 1974.

Goodbye, Charlie.   Mankato, Minnesota, Creative Education, 1974.

Ride When You're Ready.   Mankato, Minnesota, Creative Education, 1974.

The Wild Horses.   Mankato, Minnesota, Creative Education, 1974.

Dream Dancer.   Mankato, Minnesota, Creative Education, 1974.

Fiction as A.E. Bunting

Pitcher to Center Field, illustrated by Len Freas.   Chicago, Children's Press, 1974.

Surfing Country, illustrated by Dale King.   Chicago, Children's Press, 1974.

High Tide for Labrador, illustrated by Bernard Garbutt.   Chicago, Children's Press, 1975.

Springboard to Summer, illustrated by Rob Sprattler.   Chicago, Children's Press, 1975.

Verse

Scary, Scary Halloween, illustrated by Jan Brett. New York, Clarion, 1986.

Other

The Two Giants (Irish folktale), illustrated by Eric von Schmidt. Lexington, Massachusetts, Ginn, 1972.
Say It Fast (tongue twisters), illustrated by True Kelley. Lexington, Massachusetts, Ginn, 1974.
Skateboards: How to Make Them, How to Ride Them, with Glenn Bunting. New York, Harvey House, 1977.
The Sea World Book of Sharks, photographs by Flip Nicklin. San Diego, Sea World, 1979.
The Sea World Book of Whales. New York, Harcourt Brace, 1980.
The Giant Squid. New York, Messner, 1981.
The Great White Shark. New York, Messner, 1982.

*

Manuscript Collection: Kerlan Collection, University of Minnesota, Minneapolis.

Eve Bunting comments:

I began writing for children at that terrible time in my life when my own children were leaving the nest, and when I was filled with a certain panic about the remainder of my productive life. I was about forty…with, hopefully, many years to go. In the past 15 years I have written and published more than 100 books, many of them with Irish backgrounds. There is always, I believe, a certain nostalgia in the immigrant for the land of her birth. I seem, too, to have a preponderance of birds in my books. Perhaps they are a symbol of the freedom that came to me through the grace of my writing.

*   *   *

Any evaluation of Eve Bunting must be made on two levels: as a professional writer and as an artist.

As a master of the craft of writing she is probably the best in the juvenile field. The list of her published work covers all genres and age groups with particular strengths in the areas of young adult mystery and romance. High standards of writing coupled with a gift for storytelling and a unique feel for the market account for her commercial success. Bunting keeps an eye out for new trends. Many of the themes for her recent novels come from the day's headlines: surrogate parenthood (*Surrogate Sister*), teenage suicide (*Face at the Edge of the World*), runaways and teenage prostitution (*If I Asked You, Would You Stay?*). She has also cleverly exploited an opening in the picture book market with charming books about the minor holidays such as *The Mother's Day Mice* and *Scary, Scary Halloween. Karen Kepplewhite Is the World's Best Kisser* wittily depicts the traumas of junior high social life on a level only slightly below Judy Blume's *Are You There, God? It's Me, Margaret.*

Bunting, in short, is the consummate professional. This ironically is also her greatest handicap. She writes too often from her head rather than her gut, raising sensitive issues but pulling away from the risks that go with them. In *The Haunting of Kildoran Abbey* she plays with the menace of IRA terrorism, but backs off at the last minute. In *If I Asked You, Would You Stay?* she throws away what might have been a haunting romance by failing to confront the issue of sex honestly. Bunting asks the reader to believe that Crow and Valentine, teenage runaways who have learned to love and trust in the course of the book, would spend their last night alone together in a sleeping bag holding hands.

This is maddening because Bunting at her best reveals flashes of

brilliance. *Someone Is Hiding on Alcatraz Island* is a claustrophobic suspense novel with all the intensity and menace of a Hitchcock film. The images of the dying blackbirds dropping out of the sky by the thousands in *Blackbird Singing,* the eerie magic of *The Man Who Could Call Down Owls,* and the use of the parrot freed from its cage as a metaphor for the soul's flight after death in *The Empty Window* form a painful contrast to the vapidness of *Happy Birthday, Dear Duck. How Many Days to America?,* a Thanksgiving Day picture book, similarly cuts through the traditional holiday clichés by presenting a modern refugee family fleeing by boat to the United States to escape a Latin American dictatorship.

Eve Bunting, in summary, is a supremely competent writer who is capable of much more inspired work than she generally produces.

—Eric A. Kimmel

———

BURCH, Robert (Joseph). American. Born in Inman, Georgia, 26 June 1925. Educated at the University of Georgia, Athens, B.A. in agriculture 1949; Hunter College, New York, 1955. Served in the United States Army, in New Guinea and Australia, 1943–46. Worked in a commercial greenhouse, 1950; civil servant, United States Army Ordnance Depot, Atlanta, 1951–53, and in Japan, 1953–55; office worker, Muir and Company Advertising, New York, 1956–59, and Walter E. Heller and Company, New York, 1959–62. Recipient: Bread Loaf Writers Conference fellowship, 1960; Women's International League for Peace and Freedom Jane Addams award, 1967; Child Study Association of America award, 1967; George G. Stone Center for Children's Books award, 1974; Children's Literature Association Phoenix award, 1986. Address: 2021 Forest Drive, Fayetteville, Georgia 30214, U.S.A.

PUBLICATIONS FOR CHILDREN

Fiction

The Traveling Bird, illustrated by Susanne Suba. New York, McDowell Obolensky, 1959.
A Funny Place to Live, illustrated by W.R. Lohse. New York, Viking Press, 1962.
Tyler, Wilkin, and Skee, illustrated by Don Sibley. New York, Viking Press, 1963.
Skinny, illustrated by Don Sibley. New York, Viking Press, 1964; London, Methuen, 1965.
D.J.'s Worst Enemy, illustrated by Emil Weiss. New York, Viking Press, 1965.
Queenie Peavy, illustrated by Jerry Lazare. New York, Viking Press, 1966.
Renfroe's Christmas, illustrated by Rocco Negri. New York, Viking Press, 1968.
Joey's Cat, illustrated by Don Freeman. New York, Viking Press, 1969.
Simon and the Game of Chance, illustrated by Fermin Rocker. New York, Viking Press, 1970.
The Hunting Trip, illustrated by Susanne Suba. New York, Scribner, 1971.
Doodle and the Go-Cart, illustrated by Alan Tiegreen. New York, Viking Press, 1972.
Hut School and the Wartime Home-Front Heroes, illustrated by Ronald Himler. New York, Viking Press, 1974.
The Jolly Witch, illustrated by Leigh Grant. New York, Dutton, 1975.

Two That Were Tough, illustrated by Richard Cuffari. New York, Viking Press, 1976.
The Whitman Kick. New York, Dutton, 1977.
Wilkin's Ghost, illustrated by Lloyd Bloom. New York, Viking Press, 1978.
Ida Early Comes over the Mountain. New York, Viking Press, 1980.
Christmas with Ida Early, illustrated by Gail Owens. New York, Viking Press, 1983.
King Kong and Other Poets. New York, Viking Kestrel, 1986.

PUBLICATIONS FOR ADULTS

Other

Translator, *A Jungle in the Wheat Field,* by Egon Mathiesen. New York, McDowell Obolensky, 1960.

*

Manuscript Collection: University of Georgia, Athens.

Robert Burch comments:
Most of my stories are realistic. They take place in the area I know best, the rural south. Although my characters are made up, they must seem real to me before I can write about them. If I think about them until I know them quite well, they help me write the book! It becomes a matter of letting the story grow as naturally as possible out of character development and the circumstances of the time and the places in which it is set.

*   *   *

Robert Burch's fiction is set in the southern part of the United States, from the 1930's to the present. His fiction reflects its original setting because southerners have always had close ties with the land, because poverty has often been a part of southern life, and because southerners have long had love and respect for family and community.

Nearly all Burch's novels have rural settings; his characters seem to prefer country to city life, and they equate urban life with ignorance about the fundamentals of existence. In *Doodle and the Go-Cart* Mr. Maxwell says he has moved back to the country because he wants his children to know that "milk and eggs come from cows and chickens" and that vegetables do not grow in tins on grocery store shelves. In *Two That Were Tough* the country means freedom and the city imprisonment; old, feeble, and somewhat forgetful, Mr. Hilton does not want to move to the city to live with his daughter where he, like his wild rooster, Wild Wings, will have to be cooped, "fed and sheltered." In *Skinny* nine-year old Skinny thinks that the country is best because it "has that special smell to it—clear and cool, and crabappley, even when the trees were not in bloom."

Though southerners love the land, it has contributed to their poverty, so the poverty of the Great Depression was not new to them. Burch's novels often depict the poverty of the south, not only of the 1930's but also of recent times. His novels remind us that affluence may not bring joy and happiness. In *Tyler, Wilkin, and Skee* the young Coley boys rarely have money, and then only a penny or two, yet they have good times playing simple games, not manufactured, singing ballads and hymns, and telling stories. In *Doodle and the Go-Cart* Doodle has only his mule, Addie Flowers, while his cousin, Glenn Carter, has a new expensive go-cart, but Doodle is happier.

Nearly all of Burch's novels portray families either negatively or positively. Queenie, in *Queenie Peavy,* is from an unhappy home,

which causes part, if not all, of her problems. Her mother is indifferent; Queenie's father is in prison, and when briefly paroled he shows Queenie how little he cares for her by letting her walk to school while he hitches a ride in a truck with room for only one passenger. In *Simon and the Game of Chance* Simon's father, Mr. Bradley, is stern, forbidding, and uncompromising. By contrasting the Rounds and Carter families in *Doodle and the Go-Cart,* Burch presents an indifferent, uncaring, unloving family in the Carters and the converse in the Roundses. *Tyler, Wilkin, and Skee, Wilkin's Ghost, D.J.'s Worst Enemy,* and *Renfroe's Christmas* all have close and happy families; *Ida Early Comes over the Mountain* is about another happy family despite the death of the mother a few months before the novel opens.

The value and importance of community exist in several of Burch's stories, but is best reflected in *Hut School and the Wartime Home-Front Heroes* in which, because of schools made overcrowded by the war, a sixth-grade class, a figurative community, learns to pull together to make the year it has to stay in a log-cabin classroom a memorable one.

Although Burch has used a regional setting, he universalizes the action, characters, and themes of his fiction. His novels speak elemental truths: wealth does not necessarily create happiness; material progress does not change the basic needs of people; rural life and the land are important to any nation; poverty is not always degrading; and family and community, good or bad, are usually what people make them.

—Malcolm Usrey

BURGESS, Thornton Waldo. American. Born in Sandwich, Massachusetts, 14 January 1874. Educated at Sandwich High School, graduated 1891; attended business college in Boston, one year. Married 1) Nina E. Osborne in 1905 (died 1906), one son; 2) Fannie P. Johnson in 1911 (died 1950). Worked as cashier and bookkeeper in shoe store; office boy, 1895, reporter, 1895–1911, and literary and household editor for Orange Judd weeklies, Phelps Publishing Company, New York; wrote as W.B. Thornton for *Country Life in America,* New York, 1902–03; associate editor, *Good Housekeeping,* New York, 1904–11; story columnist, Associated News, 1912–20, and New York *Herald Tribune* syndicate, 1920–48; founder, and commentator for six years, Burgess Radio Nature League. Litt.D.: Northeastern University, Boston, 1938. *Died 5 June 1965.*

PUBLICATIONS FOR CHILDREN

Fiction

Mother West Wind series:
   Old Mother West Wind, illustrated by George Kerr. Boston, Little Brown, 1910; London, Lane, 1937.
   Mother West Wind's Children, illustrated by George Kerr. Boston, Little Brown, 1911; London, Lane, 1937.
   Mother West Wind's Animal Friends, illustrated by George Kerr. Boston, Little Brown, 1912; London, Lane, 1937.
   Mother West Wind's Neighbors, illustrated by George Kerr. Boston, Little Brown, 1913; London, Lane, 1950.
   Mother West Wind "Why" Stories, illustrated by Harrison Cady. Boston, Little Brown, 1915; London, Lane, 1950.
   Mother West Wind "How" Stories, illustrated by Harrison Cady.

Boston, Little Brown, 1916; London, Lane, 1950.
Mother West Wind "When" Stories, illustrated by Harrison Cady. Boston, Little Brown, 1917; London, Lane, 1950.
Mother West Wind "Where" Stories, illustrated by Harrison Cady. Boston, Little Brown, 1918; London, Lane, 1950.
Boy Scouts series:
   The Boy Scouts of Woodcraft Camp, illustrated by C.S. Corson. Philadelphia, Penn, 1912.
   The Boy Scouts on Swift River, illustrated by C.S. Corson. Philadelphia, Penn, 1913.
   The Boy Scouts on Lost Trail, illustrated by C.S. Carson. Philadelphia, Penn, 1914.
   The Boy Scouts in a Trapper's Camp, illustrated by F.A. Anderson. Philadelphia, Penn, 1915.
Bedtime Story-Books (illustrated by Harrison Cady):
   The Adventures of Reddy Fox. Boston, Little Brown, 1913; London, Lane, 1931.
   The Adventures of Johnny Chuck. Boston, Little Brown, 1913; London, Lane, 1938.
   The Adventures of Peter Cottontail. Boston, Little Brown, 1914; London, Lane, 1931.
   The Adventures of Unc' Billy Possum. Boston, Little Brown, 1914; London, Lane, 1940.
   The Adventures of Mr. Mocker. Boston, Little Brown, 1914; London, Lane, 1938.
   The Adventures of Jerry Muskrat. Boston, Little Brown, 1914.
   The Adventures of Danny Meadow Mouse. Boston, Little Brown, 1915; London, Lane, 1939.
   The Adventures of Grandfather Frog. Boston, Little Brown, 1915; London, Lane, 1931.
   The Adventures of Chatterer, The Red Squirrel. Boston, Little Brown, 1915; London, Lane, 1931.
   The Adventures of Sammy Jay. Boston, Little Brown, 1915; London, Lane, 1932.
   The Adventures of Buster Bear. Boston, Little Brown, 1916; London, Lane, 1931.
   The Adventures of Old Mr. Toad. Boston, Little Brown, 1916; London, Lane, 1932.
   The Adventures of Prickly Porky. Boston, Little Brown, 1916; London, Lane, 1932.
   The Adventures of Old Man Coyote. Boston, Little Brown, 1916; London, Lane, 1938.
   The Adventures of Paddy the Beaver. Boston, Little Brown, 1917; London, Lane, 1931.
   The Adventures of Poor Mrs. Quack. Boston, Little Brown, 1917; London, Lane, 1932.
   The Adventures of Bobby Coon. Boston, Little Brown, 1918; London, Lane, 1939.
   The Adventures of Jimmy Skunk. Boston, Little Brown, 1918; London, Lane, 1938.
   The Adventures of Bob White. Boston, Little Brown, 1919; London, Lane, 1940.
   The Adventures of Ol' Mistah Buzzard. Boston, Little Brown, 1919.
Wishing-Stone Stories, illustrated by Harrison Cady. Boston, Little Brown, 1935.
   Tommy and the Wishing Stone. New York, Century, 1915.
   Tommy's Wishes Come True. Boston, Little Brown, 1921.
   Tommy's Change of Heart. Boston, Little Brown, 1921.
The Burgess Big Book of Green Meadow Stories, illustrated by Harrison Cady. Boston, Little Brown, 1932.
   Happy Jack. Boston, Little Brown, 1918; London, Lane, 1934.
   Mrs. Peter Rabbit. Boston, Little Brown, 1919; London, Lane, 1934.
   Bowser the Hound. Boston, Little Brown, 1920; London, Lane, 1934.

   Old Granny Fox. Boston, Little Brown, 1920; London, Lane, 1934.
Green Forest series (illustrated by Harrison Cady):
   Lightfoot the Deer. Boston, Little Brown, 1921; London, Lane, 1933.
   Blacky the Crow. Boston, Little Brown, 1922; London, Lane, 1933.
   Whitefoot the Wood Mouse. Boston, Little Brown, 1922; London, Lane, 1933.
   Buster Bear's Twins. Boston, Little Brown, 1923; London, Lane, 1933.
Smiling Pool series (illustrated by Harrison Cady):
   Billy Mink. Boston, Little Brown, 1924; London, Lane, 1935.
   Little Joe Otter. Boston, Little Brown, 1925; London, Lane, 1935.
   Jerry Muskrat at Home. Boston, Little Brown, 1926; London, Lane, 1935.
   Longlegs the Heron. Boston, Little Brown, 1927; London, Lane, 1935.
Happy Jack Squirrel Helps Unc' Billy, illustrated by Harrison Cady. New York, Eggers, 1924.
Grandfather Frog Gets a Ride, illustrated by Harrison Cady. New York, Eggers, 1924.
A Great Joke on Jimmy Skunk, illustrated by Harrison Cady. New York, Eggers, 1924.
Baby Possum's Queer Voyage, illustrated by Harrison Cady. New York, Eggers, 1924.
The Neatness of Bobby Coon, illustrated by Harrison Cady. New York, Eggers, 1924.
Digger the Badger Decides to Stay, illustrated by Harrison Cady. New York, Eggers, 1924.
Animal Folk, illustrated by Harrison Cady. Akron, Ohio, Saalfield, 1925.
Friendly Animals, illustrated by Harrison Cady. Akron, Ohio, Saalfield, 1925.
Picture Book, illustrated by Harrison Cady. Akron, Ohio, Saalfield, 1925.
The Christmas Reindeer, illustrated by Rhoda Chase. New York, Macmillan, 1926.
Cubby Bear Books (*A Frightened Baby, Farmer Brown's Boy Becomes Curious, What Farmer Brown's Boy Did, Cubby Bear Has a Mind of His Own, An Imp of Mischief, Cubby in Mother Brown's Pantry, A Woe-Begone Little Bear, Cubby Gets a Bath, Milk and Honey, Cubby Finds an Open Door*), illustrated by Nina Jordan. Racine, Wisconsin, Whitman, 10 vols., 1929.
Wee Little Books (*Little Joe Otter's Slide, Betty Bear's Lesson, Unc' Billy Gets Even, Whitefoot's Secret, Jimmy Skunk's Justice, Peter Rabbit's Carrots*). Racine, Wisconsin, Whitman, 6 vols., 1929–33.
Tales from the Storyteller's House, illustrated by Lemuel Palmer. Boston, Little Brown, 1937; London, Lane, 1938.
While the Story-Log Burns, illustrated by Lemuel Palmer. Boston, Little Brown, 1938; London, Lane, 1939.
Animal Stories, illustrated by Harrison Cady. New York, Platt and Munk, 1942; as *The Animal World of Thornton Burgess,* 1961.
   Bobby Coon's Mistake. New York, Platt and Munk, 1940; as *Bobby Coon's Surprise,* 1961.
   The Three Little Bears. New York, Platt and Munk, 1940; as *A Bear Scare,* 1961.
   Peter Rabbit Proves a Friend. New York, Platt and Munk, 1940; as *Peter Rabbit Goes Scouting,* 1961.
   Reddy Fox's Sudden Engagement. New York, Platt and Munk, 1940; as *Reddy Fox Leaves in a Hurry,* 1961.
   Paddy's Surprise Visitor. New York, Platt and Munk, 1940; as *Paddy the Beaver's Visitor,* 1961.
   A Merry Coasting Party. New York, Platt and Munk, 1940; as

Fun at the Queer Trail, 1961.
Young Flash, The Deer.   New York, Platt and Munk, 1940; as
   Flash the Young Deer, 1961.
A Robber Meets His Match.   New York, Platt and Munk, 1940;
   as *Robber the Rat Loses Out*, 1961.
Little Color Classics (*Little Pete's* [*Chuck's, Red's*] *Adventure*),
   illustrated by Harrison Cady.   Springfield, Massachusetts, Mc-
   Loughlin, 3 vols., 1941–42.
Nature Stories (illustrated by Harrison Cady):
   On the Green Meadows.   Boston, Little Brown, 1944.
   At the Smiling Pool.   Boston, Little Brown, 1945.
   The Crooked Little Path.   Boston, Little Brown, 1946.
   The Dear Old Briar-Patch.   Boston, Little Brown, 1947.
   Along Laughing Brook.   Boston, Little Brown, 1949.
   At Paddy the Beaver's Pond.   Boston, Little Brown, 1950.
Baby Animal Stories, illustrated by Phoebe Erickson.   New York,
   Grosset and Dunlap, 1949.
A Thornton Burgess Picture Story Book, illustrated by Nino Carbe.
   New York, Garden City Publishing, 1950.
The Littlest Christmas Tree, illustrated by Mary and Carl Hauge.
   New York, Wonder Books, 1954.
Peter Rabbit and Reddy Fox, illustrated by Mary and Carl Hauge.
   New York, Wonder Books, 1954; as *Peter Cottontail and Reddy
   Fox*, 1974.
Aunt Sally's Friends in Fur; or, The Woodhouse Night Club,
   photographs by the author.   Boston, Little Brown, 1955.
Stories Around the Year, illustrated by Phoebe Erickson.   New York,
   Grosset and Dunlap, 1955.
Little Peter Cottontail, illustrated by Phoebe Erickson.   New York,
   Wonder Books, 1956.
Bedtime Stories, illustrated by Mary and Carl Hauge.   New York,
   Grosset and Dunlap, 1959; London, Macdonald, 1960.
Nature Stories, illustrated by Adrianna Mazza.   New York, Wonder
   Books, 1959; London, Golden Pleasure Books, 1966.
The Million Little Sunbeams, illustrated by Harrison Cady.   Toledo,
   Ohio, Six Oaks Press, 1963.
*The Burgess Book of Nature Lore: Adventures of Tommy, Sue, and
   Sammy with Their Friends of Meadow, Pool, and Forest*, il-
   lustrated by Robert Candy.   Boston, Little Brown, 1965.

Verse (illustrated by Harrison Cady)

Animal Paint Book.   Akron, Ohio, Saalfield, 1925.
Peter Cottontail's Own Paint Book.   Akron, Ohio, Saalfield, 1925.
Animal Pictures.   Akron, Ohio, Saalfield, 1925.
Mother Nature's Song and Story Book, music by Rebecca Richards,
   illustrated by Henry Johnson and Lemuel Palmer.   Boston, Wor-
   ley, 1938.

Other

Natural History series:
   The Burgess Bird Book for Children, illustrated by Louis Agassiz
      Fuertes.   Boston, Little Brown, 1919.
   The Burgess Animal Book for Children, illustrated by Louis
      Agassiz Fuertes.   Boston, Little Brown, 1920.
   The Burgess Flower Book for Children.   Boston, Little Brown,
      1923.
   The Burgess Seashore Book for Children, illustrated by W.H.
      Southwick and George Sutton.   Boston, Little Brown, 1929.
Wild Flowers We Know [*We Should Know*].   Racine, Wisconsin,
   Whitman, 2 vols., 1929.
Birds You Should Know, illustrated by Louis Agassiz Fuertes.   Bos-
   ton, Little Brown, 1933.
The Book of Animal Life, with Thora Stowell.   Boston, Little
   Brown, 1937.

The Little Burgess Animal [and *Bird*] *Book for Children*, illustrated
   by Louis Agassiz Fuertes.   Chicago, Rand McNally, 2 vols.,
   1941.
Nature Almanac, illustrated by Phoebe Erickson.   New York, Grosset and Dunlap, 1949.

PUBLICATIONS FOR ADULTS

Other

*The Bride's Primer, Being a Series of Quaint Parodies on the Ways
   of Brides...*, with others.   New York, Phelps, 1905.
Now I Remember: Autobiography of an Amateur Naturalist.   Boston, Little Brown, 1960.

*

Bibliography: *Thornton Waldo Burgess: A Descriptive Book
Bibliography* by Wayne W. Wright, Sandwich, Massachusetts,
Burgess Society, 1979.

Manuscript Collections: Burgess Society, Sandwich, Massachusetts;
Sandwich Public Library.

*   *   *

Thornton Waldo Burgess, one of the most prolific writers of
animal stories for children, published over 70 books during his
lifetime and over fifteen thousand story columns during his 44 years
of daily syndication in American newspapers. His animal stories
belong to a genre which includes, at one extreme, stories featuring
animals which are actually humans masquerading in feathers or fur,
and, at the other, stories presenting the cycles of animal life with strict
and often brutal realism. Burgess's animal stories fall somewhere
around the middle of this generic continuum. His bestiary is made
up of anthropomorphic creatures which reason, converse, and gossip.
They do not, however, ride bicycles, snooze in armchairs, or sew the
clothes they are always depicted as wearing in the whimsical Harrison Cady illustrations which accompany almost all of Burgess's
works. In short, Burgess's animals are hybrids: they operate in a
realm at once natural and yet infused with a human moral code. This
accommodation between the human and the bestial allowed Burgess
to entertain his youthful readers while offering them moral guidance
and teaching them nature lore. These three intentions inform nearly
all of Burgess's works.
   Burgess's career was determined by the success of *Old Mother
West Wind* (1910), the first of eight volumes comprising the Mother
West Wind series. Each volume offers a collection of short moral
fables and explanatory tales which focus on a particular animal's
dominant physical traits or behavioral characteristics and conclude
with a moral lesson. For example, in the tenth story of *Old Mother
West Wind*, "How Sammy Jay Was Found Out," Burgess's narrator
presents the vain, lazy Sammy Jay making fun of Johnny Chuck's
industrious preparations for winter. When Old Mother West Wind
hears that someone has been stealing Happy Jack Squirrel's store of
nuts, she convenes all the creatures, blows a stick from Sammy's
nut-filled nest, and exposes him as the thief. As a punishment for
stealing and as a sign that those who steal can no longer be trusted,
Sammy Jay is made to cry "Thief! Thief!" whenever he opens his
mouth. The uncomplicated dramatic conflicts of these tales, their
unambiguous moral truths, and their genial animal characters account for the prevailing innocence and charm which helped to make
the Mother West Wind series among Burgess's most popular works.
   In the 20 volumes of the Bedtime Story-Books series, initiated in
1913 with *The Adventures of Reddy Fox* and *The Adventures of*

Johnny Chuck, Burgess attempted to render the subject animal of each volume in the round, to delineate its habits, pursuits, and pastimes while refraining from any depiction of natural processes which might be considered unpleasant or pathetic by his child audience. In addition, the formula for the Bedtime Story-Books called for the inclusion of didactic verses and moral asides prompted by life incidents or characteristic habits of the animal depicted. This series, and the Mother West Wind volumes, comprise Burgess's best-known works.

Two other series show Burgess's intention to instruct children in nature lore. The Wishing-Stone series aimed to produce that empathy necessary to convert the child audience into protectors and conservators of wild creatures. Through the agency of the wishing stone, Tommy Brown is transformed into the various animals which he had hitherto menaced. His understanding enlarged through his experiences, Tommy retires his rifle and retrieves his traps, vowing to become a friend to nature's children. In the Bird, Animal, Flower, and Seashore Books for Children, Burgess presented illustrations and information about North American flora and fauna. In each volume, Burgess arranged this encyclopedic information in highly contrived and generally unsuccessful narrative frames involving Peter Rabbit's tuition by various instructors, from Old Mother Nature herself to the sharp-tongued Jenny Wren.

Burgess's works strike many modern readers as formulaic and didactic. His plots lack complexity, and his supra-zoological animal characters are often one-dimensional, embodying a single emblematic characteristic. Because Burgess occasionally descends into racial, sexual, and jingoistic stereotyping, his works often seem dated, though their concern for conservation is certainly current. In spite of their literary flaws, however, Burgess's works continue to be read. The animals which populate Burgess's world are charming, cuddly and gently whimsical; they live and play in a pastoral landscape which reflects the author's longing for a simpler time out of time, an edenic rural past. The world depicted is governed by a clear, unambiguous moral code framed from traditional homespun rural values. The works of Thornton Waldo Burgess thus share the appeal of all popular formulaic literature which reduces life's disturbing complexities into simple and comfortable clarity.

—Lucien L. Agosta

BURMAN, Ben Lucien. American. Born in Covington, Kentucky, 12 December 1896. Educated at Harvard University, Cambridge, Massachusetts, A.B. 1920. Served in the United States Army Field Artillery in France during World War I: wounded; Legion of Honor, for journalism, 1947. Married Alice Caddy in 1927 (died 1977). Reporter, Boston *Herald,* 1920; assistant city editor, Cincinnati *Times Star,* 1921; special writer, New York *Sunday World,* 1922; staff writer, Newspaper Enterprise Association, 1927; war correspondent, in Africa and the Middle East, 1941. *Died 12 November 1984.*

PUBLICATIONS FOR CHILDREN

Fiction (illustrated by Alice Caddy)

High Water at Catfish Bend.   New York, Messner, 1952; with *Seven Stars for Catfish Bend,* London, Kestrel, 1975.
Seven Stars for Catfish Bend.   New York, Funk and Wagnalls, 1956; with *High Water at Catfish Bend,* London, Kestrel, 1975.
The Owl Hoots Twice at Catfish Bend.   New York, Taplinger, 1961;

with *Blow a Wild Bugle for Catfish Bend,* London, Kestrel, 1975.
Blow a Wild Bugle for Catfish Bend.   New York, Taplinger, 1967; with *The Owl Hoots Twice at Catfish Bend,* London, Kestrel, 1975.
High Treason at Catfish Bend.   New York, Vanguard Press, and London, Kestrel, 1977.
The Strange Invasion of Catfish Bend.   New York, Vanguard Press, 1980.
Thunderbolt at Catfish Bend.   New York, Wieser and Wieser, 1984.

PUBLICATIONS FOR ADULTS

Novels

Mississippi.   New York, Cosmopolitan, 1929; as *Then There's Cripple Creek,* London, Butterworth, 1930.
Steamboat round the Bend.   New York, Farrar and Rinehart, 1933; London, Nelson, 1936.
Blow for a Landing.   Boston, Houghton Mifflin, 1938; London, Lutterworth Press, 1948.
Rooster Crows by Day.   New York, Dutton, 1945; London, Lutterworth Press, 1948.
Everywhere I Roam.   New York, Doubleday, 1949; London, Longman, 1957.
The Four Lives of Mundy Tolliver.   New York, Messner, 1953; London, Vallentine Mitchell, 1955.
The Street of the Laughing Camel.   New York, McGraw Hill, 1959.
The Sign of the Praying Tiger.   New York, New American Library, 1966.

Other

Big River to Cross: Mississippi Life Today.   New York, Day, 1940.
Miracle on the Congo: Report from the Free French Front.   New York, Day, 1942; London, Macmillan, 1943.
Children of Noah: Glimpses of Unknown America.   New York, Messner, 1951.
It's a Big Country: America Off the Highways.   New York, Reynal, 1956.
It's a Big Continent.   New York, McGraw Hill, 1961.
The Generals Wear Cork Hats.   New York, Taplinger, 1963; London, Harrap, 1965.
Look Down That Winding River: An Informal Profile of the Mississippi.   New York, Taplinger, and Newton Abbot, Devon, David and Charles, 1973.

*

Manuscript Collections: University of Kentucky, Lexington; Tulane University, New Orleans.

*   *   *

Ben Lucien Burman was born in the river town of Covington, Kentucky, and is most famous for his stories of the rural south, particularly his novels of the Mississippi River. He started writing in childhood, was editor of his high school paper and later had reporting jobs on several major newspapers.

Burman wrote a series of six books for children—and I would certainly recommend them for adults as well—about the talented and wise animals of Catfish Bend. Catfish Bend is located in a swampy area on the banks of the Mississippi River, and the animals who live there include Doc Raccoon, Judge Black (a black watersnake), and the frogs of the Indian Bayou Glee Club. In *High Treason at Catfish Bend* the whole lot of them are taken with the idea that the humans who are moving to Paradise Valley in California may have found paradise. Life is hard enough in Catfish Bend to warrant their making the long trek to the West Coast to find heaven-on-earth. Their difficulties along the way, and their very human ups-and-downs, are reassuring to a child reader. The Catfish Bend crowd, like the characters in Burman's books for older readers, are down and out. And their approach to the high and mighty (mostly human beings living in fancy northern states) is both understandable and sympathetic. Further, these animals know that it is important for survival to help one another, to stick together. "Fighting is the stupidest thing in the world," says the raccoon to some newcomers to the area. He then tells them about the pact the animals at Catfish signed during the big flood, when they'd found out they couldn't stay alive if they kept on quarreling.

Burman, like Mark Twain, is as popular with adult as with adolescent readers. Like Twain, he brings alive the rural poor who have few advantages and limited life experiences. These individuals, animals or human, usually looked down upon as unintelligent and dull, are shown in Burman's tales as amazingly acute, perceptive, and considerably better able to cope than are some of their more sophisticated critics. Their views of nature, of people, and of the world around them, can be excruciatingly insightful and funny. One of Burman's stories for adults, *The Sign of the Praying Tiger,* takes a Kentucky mountaineer out of his rural setting to New Orleans, all the way to Singapore, and finally to the exotic Malaysian island of "Menang," in a great, yarn-spinning adventure.

Beneath Burman's outright foolishness lies a concern and respect for individuals at the bottom, who most often remain unnoticed and unappreciated. Burman makes these individuals, human and animal, come alive and their societies—with their hopes, inconsistencies, and frustrations—come alive as well. He does this in a gentle and humorous manner, and his books provide marvelous entertainment.

—Mary Lystad

BURNETT, Frances (Eliza) Hodgson. American. Born in Cheetham Hill, Manchester, England, 24 November 1849; emigrated with her mother to New Market, Tennessee, 1865; became citizen, 1905. Educated in schools in Manchester. Married 1) Dr. Swan Moses Burnett in 1873 (divorced 1898), two sons; 2) Stephen Townesend in 1900 (separated 1901; died 1914). Lived in Knoxville, 1869–74, Europe, 1875–76, and Washington, D.C., 1877–87; after 1887 traveled frequently between the U.S. and Europe. *Died 29 October 1924.*

PUBLICATIONS FOR CHILDREN

Fiction

Little Lord Fauntleroy. New York, Scribner, and London, Warne, 1886.
Sara Crewe; or, What Happened at Miss Minchin's. London, Warne, and New York, Scribner, 1888.
Editha's Burglar. Boston, Jordan Marsh, 1888.
Editha's Burglar, and Sara Crewe. London, Warne, 1888.
Little Saint Elizabeth and Other Stories. New York, Scribner, and London, Warne, 1890.
Children I Have Known. London, Osgood McIlvaine, 1892; as *Giovanni and the Other: Children Who Have Made Stories,* New York, Scribner, 1892.
Piccino and Other Child Stories. New York, Scribner, 1894; as *The*

Captain's Youngest, Piccino, and Other Child Stories, London, Warne, 1894.
Two Little Pilgrims' Progress: A Story of the City Beautiful. New York, Scribner, and London, Warne, 1895.
A Little Princess, Being the Whole Story of Sara Crewe Now Told for the First Time. New York, Scribner, and London, Warne, 1905.
Racketty-Packetty House. New York, Century, 1906; London, Warne, 1907.
Queen Silver-Bell. New York, Century, 1906; as *The Troubles of Queen Silver-Bell,* London, Warne, 1907.
The Cozy Lion, as Told by Queen Crosspatch. New York, Century, 1907; London, Stacey, 1972.
The Spring Cleaning, as Told by Queen Crosspatch. New York, Century, 1908; London, Stacey, 1973.
The Good Wolf. New York, Moffat, 1908.
Barty Crusoe and His Man Saturday. New York, Moffat, 1909.
The Land of the Blue Flower. New York, Moffat, 1909; London, Putnam, 1912.
The Secret Garden, illustrated by Charles Robinson. New York, Stokes, and London, Heinemann, 1911.
The Lost Prince. New York, Century, and London, Hodder and Stoughton, 1915.
The Way to the House of Santa Claus: A Christmas Story. New York and London, Harper, 1916.
The Little Hunchback Zia. New York, Stokes, and London, Heinemann, 1916.

Plays

The Real Little Lord Fauntleroy, adaptation of her own novel (produced London, Boston, and New York, 1888).
Editha's Burglar, with Stephen Townesend, adaptation of the novel by Burnett (produced Neath, Glamorgan, 1890; as *Nixie,* produced London, 1890).
A Little Princess, adaptation of her novel *Sara Crewe* (as *A Little Unfairy Princess,* produced London, 1902; as *A Little Princess,* produced London and New York, 1903). Published in *Treasury of Plays for Children,* edited by Montrose J. Moses, Boston, Little Brown, 1921.
Racketty-Packetty House, adaptation of her own story (produced New York, 1912).

PUBLICATIONS FOR ADULTS

Novels

That Lass o' Lowrie's. New York, Scribner, and London, Warne, 1877.
Dolly: A Love Story. Philadelphia, Porter and Coates, and London, Routledge, 1877; as *Vagabondia,* New York, Scribner, 1883.
Haworth's. London, Macmillan, and New York, Scribner, 1879.
Louisiana. New York, Scribner, 1880; with *That Lass o' Lowrie's,* London, Macmillan, 1880.
A Fair Barbarian. Boston, Osgood, and London, Warne, 1881.
Through One Administration. Boston, Osgood, 3 vols., 1883; London, Warne, 1883.
A Woman's Will; or, Miss Defarge. London, Warne, 1887; as *Miss Defarge,* with *Brueton's Bayou,* by John Habberton, Philadelphia, Lippincott, 1888.
The Fortunes of Philippa Fairfax. London, Warne, 1888.
The Pretty Sister of José. New York, Scribner, and London, Blackett, 1889.
A Lady of Quality.... New York, Scribner, and London, Warne, 1896.

His Grace of Osmonde....   New York, Scribner, and London, Warne, 1897.
In Connection with the De Willoughby Claim.   New York, Scribner, and London, Warne, 1899.
The Making of a Marchioness.   New York, Stokes, and London, Smith Elder, 1901.
The Methods of Lady Walderhurst.   New York, Stokes, 1901; London, Smith Elder, 1902.
In the Closed Room.   London, Hodder and Stoughton, and New York, McClure, 1904.
The Dawn of a To-morrow.   New York, Scribner, 1906; London, Warne, 1907.
The Shuttle.   New York, Stokes, and London, Heinemann, 1907.
My Robin.   New York, Stokes, 1912; London, Putnam, 1913.
T. Tembarom.   New York, Century, and London, Hodder and Stoughton, 1913.
The White People.   New York, Harper, 1917; London, Heinemann, 1920.
The Head of the House of Coombe.   New York, Stokes, and London, Heinemann, 1922.
Robin.   New York, Stokes, and London, Heinemann, 1922.

Short Stories

Surly Tim and Other Stories.   New York, Scribner, and London, Ward Lock, 1877.
Theo: A Love Story.   Philadelphia, Peterson, and London, Ward Lock, 1877.
Pretty Polly Pemberton: A Love Story.   Philadelphia, Peterson, 1877; London, Routledge, 1878.
Kathleen: A Love Story.   Philadelphia, Peterson, and London, Routledge, 1878.
Miss Crespigny: A Love Story.   Philadelphia, Peterson, and London, Routledge, 1878.
Earlier Stories.   New York, Scribner, 1878; London, Routledge, 1879.
Earlier Stories, second series.   New York, Scribner, 1878; London, Chatto and Windus, 1879.
A Quiet Life, and The Tide on the Moaning Bar.   Philadelphia, Peterson, 1878; London, Routledge, 1879.
Our Neighbour Opposite.   London, Routledge, 1878.
Jarl's Daughter and Other Stories.   Philadelphia, Peterson, 1879.
Natalie and Other Stories.   London, Warne, 1879.

Plays

That Lass o' Lowrie's, with Julian Magnus, adaptation of the novel by Burnett (produced New York, 1878).
Esmeralda, with William Gillette (produced Newark, New Jersey, and New York, 1881; as *Young Folks' Ways,* produced London, 1883).   New York, French, 1881(?).
Phyllis, adaptation of her novel *The Fortunes of Philippa Fairfax* (produced London, 1889).
The Showman's Daughter, with Stephen Townesend (produced Worcester, 1891; London, 1892).
The First Gentleman of Europe, with Constance Fletcher (produced New York and London, 1897).
A Lady of Quality, with Stephen Townesend, adaptation of the novel by Burnett (produced Detroit and New York, 1897; Cambridge and London, 1899).
The Pretty Sister of José, adaptation of her own novel (produced Syracuse, New York, New York City, and London, 1903).
That Man and I, adaptation of her novel *In Connection with the De Willoughby Claim* (produced London, 1903; New York, 1904).
The Dawn of a Tomorrow, adaptation of her own novel (produced New York, 1909; Liverpool and London, 1910).

Other

The Drury Lane Boys' Club.   Washington, D.C., Moon Press, 1892.
The One I Knew the Best of All: A Memory of the Mind of a Child (autobiography).   New York, Scribner, and London, Warne, 1893.
In the Garden.   New York, Medici Society, 1925.

*

Manuscript Collection: Princeton University Library, New Jersey.

Critical Studies: *Mrs. Ewing, Mrs. Molesworth, and Mrs. Hodgson Burnett* by Marghanita Laski, London, Barker, 1950, New York, Oxford University Press, 1951; *Waiting for the Party: The Life of Frances Hodgson Burnett 1849–1924* by Ann Thwaite, London, Secker and Warburg, and New York, Scribner, 1974; *Frances Hodgson Burnett* by Phyllis Bixler, Boston, Twayne, 1984.

*   *   *

The bulk of Frances Hodgson Burnett's work for children was written in the 19th century, but her two best books—the final version of *Sara Crewe,* called *A Little Princess,* and *The Secret Garden*—both belong to the 20th. These are the two books which are still read and enjoyed by thousands of children every year, not as period pieces but in exactly the same way as they read contemporary writers. A third book, *Little Lord Fauntleroy,* is also enjoyed; but the critic, anyway, if not the child reader, is more affected in his judgment by the date it was written.

Burnett was well established as a writer for adults when she published *Fauntleroy.* Her early novels were compared with those of George Eliot, and in 1883 an article in the *Century* magazine listed her as one of those with Henry James "who hold the front rank today in general estimation." Her first stories for children were short ones, which appeared in *St. Nicholas.* It was only after the phenomenal success of *Fauntleroy* that she regularly published children's books. The quality of these was variable, and her most impressive work continued to be for adults until the publication of *A Little Princess* in 1905.

The history of this book is curious and is worth going into in some detail. Indeed, a comparison of the three versions of the story gives a rewarding insight into Burnett's working methods and her development as a children's writer. *Sara Crewe* first appeared in 1887. It was a story drawing on some of her experiences as a child at the Miss Hadfields' school in Manchester, but was set in London. Like nearly all Burnett's stories, its theme is the reversal of fortune. In *Fauntleroy* Cedric Erroll had left a small house in New York, wearing clothes made out of his mother's old gown, for the life of the heir to an earldom and an English castle. Sara Crewe had gone to school as an heiress and been reduced, after her bankrupt father's death, to living in an attic as a drudge and an outcast. In both cases, the moral is firmly drawn and cannot be missed by even the most unperceptive child reader: we are what we are, and our outward trappings and possessions have nothing to do with real nobility.

In 1902 Burnett turned the story of *Sara Crewe* into a play. The following year, her editor at Scribner's came up with the suggestion that she write a new, longer version of the book under the play's title, *A Little Princess,* incorporating the new material she had introduced in the play. He wanted the book quickly, the play was still running and sales would be splendid. Fortunately at that point Burnett was committed to two other plays. The book was not rushed and was not finally finished until November 1904.

In the original version, Sara's experiences up until her father's death took no more than four and a half pages. In *A Little Princess* they take ninety. The earlier book is little more than a series of notes for the rich rewards of the full-scale novel. The basic story is an excellent one, and the final version demonstrates with what tremendous skill Burnett was able to make the most of it. The detail is excellent too: Burnett was always good at detail. As she once said, "It is not enough to mention they have tea; you must specify the muffins."

A Little Princess is a great deal more interesting than *Fauntleroy*, partly because Sara is seen not from the adult point of view, but from her own viewpoint. *The Secret Garden* is even more interesting. "It is the most satisfying children's book I know," the critic Marghanita Laski once wrote, and countless people have shared that view. Burnett wrote much of the book in the rose garden of Great Maytham Hall in Rolvenden in Kent. All her life, she said, she had felt "a sort of curious kinship with things which grew," and *The Secret Garden* is, among many other things, an expression of this kinship.

The place is important: the atmosphere of the huge house and garden is romantic and mysterious. The small orphan from India comes to Misselthwaite across the moors. Her arrival is strongly reminiscent of that of Jane Eyre at Thornfield, and there are other points of resemblance between the two books. Burnett did not in fact know Yorkshire well, and her setting owes more to the Brontës than to real life. She stayed with Lord Crewe at Fryston Hall in 1895, but that is her only recorded visit to the area. We don't know where she acquired her knowledge of the Yorkshire dialect Dickon and his family speak so convincingly, but she had always been interested in dialect, ever since the days as a child in Manchester and Salford when one of her greatest pleasures was to sneak out and gossip with the "back street" children.

The setting, as I say, is important, but much more important are the children. The most original thing about the book is that its heroine and one of its heroes are both thoroughly unattractive children. The first sentence makes it compulsive reading: "When Mary Lennox was sent to Misselthwaite Manor to live with her uncle, everybody said she was the most disagreeable-looking child ever seen." And Colin is a hysterical hypochondriac. It is the entirely convincing transformation of these two unhappy children that gives the story its great appeal, even to readers who do not find the natural world particularly attractive.

Other Victorian writers had made deprived children behave quite inappropriately, but Burnett's instinct has since been confirmed by child psychologists. A child denied love does behave as Mary behaved. But *The Secret Garden* is far more than a parable or a demonstration of child behaviour. With Burnett the story always came first, and she was far too good a writer to spoil it with propaganda. Only at the beginning of Chapter 27 does she lapse, with explicit explanations of her symbolism and a bad definition of what the rest of the book conveys so subtly: "to let a sad thought or a bad one get into your mind is as dangerous as letting a scarlet fever germ get into your body." *The Secret Garden* was a book of the new, the 20th century. Far from encouraging the attitudes instilled in Frances as a child ("speak when you're spoken to, come when you're called..."), it suggested children should be self-reliant and have faith in themselves, that they should listen, not to their elders and betters, but to their own hearts and consciences.

The Secret Garden did not make a great impact on its first appearance, but it has never been out of print. It is this book which establishes Mrs. Burnett as undoubtedly one of the most important writers of the century.

—Ann Thwaite

BURNFORD, Sheila (Philip Cochrane, née Every). Canadian. Born in Scotland, 11 May 1918; emigrated to Canada, 1951. Educated at St. George's School, Edinburgh; Harrogate College, Yorkshire; studied in Germany. Married David Burnford in 1941; three daughters. Served in the Royal Naval Hospitals Voluntary Aid Detachment, England, 1939–41; ambulance driver, 1941–42. Recipient: Canadian Library Association Book of the Year Medal, 1963. *Died 20 April 1984.*

PUBLICATIONS FOR CHILDREN

Fiction

The Incredible Journey, illustrated by Carl Burger. Boston, Little Brown, 1961; revised edition, London, Hodder and Stoughton, 1961.
Mr. Noah and the Second Flood, illustrated by Michael Foreman. Toronto, McClelland and Stewart, London, Gollancz, and New York, Praeger, 1973.

PUBLICATIONS FOR ADULTS

Novel

Bel Ria. London, Joseph, 1977; Boston, Little Brown, 1978.

Other

The Fields of Noon (autobiographical essays). Toronto, McClelland and Stewart, Boston, Little Brown, and London, Hodder and Stoughton, 1964.
Without Reserve (on the Indians of Ontario). Toronto, McClelland and Stewart, Boston, Little Brown, and London, Hodder and Stoughton, 1969.
One Woman's Arctic. London, Hodder and Stoughton, 1972; Boston, Little Brown, 1973.

*   *   *

Of Sheila Burnford's two books for children, *The Incredible Journey* is by far the most popular. In the same genre as Anna Sewell's *Black Beauty*, the story is a sentimental account of the adventures of three pets who survive incredible hardships in an attempt to return to their owners. A young Labrador Retriever, a Siamese cat, and an old Bull Terrier regularly overcome tremendous problems—attack by wild animals, hunger, inclement weather, to name a few—and eventually do succeed in becoming reunited with their owners. Perhaps such an adventure is possible in reality, but it seems implausible that three house pets could so readily adapt to the rigours of wilderness survival in northern Ontario.

The author ascribes just about every human characteristic except speech to her protagonists. In fact, her animals could easily be three children since they think and act much more like people than animals. Allusions are made, for example, to the terrier's "irrepressible air of sly merriment" and his "apologetic grin." The relationship between the three pets seems to be unrealistically altruistic. On one occasion, the cat attacks a bear cub in an effort to save one of the dogs and later gives up his supper in order that the dog might regain his strength. References are made to the Labrador Retriever as the group's "gentle, worried leader." All of the animals, indeed, are invested with commendable traits and human-like emotions. Burnford created a memorable story but not one that is a fair representation of the true nature of animals.

Mr. Noah and the Second Flood is an entirely different type of book. Obviously the vehicle for a strong anti-pollution crusade, this overly long contemporary fable about Noah's descendents is sometimes humorous, sometimes depressing. The theme of man's carelessness in upsetting the ecological balance is very heavily stressed to the detriment of the story. The characters tend to be stereotypes—Mrs. Noah is the epitome of the befuddled, kind-hearted grandmother and Noah is ever the serene patriarch. Most of the humor is derived from observations made by the isolated Noah family on events taking place in the world outside their mountain retreat. The story would probably be more successful in a format less reminiscent of a picture book and cut down to half of its present length.

—Fran Ashdown

* * *

BURNINGHAM, John (Mackintosh). British. Born in Farnham, Surrey, 27 April 1936. Educated at Summerhill School, Leiston, Suffolk; Central School of Art, London, 1956–59, diploma. Married the illustrator Helen Oxenbury in 1964; one son and two daughters. Recipient (for illustration): Library Association Kate Greenaway Medal, 1964, 1971; Boston *Globe-Horn Book* award, 1972; Maschler award, 1984. Lives in London. Address: c/o Jonathan Cape Ltd., 32 Bedford Square, London WC1B 3EL, England.

PUBLICATIONS FOR CHILDREN (illustrated by the author)

Fiction

Borka: The Adventures of a Goose with No Feathers. London, Cape, 1963; New York, Random House, 1964.
Trubloff: The Mouse Who Wanted to Play the Balalaika. London, Cape, 1964; New York, Random House, 1965.
ABC, illustrated by the author and Leigh Taylor. London, Cape, 1964; Indianapolis, Bobbs Merrill, 1967.
Humbert, Mister Firkin and the Lord Mayor of London. London, Cape, 1965; Indianapolis, Bobbs Merrill, 1967.
Cannonball Simp. London, Cape, 1966; Indianapolis, Bobbs Merrill, 1967.
Harquin, The Fox Who Went Down to the Valley. London, Cape, 1967; Indianapolis, Bobbs Merrill, 1968.
Seasons. London, Cape, 1969; Indianapolis, Bobbs Merrill, 1971.
Mr. Gumpy's Outing. London, Cape, and New York, Holt Rinehart, 1970.
Mr. Gumpy's Motor Car. London, Cape, 1973; New York, Crowell, 1976.
Come Away from the Water, Shirley. London, Cape, and New York, Crowell, 1977.
Time to Get Out of the Bath, Shirley. London, Cape, and New York, Crowell, 1978.
Would You Rather.... London, Cape, and New York, Crowell, 1978.
The Shopping Basket. London, Cape, and New York, Crowell, 1980.
Avocado Baby. London, Cape, and New York, Crowell, 1982.
Granpa. London, Cape, and New York, Crown, 1984.
Where's Julius? London, Cape, and New York, Crown, 1986.
John Patrick Norman McHennessy: The Boy Who Was Always Late. London, Cape, and New York, Crown, 1987.

Other

Birdland: Wall Frieze. London, Cape, and New York, Braziller, 1966.
Lionland: Wall Frieze. London, Cape, 1966.
Storyland: Wall Frieze. London, Cape, 1966.
Jungleland: Wall Frieze. London, Cape, 1968.
Wonderland: Wall Frieze. London, Cape, 1968.
Around the World: Two Wall Friezes. London, Cape, 1972.
Around the World in Eighty Days. London, Cape, 1972.
Little Books (readers; *The Baby, The Rabbit, The School, The Snow, The Blanket, The Cupboard, The Dog, The Friend*). London, Cape, 8 vols., 1974–75; New York, Crowell, 8 vols., 1975–76.
Number Play (*Count Up, Read One, Ride Off, Pigs Plus, Just Cats, Five Down*). London, Walker, and New York, Viking Press, 6 vols., 1983.
First Words (*Cluck Baa, Skip Trip, Slam Bang, Sniff Shout, Wobble Pop, Jangle Twang*). London, Walker, 6 vols., 1984; New York, Viking Kestrel, 6 vols., 1984–85.
Play and Learn (*123, Opposites, Colours*). London, Sainsbury-Walker, 3 vols., 1985; as *It's Great to Learn!* (*ABC, 123, Opposites, Colors*), New York, Crown, 4 vols., 1986; *123* as *Numbers Book,* London, Walker, 1987; *ABC* as *Alphabet Book,* London, Walker, 1987.

*

Illustrator: *Chitty-Chitty Bang-Bang* by Ian Fleming, 1964; *The Extraordinary Tug-of-War* by Letta Schatz, 1968; *The Wind in the Willows* by Kenneth Grahame, 1983.

* * *

John Burningham is one of the most outstanding author-illustrators of children's books today, creating books that delight children and their teachers alike. He manages to appeal to the young child's imagination without appearing condescending, and his texts are models of what books for children learning to read should be. He uses vocabulary that is controlled but not restrictive, and his use of repetition of key phrases encourages children to join in and anticipate the sequence of the story as it is read to them, and gives them confidence as they begin to read for themselves. His books abound with humour and their subjects ensure their attraction to children.

John Burningham burst onto the children's book scene in 1963 with *Borka: The Adventures of a Goose with No Feathers,* for which he won the Kate Greenaway Medal for illustration. It is a gentle story of a goose who never develops feathers and is rejected by the other geese. It ends happily with Borka living in Kew Gardens amongst so many different species of bird that she is no longer out of place.

In the early 1970's Burningham produced a classic among picture books with *Mr. Gumpy's Outing.* The story is a simple one in which Mr Gumpy goes on a boat trip and is persuaded to take on board some children, a rabbit, a cat, a dog, a pig, a sheep, a chicken, a calf, and a goat. Despite their undertaking to behave and not to antagonise the other passengers, the inevitable happens and they all end up in the water. The tension is well built up and the ending is no less enjoyable for being predictable. The sequel, *Mr. Gumpy's Motor Car,* features the same characters; this time a car ride ends in chaos.

Two books that capture exactly what it is like to be a child are *Come Away from the Water, Shirley* and *Time to Get Out of the Bath, Shirley.* Shirley's exciting make-believe world is shown in stark contrast to her parents' drab everyday world. As her mother nags her about trivial, mundane things Shirley conjures up fantastic adventures in her imagination. Although the subject is treated humorously the underlying note is a serious one: Shirley's parents are either unable or unwilling to appreciate her fantasies and they are, by implication, the poorer for not doing so. Burningham returns to the same theme in *Where's Julius?* but on an altogether more cheerful note. Julius can never join his parents for meals because he is always doing something more important. At each meal his reasons for not joining them become more farfetched, but Mr. and Mrs. Troutbeck are able to accept and enjoy Julius's fantasy world and, uncomplaining, take his meals to him on a tray. The illustrations of Mr. Troutbeck scaling the Changa Benang mountains or Mrs. Troutbeck shooting the rapids on the Chico Neeko River, tray held aloft, are marvellous interpretations of the text. Each time the descriptions of the meals and of Julius's imaginary games are repeated to great effect.

The Shopping Basket and *Avocado Baby* also depict the stuff of children's fantasies. The latter is the story of a sickly baby born into a family of weaklings. After being fed on avocado pear he becomes progressively stronger until he is a "superbaby," carrying the shopping, frightening away burglars, and fighting off bullies in the park. The illustrations of the baby in his blue stretchsuit accomplishing these feats of strength make the book a winner. *The Shopping Basket* is, to my mind, one of the best children's books ever conceived. Not only is it a nicely moralistic tale of a rather weedy-looking boy who is able to get the better of his physically stronger assailants by using his intelligence, but it is also a near perfect book for children beginning to read. The vocabulary is controlled, there is plenty of repetition, and new words are introduced within a format that becomes familiar to the child as he reads the story. Steven is sent shopping by his mother and on his way home is accosted by a variety of greedy animals all demanding some of his shopping. He outwits them by challenging them to do something; each animal cannot resist the challenge and falls into the trap. Each time a wordless picture shows the hilarious outcome of the challenge. (Incidentally this adds a counting theme to the book as Steven has to sacrifice one item of shopping each time to escape.)

Burningham's most recent book, *John Patrick Norman Mc-Hennessy: The Boy Who Was Always Late,* is along similar lines. John Patrick is always late for school because of the extraordinary things that happen to him on the way. He manages to get out of some extremely tricky situations in a humorous way, but is always severely punished for his lateness. Although the tables are turned on the stern, unbelieving teacher in the end, the lasting impression is of the unjust punishment John Patrick has endured.

Granpa stands out as being different in style and tone to Burningham's other books. It depicts the relationship between a small girl and her grandfather in a series of interchanges between the two. The humour here is subtle, unlike the slapstick humour of previous books. For example, the little girl says "When we get to the beach can we stay there for ever?" to which her grandfather replies "Yes, but we must go back for our tea at four o'clock." The emphasis is as much on what is left unsaid as what is said, as in the spread that shows them walking away from each other and the words "That was not a nice thing to say to Granpa." The illustrations are a mixture of sepia line drawings and pastel-coloured pictures which balance the text perfectly throughout. The poignant ending with the little girl staring at an empty chair, suggesting Granpa's death, has been too much for many adult reviewers to bear, but children, it seems, cope much better.

—Fiona Lafferty

———

BURTON, Hester (Wood-Hill). British. Born in Beccles, Suffolk, 6 December 1913. Educated at Headington School, Oxford, 1925–31; Oxford University, 1932–36, B.A. (honours) in English 1936. Married Reginald W.B. Burton in 1937; three daughters. Part-time grammar school teacher; assistant editor, Oxford Junior Encyclopedia, London, 1956–61. Recipient: Library Association Carnegie Medal, 1964; Boston *Globe-Horn Book* award, 1971.

Address: Mill House, Kidlington, Oxford, England.

PUBLICATIONS FOR CHILDREN

Fiction

The Great Gale, illustrated by Joan Kiddell-Monroe. London, Oxford University Press, 1960; as *The Flood at Reedsmere,* Cleveland, World, 1968.
Castors Away!, illustrated by Victor Ambrus. London, Oxford University Press, 1962; Cleveland, World, 1963.
Time of Trial, illustrated by Victor Ambrus. London, Oxford University Press, 1963; Cleveland, World, 1964.
No Beat of Drum, illustrated by Victor Ambrus. London, Oxford University Press, 1966; Cleveland, World, 1967.
In Spite of All Terror, illustrated by Victor Ambrus. London, Oxford University Press, 1968; New York, World, 1969.
Otmoor for Ever!, illustrated by Gareth Floyd. London, Hamish Hamilton, 1968.
Thomas, illustrated by Victor Ambrus. London, Oxford University Press, 1969; as *Beyond the Weir Bridge,* New York, Crowell, 1970.
Through the Fire, illustrated by Gareth Floyd. London, Hamish Hamilton, 1969.
The Henchmans at Home, illustrated by Victor Ambrus. London, Oxford University Press, 1970; New York, Crowell, 1972.
The Rebel, illustrated by Victor Ambrus. London, Oxford University Press, 1971; New York, Crowell, 1972.
Riders of the Storm, illustrated by Victor Ambrus. London, Oxford University Press, 1972; New York, Crowell, 1973.
Kate Rider, illustrated by Victor Ambrus. London, Oxford University Press, 1974; as *Kate Ryder,* New York, Crowell, 1975.
To Ravensrigg, illustrated by Victor Ambrus. London, Oxford University Press, 1976; New York, Crowell, 1977.
Tim at the Fur Fort, illustrated by Victor Ambrus. London, Hamish Hamilton, 1977.
A Grenville Goes to Sea, illustrated by Colin McNaughton. London, Heinemann, 1977.
When the Beacons Blazed, illustrated by Victor Ambrus. London, Hamish Hamilton, 1978.
Five August Days, illustrated by Trevor Ridley. London, Oxford University Press, 1981.

Plays

Radio Play: *The Great Gale,* from her own story, 1961.

Television Play: *Castors Away!,* from her own story, 1968.

Other

A Seaman at the Time of Trafalgar, illustrated by Victor Ambrus. London, Oxford University Press, 1963.

Editor, *Her First Ball: Short Stories,* illustrated by Susan Einzig. London, Oxford University Press, 1959.

PUBLICATIONS FOR ADULTS

Other

Barbara Bodichon 1827–1891. London, Murray, 1949.

Editor, *Coleridge and the Wordsworths.* London, Oxford University Press, 1953.

Editor, *Tennyson.* London, Oxford University Press, 1954.
Editor, *A Book of Modern Stories.* London, Oxford University Press, 1959.

*

Hester Burton comments:

I have always been interested in the way ordinary people lived in times past. I love children, and I enjoy writing; hence my historical novels for young people. My method is to find some fairly small episode in history which catches my imagination such as a natural disaster, a battle, or a siege or a riot—find out all I can about it—and then plunge my imaginary young people into it and watch them struggle, usually very bravely, for honour and survival. It is the quality of the average boy and girl when put to the test which I find so surprising and inspiring.

*   *   *

Towards the end of *The Great Gale* when the flooded East Anglian village of Reedsmere has been visited both by the Queen and by the Minister of Housing, Mr. Macmillan, Mary whispers to her friend Myrtle: "I shall never forget today....Today we were part of history." Later after hearing on the radio the full extent of the havoc wrought by the gale she has a different thought. "Perhaps, after all, it was not an exciting, but a solemn and dreadful thing to be part of history." This duality of response on the part of individuals caught up in a national crisis is very characteristic of Hester Burton's novels, whether they are set in the 17th, 18th, 19th, or 20th centuries; it is not for nothing that one of her most highly praised books is called *Time of Tria.* (though in this case the "time" is 1801, and the "trial" is in one sense that of the heroine's radical book-seller father accused of sedition). Burton has modestly acknowledged a tendency to "find refuge" in history because the present age is becoming increasingly difficult to understand, whereas the past, in so far as historians have selected and interpreted the evidence, is easier to see in perspective. Moreover she has confessed that she is inclined to choose an historical event or theme because it echoes something she has experienced in her own life, and one can see, for instance, that *Castors Away!,* with its vivid and at times harrowing account of the autumn of the Battle of Trafalgar has its parallel in some events of the Second World War, while *No Beat of Drum,* with its portrayal of the harsh poverty of the English farm-labourers in 1829 to 1831, mirrors to a certain extent the divisive class-conflicts of the 1930's. Yet in fact her most successful novel of all is the one which derives most directly from lived experience. *In Spite of All Terror* evokes for us with a wonderful visual concreteness the outbreak of war in 1939, the evacuation of an East London school to the remoteness of the Oxfordshire countryside, the trauma of Dunkirk, the excitement of the Battle of Britain, and the anguish of the bombing of London in the autumn of 1940. It is moreover the most compulsively readable of her novels, its characterisation remains convincing while covering an extremely varied range of social classes, and it has in Liz Hawtin a protagonist who is at the same time the most believable and the most engaging of all Burton's heroines.

Even in this novel Burton supplemented her own recollections with the use of books, as well as other people's memories. Her more strictly historical novels have all been thoroughly and intelligently researched, using contemporary documents and diaries as well as modern scholarship, so that they recreate for us with powerful authenticity both the atmosphere and the detailed ways of life of her chosen period. (In keeping with the spirit of her self-acknowledged selectivity she has made herself particularly at home in the period of the French Revolution and the Napoleonic Wars—*The Rebel, Riders of the Storm, Time of Trial,* and *Castors Away!*—and also in the period of the English Civil War—*Thomas* and *Kate Rider.*) In general

her stories move at a brisk pace and are well supplied with incident; for the young adolescent reader their appeal is probably enhanced by a disposition to include, and even to work for, moments of strong feeling and uninhibited emotional release. An attractive example of her historical work at its best is *No Beat of Drum* in which the action moves from the impoverished countryside of southern England to the penal settlements of Van Diemen's Land. One cannot fault the generosity of the author's sympathy with the exploited and starving labourers, and she shows understanding of the "Captain Swing" riots even though she does not condone them. The portrayal of life in Tasmania is as vividly detailed as that of life in Hampshire, and one's only reservation about the latter part of the book is that the plot relies rather too much on coincidence.

The "excitement" of "being part of history" has always been strongly present in Burton's fiction, but in some of her later work the "solemn and dreadful" aspects have come more to the fore. Thus even in the relatively early *Castors Away!* the more barbarous features of the naval warfare of the time were rendered with an unflinching realism which makes some parts of the book strong meat for juvenile stomachs. A few years later in *Thomas* Burton seemed to have lost contact temporarily with her young readership by a too remorseless insistence on the hardships, miseries, and frustrations of her three protagonists; indeed her description of the Great Plague of London makes harrowing reading for an adult. Unfortunately, her next two novels, *The Rebel* and *Riders of the Storm,* were weakened by uncharacteristic elements of contrivance. However, in *Kate Rider* she returned fully to form, with a story about a Roundhead girl growing up in the early years of the Civil War. *To Ravensrigg,* set in the late 18th century, recounts how an adolescent girl confronts the discovery of her own unsuspected illegitimacy and is helped to trace her true origins by a group of Quaker anti-slave-trade campaigners one of whom falls in love with her; more than usually romantic in its story-line, it makes an absorbing and moving tale. Burton's most recent novel, *Five August Days,* is her sole venture into the strictly contemporary. The local East Anglian detail is as vivid as ever, and though plot and characterisation show rather less of her own individual distinction, they still make compulsive reading for 11 to 12 year olds of either sex.

In addition to her full-length novels Burton has also published in *The Henchmans at Home* a collection of six related stories about a country doctor's family in Victorian England which contains some of her most appealing work. There are also four shorter and more simply written books for readers in the 7–10 age-range which do not give her scope to deploy her gifts to the full, although in each case the narrative is developed with workmanlike skill and the historical background has been researched with typical care.

—Frank Whitehead

———

BURTON, Virginia Lee. American. Born in Newton Center, Massachusetts, 30 August 1909. Educated at the California School of Fine Arts, San Francisco, 1926–28; Boston Museum School, 1930. Married George Demetrios in 1931; two sons. Sketcher, Boston *Transcript,* 1928–31. Recipient: American Library Association Caldecott Medal, 1943. *Died 15 October 1968.*

PUBLICATIONS FOR CHILDREN (illustrated by the author)

Fiction

Choo Choo: The Story of a Little Engine Who Ran Away. Boston,

Houghton Mifflin, 1937; London, Faber, 1944.

Mike Mulligan and His Steam Shovel. Boston, Houghton Mifflin, 1939; London, Faber, 1941.

Calico the Wonder Horse; or, The Saga of Stewy Stinker. Boston, Houghton Mifflin, 1941; London, Faber, 1942.

The Little House. Boston, Houghton Mifflin, 1942; London, Faber, 1946.

Katy and the Big Snow. Boston, Houghton Mifflin, 1943; London, Faber, 1947.

Maybelle the Cable Car. Boston, Houghton Mifflin, 1952.

Other

Life Story. Boston, Houghton Mifflin, 1962.

*

Manuscript Collections: Free Library, Philadelphia; University of Oregon Library, Eugene.

Illustrator: *Sad-Faced Boy* by Arna Bontemps, 1937, and *The Fast Sooner Hound* by Bontemps and Jack Conroy, 1942; *Manual of American Mountaineering* edited by Kenneth A. Henderson, 1941; *Don Coyote* by Leigh Park, 1942; *Song of Robin Hood* edited by Anne Malcolmson, 1947; *The Emperor's New Clothes* by Hans Christian Andersen, 1949.

*   *   *

Writing her books was always the most difficult part, Virginia Lee Burton claimed—a hundred times harder than drawing pictures, of which she never tired. After her few ventures with illustrating stories written by others, she wanted to be in complete control of every aspect of her books, so she wrote them herself. But rather than let an idea develop freely into a story, she approached the text in terms of composing it to fit space on an illustrated page.

Despite this limitation, her texts are effective, especially when read aloud. Continual elimination of extra words plus trial-and-error to assure each word used was the best choice produced simple and strong texts. Burton found a subject she wanted to draw (a machine or a house); then she worked out a story with that subject as heroine by planning a series of drawings to enliven a thin plot thread. The text length was dictated by the number of pages available and the situations for drawings to be spread over them. The actual attention to individual words came last, as she created the text to accompany the pictures. The final step came after the text was set, when she would cut or substitute words so the shape of the type pattern would be an integral part of the page design.

That *Choo Choo* is still a success after more than 50 years says a great deal about the effectiveness of the story despite changing times. The spare but energetic text, full of read-aloud sound effects, catches the exuberant motion in the black-and-white drawings of the runaway steam engine on its dramatic adventure. A child today who has never seen nor heard a steam engine will gain a definite idea of what one was like from hearing *Choo Choo* read, and gain, too, a comforting feeling when the naughty engine is rescued and welcomed back by its crew.

Mike Mulligan and His Steam Shovel is wordier (but only because the story covers a longer span of time) and introduces more characters, and the surprise ending takes verbal as well as visual explanation. Here Burton allows her words to express more than mere accompaniment to the action of the color pictures; she introduces suspense as Mike Mulligan wonders if his long-unemployed, old-fashioned steam-shovel, Mary Anne, really can "dig as much in a day as a hundred men could dig in a week." This suspense becomes the crux of the story as Mary Anne and Mike take on a race against

time, digging the cellar for the new town hall in Popperville in just one day. Then a puzzle: how can Mike get Mary Anne out of the cellar? The entire story keeps children's interest and the ingenious ending intrigues them. This is an all-time favorite among American picture books with Mary Anne and Mike Mulligan enshrined in any Hall of Fame of children's book characters.

Burton also used the theme of machine as heroine with a snowplow in *Katy and the Big Snow* and with a cable-car in *Maybelle the Cable Car*. *Katy* has the appeal inherent in fighting a bad storm, a subject all children can understand. It is told with a strong, direct text. *Maybelle* is complicated, involving technical explanations about San Francisco's cable-cars and the citizens' vote to save them; and even introducing a villain, Big Bill the bus, doesn't make it an entertaining story.

Calico the Wonder Horse has more plot than her other books and the writing is as sharp and vivid as the drawings (some of her most exciting black-and-white work is in this book, which she drew as an antidote to the comics her sons read). It is parody of westerns and tall tales. The style, slap-bang in pace, is just right for this grand mix of funny desperados and frantic action.

A story with a lyric quality which comes partly from the repetition of words that sound well read aloud and partly from the repetition of patterns of the seasons and the years is *The Little House* who "shall never be sold for gold or silver and she will live to see our great-great-grandchildren's great-great-grandchildren living in her." Bestowing feminine genre on her like a ship, Burton also gives the house human qualities—curiosity, sadness, loneliness, fear, and finally happiness when she is rescued from the engulfing city and restored to country life. Children identify with having things happen to them that they cannot prevent and, like the welcoming back of naughty Choo Choo, they find great satisfaction in a happy ending; the little house being lived in and loved once more. They also absorb the complex concepts of times (the sun rising and setting each day; the moon waxing and waning each month; the seasons changing each year) and of change (from country to city to country) through just such a simple and moving story as *The Little House*.

Burton conceived of *Life Story*," "The Story of Life on Our Earth from Its Beginnings Up to Now," as a drama. Her carefully detailed color paintings are framed by the proscenium arch of a stage as an astronomer, a geologist, a paleontologist, a historian, a grandmother, and the author herself stand in the spotlight to show and tell. New scientific discoveries since 1962 may alter theories of creation and evolution and the date man first existed, but *Life Story* will always be brilliant presentation of infinitely complicated material. The text is specifically written to fit each illustration and the reduction of each enormous scientific era or area of study to a few brief sentences sometimes leads to obvious oversimplification. But the brevity is an invitation to a child to discover more. The last section recapitulates *The Little House* and the author's own experience. It also projects and shares emotionally with the reader Burton's deep respect for the designs of nature and the forces of life.

—Lee Kingman

————

BUTTERWORTH, Oliver. American. Born in Hartford, Connecticut, 23 May 1915. Educated at Kent School, Connecticut, 1930–33; Dartmouth College, Hanover, New Hampshire, 1933–37, A.B. 1937; Middlebury College, Vermont, M.A. 1947. Married Miriam Brooks in 1940; three sons and one daughter. Teacher, Kent School, 1937–48, and The Junior School, West Hartford, Connecticut, 1948–49. Since 1949 Instructor in English, Hartford College, Connecticut. Address: 81 Sunset Farm Road, West Hartford, Connecticut 06107, U.S.A.

PUBLICATIONS FOR CHILDREN

Fiction

The Enormous Egg, illustrated by Louis Darling.   Boston, Little
   Brown, 1956; London, Sidgwick and Jackson, 1975.
The Trouble with Jenny's Ear, illustrated by Julian de Miskey.
   Boston, Little Brown, 1960.
The Narrow Passage, illustrated by Eric Blegvad.   Boston, Little
   Brown, 1973.
The First Blueberry Pig, illustrated by the author.   Lubec, Maine,
   Stone Man Press, 1986.
A Visit to the Big House, illustrated by Vinny Collins.   Hartford,
   Connecticut, Families in Crisis, 1987.

*

Oliver Butterworth comments:

   I feel that my approach to writing for children is related to a deeply
rooted American skepticism of social institutions, and a
corresponding tendency to believe in the independent *untaught*
individual self. Mark Twain has been a strong influence on me,
especially in his book *Huckleberry Finn,* and I see my child
characters as "innocent" persons who find themselves having to
make moral or personal decisions on the basis of their own inner
feelings or instincts or convictions, much as Huck Finn has to do. I
suppose Mark Twain became a model for me in part because he lived
in Hartford, not far from my birthplace, and I felt he was my kind of
writer, because he wrote children's books for grownups.

*   *   *

   Some of the world's best-loved stories are "what ifs?" What if the
impossible were to happen in everyday, ordinary surroundings,
among ordinary folk? What if two young lads, tagging along with
an archaeological expedition exploring caves in France, were to
struggle through a tiny, narrow passage, impassable to adults, and
discover a series of wonderful prehistoric cave paintings, with the
artist still in residence? What if they struck up a wordless friendship
with him, and realized that his paintings are sacred to the old, old
man, and that he will suffer greatly if they are profaned by the eyes
of the curious outside world? Will they tell of their discovery, or keep
his secret?
   Another what if: suppose Jenny, at six years old too young to
understand its implications, had incredible powers of mental
telepathy. Suppose the child's family was in dire need of money,
immediately, and that the child, by appearing in a "whiz kid" contest,
could be eligible to win a large prize. Jenny's family are honest folk,
but their need is desperate, and the child is willing. What might be
the consequences?
   Best of all, the "what if" daydream of untold numbers of children
brought up on the fantasy of the loveable dinosaur: suppose, one fine
day, a common barn-yard hen should lay a truly *enormous* egg? What
if that egg, carefully tended over many weeks by a tremulously
hopeful young boy, should hatch into a tiny, perfect, charming
triceratops? What then if the dear little creature should double his
weight daily, threatening to eat the state of New Hampshire, never
mind the family, out of house and home? Suppose a publicity-seek-
ing senator declares that feeding the always-hungry triceratops (now
lovingly named Uncle Beasley) to be a waste of public funds,
demanding that he be stuffed and mounted as a museum exhibit?
Surely the boy who has raised him from a pup, so to speak, will hurry
to his defence, and just as surely a warm-hearted nation will rise to
defend the threatened dinosaur from extinction....
   With these three fantasies, Oliver Butterworth has earned a lasting
place in the hearts of child readers, and viewers too; for his best-loved

creation, *The Enormous Egg,* was filmed for television with great
success. Butterworth has a rare ability to recall the substance of
childhood dreams of glory; finding treasure; making contact with the
unreachable past; controlling the omnipresent adult population, and
setting it gently but firmly in its (subordinate) place. His adult figures
are a bit dated and stereotyped: Mom never sheds her apron and can't
remember difficult words like microphone, and Dad is none too sure
of himself outside the farm fence; but Butterworth's lively kids have
a lot of fun and adventure, and so do his countless child readers.

—Joan McGrath

————

BYARS, Betsy (née Cromer).   American.   Born in Charlotte,
North Carolina, 7 August 1928. Educated at Furman University,
Greenville, South Carolina, 1946–48; Queens College, Charlotte,
1948–50, B.A. in English 1950. Married Edward Ford Byars in 1950;
three daughters and one son. Recipient: American Library Association Newbery Medal, 1971; Child Study Committee award, 1977;
American Book award, 1981; Catholic Library Association Regina
Medal, 1987. Address: 4 Riverpoint, Clemson, South Carolina
29631, U.S.A.

PUBLICATIONS FOR CHILDREN

Fiction

Clementine, illustrated by Charles Wilton.   Boston, Houghton Mif-
   flin, 1962.
The Dancing Camel, illustrated by Harold Berson.   New York,
   Viking Press, 1965.
Rama, The Gypsy Cat, illustrated by Peggy Bacon.   New York,
   Viking Press, 1966.
The Groober, illustrated by the author.   New York, Harper, 1967.
The Midnight Fox, illustrated by Ann Grifalconi.   New York,
   Viking Press, 1968; London, Faber, 1970.
Trouble River, illustrated by Rocco Negri.   New York, Viking Press,
   1969.
The Summer of the Swans, illustrated by Ted CoConis.   New York,
   Viking Press, 1970; London, Hippo, 1980.
Go and Hush the Baby, illustrated by Emily McCully.   New York,
   Viking Press, 1971; London, Bodley Head, 1980.
The House of Wings, illustrated by Daniel Schwartz.   New York,
   Viking Press, 1972; London, Bodley Head, 1973.
The 18th Emergency, illustrated by Robert Grossman.   New York,
   Viking Press, 1973; London, Bodley Head, 1974.
The Winged Colt of Casa Mia, illustrated by Richard Cuffari.   New
   York, Viking Press, 1973; London, Bodley Head, 1974.
After the Goat Man, illustrated by Ronald Himler.   New York,
   Viking Press, 1974; London, Bodley Head, 1975.
The Lace Snail, illustrated by the author.   New York, Viking Press,
   1975.
The T.V. Kid, illustrated by Richard Cuffari.   New York, Viking
   Press, and London, Bodley Head, 1976.
The Pinballs.   New York, Harper, and London, Bodley Head, 1977.
The Cartoonist, illustrated by Richard Cuffari.   New York, Viking
   Press, and London, Bodley Head, 1978.
Good-bye, Chicken Little.   New York, Harper, and London, Bodley
   Head, 1979.
The Night Swimmers, illustrated by Troy Howell.   New York,
   Delacorte Press, and London, Bodley Head, 1980.
The Cybil War, illustrated by Gail Owens.   New York, Viking Press,

and London, Bodley Head, 1981.

The Animal, The Vegetable, and John D. Jones, illustrated by Ruth Sanderson. New York, Delacorte Press, and London, Bodley Head, 1982.

The Two-Thousand-Pound Goldfish. New York, Harper, and London, Bodley Head, 1982.

The Glory Girl. New York, Viking Press, and London, Bodley Head, 1983.

The Computer Nut. New York, Viking Kestrel, and London, Bodley Head, 1984.

Cracker Jackson. New York, Viking Kestrel, and London, Bodley Head, 1985.

The Blossoms Meet the Vulture Lady, illustrated by Jacqueline Rogers. New York, Delacorte Press, and London, Bodley Head, 1986.

The Golly Sisters Go West, illustrated by Sue Truesdell. New York, Harper, 1986.

The Not-Just-Anybody Family, illustrated by Jacqueline Rogers. New York, Delacorte Press, and London, Bodley Head, 1986.

A Blossom Promise, illustrated by Jacqueline Rogers. New York, Delacorte Press, and London, Bodley Head, 1987.

The Blossoms and the Green Phantom, illustrated by Jacqueline Rogers. New York, Delacorte Press, and London, Bodley Head, 1987.

Beans on the Roof, illustrated by Melodye Rosales. New York, Delacorte Press, and London, Bodley Head, 1988.

The Burning Questions of Bingo Brown. New York, Viking Kestrel, and London, Bodley Head, 1988.

Bingo Brown and the Language of Love. New York, Viking Kestrel, 1989.

*

Manuscript Collection: Clemson University, South Carolina.

Betsy Byars comments:

My books usually begin with something that really happened, a newspaper story or an event from my children's lives. But, aside from this mutual starting point, each book has been a different writing experience. My daughter once described one of my books by saying, "Mom just made it up as she went along." That was true, but in another book I wrote the end first and worked back.

It takes me about a year to write a book, but I spend another year thinking about it and polishing it. Living with my own teenagers has taught me that not only must I not write down to my readers, I must write up to them. Boys and girls are very sharp today, and when I visit classrooms and talk with students I am always impressed to find how many of them are writing stories and how knowledgeable they are about writing.

*   *   *

Betsy Byars is a prolific writer; over the past 27 years she has written over 30 books for children. Her works include books for the very young (picture books such as *The Lace Snail* and *Go and Hush the Baby*), one historical novel (*Trouble River*), and two fantasies (*The Winged Colt of Casa Mia* and *The Computer Nut*). But she is best known for her realistic novels for children, with certain similar qualities: a clear, concise prose style; likeable but often lonely or alienated protagonists trying to cope with a believable problem; an almost exclusively adolescent or pre-adolescent point of view; and humor, which is present, if only faintly, even in Byars' more serious books.

For instance, in *The Midnight Fox* Tom, the protagonist, has been temporarily abandoned by his parents; while they bicycle through Europe, he must stay on his aunt's and uncle's farm, a setting that terrifies him. He is frightened of animals, and finds the farmland and woods intimidating and lonely. Unathletic by nature and inclination, Tom is misunderstood by his very athletic parents and feels he is a disappointment to them. His fears of the cows and chickens on the farm are at once understandable and amusing. But Tom grows and changes when for the first time in his life he does a courageous thing. Ironically he does it for an animal, the creatures he has always been afraid of—he saves the beautiful midnight fox. He is still the boy who can strike out 17 consecutive times in baseball, but he is also a boy who can take courageous action to defend and preserve what he loves.

As in *The Midnight Fox,* the protagonists of many of Byars' novels feel isolated, and often unloved and abandoned by their parents. Sammy in *The House of Wings* wakes one morning to find his parents have left for Detroit and he has been left behind with a grandfather he does not know. Warren in *The Two-Thousand-Pound Goldfish* longs for his mother, who started out simply protesting government policy, but has now become involved in bombings and can't come home because she is wanted by the FBI. Warren lives with his grandmother but escapes more and more from reality by daydreaming. Carlie, Harvey, and Thomas J. in *The Pinballs* are foster children. Each has been abandoned or abused by his or her parents. Carlie initially feels like a pinball: out of control, without rights, and pushed around by others. She, like most of Byars' characters, finds that she does have choices; she is not a pinball, she can make things better for herself.

Betsy Byars often combines humor and pathos in her books while creating a complex plot. In *The Burning Questions of Bingo Brown,* Bingo, the protagonist, wants to be a writer but needs answers to the questions in his journal: "Has there ever been a successful writer with freckles?"; "Why did no one notice my mousse?"; "Am I ready for a mixed-sex conversation?" When Bingo's sixth-grade English teacher Mr. Markham begins acting strange and giving even stranger assignments, Bingo wants to help but doesn't know how. Mr. Markham has a serious motorcycle accident shortly after he has had the class, as an assignment, write a letter to a person contemplating suicide. To try to get answers as to why and how the accident happened, Bingo goes out to view the accident scene, but feels worse because he thinks Mr. Markham may have driven off the road on purpose. Bingo grows and changes when he learns that Mr. Markham has gained consciousness and is happy to be alive. He remains a boy with many questions, but he comes to realize that some questions do not have answers and never will.

As in *The Burning Questions of Bingo Brown* Byars shows that she is capable of being humorous even while writing about very difficult subjects. In *The Summer of the Swans* the frightening news that learning-disabled Charlie is missing impinges directly on the scene in which Sara, trying to dye her orange sneakers light blue, has just succeeded in turning them puce. Her distress and fear for Charlie is mixed with her comic embarrassment about the hideous color of her sneakers. In *Cracker Jackson* the trauma associated with Cracker taking his babysitter Alma to a shelter for abused women is overshadowed by the comedy of the car ride. The car is being driven by Cracker, an unlicensed and inexperienced 12 year old under the instruction of his friend Goat, who knows no more about driving than Cracker does. An even more subtle effect is achieved in *The Cartoonist,* when the mentally immature mother employs constant clichés from television advertising to try to persuade Alfie to give up the peace of his attic and his art and join her and his grandfather in the mindless consumption of television.

Byars has written and continues to write many novels for adolescents that are popular and enjoyable, with a variety of themes and memorable characters. She is at her best when writing about the child who is isolated, either by circumstances, or by his or her own nature. Byars' understanding of the traumatic impact of ordinary, often minor crises, upon the child's developing character is central to the success of her best writing. The simplicity of the language she uses to express these crucial incidents of trial and change is one of the most important elements of her success. To her readers her prolific production is also an element to be grateful for. She is (and her fans hope she will long continue to be) a reliable author whose many books illuminate the ordinary.

—Rosanne Fraine Donahue

* * *

CAMERON, Eleanor (Frances, née Butler). American. Born in Winnipeg, Manitoba, Canada, 23 March 1912. Educated at the University of California, Los Angeles, 1931–33; Art Center School, Los Angeles, one year. Married Ian Stuart Cameron in 1934; one son. Library clerk, Los Angeles Public Library, 1930–36, and Los Angeles Schools Library, 1936–42; research librarian, Foote Cone and Belding Advertising, Los Angeles, 1942–43; research assistant, Batten Barton Durstine and Osborn, Los Angeles, 1956–58; librarian, Dan B. Miner Co., advertising, Los Angeles, 1958–59. Whittall Lecturer, Library of Congress, Washington, D.C., 1977. Member of the editorial board, *Cricket* magazine, La Salle, Illinois, since 1973, and *Children's Literature in Education,* New York, since 1982; since 1977 member of the advisory board, Center for the Study of Children's Literature, Simmons College, Boston. Recipient: Boston *Globe-Horn Book* award, 1971; National Book award, 1974; University of Minnesota Kerlan award, 1985. Lives in Pebble Beach, California. Address: c/o E.P. Dutton Inc., 2 Park Avenue, New York, New York 10016, U.S.A.

PUBLICATIONS FOR CHILDREN

Fiction

The Wonderful Flight to the Mushroom Planet, illustrated by Robert Henneberger. Boston, Little Brown, 1954.
Stowaway to the Mushroom Planet, illustrated by Robert Henneberger. Boston, Little Brown, 1956.
Mr. Bass's Planetoid, illustrated by Louis Darling. Boston, Little Brown, 1958.
The Terrible Churnadryne, illustrated by Beth and Joe Krush. Boston, Little Brown, 1959.
A Mystery for Mr. Bass, illustrated by Leonard Shortall. Boston, Little Brown, 1960.
The Mysterious Christmas Shell, illustrated by Beth and Joe Krush. Boston, Little Brown, 1961.
The Beast with the Magical Horn, illustrated by Beth and Joe Krush. Boston, Little Brown, 1963.
A Spell Is Cast, illustrated by Beth and Joe Krush. Boston, Little Brown, 1964.
Time and Mr. Bass, illustrated by Fred Meise. Boston, Little Brown, 1967.
A Room Made of Windows, illustrated by Trina Schart Hyman. Boston, Little Brown, 1971; London, Gollancz, 1972.
The Court of the Stone Children. New York, Dutton, 1973.
To the Green Mountains. New York, Dutton, 1975.
Julia and the Hand of God, illustrated by Gail Owens. New York, Dutton, 1977.
Beyond Silence. New York, Dutton, 1980.
That Julia Redfern, illustrated by Gail Owens. New York, Dutton, 1982.
Julia's Magic, illustrated by Gail Owens. New York, Dutton, 1984.

The Private Worlds of Julia Redfern.   New York, Dutton, 1988.

PUBLICATIONS FOR ADULTS

Novel

Unheard Music. Boston, Little Brown, 1950.

Other

The Green and Burning Tree: On the Writing and Enjoyment of Children's Books. Boston, Little Brown, 1969.

*

Manuscript Collection: Kerlan Collection, University of Minnesota, Minneapolis.

Eleanor Cameron comments:
   Why write for children? Because, for some unexplainable reason, what the children's writer has to say, the stories he has to tell, come forth most naturally and fully and freely when related to the memories and emotions of childhood. The writer for children is most deeply released when speaking out of his own childhood (at least using autobiographical feelings), and yet his work must be as good for adults as it is for children. This cannot be stressed too much. He will, just as in writing for adults, give the best of himself and demand the best of himself. If this seems an obvious statement, it is astonishing how many otherwise intelligent people believe that it is a matter of writing down when one writes for children. This idea is, of course, insulting. Yet a young woman once told my husband very seriously that she was spending four hours a day, apart from an eight-hour job, in trying to write for children, and that she supposed the main problem was in learning how to write down properly. She should have heard Dorothy Parker's remark, concerning fiction writing in general, "It's going to be the best you can do, and it's the fact that it's the best you can do that kills you."
   Surely what we call literature must be able to give the child or adult reader revelations, an intensified sense of existence, human beings with idiosyncracies and habits and beliefs, with histories and possible futures which the reader cannot help dwelling upon when the last page is turned. That texture we call "the novel" offers, at its most treasurable, a passionate, sometimes rapturous meeting between the artist's private vision and the haunting, ambiguous, paradoxical world of feelings and objects—all interlaced. And these interlacings open up for us intimations about ourselves and the world that we had not guessed at before, or had not seen, or been able to put into words.
   Children's literature is not something separate in its requirements of excellence, but a branch of the tree of all literature, sharing the same elements and depending upon the same surge of life and artistry. It is the state of mind of the writer that determines the point of view from which he will see the world he is telling about, and respect for audience, be it child or adult, is always present in what we call literature. Therefore it holds that in writing for either of these audiences, literature can only be achieved when the author works at the top of his bent, matured enough in his craft that he is able to fuse fully realized elements into a firmly conceived whole. All of youth needs to be given, not what it already knows, but what it has not yet divined.

* * *

Eleanor Cameron has been slow to receive the recognition she deserves. Perhaps her reputation was hurt by her breaking into print initially as a writer of juvenile science fiction, a genre only now being accepted. Perhaps, too, Cameron's role as a critic of children's books unafraid of established reputations has been held against her. In any case, a look at the quality and variety of Cameron's books and the ample signs of her continuing artistic growth should suffice to convince the disinterested observer that Cameron is a major author of children's fiction.

The Mushroom Planet books, which first brought Cameron success, continue to be popular, and for good reason: they are entertainingly written, contain lively incidents, skillfully employ some of the more immediately attractive conventions of science fiction, and feature characters, e.g., David, Chuck, and Tyco Bass, easy to identify with and like. Already evident in these narratives is Cameron's skill in describing physical setting and suggesting the close relationship that can exist between place and character. The next several novels reveal an author deliberately seeking to broaden her scope and hone her narrative skills. For instance, *The Terrible Churnadryne,* a fantasy, breaks loose from the constraints of science fiction. Plotting becomes realistic, as *The Mysterious Christmas Shell* aptly illustrates, rejecting a dependence on magic and extrapolated technology. Theme moves into the foreground, most notably in *A Spell Is Cast,* and tends to focus on problems peculiar to growing up.

A Room Made of Windows marks the end of Cameron's apprenticeship and her emergence as an important writer with the first of several books centered on the character Julia Redfern. Capturing the emotional and psychological nuances of preadolescence, the novel describes Julia's learning to make her thoughts and feelings "windows" into her deepest self and then outward toward the world around her. The novel also depicts Julia's difficulty in accepting her mother's remarriage as well as her fondly remembered father's inadequacies. *Julia and the Hand of God, That Julia Redfern,* and *Julia's Magic* fill in the details of Julia's childhood that accounts for the self-discovery of *A Room Made of Windows. The Private Worlds of Julia Redfern* finds Julia at 15 still struggling to come to terms with her new stepfather. Her realization that she cannot always be center stage in her family's and friends' lives (literally as well as figuratively—she is upstaged by a rival to play Shakespeare's Juliet in the school play) insures that she is on her way to growing up.

The Court of the Stone Children and *To the Green Mountains* continue Cameron's exploration of feminine preadolescence. In the former, which combines elements of fantasy, ghost story, and mystery, Nina learns that history and art can not only give immediacy to the past but heighten her perceptions and structure her life. In *To the Green Mountains* Kath grows up against a background of small town life at its best and worst, increasingly aware of the fact that ambitions and dreams are often thwarted because of inadequate self-knowledge, that fidelity and loyalty cannot always resolve conflicts, and that sexuality, expressed as well as repressed, does sometimes destroy. Considered as a whole, what Cameron has already accomplished surely must place her among the finest contemporary authors of children's fiction.

—Francis J. Molson

CANNAN, Joanna (Maxwell). British. Born in Oxford, in 1898. Educated at Wychwood School, Oxford, and in Paris. Married H.J. Pullein-Thompson in 1918 (died 1957); three daughters, the writers Diana, Christine, and Josephine Pullein-Thompson, *qq.v.,* and one son, the writer Denis Cannan. *Died 22 April 1961.*

PUBLICATIONS FOR CHILDREN

Fiction

A Pony for Jean, illustrated by Anne Bullen. London, Lane, 1936; New York, Scribner, 1937.
We Met Our Cousins, illustrated by Anne Bullen. London, Collins, 1937; New York, Dodd Mead, 1938.
Another Pony for Jean, illustrated by Anne Bullen. London, Collins, 1938.
London Pride, illustrated by Anne Bullen. London, Collins, 1939.
More Ponies for Jean, illustrated by Anne Bullen. London, Collins, 1943.
They Bought Her a Pony, illustrated by Rosemary Robertson. London, Collins, 1944.
Hamish: The Story of a Shetland Pony, illustrated by Anne Bullen. London, Penguin, 1944.
Gaze at the Moon, illustrated by Sheila Rose. London, Collins, 1957.

Other

Editor, with M.D. and May W. Cannan, *The Tripled Crown: A Book of English, Scotch and Irish Verse for the Age of Six to Sixteen.* London, Frowde, 1908.

PUBLICATIONS FOR ADULTS

Novels

The Misty Valley. London, First Novel Library, 1922; New York, Doran, 1924.
Wild Berry Wine. London, Unwin, and New York, Stokes, 1925.
The Lady of the Heights. London, Unwin, 1926.
Sheila Both-Ways. London, Benn, 1928; New York, Stokes, 1939.
The Simple Pass On. London, Benn, 1929; as *Orphan of Mars,* Indianapolis, Bobbs Merrill, 1930.
No Walls of Jasper. London, Benn, 1930; New York, Doubleday, 1931.
Ithuriel's Hour. London, Hodder and Stoughton, 1931; New York, Doubleday, 1932.
High Table. London, Benn, and New York, Doubleday, 1931.
Snow in Harvest. London, Hodder and Stoughton, 1932.
North Wall. London, Hodder and Stoughton, 1933.
Under Proof. London, Hodder and Stoughton, 1934.
The Hills Sleep On. London, Hodder and Stoughton, 1935.
A Hand to Burn. London, Hodder and Stoughton, 1936.
Frightened Angels. London, Gollancz, and New York, Harper, 1936.
Pray Do Not Venture. London, Gollancz, 1937.
Princes in the Land. London, Gollancz, 1938.
They Rang Up the Police. London, Gollancz, 1939.
Death at The Dog. London, Gollancz, 1940; New York, Reynal, 1941.
Idle Apprentice. London, Gollancz, 1940.
Blind Messenger. London, Gollancz, 1941.
Little I Understood. London, Gollancz, 1948.
The Hour of the Angel; Ithuriel's Hour. London, Pan, 1949.
Murder Included. London, Gollancz, 1950; as *Poisonous Relations,* New York, Morrow, 1950; as *The Taste of Murder,* New York, Dell, 1951.
Body in the Beck. London, Gollancz, 1952; New York, Garland, 1983.
And All I Learned. London, Gollancz, 1952.
Long Shadows. London, Gollancz, 1955.

People to Be Found. London, Gollancz, 1956.
And Be a Villain. London, Gollancz, 1958.
All Is Discovered. London, Gollancz, 1962.

Other

I Wrote a Pony Book. London, Collins, 1950.

*   *   *

Joanna Cannan was already the author of several satirical adult novels when she wrote her first children's book. *A Pony for Jean* tells the story of Jean Leslie who, exiled from London to the country when her father loses his money "in pepper," acquires a half-starved pony nicknamed The Toastrack, nurses him back to health, learns to ride him, and scoops most of the prizes in the local gymkhana.

A Pony for Jean followed years crowded with other writers' pony biographies or autobiographies, written in the style of *Black Beauty.* Each assumed that horses were morally good, their faults due only to mistreatment; and by 1936 this procession of blameless animals scarred by humanity had become tediously repetitive. Cannan, wanting to write about the ponies she loved and seeking a new angle, shrewdly moved the focus of interest away from the pony to the rider. Nor was Jean just any rider. As the first fanatical pony addict to appear in a book, she left a lasting mark on children's literature.

Early in the story Jean goes to visit her horsy cousins. Goaded by their scorn she mounts a pony, heads for a jump—and recovers consciousness on the drawing room sofa. The fall doesn't matter; the experience of riding has, like a religious conversion, changed Jean's life forever. She staggers off the sofa so that her cousins can show her the despised Toastrack, waiting bony and unkempt in the stable. He turns and gives her "a long soft look," and it is love at first sight.

Cavalier, as the pony is renamed, is everything to Jean: her child, as she nurses him back to health; her teacher, as she learns to ride; her heroic lover, leaping a stile for her at midnight, and winning her glory in the gymkhana. He is a dream pony, yet he is always second in interest. Jean—passionate, resolute, brave, but lighthearted—dominates the book.

A Pony for Jean was an immediate success, and Cannan followed it with other pony stories. *Another Pony for Jean* and *More Ponies for Jean* show the same heroine enlarging her experience and starting her own riding school. *We Met Our Cousins* and *London Pride* also include ponies, but their importance is slighter in these two books based on Cannan's childhood visits to Scotland. *They Bought Her a Pony* proved as archetypal as *A Pony for Jean,* describing how an ignorant rider mismanages her pony until taken in hand by the horse-mad children she has previously despised.

The themes of the girl who adores her pony and the young rider learning from sad experience were well-established by the mid 1940's, taken up, and continued by Cannan's daughters—the Pullein-Thompsons—and many other writers. "Pony books," after Cannan, meant "rider books": stories of heroines struggling with ponies who may at first seem difficult but who, through schooling and cherishing, become winners in the last chapter.

Yet there is an originality and a stylishness in Cannan's books which no other pony book author achieved; and it is perhaps surprising that her work is so little valued. Unfortunately the Cannan personality glimpsed behind the pages seems nowadays uncongenial. Against the realistic, egalitarian, tolerant books of today, Cannan's appear highbrow, intolerant, perversely romantic, and glaringly snobbish.

These traits were the result of her upbringing. She was the descendant of dons and upper-class Scottish soldiers. The Cannans kept aloof from everyday society; in their lonely nursery the children steeped themselves in family tradition and historical romance, constructing stern, heroic dramas imbued with the attitudes that mark all Cannan's books. Courage, courtesy, generosity, and self-control are prized; materialism and indulgence in fantasy or emotionalism are abhorred.

Embodied in fiction, these attitudes make for an unbridgeable gulf between "good" and "bad" characters. Cannan does not, in the usual manner of snobs, prefer the rich to the poor, the thoroughbred to the moorland pony. Instead she directs her readers to empathise with the characters she approves of and scorn those she doesn't. Ideal behaviour is illustrated when Jean saves a horse's life by applying a tourniquet to its injured leg, and then rides away, with no thought of thanks or reward, grateful that her mother taught her "sensible things about arteries, instead of idiotic things about fairies."

Cannan's rigid standards, acceptable once but now outdated, inevitably jar; and that is why her books, for all their originality, passion, wit, and love of animals, are forgotten. If they were ever rediscovered as period pieces, their attractive qualities might be found to counterbalance their unattractive characteristics.

—Angela Bull

———

CARLE, Eric. American. Born in Syracuse, New York, 25 June 1929. Educated at Akademie der Bildenden Künste, Stuttgart, Germany, 1945–50. Served in the United States Army, 1952–54. Married 1) Dorothea Wohlenberg in 1954 (divorced 1964), one daughter and one son; 2) Barbara Morrison in 1973. Poster designer, United States Information Center, Stuttgart, 1950–52; graphic designer, *New York Times,* 1954–56; art director, L.W. Frohlich and Co., New York, 1956–63; guest instructor, Pratt Institute, Brooklyn, New York, 1964. Since 1963 freelance writer, illustrator, and designer. Individual shows: Frans Hals Museum, Haarlem, Netherlands, 1988; Zeeuwse Bibliotheek, Middelburg, Openbare Bibliotheek, Hengelo, and Bisschoppelijk Museum, Breda, all Netherlands, 1989; Klingspor Museum, Germany, 1989. Recipient: American Institute of Graphic Arts award, 1970 (twice); Children's Literature prize (Germany), 1970. Address: 231 Crescent Street, Northampton, Massachusetts 01060, U.S.A.

PUBLICATIONS FOR CHILDREN (illustrated by the author)

Fiction

1, 2, 3, to the Zoo. Cleveland, World, 1968; London, Hamish Hamilton, 1969.
The Very Hungry Caterpillar. Cleveland, World, and London, Hamish Hamilton, 1969.
Pancakes, Pancakes! New York, Knopf, and London, Hamish Hamilton, 1970.
Do You Want to Be My Friend? New York, Crowell, and London, Hamish Hamilton, 1971.
The Rooster Who Set Out to See the World. New York, Watts, and London, Dent, 1972; as *Rooster's Off to See the World,* London, Hodder and Stoughton, 1988.
The Secret Birthday Message. New York, Crowell, and London, Hamish Hamilton, 1972.
Have You Seen My Cat? New York, Watts, and London, Dent, 1973.
I See a Song. New York, Crowell, and London, Hamish Hamilton, 1973.
All About Arthur (an Absolutely Absurd Ape). New York, Watts, 1974; London, Dent, 1975.
My Very First Library. New York, Crowell, 1974.
The Mixed-Up Chameleon. New York, Crowell, and London, Hamish Hamilton, 1975; revised edition, Hamish Hamilton, 1985.

The Grouchy Ladybug. New York, Crowell, 1977; as *The Bad-Tempered Ladybird,* London, Hamish Hamilton, 1978.
Watch Out! A Giant! New York, Collins World, 1978; London, Hamish Hamilton, 1979.
The Honeybee and the Robber. New York, Philomel, and London, MacRae, 1981.
The Very Busy Spider. New York, Philomel, 1984; London, Hamish Hamilton, 1985.
All Around Us. Natick, Massachusetts, Picture Book Studio, 1986.
Papa, Please Get the Moon for Me. Natick, Massachusetts, Picture Book Studio, 1986; London, Hodder and Stoughton, 1987.
A House for Hermit Crab. Natick, Massachusetts, Picture Book Studio, 1987.

Other

The Say-with-Me ABC Book. New York, Holt Rinehart, 1967.
The Tiny Seed. New York, Crowell, 1970; as *The Tiny Seed and the Giant Flower,* London, Nelson, 1970.
The Very Long Tail. New York, Crowell, 1972.
The Very Long Train. New York, Crowell, 1972.
Walter the Baker (retelling). New York, Knopf, 1972.
My Very First Book of Colors [*Numbers, Shapes, Words, Food, Growth, Heads and Tails, Homes, Motion, Sounds, Tools, Touch*]. New York, Crowell, 12 vols., 1974–86.
Storybook: Seven Tales by the Brothers Grimm. New York and London, Watts, 1976.
Seven Stories by Hans Christian Andersen. New York and London, Watts, 1978.
Twelve Tales from Aesop. New York, Philomel, 1980.
Catch the Ball! New York, Philomel, and London, Collins, 1982.
Let's Paint a Rainbow. New York, Philomel, and London, Collins, 1982.
What's for Lunch? New York, Philomel, and London, Collins, 1982.

Editor, *Treasury of Classic Stories for Children.* New York, Orchard, and London, Hamish Hamilton, 1988.

*

Illustrator: *The Sun Is a Star,* 1963, and *Gravity at Work and Play,* 1963, both by Sune Engelbrektson; *If You Can Count to Ten,* 1964, *Brown Bear, Brown Bear, What Do You See?,* 1967, and *A Ghost Story,* 1970, all by Bill Martin; *Nature Thoughts,* 1965, and *On Friendship,* 1966, both edited by Louise Bachelder; *Red-Flannel Hash and Shoo-Fly Pie* by Lila Perl, 1965; *Aesop's Fables,* 1965, and *The Whale with a Jail,* 1968, both by Nora Roberts Wainer; *Indoor and Outdoor Grow-It-Book* by Samm S. Baker, 1966; *In Search of Meaning: Living Religions of the World* by Carl H. Voss, 1968; *Pandekager til Jens,* 1970, and *Vil du Vaere Min Ven?,* 1971, both by Martin Berg; *Tales of the Nimipoo* by Eleanor B. Heady, 1970; *The Boastful Fisherman* by William Knowlton, 1970; *Feathered Ones and Furry,* 1971, and *Do Bears Have Mothers Too?,* 1973, both by Aileen Fisher; *The Scarecrow Clock* by George Mendoza, 1971; *Why Noah Chose the Dove* by Isaac Bashevis Singer, 1974; *The Hole in the Dyke* by Norma B. Green, 1975; *Otter Nonsense* by Norton Juster, 1982; *Chip Has Many Brothers* by Hans Baumann, 1985; *The Foolish Tortoise* and *The Greedy Python* both by Richard Buckley, 1985; *The Mountain That Loved a Bird* by Alice McLerran, 1985; *The Lamb and the Butterfly* by Arnold Sundgaard, 1989.

*   *   *

An author-illustrator must be judged on both arts. Eric Carle is a master craftsman in words and pictures, showing boldness not only in his use of colour but also in the themes he has chosen for his picture books. Although almost all of his books feature an animal or insect, interwoven in the storyline of a humanised creature there is the real natural world, authentically depicted. Added emphasis is given by the use of fable format and humour.

Carle's most famous and probably best-loved book is *The Very Hungry Caterpillar.* Its appeal to young children and adults lies in the multiplicity of attractions within the 16 main pages. The low-key scene-setting text on the white left edge of the first double spread bold colour picture; the contrasting sunny picture on the next page, with the developing storyline, whet the appetite for the eye-catching split pages to follow, through which the caterpillar literally eats his way. Holes in the page indicate his progress through a succession of types of food. The natural aspects of growth, cocoon, and the final glorious double spread butterfly make an impact on the reader after the masterly build up of action, cause and effect, humour, and the possibility for child readers to identify with some of the proxy human similarities.

Therein lies Carle's success, the construction of story and picture providing meat for the eye and the mind while simultaneously carrying the reader forward towards a satisfying end. The same skill can be seen in many of his other books, such as *The Grouchy Ladybug,* where in 40 pages, many of them split, the ladybug meets and retreats from natural and unnatural enemies, involving the reader in recognition of size, shape, and response to her bad temper.

Carle's empathy with the natural world has led him to concentrate most of his books on that theme—he has also written about roosters, spiders, crabs, cats, chameleons, bears, and pythons. In the counting book *1, 2, 3 to the Zoo* each double double page has a railway carriage with a growing number of animals in it.

Carle's illustrative style, now well known for the use of collage, is effective and extends the reader's perception. His methods of using the physical page to add knowledge, interest, and imaginative stimulus are also admired. They include split pages in *The Grouchy Ladybug;* different lengths of page and holes in *The Very Hungry Caterpillar;* pages folding and unfolding outwards and upwards in *Papa, Please Get the Moon for Me,* in which Papa climbs up a ladder on the unfolding upwards page to bring home the moon for little Monica; and the die-cut pages with raised surfaces to feel the story in *The Very Busy Spider.* Here the spider, the spider's web, and a fly are in thermo-plastic relief, enabling both visually handicapped and sighted children to read the pictures.

The impact of Carle's dramatic illustrations may cause the adult reader to overlook the carefully designed text, brief though it is in each book. The fable format requires and receives a simple storyline, narrative flow, and both the economical use of words and evocative vocabulary with imaginative stimulus. The build up of atmosphere and tension by repetitive phrases is another feature as is the unforced message or moral inherent in the story and humorously transmitted.

Carle's books though for young children are not childish, but appeal to the child in all of us, to our curiosity, our emotions, to our interest in change, exemplified in *A House for Hermit Crab:* "'Time to move,' said Hermit Crab one day in January. 'I've grown too big for this little shell.'"

Growth is the thread running through Carle's books: growth in knowledge, understanding, concepts, and self-awareness, absorbed painlessly and enjoyably. For underlying all is the author-illustrator's capacity for entertaining through word and picture.

—Margaret R. Marshall

CARLSON, Natalie Savage. American. Born in Winchester, Virginia, 3 October 1906. Attended high school in California. Married Daniel Carlson in 1929; two daughters. Reporter, Long Beach *Morning Sun,* California, 1926–29. Recipient: Child Study Association of America award, 1966. Address: 3220 Highway 19, North Lot 17, Doral Mobile Home Villas, Clearwater, Florida 33515, U.S.A.

PUBLICATIONS FOR CHILDREN

Fiction

Alphonse, That Bearded One, illustrated by Nicolas Mordvinoff. New York, Harcourt Brace, 1954.
Wings Against the Wind, illustrated by Mircea Vasiliu. New York, Harper, 1955.
Hortense, The Cow for a Queen, illustrated by Nicolas Mordvinoff. New York, Harcourt Brace, 1957.
The Happy Orpheline, illustrated by Garth Williams. New York, Harcourt Brace, 1957; London, Blackie, 1960.
The Family under the Bridge, illustrated by Garth Williams. New York, Harper, 1958; as *Under the Bridge,* London, Blackie, 1969.
A Brother for the Orphelines, illustrated by Garth Williams. New York, Harper, 1959; London, Blackie, 1961.
Evangeline, Pigeon of Paris, illustrated by Nicolas Mordvinoff. New York, Harcourt Brace, 1960; as *Pigeon of Paris,* London, Blackie, 1972.
The Tomahawk Family, illustrated by Stephen Cook. New York, Harper, 1960; London, Hamish Hamilton, 1961.
The Song of the Lop-Eared Mule, illustrated by Janina Domanska. New York, Harper, 1961.
Carnival in Paris, illustrated by Fermin Rocker. New York, Harper, 1962; London, Blackie, 1964.
A Pet for the Orphelines, illustrated by Fermin Rocker. New York, Harper, 1962; London, Blackie, 1963.
School Bell in the Valley, illustrated by Gilbert Riswold. New York, Harcourt Brace, 1963.
Jean-Claude's Island, illustrated by Nancy Ekholm Burkert. New York, Harper, 1963; London, Blackie, 1966.
The Orphelines in the Enchanted Castle, illustrated by Adriana Saviozzi. New York, Harper, 1964; London, Blackie, 1965.
The Letter on the Tree, illustrated by John Kaufmann. New York, Harper, 1964; London, Blackie, 1967.
The Empty Schoolhouse, illustrated by John Kaufmann. New York, Harper, 1965.
Sailor's Choice, illustrated by George Loh. New York, Harper, 1966.
Chalou, illustrated by George Loh. New York, Harper, 1967; London, Blackie, 1968.
Luigi of the Streets, illustrated by Emily McCully. New York, Harper, 1967; as *The Family on the Waterfront,* London, Blackie, 1969.
Ann Aurelia and Dorothy, illustrated by Dale Payson. New York, Harper, 1968.
Befana's Gift, illustrated by Robert Quackenbush. New York, Harper, 1969; as *A Grandson for the Asking,* London, Blackie, 1969.
Marchers for the Dream, illustrated by Alvin Smith. New York, Harper, 1969; London, Blackie, 1971.
The Half Sisters, illustrated by Thomas di Grazia. New York, Harper, 1970; London, Blackie, 1972.
Luvvy and the Girls, illustrated by Thomas di Grazia. New York, Harper, 1971.
Marie Louise and Christophe, illustrated by Jose Aruego and Ariane Dewey. New York, Scribner, 1974.
Marie Louise's Heyday, illustrated by Jose Aruego and Ariane Dewey. New York, Scribner, 1975; London, MacRae, 1980.
Runaway Marie Louise, illustrated by Jose Aruego and Ariane

Dewey. New York, Scribner, 1977.
Jaky or Dodo?, illustrated by Gail Owens. New York, Scribner, 1978.
Time for the White Egret, illustrated by Charles Robinson. New York, Scribner, 1978.
The Night the Scarecrow Walked, illustrated by Charles Robinson. New York, Scribner, 1979.
A Grandmother for the Orphelines, illustrated by David White. New York, Harper, 1980.
Marie Louise and Christophe at the Carnival, illustrated by Jose Aruego and Ariane Dewey. New York, Scribner, 1981.
Spooky Night, illustrated by Andrew Glass. New York, Lothrop, 1982.
Surprise in the Mountains, illustrated by Elise Primavera. New York, Harper, 1983.
The Ghost in the Lagoon, illustrated by Andrew Glass. New York, Lothrop, 1984.
Spooky and the Ghost Cat, illustrated by Andrew Glass. New York, Lothrop, 1985.
Spooky and the Wizard's Bats, illustrated by Andrew Glass. New York, Lothrop, 1986.
Spooky and the Bad Luck Raven, illustrated by Andrew Glass. New York, Lothrop, 1988.
Spooky and the Witch's Goat, illustrated by Andrew Glass. New York, Lothrop, 1989.

Other

The Talking Cat and Other Stories of French Canada, illustrated by Roger Duvoisin. New York, Harper, 1952.
Sashes Red and Blue, illustrated by Rita Fava. New York, Harper, 1956.
King of Cats and Other Tales (Breton folktales), illustrated by David Frampton. New York, Doubleday, 1980.

*

Manuscript Collections: Kerlan Collection, University of Minnesota, Minneapolis; de Grummond Collection, University of Southern Mississippi, Hattiesburg.

*   *   *

Natalie Savage Carlson acknowledges that she sought professional training to learn to write. Though this training may account for her well-structured books, her inherent ability is reflected in her graceful style and her amused and amusing observations of human behavior. Her writing has a genial overtone, derived perhaps partly from her childhood in the American South and partly from her French-Canadian roots.

One of her early books, *The Talking Cat and Other Stories of French Canada,* consists of tales told to her mother by a French relative, Michel Meloche. Her version of a well-known French-Canadian folktale about the skunk in the kitchen is a good example of her warm style and gentle humor. Another book in the same temper is *The Song of the Lop-Eared Mule* in which Janina Domanska's illustrations synchronize nicely with the story.

Perhaps her most successful work is *The Family under the Bridge,* a story which developed during an extended stay in Paris. Here, for instance, the tramp, Armand, feeds on the rich odours from a restaurant: "For two hours, Armand sat on the curb enjoying the food smells, because that is the length of time a Frenchman allows himself for lunch in the middle of the day. Then he daintily wiped his whiskered lips with his cuff and rose...."

Another popular book which grew out of her Paris experience is *The Happy Orpheline,* with pictures by Garth Williams. The plot has a clever twist: in an orphanage outside Paris, 20 orphans don't want to be adopted—they are happy where they are!

Beginning with *Marie Louise and Christophe* in 1974, and continuing through *Surprise in the Mountains* and the *Spooky* series, Carlson has devoted her time to writing picture books. In *Spooky and the Ghost Cat* a ghost cat becomes a real one when Spooky outwits a witch. In *Spooky and the Wizard's Bats* he outwits a wizard and in *Spooky and the Bad Luck Raven* he outwits a witch's raven. The illustrations of all these stories by Andrew Glass complement the not-too-scary texts, which inform children that the mysterious elements in life add sparkle to experience.

She attempts always to tell a story which no one else has told, or at least one which she feels she is especially able to tell well. Some wry satire can be detected in *Alphonse, That Bearded One,* in which a trained bear masquerades successfully as a soldier and helps bring peace with the Indians. Less successful are her attempts to adapt her talent to social needs, as in *The Empty Schoolhouse* and *Marchers for the Dream. The Half Sisters* is semi-autobiographical, and an interesting account of how truth is adapted to the fictional form has been written by her daughter, Dr. Julie Carlson McAlpine (*Children's Literature,* 1976). In his work *The Nesbit Tradition* Marcus Crouch praises Carlson highly for her effortless lightness of touch and fine dialogue.

—Francelia Butler

CARTER, Bruce. Pseudonym for Richard Alexander Hough; has also written as Elizabeth Churchill; Pat Strong. British. Born in Brighton, Sussex, 15 May 1922. Educated at Frensham Heights School, Farnham, Surrey, 1931–40. Served in the Royal Air Force, 1941–46: Fighter Pilot. Married 1) Helen Charlotte Woodyatt (i.e., Charlotte Hough, *q.v.*), in 1943 (divorced 1980), four daughters; 2) Judy Taylor in 1980. General manager and children's books editor, The Bodley Head, London, 1947–55; managing director, Hamish Hamilton Books for Children, London, 1955–70. Chairman, Auxiliary Hospitals Committee, King Edward's Hospital Fund, 1975. Member of the Council, 1970–73 and 1975–84, and Vice-President 1977–82, Navy Records Society. Recipient: *Daily Express* Best Book of the Sea award, 1972. Agent: Heather Jeeves, 15 Campden Hill Square, London W8 7JY. Address: 31 Meadowbank, Primrose Hill Road, London NW3 1AY, England.

PUBLICATIONS FOR CHILDREN

Fiction

The Perilous Descent into a Strange Lost World, illustrated by Tony Weare. London, Lane, 1952; as *Into a Strange Lost World,* New York, Crowell, 1953.
Speed Six!, illustrated by Tony Weare. London, Lane, 1953; New York, Harper, 1956.
Peril on the Iron Road, illustrated by Charlotte Hough. London, Hamish Hamilton, 1953.
Gunpowder Tunnel, illustrated by Charlotte Hough. London, Hamish Hamilton, 1955.
Target Island, illustrated by Tony Weare. London, Hamish Hamilton, 1956; New York, Harper, 1957; revised edition, Hamish Hamilton, 1967.
Juliet in Publishing (as Elizabeth Churchill). London, Lane, 1956.
Tricycle Tim, illustrated by Prudence Seward. London, Hamish Hamilton, 1957.

The Kidnapping of Kensington, illustrated by C. Walter Hodges. London, Hamish Hamilton, and New York, Harper, 1958; as *The Children Who Stayed Behind,* London, Penguin, 1964.
Four-Wheel Drift. London, Bodley Head, and New York, Harper, 1959; revised edition, London, Heinemann, 1973.
The Night of the Flood, illustrated by Prudence Seward. London, Hamish Hamilton, 1959.
Ballooning Boy, illustrated by Prudence Seward. London, Hamish Hamilton, 1960.
The Motorway Chase, illustrated by Bernard Wragg. London, Hamish Hamilton, 1961.
The Plane Wreckers (as Pat Strong), illustrated by Bernard Wragg. London, Hamish Hamilton, 1961.
Fast Circuit. London, Hamish Hamilton, and New York, Harper, 1962.
The Playground, illustrated by Prudence Seward. London, Hamish Hamilton, 1964.
The Airfield Man. London, Hamish Hamilton, 1965; New York, Coward McCann, 1966.
The Gannet's Nest, illustrated by Constance Marshall. London, Hamish Hamilton, 1966.
B Flight. London, Hamish Hamilton, 1970; as *Flight to Victory* (as Richard Hough), New York, Dutton, 1985.
Upley United, illustrated by Harry Bloom. London, Heinemann, 1972.
The Deadly Freeze. London, Dent, 1976.
Buzzbugs. London, Dent, and New York, Warne, 1977.
Miaow! London, Dent, 1978.
Razor Eyes (as Richard Hough). London, Dent, 1981; New York, Lodestar, 1983.

Other as Richard Hough

The Battle of Midway. New York, Macmillan, and London, Collier Macmillan, 1970.
The Battle of Britain. New York, Macmillan, and London, Collier Macmillan, 1971.
Galápagos: The Enchanted Islands, illustrated by Charlotte Hough. London, Dent, and Reading, Massachusetts, Addison Wesley, 1975.

Other

Motor Racing: A Guide for the Younger Enthusiast, with Michael Frostick. London, Lane, 1955.
The Wright Brothers. London, Newnes, 1955.
Neville Duke. London, Newnes, 1955.
Tim Baker, Motor Mechanic: A Career Book. London, Chatto and Windus, 1957.
Nuvolari and the Alfa Romeo, illustrated by Raymond Briggs. London, Hamish Hamilton, and New York, Coward McCann, 1968.
Jimmy Murphy and the White Dusenberg, illustrated by Raymond Briggs. London, Hamish Hamilton, and New York, Coward McCann, 1968.
The Bike Racers (reader), illustrated by John Crawley. London, Longman, 1974; revised edition, 1979.

Editor, *Great Motor Races.* London, Weidenfeld and Nicolson, 1960; as *Great Auto Races,* New York, Harper, 1961.

PUBLICATIONS FOR ADULTS as Richard Hough

Novels

The Fighter. London, Joseph, 1963.

Angels One-Five. London, Cassell, 1978; as *Wings Against the Sky,* New York, Morrow, 1979.

The Fight of the Few. London, Cassell, 1979; New York, Morrow, 1980.

The Fight to the Finish. London, Cassell, 1979; as *Wings of Victory,* New York, Morrow, 1980.

Buller's Guns. London, Weidenfeld and Nicolson, and New York, Morrow, 1981.

Buller's Dreadnought. London, Weidenfeld and Nicolson, and New York, Morrow, 1982.

Buller's Revenge. London, Weidenfeld and Nicolson, and New York, Morrow, 1983.

Buller's Victory. London, Weidenfeld and Nicolson, and New York, Morrow, 1984.

The Raging Sky. London, Macdonald, 1989.

Other

Six Great Railwaymen: Stephenson, Hudson, Denison, Huish, Stephen, Gresley. London, Hamish Hamilton, 1955.

Tourist Trophy: The History of Britain's Greatest Motor Race. London, Hutchinson, 1957.

W.O.: An Autobiography, with Walter Owen Bentley. London, Hutchinson, 1958.

The Fleet That Had to Die. London, Hamish Hamilton, and New York, Viking Press, 1958; abridged edition, London, Chatto and Windus, 1963.

British Grand Prix: A History. London, Hutchinson, 1958.

Admirals in Collision. London, Hamish Hamilton, and New York, Viking Press, 1959.

B.P. Book of the Racing Campbells. London, Stanley Paul, 1960.

The Potemkin Mutiny. London, Hamish Hamilton, 1960; New York, Pantheon, 1961.

Sky Fever, with Geoffrey de Havilland. London, Hamish Hamilton, 1961.

A History of the World's Sports Cars, with Michael Frostick. London, Allen and Unwin, and New York, Harper, 1961.

A History of the World's Classic Cars, with Michael Frostick. London, Allen and Unwin, and New York, Harper, 1963.

The Hunting of Force Z. London, Collins, 1963; as *Death of the Battleship,* New York, Macmillan, 1963.

Dreadnought: A History of the Modern Battleship. New York, Macmillan, 1964; London, Joseph, 1965; revised edition, Cambridge, Stephens, and New York, Macmillan, 1975.

The Battle of Jutland. London, Hamish Hamilton, 1964.

A History of the World's Racing Cars, with Michael Frostick. London, Allen and Unwin, and New York, Harper, 1965.

Rover Memories: An Illustrated Survey of the Rover Car, with Michael Frostick. London, Allen and Unwin, 1966.

A History of the World's Motorcycles, with L.J.K. Setright. London, Allen and Unwin, and New York, Harper, 1966; revised edition, 1973.

The Big Battleship; or, The Curious Career of H.M.S. Agincourt. London, Joseph, 1966; as *The Great Dreadnought: The Strange Story of the H.M.S. Agincourt, The Mightiest Battleship of World War I,* New York, Harper, 1967.

Racing Cars. London, Hamlyn, 1967.

A History of the World's High Performance Cars, with Michael Frostick. London, Allen and Unwin, and New York, Harper, 1967.

Fighting Ships. London, Joseph, and New York, Putnam, 1969.

First Sea Lord: An Authorised Biography of Admiral Lord Fisher. London, Allen and Unwin, 1969; revised edition, London, Severn House, 1977; as *Admiral of the Fleet: The Life of John Fisher,* New York, Macmillan, 1970.

The Pursuit of Admiral von Spee. London, Allen and Unwin, 1969; as *The Long Pursuit,* New York, Harper, 1969.

The Blind Horn's Hate. London, Hutchinson, and New York, Norton, 1971.

Captain Bligh and Mr. Christian: The Men and the Mutiny. London, Hutchinson, 1972; New York, Dutton, 1973; revised edition, London, Cassell, 1979; revised edition as *The Bounty,* London, Corgi, 1984.

Louis and Victoria: The First Mountbattens. London, Hutchinson, 1974; as *The Mountbattens,* New York, Dutton, 1975.

One Boy's War: Per Astra Ad Ardua (autobiography). London, Heinemann, 1975.

The Great Admirals. London, Weidenfeld and Nicolson, 1977; New York, Morrow, 1978.

Man o' War: The Fighting Ship in History. London, Dent, and New York, Scribner, 1979.

The Murder of Captain James Cook. London, Macmillan, 1979; as *The Last Voyage of Captain James Cook,* New York, Morrow, 1979.

Mountbatten, Hero of Our Time. London, Weidenfeld and Nicolson, 1980; as *Mountbatten,* New York, Random House, 1981.

Nelson. London, Park Lane Press, 1980.

The Great War at Sea 1914–1918. London and New York, Oxford University Press, 1983.

Edwina: Countess Mountbatten of Burma. London, Weidenfeld and Nicolson, 1983; New York, Morrow, 1984.

Former Naval Person: Churchill and the Wars at Sea. London, Weidenfeld and Nicolson, 1985; as *The Greatest Crusade: Roosevelt, Churchill, and the Naval War,* New York, Morrow, 1986.

The Ace of Clubs: A History of the Garrick. London, Deutsch, 1986.

The Longest Battle: The War at Sea 1939–45. London, Weidenfeld and Nicolson, and New York, Morrow, 1986.

Born Royal: The Lives and Loves of the Young Windsors (1894–1937). London, Deutsch, and New York, Bantam, 1988.

The Battle of Britain: The Jubilee History, with Denis Richards. London, Hodder and Stoughton, 1989.

Editor, *First and Fastest: A Collection of the World's Great Motor Races.* London, Allen and Unwin, 1963; as *First and Fastest: A Collection of Accounts of the World's Greatest Auto Races,* New York, Harper, 1964.

Editor, *The Enzo Ferrari Memoirs: My Terrible Joys,* by Enzo Ferrari, translated by Ivan Scott. London, Hamish Hamilton, 1963.

Editor, *The Motor Car Lover's Companion.* London, Allen and Unwin, and New York, Harper, 1965.

Editor, *Advice to a Grand-daughter: Letters from Queen Victoria to Princess Victoria of Hesse.* London, Heinemann, and New York, Simon and Schuster, 1975.

*

Bruce Carter comments:

My writing for children stems directly from, first, the tastes of my own children, and, second, from my experience as an editor of children's books. (I started the Bodley Head children's list in 1947, the Hamish Hamilton list in 1955, and participated as a consultant editor in the redevelopment of the Heinemann list 1971–76.) Except for one or two educational books, my adventure books, historical novels, science fiction (my first *and* most recent), and motor racing stories reflect my own enthusiasms, which have been widely varied, from flying in the war to canoeing on old canals, from long-distance bicycling to ornithology. If they have had any success, I think it must be because I enormously enjoy writing them, and always turn back to writing them with relief and delight after a long, heavily researched adult work.

*   *   *

Most of Bruce Carter's stories centre on mechanical transport, and the amount of technical detail increases with the age range of the readers. His adult books are non-fiction on the same themes, suggesting sound knowledge.

His stories, even for the youngest readers, are vigorous and lively, and often have a strong comic line. Tim, in *Tricycle Tim,* is lost, though he hardly realises it, and Jim and Bryony in *The Gannet's Nest,* too young to appreciate the very real danger, are rescued at the vital moment. Boisterous older children fend for themselves in Robinson Crusoe situations in *Target Island* and *The Kidnapping of Kensington.* For teenage readers there are car-racing stories full of thrills and spills where the characters are all adult. *The Perilous Descent into a Strange Lost World* and *The Deadly Freeze* are both science fiction, two lively thrillers where the imaginative use of technology mixed with fantasy blends with politics.

Two historical novels—*Peril on the Iron Road* and *Gunpowder Tunnel*—are carefully researched accounts of tunnel building for an early railway and a pioneer canal. Local opposition is strong in both cases, but trouble in *Gunpowder Tunnel* comes from the rival contractor. Both have plenty of excitement—battles with and among miners and attempts to blow up the tunnels. The young people succeed in foiling the plans of the villains, but in neither book do the characters wholly convince the reader.

The car-racing stories—*Speed Six!, Four-Wheel Drift, Fast Circuit,* and the two imaginative reconstructions of real races, *Jimmy Murphy and the White Dusenberg* and *Nuvolari and the Alfa Romeo*—are good examples of the genre, by an enthusiast for enthusiasts. Team work and brilliant driving succeed against all odds, but heroism also has its place. Unfortunately, with its lower standards, big business is also involved in motor-racing; unscrupulous rivals extend the dimensions of the plot. Yet Carter shows, for instance in *Nuvolari,* that he can write a really gripping fast-moving story in quite simple language by concentrating on the race and the personality of the driver only.

Carter's best books are his air stories—*B Flight, The Airfield Man,* and *Razor Eyes.* Here technicalities are submerged beneath the personalities of the characters—Will, flying fighter planes in the First World War; Simon's father, a failure as the proprietor of the hardware shop who only really lived as a wartime pilot; the deranged farmer. War is never glorified, heroes are heroic not through bravado but through determination, and often the ending is wistful rather than happy.

—Margaret M. Tye

———

CARTER, Peter.   British.   Born in Manchester, Lancashire, 13 August 1929.   Educated at Wadham College, Oxford (mature state scholar, 1958), M.A. 1972.   Married Gudrun Willege in 1974.   Apprentice in the building trade, 1942–49; formerly teacher in Birmingham.   Freelance writer.   Recipient: *Guardian* award, 1981; *Observer* prize, 1983, 1986.   Address: c/o Oxford University Press Educational Books, Walton Street, Oxford OX2 6DP, England.

PUBLICATIONS FOR CHILDREN

Fiction

The Black Lamp, illustrated by David Harris.   London, Oxford University Press, 1973; Nashville, Nelson, 1975.
The Gates of Paradise, illustrated by Fermin Rocker.   London, Oxford University Press, 1974; New York, Oxford University Press, 1979.
Madatan, illustrated by Victor Ambrus.   London, Oxford University Press, 1974; New York, Oxford University Press, 1979.
Under Goliath, illustrated by Ian Ribbons.   London, Oxford University Press, 1977; New York, Oxford University Press, 1979.
The Sentinels.   Oxford and New York, Oxford University Press, 1980.
Children of the Book.   Oxford, Oxford University Press, 1982; New York, Oxford University Press, 1987.
Bury the Dead.   Oxford, Oxford University Press, 1986; New York, Farrar Straus, 1987.

Play

The Sea Green Man (televised 1984).   London, Heinemann, 1986.

Television Play: *The Sea Green Man,* 1984.

Other

Mao.   London, Oxford University Press, 1976; New York, Viking Press, 1979.

Translator, *The Snowman Who Went for a Walk,* by Mira Lobe, illustrated by Winifried Opgenoorth.   Oxford, Oxford University Press, 1982; New York, Morrow, 1984.
Translator, *Grimms' Fairy Tales,* illustrated by Peter Richardson.   Oxford, Oxford University Press, 1982.
Translator, *Valerie and the Good-Night Swing,* by Mira Lobe, illustrated by Winifried Opgenoorth.   New York, Oxford University Press, 1983.

*   *   *

A common theme in Peter Carter's books is the fate of the ordinary individual caught up at times of historical change in life-threatening events he can neither evade nor control. In *The Black Lamp* it is the impact of both the Napoleonic Wars and the Industrial Revolution on the lives of handloom weavers, whose attempts to combine under the Luddite banner to break the machines and protect their way of life culminate in the massacre at Peterloo in 1819. Daniel Cregg, the hero of the story, is orphaned during the massacre, and his young sister threatened with a lifetime of slavery in the mills. Daniel's fight to save them both is told with a thoughtful appreciation of the loss of work, rising taxes, and increasing poverty facing the ordinary people of that time.

Madatan is a more complex book, set this time in the eighth century. Maddah's relatively peaceful herdsman's life comes to an abrupt end when he is carried off by the fierce raiding Norsemen. He accompanies them on an unsuccessful expedition against the English, but finds protection from the monks of Northumbria. The book's main theme is the conflict generated in Madaah through his several encounters with brutal, bold, and dangerous adventurers, whether Norse or English, and with the more peaceful, meditative, apparently gentle but still potentially dangerous men of the new Christian religion. In consequence Madaah becomes both actor and victim, betrayed and betrayer, probing the uneasy mixture of self-interest and idealism in himself and others in this tough and powerful story of revenge and outlawry, but also, finally, of reconciliation.

Under Goliath is set in Belfast in 1969. Two boys, the Protestant Alan Kenton and the Catholic Fergus Riley, strike up an ambivalent, uneasy friendship in spite of the growing hostility between their two communities. But there is comedy as well as tension in the story, a close observation of the small details of life as well as action at the barricades, and a sense of the possibilities of friendship as well as bitterness at the divisive prejudices that have frustrated their ambitions and left them with a sense of tragedy, futility, and waste.

The Sentinels is dedicated to the "memory of the millions of Africans taken into slavery, and the thousands of seamen of the Royal Navy who died to free them." The story follows by turns the fortunes of Lyapo, a Yoruba sold into captivity, the American slaver *Phantom,* and the men on board the rescuing Royal Navy vessel *The Sentinel.* The British seamen are by no means as altruistic as the dedication may suggest, and the brutality of life at sea in the 1840's is vividly evoked through the eyes of the "gentleman volunteer," 15-year-old John Spencer.

Children of the Book is an account of the Siege of Vienna by the armies of the Ottoman Empire in 1783. Like *The Sentinels* this story follows several different groups of characters in a sequence requiring the reader's close attention. The overall pattern of events makes a powerful impact: the horror and futility of war, the petty personal ambitions and cruelties that affect its course, and the ironic parallels and differences of belief which both inspire and betray each side.

Another book concerned with recent history is *Bury the Dead,* a complex attempt to discuss the ways in which the Nazi past, extermination camps, anti-Semitism, and unspeakable cruelties of the war years live on for the Nordern family in East Germany. They have made valiant attempts to rebuild their lives, to work earnestly and conscientiously for the future, and to forget the past. But all, including the innocent children, find themselves implicated against their will in the plots of their ex-Nazi uncle. Through his activities readers are reminded of the horrendous consequences of the Nazi ideology still threatening those who at the time tried to avert their eyes from what was happening or to deny complicity in the violence that is inevitable in time of war.

The Gates of Paradise is an ambitious but less successful story about William Blake. The various aspects of Blake's character seen through the eyes of his young admirer, Ben, never quite come together—the moody and slightly batty visionary, the lucid poet, and the calm, compassionate man, whose clearsighted understanding of the world around him seems so remarkably penetrating and sane. This is an interesting story, but its audience will be select.

Carter's most recent publication, *The Sea Green Man,* has been adapted for amateur or school stage performance from his own television play. It concerns the Levellers, a radical group within Cromwell's armies who remained true to their belief in real equality for all. There is an intriguing feminist strand in the spirited young girl Joan, who speaks out fearlessly on behalf of her own rights as well as in defence of her fanatical and free-thinking father, the cobbler Tyler.

In all his books Carter is clearly on the side of the ordinary man, while attempting always to give a balanced picture of events, and to suggest that neither good nor evil are the monopoly of any one side or individual.

—Winifred Whitehead

———

CASSEDY, Sylvia. American. Born in Brooklyn, New York, 29 January 1930. Educated at Brooklyn College, 1946–51, B.A. 1951; Johns Hopkins University, Baltimore, 1959–60. Married 1) Leslie Verwiebe in 1949 (died 1950); 2) Edward Cassedy in 1952, three daughters and one son. Teacher of creative writing to children, Queens College, City University of New York, Flushing, 1973–74, Great Neck Public Library, New York, 1975–79, and Manhasset Public Schools, New York, 1977–84. Instructor in teaching creative writing to children, Nassau County Board of Cooperative Education, New York, 1978–79. *Died 6 April 1989.*

PUBLICATIONS FOR CHILDREN

Fiction

Little Chameleon, illustrated by Rainey Bennett. Cleveland, World, 1966.
Pierino and the Bell, illustrated by Evaline Ness. New York, Doubleday, 1966.
Marzipan Day on Bridget Lane, illustrated by Margot Tomes. New York, Doubleday, 1967.
Behind the Attic Wall. New York, Crowell, 1983; London, Bodley Head, 1984.
M.E. and Morton. New York, Crowell, and London, Bodley Head, 1987.
Lucie Babbidge's House. New York, Crowell, 1989.

Verse

Roomrimes, illustrated by Michele Chessare. New York, Crowell, 1987.

Other

In Your Own Words: A Beginner's Guide to Writing. New York, Doubleday, 1979.

Editor, and Translator with Kunihiro Suetake, *Birds, Frogs, and Moonlight,* illustrated by Vo-Dinh. New York, Doubleday, 1967.
Editor, and Translator with Parvathi Thampi, *Moon-Uncle, Moon-Uncle: Rhymes from India,* illustrated by Susanne Suba. New York, Doubleday, 1973.

*   *   *

Sylvia Cassedy wrote with the inward eye of a child. In her fiction and poetry the boundary between children and adults—a boundary often blurred or absent in literature for this age group—is firmly present. On one side are the acute perceptions, fantasies, and helplessness of being young, on the other the rigidity and misunderstanding of grown ups. In her books the children have a relationship to the physical world that adults have lost. They revel in odd, messy minutiae—smeary pink silver polish, the red strings from cigarette papers, the way a bubble of tar pops on a hot roof—and they haven't yet developed the armour to shield themselves from either the pleasant or unpleasant sensations of their world.

In particular, the author's child characters all possess the transforming power of imagination. This is most obvious in her fantasy *Behind the Attic Wall.* Orphaned Maggie is a child stripped of love and security. Appropriately, she invents a game of domineering the imaginary "Backwoods Girls," who have even less than she. The talking dolls that Maggie later discovers spring naturally out of this needy game; now she can really give, instead of just pretending to. Although the book is a fantasy, the line between how much the dolls are Maggie's own creation and how much they are "real" is very fine—which makes their existence all the more haunting. The result is a remarkably powerful novel about caring and continuity.

In *M.E. and Morton* Mary Ella—or M.E., as she prefers to call herself—also uses fantasy as a solace. In a game similar to the "Backwoods Girls," M.E. pretends that her bottles of paints are orphans. She also deludes herself into believing that she is more popular and loved than she is. Her neighbour Polly has fantasies as well—she imagines that the bugs on her ceiling are dancing or that she can shrink herself to fit into a toy train. Unlike the unhealthy fantasies of M.E., however, Polly's inventions enable her to transfer the dull reality of her poverty-stricken life into joy. M.E.'s childlike adolescent brother Morton is a perfect companion for Polly. His slowness saves him from the guilty confusion of his sister and he can engage with Polly in simple play. Although *M.E. and Morton* is realistic, the use of imagination in both books results in a similar "magic": make-believe comes true through the healing power of love.

The two novels show the strong characterizations that are Cassedy's hallmark. She carefully and gradually shows how Maggie, M.E., Polly, and Morton react in different ways to being victims of adult neglect. Desperately lonely Maggie, posturing M.E., resilient Polly, and stolid Morton—all emerge as unforgettable personalities. While the leisurely pace of her fiction may discourage readers looking for continuous action, each novel builds suspense in delicate layers to reach a surprise ending.

The elements in Cassedy's writing are so consistent that the poems in her newest book *Roomrimes* could have been written by either Maggie or M.E.. Using a variety of poetical forms, an alphabet of interior and exterior rooms and spaces is set forth in fresh and whimsical images, as if observed by a solitary, listening, watching child. Closets are inhabited by whoozits, boys live behind mirrors, and the comments on attics, parlors, and roofs especially are similar to those in her novels.

The author's precise language is another strength in her books. The carefully chosen words that are the foundation of her own and her translated poetry result in impeccable prose as well. Cassedy was a compelling writer whose work showed a unique promise.

—Kit Pearson

CATHERALL, Arthur. Also wrote as J. Baltimore; A.R. Channel; Dan Corby; Peter Hallard; Trevor Maine; Linda Peters; Margaret Ruthin. British. Born in Bolton, Lancashire, 6 February 1906. Served in the Royal Air Force, 1940–45: Staff Officer. Married Elizabeth Benson in 1936; one daughter and one son. *Died 6 January 1980.*

PUBLICATIONS FOR CHILDREN

Fiction

Rod o' the Rail. London, Pearson, 1936.
The Rival Tugboats. London, Partridge, 1937.
Adventurers, Ltd. London, A. and C. Black, 1938.
Black Gold. London, Pearson, 1939.
Vanished Whaler, illustrated by S. Drigin. London, Nelson, 1939.
Keepers of the Khyber. London, Nelson, 1940.
Lost with All Hands. London, Nelson, 1940.
Raid on Heligoland. London, Collins, 1940.
The Flying Submarine. London, Collins, 1942.
The River of Burning Sand. London, Collins, 1947.
The Bull Patrol. London, Lutterworth Press, 1949.
Riders of the Black Camel. Bath, Venturebooks, 1949.

Cock o' the Town, illustrated by Kenneth Brookes. London, Boy Scouts Association, 1950.
Wings for a Gull. London and New York, Warne, 1951.
Pirate Sealer. London, Collins, 1953.
Shanghaied! London, Collins, 1954.
Ten Fathoms Deep, illustrated by Geoffrey Whittam. London, Dent, 1954; New York, Criterion, 1968.
Jackals of the Sea, illustrated by Geoffrey Whittam. London, Dent, 1955.
The Scuttlers, illustrated by A. Bruce Cornwell and Drake Brookshaw. London, Nelson, 1955.
Sea Wraith. London, Lutterworth Press, 1955.
Wild Goose Saboteur, illustrated by Kenneth Brookes. London, Dent, 1955.
Forgotten Submarine, illustrated by Geoffrey Whittam. London, Dent, 1956.
Land under the White Robe, illustrated by Geoffrey Whittam. London, Dent, 1956.
Jamboree Challenge, illustrated by Kenneth Brookes. London, Dent, and New York, Roy, 1957.
Java Sea Duel, illustrated by Geoffrey Whittam. London, Dent, 1957.
Jungle Trap, illustrated by Paul Hogarth. London, Dent, 1958; New York, Roy, 1967.
Tenderfoot Trapper, illustrated by Edward Osmond. London, Dent, 1958; New York, Criterion, 1959.
Sea Wolves, illustrated by Geoffrey Whittam. London, Dent, 1959; New York, Roy, 1960.
Dangerous Cargo illustrated by Geoffrey Whittam. London, Dent, 1960; New York, Roy, 1961.
Lapland Outlaw, illustrated by Fred Wood. London, Dent, 1960; New York, Lothrop, 1966.
Blue Veil and Black Gold (as Trevor Maine), illustrated by Richard Kennedy. London, Odhams Press, 1961; New York, Roy, 1965.
China Sea Jigsaw, illustrated by Geoffrey Whittam. London, Dent, 1961; New York, Roy, 1962.
Orphan Otter, illustrated by N. Osten-Sacken. London, Dent, 1962; New York, Harcourt Brace, 1963.
Vagabond Ape, illustrated by N. Osten-Sacken. London, Dent, 1962.
Yugoslav Mystery, illustrated by Stuart Tresilian. London, Dent, 1962; New York, Lothrop, 1964.
Prisoners under the Sea, illustrated by Geoffrey Whittam. London, Dent, 1963.
Lone Seal Pup, illustrated by Edward Osmond. London, Dent, 1964; New York, Dutton, 1965.
The Strange Invader, illustrated by Stuart Tresilian. London, Dent, 1964; as *The Strange Intruder,* New York, Lothrop, 1965.
Tanker Trap, illustrated by Geoffrey Whittam. London, Dent, 1965; New York, Roy, 1966.
Reindeer Rescue (as Linda Peters), illustrated by F.M. Johnson. Leeds, E.J. Arnold, 1966.
Sicilian Mystery, illustrated by Stuart Tresilian. London, Dent, 1966; New York, Lothrop, 1967.
A Zebra Came to Drink, illustrated by Edward Osmond. London, Dent, and New York, Dutton, 1967.
Prisoners in the Snow, illustrated by Victor Ambrus. London, Dent, and New York, Lothrop, 1967.
Death of an Oil Rig, illustrated by Geoffrey Whittam. London, Dent, 1967; New York, Phillips, 1969.
Night of the Black Frost, illustrated by Roger Payne. London, Dent, and New York, Lothrop, 1968.
Camel Caravan, illustrated by Joseph Papin. New York, Seabury Press, 1968; as *Desert Caravan,* London, Macdonald, 1969.
Kidnapped by Accident, illustrated by Victor Ambrus. London, Dent, 1968; New York, Lothrop, 1969.

Island of Forgotten Men, illustrated by Geoffrey Whittam. London, Dent, 1968.

Duel in the High Hills, illustrated by Stanley Smith. London, Dent, 1968; New York, Lothrop, 1969.

Red Sea Rescue, illustrated by Victor Ambrus. London, Dent, 1969; New York, Lothrop, 1970.

Antlers of the King Moose, illustrated by Edward Mortelmans. London, Dent, and New York, Dutton, 1970.

The Big Tusker, illustrated by Douglas Phillips. London, Dent, and New York, Lothrop, 1970.

Keepers of the Cattle, illustrated by Bernard Brett. London, Dent, 1970.

Freedom for a Cheetah, illustrated by Shyam Varma. London, Dent, and New York, Lothrop, 1971.

Barracuda Mystery, illustrated by Gavin Rowe. London, Dent, 1971.

The Unwilling Smuggler, illustrated by Geoffrey Whittam. London, Dent, 1971.

Last Horse on the Sands, illustrated by David Farris. London, Dent, 1972; New York, Lothrop, 1973.

Cave of the "Cormorant." London, Dent, 1973.

A Wolf from the Sky, illustrated by Derek Lucas. London, Dent, 1974.

Stranger on Wreck Buoy Sands. London, Dent, 1975.

Twelve Minutes to Disaster and Other Stories, illustrated by Derek Lucas. London, Dent, 1977.

The Ghost Elephant. London, Abelard Schuman, 1977.

The Last Run and Other Stories. London, Dent, 1977.

No Surrender! and Other Stories. London, Dent, 1979.

The Thirteen Footprints and Other Stories. London, Dent, 1979.

Smuggler in the Bay. London, Dent, 1980.

Fiction as A.R. Channel

Phantom Patrol. London, Collins, 1940.

The Tunnel Busters. London, Collins, 1960.

The Million-Dollar Ice Floe, illustrated by Eric Mudge-Marriott. London, Dobson, 1961.

Operation V.2. London, Collins, 1961.

Arctic Spy, illustrated by Horace Gaffron. London, Collins, 1962.

The Forgotten Patrol. London, Collins, 1962.

The Rogue Elephant, illustrated by D.J. Watkins-Pitchford. London, Dobson, 1962; Philadelphia, Macrae Smith, 1963.

Mission Accomplished. London, Collins, 1964.

Red Ivory, illustrated by D.J. Watkins-Pitchford. London, Dobson, and Philadelphia, Macrae Smith, 1964.

Jungle Rescue, illustrated by D.J. Watkins-Pitchford. London, Dobson, 1967; New York, Phillips, 1968.

Fiction as Margaret Ruthin

Kidnapped in Kandy, illustrated by C. Cane. London, Blackie, 1951.

The Ring of the Prophet. London and New York, Warne, 1953.

White Horse of Hungary. London and New York, Warne, 1954.

Strange Safari. London and New York, Warne, 1955.

The Secret Pagoda. London and New York, Warne, 1960.

Jungle Nurse, illustrated by Hugh Marshall. London, Dobson, and New York, Watts, 1960.

Reindeer Girl, illustrated by Marie Whitby. London, Dobson, 1961; as *Elli of the Northland,* New York, Farrar Straus, 1968.

Lapland Nurse, illustrated by Marie Whitby. London, Dobson, 1962.

Secret of the Shetlands, illustrated by Gwen Gibson. London, Dobson, 1963.

Katrina of the Lonely Isles, illustrated by Gwen Gibson. London,

Dobson, 1964; New York, Farrar Straus, 1965.

Kidnapped on Stromboli. London, Dobson, 1966.

Hungarian Rebel. London, Dobson, 1970.

Fiction as Peter Hallard

Coral Reef Castaway, illustrated by Terence Greer. London, Phoenix House, 1958; New York, Criterion, 1960.

Barrier Reef Bandits, illustrated by Hugh Marshall. London, Dobson, and New York, Criterion, 1960.

Guardian of the Reef, illustrated by Hugh Marshall. London, Dobson, 1961.

Boy on a White Giraffe, illustrated by Sheila Bewley. London, Macdonald, and New York, Seabury Press, 1969.

Lost in Lapland, illustrated by Judith Ann Lawrence. London, Macdonald, 1970; as *Puppy Lost in Lapland,* New York, Watts, 1971.

Kalu and the Wild Boar, illustrated by W.T. Mars. New York, Watts, 1973.

Fiction as Dan Corby (U.S. editions as Arthur Catherall)

A Shark on the Saltings. London, Parrish, 1959.

The Little Sealer. London, Parrish, 1960; as *The Arctic Sealer,* New York, Criterion, 1961.

Lost Off the Grand Banks. London, Parrish, 1961; New York, Criterion, 1962.

Man-Eater, illustrated by Richard Lewis. London, Parrish, 1963; New York, Criterion, 1964.

Thunder Dam, illustrated by Omar Davis. London, Parrish, 1964; New York, Criterion, 1965.

Conqueror's Gold. London, Parrish, 1965.

Other

Camp-Fire Stories and How to Tell Them. London, Jenkins, 1935.

The Steam and Steel Omnibus, with George W. Blow, illustrated by Blow. London, Collins, 1950.

The Scout Story Omnibus. London, Collins, 1954.

The Young Baden-Powell, illustrated by William Randell. London, Parrish, 1961; New York, Roy, 1962.

Vanishing Lapland. New York, Watts, 1972.

PUBLICATIONS FOR ADULTS

Novels

Tomorrow's Hunter. London, Jenkins, 1950.

Vibrant Brass. London, Dent, 1954.

Singapore Sari (as J. Baltimore). Leicester, Fiction House, 1958.

No Bouquets for These. London, Tempest Press, 1958.

Play

Step in My Shoes, with David Reade (produced Southport, Lancashire, 1958).

*

Arthur Catherall commented:

(1978) As a young reader I always took for gospel whatever I got from a book. For that reason I have endeavoured throughout my life as a writer to be authentic. As far as possible I have been to the places where I set my stories. I have worked with young people for over 40 years, and I have tried to get the feel of what they look for. You don't find any unnecessary clubbing or shooting in my books. Boys can be little savages without the inspiration of a story to start them off. They look for heroes in a story. I try to give them the right kind of heroes, for boys are great imitators.

* * *

Arthur Catherall, with his many pseudonyms, must have been one of the most prolific of writers for the young, but the truly amazing thing is not so much the output as the consistently authentic standard, the fidelity to fact. The stories are all set in places which Catherall had personal knowledge of, so that although the scenes are immensely varied they are all authentic. And furthermore, he never cheated on plot, he is as clever at extricating his hero from his predicament as he is at devising it.

Catherall served in World War II in various zones of action, including the Pacific; he travelled in all parts of the British Commonwealth, Europe, North America, the Arctic. But his intimate knowledge of a region is no mere backcloth; it also provides the warp and weft of the plot. In other words, plot is intrinsic to place—that of *Red Sea Rescue* could never be adapted for a book about Sicily or Scotland, nor could *Jungle Trap* be adapted to the Arctic or Lancashire. Monsoons, floods, drug-smuggling, working elephants all belong to the India of *The Big Tusker.* Not only did the author know the climate and terrain but also the methods used by local smugglers, the behaviour of elephants, and the way they work with timber. Every detail is thoroughly studied. Catherall's mastery of the cliffhanger consisted in exploiting to the full the hazards intrinsic to the scene and situation by bringing them into the narrative at the exact point where they will maximize the drama and create the greatest surprise.

Let us take a close look at one of his best animal stories, *Freedom for a Cheetah.* First the spellbinding atmosphere of the Indian plains. Dum-dum the cheetah had spent the two years of her life in a stable with only the occasional company of pariah dogs. The air had never been really clean. When her master hunted she was sent dashing across the dusty plains in pursuit of black buck. Now, a youth with a spite against her trainer offers the cheetah her freedom. But freedom held many terrors for Dum-dum and the story follows her adventures with wild dogs, treacherous mud, hunger, tiger, cobra, bees, fire, and finally men. Pursued by a pack of wild dogs, Dum-dum finds that the river mud which had almost fatally trapped her when first she was free now became her ally, for the dogs could not trust themselves to it.

When children are the heroes, their ingenuity and intelligence are stretched to the full to deal with their predicament but always in a way that fits their young experience. In *Prisoners in the Snow* we are in the Austrian mountains. Two children are trapped with their grandfather in their farmhouse after an aeroplane crashing into the mountain causes an avalanche which buries the house in snow. Cows from the damaged cowshed have to be brought into the parlour and hay to feed them brought from the threatened hay loft; the injured pilot who bailed out has to be rescued from the roof—but the roof may collapse and it is a long fall. So they rig up a net, but the idea came quite naturally from the children's experience of a travelling circus. And the children's own excitement is yet another factor adding to the tension and excitement of the reader. It can be explicit in a way not possible in animal stories; but emotion never interferes or takes over.

Catherall in books such as the Bulldog series wrote adventures with men as heroes: Jack Frodsham and Husky Hudson of the salvage tug *Bulldog* in China seas. These resourceful fellows are always up against the same enemy, Karmey, an unscrupulous villain who is constantly balked of his plan to sink them. These are superb yarns, all the more satisfying because it is the same team of heroes being brought time and again to the brink of disaster but turning the tables on the same enemy. *Death of an Oil Rig, Island of Forgotten Men,*

and *Ten Fathoms Deep* are a few of these marvellously thrilling novels.

It is a comment on our times that a writer of exciting adventures with real believable heroes was considered a writer for young people. To exploit the same talents in the adult market today he would have to write grisly whodunnits or novels with an anti-hero like Flashman. But this would not be Catherall at all. Throughout his long writing career he always held up to his readers an image of a hero or heroine with courage, kindness, loyalty, and spirit.

—Gwen Marsh

CAUDILL, Rebecca. American. Born in Poor Fork (now Cumberland), Kentucky, 2 February 1899. Educated at Sumner County High School, Portland, Tennessee, graduated 1916; Wesleyan College, Macon, Georgia, 1916–20, B.A. in English 1920; Vanderbilt University, Nashville, 1921–22, M.A. 1922. Married James S. Ayars in 1931; one son and one daughter. English and history teacher, Sumner County High School, 1920–21; English teacher, Collegio Bennett, Rio de Janeiro, 1922–24; editor, *Torchbearer* magazine, Nashville, 1924–30. Member of the Board of Trustees, Pine Mountain Settlement School, Kentucky, 1967–85. Rebecca Caudill Public Library, Cumberland, Kentucky, named in 1965. *Died 2 October 1985.*

PUBLICATIONS FOR CHILDREN

Fiction

Barrie & Daughter, illustrated by Berkeley Williams.   New York, Viking Press, 1943.
Happy Little Family, illustrated by Decie Merwin.   Philadelphia, Winston, 1947.
Tree of Freedom, illustrated by Dorothy Bayley Morse.   New York, Viking Press, 1949.
Schoolhouse in the Woods, illustrated by Decie Merwin.   Philadelphia, Winston, 1949.
Up and Down the River, illustrated by Decie Merwin.   Philadelphia, Winston, 1951.
Saturday Cousins, illustrated by Nancy Woltemate.   Philadelphia, Winston, 1953.
The House of the Fifers, illustrated by Genia.   New York, Longman, 1954.
Susan Cornish, illustrated by E. Harper Johnson.   New York, Viking Press, 1955.
Schoolroom in the Parlor, illustrated by Decie Merwin.   Philadelphia, Winston, 1959.
Time for Lissa, illustrated by Velma Ilsley.   New York, Nelson, 1959.
Higgins and the Great Big Scare, illustrated by Beth Krush.   New York, Holt Rinehart, 1960.
The Best-Loved Doll, illustrated by Elliott Gilbert.   New York, Holt Rinehart, 1962.
The Far-Off Land, illustrated by Brinton Turkle.   New York, Viking Press, 1964; London, Hart Davis, 1965.
A Pocketful of Cricket, illustrated by Evaline Ness.   New York, Holt Rinehart, 1964; London, Harrap, 1966.
A Certain Small Shepherd, illustrated by William Pène du Bois.   New York, Holt Rinehart, 1965; Edinburgh, Oliver and Boyd, 1966.

Did You Carry the Flag Today, Charley?, illustrated by Nancy Grossman. New York, Holt Rinehart, 1966.
Contrary Jenkins, with James S. Ayars, illustrated by Glen Rounds. New York, Holt Rinehart, 1969.
Somebody Go and Bang a Drum, illustrated by Jack Hearne. New York, Dutton, 1974.

Verse

Come Along!, illustrated by Ellen Raskin. New York, Holt Rinehart, 1969.
Wind, Sand, and Sky, illustrated by Donald Carrick. New York, Dutton, 1976.

Other

Florence Nightingale, illustrated by William Neebe. Evanston, Illinois, Row Peterson, 1953.

Publications for Adults

Other

The High Cost of Writing. Cumberland, Kentucky, Southeast Community College, 1965.
My Appalachia: A Reminiscence. New York, Holt Rinehart, 1966.

*

Manuscript Collections: University of Kentucky, Lexington; Kerlan Collection, University of Minnesota, Minneapolis.

Rebecca Caudill commented:
(1978) My writing for children—even the rewriting—has been an exercise in joy. Most of my books are based on experiences of my own childhood spent in Appalachian Kentucky, and so are written from the heart. The response from children has been gratifying.

*   *   *

Significant in Rebecca Caudill's novels for older children and her stories for younger ones is the part that setting plays. Child protagonists are usually hill children from Appalachia, their lives largely determined by the setting in which they live. Pioneers and early settlers live in wild surroundings, their simple and rugged homes determining the nature of their lives. In clear descriptions that work smoothly with the action, Caudill convinces the reader of the importance of place and time—18th or 19th-century America.

Well-defined conflicts in Caudill's novels for older children, *Tree of Freedom* and *A Far-Off Land,* for example, frequently show girl protagonists, like Stephanie Venable in the latter book, struggling with a desire to be an individual, to maintain her principles without losing her friendships. The omniscient point of view keeps the reader fully informed about all that the heroine thinks. With action, suspense, and careful attention to historical detail, Caudill builds the story to a climax and leaves the reader satisfied. Although the romance is idealized and a bit sentimental, Caudill's teenage girls are individuals, clearly and believably defined. Pioneer families are warm and relationships deftly sketched; parents, who might seem stern and workridden, are human and admirable.

The most notable stylistic element in Caudill's books for older children is the authentic-sounding mountain diction of the characters. Not overdone, the dialect does not call attention to itself. Although Caudill's themes in these novels for older children are

highly moralistic—behave as conscience requires, be yourself rather than a conformist—they are not didactic.

Stories for younger children, like *Up and Down the River* and *The House of the Fifers,* as well as *Did You Carry the Flag Today, Charley?* and *A Certain Small Shepherd,* show understanding of the wondering child amused by and amazed at the ordinary, simple things. Quiet, rural children gathering pinto beans and crickets, noting snakes and pretty rocks are her characters. Caudill's use of the haiku, however, as text for some of her picture books is disappointing because the verses fail either to surprise or to intensify the vision glimpsed. Caudill was at her best in her stories of Appalachia.

—Rebecca J. Lukens

————

CAUSLEY, Charles (Stanley). British. Born in Launceston, Cornwall, 24 August 1917. Educated at Launceston National School; Horwell Grammar School; Launceston College; Peterborough Training College, 1946–47. Served in the Royal Navy, 1940–46. Clerk in builder's office and in electrical supply company, Launceston, 1933–40; teacher in Cornwall, 1947–76. Honorary Visiting Fellow in Poetry, University of Exeter, Devon, 1973–74. Literary editor of BBC radio magazines *Apollo in the West* and *Signature,* 1953–56. Member, Arts Council Poetry (later Literature) Panel, 1962–66. Vice-President, West Country Writers' Association; Vice-President, Poetry Society, London. Recipient: Society of Authors travelling scholarship, 1954, 1966; Queen's Gold Medal for Poetry, 1967; Cholmondeley award, for verse, 1971; *Signal* Poetry award, 1987; Maschler award, 1987. D. Litt.: University of Exeter, 1977; M.A.: Open University, 1982. Fellow, Royal Society of Literature, 1958. C.B.E. (Commander, Order of the British Empire), 1986. Agent: David Higham Associates, 5–8 Lower John Street, London W1R 4HA. Address: 2 Cyprus Well, Launceston, Cornwall PL15 8BT, England.

Publications for Children

Fiction

The Last King of Cornwall, illustrated by Krystyna Turska. London, Hodder and Stoughton, 1978.

Plays

The Gift of a Lamb, music by Vera Gray, illustrated by Shirley Felts. London, Robson, 1978.
The Ballad of Aucassin and Nicolette, music by Stephen McNeff, illustrated by Yvonne Gilbert (produced London, 1978). London, Kestrel, 1981.

Verse

Figure of 8: Narrative Poems, illustrated by Peter Whiteman. London, Macmillan, 1969.
Figgie Hobbin: Poems for Children, illustrated by Pat Marriott. London, Macmillan, 1970; New York, Walker, 1973.
The Tail of the Trinosaur, illustrated by Jill Gardiner. Leicester, Brockhampton Press, 1973.
As I Went Down Zig Zag, illustrated by John Astrop. London and New York, Warne, 1974.
Here We Go Round the Round House, illustrated by Stanley

Simmonds.   Leicester, New Broom Press, 1976.

The Hill of the Fairy Calf, illustrated by Robine Clignett.   London, Hodder and Stoughton, 1976.

The Animals' Carol, illustrated by Judith Horwood.   London, Macmillan, 1978.

Schondilie, illustrated by Robert Tilling.   Leicester, New Broom Press, 1982.

Quack! Said the Billy-Goat, illustrated by Barbara Firth.   London, Walker, and New York, Lippincott, 1986.

Early in the Morning: A Collection of New Poems, music by Anthony Castro, illustrated by Michael Foreman.   London, Viking Kestrel, 1986; New York, Viking Kestrel, 1987.

Jack the Treacle Eater and Other Poems, illustrated by Charles Keeping.   London, Macmillan, 1987.

Other

When Dad Felt Bad (reader), illustrated by Richard Rose.   London, Macmillan, 1975.

Dick Whittington, illustrated by Antony Maitland.   London, Penguin, 1976.

Three Heads Made of Gold (folktale), illustrated by Pat Marriott.   London, Robson, 1978.

Editor, *Dawn and Dusk: Poems of Our Time,* illustrated by Gerald Wilkinson.   Leicester, Brockhampton Press, 1962; New York, Watts, 1963.

Editor, *Rising Early: Story Poems and Ballads of the 20th Century,* illustrated by Anne Netherwood.   Leicester, Brockhampton Press, 1964; as *Modern Ballads and Story Poems,* New York, Watts, 1965.

Editor, *In the Music I Hear: Poems by Children.*   Gillingham, Kent, ARC Press, 1970.

Editor, *Oats and Beans and Barley: Poems by Children.*   Gillingham, Kent, ARC Press, 1971.

Editor, *The Puffin Book of Magic Verse,* illustrated by Barbara Swiderska.   London, Penguin, 1974.

Editor, *The Puffin Book of Salt-Sea Verse,* illustrated by Antony Maitland.   London, Kestrel, 1978.

Editor, *The Batsford Book of Stories in Verse for Children,* illustrated by Charles Keeping.   London, Batsford, and New York, Hippocrene, 1979.

Editor, *The Sun, Dancing: Christian Verse,* illustrated by Charles Keeping.   London, Kestrel, 1982.

PUBLICATIONS FOR ADULTS

Short Stories

Hands to Dance.   London, Carroll and Nicholson, 1951; augmented edition, as *Hands to Dance, and Skylark,* London Robson, 1979.

Plays

Runaway.   London, Curwen, 1936.

The Conquering Hero.   London, Curwen, and New York, Schirmer, 1937.

Benedict.   London, Muller, 1938.

How Pleasant to Know Mrs. Lear: A Victorian Comedy.   London, Muller, 1948.

Verse

Farewell, Aggie Weston.   Aldington, Kent, Hand and Flower Press,

1951.

Survivor's Leave.   Aldington, Kent, Hand and Flower Press, 1953.

Union Street.   London, Hart Davis, 1957; Boston, Houghton Mifflin, 1958.

The Ballad of Charlotte Dymond.   Privately printed, 1958.

Johnny Alleluia.   London, Hart Davis, 1961.

Penguin Modern Poets 3, with George Barker and Martin Bell.   London, Penguin, 1962.

Ballad of the Bread Man.   London, Macmillan, 1968.

Underneath the Water.   London, Macmillan, 1968.

Pergamon Poets 10, with Laurie Lee, edited by Evan Owen.   Oxford, Pergamon Press, 1970.

Timothy Winters, music by Wallace Southam.   London, Turret, 1970.

Six Women.   Richmond, Surrey, Keepsake Press, 1974.

Collected Poems 1951–1975.   London, Macmillan, and Boston, Godine, 1975.

St. Martha and the Dragon, music by Phyllis Tate.   London, Oxford University Press, 1978.

Hymn.   North Tawton, Devon, Morrigu Press, 1983.

Secret Destinations.   London, Macmillan, 1984.

Kings' Children and Other German Ballads in English Versions.   Ashington, Mid-Northumberland Arts Group, 1986.

21 Poems.   Shipston-on-Stour, Warwickshire, Celandine Press, 1986.

A Field of Vision.   London, Macmillan, 1988.

Secret Destinations: Selected Poems 1976–88.   Boston, Godine, 1988.

Recordings: *Here Today 1,* Jupiter; *The Poet Speaks 8,* Argo; British Council tapes, 1960, 1966, 1968; *Causley Reads Causley,* Sentinel, 1975; *Pushing the Business On,* Plant Life, 1977; *Secret Destinations,* Sentinel, 1984.

Published Songs: *Shore Leave,* music by Michael Hurd; *Round the Town,* music by Michael Hurd; *Cowboy Song,* music by William Bowie; *The Sheep on Blackening Fields,* music by William Bowie; *Three Masts,* music by William Bowie; *Nursery Rhyme of Innocence and Experience,* music by Betty Rice; *Daystar in Winter,* music by Geoffrey Bush; *Mary, Mary Magdalene,* music by Phyllis Tate; *Jonah,* music by William Mathias.

Other

Editor, *Peninsula: An Anthology of Verse from the West-Country.*   London, Macdonald, 1957.

Editor, *An Octave,* by Siegfried Sassoon.   London, Arts Council, 1966.

Editor, *Modern Folk Ballads.*   London, Studio Vista, 1966.

Editor, *Selected Poems,* by Frances Bellerby.   London, Enitharmon Press, 1971.

Translator, *Twenty-five Poems,* by Hamdija Demirovic.   Richmond, Surrey, Keepsake Press, 1980.

*

Manuscript Collections: State University of New York, Buffalo; University of Exeter Library, Devon.

Critical Study: *Causley at 70: Poem and Prose Tribute* edited by Harry Chambers, Calstock, Cornwall, Peterloo, 1987.

Charles Causley comments:
    If there is a "best" way to set about writing poems for children, I think it may be by concentrating first on trying to produce a *poem,*

and by deciding afterwards on its most appropriate audience. The test of an authentic "children's" poem, surely, is that it should work equally successfully with both the child and the adult. My guiding principle here has always been something I found in W.H. Auden's matchless introduction to his *A Choice of de la Mare's Verse* in which, among many other good things, he wrote "while there are some good poems which are only for adults, because they pre-suppose adult experience in their readers, there are no good poems which are only for children."

*   *   *

The poet Charles Causley, in his work for both adults and children, is above all things else a rooted man: rooted in his native Cornwall and in the best traditions of English verse. Some poets have one subject matter for adults—adulthood—and an entirely different one for children—childhood—and a manner of writing, including a separate vocabulary, for each. Other poets' work seems to encompass quite naturally the world and preoccupations of children without selfconsciously writing down to them—I think in this context not only of Causley but of Eleanor Farjeon. Causley's imagination, steeped as it is in myth, folklore, and the world of the ballad, a world which in its anonymity tends to speak for Everyman, is perpetually moving back and forth, from childhood to adulthood and back again. He is careful not to overestimate the adult taste for a sophisticated poetic veneer, nor to underestimate the extent to which narrative verse, for example, can continue to speak to us now. His most recent collections for children, *Early in the Morning* and *Jack the Treacle Eater,* are steeped in the world of children's nursery rhymes, and the poems in these books, appropriately, have bouncing, infectious rhythms and that haunting and mysterious flavour that one associates with the best kinds of Nonsense: they are a familiar Causley blend of ancient and modern. In *Jack the Treacle Eater* the modern is represented by a poem entitled "I've Never Seen the Milkman" and the ancient by the balladic "Lady Jane Grey." Both these poems have a clarity, a simplicity, and a freshness that render the notion of whether or not the subject matter is culled from the past or the present quite irrelevant—the fact is that they speak to us now. If anything it is the poem about the milkman, that spectral visitant who leaves evidence of his calls on the doorstep daily but who is never in fact seen by the child, that continues to resonate in the mind long after one has read it:

> I wonder if he's thin or fat
> Or fair or dark or bald,
> Or short or tall, and most of all
> *I wonder what he's called.*
>
> He goes to bed so early
> That not an owl has stirred
> And rises up again before
> The earliest early bird…

Causley returns again and again as a poet to the lore and legends of his native Cornwall, and this strain is represented in these collections by such poems as "At Linkinhorne" (where, it is said by those who should know, the Devil was born) and "The Twelve O'Clock Stone," a haunting poem which recounts how children who suffered from rickets were carried to a certain part of West Penwith to be laid on a logan-stone (a giant boulder with seemingly magical properties which can be rocked by the gentlest of touches) in the expectation of a cure. This particular stone could not be rocked by human hand,

but swayed of its own accord at the stroke of midnight. Causley can make the Matter of Britain come alive for children in a way that is unmatched by any other poet of his generation.

—Michael Glover

———

CAVANNA, Betty (Elizabeth Cavanna). Also writes as Betsy Allen; Elizabeth Headley. American. Born in Camden, New Jersey, 24 June 1909. Educated at local schools, Haddonfield, New Jersey; Douglass College, New Brunswick, New Jersey, 1925–29, Litt.B. in journalism 1929 (Phi Beta Kappa). Married 1) Edward Talman Headley in 1940 (died 1952), one son; 2) George Russell Harrison in 1957 (died 1979). Reporter, Bayonne *Times,* New Jersey, 1929–31; worked in the publicity and advertising departments and as art director, Westminster Press, Philadelphia, 1931–41. Address: 45 Pasture Lane, Bryn Mawr, Pennsylvania 19010, U.S.A.

PUBLICATIONS FOR CHILDREN

Fiction

Puppy Stakes. Philadelphia, Westminster Press, 1943.
The Black Spaniel Mystery. Philadelphia, Westminster Press, 1945.
Secret Passage, illustrated by Jean MacLaughlin. Philadelphia, Winston, 1946.
Going on Sixteen. Philadelphia, Westminster Press, 1946.
Spurs for Suzanna, illustrated by Virginia Mann. Philadelphia, Westminster Press, 1947; London, Lutterworth Press, 1948.
A Girl Can Dream, illustrated by Harold Minton. Philadelphia, Westminster Press, 1948.
Paintbox Summer, illustrated by Peter Hunt. Philadelphia, Westminster Press, 1949.
Spring Comes Riding. Philadelphia, Westminster Press, 1950; London, Lutterworth Press, 1952.
Two's Company, illustrated by Edward J. Smith. Philadelphia, Westminster Press, 1951.
Lasso Your Heart. Philadelphia, Westminster Press, 1952.
Love, Laurie. Philadelphia, Westminster Press, 1953.
Six on Easy Street. Philadelphia, Westminster Press, 1954.
Passport to Romance. New York, Morrow, 1955.
The Boy Next Door. New York, Morrow, 1956.
Angel on Skis, illustrated by Isabel Dawson. New York, Morrow, 1957.
Stars in Her Eyes. New York, Morrow, 1958.
The Scarlet Sail. New York, Morrow, 1959; Leicester, Brockhampton Press, 1962.
Accent on April. New York, Morrow, 1960.
A Touch of Magic, illustrated by John Gretzer. Philadelphia, Westminster Press, 1961.
Fancy Free. New York, Morrow, 1961.
A Time for Tenderness. New York, Morrow, 1962.
Almost Like Sisters. New York, Morrow, 1963.
Jenny Kimura. New York, Morrow, 1964; Leicester, Brockhampton Press, 1966.
Mystery at Love's Creek. New York, Morrow, 1965.
A Breath of Fresh Air. New York, Morrow, 1966.
The Country Cousin. New York, Morrow, 1967.
Mystery in Marrakech. New York, Morrow, 1968.
Spice Island Mystery. New York, Morrow, 1969.
Mystery on Safari, illustrated by Joseph Cellini. New York, Morrow, 1970.

The Ghost of Ballyhooly.   New York, Morrow, 1971.
Mystery in the Museum.   New York, Morrow, 1972.
Petey, illustrated by Beth and Joe Krush.   Philadelphia, Westminster Press, 1973.
Joyride.   New York, Morrow, 1974.
Ruffles and Drums, illustrated by Richard Cuffari.   New York, Morrow, 1975.
Mystery of the Emerald Buddha.   New York, Morrow, 1976.
Runaway Voyage.   New York, Morrow, 1978.
Stamp Twice for Murder.   New York, Morrow, 1981.
The Surfer and the City Girl.   Philadelphia, Westminster Press, 1981.
Storm in Her Heart.   Philadelphia, Westminster Press, 1983.
Romance on Trial.   Philadelphia, Westminster Press, 1984.
Wanted: A Girl for the Horses.   New York, Morrow, 1984.
Banner Year.   New York, Morrow, 1987.

Fiction as Elizabeth Headley

A Date for Diane, illustrated by Janet Smalley.   Philadelphia, Macrae Smith, 1946.
Take a Call, Topsy!, illustrated by Janet Smalley.   Philadelphia, Macrae Smith, 1947; revised edition, as *Ballet Fever* (as Betty Cavanna), Philadelphia, Westminster Press, 1978.
She's My Girl!   Philadelphia, Macrae Smith, 1949; as *You Can't Take Twenty Dogs on a Date* (as Betty Cavanna), Philadelphia, Westminster Press, 1977.
Catchpenny Street.   Philadelphia, Macrae Smith, 1951.
Diane's New Love.   Philadelphia, Macrae Smith, 1955.
Toujours Diane.   Philadelphia, Macrae Smith, 1957.

Fiction as Betsy Allen

Puzzle in Purple.   New York, Grosset and Dunlap, 1948.
The Secret of Black Cat Gulch.   New York, Grosset and Dunlap, 1948.
The Riddle in Red.   New York, Grosset and Dunlap, 1948.
The Clue in Blue.   New York, Grosset and Dunlap, 1948.
The Green Island Mystery.   New York, Grosset and Dunlap, 1949.
The Ghost Wore White.   New York, Grosset and Dunlap, 1950.
The Yellow Warning.   New York, Grosset and Dunlap, 1951.
The Gray Menace.   New York, Grosset and Dunlap, 1953.
The Brown Satchel Mystery.   New York, Grosset and Dunlap, 1954.
Peril in Pink.   New York, Grosset and Dunlap, 1955.
The Silver Secret.   New York, Grosset and Dunlap, 1956.
The Mystery of the Ruby Queens.   New York, Grosset and Dunlap, 1958.

Other

The First Book of Seashells, illustrated by Marguerite Scott.   New York, Watts, 1955; London, Edmund Ward, 1965.
Arne of Norway, photographs by George Russell Harrison.   New York, Watts, and London, Chatto and Windus, 1960.
The First Book of Wild Flowers, illustrated by Page Cary.   New York, Watts, 1961.
Lucho of Peru, photographs by George Russell Harrison.   New York, Watts, 1961; London, Chatto and Windus, 1962.
Paulo of Brazil, photographs by George Russell Harrison.   New York, Watts, 1962; London, Chatto and Windus, 1963.
Pepe of Argentina, photographs by George Russell Harrison.   New York, Watts, 1962; London, Chatto and Windus, 1963.
Lo Chau of Hong Kong, photographs by George Russell Harrison.   New York, Watts, and London, Chatto and Windus, 1963.
Chico of Guatemala, photographs by George Russell Harrison.   New York, Watts, and London, Chatto and Windus, 1963.

Noko of Japan, photographs by George Russell Harrison.   New York, Watts, 1964.
Carlos of Mexico, photographs by George Russell Harrison.   New York, Watts, and London, Chatto and Windus, 1964.
Tavi of the South Seas, photographs by George Russell Harrison.   New York, Watts, 1965; London, Chatto and Windus, 1967.
Doug of Australia, photographs by George Russell Harrison.   New York, Watts, and London, Chatto and Windus, 1965.
Ali of Egypt, photographs by George Russell Harrison.   New York, Watts, and London, Chatto and Windus, 1966.
Demetrios of Greece, photographs by George Russell Harrison.   New York, Watts, and London, Chatto and Windus, 1966.
The First Book of Wool, photographs by George Russell Harrison.   New York, Watts, 1966; as *Wool,* London, Watts, 1972.
The First Book of Fiji, photographs by George Russell Harrison.   New York, Watts, 1968; as *Fiji,* London, Watts, 1972.
Morocco, photographs by George Russell Harrison.   New York, Watts, 1970; London, Watts, 1972.

Editor, *Pick of the Litter: Favorite Dog Stories.*   Philadelphia, Westminster Press, 1952.

*

Manuscript Collection: de Grummond Collection, University of Southern Mississippi, Hattiesburg.

*   *   *

Betty Cavanna's books are about growing up. She has written a string of teenage romance books which follow the conventions of the junior novel, treating emotional problems of girls as they move past adolescence. The world of Cavanna's fiction is pleasant, conventional, stereotyped, with few enormous problems.

The protagonists are wholesome, pretty American girls with cute names such as Dizzy, Carlie, Marcy, Fancy, and April. These young women are well-rounded teenagers with idealized perceptions of reality. They have an innate wisdom which might take most people a lifetime of hardship to attain. Their problems are only those minor difficulties which prevent them from having a full, mature grasp of reality.

Many of the stories are humorless books with shallow characterizations of girls worried about whether to wear lipstick, but Cavanna's books have been enormously popular and in fact have been highly recommended by critics for their attention to subjects that have reflected girls' interests. However, the heroines usually cannot succeed independently and they look up to success-seeking, industrious male figures. Cavanna has a good reputation for her sensitive treatment of those awkward transition years, and her stories have been recommended for slow readers. Although her writing style tends to be formal and functional, her vocabulary is extensive.

The plots are about the heartbreaks of growing up. In *A Date for Diane* Diane is sensitive about her braces but discovers that the boy she likes also wears them. In *Going on Sixteen* a girl with artistic ambitions overcomes her shyness through her relationship with her dog. *The Boy Next Door* is a typical novel about first love. Jane and the boy next door have been good friends all their lives, but when he becomes romantic, Jane rejects his advances and a difficult period follows, especially when Jane's sister claims him for herself.

More recent stories challenge the older taboos of children's fiction. *Almost Like Sisters* treats a mother-daughter rivalry. Victoria's young, pretty, widowed mother dances with all the boys at the dance while Victoria stands in the shadows. Another story examines the effect of divorce. In *Jenny Kimura* the Tokyo-born daughter of a mixed marriage confronts racial and cultural prejudice in Kansas City and on Cape Cod. In *A Time for Tenderness* young people of different cultures and racial backgrounds intermingle when a Southern girl goes to Brazil with her mother.

Although junior novels of the 1970's incorporated contemporary problems such as slum conditions and abortion, many of Cavanna's more recent books have been mystery-adventures patterned after the popular series books. *Mystery in Marrakech,* for example, uses trite tourist trappings typical of the settings of popular mysteries (medieval mosques, ominous bazaars, nomads on camels, ancient casbahs) to tell a tale about a mysterious kidnapping in the winding alleyway of a menacing foreign city, complete with an international oil intrigue. And *Spice Island Mystery,* set on the romantic Caribbean island of Grenada, bears a strong message against marijuana as the heroine battles a smuggling ring. The heroine is in some ways atypical. She is a dark-skinned West Indian girl who has gone to school in the United States. Except for a certain sensitivity to the problems of Grenada, she is a suburban American girl in disguise. In *Stamp Twice for Murder* someone sinister tries to scare the heroine away from a hidden treasure. Jan Nelson's mother inherits a stone house with a mysterious past in a picturesque French village. Jan, who gets sick when she dares to drink champagne, solves the mystery and is rewarded with a lingering kiss from a handsome college student.

Although they are less realistic than her soap-opera style books, Cavanna's mysteries are somewhat more palatable because energetic plots are well-sustained and the heroines more forceful.

—Bobbie Ann Mason

CAWLEY, Winifred (née Cozens). British. Born in Felton, Northumberland, 24 January 1915. Educated at Western Elementary School, Wallsend, Northumberland, 1921–26; Wallsend Secondary School, 1926–33; University of Durham at Newcastle (open scholar, 1933–36; Spence Watson prize for English literature, 1936; Ellen Phoebe Wright prize for education, 1937), 1933–37, B.A. (honours) in English 1936, diploma in the theory and practice of teaching 1937; University College, London (William Black Noble student), 1937–39. Married Arthur Clare Cawley in 1939; one son. English teacher, British Institute, Romania, 1939–40, and Yugoslavia, 1940–41, and English School, Cairo, 1941–44, Leeds College of Technology, 1950–54, West Park School, Leeds, 1954–58, Leeds Girls' High School, 1958–59 and 1966–73, Lourdes Hill Convent, Brisbane, Queensland, 1960–63, and Indooroopilly High School, Brisbane, 1964–65. Recipient: *Guardian* award, 1974. Agent: Oxford University Press, Walton Street, Oxford OX2 6DP. Address: 2 Harrowby Road, West Park, Leeds, Yorkshire LS16 5HN, England.

PUBLICATIONS FOR CHILDREN

Fiction

Down the Long Stairs, illustrated by William Stobbs. London, Oxford University Press, 1964; New York, Holt Rinehart, 1965.
Feast of the Serpent, illustrated by Doreen Roberts. London, Oxford University Press, 1969; New York, Holt Rinehart, 1970.
Gran at Coalgate, illustrated by Fermin Rocker. London, Oxford University Press, 1974; New York, Holt Rinehart, 1975.
Silver Everything, and Many Mansions, illustrated by William Stobbs. London, Oxford University Press, 1976.

*

Winifred Cawley comments:

Down the Long Stairs was set in motion by a building I've been aware of all my life, Tynemouth Castle; *Feast of the Serpent* by a brief, tantalising account of a 1649 Newcastle witchcraft trial in an old book, *England's Grievance,* by Ralph Gardiner (1655), which was among the many I used to try to make the 17th-century coal-trade background of my first story as accurate as possible.

Gran at Coalgate, which won the *Guardian* Award, is also set in northeast England, but nearly 300 years later, in 1926, the year of the General Strike and the great coal strike. Yet to a young reader it probably seems as remote as the first two, for it also tells of a way of life that has vanished. I suppose it is to some extent autobiographical. Coalgate is based on Leadgate in County Durham, as I knew it. Gran is my own Gran; other characters, other people I knew there and then. Coalgate/Leadgate may seem an unlikely place to be something of an earthly paradise, yet such it was to me. I wanted present day children to catch a glimpse of its quality. *Silver Everything* and *Many Mansions* are again based on my memories, this time of life in Wallsend-on-Tyne where I grew up. Most of the events in the stories actually happened.

In the first two books I tried to imagine what it was like to be an ordinary boy or girl in long ago extraordinary times. In the next two I tried to record what it was like to be an ordinary child in very ordinary and very humble circumstances 50 years ago.

*   *   *

Winifred Cawley's books are set in Northumberland. *Down the Long Stairs* is a first person narrative, in which Ralph Cole, now an old man, reflects on the events and personalities he met during his panic-stricken flight from the Roundheads in 1648. After a slow start, the excitement of the chase, the quieter yet vivid detail of the Border country, and the warm and moving memories of the people who helped him will capture the young reader's attention. But the heart of the novel is Ralph's slowly growing awareness of the complexity of life. At 15 his future seemed assured: this security he loses, not merely through his own wilfulness, but also through his subsequent discovery of what life down the mines was really like. He learns, too, that Royalist and Roundhead, Papist and Puritan, coalowner and coalminer are not labels which divide people straightforwardly into good and bad; and that his own attitudes and behavior are more complex and less creditable than he has supposed, and are fraught with danger to others besides himself. These lessons on the road to maturity, in themselves a common enough theme in children's books, are here presented in a clearly realised historical setting.

In *Feast of the Serpent,* set a year later in 1649, the heroine's difficulties are compounded by a growing alienation both from her mother's Romany world and her father's Border kinsfolk; and when she also becomes involved in the Roundheads' hysterical witchhunts, the pressures of her own inner conflicts added to her terrifying prison experience bring her perilously close to accepting their accusations as justified. There is good writing here, too, and a moving analysis of the girl's predicament, but the handling of the narrative is less assured. The story is told in the third person, but from shifting viewpoints, and the unwary young reader is sometimes left bewildered by the attempt to reflect both the confusions and uncertainties of the heroine and the suspicions and hostilities of the people around her.

The third story, *Gran at Coalgate,* is set in a Northumbrian mining town of the 1920's, a time remote enough to make the young reader view this as an historical novel, too. Jinnie's father is a rigid, Puritanical man who does not hold with the Goings-on at Coalgate. When Jinnie goes there to stay with Gran she is understandably bored by her cousin's Getting-Worked-Up over the lads, but is agonised fascinated by the Sins-of-Dancing-and-Going-to-the-Pictures, and is also naively and unbelievably puzzled by the activities of Aunt Polly, who is No-Better-Than-She-Should-Be. The style is not entirely successful, a mixture of straightforward narrative and a reported-speech reflection of Jinnie's bewildered thoughts, which is racy and idiomatic, but too insistently sprinkled with the Capital Letters with which she views life. A melodramatic ending seems to endorse Father's dire warnings about the Sinfulness of Pleasure and the Coalgate relations, and deflects attention from the realities of Jinnie's difficulties in understanding conflicting adult values and in reconciling her strict and repressive upbringing with the laxer morals of the outside world. In *Silver Everything, and Many Mansions* Jinnie is younger, the narrative is correspondingly more restrained, and the capital letters less insistent. Whereas the earlier books require a relatively sophisticated readership, this detailed, lively, sympathetic, and sometimes poignant account of a time of hardship, uncertainty, and change for Jinnie and her family would appeal, on different levels, to readers from ten upwards.

—Winifred Whitehead

CHALMERS, Mary (Eileen). American. Born in Camden, New Jersey, 16 March 1927. Educated at the Philadelphia College of Art, 1945–48, graduated 1948; Barnes Foundation, Merion, Pennsylvania, 1949–50. Commercial artist in the 1950's. Address: 1644 Oak Avenue, Haddon Heights, New Jersey 08035, U.S.A.

PUBLICATIONS FOR CHILDREN (illustrated by the author)

Fiction

Come for a Walk with Me.   New York, Harper, 1955.
Here Comes the Trolley Car.   New York, Harper, 1955.
A Hat for Amy Jean.   New York, Harper, 1956.
A Christmas Story.   New York, Harper, 1956.
George Appleton.   New York, Harper, 1957.
Kevin.   New York, Harper, 1957.
Boats Finds a House.   New York, Harper, 1958.
Throw a Kiss, Harry.   New York, Harper, 1958.
The Cat Who Liked to Pretend.   New York, Harper, 1959.
Mr. Cat's Wonderful Surprise.   New York, Harper, 1961.
Take a Nap, Harry.   New York, Harper, 1964.
Be Good, Harry.   New York, Harper, 1967.
Merry Christmas, Harry.   New York, Harper, 1977.
Come to the Doctor, Harry.   New York, Harper, 1981.
Six Dogs, Twenty-Three Cats, Forty-Five Mice, and One Hundred Sixteen Spiders.   New York, Harper, 1986.
The Easter Parade.   New York, Harper, 1987; London, Methuen, 1988.

*

Manuscript Collection: Kerlan Collection, University of Minnesota, Minneapolis.

Illustrator: *The Secret Language* by Ursula Nordstrom, 1960; *Big Brother,* 1960, and *The Three Funny Friends,* 1961, both by Charlotte Zolotow; *The Happy Birthday Present* by Joan Heilbroner, 1962; *The House of Thirty Cats* by Mary Calhoun, 1965; *Three to Get Ready* by Betty Boegehold, 1965; *The Crystal Tree* by Jenny D. Lindquist, 1966; *Goodnight Andrew Goodnight Craig* by Marjorie Weinman Sharmat, 1969; *I Write It* by Ruth Krauss, 1970; *When Will*

It Snow by Syd Hoff, 1971; *The Snuggle Bunny* by Nancy Jewell, 1972; *Letitia Rabbit's String Song* by Russell Hoban, 1973; *Crickety Cricket! The Best-Loved Poems of James S. Tippett,* 1973; *When Daisies Pied, and Violets Blue: Songs from Shakespeare,* 1974; *The Day after Christmas* by Alice Bach, 1975; *Oh No, Cat!* by Janice Udry, 1976; *Mule in the Mail* by Stephen Manes, 1978; *Home at Last* by Patricia Lauber, 1980.

Mary Chalmers comments:

The books of which I am both author and illustrator are all for the very young child—they are "picture books." The books by other authors that I have illustrated range from picture books to stories for young teenagers. There is a different ratio of pictures to words in these books. For instance, Jenny D. Lindquist's *The Crystal Tree* is nearly 300 pages long and has 20 illustrations by me; Russell Hoban's *Letitia Rabbit's String Song* has a picture on every page. I have worked almost entirely with pen and ink, pencil and water color.

*   *   *

Mary Chalmers is best known for Harry, the beguiling, anthropomorphic cat who has appeared in five tiny books which span 23 years. However, a handful of other small books, which present a childlike point of view, predate and presage Harry. With leisurely language and an artless fusion of fantasy and reality, they describe the simplest of adventures which begin and end in the cozy, nurturing climate of home. Trilby, the cat in *George Appleton,* wakes in human fashion in a fourposter with his head on a pillow but later huddles in classic cat position under the family car; he meets a peaceful, lonely dragon in the woods and they have a "perfectly marvelous time" playing together all day. In *Come for a Walk with Me* Susan invites Will Rabbit to accompany her to Mrs. Horseyfeather's house to borrow molasses; upon arrival they "had had such a lovely walk and they were so happy that they did a little dance." In these narratives there is time for hellos and goodbyes, cups of hot chocolate, and smelling flowers—time for exploration, reflection, communion, and celebration.

Harry demanded a new style. With condensed prose, the elimination of precious words such as "little" and names such as "Harry Hop Toad," and with the whimsy sharpened into wit, the tranquil, domestic happiness is stretched to incorporate conflict and resolution. A more pungent happiness emerges through Harry's first small struggles for autonomy. Familiar parental commands, signalized in titles like *Throw a Kiss, Harry* and *Take a Nap, Harry,* rouse these minor mutinies. Harry throws a kiss to the fireman who rescues him from a rooftop—but only after his mother stops cajoling him to do so and disappears; then he throws an independent, heartfelt kiss. Similarly, he takes a nap, not when his mother, eager to get on with making a cake, rushes him to bed, but later, when a yawn comes after they begin the cake. These are small struggles, but eminently important to a small cat...and a small child.

Despite their young ages, Harry and Chalmers's other protagonists operate with an appealing aplomb and assiduously overcome obstacles. When a star is needed to complete the tree in *A Christmas Story,* tiny Elizabeth states matter-of-factly, "I'll go get one," and does so, returning with the simple, self-satisfied pronouncement, "There," as the star shines from atop the tree. Harry enters the doctor's office with considerable trepidation in *Come to the Doctor, Harry,* but emerges unimpaired, proudly waving his tail bandage. These attributes are missing in *Merry Christmas, Harry,* Chalmer's least successful Harry book; an uncharacteristically passive role—requesting and receiving a baby kitten from Santa Claus—places Harry in a disappointingly dependent position.

In the early books the illustrations are decorative accessories; in the Harry series they carry the feelings and drama. All but the essentials are eliminated in the sketches and sufficient empty space surrounds Harry so attention is directed to the tiny soft-pencil lines that animate and denote changes in his expressions and actions. When combined judiciously with an understated text that effectively uses silences and pauses, Harry's small powers loom large.

—Nancy C. Hammond

———

CHAMBERS, Aidan. Also writes as Malcolm Blacklin. British. Born in Chester-le-Street, County Durham, 27 December 1934. Educated at Queen Elizabeth I Grammar School, Darlington, County Durham, 1948–53; Borough Road College, London, 1955–57. Served in the Royal Navy, 1953–55. Married Nancy Harris Lockwood in 1968. Teacher of English and drama in English schools, 1957–68. Since 1970 proprietor and publisher, Thimble Press, and publisher, *Signal: Approaches to Children's Books,* South Woodchester, Gloucestershire; since 1970 tutor, Further Professional Studies Department, University of Bristol. Columnist ("Young Reading"), *Times Educational Supplement,* London, 1970–72; columnist ("Letter from England"), *Horn Book,* Boston, 1972–84; writer and presenter, with Nancy Chambers, *Bookbox* programme, Radio Bristol, 1973–75; writer and presenter, *Children and Books* programme, BBC Radio, 1976. General editor, Topliners, Club 75, and Rockets series, 1967–81, and since 1977 M Books series, Macmillan, publishers, London. Recipient: Children's Literature Association award, for criticism, 1978; Eleanor Farjeon award, 1982; Silver Pencil award (Netherlands), 1985, 1986. Agent: Pat White, Deborah Rogers Ltd., 20 Powis Mews, London W11 1JN. Address: Lockwood, Station Road, South Woodchester, Stroud, Gloucestershire GL5 5EQ, England.

PUBLICATIONS FOR CHILDREN

Fiction

Cycle Smash. London, Heinemann, 1967.
Marle. London, Heinemann, 1968.
Mac and Lugs, illustrated by Barbara Swiderska. London, Macmillan, 1971.
Don't Forget Charlie and the Vase, illustrated by Clyde Pearson. London, Macmillan, 1971.
Ghosts 2 (short stories). London, Macmillan, 1972.
Snake River, illustrated by Peter Morgan. Stockholm, Almqvist och Wiksell, 1975; London, Macmillan, 1977.
Ghost Carnival: Stories of Ghosts in Their Haunts, illustrated by Peter Wingham. London, Heinemann, 1977.
Breaktime. London, Bodley Head, 1978; New York, Harper, 1979.
Fox Tricks (short stories), illustrated by Robin and Jocelyn Wild. London, Heinemann, 1980.
Seal Secret. London, Bodley Head, 1980; New York, Harper, 1981.
Dance on My Grave. London, Bodley Head, 1982; New York, Harper, 1983.
The Present Takers. London, Bodley Head, and New York, Harper, 1983.
Now I Know. London, Bodley Head, 1987; as *NIK: Now I Know,* New York, Harper, 1988.

Plays

Johnny Salter (produced Stroud, Gloucestershire, 1965). London,

Heinemann, 1966.
The Car (produced Stroud, Gloucestershire, 1966). London, Heinemann, 1967.
The Chicken Run (produced Stroud, Gloucestershire, 1967). London, Heinemann, 1968.
The Dream Cage: A Comic Drama in Nine Dreams (produced Stroud, Gloucestershire, 1981). London, Heinemann, 1982.

Television Series: *Ghosts,* 1980; *Long, Short and Tall Stories,* 1980–81.

Other

Haunted Houses, illustrated by John Cameron Jarvies. London, Pan, 1971.
Book of Ghosts and Hauntings, illustrated by Antony Maitland. London, Longman, 1973.
More Haunted Houses, illustrated by Chris Bradbury. London, Pan, 1973.
Great British Ghosts, illustrated by Barry Wilkinson. London, Pan, 1974.
Great Ghosts of the World, illustrated by Peter Edwards. London, Pan, 1974.
Book of Flyers and Flying, illustrated by Trevor Stubley. London, Kestrel, 1976.
Book of Cops and Robbers, illustrated by Allan Manham. London, Kestrel, 1977.

Editor, with Nancy Chambers, *Ghosts.* London, Macmillan, 1969.
Editor, with Nancy Chambers, *World Zero Minus: An SF Anthology.* London, Macmillan, 1971.
Editor, *I Want to Get Out: Stories and Poems by Young Writers.* London, Macmillan, 1971.
Editor, with Nancy Chambers, *Hi-Ran-Ho: A Picture-Book of Verse,* illustrated by Barbara Swiderska. London, Longman, 1971.
Editor, with Nancy Chambers, *In Time to Come: An SF Anthology.* London, Macmillan, 1973.
Editor, *Fighters in the Sky.* London, Macmillan, 1976.
Editor, *Funny Folk: A Book of Comic Tales,* illustrated by Trevor Stubley. London, Heinemann, 1976.
Editor, *Men at War.* London, Macmillan, 1977.
Editor, *Escapers.* London, Macmillan, 1978.
Editor, *War at Sea.* London, Macmillan, 1978.
Editor (as Malcolm Blacklin), *Ghosts 4.* London, Macmillan, 1978.
Editor, *Animal Fair,* illustrated by Anthony Colbert. London, Heinemann, 1979.
Editor, *Ghosts That Haunt You,* illustrated by Gareth Floyd. London, Kestrel, 1980.
Editor, *Loving You Loving Me.* London, Macmillan, 1980.
Editor, *Ghost after Ghost,* illustrated by Bert Kitchen. London, Kestrel, 1982.
Editor, *Plays for Young People to Read and Perform.* Stroud, Gloucestershire, Thimble Press, 1982.
Editor, with Jill Bennett, *Poetry for Children.* Stroud, Gloucestershire, Thimble Press, 1984.
Editor, *Out of Time: Stories of the Future.* London, Bodley Head, 1984; New York, Harper, 1985.
Editor, *Shades of Dark: Ghost Stories.* London, Hardy, 1984; New York, Harper, 1986.
Editor, *A Sporting Chance: Stories of Winning and Losing.* London, Bodley Head, 1985.
Editor, *A Quiver of Ghosts.* London, Bodley Head, 1987.
Editor, *A Haunt of Ghosts.* New York, Harper, 1987.
Editor, *Love All.* London, Bodley Head, 1988.

PUBLICATIONS FOR ADULTS

Play

Everyman's Everybody (produced London, 1957).

Other

The Reluctant Reader. Oxford, Pergamon Press, 1969.
Introducing Books to Children. London, Heinemann, 1973; revised edition, Boston, Horn Book, 1983, London, Heinemann, 1984.
Axes for Frozen Seas (lecture). Huddersfield, Yorkshire, Woodfield and Stanley, 1981.

Editor, *The Tenth* [and *Eleventh*] *Ghost Book.* London, Barrie and Jenkins, 2 vols., 1975–76; published together as *The Bumper Book of Ghost Stories,* London, Pan, 1976.
Editor, *Booktalk: Occasional Writing on Literature and Children.* London Bodley Head, and New York, Harper, 1985.

*   *   *

Aidan Chambers's contribution to children's literature is extraordinarily wide. He is well known as anthologist, publisher, lecturer, critic, and theorist, particularly for his two studies *The Reluctant Reader* and *Introducing Books to Children.* In concentrating here on his novels, it has to be said that although he may not be one of the top sellers he is certainly one of the most challenging and influential writers for young people. His work implicitly denies any firm distinction between adult and juvenile fiction. Thematically he is prepared to tackle whatever his adolescent characters might experience, be it Ditto's sexual encounter with Helen or Hal's homosexuality, and not all reviewers have approved. Technically his work reveals the influence of the major experimental novelists, particularly B.S. Johnson (more, perhaps, in *Albert Angelo* than in *The Unfortunates,* about which Chambers has spoken glowingly). In talking and writing about literature, Chambers has always emphasised the significance of stories as a way of discovering meaning, of changing lives. Barthes, Iser, and other "reader response" critics have helped to shape what he instinctively knew from the act of composing: that readers must construct the meaning of stories for themselves, that authors do not always know what is "there" in the stories they have written.

Breaktime, his first important novel about the adolescent quest for independence, is about ways of telling. Ditto is challenged by Morgan, a fellow sixth-former, who claims that fiction is a lie, a game, not life. In one sense the book is Ditto's response: the story of his holiday break, camping, disturbing a political meeting, being involved in a burglary, losing his virginity. Like Morgan at the end, readers have to make their own sense of the narrative, to decide how much of it is "true." The story is told in a mixture of external third-person and internal stream-of-consciousness styles, interspersed with headlines, typescript and handwriting, playtext, cartoons, lists, and quotations. The effect is rather like Joyce or Vonnegut for adolescents. The climactic scene with Helen is a three-part counterpoint: the events, Ditto's thoughts, and—in a separate column—a section from a textbook describing the act of intercourse. Such devices and the fact that Ditto's story also incorporates the stories of others (like Helen and his father) mean that the reader feels simultaneously involved in and detached from the events described.

Dance on My Grave is also narrated in a cinematic montage of different documents, presenting Hal's account of his life as given to a social worker, but involving the reader in evaluating the validity of what is being told. Hal capsizes a dinghy on the Thames and is rescued by the rather older Barry Gorman. The two become friends and lovers, but when Barry sleeps with someone else the boys quarrel, and Barry goes off on his motorbike and is killed. Hal finally keeps the promise (apparently drawn from an actual incident) that the survivor of the pair will dance on the other's grave. The subtlety of the narration cannot be conveyed by such a bald outline, and summary would be even more fruitless as a way of conveying the qualities of *Now I Know,* another complex mixture of modes and parallel texts, this time centred on the nature of religious belief and different ways of "investigating" life. A youth group is making a film about the second coming of Christ; Nick encounters Julie, who is blinded in an accident; the eternal question "How can God let this happen?" is raised.

Chambers has also written two more straightforward novels for younger readers, *Seal Secret* and *The Present Takers,* though each can also be read at deeper levels. The first of these examines the conflict between sensitive, artistic William and Gwyn, the practical farmer's son he meets on holiday. Gwyn plans to farm seals for their skins and meat. William's idealistic attempt to save the seal pup hidden in a cave ends in disaster. Through the excitement of this narrative run other stories about relationships with parents and friends, moral choice, and self-understanding.

In a similar way *The Present Takers* can be seen as a tale in which Lucy, victim of school bullying, learns to overcome her adversary Melanie. In another way, though, against her home background, Melanie can be seen as the real victim. The story is more concerned with what is said than what is done, and with its hidden messages and metaphors it can be read as demonstrating the power of language. The "simple" tale of a gang of bullies opens up for reflection powerful questions about violence, the motivation of those who use it and those who permit it, and the problems it poses for any society.

—Robert Protherough

———

CHANCE, Stephen. See **TURNER, Philip.**

———

CHANEY, Jill. British. Born in Radlett, Hertfordshire, 5 June 1932. Educated at Downs School, Seaford, Sussex, graduated 1947; Waterperry Horticultural School, Oxfordshire, 1948–50, Royal Horticultural Society diploma 1950. Married Walter Leeming in 1960; one daughter and one son. Gardener, Jewish Board of Guardians, London, 1954–59; director, Chorleywood Bookshop, Hertfordshire, 1971–88. Address: Glen Rosa, Colleyland, Chorleywood, Hertfordshire, England.

PUBLICATIONS FOR CHILDREN

Fiction

On Primrose Hill, illustrated by Jane Paton. London, Methuen, 1962.
Half a Candle, illustrated by Carolyn Dinan. London, Dobson, 1968; New York, Crown, 1969.
A Penny for the Guy, illustrated by John Dyke. London, Dobson, 1970.
Mottram Park, illustrated by Carolyn Dinan. London, Dobson, 1971.

Christopher's Dig, illustrated by John Dyke. London, Dobson, 1972.
Taking the Woffle to Pebblecombe-on-Sea, illustrated by Elizabeth Ogan. London, Dobson, 1974.
Return to Mottram Park, illustrated by Carolyn Dinan. London, Dobson, 1974.
Christopher's Find, illustrated by John Dyke. London, Dobson, 1975.
Woffle, R.A., illustrated by Catherine Leeming. London, Dobson, 1976.
The Buttercup Field, illustrated by Elizabeth Ogan. London, Dobson, 1976.
Canary Yellow, illustrated by Carolyn Dinan. London, Dobson, 1977.
Angel Face, illustrated by Carolyn Dinan. London, Dobson, 1979.
Vectis Diary, illustrated by Catherine Leeming. London, Dobson, 1979.
Leaving Mottram Park, illustrated by Carolyn Dinan. Lewes, Sussex, Book Guild, 1989.

*

Jill Chaney comments:

Each of my books, even if it is part of a series, is an entity in itself. The books are usually set in an actual place, although these are not always named: I have written one set in East Anglia, several in London, two on the Isle of Wight, one in Oxfordshire. The characters are always entirely fictitious, and what is described is usually a momentous time in the lives of the characters, although to an outsider the incidents might appear unremarkable. It is only now, looking back at the 14 books, that I can discern a pattern common to them all. They seem to be about people trying to get on well with each other, not wanting to quarrel. The books for older children are also about bridging the gap between childish expectations and adult reality. I see this now, but each time I embark on a new book I am only concerned with writing a story about a group of people, many of whom happen to be between the ages of 10 and 20.

*   *   *

Jill Chaney writes equally successfully for the eight-year-old level and the older adolescent reader. One of her most appealing stories in the former category is *Christopher's Dig,* in which a young boy, after a visit to the Natural History Museum, is fired by enthusiasm to emulate Mary Anning, the 19th-century Dorset girl who dug up a dinosaur. Christopher, who lives in a small London flat, has to borrow a spade from an elderly gardener, but his main problem is finding somewhere to dig. He gets into trouble when he starts excavating the London parks, the Square gardens, and even disused building sites. Eventually he starts work by a sewer outlet on the Thames embankment and finds not a fossilised dinosaur but a box of jewels and gold coins. With the proceeds he takes his family on holiday to the Dorset coast to continue his hunt. The second book, *Christopher's Find,* is equally satisfactory, with the single-minded boy again triumphing over his disbelieving elders. The Woffle stories are for younger readers and make good bedtime tales.

As a writer of teenage fiction, Chaney appeals mainly to girls. *Canary Yellow* is the story of 16-year-old Julia who leaves home because of the incessant squabbling of her parents. She makes friends with a lonely old man living on a canal boat and when he has to go into hospital she moves in to look after his canary. A homeless young couple with small children camping out in a derelict cottage seem to have even greater problems than she has, and she offers to babysit while Dave takes his young wife to the hospital. Eventually the children get put into care and Julia's sympathy for Dave blossoms into love. He takes advantage of this and her initiation is painful.

Vectis Diary is also the story of a girl on her own for the first time, working in a hotel on the Isle of Wight and writing her diary each night, exploring her feelings as she fumbles her way through the complications of growing up. These are sensitively handled stories and the teenager will not feel "talked-down-to" as she reads them.

—Ann G. Hay

————

CHANNEL, A.R. See **CATHERALL, Arthur.**

————

CHAUNCY, Nan(cen Beryl, née Masterman). British. Born in Northwood, Middlesex, 28 May 1900. Educated at St. Michael's Collegiate School, Hobart, Tasmania. Married Antony Chauncy in 1938; one daughter. Recipient: Australian Children's Book award, 1958, 1959, 1961. *Died 1 May 1970.*

<small>PUBLICATIONS FOR CHILDREN</small>

Fiction

They Found a Cave, illustrated by Margaret Horder. Melbourne and London, Oxford University Press, 1948; New York, Watts, 1961.
World's End Was Home, illustrated by Shirley Hughes. Melbourne and London, Oxford University Press, 1952; New York, Watts, 1961.
A Fortune for the Brave, illustrated by Margaret Horder. Melbourne and London, Oxford University Press, 1954; New York, Watts, 1961.
Tiger in the Bush, illustrated by Margaret Horder. London, Oxford University Press, 1957; New York, Watts, 1961.
Devil's Hill, illustrated by Geraldine Spence. London, Oxford University Press, 1958; New York, Watts, 1960.
Tangara: "Let Us Set Off Again," illustrated by Brian Wildsmith. London, Oxford University Press, 1960; as *The Secret Friends,* New York, Watts, 1962.
Half a World Away, illustrated by Annette Macarthur-Onslow. London, Oxford University Press, 1962; New York, Watts, 1963.
The "Roaring 40," illustrated by Annette Macarthur-Onslow. London, Oxford University Press, and New York, Watts, 1963.
High and Haunted Island, illustrated by Victor Ambrus. London, Oxford University Press, 1964; New York, Norton, 1965.
The Skewbald Pony, illustrated by David Parry. London, Nelson, 1965.
Panic at the Garage, illustrated by Peter Lloyd. Edinburgh, Oliver and Boyd, 1965.
Mathinna's People, illustrated by Victor Ambrus. London, Oxford University Press, 1967; as *Hunted in Their Own Land,* New York, Seabury Press, 1973.
Lizzie Lights, illustrated by Judith White. London, Oxford University Press, 1968.
The Lighthouse Keeper's Son, illustrated by Victor Ambrus. London, Oxford University Press, 1969.

Other

Beekeeping, illustrated by Jane Walker. Melbourne, Oxford

University Press, 1967.

*

Manuscript Collection: State Archives, Hobart, Tasmania.

*   *   *

Nan Chauncy began writing at a time when Australian children's literature was dominated by melodramatic and romantic post-war fiction. Her early stories for children were in the existing mode except that *They Found a Cave,* although retaining conventional eccentric adult characters and exploiting a strong story line, was about a group of children who emerged as dynamic interacting individuals. They exist in a strong family relationship, and the Tasmanian bush setting is recognisably real. These two characteristics were so refined and strengthened in *Tiger in the Bush* and *Devil's Hill* that both books won the Australian Children's Book of the Year award in successive years and established the author's reputation as a realist. Indeed it can well be claimed that she established the contemporary realistic novel for children in Australia which has now been extended and developed in style and technique, as well as in content, by writers such as Patricia Wrightson and Ivan Southall.

In *Tiger in the Bush, Devil's Hill* and *The "Roaring 40"* Nan Chauncy explores the personal relationships of the Lorenny family. Badge Lorenny, "the little boy, the odd man out, the pest and the hanger-on" whom his older brother Lance and his sister Iggy call a "Bidgee burr" and a "wattle tick" because they can't do anything without his irritating presence, is the stalwart younger son of a strongly drawn family. There is Liddle-ma, a big woman in every way with strong principles and a warm heart, Dad, of few words but inspiring utter confidence in his offspring, the children, and their cousins from "outside." For "the world as Badge Lorenny knew it was just home—home tucked between the rough-wrought mountains of Tasmania like a drop of dew between cabbage leaves." To each of the children "home was home...as soon as you opened the door you saw the great blaze of the fire in the wide black hearth...you saw Dad slowly put down his newspaper—Liddle-ma's comforting smile." Home was a valley sanctuary hewn from the bush and accessible only by flying-fox—"The Wire." Here Badge learns that honesty and loyalty are more important than possessions or popularity, and that retaining his integrity brings a glow "greater than any sunset, uplifting him with joy and pride and a great relief." Through the incident of the lost cow in *Devil's Hill,* which had actually happened to the writer and one of her brothers, Badge's cousin, Sam, the Skite, the blusterer, and the shirker, learns the value of honest toil and the necessity for interdependence as well as independence to weld a family into an enduring unit.

Tangara made a different contribution to Australian children's literature. Perhaps for the first time there was a successful blending of realism with fantasy, and the plight of the aborigines who had been exterminated by white settlers in the early days of the colony of Tasmania was treated with dignity and spirituality. *Tangara* is a journey in time, a psychic rediscovery of the life of the Tasmanian aborigines through the "vision" of Lexie Pavemont whose deep affinity with her great-great-aunt Rita summons the aboriginal girl, Merrina, Rita's friend, from the past to prevent a latter-day tragedy, so that yet another debt is added to the past. The novel moves by implication and imagery to evoke insight into the unspeakable past and ends elegiacally with Merrina keening, "her thin arms reaching up imploringly," "alone and calling to her dead." A more formal lament was to be sung by Chauncy in *Mathinna's People,* a series of tableaux from the day that the young chief Wyrum gazed with awe at the white sails of the *Heemskerck* in 1642 to the death of Towterer, the chief, who went to the Old Ones broken in body and spirit by the

contamination of white culture. Ironically the white man, George Robinson, who sought to do good from the highest motives is the one most responsible for a psychological affliction that was far more traumatic than bodily hurt.

Mathinna's People is Chauncy's finest composition. In *The "Roaring 40"* and *High and Haunted Island* she had written evocatively of Tasmania's lonely and threatening South-West coast, and had then created a fictitious island where a colony of Circlists act out the rituals of their religious faith. Even here, where there is a hint of the mysterious, Chauncy's writing is poetically realistic and convincing. Her last two stories, *Lizzie Lights* and *The Lighthouse Keeper's Son,* were less satisfying in that her work had come almost full circle with a return to some early weaknesses of plotting and characterisation.

In spite of a changing society and a greater sophistication in more recent writers, Nan Chauncy, through the Lorenny books and her aboriginal studies in particular, remains among the foremost Australian writers for children.

—H.M. Saxby

CHAUNDLER, Christine. British. Born in Biggleswade, Bedfordshire, 5 September 1887. Educated at Queen Anne's School, Caversham, Berkshire; St. Winifred's School, Bangor, Wales. Editor, *Little Folks* magazine, London, 1914–17; children's editor, Nisbet, publishers, London, 1919–23; book reviewer, *Quiver* magazine, London, 1923–48; reader, Robert Hale, publishers, London, from 1939. *Died in December 1972.*

PUBLICATIONS FOR CHILDREN

Fiction

The Magic Kiss. London, Cassell, 1916.
Little Squirrel Tickletail, illustrated by Harry Rountree. London, Cassell, 1917; New York, Stokes, 1918.
Ronald's Burglar, illustrated by Helen Stratton. London, Nelson, 1919; New York, Nelson, 1921.
The Reputation of the Upper Fourth. London, Nisbet, 1919.
Pat's Third Term, illustrated by Harold Earnshaw. London, Oxford University Press, 1919.
The Thirteenth Orphan, illustrated by Honor Appleton. London, Nisbet, 1920; New York, Stokes, 1921.
Just Gerry. London, Nisbet, 1920.
The Right St. John's, illustrated by Savile Lumley. London, Oxford University Press, 1920.
The Binky Books (The Motor Bandits, The Circus Lion), illustrated by Will Owen. London, Nisbet, 2 vols., 1920.
Snuffles for Short, illustrated by Honor Appleton. London, Nisbet, 1921.
The Fourth Form Detectives. London, Nisbet, 1921.
The Reformation of Dormitory Five. London, Nisbet, 1921.
A Fourth Form Rebel. London, Nisbet, 1922.
Captain Cara. London, Nisbet, 1923.
Jan of the Fourth. London, Nisbet, 1923.
Tomboy Toby. London, Partridge, 1923.
Dickie's Day. London, Nelson, 1924.
Winning Her Colours. London, Nisbet, 1924.
Sally Sticks It Out. London, Partridge, 1924.
Judy the Tramp. London, Nisbet, 1924.
Princess Carroty-Top and Timothy. London, Warne, 1924.

Jill the Outsider, illustrated by Elizabeth Earnshaw.   London, Cassell, 1924.
An Unofficial Schoolgirl.   London, Nisbet, 1925.
Bunty of the Blackbirds.   London, Nisbet, 1925.
The Adopting of Mickie, illustrated by T. Peddie.   London, Religious Tract Society, 1925.
A Credit to Her House.   London, Ward Lock, 1926.
Twenty-Six Christine Chaundler School Stories for Girls, illustrated by Arthur Twidle.   London, Religious Tract Society, 1926.
The Exploits of Evangeline.   London, Nisbet, 1926.
Reforming the Fourth.   London, Ward Lock, 1927.
The Chivalrous Fifth, illustrated by Anne Rochester.   London, Nelson, 1927.
Philippa's Family.   London, Nisbet, 1927.
Meggy Makes Her Mark.   London, Nisbet, 1928.
The Games Captain.   London, Ward Lock, 1928.
Friends in the Fourth.   London, Ward Lock, 1929.
The Technical Fifth.   London, Ward Lock, 1930.
A Disgrace to the Fourth, illustrated by M.D. Swales.   London, Nelson, 1930.
The New Girl in Four A.   London, Nisbet, 1930.
The Madcap in the School.   London, Nelson, 1930.
Two in Form Four.   London, Cassell, 1931.
The Junior Prefect.   London, Ward Lock, 1931.
The Story-Book School.   London, Oxford University Press, 1931.
Jill of the Guides.   London, Nisbet, 1932.
Five B and Evangeline.   London, Newnes, 1932.
The Feud with the Sixth.   London, Nisbet, 1932.
Cinderella Ann.   London, Ward Lock, 1932.
The Amateur Patrol.   London, Nisbet, 1933.
The Lonely Garden, and Ronald's Burglar.   London, Nelson, 1934.
Tales of Nicky-Nob.   London, Chambers, 4 vols., 1937.
The Children's Story Hour, illustrated by Alfred E. Kerr.   London, Evans, 1938.
The Odd Ones, illustrated by Harry Rountree.   London, Country Life, 1941.
Winkie Wee and the Silver Sixpence.   London, Museum Press, 1947.
Winkie-Wee's Spring Cleaning.   London, Museum Press, 1947.
Prize for Gardening, illustrated by L.M. Dufty.   London, Nelson, 1948.
More Stories for the Children's Hour, illustrated by Cyril Foster.   London, Hale, 1949.

Play

A Child Is Born: A Nativity Play.   London, Evans, 1949.

Verse

Curious Creatures, illustrated by Fred Robinson.   London, The Naturist, 1944.
The Golden Years: Some Verses for Nurseries.   London, Hale, 1950.

Other

My Book of Beautiful Legends, with Eric Wood, illustrated by A.C. Michael.   London, Cassell, and New York, Funk, 1916.
My Book of Stories from the Poets, illustrated by A.C. Michael.   London, Cassell, 1919; New York, Funk, 1920.
Arthur and His Knights, illustrated by Mackenzie.   London, Nisbet, 1920; as *Legends and Tales of King Arthur,* New York, Stokes, 1920.
The Children's Christmas Book.   London, Mowbray, 1949.
The Blue [Brown, Red] Book of Saints' Stories, Retold.   London, Mowbray, 3 vols., 1952.

A Year-Book of Legends [*Fairy Tales, the Stars, Customs, Saints, Folk-lore, Nursery Tales*], illustrated by Tom Godfrey.   London, Mowbray, 7 vols., 1954–63; *A Year-Book of Customs* published New York, Morehouse Gorham, 1957.
The End of the Rainbow (reader), illustrated by Hilda Boswell.   Edinburgh, McDougall, 1958.
Through the Christian Year.   London, Mowbray, 1960.
Great Saints Library: Simply-Written Lives for Christian Reading (*St. Bridget, St. Christopher, St. Elizabeth and St. Teresa, St. Francis of Assisi, St. George and St. Alban, St. Hilda of Whitby, St. Hugh of Lincoln, St. Joan of Arc, St. Margaret of Scotland, St. Martin of Tours, St. Nicholas, St. Vincent de Paul*), illustrated by Jennifer Miles.   London, Mowbray, 12 vols., 1961.
Everyman's Book of Legends.   London, Mowbray, 1963.
Everyman's Book of Ancient Customs.   London, Mowbray, 1968.
Every Man's Book of Superstitions, illustrated by Margaret Francis.   London, Mowbray, and New York, Philosophical Library, 1970.

PUBLICATIONS FOR ADULTS

Other

The Children's Author: A Writer's Guide to the Juvenile Market.   London, Pitman, 1934.

*   *   *

Christine Chaundler was a colourful writer who, for several decades, contributed stories on school, Girl Guide, and fairy themes to many children's magazines and annuals, as well as producing full-length books. She was an editor of *Little Folks* from 1914 to 1917, and some of her most memorable works (*Meggy Makes Her Mark, Jill of the Guides,* etc.) were first published in that periodical. Her fairy poems and stories for younger children were refreshingly unsentimental. She was best known during the 1920's and 1930's, however, for her school stories. These were variations on classic themes of the genre established by Angela Brazil and developed by Dorita Fairlie Bruce. But Chaundler failed to achieve a comparable degree of recognition—possibly because her charactizations were less acute, and because she never extended the adventures of any of her heroines beyond a single novel into a series.

She managed to inject a strong sense of realism into her books, even when exploiting vivid and dramatic situations. One of the most distinctive elements of her writing was the capacity to deal with the girl who finds herself suddenly against the tide of popular standards and opinion. She first used this theme persuasively in *Pat's Third Term* with a junior who refused to make the expected gestures of homage to the generally idolized Head Girl; she developed and refined it in *Jill the Outsider* and *A Disgrace to the Fourth,* and, with considerable wit and style, in *The Chivalrous Fifth.* This was an attack on the type of snobbery that was so often associated with traditional, elitist boarding-schools: a new girl, Jane, is tolerated rather than accepted because she has told her form-mates that her mother keeps a second-hand shop, but this turns out to be a Bond Street antique gallery, and Jane's mother is a Viscountess!

Chaundler wrote numerous stories that catered for the enormous enthusiasm that surrounded the early days of the Girl Guide Movement. Here again, however, she was careful to steer clear of high-flown sentiment; her Girl Guides were not always the epitomes of efficiency and preparedness that they were in stories by many other Guiding writers. In *Bunty of the Blackbirds,* for example, one girl is shown as unable to light a campfire without setting the common alight, ripping her skirt from hem to waist, and burning a hole in her knickers. Similar uninflated realism was the keynote of her excellent 1919 series of *Little Folks* short stories, "How We Won the War," in which the over-ambitious patriotic efforts of a family of children repeatedly and entertainingly misfire.

Christine Chaundler continued to produce inventive fiction well into the 1930's. Later, in the 1950's and 1960's, she concentrated on writing a series of informative, religious non-fiction books, and "re-tellings" for younger children.

—Mary Cadogan

———

CHEETHAM, Ann. See **PILLING, Ann.**

———

CHILDRESS, Alice. American. Born in Charleston, South Carolina, 12 October 1920. Educated at schools in Harlem, New York; Radcliffe Institute for Independent Study (scholar), 1966–68, graduated 1968. Married the musician Nathan Woodard; one daughter. Actress and director, American Negro Theatre, New York, 1941–52; columnist ("Here's Mildred"), Baltimore *Afro-American*, 1956–58. Artist-in-residence, University of Massachusetts, Amherst, 1984. Recipient: Obie award, 1956; Woodward School Book award, 1975; Paul Robeson award, for screenplay, 1977; Virgin Islands Film Festival award, 1977; Radcliffe Graduate Society medal, 1984; African Poets Theatre award, 1985; Audelco award, 1986; Harlem School of the Arts Humanitarian award, 1987. Agent: Flora Roberts Inc., 157 West 57th Street, New York, New York 10019, U.S.A.

PUBLICATIONS FOR CHILDREN

Fiction

A Hero Ain't Nothin' But a Sandwich. New York, Coward McCann, 1973.
Rainbow Jordan. New York, Coward McCann, 1981.
Those Other People. New York, Putnam, 1989.

Plays

When the Rattlesnake Sounds, illustrated by Charles Lilly. New York, Coward McCann, 1975.
Let's Hear It for the Queen, illustrated by Loring Eutemey. New York, Coward McCann, 1976.

Screenplay: *A Hero Ain't Nothin' But a Sandwich,* 1977.

PUBLICATIONS FOR ADULTS

Novel

A Short Walk. New York, Coward McCann, 1979.

Plays

Florence (also director: produced New York, 1949). Published in *Masses and Mainstream* (New York), October 1950.
Just a Little Simple, adaptation of stories by Langston Hughes

(produced New York, 1950).
Gold Through the Trees (produced New York, 1952).
Trouble in Mind (produced New York, 1955). Published in *Black Theatre: A Twentieth-Century Collection of the Work of Its Best Playwrights,* edited by Lindsay Patterson, New York, Dodd Mead, 1971.
Wedding Band (produced Ann Arbor, Michigan, 1966; New York, 1972). New York, French, 1974.
The World on a Hill, in *Plays to Remember.* New York, Macmillan, 1968.
Young Martin Luther King (produced on tour, 1969).
String, adaptation of a story by Maupassant (produced New York, 1969). With *Mojo,* New York, Dramatists Play Service, 1971.
Wine in the Wilderness (televised 1969; produced New York, 1976). New York, Dramatists Play Service, 1970.
Mojo (produced New York, 1970). With *String,* New York, Dramatists Play Service, 1971.
Sea Island Song (produced Charleston, South Carolina, 1977).
Gullah (produced Amherst, Massachusetts, 1984).
Moms: A Praise Play for a Black Comedienne, music and lyrics by Childress and Nathan Woodard (produced New York, 1987).

Television Play: *Wine in the Wilderness,* 1969.

Other

Like One of the Family: Conversations from a Domestic's Life. New York, Independence, 1956.

Editor, *Black Scenes: Collections of Scenes from Plays Written by Black People about Black Experience.* New York, Zenith, 1971.

*

Theatrical Activities:
Director: **Play**—*Florence,* New York, 1949.
Actress: **Plays**—Dolly in *On Strivers Row* by Abram Hill, New York, 1940; Polly Ann in *Natural Man* by Theodore Browne, 1941; Blanche in *Anna Lucasta* by Philip Yordan, New York, 1944.

*   *   *

When the social agitation of the 1960's brought about the development of a new genre of hard-hitting problem novels aimed specifically at teenage readers, editor F. N. Monjo challenged dramatist Alice Childress to devote her writing skills to a book for young readers. The result was *A Hero Ain't Nothin' But a Sandwich,* which is such a powerful book that it helped shape the new genre as well as bring it respect.

The story circles around 13-year-old Benjie, a heroin addict, who may or may not make it out of the vicious cycle in which he finds himself. The 23 chapters consist of monologues from a dozen characters—Benjie, his mother, his stepfather, his teachers, his pusher, his grandmother, his friend. On the first page Benjie compares his life where "You best get over being seven or eight right soon" because "My block ain't no place to be a chile in peace," to that of a "rich chile like in some movin picture or like on TV—where everybody is livin it up and their room is perfect-lookin and their swimmin pool and their block and their house...." Benjie's comparison aptly illustrates the differences between the new realistic problem novel and the old romanticized fiction commonly offered to young readers. In the new books it was acceptable to have characters from lower-class families who lived in harsh and difficult settings rather than in idyllic and pleasant suburbia. These characters faced major problems and used colloquial and sometimes vulgar language. Many of the books had unhappy endings.

Some adults were shocked at this new realism, and *A Hero Ain't Nothin' But a Sandwich* was widely censored, eventually coming before the Supreme Court in *Pico v. Bd. of Ed., Island Trees.* But as movies, television, rock music, videos, magazines, and even the daily news made commonplace much that used to be considered obscene or at least inappropriate for young readers, critics began paying less attention to the controversial language in Childress's writing and more to its substance.

Childress uses the same dramatic technique of switching first-person viewpoints from chapter to chapter in *Rainbow Jordan* and *Those Other People.* The technique lets readers get into the minds of characters in ways that are more credible than if an omniscient narrator were describing the events. Since there's no narrator to tie together all the pieces, readers have to draw their own conclusions—a responsibility that censors fear teenage readers may not be prepared for.

Childress's greatest strength is in developing characters that make readers see such social issues as racism, sexism, drugs, and child abuse in personal terms. Few readers will forget the heroic Butler Craig, Benjie's unconventional stepfather, or 14-year-old Rainbow Jordan and 57-year-old Josephine who suffer together when Rainbow's childlike mother leaves for an out-of-town gig.

Childress has also written two one-act plays. *Let's Hear It for the Queen* is a humorous play for children that parodies the "Queen of Hearts" nursery rhyme. *When the Rattlesnake Sounds,* written for young adults, has a more serious intent. It takes viewers and performers beyond the stereotype of Harriet Tubman leading slaves through wilderness swamps to freedom. The setting is a hotel in Cape May, New Jersey, where Tubman is scrubbing, with two other young women, the hotel's linens and the guests' clothing to earn money for the support of the underground railway.

—Alleen Pace Nilsen

CHIPPERFIELD, Joseph E(ugene). Also wrote as John Eland Craig. British. Born in St. Austell, Cornwall, 20 April 1912. Educated privately. Married Mary Anne Tully in 1936. Editor, Author's Literary Service, London, 1930–34; editor and scriptwriter for documentary films, 1934–40. *Died 3 January 1976.*

PUBLICATIONS FOR CHILDREN

Fiction

Two Dartmoor Interludes. London, Boswell Press, 1935.
An Irish Mountain Tragedy. London, Boswell Press, 1936.
Three Stories (includes *Two Dartmoor Interludes, An Irish Mountain Tragedy, The Ghosts from Baylough*). London, Boswell Press, 1936.
This Earth—My Home: A Tale of Irish Troubles. Dublin, Padraic O'Follain, 1937.
Storm of Dancerwood, illustrated by C. Gifford Ambler. London, Hutchinson, 1948; New York, Longman, 1949; revised edition, Hutchinson, 1967.
Greatheart, The Salvation Hunter: The Epic of a Shepherd Dog, illustrated by C. Gifford Ambler. London, Hutchinson, 1950; New York, Roy, 1953.
Beyond the Timberland Trail, illustrated by Raymond Shepard. London, Hutchinson, 1951; New York, Longman, 1953.
Windruff of Tor Links, illustrated by Helen Torrey. New York, Longman, 1951; London, Hutchinson, 1954.

Grey Chieftain, illustrated by C. Gifford Ambler. London, Hutchinson, 1952; New York, Roy, 1954.
The Dog of Castle Crag (as John Eland Craig), illustrated by Leslie Atkinson. London, Nelson, 1952.
Silver Star, Stallion of the Echoing Mountain, illustrated by C. Gifford Ambler. London, Hutchinson, 1953; New York, Roy, 1955.
Greeka, Eagle of the Hebrides, illustrated by C. Gifford Ambler. London, Hutchinson, 1953; New York, Longman, 1954; revised edition, Hutchinson, 1962.
Rooloo, Stag of the Dark Water, illustrated by C. Gifford Ambler. London, Hutchinson, 1955; New York, Roy, 1962; revised edition, Hutchinson, 1962, Roy, 1963.
Dark Fury, Stallion of Lost River Valley, illustrated by C. Gifford Ambler. London, Hutchinson, 1956; New York, Roy, 1957.
Wolf of Badenoch: Dog of the Grampian Hills, illustrated by C. Gifford Ambler. London, Hutchinson, 1958; New York, Longman, 1959.
Ghost Horse: Stallion of the Oregon Trail, illustrated by C. Gifford Ambler. London, Hutchinson, 1959; New York, Roy, 1962.
Grasson, Golden Eagle of the North, illustrated by C. Gifford Ambler. London, Hutchinson, 1960.
Petrus, Dog of the Hill Country, illustrated by Stuart Tresilian. London, Heinemann, and New York, Longman, 1960.
Seokoo of the Black Wind, illustrated by C. Gifford Ambler. London, Hutchinson, 1961; New York, McKay, 1962.
The Grey Dog from Galtymore, illustrated by Stuart Tresilian. London, Heinemann, 1961; New York, McKay, 1962.
Sabre of Storm Valley, illustrated by C. Gifford Ambler. London, Hutchinson, 1962; New York, Roy, 1965.
A Dog Against Darkness, illustrated by F.R. Exell. London, Heinemann, 1963; as *A Dog to Trust: The Saga of a Seeing-Eye Dog,* New York, McKay, 1964.
Checoba, Stallion of the Comanche, illustrated by C. Gifford Ambler. London, Hutchinson, 1964; New York, Roy, 1966.
Boru, Dog of the O'Malley, illustrated by C. Gifford Ambler. London, Hutchinson, 1965; New York, McKay, 1966.
The Two Fugitives, illustrated by John Lathey. London, Heinemann, 1966.
Lone Stands the Glen, illustrated by Barry Driscoll. London, Hutchinson, 1966.
The Watcher on the Hills. London, Heinemann, 1968.
Rex of Larkbarrow, illustrated by Robert Hales. London, Hutchinson, 1969.
Storm Island, illustrated by Gareth Floyd. London, Hutchinson, 1970.
Banner, The Pacing White Stallion, illustrated by Robert Hales. London, Hutchinson, 1972.
Lobo, Wolf of the Wind River Range, illustrated by Robert Hales. London, Hutchinson, 1974.
Hunter of Harter Fell, illustrated by Victor Ambrus. London, Hutchinson, 1976.

Other

The Story of a Great Ship: The Birth and Death of the Steamship Titanic, illustrated by Charles King. London, Hutchinson, 1957; New York, Roy, 1959.

*   *   *

Joseph E. Chipperfield's *Storm of Dancerwood* has been revised and reprinted and is probably his best book. It tells of an alsatian dog and a blind vixen who have a curious, gentle relationship which ends in her death. The dog becomes gradually attached to a man who succeeds in winning his confidence. So develops that extraordinary empathy between human and animal that this author understood so well. Children understand this too because so many of them have just such close ties with their pets.

Often Chipperfield's dogs, or horses, are wild, intractable, or misunderstood, which adds spice to the stories. He has been said to "revive nostalgically the dramatic quality of Jack London," and this is a fair comparison. He had the same gift for interpreting animals' reactions without becoming too anthropomorphic. Only in *A Dog Against Darkness* does one have doubts about the subtlety of the thoughts that run through Arno's brain as he is being trained to be a guide dog for the blind. But this book has its own peculiar fascination, for readers of any age, because of the descriptions of this very special training.

The horse stories are violent and vivid and greatly enriched by the background of pioneering days in America. *Banner* is a tale of men obsessively determined to capture a horse that has become a legend. Banner is the last of the wild white stallions driven up the Colorado Rockies into a country being ravaged by men and their new railroads. He finally escapes his most persistent and crazy pursuer, leaving man and horse to the vultures. But there is no doubt left in the reader's mind that the frontiers of the west are pushing on and destroying the old ways of life.

Many of Chipperfield's books have remained in print, and *Ghost Horse* is available also in paperback. Children love animal stories. You will not find Chipperfield books learnedly analysed in manuals on children's literature, or hear them seriously discussed at conferences, but neither will you find them sitting unread on library shelves.

—Cecilia Gordon

CHORPENNING, Charlotte (Lee Barrows). American. Born 3 January 1872. Educated at Iowa Agricultural College, Ames; Cornell University, Ithaca, New York, 1892–94, B.L. 1894; Harvard University, Cambridge, Massachusetts (John Craig prize, 1915), 1913–15. Married John C. Chorpenning. Teacher, Wolf Hall school, Denver, 1901–04; English teacher, Winona Normal School, Minnesota, 1904–13, and 1915 to early 1920's; dramatic director, Recreation Training School, Hull House, Chicago; member of the Speech Department, Northwestern University, Evanston, Illinois; head of the Children's Theatre, Goodman Theatre, Art Institute of Chicago, 1931–52; worked with the U.S.O. during World War II. Co-founder, Children's World Theatre, late 1940's. *Died in January 1955.*

PUBLICATIONS FOR CHILDREN

Plays

The Emperor's New Clothes, adaptation of the story by Hans Christian Andersen (produced New York, 1935). New York, French, 1932.
Rhodopis, The First Cinderella. Chicago, Coach House Press, 1934.
Jack and the Beanstalk (produced New York, 1937). Anchorage, Kentucky, Children's Theatre Press, 1935.
The Indian Captive (produced Chicago, 1936). Anchorage, Kentucky, Children's Theatre Press, 1937.
Tom Sawyer's Treasure Hunt, adaptation of the story *Tom Sawyer* by Mark Twain. New York, French, 1937.
Hans Brinker and the Silver Skates, adaptation of the story by Mary Mapes Dodge. Anchorage, Kentucky, Children's Theatre Press, 1938.
Little Black Sambo and the Tigers, adaptation of the story by Helen Bannerman (produced New Orleans, 1939). New York, Dramatists Play Service, 1938; as *Rama and the Tigers,* Chicago, Coach House Press, 1954.
The Prince and the Pauper, adaptation of the story by Mark Twain. New York, Dramatists Play Service, 1938.
Radio Rescue (produced London, 1958). New York, Dramatists Play Service, 1938.
The Return of Rip Van Winkle, adaptation of the story "Rip Van Winkle" by Washington Irving. New York, Dramatists Play Service, 1938; as *Rip Van Winkle,* Chicago, Coach House Press, 1954.
Cinderella, adaptation of the story by Charles Perrault. Anchorage, Kentucky, Children's Theatre Press, 1940.
Abe Lincoln—New Salem Days (produced Chicago, 1941). Chicago, Coach House Press, 1954.
Rumpelstiltskin (produced New York, 1947). Anchorage, Kentucky, Children's Theatre Press, 1944.
The Secret Weapon. Washington, D.C., National Education Association, 1944.
Alice in Wonderland, adaptation of the story by Lewis Carroll. Chicago, Dramatic Publishing Company, 1946.
The Adventures of Tom Sawyer, adaptation of the story by Mark Twain. Chicago, Dramatic Publishing Company, 1946.
Many Moons, adaptation of the story by James Thurber (produced New York, 1947). Chicago, Dramatic Publishing Company, 1946.
The Elves and the Shoemaker, with Nora Tully (produced Chicago, 1946). Anchorage, Kentucky, Children's Theatre Press, 1946.
Little Red Riding Hood; or, Grandmother Slyboots (produced New York, 1947). Anchorage, Kentucky, Children's Theatre Press, 1947.
The Sleeping Beauty. Anchorage, Kentucky, Children's Theatre Press, 1947.
Little Lee Bobo, Chinatown Detective, with R.H. Lee. Anchorage, Kentucky, Children's Theatre Press, 1948.
The Three Bears. Anchorage, Kentucky, Children's Theatre Press, 1949.
King Midas and the Golden Touch. Anchorage, Kentucky, Children's Theatre Press, 1950.
Flibbertygibbet (His Last Chance), with Nora Tully MacAlvay. Anchorage, Kentucky, Children's Theatre Press, 1952.
Robinson Crusoe, adaptation of the novel by Daniel Defoe. Anchorage, Kentucky, Children's Theatre Press, 1952.
The Magic Horn: A Story of Roland and Charlemagne, with Anne Nicholson. Chicago, Coach House Press, 1954.
Lincoln's Secret Messenger—Boy Detective to a President. Chicago, Coach House Press, 1955.
Hansel and Gretel, adaptation of the story by the Grimm Brothers. Chicago, Coach House Press, 1956.
Three Adventure Plays (includes *The Adventures of Tom Sawyer, Radio Rescue, The Magic Horn*). Chicago, Coach House Press, 1972.

PUBLICATIONS FOR ADULTS

Other

Twenty One Years with Children's Theatre. Anchorage, Kentucky, Children's Theatre Press, 1954.

*   *   *

Charlotte Chorpenning is acknowledged as the first lady of

children's theatre in the United States; both as playwright and producer, her influence has been immeasurable. Her plays are chiefly adaptations of fairy tales and children's literary classics but include dramatizations of history and legend. The dramas demonstrate the principles she preached about writing plays for children in *Twenty One Years with Children's Theatre,* such as the need for conventionally constructed plots allowing physical action, central characters with whom the child could identify, moral values, and colorful settings.

Adaptations of well-known fairy tales such as *Jack and the Beanstalk* and *Rumpelstiltskin* constitute the largest body of the Chorpenning canon. The hero of *Jack and the Beanstalk* aids his mother and neighbors by outwitting a cruel giant after climbing a magic beanstalk into the sky and returning with riches courageously won. Despite the characters' one-dimensionality, the fanciful plot provides imaginative action and theatricality that make this early play continually popular. The characters in *Rumpelstiltskin* assume more dimension in a tale of a miller's daughter who wins a prince by spinning straw into gold through the proffered magical services of an evil dwarf who demands a cruel bargain from which she only narrowly escapes. Also representative is a charming dramatization of Thurber's *Many Moons,* in which a spoiled princess maturely accepts that she does not possess the only moon. Evident in all three plays is a well-structured plot projecting appealing characters, fanciful settings, and a traditional moral.

Children's literary classics are another Chorpenning source. One example is *The Return of Rip Van Winkle,* whose title character is sensitively portrayed with his frailties and warmheartedness. Rip's adventures in fleeing from an exasperated wife, meeting Henry Hudson's crew, and waking up after a 20 year sleep are both affecting and stageworthy. In *Hans Brinker and the Silver Skates,* to give another example, the young hero's courageous efforts save his family's sanity and security, and enable his sister to win a skating match on the Holland canals. Characteristic of these audience-appealing adaptations is the presence of familiar scenes from the original stories and a theatrically efficacious *pièce bien faite* plot pattern.

Three plays exemplify Chorpenning dramas trotting out the material of history and legend. A pioneer girl actually captured and adopted by the Seneca Indians is the protagonist of *The Indian Captive* who is forbidden by a loving but possessive Chief to reveal herself to her mother come in search of her, but is finally returned to her own people. The drama credibly depicts Indian life and theatrically interprets historical incident. Young Abe is convincingly recreated amid Lincoln lore in *Abe Lincoln—New Salem Days* as a debt-ridden Illinois storekeeper. Also successfully portrayed, President Lincoln is saved by a boy from a Copperhead kidnapping plot in *Lincoln's Secret Messenger.* These stageworthy dramas hold particular appeal for young adults.

The plotting and production requirements of many of Chorpenning's plays seem out of fashion today. Yet that her plays continue to be performed attests to their durability and to their author's craftsmanship and merited reputation.

—Christian H. Moe

CHRISMAN, Arthur Bowie. American. Born near White Post, Virginia, 16 July 1889. Educated at the Virginia Polytechnic Institute, Blacksburg, 1906–08. Schoolteacher for two years; also worked as farmer, draftsman, movie extra, and lecturer. Recipient: American Library Association Newbery Medal, 1926. *Died 24 February 1953.*

PUBLICATIONS FOR CHILDREN

Fiction (illustrated by Else Hasselriis)

Shen of the Sea. New York, Dutton, 1925; London, Dent, 1926.
The Wind That Wouldn't Blow: Stories of the Merry Middle Kingdom. New York, Dutton, and London, Dent, 1927.

Other

Treasures Long Hidden: Old Tales and New Tales of the East, illustrated by Weda Yap. New York, Dutton, 1941.

PUBLICATIONS FOR ADULTS

Other

Clarke County 1836–1936. Berryville, Virginia, Clarke Courier Press, 1936.

* * *

Arthur Bowie Chrisman was by many accounts a born storyteller who from childhood made up elegant tales of men and animals and demons for his own and others' benefit. He was fascinated by Chinese customs and folk tales, and as luck would have it, met a Chinese shopkeeper who was persuaded to share stories and profundities from his native land. Several years after this, *Shen of the Sea* was written; it won the Newbery Medal. He wrote two other books of Chinese stories for children, *The Wind That Wouldn't Blow* and *Treasures Long Hidden.*

Chrisman's short stories are stylistic gems. His prose is clear and crisp and marvelously funny. They are the work of someone keenly sensitive to the human condition, to human needs and human attempts to satisfy such needs. While they are spoken of as "Chinese" stories, they are in reality universal tales with a Chinese background—for they deal with loves and hates, greeds and grievances, hopes and dreams. *Shen of the Sea* consists of 16 short stories which must be read carefully in order to discover all the humor and wisdom therein. The first story, "Ah Mee's Invention," concerns an age-old problem of how to socialize the erring child, a son so disobedient of a father so loving. Perhaps it is the father's great tolerance of the son's impossible mischief that enables the son to invent the art of printing; perhaps, but is this necessarily so? Another story, "Shen of the Sea," concerns the first King of Wa Tien and his encounters with the shen (or water devils). Twice the good King successfully seals up the shen in bottles so as to save his people from drowning. It is obvious from the beginning that the good King will triumph over the evil devils, for good almost always triumphs in folk tales, but the King's excellence in confusing and distracting his adversaries makes a rollicking yarn. A third story, "Chop-sticks," focuses on two important needs of man: food and fortitude. Did you know that in the olden days the Chinese used knives and forks and spoons like us? That this was only changed when King Cheng Chang had been attacked, not once, not twice, but three times: with a knife, with a fork, and with a spoon? From then on he ate rice and duck with the aid of two harmless little sticks which could not be used by others to hurt him.

It is said that throughout his life Chrisman enjoyed telling stories and that generations of children, relatives and neighbors, enjoyed hearing them. He is remembered as an unassuming, imaginative, and caring man; his works reflect such a person.

—Mary Lystad

———

CHRISTOPHER, John. Pseudonym for Christopher Samuel Youd; has also written as Hilary Ford; William Godfrey; Peter Graaf; Peter Nichols; Anthony Rye. British. Born in Knowsley, Lancashire, 16 April 1922. Educated at Peter Symonds' School, Winchester. Served in the Royal Signals, 1941–46. Married twice; four daughters and one son from first marriage. Since 1958 full-time writer. Recipient: Rockefeller-Atlantic award, 1946; Christopher award, 1971; *Guardian* award, 1971; Children's Literature prize (Germany), 1976; George G. Stone Center for Children's Books award, 1977. Address: La Rochelle, Rye, East Sussex TN31 7JY, England.

PUBLICATIONS FOR CHILDREN

Fiction

The Caves of Night. London, Eyre and Spottiswoode, and New York, Simon and Schuster, 1958.
The Long Voyage. London, Eyre and Spottiswoode, 1960; as *The White Voyage,* New York, Simon and Schuster, 1961.
The Tripods Trilogy. New York, Macmillan, 1980.
  The White Mountains. London, Hamish Hamilton, and New York, Macmillan, 1967.
  The City of Gold and Lead. London, Hamish Hamilton, and New York, Macmillan, 1967.
  The Pool of Fire. London, Hamish Hamilton, and New York, Macmillan, 1968.
The Lotus Caves. London, Hamish Hamilton, and New York, Macmillan, 1969.
The Guardians. London, Hamish Hamilton, and New York, Macmillan, 1970.
The Sword of the Spirits Trilogy. New York, Macmillan, 1980; as *The Prince in Waiting Trilogy,* London, Penguin, 1983.
  The Prince in Waiting. London, Hamish Hamilton, and New York, Macmillan, 1970.
  Beyond the Burning Lands. London, Hamish Hamilton, and New York, Macmillan, 1971.
  The Sword of the Spirits. London, Hamish Hamilton, and New York, Macmillan, 1972.
In the Beginning (reader for adults). London, Longman, 1972; revised edition (for children), as *Dom and Va,* London, Hamish Hamilton, and New York, Macmillan, 1973.
A Figure in Grey (as Hilary Ford). Kingswood, Surrey, World's Work, 1973.
Wild Jack. London, Hamish Hamilton, and New York, Macmillan, 1974; original version (reader for adults), London, Longman, 1974.
Empty World. London, Hamish Hamilton, 1977; New York, Dutton, 1978.
Fireball. London, Gollancz, and New York, Dutton, 1981.
New Found Land. London, Gollancz, and New York, Dutton, 1983.
Dragon Dance. London, Viking Kestrel, and New York, Dutton, 1986.
When the Tripods Came. New York, Dutton, 1988.

PUBLICATIONS FOR ADULTS

Novels

The Year of the Comet. London, Joseph, 1955; as *Planet in Peril,* New York, Avon, 1959.
The Death of Grass. London, Joseph, 1956; as *No Blade of Grass,* New York, Simon and Schuster, 1957.
Giant's Arrow (as Anthony Rye). London, Gollancz, 1956; as Samuel Youd, New York, Simon and Schuster, 1960.
Malleson at Melbourne (as William Godfrey). London, Museum Press, 1956.
The Friendly Game (as William Godfrey). London, Joseph, 1957.
A Scent of White Poppies. London, Eyre and Spottiswoode, and New York, Simon and Schuster, 1959.
The World in Winter. London, Eyre and Spottiswoode, 1962; as *The Long Winter,* New York, Simon and Schuster, 1962.
Sweeney's Island. New York, Simon and Schuster, 1964; as *Cloud on Silver,* London, Hodder and Stoughton, 1964.
The Possessors. London, Hodder and Stoughton, and New York, Simon and Schuster, 1965.
A Wrinkle in the Skin. London, Hodder and Stoughton, 1965; as *The Ragged Edge,* New York, Simon and Schuster, 1966.
Patchwork of Death (as Peter Nichols). New York, Holt Rinehart, 1965; London, Hale, 1967.
The Little People. London, Hodder and Stoughton, and New York, Simon and Schuster, 1967.
Pendulum. London, Hodder and Stoughton, and New York, Simon and Schuster, 1968.

Novels as Samuel Youd

The Winter Swan. London, Dobson, 1949.
Babel Itself. London, Cassell, 1951.
Brave Conquerors. London, Cassell, 1952.
Crown and Anchor. London, Cassell, 1953.
A Palace of Strangers. London, Cassell, 1954.
Holly Ash. London, Cassell, 1955; as *The Opportunist,* New York, Harper, 1957.
The Choice. New York, Simon and Schuster, 1961; as *The Burning Bird,* London, Longman, 1964.
Messages of Love. New York, Simon and Schuster, 1961; London, Longman, 1962.
The Summers at Accorn. London, Longman, 1963.

Novels as Peter Graaf

Dust and the Curious Boy. London, Joseph, 1957; as *Give the Devil His Due,* New York, Mill, 1957.
Daughter Fair. London, Joseph, and New York, Washburn, 1958.
Sapphire Conference. London, Joseph, and New York, Washburn, 1959.
The Gull's Kiss. London, Davies, 1962.

Novels as Hilary Ford

Felix Walking. London, Eyre and Spottiswoode, and New York, Simon and Schuster, 1958.
Felix Running. London, Eyre and Spottiswoode, 1959.
Bella on the Roof. London, Longman, 1965.
Sarnia. London, Hamish Hamilton, and New York, Doubleday, 1974.
Castle Malindine. London, Hamish Hamilton, and New York, Harper, 1975.
A Bride for Bedivere. London, Hamish Hamilton, 1976; New York, Harper, 1977.

Short Stories

The Twenty-Second Century. London, Grayson, 1954; New York, Lancer, 1962.

*   *   *

Publication in 1967 of *The White Mountains,* John Christopher's first important book for children, was arguably the point at which science fiction began to take its proper place in English children's literature. Previously in this country it had probably been the least-esteemed form of writing for children, associated by unsympathetic adults with pulp comics and the sillier side of television, and featuring (it was supposed) super-heroes, bug-eyed monsters, and ray-gun battles in space. *The White Mountains,* written in cool clear prose and intelligently thought out, was unmistakably a "quality" book as well as a highly readable one; and with the two titles that followed, *The City of Gold and Lead* and *The Pool of Fire,* it made up a trilogy which was successful with children and critics alike.

The books tell how three boys join the struggle of a handful of free men against the Masters, a ruling elite from a distant world who look on humans as inferior, expendable creatures—rather, in fact, as we look on animals. A second trilogy—*The Prince in Waiting, Beyond the Burning Lands,* and *The Sword of the Spirits*—is set in a different kind of post-cataclysmic England, now divided into warring city-states. The hero, Luke, has a mission to unite his fragmented country, but in the end turns against his own people: a disconcerting twist which would be unimaginable in the old-fashioned boys' adventure story.

Indeed, Christopher does not simplify any issue for the sake of young readers. *The Lotus Caves, The Guardians,* and *Wild Jack,* which are three separate books and not a trilogy, present in different forms a choice for their heroes between lives of comfort but restricted liberty on one hand and of harsh, dangerous freedom on the other; and it is not pretended that this choice is an easy one. *Empty World* is a post-cataclysm story, the cataclysm being of a singularly gruesome kind: a virus that kills off entire populations by immensely accelerating the ageing process.

With *Fireball* Christopher began a third trilogy. The fireball is "a shimmering white sphere of light" through which English Simon and his American cousin Brad are sucked into a parallel time in which the world has developed differently. Present-day Britain is still in the Roman Empire; but Brad and Simon, by introducing the stirrup and the longbow, contribute to the empire's downfall. A Christian revolution however brings its own tyranny, and the two make their way to the undiscovered New World. In *New Found Land* they meet unfriendly Indians, carousing Vikings who would happily sacrifice them to Odin, and callously cruel Aztecs; and in *Dragon Dance* they cross the Pacific to a China in which they confront occult and illusion-creating powers, and are involved in palace revolution and civil war.

Though the notion of parallel time is interesting, and a good deal of information is imparted along the way, this trilogy did not, to my mind, add to Christopher's reputation. The action is largely a matter of constant peril and hairbreadth escapes, occasionally bringing to mind the famous resource of the hard-pressed adventure-story writer: "With one bound Jack was free." It is spiced with rivalry between Brad and Simon and a few indecisive encounters with pretty teenage girls. Christopher then, in a sense, brought his fiction for young readers round full circle by writing *When the Tripods Came,* which tells how the state of affairs at the opening of *The White Mountains* came about. Unfortunately *When the Tripods Came* is thinner and

less convincing than the trilogy to which it is a forerunner.

—John Rowe Townsend

CHURCH, Richard (Thomas). British. Born in London, 26 March 1893. Educated at Dulwich Hamlet School, London, 1905–08. Married 1) Caroline Parfett in 1915; 2) Catherina Schimmer in 1930 (died 1965); 3) Dorothy Beale in 1967; three daughters and one son. Civil servant, London, 1909–33; editor, J.M. Dent, publishers, London, 1933–51. Co-founder, the *Criterion,* London, 1921; regular contributor to the *Spectator* and *New Statesman,* London; for 40 years contributor of a monthly essay to the "Home Forum Page" of the *Christian Science Monitor,* Boston. Director, English Festival of Spoken Poetry, until it merged with the Arts Council Poetry Panel. President, PEN, 1958–59, and the English Association, 1964–65. Recipient: Femina Vie Heureuse prize, 1938; *Sunday Times* Gold Medal, 1955; Foyle Poetry prize, 1957. Fellow, 1950, and Vice-President, 1968, Royal Society of Literature; Fellow, Royal Society of Art, 1970. C.B.E. (Commander, Order of the British Empire), 1957. *Died 4 March 1972.*

PUBLICATIONS FOR CHILDREN

Fiction

A Squirrel Called Rufus, illustrated by John Skeaping. London, Dent, 1941; Philadelphia, Winston, 1946.
The Cave, illustrated by Clarke Hutton. London, Dent, 1950; as *Five Boys in a Cave,* New York, Day, 1951; revised edition, Dent, 1953.
Dog Toby: A Frontier Tale, illustrated by Laurence Irving. London, Hutchinson, 1953; New York, Day, 1958.
Down River, illustrated by Laurence Irving. New York, Day, 1957; London, Heinemann, 1958.
The Bells of Rye. London, Heinemann, 1960; New York, Day, 1961.
The White Doe, illustrated by John Ward. London, Heinemann, 1968; New York, Day, 1969.
The French Lieutenant: A Ghost Story. London, Heinemann, 1971; New York, Day, 1972.

PUBLICATIONS FOR ADULTS

Novels

Oliver's Daughter: A Tale. London, Dent, 1930.
High Summer. London, Dent, 1931; New York, Smith, 1932.
The Prodigal Father. London, Dent, and New York, Day, 1933.
The Apple of Concord. London, Dent, 1935.
The Porch. London, Dent, 1937.
The Stronghold. London, Dent, 1939.
The Room Within. London, Dent, 1940.
The Sampler. London, Dent, 1942.
The Nightingale. London, Hutchinson, 1952.
The Dangerous Years. London, Heinemann, 1956; New York, Dutton, 1958.
The Crab-Apple Tree. London, Heinemann, 1959.
Prince Albert. London, Heinemann, 1963.

Little Miss Moffatt: A Confession.   London, Heinemann, 1969.

Play

The Prodigal: A Play in Verse (produced Canterbury, 1953).   London, Staples Press, 1953.

Verse

The Flood of Life and Other Poems.   London, Fifield, 1917.
Hurricane and Other Poems.   London, Selwyn and Blount, 1919.
Philip and Other Poems.   Oxford, Blackwell, 1923.
The Portrait of the Abbot: A Story in Verse.   London, Benn, 1926; New York, Dial Press, 1927.
The Dream and Other Poems.   London, Benn, 1927.
Mood Without Measure.   London, Faber and Gwyer, 1927.
Theme with Variations.   London, Benn, 1928.
The Glance Backward: New Poems.   London, Dent, 1930.
News from the Mountain.   London, Dent, 1932.
Twelve Noon.   London, Dent, 1936.
The Solitary Man and Other Poems.   London, Dent, 1941.
Twentieth-Century Psalter.   London, Dent, 1943.
The Lamp.   London, Dent, 1946.
Collected Poems.   London, Dent, 1948; New York, AMS Press, 1976.
Selected Lyrical Poems.   London, Staples Press, 1951.
The Inheritors: Poems 1948–1955.   London, Heinemann, 1957.
(Poems).   London, Hulton, 1959.
North of Rome.   London, Hutchinson, 1960.
The Burning Bush: Poems 1958–1966.   London, Heinemann, 1967.
25 Lyrical Poems.   London, Heinemann, 1967.

Other

Mary Shelley.   London, Howe, and New York, Viking Press, 1928.
An Essay in Estimation of Dorothy Richardson's "Pilgrimage."   London, Dent-Cresset Press, 1938.
Calling for a Spade.   London, Dent, 1939.
Eight for Immortality.   London, Dent, 1941; Freeport, New York, Books for Libraries Press, 1969.
Plato's Mistake.   London, Routledge, 1941.
British Authors: A Twentieth Century Gallery.   London, Longman, 1943; revised edition, 1948; Freeport, New York, Books for Libraries Press, 1969.
Green Tide.   London, Country Life, 1945.
Richard Jefferies Centenary 1848–1948: Memorial Lecture.   Swindon, Council of the Borough of Swindon, 1948.
Kent.   London, Hale, 1948.
A Window on a Hill.   London, Hale, 1951.
The Growth of the English Novel.   London, Methuen, 1951; New York, Barnes and Noble, 1961.
A Portrait of Canterbury.   London, Hutchinson, 1953; revised edition, 1968.
Over the Bridge: An Essay in Autobiography.   London, Heinemann, 1955; as *Over the Bridge: An Autobiography,* New York, Dutton, 1956.
The Royal Parks of London.   London, Ministry of Works, 1956.
Small Moments.   London, Hutchinson, 1957; New York, Dutton, 1958.
The Golden Sovereign: A Conclusion to "Over the Bridge."   London, Heinemann, and New York, Dutton, 1957.
A Country Window: A Round of Essays.   London, Heinemann, 1958.
Calm October: Essays.   London, Heinemann, 1961.
The Voyage Home (autobiography).   London, Heinemann, 1964; New York, Day, 1966.

A Stroll Before Dark: Essays.   London, Heinemann, 1965.
A Look at Tradition.   London, Oxford University Press, 1965.
London: Flower of Cities All.   London, Heinemann, and New York, Day, 1966.
Speaking Aloud.   London, Heinemann, 1968.
A Harvest of Mushrooms and Other Sporadic Essays.   London, Heinemann, 1970.
The Wonder of Words.   London, Hutchinson, 1970.
London in Colour.   London, Batsford, and New York, Norton, 1971.
Kent's Contribution.   Bath, Adams and Dart, 1972.

Editor, *Poems and Prose,* by Swinburne.   London, Dent, and New York, Dutton, 1940.
Editor, with M.M. Bozman, *Poems of Our Time 1900–1942.*   London, Dent, 1945.
Editor, *John Keats: An Introduction and a Selection.*   London, Phoenix House, 1948.
Editor, *Poems,* by Shelley.   London, Folio Society, 1949.
Editor, *Poems for Speaking.*   London, Dent, 1950.
Editor, *A Selection of Poems,* by Spenser.   London, Grey Walls Press, 1954.
Editor, *Out of the Dark: New Poems,* by Phoebe Hesketh.   London, Heinemann, 1954.
Editor, *The Spoken Word: A Selection from Twenty-Five Years of "The Listener."*   London, Collins, 1955; revised edition, 1960.
Editor, *The Little Kingdom: A Kentish Collection.*   London, Hutchinson, 1964.
Editor, *Essays by Divers Hands.*   London, Oxford University Press, 1965.

*

Manuscript Collection: University of Texas, Austin.

*   *   *

Unlike many authors Richard Church is not easy to categorize; he belongs to no obvious group or movement, apparently owes nothing to older writers, and was content every so often to publish a skilful, polished, craftsmanlike story, capable of catching the attention on more than one level, that of the younger reader who might possibly remain unaware of a deeper significance, and that of the adult who is not afraid to dip into what ostensibly is a story for children and find there a satisfying and perceptive commentary on the human condition. *Dog Toby* is such a story, a moving and poignant tale which takes place on both sides of a barbed wire frontier. Three children and their two dogs, innocently oblivious of the significance of the wire, ignore the division it represents, and reach a close understanding with ordinary people on the other side. A simple allegory but none the less effective.

Similarly, *A Squirrel Called Rufus* is the story of an old-established family of red squirrels, secure in the heart of a forest, who are confronted by a deadly and ruthless enemy, a horde of grey squirrels invading their home, threatening to usurp their rights and freedoms. After a great battle, the climax of the struggle, the invaders are hurled back, to leave the red squirrels triumphant. Once again to all intents and purposes this is nothing more than an unpretentious if exciting and dramatic adventure story, but then we notice the date of publication—1941, and so presumably written when England itself stood in the same perilous situation.

The world of nature also provides the backcloth to *The White Doe,* about Tom Winter's concern for a white doe and her fawn he befriends in the forest where his father is woodman. At the same time Tom is troubled in his mind by the effect of his parting with his close friend Billy Lander, the Squire's son away for the first time at boarding school. And then another complicating factor enters his life, the arrival of snobbish Harold Sims into the locality, with whom Tom immediately crosses swords, and whose determination to hunt the deer occasions the life-and-death climax. In this instance the angry thread of human relationships, entangled even further by Tom's friendship with Harold's sister, is thrown into sharp contrast with the orderly passing of the seasons in the forest and on the shore.

The Cave relates the exploration by a group of five boys who call themselves the Tomahawk Club of a limestone cave one of them stumbles across. Again Church focuses attention on human relationships: when danger comes the dominating Alan Hobbs fails to measure up to it and another of the group, George Reynolds, assumes authority and responsibility, and displays the qualities of leadership. Compared to this compelling series of character studies, *Down River,* the further adventures of the Tomahawk Club, is slightly pedestrian. But no author can sustain such a high level of excellence indefinitely, not even Richard Church.

—Alan Edwin Day

CHUTE, Marchette (Gaylord). American. Born in Wayzata, Minnesota, 16 August 1909. Educated at Central High School, Minneapolis, 1921–25; Minneapolis School of Art, 1925–26; University of Minnesota, Minneapolis, 1926–30, B.A. 1930 (Phi Beta Kappa). President, American PEN, 1955–57. Recipient: Poetry Society of America Chap-Book award, 1954; University of Minnesota Achievement award, 1958; Women's National Book Association Constance Lindsay Skinner award, 1959. Litt.D.: Western College, Oxford, Ohio, 1952; Carleton College, Northfield, Minnesota, 1957; Dickinson College, Carlisle, Pennsylvania, 1964. Vice-President, 1961, and Secretary, 1962, National Institute of Arts and Letters; Member, American Academy; Benjamin Franklin Fellow, Royal Society of Arts. Address: c/o Elizabeth M. Roach, 66 Glenbrook Road, Morris Plains, New Jersey 07950, U.S.A.

PUBLICATIONS FOR CHILDREN

Fiction

The Innocent Wayfaring, illustrated by the author. New York, Scribner, 1943; London, Phoenix House, 1956.
The Wonderful Winter, illustrated by Grace Golden. New York, Dutton, 1954; London, Phoenix House, 1956.

Verse (illustrated by the author)

Rhymes about Ourselves. New York, Macmillan, 1932.
Rhymes about the Country. New York, Macmillan, 1941.
Rhymes about the City. New York, Macmillan, 1946.
Around and About. New York, Dutton, 1957.
Rhymes about Us. New York, Dutton, 1974.

Other

An Introduction to Shakespeare. New York, Dutton, 1951; as *Shakespeare and His Stage,* London, University of London Press, 1953.
Stories from Shakespeare. Cleveland, World, 1956; London, Murray, 1960.
Jesus of Israel. New York, Dutton, 1961; London, Gollancz, 1962.
The Green Tree of Democracy. New York, Dutton, 1971.

PUBLICATIONS FOR ADULTS

Plays

Sweet Genevieve, with M.G. Chute (produced New York, 1945).
The Worlds of Shakespeare, with Ernestine Perrie (produced New York, 1963). New York, Dutton, 1963.

Other

The Search for God. New York, Dutton, 1941; London, Benn, 1946.
Geoffrey Chaucer of England. New York, Dutton, 1946; London, Hale, 1951.
The End of the Search. New York, North River Press, 1947.
Shakespeare of London. New York, Dutton, 1950; London, Secker and Warburg, 1951.
Ben Jonson of Westminster. New York, Dutton, 1953; London, Hale, 1954.
Two Gentle Men: The Lives of George Herbert and Robert Herrick. New York, Dutton, 1959; London, Secker and Warburg, 1960.
The First Liberty: A History of the Right to Vote in America 1619–1850. New York, Dutton, 1969; London, Dent, 1970.
P.E.N. American Center: A History of the First Fifty Years. New York, P.E.N. American Center, 1972.

*

Manuscript Collections: New York Public Library; Kerlan Collection, University of Minnesota, Minneapolis.

Marchette Chute comments:

I enjoy doing historical research and the past is very real to me, but the subject chooses me rather than my choosing the subject. I have written adult books on Shakespeare, on the Bible, and on American political history, and in each case, when long years of research have brought me the necessary perspective, I have then felt able to write non-fiction books on these subjects for young people. I have also written two novels for young people with backgrounds in English history, one in Chaucer's day and the other in Shakespeare's. The only contemporary work I have done is my verse for young children, in which I have had no research to do except to remember my own fortunate childhood.

*   *   *

Marchette Chute is a scholarly writer who specialises in the 16th century. She is known for her books on Shakespeare and Ben Jonson, also Geoffrey Chaucer and a children's information book on the life and times of Shakespeare and his fellow players. Her gifts for bringing factual material to life and putting her readers into the picture have been channelled into producing fictional tales of the places and people of whom she knows so much.

In *The Innocent Wayfaring* two young people run away from home and set off across country towards London. The Merrie England of Chaucer's day had its dark side too, and their eyes are opened to the realities of life. They visit the great trade fairs, one of the stately homes of England, and fall in with all kinds of travellers on the roads and in the boisterous inns. There is a wonderful sense of period and, though at no time does the author seem to be "teaching," every detail in the story can be substantiated by documentary evidence, even down to the recipe for face cream.

With *The Wonderful Winter* she moves us back into Elizabethan London. A youthful nobleman runs away with his puppy and gets taken on by Shakespeare's company of players. He becomes a boy actor and helps behind the scenes, and we learn a lot, incidentally, about the conditions of life at the Globe Theatre. At last, conscience pricking him, he confesses his true identity and returns home, a mature young man.

Informative, amusing, though not all that exciting, these stories are full of character and life and could do much to give a child a taste for historical fiction, and bring him to share the author's love for the rumbustious past of England about which Chute writes so affectionately.

—Ann G. Hay

CIARDI, John (Anthony). American. Born in Boston, Massachusetts, 24 June 1916. Educated at Bates College, Lewiston, Maine, 1934–36; Tufts College, Medford, Massachusetts, B.A. (magna cum laude) 1938 (Phi Beta Kappa); University of Michigan, Ann Arbor (Hopwood award, 1939), A.M. 1939. Served in the United States Army Air Corps, 1942–45: Air Medal, Oak Leaf Cluster. Married Myra Judith Hostetter in 1946; one daughter and two sons. Instructor, University of Kansas City, Missouri, 1940–42 and 1945–46; Briggs Copeland Instructor in English, 1946–48, and Assistant Professor, 1948–53, Harvard University, Cambridge, Massachusetts; Lecturer, 1953–54, Associate Professor, 1954–56, and Professor of English, 1956–61, Rutgers University, New Brunswick, New Jersey; Lecturer, 1947–73, and Director, 1956–72, Bread Loaf Writers Conference, Vermont. Editor, Twayne Publishers, New York, 1949; lecturer, Salzburg Seminar in American Studies, 1951; poetry editor, 1956–73, and contributing editor, 1973–80, *Saturday Review,* New York; host, *Accent* program, CBS-TV, 1961–62; contributing editor, *World Magazine,* New York, 1972–73. Director, 1955–57, and President, 1958–59, National College English Association. Recipient: Bread Loaf Writers Conference fellowship, 1940; Oscar Blumenthal prize, 1943, Eunice Tietjens Memorial prize, 1944, Levinson prize, 1946, and Harriet Monroe Memorial prize, 1955 (*Poetry,* Chicago); New England Poetry Club Golden Rose, 1948; American Academy in Rome fellowship, 1956; National Council of Teachers of English award, for poetry, 1982. D. Litt.: Tufts College, 1960; Ohio Wesleyan University, Delaware, 1971; Washington University, St. Louis, 1971; Hum.D.: Wayne State University, Detroit, 1963; LL.D.: Ursinus College, Collegeville, Pennsylvania, 1964; D.L.H.: Kalamazoo College, Michigan, 1964; Bates College, 1970; Honorary Doctorate: Kean College, Union, New Jersey, 1977. Member, American Academy, and American Academy of Arts and Sciences. *Died 30 March 1986.*

PUBLICATIONS FOR CHILDREN

Fiction

The Wish-Tree, illustrated by Louis Glanzman.   New York, Crowell Collier, 1962.

Verse

The Reason for the Pelican, illustrated by Madeleine Gekiere. Philadelphia, Lippincott, 1959.
Scrappy the Pup, illustrated by Jane Miller.   Philadelphia, Lippincott, 1960.
I Met a Man, illustrated by Robert Osborn.   Boston, Houghton Mifflin, 1961.
The Man Who Sang the Sillies, illustrated by Edward Gorey. Philadelphia, Lippincott, 1961.

You Read to Me, I'll Read to You, illustrated by Edward Gorey. Philadelphia, Lippincott, 1962.
John J. Plenty and the Fiddler Dan: A New Fable of the Grasshopper and the Ant, illustrated by Madeleine Gekiere.   Philadelphia, Lippincott, 1963.
You Know Who, illustrated by Edward Gorey.   Philadelphia, Lippincott, 1964.
The King Who Saved Himself from Being Saved, illustrated by Edward Gorey.   Philadelphia, Lippincott, 1965.
The Monster Den; or, Look What Happened at My House—and to It, illustrated by Edward Gorey.   Philadelphia, Lippincott, 1966.
Someone Could Win a Polar Bear, illustrated by Edward Gorey. Philadelphia, Lippincott, 1970.
Fast and Slow: Poems for Advanced Children and Beginning Parents, illustrated by Becky Gaver.   Boston, Houghton Mifflin, 1975.
Doodle Soup, illustrated by Merle Nacht.   Boston, Houghton Mifflin, 1985.
The Hopeful Trout and Other Limericks, illustrated by Susan Meddaugh.   Boston, Houghton Mifflin, 1989.

PUBLICATIONS FOR ADULTS

Verse

Homeward to America.   New York, Holt, 1940.
Other Skies.   Boston, Little Brown, 1947.
Live Another Day.   New York, Twayne, 1949.
From Time to Time.   New York, Twayne, 1951.
As If: Poems New and Selected.   New Brunswick, New Jersey, Rutgers University Press, 1955.
I Marry You: A Sheaf of Love Poems.   New Brunswick, New Jersey, Rutgers University Press, 1958.
39 Poems.   New Brunswick, New Jersey, Rutgers University Press, 1959.
In the Stoneworks.   New Brunswick, New Jersey, Rutgers University Press, 1961.
In Fact.   New Brunswick, New Jersey, Rutgers University Press, 1962.
Person to Person.   New Brunswick, New Jersey, Rutgers University Press, 1964.
This Strangest Everything.   New Brunswick, New Jersey, Rutgers University Press, 1966.
An Alphabestiary: Twenty-Six Poems.   Philadelphia, Lippincott, 1967.
A Genesis: 15 Poems.   New York, Touchstone, 1967.
The Achievement of John Ciardi: A Comprehensive Selection of His Poems with a Critical Introduction, edited by Miller Williams. Chicago, Scott Foresman, 1969.
Lives of X.   New Brunswick, New Jersey, Rutgers University Press, 1971.
The Little That Is All.   New Brunswick, New Jersey, Rutgers University Press, 1974.
Limericks: Too Gross, with Isaac Asimov.   New York, Norton, 1978.
For Instance.   New York, Norton, 1979.
A Grossery of Limericks, with Isaac Asimov.   New York, Norton, 1981.
Selected Poems.   Fayetteville, University of Arkansas Press, 1984.
The Birds of Pompeii.   Fayetteville, University of Arkansas Press, 1985.
Ciardi, Measure of the Man, edited by Vince Clemente.   Fayetteville, University of Arkansas Press, 1987.

Recordings: *As If,* Folkways; *John Ciardi,* Everett Edwards, 1972.

Other

Dialogue with an Audience. Philadelphia, Lippincott, 1963.
Dante Alighieri: Three Lectures, with J.C. Mathews and Francis Fergusson. Washington, D.C., Library of Congress, 1965.
On Poetry and the Poetic Process, with Joseph B. Roberts, Jr. Troy, Alabama, Troy State University Press, 1972.
Manner of Speaking (*Saturday Review* columns). New Brunswick, New Jersey, Rutgers University Press, 1972.
A Browser's Dictionary and Native's Guide to the Unknown American Language. New York, Harper, 1980; *A Second Browser's Dictionary,* New York, Harper, 1983.
Plain English in a Complex Society, with Laurence Urdang and Frederick Dickerson. Bloomington, Indiana University Poynter Center, 1980.
Good Words to You: An All-New Dictionary and Native's Guide to the Unknown American Language. New York, Harper, 1987.
Saipan: The War Diary of John Ciardi. Fayetteville, University of Arkansas Press, 1988.

Editor, *Mid-Century American Poets.* New York, Twayne, 1950.
Editor, *How Does a Poem Mean?* Boston, Houghton Mifflin, 1960; revised edition, with Miller Williams, 1975.
Editor, with James M. Reid and Laurence Perrine, *Poetry: A Closer Look.* New York, Harcourt Brace, 1963.

Translator, *The Divine Comedy,* by Dante. New York, Norton, 1977.
  The Inferno. New Brunswick, New Jersey, Rutgers University Press, 1954.
  The Purgatorio. New York, New American Library, 1961.
  The Paradiso. New York, New American Library, 1970.

*

Bibliography: *John Ciardi: A Bibliography* by William White, Detroit, Wayne State University Press, 1959.

Manuscript Collections: Wayne State University, Detroit; Library of Congress, Washington, D.C.; Lockwood Library, State University of New York, Buffalo.

Critical Study: *John Ciardi* by Edward Francis Krickel, Boston, Twayne, 1980.

John Ciardi commented:

(1978) I gather that there is a professionalism about writing for children. The professionals I have met seem to have rules, some of which make me uneasy. I began writing children's poems first as a game with my nephews, then with my own children. I do not know how to do it by rule, only by ear. I know I am happy when I reach children. I want the contact to be *fun.* A few years ago the National Council of Teachers of English surveyed American school children and had them vote for their 25 favorite poems. The poem they put at the top of the list was my "Mummy Slept Late and Daddy Fixed Breakfast." No citation has ever given me more pleasure, especially as evidence that my amateur sense of it has been right, that I am reaching children where it is fun.

*   *   *

It is one thing to write nonsense verse for children, as many do, with outrageously silly situations, concocted creatures, and humorous story lines as well as attention to contemporary concerns—but quite another matter when a poet, in command of his craft, puts his mind and heart to it. John Ciardi, whose background

was that of a scholar, critic, and adult poet, was such a craftsman who kept in touch with the matters that delight the young and, through numerous books, presented them with a wealth of observations, creatures, and situations deriving their strength from pattern and rhyme that ring clear and true to the ear and often invite active participation and much laughter.

Ciardi's imagination was in tune with the young who enjoy the absurdity of ridiculous names; he, in a sense, updated Edward Lear for the contemporary child with his "Brobinyak" who lives in the "Forest of Foffenzee/In the land of the Pshah of Psham," where one might also meet "Radio Eeels" or the "Banjo Tern" or the "Scrawny Shank," or the "Saginsack" whose "Radio Horns/And Aerials for ears" could "be listening to you." Again, in the story of "The Army Horse and the Army Jeep" there are echoes of the inanimate table and chair of Lear. Yet Ciardi was not imitating; he was his own man, unlike others writing for children who seize nonsense and preposterous names and situations and who do not, in craft or in use of symbol, measure up to Lear.

Ciardi's interest in animals, the shark, python, whale, crow, ape, boa constrictor, and others, permeates his books in an imaginative series of short-story poems. Nature is also given emphasis in "How to Tell the Top of a Hill" or "The River Is a Piece of Sky." Ecological concerns crop up in "And They Lived Happily Ever After for a While," all of which focus on the same wonder and imaginative speculation as in "The Reason for the Pelican" or "Fast and Slow" where the "fast young crow" does not know "…Where to go."

The occasional cuteness of "Mummy Slept Late and Daddy Fixed Breakfast" or "Prattle," although these poems are popular, seems to me to show Ciardi at less than his best. The strength and haunting quality of "There once was an Owl perched on a shed./Fifty years later the Owl was dead./Some say mice are in the corn./Some say kittens are being born" prove his ability to soar beyond mere childishness.

In whatever form he chose to write, his control was always admirable; his couplets, tercets, quatrains, limericks attest to his carefully constructed meter and rhyme; his technique went happily beyond what he himself called "spillage of raw emotion." Ciardi wrote to entertain in a rhythm to which the young respond, and if occasional morals creep in now and again, they are done with a sophistication and humor that are so carefully worked into the poem that they cannot be faulted.

—Myra Cohn Livingston

CLAPP, Patricia. American. Born in Boston, Massachusetts, 9 June 1912. Attended Kimberley School, Montclair, New Jersey; Columbia University School of Journalism, New York, 1932. Married Edward della Torre Cone in 1933; one son and two daughters. Since 1940 member of the Board of Managers, Studio Players, Upper Montclair, New Jersey. Address: 83 Beverley Road, Upper Montclair, New Jersey 07043, U.S.A.

PUBLICATIONS FOR CHILDREN

Fiction

Constance: A Story of Early Plymouth. New York, Lothrop, 1968.
Jane-Emily. New York, Lothrop, 1969.
King of the Dollhouse, illustrated by Judith Gwyn Brown. New York, Lothrop, 1974.
I'm Deborah Sampson: A Soldier in the War of the Revolution. New York, Lothrop, 1977.
Witches' Children: A Story of Salem. New York, Lothrop, 1982.

The Tamarack Tree.   New York, Lothrop, 1986.

Plays

Peggy's on the Phone.   Chicago, Dramatic Publishing Company, 1956.
Smart Enough to Be Dumb.   Chicago, Dramatic Publishing Company, 1956.
The Incompleted Pass.   Chicago, Dramatic Publishing Company, 1957.
Her Kissin' Cousin.   Cedar Rapids, Iowa, Heuer, 1957.
The Girl Out Front.   Chicago, Dramatic Publishing Company, 1958.
The Ghost of a Chance.   Cedar Rapids, Iowa, Heuer, 1958.
The Curley Tale.   Cedar Rapids, Iowa, Art Craft, 1958.
Inquire Within.   Evanston, Illinois, Row Peterson, 1959.
The Girl Whose Fortune Sought Her, in *Children's Plays from Favorite Stories,* edited by Sylvia E. Kamerman.   Boston, Plays Inc., 1959.
Edie-Across-the-Street.   Boston, Baker, 1960.
The Honeysuckle Hedge.   Franklin, Ohio, Eldridge, 1960.
Never Keep Him Waiting.   Chicago, Dramatic Publishing Company, 1961.
Red Heels and Roses.   New York, McKay, 1962.
If a Body Meets a Body.   Cedar Rapids, Iowa, Heuer, 1963.
Now Hear This.   Franklin, Ohio, Eldridge, 1963.
The Magic Bookshelf, and *The Other Side of the Wall,* in *Fifty Plays for Junior Actors,* edited by Sylvia E. Kamerman.   Boston, Plays Inc., 1966.
The Do-Nothing Frog, in *100 Plays for Children,* edited by A.S. Burack.   Boston, Plays Inc., 1970.
The Invisible Dragon.   Chicago, Dramatic Publishing Company, 1971.
The Toys Take Over Christmas.   Chicago, Dramatic Publishing Company, 1977.
The Mudcake Princess.   Chicago, Dramatic Publishing Company, 1979.
The Truly Remarkable Puss-in-Boots.   Chicago, Dramatic Publishing Company, 1979.

Other plays: *Susan and Aladdin's Lamp,* 1957, *The Signpost,* 1962, *The Friendship Bracelet,* 1963, *Christmas in Old New England,* 1964, and *Yankee Doodle Came to Cranetown,* 1975, all in the magazine *Plays* (Boston); *A Feather in His Cap,* 1957, *The Wonderful Door,* 1961, and *A Wish Is for Keeping,* 1967, all in the magazine *Instructor* (Dansville, New York); *A Straight Line from Somewhere,* in the magazine *Grade Teacher* (Greenwich, Connecticut), 1960.

Verse

Popsical Song.   Chicago, Encyclopaedia Britannica Educational Corporation, 1972.
A Specially Wonderful Day.   Chicago, Encyclopaedia Britannica Educational Corporation, 1972.

Other

Dr. Elizabeth: The Story of the First Woman Doctor.   New York, Lothrop, 1974.

PUBLICATIONS FOR ADULTS

Plays

A Candle on the Table.   Boston, Baker, 1972.

The Retirement.   Franklin, Ohio, Eldridge, 1972.

*

Manuscript Collections: Kerlan Collection, University of Minnesota, Minneapolis; de Grummond Collection, University of Southern Mississippi, Hattiesburg.

Patricia Clapp comments:

Having spent many years working in a theatre it was probably natural that my first writings were plays. I had observed innumerable audiences of children, and I wrote what they enjoyed: action, uncomplicated dialogue, color, and sometimes music. Later, when family records introduced me to an ancestor of my husband's—one Constance Hopkins, a passenger on the Mayflower—I was caught up in the settling of Plymouth, Massachusetts in 1620. My first book, *Constance,* was the result. It has brought me to other highlights of American history and the people who made it. In the 1920's history was taught as an endless list of dates and forgettable names. None of it seemed real. It wasn't until I realized that history was only a record of what people had done that it began to excite me. People fascinate me and now, whenever possible, I find or create a heroine whose shoes I can step into and understand why she did whatever she did. It seems to work for my readers as well as for me.

*   *   *

Although most of Patricia Clapp's writing for children and young people is in the form of plays, her first novel made more impact than her earlier dramatic work in the field of children's literature, winning a place as one of the runners-up for the National Book award in the first year there was a category for children's books. *Constance* is in journal form, and Clapp uses this literary device brilliantly in one of the most outstanding books set in the colonial period of the United States—and there are many. Constance has come over on the *Mayflower,* and she is an outspoken, lively girl of 14 who finds America "cold, grey, hard, bleak, unfriendly," and the first winter in the Plymouth colony grim. She misses London, and she is apprehensive about her future. But, like any adolescent, she is resilient and soon becomes immersed in the affairs of the colony, in relationships with Native Americans and struggles with English backers, and, as she grows older, in the man she marries at the close of the story. The last diary entry begins "How Beautiful Plymouth is, held tight in winter!" Clapp's research is not obtrusive in historical details, but emerges in the thorough identification with the period, and her heroine is both a girl of her time and a character with universality in a story that is smoothly written, historically accurate, and vivid in its characterization.

The skillful blending of fact and fiction is also evident in *Witches' Children* and *The Tamarack Tree,* again through the voice of a young girl. In the story of Tituba and the witch-hunting of Salem there are few new facts; what Clapp does is make the role of the participants more comprehensible. In *The Tamarack Tree* the protagonist is an English visitor, and it is through her objectivity and empathy that the book achieves perspective in interpreting the conflicting views of North and South in the internecine conflict of the Civil War.

In *Jane-Emily* and *King of the Dollhouse* Clapp turns to fantasy. The first is told by Louisa, 18, who expects a quiet summer with her orphaned niece Jane and Jane's grandmother, but Jane becomes obsessed by the spirit of Emily, an aunt who had died at Jane's age and whose malice is made increasingly apparent as the story develops. The realism and fantasy are nicely blended and the story builds in suspense, albeit at a slow pace. The second book is somewhat less effective, since there is no real story line and the fantasy is not as well combined with its realistic base as it is in *Jane-Emily.* A small girl discovers that her dollhouse is inhabited by a tiny, plump king who takes care of 11 babies of identical size while their mother the queen is off riding and hunting. The incidents are episodic rather than cohesive, and the book needs either humor or action to compensate for its static quality, although the style of the writing is competent.

As she did in *Constance,* Clapp uses first person to gain immediacy in her one biography, *Dr. Elizabeth,* the life story of Elizabeth Blackwell, the first woman to get a medical degree in the United States. Clapp avoids two of the pitfalls to which many biographers for young readers succumb: there is no note of adulation in the writing, and there is no undue attention to the subject's childhood. Blackwell emerges as a vivid character, and her story is valuable both as a segment of medical history and as a chapter in the long struggle for women's rights.

—Zena Sutherland

CLARE, Helen. See **CLARKE, Pauline.**

CLARK, Ann Nolan. American. Born in Las Vegas, New Mexico, 5 December 1896. Educated at New Mexico Highlands University, Las Vegas, graduated 1919. Married Thomas Patrick Clark in 1919 (died); one son (deceased). Schoolteacher near Las Vegas, 1917 and 1919; worked in Tacoma, Washington, 1918; assistant English teacher, Highlands University; educational supervisor, Bureau of Indian Affairs, 1920–62; trained teachers in Latin America, 1945–50; education consultant, Institute of Latin-American Affairs, 1946–62. United States delegate to Unesco Conference, Brazil. Recipient: American Library Association Newbery Medal, 1953; United States Bureau of Indian Affairs Distinguished Service award, 1962; Catholic Library Association Regina Medal, 1963. Address: Tucson Terrace, Apartment 139, 201 North Jessica, Tucson, Arizona 85710, U.S.A.

PUBLICATIONS FOR CHILDREN

Fiction

Buffalo Caller: The Story of a Young Sioux Boy of the Early 1700's, Before the Coming of the Horse, illustrated by Marian Hulsizer. Evanston, Illinois, Row Peterson, 1942.
Young Hunter of Picuris, illustrated by Velino Herrara. Chilocco, Oklahoma, Bureau of Indian Affairs, 1943.
Little Navajo Bluebird, illustrated by Paul Lantz. New York, Viking Press, 1943.
Magic Money, illustrated by Leo Politi. New York, Viking Press, 1950.
Secret of the Andes, illustrated by Jean Charlot. New York, Viking Press, 1952; London, Penguin, 1976.
Looking-for-Something: The Story of a Stray Burro of Ecuador, illustrated by Leo Politi. New York, Viking Press, 1952.
Blue Canyon Horse, illustrated by Allan Houser. New York, Viking Press, 1954.
Santiago, illustrated by Lynd Ward. New York, Viking Press, 1955.
A Santo for Pasqualita, illustrated by Mary Villarejo. New York, Viking Press, 1959.
World Song, illustrated by Kurt Wiese. New York, Viking Press, 1960.

Paco's Miracle, illustrated by Agnes Tait. New York, Farrar Straus, 1962.
Tia Maria's Garden, illustrated by Ezra Jack Keats. New York, Viking Press, 1963.
Medicine Man's Daughter, illustrated by Don Bolognese. New York, Farrar Straus, 1963.
This for That, illustrated by Don Freeman. San Carlos, California, Golden Gate Books, 1965.
Summer Is for Growing, illustrated by Agnes Tait. New York, Farrar Straus, 1968.
Hoofprint on the Wind, illustrated by Robert Andrew Parker. New York, Viking Press, 1972.
Year Walk. New York, Viking Press, 1975.
All This Wild Land. New York, Viking Press, 1976.
To Stand Against the Wind. New York, Viking Press, 1978.

Verse

In My Mother's House, illustrated by Velino Herrara. New York, Viking Press, 1941.
Third Monkey, illustrated by Don Freeman. New York, Viking Press, 1956.
Bear Cub, illustrated by Charles Fracé. New York, Viking Press, 1965.

Other

Who Wants to Be a Prairie Dog? (reader), illustrated by Van Tishnahjinnie. Phoenix, Office of Indian Affairs, 1940.
Little Herder in Spring [Autumn, Winter, Summer] (readers), illustrated by Hoke Denetsosie. Phoenix, Office of Indian Affairs, 4 vols., 1940–42.
Little Boy with Three Names: Stories of Taos Pueblo (reader), illustrated by Tonita Lujan. Chilocco, Oklahoma, Office of Indian Affairs, 1940.
The Pine Ridge Porcupine (reader), illustrated by Andrew Standing Soldier. Lawrence, Kansas, Office of Indian Affairs, 1941.
A Child's Story of New Mexico, with Frances Carey. Lincoln, Nebraska, University Publishing, 1941.
There Still Are Buffalo (reader), illustrated by Andrew Standing Soldier. Lawrence, Kansas, Office of Indian Affairs, 1942.
About the Slim Butte Raccoon (reader), illustrated by Andrew Standing Soldier. Lawrence, Kansas, Office of Indian Affairs, 1942.
About the Grass Mountain Mouse (reader), illustrated by Andrew Standing Soldier. Lawrence, Kansas, Office of Indian Affairs, 1942.
About the Hen of Wahpeton (reader), illustrated by Andrew Standing Soldier. Lawrence, Kansas, Office of Indian Affairs, 1943.
Bringer of the Mystery Dog (reader), illustrated by Oscar Howe. Lawrence, Kansas, Office of Indian Affairs, 1943.
Brave Against the Enemy: A Story of Three Generations—of the Day Before Yesterday, of Yesterday, and of Tomorrow (reader), illustrated by Helen Post. Lawrence, Kansas, Office of Indian Affairs, 1944.
Sun Journey: A Story of the Zuñi Pueblo (reader), illustrated by Percy T. Sandy. Chilocco, Oklahoma, Office of Indian Affairs, 1945.
Singing Sioux Cowboy Reader, illustrated by Andrew Standing Soldier. Lawrence, Kansas, United States Indian Service, 1947.
Linda Rita (reader). Washington, D.C., Government Printing Office, 1948.
Los Patos Son Diferentes (reader). Washington, D.C., Government Printing Office, 1948.
El Buey Que Quería Vivir en la Casa (reader). Washington, D.C., Government Printing Office, 1948.
Juan el Poblano (reader). Washington, D.C., Government Printing Office, 1949.

El Cerdito Que Fué al Mercado (reader).   Washington, D.C.,
     Government Printing Office, 1949.
El Maestro Rural en la Comunidad, with Manuel Arce and Miguel
     Gordillo.   Guatemala, Ministerio de Educacibon Publica, 1955.
The Little Indian Pottery Maker, illustrated by Don Perceval.   Los
     Angeles, Melmont, 1955.
Third Monkey, illustrated by Don Freeman.   New York, Viking
     Press, 1956.
The Little Indian Basket Maker, illustrated by Harrison Begay.   Los
     Angeles, Melmont, 1957.
The Desert People, illustrated by Allan Houser.   New York, Viking
     Press, 1962.
Father Kino: Priest to the Pimas, illustrated by H. Lawrence Hoff-
     man.   New York, Farrar Straus, and London, Burns Oates, 1963.
Brother Andre of Montreal, illustrated by Harold Lang.   New York,
     Vision Books, and London, Burns Oates, 1967.
Arizona Is for Young People, with Glenna Craw.   Lincoln, Nebras-
     ka, University Publishing, 1968.
Along Sandy Trails, illustrated by Alfred A. Cohn.   New York,
     Viking Press, 1969.
Circle of Seasons, illustrated by W.T. Mars.   New York, Farrar
     Straus, 1970.
In the Land of Small Dragon: A Vietnamese Folktale, with Dang
     Manh Kha, illustrated by Tony Chen.   New York, Viking Press,
     1979.

PUBLICATIONS FOR ADULTS

Other

Journey to the People.   New York, Viking Press, 1969.
These Were the Valiant: A Collection of New Mexico Profiles.   Al-
     buquerque, Horn, 1969.

                                          *

Manuscript Collections: Kerlan Collection, University of Min-
nesota, Minneapolis; de Grummond Collection, University of
Southern Mississippi, Hattiesburg; University of Oregon Library,
Eugene.

Ann Nolan Clark comments:
     When I entered the Bureau of Indian Affairs (B.I.A.) in the 1920's,
I quickly realized that there were no textbooks which Indian children
could relate to—vocabulary, background, and values in the books
then available were foreign to them and could not be understood. I
wrote what was then called "Third Grade Geography" which I
thought would help to build concepts of people in relation to places
and modes of living. Each child bound (in Indian calico) his own
book and illustrated it. Someone from the B.I.A. Washington office
showed a copy to May Massee at Viking Press, and the book was
published as *In My Mother's House.* This led the B.I.A. to encourage
me to write Indian readers for Indian children. These were illustrated
by Indian students and published at Indian schools where printing
was being taught. I did a series of Pueblo, Navajo, Sioux, and Papago
stories, but World War II cut off our appropriation for printing. After
that I continued to work for the B.I.A., and tried to write a book every
year.

                         *   *   *

     In My Mother's House is one of the most unusual books ever
written for children in the United States. Ann Nolan Clark wrote it
so that her small class of third graders in the tiny Tewa Indian village
of Tesuque, New Mexico, would have a book that they could read

and understand about the everyday life of their people.
     It is no wonder the five Indian children took the book to their
hearts. It is a book filled with their ways, their world, their words;
and said in a way that they would say it. Yes, the book must be *said.*
If one just looks at the words it could easily be mistaken for any other
primer for early readers, but when the words are given sound, the
Indian child's deep feeling for nature and love of family are poetically revealed.
     Ordinarily teaching children and writing for them doesn't mix
well, but then Clark is no ordinary woman. Like that of Sylvia
Ashton-Warner, the remarkable teacher-writer who worked among
the Maori children of New Zealand, Clark's writing is extraordinary
because her approach to teaching was extraordinary. For instance,
she found in the written work of older Indian children the quiet
beauty of straightforward "Talk" that comes naturally to a person
raised in the oral tradition. Here, in "Sleep," is but one of those she
shares in *Journey to the People:*

              The sun goes down
                 and night falls.
              Then I close my eyes
                 and go to sleep
                 in my bed under the trees.

     These served as her models when she turned to writing books for
their younger brothers and sisters, who could not as yet read or write,
but whose minds and hearts she knew and understood, books like
Blue Canyon Horse and *The Desert People* (a companion piece to
In My Mother's House). It begins:

              I am a boy
                 of the Desert People.

              White men call me Indian
              White men call me Papago
                 but the wild animals
                 call me Brother
                 because they know me
                 and love me.

     Simple beauty remains the most succinct and apt description of
Clark's books, even when one considers those that are addressed to
more sophisticated readers. The plots of books like *Secret of the
Andes* and *Santiago* revolve around the difficulties faced by young
Indians in meeting the demands of two conflicting cultures. These
works appeal most to those readers who appreciate the special
delights of atmosphere and mood that are captured only by a writer
who not only knows the cultures of the Indians of the Americas but
who also has a reverential understanding for the people and their
ways, all gained through a lifetime of living with them.
     As she says: "children need children's books that have been
written with honesty, accuracy, and reality. They need books that
develop deeper understandings and broader acceptances, that enrich
imagination. Their need is my challenge." Ann Nolan Clark has met
that challenge.

                                              —James E. Higgins

                         ————

CLARK, Catherine Anthony (née Smith).   British.   Born in
London, 5 May 1892; emigrated to Canada, 1914. Educated at the
Convent of Jesus and Mary, Ipswich, Suffolk. Married Leonard
Clark in 1919; one son and one daughter. Columnist, *Prospector,*

Nelson, British Columbia. Recipient: Canadian Library Association Book of the Year medal, 1952. *Died 24 February 1977.*

PUBLICATIONS FOR CHILDREN

Fiction

The Golden Pine Cone, illustrated by Clare Bice. Toronto, Macmillan, 1950.
The Sun Horse, illustrated by Clare Bice. Toronto, Macmillan, 1951.
The One-Winged Dragon, illustrated by Clare Bice. Toronto, Macmillan, 1955.
The Silver Man, illustrated by Clare Bice. Toronto, Macmillan, 1958; London, Macmillan, 1959.
The Diamond Feather; or, The Door in the Mountain: A Magic Tale for Children, illustrated by Clare Bice. Toronto and London, Macmillan, 1962.
The Man with the Yellow Eyes, illustrated by Gordon Raynor. Toronto, Macmillan, and New York, St. Martin's Press, 1963; London, Macmillan, 1964.
The Hunter and the Medicine Man, illustrated by Clare Bice. Toronto, Macmillan, 1966.

*   *   *

As the author of six books of fantasy Catherine Anthony Clark was an important contributor to a field of writing sparsely represented in Canadian children's literature. Her books are set in British Columbia and the magic adventures they recount take place in wilderness areas and the foothills of the Rocky Mountains where the spirits of the land and the people who have inhabited it are alive. They draw strongly on the legendary figures and the beliefs of the Indians of the Pacific Northwest, and indeed native peoples play an important role in all the stories. Clark has created folk spirits of the countryside, the Lake Snake, the Head Canada Goose, which add humour and imaginative vigour. On the periphery of the enchanted lands are prospectors and settlers. It is often through these characters, for whom the boundaries of reality have become blurred, that the spirits are introduced.

The protagonists are children, generally a boy and girl. At odds with their lives, they are drawn to fantastic adventures in which they undertake a quest. In following it they come to a better understanding of themselves and the problems with which they must contend. While this forms the unifying theme of the plots, the author's purpose is more closely involved in portraying the land and its inheritance. Her strength as a descriptive writer is a major factor in her success. There is a marked similarity between the stories. *The Golden Pine Cone* relates the magic adventures of two children who find a golden pine cone belonging to the ruler of the lands, lakes, and the forests and must withstand those who seek the power it holds. In *The Sun Horse* a boy and girl search for their father who has been lured by a golden stallion into the idyllic valley of forgetfulness. The Chinese and Indian strains in British Columbia's past are brought together in *The One-Winged Dragon,* the story of an old Chinese farmer who keeps a dragon in his well and the children who, with the dragon's help, return his daughter to him. The life of native peoples of the Pacific Northwest is well reflected in their adventures. The book is more well constructed than the earlier fantasies, its characterization is fuller and more sympathetic. *The Silver Man* tells of a troubled boy who, in his dazed contemplation of a rock crystal, experiences an adventure in which he restores a lost young chieftain to his tribe. Clark's last two novels are weakened by a plethora of incident and plot. In *The Diamond Feather* an orphaned brother and sister go through the door in a mountain to the Valley at the Edge of Time in

search of the children of a bitter old prospector. *The Hunter and the Medicine Man* tells of two children who explore a haunted mountain and become involved in an evil medicine man's attempt to usurp the position of a tribe's rightful chief.

The books are limited in their imaginative scope. There is often little distinction between the real world and the fantastic. Although the children are believable, their dialogue natural and colloquial, the conduct clearly expected of them is very exacting. Written with ease and inventiveness the stories are, however, entertaining reading.

Clark also produced a book of historical fiction for early readers, *The Man with the Yellow Eyes.* Set near Nelson, British Columbia, at the turn of the century it tells of a boy's race against an unscrupulous prospector to stake his father's claim to land containing rich deposits of silver. The handling of the plot is banal but the descriptions of the foothills and the practical ways of the hardworking settlers are here, as in the other books, noteworthy.

—Ruth Osler

———

CLARK, David.   See **HARDCASTLE, Michael.**

———

CLARK, Leonard.   British.   Born in St. Peter Port, Guernsey, 1 August 1905. Educated at Monmouth School, 1917–22; Normal College, Bangor, Caernarvonshire, 1928–30, Cert. Ed. 1930. Served in the Home Guard, Devon Regiment, 1940–43. Married Jane Callow in 1954; one son and one daughter. Teacher in Gloucestershire, 1922–28, and London, 1930–36; Assistant Inspector, 1936–45, and Inspector of Schools, 1945–70, Board of Education, later Ministry of Education, in Devon, Yorkshire, and London; from 1970 editor, Longmans Poetry Library series; consultant editor, Chatto and Windus Poetry Books for the Young, London, and Thornhill Press, Gloucester. Member, Arts Council Literature panel, 1965–69, and Westminster Diocesan Schools Commission, 1970–76. Recipient: Children's Literature Association award, for criticism, 1979. Liveryman of Haberdashers' Company, 1965; Freeman of City of London, 1965. Honorary Associate, London Academy of Music and Dramatic Art, 1969. Fellow, Royal Society of Literature, 1953. Knight of the Order of St. Sylvester, 1970. O.B.E. (Officer, Order of the British Empire), 1966. *Died 10 September 1981.*

PUBLICATIONS FOR CHILDREN

Fiction

Robert Andrew Tells a Story [*and Tiffy, by the Sea, and the Holy Family, and the Red Indian Chief, and Skippy, in the Country*], illustrated by James Scargill. Leeds, E.J. Arnold, 7 vols., 1965–66.
Mr. Pettigrew's Harvest Festival, illustrated by Toffee Sanders. Gloucester, Thornhill Press, 1974.
Mr. Pettigrew's Train, illustrated by Toffee Sanders. Gloucester, Thornhill Press, 1975.
Mr. Pettigrew and the Bell-ringers, illustrated by Toffee Sanders. Gloucester, Thornhill Press, 1976.

Verse

Daybreak: A First Book of Poems, illustrated by Selma Nankivell. London, Hart Davis, 1963.

The Year Round: A Second Book of Poems, illustrated by Edward Ardizzone. London, Hart Davis, 1966.
Fields and Territories. London, Turret, 1967.
Good Company, illustrated by Jennie Corbett. London, Dobson, 1968.
Near and Far, illustrated by Kozo Kakimoto and others. London, Hamlyn, 1968.
Here and There, illustrated by Kuniro Fukazawa. London, Hamlyn, 1969.
Secret as Toads. London, Chatto and Windus, 1972.
Singing in the Streets: Poems for Christmas. London, Dobson, 1972.
The Broad Atlantic. London, Dobson, 1974.
Four Seasons, illustrated by Jennie Corbett. London, Dobson, 1975.
Collected Poems and Verses for Children. London, Dobson, 1975.
The Tale of Prince Igor, illustrated by Charles Keeping. London, Dobson, 1979.
Stranger Than Unicorns, illustrated by Jennie Corbett. London, Dobson, 1979.
The Singing Time: Poems and Verses for Children, illustrated by Doreen Caldwell. London, Hodder and Stoughton, 1980.
The Corn Growing, illustrated by Lisa Kopper. London, Hodder and Stoughton, 1982.

Other

When They Were Children, illustrated by William Randell. London, Parrish, and New York, Roy, 1964.
St. Felix and the Spider. London, Catholic Truth Society, 1974.
St. Patrick. London, Catholic Truth Society, 1974.
St. Anthony of Egypt. London, Catholic Truth Society, 1974.
St. Dorothea and the Flowers of Paradise. London, Catholic Truth Society, 1974.
Tales from the Panchatantra, illustrated by Jeroo Roy. London, Evans, 1979.

Editor, *The Magic Kingdom: An Anthology of Verse for Seniors.* London, Mathews and Marrot, 1937.
Editor, *The Open Door: An Anthology of Verse for Juniors.* London, Mathews and Marrot, 1937.
Editor, *Quiet as Moss: Thirty Six Poems,* by Andrew Young. London, Hart Davis, 1959.
Editor, *Drums and Trumpets: Poetry for the Youngest,* illustrated by Heather Copley. London, Bodley Head, 1962.
Editor, *Common Ground: An Anthology for the Young,* illustrated by M.E. Eldridge. London, Faber, 1964.
Editor, *Selected Poems by John Clare 1793–1864.* Leeds, E.J. Arnold, 1964.
Editor, *All Things New: An Anthology,* illustrated by Ann Tout. London, Constable, 1965.
Editor, *The Poetry of Nature.* London, Hart Davis, 1965.
Editor, *Following the Sun: Poems by Children,* illustrated by Tony Dyson. London, Odhams Press, 1967.
Editor, *Burning as Light: Thirty Seven Poems,* by Andrew Young, illustrated by Joan Hassall. London, Hart Davis, 1967.
Editor, *Flutes and Cymbals: Poetry for the Young,* illustrated by Shirley Hughes. London, Bodley Head, 1968; New York, Crowell, 1969.
Editor, *Sound of Battle,* illustrated by Ewart Oakeshott. Oxford, Pergamon Press, 1969.
Editor, *Poems by Children.* London, Studio Vista, 1970.
Editor, *All Along, Down Along: A Book of Stories in Verse,* illustrated by Pauline Baynes. London, Longman, 1971.
Editor, *Fire of Spring: Prose and Poetry from IAPS Schools.* Tunbridge Wells, Kent, Fenrose, 1974.

Editor, *The Way the Wind Blows: A Book of Verse,* illustrated by Lisa Kopper. London, Evans, 1979.

PUBLICATIONS FOR ADULTS

Verse

Poems. London, Fortune Press, 1940.
Passage to the Pole and Other Poems. London, Fortune Press, 1944.
Rhandanim. Leeds, Salamander Press, 1945.
The Mirror and Other Poems. London, Wingate, 1948.
XII Poems. Birmingham, City of Birmingham School of Printing, 1948.
English Morning and Other Poems. London, Hutchinson, 1953.
Selected Poems 1940–1957. London, Hutchinson, 1958.
Walking with Trees. London, Enitharmon Press, 1970.
Every Voice. Guildford, Surrey, Words Press, 1971.
The Hearing Heart. London, Enitharmon Press, 1974.
Winter to Winter and Other Poems. London, Dobson, 1977.
Silence of the Morning. London, Enitharmon Press, 1977.
Twelve Poems from St. Bartholomew's. Privately printed, 1978.
As I Looked Over Jordan: Sixteen Poems. Kinnesswood, Kinross, Lomond Press, 1984.

Other

Alfred Williams: His Life and Work. Oxford, Blackwell, 1945; New York, Kelley, 1969.
Ideas in Poetry. Birmingham, City of Birmingham School of Printing, 1947.
Sark Discovered: The Prospect of an Island, Being a Literary and Pictorial Record of the Island of Sark. London, Dent, 1956; revised edition, London, Dobson, 1971, 1979.
Walter de la Mare: A Checklist. Cambridge, University Press, 1956.
Walter de la Mare. London, Bodley Head, 1960; New York, Walck, 1961.
Green Wood: A Gloucestershire Childhood. London, Parrish, 1962.
Andrew Young. London, Longman, 1964.
A Fool in the Forest (autobiography). London, Dobson, 1965.
Prospect of Highgate and Hampstead. London, Highgate Press, 1967.
Grateful Caliban (autobiography). London, Dobson, 1968.
A Tribute to Walter de la Mare, with Edmund Blunden. London, Enitharmon Press, 1974.
Three Poets, Two Children, with Vernon Scannell and Dannie Abse, edited by Desmond Badham-Thornhill. Gloucester, Thornhill Press, 1975.
The Inspector Remembers: A Diary of One of Her Majesty's Inspectors of Schools 1936–1970. London, Dobson, 1976.
Writing for the Public. Gloucester, Thornhill Press, 1976.
The Story of Rahere. Privately printed, 1978.
An Intimate Landscape. London, Nottingham Court Press, 1981.

Editor, *The Kingdom of the Mind: Essays and Addresses 1903–1937 of Albert Mansbridge.* London, Dent, 1944.
Editor, *Andrew Young: Prospect of a Poet: Essays and Tributes by Fourteen Writers.* London, Hart Davis, 1957.
Editor, *The Collected Poems of Andrew Young.* London, Hart Davis, 1960.
Editor, *(Poems),* by Robert Graves and D.H. Lawrence. London, Longman, 1967.
Editor, with others, *The Complete Poems of Walter de la Mare.*

London, Faber, 1969; New York, Knopf, 1970.
Editor, *Poems of Ivor Gurney 1890–1937.* London, Chatto and Windus, 1973.
Editor, *Complete Poems of Andrew Young.* London, Secker and Warburg, 1974.
Editor, *Great and Familiar: The Heritage of English Poetry.* Tunbridge Wells, Kent, Fenrose, 1974.
Editor, *They Looked at Gloucestershire: An Anthology of Poetry and Prose.* London, Dobson, 1980.

Translator, with Iris Allam, *The Zemganno Brothers,* by E.L.A. Goncourt. London, Redman, 1957.

*

Leonard Clark commented:

(1978) It is natural that, as the father of two children, a former teacher, and one of Her Majesty's Inspectors of Schools for many years, I should write prose and poetry for the young. In addition, as editor of many anthologies of poetry for the young, I have seen the need for providing for them, in attractive form, collections of poetry by other poets. In essence, my poetry for the young does not differ greatly from any other poetry I write, for I have always believed that a good poem for children must be a good poem for everybody else. This poetry, which has largely concerned itself with nature, and with the thoughts and feelings of children as they grow up and inherit the world, is successful, perhaps, because I believe I am the child for whom the poems have been written. Although I owe a great deal to Walter de la Mare's advice and guidance, my voice is my own. It is a very English voice which tries to speak of things eternal, without any condescension, sentimentality, or undue nostalgia. It faces up to life as life is lived imaginatively, with always an eye on the visionary and mystical.

*   *   *

Despite his popular Mr. Pettigrew stories Leonard Clark was best known for poetry. Teaching experience enabled him to speak directly to children. "You are the child for whom the poem is written," Kathleen Raine told him. He was also the only Inspector of Schools since Matthew Arnold to publish a substantial body of verse. After de la Mare, only he and James Reeves produced their collected children's poems. His influence on educational literary policy has been considerable, and he originated the Arts Council's "Writers in Schools" project. He edited many anthologies, some of poems by children themselves. All his books are very carefully designed. In *Following the Sun* the chapter headings from Traherne make a continuous and developing accompaniment to the poems themselves. In *All Things New,* seasonal changes, the Six Days and varied manifestations of Creation, the illustrations, link the verse to a subtle whole. His own poem "Earthworm" is shaped like a worm, the rhythms of "Snow" approximate that of the fall of snow itself. Clark was particularly sympathetic to the 5–12 age group but always "a poem for children must be a good poem." He never hesitated to include a difficult work, confident that even a small response is ample justification. Too much easy reading rots the imagination; a poem, wrote T.S. Eliot, can communicate before it is understood.

Clark's range was wide: the undeservedly obscure, neglected, and forgotten may flank some famous name, testifying not to the insignificance but unimportance of fashion. Throughout, originality of theme is rated less than originality of perception. He was quick to notice the child who sees the ocean as an angry cat but who may yet allow people to lie on its wet back: and the teenager who sadly, memorably, wonders whether her own indifference has killed a baby. His concern with tradition placed poems and individual words against total history, the changing values and perspectives. "Sleep"

is shown treated by John Fletcher, Wordsworth, Tennyson, Edward Thomas, Auden. This concern informed his choices among contemporaries. When an Inspector, he set himself to remedy their neglect in schools. His *The Poetry of Nature,* starting with Chaucer and Lydgate, ends with Wain, Thwaite, Kirkup, Ted Hughes. A teacher, he realised that little can be taught, much implied. He seldom wrote a "children's poem," but first wrote, then decided the audience. His own verse included lyrics, narratives of travel and adventure, and, above all, nature poetry in the tradition of Clare, Christina Rossetti, Frost, and Edward Thomas, with affinities to de la Mare and Andrew Young, on both of whom he was an authority. It is not the slack pastoral of nymphs and shepherds, but of observation, precise, sharp, at times ironic. Edith Sitwell once called him "a practical mystic." He saw not Man and Nature but Man with Nature. There are also echoes of Blake and Samuel Palmer. His most consistent influence was the English countryside, its centuries of order, work—he enjoyed *things* in action—conflict, and evolution, landscapes of peace made strong despite inescapable present pollutions and past cruelties. Quiet Somerset contains sad, once-bloody Sedgemoor. With little violence but much intensity his is a poetry of special places, private dreams, secret sounds, the precious autonomy of field and wood, the gaps within silence of an abandoned house. Conflict is suggested, not between Science and Nature, but irresponsible bits of Science exploiting or ruining a Nature which, if left wholly to itself, would likewise distort and overwhelm. Clark spoke to those for whom trees are more than timber, hedges more than barriers. Birds are simultaneously remote and personal: they are pattern and colour, carrion and myth, pet and victim.

He recorded the permutations of the child's day, the complex gradations of light and emotion, overlappings of morning, afternoon, and evening, of play and dream. He largely ignored current events but not history: was grieved and angered by the murder both of the Inca Atahualpa and of J.F. Kennedy. He knew that for certain minds a cave painting or Spanish ingot can be more contemporary than a transistor. Many poems, ostensibly simple, can ultimately reveal the unexpected. In his long writing life—he began publishing at 18—he kept an evenness of texture which may have prevented many obvious anthology pieces. This at least leaves much to be discovered. That he always wanted to delight gently rather than bruise and crudely shock may have robbed him of some critical esteem but undeniably won him a very wide readership.

—Peter Vansittart

———

CLARK, Mavis Thorpe. Has also written as M.R. Clark. Australian. Born in Melbourne Victoria, in 1912 (?). Educated at Methodist Ladies College, Melbourne. Married Harold Latham (died); two daughters. Member of Committee of Management, Australian Society of Authors, 15 years. President, International PEN, Melbourne (two terms). Member of Committee, National Book Council, seven years. Recipient: Australian Children's Book Council Book of the Year award, 1967. Address: 1/22 Rochester Road, Canterbury, Victoria 3126, Australia.

PUBLICATIONS FOR CHILDREN

Fiction

Hatherly's First Fifteen (as M.R. Clark), illustrated by F.E. Wiley. Sydney, Whitcombe and Tombs, and London, Oxford University Press, 1930.

Dark Pool Island. Melbourne, Oxford University Press, 1949.

The Twins from Timber Creek. Melbourne, Oxford University Press, 1949.

Home Again at Timber Creek. Melbourne, Oxford University Press, 1950.

Missing Gold. London, Hutchinson, 1951.

Jingaroo. Melbourne, Oxford University Press, 1951.

The Brown Land Was Green, illustrated by Harry Hudson. Melbourne and London, Heinemann, 1956.

Gully of Gold, illustrated by Anne Graham. Melbourne and London, Heinemann, 1958.

Pony from Tarella, illustrated by Jean M. Rowe. Melbourne and London, Heinemann, 1959.

They Came South, illustrated by Joy Murray. Melbourne and London, Heinemann, 1963.

The Min-Min, illustrated by Genevieve Melrose. Melbourne, Lansdowne Press, 1966; London, Angus and Robertson, 1967; New York, Macmillan, 1969.

Blue above the Trees, illustrated by Genevieve Melrose. Melbourne, Lansdowne Press, 1967; London, Angus and Robertson, 1968; New York, Meredith Press, 1969.

Spark of Opal, illustrated by Genevieve Melrose. Melbourne, Lansdowne Press, 1968; London, Methuen, 1971; New York, Macmillan, 1973.

Nowhere to Hide, illustrated by Genevieve Melrose. Melbourne, Lansdowne Press, 1969.

Iron Mountain, illustrated by Ronald Brooks. Melbourne, Lansdowne Press, 1970; New York, Macmillan, 1971; London, Methuen, 1972.

New Golden Mountain. Melbourne, Lansdowne Press, 1973; as *If the Earth Falls In,* New York, Seabury Press, 1975.

Wildfire. Sydney, Hodder and Stoughton, and Leicester, Brockhampton Press, 1973; New York, Macmillan, 1974.

The Sky Is Free. Sydney, Hodder and Stoughton, 1974; Leicester, Brockhampton Press, and New York, Macmillan, 1976.

The Hundred Islands, illustrated by Astra Lacis. Sydney and London, Hodder and Stoughton, 1976; New York, Macmillan, 1977.

The Lilly-Pilly, illustrated by Prue Chammen. Adelaide, Rigby, 1979.

A Stranger Came to the Mine, illustrated by Jane Walker. Richmond, Victoria, Hutchinson, 1980.

Solomon's Child. Richmond, Victoria, and London, Hutchinson, 1981.

Soft Shoe, illustrated by Iiba Wentenberg. Melbourne, Martin Educational, 1988.

Radio Series, from her own stories: *The Brown Land Was Green,* 1961; *Gully of Gold,* 1962; *They Came South,* 1965.

Other

Fishing (as Mavis Latham), illustrated by Joy Murray. Melbourne, Oxford University Press, 1963.

A Pack-Tracker, illustrated by Shirley Turner. Melbourne, London, and New York, Oxford University Press, 1968.

Opal Mining, illustrated by Barbara Taylor. Melbourne, Oxford University Press, 1969.

Iron Ore Mining, illustrated by Jocelyn Bell. Melbourne, Oxford University Press, 1971.

Spanish Queen (reader), illustrated by Joan Saint. Sydney and London, Hodder and Stoughton, 1977.

The Boy from Cumeroogunga: The Story of Sir Douglas Nicholls, Aboriginal Leader. Sydney, Hodder and Stoughton, 1979.

Joey (reader), illustrated by Joanna McKeown. Mount Gravatt, Queensland, Mount Gravatt College of Advanced Education, 1980.

Boo to a Goose (reader), illustrated by Bruce Riddell. Mount Gravatt, Queensland, Mount Gravatt College of Advanced Education, 1981.

The Thief Who Came Quietly. Mount Gravatt, Queensland, Mount Gravatt College of Advanced Education, 1982.

Young and Brave. Sydney, Hodder and Stoughton, 1984.

PUBLICATIONS FOR ADULTS

Other

John Batman (as Mavis Latham). Melbourne, Oxford University Press, 1962.

Pastor Doug: The Story of an Aboriginal Leader. Melbourne, Lansdowne Press, 1965; London, Newnes, 1966; revised edition, as *Pastor Doug: The Story of Sir Douglas Nicholls, Aboriginal Leader,* Lansdowne Press, 1972.

Jane and Betty Rayner, Strolling Players. Melbourne, Lansdowne Press, 1972.

No Mean Destiny: The Story of the War Widows' Guild of Australia 1945–1985. Melbourne, Hyland House, 1986.

*

Manuscript Collection: National Library of Australia, Canberra.

Mavis Thorpe Clark comments:

Individual writers concentrate their work effort, usually, on a particular category of literature. Among the many forms, he or she may be a novelist, an historian, an essayist, a playwright, a biographer, a poet, a writer for children. The genre, I believe, "chooses" its exponents. I began to write in my early school years, about children, for children. These first steps revealed my path. As a result my main body of work has been for young people, though I have written biographies and factual books for adults.

As a writer for today's youth, I am writing for the most important generation ever born. Today's young ones will be the caretakers of the world's uncertain future, and responsible for its preservation, even survival. It is a sobering thought, but an honour and a privilege to be "chosen" to work in this field of literature.

*   *   *

Mavis Thorpe Clark is a prolific and well-organized writer; her teenage novels are set in different parts of Australia, and she first investigates these backgrounds very thoroughly before she begins to write. In *Blue above the Trees* and *The Brown Land Was Green,* two early novels, she relates the experiences of two (fictional) pioneer families. In these two stories, plot and characterization can be more readily separated than in her later novels, when her skill in characterization increases to the point where events and characters interact upon each other. Her plots, however, are always strong, with events and their outcome a vital force in each story. *Nowhere to Hide,* another earlier work, is interesting as being one of the few novels for young readers which has a background of Australia during the second world war.

The Min-Min (Australian Children's Book of the Year, 1967) is undoubtedly Clark's most outstanding work; in telling the story of an outback railway settler's family, living cut off from civilization, she displays a degree of conviction and compassion which she has not quite achieved since, perhaps because in *The Min-Min* she was content to pursue one outstanding theme. In several of her other novels, by contrast, she tends to introduce a number of parallel or sub-themes, diffusing the reader's interest between characters of almost equal importance. *The Sky Is Free* and *The Hundred Islands* are each concerned with topical and social questions, which tend now and then to dominate characterization and plot. In *The Sky Is Free,* the young hero runs away from a comfortable suburban home to the opal fields; on the way he teams up with a boy who is also on the run, from an institutional home. While this novel has many admirable qualities, including well-assimilated information about the opal fields, the plot is perhaps too neatly contrived. Conservation, especially that of the fauna of the Bass Strait islands, is the theme of *The Hundred Islands,* which contains fascinating first-hand observation of the mutton-bird, in particular; but in this novel, too, the author tends to subject characterization to the theme, and manipulate the plot a little too firmly.

Solomon's Child, again a purposeful novel, is concerned with present-day social issues. It tells how the teenage daughter of separated parents comes to terms with the decision of which parent will have custody, and describes the anti-social behaviour induced in her by her emotional conflict.

—Barbara Ker Wilson

CLARKE, Pauline. Has also written as Helen Clare. British. Born in Kirkby-in-Ashfield, Nottinghamshire, 19 May 1921. Educated at Somerville College, Oxford, B.A. (honours) in English 1943. Married the historian Peter Hunter Blair in 1969 (died 1982). Recipient: Library Association Carnegie Medal, 1963; Children's Literature prize (Germany), 1968. Agent: Curtis Brown, 162–168 Regent Street, London W1R 5TB. Address: Church Farm House, Bottisham, Cambridgeshire CB5 9BA, England.

PUBLICATIONS FOR CHILDREN

Fiction

The Pekinese Princess, illustrated by Cecil Leslie. London, Cape, 1948.
The Great Can, illustrated by Cecil Leslie. London, Faber, 1952.
The White Elephant, illustrated by Richard Kennedy. London, Faber, 1952; New York, Abelard Schuman, 1957.
Smith's Hoard, illustrated by Cecil Leslie. London, Faber, 1955; as *Hidden Gold,* New York, Abelard Schuman, 1957; as *The Golden Collar,* Faber, 1967.
Sandy the Sailor, illustrated by Cecil Leslie. London, Hamish Hamilton, 1956.
The Boy with the Erpingham Hood, illustrated by Cecil Leslie. London, Faber, 1956.
James the Policeman [*and the Robbers, and the Smugglers, and the Black Van*], illustrated by Cecil Leslie. London, Hamish Hamilton, 4 vols., 1957–63.
Torolv the Fatherless, illustrated by Cecil Leslie. London, Faber, 1959.
The Lord of the Castle, illustrated by Cecil Leslie. London, Hamish Hamilton, 1960.
The Robin Hooders, illustrated by Cecil Leslie. London, Faber, 1960.
Keep the Pot Boiling, illustrated by Cecil Leslie. London, Faber, 1961.
The Twelve and the Genii, illustrated by Cecil Leslie. London, Faber, 1962; as *The Return of the Twelves,* New York, Coward McCann, 1964.
The Bonfire Party, illustrated by Cecil Leslie. London, Hamish Hamilton, 1966.

The Two Faces of Silenus. London, Faber, and New York, Coward McCann, 1972.

Fiction as Helen Clare (illustrated by Cecil Leslie)

Five Dolls in a House. London, Lane, 1953; Englewood Cliffs, New Jersey, Prentice Hall, 1965.
Merlin's Magic. London, Lane, 1953.
Bel the Giant and Other Stories, illustrated by Peggy Fortnum. London, Lane, 1956; as *The Cat and the Fiddle, and Other Stories,* Englewood Cliffs, New Jersey, Prentice Hall, 1968.
Five Dolls and the Monkey. London, Lane, 1956; Englewood Cliffs, New Jersey, Prentice Hall, 1967.
Five Dolls in the Snow. London, Bodley Head, 1957; Englewood Cliffs, New Jersey, Prentice Hall, 1967.
Five Dolls and Their Friends. London, Bodley Head, 1959; Englewood Cliffs, New Jersey, Prentice Hall, 1968.
Seven White Pebbles, illustrated by Cynthia Abbott. London, Bodley Head, 1960.
Five Dolls and the Duke. London, Bodley Head, 1963; Englewood Cliffs, New Jersey, Prentice Hall, 1968.

Verse

Silver Bells and Cockle Shells, illustrated by Sally Ducksbury. London and New York, Abelard Schuman, 1962.

Other

Crowds of Creatures, illustrated by Cecil Leslie. London, Faber, 1964.

PUBLICATIONS FOR ADULTS

Other

Editor (as Pauline Hunter Blair), with Michael Lapidge, *Anglo-Saxon Northumbria,* by Peter Hunter Blair. London, Variorum, 1984.

*   *   *

The greatest single achievement of Pauline Clarke is undoubtedly her original fantasy *The Twelve and the Genii.* Once the concept is accepted that the toy soldiers given to Branwell Brontë when he was eight might be rediscovered and brought to life by another young boy in the present, the rest follows with compelling and inevitable logic. The Twelve are sharply individualised characters but always retain their soldierly nature, and the saga of their final journey, helped by children, is full of fascinating detail. Her other stories can be grouped for convenience into historical novels, contemporary adventures, and first readers. Among the historical stories, *Torolv the Fatherless* is a striking example of her skill in combining a feeling of period with a strong narrative and the ability to create character. The conflict between Torolv's loyalty to his Saxon foster family and to the Viking raider to whom he owed his first allegiance is shown with compassion. Life in medieval Norwich is vividly described in *The Boy with the Erpingham Hood* and the everyday detail is combined with the excitement and heartbreak of action at Agincourt and Harfleur.

Her contemporary stories such as *Keep the Pot Boiling,* a collection of nostalgic episodes about a family trying to make money, *The White Elephant,* a fast-moving but unlikely thriller about jewel thieves in London, and *Smith's Hoard,* in which children fight to save some Iceni treasures from the scrap merchant, are mostly well-written and full of vitality with authentic backgrounds and straightforward narrative style. *The Two Faces of Silenus* is a fantasy for older readers—a difficult undertaking—in which she captures the transition between childhood and adult emotions. Clarke has a special ability in writing for the very young which sparkles from her James stories, *Sandy the Sailor,* and *The Bonfire Party,* for instance. She uses simple vocabulary and repetition to create interesting stories in which her knowledge of children and her ability to capture them on paper are ably demonstrated. However remote the historical setting or bizarre the fantasy, her books are enriched and given plausibility by the description of everyday events and characters: the children in *The Twelve,* the detail of London in *The White Elephant,* the skills and rivalries in *Torolv* and the factual research in *Erpingham Hood.* Above all, she has that most essential talent for writers for children: the ability to tell a story.

—Valerie Brinkley-Willsher

———

CLEARY, Beverly (née Bunn). American. Born in McMinnville, Oregon, 12 April 1916. Educated at the University of California, Berkeley, B.A. 1938; University of Washington, Seattle, B.A. in librarianship 1939. Married Clarence Cleary in 1940; twin daughter and son. Children's librarian, Yakima Public Library, Washington, 1939–40; post librarian, United States Army Hospital, Oakland, California, 1942–45. Recipient: American Library Association Laura Ingalls Wilder award, 1975; Catholic Library Association Regina Medal, 1980; American Book Award, for paperback, 1981; University of Southern Mississippi award, 1982; George G. Stone Center for Children's Books award, 1983; Society of Children's Writers Golden Kite award, 1983; Christopher award, 1984; American Library Association Newbery Medal, 1984. Lives in Carmel, California. Address: c/o William Morrow Inc., 105 Madison Avenue, New York, New York 10016, U.S.A.

PUBLICATIONS FOR CHILDREN

Fiction

Henry Huggins, illustrated by Louis Darling. New York, Morrow, 1950.
Ellen Tebbits, illustrated by Louis Darling. New York, Morrow, 1951.
Henry and Beezus, illustrated by Louis Darling. New York, Morrow, 1952; London, Hamish Hamilton, 1982.
Otis Spofford, illustrated by Louis Darling. New York, Morrow, 1953.
Henry and Ribsy, illustrated by Louis Darling. New York, Morrow, 1954; London, Hamish Hamilton, 1979.
Beezus and Ramona, illustrated by Louis Darling. New York, Morrow, 1955; London, Hamish Hamilton, 1978.
Fifteen, illustrated by Beth and Joe Krush. New York, Morrow, 1956; London, Penguin, 1962.
Henry and the Paper Route, illustrated by Louis Darling. New York, Morrow, 1957.
The Luckiest Girl. New York, Morrow, 1958.
Jean and Johnny, illustrated by Beth and Joe Krush. New York, Morrow, 1959.
Leave It to Beaver (fictionalization of tv series). New York, Berkley, 1960.
The Real Hole, illustrated by Mary Stevens. New York, Morrow, 1960; London, Collins, 1962.

Two Dog Biscuits, illustrated by Mary Stevens. New York, Morrow, 1961; London, Collins, 1963.
Emily's Runaway Imagination, illustrated by Beth and Joe Krush. New York, Morrow, 1961.
Henry and the Clubhouse, illustrated by Louis Darling. New York, Morrow, 1962; London, Hamish Hamilton, 1981.
Sister of the Bride, illustrated by Beth and Joe Krush. New York, Morrow, 1963.
Ribsy, illustrated by Louis Darling. New York, Morrow, 1964.
The Mouse and the Motorcycle, illustrated by Louis Darling. New York, Morrow, 1965; London, Hamish Hamilton, 1974.
Mitch and Amy, illustrated by George Porter. New York, Morrow, 1967.
Ramona the Pest, illustrated by Louis Darling. New York, Morrow, 1968; London, Hamish Hamilton, 1974.
Runaway Ralph, illustrated by Louis Darling. New York, Morrow, 1970; London, Hamish Hamilton, 1974.
Socks, illustrated by Beatrice Darwin. New York, Morrow, 1973.
Ramona the Brave, illustrated by Alan Tiegreen. New York, Morrow, and London, Hamish Hamilton, 1975.
Ramona and Her Father, illustrated by Alan Tiegreen. New York, Morrow, 1977; London, Hamish Hamilton, 1978.
Ramona and Her Mother, illustrated by Alan Tiegreen. New York, Morrow, and London, Hamish Hamilton, 1979.
Ramona Quimby, Age 8, illustrated by Alan Tiegreen. New York, Morrow, and London, Hamish Hamilton, 1981.
Ralph S. Mouse, illustrated by Paul O. Zelinsky. New York, Morrow, and London, Hamish Hamilton, 1982.
Dear Mr. Henshaw, illustrated by Paul O. Zelinsky. New York, Morrow, and London, MacRae, 1983.
Lucky Chuck, illustrated by J. Winslow Higginbottom. New York, Morrow, and London, MacRae, 1984.
Ramona Forever, illustrated by Alan Tiegreen. New York, Morrow, and London, MacRae, 1984.
Janet's Thingamajigs, illustrated by DyAnne DiSalvo-Ryan. New York, Morrow, 1987.
The Growing-Up Feet, illustrated by DyAnne DiSalvo-Ryan. New York, Morrow, 1987.

Play

The Sausage at the End of the Nose. New York, Children's Book Council, 1974.

Verse

The Hullabaloo ABC, illustrated by Earl Thollander. Berkeley, California, Parnassus Press, 1960.

Other

The Ramona Quimby Diary, illustrated by Alan Tiegreen. New York, Morrow, 1984.
The Beezus and Ramona Diary, illustrated by Alan Tiegreen. New York, Morrow, 1986.
A Girl from Yamhill: A Memoir. New York, Morrow, 1988.

*

Beverly Cleary comments:
As a child I had difficulty learning to read. The discovery, when I was about eight years old, that I could actually read, and read with pleasure, was one of the most exciting moments of my life. From that moment on, as I read through the shelves of the library, I searched for, but was unable to find, the books I wanted to read most of all: books about the sort of children who lived in my neighborhood,

books that would make me laugh. The stories I write are the stories I wanted to read as a child, and the experience I hope to share with children is the discovery that reading is one of the pleasures of life and not just something one must do in school.

*   *   *

As *Henry Huggins* approaches its 40th birthday Beverly Cleary's impact as a children's book writer cannot be overestimated. Her global popularity with four generations of reading children is rivalled only by the critical acclaim her books have garnered. The appeal of Cleary's work can be attributed to her extraordinary talent in creating memorable young characters whose exuberant spirit and zest for life attract young and old readers alike.

Perhaps the most significant statement one can make about Cleary's children's books is that they are read, over and over again, aloud and alone; they are shared by adults and children, and passed from child to child. Her creation of picture books, young adult novels, books about animals, fantasy, and realism attest to her versatility as an author. Reading, the library, and the power of literature are recurring elements in her novels. Humor and clarity characterize her writing style no matter what the genre. Marked by plot-intensive episodes usually recounted in chapter format, her stories revolve around the antics and adventures of engaging characters. Primary attributes of Cleary's characters remain their highly creative play, their dominant ties to neighborhood friends, and a strong sense of community. Still, these characters struggle, not with heavy-handed issues which threaten to consume their naïve lives, but with emotions and concerns familiar to young and intermediate readers. Their universal experiences range from Henry Huggins's challenge to demonstrate his ability to manage a paper route to the often physical and emotionally trying sibling rivalry between Beezus and Ramona Quimby.

Cleary's four picture books stand as the least successful of her work. *The Real Hole* and *The Growing-Up Feet* focus on twins Jimmy and Janet as they investigate the world around them. Told in static, at times forced rhyme, *The Hullabaloo ABC* features nameless twins exploring a farm in the morning. *Lucky Chuck* represents a change both for Cleary and in the expectations of a picture book: uncharacteristically the book focuses on a teenaged boy who must suffer the consequences of his carefree recklessness while riding a motorcycle. The illustrations detail Chuck's motorcycle, its parts, and his loving attention to its maintenance.

Motorcycles also figure prominently in three books about Ralph S. Mouse. *The Mouse and the Motorcycle, Runaway Ralph,* and *Ralph S. Mouse* exemplify Cleary's most successful ventures into fantasy as they trace a mouse's first communication with a human, his acquisition of a motorcycle, his ensuing journey into the dangers away from his family, and his satisfying return home. The worlds of fantasy and realism co-exist; their interaction is governed by clearly prescribed rules which are strictly observed. The combination results in a tantalizing tale of an adventurous mouse.

Without question Beverly Cleary's best known and most loved characters reside on or near Klickitat Street in Portland, Oregon, the bustling neighborhood of Henry Huggins, Ellen Tebbits, Otis Spofford, and the unforgettable Beezus and Ramona Quimby. Above all these children are normal; they genuinely care for their parents and friends and their love is fully returned. They act as real children act. Sometimes they misunderstand or are misunderstood. Readers closely identify with the older children feeling pestered by their younger friends as they simultaneously recognize the younger child's attraction to the stimulating games enjoyed by older counterparts. While some aspects of the wholesome lifestyle Cleary depicts now appear dated, her sensitive, penetrating awareness of individual children and their needs endures. She must be commended for writing about real children faced with difficult circumstances without becoming

fixated on the issues themselves. Published in 1953, *Otis Spofford* depicts one of the first latchkey, single-parent children in children's literature. Yet the story is about Otis, his pleasures and pains, his friends, and his feelings; it is not about his stereotyped problems.

The earlier books shift focus from character to character, developing a community of individual children with unique attributes and interests. With a greater number of books focusing on Henry and his dog Ribsy, Beezus, and Ramona, readers form strong alliances with these three special characters. Of them, Ramona emerges most fully. She makes her first appearance in *Henry Huggins* and immediately threatens to steal the spotlight from well-meaning, reliable Henry. Ramona's spunk, her impermeable but often ambivalent bond to Beezus, and her unsurpassed creativity intrigue and entertain readers. Cleary never cheapens her characters; she never sacrifices Ramona's integrity or intelligence for a laugh. Through Ramona, Cleary touches young readers on an emotional level which engages and challenges, but does not overwhelm. Her ability to sustain their attention over time, from book to book, remains an accomplishment beyond evaluation.

Cleary's novels for young adults, especially adolescent girls, do not possess the timeless qualities of the Ramona and Henry books. *Fifteen, Jean and Johnny,* and *The Luckiest Girl* do not speak to contemporary young adults. Partly thanks to spirited Ramona, 15-year-old girls no longer define themselves solely by their boyfriends or lack of boyfriends. Their future aspirations extend beyond wife and mother to include careers in a range of professions. Despite such limitations these novels are historically interesting as they recall social practices and attitudes less prevalent in contemporary times.

In *Dear Mr. Henshaw* Cleary definitively enters the 1980's. The story opens as Leigh M. Botts writes to his favorite author in fulfillment of a school assignment. The letters gradually move into revealing diary entries as Leigh gains confidence in himself and demonstrates greater writing skill. With tenacity characteristic of Ramona, Leigh struggles with his parents' divorce, his working mother's absence, his father's emotional absence, and adjustment to a new school and town. The atypical shape of the narrative successfully breaks from Cleary's usual form as she stakes out new territory as a writer. Unlike earlier books *Dear Mr. Henshaw* turns not on dramatic episodes but on Leigh's introspection.

If *Dear Mr. Henshaw* reveals Leigh Botts in personal dialogue with himself, *A Girl from Yamhill* represents Cleary's self-contemplation. This candid autobiography traces the author from her early childhood through young adolescence. Cleary deftly portrays herself as an animated, curious, and often misunderstood little girl, a kindred spirit of Ramona. The book reveals the author's ongoing struggle to resolve troublesome issues about her possessive mother and their less-than-perfect relationship. Voracious readers and avid Cleary fans will recognize here familiar sights, sounds, names, and happenings which have been disclosed in stories. As in all her work, Cleary moves readers with humorous but controlled prose emanating from genuine emotion and familiar experience.

—Cathryn M. Mercier

CLEAVER, Vera and Bill. Americans. **CLEAVER, Vera (née Allen):** Born in Virgil, South Dakota, 6 January 1919. Educated at schools in Kennebec, South Dakota, and Perry and Tallahassee, Florida. Married Bill Cleaver in 1945. Freelance accountant, 1945–54; accountant (civilian), United States Air Force, Tachikawa, Japan, 1954–56, and Chaumont, France, 1956–58. Address: c/o Harper Junior Books Group, Harper and Row Publishers, 10 East 53rd Street, New York, New York 10022, U.S.A. **CLEAVER, Bill** (William Joseph Cleaver): Born in Hugo, Oklahoma, 24 March 1920. Educated at schools in Vancouver and Seattle. Served in the United States Army Air Corps, in Italy, 1942–45; United States Air Force, in Japan, 1954–56, and in France, 1956–58. Jeweler and watchmaker, 1950–54. *Died 20 August 1981.* Recipients: Western Writers of America Spur award, 1976.

PUBLICATIONS FOR CHILDREN

Fiction

Ellen Grae, illustrated by Ellen Raskin. Philadelphia, Lippincott, 1967; with *Lady Ellen Grae,* London, Hamish Hamilton, 1973.
Lady Ellen Grae, illustrated by Ellen Raskin. Philadelphia, Lippincott, 1968; with *Ellen Grae,* London, Hamish Hamilton, 1973.
Where the Lilies Bloom, illustrated by Jim Spanfeller. Philadelphia, Lippincott, 1969; London, Hamish Hamilton, 1970.
Grover, illustrated by Frederic Marvin. Philadelphia, Lippincott, 1970; London, Hamish Hamilton, 1971.
The Mimosa Tree. Philadelphia, Lippincott, 1970; London, Oxford University Press, 1977.
The Mock Revolt. Philadelphia, Lippincott, 1971; London, Hamish Hamilton, 1972.
I Would Rather Be a Turnip. Philadelphia, Lippincott, 1971; London, Hamish Hamilton, 1972.
Delpha Green and Company. Philadelphia, Lippincott, 1972; London, Collins, 1975.
Me Too. Philadelphia, Lippincott, 1973; London, Collins, 1975.
The Whys and Wherefores of Littabelle Lee. New York, Atheneum, 1973; London, Hamish Hamilton, 1974.
Dust of the Earth. Philadelphia, Lippincott, 1975; London, Oxford University Press, 1977.
Trial Valley. Philadelphia, Lippincott, and London, Oxford University Press, 1977.
Queen of Hearts. Philadelphia, Lippincott, 1978.
A Little Destiny. New York, Lothrop, 1979.
The Kissimmee Kid. New York, Lothrop, 1981.
Hazel Rye. New York, Lippincott, 1983.

Fiction by Vera Cleaver

Sugar Blue, illustrated by Eric Nones. New York, Lothrop, 1984.
Sweetly Sings the Donkey. New York, Lippincott, 1985.
Moon Lake Angel. New York, Lothrop, 1987.
Belle Pruitt. New York, Lippincott, 1988.

PUBLICATIONS FOR ADULTS by Vera Cleaver

Novel

The Nurse's Dilemma. New York, Bouregy, 1966.

*

Manuscript Collections: Kerlan Collection, University of Minnesota, Minneapolis; University of North Carolina, Chapel Hill.

Vera Cleaver comments:
   To strive for stature, to attempt to offer the unhackneyed, to arouse curiosity and compassion—that is the goal.

*   *   *

Vera and Bill Cleaver were a wife-and-husband writing team for many years until Bill Cleaver's death in 1981. As a partnership they were reluctant to be divided. One of them (carefully not saying which) wrote in 1979: "We are joint and so all of our endeavors and opinions are joint." But it can be assumed that Vera was the principal writing partner; and after her husband's death she continued to produce books of much the same kind and quality as before.

Most of the Cleaver novels show young people—usually girls—grappling with situations that test them to the limit. The Cleaver gallery of idiosyncratic and rather alarming heroines is noteworthy. It begins with Ellen Grae Derryberry in their much acclaimed first novel *Ellen Grae.* Ellen, a highly articulate 11-year-old with a distinctive tone of voice, is a notorious inventor of tall stories; and when she comes into unhappy possession of a dreadful secret and has to disclose it to Authority, Authority refuses to believe her. The book, like life, is both serious and funny and has many acute perceptions of character. Ellen herself dominates it: an imaginative eccentric, cleverly contrasted with the ordinary and complacent Rosemary who shares her room. Ellen reappears in a sequel, *Lady Ellen Grae,* in which she attempts with predictable lack of success to become ladylike.

Ellen Grae is instantly likeable, but this is not true of all the Cleaver heroines. They are fierce and determined; they cope, impressively, with appalling problems; but they don't have much time for radiating sweetness and light. In *Where the Lilies Bloom,* set in well-named Trial Valley in the Appalachian region of the United States, 14-year-old Mary Call Luther finds herself in charge of a family of four, including "cloudy-headed" older sister Devola, when their parents have died. They scrape a precarious living by wildcrafting—harvesting wild buds, roots, leaves, and bark—and Mary Call bullies the others unmercifully, compelling them to work out of doors for long hours in all weathers. They complain, calling her mean and ugly; but, thanks to her, they survive together through a hard winter, and the arrival of spring brings relief and hope. In *Trial Valley,* two years on, Mary Call has another problem: a small abandoned boy who is an extra mouth to feed, an extra responsibility, a painful joy. She wins through again, though not to some improbable happy ending. Her triumph and reward is that life goes on.

Annie Jelks in *I Would Rather Be a Turnip* is a particularly memorable Cleaver heroine. She resents, and behaves unpleasantly to, her sister's illegitimate child, the mild bright eight-year-old Calvin, whose existence provokes small-town censoriousness. Poor, uncomplaining Calvin has a hard time; and when, reluctantly reconciled, Annie bad-temperedly saves his life, she can't bear his gratitude: "Oh, be quiet, Calvin. You get on my nerves. Did I ever tell you that? Well, you do. You get on my nerves." Yet by the end of the book one likes and admires Annie and realizes that her loyalty, if grudging, would be unbounded; this resourceful, awful, splendid child is a true heroine.

The trials of Cleaver heroines are many. Lydia in *Me Too* has a mentally deficient twin sister, Lorna, and in spite of all efforts can do little or nothing to help her; in *The Mimosa Tree* the Proffitt family cannot find a way to survive in a Chicago slum; Littabelle in *The Whys and Wherefores of Littabelle Lee* and Wilma in *Queen of Hearts* find themselves looking after aged grandparents; Evelyn in *The Kissimmee Kid* faces an appalling conflict between her integrity and her loyalty to her family. *Sugar Blue*—Vera Cleaver's first book since the death of her husband—has strong parallels with *I Would Rather Be a Turnip.* Amy Blue is, like Annie Jelks, a reluctant aunt. Neglected by her busy parents she has built a hard, isolating shell around herself. Unaccountably she is loved by the four-year-old niece who comes to stay and who calls her Sugar Blue; and though Ella has to leave and go home it is clear that Amy will find a way out of her prison of self.

Though most of the Cleaver protagonists are girls, there are heroes too; and they likewise have their trials. Grover, the loyal friend of

Ellen Grae, must contend, in the book that bears his name, with his mother's death; Ussy Mock in *The Mock Revolt* is more irritated and imposed upon than suffering, but has to realize that his dreams of escaping from his small-town ambience are no more than dreams.

The Cleaver world is in the main a rural one, and ways of life are down-to-earth. Settings are obviously important, and graphically portrayed, from Ellen Grae's small Florida town of Thicket, "as neat and as beautiful as a rose garden," to the badlands of South Dakota in *Dust of the Earth*, where "the coyotes howl at night in the awful raw stillness." It is in many ways a harsh world. The blows that life delivers to innocent and guilty alike are never dodged or diminished. Battles are sometimes won, sometimes lost; it is never safe to assume that the protagonist will succeed; victory if it comes does not come easily and does not bring glory. Yet the Cleaver books, though demanding, are not depressing. The protagonists are fighters, with strength and endurance, and even when they are defeated the human spirit is unbowed.

—John Rowe Townsend

CLEMENTS, Bruce. American. Born in New York City, 25 November 1931. Educated at Columbia University, New York, A.B. 1954; Union Theological Seminary, New York, B.D. 1956; State University of New York, Albany, M.A. 1962. Married Hanna Kiep in 1954; one son and three daughters. Ordained Minister of the United Church of Christ: pastor in Schenectady, New York, 1957–64; instructor, Union College, Schenectady, 1964–67. Since 1967 member of the Department of English, Eastern Connecticut State College, Willimantic. Address: Department of English, Eastern Connecticut State College, Willimantic, Connecticut 06226, U.S.A.

PUBLICATIONS FOR CHILDREN

Fiction

Two Against the Tide. New York, Farrar Straus, 1967.
The Face of Abraham Candle. New York, Farrar Straus, 1969.
I Tell a Lie Every So Often. New York, Farrar Straus, 1974.
Prison Window, Jerusalem Blue. New York, Farrar Straus, 1977.
Anywhere Else But Here. New York, Farrar Straus, 1980.
Coming About. New York, Farrar Straus, 1984.
The Treasure of Plunderell Manor. New York, Farrar Straus, 1987.

Other

From Ice Set Free: The Story of Otto Kiep. New York, Farrar Straus, 1972.
Coming Home to a Place You've Never Been Before, with Hanna Clements. New York, Farrar Straus, 1975.

* * *

Bruce Clements's concern with moral order (he is an ordained minister) and his interest in teaching come through very clearly in his writings for young persons. Both his fiction and non-fiction strongly emphasize man's responsibility to his fellow man, society's need to support other societies. His writing style is crisp and clear; in a few words and phrases Clements conjures up vivid images of people and places and times in conflict.

His novel *The Face of Abraham Candle* is set in the Colorado of silver-mining days and focuses upon a young adolescent, suddenly orphaned, restless for adventure, who explores the caves of Mesa Verde in search of Indian relics. *Prison Window, Jerusalem Blue* focuses on a 9th-century English girl and her brother who are captured by Viking sailors and carried away to Denmark to become slaves. *Coming About,* set in the present, is a story of a young adolescent who is a loner and a mechanical genius, who thinks a lot about war and peace. To most of his peers he is "weird," but to one who becomes his friend he is a complex individual trying to find, amidst good and evil, a meaningful place in his world.

Among the works of non-fiction, *From Ice Set Free* is a biography of Clements's father-in-law, a German raised in Scotland who was hanged by the Nazis in Berlin in 1944 as a resister to their regime. *Coming Home to a Place You've Never Been Before* is a documentary account of 24 hours in a halfway house for ex-junkies and ex-drug pushers.

Each of Clements's books shows considerable research; the backgrounds are detailed and complex. But more, the books show an understanding of persons living out their lives within the boundary of special cultures, with their own needs and goals placed in juxtaposition to group demands and limitations. Clements is not easy reading, but he is worth the effort. His stories are powerful, with strong characters facing basic human choices.

—Mary Lystad

CLEWES, Dorothy (Mary, née Parkin). British. Born in Nottingham, 6 July 1907. Educated privately in Nottingham; at University of Nottingham. Married Winston David Armstrong Clewes in 1932 (died 1957). Secretary and physician's dispenser, Nottingham, 1924–32. Agent: Curtis Brown, 162–168 Regent Street, London WIR 5TB. Address: Soleig, Kings Ride, Alfriston, Sussex BN26 5XP, England.

PUBLICATIONS FOR CHILDREN

Fiction

The Rivals of Maidenhurst. London, Nelson, 1925.
The Cottage [Stream, Treasure, Fair] in the Wild Wood, illustrated by Irene Hawkins. London, Faber, 4 vols. 1945–49.
The Wild Wood (includes *The Cottage in the Wild Wood* and *The Stream in the Wild Wood*), illustrated by Irene Hawkins. New York, Coward McCann, 1948.
Henry Hare's Boxing Match, illustrated by Patricia W. Turner. London, Chatto and Windus, and New York, Coward McCann, 1950.
Henry Hare's Earthquake, illustrated by Patricia W. Turner. London, Chatto and Windus, 1950; New York, Coward McCann, 1951.
Henry Hare, Painter and Decorator, illustrated by Patricia W. Turner. London, Chatto and Windus, 1951.
Henry Hare and the Kidnapping of Selina Squirrel, illustrated by Patricia W. Turner. London, Chatto and Windus, 1951.
The Adventure of the Scarlet Daffodil, illustrated by R.G. Campbell. London, Chatto and Windus, 1952; as *The Mystery of the Scarlet Daffodil,* New York, Coward McCann, 1953.
The Mystery of the Blue Admiral, illustrated by J. Marianne Moll. New York, Coward McCann, 1954; London, Collins, 1955.
The Secret, illustrated by Peggy Beetles. London, Hamish Hamilton, and New York, Coward McCann, 1956.
The Runaway, illustrated by Peggy Beetles. London, Hamish Hamilton, and New York, Coward McCann, 1957.

Adventure on Rainbow Island, illustrated by Shirley Hughes. London, Collins, 1957; as *Mystery on Rainbow Island,* New York, Coward McCann, 1957.

The Jade Green Cadillac, illustrated by Shirley Hughes. London, Collins, 1958; as *The Mystery of the Jade-Green Cadillac,* New York, Coward McCann, 1958.

The Happiest Day, illustrated by Peggy Beetles. London, Hamish Hamilton, 1958; New York, Coward McCann, 1959.

The Old Pony, illustrated by Peggy Beetles. London, Hamish Hamilton, 1959; New York, Coward McCann, 1960.

Hide and Seek, illustrated by Peggy Beetles. London, Hamish Hamilton, 1959; New York, Coward McCann, 1960.

The Lost Tower Treasure, illustrated by Shirley Hughes. London, Collins, 1960; as *The Mystery of the Lost Tower Treasure,* New York, Coward McCann, 1960.

The Hidden Key, illustrated by Peggy Beetles. London, Hamish Hamilton, 1960; New York, Coward McCann, 1961.

The Singing Strings, illustrated by Shirley Hughes. London, Collins, 1961; as *Mystery of the Singing Strings,* New York, Coward McCann, 1961.

All the Fun of the Fair, illustrated by Juliette Palmer. London, Hamish Hamilton, 1961; New York, Coward McCann, 1962.

Wilberforce and the Slaves, illustrated by Peter Edwards. London, Hutchinson, 1961.

Skyraker and the Iron Imp, illustrated by Peter Edwards. London, Hutchinson, 1962.

The Purple Mountain, illustrated by Robert Broomfield. London, Collins, 1962; as *The Golden Eagle,* New York, Coward McCann, 1962.

The Birthday, illustrated by Juliette Palmer. London, Hamish Hamilton, 1962; New York, Coward McCann, 1963.

The Branch Line, illustrated by Juliette Palmer. London, Hamish Hamilton, and New York, Coward McCann, 1963.

Operation Smuggle, illustrated by Shirley Hughes. London, Collins, 1964; as *The Mystery of the Midnight Smugglers,* New York, Coward McCann, 1964.

Boys and Girls Come Out to Play, illustrated by Jane Paton. London, Hamish Hamilton, 1964.

The Holiday, illustrated by Janet Duchesne. London, Hamish Hamilton, and New York, Coward McCann, 1964.

Guide Dog, illustrated by Peter Burchard. London, Hamish Hamilton, and New York, Coward McCann, 1965; as *Dog for the Dark,* London, White Lion, 1974.

Red Ranger and the Combine Harvester, illustrated by Peter Edwards. London, Hutchinson, 1966.

Roller Skates, Skooter and Bike, illustrated by Constance Marshall. London, Hamish Hamilton, and New York, Coward McCann, 1966.

A Boy like Walt. London, Collins, and New York, Coward McCann, 1967.

A Bit of Magic, illustrated by Robert Hales. London, Hamish Hamilton, 1967.

A Girl like Cathy. London, Collins, 1968.

Adopted Daughter. New York, Coward McCann, 1968.

Upsidedown [*Special Branch, Fire-Brigade*] *Willie,* illustrated by Edward Ardizzone. London, Hamish Hamilton, 3 vols., 1968–70.

Peter and the Jumbie, illustrated by Robert Hales. London, Hamish Hamilton, 1969.

Library Lady, illustrated by Robert Hales. London, Chatto Boyd and Oliver, 1970; as *The Library,* New York, Coward McCann, 1971.

Two Bad Boys, illustrated by Lynette Hemmant. London, Hamish Hamilton, 1971.

The End of Summer. New York, Coward McCann, 1971.

Storm over Innish. London, Heinemann, 1972; Nashville, Nelson, 1973.

A Skein of Geese, illustrated by Janet Duchesne. London, Chatto Boyd and Oliver, 1972.

Ginny's Boy. London, Heinemann, 1973.

Hooray for Me, illustrated by Michael Jackson. London, Heinemann, 1973.

Wanted—A Grand, illustrated by Robert Micklewright. London, Chatto and Windus, 1974.

Missing from Home. London, Heinemann, 1975; New York, Harcourt Brace, 1978.

Nothing to Declare. London, Heinemann, 1976.

The Testing Year. London, Heinemann, 1977.

Other

The Brown Burrows Books, illustrated by Patricia W. Turner. London, Chatto and Windus, 4 vols., 1950–51.

Guide Dogs for the Blind. London, Hamish Hamilton, 1966.

Editor, *The Secret of the Sea: An Anthology of Underwater Exploration and Adventure,* illustrated by Jeroo Roy. London, Heinemann, 1973.

PUBLICATIONS FOR ADULTS

Novels

She Married a Doctor. London, Jenkins, 1943; as *Stormy Hearts,* New York, Arcadia House, 1944.

Shepherd's Hill. London, Sampson Low, 1945.

To Man Alone. London, Jenkins, and New York, Arcadia House, 1945.

A Stranger in the Valley. London, Harrap, 1948.

The Blossom on the Bough. London, Harrap, 1949.

Summer Cloud. London, Harrap, 1951.

Merry-Go-Round. London, Hodder and Stoughton, 1954.

I Came to a Wood. London, Hale, 1956.

* * *

Dorothy Clewes writes for a variety of ages. Her work for younger children, the stories of preschool Willie, or Penny and her friends, are undemanding tales in everyday settings, with children who get up to amusing little naughtiness. In another series the Hadley children, who seem to enjoy eternal summer holidays, spend them in detecting crimes; it is important to score off the adult world. The trouble with these stories is that the characters are not sufficiently well drawn or interesting enough to get the reader "hooked" on the series, and anyone finding them safe, comfortable reading would quickly find his palate cloying. It is a case of "read one, you've read them all."

Her books for teenagers are rather more successful, apart from the everpresent premise that problem teenagers will be helped by reading about fictional characters with the same problems. That sort of child does not read that sort of book. *Nothing to Declare* tells of Dave, not very bright at school, who takes on a cross-channel driving job. He quickly realises that it involves smuggling, and starts to worry not just about getting caught but about the moral aspects of his actions. He has to choose between the easy money and his conscience, complicated by the fact that other people do not seem to think it is wrong. *Ginny's Boy* is a story of young love, though Ginny tries to blind herself to the fact that her boyfriend is irresponsible and selfish, and that the love is mostly on her side. *Storm over Innish* is her most successful book. Her heroine Letty, a highly imaginative girl who escapes into a secret world of writing, loses her brother in a boating accident. A few years later a boy of the same age is washed up unconscious on the same beach, suffering from amnesia. Letty looks after him and tries to help him recover his identity, fearing all the while that when he does so she will lose him. It is not quite a love story but very nearly so, a tentative reaching-out into uncharted waters.

In some ways it is difficult to make a satisfying meal out of Clewes's books. Perhaps it is because she tries so hard to help us to identify and emphathise with the protagonists that other figures in her stories, particularly the adults, become stereotypes. Children prefer adults to be real and recognisable; maybe it would be better for Clewes to use Arthur Ransome as a model and keep them out of the way.

—Ann G. Hay

CLIFFORD, Martin.   See RICHARDS, Frank.

CLIFTON, (Thelma) Lucille (née Sayles).   American.   Born in Depew, New York, 27 June 1936. Educated at Howard University, Washington, D.C., 1953–55; Fredonia State Teachers College, New York, 1955. Married Fred J. Clifton in 1958; four daughters and two sons. Claims clerk, New York State Division of Employment, Buffalo, 1958–60; literature assistant, U.S. Office of Education, Washington, D.C., 1969–71. Visiting writer, Columbia University School of the Arts; poet-in-residence, Coppin State College, Baltimore, 1972–76; visiting writer, George Washington University, Washington, D.C., 1982–83. Recipient: YM-YWHA Poetry Center Discovery award, 1969; National Endowment for the Arts grant, 1970, 1972; Juniper prize, 1980; American Library Association Coretta Scott King award, 1984. Agent: Marilyn Marlow, Curtis Brown, 10 Astor Place, New York, New York 10003, U.S.A.

PUBLICATIONS FOR CHILDREN

Fiction

All Us Come Cross the Water, illustrated by John Steptoe. New York, Holt Rinehart, 1973.
Don't You Remember?, illustrated by Evaline Ness. New York, Dutton, 1973.
The Boy Who Didn't Believe in Spring, illustrated by Brinton Turkle. New York, Dutton, 1973.
The Times They Used to Be, illustrated by Susan Jeschke. New York, Holt Rinehart, 1974.
My Brother Fine with Me, illustrated by Moneta Barnett. New York, Holt Rinehart, 1975.
Three Wishes, illustrated by Stephanie Douglas. New York, Viking Press, 1976.
Amifika, illustrated by Thomas di Grazia. New York, Dutton, 1977.
The Lucky Stone, illustrated by Dale Payson. New York, Delacorte Press, 1979.
My Friend Jacob, illustrated by Thomas di Grazia. New York, Dutton, 1980.
Sonora Beautiful, illustrated by Michael Garland. New York, Dutton, 1981.

Verse

Some of the Days of Everett Anderson, illustrated by Evaline Ness. New York, Holt Rinehart, 1970.

Everett Anderson's Christmas Coming, illustrated by Evaline Ness. New York, Holt Rinehart, 1971.
Good, Says Jerome, illustrated by Stephanie Douglas. New York, Dutton, 1973.
Everett Anderson's Year, illustrated by Ann Grifalconi. New York, Holt Rinehart, 1974.
Everett Anderson's Friend, illustrated by Ann Grifalconi. New York, Holt Rinehart, 1976.
Everett Anderson's 1—2—3, illustrated by Ann Grifalconi. New York, Holt Rinehart, 1977.
Everett Anderson's Nine Month Long, illustrated by Ann Grifalconi. New York, Holt Rinehart, 1978.
Everett Anderson's Goodbye, illustrated by Ann Grifalconi. New York, Holt Rinehart, 1983.

Other

The Black BC's, illustrated by Don Miller. New York, Dutton, 1970.

PUBLICATIONS FOR ADULTS

Novel

Generations of Americans: A Memoir. New York, Random House, 1976.

Verse

Good Times. New York, Random House, 1969.
Good News about the Earth. New York, Random House, 1972.
An Ordinary Woman. New York, Random House, 1974.
Two-Headed Woman. Amherst, University of Massachusetts Press, 1980.

*   *   *

Lucille Clifton writes both poetry and prose for children. In her six picture books about Everett Anderson, which have won steady acclaim, she has developed a free-flowing poetic style in which she tells us a good deal about this little black boy in just a few rhythmical lines. We first know him when he is six and missing his Daddy, who has gone away; we learn that he lives alone with his Mama; we see him make a new friend; and we feel with him when Mr. Tom Perry enters the scene and eventually marries his Mama; and yes—along comes a new baby. Readers are no doubt hoping to find out what will happen next to this little boy who is now like a real person to them.

Six other picture books, suitable for preschoolers up to about age seven, tell their stories not in poetry but in colorful, easy-spoken words that often reflect the language of the black children Clifton knows. For instance, from *All Us Come Cross the Water:* "I got this teacher name Miss Wills. This day she come asking everybody to tell where they people come from."

These six picture books, all about black children, include the above-named and *Amifika, Don't You Remember?, Good, Says Jerome, My Brother Fine with Me,* and *The Boy Who Didn't Believe in Spring.* The stories are about some of the things that concern and puzzle children—their feelings about themselves and their relationships with parents and brothers and sisters. All are eye-catching books, illustrated by well-known artists in either soft black and white or in bright colors.

For children a little older, there are two other picture books, both about friendship, *Three Wishes* and *My Friend Jacob.* The latter book is unusual in that it deals with a highly valued friendship between an 8-year-old black boy and his neighbor, a 17-year-old white boy who is in some ways retarded, but can be helped to learn.

Three more books, for still older children, are abundantly illustrated but are not in picture-book format. In *The Times They Used to Be* Mama tells, in a prose poem, about happenings way back in 1948. In *The Lucky Stone* a great-grandmother weaves four stories around a little black stone that brought luck to its owners, from slave times up to the present. *The Black BC's* also gives a glimpse of black history. The letters of the alphabet are used to introduce discussions, in prose and poetry, of the contributions of black men and women to American life.

Also for older children is *Sonora Beautiful,* published as a "Skinny Book"—that is, a short, easily read book to interest children of junior or senior high age. The story's 22 pages, including 10 full-page illustrations, give the reader an intriguing glimpse of a teenage white girl who is struggling to feel good about herself and her individualistic family.

—Claudia Lewis

CLYMER, Eleanor (née Lowenton). Also writes as Janet Bell; Elizabeth Kinsey. American. Born in New York City, 7 January 1906. Educated at Barnard College, New York, 1923–25; University of Wisconsin, Madison, B.A. 1927; New York University; Bank Street College of Education, New York. Married Kinsey Clymer in 1933; one son. Teacher in camps and nursery schools. Worked for Dodd Mead, publishers, 1928–32. Recipient: Child Study Association of America award, 1975. Address: 11 Nightingale Road, Katonah, New York 10536, U.S.A.

PUBLICATIONS FOR CHILDREN

Fiction

A Yard for John, illustrated by Mildred Boyle. New York, McBride, 1943.
Here Comes Pete, illustrated by Mildred Boyle. New York, McBride, 1944.
The Grocery Mouse, illustrated by Jeanne Bendick. New York, McBride, 1945.
Little Bear Island, illustrated by Ursula Koering. New York, McBride, 1945.
Sunday in the Park (as Janet Bell), illustrated by Aline Appel. New York, McBride, 1946.
Monday–Tuesday–Wednesday Book (as Janet Bell), illustrated by Mary Stevens. New York, McBride, 1946.
The Country Kittens, illustrated by Jeanne Bendick. New York, McBride, 1947.
The Trolley Car Family, illustrated by Ursula Koering. New York, McKay, 1947.
The Latch Key Club, illustrated by Corinne Dillon. New York, McKay, 1949.
Treasure at First Base, illustrated by Jean MacDonald Porter. New York, Dodd Mead, 1950.
Tommy's Wonderful Airplane, illustrated by Kurt Wiese. New York, Dodd Mead, 1951.
Thirty-Three Bunn Street, illustrated by Jane Miller. New York, Dodd Mead, 1952.
Chester, illustrated by Ezra Jack Keats. New York, Dodd Mead, 1954.
Not Too Small after All, illustrated by Tom O'Sullivan. New York, Watts, 1955.

Sociable Toby, illustrated by Ingrid Fetz. New York, Watts, 1956.
Mr. Piper's Bus, illustrated by Kurt Wiese. New York, Dodd Mead, 1961.
Benjamin in the Woods. New York, Wonder Books, 1962.
Now That You Are Seven, illustrated by Ingrid Fetz. New York, Association Press, 1963.
Harry, The Wild West Horse, illustrated by Leonard Shortall. New York, Atheneum, 1963; London, Hamish Hamilton, 1964.
The Tiny Little House, illustrated by Ingrid Fetz. New York, Atheneum, 1964.
Chipmunk in the Forest, illustrated by Ingrid Fetz. New York, Atheneum, 1965.
The Adventure of Walter, illustrated by Ingrid Fetz. New York, Atheneum, 1965.
My Brother Stevie. New York, Holt Rinehart, 1967.
The Big Pile of Dirt, illustrated by Robert Shore. New York, Holt Rinehart, 1968.
Horatio, illustrated by Robert Quackenbush. New York, Atheneum, 1968.
Belinda's New Spring Hat, illustrated by Gioia Fiammenghi. New York, Watts, 1969.
We Lived in the Almont, illustrated by David Stone. New York, Dutton, 1970.
The House on the Mountain, illustrated by Leo Carty. New York, Dutton, 1971.
The Spider, The Cave, and the Pottery Bowl, illustrated by Ingrid Fetz. New York, Atheneum, 1971.
Me and the Eggman, illustrated by David Stone. New York, Dutton, 1972.
How I Went Shopping and What I Got, illustrated by Trina Schart Hyman. New York, Holt Rinehart, 1972.
Santiago's Silver Mine, illustrated by Ingrid Fetz. New York, Atheneum, 1973.
Luke Was There, illustrated by Diane de Groat. New York, Holt Rinehart, 1973.
Leave Horatio Alone, illustrated by Robert Quackenbush. New York, Atheneum, 1974.
Take Tarts as Tarts Is Passing, illustrated by Roy Doty. New York, Dutton, 1974.
Engine Number Seven, illustrated by Robert Quackenbush. New York, Holt Rinehart, 1975.
Hamburgers—And Ice Cream for Dessert, illustrated by Roy Doty. New York, Dutton, 1975.
Horatio's Birthday, illustrated by Robert Quackenbush. New York, Atheneum, 1976.
Horatio Goes to the Country, illustrated by Robert Quackenbush. New York, Atheneum, 1978.
The Get-Away Car. New York, Dutton 1978.
Horatio Solves a Mystery, illustrated by Robert Quackenbush. New York, Atheneum, 1980.
A Search for Two Bad Mice, illustrated by Margery Gill. New York, Atheneum, 1980.
My Mother Is the Smartest Woman in the World, illustrated by Nancy Kincade. New York, Atheneum, 1982.
The Horse in the Attic, illustrated by Ted Lewin. Scarsdale, New York, Bradbury Press, 1983.

Fiction as Elizabeth Kinsey

Teddy, illustrated by Jeanne Bendick. New York, McBride, 1945.
Patch, illustrated by James Davis. New York, McBride, 1946.
Sea View Secret, illustrated by Mary Stevens. New York, Watts, 1952.
Donny and Company, illustrated by Mary Stevens. New York, Watts, 1953.
This Cat Came to Stay!, illustrated by Don Sibley. New York,

Watts, 1955.

Other

Make Way for Water, illustrated by J.C. Wonsetler. New York, Messner, 1953.
Modern American Career Women, with Lillian Erlich. New York, Dodd Mead, 1959.
The Case of the Missing Link, illustrated by Robert Macguire. New York, Basic Books, 1962; revised edition, 1968.
Search for a Living Fossil: The Story of the Coelacanth, illustrated by Joan Berg. New York, Holt Rinehart, 1963; London, Lutterworth Press, 1965.
Communities at Work. Boston, Heath, 1964; revised edition, 1969.
Wheels, illustrated by Charles Goslin. New York, Holt Rinehart, 1965.
The Second Greatest Invention: Search for the First Farmers, illustrated by Lili Réthi. New York, Holt Rinehart, 1969.

PUBLICATIONS FOR ADULTS

Other

Management in the Home, with Lillian Gilbreth. New York, Dodd Mead, 1954.

*

Manuscript Collections: Kerlan Collection, University of Minnesota, Minneapolis; de Grummond Collection, University of Southern Mississippi, Hattiesburg.

Eleanor Clymer comments:

I began writing for children under the guidance of Lucy Sprague Mitchell, who is not so well remembered now, but in the 1930's revolutionized children's literature with her "Here and Now" realistic approach. My first books were based on the everyday familiar world of my young son and his friends. As they grew older I wrote stories about their interests: baseball, airplanes, exploring, photography, pets. I also wrote about the history of science, an earlier interest of mine. In the 1950's and 1960's, however, the world was changing. My child was grown up, but there were other children to write for. I wanted to say something about the emotions and problems of children dealing with a sometimes hostile world. In *My Brother Stevie* I tried to tell what a child of the "inner city" might have said in talking about her own life. I tried to write simply enough not to put off older children who might not be facile readers but who had already had difficult life experience. I had moved from the city to a small country village, but that was the first of a number of books about the city I had known well. After traveling in the Southwest and Mexico I became interested in the life of present-day Native Americans and wrote *The Spider, The Cave and the Pottery Bowl* and *Santiago's Silver Mine.* More recently I have been writing about life in a small town. *My Mother Is the Smartest Woman in the World* is about small-town politics and how much women are needed to participate in them. *The Get-Away Car* is based partly on the village where I live. *The Horse in the Attic* is a mystery story but its central theme is that of a loving family.

It has been a long road. I have several more books which I hope to write in the time remaining.

*   *   *

Eleanor Clymer has written 50 books for children, enough surely to earn her the label of a prolific writer. But there are other writers

who turn out books regularly; the difference is that Clymer is an *excellent* as well as a prolific writer of children's books. She exhibits the same fine literary quality in a non-fiction book such as *Search for a Living Fossil: The Story of the Coelacanth* as she does in her renowned works of fiction such as *My Brother Stevie, The House on the Mountain,* and *Luke Was There.*

Clymer writes both for the picture book crowd, young readers, and older readers from 10 up. While *My Brother Stevie* and *Luke Was There* may be catalogued for an audience of 9 to 11, adults will be as deeply moved as children by these books. Both books throw doubt on the claim that only ethnic writers can know the ethnic experience, for one of these stories is from the viewpoint of a young black girl, the other from that of a young black boy. And in both tales, the reader intensely identifies with the characters. Clymer doesn't let the environment and life style of the protagonists occupy the foreground. She is unsparing in her depiction of the problems facing the children, of the less-than-ideal treatment they receive both from their situations and from the people surrounding them. In her books, the facts of reality must be accepted; what is important to the reader is how the children cope with them. In the coping, they reveal to us some important truths about ourselves. Clymer never *tells* us; the characters and their actions *show* us. When we see Stevie's negative responses to his grandmother's punishing attitudes, and his loving response to his understanding teacher, we learn something about helping human needs. In *Luke Was There* we live in the skin of an institutionalized child and feel in our bones his despair and anger as adults betray his trust again and again. After experiencing these books (and *The House on the Mountain*), we can never again view ghetto children as before; we have walked in their shoes. These three books alone place Clymer in the foremost rank of children's writers.

Clymer's style is deceptively simple; but it is the simplicity that results from the painstaking paring away of superfluous or extraneous words and thoughts. Her characters' speech seems to be their natural speech; in actuality, it is Clymer's skill in subtly deleting all but the important prose yet retaining the flavor and rhythm of natural speech that allows us to understand the needs and personalities of the characters. For instance, these two lines from *The House on the Mountain:* "I tell Gloria, 'Why don't you watch the kids?' She says, 'Why don't you leave me alone?'" Here we glimpse the concern of the 10-year-old "I" who is relating the story, and his teenage sister's indifference—in just seventeen words!

Clymer's recent books about Horatio the cat, for younger children, are much more amusing and lighter in theme. Parents who are inveigled into reading them aloud will chuckle in recognition of the "characteristic cat" that is Horace. Only an appreciative watcher of cats could so unerringly portray Horace in all his set ways! Clymer must have as much fun in creating these adventures as children will in listening to them.

—Betty Boegehold

————

COATSWORTH, Elizabeth (Jane). American. Born in Buffalo, New York, 31 May 1893. Educated at Park Street School, 1899–1907; Los Robles School, Pasadena, California, 1907–09; Buffalo Seminary, 1909–11; Vassar College, Poughkeepsie, New York, B.A. 1915 (Phi Beta Kappa); Columbia University, New York, M.A. 1916; Radcliffe College, Cambridge, Massachusetts. Married the writer Henry Beston in 1929 (died 1968); two daughters. Recipient: American Library Association Newbery Medal, 1931; New England Poetry Club Golden Rose, 1967; University of Minnesota Kerlan award, 1975. Litt.D.: University of Maine, Orono, 1955; L.H.D.: New England College, Henniker, New Hampshire,

1958. *Died 2 September 1986.*

PUBLICATIONS FOR CHILDREN

Fiction

The Cat and the Captain, illustrated by Gertrude Kaye. New York, Macmillan, 1927.

Toutou in Bondage, illustrated by Thomas Handforth. New York, Macmillan, 1929.

The Boy with the Parrot, illustrated by Wilfred Bronson. New York, Macmillan, 1930.

The Cat Who Went to Heaven, illustrated by Lynd Ward. New York, Macmillan, 1930; London, Dent, 1949.

Knock at the Door, illustrated by F.D. Bedford. New York, Macmillan, 1931.

Cricket and the Emperor's Son, illustrated by Weda Yap. New York, Macmillan, 1932; revised edition, Kingswood, Surrey, World's Work, 1962.

Away Goes Sally, illustrated by Helen Sewell. New York, Macmillan, 1934; London, Woodfield, 1955.

The Golden Horseshoe, illustrated by Robert Lawson. New York, Macmillan, 1935; revised edition, as *Tamar's Wager,* London, Blackie, 1971.

Sword of the Wilderness, illustrated by Harve Stein. New York, Macmillan, 1936; London, Blackie, 1972.

Alice-All-by-Herself, illustrated by Marguerite de Angeli. New York, Macmillan, 1937; London, Harrap, 1938.

Dancing Tom, illustrated by Grace Paull. New York, Macmillan, 1938; London, Combridge, 1939.

Five Bushel Farm, illustrated by Helen Sewell. New York, Macmillan, 1939; London, Woodfield, 1958.

The Littlest House, illustrated by Marguerite Davis. New York, Macmillan, 1940; Kingswood, Surrey, World's Work, 1958.

The Fair American, illustrated by Helen Sewell. New York, Macmillan, 1940; London, Blackie, 1970.

A Toast to the King, illustrated by Forrest Orr. New York, Coward McCann, 1940; London, Dent, 1941.

Tonio and the Stranger, illustrated by Wilfred Bronson. New York, Grosset and Dunlap, 1941.

You Shall Have a Carriage, illustrated by Henry Pitz. New York, Macmillan, 1941.

Forgotten Island, illustrated by Grace Paull. New York, Grosset and Dunlap, 1942.

Houseboat Summer, illustrated by Marguerite Davis. New York, Macmillan, 1942.

The White Horse, illustrated by Helen Sewell. New York, Macmillan, 1942; as *The White Horse of Morocco,* London, Blackie, 1973.

Thief Island, illustrated by John Wonsetler. New York, Macmillan, 1943; Kingswood, Surrey, World's Work, 1960.

Twelve Months Make a Year, illustrated by Marguerite Davis. New York, Macmillan, 1943.

The Big Green Umbrella, illustrated by Helen Sewell. New York, Grosset and Dunlap, 1944.

Trudy and the Tree House, illustrated by Marguerite Davis. New York, Macmillan, 1944.

The Kitten Stand, illustrated by Kathleen Keeler. New York, Grosset and Dunlap, 1945.

The Wonderful Day, illustrated by Helen Sewell. New York, Macmillan, 1946; London, Blackie, 1973.

Plum Daffy Adventure, illustrated by Marguerite Davis. New York, Macmillan, 1947; Kingswood, Surrey, World's Work, 1965.

Up Hill and Down: Stories, illustrated by James Davis. New York, Knopf, 1947.

The House of the Swan, illustrated by Kathleen Voute. New York, Macmillan, 1948; Kingswood, Surrey, World's Work, 1959.

The Little Haymakers, illustrated by Grace Paull. New York, Macmillan, 1949.

The Captain's Daughter, illustrated by Ralph Ray. New York, Macmillan, 1950; London, Collier Macmillan, 1963.

American Adventures 1620–1945, illustrated by Robert Frankenburg. New York, Macmillan, 1968.
  First Adventure, illustrated by Ralph Ray. New York, Macmillan, 1950.
  The Wishing Pear, illustrated by Ralph Ray. New York, Macmillan, 1951.
  Boston Bells, illustrated by Manning Lee. New York, Macmillan, 1952.
  Aunt Flora, illustrated by Manning Lee. New York, Macmillan, 1953.
  Old Whirlwind: A Story of Davy Crockett, illustrated by Manning Lee. New York, Macmillan, 1953.
  The Sod House, illustrated by Manning Lee. New York, Macmillan, 1954.
  Cherry Ann and the Dragon Horse, illustrated by Manning Lee. New York, Macmillan, 1955.

Door to the North, illustrated by Frederick Chapman. Philadelphia, Winston, 1950; Kingswood, Surrey, World's Work, 1960.

Dollar for Luck, illustrated by George and Doris Hauman. New York, Macmillan, 1951; as *The Sailing Hatrack,* London, Blackie, 1972.

The Last Fort, illustrated by Edward Shenton. Philadelphia, Winston, 1952; London, Hamish Hamilton, 1953.

Cat Stories, illustrated by Feodor Rojankovsky. New York, Simon and Schuster, 1953; London, Publicity Products, 1955.

Dog Stories, illustrated by Feodor Rojankovsky. New York, Simon and Schuster, 1953; London, Publicity Products, 1954.

Horse Stories, with Kate Barnes, illustrated by Feodor Rojankovsky. New York, Simon and Schuster, 1954.

Hide and Seek, illustrated by Genevieve Vaughan-Jackson. New York, Pantheon, 1956.

The Peddler's Cart, illustrated by Zhenya Gay. New York, Macmillan, 1956; as *The Pedlar's Cart,* London, Blackie, 1971.

The Dog from Nowhere, illustrated by Don Sibley. Evanston, Illinois, Row Peterson, 1958.

Down Tumbledown Mountain, illustrated by Aldren Watson. Evanston, Illinois, Row Peterson, 1958.

The Cave, illustrated by Allan Houser. New York, Viking Press, 1958; as *Cave of Ghosts,* London, Hamish Hamilton, 1971.

You Say You Saw a Camel!, illustrated by Brinton Turkle. Evanston, Illinois, Row Peterson, 1958.

Pika and the Roses, illustrated by Kurt Wiese. New York, Pantheon, 1959.

Desert Dan, illustrated by Harper Johnson. New York, Viking Press, 1960; London, Harrap, 1963.

Lonely Maria, illustrated by Evaline Ness. New York, Pantheon, 1960; London, Hamish Hamilton, 1967.

The Noble Doll, illustrated by Leo Politi. New York, Viking Press, 1961.

Ronnie and the Chief's Son, illustrated by Stefan Martin. New York and London, Macmillan, 1962.

Jock's Island, illustrated by Lilian Obligado. New York, Viking Press, 1963; London, Angus and Robertson, 1965.

Jon the Unlucky, illustrated by Esta Nesbitt. New York, Holt Rinehart, 1964; Chalfont St. Giles, Buckinghamshire, Sadler, 1968.

The Secret, illustrated by Don Bolognese. New York, Macmillan, 1965; Kingswood, Surrey, World's Work, 1967.

The Hand of Apollo, illustrated by Robin Jacques. New York, Viking Press, 1965; Kingswood, Surrey, World's Work, 1967.

The Place, illustrated by Marjorie Auerbach. New York, Holt Rinehart, 1966.

The Fox Friend, illustrated by John Hamberger. New York, Macmillan, 1966.

Chimney Farm Bedtime Stories, with Henry Beston, illustrated by Maurice Day. New York, Holt Rinehart, 1966.

Bess and the Sphinx (includes verse), illustrated by Bernice Loewenstein. New York, Macmillan, 1967; London, Blackie, 1974.

Troll Weather, illustrated by Ursula Arndt. New York, Macmillan, 1967; Kingswood, Surrey, World's Work, 1968.

The Ox-Team, illustrated by Peter Warner. London, Hamish Hamilton, 1967.

Bob Bodden and the Good Ship "Rover," illustrated by Ted Schroeder. Champaign, Illinois, Garrard, 1968; London, Watts, 1972.

The Lucky Ones: Five Journeys Toward a Home, illustrated by Janet Doyle. New York, Macmillan, 1968.

Lighthouse Island, illustrated by Symeon Shimin. New York, Norton, 1968.

George and Red, illustrated by Paul Giovanopoulos. New York, Macmillan, 1969.

They Walk in the Night, illustrated by Stefan Martin. New York, Norton, 1969.

Indian Mound Farm, illustrated by Fermin Rocker. New York, Macmillan, and London, Collier Macmillan, 1969.

Grandmother Cat and the Hermit, illustrated by Irving Boker. New York, Macmillan, 1970.

Bob Bodden and the Seagoing Farm, illustrated by Frank Aloise. Champaign, Illinois, Garrard, 1970; London, Watts, 1972.

The Snow Parlor and Other Bedtime Stories, illustrated by Charles Robinson. New York, Grosset and Dunlap, 1971.

Under the Green Willow, illustrated by Janina Domanska. New York, Macmillan, 1971.

Good Night, illustrated by Jose Aruego. New York, Macmillan, 1972.

The Wanderers, illustrated by Trina Schart Hyman. New York, Four Winds Press, 1972.

Daisy, illustrated by Judith Gwyn Brown. New York, Macmillan, 1973.

Pure Magic, illustrated by Ingrid Fetz. New York, Macmillan, 1973; as *The Were-fox,* New York, Collier, 1975; as *The Fox Boy,* London, Blackie, 1975.

All-of-a-Sudden Susan, illustrated by Richard Cuffari. New York, Macmillan, 1974.

Marra's World, illustrated by Krystyna Turska. New York, Greenwillow, 1975.

Verse

Night and the Cat, illustrated by Foujita. New York, Macmillan, 1950.

Mouse Chorus, illustrated by Genevieve Vaughan-Jackson. New York, Pantheon, 1955.

The Peaceable Kingdom and Other Poems, illustrated by Fritz Eichenberg. New York, Pantheon, 1958.

The Children Come Running, illustrated by Roger Duvoisin. New York, Golden Press, 1960.

The Sparrow Bush: Rhymes, illustrated by Stefan Martin. New York, Norton, 1966.

Down Half the World, illustrated by Zena Bernstein. New York, Macmillan, 1968.

Other

Runaway Home (reader), illustrated by Gustaf Tenggren.

Evanston, Illinois, Row Peterson, 1942.

The Princess and the Lion, illustrated by Evaline Ness. New York, Pantheon, 1963.

Daniel Webster's Horses, illustrated by Cary. Champaign, Illinois, Garrard, 1971.

Editor, *Tales of the Gauchos,* by W.H. Hudson, illustrated by Henry Pitz. New York, Knopf, 1946.

Editor, *Indian Encounters: An Anthology of Stories and Poems,* illustrated by Frederick Chapman. New York, Macmillan, 1960.

PUBLICATIONS FOR ADULTS

Novels

Here I Stay. New York, Coward McCann, 1938; London, Harrap, 1939.

The Trunk. New York, Macmillan, 1941.

The Enchanted. New York, Pantheon, 1951; London, Dent, 1952.

Silky: An Incredible Tale. New York, Pantheon, and London, Gollancz, 1953.

Mountain Bride: An Incredible Tale. New York, Pantheon, 1954.

The White Room. New York, Pantheon, 1958; London, Dent, 1959.

Verse

Fox Footprints. New York, Knopf, 1923.

Atlas and Beyond. New York, Harper, 1924.

Compass Rose. New York, Coward McCann, 1929.

Country Poems. New York, Macmillan, 1942.

Summer Green. New York, Macmillan, 1948.

The Creaking Stair. New York, Coward McCann, 1949.

Poems. New York, Macmillan, 1957.

Other

The Sun's Diary: A Book of Days for Any Year. New York, Macmillan, 1929.

Country Neighborhood. New York, Macmillan, 1944.

Maine Ways. New York, Macmillan, 1947.

South Shore Town. New York, Macmillan, 1948.

Maine Memories. Brattleboro, Vermont, Stephen Greene Press, 1968.

Personal Geography: Almost an Autobiography. Brattleboro, Vermont, Stephen Greene Press, 1976; London, Prior, 1979.

Editor, *Especially Maine: The Natural World of Henry Beston from Cape Cod to the St. Lawrence.* Brattleboro, Vermont, Stephen Greene Press, 1970.

*

Manuscript Collections: Kerlan Collection, University of Minnesota, Minneapolis; Bowdoin College Library, Brunswick, Maine.

*   *   *

Elizabeth Coatsworth wrote about "things which touch my imagination." Her imagination was as boundless as her pen was prolific. The author of some 90 books for children, Coatsworth wrote on such diverse subjects as Viking-raided Ireland (*The Wanderers*), the ancient inhabitants of the fjords and mountains in Norway (*Troll Weather*), and a city boy's summer in *Lighthouse Island.* Her vision encompassed lonely children and their search for independence, magic dolls, refugees, forests where animals can turn into people, and, above all, nature.

Although she travelled widely, the bulk of her work concerns America in all its phases. History books aside, she wrote of the desert, the plains, the mountains, Indians, pioneers, immigrants. But it is from Maine that her finest books have come, and in Maine that she found for decades the resources to create one lapidary tale after another.

Although born in 1893, the author continued to understand the perceptions of the young throughout her long writing career. One of her most successful themes is that of the lonely and different child learning to cope in an adverse world. *Lonely Maria* and *Grandmother Cat and the Hermit* both deal with this idea, as does *Marra's World* which combines the theme with Coatsworth's favorite setting—an island off the Maine Coast. With the subtle use of magic and fantasy it conveys the mood of a legend. Marra is regarded as hopeless by her teacher and schoolmates and even by her father and grandmother: "Everything about her life bewildered her." But when it comes to nature, Marra excels. She knows everything about the island. Gradually, with the help of a friend, she accepts herself as different, and the enchantment begins. Marra's mother is Nerea, a seal who was human for a time and who returned to the sea. Here, and in *The Enchanted,* Coatsworth touches on the ancient mythic theme where one being is able to work extraordinary changes for love of another.

Coatsworth reached her apogee in her nature writing, notably "The Incredible Tales" tetralogy about New England originally written for adults. As critic Edmund Fuller observes: "As with all Miss Coatsworth's work, *Silky* is a poet's book, mystic, delicate, lovely. With these 'Incredible Tales' she has created a rich, fresh medium that is at once original and yet the revival of a tradition neglected or distorted in this material age." *The Enchanted,* the best of the four, begins: "There is in northern Maine a township or, as they say here, a 'plantation,' called the Enchanted. It lies in the heart of the forest country and is seldom entered except by lumbermen bound for some winter logging camp from which they return with curious stories." A young man, David Ross, decides to try farming and buys a place right next to the Enchanted. His neighbors are a warm, closely knit family named Perdry, and he falls in love with one of the daughters and marries her. For their honeymoon they camp in the forest: "The stream seemed to sing its continual braided song especially for them, and the big pine sheltered them as though it liked them. They sat for many hours between its curving roots, their backs to its wide trunk, looking out at the water flowing by, always new water, and new ripples of light, yet always essentially the same stream catching the sunlight in the same net of motion." The magic in this tale and in Coatsworth's others is not arbitrary. It is all planned, provided for. Her special gift was the weaving together of a local story and her own vivid characters. The events that conclude *The Enchanted,* the metamorphosis of the Perdrys, are at once anticipated and surprising.

It was Coatsworth's intention to instruct through her stories, but she was never pedantic. The works do not come together with quite the ease of a folk tale that has been repeated from generation to generation, but are a combination of good New England common sense and modern legend. In *All-of-a-Sudden Susan,* building a feeling of danger, Coatsworth writes: "Everything was uneasy, except people, who are always the last to notice what's happening around them." A weakened dam bursts in a storm and Susan is carried away on the flood with her magic doll, Emelida, who talks to her. Susan sees uprooted houses, bloated animals, even a dead woman. "You can't keep people from dying," Emelida comforts her. "They do it all the time and we may be doing it, too, for all we know. But meantime, enjoy yourself."

The Sod House follows immigrants from their arrival in Boston to the settling of a community in Kansas. The New England Emigrant Aid Society helps the Traubels buy land on the Osage River. They are not welcome as northerners at a time when North and South are angling for control of the territory. Political reasons are carefully explained. The Indians the Traubels meet are portrayed solemnly and informatively (Coatsworth was always interested in their way of life), and Ilse, the child in the story, is allowed to fulfill her possibilities, as are most of Coatsworth's fictive children.

The Lucky Ones, a collection of five stories about the homeless and the stateless from different parts of the world—Tibet, Algeria, Rwanda, Hungary, and Hong Kong—explains why they are refugees, and describes the adversity they meet in trying to adjust to another way of life. Each story is preceded by a poem, and while in some cases the political background is not given enough detail, the children in the stories, and the children who read them, are treated with the respect that marks all Coatsworth's work.

Using her considerable creativeness and knowledge, her love of the natural world and her regard for children, Coatsworth was responsible for consistently fine literature for readers whose imaginations are as young and fresh as her own was.

—Angela Wigan

———

COCKETT, Mary. British. Born in Yorkshire in 1915. Educated at Bedford College, University of London; Institute of Education, London. Married to Reginald Cockett; one son and one daughter. Editor, National Institute of Industrial Psychology, 1943–48, and International Congress of Mental Health, 1948–49. Address: 24 Benville Avenue, Bristol BS9 2RX, England.

PUBLICATIONS FOR CHILDREN

Fiction

Jonathan on the Farm, illustrated by Joan and Dick Robinson. London, Harrap, 1954.
Jonathan and Felicity, illustrated by Joan and Dick Robinson. London, Harrap, 1955.
Fourteen Stories about Jonathan, illustrated by Sheila Connelly. London, Harrap, 1956.
More about Jonathan, illustrated by Dick Robinson. London, Harrap, 1957.
Jan the Market Boy, illustrated by Peggy Beetles. Leicester, Brockhampton Press, 1957.
Bouncing Ball, illustrated by Peggy Beetles. London, Hamish Hamilton, 1958.
Jasper Club, illustrated by Mary Shillabeer. London, Heinemann, 1959.
When Felicity Was Small, illustrated by Dick Robinson. London, Harrap, 1959.
Rolling On, illustrated by Shirley Hughes. London, Methuen, 1960.
Seven Days with Jan, illustrated by Peggy Beetles. Leicester, Brockhampton Press, 1960.
Mary Ann Goes to Hospital, illustrated by Shirley Hughes. London, Methuen, 1961.
Out with Felicity and Jonathan, illustrated by Dick Robinson. London, Harrap, 1962.
Cottage by the Lock, illustrated by Shirley Hughes. London, Methuen, 1962.
Benny's Bazaar, illustrated by Jennifer Cook. Edinburgh, Oliver and Boyd, 1964.
Acrobat Hamster, illustrated by Lynette Hemmant. London, Hamish Hamilton, 1965.

The Birthday Ride, illustrated by W.F. Phillipps. Edinburgh, Oliver and Boyd, 1965.

Sunflower Giant, illustrated by Lynette Hemmant. London, Hamish Hamilton, 1966.

There for the Picking, illustrated by Maureen Eckersley. Edinburgh, Oliver and Boyd, 1966.

Ash Dry, Ash Green, illustrated by Diana Stanley. Edinburgh, Oliver and Boyd, 1966; New York, Criterion, 1968.

Strange Valley, illustrated by Mary Dinsdale. Edinburgh, Oliver and Boyd, 1967.

Twelve Gold Chairs, illustrated by Margery Gill. Edinburgh, Oliver and Boyd, 1967.

Something Big, illustrated by Robert Hales. Edinburgh, Oliver and Boyd, 1968.

The Wild Place, illustrated by Margery Gill. Edinburgh, Oliver and Boyd, 1968.

Rosanna the Goat, illustrated by Reginald Gray. London, Chatto Boyd and Oliver, 1969; Indianapolis, Bobbs Merrill, 1970.

Pelican Park, illustrated by Frank Francis. London, Harrap, and New York, Warne, 1969.

Another Home, Another Country, illustrated by Sandra Archibald. London, Chatto Boyd and Oliver, 1969.

Farthing Bundles, illustrated by Jane Paton. London, Chatto Boyd and Oliver, 1970.

The Joppy Stories (Joppy Crawling, and Joppy on His Feet; Joppy Steps Out, and Caught on a Tree Stump; Joppy in a Bucket, and The Moving Cat), illustrated by Mary Cossey. London, Chatto and Windus, 3 vols., 1972.

Boat Girl, illustrated by Gareth Floyd. London, Chatto and Windus, 1972.

As Big as the Ark, illustrated by Barry Wilkinson. London, Methuen, 1974.

Look at the Little One, illustrated by Margaret Palmer. London, Hodder and Stoughton, 1974; Chicago, Children's Press, 1976.

Snake in the Camp, illustrated by Joan Beales. Leicester, Brockhampton Press, 1975; Chicago, Children's Press, 1976.

Tower Raven, illustrated by Sally Launder. London, Abelard Schuman, 1975.

Backyard Bird Hospital, illustrated by Gareth Floyd. London, Hodder and Stoughton, 1976.

The Balloon That Brought Luck, illustrated by Mary Dinsdale. London, Kaye and Ward, 1978.

The Drowning Valley, illustrated by Trevor Stubley. London, Hodder and Stoughton, 1978.

Monster in the River, illustrated by Mary Dinsdale. Exeter, Devon, Wheaton, 1979.

Pig at the Market, illustrated by David Anstey. Exeter, Devon, Wheaton, 1979.

Ladybird at the Zoo, illustrated by Caroline Sharpe. Exeter, Devon, Wheaton, 1979.

The Birthday, illustrated by Doreen Caldwell. London, Hodder and Stoughton, 1979.

The Christmas Tree, illustrated by Carol Walklin. London, Collins, 1979.

Enough Is Enough, illustrated by Nancy Petley-Jones. London, Hodder and Stoughton, 1980.

Shadow at Applegarth, illustrated by Gavin Rowe. London, Hodder and Stoughton, 1981.

Witch of Candlewick, illustrated by Janet Duchesne. London, Kaye and Ward, 1981.

Hoo-Ming's Discovery, illustrated by Valerie Littlewood. London, Hamish Hamilton, 1982.

The Cat and the Castle, illustrated by Doreen Caldwell. London, Hodder and Stoughton, 1982.

The School Donkey, illustrated by Valerie Littlewood. London, Hamish Hamilton, 1982.

Strange Hill, illustrated by Mark Peppé. London, Hodder and Stoughton, 1984.

Tracker, illustrated by Maria Majewska. London, Hamish Hamilton, 1984.

Better Than a Party, illustrated by Karen Heywood. London, Hamish Hamilton, 1985.

Zoo Ticket, illustrated by Doreen Caldwell. London, Hodder and Stoughton, 1985.

Rescue at the Zoo, illustrated by Colin Threadgall. London, Hamish Hamilton, 1986.

The Day of the Squirrels, illustrated by Doreen Caldwell. London, Hodder and Stoughton, 1987.

Kate of Candlewick, illustrated by Janet Duchesne. London, Hodder and Stoughton, 1987.

The Little Leaf and the Loose Tooth, with Rosalie Eisenstein. London, Macmillan, 1987.

The Paper Boy and Other Stories. London, Macmillan, 1987.

Bridesmaids, illustrated by Annabel Spenceley. London, Hodder and Stoughton, 1988.

Mystery on the Farm, illustrated by Janet Duchesne. London, Hamish Hamilton, 1988.

Other

Roads and Travelling, illustrated by Trevor Stubley. Oxford, Blackwell, 1964.

Bridges, illustrated by Diana Stanley. Edinburgh, Oliver and Boyd, 1965.

Tufty (reader), illustrated by George Adamson. London, Macmillan, 1968.

Frankie's Country Day (reader), illustrated by Mary Dinsdale. London, Macmillan, 1968.

The Lost Money (reader), illustrated by Mary Dinsdale. London, Macmillan, 1968.

The Wedding Tea (reader), illustrated by Mary Dinsdale. London, Macmillan, 1970.

Magic and Gold: Tales from Northern Europe, illustrated by Peter Kesteven. Oxford and New York, Pergamon Press, 1970.

Towns. Oxford, Blackwell, 1971.

The Marvellous Stick (reader), illustrated by Mary Dinsdale. London, Macmillan, 1972.

Bells in Our Lives, illustrated by Janet Duchesne. Newton Abbot, Devon, David and Charles, 1973.

Treasure, illustrated by Desmond Knight. London, Dent, 1973.

The Rainbow Walk (reader), illustrated by Prudence Seward. London, Burke, 1973.

An Armful of Sparrows (reader), illustrated by George Adamson. London, Macmillan, 1973.

Dolls and Puppets. Newton Abbot, Devon, David and Charles, 1974.

Walls, illustrated by W.G.D. Hill. Oxford, Blackwell, 1974.

He Cannot Really Read (reader), illustrated by Prudence Seward. London, Oxford University Press, 1975.

The Story of Cars, illustrated by Ralph Hodgson. Oxford, Blackwell, 1976.

The Magician (reader), illustrated by Richard Rose. London, Oxford University Press, 1976.

Fly High, Magpie (reader), illustrated by Jeroo Roy. London, Macmillan, 1977.

Missing (reader), illustrated by Peter Edwards. London, Oxford University Press, 1978.

For Children on Wheels, with A.M.L. Miller, illustrated by Edward Carr. London, Royal Automobile Club, 1979.

The Bell (reader), illustrated by Pat Nessling. London, Macmillan, 1980.

Money to Spend (reader), illustrated by Chris Masters. London,

Macmillan, 1980.
At the Tower (reader). London, Macmillan, 1984; Cleveland, Modern Curriculum Press, 1985.
Crab Apples (reader). London, Macmillan, 1984; Cleveland, Modern Curriculum Press, 1985.
Paper Boys (reader). London, Macmillan, 1985.
A Place of His Own (reader). London, Macmillan, 1987.
Winning All the Way (reader). London, Macmillan, 1987.

*   *   *

Mary Cockett is one of those figures familiar in all fields of literary endeavour, the conscientious professional more noted for reliability than outstanding talent. Her output is considerable, numbering some 70 books as well as stories for radio and television. Over three decades she has worked for several publishers, producing fiction for many different age groups, information books, and supplementary readers. However, she is best known for series books intended for 5–9-year-olds. Recent titles such as *The Day of the Squirrels* or *Tracker* show her ability to write satisfying stories within the length and language restraints of series requirements. While her books have attracted little critical attention, they are of the kind likely to form the bulk of the average child's reading, and as such deserve closer assessment.

Reading a whole batch at a time makes one aware that there has been neither significant development nor a falling off over the years, but rather the maintenance of a dependable standard. The peak of recognition probably came in 1961 when *Rolling On*, a predictable but warmhearted tale of one summer Dan spends with his grandfather, was one of the three British titles considered for the Hans Andersen award. One can find in it, as in some of the other non-series titles such as *Shadow at Applegarth*, a greater freedom in the writing and a sense of personal engagement. Mary Cockett's work in general shows a recognition of contemporary issues and interests, for example in the world of *Hoo-Ming's Discovery* or *Kate of Candlewick* with its bridges between old age and childhood, but she never allows the story to be lost in didacticism.

Most stories are set in the present and treat everyday happenings, relying for success on traditional factors: a clear, simple plot, sympathetic characters, and perception of children's interests, the whole imbued with a belief in kindness, courage, and perseverance. The shortage of accessible stories for children at the post-picture book stage is often deplored, and Cockett has made a substantial contribution to this area, managing to achieve credible characters and a fresh style within the series format. The ability to compose a spare text resonant with meaning and close to children's interests is seen in some of the picture books, for instance *Monster in the River*, the tall tale which turns out to be true, and similar features characterise the supplementary readers such as *The Rainbow Walk*, diminishing current arguments which polarise "real books" and "readers."

—Peggy Heeks

———

COHEN, Barbara (née Kauder). American. Born in Asbury Park, New Jersey, 15 March 1932. Educated at Barnard College, New York, 1950–54, B.A. 1954; Rutgers University, New Brunswick, New Jersey, 1954–55, M.A. 1957. Married Gene Cohen in 1954; three daughters. English teacher in New Jersey public high schools, Tenafly, 1955–57, Somerville, 1958–60, and Hillsborough, 1970–78. Recipient: Association of Jewish Libraries Best Book award and Sydney Taylor award, 1982; National Jewish Book award, 1983 (twice). Agent: Dorothy Markinko, McIntosh and Otis, 310 Madison Avenue, New York, New York 10017. Address: 540 Foothill Road, Bridgewater, New Jersey 08807, U.S.A.

PUBLICATIONS FOR CHILDREN

Fiction

The Carp in the Bathtub, illustrated by Joan Halpern. New York, Lothrop, 1972.
Thank You, Jackie Robinson, illustrated by Richard Cuffari. New York, Lothrop, 1974.
Bitter Herbs and Honey. New York, Lothrop, 1976.
Where's Florrie?, illustrated by Joan Halpern. New York, Lothrop, 1976.
Benny. New York, Lothrop, 1977.
R, My Name Is Rosie. New York, Lothrop, 1978.
The Innkeeper's Daughter. New York, Lothrop, 1979.
Fat Jack. New York, Atheneum, 1980.
I Am Joseph, illustrated by Charles Mikolaycak. New York, Lothrop, 1980.
Unicorns in the Rain. New York, Atheneum, 1980.
Queen for a Day. New York, Lothrop, 1981.
Gooseberries to Oranges, illustrated by Beverly Brodsky. New York, Lothrop, 1982.
King of the Seventh Grade. New York, Lothrop, 1982.
Seven Daughters and Seven Sons, with Bahija Lovejoy. New York, Atheneum, 1982.
Lovers' Games. New York, Atheneum, 1983.
Molly's Pilgrim, illustrated by Michael Deraney. New York, Lothrop, 1983.
Here Come the Purim Players!, illustrated by Beverly Brodsky. New York, Lothrop, 1984.
Roses, illustrated by John Steptoe. New York, Lothrop, 1984.
Coasting. New York, Lothrop, 1985.
The Secret Grove, illustrated by Michael Deraney. New York, Union of American Hebrew Congregations, 1985.
The Christmas Revolution, illustrated by Diane de Groat. New York, Lothrop, 1987.
First Fast. New York, Union of American Hebrew Congregations, 1987.
People Like Us. New York, Bantam, 1987.
The Orphan Game, illustrated by Diane de Groat. New York, Lothrop, 1988.
Tell Us Your Secret. New York, Bantam, 1989.

Other (retellings)

The Binding of Isaac, illustrated by Charles Mikolaycak. New York, Lothrop, 1978.
Lovely Vassilisa, illustrated by Anatoly Ivanov. New York, Atheneum, 1980.
Yussel's Prayer, illustrated by Michael Deraney. New York, Lothrop, 1981.
The Demon Who Would Not Die, illustrated by Anatoly Ivanov. New York, Atheneum, 1982.
Even Higher, illustrated by Anatoly Ivanov. New York, Lothrop, 1987.
The Donkey's Story: A Bible Story, illustrated by Susan Jeanne Cohen. New York, Lothrop, 1988.
Canterbury Tales, illustrated by Trina Schart Hyman. New York, Lothrop, 1988.

*

Manuscript Collection: Rutgers University Library, New Brunswick, New Jersey.

Barbara Cohen comments:
I've loved stories for as long as I can remember—nursery tales my

mother told me, family anecdotes recounted by relatives around countless holiday dinner tables, books of all kinds that I consumed voraciously on my own. I decided as soon as they taught me to form letters that writing stories was a good thing to do, and I still think so. I write children's stories because inside my own head I'm stuck at 12 years old. That's OK. It's worked out.

*   *   *

Barbara Cohen is best known as a writer of stories reflecting her Jewish heritage, but she is far more than just a Jewish writer. She is a master storyteller who deals with universal themes, drawing on her own childhood experiences and those of friends and family members to create stories that reveal commonalities among people from different times, places, and cultural and religious backgrounds. Although the family is of paramount importance, most of Cohen's protagonists are struggling to maintain their unique identities and to fit into a larger world outside the family.

Cohen is especially strong writing for 6–9-year-olds who want to read alone but are not ready for a full-length novel. *The Carp in the Bathtub* centers around the preparation of gefilte fish for Passover, but all youngsters can identify with Leah and Harry who refuse to eat the carp their mother has kept in the bathtub. *Molly's Pilgrim* is about a young Russian immigrant who after much anguish as an outsider eventually helps her third-grade class appreciate what it means to be a pilgrim. *The Secret Grove*, based on a true story, tells of a Jewish boy and an Arab boy who meet in an orange grove between their lands, share an orange, and plant the seeds. Years later after many wars between their two nations the Jewish boy, now a former soldier, returns to the grove and wonders about the fate of his Arab friend.

The young adult novel *Bitter Herbs and Honey* takes place in 1916 and captures the essence of Orthodox Jewish family life at the beginning of this century. Becky, the daughter of Jewish immigrants, is struggling with her family's resistance to her friendship with Peter, a "goy." *The Innkeeper's Daughter* is the story of 16-year-old Rachel Gold whose father died in 1941 and who now is living with her mother and younger siblings, Dan and Rosie in the Waterbridge Inn the family owns. *King of the Seventh Grade* moves to a more contemporary time to share Vic Abrams's resentment of Hebrew School and his Bar Mitzvah which he sees primarily as ways to separate him from his non-Jewish friends. Each of these stories, set in different times, deals with the problem of a young person whose religious and cultural heritage sets him/her apart from schoolmates and friends.

In her books Cohen uses the power of her own language and her voice as a storyteller to bring what might appear to be foreign or strange to today's young people and makes it familiar and worthy of thoughtful consideration.

—Kay E. Vandergrift

———————

COLE, Babette. British. Born in Jersey, Channel Islands. Educated at Canterbury College of Art, graduated 1973. Has worked as an animator for television and illustrator of greeting cards. Lives in Kent. Address: c/o Hamish Hamilton, 27 Wrights Lane, London W8 5TZ, England.

PUBLICATIONS FOR CHILDREN (illustrated by the author)

Fiction

Basil Brush of the Yard. London, Purnell, 1977.

Promise Solves the Problem. London, Kaye and Ward, 1977.
Nungu and the Crocodile. London, Purnell, 1978; New York, McGraw Hill, 1979.
Nungu and the Hippopotamus. London, Macdonald, 1978.
Nungu and the Elephant. London, Macdonald, and New York, McGraw Hill, 1980.
Promise and the Monster. London, Granada, 1981.
Beware of the Vet. London, Hamish Hamilton, 1982.
Don't Go Out Tonight. London, Hamish Hamilton, 1982.
The Trouble with Mum. Kingswood, Surrey, Kaye and Ward, 1983; as *The Trouble with Mom,* New York, Coward McCann, 1984.
The Hairy Book. London, Cape, 1984; New York, Random House, 1985.
The Slimy Book. London, Cape, 1985; New York, Random House, 1986.
The Trouble with Dad. London, Heinemann, 1985; New York, Putnam, 1986.
Princess Smartypants. London, Hamish Hamilton, 1986; New York, Putnam, 1987.
Prince Cinders. London, Hamish Hamilton, 1987; New York, Putnam, 1988.
The Smelly Book. London, Cape, 1987; New York, Simon and Schuster, 1988.
The Trouble with Gran. London, Heinemann, and New York, Putnam, 1987.
The Trouble with Grandad. London, Heinemann, 1988.
King Change-a-Lot. London, Hamish Hamilton, 1988; New York, Putnam, 1989.
Three Cheers for Errol. London, Heinemann, 1988; New York, Putnam, 1989.

*

Illustrator: *Your Dog* by Joan Tate, 1975; *Daisy* by Jenny Butterworth, 1976; *The Unicorn Drum* by Annabel Farjeon, 1976; *Mice and Mendelson* by Joan Aiken, 1978; *A Flying Bird* and *The Marrow Boat,* both by Oliver Postgate, 1978; *Count Bakwerdz on the Carpet,* 1979, and *Sneeze and Be Slain,* 1980, both by Norman Hunter; *Grasshopper and the Unwise Owl* [*Pickle Factory, Poisoned River*], all by Jim Slater, 3 vols., 1979–82; *The Last Vampire,* 1982, and *The Inflatable Shop,* 1984, both by Willis Hall; *The Wind in the Willows* by Kenneth Grahame, 1983; *Hocus Pocus* edited by Lesley Young, 1983.

*   *   *

Text and illustration are inseparable in Babette Cole's picture books, which all demonstrate her uniquely quirky sense of humour. Zany is the word that most succinctly describes her output and it is this unpredictability that makes the humour almost anarchic in places and ensures her appeal to children. The characters she writes about are larger than life and her cartoonlike illustrations capture their grotesqueness. Her imagination almost runs away with her at times as she creates ever more bizarre situations, as, for example, in *Beware of the Vet* in which the vet Mr. MacPlaster mistakes cow hormone accelerator tablets for aspirin and grows horns and a tail. The resulting series of ridiculous encounters includes puncturing a bloated hippo with his horns and frightening a vicar who thinks he is the devil.

In *The Trouble with Mum* Cole exaggerates every schoolchild's fear that his or her mother is different. Here the mother is a witch, complete with a witch's hat, and brings her child to school on a broomstick. The embarrassment caused by this mother will make any normal child's fears pale into insignificance. This book was followed by three more in similar vein. *The Trouble with Dad* features a father whose boring job makes him seek excitement by making robots that never quite work as one might expect them to. The grandad in *The Trouble with Grandad* grows giant vegetables that unfortunately produce giant caterpillars that cause chaos, and *The Trouble with Gran* is that she's an alien! This gran livens up the OAPs' outing and ends up having to transport everyone home in the bus shelter, but not before taking them on a quick visit to her planet. The humour in all these books is wonderfully underplayed in the text and hilariously depicted in the pictures. For example, on the final page of *The Trouble with Gran* the text says "When she got home she opened up her own travel agency...in Dad's garage!"—a straightforward statement one might think—but the illustration shows a garage packed with holidaymakers flying over houses and piloted by a strange-looking old lady!

Babette Cole delights in turning language and situations upside down. She inverts the traditional role of the fairytale princess in *Princess Smartypants,* in which the princess wears dungarees and wants to remain unmarried. All her suitors fail the classic ordeals she sets them until Prince Swashbuckle comes along. He successfully feeds her revolting pets, rides pillion on her motorbike, outlasts her at the roller-disco, and finally wins a kiss from the princess, which turns him into a toad. This ensures the princess's future as a single woman as no other suitors want to risk winning her hand. Similarly in *Prince Cinders* she turns the Cinderella story on its head with her tale of the prince who is "small, spotty, scruffy and skinny" and who is persecuted by his three big hairy brothers. He finally wins the hand of Princess Lovelypenny (no thanks to the dirty fairy, however) by being able to fit into, not a glass slipper, but some tight blue jeans.

Cole is expert at portraying the revolting or disgusting—the things that young children revel in reading about—and does so most effectively and amusingly in her trio *The Hairy Book, The Slimy Book,* and *The Smelly Book.* Each of these has children squealing with delight as the rhyming texts list the ever more revolting subjects. *The Slimy Book,* for example, begins "Sticky, sludgy, slippy slime, the sloppy, ploppy, creepy kind." The humour is extended in the illustrations which are equally disgusting and feature grotesque noses, monsters, and the like. However, despite the distasteful nature of the subject matter, none of these books is in any way offensive. Cole's humour has a lightness of touch that makes the whole simply fun.

Although her books are not serious in design they can have an underlying moral. In her recent book *Three Cheers for Errol,* for example, Errol the rat is bad at sums, spelling, science, and art. He is, however, good at sport and is chosen to represent his school in the Inter-school Ratathalon. When other competitors from "better" schools play a dirty trick on Errol it looks as though he will not be able to take part in the contest. However, he is inspired by the feats of some busking acrorats spinning on their tails and finally wins all the events by using his tail. In other words, you don't have to be academically clever to have brains. This book is also a good example of the way Cole plays with words, and apart from the obvious words in the text—"Ratathalon," "acrorat"—children should enjoy spotting others in the pictures, like the poster advertising a "Ratmaninov" concert, or the cheering at the end which includes the odd "hoorat."

Humour can often attract those who are less keen to read. Cole's brand of infectious humour can show such children that reading can be as much fun as watching television, for example. For this reason alone her books are to be enthusiastically recommended.

—Fiona Lafferty

COLLIER, James Lincoln. American. Born in New York City, 27 June 1928. Educated at Hamilton College, Clinton, New York, A.B. 1950. Served in United States Army, 1950–51. Married 1) Carol Burrows in 1952 (divorced), two sons; 2) Ida Karen Potash in 1983. Freelance writer. Recipient: Child Study Committee award, 1971; National Foundation for the Humanities fellowship, 1982; Institute for Studies in American Music fellowship, 1985; Christopher award, 1986. Address: c/o Macmillan Publishing Company, 866 Third Avenue, New York, New York 10022, U.S.A.

PUBLICATIONS FOR CHILDREN

Fiction

The Teddy Bear Habit, illustrated by Lee Lorenz. New York, Norton, 1967.
Rock Star. New York, Four Winds Press, 1970.
Why Does Everybody Think I'm Nutty? New York, Grosset and Dunlap, 1971.
It's Murder at St. Basket's. New York, Grosset and Dunlap, 1972.
My Brother Sam Is Dead, with Christopher Collier. New York, Four Winds Press, 1974.
Rich and Famous. New York, Four Winds Press, 1975.
The Bloody Country, with Christopher Collier. New York, Four Winds Press, 1976.
Give Dad My Best. New York, Four Winds Press, 1976.
The Winter Hero, with Christopher Collier. New York, Four Winds Press, 1978.
Jump Ship to Freedom, with Christopher Collier. New York, Delacorte Press, 1981.
Planet Out of the Past. New York, Macmillan, 1983.
War Comes to Willie Freeman, with Christopher Collier. New York, Delacorte Press, 1983.
Who Is Carrie?, with Christopher Collier. New York, Delacorte Press, 1984.
When the Stars Begin to Fall. New York, Delacorte Press, 1986.
Outside Looking In. New York, Macmillan, 1987.
The Winchesters. New York, Macmillan, 1988.

Other

Battleground: The United States Army in World War II. New York, Norton, 1965.
A Visit to the Firehouse, photographs by Yale Joel. New York, Norton, 1967.
Which Musical Instrument Shall I Play?, photographs by Yale Joel. New York, Norton, 1969.
Danny Goes to the Hospital, photographs by Yale Joel. New York, Norton, 1970.
Practical Musical Theory: How Music Is Put Together from Bach to Rock. New York, Norton, 1970.
The Hard Life of the Teenager. New York, Four Winds Press, 1972.
Inside Jazz. New York, Four Winds Press, 1973.
Jug Bands and Handmade Music. New York, Grosset and Dunlap, 1973.
The Making of Man. New York, Four Winds Press, 1974.
Making Music for Money. New York, Watts, 1976.
CB. New York, Watts, 1977.
The Great Jazz Artists, illustrated by Robert Andrew Parker. New York, Four Winds Press, 1977.
Louis Armstrong: An American Success Story. New York, Macmillan, 1985.

PUBLICATIONS FOR ADULTS

Novels

Cheers. New York, Avon, 1960.

Somebody Up There Hates Me. New York, Macfadden, 1962.
Fires of Youth. London, Penguin, 1968.

Other

The Hypocritical American: An Essay on Sex Attitudes in America. Indianapolis, Bobbs Merrill, 1964.
The Fine Art of Swindling, with others, edited by Walter Brown Gibson. New York, Grosset and Dunlap, 1966.
Sex Education U.S.A.: A Community Approach, with others. New York, Sex Information and Education Council of the United States, 1968.
The Making of Jazz: A Comprehensive History. Boston, Houghton Mifflin, and London, Hart Davis MacGibbon, 1978.
Louis Armstrong, An American Genius. New York, Oxford University Press, 1983; as *Louis Armstrong: A Biography,* London, Joseph, 1984.
Decision in Philadelphia: The Constitutional Convention of 1787, with Christopher Collier. New York, Random House, 1986.
Duke Ellington. New York, Oxford University Press, and London, Joseph, 1987.

*

Manuscript Collection: Kerlan Collection, University of Minnesota, Minneapolis.

James Lincoln Collier comments:

Although I have written many different types of books for children, I think that I am best-known for works with social and political themes, such as *My Brother Sam is Dead, When the Stars Begin to Fall,* and *The Winchesters.* The point of these books is both to give readers a strong and exciting story, and to make them think about issues which face children growing up in a complex world, filled with difficult moral choices.

* * *

James Lincoln Collier is best known as one half of the writing team that has produced *My Brother Sam Is Dead* and the Arabus family trilogy. However, Collier wrote a number of books prior to the publication of the jointly authored historical novels, and has continued to publish adolescent novels. *The Teddy Bear Habit* is perhaps the most representative of his early work, and includes several recurring themes in Collier's novels. The first is the role of music. Collier's own experience as a musician helps him to portray aspects of the musical scene with a realistic touch. In *The Teddy Bear Habit,* a young boy's interest in music involves him in a jewel theft. In *Give Dad My Best* a father's passion for his music almost destroys his family, while the desire to play an instrument is one factor in Collier's more recent work, *Outside Looking In.*

A second theme is the inability of parents to function as effective moral and emotional guides for their children. Collier regularly creates cruel and ineffectual parents. The fathers in *Give Dad My Best* and *Outside Looking In* are thieves and hucksters who abuse their children. Their wives are not able to protect their children, and allow their lives to be buried in dirt, dishonesty, and poverty. Even the father in *The Teddy Bear Habit,* while neither cruel nor dishonest, is generally ineffectual. As his son explains, "I hate to say it about my own pop, but frankly, I think the whole thing [his father's art] is a lot of baloney." It is interesting to note, too, that several of these fathers are described in almost the same words: "kind of fat and had a big, brown mustache." They tend to think that "ripping off the system" is acceptable because the "system" is dishonest and corrupt.

The third distinguishing mark of these novels is the first-person male narrator. Sometimes this is a very effective technique. It works

especially well in *My Brother Sam Is Dead* where the narrator represents a middle ground between the warring factions in his own family and in his country. It becomes repetitive, however, in the more contemporary novels where the voices begin to sound like the same 14-year-old boy in each book.

Endings are also a problem for Collier. In *When the Stars Begin to Fall* the misused son declares at the end of the book that someday he will kill his father. In *Outside Looking In* everything will "work out in the end" in spite of a possible prison sentence and an abusive father on the loose. This type of ending is typical of Collier's books. In *Who Is Carrie?*, for instance, the book's final chapter is an epilogue. This technique was used quite successfully in *My Brother Sam Is Dead,* but in this case it has the feel of air slowly escaping from a balloon—a real letdown. The ending is simply a speculation on what might have happened to Carrie if she had been a real person. The authors invented Carrie—they need to have chosen an ending, and discussed other possibilities in an afterward. *Jump Ship to Freedom,* fizzles too. We are led to believe that after running away, defying death, and discovering his own self-worth, the slave Daniel Arabus would be content to wait three years more for his freedom.

Yet each of these books contains elements that will appeal to adolescent readers. There is courage in the protagonists' fight against the cruel circumstances of their lives, and a sense that dignity can be won in the face of adversity. There is a recognition that the system doesn't always work and that while corruption often wins individuals do not have to be corrupted. These themes are especially well done in the historical novels that represent the collaboration between James and Christopher Collier. The Arabus trilogy, for instance, is an interesting attempt to tell the story of black Americans in the early days of the United States.

The most interesting of Collier's books is *My Brother Sam Is Dead,* co-authored with Christopher Collier. This book represents a breakthrough in historical novels for children. Its graphic depiction of the brutality of both sides during the American Revolution, and the protagonist's ability to see the good and evil on both sides marks it as a real departure from such nationalistic novels as Esther Forbes's *Johnny Tremain.* In terms of historiography, this book is a post-Vietnam approach to America's involvement in wars, and to what children should learn about war and history. It is also moving, thought-provoking and fast-paced—a rare combination in historical fiction.

—Linda S. Levstik

————————

COLMAN, Hila (née Crayder). Also writes as Teresa Crayder. American. Born in New York City. Educated at Radcliffe College, Cambridge, Massachusetts, 2 years. Married Louis Colman in 1945; two sons. Publicity/promotion officer, Russian War Relief, New York, 1940–45; executive director, Labor Book Club, New York, 1945–47. Since 1949 freelance writer. Recipient: Child Study Committee award, 1962. Address: P.O. Box 95, Bridgewater, Connecticut 06752, U.S.A.

PUBLICATIONS FOR CHILDREN

Fiction

The Big Step. New York, Morrow, 1957.
A Crown for Gina. New York, Morrow, 1958.
Julie Builds Her Castle. New York, Morrow, 1959.
The Best Wedding Dress. New York, Morrow, 1960.

The Girl from Puerto Rico.   New York, Morrow, 1961.
Mrs. Darling's Daughter.   New York, Morrow, 1962.
Watch That Watch.   New York, Morrow, 1962; Kingswood, Surrey, World's Work, 1963.
Peter's Brownstone House.   New York, Morrow, 1963.
Phoebe's First Campaign.   New York, Morrow, 1963.
Cathy and Lisette (as Teresa Crayder), illustrated by Evelyn Copelman.   New York, Doubleday, 1964.
Classmates by Request.   New York, Morrow, 1964.
The Boy Who Couldn't Make Up His Mind.   New York, Macmillan, 1965.
Christmas Cruise.   New York, Morrow, 1965.
Bride at Eighteen.   New York, Morrow, 1966.
Dangerous Summer.   New York, Bantam, 1966.
Sudden Fame (as Teresa Crayder).   New York, Macmillan, 1966.
Car-Crazy Girl.   New York, Morrow, 1967.
Thoroughly Modern Millie (novelization of screenplay).   New York, Bantam, 1967.
Mixed-Marriage Daughter.   New York, Morrow, 1968.
Something Out of Nothing, illustrated by Sally Trinkle.   New York, Weybright and Talley, 1968.
Andy's Landmark House, illustrated by Fermin Rocker.   New York, Parents' Magazine Press, 1969.
Claudia, Where Are You?   New York, Morrow, 1969.
The Happenings at North End School.   New York, Morrow, 1970.
Daughter of Discontent.   New York, Morrow, 1971.
End of the Game, photographs by Milton Charles.   Cleveland, World, 1971.
The Family and the Fugitive.   New York, Morrow, 1972.
Benny the Misfit, illustrated by Elaine Raphael.   New York, Crowell, 1973.
Chicano Girl.   New York, Morrow, 1973.
Diary of a Frantic Kid Sister.   New York, Crown, 1973.
Friends and Strangers on Location.   New York, Morrow, 1974.
After the Wedding.   New York, Morrow, 1975.
Ethan's Favorite Teacher, illustrated by John Wallner.   New York, Crowell, 1975.
That's the Way It Is, Amigo.   New York, Crowell, 1975.
The Amazing Miss Laura.   New York, Morrow, 1976.
Nobody Has to Be a Kid Forever.   New York, Crowell, 1976.
The Case of the Stolen Bagels, illustrated by Pat Grant Porter.   New York, Crown, 1977.
Sometimes I Don't Love My Mother.   New York, Morrow, 1977.
Rachel's Legacy.   New York, Morrow, 1978.
The Secret Life of Harold, The Bird Watcher, illustrated by Charles Robinson.   New York, Crowell, 1978.
Tell Me No Lies.   New York, Crown, 1978.
Ellie's Inheritance.   New York, Morrow, 1979.
Accident.   New York, Morrow, 1980.
What's the Matter with the Dobsons?   New York, Crown, 1980.
Confessions of a Storyteller.   New York, Crown, 1981.
The Family Trap.   New York, Morrow, 1982.
Not for Love.   New York, Morrow, 1983.
Just the Two of Us.   New York, Scholastic, 1984.
Nobody Told Me What I Need to Know.   New York, Morrow, 1984.
Weekend Sisters.   New York, Morrow, 1985.
Suddenly.   New York, Morrow, 1987.
The Double Life of Angela Jones.   New York, Morrow, 1988.
Rich and Famous Like My Mom.   New York, Crown, 1988.

Other

Beauty, Brains, and Glamour: A Career in Magazine Publishing, illustrated by Jacqueline Tomes.   Cleveland, World, 1968.
A Career in Medical Research, illustrated by Edna Mason Kaula.   Cleveland, World, 1968.

Making Movies: Student Films to Features.   Cleveland, World, 1969.
City Planning: What It's All About—In the Planners' Own Words.   Cleveland, World, 1971.

PUBLICATIONS FOR ADULTS

Other

The Country Weekend Cookbook, with Louis Colman.   New York, Barrows, 1961.
Cleopatra (as Teresa Crayder).   New York, Coward McCann, 1969.
Hanging On.   New York, Atheneum, 1977.

*   *   *

Hila Colman writes books for young adolescents about interpersonal problems at home and with peers. She does this with clarity and directness, dealing with intergenerational and intragenerational concerns of grandparents, parents, and children. Her grandmothers are usually strong people, some with traditional and some with modern views of social behavior. Her parents are shown with strengths, frailties, and self-doubts. Teenagers wrestle with the multiple social and personal crises that are part of growing up.

What's the Matter with the Dobsons? portrays a family in which the parents separate and come together again, menstruation and menopause are dealt with matter-of-factly, and problems of teenage dating as well as dating of elderly widows are discussed.

Tell Me No Lies concerns a single-parent family in which the teenage daughter sets out to find her biological father, despite her mother's misgivings. Once she gets to know her father she is more able to accept her mother's affection for her and her mother's new husband's desire to adopt her.

Diary of a Frantic Kid Sister focuses on a younger sister's rage against her older sister, whom she perceives as more loved, more popular, and more accomplished. Rage gives way over time to understanding of her sister's own problems in living and of their ability to co-exist.

Mixed-Marriage Daughter concerns the child of a Jewish mother and a Protestant father. Her Jewish grandmother desperately wants the child to believe in and to practice the orthodox Jewish faith. The child questions, rebels, and makes peace with her extended family. She manages in the end to be a friend of, but not bound to, her grandmother.

Rachel's Legacy, set in the Jewish East Side of New York City in the early 1900's, is about the immigrant experience. The Ginsbergs arrive at Ellis Island from their Russian village with great hopes and expectations for the future. Their story, spanning three generations of family life, is full of strong and complex emotions, of successes and failures, of support and betrayal, as family members reach out, in diverse ways, to make their place in the new world.

Colman's families and family members have real feelings and real problems. They do not all live happily ever after. But they are able to deal with adversity, alter courses in their lives, and provide comfort to those close to them. Colman's works reflect more accurately than most American books for adolescents changing family structures and functions, and the meaning of these changes to family members. As such they are possible sources of comfort for some readers in personal and familial crises, who will glean from these books identification, understanding, and support.

—Mary Lystad

COLUM, Padraic. Irish. Born in Longford, 8 December 1881. Educated at Glasthule National School, Sandycove, County Dublin. Married the writer Mary Catherine Gunning Maguire in 1912 (died 1957). Clerk, Irish Railway Clearing House, Dublin, 1898–1904; member of the National Theatre Society and associated with the founding of the Abbey Theatre, Dublin; founder, with others, 1911, and editor, 1912–13, *Irish Review,* Dublin; moved to the United States, 1914, and lived in Pittsburgh, Connecticut, and New York; lived in France, 1930–33; lecturer, Columbia University, New York, from 1939. President, James Joyce Society, New York, and Poetry Society of America, 1938–39. Recipient: Academy of American Poets fellowship, 1952; Irish Academy of Letters Gregory medal, 1953; Catholic Library Association Regina Medal, 1961; Georgetown University medal, 1964. Litt.D: Columbia University, New York, 1958; Trinity College, Dublin, 1958. Member, Irish Academy of Letters, and American Academy. *Died 11 January 1972.*

PUBLICATIONS FOR CHILDREN

Fiction

A Boy in Eirinn, illustrated by Jack B. Yeats. New York, Dutton, 1913; London, Dent, 1915.
The Boy Apprenticed to an Enchanter, illustrated by Dugald Stuart Walker. New York, Macmillan, 1920.
The Peep-Show Man, illustrated by Lois Lenski. New York, Macmillan, 1924; London, Macmillan, 1932.
The White Sparrow, illustrated by Joseph Low. New York, Macmillan, 1933; as *Sparrow Alone,* London, Blackie, 1975.
Where the Winds Never Blew and the Cocks Never Crew, illustrated by Richard Bennett. New York, Macmillan, 1940.

Play

The Destruction of the Hostel (produced Dublin, 1910).

Other

The King of Ireland's Son, illustrated by Willy Pogány. New York, Macmillan, 1916; London, Harrap, 1920.
The Boy Who Knew What the Birds Said, illustrated by Dugald Stuart Walker. New York, Macmillan, 1918.
The Adventures of Odysseus and the Tale of Troy, illustrated by Willy Pogány. New York, Macmillan, 1918; London, Harrap, 1920; as *The Children's Homer,* Macmillan, 1946.
The Girl Who Sat by the Ashes, illustrated by Dugald Stuart Walker. New York, Macmillan, 1919; London, Collier Macmillan, 1968.
The Children of Odin: A Book of Northern Myths, illustrated by Willy Pogány. New York, Macmillan, 1920; London, Harrap, 1922.
The Golden Fleece and the Heroes Who Lived Before Achilles, illustrated by Willy Pogány. New York, Macmillan, 1921.
The Children Who Followed the Piper, illustrated by Dugald Stuart Walker. New York, Macmillan, 1922.
The Six Who Were Left in a Shoe, illustrated by Dugald Stuart Walker. Chicago, Volland, 1923; London, Brentano, 1924.
Tales and Legends of Hawaii: At the Gateways of the Day, and *The Bright Islands,* illustrated by Juliette May Fraser. New Haven, Connecticut, Yale University Press, 2 vols., 1924–25; as *Legends of Hawaii,* Yale University Press, and London, Oxford University Press, 1937.
The Island of the Mighty, Being the Hero Stories of Celtic Britain Retold from the Mabinogion, illustrated by Wilfred Jones. New York, Macmillan, 1924.
The Voyagers, Being Legends and Romances of Atlantic Discovery, illustrated by Wilfred Jones. New York, Macmillan, 1925.

The Forge in the Forest, illustrated by Boris Artzybasheff. New York, Macmillan, 1925.
The Fountain of Youth: Stories to Be Told, illustrated by Jay Van Everen. New York, Macmillan, 1927.
Orpheus: Myths of the World, illustrated by Boris Artzybasheff. New York, Macmillan, 1930; as *Myths of the Old World,* New York, Universal Library, n.d.
The Big Tree of Bunlahy: Stories of My Own Countryside, illustrated by Jack B. Yeats. New York, Macmillan, 1933; London, Macmillan, 1934.
The Frenzied Prince, Being Heroic Stories of Ancient Ireland, illustrated by Willy Pogány. Philadelphia, McKay, 1943.
The Stone of Victory and Other Tales, illustrated by Judith Gwyn Brown. New York, McGraw Hill, 1966.

Editor, *Gulliver's Travels,* by Swift, illustrated by Willy Pogány. New York, Macmillan, 1917; London, Harrap, 1919.
Editor, *The Arabian Nights, Tales of Wonder and Magnificence,* illustrated by Lynd Ward. New York, Macmillan, 1953.

PUBLICATIONS FOR ADULTS

Novels

Castle Conquer. New York, Macmillan, 1923.
The Flying Swans. New York, Crown, 1957.

Short Stories

Three Men: A Tale. London, Mathews and Marrot, 1930.
Selected Short Stories of Padraic Colum, edited by Sanford Sternlicht. Syracuse, New York, Syracuse University Press, 1985.

Plays

The Children of Lir, and *Brian Boru* in *Irish Independent* (Dublin), 1902.
The Kingdom of the Young (produced 1902). Published in *United Irishman* (Dublin), 1903.
The Foleys, and *Eoghan's Wife,* in *United Irishman* (Dublin), 1903.
The Saxon Shillin' (produced Dublin, 1903). Published in *Lost Plays of the Irish Renaissance,* edited by Robert Hogan and James Kilroy, Dixon, California, Proscenium Press, 1970.
The Fiddler's House (as *Broken Soil,* produced Dublin, 1903; London, 1904; revised version, as *The Fiddler's House,* produced Dublin, 1907; New York, 1941). Dublin, Maunsel, 1907; in *Three Plays,* 1916.
The Land (produced Dublin and London, 1905). Dublin, Abbey Theatre, 1905; in *The Three Plays,* 1916.
The Miracle of the Corn: A Miracle Play (produced Dublin, 1908; London, 1911). Included in *Studies,* 1907; in *Dramatic Legends and Other Poems,* 1922.
Thomas Muskerry (produced Dublin and London, 1910). Dublin, Maunsel, 1910; in *Three Plays,* 1916.
The Desert. Dublin, Devereux, 1912; as *Mogu the Wanderer; or, The Desert: A Fantastic Comedy,* Boston, Little Brown, 1917; as *Mogu of the Desert* (produced Dublin, 1931).
The Betrayal (produced Manchester, 1913; Pittsburgh, 1914). Published in *One-Act Plays of To-Day 4,* edited by J.W. Marriott, London, Harrap, 1928; in *Selected Plays,* 1986.
Three Plays: The Fiddler's House, The Land, Thomas Muskerry. Boston, Little Brown, 1916; Dublin and London, Maunsel, 1917; revised edition, New York, Macmillan, 1925.
The Grasshopper, with F.E. Washburn-Freund, adaptation of a play

by Count Keyserling (produced New York, 1917).
Balloon (produced Ogunquit, Maine). New York, Macmillan, 1929.
The Show-Booth, adaptation of a play by Alexander Blok (produced Dublin, 1948).
Moytura: A Play for Dancers. Dublin, Dolmen Press, 1963.
The Challengers: Monasterboice, Glendalough, Cloughoughter (produced Dublin, 1966). *Monasterboice* and *Glendalough* included in *Selected Plays,* 1986.
The Road round Ireland, with Basil Burwell, adaptation of works by Colum (produced Norwalk, Connecticut, 1967; as *Carricknabauna,* produced New York, 1967).
Selected Plays of Padraic Colum (includes *The Land, The Betrayal, Glendalough, Monasterboice*), edited by Sanford Sternlicht. Syracuse, New York, Syracuse University Press, 1986.

Verse

Heather Ale. Privately printed, 1907.
Wild Earth. Dublin, Maunsel, 1907; revised edition, as *Wild Earth and Other Poems,* Maunsel, and New York, Holt, 1916.
Dramatic Legends and Other Poems. New York, Macmillan, 1922.
The Way of the Cross: Devotions on the Progress of Our Lord Jesus Christ from the Judgment Hall to Calvary. Chicago, Seymour, 1926.
Creatures. New York, Macmillan, 1927.
Old Pastures. New York, Macmillan, 1930.
Poems. New York, Macmillan, and London, Macmillan, 1932; revised edition, as *The Collected Poems of Padraic Colum,* New York, Devin Adair, 1953.
The Story of Lowry Maen. New York, Macmillan, 1937.
Flower Pieces: New Poems. Dublin, Orwell Press, 1938.
The Jackdaw. Dublin, Gayfield Press, 1939.
The Vegetable Kingdom. Bloomington, Indiana University Press, 1954.
Ten Poems. Dublin, Dolmen Press, 1957.
Garland Sunday. Dublin, Dolmen Press, 1958.
Irish Elegies. Dublin, Dolmen Press, 1958; revised edition, 1961, 1966; London, Oxford University Press, 1963.
The Poet's Circuits: Collected Poems of Ireland. London, Oxford University Press, 1960.
Images of Departure. Dublin, Dolmen Press, 1969.

Other

Studies (miscellany). Dublin, Maunsel, 1907.
My Irish Year. London, Mills and Boon, and New York, Pott, 1912.
The Irish Rebellion of 1916 and Its Martyrs: Erin's Tragic Easter, with others, edited by Maurice Joy. New York, Devin Adair, 1916.
The Road round Ireland. New York, Macmillan, 1926.
Cross-Roads in Ireland. New York, Macmillan, 1930.
Ella Young: An Appreciation. London and New York, Longman, 1931.
A Half-Day's Ride: or, Estates in Corsica. New York, Macmillan, 1932.
The Legend of Saint Columba. New York, Macmillan, 1935; London, Sheed and Ward, 1936.
Our Friend James Joyce, with Mary Colum. New York, Doubleday, 1958; London, Gollancz, 1959.
Arthur Griffith. Dublin, Browne and Nolan, 1959; as *Ourselves Alone! The Story of Arthur Griffith and the Origin of the Irish Free State,* New York, Crown, 1959.
Story Telling Old and New. New York, Macmillan, 1961.

Editor, *Oliver Goldsmith.* London, Herbert and Daniel, and Chicago, Browne, 1913.
Editor, *Broad-Sheet Ballads, Being a Collection of Irish Popular Songs.* Dublin and London, Maunsel, 1913; Baltimore, Remington, 1914.
Editor, with Edward J. O'Brien, *Poems of the Irish Revolutionary Brotherhood.* Boston, Small Maynard, 1916; revised edition, 1916.
Editor, *Anthology of Irish Verse.* New York, Boni and Liveright, 1922; revised edition, New York, Liveright, 1948.
Editor, *A Treasury of Irish Folklore: The Stories, Traditions, Legends, Humor, Wisdom, Ballads, and Songs of the Irish People.* New York, Crown, 1954; revised edition, 1962, 1967.
Editor, with Margaret Freeman Cabell, *Between Friends: Letters of James Branch Cabell and Others.* New York, Harcourt Brace, 1962.
Editor, *The Poems of Samuel Ferguson.* Dublin, Figgis, 1963.
Editor, *Roofs of Gold: Poems to Read Aloud.* New York, Macmillan, and London, Collier Macmillan, 1964.

*

Manuscript Collection: Berg Collection, New York Public Library.

Critical Study: *Padraic Colum: A Biographical-Critical Introduction* by Zack R. Bowen, Carbondale, Southern Illinois University Press, 1970.

Theatrical Activities:
Actor: **Plays**—Buinne in *Deirdre* by AE, Dublin, 1902; Pupil in *The Hour-Glass* by W.B. Yeats, Dublin, 1903; A Cripple in *The King's Threshold* by W.B. Yeats, Dublin, 1903.

*   *   *

Padraic Colum's fictional work for the young ranges from the retelling of traditional tales, like his Cinderella story *The Girl Who Sat by the Ashes* to the partially autobiographical novel *A Boy in Eirinn.* Working in collaboration with many different artists his picture books vary greatly in their length and complexity. The bulk of his output lies in the period 1914 to 1939, and much of it is now unavailable to the general British public.
It is in *A Boy in Eirinn* that Colum's version of the Ancient Mariner first appears. Carrying the tiny closed theatre on his back like a hunch, the peep-show man with his fund of stories and concealed pictures both anticipates Ray Bradbury's Illustrated Man in having been terrified by his own exhibits, and more directly represents the author himself, accompanied by his Muse. This equivocal figure is developed further in the three short stories titled *The Peep-Show Man*; while, by the simple expedient of never revealing its contents, the portable theatre projects itself to the reader as a Pandora's Box of unconscious images, its owner narrates to a young boy, outside whose house he has paused, the first two tales, which concern noble young men brought low by fickle women. But of greater significance in the totality of Colum's work is the third tale. The peep-show man here switches roles to become an off-stage character, who has given the same lonely boy a caged white blackbird. The bird, which must be free to sing on Easter morning, is released in spiritual exchange for the return of the boy's missing father. In its employment of bird symbolism, in its portrayal by analogy of a specially gifted child, and in its moving scene of paternal reunion, this episode draws together three of the author's most abiding motifs. The latter two, very Joycean in their sympathies (Colum and Joyce were long-standing friends), certainly have their origin in the three years Colum spent in the care of an uncle, while Colum senior ineffectually sought his fortune in America. Such figures as the peep-show man, the entertainer in *The White Sparrow,* and the evil guardian magician in *The*

Boy Apprenticed to an Enchanter may therefore be partially regarded as ambivalent father surrogates. Even such a mundane story as *The Six Who Were Left in a Shoe* is elevated by the keenly conveyed desolation of the deserted animals. And at the end of *Where the Winds Never Blew and the Cocks Never Crew* the characters pass away across the edge of the world, as one figuratively would when leaving Ireland for America.

Through the fictional persona of Finn O'Donnell these crucial years are explored most candidly in *A Boy in Eirinn.* This *bildungsroman*, illustrated by Jack B. Yeats in his naturalistic phase, is both a summing up of the author's Irish childhood and an introduction to the mother country for Irish-American boys. The dissolute elder Colum is here transformed as Finn's father into a political prisoner of the British. Like his author, the child hero is farmed out to an uncle and grandfather. Cleverly interleaved with a calendar of country customs and the adventures of Finn and his friend Tim (another boy without a father) on a set-piece visit to the Dublin of horse trams and gaslight are mythical stories like the Children of Ler and patriotic lessons in Irish history. Although one would not particularly expect a child to read it today, *A Boy in Eirinn,* with its whitewashed houses and long dusty roads full of tinkers and show people, has not lost its period charm. While that book, with among others its caged goldfinch and tame jackdaw, abounds in birds, and birds figure prominently as the guardian angel starlings of *The Girl Who Sat by the Ashes* and in *The Boy Who Knew What the Birds Said,* it is with *The White Sparrow* that they crowd out the landscape and reach their apogee. Here the famous flock of starlings in the Luxembourg Gardens are ingeniously equated with western city dwellers who have sold their souls for industry and gossip. In their midst and identifying himself with more melodious and solitary species is the White Sparrow. Spurned by his fellows, conscious of his difference from the herd, the hero in temperament and some of his adventures is really another incarnation of the fair-haired Finn. This 60-page book is Colum's most enduring creation in the genre.

—John Churcher

CONFORD, Ellen (née Schaffer). American. Born in New York City, 20 March 1942. Attended Hofstra University, Hempstead, New York, 1959–62. Married David H. Conford in 1960; one son. Agent: McIntosh and Otis Inc., 310 Madison Avenue, New York, New York 10017. Address: 26 Strathmore Road, Great Neck, New York 11023, U.S.A.

PUBLICATIONS FOR CHILDREN

Fiction

Impossible, Possum, illustrated by Rosemary Wells. Boston, Little Brown, 1971.
Why Can't I Be William?, illustrated by Philip Wende. Boston, Little Brown, 1972.
Dreams of Victory, illustrated by Gail Rockwell. Boston, Little Brown, 1973.
Felicia the Critic, illustrated by Arvis Stewart. Boston, Little Brown, 1973; London, Hamish Hamilton, 1975.
Me and the Terrible Two, illustrated by Charles Carroll. Boston, Little Brown, 1974.
Just the Thing for Geraldine, illustrated by John Larrecq. Boston, Little Brown, 1974.
The Luck of Pokey Bloom, illustrated by Bernice Lowenstein. Boston, Little Brown, 1975.

Dear Lovey Hart, I Am Desperate. Boston, Little Brown, 1975.
The Alfred G. Graebner Memorial High School Handbook of Rules and Regulations. Boston, Little Brown, 1976.
And This Is Laura. Boston, Little Brown, 1977.
Eugene the Brave, illustrated by John Larrecq. Boston, Little Brown, 1978.
Hail, Hail Camp Timberwood, illustrated by Gail Owens. Boston, Little Brown, 1978.
Anything for a Friend. Boston, Little Brown, 1979.
We Interrupt This Semester for an Important Bulletin. Boston, Little Brown, 1979.
The Revenge of the Incredible Dr. Rancid and His Youthful Assistant, Jeffrey. Boston, Little Brown, 1980.
Seven Days to a Brand-New Me. Boston, Little Brown, 1981.
To All My Fans, With Love, From Sylvie. Boston, Little Brown, 1982.
Lenny Kandell, Smart Aleck, illustrated by Walter Gaffney-Kessell. Boston, Little Brown, 1983.
If This Is Love, I'll Take Spaghetti. New York, Four Winds Press, 1983; London, Fontana, 1984.
You Never Can Tell. Boston, Little Brown, 1984.
Strictly for Laughs. New York, Putnam, 1985.
Why Me? Boston, Little Brown, 1985.
A Royal Pain. New York, Scholastic, 1986.
The Things I Did for Love. New York, Bantam, 1987.
A Case for Jenny Archer, illustrated by Diane Palmisciano. Boston, Little Brown, 1988.
A Job for Jenny Archer, illustrated by Diane Palmisciano. Boston, Little Brown, 1988.
Genie with the Light Blue Hair. New York, Bantam, 1989.
Jenny Archer, Author, illustrated by Diane Palmisciano. Boston, Little Brown, 1989.
What's Cooking, Jenny Archer?, illustrated by Diane Palmisciano. Boston, Little Brown, 1989.

*

Manuscript Collection: Kerlan Collection, University of Minnesota, Minneapolis.

Ellen Conford comments:
I write primarily to entertain. When I was a child reading was the thing I most loved to do. I hope that my books provide something of that same enjoyment for today's readers.

*   *   *

Ellen Conford has explained that she writes books she hopes will "wrest a child away from the TV set for a couple of hours," and her books are designed to do just that—compete with the streamlined world of television. Fast-paced and optimistic, Conford's stories offer engaging, sometimes quirky characters, uncomplicated plots, and simple solutions, complete with a generous dose of humor. Written in a style best described as comic realism, the majority of the books deal with the lighter problems of childhood and adolescence, as seen through the eyes of preteen and teenage girls.

Conford's works can be grouped chronologically into four categories, each with a slightly different audience or approach. Her early publications consist of picture books and stories for junior readers, usually dealing with characters discovering that questionable qualities can be assets or learning to develop their own abilities. The second group, embracing most of the publications from *Dear Lovey Hart, I Am Desperate* to *Anything for a Friend,* treats the transition from childhood to adolescence, often incorporating romance as a plot complication. Most of these also include a change in the protagonist's surroundings and use her gradual adjustment as a way of illustrating emotional growth.

Love and the attendant complications become progressively more important in the books from 1979 on, culminating in *The Things I Did for Love*, which humorously explores why people fall in love. The books from this period are a logical continuation of Conford's previous works: it is as if the heroines of the earlier stories have grown older and are now confronting a new set of problems. In contrast, the final group of books, also published during the 1980's, experiments with plots, characters, or settings. Three stories use male protagonists, although the boys are essentially the male equivalent of the typical Conford heroine. Several vary the setting: *Lenny Kandell, Smart Aleck* and *To All My Fans, With Love, From Sylvie*—the latter, Conford's attempt at a more somber "problem novel"—are set in the 1950's; *A Royal Pain*, a strained variation of *The Prince and the Pauper*, takes place in a fictitious European country.

The cast of characters remains much the same from book to book. Most protagonists are average girls, mildly pretty, reasonably intelligent, and possessed of a wry sense of humor. Their biggest problem is unrequited love or a lack of self-confidence. Usually the heroine has one or more close friends. Practical and passive, they serve as a sounding board for her woes but rarely emerge as strong characters. In stories featuring a love interest, the boy, too, is virtually faceless—attractive in a vague sort of way, but with little personality. Except for Lenny and Sylvie, the protagonists come from happy, healthy families, complete with father, mother, and one or two siblings. Firmly ensconced in the middle class, they live in comfortable houses in suburbia, spending their time at school and shopping malls.

Plots are streamlined, with few scenes devoted to developing character or setting. This works well in books like *The Alfred G. Graebner Memorial High School Handbook of Rules and Regulations* and *Dreams of Victory*, where the story advances through a series of well-chosen vignettes and the action occurs in a familiar environment, and with books like *Dear Lovey Hart* and *We Interrupt This Semester for an Important Bulletin*, where strong secondary characters and/or subplots provide the necessary depth. It occasionally backfires in some young adult novels where the subject matter could benefit from more complex plots and characterizations.

Conford deals with surfaces and the visible rather than complex psychological studies. Accordingly, her heroines usually have fairly straightforward goals: they want to be popular or they want a particular boy's affection. The actions taken to achieve this also effect exteriors—buying new clothes, trying new makeup, or learning to make small talk. Social success and physical attractiveness are important to them and indeed are sometimes equated. This is ironic since an underlying theme in many of the books is developing self-confidence by recognizing inner qualities. Occasionally Conford tries to invert the message: *Why Me?* and *You Never Can Tell* touch on the perils of loving someone for appearance rather than self. Unfortunately neither story has the impact it should, perhaps because, like the protagonists themselves, Conford settles for surface rather than substance and neither develops the characters nor delves into the issues.

Conford's greatest asset is her humor, whether it be the wry commentary of her narrators, the one-liners in the dialogue, or the cleverly constructed incidents that leave the heroine bewildered and the reader delighted. One of Conford's favorite and most effective techniques for treating a subject is to juxtapose the real and the imaginary. In *Dreams of Victory* Victory daydreams to compensate for her failures; the exaggerated fantasies show another side of her character and counterpoint her all-too-normal life. Similarly, *Seven Days to a Brand-New Me* rests on the humorous contrast between the effervescent advice given in a self-help book, the exotic adventures described in a paperback romance, and the everyday life and frustrations of the narrator, a high school girl struggling to overcome her shyness and gain the attention and affection of the boy at the next locker.

At her worst, Conford produces readable but forgettable books; at her best, warm and funny tales illustrating the pitfalls of growing up—well worth missing a few television shows to read.

—Deidre Johnson

COOPER, Gordon (John Llewellyn). British. Born in Melksham, Wiltshire, 27 March 1932. Educated at St. Michael's School, Melksham, 1937–43; High School for Boys, Trowbridge, Wiltshire, 1943–48. Civil servant, 1967. Address: 6 Beanacre Road, Melksham Wiltshire, England.

PUBLICATIONS FOR CHILDREN

Fiction

An Hour in the Morning, illustrated by Philip Gough. London, Oxford University Press, 1971;.New York, Dutton, 1974.
A Time in a City, illustrated by Robin Jacques. London, Oxford University Press, 1972; New York, Dutton, 1975.
A Second Springtime, illustrated by Robin Jacques. London, Oxford University Press, 1973; Nashville, Nelson, 1975.
Hester's Summer, illustrated by Robin Jacques. London, Oxford University Press, 1974.
A Certain Courage, illustrated by Robin Jacques. London, Oxford University Press, 1975.

*

Gordon Cooper comments:

An Hour in the Morning began life as a short poem, "Country Girl," which I had written after seeing an old brown photograph of a group of girls with their teacher outside a village school in 1914.

I began writing *A Second Springtime* after seeing a paragraph in a local newspaper from a "March of Time" column which stated that in 1870 six girls had appeared before the magistrates in order to obtain necessary certificates authorizing their departure to Canada under a special welfare scheme.

Settings and real-life circumstances play an important part in all the books. At the end of writing each story I have always felt a deep sense of admiration for the people whose lives I have tried to portray.

*   *   *

The quiet chronicle of everyday events has a secure place in adult fiction but it is in many ways the antithesis of what children demand of a story. Adventure regularly comes top of polls of children's reading tastes, with humour, fantasy, and school themes fairly close behind, and it is difficult to recall a contemporary best-selling children's author whose work does not fall into one of these categories. It cannot be claimed that Gordon Cooper's books slot in to any of these groups, or that his careful reconstructions of times just past have achieved great popularity among library borrowers. It is the adults, especially the critics, who have discerned the fascination of detail when built into a credible background, and the potential emotional richness of the everyday.

The tone of the stories is thoughtful; the chief characters live restricted domestic lives on which world events impinge but are only half understood. Duty plays a large part. Kate in *An Hour in the Morning* rises at six, lights fires, carries hot water, cleans shoes, and is never resentful of her labour-filled life. The six-year-old twins walk three miles to school and three back and never consider this a hardship.

We do, of course, meet unpleasant characters—Aunt Em in *A Time in a City,* continually complaining and critical, or brusque Mr. Pritchard and his wife—and problems, such as Ben's unfriendliness and the accusation of theft in *A Second Springtime.* There are hints of deep thoughts and moral problems, as in the whole sequence in *A Second Springtime* when Hester decides how to meet Mrs. Pollitt's attempts to make amends. Rarely, though, do we glimpse the dark side of human nature. It is fascinating to compare Nina Bawden's view of Edwardian family life in *The Peppermint Pig* and of wartime evacuation in *Carrie's War* with *An Hour in the Morning* and *A Certain Courage,* respectively, and assess which is nearer the truth.

The basic structure of a Cooper novel is usually simple, the chronicling of life for one central character over a year or so, filled in with a fairly large supporting cast of neighbourhood acquaintance, the charting of a course from tribulation to achievement via hard work and honesty. There is no attempt to probe deeply into motives, desires, frustrations, and the style has a flat tranquillity which makes even the small emotions described hard to transmit. "'Happy birthday Hester' Mrs. Clarke said, 'Thank you Ma,' said Hester excitedly" (*A Second Springtime*) is one of many examples of language failing to meet situation. Yet the stories have the same ring of truth which Judith St. John's reminiscences of her Canadian childhood have; they make compulsive reading just as *The Archers* makes compulsive listening. The simple structure—this happened, then that—the untraumatic experiences, the optimism, the detailed guide to times within living memory, combine to make satisfying stories which leave their readers more grateful for the conditions and opportunities of the present.

—Peggy Heeks

COOPER, Lettice (Ulpha). British. Born in Eccles, Lancashire, 3 September 1897. Educated at St. Cuthbert's School, Southbourne; Lady Margaret Hall, Oxford, 1916–18, B.A. Editorial assistant and drama critic, *Time and Tide,* London, 1939–40. Public relations officer, Ministry of Food, London, 1940–45. President, Robert Louis Stevenson Club, 1958–74; Vice-Chairman, 1975–78, and President, 1979–81, English PEN Club. Recipient: Arts Council bursary, 1968, 1979; Eric Gregory travelling scholarship, 1977. O.B.E. (Officer, Order of the British Empire), 1980. Agent: A.P. Watt Ltd., 20 John Street, London WC1N 2DL. Address: 95 Canfield Gardens, London NW6 3DY, England.

PUBLICATIONS FOR CHILDREN

Fiction

Blackberry's Kitten, illustrated by Mary Shillabeer. Leicester, Brockhampton Press, 1961; New York, Vanguard Press, 1963.
The Bear Who Was Too Big, illustrated by Nicholas Fisk. London, Parrish, 1963; Chicago, Follett, 1966.
Bob-a-Job, illustrated by Mary Dinsdale. Leicester, Brockhampton Press, 1963.
Contadino, illustrated by Antony Maitland. London, Cape, 1964.
The Twig of Cypress, illustrated by W.F. Phillipps. London, Deutsch, 1965; New York, Washburn, 1966.
We Shall Have Snow. Leicester, Brockhampton Press, 1966.
Robert the Spy Hunter. London, Kaye and Ward, 1973.
Parkin, illustrated by Rosie Evans. London, Harrap, 1977.

Other

Great Men of Yorkshire (West Riding). London, Lane, 1955.
The Young Florence Nightingale, illustrated by Denise Brown. London, Parrish, 1960; New York, Roy, 1961.
The Young Victoria, illustrated by Denise Brown. London, Parrish, 1961; New York, Roy, 1962.
James Watt, illustrated by W.F. Phillipps. London, A. and C. Black, 1963.
Garibaldi, illustrated by Ronald Ferns. London, Methuen, 1964; New York, Roy, 1966.
The Young Edgar Allan Poe, illustrated by William Randell. London, Parrish, 1964; New York, Roy, 1965.
The Fugitive King, illustrated by Denise Brown. London, Parrish, 1965.
A Hand upon the Time: A Life of Charles Dickens. New York, Pantheon, 1968; London, Gollancz, 1971.
Robert Louis Stevenson. London, Burns and Oates, 1969.
Gunpowder: Treason and Plot, illustrated by Elisabeth Grant. London, Abelard Schuman, 1970.

PUBLICATIONS FOR ADULTS

Novels

The Lighted Room. London, Hodder and Stoughton, 1925.
The Old Fox. London, Hodder and Stoughton, 1927.
Good Venture. London, Hodder and Stoughton, 1928.
Likewise the Lyon. London, Hodder and Stoughton, 1928.
The Ship of Truth. London, Hodder and Stoughton, and Boston, Little Brown, 1930.
Private Enterprise. London, Hodder and Stoughton, 1931.
Hark to Rover! London, Hodder and Stoughton, 1933.
We Have Come to a Country. London, Gollancz, 1935.
The New House. London, Gollancz, and New York, Macmillan, 1936.
National Provincial. London, Gollancz, and New York, Macmillan, 1938.
Black Bethlehem. London, Gollancz, and New York, Macmillan, 1947.
Fenny. London, Gollancz, 1953.
Three Lives. London, Gollancz, 1957.
A Certain Compass. London, Gollancz, 1960.
The Double Heart. London, Gollancz, 1962.
Late in the Afternoon. London, Gollancz, 1971.
Tea on Sunday. London, Gollancz, 1973.
Snow and Roses. London, Gollancz, 1976.
Desirable Residence. London, Gollancz, 1980.
Unusual Behaviour. London, Gollancz, 1986.

Other

Robert Louis Stevenson. London, Home and Van Thal, 1947; Denver, Alan Swallow, 1948.
Yorkshire: West Riding. London, Hale, 1950.
George Eliot. London, Longman, 1951; revised edition, 1960, 1964.

*

Manuscript Collection: Eccles Public Library, Lancashire.

Lettice Cooper comments:
I want to write books that children will *enjoy,* and I hope the books will stimulate their imaginations. I should like to write them so that

they give children an example of good English.

*   *   *

Lettice Cooper is known to adults both as a novelist and for her scholarly but readable biography of Dickens, *A Hand upon the Time*, but she has also written delightful books for the very young and some intended for the newly independent reader. The child who is just beginning to master this new skill and can cope with a limited vocabulary will have great fun with the adventures of Robert the spy hunter, and will identify joyfully with the heroic Robert as he survives exciting perils like a mini-James Bond. Young children love stories where the small and underprivileged score over the large and powerful, and this is one of the book's great charms.

Blackberry's Kitten and *Parkin* are further tales for this age group. They read aloud well and provide a good vehicle for shared appreciation as books for bedtime. *Bob-a-Job* is the story of a couple of attractive but incompetent small boys attempting to do their good deeds for Scout Week; the humour here will appeal to young readers as the situations are familiar and the escapades only slightly over-the-top. The improbably plausible is the style of comedy that nines-to-elevens relish. *We Shall Have Snow* is in a more serious vein, telling how a lonely little girl left with relatives comes to terms with her difficulties.

Cooper's work for older children is set in the Italian countryside which is described in loving detail. She knows Tuscany and its people well, and in *Contadino* we see the region through the eyes of a young American boy coming to live with his Italian grandparents, exploring the totally new way of life and beliefs. There is some plot excitement to spice the descriptive writing when young Nicolo is instrumental in persuading the local landlord against the eviction of his grandfather from the family home. *The Twig of Cypress* takes us back to the 19th century, and we follow the story of a youngster who supports Garibaldi and his freedom fighters in an exciting adventure story.

Apart from the last-mentioned story her books could be said to sacrifice plot to description and character delineation. We learn a lot about appearances, scenery, motives and feelings, but the why seems more important than the what. Perhaps this is oversimplification, but the stories have a candyfloss quality, a frothy delicacy that is so evanescent that as soon as you put the book down you wonder whether you really enjoyed it after all. With the tales for the little ones this does not really matter.

—Ann G. Hay

COOPER, Susan (Mary).   British.   Born in Burnham, Buckinghamshire, 23 May 1935. Educated at Slough High School, Buckinghamshire; Somerville College, Oxford, 1953–56, M.A. 1956. Married Nicholas J. Grant in 1963 (divorced 1982); one son and one daughter. Moved to the United States in 1963. Reporter and feature writer, *Sunday Times*, London, 1956–63; U.S. columnist, Cardiff *Western Mail*, 1963–72. Recipient: Boston *Globe-Horn Book* award, 1973; American Library Association Newbery Medal, 1976; Welsh Arts Council Tir na n'Og award, 1976, 1978; B'nai B'rith Janusz Korczak award, 1984. Address: c/o Atheneum Publishers, 115 Fifth Avenue, New York, New York 10003, U.S.A.

PUBLICATIONS FOR CHILDREN

Fiction

The Dark Is Rising:
   Over Sea, Under Stone, illustrated by Margery Gill.   London,
      Cape, 1965; New York, Harcourt Brace, 1966.
   The Dark Is Rising, illustrated by Alan Cober.   London, Chatto
      and Windus, and New York, Atheneum, 1973.
   Greenwitch.   London, Chatto and Windus, and New York,
      Atheneum, 1974.
   The Grey King, illustrated by Michael Heslop.   London, Chatto
      and Windus, and New York, Atheneum, 1975.
   Silver on the Tree.   London, Chatto and Windus, and New York,
      Atheneum, 1977.
Dawn of Fear, illustrated by Margery Gill.   New York, Harcourt
      Brace, 1970; London, Chatto and Windus, 1972.
Jethro and the Jumbie, illustrated by Ashley Bryan.   New York,
      Atheneum, 1979; London, Chatto and Windus, 1980.
Seaward.   New York, Atheneum, and London, Bodley Head, 1983.

Other

The Silver Cow: A Welsh Tale, illustrated by Warwick Hutton.   New
      York, Atheneum, and London, Chatto and Windus, 1983.
The Selkie Girl, illustrated by Warwick Hutton.   New York, Mc-
      Elderry, 1986; London, Hodder and Stoughton, 1987.

PUBLICATIONS FOR ADULTS

Novel

Mandrake.   London, Hodder and Stoughton, 1964.

Plays

Foxfire, with Hume Cronyn, music by Jonathan Holtzman, adapta-
      tion of the *Foxfire* books edited by Eliot Wigginton (produced
      Stratford, Ontario, 1980; Minneapolis and New York, 1982).
      New York and London, French, 1983.

Television Plays: *Dark Encounter*, 1976; *The Dollmaker*, with Hume
Cronyn, from the novel by Harriette Arnow, 1983.

Other

Behind the Golden Curtain: A View of the U.S.A.   London, Hodder
      and Stoughton, 1965; New York, Scribner, 1966.
J.B. Priestley: Portrait of an Author.   London, Heinemann, 1970;
      New York, Harper, 1971.

Editor, *Essays of Five Decades*, by J. B. Priestley.   Boston, Little
      Brown, 1968; London, Heinemann, 1969.

*

Manuscript Collection: Osborne Collection, Toronto Public Library.

Susan Cooper comments:
   (1978) Although *Dawn of Fear* is a realistic novel the remaining
five books for children constitute a sequence with the overall title of
The Dark Is Rising. This is a fantasy dealing with the pressures of
good and evil in the world, which appears to be read by children from
the age of 10 upwards, by university students, and by assorted adults.

*   *   *

Susan Cooper has come to be be recognized as a major author of
books for children and young adults. Her first work for children,
Over Sea, Under Stone, came as a response to a contest designed to
honor the memory of E. Nesbit. Set in Cornwall, this is a family

adventure story concerning Simon, Barnabus, and Jane's search for a mysterious grail. The magic and myth, so much a part of the subsequent books of *The Dark Is Rising* series, is only hinted at here. The story draws upon the King Arthur legend and suggests connections to a world outside that of the contemporary environment.

Dawn of Fear calls upon the actual experiences of English childhood during World War II, but recasts them in the form of the fictional story of Derek and his friends Peter and Geoffrey. One of the strengths of this work lies in its ability to contrast the world of childhood play with the horrors of war without either losing the sense of innocent play or minimizing the atrocities of the world conflict.

Cooper's major contribution thus far has been *The Dark Is Rising* series, which greatly expands the mythical theme suggested in *Over Sea, Under Stone* and reveals Cooper's extraordinary prowess as an author of fantasy. *The Dark Is Rising,* set in Buckinghamshire, is the second work in the sequence. Here the battle lines between good and evil are formally established as the forces of Light and Dark are drawn into conflict. The Light, aided by Will Stanton, youngest of the Old Ones, seeks to gather together the Six Signs of the Light that will enable Light to overcome Dark. Yet the drawing of lines between good and evil, Light and Dark, rather than completely clarifying the conflict, serves as a mechanism to cast doubt upon the nature of good and evil as concepts. The shadowy aspect of the conflict and the inability to "read" clearly the motivations of some of the characters are areas in which Cooper has been criticized. However, I feel that the ambiguity of protagonists and antagonists is a deliberate literary device. Rather than succumbing to artistic flaw, Cooper goes beyond the conventional expectations of her readers by inviting them to glimpse the complex, the unexplainable, and often the threatening aspects of mankind's nature. By offering the thesis that the human psyche may manifest itself in explicit actions or present itself in a mysterious and often frustrating manner, Cooper exceeds the traditional presentations of good versus evil often found in fantasy literature.

Greenwitch, the third book in the series, is quite different in mood from the earlier books. In this dreamlike novel set in Cornwall, magic often occurs during the hours of darkness and yet readers are not left with the feeling that experiences have been merely imagined. The Greenwitch, a figure created by village women, comes into possession of a great secret coveted by the powers of Light and Dark. Young Jane's innocence moves the creature to release the secret. Jane is an interesting figure because at first she appears to be a rather flat character who reacts according to convention. Yet as the story progresses, we learn that even those who are skilled and knowledgeable in fighting the powers of the Dark are powerless in this instance. Ironically it is Jane who is successful, not through dramatic means, but rather through communicating her compassion for the Greenwitch. Indeed, irony is a convention used to great effectiveness by Cooper here, and one that helps intensify the conflict.

Will Stanton is the central figure in *The Grey King,* set in Wales, the fourth part of the Sequence. He is assisted in his quest for a golden harp by several people, including Bran, son of King Arthur, brought forward in time. Cooper continues her exploration of the many guises of evil and reiterates the theme that the Dark is a wily foe, capable of taking many forms. The sense of danger in this book, set during the period of Halloween, is very real, and the menacing setting of the mountainous Wales serves to heighten the suspense.

Silver on the Tree rivals *The Dark Is Rising* in complexity. Set in Buckinghamshire, the book functions as the grand final conclusion of the series, with intricate themes borrowed from earlier books sounding forth. The five children Simon, Jane, Barnabus, Will, and Bran are called together to assist in resolving the dramatic conflict between Light and Dark. In this book Cooper is at her most powerful, drawing upon the full range of her creative genius. Characterizations are complex and there are surprises in store for both the reader and the characters.

Cooper's subsequent works are major departures from the preceding series. *Jethro and the Jumbie, The Silver Cow: A Welsh Tale,* and *The Selkie Girl* are compact, imaginative works intended for a younger audience. In the the first book set on a Carribean Island, Cooper introduces a black protagonist who must deal with the mischievous spirit called the Jumbie. The other two books both return to the Celtic mythic material used in Cooper's earlier works. In *The Silver Cow* a fairy cow given as a gift is misused by a young boy's father, with consequences to follow. *The Selkie Girl* is the tragic love story of the marriage of a mortal man and a Selkie girl. This is a story of transformation, a theme that intrigues Cooper and appears in many of her works.

Cooper's most recent full length work to date is *Seaward,* which is perhaps the most complex and least clearcut of all of her works. Here she appears purposely to avoid explanations and instead chooses to offer the reader a world of possibilities, so many in fact that they create an extremely ambiguous text. This is a challenging novel, with subtleties which may perhaps be best appreciated by an adult audience. The protagonists, Cally and West, are adolescents caught up in the drama of having to cope with the deaths of their parents, events around which swirl mystery and innuendo. At the height of their personal tragedy they are transported to a Celtic world ruled by the old gods who would use the children should they be unable to resist the temptations placed before them. This is an allegorical tale about coming of age in a hostile world.

Susan Cooper's work is fully illustrative of a richly creative imagination. Throughout her books major themes resurface, allowing the reader to experience and internalize the depth of her commitment to her social ideals as well as to her art. While she freely acknowledges her debt to the past, her fantasy writing for children offers readers original perspectives in an area which continues to maintain a firm grasp upon the hearts of readers and authors alike.

—Karen Patricia Smith

CORBETT, (Winfield) Scott. American. Born in Kansas City, Missouri, 27 July 1913. Educated at Kansas City Junior College, 1930–32; University of Missouri, Columbia, bachelor of journalism 1934. Served as a correspondent, United States Army 42nd (Rainbow) Infantry Division, 1943–46. Married Elizabeth Grosvenor Pierce in 1940; one daughter. Part-time teacher, Moses Brown School, Providence, 1957–65. Recipient: Mystery Writers of America Edgar Allan Poe award, 1963. Agent: Curtis Brown, 10 Astor Place, New York, New York 10003. Address: 149 Benefit Street, Providence, Rhode Island 02903, U.S.A.

PUBLICATIONS FOR CHILDREN

Fiction

Susie Sneakers, illustrated by Leonard Shortall. New York, Crowell, 1956.
Midshipman Cruise. Boston, Little Brown, 1957.
Tree House Island, illustrated by Gordon Hansen. Boston, Little Brown, and London, Dent, 1959.
Dead Man's Light, illustrated by Leonard Shortall. Boston, Little Brown, 1960.
The Lemonade [*Mailbox, Disappearing Dog, Limerick, Baseball, Turnabout, Hairy Horror, Hateful Plateful, Home Run, Hockey, Black Mask, Hangman's Ghost*] *Trick,* illustrated by Paul Galdone. Boston, Little Brown, 12 vols., 1960–77.

Cutlass Island, illustrated by Leonard Shortall. Boston, Little Brown, 1962; London, Dent, 1964.

Danger Point: The Wreck of the "Birkenhead." Boston, Little Brown, 1962.

One by Sea, illustrated by Victor Mays. Boston, Little Brown, 1965.

The Cave above Delphi, illustrated by Gioia Fiammenghi. New York, Holt Rinehart, 1965.

Pippa Passes, illustrated by Judith Gwyn Brown. New York, Holt Rinehart, 1966.

The Case of the Gone Goose, illustrated by Paul Frame. Boston, Little Brown, 1966.

Diamonds Are Trouble. New York, Holt Rinehart, 1967; revised edition as *The Trouble with Diamonds,* New York, Dutton, 1985.

Cop's Kid, illustrated by Jo Polseno. Boston, Little Brown, 1968.

Ever Ride a Dinosaur?, illustrated by Mircea Vasiliu. New York, Holt Rinehart, 1969.

The Case of the Fugitive Firebug, illustrated by Paul Frame. Boston, Little Brown, 1969.

Diamonds Are More Trouble. New York, Holt Rinehart, 1969.

Steady, Freddie, illustrated by Lawrence Beall Smith. New York, Dutton, 1970.

The Baseball Bargain, illustrated by Wallace Tripp. Boston, Little Brown, 1970.

The Mystery Man, illustrated by Nathan Goldstein. Boston, Little Brown, 1970.

The Case of the Ticklish Tooth, illustrated by Paul Frame. Boston, Little Brown, 1971.

The Big Joke Game, illustrated by Mircea Vasiliu. New York, Dutton, 1972.

The Red Room Riddle, illustrated by Geff Gerlach. Boston, Little Brown, 1972.

Dead Before Docking, illustrated by Paul Frame. Boston, Little Brown, 1972.

Run for the Money, illustrated by Bert Dodson. Boston, Little Brown, 1973.

Dr. Merlin's Magic Shop, illustrated by Joe Mathieu. Boston, Little Brown, 1973.

Take a Number. New York, Dutton, 1974.

Here Lies the Body, illustrated by Geff Gerlach. Boston, Little Brown, 1974.

The Case of the Silver Skull, illustrated by Paul Frame. Boston, Little Brown, 1974.

The Great Custard Pie Panic, illustrated by Joe Mathieu. Boston, Little Brown, 1974.

The Boy with Will Power, illustrated by Ed Parker. Boston, Little Brown, 1975.

The Case of the Burgled Blessing Box, illustrated by Paul Frame. Boston, Little Brown, 1975.

The Boy Who Walked on Air, illustrated by Ed Parker. Boston, Little Brown, 1975.

The Great McGoniggle's Gray Ghost, illustrated by Bill Ogden. Boston, Little Brown, 1975.

The Great McGoniggle's Key Play, illustrated by Bill Ogden. Boston, Little Brown, 1976.

The Hockey Girls. New York, Dutton, 1976.

Captain Butcher's Body, illustrated by Geff Gerlach. Boston, Little Brown, 1976.

The Great McGoniggle Rides Shotgun, illustrated by Bill Ogden. Boston, Little Brown, 1977.

The Foolish Dinosaur Fiasco, illustrated by Jon McIntosh. Boston, Little Brown, 1978.

The Discontented Ghost. New York, Dutton, 1978.

The Donkey Planet, illustrated by Troy Howell. New York, Dutton, 1979.

The Mysterious Zetabet, illustrated by Jon McIntosh. Boston, Little Brown, 1979.

The Great McGoniggle Switches Pitches, illustrated by Bill Ogden. Boston, Little Brown, 1980.

The Deadly Hoax. New York, Dutton, 1981.

Grave Doubts. Boston, Little Brown, 1982.

Down with Wimps!, illustrated by Larry Ross. New York, Dutton, 1984.

Witch Hunt. Boston, Little Brown, 1985.

Other

What Makes a Car Go?, illustrated by Len Darwin. Boston, Little Brown, 1963; London, Muller, 1968.

What Makes TV Work?, illustrated by Len Darwin. Boston, Little Brown, 1965; London, Muller, 1968.

What Makes a Light Go On?, illustrated by Len Darwin. Boston, Little Brown, 1966; London, Muller, 1968.

What Makes a Plane Fly?, illustrated by Len Darwin. Boston, Little Brown, 1967.

Rhode Island. New York, Coward McCann, 1969.

What Makes a Boat Float?, illustrated by Victor Mays. Boston, Little Brown, 1970.

What about the Wankel Engine?, illustrated by Jerome Kühl. New York, Four Winds Press, 1974.

Bridges, illustrated by Richard Rosenblum. New York, Four Winds Press, 1978.

Jokes to Read in the Dark, illustrated by Annie Gusman. New York, Dutton, 1980.

Home Computers: A Simple and Informative Guide. Boston, Little Brown, 1980.

Jokes to Tell Your Worst Enemy, illustrated by Annie Gusman. New York, Dutton, 1984.

PUBLICATIONS FOR ADULTS

Other

The Reluctant Landlord. New York, Crowell, 1950.

Sauce for the Gander. New York, Crowell, 1951.

We Chose Cape Cod. New York, Crowell, 1953.

Cape Cod's Way: An Informal History. New York, Crowell, 1955.

The Sea Fox: The Adventures of Cape Cod's Most Colorful Rumrunner, with Manuel Zora. New York, Crowell, 1956; London, Hale, 1957.

*

Manuscript Collections: de Grummond Collection, University of Southern Mississippi, Hattiesburg; Kerlan Collection, University of Minnesota, Minneapolis.

Scott Corbett comments:

I am a storyteller devoted to the proposition that suspense and humor are a worthwhile combination. My books, especially the Trick books, have been widely used in schools to trap reluctant readers and get them started on books. My most successful efforts of late have been ghost stories of a slightly more modern flavor than those Victorian chillers which today are not only period pieces but, all too often, semi-colon pieces. The What Makes It Work books were successful in explaining difficult subjects to beginning readers—mainly because I started with no knowledge of the subjects myself and thus did not make the expert's mistake of assuming too much basic understanding on the part of his readers. *What Makes a Car Go?* was published in an Arabic edition, not for children but as a workable introduction to the internal combustion engine for adult

Arabs. Perhaps this was a mistake—I may have let something slip about the importance of all that oil. An interest in computers led me to write about them—and now I write all my books *on* my computer, while my typewriter gathers dust.

* * *

A strange old lady gave Kerby Maxwell a magic chemistry set. Think what different comic authors might do with this beginning. What Scott Corbett did was to have Kerby and his friend Fenton concoct a lemonade that made whoever drank it *good*. There are humorous consequences for Kerby's relationships with his surprised parents, the bully next door, and for the school play. *The Lemonade Trick* turned out to be the first of the successful series of "trick books" for which Corbett is best known.

In these and many of his other stories, Corbett blends a little magic and plot with a lot of boyish humor. *Ever Ride a Dinosaur?* begins "I don't know how you feel about garbage. Personally, I agree with the fellow who said 'I can take it out, or leave it alone.' The only trouble was at my cousin Charlie's house, I seemed to do the taking out, and he did the leaving alone." As this opening suggests, Corbett establishes an amiable relationship with the reader and gets on with his story. His themes are basic ones for the pre-adolescent boy. Corbett treats these themes in such a way as to keep them fun but non-threatening. "As usual," he writes in *The Limerick Trick* "when [Kerby] secretly worked with his chemistry set, he felt a bit guilty. What would his parents think if they knew?" In the work of Sendak, du Bois, or Dahl the explosive potential of this chemistry set would become apparent. In Corbett's stories the chemicals are used in a pro-social way. The lemonade trick makes one good, the hockey trick must be used to maintain a fair balance between the rival Panthers and Wildcats, etc.

Corbett has applied his skills to a non-fiction series, ranging from *What Makes a Car Go?* and *What Makes a Boat Float?* to a book on home computers. He has also written easy-to-read adventures, ghost stories, mysteries, and science fiction. In the quarter of a century from 1960 to 1985 he published an average of two to three books a year. In some of his stories the main characters are older than Kerby Maxwell. For example, two 16-year-olds, Wally and Les, are sleuths in the fairly complex mysteries *Grave Doubts* and *Witch Hunt.* Two young male scientists are the heroes of *The Donkey Planet,* but to disguise them for a secret mission their boss turns the pair into a 14-year-old boy with horns on his head and a donkey. The donkey has to resist the advances of female donkeys while the boy outwits the villain. When the boss commends them after their return to Earth, they tell him that "any ass could do it."

The chemistry of Corbett's appeal shows consistencies over time. He is a skilled craftsman but not a perfectionist. Though his humor and invention lack the brilliance of authors who are more daring and more invested in their creativity, he is a friendly and enjoyable author for pre-adolescent boys.

—Ravenna Helson

—

CORBETT, W(illiam) J(esse). British. Born in Birmingham, Warwickshire, 21 February 1938. Educated at Billesley Secondary School, Birmingham, 1942–53. Served as a physical training instructor in the British Army. Has worked as a merchant seaman, baker's assistant, furniture removal man, slaughterman, and builder. Recipient: Whitbread award, 1983. Agent: Murray Pollinger, 4 Garrick Street, London WC2B 9BH. Address: 6 Selborne Grove, Billesley, Birmingham, England.

PUBLICATIONS FOR CHILDREN

Fiction

The Song of Pentecost, illustrated by Martin Ursell. London, Methuen, 1982; New York, Dutton, 1984.
Pentecost and the Chosen One, illustrated by Martin Ursell. London, Methuen, 1984; New York, Delacorte Press, 1987.
The End of the Tale and Other Stories, illustrated by Tony Ross. London, Methuen, 1985.
Pentecost of Lickey Top, illustrated by Martin Ursell. London, Methuen, 1987.
The Bear Who Stood on His Head, illustrated by Martin Ursell. London, Methuen, 1988.
Dear Grumble. London, Methuen, 1989.

*

W.J. Corbett comments:
Although my books are classed as children's, I like to think that they can be enjoyed by a wide age group. My publications to date have all had animal characters with human parallels.
I never write down to children. I believe that they can grasp situations very quickly, and can enjoy sadness as well as humour in a book. I try to keep the ending under wraps as long as possible, allowing the reader's own imagination full play.
My latest work, *Dear Grumble,* is a change for readers as children are involved in the story.

* * *

W.J. Corbett's first book *The Song of Pentecost* was a deserved winner of the Whitbread award. It is a splendid saga story, telling of the journey of a group of assorted animals across a dangerous country to a new home in the Lickey Hills. An ingenuous snake is cheated of his inheritance, a beautiful pond, and is helped by harvest mice, led by their hereditary chief Pentecost. They agree to help the snake regain his home in return for a place to live, since their own dwellings have become hazardous through slum clearance plans. The characters are lively, the wit is adult, and we follow with keen interest their adventures, stirred up by a frog who is a pathological liar, an untrustworthy fox, and a strange seven-legged bug who is a born troublemaker.

The sequels, *Pentecost and the Chosen One* and *Pentecost of Lickey Top,* continue the adventure of Pentecost, his family, and the various animals living in the Lickey Hills. These books are less successful, however; most of the new characters are far less attractive, and the adult reader at least is aware of disturbing overtones.

Obviously comparisons with *Watership Down* are bound to be made, but though the theme is similar, there it ends. There are more different species among the characters, there are no legends, and over all there is a disturbing feeling not resolved as it is to some extent in *Watership Down.* No one character is really admirable, and children do like their heroes to be uncluttered by feet of clay.

—Ann G. Hay

—

CORBY, Dan. See CATHERALL, Arthur.

—

CORDELL, Alexander. Pseudonym for George Alexander

Graber. British. Born in Colombo, Ceylon (now Sri Lanka), 9 September 1914. Educated privately, and at Marist Brothers' College, 1921–30. Served in the British Army, 1932–36; Royal Engineers, 1939–45: Major. Married 1) Rosina Wells in 1937 (died 1972), one daughter; 2) Elsie May Donovan. Quantity surveyor in Wales, 1936–68. Since 1968 fulltime writer. Address: The Conifers, Railway Road, Rhosddu, Wrexham, Clwyd, Wales.

PUBLICATIONS FOR CHILDREN

Fiction

The White Cockade. Leicester, Brockhampton Press, and New York, Viking Press, 1970.
Witches' Sabbath. Leicester, Brockhampton Press, and New York, Viking Press, 1970.
The Healing Blade. Leicester, Brockhampton Press, and New York, Viking Press, 1971.
The Traitor Within, illustrated by Victor Ambrus. Leicester, Brockhampton Press, 1971; Nashville, Nelson, 1973.
Sea-Urchin. London, Collins, 1979.

PUBLICATIONS FOR ADULTS

Novels

A Thought of Honour. London, Museum Press, 1954; as *The Enemy Within,* London, Coronet, 1974.
Rape of the Fair Country. London, Gollancz, and New York, Doubleday, 1959.
The Hosts of Rebecca. London, Gollancz, 1960; as *Robe of Honor,* New York, Doubleday, 1960.
Race of the Tiger. London, Gollancz, 1963.
The Sinews of Love. London, Gollancz, 1965; New York, Doubleday, 1966.
The Bright Cantonese. London, Gollancz, 1967; as *The Deadly Eurasian,* New York, Weybright and Talley, 1968.
Song of the Earth. London, Gollancz, 1969; New York, Simon and Schuster, 1970.
The Fire People. London, Hodder and Stoughton, 1972.
If You Believe the Soldiers. London, Hodder and Stoughton, 1973; New York, Doubleday, 1974.
The Dream and the Destiny. London, Hodder and Stoughton, and New York, Doubleday, 1975.
This Sweet and Bitter Earth. London, Hodder and Stoughton, 1977; New York, St. Martin's Press, 1978.
To Slay the Dreamer. London, Hodder and Stoughton, and New York, St. Martin's Press, 1980.
Rogue's March. London, Hodder and Stoughton, 1981.
Land of My Fathers. London, Hodder and Stoughton, 1983.
Peerless Jim. London, Hodder and Stoughton, 1984.
Tunnel Tigers. London, Weidenfeld and Nicolson, 1986.
This Proud and Savage Land. London, Weidenfeld and Nicolson, 1987.
Requiem for a Patriot. London, Weidenfeld and Nicolson, 1988.
Moll Walbee. London, Weidenfeld and Nicolson, 1989.

Short Stories

Tales from Tiger Bay. Abergavenny, Blorenge Press, 1986.

*

Manuscript Collection: Boston University.

Alexander Cordell comments:

Children are small adults. To write down to them is insulting; their philosophy and outlook are usually mature, and their characters more honest. My intention in writing for them, certainly in respect of the historical trilogy of the '98 Irish Rebellion, was to give them an insight into the real reasons for the Irish troubles we experience today. *The Traitor Within* gives them a "peeping over the wall" glance at the great sleeping giant of China, at whose universities I lectured in 1958; *Sea-Urchin* creates for them the fairy-like quality of the Isle of Man, where Little People actually exist. My last published novel—*This Proud and Savage Land*—is dedicated to children everywhere, and tells this generation of the suffering and contributions to Britain's wealth of the children of the Industrial Revolution.

*   *   *

Alexander Cordell's transition from writing adult novels to writing for children was in a way a natural one, but he accepted the challenge, for challenge it was, with the same dedication and seriousness he had brought to writing for adults. He had already represented the oppressed people of Wales in the trilogy which began with *Rape of the Fair Country.* In his first essay in writing for children he chose to do the same for Ireland, taking as his focal point the 1798 rebellion. *The White Cockade, Witches' Sabbath,* and *The Healing Blade* are on one level swashbuckling spy-stories, chock-full of changes of fortune, as young John Regan takes on the mantle of his dead father as an agent for the United Irishmen, and the pace is as fast as his splendid mare Mia who carries him on his adventures. But Regan is not quite the super-human figure of romantic fantasy. He has feelings, and through his eyes too is reflected the quandary of the ordinary folk, pushed to arms against the British only because there was no alternative.

In *The White Cockade* the historical situation is set as Regan takes a message to the leader of the imminent rebellion, Lord Edward Fitzgerald. Of the three, this is the most "fictional," and the plot has twist after twist before Regan, having at one point been press-ganged into the British navy, succeeds in his mission. In *Witches' Sabbath* there is greater attention to the interpretation of historical personages and events, as Regan joins Father John Murphy, that mystical figure driven by circumstances to start the revolution before its leaders are ready. At the start of *The Healing Blade* the Wexford Rebellion has been crushed. Regan is sent to France to penetrate the English spy-ring and to protect Wolfe Tone, the man who was Ireland's last hope if she was to rise again. At the end of the book the fictional character and historical fact come together when Regan is the means whereby the knife with which the captured Tone committed suicide is put into Tone's hands. All three stories are particularly distinguished for their glorious, passionate Irish prose.

The Traitor Within reflects Cordell's great interest in the East, of which he has first-hand experience. The setting is a modern Chinese commune repeatedly threatened from Taiwan. Through the boy Ling's doubts and fears we learn of the conflict between the old Chinese culture and the new, and read the underlying message that young people, for all their different upbringings, are basically the same the world over. This utterly successful and moving story, told with humour and in language which catches admirably the Far Eastern way of speech and thought, is one of the most significant but under-rated children's novels of its time.

—Antony Kamm

CORLETT, William. British. Born in Darlington, County Durham, 8 October 1938. Educated at St. Olave's School, Ripon, Yorkshire; Fettes College, Edinburgh; Royal Academy of Dramatic Art, London, 1956–58, diploma. Repertory and television actor in London and the provinces. Recipient: Pye award, for television play, 1978. Address: Churchfields, Hope Mansell, near Ross-on-Wye, Herefordshire HR9 5TA, England.

PUBLICATIONS FOR CHILDREN

Fiction

The Gate of Eden. London, Hamish Hamilton, 1974; Scarsdale, New York, Bradbury Press, 1975.
The Land Beyond. London, Hamish Hamilton, 1975; Scarsdale, New York, Bradbury Press, 1976.
Return to the Gate. London, Hamish Hamilton, 1975; Scarsdale, New York, Bradbury Press, 1977.
The Dark Side of the Moon. London, Hamish Hamilton, 1976; Scarsdale, New York, Bradbury Press, 1977.
Barriers. London, Hamish Hamilton, 1981.
Bloxworth Blue. London, MacRae, 1984; New York, Harper, 1985.
The Secret Line. London, Walker, 1988.

Plays

Orlando the Marmalade Cat Buys a Cottage, adaptation of the story by Kathleen Hale (produced London, 1975).
Orlando's Camping Holiday, adaptation of the story by Kathleen Hale (produced London, 1976).

Television Plays: *Stephen,* 1979; *Barriers* series, 1980; *The Machine-Gunners,* from the story by Robert Westall, 1983.

Verse

The Ideal Tale, illustrated by Maria Lancaster. Salisbury, Compton Russell, 1975.
The Once and Forever Christmas, with John Moore. Tisbury, Wiltshire, Compton Russell, 1975.

Other

Questions series (*The Question of Religion, The Christ Story, The Hindu Sound, The Judaic Law, The Buddha Way, The Islamic Space*), with John Moore. London, Hamish Hamilton, 6 vols., 1978–79; as *Their Questions,* Scarsdale, New York, Bradbury Press, 6 vols., 1980.

PUBLICATIONS FOR ADULTS

Plays

The Gentle Avalanche (produced Farnham, Surrey, 1962; London, 1963). London, French, 1964.
Another Round (produced Farnham, Surrey, 1962). London, French, 1963.
Return Ticket (produced Farnham, Surrey, 1962; London, 1965). London, English Theatre Guild, 1966.
The Scallop Shell (produced Farnham, Surrey, 1963).
Flight of a Lone Sparrow (produced Farnham, Surrey, 1965).
The Scourging of Matthew Barrow (produced Leicester, 1966).
Tinker's Curse (produced Nottingham, 1968). Published in *Plays of the Year 34,* London, Elek, 1968; New York, Ungar, 1969.
We Never Went to Cheddar Gorge (televised 1968; produced Perth, 1969).
The Illusionist (produced Perth, 1969).
National Trust (produced Perth, 1970).
The Deliverance of Fanny Blaydon (produced Perth, 1971).

Television Plays: *Dead Set at Dream Boy,* 1965; *We Never Went to Cheddar Gorge,* 1968; *The Story Teller,* 1969; *A Memory of Two Loves,* 1972; *Conversations in the Dark,* 1972; *Mr. Oddy,* from story by Hugh Walpole, 1975; *The Orsini Emeralds,* from story by G.B. Stern, 1975; *Emmerdale Farm* series, 1975–77; *Philip,* 1979; *Going Back,* 1979; *The Red Signal,* from a work by Agatha Christie, 1982; *Dearly Beloved,* 1984; *The Christmas Tree,* from the novel by Jennifer Johnston, 1986; *Dreams Lost, Dreams Found,* from a work by Pamela Wallace, 1987.

*   *   *

William Corlett works at the boundary between teenage and adult fiction. His first novel, *The Gate of Eden,* appeared before publishers began using labels such as "Young Adult" to categorise novels that seem suitable for mid to late adolescence. Classification at this level is often difficult. Corlett's writing does not fit easily in such a slot, despite the usual presence of young adult characters. They are not late adolescents preoccupied by their own world, but people in a larger world of children and adults. Corlett's novels are serious and "adult" in a way that defies attempts to categorise possible readership.

The Gate of Eden is, apparently, a simple story about a teenage schoolboy who makes friends with an eccentric retired bachelor school teacher. This is the boy's first step beyond the confines of home and school. By the end of the book the boy has found his first girlfriend and rejects the old man in favour of the young woman. But there is much more. The character of the vulnerable old man is presented as vividly as that of the boy, the unnamed first-person narrator, who tells the story—recalling, quoting from letters, and commenting on his own memories and failings—long after the events. The balance of interest between youth and old age is equal and the point of view is strictly adult, tinged with bittersweet nostalgia and regret, poetically told.

Taken on its own *The Gate of Eden,* with its symbolic title, poetic writing, vigorous dialogue, compelling characterisation, and penetrating insight, compares very well with other outstanding books about complex relationships between teenagers and old people, such as John Branfield's *The Fox in Winter* and Penelope Lively's *The House in Norham Gardens,* where ideas about the start of adult life are balanced by thoughts of old age and death. But Corlett's first novel is actually the beginning of a trilogy.

The Land Beyond takes the unnamed young man through the aftermath of a three-year relationship with a different girl. Although the end of an affair can be of interest to teenagers, all the characters are adult. The narrative progresses through several different styles and levels: stream of consciousness, notebook, diary, TV screenplay, meditation, memory, a time-slip narrative as the man explores the temples at Delphi, and metaphysical speculation about life. There is a rebirth of the individual, framed within a confrontation or mutual haunting between the young man and the young Greek who was the model for the famous statue of the charioteer of Delphi. This use of time fantasy and living mythology links the book with the recently popular children's genre of a modern story haunted by the presence of ancient mythology. However the experimental nature of the writing demands far more than is usual with children's books.

Return to the Gate presents the unnamed narrator as an old man, surviving alone in an era of political collapse and economic scarcity. The old man meets a young woman. They establish a tentative relationship and help each other try to cope with the violence of the authoritarian society they live in. This subtly reworks the structure of relationships in *The Gate of Eden*. Although the book can be described as a kind of political science fiction, its characters are concerned to find some purpose in being alive, some way to make sense of life, and to know who they are and what they value. Corlett's vision is religious, broadly and humanely, rather than political.

After the trilogy, Corlett has worked on a more compressed scale. *The Dark Side of the Moon* interweaves three stories: an innocent(?) school boy is kidnapped as a philosophical protest against confining social values; a policeman tries to investigate the kidnapping; and an astronaut breaks down on the first trip behind the moon. Each story reflects on the other, and each raises serious questions about the meaning of life, madness, identity, good and evil, and social decay—questions which cannot reasonably be answered but deserve to be considered. The boy and the policeman are well realised, but the moon story does not integrate convincingly, despite its metaphorical significance. Much of the book's poetic speculative questioning resembles Corlett's non-fictional *Questions* series on religions. It is a brave experiment, deserving comparison with John Fowles's *The Collector* and William Golding's *Free Fall*.

Bloxworth Blue (named after a species of rare butterfly), much less experimental in prose style, explores many of Corlett's usual themes through five related strands of story. There is a medieval legend of two imps and Lincoln Cathedral, memories of the very elderly uncle, marital crisis of the mother, first sexual encounter of the daughter, and adventures of the son as he explores the cathedral, relives the legend, and discovers his uncle's bitter secret. Guilt, death, love, betrayal, murder, pain, lust, youth, old age, time, and God: a strong mixture—but "children's," "Young Adult," or adult? At times there is more telling than showing, but counterbalanced by insight and honesty, strong dialogue, complex emotion, and a range of interesting characters.

Corlett may not be to everyone's taste, but his individual voice, intelligence, and undeniable skill are always challenging and he deserves serious attention.

—John Gough

CORMIER, Robert (Edmund). American. Born in Leominster, Massachusetts, 17 January 1925. Educated at St. Cecilia's Parochial School, Leominster; Leominster High School, graduated 1942; Fitchburg State College, Massachusetts, 1943–44. Married Constance B. Senay in 1948; three daughters and one son. Scriptwriter, WTAG Radio, Worcester, Massachusetts, 1946–48; reporter and columnist ("And So On"), Worcester *Telegram and Gazette,* 1948–55; reporter, columnist (as John Fitch IV), and associate editor, Fitchburg *Sentinel and Enterprise,* 1955–78. Recipient: Bread Loaf Writers Conference fellowship, 1968; Associated Press award, for journalism, 1959, 1973; ALAN award, 1982. D.Litt.: Fitchburg State College, 1977. Agent: Curtis Brown, 10 Astor Place, New York, New York 10003. Address: 1177 Main Street, Leominster, Massachusetts 01453, U.S.A.

PUBLICATIONS FOR CHILDREN

Fiction

The Chocolate War. New York, Pantheon, 1974; London, Gollancz, 1975.
I Am the Cheese. New York, Pantheon, and London, Gollancz, 1977.
After the First Death. New York, Pantheon, and London, Gollancz, 1979.

Eight Plus One (short stories). New York, Pantheon, 1980.
The Bumblebee Flies Anyway. New York, Pantheon, and London, Gollancz, 1983.
Beyond the Chocolate War. New York, Knopf, and London, Gollancz, 1985.
Fade. London, Gollancz, and New York, Delacorte Press, 1988.

PUBLICATIONS FOR ADULTS

Novels

Now and at the Hour. New York, Coward McCann, 1960.
A Little Raw on Monday Mornings. New York, Sheed and Ward, 1963.
Take Me Where the Good Times Are. New York, Macmillan, 1965.

*

Manuscript Collection: Fitchburg State College, Massachusetts.

Critical Study: *Presenting Robert Cormier* by Patricia J. Campbell, Boston, Twayne, 1985.

Robert Cormier comments:

My books have been accepted by young readers for which I am grateful because young readers are a marvelous audience, open and responsive. I do not, however, write books for young people but about them. I write for the intelligent reader and this intelligent reader is often 12 or 14 or 16 years old. A work of fiction, if true to itself, written honestly, will set off shocks of recognition in the sensitive reader no matter what age that reader is. And I write for that reader.

* * *

Robert Cormier's novels for teenage readers have had an impact on the field of adolescent literature well out of proportion to their number. Cormier has brought a reporter's straightforward prose style and strong narrative sense to three searing stories of contemporary American life, causing waves of shock among reviewers accustomed to milder conventions and more reassuring messages. Unlike most novels written for a young audience, Cormier's are political rather than personal; they carry a narrative to a logical if bitter end, rather than suggesting (as many teen novels do) that adjustment and acceptance offer workable solutions to all human dilemmas.

The Chocolate War, first of Cormier's novels to be published for young readers (he had written three well-received adult novels previously), can be read on two levels. As a realistic tale of power and corruption in a Catholic boys high school, it is a tough, taut narrative that moves relentlessly toward a profoundly pessimistic ending. As a metaphor for society at large, it is a commentary on the sources of political power, the machinery of corruption, the costs of passivity, and the price of resistance. At either level, it is a challenging, unsettling story.

The next two novels carry their political themes without metaphor. *I Am the Cheese* tells the harrowing tale of a young boy trapped in a war between organized crime on one side and an equally ruthless government bureaucracy on the other. It is a terribly bleak story, without an escape route for its protagonist. The point made—among others—is that size alone is fearsome: losing human scale, organizations also lose human meaning. The style is terse, even elliptical; the events must be pieced together by the reader who thus makes the awful discoveries of the tale for himself. In *After the First Death,* terrorists hijack a school bus in order to confront the U.S. military establishment with political demands. Once again, the narrative is firmly paced and compelling, the mood intense, the underlying questions political and profound. Cormier asks his readers to consider the fragility of the distinction between patriotism and fanaticism, the responsibility of the individual citizen for the decisions of government, the moral dimensions of authority, power, and privileged information. At the center of a journalistic tale of suspense lie some of the hardest questions of our time.

Cormier's first three novels brought him great attention, if not always acclaim. Even reviewers appalled by the relentlessly stark conclusions of the narratives admitted their power and readability. As the books were quickly adopted by adolescent readers and even more discussed in professional literature, Cormier became a frequent speaker on the conference circuit.

His next three publications suggest that, for a while, at least, he may have listened to the critics who so often deplored the pessimism of his stories. *Eight Plus One,* a collection of short stories, although competent, lacks the impact of the novels. Each story is introduced by a brief forword in which Cormier describes the genesis of the tale, sometimes offering as well his own judgment about how he has succeeded in conveying the original idea. The book gives some insight into the craft of writing, but the stories themselves are neither as strongly written nor as subtle as the novels.

If *Eight Plus One* is bland by Cormier standards, *Beyond the Chocolate War* is unsatisfying in other ways. While both language and events match the original in shock value, the novel as a whole has a weakening strain of apology running through it. Instead of letting his story speak for itself and his readers work out the underlying themes for themselves, Cormier seems to want to redeem the profound pessimism of the earlier book with explicit messages about the power of nonviolence and the possibility of individual dissent from collective evil. Indeed, there are numerous passages that come alarmingly close to preaching. Adolescent readers will doubtless find many episodes gripping, especially in their tense potential for violence, but the novel has neither the haunting political overtones nor the subtle, persistent pressure to *think* that made *The Chocolate War* remarkable.

The Bumblebee Flies Anyway looks at first like the old Cormier. The narrative form takes puzzling out. As in *Cheese,* it isn't always apparent who is villain, who victim, or what ethic, if any, guides this mechanistic medical institution in which all the patients are terminal except for Barney, the young narrator. Barney doesn't know why he is there, since he believes himself entirely healthy. By the time he learns differently, he and readers alike are deeply enmeshed in the dwindling lives of the adolescent patients around him. And by the time Barney works out his complicated plan to retrieve some dignity from death by staging a spectacular multiple suicide, even a horrified reader is empathetic.

But at the last possible moment, Cormier swerves. The flight of the wooden automobile (The Bumblebee) from the hospital roof goes ahead, but without passengers; the sickest and most despairing of the boys dies there on the roof, but of disease, not volition, and Barney delivers himself of some highly conventional thoughts to the effect that the intent is equal to the deed—not a sentiment one expects from Cormier.

His most recent novel, however, demonstrates that the tough-minded Cormier has not retired. *Fade* operates at the farthest margin of the "young adult" category. It is a mesmerizing, psychologically complex story about Paul Moreaux, who discovers at 13 that he can make himself disappear. The power is hereditary, passing from uncle to nephew, a dark secret shared only by the unhappy inheritors. "Unhappy" is the key word. Paul's education as an unseen observer teaches him nothing joyous or uplifting; incest and treachery are only the beginnings of the awful revelations his power brings him. By midpoint in the novel, Paul knows too well the dark side of human nature, including his own.

The second half of the story is less tightly held together. Cormier constructs a distracting frame story about a manuscript written by

Paul (now a famous novelist) to finish the tale. In the manuscript Paul tells of searching for the nephew who is his successor to the "fade." He finds him, a terrified, raging, psychotic boy who has already begun to exact dreadful payment for the abuses of his childhood. Their meeting brings about the violent climax of the novel, leaving the reader to ponder the nature and source of human evil. *Fade* is Cormier at full power. The writing is strong, the narrative compelling, the vision dark yet compassionate, and painfully convincing. Reviewers will find it difficult to classify this novel as anything but fully adult, but young adults will read it, as they read Stephen King. And if it is about as savage as King's fantasies, it is far more thought-provoking.

—Anne Scott MacLeod

COWLEY, (Cassia) Joy. New Zealander. Born 7 August 1936. Educated at the Girls' High School, Palmerston North, Wellington. Married Malcolm Mason; two daughters and two sons (from a previous marriage). Pharmacist's apprentice, 1953–56. Recipient: New Zealand Children's Book of the Year award, 1983. Address: c/o Shortland Publications, P.O. Box 56–133, Auckland 3, New Zealand.

PUBLICATIONS FOR CHILDREN

Fiction

The Duck in the Gun, illustrated by Edward Sorel. New York, Doubleday, 1969.
The Silent One, illustrated by Hermann Greissle. New York, Knopf, 1981; London, Methuen, 1982.
The Terrible Taniwha of Timberditch, illustrated by Rodney McRae. Auckland, Oxford University Press, 1982.
Two of a Kind: Stories, with Mona Williams, illustrated by Jane Amos. Upper Hutt, Blackberry Press, 1984.
Salmagundi, illustrated by Philip Webb. Auckland and Oxford, Oxford University Press, 1985.
Captain Felonius, illustrated by Elizabeth Fuller. Auckland, Shortland, 1986.
The Lucky Feather, illustrated by Philip Webb. Auckland, Shortland, 1986.
My Tiger (stories), illustrated by Jan van der Voo. Auckland, Shortland, 1986.

Other (readers)

Fish in the Trough [*A New Friend, Johnny's Guitar, The Fire-Fighters, The Meeting House, Wendy Makes a Poi*], all illustrated by Nancy Parker. Wellington, Kea Press, 6 vols., 1968; as *The Tui and Sis Books,* Wellington, 6 vols., Price Milburn, 1977.
Story Chest Read-Together Books (*Mrs. Wishy-Washy, Smarty Pants, The Big Toe, Boo-Hoo, Grandpa Grandpa, Hairy Bear, The Hungry Giant, In a Dark Dark Wood, Lazy Mary, Obadiah!, One Cold Wet Night, Poor Old Polly, Sing a Song, Three Little Ducks, Woosh!, Yes Ma'am, The Red Rose, To Town, Dan the Flying Man, The Farm Concert, The Jigaree, Meanies, The Monster's Party, Who Will Be My Mother?*), with June Melser, illustrated by Elizabeth Fuller, Murray Grimsdale, Philip Webb, Martin Bailey, Andrew Reid, David Cowe, Deirdre Gardiner, Jenny Cochrane, Christine Ross, Jo Davies, Gary Hebley, Rosemary Turner, Annie Dickeson, Isabel Lowe, and Rita Parkinson. Auckland,

Shortland, 24 vols., 1980–83; Leeds, Arnold Wheaton, 24 vols., 1982–83.

Story Chest Books (*The Birthday Cake, The Dragon, A Terrible Fright, A Barrel of Gold, Clever Mr. Brown, Hungry Monster, Jack-in-the-Box, The Kick-a-Lot Shoes, The Pirates, Wet Grass, Where Is My Spider?, Yum and Yuk, Captain Bumble, Countdown, A Day in Town, The Big Tease, Cat on the Roof, The Ghost and the Sausage, Grandma's Stick, Hatupatu and the Birdwoman, Little Brother's Haircut, The Sunflower That Went FLOP, Tell-Tale, Sun Smile*), with June Melser, illustrated by Philip Webb, Martin Bailey, David Cowe, Deirdre Gardiner, Glenda Jones, Murray Grimsdale, Annie Dickeson, Robyn Kahukiwa, Helen Humphries, Sherryl Jordan, Isabel Lowe, and Christine Ross. Auckland, Shortland, 24 vols., 1981–82; Leeds, Arnold Wheaton, 24 vols., 1982.

Story Chest Ready-Set-Go Books (*The Bee, The Chocolate Cake, Come with Me, Copy-Cat, Flying, I Want an Ice Cream, Little Pig, Lost, My Home, Plop!, Round and Round, Splosh, To New York, Who Lives Here?, Where Are They Going?, Who's Going to Lick the Bowl?, Horace, The Night Train, The Pumpkin, Rum-Tum-Tum, Sleeping Out, Too Big for Me, What a Mess!, Look for Me*), with June Melser, illustrated by Christine Ross, Robyn Belton, Deirdre Gardiner, Murray Grimsdale, Jenni Webb, Philip Webb, Isabel Lowe, David Cowe, Martin Bailey, Annie Dickeson, Robyn Kahukiwa, Lynette Vondruska, and Rodney McRae. Auckland, Shortland, 24 vols., 1981–82; Leeds, Arnold Wheaton, 24 vols., 1982.

Story Chest Books (*Cooking Pot, Fast and Funny, Roly-Poly, Sing to the Moon, Tiddalik*), with June Melser and Margaret Mahy, illustrated by Deirdre Gardiner, Lynette Vondruska, Jo Davies, Isabel Lowe, Annie Dickeson, Philip Webb, and others. Auckland, Shortland, and Leeds, Arnold Wheaton, 5 vols., 1982.

Story Box Books (*The Pie Thief, The Tale of the Cook, The Trader from Currumbin, The War of the Winds, Poor Old Robot*), illustrated by Robyn Belton, David Cowe, and Jan van der Voo. Auckland, Shortland, 5 vols., 1982–85; first vol. published Leeds, Arnold Wheaton, 1982.

Story Chest Ready-to-Read Books (*Number One, The Biggest Cake in the World, Fasi Sings; Fasi's Fish, Greedy Cat, Our Teacher Miss Pool, Rain Rain, Words, I'm the King of the Mountain, Rosie at the Zoo, The Wild Wet Wellington Wind, Did You Say Five?, The Smile, Where Is Miss Pool?*), illustrated by Jill McDonald, Diane Perham, Murray Grimsdale, Robyn Belton, Nina Price, Lesley Moyes, Dick Frizzell, Christine Ross, Clare Bowes, and Penny Newman. Wellington, Department of Education School Publications Branch, 13 vols., 1982–87.

Story Chest Get Ready Books (*The Bicycle, The Big Hill, Feet, The Ghost, Go Go Go, Houses, If You Meet a Dragon, In the Mirror, A Monster Sandwich, Mouse, Night-Time, On a Chair, Painting, The Party, The Storm The Tree-House*), with June Melser, illustrated by Debbie Britten, Rita Parkinson, Sandra Morris, Robyn Belton, Rodney McRae, Elizabeth Fuller, Deirdre Gardiner, Glenda Jones, Sherryl Jordan, Isabel Lowe, Annie Dickeson, Jo Davies, and Rachel Waddy. Leeds, Arnold Wheaton, 16 vols., 1983.

The Fierce Little Woman and the Wicked Pirate, illustrated by Jo Davies. Auckland, Shortland, 1984.

Old Tuatara, illustrated by Clare Bowes. Wellington, Department of Education School Publications Branch, 1983; as *Old Lizard*, Melbourne, Nelson, 1985.

Jellybeans (*Don't Wake the Baby, The Kangaroo from Wool-loomooloo, Lavender the Library Cat, Let's Get a Pet, The Little Brown House, The Magician's Lunch, Morning Dance, The Most Scary Ghost, Mouse Monster, The Plants of My Aunt, Ten Loopy Caterpillars, The Terrible Armadillo, The Train That Ran Away, The Yukadoos, Monster, The Amazing Popple Seed, The Bull and the Matador, Cow Up a Tree, The Difficult Day, The Gumby Shop,*

A Handy Dragon, The Horrible Thing with Hairy Feet, Mr. Beep, Boggity-Bog, Do-Whacky-Do, The Shoe Grabber, A Silly Old Story, A Walk with Grandpa, The Wonder-Whizz, The Wild Woolly Child), illustrated by Elizabeth Fuller, Philip Webb, Rodney McRae, Jo Davies, Murray Grimsdale, Sherryl Jordan, David Cowe, Mary Davy, Rita Parkinson, Jan van der Voo, Kelvin Hawley, Martin Bailey, and Ian McNee. Auckland, Shortland, 30 vols., 1985–88; first 23 vols. published Leeds, Arnold Wheaton, 1986–87.

The King's Pudding, illustrated by Martin Bailey. Auckland, Shortland, 1986.

Turnips for Dinner, illustrated by Jan van der Voo. Auckland, Shortland, 1986; Leeds, Arnold Wheaton, 1987.

Mrs. Grindy's Shoes, illustrated by Val Biro. Auckland, Shortland, and Leeds, Arnold Wheaton, 1986.

Sunshine Books (*Yuk Soup, Baby Gets Dressed, Big and Little, Buzzing Flies, Dinner!, Down to Town, A Hug Is Warm, Huggles' Breakfast, Huggles Can Juggle, Huggles Goes Away, I Am a Bookworm, I Can Fly, I Can Jump, I Love My Family, Ice Cream, Little Brother, The Long Long Tail, Major Jump, My Home, My Puppy, Our Granny, Our Street, The Race, Scat! Said the Cat, Shark in a Sack, Shoo!, Snap!, Uncle Buncle's House, Up in a Tree, What Is a Huggles?, When Itchy Witchy Sneezes, Along Comes Jake, Bread, Come for a Swim, The Cooking Pot, Dad's Headache, Don't You Laugh at Me!, The Giant's Boy, Good for You, Goodbye Lucy, I'm Bigger Than You!, Let's Have a Swim!, Little Car, The Monkey Bridge, Mr. Grump, Mr. Whisper, My Boat, My Sloppy Tiger, Noise, Nowhere and Nothing, Old Grizzly, One Thousand Currant Buns, The Poor Sore Paw, Ratty-Tatty, Red Socks and Yellow Socks, The Seed, Spider Spider, The Terrible Tiger, The Tiny Woman's Coat, Wake Up, Mum!, What Would You Like?, Where Are You Going Aja Rose?, The Wind Blows Strong*), illustrated by Rodney McRae, Robyn Belton, Miranda Witford, Rita Parkinson, Judith Cowley, Isabel Lowe, Philip Webb, Sandy Nightingale, Jill Allpress, Madeline Beasley, Jan van der Voo, Susan Moxley, Annie Dickeson, Korky Paul, Val Biro, Wendy Hodder, Lynn Breeze, Terry Burton, Nick Price, Martin Bailey, Eric Kincaid, Peter Stevenson, Astrid Matijasevic, Jeff Fowler, Michelle Stuart, John Francis, Rosemary Murphy, and Vicki Smillie-McItoull. Auckland, Heinemann, 63 vols., 1986–87.

Windmill Books (*Growing, The Little Red Hen, My Little Brother, Splish Splash!, Where Can We Put an Elephant?, Where's the Egg Cup, Lucy's Sore Knee, My Wonderful Chair*), illustrated by Miranda Witford, Wendy Hodder, Judith Trevelyan, Dawn Johnston, Dick Frizzell, Jan van der Voo, and Trevor Pye. Auckland, Heinemann, 8 vols., 1986–88.

The Train Ride Story, illustrated by Val Biro. Auckland, Shortland, and Leeds, Arnold Wheaton, 1987.

Giant on the Bus, illustrated by Ian McNee. Auckland, Shortland, 1987.

Seventy Kilometers from Ice Cream, photographs by Winton Cleal. Wellington, Department of Education School Publications Branch, 1987.

PUBLICATIONS FOR ADULTS

Novels

Nest in a Falling Tree. New York, Doubleday, and London, Secker and Warburg, 1967.

Man of Straw. New York, Doubleday, 1970; London, Secker and Warburg, 1971.

Of Men and Angels. New York, Doubleday, 1972; London, Hodder and Stoughton, 1973.

The Mandrake Root. New York, Doubleday, 1975; London, Hodder and Stoughton, 1976.
The Growing Season. New York, Doubleday, 1978; London, Hodder and Stoughton, 1979.

Short Stories

Heart Attack and Other Stories. Auckland, Hodder and Stoughton, 1985; London, Hodder and Stoughton, 1986.

Other

Editor, with Thelma France, *Women Writers of New Zealand 1932–1982.* Wellington, Colonial, 1982.

*   *   *

Joy Cowley had her first stories (for adults) published in the New Zealand *Listener* in the 1960's. Since then she has published five novels for adults and a book of collected short stories. This body of writing is significant and valuable. In addition, however, she has established herself as one of New Zealand's finest writers for children. Not only has she had her work published in the public arena but has also made a tremendous contribution to series directed specifically to schools.

Cowley has said that "Reading should be 'magic.' Humour is valuable (children can't be tense when they are laughing) and also rhyme, rhythm, alliteration, etc. The two crimes in early reading are giving children books which are dull, and books which are difficult." The author follows her own advice exactly in the scores of stories she has written for children.

The Duck in the Gun first appeared in an American edition in 1969 and did not receive the attention it deserved until the 1984 New Zealand publication illustrated by Robyn Belton. The superb pictures underline the comic irony of a story in which the foolishness of war is gently derided.

In a picture book designed for older children, *Salmagundi,* the tone is sharper and the satire more direct. Even after the rival arms manufacturers, Dr. Foster and Major Brassblow, have replaced their factories with trees, gardens, and playgrounds their wickedness lives on.

The Terrible Taniwha of Timberditch goodhumouredly dramatises Josephine's search for the mysterious Maori monster, and her discovery of the mythical creatures of other countries such as trolls, gorgons, and the Loch Ness monster.

Pirates are the protagonists of *The Lucky Feather* and *The Fierce Little Woman and the Wicked Pirate.* In the first, Captain Castor discovers after a nasty accident that he needs no talisman but only his own independent judgement to keep himself out of trouble. The delightfully fierce little woman who lives in a cottage on the end of a jetty knits socks for sailors and plays her bagpipes to the seagulls. When the pirate finds humility, and she finds love, they live happily ever after.

Short stories in a volume shared with Mona Williams entitled *Two of a Kind* and the novel *The Silent One* demonstrate Cowley's deep, compassionate, and realistic knowledge of human values and behavior. *The Silent One* deserves the critical acclaim it has received. Set on a tropical island in the South Pacific, the story describes the ordeal of the deaf child Jonasi. Ostracised by the people of the village because of their superstition, he has only the love of his stepmother, and of the chief and his son. He spends most of his time fishing in the lagoon where he discovers and makes friends with the mysterious white turtle, who is the spirit of age-old wisdom and of light and grace. The story is mythic in quality, in style poetic, and simple and direct in the telling.

Cowley comes to her writing from a background of varied ex-periences. As a writer she is gifted and committed. Her imagination, her depth of understanding, her sense of fun, and her exhilaration give her books lasting qualities.

—Tom Fitzgibbon

———

CRAIG, John (Ernest). Canadian. Born in Peterborough, Ontario, 2 July 1921. Educated at the University of Manitoba, Winnipeg (King fellow), B.A. 1951; University of Toronto, M.A. in Canadian history. Served in the Royal Canadian Naval Volunteer Reserve, 1941–45. Married Frances Patten Morrison in 1945; three sons and one daughter. Market researcher, Canadian Facts Company, 1952–69, and ORC International, 1969–71, both Toronto. Recipient: Vicky Metcalf award, 1980. *Died 23 January 1982.*

PUBLICATIONS FOR CHILDREN

Fiction

Wagons West, illustrated by Stanley Wyatt. Toronto, Dent, 1955; London, Dent, and New York, Dodd Mead, 1956.
The Long Return, illustrated by Robert Doremus. Toronto, Mc-Clelland and Stewart, and Indianapolis, Bobbs Merrill, 1959.
No Word for Good-bye, illustrated by Harri Aalto. Toronto, Peter Martin Associates, 1969; New York, Coward McCann, 1971.
Zach. New York, Coward McCann, 1972; London, Gollancz, 1973.
Who Wants to Be Alone? New York, Scholastic, 1974.
The Wormburners. New York, Scholastic, 1976.

Other

Track and Field, with Frances Craig. New York, Watts, 1979.

PUBLICATIONS FOR ADULTS

Novels

By the Sound of Her Whistle. Toronto, Peter Martin Associates, 1966.
The Pro. Toronto, Peter Martin Associates, 1968; as *Power Play,* New York, Dodd Mead, 1973.
In Council Rooms Apart. New York, Putnam, 1971.
If You Want to See Your Wife Again.... New York, Putnam, 1971; London, Cassell, 1973.
Superdude. New York, Warner, 1974.
How Far Back Can You Get? Toronto and New York, Doubleday, 1974.
The Clearing. London, Constable, 1975.
Close Doesn't Count. Toronto, Macmillan, and London, Macdonald and Jane's 1975.
All G.O.D.'s Children. New York, Morrow, 1975.
Some of My Best Friends Are Fishermen. Toronto, McClelland and Stewart, 1976.
Chappie and Me. New York, Dodd Mead, 1979; as *Ain't Lookin',* Richmond Hill, Ontario, Scholastic, 1983.
The Last Canoe. Toronto, Peter Martin Associates, 1979.

Plays

Television Series: *Adventures in Rainbow Country,* 1970–71; *The*

Starlost, 1973; *Matt and Jenny.*

Other

Canada's Olympic Chances, with David Steen.   Markham, Ontario, Simon and Schuster, 1976.
The Noronic Is Burning.   Don Mills, Ontario, General Publishing, 1976.
Simcoe County: The Recent Past.   Midhurst, Ontario, Corporation of the County of Simcoe, 1977.
The Years of Agony 1910–1920.   Toronto, Natural Science of Canada, 1977.
The Crazy Twenties 1920–1930.   Toronto, Natural Science of Canada, 1978.

*

Manuscript Collection: University of Texas, Austin.

*   *   *

The most beautiful, perhaps, of John Craig's books for young readers is *No Word for Good-bye,* the haunting story of a friendship, and of its power to bridge the gulf of prejudice and misunderstanding. Ken is a white city boy who has "everything"; Paul an Ojibway Indian whose family is about to be driven from the shack which is their home. Ken is inquisitive, articulate; Paul is silent and remote. But somehow sympathy and generosity narrow the gap between their two worlds, and the boys become friends and allies in a hopelessly outmatched battle with big business. At summer's end life tears them apart, perhaps never to meet again, and Paul has no word with which to say goodbye to Ken; but their friendship has never relied upon words.

Another of Craig's young Indian heroes, Zach of *Who Wants to Be Alone?,* is literally alone in the world, for he is the last surviving Agawa. He finds no trace of his vanished tribe though he searches through much of Canada and the American midwest. All but resigned to a life alone, he falls in with others who share his sense of dislocation—Willie, a black badly hurt by the white college world of athletic scholarships, and D.J., a white girl fleeing a comfortable middle-class home whose values are totally inimical to her. Gradually they find themselves belonging somewhere—they have become a family.

As a change of pace from wilderness settings, *The Wormburners* is the heartening story of an inner-city cross-country team (who run "fast enough to burn the worms in the ground"); they are short of funds but well supplied with spirit and determination. This is a warmly satisfying story of underdogs coming from behind to win the national championship, and it has the kind of old-fashioned happy ending that leaves the reader with a warm glow of satisfaction.

Craig writes for the mature young reader, able to interpret subtle shadings and relationships without requiring exhaustive explanation. His girls and women are sketchy creations at best, but his boys and young men are painfully real: their bruises of the spirit are more poignant than the cuts and slashes of more boisterous fiction for young people.

A favorite device in Craig's work is the use of a summer place in the bush country to illustrate a deepening awareness of the realities of life with advancing years. Where the child sees only the sparkling lake and the picnic grounds, the youth begins to envision that same smiling landscape in its unwelcoming winter guise, and to speculate about the lives of those who must live the year round where others come only to holiday.

Craig's ability to discern and to convey to others the special beauty that is so often a part of lives of rugged privation, and his generous admiration of the fortitude with which such lives are undertaken, are praiseworthy qualities.

—Joan McGrath

———

CRAYDER, Teresa.   See **COLMAN, Hila.**

———

CRESSWELL, Helen.   British.   Born in Nottinghamshire, 11 July 1934. Educated at Nottingham Girls' High School; King's College, University of London, B.A. (honours) in English 1955. Married Brian Rowe in 1962; two daughters. Worked as a literary assistant, fashion buyer, teacher. Agent: A.M. Heath, 79 St. Martin's Lane, London WC2N 4AA. Address: Old Church Farm, Eakring, Newark, Nottinghamshire NG22 0DA, England.

PUBLICATIONS FOR CHILDREN

Fiction

Sonya-by-the-Shore, illustrated by Robin Jane Wells.   London, Dent, 1960.
Jumbo Spencer, illustrated by Clixby Watson.   Leicester, Brockhampton Press, 1963; Philadelphia, Lippincott, 1966.
The White Sea Horse, illustrated by Robin Jacques.   Edinburgh, Oliver and Boyd, 1964; Philadelphia, Lippincott, 1965.
Jumbo Back to Nature, illustrated by Leslie Wood.   Leicester, Brockhampton Press, 1965.
Pietro and the Mule, illustrated by Maureen Eckersley.   Edinburgh, Oliver and Boyd, and Indianapolis, Bobbs Merrill, 1965.
Jumbo Afloat, illustrated by Leslie Wood.   Leicester, Brockhampton Press, 1966.
Where the Wind Blows, illustrated by Peggy Fortnum.   London, Faber, 1966; New York, Funk and Wagnalls, 1968.
The Piemakers, illustrated by V.H. Drummond.   London, Faber, 1967; Philadelphia, Lippincott, 1968.
A Day on Big O, illustrated by Shirley Hughes.   London, Benn, 1967; Chicago, Follett, 1968.
A Tide for the Captain, illustrated by Robin Jacques.   Edinburgh, Oliver and Boyd, 1967.
The Signposters, illustrated by Gareth Floyd.   London, Faber, 1968.
Jumbo and the Big Dig, illustrated by Leslie Wood.   Leicester, Brockhampton Press, 1968.
The Barge Children, illustrated by Lynette Hemmant.   London, Hodder and Stoughton, 1968.
The Sea Piper, illustrated by Robin Jacques.   Edinburgh, Oliver and Boyd, 1968.
The Night-Watchmen, illustrated by Gareth Floyd.   London, Faber, and New York, Macmillan, 1969.
A Gift from Winklesea, illustrated by Janina Ede.   Leicester, Brockhampton Press, 1969.
A Game of Catch, illustrated by Gareth Floyd.   London, Chatto Boyd and Oliver, 1969; New York, Macmillan, 1977.
A House for Jones, illustrated by Margaret Gordon.   London, Benn, 1969.
The Outlanders, illustrated by Doreen Roberts.   London, Faber, 1970.
Rainbow Pavement, illustrated by Shirley Hughes.   London, Benn, 1970.
The Wilkses, illustrated by Gareth Floyd.   London, BBC Publications, 1970; as *Time Out,* Cambridge, Lutterworth Press, 1987.
The Bird Fancier, illustrated by Renate Meyer.   London, Benn, 1971.

Up the Pier, illustrated by Gareth Floyd. London, Faber, 1971; New York, Macmillan, 1972.

The Weather Cat, illustrated by Margery Gill. London, Benn, 1971.

The Beachcombers, illustrated by Errol Le Cain. London, Faber, and New York, Macmillan, 1972.

Bluebirds over Pit Row, illustrated by Richard Kennedy. London, Benn, 1972.

Jane's Policeman, illustrated by Margery Gill. London, Benn, 1972.

The Long Day, illustrated by Margery Gill. London, Benn, 1972.

Roof Fall!, illustrated by Richard Kennedy. London, Benn, 1972.

Short Back and Sides, illustrated by Richard Kennedy. London, Benn, 1972.

The Beetle Hunt, illustrated by Anne Knight. London, Longman, 1973.

The Bongleweed, illustrated by Ann Strugnell. London, Faber, 1973; New York, Macmillan, 1974.

The Bower Birds, illustrated by Margery Gill. London, Benn, 1973.

Lizzie Dripping, illustrated by Jenny Thorne. London, BBC Publications, 1973.

Lizzie Dripping by the Sea, illustrated by Faith Jaques. London, BBC Publications, 1974.

Lizzie Dripping and the Little Angel, illustrated by Faith Jaques. London, BBC Publications, 1974.

Lizzie Dripping Again, illustrated by Faith Jaques. London, BBC Publications, 1974.

Two Hoots [*Go to Sea, in the Snow, and the Big Bad Bird, and the King, Play Hide-and-Seek*], illustrated by Martine Blanc. London, Benn, 6 vols., 1974–77; New York, Crown, 6 vols., 1978.

More Lizzie Dripping, illustrated by Faith Jaques. London, BBC Publications, 1974.

Butterfly Chase, illustrated by Margery Gill. London, Kestrel, 1975.

The Winter of the Birds. London, Faber, 1975; New York, Macmillan, 1976.

The Bagthorpe Saga, illustrated by Jill Bennett:
  Ordinary Jack. London, Faber, and New York, Macmillan, 1977.
  Absolute Zero. London, Faber, and New York, Macmillan, 1978.
  Bagthorpes Unlimited. London, Faber, and New York, Macmillan, 1978.
  Bagthorpes v. the World. London, Faber, and New York, Macmillan, 1979.
  Bagthorpes Abroad. London, Faber, and New York, Macmillan, 1984.
  Bagthorpes Haunted. London, Faber, and New York, Macmillan, 1985.
  Bagthorpes Liberated. London, Faber, and New York, Macmillan, 1989.

Donkey Days, illustrated by Shirley Hughes. London, Benn, 1977.

Awful Jack, illustrated by Joanna Stubbs. London, Hodder and Stoughton, 1977.

The Flyaway Kite, illustrated by Bridget Clarke. London, Kestrel, 1979.

My Aunt Polly by the Sea, illustrated by Margaret Gordon. Exeter, Wheaton, 1980.

Dear Shrink. London, Faber, and New York, Macmillan, 1982.

The Secret World of Polly Flint, illustrated by Shirley Felts. London, Faber, 1982; New York, Macmillan, 1984.

Ellie and the Hagwitch, illustrated by Jonathan Heap. London, Hardy, 1984.

Petticoat Smuggler, illustrated by Shirley Bellwood. London, Macmillan, 1985.

Greedy Alice, illustrated by Martin Honeysett. London, Deutsch, 1986.

Whodunnit?, illustrated by Caroline Browne. London, Cape, 1986.

Dragon Ride, illustrated by Liz Roberts. London, Kestrel, 1987.

Moondial. London, Faber, and New York, Macmillan, 1987.

Trouble, illustrated by Margaret Chamberlain. London, Gollancz, 1987; New York, Dutton, 1988.

Rosie and the Boredom Eater. London, Heinemann, 1989.

Hokey Pokey Did It! Loughborough, Ladybird, 1989.

Plays

Lizzie Dripping and the Witch (produced London, 1977).

Television Plays: *Lizzie Dripping* series, from her own stories, 1973, 1975; *Dick Whittington,* 1974; *Jumbo Spencer,* from her own story, 1976; *The Secret World of Polly Flint* series, from her own story, 1987; *Moondial,* 1988.

Other (readers)

Rug Is a Bear, illustrated by Susanna Gretz. London, Benn, 1968.

Rug Plays Tricks, illustrated by Susanna Gretz. London, Benn, 1968.

Rug Plays Ball, illustrated by Susanna Gretz. London, Benn, 1969.

Rug and a Picnic, illustrated by Susanna Gretz. London, Benn, 1969.

John's First Fish, illustrated by Prudence Seward. London, Macmillan, 1970.

At the Stroke of Midnight: Traditional Fairy Tales Retold, illustrated by Carolyn Dinan. London, Collins, 1971.

The Key, illustrated by Richard Kennedy. London, Benn, 1973.

Cheap Day Return, illustrated by Richard Kennedy. London, Benn, 1974.

Shady Deal, illustrated by Richard Kennedy. London, Benn, 1974.

The Trap, illustrated by Richard Kennedy. London, Benn, 1974.

Nearly Goodbye, illustrated by Tony Morris. London, Macmillan, 1980.

Penny for the Guy, illustrated by Nicole Goodwin. London, Macmillan, 1980.

The Story of Grace Darling, illustrated by Paul Wright. London, Viking, 1988.

PUBLICATIONS FOR ADULTS

Play

Television Play: *For Bethlehem Read Little Thraves,* 1977.

*   *   *

Although Helen Cresswell began her career as a writer of delicate poetic fantasies, her reputation was made of stronger stuff. Her major books have something fantastic, if not always fantasy, in them. *The Piemakers,* her first outstanding success, includes no magical elements; the fantasy comes from telling a story larger than life. *The Signposters* was from a similar mould. With *The Night-Watchmen* in 1969 her work changed direction. The scene was still an enlarged version of the ordinary world, but the supernatural crept in, and it has stayed with her ever since. From *The Outlanders* to *The Winter of the Birds* her stories have occupied the frontier country between a world of commonplace niceness and nastiness and the terrors and wonders which lurk just out of sight. Part of the strength of the novels lies in their implications; she rarely brings the reader face to face with magic.

In her Lizzie Dripping stories, originally designed for television, Cresswell leaves it to the reader to decide whether the supernatural exists. Lizzie is a very ordinary girl in an ordinary family. Does she really have adventures with a witch? Television is a medium which by its nature cannot deal effectively with implications. The viewer has to see the witch as Lizzie does. In the more subtle written version options are left open. That gloriously colourful and embarrassing witch may be real, or she may exist only in Lizzie Dripping's inventive head.

Attractive as they are, the Lizzie Dripping stories are a byproduct of the major novels. So too are the Jumbo Spencer stories, and the disciplined brief texts which Cresswell has written for reluctant older readers, these latter perhaps the finest examples of a creative artist accepting restrictions on vocabulary, syntax, and subject-matter. It is as a writer of humorous and poetic fantasies that Cresswell is best known and is likely to be best remembered.

The Piemakers is the real foundation-stone of her work. This is a story of the Roller family, hereditary piemakers of Danby Dale in Yorkshire. A recurrent theme in all Cresswell's books is that of craftsmanship, of work done with skill and pride. The Rollers, like the Signposters and the entertainers in *Up the Pier* and even the scavengers and beachcombers, like to do a job well. Even Gravella Roller, who hates the family trade and wants to go on the stage, recognizes her father's supreme artistry. Faced with the newly baked royal pie "faintly golden, smooth and yet promising a rough, satisfying crustiness, and decorated with the Royal Coat of Arms, a slightly deeper gold, perfect as if it had been carved from stone by the chisel of a master," Gravella breathes: "Oh, it's beautiful!" and her mother dabs her eyes with "the pinafore that wasn't there."

The Piemakers is a funny book, but it takes the fun quite seriously. It is a comedy of incongruity, achieved by blowing a commonplace situation up to gigantic proportions. Baking a pie is not funny. Baking a pie for two thousand eaters *is,* the more so because the logistics of the operations are worked out in detail. Cresswell sets her very tall story neatly in a pseudo-historical context, producing archival evidence. Archaeological too; in an exquisite epilogue she takes sceptical readers back to Danby Dale to look at the duck pond on the village green. Yes, it *is* the pie-dish.

Funny as the book is, real life is sometimes funnier. Having spun *The Piemakers* out of her imagination, Cresswell discovered that the piemakers of Danby Dale had really existed. Documentary evidence was to be had, and earnest historical researchers sought her acquaintance and co-operation.

In *The Signposters* Helen Cresswell pursued a similar theme, but with a little less gusto. Again the emphasis is on craftsmanship, but the crafts are many and the effect diffuse. This is a story of the open road, and the best of it is the atmosphere and the pervasive happiness.

She is at her best in drawing eccentrics, and this is perhaps a small criticism of her work. Every fantasy needs a touchstone of reality. In *The Night-Watchmen* the story turns on a very normal little boy who lacks the sharp individuality of, for example, Alice. Consequently, instead of providing a bridge between the real and the fantastic worlds, Henry tends to be an obstacle to one's acceptance of the fantasy. The same is true, in a lesser degree, of the small lodger in *The Beachcombers.*

This apart, *The Night-Watchmen* is an absorbing novel as well as a key to Cresswell's later work. The central idea is marvellous in its originality and simplicity. Josh and Caleb are tramps who have devised the perfect protection against being moved on by the police. A hole in the ground, a Danger Men at Work sign, and tramps become night-watchmen, part of the scenery and not worth a second glance. A whole comic novel could be grown from this seed, and this writer could have brought it off splendidly with such richly humorous characters as Josh and Caleb. But Cresswell had already written two purely funny books, and she was pushing outwards the frontiers of her craft. So the night-watchmen are threatened by Greeneyes, a half-explained and less than half-seen terror of the night. Henry helps to frustrate the Greeneyes and Josh and Caleb catch the night train to There. The story is masterly in its rise to a climax and a swift

resolution, but some readers are left with the vague feeling that they have been cheated.

The Winter of the Birds is the latest of her stories in the category of poetic and grotesque fantasy. It is perhaps her cleverest book, but it is not necessarily for that reason more original and important than the earlier work. There are signs that with greater maturity she is becoming more serious, or more sober. There is not much sheer fun in *The Winter of the Birds.* Edward Flack, who has dedicated his life to the achievement of heroism, is a nice invention but he barely raises a smile. Patrick Finn, who *is* a hero, is one of Cresswell's larger-than-life people; he is very noisy but hardly very amusing. The best touches of Cresswell humour come from the terrible MacKays, enormously antisocial small boys.

The power and seriousness of much of *The Winter of the Birds* may have led some admirers to think that Cresswell was turning away from humour. They were reassured by the Bagthorpe books. In one of those abrupt changes of direction in which she delights, she turned to uproarious situation comedy. The Bagthorpes are a family of geniuses, all, that is, except Jack who is ordinary. They are also lacking in the ordinary faculties of commonsense and self-preservation, and their brilliance leads them into ever more hilarious dilemmas. Take, for example, the great competition phase. The family decide to make capital out of their preternatural intelligence by entering for every available competition. To this end Father removes all the labels from the food tins in the larder. Thereafter every meal in the Bagthorpe household becomes a matter of high adventure as each member of the family in turn takes pot-luck among the anonymous cans. Fostered by a television series the Bagthorpes have become something of a cult, good for sales but not so good for creativity. Indeed there was a sad failure of imagination in the last two books of the series, when the author strove hard to inject some of the old humour into contrived situations and tired characters.

Before this Cresswell had made another of her abrupt changes of direction. In *Dear Shrink* she entered an area so far unfamiliar to her, that of the sociological novel. The sensitive, cultured, and reasonably affluent Saxon children find themselves, through an unforeseen change in their parents' plans, at the mercy of the Social Services Department. They are put into "care," first with a foster mother of positively Dickensian horror, then in a children's home. In his distress Oliver Saxon, who tells the story, takes to confiding his inmost thoughts to Carl Jung, whom he addresses in his journal as "Dear Shrink." The writer strains probability, both in the basic situation and in some of the details, but she paints a memorable picture of a modern human problem, the more effective because it comes through the words of an articulate small boy.

The most successful of her later work has come from a renewed interest in the possibilities offered by television drama. *Moondial* was written simultaneously for television and as a novel, and it proved outstandingly excellent in both forms. In the reality of Belton House, a recent acquisition of the National Trust, Cresswell tapped a powerful source of imaginative energy. Her purely fictional story of a young girl who solves her own personal problem by taking to herself the troubles of long-dead children in the great house carries particular conviction because it is so closely related to the topography of a real house and its landscape. *Moondial* is the most moving, as it is the most personal, of her writings to date. It may prove to be a turning point in her development. It certainly confirms that she is among the most unpredictable as well as the most exciting of the writers of her generation.

—Marcus Crouch

———

CROCKETT, Samuel Rutherford. British. Born in Little Duchrae, Balmaghie, Kirkcudbrightshire, 24 September 1860. Educated at Laurieston Free Church School, 1865–67; Cowper's Free Church School, Castle Douglas, Kirkcudbrightshire, 1867–76; Edinburgh University, 1876–79; Heidelberg University; New College, Edinburgh, 1882–86. Married Ruth Mary Milner in 1887; two sons and two daughters. Travelling tutor in Germany, Sicily, and Italy, 1879–82. Entered the Free Church of Scotland and ordained minister, 1886: minister, Penicuik, Midlothian, 1886–95 (resigned). Editor, *Worker's Monthly,* London, 1890–91. *Died 21 April 1914.*

PUBLICATIONS FOR CHILDREN

Fiction

Sweetheart Travellers: A Child's Book for Children, for Women, and for Men, illustrated by Gordon Browne and W.H.C. Groome. London, Wells Gardner Darton, and New York, Stokes, 1895.
The Surprising Adventures of Sir Toady Lion with Those of General Napoleon Smith: An Improving History for Old Boys, Young Boys, Good Boys, Bad Boys, Little Boys, Cowboys, and Tom-Boys, illustrated by Gordon Browne. London, Wells Gardner Darton, and New York, Stokes, 1897.
Sir Toady Crusoe, illustrated by Gordon Browne. London, Wells Gardner Darton, and New York, Stokes, 1905.
Sweethearts at Home: Assisted by Sweetheart Herself, and with Additions and Corrections by Hugh John, Sir Toady Lion, Maid Margaret, and Miss Elizabeth Fortinbras, illustrated by C.E. Brock. London and New York, Hodder and Stoughton, 1912.

Other

Editor, *Red Cap Tales Told from Ivanhoe* [*The Fortunes of Nigel, Quentin Durward, Guy Mannering, Rob Roy, The Antiquary, Waverley, The Pirate,* and *A Legend of Montrose*], by Walter Scott. London, A. and C. Black, and New York, Macmillan, 8 vols., 1904–10.

PUBLICATIONS FOR ADULTS

Novels

The Play-Actress. London, Unwin, and New York, Putnam, 1894.
The Lilac Sunbonnet. London, Unwin, and New York, Appleton, 1894.
Mad Sir Uchtred of the Hills. London, Unwin, and New York, Macmillan, 1894.
The Raiders, Being Some Passages in the Life of John Faa, Lord and Earl of Little Egypt. London, Unwin, and New York, Macmillan, 1894.
The Men of the Moss Hags. London, Isbister, and New York, Macmillan, 1895.
A Galloway Herd. New York, Fenno, 1895.
The Grey Man. London, Unwin, and New York, Harper, 1896.
Cleg Kelly, Arab of the City. London, Smith Elder, and New York, Appleton, 1896.
Lochinvar. London, Methuen, 1897; New York, Harper, 1898.
The Standard Bearer. London, Methuen, and New York, Appleton, 1898.
The Red Axe. London, Smith Elder, 1898; New York, Harper, 1899.
The Silver Skull. New York, Stokes, 1898; London, Smith Elder, 1901.
The Black Douglas. London, Smith Elder, and New York, Doubleday, 1899.
Kit Kennedy, Country Boy. London, Clarke, and New York, Harper, 1899.

Ione March. London, Hodder and Stoughton, and New York, Dodd Mead, 1899.
Joan of the Sword Hand. London, Ward Lock, and New York, Dodd Mead, 1900.
Little Anna Mark. London, Smith Elder, 1900; as *The Isle of the Winds: An Adventurous Romance,* New York, Doubleday, 1900.
Cinderella. London, Clarke, and New York, Dodd Mead, 1901.
The Firebrand. London, Macmillan, and New York, McClure, 1901.
The Dark o' the Moon, Being Certain Further Histories of Folk Called "Raiders." London, Macmillan, and New York, Harper, 1902.
The Banner of Blue. New York, McClure, 1902; London, Hodder and Stoughton, 1903.
Flower o'-the-Corn. London, Clarke, 1902; New York, McClure, 1903.
The Adventurer in Spain. London, Isbister, and New York, Stokes, 1903.
The Loves of Miss Anne. London, Clarke, and New York, Dodd Mead, 1904.
Strong Mac. London, Ward Lock, and New York, Dodd Mead, 1904.
Raiderland: All about Grey Galloway. London, Hodder and Stoughton, and New York, Dodd Mead, 1904.
Maid Margaret of Galloway. London, Hodder and Stoughton, 1905; as *May Margaret: Called "The Fair Maid of Galloway,"* New York, Dodd Mead, 1905.
The Cherry Ribband. London, Hodder and Stoughton, and New York, Barnes, 1905.
Kid McGhie: A Nugget of Dim Gold. London, Clarke, 1906.
Fishers of Men. New York, Appleton, 1906.
The White Plumes of Navarre: A Romance of the Wars of Religion. London, Religious Tract Society, 1906; as *The White Plume,* New York, Dodd Mead, 1906.
Me and Myn. London, Unwin, 1907.
Vida; or, The Iron Lord of Kirktown. London, Clarke, 1907; as *The Iron Lord,* New York, Empire Book Company, 1907.
Little Esson. London, Ward Lock, 1907.
Deep Moat Grange. London, Hodder and Stoughton, and New York, Appleton, 1908.
Princess Penniless. London, Hodder and Stoughton, 1908.
The Bloom o' the Heather. London, Nash, 1908.
The Men of the Mountain. London, Religious Tract Society, and New York, Harper, 1909.
Rose of the Wilderness. London, Hodder and Stoughton, 1909.
The Seven Wise Men. London, Religious Tract Society, 1909.
Love's Young Dream. New York, Macmillan, 1910.
The Dew of Their Youth. London, Hodder and Stoughton, 1910.
The Smugglers. London, Hodder and Stoughton, 1911.
The Lady of the Hundred Dresses. London, Nash, 1911.
Love in Pernicketty Town. London and New York, Hodder and Stoughton, 1911.
Patsy. New York, Macmillan, 1912.
Anne of the Barricades. London and New York, Hodder and Stoughton, 1912.
The Moss Troopers. London and New York, Hodder and Stoughton, 1912.
Sandy's Love Affair. London, Hutchinson, 1913; as *Sandy,* New York, Macmillan, 1914.
A Tatter of Scarlet. London, Hodder and Stoughton, 1913.
Silver Sand. London, Hodder and Stoughton, and Chicago, Revell, 1914.
Hal o' the Ironsides. London, Hodder and Stoughton, and New York, Revell, 1915.
The Azure Hand. London and New York, Hodder and Stoughton, 1917.

The White Pope, Called "The Light Out of the East." Liverpool,
Books Ltd., 1920; as *The Light Out of the East,* New York, Doran,
1920.
Rogues' Island. London, Faber, 1926.

Short Stories

The Stickit Minister and Some Common Men. London, Unwin,
1893; New York, Macmillan, n.d.
Bog-Myrtle and Peat: Tales, Chiefly of Galloway. London, Bliss
Sands, and New York, Appleton, 1895.
Lad's Love: Tales. London, Bliss Sands, and New York, Appleton,
1897.
The Stickit Minister's Wooing and Other Galloway Stories. Lon-
don, Hodder and Stoughton, and New York, Doubleday, 1900.
Love Idylls. London, Murray, and New York, Dodd Mead, 1901.
Young Nick and Old Nick: Yarns for the Year's End. London,
Stanley Paul, 1910.

Verse

Dulce Cor, Being the Poems of Ford Berêton. London, Kegan Paul,
1886.

Other

My Two Edinburghs: Searchlights Through the Mists of Thirty Years.
London, Cedar Press, 1909.

*   *   *

Sir Toady Lion, otherwise Arthur George Picton Smith—the *nom
de guerre* derives from his early attempts to twist his tongue round
the name of his favorite character in history, Richard *Coeur de
Lion*—is the younger brother of Hugh John Smith who assumes the
imperial title of General Napoleon Smith at the age of twelve before
leading his army in a campaign against the town "Smoutchies" who
are holding a pet lamb hostage in the Black Sheds, the slaughterhouse
yard, and who are trespassing in the grounds of The House of Windy
Standard, Sir Toady's home in the Scottish border country. The army
musters in its ranks their literary sister Priscilla, Sammy and Cissy
Carter from the neighbouring estate of Oaklands, and two stable
boys, Mike O'Donelly and Peter Greg. And it is Sir Toady himself
who stealthily rescues the lamb for all the military ardour, staffwork,
and planning of the commander-in-chief after the first set encounter
with the enemy had decidedly ended in the Smoutchies' favour.
    Nevertheless Samuel Rutherford Crockett's *The Surprising Ad-
ventures of Sir Toady Lion with Those of General Napoleon Smith*
really belongs to the elder brother as he emerges from a series of
adventures with honour unblemished and his sense of duty undiminished in true romantic fashion whereas Sir Toady demands a
fair measure of patience and toleration in the reader. He appears as
a more sympathetic and engaging character in *Sir Toady Crusoe*
when befriending an Australian boy searching for his sister, but even
here his precocious cunning is in no way alleviated by the mawkish
sentimentality constantly surrounding him. In many respects this is
a pity because Crockett writes with a fresh and affectionate nostalgia
in the earlier volume which is largely based on his own childhood
upbringing. Of *Sweetheart Travellers* and *Sweethearts at Home,*
described by the author as "vagrom chronicles," little need be said;
their excessively sentimental approach has earned for them a truly
deserved and lasting oblivion.

—Alan Edwin Day

CROMPTON, Richmal. British. Born Richmal Crompton
Lamburn in Bury, Lancashire, 15 November 1890. Educated at St.
Elphin's Clergy Daughters' School, Warrington, Lancashire, later
Darley Dale, Derbyshire; Royal Holloway College, University of
London 1911–14 (Driver scholar, 1914), B.A. (honours) in classics
1914. Teacher, St. Elphin's, 1915–17; classics mistress, Bromley
High School for Girls, Kent, 1917–24. Crippled by poliomyelitis in
1923. Served as a volunteer in the Auxiliary Fire Service, Bromley,
during World War II. *Died 11 January 1969.*

PUBLICATIONS FOR CHILDREN

Fiction (William books illustrated by Thomas Henry through 1962)

Just—William. London, Newnes, 1922.
More William. London, Newnes, 1922.
William Again. London, Newnes, 1923.
William the Fourth. London, Newnes, 1924.
Still William. London, Newnes, 1925.
William the Conqueror. London, Newnes, 1926.
William the Outlaw. London, Newnes, 1927.
William in Trouble. London, Newnes, 1927.
William the Good. London, Newnes, 1928.
William. London, Newnes, 1929.
William the Bad. London, Newnes, 1930.
William's Happy Days. London, Newnes, 1930.
William's Crowded Hours. London, Newnes, 1931.
William the Pirate. London, Newnes, 1932.
William the Rebel. London, Newnes, 1933.
William the Gangster. London, Newnes, 1934.
William the Detective. London, Newnes, 1935.
Sweet William. London, Newnes, 1936.
William the Showman. London, Newnes, 1937.
William the Dictator. London, Newnes, 1938.
William and A.R.P. London, Newnes, 1939; as *William's Bad
Resolution,* 1956.
Just William: The Story of the Film. London, Newnes, 1939.
William and the Evacuees. London, Newnes, 1940; as *William the
Film Star,* 1956.
William Does His Bit. London, Newnes, 1941.
William Carries On. London, Newnes, 1942.
William and the Brains Trust. London, Newnes, 1945; abridged
edition, as *William the Hero,* London, Collins, 1972.
Just William's Luck. London, Newnes, 1948.
Jimmy. London, Newnes, 1949.
William the Bold. London, Newnes, 1950.
Jimmy Again, illustrated by Lunt Roberts. London, Newnes, 1951.
William and the Tramp. London, Newnes, 1952.
William and the Moon Rocket. London, Newnes, 1954.
William and the Space Animal. London, Newnes, 1956.
William's Television Show. London, Newnes, 1958.
William the Explorer. London, Newnes, 1960.
William's Treasure Trove. London, Newnes, 1962.
William and the Witch, illustrated by Thomas Henry and Henry Ford.
London, Newnes, 1964.
Jimmy the Third, illustrated by Lunt Roberts. London, Armada,
1965.
William and the Monster, illustrated by Peter Archer and Thomas
Henry. London, Armada, 1965.
William the Ancient Briton, illustrated by Peter Archer and Thomas
Henry. London, Armada, 1965.
William the Cannibal, illustrated by Peter Archer and Thomas Henry.
London, Armada, 1965.
William the Globetrotter, illustrated by Peter Archer and Thomas
Henry. London, Armada, 1965.

William and the Pop Singers, illustrated by Henry Ford. London, Newnes, 1965.
William and the Masked Ranger, illustrated by Henry Ford. London, Newnes, 1966.
William the Superman, illustrated by Henry Ford. London, Newnes, 1968.
William the Lawless, illustrated by Henry Ford. London, Newnes, 1970.

Play

William and the Artist's Model. London, J. Garnet Miller, 1956.

PUBLICATIONS FOR ADULTS

Novels

The Innermost Room. London, Melrose, 1923.
The Hidden Light. London, Hodder and Stoughton, 1924.
Anne Morrison. London, Jarrolds, 1925.
The Wildings. London, Hodder and Stoughton, 1925.
David Wilding. London, Hodder and Stoughton, 1926.
The House. London, Hodder and Stoughton, 1926; as *Dread Dwelling,* New York, Boni and Liveright, 1926.
Millicent Dorrington. London, Hodder and Stoughton, 1927.
Leadon Hill. London, Hodder and Stoughton, 1927.
Enter—Patricia. London, Newnes, 1927.
The Thorn Bush. London, Hodder and Stoughton, 1928.
Roofs Off! London, Hodder and Stoughton, 1928.
The Four Graces. London, Hodder and Stoughton, 1929.
Abbot's End. London, Hodder and Stoughton, 1929.
Blue Flames. London, Hodder and Stoughton, 1930.
Naomi Godstone. London, Hodder and Stoughton, 1930.
Portrait of a Family. London, Macmillan, 1932.
The Odyssey of Euphemia Tracy. London, Macmillan, 1932.
Marriage of Hermione. London, Macmillan, 1932.
The Holiday. London, Macmillan, 1933.
Chedsy Place. London, Macmillan, 1934.
The Old Man's Birthday. London, Macmillan, 1934; Boston, Little Brown, 1935.
Quartet. London, Macmillan, 1935.
Caroline. London, Macmillan, 1936.
There Are Four Seasons. London, Macmillan, 1937.
Journeying Wave. London, Macmillan, 1938.
Merlin Bay. London, Macmillan, 1939.
Steffan Green. London, Macmillan, 1940.
Narcissa. London, Macmillan, 1941.
Mrs. Frensham Describes a Circle. London, Macmillan, 1942.
Weatherley Parade. London, Macmillan, 1944.
Westover. London, Hutchinson, 1946.
The Ridleys. London, Hutchinson, 1947.
Family Roundabout. London, Hutchinson, 1948.
Frost at Morning. London, Hutchinson, 1950.
Linden Rise. London, Hutchinson, 1952.
The Gypsy's Baby. London, Hutchinson, 1954.
Four in Exile. London, Hutchinson, 1955.
Matty and Dearingroydes. London, Hutchinson, 1956.
Blind Man's Buff. London, Hutchinson, 1957.
Wiseman's Folly. London, Hutchinson, 1959.
The Inheritor. London, Hutchinson, 1960.

Short Stories

Kathleen and I, and, of Course, Veronica. London, Hodder and Stoughton, 1926.

A Monstrous Regiment. London, Hutchinson, 1927.
Mist and Other Stories. London, Hutchinson, 1928.
The Middle Things. London, Hutchinson, 1928.
Felicity Stands By. London, Newnes, 1928.
Sugar and Spice and Other Stories. London, Ward Lock, 1929.
Ladies First. London, Hutchinson, 1929.
The Silver Birch and Other Stories. London, Hutchinson, 1931.
The First Morning. London, Hutchinson, 1936.

*

Bibliography: *William: A Bibliography* by W.O.G. Lofts and Derek J. Adley, privately printed, 1980.

Critical Studies: *Richmal Crompton: The Woman Behind William* by Mary Cadogan, London, Allen and Unwin, 1986; *Just Richmal: The Life Work of Richmal Crompton* by Kay Williams, Guildford, Surrey, Genesis, 1986.

*   *   *

Richmal Crompton never achieved distinction as a writer of adult novels, but ironically her success as a children's author rests almost entirely on her William stories which were originally created for mature readers. William Brown first appeared in the February 1919 issue of *Home Magazine* in a story called "Rice Mould," which was later included in the book *More William* (1922). Nearly all the William books (the exception is the full length *Just William's Luck*) comprise a series of separate episodes; this pattern was established because up to the publication of *William and the Evacuees* in 1940 each chapter was a reprint of a short story that had first been published in the *Home* or *Happy* magazines.

The books work on several levels and interest readers of differing ages and tastes. If the irony and subtlety of the early episodes were over the heads of juvenile readers, they were still bound to respond to the absurd situations in which William finds himself and to the facetious tone which Crompton uses to describe these. The stories lost something of their satirical edge when, after 1940, Crompton began to write them specifically for children, but they remained inventive and anarchic.

In the early 1920's William, the anti-hero, emerged as something new in children's fiction, a welcome departure from the impeccably honourable boys and girls who had for so long been leading characters in juvenile books. William is not particularly truthful; he carries untidiness and dirtiness almost to the point of fetishism; he is intellectually lazy, acquisitive, and belligerent. But in the stories these traits are appealing rather than repulsive. William's boisterous proclivities seem natural and require no justification (though he is always complaining that grown-ups misunderstand his good intentions). He is the ultimate unbookish, adventurous, outdoor child. Crompton, whose main ambition was to produce serious adult novels, had without realizing it made the character that she called her "pot-boiler" into an archetype, and today the name of William Brown—like Cinderella or Billy Bunter—has symbolic meaning even for people who have never read the stories.

The William books are almost parodies of Crompton's adult family sagas. The genre is drawing-room comedy, with William as the ingenuous initiator of social chaos and embarrassment for his elders. His family belongs to the cook-gardener-and-house-maid-employing class, and by placing William in a genteel environment Crompton makes his rugged non-conformity and rebelliousness more effective than if he came from a working-class home.

Although Crompton had been a supporter of the campaign for women's suffrage, there is little evidence of feminism in the books. The "Outlaws" (William and his friends Ginger, Henry, and Douglas) firmly despise women and girls. Of course, the females in William's world tend to be stereotypes. Mrs. Brown is the typical wife who always concurs with her husband's opinions by absently reiterating "Yes dear," as she constantly darns the socks of her menfolk. (In one book she is described as darning on five separate occasions.) William's sister Ethel is a bright but useless young thing (she never works except in times of National Emergency when she becomes a fetching V.A.D.), a flirt whose red-gold hair and eyelash-fluttering techniques eventually take their toll of every male in the village. Violet Elizabeth Bott, the rather vulgar sauce-magnate's daughter, is the only interesting girl character in the stories, and William frequently meets his match in this six-year-old bundle of frills, fluffiness, and precocious obstinacy who gets her own way so often by threatening to "thcream and thcream" till she's "thick." Of course Crompton is not usually concerned with complex presentation of character, either male or female; she simply exploits stereotypes, like the outraged clergyman, the batty artist, the ageing spinster apostle of higher thought, to trigger off a series of preposterous situations— which nevertheless in the William context are somehow believable.

The character of William was partly inspired by events in the lives of Crompton's own family. She drew on memories of the childhood of her brother and, later, that of her nephew. Her stories featuring Jimmy were less addictive and ran only to three books. Several years younger than the 11-year-old William, Jimmy engaged in less memorable adventures that were described in lively but very short and simple stories.

It appears that Crompton made one or two unsuccessful attempts to create a female character who would have something of William's irrepressible nature. However, Veronica, in *Kathleen and I, and, of Course, Veronica* (1926), is a little girl whose amusing antics are merely cute, and the determinedly bouncy heroines of *Enter—Patricia* (1927) and *Felicity Stands By* (1928) are young adults rather than juveniles.

—Mary Cadogan

CROSS, Gillian (Clare, née Arnold) British. Born in London, 24 December 1945. Educated at North London Collegiate School, 1957–64; Somerville College, Oxford, 1965–69, B.A. 1969, M.A. 1972; University of Sussex, Brighton, 1970–73, D. Phil. in English 1974. Married Martin Cross in 1967; two sons and two daughters. Address: 41 Essex Road, Gravesend, Kent DA11 0SL, England.

<small>PUBLICATIONS FOR CHILDREN</small>

Fiction

The Runaway, illustrated by Reginald Gray. London, Methuen, 1979.
The Iron Way, illustrated by Tony Morris. London and New York, Oxford University Press, 1979.
Revolt at Ratcliffe's Rags, illustrated by Tony Morris. Oxford and New York, Oxford University Press, 1980.
Save Our School, illustrated by Gareth Floyd. London, Methuen, 1981.
A Whisper of Lace. Oxford and New York, Oxford University Press, 1981.
The Dark Behind the Curtain, illustrated by David Parkins. Oxford, Oxford University Press, 1982; New York, Oxford University Press, 1984.
The Demon Headmaster, illustrated by Gary Rees. Oxford and New York, Oxford University Press, 1982.

The Mintyglo Kid, illustrated by Gareth Floyd. London, Methuen, 1983.
Born of the Sun. Oxford, Oxford University Press, 1983; New York, Holiday House, 1984.
On the Edge. Oxford, Oxford University Press, 1984; New York, Holiday House, 1985.
The Prime Minister's Brain, illustrated by Sally Burgess. Oxford, Oxford University Press, 1985.
Swimathon!, illustrated by Gareth Floyd. London, Methuen, 1986.
Chartbreak. Oxford, Oxford University Press, 1986; as *Chartbreaker,* New York, Holiday House, 1987.
Roscoe's Leap. Oxford, Oxford University Press, and New York, Holiday House, 1987.
A Map of Nowhere. Oxford, Oxford University Press, 1988; New York, Holiday House, 1989.

*

Gillian Cross comments:

My books have had varying backgrounds, from the building of the railways in the 1840's to a strike in a modern clothing factory and from lace smuggling in the 18th century to life in 20th-century schools. My aim is to try to reveal character through action rather than through analysis and to show how people react in stressful, exciting situations. I try also to show how the particular story I am telling fits into a wider social context. But, above all, I want not to be as boring as all that sounds—I want to entertain, to amuse, and to move my readers.

*   *   *

Gillian Cross is a versatile author who has written successfully for widely differing age groups and reading capabilities, and her books for older and more experienced readers represent several of the most prominent sub-genres in modern writing for children. Her early books showed a strong bent towards the historical novel. *The Iron Way,* for example, is set in the period of railway expansion, when gangs of itinerant navvies were opening up the English countryside to the age of steam and rapid transport. Despite the meticulous exactness of historical place and period, however, the book's implicit messages concerning destructive intolerance, resistance to change, and the strength and weakness of closed communities have a relevance to modern society which children can readily observe.

The relationship between past and present takes more overt and sinister forms in two of her more recent books, *The Dark Behind the Curtain* and *Roscoe's Leap.* Both stories are set in the present day, but the activities of modern characters reactivate malign influences lying dormant in the past. *The Dark Behind the Curtain* is both a school story and a tale of the supernatural, in which a school production of *Sweeney Todd* summons the ghostly presences of frightened, tormented Victorian children. Their sufferings under cruel and repressive masters have a modern parallel in the main character's acquiescent, passive, self-destructive relationship with another boy, whose spiteful dominance has gained acceptance because family expectations reinforce it. As the plot unfolds and the suffering dead children at last escape into delighted freedom, so the present-day mould is broken and the boy Jackus, rejecting the bond of spurious friendship, finally wins psychological liberty.

In *Roscoe's Leap* the past does not manifest itself in supernatural forms, but is just as threatening and destructive. Roscoe's Leap, the family home of Stephen and Hannah, is a strange Gothic house built on both sides of a river, the two buildings connected by a long bridging gallery. The two houses embody the enigmatic division of the children's family, and a strange, disordered pattern of relationships is gradually revealed. A sinister past is reanimated when the children restore a collection of automata gathered by their ancestor

Samuel Roscoe, the builder of the house. The pride of his collection is the French Terror, a macabre automaton replaying endlessly the grisly ritual of the guillotine. Only by much subterfuge, tension, and ultimate danger do the children achieve the metaphorical (and literal) "leap" that joins their split family together and lays the cruel past to rest.

Despite the striking imaginative conception of these historical or "Gothic" stories, however, the general trend of Cross's work has been towards novels with naturalistic plots, modern settings, and contemporary social themes. An early example was *Revolt at Ratcliffe's Rags,* in which schoolchildren become entangled in the world of labour relations, strikes, and unscrupulous capitalism. More recently she has published *Chartbreak.* Set in the glamorous world of rock music, this is a powerful atmospheric story which unsparingly reveals the human cost as well as the potential rewards of the life so many readers envy. Finch is a 17-year-old rock star as the novel opens, but the story of her success is one of family conflict and pain, fierce working loyalties and antagonisms, and a savagely committed discipline as well as episodes of therapeutic anger, high excitement, and euphoria. By the end of the novel Finch, like other protagonists of Cross's novels, has found her own identity by a tough route.

The finding of identity through crisis is the theme of Cross's best novel to date, *On the Edge.* In this original and remarkable story the very concept of the family is challenged, ideologically, by a group of terrorists. Tug, a teenage schoolboy, is kidnapped by the group because his mother is an influential journalist, and is not only imprisoned and threatened with death but subjected to ruthless brainwashing techniques designed to dislocate his sense of identity and relationship. This outstanding novel explores some complex, provocative, and important ideas in a situation of unremitting tension and suspense.

For younger readers Gillian Cross has written a particularly attractive series of short comic novels about inter-school rivalries, with an engaging West Indian girl, Clipper, as the leading character. The best of these is *Swimathon!,* where mayhem is caused by the otherwise athletic Clipper's inability to swim. In her full-length novels, however, Gillian Cross is becoming a steadily bolder and more challenging writer. Her recurrent theme, most recently exemplified in the taut and original *A Map of Nowhere,* is that personal freedom is inseparable from self-knowledge and secure identity. These are not life's automatic gifts but are won by hard choices and must often be fought for in the teeth of inner waverings and external threats. Such fights are memorably depicted in these strongly plotted and exciting novels.

—Peter Hollindale

CROSSLEY-HOLLAND, Kevin (John William). British. Born in Mursley, Buckinghamshire, 7 February 1941. Educated at Bryanston School; St. Edmund Hall, Oxford, B.A. (honours) in English language and literature 1962. Married 1) Caroline Fendall Thompson in 1963, two sons; 2) Ruth Marris in 1972; 3) Gillian Cook in 1982, two daughters. Editor, Macmillan, publishers, London, 1962–71; Gregory Fellow, University of Leeds, 1969–71; talks producer, BBC, London, 1972; editorial director, Victor Gollancz Ltd., publishers, London, 1972–77; English Lecturer, University of Regensburg, 1978–80. Since 1975 general editor, Mirror of Britain series, André Deutsch Ltd., publishers, London; since 1983 editorial consultant, Boydell and Brewer, publishers, Woodbridge, Suffolk. Lecturer in English, Tufts in London programme, 1967–78; Arts Council Fellow in English, Winchester School of Art, 1983, 1984; Visiting Fulbright Professor of English, St. Olaf College, Northfield, Minnesota, 1987–88. Since 1986 Chairman of the Literature Panel,

Eastern Arts Association. Recipient: Arts Council award, 1968, 1977, 1978; Library Association Carnegie Medal, 1986. Agent: Rogers Coleridge and White, 20 Powis Mews, London W11 1JN. Address: The Old Vicarage, Walsham-le-Willows, Bury St. Edmunds, Suffolk, England.

PUBLICATIONS FOR CHILDREN

Fiction

Havelok the Dane, illustrated by Brian Wildsmith. London, Macmillan, 1964; New York, Dutton, 1965.
King Horn, illustrated by Charles Keeping. London, Macmillan, 1965; New York, Dutton, 1966.
The Sea-Stranger, illustrated by Joanna Troughton. London, Heinemann, 1973; New York, Seabury Press, 1974.
The Fire-Brother, illustrated by Joanna Troughton. London, Heinemann, and New York, Seabury Press, 1975.
The Earth-Father, illustrated by Joanna Troughton. London, Heinemann, 1976.
The Wildman, illustrated by Charles Keeping. London, Deutsch, 1976.
Storm, illustrated by Alan Marks. London, Heinemann, 1985.

Other

The Green Children, illustrated by Margaret Gordon. London, Macmillan, 1966; New York, Seabury Press, 1968.
The Callow Pit Coffer, illustrated by Margaret Gordon. London, Macmillan, 1968; New York, Seabury Press, 1969.
Wordhoard: Anglo-Saxon Stories, with Jill Paton Walsh. London, Macmillan, and New York, Farrar Straus, 1969.
The Pedlar of Swaffham, illustrated by Margaret Gordon. London, Macmillan, 1971; New York, Seabury Press, 1972.
Green Blades Rising: The Anglo-Saxons. London, Deutsch, 1975; New York, Seabury Press, 1976.
The Dead Moon and Other Tales from East Anglia and the Fen Country, illustrated by Shirley Felts. London, Deutsch, 1982.
Tales from the Mabinogion, with Gwyn Thomas, illustrated by Margaret Jones. London, Gollancz, 1984; Woodstock, New York, Overlook Press, 1985.
Axe-Age, Wolf-Age: A Selection from the Norse Myths, illustrated by Hannah Firmin. London, Deutsch, 1985.
The Fox and the Cat: Animal Tales from Grimm, with Susan Varley, illustrated by Varley. London, Andersen Press, 1985; New York, Lothrop, 1986.
British Folk Tales: New Versions. London and New York, Orchard, 1987; selections as *Boo!, Dathera Dad, Piper and Pooka,* and *Small-Tooth Dog,* illustrated by Peter Melnyczuk, London, Orchard, 4 vols., 1988.
Northern Lights: Legends, Sagas and Folk-Tales, illustrated by Alan Howard. London, Faber, 1987.
The Quest for Olwen, with Gwyn Thomas, illustrated by Margaret Jones. Cambridge, Lutterworth Press, 1988.
Wulf. London, Faber, 1988.

Editor, *Winter's Tales for Children 3.* London, Macmillan, 1967.
Editor, *The Faber Book of Northern Legends* [*Northern Folktales*], illustrated by Alan Howard. London, Faber, 2 vols., 1977–80.
Editor, *The Riddle Book,* illustrated by Bernard Handelsman. London, Macmillan, 1982.

Translator, *Storm and Other Old English Riddles,* illustrated by Miles Thistlethwaite. London, Macmillan, and New York, Farrar Straus, 1970.

Translator, *Beowulf,* illustrated by Charles Keeping. London, Oxford University Press, 1982.

PUBLICATIONS FOR ADULTS

Verse

On Approval. London, Outposts, 1961.
My Son. London, Turret, 1966.
Alderney: The Nunnery. London, Turret, 1968.
Confessional. Frensham, Surrey, Sceptre Press, 1969.
Norfolk Poems. London, Academy, 1970.
A Dream of a Meeting. Frensham, Surrey, Sceptre Press, 1970.
More Than I Am. London, Steam Press, 1971.
The Wake. Richmond, Surrey, Keepsake Press, 1972.
The Rain-Giver. London, Deutsch, 1972.
Petal and Stone. Knotting, Bedfordshire, Sceptre Press, 1975.
The Dream-House. London, Deutsch, 1976.
Between My Father and My Son. Minneapolis, Black Willow Press, 1982.
Time's Oriel. London, Hutchinson, 1983.
Waterslain and Other Poems. London, Hutchinson, 1986.
The Painting-Room and Other Poems. London, Century Hutchinson, 1988.
East Anglian Poems. Colchester, Jardine, 1988.

Other

Pieces of Land: Journeys to Eight Islands. London, Gollancz, 1972.
The Norse Myths: A Retelling. London, Deutsch, and New York, Pantheon, 1980.
The Stones Remain, with Andrew Rafferty. London, Rider, 1989.

Editor, *Running to Paradise: An Introductory Selection of the Poems of W.B. Yeats.* London, Macmillan, 1967; New York, Macmillan, 1968.
Editor, *Winter's Tales 14.* London, Macmillan, 1968.
Editor, with Patricia Beer, *New Poetry 2.* London, Arts Council, 1976.
Editor, *Folk-Tales of the British Isles.* London, Folio Society, 1985; New York, Pantheon, 1988.
Editor, *The Oxford Book of Travel Verse.* Oxford and New York, Oxford University Press, 1986.
Editor, *Medieval Lovers: A Book of Days.* London, Century Hutchinson, and New York, Weidenfeld and Nicolson, 1988.

Translator, *The Battle of Maldon and Other Old English Poems,* edited by Bruce Mitchell. London, Macmillan, and New York, St. Martin's Press, 1965.
Translator, *Beowulf.* London, Macmillan, and New York, Farrar Straus, 1968.
Translator, *The Exeter Riddle Book.* London, Folio Society, 1978; as *The Exeter Book of Riddles,* London, Penguin, 1979.
Translator, *The Anglo-Saxon World.* Woodbridge, Suffolk, Boydell Press, 1982; New York, Barnes and Noble, 1983.
Translator, *The Wanderer.* Colchester, Jardine, 1986.
Translator, *The Old English Elegies.* London, Folio Society, 1988.

*

Manuscript Collection: Brotherton Collection, University of Leeds.

* * *

Kevin Crossley-Holland's work for children seems limited only by his predilection for the re-telling of an ancient story. So far, he has avoided the challenge of the purely original, imaginative tale. But, among his contemporaries, he has few rivals as an exponent of the traditional narrative re-told.

The stories are of long ago; but character, situation, landscape—however strange and remote they may at first appear—soon declare themselves as being not merely of their own, but of all time. The narrative skill, freshness and aptness of language, quietly direct mode of address, all compel the attention, awaken the imagination, remain in the mind. It is a voice as old, and as new, as poetry. Even the most insignificant-seeming characters are never remote, lay figures. They live, breathe, and move. At the same time, they retain their mythic, mystic qualities. The underlying themes and *motifs,* the subtly revealed eternal truths beating at the heart of all great folk-literature, are always delicately but firmly indicated.

These vital components are particularly well-represented by the quartet of medieval stories written primarily for young readers (or listeners), beginning with *The Green Children.* In each case, the basic structure is thoroughly established; and not the smallest detail is lost or distorted in the process of the story's realization. The voice of the narrator remains as anonymous an instrument as that of the minstrel or ballad-singer. The emphasis, very properly, is not on the singer but on the song. The verbal furnishing is spare, but chosen with great precision; the dramatic movement cunningly sited and sprung. Mind and imagination are continuously stimulated and fed as the tales are resolved.

In the dark legend of *The Callow Pit Coffer,* two young brothers suddenly find "strength in themselves" to resist the powers of darkness. At the mysterious close of *The Green Children,* we learn that "nobody knows—unless you do—whether the green girl lived on earth to the end of her days: or whether, one day, near the Wolfpits, she simply disappeared." The painful, but ultimately peaceful Suffolk myth *The Wildman,* telling of a merman's capture, suffering, and escape, also suggests—among much else—a near-parable of each individual's entrance into this world from a bag of waters. In the more solidly grounded *The Pedlar of Swaffham,* on the other hand, the central figure takes the Gold Road to London in pursuit of his own dream, but returns with (and resolves happily) that of another: discovering, in the process, how many of us are "foreigners in our own country."

Splendidly complementary to the stories are Crossley-Holland's translations of Early English riddles collected in *Storm:* poems dazzlingly new-minted, witty, imaginatively refreshing. (This volume should not be confused with Crossley-Holland's ghost story of the same title, which won the 1985 Carnegie Medal.) Again, as in so much of his work, the people and moods of a period apparently remote in time are vitalized and gently brought near. In the writer, and by attrition, in the reader, past, present, and future meet. Such writing, to such effect, is a rare and notable achievement.

—Charles Causley

————

CUMMING, Primrose (Amy). British. Born on the Isle of Thanet, Kent, 7 April 1915. Educated privately. Served in an anti-aircraft unit of the Auxiliary Territorial Service, 1940–45: Defence Medal. Address: Wynberg, Sandhurst, Hawkhurst, Kent TN18 5JU, England.

PUBLICATIONS FOR CHILDREN

Fiction

Doney, illustrated by Allen Seaby. London, Country Life, 1934.

Spider Dog, illustrated by Barbara Turner. London, Country Life, 1936.

Silver Snaffles, illustrated by Stanley Lloyd. London, Blackie, and New York, Mill, 1937.

The Silver Eagle Riding School, illustrated by Cecil Trew. London, A. and C. Black, 1938.

Rachel of Romney, illustrated by Nina Scott Langley. London, Country Life, 1939; New York, Scribner, 1940.

The Wednesday Pony, illustrated by Stanley Lloyd. London, Blackie, and New York, Mill, 1939.

Ben: The Story of a Cart-Horse, photographs by Harold Burdekin. London, Dent, 1939; New York, Dutton, 1940.

The Chestnut Filly. London, Blackie, and New York, Mill, 1940.

Silver Eagle Carries On, illustrated by Cecil Trew. London, A. and C. Black, 1940.

Owls Castle Farm, illustrated by Veronica Baker. London, A. and C. Black, 1942.

The Great Horses, illustrated by Lionel Edwards. London, Dent, 1946.

Trouble at Trimbles, illustrated by Geoffrey Whittam. London, Country Life, 1949.

Four Rode Home, illustrated by Maurice Tulloch. London, Dent, 1951.

Rivals to Silver Eagle, illustrated by Eve Gosset. London, A. and C. Black, 1954.

No Place for Ponies, illustrated by Maurice Tulloch. London, Dent, 1954; as *The Mystery Pony,* New York, Criterion, 1957.

The Deep-Sea Horse, illustrated by Mary Shillabeer. London, Dent, 1956.

Flying Horseman, illustrated by Sheila Rose. London, Dent, 1959.

The Mystery Trek, illustrated by Sheila Rose. London, Dent, 1964.

Foal of the Fjords, illustrated by Wendy Marchant. London, Dent, 1966.

Penny and Pegasus, illustrated by Mary Gernatt. London, Dent, 1969.

*

Primrose Cumming comments:

I write for children because I was still a child when my first story was printed, and a teenager when my first book was published—and so carried on. My fiction is based on fact, and I aim to be consistent with my observations of country life and to share my pastoral pleasures with my readers.

*   *   *

For Primrose Cumming, writing books for children was a part of the wider and more absorbing business of being a countrywoman. She had a profound enjoyment of all that this implies: the society of others in the village, young and old, the pattern of the seasons, walking, and, above all, riding. When in the mid-1930's she turned to writing it was inevitable that these activities should provide the subject-matter of her books.

This was the age of the "pony book." With Joanna Cannan, Cumming can claim to have been a leading pioneer of this genre, and unlike some other practitioners she quickly recognised its limitations. If *Silver Eagle Riding School* was content to remain within the conventions which she and her contemporaries had established she was always very ready to depart from them in the interests of a good story and convincing view of life. In her first book, *Doney,* she went to the—in pony-book terms—unfashionable setting of the Border country. *Rachel of Romney* showed her (to use an appropriate metaphor) firmly in the saddle, drawing upon the countryside that she knew best as an essential ingredient in the action and painting a set of neat portraits of characters as recognisable as they are attrac-

tive. This book set a standard which she maintained but did not surpass in the next ten years. *Four Rode Home* marks probably her highest achievement in this field. The setting was again that of her own country of the Kentish weald and marsh, the situation was entirely credible and productive of tension and action, the principals clearly drawn and well differentiated. Later books, although as carefully researched and competently written, showed a little falling off in invention.

While she wrote books about pony-worship and pony-mad children for more that 30 years, Cumming was always aware of the dangers of becoming identified with a limited byway of literature. Moreover, much as she delighted in riding, she was deeply interested in the working countryside and its animals. As early as 1939 she had collaborated with the photographer Harold Burdekin in *Ben,* a sympathetic study of the life of a farm horse, presented in picture-book format. She thought much about these huge gentle animals which had descended, she was convinced, from the war horses of the middle ages. Out of this idea came what is arguably her best, as it is her least typical, book, *The Great Horses.* Choosing three key periods in history she showed, in fictional form, how the horses which the Normans brought with them to the conquest of England developed into the patient draught horses of yesterday. It was a big subject calling for heroic treatment and for rather more eloquence than this writer was master of. *The Great Horses* must perhaps be classed as a brave failure, but in failing Primrose Cumming lifted herself into an altogether higher society of writers.

—Marcus Crouch

———

CUNLIFFE, John (Arthur). British. Born in Colne, Lancashire, 16 June 1933. Educated at The Grammar School, Colne, 1944–50; Leeds School of Librarianship, 1954–55; A.L.A. 1955; Northwest London Polytechnic School of Librarianship, 1956–57; F.L.A. 1957; Charlotte Mason College of Education, Ambleside, Westmorland, 1973–75, Cert. Ed. 1975. Married Sylvia May Thompson in 1960; one son. Branch librarian, Earby, Yorkshire, 1951–54; mobile librarian, Wooler, Northumberland, 1955–56; deputy information officer, Decca Radar Research Laboratories, Tolworth, Surrey, 1957–58; senior assistant librarian, Hendon, London, 1958; manager, rare books department, Foyle's booksellers, London, 1958–59; regional children's librarian, Bletchley, Buckinghamshire, 1959–62; librarian in charge of work with young people, Reading, Berkshire, 1962–64, and Brighton, 1967–73; librarian, British Council, Belgrade, Yugoslavia, 1964–66; education librarian, Newcastle-upon-Tyne, 1966–67; teacher, Castle Park School, Kendal, Cumbria, 1975–79; teacher-organiser, Manchester Education Committee, 1979–80. Since 1981 deputy head teacher, Crowcroft Park Primary School, Manchester. Address: 64 Goulden Road, Withington, Manchester M20 9YF, England.

PUBLICATIONS FOR CHILDREN

Fiction

Farmer Barnes Buys a Pig, illustrated by Carol Barker. London, Deutsch, 1964; New York, Lion Press, 1968.

Farmer Barnes and Bluebell, illustrated by Carol Barker. London, Deutsch, 1966.

Farmer Barnes at the County Show, illustrated by Jill McDonald. London, Deutsch, 1969; as *Farmer Barnes at the County Fair,* New York, Lion Press, 1969.

The Adventures of Lord Pip, illustrated by Robert Hales. London,

Deutsch, 1970.

The Giant Who Stole the World, illustrated by Faith Jaques. London, Deutsch, 1971.

Farmer Barnes and the Goats, illustrated by Jill McDonald. London, Deutsch, 1971.

Riddles and Rhymes and Rigamaroles, illustrated by Alexy Pendle. London, Deutsch, 1971.

The Giant Who Swallowed the Wind, illustrated by Faith Jaques. London, Deutsch, 1972.

Farmer Barnes Goes Fishing, illustrated by Jill McDonald. London, Deutsch, 1972.

Giant Kippernose and Other Stories, illustrated by Fritz Wegner. London, Deutsch, 1972.

The King's Birthday Cake, illustrated by Faith Jaques. London, Deutsch, 1973.

The Great Dragon Competition and Other Stories, illustrated by Alexy Pendle. London, Deutsch, 1973.

The Farmer, The Rooks, and the Cherry Tree, illustrated by Prudence Seward. London, Deutsch, 1974.

Small Monkey Tales, illustrated by Gerry Downes. London, Deutsch, 1974.

Farmer Barnes and the Snow Picnic, illustrated by Joan Hickson. London, Deutsch, 1974.

Giant Brog and the Motorway, illustrated by Alex Pendle. London, Deutsch, 1976.

Farmer Barnes Fells a Tree, illustrated by Joan Hickson. London, Deutsch, 1977.

Farmer Barnes and the Harvest Doll, illustrated by Joan Hickson. London, Deutsch, 1977.

Mr. Gosling and the Runaway Chair, illustrated by William Stobbs. London, Deutsch, 1978.

Farmer Barnes' Guy Fawkes Day, illustrated by Joan Hickson. London, Deutsch, 1978.

Mr. Gosling and the Great Art Robbery, illustrated by William Stobbs. London, Deutsch, 1979.

Sara's Giant and the Upside-Down House, illustrated by Hilary Abrahams. London, Deutsch, 1980.

Our Sam: The Daftest Dog in the World, illustrated by Maurice Wilson. London, Deutsch, 1980.

Postman Pat and the Mystery Thief [*Takes a Message, Goes Sledging, to the Rescue*], illustrated by Celia Berridge. London, Deutsch, 4 vols., 1981–86.

Postman Pat's Treasure Hunt [*Secret, Rainy Day, Difficult Day, Foggy Day, Tractor Express, Thirsty Day, Letters on Ice, Breezy Day*], illustrated by Celia Berridge. London, Deutsch, 9 vols., 1981–85.

Postman Pat Easy Readers (*Postman Pat's Wet Day* [*Messy Day, Safari, Day in Bed, Washing Day, Sore Tooth*], *Postman Pat Plays for Greendale* [*and the Christmas Puddings, and the Greendale Ghost, Makes a Splash, and the Dinosaur Bone, and the Cleaning-Day, and the Pet Show, and the Bees*]), illustrated by Joan Hickson. London, Deutsch, 14 vols., 1986–89.

Postman Pat Beginners (*Postman Pat's 123 Story* [*ABC Story, Three Wishes*], *Postman Fat*), illustrated by Joan Hickson. London, Deutsch, 4 vols., 1986–89.

Postman Pat's Summer Storybook [*Winter Storybook*], illustrated by Celia Berridge. London, Deutsch, 2 vols., 1987.

Postman Pat's Parcel of Fun, illustrated by Stuart Trotter. London, Deutsch, 1987.

My Postman Pat Storytime Book. London, Treasure, 1987.

Fog Lane School and the Great Racing Car Disaster, illustrated by Andrew Tiffen. London, Deutsch, 1988.

Plays

Postman Pat's Adventures (produced Wimbledon, 1987).

Television Plays: *Postman Pat* series, from 1981.

Verse

Standing on a Strawberry and Other Poems, illustrated by David Parkins. London, Deutsch, 1987.

Other

Fun and Games with Postman Pat: An Activity Book, with Ivor Wood, illustrated by Joan Hickson. London, Deutsch, 1983.

Play Logo. London, Deutsch, 1984.

The Postman Pat Fun Book, illustrated by Celia Berridge. London, Deutsch, 1987.

*

John Cunliffe comments:

I write stories for young children in the clearest and simplest prose that I can manage. They are realistic stories about country life, or fantasies about giants and dragons. I have also written some books of verse.

*   *   *

John Cunliffe is a well-established storyteller who has written a number of charming picture book stories and some original fairy tales. His earliest picture books, about Farmer Barnes, are simple, appealing stories, written at a slow measured pace, about a somewhat harassed farmer and his family. They are rather long for reading aloud, but the language is simple enough for children of about seven with a reasonable reading ability. Unfortunately, these pleasant stories lack visual uniformity as a series by having three illustrators, Jill McDonald, Joan Hickson, and Carol Barker.

Cunliffe has been a storyteller to groups of children of different ages for a number of years, and has used this experience very effectively in his various collections of original tales. The giant stories are to my mind the most pleasing. "Giant Kippernose" is a very amusing story about a kindly giant who gets very lonely because the people in the village always run away from him. It is only one day when everyone has a streaming cold that the truth is revealed: he stinks! He turns the cheese green, the milk sour, the butter rancid (children revel in such details!). When Giant Kippernose turns over a new leaf and starts having a bath, washing his hair and beard and socks, the villagers are happy to talk to him again. These are all nicely written tales, in the folk tradition, although often with a distinctly modern flavour. *The Great Dragon Competition and Other Stories* is in a similar vein, with some nicely controlled stories, again suitable for reading aloud.

Undoubtedly Cunliffe's most well-received venture has been his stories about Postman Pat and his black and white cat and the residents of a slightly sleepy small valley called Greendale. Part of a television series as well as published books, the stories have had wide exposure and proved immensely popular with preschool aged children. They are competently written, using lively language, short sentences, and simple dialogue. They draw upon a stock of characters peopling Greendale, and present an innocent, fanciful view of small-town life where Pat is given cups of tea and cake on his rounds, collects stamps from the letters he delivers, and bats and bowls the town's cricket team to victory (celebrated with nothing stronger than rhubarb wine). While seeming to look to the past, the stories have amusing touches of the 1980's—in *Postman Pat's Day in Bed*, for instance, Pat's replacement while he is ill is a young woman with wonderful spiky green and pink hair.

—Judith Elkin

CUNNINGHAM, Julia (Woolfolk). American. Born in Spokane, Washington, 4 October 1916. Educated at St. Anne's School, Charlottesville, Virginia, graduated 1933. Clerk, Guaranty Trust Company, New York, 1937–40; co-ordinating editor, G. Schirmer, music publishers, New York, 1940–44; associate editor, Dell Publishing Company, New York, 1944–47; secretary, Air Reduction Company, New York, 1947–49; assistant to the advertising manager, Sherman Clay and Company, San Francisco, 1950–51; free-lance writer, France, 1952; salesperson, Metropolitan Museum of Art, New York, 1953–56; bookseller and children's book buyer, Tecolote Book Shop, Santa Barbara, California, 1960–76. Recipient: Christopher award, 1978. Agent: Bill Berger Associates, 444 East 58th Street, New York, New York 10022. Address: 122-A West Valerio Street, Santa Barbara, California 93101, U.S.A.

PUBLICATIONS FOR CHILDREN

Fiction

The Vision of François the Fox, illustrated by Nicholas Angelo. Boston, Houghton Mifflin, 1960.
Dear Rat, illustrated by Walter Lorraine. Boston, Houghton Mifflin, 1961.
Macaroon, illustrated by Evaline Ness. New York, Pantheon, 1962; London, Harrap, 1963.
Candle Tales, illustrated by Evaline Ness. New York, Pantheon, 1964.
Dorp Dead, illustrated by James Spanfeller. New York, Pantheon, 1965; London, Heinemann, 1967.
Viollet, illustrated by Alan Cober. New York, Pantheon, 1966.
Onion Journey, illustrated by Lydia Cooley. New York, Pantheon, 1967.
Burnish Me Bright, illustrated by Don Freeman. New York, Pantheon, 1970; London, Heinemann, 1971.
Wings of the Morning, photographs by Katy Peake. San Carlos, California, Golden Gate Books, 1971.
Far in the Day, illustrated by Don Freeman. New York, Pantheon, 1972.
The Treasure Is the Rose, illustrated by Judy Graese. New York, Pantheon, 1973.
Maybe, A Mole, illustrated by Cyndy Szekeres. New York, Pantheon, 1974.
Come to the Edge. New York, Pantheon, 1977.
Tuppenny. New York, Dutton, 1978.
A Mouse Called Junction, illustrated by Michael Hague. New York, Pantheon, 1980.
Flight of the Sparrow. New York, Pantheon, 1980.
The Silent Voice. New York, Dutton, 1981.
Wolf Roland. New York, Pantheon, 1983.
Oaf, illustrated by Peter Sis. New York, Knopf, 1986.

*

Manuscript Collections: Kerlan Collection, University of Minnesota, Minneapolis; University of Oregon Library, Eugene.

*   *   *

Since the publication of her first children's book in 1960, Julia Cunningham's works for children have been praised for their originality and for their carefully crafted, highly concentrated, indeed poetic, prose. Cunningham has written such appealing animal fables as *Maybe, A Mole, Macaroon,* and *The Vision of François the Fox* and quasi-gothic stories in the manner of *The Treasure Is the Rose* and *Tuppenny.* In several spare, fable-like stories which feature lost children in search of home, identity, love, and self-worth, Cunningham has brought her work to a high level of excellence.

Among Cunningham's most memorable creations are her anthropomorphic animal characters. Most often in her animal fables Cunningham reveals the power of love to bring forth the highest and the best self. In *The Vision of François the Fox* François begins his adventures as a pleasure-loving and urbane trickster. But when he enters a cathedral, he is awed by the stained-glass vision of a saint. Thenceforth, he surrenders his life of pleasure and aesthetic enjoyment, devoting himself to self-sacrifice. In reversing her readers' expectations about fox behavior, Cunningham suggests that we may break out of conventional molds which limit our possibilities. In *Macaroon* Cunningham depicts a spoiled raccoon who loves only his own pleasure until he finds a little girl, Erika, who truly needs him. This charming animal story reveals Cunningham's gifts for writing descriptions of the natural world and for creating character. *Maybe, A Mole* features a lovable mole who is nevertheless an outsider because he loves the light. Maybe's capacity for loyalty and friendship transforms the worldly fox, who realizes that Maybe is "someone to be trusted, to be company, to be loved." This delightful story provides fine examples of Cunningham's talent for writing droll dialogue. In *A Mouse Called Junction* Cunningham presents an over-protected child mouse who lives in perfect security in a large family. Character motives remain ambiguous in this animal story; the tale strains to realize allegorical significance which remains obscure.

Cunningham's animal characters please the reader with their memorable and vividly depicted personalities, their amusing dialogue, and their capacity for friendship. At times, however, readers may feel that the allegory in the animal fables is strained, that the design upon the reader is perhaps too palpable. At their best, then, Cunningham's stories please with wry humor and vivid characterization; at their worst, they are excessively didactic.

One of Cunningham's most popular children's books is *Dear Rat* which features Andrew the Rat. Cunningham clearly enjoys blending the conventions of detective fiction with the romance of fairy tale in this tale of Andrew the detective from Hampton, Wyoming, who encounters and successfully defeats a tough gangster, Groge, and his muscled goons, Snatch and Flicker. When Andrew arrives in France, he finds that these three gangsters are involved in stealing jewels from the Lady's crown in Chartres Cathedral. Outwardly tough but inwardly honest and tender, Andrew makes friends with Richet, a sensitive and cultivated bird. Through his tenacious powers of ratiocination, Andrew succeeds in returning the jewels to Chartres Cathedral and in winning the hand of the delicately lovely princess rat, Angelique.

Several of Cunningham's works for children reveal strongly gothic elements. In *Viollet* a lovely thrush is a gifted singer who can perform only when she is alone, despite the encouragement of her friends, Warwick the fox and Oxford the hound. An innocent and kind-hearted Count, owner of a vineyard, is keenly in tune with nature and hears the lovely song of the thrush. The setting of this tale with its ruined castle and its lush ripening grapes is powerfully depicted. Tressac, the villainous foreman, is duly thwarted by Viollet, Warwick, and Oxford when he tries to murder the Count and to seize the estate by means of a forged will. Another gothic tale, *The Treasure Is the Rose,* is set in the medieval world of 1100. This tale combines the terrors of the gothic with the charms of medieval romance: love again redeems spiritual and emotional paralysis. In *Tuppenny* Cunningham creates the powerful story of Tuppenny, a lovely and mysterious young girl who enters the lives of three families, each of which hides unspeakable dark secrets from the past. Tuppenny, who strongly suggests that she is a supernatural agent, quite literally rids the town of a horrifying nightmare. *Tuppenny* makes use of more sophisticated gothic dimensions; it conveys a remarkable sense of moral and psychological horror.

One of Cunningham's most significant achievements is her use of what critics have called the "Romantic child." This child is characterized by innocence, affinity with the imagination and with nature. In many of her most compelling children's books Cunningham places this homeless, outcast child in a hostile, sometimes insane, world. This child character not only endures and prevails but brings blessedness and reconciliation to all who are able to receive these gifts.

Certainly Cunningham's most famous and controversial book of this kind is *Dorp Dead*. In this troubling, intensely allegorical work, the first-person narrator, Gilly Ground, hides his intelligence and sensitive nature in the gray, prison-like atmosphere of an orphanage. Driven to distraction by this existence, Gilly runs away for a day to his haven, an ancient crumbling tower "in the center of a tall stand of pines." Gilly regards this isolated pastoral tower as his home, his kingdom; it is the shelter for his dreaming and imagining. On the day when Gilly has fled, Mrs. Heister, the director, has placed him in the foster home of Master Kobalt, an eccentric carpenter who makes ladders. At the tower, Gilly meets a hunter whose gun carries no bullets. The Hunter explains to Gilly that he "hunts to see." Once he finds himself caught up in Master Kobalt's rigid routine, he barely remembers the hunter. At first Gilly is attracted to Kobalt's regimented ways, for Gilly enjoys the benefits of good food, warm clothing, and a comfortable house for the first time in his life. Gradually, however, he learns that Kobalt is not a caring parent, but a mad tyrant, who plans to enslave Gilly in a cage, just as he has enslaved his dog Mash. Gilly narrowly escapes death at Kobalt's hands. As he escapes from his prison with Kobalt (what the Hunter has called Gilly's "bewitchment"), Gilly is encouraged by the vision of a star, by the chorusing of birds in the garden, and by his love for Mash. In this powerful story Cunningham suggests that the Hunter represents the questing, imagining human spirit which perceives its oneness with the universe yet dares to be itself. Kobalt, a fixed element with destructive connotations, seems to represent the regimentation and life-denying aspects of the technological world which values only the practical. Happily Gilly chooses the Hunter's way even at the risk of his life, leaving an unequivocal message to Kobalt, "Dorp Dead." Gilly has not mastered his spelling problems, but he has made the right and the human choice.

In *Flight of the Sparrow* Cunningham reveals a young, homeless girl's attempts to survive on her own in the streets of Paris. "Little Cigarette" is adopted by the boy, Mago, who provides for several homeless children. Eventually Little Cigarette finds herself caught between her loyalty for Mago and her own ideals and values. Cunningham explores a similar theme in the novel *Come to the Edge*.

In her three books about Auguste, the gifted deaf-mute mime artist, Cunningham reveals her creative talent at its best. Her feeling for art and the imagination, her belief that beauty and innocence can survive and even change the worst cruelty and evil, her conviction that human love can exert a powerful moral and spiritual force all find expression in these highly poetic and beautifully crafted books— *Burnish Me Bright, Far in the Day,* and *The Silent Voice*.

In sum, Cunningham has created a distinctive place for herself in 20th-century American children's literature. Her stories present a powerful vision of human possibility and only occasionally strain for allegorical significance or lapse into melodramatic sentimentality. She affirms that innocence, love, human art, and the imagination can prevail in the face of moral blindness, human cruelty, and ignorance.

—Anita Moss

CURRY, Jane Louise. American. Born in East Liverpool, Ohio, 24 September 1932. Educated at Pennsylvania State University, State College, 1950–51; Indiana State College (now Indiana University of Pennsylvania), 1951–54, B.S. in education 1954; University of California, Los Angeles, 1957–59; Stanford University, California (teaching assistant), 1959–61, 1964–65, 1967–68, M.A. 1962, Ph.D. 1969; Royal Holloway College, University of London (Fulbright fellow), 1961–62; University College, University of London (Leverhulme fellow), 1965–66. Art instructor, East Liverpool, 1955, and Los Angeles city schools, 1955–59; shop assistant, Vroman's Bookstore, Pasadena, California, 1963; acting instructor, 1967–68, and lecturer, 1984, 1987, Stanford University. Lives in Los Angeles. Address: c/o Margaret K. McElderry Books, Macmillan Children's Book Group, 866 Third Avenue, New York, New York 10022, U.S.A.

PUBLICATIONS FOR CHILDREN

Fiction

Beneath the Hill, illustrated by Imero Gobbato. New York, Harcourt Brace, 1967; London, Dobson, 1968.
The Sleepers, illustrated by Gareth Floyd. New York, Harcourt Brace, 1968; London, Dobson, 1969.
The Change-Child, illustrated by Gareth Floyd. New York, Harcourt Brace, 1969; London, Dobson, 1970.
The Daybreakers, illustrated by Charles Robinson. New York, Harcourt Brace, and London, Longman, 1970.
Mindy's Mysterious Miniature, illustrated by Charles Robinson. New York, Harcourt Brace, 1970; as *The Housenapper,* London, Longman, 1971.
Over the Sea's Edge, illustrated by Charles Robinson. New York, Harcourt Brace, and London, Longman, 1971.
The Ice Ghosts Mystery. New York, Atheneum, 1972; London, Longman, 1973.
The Lost Farm, illustrated by Charles Robinson. New York, Atheneum, and London, Longman, 1974.
Parsley Sage, Rosemary and Time, illustrated by Charles Robinson. New York, Atheneum, 1975.
The Watchers. New York, Atheneum, 1975; London, Kestrel, 1976.
The Magical Cupboard, illustrated by Charles Robinson. New York, Atheneum, 1976.
Poor Tom's Ghost, illustrated by Janet Archer. New York, Atheneum, and London, Kestrel, 1977.
The Birdstones. New York, Atheneum, 1977; London, Kestrel, 1978.
The Bassumtyte Treasure. New York, Atheneum, and London, Kestrel, 1978.
Ghost Lane. New York, Atheneum, 1979.
The Wolves of Aam. New York, Atheneum, 1981.
Shadow Dancers. New York, Atheneum, 1983.
The Great Flood Mystery. New York, Atheneum, and London, Hippo, 1985.
The Lotus Cup. New York, Atheneum, 1986.
Me, Myself and I. New York, McElderry, 1987.

Other

Down from the Lonely Mountain: California Indian Tales, illustrated by Enrico Arno. New York, Harcourt Brace, 1965; illustrated by the author, London, Dobson, 1968.
Back in the Beforetime: Tales of the Californian Indians, illustrated by James Watts. New York, McElderry, 1987.

*

Manuscript Collection: Kerlan Collection, University of Minnesota, Minneapolis.

Jane Louise Curry comments:

Most of my novels for children, whether for younger or older readers, are adventures—often, in part or in whole, fantasies—which in one way or another involve children of the present in events of the past. This is not always an essentially historical past, as it is in *Poor Tom's Ghost.* In the Abáloc stories (*Beneath the Hill, The Daybreakers, Over the Sea's Edge, The Watchers,* and *The Birdstones*), it is one that draws as much or more from both Old and New World legend and myth as from archaeology and history.

I find great satisfaction in involving children in other places, people and times—but from time to time I also enjoy writing a story like *The Housenapper,* for sheer fun.

*   *   *

Since publication of her first book in 1965, Jane Louise Curry has produced works of fantasy and modern fiction, each imbued with the sense of a past that may be gone but certainly is not dead or forgotten. In works like *The Lotus Cup* and *The Great Flood Mystery* the protagonists, intrigued by mysteries and artifacts from the past, seek to learn more; in the course of solving the mystery they realize that history is not barren but made up of the stories of lively, interesting people whose lives still touch their own. Most of Curry's many fantasies concern time and time travel. They are rich with a sense that time past and time present are not separate; the present and the past resonate, each affecting the other, as children of the 20th century help those in earlier times and are themselves helped in return. This resonance is strongest in *Poor Tom's Ghost,* a time fantasy set as much in the England of Elizabeth I as in that of Elizabeth II, as a young boy seeks to alter the destiny of an Elizabethan actor who haunts the boy's father in the 20th century.

Central among Curry's works are her Abáloc novels, eight loosely connected works of high fantasy set on the North American continent. *The Wolves of Aam* and *Shadow Dancers* postulate that magical beings lived here in prehistoric times; *The Watchers, The Birdstones, The Daybreakers, Over the Sea's Edge, The Change-Child,* and *Beneath the Hill* chronicle the remains of that magic in historical times. These works are as much about time and its passage as they are about the struggle between good and evil, as lands and peoples replace earlier lands and peoples. Before the Ice Age, eastern North America is inhabited by the magical Silvrin, who move on and leave the land to the Aldar, an equally magical people. During the Ice Age the region, populated by giants and men and the nomadic Tiddi, is called Astarlind. By the 4th century, when the Aldar have traveled to a land beyond the world, what remains has been replaced by Ebhélic. Ebhélic becomes Abáloc long before the 12th century; by the 20th century, even Abáloc has been forgotten, though Apple Lock, West Virginia, has grown up in the area. Each age forgets what has gone before—the shy, long-established families of 20th-century Twilly's Green, West Virginia, have no knowledge of the Aldar from whom they are descended, and the 12th-century Abalockians cannot read the ancient book of history preserved from 4th-century Ebhélic. But the magic has lived on in the land: each period feels the touch of evil powers imprisoned beneath the mountains in the first age of Astarlind; and in the 20th century an ancient ammarn tree remains from the powerful groves that protected the land long before the 4th century. Time is a real presence in those novels. Represented as an endless ring surrounding a tree, it appears several places in the novels: the gentle Abalockians see it as the ring of eternity cradling the fruitfulness of life, while the savage people of Cibotlán see it as the ring of death binding the life inside.

Ultimately the past, in almost all Curry's novels, is something we ignore at our peril. Destroying the writings of earlier ages, the people of Ebhélic are defenseless against those who use knowledge to hold them in thrall; the evil forces held beneath the mountains almost destroy the descendants of their keepers, who are ignorant of earlier events. In *Poor Tom's Ghost,* Roger Nicholas, happy when his family finally settles in the house his father has inherited, finds that its history may destroy the security he has built. In several works—including Curry's modern fiction—the protagonists find in the past a sort of saving grace. In *The Daybreakers* artifacts of Abáloc when sold will bolster the Apple Lock school system's sagging budget and help reopen the schools. In *The Lotus Cup* Corry Tipson finds the key to her future in her family's past: reconstructing a porcelain-making process, she discovers both her true talents and confidence in herself.

Curry's work is graceful and evocative, her characters lively, especially in *The Lotus Cup* and *Poor Tom's Ghost.* Her attempt to create for North America a mythical past is especially interesting for the reader of fantasy. Reading the Abáloc novels in order of publication is like watching an archaeological dig: having "discovered" the artifacts of Astarlind in *Beneath the Hill,* Curry seems to have dug deeper and deeper into her mythical past with each successive book, and part of the reader's pleasure is in fitting together the history of the land.

—Pat Pflieger

———

CUTT, W(illiam) Towrie. Canadian. Born in Orkney, Scotland, 26 January 1898. Educated at Kirkwall Grammar School, Orkney; University of Alberta, Edmonton, B.A. 1942, B.Ed. 1947, M.A. 1950. Served in the Gordon Highlanders in France, 1916–19: Private; instructor, Royal Canadian Air Force, 1942–44. Married Margaret Nancy Davis in 1948. Teacher, Alberta, 1928–63. *Died 25 August 1981.*

PUBLICATIONS FOR CHILDREN

Fiction

On the Trail of Long Tom, illustrated by Sheila Dorrell. Toronto, Collins, and London, Deutsch, 1970.
Message from Arkmae. Toronto, Collins, 1972; edited by Madean Stewart, London, Deutsch, 1972.
Seven for the Sea. London, Deutsch, 1972; Chicago, Follett, 1974.
Carry My Bones Northwest. London, Deutsch, 1973.

Other

Faraway World: An Orkney Boyhood, illustrated by Joseph Sloan. London, Deutsch, 1977.
The Hogboon of Hell and Other Strange Orkney Tales, with Nancy Cutt, illustrated by Richard Kennedy. London, Deutsch, 1979.

*

Manuscript Collection: W. Towrie Cutt Library, Sanday, Orkney, Scotland.

W. Towrie Cutt commented:

(1978) Writers of children's books are advised to keep the child in view—to connect. Which children? Out of 10,000,000 Canadian and British children, 4,000 will, if I am lucky, read my book—one out of 2,000. Which one am I writing for? I have written for children who may be led to take an interest in the humble unrecorded makers of Canadian history and interested in the preservation of animal life, especially sea mammals. I deal with two half-breed boys in my Canadian historicals, one who went the way of the white man and the other who went the way of the Indian—a choice such boys had to make at one time. In my seal stories, I seek to recall Orkney folk lore. I am against books understood only by gifted youths being labelled as "children's books."

*   *   *

W. Towrie Cutt's *Message from Arkmae* and *Seven for the Sea* are really one book broken in two, though each can be read independently. Both books are an impassioned plea for the protection of wild life in the Orkneys, written with the observation and insight of a man who was born and spent his childhood in the islands and who, figuratively speaking, never left.

Set on the isle of Sanday, both books concern the Ward family. Father and two sons have the distinguishing feature of a hard skin between their fingers and a red tinge on the neck which is said to denote their descent from a Ward who married a seal woman. Thus the legend. Two younger Wards, cousins, Erchie and Mansie, who spend days in their rowing boat fishing and beach combing, find themselves one day in an underground cavern where they meet a merman. It is this character who articulates the author's plea for the conservation of the island, and above all of the seals. In the sequel, the two boys, rowing to Sanday, are held up by fog and accept a lift from a strange boatman. Slowly they realise that the boatman has taken them back into the past where they witness what actually happened to their great-great grandfather, Selkie Ward, when, through his own fault, he lost his seal wife. Even though not sure afterwards whether it was perhaps only a dream, the two boys now accept as true the local legend about Selkie Ward.

The quality of life on the Orkneys a hundred years ago is beautifully captured and the freshly remembered detail firmly anchors the old Celtic fairy tale, which, in both books, is told with a strong sense of mystery and suspense.

—James Roose-Evans

———

DAHL, Roald. British. Born in Llandaff, Glamorgan, Wales, 13 September 1916. Educated at Repton School, Yorkshire. Served in the Royal Air Force, 1939–45: in Nairobi and Habbanyah, 1939–40; with a fighter squadron in the Western Desert, 1940 (wounded); in Greece and Syria, 1941; assistant air attaché, Washington, D.C., 1942–43; wing commander, 1943; with British Security Co-ordination, North America, 1943–45. Married 1) the actress Patricia Neal in 1953 (divorced 1983), one son and four daughters (one deceased); 2) Felicity Ann Crosland in 1983. Member of the Public Schools Exploring Society expedition to Newfoundland, 1934; member of the Eastern staff, Shell Company, London, 1933–37, and Shell Company of East Africa, Dar-es-Salaam, 1937–39. Recipient: Mystery Writers of America Edgar Allan Poe award, 1953, 1959, 1980; Federation of Children's Book Groups award, 1983; Whitbread award, 1983; World Fantasy Convention award, 1983. D.Litt.: University of Keele, Staffordshire, 1988. Agent: Murray Pollinger, 4 Garrick Street, London WC2E 9BH; or, Watkins Loomis Agency, 150 East 35th Street, New York, New York 10016, U.S.A. Address: Gipsy House, Great Missenden, Buckinghamshire HP16 0PB, England.

PUBLICATIONS FOR CHILDREN

Fiction

The Gremlins, illustrated by Walt Disney Studio. New York, Random House, 1943; London, Collins, 1944.
James and the Giant Peach, illustrated by Nancy Ekholm Burkert. New York, Knopf, 1961; London, Allen and Unwin, 1967.
Charlie and the Chocolate Factory, illustrated by Joseph Schindelman. New York, Knopf, 1964; London, Allen and Unwin, 1967.
The Magic Finger, illustrated by William Pène du Bois. New York, Harper, 1966; London, Allen and Unwin, 1968.
Fantastic Mr. Fox, illustrated by Donald Chaffin. New York, Knopf, and London, Allen and Unwin, 1970.
Charlie and the Great Glass Elevator, illustrated by Joseph Schindelman. New York, Knopf, 1972; London, Allen and Unwin, 1973.
Danny, The Champion of the World, illustrated by Jill Bennett. London, Cape, and New York, Knopf, 1975.
The Wonderful Story of Henry Sugar and Six More. London, Cape, 1977; as *The Wonderful World of Henry Sugar,* New York, Knopf, 1977.
The Complete Adventures of Charlie and Mr. Willy Wonka (omnibus), illustrated by Faith Jaques. London, Allen and Unwin, 1978.
The Enormous Crocodile, illustrated by Quentin Blake. London, Cape, and New York, Knopf, 1978.
The Twits, illustrated by Quentin Blake. London, Cape, 1980; New York, Knopf, 1981.
George's Marvellous Medicine, illustrated by Quentin Blake. London, Cape, 1981; New York, Knopf, 1982.
The BFG, illustrated by Quentin Blake. London, Cape, and New York, Farrar Straus, 1982.
The Witches, illustrated by Quentin Blake. London, Cape, and New York, Farrar Straus, 1983.
The Giraffe and the Pelly and Me, illustrated by Quentin Blake. London, Cape, and New York, Farrar Straus, 1985.
Matilda, illustrated by Quentin Blake. London, Cape, and New York, Viking Kestrel, 1988.

Verse

Revolting Rhymes, illustrated by Quentin Blake. London, Cape, 1982; New York, Knopf, 1983.
Dirty Beasts, illustrated by Rosemary Fawcett. London, Cape, 1983; New York, Farrar Straus, 1984.

Other (autobiography)

Boy: Tales of Childhood. London, Cape, and New York, Farrar Straus, 1984.
Going Solo. London, Cape, and New York, Farrar Straus, 1986.

PUBLICATIONS FOR ADULTS

Novels

Sometime Never: A Fable for Supermen. New York, Scribner, 1948; London, Collins, 1949.
My Uncle Oswald. London, Joseph, 1979; New York, Knopf, 1980.

Short Stories

Over to You: 10 Stories of Flyers and Flying. New York, Reynal,

1946; London, Hamish Hamilton, 1947.
Someone Like You. New York, Knopf, 1953; London, Secker and Warburg, 1954; revised edition, London, Joseph, 1961.
Kiss, Kiss. New York, Knopf, and London, Joseph, 1960.
Twenty-Nine Kisses. London, Joseph, 1969.
Selected Stories. New York, Random House, 1970.
Penguin Modern Stories 12, with others. London, Penguin, 1972.
Switch Bitch. New York, Knopf, and London, Joseph, 1974.
The Best of Roald Dahl. New York, Random House, 1978; London, Joseph, 1983.
Tales of the Unexpected. London, Joseph, and New York, Vintage, 1979.
More Tales of the Unexpected. London, Joseph, 1980; as *Further Tales of the Unexpected,* Bath, Chivers, 1981.
A Roald Dahl Selection: Nine Short Stories, edited by Roy Blatchford. London, Longman, 1980.
Two Fables. London, Viking, 1986; New York, Farrar Straus, 1987.
A Second Roald Dahl Selection: Eight Short Stories, edited by Hélène Fawcett. London, Longman, 1987.

Plays

The Honeys (produced New York, 1955).

Screenplays: *You Only Live Twice,* with Harry Jack Bloom, 1967; *Chitty-Chitty-Bang-Bang,* with Ken Hughes, 1968; *The Night-Digger,* 1970; *The Lightning Bug,* 1971; *Willy Wonka and the Chocolate Factory,* 1971.

Television Play: *Lamb to the Slaughter* (*Alfred Hitchcock Presents* series), 1955.

Other

Editor, *Roald Dahl's Book of Ghost Stories.* London, Cape, and New York, Farrar Straus, 1983.

*

Critical Study: *Roald Dahl* by Chris Powling, London, Hamish Hamilton, 1983.

*   *   *

In his autobiographical piece "Lucky Break—How I Became a Writer" Roald Dahl remarks, "the most important and difficult thing about writing fiction is to find the plot. Good original plots are very hard to come by." He speaks too of what "slender threads" a children's book must ultimately be woven. The interesting thing about Dahl as a children's writer is *how* slender those threads have always been and continue to be. Indeed lately he has become so sure of his audience that the "slenderness" has been openly admitted: "But that's enough of that. We can't go on forever watching these two disgusting people doing disgusting things to each other. We must get ahead with the story." By the time this announcement comes we are already halfway through *The Twits* and "two disgusting people doing disgusting things to each other" is a fair summary of the plot.

Dahl's appeal lies in this kind of aplomb—the sense that you can do anything and make anything happen if you really want to. You are jerked along through the story by your wonderment at what new outrage can be perpetrated next and certainly not out of any sense of "development." Though Dahl speaks of his stories "building" or "expanding," the building has to do with the addition of events strung like beads on the thread of the plot. He has made a virtue for himself out of this kind of panache—his stories are strewn with characters who make an appearance and are then sharply dealt with—like

James's parents and Aunts Spicer and Sponge in *James and the Giant Peach* or the awful children in *Charlie and the Chocolate Factory.*

Mr. Wonka is in fact the embodiment of Dahl's approach to story-telling. He holds both the Charlie books together, manipulating people and events—always breathless, always in a hurry—and Charlie, like the reader, is dazzled by the performance. There can be no time for questions—otherwise, the magic won't work.

The problem for the writer, of course, is that "good original plots are hard to come by," that the invention flags. That seems to me the case in both *The Twits* and *George's Marvellous Medicine,* and it's interesting that the seeds of *The BFG* lie in an earlier book, *Danny, The Champion of the World.* A writer of Dahl's immense popularity makes the most of his ideas.

However, it is important not to become too complicated in talking about Dahl because keeping the stories simple and uncluttered is what he is about. What his child readers dwell on is their relish of his bizarre inventions—"I liked that bit where Augustus Gloop went up the tube"—and his slightly risqué irreverence, usually at the expense of adults. Dahl says the things that would get you into trouble if you said them: "What I'm trying to tell you is that Mr. Twit was a foul and smelly old man." Because he addresses his audience so directly they have the pleasure of feeling that they are in on a tremendous joke; although this always goes with the slightly uncomfortable sense that the joke might be turned on you. This sense of sharing, of joining with Dahl in a game or plot, is crucial: you admire him and his cleverness, *not* his characters. He reminds me of those clever boys who haunted my childhood who were great talkers and storytellers and who told rude jokes to an admiring audience, the ones who seemed mysteriously to have more experience and who dared to "say things." The best example of his appeal to that sense of daring is *The Magic Finger:* "'You are a stupid little girl!' Mrs. Winter said. 'I am not a stupid little girl!' I cried. 'I am a very nice little girl.' Then I got cross, and I saw red, and I put the Magic Finger on Mrs. Winter.…" I have to admit that *The Magic Finger* is my least favorite story—it illustrates best the narrowness of the ground Dahl works.

In only one story does he risk something larger—*Danny, The Champion of the World:* "When I was four months old, my mother died suddenly and my father was left to look after me all by himself." The opening chapters are full of simple affection and tenderness, and, although there's no falling off of outrageous invention and satire, what holds the book together is the relationship between father and son, treated without irony. It is an oddity among the stories because the reader is asked very directly to care for and sympathise with the two main characters. It is—and none the worse for that—Dahl's only sentimental story: "What I have been trying so hard to tell you all along is simply that my father…was the most marvellous and exciting father any boy ever had."

—Eric Hadley

———

DALGLIESH, Alice. American. Born in Trinidad, West Indies, 7 October 1893; emigrated to the United States, 1902; naturalized citizen. Educated at the Pratt Institute, Brooklyn, New York, diploma in kindergarten teaching; Teachers College, Columbia University, New York, A.B. in English and education, M.A. Teacher of kindergarten and elementary education for 17 years; teacher at Horace Mann School, New York; editor, Books for Young Readers, Charles Scribner's Sons, New York, 1934–60. Contributing editor, *Saturday Review,* New York, 1960–66. *Died 11 June 1979.*

PUBLICATIONS FOR CHILDREN

Fiction

West Indian Play Days, illustrated by Margaret Evans Price. Chicago, Rand McNally, 1926.
The Little Wooden Farmer, and The Story of the Jungle Pool, illustrated by Theodora Baumeister. New York, Macmillan, 1930; revised edition, 1968; London, Hamish Hamilton, 1969.
The Blue Teapot: Sandy Cove Stories, illustrated by Hildegard Woodward. New York, Macmillan, 1931.
The Choosing Book, illustrated by Eloise Burns Wilkin. New York, Macmillan, 1932.
Relief's Rocker, illustrated by Hildegard Woodward. New York, Macmillan, 1932.
Roundabout, illustrated by Hildegard Woodward. New York, Macmillan, 1934.
Sailor Sam, illustrated by the author. New York, Scribner, 1935.
The Smiths and Rusty, illustrated by Berta and Elmer Hader. New York and London, Scribner, 1936.
Wings for the Smiths, illustrated by Berta and Elmer Hader. New York and London, Scribner, 1937.
The Young Aunts, illustrated by Charlotte Becker. New York and London, Scribner, 1939.
The Hollyberrys, illustrated by Pru Herric. New York and London, Scribner, 1939.
Wooden Shoes in America, illustrated by Lois Maloy. New York, Scribner, 1940.
A Book for Jennifer: A Story of London Children in the Eighteenth Century and of Mr. Newbery's Juvenile Library, illustrated by Katherine Milhous. New York, Scribner, 1940.
Three from Greenways, illustrated by Gertrude Howe. New York, Scribner, and London, Hodder and Stoughton, 1941.
Gulliver Joins the Army, illustrated by Ellen Segner. New York, Scribner, 1942.
The Little Angel, illustrated by Katherine Milhous. New York, Scribner, 1943.
The Silver Pencil, illustrated by Katherine Milhous. New York, Scribner, 1944.
Along Janet's Road, illustrated by Katherine Milhous. New York, Scribner, 1946.
Reuben and His Red Wheelbarrow, illustrated by Ilse Bischoff. New York, Grosset and Dunlap, 1946.
The Davenports Are at Dinner, illustrated by Flavia Gág. New York, Scribner, 1948.
The Davenports and Cherry Pie, illustrated by Flavia Gág. New York, Scribner, 1949.
The Bears on Hemlock Mountain, illustrated by Helen Sewell. New York, Scribner, 1952; London, Epworth Press, 1965.
The Courage of Sarah Noble, illustrated by Leonard Weisgard. New York, Scribner, 1954; London, Hamish Hamilton, 1970.
Adam and the Golden Cock, illustrated by Leonard Weisgard. New York, Scribner, 1959.

Other

A Happy School Year (reader), illustrated by Mary Spoor Brand. Chicago, Rand McNally, 1924.
Peregrin and the Goldfish, illustrated by Tom Seidmann-Freud. New York, Macmillan, 1929.
First Experiences with Literature (textbook). New York, Scribner, 1932.
America Travels: The Story of a Hundred Years of Travel in America, illustrated by Hildegard Woodward. New York, Macmillan, 1933; revised edition, 1961.
Long Live the King! A Story Book of English Kings and Queens, illustrated by Lois Maloy. New York, Scribner, 1937.
America Begins: The Story of the Finding of the New World, illustrated by Lois Maloy. New York, Scribner, 1938; revised edition, 1959.
America Builds Homes: The Story of the First Colonies, illustrated by Lois Maloy. New York, Scribner, 1938.
Wings Around South America, illustrated by Katherine Milhous. New York, Scribner, 1941.
The True Story of Fala, with Margaret Suckley. New York, Scribner, 1942.
They Live in South America, illustrated by Katherine Milhous and Frances Lichten. New York, Scribner, 1942.
The Thanksgiving Story, illustrated by Helen Sewell. New York, Scribner, 1954.
The Columbus Story, illustrated by Leo Politi. New York, Scribner, 1955.
The Fourth of July Story, illustrated by Marie Nonnast. New York, Scribner, 1956.
Ride the Wind (on Charles Lindbergh), illustrated by Georges Schreibner. New York, Scribner, 1956.

Editor, *Christmas: A Book of Stories New and Old,* illustrated by Hildegard Woodward. New York, Scribner, 1934; as *A Christmas Holiday Book,* London, Dent, 1934.
Editor, *Once on a Time* (folktales), illustrated by Katherine Milhous. New York, Scribner, 1938.
Editor, with Françoise, *The Gay Mother Goose,* illustrated by Françoise. New York, Scribner, 1938.
Editor, *The Will James Cowboy Book.* New York, Scribner, 1938.
Editor, *Happily Ever After: Fairy Tales,* illustrated by Katherine Milhous. New York, Scribner, 1939.
Editor, *St. George and the Dragon,* by Richard Johnson, illustrated by Lois Maloy. New York, Scribner, 1941.
Editor, *The Enchanted Book,* illustrated by Concetta Cacciola. New York, Scribner, 1947.

PUBLICATIONS FOR ADULTS

Other

Selected Books for Young Children, with *Selected Pictures for Young Children,* by Rita Scherman. New York, Educational Playthings, 1934.
The Horace Mann Kindergarten for Five-Year-Old Children, with Charlotte Garrison and Emma Sheehy. New York, Columbia University Teachers College, 1937.

Editor, with Annis Duff, *Aids to Choosing Books for Your Children.* New York, Children's Book Council, 1957.

* * *

Alice Dalgliesh's rich background as a British and American subject, as a kindergarten and elementary school teacher, and as a children's book editor are all reflected in her many different types of children's books, with their wide variety of locale, period, and subject matter. Perhaps Dalgliesh's information books are her most popular ones; many have gone through various editions, and, in the case of *America Travels,* the second edition is revised and enlarged. This work is characteristic of Dalgliesh's competent treatment of information and history. The style is casual, with a strong emphasis on dialogue, factual exposition, and indirect characterization. This particular work contains eight "traveling tales," as diverse as the story about a young pioneer child who travels alone by stage coach, and a story about "two boys and the first automobile that came to town." The intent of the author is to give a young reading audience a taste of a broad range of accurate subject matter related to travel.

This attention to accuracy, detail, and diversity is also characteristic of *The Thanksgiving Story, The Fourth of July Story,* and *Christmas: A Book of Stories New and Old.* The exactness of detail and perspective in the information books is reflected in Dalgliesh's juvenile historical novels, such as *Adam and the Golden Cock,* based on a true story that occurred around Newton, Connecticut, in 1781, and *The Courage of Sarah Noble,* also a true story, about an eight-year-old child who travels through the wilderness into Indian country to cook for her father while he builds a new home. Sarah's perceptions about the Indian community and the "humanness" of its members are of real value to the child who grows up with a demeaning and stereotyped impression of American Indians superimposed on him from all sides.

Alice Dalgliesh's characters and stories are all given life and moment because of the author's attention to image, detail, and believability. For this reason, two of Dalgliesh's picture books for young children have remained perennial favorites. *The Little Wooden Farmer,* in a 1968 edition with fine illustrations by Anita Lobel, is a repetition book emphasizing the progressive steps one takes to produce a well-appointed farm. Because of the dialogue, repetition, and progression, the book reads well aloud. Dalgliesh apparently realized this when she first published the story in 1930 as one "to read and play." The dramatic quality of Dalgliesh's picture books is seen best in *The Bears on Hemlock Mountain.* This is a tense, suspenseful, and characteristically imaginative tale that lends itself both to reading aloud and acting out. Behind all of Dalgliesh's work is a strong sense of the child audience for which it is written, and a delight in language, detail, situation, and action.

—Rachel Fordyce

DALLAS, Ruth. Pseudonym for Ruth Mumford. New Zealander. Born in Invercargill, 29 September 1919. Educated at Southland Technical College, Invercargill. Recipient: New Zealand Literary Fund achievement award, 1963; University of Otago Robert Burns fellowship, 1968; New Zealand Book award, for poetry, 1977; Buckland award, for poetry, 1977. Litt.D.: University of Otago, Dunedin, 1978. Address: 448 Leith Street, Dunedin, New Zealand.

PUBLICATIONS FOR CHILDREN

Fiction

The Children in the Bush, illustrated by Peter Campbell. London, Methuen, 1969.
Ragamuffin Scarecrow, illustrated by Els Noordhof. Dunedin, University of Otago Bibliography Room, 1969.
A Dog Called Wig, illustrated by Edward Mortelmans. London, Methuen, 1970.
The Wild Boy in the Bush, illustrated by Peter Campbell. London, Methuen, 1971.
The Big Flood in the Bush, illustrated by Peter Campbell. London, Methuen, 1972; New York, Scholastic, 1974.
The House on the Cliffs, illustrated by Gavin Rowe. London, Methuen, 1975.
Shining Rivers, illustrated by Gareth Floyd. London, Methuen, 1979.
Holiday Time in the Bush, illustrated by Gary Hebley. London, Methuen, 1983.

Other

Sawmilling Yesterday, illustrated by Juliet Peter. Wellington, Department of Education, 1958.

PUBLICATIONS FOR ADULTS

Verse

Country Road and Other Poems 1947–1952. Christchurch, Caxton Press, 1953.
The Turning Wheel. Christchurch, Caxton Press, 1961.
Experiment in Form. Dunedin, University of Otago Bibliography Room, 1964.
Day Book: Poems of a Year. Christchurch, Caxton Press, 1966.
Shadow Show. Christchurch, Caxton Press, 1968.
Song for a Guitar and Other Songs, edited by Charles Brasch. Dunedin, University of Otago Press, 1976.
Walking on the Snow. Christchurch, Caxton Press, 1976.
Steps of the Sun. Christchurch, Caxton Press, 1979.
Collected Poems. Dunedin, University of Otago Press, 1987.

*

Manuscript Collection: Hocken Library, University of Otago, Dunedin, New Zealand.

Ruth Dallas comments:

In New Zealand when I was a child, the books I read came from England and were to a certain extent foreign, in that I had never seen the environment I was reading about: big cities, attached houses, upstairs bedrooms, nurseries, nannies, fathers who were abroad, English villages, gamekeepers, and all historical material, including very old houses—in short, the common paraphernalia of children's fiction as I first encountered it. Even the elderly people in my family had grown up in a setting that was quite different from the "old country." Between the oral New Zealand tales I heard and storybook stories from overseas, there was a gap that disturbed me for a long time. I began to write stories about New Zealand children for the school journals in 1958. My first children's novel was published in London in 1969 and was based on tales I had heard in my own family. I had noticed that children were growing up who did not know that much of their green farmland was once covered with the forest that is now found in reserves and that not only old pioneers had lived in the bush but children, too. I plan to continue writing New Zealand stories, both historical and contemporary, as well as poetry.

*   *   *

Ruth Dallas is best known in her own country as a poet who particularly evokes the landscape of southern South Island. Both her prose and poetry for children have been made available to numerous young New Zealanders through the School Journals, enlightened publications put out by the Department of Education for reading in schools.

The connection with educational purpose may in part contribute to the slightly didactic nature of her earlier works. *The Children in the Bush, The Wild Boy in the Bush,* and *The Big Flood in the Bush* all rather self-consciously teach about the life of the early settlers but are made vivid by the liveliness of their characterization. All three books feature a family of four 19th-century children whose vigour, enthusiasm, and propensity for getting into not unlikely scrapes in the absences of their widowed mother, the Settlement's nurse, are reminiscent of E. Nesbit's. Ruth Dallas has the rare gift of conveying a "child's eye view," and these books are recounted by the youngest—8-year-old Jean. The angle of the narrative is convincingly hers, whether she describes laughing and talking after bedtime so that "Mrs. Bain came into the room in her petticoat" or the frequent crises with their cow, who rejoiced in the inspired name of "Hokey-Pokey."

The numerous animal stories, plays, and poems published in the "Journals" reached fruition in *A Dog Called Wig*, which must be one of the most unusual of all animal stories. Here a boy, who initially has to plead with his parents to keep the stray dog which has appeared in the garden, subsequently feels betrayed and disillusioned by the animal's attachment to his father. Only after the dog is badly injured and the boy involved in an exciting adventure with escaped Borstal inmates, is the relationship restored.

These books are all in an "easy to read" format which, while most suitable to the less confident reader, are stylistically cramping. In *The House on the Cliffs,* however, Dallas has profited by a longer book for an older reader. In this evocative story the images of shells, wind, rocks, and solitary sea-birds, which occur so frequently in her poems, become symbols of the delicate balance between loneliness and independence in the relationship between eccentric old Biddy Bristow and two present-day schoolgirls. This story has the different levels of meaning so characteristic of both good poetry and good children's literature, and in Biddy's single-minded beach searchings for "a bell to ring when the wind blows" we learn something of the nature of creative seeking.

Friendship between old and young is again central in *Shining Rivers,* set in the Otago goldfields of the 1860's, in which a young immigrant boy leaves a safe bakery job to go to "the diggings," lured by prospects of speedy wealth. His disenchantment with the rough scene there is tempered by the guidance and generosity of an old miner, and this carefully researched novel presents a thoughtful and convincing picture of the past.

—Betty Gilderdale

DALY, Maureen. American. Born in Castle Caulfield, County Tyrone, Ireland, in 1922(?). Educated at St. Mary Springs Academy, Fond du Lac, Wisconsin; Rosary College, River Forest, Illinois, B.A. Married the writer William P. McGivern in 1948 (died 1982); one daughter (deceased) and one son. Police reporter and columnist, Chicago *Tribune,* 1946–48; associate editor, *Ladies' Home Journal,* Philadelphia, 1948–54; editorial consultant, *Saturday Evening Post,* Philadelphia, 1960–69. Since 1970 film and television writer, Hollywood. Agent: Eleanor Wood, Blassingame McCauley and Wood, 432 Park Avenue South, Suite 1205, New York, New York 10016. Address: P.O. Box 3875, Palm Desert, California 92260, U.S.A.

PUBLICATIONS FOR CHILDREN

Fiction

Seventeenth Summer. New York, Dodd Mead, 1942; London, Hollis and Carter, 1947.
Patrick Visits the Farm, illustrated by Ellie Simmons. New York, Dodd Mead, 1959.
Patrick Takes a Trip, illustrated by Ellie Simmons. New York, Dodd Mead, 1960.
Sixteen and Other Stories, illustrated by Kendall Rossi. New York, Dodd Mead, 1961.
Patrick Visits the Library, illustrated by Paul Lantz. New York, Dodd Mead, 1961.

Patrick Visits the Zoo, illustrated by Sam Savitt. New York, Dodd Mead, 1963.
The Ginger Horse, illustrated by Wesley Dennis. New York, Dodd Mead, 1964.
The Small War of Sergeant Donkey, illustrated by Wesley Dennis. New York, Dodd Mead, 1966.
Rosie, The Dancing Elephant, illustrated by Lorence Bjorklund. New York, Dodd Mead, 1967.
Acts of Love. New York, Scholastic, 1986; London, Gollancz, 1987.

Other

What's Your P.Q. (Personality Quotient)?, illustrated by Ellie Simmons. New York, Dodd Mead, 1952; revised edition, 1966.
Twelve Around the World, illustrated by Frank Kramer. New York, Dodd Mead, 1957.
Spain: Wonderland of Contrasts. New York, Dodd Mead, 1965.

Editor, *My Favorite Mystery [Suspense] Stories.* New York, Dodd Mead, 2 vols., 1966–68.

PUBLICATIONS FOR ADULTS

Other

Smarter and Smoother: A Handbook on How to Be That Way. New York, Dodd Mead, 1944.
The Perfect Hostess: Complete Etiquette and Entertainment for the Home. New York, Dodd Mead, 1948.
Mention My Name in Mombasa: The Unscheduled Adventures of an American Family Abroad (as Maureen Daly McGivern), with William P. McGivern. New York, Dodd Mead, 1958.
Spanish Roundabout. New York, Dodd Mead, 1960.
Moroccan Roundabout. New York, Dodd Mead, 1961.

Editor, *My Favorite Stories.* New York, Dodd Mead, 1948.
Editor, *Profile of Youth.* Philadelphia, Lippincott, 1951.

*

Manuscript Collection: University of Oregon Library, Eugene.

Maureen Daly comments:
I cannot remember the exact names of the streets I walked on my way to school. I cannot remember the color of the bedroom walls in the house in which I spent my childhood. But I do remember with warmth and clarity the names of the three librarians in charge of our public library during my growing-up years in the small lake town of Fond du Lac, Wisconsin: Miss Janes, Miss Shepherd, and Miss Kramer. Each was a generous conspirator in introducing me to the hidden magic of rows and rows of books in that little greystone library. Later, as a journalist and a traveller, I had a plan of my own when I began to write books for children. I would try to invent some magic in plot and characters—and then add the special magic of fact to my stories. So everything I write for children has a touch of the *real*—the look of a foreign country, the sounds and smells of a desert, the color, shapes, and skills of horses and birds and elephants.

Laugh, perhaps, and dream, and let your heart beat faster while you read, but learn a little truth along the way. Miss Janes made me believe that, or maybe it was Miss Shepherd. Or then again, was it Miss Kramer?

*   *   *

"In almost everything I write," Maureen Daly has said, "I seem to travel far for the subject—or else write microscopically about things that happen right at home." She has traveled thousands of miles preparing her book on teenagers, *Twelve Around the World,* and her other travel books. Closer to home are her books on etiquette and the social properties.

And right from her own home town, by the shores of Lake Winnebago in Fond du Lac, Wisconsin, came her first and most lasting stories. As a sophomore in high school, she learned, along with her classmates, to appreciate good writing under the tutelage of a gifted enthusiastic teacher. "The entire class soon wanted to become authors," she remembers. At fifteen, with a story entitled "Fifteen," she won fourth place in a national short story contest conducted by *Scholastic Magazine.* The next year, she won first place with "Sixteen," a story reprinted in the 1938 annual O. Henry Memorial award volume. "Sixteen" is a spare first-rate story that says more in seven pages than most say in seventy. "You Can't Kiss Caroline" is memorable for its lovely surprise ending; and the true story of a nun from the nursing order of Sisters on the island of Ibiza, just off the coast of Barcelona, elicited a response from a doctor who wanted to contribute money to the good work carried on by the nuns. "Love Is a Summer Word" is an excerpt from Maureen Daly's first novel and most successful work, *Seventeenth Summer.*

Seventeenth Summer is a sensitively written sincere story of an adolescent's awakening to the raptures and anxieties of a first young love. It was an instantaneous hit. Teenagers claimed it at once as their own. There had been teenage books but, magically, this one was written by one of their own crowd, then a sophomore in college, who intuitively sensed the fears and doubts, the heights and depths of their emotions at that moment. The novel's personal viewpoint reflected their feeling· of insecurity, of humiliation, of heavenly exhilaration; their daydreams and endless streams of speculation about themselves and their codes of behavior. For the lonely outsider, the unsophisticated girl who did not smoke or drink or pet, the heroine's innocence and natural artlessness were immensely reassuring. It was a time of blossoming, of new beginnings, of discovering values, forming relationships and growing up to one's own responsibilities.

Maureen Daly had heeded well the advice of her high school teacher who had urged her students to try to look honestly at themselves and to write what they knew about. *Seventeenth Summer* is a story written "microscopically," with distinction.

Daly's second novel for young adults, *Acts of Love,* was published in 1986, 44 years after *Seventeenth Summer.* Inspired by the "deepest joys" of her daughter, Megan, the author has again written a story of the wonder and magic and heartache of first love. Henrietta (Retta) Caldwell is a high school junior whose sheltered middle-class life is shattered by two irresistible forces: the building of a six-lane highway through part of her family's property in Pennsylvania, and an overwhelming attraction for Dallas, the rangy young Texan, a newcomer in town. Dallas is two years older than Retta, cryptic and proud, but the two soon share many feelings and interests. Even when the Caldwells move to California, their friendship continues for, with Retta's help, Dallas gets a summer job doing what he knows best—caring for Arabian horses on a California ranch. *Acts of Love* touches sketchily on changing patterns of adolescence and on family relationships. By coincidence, Retta's mother had had a consuming passion for Dallas's father when she was 16. The book's romance will appeal to early teens, but the story is slight in substance and significance for young adults of the 1980's.

—Mary Silva Cosgrave

———

DANIELL, David Scott. Pseudonym for Albert Scott Daniell; also wrote as Richard Bowood; John Lewesdon. British. Born in London, 1 July 1906. Educated at Bedford Modern School. Served in the Royal Engineers, Eighth Army, in Sicily and Italy, 1941–46: Captain; mentioned in despatches. Married Elizabeth Mary Thirlby in 1939; one son. Worked for the Commonwealth Trust, Gold Coast, 1929–30. *Died 29 August 1965.*

PUBLICATIONS FOR CHILDREN

Fiction

Mission for Oliver, illustrated by William Stobbs. London, Cape, 1953.
Polly and Oliver, illustrated by William Stobbs. London, Cape, 1954.
The Dragon and the Rose, illustrated by Sheila Stratton. London, Cape, 1955; New York, Abelard Schuman, 1957.
Hunt Royal, illustrated by William Stobbs. London, Cape, 1958.
Hideaway Johnny, illustrated by Val Biro. Leicester, Brockhampton Press, 1959.
The Boy They Made King, illustrated by William Stobbs. London, Cape, 1959; New York, Duell, 1960.
Polly and Oliver at Sea, illustrated by William Stobbs. London, Cape, 1960.
The Rajah's Treasure, illustrated by William Stobbs. New York, Duell, 1960.
Sandro's Battle, illustrated by Colin Spencer. London, Cape, and New York, Duell, 1962.
By Jiminy, illustrated by D.G. Valentine. Leicester, Brockhampton Press, 1962.
Saved by Jiminy, illustrated by D.G. Valentine. Leicester, Brockhampton Press, 1963.
Polly and Oliver Besieged, illustrated by William Stobbs. London, Cape, 1963.
By Jiminy Ahoy, illustrated by D.G. Valentine. Leicester, Brockhampton Press, 1963.
By Jiminy in the Jungle, illustrated by D.G. Valentine. Leicester, Brockhampton Press, 1964.
Polly and Oliver Pursued, illustrated by William Stobbs. London, Cape, 1964.
Horsey and Co. and the Bank Robbers (as Richard Bowood), illustrated by A. Oxenham. London, Golden Pleasure Books, 1965.
By Jiminy in the Highlands, illustrated by D.G. Valentine. Leicester, Brockhampton Press, 1966.
Red Gaskell's Gold (as Richard Bowood), illustrated by Peter Kesteven. London, Macmillan, and New York, St. Martin's Press, 1966.

Plays

Children's Theatre Plays (includes *Hide-and-Seek; The Queen and Mr. Shakespeare; The King's Messenger; Stand and Deliver; The Adventure; The Jester, The Queen, and the Hen*). London, Harrap, 1948.
More Children's Theatre Plays (includes *Hereward the Wake, The Gascon Ring, The Stowaway, The Silver Snuff Box*), illustrated by Elizabeth Thirlby. London, Harrap, 1951.
Costume Plays for Schools (includes *Hunt Royal, The Ring of Gold, Roses for the Queen, Tyger's Hart, Treasure Hunt*). London, Harrap, 1955.
Faith of Our Fathers: The Story of Christianity in Britain (includes *A.D. 150–878: Go Preach in Heathen Britain, 1100–1382: The Glory of the Medieval Church, 1537–1620: The Years of Conflict,*

1662–1960: Freely to Worship), with G.W.H. Lampe. London, University of London Press, 4 vols., 1961.
Letters for the Prince, in *Junior One-Act Plays of To-Day, Fourth Series,* edited by Harold Gardiner. London, Harrap, 1963.

Other

Flight One to Six: Australia, Canada, United States of America, India, Africa, and *The Holy Land,* illustrated by Jack Matthew. Loughborough, Leicestershire, Wills and Hepworth, 6 vols., 1958–62.
The Golden Pomegranate, illustrated by George Adamson. London, University of London Press, 1960.
Ladybird Book of London (as John Lewesdon). Loughborough, Leicestershire, Wills and Hepworth, 1961.
Battles and Battlefields, illustrated by William Stobbs. London, Batsford, 1961.
Discovering the Bible, with G.W.H. Lampe, illustrated by Graham Oakley. London, University of London Press, 1961; Nashville, Abingdon Press, 1966.
Explorers and Exploration, illustrated by William Stobbs. London, Batsford, 1962.
Discovering the Army, illustrated by Crispin Fisher. London, University of London Press, 1965.
Sea Fights. London, Batsford, 1966.
Your Body, illustrated by Robert Ayton. Loughborough, Leicestershire, Wills and Hepworth, 1967.

Other as Richard Bowood

The Story of Flight [*Railways, Ships, Houses and Homes, Clothes and Costume, Our Churches and Cathedrals*], illustrated by Robert Ayton. Loughborough, Leicestershire, Wills and Hepworth, 6 vols., 1960–64.
Great Inventions, illustrated by Robert Ayton. Loughborough, Leicestershire, Wills and Hepworth, 1961.
The Weather, with F.E. Newing, illustrated by J.H. Wingfield. Loughborough, Leicestershire, Wills and Hepworth, 1962.
Magnets, Bulbs and Batteries, with F.E. Newing, illustrated by J.H. Wingfield. Loughborough, Leicestershire, Wills and Hepworth, 1962.
Lights, Mirrors and Lenses, with F.E. Newing, illustrated by J.H. Wingfield. Loughborough, Leicestershire, Wills and Hepworth, 1962.
Levers, Pulleys and Engines, with F.E. Newing, illustrated by J.H. Wingfield. Loughborough, Leicestershire, Wills and Hepworth, 1963.
Air, Wind and Flight, with F.E. Newing, illustrated by J.H. Wingfield. Loughborough, Leicestershire, Wills and Hepworth, 1963.
Naples Ahead, illustrated by David Knight. London, Macmillan, and New York, St. Martin's Press, 1964.
Soldiers. London, Hamlyn, 1965.
Animals [and *Birds*] *and How They Live,* with F.E. Newing, illustrated by Ronald Lampitt. Loughborough, Leicestershire, Wills and Hepworth, 2 vols., 1965–66.
Plants and How They Grow, with F.E. Newing, illustrated by Ronald Lampitt. Loughborough, Leicestershire, Wills and Hepworth, 1965.
Our Land in the Making: Earliest Times to the Norman Conquest and *Norman Conquest to Present Day,* illustrated by Ronald Lampitt. Loughborough, Leicestershire, Wills and Hepworth, 2 vols., 1966.
Underwater Exploration, illustrated by B. Knight. Loughborough, Leicestershire, Wills and Hepworth, 1967.

PUBLICATIONS FOR ADULTS

Novels

Young English. London, Cape, 1931.
Morning's at Seven. London, Cape, 1940.
The Time of the Singing. London, Cape, 1941.
Nicholas Wilde. London, Cape, 1948.
Fifty Pounds for a Dead Parson. London, Cape, 1960.

Other

Cap of Honour: The Story of the Gloucestershire Regiment (the 28th/61st Foot) 1694–1950. London, Harrap, 1951.
Royal Hampshire Regiment 1918–1950, vol. 3. Aldershot, Hampshire, Gale and Polden, 1955.
History of the East Surrey Regiment 1920–1952, vol. 4. London, Benn, 1957.
4th Hussar: The Story of the 4th Queen's Own Hussars 1685–1958. Aldershot, Hampshire, Gale and Polden, 1959.
World War 1 and *2: An Illustrated History.* London, Benn, 2 vols., 1965–66.

*   *   *

David Scott Daniell was a full-time professional writer with many interests. Whatever he wrote is distinctive for the enthusiasm he brought to his subject and for the desire to share that enthusiasm with his readers. As a storyteller he tends to stand outside the action, so that the effect is as if we were watching a film or a play. Indeed his first published work for children was a collection of some of the costume plays he had written for Bertha Waddell's theatre, and from these and his work for radio come his ability to handle dialogue and his penchant for dramatic happenings and swift change of fortune.

The five Polly and Oliver stories, two of which were originally written as radio plays, are in effect costume dramas in narrative form. Oliver is a drummer boy in the 111th Regiment of Foot at the time of the Napoleonic Wars. His long-suffering sergeant is also his uncle, whose daughter Polly accompanies the regiment everywhere and Oliver most places. The adventures of the pair of them take place on land and sea in Sicily, Spain, and India, and involve soldiers and bandits, spies and subterfuges, chases and captures, misunderstandings and mistaken identities. They are fun to read and are also full of authentic military and nautical detail.

Another series of adventure stories is that woven round the lively and resourceful By Jiminy, a modern Neapolitan shoeshine boy, and his English friends, the twins Tom and Sukie, children of an archaeologist. Though basically these are straightforward and easily assimilable variations on the theme of children versus crooks, there are sufficient characterisation, genuine humour, and accurate archaeological background to lift them above many other stories of this kind.

Of the individual historical novels *The Boy They Made King* successfully illuminates the story of Lambert Simnel. The character of Lambert himself is especially well drawn, and his transition from shoe-maker's son to royal imposter and back again to ordinary boy is completely convincing. *Hunt Royal,* about the flight of Charles II, is along more conventional lines, but Daniell is a good enough writer to make Charles a character in his own right and to take advantage of opportunities for dramatic irony. A particularly good scene is that in which three boys staying in the house in which Charles is hiding are interrogated by Cromwell's officers.

In *Sandro's Battle* a boy, living with his composer father and a beloved donkey in a castle in Italy during World War II, is involved with soldiers on both sides when the area becomes a no-man's land between the two armies and the castle a strategic position. The dialogue sparkles and the fun is fast, but the underlying message is serious—war destroys innocent bystanders and causes them to lose their homes and possessions; it also makes ordinary and friendly people range themselves against each other to kill.

—Antony Kamm

DANZIGER, Paula. American. Born in Washington, D.C., 18 August 1944. Former teacher in a junior high school. Recipient: Child Study Committee award, 1978. Address: c/o Delacorte Press, 1 Dag Hammarskjold Plaza, 245 East 47th Street, New York, New York 10017, U.S.A.

PUBLICATIONS FOR CHILDREN

Fiction

The Cat Ate My Gymsuit. New York, Delacorte Press, 1974; London, Heinemann, 1986.
The Pistachio Prescription. New York, Delacorte Press, 1978; London, Heinemann, 1986.
Can You Sue Your Parents for Malpractice? New York, Delacorte Press, 1979; London, Heinemann, 1986.
There's a Bat in Bunk Five. New York, Delacorte Press, 1980.
The Divorce Express. New York, Delacorte Press, 1982; London, Heinemann, 1986.
It's an Aardvark-Eat-Turtle World. New York, Delacorte Press, 1985.
This Place Has No Atmosphere. New York, Delacorte Press, 1986.
Remember Me to Harold Square. New York, Delacorte Press, 1987.

*   *   *

In 1974 when *The Cat Ate My Gymsuit* appeared, Paula Danziger's fresh and funny fiction grabbed teenagers' attention because it was so different from the serious realistic novels that adult critics were raving over. Even though the focus is on overweight and unhappy Marcy, it's nevertheless a lightweight book when compared to such other 1974 titles as Robert Cormier's *The Chocolate War,* William Sleator's *House of Stairs,* James Baldwin's *If Beale Street Could Talk,* and Virginia Hamilton's *M. C. Higgins, The Great.* Danziger's plots center around young teenage girls faced with the problems of establishing a grownup identity, separate from their parents and different from what they were as children yet pleasing to all concerned. She treats this basically serious theme with enough humor that teenagers begin to smile at themselves and come away from her books a little more confident that they too will make it.

Danziger is probably never going to win the Newbery award, but if a prize were to be given for intriguing titles she ought to win hands down. "The cat ate my gymsuit," is one of the excuses that overweight Marcy gives the P. E. teacher so that she won't have to get undressed in gym class. *The Pistachio Prescription* gets its name from Cassie Stephen's self-prescribed cure for feeling insecure—she pigs out on pistachio nuts. The "Divorce Express" is what Rosie calls the bus that she rides back and forth on weekends between Greenwich Village where her father lives and Woodstock where her mother lives.

Danziger uses some unusual settings to keep her books from being all the same. *There's a Bat in Bunk Five* is set at summer camp. *Remember Me to Harold Square* is set in New York City and *This*

Place Has No Atmosphere is a science fiction spoof set on the moon in the year 2057. Especially in these last two titles, Danziger relies for her appeal on the kind of wish fulfillment that appears in formula romances for teenage girls. The protagonists have problems, but they are the kinds of problems that most teenage girls would love to solve. The problems are made easier to bear by the friendship of some wonderful boys that Danziger drops into her books much like ancient script writers used *deux ex machina.*

In *This Place Has No Atmosphere* Aurora doesn't want to leave Monolith Mall and her group the "Turnips," so named because they always turn up to make an appearance. (They also turn up their noses at kids they judge to be uncool.) Despite Aurora's protests, readers may think it would be kind of exciting and fun to be a space pioneer. And what girl hasn't dreamed of being forced to spend a summer with a handsome older boy in need of friendship and comfort, which is the plot in *Remember Me to Harold Square.* 15-year-old Frank, the son of Kendra's parents' best friends, comes from Wisconsin to stay for the summer with Kendra's New York City family. To keep Kendra and Frank and Kendra's little brother, Oscar Kaye ("That means I'm O.K. and you're not") happily and constructively occupied, the two sets of parents devise a six-week-long scavenger hunt. What keeps the book from falling into one of those old-fashioned travel guides where a doting uncle explains everything to an enthusiastic nephew is the fact that the kids are on their own, wisecracking their way through the summer with the kind of wit young readers like to imagine themselves using.

Danziger also achieves her efficient brand of humor through funny names. Characters in *This Place Has No Atmosphere* include Juna Jamieson, Cosmosa Lloyd, Julie Verne, Rita Retrogade, and a poet named Emily Doowinkle. Danziger plays with words and rhyming, and she isn't afraid to have her characters touch on the gross parts of life. For example, Kendra says they will have to rename their rug Spot if Frank brings his pet cow from Wisconsin, and then she warns her little brother that if he doesn't quit eating so much, when he's a teenager he will change from the bottomless pit to the bottomless zit. Danziger also taps into the ongoing tension between children and parents with such jokes as the title *Can You Sue Your Parents for Malpractice?.* School teachers get a similar treatment as when in *This Place Has No Atmosphere,* Aurora explains that the electric power for the school comes from recycled garbage: "Everyone seems to be amazed that garbage is being used to run the school, but I don't see what's so unusual about that. The same can be said about Mr. Finsterwald, the principal." This kind of humor is undoubtedly one of the factors that makes Danziger's books more popular with teens than with adults.

—Alleen Pace Nilsen

DARKE, Marjorie (Sheila). British. Born in Birmingham, Warwickshire, 25 January 1929. Educated at Worcester Grammar School for Girls, 1938–46; Leicester College of Art and Technology, 1946–50; Central School of Art, London, 1950. Married in 1952; two sons and one daughter. Textile designer, John Lewis Partnership, London, 1951–54. Lives in Somerset. Agent: Rogers Coleridge and White, 20 Powis Mews, London W11 1JN, England.

PUBLICATIONS FOR CHILDREN

Fiction

Ride the Iron Horse, illustrated by Michael Jackson. London,

Longman, 1973.

The Star Trap, illustrated by Michael Jackson. London, Longman, 1974.

Mike's Bike, illustrated by Jim Russell. London, Kestrel, 1974.

A Question of Courage, illustrated by Janet Archer. London, Kestrel, and New York, Crowell, 1975.

What Can I Do?, illustrated by Barry Wilkinson. London, Kestrel, 1975.

The Big Brass Band, illustrated by Charles Front. London, Kestrel, 1976.

Kipper's Turn, illustrated by Mary Dinsdale. London, Blackie, 1976.

My Uncle Charlie, illustrated by Jannat Houston. London, Kestrel, 1977.

The First of Midnight, illustrated by Anthony Morris. London, Kestrel, 1977; New York, Seabury Press, 1978.

A Long Way to Go. London, Kestrel, 1978.

Kipper Skips, illustrated by Thelma Lambert. London, Blackie, 1979.

Carnival Day, illustrated by Nita Sowter. London, Kestrel, 1979.

Comeback. London, Kestrel, 1981.

Tom Post's Private Eye. London, Macmillan, 1983.

Messages: A Collection of Shivery Tales. London, Viking Kestrel, 1984.

Imp, illustrated by Margaret Chamberlain. London, Heinemann, 1985.

The Rainbow Sandwich, illustrated by Joanna Worth. London, Methuen, 1989.

*

Marjorie Darke comments:

Unlike many writers I came to the craft late. Although I have always been an avid reader, the idea of writing stories did not occur until greater leisure—when my children went to school—made me aware of an ever-growing need to do something more creative and demanding than housework. Writing specifically for children was not a conscious choice. In my opinion too much emphasis is placed on the dividing line between stories for children and those for adults. I write for myself, the characters and storyline often beginning with a chance conversation, a few words overheard in the street, something read in a book or seen on television. Once born, the people in my imagination have a curious knack of assuming a life of their own, their actions often veering away from paths I have planned for them. I find it difficult to pin-point the reasons why I have often chosen historical backgrounds for my books. They may stem from a lifelong love of hearing tales told by my mother and grandmother of "when I was a girl." Certainly it had nothing to do with school history which I found dry and boring except for the rare times we studied the lives of ordinary people. People, in fact, are my main concern—whether in past or present-day settings—trying to make them live and be as real as I possibly can.

Short stories were a later development in my writing career, as were stories written specially for very young children. Both need a refreshingly different approach, I find, although the writing of novels remains my first love. But whatever the length of the story, because children are clear-sighted and perceptive, endeavouring to entertain them continues to be a great challenge and an ever-growing pleasure.

*   *   *

Marjorie Darke has largely confined herself to writing historical novels for older children, concentrating on late 18th-, 19th-, and early 20th-century British history. In many of her stories she demonstrates a very sympathetic understanding of how ordinary working people cope in difficult and often rapidly changing circumstances. In this way she has tackled a number of "problem" areas, such as the effects in urban and rural areas of the Industrial Revolution, the brutalising effects of the slave trade, and the growing consciousness of women through the Suffragette movement. The background historical detail is carefully researched and has an authentic feel to it, the settings and stories are realistic, and the characters drawn with a conviction that gives credence to the story and a real "feel" for that particular period of history.

Her earliest book, *Ride the Iron Horse,* looks at a rural community threatened by the advent of machines in the mid-19th century. In it she carefully contrasts, through the eyes of the main character, the potential benefits of the new machines with the disastrous effects on the local employment rate. The villagers' fear and loathing of the great steam engines are portrayed with great understanding. *A Question of Courage* is set in a working-class urban community in the 1900's, initially in Birmingham, then in London. The book gives a warm and convincing picture of what life was like for a poor seamstress and her family and shows a young girl's growing involvement with, and understanding of, the Suffragette movement.

But *The First of Midnight* is probably her most powerful novel. The story revolves round the slave trade in Bristol at the end of the 18th century. It provides an interesting contrast between the life of a black ex-slave, Midnight, and the orphan wench, Jess, showing how both are treated as almost worthless chattels by their "owners." The growing love between Midnight and Jess, despite all the taboos against a black/white relationship, is sensitively drawn, capturing Midnight's inherent pride in his African background and Jess's gentle but stubborn nature very effectively. The characterisation is good and the details of the brutality of slavery well handled. Together with *A Long Way to Go* and *Comeback,* it forms part of a loosely connected trilogy spanning almost two centuries. *A Long Way to Go* is set during World War I, and looks in particular at the arguments for and against being a conscientious objector. But it lacks the emotional impact and depth of feeling of *The First of Midnight.* *Comeback* is set in contemporary times and explores the world of competitive gymnastics, showing honestly the absolute dedication required of a top gymnast.

Darke has also written a number of books for younger early readers, the most successful being *Carnival Day.* Two stories for slightly older children which provide a useful early introduction to historical novels are *Kipper's Turn* and *Kipper Skips,* both set in Birmingham in the 1880's. Young Kipper works for a jeweller earning enough money to pay for his board and lodging. By law he should be at school. But if he cannot work he cannot pay his way and will be sent to the workhouse. Kipper's dilemma and desperate attempts to remain honest while needing to survive are well portrayed. These are very readable short novels, written in an economical and carefully controlled language.

—Judith Elkin

———

DAUGHERTY, James (Henry). American. Born in Asheville, North Carolina, 1 June 1889. Educated at Corcoran School of Art, Washington, D.C.; Pennsylvania Academy of Fine Arts, Philadelphia; London School of Art. Worked as a ship camouflager during World War I. Married Sonia Medvedeva in 1913; one son. Artist and illustrator: murals in Cleveland, and in Weston, Fairfield, and Stamford, Connecticut; retrospective exhibition, New York, 1971. Recipient: American Library Association Newbery Medal, 1940. *Died 12 February 1974.*

PUBLICATIONS FOR CHILDREN (illustrated by the author)

Fiction

Andy and the Lion. New York, Viking Press, 1938.
The Picnic. New York, Viking Press, 1958.

Verse

The Wild, Wild West. Philadelphia, McKay, 1948.
West of Boston. New York, Viking Press, 1956.

Other

Daniel Boone. New York, Viking Press, 1939.
Poor Richard. New York, Viking Press, 1941.
Abraham Lincoln. New York, Viking Press, 1943.
The Landing of the Pilgrims. New York, Random House, 1950.
Of Courage Undaunted: Across the Continent with Lewis and Clark.
  New York, Viking Press, 1951.
Trappers and Traders of the Far West. New York, Random House,
  1952.
Marcus and Narcissa Whitman, Pioneers of Oregon. New York,
  Viking Press, 1953.
The Magna Charta. New York, Random House, 1956.
William Blake. New York, Viking Press, 1960.

Editor, *The Kingdom and the Power and the Glory: Stories of Faith
  and Marvel.* New York, Knopf, 1929.
Editor, *Their Weight in Wildcats: Tales of the Frontier.* Boston,
  Houghton Mifflin, 1936.
Editor, *In the Beginning, Being the First Chapter of Genesis from
  the King James Version.* New York and London, Oxford Univer-
  sity Press, 1941.
Editor, *Walt Whitman's America* (selections). Cleveland, World,
  1964.
Editor, *Henry David Thoreau, A Man of Our Time.* New York,
  Viking Press, 1967.
Editor, *The Sound of Trumpets: Selections from Ralph Waldo Emer-
  son.* New York, Viking Press, 1971.

PUBLICATIONS FOR ADULTS

Other

An Outline of Government in Connecticut, edited by Philip E.
  Curtiss. Hartford, Connecticut, House Committee on Public Information, 1944.

*

Bibliography: "James Henry Daugherty: A Bibliography" by
Edward and Elaine Kemp, in *Imprint: Oregon* (Eugene), Fall 1975.

Manuscript Collections: University of Oregon Library, Eugene; May
Massee Collection, Emporia State University, Kansas.

Illustrator: *Tad Sheldon, Boy Scout* by John Fleming Wilson, 1913;
King Penguin by Richard Henry Horne, 1925; *The Lost Gospel* by
Arthur Cheney Train, 1925; *The Plucky Allens* by Clara Pierson,
1925; *The Adventures of Johnny T. Bear* by Margaret McElroy, 1926;
Daniel Boone, Wilderness Scout by Stewart Edward White, 1926;
The Mountain of Jade by Violet Irwin and Vilhjalmur Stefansson,
1926; *Drake's Quest* by Cameron Rogers, 1927; *Kris and Kristina*
by Marie Bruce, 1927; *The Splendid Spur* edited by Arthur
Quiller-Couch, 1927; *The Story of Bread,* 1927, *The Story of Milk,*

1927, and *The Story of Textiles,* 1928, all by Elizabeth Watson; *Abe
Lincoln Grows Up* 1928, and *Early Moon,* 1930, both by Carl
Sandburg; *The Blacksmith and the Blackbirds* by Edith Rickert,
1928; *The Conquest of Montezuma's Empire* by Andrew Lang, 1928;
Hugh Gwyeth by Beulah Dix, 1928; *Irene of Tundra Towers,* 1928,
and *Judy of the Whale Gates,* 1930, both by Elizabeth Burrows;
Knickerbocker's History of New York, 1928, and *The Bold Dragoon,*
1930, both by Washington Irving; *The Stream of History* by Geoffrey
Parsons, 1928; *Tuftoo, The Clown* by Howard Garis, 1928; *The White
Company* by Arthur Conan Doyle, 1928; *Wulnoth, The Wanderer* by
Herbert Inman, 1928; *Courageous Companions* by Charles J. Finger,
1929; *Three Comedies* by William Shakespeare, 1929; *Uncle Tom's
Cabin* by Harriet Beecher Stowe, 1929; *The Adventures of Johnny
Appleseed* by Henry Chapin, 1930; *John Brown's Body* by Stephen
Vincent Benét, 1930; *The Oregon Trail* by Francis Parkman, 1931;
The Adventures of Tom Sawyer by Mark Twain, 1932; *Mashinka's
Secret,* 1932, *All Things New,* 1936, *Vanka's Donkey,* 1940, *Wings of
Glory,* 1940, *The Way of an Eagle,* 1941, *Ten Brave Men,* 1951, *Ten
Brave Women,* 1953, and *Thomas Jefferson,* 1963, all by Sonia
Medvedeva Daugherty; *The Memoirs of Benvenuto Cellini,* 1932;
The Railroad to Freedom, by Hildegarde Swift, 1932; *The Sign of
the Buffalo Skull* by Peter O. Lamb, 1932; *Windows on Henry Street*
by Lillian D. Wald, 1934; *Girls of Glen Hazard,* 1937, and *Clue of
the Faded Dress,* 1938, both by Maristan Chapman; *Green Gravel*
by Dora Aydelotte, 1937; *Over the Blue Wall* by Etta Lane Matthews,
1937; *Call of the Mountain* by Cornelia Meigs, 1940; *Morgan's
Fourth Son* by Margaret Isabel Ross, 1940; *Almanac for Americans*
by Willis Thornton, 1941, 1954; *Barnaby Rudge* by Charles Dickens,
1941; *A Treasury of Best-Loved Hymns* edited by Daniel Poling,
1942; *Yankee Thunder,* 1944, *John Henry and the Double-Jointed
Steam Drill,* 1945, *Joe Magarac and His U.S.A. Citizen Papers,*
1948, and *Heroes in American Folklore,* 1962, all by Irwin Shapiro;
Lincoln's Gettysburg Address, 1947; *American Folklore and Its
Old-World Backgrounds* by Carl Lamsen Carmer, 1949; *American
Life in Literature* edited by Jay Hubbell, 1949; *The Authentic
Revolution* by Erwin Canham, 1950; *Better Known as Johnny
Appleseed* by Mabel Leigh Hunt, 1950; *Comanche* by David Appel,
1951; *A Long Way to Frisco* by Alfred Powers, 1951; *The Loudest
Noise in the World,* 1954, and *Gillespie and the Guards,* 1956, both
by Benjamin Elkin; *The Rainbow Book of American History* by Earl
Schenck Miers, 1955, 1968; *The Last of the Mohicans* by James
Fenimore Cooper, 1957; *Wisher,* 1960, and *Robert Goddard,* 1964,
both by Charles Michael Daugherty; *A Promise to Our Country* by
James Francis Calvert, 1961; *The Three Musketeers* by Alexandre
Dumas, 1962.

*   *   *

Only an occasional page, such as James Daugherty's salute as
illustrator to Father Knickerbocker in *Knickerbocker's History of
New York,* foretells the remarkable command of English, the talent
for melodic lines, exhibited privately in the journals young Daugherty kept while traveling as an art student of 16 in England. That one
page, along with bold, witty illustrations of typical Daugherty
women and men with keen eyes, thrust jaws, and angular bodies,
presaged Daugherty the writer.

Daugherty was nearly fifty when he became established as a
writer, and perhaps because this talent had been dammed up for so
many years, it seemed to pour forth rapidly after Daugherty completed his first book as author and illustrator, *Andy and the Lion.* The
illustrations in *Andy* stand independently of the text, and, indeed,
Daugherty had submitted them to his editor at Viking without words.
However, with the addition of a simple, charming narration, he
secured a balance between words and illustrations.

His second book, the first in which his talents as a writer are fully
displayed, was *Daniel Boone.* Daugherty's appreciation, under-

standing, and admiration of this typically American figure are constantly evident. The prose, illustrations, and subject are a successful blend, and introduce the qualities which appear in nearly every book written by this artist, a major exponent of the Synchromist art school in the 1910's.

Daugherty's love of country, of American life and customs, the expanding frontier in American history, and of heroes, both legendary and historic, became the source for many books. Like the poet Walt Whitman, he celebrated many national events and people, but unlike Whitman, he did not sing of himself nor did he accept all American history at face value. He combined a serious regard for human values, when writing of Thoreau, Emerson, or Lincoln, with a somewhat sceptical view of the possible motivation of some American patriots. His sincere admiration for the Pilgrims (*The Landing of the Pilgrims*), the exploration of the American west (*Of Courage Undaunted: Across the Continent with Lewis and Clark*), and the hardy pioneer (*Marcus and Narcissa Whitman, Pioneers of Oregon*) is exemplified by his warm descriptions in prose and illustration. While he proclaimed in resonant prose or poetry, or both in combination, the deeds of his forebears, Daugherty was a good critic, with a turn of phrase or malicious facial expression shared with the reader; *West of Boston, The Wild, Wild West,* and *Their Weight in Wildcats* are good examples. Concern for fellow man, for the honest, self-reliant individual is expressed as Daugherty writes of Lincoln or introduces the transcendental philosophy of Emerson and Thoreau. Daugherty accepts the philosophy, which appears as an underlying theme in his work, while warning his reader that meditation cannot demand inward commitment: Thoreau and Emerson have obligations to their society. The matter is cause for comment in *West of Boston.*

Daugherty's place as a writer is assured. Although his subjects are American by birth or nature, their appeal is universal. Daugherty's mastery of language and humor, his appeal to the senses, his celebration of life, understanding of mankind, and his love of all things fill each book. As a writer and illustrator with a good editorial sense, he knew how to combine, balance, and strengthen the art of writing and of illustration.

—Edward Kemp

---

d'AULAIRE, Edgar and Ingri Parin. Americans.
d'AULAIRE, Edgar Parin: Born in Munich, Germany, 30 September 1898; emigrated to the United States, 1929; became citizen, 1939. Educated at the Institute of Technology, 1917–19, and School of Applied Arts, 1919–22, Munich; studied art with Hans Hofmann, Munich, 1922–24, and with Andre Lhote and Pola Gauguin, Paris, 1925–29. Married Ingri Maartenson (i.e., Ingri d'Aulaire) in 1925 (died 1980); two children. Artist: book illustrator, 1922–26; painted frescoes, Norway, 1926–27; graphic work exhibited in United States, Italy, Norway, Czechoslovakia, France. *Died 1 May 1986.*
d'AULAIRE, Ingri (Maartenson) Parin: Born in Kongsberg, Norway, 27 December 1904; emigrated to the United States, 1929; became citizen, 1940. Educated at Kongsberg Junior College, 1918–23; Institute of Arts and Crafts, Oslo, 1923–24; studied art with Hans Hofmann, Munich, 1924–25, and with Andre Lhote and Pola Gauguin, Paris, 1925–29. Portrait artist. *Died 24 October 1980.*
Recipients: American Library Association Caldecott Medal, 1940; Catholic Library Association Regina Medal, 1970.

PUBLICATIONS FOR CHILDREN (illustrated by the authors)

Fiction

The Magic Rug. New York, Doubleday, 1931.

Ola. New York, Doubleday, 1932.
Ola and Blakken and Line, Sine, Trine. New York, Doubleday, 1933; revised edition, as *The Terrible Troll-Bird,* 1976.
Children of the Northlights. New York, Viking Press, 1935; London, Woodfield, 1960.
Animals Everywhere. New York, Doubleday, 1940; revised edition, 1954.
Don't Count Your Chicks. New York, Doubleday, 1943.
Wings for Per. New York, Doubleday, 1944.
Too Big. New York, Doubleday, 1945.
Nils. New York, Doubleday, 1948.
Foxie. New York, Doubleday, 1949; revised edition, as *Foxie, The Singing Dog,* 1969.
The Two Cars. New York, Doubleday, 1955.
The Magic Meadow. New York, Doubleday, 1958.

Other

The Conquest of the Atlantic. New York, Viking Press, 1933.
George Washington. New York, Doubleday, 1936.
Abraham Lincoln. New York, Doubleday, 1939; Birmingham, Combridge, 1957; revised edition, New York, Doubleday, 1957.
Leif the Lucky. New York, Doubleday, 1941.
Pocahontas. New York, Doubleday, 1946.
Benjamin Franklin. New York, Doubleday, 1950.
Buffalo Bill. New York, Doubleday; 1952.
Columbus. New York, Doubleday, 1955.
Book of Greek Myths. New York, Doubleday, 1962.
Norse Gods and Giants. New York, Doubleday, 1967.
Trolls (Norwegian folktales). New York, Doubleday, 1972.

Translator, *East of the Sun and West of the Moon: Twenty-One Norwegian Folktales,* by Peter Christen Asbjørnsen. New York, Viking Press, 1938; revised edition, 1966.

*

Manuscript Collections: Dartmouth College, Hanover, New Hampshire; University of Oregon Library, Eugene; Kerlan Collection, University of Minnesota, Minneapolis; de Grummond Collection, University of Southern Mississippi, Hattiesburg.

Illustrator (Edgar Parin d'Aulaire): 17 books in Germany, 1922–26; *Rama, The Hero of India* by Dhan Gopal Mukerji, 1930; *Blood* by Hanns J. Ewers, 1930; *Needle in a Haystack* by John Mattheson, 1930; *Coming of the Dragon Ships* by Florence McClurg Everson, 1931; *Kari* by Gabriel Scott, 1931; *Gao of the Ivory Coast* by Katherine Seabrook, 1931; with Ingri Parin d'Aulaire: *The Lord's Prayer,* 1934; *Sidsel Longskirt,* 1935, and *Solve Suntrap,* 1936, both by Hans Aanrud, translated by Margery Williams Bianco and Dagay Mortenson; *The Star Spangled Banner* by Francis Scott Key, 1942; *Johnny Blossom* by Dikken Zwilgmeyer, 1948.

Edgar and Ingri Parin d'Aulaire commented:
(1978) For almost 50 years we have been working together on picture books, and still like it as much as when we first began. But when a book is finished we return to our individual paintings—which are still as different as when we first met. We have created a third personality for our books—it is not Edgar, it is not Ingri—it is a mixture of us both. We have no intention of ever becoming a monster with one head and four hands.

*   *   *

Working as a couple Edgar and Ingri Parin d'Aulaire created over 20 picture books for children from their extensive research and travel. They become "one unity with two heads, four hands, and one handwriting when working." Producing books with Norwegian and American backgrounds predominantly, they steeped themselves in the subject and locale for about a year prior to executing each one.

The most authoritative books are the seven with Norwegian settings. *Ola* incorporates Norwegian folklore motifs, customs, and local color in the realistic story about a contemporary child. The sequel, *Ola and Blakken and Line, Sine, Trine,* is more fanciful (and was reworked for a new edition called *The Terrible Troll-Bird*). Laplanders are followed through a year of seasonal activities in *Children of the Northlights.* *Norse Gods and Giants* treats mythology, and folklore is the source of *East of the Sun and West of the Moon* and *Trolls.* Three books link Norway and the United States. *Leif the Lucky* is a biography of the man who discovered Vineland on the American shores, and *The Conquest of the Atlantic* describes voyages from the Vikings to Balboa. The countries are not specifically identified in *Wings for Per,* which juxtaposes traditional law and justice with tyranny and occupation. In *Nils* a school boy is called a sissy when he wears hand-knit stockings to school, but this second generation Norwegian-American eventually achieves acceptance and respect among his classmates. Edgar was generally credited for the dramatic quality in the texts, Ingri for the humor.

As immigrants to the United States, the d'Aulaires selected national heroes and patriotic subjects. *George Washington, Abraham Lincoln, Pocahontas, Benjamin Franklin, Buffalo Bill,* and *Columbus* were published in a span of 19 years. These biographies are propelled by the chronological action and seem stiff when compared to *Ola* and the more imaginative books. The d'Aulaires came to American themes "as children," offering a fresh approach to the national anthem, *The Star Spangled Banner.* Even *The Lord's Prayer* was interpreted from the viewpoint of an American child, which annoyed Bertha E. Mahony and Marguerite M. Mitchell, who felt that children's imagination should provide the images. *Don't Count Your Chicks,* though based on the Danish Hans Christian Andersen work, has an early American interpretation.

The d'Aulaires used research and travel to ensure the accuracy of their books. Their first book, *The Magic Rug,* was written in the style of a travelogue in response to a Norwegian child's request for information about their winter stay in Kairawan in Tunisia. To write *The Conquest of the Atlantic,* they studied in the New York Public Library and University of Norway in Oslo, and viewed ship models and costumes in the Musée de la Marine in the Louvre in Paris. They established a base in Geneva, and become acquainted with Swiss history, literature, and art before beginning *The Magic Meadow.* The authors once remarked that a thousand pages of research may be compressed into each picture book, and that they may rework a manuscript ten or twenty times before being satisfied. In an interview with Art Buchwald (*Herald Tribune,* 30 October 1956), Ingri d'Aulaire said: "We found out many wicked stories about Mr. Franklin and we were tempted to use them, but we were afraid because it would spoil the market for the children's books. The mothers and grandmothers would say 'no.'" As well as accumulating notes, the couple visited the locales they wrote about: while working on *Buffalo Bill,* they spent six weeks camping out on the midwest plains; they walked over George Washington's Virginia, and pitched tents along the Lincoln trail.

Unlike the biographies, which have little dialogue, the imaginative books have lively conversation. *Foxie* is based in part on Anton Chekhov's *Kashtanka,* about a performing theatrical dog. While Kashtanka's master is a poor carpenter and her fellow performers are a cat, a gander, and a pig, Foxie's master is a boy and her co-performers a cat and a rooster. Ingri's humor is apparent in *The Two Cars,* one of which remarks, "My paint is hardly dry behind my fenders," while the other states, "I am one hundred thousand miles old." A statement in this book, published midway in their career, is indicative of the manner in which the couple worked—"you won the race but not the praise." Striving for perfection, they produced both quantity and quality.

—Karen Nelson Hoyle

DAVIES, Andrew (Wynford). British. Born in Cardiff, Glamorgan, 20 September 1936. Educated at Whitchurch Grammar School, Glamorgan; University College, London, B.A. in English 1957. Married Diana Huntley in 1960; one son and one daughter. Teacher, St. Clement Danes Grammar School, 1958–61, and Woodberry Down School, 1961–63, both London; lecturer, Coventry College of Education and University of Warwick, Coventry, 1963–87. Recipient: *Guardian* award, 1979; Boston *Globe-Horn Book* award, 1980; Broadcasting Press Guild award, for television play, 1981; Pye award, for television play, 1982; Royal Television Society award, for television series, 1987. Agent: Harvey Unna and Stephen Durbridge Ltd., 24–32 Pottery Lane, London W11 4LZ. Address: 21 Station Road, Kenilworth, Warwickshire CV8 1JJ, England.

<small>PUBLICATIONS FOR CHILDREN</small>

Fiction

The Fantastic Feats of Doctor Boox, illustrated by Tony Escott. London, Collins, 1972; Scarsdale, New York, Bradbury Press, 1973.
Conrad's War. London, Blackie, 1978; New York, Crown, 1980.
Marmalade and Rufus, illustrated by John Laing. London, Abelard Schuman, 1979; New York, Crown, 1983; as *Marmalade Atkins' Dreadful Deeds,* London, Abelard Schuman, 1982.
Marmalade Atkins in Space, illustrated by John Laing. London, Abelard Schuman, 1982.
Educating Marmalade, illustrated by John Laing. London, Abelard Schuman, 1983.
Badger Girl. London, BBC Publications, 1984.
Danger: Marmalade at Work, illustrated by John Laing. London, Abelard Schuman, 1984.
Marmalade Hits the Big Time, illustrated by John Laing. London, Blackie, 1984.
Alfonso Bonzo, illustrated by Tony Ross. London, Methuen, 1986.

Plays

Marmalade Atkins in Space (televised 1981). London, Abelard Schuman-Methuen, 1982.

Radio Play: *Hey Jude,* 1982.

Television Plays: *The Legend of King Arthur,* 1979; *Marmalade Atkins in Space,* 1981; *Educating Marmalade,* 1982; *Danger: Marmalade at Work,* 1984.

Other

The Legend of King Arthur, illustrated by Peter Archer. London, Armada, 1979.

<small>PUBLICATIONS FOR ADULTS</small>

Novels

A Very Peculiar Practice (novelization of television series).

London, Methuen, 1986.
A Very Peculiar Practice: The New Frontier (novelization of
    television series).   London, Methuen, 1988.
Getting Hurt.   London, Methuen, 1989.

Plays

Can Anyone Smell Gas? (produced Richmond, Surrey, 1972).
The Shortsighted Bear (broadcast 1972; produced Coventry, 1979).
Filthy Fryer and the Woman of Mature Years (produced Richmond,
    Surrey, 1974).
Linda Polan: Can You Smell Gas?, What Are Little Girls Made Of?
    (produced Leicester, 1975).
Rohan and Julie (produced London, 1975).
Randy Robinson's Unsuitable Relationship (produced London,
    1976).
Teacher's Gone Mad (produced Richmond, Surrey, 1977).
Going Bust (produced Coventry, 1977).   London, French, 1982.
Fearless Frank (televised 1978; revised version, music by Dave
    Brown, produced London, 1979; New York, 1980).
Brainstorming with the Boys (produced Richmond, Surrey, 1978).
Battery (produced Coventry, 1979).
Diary of a Desperate Woman (produced Coventry, 1979).
Rose (produced London, 1980; New York, 1981).   London, French,
    1980; New York, French, 1981.

Radio Plays: *The Hospitalisation of Samuel Pellett*, 1964; *Getting
the Smell of It*, 1967; *A Day in Bed*, 1967; *Curse on Them, Astonish
Me!*, 1970; *Steph and the Man of Some Distinction*, 1971; *The
Innocent Eye*, 1971; *The Shortsighted Bear*, 1972; *Steph and the
Simple Life*, 1972; *Steph and the Zero Structured Life Style*, 1976;
Accentuate the Positive, 1980; *Campus Blues*, 1984.

Television Plays: *Who's Going to Take Me On?*, 1967; *Is That Your
Body, Boy?*, 1970; *The Christmas Present*, 1970; *No Good Unless It
Hurts*, 1973; *The Water Maiden*, 1974; *Grace*, 1975; *The Imp of the
Perverse*, 1975; *The Signalman*, 1976; *A Martyr to the System*, 1976;
Eleanor Marx, 1977; *Happy in War*, 1977; *The Velvet Glove*, 1977;
Fearless Frank, 1978; *Renoir My Father*, 1978; *To Serve Them All
My Days*, from the novel by R.F. Delderfield, 1980; *Bavarian Night*,
1981; *Heartattack Hotel*, 1983; *Diana*, from the novel by R.F.
Delderfield, 1984; *Pythons on the Mountain*, 1985; *A Very Peculiar
Practice* series, 1986, 1988; *Inappropriate Behaviour*, 1987; *Lucky
Sunil*, 1988; *Baby, I Love You*, 1988.

*   *   *

It was the smooth veneer of genteel unreality over much of what
has been written for children that irritated Andrew Davies into
making his own robust scratch marks. Children's emotional relationships, particularly with their families, their private opinions, and,
most of all, their sense of humour, were all rougher and tougher than
it seemed to him were reflected in the sensitive well-meaning works
that they were being offered. And in *Conrad's War* he did create a
true original.
    It's a skilfully constructed little book, written in a direct, simple
style (deceptively so, for beneath the simplicity and slapstick are
some provocative and subtle ideas for ten-to-twelves to tackle), and
it knits together realism and Monty Python-type fantasy, farce, and
genuine emotions into a neat seamless unit. It tells of how a small
boy's consuming passion for war—for war toys, games, comics,
defiant heroism, all the clichés of war, in fact—is distinctly cooled
by finding himself (and his dog, his Airfix Lancaster, and his fat,
absent-minded Dad) in a series of grotesque time-leaks into World
War II, episodes that begin as hilarious parodies of Conrad's fantasies
but alarmingly become more and more realistic. The attitude of

Conrad to his father, suggested (but never explained) in all its tangled
reality of simmering rage, frustration, affectionate contempt, dependence, and love, is both very funny and instantly recognisable. I
can think of no other like it in British fiction for children.
    Conrad's War is a hugely successful joke, but a joke with a real
punch to its punchline, and it is the—admittedly deliberate—lack of
weight behind the punch that keeps the bad girl Marmalade Atkins
stories on the levels of jolly farce. Some of the happiest effects are
familiar from *Conrad*: there is the same teasing warping of dreams
by real life; the same energetic dialogue, effortlessly heard in the
reader's head—no accident that Davies, the adult dramatist, introduced Marmalade so successfully to children's television. There are
some memorably daft characters who are marvellously alive in their
own right—Rufus, the tough old chauvinist donkey, who aids and
abets Marmalade in her wicked ways, and Sister Conception, she of
the moustache and the great hairy hands and the baseball bat, who
tries to teach Marmalade at the Convent of the Blessed Limit. But
there are also more predictable caricatures, painted with a very broad
brush indeed and jokey Capital Letters, who would be at home in
Conrad's *Beano*. And indeed, the welcome energy and gutsy bounce
of Davies's writing owe much to the spirit of traditional comics.
    The later *Alfonso Bonzo*, though powered by the same high spirits,
echoes the tensions and sense of shadows lurking behind the fun of
Conrad's War: a young boy finds more than he bargained for (literally—with an enchantingly mysterious doorstep salesman) when
magical wish-fulfilment transports him into what's happening on the
TV screen. At his best, Davies pans the comic rough stuff through a
mesh of dramatic skill and an understanding of young minds to
produce literary gems glinting with sharp edges.

—Stephanie Nettell

DAWLISH, Peter.   Pseudonym for James Lennox Kerr; also wrote
as Lennox Kerr. British. Born in Paisley, Renfrewshire, 1 July
1899. Educated at North School, Paisley. Served in the Royal Naval
Volunteer Reserve, 1915–19 and 1942–46: mentioned in despatches.
Married Elizabeth Lamorna Birch in 1932; one son. Gold prospector;
member of the British Mercantile Marine, 1919–29, 1939–42. *Died
11 March 1963.*

PUBLICATIONS FOR CHILDREN

Fiction

The Blackspit Smugglers (as Lennox Kerr), illustrated by Rowland
    Hilder. London, Nelson, 1935.
The Eye of the Earth (as James Lennox Kerr), illustrated by F.P.
    Paterson. London, Nelson, 1936.
Peg-Leg and the Fur Pirates, illustrated by Norman Hepple.   Lon-
    don, Oxford University Press, 1939.
Captain Peg-Leg's War, illustrated by J.D. Evans.   London, Oxford
    University Press, 1939.
Peg-Leg and the Invaders, illustrated by Jack Matthew.   London,
    Oxford University Press, 1940.
Peg-Leg Sweeps the Sea, illustrated by Leonard Boden.   London,
    Oxford University Press, 1940.
Dauntless Finds Her Crew, illustrated by P.A. Jobson.   London,
    Oxford University Press, 1947; as *Dauntless Finds a Crew,* Wen-
    dover, Buckinghamshire, Goodchild, 1984.
The First Tripper, illustrated by P.A. Jobson.   London, Oxford
    University Press, 1947.
Dauntless Sails Again, illustrated by P.A. Jobson.   London, Oxford

University Press, 1948; as *Dauntless and the Smugglers,* Wendover, Buckinghamshire, Goodchild, 1984.

Dauntless and the Mary Baines, illustrated by P.A. Jobson.   London, Oxford University Press, 1949; as *Dauntless and the Wreck of the Mary Baines,* Wendover, Buckinghamshire, Goodchild, 1985.

North Sea Adventure, illustrated by P.A. Jobson.   London, Oxford University Press, 1949.

Dauntless Takes Recruits, illustrated by P.A. Jobson.   London, Oxford University Press, 1950; as *Dauntless and the Poplar Pirates,* Wendover, Buckinghamshire, Goodchild, 1985.

MacClellan's Lake, illustrated by Roy Sharp.   London, Oxford University Press, 1951.

Aztec Gold, illustrated by P.A. Jobson.   London, Oxford University Press, 1951.

Dauntless Sails In, illustrated by P.A. Jobson.   London, Oxford University Press, 1952.

The Bagodia Episode, illustrated by P.A. Jobson.   London, Oxford University Press, 1953.

Dauntless in Danger, illustrated by P.A. Jobson.   London, Oxford University Press, 1954.

Way for a Soldier.   London, Oxford University Press, 1955.

He Went with Drake, illustrated by P.A. Jobson.   London, Harrap, 1955.

Sailors All.   Oxford, Blackwell, 1958.

The Race for Gowrie Bay, illustrated by Christopher Brooker.   London, Oxford University Press, 1959.

Dauntless Goes Home, illustrated by P.A. Jobson.   London, Oxford University Press, 1960.

The Boy Jacko, illustrated by William Stobbs.   London, Oxford University Press, 1962; New York, Watts, 1963.

Other

Young Drake of Devon.   London, Oxford University Press, 1954.

Martin Frobisher, illustrated by William Stobbs.   London, Oxford University Press, 1956.

Johnno the Deep-Sea Diver: The Life Story of Diver John Johnstone as Told to Peter Dawlish.   London, Harrap, and New York, Watts, 1960.

The Royal Navy, illustrated by Victor Ambrus.   London, Oxford University Press, 1963.

The Seas of Britain, illustrated by Val Biro.   London, Benn, 1963.

The Merchant Navy, illustrated by Victor Ambrus.   London, Oxford University Press, 1966.

Editor (as James Lennox Kerr), *On—and Under—the Ocean Wave: A Book of Modern Sea Stories.*   London, Nelson, 1933.

PUBLICATIONS FOR ADULTS as James Lennox Kerr

Novels

Old Ship.   London, Constable, 1930; New York, Macmillan, 1931.
Glenshiels.   London, Lane, 1932.
Ice: A Tale of Effort.   London, Lane, 1933.
Woman of Glenshiels.   London, Collins, 1935.
The Fool and the Tractor.   London, Collins, 1936.

Other

Backdoor Guest.   London, Constable, and Indianapolis, Bobbs Merrill, 1930.

The Young Steamship Officer.   London, Nelson, 1933.

Cruising in Scotland: The Log of the Migrant, Describing How a

£35 Cruiser Gave Pleasure to a Distinguished Artist and His Family.   London, Collins, 1938.

The Eager Years: An Autobiography.   London, Collins, 1949.

The Great Storm, Being the Authentic Story of the Loss at Sea of the "Princess Victoria" and Other Vessels Early in 1953.   London, Harrap, 1954.

The R.N.V.R.: A Record of Achievement, with Wilfred Granville.   London, Harrap, 1957.

Wilfred Grenfell: His Life and Work.   London, Harrap, and New York, Dodd Mead, 1959.

The Unfortunate Ship: The Story of H.M. Troopship Birkenhead.   London, Harrap, 1960.

Harbour Spotter.   London, Newman Neame, 1962.

The Yachtsman's Log and Astronomical Position Line Formula.   Privately printed, 1963.

Editor, *A Modern Sinbad: An Autobiography,* by Aylward Edward Dingle.   London, Harrap, 1948.

Editor, with David James, *Wavy Navy by Some Who Served.*   London, Harrap, 1950.

Editor, *Touching the Adventures of Merchantmen in the Second World War.*   London, Harrap, 1953.

*   *   *

Peter Dawlish's books for boys, along with many others of the 1930–60 period, are now regrettably considered outdated and outmoded. Contemporary trends and standards have retreated from his stern and exacting regard for duty and service. Sociological cries protesting against the slightest taint of "elitism" wherever it can be discerned, or imagined where it cannot, contrast painfully with his disciplined, salt-crusted yarns. His books are in fact as dated as the wireless, Saturday morning cinemas, or stop-me-and-buy-one cyclists. Not surprisingly, most of them are long out of print.

His first fictional hero was the formidable figure of Captain Peg-Leg, a nautical equivalent to Biggles, admirably suited to the mood of wartime Britain. Unlike Biggles, however, Captain Peg-Leg was pensioned off at the end of hostilities in 1945. So Dawlish embarked upon series of books about the voyages of a 45-foot schooner, *Dauntless,* which when first encountered was apparently destined for the breaker's yard. Reconditioned and recommissioned by a group of school boys under the command of a former naval captain, *Dauntless* eventually put to sea. Dawlish's own extensive marine experience and know-how were evident on every page, and no boy with salt in his veins could resist the authentic tang of the sea. Landlubbers might find themselves in difficulties wading through oceans of seafaring terminology but they too could wallow in these exhilarating and intoxicating sea stories.

Subsequently Dawlish took to historical adventures set in Tudor and Stuart times. *Aztec Gold* narrates the fortunes of an expedition mounted by a Devon farmer to rescue his brother, reported to be held captive on an isolated Aztec island stronghold. *He Went with Drake* is a return to the Henty tradition of enlisting a young hero in the company of a great captain, while *The Boy Jacko* tells of a voyage to Virginia in response to a summons from a rich uncle, hindered by villainy and skulduggery at every turn which a London street urchin is instrumental in thwarting.

In the not-so-distant past sea stories were a recognizable and respected genre of both adult and junior fiction. Why they should have almost totally disappeared from publishers' lists is not altogether clear, unless it is because many of them, especially those written for children, were set in times of war or in historical periods when the prevailing national mood and temper was one of expansion, a concept now regarded as neither practical nor creditable. Possibly the English Tourist Board's Maritime England promotion of might encourage enterprising publishers to reprint titles from their back-lists. Should this prove feasible Peter Dawlish's books must surely be among the first to re-emerge from the shadows. Their refreshing, open-air, good-natured comradeship has a lot to offer present day readers.

—Alan Edwin Day

DAY LEWIS, C(ecil). Also wrote as Nicholas Blake. British. Born in Ballintubbert, Queen's County (now County Laois), Ireland, 27 April 1904; brought to England in 1905. Educated at Wilkie's Preparatory School, London, 1912–17; Sherborne School, Dorset, 1917–23; Wadham College, Oxford, 1923–27, B.A. 1927, M.A. Served as an editor in the Ministry of Information, London, 1941–46. Married 1) Mary King in 1928 (divorced 1951), two sons; also one other son; 2) Jill Balcon in 1951, one daughter and one son. Assistant master, Summer Fields School, Oxford, 1927–28; master, Larchfield School, Helensburgh, Dunbartonshire, 1928–30, and Cheltenham Junior School, Gloucestershire, 1930–35; reader from 1946, and Director from 1954, Chatto and Windus, publishers, London. Professor of Poetry, Oxford University, 1951–56; Norton Professor of Poetry, Harvard University, Cambridge, Massachusetts, 1964–65. Clark Lecturer, 1946, and Sidgwick Lecturer, 1956, Cambridge University; Warton Lecturer, British Academy, London, 1951; Byron Lecturer, University of Nottingham, 1952; Chancellor Dunning Lecturer, Queen's University, Kingston, Ontario, 1954; Compton Lecturer, University of Hull, Yorkshire, 1968. Member, Arts Council of Great Britain, 1962–67: Chairman of the Poetry, later Literature, Panel. Honorary Fellow, Wadham College, 1968. D.Litt.: University of Exeter, 1965; University of Hull, 1970; Litt.D.: Trinity College, Dublin, 1968. Fellow, 1944, Vice-President, 1959, and Companion of Literature, 1965, Royal Society of Literature; Honorary Member, American Academy, 1966; Member, Irish Academy of Letters, 1968. C.B.E. (Commander, Order of the British Empire), 1950. Poet Laureate, 1968. *Died 22 May 1972.*

PUBLICATIONS FOR CHILDREN

Fiction

Dick Willoughby. Oxford, Blackwell, 1933; New York, Random House, 1938.
The Otterbury Incident, illustrated by Edward Ardizzone. London, Putnam, 1948; New York, Viking Press, 1949.

Other

Poetry for You: A Book for Boys and Girls on the Enjoyment of Poetry. Oxford, Blackwell, 1944; New York, Oxford University Press, 1947.

Editor, *The Echoing Green: An Anthology of Verse.* Oxford, Blackwell, 3 vols., 1937.
Editor, *The Midnight Skaters: Poems for Young Readers,* by Edmund Blunden, illustrated by David Gentleman. London, Bodley Head, 1968.

PUBLICATIONS FOR ADULTS

Novels

The Friendly Tree. London, Cape, 1936; New York, Harper, 1937.

Starting Point. London, Cape, 1937; New York, Harper, 1938.
Child of Misfortune. London, Cape, 1939.

Novels as Nicholas Blake

A Question of Proof. London, Collins, and New York, Harper, 1935.
Thou Shell of Death. London, Collins, 1936; as *Shell of Death,* New York, Harper, 1936.
There's Trouble Brewing. London, Collins, and New York, Harper, 1937.
The Beast Must Die. London, Collins, and New York, Harper, 1938.
The Smiler with the Knife. London, Collins, and New York, Harper, 1939.
Malice in Wonderland. London, Collins, 1940; as *The Summer Camp Mystery,* New York, Harper, 1940; as *Malice with Murder,* New York, Pyramid, 1964.
The Case of the Abominable Snowman. London, Collins, 1941; as *The Corpse in the Snowman,* New York, Harper, 1941.
Minute for Murder. London, Collins, 1947; New York, Harper, 1948.
Head of a Traveller. London, Collins, and New York, Harper, 1949.
The Dreadful Hollow. London, Collins, and New York, Harper, 1953.
The Whisper in the Gloom. London, Collins, and New York, Harper, 1954; as *Catch and Kill,* New York, Bestseller, 1955.
A Tangled Web. London, Collins, and New York, Harper, 1956; as *Death and Daisy Bland,* New York, Dell, 1960.
End of Chapter. London, Collins, and New York, Harper, 1957.
A Penknife in My Heart. London, Collins, 1958; New York, Harper, 1959.
The Widow's Cruise. London, Collins, and New York, Harper, 1959.
The Worm of Death. London, Collins, and New York, Harper, 1961.
The Deadly Joker. London, Collins, 1963.
The Sad Variety. London, Collins, and New York, Harper, 1964.
The Morning after Death. London, Collins, and New York, Harper, 1966.
The Private Wound. London, Collins, and New York, Harper, 1968.

Plays

Screenplays (documentaries): *The Colliers,* 1939; *The Green Girdle,* 1940.

Radio Play: *Calling James Braithwaite,* 1940.

Verse

Beechen Vigil and Other Poems. London, Fortune Press, 1925.
Country Comets. London, Hopkinson, 1928.
Transitional Poem. London, Hogarth Press, 1929.
From Feathers to Iron. London, Hogarth Press, 1931.
The Magnetic Mountain. London, Hogarth Press, 1933.
Collected Poems 1929–1933. London, Hogarth Press, 1935; with *A Hope for Poetry,* New York, Random House, 1935.
A Time to Dance and Other Poems. London, Hogarth Press, 1935.
Noah and the Waters. London, Hogarth Press, 1936.
A Time to Dance, Noah and the Waters, and Other Poems, with an Essay, Revolution in Writing. New York, Random House, 1936.
Overtures to Death and Other Poems. London, Cape, 1938.
Poems in Wartime. London, Cape, 1940.
Selected Poems. London, Hogarth Press, 1940.

Word over All. London, Cape, 1943; New York, Transatlantic, 1944.

(Poems). London, Eyre and Spottiswoode, 1943.

Short Is the Time: Poems 1936–1943 (includes *Overtures to Death* and *Word over All*). New York, Oxford University Press, 1945.

Poems 1943–1947. London, Cape, and New York, Oxford University Press, 1948.

Collected Poems 1929–1936. London, Hogarth Press, 1949.

Selected Poems. London, Penguin, 1951; revised edition, 1957, 1969, 1974.

An Italian Visit. London, Cape, and New York, Harper, 1953.

Collected Poems. London, Cape-Hogarth Press, 1954.

Christmas Eve. London, Faber, 1954.

The Newborn: D.M.B., 29th April, 1957. London, Favil Press of Kensington, 1957.

Pegasus and Other Poems. London, Cape, 1957; New York, Harper, 1958.

The Gate and Other Poems. London, Cape, 1962.

Requiem for the Living. New York, Harper, 1964.

On Not Saying Everything. Privately printed, 1964.

A Marriage Song for Albert and Barbara. Privately printed, 1965.

The Room and Other Poems. London, Cape, 1965.

C. Day Lewis: Selections from His Poetry, edited by Patric Dickinson. London, Chatto and Windus, 1967.

Selected Poems. New York, Harper, 1967.

The Abbey That Refused to Die: A Poem. County Mayo, Ireland, Ballintubber Abbey, 1967.

The Whispering Roots. London, Cape, 1970; as *The Whispering Roots and Other Poems,* New York, Harper, 1970.

Going My Way. London, Poem-of-the-Month Club, 1970.

Poems of C. Day Lewis 1925–1972, edited by Ian Parsons. London, Cape-Hogarth Press, 1977.

Posthumous Poems. Andoversford, Gloucestershire, Whittington Press, 1979.

Recording: *Poems,* Argo, 1974.

Other

A Hope for Poetry. Oxford, Blackwell, 1934; with *Collected Poems,* New York, Random House, 1935.

Revolution in Writing. London, Hogarth Press, 1935; New York, Random House, 1936.

Imagination and Thinking, with L. Susan Stebbing. London, British Institute of Adult Education, 1936.

We're Not Going to Do Nothing: A Reply to Mr. Aldous Huxley's Pamphlet "What Are You Going to Do about It?" London, Left Review, 1936.

The Poetic Image. London, Cape, and New York, Oxford University Press, 1947.

Enjoying Poetry: A Reader's Guide. London, National Book League, 1947.

The Colloquial Element in English Poetry. Newcastle-upon-Tyne, Literary and Philosophical Society, 1947.

The Poet's Task. Oxford, Clarendon Press, 1951.

The Grand Manner. Nottingham, University of Nottingham, 1952.

The Lyrical Poetry of Thomas Hardy. London, Oxford University Press, 1953.

Notable Images of Virtue: Emily Brontë, George Meredith, W.B. Yeats. Toronto, Ryerson Press, 1954.

The Poet's Way of Knowledge. Cambridge, University Press, 1957.

The Buried Day (autobiography). London, Chatto and Windus, and New York, Harper, 1960.

The Lyric Impulse. Cambridge, Massachusetts, Harvard University Press, and London, Chatto and Windus, 1965.

Thomas Hardy, with R.A. Scott-James. London, Longman, 1965.

A Need for Poetry? Hull, University of Hull, 1968.

On Translating Poetry: A Lecture. Abingdon-on-Thames, Berkshire, Abbey Press, 1970.

Editor, with W.H. Auden, *Oxford Poetry 1927.* Oxford, Blackwell, 1927.

Editor, with John Lehmann and T.A. Jackson, *A Writer in Arms,* by Ralph Fox. London, Lawrence and Wishart, 1937.

Editor, *The Mind in Chains: Socialism and the Cultural Revolution.* London, Muller, 1937.

Editor, with Charles Fenby, *Anatomy of Oxford: An Anthology.* London, Cape, 1938.

Editor, with L.A.G. Strong, *A New Anthology of Modern Verse 1920–1940.* London, Methuen, 1941.

Editor, with others, *Orion 2–3.* London, Nicholson and Watson, 2 vols., 1945–46.

Editor, *The Golden Treasury of the Best Songs and Lyrical Poems in the English Language,* by Francis Turner Palgrave. London, Collins, 1954.

Editor, with John Lehmann, *The Chatto Book of Modern Poetry 1915–1955.* London, Chatto and Windus, 1956.

Editor, with Kathleen Nott and Thomas Blackburn, *New Poems 1957.* London, Joseph, 1957.

Editor, *A Book of English Lyrics.* London, Chatto and Windus, 1961; as *English Lyric Poems 1500–1900,* New York, Appleton Century Crofts, 1961.

Editor, *The Collected Poems of Wilfred Owen.* London, Chatto and Windus, 1963; New York, New Directions, 1964.

Editor, *The Poems of Robert Browning.* Cambridge, Limited Editions Club, 1969; New York, Heritage Press, 1971.

Editor, *A Choice of Keats's Verse.* London, Faber, 1971.

Editor, *Crabbe.* London, Penguin, 1973.

Editor, *A Lasting Joy: An Anthology.* London, Allen and Unwin, 1973.

Translator, *The Georgics of Virgil.* London, Cape, 1940; New York, Oxford University Press, 1947.

Translator, *The Graveyard by the Sea,* by Paul Valéry. London, Secker and Warburg, 1947.

Translator, *The Aeneid of Virgil.* London, Hogarth Press, and New York, Oxford University Press, 1952.

Translator, *The Eclogues of Virgil.* London, Cape, 1963; with *The Georgics,* New York, Doubleday, 1964.

Translator, with Mátyás Sárközi, *The Tomtit in the Rain: Traditional Hungarian Rhymes,* by Erzsi Gazdas. London, Chatto and Windus, 1971.

*

Bibliography: *C. Day Lewis, The Poet Laureate: A Bibliography* by Geoffrey Handley-Taylor and Timothy d'Arch Smith, London and Chicago, St. James Press, 1968.

Manuscript Collections: New York Public Library; State University of New York, Buffalo; British Library, London; University of Liverpool.

Critical Studies: *C. Day Lewis* by Clifford Dyment, London, Longman, 1955, revised edition, 1963; *C. Day Lewis* by Joseph N. Riddel, New York, Twayne, 1971; *C. Day-Lewis: An English Literary Life* by Sean Day-Lewis, London, Weidenfeld and Nicolson, 1980.

Theatrical Activities:
Actor: **Radio**—Tom Moore in *Blame Not the Bard*, 1942.

*   *   *

C. Day Lewis is best known as a children's writer for *The Otterbury Incident*. It has been "one of those books that work" to grateful teachers and librarians in the United Kingdom for some 40 years.

His heroes attend a day school in post-war England, a departure from the timeless cloisters of boarding schools which were still a feature of boys' comics of the period. Their exploits are described by George, himself a participant in the kids-catch-crooks adventure—a device which allows confidential asides to his reader and a mock-heroic style as the boys go into action with the discipline of a commando unit. His idiom is firmly middle-class and, inevitably, of its time: chaps in the company shut up "j. quick" when their leader tells them off; a couple of spivs are "a pair of blisters" or "fearful outsiders." There are unselfconscious references to a search proving as difficult as looking for "a nigger in a dark cellar" and to a pawnbroker "jewing" the boys, and a carefree objectivity about "females."

The abiding success of the book lies in the fact that it reworks, in a particularly lively way, a situation of unfailing appeal to children. A group of kids, unaided, outwit a trio of grown-ups; and since the grown-ups are criminals, the children earn the gratitude and admiration of adult society, embodied in a police inspector and their headmaster.

The basic formula was well-tried even in 1948. Day Lewis's story is distinguished by the rapid and entertaining ride he offers over a steeplechase of a plot. Each hurdle requires ingenious negotiation: inventive and comic fund-raising to pay for a broken window; bizarre detection by the local newsagent, E. Sidebotham, who suffers periodic delusions that he is Sherlock Holmes; and a satisfying denouement as the boys' practised military strategies are brought into play against a criminal with a cut-throat razor he means to use.

Characters are simply sketched, but for many children the stereotypes may provide readier access to the narrative than subtler portraits. Day Lewis had already demonstrated his control of an exciting plot peopled by boldly drawn figures in *Dick Willoughby,* where he charted the progress of a young Elizabethan. Secret tunnels, sword-play on the Spanish Main, an evil Catholic kinsman, and a dash of innocent romance spice the mixture. The dialogue is entangled in what Geoffrey Trease calls "tushery": "Marry, come up, thou tun of a booby, that hairy comet of thine, that holly-bush thou grow'st to keep thy neck warm for the rope med frighten Spaniards but not a Dorset maiden," cries a serving maid to a bluff retainer "in high glee."

Even in *Dick Willoughby,* however, there are many of the qualities which mark *The Otterbury Incident*: the clarity of the issues at stake, the pace of the action, and a pervading high spiritedness.

—Geoff Fox

————

de ANGELI, Marguerite (née Lofft). American. Born in Lapeer, Michigan, 14 March 1889. Educated at schools in Lapeer and Philadelphia. Married John de Angeli in 1910 (died 1969); four sons and one daughter. Professional singer, 1904–21. Recipient: American Library Association Newbery Medal, 1950; Catholic Library Association Regina Medal, 1968. Marguerite de Angeli Library, Lapeer, Michigan, named in 1981. *Died 16 June 1987.*

PUBLICATIONS FOR CHILDREN (illustrated by the author)

Fiction·

Ted and Nina Go to the Grocery Store. New York, Doubleday, 1935.
Ted and Nina Have a Happy Rainy Day. New York, Doubleday, 1936.
Henner's Lydia. New York, Doubleday, 1936; Kingswood, Surrey, World's Work, 1965.
Petite Suzanne. New York, Doubleday, 1937.
Copper-Toed Boots. New York, Doubleday, 1938; Kingswood, Surrey, World's Work, 1965.
Skippack School. New York, Doubleday, 1939; Kingswood, Surrey, World's Work, 1964.
A Summer Day with Ted and Nina. New York, Doubleday, 1940.
Thee, Hannah! New York, Doubleday, 1940; Kingswood, Surrey, World's Work, 1962.
Elin's Amerika. New York, Doubleday, 1941; Kingswood, Surrey, World's Work, 1964.
Up the Hill. New York, Doubleday, 1942.
Yonie Wondernose. New York, Doubleday, 1944.
Turkey for Christmas. Philadelphia, Westminster Press, 1944.
Bright April. New York, Doubleday, 1946.
Jared's Island. New York, Doubleday, 1947.
The Door in the Wall. New York, Doubleday, 1949; Kingswood, Surrey, World's Work, 1959.
Just Like David. New York, Doubleday, 1951.
Black Fox of Lorne. New York, Doubleday, 1956; Kingswood, Surrey, World's Work, 1959.
Fiddlestrings. New York, Doubleday, 1974.
The Lion in the Box. New York, Doubleday, 1975.
Whistle for the Crossing. New York, Doubleday, 1977.

Other

A Pocket Full of Posies: A Merry Mother Goose. New York, Doubleday, 1961.
The Goose Girl. New York, Doubleday, 1964.

Editor, *Book of Nursery and Mother Goose Rhymes.* New York, Doubleday, 1954.
Editor, *The Old Testament.* New York, Doubleday, 1960.
Editor, *Book of Favorite Hymns.* New York, Doubleday, 1963.

PUBLICATIONS FOR ADULTS

Other

Libraries and Reading: Their Importance in the Lives of Famous Americans, with others, edited by Donald H. Hunt. Philadelphia, Drexel Press, 1964.
Butter at the Old Price: The Autobiography of Marguerite de Angeli. New York, Doubleday, 1971.

*

Manuscript Collection: Free Library, Philadelphia.

Illustrator: *The New Moon,* 1924, and *The Covered Bridge,* 1936, both by Cornelia Meigs; *Meggy MacIntosh* by Elizabeth Janet Gray, 1930; *A Candle in the Mist* by Florence Crannell Means, 1931; *The Christmas Nightingale* by Eric Kelly, 1932; *Joan Wanted a Kitty* by Jane Brown Gemmill, 1937; *Alice-All-by-Herself* by Elizabeth Coatsworth, 1937; *Red Sky over Rome* by Anne D. Kyle, 1938; *The*

Princess and the Gypsy by Jean Rosmer, 1938; *Prayers and Graces for Little Children* edited by Quail Hawkins, 1941; *They Loved to Laugh* by Kathryn Worth, 1942; *In and Out: Verses* by Tom Robinson, 1943; *The Empty Barn,* 1966, and *The Door in the Wall: A Play,* 1968, both by Arthur C. de Angeli.

*   *   *

Most famous of all Marguerite de Angeli's long list of titles is *The Door in the Wall,* which won for her the Newbery Medal. Set in the England of Edward III, it is a beautifully realized piece of historical fiction: the young hero's brave acceptance of his handicap and his determination to fight on against all but insuperable hardship have an inspiring message for youngsters of any era. The writer conveys with jewel-like clarity both the differences and the similarities of that distant time and this: green, wild England with its glorious, comfortless castles and noisome narrow streets, and the inhabitants in so many ways like their counterparts of today. Robin is a boy of the 13th century, but he speaks very clearly to the 20th-century reader.

De Angeli had a gift for making the exotic, peculiar, or particular seem universal and unthreatening to young readers, who are often xenophobic in their rejection of the unfamiliar. She wrote with equal sympathy and understanding of families of varied ethnic backgrounds and creeds; and just as her illustrations bring their outward appearances vividly to life, her gentle, simple stories make their daily lives and the small concerns of their children those of all loving families everywhere. If at first glance her works seem concerned with contrasting cultures, in fact her study was that of the universality of happy childhood.

She reserved the larger dramatic themes, such as war and revenge, for her few tales of the remote past; young Robin of *The Door in the Wall* is the saviour of his besieged castle in the mist; in *Black Fox of Lorne* Jan and Brus, twin Viking lads of the 10th century, avenge their father's death by treachery; but these ambitious novels for older children are atypical. De Angeli was best known and loved for her shorter stories of ordinary, day-to-day childhood concerns; of the boy who longs above all things for a pair of copper-toed boots; the working lad whose stern but loving father must be made to see that there is a place for artists as well as for miners; little Hannah who painfully discovers for herself the meaning of her drab Quaker bonnet and learns to wear it with pride; and all her other believable, loveable children.

Many of her stories and their illustrations are based upon de Angeli's own family and its folklore, and have both the strength and weakness of family tradition revealed to the outsider. There is a suggestion of the "separateness" enveloping any close-knit family, however large-hearted its members, and a natural tendency to overrate family stories and catch-phrases that have meaning only to the inner circle of intimates. But more than offsetting the effect of partiality is the depth of love, trust, and understanding that informs de Angeli's writings with the glow of happiness remembered and preserved.

—Joan McGrath

---

de GRAFT-HANSON, J(ohn) O(rleans). Ghanaian. Born in Sunyani, 7 October 1932. Educated at Mfantsipim School, Cape Coast, 1947–50; University College of Gold Coast (now Ghana), 1951–56, B.A. (honours) in classics 1956; Cambridge University, England, 1957–61, B.A. 1959, M.Litt. in classics 1961. Married; 10 children. Lecturer, 1960–65, Senior Lecturer, 1965–74, and Associate Professor of Classics, 1974–82, University of Ghana, Legon;

Associate Professor of Classics, Fourah Bay College, University of Sierra Leone, Freetown, 1982–86. Since 1987 Professor of Classics, University of Cape Coast. Dean, Faculty of Arts, University of Ghana, Legon, 1970–76; member of the Board of Directors, Graphic Corporation, 1971–72, and Museums and Monuments, 1973–74; visiting lecturer, University of British Columbia, Vancouver, 1976–77; President, Council of the Children's Literature Foundation (Ghana), 1978–82; Vice-Chairman, Ghana Book Development Board, 1980–82. Recipient: Ghana Book Development award, 1979. Fellow, Ghana Academy of Arts and Sciences, 1979. Lives in Cape Coast. Address: c/o Department of Classics, University of Cape Coast, Cape Coast, Ghana.

PUBLICATIONS FOR CHILDREN

Fiction

The Secret of Opokuwa, illustrated by John Kedjani.   Accra, Ghana, Anowuo, 1967.
The Little Sasabonsam.   Tema, Ghana Publishing Corporation, 1972.
Papa Ewusi and the Magic Marble.   Tema, Ghana Publishing Corporation, 1973.
Papa and the Animals.   Tema, Ghana Publishing Corporation, 1973.
The Fetish Hide-Out.   Tema, Ghana Publishing Corporation, 1975.
The People from the Sea.   Tema, Ghana Publishing Corporation, 1988.

Other

Ancient Greek Stories About Africa, illustrated by Fred Odametey. Accra, Adwinsa Publications, 1982.

*

J. O. de Graft-Hanson comments:
In my children's books I aim at utilizing our rich heritage of traditional stories, mainly folktales and legends, for original creative writing for our children—to stimulate their curiosity and imagination, to thrill them with a sense of adventure and discovery, and also to give them a feeling for literature.

The traditional stories are not simply retold; rather they serve as sources of inspiration from which my own stories take off or, where appropriate, as content material around which they are woven. For example, from our folktales comes *The Little Sasabonsam*: a child hears a story about the Sasabonsam, a forest demon of our Ananse tales, just before bedtime, and he sets out to find a little one, his adventures taking the form of a dream that is almost nightmarish. But in *Papa and the Animals* a substantial portion is taken up by a number of animals who come to console a child weeping for the loss of his marbles by narrating, each in turn, their own stories of how they too lost some precious possession. Their stories are essentially from well-known Akan folktales of the "why or how so?" kind, but are made more dramatic by being told by the animals themselves.

On the other hand *The Secret of Opokuwa* has its germ in the alleged historical attempt to get possession of the famous sacred Golden Stool of Ashanti by a British Governor of the Gold Coast (now Ghana). Similarly *The Fetish Hide-Out* is woven around the legend of the destruction of what was once the most famous oracular shrine of the Fanti states; while in *The People from the Sea* a group of children in search of information for a history lesson get involved in tracking down the perpetrators of a burglary and helping to effect their capture.

de HAMEL 273

In all my books I try as much as possible to make the language simple and direct, bearing in mind that my target readership is children between the ages of 8 and 14.

* * *

J.O. de Graft-Hanson believes that folklore provides important source material for Ghanaian children's literature. In all of his fiction he places contemporary children in contact with persons or places that are important in Fante or Akan folklore or tells folk tales in the context of the story. His fiction, like the folklore upon which it is based, includes implicit and sometimes explicit morals.

Papa Ewusi is the young, highly imaginative boy hero of a series of stories that make extensive use of folk tales and well-known characters in Ghanaian folklore such as Sasabonsam and dwarves. In *The Little Sasabonsam* Papa Ewusi becomes very curious about the fierce, gigantic, hairy, scaly Sasabonsam about which his grandfather told him. In his dreams he enters the forest, talks with birds and animals, plays and sings with dwarves, and meets and befriends a baby Sasabonsam. However, the father Sasabonsam is not friendly and chases and breathes fire on Papa when he wakes up. In *Papa Ewusi and the Magic Marble* Papa obtains a magic marble from dwarves in their forest home. When the marble is lost (actually stolen by another boy) the dwarves help Papa find it. They also help Papa with his household chores and provide his grandparents with food. However, Papa's good fortune is short-lived, for he really loses the magic marble in a well.

In the final story in the series, *Papa and the Animals,* Papa becomes bored and cries. When a mouse laughs at him, Papa tells the mouse a story, and the mouse reciprocates. The same events occur with a pig, monitor lizard, and vulture. As a result Papa hears four explanatory tales including how vulture became bald and how monitor lizard lost his hearing. De Graft-Hanson includes few details about the folkloric characters that appear in the Papa Ewusi series, for they are familiar to the Ghanaian children for whom he writes.

De Graft-Hanson's historical adventure stories are based on oral traditions about real historical events or on legends about the distant past. *The People from the Sea* takes place at the time of the Cape Coast earthquake of 1939. The hero hears the legend of Asebu told by his uncle and learns that it has contemporary relevance in the robbery of a store, which he helps to solve. *The Secret of Opokuwa* is based on a well-known event in Ghanaian history, the "theft" of the Ashanti golden stool by British colonial officials. In the context of the story, part of a yam festival is performed and children tell ananse stories to entertain themselves. The three child heroes and heroines actually save the state stool by substituting a newly made facsimile. The same three children are the main characters in *The Fetish Hide-Out* which is based on a legend about the Fante shrine of Nananompow. This story also includes rituals associated with "traditional" rulers. The children save Nana Otei's pet lamb, and in the process find a fetish hide-out where "bad" medicine is made. The hide-out is eventually destroyed after one of the children who was being held captive there is rescued, and the "good" medicine of the chief priest prevails bringing rain to end a drought.

In de Graft-Hanson's stories the past lives in the present. His written stories continue an old African storytelling tradition in which each storyteller creates well-known stories anew for a contemporary audience.

—Nancy J. Schmidt

_____

de HAMEL, Joan (Littledale, née Pollock). British. Born in London, 31 March 1924; emigrated to New Zealand, 1955. Educated at Queen's Gate School, London, 1932–40; Ecole S. Georges (Switzerland) at Onslow Hall, Shrewsbury, 1940–42; Lady Margaret Hall, Oxford, 1942–44, B.A. (honours) in modern languages 1944, M.A. 1949. Married Francis de Hamel in 1948; five sons. Assistant mistress, St. Nicholas School, Hemel Hempstead, Hertfordshire, 1944–45; head of languages, Francis Holland School, London, 1945–48; Lecturer in French, Teachers College, Dunedin, 1967–79. Recipient: New Zealand Library Association Esther Glen award, 1979; Reed Memorial award, 1985. Agent: Ray Richards, 3/43 Aberdeen Road, Castor Bay, Auckland; or, A.P. Watt Ltd., 20 John Street, London WC1N 2DL, England. Address: 25 Howard Street, Macandrew Bay, Dunedin, New Zealand.

PUBLICATIONS FOR CHILDREN

Fiction

X Marks the Spot, illustrated by the author. Guildford, Surrey, Lutterworth Press, 1973.
Take the Long Path, illustrated by Gareth Floyd. Guildford, Surrey, Lutterworth Press, 1978.
Hemi's Pet, illustrated by Christine Ross. Auckland, Reed Methuen, and London, Angus and Robertson, 1985; Boston, Houghton Mifflin, 1987.
The Third Eye. Auckland, Viking Kestrel, 1987.

*

Joan de Hamel comments:
X Marks the Spot is an adventure story about three children surviving under difficult circumstances after a helicopter crash in the New Zealand bush. There is a strong slant towards natural history and survival techniques—in addition to the mystery of "X." *Take the Long Path* is set on Otago Peninsula. David lives on an isolated farm and follows the fortunes of the local yellow-eyed penguins. He meets an old Maori and finds his own life is mysteriously bound up with the history of the Maoris on the peninsula and paralleled by the lives of the penguins he protects. *Hemi's Pet* is a picture story book. If a pet is something alive that you love and look after, why not enter your little sister in the school pet show? *The Third Eye* is a story of intrigue for the older age group. The secret work of a scientist on the rare tuatara, the prophecies of the Maori ancestors, and the plans of a property developer involve the three children from *X Marks the Spot* (now four years older) during a working holiday in the mountains near Takaka, New Zealand.

* * *

Joan de Hamel is an English immigrant to New Zealand whose great strength is her freshness of vision in interpreting the local scene. Her three novels show an awareness of current New Zealand issues such as the conservation of rare species and the human problems inherent in a multi-racial society. But above all they demonstrate her exuberant response to the New Zealand landscape, which assumes as great an importance to her canvases as her convincingly portrayed human relationships.

X Marks the Spot is a celebration of the remote southwestern forests of the South Island in which a family of children have to survive after a plane crash. Against all the beauty of the clear atmosphere and the exhilaration of the high peaks are set the discomfort of sandflies and the real dangers of rushing rivers. When their backpacks are swept away and they are left with only a gun and matches, these city-bred children realize that they will have to kill a deer to avoid starvation and their ensuing agony of mind is memorably portrayed. The sub-plot is the discovery of South American poachers out to capture the rare kakapo parrot.

The landscape alters in *Take the Long Path* to the bare sheep country of southeastern Otago flanked by lupin-clad sand dunes and the treacherously beautiful Pacific. It is a much more complex book than *X Marks the Spot,* and deservedly won the Esther Glen Medal. Its three themes are all deftly interwoven. The main one is that of the boy David's relationships with his parents, but it has strong Maori and animal story components. David, loving his rather disorganised mother, but fearing his forbidding sheep-farming father, turns for consolation to the penguins that nest in the sand dunes, adopting one family of them in particular as his own. It is there that he meets an old Maori man, who tells him that he is there on "family business" to find an ancient whalebone club which had belonged to one of his ancestors. David discovers the club, only to find that he had been talking to the ghost of his own grandfather, who had "taken the long path" from the spirit world. David then realizes that he himself is half-Maori and that the man he has thought of as his father is in fact his stepfather. He is able to come to terms with the situation when he sees it parallels the plight of his penguin family, whose father has been killed but whose rather feckless mother—like his own—needs a mate to protect her. David too has taken the long path to self-knowledge in a book that portrays at individual level the struggle between differing attitudes of Maori and European as a new nation emerges.

In *The Third Eye* the children of *X Marks the Spot* are now in their late teens and become involved in a conservation issue as they discover that rare lizards—tuataras—are being smuggled out of the country by an American woman scientist. She suspects that their pineal (or third) eye may hold the secret of their survival on barren rocks—information that might be relevant to human beings after a nuclear war. Unobtrusively the novel raises the whole question of whether bad means are justified by laudable ends. Another underlying issue is whether remote areas should be developed if doing so would create local employment. There are never easy answers, but within the framework of well-written, highly readable adventure stories, Joan de Hamel offers food for thought on current issues.

She does, however, present an unusual solution to a problem in her only picture book text. In the engagingly related *Hemi's Pet* a seven-year-old Maori boy has no animal to show at the school pet show until he realizes that his little sister fits all the criteria for a "pet" and he wins first prize for originality.

—Betty Gilderdale

DEHN, Olive. British. Born in Manchester, Lancashire, 29 September 1914; sister of the writer Paul Dehn. Educated at Downs School, Seaford, Sussex, 1926–31. Married David Markham in 1937 (died 1983); four children. Freelance writer; scriptwriter and broadcaster, *Children's Hour* programme, BBC Radio, London, 1933–37. Agent: Judy Daish Associates, 83 Eastbourne Mews, London W2 6LQ. Address: Lear Cottage, Colemans Hatch, Hartfield, Sussex, England.

PUBLICATIONS FOR CHILDREN

Fiction

Tales of Sir Benjamin Bulbous, Bart, illustrated by Harry Rountree. Oxford, Blackwell, 1935.
The Basement Bogle. Oxford, Blackwell, 1935.
The Nixie from Rotterdam, illustrated by Harry Rountree. Oxford, Blackwell, 1937.
Tales of the Taunus Mountains, illustrated by Charles Folkard. Oxford, Blackwell, 1937.
The Well-Behaved Witch, illustrated by Frances Murray. Oxford, Blackwell, 1937.
Come In, illustrated by Kathleen Gell. Oxford, Shakespeare Head Press, 1946.
Higgly-Piggly Farm, illustrated by Holly Bourne. London, Hamish Hamilton, 1957.
The Pike Dream, illustrated by Sonia Markham. London, Hamish Hamilton, 1958.
The Caretakers [*and the Poacher, and the Gipsy, to the Rescue, of Wilmhurst*], illustrated by Dorothy Clark. London, Burke, 5 vols., 1960–67.
Spectacles for the Mole, illustrated by Sonia Markham. London, Gollancz, 1968.
Good-bye Day. London, Gollancz, 1980.

Other

Folk Tales, illustrated by Hilda Figorski. Leeds, E.J. Arnold, 1948.

*

Olive Dehn comments:
I believe I started inventing stories when I was very young—because I was frightened of the dark and wanted to keep my youngest brother (with whom I shared a room) awake. I couldn't bear to think he might fall asleep before I did. I think I always preferred writing for children because you have to be honest with children and also because I have always had a strong childish streak in me—even now.

*   *   *

The characteristics of Olive Dehn's work are a variety of themes but a constant style of dry humour, succinct phrases, and well-rounded plot. The early 1930's books are centered on fantasy creatures like the pixie in *The Basement Bogle* and *The Well-Behaved Witch*; then came family adventures in a rural background; the most recent work is social realism in an urban setting.

Humour and an ear for children's conversations are the keynotes of the five books involving the Caretakers, intended for readers aged seven to ten. A family of children whose mother is the caretaker of a large house belonging to the National Trust become involved in adventures in and around their village and school. In *The Caretakers of Wilmhurst* the Meredith children become enthusiastically active in a Best Kept Village competition. Almost 30 years after first publication the books are still relevant in their depiction of village life, childhood interests, and children's perception of adults. There are not many English children's books with rural settings and plenty of action and humour, but this saga creates a believable locality with believable characters doing believable things, and deserves a wider readership.

The Nixie from Rotterdam contains a tongue-in-cheek humour which may be of curiosity value to young readers but which speaks powerfully to the older and adult reader. When a small boy falls into the canal in Rotterdam his nurse blames herself for both the accident and the encounter with a water sprite. While under the water little Carel is bewitched with subsequent hilarious results, made all the more telling by the crisp succinct style. The story has pace, the dialogue is realistic, the humour has several levels, and the work has an enjoyable originality. A similarly original view of seemingly ordinary places and events is to be found in *Spectacles for the Mole*.

But the most recent book, *Good-bye Day,* is quite different from the other works. A novel for the age range nine to thirteen plus, it concerns the Sands family seen through the eyes of daughter Coral as she tries to trace her father, who seems to have abandoned the family. There is much perception in the series of incidents leading to her discovery of him at Manchester Docks—the anxieties of childhood, the vulnerability of a grieving girl, the jokey repartee among the characters, the use of language as it is spoken.

Though there is an span of some 45 years between her first book and her most recent, Olive Dehn has consistently attended to the little details loved by children and to children's use of language. Constant also is the quiet, understated verbal humour.

—Margaret R. Marshall

———

DE JONG, Meindert. American. Born in Wierum, Netherlands, 4 March 1906; brought to the United States at age eight. Educated at Calvin College, Grand Rapids, Michigan, A.B. 1928; University of Chicago. Served in the United States Army Air Corps during World War II: historian of the Chinese-American Wing, 14th Air Force. Married 1) Hattie Overeinter in 1932; 2) Beatrice DeClaire McElwee in 1962 (died 1969), five stepchildren. College teacher, then farmer, in Iowa, 1928–38; worked with the Federal Writers Project, Grand Rapids, Michigan. Lived in Mexico, 1962–67. Recipient: American Library Association Newbery Medal, 1955; Child Study Committee award, 1957; Hans Christian Andersen International Medal, 1962; National Book award, 1969; Catholic Library Association Regina Medal, 1972. Address: 351 Grand Street, Allegan, Michigan 49010, U.S.A.

PUBLICATIONS FOR CHILDREN

Fiction

The Big Goose and the Little White Duck, illustrated by Edna Potter. New York, Harper, 1938; London, Heinemann, 1939.
Dirk's Dog Bello, illustrated by Kurt Wiese. New York, Harper, 1939; London, Lutterworth Press, 1960.
Wheels over the Bridge, illustrated by Aldren Watson. New York, Harper, 1941.
Bells of the Harbor, illustrated by Kurt Wiese. New York, Harper, 1941.
The Cat That Walked a Week, illustrated by Tessie Robinson. New York, Harper, 1943; London, Lutterworth Press, 1965.
The Little Stray Dog, illustrated by Edward Shenton. New York, Harper, 1943.
Billy and the Unhappy Bull, illustrated by Marc Simont. New York, Harper, 1946; London, Lutterworth Press, 1966.
Good Luck Duck, illustrated by Marc Simont. New York, Harper, and London, Hamish Hamilton, 1950.
Tower by the Sea, illustrated by Barbara Comfort. New York, Harper, and London, Hamish Hamilton, 1950.
Smoke above the Lane, illustrated by Girard Goodenow. New York, Harper, 1951.
Shadrach, illustrated by Maurice Sendak. New York, Harper, 1953; London, Lutterworth Press, 1957.
Hurry Home, Candy, illustrated by Maurice Sendak. New York, Harper, 1953; London, Lutterworth Press, 1962.
The Wheel on the School, illustrated by Maurice Sendak. New York, Harper, 1954; London, Lutterworth Press, 1956.
The Little Cow and the Turtle, illustrated by Maurice Sendak. New York, Harper, 1955; London, Lutterworth Press, 1961.

The House of Sixty Fathers, illustrated by Maurice Sendak. New York, Harper, 1956; London, Lutterworth Press, 1958.
Along Came a Dog, illustrated by Maurice Sendak. New York, Harper, 1958; London, Lutterworth Press, 1959.
The Last Little Cat, illustrated by Jim McMullen. New York, Harper, 1961; London, Lutterworth Press, 1962.
The Singing Hill, illustrated by Maurice Sendak. New York, Harper, 1962; London, Lutterworth Press, 1963.
Nobody Plays with a Cabbage, illustrated by Tom Allen. New York, Harper, 1962; London, Lutterworth Press, 1963.
Far Out the Long Canal, illustrated by Nancy Grossman. New York, Harper, 1964; London, Lutterworth Press, 1965.
Puppy Summer, illustrated by Anita Lobel. New York, Harper, and London, Lutterworth Press, 1966.
Journey from Peppermint Street, illustrated by Emily McCully. New York, Harper, 1968; London, Lutterworth Press, 1969.
A Horse Came Running, illustrated by Paul Sagsoorian. New York, Macmillan, and London, Lutterworth Press, 1970.
The Easter Cat, illustrated by Lillian Hoban. New York, Macmillan, 1971; Guildford, Surrey, Lutterworth Press, 1972.
The Almost All-White Rabbity Cat, illustrated by H.B. Vestal. New York, Macmillan, and Guildford, Surrey, Lutterworth Press, 1972.

Other

Bible Days, illustrated by Kreigh Collins. Grand Rapids, Michigan, Fideler, 1949.
The Mighty Ones: Great Men and Women of Early Bible Days, illustrated by Harvey Schmidt. New York, Harper, 1959; London, Lutterworth Press, 1960.

*

Manuscript Collections: Kerlan Collection, University of Minnesota, Minneapolis; Park Library, Central Michigan University, Mount Pleasant.

*   *   *

Great writers have a quality far more important than facility with words, more than observation and a graphic portrayal of what is observed. It is a quality that might be called compassionate perception. Certain writers of children's literature have this characteristic. Children are often loving by nature, perceptive, sensitive, and they respond to an author who is spiritually akin to them.

Meindert De Jong, whose books span many years and assorted ages, is such a writer. That De Jong likes animals can be quickly seen from his titles: *Puppy Summer, The Last Little Cat, The Cat That Walked a Week, A Horse Came Running, Good Luck Duck.* But titles do not reveal his wonderful ability to describe sensitively but without sentimentality the shimmering love which sometimes springs up between a child and a pet.

The Easter Cat is the story of Millicent, a little girl who adored cats but was prevented from having one of her own by her Mother's allergy. Gradually the reader learns that Millicent is the only small person in a world of adults. Her desire for a kitten is really her need for a being smaller than herself who depends upon her love and care. How universal a situation from a child's eye level! In solving the problem, De Jong uses carefully selected diction. Note this description of a clock at night—"The white dial of the big clock was a murky nothing sending out its heavy tick-tocks"—or the description of an emotional reaction—"Your heart sort of gets like cheap ice cream when it melts—all watery and mushy." The vocabulary of *The Easter Cat* is familiar to little children—ice cream and tick-tocks and mush—yet De Jong's artistry is obvious. Adults may forget the pain of being always too small or too weak, but a child recognizes the feeling readily, and, in Millicent, finds a heroine who learns to cope and conquer.

In *The Wheel on the School*, written for older children, De Jong begins his story in a sleepy Dutch school with a little girl's composition about storks. Storks may not be familiar to the average child, but school rooms and compositions are and so he slips easily into the barren seaside community of Shora whose children desire the return of the great birds to nest upon their roofs as they did in the past. Now the roofs of Shora are all sharp, too slippery for nesting, but the children intend to entice the storks by placing a wheel on the school house roof. This simple plot becomes complicated because the children must overcome hostility from adults, violent storms, and finally a close brush with death to rescue two bedraggled storm-weakened birds. *The Wheel on the School* is an absorbing adventure story but it has a larger meaning. It is a monumental struggle which touches a whole community. A fisherman learns that his mind and his courage can supplement the use of legs; the children find that physical strength is second to spiritual tenuousness; the whole village encounters elemental forces of wind and tide but the common project causes a deep emotional stirring which finally washes away petty feelings and unifies Shora's people. It is a lovely story and one which shows a child that he need not be unimportant just because he is not an adult.

Shadrach is a classic and as such is confined to no age group. *Shadrach* is about the finding of identity, the nucleus of being which a child must discover so that his own uniqueness may stand forth. Grandfather has promised Davie a rabbit—not just any rabbit—a black rabbit. Perceiving its specificity even before it is a reality, Davie names his rabbit carefully—a wonderful name with Biblical undertones—Shadrach. Like Millicent in *The Easter Cat*, this child needs a smaller being to care for, and his affection for his rabbit is very deep. When the rabbit is lost, the family suggests a replacement (as families do) but Davie becomes ill at the thought. He understands the animal's uniqueness. There can be no casual substitution. This child is "all-children." Will no one *see*? At last the busy adults pause and try to comprehend what a small voice is saying. At last they listen. *Shadrach* is a definition of love—perceptive, sensitive love because it rests on the ability to understand and accept each individual as special.

Meindert De Jong's books are important contributions to literature, examining problems of childhood with depth and beauty.

—Carolyn T. Kingston

———

de la MARE, Walter. Also wrote as Walter Ramal. British. Born in Charlton, Kent, 25 April 1873. Educated at St. Paul's Cathedral Choristers' School, London (founder, *Choristers Journal*, 1889). Married Constance Elfrida Ingpen in 1899 (died 1943); two sons and two daughters. Clerk, Anglo-American Oil Company, London, 1890–1908. Reviewer for the *Times, Westminster Gazette, Bookman,* and other journals, London. Recipient: Royal Society of Literature Polignac prize, 1911; James Tait Black Memorial prize, for fiction, 1922; Library Association Carnegie Medal, 1948; Foyle Poetry prize, 1954. D.Litt.: Oxford, Cambridge, Bristol, and London universities; LL.D.: University of St. Andrews. Honorary Fellow, Keble College, Oxford. Granted Civil List pension, 1908; Companion of Honour, 1948; Order of Merit, 1953. *Died 22 June 1956.*

PUBLICATIONS FOR CHILDREN

Fiction

The Three Mulla-Mulgars, illustrated by Dorothy P. Lathrop. Lon-

don, Duckworth, 1910; New York, Knopf, 1919; as *The Three Royal Monkeys; or, The Three Mulla-Mulgars,* London, Faber, 1935.
Story and Rhyme: A Selection from the Writings of Walter de la Mare, Chosen by the Author. London, Dent, and New York, Dutton, 1921.
Broomsticks and Other Tales, illustrated by Bold. London, Constable, and New York, Knopf, 1925.
Miss Jemima, illustrated by Alec Buckels. Oxford, Blackwell, 1925; Poughkeepsie, New York, Artists and Writers Guild, 1935.
Old Joe, illustrated by C. T. Nightingale. Oxford, Blackwell, 1927.
The Dutch Cheese and the Lovely Myfanwy, illustrated by Dorothy P. Lathrop. New York, Knopf, 1931.
The Lord Fish and Other Tales, illustrated by Rex Whistler. London, Faber, 1933.
The Old Lion and Other Stories, illustrated by Irene Hawkins. London, Faber, 1942.
Mr. Bumps and His Monkey, illustrated by Dorothy P. Lathrop. Philadelphia, Winston, 1942.
The Magic Jacket and Other Stories, illustrated by Irene Hawkins. London, Faber, 1943.
The Scarecrow and Other Stories, illustrated by Irene Hawkins. London, Faber, 1945.
The Dutch Cheese and Other Stories, illustrated by Irene Hawkins. London, Faber, 1946.
Collected Stories for Children, illustrated by Irene Hawkins. London, Faber, 1947.
A Penny a Day, illustrated by Paul Kennedy. New York, Knopf, 1960.

Play

Crossings: A Fairy Play, music by C. Armstrong Gibbs, illustrated by Randolph Schwabe (produced Hove, Sussex, 1919; London, 1925). London, Beaumont Press, 1921; New York, Knopf, 1923.

Verse

Songs of Childhood (as Walter Ramal). London, Longman, 1902; New York, Garland, 1976; revised edition, as Walter de la Mare, Longman, 1916, 1923.
A Child's Day: A Book of Rhymes, illustrated by Carine and Will Cadby. London, Constable, 1912; New York, Holt, 1923.
Peacock Pie: A Book of Rhymes. London, Constable, 1913; New York, Holt, 1917.
Down-Adown-Derry: A Book of Fairy Poems, illustrated by Dorothy P. Lathrop. London, Constable, and New York, Holt, 1922.
Stuff and Nonsense and So On, illustrated by Bold. London, Constable, and New York, Holt, 1927; revised edition, London, Faber, 1946.
Poems for Children. London, Constable, and New York, Holt, 1930.
This Year, Next Year, illustrated by Harold Jones. London, Faber, and New York, Holt, 1937.
Bells and Grass: A Book of Rhymes, illustrated by Rowland Emett. London, Faber, 1941; New York, Viking Press, 1942.
Collected Rhymes and Verses, illustrated by Berthold Wolpe. London, Faber, 1944.
Rhymes and Verses: Collected Poems for Children, illustrated by Elinore Blaisdell. New York, Holt, 1947.
Poems, edited by Eleanor Graham, illustrated by Margery Gill. London, Penguin, 1962.
The Voice, edited and illustrated by Catherine Brighton. London, Faber, 1986; New York, Delacorte Press, 1987.

Other

Told Again: Traditional Tales, illustrated by A.H. Watson. Oxford, Blackwell, 1927; as *Told Again: Old Tales Told Again,* New York, Knopf, 1927; as *Tales Told Again,* London, Faber, and Knopf, 1959.

Stories from the Bible, illustrated by Theodore Nadejen. London, Faber, and New York, Cosmopolitan, 1929.

Letters from Mr. Walter de la Mare to Form Three. Privately printed, 1936.

Animal Stories, Chosen, Arranged, and in Some Part Re-Written. London, Faber, 1939; New York, Scribner, 1940.

Selected Stories and Verses, edited by Eleanor Graham. London, Penguin, 1952.

Molly Whuppie, illustrated by Errol Le Cain. London, Faber, and New York, Farrar Straus, 1983.

Editor, *Come Hither: A Collection of Rhymes and Poems for the Young of all Ages,* illustrated by Alec Buckels. London, Constable, and New York, Knopf, 1923; revised edition, 1928.

Editor, with Thomas Quayle, *Readings: Traditional Tales Told by the Author,* illustrated by A.H. Watson and C. T. Nightingale. Oxford, Blackwell, 6 vols., 1925–28; New York, Knopf, 1 vol., 1927.

Editor, *Tom Tiddler's Ground: A Book of Poetry for the Junior and Middle Schools.* London, Collins, 3 vols., 1932; New York, Knopf, 1 vol., 1962.

Editor, *Old Rhymes and New, Chosen for Use in Schools.* London, Constable, 2 vols., 1932.

PUBLICATIONS FOR ADULTS

Novels

Henry Brocken: His Travels and Adventures in the Rich, Strange, Scarce-Imaginable Regions of Romance. London, Murray, 1904; New York, Knopf, 1924.

The Return. London, Arnold, 1910; New York, Putnam, 1911; revised edition, London, Collins, and New York, Knopf, 1922; London, Faber, 1945.

Memoirs of a Midget. London, Collins, 1921; New York, Knopf, 1922.

Short Stories

Lispet, Lispett, and Vaine. London, Bookman's Journal, 1923.

The Riddle and Other Stories. London, Selwyn and Blount, 1923; as *The Riddle and Other Tales,* New York, Knopf, 1923.

Ding Dong Bell. London, Selwyn and Blount, and New York, Knopf, 1924.

Two Tales: The Green-Room, The Connoisseur. London, Bookman's Journal, 1925.

The Connoisseur and Other Stories. London, Collins, and New York, Knopf, 1926.

At First Sight. New York, Crosby Gaige, 1928.

On the Edge: Short Stories. London, Faber, 1930; New York, Knopf, 1931.

Seven Short Stories. London, Faber, 1931.

A Froward Child. London, Faber, 1934.

The Nap and Other Stories. London, Nelson, 1936.

The Wind Blows Over. London, Faber, and New York, Macmillan, 1936.

The Picnic and Other Stories. London, Faber, 1941.

Best Stories of Walter de la Mare. London, Faber, 1942.

The Collected Tales of Walter de la Mare, edited by Edward Wagenknecht. New York, Knopf, 1950.

A Beginning and Other Stories. London, Faber, 1955.

Ghost Stories. London, Folio Society, 1956.

Some Stories. London, Faber, 1962.

Eight Tales. Sauk City, Wisconsin, Arkham House, 1971.

Verse

Poems. London, Murray, 1906.

The Listeners and Other Poems. London, Constable, 1912; New York, Holt, 1916.

The Old Men. London, Flying Fame, 1913.

The Sunken Garden and Other Poems. London, Beaumont Press, 1917.

Motley and Other Poems. London, Constable, and New York, Holt, 1918.

Flora, drawings by Pamela Bianco. London, Heinemann, and Philadelphia, Lippincott, 1919.

Poems 1901 to 1918. London, Constable, 2 vols., 1920; as *Collected Poems 1901 to 1918,* New York, Holt, 2 vols., 1920.

The Veil and Other Poems. London, Constable, 1921; New York, Holt, 1922.

Thus Her Tale: A Poem. Edinburgh, Porpoise Press, 1923.

A Ballad of Christmas. London, Selwyn and Blount, 1924.

The Hostage. London, Selwyn and Blount, 1925.

St. Andrews, with Rudyard Kipling. London, A. and C. Black, 1926.

(Poems). London, Benn, 1926.

Alone. London, Faber, 1927.

Selected Poems. New York, Holt, 1927.

The Captive and Other Poems. New York, Bowling Green Press, 1928.

Self to Self. London, Faber, 1928.

A Snowdrop. London, Faber, 1929.

News. London, Faber, 1930.

To Lucy. London, Faber, 1931.

The Sunken Garden and Other Verses. Birmingham, Birmingham School of Printing, 1931.

Two Poems. Privately printed, 1931.

The Fleeting and Other Poems. London, Constable, and New York, Knopf, 1933.

Poems 1919 to 1934. London, Constable, 1935; New York, Holt, 1936.

Poems. London, Corvinus Press, 1937.

Memory and Other Poems. London, Constable, and New York, Holt, 1938.

Two Poems, with Arthur Rogers. Privately printed, 1938.

Haunted: A Poem. London, Linden Press, 1939.

Collected Poems. New York, Holt, 1941; London, Faber, 1942.

Time Passes and Other Poems, edited by Anne Ridler. London, Faber, 1942.

The Burning-Glass and Other Poems, Including The Traveller. New York, Viking Press, 1945.

The Burning-Glass and Other Poems. London, Faber, 1945.

The Traveller. London, Faber, 1946.

Two Poems: Pride, The Truth of Things. London, Dropmore Press, 1946.

Inward Companion. London, Faber, 1950.

Winged Chariot. London, Faber, 1951.

Winged Chariot and Other Poems. New York, Viking Press, 1951.

O Lovely England and Other Poems. London, Faber, 1953.

The Winnowing Dream. London, Faber, 1954.

Selected Poems, edited by R.N. Green-Armytage. London, Faber, 1954.

The Morrow. Privately printed, 1955.

(Poems), edited by John Hadfield. London, Vista Books, 1962.

A Choice of de la Mare's Verse, edited by W.H. Auden.   London, Faber, 1963.

Envoi.   Privately printed, 1965.

The Complete Poems of Walter de la Mare, edited by Leonard Clark and others.   London, Faber, 1969; New York, Knopf, 1970.

The Collected Poems of Walter de la Mare.   London, Faber, 1979.

Other

M.E. Coleridge: An Appreciation.   London, The Guardian, 1907.

Rupert Brooke and the Intellectual Imagination (lecture).   London, Sidgwick and Jackson, and New York, Harcourt Brace, 1919.

Some Thoughts on Reading (lecture).   Bembridge, Isle of Wight, Yellowsands Press, 1923.

Some Women Novelists of the 'Seventies.   London, Cambridge University Press, 1929.

The Printing of Poetry (lecture).   London, Cambridge University Press, 1931.

The Early Novels of Wilkie Collins.   London, Cambridge University Press, 1932.

Lewis Carroll.   London, Faber, 1932.

Early One Morning in the Spring: Chapters on Children and on Childhood as It Is Revealed in Particular in Early Memories and in Early Writings.   London, Faber, and New York, Macmillan, 1935.

Poetry in Prose (lecture).   London, Oxford University Press, 1936; New York, Oxford University Press, 1937.

Arthur Thompson: A Memoir.   Privately printed, 1938.

An Introduction to Everyman.   London, Dent, 1938.

Stories, Essays, and Poems, edited by M.M. Bozman.   London, Dent, 1938.

Pleasures and Speculations.   London, Faber, 1940; Freeport, New York, Books for Libraries Press, 1969.

Private View (essays).   London, Faber, 1953; Westport, Connecticut, Hyperion, 1979.

Walter de la Mare: A Selection from His Writings, edited by Kenneth Hopkins.   London, Faber, 1956.

Editor, *Desert Islands and Robinson Crusoe.*   London, Faber, and New York, Fountains Press, 1930; revised edition, Faber, 1932.

Editor, *Poems,* by Christina Rossetti.   Newtown, Wales, Gregynog Press, 1930.

Editor, *The Eighteen-Eighties: Essays by Fellows of the Royal Society of Literature.*   London, Cambridge University Press, 1930.

Editor, *Behold, This Dreamer! Of Reverie, Night, Sleep, Dream, Love-Dreams, Nightmare, Death, The Unconscious, The Imagination, Divination, The Artist, and Kindred Subjects.*   London, Faber, and New York, Knopf, 1939.

Editor, *Love.*   London, Faber, 1943; New York, Morrow, 1946.

*

Bibliography: in *L'Oeuvre de Walter de la Mare: Une Aventure Spirituelle* by Luce Bonnerot, Paris, Didier, 1969.

Manuscript Collections: Syracuse University, New York; Temple University, Philadelphia; University of Chicago; King's College, Cambridge.

Critical Studies (selection): *Walter de la Mare: A Critical Study* by Forrest Reid, London, Faber, and New York, Holt, 1929; *Walter de la Mare: An Exploration* by John Atkins, London, Temple, 1947; *Walter de la Mare* by Kenneth Hopkins, London, Longman, 1953; *Tea with Walter de la Mare* by Russell Brain, London, Faber, 1957; *Walter de la Mare* by Leonard Clark, London, Bodley Head, 1960,

New York, Walck, 1961; *Walter de la Mare* by Doris Ross McCrosson, New York, Twayne, 1966.

*   *   *

Walter de la Mare, though one of the most gifted and original writers of the 20th century, is currently one of the most neglected. His poetry, much admired on its first appearance, has steadily lost ground and is now regarded as incontrovertibly minor. The preference for traditional forms and refusal to tackle contemporary social problems or to indulge in the direct expression of personal feeling have condemned it. His prose never received due appreciation, the dated settings, sexual reticence, and determined rejection of contemporary life mitigating against success; yet, like Kipling, de la Mare was arguably at his best in the short story. He wrote a great deal specifically for children, and this has been more consistently admired since here his supposed deficiencies might be felt to be advantages. It is more rewarding, however, to treat his work for adults and children as a whole, in which the child's apprehension of the world represents a central and passionate mode of experience. De la Mare held strong and slightly odd convictions about childhood, associating it with intuition and a natural physical grace that was subsequently lost; like dreams, it afforded fresher, more intense visions whose ultimate source might lie beyond, as well as within the individual. A profoundly platonic thinker, de la Mare felt that children lived closer to primal truths, being as yet unshadowed by the miseries and burdens of adult life. He resisted the temptation to idealise, and several stories (e.g., "In the Forest") reveal the callousness, even cruelty of the young; but despite their prevailing self-absorption, children seemed to him powerfully, if only too briefly, in contact with underlying spiritual truths.

De la Mare's most sustained work for children is *The Three Mulla-Mulgars,* later reprinted as *The Three Royal Monkeys,* and written to amuse his own. It is a powerfully original creation, a complete and consistent secondary world, with its own powers for good and evil, invented cultures, hierarchies, even language. This world is inhabited primarily by the various races of monkeys ("Mulgars"), among whom man is only another sub-species (or "Oomgar-Mulgar"). The highest in rank are the "Mulla-Mulgars" or royal monkeys such as the book's heroes, the brothers Thumb, Thimble, and Nod. Their quest for the paradisal land of Tishnar, their destined home, provides the main narrative thread. Although most of the book's denizens are familiar enough—zebras, jackals, eagles—everything that appears is endowed with a new significance, being changed "into something rich and strange." The tropical forest is altered beyond recognition by heavy falls of snow, the panther Immanâla becomes the very principle of evil itself, the zebras are "the Little Horses of Tishnar." The youngest brother, Nod, has the standard folkloric virtues of luck, pluck, and determination to carry him through his various adventures—his digressive stay with the shipwrecked sailor Andy Battle, the near loss of his talismanic Wonderstone to the enchantingly beautiful Water Midden, and the final underground journey to the very borders of Tishnar. De la Mare continually echoes traditional folk tales and as continually transforms them.

Like Tolkien's hobbits, the brothers are at once human in their ways of thinking and responding, and yet distinctively alien in their habits and instincts; their mother has taught them that, as royal monkeys, they must never walk on all fours, taste blood, nor, unless in danger and despair, climb trees or grow a tail. De la Mare seems to have been intrigued by the human potentiality within the simian. A later story, "The Old Lion," relates the experiences of a uniquely intelligent monkey, Jasper, his friendship with the first mate of "The Old Lion," and his later exploitation as a music-hall turn. Human greed and cruelty are sharply contrasted to Jasper's trust and innocence, and his role within the story resembles that of the child observer in the world of adults, a device de la Mare used particularly effectively. This is one of 17 stories selected from *Broomsticks* and *The Lord Fish* to form *Collected Stories for Children*. In subject matter these are surprisingly heterogeneous. Most make use of magic or folklore motifs in one way or another, but some openly inhabit a fairytale world ("Dick and the Beanstalk," "A Penny a Day," "The Three Sleeping Boys of Warwickshire"), others approach it obliquely ("Lucy," "Alice's Godmother," "Miss Jemima," "The Scarecrow"), while others barely glance at it ("Maria-Fly," "Visitors"). All are illuminated by an instinctive grasp of the child's imaginative life and an intense apprehension of unknown modes of being which make them deeply rewarding for adult readers. It is, however, rare to find a child who has read them with real pleasure because their subtle, understated, and indirect approach creates delays and difficulties avoided in the more obviously exciting adventures of the travellers to Tishnar.

If de la Mare's short stories for children inadvertently erect barriers, his children's verse has an irresistible rhythmic force and immediacy. With the exception of Blake and Carroll, no poet has more effectively recaptured the direct appeal of the nursery-rhyme, at its most hypnotic when at its most incantatory:

> *Applecumjocaby,* blindfold eye!
> How many rooks come sailing by;
> Caw—caw in the deep blue sky?
> Eeka, Neeka, Leeka, Lee—
> Here's a lock without a key...
> Do diddle di do
> Poor Jim Jay
> Got stuck fast
> In Yesterday.

Like his short stories, de la Mare's verse for children ranges over a wide variety of subjects, combining an extraordinary degree of technical virtuosity with a characteristic complexity. The moods comprehended include terror, enchantment, laughter and tears, while time passing, evil, unhappiness, and cruelty are as often present as the pleasures and energies of nature. These are poems that should be part of every child's reading experience.

In addition to these achievements, de la Mare edited *Come Hither* and *Tom Tiddler's Ground,* delightful anthologies of children's verse, as well as retelling fairy stories (*Told Again*), and Bible stories, and collecting *Animal Stories,* many of which were of his own invention.

—Julia Briggs

---

de PAOLA, Tomie (Thomas Anthony de Paola). American. Born in Meriden, Connecticut, 15 September 1934. Educated at the Pratt Institute, Brooklyn, New York, B.F.A. 1956; California College of Arts and Crafts, Oakland, M.F.A. 1969; Lone Mountain College, San Francisco, doctoral equivalency 1970. Since 1956 freelance artist and designer: paintings and murals for churches and monasteries in New England; set designer for night clubs and theatres; several individual shows since 1961, and numerous group shows. Instructor, 1962–63, and Assistant Professor of Art, 1963–66, College of the Sacred Heart, Newton, Massachusetts; Assistant Professor of Art, San Francisco College for Women (now Lone Mountain College), 1967–70; Instructor in Art, Chamberlayne Junior College, Boston, 1972–73; Associate Professor, designer, and technical director in the Speech and Theatre departments, Colby College, New London, New Hampshire, 1973–76; Associate Profes-

sor of Art, 1976–78, and artist-in-residence, 1978–79, New England College, Henniker, New Hampshire. Recipient: Boston Art Directors' Club award, 1968; Franklin Typographers award, 1969; University of Minnesota Kerlan award, 1981; Society of Children's Book Writers Golden Kite award, for illustration, 1983; Catholic Library Association Regina Medal, 1983. Agent: Florence Alexander, 80 Park Avenue, New York, New York 10016. Address: c/o Putnam's Sons, 200 Madison Avenue, New York, New York 10016, U.S.A.

PUBLICATIONS FOR CHILDREN (illustrated by the author)

Fiction

The Wonderful Dragon of Timlin. Indianapolis, Bobbs Merrill, 1966.
Fight the Night. Philadelphia, Lippincott, 1968.
Joe and the Snow. New York, Hawthorn, 1968.
Parker Pig, Esquire. New York, Hawthorn, 1969.
The Journey of the Kiss. New York, Hawthorn, 1970.
The Monsters' Ball. New York, Hawthorn, 1970.
Nana Upstairs and Nana Downstairs. New York, Putnam, 1973; London, Methuen, 1983.
Andy (That's My Name). Englewood Cliffs, New Jersey, Prentice Hall, 1973.
The Unicorn and the Moon. Lexington, Massachusetts, Ginn, 1973.
Charlie Needs a Cloak. Englewood Cliffs, New Jersey, Prentice Hall, 1974; London, Collins, 1975.
Watch Out for the Chicken Feet in Your Soup. Englewood Cliffs, New Jersey, Prentice Hall, 1974.
Michael Bird-Boy. Englewood Cliffs, New Jersey, Prentice Hall, 1975.
When Everyone Was Fast Asleep. New York, Holiday House, 1976.
Four Stories for Four Seasons. Englewood Cliffs, New Jersey, Prentice Hall, 1977.
Helga's Dowry: A Troll Love Story. New York, Harcourt Brace, 1977.
Bill and Pete. New York, Putnam, 1977; Oxford, Oxford University Press, 1982.
Pancakes for Breakfast. New York, Harcourt Brace, 1978.
Oliver Button Is a Sissy. New York, Harcourt Brace, 1979; London, Methuen, 1981.
Big Anthony and the Magic Ring. New York, Harcourt Brace, 1979.
Flicks. New York, Harcourt Brace, 1979.
Songs of the Fog Maiden. New York, Holiday House, 1979.
The Knight and the Dragon. New York, Putnam, and London, Methuen, 1980.
The Hunter and the Animals. New York, Holiday House, 1981; London, Andersen Press, 1982.
Now One Foot, Now the Other. New York, Putnam, 1981; London, Methuen, 1982.
The Friendly Beasts: An Old English Christmas Carol. New York, Putnam, 1981; London, Methuen, 1984.
Marianna May and Nursey. New York, Holiday House, 1983.
Sing, Pierrot, Sing (wordless book). New York, Harcourt Brace, and London, Methuen, 1983.
Merry Christmas, Strega Nona. San Diego, Harcourt Brace, 1986; London, Methuen, 1987.
Bill and Pete Go Down the Nile. New York, Putnam, and Oxford, Oxford University Press, 1987.
An Early American Christmas. New York, Holiday House, 1987.
Baby's First Christmas. New York, Putnam, 1988.
The Art Lesson. New York, Putnam, 1989.

Haircuts for the Woolseys.   New York, Putnam, 1989.
Too Many Hopkins.   New York, Putnam, 1989.

Play

A Rainbow Christmas (puppet play; also director and designer: produced Cambridge, Massachusetts, 1971).

Verse

Book of Poems.   New York, Putnam, 1988; London, Methuen, 1989.

Other

The Wind and the Sun (tale from Aesop).   Lexington, Massachusetts, Ginn, 1972.
The Cloud [Quicksand, Popcorn, Kids' Cat, Family Christmas Tree] Book.   New York, Holiday House, 5 vols., 1975–80.
Strega Nona: An Old Tale.   Englewood Cliffs, New Jersey, Prentice Hall, 1975; as *The Magic Pasta Pot,* London, Hutchinson, 1979.
Things to Make and Do for Valentine's Day.   New York, Watts, 1976.
The Clown of God: An Old Story.   New York, Harcourt Brace, 1978; London, Methuen, 1979.
Criss-Cross, Applesauce, photographs by B.A. King.   New York, Addison House, 1979.
The Lady of Guadalupe.   New York, Holiday House, 1980.
The Prince of the Dolomites: An Old Italian Tale.   New York, Harcourt Brace, 1980; London, Methuen, 1981.
The Legend of Old Befana: An Italian Christmas Story.   New York, Harcourt Brace, 1980.
Fin M'Coul: The Giant of Knockmany Hill.   New York, Holiday House, and London, Andersen Press, 1981.
The Comic Adventures of Old Mother Hubbard and Her Dog.   New York, Harcourt Brace, and London, Methuen, 1981.
Giorgio's Village.   New York, Putnam, and London, Methuen, 1982.
Francis, The Poor Man of Assisi.   New York, Holiday House, 1982.
Strega Nona's Magic Lessons.   New York, Harcourt Brace, 1982; London, Methuen, 1983.
Bible Story Cut-Outs (Noah and the Ark, David and Goliath).   Minneapolis, Winston Press, 2 vols., 1983–84.
The Legend of the Bluebonnet: An Old Tale of Texas.   New York, Putnam, and London, Methuen, 1983.
The Story of the Three Wise Kings.   New York, Putnam, and London, Methuen, 1983.
The Mysterious Giant of Barletta.   New York, Harcourt Brace, 1984; London, Andersen Press, 1985.
Queen Esther.   New York, Harper, 1986.
The Miracles of Jesus.   New York, Holiday House, 1987.
The Parables of Jesus.   New York, Holiday House, 1987.
The Legend of the Indian Paintbrush.   New York, Putnam, 1988.

Editor, *Mother Goose.*   New York, Putnam, and London, Methuen, 1985.
Editor, *Favorite Nursery Tales.*   New York, Putnam, and London, Methuen, 1986.
Editor, *Book of Christmas Carols.*   New York, Putnam, and London, Methuen, 1987.

*

Manuscript Collection: Kerlan Collection, University of Minnesota, Minneapolis.

Illustrator: *Sound,* 1965, and *Wheels,* 1965, both by Lisa Miller; *The Tiger and the Rabbit and Other Tales* by Pura Belpré, 1965; *Tricky Peik and Other Picture Tales* edited by Jeanne B. Hardendorff, 1967; *Finders Keepers, Losers Weepers* by Joan M. Lexau, 1967; *Sound Science,* 1968, and *Light and Sight,* 1969, both by Melvin L. Alexenberg; *The Cabinet of the President of the United States* by James A. Eichner, 1968; *Poetry for Chuckles and Grins* edited by Leland Blair Jacobs, 1968; *Take This Hammer,* 1969, *Who Needs Holes?,* 1970, *Pick It Up,* 1971, *Hold Everything,* 1973, and *Look in the Mirror,* 1973, all by Samuel and Beryl Epstein; *The Rocking-Chair Ghost* by Mary C. Jane, 1969; *Hercules, The Gentle Giant* by Nina Schneider, 1969; *The Morning Glory* by Robert Bly, 1969; *How to Be a Puppeteer* by Eleanor Boylan, 1970; *Rutherford T. Finds 21 B* by Barbara Rinkoff, 1970; *The Folklore of Love and Courtship* and *The Folklore of Weddings and Marriage* both edited by Duncan Emrich, 1970; *Hot as an Ice Cube* by Philip Balestrino, 1971; *John Fisher's Magic Book* by John Fisher, 1971; *Monsters of the Middle Ages* by William Wise, 1971; *Authorized Autumn Charts of the Upper Red Canoe River Country* by Peter Zachary Cohen, 1972; *What Is Fear* by Jean Rosenbaum and Lutie McAuliffe, 1972; *Mario's Mystery Machine* by Sibyl Hancock, 1972; *The Franklin Watts Concise Guide to Baby-Sitting* by Rubie Saunders, 1972; *Let's Find Out about Communications* by Valerie Pitt, 1973; *Danny and His Thumb* by Kathryn F. Ernst, 1973; *David's Windows* by Alice Low, 1974; *The Star-Spangled Banana* edited by Charles Keller and Richard Baker, 1974; *Let's Find Out about Houses* by Martha and Charles Shapp, 1975; *Old Man Whickutt's Donkey* by Mary Calhoun, 1975; *This Is the Ambulance Leaving the Zoo,* 1975, and *Six Impossible Things Before Breakfast,* 1977, both by Norma Farber; *The Tyrannosaurus Game,* 1976, *Santa's Crash-Bang Christmas,* 1978, and *Fat Magic,* 1978, all by Steven Kroll; *If He's My Brother* by Barbara Williams, 1976; *Good Morning to You, Valentine,* 1976, *Beat the Drum, Independence Day Has Come,* 1977, and *Easter Buds Are Springing,* 1979, all edited by Lee Bennett Hopkins; *I Love You, Mouse* by John Graham, 1976; *The Whatchamacallit Book* by Bernice Kohn Hunt, 1976; *The Mixed-Up Mystery Smell* by Eleanor Coerr, 1976; *Let's Find Out about Summer* by Martha Shapp, 1976; *Can't You Make Them Behave, King George?,* 1977, *The Good Giants and the Bad Pukwudgies,* 1982, and *Shh! We're Writing the Constitution,* 1987, all by Jean Fritz; *Once upon a Dinkelsbühl,* 1977, and *The Little Friar Who Flew,* 1980, both by Patricia Lee Gauch; *The Ghost with the Halloween Hiccups,* 1977, *Funnyman's First Case,* 1981, and *Funnyman and Penny Dodo,* 1984, all by Stephen Mooser; *Simple Pictures Are Best,* 1977, and *The Mountains of Quilt,* 1987, both by Nancy Willard; *Odd Jobs,* 1977, *Four Scary Stories,* 1978, *Odd Jobs and Friends,* 1982, *The Vanishing Pumpkin,* 1983, *The Quilt Story,* 1985, and *Pages of Music,* 1988, all by Tony Johnston; *The Surprise Party,* 1977, *The Spooky Halloween Party,* 1981, and *Party Time for Nicky,* 1983, all by Annabelle Prager; *Solomon Grundy, Born on Oneday* by Malcolm E. Weiss, 1977; *The Giants' Farm,* 1977, and *The Giants Go Camping,* 1979, both by Jane Yolen; *The Christmas Pageant* (text from Bible), 1978; *Oh, Such Foolishness!* edited by William Cole, 1978; *Jamie's Tiger* by Jan Wahl, 1978; *Marc the Magnificent* by Sue Alexander, 1978; *Ghost Poems* edited by Daisy Wallace, 1979; *The Cat on the Dovrefell* translated by George Webbe Dasent, 1979; *My Daddy's Mustache* by Naomi Panush Salus, 1979; *The Triumphs of Fuzzy Fogtop* by Anne K. Rose, 1979; *The Night Before Christmas* by Clement C. Moore, 1980; *The Walking Coat* by Pauline Watson, 1980; *The Wuggie Norple Story* by Daniel Pinkwater, 1980; *Moon, Stars, Frogs, and Friends* by Patricia MacLachlan, 1980; *Edward, Benjamin, and Butter* by Malcolm Hall, 1981; *Robin Goodfellow and the Giant Dwarf* by Michael Jennings, 1981; *The Friendly Beasts: An Old English Christmas Carol,* 1981; *Nicholas Bentley Stoningpot III* by Ann McGovern, 1982; *Tattie's River Journey* by Shirley Rousseau Murphy, 1983; *The Carsick Zebra and Other*

Animal Riddles by David A. Adler, 1983; *The Mother Goose Frieze*, 1984; *Mother Goose Story Streamers*, 4 vols., 1984; *Mary Had a Little Lamb* by Sarah Josepha Hale, 1984; *The First Christmas*, 1984; *Country Farm*, 1984; *Miracle on 34th Street* by Valentine Davies, 1984; *Teeny Tiny* retold by Jill Bennett, 1986; *For Every Child a Star* by Thomas Yeomans, 1986; *The Kitten Kids*, 4 vols., 1986; *Maggie and the Monster* by Elizabeth Winthrop, 1987; *What the Mailman Brought* by Carolyn Craven, 1987; *Who's a Friend of the Water-Spurting Whale?* by Sanna Anderson Baker, 1987; *Petook* by Caryll Houselander, 1988; *Cookie's Week*, 1988, and *Caspar's Week*, 1989, both by Cindy Ward.

*   *   *

Tomie de Paola's creative brush and pen have fashioned more than 140 informational books, imaginative stories, realistic picture books, and folktales, gaining him recognition as a creative writer and illustrator and as a favorite choice of children. Though de Paola has been criticized for being too prolific, a close inspection signals versatility and a distinct style as the significant hallmarks of his work.

Humor, often an innate part of de Paola books, surfaces even in his concept books, a genre where amusement is too rarely found. Evidence can be noted in *The Quicksand Book*, which, while giving concise and factual details about Jungle Girl and her particular dilemma in the sinking mud, also tells a funny story. *The Popcorn Book* and *The Kids' Cat Book* are patterned in that same tradition.

De Paola's imaginative stories, such as the early *Helga's Dowry* and the more recent *Bill and Pete Go Down the Nile* also provide a showcase for the author-artist's nimble wit. A newly launched series for very young children entitled The Friendly Families of Fiddle-Dee-Dee Farms uses wordplay in both straightforward and subtle ways: the titles *Haircuts for the Woolseys* (about a family of sheep who get "haircuts" too early in the spring) and *Too Many Hopkins* (a large rabbit family who get in each other's way during spring planting) gives evidence of de Paola's delight in making children laugh.

But de Paola also has a serious side to his nature. This can be noted in his religious titles, *The Clown of God, Francis, The Poor Man of Assisi*, and *The Miracles of Jesus*, which are sensitive but not sentimental, thoughtful but not didactic. Recent folktales also demonstrate a somber note. *The Legend of the Bluebonnet* and *The Legend of the Indian Paintbrush*, both Indian legends, deal with sacrifice and personal courage. *Bluebonnet*, in which a young girl throws her doll into the fire to help bring rain to her starving people, is particularly compelling.

This serious strain also can be found in his realistic stories, which tend to be autobiographical. *Nana Upstairs and Nana Downstairs* and *Now One Foot, Now the Other* deal with aging and death and are based on childhood relationships with his own grandparents. *Oliver Button Is a Sissy* and *The Art Lesson* address name calling and student-teacher confrontations. It is rare for a children's author to reveal such personal details; it is to de Paola's credit that he does so, yet without any self-aggrandizement.

His folktales have not only generated some of the most serious attention accorded de Paola but also provide a generous stage for his wide-ranging talents. *Strega Nona* brought early recognition with a Caldecott Honor award. He has retold and illustrated folktales from both the Italian and Irish sides of his heritage and has also incorporated his own New England background into his Americana works. *The Night Before Christmas* and *Mary Had a Little Lamb*, which he illustrated, and *An Early American Christmas* evoke his interest in antique quilts, old houses, and 19th-century decorative objects. Concern with authenticity can be seen in the source notes provided, and in the latter book his careful choice of words and dialogue results in a tale that rings true.

The last years have seen three major anthologies, with material selected and illustrated by this prolific artist. Besides a collection of Christmas carols, he issued *Mother Goose* and *Favorite Nursery Tales*, as well as his own *Book of Poems*. Large diverse collections, they are all generously and lavishly illustrated with meaningful artwork that extends the written words. Perusal of these books shows the selections have been made carefully and thoughtfully, with the attention span, interest, and appeal of readers clearly in mind. The child de Paola once was shines through all his works, captivating readers and enriching the field of children's books.

—Barbara Elleman

---

de REGNIERS, Beatrice Schenk (née Freedman). Also writes as Tamara Kitt. American. Born in Lafayette, Indiana, 16 August 1914. Educated at the University of Illinois, Urbana, 1931–33; University of Chicago, Ph. B. 1935, and graduate student, 1936–37; University of Toulouse, 1935; the Sorbonne, Paris, 1935–36; Winnetka Graduate Teachers College, Illinois, M.Ed. 1941. Married Francis de Regniers in 1953. Member of the Eloise Moore Dance Group, Chicago, 1942–43; copywriter, Scott Foresman, publishers, Chicago, 1943–44; welfare officer, UNRRA, Egypt, 1944–46; copywriter, American Book Company, New York, 1948–49; director of educational materials, American Heart Association, New York, 1949–61; editor, Lucky Book Club, Scholastic Book Services, New York, 1961–81. Address: 180 West 58th Street, Apartment 5-A, New York, New York 10019, U.S.A.

PUBLICATIONS FOR CHILDREN

Fiction

The Giant Story, illustrated by Maurice Sendak.   New York, Harper, 1953.
A Little House of Your Own, illustrated by Irene Haas.   New York, Harcourt Brace, 1954; London, Collins, 1957.
A Child's Book of Dreams, illustrated by Bill Sokol.   New York, Harcourt Brace, 1957.
The Snow Party, illustrated by Reiner Zimnik.   New York, Pantheon, 1959; London, Faber, 1961.
What Happens Next: Adventures of a Hero, illustrated by Remo.   New York, Macmillan, 1959.
Who Likes the Sun?, illustrated by Leona Pierce.   New York, Harcourt Brace, 1961; London, Collins, 1962.
The Little Book, illustrated by the author.   New York, Walck, 1961; as *Going for a Walk*, New York, Harper, 1982.
The Little Girl and Her Mother, illustrated by Esther Gilman.   New York, Vanguard Press, 1963.
How Joe the Bear and Sam the Mouse Got Together, illustrated by Brinton Turkle.   New York, Parents' Magazine Press, 1965.
Penny, illustrated by Marvin Bileck.   New York, Viking Press, 1966.
The Giant Book, illustrated by William Lahey Cummings.   New York, Atheneum, 1966.
The Day Everybody Cried, illustrated by Nonny Hogrogian.   New York, Viking Press, 1967.
The Boy, The Rat, and the Butterfly, illustrated by Haig and Regina Shekerjian.   New York, Atheneum, 1971.
Laura's Story, illustrated by Jack Kent.   New York, Atheneum, 1979.
Waiting for Mama.   New York, Clarion, 1984.

Fiction as Tamara Kitt

The Adventures of Silly Billy, illustrated by Jill Elgar.   New York, Grosset and Dunlap, 1961; London, Muller, 1966.
The Secret Cat, illustrated by William Russell.   New York, Grosset and Dunlap, 1961.
Billy Brown Makes Something Grand, illustrated by Rosalind Welcher.   New York, Grosset and Dunlap, 1961; London, Muller, 1970.
Billy Brown the Baby Sitter, illustrated by Rosalind Welcher.   New York, Grosset and Dunlap, 1962; London, Muller, 1970.
The Surprising Pets of Billy Brown, illustrated by Rosalind Welcher.   New York, Grosset and Dunlap, 1962.
The Boy Who Fooled the Giant, illustrated by William Russell.   New York, Grosset and Dunlap, 1963; London, Muller, 1968.
The Boy, The Cat, and the Magic Fiddle, illustrated by William Russell.   New York, Grosset and Dunlap, 1964.
A Special Birthday Party for Someone Very Special, illustrated by Brinton Turkle.   New York, Norton, 1966.
Sam and the Impossible Thing, illustrated by Brinton Turkle.   New York, Norton, 1967.
Jake, illustrated by Brinton Turkle.   New York and London, Abelard Schuman, 1969.

Plays

Picture Book Theater: The Mysterious Stranger, and The Magic Spell, illustrated by William Lahey Cummings.   New York, Clarion, 1982.
Everyone Is Good for Something, from her own retelling of a Russian folktale (produced Louisville, Kentucky, 1986).

Verse

What Can You Do with a Shoe?, illustrated by Maurice Sendak.   New York, Harper, 1955.
Was It a Good Trade?, illustrated by Irene Haas.   New York, Harper, 1956; London, Collins, 1957.
Something Special, illustrated by Irene Haas.   New York, Harcourt Brace, 1958; London, Collins, 1959.
Cats Cats Cats Cats Cats, illustrated by Bill Sokol.   New York, Pantheon, 1958.
May I Bring a Friend?, illustrated by Beni Montresor.   New York, Atheneum, 1964; London, Collins, 1966.
Circus, photographs by Al Giese.   New York, Viking Press, 1966.
Willy O'Dwyer Jumped in the Fire: Variations on a Folk Rhyme, illustrated by Beni Montresor.   New York, Atheneum, 1968; London, Collins, 1970.
Catch a Little Fox: Variations on a Folk Rhyme, illustrated by Brinton Turkle.   New York, Seabury Press, 1970; London, Hamish Hamilton, 1971.
It Does Not Say Meow and Other Animal Riddle Rhymes, illustrated by Paul Galdone.   New York, Seabury Press, 1972; Kingswood, Surrey, World's Work, 1973.
Red Riding Hood, Retold in Verse..., illustrated by Edward Gorey.   New York, Atheneum, 1972; London, Collins, 1973.
A Bunch of Poems and Verses, illustrated by Mary Jane Dunton.   New York, Seabury Press, 1977.
Jack and the Beanstalk Retold in Verse, illustrated by Anne Wilsdorf.   New York, Atheneum, 1985.
So Many Cats!, illustrated by Ellen Weiss.   New York, Clarion, 1985.
This Big Cat, and Other Cats I've Known, illustrated by Alan Daniel.   New York, Crown, 1985.
A Week in the Life of Best Friends and Other Poems of Friendship, illustrated by Nancy Doyle.   New York, Atheneum, 1986.

Jack the Giant-Killer Retold in Verse, illustrated by Anne Wilsdorf.   New York, Atheneum, 1987.
The Way I Feel...Sometimes, illustrated by Susan Meddaugh.   New York, Clarion, 1988.

Other

The Shadow Book, photographs by Isabel Gordon.   New York, Harcourt Brace, 1960.
The Abraham Lincoln Joke Book, illustrated by William Lahey Cummings.   New York, Random House, 1965.
David and Goliath, illustrated by Richard Powers.   New York, Viking Press, 1965.
The Enchanted Forest: From a Story by La Comtesse de Ségur, illustrated by Gustave Doré and others.   New York, Atheneum, 1974.
Little Sister and the Month Brothers (Slav folktale), illustrated by Margot Tomes.   New York, Seabury Press, and London, Hamish Hamilton, 1976.
Everyone Is Good for Something (Russian folktale), illustrated by Margot Tomes.   New York, Clarion, 1980.

Editor, with Eva Moore and Mary M. White, *Poems Children Will Sit Still For: A Selection for Primary Grades.*   New York, Citation Press, 1969; revised edition, as *Sing a Song of Popcorn: Every Child's Book of Poems,* New York, Scholastic, 1988.

*   *   *

"Sometimes you just want everyone to leave you alone. No children. No grownups. Then it is a good thing to have a little house. A false face is a little house for your face."

Those lines from Beatrice Schenk de Regniers's *A Little House of Your Own* are marked by the deceptively simple style that characterizes her writing. On closer examination, one becomes aware of the pleasing rhythm, the precise choice of words, the genuinely childlike point-of-view, and the *speakability* of the lines. These are qualities that distinguish most of the more than 30 books for young children that de Regniers has written and published since 1953.

While unified in style, her output can be separated into several distinct categories. First there are the concept books, of which *A Little House of Your Own* is a notable example. Others in this group would include the poetic *Who Likes the Sun?, The Shadow Book* with its lovely blend of photographs and text, and *The Little Girl and Her Mother,* which gently describes what each can, and cannot, do and ends with the little girl growing up and becoming a mother herself.

Another category to which de Regniers has made some important contributions is that of the retold folk tale. In *Everyone Is Good for Something, Little Sister and the Month Brothers,* and *Red Riding Hood* she employs her gift for simple directness to achieve texts that young children can read by themselves, while at the same time maintaining an unobtrusive elegance—no mean accomplishment. And her original story *The Snow Party* adheres to many of the classic folk tale patterns as it recounts what happened when a bunch of snowbound people—and animals—turned what might have been a disaster into a frolic. *The Snow Party* is one of de Regniers's most unbridled, and most zestful, books.

The largest section in her body of work is comprised of picture book variations on folk rhymes, and original texts with the same lilting, musical quality. *What Can You Do with a Shoe?* is one of the most amusing and imaginative examples, and *Was It a Good Trade?, Catch a Little Fox,* and *It Does Not Say Meow* have their share of sparkling moments too. *Willy O'Dwyer Jumped in the Fire* seems too frail as a text, however, perhaps because Beni Montresor's pictures for it are so dark and heavy. Earlier, Montresor won the Caldecott Medal with another of de Regniers's texts in the folk rhyme genre, *May I Bring a Friend?* While this sustains a pleasingly gentle tone as it tells of all the animals that accompany a little boy on his visits to the King and Queen, it lacks some of the energy that infuses de Regniers's other songlike picture books.

In the 1980's de Regniers concentrated her energies on collections of original poems for children, most notably *A Week in the Life of Best Friends and Other Poems of Friendship* and *The Way I Feel...Sometimes.* The latter is a refreshingly honest exploration of the strong emotions, ranging from anger to jealousy to joy, that all children experience at one time or another. Her lasting affection for cats and their ways reveals itself in another collection of this period, *This Big Cat, and Other Cats I've Known,* and in her counting story told in verse, *So Many Cats!.*

Occupying a special place in de Regniers's *oeuvre* are the exceptions, books that fit into no particular category as they experiment with new forms and themes. *The Day Everybody Cried* explores feelings of sadness and happiness but stays on too abstract a level to make its point successfully. *Penny,* a modern reworking of the Thumbelina theme, is a fascinating attempt to create a miniature novel. And *The Boy, The Rat, and the Butterfly* attempts even more—a parable of life, death, and rebirth expressed through the relationship of the three title characters, all of whom are named Peter. "Now they are going down the road," the book ends. "The boy, the rat, and the butterflies. They don't seem to be going very far. And wherever they are going, they are not getting there very fast. And it doesn't matter, really."

There it is again—the deceptive simplicity that stamps so many of Beatrice de Regniers's books for children.

—James Cross Giblin

————

de ROO, Anne (Louise). New Zealander. Born in Gore in 1931. Educated at New Plymouth Girls' High School; University of Canterbury, Christchurch, 1949–52, B.A. 1952. Library assistant, Dunedin Public Library, 1956; assistant librarian, Dunedin Teachers' College, 1957–59; governess and part-time gardener, Church Preen, Shropshire, England, 1962–68; part-time secretary, Barkway, Hertfordshire, England, 1969–73; part-time medical typist, Palmerston North, New Zealand, 1974–78. Since 1978 full-time writer. Recipient: ICI bursary, 1981. Agent: A.P. Watt Ltd., 20 John Street, London WC1N 2DL, England. Address: 38 Joseph Street, Palmerston North, New Zealand.

PUBLICATIONS FOR CHILDREN

Fiction

The Gold Dog. London, Hart Davis, 1969.
Moa Valley. London, Hart Davis, 1969.
Boy and the Sea Beast, illustrated by Judith Anson. London, Hart Davis, 1971; New York, Scholastic, 1974.
Cinnamon and Nutmeg. London, Macmillan, 1972; Nashville, Nelson, 1974.
Mick's Country Cousins. London, Macmillan, 1974.
Scrub Fire. London, Heinemann, 1977; New York, Atheneum, 1980.
Traveller. London, Heinemann, 1979.
Because of Rosie. London, Heinemann, 1980.
Jacky Nobody. Auckland, Methuen, 1983; London, Methuen, 1984.

The Bats' Nest. Auckland and London, Hodder and Stoughton, 1986.
Friend Troll, Friend Taniwha, illustrated by R.H.G. Jahnke. Auckland and London, Hodder and Stoughton, 1986.

Plays

The Dragon Master, music by John Schwabe (produced Palmerston North, 1978).
The Silver Blunderbuss, music by John Schwabe (produced Palmerston North, 1984).

*

Anne de Roo comments:

As a child in New Zealand I had only books that told of strange faraway places where Christmas came in midwinter and children gathered bluebells in the woods in May. Books in fact that had nothing to do with the world I saw about me. Tales of strange distant places are fine and exciting and I like to think I provide them for English and American children—New Zealand is a new, wild place in which exciting things can still happen. But much more important to me are the New Zealand children who as well as strange stories of Christmas by the fireside instead of in the summer sunshine have a right to stories that belong to the world they see about them and to parts of their country they have not yet explored for themselves.

*   *   *

Anne de Roo's first book reveals a style which is unpretentious and sparing. *The Gold Dog* is a good, lively "yarn," skilfully constructed with vigorous scenes of outdoor adventure as children, following their own hunches, perform feats of courage. Set in a very authentic and distinctive part of New Zealand, the mountainous district of Central Otago, scene of the gold discoveries of Gabriel Read in 1861, the book describes a search for lost treasure. The most interesting part of the story concerns the reverberations of the area's romantic past when the old digger, Seb, wins the love and respect of the little community of Marston on the Oxburn.

Moa Valley is also set in the mountains in the southern part of the South Island of New Zealand. The book describes courage in the face of hardship when young people become lost in unexplored territory. An older man is again the focus of the story: Mr. Peacock dreams he will find a living moa, a giant flightless bird, long thought extinct.

Boy and the Sea Beast marks a stage when a new dimension enters her work. Up to this point, it is clear that de Roo is technically very effective but while the quality of suspense is strong, the solution to the action comes too easily and character is subordinated to the need for a happy ending. This is much less so in *Boy and the Sea Beast* which is about a child's friendship with a dolphin. The book is inspired by the charming stories of two famous dolphins, Pelorous Jack and Opo, who have been friends to man in New Zealand. Despite the very indifferent illustrations which in no way convey with accuracy the Maori or his environment, Boy-at-Last Rangi and his family who live in the far North of the North Island of New Zealand are spontaneous and vital people. The delightful dolphin, Thunder, is saved by Boy from exploitation but must finally leave for the free and wild life with his own kind.

This theme is extended and deepened in *Cinnamon and Nutmeg* and *Mick's Country Cousins,* two closely related stories of the lush rolling dairy lands of the North Island province of Taranaki in which characters matter far more than the adventures which follow from their predicaments. In the second novel, Mick has no father and, as a consequence, becomes unmanageable. Sent to wholesome surroundings in the country, he feels the tension between his old values and the newer ones on the farm. Significantly, it is the love of animals which has a large part in the development of a feeling for those around him.

Traveller and *Because of Rosie* show the author's mastery of the writing of the historical novel for children. *Traveller* is the effortlessly told story of the highly intelligent sheep dog which the legendary Mackenzie used in the South Island High Country of the 1850's. *Because of Rosie* describes a very different scene—that of the North Island bush of the Manawatu Plain in 1872. Though the theme is a well-used one—an orphaned family surviving amid the hardships of pioneering days in the bush—the author brings to it a sense of fresh vigour.

Scrub Fire is based on the wellworn theme of children lost in the bush. However, the author handles her material with a light touch even including humour within a tense drama of survival in the rugged North Island bush. Surehanded as ever in her characterisation, she does not fudge the near-fatal consequences of such a plight as the children struggle to conquer their fears and overcome their mistakes.

De Roo returned to history in the award-winning *Jacky Nobody* and its sequel *The Bats' Nest*. When the chief Hone Heke refers to Jacky as a relative he begins to realise he is not a *pakeha* boy who is kept and educated by a missionary as one of his own family. He is Maori, the son of an English sailor and a highborn Maori mother. Despite the pain of parting Jacky finally joins the Maori warriors and recognises them as his own people. The reader sees through the eyes of Jacky the frustrations that the Maori had with the Treaty of Waitangi, the cutting of the flag pole at Kororareka, defeat of the Redcoats at Ohaeawai, and the Maori defeat on a Sunday at Ruapekapeka. Frustrated by and disillusioned with the Treaty of Waitangi, Hone Heke takes what he considers to be peaceful means of protest. In the course of misunderstandings between Maori and European, violence erupts and many innocent people suffer. These carefully researched novels bring the past vividly back and show us how relevant such events are to the state of society in New Zealand today.

Friend Troll, Friend Taniwha demonstrates de Roo's versatility, for here she succeeds with fantasy firmly based on New Zealand soil. She brings together the Scandanavian giant and the Maori sea beast who enlist the support of the dolphins and the cheeky keas. Children will love the humour.

De Roo has moved a long distance from her early novels of adventure to works that delve deeply into the most important elements of life—love and laughter, loyalty and courage, peace and forgiveness.

—Tom Fitzgibbon

———

DESAI, Anita (née Mazumbar). Indian. Born in Mussoorie, 24 June 1937. Educated at Queen Mary's Higher Secondary School, New Delhi; Miranda House, Delhi University, B.A. (honours) in English literature 1957. Married Ashvin Desai in 1958; two sons and two daughters. Since 1972 member of the Sahitya Academy English Board. Recipient: Royal Society of Literature Winifred Holtby prize, for adult fiction, 1978; Sahitya Academy award, 1979; *Guardian* award, 1982. Fellow, Royal Society of Literature, 1978. Agent: Deborah Rogers Ltd., 20 Powis Mews, London W11 1JN, England.

PUBLICATIONS FOR CHILDREN

Fiction

The Peacock Garden.   Bombay, India Book House, 1974; London, Heinemann, 1979.

Cat on a Houseboat.   Bombay, Orient Longman, 1976.
The Village by the Sea.   London, Heinemann, 1982.

PUBLICATIONS FOR ADULTS

Novels

Cry, The Peacock.   Calcutta, Rupa, n.d.; London, Owen, 1963.
Voices in the City.   London, Owen, 1965.
Bye-Bye, Blackbird.   New Delhi, Hind, and Thompson, Connecticut, InterCulture, 1971.
Where Shall We Go This Summer?   New Delhi, Vikas, 1975.
Fire on the Mountain.   New Delhi, Allied, London, Heinemann, and New York, Harper, 1977.
Clear Light of Day.   New Delhi, Allied, London, Heinemann, and New York, Harper, 1980.
In Custody.   London, Heinemann, 1984; New York, Harper, 1985.
Baumgartner's Bombay.   London, Heinemann, 1988.

Short Stories

Games at Twilight and Other Stories.   New Delhi, Allied, and London, Heinemann, 1978; New York, Harper, 1980.

*

Critical Studies: *Indian Writing in English* by Paul Verghese, Bombay, Asia Publishing House, 1970; *Anita Desai: A Study of Her Fiction* by Meena Belliappa, Calcutta, Writers Workshop, 1971; *The Twice-Born Fiction* by Meenakshi Mukherjee, New Delhi, Arnold-Heinemann, 1972; *Indian Writing in English* by Srinivas Iyyengar, Bombay, Asia Publishing House, 1972; *The Novels of Mrs. Anita Desai* by B.R. Rao, New Delhi, Kalyani, 1977; *Anita Desai the Novelist* by Madhusudan Prasad, Allahabad, New Horizon, 1981; *Perspectives on Anita Desai,* edited by Ramesh K. Srivastava, Ghaziabad, Vimal, 1984.

*   *   *

Anita Desai is one of India's best contemporary writers. Her lucid and intelligent novels, such as *Clear Light of Day,* vividly evoke the atmosphere and landscape of India, but tend to focus more on the psychological and spiritual problems of her characters rather than social issues. Her children's books, on the other hand, change this emphasis slightly, and to good dramatic effect, while remaining faithful to a sympathetic appreciation of the inner lives of her characters.

The Peacock Garden, for example, tells the story of little Zuni and her Muslim family, who are forced to flee from their village in the race riots in Punjab in 1947. After a friendly Hindu leads them to the safety of a mosque, where the family contrives to make a temporary life for themselves, Zuni in particular discovers that what was apparently a place of confinement in the "silent walled garden" is in fact a place of interest and beauty. Though there is still much tragic news in store for Zuni's family, life gradually returns to normal, and it is both realistically and symbolically appropriate that the story should end after the garden's pea-hen has produced chicks, with a richly described party of royal peacocks. This is a charming book with deeper resonances than its apparently simple format in Longman's *Long Ago* series would suggest.

The Village by the Sea is even more socially explicit, for this is the story of the tribulations of Lila and Hari, the eldest daughter and the only son of a poor family living in a small fishing village on the west coast of India. Their mother is seriously ill and their out-of-work father spends most of his time drunk. Seeing no way out of their poverty, Lila and Hari struggle desperately to keep their family together. Faced with a choice between joining the declining fishing industry or waiting for a new factory to open, Hari escapes to Bombay and, though overwhelmed by his initial experiences, gradually learns to survive, while his gentle sister Lila manages to cope at home by working as a servant for a family of wealthy holiday visitors. Matters gradually improve, and when Hari returns from the city with plans for the future, the story comes to a satisfactory conclusion.

Desai sets her simple but absorbing story in a deftly realised social context where a primitive economy will be followed by an equally harsh industrial one unless people can learn to adapt to the changes and master them. The story creates a vivid picture both of family life and the struggle to survive in a small village, and the hustle and bustle of Bombay whose slums are described in almost Dickensian terms. The central characters command complete sympathy, and the minor characters—Biju the rich fisherman, Jagu the restaurant owner, Mr. Panwallah the clock mender—gradually take on a life of their own. If the need to adapt is insisted upon a little too didactically in places, and the philanthropic de Silva family are a little too good to be true, there is an overall honesty and warmth about the story which more than compensates.

An intelligent, compassionate, perceptive, Indian novelist, more complex than R.K. Narayan, more direct than Salman Rushdie, Desai has written attractive children's books which engage with some of the most difficult problems of our time, issues that extend beyond the Third World.

—Dennis Butts

de TREVIÑO, Elizabeth Borton. American. Born in Bakersfield, California, 2 September 1904. Educated at Stanford University, California, B.A. 1925 (Phi Beta Kappa); Boston Conservatory of Music. Married Luis Treviño Gomez in 1935; two sons (one deceased). Reporter, *Jamaica Plain Journal,* Boston, 1927–28; apprentice in production and advertising, Ginn and Company, publishers, Boston, 1928–31; interviewer, Boston *Herald American,* 1930–34; publicist, Mexico City Tourist Department, Mexican National Railways, and Mexican National Symphony, 1942–52; violinist, Vivaldi Orchestra, Mexico City, 1962–67. Recipient: American Library Association Newbery Medal, 1966. Agent: Mrs. Ray Pierre Corsini, 12 Beekman Place, New York, New York 10022, U.S.A. Address: Apartado Postal 827, Cuernavaca, Morelos, Mexico.

PUBLICATIONS FOR CHILDREN

Fiction

Pollyanna in Hollywood, illustrated by H. Weston Taylor. Boston, Page, 1931.
Our Little Aztec Cousin of Long Ago, Being the Story of Coyotl and How He Won Honor under His Kings, illustrated by Harold Cue. Boston, Page, 1934.
Pollyanna's Castle in Mexico, illustrated by Harold Cue. Boston, Page, 1934.
Our Little Ethiopian Cousin: Children of the Queen of Sheba. Boston, Page, 1935.
Pollyanna's Door to Happiness, illustrated by Harold Cue. Boston, Page, 1936.
Pollyanna's Golden Horseshoe, illustrated by Griswold Tyng.

Boston, Page, 1939.
About Bellamy, illustrated by Jessie Robinson. New York, Harper, 1940.
Pollyanna and the Secret Mission, illustrated by Harold Cue. Boston, Page, 1951.
A Carpet of Flowers, illustrated by Alan Crane. New York, Crowell, 1955; Kingswood, Surrey, World's Work, 1956.
Nacar, The White Deer, illustrated by Enrico Arno. New York, Farrar Straus, 1963; Kingswood, Surrey, World's Work, 1964.
I, Juan de Pareja. New York, Farrar Straus, 1965; London Gollancz, 1966.
Casilda of the Rising Moon: A Tale of Magic and of Faith, of Knights and a Saint in Medieval Spain. New York, Farrar Straus, 1967; London, Gollancz, 1968.
Turi's Poppa. New York, Farrar Straus, 1968; as *Turi's Papa,* London, Gollancz, 1969.
Beyond the Gates of Hercules: A Tale of the Lost Atlantis. New York, Farrar Straus, and London, Gollancz, 1971.
El Güero. New York, Farrar Straus, 1989.

Other

Here Is Mexico. New York, Farrar Straus, 1970.

PUBLICATIONS FOR ADULTS

Novels

Even As You Love. New York, Crowell, 1957.
The Greek of Toledo: A Romantic Narrative about El Greco. New York, Crowell, 1959.
The Fourth Gift. New York, Doubleday, 1966.
The House on Bitterness Street. New York, Doubleday, 1970.
The Music Within. New York, Doubleday, 1973.
The Heart Possessed: A Love Story. New York, Doubleday, 1978.
Among the Innocent. New York, Doubleday, 1981.

Other

My Heart Lies South: The Story of My Mexican Marriage. New York, Crowell, 1953.
Where the Heart Is (memoirs). New York, Doubleday, 1962.
Juarez, Man of Law. New York, Farrar Straus, 1974.
The Hearthstone of My Heart (memoirs). New York, Doubleday, 1977.

*

Manuscript Collection: Boston University Library.

Critical Study: *Mexico in the Work of Elizabeth Borton de Treviño* by Patricia Vickers, unpublished dissertation, Christian College, Lubbock, Texas, 1976.

Elizabeth Borton de Treviño comments:

All my books enclose a little kernel of truth … something that really happened. *Nacar, The White Deer* enlarges upon a note in the history of the Manila galleon, the Spanish vessel that plied between the Orient and Acapulco, New Spain (now Mexico). According to the note, at one time the great ship carried across the Pacific a beautiful albino deer, which was reshipped from Veracruz to Spain as a gift for the king. *I, Juan de Pareja* retells the story of the lifelong friendship and regard of the famous Spanish painter Velasquez and his Negro slave, Juan; Juan taught himself to paint, in secret, and later Velasquez freed him and made him his assistant. *Casilda of the Rising Moon* recounts the story of a young Moorish princess of Spain in the 11th century who became a Christian convert and a saint. *Turi's Poppa* is the tale of a small boy and his father who walked halfway across Europe so that the father could take up a position as a violin-maker in Cremona, Italy. *Here Is Mexico* explores historical and contemporary Mexico, revealing a potpourri of truths and legends which combine to give this country its unique flavor.

At the same time, each of my stories tries to show some phase of love, that powerful emotion "which makes the world go round." *Nacar, The White Deer* portrays the love between a child and a gentle wild creature, the deer. *I, Juan de Pareja* shows the strong affection and esteem that can exist between persons of different races. *Casilda of the Rising Moon* is a study of the way in which the love of God may express itself in compassion for all living things. *Turi's Poppa* tells of the love between a boy and his father, and *Here Is Mexico* is an account of my beloved adopted country.

*   *   *

"All my life," writes Elizabeth Borton de Treviño, "I have been fascinated by imaginative speculation," and each of her stories is such a speculation, triggered off by some legend or historical incident.

Of her books, *I, Juan de Pareja* has had most acclaim. It is based on Velasquez's paintings, and on the known facts of his life, but the hero is Juanico, his slave, who tells the story. It is an unusual and memorable book, concerned with the problems and frustrations of slavery, and the parallel constraints imposed on artistic freedom by the requirements of court convention. Tolerance, understanding, and love of art and truth are its moral values, as exemplified by Velasquez himself, whose words, "Art should be Truth, and Truth, unadorned, unsentimentalised, is Beauty," lie at the centre of the book.

This attitude is explicit also in *Beyond the Gates of Hercules*, a tale of the lost Atlantis which becomes, finally, a modern moral fable. The Atlanteans are deeply religious, and committed to the civilised peaceful way of life, though one might question here their uncritical acceptance of voluntary human sacrifice to the angry Seagod. The story elaborates the idyllic life of Atlantis in a Golden Age of mutual understanding and co-operation, though its happiness is soon shot through with trouble and anxiety as events move inexorably forward. For Baka, lacking the intuitive thought-reading powers of his people, becomes a scientist, and eventually, to compensate for his increasing alienation from his family, an aggressive powerseeker. He turns his master's potentially good invention to evil use, becomes a military dictator, and Atlantis is destroyed. Its fate is clearly a warning to the Atomic Age, but the diagnosis of its ills is too superficial and simplistic. The book has charm, all the same.

Turi's Poppa, though set in post-war Europe, with echoes of its confusions and distresses, is less fraught with warnings. Turi is half gypsy. After his mother's death he and his father, a penniless violin-maker, walk to Italy where work is waiting. Turi's gypsy lore and cunning, though of great help on the journey and in encounters with border guards, are also a source of trouble and distress: the conflicting attitudes and values of father and son are recounted with engaging simplicity, though with some of the lapses into sentimentality which so mar *Casilda of the Rising Moon.* This latter book tells the legendary story of a frail, suffering, sensitive Moorish princess, whose faith transforms her into an incredibly enduring and miracle-working saint. But the writing is strained and over-insistent, and the story remains a fervidly romantic idealisation which contrasts unfavourably with the calmer achievements of the other books. *Nacar, The White Deer* is a more appealing story, with its loving and detailed account of pastoral life in 17th-century Mexico, exciting encounters with snakes and brigands, a voyage to Spain, and a climax in which the hitherto dumb hero makes an impassioned plea for the life of his

deer, now threatened with a sacrificial role in a glorious royal hunt. This story, too, is concerned to extol and defend the gentler things of life against violence and greed: a theme which runs through all these stories, and which, in spite of the sentimentality which sometimes creeps in, remains refreshing and appealing to the sensitive, thoughtful young reader.

—Winifred Whitehead

DHONDY, Farrukh. Indian. Born in Poona, Bombay, in 1944. Educated at Wadia College, Poona, B.Sc.; Cambridge University, 1964–67, B.A. in English 1967; University of Leicester, M.A. in English. English teacher, Henry Thornton comprehensive school, Clapham, London; teacher, later head of English, Archbishop Temple School, Lambeth, London, 1974–80. Since 1985 commissioning editor, Channel Four Television, London. Recipient: Children's Rights Workshop Other award, 1977, 1979; Beckett prize, for television play, 1984. Address: c/o Channel Four, 60 Charlotte Street, London W1P 2AX, England.

PUBLICATIONS FOR CHILDREN

Fiction

East End at Your Feet. London, Macmillan, 1976.
The Siege of Babylon. London, Macmillan, 1978.
Come to Mecca and Other Stories. London, Collins, 1978.
Poona Company. London, Gollancz, 1980.
Trip Trap. London, Gollancz, 1982.

PUBLICATIONS FOR ADULTS

Plays

Mama Dragon (produced London, 1980).
Shapesters (produced London, 1981).
Trojans, adaptation of a play by Euripides (produced London, 1982).
Kipling Sahib (produced London, 1982).
Romance, Romance; and The Bride. London, Faber, 1985.
Vigilantes (produced London, 1985). London, Hobo, 1988.
All the Fun of the Fair, with John McGrath and others (produced London, 1986).
Film, Film, Film (produced London, 1986).

Television Plays: *Maids the Mad Shooter,* 1981; *No Problem* series, with Mustapha Matura, 1983; *Good at Art,* 1983; *Dear Manju,* 1983; *The Bride,* 1983; *Salt on a Snake's Tail,* 1983; *Come to Mecca,* 1983; *Romance, Romance,* 1983; *The Empress and the Munshi,* 1984; *Tandoori Nights* series, 1985; *King of the Ghetto,* 1986; *To Turn a Blind Eye,* 1986.

Other

The Black Explosion in British Schools, with Barbara Beese and Leila Hassan. London, Race Today, 1982.

*   *   *

Farrukh Dhondy established a formidable reputation with his first three books as an accurate and incisive recorder of café and street life in multi-cultural Britain. In the stories of *East End at Your Feet* and *Come to Mecca* and his novel *The Siege of Babylon* he demonstrated a rare ability to express racial differences in the texture of his language, and to make them his subject matter without becoming strident or simplistic. He is, indeed, one of the few writers in Britain who has been able to approach such subjects unselfconsciously. The spare, laconic style he adopts enables him to imply much which other writers would feel the need to explain, defend, or discuss. Instead he takes his reader inside a situation, inviting him to overhear the story as one might eavesdrop on the speakers at a neighbouring table. He has an acute ear for dialogue, but his success depends most on his gift for construction, shaping his stories as a series of interrelated scenes rather than as a steady progression to a climax. The result is poetic intensity combined with compulsive readability. There is also a certain teasing relationship with the reader, which in *Trip Trap* has degenerated into sterile formal games and narrative twists.

The title story of *Come to Mecca* is typical in its range and economy. Bengali youths on strike against a wage-cut in the East End rag trade sweatshop in which they work are taken up by a radical white girl, Betty. Shahid, who organised the strike, falls innocently in love with her, only to discover that he has misinterpreted all her gestures of friendship. She sees him, with infinite patronage, as a representative of his race, not as an individual. She is just as much an exploiter as his mercenary employer. All this is conveyed with great subtlety and restraint: there is no sloganising, because Dhondy, unlike Betty, is more interested in the individual than the cause. And concentrating on individuals brings, inevitably, a refreshing humour in even his most troubled stories.

But in *The Siege of Babylon*—a tense, passionately felt, and tightly organised story about black youths at the end of their tether holding four hostages after a failed robbery—Dhondy finds no cause to smile. His depiction of the suppressed violence underlying the aimless, frustrated lives of his characters is entirely convincing, in a narrative which is brilliantly layered to explore the implications and resonances of what could have been either a political tract or a mindless police drama. In the end the only moral is that of all Dhondy's writing: "Language is identity."

Dhondy's fourth and best book, *Poona Company*, is set in India, and draws on his own childhood memories. It is an intelligent, strictly disciplined book, in which not a word is wasted. But more than that it is told with real flair and enjoyment, so that the busy, spicy atmosphere of the Chowk, the Poona bazaar, and the musty eccentricity of the stiff parody of an English public school which Dhondy attended come across with vivid force. "Black Dog" is a typically sure story, with a supernatural tinge: details of the feud between a local family and blind beggar and his dog are relayed through the scabrous, scrupulously notated voices of Chowk gossip.

Dhondy's current energies seem directed more towards theatre and television than prose fiction, and his subsequent collection *Trip Trap* has little of the concentration and verve of *Poona Company*.

—Neil Philip

DICKINSON, Peter (Malcolm de Brissac). British. Born in Livingstone, Northern Rhodesia (now Zambia), 16 December 1927. Educated at Eton College (King's scholar), 1941–46; King's College, Cambridge (exhibitioner), B.A. 1951. Served in the British Army, 1946–48. Married Mary Rose Barnard in 1953 (died 1988); two daughters and two sons. Assistant editor and reviewer, *Punch*, London, 1952–69. Chairman, Society of Authors Management Committee, 1978–80. Recipient: Crime Writers Association Gold Dagger, 1968, 1969; *Guardian* award, 1977; Boston *Globe-Horn*

Book award, for non-fiction, 1977; Whitbread award, 1979; Library Association Carnegie Medal, 1980, 1981. Agent: A.P. Watt Ltd., 20 John Street, London WC1N 2DL. Address: Brendeen Lodge, near Alresford, Hampshire SO24 0JN, England.

PUBLICATIONS FOR CHILDREN

Fiction

The Changes. London, Gollancz, 1975.
    The Weathermonger. London, Gollancz, 1968; Boston, Little Brown, 1969.
    Heartsease, illustrated by Robert Hales. London, Gollancz, and Boston, Little Brown, 1969.
    The Devil's Children, illustrated by Robert Hales. London, Gollancz, and Boston, Little Brown, 1970.
Emma Tupper's Diary. London, Gollancz, and Boston, Little Brown, 1971.
The Dancing Bear, illustrated by David Smee. London, Gollancz, 1972; Boston, Little Brown, 1973.
The Iron Lion, illustrated by Marc Brown. Boston, Little Brown, 1972; London, Allen and Unwin, 1973.
The Gift, illustrated by Gareth Floyd. London, Gollancz, 1973; Boston, Little Brown, 1974.
The Blue Hawk, illustrated by David Smee. London, Gollancz, and Boston, Little Brown, 1976.
Annerton Pit. London, Gollancz, and Boston, Little Brown, 1977.
Hepzibah, illustrated by Sue Porter. Twickenham, Middlesex, Eel Pie, 1978; Boston, Godine, 1980.
Tulku. London, Gollancz, and New York, Dutton, 1979.
The Seventh Raven. London, Gollancz, and New York, Dutton, 1981.
Healer. London, Gollancz, 1983; New York, Delacorte Press, 1985.
Giant Cold, illustrated by Alan Cober. London, Gollancz, and New York, Dutton, 1984.
A Box of Nothing, illustrated by Ian Newsham. London, Gollancz, 1985; New York, Delacorte Press, 1987.
Mole Hole, illustrated by Jean Claverie. London, Blackie, and New York, Bedrick, 1987.
Eva. London, Gollancz, 1988; New York, Delacorte Press, 1989.
Merlin Dreams, illustrated by Alan Lee. London, Gollancz, and New York, Delacorte Press, 1988.

Plays

Television Series: *Mandog,* 1972.

Other

Chance, Luck and Destiny (miscellany), illustrated by David Smee and Victor Ambrus. London, Gollancz, 1975; Boston, Little Brown, 1976.
City of Gold and Other Stories from the Old Testament, illustrated by Michael Foreman. London, Gollancz, and New York, Pantheon, 1980.

Editor, *Presto! Humorous Bits and Pieces.* London, Hutchinson, 1975.
Editor, *Hundreds and Hundreds.* London, Penguin, 1984.

PUBLICATIONS FOR ADULTS

Novels

Skin Deep. London, Hodder and Stoughton, 1968; as *The Glass-*

Sided Ants' Nest, New York, Harper, 1968.

A Pride of Heroes.   London, Hodder and Stoughton, 1969; as *The Old English Peep Show,* New York, Harper, 1969.

The Seals.   London, Hodder and Stoughton, 1970; as *The Sinful Stones,* New York, Harper, 1970.

Sleep and His Brother.   London, Hodder and Stoughton, and New York, Harper, 1971.

The Lizard in the Cup.   London, Hodder and Stoughton, and New York, Harper, 1972.

The Green Gene.   London, Hodder and Stoughton, and New York, Pantheon, 1973.

The Poison Oracle.   London, Hodder and Stoughton, and New York, Pantheon, 1974.

The Lively Dead.   London, Hodder and Stoughton, and New York, Pantheon, 1975.

King and Joker.   London, Hodder and Stoughton, and New York, Pantheon, 1976.

Walking Dead.   London, Hodder and Stoughton, 1977; New York, Pantheon, 1978.

One Foot in the Grave.   London, Hodder and Stoughton, 1979; New York, Pantheon, 1980.

A Summer in the Twenties.   London, Hodder and Stoughton, and New York, Pantheon, 1981.

The Last House-Party.   London, Bodley Head, and New York, Pantheon, 1982.

Hindsight.   London, Bodley Head, and New York, Pantheon, 1983.

Death of a Unicorn.   London, Bodley Head, and New York, Pantheon, 1984.

Tefuga.   London, Bodley Head, and New York, Pantheon, 1986.

Perfect Gallows.   London, Bodley Head, and New York, Pantheon, 1988.

Other

The Flight of Dragons, illustrated by Wayne Anderson.   London, Pierrot, and New York, Harper, 1979.

*

Peter Dickinson comments:

My purpose in writing a children's book is to tell a story, and everything else is secondary to that; but when secondary considerations arise they have to be properly dealt with. Apart from that I like my stories exciting and as different as possible from the one I wrote last time. When I write for children I'm conscious of doing a different sort of thing from what I do when I write for adults, but that doesn't mean I'm writing down. Place and feel, even of imaginary landscapes, are important to me, nuances of character less so. Most of my books have an element of fantasy in them, but where this happens I try to deal with the subject in as practical and logical a way as possible.

*   *   *

Peter Dickinson arrived on the children's book scene in 1969, and by spring of the following year could be regarded as established and successful. His first three books were published within a few months of one another and were received with the highest praise. Perhaps they were overpraised. Yet this acclamation, if not entirely justified at the time, has been fully earned by Dickinson's later work, which has increased in depth and power.

The first three books were all about the Changes: a time which the author describes as "now, or soon," when people in England have turned against machinery and gone back to a dark age of ignorance and malice. The three could be called a trilogy in reverse, for the first, *The Weathermonger,* tells how the Changes ended; the second,

Heartsease, comes in the middle, and the last, *The Devil's Children,* describes what happened at the beginning. In *The Weathermonger* two children, Geoffrey and Sally, having escaped from benighted England to France, are sent back to find out what is going on. After a dash across country in a superb 1909 Rolls-Royce, borrowed from the Beaulieu motor museum, they track down the source of the Changes. This, implausibly, is the famous magician Merlin of Arthurian legend, who has been revived but is lying in a drug-sick condition, in which his powerful but distorted mind is having drastic effects on the land and on the mentality of its people. The children persuade him to give up the drug, and he returns to his long rest. Wisely, in the other two books the author says no more about Merlin, and presents the Changes without explanation, as a background for adventure and for some shrewd perceptions about human nature. *Heartsease,* the best of the three, tells how a group of young people rescue a "witch"—a young man who has been stoned and left for dead—and smuggle him away on board an old tugboat. In *The Devil's Children* a girl called Nicola, who herself experiences the revulsion against machinery which in the other books has been seen from outside, is adopted by a group of Sikhs who are unaffected by the Changes but are in danger from the hostility of those around them.

Taken together, these three books form rather a mixed achievement; so do a further three of Dickinson's novels, all of which have contemporary settings but are tinged in varying degrees with fantasy. *Emma Tupper's Diary* is a holiday adventure story in which an attempt to hoax the television people by producing a phoney monster in a loch is overtaken by the discovery that the loch does in fact have astonishing unknown inhabitants. In *The Gift* a boy with a form of second sight sees the pictures formed in the minds of people near him, and finds himself looking at the contents of a violently disordered, criminal mind; in *Annerton Pit* a blind boy, his blindness now no handicap, leads his brother and grandfather to safety from abandoned mine-workings, and in the course of the escape appears to make mental contact with an infinitely strange being that inhabits the mined land.

Peter Dickinson's best work for young people in the 1970's consisted of three novels with distant and indeed exotic settings. *The Dancing Bear* opens in Byzantium in the 6th century A.D. After a great household has been raided by Huns, a young slave called Silvester sets out with Holy John, the dirty old resident saint, and Bubba the bear, on a perilous mission to Hunnish lands. This is a close-textured, vigorous, and often very funny story; and the contrast between the devious intricacies of Byzantium and the brutal simplicity of life among the Huns is effectively drawn. Silvester, though able and resourceful, thinks as a slave and knows his place. It takes a formal manumission to persuade him that in his adventurings he has become a free man and can have the girl he wants.

The setting of *The Blue Hawk* is a country that strongly suggests ancient Egypt, though the time (unstated) seems more likely to be the remote future than the remote past. It is a society run largely by priests in the name of the Gods: a society in which there are rigid rules for everything, and nothing can ever change. A boy priest called Tron, rashly interrupting the ritual sacrifice of a blue hawk, comes into companionship with the young, active, but threatened King, and helps to open up the sealed, static land. There is deep ambiguity in Tron, a boy unsure to whom he owes his allegiance; and there are even deeper mysteries surrounding the Gods. Do they exist, and, if so, what are they really like?

Concern with the nature of religious belief is also a feature of *Tulku,* winner of the Carnegie Medal and of a Whitbread award. Theodore, escaping from a gutted missionary settlement in China at the time of the Boxer Rebellion, accompanies rich flower-collector Mrs. Jones and her guide Lung, soon to be her lover, to Tibet. At the great monastery of Dong Pe, Mrs. Jones's unborn child is declared by the ruling Lama Amchi to be the Tulku, reincarnation of a great lama. Attempts at escape and assassination are among the complex action that follows; the book is compelling enough if simply read at surface level; but even more complex than the action are the questions of truth and illusion, belief and pretence, sincerity and cynical manipulation.

With *The Seventh Raven* Dickinson returns to the contemporary world. Kensington children, rehearsing in church an original opera based on the story of the prophet Elijah, are held hostage by revolutionaries from a repulsive South American dictatorship. The subject was, and remains, topical, but after the hostages are seized the situation becomes too static and there is too much talk. Oddly perhaps, the best feature of this book is a brilliant evocation of the excitement and chaos of an amateur production.

Healer, like the earlier *The Gift* and *Annerton Pit,* exemplifies Dickinson's interest in the paranormal. A small girl called Pinkie Proudfoot has a gift of healing and is exploited by a charlatan called Freeman, who gets large sums from afflicted people for his phony Foundation of Harmony. 16-year-old Barry, whom Pinkie cured of his migraines years ago, plans to rescue her, and his doing so is the main action of the plot. But there is also an inner drama of Barry's personality, for he feels he has another being inside himself, whom he calls Bear: animal, violent, liable to get out of control, and almost causing him to kill Freeman. Pinkie's parting gift to Barry is to make whole his divided personality; a fine concluding passage shows that he has integrated Bear into himself.

The human-animal dichotomy, in starker form, is at the heart of *Eva*; for 13-year-old Eva, her body wrecked in a car crash some time in the future, has had her mind transferred into the body of a chimpanzee. She is human yet partly chimp, with a chimp's instincts and behaviour patterns and a need to be with other chimps. This is an ingenious piece of speculative writing that makes convincing the perilous imaginative leap into the animal consciousness.

In *Merlin Dreams* Dickinson returns after 20 years to the great magician who figured in his first book for young people. Brief poetic chapters in which, from time to time, the old enchanter stirs in his sleep beneath the rock where he is forever buried are interleaved with longer chapters, presumably his dreams. These tell vivid tales of the age of chivalry in which familiar themes—knightly encounters, rescues of damsels, combats with monsters—are enacted by credible, flesh-and-blood people. It is a handsome, large-format book to which evocative and splendidly atmospheric illustrations by Alan Lee make a major contribution.

—John Rowe Townsend

DILLON, Eilís. Irish. Born in Galway, 7 March 1920. Educated at Ursuline Convent, Sligo. Married 1) Cormac O Cuilleanain in 1940 (died 1970), one son and two daughters; 2) the writer Vivian Mercier in 1974. Lecturer in Creative Writing, Trinity College, Dublin, 1971–72. Fellow, Royal Society of Literature. Agent: David Bolt Associates, 12 Heath Drive, Send, Surrey GU23 7EP, England; or, Georges Borchardt Inc., 136 East 57th Street, New York, New York 10022, U.S.A. Address: 7 Templemore Avenue, Rathgar, Dublin 6, Ireland.

PUBLICATIONS FOR CHILDREN

Fiction

An Choill Bheo (The Live Forest). Dublin, Government Publication Sale Office, 1948.
Midsummer Magic, illustrated by Stuart Tresilian. London, Macmillan, 1950.
Oscar agus an Cóiste Sé nEasóg (Oscar and the Six-Weasel Coach).

Dublin, Government Publication Sale Office, 1952.
The Lost Island, illustrated by Richard Kennedy. London, Faber, 1952; New York, Funk and Wagnalls, 1954.
The San Sebastian, illustrated by Richard Kennedy. London, Faber, 1953; New York, Funk and Wagnalls, 1954.
Ceol na Coille (The Song of the Forest). Dublin, Government Publication Sale Office, 1955.
The House on the Shore, illustrated by Richard Kennedy. London, Faber, 1955; New York, Funk and Wagnalls, 1956.
The Wild Little House, illustrated by V.H. Drummond. London, Faber, 1955; New York, Criterion, 1957.
The Island of Horses, illustrated by Richard Kennedy. London, Faber, 1956; New York, Funk and Wagnalls, 1957.
Plover Hill, illustrated by Prudence Seward. London, Hamish Hamilton, 1957.
Aunt Bedelia's Cats, illustrated by Christopher Brooker. London, Hamish Hamilton, 1958.
The Singing Cave, illustrated by Richard Kennedy. London, Faber, 1959; New York, Funk and Wagnalls, 1960.
The Fort of Gold, illustrated by Richard Kennedy. London, Faber, and New York, Funk and Wagnalls, 1961.
King Big-Ears, illustrated by Kveta Vanecek. London, Faber, 1961; New York, Norton, 1963.
A Pony and a Trap, illustrated by Monica Brasier-Creagh. London, Hamish Hamilton, 1962.
The Cats' Opera, illustrated Kveta Vanecek. London, Faber, 1962; Indianapolis, Bobbs Merrill, 1963.
The Coriander, illustrated by Richard Kennedy. London, Faber, 1963; New York, Funk and Wagnalls, 1964.
A Family of Foxes, illustrated by Richard Kennedy. London, Faber, 1964; New York, Funk and Wagnalls, 1965.
The Sea Wall, illustrated by Richard Kennedy. London, Faber, and New York, Farrar Straus, 1965.
The Lion Cub, illustrated by Richard Kennedy. London, Hamish Hamilton, 1966; New York, Duell, 1967.
The Road to Dunmore, illustrated by Richard Kennedy. London, Faber, 1966.
The Cruise of the Santa Maria, illustrated by Richard Kennedy. London, Faber, and New York, Funk and Wagnalls, 1967.
The Key, illustrated by Richard Kennedy. London, Faber, 1967.
Two Stories: The Road to Dunmore and The Key, illustrated by Richard Kennedy. New York, Meredith Press, 1968.
The Seals, illustrated by Richard Kennedy. London, Faber, 1968; New York, Funk and Wagnalls, 1969.
Under the Orange Grove, illustrated by Richard Kennedy. London, Faber, 1968; New York, Meredith Press, 1969.
A Herd of Deer, illustrated by Richard Kennedy. London, Faber, 1969; New York, Funk and Wagnalls, 1970.
The Wise Man on the Mountain, illustrated by Gaynor Chapman. London, Hamish Hamilton, 1969; New York, Atheneum, 1970.
The Voyage of Mael Duin, illustrated by Alan Howard. London, Faber, 1969.
The King's Room, illustrated by Richard Kennedy. London, Hamish Hamilton, 1970.
The Five Hundred, illustrated by Gareth Floyd. London, Hamish Hamilton, 1972.
The Shadow of Vesuvius. New York, Nelson, 1977; London, Faber, 1978.
Down in the World, illustrated by Richard Kennedy. London, Hodder and Stoughton, 1983.
The Horse-Fancier. London, Macmillan, 1985.
The Seekers. New York, Scribner, 1986.

Play

The Cats' Opera, adaptation of her own story (produced Dublin, 1981).

Other

Living in Imperial Rome, illustrated by Richard Kennedy. London, Faber, 1974; as *Rome under the Emperors,* Nashville, Nelson, 1975.

Editor, *The Hamish Hamilton Book of Wise Animals,* illustrated by Bernard Brett. London, Hamish Hamilton, 1975.
Editor, with others, *The Lucky Bag: Classic Irish Children's Stories,* illustrated by Martin Gale. Dublin, O'Brien Press, 1985.

PUBLICATIONS FOR ADULTS

Novels

Death at Crane's Court. London, Faber, 1953; New York, Walker, 1963.
Sent to His Account. London, Faber, 1954; New York, Walker, 1969.
Death in the Quadrangle. London, Faber, 1956; New York, Walker, 1968.
The Bitter Glass. London, Faber, 1958; New York, Appleton Century Crofts, 1959.
The Head of the Family. London, Faber, 1960.
Bold John Henebry. London, Faber, 1965.
Across the Bitter Sea. New York, Simon and Schuster, 1973; London, Hodder and Stoughton, 1974.
Blood Relations. London, Hodder and Stoughton, and New York, Simon and Schuster, 1978.
Wild Geese. New York, Simon and Schuster, 1980; London, Hodder and Stoughton, 1981.
Citizen Burke. London, Hodder and Stoughton, 1984.
The Interloper. London, Hodder and Stoughton, 1987.

Plays

A Page of History (produced Dublin, 1966).

Radio Play: *Manna,* 1960.

Other

Inside Ireland, photographs by Tom Kennedy. London, Hodder and Stoughton, 1982; New York, Beaufort, 1984.

*

Eilís Dillon comments:

I began to write at a very early age and so unselfconsciously that it was almost inevitable that I should begin by writing children's books. I work on them exactly as I do on adult fiction, concentrating on character and background rather than on plot, but usually find that a strong story soon develops. Almost all of my books for children have a strong Irish background and have their source in my knowledge of the Irish language. The exceptions are set in Italy, where I lived for six years.

*   *   *

Though some of her books for younger readers, notably *Under the Orange Grove* and *The Five Hundred,* are set in Italy, Eilís Dillon is best known as a writer of Irish adventure stories appealing especially to boys of about 9 to 13. This description alone, however, does not adequately reflect her quality, for in her authentic picture of life on the west coast of Ireland, with a sensitive portrayal of human motives and emotions, Dillon has raised the conventional adventure story to a level of seriousness that is rare in children's books. Some of her subjects—boats, deserted islands, storms, wrecks, caves, assorted land and sea creatures, tinkers, horse-thieves, eccentric men and women—may not be particularly bold or original; in less skillful hands they could well receive banal and melodramatic treatment. But if her earliest books such as *The Lost Island* and *The San Sebastian* should strain credulity in places, their successors are well-constructed stories of originality and realism, with credible characters and events arising naturally out of everyday life in Connemara. What gives Dillon's novels their distinctive depth is her ability to invest her material with mature significance as well as youthful excitement, and to treat important human themes in an unforced, undidactic way.

A recurrent theme is misunderstanding, discord, and ultimate reconciliation. Bad blood exists within or between families, between island and island, islanders and the mainland, or the local inhabitants and a foreign newcomer. Tension arises from superstition, suspicion, stupidity, pride, or obstinacy, and often harks back to some trivial incident or apocryphal tale in the distant past, such as the feud in *The Coriander* between the islanders of Inishgillan and those of Inishthorav over the alleged extinction of the Killaney light long ago in order to cause a lucrative wreck, or the alleged betrayal of the priest in the rebellion of 1795 that is still the occasion of bitterness between the men of Rossmore and those of Inishrone in *The Island of Horses.* Without making light of the consequences, the author plays a gentle if pointed humour upon these human foibles. It usually takes an alliance of boys and older women to bring the men to their senses, despite the men's obstructive attitudes on the place of boys, and women, in their society. As Sally MacDonagh says in *The Sea Wall,* "It happens that way in the world, that the young people have more courage than the grown-up ones." The heroes of the stories are boys of 15 or 16, approaching manhood and ready to test their growing powers in response to challenging situations, yet close enough in age and status to form a link between the boy reader and the world of adults. For in the course of their adventures with currachs and hookers which enact and match children's fantasies, these heroes encounter the harsh realities of life, including conflict of loyalties and adult unreliability. The reality of Dillon's fiction is moral, social, and emotional, as well as physical.

In Connemara and the islands of Galway Bay, families have dwindled and declined through emigration to America. Few return with their new skills and prosperity. Islands that once thrived are now inhabited only by animals grazing among the derelict homes. Old men remember with wild glee their deeds against the Black and Tans. The sense of community is very strong, and the power of customs and traditional beliefs is ever present. The physical scene is vividly recreated, from the populous, jostling Galway Horse Fair to the bleak tracts of moorland where the turfs are cut for the fires. Each story is separate, without formal links with any other, yet they share a distinctive atmosphere that is powerfully and sensitively evoked in language that does not strain after figurative effect or portentous symbolism but works directly. The deceptively simple drawings, contributed by Richard Kennedy throughout a remarkable 25-year partnership, subtly complement the keen sense of place and character established in the writing. Dillon's books are marked for their restraint and under-statement, and for their total lack of quaintness and sentimentality.

Dillon's adult characters, unlike those in so many children's books, are as convincing as the younger ones. Particularly well drawn are the irascible, alienated, or eccentric older men, such as the shipwrecked doctor in *The Coriander,* chafing at his enforced stay on Inishgillan; the grandfather and Colman Flaherty, both in *The Cruise of the Santa Maria,* who drive away those close to them by their fierce independence and insults; the remote figure of Michael Joyce in *A Herd of Deer,* mystified by his neighbours' hostility to his unwitting flouting of local custom. But Dillon excels in creating strong-minded, highly individual women who have in them "the stored wisdom and charity of years," such as old Mrs. Conroy in *The Island of Horses,* making her affecting but unsentimental journey to the abandoned island where she was born; Mamó in *The Coriander,* whose patient hospitality and caring good sense win over the doctor to the islanders; Sally MacDonagh in *The Sea Wall,* striving against obstinacy and superstition to prevent another disaster; and the silent, redhaired Maggie in *The Cruise of the Santa Maria,* devotedly finishing her dead father's half-built hooker. Dillon sensitively reveals as the narrative unfolds the motives and feelings of each character, major or minor, good or bad, man, woman, or child, so that the moments of high drama or pathos, such as when the men of Inishgillan arrive off Inishthorav to retrieve their stolen sheep, or when Sarah is reunited with her old father, Colman Flaherty, need no elaboration but rely on an imaginative response from the reader.

Pervading the swift action and wide-ranging adventure is Dillon's wise, moral, sometimes gently mocking, always compassionate reflection upon the life and lives she so perceptively observes. To have fashioned out of the child's adventure story a natural vehicle for moral significance, without obtrusive moralising, and without loss of narrative interest and excitement, is a major achievement.

—Graham Hammond

DODD, Lynley (Stuart, née Weeks). New Zealander. Born in Rotorua, 5 July 1941. Educated at Tauranga College, 1954–57; Elam School of Fine Arts, Auckland University, 1959–61, diploma in fine arts 1962; Auckland Teachers College, 1962. Married Anthony R.F. Dodd in 1965; one son and one daughter. Art mistress, Queen Margaret College, Wellington, 1963–68; freelance illustrator, 1968–83. Recipient: New Zealand Library Association Esther Glen award, 1975; Choysa bursary, 1978; New Zealand Book award, for illustration, 1981; New Zealand Picture Book of the Year award, 1984, 1986, 1988. Address: 60 Pomare Road, Belmont, Lower Hutt, New Zealand.

PUBLICATIONS FOR CHILDREN

Fiction (illustrated by the author)

Titimus Trim. Auckland, Hodder and Stoughton, and London, Hamish Hamilton, 1979.
The Apple Tree. Wellington, Mallinson Rendel, 1982; Milwaukee, Stevens, 1985.
The Smallest Turtle. Wellington, Mallinson Rendel, and Barnstaple, Devon, Spindlewood, 1982; Milwaukee, Stevens, 1985.
Hairy Maclary from Donaldson's Dairy. Wellington, Mallinson Rendel, and Barnstaple, Devon, Spindlewood, 1983; Milwaukee, Stevens, 1985.
Hairy Maclary's Bone. Wellington, Mallinson Rendel, and Barnstaple, Devon, Spindlewood, 1984; Milwaukee, Stevens, 1985.
Hairy Maclary, Scattercat. Wellington, Mallinson Rendel, and Barnstaple, Devon, Spindlewood, 1985; Milwaukee, Stevens, 1987.
Wake Up, Bear. Wellington, Mallinson Rendel, and Barnstaple, Devon, Spindlewood, 1986; Milwaukee, Stevens, 1988.
Hairy Maclary's Caterwaul Caper. Wellington, Mallinson Rendel,

and Barnstaple, Devon, Spindlewood, 1987.
A Dragon in a Wagon. Wellington, Mallinson Rendel, and Barnstaple, Devon, Spindlewood, 1988.
Hairy Maclary's Rumpus at the Vet. Wellington, Mallinson Rendel, and Barnstaple, Devon, Spindlewood, 1989.

Other

The Nickle Nackle Tree. London, Hamish Hamilton, 1976; New York, Macmillan, 1978.

*

Illustrator: *My Cat Likes to Hide in Boxes* by Eve Sutton, 1973; *Pussyfooting* by Jillian Squire, 1978; *I'm a Tree* by James K. Baxter, 1979; *Druscilla* by Clarice England, 1980; *Kindness* and *Barnyard Song* (traditional rhymes), 1981; *Pop Pop Pop* (adaptation of traditional rhyme), and *One Big Dinosaur,* both by Beverley Randell, 1981; *The Pesky Paua* by Robin Cunningham and Fran Hunia, 1983.

Lynley Dodd comments:
I came to writing late. It was through my illustrating work for *My Cat Likes to Hide in Boxes* that I became hooked on picture books; the heady excitement of a first publication, plus the fact that my own two children were active "consumers" at that stage, meant that ideas began germinating and with the confidence of ignorance I decided to give writing a try. The result, after much sweated labour, was *The Nickle Nackle Tree.* Since then I have written and illustrated my own books.

The big advantage of being author and illustrator lies in being able to plan the whole book from scratch. There is no conflict over interpretation and from the first rough rhythms and images in the head through to final result, words and pictures can evolve together in mood, balance, style, and sympathy.

I don't set out with earnest messages in mind. I like to have fun with words and characters and I aim to amuse and entertain—if a little learning creeps in occasionally, that's fine. I keep an eye and ear open for the whimsical; my "ideas" book is full of things earmarked for possible future use, from improbable names on a Royal Banquet guest list to a sketch of my mother's cat wearing an upturned supermarket bag.

Children often ask, "Will you write 'chapter' books?" That would probably mean giving up "writing the pictures," as a two-year-old friend once put it. I think I'll stick with picture books.

*   *   *

If the mantle of Beatrix Potter has descended on any one contemporary picture book author it must surely be upon Lynley Dodd. Both writers have created unforgettable animal characters, and both achieve equal excellence in text and pictures with a total cohesion between the two. But there the similarities end. Dodd's books are not pale imitations of Potter's; their individuality and vigour are totally original.

Undoubtedly Dodd's success rests largely upon the sequence of stories which begins with *Hairy Maclary from Donaldson's Dairy* and which hopefully is not yet ended. Within these books she has created a range of canine and feline protagonists who inhabit the world of the small shaggy terrier-like Hairy Maclary. His friends include the mastiff "Hercules Morse as big as a horse," Dalmatian "Bottomley Potts covered in spots," old English sheep dog "Muffin McLay like a bundle of hay," the greyhound-like "Bitzer Maloney, all skinny and bony," and the dachshund "Schnitzel von Krumm, with the very low tum." In the first book they are all routed by the "toughest tom in town," the formidable Scarface Claw, who also defeats Hairy Maclary in *Hairy Maclary, Scattercat,* but the dogs gain something of a revenge in *Hairy Maclary's Caterwaul Caper* when Scarface Claw is stuck up a tree. It is the dogs' turn to get stuck at various obstacle points when they are trying to divest Hairy Maclary of his bone in *Hairy Maclary's Bone*. The books owe their success to the vivacity and humour of both the cumulative texts and the pictures in which a dog's eye view of vanishing tails, pavements, plants, walls, and feet has been created.

Although Dodd's animals have marked personalities she is never tempted into anthropomorphism. Her characters stay within the limitations of their species. Her earlier books *The Apple Tree* and *The Smallest Turtle* are virtually non-fiction as in the former a possum steals apples and in the latter a young turtle newly hatched from his egg has to make his way to the sea. In the later *Wake Up, Bear* a succession of animals are unable to waken Bear from his hibernation until a passing bee reminds him of honey and succeeds where everyone else has failed.

In her recent book *A Dragon in a Wagon* a small girl, Susie Fogg, daydreams that her dog Sam becomes something more exciting, like a "dragon in a wagon" or "a gnu with 'flu." She herself plays an active part in these Walter Mitty-like departures from reality, but is delighted when she falls over to find the real Sam with his "friendly doggy face" ready to comfort her.

There has been a steady development in Dodd as an artist. Her earlier books, the pictures in Eve Sutton's *My Cat Likes to Hide in Boxes* and her own *The Nickle Nackle Tree* and *Titimus Trim* (the story of an old man who muddles his routine), display a strong decorative element, with much flat use of primary colour. Her later stories, although still exhibiting a marked ability in drawing and design, rely more upon her own visual experiences to produce greater subtlety of atmosphere and colour with a correspondingly stronger sense of space and realism.

From *The Nickle Nackle Tree* (a splendidly alliterative counting book) onwards, she has always shown a command of the sound and rhythms of language. These are excellent books to read aloud to children. The names, rhymes, repetition, and cumulative effects all invite participation, and the total unity of text and pictures ensures an economical, disciplined, and artistic entity.

—Betty Gilderdale

DOHERTY, Berlie. British. Born in Liverpool, Lancashire, 6 November 1943. Educated at Durham University, 1961–64, B.A. (honours) in English; Liverpool University, 1964–65, postgraduate certificate in social science; Sheffield University, 1977–78. postgraduate certificate in education. Married Gerard Adrian Doherty in 1966; two daughters and one son. Social worker, Leicestershire County Council, 1966–67; English teacher, schools in Sheffield, 1978–80; teacher with BBC Radio, Sheffield, 1980–82. Recipient: Library Association Carnegie Medal, 1987. Address: 38 Banner Cross Road, Sheffield, Yorkshire S11 9HR, England.

PUBLICATIONS FOR CHILDREN

Fiction

How Green You Are!, illustrated by Elaine McGregor Turney. London, Methuen, 1982.
The Making of Fingers Finnigan, illustrated by John Haysom. London, Methuen, 1983.
Tilly Mint Tales, illustrated Thelma Lambert. London, Methuen, 1984.

White Peak Farm. London, Methuen, 1984.
Children of Winter, illustrated by Ian Newsham. London, Methuen, 1985.
Granny Was a Buffer Girl. London, Methuen, 1986; New York, Orchard, 1988.
Tough Luck. London, Hamish Hamilton, 1987.
Tilly Mint and the Dodo, illustrated by Janna Doherty. London, Methuen, 1988.
Paddiwak and Cosy, illustrated by Teresa O'Brien. London, Methuen, 1988; New York, Dial Press, 1989.
Spellhorn. London, Hamish Hamilton, 1989.

Plays

Smells and Spells (produced Sheffield, 1978).
Howard's Field (produced Sheffield, 1979).
The Amazing Journey of Jazz O'Neill (produced Hull, 1984).
A Case for Probation, in *Studio Scripts*, edited by David Self. London, Hutchinson, 1986.
Tilly Mint and the Dodo, adaptation of her own story (produced Doncaster, 1986).
How Green You Are!, adaptation of her own story, in *Drama 1*, edited by John Foster. London, Macmillan, 1987.
Matthew, Come Home, in *Drama 2*, edited by John Foster. London, Macmillan, 1987.
Tribute to Tom, in *Drama 3*, edited by John Foster. London, Macmillan, 1988.
Home, in *Stage Write*, edited by Gervase Phinn. London, Unwin Hyman, 1988.

Radio Play: *The Mouse and His Child*, from the story by Russell Hoban, 1987.

Television Series: *White Peak Farm*, from her own story, 1988.

PUBLICATIONS FOR ADULTS

Plays

A Growing Girl's Story (produced Hartlepool, Yorkshire, 1980).
Return to the Ebro (produced Manchester, 1986).

Radio Plays: *The Drowned Village*, 1978; *Requiem*, 1982; *Sacrifice*, 1986; *Miss Elizabeth*, 1986; *Dream of Unicorns*, 1988; *Children of Winter*, 1989.

*

Berlie Doherty comments:
Although most of my writing has been in the form of fiction for children, I like the freedom and challenge of moving from one medium to another and across the full age range. I love the short story form and many of my novels contain chapters which are free-standing and self-contained as short stories, but which knit into their neighbouring chapters as part of the novel's narrative. Many of my books began as radio series and I still think of radio as being the finest medium for imaginative writing. Above all I am interested in characters, and like to feel that whether my novel is a realistic one like *Granny Was a Buffer Girl* or a fantasy like *Spellhorn* there is a quiet emotional energy driving the story home.

* * *

Berlie Doherty writes for a wide age range. Her work usually consists of short stories centred round a family group or a gang of friends. She is interested in youngsters themselves, in their friendships with people of their grandparents' generation, and in their acceptance of the physically and mentally handicapped. Her work, set mainly near Liverpool and Sheffield, has a strong sense of place.

How Green You Are! is lively and often funny. It describes the activities of friends, first years at secondary school, life in a terraced street in a seaside town. The early stories, in which Julie, going to a convent school, is teased, Kevin makes friends with an old lady because he wants to stroke her cat, and Weird George comes to live in the street, show Doherty's care for the children about whom she is writing; they ring true. Characterisation is clean, sharp, and immediate. The later, more dramatic stories have little depth, but are still enjoyable on a superficial level. Vividness is sometimes lost by a lack of description. The sequel, *The Making of Fingers Finnigan,* is a series of stories linked by the theme of the youngsters' campaign to have a local swimming pool re-opened.

Tilly Mint Tales, for younger children, is a collection of short stories, good for bed-time reading, about Tilly and Mrs. Hardcastle, who looks after her when her mother is at work. When Mrs. Hardcastle falls asleep "something magic always seems to happen to Tilly Mint." The stories are cosy and secure, with no real excitement to the adventures. Tilly's victories are always quick and easy. Their sequel, *Tilly Mint and the Dodo,* is didactic, targeted at an older age group, and doesn't work. Its theme is conservation, the "terrible things" people do to animals, and the fact that "the world belongs to all of us."

It is in her books for teenagers where Doherty's strength lies. *White Peak Farm* is a vivid evocation of life on a Derbyshire farm, narrated by Jeannie. The first two stories are gentle, with the dying grandmother setting the underlying theme: "The only harm you can do yourself is to waste your life." Then the father begins to dominate. His hatred, loneliness and bad temper "divided him from the rest of us and us from each other." Theirs is "a house of secrets," of strong suppressed emotions, each person living in their own world. Extremely movingly, Doherty tells how Jeannie's older brother and sister, and finally Jeannie herself, assert their independence and make the painful break from family and from the land that they have loved. *White Peak Farm* shows Doherty's greatest commitment to her characters and their setting.

The framework to Carnegie-Medal-winning *Granny Was a Buffer Girl* is narrator Jess's family party as she is about to leave Sheffield for a year at university in France. It is a collection of the love stories—not all romantic—of the three generations of Jess's family. Particularly enjoyable is "The Buffer Girl," an account of grandmother Dorothy's failed Cinderella-like attachment to her boss's son, and her making do with neighbour Albert. Particularly moving is "Danny," the story of Jess's handicapped older brother who dies when he is 17; its moods change from anxiety to joy to grief. *Granny Was a Buffer Girl* lacks the cohesion and depth of *White Peak Farm* but it is compelling reading.

—Maggie Freeman

DONKIN, Nance (Clare, née Pender). Australian. Born in West Maitland, New South Wales, in 1915. Married Victor Donkin in 1939; one son and one daughter. Journalist, Maitland *Daily Mercury,* 1932–35, and Newcastle *Morning Herald,* 1935–39. Since 1970 children's books reviewer, Melbourne *Herald;* since 1975 tutor, Council of Adult Education, Melbourne. President, 1968–75, and Vice-President, 1975–79, Children's Book Council, Victoria. Recipient: Australian Arts Council travel grant, 1974, and senior fellowship, 1980. A.M. (Member, Order of Australia), 1986. Address: 8/8 Mooltan Avenue, Balaclava, Victoria 3183, Australia.

PUBLICATIONS FOR CHILDREN

Fiction

Araluen Adventures, illustrated by Edith B. Bowden. Melbourne, Cheshire, 1946.
No Medals for Meg, illustrated by Edith B. Bowden. Melbourne, Cheshire, 1947.
Julie Stands By, illustrated by Joan Turner. Melbourne, Cheshire, 1948.
Blue Ribbon Beth. Melbourne, Oxford University Press, 1951.
House by the Water, illustrated by Astra Lacis Dick. London, Angus and Robertson, 1969.
Johnny Neptune. Sydney, Angus and Robertson, 1971; London, Angus and Robertson, 1972.
The Cool Man. London, Angus and Robertson, 1973.
A Friend for Petros, illustrated by Gavin Rowe. London, Hamish Hamilton, 1974.
Patchwork Grandmother, illustrated by Mary Dinsdale. London, Hamish Hamilton, 1975; as *Patchwork Mystery,* London, Beaver, 1978.
Green Christmas, illustrated by Gavin Rowe. London, Hamish Hamilton, 1976.
Yellowgum Girl, illustrated by Margaret Loxton. London, Hamish Hamilton, 1976.
A Handful of Ghosts. London, Hodder and Stoughton, 1976.
The Best of the Bunch, illustrated by Edwina Bell. Sydney, Collins, 1978; London, Collins, 1979.
The Maidens of Pefka, illustrated by Bruce Treloar. Sydney, Methuen, 1979.
Nini. Adelaide, Rigby, 1979.
Two at Sullivan Bay, illustrated by Margaret Senior. Kenthurst, New South Wales, Kangaroo Press, 1985.
A Family Affair, illustrated by Lyn Sikiotis. Cammeray, New South Wales, Martin, 1988.

Other

Sheep, illustrated by Jocelyn Jones. Melbourne, Oxford University Press, 1967.
Sugar, illustrated by Jocelyn Jones. Melbourne, Oxford University Press, 1967.
An Emancipist, illustrated by Jane Robinson. Melbourne, Oxford University Press, 1968.
A Currency Lass, illustrated by Jane Walker. Melbourne, Oxford University Press, 1969.
An Orphan, illustrated by Anne Culvenor. Melbourne, Oxford University Press, 1970.
Margaret Catchpole, illustrated by Edwina Bell. Sydney and London, Collins, 1974.
We of the Never Never (retelling). Hawthorne, Victoria, Hutchinson, 1983.
Blackout (reader), illustrated by Dandra Laroche. Melbourne, Macmillan, 1987.

Editor, *The Australian Children's Annual.* Melbourne, Lothian, 1963.

PUBLICATIONS FOR ADULTS

Other

A Writer at Work (lecture). Reid, Australian Capital Territory, Children's Book Council of Australia, 1975.
Stranger and Friend: The Greek-Australian Experience. Blackburn, Victoria, Dove, 1983.
The Women Were There: Some Ladies and Others in Australia's History. Blackburn, Victoria, Collins Dove, 1988.

*

Manuscript Collections: Dromkeen Trust Collection, Melbourne; Lu Rees Archives, Canberra College of Advanced Education.

Nance Donkin comments:

Digging into Australia's rough, tough, sad, bad past has been a satisfying and stimulating occupation. In trying to picture the past for children I hope to help them to see, even vaguely, that "history is people like you." My several books for younger children I enjoyed writing very much because I enjoy the company and the conversation of young children and have been pleased that I am apparently able to communicate with them in this other way.

Migrants are also a deep personal interest, particularly Greek people. As a result of living in a Greek village for six months, I have written an adult book about the Greek-Australian experience.

My latest book, also for adults, is my way of putting women back in Australian history where they most certainly belong but were almost entirely omitted in official records as anything other than statistics. I expect to keep on with this kind of historical "digging" for the rest of my writing life. There is buried treasure there in fabulous nuggets.

*   *   *

Perhaps the mood of Nance Donkin's writing was fashioned by—in her own words—the "web of words spun by my father, a natural story-teller of the yarn and tall story ender." Her reason for writing her books, she once said, is because "I have found writing for children gives me great satisfaction and I think there is an enormous vacuum in Australian children's writing which should be filled with lots of well-written books about ordinary lives and occasionally making extraordinary discoveries, though not of buried treasures or smugglers' caches." How far has she succeeded in attaining this goal? In her books ordinary lives abound; there is a scarcity of extraordinary discoveries.

Her early books deal with middle-class suburban and country life. *Araluen Adventures, No Medals for Meg,* and *Julie Stands By* have uninspired plots and much digressive conversation. "Elsie's a good stick," said Kate, "but she does get rattled, doesn't she?" Except in *Blue Ribbon Beth* where two girls assist the home help to recover his memory, there are no really dramatic moments.

Her later books are more interesting, and she shows a genuine feeling for her Australian background. In *House by the Water* there is a real family, and the dialogue is stronger and more convincing. May Reibey, having told her sons that she is an ex-convict, adds, "There's something else boys," she winked at them and put a finger up in warning, "Now you know how I was boned, don't turn conk! No whidding to the girls." *Johnny Neptune,* set in Sydney in 1790, describes the fortunes of an orphan fighting for existence in the rough life of the new colony and, although sometimes rambling, is a pioneer story that holds one's interest.

Two later books show an appreciation and knowledge of the Australian Bush. *Yellowgum Girl* is an enjoyable story about a city boy's holiday near a nature reserve where "Desert mice that move

quicker than a flash nibble silky tea tree blossom and the emu's favourite food is the bright red tops of greeny flame heath bushes." In *Green Christmas* a family spending their first camping Christmas are shown, in this so-called new country, a secret cave where the wall paintings are thousands of years old.

—Nancy Shepherdson

———

DONOVAN, John. American. Born in 1928. President, Children's Book Council, New York. Address: c/o Children's Book Council Inc., 67 Irving Place North, New York, New York 10003, U.S.A.

PUBLICATIONS FOR CHILDREN

Fiction

The Little Orange Book, illustrated by Mauro Caputo. New York, Morrow, 1961.
I'll Get There. It Better Be Worth the Trip. New York, Harper, 1969; London, Macdonald, 1970.
Wild in the World. New York, Harper, 1971.
Remove Protective Coating a Little at a Time. New York, Harper, 1973.
Good Old James, illustrated by James Stevenson. New York, Harper, 1975.
Family. New York, Harper, 1976.

PUBLICATIONS FOR ADULTS

Play

Riverside Drive (produced New York, 1964).

*   *   *

John Donovan's novels stand apart from each other and from most of children's literature. His characters live in a lonely world, but in each book they find a close friend to redeem them from emotional extinction. These friends are thorny and independent, giving their love with integrity, without obligation.

In *I'll Get There. It Better Be Worth the Trip* Dave Ross is isolated by his grandmother's death. His divorced parents do not really want either him or his dog Fred, unless by occasional arrangement. The one classmate Dave is drawn to in his new school still suffers too much from the death of a best friend to let Dave near. Later, the love both boys need and begin to feel toward each other leads to a brief sexual encounter, and after Dave's beloved dog is killed, firm companionship.

Where *I'll Get There* intones the casual language of first-person narrative, *Wild in the World* is stark, tight, and concentrated. A brief first chapter dispenses with twelve members of a mountain family, leaving only one teenage boy alive. He survives physically by his own strength and knowledge and emotionally with the help of a wild dog whom he calls Son. The two discover and care for each other with growing joy. Son endures a rattlesnake bite, but John dies of pneumonia, leaving to the dog his heritage of free affection and to readers an intensely moving memory.

Remove Protective Coating a Little at a Time returns to the desperately sophisticated New York City boy who has everything materially and very little else. Harry caused his parents' marriage by being conceived, and the marriage dictates a predictable but empty path for both his mother, an ex-prom queen whose life means nothing as her son grows older, and his father, a high-school baseball star who has succeeded in the advertising business and in staying away from home to avoid his wife's disintegration. None of Harry's peers seem to stray across his path: an old woman does—briefly and meaningfully. Amelia is a derelict but she speaks her mind and lives by it as well. By the time she disappears. Harry has finally connected with somebody for the first time in his life, deeper than surface. One knows it will happen again.

Family is beautifully written. It blends wit with tragedy, a tight plot with unforgettable characterizations, a perfectly trimmed style with an ambitiously extended theme, and an experimental mixture of genres—science fiction, fantasy, realism, and allegory. Several captive apes, more or less strangers to each other, escape from what one of them suspects will be a mutilating experiment. In finding and establishing a wild home, they revert to a natural allegiance of warmth and loyalty. A gentle Man, who symbolizes human integrity, joins them briefly, but the next visitors are late fall hunters. With the leader and baby slain, the animal narrator and his pregnant companion return to the science lab, forced to trust the mercy of man. The reader is forced to respond with compassion as a member of the universal family.

Donovan creates scenes of great impact. His ideal of the respectful common bond reaches straight and simply toward adolescents struggling with the pain of both loneliness and relationships. He has been there, and made the trip worthwhile.

—Betsy Hearne

———

DOUGLAS, Michael.   See BRIGHT, Robert.

———

DOWNIE, Mary Alice (Dawe, née Hunter).   Canadian.   Born in Alton, Illinois, United States, 12 February 1934; moved to Canada, 1940. Educated at St. Clement's School, Toronto; Trinity College, University of Toronto, 1951–55, B.A. (honours) in English 1955. Married John Downie in 1959; three daughters. Stenographer, Maclean-Hunter, Toronto, 1955; reporter, *Marketing* magazine, Toronto, 1955–56; editorial assistant, *Canadian Medical Association Journal*, Toronto, 1956–57; librarian, later publicity manager, Oxford University Press, Toronto, 1958–59; book review editor, Kingston *Whig-Standard*, Ontario, 1973–78. Founding editor, Kids Canada series, Kids Can Press, Toronto, and Northern Lights series, Peter Martin Associates, Toronto. Recipient: Ontario Arts Council award, 1970, 1975, 1981, 1987; Canada Council bursary, 1971, 1981, 1987. Address: 190 Union Street, Kingston, Ontario K7L 2P6, Canada.

PUBLICATIONS FOR CHILDREN

Fiction

Honor Bound, with John Downie, illustrated by Joan Huffman. Toronto, Oxford University Press, and New York, Walck, 1971.
Scared Sarah, illustrated by Laszlo Gal.   Toronto, Nelson, 1974.
Dragon on Parade, illustrated by Mary Lynn Baker.   Toronto, Peter

Martin Associates, 1974.
The King's Loon, illustrated by Ron Berg.   Toronto, Kids Can Press, 1979.
The Last Ship, illustrated by Lissa Calvert.   Toronto, Peter Martin Associates, 1980.
A Proper Acadian, with George Rawlyk, illustrated by Ron Berg. Toronto, Kids Can Press, 1981.
Jenny Greenteeth, illustrated by Ann Powell.   Toronto, Rhino, 1981.
Alison's Ghosts, with John Downie.   Toronto, Nelson, 1984; Independence, Ohio, Schoolhouse Press, 1986.

Other

The Magical Adventures of Pierre (French-Canadian fairy tale), illustrated by Yüksel Hassan.   Toronto, Nelson, 1974.
The Witch of the North: Folk Tales of French Canada, illustrated by Elizabeth Cleaver.   Ottawa, Oberon Press, 1975.
Seeds and Weeds: A Book of Country Crafts, with Jillian Hulme Gilliland.   Toronto, North Winds Press, 1981.
The Wicked Fairy-Wife: A French-Canadian Folktale, illustrated by Kim Price.   Toronto, Kids Can Press, 1983.
Stones and Cones: Country Crafts for Kids, with Jillian Hulme Gilliland.   Toronto, Scholastic, 1984.
How the Devil Got His Cat (French-Canadian folktale), illustrated by Jillian Hulme Gilliland.   Kingston, Ontario, Quarry Press, 1988.

Editor, with Barbara Robertson, *The Wind Has Wings: Poems from Canada,* illustrated by Elizabeth Cleaver.   Toronto, Oxford University Press, and New York, Walck, 1968; London, Oxford University Press, 1969.
Editor, with Mary Hamilton, *And Some Brought Flowers: Plants in a New World,* illustrated by E.J. Revell.   Toronto, University of Toronto Press, 1980.
Editor, with Barbara Robertson, *The New Wind Has Wings: Poems from Canada,* illustrated by Elizabeth Cleaver.   Toronto and London, Oxford University Press, 1984; New York, Oxford University Press, 1985.
Editor, with Elizabeth Greene and M.-A. Thompson, *The Window of Dreams: New Canadian Writing for Children.*   Toronto, Methuen, 1986.
Editor, with Barbara Robertson, *The Well-Filled Cupboard: Everyday Pleasures of Home and Garden.*   Toronto, Lester and Orpen Dennys, 1987.

*

Mary Alice Downie comments:

My books are for children, and my themes are usually drawn from the Canadian past. It's a short past when you consider the country but stretches out when the heritage of the immigrant is included.

The books have resulted from a mixture of writing, translating, retelling, and rediscovery of little-known materials. My aim is to entertain and occasionally inform young Canadians. My hope is that the stories and poems will appeal beyond the borders of the country and the age of childhood.

*   *   *

Mary Alice Downie's junior fiction breathes life into distant periods of Canadian history. Her youthful Canadians of long ago are irresistible creations: believably of their period, yet as lively and full of fun as their distant descendants who people the playgrounds of today.

Her most ambitious historical fiction to date, written in collaboration with her husband, is *Honor Bound,* set in 1784. This suspenseful story depicts the terrifying times that brought an important segment of the Canadian population—the United Empire Loyalists—to strengthen a struggling new nation.

The Averys of Philadelphia are Loyalists, faithful to England's King George III. The War of Independence is now over, but the persecution of the defeated goes on unabated. Unwilling "Americans" who doggedly remain faithful to the King to whom they had sworn allegiance are being persecuted in the name of freedom. Many, like the Averys, left homes and possessions to make their hazardous way to Canada; and in those days, going to Canada meant going to the wilderness.

Unused as they are to rough backwoods ways, the Averys make Cataraqui (now Kingston) a haven and a home. The heaviest burden the family has to bear is that of separation from Honor, the 17-year-old eldest daughter of the family, who had been visiting an aunt in upstate New York when the Yankee vigilantes struck, and of whom they have since had no word. If only Honor can be found, these proud new Canadians will be very content in their "uncivilized" home.

A Proper Acadian, for younger readers, simplifies a complex tragedy into dimensions within the grasp of children. 12-year-old Timothy is an orphaned Bostonian of the 1750's, sent to live with his dead mother's sister to keep him out of the trouble for which he shows too much aptitude. Thus it happens that he is living with his Acadian kinsfolk in Minas when in 1775 the dread order for the deportation of all Acadians is carried out.

Timothy elects to accompany his aunt's family into exile rather than return to his home in Boston. The lives of the puritanical Bostonians and the warm-hearted, happy-go-lucky Acadians are nicely contrasted, and it is easy to understand Timothy's choice. The story is vividly told from the perspective of a young lad torn between loyalties to his New England birthplace and to his beloved adoptive family.

In *The King's Loon* the thankless foundling Andre learns through the ungrateful behavior of the captive loon he releases to freedom exactly how hurtful his own carelessness has been to his adoptive parent, Tante Louet. The appealing story is imbedded in a mini-history lesson of the expedition of Count Frontenac, the haughty new Governor of New France, to make himself known to the Iroquois and impress them with his power.

The Last Ship, too, is a tiny, well-sugared lesson in Canadian history. The departure of the last supply ship of the year to leave New France before winter ends all navigation has always signalled a time of deep gloom to the exiles in this bleak place now cut off from all they hold dear for long, empty months: yet somehow this year, *real* life goes on just as before, for suddenly Quebec, not the France of Louis XIV, is where Madeleine's life, and the lives of her family and friends, are really lived. Quebec is no longer exile, but home.

Contemporary in setting, yet evoking the past, *Alison's Ghosts* is the mildly otherwordly story of a youngster troubled by the possession of an Indian artifact, the bowl of an ancient medicine pipe. She becomes convinced that it is necessary for her to locate the missing stem, and to restore the pipe intact to the questing spirit of a Micmac shaman. In her search for the spirit pipe, Alison uncovers the story of its haunted history.

Her interest in history probably influenced Downie's adapted versions of two French-Canadian folktales, the slightly chilling *The Wicked Fairy-Wife,* and the more cheerful *How the Devil Got His Cat,* in which a clever Mother Superior plays a sly trick upon the mysterious stranger who has tried to trick *her,* in volunteering to build the bridge the convent needs, if he may claim for his own the first thing to cross that bridge when it is completed.

For much younger readers, *Dragon on Parade* is a small-town summer idyll of three little girls who want to be the hit of the Bayfield Lions Club Carnival by creating a stunning dragon costume out of cardboard boxes, drapery, paint, and sequins, in every child's dress-up dream come true.

Downie is a writer who understands children, and has a rare talent for speaking directly to them by focussing upon that carefully selected aspect of her subject most surely calculated to appeal to the hearts of young readers.

—Joan McGrath

DOYLE, Brian. Canadian. Born in Ottawa, Ontario, 12 August 1935. Educated at York Street Public School, Ottawa; Glebe Collegiate Institute, Ottawa; Carleton University, Ottawa, B.A. and degree in journalism. Married Jackie Doyle; one daughter and one son. Journalist, Toronto *Telegram.* Since 1969 teacher and head of English department, Glebe Collegiate Institute. Lives in Ottawa. Address: c/o Groundwood Books, 26 Lennox Street, Third Floor, Toronto, Ontario M6G 1J4, Canada.

PUBLICATIONS FOR CHILDREN

Fiction

Hey, Dad! Toronto, Groundwood, 1978.
You Can Pick Me Up at Peggy's Cove. Toronto, Groundwood, 1979.
Up to Low. Toronto, Groundwood, 1982.
Angel Square. Toronto, Groundwood, 1984; New York, Bradbury Press, 1986.
Easy Avenue. Toronto, Groundwood, 1988.

* * *

Brian Doyle is a rarity among Canadian children's authors—a serious writer of comedy. His seriousness is evident in his themes, which he calls "the classic concerns, the ones with the capital letters." In each of his five first-person novels, an adolescent matures by struggling to understand ideas about death, love, and reconciliation. Doyle, however, recognizes the comic side of this often painful struggle: "When I work on a serious question, a mirror of humour always presents itself." This mirror, like that in a funhouse, reflects characters as comic grotesques and eccentrics. It also gives the action proportions more common in tall tales than adolescent maturation novels.

Doyle's novels form two groups. *Hey, Dad!* and *You Can Pick Me Up at Peggy's Cove* are contemporary stories inspired by Doyle's relationship with his children. *Hey, Dad!,* the superior work, set the pattern for later books. It uses a family's vacation journey to symbolize a girl's inward journey to maturation. 13-year-old Megan hates her father for forcing her to come, and even tries running away. Although episodic, like subsequent books, *Hey, Dad!* is unified by a motif. The majority of episodes present ideas about death. Some do this comically, as when a terminally ill boy insists that Megan is dying, for that is the only reason a family undertakes such a vacation. Others are serious, as when Megan mistakes a dying man for her father. Eventually Megan is reconciled to her father, who teaches her that love and memories defeat time. As in later books, the conclusion is symbolic. Now mature enough to accept life, Megan wades with her father into the ocean, a unifying symbol of both life and eternity.

You Can Pick Me Up at Peggy's Cove contains some effective satire of tourists, but it is a more conventional book. Its episodes dramatize either the pain of loss or the power of love. Megan's brother, Ryan, sent to Peggy's Cove when his father temporarily leaves the family, tries to coerce his father's love by taking up with a thief. Ryan learns that love is a gift and in the symbolic ending leans against his father, the still centre of love in a whirl of activity.

Doyle's other novels, inspired by his own childhood, are set in the period following World War II. These mix tragedy and comedy far more effectively than the novels of contemporary life. *Up to Low,* his most successful work, contains more eccentrics and tall tale elements. Like *Hey, Dad!* it uses physical journeys to symbolize spiritual journeys. In this case, however, the structure is complex, dividing into two sections. The first, a tall tale of a drunken auto trip, emphasizes the personal destructiveness when an alcoholic gradually destroys his new car. The second is Bridget's river journey to visit her father, Mean Hughie, who was responsible for her loss of an arm. After confessing his sorrow, Mean Hughie dies. The Faulknerian return trip, in which his coffin is precariously balanced across the boat to form a cross, symbolizes the redemption of Mean Hughie, Bridget, and Tommy, the narrator. This redemptive power of love, which overcomes destruction, is further emphasized when Tommy, finally seeing Bridget as a woman instead of a mutilated girl, kisses her.

Doyle's other novels chronicle life among the poor. *Angel Square* is a "prequel" to *Up to Low.* Constantly switching sides in the daily fights among Catholics, Jews, and Protestants, "Because I'm not anything," Tommy seeks meaningful identity in the role of a radio character, the Shadow. When he successfully solves a crime, he establishes himself as a hero and temporarily brings peace to the neighbourhood. As with *Hey, Dad!,* the theme develops through motifs. Here the word "mystery" connects the crime story to Tommy's contemplation of puzzling religious and social questions.

Similarly, *Easy Avenue* explores various definitions of the term "success." A poor boy who comes into some money, Hubbo O'Driscoll learns that financial success does not ensure success as a human being. His moral triumph comes when he finally expresses publicly his love for the cleaning woman who raised him. More heavyhanded in its repeated jokes and comic eccentrics, it lacks the thematic depth of the two previous novels. Nevertheless, like them it affirms the redemptive power of love, for Hubbo's rejection of the arrogant materialism of the rich kids at school unites him with both his foster mother and a neighbouring girl, from whom he was estranged.

Doyle occasionally belabours comic effects and sometimes loses theme in anecdote. His novels are, however, genuinely humourous, and they contain, beneath deceptively simple surfaces, depths unplumbed in most other contemporary Canadian works.

—Raymond E. Jones

DRUMMOND, V(iolet) H(ilda). British. Born in London, 30 July 1911. Educated at The Links, Eastbourne, Sussex; St. Martin's School of Art, London. Married Anthony Swetenham in 1948; one son by previous marriage. Since 1960 Chairman, V.H. Drummond Productions. Recipient: Library Association Kate Greenaway Medal, for illustration, 1957. Address: 24 Norfolk Road, London NW8 6HG, England.

PUBLICATIONS FOR CHILDREN (illustrated by the author)

Fiction

Phewtus the Squirrel. London, Oxford University Press, 1939; revised edition, London, Constable, 1966; New York, Lothrop,

1987.
Mrs. Easter's Parasol. London, Faber, 1944.
Miss Anna Truly. London, Faber, 1945; Boston, Houghton Mifflin, 1949.
Lady Talavera. London, Faber, 1946.
Tidgie's Innings. London, Faber, 1947.
The Charming Taxi-cab. London, Faber, 1947.
The Mountain That Laughed. London, Grey Walls Press, 1947.
The Flying Postman. London, Penguin, 1948; Boston, Houghton Mifflin, 1949.
Mr. Finch's Pet Shop. London, Faber, 1953; New York, Oxford University Press, 1954.
Mrs. Easter and the Storks. London, Faber, 1957; New York, A.S. Barnes, 1960.
Little Laura's Cat. London, Faber, 1960.
Little Laura on the River. London, Faber, 1960.
Little Laura and the Thief. London, Nelson, 1963.
Little Laura and Her Best Friend. London, Nelson, 1963.
Little Laura and the Lonely Ostrich. London, Nelson, 1963.
Miss Anna Truly and the Christmas Lights. London, Longman, 1968.
Mrs. Easter and the "Golden Bounder." London, Faber, 1970.
Mrs. Easter's Christmas Flight. London, Faber, 1972.

Plays

Television Series: *Little Laura,* 1963.

Other

I'll Never Be Asked Again. London, Debrett's, 1979.

*

Illustrator: *The Twelfth* by J.K. Stanford, 1944; *Here and There a Lusty Trout* by Thomas A. Powell, 1947; *Verse and Worse* by Arnold Silcock, 1947; *The Shaggy Dog Story* by Eric Partridge, 1948; *Carbonel* by Barbara Sleigh, 1955; *The Wild Little House* by Eilís Dillon, 1955; *Esprit de Corps* by Lawrence Durrell, 1957; *The Piemakers* by Helen Cresswell, 1967.

V.H. Drummond comments:

I wrote my first children's book for my son aged four; the idea for my next book, *Mrs. Easter's Parasol,* came to me while walking with him in Kensington Gardens. In 1963 I drew the pictures and wrote the stories for the *Little Laura* series on BBC "Children's Hour," and my last three children's books were written for my three grandchildren.

*   *   *

V.H. Drummond won the Kate Greenaway medal in 1957, but her talent as an imaginative and original writer of stories for young children is at least as great as her talent as an illustrator. Her characters, Little Laura and her beloved Nannie, Laura's best friend, Billie Guftie, his Aunt Mrs. Easter, even Miss Anna Truly (though she hates washing-up) inhabit a world which has so little connection with reality that surely no one could call it dated or class-ridden. Certainly, Drummond has a decided preference for things that are not new-fangled and automatic, useful as the escalator is in disposing of Vilewort the Villain. And Laura may cry "What larking fun!" This is hardly the expression of a contemporary child, but one with as much appeal for such children as her ride on the swan's back and her unselfconscious converse with the King.

Drummond's characters are all tremendously spirited. The King reacts to the story of Mrs. Easter and the storks with "What courage!

What a tale of romance!" We can only say the same. One of Drummond's favourite words is elegant. The King's tea table is, of course, elegant. So is the main lodge in *Lady Talavera*. More surprisingly, so is the ice cream in *The Flying Postman*. And Drummond's style and language are never less than elegant: "So they descended from the roof and made their way towards the harbour, followed by the grieving bird."

The Flying Postman is the best of all these delightful books. Shorter than most, with bolder yet softer artwork, the story tells of Mr. Musgrove, who delivered letters by helicopter and foolishly crashed into the church when entertaining the children with his aerobatics. The Postal Authorities dismiss him and Mr. Musgrove is forced to make a living by selling pink ice cream. Fortunately one day the Post Master General has an accident outside Mr. Musgrove's house and, in return for his kindness and the reviving elegant ice cream, reinstates him in his job—a logical, unbureaucratic procedure any child would applaud.

—Ann Thwaite

---

du BOIS, William Pène. American. Born in Nutley, New Jersey, 9 May 1916. Educated at Miss Barstow's School, New York; Lycée Hoche, Versailles, 1924–28; Lycée de Nice, 1928–29; Morristown School, New Jersey, 1930–34. Served in the United States Army, 1941–45: correspondent, *Yank* magazine. Married 1) Jane Bouché in 1943; 2) Willa Kim in 1955. Art editor and designer, *Paris Review*. Recipient: American Library Association Newbery Medal, 1948. Agent: Watkins/Loomis Agency, 150 East 35th Street, New York, New York 10016. Address: 60 Boulevard Franck Pilatte, 06300 Nice, France.

PUBLICATIONS FOR CHILDREN (illustrated by the author)

Fiction

Elisabeth, The Cow Ghost. New York, Nelson, 1936; London, Museum Press, 1944.
Giant Otto. New York, Viking Press, 1936; London, Harrap, 1937; revised edition, as *Otto in Africa*, New York, Viking Press, 1961, Leicester, Brockhampton Press, 1962.
Otto at Sea. New York, Viking Press, 1936; London, Harrap, 1937.
The Three Policemen; or, Young Bottsford of Farbe Island. New York, Viking Press, 1938.
The Great Geppy. New York, Viking Press, 1940; London, Hale, 1942.
The Flying Locomotive. New York, Viking Press, 1941; London, Museum Press, 1946.
The Twenty-One Balloons. New York, Viking Press, 1947; London, Hale, 1950.
Peter Graves. New York, Viking Press, 1950; Kingswood, Surrey, World's Work, 1974.
Bear Party. New York, Viking Press, 1951; Kingswood, Surrey, World's Work, 1975.
Squirrel Hotel. New York, Viking Press, 1952.
The Giant. New York, Viking Press, 1954.
Lion. New York, Viking Press, 1956.
Otto in Texas. New York, Viking Press, 1959; Leicester, Brockhampton Press, 1961.
The Alligator Case. New York, Harper, 1965.
Lazy Tommy Pumpkinhead. New York, Harper, 1966.
The Horse in the Camel Suit. New York, Harper, 1967.

Pretty Pretty Peggy Moffitt. New York, Harper, 1968.
Porko Von Popbutton. New York, Harper, 1969.
Call Me Bandicoot. New York, Harper, 1970.
Otto and the Magic Potatoes. New York, Viking Press, 1970.
Bear Circus. New York, Viking Press, 1971; Kingswood, Surrey, World's Work, 1975.
Mother Goose for Christmas. New York, Viking Press, 1973.
The Forbidden Forest. New York, Harper, and London, Chatto and Windus, 1978.
Gentleman Bear. New York, Farrar Straus, 1985.

Other

The Hare and the Tortoise, and The Tortoise and the Hare/La Liebre y la Tortuga, & la Tortuga y la Liebre (bilingual edition), with Lee Po. New York, Doubleday, 1972.

*

Manuscript Collection: May Massee Collection, Emporia State University, Kansas.

Illustrator: *S.O.S. Geneva* by Richard Plant and Oskar Seidlin, 1939; *Harriet* by Charles McKinley, Jr., 1946; *The Witch of Scrapfaggot Green* by Patricia Gordon, 1948; *The Mousewife* by Rumer Godden, 1951; *The Young Visiters* by Daisy Ashford, 1951; *Moon Ahead* by Leslie Greener, 1951; *Twenty and Ten* by Claire Huchet Bishop, 1952; *My Brother Bird* by Evelyn Ames, 1954; *The Rabbit's Umbrella* by George Plimpton, 1955; *In France* by Marguerite Clement, 1956; *Jexium Island* by Madeleine Grattan, 1957; *Castles and Dragons* edited by the Child Study Association, 1958; *Fierce John* by Edward Fenton, 1959; *Billy the Barber* by Dorothy Kunhardt, 1961; *The Owl and the Pussycat* by Edward Lear, 1962; *The Light Princess* by George MacDonald, 1962; *The Three Little Pigs,* 1962; *Dr. Ox's Experiment* by Jules Verne, 1963; *The Poison Belt* by Arthur Conan Doyle, 1964; *A Certain Small Shepherd* by Rebecca Caudill, 1965; *The Magic Finger* by Roald Dahl, 1966; *The Tiger in the Teapot* by Betty Yurdin, 1968; *Digging for China: A Poem* by Richard Wilbur, 1970; *The Topsy-Turvy Emperor of China* by Isaac Bashevis Singer, 1971; *Seal Pool* by Peter Matthiessen, 1972; *William's Doll,* 1972, *My Grandson Lew,* 1974, *The Unfriendly Book,* 1975, and *It's Not Fair,* 1976, all by Charlotte Zolotow; *Where's Gomer?* by Norma Farber, 1974; *Moving Day* by Tobi Tobias, 1976; *The Runaway Flying Horse* by Paul J. Bonzon, 1976; *We Came A-Marching—One, Two, Three* by Mildred Hobzek, 1978; *The Sick Day* by Patricia MacLachlan, 1979; *The Planet of Lost Things,* 1982, and *The Night Book,* 1985, both by Mark Strand; *Anna Witch* by Madeleine Edmondson, 1982; *Bear in Mind,* edited by Bobbye S. Goldstein, 1989.

*   *   *

If the prolific writings of William Pène du Bois suggest any common theme, it would have to be the celebration of eccentricity. His Newbery Medal winner, *The Twenty-One Balloons,* begins with a retired arithmetic teacher being retrieved from the Atlantic Ocean where he clung for dear life to the workings of twenty-one deflated balloons. But instead of pursuing the reason why, the author focuses instead upon outrageously idiosyncratic Professor Sherman as he rebuffs entreaties of benefactors and dignitaries—even the President of the United States—rather than relate his experiences prior to addressing the Western American Explorer's Club. His accidental landing on the island of Krakatoa had brought him into contact with people whose proclivities were if anything more peculiar than his own. The gentleman who originally discovered Sherman unconscious and naked upon the beach, waits in a stolid, butler-like stance to provide the survivor with spats, a detachable collar, and a starched white dickey in order to commence a brief expedition through tropical brush and into the society of Krakatoa.

Although the virtues of loyalty and perseverence are implicitly applauded throughout du Bois's writings, overbearing commitment to excess commands the essential spotlight. In separate studies of the seven deadly sins (four of these theological fictions for children have appeared so far) he parades impish delight in excess with one central character demonstrating comic ingenuity in perpetuating an obvious psychological imbalance. There is no denunciation of vice. Porko von Popbutton's swelled belly and voracious gastronomic compulsion cast him ultimately as unlikely hero as victorious goalie against an arch rival school. Ermine Bandicoot, the youthful miser, is as well a charming teller of tales who eschews cigarettes because they are too costly. He does, however, collect the butts with the intention of reprocessing valuable tobacco. His comic lust for gain provokes the ingenious venture of using the Statue of Liberty as an advertising pedestal and he later uses a football field to roll the world's largest cigarette. *Peter Graves* features two eccentrics, Peter the fearless, who urges his school gang across the bay via sharply peaking and declining bridge cables, and Houghton F. Furlong whose horrible house and preposterous inventions scare off even the authorities. Furlong's latest concoction defies the inventor and his youthful accomplice in the search for a possible use. Five small books concern Otto, a Bunyanesque otterhound who can snuggle up to the Sphinx, fan a windmill with his tail, and casually bury 171 Arab warriors in the sand. *The Alligator Case* and its sequel, *The Horse in the Camel Suit,* concern a young boy's preoccupation with being a detective. His over zealous imagination is matched by equally peculiar villains, one of whom knocks bullet peas into the air with pork chop mallets, each time adroitly retrieving the vegetables in his open mouth. The comedy of humours continues throughout the du Bois opus.

After a seven-year absence, du Bois returned to writing with the most preposterous theme of them all—himself. Any devotee of du Bois, and there are many of them, might suspect that his own life would provide a stream of fictional excesses quite exceeding any of the idiosyncratic figures in the du Bois canon. To assure that the tale not be constrained by an undue focus upon the author, the major personage in *Gentleman Bear* is not Sir Billy Browne-Browne, but a teddybear named Bayard. After all, the achievements of flesh and blood are all too tame a preoccupation when compared with activating the personality of a stuffed creature. That's why few writers would want to confine themselves with uncovering the mundane realities of the man on the street. In the life of the fictional du Bois, only the dates, some of the names, and the superabundance of absurdities sustain a connection with the author. Certainly the real Billy Browne-Browne is so truly and grandly ridiculous in his whims and accomplishments that he would be a hard act to follow. True allegiance, after all, is spiritual not biological. The book provides a steady stream of studied excessiveness, and the most ludicrous revelation of all is that the compounding of excessive improbables turns out to be so calmly rational. The sustained laughter notwithstanding, *Gentleman Bear* makes one wonder if the true absurdities do not reside in the literal reading of one's own pursuits and achievements. Most readers are likely to be convinced, as are all the characters in the book, that we all need the attendance of a stuffed bear, at least through the seemingly important junctures of what we are apt to call life.

—Leonard R. Mendelsohn

DUDER, Tessa (née Staveley). New Zealander. Born in Auckland, 13 November 1940. Educated at Diocesan High School for Girls, Auckland, 1946–57; University of Auckland. Married John Nelson Duder in 1964; four daughters. Journalist, Auckland *Star,* 1959–64; feature writer, *Daily Express,* London, 1964–66. Since 1986 editor, Spirit of Adventure Trust, Auckland, and book reviewer, *Dominion Sunday Times,* Wellington. Recipient: Cardiff Empire Games silver medal, for swimming, 1958; Choysa bursary, 1985; New Zealand Library Association Esther Glen award, 1988; New Zealand Children's Book of the Year award, 1988; New Zealand Literary Fund travel grant, 1989. Agent: Ray Richards, Richards Literary Agency, 3/43 Aberdeen Road, Castor Bay, Auckland. Address: 94-A Shakespeare Road, Milford, Auckland, New Zealand.

PUBLICATIONS FOR CHILDREN

Fiction

Night Race to Kawau. Auckland, Oxford University Press, 1982; London, Penguin, 1985.
Jellybean. Auckland and Oxford, Oxford University Press, 1985; New York, Viking Kestrel, 1986.
Alex. Auckland, Oxford University Press, 1987; Oxford, Oxford University Press, 1988; Boston, Houghton Mifflin, 1989.

Other

The Book of Auckland. Auckland, Oxford University Press, 1985.
Play It Again, Sam (reader), illustrated by Kelvin Hawley. Auckland, Shortland, 1987.
Dragons (reader), illustrated by Kelvin Hawley. Auckland, Shortland, 1987.
Simply Messing About in Boats (reader). Auckland, Shortland, 1988.

PUBLICATIONS FOR ADULTS

Other

Kawau. Auckland, Bush Press, 1980; revised edition, as *Discover Kawau,* 1984.
Spirit of Adventure: The Story of New Zealand's Sail Training Ship. Auckland, Century Hutchinson, 1985.
Waitemata: Harbour of Sail. Auckland, Century Hutchinson, 1989.

*

Tessa Duder comments:

I began as a writer of novels for children and intend to continue that way, but with various other areas opening up—musical plays, educational readers, television scripting, radio stories—and the occasional foray into adult non-fiction. A pattern has emerged—three novels which focus on the special problems of girls in contemporary society (identity, expectations, pressures and prejudices); exploring deliberately but not aggressively, since I see myself as a realist/feminist, the dynamics of growing up and family life. It has been a special pleasure that my work has found readers in England, America, Holland, among others; part of an international recognition of the quality of New Zealand writing, with Margaret Mahy pre-eminent. Like her, I've become involved in writing educational material (school readers) for which New Zealand has developed a well-deserved reputation for excellent and innovation. Across the whole spectrum, New Zealand writing and publishing for children is entering the 1990's in good heart.

*　　*　　*

Tessa Duder's wide experiences have contributed to the growth of her ability to write with convincing power, and to her constant concern with the struggle and triumph of strong female characters. In *Night Race to Kawau,* when Sam's father is knocked unconscious while trying to haul down the spinnaker, Sam, her mother, and young sister Jane have to sail their yacht through the stormy night of the race from Auckland to Kawau Island in the Hauraki Gulf. Then Sam and Jane have to hike over the bush-clad hills of Kawau Island for help. Fluent readers find this an exciting story of achievement with already tense family relationships frayed through stress, danger, and exhaustion. For yachting enthusiasts there is the added pleasure of authentic nautical details.

"Musicians are never ordinary, least of all conductors." Beautifully controlled and moving, *Jellybean* captures agony and ecstasy in a fine study of a musical child set apart from society by her "impossible yearning," and reveals with compassion the emotional conflicts of a busy solo mother and daughter. Geraldine, alias Jellybean, aged 10, often goes reluctantly with her cellist mother when she plays in the orchestra and, as well, in pubs for extra money. Yet by going to her mother's rehearsals and concerts, Jellybean develops a longing to be a conductor of the "real music" she hears there. At the attainable level of a school performance, Jellybean's achievement is credible and triumphant. The arrival of Gerald, the mysterious cellist, adds mystery to the storyline. Could he be Jellybean's father? She doesn't want to know. Images spring clear in the immediacy of the narrative's present tense. Humour enhances several occasions, notably Jellybean's unofficial orchestra-pit-eye view of a ballet dress rehearsal. The frightful "competition mum" is the only stereotype in a story where women can achieve even as conductors, and a man can be sensitive and caring. The whole story is illuminated by the music and ballet of Tchaikovsky's *The Nutcracker.*

Duder's first two novels use a simple chronological timeline. The development of a double timeline gives *Alex* an appropriately complex structure for, again, a study of female achievement, with risk-taking, unashamed ambition, and punishing hard work. Alex, aged 15 and very mature, is a competitive swimmer, aiming for the 1960 Olympic Games in Rome. The prologue in italics introduces her at the crisis of being called to the blocks for the final selection race: "In a few minutes I will dive into that artificially turquoise water waiting at my feet. A minute later I'll be either ecstatic or a failure." That minute lasts the length of the novel. Between each phase of the race printed in italics, Alex's life is recounted in chronological flashbacks printed in ordinary type. Both timelines maintain tension as they move forward through humorous and dramatic happenings, disaster and despair, to the climatic moment of success. To add to the complexity, Alex bears in her mind throughout the race the voice of Andy, the young man she has fallen in love with, who meets his death with the unexpectedness of real life.

Because of its strong structure, *Alex* can fully embrace the teenage world of family, school, friends, and society. Alex is multi-talented—on the school stage, in class, on the hockey field as well as in the swimming pool. Her poignant love affair with the also talented Andy is handled with tenderness and passion. Attitudes and issues are confronted—dangerous driving, alcohol, parental and peer pressure, group dynamics, comradeship in competition, society's expectations of girls, and concepts of femaleness and femininity. Adults are portrayed mainly as generous and supportive. A few have their own suffering to deal with; a few are insensitive and scheming. Setting a precedent by winning both the Esther Glen award and the Government Printer's award of 1988, and with rights to TV already sold, this skilful and most moving novel seems certain to reach the readership it deserves. A sequel is already in progress to cover the

Olympic Games themselves.

Duder's writing also includes impressive short stories and, in non-fiction, *The Book of Auckland* and *Spirit of Adventure,* all a valuable contribution to our indigenous literature in which we express "our identity as a nation, something very precious."

—Diane Hebley

DUGGAN, Maurice (Noel). New Zealander. Born in Auckland, 25 November 1922. Educated at the University of Auckland. Married Barbara Platts in 1945; one child. Worked in advertising from 1961: with J. English Wright (Advertising) Ltd. Auckland, 1965–72. Recipient: Hubert Church Prose award, 1957; New Zealand Library Association Esther Glen award, 1959; Katherine Mansfield Memorial award, for short story, 1959; University of Otago Robert Burns fellowship, 1960; New Zealand Literary Fund scholarship, 1966; Buckland award, 1969. *Died 11 December 1974.*

PUBLICATIONS FOR CHILDREN

Fiction

Falter Tom and the Water Boy, illustrated by Kenneth Rowell. Auckland, Blackwood and Janet Paul, 1957; London, Faber, and New York, Criterion, 1958.
The Fabulous McFanes and Other Children's Stories, illustrated by Richard Kennedy. Whatamongo Bay, Cape Catley, 1974.

PUBLICATIONS FOR ADULTS

Short Stories

Immanuel's Land. Auckland, Pilgrim Press, 1956.
New Authors: Short Story 1, with others. London, Hutchinson, 1961.
Summer in the Gravel Pit. Auckland, Blackwood and Janet Paul, and London, Gollancz, 1965.
O'Leary's Orchard and Other Stories. Christchurch, Caxton Press, 1970.
Collected Stories, edited by C.K. Stead. Auckland, Auckland University Press-Oxford University Press, 1981.

*　　*　　*

Maurice Duggan's claim to distinction as a children's author stems undoubtedly from his award-winning novel *Falter Tom and the Water Boy.* A collection of three short stories, *The Fabulous McFanes,* reveals a capacity for energetic storytelling and considerable insight into the concerns of childhood; but to *Falter Tom* must go the ultimate tribute. It remains, without doubt, the most distinguished work to have emerged so far from the pen of a New Zealand author for children.

The story is a fantasy, told in simple, almost faultless prose, the whole a mere 64 pages long. Falter Tom, an old, tale-spinning sailor whose nickname derives from a stiff leg which imparts "a peculiar style to his walk" is enticed into the underwater world by the water boy, and ageless child of the sea, a mixture of wisdom and innocence, gravity and gaiety. Duggan's sea-world is a timeless one, a setting in which the old man's age is irrelevant, his lameness unhampering. It is simultaneously a real world, inhabited by live fish, furnished with ghostly wrecks of ancient and modern ships, embellished here and there with lost treasure and spilled cargo. Duggan invents a minimum of artificial detail; even the Sea Kings, who must be consulted, ultimately, as to Falter Tom's destiny, are heard but not seen, their awesome voices intoning the conditions in unison. The boy himself is at once all-child and all-spirit, humanity and immortality.

It would be possible to theorize that Duggan, a man of robust, outdoor temperament to whom the loss of a leg was a major tragedy, and who before his early death suffered in turn a series of debilitating illnesses, saw in Falter Tom's story the enactment of his own wish fulfilment—deliverance from a world in which pain and despair must often have threatened to extinguish the wit and humour that were his by nature. Certainly, the underwater world as Falter Tom, escorted by the boy, experiences it, seems to contain all of eternity. There, the old become young, the halt and the lame are made whole.

But to the child reader, preoccupied quite properly with his own enjoyment of the story, such speculation is irrelevant. The pace and shape of the tale, the humanity of the characters, the green reality of the underwater world, and the mounting of the tension are all. Falter Tom's agony of choice (to remain forever, or to leave and resume mortal life) elevates his story to the level of high drama. His decision is an affirmation of life, his story heroic.

—Dorothy Butler

———

DUNCAN, Jane. Pseudonym for Elizabeth Jane Cameron; also wrote as Janet Sandison. British. Born in Dunbartonshire, Scotland, 10 March 1910. Educated at Lenzie Academy, Dumbarton; University of Glasgow, M.A. 1930. Served in the photographic intelligence division of the Women's Auxiliary Air Force, 1939–45: Flight Officer. Worked in various jobs, mainly secretarial, 1931–39; worked in the Bahamas, 1945–58. *Died 20 October 1976.*

PUBLICATIONS FOR CHILDREN

Fiction

Camerons on the Train, illustrated by Victor Ambrus. London, Macmillan, 1963.
Camerons on the Hills, illustrated by Victor Ambrus. London, Macmillan, 1963.
Camerons at the Castle, illustrated by Victor Ambrus. London, Macmillan, 1964; New York, St. Martin's Press, 1965.
Camerons Calling, illustrated by Victor Ambrus. London, Macmillan, and New York, St. Martin's Press, 1966.
Camerons Ahoy!, illustrated by Victor Ambrus. London, Macmillan, and New York, St. Martin's Press, 1968.
Herself and Janet Reachfar, illustrated by Mairi Hedderwick. London, Macmillan, 1975; as *Brave Janet Reachfar,* New York, Seabury Press, 1975.
Janet Reachfar and the Kelpie, illustrated by Mairi Hedderwick. London, Macmillan, and New York, Seabury Press, 1976.
Janet Reachfar and the Chickabird, illustrated by Mairi Hedderwick. London, Macmillan, and New York, Seabury Press, 1978.

PUBLICATIONS FOR ADULTS

Novels

My Friends the Miss Boyds. London, Macmillan, and New York, St. Martin's Press, 1959.

My Friend Muriel. London, Macmillan, 1959; New York, St. Martin's Press, 1960.
My Friend Monica. London, Macmillan, and New York, St. Martin's Press, 1960.
My Friend Annie. London, Macmillan, and New York, St. Martin's Press, 1961.
My Friend Sandy. London, Macmillan, 1961; New York, St. Martin's Press, 1962.
My Friend Martha's Aunt. London, Macmillan, and New York, St. Martin's Press, 1962.
My Friend Flora. London, Macmillan, 1962; New York, St. Martin's Press, 1963.
My Friend Madame Zora. London, Macmillan, and New York, St. Martin's Press, 1963.
My Friend Rose. London, Macmillan, and New York, St. Martin's Press, 1964.
My Friend Cousin Emmie. London, Macmillan, 1964; New York, St. Martin's Press, 1965.
My Friends the Mrs. Millers. London, Macmillan, and New York, St. Martin's Press, 1965.
My Friends from Cairnton. London, Macmillan, and New York, St. Martin's Press, 1966.
My Friend My Father. London, Macmillan, 1966; New York, St. Martin's Press, 1967.
My Friends the MacLeans. London, Macmillan, and New York, St. Martin's Press, 1967.
My Friends the Hungry Generation. London, Macmillan, and New York, St. Martin's Press, 1968.
My Friend the Swallow. London, Macmillan, and New York, St. Martin's Press, 1970.
My Friend Sashie. London, Macmillan, and New York, St. Martin's Press, 1972.
My Friends the Misses Kindness. London, Macmillan, and New York, St. Martin's Press, 1974.
My Friends George and Tom. London, Macmillan, and New York, St. Martin's Press, 1976.

Novels as Janet Sandison

An Apology for the Life of Jean Robertson:
Jean in the Morning. London, Macmillan, and New York, St. Martin's Press, 1969.
Jean at Noon. London, Macmillan, 1971; New York, St. Martin's Press, 1972.
Jean in the Twilight; or, The Mists of Autumn. London, Macmillan, 1972; New York, St. Martin's Press, 1973.
Jean Towards Another Day; or, Can Spring Be Far Away? London, Macmillan, and New York, St. Martin's Press, 1975.

Other

Letter from Reachfar (memoir). London, Macmillan, 1975; New York, St. Martin's Press, 1976.

*   *   *

Jane Duncan's chief contribution to children's literature is a series of five books written about the Cameron family. These imaginary children are based on the author's own nieces and nephews—one sister (the eldest), two brothers a little younger, and a much smaller brother, Iain. Iain—or Nink as he is known to his relatives and friends—is retarded, and the loving relationship between Nink and the rest of the family may well prove most helpful to many readers in a similar situation.

The Cameron children are accustomed to spending their summer holidays with an aunt in Scotland; although they themselves live north of the Border, Aunt Liz lives much further north. Each time they visit her, fresh excitements occur. They become very attached to a Scottish stately home called "Castle Vannich," which in one story is being turned into a hotel to make ends meet, but whatever is happening there becomes part of the tale. As one might expect, there are legends concerning Castle Vannich, notably one around the disappearance of the White Hart of Vannich, and it is little Nink who accidentally solves this mystery.

The characters of the children are cleverly drawn, and the Scottish countryside adds a great deal to the background of the stories. The author weaves a blend of history into each narrative. For example, it may be a professor friend of Aunt Liz who is an expert on Viking ships, so imagine the delight when it seems likely that the remains of a Viking ship may lie buried nearby. It may be the discovery of the stone of Strathdonan, but whatever it is, Jane Duncan's family stories have this additional quality which gives them a certain appeal for historically minded young readers.

It must be borne in mind, however, that these family stories were written in the 1960's and reflect a style of family holiday which, sadly enough, is less common today. Nowadays, individual members of a family tend to go their separate ways. This in no way detracts from the sound values inherent in the Cameron series, and their very difference may well provide an added attraction to some readers.

In 1975 Duncan wrote the first of three picture books which have the same setting—Black Isle in Ross-shire—as her popular novels for adult readers. In *Herself and Janet Reachfar* Janet is the little granddaughter living on the farm, and Herself is, of course, Janet's grandmother. Granny is a wonderful combination of stern attitude and overwhelming warmth. One day there is a sudden snowstorm, and against orders Janet goes with her sheepdog Fly to rescue the sheep marooned on East Hill. Not only does she save the sheep, but finds the first lamb of the spring as well! This is a picture book for younger readers, but ideally it should be read to them, as the author has made no concessions in the text to lack of reading ability.

—Berna C. Clark

DUNCAN, Lois (née Steinmetz). Also writes as Lois Kerry. American. Born in Philadelphia, Pennsylvania, 28 April 1934. Educated at Duke University, Durham, North Carolina, 1952–53; University of New Mexico, Albuquerque, B.A. (cum laude) in English 1977 (Phi Beta Kappa). Married Donald Arquette in 1966; five children. Lecturer in Journalism, University of New Mexico, 1970–81. Agent: Clare Smith, Harold Ober Associates, 40 East 49th Street, New York, New York 10017. Address: 1112 Dakota, N.E., Albuquerque, New Mexico 87110, U.S.A.

PUBLICATIONS FOR CHILDREN

Fiction

Debutante Hill. New York, Dodd Mead, 1958.
Love Song for Joyce (as Lois Kerry). New York, Funk and Wagnalls, 1958.
A Promise for Joyce (as Lois Kerry). New York, Funk and Wagnalls, 1959.
The Littlest One in the Family, illustrated by Suzanne Larsen. New York, Dodd Mead, 1960.
The Middle Sister. New York, Dodd Mead, 1960.

Silly Mother, illustrated by Suzanne Larsen. New York, Dial Press, 1962.
Game of Danger. New York, Dodd Mead, 1962.
Giving Away Suzanne, illustrated by Leonard Weisgard. New York, Dodd Mead, 1963.
Season of the Two-Heart. New York, Dodd Mead, 1964.
Ransom. New York, Doubleday, 1966; as *Five Were Missing,* New York, New American Library, 1972.
They Never Came Home. New York, Doubleday, 1969.
Hotel for Dogs, illustrated by Leonard Shortall. Boston, Houghton Mifflin, 1971.
A Gift of Magic, illustrated by Arvis Stewart. Boston, Little Brown, 1971.
I Know What You Did Last Summer. Boston, Little Brown, 1973; London, Hamish Hamilton, 1982.
Down a Dark Hall. Boston, Little Brown, 1974.
Summer of Fear. Boston, Little Brown, 1976; London, Hamish Hamilton, 1981.
Killing Mr. Griffin. Boston, Little Brown, 1978; London, Hamish Hamilton, 1980.
Daughters of Eve. Boston, Little Brown, 1979.
Stranger with My Face. Boston, Little Brown, 1981; London, Hamish Hamilton, 1983.
The Third Eye. Boston, Little Brown, 1984; as *The Eyes of Karen Conners,* London, Hamish Hamilton, 1985.
Locked in Time. Boston, Little Brown, 1985; London, Hamish Hamilton, 1986.
The Twisted Window. New York, Delacorte Press, and London, Hamish Hamilton, 1987.
Wonder Kid Meets the Evil Lunch Snatcher, illustrated by Margaret Sanfilippo. Boston, Little Brown, 1988.
Don't Look Behind You. New York, Delacorte Press, and London, Hamish Hamilton, 1989.

Verse

From Spring to Spring, photographs by the author. Philadelphia, Westminster Press, 1982.
The Terrible Tales of Happy Days School. Boston, Little Brown, 1983.
Horses of Dreamland, illustrated by Donna Diamond. Boston, Little Brown, 1985; London, Hamish Hamilton, 1986.
Songs from Dreamland, music by Robin Arquette, illustrated by Kay Chorao. New York, Knopf, 1989.
The Birthday Moon, illustrated by Susan Davis. New York, Viking, 1989.

Other

Major André, Brave Enemy, illustrated by Tran Mawicke. New York, Putnam, 1969.
Peggy (on Margaret Arnold). Boston, Little Brown, 1970.

PUBLICATIONS FOR ADULTS

Novels

Point of Violence. New York, Doubleday, 1966; London, Hale, 1968.
When the Bough Breaks. New York, Doubleday, 1973.

Other

How to Write and Sell Your Personal Experiences. Cincinnati, Writer's Digest, 1979.

Chapters: My Growth as a Writer. Boston, Little Brown, 1982.

*

Manuscript Collection: Kerlan Collection, University of Minnesota, Minneapolis.

Lois Duncan comments:

During my lengthy career as a writer, I have written many different kinds of books. My earliest were romances, and then I moved to mysteries. I produced a humorous book about dogs, two biographies of historical figures, two books of children's verse, an autobiography called *Chapters,* and a how-to book for people who aspire to be professional writers. My most recent books and the ones that I am best known for are psychological suspense novels. In all cases, I write the sort of books that I myself enjoy reading, use for my characters people who are much like the ones in my family, and lay my stories in settings with which I am familiar.

Writing is my work, my hobby; my agony and my joy. I cannot imagine ever wanting to do anything else.

*   *   *

Lois Duncan began her writing career very early in life, shortly after she learned to print at age five or so. At age 10 she submitted her first typed manuscript to *Ladies' Home Journal.* The editor did not publish it but his kindly rejection letter encouraged her to keep trying. Some sage advice from a new neighbor, who turned out to be MacKinley Kantor, led her to stop writing what he called romantic "trash" and write about what she knew. She did, and as a result sold her first short story to a teen magazine at age 13. A decade later Duncan's first novel *Debutante Hill,* a piece of "sweet and sticky...pap," won a literary competition that awarded her $1000 and a book contract from Dodd Mead.

The world of adolescent fiction by the mid 1960's was not a world of books like *Debutante Hill,* however. Fiction of this period was characterized by an often gritty realism; plots were no longer concerned solely with sports and dating and horses but used as their subject matter things that were happening in the real world—drugs, peer pressure, social and psychological problems, sex, divorce, etc. This new freedom to write more realistically for young readers appealed to Duncan, and her first novel written "under the new set of ground rules" was *Ransom,* a taut adventure story about a group of teenagers kidnapped by their school bus driver. How different *Ransom* was from Duncan's earlier teen novels is indicated by the fact that Dodd Mead refused to publish it because it "wasn't Duncan's style;" Doubleday then took it on and it become a runnerup for the Edgar Allan Poe award. A second realistic teen novel, *They Never Came Home,* was also an Edgar runnerup, and Duncan was firmly set in the writing style that was to prove so successful for her over the next two decades.

The style Duncan has used is a simple one. She places an individual or a group of normal, believable young people in what appears to be a prosaic setting such as a suburban neighborhood or an American high school; on the surface everything is as it should be, until Duncan introduces an element of surprise that gives the story an entirely new twist. In her novel *Down a Dark Hall,* for example, a young woman goes off to what appears to be a normal boarding school. It proves however to be run by a headmistress who is herself a medium, and the school is haunted by malevolent ghosts of artists and writers who invade the minds and bodies of the innocent students. *Summer of Fear* is about an average family in Albuquerque, New Mexico, who "inherit" a 17-year-old girl, Julia, from relatives who have died in a car crash. Rachael, the narrator, first suspects Julia of being strangely sinister, but when she finds out that Julia cannot be photographed, Rachael begins to realize that Julia is not

merely different but is a witch and an evil one at that. *Stranger with My Face* introduces astral projection when an evil young woman tries to take over the mind and body of her identical twin sister. *The Third Eye* tells the story of Karen, who must summon the courage to use her gift of E.S.P. to stop the evil machinations of an older couple who kidnap babies to sell them on the baby market. One of Duncan's most exciting and sophisticated novels, *Locked in Time,* finds Nore spending the summer with her new step-relations and her father on her stepmother's Louisiana plantation. Strange events and unlikely occurrences lead her to believe her new relatives are "locked in time"—ageless—but her discovery of their secret leads to terrible danger for Nore. In each of these books, an element of the occult is an integral part of a fast-moving plot, but it is always believable because Duncan never carries her depiction of the supernatural into the sometimes goofy realms that a writer such as Stephen King does. Character and plot are always predominant; the books are first and foremost good mysteries made even more interesting for young readers by some aspect of the unusual.

Not all Duncan's novels depend on use of the supernatural, however. Some of her best works for young adults use the depths of human nature as an unexpected fillip that raises them above the level of the average teen novel. In *I Know What You Did Last Summer* four teenage friends riding in a car which is going too fast on a dark road hit and kill a young boy on a bike. Barry, the driver, persuades the others that nothing will be gained by confessing what they have done, especially since they'd been coming from a party where they had smoked a little pot and drunk some beer. They all manage to put the incident out of their minds until a year later, when each receives a letter saying simply, "I know what you did last summer." A succession of letters follows, each more threatening than the last, until the young people realize that their very lives are in danger from a psychopath bent on revenge.

In *Killing Mr. Griffin,* a group of high school students set out to scare a hated English teacher into being a little more reasonable by taking him to a remote spot in a woods, tying him to a tree, and leaving him overnight. It soon becomes apparent that Mark, the charismatic leader of the group, would like to go even further than frightening Mr. Griffin, but the rest refuse to go along with him. The next morning when they go to release the teacher they find him dead; without his life-sustaining medication he has succumbed to a heart attack. This time Mark does prevail by convincing the others that nothing is to be gained by telling the truth about what has happened. It is only when Mark begins to pressure the group to kill again that they recognize him for the evil person he is, but by then it's almost too late.

One of Duncan's most chilling examples of the power of an evil person is in her portrayal of Irene Stark in *Daughters of Eve,* who uses the members of a high school girls' service club as instruments of revenge on all men. Her pathological hatred results in tragic consequences for the naïve young women she is ostensibly guiding as the club's advisor and mentor. In *The Twisted Window,* Tracy Lloyd, abandoned by her father after her mother's death, is drawn into helping a strange young man, Brad Johnson, rescue his baby sister, kidnapped by their stepfather and now living in the same town as Tracy. The plot backfires for Tracy, though, when she begins to realize that Brad is seriously disturbed and she finds herself and the child in terrible danger.

In each of these novels it is a mark of Duncan's ability as a writer that the evils she describes are perfectly plausible and believable. As in her use of the occult, her use of warped human nature as a tool to move the plot along briskly never seems contrived or used solely for shock effect, but is integral to the story. In this respect, Duncan is strongly reminiscent of Robert Cormier in her no-holds-barred portraits of the consequences of human evil and perversity. For that very reason Duncan is shocking to many adult critics, but her youthful readers enjoy the fast-moving plots, fine characterization, and excruciating suspense that characterize most of her fiction and make her one of the most popular writers for this group on the contemporary scene.

—Audrey Eaglen

————

DUNCAN, Norman (McLean). Canadian. Born in Brantford, Ontario, 2 July 1871. Educated at the University of Toronto, 1891–95. Journalist, Auburn *Bulletin,* New York, 1895–97, and New York *Evening Post,* 1897–1900; Newfoundland and Labrador correspondent, *McClure's* magazine, New York, 1900–04; Professor of Rhetoric, Washington and Jefferson College, Washington, Pennsylvania, 1901–06; Middle and Far East correspondent, *Harper's* magazine, New York, 1907, 1912–13; Professor of English, University of Kansas, Lawrence, 1909–11. *Died 18 October 1916.*

PUBLICATIONS FOR CHILDREN

Fiction

The Adventures of Billy Topsail. New York, Revell, and London, Hodder and Stoughton, 1906.
Billy Topsail and Company. New York, Revell, 1910.
Billy Topsail, M.D.: A Tale of Adventure with Doctor Luke of the Labrador. New York, Revell, 1916; London, Hodder and Stoughton, 1917.

PUBLICATIONS FOR ADULTS

Novels

The Way of the Sea. New York, McClure, 1903; London, Hodder and Stoughton, 1904.
Doctor Luke of the Labrador. New York, Revell, and London, Hodder and Stoughton, 1904.
The Mother. New York, McClure, and London, Hodder and Stoughton, 1905.
The Cruise of the Shining Light. Toronto, Oxford University Press, and New York, Harper, 1907.
Every Man for Himself. New York, Harper, 1908.
The Suitable Child. New York, Revell, 1909.
The Measure of a Man: A Tale of the Big Woods. New York, Revell, 1911; London, Hodder and Stoughton, 1912.
The Best of a Bad Job: A Hearty Tale of the Sea. Toronto, Oxford University Press, and New York, Revell, 1912.
Finding His Soul. New York, Harper, 1913.
The Bird-Store Man: An Old-Fashioned Story. New York, Revell, 1914.
Christmas Eve at Swamp's End. New York, Revell, 1915.
Battles Royal Down North. New York, Revell, 1918.
Harbour Tales Down North. New York, Revell, 1918.

Short Stories

The Soul of the Street: Correlated Stories of the New York Syrian Quarter. New York, McClure, 1900.

Other

Dr. Grenfell's Parish: The Deep Sea Fisherman. Toronto and New

York, Revell, and London, Hodder and Stoughton, 1905.
Higgins: A Man's Christian. New York, Harper, 1909.
Going Down from Jerusalem: The Narrative of a Sentimental Traveller, illustrated by Lawren S. Harris. New York, Harper, 1909.
Australian Byways: The Narrative of a Sentimental Traveller, illustrated by George Harding. New York, Harper, 1915.

*   *   *

Norman Duncan wrote more than twenty books, most of which can be categorized as popular fiction for adults. However, a number of these adult books, such as *The Cruise of the Shining Light,* were read by adolescents as well as by adults. Although the characters in Duncan's books for adults are drawn from subjects as diverse as New York prostitution and the fishermen of Labrador and Newfoundland, it is generally agreed that he is as his best when writing stories of the sea. His technique is to employ a mixture of sentimentality and sharply focused realism, and his emphasis is usually on action and the documentary presentation of a particular region rather than on an in-depth exploration of character.

The popular Billy Topsail novels, which Duncan wrote specifically for young readers, are episodic adventure stories set on the Newfoundland and Labrador coast. The early years of the boy protagonist Billy Topsail are the focus of *The Adventures of Billy Topsail;* the sequel, *Billy Topsail and Company* covers some of the same time-span, but focuses on a merchant-trading venture of Billy's adolescent years; *Billy Topsail, M.D.* again reworks some of the earlier material, but it focusses on Billy's later teen years, during which time he assists Duncan's famous Dr. Luke and decides to become a doctor himself. (The fictional Dr. Luke, based partly on the real Dr. Wilfred T. Grenfell, is the protagonist of *Doctor Luke of the Labrador,* one of Duncan's well-known works for adults.)

Despite some repetition, the novels are exciting to read, and they give the reader a sense of what it was like to grow up on the rugged, sparsely populated Canadian coast around the turn of the century. Billy Topsail is a lively, red-blooded little boy whose curiosity and sense of adventure often take him into danger on either land or sea, but his pluck, common sense, and courage always save him. One memorable portion of the first book, for instance, describes Billy and a friend's encounter with a giant squid who plays dead until the curious boys bring their boat near him; then his ubiquitous tentacles appear from all angles, behind and under their punt, and the terrified boys fight for their lives. Another scene which appears in many variations in the Topsail series is that in which Billy (or someone else, like Dr. Luke) takes a shortcut across the cove on floating ice pans in order to save a life or to do a good deed. These perilous trips, so dangerous because the boys (or men) either may slip off the ice and drown, or fall through "rotten" ice and suffocate, or float out to sea and freeze, serve to underline Duncan's admiration for the hardiness and bravery of these people of Newfoundland and Labrador. *Billy Topsail, M.D.,* for example, includes an extraordinarily effective long episode in which Billy is rushing a little lame boy across the ice in the huge bay on the fateful night that the spring ice breaks up and begins drifting out to sea. The two boys are left helplessly marooned on an ice pan with the starving, vicious, part-wolf sled dogs who try to attack and eat the weakening boys.

Duncan stresses bravery, loyalty, kindness, humour, manners, friendliness, and helpfulness to others, especially weaker people. Although he often lapses into didacticism and sentimental idealization of character, Duncan reveals remarkable narrative and descriptive powers in the Billy Topsail series.

—Mary Rubio

————

DUNLOP, Eileen (Rhona). British. Born in Alloa, Clackmannan, Scotland, 13 October 1938. Educated at Alloa Academy, 1943–56; Moray House College of Education, Edinburgh, 1956–59, diploma (honours) in primary education 1959. Married Antony Kamm in 1979. Assistant teacher, Eastfield School, Penicuik, Midlothian, 1959–61, and Abercromby School, Tullibody, Clackmannan, 1961–63; deputy headmistress, Sunnyside School, Alloa, 1963–79. Since 1980 teacher, Preparatory School of Dollar Academy, Clackmannan. Recipient: Scottish Arts Council award, 1983, 1986. Address: 46 Tarmangie Drive, Dollar, Clackmannan FK14 7BP, Scotland.

PUBLICATIONS FOR CHILDREN

Fiction

Robinsheugh, illustrated by Peter Farmer. London, Oxford University Press, 1975; as *Elizabeth Elizabeth,* New York, Holt Rinehart, 1977.
A Flute in Mayferry Street, illustrated by Phillida Gili. London, Oxford University Press, 1976; as *The House on Mayferry Street,* New York, Holt Rinehart, 1976.
Fox Farm. London, Oxford University Press, 1978; New York, Holt Rinehart, 1979.
The Maze Stone, illustrated by Martin White. Oxford, Oxford University Press, 1982; New York, Coward McCann, 1983.
Clementina. Oxford, Oxford University Press, 1985; New York, Holiday House, 1987.
The House on the Hill. Oxford, Oxford University Press, and New York, Holiday House, 1987.
The Valley of Deer. Oxford, Oxford University Press, and New York, Holiday House, 1989.

Other (with Antony Kamm)

Edinburgh, illustrated by Helen Herbert. Cambridge, Cambridge University Press, 1982.
Kings and Queens of Scotland, illustrated by Maureen and Gordon Gray. Glasgow, Drew, 1984.
Scottish Heroes and Heroines of Long Ago, illustrated by Maureen and Gordon Gray. Glasgow, Drew, 1984.
The Story of Glasgow, illustrated by Maureen and Gordon Gray. Glasgow, Drew, 1984.
Scottish Homes Through the Ages, illustrated by John Harrold. Glasgow, Drew, 1985.

Editor, *Scottish Traditional Rhymes,* illustrated by Maureen and Gordon Gray. Glasgow, Drew, 1985.

PUBLICATIONS FOR ADULTS

Other

Editor, with Antony Kamm, *A Book of Old Edinburgh.* Edinburgh, Macdonald, 1983.
Editor, with Antony Kamm, *The Scottish Collection of Verse to 1800.* Glasgow, Drew, 1985.

*

Eileen Dunlop comments:
From time to time I am asked whether I have ever had the kind of experience which I describe in my books. This surprises me, since I believe in a reasoned universe, and subscribe to Coleridge's dictum, *The imagination is the servant of reason.* I believe that our experience of the past must be cerebral, or imaginative, or both. I do not believe that ghosts have any objective validity; if they exist at all, they must be products of minds and imaginations pushed by abnormal stress to their limits. This is the symbolic function they have in my work.

I choose to write in the way I do for two reasons. The first is simple. Children love a ghost story. Whether or not they admit to believing in ghosts, they enjoy being frightened within a secure environment. They also love the idea of being able to go back into the past. Any of my books can be read on the level of a weird tale; I have suspended my disbelief in writing it, and the measure of my success is the extent to which young readers can do the same.

The second reason is more complex. Although I write in the first instance for children, for my own satisfaction I try to enrich my work by employing a wide range of symbolism and allusion. In *The House on the Hill,* for example, many of the motifs echo the *Four Quartets* of T.S. Eliot, a writer whose ideas of time and its significance have greatly influenced my own. I am interested also in adult, as well as child psychology, in the relation of children to adults, and of childhood to adult experience. I am fascinated by the past, and how the influence of the past makes us what we are, as individuals, as families, as a nation. The ghosts in my books are symbolic of the power of imagination to evoke the most vivid images, and excursions into the past are to be understood as feats of imagination taken—for conventional and artistic reasons—far beyond the limits of normal possibility. The suggestion in my fiction that a child's "occult" experience may arise from some tumult in the mind of an adult character, as in the relationship between Kate and Elizabeth in *Robinsheugh,* or between Jane and Philip in *The House on the Hill,* underlines the close affinity there may be between different generations of one family. It also emphasises the fact that, while an openness of response may be one of the blessings of youth, an informed mind and the power of recall are among the compensations of maturity.

I am a Scottish writer. While I am aware of the dangers of narrowness and insularity, I find that I can write with greatest conviction when I choose Scottish themes and settings; my sense of the "spirit of place" is very strong. A strongly-imagined, realistic beackground seems to me indispensable, if I am to achieve in my readers the "willing suspension of disbelief" which fantasy writing requires. The intertwining of fantasy with humdrum reality, and the evocation of real places, is a common facet of Scottish folklore and literature; from Burns's *Tam O' Shanter* to Fred Urquhart's *Proud Lady in a Cage,* the chilling effect of the magical and macabre arises from its juxtaposition with the utterly commonplace. I should like to feel that my writing finds a place in this tradition.

*   *   *

Eileen Dunlop is haunted by the past—the dark, sinister, yet compellingly romantic past of her native Scotland. And so too are the characters in her novels. They become possessed by the past, sometimes drawn into it by magic talismans, sometimes just by being in the right place at the right time; and once there, they experience for themselves its glamour and terror.

Robinsheugh, Dunlop's first and most substantial story, introduces her theme. Prickly Elizabeth, the reluctant guest of a scholarly aunt who is pursuing her researches in an ancient Borders house, finds a silver looking glass, which transports her back into the 18th century. At first she is delighted, but enjoyment turns to fear as the power of the long-ago family tightens round her. This is a rich, many-layered book, hinting too at the perilous Scottish fairy world behind its actual past. Was she "awa' wi' the fairies," Elizabeth is asked; and both her enchanted mirror and the spellbinding boy who compels her return, suggest that she has been.

The fairy theme is developed in *The Maze Stone,* where a cold-eyed Tam Lin figure, masquerading as a teacher in a Lanarkshire comprehensive, lures lovesick Hester into his pale fairy world under the traditional green hill.

A Flute in Mayferry Street presents a gentler version of the past, as two children learn the story of some former inhabitants of their Edinburgh home; but *Clementina* gives a darker picture, in which three teenage girls, unwillingly linked in a timeshare (the word is significant) holiday in the Trossachs, find themselves re-enacting a Jacobite drama of love and murder.

Elizabeth, in *Robinsheugh* went into the past, "because she had to." Her mirror, the ghostly flute of Mayferry Street, and Clementina's ruined tower exert their influence unbidden over their destined objects. So there is a surprise in Dunlop's latest book, *The Valley of Deer.* Modern Anne, having relived the terrors of a white witch murdered in 1726, is prompted to try a little magic herself, to help a crippled friend. The rejection of her potion leads Anne herself to reject, utterly and decisively, the fey power of the past, and choose raw, unglamourous reality instead. Perhaps Dunlop too is preparing to break the old spell, and move to new fields.

Dunlop's books will appeal most to serious, historically-minded readers. They require quite a high degree of concentration, with their preponderance of narrative, analysis, and explanation over dialogue. The accumulation of historical detail, especially in *Robinsheugh,* gives great authenticity but slows down the action. Recurrent themes seem literary and old-fashioned—the helpless invalid girl, the orphan to whom charity is extended, the preoccupied academics and landed families, the clues derived from books and letters. Although Dunlop achieves sharp characterization, and casts an ominous, brooding shadow over her stories, there is a stiffness, a—perhaps Scottish—reserve about them, which prevents her exciting plots from always catching fire. She often hurries her climaxes—the journey under the fairy hill in *The Maze Stone,* the fatal fire in *Clementina*—in a way that muffles them, as if either her courage, or her technique, cannot quite match her dramatic imagination.

In the end, her most completely satisfactory book is her simplest, *Fox Farm.* This too is a story of possession, but not by the past; although, as in any Dunlop book, the past cannot be wholly ignored, and she includes another ruined tower, and a stolen chalice which still throws a curse over the descendants of the thief. But this is of minor importance. The real story concerns Adam, abandoned by his father, yet refusing to trust the kind family who has fostered him; and who, instead, lavishes an obsessive love on the orphaned fox cub he himself is secretly fostering. Dunlop's portrayal of characters and relationships is unerring. The tension rises quite as grippingly as in her more ambitious novels, and the book ends with an unexpected and truly delightful surprise. It is hard to imagine any child who would not enjoy *Fox Farm.*

—Angela Bull

DURACK, (Dame) Mary. Australian. Born in Adelaide, South Australia, 20 February 1913. Educated at Loreto Convent, Perth. Married Horace Clive Miller in 1938 (died 1980); four daughters (two deceased) and two sons. Columnist (as "Virgilia"), Western Australian Newspapers, Perth, 1937–38; worked for Australian Broadcasting Corporation. President, Western Australian Branch, Fellowship of Australian Writers, Swanbourne, 1958–63; from 1983 Emeritus Fellow, Literature Board of Australia. Recipient: Commonwealth Literary Fund grant, 1973, 1977; Australian Research Committee grant, 1980, 1984; Australian Society of Women Writers Alice award, 1982; Australian Council fellowship, 1983. D.Litt.: University of Western Australia, Nedlands, 1978. O.B.E. (Officer,

Order of the British Empire), 1966; D.B.E. (Dame Commander, Order of the British Empire), 1978. Agent: Curtis Brown (Australia) Pty. Ltd., 86 William Street, Paddington, New South Wales 2021. Address: 12 Bellevue Avenue, Nedlands, Western Australia 6009, Australia.

PUBLICATIONS FOR CHILDREN

Fiction

The Way of the Whirlwind, illustrated by Elizabeth Durack. Sydney, Consolidated Press, 1941; London, Angus and Robertson, 1956; revised edition, Angus and Robertson, 1979.

Plays

The Ship of Dreams (produced Fremantle, Western Australia, 1968).
The Way of the Whirlwind, adaptation of her own story (produced Broome, Western Australia, 1970).

Verse

Little Poems of Sunshine by an Australian Child. Perth, Sampson, 1923.
Piccaninnies, illustrated by Elizabeth Durack. Sydney, Offset Printing, 1940.
The Magic Trumpet, illustrated by Elizabeth Durack. Melbourne, London, and New York, Cassell, 1946.
Kookanoo and Kangaroo, illustrated by Elizabeth Durack. Adelaide, Rigby, 1963; London, Angus and Robertson, 1964; Minneapolis, Lerner, 1966.
Red Jack, illustrated by Michael Wilkin. Melbourne, Macmillan, 1987; London, Macmillan, 1988.

Other

All-About: The Story of a Black Community on Argyle Station, Kimberley, illustrated by Elizabeth Durack. Sydney, The Bulletin, 1935.
Chunuma, illustrated by Elizabeth Durack. Sydney, The Bulletin, 1936.
Son of Djaro, illustrated by Elizabeth Durack. Sydney, The Bulletin, 1938.
To Ride a Fine Horse, illustrated by Elizabeth Durack. Melbourne and London, Macmillan, and New York, St. Martin's Press, 1963.
The Courteous Savage: Yagan of Swan River, illustrated by Elizabeth Durack. Melbourne and London, Nelson, 1964; as *Yagan of the Bibbulmun,* Melbourne, Nelson, 1976.
An Australian Settler, illustrated by David Parry. Melbourne and London, Oxford University Press, 1964; as *A Pastoral Emigrant,* Melbourne, London, and New York, Oxford University Press, 1965.
Tjakamarra: Boy Between Two Worlds. Perth, Vanguard, 1977.

PUBLICATIONS FOR ADULTS

Novel

Keep Him My Country. Sydney, Angus and Robertson, and London, Constable, 1955.

Plays

Dalgerie, music by James Penberthy (produced Perth, 1966).

Swan River Saga (produced Perth, 1971). Perth, Service Printing, 1975.

Radio Play: *The Dallying Llama,* 1959.

Other

Child Artists of the Australian Bush, with Florence Rutter. London, Harrap, 1950.
Kings in Grass Castles. London, Constable, 1959.
The Rock and the Sand. London, Constable, 1969.
To Be Heirs Forever (biography of Eliza Shaw). London, Constable, 1976.
The Aborigines in Australian Literature. Perth, Western Australian Institute of Technology, 1978.
A Legacy of Love, with B. Mulholland. Perth, Artlook, 1981.
Sons in the Saddle. London, Constable, 1983.
The Land Beyond Time, with others. Sydney, Lansdowne Press, 1984.
The Stockman, with others. Sydney, Lansdowne Press, 1984.

Editor, *The Fifth Sparrow,* by M.L. Skinner. Sydney, Sydney University Press, 1972.
Editor, *The End of Dreaming,* by Ingrid A. Drysdale. Adelaide, Rigby, 1974; London, Hale, 1975.

*   *   *

Mary Durack and her sister Elizabeth, whose illustrations form an integral part of all her books, have a unique position in Australian children's literature. As the grandchildren of one of Australia's most picturesque pioneers who drove his flocks and herds thousands of miles through unexplored country in one of the greatest pioneering feats of the 19th century, their name was already known when the *Bulletin* in Sydney published their first book in 1935. This and two subsequent books depicted life on Argyle Station in remote northwestern Australia, telling of the day-to-day events of the aborigines living on the station. Though the books often told of the doings of aboriginal children, they are not necessarily books *for* children. Several years later, in 1941, they produced a real fairy story, *The Way of the Whirlwind.* In the old fairy tale tradition it told of two children who set out on a quest, their adventures, and the ultimate success of their search. But in this story the children were aborigines, whose baby brother had been stolen by a whirlwind. Their search involved them with such creatures, of the spirit or animal world, that imaginary aboriginal children could possibly have encountered. The young children, for whom the book was written, could identify with the aboriginal hero and heroine, and the story was skilfully told, the suspense being maintained throughout. This was at the time the most successful attempt to create a fantasy based on aboriginal life. Though it did not purport to interpret aboriginal mythology, the device lent a new dimension to the conventional fairy story, and it enabled Australian children to relate to the aboriginal children they had probably never seen, and the country and creatures who formed their environment. This story has not the richness or conviction of imaginative power to move the reader as do the great works of the imagination, but its liveliness and originality still appeal to young children. It advanced children's stories in Australia through the author's unselfconscious acceptance of aboriginal characters and a primitive setting, which was then an innovation.

The Magic Trumpet, a lyrical fantasy in verse, was imaginatively illustrated throughout with some of her sister's most successful drawings printed both in colour and in sepia. *The Courteous Savage* is a sympathetic account of the tragic relations between the early white settlers in Western Australia and the aboriginal inhabitants. Mary Durack has interpreted aboriginal life in many books for Australian children with understanding and imagination.

—Marcie Muir

————

DUVOISIN, Roger (Antoine). American. Born in Geneva, Switzerland, 28 August 1904; emigrated to the United States, 1927; naturalized citizen, 1938. Educated at Ecole Professionelle, Geneva, 1915–17; Ecole des Arts Decoratifs, Geneva, 1917–23, teaching diploma. Married Louise Fatio, *q.v.,* in 1925; two sons. Stage designer, Geneva Opera, 1922–24; manager of a ceramics firm, Ferney-Voltaire, France, 1924–25; textile designer, in Lyon and Paris, 1927, and for Mallinson Silk Company, New York, 1927–32; Visiting Professor, Parsons School of Art, New York, 1942–50. Freelance illustrator, 1932–60. Group shows: Art Alliance Gallery, Philadelphia, 1946; Museum of Modern Art, New York, 1946; Durand Rue Gallery, New York, 1949; Philadelphia Museum School of Art, 1953; "Graphic Art in the U.S.A.," European tour, 1963; Bratislava Biennale; Rutgers University Museum of Art, 1973. Recipient: American Library Association Caldecott Medal, for illustration, 1948; Society of Illustrators award, 1961; University of Southern Mississippi award, 1971; New York Academy of Science award, for non-fiction, 1975; University of Minnesota Kerlan award, 1976. Honorary Doctorate: Kean College, Union, New Jersey, 1978. *Died 30 June 1980.*

PUBLICATIONS FOR CHILDREN (illustrated by the author)

Fiction

A Little Boy Was Drawing. New York, Scribner, 1932.
Donkey-Donkey: The Troubles of a Silly Little Donkey. Racine, Wisconsin, Whitman, 1933; London, Chatto Boyd and Oliver, 1969.
All Aboard! New York, Grosset and Dunlap, 1935.
The Christmas Cake in Search of Its Owner. New York, American Artists Group, 1941.
The Christmas Whale. New York, Knopf, 1945.
Chanticleer. New York, Grosset and Dunlap, 1947.
Petunia. New York, Knopf, 1950; London, Lane, 1958.
Petunia and the Song. New York, Knopf, 1951.
A for the Ark. New York, Lothrop, 1952; London, Bodley Head, 1961.
Petunia's Christmas. New York, Knopf, 1952; London, Bodley Head, 1960.
Petunia Takes a Trip. New York, Knopf, 1953; London, Bodley Head, 1959.
Easter Treat. New York, Knopf, 1954.
One Thousand Christmas Beards, See Smith Toy Shop, Eat at Joe's. New York, Knopf, 1955; Kingswood, Surrey, World's Work, 1975.
Two Lonely Ducks: A Counting Book. New York, Knopf, 1955; London, Bodley Head, 1966.
The House of Four Seasons. New York, Lothrop, 1956; Leicester, Brockhampton Press, 1960.
Petunia, Beware! New York, Knopf, 1958; London, Bodley Head, 1962.
Day and Night. New York, Knopf, 1960.
The Happy Hunter. New York, Lothrop, 1961; Edinburgh, Oliver and Boyd, 1962.
Veronica. New York, Knopf, 1961; London, Bodley Head, 1962.

Our Veronica Goes to Petunia's Farm. New York, Knopf, 1962; as *Veronica Goes to Petunia's Farm,* London, Bodley Head, 1963.

Lonely Veronica. New York, Knopf, 1963; London, Bodley Head, 1964.

Spring Snow. New York, Knopf, 1963; Kingswood, Surrey, World's Work, 1966.

Veronica's Smile. New York, Knopf, 1964; London, Bodley Head, 1965.

Petunia, I Love You. New York, Knopf, 1965; London, Bodley Head, 1966.

The Missing Milkman. New York, Knopf, 1967; Kingswood, Surrey, World's Work, 1968.

What Is Right for Tulip. New York, Knopf, 1969.

Veronica and the Birthday Present. New York, Knopf, 1971; London, Bodley Head, 1972.

The Crocodile in the Tree. London, Bodley Head, 1972; New York, Knopf, 1973.

Jasmine. New York, Knopf, 1973; London, Bodley Head, 1974.

Petunia's Treasure. New York, Knopf, 1975; London, Bodley Head, 1977.

Periwinkle. New York, Knopf, 1976.

Crocus. New York, Knopf, and London, Bodley Head, 1977.

Snowy and Woody. New York, Knopf, 1979.

The Importance of Crocus. London, Bodley Head, 1980; New York, Knopf, 1981.

Other

And There Was America. New York, Knopf, 1938.

The Three Sneezes and Other Swiss Tales. New York, Knopf, 1941; London, Muller, 1943; as *Fairy Tales from Switzerland,* Muller, 1958.

They Put Out to Sea: The Story of the Map. New York, Knopf, 1943; London, University of London Press, 1947.

The Four Corners of the World. New York, Knopf, 1948.

The Miller, His Son, and Their Donkey. New York, McGraw Hill, 1962; London, Bodley Head, 1963.

See What I Am. New York, Lothrop, 1974; Kingswood, Surrey, World's Work, 1977.

*

Bibliography: *A Roger Duvoisin Bibliography* by Irvin Kerlan, Charlottesville, Bibliographic Society of the University of Virginia, 1958.

Manuscript Collections: Kerlan Collection, University of Minnesota, Minneapolis; University of Oregon Library, Eugene; Rutgers University Library, New Brunswick, New Jersey; de Grummond Collection, University of Southern Mississippi, Hattiesburg.

Illustrator: *Mother Goose* edited by William Rose Benét, 1936; *The Pied Piper of Hamelin* by Robert Browning, 1936; *Riema, Little Brown Girl of Java,* 1937, *Soomoon, Boy of Bali,* 1938, and *Jo-Yo's Idea,* 1939, all by Kathleen Morrow Elliot; *The Feast of Lamps* by Charlet Root, 1938; *Tales of the Pampas* by W.H. Hudson, 1939; *Rhamon, A Boy of Kashmir* by Heluiz Washburne, 1939; *Language Arts for Modern Youth,* 1939; *The Dog Cantbark* by Marjorie Fischer, 1940; *Petits Contes Vrais* by Mary Riley and Andre Humbert, 1940; *Military French,* n.d.; *At Our House* by John G. McCullough, 1943; *A Child's Garden of Verses,* 1944, and *Travels with a Donkey,* 1957, both by Robert Louis Stevenson; *Fair, Fantastic Paris* by Harold Ettlinger, 1944; *Jumpy the Kangaroo* by Janet Howard, 1944; *The Christmas Book of Legends and Stories,* by Elva Smith and Alice Hazeltine, 1944; *Virgin with Butterflies* by

Tom Powers, 1945; *The Happy Time* by Robert Fontaine, 1945; *Bhimsa the Dancing Bear* by Christine Weston, 1945; *"I Won't,"* *Said the King* by Mildred Jordan, 1945; *The Life and Adventures of Robinson Crusoe* by Daniel Defoe, 1946; *The Successful Secretary* by Margaret Pratt, 1946; *At Daddy's Office* by Robert Jay Misch, 1946; *Daddies: What They Do All Day,* 1946, and *The Sitter Who Didn't Sit,* 1949, both by Helen Walker Puner; *Moustachio* by Douglas Rigby, 1947; *White Snow, Bright Snow,* 1947, *Johnny Maple-Leaf,* 1948, *Sun Up,* 1949, *Follow the Wind,* 1950, *Hi, Mr. Robin!,* 1950, *Autumn Harvest,* 1951, *Follow the Road,* 1953, *I Saw the Sea Come In,* 1954, *Wake Up, Farm!,* 1955, *Wake Up, City!,* 1957, *The Frog in the Well,* 1958, *Timothy Robbins Climbs the Mountain,* 1960, *Under the Trees and Through the Grass,* 1962, *Hide and Seek Fog,* 1965, *The World in the Candy Egg,* 1967, *It's Time Now!,* 1969, *The Beaver Pond,* 1970, and *What Did You Leave Behind?,* 1978, all by Alvin Tresselt; *The Steam Shovel That Wouldn't Eat Dirt* by George Walters, 1948; *Christmas Pony,* 1948, and *Winkie's World,* 1958, both by William Hall; *The Little Whistler* by Frances Frost, 1949; *The Man Who Could Grow Hair* by William Attwood, 1949; *Dozens of Cousins* by Mabel Watts, 1950; *Vavache, The Cow Who Painted Pictures* by Frederic Attwood, 1950; *Love and Dishes* by Niccolo de Quattrociocchi, 1950; *The Christmas Forest,* 1950, *Anna the Horse,* 1951, *The Happy Lion,* 1954, *The Happy Lion in Africa,* 1955, *The Happy Lion Roars,* 1957, *A Doll for Marie,* 1957, *The Three Happy Lions,* 1959, *The Happy Lion's Quest,* 1961, *Red Bantam,* 1963, *The Happy Lion and the Bear,* 1964, *The Happy Lion's Vacation,* 1967, *The Happy Lion's Treasure,* 1971, *Hector Penguin,* 1973, *The Happy Lion's Rabbits,* 1974, *Marc and Pixie and the Walls in Mrs. Jones's Garden,* 1975, *Hector and Christina,* 1977, and *The Happy Lioness,* 1980, all by Louise Fatio; *The Camel Who Took a Walk,* 1951, and *Tigers Don't Bite,* 1956, both by Jack Tworkov; *Farm Wanted* by Helen Hilles, 1951; *Gian-Carlo Menotti's Amahl and the Night Visitors,* 1952; *The Talking Cat and Other Stories of French Canada* by Natalie Savage Carlson, 1952; *Busby and Co.* by Herbert Coggins, 1952; *Chef's Holiday* by Idwal Jones, 1952; *Tell Me, Little Boy* by Doris Van Liew Foster, 1953; *The Night Before Christmas* by Clement C. Moore, 1954; *Sophocles the Hyena* by James Moran, 1954; *Flash of Washington Square* by Margaret Pratt, 1954; *Little Red Nose* by Miriam Schlein, 1955; *One Step, Two...,* 1955, *Not a Little Monkey,* 1957, *In My Garden,* 1960, and *The Poodle Who Barked at People,* 1964, all by Charlotte Zolotow; *Ride with the Sun* edited by Harold Courlander, 1955; *Trillium Hill* by E.L. Marsh, 1955; *Christmas on the Mayflower* by Wilma Pitchford Hays, 1956; *Bennie, The Bear Who Grew Too Fast* by Beatrice and Ferrin Frasher, 1956; *The Sweet Pattotie Doll,* 1957, *Wobble the Witch Cat,* 1958, *Houn' Dog,* 1959, *The Nine Lives of Homer C. Cat,* 1961, and *The Hungry Leprechaun,* 1962, all by Mary Calhoun; *Does Poppy Live Here?* by Arthur Gregor, 1957; *Wait Till Sunday* by Susan Dorritt, 1957; *The Little Church on the Big Rock* by Hazel Allen, 1958; *Favorite Fairy Tales Told in France* edited by Virginia Haviland, 1959; *A Fish Is Not a Pet* by May Natalie Tabak, 1959; *The Pointed Brush* by Patricia Miles Martin, 1959; *The Three-Cornered Hat* by Pedro Antonio de Alarcón, 1959; *Please Pass the Grass* by Leone Adelson, 1960; *The Children Come Running* by Elizabeth Coatsworth, 1960; *Angelique,* 1960, and *Mr. and Mrs. Button's Wonderful Watchdogs,* 1978, both by Janice; *The Wishing Well in the Woods,* 1961, and *The April Umbrella,* 1963, both by Priscilla and Otto Friedrich; *Lisette,* 1962, *The Rain Puddle,* 1965, and *The Remarkable Egg,* 1968, all by Adelaide Holl; *The Lamb and the Child,* 1963, and *Days of Sunshine, Days of Rain,* 1965, both by Dean Frye; *Teddy* by Grete Janus Hertz, 1964; *Around the Corner* by Jean B. Showalter, 1966; *Nubber Bear* by William Lipkind, 1966; *Poems from France* edited by William Jay Smith, 1967; *The Old Bullfrog,* 1968, and *The Web in the Grass,* 1972, both by Berniece Freschet; *Earth and Sky* by Mona Dayton, 1969; *The Owl Book* edited by Richard Shaw, 1970; *Which Is the*

Best Place? translated by Mirra Ginsburg, 1976; *What Ever Happened to the Baxter Place?* by Pat Ross, 1976; *Heinz Hobnail and the Great Shoe Hunt* by Anne Duvoisin, 1976.

Roger Duvoisin commented:

(1978) The childhood impressions that are still alive in Louise Fatio and me help us to understand children and to communicate with them. I love the lively curiosity children show toward their surroundings; I love their questions, and the free way they have of expressing their reactions in their conversation, in their drawings and paintings, and even in their poems and letters. Adults often lose this refreshing freedom and curiosity as they form set, conventional opinions about their world. That is why it is so interesting to converse with children, to learn from them as well as to teach them.

It is good to observe that children are now more and more encouraged to express themselves, to create, and that they are taken more seriously. Because of this, making books for children is a more captivating form of art for the writer and illustrator.

*   *   *

Whether illustrating his own stories or those by others (including his wife, Louise Fatio), Roger Duvoisin's pictures became part of the whole. It's almost impossible to separate his visuals from the texts because Duvoisin's innate and professionally developed gifts insured that his illustrations complement the tales. And this sense of design served him as well in the construction of a narrative; he was an artist with words as well as with his brush. Most critics would agree, however, that the reason for the author-illustrator's lasting appeal is that readers knew he cared, about them and his subjects.

Specifically he was appreciated for his delicious sense of humor, the playfulness which infuses a Duvoisin production even on a serious theme. Everyone loves to laugh at Petunia, the silly goose who convinces herself and the other farm animals that she knows everything because she owns a book. After a succession of convulsive mishaps based on Petunia's pretensions as an expert, she learns: "I can't carry wisdom under my wing…I must learn to read." Another of Duvoisin's charming characters is the cow Jasmine, who argues the case for individuality. Finding a fancy hat, she wears it and sticks to her principles even when the chapeau makes her the laughing-stock of the barnyard.

Jasmine, Petunia, and their companions are well known to millions of children as are Duvoisin's other animal stars—cats, dogs, and more exotic fauna like the hippo and the giraffe. *A for the Ark*—one of the catchiest alphabet books for beginners to cut their literary teeth on—brings a whole menagerie to joyous life. And sometimes his plots involve humans as well. In *The House of Four Seasons* Suzy and Billy are helping their parents paint their house, a task which gives Duvoisin the chance to present a nifty lesson in how to create various colors and, not incidentally, to tell a suspenseful story. *The Missing Milkman* invigorates the maxim concerning all work and no play and vice versa. Here we follow the adventures of a dairy worker who runs away to spend a bucolic holiday until idleness palls and duty calls.

In all the original and witty books which Roger Duvoisin conjured up for 50 years, he taught implicitly while he entertained. That characteristic is no small part of his appeal.

—Jean F. Mercier

EAGER, Edward (McMaken). American. Born in Toledo, Ohio, in 1911. Educated at Harvard University, Cambridge, Mas-

sachusetts. Married Jane Eberly in 1938; one son. *Died 23 October 1964.*

PUBLICATIONS FOR CHILDREN

Fiction

Mouse Manor, illustrated by Beryl Bailey-Jones.   New York, Farrar Straus, 1952.
Half Magic, illustrated by N.M. Bodecker.   New York, Harcourt Brace, and London, Macmillan, 1954.
Playing Possum, illustrated by Paul Galdone.   New York, Putnam, 1955.
Knight's Castle, illustrated by N.M. Bodecker.   New York, Harcourt Brace, and London, Macmillan, 1956.
Magic by the Lake, illustrated by N.M. Bodecker.   New York, Harcourt Brace, and London, Macmillan, 1957.
The Time Garden, illustrated by N.M. Bodecker.   New York, Harcourt Brace, 1958; London, Macmillan, 1959.
Magic or Not?, illustrated by N.M. Bodecker.   New York, Harcourt Brace, and London, Macmillan, 1959.
The Well-Wishers, illustrated by N.M. Bodecker.   New York, Harcourt Brace, 1960; London, Macmillan, 1961.
Seven-Day Magic, illustrated by N.M. Bodecker.   New York, Harcourt Brace, 1962; London, Macmillan, 1963.

Verse

Red Head, illustrated by Louis Slobodkin.   Boston, Houghton Mifflin, 1951.

PUBLICATIONS FOR ADULTS

Plays

Pudding Full of Plums (produced Cambridge, Massachusetts).
Dream with Music (lyrics only), book by Sidney Sheldon, Dorothy Kilgallen, and Ben Roberts, music by Clay Warnick (produced New York, 1944).
The Liar, with Alfred Drake, music by John Mundy, lyrics by Eager, adaptation of a play by Goldoni (produced New York, 1950).
The Gambler, with Alfred Drake, adaptation of a play by Ugo Betti (produced New York, 1952).
The Adventures of Marco Polo: A Musical Fantasy (lyrics only), book by William Friedberg and Neil Simon, music by Clay Warnick and Mel Pahl (televised, 1956).   New York, French, 1959.
Call It Virtue, adaptation of a play by Luigi Pirandello (produced New York, 1963).
Gentlemen, Be Seated, with Jerome Moross, music by Moross, lyrics by Eager (produced New York, 1963).
Rugantino (lyrics only), book by Alfred Drake, music by Armando Trovaioli, adaptation of a play by Pietro Garinei, Sandro Giovanini, Festa Campanile, and Franciosa (produced New York, 1964).
The Happy Hypocrite, music by James Bredt, adaptation of the story by Max Beerbohm (produced New York, 1968).

Television Plays: *The Marriage of Figaro,* from the libretto by Lorenzo da Ponte, music by Mozart, 1954; *The Adventures of Marco Polo* (lyrics only), 1956.

*   *   *

Seldom has a major author been imitated so blatantly and in many ways so successfully as E. Nesbit by Edward Eager. In *Half Magic* and its sequels, Eager's indebtedness is gracefully acknowledged; Nesbit is his group of children's favorite author, and they want the sort of real magic that came into her characters' ordinary lives to enter theirs. This magic has rules that enable you to direct it, or, if they are not respected, cause the magic to thwart you.

This basic paradigm Eager takes from Nesbit, along with the family of four or five clever but believable children. The coin of *Half Magic* recalls Nesbit's amulet, *Knight's Castle* the Magic City, the Natterjack of *The Time Garden* is her Psammead, etc. The adventures are like hers and the humor is like hers, perhaps even more abundant. Sometimes there is also a scene, setting, or mood from Baum, Boston, or Carroll. Eager loved books and was a natural at entering the literary worlds of others with appreciation and zest.

Eager's experience of "magic" was almost certainly less deep than Nesbit's. Perhaps he resembled Mr. Smith in *Half Magic,* who says: "The trouble with life is that not enough impossible things happen for us to believe in, don't you agree?" In some of his best books, *Magic or Not?* and *The Well-Wishers,* Eager uses the device of tantalizing uncertainty about the reality of the magic. Nowhere in Eager's books is there the powerful force field of inner psychic happenings that Nesbit can create.

As a fantasist, Eager is looser and less compelling than his model. On the other hand, he is more interested in his characters as people in real relationships. Compare Mr. Smith in *Half Magic* with "the gentleman upstairs" in *The Story of the Amulet.* Eager is at his best when he uses his affection and perceptiveness to delineate his characters and integrate his story at the level of real life. In other books, such as *Seven-Day Magic,* he remains witty and inventive but seems to be repeating his own adaptations.

—Ravenna Helson

EDMONDS, Walter D(umaux). American. Born in Boonville, New York, 15 July 1903. Educated at Cutler School, New York, 1914–16; St. Paul's School, Concord, New Hampshire, 1916–19; Choate School, Wallingford, Connecticut, 1919–21; Harvard University, Cambridge, Massachusetts (staff member, from 1922, secretary, 1924–25, and president, 1925–26, *Harvard Advocate*), 1921–26, A.B. 1926 (Phi Beta Kappa). Married 1) Eleanor Livingston Stetson in 1930 (died 1956), one son and two daughters; 2) Katharine Howe Baker-Carr in 1956. Member of the Board of Overseers, Harvard College, 1945–50; director, 1955–72, and president and publisher, 1957–66, *Harvard Alumni Bulletin*. Recipient: American Library Association Newbery Medal, 1942; National Book award, 1976; Christopher award, 1976. Litt.D.: Union College, Schenectady, New York, 1936; Rutgers University, New Brunswick, New Jersey, 1940; Colgate University, Hamilton, New York, 1947; Harvard University, 1952. Member, American Academy of Arts and Sciences. Agent: Harold Ober Associates, 40 East 49th Street, New York, New York 10017. Address: 27 River Street, Concord, Massachusetts 01742, U.S.A.

PUBLICATIONS FOR CHILDREN

Fiction

The Matchlock Gun, illustrated by Paul Lantz. New York, Dodd Mead, 1941.
Tom Whipple, illustrated by Paul Lantz. New York, Dodd Mead, 1942.
Two Logs Crossing: John Haskell's Story, illustrated by Tibor Gergely. New York, Dodd Mead, 1943.
Wilderness Clearing, illustrated by John de Martelly. New York, Dodd Mead, 1944.
Cadmus Henry, illustrated by Manning Lee. New York, Dodd Mead, 1949.
Mr. Benedict's Lion, illustrated by Doris Lee. New York, Dodd Mead, 1950.
Corporal Bess, illustrated by Manning Lee. New York, Dodd Mead, 1952.
Hound Dog Moses and the Promised Land, illustrated by William Gropper. New York, Dodd Mead, 1954.
Uncle Ben's Whale, illustrated by William Gropper. New York, Dodd Mead, 1955.
They Had a Horse, illustrated by Douglas Gorsline. New York, Dodd Mead, 1962.
Time to Go House, illustrated by Joan Berg Victor. Boston, Little Brown, 1969.
Seven American Stories, illustrated by William Sauts Bock. Boston, Little Brown, 1970.
Wolf Hunt, illustrated by William Sauts Bock. Boston, Little Brown, 1970.
Beaver Valley, illustrated by Leslie Morrill. Boston, Little Brown, 1971.
The Story of Richard Storm, illustrated by William Sauts Bock. Boston, Little Brown, 1974.
Bert Breen's Barn. Boston, Little Brown, 1975.
The Night Raider and Other Stories. Boston, Little Brown, 1980.

PUBLICATIONS FOR ADULTS

Novels

Rome Haul. Boston, Little Brown, and London, Sampson Low, 1929.
The Big Barn. Boston, Little Brown, 1930; London, Sampson Low, 1931.
Erie Water. Boston, Little Brown, 1933; London, Hurst and Blackett, 1934.
Drums along the Mohawk. Boston, Little Brown, and London, Jarrolds, 1936.
Chad Hanna. Boston, Little Brown, and London, Collins, 1940.
Young Ames. Boston, Little Brown, and London, Collins, 1942.
In the Hands of the Senecas. Boston, Little Brown, and London, Collins, 1947; as *The Captive Woman,* New York, Bantam, 1962.
The Wedding Journey. Boston, Little Brown, 1947.
The Boyds of Black River. New York, Dodd Mead, and London, Collins, 1953.
The South African Quirt. Boston, Little Brown, 1985.

Short Stories

Mostly Canallers: Collected Stories. Boston, Little Brown, 1934.

Other

Moses. Privately printed, 1939.
The First Hundred Years, 1848–1948: 1848, Oneida Community; 1880, Oneida Community Limited; 1935, Oneida Ltd. Oneida, New York, Oneida Ltd., 1948; revised edition, 1958.
They Fought with What They Had: The Story of the Army Air Forces in the Southwest Pacific 1941–1942. Boston, Little Brown, 1951.
The Erie Canal: The Story of the Digging of Clinton's Ditch. Utica,

New York, Munson Williams Proctor Institute, 1960.
The Musket and the Cross: The Struggle of France and England for North America. Boston, Little Brown, 1968.

*

Critical Study: *Walter D. Edmonds, Storyteller* by Lionel D. Wyld, Syracuse, New York, Syracuse University Press, 1982.

Walter D. Edmonds comments:

I am no good at this sort of thing, but perhaps my remarks accepting the National Book award for *Bert Breen's Barn* may be apropos.

"It's a fine thing to be given a National Book award, and I am deeply grateful—though I'm not sure my book deserves recognition as a book for children. I'm not sure there really is such a book, anyway. The great children's classics belong equally to adults. Though I have no classics to my name, all but three of my children's books' appeared originally in adult magazines or were written for adult readers. The three I started out deliberately to write for children seem to me not much more so than the others—which may, I see, be a commentary on my writing. So I think categories do not mean a great deal. The story is the important thing.

"In *Bert Breen's Barn* I set out to make a story about an occurrence that happened on our place and neighborhood in upstate New York when I was a very small boy, just learning to tie my own shoes. As a matter of fact it was an old man on whom I modelled the character of Birdy Morris who showed me how to tie the laces so they never came undone, until you wanted them to. I did not write the story for children but for my own pleasure, finding myself, in the process, overwhelmed with remembrances of how things were just after the turn of the century and by the qualities of life we were brought up to think valuable.

"So to be given a National Book award near the end of fifty years of writing means a great deal more than I can put into words. Especially as I never have been much of a hand to win a prize. Except in marriage."

*   *   *

Although Walter D. Edmonds has been known as a fine writer of adult books, his work for children has been equally well received. His first, *The Matchlock Gun,* won the Newbery Medal; a later novel, and his best so far, *Bert Breen's Barn,* won the 1976 National Book Award.

Edmonds now lives in Concord, Massachusetts, but it is the Boonville area of New York in the Mohawk Valley, the place he returns to each summer, that he uses for the settings for most of his books. Through his skill as a writer, he recreates the past there, thoroughly immersing the reader in various periods with his clear prose. In *The Matchlock Gun,* set in the 18th century, savage Indians on the warpath attacking innocent people may now seem one-sided from the perspective of the 1980's because social attitudes have changed a great deal in the last 40 years. Time has a way of giving a different view, but the book remains effective.

Bert Breen's Barn, set around Boonville at the beginning of the 20th century, is quality writing for young adults. The simple but eloquent prose, laced with country imagery ("like a raccoon peering sideways through the slats of a chicken coop") and vernacular, first catches the reader and then absorbs him completely in the narrative. The pace is steady, but suspense builds as the characters become more sharply defined and the plot unfolds. Although there is a search for buried treasure, this is no run-of-the-mill mystery story and hunt, but a well-crafted book that improves with each rereading. With its strong emphasis on characterization, the novel should appeal to readers for generations to come.

All of Edmonds's books contain strong characterizations that have much in common: many of the protagonists have an indomitable, unquenchable spirit that keeps them going even in the face of adversity, and that determination, combined with a strong moral fiber, creates a sure knowledge in the reader that the character will succeed. Edward, in *The Matchlock Gun,* kills the Indians and saves his mother and sister; Tom, in *Bert Breen's Barn,* gains his family a fine reputation (they had been considered shiftless) through his hard work and honesty; in two shorter works, *Two Logs Crossing* and *They Had a Horse,* each protagonist's determination brings success out of failure. The successes are hard-won, often preceded by tears and discouragement, but these weaknesses make the characters more convincing. In *They Had a Horse* the final scene where Jacob's tears mingle with his wife's remains with the reader long after the tale has been finished. In most of the books, too, the protagonists are willing to heed the advice of others.

Edmonds has said that, except for three books, he has not intentionally written for children. His latest book perhaps demonstrates that best, for *The Night Raider and Other Stories* contains four tales for older readers or adults. Set in the Boonville area, each is very different from the others, even the humorous ones: "Perfection of Orchard View" includes great comic correspondence between a gentleman farmer and his hired hand about a prize pig, and "Charlie Phister's Famous Bee Shot" demonstrates how gullible people can be. The other two tales are much more somber, especially "Raging Canal," which reveals the brutality that many boy canallers had to face. "The Night Raider" gradually discloses a mystery: something is killing the guinea hens. When the raiding owl is discovered and caught, but not killed, the result is a moving one.

In all of his books, for children or for adults, Edmonds displays his skill with words. He has an ear carefully tuned to each situation, and he plays with the language accordingly. He can be detailed in his description when it serves his purpose, or spare, and simple; his humor can be tongue-in-cheek or satirical; and he ably uses dialogue to reveal character as well as to further the action. His books stand up well to rereading, the ultimate test of any writer.

—Marilyn F. Apseloff

———

EDWARDS, Dorothy (née Brown). British. Born in Teddington, Middlesex, 6 November 1914. Educated at schools in Teddington and Sunbury. Married Francis P. Edwards in 1942; one daughter and one son. Secretary for Odeon cinemas; freelance editor for many years, and producer of *Listen with Mother* series, 1969–70, BBC, London; lecturer and broadcaster. Recipient: Children's Rights Workshop Other award, 1975, 1981. *Died 9 August 1982.*

PUBLICATIONS FOR CHILDREN

Fiction

My Naughty Little Sister: Stories from "Listen with Mother," illustrated by Henrietta Garland. London, Methuen, 1952.
My Naughty Little Sister and Some Others, illustrated by Caroline Guthrie. London, Methuen, 1957.
My Naughty Little Sister's Friends, illustrated by Una J. Place. London, Methuen, 1962.
When My Naughty Little Sister Was Good, illustrated by Shirley Hughes. London, Methuen, 1968.
Tales of Joe and Timothy, illustrated by Reintje Venema. London, Methuen, 1969.

All about My Naughty Little Sister, illustrated by Shirley Hughes. London, Methuen, 1969.

Listen, Listen!, illustrated by Elizabeth Davies. London, BBC Publications, 1970.

More Naughty Little Sister Stories, illustrated by Shirley Hughes. London, Methuen, 1970.

Peter Nick-Nock and the Cuckoo Clock, illustrated by Alexy Pendle. London, Transworld, 1971.

Roger's Trains, illustrated by Alexy Pendle. London, Transworld, 1971.

Joe and Timothy Together, illustrated by Reintje Venema. London, Methuen, 1971.

Janie's Cooking Day, illustrated by Elizabeth Davies. London, Transworld, 1973.

Sam's Woolly Hat, illustrated by Elizabeth Davies. London, Transworld, 1973.

My Naughty Little Sister and Bad Harry, illustrated by Shirley Hughes. London, Methuen, 1974.

The Magician Who Kept a Pub and Other Stories, illustrated by Jill Bennett. London, Kestrel, 1975.

A Wet Monday, illustrated by Jenny Williams. London, Methuen, 1975; New York, Morrow, 1976.

Dad's New Car, illustrated by John Dyke. London, Methuen, 1976.

My Naughty Little Sister Goes Fishing, illustrated by Shirley Hughes. London, Methuen, 1976.

My Naughty Little Sister and Bad Harry's Rabbit, illustrated by Shirley Hughes. London, Methuen, 1977; Englewood Cliffs, New Jersey, Prentice Hall, 1981.

My Naughty Little Sister at the Fair, illustrated by Shirley Hughes. London, Methuen, 1979.

Here's Sam, illustrated by David Higham. London, Methuen, 1979.

A Strong and Willing Girl, illustrated by Robert Micklewright. London, Methuen, 1980.

Crash!!, illustrated by Lynne Cousins. London, Hippo, 1980.

The Witches and the Grinnygog. London, Faber, 1981.

My Naughty Little Sister and *My Naughty Little Sister's Friends* (collections), illustrated by Shirley Hughes. London, Methuen, 2 vols., 1982.

The Old Man Who Sneezed: Read Aloud Stories, illustrated by Thelma Lambert. London, Methuen, 1983.

Mark the Drummer-Boy. London, Methuen, 1983.

Emmie and the Purple Paint, illustrated by Priscilla Lamont. London, Methuen, 1984.

Robert Goes to Fetch a Sister, illustrated by Carolyn Dinan. London, Methuen, 1986.

King Dicky Bird and the Bossy Princess. London, Methuen, 1987.

Plays

Radio Plays: *The Girl Who Wanted to Eat Boys,* 1974; *The Old Woman Who Lived in a Real Glass Vinegar Bottle,* 1976; *Listen with Mother* series.

Television Scripts: *Playschool* series.

Verse

Listen and Play Rhymes 1–2, illustrated by Prudence Seward. London, Methuen, 2 vols., 1973.

Other

Look, Look, A Cookery Book, illustrated by Prudence Seward. London, Methuen, 1973.

Look, Look, My Garden Book, illustrated by Prudence Seward. London, Methuen, 1973.

A Look, See and Touch Book, illustrated by Peter Edwards. London, Methuen, 1976.

A Walk Your Fingers Story, illustrated by Peter Edwards. London, Methuen, 1976.

My Naughty Little Sister's Birthday Book, illustrated by Shirley Hughes. London, Methuen, 1982.

Editor, *"Listen with Mother" Stories,* illustrated by Caroline Sharpe. London, BBC Publications, 1972.

Editor, *The Read-to-Me Story Book,* illustrated by Lynnette Hemmant. London, Methuen, 1974.

Editor, *The Read-to-Me-Another Story Book,* illustrated by Jenny Williams. London, Methuen, 1976.

Editor, *Once, Twice, Thrice upon a Time,* illustrated by Juliette Palmer. Guildford, Surrey, Lutterworth Press, 1976.

Editor, *Once, Twice, Thrice and Then Again,* illustrated by Juliette Palmer. Guildford, Surrey, Lutterworth Press, 1976.

Editor, *Ghosts and Shadows,* illustrated by Jane Walmsley. Guildford, Surrey, Lutterworth Press, 1980.

Editor, *Mists and Magic,* illustrated by Jill Bennett. Guildford, Lutterworth Press, 1983.

* * *

Children delight in tales of bad behaviour in their peers and who could sound more promising than "My Naughty Little Sister" and her boon companion Bad Harry. The enormous following and affection for the Naughty Little Sister stories, Dorothy Edwards's chief success, stem from several masterly devices. The first must be the use of the first person throughout. There is the obvious connotation of once upon a time when Mummy (or Granny or whoever is reading the story) was young and all the implications of the story unfolding with the added bonus of the closeness of the relationship. There is the marvellous mixture of envy, respect, and disapproval evinced by the older sister—somehow above such bad behaviour and yet longing to be young and carefree again. The stories are just the right length for reading aloud, and there is enough action and development to satisfy both reader and listener. The style is conversational (very suited to the late lamented *Listen with Mother* which first broadcast many of the stories), and the stories of simple everyday adventures. Above all else there are the warmth and security of the family. Whatever awful thing My Naughty Little Sister does, all ends well, on the "and they all lived happily ever after" note.

Joe and Timothy, and Sam, are less successful creations, lacking the character and indomitable will of the Naughty Little Sister, but well worth closer attention is *A Strong and Willing Girl,* winner of the Other Award. The girl in question was Edwards's own Auntie Nan, and the book portrays in fascinating detail what it was like to be in service in Victorian times. Again the style is conversational, confiding, but richly humorous and full of life. The picture painted is realistic without being melodramatic or sentimental, and the book eminently readable.

All Edwards's books are full of domestic detail, and herein lies much of their appeal—the familiar and the recognizable, bound together in day-to-day adventures.

—Fiona Waters

EDWARDS, Monica (le Doux). British. Born in Belper, Derbyshire, 8 November 1912. Educated at Wakefield High School; Thornes House School, Wakefield; St. Brandon's School for the

Daughters of the Clergy, Bristol. Married William Edwards in 1933; one son and one daughter. Agent: Curtis Brown Ltd., 162–168 Regent Street, London W1R 5TB. Address: Cowdray Cross, Thursley, Godalming, Surrey, England.

PUBLICATIONS FOR CHILDREN

Fiction

Wish for a Pony, illustrated by Anne Bullen. London, Collins, 1947.
No Mistaking Corker, illustrated by Anne Bullen. London, Collins, 1947.
The Summer of the Great Secret, illustrated by Anne Bullen. London, Collins, 1948.
The Midnight Horse, illustrated by Anne Bullen. London, Collins, 1949; New York, Vanguard Press, 1950.
The White Riders, illustrated by Geoffrey Whittam. London, Collins, 1950.
Black Hunting Whip, illustrated by Geoffrey Whittam. London, Collins, 1950.
Punchbowl Midnight, illustrated by Charles Tunnicliffe. London, Collins, 1951.
Cargo of Horses, illustrated by Geoffrey Whittam. London, Collins, 1951.
Spirit of Punchbowl Farm, illustrated by Joan Wanklyn. London, Collins, 1952.
Hidden in a Dream, illustrated by Geoffrey Whittam. London, Collins, 1952.
The Wanderer, illustrated by Joan Wanklyn. London, Collins, 1953.
Storm Ahead, illustrated by Geoffrey Whittam. London, Collins, 1953.
No Entry, illustrated by Geoffrey Whittam. London, Collins, 1954.
Punchbowl Harvest, illustrated by Joan Wanklyn. London, Collins, 1954.
The Nightbird, illustrated by Geoffrey Whittam. London, Collins, 1955.
Frenchman's Secret, illustrated by Geoffrey Whittam. London, Collins, 1956.
Strangers to the Marsh, illustrated by Geoffrey Whittam. London, Collins, 1957.
Operation Seabird, illustrated by Geoffrey Whittam. London, Collins, 1957.
The Cownappers, illustrated by Geoffrey Whittam. London, Collins, 1958.
Killer Dog, illustrated by Sheila Rose. London, Collins, 1959.
No Going Back, illustrated by Geoffrey Whittam. London, Collins, 1960.
The Outsider, illustrated by Geoffrey Whittam. London, Collins, 1961.
The Hoodwinkers, illustrated by Geoffrey Whittam. London, Collins, 1962.
Dolphin Summer, illustrated by Geoffrey Whittam. London, Collins, 1963; New York, Hawthorn, 1971.
Fire in the Punchbowl, illustrated by Geoffrey Whittam. London, Collins, 1965.
The Wild One, illustrated by Geoffrey Whittam. London, Collins, 1967.
Under the Rose, illustrated by Richard Kennedy. London, Collins, 1968.
A Wind Is Blowing. London, Collins, 1969.

Play

Screenplay: *The Dawn Killer,* 1958.

Other

Joan Goes Farming. London, Lane, 1954.
Rennie Goes Riding. London, Lane, 1956.

PUBLICATIONS FOR ADULTS

Other

The Unsought Farm. London, Joseph, 1954.
The Cats of Punchbowl Farm. London, Joseph, and New York, Doubleday, 1964.
The Badgers of Punchbowl Farm. London, Joseph, 1966.
The Valley and the Farm. London, Joseph, 1971.
Badger Valley. London, Joseph, 1976.

*

Monica Edwards comments:
My books for children are all based on fact. They form two series: one ("Romney Marsh") was inspired by my own youth in a Sussex fishing village, the other ("Punchbowl Farm") by my children's life on a Surrey farm. Both places are real, and the events can be followed on Ordnance Survey maps for the areas.

*   *   *

From a seemingly inauspicious start in the late 1940's, with the publication of *Wish for a Pony* and *No Mistaking Corker,* Monica Edwards developed two very real and memorable series in the "Romney Marsh" and "Punchbowl" books. In spite of the heavy emphasis on the pony-lovers in the first two books, there was even then a noticeable depth of character in the children, usually missing from the horse-show-and-rosette story which was published in such great numbers in the late 1940's and 1950's. Edwards takes each character and builds identity within a setting she knows and, obviously, loves.

Tamzin, Rissa, Roger, and Meryon love the Romney Marsh, with its sheep and wide sky and distant sea, and their adventures in and around it often arise out of the plight of one aspect of their way of life: the fishing in *The Nightbird,* or sheep farming in *The White Riders* and *No Entry.* The author is not afraid of blood and fighting as in *Cargo of Horses,* or of the emotional problems of growing up, in *No Going Back* and *A Wind Is Blowing.*

The Thorntons of Punchbowl Farm move from Hampshire into Surrey after the caravan holiday described in the first person by Lindsey in *No Mistaking Corker.* These are much more family stories, with Andrea, Dion, Lindsey, and Peter leading normal, bickering, loving family lives in the setting of the wild Devil's Punchbowl and the derelict farm they own beside it. Most of the adventures in this series arise out of normal farming crises, like the animals poisoned by yew in *Spirit of Punchbowl Farm,* or the escaping animals in *The Wanderer.* Andrea is followed through her adolescent years, Lindsey remains staunch in her defence of wild creatures and the old ways, and Dion's ever-present determination to farm the wild acres is seen to reach fruition by the last in the series—*The Wild One.* Peter alone plays no major part in any of the stories, except to preserve normality by being the imitating younger brother whose mice have always got out or who needs looking after. Touches of time travel and fantasy (in *Black Hunting Whip* and *Spirit of Punchbowl Farm*) add to the exceptional quality of these realistic tales of farm life.

As Monica Edwards herself shows from the beginning of her writing a touch of the qualities of Arthur Ransome, whose titles are often mentioned in her text, so is she now being seen to influence the writings of younger authors. Much of her style of writing is apparent in the books by Tasmanian author Anne Farrell, who quotes Edwards titles as Edwards quoted Ransome. Such developments are proof of the author's quality: that her writing ability is admirable, and that her stories are memorable.

—Mary Nettlefold

* * *

EHRLICH, Bettina.   See BETTINA.

* * *

EKWENSI, Cyprian (Odiatu Duaka). Nigerian. Born in Minna, Niger State, 26 September 1921. Educated at Government School, Jos, 1931–36; Government College, Ibadan, 1936–41; Higher College, Yaba, 1941–43; School of Forestry, Ibadan, 1942–45; Achimota College, Gold Coast, 1943; School of Pharmacy, Yaba, 1947–49; Chelsea School of Pharmacy, University of London, 1951–56; University of Iowa, Iowa City, 1974. Married to Eunice Anyiwo; five children. Teacher, Igbobi College, Yaba, 1947–49; lecturer, School of Pharmacy, Lagos, 1949–51; pharmacist superintendent, Nigerian Medical Services, 1956–57; head of features, Nigerian Broadcasting Corporation, 1957–61; director, Federal Information Services, 1961–67; director-general, Broadcasting Corporation of Biafra, during Nigerian civil war, 1967–70; proprietor, East Niger Chemists and East Niger Trading Company, from 1970; chairman, East Central State Library Board, 1972–75; managing director, Star Printing and Publishing Company, 1975–79; consultant, *Weekly Trumpet* and *Daily News,* both Anambra State, and *Weekly Eagle,* Imo State, 1980–81; commissioner for information, Anambra State, 1983. Member of the Board of Governors, Federal Radio Corporation, Lagos, 1985; chairman, Anambra State Hospitals Board, 1986–88. Recipient: Dag Hammarskjöld International award, 1968. Agent: David Bolt Associates, 12 Heath Drive, Send, Surrey GU23 7EP, England. Address: 12 Hillview, P.O. Box 317, Enugu, Anambra State, Nigeria.

PUBLICATIONS FOR CHILDREN

Fiction

When Love Whispers.   Onitsha, Nigeria, Tabansi Bookshop, 1947.
The Leopard's Claw.   London, Longman, 1950.
The Drummer Boy.   London, Cambridge University Press, 1960.
The Passport of Malam Ilia.   London, Cambridge University Press, 1960.
Yaba Roundabout Murder.   Lagos, Tortoise, 1962.
The Rainmaker and Other Stories.   Lagos, African Universities Press, 1965.
Trouble in Form Six, illustrated by Prue Theobalds.   London, Cambridge University Press, 1966.
Juju Rock, illustrated by Bruce Onabrakpeya.   Lagos, African Universities Press, 1966.
Coal Camp Boy.   Lagos, Longman, 1973.
Samankwe in the Strange Forest.   Ikeja, Longman Nigeria, 1973.
The Rainbow-Tinted Scarf and Other Stories, illustrated by Gay Galsworthy.   London, Evans, 1975.

Samankwe and the Highway Robbers.   London, Evans, 1975.
Motherless Baby.   Enugu, Fourth Dimension, 1980.

Other

Ikolo the Wrestler and Other Ibo Tales.   London, Nelson, 1947.
An African Night's Entertainment: A Tale of Vengeance, illustrated by Bruce Onabrakpeya.   Lagos, African Universities Press, and London, Deutsch, 1962.
The Great Elephant-Bird (folktale), illustrated by Rosemary Tonks and John Cottrell.   London, Nelson, 1965.
The Boa Suitor, illustrated by John Cottrell.   London, Nelson, 1966.

PUBLICATIONS FOR ADULTS

Novels

People of the City.   London, Dakers, 1954; revised edition, London, Heinemann, 1963; New York, Fawcett, 1969.
Jagua Nana.   London, Hutchinson, 1961; New York, Fawcett, 1969.
Burning Grass: A Story of the Fulani of Northern Nigeria.   London, Heinemann, 1962.
Beautiful Feathers.   London, Hutchinson, 1963.
Iska.   London, Hutchinson, 1966.
Survive the Peace.   London, Heinemann, 1976.
Divided We Stand.   Enugu, Fourth Dimension, 1980.
Jagua Nana's Daughter.   Ibadan, Spectrum, 1986.
For a Roll of Parchment.   Ibadan, Heinemann, 1987.

Short Stories

Lokotown and Other Stories.   London, Heinemann, 1966.
Restless City and Christmas Gold with Other Stories.   London, Heinemann, 1975.

Other

Editor, *Festac Anthology of Nigerian New Writing.*   Lagos, Federal Ministry of Information, 1977.

*

Critical Study: *Cyprian Ekwensi* by Ernest Emenyona, London, Evans, 1974.

* * *

Cyprian Ekwensi is one of the most prolific children's writers in Africa and an acknowledged pioneer in writing Nigerian youth literature. He is nearly unique among African writers in publishing stories for children as early as the 1940's, in *West African Review* and T. Cullen Young's *African New Writing,* before children's literature was emphasized, and in continuing to write for children even after becoming internationally known as a novelist. The reissue of his stories in collections and new editions attests to his popularity among young readers.

Ekwensi's writing for children is thoroughly grounded in the realities of contemporary life in the three main geographical regions of Nigeria. Folk tales, including *An African Night's Entertainment,* and adventure stories, such as *Juju Rock* and *The Passport of Malam Ilia,* are set in northern Nigeria among the Hausa and Fulani people. Most of the stories in *The Rainbow-Tinted Scarf* take place in western Nigeria among the Yoruba people, while *Coal Camp Boy* and the new series about Samankwe are set in eastern Nigeria among the

Igbo people. *The Drummer Boy* and many of the stories in *The Rainmaker* have urban settings. Ekwensi is truly a national writer, yet his work is not so localized as to prevent its being enjoyed by children outside Nigeria.

Ekwensi's folklore, like his fiction, is told in contemporary Nigerian idiom. The folk tales reflect some of the diversity of Nigerian folklore by including tales told by several ethnic groups, tales with human as well as animal characters, and long tales like the one in *An African Night's Entertainment.* Versions of widespread themes in West African folklore, such as a woman who marries an animal, melting girl, a king who refuses to let his beautiful daughter marry, and tortoise trickster tales are found in his collections, along with local themes. Numerous stylistic features of oral narratives such as epigrammatic naming, proverbs, songs, choral responses, and extensive dialogue are used, though considerably simplified for children. Ekwensi has chosen to retell folk tales with implicit or explicit morals, reflecting the strong didactic emphasis in all his writing for children.

Ekwensi's fiction includes the same elements which he enjoyed reading as a youth: truth, poetic justice, heroism, romance, folkloric mystery, and adventure. His stories, most of which are about the adventures of boys and men, reflect real experiences such as going to school in the colonial and post-colonial eras, poverty in urban areas, and the aftermath of the Nigerian Civil War, as well as fictional experiences prominent in the mass media, such as capturing thieves and searching for lost treasure.

Adventure is a focus of all Ekwensi's fiction, regardless of its setting. The adventure may be sheer fun, as when school boys play pranks in *Trouble in Form Six,* but more often it involves apprehending wrong-doers. The blind hero of *The Drummer Boy* unknowingly becomes involved with thieves who purport to be his friends, while the hero of *Coal Camp Boy* who resettles near Enugu after the Nigerian Civil War discovers looters who are reselling property stolen from war victims. In *Juju Rock* a search for a man lost in a boat crash leads to the discovery of a gold mine whose riches are being concealed by a group of men who use secret society rituals to frighten away potential discoverers of their wealth. In his various adventures, Samankwe encounters highway robbers, kidnappers, money doublers, and illicit palm-wine makers. The adventures often include fighting and violence, but those who do wrong always are punished and the heroes receive praise for their bravery and attempts to uphold justice.

—Nancy J. Schmidt

———

ELLIN E(lizabeth) M(uriel). New Zealander. Born in Waiuku, 22 March 1905. Educated at a secondary school in Auckland. Agent: Minerva Bookshop Ltd., C.P.O. Box 2597, 13 Commerce Street, Auckland 1, New Zealand.

PUBLICATIONS FOR CHILDREN

Fiction

The Children of Clearwater Bay, illustrated by Garth Tapper. Auckland, Minerva, and London, Macmillan, 1969.
The Greenstone Axe, illustrated by Elizabeth Sutherland. Albany, New Zealand, Stockton House, 1975.

*   *   *

E.M. Ellin's two published novels have, in high degree, what educationists currently call "readability." Both books show children

coping with situations which are dangerous in a very real sense; both, by the use of a deceptively simple prose style, a swift evocation of setting and character, and sure handling of energetic narrative, ensure reader attention to the last page.

The Children of Clearwater Bay is a tale of endurance, of desperate measures taken to ensure survival in the face of catastrophe. The Cameron children, six of them ranging in age from 14 to two-year-old twins, are real children: quarrelsome, joyful, and, in the face of danger, sensibly dismayed. This dismay emphasises their subsequent resourcefulness; in common with their counterparts in *The Greenstone Axe* (the three Archer children) they demonstrate a proper balance of anxiety evoked by consciousness of their own immaturity, and determination to do the best in the circumstances.

This capacity for bringing the characters alive and bestowing credibility on the action is the hallmark of Ellin's writing. One senses in her prose—particularly in the dialogue—a memory for the preoccupations of childhood, an effortless recapturing of childish reaction to circumstance, as well as a retention of that particular quality of zest and resilience which belongs, alone, to the healthy child.

Ellin's childhood, spent on a farm in the far north of New Zealand, obviously equipped her with a strong sense of place. This she transmits smoothly to her books, which are both set in this area. The isolation of pioneer life, the necessity for children to behave responsibly and independently, while yet retaining the ebullience of childhood, the ever-present influence of the bush and the sea, all emerge strongly.

The historical details in Ellin's stories are accurately researched and presented without comment. There are friendly Maoris and hostile Maoris; the author sees as her concern the recounting of the children's adventures against an authentic background rather than the espousal of any cause. In this—and in her predilection for banishing parents so that the action centres around her children, unencumbered and unassisted—she reflects a tradition earlier than her own in children's writing though several other modern authors (notably Southall in his earlier work) favoured this device.

If one is to believe (with Geoffrey Trease) that "whatever the other valuable elements in a story, the single indispensable one is entertainment," one must acknowledge Ellin's achievement. Her characters interact vigorously against a background which exists. The result is entertainment of a high order.

—Dorothy Butler

———

EMECHETA, (Florence Onye) Buchi. British. Born in Lagos, Nigeria, 21 July 1944. Educated at Methodist Girls' High School, Lagos; University of London, B.Sc. (honours) in sociology 1972. Married Sylvester Onwordi in 1960 (separated 1969); two sons and three daughters. Librarian, 1960–64; library officer, British Museum, London, 1965–69; youth worker and resident student, Race, 1974–76; community worker, Camden Council, London, 1976–78; visiting lecturer at 11 universities in the United States, 1979; Senior Research Fellow and Visiting Professor of English, University of Calabar, Nigeria, 1980–81; Lecturer, Yale University, New Haven, Connecticut, 1982. Since 1982 Lecturer, University of London. Proprietor, Ogwugwu Afo Publishing Company, London; since 1979 member of the Home Secretary's Advisory Council on Race. Address: 7 Briston Grove, London N8 9EX, England.

PUBLICATIONS FOR CHILDREN

Fiction

The Bride Price. London, Allison and Busby, and New York,

Braziller, 1976.
Titch the Cat, illustrated by Thomas Joseph. London, Allison and Busby, 1979.
Nowhere to Play, illustrated by Peter Archer. London, Allison and Busby, 1980.
The Moonlight Bride. Oxford, Oxford University Press, 1980.
The Wrestling Match. Oxford, Oxford University Press, 1981; New York, Braziller, 1983.
Naira Power. London, Macmillan, 1982.

PUBLICATIONS FOR ADULTS

Novels

Adah's Story. London, Allison and Busby, 1983.
  In the Ditch. London, Barrie and Jenkins, 1972.
  Second-Class Citizen. London, Allison and Busby, 1974; New York, Braziller, 1975.
The Slave Girl. London, Allison and Busby, and New York, Braziller, 1977.
The Joys of Motherhood. London, Allison and Busby, and New York, Braziller, 1979.
Destination Biafra. London, Allison and Busby, 1982.
Double Yoke. London, Ogwugwu Afo, 1982; New York, Braziller, 1983.
The Rape of Shavi. London, Ogwugwu Afo, 1983; New York, Braziller, 1985.
A Kind of Marriage. London, Macmillan, 1986.

Plays

Television Plays: *A Kind of Marriage,* 1976; *The Ju Ju Landlord,* 1976.

Other

Our Own Freedom, photographs by Maggie Murray. London, Sheba, 1981.
Head above Water (autobiography). London, Ogwugwu Afo, 1986.

*   *   *

Buchi Emecheta today is one of Africa's most prolific writers, who writes for adults as well as for children. She lives in London, and her two picture books for children, *Titch the Cat* and *Nowhere to Play,* are set there as well, and concern the lives of families of Nigerian origin but English upbringing. Her most successful adolescent works, however—*The Bride Price* and *Naira Power*—are both set in Nigeria and address distinctly Nigerian themes.

The adolescent novel *The Bride Price* stands apart from conventional didactic novels and covers some burning issues—polygamy, marriage, true and false love, sincerity and pretense, and the relations between the sexes. In *The Bride Price* one glimpses that young womanhood (and womanhood in general) has been inadequately served by African male writers in their works. What distinguishes this novel from many young adult works is its satiric and non-didactic stance. The narrator does not say anything positive about traditional ways of life discussed in the novel. Emecheta sees the custom of Bride Price as the barbaric reduction of marriage to buying of wives, and the custom of "Osu," or outcast, as barbaric and inhuman. In spite of the fact that Chike's father is one of the wealthiest and most educated people in Ibuza Community, he and his family are regarded as slaves since one of his ancestors had been sold into slavery. As far as Emecheta is concerned, these are customs humans

should mercilessly fight against, but she makes the narrator hold back when it comes to direct criticism. For all its protest, *The Bride Price* is non-didactic.

She switches from a focus on tradition to contemporary times in *Naira Power,* a more didactic work. The novel explores the decadence and corruption which excessive love of money can unleash on a society. The plot unfolds mainly through flashback spanning colonial days through the present and is narrated by Amina to Bintu as they sit in a car during a strong tropical rainstorm. The major didactic element in *Naira Power* concerns limitation of Nigerian currency (the naira) and the general limitation of the power of money; as Bintu tells Amina, "I am glad to hear that there are instances in which naira can't ferry one through."

In the novel young Ramonu's robbery career ends in disgrace: he is burnt to death when the community who knows him mistakes him for an actual robber. Ramonu's moral degeneration begins precisely after his expulsion from home by his father. Lacking parental guidance he easily drifts into a bad group of business associates. Unlike Amina's father, who is quite concerned with the welfare and progress of his children and the company they keep, Ramonu's father does not seem to worry about his son's associates and how he makes his money. Instead, he glories in enjoying his son's ill-gotten money. Emecheta uses Ramonu's father's relationship with his son and Amina's father's relationship with his children to stress the need for parental guidance of children.

Naira Power also addresses the issue of overpopulation, a serious problem which has the potential to ruin Nigeria. Part of the novel is set in contemporary Lagos, and the congestion of the city and the physical squalor are reflected in the moral decadence of many of the characters. Most of the problems in the novel arise either from a singular lack of moral integrity or an ignoble lust for possession of the naira.

—Osayimwense Osa

———

ENGDAHL, Sylvia (Louise). American. Born in Los Angeles, California, 24 November 1933. Educated at Pomona College, Claremont, California, 1950; Reed College, Portland, Oregon, 1951; University of Oregon, Eugene, 1951–52, 1956–57; University of California, Santa Barbara, B. A. in education 1955; graduate work in anthropology, Portland State University, Oregon, 1978–80. Elementary school teacher, Portland, 1955–56; programmer, then computer systems specialist, SAGE Air Defense System, Lexington, Massachusetts, Madison, Wisconsin, Tacoma, Washington, and Santa Monica, California, 1957–67; full-time writer, 1968–80; self-employed developer and vendor of home computer software, 1981–84. Since 1985 staff member, Connected Education Inc., New York. Recipient: Christopher award, 1973. Address: 3088 Delta Pines Drive, Eugene, Oregon 97401, U.S.A.

PUBLICATIONS FOR CHILDREN

Fiction

Enchantress from the Stars, illustrated by Rodney Shackell. New York, Atheneum, 1970; London, Gollancz, 1974.
Journey Between Worlds, illustrated by James and Ruth McCrea. New York, Atheneum, 1970.
The Far Side of Evil, illustrated by Richard Cuffari. New York, Atheneum, 1971; London, Gollancz, 1975.
This Star Shall Abide, illustrated by Richard Cuffari. New York,

Atheneum, 1972; as *Heritage of the Star,* London, Gollancz, 1973.
Beyond the Tomorrow Mountains, illustrated by Richard Cuffari. New York, Atheneum, 1973.
The Doors of the Universe. New York, Atheneum, 1981.

Other

The Planet-Girded Suns: Man's View of Other Solar Systems, illustrated by Richard Cuffari. New York, Atheneum, 1974.
The Subnuclear Zoo: New Discoveries in High Energy Physics, with Rick Roberson. New York, Atheneum, 1977.
Tool for Tomorrow: New Knowledge about Genes, with Rick Roberson. New York, Atheneum, 1979.
Our World Is Earth, illustrated by Don Sibley. New York, Atheneum, 1979.

Editor, with Rick Roberson, *Universe Ahead: Stories of the Future,* illustrated by Richard Cuffari. New York, Atheneum, 1975.
Editor, *Anywhere, Anywhen: Stories of Tomorrow.* New York, Atheneum, 1976.

*

Sylvia Engdahl comments:

Though my novels are set in future or hypothetical worlds, they are directed toward a general audience rather than toward fans of genre-oriented science fiction. They are intended primarily for older teenagers, but are enjoyed by preadolescents who are advanced readers and also by many adults. Their main emphasis is on the significance of space exploration, man's place in the universe, and human values that I consider universal: all themes in which I believe today's young people are seriously interested. My chief concern is to place the future in perspective in relation to the past and present, as well as to offer an affirmative outlook toward that future, and toward a wider universe than the single planet Earth.

* * *

Sylvia Engdahl has written only science fiction so far in her career. SF would appear, then, to be no passing interest but the focus of virtually all her creativity. This deep commitment may account for the shape and quality of Engdahl's fiction, for she does not go out of her way to accommodate the general reader. Engdahl's SF is not easy to read: it tends to be lengthy, eschews lively incident in favor of dialogue, and prefers analysis and commentary. Although several novels include romance, perhaps in an attempt to wed a popular young adult element to SF, Engdahl's primary intent remains presenting the latter as undiluted as possible. At the same time, her SF is neither "Buck Rogerish" nor "Star Trekky"; that is, there is no heavy emphasis on nuts and bolts procedures, futuristic technological innovations, and the conventions of "space opera." Engdahl's subjects are less glamorous but more significant: the possibility of life in outer space, the attraction of travel to the stars upon human curiosity and daring, the rigorous challenge of space colonization, and the relationship between two races and cultures, one technologically superior, the other, primitive.

Enchantress from the Stars and *The Far Side of Evil* best represent Engdahl's method and achievement. Both are detailed and overly long narratives that describe the ways a much older, more advanced, and, presumably, wiser race handles a younger and technologically inferior race it encounters in space. In the first novel members of the Anthropological Service from the Foundation seek to prevent the Imperial Exploration Corps of a young, still aggressive and materialistic planet from subjugating and colonizing an even younger planet. In the second novel members of the Service become involved in a struggle between two super powers on Toris. Elana, a

young woman member of the Service, figures prominently in both narratives. In *Enchantress from the Stars* Georyn, a native of the planet, believes Elana an enchantress and falls in love with her, unexpectedly complicating her mission; in *The Far Side of Evil* Elana is captured and tortured because another Federation agent unwisely falls in love and decides to interfere in Torrian affairs. Neither novel contains much overt action; what does occur is primarily psychological and emotional. Engdahl too obviously prefers to work on a relatively small and intimate scale. In this way, she trusts she can bring home quietly and persuasively, if not dramatically and excitingly, her major theme: new ideas, attitudes, and values must not be forced upon a society but allowed and encouraged to affect, first, one individual and then, gradually and naturally, others.

This theme, along with a fondness for working on a small scale, appears in the trilogy *This Star Shall Abide, Beyond the Tomorrow Mountains,* and *The Doors of the Universe,* concerning Noren, greatest of Scholars and heroes, on a human-colonized planet lacking metal and, hence, the capacity to build machinery. Even more than the Elana novels, the Noren novels are long, worked out in detail, and heavily dependent upon dialogue and commentary. Because Engdahl insists upon her kind of science fiction that uncompromisingly stresses ideas over action and even character, one wonders how much longer she can go on writing before her small audience and consequent small sales will silence her.

—Francis J. Molson

———

ENRIGHT, Elizabeth (Wright). American. Born in Oak Park, Illinois, 17 September 1909. Educated at Edgewood School, Greenwich, Connecticut; Art Students' League, New York, 1927–28; in Paris, 1928; Parsons School of Design, New York. Married Robert Marty Gillham in 1930; three sons. Teacher of creative writing, Barnard College, New York, 1960–62. Recipient: American Library Association Newbery Medal, 1939. LL.D.: Nasson College, Springvale, Maine, 1966. *Died 8 June 1968.*

PUBLICATIONS FOR CHILDREN (illustrated by the author)

Fiction

Kintu: A Congo Adventure. New York, Farrar and Rinehart, 1935.
Thimble Summer. New York, Farrar and Rinehart, 1938; London, Heinemann, 1939.
The Sea Is All Around. New York, Farrar and Rinehart, 1940; London, Heinemann, 1959.
The Saturdays. New York, Farrar and Rinehart, 1941; London, Heinemann, 1955.
The Four-Story Mistake. New York, Farrar and Rinehart, 1942; London, Heinemann, 1955.
Then There Were Five. New York, Farrar and Rinehart, 1944; London, Heinemann, 1956.
The Melendy Family (includes *The Saturdays, The Four-Story Mistake, Then There Were Five*). New York, Farrar and Rinehart, 1947.
A Christmas Tree for Lydia. New York, Rinehart, 1951.
Spiderweb for Two: A Melendy Maze. New York, Rinehart, 1951; London, Heinemann, 1956.
Gone-Away Lake, illustrated by Beth and Joe Krush. New York, Harcourt Brace, and London, Heinemann, 1957.
Return to Gone-Away, illustrated by Beth and Joe Krush. New York, Harcourt Brace, 1961; London, Heinemann, 1962.

Tatsinda, illustrated by Irene Haas. New York, Harcourt Brace, 1963; London, Heinemann, 1964.
Zeee, illustrated by Irene Haas. New York, Harcourt Brace, 1965; London, Heinemann, 1966.

PUBLICATIONS FOR ADULTS

Short Stories

Borrowed Summer and Other Stories. New York, Rinehart, 1946; as *The Maple Tree and Other Stories,* London, Heinemann, 1947.
The Moment Before the Rain. New York, Harcourt Brace, and London, Heinemann, 1955.
The Riddle of the Fly and Other Stories. New York, Harcourt Brace, 1959; London, Heinemann, 1960.
Doublefields: Memories and Stories. New York, Harcourt Brace, 1966; London, Heinemann, 1967.

*

Illustrator: *Kees,* 1930, *Amnon, A Lad of Palestine,* 1931, and *Kees and Kleintje,* 1934, all by Marian King; *The Crystal Locket* by Nellie M. Rowe, 1935.

*   *   *

Elizabeth Enright's keen perception of childhood and her remarkable gifts as a writer place her books among the select few that are timeless and enduring. In *The Sea Is All Around* one of her characters says, "I like people to look at things wholeheartedly...learning and absorbing them so that their memories are full of accurate impressions." Her books are full of "accurate impressions"; they ring true. The children in her books, too, have this ability to look, learn, and absorb wholeheartedly. They are interesting and full of life.

The heroine of *Thimble Summer* is 10-year-old Garnet Linden. Her Wisconsin summer starts out to be dull and hopeless; her family's farm is in serious trouble because of drought, and it is the time of the great depression. Soon after she finds a silver thimble in a dried up river bed, the rains come and a lovely summer of adventure begins. The book is full of the feel of a midwest farm and the dry little towns nearby, and the mood of America in the 1930's. A child of the depression, an orphan named Eric whose life has been lonely wandering, accidentally finds his way to the Linden family and is cared for and eventually adopted by them. There is a tree-house adventure, a wonderful chapter about being locked in the town library after closing time, a rebellious trip to a distant city. The summer, and the book, come to an end on a note of joy when Garnet's own personal pig whom she has raised from babyhood wins the blue ribbon at the county fair.

The Sea Is All Around is full of the mood of a storm-swept wintery island thirty miles out in the Atlantic. Once a busy port and home for prosperous whaling captains, the island is rich in tradition, scenery, and characters as well. Mab Kendall is an orphan who comes from Iowa to live with an aunt on Pokenick Island. This book is unforgettable for its description of loneliness and the awakening of contentment in a child. There are many lovely old people: "They carry with them memories of a long life starred with adventures." Her warm descriptions are delightful—she makes us see and feel storms and cold, snow and spring, the presence of the sea, northern lights, dune plants, swamp flowers and mosses, always called by their right names and more vivid as a result.

In the Melendy books the children are satisfying characters, particularly now when television gives ready-made dreams and makes watchers of us. All Enright children do things that children dream of doing. In *The Saturdays* they contrive ways of making New

York City their private source of joy. *The Four-Story Mistake* takes Mona, Rush, Randy, and Oliver Melendy out of the city and into an old house in the country, full of secrets and mysteries. The grounds are "thirty acres of land that hold a sample of everything delightful short of an active volcano and an ocean that one could want on his own territory: brook, woods, stable, hollow tree and summer house."

Then There Were Five continues Melendy life in the country. World War Two plays a part in this book, with Father in Washington and the children involved in at-home war efforts. The Melendy children have many talents and use them in fascinating ways. They also love to talk, and say things the way one wishes one could, and they are funny. A new Melendy comes on the scene, Mark, a young boy with no home, who adds much to the family and the book. *Spiderweb for Two* finds the older children away and Randy and Oliver home alone. For a little while their lives are empty. Then the mail brings the first of a series of clues in the form of cryptic poems, which, when deciphered, lead the children to strange hiding places and many adventures.

Gone-Away Lake and *Return to Gone-Away* are about two realistically drawn families who live in the country. Witty, original old people give a sense of history with stories of the past. Animals abound, and secrets and clubs, danger and daring, and always nature, authentic and fascinating, accessible and an accessory to what happens.

Tatsinda is a "once-upon-a-time" fairy tale, traditional in feeling. But Enright's knowing characterizations and lovely language make it special and fresh. *Zeee* is a funny down-to-earth fairy tale about a "bad" fairy, the size of a bee, who lives in the present and has personality problems. Zeee eventually finds a home and a friend and makes peace with herself and the cruel world which looms around her.

These are all beautiful books, to become deeply involved in, to absorb easily and happily and to remember always.

—Irene Haas

———

ESTES, Eleanor (Ruth, née Rosenfeld). American. Born in West Haven, Connecticut, 9 May 1906. Educated at Union Grammar School, West Haven; West Haven High School, graduated 1923; Pratt Institute Library School, New York (Hewins scholar), 1931–32. Married Rice Estes in 1932; one daughter. Children's librarian, Free Public Library, New Haven, Connecticut, 1924–31, and branches of the New York Public Library, 1932–40. Recipient: American Library Association Newbery Medal, 1952; Pratt Institute Alumni Medal, 1968. *Died 15 July 1988.*

PUBLICATIONS FOR CHILDREN

Fiction

The Moffats, illustrated by Louis Slobodkin. New York, Harcourt Brace, 1941; London, Bodley Head, 1959.
The Middle Moffat, illustrated by Louis Slobodkin. New York, Harcourt Brace, 1942; London, Bodley Head, 1960.
Rufus M., illustrated by Louis Slobodkin. New York, Harcourt Brace, 1943; London, Bodley Head, 1960.
The Sun and the Wind and Mr. Todd, illustrated by Louis Slobodkin. New York, Harcourt Brace, 1943.
The Hundred Dresses, illustrated by Louis Slobodkin. New York, Harcourt Brace, 1944.
The Sleeping Giant and Other Stories, illustrated by the author. New York, Harcourt Brace, 1948.

Ginger Pye, illustrated by the author. New York, Harcourt Brace, 1951; London, Bodley Head, 1961.

A Little Oven, illustrated by the author. New York, Harcourt Brace, 1955.

Pinky Pye, illustrated by Edward Ardizzone. New York, Harcourt Brace, 1958; London, Constable, 1959.

The Witch Family, illustrated by Edward Ardizzone. New York, Harcourt Brace, 1960; London, Constable, 1962.

The Alley, illustrated by Edward Ardizzone. New York, Harcourt Brace, 1964.

Miranda the Great, illustrated by Edward Ardizzone. New York, Harcourt Brace, 1967.

The Tunnel of Hugsy Goode, illustrated by Edward Ardizzone. New York, Harcourt Brace, 1971.

The Coat-Hanger Christmas Tree, illustrated by Susanne Suba. New York, Atheneum, 1973; London, Oxford University Press, 1976.

The Lost Umbrella of Kim Chu, illustrated by Jacqueline Ayer. New York, Atheneum, 1978; London, Oxford University Press, 1980.

The Moffat Museum. New York, Harcourt Brace, 1983.

The Curious Adventures of Jimmy McGee, illustrated by John O'Brien. San Diego, Harcourt Brace, 1987.

Play

The Lollipop Princess: A Play for Paper Dolls, illustrated by the author. New York, Harcourt Brace, 1967.

PUBLICATIONS FOR ADULTS

Novel

The Echoing Green. New York, Macmillan, 1947.

*

Manuscript Collection: Kerlan Collection, University of Minnesota, Minneapolis.

Eleanor Estes commented:

(1983) I have no aim other than to entertain, and to do this in the most complete and artistic way that I can.

*   *   *

Eleanor Estes's most exceptional feat, in her long and much-lauded career as an author of books for children, was her ability to distill the very essence of childhood. Estes's prose, simple and direct, and written with a rare authenticity of voice, never for an instant betrays her adult perceptions and perspectives. Estes wrote as a child writing for children, not as an adult writing for children, capturing with keen insight and sharp observation the vibrancy and vitality of that which is "long ago and far away" for many adults, but everyday reality for the child.

Perhaps Estes's best-known and best-loved creation is the Moffat family of Cranbury, Connecticut. *The Moffats* centers around bashful Joey, inspired Jane, irrepressible Rufus, and big sister Sylvie. Estes paints a portrait of each child as special and individual, and simultaneously gives them a firm grounding as part of a cohesive family unit. A string-of-pearls format characterizes the book—episodic in nature, each chapter focuses on a single event or incident, rather than having a formal plot structure. This lack of plot movement does not detract from the strength of the book, however. Estes's finesse at powerfully evoking the sights and sounds and the pleasures and pains of childhood is unwavering. The ebullient and energetic adventures of the indomitable Moffat family spill across every page of the

Moffat book and its successors, *The Middle Moffat, Rufus M.,* and finally, *The Moffat Museum,* written 42 years after the first Moffat story.

Ginger Pye, the 1952 Newbery Medal winner, and *Pinky Pye* are also set in Cranbury. Warm family stories, they are written with the same realistic humor and understanding of the child psyche that plays such an integral role in the Moffat books. Pets are important in the lives of the Pye children—in *Ginger Pye* Jerry and Rachel, with the special tenacity of children, spend months searching for their new puppy Ginger after she disappears on Thanksgiving Day. *Pinky Pye* combines fantasy and reality in the account of an extraordinary black kitten who, after being adopted by the family, learns to type on Mr. Pye's typewriter.

Connie Ives and her best friend Billy Maloon spring to life in *The Alley,* a mystery story set in Brooklyn, New York. When Connie's house is burglarized Connie and Billy turn detective, determined to solve the crime. Shot through with charm and originality, *The Alley* is all "cops and robbers," and distinguished by a stronger plot design than the Moffat and Pye stories.

The Hundred Dresses, like *The Alley,* is more solidly plotted than much of Estes's work, and also has a more serious theme than a great deal of her writing. Told with Estes's trademark sensitivity to and understanding of child character, it stands as a tribute to the invincibility of the human spirit. Wanda Petronski wears the same faded blue dress to school every day, but tells her classmates she has one hundred dresses at home. After becoming the subject of incessant teasing and prejudiced remarks, Wanda drops out of school and her family moves away. In an emotional, cathartic ending, Wanda's disconsolate and guilt-ridden persecutors are taught an enduring lesson in compassion and forgiveness.

With *The Witch Family* Estes again ventures into the realm of fantasy. By drawing pictures, best friends Amy and Clarissa create and manipulate Old Witch, head witch of all the witches, Little Witch Girl, Weeny Witch, and Malachi, the spelling bee. Filled with wit, wordplay, and plenty of "hurly-burlies," the book is a salute to the transforming power of a child's imagination. A less successful fantasy than *The Witch Family, The Curious Adventures of Jimmy McGee* reintroduces the reader to Amy and Clarissa, but the hero of the story is Jimmy McGee, a plumber who wears a stovepipe hat and a bombazine suit. The melding of fantasy and reality is not accomplished seamlessly, and Jimmy McGee and his antics are not as engrossing as are those of the witch family.

The reader does become involved in *The Lost Umbrella of Kim Chu,* however. Estes impeccably captures the ethnic flavor of New York, in particular Manhattan's Chinatown, in the early years of the 20th century. At the library, Kim Chu forgets her father's unique umbrella, which contains a scroll hidden in a secret compartment in the handle. Her grandmother sends Kim Chu on a quest in search of the umbrella, and she becomes involved in a chase on an elevated train and the Staten Island ferry before it is retrieved. At times the story seems manipulated to suit the author's intentions, but the direct prose style and sure eye for telling detail is distinctive of all of Estes's writing.

Estes was a celebrant of childhood. She moved in the kingdom of the young as if her passport for that country had never expired—indeed, in her mind it had not. Her books are immediate and have kept their appeal despite spanning four generations of readers. They have the kind of staying power springing from the authenticity of recreated experience that begins, and ends, in the joy that is so characteristic of childhood.

—Carolyn Shute

ESTORIL, Jean.   See **ALLAN, Mabel Esther.**

———

ETS, Marie Hall.   American.   Born in North Greenfield, Wisconsin, 16 December 1893. Educated at Lawrence College, Appleton, Wisconsin, 1915–16; New York School of Fine and Applied Art, 1916–17; University of Chicago, Ph.B. 1924, and graduate work; Art Institute, Chicago; Columbia University, New York. Married 1) Milton T. Rodig in 1917 (died 1918); 2) Harold N. Ets in 1929 (died 1943). Artist for San Francisco and Los Angeles decorating firms, 1917–18; social worker, Department of the Navy, 1918; part-time volunteer resident, Chicago Commons Settlement House, 1919–29; child health worker for the American Red Cross in Pilsen, Czechoslovakia, 1921–22; agent, United States Coal Commission in West Virginia and Illinois, 1923. Individual show (drawings): Columbia University Teachers College, New York, 1963. Recipient: American Library Association Caldecott Medal, 1960; University of Minnesota Kerlan award, 1975. Address: c/o Viking Penguin, 40 West 23rd Street, New York, New York 10010, U.S.A.

PUBLICATIONS FOR CHILDREN (illustrated by the author)

Fiction

Mister Penny.   New York, Viking Press, 1935; London, Woodfield, 1957.
In the Forest.   New York, Viking Press, 1944; London, Faber, 1955.
My Dog Rinty, with Ellen Tarry, illustrated by Alexander and Alexandra Alland.   New York, Viking Press, 1946.
Oley, The Sea Monster.   New York, Viking Press, 1947.
Little Old Automobile.   New York, Viking Press, 1948.
Mr. T.W. Anthony Woo: The Story of a Cat and a Dog and a Mouse.   New York, Viking Press, 1951.
Another Day.   New York, Viking Press, 1953; London, Faber, 1956.
Play with Me.   New York, Viking Press, 1955; London, Penguin, 1976.
Mister Penny's Race Horse.   New York, Viking Press, 1956; London, Woodfield, 1958.
Cow's Party.   New York, Viking Press, 1958; London, Faber, 1959.
Nine Days to Christmas, with Aurora Labastida.   New York, Viking Press, 1959.
Mister Penny's Circus.   New York, Viking Press, 1961.
Gilberto and the Wind.   New York, Viking Press, 1963.
Automobiles for Mice.   New York, Viking Press, 1964.
Just Me.   New York, Viking Press, 1965; London, Angus and Robertson, 1966.
Bad Boy, Good Boy.   New York, Crowell, 1967.
Talking Without Words: I Can, Can You?   New York, Viking Press, 1968.
Elephant in a Well.   New York, Viking Press, 1972.
Jay Bird.   New York, Viking Press, 1974.

Verse

Beasts and Nonsense.   New York, Viking Press, 1952.

Other

The Story of a Baby.   New York, Viking Press, 1939.

PUBLICATIONS FOR ADULTS

Other

Rosa: The Life of an Italian Immigrant.   Minneapolis, University of Minnesota Press, 1970.

*

Manuscript Collection: Kerlan Collection, University of Minnesota, Minneapolis.

Marie Hall Ets comments:

I lived in a family with several children who loved to hear stories and have me draw for them. I found it to be as enjoyable for me as for my nieces and nephew, so have tried to entertain children with my stories and pictures ever since.

*   *   *

The best work of Marie Hall Ets is deceptively simple. Most picture books that speak directly to the young child of nursery school age stand the risk of not at first impressing the adult who selects it. Very often it is only after the adult witnesses the secret appeal that such books hold for children that he returns to examine and appreciate the subtle craftsmanship of the author-illustrator.

A book like *In the Forest* or *Play with Me* is so simple in construction and syntax that one may be tempted to say that it wouldn't be very hard to write a book like that—when in fact these are the most difficult books of all to write. The distance in years and experience between the writer and the young child is so great that only a special few, like Ets, have been successful in creating picture books that the child intuitively recognizes as having been written expressly for him.

In these books Ets daringly selects a first person telling. In order for her to do this she not only must feel comfortable with the mental furniture of the young child's mind, but she must also be sure to select a content and a style with which the child is both familiar and comfortable. She skillfully blends fancifulness with matter-of-factness: both are integral ingredients of a child's imaginative play. Repetition, artfully employed, gives the effect of the muted chant that a child often creates when he plays alone:

> I had a new horn and a paper hat
> And I went for a walk in the forest.
> A big wild lion was taking a nap.
> But he woke up when he heard my horn.
> "Where are you going?" he said to me.
> "May I go too, if I comb my hair?"
> So he combed his hair and he came too
> When I went for a walk in the forest.

Her longer stories, like *Mister Penny* and *Mr. T.W. Anthony Woo,* are reminiscent of the earlier stories of Hugh Lofting. Like Doctor Dolittle in fiction (and Doctor Schweitzer in life), Mr. Penny and the cobbler of Shooshko are superb adult models for children. They show a great love and reverence for all God's creatures, and they demonstrate great patience towards them, no matter how mischievous they may be. These books are alive with silly names and slapstick humor that make children laugh out loud, but beneath all the fun, and devoid of moralistic pronouncement, are such notions as: "People always hate the things they are afraid of" and "How nice it is to have peace."

The works of Ets are perfect for sharing: there is much to savor for both child and adult.

—James E. Higgins

———

EVANS, Hubert (Reginald). Canadian. Born in Vankleek Hill, Ontario, 9 May 1892. Educated at Galt Collegiate, Ontario, graduated 1909. Served in the Kootenay Battalion, Rocky Mountain Rangers, in France and Flanders, 1915–19. Married Anna Winter in 1920 (died 1960); three children. Newspaper reporter, Toronto and British Columbia, 1910–14; worked for commercial fisheries and on salmon conservation as a fisheries officer; lived in Indian villages, Northern British Columbia, 1946–53. *Died 17 June 1986.*

PUBLICATIONS FOR CHILDREN

Fiction

Forest Friends: Stories of Animals, Fish and Birds West of the Rockies. Philadelphia, Judson Press, 1926.
Derry, Airedale of the Frontier. New York, Dodd Mead, 1928.
Derry's Partner, illustrated by Frank E. Schoonover. New York, Dodd Mead, 1929.
Derry of Totem Creek, illustrated by H.E.M. Sellen. New York, Dodd Mead, 1930.
The Silent Call. New York, Dodd Mead, 1930.
Mountain Dog. Philadelphia, Westminster Press, 1956; as *Son of the Salmon People,* Madeira Park, British Columbia, Harbour, 1981.

Other

North to the Unknown: The Achievement and Adventures of David Thompson, illustrated by Ruth Collins. Toronto, McClelland and Stewart, and New York, Dodd Mead, 1949.

PUBLICATIONS FOR ADULTS

Novels

The New Front Line. Toronto, Macmillan, 1927.
Mist on the River. Toronto, Copp Clark, 1954.
O Time in Your Flight. Madeira Park, British Columbia, Harbour, 1979.

Verse

Whittlings. Madeira Park, British Columbia, Harbour, 1976.
Endinas. Madeira Park, British Columbia, Harbour, 1978.
Mostly Coast People. Madeira Park, British Columbia, Harbour, n.d.

*   *   *

Hubert Evans's writings are concerned for the most part with the Skeena River area of British Columbia, an area whose facets he knew very well from his life there working first in the commercial fisheries and later as a fisheries officer. This background is evident in his writing for adults, which reflects his knowledge of life in the province, particularly the life of the Indians.

In his children's books Evans drew on much of his own experience of close contact with the outdoors for his material. His two collections of animal stories, *Forest Friends* and *The Silent Call,* are told in a familiar, anecdotal style. Their chief interest is their reflection of the natural world Evans appeared to know very well. His fictionalized biography of David Thompson (1770–1857), *North to the Unknown,* written for teenagers, is marred by his lack of familiarity with the historical period about which he wrote.

Perhaps his most successful writing is to be seen in his novels

about Derry, an Airedale terrier, which appeared in Grosset's *Famous Dog Stories* series, and *Mountain Dog.* In these, Evans writes animal biographies against a background of carefully described and obviously well-loved settings in British Columbia. His love of nature and his desire for its conservation are evident throughout these books. Like most attempts at rendering intelligible the thoughts and activities of animals, these books could be accused of, at times, sentimentalizing and anthropomorphizing dogs. While Evans can at times be accused of both practices, the stories, with their well-observed detail and their exciting and imaginative plots, sustain interest very well. As a writer of nature stories, and particularly of dog stories, Evans was quite successful, and much of his work bears favourable comparison with that of the two most prominent Canadian writers of the genre, Ernest Thompson Seton and Charles G.D. Roberts.

—Janet E. Baker

———

FARBER, Norma (née Holzman). American. Born in Boston, Massachusetts, 6 August 1909. Educated at Girls' Latin School, Boston, graduated 1926; Wellesley College, Massachusetts, A.B. 1931 (Phi Beta Kappa); Radcliffe College, Cambridge, Massachusetts, M.A. in comparative literature 1932. Married Sidney Farber in 1928 (died); two daughters and two sons. Professional singer. Recipient: Jury Central des Études Musicales (Belgium) diploma, 1936; Borestone Mountain Poetry award, 1957, 1973, 1975, 1976; New England Poetry Club Golden Rose, 1958; Poetry Society of America Reynolds award, 1959, award, 1961, Sloane award, 1961, Markham award, 1963, Reedy award, 1969, Morley award, 1973, and Davidson award, 1978; Children's Book Council award, 1976. D.H.L.: Framingham State College, Massachusetts, 1984. *Died 21 March 1984.*

PUBLICATIONS FOR CHILDREN

Fiction

This Is the Ambulance Leaving the Zoo, illustrated by Tomie de Paola. New York, Dutton, 1975.
Six Impossible Things Before Breakfast: Stories and Poems, illustrated by Tomie de Paola and others. Reading, Massachusetts, Addison Wesley, 1977.
Three Wanderers from Wapping, illustrated by Charles Mikolaycak. Reading, Massachusetts, Addison Wesley, 1978.
A Night on Gars Mountain, illustrated by Allen Atkinson. Boston, Houghton Mifflin, 1981.
Mercy Short: A Winter Journal, North Boston 1692–93. New York, Dutton, 1982.

Verse

Did You Know It Was the Narwhale?, illustrated by Carole Vizbara. New York, Atheneum, 1967.
Where's Gomer?, illustrated by William Pène du Bois. New York, Dutton, 1974.
As I Was Crossing Boston Common, illustrated by Arnold Lobel. New York, Dutton, 1975.
A Ship in a Storm on the Way to Tarshish, illustrated by Victoria Chess. New York, Greenwillow, 1977.
There Once Was a Woman Who Married a Man, illustrated by Lydia Dabcovich. Reading, Massachusetts, Addison Wesley, 1978.
How the Left-Behind Beasts Built Ararat, illustrated by Antonio

Frasconi. New York, Walker, 1978.

Never Say Ugh to a Bug, illustrated by Jose Aruego. New York, Greenwillow, 1979.

Small Wonders, illustrated by Kazue Mizumura. New York, Coward McCann, 1979.

There Goes Feathertop!, illustrated by Marc Brown. New York, Dutton, 1979.

How Does It Feel to Be Old?, illustrated by Trina Schart Hyman. New York, Dutton, 1979.

Up the Down Elevator, illustrated by Annie Gusman. Reading, Massachusetts, Addison Wesley, 1979.

How the Hibernators Came to Bethlehem, illustrated by Barbara Cooney. New York, Walker, 1980.

How to Ride a Tiger, illustrated by Claire Schumacher. Boston, Houghton Mifflin, 1983.

All Those Mothers at the Manger, illustrated by Megan Lloyd. New York, Harper, 1985.

Other

I Found Them in the Yellow Pages, illustrated by Marc Brown. Boston, Little Brown, 1973.

Editor, with Myra Cohn Livingston, *These Small Stones.* New York, Harper, 1987.

PUBLICATIONS FOR ADULTS

Play

Mary Chesnut's Diary (produced Cambridge, Massachusetts, 1961).

Verse

Poets of Today 2, with Robert Pack and Louis Simpson. New York, Scribner, 1955.

Look to the Rose. Boston, Fandel, 1958.

A Desperate Thing: Marriage Is a Desperate Thing. Boston, Plowshare Press, 1973.

Household Poems. Belmont, Massachusetts, Hellric, 1975.

Something Further. Ann Arbor, Michigan, Kylix Press, 1979.

Shekhina: Forty Poems. Tucson, Capstone, 1984.

Other

Translator, with Edith Helman, *To Live in Pronouns: Selected Love Poems,* by Pedro Salinas. New York, Norton, 1974.

*

Manuscript Collection: Kerlan Collection, University of Minnesota, Minneapolis.

Norma Farber commented:

(1983) I have always written poems, as far back as I can remember. In 1926 I was Class Poet at our Girls' Latin School graduation. Spenserian stanzas, no less! I have since graduated from *that.*

*   *   *

It was the wonders and miracles of life that captured Norma Farber's imagination in her work for young people, a devotion to the seemingly obscure to which she held a glittering magnifying glass. This celebration of life is an unending invitation to marvel at both the commonplace and the extraordinary, brought into focus by startling metaphor and rich patterns of form and rhythm.

Nowhere is this more evident than in her poems of the Nativity—a theme she explored constantly in some of her finest work for adults. With tenderness she wrote of Joseph and Mary, of the Holy Child, the three kings, and the surrounding mysteries of one night almost 2000 years ago. But she directed her reader

> To think of all the kings who were not there, who never
> dropped their crowns and cares of state
> unceremoniously…

For children she also turned "to think of those absent" in fresh and vivid imagery. Here are the sea creatures who could not make the journey, as well as the hibernators, animals, insects, and people who do. It is the ladybug who is "Worn like a jewel,/a fiery pin,/a ruby sequin" over the baby's heart, and the dove who asks "What thing/should I sing/little king?/*Coo-roo?*" Her use of synesthesia was remarkable in numerous poems, but reached a pinnacle when the spider speaks to the Holy Child: "I loop my wiring silver-clear,/to light your manager chandelier./Listen! My web is what you hear."

In *Small Wonders* creatures and objects, in varying poetic forms, force the reader to see and think anew. Maggots are transformed into "coral strings" or "grains of glistening rice." The caterpillar is a "concertina," the turtle a "creeping stone." A walnut becomes a "tiny wizened tot" in his cradle of shell, and a dandelion a "white pincushion." Leaves from a rich autumn tree fall as coins in "Spendthrift."

Farber's poetic craft enabled her to give readers a continual wealth of assonance, consonance, and alliteration, weaving in and out of rhythms through which her readers may listen to many a song unsung. "Softer than the breath of woolly bears, sleeping,/the sound of my velvet bellows, creeping…" begins the "Caterpillar Carol" in *Never Say Ugh to a Bug,* a collection that brings to life arresting portraits of the insect world, mixed with humor. Wit and imagination are found in *As I Was Crossing Boston Common* with its splendid refrain of "how uncommon" to the nonsense creatures who parade before the reader. Yet she is equally adept at the serious. In *How Does It Feel to Be Old?* the woman tells a child who asks, "I'm dreaming the past/as though it never was over…"

Farber's talents were far-ranging. She brought to the world of poetry written for children a gift of music and of observation, expanding horizons of reality and of fantasy. We are all the richer for her poetry.

—Myra Cohn Livingston

FARJEON, Eleanor. Also wrote as Tomfool. British. Born in London, 13 February 1881; daughter of the novelist Benjamin Leopold Farjeon; sister of the writers Herbert and Joseph Jefferson Farjeon and the composer Harry Farjeon. Educated privately. Regular contributor to *Punch,* London, 1914–17; wrote verse (as Tomfool) for the London *Daily Herald,* 1917–30; staff member and verse contributor (as Chimaera), *Time and Tide,* London, in the 1920's. Recipient: Hans Christian Andersen International Medal, 1956; Library Association Carnegie Medal, 1956; Catholic Library Association Regina Medal, 1959. *Died 5 June 1965.*

PUBLICATIONS FOR CHILDREN

Fiction

Martin Pippin in the Apple-Orchard, illustrated by C.E. Brock. London, Collins, 1921; New York, Stokes, 1922.
Tom Cobble, illustrated by M. Dobson. Oxford, Blackwell, 1925.
Nuts and May: A Medley for Children, illustrated by Rosalind Thornycroft. London, Collins, 1926.
Italian Peepshow and Other Tales, illustrated by Rosalind Thornycroft. New York, Stokes, 1926; as *Italian Peepshow and Other Stories,* Oxford, Blackwell, 1934; revised edition as *Italian Peepshow,* London, Oxford University Press, 1960.
The Wonderful Knight, illustrated by Doris Pailthorpe. Oxford, Blackwell, 1927.
The King's Barn; or, Joan's Tale. London, Collins, 1927.
The Mill of Dreams; or, Jennifer's Tale. London, Collins, 1927.
Young Gerard; or, Joyce's Tale. London, Collins, 1927.
A Bad Day for Martha, illustrated by Eugenie Richards. Oxford, Blackwell, 1928.
Kaleidoscope. London, Collins, 1928; New York, Stokes, 1929.
The Perfect Zoo. London, Harrap, and Philadelphia, McKay, 1929.
The King's Daughter Cries for the Moon, illustrated by May Smith. Oxford, Blackwell, 1929.
The Tale of Tom Tiddler, illustrated by Norman Tealby. London, Collins, 1929; New York, Stokes, 1930.
Westwoods, illustrated by May Smith. Oxford, Blackwell, 1930; Poughkeepsie, New York, Artists and Writers Guild, 1935.
The Old Nurse's Stocking Basket, illustrated by E. Herbert Whydale. London, University of London Press, and New York, Stokes, 1931.
Perkin the Pedlar, illustrated by Clare Leighton. London, Faber, 1932.
Katy Kruse at the Seaside; or, The Deserted Islanders. London, Harrap, and Philadelphia, McKay, 1932.
Ameliaranne's Prize Packet, illustrated by S.B. Pearse. London, Harrap, 1933; as *Ameliaranne and the Magic Ring,* Philadelphia, McKay, 1933.
Pannychis, illustrated by Clare Leighton. Shaftesbury, Dorset, High House Press, 1933.
Ameliaranne's Washing Day, illustrated by S.B. Pearse. London, Harrap, and Philadelphia, McKay, 1934.
Jim at the Corner and Other Stories, illustrated by Irene Mountfort. Oxford, Blackwell, 1934; as *The Old Sailor's Yarn Box,* New York, Stokes, 1934.
The Clumber Pup, illustrated by Irene Mountfort. Oxford, Blackwell, 1934.
And I Dance Mine Own Child, illustrated by Irene Mountfort. Oxford, Blackwell, 1935.
Jim and the Pirates, illustrated by Roger Naish. Oxford, Blackwell, 1936.
Martin Pippin in the Daisy-Field, illustrated by Isobel and John Morton-Sale. London, Joseph, 1937; New York, Stokes, 1938.
One Foot in Fairyland: Sixteen Tales, illustrated by Robert Lawson. London, Joseph, and New York, Stokes, 1938.
The Silver Curlew, from her own play, illustrated by Ernest H. Shepard. London, Oxford University Press, 1953; New York, Viking Press, 1954.
The Little Book-Room, illustrated by Edward Ardizzone. London, Oxford University Press, 1955; New York, Oxford University Press, 1956.
The Glass Slipper, from the play by Eleanor and Herbert Farjeon, illustrated by Ernest H. Shepard. London, Oxford University Press, 1955; New York, Viking Press, 1956.
Mr. Garden, illustrated by Jane Paton. London, Hamish Hamilton, and New York, Walck, 1966.

Plays

Grannie Gray: Children's Plays and Games with Music and Without, illustrated by Joan Jefferson Farjeon. London, Dent, 1939.
The Glass Slipper, with Herbert Farjeon, music by Clifton Parker, illustrated by Hugh Stevenson (produced London, 1944). London, Wingate, 1946.
The Silver Curlew: A Fairy Tale, music by Clifton Parker (produced London, 1949). London, French, 1953.

Verse

Nursery Rhymes [and *More Nursery Rhymes*] *of London Town,* illustrated by Macdonald Gill. London, Duckworth, 2 vols., 1916–17; with music by the author, London, Oxford University Press, 4 vols., 1919–26.
All the Way to Alfriston, illustrated by Robin Guthrie. London, Morland Press, 1918.
Singing Games for Children, illustrated by J. Littlejohns. London, Dent, and New York, Dutton, 1919.
A First [and *Second*] *Chap-Book of Rounds,* music by Harry Farjeon, illustrated by John Garside. London, Dent, and New York, Dutton, 2 vols., 1919.
Tunes of a Penny Piper, illustrated by John Aveten. London, Selwyn and Blount, 1922.
Songs for Music and Lyrical Poems, illustrated by John Aveten. London, Selwyn and Blount, 1922.
All the Year Round. London, Collins, 1923; as *Around the Seasons,* London, Hamish Hamilton, and New York, Walck, 1969.
The Country Child's Alphabet, illustrated by William Michael Rothenstein. London, Poetry Bookshop, 1924.
The Town Child's Alphabet, illustrated by David Jones. London, Poetry Bookshop, 1924.
Songs from "Punch" for Children, music by the author. London, Saville, 1925.
Young Folk and Old. Shaftesbury, Dorset, High House Press, 1925.
Joan's Door, illustrated by Will Townsend. London, Collins, 1926; New York, Stokes, 1927.
Singing Games from Arcady, music by the author. Oxford, Blackwell, 1926.
Come, Christmas, illustrated by Molly McArthur. London, Collins, 1927; New York, Stokes, 1928.
An Alphabet of Magic, illustrated by Margaret Tarrant. London, Medici Society, 1928.
Poems for Children. Philadelphia, Lippincott, 1931.
Kings and Queens, with Herbert Farjeon, illustrated by Rosalind Thornycroft. London, Gollancz, and New York, Dutton, 1932; revised edition, London, Dent, 1953; Philadelphia, Lippincott, 1955.
Heroes and Heroines, with Herbert Farjeon, illustrated by Rosalind Thornycroft. London, Gollancz, and New York, Dutton, 1933.
Over the Garden Wall, illustrated by Gwendolen Raverat. London, Faber, and New York, Stokes, 1933.
Sing for Your Supper, illustrated by Isobel and John Morton-Sale. London, Joseph, and New York, Stokes, 1938.
Songs of Kings and Queens, with Herbert Farjeon, music by Eleanor Farjeon. London, Arnold, 1938.
A Sussex Alphabet, illustrated by Sheila M. Thompson. Bognor Regis, Sussex, Pear Tree Press, 1939.
Cherrystones, illustrated by Isobel and John Morton-Sale. London, Joseph, 1942; Philadelphia, Lippincott, 1944.
A Prayer for Little Things, illustrated by Elizabeth Orton Jones. Boston, Houghton Mifflin, 1945.
The Mulberry Bush, illustrated by Isobel and John Morton-Sale. London, Joseph, 1945.
The Starry Floor, illustrated by Isobel and John Morton-Sale. Lon-

don, Joseph, 1949.
Mrs. Malone, illustrated by David Knight.   London, Joseph, 1950; New York, Walck, 1962.
Silver-Sand and Snow.   London, Joseph, 1951.
The Children's Bells: A Selection of Poems, illustrated by Peggy Fortnum.   London, Oxford University Press, 1957; New York, Walck, 1960.
A Puffin Quartet of Poets, with others, edited by Eleanor Graham, illustrated by Diana Bloomfield.   London, Penguin, 1958.
Then There Were Three, Being Cherrystones, The Mulberry Bush, The Starry Floor, illustrated by Isobel and John Morton-Sale.   London, Joseph, 1958; Philadelphia, Lippincott, 1965.
Morning Has Broken, illustrated by Gordon Stowell.   Oxford, Mowbray, 1981.
Invitation to a Mouse and Other Poems, edited by Annabel Farjeon, illustrated by Antony Maitland.   London, Pelham, 1981.
Something I Remember, edited by Anne Harvey, illustrated by Alan Marks.   London, Blackie, 1987.

Other

Mighty Men: Achilles to Julius Caesar, Beowulf to Harold, illustrated by Hugh Chesterman.   Oxford, Blackwell, 2 vols., 1924–25; New York, Appleton, 2 vols., 1925.
Tales from Chaucer: The Canterbury Tales Done into Prose, illustrated by W. Russell Flint.   London, Medici Society, and New York, Cape and Smith, 1930.
Ten Saints, illustrated by Helen Sewell.   New York, Oxford University Press, 1936; London, Oxford University Press, 1953.
Lector Readings (reader), illustrated by Ruth Westcott.   London, Nelson, 1936.
The Wonders of Herodotus, illustrated by Edmund Nelson.   London, Nelson, 1937.
Paladins in Spain..., illustrated by Katharine Tozer.   London, Nelson, 1937.
The New Book of Days, illustrated by Philip Gough and Meredith W. Hawes.   London, Oxford University Press, 1941; New York, Walck, 1961.
Eleanor Farjeon's Book: Stories, Verses, Plays, edited by Eleanor Graham, illustrated by Edward Ardizzone.   London, Penguin, 1960.

Editor, with William Mayne, *The Hamish Hamilton Book of Kings,* illustrated by Victor Ambrus.   London, Hamish Hamilton, 1964; as *A Cavalcade of Kings,* New York, Walck, 1965.
Editor, with William Mayne, *The Hamish Hamilton Book of Queens,* illustrated by Victor Ambrus.   London, Hamish Hamilton, 1965; as *A Cavalcade of Queens,* New York, Walck, 1965.
Editor, *The Green Roads: Poems for Young Readers,* by Edward Thomas, illustrated by Bernard Brett.   London, Bodley Head, and New York, Holt Rinehart, 1965.

PUBLICATIONS FOR ADULTS

Novels

The Soul of Kol Nikon.   London, Collins, and New York, Stokes, 1923.
Ladybrook.   London, Collins, and New York, Stokes, 1931.
The Fair of St. James: A Fantasia.   London, Faber, and New York, Stokes, 1932.
The Humming Bird.   London, Joseph, 1936; New York, Stokes, 1937.
Miss Granby's Secret.   London, Joseph, 1940; as *Miss Granby's*

Secret; or, The Bastard of Pinsk, New York, Simon and Schuster, 1941.
Brave Old Woman.   London, Joseph, 1941.
The Fair Venetian.   London, Joseph, 1943.
Golden Coney.   London, Joseph, 1943.
Ariadne and the Bull.   London, Joseph, 1945.
Love Affair.   London, Joseph, 1947; New York, Macmillan, 1949.
The Two Bouquets, from the play by Eleanor and Herbert Farjeon.   London, Joseph, 1948.

Short Stories

Gypsy and Ginger.   London, Dent, and New York, Dutton, 1920.
Faithful Jenny Dove and Other Tales.   London, Collins, 1925; revised edition, as *Faithful Jenny Dove and Other Illusions,* London, Joseph, 1963.

Plays

Floretta (opera), music by Harry Farjeon (produced London, 1899).   London, Henderson and Spalding, 1899.
The Registry Office (opera), music by Harry Farjeon (produced London, 1900).   London, Henderson and Spalding, 1900.
A Gentleman of the Road (operetta), music by Harry Farjeon (produced London, 1902).   London, Boosey and Hawkes, 1903.
St. John's Eve, music by Alexander C. Mackenzie (produced Liverpool, 1924).
The Two Bouquets: A Victorian Comedy with Music, with Herbert Farjeon, music by the authors (produced London, 1936).   London, Gollancz, 1936.
An Elephant in Arcady, with Herbert Farjeon, music by Ernest Irving (produced London, 1938).
A Room at the Inn: A Christmas Masque, with Herbert Farjeon, music by Harry Farjeon (broadcast, 1938).   Privately printed, 1956.
Aucassin and Nicolette, with Herbert Farjeon, music by Clifton Parker.   London, Chappell, 1952.

Radio Play: *A Room at the Inn: A Christmas Masque,* with Herbert Farjeon, 1938.

Verse

Pan-Worship and Other Poems.   London, Elkin Mathews, 1908.
Dream-Songs for the Beloved.   London, Orpheus Press, 1911.
Sonnets and Poems.   Oxford, Blackwell, 1918.
Tomfooleries (as Tomfool).   London, Daily Herald, 1920.
Moonshine (as Tomfool).   London, Labour Publishing-Allen and Unwin, 1921.
The ABC of the B.B.C.   London, Collins, 1928.
Snowfall.   London, Favil Press, 1928.
A Collection of Poems.   London, Collins, 1929.
First and Second Love: Sonnets.   London, Joseph, 1947.

Other

Arthur Rackham: The Wizard at Home.   New York, Century, 1914.
Trees.   London, Batsford, 1914.
A Nursery in the Nineties (autobiography).   London, Gollancz, 1935; as *Portrait of a Family,* New York, Stokes, 1936.
Magic Casements (essays).   London, Allen and Unwin, 1941.
Dark World of Animals.   London, Sylvan Press, 1945.
Elizabeth Myers.   Aylesford, Kent, St. Albert's Press, 1957.
Edward Thomas, The Last Four Years: The Memoirs of Eleanor Farjeon, Book One.   London, Oxford University Press, 1958.

Translator, with Herbert Farjeon, *The Fan,* in *Four Comedies,* by

Carlo Goldoni, edited by Clifford Bax. London, Cecil Palmer, 1922.

*

Critical Studies: *Eleanor Farjeon* by Eileen Colwell, London, Bodley Head, and New York, Walck, 1961; *The Eleanor Farjeon Book: A Tribute to Her Life and Work 1881–1965*, London, Hamish Hamilton, 1966, as *A Book for Eleanor Farjeon*, New York, Walck, 1966; *Eleanor: Portrait of a Farjeon*, London, Gollancz, 1966, and *In Search of Elsie Piddock*, London, Favil Press, 1967, both by Denys Blakelock; *Morning Has Broken: A Biography of Eleanor Farjeon* by Annabel Farjeon, London, MacRae, and New York, Watts, 1986.

* * *

Eleanor Farjeon's writing was so much part of her own bubbling, enthusiastic personality that it is impossible not to see her as one of her own characters. She is, without doubt, the motherly, generous animal-lover Mrs. Malone "Whose heart was so big/It had room for us all...." And she is the Nurse in *The Old Nurse's Stocking Basket*. Old Nurse has been around a long while and nursed such charges as King Neptune, the Brothers Grimm, the Spanish Infanta "who had to be best at everything," and tiny Lipp the Lapp "who was so small his mother couldn't find him." She tells wise and witty stories to her present family.

Farjeon enjoyed this device of circling stories around a central character, and it also works well in *Jim at the Corner*, in which Sailor Jim spins yarns for the boy Derry. She first used it in *Martin Pippin in the Apple-Orchard*, a romantic pastoral originally intended for adults. It caught the imaginations of young girls in the 1920's, though its whimsical charm has dated. The sequel, *Martin Pippin in the Daisy-Field*, is a sturdier book for a younger age group, where the batch of tales told by the minstrel are also Sussex-based, and well plotted and sustained. One story, "Elsie Piddock Skips in Her Sleep," stands out, and was the writer's own favorite.

In later life Farjeon wrote that it was her absorption in imaginative play that led to "that flow of ease that makes writing a delight." She was also fortunate in her unorthodox father's dislike of formal education and encouragement to read freely in his well-stocked library. "That little bookroom," she wrote, "opened magic casements for me through which I looked out on other worlds and times than those I lived in." *The Little Book-Room* was an apt title for the 1955 collection she made from her own stories. It is her finest work, and a worthy winner of the Andersen and Carnegie medals. The range is wide, the stories are amusing and unsentimental; fantasy combines with sharp observation, lit by unexpected twists and turns. Reading these 27 stories one learns of her own experience and values. Trust, friendship, and justice are more important than rank or material possessions. She is never far away from her own childhood, and the wisest of her adult characters know the importance of "a life kept always young." The humour is rich and firm, but she never glosses over death, old age, or disappointment. It is a collection of quality, of depth, of ageless appeal, to return to over and over again.

Among the stories *And I Dance Mine Own Child* is unusual. The two main characters, Griselda and her Great Grandmother, separated by a span of 100 years, have reversed roles. The old lady enjoys sorting beads, playing with Bella the doll, and stealing currants. Her eyes grow bright and greedy for sweets to take with the medicine Grissie doses her with. Grissie is capable, wise to Gramma's ways, adept at tucking her up and telling her stories. They are descendants of the poet, Thomas Dekker, and own an ancient book of his; Bella sits by it—"it props her up beautiful"—but it turns out to be so valuable that Gramma need not go to the Almshouse and Grissie can go on singing her the song Dekker wrote for that other, long ago

Griselda: "Hush...hush...hush....And I dance mine own child."

Farjeon was the friend of many poets, among them D.H. Lawrence, Robert Frost, and Edward Thomas, and in her youth she too "dreamed of being a real poet, but half way through my life the dream died and whatever figments of it remained went into writing songs and verses for children." The best of her poetry matches the best of her prose, but at times she allowed her delight in words, rhyme, and rhythm to dance along into slight, rather tripping verse. She never quite caught the chilling edge, the sense of menace, of her friend Walter de la Mare; but her work offers amazing variety and craftsmanship. The two stand together as the most important English children's poets of the 20th century. She drew on a vast store of knowledge, and wrote of town and country, good and bad children, old folk, magic and the sea, school and home. She liked to weave poems around the alphabet letters, or a theme like the zodiac or party games. Her poems on kittens, on a special golden cat, on the cats that "Sleep anywhere,/Any table, any chair..." are very popular. She practiced no formal religion until she became a Catholic in old age, but "Morning Is Broken" is sung as a hymn, she wrote much on saints, and no-one captures the holiness, as well as the festivity, of Christmas as she did. *Nursery Rhymes of London Town*, includes inventive and quirky play on London place names: "King's Cross! What shall we do?/Leave him alone for a minute or two"; "Wormwood scrubs the City streets,/Wormwood scrubs St. Paul's." Herbert Farjeon's collaboration with his sister was a happy one; his more caustic humour combined well with her light-hearted touch. Their masterpiece, *Kings and Queens*, offers a tongue in cheek glimpse at the monarchy, with such observations as:

> Bluff King Hal was full of beans,
> He married half a dozen Queens,
> For three called Kate they cried the banns
> And one called Jane, and a couple of Anne's....

They also collaborated on a play, *The Glass Slipper*, and later she wrote one on her own, *The Silver Curlew*. Both are highly professional theatre pieces, with attractive characters and sparkling dialogue, and are far less dated than one would expect.

Farjeon's final piece of writing, the perceptive introduction to a selection of Edward Thomas's poems for young readers, was completed the day before her 84th birthday. This closed a career that is recognised annually when the Children's Book Circle give the Eleanor Farjeon award in her memory. In the 1930's she told would-be children's writers: "Don't write down to children...don't try to be on their level...don't think there is a special tone they will respond to. Don't be afraid of words and things you think they can't yet grasp...." It was advice she always followed herself.

—Anne Harvey

———

FARLEY, Walter (Lorimer). American. Born in Syracuse, New York, 26 June 1915. Educated at Erasmus High School, Brooklyn, New York; Mercersburg Academy, Pennsylvania, 1931–35; Columbia University, New York, 1941. Served in the Fourth Armored Division, and as staff member of *Yank* magazine, United States Army, 1942–46. Married Rosemary Lutz in 1945; two daughters (one deceased) and two sons. Advertising copywriter, Batten Barton Durstine and Osborn, New York, 1941; horse breeder, Earlville, Pennsylvania, 1946–65. Lives in Pennsylvania and Florida. Address: c/o Random House Inc., 201 East 50th Street, New York, New York 10022, U.S.A.

PUBLICATIONS FOR CHILDREN

Fiction

The Black Stallion, illustrated by Keith Ward. New York, Random
House, 1941; London, Lunn, 1947; abridged edition, as *The Black
Stallion Picture Book,* Random House, 1979.
Larry and the Undersea Raider, illustrated by P.K. Jackson. New
York, Random House, 1942; London, Muller, 1944.
The Black Stallion Returns, illustrated by Harold Eldridge. New
York, Random House, 1945; London, Lunn, 1947.
Son of the Black Stallion, illustrated by Milton Menasco. New
York, Random House, 1947; London, Collins, 1950.
The Island Stallion, illustrated by Keith Ward. New York, Random
House, 1948; London, Hodder and Stoughton, 1973.
The Black Stallion and Satan, illustrated by Milton Menasco. New
York, Random House, 1949; revised edition, London, Hodder and
Stoughton, 1974.
The Blood Bay Colt, illustrated by Milton Menasco. New York,
Random House, 1950.
The Island Stallion's Fury, illustrated by Harold Eldridge. New
York, Random House, 1951; London, Knight, 1975.
The Black Stallion's Filly, illustrated by Milton Menasco. New
York, Random House, 1952; London, Knight, 1979.
The Black Stallion Revolts, illustrated by Harold Eldridge. New
York, Random House, 1953; London, Knight, 1978.
The Black Stallion's Sulky Colt, illustrated by Harold Eldridge.
New York, Random House, 1954.
The Island Stallion Races, illustrated by Harold Eldridge. New
York, Random House, 1955.
The Black Stallion's Courage. New York, Random House, 1956;
London, Knight, 1978.
The Black Stallion Mystery, illustrated by Mal Singer. New York,
Random House, 1957; London, Hodder and Stoughton, 1973.
The Horse-Tamer, illustrated by James Schucker. New York, Ran-
dom House, 1958.
The Black Stallion and Flame, illustrated by Harold Eldridge. New
York, Random House, 1960; revised edition, London, Hodder and
Stoughton, 1974.
Little Black, A Pony, illustrated by James Schucker. New York,
Random House, 1961; London, Collins, 1963.
Little Black Goes to the Circus, illustrated by James Schucker. New
York, Random House, 1963; London, Collins, 1965.
The Black Stallion Challenged!, illustrated by Angie Draper. New
York, Random House, 1964.
The Horse That Swam Away, illustrated by Leo Summers. New
York, Random House, 1965.
The Great Dane, Thor, illustrated by Joseph Cellini. New York,
Random House, 1966.
The Little Black Pony Races, illustrated by James Schucker. New
York, Random House, 1968.
The Black Stallion's Ghost, illustrated by Angie Draper. New York,
Random House, 1969.
The Black Stallion and the Girl, illustrated by Angie Draper. New
York, Random House, 1971.
The Black Stallion Picture Book. New York, Random House, 1979.
The Black Stallion Legend. New York, Random House, 1983.

Other

Man o' War, illustrated by Angie Draper. New York, Random
House, 1962.
How to Stay Out of Trouble with Your Horse, photographs by Tim
Farley. New York, Doubleday, 1981.
The Black Stallion Returns Movie Storybook. New York, Random
House, 1983.

*

Manuscript Collections: Butler Library, Columbia University, New
York; Venice Area Public Library, Venice, Florida.

*   *   *

Beginning with *The Black Stallion* in 1941, the story of a shipwrecked stallion of Arabian origins and unknown parentage, Walter
Farley built a series of stories around the Black Stallion. The fillies
and colts that the Black Stallion sires are the subjects of books that
tell of Flame, Satan, Black Minx, Bonfire, and others.

Farley's early style is choppy, rough, and occasionally awkward. In
addition to frequent exclamation points to force excitement and
suspense, Farley over-uses simple, regular sentences in subject-
predicate order. The later books, however, are varied in style, using
complex sentence forms as well as vivid fragments. Always realistic
in details about horse farms, stables, and race tracks, Farley successfully pictures his setting, giving each book a strong sense of place;
The Black Stallion Returns, for example, clearly shows the horse's
original Arabian habitat.

While early Black Stallion books show a minimum of distinction
between human characters, Farley's later stories develop the character of Alec Ramsay, the Black's master, into a credible boy who is
skillful with horses and a natural rider, as in *The Black Stallion and
Flame.* Although many of the racetrack and stable characters seem
interchangeable, occasionally some are endowed with more life and
become distinctive and memorable. Characterization of the Black
Stallion and the other race horses also changes throughout the series.
Individual horses acquire personality, but not without Farley's lapsing into an omniscient point of view that pretends to know a horse's
thoughts, as in *The Blood Bay Colt.*

The strongest feature of Farley's stories is the successful involvement of the reader in admiration for the horses, his true subjects;
whatever the plot, the horse is the focus. Alec Ramsay may be the
protagonist, but life to Alec is the Black. Like most series books, the
Black Stallion stories tend to melt into one another, and one of his
later books may be as good as another. The Black Stallion and his
offspring remain alive, more memorable than plots or people.

—Rebecca J. Lukens

———————

FARMER, Penelope. British. Born in Westerham, Kent, 14
June 1939. Educated privately, 1945–56; at St. Anne's College,
Oxford, 1957–60, B.A. (honours) in history 1960; Bedford College,
University of London, diploma of social studies 1962. Married
Michael John Mockridge in 1962 (divorced 1977); one daughter and
one son. Teacher, London County Council, 1961–63. Agent:
Deborah Owen, 78 Narrow Street, London E14 8BP. Address: 39
Mount Ararat Road, Richmond, Surrey, England.

PUBLICATIONS FOR CHILDREN

Fiction

The China People, illustrated by Pearl Falconer. London, Hutchin-
son, 1960.
The Summer Birds, illustrated by James Spanfeller. London, Chat-
to and Windus, and New York, Harcourt Brace, 1962.
The Magic Stone, illustrated by John Kaufmann. New York, Har-
court Brace, 1964; London, Chatto and Windus, 1965.
Saturday Shillings, illustrated by Prudence Seward. London,
Hamish Hamilton, 1965; as *Saturday by Seven,* London, Penguin,

1978.

The Seagull, illustrated by Ian Ribbons. London, Hamish Hamilton, 1965; New York, Harcourt Brace, 1966.

Emma in Winter, illustrated by Laszlo Acs. London, Chatto and Windus, and New York, Harcourt Brace, 1966.

Charlotte Sometimes, illustrated by Chris Connor. London, Chatto and Windus, and New York, Harcourt Brace, 1969.

Dragonfly Summer, illustrated by Tessa Jordan. London, Hamish Hamilton, 1971.

A Castle of Bone. London, Chatto and Windus, and New York, Atheneum, 1972.

William and Mary. London, Chatto and Windus, and New York, Atheneum, 1974.

August the Fourth, illustrated by Jael Jordan. London, Heinemann, 1975; Los Angeles, Parnassus Press, 1976.

Year King. London, Chatto and Windus, and New York, Atheneum, 1977.

The Coal Train, illustrated by William Bird. London, Heinemann, 1977.

The Runaway Train, illustrated by William Bird. London, Heinemann, 1980.

Other

Daedalus and Icarus, illustrated by Chris Connor. London, Collins, and New York, Harcourt Brace, 1971.

The Serpent's Teeth: The Story of Cadmus, illustrated by Chris Connor. London, Collins, 1971; New York, Harcourt Brace, 1972.

The Story of Persephone, illustrated by Graham McCallum. London, Collins, 1972; New York, Morrow, 1973.

Heracles, illustrated by Graham McCallum. London, Collins, 1975.

Editor, *Beginnings: Creation Myths of the World,* illustrated by Antonio Frasconi. London, Chatto and Windus, 1978; New York, Atheneum, 1979.

Translator, with Amos Oz, *Soumchi,* by Oz, illustrated by William Papas. London, Chatto and Windus, 1980; New York, Harper, 1981.

PUBLICATIONS FOR ADULTS

Novels

Standing in the Shadow. London, Gollancz, 1984.

Eve: Her Story. London, Gollancz, 1985; San Francisco, Mercury House, 1988.

Away from Home. London, Gollancz, 1987.

Glasshouses. London, Gollancz, 1988.

Play

Television Play: *The Suburb Cuckoo,* 1961.

*   *   *

It may be that Penelope Farmer's most considerable work is already over—in the complex allegory, *A Castle of Bone*—and this not because of fading gifts but because the preoccupations informing the major books over the decade 1962–72 have reached a stage of resolution. While some authors say "I write for myself" somewhat hypocritically, the feeling of personal involvement in Farmer's novels is particularly strong, the images, landscapes, and characters

seeming spun out of her own life threads.

To reduce the stories to precis is as difficult as reducing lyric poems to one sentence summaries and as irrelevant. Farmer has classified herself as a writer of introvert fantasies, concerned with "the process of consciousness or of dream," and one traces these concerns in the hallucinatory flying episodes in *The Summer Birds,* the dream sequences in *Emma in Winter,* and Hugh's dreams in *A Castle of Bone* of the forest beyond which is the castle it is his task to claim. Even the settings and landscapes have a hypnotic quality— the downs at night in full moonlight, the silver gorse flowers, the turf cold and gray, the evening star cold and white; or the somnolent heat of midsummer meadows pictured in *The Summer Birds,* the mysterious blue shadows and luminosity of a snowbound world in *Emma in Winter,* and the dark cedar tree in *Charlotte Sometimes.* Buildings match landscape in these three books, the decaying Victorian mansion, the archaic flavour of the village school with its chalk smell, noisy desk lids, round of monitorial duties, and the "Silence, children, silence" fussing of Miss Hallibutt. The characters, in contrast, are sharply contemporary and clearly defined. The unpredictable nature of adults, the tensions of shifting classroom relationships ("Shall I be chosen?"; "Why did she snub me?"), the helplessness of being a child in a grown-up world, and the shadows cast by the transitory nature of childhood are presented with tact and a lightness of touch which bring fantasy and reality into equipoise.

Some fantasies grow from darkness, but the three stories of Charlotte and Emma Makepeace have a white beneficent magic. The most popular of the three, *Charlotte Sometimes,* shows a brilliant handling of the time-switch technique and a sincerity which rejects slick solutions to the dilemmas of the two heroines. The dreams of *A Castle of Bone* are of another quality, more powerful and more painful, both fantasy and reality realised with raw intensity as uncompromising as Garner's *The Owl Service.*

In addition to these major works Farmer has given her own touch of distinction to contributions to Hamish Hamilton's Antelope series, to crisp retellings of heroic tales, and to collections of short stories.

—Peggy Heeks

———

FARROW, G(eorge) E(dward). British. Born in Ipswich, Suffolk, 17 March 1862. Educated in the United States and London. *Died in 1920(?).*

PUBLICATIONS FOR CHILDREN

Fiction

The Wallypug of Why, illustrated by Harry and Dorothy Furniss. London, Hutchinson, 1895; New York, Dodd Mead, 1896.

The King's Gardens: An Allegory, illustrated by A.L. Bowley. London, Hutchinson, 1896.

The Missing Prince, illustrated by Harry and Dorothy Furniss. London, Hutchinson, 1896; New York, Dodd Mead, 1897.

The Wallypug in London, illustrated by Alan Wright. London, Methuen, 1897.

Adventures in Wallypug-Land, illustrated by Alan Wright. London, Methuen, 1898; New York, Burt, 1900.

The Little Panjandrum's Dodo, illustrated by Alan Wright. London, Skeffington, and New York, Stokes, 1899; as *Dick, Marjorie, and Fidge: The Adventures of Three Little People,* New York, Burt, 1901.

The Mandarin's Kite, illustrated by Alan Wright. London, Skeffington, 1900.

Baker Minor and the Dragon, illustrated by Alan Wright. London, Pearson, 1901.

The New Panjandrum, illustrated by Alan Wright. London, Pearson, 1901; New York, Dutton, 1902.

In Search of the Wallypug, illustrated by Alan Wright. London, Pearson, 1902.

All About the Wallypug. London, Tuck, 1903.

Professor Philanderpan. London, Pearson, 1903.

The Cinematograph Train and Other Stories, illustrated by Alan Wright. London, Johnson, 1904.

Pixie Pickles: The Adventures of Pixene and Pixette in Their Woodland Haunts, illustrated by Harry B. Neilson. London, Skeffington, 1904; New York, Warne, 1906.

The Wallypug Birthday Book, illustrated by Alan Wright. London, Routledge, 1904.

The Wallypug in Fog-land, illustrated by Alan Wright. London, Pearson, and Philadelphia, Lippincott, 1904.

The Mysterious "Mr. Punch." London, S.P.C.K., 1905.

The Wallypug Book, illustrated by Harry Furniss. London, Treherne, 1905.

The Wallypug in the Moon; or, His Badjesty, illustrated by Alan Wright. London, Pearson, and Philadelphia, Lippincott, 1905.

Ruff and Ready: The Fairy Guide, with May Byron, illustrated by John Hassall. London, Cooke, 1905.

Ten Little Jappy Chaps, illustrated by John Hassall. London, Treherne, 1905.

The Adventures of Ji, illustrated by G.C. Tresidder. London, Partridge, 1906.

The Escape of the Mullingong: A Zoological Nightmare, illustrated by Gordon Browne. London, Blackie, 1906.

The Adventures of a Dodo, illustrated by Willy Pogány. London, Unwin, 1907; New York, Wessels, 1908; as *A Mysterious Voyage,* London, Partridge, 1910.

Zoo Babies, illustrated by Cecil Aldin. London, Hodder and Stoughton, 1907; New York, Stokes, 1908.

The Dwindleberry Zoo, illustrated by Gordon Browne. London, Blackie, 1908.

Don't Tell, illustrated by John Hassall. New York, Stokes, n.d.

The Mysterious Shin Shira. London, Hodder and Stoughton, 1913.

Verse

An A.B.C. of Every-Day People, illustrated by John Hassall. London, Blackie, 1902.

Absurd Ditties, illustrated by John Hassall. London, Routledge, and New York, Dutton, 1903.

Wallypug Tales. London, Tuck, 1903.

Round the World A.B.C., illustrated by John Hassall. London, Nister, and New York, Dutton, 1904.

PUBLICATIONS FOR ADULTS

Other

Lovely Man, Being the Views of Mistress A. Crosspatch. London, Skeffington, 1904.

Food of the Dogs and What Became of It: A Travesty, with Ample Apologies to Mr. H.G. Wells. London, Johnson, 1904.

Editor, *Essays in Bacon: An Autograph Book.* London, Treherne, 1906.

*   *   *

G.E. Farrow was perhaps the best, and certainly the most prolific, of the many Victorian and Edwardian Lewis Carroll imitators, who felt they too had an aptitude for paradox, puns, and versifying, and that a dream setting was a convenient excuse for a loose and inconsequential plot. It is startling now to observe how closely they followed their model: *The Wallypug of Why,* Farrow's first and most popular book, begins, like *Alice in Wonderland,* with its heroine (who greatly resembles Alice) waking in a dreamland filled with strange and combative creatures against whom she struggles to assert herself. But the Wallypug himself is genuinely original, a nervous little nonentity who in theory rules the land of Why but in practice is ruled by his subjects whom he addresses as "Your Majesty." Harry Furniss's drawings of this pathetic little being with his crown tipped over one eye were so apt that they were followed by subsequent illustrators of Wallypug sequels. There were many of these. The Wallypug and his entourage are brought to London in *The Wallypug in London* to see the sights of Queen Victoria's Diamond Jubilee; sent to Fog-land in 1904, and to the Moon in 1905, adventures which lack the spontaneity and sprightliness of the first book.

The Little Panjandrum's Dodo, his best book, is better constructed than any of these, and much his most original writing. Three children float away on a high tide to a land ruled by the Little Panjandrum who sends them, under pain of "subtransex-districation," to find his Dodo. The Dodo himself is an endearing character for all his vanity, touchiness, and consequential airs. "It's lovely being extinct. Have you ever tried it?.... It's most convenient, if anyone calls whom you don't wish to see, just tell the servant to say that you're extinct, and there is an end of the matter." The Dodo's final arrival in London, his attempt to take a job as a "typewriter," and his disappearance are depicted with a light humour that Farrow never achieved anywhere else, and certainly not in the two subsequent stories of the Dodo's adventures.

—Gillian Avery

———

FATCHEN, Max. Australian. Born in Adelaide, South Australia, 3 August 1920. Educated at Angle Vale Primary School; Gawler High School. Served in the Royal Australian Air Force, 1940–45. Married Jean Wohlers in 1942; two sons and one daughter. Journalist, Adelaide *News* and *Sunday Mail,* 1946–55; journalist, 1955–84, literary editor, 1971–81, and special writer, 1981–84, Adelaide *Advertiser.* A.M. (Member, Order of Australia), 1980. Agent: John Johnson Ltd., 45–47 Clerkenwell Green, London ECIR 0HT, England. Address: 15 Jane Street, Smithfield, South Australia 5114, Australia.

PUBLICATIONS FOR CHILDREN

Fiction

The River Kings, illustrated by Clyde Pearson. Sidney, Hicks Smith, and London, Methuen, 1966; New York, St. Martin's Press, 1968.

Conquest of the River, illustrated by Clyde Pearson. Sydney, Hicks Smith, and London, Methuen, 1970.

The Spirit Wind, illustrated by Trevor Stubley. Sydney, Hicks Smith, and London, Methuen, 1973.

Chase Through the Night, illustrated by Graham Humphreys. Sydney and London, Methuen, 1977.

The Time Wave, illustrated by Edward Mortelmans. Sydney and London, Methuen, 1978.

Closer to the Stars.   Sydney and London, Methuen, 1981.
Had Yer Jabs?   Sydney, Methuen, 1987.

Verse

Songs for My Dog and Other People, illustrated by Michael
   Atchison.   London, Kestrel, 1980.
Wry Rhymes for Troublesome Times, illustrated by Michael Atchison.
   London, Kestrel, 1983.
A Paddock of Poems, illustrated by Kerry Argent.   Adelaide, Om-
   nibus, 1987.
A Pocketful of Rhymes, illustrated by Kerry Argent.   Adelaide,
   Omnibus, 1989.

Other (in verse)

Drivers and Trains, illustrated by Iris Millington.   Melbourne,
   Longman, 1963.
Keepers and Lighthouses, illustrated by Iris Millington.   Mel-
   bourne, Longman, 1963.
The Plumber, illustrated by Iris Millington.   Melbourne, Longman,
   1963.
The Electrician, illustrated by Iris Millington.   Melbourne,
   Longman, 1963.
The Transport Driver, illustrated by Iris Millington.   Melbourne,
   Longman, 1965.
The Carpenter, illustrated by Iris Millington.   Melbourne,
   Longman, 1965.

PUBLICATIONS FOR ADULTS

Verse

Peculia Australia: Verses.   Privately printed, 1965.

Other

*Just Fancy, Mr. Fatchen! A Collection of Verse, Prose and Fate's
   Cruel Blows.*   Adelaide, Rigby, 1967.
Forever Fatchen.   Adelaide, Advertiser, 1983.

*

Manuscript Collection: South Australia State Library, Adelaide.

Max Fatchen comments:
   My work as a journalist has taken me along Australia's river
systems, particularly the Murray. I have covered its floods, talked to
its oldtimers, ridden on some of the last of its riverboats and thus
gathered material for my two books on the Murray—*The River Kings*
and *Conquest of the River.* I have also seen the Mississippi, and it
was a visit there in 1963 that helped to trigger my interest in writing
books myself. My assignments have also taken me to sea aboard
lighthouse ships and landing servicing crews by boat and helicopter
on lonely islands of the southern Australian coast. I have also been
at sea with trawlermen, naval surveyors, and lobster fishermen. I
know particularly the windy coastline of South Australia where the
last squareriggers came to load grain for their race around the Horn.
I have also roamed over Australia's outback, particularly in the area
under the Gulf of Carpentaria and across the lonely rivers and
coastline of Arnhem Land in the Northern Territory. Here again I
have found material for my books. The sea and the land are not just
background but characters in my books because I feel they are alive,
have a personality of their own and react on the people I write about.
So I describe weather, the moods of landscape and climate, the fact

that in the loneliness of the outback, particularly at night, the land
can be felt like a presence padding around in the darkness outside. I
feel that children like a strong storyline, action, character, good
dialogue, and no humbug. I find them honest, attentive, and
perceptive once their interest is captured. A book is a voyage, and I
don't want them just to be passengers but members of the crew.

*   *   *

   The sea, rivers, and sailing craft, combined with his deep feeling
for his native South Australia, lie at the heart of Max Fatchen's
writing for young readers. His first two novels (for younger
teenagers) formed a slightly tentative approach into the area of
children's literature. *The River Kings* and *Conquest of the River,* set
in South Australia's pioneering days when riverboats used to trade
and cruise along the Murray River, both follow the fortunes of
teenaged Shane, who runs away from an unhappy home and becomes
a member of a riverboat crew. Both stories are well constructed,
though perhaps a little too tightly organized, and they are filled with
dramatic and humorous incident and deft characterization of typical
riverboat people—a tough but kindly Cap'n, a Chinese cook, Scottish engineer, and so forth. They are also soundly based on riverboat
knowledge and research. The choice of incidents and their outcome
tend to be predictable, but, given the riverboat setting, this is to some
extent inevitable—fire, flood, bunyips, and races between one riverboat and another are obvious ingredients of stories set on the Murray—and Fatchen was one of the first to choose this setting for junior
fiction. Well in the background lurks the author's almost mystic and
certainly poetic feeling for the great river. Here is a sound professional journalist producing exciting and very readable fiction, with
just a hint of more significant power behind him. His narrative style
is exceptionally clear-cut, free of any excess verbiage.
   The publication of *The Spirit Wind* marked an important new
departure for Fatchen. This is a much deeper and more ambitious
work, in which the strain of poetry and mysticism emerges strongly,
linked to Aboriginal lore through the character of Nunganee, an
outcast from his tribe because he once "sang" a man's death. This
book is set, once again, in the last century; the central character is
15-year-old Jarl Hansen, deckhand aboard the *Hootzen,* a squarerig-
ger out of Norway bound for Australia, and ruled by a sadistic Mate.
Jarl encounters Nunganee when he jumps ship in South Australia;
their destinies, as well as that of the Mate and of the *Hootzen* herself,
become entwined and are eventually fulfilled during a night of fierce
storm when the mysterious Spirit Wind is unleashed. In this work
Fatchen shows new powers and has launched his writing beyond the
shallower seas of predictable incident and nicely observed characterization.

—Barbara Ker Wilson

———

FATIO, Louise.   American.   Born in Lausanne, Switzerland, 18
August 1904. Educated at a boarding school, Basel, Switzerland;
Collège des Jeunes Filles, Geneva. Married Roger Duvoisin, *q.v.,* in
1925 (died 1980); two sons. Emigrated to the United States in 1925;
naturalized citizen, 1938. Address: P.O. Box 116, Gladstone, New
Jersey 07934, U.S.A.

PUBLICATIONS FOR CHILDREN (illustrated by Roger Duvoisin)

Fiction

The Christmas Forest.   New York, Aladdin, 1950.
Anna the Horse.   New York, Aladdin, 1951.

The Happy Lion. New York, McGraw Hill, 1954; London, Lane, 1955.

The Happy Lion in Africa. New York, McGraw Hill, 1955; London, Bodley Head, 1963.

The Happy Lion Roars. New York, McGraw Hill, 1957; London, Bodley Head, 1959.

A Doll for Marie. New York, McGraw Hill, 1957.

The Three Happy Lions. New York, McGraw Hill, 1959; London, Bodley Head, 1960.

The Happy Lion's Quest. New York, McGraw Hill, 1961; London, Bodley Head, 1962.

Red Bantam. New York, McGraw Hill, and London, Bodley Head, 1963.

The Happy Lion and the Bear. New York, McGraw Hill, 1964; London, Bodley Head, 1965.

The Happy Lion's Vacation. New York, McGraw Hill, 1967; as *The Happy Lion's Holiday,* London, Bodley Head, 1968.

The Happy Lion's Treasure. New York, McGraw Hill, and London, Bodley Head, 1971.

Hector Penguin. New York, McGraw Hill, and London, Bodley Head, 1973.

The Happy Lion's Rabbits. New York, McGraw Hill, 1974; London, Bodley Head, 1975.

Marc and Pixie and the Walls in Mrs. Jones's Garden. New York, McGraw Hill, 1975; London, Hodder and Stoughton, 1977.

Hector and Christina. New York, McGraw Hill, 1977; London, Bodley Head, 1978.

The Happy Lioness. New York, McGraw Hill, 1980.

*

Manuscript Collection: Kerlan Collection, University of Minnesota, Minneapolis.

Louise Fatio comments:

(1978) As in the case of most of those who translate their thoughts and beliefs into books, my books are an extension of my life. Or, I should say, our lives, my husband's and mine, for we have similar backgrounds, share the same tastes, and collaborate on many of our books.

Our love of people, of nature, our respect for animals—all often expressed in my books—date from our childhoods. We spent many summer vacations on farms or in villages, my husband in a Savoy village or a fishing village on the Mediterranean, I in a French-Swiss village. The need for a full country life not too far from a civilized city led us to settle in New Jersey (then a farming land which deserved its name of garden state) when we came to America. It is in this country atmosphere that we composed most of our books and brought up our children.

*   *   *

Louise Fatio is best known for her Happy Lion picture books, a series with general unifying qualities, perhaps the most significant the characterization of the genial lion and the quiet themes of friendship and acceptance.

The Happy Lion lives in the zoo, but, thanks to his friendship with François, the zookeeper's son, is able to wander out of the zoo whenever it suits him. Uncharacteristically gentle and thoroughly kind, the Happy Lion shows great concern for others—visitors as well as fellow zoo-dwellers. He is pensive, restless, lonely, helpful; when he is free, he occasionally frightens townspeople, but not by his fierceness.

In addition to the memorable character of the Happy Lion, the themes of the books are important. To love and be loved is a treasure. We need someone like ourselves, as the Happy Lion discovers when

he finds a mate in *The Happy Lion Roars.* Where we live is home, not where we come from, the Happy Lion discovers in *The Happy Lion in Africa.* He challenges rules and finds that sometimes new rules are needed, and in another story he discovers that befriending others makes one happy. Aggressive behavior is rewarded with aggression, kind behavior with kindness, as in *Red Bantam.* Hector in *Hector Penguin* finds it important to be what you are; don't conform.

These direct, straightforward stories with little imagery or stylistic complexity, illustrated by Roger Duvoisin, have warmth and acceptance in their tone: they are important as comfortable affirmations of love and loyalty.

—Rebecca J. Lukens

————

FAULKNOR, (Chauncey) Cliff(ord Vernon). Canadian. Born in Vancouver, British Columbia, 3 March 1913. Educated at the University of British Columbia, Vancouver, B.S.A. (honours) 1949. Served as a gunner, Royal Canadian Artillery, Victoria, 1937–39; marine engineer sergeant, Canadian Army Water Transport, 1939–45. Married Elizabeth Harriette Sloan in 1943; one son and one daughter. Ledger keeper, Royal Bank of Canada, Vancouver, 1929–31; machine operator, Alberni Pacific Lumber, Port Alberni, and assistant ranger, British Columbia Forest Service; land inspector, 1949–54, and since 1949 agrologist, British Columbia Department of Lands and Forests, Land Utilization Research and Survey Division, Victoria; associate editor, *Country Guide* magazine, Winnipeg, 1954–55, and Calgary, 1955–75. Since 1976 land appraiser, Calgary. Since 1978 member, Alberta Land Compensation Board. Past president, Alberta Farm Writers Association. Recipient: Canadian Farm Writers Federation award, 1961, 1968, 1969, 1973, 1974, 1975; Canadian Children's Book award, 1965; Vicky Metcalf award, 1979. Address: 2919 14th Avenue N.W., Calgary, Alberta T2N 1N3, Canada.

PUBLICATIONS FOR CHILDREN

Fiction

The White Calf: The Story of Eagle Child, The Piegan Boy, Who Found a White Buffalo Calf Said to Have Been Sent by the Above Ones, illustrated by Gerald Tailfeathers. Toronto and Boston, Little Brown, 1965; London, Dent, 1966.

The White Peril, illustrated by Gerald Tailfeathers. Toronto and Boston, Little Brown, 1966; London, Dent, 1968.

The In-Betweener, illustrated by Leonard Shortall. Toronto and Boston, Little Brown, 1967.

The Smoke Horse, illustrated by W.F. Phillipps. Toronto, McClelland and Stewart, and London, Dent, 1968.

West to Cattle Country, illustrated by Gordon McLean. Toronto, McClelland and Stewart, 1975.

Johnny Eagleclaw, illustrated by Richard A. Conroy. Edmonton, Alberta, LeBel, 1982.

PUBLICATIONS FOR ADULTS

Other

The Romance of Beef. Winnipeg, Public Press, 1966.

Pen and Plow. Winnipeg, Public Press, 1976.
Turn Him Loose! Herman Linder, Canada's Mr. Rodeo. Saskatoon, Western Producer Prairie Books, 1977.
Alberta Hereford Heritage. Red Deer, Alberta, Adviser Graphics, 1982.

*

Manuscript Collections: University of Calgary; Kerlan Collection, University of Minnesota, Minneapolis.

Cliff Faulknor comments:

I don't consciously set out to write for children. When an idea comes to me I just sit down at my typewriter and let it work itself out. I have found that once you have created a genuine character he or she will act and react according to the natures you have given them, and the story will flow from these actions.

As for the story setting and background information, I research this very carefully. And if I am dealing with the past, my story must be true to the history of that period, and the setting must be as it was during that period.

For instance, in my Indian books, a rider cannot have his horse nibbling on a grass or shrub species not native to that area or have him swim a river in a year history records as a time of intense drought. I have read some books where the main character describes the scene from a certain mountain, and I have gone up that mountain only to find it would be impossible for him to do so. I wouldn't want that to happen in any of my books. For my western books I went "on location," plotting the movements of my characters and locating the battle scenes. I don't attempt to be very profound in any of my writings; I like to entertain and inform.

* * *

Cliff Faulknor's *The White Calf, The White Peril,* and *The Smoke Horse* comprise a trilogy focussed on the life of a Piegan Blackfoot boy as he grows to manhood in the mid-19th century. *The White Calf* introduces Eagle Child at age 12, when he saves an orphaned white buffalo calf—believed to be sacred because of its colour—and raises it to near-yearling status. The novel ends with the buffalo's release and its return to the herd. In the interval, the calf fills the role of a wilful spirit, sometimes bringing good in its wake, sometimes ill. Its primary significance is as a mark of Eagle Child's own maturing process; he learns that the acclaim the calf brings him carries with it a duty, and that internalization of this sense of duty is part of what makes a man. Indeed, as the subsequent books reveal, it is through the eventual necessary retaking of the full-grown buffalo's life that Eagle Child earns his warrior name, White Bull.

The White Calf also shows Eagle Child's band on the hunt, in struggles with other tribes (wherein his older brother Tailfeathers earns his adult name, War Bonnet), and at the Sun Dance. The events are exciting, and the details of Blackfoot life are authentic, but the book suffers a little from the presence of two heroes, Eagle Child and War Bonnet. Some of the most exciting events are seen through the latter's eyes, not the former's, and this can lead to problems of reader-identification.

The White Peril opens five winters later, again beginning and ending with encounters between Eagle Child and the white buffalo, now a rogue killer. The title refers not only to the animal, however; it also implies the encroachment of white men. This danger is repeatedly mentioned, and at one point the possibility of forming an Indian confederation to war against the whites is raised. White weapons and disease make this impractical. As before, the adventures of the hunt and inter-tribal raiding parties comprise much of the novel's excitement, but the most important event is a deadly epidemic of measles. Concomitantly, the white buffalo—at one point

a symbol of Indian hopes for the favour of the Above Ones—is also killed. In everything, the manifold unforeseen consequences of human acts are evident. Thus the book contains a realistic admixture of sadness and joys, with the coming of the whites viewed from an Indian perspective. This novel is carefully constructed, and the previous work's problem with dual viewpoints does not occur.

In *The Smoke Horse,* set later the same year, Eagle Child (now White Bull) learns the quality of mercy—a quality that marks his inner maturity and true manhood. The action focuses on horse raids, captures, escapes, battles—all very well depicted. It's a fine story, well-crafted and gripping, with many flashes of Faulknor's subtle humour and adept dialogue. It provides a fitting conclusion to the trilogy.

The In-Betweener also deals with the maturing process—and its difficulties—in an adolescent boy, Chad. The white protagonist and the 20th-century British Columbia setting are changes for Faulknor, and Chad's problems—compared to those of Eagle Child—reflect the less integral society to which he belongs. Cheating, stealing, murder, imprisonment, and domestic difficulties are all present; however, in the end, right wins out, and communication between father and son is restored. *Johnny Eagleclaw,* too, has a contemporary setting. The protagonist is an Indian rodeo competitor who, in an extended flashback, reviews his adolescent experiences at a white school, working on a ranch, and competing in his first rodeos. There is a good depiction of cross-cultural differences and of how cultural misunderstandings arise and can be corrected. Like the trilogy, these later novels are exciting, basically realistic, and enjoyable to read.

—John Robert Sorfleet

FENTON, Edward. American. Born in New York City, 7 July 1917. Attended Amherst College, Massachusetts. Served in the American Field Service and the British 8th Army in North Africa during World War II. Married Sophia Harvati in 1963. Staff member in the print department, Metropolitan Museum of Art, New York, 1950–55. Recipient: Mystery Writers of America Edgar Allan Poe award, 1962; Batchelder award, for translation, 1970, 1974, 1980. Address: 24 Evrou Street, Athens 610, Greece.

PUBLICATIONS FOR CHILDREN

Fiction

Us and the Duchess, illustrated by Reisie Lonette. New York, Doubleday, 1947.
Aleko's Island, illustrated by Dimitris Davis. New York, Doubleday, 1948; London, Oxford University Press, 1953.
Hidden Trapezes, illustrated by Reisie Lonette. New York, Doubleday, 1950.
Nine Lives; or, The Celebrated Cat of Beacon Hill, illustrated by Paul Galdone. New York, Pantheon, 1951.
The Golden Doors, illustrated by Gioia Fiammenghi. New York, Doubleday, 1957; as *Mystery in Florence,* London, Constable, 1959.
Once upon a Saturday, illustrated by Rita Fava. New York, Doubleday, 1958.
Fierce John, illustrated by William Pène du Bois. New York, Doubleday, 1959.
The Nine Questions, illustrated by C. Walter Hodges. New York,

Doubleday, 1959; Kingswood, Surrey, World's Work, 1962.

The Phantom of Walkaway Hill, illustrated by Jo Ann Stover. New York, Doubleday, 1961.

An Island for a Pelican, illustrated by Dimitris Davis. New York, Doubleday, and Kingswood, Surrey, World's Work, 1963.

The Riddle of the Red Whale. New York, Doubleday, 1966.

The Big Yellow Balloon, illustrated by Ib Ohlsson. New York, Doubleday, 1967.

A Matter of Miracles. New York, Holt Rinehart, 1967.

Penny Candy, illustrated by Edward Gorey. New York, Holt Rinehart, 1970.

Duffy's Rocks. New York, Dutton, and London, Hamish Hamilton, 1974.

The Refugee Summer. New York, Delacorte Press, 1982; London, MacRae, 1983.

The Morning of the Gods. New York, Delacorte Press, and London, MacRae, 1987.

Other

Translator, *Wildcat under Glass,* by Alki Zei. New York, Holt Rinehart, 1968; London, Gollancz, 1969.

Translator, *Petros' War,* by Alki Zei. New York, Dutton, and London, Gollancz, 1972.

Translator, *The Sound of the Dragon's Feet,* by Alki Zei. New York, Dutton, 1979.

PUBLICATIONS FOR ADULTS

Novels

The Double Darkness. New York, Doubleday, 1947; London, Cresset Press, 1948.

Anne of the Thousand Days (novelization of screenplay). New York, New American Library, 1970.

Verse

Soldiers and Strangers. New York, Macmillan, 1945.

Other

Translator, *Greek Shop Signs,* by George Vakirtzis and others. Athens, Papastratos, 1974.

*

Manuscript Collection: de Grummond Collection, University of Southern Mississippi, Hattiesburg.

*   *   *

Through a writing career stretching over a period of 40 years, Edward Fenton has written books in a wide range of styles for young readers. His many novels have been published in numerous languages, and it is this cosmopolitan appeal that is unusual in a children's writer. Although American born, Fenton now considers himself a Greek by adoption, while retaining his sense of *kosmos* in his themes. *The Morning of the Gods,* his latest work, is set in a Greece repressed by the rule of the Colonels, a repressive military junta. Fenton identifies in exact detail the Greece of the mind's eye: "There was hardly anything to see: a small square with a couple of stunted palm trees in the middle of it and some yellowish houses clutching the dry rocks; the sea behind them; and then, the vast sky." Location clarified, the reader is not allowed to lose this shared vision

of the colour and beauty of the land, a daily life of encounters and experience, where myth and poetry are still vital elements. This is Carla's first visit home. Her, and Fenton's, native New York is a world removed from her mother's birthplace. However, she soon comes to empathise with the people—their warmth, heritage, and loathing of the Colonels. "Colonels, generals, they all come, and eventually they all go away again. We are the ones who remain." Carla soon finds a practical way to share this mutual abhorrence of the military rule, and contribute a step, albeit a small one, on the return to the fields of Asphodel.

Fenton's time living in both Greece and Italy has naturally been a major influence on his writing, giving him a breadth of experience that allows his books to transcend the restrictive themes of much modern writing for young readers. *Aleko's Island, An Island for a Pelican, The Golden Doors,* as well as *The Morning of the Gods,* are all triumphant testaments to his travels. The atmospheric and descriptive writing has a stamp of authority that surpasses the vividest of imaginations or depth of research. Naturally because of his strong American roots much of Fenton's work is based on his early experiences growing up in and around New York City. One of these, *The Phantom of Walkaway Hill,* first gained him public recognition through its selection as winner of the prestigious Edgar Allen Poe award in 1962. Others to recommend from this period include *Once upon a Saturday,* based upon his own adolescence, *Fierce John,* and *The Riddle of the Red Whale.* An extension of the American experience theme is attempted successfully in *Duffy's Rocks.* Although Fenton was New York born and bred, he manages to convey the Depression years in industrial Pittsburgh in an inspired piece of imagined-experience writing.

Penny Candy, a magical picture book, shows Fenton's skills in yet further areas of the writer's art. Widow Shinn has a candy store. But, is she really a witch? Who's going to hang around long enough to put her to the test? Those tempted to sneak in and try the candy tend to find they turn a strange colour—a bit of a giveaway.

Carla's mother had told her that "You will see it all for yourself when I take you there." With Fenton that promise is never made, but the result is certainly achieved. Fenton's settings, whether they are in New York or Greece, or indeed wherever, fill the mind's imaginings. To say that he is a word photographer in sympathy with his locations undervalues the writer. To visit, to experience, to inhabit even, does not mean at all that you can capture the essence for the delight of the reader. Fenton has that gift, not just for the physical appearances of terrain, but for the capturing of the soul, the spirit, the sense of any place he portrays.

—Bill Boyle

FIDLER, Kathleen (Annie). British. Born in Coalville, Leicestershire, 10 August 1899. Educated at Girls' High School, Wigan, Lancashire, 1911–18; St. Mary's College, Bangor, North Wales, 1918–20, Teacher's Certificate 1920. Married J.H. Goldie in 1930 (died); one son and one daughter. Headmistress, Scot Lane Evening Institute, 1924–30, and St. Paul's Girls' School, Wigan, 1925–30; script writer, Authors' Panel for Schools Broadcasting in Scotland, 1938–62. Recipient: Moscow Film Festival award, 1967. *Died in 1980.*

PUBLICATIONS FOR CHILDREN

Fiction

The Borrowed Garden. London, Lutterworth Press, 1944.

St. Jonathan's in the Country: A Sequel to "The Borrowed Garden," illustrated by Charles Koolman. London, Lutterworth Press, 1945; revised edition, 1952.

Fingal's Ghost. London, John Crowther, 1945.

The Brydons at Smugglers' Creek, illustrated by H. Tilden Reeves. London, Lutterworth Press, 1946.

The White Cockade Passes. London, Lutterworth Press, 1947.

The Mysterious Mr. Simister. London, Lutterworth Press, 1947.

More Adventures of the Brydons, illustrated by Victor Bertoglio. London, Lutterworth Press, 1947; revised edition, London, Hodder and Stoughton, 1971.

The Brydons Go Camping, illustrated by A.H. Watson. London, Lutterworth Press, 1948.

Mr. Simister Appears Again, illustrated by Margaret Horder. London, Lutterworth Press, 1948.

Mr. Simister Is Unlucky, illustrated by Margaret Horder. London, Lutterworth Press, 1949.

The Brydons Do Battle, illustrated by A.H. Watson. London, Lutterworth Press, 1949.

The Brydons in Summer, illustrated by A.H. Watson. London, Lutterworth Press, 1949.

Guest Castle. London, Lutterworth Press, 1949.

I Rode with the Covenanters, illustrated by E. Boyce Uden. London, Lutterworth Press, 1950.

The Brydons Look for Trouble, illustrated by T.R. Freeman. London, Lutterworth Press, 1950.

The Brydons in a Pickle, illustrated by T.R. Freeman. London, Lutterworth Press, 1950.

Surprises for the Brydons, illustrated by T.R. Freeman. London, Lutterworth Press, 1950.

The White-Starred Hare and Other Stories, illustrated by A.H. Watson. London, Lutterworth Press, 1951.

The Brydons Get Things Going, illustrated by T.R. Freeman. London, Lutterworth Press, 1951; revised edition, Hodder and Stoughton, 1971.

The Brydons Hunt for Treasure, illustrated by T.R. Freeman. London, Lutterworth Press, 1951.

The Brydons Catch Queer Fish, illustrated by T.R. Freeman. London, Lutterworth Press, 1952.

The Brydons Stick at Nothing, illustrated by T.R. Freeman. London, Lutterworth Press, 1952.

Fedora the Donkey, illustrated by Iris Gillespie. London, Lutterworth Press, 1952.

The Stallion from the Sea, illustrated by G.S. Ronald. London, Lutterworth Press, 1953.

The Brydons Abroad, illustrated by T.R. Freeman. London, Lutterworth Press, 1953.

The Deans Move In, illustrated by Reg Forster. London, Lutterworth Press, 1953.

Pete, Pam and Jim, the Investigators, illustrated by Lunt Roberts. London, Lutterworth Press, 1954.

The Deans Solve a Mystery, illustrated by Reg Forster. London, Lutterworth Press, 1954.

The Deans Follow a Clue, illustrated by Reg Forster. London, Lutterworth Press, 1954.

The Bank House Twins, illustrated by Frank Bellamy. London, Lutterworth Press, 1955.

The Droving Lad, illustrated by Geoffrey Whittam. London, Lutterworth Press, 1955.

The Deans Defy Danger, illustrated by Reg Forster. London, Lutterworth Press, 1955.

The Brydons on the Broads, illustrated by T.R. Freeman. London, Lutterworth Press, 1955; revised edition, London, Hodder and Stoughton, 1971.

Challenge to the Brydons, illustrated by T.R. Freeman. London, Lutterworth Press, 1956.

Mr. Punch's Cap, illustrated by Shirley Hughes. London, Lutterworth Press, 1956.

The Deans Dive for Treasure, illustrated by Reg Forster. London, Lutterworth Press, 1956.

The Deans to the Rescue, illustrated by Reg Forster. London, Lutterworth Press, 1957.

The McGills at Mystery Farm, with Jack Gillespie, illustrated by Leo Davy. London, Lutterworth Press, 1958.

Lanterns over the Lune, illustrated by David Walsh. London, Lutterworth Press, 1958.

The Deans' Lighthouse Adventure, illustrated by Reg Forster. London, Lutterworth Press, 1959.

More Adventures of the McGills, with Jack Gillespie, illustrated by Hodgson. London, Lutterworth Press, 1959.

The Deans and Mr. Popple, illustrated by Reg Forster. London, Lutterworth Press, 1960.

The Brydons at Blackpool, illustrated by T.R. Freeman. London, Lutterworth Press, 1960.

Escape in Darkness, illustrated by Geoffrey Whittam. London, Lutterworth Press, 1961.

The Deans' Dutch Adventure, illustrated by Reg Forster. London, Lutterworth Press, 1962.

The Brydons Go Canoeing, illustrated by T.R. Freeman. London, Lutterworth Press, 1963.

The Little Ship Dog, illustrated by Antony Maitland. London, Lutterworth Press, 1963.

The Desperate Journey, illustrated by Michael Charlton. London, Lutterworth Press, 1964.

Flash the Sheep Dog, illustrated by Antony Maitland. London, Lutterworth Press, 1965.

Police Dog, illustrated by Sheila Rose. London, Lutterworth Press, 1966.

The Boy with the Bronze Axe, illustrated by Edward Mortelmans. Edinburgh, Oliver and Boyd, 1968.

Haki the Shetland Pony, illustrated by Victor Ambrus. London, Lutterworth Press, 1968; Chicago, Rand McNally, 1970.

Treasure of Ebba, illustrated by Trevor Ridley. London, Lutterworth Press, 1968.

Mountain Rescue Dog, illustrated by Mary Russon. London, Lutterworth Press, 1969.

School at Sea, illustrated by David Grice. London, Epworth Press, 1970.

The Gold of Fast Castle, illustrated by Trevor Ridley. London, Lutterworth Press, 1970.

The Thames in Story. London, Epworth Press, 1971.

Turk, The Border Collie, illustrated by Mary Dinsdale. Guildford, Surrey, Lutterworth Press, 1975.

The Railway Runaways, illustrated by Terry Gabbey. London, Blackie, 1977.

The Lost Cave. London, Blackie, 1978.

Seal Story, illustrated by Douglas Phillips. Guildford, Surrey, Lutterworth Press, 1979.

Pablos and the Bull. London, Blackie, 1979.

The Ghosts of Sandeel Bay, illustrated by Annabel Large. London, Blackie, 1981.

Plays

Screenplay: *Flash the Sheepdog,* 1968.

Radio Plays: *Children's Hour* series.

Television Play: *Haki the Shetland Pony,* from her own story, 1970.

Other

Stories from Scottish Heritage, with Lennox Milne. Edinburgh,

Chambers, 3 vols., 1951.

Tales of the North Country, illustrated by Jack Matthew. London, Lutterworth Press, 1952.

To the White North: The Story of Sir John Franklin, illustrated by F. Furnivall. London, Lutterworth Press, 1952.

Tales of London, illustrated by Douglas Relf. London, Lutterworth Press, 1953.

Tales of the Midlands, illustrated by Douglas Relf. London, Lutterworth Press, 1954.

The Man Who Gave Away Millions: The Story of Andrew Carnegie, illustrated by Hodgson. London, Lutterworth Press, 1955; New York, Roy, 1956.

Tales of Scotland, illustrated by Douglas Relf. London, Lutterworth Press, 1956.

Look to the West: Tales of Liverpool, illustrated by Henry Toothill. London, Lutterworth Press, 1957.

Tales of the Islands, illustrated by Douglas Relf. London, Lutterworth Press, 1959.

Tales of Pirates and Castaways, illustrated by Charles Keeping. London, Lutterworth Press, 1960.

Tales of the West Country, illustrated by Charles Keeping. London, Lutterworth Press, 1961.

True Tales of Treasure, illustrated by W.F. Phillipps. London, Lutterworth Press, 1962.

Tales of the South Country, illustrated by W.F. Phillipps. London, Lutterworth Press, 1962.

True Tales of Escapes, illustrated by W.F. Phillipps. London, Lutterworth Press, 1965.

New Lamps for Old (reader), illustrated by John Dugan. Edinburgh, Oliver and Boyd, 1965.

Adventure Underground (reader), illustrated by Forth Studios. Edinburgh, Oliver and Boyd, 1966.

Forest Fire (reader), illustrated by Laszlo Acs. Edinburgh, Oliver and Boyd, 1966.

True Tales of Mystery, illustrated by Bonar Dunlop. London, Lutterworth Press, 1967.

True Tales of Castles, illustrated by Imre Hofbauer. London, Lutterworth Press, 1969.

Flodden Field, September 9, 1513, illustrated by F.R. Exell. London, Lutterworth Press, 1971.

Diggers of Lost Treasure. London, Epworth Press, 1972.

Stories of Old Inns. London, Epworth Press, 1973.

The '45 and Culloden, July 1745 to April 1746, illustrated by F.R. Exell. Guildford, Surrey, Lutterworth Press, 1973.

Pirate and Admiral: The Story of John Paul Jones, illustrated by Bernard Brett. Guildford, Surrey, Lutterworth Press, 1974.

Wrecks, Wreckers and Rescuers, with Ian Morrison, illustrated by Morrison. Guildford, Surrey, Lutterworth Press, 1977.

*

Kathleen Fidler commented:

(1978) My writing first began for my own children's interest and amusement. The "Brydon Family" books, written first as broadcasts, later as books, reflected my own happy and simple family life. As my children grew, my writing expanded into historical, biographical, and archaeological fields, representing my and their varied interests. I now write to interest my grandchildren. Broadcasting has been a large part of my writing, and this sharpened the focus of books and dialogue. I also give talks to children in schools and libraries, and this keeps me actively in touch with children.

* * *

To remark that Kathleen Fidler earned an enviable reputation for good stories well told is not to damn with faint praise but to place her firmly in the mainstream of professional children's writers who year in, year out continue to publish well constructed books that satisfy an ever widening circle of readers. During her long writing career, spanning four decades, she confirmed her craftsmanlike ability to come to grips with most types of children's fiction. With undiminished skill she fashioned good, honest plots, moving at a brisk pace, in two family series, the Brydons and the Deans; holiday adventures, usually set in remote and isolated countryside; imaginative historical fiction; and in her extremely popular animal stories. Authors who turn to this last category, especially those favouring dog tales, sometimes find it difficult to avoid that mawkish sentimentality so easily aroused in doggie people, young or old. Aware of the danger, she was careful to write only about working dogs mostly in a harsh environment: *Police Dog*; *Mountain Rescue Dog,* an authentic account of training in the Scottish Highlands; and *The Little Ship Dog,* who guards a valuable cargo voyaging up the Grand Union Canal. *Turk, The Border Collie* relates what might have happened to the dog actually given the starring role in the filming of her earlier book, *Flash the Sheep Dog,* whose inconsolable grief caused him to slip away from his farm when his master died. At the end Turk returns, a rare move away from reality, but in this case her readers would expect no less.

Fidler's amateur knowledge of archaeology was sometimes enlisted to good effect, nowhere more so than in *The Boy with the Bronze Axe,* inspired by a visit to the Stone Age settlement of Skara Brae, in the Orkneys. The events following the arrival of a strange boy from over the sea, equipped with a bronze axe, and the impact this advance in technology had on a backward and pastoral community, are unveiled with a deceptively light and easy touch. Her enthusiasm for archaeology is also evident in *Treasure of Ebba,* the holiday adventures of a group of four, two families of brother and sister, a typical Fidler cast, who reappear in *The Gold of Fast Castle.* Purists might object to adding the glamorous concept of treasure: the realist author would reply that treasure is indispensable if life is to be breathed into archaeology for children.

This sense of realism is the hallmark of Fidler's contribution to children's literature. Essentially she portrays ordinary people caught up in slightly extraordinary circumstances, in exciting but not unduly perilous adventures, usually arising out of everyday, matter-of-fact occurrences. The unlikely attains credibility by contrast with its mundane surroundings. This is not an easy balance to achieve, or to maintain: Fidler achieved it, and maintained it.

—Alan Edwin Day

———

FIELD, Rachel (Lyman). American. Born in New York City, 19 September 1894. Educated at Springfield High School, Massachusetts; Radcliffe College, Cambridge, Massachusetts, 1914–18. Married Arthur Siegfried Pederson in 1935; one adopted daughter. Member of the editorial department, Famous Players-Lasky film company, Hollywood, 1918–23. Recipient: Drama League of America prize, 1918; American Library Association Newbery Medal, 1930. *Died 15 March 1942.*

Publications for Children

Fiction

Eliza and the Elves, illustrated by Elizabeth MacKinstry. New York, Macmillan, 1926.

The Magic Pawnshop: A New Year's Eve Fantasy, illustrated by

Elizabeth MacKinstry.   New York, Dutton, 1927; London, Dent, 1928.
Little Dog Toby, illustrated by the author.   New York, Macmillan, 1928.
Polly Patchwork, illustrated by the author.   New York, Doubleday, 1928.
Hitty, Her First Hundred Years, illustrated by Dorothy P. Lathrop. New York, Macmillan, 1929; as *Hitty: The Life and Adventures of a Wooden Doll,* London, Routledge, 1932.
Pocket-Handkerchief Park, illustrated by the author.   New York, Doubleday, 1929.
Calico Bush, illustrated by Allen Lewis.   New York, Macmillan, 1931; London, Collier Macmillan, 1966.
The Yellow Shop, illustrated by the author.   New York, Doubleday, 1931.
The Bird Began to Sing, illustrated by Ilse Bischoff.   New York, Morrow, 1932.
Hepatica Hawkes, illustrated by Allen Lewis.   New York, Macmillan, 1932.
Just Across the Street, illustrated by the author.   New York, Macmillan, 1933.
Susanna B. and William C., illustrated by the author.   New York, Morrow, 1934.
The Rachel Field Story Book (includes *The Yellow Shop, Pocket-Handkerchief Park, Polly Patchwork*), illustrated by Adrienne Adams.   New York, Doubleday, 1958; Kingswood, Surrey, World's Work, 1960.

Plays

Everygirl, in *St. Nicholas* (New York), October 1913.
Three Pills in a Bottle (produced Cambridge, Massachusetts, 1917; New York, 1923).   Included in *Six Plays,* 1924.
Rise Up, Jennie Smith (produced Cambridge, Massachusetts, 1918).   New York, French, 1918.
Time Will Tell (produced Cambridge, Massachusetts, 1920).
The Fifteenth Candle.   New York, French, 1921.
Six Plays (includes *Cinderella Married, Three Pills in a Bottle, Columbine in Business, The Patchwork Quilt, Wisdom Teeth, Theories and Thumbs*).   New York, Scribner, 1924; *The Patchwork Quilt* published in *One-Act Plays of Today,* edited by J.W. Marriott, London, Gollancz, 1928.
The Cross-Stitch Heart and Other Plays (includes *Greasy Luck, The Nine Days' Queen, The Londonderry Air, At the Junction, Bargains in Cathay*).   New York, Scribner, 1927.
Patchwork Plays (includes *Polly Patchwork; Little Square-Toes; Miss Ant, Miss Grasshopper, and Mr. Cricket; Chimney Sweeps' Holiday; The Sentimental Scarecrow*), illustrated by the author. New York, Doubleday, 1930.
First Class Matter.   New York, French, 1936.
The Bad Penny.   New York, French, 1938.

Verse (illustrated by the author)

The Pointed People: Verses and Silhouettes.   New Haven, Connecticut, Yale University Press, and London, Oxford University Press, 1924.
An Alphabet for Boys and Girls.   New York, Doubleday, and London, Heinemann, 1926.
Taxis and Toadstools: Verses and Decorations.   New York, Doubleday, and London, Heinemann, 1926.
A Little Book of Days.   New York, Doubleday, and London, Heinemann, 1927.
Christmas Time.   New York, Macmillan, 1941.
Poems.   New York, Macmillan, 1957.
Poems for Children, illustrated by Lynette Hemmant.   Kingswood, Surrey, World's Work, 1978.

Other

Fortune's Caravan, from translation by Marion Saunders of a work by Lily Jean-Javal, illustrated by Maggie Salcedo.   New York, Morrow, 1933; London, Oxford University Press, 1935.
All Through the Night, illustrated by the author.   New York, Macmillan, 1940; London, Collins, 1954.
Prayer for a Child, illustrated by Elizabeth Orton Jones.   New York, Macmillan, 1944.

Editor, *The White Cat and Other Old French Fairy Tales,* by Marie Catherine d'Aulnoy, illustrated by Elizabeth MacKinstry.   New York, Macmillan, 1928.
Editor, *American Folk and Fairy Tales,* illustrated by Margaret Freeman.   New York, Scribner, 1929.
Editor, *People from Dickens: A Presentation of Leading Characters from the Books of Charles Dickens,* illustrated by Thomas Fogarty. New York, Scribner, 1935.

PUBLICATIONS FOR ADULTS

Novels

Time Out of Mind.   New York, Macmillan, 1935; London, Macmillan, 1937.
To See Ourselves, with Arthur Pederson.   New York, Macmillan, 1937; London, Collins, 1939.
All This and Heaven Too.   New York, Macmillan, 1938; London, Collins, 1939.
And Now Tomorrow.   New York, Macmillan, 1942; London, Collins, 1943.

Short Story

Christmas in London.   Privately printed, 1946.

Verse

Points East: Narratives of New England.   New York, Brewer and Warren, 1930.
A Circus Garland.   Washington, D.C., Winter Wheat Press, 1930.
Branches Green.   New York, Macmillan, 1934.
Fear Is the Thorn.   New York, Macmillan, 1936.

Other

God's Pocket: The Story of Captain Samuel Hadlock, Junior, of the Cranberry Isles, Maine.   New York, Macmillan, 1934; London, Macmillan, 1937.
Ave Maria: An Interpretation from Walt Disney's "Fantasia" Inspired by the Music of Franz Schubert.   New York, Random House, 1940.

*

Illustrator: *Punch and Robinetta* by Ethel May Gate, 1923; *Come, Christmas* by Eleanor Farjeon, 1928; *The House That Grew Smaller* by Margery Williams Bianco, 1931.

*   *   *

Rachel Field's reputation as a children's book author today rests almost solely on her book *Hitty, Her First Hundred Years* which won the Newbery Medal in 1930. The book is a picaresque, first-person narrative of the memoirs of the doll Mehitabel's first hundred years. The strong personality of the doll binds the narration together, although individual scenes and a wide variety of characters are given considerable dimension. The setting ranges from New England to India and eventually back again, with realistic scenes devoted to plantation life, whale sightings, the singing of Jenny Lind, and sitting for a daguerreotypist intermixed. The book is enhanced by illustrations by Dorothy P. Lathrop who frequently illustrated for Field. For a discussion of Field's work habits and how *Hitty* came into being, one should consult Louise Bechtel's *Books in Search of Children.*

Field was also an illustrator of books for children and adults, but she is best known for her literary canon which includes fantasy, historical fiction, non-fiction, poetry, and plays, as well as a selected edition of Mme. d'Aulnoy's fairy tales and a slightly saccharine *Prayer for a Child.* One aspect of her work that is largely ignored today, but merits attention, is her playwriting for children. Her best known works in this genre are five diverse plays anthologized in a volume entitled *Patchwork Plays.* These plays are good in that they are all playable, making few highly technical demands on child players but considerable demands on the child audience's imagination. Each of the plays is packed with action and believability. Perhaps a distance of fifty years precludes immediacy and dramatic impact on a modern audience of a play about a sentimental scarecrow, but Field would capture a modern audience with her play *Little Square-Toes.* This short work is about a young girl who is captured by Indians during King Philip's war and who is reluctant to return to "civilization" when given the chance. It is marked by highly realistic dialogue, swift action, and a strong, developmental plot. Field's best-known book of poetry for children is *Taxis and Toadstools,* a town-and-country anthology on subjects as diverse as the conjunction of the two subjects in the title would suggest. The best poems read naturally with flowing enjambment; the weakest scan methodically and almost monotonously, though the latter are much in the minority.

—Rachel Fordyce

FINE, Anne. British. Born in Leicester, 7 December 1947. Educated at Northampton High School for Girls, 1958–65; University of Warwick, Coventry, 1965–68, B.A. (honours) in history and politics 1968. Married Kit Fine in 1968; two daughters. Teacher, Cardinal Wiseman Secondary School, Coventry, 1968–69, and Saughton Prison, Edinburgh, 1971–72; information officer, Oxfam, Oxford, 1969–71. Recipient: Scottish Arts Council award, 1986. Lives in Edinburgh. Agent: Murray Pollinger, 4 Garrick Street, London WC2E 9BH, England.

PUBLICATIONS FOR CHILDREN

Fiction

The Summer-House Loon. London, Methuen, 1978; New York, Crowell, 1979.
The Other, Darker Ned. London, Methuen, 1979.
The Stone Menagerie. London, Methuen, 1980.
Round Behind the Ice-House. London, Methuen, 1981.
The Granny Project. London, Methuen, and New York, Farrar Straus, 1983.
Scaredy-Cat, illustrated by Vanessa Julian-Ottie. London, Heinemann, 1985.

Anneli the Art Hater. London, Methuen, 1986.
Madame Doubtfire. London, Hamish Hamilton, 1987; as *Alias Madame Doubtfire,* Boston, Little Brown, 1988.
Crummy Mummy and Me, illustrated by David Higham. London, Deutsch, 1988.
A Pack of Liars. London, Hamish Hamilton, 1988.
Goggle Eyes. London, Hamish Hamilton, 1989; as *My War with Goggle Eyes,* Boston, Little Brown, 1989.
Stranger Danger, illustrated by Jean Baylis. London, Hamish Hamilton, 1989.
Bill's New Frock, illustrated by Philippe Dupasquier. London, Methuen, 1989.

Play

The Granny Project, adaptation of her own story. London, Collins, 1986.

PUBLICATIONS FOR ADULTS

Novel

The Killjoy. London, Bantam, 1986; New York, Mysterious Press, 1987.

Play

Radio Play: *The Captain's Court Case,* 1987.

*

Anne Fine comments:

I find I write mostly about that period during which the stability of childhood, when almost all decisions are made by others, is giving way to a wider world. A sense of the need for a sort of personal elbow-room is developing, and people outside the family seem to be showing other ways to go. Growing through to full autonomy is, for anyone, a long and doggy business; for some, more sabotaged than others by their nature or upbringing, it can seem impossible. I try to show that the battle through the chaos and confusions is worthwhile and can, at times, be seen as very funny.

*   *   *

Anne Fine's first three books are 20th-century comedies of manners. They are not for everyone, requiring a certain amount of sophistication in the reader, but for those in command of that sophistication they are stylishly lighthearted entertainment. Academic passions running high over early Sardinian trade routes, in *The Summer-House Loon,* make a change from the earnest social relevance of many contemporary teenage novels. Ione Muffet, the book's heroine, has to sort out the romantic affairs of a promising young academic and her father's secretary, as well as dealing with her father himself, a blind professor of history who is a pleasing variation on the eccentric professor of popular mythology. The same characters return with further complications in the book's sequel, *The Other, Darker Ned,* where Ione, social conscience aroused, organizes a fete in aid of Oxfam, and finds new adolescent emotions emerging in her.

In her third book, *The Stone Menagerie,* Fine takes as her central figures another young person, the boy Ally, and another young couple, Flora and Riley, squatters in the disused menagerie buildings of a mental hospital. The captivating Flora—vegetarian, wholefoods enthusiast, and basket weaver—and her lover are an attractive pair, and the spirit of comedy hovers over the book, pushing Ally's own family difficulties into the background.

Round Behind the Ice-House is the most overtly serious of Fine's books: a study of the difficulties of young people growing up, complicated by the fact that two of the central figures are twins who have previously been very close. In subsequent novels, however, while moving closer to the genre of the social-problem novel, Fine has turned her gift for comedy to good account again. *Madame Doubtfire* hinges on the problem of divorce, and *The Granny Project* on the problem of old age, with their effects on an entire family. *A Pack of Liars,* beneath the entertaining surface sparkle common to both her first books and these later titles, conducts a debate on the nature and consequences of veracity. Details of the plots, though neatly worked out, may sometimes seem a little farfetched in the abstract; in practice, however, the sheer comic verve of the writing carries them off. Gentle irony about such standard phenomena of the modern child's experience as school projects is matched by a perceptive warmth in the description of friendships between children, whether within the family (*The Granny Project*) or unrelated (*A Pack of Liars* and *Anneli the Art Hater*). Most of Fine's books are for children approaching adolescence, but in *Anneli the Art Hater* she writes for a younger age group without in any way compromising her idiosyncratic approach and style, and she is able to write for those just past picture-book age as well, as in *Bill's New Frock.*

—Anthea Bell

FINGER, Charles J(oseph). American. Born in Willesden, Middlesex, England, 25 December 1869; emigrated to the United States, 1887; became American citizen, 1896. Educated at a private school; King's College, London; studied music in Frankfurt. Married Nellie B. Ferguson in 1902; three sons and two daughters. Worked in South America, Mexico, and Africa for five years, including jobs as a sailor and as a guide on an ornithological expedition to Tierra del Fuego; prospector in the Klondike gold fields; director, Conservatory of Music, San Angelo, Texas, 1898–1900; boilermaker's helper, later auditor and general manager, Ohio Southeastern Railroad, 1906–20; also receiver for several railroads; editor, *Reedy's Mirror,* St. Louis, 1919; proprietor and editor, *All's Well* magazine, Fayetteville, Arkansas, 1920–35; managing editor, Bellows-Reeve Company, Chicago, 1933. Member of the Editorial Board, *Story Parade* magazine, New York. Recipient: American Library Association Newbery Medal, 1925. D. Litt.: Knox College, Galesburg, Illinois, 1921; LL.D.: University of Arkansas, Fayetteville, 1931. *Died 7 January 1941.*

PUBLICATIONS FOR CHILDREN

Fiction

The Spreading Stain, illustrated by Paul Honoré. New York, Doubleday, and London, Heinemann, 1927.
Courageous Companions, illustrated by James Daugherty. New York, Longman, 1929.
The Magic Tower, illustrated by Helen Finger. New York, Kings Arms Press, 1933.
A Dog at His Heel, illustrated by Henry Pitz. Philadelphia, Winston, 1936; London, Harrap, 1937.
When Guns Thundered in Tripoli, illustrated by Henry Pitz. New York, Holt, 1937.
Bobbie and Jock and the Mailman, illustrated by Helen Finger. New York, Holt, 1938.
Give a Man a Horse, illustrated by Henry Pitz. Philadelphia,

Winston, 1938; London, Harrap, 1939.
Cape Horn Snorter, illustrated by Henry Pitz. Boston, Houghton Mifflin, 1939.
The Yankee Captain in Patagonia, illustrated by Henry Pitz. New York, Grosset and Dunlap, 1941.
High Water in Arkansas, illustrated by Henry Pitz. New York, Grosset and Dunlap, 1943.

Other

Tales from Silver Lands, illustrated by Paul Honoré. New York, Doubleday, and London, Heinemann, 1924.
Robin Hood and His Merry Men. Girard, Kansas, Haldeman Julius, 1924.
Tales Worth Telling, illustrated by Paul Honoré. New York, Century, 1927.
David Livingstone, illustrated by Arthur Zaidenberg. New York, Doubleday, 1930.
A Paul Bunyan Geography, illustrated by Helen Finger. Privately printed, 1931.
Our Navy: An Outline History for Young People, illustrated by Henry Pitz. Boston, Houghton Mifflin, 1936.
Golden Tales from Faraway, illustrated by Helen Finger. Philadelphia, Winston, 1940.

Editor, *Heroes from Hakluyt,* illustrated by Paul Honoré. New York, Holt, 1928.

PUBLICATIONS FOR ADULTS

Short Stories

In Lawless Lands. New York, Kennerley, 1924.
The Affair at the Inn, as Seen by Philo the Innkeeper and the Tax-Gatherer of Rome. Westport, Connecticut, Georgian Press, 1931.

Other

Henry David Thoreau: The Man Who Escaped from the Herd. Girard, Kansas, Haldeman Julius, 1922.
Hints on Writing Short Stories [One-Act Plays]. Girard, Kansas, Haldeman Julius, 2 vols., 1922–23.
Historic Crimes and Criminals. Girard, Kansas, Haldeman Julius, 1922.
Lost Civilizations. Girard, Kansas, Haldeman Julius, 1922.
The Ice Age. Girard, Kansas, Haldeman Julius, 1922.
Joseph Addison and His Time. Girard, Kansas, Haldeman Julius, 1922.
The Essence of Confucianism. Girard, Kansas, Haldeman Julius, 1923.
Life of Napoleon. Girard, Kansas, Haldeman Julius, 1923.
Mahomet. Girard, Kansas, Haldeman Julius, 1923.
My View of William Feather. Cleveland, William Feather Company, 1923.
Oscar Wilde in Outline. Girard, Kansas, Haldeman Julius, 1923.
The Tragic Story of Oscar Wilde's Life. Girard, Kansas, Haldeman Julius, 1923.
Highwaymen: A Book of Gallant Rogues. New York, McBride, 1923; London, Harrap, 1925.
Bushrangers. New York, McBride, 1924; London, Harrap, 1925.
Free Fantasia on Books and Reading. Girard, Kansas, Haldeman Julius, 1924.
The Gist of Burton's Anatomy of Melancholy. Girard, Kansas, Haldeman Julius, 1924.

Life of Barnum: The Man Who Lured the Herd. Girard, Kansas, Haldeman Julius, 1924.

Life of Theodore Roosevelt. Girard, Kansas, Haldeman Julius, 1924.

Magellan and the Pacific. Girard, Kansas, Haldeman Julius, 1924.

Mark Twain: The Philosopher Who Laughed at the World. Girard, Kansas, Haldeman Julius, 1924.

Great Pirates. Girard, Kansas, Haldeman Julius, 1924.

The Travels of Marco Polo. Girard, Kansas, Haldeman Julius, 1924.

A Book of Strange Murders. Girard, Kansas, Haldeman Julius, 1925.

David Livingstone: Explorer and Prophet. New York, Doubleday, and London, Heinemann, 1927.

Ozark Fantasia, edited by Charles Morrow Wilson. Fayetteville, Arkansas, Golden Horseman Press, 1927.

A Note on Texas. Privately printed, 1927.

Romantic Rascals. New York, McBride, 1927.

A Man for a' That: The Story of Robert Burns. Boston, Stratford, 1929.

Seven Horizons (autobiography). New York, Doubleday, 1930.

Adventure under Sapphire Stars (travel). New York, Morrow, 1931.

Foot-loose in the West, Being an Account of a Journey to Colorado and California and Other Western States. New York, Morrow, 1932.

After the Great Companions: A Free Fantasia on a Lifetime of Reading. New York, Dutton, 1935.

The Distant Prize: A Book about Rovers, Rangers, and Rascals. New York, Appleton Century, 1935.

Valiant Vagabonds. New York, Appleton Century, 1938.

Editor, *The Choice of the Crowd* (anthology of poetry). Fayetteville, Arkansas, Golden Horseman Press, 1922.

Editor, *Pepys' Diary.* Girard, Kansas, Haldeman Julius, 1922.

Editor, *Autobiography of Benvenuto Cellini.* Girard, Kansas, Haldeman Julius, 1923.

Editor, *Boswell's Life of Johnson.* Girard, Kansas, Haldeman Julius, 1923.

Editor, *The Privateersman,* by Frederick Marryat. Girard, Kansas, Haldeman Julius, 1923.

Editor, *Sailor Chanties and Cowboy Songs.* Girard, Kansas, Haldeman Julius, 1923.

Editor, *Thirteenth Century Prose Tales,* by William Morris. Girard, Kansas, Haldeman Julius, 1923.

Editor, *Book of Real Adventures.* Girard, Kansas, Haldeman Julius, 1925.

Editor, *Frontier Ballads.* New York, Doubleday, and London, Heinemann, 1927.

Translator, *Five Weeks in a Balloon,* by Jules Verne. Girard, Kansas, Haldeman Julius, 1923.

Translator, *A Voyage to the Moon,* by Jules Verne. Girard, Kansas, Haldeman Julius, 1923.

* * *

Charles J. Finger was an adventurer. Imbued with high spirits and great curiosity, he set off to sea while still in his teens. He traveled throughout Africa and the Americas before settling in Arkansas. He wrote fiction as well as non-fiction, for adult and for child audiences. His autobiography, *Seven Horizons,* is a vivid account of a colorful life lived on several continents. He produced books on literature and travel, and a collection of sailor chanties and cowboy songs learned from companions of earlier years (*Frontier Ballads*). He wrote several sea adventures, such as *Courageous Companions,* the story

of an English boy who sailed with Magellan around the world. This and other sea tales provide humanistic portrayals of individual men embarked on voyages of great discovery.

Finger is most noted for two books of folktales: *Tales from Silver Lands* and *Tales Worth Telling.* He had learned many legends and folktales in his ten years of travel in South America and had told and retold them to his own children. His children in turn as teenagers chose particular stories to be put in book form. After he had grandchildren, Finger turned his attention to a younger audience and wrote books specifically for them: *Bobbie and Jock and the Mailman, High Water in Arkansas,* and *Golden Tales from Faraway. Tales from Silver Lands* won the Newbery Medal for 1925. It is a collection of 19 stories Finger learned from various Indian tribes in South America while traveling from one "silver land" to another, far from railroads or main lines of transportation. There are tales from tribes as far north as Colombia and as far south as Cape Horn. The tales tell of powerful and wise persons, of gentle flowers and birds and animals, and of supernatural beings—witches, giants, magicians, wild men, fairy folk, and under-sea people—all of whom have extraordinary abilities and behave in most unpredictable ways.

Finger is important in 20th-century literature on two counts. First, he provides children with riveting stories of around the world adventure, to fulfill endless desire for new experiences and new discoveries. Second, he provides children with tales of human needs and longings, social fabrics and beliefs, from a wide variety of old and new cultures. His insights are well matched by imaginative storytelling.

—Mary Lystad

FINKEL, George (Irvine). British. Born in South Shields, County Durham, 13 May 1909. Educated at public primary schools; Bede Collegiate School, Sunderland, County Durham, 1919–26. Served in the Royal Auxiliary Air Force, 1930–34; Sub-Lieutenant, Royal Naval Volunteer Reserve, 1939–45; Lieutenant Commander, Royal Navy, 1945–50; Technical Training Officer, Australian Fleet Air Arm, Nowra, New South Wales, during the Korean War; Engineer Officer, Naval Air Base, Nowra, 1952–58. Married Lena Almond in 1930; three sons and one daughter. Cadet chemical engineer, 1927–34; aviator, Imperial Airways, England, Europe, and Africa, 1934–39; professional officer and later teaching hospitals planning officer, University of New South Wales, Kensington, 1958–69. *Died in March 1975.*

PUBLICATIONS FOR CHILDREN

Fiction

The Mystery of Secret Beach. Sydney, Angus and Robertson, 1962; London, Angus and Robertson, 1963.

Ship in Hiding. Sydney, Angus and Robertson, 1963.

Cloudmaker. Sydney and London, Angus and Robertson, and New York, Roy, 1965.

The Singing Sands. Sydney and London, Angus and Robertson, 1966.

The Long Pilgrimage, illustrated by George Tetlow. Sydney and London, Angus and Robertson, 1967; New York, Viking Press, 1969.

Twilight Province, illustrated by George Tetlow. Sydney and London, Angus and Robertson, 1967; as *Watch Fires to the North,* New York, Viking Press, 1967.

The "Loyall Virginian." Sydney and London, Angus and
Robertson, and New York, Viking Press, 1968.
Journey to Jorsala. Sydney and London, Angus and Robertson,
1969.
The Peace Seekers. Sydney and London, Angus and Robertson,
1970.
The Stranded Duck, illustrated by Andrew Parnell. Sydney, Angus
and Robertson, 1973.
Operation Aladdin, illustrated by Walter Stackpool. Sydney and
London, Hodder and Stoughton, 1976.

Other

Navigator and Explorer: James Cook, illustrated by Amnon
Sadubin. Sydney, Wentworth Press, 1969.
James Cook, Royal Navy, illustrated by Amnon Sadubin. Sydney
and London, Angus and Robertson, 1970.
Community Services: Power, Transport. Melbourne, Nelson, 2
vols., 1970.
Laws: Making and Keeping Them. Melbourne, Nelson, 1970.
Migrants of Legend [*Who Changed the World, Who Had No Choice,
Who Made Britain*]. Melbourne, Nelson, 4 vols., 1970.
Producing Food: Cereals, Fish, Fruit, Meat. Melbourne, Nelson,
4 vols., 1970.
William Light. Sydney, Angus and Robertson, 1972.
Matthew Flinders, Explorer and Scientist, illustrated by Victor
Hatcher. Sydney and London, Collins, 1973.
New South Wales 1788–1900. Melbourne, Nelson, 1974.
Victoria 1834–1900. Melbourne, Nelson, 1974.
The Dutchman Bold: The Story of Abel Tasman. Sydney and Lon-
don, Angus and Robertson, 1975.
Governor Lachlan Macquarie. Melbourne, Nelson, 1975.
South Australia 1836–1900. Melbourne, Nelson, 1975.
Queensland 1824–1900. Melbourne, Nelson, 1975.
Antarctica: The Heroic Age. Sydney and London, Collins, 1976.
Tasmania 1803–1900. Melbourne, Nelson, 1976.
Western Australia 1829–1900. Melbourne, Nelson, 1976.

* * *

George Finkel began his literary career by writing a few well-
structured adventure stories for boys. He then became absorbed in a
much deeper vein of creative fiction, and produced a number of
originally researched historical novels, as well as fictional
biographies. In both novels and biographies he often presents ingenious theories and fresh viewpoints on the significance of certain
events or character motivation. Thus, in *Twilight Province* he
presents his view of the Arthur legend; *The "Loyall Virginian"*
explores an unusual aspect of the secession of the North American
colonies from Britain; *The Peace Seekers* attempts an explanation of
the infiltration of a North American Indian tribe by men of Celtic
stock. Attention to detail and exact explanation of, for example,
mechanical parts is a recognizable facet of his writing, reflecting his
own inquiring mind. The careful plotting of his novels tends to
occupy first place in the scheme of work; characterization is not the
dominant aspect. George Finkel's fictional biographies, especially
James Cook, Royal Navy (he felt a particular empathy in relation to
Cook for they belonged to the same part of England, and Finkel's
own seagoing experience was considerable) and *William Light*—the
gallant, artistic ex-Army officer who became first Surveyor General
for South Australia—are clear-cut and strike a happy balance between fiction and fact. They are neither romanticized nor are they
bereft of the attribute of story.

Latterly, Finkel turned to a new form of fiction: short, compelling
novels set in the present day whose main appeal is to boys in the
10–14 age group. In *The Stranded Duck* and *Operation Aladdin* he
related two stories concerning salvage operations carried out by a
family of cousins and their grandfather. But for the author's untimely
death, these stories might well have developed into a continuing
series. They are tightly structured, told with economy of narrative,
and show a considerably deeper degree of characterization than do
his longer novels.

—Barbara Ker Wilson

———

FINLAY, Winifred (Lindsay Crawford). British. Born in
Newcastle-upon-Tyne, Northumberland, 27 April 1910. Educated at
High School for Girls, Whitley Bay, Northumberland; King's Col-
lege, University of Newcastle, 1928–33, M.A. (honours) in English.
Married Evan Finlay in 1935; one daughter. Schoolmistress and
college lecturer, Newcastle-upon-Tyne, 1933–35, Stratford-on-
Avon, 1941–44, Leeds, 1944–48, and Northampton, 1948–50.
Regular contributor, *Child Education,* London. Recipient: Mystery
Writers of America Edgar Allan Poe award, 1970. Address: The Old
House, Walgrave, Northamptonshire NN6 9QN, England.

PUBLICATIONS FOR CHILDREN

Fiction

The Witch of Redesdale. London, Harrap, 1951.
Peril in Lakeland. London, Harrap, 1953.
Peril in the Pennines. London, Harrap, 1953.
Cotswold Holiday, illustrated by Shirley Macgregor. London, Har-
rap, 1954.
The Lost Silver of Langdon. London, Harrap, 1955.
Storm over Cheviot. London, Harrap, 1955.
Judith in Hanover. London, Harrap, 1955.
Canal Holiday. London, Harrap, 1957.
The Cruise of the "Susan." London, Harrap, 1958.
The Castle and the Cave, illustrated by John S. Goodall. London,
Harrap, 1960.
The Lost Emeralds of Black Howes. London, Harrap, 1961.
Alison in Provence, illustrated by John S. Goodall. London, Har-
rap, 1963.
Mystery in the Middle Marches. London, Harrap, 1964.
Castle for Four. London, Harrap, 1966.
Adventure in Prague. London, Harrap, 1967.
Danger at Black Dyke. London, Harrap, and New York, Phillips,
1968.
The Cry of the Peacock. London, Harrap, 1969.
Summer of the Golden Stag. London, Harrap, 1969.
Singing Stones. London, Harrap, 1970.
Beadbonny Ash. London, Harrap, 1973; Nashville, Nelson, 1975.

Plays

Radio Plays: *Children's Hour* series, 1947–63, including *The Clues
of the Sickle Moon,* 1961, *Mystery in the Middle Marches,* 1962,
Castle for Four, 1963.

Other

Folk Tales from the North, illustrated by Victor Ambrus. London,
Kaye and Ward, 1968; New York, Watts, 1969.
Folk Tales from Moor and Mountain, illustrated by Victor Ambrus.
London, Kaye and Ward, 1969; New York, Roy, 1970.

Cap o' Rushes and Other Folk Tales, illustrated by Victor Ambrus. London, Kaye and Ward, and Eau Claire, Wisconsin, Hale, 1974.

Tattercoats and Other Folk Tales, illustrated by Shirley Hughes. London, Kaye and Ward, 1976; New York, Harvey House, 1977.

Ghosts, Ghouls, and Spectres: English Ghost Stories, with Gillian Hancock, illustrated by Gavin Rowe. London, Kaye and Ward, 1976.

Spies and Secret Agents, with Gillian Hancock, illustrated by Gavin Rowe. London, Kaye and Ward, 1977.

Treasure Hunters, with Gillian Hancock, illustrated by Edward Mortelmans. London, Kaye and Ward, 1978.

Tales from the Hebrides and Highlands, illustrated by Bernadette Watts. London, Kaye and Ward, 1978.

Clever and Courageous Dogs, with Gillian Hancock, illustrated by Gavin Rowe. London, Kaye and Ward, 1978.

Famous Flights of Airships and Balloons, with Gillian Hancock, illustrated by David Armitage. London, Kaye and Ward, 1979.

Tales from the Borders, illustrated by Victor Ambrus. London, Kaye and Ward, 1979.

Tales of Sorcery and Witchcraft, illustrated by Laszlo Acs. London, Kaye and Ward, 1980.

Tales of Fantasy and Fear, illustrated by Victor Ambrus. London, Kaye and Ward, 1981.

Fight for Life, illustrated by Gavin Rowe. London, Kaye and Ward, 1981.

Secret Rooms and Hiding Places, illustrated by Gavin Rowe. London, Kaye and Ward, 1982.

Vampires, Werewolves and Phantoms of the Night: Demonic Tales from Different Lands, illustrated by Kate Mellor. London, Methuen, 1983.

*

Winifred Finlay comments:

I have written stories ever since I can remember. I first wrote professionally for my own daughter during the war when there was a shortage of suitable books. My stories and plays are set in real places which I know well: Britain, France, Germany, Czechoslovakia. I have tried to show that, because of the action in which they were involved, my principal characters have developed in their understanding of themselves and other people.

As a Northumbrian with Scottish parents, I have often drawn on areas I knew when young: the Roman Wall, the Border Country, and the Scottish Highlands and Islands. For my later work I have collected fascinating folk and ghost tales, ballads and legends. I was taught to have a healthy respect for the English language, and I have always tried to maintain sound literary standards as I feel very strongly that only the best is good enough for children.

*   *   *

Winifred Finlay has had a prolific career as a writer of children's books and radio plays. Most of her novels have followed the same pattern: some children on holiday are involved in a mystery which they eventually solve, finding after dramatic and often dangerous events that the mystery itself was not as spectacular as they had thought. The anti-climactic conclusion keeps her stories realistic and sensible, and the hordes of international crooks and caves stuffed with treasure remain firmly in the children's imaginations.

She narrates not only a story, but also the emotional journey taken by one or more children who have to come to terms with a difficult relationship or one of the problems of growing up. From her observation and experience Finlay is best qualified to describe the adolescent girl, and though her heroines are from the same mould, the different situations they face bring plenty of variety to the basic theme of a girl growing up, finding out how to relate to her mother

and to boyfriends, finding a suitable career and perhaps going against her parents wishes.

Several of her books, like *Summer of the Golden Stag* and *Adventure in Prague,* deal with a teenage girl alone, abroad. As she copes with foreigners, plus the inevitable mystery, she learns about her own personality and needs. Whether abroad or at home, the mystery element is usually associated with a genuine historical background. Finlay is especially sympathetic to the scenery and antiquities of North Britain—the lakes, the Roman Wall, ancient stones, etc., which are described in detail, while she also ridicules childish fantasies, e.g., of Druids: "Stonehenge and mistletoe and long white beards."

In 1970 Finlay deserted the typical adventure story for full-blooded fantasy of the Alan Garner kind, where supernatural creatures from the past come alive now. *Singing Stones* and *Beadbonny Ash* are magical adventures in Scotland's Celtic past. They resemble the earlier books in their well-drawn family relationships and historical detail, but they abandon the cynical attitude to mystery for a genuine commitment to the power of the supernatural and the war between Good and Evil.

Singing Stones is about the discovery of the ancient carved coronation stone of Scotland; *Beadbonny Ash* about a girl's rediscovery of her love for her mother, through a journey in time to the days when the Old Gods were replaced by Christ. The girl's mother is identified with the great Celtic goddess, Ugly Hag and Beautiful Lady in one, just as in real life her daughter loves and hates her.

Recently she has written several collections of folk-tales from oral and literary sources. Her retellings are not mere paraphrases, but expansions of the old tales with detail and humour. Several collections of ghost and spy stories have extended her work. But *Beadbonny Ash* is her masterpiece.

—Jessica Yates

———

FISHER, Aileen (Lucia). American. Born in Iron River, Michigan, 9 September 1906. Educated at the University of Chicago, 1923–25; University of Missouri, Columbia, Bachelor of Journalism 1927. Director, Women's National Journalistic Register, Chicago, 1929–32; research assistant, Labor Bureau of the Middle West, Chicago, 1931–32. Recipient: Western Writers of America award, for non-fiction, 1967; National Council of Teachers of English award, for poetry, 1978. Address: 505 College Avenue, Boulder, Colorado 80302, U.S.A.

PUBLICATIONS FOR CHILDREN

Fiction

Over the Hills to Nugget, illustrated by Sandra James. New York, Aladdin, 1949.

Trapped by the Mountain Storm, illustrated by J. Fred Collins. New York, Aladdin, 1950.

Homestead of the Free: The Kansas Story. New York, Aladdin, 1953.

Timber! Logging in Michigan, illustrated by Pers Crowell. New York, Aladdin, 1955.

Off to the Gold Fields, illustrated by R.M. Powers. New York, Nelson, 1955; as *Secret in the Barrel,* New York, Scholastic, 1965.

Cherokee Strip: The Race for Land, illustrated by Walt Reed. New York, Aladdin, 1956.

A Lantern in the Window, illustrated by Harper Johnson.   New York, Nelson, 1957.

Skip, illustrated by Genevieve Vaughan-Jackson.   New York, Nelson, 1958.

Fisherman of Galilee, illustrated by John De Pol.   New York, Nelson, 1959.

Summer of Little Rain, illustrated by Gloria Stevens.   New York, Nelson, 1961.

My Cousin Abe, illustrated by Leonard Vosburgh.   New York, Crowell, 1962.

Arbor Day, illustrated by Nonny Hogrogian.   New York, Crowell, 1965.

Human Rights Day, with Olive Rabe, illustrated by Lisl Weil.   New York, Crowell, 1966.

Plays

The Squanderbug's Christmas Carol.   Washington, D.C., United States Treasury Department, 1943.

The Squanderbug's Mother Goose.   Washington, D.C., United States Treasury Department, 1944.

A Tree to Trim: A Christmas Play.   Evanston, Illinois, Row Peterson, 1945.

What Happened to Toyland.   Evanston, Illinois, Row Peterson, 1945.

Nine Cheers for Christmas: A Christmas Pageant.   Evanston, Illinois, Row Peterson, 1945.

Before and After: A Play about the Community School Lunch Program.   Washington, D.C., War Food Administration, 1945.

All Set for Christmas.   Evanston, Illinois, Row Peterson, 1946.

Here Comes Christmas! A Varied Collection of Christmas-Program Materials for Elementary Schools.   Evanston, Illinois, Row Peterson, 1947.

Witches, Beware: A Hallowe'en Play.   New York, Play Club, 1948.

Set the Stage for Christmas: A Collection of Pantomimes, Skits, Recitations, Readings, Plays and Pageants.   Evanston, Illinois, Row Peterson, 1948.

Christmas in Ninety-Nine Words (lyrics only), music by Rebecca Welty Dunn.   Evanston, Illinois, Row Peterson, 1949.

Angel in the Looking-Glass, in *Plays* (Boston), ix, 1950.

The Big Book of Christmas: A Collection of Plays, Songs, Readings, Recitations, Pantomimes, Skits, and Suggestions for Things to Make and Do for Christmas.   Evanston, Illinois, Row Peterson, 1951.

Health and Safety Plays and Programs.   Boston, Plays Inc., 1953.

Holiday Programs for Boys and Girls.   Boston, Plays Inc., 1953; revised edition, 1980.

United Nations Plays and Programs, with Olive Rabe.   Boston, Plays Inc., 1954.

Patriotic Plays and Programs, with Olive Rabe.   Boston, Plays Inc., 1956.

Christmas Plays and Programs.   Boston, Plays Inc., 1960.

Plays about Our Nation's Songs.   Boston, Plays Inc., 1962.

The King's Toothache, and *One-Ring Circus,* in *Thirty Plays for Classroom Reading,* edited by Donald D. Durrell.   Boston, Plays Inc., 1965.

Time for Mom, and *Young Abe Lincoln,* in *Fifty Plays for Holidays,* edited by Sylvia E. Kamerman.   Boston, Plays Inc., 1969.

Bicentennial Plays and Programs.   Boston, Plays Inc., 1975.

Year-Round Programs for Young Players.   Boston, Plays Inc., 1985.

Verse

The Coffee-Pot Face, illustrated by the author.   New York, McBride, 1933.

Inside a Little House, illustrated by the author.   New York, McBride, 1938.

That's Why, illustrated by the author.   New York, Nelson, 1946.

Up the Windy Hill: A Book of Merry Verse with Silhouettes, illustrated by the author.   New York, Abelard Press, 1953; London, Abelard Schuman, 1958.

Runny Days, Sunny Days: Merry Verses, illustrated by the author.   New York and London, Abelard Schuman, 1958.

Going Barefoot, illustrated by Adrienne Adams.   New York, Crowell, 1960.

Where Does Everyone Go?, illustrated by Adrienne Adams.   New York, Crowell, 1961.

I Wonder How, I Wonder Why, illustrated by Carol Barker.   New York and London, Abelard Schuman, 1962.

Like Nothing at All, illustrated by Leonard Weisgard.   New York, Crowell, 1962.

I Like Weather, illustrated by Janina Domanska.   New York, Crowell, 1963.

Cricket in a Thicket, illustrated by Feodor Rojankovsky.   New York, Scribner, 1963.

Listen, Rabbit, illustrated by Symeon Shimin.   New York, Crowell, 1964.

In the Middle of the Night, illustrated by Adrienne Adams.   New York, Crowell, 1965.

In the Woods, In the Meadow, In the Sky, illustrated by Margot Tomes.   New York, Scribner, 1965; Kingswood, Surrey, World's Work, 1967.

Best Little House, illustrated by Arnold Spilka.   New York, Crowell, 1966.

Skip Around the Year, illustrated by Gioia Fiammenghi.   New York, Crowell, 1967.

My Mother and I, illustrated by Kazue Mizumura.   New York, Crowell, 1967.

Up, Up the Mountain, illustrated by Gilbert Riswold.   New York, Crowell, 1968.

We Went Looking, illustrated by Marie Angel.   New York, Crowell, 1968.

Clean as a Whistle, illustrated by Ben Shecter.   New York, Crowell, 1969.

In One Door and Out the Other: A Book of Poems, illustrated by Lillian Hoban.   New York, Crowell, 1969.

Sing, Little Mouse, illustrated by Symeon Shimin.   New York, Crowell, 1969.

But Ostriches..., illustrated by Peter Parnall.   New York, Crowell, 1970.

Feathered Ones and Furry, illustrated by Eric Carle.   New York, Crowell, 1971.

Do Bears Have Mothers Too?, illustrated by Eric Carle.   New York, Crowell, 1973.

My Cat Has Eyes of Sapphire Blue, illustrated by Marie Angel.   New York, Crowell, 1973.

Once We Went on a Picnic, illustrated by Tony Chen.   New York, Crowell, 1975.

I Stood upon a Mountain, illustrated by Blair Lent.   New York, Crowell, 1979.

Anybody Home?, illustrated by Susan Bonners.   New York, Crowell, 1980.

Out in the Dark and Daylight, illustrated by Gail Owens.   New York, Harper, 1980.

Rabbits, Rabbits, illustrated by Gail Niemann.   New York, Harper, 1983.

In Summer, with Jane Belk Moncure, illustrated by Marie-Claude Monchaux.   Elgin, Illinois, Children's World, 1985.

When It Comes to Bugs, illustrated by Chris and Bruce Degen.   New York, Harper, 1986.

The House of a Mouse, illustrated by Joan Sandin.   New York,

Harper, 1988.

Other

Guess Again! (riddles). New York, McBride, 1941.
All on a Mountain Day, illustrated by Gardell Christensen. New York, Nelson, 1956.
We Dickinsons: The Life of Emily Dickinson as Seen Through the Eyes of Her Brother Austin, with Olive Rabe, illustrated by Ellen Raskin. New York, Atheneum, 1965.
Valley of the Smallest: The Life Story of a Shrew, illustrated by Jean Zallinger. New York, Crowell, 1966.
We Alcotts: The Life of Louisa May Alcott as Seen Through the Eyes of "Marmee"..., illustrated by Ellen Raskin. New York, Atheneum, 1968.
Easter, illustrated by Ati Forberg. New York, Crowell, 1968.
Jeanne d'Arc, illustrated by Ati Forberg. New York, Crowell, 1970.
The Ways of Animals (in verse) (*Animal Houses,* illustrated by Jan Wills; *Animal Jackets,* illustrated by Muriel Wood; *Filling the Bill,* illustrated by Betty Fraser; *No Accounting for Taste,* illustrated by Gloria Gaulke; *Now That Days Are Colder,* illustrated by Gordon Laite; *Sleepy Heads,* illustrated by Phero Thomas; *"You Don't Look Like Your Mother," Said the Robin to the Fawn,* illustrated by Ati Forberg; *Tail Twisters,* illustrated by Albert John Pucci; *Going Places,* illustrated by Midge Quenell; *Animal Disguises,* illustrated by Tim and Greg Hildebrandt). Glendale, California, Bowmar, 10 vols., 1973–74.
The Ways of Plants (in verse) (*Plant Magic,* illustrated by Barbara Cooney; *Mysteries in the Garden,* illustrated by Ati Forberg; *Swords and Daggers,* illustrated by James Higa; *And a Sunflower Grew,* illustrated by Trina Schart Hyman; *Petals Yellow and Petals Red,* illustrated by Albert John Pucci; *Now That Spring Is Here,* illustrated by Symeon Shimin; *As the Leaves Fall Down,* illustrated by Barbara Smith; *Prize Performances,* illustrated by Margot Tomes; *A Tree with a Thousand Uses,* illustrated by James Endicott; *Seeds on the Go,* illustrated by Hans Zander). Glendale, California, Bowmar, 10 vols., 1977.

*

Manuscript Collection: Kerlan Collection, University of Minnesota, Minneapolis.

Aileen Fisher comments:

I enjoy writing for children. I especially enjoy writing verse. It gives me such a good chance for remembering how things looked and felt and *were* when I was a child.

*   *   *

Aileen Fisher draws upon observation and research to produce children's literature in various genres. She has written poetry, prose in the form of nature stories, and biographies, nonfiction, and plays.

Poetry has been her most significant contribution; as one *New York Times* reviewer wrote, "She lights the commonplace moment with wonder." While in college, she published her first collection, *The Coffee-Pot Face.* Subjects which she would treat for a lifetime were here—nature, such as a ladybug and icicles, objects such as a chair, childhood conditions such as a tummy-ache, and seasons. Well-known illustrators were selected to interpret her one-poem picture books, such as *In the Middle of the Night* and *Once We Went on a Picnic.* Inspired by her verse, Adrienne Adams, Marie Angel, and Symeon Shimin earned honors for their work. While praising *Going Barefoot* for its "rare synthesis of information and imagination," a reviewer considered it too long for one sitting with a small child.

Fisher's rhymed verses may be short (*Sing, Little Mouse*), or

sustained as a story (*My Mother and I* and *Where Does Everyone Go?*). Many of them open with a query (*Anybody Home?*), or musing (*In the Middle of the Night*), and expand to include observations on many animals. Fisher uses a light and lilting tone and often injects humor, as in the description of a skunk who investigates animal homes. Her special experiences with northern climes make the anticipation of "the wonderful month of the Barefoot Moon" convincing.

Close observation of nature and research on the Upper Peninsula in Michigan are the basis of *Timber! Logging in Michigan.* Colorado mountains are the setting for a number of books, such as *Trapped by the Mountain Storm* and *Valley of the Smallest: The Life Story of a Shrew.* The shrew was an unusual selection of an animal for a full-length narrative, but the author introduces other animals to show the natural interrelationships, and the author acknowledged a British zoologist who had published a book on the behaviour of a shrew. Virginia Haviland wrote in the *Horn Book* (December 1966): "A sharp observer, with a poet's imagination, the author records what she has seen near her mountain home. Her account is both more vivid and more suspenseful than most nature books...."

Her biographies have fared less well under the scrutiny of reviewers. By having Simon Peter, the brother of Emily Dickinson, and the mother of the March girls tell the stories of *Fisherman of Galilee, We Dickinsons,* and *We Alcotts,* she ensures a fresh approach. But despite direct quotations from primary sources, the books pale when compared to the Biblical narrative and authors' autobiographical writing. *Jeanne d'Arc,* according to the reviewer Barbara Wersba in the *New York Times Review* (24 May 1970), lacks passion, and "remains less of the journey of a saint than a biography of a very nice girl." Fisher's other non-fiction publications are the result of the same research, observation, and literary style. The collections of plays have the usefulness of being free of royalty fees for the performers, but, perhaps for the same reason, are unimpressive.

—Karen Nelson Hoyle

———

FISHER, Dorothy Canfield. American. Born Dorothea Frances Canfield in Lawrence, Kansas, 17 February 1879. Educated at Ohio State University, Columbus, Ph.B. 1899; the Sorbonne, Paris; Columbia University, New York, Ph.D. in romance languages 1905. Married John Redwood Fisher in 1907; one daughter and one son. Secretary, Horace Mann School, New York, 1902–05; relief worker in France, 1916–19. Member of the Vermont Board of Education, 1921–23. Recipient: Delta Kappa Gamma Society Educator's award, 1946; Women's National Book Association Skinner award, 1951; Sarah Josepha Hale Special award, 1958. D.Litt.: Middlebury College, Vermont, 1921; Dartmouth College, Hanover, New Hampshire, 1922; University of Vermont, Burlington, 1922; Columbia University, 1929; Northwestern University, Evanston, Illinois, 1931; Rockford College, Illinois, 1934; Ohio State University, 1935; Williams College, Williamstown, Massachusetts, 1935; Swarthmore College, Pennsylvania, 1935; University of Nebraska, Lincoln, 1936; Mount Holyoke College, South Hadley, Massachusetts, 1936; Marlboro College, Vermont, 1951; Smith College, Northampton, Massachusetts, 1954. *Died 9 November 1958.*

PUBLICATIONS FOR CHILDREN

Fiction

Understood Betsy, illustrated by Ada C. Williamson. New York,

Holt, 1917; London, Constable, 1922; as *Betsy,* London, Bodley Head, 1962; revised edition, New York, Holt Rinehart, 1972.

Made-to-Order Stories, illustrated by Dorothy P. Lathrop. New York, Harcourt Brace, 1925; London, Cape, 1926.

Tell Me a Story: A Book of Stories to Tell to Children, illustrated by Tibor Gergely. Lincoln, Nebraska, University Publishing Company, 1940; London, Mitre Press, n.d.

Nothing Ever Happens and How It Does, with Sarah N. Cleghorn, illustrated by Esther Boston Bristol. Boston, Beacon Press, 1940.

Something Old, Something New: Stories of People Who Are America, illustrated by Mary D. Shipman. Chicago, Scott Foresman, 1949.

Plays

A Family Talk about War. New York, Children's Crusade for Children, 1940.

Liberty and Union, with Sarah N. Cleghorn. New York, Book of the Month Club, 1940.

Other

What Shall We Do Now? Five Hundred Games and Pastimes, with others. New York, Stokes, 1907.

On a Rainy Day, with Sarah Fisher Scott. New York, A.S. Barnes, 1938.

In the City and on the Farm (reader), with Eunice Crabtree and Lu Verne Walker, illustrated by Terry Townsend. Lincoln, Nebraska, University Publishing Company, 1940; London, Mitre Press, n.d.

My First Book: A Reading Readiness Book, with Eunice Crabtree and Lu Verne Walker. Lincoln, Nebraska, University Publishing Company, 1940.

Runaway Toys (reader), with Eunice Crabtree and Lu Verne Walker, illustrated by Terry Townsend. Lincoln, Nebraska, University Publishing Company, 1940.

To School and Home Again (reader), with Eunice Crabtree and Lu Verne Walker, illustrated by Terry Townsend. Lincoln, Nebraska, University Publishing Company, 1940; London, Mitre Press, n.d.

More about the City and the Farm (reader), with Eunice Crabtree and Lu Verne Walker, illustrated by Terry Townsend. Lincoln, Nebraska, University Publishing Company, 1941.

Under the Roof (reader), with Eunice Crabtree and Lu Verne Walker, illustrated by Terry Townsend. Lincoln, Nebraska, University Publishing Company, 1941; London, Mitre Press, n.d.

Under the Sun (reader), with Eunice Crabtree and Lu Verne Walker, illustrated by Terry Townsend. Lincoln, Nebraska, University Publishing Company, 1941; London, Mitre Press, n.d.

Highroads and Byroads (reader), with Eunice Crabtree and Lu Verne Walker, illustrated by Mary Royt and George Buctel. Lincoln, Nebraska, University Publishing Company, 1948; London, Mitre Press, n.d.

Next Door (reader), with Eunice Crabtree and Lu Verne Walker. Lincoln, Nebraska, University Publishing Company, 1949.

Paul Revere and the Minute Men, illustrated by Norman Price. New York, Random House, 1950.

Our Independence and the Constitution, illustrated by Robert Doremus. New York, Random House, 1950.

A Fair World for All: The Meaning of the Declaration of Human Rights, illustrated by Jeanne Bendick. New York, McGraw Hill, 1952.

And Long Remember: Some Great Americans Who Have Helped Me, illustrated by Ezra Jack Keats. New York, McGraw Hill, 1959.

PUBLICATIONS FOR ADULTS

Novels

Gunhild: A Norwegian-American Episode. New York, Holt, 1907.

The Squirrel-Cage. New York, Holt, and London, Constable, 1912.

The Bent Twig. New York, Holt, 1915, and London, Constable, 1916.

The Brimming Cup. New York, Harcourt Brace, and London, Cape, 1921.

Rough-Hewn. New York, Harcourt Brace, 1922; London, Cape, 1923.

Raw Material. New York, Harcourt Brace, 1923.

The Home-Maker. New York, Harcourt Brace, and London, Cape, 1924.

Her Son's Wife. New York, Harcourt Brace, and London, Cape, 1926.

The Deepening Stream. New York, Harcourt Brace, and London, Cape, 1930.

Bonfire. New York, Harcourt Brace, and London, Cape, 1933.

Seasoned Timber. New York, Harcourt Brace, and London, Cape, 1939.

Short Stories

Hillsboro People, verse by Sarah N. Cleghorn. New York, Holt, 1915; London, Cape, 1923.

The Real Motive. New York, Holt, and London, Constable, 1916.

Home Fires in France. New York, Holt, 1918; London, Constable, 1919.

Basque People. New York, Harcourt Brace, and London, Cape, 1931.

Fables for Parents. New York, Harcourt Brace, 1937; London, Cape, 1938.

Four-Square. New York, Harcourt Brace, 1949.

A Harvest of Stories, from a Half Century of Writing. New York, Harcourt Brace, 1956.

Other

Emile Angier, Playwright-Moralist-Poet: A Study. Columbus, Ohio State University, 1899.

Corneille and Racine in England: A Study of the English Translations of the Two Corneilles and Racine, with Especial Reference to Their Presentation on the English Stage. New York, Columbia University Press, and London, Macmillan, 1904.

Elementary Composition, with George R. Carpenter. New York and London, Macmillan, 1906.

A Montessori Mother. New York, Holt, 1912; London, Constable, 1913; as *Montessori for Parents,* Cambridge, Massachusetts, Bentley, 1965.

The Montessori Manual, in Which Dr. Montessori's Teachings and Educational Occupations Are Arranged in Practical Exercises or Lessons.... Chicago, Richardson, 1913; London, Kegan Paul, 1914.

Mothers and Children. New York, Holt, 1914; London, Constable, 1915.

A Peep into the Educational Future. Buffalo, New York, Park School, 1915.

Self-Reliance: A...Discussion of Teaching Self-Reliance...to Modern Children. Indianapolis, Bobbs Merrill, 1916; London, Constable, 1917.

Fellow Captains!, with Sarah N. Cleghorn. New York, Holt, 1916.

The Day of Glory. New York, Holt, 1919.

What Grandmother Did Not Know. Boston, Pilgrim Press, 1922.

The French School at Middlebury. Middlebury, Vermont,

Middlebury College, 1923.

Why Stop Learning? New York, Harcourt Brace, 1927.

Learn or Perish (lecture). New York, Liveright, and London, Oxford University Press, 1930.

Vermont Summer Homes. Montpelier, Vermont Bureau of Publicity, 1932.

Moral Pushing and Pulling (lecture). Townsend, Vermont, Leland and Gray Seminary, 1933.

Tourists Accommodated: Some Scenes from Present Day Summer Life in Vermont. New York, Harcourt Brace, 1934.

Wells College Phi Beta Kappa Address. Aurora, New York, Wells College, 1936.

Another Night for America. New York, Harrison, 1942.

Our Young Folks. New York, Harcourt Brace, 1943.

American Portraits. New York, Holt, 1946.

Book Clubs (lecture). New York, New York Public Library, 1947.

Vermont Traditions: The Biography of an Outlook on Life. Boston, Little Brown, 1953.

Memories of My Home Town. Privately printed, 1956.

Memories of Arlington, Vermont. New York, Duell, 1957.

Editor, with Sidonie Matsner Grunberg, *Our Children: A Handbook for Parents.* New York, Viking Press, 1932.

Translator, *Life of Christ,* by Giovanni Papini. New York, Harcourt Brace, 1923.

Translator, *Work: What It Has Meant to Men Through the Ages,* by Adriano Tilgher. New York, Harcourt Brace, and London, Harrap, 1931.

*

Critical Studies: *Pebble in a Pool: The Widening Circles of Dorothy Canfield Fisher's Life* by Elizabeth Yates, New York, Dutton, 1958, as *The Lady from Vermont,* Brattleboro, Vermont, Stephen Greene Press, 1971; *Dorothy Canfield Fisher: A Biography* by Ida H. Washington, Shelburne, Vermont, New England Press, 1981.

*   *   *

Dorothy Canfield Fisher used her own background as a basis for her written work. Her unusual ability to create realistic tales was based on her own experiences as a girl and young woman. She was a professor's daughter, born in Kansas of strong New England heritage. The atmosphere of learning and the familiarity with her family history shaped her character. She had a privileged position from which to view her surroundings. Yet her Vermont values, strengthened and broadened by education and travel, helped mold an individual sensitive to the needs and aspirations of human beings.

Understood Betsy certainly reflects all of her powers of observation as well as her biases and interests. In this book a young girl, raised by two aunts in a midwestern city, must spend time with distant relatives in Vermont. Two prim, affluent, city-dwelling aunts have provided for their niece, but they have turned her into a dependent, nervous, and neurotic being. It is not a pleasant view of urban life. The Vermonters who take Betsy in are deftly characterized. Uncle Harry is a taciturn yet warm-hearted man the likes of whom are disappearing from New England. Cousin Ann and Aunt Abigail are the very embodiment of the stern, upright, resourceful, yet loving Yankee. In this new atmosphere, Betsy learns to adjust, adapt, and grow in self-reliance and warm personal relationships. One is impressed with the characters and background in the story: they are psychologically and historically accurate. The theme of learning to overcome problems and adjust has been accomplished without becoming overbearing or maudlin.

Made-to-Order Stories is more unusual. These stories originated in tales made up for Fisher's ten-year-old son who disliked trite and usual plots. All of the stories are based on diverse objects. For example, a ship's anchor, a library, a woodchuck, a spider, a bed, a doorknob and usually a little boy are woven into an exciting and unusual tale. Only when one reads through the innumerable stories can one fathom the incredible well of creativity from which she drew.

Fisher's stories have entertained children for generations. Her writing, of course, reflects the rural attitudes and values of her era as well as her respect for children and their intelligence. Her characters are always real and the author never talks down to her readers. Teachers and parents who want accurate American historical and cultural material in children's literature will want to see her work on every library shelf. It is interesting to note that *Understood Betsy,* with a setting that may be unfamiliar to a late-20th-century urban child, is most unusual. This book about a girl growing up in the early 20th century stresses Betsy's human rather than her feminine identity. The author's creativity, humor, insight, and observation have been used to construct tales which have held and will continue to hold the attention of children from 8 to 12.

—Dorothy D. Siles

————

FISK, Nicholas. Pseudonym for David Higginbottom. British. Born in London, 14 October 1923. Educated at Ardingly College, Sussex. Served in the Royal Air Force during World War II. Married Dorothy Antoinette Richold in 1949; twin daughters and two sons. Has worked as an actor, journalist, musician, editor, and publisher; former advertising creative director and consultant. Agent: Laura Cecil, 17 Alwyne Villas, London N1 2HG. Address: 59 Elstree Road, Bushey Heath, Hertfordshire WD2 3QX, England.

PUBLICATIONS FOR CHILDREN

Fiction

The Bouncers, illustrated by the author. London, Hamish Hamilton, 1964.

The Fast Green Car, illustrated by Bernard Wragg. London, Hamish Hamilton, 1965.

There's Something on the Roof!, illustrated by Dugald Macdougall. London, Hamish Hamilton, 1966.

Space Hostages. London, Hamish Hamilton, 1967; New York, Macmillan, 1969.

Trillions. London, Hamish Hamilton, 1971; New York, Pantheon, 1973.

Grinny. London, Heinemann, 1973; Nashville, Nelson, 1974.

High Way Home. London, Hamish Hamilton, 1973.

Emma Borrows a Cup of Sugar, illustrated by Carol Barker. London, Heinemann, 1973.

Little Green Spaceman, illustrated by Trevor Stubley. London, Heinemann, 1974.

The Witches of Wimmering, illustrated by Trevor Stubley. London, Pelham, 1976.

Time Trap. London, Gollancz, 1976.

Wheelie in the Stars. London, Heinemann, 1976.

Antigrav. London, Kestrel, 1978.

Escape from Splatterbang. London, Pelham, 1978; New York, Macmillan, 1979; as *Flamers,* London, Knight, 1979.

Monster Maker. London, Pelham, 1979; New York, Macmillan, 1980.

A Rag, A Bone, and a Hank of Hair. London, Kestrel, 1980; New York, Crown, 1982.
The Starstormer Saga (Starstormers, Sunburst, Catfang, Evil Eye, Volcano). London, Knight, 5 vols., 1980–83.
Leadfoot. London, Pelham, 1980.
Robot Revolt. London, Pelham, 1981.
Sweets from a Stranger and Other Science Fiction Stories, illustrated by David Barlow. London, Kestrel, 1982.
Snatched. London, Hodder and Stoughton, 1983.
On the Flip Side. London, Kestrel, 1983.
You Remember Me! London, Viking Kestrel, 1984; Boston, Hall, 1987.
Bonkers Clocks, illustrated by Colin West. London, Viking Kestrel, 1985.
Dark Sun, Bright Sun, illustrated by Brigid Marlin. London, Blackie, 1986.
Mindbenders. London, Viking Kestrel, 1987.
Backlash. London, Walker, 1987.
Living Fire. London, Corgi, 1987.
The Talking Car, illustrated by Ann John. London, Macmillan, 1988.
The Worm Charmers. London, Walker, 1989.

Other

Look at Cars, illustrated by the author. London, Hamish Hamilton, 1959; revised edition, London, Panther, 1969.
Look at Newspapers, illustrated by Eric Thomas. London, Hamish Hamilton, 1962.
Cars. London, Parrish, 1963.
The Young Man's Guide to Advertising. London, Hamish Hamilton, 1963.
Making Music, illustrated by Donald Green. London, Joseph, 1966; Boston, Crescendo, 1969.
Lindbergh the Lone Flier, illustrated by Raymond Briggs. London, Hamish Hamilton, and New York, Coward McCann, 1968.
Richthofen the Red Baron, illustrated by Raymond Briggs. London, Hamish Hamilton, and New York, Coward McCann, 1968.

*

Illustrator: *A Fishy Tale* by Beryl Cooke, 1957; *Look at Aircraft* by Sir Philip Joubert de la Ferte, 1960; *The Bear Who Was Too Big* by Lettice Cooper, 1963; *Tea with Mr. Timothy* by Geoffrey Morgan, 1966; *Menuhin's House of Music* by Eric Fenby, 1969; *Skiffy* by William Mayne, 1972.

*   *   *

Nicholas Fisk caters for children bred on television. Much of his work ends up on television, like Jim Hensen's 1989 film of *Monster Maker.* His style is punchy and to the point as you might expect from a man who once commuted to London on his motorbike to head the creative department of a leading printing and publishing firm. Ex RAF, occasional jazz musician, lecturer, illustrator, and photographer, Fisk understands and relishes today's computerised world, its pressures and promises. When he writes his children's books he draws extensively on his technical knowledge. He subscribes to the convention that children identify best with other children, but he makes few concessions to a child readership in his range of vocabulary and the sophistication of his ideas. He says that it is television that has made this possible. Today's children have been brought up on the conventions of flashback and fast cutting, so they understand the equivalent tricks he employs in his writing.

It is Fisk's particular contribution to take something ordinary and develop it into something quite extraordinary; the salvaged motorbike in *Wheelie in the Stars* becomes a symbol of freedom and individuality; the old lady in *Grinny* turns out to be a sinister robot from outer space. In his essay in *The Thorny Paradise* (edited by Edward Blishen, 1975) he writes: "How much more exciting the microscope's or telescope's viewpoint than one's own. How much more interesting the possibility than the fact..." This attitude has evolved over the years—he started by writing realistic novels like *The Bouncers* and *The Fast Green Car,* drawing affectionately and humorously on his own experience of family life.

Then in 1967 came *Space Hostages.* The story follows the fortunes of a group of children hijacked in a spaceship by a fanatical, dying airman. Like their counterparts in *Lord of the Flies,* they are forced to sort out their pecking order *in extremis.* It was Fisk's first science-fiction offering, and it made an immediate impact. He continued to experiment with different kinds of children's books. Within a year of each other he produced *Grinny; High Way Home,* a practical account of three adolescents shipwrecked on a remote island who make their way back to civilisation by constructing an air balloon; and *Emma Borrows a Cup of Sugar,* a wry nursery tale. But by the end of the 1970's he was specialising more and more in science-fiction novels like *Time Trap,* set in a future when the worst fears of the environmentalists have been realised. He continues to develop his science-fiction ideas by suggesting new possibilities for everyday objects. *A Rag, A Bone, and a Hank of Hair* is about cloning; *The Starstormer Saga* is about children who, bored with life on a decrepit Earth, try to join their parents Out There by building their own spaceship from junk components in the local scrapyard. In *Mindbenders* a brother and sister acquire mind-over-matter powers. This is not a Uri Geller trick. They really can will glass to smash. But their power takes on frightening dimensions when a present of a formicarium accidentally breaks. *Sweets from a Stranger* and *Living Fire* are collections of short stories, similarly inspired.

Fisk is prolific. His characters are mostly stereotypes but his plots are inexhaustibly original and thought-provoking. In *You Remember Me!,* the chilling sequel to *Grinny,* he utilises familiar aspects of malaise in contemporary society—hooliganism, cult worship, and political apathy. One of his own favourites is *Backlash,* about a manufactured, almost-human princess on another planet. A most entertaining writer, Fisk could be described as the Huxley-Wyndham-Golding of children's literature scaled but not watered down.

—Joy Whitby

———

FITZGERALD, John D(ennis). American. Born in Utah, in 1906. Worked as a journalist and musician. *Died 21 May 1988.*

PUBLICATIONS FOR CHILDREN (illustrated by the author)

Fiction (Great Brain series illustrated by Mercer Mayer)

The Great Brain. New York, Dial Press, 1967; London, Dent, 1969.
More Adventures of the Great Brain. New York, Dial Press, 1969; London, Dent, 1972.
Me and My Little Brain. New York, Dial Press, 1971; London, Dent, 1974.
The Great Brain at the Academy. New York, Dial Press, 1972.
The Great Brain Reforms. New York, Dial Press, 1973.
Brave Buffalo Fighter (Waditaka Tatanka Kisisohitka), illustrated by John Livesay. Independence, Missouri, Independence Press,

1973.
Private Eye.   Nashville, Nelson, 1974.
The Return of the Great Brain.   New York, Dial Press, 1974.
The Great Brain Does It Again.   New York, Dial Press, 1975; London, Dent, 1976.

PUBLICATIONS FOR ADULTS

Novels

Papa Married a Mormon.   Englewood Cliffs, New Jersey, Prentice Hall, 1955; London, W.H. Allen, 1956.
Mamma's Boarding House.   Englewood Cliffs, New Jersey, Prentice Hall, and London, W.H. Allen, 1958.
Uncle Will and the Fitzgerald Curse.   Indianapolis, Bobbs Merrill, 1961; London, W. H. Allen, 1962.

Other

The Professional Story Writer and His Art, with Robert C. Meredith. New York, Crowell, 1963.
Structuring Your Novel: From Basic Idea to Finished Manuscript, with Robert C. Meredith.   New York, Barnes and Noble, 1972.

*

Manuscript Collection: Kerlan Collection, University of Minnesota, Minneapolis.

*   *   *

The Great Brain series, for which John D. Fitzgerald is best known, focuses on the lives—part fictional, part real—of the Fitzgerald family in southern Utah between 1896 and 1899. The main characters are John D. and Tom D. Fitzgerald, aged seven and 10 respectively at the beginning of the series. John is the narrator, but it is his brother Tom's activities as the Great Brain which provide most of the interest and plot action.

The genesis of the series lies in the real John D. Fitzgerald's origins and childhood, detailed in his early biographical novel *Papa Married a Mormon.* Indeed, much of the second half of *Papa* recounts various real-life exploits of the Great Brain and family. In tone, style, phraseology, and ethics these tales are very similar to those in the subsequent works of fiction, but there are also some important differences: for example, Fitzgerald's real-life sister, Katie, and his Uncle Will and Aunt Queenie (a former saloon owner and dance-hall girl), though very prominent in the family history, have no place in the children's novels; even more striking, the real Tom, unlike his brothers, became a Mormon, attended a Mormon, not a Catholic, academy, and eventually (surprise!) went to the Orient as a Mormon missionary.

However, it is the children's books which are the most important works, and they show Fitzgerald's creativity transcending autobiography and reaching into the realms of the tall tale and the American myth. Typically, in the fiction, Tom, stimulated by a particular situation to use his Great Brain, develops an ingenious scheme or idea and recruits J.D. as his assistant (frequently to J.D.'s at least partial disadvantage). Sometimes Tom will tackle a community problem (the Alkali Flats Stock Swindle, the Adenville Bank Robbery). Sometimes he'll provide a service (the education of Britches Dotty, the Americanizing of a Greek immigrant boy). Sometimes he'll con his companions into accepting what amount to sure bets on his part (the Magnetic Stick Swindle, the Tin Can Swindle). And, almost always, he is on watch for the opportunity to make a profit from the situation via rewards, pay for services rendered, kickbacks,

and outright con-artist cheating.

J.D. describes the problem as Tom's Great Brain plus his money-loving heart, but the reality is a bit more subtle than this. As events prove time and again, the problem is not really Tom's Great Brain but, instead, the conflict within his heart between, on the one hand, the money-loving impulse (self-interest and perhaps, in a larger metaphor, the capitalist element in American society) and, on the other hand, the ethical sense, compassion for one's fellow man, the kind of cooperative neighbourliness which did much to build American society. This conflict is the key to Tom's character. His dilemma is not brain versus heart but rather the uses to which the heart, motivated two conflicting ways, puts the powers of his brain. Thus, in many instances, Tom's sheer conniving impulse, his pride, and his desire to make a profit bring his brain into play with these goals alone in mind. Yet in other instances his brain is harnessed not primarily by the need for profit but instead by compassion: two good instances are his rehabilitation (with fee refunded) of one-legged Andy Anderson and his organization of a funeral for Old Butch, a mongrel loved by the dogless children. Then of course there are the various times both impulses work together to benefit both society and Tom himself; for example, solving various robberies and finding two boys lost in a labyrinthine cave. This is as it should be in American society, and indeed the books in many ways are quintessentially American: the profit motive and the ethic of helpfulness mutually reinforcing one another, all held together under the aegis of the democratic ideal, best exemplified in the story of the starving Paiute Indians in the seventh book. Here, conviction of the rightness of the American ideal leads Tom to write to the President when he feels that ideal is being violated. And, by exercising this very basic American concept of free speech to call for redress of grievances he in fact achieves just that, a redress of Indian grievances and a cleansing of a slightly corrupt system. Right triumphs here, and it is because of Tom's ethical values, his intelligence (his Great Brain), and his self-confident willingness to act.

The books are all of a kind, with little to separate one from its fellows. Though somewhat episodic, they yet retain one or more narrative threads integrating each book and connecting the series as a whole. As individual works, probably the most satisfactory overall are *The Great Brain* and *More Adventures of the Great Brain,* while *Me and My Little Brain*—though still a good read—is the least humorous and therefore least satisfactory.

The strengths of the series are its portrayal of close-knit family and community life in the late 19th-century American west, its ecumenical aspects, its very American value system, and its humour—deriving partly from the American tradition of the tall tale and partly from a form of dramatic irony: the contrast between J.D.'s over-naive attitude in the stories and the reader's larger perspective. In addition, Fitzgerald treats childhood with respect, as an arena of life where good and evil are present and where real choices must be made as part of the growing-up process, but also an arena where courage, intelligence, and ethical action, in the end, prevail.

—John Robert Sorfleet

———

FITZHUGH, Louise.   American.   Born in Memphis, Tennessee, 5 October 1928. Educated at Hutchison School, Memphis; Southwestern College, Memphis; Florida Seminary College, Lakeland; New York University School of Education; Bard College, Annandale-on-Hudson, New York; Art Students' League, New York; Cooper Union, New York. Recipient: Children's Rights Workshop Other award, 1976. *Died 19 November 1974.*

PUBLICATIONS FOR CHILDREN (illustrated by the author)

Fiction

Harriet the Spy. New York, Harper, 1964; London, Gollancz, 1974.
The Long Secret. New York, Harper, 1965; London, Gollancz, 1975.
Bang, Bang, You're Dead, with Sandra Scoppettone. New York, Harper, 1969.
Nobody's Family Is Going to Change. New York, Farrar Straus, 1974; London, Gollancz, 1976.
I Am Five. New York, Delacorte Press, 1978.
Sport. New York, Delacorte Press, 1979.
I Am Three, illustrated by Susanna Natti. New York, Delacorte Press, 1982.
I Am Four, illustrated by Susan Bonners. New York, Delacorte Press, 1982.

*

Illustrator: *Suzuki Beane* by Sandra Scoppettone, 1961.

*   *   *

During her brief career as a children's writer Louise Fitzhugh was perhaps most well known for creating memorable and psychologically realistic characterizations of upper-middle-class urban children. Zena Sutherland called *Harriet the Spy* a "milestone" in children's literature because of the power with which Fitzhugh reveals the emotional anguish of the contemporary American child. Other critics agree that the book's artistry makes it a masterpiece. At her best, certainly, Fitzhugh created a moving vision of lonely intelligent urban children caught in the complexities of modern life and fragmented families, thrown painfully upon their own emotional resources.

In *Harriet the Spy* Fitzhugh delineates the character of a highly intelligent and imaginative child living in an affluent home. Though imaginative and resourceful, Harriet is nevertheless lonely; to assuage her insecurities, she leads an obsessively regimented existence: she writes compulsively in her "spy" notebook; she eats only tomato sandwiches at precisely the same time each day; she insists upon cake and milk on the dot each day after school. Fitzhugh makes it clear almost at once that Harriet is misusing her talent for writing by spying on others and by writing unkind remarks about her friends. Yet Harriet has no one to offer real guidance to her.

Harriet's father is a highly pressured television executive, who is too exhausted at the end of the day to do anything but sip martinis and slump in front of the television. Her mother is preoccupied with social activities and asks Harriet only the most inane questions about school life. Harriet's teachers are apparently oblivious to her obvious talent for writing and her imagination; they give her an appallingly unimaginative role in the school Thanksgiving play, that of an onion. Only Harriet's nurse, "Ole Golly," understands anything about the inner life of this vibrant, intelligent child. Yet Ole Golly is herself not entirely emotionally whole. In response to Harriet's incessant questions, her voracious need to know everything, Ole Golly can only quote in pedantic fashion from her enormous store of reading— everything from Dostoevsky to Emerson. Sometimes Ole Golly's continual quoting irritates Harriet, who wishes that she "would just shut up."

Yet the nurse is Harriet's lifeline. When Ole Golly marries Mr. Waldenstein, Harriet's emotional problems began to mount. When her friends discover her notebook and the unkind remarks she has written about them, they give her the silent treatment, and the notebook is taken away from her. When the notebook is removed, Harriet no longer possesses the smallest stay against confusion. She

rapidly declines into an emotional breakdown. Finally, psychotherapy, a letter from Ole Golly reminding Harriet that the purpose of writing is "to put love in the world, not to use against your friends," and a job on the school paper help to make Harriet whole again.

In some respects Harriet's character reminds the reader of such conventional naughty, imaginative, high-spirited children as Twain's Tom Sawyer. Such children seem to realize their imaginative and creative potentiality most fully apart from the intrusion of adults. Yet such a vision of childhood assumes a safe and secure home and community. Harriet's isolation from adults conveys a sense of painful alienation, not joyous anarchy. *Harriet the Spy,* despite its delightful characterizations and humorous dialogue, shocks the reader with its insight into the dreadful freedom of contemporary children.

The Long Secret is ostensibly a sequel to *Harriet the Spy* but actually centers upon the character of shy, wealthy Beth Ellen Hansen. Beth Ellen and Harriet both spend their summers in Water Mill, New York. Two events bring Beth Ellen's smoldering emotional problems to a crisis. First, Harriet is determined to track down the notewriter who has been leaving shocking notes around town (a grocery store clerk receives the message "Jesus hates you"). At the same time Beth Ellen discovers that her wealthy, vain, and spoiled mother, Zeebey, and her equally shallow husband, Wallace, are coming to visit her for the first time since she was a small child. As a counterpoint to the inane and trivial socializing of the idle rich, Fitzhugh creates an unlikely family of religious fanatics from Mississippi. Mama Jenkins, the mother of this family, is making her fortune manufacturing toe medicine from watermelons. Fitzhugh is clearly interested in Mama Jenkins's capacity to blend her religious doctrine with her greed for money. The purpose of this family in the fabric of the novel remains ambiguous, although it does lead Harriet to ask her father some hard religious questions. In the denouement of *The Long Secret* Beth Ellen finally expresses her repressed anger towards her narcissistic mother and experiences emotional liberation, and Harriet figures out that Beth Ellen has written the notes, clearly as an outlet for her anger.

One of Fitzhugh's most disturbing novels (and in the minds of some readers, her best) is *Nobody's Family Is Going to Change.* In this novel Fitzhugh focuses upon 11-year old, overweight Emma Sheridan, the daughter of an ambitious middle-class black lawyer. Emma desperately wishes to become a lawyer and to win her father's approval. Her little brother, Willis, is a gifted dancer. Mrs. Sheridan exists in the shadow of her husband, a domineering patriarch, who dislikes Emma for her intelligence and her ambitions to be a lawyer. Likewise he harshly refuses to accept Willie's identity as a dancer. Emma tries many tactics to win her father's love; at one point she even joins the Children's Army to fight for children's rights. All of her attempts signally fail. In a riveting and shocking illumination, Emma recognizes the bitter fact that her father hates her, "that fathers and mothers don't change. It's up to us to change.... We have to stop trying to make them love us." Emma's painful insight perhaps strains credibility; yet the novel attests to Fitzhugh's tough-minded vision of the family. A family, she suggests unequivocally, may be a trap and a tomb, where children are doomed to shrink and to die rather than to grow. Despite the novel's dark implications, Emma's final word is triumphant and assertive. If the father cannot accept who she is, what her talents are, "That," she says emphatically, "is your problem."

Sport, published posthumously in 1979, centers upon Harriet's friend, Simon Rocque ("sport"). Despite its rather improbable plot, this novel features another memorable portrait of a tough child who survives because of his own resourcefulness and because of the support of his father and friends. The relationship between Sport and his father is moving and tender; Sport's growing love and acceptance of his new step-mother, Kate, is also convincingly presented.

Fitzhugh's picture book, *Bang, Bang, You're Dead,* was a controversial book prominently associated with the so-called "New Realism" in children's literature. Published in the Vietnam War era, the book conveyed a vehement message against the folly of war and violence. Part of the controversy over the book occurred because of its graphic language (including such expressions as "puke-face") and its graphic depiction of violence. In this book, the message overshadows everything else; the characters are barely developed.

Flannery O'Connor has written that to reach a morally blind audience, the writer must exaggerate and distort. Fitzhugh's works resonate with social consciousness and with just indignation against human selfishness, greed, and ignorance. She sometimes creates grotesque characterizations, apparently in an attempt to shock her readers into an awareness that middle-class, affluent children may be lost in the wilderness, the emotional and moral chaos of contemporary urban life. Fitzhugh's mastery in writing witty dialogue, her gift for creating memorable characters, and her moral honesty in relentlessly depicting psychologically realistic portraits of contemporary American children have earned for her a lasting place in children's literature.

—Anita Moss

FLACK, Marjorie. American. Born in Greenport, Long Island, New York, 23 October 1897. Educated at the Art Students' League, New York, 1918–20. Married 1) the artist Karl Larsson in 1919 (divorced 1940), one daughter; 2) the poet William Rose Benét in 1941 (died 1950). Art teacher, Bronxville, New York. *Died 29 August 1958.*

PUBLICATIONS FOR CHILDREN

Fiction (illustrated by the author)

Taktuk, An Arctic Boy, with Helen Lomen. New York, Doubleday, 1928; London, Lane, 1956.
All Around the Town. New York, Doubleday, 1929.
Angus and the Ducks. New York, Doubleday, 1930; London, Lane, 1933.
Angus and the Cat. New York, Doubleday, 1931; London, Lane, 1933.
Angus Lost. New York, Doubleday, 1932; London, Lane, 1933.
Ask Mr. Bear. New York, Macmillan, 1932.
The Story about Ping, illustrated by Kurt Wiese. New York, Viking Press, 1933; London, Lane, 1935.
Wag-Tail Bess. New York, Doubleday, 1933; as *Angus and Wag-Tail Bess,* London, Lane, 1935.
Tim Tadpole and the Great Bullfrog. New York, Doubleday, 1934.
Humphrey: One Hundred Years Along the Wayside with a Box Turtle. New York, Doubleday, 1934.
Christopher. New York, Scribner, 1935.
Topsy. New York, Doubleday, 1935; as *Angus and Topsy,* London, Lane, 1935.
Up in the Air, illustrated by Karl Larsson. New York, Macmillan, 1935.
Wait for William. Boston, Houghton Mifflin, 1935.
What to Do about Molly, illustrated by the author and Karl Larsson. Boston, Houghton Mifflin, 1936; London, Lane, 1938.
Willy Nilly. New York, Macmillan, 1936; London, Lane, 1939.
Lucky Little Lena. New York, Macmillan, 1937.
The Restless Robin. Boston, Houghton Mifflin, 1937.
Walter, The Lazy Mouse. New York, Doubleday, 1937; Edinburgh,

Chambers, 1964.
William and His Kitten. Boston, Houghton Mifflin, 1938; London, Lane, 1939.
Pedro, with Karl Larsson, illustrated by Larsson. New York, Macmillan, 1940.
The New Pet. New York, Doubleday, 1943; London, Lane, 1956.
I See a Kitty, illustrated by Hilma Larsson. New York, Doubleday, 1943.
The Boats on the River, illustrated by Jay Hyde Barnum. New York, Viking Press, 1946.

Verse

Adolphus; or, The Adopted Dolphin and the Pirate's Daughter, with William Rose Benét. Boston, Houghton Mifflin, 1941.
Away Goes Jonathan Wheeler, illustrated by Hilma Larsson. New York, Doubleday, 1944.

Other

Neighbors on the Hill, with Mabel O'Donnell, illustrated by Florence and Margaret Hoopes. Evanston, Illinois, Row Peterson, 1943.

*

Manuscript Collection: University of Oregon Library, Eugene.

Illustrator: *Knights, Goats, and Battleships* by Terry Strickland Colt, 1930; *Scamper, The Bunny Who Went to the White House,* 1934, and *Scamper's Christmas,* 1934, both by Anne Roosevelt Dall; *Here, There, and Everywhere,* 1936, and *All Together,* 1952, both by Dorothy Aldis; *The Country Bunny and the Little Gold Shoes* by DuBose Heyward, 1939; *A Black Velvet Story* by Dee Smith, 1940; *Olaf, Lofoten Fisherman* by Fru Constance Schram, 1940.

*　　*　　*

Marjorie Flack's picture books are good for reading aloud to small children. Angus is a Scottie dog who chases ducks, strongly objects to sharing his home with a cat, gets lost, and helps to overcome the excessive timidity of Bess the airedale and to solve the problems of the spaniel Topsy. Each simple story is illustrated with clear realistic line drawings and told with a good eye for the detail of a lively young dog's life. The young child will enjoy Angus's experiences as they are also his own: the "Things Which Come Apart" though clearly they shouldn't; the fascination of things on the other side of the hedge; the terrors of being lost; and the jealousy when a rival appears in the household. There is a comforting progression in the books, too; the alarums and excursions with the ducks in the first book are followed by later episodes in which the same ducks are routed by an older and more confident Angus. These stories are for under-fives; *The Story about Ping* is a favorite with five to six-year-olds. Ping is a duckling who lives on a Chinese boat on the Yangtze River. He runs away to escape punishment, but after a frightening day alone on the river returns thankfully to the safety of his wise-eyed boat, along with his father, mother, and all his other relations. This is a varied and entertaining story, with a touch of fantasy and the exotic, illustrated with bright, quaint, and intriguing pictures by Kurt Wiese.

Walter, The Lazy Mouse is a longer story for five to seven-year-olds. Walter is so lazy that he is perpetually out of phase with both home and school. Eventually, when his family forget his existence altogether and move house without him he finds refuge with a family of bullfrogs who are even more happy-go-lucky than himself. Rather perversely, he is so anxious to establish himself in their singularly unretentive memories that he becomes punctual, active, and hardworking, labouring at a more-than-usually thankless task of perpetually teaching these frogs what they don't need to know and will inevitably forget. The illogicality of this teacher's nightmare, however, will not be apparent or important to the child reader, for whom the amusing detail of Walter's efforts at swimming and furniture-making and his wholly delightful first encounter with the chorus of frogs will make this a memorable tale.

Taktuk, An Arctic Boy, written in collaboration with Helen Lomen, is a very different kind of book. It gives an informative picture of the life of a ten-year-old Eskimo boy, but though the detail is good and the story simply told, the tone is a little condescending, and amid the welter of information and the rather wooden prose the Eskimo family never comes alive. It is a useful rather than an enthralling book.

—Winifred Whitehead

FLEISCHMAN, Paul. American. Born in Monterey, California, 5 September 1952; son of Sid Fleischman, *q.v.* Educated at the University of California, Berkeley, 1970–72; University of New Mexico, Albuquerque, 1975–77, B. A. in university studies 1977. Married Becky Mojica in 1978. Has worked as janitor, bagel baker, bookstore clerk, and proofreader. Recipient: American Library Association Newbery Medal, 1989. Address: 855 Marino Pines Road, Pacific Grove, California 93950, U.S.A.

PUBLICATIONS FOR CHILDREN

Fiction

The Birthday Tree, illustrated by Marcia Sewall. New York, Harper, 1979.
The Half-a-Moon Inn, illustrated by Kathy Jacobi. New York, Harper, 1980.
Graven Images: Three Stories, illustrated by Andrew Glass. New York, Harper, 1982.
Animal Hedge, illustrated by Lydia Dabcovich. New York, Dutton, 1983.
Finzel the Farsighted, illustrated by Marcia Sewall. New York, Dutton, 1983.
Path of the Pale Horse. New York, Harper, 1983.
Phoebe Danger, Detective, in the Case of the Two-Minute Cough, illustrated by Margot Apple. Boston, Houghton Mifflin, 1983.
Coming-and-Going Men: Four Tales of Itinerants, illustrated by Randy Gaul. New York, Harper, 1985.
Rear-View Mirrors. New York, Harper, 1986.
Rondo in C, illustrated by Janet Wentworth. New York, Harper, 1988.

Verse

I Am Phoenix: Poems for Two Voices, illustrated by Ken Nutt. New York, Harper, 1985.
Joyful Noise: Poems for Two Voices, illustrated by Eric Beddows. New York, Harper, 1988.

* * *

Remarkable versatility distinguishes Paul Fleischman's current contribution to children's literature. At present his body of work, bookended with two picture books, includes two collections of short stories, novels of intrigue and suspense for young readers, a young

adult novel, and two extraordinary, groundbreaking collections of poetry. What binds all these works together is Fleischman's profound sense of the power of sound. Fleischman claims had he the talent he would have written music; his readers know he has done precisely that. All his books are truly constructed with attention to sound. Yet sound is ever the handmaiden of sense: we are first drawn into a story, then we experience a heightening of that story through the sensual use of language. Fleischman acknowledges the roots of his education in sound: his father Sid Fleischman read aloud his own rollicking tales rich in aural pleasures, and the Fleischman family all played musical instruments. *Rondo in C* brings together Fleischman's love of music and literature. A young girl's recital of Beethoven's piece evokes different memories in each member of the audience, and Fleischman uses the nostalgic occasion to create poetry in which rhythm and rhyme combine with linguistic devices to speak for that "lovely piece."

His "metrical prose," resonating with this same aural element, tells visually exciting tales. To read his *Graven Images* is to be treated to three imaginative stories whose mysteries are all experienced through various actual sculpted images. In his first tale, "The Binnacle Boy," a life-sized carving of a sailor boy is the sole witness aboard ship of the death of the entire crew. Harboring the secret of how the crew died, the Binnacle boy becomes the townspeople's chosen repository for their own secrets. A mute servant girl who communicates solely by lipreading learns the awful circumstances of the crew's death when that truth is revealed to the Binnacle boy. His other collection of tales, *Coming-and-Going Men,* extends his imaginative scope. Here the four tales are grounded in the same geography and time as four different traveling men pass through New Canaan, Vermont in 1800. Seasonal changes echo more significant changes as the men both affect and are affected by the characters and events in the town. Ironic twists and haunted turnings in both collections evoke Hawthorne and Poe, earlier New England masters of the short story.

The Half-a-Moon Inn and *Path of the Pale Horse* present two righteous youthful protagonists whose dramatic journeys in the name of good bring them up against villainy of all sorts. The hero of *Half-a-Moon Inn,* another mute character, communicates by writing on a chalkboard. The strength of Fleischman's attention to sound is manifest also in his conscious absence of sound. Sobriety is tempered here as elsewhere with wry humor and colorful characters.

All his crafted stories brim with images of crows and mosquitoes, whippoorwills and butterflies. Birds and insects with their various noises punctuate his tales. In his earliest *The Birthday Tree,* a meadowlark and a gull nesting in a tree serve as harbingers to parents who look to the tree for signs of their son's wellbeing. The protagonist father in *Rear-View Mirrors* is an obsessive stalker and collector of moths and butterflies; even a lighthearted detective story features a young binocular birdwatcher.

His fascination with the sound and sights of birds and insects culminates in his two companion poetry books, *I Am Phoenix* and *Joyful Noise,* in which Fleischman the musician orchestrates his singular creative vision. Here he invents lyrical poems "to be read aloud by two readers at once, one taking the lefthand part, the other the righthand part" with both parts "meshing as in a musical duet." The 1989 Newbery winner, *Joyful Noise* features 14 different insects, each which becomes a personality through the force of Fleischman's language. The poems vary appropriately in tone and treatment, from the lighthearted "Book Lice" in which two book lice maintain a meaningful relationship in spite of different reading tastes, to the poignant final "Chrysalis Diary" in whose final entry on March 28 are the nascent butterfly's dreams of flying. Fleischman takes advantage of all the techniques of artful writing to which he is so apparently dedicated: alliteration, figurative language, rhythm, and meter. The patterned results are incandescent: a broadening and deepening of our knowledge and appreciation of the worlds of birds and insects as we experience them through participation.

—Susan P. Bloom

FLEISCHMAN, (Albert) Sid(ney). Has also written as Carl March. American. Born in Brooklyn, New York, 16 March 1920. Educated at San Diego State College, B.A. 1949. Served in the United States Naval Reserve, 1941–45. Married Betty Taylor in 1942; two daughters and one son, Paul Fleischman, *q.v.* Magician in vaudeville and night clubs, 1938–41; reporter, San Diego *Daily Journal,* 1949–50; associate editor, *Point* magazine, San Diego, 1950–51. Recipient: Western Writers of America Spur award, 1964; George G. Stone Center for Children's Books award, 1972; Society of Children's Book Writers Golden Kite award, 1974; Boston *Globe-Horn Book* award, 1979; American Library Association Newbery Medal, 1987. Agent: Bill Berger Associates, 444 East 58th Street, New York, New York 10022. Address: 305 Tenth Street, Santa Monica, California 90402, U.S.A.

PUBLICATIONS FOR CHILDREN

Fiction

Mr. Mysterious and Company. Boston, Little Brown, 1962; London, Hutchinson, 1963.
By the Great Horn Spoon!, illustrated by Eric von Schmidt. Boston, Little Brown, 1963; London, Hamish Hamilton, 1965; as *Bullwhip Griffin,* New York, Avon, 1967.
The Ghost in the Noonday Sun, illustrated by Warren Chappell. Boston, Little Brown, 1965; London, Hamish Hamilton, 1966.
McBroom Tells the Truth, illustrated by Kurt Werth. New York, Norton, 1966.
Chancy and the Grand Rascal, illustrated by Eric von Schmidt. Boston, Little Brown, 1966; London, Hamish Hamilton, 1967.
McBroom and the Big Wind, illustrated by Kurt Werth. New York, Norton, 1967.
McBroom's Ear, illustrated by Kurt Werth. New York, Norton, 1969.
Longbeard the Wizard, illustrated by Charles Bragg. Boston, Little Brown, 1970.
Jingo Django, illustrated by Eric von Schmidt. Boston, Little Brown, and London, Hamish Hamilton, 1971.
McBroom's Ghost, illustrated by Robert Frankenberg. New York, Grosset and Dunlap, 1971.
The Wooden Cat Man, illustrated by Jay Yang. Boston, Little Brown, 1972.
McBroom's Zoo, illustrated by Kurth Werth. New York, Grosset and Dunlap, 1972.
McBroom's Wonderful One-Acre Farm (includes *McBroom Tells the Truth, McBroom and the Big Wind, McBroom's Ghost*), illustrated by Quentin Blake. London, Chatto and Windus, 1972.
McBroom the Rainmaker, illustrated by Kurt Werth. New York, Grosset and Dunlap, 1973.
The Ghost on Saturday Night, illustrated by Eric von Schmidt. Boston, Little Brown, 1974; London, Heinemann, 1975.
McBroom Tells a Lie, illustrated by Walter Lorraine. Boston, Little Brown, 1976.
Here Comes McBroom (includes *McBroom Tells a Lie, McBroom the Rainmaker, McBroom's Zoo*), illustrated by Quentin Blake. London, Chatto and Windus, 1976.
Me and the Man on the Moon-Eyed Horse, illustrated by Eric von

Schmidt. Boston, Little Brown, 1977; as *The Man on the Moon-Eyed Horse,* London, Gollancz, 1980.
Kate's Secret Riddle Book, illustrated by Barbara Bottner. New York and London, Watts, 1977.
McBroom and the Beanstalk, illustrated by Walter Lorraine. Boston, Little Brown, 1978.
Jim Bridger's Alarm Clock and Other Tall Tales, illustrated by Eric von Schmidt. New York, Dutton, 1978.
Humbug Mountain, illustrated by Eric von Schmidt. Boston, Little Brown, 1978; London, Gollancz, 1980.
The Hey Hey Man, illustrated by Nadine Bernard Westcott. Boston, Little Brown, 1979.
McBroom and the Great Race, illustrated by Walter Lorraine. Boston, Little Brown, 1980; London, Chatto and Windus, 1981.
The Case of the Cackling Ghost, illustrated by Anthony Rao. New York, Random House, 1981.
The Case of the Flying Clock, illustrated by William Harmuth. New York, Random House, 1981.
The Case of Princess Tomorrow, illustrated by Bill Morrison. New York, Random House, 1981.
The Case of the Secret Message, illustrated by William Harmuth. New York, Random House, 1981.
The Case of the 264-Pound Burglar, illustrated by Bill Morrison. New York, Random House, 1982.
The Bloodhound Gang's Secret Code Book, illustrated by Bill Morrison. New York, Random House, 1983.
McBroom's Almanac, illustrated by Walter Lorraine. Boston, Little Brown, 1984.
The Whipping Boy, illustrated by Peter Sis. New York, Greenwillow, 1986; London, Methuen, 1988.
The Scarebird, illustrated by Peter Sis. New York, Greenwillow, 1988.

Other

Mr. Mysterious's Secrets of Magic, illustrated by Eric von Schmidt. Boston, Little Brown, 1975; as *Secrets of Magic,* London, Chatto and Windus, 1976.

PUBLICATIONS FOR ADULTS

Novels

The Straw Donkey Case. New York, Phoenix Press, 1948.
Murder's No Accident. New York, Phoenix Press, 1949.
Shanghai Flame. New York, Fawcett, 1951; London, Fawcett, 1957.
Look Behind You, Lady. New York, Fawcett, 1952; London, Muller, 1953; as *Chinese Crimson,* London, Jenkins, 1962.
Danger in Paradise. New York, Fawcett, 1953; London, Muller, 1954.
Counterspy Express. New York, Ace, 1954.
Malay Woman. New York, Fawcett, 1954; London, Fawcett, 1955; as *Malaya Manhunt,* London, Jenkins, 1965.
Blood Alley. New York, Fawcett, 1955; London, Fawcett, 1956.
Yellowleg. New York, Fawcett, and London, Muller, 1960.
The Venetian Blonde. New York, Fawcett, 1963; London, Muller, 1964.

Plays

Screenplays: *Blood Alley,* 1955; *Good-bye My Lady,* 1956; *Lafayette Escadrille,* with William A. Wellman, 1958; *The Deadly Companions,* 1961; *Scalawag,* 1972.

Other

Between Cocktails. N.p., Abbott Magic Company, 1939.
Magic Made Easy (as Carl March). N.p., Croydon, 1953.

*

Manuscript Collection: Kerlan Collection, University of Minnesota, Minneapolis.

Sid Fleischman comments:

While my books rarely draw upon direct personal experience, I catch ghostly glimpses of my presence on almost every page. The stories inevitably reveal my interests and enthusiasms—my taste for the comic in life, my love of adventure, the seductions (for me) of the 19th-century American frontier, and my enchantment with the folk speech of that period. Language is a wondrous toy and I have great literary fun with it.

Since I don't plot my stories in advance, the experience of writing a book is, for me, very much the same as reading a book. I rarely know what is going to happen next and have to sit at the typewriter to find out. My starting point is almost always a background, such as the California gold rush in *By the Great Horn Spoon!* or the age of piracy in *The Ghost in the Noonday Sun.* On other occasions I begin with an idea for a character: the magician in *Mr. Mysterious and Company,* for example, or a midwest teller of tall tales as in the McBroom stories.

*   *   *

The tall tale is a special branch of folklore. It has its own language, its own pacing, its own outrageous logic. But it is also tied to a specific place: rural America. Coming out of the European Munchausen tradition, the tall tale found a permanent home on the American frontier where it was frontier in spirit, style, and tone. The tall tale can still be found in its oral form in the rural southern and western United States. In its literary form it can be found, occasionally, in children's books.

Sid Fleischman comes neither from the south or west, nor from the country at all. He is a product of the urban East. Yet he has made the particular voice of the tall tale so much his own that, if any one author can be said to be master of the genre, it is he. His oddball characters include Chancy, so skinny he has to stand twice to cast a shadow; McBroom, who owns the richest one-acre farm in the world; Jingo Hawks, the biggest liar in Mrs. Duggart's Beneficent Orphan Home—and proud of it; the irrepressible Hey-Hey man; and hosts of others.

Fleischman's wit and style are deceptive. His flagrant humor disguises the fact that he is a careful craftsman who chooses each scene with infinite care and sets it down straight-facedly. He may be pulling your leg, but he does it with a pokerface. His slangy style, with its tall tale helpings of grandiloquence, hyperbole, and exaggeration, are the result of impeccable research. He fills looseleaf notebooks with data on names, phrases, places, all culled from period novels, newspapers, and other primary sources. For Fleischman, the tall tale is both a literary dialect and a literary folklore. He takes it seriously.

Fleischman's many novels combine adventure with history, humor with serious statement. But the stories themselves are told at such a breakneck pace that the reader is given little time to consider how finely drawn the strange characters are, how definitively rendered are the villains. Instead it seems, at first reading, that story is all. Nowhere does this craftsmanship, this use of language, this swiftness of pace show more clearly than in *Chancy and the Grand Rascal.* One part quest story, two parts braggadocio, it concerns the travels of young Chancy Dundee and his uncle (the grand rascal) by

foot, by raft, by train, by steamboat, and by will power through the U.S.A. as they look for the scattered remnants of their family. There are tall tales within tall tales, whoppers told offhandedly by Chancy, his Uncle Will, his sister Indiana, and others. And by the time the book is through, the reader has laughed a lot, learned a great deal about frontier life, and added some marvelous new/old words to his vocabulary like yawhawin', pineries, mudshoes, jayhawkers, and beeves.

Fleischman writes for television and has done riddle books, young mysteries, and adult westerns, but it is in the tall tale that he throws a shadow—singular and irresistible.

In 1986 Fleischman published *The Whipping Boy,* a novel that is more historical and less flamboyant than some of his tall tales. But his command of story is so strong, the characters so engaging, that the book won the Newbery Medal, a tribute not just to that one book, but to his highly original contributions to the literature of childhood, at least in this critic's opinion.

—Jane Yolen

———

FLORA, James (Royer). American. Born in Bellefontaine, Ohio, 25 January 1914. Educated at Urbana College, Ohio, 1931–33; Art Academy of Cincinnati, 1934–39. Married Jane Sinnickson in 1941; five children. Co-founding publisher, Little Man Press, Cincinnati, 1939–42; art director and sales promotion manager, Columbia Recording Corporation, New York and Bridgeport, Connecticut, 1942–50; lived in Mexico 1950–52; consultant art director and board member, Benwill Publishing Corporation, Boston, 1957–62; art director and board member, Computer Design Publishing Company, 1962–80. Freelance magazine illustrator, 1952–80. Address: St. James Place, Bell Island, Rowayton, Connecticut 06853, U.S.A.

PUBLICATIONS FOR CHILDREN (illustrated by the author)

Fiction

The Fabulous Firework Family. New York, Harcourt Brace, 1955.
The Day the Cow Sneezed. New York, Harcourt Brace, 1957.
Charlie Yup and His Snip-Snap Boys. New York, Harcourt Brace, 1959.
Leopold, The See-Through Crumbpicker. New York, Harcourt Brace, 1961.
Kangaroo for Christmas. New York, Harcourt Brace, 1962.
My Friend Charlie. New York, Harcourt Brace, 1964.
Grandpa's Farm: Four Tall Tales. New York, Harcourt Brace, 1965.
Sherwood Walks Home. New York, Harcourt Brace, 1966.
Fishing with Dad. New York, Harcourt Brace, 1967.
The Joking Man. New York, Harcourt Brace, 1968.
Little Hatchy Hen. New York, Harcourt Brace, 1969.
Pishtosh, Bullwash, and Wimple. New York, Atheneum, 1972.
Stewed Goose. New York, Atheneum, 1973.
The Great Green Turkey Creek Monster. New York, Atheneum, 1976.
Grandpa's Ghost Stories. New York, Atheneum, 1978.
Wanda and the Bumbly Wizard. New York, Atheneum, 1980.
Grandpa's Witched-Up Christmas. New York, Atheneum, 1982.

Plays

Screenplays (animated films): *The Fabulous Firework Family,* 1959;

Leopold, The See-Through Crumbpicker, 1972.

PUBLICATIONS FOR ADULTS

Other

New Orleans Wood Engravings in Portfolio. Cincinnati, Little Man Press, n.d.

*

Manuscript Collection: Kerlan Collection, University of Minnesota, Minneapolis.

Illustrator: *3 Fragments and a Story* by William Saroyan, 1939; *Murderpie,* 1939, *I'll Never Be the Same,* 1939, and *Gup,* 1942, all by Robert Lowry; *The Talking Dog and the Barking Man* by Elizabeth Seeman, 1960; *101 Words and How They Began,* 1979, and *101 More Words and How They Began,* 1980, both by Arthur Steckler.

James Flora comments:

Aside from my own personal pleasure in writing and illustrating for children my only aim is entertainment. I always try to write a bang-up good story that will intrigue a child and demonstrate how much fun reading can be. The process of learning to read is so protracted, difficult, and boring in our schools that many children find it distasteful and never learn at all.

I keep my work light and rollicking and my reward is the letters I get from children telling me how much they *enjoy reading* my books. To impart the joy of reading is the single thread that runs through all my stories.

*   *   *

Hyperbole, humor, action, and invention are hallmarks of James Flora's cumulative and tall tales and fanciful adventures. Elaborating on what might happen if a seed company sent the wrong order, a hen could hatch anything, or the North Pole was stolen, he lets his imagination run rampant. In *The Day the Cow Sneezed* the sneeze exposes a mouse, which eludes a cat, who claws a goat, and on and on until breathtaking rides involving a policeman's motorcycle, a steam roller, a Ferris wheel, and a truck loaded with fireworks, they roll—shooting rockets and all—onto a boat; whereupon the fireworks are extinguished and Fletcher, the boy protagonist, is summarily punished for allowing the cow to get chilled and wet. In *The Great Green Turkey Creek Monster* a Hooligan vine, which grows so fast "you had to run to keep ahead of it," rampages through Turkey Creek, its multitudinous tendrils invading town buildings. Causing chaos, confusion, and eventually consternation, it opens fireplugs to take a shower, pushes the garbage truck into the movie theater (patrons rush out exclaiming, "Hoo boy! What a stinky picture") and forces the school principal into the girl's room, eliciting the shocked pronouncement, *"and he isn't a girl."* Fun, funny, fast-paced, and exuberant, these stories show events and objects appealing out of control.

Flora loses control, however, in stories which ignore logic while building nonsense. In *Stewed Goose,* which smacks of animated cartoons, the action is frenetic rather than funny as a bear contrives endlessly to catch a goose that he could in reality snare with one swat of his paw. Similarly, in *The Joking Man,* the final revelation that the two boy protagonists are, in fact, the mysterious joking man, undermines the plot when there is no accounting for their ability to perform the impossible pranks. These books, like *Pishtosh, Bullwash, and*

Wimple and *My Friend Charlie,* have ⌐lot or characterization to sustain them; they rise and fall ⌐ ⌐ne invention and silliness concocted upon each page.

The most successful narratives such as *Little Hatchy Hen, Grandpa's Farm,* and *Grandpa's Ghost Stories,* with their emphasis on superlatives, invincibility, growth, and invention, are in the mode of traditional American folklore and benefit from its structure. Their conversational storytelling tone and direct authorial appeals, like "Did you ever hear…?" and "You don't believe…?," draw readers into the tall tales about the hen who is kidnapped by the world's champion chicken thief, and the farm where cornstalks grow so fast Grandpa can't chop them down because he can "never chop twice in the same place." The "too terrible to tell" ghost stories ghoulishly reek of "shrouds that smell like a toad's underwear," and promote "goosebumps in between…goosebumps."

At his best Flora communes with the roguish, playful qualities in children. His aim is to entertain; his method is boisterous, zany action and clever invention. His flat, stylized cartoon drawings animate and extend the hilarity even onto the title pages.

—Nancy C. Hammond

————

FOON, Dennis. American. Born in Detroit, Michigan, 18 November 1951. Educated at the University of Michigan, Ann Arbor (Hopwood award, 1972), 1969–73, B.A. (honors) in religious studies and creative writing 1973; University of British Columbia, Vancouver, 1973–75, M.F.A. in playwriting 1975. Married Jane Howard Baker in 1975 (divorced); one daughter. Instructor in Playwriting, University of British Columbia Centre for Continuing Education, 1974–79. Since 1975 co-founder and artistic director, Green Thumb Theatre for Young People, Vancouver. Playwright-in-residence, Young People's Theatre, Toronto, 1983–84. Canadian Vice-President, International Association of Theatres for Children and Youth, 1979–82. Recipient: *Writers Digest* award, 1973; Jesse award, for directing, 1984, 1985, 1986, 1987; Canadian Broadcasting Corporation award, 1985; British Theatre award, 1986; Chalmers award, 1987. Agent: Great North Artists Management, 350 Dupont Street, Toronto, Ontario M5R 1V9; or, Green Thumb Theatre, 1885 Venables, Vancouver, British Columbia V5L 2H6. Address: 647 East 12th Avenue, Vancouver, British Columbia V5T 2H7, Canada.

PUBLICATIONS FOR CHILDREN

Fiction

The Short Tree and the Bird That Could Not Sing, illustrated by John Bianchi. Vancouver, Douglas and McIntyre, 1986.

Plays

The Last Days of Paul Bunyan (puppet play; produced Vancouver, 1977). With *The Windigo,* Toronto, Playwrights, 1978.
Heracles (produced Vancouver, 1978). Vancouver, Talonbooks, 1978.
Raft Baby (produced Vancouver, 1978).
The Windigo (produced Vancouver, 1979; London, 1980). With *The Last Days of Paul Bunyan,* Toronto, Playwrights, 1978.
La Malice, Voyageur (produced Vancouver and Seattle, 1979).
The Hunchback of Notre Dame, adaptation of a novel by Victor Hugo (produced Vancouver, 1981). Toronto, Playwrights, 1983.

New Canadian Kid (produced Vancouver, 1981; London, 1985). Vancouver, Pulp Press, 1982.
Trummi Kaput, adaptation of the play by Volker Ludwig (produced Vancouver, 1982; New York, 1983). Published in *Canadian Theatre Review* (Toronto), Spring 1983.
Feeling Yes, Feeling No (produced Vancouver, 1982).
Skin (produced Vancouver, 1984; revised version, also director: produced Toronto, 1986). With *Liars,* Toronto, Playwrights, 1988.
Invisible Kids (also director: produced London, 1985).
Liars (produced Vancouver, 1986). With *Skin,* Toronto, Playwrights, 1988.
Bedtimes and Bullies, adaptation of a play by Volker Ludwig (also director: produced Toronto, 1987).
Mirror Game (also director: produced Quebec City, 1988).

Other

Am I the Only One? A Young People's Book about Sex Abuse, with Brenda Knight. Vancouver, Douglas and McIntyre, 1985.

PUBLICATIONS FOR ADULTS

Plays

Hotsy Totsy, with others (produced Vancouver, 1978).
Children's Eyes (produced Vancouver, 1983).
Afternoon Tea (produced Vancouver, 1986).
Zaydok (produced Vancouver, 1987; New York, 1988).

Screenplay: *Differences,* 1986.

Television Plays: *Boogeymen* and *Wheels* (both in *Lies from Lotusland* series), 1987.

*

Theatrical Activities:
Director: **Plays**—many of his own plays, and *Portrait of an Adult as a Young Kid* by John Carroll, Vancouver, 1980; *Schoolyard Games* by John Lazarus, Vancouver, 1981; *The Bittersweet Kid* by Peggy Thompson, Vancouver, 1982, and subsequent tours; *One Thousand Cranes* by Colin Thomas, Vancouver, 1983, and Pacific tour, 1985; *Not So Dumb* by John Lazarus, Vancouver, 1984, and Canadian tour, 1985; *Herot,* Adelaide, Australia, 1985; *Secrets of an Usherette* by Gordon Armstrong, Vancouver, 1986; *Nightlight* by John Lazarus, Vancouver, 1986; *One in a Million* by David Holman, Vancouver, 1987; *No Worries* by David Holman, Toronto, 1989.

Dennis Foon comments:
When I was growing up in Detroit I used to spend my summers in Algonquin Park, Ontario. The tranquility of those lakes and forests always served as an antidote to the rising racial tension I was experiencing in my home town. Some years later when I was invited to pursue my M.F.A. at the University of British Columbia I jumped at the chance. I hated Detroit, hated the fact that things had become so polarized, so far gone that I couldn't see an end to the social problems. Canada had always represented a kind of Mecca to me. I had always sworn I'd get here somehow.

When I finished my degree and we started Green Thumb Theatre, I had little idea in the beginning what theatre for young people could be. But very soon it became clear to me that theatre could be a way to communicate ideas, a way to work toward change.

By comparison with the violence and chaos in Detroit, Vancouver is a very calm and sensible place. But it is clear that the seeds of many of the same problems that I experienced in Detroit are pervasive in Canada. To me they are like St. Exupery's baobab seeds: if we ignore them, they will destroy us.

I believe in the possibility for change and that it is up to each of us to make it happen, both inside and outside. My plays and other writings are a vote for the future.

*   *   *

The written products of Dennis Foon, playwright and director of theatre for children and young adults, have been both consistent and changing over the last decade. His plays, which generally contain few characters and require little elaborate staging, are available to small companies and can reach wide audiences. Foon's subject matter has undergone transformation: many of his early plays are plot- or character-oriented, but more recently they have focused on contemporary social issues.

Among the "story" plays is *The Last Days of Paul Bunyan,* a puppet play in which Paul, tall tale hero, is told "The thing you cannot fight has come." While seeking this thing Paul overcomes other challenges but, unable to defeat the reality that "the big trees are gone" and his days as a lumberjack are over, Paul and his blue ox Babe go to the Land of Tall Tales.

An Ojibwa Indian belief regarding a spirit, the Windigo, which drives starving hunters mad and leads them into cannibalism, is the basis for *The Windigo.* Red Bird, a shaman, wants Sweet Grass to be his wife. When she chooses Half Sky instead, Red Bird places a curse on him. During a harsh winter, the pregnant Red Bird risks murder by a starving Half Sky unless he defeats the Windigo.

Raft Baby is a dramatized version of an event that ostensibly happened in British Columbia in the late 19th century. As a white man and his Blackfoot wife are dying they place their infant daughter on a raft which they float down the Peace River. By chance the woman's brother rescues the child but, not recognizing her parentage, gives her to a couple to raise. Some two decades later, the brother recovers his brother-in-law's diary, realizes the child's identity, and searches for his niece, discovering her on her wedding day.

The Hunchback of Notre Dame provides the essential storyline around the relationships of Esmerelda, Frollo, Quasimodo, Phoebus, and Gringoire. *Heracles,* which commences following the death of the mythical Greek hero of enormous strength, reviews the events leading up to Heracles's death caused by his donning the poisoned shirt given him by his wife. *Bedtimes and Bullies* examines children's fears and the quality of communication between parents and children.

Probably the most recognized of Foon's plays treating social issues is *New Canadian Kid,* which reflects the immigrant experience, especially its impact on children. Audiences can participate in what a new Canadian might experience because Nick, the boy from Homeland, speaks English while the Canadian characters speak "gibberish." Anxious about lost friends and learning a new language, Nick is reassured by his mother that "It won't even take a week." Nick interacts principally with Mug and Mench. Focusing on Nick's differences, Mug mocks Nick's smelly food and inability to speak "English." Mench, a girl, supports Nick and becomes his first Canadian friend.

Mirror Game portrays the destructive cycle of child and spouse abuse. Luke, physically abused by his father, becomes an abuser of his girlfriend Sara. She in turn allows the mistreatment because she observes her mother's submission to her live-in boyfriend's battering. Foon shows that appearances are not reality. Luke and Sara, "the beautiful people" on the outside, are tormented by inner blemishes; Bob and Maggie, the seemingly "normal kids" with exterior imperfections of zits and excess weight, have been emotionally abused by parents and carry into relationships the effects of diminished self-respect. By the play's end all but Luke have apparently broken the cycle.

As five preteens play in *Invisible Kids,* listeners learn that Georgie's parents are saving money to bring her older sister from Jamaica. Achieving the needed amount, the family discovers their daughter must wait two further years for her papers. The children conclude the delay is because "we're the wrong colour" since European applicants are delayed but months while Asians, South Americans, and Africans wait years. Deciding they are neither powerless nor invisible, the children create a petition demanding equality of treatment and send one copy to the prime minister and another to a television network since politicians "won't listen to us. We're just kids."

Skin and *Liars* are published together. *Skin* deals with racial prejudice, especially its expression within schools. A Canadian-born girl of West Indian parents hears a teacher categorizing her as lazy and capable of no higher aspirations than vocational school. Fearing rejection of her heritage, Bombay-born Phiroza describes herself as Persian to a boy she likes. Tuan, a Vietnamese boatperson, is physically harassed in the halls and loses his part-time job because of being Asian. In *Liars* a pair of 16-year-olds, Jace, a headbanger, and Lenny, a preppy girl, share a problem—parental alcoholism. Jace's father is a physically abusive drunk while Lenny's mother is the protected, hidden alcoholic. Initially Jace and Lenny provide mutual emotional support, but Jace eventually escapes into drugs.

In addition to his plays Foon has co-edited a book and authored a picture book. With Brenda Knight, Foon created *Am I the Only One? A Young People's Book about Sex Abuse.* Some two dozen boys and girls, in prose, poetry, and art, powerfully share their experiences of being abused by parents, relatives, babysitters, and neighbors. As the title implies, the contents attempt to reassure abused readers they are not alone in having experienced sexual abuse, and the text offers suggestions for obtaining help. The theme of friendship, which recurs in many of Foon's plays, appears in *The Short Tree and the Bird That Could Not Sing.* Being short, the tree could not see the world's goings-on. A bird with an atrocious voice begins roosting in the tree's branches and becomes the tree's eyes to the wider world. Their friendship grows until autumn migration when the tree is convinced he will lose his friend forever, but spring brings the bird back. While the text carries the storyline, John Bianchi's illustrations reinforce the book's emotions.

Perhaps it is the fate of playwrights to have their names forgotten because, while audiences see plays and may remember their titles, they do not carry away a script bearing the playwright's name. Foon's plays have won awards and been performed internationally, but in Canada his name might first be connected to one of his books rather than to his principal literary vehicle, plays.

—David H. Jenkinson

FORBES, Esther. American. Born in Westborough, Massachusetts, 28 June 1891. Educated at Bradford Junior College, graduated 1912; University of Wisconsin, Madison, 1916–18. Married Albert Learned Hoskins in 1926 (divorced 1933). Staff member, Houghton Mifflin Company, publishers, Boston, 1920–26, 1942–46. Recipient: Pulitzer prize, for history, 1943; American Library Association Newbery Medal, 1944. Litt.D.: Clark University, Worcester, Massachusetts, 1943; University of Maine, Orono, 1943; University of Wisconsin, Madison, 1949; Northeastern University, Boston, 1949; Wellesley College, Massachusetts, 1959; LL.D.: Tufts University, Medford, Massachusetts. Member, American Academy of Arts and Sciences. *Died 12 August 1967.*

PUBLICATIONS FOR CHILDREN

Fiction

Johnny Tremain, illustrated by Lynd Ward. Boston, Houghton Mifflin, 1943; London, Chatto and Windus, 1944.

Other

America's Paul Revere, illustrated by Lynd Ward. Boston, Houghton Mifflin, 1946.

PUBLICATIONS FOR ADULTS

Novels

O Genteel Lady! Boston, Houghton Mifflin, 1926; London, Heinemann, 1927.
Miss Marvel. Boston, Houghton Mifflin, 1935.
Paradise. New York, Harcourt Brace, and London, Chatto and Windus, 1937.
The General's Lady. New York, Harcourt Brace, 1938; London, Chatto and Windus, 1939.
The Running of the Tide. Boston, Houghton Mifflin, 1948; London, Chatto and Windus, 1949.
Rainbow on the Road. Boston, Houghton Mifflin, 1954; London, Chatto and Windus, 1955.

Other

Ann Douglas Sedgwick: An Interview. Boston, Houghton Mifflin, 1928.
A Mirror for Witches, in Which Is Reflected the Life, Machinations, and Death of Famous Doll Bilby, Who, with a More Than Feminine Perversity, Preferred a Demon to a Mortal Lover. Boston, Houghton Mifflin, and London, Heinemann, 1928.
Paul Revere and the World He Lived In. Boston, Houghton Mifflin, 1942.
The Boston Book. Boston, Houghton Mifflin, 1947.

*

Manuscript Collections: American Antiquarian Society, Worcester, Massachusetts; Clark University Library, Worcester, Massachusetts.

Critical Study: *Esther Forbes* by Margaret Erskine, Worcester, Massachusetts, Worcester Bicentennial Committee, 1976.

*   *   *

The reputation of Esther Forbes as a writer for children has been established by one book—*Johnny Tremain.* It is her only work of fiction for children. Young people who are interested in historical fiction, however, would enjoy her other work, particularly *Rainbow on the Road.*

Forbes had several unique advantages in writing *Johnny Tremain* which helped to make the book one of the most solid choices to win the Newbery Medal in the history of the award; they have also helped to make the book still worthwhile—even enabling it to survive the trauma of being required reading in many a school system.

The first advantage was her detailed knowledge of Paul Revere's world—its physical conditions, its contemporary events, its political figures and their influences. Information of all kinds, gathered in her exhaustive research for her earlier *Paul Revere* was so firm in her mind that complete scenes for *Johnny Tremain,* accurately detailed and furnished, could arise spontaneously. The creative process did not have to be interrupted and reaffirmed by research. The richness and liveliness added to the story by this ability are as rewarding as the plot and characters.

The second advantage derived also from her historical research: the curiosity and insight with which she considered people and the reasons for their behavior. She was always titillated by the quirk of thought or misunderstanding which could precipitate an historical incident. As she studied the Boston of the 1760's and 1770's, the role played by apprentices of all trades intrigued her—and she promised herself the indulgence of writing a piece of fiction about them in time.

When World War II brought the issue of freedom and fighting for it once more into daily consciousness, she found the crux for her story. She could reveal the universal and timeless problems of making difficult choices, believing in a cause, being responsible for one's actions, overcoming a handicap (Johnny's burned hand), and facing grief and loss (the death of Rab) by telling the story of Johnny Tremain, apprentice to a silversmith in Boston during the American Revolution. In her Newbery Medal acceptance speech, Forbes said, "I was anxious to show young readers something of the excitement of human nature, never static, always changing, often unpredictable, and endlessly fascinating." She might well have been defining the elements needed to produce a classic—which is what she did.

The text for *America's Paul Revere* is a distillation of the man and the most important facts of his life and times, prepared for younger readers as a counterpart for Lynd Ward's illustrations.

—Lee Kingman

———

FORD, Hilary.   See **CHRISTOPHER, John.**

———

FOREMAN, Michael. British. Born in Pakefield, Suffolk, 21 March 1938. Educated at Notley Road Secondary Modern School, Lowestoft, Suffolk; Lowestoft School of Art, National Diploma in Design 1958; Royal College of Art, London (Silver Medal, 1963), A.R.C.A. (honours) 1963. Married 1) Janet Charters in 1959 (divorced 1966), one son; 2) Louise Phillips in 1980, two sons. Lecturer, St. Martin's School of Art, London, 1963–65, London School of Printing, 1967, Royal College of Art, 1968–70, and Central School of Art, London, 1971–72. Art director, *Playboy*, Chicago, 1965, and *King*, London, 1966. Since 1960 art director, *Ambit*, London. Individual show: Royal Festival Hall, London, 1985. Recipient (for illustration): Schweppes travelling scholarship, 1961–63; Festival International du Livre Silver Eagle award (Nice), 1972; Victoria and Albert Museum Francis Williams prize, 1972, 1977; Graphics prize (Bologna), 1982; Maschler award, 1982; Library Association Kate Greenaway Medal, 1983; Federation of Children's Books Group award, 1984; *Signal* Poetry award, 1987. Agent: John Locke, 15 East 76th Street, New York, New York 10021, U.S.A. Address: 5 Church Gate, London, S.W.6, England.

Publications for Children (illustrated by the author)

Fiction

The Perfect Present.   London, Hamish Hamilton, and New York, Coward McCann, 1967.

The Two Giants.   Leicester, Brockhampton Press, and New York, Pantheon, 1967.

The Great Sleigh Robbery.   London, Hamish Hamilton, 1968; New York, Pantheon, 1969.

Horatio.   London, Hamish Hamilton, 1970; as *The Travels of Horatio,* New York, Pantheon, 1970.

Moose.   London, Hamish Hamilton, 1971; New York, Pantheon, 1972.

Dinosaurs and All That Rubbish.   London, Hamish Hamilton, 1972; New York, Crowell, 1973.

War and Peas.   London, Hamish Hamilton, and New York, Crowell, 1974.

All the King's Horses.   London, Hamish Hamilton, 1976; Scarsdale, New York, Bradbury Press, 1977.

Panda's Puzzle, and His Voyage of Discovery.   London, Hamish Hamilton, 1977; Scarsdale, New York, Bradbury Press, 1978.

Winter's Tales, illustrated by Freire White.   London, Benn, and New York, Doubleday, 1979.

Trick a Tracker.   London, Gollancz, and New York, Philomel, 1981.

Panda and the Odd Lion.   London, Hamish Hamilton, 1981.

Land of Dreams.   London, Andersen Press, and New York, Holt Rinehart, 1982.

Cat and Canary.   London, Andersen Press, 1984; New York, Dial Press, 1985.

Panda and the Bunyips.   London, Hamish Hamilton, 1984; New York, Schocken, 1987.

Private Zoo.   London, Methuen, 1985.

Panda and the Bushfire.   London, Hamish Hamilton, and Englewood Cliffs, New Jersey, Prentice Hall, 1986.

Ben's Box (pop-up).   London, Hodder and Stoughton, 1986.

Ben's Baby.   London, Andersen Press, 1987; New York, Harper, 1988.

The Angel and the Wild Animal.   London, Andersen Press, 1988; New York, Atheneum, 1989.

*

Illustrator: *The General* by Janet Charters, 1961; *Making Music* by Gwen Clemens, 1966; *I'm for You and You're for Me* by Mabel Watts, 1967; *Let's Fight and Other Russian Fables* by Sergei Vladimirovich Mikhalkov, 1968; *Adam's Balm* by William Ivan Martin, 1970; *The Birthday Unicorn,* 1970, and *Alexander in the Land of Mog,* 1973, both by Janet Elliott; *The Living Arts of Nigeria* edited by William Fagg, 1971; *Fischer v. Spassky* by C.O. Alexander, 1972; *The Living Treasures of Japan* by Barbara Adachi, 1973; *Mr. Noah and the Second Flood* by Sheila Burnford, 1973; *Rainbow Rider* by Jane Yolen, 1974; *Private Zoo* by Georgess McHargue, 1975; *Teeny-Tiny and the Witch Woman* by Barbara K. Walker, 1975; *The Stone Book,* 1976, *Tom Fobble's Day,* 1977, *Granny Reardun,* 1977, *The Aimer Gate,* 1978, and *Fairy Tales of Gold,* 4 vols., 1979, all by Alan Garner; *The Pushcart War* by Jean Merrill, 1976; *Hans Christian Andersen: His Classic Fairy Tales* translated by Erik Haugaard, 1976; *Monkey and the Three Wizards* translated by Peter Harris, 1976; *Borrowed Feathers and Other Fables* retold by Bryna Stevens, 1978; *The Selfish Giant,* 1978, and *The Nightingale and the Rose,* 1981, both by Oscar Wilde; *The Brothers Grimm: Popular Folk Tales* translated by Brian Alderson, 1978; *Mickey's Kitchen Contest* by Kurt Baumann, 1978; *Seven in One Blow,* 1978; *How to Catch a Ghost* by Noodles, 1979; *The Faithful Bull* by Ernest Hemingway, 1980; *The Tiger Who Lost His Stripes* by Anthony Paul, 1980; *City of Gold* by Peter Dickinson, 1980; *The Pig Plantagenet* by Allen Andrews, 1980; *After Many a Summer* by Aldous Huxley, 1980; *Over the Bridge* edited by John Loveday, 1981; *Fairy Tales,* 1981,

The Saga of Eric the Viking, 1983, *Nicobobinus,* 1985, and *The Curse of the Vampire's Socks,* 1988, all by Terry Jones; *The Magic Mouse and the Millionaire,* 1982, *The Brontosaurus Birthday Cake,* 1983, and *Brontosaurus Superstar!,* 1985, all by Robert McCrum; *Sleeping Beauty and Other Favourite Fairy Tales* retold by Angela Carter, 1982; *Long Neck and Thunder Foot* by Helen Piers, 1982; *The Crab That Played with the Sea,* 1982, *The Jungle Book,* 1987, and *Just So Stories,* 1987, all by Rudyard Kipling; *A Christmas Carol* by Dickens, 1983; *Poems for 7-Year-Olds and Under* edited by Helen Nicoll, 1983; *Poems for 9-Year-Olds and Under* [*10-Year-Olds and Over*] edited by Kit Wright, 2 vols., 1984; *A Cat and Mouse Love Story* by Nanette Newman, 1984; *A Child's Garden of Verses* by Robert Louis Stevenson, 1985; *Charlie and the Chocolate Factory* by Roald Dahl, 1985; *Shakespeare Stories* by Leon Garfield, 1985; *Seasons of Splendour: Tales, Myths and Legends of India* by Madhur Jaffrey, 1985; *I'll Take You to Mrs. Cole* by Nigel Gray, 1985; *Letters from Hollywood* by Michael Moorcock, 1986; *The Magic Ointment and Other Cornish Legends* by Eric Quayle, 1986; *Tales for the Telling: Irish Folk and Fairy Stories* by Edna O'Brien, 1986; *Fun* by Jan Mark, 1987; *Classics of the Macabre* by Daphne du Maurier, 1987; *The Night Before Christmas* by Clement C. Moore, 1988; *Peter Pan and Wendy* by J.M. Barrie, 1988; *Worms Wiggle* by David Pelham, 1989; *The Sand Horse* by Ann Turnbull, 1989; *Edmond Went Far Away* by Martin Bax, 1989.

* * *

As a writer and illustrator of picture books, Michael Foreman displayed almost from the start the ability to wrap up a political point or social theme in an engaging story with stylish illustrations and considerable appeal to children. If *The Great Sleigh Robbery,* in which a gang of robbers kidnaps Father Christmas, is an amusing story with no particular moral, *Horatio,* which features a hippopotamus dissatisfied with squelching in mud and longing for "fields of corn and marigolds," makes a point both about the world and man's nature, for Horatio has to discover for himself that there are houses on the corn fields and roads built on the marigolds.

Moose takes a more political theme: the gentle moose, caught in the middle of a flaming row between Bear and Eagle who hurl abuse and sticks and stones at each other, builds himself a shelter which creates his own haven of peace and which the other animals come to share. Cartoon-like elements indicate Bear (in his yellow dictator's uniform) and Eagle as the superpowers. At the same time there is play on words to relish ("Very amoosing...I'll shout at you if you don't vamoose, Moose"). *War and Peas* (a play of course on the word peace) contrasts, very graphically, overconsumption with poverty as the enormously fat king of a country groaning with food—giant cakes and jellies which fill the page—refuses help to his starving neighbour King Lion. The effects of pollution are demonstrated in *Dinosaurs and All That Rubbish,* but the dinosaurs who come to clear the planet are jolly creatures and full of fun.

All the King's Horses was one of the first fairytales to be stood on its conventional head: the princess, far from "the milk-white, golden-haired, pink little number princesses are supposed to be," throws her prospective husbands at wrestling and gallops away "rushing through the nightmares of kings and the dreams of princesses"— prophetic words, as princesses in picture books have not looked back since.

Panda's Puzzle was one of the first "searches for identity" in picture books, and is rated as a modern classic. Panda travels the world to find out whether he is a white bear with black bits or a black bear with white bits, and faced with conflicting advice finally discovers it does not matter. Panda features in three further titles in which he shares adventures with the Odd (because he is winged) Lion, set against vibrant Australian landscapes.

Foreman's prolific output as an illustrator of other writers' books,

for which he has developed a distinctive style of flowing and atmospheric watercolour, has possibly had an effect on his approach as a writer in that his later picture books are more whimsical in nature. *Cat and Canary* is a fantasy set against the glimmering skyline of New York as Cat is blown about at the end of a kite high above the streets—the opportunity for some dazzling perspectives.

Two recent books are firmly child centred, and both were inspired by his own son. In *Ben's Baby* a small boy looks forward to the birth of a baby brother in a warm and realistic story, while *The Angel and the Wild Animal* features a small boy in his many moods, with a spare text ("Sometimes we have an Angel in our house. Most times at night, and mostly asleep...").

For the future Foreman says he intends to concentrate on writing his own texts for picture books and, having explored personal and domestic themes, he plans to return to more universal ones, not set in any particular time or place. Of his output he chooses *War and Peas* and *Dinosaurs and All That Rubbish* as having "stood the test of time," and *Dinosaurs* was indeed reissued 15 years after first publication.

With any serious content always presented with a sense of fun, Foreman is a writer who can be enjoyed by a wide age range. He describes his forthcoming work *War Boy,* which recounts his memories of boyhood in wartime Suffolk, as a book for all ages.

—Jennifer Taylor

FOREST, Antonia. British. Born in London. Address: c/o Faber and Faber Ltd., 3 Queen Square, London WC1N 2AU, England.

Fiction

Autumn Term, illustrated by Marjorie Owens. London, Faber, 1948.
The Marlows and the Traitor, illustrated by Doritie Kettlewell. London, Faber, 1953.
Falconer's Lure: The Story of a Summer Holiday, illustrated by Tasha Kallin. London, Faber, 1957.
End of Term. London, Faber, 1959.
Peter's Room. London, Faber, 1961.
The Thursday Kidnapping. London, Faber, 1963; New York, Coward McCann, 1965.
The Thuggery Affair. London, Faber, 1965.
The Ready-Made Family. London, Faber, 1967.
The Player's Boy. London, Faber, 1970.
The Players and the Rebels. London, Faber, 1971.
The Cricket Term. London, Faber, 1974.
The Attic Term. London, Faber, 1976.
Run Away Home. London, Faber, 1982.

* * *

Although four of Antonia Forest's books are primarily school stories, the rest of her series about the Marlow family is set mainly outside school in holiday periods. In all these stories the upper middle-class background is evident, particularly in the stories set at home, which have casual references to servants, hunting, parties, and private chapels, more akin to children's books of the 1930's than to the 1980's.

The most original and outstanding plot in the series is that of *Peter's Room,* a brilliant blend of reality and fantasy woven around the intense fascination of the Brontë kingdoms of Gondal and Angria for the young Marlows. The interest in these imaginary kingdoms is aroused when one of the sisters, Ginty, has to produce an essay on some aspect of the Brontës' life or work. The Marlows create their own kingdom of Angora and become utterly absorbed in it for an entire Christmas holiday. This highly successful book well deserved the commendation it received from the Library Association in 1961.

In 1982 *Run Away Home* was a welcome addition to the Marlow saga. Set in a Christmas holiday period, it introduces an original approach to the ever popular running-away theme with the gripping sailing incident which reaches a peak of suspense. This book will delight devotees of the Marlow family with its totally consistent evolution of the characters of the sisters Rowena, Ann, Nicola, and Lawrie. It also continues the tradition of eloquent dialogue for which Forest is noted.

. However, Forest is likely to be remembered primarily for her school stories in which she follows accepted formulae, but gives the Marlows a rare form of immortality with school years spanning a period of nearly 30 years, and also introduces ingenious variations. The twins' hopes of academic triumph are doomed to failure. Running away is an ignominious experience for Nick who is immediately sent back to school by her elder brother, and has not even been missed in her absence. Starts of term are highlighted by the incident of the pulling of the communication cord in the train or a bolt across the fields to catch an escaped merlin. Dramatics perhaps occupy an undue proportion of certain plots, but this is acceptable to the wariest reader because of Forest's enthusiastic details.

It is not Forest's skilful handling of the school story plot that ensures her success, but her positive flair for characterisation, her presentation of violent clashes of personality, her understanding of the fluctuations of schoolgirl friendships, and her insight into sisterly relationships.

Antonia Forest's able handling of plot and character, combined with sound literary style, enable her to present the traditional school story in a new and lasting dimension, unlikely to have many if any successful imitators.

—Anne W. Ellis

FOX, Paula. American. Born in New York City, 22 April 1923; daughter of the writer Paul Hervey Fox. Attended Columbia University, New York, 1955–58. Married 1) Richard Sigerson in 1948 (divorced 1954), two sons; 2) Martin Greenberg in 1962. News service correspondent, Paris and Warsaw, late 1940's; from 1963 teacher of writing workshops, University of Pennsylvania, Philadelphia. Recipient: Guggenheim fellowship, 1972; American Academy award, 1972; American Library Association Newbery Medal, 1974; National Endowment for the Arts award, 1974; Hans Christian Andersen International Medal, 1978; American Book award, for paperback fiction, 1983; Child Study Committee award, 1984; Christopher award, 1985; University of Southern Mississippi award, 1987. Lives in Brooklyn, New York. Agent: Robert Lescher, Lescher and Lescher, 67 Irving Place, New York, New York 10009, U.S.A.

PUBLICATIONS FOR CHILDREN

Fiction

Maurice's Room, illustrated by Ingrid Fetz.   New York, Macmillan,

1966.
A Likely Place, illustrated by Edward Ardizzone.   New York, Macmillan, 1967; London, Macmillan, 1968.
How Many Miles to Babylon?, illustrated by Paul Giovanopoulos.   New York, David White, and London, Macmillan, 1967.
Dear Prosper, illustrated by Steve McLachlin.   New York, David White, 1968.
The Stone-Faced Boy, illustrated by Donald Mackay.   Englewood Cliffs, New Jersey, Bradbury Press, 1968; London, Macmillan, 1969.
The King's Falcon, illustrated by Eros Keith.   Englewood Cliffs, New Jersey, Bradbury Press, 1969; London, Macmillan, 1970.
Portrait of Ivan, illustrated by Saul Lambert.   Englewood Cliffs, New Jersey, Bradbury Press, 1969; London, Macmillan, 1970.
Hungry Fred, illustrated by Rosemary Wells.   Englewood Cliffs, New Jersey, Bradbury Press, 1969.
Blowfish Live in the Sea.   Englewood Cliffs, New Jersey, Bradbury Press, 1970.
Good Ethan, illustrated by Arnold Lobel.   Scarsdale, New York, Bradbury Press, 1973.
The Slave Dancer, illustrated by Eros Keith.   Scarsdale, New York, Bradbury Press, 1973; London, Macmillan, 1974.
A Place Apart.   New York, Farrar Straus, 1980; London, Dent, 1981.
One-Eyed Cat.   New York, Bradbury Press, 1984; London, Dent, 1985.
The Moonlight Man.   New York, Bradbury Press, and London, Dent, 1986.
Lily and the Lost Boy.   New York, Orchard, 1987; as *The Lost Boy,* London, Dent, 1987.
The Village by the Sea.   New York, Orchard, 1988.
In a Place of Danger.   New York, Orchard, 1989.

Other

The Little Swineherd and Other Tales, illustrated by Leonard Lubin.   New York, Dutton, 1978; London, Dent, 1979.

PUBLICATIONS FOR ADULTS

Novels

Poor George.   New York, Harcourt Brace, and London, Bodley Head, 1967.
Desperate Characters.   New York, Harcourt Brace, and London, Macmillan, 1970.
The Western Coast.   New York, Harcourt Brace, 1972; London, Macmillan, 1973.
The Widow's Children.   New York, Dutton, 1976.
A Servant's Tale.   Berkeley, California, North Point Press, 1984; London, Virago Press, 1986.

*   *   *

Paula Fox is an unusually perceptive writer who has a remarkable ability to portray a world as it exclusively appears through the eyes of a youthful protagonist. She captures the intensity of young emotions through carefully crafted stories which unravel with a quiet precision, and ultimately culminate in some new found wisdom. Many of Fox's children live in a confusing and mysterious world, a world in which, for some unknown reason, one must learn to spell and multiply, and where adults ask meaningless questions and make incomprehensible statements. In this bewildering, sometimes funny, sometimes depressing environment, young people grope for a clue that might make some sense of the chaos that surrounds them. This groping process often takes the form of a journey, a recurring theme in Fox's work. Sometimes the journey is taken willingly, as in *Portrait of Ivan*. Here the life of a lonely, introspective child is touched by an artist who takes Ivan with him on a trip to Florida. The artist is painting Ivan's portrait, and as the portrait evolves, so does Ivan's sense of identity, a process aided by new experiences and new communications.

The journey in *Blowfish Live in the Sea* is also made willingly, but with some trepidation. 12-year-old Carrie accompanies Ben, her 18-year-old half-brother, on a visit to Ben's father, a drifter who has not been heard from for 12 years. Carrie's perspective offers a striking portrayal of a troubled, uncommunicative young man, and an acute vision of the state of loneliness that provokes a variety of behaviors. Another traveler with mixed emotions appears in *The Stone-Faced Boy*. 10-year-old Gus is a pensive, withdrawn boy who has devised a stoic exterior to protect himself from obstreperous siblings and a complacent family in which he feels out of place. Persuaded by a younger sister and an eccentric aunt to go out into the cold night in search of a lost dog, his little journey forms a symbolic representation of a personal search, a search for means to realize and articulate his own feelings. The plot is thin, but serves sufficiently as a frame for a penetrating portrait.

Sometimes the journey is made with great reluctance, with the protagonist in the position of unwilling victim. Such is the case in *How Many Miles to Babylon?*, where the basic confusion of a child's world is compounded by the harsh, bleak reality of life in a Brooklyn ghetto. 10-year-old James is forced to accompany a trio of young dog thieves and assist them in their racket. Through his journey and ultimate escape, the bewildered child is forced to confront a frightening situation and discovers his own ability to survive. An even more dramatic kidnapping occurs in Fox's Newbery Medal-winning *The Slave Dancer*, a profoundly vivid evocation of one of history's more sordid chapters. Set in 1840, the story follows the adventure of 13-year-old Jessie Bollier, captured on the streets of New Orleans to play the fife aboard a slave ship. In this moving portrayal of human suffering, Jessie is brutally shoved from childhood into manhood as he observes the dehumanization of the African slaves. Some reviewers have criticized the book for what they perceive to be racist implications; their complaints are based on a belief that the white captors are not clearly blamed for the tragic situation, and the black characters are not fully developed. But the work is not designed to serve either as an indictment or a polemic; it is merely the honest observations of one young boy, and, as such, becomes a compelling and gripping story.

Lily and the Lost Boy is set on a Greek island, where 11-year-old Lily, her brother, and their parents are spending three months. When another American boy intrudes on the close relationship Lily has recently established with her brother, she becomes resentful. But a tragic event involving the adolescents forces Lily and her brother to move toward more mature levels of sensitivity and courage, and they leave the island with a heightened awareness of the human condition.

In *The Village by the Sea* 10-year-old Emma has been sent to stay with her Uncle Crispin and Aunt Bea while her father is hospitalized. Aunt Bea is a peculiarly hostile woman, whose coldness and sarcasm are only tempered by the uncle's mild-mannered kindness. Emma makes a friend with whom she builds a stone and shell village on the beach. This experience provides Emma with some sense of escape and security—until the village is inexplicably destroyed by Aunt Bea. The peculiar relationships displayed in this work may seem puzzling, even bizarre, but as Aunt Bea's character is slowly revealed in all its sadness, Emma becomes aware of the potential emotional complexities that can evolve in a disturbed human being.

The emotionally isolated child appears in many of the author's books. *Maurice's Room* is the charming tale of an 8-year-old collector of odds and ends. Maurice cannot understand why his family is distressed by his penchant for "things," and blithely disregards their attempts to distract him. There's a sense of warmth and humor in this account of a small predicament, and this tone is also evident in *A Likely Place*. Here, an uncommunicative 9-year-old strikes up a rewarding friendship with an elderly man who also has difficulty communicating his needs to his family. Both of these works are understated, imaginative stories with deeper meanings that lie just beneath the surface of their deceptive simplicity.

A Place Apart is a strong articulate work in which Fox's sophisticated use of language is clearly evident in striking descriptions and vivid dialogue. A few months after her father's sudden death, 13-year-old Victoria and her mother move from Boston to a small Massachusetts town. There, Victoria strikes up an unlikely friendship with Hugh, a wealthy, rather arrogant classmate who seems to admire a play Victoria is writing for an English class. The play, however, is the only basis for their relationship. Hugh is only interested in people who are "special" in some way; Victoria's writing puts her in that category. Victoria's gradual realization of Hugh's attempts to manipulate her, and others, forces her to explore her own feelings about herself and the ways in which people seek to fulfill their own personal needs.

In *One-Eyed Cat* 11-year-old Ned receives as a gift from his uncle a rifle, which is taken away by his minister father. One night Ned retrieves the rifle and fires it. A fear that he may have hit something intensifies when he sees a one-eyed cat. His guilt over this is overwhelming, and affects his relationships with family and friends. This psychologically complex work rings true in its examination of right and wrong, and the nature of personal responsibility.

The Moonlight Man focuses on the confused relationship between 15-year-old Catherine and her barely-known father, an alcoholic poet. In her attempts to understand her father's erratic behavior and attitude, Catherine runs the gamut of emotions, from pity to anger, and ultimately to a tentative acceptance. Fox's unique treatment raises this novel from a didactic treatise on alcoholism to a distinctive study of a unique situation.

Fox has an uncommon talent for capturing and exposing intense emotions without resorting to melodrama or "problem novel" formats. Her unpretentious, almost detached narratives give her novels an integrity which demonstrates a respect for her juvenile audience. While there are recurring elements of theme and characterization in her books, each work remains a thoughtful exploration of a unique identity.

—Marilyn Kaye

FREEMAN, Barbara C(onstance). British. Born in Ealing, Middlesex, 29 November 1906. Educated at Tiffin Girls' School, Kingston-upon-Thames, Surrey; Kingston School of Art. Painter, Green and Abbott, wallpaperers, London, 1926–27; then freelance illustrator and writer. Artist: individual show at the Heritage Centre, Kingston-upon-Thames Museum, 1989. Address: 62 Hook Road, Surbiton, Surrey KT6 5BH, England.

PUBLICATIONS FOR CHILDREN (illustrated by the author)

Fiction

Timi. London, Faber, 1961; New York, Grosset and Dunlap, 1970.
Two-Thumb Thomas. London, Faber, 1961.
A Book by Georgina. London, Faber, 1962; New York, Norton, 1968.
Broom-Adelaide. London, Faber, 1963; Boston, Little Brown,

1965.

The Name on the Glass.   London, Faber, 1964; New York, Norton, 1966.

Lucinda.   London, Faber, 1965; New York, Norton, 1967.

Tobias.   London, Faber, 1967.

The Forgotten Theatre.   London, Faber, 1967.

The Other Face.   London, Macmillan, 1975; New York, Dutton, 1976.

A Haunting Air.   London, Macmillan, 1976; New York, Dutton, 1977.

A Pocket of Silence.   London, Macmillan, 1977; New York, Dutton, 1978.

The Summer Travellers.   London, Macmillan, 1978.

Snow in the Maze.   London, Macmillan, 1979.

Clemency in the Moonlight.   London, Macmillan, 1981.

*

Manuscript Collection: de Grummond Collection, University of Southern Mississippi, Hattiesburg.

Illustrator: *Stories from Hans Andersen,* 1949; *Stories from Grimm,* 1949; *Jan and His Clogs,* 1951, *Jan Klaassen Cures the King,* 1952, *Puppet Plays for Children,* 1953, and *Never Run from the Lion and Another Story,* 1958, all by Antonia Ridge; *The Magic Candles* by Mary Steward, 1954; *The Sleeping Beauty and Other Tales* by Charles Perrault, 1954; *Granny's Wonderful Chair* by Frances Browne, 1955; pictures for *The Children's Encyclopedia.*

Barbara C. Freeman comments:

I write, I suppose, chiefly because I enjoy writing and I like living in two worlds: the one I was born into and the other (which becomes entirely real) which I write about. I'm deeply interested in the way ordinary people lived in the past and the way in which the past thrusts into the present. I believe that most writers find that their characters develop lives of their own and sometimes take charge of both conversations and plots. This, for me, is pure delight, and I allow my people all the freedom that is possible.

At art school I was trained to observe details of every kind, and it is a habit that one never grows out of. Details, especially those of the past, fascinate me.

*   *   *

"Don't you understand? *I must take charge of my own life.* If I don't, I don't know what will happen to me." Rose, the heroine of *Snow in the Maze,* sums up the underlying theme of all of Barbara C. Freeman's work, whether fantasy, like the early novels *Timi* and *Two-Thumb Thomas,* or historical, like *The Name on the Glass* or *The Summer Travellers,* or ghost stories, the most recent of which are *Snow in the Maze* and *Clemency in the Moonlight.* The heroines (or hero, in *Two-Thumb Thomas*) tend to be rather lonely people for whom it is an effort to resist outside pressures and be decisive. It is cheerful to know that they can and do succeed. In the case of the ghost stories, success comes through contact with the past, where an older unhappiness to be righted gives the heroine an absorbing interest—and the necessary impetus to help herself.

Freeman's handling of these ghostly episodes is masterly. They are never frightening, but the sense of a place and of the people who inhabited that place are conveyed so strongly that the reader is taken quite naturally into the "other" part of the plot. Indeed, in one book, *Snow in the Maze,* Freeman has depicted a most interesting combination of place (Briarcourt House) and a ghost who isn't—the rather splendid, definitely flesh-and-body young caretaker turns out to be the original 18th-century owner, trapped in time. It is particularly satisfying to find that he can mend a bike. The most memorable

character of all is undoubtedly Linette, the school cat, in *Two-Thumb Thomas.* Thomas himself is rather a timid boy (hardly surprising in one raised in the school stationery cupboard), but Linette, who looks after him, is a great personality, full of resource and warmth.

All the novels show the author's love of gardens, of art, and of many crafts, some now almost forgotten. Lacemaking, the cutting of silhouettes, and fanmaking, for example, contribute substantially to the plots of those books in which they appear, while the reader takes in, almost without realizing, some interesting details of how these things were done. Her love of such things is also evident in the author's pictures, which decorate every book.

Barbara C. Freeman is a gentle writer, with a particular appeal to girls. She makes no great demands on her readers, but does provide good entertainment. Anyone wanting easy, fluent, romantic stories would do well to consider her work.

—Felicity Trotman

———

FREEMAN, Bill (William Bradford Freeman).   Canadian.   Born in London, Ontario, 21 October 1938. Educated at Acadia University, Wolfville, Nova Scotia, B.A. in philosophy 1964; McMaster University, Hamilton, Ontario, M.A. 1970, Ph.D. in sociology 1979. Married Marsha Hewitt (divorced); two sons and two daughters. Probation officer, Hamilton, Ontario, 1964–69; community organizer, Hamilton Welfare Rights, 1970; Lecturer, McMaster University, 1971–73; teacher, Vanier College, Montreal, 1977–86. Since 1988 financial consultant, 3rd Street Funding, Toronto. Recipient: Canada Council prize, 1976; Vicky Metcalf award, 1984. Address: 16 Third Street, Ward's Island, Toronto, Ontario M5J 2B2, Canada.

PUBLICATIONS FOR CHILDREN

Fiction

Shantymen of Cache Lake.   Toronto, Lorimer, 1975.

The Last Voyage of the Scotian.   Toronto, Lorimer, 1976.

Cedric and the North End Kids, photographs by Lutz Lille.   Toronto, Lorimer, 1978.

First Spring on the Grand Banks.   Toronto, Lorimer, 1978.

Trouble at Lachine Mill.   Toronto, Lorimer, 1983.

Harbour Thieves.   Toronto, Lorimer, 1984.

Danger on the Tracks.   Toronto, Lorimer, 1987.

Play

Ghosts of the Madawaska (produced Ottawa, 1985).

PUBLICATIONS FOR ADULTS

Play

Glorydays (produced Hamilton, Ontario, 1988).

Other

1005: Political Life of a Local Union.   Toronto, Lorimer, 1982.

Editor, with Marsha Hewitt, *Their Town: The Mafia, The Media, and the Party Machine.* Toronto, Lorimer, 1979.

*

Bill Freeman comments:

I am perhaps best known for my series of books that have come to be called "Adventures in Canadian History." These books are an attempt to portray the life of ordinary Canadians in the 1870's. Each book, in a different setting, is an adventure story that is engaging and fast moving. The Bains children, heroes of the stories, are not "superkids" but they have learned to struggle against odds for their survival.

* * *

Adventures in Canadian History, the series title of Bill Freeman's novels for children, reflects one of his purposes in writing for younger Canadian readers: a desire to introduce them to the excitement of their country's past. A more important, underlying purpose is revealed in his statement that "economic factors shaped ordinary people's lives." The difficulties faced by members of the working class and the pressures placed on them by the controllers of society are revealed in each story.

The central characters in the series are John and Meg Bains, young teenagers, and later Jamie, their little brother. In *Shantymen of Cache Lake,* set in the Ottawa Valley in the 1870's, the two older siblings seek work at a lumber camp to aid their impoverished and widowed mother. In addition to the dangers of logging and the harshness of the elements, they must confront a selfish and evil foreman and overcome the skepticism of their co-workers. In the later books they work on a schooner carrying immigrants to the New World, on a Newfoundland fishing boat, in a Quebec textile mill, and on the newly built railroad in southern Ontario. Each adventure tests their courage and their resolve to provide financial aid to their mother; and in each the children learn about the dignity of the common laborers and about the economic forces and personal selfishness threatening these people.

For the novels Freeman has done extensive historical research and incorporated his findings smoothly into the narratives. As Meg, John, and Jamie enter a new job they experience difficulties which give Freeman the opportunity to explain techniques and, equally important, the dangers that all the workers must face. Included are diagrams and rare historical photographs enabling readers to visualize clearly the different occupations.

While his contention that a rich few controlled the lives of the impoverished laborers is quite likely true, his presentation of this theme is awkward. Foremen become stereotypical villains, while owners are incredibly ignorant of the hardships endured by those who make their wealth possible. Although each new book introduces a new area of Canada, the plot structures and character types become predictably similar. Having clearly and vividly presented his thesis in the first book, Freeman does little more than expound it in the rest of the series. Moreover, the characters of the children seem to develop very little: John is somewhat timid, Meg combines assertiveness and motherly concern, and Jamie reveals his talent for getting into scrapes.

In spite of these limitations, Freeman's historical novels have earned a significant place in Canadian children's literature, exploring as they do aspects of Canadian history frequently ignored by writers: the difficult lives of ordinary people struggling to make their lives worthwhile while laboring in occupations generally little known by younger readers of today.

—Jon C. Stott

———

FREEMAN, Don. American. Born in San Diego, California, 11 August 1908. Educated at Principia High School, St. Louis; San Diego School of Fine Arts; Art Students' League, New York. Served in the United States Army Infantry, Rainbow Division, for two years. Married Lydia Cooley in 1931; one son. Trumpeter in jazz band; drama artist, *New York Times,* 1934–52. Individual show: Margo Feiden Galleries, New York, 1975. *Died 1 February 1978.*

PUBLICATIONS FOR CHILDREN (illustrated by the author)

Fiction

Chuggy and the Blue Caboose, with Lydia Freeman. New York, Viking Press, 1951.
Pet of the Met, with Lydia Freeman. New York, Viking Press, 1953.
Beady Bear. New York, Viking Press, 1954; London, Penguin, 1977.
Mop Top. New York, Viking Press, 1955.
Fly High, Fly Low. New York, Viking Press, 1957.
The Night the Lights Went Out. New York, Viking Press, 1958.
Norman the Doorman. New York, Viking Press, 1959; Leicester, Brockhampton Press, 1972.
Space Witch. New York, Viking Press, 1959.
Cyrano the Crow. New York, Viking Press, 1960.
Come Again, Pelican. New York, Viking Press, 1961.
Botts, The Naughty Otter. San Carlos, California, Golden Gate Books, 1963.
Ski Pup. New York, Viking Press, 1963.
Dandelion. New York, Viking Press, 1964; Kingswood, Surrey, World's Work, 1965.
The Turtle and the Dove. New York, Viking Press, 1964; Kingswood, Surrey, World's Work, 1965.
A Rainbow of My Own. New York, Viking Press, 1966; Kingswood, Surrey, World's Work, 1967.
The Guard Mouse. New York, Viking Press, 1967; Kingswood, Surrey, World's Work, 1970.
Corduroy. New York, Viking Press, 1968; London, Penguin, 1976.
Quiet! There's a Canary in the Library. San Carlos, California, Golden Gate Books, 1969.
Tilly Witch. New York, Viking Press, 1969.
Forever Laughter. San Carlos, California, Golden Gate Books, 1970.
Hattie the Backstage Bat. New York, Viking Press, 1970.
Penguins of All People! New York, Viking Press, 1971.
Inspector Peckit. New York, Viking Press, 1972; Kingswood, Surrey, World's Work, 1973.
Flash the Dash. Chicago, Children's Press, 1973.
The Seal and the Slick. New York, Viking Press, 1974; as *The Sea Lion and the Slick,* Kingswood, Surrey, World's Work, 1976.
The Paper Party. New York, Viking Press, 1974; Kingswood, Surrey, World's Work, 1977.
Will's Quill. New York, Viking Press, 1975.
Bearymore. New York, Viking Press, 1976.
The Chalk Box Story. Philadelphia, Lippincott, 1976.
A Pocket for Corduroy. New York, Viking Press, and London, Penguin, 1978.
Corduroy's Toys [*Party Day*], illustrated by Lisa McCue. New York, Viking Kestrel, 2 vols., 1985.

Plays

Screenplays (short films): *Lollipop Opera,* 1970; *Storymaker,* 1972.

Television Play: *The Baker* (*Sesame Street* series), 1971.

Other

Add-a-Line Alphabet. San Carlos, California, Golden Gate Books, 1968.

PUBLICATIONS FOR ADULTS

Other

It Shouldn't Happen. New York, Harcourt Brace, 1945.
Come One, Come All! New York, Rinehart, 1949.

*

Bibliography: *The Prints of Don Freeman: A Catalogue Raisonné* by Edith McCulloch, Charlottesville, University Press of Virginia, 1987.

Manuscript Collection: May Massee Collection, Emporia State University, Kansas.

Illustrator: *My Name Is Aram,* 1940, and *The Human Comedy,* 1943, both by William Saroyan; *Diedrich Knickerbocker's History of New York* by Washington Irving, 1940; *The White Deer* by James Thurber, 1945; *Once Around the Sun* by Brooks Atkinson, 1951; *Sauce for the Gander* by Scott Corbett, 1951; *Mike's House* by Julia Sauer, 1954; *Third Monkey,* 1956, and *This for That,* 1965, both by Ann Nolan Clark; *The Uninvited Donkey* by Anne H. White, 1957; *Ghost Town Treasure* by Clyde Robert Bulla, 1957; *Angelenos, Then and Now,* 1966; *Best Friends,* 1967, and *Best of Luck,* 1969, both by Myra Brown; *Voltaire's Micromegas* by Elizabeth Hall, 1967; *California Indian Days* by Helen Bauer, revised edition 1968; *Seven in a Bed* by Ruth Sonneborn, 1968; *Joey's Cat* by Robert Burch, 1969; *Burnish Me Bright,* 1970, and *Far in the Day,* 1972, both by Julia W. Cunningham; *Edward and the Night Horses* by Jacklyn Matthews, 1971; *The Wild Cats of Rome* by Elizabeth Cooper, 1972; *The Christmas Strangers,* 1976, and *The April Foolers,* 1978, both by Marjorie Thayer; *Monster Night at Grandma's House* by Richard Peck, 1977; *Dinosaur, My Darling* by Edith Thacher Hurd, 1978; *The Day Is Waiting* by Linda Z. Knab, 1980; *Uncle Sam Presents* by Tony Buttitta and Barry B. Witham, 1982.

* * *

Don Freeman's picture books sing out with a playfulness that strikes the child's imagination. He sees his themes and subjects with an artist's eye from which comes a flow of pictures followed by a stream of words.

Pet of the Met, one of his first books (written in collaboration with his wife, Lydia), set a high standard for his work. He blends his intimate knowledge of the Opera House and Mozart's *The Magic Flute* with mouse and cat antics. Mr. Petrini, the page turner at the opera house, and a *Magic Flute* enthusiast, deftly confronts a mouse's traditional enemy, Mefisto, the cat. There is a jauntiness of writing that gives the book a lasting spirit.

Norman the Doorman is a master at collecting mousetraps set for him in the museum where he is the doorman and guide to his relatives, including Maestro Petrini and family. He hears of a sculpture competition, enters his sculpture *Trapeese,* and wins first prize. This is a caper to be enjoyed for what it is, with an implicit commentary on the meaning of art exhibits to be detected by the more sophisticated reader. *The Guard Mouse* continues the fanciful escapades of the Petrini family. Their cousin, Clyde, a Grenadier guard at Buckingham Palace, welcomes the Petrinis. The children, Do, Re, Mi, tired after their long trip from New York, are left behind as Clyde

takes the parents on a tour of London, a light-hearted romp that indicates more than a chance acquaintance with the city. In each of these books an element of surprise adds marked interest to the story. Freeman is an effective storyteller, interweaving information that can arouse the undiscovered interests of the young child.

Freeman's imagination reaches out into unlikely areas. Peary B. Penguin, in *Penguins of All People!,* is urgently requested to attend a special meeting of the United Nations, to share with the members the secret of how penguins live together so peacefully. Might the U.N. members learn from him? In *Will's Quill* Willoughby, a country goose, is rescued by Young Will, and, to show his gratefulness for Will's kindness, tells the story with overtones of archaic language about a country goose who helped William Shakespeare in the writing of his plays.

Freeman also created books that capture spontaneously, without ulterior motive, the imaginative world to which the young child responds. *Mop Top* is the story of a little boy who will not have his hair cut until he is mistaken for a mop. In *Dandelion* a lion receives an invitation to a tea-and-taffy party from Jennifer Giraffe, and sets about with meticulous preparation to look his best. The results are preposterous, sustained by Freeman's clear vision and obvious zest for the development of this situation. Children can identify with the implicit, gentle wisdom. In *Corduroy* a shopworn bear yearns for a home in which his sense of belonging can be satisfied. Lisa sees Corduroy, the bear, and empties her piggy bank to buy him. He must belong to her. Freeman develops the not-uncommon theme of a stuffed animal and a child with understanding and compassion.

Freeman's visual sense gave strength to his picture books even when his text did not reach the same height. At his best, he offers rich visual experiences with sparkle and harmony in his writing.

—Mae Durham Roger

———

FRENCH, Fiona (Mary). British. Born in Bath, Somerset, 27 June 1944. Educated in Devon; at Croydon College of Art, Surrey, 1961–66, National Diploma in Design for painting and lithography 1966. Children's art therapy teacher, Long Grove Psychiatric Hospital, Epsom, Surrey, 1967–69; design teacher, Wimbledon School of Art, 1970–71, and Leicester and Brighton polytechnics, 1973–74. Assistant to the painter Bridget Riley, 1967–72. Since 1974 freelance illustrator. Recipient: Library Association Kate Greenaway Medal, 1987. Agent: Pat White, Rogers Coleridge and White, 20 Powis Mews, London W11 1JN. Address: 33 Hungate Street, Aylsham, Norfolk NR11 6AA, England.

PUBLICATIONS FOR CHILDREN (illustrated by the author)

Fiction

Jack of Hearts. London, Oxford University Press, and New York, Harcourt Brace, 1970.
Huni. London, Oxford University Press, 1971.
The Blue Bird. London, Oxford University Press, and New York, Walck, 1972.
King Tree. London, Oxford University Press, and New York, Walck, 1973.
City of Gold. London, Oxford University Press, and New York, Walck, 1974.
Aio the Rainmaker. London, Oxford University Press, 1975; New York, Oxford University Press, 1978.
Matteo. London, Oxford University Press, 1976; New York,

Oxford University Press, 1978.
Hunt the Thimble. London and New York, Oxford University Press, 1978.
The Princess and the Musician. London, Evans, 1981.
Future Story. Oxford, Oxford University Press, 1983; New York, Bedrick, 1984.
Maid of the Wood. Oxford, Oxford University Press, 1985.
Snow White in New York. Oxford, Oxford University Press, 1986; New York, Oxford University Press, 1987.
The Song of the Nightingale. London, Blackie, 1986.

Other

John Barleycorn (retelling). London, Abelard Schuman, 1982.
Cinderella (retelling). Oxford, Oxford University Press, 1987; New York, Oxford University Press, 1988.
Rise, Shine! London, Methuen, 1989.

PUBLICATIONS FOR ADULTS

Short Stories

Un-Fairy Tales. Privately printed, 1966.

*

Illustrator: *Book of Magical Birds* by Margaret Mayo, 1977; *Fabulous Beasts* by Richard Blythe, 1977; *The Star Child* by Oscar Wilde, abridged by Jennifer Westwood, 1979; *The Necklace of Princess Fiorimonde* by Mary de Morgan, 1980; *Clowns and Clowning* by Carol Crowther, 1980; *Hidden Animals* by Josephine Karavasil, 1982; *Fat Cat,* 1984, and *Going to Squintum's,* 1985, both by Jennifer Westwood.

*   *   *

By steeping herself in the culture or period content of her picture books, Fiona French produces not only authentic detail but an almost tangible atmosphere, a feat perceiveable in her gloriously rich illustrative style and in the entirely suitable economy and relevance of the texts.

All her books are full of the powerful elemental themes found in myth and fairy tale. Envy, greed, and power appear in the first book, *Jack of Hearts,* based on the playing card Kings of Hearts, Diamonds, Clubs, and Spades, represented as happy, rich, warlike, and evil respectively and the 18th birthday feast of Jack of Hearts. Research shows in the description of the feast, including "wild boar and peacock and paradise sauce and herring pie and hedgehog, gingerbread, sea-holly candy and rich red wine." Elemental emotions appear also in *King Tree,* in a Louis XIV Garden of Versailles setting, where Orange Tree organises nominations for king, and the oak, laurel, pomegranate, olive, and vine vie with each other in election promises; but the ladies choose Orange Tree as King. Pride and the fight between good and evil appear in *City of Gold,* a medieval, Biblical style tale of John and Thomas, brothers journeying on the roads easy and hard, thwarting the Devil in a series of encounters. *The Blue Bird* reveals the evil Enchantress when the Chinese girl Blue Jade seeks a cure for her pet bird's loss of voice, a revelation spectacularly accomplished in transition from Wedgwood blue illustration to a burst of colour when the Enchantress is demolished and her victims freed. *Matteo,* too, follows the practical jokers through apparent success to just retribution.

Survival and proving oneself to the gods are the themes of *Huni* and *Aio the Rainmaker.* Huni, possible successor to Pharaoh, meets some of the gods from Egyptian mythology—Ra, the cat, the serpent,

Osiris—survives ordeals to prove health and strength, and is deemed fit to be the new Pharaoh. In *Aio* African tribal art and legend are interwoven to form an African "experience" of a parched land, of Aio's powers to call on the Ancestors for rain to relieve the thirsty animals, graphically described in text and pictures.

These simple but strong emotions lend themselves to a textual treatment in which French retains the essence of the concept in short yet strongly phrased sentences with the narrative flow and the underlying moral message of the oral tradition. The striking use of colour is a feature of her powerful illustrative style: playing cards based on a real design, medieval stained glass windows in *City of Gold,* Egyptian art in *Huni,* Chinese style in *The Blue Bird,* French mannered style in *King Tree,* African art in *Aio,* and Florentine style in *Matteo.* Sombre shades to stunning colours match the events in *The Song of the Nightingale* which, with St. Francis, brings peace and new life to war-torn Assisi. *Maid of the Wood,* a wooden doll into whom life is breathed with unexpected results, carries on the bold colour and simple text story.

Two departures from traditional themes are first, the extraordinary *Future Story* in which the influence of space photography and high tech form the basis of life and relationships in future times and places—a strong and beautiful space age theme. The second example also has strength of line and colour. *Snow White in New York,* which won a Greenaway award, is a retelling with a 1920's setting and jazz musicians instead of the seven dwarfs. The illustrations are in perfect harmony with the 1920's-style humorous text.

After transposing that fairy tale into the 20th century French reverted to traditional treatment with *Cinderella,* giving prominence to the characters rather than the scenery, with sumptuous detailed costume and brief text set on multicoloured wash backgrounds.

French's picture books are not, in theme and style, for the young child, but for those over eight, for young people, and for adults who see the masterly relationships between the verbal and visual concept of each book.

—Margaret R. Marshall

FRENCH, Simon. Australian. Born in Sydney, New South Wales, 26 November 1957. Educated at Mitchell College, Bathurst, New South Wales, 1976–79, diploma in teaching 1979. Has worked as library clerical assistant and fruitpicker; infants' teacher, in Willow Tree, 1980, and St. Clair, 1981–84, both New South Wales; youth worker, 1984–87. Since 1988 teacher in New South Wales. Recipient: Australian Children's Book of the Year award, 1987. Address: 24 Burdekin Road, Wilberforce, New South Wales 2756, Australia.

PUBLICATIONS FOR CHILDREN

Fiction

Hey, Phantom Singlet, illustrated by Alex Nicholas. Sydney and London, Angus and Robertson, 1975.
Cannily, Cannily. Sydney and London, Angus and Robertson, 1981.
All We Know. Sydney and London, Angus and Robertson, 1986.

*   *   *

Simon French writes about people and situations he knows well. Although his books are fiction they are an authentic representation of the speech, outlook, and actions of some Australians, most particularly schoolchildren. As a schoolboy writing *about* schoolboys in *Hey, Phantom Singlet* this authenticity is to be expected, but as an adult he has maintained an ability to create convincing dialogue and believable settings. There is little action in French's novels; rather the protagonists, always outsiders, come to learn about themselves and their world. Being an outsider is depicted in a positive light as a potential situation for creativity. In all three novels the same values are upheld. There is respect for creativity of any type, even if expressed principally in how a person dresses, and scorn for the type of conformity best described as arid respectability. Homes and their comforts are central to all the novels, and emphasis is placed on objects that have little monetary value but reflect something of their owner's personality.

In *Hey, Phantom Singlet* Math's orange singlet (vest) and Russian bear cap set him apart from his friends, suggesting both self-confidence and self-sufficiency. Math's reflections on his friends, the habits of his brothers, and his affection for Steve, an artist neighbour, reveal that far from being confident Math feels an outsider and misses his absent father. We find in the last pages of the book that the father has been in gaol, but a teacher helps Math to view his own actions and those of his father in a more positive light. In *Cannily, Cannily* the small town setting emphasises Trevor's awareness of the differences between the lives of the townsfolk and his own roving existence. In an ironic twist to the usual fictional situation of rebel children, Trevor's parents, Buckley and Kath, have cut their ties with a settled home and wander the country in their Kombi van, going from job to job. Central to this story is how Trevor cannily copes with a hostile school environment (hence the title). Sport and male aggression is a concern, and there is a fine parody of the Boy's Own set piece of a new boy's role in a vital game. Also prominent are questions about the nature of adult authority. Even kindly Buckley and Kath are shown to have been forgetful of Trevor's needs. A continuing emphasis on family relationships is tied to notions of time and change in *All We Know*, winner of an Australian Children's Book of the Year award. Because of changes in some of her own relationships the heroine Arkie starts to look closely at the connections between other people's lives, using her camera as another, different eye. French's empathy with children is apparent in this convincing portrayal of the fascination adolescents have with how others have managed to grow up.

French has said he "doesn't push a barrow," but his interest in relations between adults and children and a deep-felt concern for a more accepting world are evident in all his writing.

—Kerry White

FRITZ, Jean (née Guttery). Has also written as Ann Scott. American. Born in Hankow, China, 16 November 1915; lived in China until 1928. Educated at Wheaton College, Norton, Massachusetts, 1933–37 (associate editor, Wheaton *News*), B.A. 1937; Columbia University Teachers College, New York, 1938–39. Married Michael G. Fritz in 1941; one son and one daughter. Research assistant, Silver Burdett, publishers, New York, 1938–41; researcher, Boy Scouts of America, New York, 1941; reviewer, San Francisco *Chronicle,* and Tacoma *Ledger-News-Tribune,* Washington, and freelance writer, Macmillan and Prang publishers, 1940's– early 1950's; children's librarian, Dobbs Ferry Library, New York, 1955–57; teacher, Jean Fritz Writers' Workshop, Katonah, New York, 1962–70, Board of Cooperative Educational Services, Westchester County, New York, 1971–75, and Appalachian State University, Boone, North Carolina, summers 1981–83. Book reviewer, *New*

York Times and Washington *Post.* Recipient: Children's Book Guild award, for non-fiction, 1979; Child Study Committee award, 1982; American Book award, 1983; Christopher award, 1983; Boston *Globe-Horn Book* award, for non-fiction, 1984; Catholic Library Association Regina Medal, 1985; American Library Association Laura Ingalls Wilder award, 1986; University of Southern Mississippi award, 1988. D.Litt: Washington and Jefferson College, Washington, Pennsylvania, 1982; LL.D.: Wheaton College, 1987. Agent: Gina Maccoby Literary Agency, 124 West 24th Street, New York, New York 10011. Address: 50 Bellewood Avenue, Dobbs Ferry, New York 10522, U.S.A.

PUBLICATIONS FOR CHILDREN

Fiction

Bunny Hopwell's First Spring, illustrated by Rachel Dixon.   New York, Wonder Books, 1954.
Help Mr. Willy Nilly, illustrated by Jean Tamburine.   New York, Treasure Books, 1954.
Fish Head, illustrated by Marc Simont.   New York, Coward McCann, 1954; London, Faber, 1956.
121 Pudding Street, illustrated by Sofia.   New York, Coward McCann, 1955.
Hurrah for Jonathan!, illustrated by Violet La Mont.   Racine, Wisconsin, Whitman, 1955.
The Late Spring, illustrated by Erik Blegvad.   New York, Coward McCann, 1957.
The Cabin Faced West, illustrated by Feodor Rojankovsky.   New York, Coward McCann, 1958.
Champion Dog, Prince Tom, with Tom Clute, illustrated by Ernest Hart.   New York, Coward McCann, 1958.
How to Read a Rabbit, illustrated by Leonard Shortall.   New York, Coward McCann, 1959.
Brady, illustrated by Lynd Ward.   New York, Coward McCann, 1960; London, Gollancz, 1966.
December Is for Christmas (as Ann Scott), illustrated by Alcy Kendrick.   New York, Wonder Books, 1961.
Tap, Tap, Lion—One, Two, Three, illustrated by Leonard Shortall. New York, Coward McCann, 1962.
I, Adam, illustrated by Peter Burchard.   New York, Coward McCann, 1963; London, Gollancz, 1965.
Magic to Burn, illustrated by Beth and Joe Krush.   New York, Coward McCann, 1964.
Early Thunder, illustrated by Lynd Ward.   New York, Coward McCann, 1967; London, Gollancz, 1969.
George Washington's Breakfast, illustrated by Paul Galdone.   New York, Coward McCann, 1969.
The Secret Diary of Jeb and Abigail: Growing Up in America 1776–1783, illustrated by Kenneth Bald and Neil Boyle. Pleasantville, New York, Reader's Digest, 1976.

Other

Growing Up, illustrated by Elizabeth Webbe.   Chicago, Rand McNally, 1956.
The Animals of Dr. Schweitzer, illustrated by Douglas Howland. New York, Coward McCann, 1958; Edinburgh, Oliver and Boyd, 1962.
San Francisco, illustrated by Emil Weiss.   Chicago, Rand McNally, 1962.
Surprise Party (reader), illustrated by George Wiggins.   New York, Initial Teaching Alphabet Publications, 1965.
The Train (reader), illustrated by Jean Simpson.   New York, Grosset and Dunlap, 1965.

And Then What Happened, Paul Revere?, illustrated by Margot Tomes. New York, Coward McCann, 1973.

Why Don't You Get a Horse, Sam Adams?, illustrated by Trina Schart Hyman. New York, Coward McCann, 1974.

Where Was Patrick Henry on the 29th of May?, illustrated by Margot Tomes. New York, Coward McCann, 1975.

Who's That Stepping on Plymouth Rock?, illustrated by J.B. Handelsman. New York, Coward McCann, 1975.

Will You Sign Here, John Hancock?, illustrated by Trina Schart Hyman. New York, Coward McCann, 1976.

What's the Big Idea, Ben Franklin?, illustrated by Margot Tomes. New York, Coward McCann, 1976.

Can't You Make Them Behave, King George?, illustrated by Tomie de Paola. New York, Coward McCann, 1977.

Brendan the Navigator, illustrated by Enrico Arno. New York, Coward McCann, 1979.

Stonewall, illustrated by Stephen Gammell. New York, Putnam, 1979.

Back to Early Cape Cod. Washington, D.C., National Park Service, 1979.

Where Do You Thing You're Going, Christopher Columbus?, illustrated by Margot Tomes. New York, Putnam, 1980.

The Man Who Loved Books (on St. Columba), illustrated by Trina Schart Hyman. New York, Putnam, 1981.

Traitor: The Case of Benedict Arnold, illustrated by John André. New York, Putnam, 1981.

The Good Giants and the Bad Pukwudgies (folktale), illustrated by Tomie de Paola. New York, Putnam, 1982.

Homesick: My Own Story, illustrated by Margot Tomes. New York, Putnam, 1982.

The Double Life of Pocahontas, illustrated by Ed Young. New York, Putnam, 1983.

China Homecoming, photographs by Michael Fritz. New York, Putnam, 1985.

Make Way for Sam Houston, illustrated by Elise Primavera. New York, Putnam, 1986.

Shh! We're Writing the Constitution, illustrated by Tomie de Paola. New York, Putnam, 1987.

China's Long March: 6000 Miles of Danger, illustrated by Yang Zhr Cheng. New York, Putnam, 1988.

PUBLICATIONS FOR ADULTS

Other

Cast for a Revolution: Some American Friends and Enemies 1728–1814. Boston, Houghton Mifflin, 1972.

*

Manuscript Collections: Kerlan Collection, University of Minnesota, Minneapolis; University of Oregon Library, Eugene.

Critical Study: *Jean Fritz: A Critical Biography* by Elizabeth Hostetler, unpublished dissertation, University of Toledo, 1981.

Jean Fritz comments:

Although I experiment in various kinds of writing, my curiosity, I suppose, drives me most often to the past where there are more people, more stories, more truths, more secrets than I can ever hope to exhaust. I like having more than one century at my disposal. And I seem to need to put my roots down deeper and deeper into my own country.

*   *   *

Early in the 1970's Jean Fritz began to write the short, beguiling biographies which promise to make her as famous literarily as her subjects are historically. For readers aged 7 through 11 years, the books bear such jaunty titles as, *And Then What Happened, Paul Revere?, Will You Sign Here, John Hancock?,* and *Where Do You Think You're Going, Christopher Columbus?* These mini-lives include a zesty account of Plymouth Rock, a work which proves that the author can infuse even a stone with personality.

The little histories have been applauded by critics and read eagerly—not just by children but by adults who are amused by Fritz's lighthearted approach to weighty subjects. But the author is in no way guilty of debunking heroes. On the contrary, she is one of the few writers who convince us, by stressing their humanity, that the American Founding Fathers were even more remarkable than we had realized.

These books are the logical culmination of Fritz's background and interests. During the 1950's, she began to invent characters to people stories rooted in actuality. (Even her fantasies, like the adventurous *Magic to Burn,* center around British/American relations.) *The Cabin Faced West* is an affectionate *roman à clef* about her own great-great grandmother, Ann Hamilton. When Ann was a child, her father moved his family from their staid home in Gettysburg across the Allegheny Mountains into trackless Western Pennsylvania. The little girl's initial loneliness and growing love for her new home in the wilds are the backbone of an appealing novel. Readers can't help feeling Ann's joyous excitement when George Washington stops on his travels to dine with her family in the rough cabin on Hamilton Hill in 1784.

It isn't surprising that a gifted woman author can capture and convey the days of a girl child seeking cheer in bleak, strange surroundings. But Fritz does equally well by her boy heroes. During the 1960's, she created several historical novels in which young men were featured, teenagers whose involvement in chaotic events have made the past real and interesting to modern readers. Daniel West battles split loyalties during the tense days of 1765 in Salem in *Early Thunder,* when the town in Massachusetts suffered from the conflicts between Whigs and Tories that presaged the storm which began raging in 1776. In *I, Adam* the suspenseful adventures of Adam Crane convince him that coming of age in 1850 doesn't equal attaining manhood, that part of his destiny is to work for the shaping of the young nation. Brady Minton of *Brady* is a kid who learns the hard way not to tell everything he knows. His father is helping slaves to escape, just before the outbreak of the Civil War, a secret Mr. Minton can't trust his son to keep until Brady comes through a crisis and proves he has grown reliable.

The hallmarks of all Fritz's books are literary quality, authenticity, empathy with her characters, and respect for her young readers—the latter quality clearly visible in writing with no hint of condescension. And her natural, unforced sense of humor doesn't hurt a bit either.

—Jean F. Mercier

FRY, Rosalie K(ingsmill). British. Born on Vancouver Island, British Columbia, Canada, 22 April 1911. Educated at St. Margarets P.N.E.U. School, Swansea; Central School of Art, London, 1929–34. Served in the Women's Royal Naval Service, 1939–45. Address: 15 East Cliff, Southgate, Swansea SA3 2AS, Wales.

PUBLICATIONS FOR CHILDREN (illustrated by the author)

Fiction

Bumblebuzz. New York, Dutton, 1938.

Ladybug! Ladybug! New York, Dutton, 1940.
Bandy Boy's Treasure Island. New York, Dutton, 1941.
Adventure Downstream. London, Hutchinson, 1946.
In a Rock Pool. London, Hutchinson, 1947.
Cherrywinkle. London, Hutchinson, 1951.
The Little Gypsy. London, Hutchinson, 1951.
Pipkin Sees the World. New York, Dutton, 1951; as *Pipkin the Woodmouse,* London, Dent, 1953.
Deep in the Forest. London, Hutchinson, 1955; New York, Dodd Mead, 1956.
The Wind Call. London, Dent, and New York, Dutton, 1955.
Lucinda and the Painted Bell. London, Dent, 1956; as *A Bell for Ringelblume,* New York, Dutton, 1957.
Child of the Western Isles. London, Dent, 1957; as *Secret of the Ron Mor Skerry,* New York, Dutton, 1959.
Secret of the Forest. London, Hutchinson, 1958.
Matelot, Little Sailor of Brittany. New York, Dutton, 1958; as *Lucinda and the Sailor Kitten,* London, Dent, 1959.
Fly Home Colombina. London, Dent, and New York, Dutton, 1960.
The Mountain Door. London, Dent, 1960; New York, Dutton, 1961.
Princess in the Forest. London, Hutchinson, 1961.
The Echo Song. London, Dent, and New York, Dutton, 1962.
The Riddle of the Figurehead. London, Dent, and New York, Dutton, 1963.
September Island, illustrated by Margery Gill. London, Dent, and New York, Dutton, 1965.
The Castle Family, illustrated by Margery Gill. London, Dent, 1965; New York, Dutton, 1966.
Promise of the Rainbow, illustrated by Robin Jacques. New York, Bell, 1965; London, Dent, 1967.
Whistler in the Mist, illustrated by Robin Jacques. New York, Farrar Straus, 1968.
Gypsy Princess, illustrated by Philip Gough. London, Dent, and New York, Dutton, 1969.
Snowed Up, illustrated by Robin Jacques. New York, Farrar Straus, 1970; London, Dent, 1971.
Mungo, illustrated by Velma Ilsley. New York, Farrar Straus, 1972.
Secrets. London, Dent, 1973.

Other

Baby's Progress Book. Cardiff, W.H. Smith, 1944.
Lost in the Dew. Cardiff, W.H. Smith, 1944.
Many Happy Returns (birthday book). Cardiff, W.H. Smith, 1944.
Two Little Pigs (readers). London, Hutchinson, 3 vols., 1953.
Cinderella's Mouse and Other Fairy Tales. New York, Dutton, 1953.

*

Manuscript Collection: de Grummond Collection, University of Southern Mississippi, Hattiesburg.

Illustrator: *The Land of Lost Handkerchiefs,* by Marjorie Knight, 1954; *Jan Perry* series by Modwena Sedgwick, 3 vols., 1955–59; *The Water-Babies* by Charles Kingsley, 1957.

*   *   *

Rosalie K. Fry trained as an artist, but from the beginning she wrote her own stories to illustrate. In the 1940's and early 1950's she wrote stories for the very young with delicately coloured illustrations. She succeeded in personalizing even such unlikely creatures as hawk moths (*Cherrywinkle*) and crabs. *In a Rock Pool,* a story of the two crab friends Captain and Crusty, is a model of simple storytelling and presentation with not a word wasted.

With *Pipkin Sees the World* Fry began storytelling at greater length for an age level of about 8 or 9. While still humanising animals, she gives more detail from nature; dramatic incidents arise from Pipkin's natural fear of the owl or from his liking for garden peas. Her line illustrations demonstrate her love of small wild animals and all the (to us) miniature splendours of their habitat. Pipkin himself is gently sentimentalized, with a hint of humour in the drawings.

Jokle, the baby bear in *Deep in the Forest,* is another cuddly animal—more so than Pipkin, for he is that dream of every child: a live toy. This little book with Fry's lovely pictures in colour and line has everything that we think of as particularly pleasing to little girls: a spirited little heroine called Katinka plays houses, loves a pet, explores natural surroundings by herself but from the secure base of a loving home. She is moved by a lyrical feeling for the countryside and by a sense of beauty and mystery. The word "pretty" is often apt for this author's work, not used, as too often by grownups, patronizingly, but simply as a more modest and childlike word than beautiful. Fry knows exactly what children mean by "pretty."

The Wind Call is a full-length tale of a fairy child and the last that could be produced with coloured illustrations, but at about this time she illustrated in the same charming style the Dent/Dutton edition of *The Water-Babies.* She went on to write and illustrate in line slightly older books, three for instance about Lucinda who, though only 8, went abroad with her artist parents and appreciated the landscapes, lore, and crafts of Brittany and Italy. Then, from *The Echo Song* onwards, her books were about children of 10 or more and were illustrated by other artists (except *Secrets*).

In these later works, which no longer draw upon fantasy, her style is still a model of clarity: thoughtful and telling details make the plots absorbing and convincing, and the characters and settings have a charm that appeals strongly to children, especially girls entering their teens. Boating is a favourite theme but there is a variety of others, all inspired by her own experience of places: song contest and bird preservation in Wales (*The Echo Song*), exploration of a flooded estuary (*September Island*), a family mystery in Devon (*The Riddle of the Figurehead*), with, always, the interplay of character sympathetically developed.

Secrets are very well handled: secret news, secret presents, secret ambitions, or vague secrets with the charm of enchantment, such as unexplored mysterious places full of secret wild life and shadowy legends—all the secrets and private discoveries a child loves to cherish. They provide the natural suspense of the story and, in emotional terms, they provide a significant aid in a child's progress towards a strong self-image. The young reader knows the importance of lone experiences which he can keep to himself, so he responds to secrets in stories.

One secret in *Gypsy Princess* actually turns out to tell Zilda who she is. The story starts with Robert and Zilda discovering a passage running the whole length of a row of houses under the roofs. It leads to an old coach-house used by Robert's uncle as a store for antiques, and here, in a dark corner, Zilda finds a gypsy living-wagon with a bed-place, sliding panels, built-in-furniture and beautiful amber glass handles and knobs. The gypsy who left it had said he would come back one day to give it to the princess to whom it rightfully belonged. When Zilda found her own name carved beneath the wagon with the words "My princess," the whole story of her own dead parents comes out. Zilda herself was, to her father at least, a princess.

The gypsy wagon, lovingly described, is irresistible. Fry made just such a discovery of a gypsy wagon herself and owns it as an annex to her home.

—Gwen Marsh

FULLER, Roy (Broadbent). British. Born in Failsworth, Lancashire, 11 February 1912. Educated at Blackpool High School, Lancashire; qualified as a solicitor, 1934. Served in the Royal Navy, 1941–46; Lieutenant, Royal Naval Volunteer Reserve. Married Kathleen Smith in 1936; one son, the writer John Fuller. Staff member of various legal firms, 1934–38; assistant solicitor, 1938–58, solicitor, 1958–69, and director, 1969–88, Woolwich Equitable Building Society, London. Chairman of the Legal Advisory Panel, 1958–69, and a Vice-President, 1969–87, Building Societies Association. Professor of Poetry, Oxford University, 1968–73. Chairman, Poetry Book Society, London, 1960–68; a Governor, BBC, 1972–79; member, Arts Council of Great Britain, and Chairman of the Literature Panel, 1976–77; member, Library Advisory Council, 1977–79. Recipient: Arts Council Poetry award, 1959; Duff Cooper Memorial prize, for poetry, 1968; Queen's Gold Medal for Poetry, 1970; Cholmondeley award, for poetry, 1980. M.A.: Oxford University; D.Litt.: University of Kent, Canterbury, 1986. Fellow, Royal Society of Literature, 1958. C.B.E. (Commander, Order of the British Empire), 1970. Address: 37 Langton Way, Blackheath, London S.E.3, England.

PUBLICATIONS FOR CHILDREN

Fiction

Savage Gold, illustrated by Robert Medley. London, Lehmann, 1946.
With My Little Eye, illustrated by Alan Lindsay. London, Lehmann, 1948; New York, Macmillan, 1957.
Catspaw, illustrated by David Gollins. London, Alan Ross, 1966.
The Other Planet and Three Other Fables, illustrated by Paul Peter Piech. Richmond, Surrey, Keepsake Press, 1979.

Verse

Seen Grandpa Lately?, illustrated by Joan Hickson. London, Deutsch, 1972.
Poor Roy, illustrated by Nicolas Bentley. London, Deutsch, 1977.
More about Tompkins and Other Light Verse. Edinburgh, Tragara Press, 1981.
Upright, Downfall, with Barbara Giles and Adrian Rumble. Oxford and New York, Oxford University Press, 1983.
The World Through the Window: Collected Poems for Children, illustrated by Nick Duffy. London, Blackie, 1989.

PUBLICATIONS FOR ADULTS

Novels

The Second Curtain. London, Verschoyle, 1953; New York, Macmillan, 1956.
Fantasy and Fugue. London, Verschoyle, 1954; New York, Macmillan, 1956; as *Murder in Mind,* Chicago, Academy, 1986.
Image of a Society. London, Deutsch, 1956; New York, Macmillan, 1957.
The Ruined Boys. London, Deutsch, 1959; as *That Distant Afternoon,* New York, Macmillan, 1959.
The Father's Comedy. London, Deutsch, 1961.
The Perfect Fool. London, Deutsch, 1963.
My Child, My Sister. London, Deutsch, 1965.
The Carnal Island. London, Deutsch, 1970.

Verse

Poems. London, Fortune Press, 1940.
The Middle of a War. London, Hogarth Press, 1942.
A Lost Season. London, Hogarth Press, 1944.
Epitaphs and Occasions. London, Lehmann, 1949.
Counterparts. London, Vershoyle, 1954.
Brutus's Orchard. London, Deutsch, 1957; New York, Macmillan, 1958.
Collected Poems 1936–1961. London, Deutsch, 1962.
Buff. London, Deutsch, 1965.
New Poems. London, Deutsch, 1968.
Pergamon Poets 1, with R.S. Thomas, edited by Evan Owen. Oxford, Pergamon Press, 1968.
Off Course. London, Turret, 1969.
Penguin Modern Poets 18, with A. Alvarez and Anthony Thwaite. London, Penguin, 1970.
To an Unknown Reader. London, Poem-of-the-Month Club, 1970.
Song Cycle from a Record Sleeve. Oxford, Sycamore Press, 1972.
Tiny Tears. London, Deutsch, 1973.
An Old War. Edinburgh, Tragara Press, 1974.
Waiting for the Barbarians: A Poem. Richmond, Surrey, Keepsake Press, 1974.
From the Joke Shop. London, Deutsch, 1975.
The Joke Shop Annexe. Edinburgh, Tragara Press, 1975.
An Ill-Governed Coast. Sunderland, Ceolfrith Press, 1976.
Re-treads. Edinburgh, Tragara Press, 1979.
The Reign of Sparrows. London, London Magazine Editions, 1980.
The Individual and His Times: A Selection of the Poetry of Roy Fuller, edited by V.J. Lee. London, Athlone Press, 1982.
House and Shop. Edinburgh, Tragara Press, 1982.
As from the Thirties. Edinburgh, Tragara Press, 1983.
Mianserin Sonnets. Edinburgh, Tragara Press, 1984.
New and Collected Poems 1934–1984. London, Secker and Warburg, 1985.
Subsequent to Summer. Edinburgh, Salamander Press, 1985.
Outside the Canon. Edinburgh, Tragara Press, 1986.
Consolations. London, Secker and Warburg, 1987.
Available for Dreams. London, Collins, 1989.

Other

Owls and Artificers: Oxford Lectures on Poetry. London, Deutsch, and New York, Library Press, 1971.
Professors and Gods: Last Oxford Lectures on Poetry. London, Deutsch, 1973; New York, St. Martin's Press, 1974.
Souvenirs (memoirs). London, London Magazine Editions, 1980.
Vamp Till Ready: Further Memoirs. London, London Magazine Editions, 1982.
Home and Dry: Memoirs 3. London, London Magazine Editions, 1984.
Twelfth Night: A Personal View. Edinburgh, Tragara Press, 1985.

Editor, *Byron for Today.* London, Porcupine Press, 1948.
Editor, with Clifford Dyment and Montagu Slater, *New Poems 1952.* London, Joseph, 1952.
Editor, *The Building Societies Acts 1874–1960: Great Britain and Northern Ireland,* 5th edition. London, Franey, 1961.
Editor, *Supplement of New Poetry.* London, Poetry Book Society, 1964.
Editor, *Fellow Mortals: An Anthology of Animal Verse.* Plymouth, Macdonald and Evans, 1981.
Editor, with John Lehmann, *The Penguin New Writing 1940–1950: An Anthology.* London, Penguin, 1985.

*

Manuscript Collections: Brotherton Collection, Leeds University; State University of New York, Buffalo; British Library, London.

Critical Study: *Roy Fuller* by Allan E. Austin, Boston, Twayne, 1979.

Roy Fuller comments:

Though writing for children has always given me a certain sense of freedom, I have never thought of my children's books as "written down" to an audience. Indeed, possibly I have erred the other way; *With My Little Eye* was published in the United States as an adult crime novel! The separation in time between the two groups of children's books is to be accounted for by the fact that I was stimulated to write them first by my son's childhood, then my grandchildren's. I spoke about (*inter alia*) my own writings for children and their relation to my other work in a Sidney Robbins Memorial Fund lecture in 1975 (printed in *Children's Literature in Education,* Spring 1976) called "The Influence of Children on Books."

* * *

Savage Gold, written for Roy Fuller's son, is the story of two lads who find themselves caught up in a clash of interests between rival mining corporations in East Africa. It is well told, its setting is an attractive one, the action comes at a fast and exciting pace, but in the end Fuller's literariness leaves doubts as to whether his talents are really suitable for the writing of junior fiction. These misgivings are reinforced by *With My Little Eye,* a boy's detective novel which examines the effects of a court-room murder on the mind of an exceptionally intellectual and literate adolescent, Frederick French, only son of a County Court judge, and which follows his peripatetic efforts to hunt down the killer.

French bears an undoubted resemblance to Michael Innes's erudite sleuth John Appleby—he finds his first clue in Sir Walter Scott's *The Black Dwarf*—and in general *With My Little Eye* contains the same bizarre mixture of intellectual cerebration and outlandish adventures that characterize the early Innes detective novels. But in all seriousness we can only conclude that Fuller sadly misdirected his inventiveness; even in 1948 the market for this type of story, aimed at that almost indefinable range of reader between 12 and 17, could not have been very large, and although the book attracted much praise from the critics, it is difficult to believe it held much interest for that age group. Take this passage, for example, which comes from a discussion between father and son:

> Well, on the highest level I think that the hunt for a murderer—fictional or in real life—satisfied a moral longing. It is all part of a revolution of our time. We—my generation—have no general and dogmatic views about right and wrong. And yet we want good to be rewarded and evil punished. Murder is a happening which usually is quite unarguably evil even from our disillusioned viewpoint. And so in that little limited sphere we have a disproportionate interest. On a lower level, of course, the pursuit of a murderer has the interest of a puzzle. But if you go on to ask me why men are fascinated by puzzles, I am afraid I cannot answer you.

Few teenage readers, either then or now, will surely continue for very long to read even a detective novel if it stops the action to moralize in this fashion, especially when the son, whose speech it is, and who also tells the story in the first person, is demonstrably in today's terms an unashamed, unrepentent elitist in his language and attitude.

Catspaw belongs to the verges of science fiction: Victoria, a little girl, wanders into a country inhabited solely by dogs who somewhat improbably are living in constant fear of Pussia the land of the cats. A clever parable about the cold war, the whole ghastly twilight world of espionage, intelligence, and security is mirrored there in fantasy, but again the message is wasted on the wrong audience.

—Alan Edwin Day

———

FYLEMAN, Rose. British. Born Rose Amy Feilmann in Basford, Nottinghamshire, 6 March 1877. Educated at University College, Nottingham; Royal College of Music, London, diploma; studied singing in Germany and Paris. Singer: first public performance, Queen's Hall, London, 1903. Teacher and lecturer; regular contributor to *Punch,* London; founding editor, *Merry-Go-Round* children's magazine, Oxford 1923–24. *Died 1 August 1957.*

PUBLICATIONS FOR CHILDREN

Fiction

The Rainbow Cat and Other Stories, illustrated by Thelma Cudlipp Grosvenor. London, Methuen, 1922; New York, Doran, 1923.
Forty Good-Night Tales, illustrated by Thelma Cudlipp Grosvenor. London, Methuen, 1923; New York, Doran, 1924.
The Adventure Club, illustrated by A.H. Watson. London, Methuen, 1925; New York, Doran, 1926.
Letty: A Study of a Child, illustrated by Lisl Hummel. London, Methuen, 1926; New York, Doran, 1927.
Forty Good-Morning Tales. London, Methuen, 1926; New York, Doran, 1929.
Twenty Tea-Time Tales. London, Methuen, 1929; as *Tea Time Tales,* New York, Doubleday, 1930.
The Dolls' House, illustrated by Margaret Tempest. London, Methuen, 1930; New York, Doubleday, 1931.
The Katy Kruse Play Book, illustrated by Katy Kruse. London, Harrap, and Philadelphia, McKay, 1930.
The Strange Adventures of Captain Marwhopple, illustrated by Gertrude Lindsay. London, Methuen, 1931; New York, Doubleday, 1932.
The Easter Hare and Other Stories, illustrated by Decie Merwin. London, Methuen, 1932.
Jeremy Quince, Lord Mayor of London, illustrated by Cecil Leslie. London, Cape, 1933.
The Princess Dances, illustrated by Cecil Leslie. London, Dent, 1933.
Timothy's Conjuror. London, Methuen, 1942.
The Timothy Boy Trust, illustrated by Marjorie Wratten. London, Methuen, 1944.
Hob and Bob: A Tale of Two Goblins, illustrated by Charles Stewart. London, Hollis and Carter, 1944.
Adventures with Benghazi, illustrated by Peggy Fortnum. London, Eyre and Spottiswoode, 1946.
The Smith Family 4–6 (At the Seaside, In the Country, In Town). Leeds, E.J. Arnold, 3 vols., 1947.
Nursery Stories. London, Evans, 1949.
Lucy the Lamb. London, Eyre and Spottiswoode, 1951.
Neddy the Donkey. London, Eyre and Spottiswoode, 1951.
The Sparrow and the Goat. London, Eyre and Spottiswoode, 1951.
The Starling and the Fox. London, Eyre and Spottiswoode, 1951.
White Flower, illustrated by M.E. Stewart. Leeds, E.J. Arnold, 1953.

Plays

Eight Little Plays for Children (includes *Darby and Joan, The Fairy Riddle, Noughts and Crosses, The Weather Clerk, The Fairy and the Doll, Cabbages and Kings, In Arcady, Father Christmas*). London, Methuen, 1924; New York, Doran, 1925.

Seven Little Plays for Children (includes *The Princess and the Pirate; The Butcher, The Baker, The Candlestickmaker; The Mermaid; Peter Coffin; The Arm-Chair; Mother Goose's Party; The Coming of Father Christmas*). London, Methuen, 1928.

Happy Families: A Comic Opera, music by Thomas F. Dunhill (produced Guildford, Surrey, 1933). London, Methuen, 1933.

Nine New Plays for Children (includes *The Whisker; The Moon; Cinderella "At Home"; The Sampler; Three Naughty Imps; Surprise, The Imp; The Test; Sleeping Beauty; Father Christmas Comes to Supper*), illustrated by Eleanor L. Halsey. London and New York, Nelson, 1934.

Six Longer Plays for Children (includes *Snow-White, Porridge, Pork-Pie Night, The Bear, The Gus-Plug, The Angry Brownies*), illustrated by Eleanor L. Halsey. London, Nelson, 1936.

The Magic Pencil and Other Plays from My Tales (includes *The Carpet of Truth, Captain Marwhopple, The Rhyming Prince, The Chestnut Man, The Three Princesses, Troodle, A Legend of St. Nicholas*). London, Methuen, 1938.

The Spanish Cloak. London, Methuen, 1939.

Red-Riding-Hood, music by Will Grant. London, Oxford University Press, 1949.

Verse

The Sunny Book, illustrated by Millicent Sowerby. London, Oxford University Press, 1918.

Fairies and Chimneys. London, Methuen, 1918; New York, Doran, 1920.

The Fairy Green. London, Methuen, 1919; New York, Doran, 1923.

The Fairy Flute. London, Methuen, 1921; New York, Doran, 1923.

A Small Cruse, illustrated by Katy Kruse. London, Methuen, 1923.

The Rose Fyleman Fairy Book. London, Methuen, and New York, Doran, 1923.

Fairies and Friends. London, Methuen, 1925; New York, Doran, 1926.

The Rose Fyleman Calendar, illustrated by Lisl Hummell. London, Methuen, 1927.

Joy Street Poems, with others. Oxford, Blackwell, 1927.

A Princess Comes to Our Town, illustrated by Gertrude Lindsay. London, Methuen, 1927; New York, Doubleday, 1928.

Old-Fashioned Girls and Other Poems, illustrated by Ethel Everett. London, Methuen, 1928.

A Garland of Rose's: Collected Poems of Rose Fyleman, illustrated by René Bull. London, Methuen, 1928.

Gay Go Up, illustrated by Decie Merwin. London, Methuen, 1929; New York, Doubleday, 1930.

Fifty-One New Nursery Rhymes, illustrated by Dorothy Burroughes. London, Methuen, 1931; New York, Doubleday, 1932.

The Blue Rhyme Book, music by Thomas F. Dunhill, illustrated by M. Bantock. London, Boosey-Methuen, 1933.

Runabout Rhymes, illustrated by Margaret Tempest. London, Methuen, 1941.

Number Rhymes. Leeds, E.J. Arnold, 1946.

Rhyme Book for Adam. London, Methuen, 1949.

Other

A Little Christmas Book, illustrated by Lisl Hummel. London, Methuen, 1926; New York, Doran, 1927.

The Katy Kruse Dolly Book, illustrated by Katy Kruse. London, Harrap, and New York, Doran, 1927; *The Second Katy Kruse Dolly Book,* Harrap, 1930.

Hey! Ding-a-Ding. London, University of London Press, 1931.

The Rose Fyleman Birthday Book, illustrated by Muriel Dawson and Margaret Tarrant. London, Medici Society, 1932.

Bears, illustrated by Stuart Tresilian. London and New York, Nelson, 1935.

Monkeys. London and New York, Nelson, 1936.

Billy Monkey: A True Tale of a Capuchin, with E.M.D. Wilson, illustrated by Cecil Leslie. London, Nelson, 1936; New York, Nelson, 1937.

A Book of Saints: Joan of Arc to St. Nicholas, illustrated by Gertrude Mittelman. London, Methuen, 1939.

Folk-Tales from Many Lands. London, Methuen, 1939.

Daphne and Dick (An Uncle from Canada, Round and About, Adventures), illustrated by Jeannetta Vise. London, Macdonald, 3 vols., 1952.

Editor, *Round the Mulberry Bush, Being a Book of Stories and Verse for Children.* London, Partridge, and New York, Dodd Mead, 1928.

Editor, *Sugar and Spice: A Collection of Nursery Rhymes, New and Old,* illustrated by Janet Laura Scott. Racine, Wisconsin, Whitman, 1935.

Editor, *Here We Come A'Piping* (verse), illustrated by Irene Mountfort. Oxford, Blackwell, 4 vols., 1936–37; New York, Stokes, 1 vol., 1937.

Editor, *A'Piping Again* (verse), illustrated by Irene Mountfort. Oxford, Blackwell, 1936; New York, Stokes, 1938.

Editor, *Bells Ringing: An Anthology of Verse for Young Children,* illustrated by Irene Mountfort. Oxford, Blackwell, 1938; New York, Stokes, 1939.

Editor, *Pipe and Drum: An Anthology of Verse for Young Children,* illustrated by Irene Mountfort. Oxford, Blackwell, 1939; New York, Stokes, 1940.

Editor, *Let's Play.* London, Grout, 1943.

Editor, *Punch and Judy,* illustrated by Paul Henning. London, Methuen, 1944.

Editor, *Over the Tree Tops: Nursery Rhymes from Many Lands.* Oxford, Blackwell, 1949.

Translator, *Bibi,* by Karin Michaelis, illustrated by Hedvig Collin. London, Allen and Unwin, 1933.

Translator, *Bibi Goes Travelling,* by Karin Michaelis, illustrated by Hedvig Collin. London, Allen and Unwin, 1934.

Translator, *Widdy-Widdy-Wurkey: Nursery Rhymes from Many Lands,* illustrated by Valerie Carrick. Oxford, Blackwell, 1934; as *Picture Rhymes from Foreign Lands,* New York, Stokes, 1935; as *Nursery Rhymes from Many Lands,* New York, Dover, 1971.

Translator, *Green Island,* by Karin Michaelis, illustrated by Hedvig Collin. London, Allen and Unwin, 1936.

Translator, *Père Castor's Wild Animal Books (Bourru, The Brown Bear; Frou, The Hare; Mischief, The Squirrel; Plouf, The Wild Duck; Scaf, The Seal; Quipic, The Hedgehog; Martin, The Kingfisher; Cuckoo),* by Lida, illustrated by Rojan. London, Allen and Unwin, 8 vols., 1937–42.

Translator, *Fireflies,* by Jan Karafiat, illustrated by Emil Weiss. London, Allen and Unwin, 1942.

Translator, *Tuck, The Story of a Snow Hare,* by Alfred Flueckiger, illustrated by Grace Huxtable. London, Lane, 1949.

Translator, *Simone and the Lilywhites,* by Marie-Louise Ventteclaye. London, Museum Press, 1949.

Translator, *The Adventures of Tommy, The Cat Who Went to Sea,* by Lillian Miozzi, illustrated by Charlotte Hough. London, Lane, 1950.

Translator, *Peter and His Friend Toby,* by Lily Martini, illustrated by Wolfgang Felten.   London, Lane, 1955.

PUBLICATIONS FOR ADULTS

Play

After All.   London, Methuen, 1939.

Other

Translator, *Songs.*   London, Curwen, 1927.

*   *   *

Rose Fyleman is one of the people responsible for the modern tiny fairy, as distinct from the Elizabethan kind like Puck, who were full-sized, often grotesque, and capable of metamorphosis. Her first poem, "There are fairies at the bottom of my garden," established for all time the tiny flower-fairies, dainty, gossamer-winged, and glamorous, wearing crowns and gaily-coloured dresses. Yet they live in surroundings familiar to her young readers, as in the poem called "The Fairy House," where a little girl discovers a tiny house with

> Teeny weeny carpets
> On shiny polished floors
> Teeny weeny handles
> On little painted doors

and the rest of its furnishings to match. Fairies are at the same time wonderful and understandable.

As a teacher she knew what appealed to little children. Some of the earlier work she produced was adapted from French and German folk tales and poems, and other work, though original, has a continental flavour, such as the tale called "The Broom," where the poor crossing-sweeper gets a witch's broom by mistake and becomes rich by hiring it out for journeys, until a scientist rents it to go to the moon and meets its rightful owner.

A skilled musician, she turned many of her poems into songs and indeed composed a children's opera. Though the present taste for magic in fiction tends to be darker and more sinister, there is still a place for Fyleman to give small children their first taste of the supernatural world.

—Ann G. Hay

———————

FYSON, J(enny) G(race, née Harrison). British. Born in Bromley, Kent, 3 October 1904. Educated at St. Swithens School, Winchester, 1918–21. Married Christopher Fyson in 1940 (died 1945); one son. Painter, 1921–37, and weaver. Address: c/o Oxford University Press, Walton Street, Oxford OX2 6DP, England.

PUBLICATIONS FOR CHILDREN

Fiction

The Three Brothers of Ur, illustrated by Victor Ambrus.   London, Oxford University Press, 1964; New York, Coward McCann, 1967.

The Journey of the Eldest Son, illustrated by Victor Ambrus.   London, Oxford University Press, 1965; New York, Coward McCann, 1967.
Friend Fire and the Dark Wings, illustrated by Annabel Large.   Oxford, Oxford University Press, 1983.

Play

Radio Play: *Saul and David,* 1952.

*

J.G. Fyson comments:
In my first two published books I have tried to fill in the background of the time of Abraham from archaeological discoveries. The pitfall that one meets in trying to write religious books for children is the snare of becoming a religious propagandist: of manufacturing facts and twisting behaviour to fit a theory. I have tried all the time to let the facts speak for themselves and to make my characters complete human beings, then found they inevitably led me to conclusions unthought of.
In *The Journey of the Eldest Son* it became clear that there was no way of freeing man from the load of guilt that his imagination has cooked up except by the intervention of the New Testament. As when a man recovers from a neurosis he sees God and is cured. The "dark wings" of the third book are primeval fears which still affect our judgment.

*   *   *

Which is the more difficult historical novel to write, one of a period which is fully documented, or one where the documentation is so thin as to be virtually invisible? J.G. Fyson chose the latter and made it seem an easy matter to recreate a 4000-year-old scene. The setting of her two linked novels is Ur of the Chaldees. Here is a sophisticated society, a city-state which has achieved a highly developed form of government, fine crafts, and a system of trade. Outside the city walls lies the wilderness where savages threaten the trade routes. The wealth of Teresh the Stern and the welfare of his family depend on the courage of those who will dare the dangers and trade in distant parts.
The Three Brothers of Ur is largely a family story. Haran the youngest son is a harum-scarum, "that king of all the jackdaws of Ur," as Mushinti the Beautiful puts it neatly. His flair for mischief is the motive-force of much of the story. The malice of Maychor, the middle son, also plays a part. Shamashazir is above mischief and malice. As the elder son he is head of the house when Teresh is away; moreover, he needs to have his father's agreement to travel on the next trade journey. But father will give no permission without a favourable sign from the Teraphim, the household god. Haran manages to break the Teraphim, but Shamashazir receives messages from someone greater than a clay image, a voice coming out of the White Mountains.
In *The Journey of the Eldest Son* Shamashazir takes the trail over the mountains and is able to test both his courage and endurance and the relative power of the gods of the tribes he meets. He also meets the Lord of All the Earth and realizes the source of the voice which he had heard from the mountains.
The advent of monotheism seems an unlikely theme on which to base two stories for children. In Fyson's hands adventure and character and philosophy become one. Many readers who delight in the fun and the excitement remain unaware that in another book Shamashazir is called Abraham, and that they are reading the story of a great turning-point in history. It is not important. No reader can be unaware that on his adventurous journey Shamashazir discovers a great truth, even if the nature of that truth remains hidden for a time.

These are not the only children's books whose true meaning is understood only in adult life.

A gap of nearly 20 years separates the Ur stories from Fyson's next book. In that time she gave much thought to the mystery of man's origins and to the biology and philosophy of evolution (expressing these thoughts most precisely in a long as-yet-unpublished poem). For her next book she went back to the emergence of homo sapiens, the "Wise-Animal" who is the central figure of *Friend Fire and the Dark Wings*. The small cave boy Lari carelessly breaks the tip of his father's precious hunting spear. While making a new one he inadvertently discovers the secret of fire and so transforms the lives of his family and changes the course of prehistory. It is a great theme. Instead of treating it with due solemnity Fyson develops it in human terms, dwelling on the impact of a major invention on a few primitive people. She avoids the common weakness of most stories about early man—hindsight. Lari and his family are inarticulate, almost without benefit of language, and the reader sees their situation through their eyes. The book is as honest as it is sensitive. The warmth that pervades it comes as much from love as from fire.

—Marcus Crouch

GÁG, Wanda (Hazel). American. Born in New Ulm, Minnesota, 11 March 1893. Educated at New Ulm High School, graduated 1912; St. Paul Art School, 1913–14; Minneapolis Art School, 1914–17; Art Students' League, New York, 1917–18. Married Earle Marshall Humphreys in 1931. Schoolteacher, 1912–13; commercial artist, 1918–23. Individual shows: New York Public Library, 1923; Weyhe Gallery, New York, 1926, 1930, 1940 (retrospective); group shows: Museum of Modern Art, New York, 1939; Metropolitan Museum, New York, 1943. Recipient: University of Minnesota Kerlan award, 1977. *Died 27 June 1946.*

PUBLICATIONS FOR CHILDREN (illustrated by the author)

Fiction

Millions of Cats. New York, Coward McCann, 1928; London, Faber, 1929.
The Funny Thing. New York, Coward McCann, 1929; London, Faber, 1962.
Snippy and Snappy. New York, Coward McCann, 1931; London, Faber, 1932.
The ABC Bunny. New York, Coward McCann, 1933; London, Faber, 1962.
Storybook. New York, Coward McCann, 1940.
Nothing at All. New York, Coward McCann, 1941; London, Faber, 1942.

Other

Gone Is Gone; or, The Story of a Man Who Wanted to Do Housework. New York, Coward McCann, 1935; London, Faber, 1936.
Tales from Grimm. New York, Coward McCann, 1936; London, Faber, 1937.
Snow White and the Seven Dwarfs. New York, Coward McCann, and London, Faber, 1938.
Three Gay Tales from Grimm. New York, Coward McCann, 1943; London, Heinemann, 1946.
More Tales from Grimm. New York, Coward McCann, 1947; London, Faber, 1962.

PUBLICATIONS FOR ADULTS

Other

Growing Pains: Diaries and Drawings for the Years 1908–1917. New York, Coward McCann, 1940.

*

Manuscript Collections: Kerlan Collection, University of Minnesota, Minneapolis; New York Public Library; Free Library, Philadelphia; Minneapolis Institute of Art.

Critical Studies: *Wanda Gág: The Story of an Artist* by Alma Scott, Minneapolis, University of Minnesota Press, 1949; *50 Years of Wanda Gág's Millions of Cats 1928–1978* by Michael Patrick Hearn, New York, Coward McCann, 1978.

Illustrator: *The Day of Doom* by Michael Wigglesworth, 1929.

*   *   *

Wanda Gág's undertakings supply an enchanting course in aesthetics for the young, as well as a display of what is good in children's fiction. *Nothing at All* articulates through simple narrative the process by which an airy notion achieves apprehensible form. An invisible puppy, whose existence is suggested by nothing more than a dog house and a name which defines his condition, emerges through desire, design, and poetry to acquire outline, colour, and form, and finally to become a bona fide pet. Cohesion and limitless possibility are key concepts for comprehending the achievement of Gág's classic, *Millions of Cats*. Primitive woodcuts mingle with a hand-lettered narrative, and serve as a means to expand narration, instead of lapsing into illustration's habitual role of incidental ornamentation. All things cohere, as a simple peasant longing soon becomes over-abundant fulfillment. Straightforward prose erupts into unforgettable lyric outbursts as the author delves into the mundane and emerges with the marvellous. The cottage environs, serene, secure, and clean, yet require a cat to love. Absolute contentment is but a wish away, a dream whose reality is induced by nothing more than a jaunt over hills, through villages to a nearby place where fancy yields surcharged plenty. The avalanche of lovely felines laps up ponds and eats the grass lands bare until the too-much becomes resolved into one straggly kitten. This homely residue, through care and love, rises in time to become the embodiment of beauty.

In *The ABC Bunny* individual images resist every static tendency and break forth into activity. Instead of the usual abcederia where each letter has its calligraphic moment and then is seen no more, here A's apple becomes C's crash which propels B's bunny into D's dash towards E's everywhere. Interlacing objects with activity, the sounds, basic segments of language, lead onward to boundless possibility. Infinite growth rather than happy end is likewise the final scene in the tale *The Funny Thing,* where a fanciful diet of jum jills causes a ceaseless succession of segments to append themselves to the tail of an already improbable creature who defies a name and must be termed an *aminal* since he fits no genus at all.

Gág's attitude toward characters, as well as author and audience, appears to be fascinated involvement. Even the plot seems susceptible to enchantment. Her 52 fairy tales, translations from the brothers Grimm, are tempered to sustain the magic of the story-telling experience recalled from her own childhood. Where literal renderings will serve, so much the better. Where phrasing, episodes, and endings must be altered, the sensibility of the narrator becomes, as it did with the ancient bards, the ultimate arbiter. However much her tamperings might dismay the folklorist, her heart is with her auditors. The lyric sound leads to a mood of distilled wonderment.

The tale is no mere narrative sequence. Above all, it is an atmosphere.

—Leonard R. Mendelsohn

———

GAGE, Wilson.   See STEELE, Mary Q.

———

GANNETT, Ruth Stiles.   American.   Born in New York City, 12 August 1923. Educated at City and Country School; George School, Pennsylvania; Vassar College, Poughkeepsie, New York, B.A. 1944. Married Peter Kahn in 1947; seven children. Medical technician, Boston City Hospital; radar research technician, Massachusetts Institute of Technology, Cambridge; staff member, Children's Book Council, New York. Address: BD-2, Box 334, Trumansburg, New York 14886, U.S.A.

PUBLICATIONS FOR CHILDREN

Fiction

My Father's Dragon, illustrated by Ruth Chrisman Gannett.   New York, Random House, 1948; London, Macmillan, 1957.
The Wonderful House-Boat-Train, illustrated by Fritz Eichenberg. New York, Random House, 1949.
Elmer and the Dragon, illustrated by Ruth Chrisman Gannett.   New York, Random House, 1950.
The Dragons of Blueland, illustrated by Ruth Chrisman Gannett. New York, Random House, 1951.
Katie and the Sad Noise, illustrated by Ellie Simmons.   New York, Random House, 1961.

*

Manuscript Collections: May Massee Collection, Emporia State University, Kansas; Kerlan Collection, University of Minnesota, Minneapolis.

*   *   *

In her trilogy (*My Father's Dragon, Elmer and the Dragon, The Dragons of Blueland*), Ruth Stiles Gannett sets her pace with verve and freshness, with a childlike matter-of-factness, and an inherent logic. Her use of the fantastic reflects a sensibility for the imagination of young children. So skillfully does she develop Elmer Elevator that the incredible becomes credible without strain. In *My Father's Dragon* her understanding of what little boys are like, especially Elmer, is apparent. The reader accepts, without question, Elmer's decision to make the journey to Wild Island to free the baby dragon. Unafraid of words, Gannett selects exactly the right ones for her tale. Clearly American in spirit, her language takes on universality.

Elmer and the Dragon continues naturally Elmer's high adventure. The humor and the nonsense are typical of the imaginative world of any child. She offers details that indicate an intuitive understanding of a child's curiosity. Whether it is food or history or even the contents of a treasure chest, everything is described with relish.

The Dragons of Blueland brings to an end Elmer's adventures as he sets out with Boris, the baby dragon, to rescue Boris's family entrapped in a cave. Although the humor and excitement are not so well sustained as in the two earlier books, this is a finale for a saga

that reflects completely the child's world. One is reminded of the world of Christopher Robin. There is the same kind of naturalness, believability, and whimsey.

The author's mother, Ruth Chrisman Gannett, illustrated the books. Her work interprets the text perfectly; they complement the text so that there is not only reading but visual pleasure.

The Wonderful House-Boat-Train, the story of the search by Pops Pops, the retired railroad engineer, and his four grandchildren for a home, is more deliberate and lacks the quality that is associated with a natural, creative flow. *Katie and the Sad Noise* appears to be a book for the beginning reader. Katie hears strange noises and tells her parents of them. Their concern leads to a consultation with Katie's teachers. One situation follows another, building up a sense of mystery. The resolution is neatly presented, and ends with a Christmas surprise, but the complexity of plot tends to throw off course the simplicity of text.

Gannett will be remembered for her singular approach to creativity. Children, hearing or reading the Elmer Elevator books, can say, "Of course!" The cultivated adult will recognize the touch of the real storyteller who has accomplished what she has set out to do—to tell her tales with grace, childlike humor, and literary style.

—Mae Durham Roger

———

GARD, Joyce.   Pseudonym for Joyce Reeves.   British.   Born in London, 13 January 1911; sister of James Reeves, *q.v.* Educated at Wycombe Abbey School, Buckinghamshire, 1924–29; Lady Margaret Hall, Oxford, 1930–33, B.A. (honours) in English 1933. Assistant, Foreign Rights Department, Curtis Brown Ltd., London, 1934–35; teacher, Varndean School for Girls, Brighton, 1935–37; lived in Paris, 1937–39; temporary administrative assistant, Ministry of Economic Warfare, London, 1939–45; civil servant, Frankfurt and Hamburg, 1945–47; apprentice, Winchcombe Pottery, Gloucestershire, 1947–48; studio potter, London and Newhaven, Sussex, 1948–56; part-time private secretary and research assistant to Sir Roland Penrose, London, 1956–72. Translator and contributor, *XX Siècle* art review, Paris, 1939–70. Address: 1 Eliza Cottages, Charing, Ashford, Kent TN27 0JG, England.

PUBLICATIONS FOR CHILDREN

Fiction

Woorroo, illustrated by Ronald Benham.   London, Gollancz, 1961.
The Dragon of the Hill.   London, Gollancz, 1963.
Talargain, The Seal's Whelp.   London, Gollancz, 1964; New York, Holt Rinehart, 1965.
Smudge of the Fells.   London, Gollancz, 1965; New York, Holt Rinehart, 1966.
The Snow Firing.   London, Gollancz, 1967; New York, Holt Rinehart, 1968.
The Mermaid's Daughter.   London, Gollancz, and New York, Holt Rinehart, 1969.
Handysides Shall Not Fall, illustrated by Carolyn Dinan.   London, Kaye and Ward, 1975.
The Hagwaste Donkeys, illustrated by Gareth Floyd.   London, Pelham, 1976.

Other

Translator, *Journey to the Centre of the Earth,* by Jules Verne, illustrated by Dick Hart.   London, Hutchinson, 1961.

PUBLICATIONS FOR ADULTS

Other

Translator (as Joyce Reeves), *Marc Chagall: Drawings and Water Colors for the Ballet,* by Jacques Lassaigne.   Paris, XX Siècle, and New York, Tudor, 1969.

*

Joyce Gard comments:

(1978) The only way I can write for children is to write for myself as a child—to become a child again, the person I was and still essentially am.

My books are not easy to introduce or categorize briefly. However, I think the basic essentials of any children's fiction, which I have tried to provide, are: 1) a good story, 2) good writing, 3) credible, interesting people, not too complex, 4) a sound setting—an individual and distinctive *place,* and 5) something *extra.*

This "extra" could be an unusual insight into a particular way of life, for instance, or a special magic or mystery. In my first children's books I attempted to recapture the ecstasy of pure physical sensation which only children, I believe, can experience unmixed: either imagined—flying like a bird in *Woorroo*—or real—ocean-swimming in *Talargain,* here enhanced by communion with the seals.

I explored other childhood dreams and obsessions, such as finding buried treasure, confronting dragons, entering into the lives of beautiful people of the past—*The Dragon of the Hill* and *Talargain.* Then I turned to practical lives I would have liked to live—a sheep farmer in the Lake District in *Smudge of the Fells*—or had myself lived—a studio potter in *The Snow Firing.* There is as much technical know-how in these two books as I could squeeze in without, I hope, giving up the first requisite of a good story.

The Mermaid's Daughter is for an older age-group; it is the story of a girl growing up in the Scilly Isles in Roman times and her adventures as she strives to reconcile her two roles—that of the chosen mortal embodiment of the Sea Goddess of the islands and of a flesh-and-blood human being and her relationships with family and lovers, friends and enemies.

I don't believe in an explicit "message"; in my experience this causes an automatic switch-off of interest in a healthy child. I believe strongly, however, that worthwhile fiction is a power for good and feeds the imagination—in the same way that Shelley claimed for poetry.

(1983) I am not writing for children any more. That vein ran out after I went to the Orkneys and Shetlands some years ago looking for a children's book and became so severely infected with the archaeological virus that the resulting book was unpublishable even after two rewritings. For a long time now I have been researching and am now writing a book which no serious archaeologist would dare to undertake, as it consists of an attempt to reconstruct a lost period of our history for which the evidence is all too scanty. However, the editor of *Current Archaeology,* Andrew Selkirk, has been good enough to publish a few short pieces of mine in a similar speculative vein, of course taking no responsibility.

*   *   *

Joyce Gard writes for children prepared to savour a book rather than romp through it for the sake of the story. Her novels are strongly rooted in place—the English Lakes, Gloucestershire, the Scillies—often luminously evoked. In each the author explores one of her many interests, which include pottery, sheep-farming, and archaeology, and these are the real focus of the story. Though they may begin with exciting action, such as the memorable horror and beauty of the dragon's flight, successive events move more slowly and are some-

times impeded by a straight recapitulation of events that the reader has not shared. The characters also are usually subordinate to the theme or plot, perfectly satisfactory for their purpose but not explored in any great depth and not much changed or developed by the things that happen to them. Gard's best gift is that of sensory perception. *Woorroo* shares the wild joy and freedom of winged flight, *Talargain* the physical sensation, the delight and fear, of swimming with the seals, and the boy's relationship with them. In *The Snow Firing* one can feel the smooth wet clay and the warmly sensuous beauty of the finished pots.

The stories intended for younger readers will appeal only to a limited audience of rather sheltered children. But in the present spate of books for the mass there may still be a need for a few for minority groups.

It is in the novels dealing with the past that the writer shows her real quality. *The Dragon of the Hill, Talargain,* and *The Mermaid's Daughter* are all wholly or partly set in the period of Roman Britain. The life and manners of the time are handled convincingly and lightly; the reader can share in them without feeling burdened by conscientious social history. Gard is particularly interested in ancient cults and can identify herself imaginatively with the religious feeling of other times and countries. *Woorroo*'s aboriginal magic, as he chants and paints in the dawn at the edge of the lake, is one of the most memorable moments in the novel. *The Mermaid's Daughter,* by far her most ambitious and successful book, attempts to recreate the cult of the Great Mother, the Sea Goddess, as it may once have existed in the Scilly Islands. The heroine, Astria, is the secret representative of the goddess among her people. The story moves between the islands and the Roman fortress at Caerleon, both vividly evoked. It develops slowly despite times of excitement, of romantic love and tragedy, but it immerses the reader completely in its own world. Individual episodes remain most vividly in the mind—the ritual marriage in the dark cave by the sea, Astria dancing on the bright spring grass beyond Caerleon, watched by the wild, shy hill people, the meeting with St. Alban in the Roman garrison. But above all one is haunted by the images of sea and sky and flowers, a sense of grace and light. This is a book of unusual quality.

—Margaret Greaves

———

GARDAM, Jane (née Pearson). British. Born in Coatham, Yorkshire, 11 July 1928. Educated at Saltburn High School for Girls; Bedford College, London, 1946–49, B.A. (honours) 1949, graduate study, 1949–52. Married David Gardam in 1952; two sons and one daughter. Red Cross librarian, 1951; sub-editor, *Weldons Ladies Journal,* London, 1952–53; assistant literary editor, *Time and Tide,* London, 1952–54. Recipient: David Higham prize, for fiction, 1975; Winifred Holtby Memorial prize, for fiction, 1976; Whitbread award, 1981; Katherine Mansfield-Menton prize, 1985. Fellow, Royal Society of Literature, 1976. Agent: Bruce Hunter, David Higham Associates, 5–8 Lower John Street, London W1R 4HA. Address: Haven House, Sandwich, Kent, England.

PUBLICATIONS FOR CHILDREN

Fiction

A Few Fair Days, illustrated by Peggy Fortnum.   London, Hamish Hamilton, 1971; New York, Macmillan, 1972.
A Long Way from Verona.   London, Hamish Hamilton, and New

York, Macmillan, 1971.
The Summer after the Funeral.   London, Hamish Hamilton, and New York, Macmillan, 1973.
Bilgewater.   London, Hamish Hamilton, 1976; New York, Greenwillow, 1977.
The Hollow Land, illustrated by Janet Rawlins.   London, MacRae, 1981; New York, Greenwillow, 1982.
Bridget and William, illustrated by Janet Rawlins.   London, MacRae, 1981.
Horse, illustrated by Janet Rawlins.   London, MacRae 1982.
Kit, illustrated by William Geldart.   London, MacRae, 1983.
Kit in Boots, illustrated by William Geldart.   London, MacRae, 1986.
Through the Dolls' House Door.   London, MacRae, and New York, Greenwillow, 1987.
Swan, illustrated by John Dillow.   London, MacRae, 1987.

PUBLICATIONS FOR ADULTS

Novels

Black Faces, White Faces.   London, Hamish Hamilton, 1975; as *The Pineapple Bay Hotel,* New York, Morrow, 1976.
God on the Rocks.   London, Hamish Hamilton, 1978; New York, Morrow, 1979.
Crusoe's Daughter.   London, Hamish Hamilton, 1985; New York, Atheneum, 1986.

Short Stories

The Sidmouth Letters.   London, Hamish Hamilton, and New York, Morrow, 1980.
The Pangs of Love and Other Stories.   London, Hamish Hamilton, 1983.
Showing the Flag.   London, Hamish Hamilton, 1989.

*   *   *

Jane Gardam's comment about one of her characters that "really she saw the world as a lovely mad sort of place underneath" highlights two motifs that are always beneath the surface of her own fictional worlds: the beauty of the northern English landscape and the absurdity of adult society. These elements are made even more memorable by the author's distinctive style. Her fiction contains three often overlapping, and usually feminine, voices: those of childhood, adolescence, and adulthood. The overlapping makes many of her children's books suitable for all ages, including adult.

Her first book, *A Few Fair Days,* is entirely from the point of view of a child aged about four to 11; but there is also present a nostalgic, although never sentimental, tone of an adult looking back. The outstanding characteristic of this work is its evocative prose, depicting a small East Yorkshire town in the 1930's and a bright, sensitive child who is often at odds with the adults around her. As the coming war casts its shadow, Lucy's—and the town's—tranquil existence is gradually threatened. Thus the book conveys a sense of loss for both a past childhood and another time. The author already demonstrates here the stylistic techniques that are her trademark. Nothing is stated that is not exact and necessary, and what is left out gives resonance and tension to her writing; this is one reason why her best books are so rereadable. Her use of specific physical details and her adeptness at summing things up in quick phrases make almost every sentence quotable. Within the short space of the book a whole childhood is perfectly captured.

Another trait of Gardam's writing, her ironic humour, flowers in *A Long Way from Verona,* the first of her books with an adolescent voice. Jessica Vye tries to make sense of being at an awkward age and of living in a world thrown out of kilter by the war. The first-person technique is supremely suitable: 13 is an age of self-absorption and Jessica is a gifted writer. But because, on the whole, one only sees the events through her eyes, the death of her mentor-teacher, Miss Philemon, is problematic. It is difficult to decide whether the obscurity of this incident is a flaw in the book or a brilliant example of showing, and not telling, that the result of the air raid is too painful for Jessica to set down. A possible danger of having such an articulate young writer tell the story is that she tends to go on and on, but the novel is saved from garrulousness by the careful structure Gardam imposes on Jessica's rush of words. The three sections are built around the three dramatic events in the book and also reflect Jessica's concerns in a progression natural to her age. First she discusses herself as a writer, then her school and friends, and only then describes her family and external events. Like Lucy, Jessica is striving to be herself. In one way she is a normal 13-year-old with the usual confusions about school, parents, and first love experiences, but she also learns to accept her special talent. The book is a complex and unforgettable character study of both a young girl and a young writer—the most memorable portrayal of a preadolescent female since Carson McCullers's *The Member of the Wedding.*

In *The Summer after the Funeral* Gardam moves along in time to a post-war period and a 16-year-old heroine. This book is her most tightly controlled and plotted. The structure revolves around Athene's three visits and her increasing sense of loss of identity resulting from the shock, not so much of her father's death, but of being homeless. Having a heroine who appears perfect, but who is quite different underneath, makes the story compelling from the start. Like Lucy and Jessica, Athene just wants to be herself; unlike them, she has no idea who that self is. Instead she clings to the fantasy that she is Emily Brontë; such a passionate alter ego seems to be a way to absorb all the feelings she won't let herself show. Setting the book in the 1940's enables the author to make Athene's feminine rites of passage both poignant and humourous. Her worry that she may have lost her virginity while she was asleep, and the blind overprotectiveness of her mother, are appropriate to a more innocent time. Athene's first experience of falling in love, and her independent stance about school, however, are universal experiences. Perhaps because she is much more ordinary than the author's other characters, she is the easiest of them to identify with.

Bilgewater is Gardam's funniest book but in some ways also her weakest. Having a modern setting and a 17-year-old heroine enables the author to write more openly about sex, and Marigold's confusions about the subject are comic and refreshing. But the early sections of the book are sometimes self-indulgent. Here the first-person voice becomes sloppy, an undifferentiated commentary instead of one that is distinctively Marigold's. However, the controlled description of the trip to Durham near the end balances to some extent the rambling quality of the beginning; and the surprising finale gives the book more structure than it first promises.

The Hollow Land returns to many of the concerns of *A Few Fair Days*: the influence of the land in people's lives and the continuity of generations. The linked stories move on in time as they do in Gardam's first book, but here there is a stronger connecting theme: the gradual and mutual acceptance by the "incomers" and the local inhabitants of each other. This theme bursts to the surface in the longer last story. Like the last chapter in *Bilgewater,* the future setting allows the author to tie up many loose ends. The very fullness of its many connections, however, makes it awkward; the other chapters lose their independence as the last one tries to answer too many questions. The book's mixture of both children's and adults' points of view makes it difficult to classify, but universal in its appeal. Above all else in this work rises the beauty of its language. The lucid descriptions make the Cumbrian Fells setting as much of a character as the people.

After her first five books Gardam turned to a series of readers written specifically for younger children. Each is a gentle, rural story that usually involves a heroic little girl. The author's spare style enables her to compress many riches into a limited space. The best of these novellas is the small gem, *Bridget and William,* and the tender story of *Kit in Boots.*

Through the Dolls' House Door, the author's first fantasy, is an entirely new departure. Ostensibly for younger children with its plot about the fate of the inhabitants of a dolls' house, this novel has much more to it than appears on the surface. As the dolls are abandoned, the stories within the story told, and the compelling, startling secret of the doll Sigger revealed, the book takes on the timeless qualities of a classic.

Gardam's strengths are her humour, her strong sense of place, the vividness of her characters, and above all her crystalline language. She is painfully accurate about the trials of being a female child or adolescent, although occasionally her own articulateness takes over and her characters sound both fey and precocious. She is at her best when, as in her first three books, she is presenting the details of a just recently past world, especially its class proprieties and peculiar inhabitants. An ambitious, utterly original writer, Gardam is beyond pigeonholing. Whether her books are most appreciated by children, teenagers, or adults is irrelevant, for she remains one of our best chroniclers of the misadventures and comedy of being young.

—Kit Pearson

GARFIELD, Leon. British. Born in Brighton, Sussex, 14 July 1921. Educated at Brighton Grammar School. Served in the Royal Army Medical Corps, 1940–46: private. Married Vivien Alcock, *q.v.,* in 1948; one daughter. Biochemical technician, Whittington Hospital, London, 1946–69. Recipient: *Guardian* award, 1967; Library Association Carnegie Medal, 1971; Whitbread award, 1980; Federation of Children's Book Groups award, 1982; Prix de la Fondation de France, 1984; Golden Cat award (Sweden), 1985; Children's Literature Association Phoenix award, 1987. Fellow, Royal Society of Literature, 1985. Agent: John Johnson Ltd., 45–47 Clerkenwell Green, London EC1R 0HT; or, International Creative Management, 40 West 57th Street, New York, New York 10019, U.S.A. Address: 59 Wood Lane, London N.6, England.

PUBLICATIONS FOR CHILDREN

Fiction

Jack Holborn, illustrated by Antony Maitland. London, Constable, 1964; New York, Pantheon, 1965.
Devil-in-the-Fog, illustrated by Antony Maitland. London, Constable, and New York, Pantheon, 1966.
Smith, illustrated by Antony Maitland. London, Constable, and New York, Pantheon, 1967.
Black Jack, illustrated by Antony Maitland. London, Longman, 1968; New York, Pantheon, 1969.
Mister Corbett's Ghost, illustrated by Alan E. Cober. New York, Pantheon, 1968.
Mr. Corbett's Ghost and Other Stories, illustrated by Antony Maitland. London, Longman, 1969.
The Drummer Boy, illustrated by Antony Maitland. New York, Pantheon, 1969; London, Longman, 1970.
The Restless Ghost: Three Stories, illustrated by Saul Lambert. New York, Pantheon, 1969.
The Boy and the Monkey, illustrated by Trevor Ridley. London, Heinemann, 1969; New York, Watts, 1970.
The Strange Affair of Adelaide Harris, illustrated by Fritz Wegner.

London, Longman, and New York, Pantheon, 1971.
The Captain's Watch, illustrated by Trevor Ridley. London, Heinemann, 1972.
The Ghost Downstairs, illustrated by Antony Maitland. London, Longman, and New York, Pantheon, 1972.
Lucifer Wilkins, illustrated by Trevor Ridley. London, Heinemann, 1973.
The Sound of Coaches, illustrated by John Lawrence. London, Kestrel, and New York, Viking Press, 1974.
The Prisoners of September. London, Kestrel, and New York, Viking Press, 1975.
The Pleasure Garden, illustrated by Fritz Wegner. London, Kestrel, and New York, Viking Press, 1976.
The Apprentices. New York, Viking Press, 1978; London, Heinemann, 1982.
  The Lamplighter's Funeral, illustrated by Antony Maitland. London, Heinemann, 1976.
  Mirror, Mirror, illustrated by Antony Maitland. London, Heinemann, 1976.
  Moss and Blister, illustrated by Faith Jaques. London, Heinemann, 1976.
  The Cloak, illustrated by Faith Jaques. London, Heinemann, 1976.
  The Valentine, illustrated by Faith Jaques. London, Heinemann, 1977.
  Labour in Vain, illustrated by Faith Jaques. London, Heinemann, 1977.
  The Fool, illustrated by Faith Jaques. London, Heinemann, 1977.
  Rosy Starling, illustrated by Faith Jaques. London, Heinemann, 1977.
  The Dumb Cake, illustrated by Faith Jaques. London, Heinemann, 1977.
  Tom Titmarsh's Devil, illustrated by Faith Jaques. London, Heinemann, 1977.
  The Filthy Beast, illustrated by Faith Jaques. London, Heinemann, 1978.
  The Enemy, illustrated by Faith Jaques. London, Heinemann, 1978.
An Adelaide Ghost. London, Ward Lock, 1977.
The Confidence Man. London, Kestrel, 1978; New York, Viking Press, 1979.
Bostock and Harris; or, The Night of the Comet, illustrated by Martin Cottam. London, Kestrel, 1979; as *The Night of the Comet,* New York, Delacorte Press, 1979.
John Diamond, illustrated by Antony Maitland. London, Kestrel, 1980; as *Footsteps,* New York, Delacorte Press, 1980.
Fair's Fair, illustrated by Margaret Chamberlain. London, Macdonald, 1981; New York, Doubleday, 1983.
King Nimrod's Tower, illustrated by Michael Bragg. London, Constable, and New York, Lothrop, 1982.
The Writing on the Wall, illustrated by Michael Bragg. London, Methuen, and New York, Lothrop, 1983.
The King in the Garden, illustrated by Michael Bragg. London, Methuen, 1984; New York, Lothrop, 1985.
Guilt and Gingerbread, illustrated by Fritz Wegner. London, Viking Kestrel, 1984.
The Wedding Ghost, illustrated by Charles Keeping. Oxford, Oxford University Press, 1985; New York, Oxford University Press, 1987.
The December Rose (novelization of his own television series). London, Viking Kestrel, 1986; New York, Viking Kestrel, 1987.
Blewcoat Boy. London, Gollancz, 1988.
The Empty Sleeve. London, Viking Kestrel, and New York, Delacorte Press, 1988.
Revolution! London, Collins, 1989.

Plays

Television Plays: *Jack Holborn,* from his own story, 1983; *The December Rose* series, 1986.

Other

The God Beneath the Sea, with Edward Blishen, illustrated by Charles Keeping.   London, Longman, 1970; New York, Pantheon, 1971.
Child o' War: The True Story of a Boy Sailor in Nelson's Navy, with David Proctor, illustrated by Antony Maitland.   London, Collins, and New York, Holt Rinehart, 1972.
The Golden Shadow, with Edward Blishen, illustrated by Charles Keeping.   London, Longman, and New York, Pantheon, 1973.
The House of Hanover: England in the Eighteenth Century.   London, Deutsch, and New York, Seabury Press, 1976.
Shakespeare Stories, illustrated by Michael Foreman.   London, Gollancz, and New York, Schocken, 1985.

Editor, *Baker's Dozen: A Collection of Stories.*   London, Ward Lock, 1973; as *Strange Fish and Other Stories,* New York, Lothrop, 1974.
Editor, *The Book Lovers: A Sequence of Love-Scenes.*   London, Ward Lock, 1976; New York, Avon, 1978.
Editor, *A Swag of Stories: Australian Stories,* illustrated by Caroline Harrison.   London, Ward Lock, 1977.

PUBLICATIONS FOR ADULTS

Novels

The Mystery of Edwin Drood (completion of the novel by Dickens).   London, Deutsch, 1980; New York, Pantheon, 1981.
The House of Cards.   London, Bodley Head, 1982; New York, St. Martin's Press, 1983.

Other

Editor, *Sketches from Bleak House,* with Mervyn Peake and Edward Blishen.   London, Methuen, 1983.

*   *   *

Since the publication of his first novel, *Jack Holborn,* a vigorous tale of piracy and adventure, Leon Garfield has produced a very considerable body of work for young people, remarkable for its high imaginative quality and individual style. His next few books, like the first, had 18th-century settings: *Devil-in-the-Fog* concerned a family of strolling actors, *Smith* was the story of a sharp little London pickpocket, *Black Jack* took its young hero Tolly out into the countryside of the same period with a group of travelling fairground folk, and *The Drummer Boy* was a powerful war story. With *The Strange Affair of Adelaide Harris* and its sequel, *Bostock and Harris,* Garfield moved forward in time to the early 19th century and turned to high comedy. *The Sound of Coaches* reflects the everyday lives of people engaged in working the stage coaches in their heyday. *The Prisoners of September* follows the fate of two young men of widely differing temperaments at the time of the French Revolution; in *The Pleasure Garden* a young clergyman's love affair becomes entangled with mystery, blackmail, and murder; the young hero of *John Diamond* finds himself among further mysteries in Garfield's favorite London back streets; and Hans Ruppert, the 14-year-old German Protestant boy in *The Confidence Man,* is stranded in Whitechapel along with his family and neighbours on their way to emigrate to 18th-century America.

Besides these full-length novels Garfield has written shorter stories, including ghost stories and others mingling adventure, romance, and comedy in the manner of his longer works. His series of "Apprentices," now collected into one volume, resembles a long picturesque novel if read as a whole, the London tradespeople who are its characters occasionally surfacing in one another's stories, or linking the end of one tale to the beginning of another. There is no diminution of imaginative power in these shorter books, still less in the award-winning *The God Beneath the Sea* and its successor, *The Golden Shadow,* both written in collaboration with Edward Blishen. These two books are not just retellings of Greek myths, but genuinely creative works, the first concentrating upon myths of the gods, with Hephaestus as central figure, and the second on legends of men, taking Heracles as focal point and making a sympathetic human figure of one of the less immediately appealing of the Greek heroes. Garfield has also written the text of a picture book, *King Nimrod's Tower.*

Apart from the two books of Greek legends, Garfield's work is usually placed under the heading of Historical Novels, but it is far from being that well-meaning type of historical writing where the painstakingly researched background is all-important. History lies lightly on these novels. Garfield has certainly done his research, but the background is transmuted so that we see it as it affects the inner lives of his characters. Now and then he may particularize: *The Confidence Man* is expanded from a small incident in contemporary records, and in *The Prisoners of September* the September Massacres are basic to the ironically twisting plot. But often he does not pinpoint actual time or (outside his vividly detailed London) even place; we feel no need to know the site and date of the battle in France where the Drummer Boy, Charlie, beats his drum, nor what duke commanded the army.

Certain important themes recur: notably, that all is not what it seems. In *Jack Holborn* the ambiguous and amoral figure of Solomon Trumpet starts as a villain and ends up befriending the hero. The supposedly wicked uncle in *Devil-in-the-Fog* turns out more pathetic than sinister. The terrifying criminal Black Jack becomes the ally of Tolly and his Belle; Charlie not only learns to see that military glory is hollow, but finds that the fat army surgeon he despised is right-thinking if unheroic. *The Pleasure Garden* has many layers of shifting illusion, to be stripped away by the reader as well as the clerical protagonist so as to come to the compassionate study of aspects of human love underneath. The narrator of *John Diamond* does not know what to make of the dwarf, Mr. Seed, or many of the other characters he meets in his wanderings, until at last all is revealed.

With illusion and disillusion so marked as themes, it is not surprising to find an element of the supernatural present too. Explicit if properly mysterious in Garfield's short ghost stories, it is present in some of the longer novels, half-glimpsed and half-felt rather than spelt out. It even surfaces briefly in the bright comic world of *Adelaide Harris,* where the old nurse's spell to summon the baby's kidnapper successfully conjures up the infant's enterprising brother who "exposed" her in ancient Roman fashion and was subsequently left with the wrong baby—only the success of the spell is lost on all concerned. Elsewhere a rational explanation usually dispels such mysteries: the trickster in *The Confidence Man,* who has about him an aura of the Devil of folktale, is shown in the end to have none but pitiful human failings. However, a whiff of the supernatural persists and is never quite explained away in the apprentice Peter Gannet's haunting by a phantom in *The Empty Sleeve,* a novel all the more powerful for the fact that the greatest evils in it turn out, in a full-blooded dramatic climax, to be of human devising.

Comedy, predominant in *Adelaide Harris* and its sequel, emerges sporadically or is present in the form of irony in most of Garfield's other books. A combination of comedy, high adventure, romance, mystery, and an eye for intriguing detail is the hallmark of Garfield's vigorously individual style. His early novel *Jack Holborn* has been described as Stevensonian, many of his others as Dickensian (and certainly a Dickensian gusto is very evident, the more so when one bears in mind Garfield's interesting completion of *Edwin Drood*). But these are parallels only, and he writes no pale imitations; one could continue to find other parallels and say there is a Keatsian touch in the two books of Greek tales, with their sense of the numinous pervading nature; or that Thomas Love Peacock would have liked the posturing of Ralph Bunnion in *Adelaide Harris,* a fashionable young sprig who thinks himself irresistible to women. Garfield's style is his own, and when he strikes notes that briefly remind one of other notes struck memorably elsewhere he does it in his own fashion. He is able to apply that style with equal success to a "novelization" of his own script for a television serial, *The December Rose,* and to a work specially commissioned in association with the National Trust, *Blewcoat Boy,* both of which vividly evoke scenes from the London underworld of the past, have sharp and knowing young heroes, and end on a pleasingly optimistic note. In a rather different vein, he has also written a fairytale novella, *Guilt and Gingerbread,* with a German Baroque setting and in a style which successfully translates material reminiscent of Brentano or Hoffman into genuine Garfield.

Beyond the sheer narrative entertainment of the books, which is very great, there is always a search, conscious or otherwise, on the part of Garfield's young heroes for true and lasting values. This shows through the vivid surface texture of the books, which is often very rich. For example, one may trace Garfield's striking use of imagery to describe the sky from *Jack Holborn,* with its storm cloud "like a great black tiger in the sky…long tail and a great paw dripping down into the sea," to *The God Beneath the Sea,* where the baby god falls "like a golden needle stitching the heavens," through to a moment at the end of *The Pleasure Garden* where the Cosmic Effect promised by the purveyor of fireworks at the end of his display finally arrives: "The blackness thinned and beyond, calm and distinct, shone the stars of heaven. Here was an unmasking indeed!" The synthesis of vivid language with a quiet revelation of simplicity beyond the complex structures is part of Garfield's wide-ranging talent.

—Anthea Bell

GARNER, Alan. British. Born in Congleton, Cheshire, 17 October 1934. Educated at Alderley Edge Primary School, Cheshire; Manchester Grammar School; Magdalen College, Oxford. Served in the Royal Artillery: Second Lieutenant. Married 1) Ann Cook in 1956 (marriage dissolved), one son and two daughters; 2) Griselda Greaves in 1972, one son and one daughter. Recipient: Library Association Carnegie Medal, 1968; *Guardian* award, 1968; Chicago International Film Festival prize, 1981. Address: Blackden, Holmes Chapel, Crewe, Cheshire CW4 8BY, England.

PUBLICATIONS FOR CHILDREN

Fiction

The Weirdstone of Brisingamen: A Tale of Alderley. London, Collins, 1960; as *The Weirdstone,* New York, Watts, 1961; revised edition, London, Penguin, 1963; New York, Walck, 1969.
The Moon of Gomrath. London, Collins, 1963; New York, Walck, 1967.
Elidor, illustrated by Charles Keeping. London, Collins, 1965; New York, Walck, 1967.
The Old Man of Mow, photographs by Roger Hill. London, Collins, 1967; New York, Doubleday, 1970.
The Owl Service. London, Collins, 1967; New York, Walck, 1968.
Red Shift. London, Collins, and New York, Macmillan, 1973.
The Breadhorse, illustrated by Albin Trowski. London, Collins, 1975.
The Stone Book Quartet, illustrated by Michael Foreman:
  The Stone Book. London, Collins, 1976; New York, Collins World, 1978.
  Tom Fobble's Day. London, Collins, 1977; New York, Collins World, 1979.
  Granny Reardun. London, Collins, 1977; New York, Collins World, 1978.
  The Aimer Gate. London, Collins, 1978; New York, Collins World, 1979.
Fairy Tales of Gold (The Girl of the Golden Gate, The Golden Brothers, The Princess and the Golden Mane, The Three Golden Heads of the Well), illustrated by Michael Foreman. London, Collins, 4 vols., 1979; 1 vol. edition, Collins, and New York, Philomel, 1980.
A Bag of Moonshine, illustrated by Patrick James Lynch. London, Collins, and New York, Delacorte Press, 1986.

Plays

Holly from the Bongs: A Nativity Play, music by William Mayne, photographs by Roger Hill (produced Goostrey, Cheshire, 1965). London, Collins, 1966; revised version, music by Gordon Crosse (produced London, 1974), published in *Labrys 7* (Frome, Somerset), 1981.
The Belly Bag, music by Richard Morris (produced London, 1971).
Potter Thompson, music by Gordon Crosse (produced London, 1975). London, Oxford University Press, 1975.
To Kill a King (televised, 1980). Published in *Labrys 7* (Frome, Somerset), 1981.
The Green Mist, in *Labrys 7* (Frome, Somerset), 1981.

Screenplays: *Places and Things,* 1978; *Images,* 1981.

Radio Plays: *Have You Met Our Tame Author?,* 1962; *Elidor,* 1962; *The Weirdstone of Brisingamen,* from his own story, 1963; *Thor and the Giants,* 1965, revised version, 1979; *Idun and the Apples of Life,* 1965, revised version, as *Loki and the Storm Giant,* 1979; *Baldur the Bright,* 1965, revised version, 1979; *The Stone Book, Granny Reardun, Tom Fobble's Day,* and *The Aimer Gate,* from his own stories, 1980.

Television Plays: *The Owl Service,* from his own story, 1969; *Red Shift,* from his own story, 1978; *Lamaload,* 1979; *To Kill a King* (*Leap in the Dark* series), 1980; *The Keeper,* 1982.

Other

The Guizer: A Book of Fools. London, Hamish Hamilton, 1975; New York, Greenwillow, 1976.
The Lad of the Gad (folktales). London, Collins, 1980; New York, Philomel, 1981.
Book of British Fairytales (retellings), illustrated by Derek Collard. London, Collins, 1984; New York, Delacorte Press, 1985.

Editor, *The Hamish Hamilton Book of Goblins: An Anthology of Folklore,* illustrated by Krystyna Turska. London, Hamish Hamilton, 1969; as *A Cavalcade of Goblins,* New York, Walck,

1969; as *A Book of Goblins,* London, Penguin, 1972.

*

Manuscript Collection: Brigham Young University, Provo, Utah.

Critical Studies: *A Fine Anger: A Critical Introduction to the Work of Alan Garner* by Neil Philip, London, Collins, and New York, Philomel, 1981; "Alan Garner Issue" of *Labrys 7* (Frome, Somerset), 1981.

*   *   *

Alan Garner is an intensely individual writer whose idiosyncrasies result in books which are few but varied, of a recognizable tradition yet unique in themselves, seemingly without precedent.

After a conventional beginning which can be seen as Tolkienlike (*The Weirdstone of Brisingamen* and *The Moon of Gomrath*), Garner's acceptance was such that he could afford to start expressing powerful ideas about life and relationships in his own peculiar way, making his own rules of style as he saw fit. This has perplexed those adults who have preconceived ideas of what books should be like. An older pre-television generation might have difficulty in understanding the visual messages carried in a bombardment of the short, sharp shocks of changing pictures in a film which their grandchildren can understand with ease. Garner's recent books are something of a counterpart to such films, with emphasis on dialogue rather than narrative, with the abrupt tentativeness of ordinary discourse replacing the artificial conventions of literary speeches. With much of the rapid action, ideas, and words being unexplained, the reader is forced to concentrate and participate if he is to share in the experience and to extract meaning.

Garner has said that his stories "have to work for *me,* to say what I want to express. In fact, I must write poetry, making words work on more than one level." For him, the discursive novelist's techniques are inappropriate, and compact images and ideas have to work implicitly and by association, thus demanding effort from the reader. *Red Shift,* for instance, observes none of the usual criteria for children's books. There are no explanations, not a single character is described, there is almost no narrative, there are no chapter divisions, the "he said"/"she replied" convention has been largely abandoned, and the dialogue, on which comprehension depends, is cryptic and fractured. *Red Shift* is thus more like a film or a poem, in which the realisation must take place in the reader's mind. It demands effort, but the rewards are great; the emotional impact can be considerable for those willing to experience it. *Red Shift* contains three parallel stories, which are pursued bit by bit, a small break in the type separating one time shift from another—for they take place in different centuries but in the same location. The people are interchangeable, as are their actions and words. Yet the first change is made abruptly without indication and by the last few pages the text so runs together that the reader cannot say with any certainty where he is at.

Those who find difficulty in extracting meaning from *Red Shift* probably find the peculiar scrambled medium distracting. They miss the essential point that this medium *is* the message, for Garner's overriding theme, as in *The Owl Service,* is that we are all caught up in a dimension of time that is only relative. It is not a continuum. *It all exists all at once.* Tom in *Red Shift* says "We're bits of other futures" and "Nothing I say is original." Just as the relationships and events are repeated (or happen simultaneously) in *Red Shift,* so are Gwyn, Alison, and Roger in *The Owl Service* caught in a conflict which has been re-enacted, with variations, century after century. The relentlessness, the irresistible inevitability of events is, thus, a determinist view of human behaviour, and one that Garner shares with Thucydides, not over a 2000-year gap but *now.* As Tom says in

Red Shift, "I see everything at once."

Garner's earlier, simpler books allowed children to slip in and out of local legend, participating in it, sharing in the ancient life of their environment. Whereas the movement is "back" into a co-existing past in *The Weirdstone of Brisingamen* and *The Moon of Gomrath,* the forces of another time and place in *Elidor* also intrude on the Manchester of the present, upsetting television sets and burning out washing machines. Even in miniature works, *The Breadhorse* and *The Stone Book,* we see children experiencing the mystical power of the past; their heritage is a tremendous source of comfort and strength.

Garner's books provide absorbing experiences. In spite of all the critical agonising over them, they are basically simple stories which, in cases like *Elidor* or *The Owl Service,* build up to an overwhelming climax on the very last page or two, leaving one thrilled yet stunned. After all, Garner wants the reader to keep reading to find out what happens next.

Garner's formal education removed him from his natural background of rural Cheshire craftsmen, with their ancient skills, their language, traditions, stories. In his *Stone Book* quartet—perhaps his masterpiece—he has attempted to resolve his own tensions, re-establishing himself, in his own way, as a writer/craftsman, in his own local culture, and establishing his own identity and place in his long family history. He says, "If you did a *Desert Island Discs* on me, I would say give me *Tom Fobble's Day* as my one book, and particularly the last two pages. Because that is acceptance."

In such books as *The Lad of the Gad* and *A Bag of Moonshine,* Garner's unfailing ear has captured perfectly the idiosyncratic voice of the oral storyteller, in retellings which are powerfully direct and engaging: "At some time or other, but not long since, there was an old man who kept a cat and a cock…I'm going to tell you about Billy Bowker. He was a hobthrust who went boggart…If you don't like, don't listen; but there were once three brothers; two were clever, and one was Jack…" In *A Bag of Moonshine,* Garner quotes John Maruskin: "…it is in the speech of carters and housewives, in the speech of blacksmiths and old women, that one discovers the magic that sings the claim of the voice in the shadow, or that chants the rhyme of the fish in the well." Garner's task, it seems, is to reconcile his formal academic training in linguistics with a need to reclaim the right, and the ability, to sing and chant the stories of his own people, but in his own way, afresh.

—Walter McVitty

GARNETT, Eve. British. Born in Worcestershire. Educated at The Convent, Bideford, Devon; West Bank School, Devon; Alice Ottley School, Worcester; Chelsea Polytechnic School of Art, London; Royal Academy Schools, London (studentship; Creswick Prize and Silver Medal). Artist: murals for Children's House, Bow, London; exhibitions at the Tate Gallery, 1939, Le Fevre Gallery, and New English Art Club, all London. Recipient: Library Association Carnegie Medal, 1938. Address: c/o Lloyds Bank, 29–31 Grosvenor Gardens, London SW1 0BU, England.

PUBLICATIONS FOR CHILDREN (illustrated by the author)

Fiction

The Family from One End Street and Some of Their Adventures. London, Muller, 1937; New York, Vanguard Press, 1939.
In and Out and Roundabout: Stories of a Little Town. London,

Muller, 1948.

Further Adventures of the Family from One End Street. London, Heinemann, and New York, Vanguard Press, 1956.

Holiday at the Dew Drop Inn: A One End Street Story. London, Heinemann, 1962; New York, Vanguard Press, 1963.

Lost and Found: Four Stories. London, Muller, 1974.

Other

To Greenland's Icy Mountains: The Story of Hans Egede, Explorer, Coloniser, Missionary. London, Heinemann, and New York, Roy, 1968.

Editor, *A Book of Seasons: An Anthology.* London, Oxford University Press, 1952; Boston, Bentley, 1953.

PUBLICATIONS FOR ADULTS

Other

"Is It Well with the Child?", illustrated by the author. London, Muller, 1938.

First Affections: Some Autobiographical Chapters of Early Childhood. London, Muller, 1982.

*

Illustrator: *The London Child* by Evelyn Sharp, 1927; *The Bad Barons of Crashbania* by Norman Hunter, 1932; *A Child's Garden of Verses* by Robert Louis Stevenson, 1948; *A Golden Land* edited by James Reeves, 1958.

*   *   *

Eve Garnett wrote *The Family from One End Street* as a shot in the battle against slums, one of the first attempts to show a working-class family from within the four walls of their home rather than as stereotypes seen from outside. It was rejected by eight publishers in all as "unsuitable for children" before being accepted.

Fifty years on, the Ruggles family are still refreshingly real. They face poverty with good sense and cheerfulness; it is an accepted part of their way of living. The mother, Rosie, is particularly well drawn: fiercely angry with her children over any waste of money—the loss of a new school hat by daughter Kate is the occasion of uncompromising fury—but immensely warm and loving at the same time. It is still rare in children's books to find parents so roundly drawn or the tug-of-war relationships between parents and children so realistically treated; and it is this as much as the class dimension which makes the family from One End Street memorable. If the children are less original, if one has met fat responsible Lily, the eldest child, before, or thin studious dreamy Kate (why are clever children in children's literature always *thin?*), they are wonderfully accurately observed. Garnett writes from inside her characters, with a gentle sense of comedy.

Take John, walking along a river bank: "The river was a wonderful place: it breathed adventure!…strange and patient men fished from its muddy banks and…flowers grew beside it in beautifully squishy mud that was a delight to walk in. Above all things it was strictly forbidden by Mrs. Ruggles, and therefore doubly attractive—a sort of adventure in itself." Or this scene in the Ruggles' kitchen: "'Will you go,' cried Rosie, 'can't you see we're worried!' The little Ruggles looked wise. 'Worried' in their experience was another name for what in a child was called 'in a shocking temper.' They scuttled off like rabbits." These are real parents up against real pressures and children who know and recognize the danger signals.

Construction is not Garnett's strong point. For example, *The Family from One End Street* strings a series of events together without any overall sense of climax, and in *Further Adventures of the Family from One End Street* she devotes two-thirds of the book to Kate's visit to the country with her younger brother and sister, and then switches completely in the final third to the rest of the family back in town; it is almost two books.

However, this is of no great importance. She writes vividly and economically with a sharp feel for people and place and with a delightful sense of humour, and no amount of clever craftsmanship will ever substitute for that.

—Mary Rayner

GATES, Doris. American. Born in Mountain View, California, 26 November 1901. Educated at Fresno State Teachers College, California, 1924–26; Los Angeles Library School, 1926–27; Western Reserve University, Cleveland, 1929–30. Children's Librarian, Fresno County Library, 1930–40; Instructor, San Jose State College, California, 1940–43, 1951; Visiting Lecturer, University of California, Berkeley, 1943–45, University of Southern California, Los Angeles, 1947, and University of San Francisco, 1956–60. Advisory editor and co-author, Basic Readers series, 1955–62, and 360 reading series, 1970–73, Ginn and Company, Boston. *Died 3 September 1987.*

PUBLICATIONS FOR CHILDREN

Fiction

Sarah's Idea, illustrated by Marjorie Torrey. New York, Viking Press, 1938; London, Muller, 1947.

Blue Willow, illustrated by Paul Lantz. New York, Viking Press, 1940; London, Muller, 1942.

Sensible Kate, illustrated by Marjorie Torrey. New York, Viking Press, 1943; London, Muller, 1947.

Trouble for Jerry, illustrated by Marjorie Torrey. New York, Viking Press, 1944; London, Muller, 1954.

North Fork. New York, Viking Press, 1945; London, Muller, 1950.

My Brother Mike. New York, Viking Press, 1948.

River Ranch, illustrated by Jacob Landau. New York, Viking Press, 1949.

Little Vic, illustrated by Kate Seredy. New York, Viking Press, 1951.

The Cat and Mrs. Cary, illustrated by Peggy Bacon. New York, Viking Press, 1962; London, Methuen, 1964.

The Elderberry Bush, illustrated by Lilian Obligado. New York, Viking Press, 1967.

A Morgan for Melinda. New York, Viking Press, 1980; as *A Horse for Melinda,* London, Carousel, 1981.

A Filly for Melinda. New York, Viking, 1984.

Other

Becky and the Bandit (reader), illustrated by Paul Lantz. Boston, Ginn, 1952.

May I Come In? (reader), with Theodore Clymer. Boston, Ginn, 1969.

The Sun That Warms (reader), with Theodore Clymer and Constance M. McCullough. Boston, Ginn, 1970.

Lord of the Sky: Zeus, illustrated by Robert Handville. New York,

Viking Press, 1972.
The Warrior Goddess: Athena, illustrated by Don Bolognese.   New
    York, Viking Press, 1972.
The Golden God: Apollo, illustrated by Constantinos CoConis.
    New York, Viking Press, 1973; as *Apollo, Tale of the Golden God,*
    London, Penguin, 1984.
Two Queens of Heaven: Aphrodite, Demeter, illustrated by Trina
    Schart Hyman.   New York, Viking Press, 1974.
Mightiest of Mortals: Heracles, illustrated by Richard Cuffari.
    New York, Viking Press, 1975.
A Fair Wind for Troy, illustrated by Charles Mikolaycak.   New
    York, Viking Press, 1976.

PUBLICATIONS FOR ADULTS

Other

Helping Children Discover Books.   Chicago, Science Research As-
    sociates, 1956.

*

Manuscript Collection: University of Oregon Library, Eugene.

*   *   *

The writings of Doris Gates cover a variety of subjects: classical
mythology, the dust bowl era in the San Joaquin Valley, lumbering
in the High Sierras, and horse racing across the United States, to
name but a few. However, in each of her books, one is aware of her
strong sense of story structure through her handling of plot, setting,
and character development. In a way, it is no accident that several of
her later books were retellings of the classical myths, for the structures of traditional stories—myths and romances—have been implicit in all her writings. This can best be illustrated by looking in
detail at two of her novels for children, *Little Vic,* representative of
her animal stories, and *Blue Willow,* representative of her California-
based stories.

Little Vic is the story of Pony Rivers and his love for Little Vic,
grandson of the famous race horse Man o' War. Basically it is a simple
story, tracing the progress of the orphaned Pony Rivers from New
York City, to the winner's circle at California's Santa Anita Race
Track. He reaches this destination because of his love for Little Vic,
whom he has been with throughout the horse's young life, and in
whom he had kept faith when all others had given up. Early in the
book, Pony thinks about the horse: "He isn't ever going to do
anything the way the people think he will. But he's going to be great
just the same." Both boy and horse prove themselves when, riding
at night on the Arizona ranch to which the horse has been sent for
training, they rescue a group of campers from a flash flood. It is at
this point that the boy truly understands the horse's greatness, and
the victory in the Santa Anita Handicap follows quickly. One sees
the age-old structure of romance, the journey of wish fulfillment to
a promised land, take the typical American form of the rags-to-riches
success story.

In *Little Vic* this romance pattern is handled very simply, with plot
and character development being very straightforward. In *Blue Willow,* justly considered a minor children's classic, the pattern is more
complex and more artistically presented. The plot concerns a family
of migrant farm workers, the Larkins, once prosperous Texas
ranchers, who escape the dust bowl to find happiness on a California
ranch. The heroine, young Janey, discovers the courage necessary to
help her family discover a home. Gates makes careful use of setting,
creating a series of symbolic scenes which reflect the family's

movement to peace and security. Of the Larkins's early Texas home
we are told little. Irretrievably past, it represents the security Janey
now lacks and so desires. The dust-bowl area containing the shack
in which the Larkins live represents the wasteland of poverty in
which the Larkins now live. It is like the wilderness through which
the children of Israel had to pass to reach their goal, or the nightmare
landscape that threatened to engulf the questing knight. The third
major symbolic setting is the river that Janey and her family visit. As
her mother, quoting Isaiah, says, it is as "rivers of water in a dry
place." It offers the family a sense of release, a few hours of hope to
offset their position as migrant workers. The Anderson farm represents the security which the Larkins once possessed and to which
they ultimately return. However, the farm, like the promised land in
many fairytales and romances, is guarded by the evil ogre who must
be defeated if it is to be achieved—in this case, it is Bounce Reyburn,
the shady ranch foreman whom Janey courageously confronts at the
climax of the novel.

Of course, the major symbol of the novel is the blue willow plate
itself. Gates uses Janey's changing attitudes toward the plate to
indicate her growth as a person. At first it serves as her means of
fighting a feeling of inferiority and she frequently escapes into
reveries about it. However, with the illness of her stepmother, she
realizes that she is willing to give up the plate and her dream world
to pay for a doctor. At the end of the story, she recovers the plate and
places it on the mantle of the fireplace in the family's new home on
the Anderson ranch. The romance journey has been completed, the
land of heart's desire has been achieved—mainly through the
courage of young Janey and her mother and father.

One sees in *Blue Willow* a perfect combination of realistic description of setting, careful study of character, and the structural patterns
of romance, the linear journey to fulfillment. The book is Gates's
major literary achievement and an important contribution to
American children's literature. Not only is it an excellent presentation of the migrant workers' lives of the 1930's; it is a universal story
of how courage can lead one to success and happiness.

—Jon C. Stott

GAY, Amelia.   See HOGARTH, Grace.

GEE, Maurice (Gough).   New Zealander.   Born in Whakatane,
22 August 1931. Educated at Avondale College, Auckland, 1945–49;
University of Auckland, 1950–53, M.A. (honours) in English 1953;
Auckland Teachers College, 1954. Married Margaretha Garden in
1970; one son (from previous marriage) and two daughters. School-
teacher, 1955–57; held various jobs, 1958–66; assistant librarian,
Alexander Turnbull Library, Wellington, 1967–69; city librarian,
Napier Public Library, 1970–72; deputy librarian, Teachers Colleges
Library, Auckland, 1974–76. Since 1976 full-time writer. Recipient:
New Zealand Literary Fund scholarship, 1962, 1976, and Award of
Achievement, 1967, 1973; University of Otago Robert Burns fellowship, 1964; Hubert Church Prose award, 1973; New Zealand Book
award, 1976, 1979, 1982, 1984; James Tait Black Memorial prize,
1979; Sir James Wattie award, 1979; New Zealand Children's Book
of the Year award, 1984; New Zealand Library Association Esther
Glen award, 1986. D.Litt.: Victoria University, Wellington, 1987.
Agent: Richards Literary Agency, P.O. Box 31240, Milford, Auckland 9. Address: 125 Cleveland Terrace, Nelson, New Zealand.

PUBLICATIONS FOR CHILDREN

Fiction

Under the Mountain.   Wellington, London, and New York, Oxford University Press, 1979.
The World Around the Corner, illustrated by Gary Hebley.   Wellington, Oxford University Press, 1980; Oxford and New York, Oxford University Press, 1981.
The Halfmen of O.   Auckland and Oxford, Oxford University Press, 1982; New York, Oxford University Press, 1983.
The Priests of Ferris.   Auckland and Oxford, Oxford University Press, 1984; New York, Oxford University Press, 1985.
Motherstone.   Auckland and Oxford, Oxford University Press, 1985.
The Fire-Raiser.   Auckland, Oxford University Press, 1986.

Plays

Television Series: *The Fire-Raiser,* from his own story, 1986.

PUBLICATIONS FOR ADULTS

Novels

The Big Season.   London, Hutchinson, 1962.
A Special Flower.   London, Hutchinson, 1965.
In My Father's Den.   London, Faber, 1972.
Games of Choice.   London, Faber, 1976.
Plumb.   London, Faber, 1978.
Meg.   London, Faber, 1981; New York, St. Martin's Press, 1982.
Sole Survivor.   London, Faber, and New York, St. Martin's Press, 1983.
Prowlers.   London, Faber, 1987.

Short Stories

A Glorious Morning, Comrade.   Auckland, Auckland University Press-Oxford University Press, 1975.
Collected Stories.   Auckland and London, Penguin, 1986; New York, Penguin, 1987.

Plays

Television Series: *Mortimer's Patch,* 1980.

Other

Nelson Central School: A History.   Nelson, Nelson Central School Centennial Committee, 1978.

*

Critical Studies: *Introducing Maurice Gee* by David Hill, Auckland, Longman Paul, 1981; *Maurice Gee* by Bill Manhire, Auckland and Oxford, Oxford University Press, 1986.

*   *   *

Maurice Gee, in his vision of the traditional fantasy struggle between good and evil, sees evil as the abuse of power, with pollution and devastation as a result. *Under the Mountain* portrays huge, worm-like creatures lurking under Auckland's volcanic cones. When activated by metamorphosing alien slugs, they will destroy Earth.

The World Around the Corner describes a band of goblin-like Grimbles, championed by a dragon cloud of poisonous gas. *The Halfmen of O, The Priests of Ferris,* and *Motherstone* as a trilogy examine at length the corruption of absolute power—political, religious, royal, and military. In turn, the satanic Otis Claw, the Paingiver, rules with his Deathguards in his spreading hell of a city; the High Priest and his police-priests use cruelty and killing in their religious rites to keep order ("There is no other way to run the State"); mad Osro is determined to be king, and mad Widd is determined to fight him, even though they each have the ultimate weapon to destroy all.

Against these evil characters are the child-protagonists. Helped by Nature, their special gifts, each other, and sympathetic, sometimes symbolically drawn adults, all discover the necessary strength to meet each challenge. The red-haired twins Rachel and Theo develop telepathic powers and control of magic stones to make the volcanoes erupt just in time. Caroline saves the magic glasses from the Grimbles and returns them, revitalised by the sun, to the elvish Moon-girl who can then win the yearly fight against the dragon. Nicholas supports his cousin Susan Ferris on her long journeys in her quest for the magic charms. With help she succeeds in destroying each set of oppressive rulers and, as a final solution, wipes out all memory so that life on O returns to the Neanderthal stage.

But this struggle demands sacrifice. Gee's "colouring" shows that in the overthrow of evil, because of human imperfections, innocent people must suffer, for which we "do right to grieve." Since "Good must be won daily in the battle that never ends," some repetition in the trilogy is inevitable, but each story ends successfully. And Gee underlines the duality of his vision by pairing and paralleling characters, creatures (notably cats, domestic and wild), magic stones, and images.

The storylines are carried by an assurance of tone and dialogue. Danger builds effectively to its climax. Humour, a shorter length, and a lighter touch make Gee's polished second title suitable for younger readers. Humour also relieves the grimness of the trilogy, mainly through greedy, shifty, garrulous Jimmy Jaspers: "Cling...I'm gunner ram yer skinny legs down yer throat." Jimmy is indeed a "Mixie...in Balance...probably more bad than good, that is the way with men." But he chooses to repent (an important theme in Gee's adult writing) and to fight against evil. Besides Jimmy Jaspers, the trilogy embraces an imaginative cast of helpful and hindering creatures.

Like other fantasy writers, Gee brings credibility to his stories through detail. He moves his settings from explicit Auckland to unnamed Nelson (where he is supported by nine full-page pencil drawings), to his Otherworld of O which is entered through a drug-induced, time-space flip. He appeals to the senses—the pervading stink of the slugs, the constantly recurring screams in O. To clarify his details, however, he leans on similes which are sometimes unnecessary, even distracting. For example, when in O the living hill dies, the awesome quality is diminished through comparison with house-timbers, herds, trucks, and battleships. Some pages lack editorial polish as well.

For his television-linked historical novel, *The Fire-Raiser,* Gee turns to the realistic world of his adult fiction. He sets the action in Jessop, a small town based on Nelson but reflecting any small New Zealand town during World War I. In a penetratingly taut opening chapter, on the night of 23 March 1915 the fire-raiser strikes again. The four children know who the fire-raiser is before the adults do. Unlike children in Blyton formula stories, these children tell the police, which doesn't reduce tension and does increase credibility.

Standing out as characters are the eccentric, tyrannical, Dickensian Mrs. Marwick and her unbalanced, middle-aged son Edgar. Refreshingly, teacher Clippy Hedges is one who likes children, has a sense of humour, and is cheerful though aware of "meanness, cruelty and pain," and colonial snobbery in the community. Patriotic fervour turns ugly in war-fanned mob hysteria that explodes in an attack on the gentle German piano teacher. The dramatic rhythms and quick scene cuts of television techniques influence the shaping of this novel, but it is handled with power and skill. As it encompasses human strengths, weaknesses, and social comment, it adds considerably to Gee's compelling, thought-provoking contribution to children's literature in New Zealand.

—Diane Hebley

GEISEL, Theodor Seuss.   See **SEUSS, Dr.**

GEORGE, Jean Craighead.   American. Born in Washington, D.C., 2 July 1919. Educated at Pennsylvania State University, State College, B.A. 1941; Louisiana State University, Baton Rouge; University of Michigan, Ann Arbor. Married John L. George in 1944 (divorced 1963); one daughter and two sons. Reporter, International News Service, 1942–44, and Washington *Post,* 1943–44, both in Washington, D.C., and United Features, 1945–46; artist, *Pageant Magazine,* New York, 1945; teacher, Chappaqua, New York, 1960–68; staff writer, 1969–74, and roving editor, 1974–82, *Reader's Digest,* Pleasantville, New York. Recipient: George G. Stone Center for Children's Books award, 1969; American Nature Society Gordon award, 1970; American Library Association Newbery Medal, 1973; University of Minnesota Kerlan award, 1982; University of Southern Mississippi award, 1986. Agent: Curtis Brown Ltd., 10 Astor Place, New York, New York 10003. Address: 20 William Street, Chappaqua, New York 10514, U.S.A.

PUBLICATIONS FOR CHILDREN

Fiction (illustrated by the author)

Vulpes the Red Fox, with John L. George.   New York, Dutton, 1948.
Vison the Mink, with John L. George.   New York, Dutton, 1949.
Masked Prowler: The Story of a Raccoon, with John L. George. New York, Dutton, 1950.
Meph, The Pet Skunk, with John L. George.   New York, Dutton, 1952.
Bubo the Great Horned Owl, with John L. George.   New York, Dutton, 1954.
Dipper of Copper Creek, with John L. George.   New York, Dutton, 1956.
The Hole in the Tree.   New York, Dutton, 1957.
Snow Tracks.   New York, Dutton, 1958.
My Side of the Mountain.   New York, Dutton, 1959; London, Bodley Head, 1962.
The Summer of the Falcon.   New York, Crowell, 1962; London, Dent, 1964.
Red Robin Fly Up!   Pleasantville, New York, Reader's Digest, 1963.
Gull Number 737.   New York, Crowell, 1964.
Hold Zero!   New York, Crowell, 1966.
Coyote in Manhattan, illustrated by John Kaufman.   New York, Crowell, 1968.
All upon a Stone, illustrated by Don Bolognese.   New York, Crowell, 1971.
Who Really Killed Cock Robin? An Ecological Mystery.   New York, Dutton, 1971.
Julie of the Wolves, illustrated by John Schoenherr.   New York, Harper, 1972; London, Hamish Hamilton, 1973.

All upon a Sidewalk, illustrated by Don Bolognese.   New York, Dutton, 1974.
Hook a Fish, Catch a Mountain.   New York, Dutton, 1975.
Going to the Sun.   New York, Harper, 1976.
The Wentletrap Trap, illustrated by Symeon Shimin.   New York, Dutton, 1978.
The Wounded Wolf, illustrated by John Schoenherr.   New York, Harper, 1978.
River Rats, Inc.   New York, Dutton, 1979.
The Cry of the Crow.   New York, Harper, 1980.
The Grizzly Bear with the Golden Ears, illustrated by Tom Catania. New York, Harper, 1982.
The Talking Earth.   New York, Harper, 1983.
Water Sky.   New York, Harper, 1987.
Shark Beneath the Reef.   New York, Harper, 1989.

Play

Tree House, music by Saul Aarons (produced).

Other

Animals from A to Z.   Pleasantville, New York, Readers Digest, 1964.
Spring Comes to the Ocean, illustrated by John Wilson.   New York, Crowell, 1966.
The Thirteen Moons (The Moon of the Owls, Bears, Salamander, Chickarees, Monarch Butterfly, Fox Pups, Wild Pigs, Mountain Lion, Deer, Alligator, Wolves, Winter Bird, and Mole), illustrated by John Schoenherr and others.   New York, Crowell, 13 vols., 1967–69.
Beastly Inventions: A Surprising Investigation into How Smart Animals Really Are, illustrated by the author.   New York, McKay, 1970; as *Animals Can Do Anything,* London, Souvenir Press, 1972.
The Wild, Wild Cookbook: A Guide for Young Wild-Food Foragers, illustrated by Walter Kessell.   New York, Crowell, 1982.
One Day in the Desert, illustrated by Fred Brenner.   New York, Crowell, 1983.
One Day in the Alpine Tundra, illustrated by Walter Gaffney-Kessell. New York, Crowell, 1984.
One Day in the Prairie, illustrated by Bob Marstall.   New York, Crowell, 1986.
One Day in the Woods, illustrated by Gary Allen.   New York, Crowell, 1988.

PUBLICATIONS FOR ADULTS

Other

Wildguide to the Everglades.   Washington, D.C., National Park Service, 1972.
New York in Maps 1972–73, with Toy Lasker.   New York, New York Magazine, 1974.
New York in Flashmaps 1974–75, with Toy Lasker.   Chappaqua, New York, Flashmaps, 1976.
The American Walk Book: An Illustrated Guide to the Country's Major Historical and Natural Walking Trails from New England to the Pacific Coast.   New York, Dutton, 1978.
Journey Inward (autobiography).   New York, Dutton, 1982.
How to Talk to Your Animals.   San Diego, Harcourt Brace, 1985; London, Hodder and Stoughton, 1986.

*

Manuscript Collection: Kerlan Collection, University of Minnesota, Minneapolis.

Illustrator: *Hawks, Owls, and Wildlife* by John Johnson Craighead, 1969.

Jean Craighead George comments:

As a naturalist I have a profound respect for a holistic view of the Earth, and so I write about children in nature and their relationship to the complex web of life of which we are but one small part. Knowledge of the scheme of things brings security and satisfaction to the human child. I call my books "documentary novels" for the investigations into nature are scientific and carefully researched. Today a work for children must be accurate and faithful to the truth.

*   *   *

The novels of Jean Craighead George are stories about nature. Though diverse in setting, characterization, and plot, her books have many themes in common. Her characters observe the mysteries of nature and seek answers that help them understand these mysteries. As they seek answers, they reflect on the secrets that nature holds. Typical of this reflection is that done by June, the main character in *The Summer of the Falcon* as she searches for answers: "There is something that all life has in common, and when I know what it is I shall know myself." This states a theme common in George's books. Sam, a teenage boy from the city, leaves his home to live in the wilderness in *My Side of the Mountain.* He attempts to understand nature in a search for ways he can live in harmony with it. Similarly, Billie Wind in *The Talking Earth* goes out alone into the Everglades to learn the secrets of nature that the Seminole Indians know. While she had doubted the ancient legends of her people, she learns to understand the language of animals as they help her survive.

Thorough scientific investigation is used to solve the mystery of the dead robins in *Who Really Killed Cock Robin?,* which has a plot designed in the manner of a murder mystery. George explores a different kind of mystery in *The Wounded Wolf,* a 32-page book intended for young children. In this story the suspense in nature is portrayed as the animals await the death of the wounded animal, but he is mysteriously saved by the leader of the wolf pack. Other mysteries of nature are presented in studies of the behavior of sea gulls in *Gull Number 737* and of wolves in *Julie of the Wolves,* the ecology of a mountain stream in *Hook a Fish, Catch a Mountain,* the life of mountain goats in *Going to the Sun* and the harsh surroundings of the Nevada desert in *River Rats, Inc.*

As important as the realization of nature's mysteries is the use of the scientific method to uncover them. George weaves the background of scientific data into the story, often with reference to actual scientific experiments to substantiate the facts. Throughout all her books, the collection of facts and the observation of data in the scientific method are important. In *Gull Number 737* Dr. Rivers, a professor of biology, is collecting data about the seagulls. Young Luke Rivers's impatience at the slowness of this process is contrasted with his father's thoroughness. "His father had taught him to write down all observations. Eventually many, many notes and hours and days and times would tell the story."

Spinner, a young girl from New York City, is introduced to the scientific research when she and her cousin Alligator attempt to solve the mystery of the large cut-throat trout she caught in *Hook a Fish, Catch a Mountain:* "The cards read: date, locale, time, water temperature, oxygen content, wind and water color. Spinner was aghast. Ecological spies were very scientific."

This thorough study of nature results in more than knowledge. The characters' love of the creations of nature comes through in the books. In *Gull Number 737* Luke Rivers watches the hatching of a gull and says, "I can't believe it," so impressed is he by this work of nature. Later his father adds: "You may be amazed by birth...but I never fail to be amazed by instinct. This little bird has never seen its mother....It could not possibly know that pecking that spot could make its mother choke up food...and yet [he] does it." In *The Talking Earth* Billie Wind exhibits a similar appreciation when she notices the pitcher plant. Observing its unique nature, Billie wonders if another planet somewhere in the universe might have a miraculous sundew plant living on it. "Will it?" she muses. "For it would be dull there without one."

Another important feature of these books is the comment on the place man has in the world of nature. In George's books, man is a part of ecology. The most important lesson for Sam is his realization that he can not live in conflict with, but has to learn to use, the elements of nature, not changing them, but accepting them as they are. Likewise, when Lincoln Noah Stonewright in *Water Sky* leaves Massachusetts to live with Eskimo whalers in the Arctic, he learns of the Eskimo belief that "The animals give themselves to the Eskimo. They let us kill them. They then become us: our blood, our voices, our spirits. They join us in our bodies. That is what they wish."

The characters show an understanding of nature and a desire to protect its creatures. Many people come to the aid of the coyote who hides in Central Park in *Coyote in Manhattan.* In the words of Miss Landry who feeds the birds in Central Park, "If birds and mice and coyotes are in the Park, they're here for a reason. They have as much right as we do." In *The Cry of the Crow,* set in the Florida Everglades, Mandy uses her knowledge of instinct and imprinting to protect her pet crow, Nina, from being shot.

Man sometimes interferes with the way of nature, a fact commented on in *The Summer of the Falcon:* "Nature had a way, the children learned at Pritchard's, of accommodating itself to the comings-and-goings of human beings." Mice and bees were left "to tolerate the people in summer and assume their rightful ownership of the house when the people were gone."

Sometimes there is an exasperation with the way man acts, as when Rob surveys the newly formed dump near Saddleboro in *Who Really Killed Cock Robin?* "Eight years ago...this dump was a half-acre hole surrounded by woods....An orchid called a pitcher plant once grew under this tree....The orchids are gone, the tree is dead, and the dump covers over ten acres. We are a very intelligent beast." This is balanced, later in the story, when Tony reflects on his job in the Conservation Service and considers the hope for educating people: "People *will* stop polluting the earth when they see what they're doing." And the book ends on this hopeful note: "A team of people killed Cock Robin and a team of people solved the crime. And that's how it's going to be from now until the day we live in balance with all beasts and plants, and air and water."

George explores the conflict between man and nature in *Going to the Sun,* as Marcus learns about mountain goats and changes his beliefs about hunting. Marcus had accepted that hunting was a way to achieve balance, but when he studies the goats he realizes he has to reject this belief.

The conflict between civilized man and nature is probably greatest in *Julie of the Wolves.* The two names used for the main character emphasize this conflict. She is part Miyax, the part that stands for the old ways of the Eskimos, and she is part Julie, her "white man's name" which depicts a changing attitude in Alaska. This contrast focuses on her two opposing desires, to join her pen pal in San Francisco, and to live in the wilderness. This dilemma is heightened when the wolf is killed. "Miyax buried her fingers in Kapu's fur. 'They did not even stop to get him!' she cried. 'They did not even kill him for money. I don't understand. I don't understand. Ta vun ga vun ga,' she cried. 'Pisupa gasu punga.' She spoke of her sadness in Eskimo, for she could not recall any English."

George returns to the Alaskan setting in *Water Sky.* Lincoln Stonewright, from Massachusetts, goes to Alaska and becomes involved in an Eskimo whale hunt. Even though he has learned much of the Eskimo tradition and appreciates the culture, he must come to terms with the fact that he is doomed to be an outsider. "…it was their songs that drew a circle and left him out…Even if he learned the words and the music, he still would be on the outside of the circle because, he knew, he could never sing with the deep feelings for the 'giving' that he had been hearing."

George has provided readers an opportunity to experience nature with a guide who understands its workings and appreciates its ways. Only occasionally do literary critics question some element of the human characterizations or the story structure. The fact that she weaves good stories while describing nature in an accurate, detailed, and exciting fashion is never challenged.

—Mary J. Lickteig

———

GERAS, Adèle (Daphne, née Weston). British. Born in Jerusalem, Israel, 15 March 1944. Educated at St. Hilda's College, Oxford, 1963–66, B.A. (honours) in modern languages 1966. Married Norman Geras in 1967; two daughters. French teacher, Fairfield High School, Droylsden, Lancashire, 1968–71. Agent: Laura Cecil, 17 Alwyne Villas, London N1 2HG. Address: 10 Danesmoor Road, Manchester M20 9JS, England.

PUBLICATIONS FOR CHILDREN

Fiction

Tea at Mrs. Manderby's, illustrated by Doreen Caldwell. London, Hamish Hamilton, 1976.
Apricots at Midnight and Other Stories from a Patchwork Quilt, illustrated by Doreen Caldwell. London, Hamish Hamilton, 1977; New York, Atheneum, 1982.
Beyond the Cross Stitch Mountains, illustrated by Mary Wilson. London, Hamish Hamilton, 1977.
The Girls in the Velvet Frame. London, Hamish Hamilton, 1979.
The Painted Garden, illustrated by Doreen Caldwell. London, Hamish Hamilton, 1979.
A Thousand Yards of Sea, illustrated by Joanna Troughton. London, Hodder and Stoughton, 1981.
The Rug That Grew, illustrated by Priscilla Lamont. London, Hamish Hamilton, 1981.
The Green Behind the Glass. London, Hamish Hamilton, 1982; as *Snapshots of Paradise: Love Stories,* New York, Atheneum, 1984.
Other Echoes. New York, Atheneum, 1982.
The Christmas Cat, illustrated by Doreen Caldwell. London, Hamish Hamilton, 1983.
Voyage. London, Hamish Hamilton, and New York, Atheneum, 1983.
Letters of Fire and Other Unsettling Stories. London, Hamish Hamilton, 1984.
Happy Endings. London, Hamish Hamilton, 1986.
Little Elephant's Moon, illustrated by Linda Birch. London, Hamish Hamilton, 1986.
Ritchie's Rabbit, illustrated by Vanessa Julian-Ottie. London, Hamish Hamilton, 1986; New York, Random House, 1987.
Finding Annabel, illustrated by Alan Marks. London, Hamish Hamilton, 1987.
Fishpie for Flamingoes, illustrated by Linda Birch. London, Hamish Hamilton, 1987.

The Fantora Family Files, illustrated by Tony Ross. London, Hamish Hamilton, 1988.
The Strange Bird, illustrated by Linda Birch. London, Hamish Hamilton, 1988.
The Coronation Picnic, illustrated by Frances Wilson. London, Hamish Hamilton, 1989.

PUBLICATIONS FOR ADULTS

Verse

Up on the Roof, with Pauline Stainer. Huddersfield, Smith Doorstop, 1987.

*

Theatrical Activities:
Actress: **Play**—in *Four Degrees Over* by David Wood and John Gould, London, 1966.

Adèle Geras comments:
I find it difficult to introduce my work because each book is so much a separate item. Generally speaking, I write novels and short stories for older readers which centre on the family and relationships between small groups of people. My short stories for younger children are quite often spooky, and my picture books are about domestic situations for the most part. I enjoy stories with a strong emotional content and I like details of setting, dress, food and so forth very much.

*   *   *

Adèle Geras can and does write for all ages. While her best writing is for older children she is equally surefooted in her picture-book texts and stories for younger readers. This confidence comes from her ability to pitch her stories directly at an audience. At whatever level she never talks down to her readers. Most of her books have a firm base and are full of close observation of people's lives and feelings. Her characters at all ages have a tendency to be intelligently reflective. Geras is a sympathetic writer who writes of moods and feeling more readily than action.

The power of particular objects absorbs her too. In *The Rug That Grew* Charlie is determined that a rug he is given is magic, and indeed strange things do happen. The beautiful cat at the centre of a classroom display is fought over by Joanna and Eddie in *The Christmas Cat.* There is an element of carefully controlled fantasy in each.

Geras's best writing is for teenagers, where her gift for conveying an atmosphere, a time, and a place can be most extensively developed. The intense and hectic excitement of an amateur dramatic company putting on a play is given vivid life in *Happy Endings.* The love story aspect is a little cliché but Geras herself makes fun of it too. Love is handled better and with interesting variation in *The Green Behind the Glass,* a collection of love stories reflecting the many and complex angles of loving relationships.

Geras's two warmest books are *The Girls in the Velvet Frame* and *Voyage.* In both she picks up on her own Jewish heritage, showing her understanding of and affection for the Jewish way of life. Her characters are convincing and, for the most part, sympathetically and humorously portrayed. *The Girls in the Velvet Frame* is set in Jerusalem in 1913. The action is minimal. The plot, insofar as there is one, centres around the plan Sarah Bernstein's five daughters concoct with their aunt Mimi to have their photograph taken and send it to their brother who has gone to America to find a better life but who has not kept in touch. The real drama comes from the interaction between the sisters and their aunt and from the vignettes of the society of the time—a young girl's first meeting with her prospective husband, the need to keep up appearances to neighbours, the oppressive heat of a Jerusalem summer.

Voyage has much the same feel—while there are more characters there is still very little action and again it is set in a small, controlled environment. A shipload of refugees from Eastern Europe is on its way to America. The story follows the different passengers, looking at how they cope with their hopes and fears and with each other. The range of characters is wide. Geras moves easily from a spoilt boy who gets his pleasure from hurting others to a young mother struggling to keep her a baby alive in terrible conditions. She is convincing about both.

Geras has also written a fantasy picture book, *A Thousand Yards of Sea,* which is a satisfyingly unusual story of a fisherman who catches a mermaid and lets her go in return for a thousand yards of sea, an apparently useless present which he puts to surprisingly good effect; a collection of quite nasty stories, each based on the idea of one individual taking over another, in *Letters of Fire and Other Unsettling Stories*; and a family story of an original and highly amusing nature in *The Fantora Family Files.*

Geras is interested in people and understands them, especially girls. Her books have an emotional integrity which makes them satisfying. Though not challenging or highly plotted they are all very well constructed and the fluent writing makes them easy to read and enjoy.

—Julia Eccleshare

GIBBS, (Cecilia) May. Australian. Born in Surrey, England, 1877; emigrated to Australia, 1881. Educated at Church of England Girls' School, Perth, Cope and Nichol School, Chelsea Polytechnic, and Henry Blackburn School of Black and White Art, London. Married B.J. Ossoli Kelly in 1913. M.B.E. (Member, Order of the British Empire). *Died 27 November 1969.*

PUBLICATIONS FOR CHILDREN (illustrated by the author)

Fiction

About Us. London, Nister, and New York, Dutton, 1912.
Gum Blossom Babies. Sydney, Angus and Robertson, 1916.
Gumnut Babies. Sydney, Angus and Robertson, 1916.
Boronia Babies. Sydney, Angus and Robertson, 1917.
Flannel Flowers and Other Bush Babies. Sydney, Angus and Robertson, 1917.
Wattle Babies. Sydney, Angus and Robertson, 1918.
Snugglepot and Cuddlepie: Their Adventures Wonderful. Sydney, Angus and Robertson, 1918.
Little Ragged Blossom, and More about Snugglepot and Cuddlepie. Sydney, Angus and Robertson, 1920.
Little Obelia, and Further Adventures of Ragged Blossom, Snugglepot and Cuddlepie. Sydney, Angus and Robertson, 1921.
Nuttybub and Nittersing. Melbourne, Osboldstone, 1923.
Chucklebud and Wunkydoo. Melbourne, Osboldstone, 1924; as *Two Little Gumnuts,* Sydney, Cornstalk, 1929.
Scotty in Gumnut Land. Sydney, Angus and Robertson, 1941; London, Angus and Robertson, 1956.
Mr. and Mrs. Bear and Friends. Sydney, Angus and Robertson, 1943; London, Angus and Robertson, 1957.
Prince Dande Lion: A Garden Whim-Wham. Sydney, Ure Smith,

1953; London, Angus and Robertson, 1954.
The May Gibbs Collection: Gumnut Classics, edited by Maureen Walsh. Sydney, Angus and Robertson, 1985.

Verse

Bib and Bub: Their Adventures. Sydney, Cornstalk, 2 vols., 1925.
The Further Adventures of Bib and Bub. Sydney, Cornstalk, 1927.
More Funny Stories about Old Friends Bib and Bub. Sydney, Cornstalk, 1928.
Bib and Bub in Gumnut Town. Waterloo, New South Wales, Halstead, 1929.
Bib and Bub Painting Book: New Stories. Sydney, Penfold, n.d.
Gumnuts. Sydney, Angus and Robertson, 1940.

Other

Alphabet Frieze. Sydney, Angus and Robertson, 1984.

*

Manuscript Collection: Mitchell Library, Sydney.

Critical Studies: *May Gibbs and Her Fantasy World* (exhibition catalogue) by Robert Holden, Sydney, Royal Botanic Gardens, 1985; *The May Gibbs Collection: Mother of the Gumnuts, Her Life and Work* by Maureen Walsh, Sydney, Angus and Robertson, 1985.

Illustrator: *Barons and Kings (1215–1485)* by Estelle Ross, 1912; *Scribbling Sue and Other Stories* by Amy Eleanor Mack, 1913; *Gem of the Flat* by Constance Mackness, 1914; *A Little Bush Poppy* by Edith Graham, 1915.

*   *   *

May Gibbs gave Australian children a sense of identity with their own land. She told them amusing stories about the wild creatures of the "bush," and of appealing "buds" and "blossoms"—imaginary figures evoked from the unique Australian flora. Like Beatrix Potter, she was a talented artist before she turned to writing. Having dwelt in her childhood amid the enchantingly beautiful West Australian bushland, she spent most of her life recreating its charm for children. She was an excellent draftswoman, and meticulous in her attention to detail. After producing calendars, post-cards, and the like during World War I, she wrote and illustrated some exquisite little booklets, beginning with *Gum Blossom Babies* in 1916. Their success encouraged her to create her best-known book, *Snugglepot and Cuddlepie,* which became a favourite, especially when it was later combined with two subsequent books to form *The Complete Adventures of Snugglepot and Cuddlepie.*

She also began to produce a comic strip, with the two main characters, Bib and Bub, closely resembling the gum-nuts in her stories. Each strip told a simple story in doggerel, but they were loved by children, and appeared weekly in Australian newspapers from 1925 for over 40 years, so that most Australians of different generations shared one childhood experience. Her humour and invention were always entertaining, though the strips in later years were sometimes reprinted. She was not fortunate in the production of her books, though the first editions of the earlier ones were well-produced with a generous number of illustrations. Later production was of a crude quality on poor paper with blurred or faint illustrations. Some of her stories were rewritten and illustrations redrawn with the addition of garish colour. However recent years have seen more sensitive reproductions of her work in response to widely attended exhibitions of her original drawings. A beautifully produced two-volume set, comprising a compendium volume of her main books together with a biography illustrated with many hitherto unpublished drawings and watercolours was published in 1985. This reflects the wider appreciation of her stature as one of Australia's finest authors and illustrators for children. The charm, gentleness, and fun of her stories and illustrations and their originality is appreciated as never before. A nationwide campaign is at present afoot to preserve her Sydney harbourside home "Nutcote" as part of the nation's heritage.

—Marcie Muir

GIPSON, Fred(erick Benjamin). American. Born in Mason, Texas, 7 February 1908. Educated at Mason High School, graduated 1926; University of Texas, Austin, 1933–37. Married Tommie Eloise Wynn in 1940 (divorced 1964); two sons. Farm and ranch hand, and clerk, 1926–33; reporter and columnist, Corpus Christi *Caller-Times,* San Angelo *Standard-Times,* and Paris *News,* all in Texas, 1938–40; associate editor, *True West* magazine, Austin, 1953–59; editorial director, *Frontier Times,* Bandera, Texas, 1958–59. President, Texas Institute of Letters, 1960. *Died 14 August 1973.*

PUBLICATIONS FOR CHILDREN

Fiction

The Trail-Driving Rooster. New York, Harper, 1955.
Old Yeller, illustrated by Carl Burger. New York, Harper, 1956; London, Hodder and Stoughton, 1957.
Savage Sam, illustrated by Carl Burger. New York, Harper, and London, Hodder and Stoughton, 1962.
Little Arliss, illustrated by Ronald Himler. New York, Harper, 1978.
Curly and the Wild Boar, illustrated by Ronald Himler. New York, Harper, 1979.

PUBLICATIONS FOR ADULTS

Fiction

Hound-Dog Man. New York, Harper, 1949.
The Home Place. New York, Harper, 1950; London, Joseph, 1951; abridged edition, as *Return of the Texan,* Edinburgh, Oliver and Boyd, 1962.
Recollection Creek. New York, Harper, 1955; revised edition, for children, 1959.

Plays

Screenplays: *Old Yeller,* with William Tunberg, 1957; *Hound Dog Man,* with Winston Miller, 1959; *Savage Sam,* with William Tunberg, 1962.

Television Play: *Brush Roper.*

Other

Fabulous Empire: Colonel Zack Miller's Story. Boston, Houghton Mifflin, 1946; as *Circles round the Wagon,* London, Joseph, 1949.
Big Bend, with J. Oscar Langford. Austin, University of Texas Press, 1952.
Cowhand: The Story of a Working Cowboy. New York, Harper,

1953; London, Corgi, 1957.
The Cow Killers: With the Aftosa Commission in Mexico. Austin, University of Texas Press, 1956.
An Acceptance Speech. New York, Harper, 1960.

*

Critical Studies: *Fred Gipson* by Sam H. Henderson, Austin, Texas, Steck Vaughn, 1967; *Fred Gipson, Texas Storyteller* by Mike Cox, Austin, Texas, Shoal Creek, 1980.

*   *   *

Fred Gipson published *The Trail-Driving Rooster,* his first book specifically for children, in 1955. He had already published three well-received books of non-fiction, a number of short stories, and three novels of somewhat uneven quality. Gipson seems to have sensed at about the time of *Rooster* that his forte was fiction for children. All of his remaining fiction is aimed, essentially, at children, although some consider it equally appealing to adults.

Gipson spoke very little about the craft of writing, but in "Writing for Young People," published in *Library Journal,* he unburdened himself on a number of points. "It just happens that I love boys and dogs and horses and the wild creatures in their natural habitat....To me, these things have meaning. They give me a lift of spirit...." In the same article, he makes clear that it is not only a certain subject matter that he finds congenial but a particular audience as well. "Children not only accepted what I had to say, but felt that it had meaning....All they ask is that [the author] write a simple and honest tale...."

Rooster, in fact, cannot be called "a simple and honest tale." It is a series of tall tales focusing on a rooster who refuses to be put in the stew pot. This element of hyperbole Gipson never gets completely away from, but in the two major works that soon follow, *Old Yeller* and *Savage Sam,* he captures those qualities he so much admires and succeeds in writing what most critics consider to be children's classics.

All of Gipson's works of fiction are imbued with a strong feel for the land and nostalgia for a past where simple human virtues helped man work in harmony with his surroundings. The hound-dog men of Gipson's world are being displaced irrevocably by the mercenary. It is in the young that Gipson most often finds those sterling qualities that have not, as yet, been "corrupted." It is no accident that the focus is on the young, even in Gipson's adult fiction.

Old Yeller is typical. A post-Civil War rancher in the frontier hill country of Texas leaves his wife and two young sons to look after the place while he is on a cattle drive. The burden falls on the teenage son, Travis, whose courage and ingenuity enable the family to overcome various bucolic vicissitudes, with the help of his plucky mother and an extraordinary loyal and stubborn dog. A somewhat similar pattern is followed in *Savage Sam,* a sequel which takes place about a year later. The sense of adventure is heightened in the fact that the boys and a neighboring girl are captured by a roving band of Indians, who, though hostile on the whole, live in harmony with and understand the environment.

For all practical purposes, Gipson's narrative vein played out soon after *Savage Sam.* He recognized this himself, and talked vaguely of moving to Mexico or somewhere else, hoping to recapture inspiration. It was not to be. *Little Arliss* and *Curly and the Wild Boar,* the latest works ascribed to him, are largely tired reworkings of previously used materials. They do nothing to enhance the reputation of his work in children's literature.

—Sam H. Henderson

GODDEN, (Margaret) Rumer. British. Born in Sussex, 10 December 1907. Educated privately and at Moira House, Eastbourne, Sussex. Married 1) Laurence Sinclair Foster in 1934 (died), two daughters; 2) James Lesley Haynes Dixon in 1949 (died 1973). Director of a children's ballet school, Calcutta, in the 1930's. Recipient: Whitbread award, 1973. Agent: Curtis Brown, 162–168 Regent Street, London W1R 5TA, England; or, 10 Astor Place, New York, New York 10003, U.S.A. Address: Ardnacloich, Moniaive, Thornhill, Dumfries and Galloway DG3 4HZ, Scotland.

PUBLICATIONS FOR CHILDREN

Fiction

The Dolls' House, illustrated by Dana Saintsbury. London, Joseph, 1947; New York, Viking Press, 1948; as *Tottie,* London, Penguin, 1983.
The Mousewife, illustrated by Dana Saintsbury. London, Macmillan, and New York, Viking Press, 1951.
Four Dolls, illustrated by Pauline Baynes. London, Macmillan, 1983; New York, Greenwillow, 1984.
  Impunity Jane: The Story of a Pocket Doll, illustrated by Adrienne Adams. New York, Viking Press, 1954; London, Macmillan, 1955.
  The Fairy Doll, illustrated by Adrienne Adams. London, Macmillan, and New York, Viking Press, 1956.
  The Story of Holly and Ivy, illustrated by Adrienne Adams. London, Macmillan, and New York, Viking Press, 1958.
  Candy Floss, illustrated by Adrienne Adams. London, Macmillan, and New York, Viking Press, 1960.
Mouse House, illustrated by Adrienne Adams. New York, Viking Press, 1957; London, Macmillan, 1958.
Miss Happiness and Miss Flower, illustrated by Jean Primrose. London, Macmillan, and New York, Viking Press, 1961.
Little Plum, illustrated by Jean Primrose. London, Macmillan, and New York, Viking Press, 1963.
Home Is the Sailor, illustrated by Jean Primrose. London, Macmillan, and New York, Viking Press, 1964.
The Kitchen Madonna, illustrated by Carol Barker. London, Macmillan, and New York, Viking Press, 1967.
Operation Sippacik, illustrated by James Bryan. London, Macmillan, and New York, Viking Press, 1969.
The Old Woman Who Lived in a Vinegar Bottle, illustrated by Mairi Hedderwick. London, Macmillan, and New York, Viking Press, 1972.
The Diddakoi, illustrated by Creina Glegg. London, Macmillan, and New York, Viking Press, 1972.
Mr. McFadden's Hallowe'en, illustrated by Ann Strugnell. London, Macmillan, and New York, Viking Press, 1975.
The Rocking Horse Secret, illustrated by Juliet Stanwell Smith. London, Macmillan, 1977; New York, Viking Press, 1978.
A Kindle of Kittens, illustrated by Lynne Byrnes. London, Macmillan, 1978; New York, Viking Press, 1979.
The Dragon of Og, illustrated by Pauline Baynes. London, Macmillan, and New York, Viking Press, 1981.
The Valiant Chatti-Maker, illustrated by Jeroo Roy. London, Macmillan, and New York, Viking Press, 1983.
Fu-Dog, illustrated by Valerie Littlewood. London, MacRae, 1989.

Verse

In Noah's Ark. London, Joseph, and New York, Viking Press, 1949.
St. Jerome and the Lion, illustrated by Jean Primrose. London, Macmillan, and New York, Viking Press, 1961.

Other

Editor, *Round the Day, Round the Year, The World Around: Poetry Programmes for Classroom or Library.* London, Macmillan, 6 vols., 1966–67.
Editor, *A Letter to the World: Poems for Young Readers,* by Emily Dickinson, illustrated by Prudence Seward. London, Bodley Head, 1968; New York, Macmillan, 1969.

PUBLICATIONS FOR ADULTS

Novels

Chinese Puzzle. London, Davies, 1936.
The Lady and the Unicorn. London, Davies, 1937.
Black Narcissus. London, Davies, and Boston, Little Brown, 1939.
Gypsy, Gypsy. London, Davies, and Boston, Little Brown, 1940.
Breakfast with the Nikolides. London, Davies, and Boston, Little Brown, 1942.
A Fugue in Time. London, Joseph, 1945; as *Take Three Tenses: A Fugue in Time,* Boston, Little Brown, 1945.
The River. London, Joseph, and Boston, Little Brown, 1946.
A Candle for St. Jude. London, Joseph, and New York, Viking Press, 1948.
A Breath of Air. London, Joseph, 1950; New York, Viking Press, 1951.
Kingfishers Catch Fire. London, Macmillan, and New York, Viking Press, 1953.
An Episode of Sparrows. New York, Viking Press, 1955; London, Macmillan, 1956.
The Greengage Summer. London, Macmillan, and New York, Viking Press, 1958.
China Court: The Hours of a Country House. London, Macmillan, and New York, Viking Press, 1961.
The Battle of the Villa Fiorita. London, Macmillan, and New York, Viking Press, 1963.
In This House of Brede. London, Macmillan, and New York, Viking Press, 1969.
The Peacock Spring. London, Macmillan, 1975; New York, Viking Press, 1976.
Five for Sorrow, Ten for Joy. London, Macmillan, and New York, Viking Press, 1979.
The Dark Horse. London, Macmillan, 1981; New York, Viking Press, 1982.
Thursday's Children. London, Macmillan, and New York, Viking, 1984.

Short Stories

Mooltiki and Other Stories and Poems of India. London, Macmillan, and New York, Viking Press, 1957.
Swans and Turtles: Stories. London, Macmillan, 1968; as *Gone: A Thread of Stories,* New York, Viking Press, 1968.

Plays

Screenplays: *The River,* with Jean Renoir, 1951; *Innocent Sinners,* with Neil Patterson, 1958.

Other

Rungli-Rungliot (Thus Far and No Further). London, Davies, 1943; as *Rungli-Rungliot Means in Paharia, Thus Far and No Further,* Boston, Little Brown, 1946; as *Thus Far and No Further,* London, Macmillan, 1961.

Bengal Journey: A Story of the Part Played by Women in the Province 1939–1945.   London, Longman, 1945.

Hans Christian Andersen: A Great Life in Brief.   London, Hutchinson, and New York, Knopf, 1955.

Two under the Indian Sun (autobiography), with Jon Godden.   London, Macmillan, and New York, Knopf, 1966.

The Tale of the Tales: The Beatrix Potter Ballet.   London, Warne, 1971.

Shiva's Pigeons: An Experience of India, with Jon Godden.   London, Chatto and Windus, and New York, Viking Press, 1972.

The Butterfly Lions: The Story of the Pekingese in History, Legend, and Art.   London, Macmillan, 1977; New York, Viking Press, 1978.

Gulbadan: Portrait of a Rose Princess at the Mughal Court.   London, Macmillan, 1980; New York, Viking Press, 1981.

A Time to Dance, No Time to Weep (autobiography).   London, Macmillan, and New York, Morrow, 1987.

A House with Four Rooms (autobiography).   London, Macmillan, 1989.

Editor, *Mrs. Manders' Cookbook,* by Olga Manders.   London, Macmillan, and New York, Viking Press, 1968.

Editor, *The Raphael Bible.*   London, Macmillan, and New York, Viking Press, 1970.

Translator, *Prayers from the Ark* (verse), by Carmen de Gasztold.   New York, Viking Press, 1962; London, Macmillan, 1963.

Translator, *The Creatures' Choir* (verse), by Carmen de Gasztold.   New York, Viking Press, 1965; as *The Beasts' Choir,* London, Macmillan, 1967.

*

Manuscript Collection: Mugar Memorial Library, Boston University.

Critical Study: *Rumer Godden* by Hassell A. Simpson, New York, Twayne, 1973.

*   *   *

"Books are meant to give a child pleasure, sheer enjoyment, and it seems to me in the writing of books nowadays, something has been lost, something that children have always wanted, obviously wanted. I believe that 'something' is the story." So Rumer Godden gave her audience a key to her own writing when she opened the 1976 Children's Book of the Year Exhibition in London. For Godden is above all else a storyteller. Her first children's story, *The Dolls' House,* was written because she wanted to see if she could produce a novel in miniature. Her success in writing for both adults and children has shown how well she has mastered the discipline of not producing a simplified adult novel for children, but having that clarity of thought which enables an author to stick to the story "and not philosophise."

Many of her books for children are about dolls, and the dolls house shows a tiny version of the adult world, the dolls serving to give a child's-eye view of relationships, personalities, and situations that come frighteningly near to reality. *Candy Floss,* about a doll stolen by a spoilt child, provides enough drama to make the reader hold his breath until he sees her safely returned. While her doll characters reflect the complexities of family life, they never lose their doll-like characteristics. In *The Story of Holly and Ivy* the much coveted doll in the toyshop which gladdens the orphan child on Christmas morning is very much a doll to be dressed and played with. Tottie Plantagenet, the farthing doll heroine of *The Dolls' House,* is a real person, and the malice which the kid-and-china doll Marchpane shows her is as bitter and acid as any fishwife's.

Godden's stories are not all as emotional or poignant as that of Tottie. Miss Happiness and Miss Flower, two Japanese dolls, achieve great joy when Nona makes them a proper little Japanese house and a whole Japanese garden to themselves. Friendship is the theme of another story about Miss Happiness and Miss Flower when they win the heart of the round cosy little doll, Little Plum, who sits on Gem's window sill next door.

It has been said that Godden's books steer a steady course between sensitivity and sentimentality. Certainly her books reflect her early childhood in India in a beautiful house with many servants: "our life did evoke a princess quality." She has that rare gift in a writer of not overstating her case, leaving the reader to discover the people behind the characters. She is always sincere and always just. Her most outstanding children's book, *The Diddakoi,* is sentimental, emotional, middle-class, and romantic; but it also and far more importantly has a timeless quality enjoyed by all children regardless of status, race, or class, because essentially it is a story about people. It is people who matter to Godden, the people who, like herself when she was sent to school in England, feel out of step with the rest of the crowd. Kizzy, the half-gypsy girl, loses her home after her Gran dies and their wagon is burnt. She is determined not to conform, to go to school; but she will look after the horse Joe, and never "go into brick." Her story, woven with that of the crusty old Admiral with his unspoken love of Miss Brooke, the magistrate who befriends Kizzy, evokes the fullness and rightness of things that children need in their tales. Children do not see the cottage fire at the climax of the book as unrealistic; they see it as logical, since it sets the scene for the happy-ever-after ending.

Although Godden's books are essentially about people and their feelings, her three royal Pekinese ruling her home amply testify to her love and understanding of animals. From an anecdote in Dorothy Wordsworth's *Journal* about the friendship between a mouse and a caged dove, she has written the parable *The Mousewife,* a delicate, tender story, just as memorable in its telling as the tragedy of many far larger heroines.

Not all Godden's writings can be called "tender and evocative"; as in all good stories, there is a hard core beneath, and also a large smattering of humour. *Operation Sippacik* is an adventure story with the unusual setting of Cyprus during the EOKA troubles. In *Mr. McFadden's Hallowe'en* she writes a jolly good horse story in every sense of the word, with a stubborn and determined heroine riding an even more stubborn and determined pony. Haggis loves Mr. McFadden's turnip field, but Mr. McFadden loves no one, least of all Selina and her pony. It is a humorous and witty story with great insight into human and animal behaviour in a small village.

Virginia Haviland has called Godden "a genuine writer for adults and children unaffected by pressures from without." This was shown to perfection when Godden published the much celebrated article in the *Horn Book* called "An Imaginary Correspondence." It was between Mr. V. Andal, a publisher, and the ghost of Beatrix Potter, and concerned possible publication of a modern retelling of the Peter Rabbit story. "Are children nowadays so much less intelligent than their parents?" she wrote. "I think I write carefully because I enjoy my writing and enjoy taking pains over it. I write to please myself: my usual way is to scribble and cut out and write it again and again. The shorter, the plainer—the better. And to read the Bible (unrevised version and Old Testament) if I feel my style wants chastening…[our] real work is to enrich a child's heritage of words—not diminish it." And enrich it she certainly does.

—Jean Russell

GORDON, John (William). British. Born in Jarrow, County Durham, 19 November 1925. Educated at Wisbech Grammar School, Cambridgeshire. Served in the Royal Navy, 1943–47. Married Sylvia Ellen Young in 1954; one son and one daughter. Reporter, 1947–49, and sub-editor, 1949–51, *Isle of Ely and Wisbech Advertiser*; chief reporter and sub-editor, *Bury Free Press,* Bury St. Edmunds, Suffolk, 1951–58; sub-editor, *Western Evening Herald,* Plymouth, 1958–62; sub-editor and columnist, *Eastern Evening News,* Norwich, 1962–73; sub-editor, *Eastern Daily Press,* Norwich, 1973–85. Address: 99 George Borrow Road, Norwich, Norfolk NR4 7HU, England.

PUBLICATIONS FOR CHILDREN

Fiction

The Giant under the Snow. London, Hutchinson, 1968; New York, Harper, 1970.
The House on the Brink. London, Hutchinson, 1970; New York, Harper, 1971.
The Ghost on the Hill. London, Kestrel, 1976; New York, Viking Press, 1977.
The Waterfall Box. London, Kestrel, 1978.
The Spitfire Grave and Other Stories. London, Kestrel, 1979.
The Edge of the World. London, Hardy, and New York, Atheneum, 1983.
Catch Your Death, illustrated by Jeremy Ford. London, Hardy, 1984.
The Quelling Eye. London, Bodley Head, 1986.
The Grasshopper. London, Bodley Head, 1987.
Ride the Wind. London, Bodley Head, 1989.
Blood Brothers. London, Signpost, 1989.

*

John Gordon comments:

There's no better place than the Fens of East Anglia for stirring the imagination—a land so flat and open must have secrets, and it has—so the stories I write come from there or thereabouts. I like the land and I like the people, and I often write about the supernatural because it is always there, beyond the edge of things. One of the pleasures of storytelling is turning things upside down. In *The Edge of the World* the Fens become a desert of red sand, village people are not at all what they seem, a palace of glass stands in the burning desert—and only those with the knack of seeing have any idea what is there all the time. G.K. Chesterton, writing about the pleasure of holding a conversation on the top deck of a tramcar, said: "To talk on the top of a hill is superb, but to talk on the top of a flying hill is a fairy tale." I would like my stories to be flying hills.

*   *   *

The best introduction to John Gordon's work was provided by Gordon himself in a brief but admirable essay in Edward Blishen's collection *The Thorny Paradise.* "For me," he wrote, "writing is always an attempt to get to the edge of things, to reach that strangest of all places where one thing ends and another begins…The boundary between imagination and reality, and the boundary between being a child and being an adult are border country, a passionate place in which to work."

Gordon's novels live and move in that border country. They are about adolescents and concerned with adolescence. They are also concerned with the supernatural and, frequently, the possibly-supernatural, when there are happenings that might have a rational explanation but might not. Gordon is particularly good at building up

tension and generating the electric shudder that comes from an uncanny event in an everyday world.

His first book, *The Giant under the Snow,* is more a children's and less a teenage novel than its successors. It is a fantasy based on the splendid idea of a Green Man—a huge legendary figure from a hillside—that once walked and now lies buried: a strange shape of mounds and ridges in the landscape. Three youngsters are caught up in the last act of a struggle between light and dark, in which an attempt is made to bring the giant to life. There is powerful material here, but too much of it; the book is overcrowded with action and not well enough organized. *The House on the Brink* is a great advance. An evil-looking log is found lying in Fenland mud. Does it move, does it leave a foul and sluglike, though invisible, trail? Could it be—or was it once—human? Is it dangerous, or is the menace in someone's mind? Or both? Dick and Helen are drawn into a quest to find out; and the answers have emotional rather than strictly factual logic.

The Ghost on the Hill is set in an isolated village; at its heart is an unquiet grave whose occupant cannot rest until repetition of an old tragedy has been averted. The style is taut, the suspense compelling, and the drawing of personal relationships precise.

The Spitfire Grave, a story collection, strikingly confirms Gordon's ability to evoke the intense feelings of adolescence, but his fourth and fifth novels are less successful. In *The Waterfall Box* the exploration of class and sexual tensions among a group of teenagers fails to mesh with a story about a sinister antique dealer and his interest in the box and phial left behind many generations ago by Silas Waterfall, potter and alchemist. *The Edge of the World* is based on the notion that if you could break through the (sometimes and to some people) thin skin of this world, you would arrive in another. A boy and girl find they can cross into a perilous fantasy realm, in which however their actions dramatically affect events in our own. The idea is good, but the fantasy world has too many second-rate elements, and its relationship to the real one does not convince.

In *The Quelling Eye* crazy old Peregrine Falconer believes he has occult powers inherited from the forebears who owned a village and its valley; believes that at the full moon and the summer solstice he will be able to fly like a hawk. And Chuck and Tessa feel themselves made tiny and carried off by a great bird of prey, which they cause to dive to its death. Mr. Falconer is found dead the next day, and the young people are sure they know why; but all that the adults have seen is a primitive form of hang glider or a tree thrashing in the wind. Can Mr. Falconer really fly? It's impossible to say. We are in border country again, between imagination and reality. *The Grasshopper,* exceptionally, has nothing supernatural in it, but the monstrous mechanical creature devised many years ago is a haunting invention, and the climax to a story of small-town intrigue comes when it is reactivated by old Josh and ridden, for the first time ever, by schoolgirl Charlotte.

Gordon has fine gifts of imagination and perception. He has not yet produced the outstanding book promised by his early work; but the promise and the power to fulfil it are still there.

—John Rowe Townsend

GOUDGE, Elizabeth (de Beauchamp). British. Born in Wells, Somerset, 24 April 1900. Educated at Grassendale School, Southbourne, Hampshire; Reading University School of Art. Taught design and applied art, Ely and Oxford, 1922–32. Recipient: Library Association Carnegie Medal, 1947. Fellow, Royal Society of Literature, 1945. *Died 1 April 1984.*

PUBLICATIONS FOR CHILDREN

Fiction

The Fairies' Baby and Other Stories. Amersham, Buckinghamshire, and London, Morland-Foyle, 1920.
Sister of the Angels: A Christmas Story, illustrated by C. Walter Hodges. London, Duckworth, and New York, Coward McCann, 1939.
Smoky-House, illustrated by C. Walter Hodges. London, Duckworth, and New York, Coward McCann, 1940.
The Well of the Star. New York, Coward McCann, 1941.
Henrietta's House, illustrated by Lorna R. Steele. London, University of London Press-Hodder and Stoughton, 1942; as *The Blue Hills,* New York, Coward McCann, 1942.
The Little White Horse, illustrated by C. Walter Hodges. London, University of London Press, 1946; New York, Coward McCann, 1947.
Make-Believe, illustrated by C. Walter Hodges. London, Duckworth, 1949; Boston, Bentley, 1953.
The Valley of Song, illustrated by Steven Spurrier. London, University of London Press, 1951; New York, Coward McCann, 1952.
Linnets and Valerians, illustrated by Ian Ribbons. Leicester, Brockhampton Press, and New York, Coward McCann, 1964.
I Saw Three Ships, illustrated by Richard Kennedy. Leicester, Brockhampton Press, and New York, Coward McCann, 1969.

Other

God So Loved the World: A Life of Christ. London, Hodder and Stoughton, and New York, Coward McCann, 1951.

PUBLICATIONS FOR ADULTS

Novels

Island Magic. London, Duckworth, and New York, Coward McCann, 1934.
The Middle Window. London, Duckworth, 1935; New York, Coward McCann, 1939.
A City of Bells. London, Duckworth, and New York, Coward McCann, 1936.
Towers in the Mist. London, Duckworth, and New York, Coward McCann, 1938.
The Bird in the Tree. London, Duckworth, and New York, Coward McCann, 1940.
The Castle on the Hill. London, Duckworth, and New York, Coward McCann, 1941.
Green Dolphin Country. London, Hodder and Stoughton, 1944; as *Green Dolphin Street,* New York, Coward McCann, 1944.
The Herb of Grace. London, Hodder and Stoughton, 1948; as *Pilgrim's Inn,* New York, Coward McCann, 1948.
Gentian Hill. London, Hodder and Stoughton, and New York, Coward McCann, 1949.
The Heart of the Family. London, Hodder and Stoughton, and New York, Coward McCann, 1953.
The Rosemary Tree. London, Hodder and Stoughton, and New York, Coward McCann, 1956.
The White Witch. London, Hodder and Stoughton, and New York, Coward McCann, 1958.
The Dean's Watch. London, Hodder and Stoughton, and New York, Coward McCann, 1960.
The Scent of Water. London, Hodder and Stoughton, and New York, Coward McCann, 1963.
The Child from the Sea. London, Hodder and Stoughton, and New York, Coward McCann, 1970.

Short Stories

A Pedlar's Pack and Other Stories. London, Duckworth, and New York, Coward McCann, 1937.
The Golden Skylark and Other Stories. London, Duckworth, and New York, Coward McCann, 1941.
The Ikon on the Wall and Other Stories. London, Duckworth, 1943.
The Reward of Faith and Other Stories. London, Duckworth, 1950; New York, Coward McCann, 1951.
White Wings: Collected Short Stories. London, Duckworth, 1952.
The Lost Angel. London, Hodder and Stoughton, and New York, Coward McCann, 1971.

Plays

The Brontës of Haworth (produced London, 1932). Included in *Three Plays,* 1939.
Joy Will Come Back (produced London, 1937).
Suomi (produced London, 1938). Included in *Three Plays,* 1939.
Three Plays: Suomi, The Brontës of Haworth, and Fanny Burney. London, Duckworth, 1939.
Fanny Burney (produced Oldham, Lancashire, 1949). Included in *Three Plays,* 1939.

Verse

Songs and Verses. London, Duckworth, 1947; New York, Coward McCann, 1948.

Other

The Elizabeth Goudge Reader, edited by Rose Dobbs. New York, Coward McCann, 1946; as *At the Sign of the Dolphin: An Elizabeth Goudge Anthology,* London, Hodder and Stoughton, 1947.
Saint Francis of Assisi. London, Duckworth, 1959; as *My God and My All: The Life of St. Francis of Assisi,* New York, Coward McCann, 1959.
The Chapel of the Blessed Virgin Mary, Buckler's Hard, Beaulieu. Privately printed, 1966.
A Christmas Book (anthology). London, Hodder and Stoughton, and New York, Coward McCann, 1967.
The Ten Gifts (anthology), edited by Mary Baldwin. London, Hodder and Stoughton, and New York, Coward McCann, 1969.
The Joy of the Snow: An Autobiography. London, Hodder and Stoughton, and New York, Coward McCann, 1974.
Pattern of People: An Elizabeth Goudge Anthology, edited by Muriel Grainger. London, Hodder and Stoughton, 1978; New York, Coward McCann, 1979.

Editor, *A Book of Comfort: An Anthology.* London, Joseph, and New York, Coward McCann, 1964.
Editor, *A Diary of Prayer.* London, Hodder and Stoughton, and New York, Coward McCann, 1966.
Editor, *A Book of Peace: An Anthology.* London, Joseph, 1967; New York, Coward McCann, 1968.
Editor, *A Book of Faith.* London, Hodder and Stoughton, and New York, Coward McCann, 1976.

*

Elizabeth Goudge commented:
(1978) I have always loved writing for children; I have enjoyed writing my children's books even more than writing my novels. Of

all my books the two I care for most are *The Little White Horse* and *The Valley of Song*. And I have enjoyed the children themselves, both receiving their letters and being visited by them. They have been one of the greatest joys of my life.

*   *   *

Elizabeth Goudge was in many ways a writer born out of her time, and always liable to be judged old-fashioned. Young readers, however, are themselves strongly inclined to have old-fashioned tastes, so that the best of her works, like the best of Victorian work, are unlikely to lose their appeal. The openly religious, sometimes Anglican, element which runs through all her writing may perhaps seem increasingly strange if the habit of church-going continues to decline, but her highly evocative powers of description, her gift for creating memorable characters, and her ability to work through an intricately woven plot and bring it to a satisfactory conclusion, are virtues which will surely survive. Among her other qualities one may note Goudge's habit of surrounding her child characters with interesting adults, often advanced in years, and her flair for giving personality to animals, especially dogs and horses.

At their best Goudge's stories are strongly rooted in everyday reality, with magic and fantasy used only to enliven; similarly, her much-criticised lapses into sentimentality and sickly-sweetness are quite rare in the two or three books on which her reputation depends. Little need be said here about *Smoky-House* and *The Valley of Song*. The former is an odd mixture of smuggling adventure, fairy-story, and cosy moralizing, while the latter, though palpably sincere, is too much concerned with the author's personal vision of heaven, and not enough with the child's normal interests. Two other books are interesting but uneven. *Sister of the Angels* is very sentimental, though redeemed by flashes of humour and a fine portrayal of an artist's dedication; and the collection called *Make-Believe* contains one story—"The Forester's Ride"—which one might recommend for any high-spirited ten-year-old, but otherwise it seems more suitable for nostalgic adults than for children.

Most of Goudge's children's books came in the earlier part of her writing career. One exception, *Linnets and Valerians*, also happens to be in her very best vein, with a plot of nicely judged complexity and a sparkling cast of heroes, villains, and eccentrics. Ezra Oake, the one-legged sailor-servant, is certainly among her finest creations. Possibly, however, her two previous great successes, *The Little White Horse* and *Henrietta's House*, deserve higher praise by virtue of their originality. *Henrietta's House* must be almost unique in giving pride of place to a group of elderly clergymen, and the combination in this book of rollicking entertainment with a deep religious purpose is a notable achievement. *The Little White Horse* is lengthy, complicated, and concerned with emotions such as sexual passion, pride, jealousy, and loneliness; yet the principal characters and incidents are exceptionally captivating, and an atmosphere of joyous enchantment persists throughout. Goudge's reputation could stand on this book alone.

—Alasdair K.D. Campbell

———

GRAHAM, Bob (Robert Graham). Australian. Born in Sydney, New South Wales, 20 October 1942. Educated at Julian Ashton Art School, Sydney, 1964–68. Married Carolyn Smith in 1968; one daughter and one son. Artist, New South Wales Government printers, Sydney, 1973–75; resource designer, Department of Technical Education, Sydney, 1975–82; illustrator, Five Mile Press, Melbourne, 1982–85. Recipient: Australian Children's Book Council Picture Book of the Year award, 1988. Agent: Anne Bower Ingram, 4/6 Boronia Street, Wollstonecraft, New South Wales 2065. Address: Lot 8, Mt. Dandenong Road, Mt. Dandenong, Victoria 3767, Australia.

PUBLICATIONS FOR CHILDREN (illustrated by the author)

Fiction

A Boggle of Bunyips.   Sydney, Hodder and Stoughton, 1981.
Pete and Roland.   Sydney, Collins, 1981; London, Collins, 1982; New York, Viking, 1984.
Here Comes John.   Adelaide, Omnibus, 1983; London, Hamish Hamilton, 1984; Boston, Little Brown, 1988.
Here Comes Theo.   Adelaide, Omnibus, 1983; London, Hamish Hamilton, 1984; Boston, Little Brown, 1988.
Pearl's Place.   Melbourne, Lothian, and London, Blackie, 1983; New York, Bedrick, 1985.
Libby, Oscar and Me.   Melbourne, Lothian, 1984; London, Blackie, and New York, Bedrick, 1985.
Bath Time for John.   Adelaide, Omnibus, and London, Hamish Hamilton, 1985; Boston, Little Brown, 1988.
First There Was Frances.   Melbourne, Lothian, and London, Blackie, 1985; New York, Bradbury Press, 1986.
Where Is Sarah?   Adelaide, Omnibus, and London, Hamish Hamilton, 1985; Boston, Little Brown, 1988.
The Wild.   Melbourne, Lothian, 1986; London, Blackie, and New York, Bedrick, 1987.
The Adventures of Charlotte and Henry.   Paris, Centurion, and London and New York, Viking Kestrel, 1987.
Crusher Is Coming!   Melbourne, Lothian, and London, Collins, 1987; New York, Viking Kestrel, 1988.
The Red Woollen Blanket.   London, Walker, 1987; Boston, Little Brown, 1988.
Has Anyone Seen William?   London, Walker, 1988; Boston, Little Brown, 1989.

Other (readers)

I Can series (*Actions 1, Actions 2, Babies, Bikes, Colour, Families, Helping, In the Water, My Senses, Pets, School, Shopping*). Fitzroy, Victoria, Five Mile Press, 12 vols., 1984; as *Reading Is Fun* series, London, Blackie, 12 vols., 1986.
Science Early Learners series (*Heat, Moving, Push, Senses, Sound, Water, Wheels*).   Fitzroy, Victoria, Five Mile Press, and London, Blackie, 7 vols., 1985–86.
Busy Day Board Books (*Playing, Sleeping, Waking*).   Fitzroy, Victoria, Five Mile Press, 3 vols., 1988.

Editor, *A First Australian Poetry Book*. Melbourne, Oxford University Press, 1983.

*

Illustrator: *Jenny's Baby Brother* by Peter Smith, 1981; *Sing Together*, 1982; *Time to Sing!*, 1982; *Second Ever Book of Things to Make and Do* by Roland Harvey, 1983; *Microwave Cooking for Kids,* 1984, and *The Second Microwave Cooking for Kids,* 1985, both by Judith Ryles; *How Does Your Garden Grow?* by Kevin Heinze, 1985; *More Free Stuff for Kids,* 1985; *Ford Family Car Fun Book* edited by Anne Bower Ingram and Peggy O'Donnell, 1986; *Camping: Let's Do It Together,* and *Making a Picture Book,* both by Anne

Bower Ingram, 1987.

*   *   *

Bob Graham's picture books always feature young children, their toys, and pets in family situations. His stories are most often about something very important to the major child character. In *Pete and Roland* a brief but warm relationship grows between a little blue budgerigar and a young boy. The restrictions of flat dwelling compared to what Graham obviously considers a "proper home" are contrasted in *Pearl's Place*. *The Red Woollen Blanket* traces the life and times of a much loved security blanket and in *The Wild* a child sees his pets choose between domesticity and the lure of the bush surrounding his home. In *Crusher Is Coming!* a young boy worries that his home life may show him up as not as tough as he would like to appear to the school football star, and *Has Anyone Seen William?* depicts the extraordinary curiosity of a newly mobile toddler. A continuing theme is the affection children have for animals. With a skill reminiscent of other highly regarded author-illustrators such as Shirley Hughes and John Burningham, Graham presents childhood concerns with dignity and humour. His portrayal of very young children has been particularly successful, and no doubt part of his popularity and success is due to the pleasure both child readers and their parents find in Graham's depiction of familiar home situations.

In the author's best books the economical text and cartoon-like illustrations appear spontaneous and uncontrived. The illustrations are ink with colour wash, and Graham uses a variety of quarter-, half-, full-, and double-page illustrations, constantly altering perspective to enlarge on the text. In *Pearl's Place* the block of flats where Arthur lives unhappily with his mother leans threateningly over diminutive figures while at Pearl's house Arthur and Jessica can easily climb on the roof. Similarly in *The Wild*, human figures fill the foreground in domestic scenes but outside towering eucalypts make them seem vulnerable. *Crusher Is Coming!* is the best example to date of the ironic relationship Graham sets up between his somewhat understated text and his illustrations. Peter has invited local tough boy Crusher to tea. Desperate to appear tough himself he hides away his teddies and plans "boyish" activities, but Crusher is beguiled by Peter's toddler sister Claire and enjoys a tea party with her and a family of stuffed toys. The dialogue gives us Peter's perception of Crusher, contradicting the illustrations (for example, of a large red-haired boy feeding a toy duck from a teacup), and providing a multi-layered text usually associated with more obviously sophisticated writing. This technique has been used with considerable success by Graham in a number of illustrated readers. One of the best is *Here Comes Theo*, where a deliberate echo of old school readers—"Here comes Theo. Look at him go—" is undercut, both by less conventional text—"Down she goes, and gets the licking treatment"—and by the funny illustrations of a manic dog knocking over his child friends with his overenthusiastic greetings. The effect is affectionate and humorous, the distinctive features of Graham's books.

—Kerry White

————

GRAHAM, Eleanor. British. Born in Walthamstow, Essex, 9 January 1896. Educated at Chingford High School, Essex, 1902–09; North London Collegiate School for Girls, 1910–14; London School of Medicine, 1914–16. Worked at Bumpus' children's book room, London, 1926–30; children's book editor, William Heinemann, Ltd., publishers, London, 1930–33, and Methuen Ltd., publishers, London, 1933–36; librarian, private children's lending library, 1936–37; children's book editor and founder of the Puffin series, Penguin Books Ltd., London, 1939–61. Children's book reviewer, *Sunday Times* and the *Bookman*, both London, 1930's. Recipient: Children's Book Circle Eleanor Farjeon award, 1973. *Died 8 March 1984.*

PUBLICATIONS FOR CHILDREN

Fiction

The Night Adventures of Alexis, illustrated by Winifred Langlands. London, Faber, 1925.
Six in a Family, illustrated by Alfred Sindall. London, Nelson, 1935.
The Children Who Lived in a Barn, illustrated by J.T. Evans. London, Routledge, 1938; revised edition, London, Penguin, 1955.
Head o' Mey, illustrated by Arnold Bond. London, Benn, 1947.

Other

High Days and Holidays: Stories, Legends and Customs of Red-Letter Days and Holidays, illustrated by Priscilla M. Ellingford. London, Benn, 1932; as *Happy Holidays: Stories, Legends and Customs of Red-Letter Days and Holidays*, New York, Dutton, 1933.
Change for Sixpence. London, University of London Press, 1937.
When the Fun Begins. London, University of London Press, 1937.
Adventure in Natal: A Book for Boys of Early Hunting Adventures in Natal, with George Gordon Campbell. London, Pitman, 1938.
The Making of a Queen: Victoria at Kensington Palace. London, Cape, 1940.
The Story of "The Wind in the Willows": How It Came to Be Written. London, Methuen, 1950.
True Dog Stories, with Lillian Gask. London, Harrap, 1950.
The Story of Charles Dickens, illustrated by Norman Meredith. London, Methuen, 1952; New York, Abelard Schuman, 1954.
The Story of Jesus, illustrated by Brian Wildsmith. London, Penguin, 1959.
J.M. Barrie's Peter Pan: The Story of the Play, illustrated by Edward Ardizzone. Leicester, Brockhampton Press, and New York, Scribner, 1962.

Editor, *Welcome Christmas! Legends, Carols, Stories, Riddles*, illustrated by Priscilla M. Ellingford. London, Benn, 1931; New York, Dutton, 1932.
Editor, *Tents in Mongolia: A Youth Edition*, by Henning Haslund-Christensen. London, Kegan Paul, 1935.
Editor, *More Travels and Adventures in Mongolia: A Youth Edition of "Men and Gods in Mongolia,"* by Henning Haslund-Christensen. London, Kegan Paul, 1936.
Editor, *Selected Stories and Verses*, by Walter de la Mare. London, Penguin, 1952.
Editor, *A Puffin Book of Verse*, illustrated by Claudia Freedman. London, Penguin, 1953.
Editor, *A Puffin Quartet of Poets*, illustrated by Diana Bloomfield. London, Penguin, 1958.
Editor, *Eleanor Farjeon's Book: Stories, Verses, Plays*, illustrated by Edward Ardizzone. London, Penguin, 1960.
Editor, *Poems*, by Walter de le Mare, illustrated by Margery Gill. London, Penguin, 1962.
Editor, *Secret Laughter* (anthology). London, Penguin, 1964.
Editor, *A Thread of Gold: An Anthology of Poetry*, illustrated by Margery Gill. London, Bodley Head, 1964; Freeport, New York, Books for Libraries Press, 1969.
Editor, *The Music of the Feast: Poems for Young Readers*, by Robert Herrick, illustrated by Lynton Lamb. London, Bodley Head,

1969.

PUBLICATIONS FOR ADULTS

Other

Kenneth Grahame. London, Bodley Head, and New York, Walck, 1963.

*   *   *

Eleanor Graham's most notable contribution to children's fiction is *The Children Who Lived in a Barn.* It merits serious consideration, as the plot offers a complete contrast to the highly successful holiday adventure plot initiated by Arthur Ransome and imitated by M.E. Atkinson, Aubrey de Selincourt, M. Pardoe, and many other writers. Graham accepts the convention of disposing of parents by means of an air crash, but this does not ensure a carefree, parentless existence. Instead, it highlights the stark realities which face a group of children left temporarily without parents. It does not prove possible to dispense with adults, and an incredibly large number of adults, pleasant and unpleasant, interfere helpfully and unhelpfully with the children's affairs. In the best tradition of Arthur Ransome, Graham extols the virtues of self-reliance. She perhaps differs from him in her relentless emphasis on the unromanticized mechanics of everyday life. It is inevitable that some of these details are now obsolete, e.g., the wash day procedure. Perhaps the greatest weakness of the plot is the return of the parents, but these are minor criticisms of an original story.

Unlike numerous forgotten writers of the period whose characterization was so nominal as to be nonexistent, Graham succeeds with the Dunnett children in creating five individual and consistent personalities. She gives convincing details of their relationships with each other, of their quarrels, and of the problems which arise in the absence of parents. She also succeeds in giving a valid account of family solidarity in a time of crisis. The strains imposed on the eldest girl, Susan, who is only 13 years old, are particularly well handled.

By the post-World War II period a family in a similar situation would normally be caught in the safety net of the social services, although John Rowe Townsend offered an alternative in *Gumble's Yard* (1961). The young reader of today might feel that the family situation of *The Children Who Lived in a Barn* has little resemblance to any situation known to him, but he might also admire the Dunnetts' success in coming to terms with a crisis, and he might even envy them a degree of freedom unlikely today. This book was a deliberate antidote to the often far-fetched holiday adventure stories of the 1930's, and Graham might be said to have had a definite didactic purpose in writing it. It is easy to understand that with her wide experience in the field of children's publishing, she must have felt deep concern over the proliferation of second-rate material for children, particularly in the 1920's. Her serious endeavours in the fields of publishing and editing led to an improvement in the quality of children's books in the 1930's, and ensures her a lasting place in the history of children's literature.

—Anne W. Ellis

———

GRAHAM, Harry (Jocelyn Clive). Also wrote as Coldstreamer; Col. D. Streamer. British. Born in London, 23 December 1874. Educated at Eton College; Royal Military College, Sandhurst, Surrey. Joined the Coldstream Guards, 1895: Aide-de-Camp to the Earl

of Minto, Governor-General of Canada, 1898; served in South Africa, 1901–02; rejoined Coldstream Guards, 1914: Captain. Married Dorothy Fraser in 1910; one daughter, Journalist. Trustee, British Museum. *Died 30 October 1936.*

PUBLICATIONS FOR CHILDREN

Fiction

Happy Families: A Story for the Young of All Ages. London, Cape, 1934.

Verse

Ruthless Rhymes for Heartless Homes (as Col. D. Streamer), illustrated by G.H. London, Arnold, 1899; New York, Russell, 1901.
A Song-Garden for Children: A Collection of Children's Songs (adaptations of French and German songs), with Rosa Newmarch, music by Norman O'Neill. London, Arnold, and New York, Longman, 1906.
More Ruthless Rhymes for Heartless Homes, illustrated by Ridgewell. London, Arnold, and New York, Putnam, 1930.
When Grandmamma Fell Off the Boat: The Best of Harry Graham. London, Methuen, 1986.

PUBLICATIONS FOR ADULTS

Novels

Lord Bellinger. London, Arnold, and New York, Duffield, 1911.
Biffin and His Circle. London, Mills and Boon, 1919.
The Last of the Biffins. London, Methuen, 1925.
The Biffin Papers. London, Lane, 1933.
The Private Life of Gregory Gorm. London, Davies, 1936.

Plays

Little Miss Nobody. London, Hopwood and Crew, 1901.
The "Mind the Gates" Girl, with others (produced London, 1912).
The Cinema Star. London, Chappell, 1914.
State Secrets (produced London, 1914). London, French, 1924.
Tina, with Paul A. Rubens (produced London, 1915).
Sybil, music by Victor Jacobi, adaptation of a play by Max Brody and Ferenc Martos (produced Baltimore and New York, 1916; Manchester, 1920; London, 1921). London, Chappell, 1915.
The Maid of the Mountains (lyrics only, with others), book by Frederick Lonsdale, music by Harold Fraser-Simson (produced Manchester, 1916; London, 1917; New York, 1918).
A Southern Maid, with D.C. Calthorp, music by Harold Fraser-Simson (produced Manchester, 1917; London, 1920). London, Ascherberg, 1920.
A Little Dutch Girl, with Seymour Hicks, music by E. Kalman (produced London, 1920). London, Chappell, 1920.
The Lady of the Rose (lyrics only), book by Frederick Lonsdale, music by Jean Gilbert, adaptation of a work by Rudolf Schanzer and Ernest Welisch (produced Manchester, 1921; London, 1922). London, Ascherberg Hopwood, 1922; as *The Lady in Ermine* (produced New York, 1922).
Our Nell (lyrics only), book by Louis N. Parker and Reginald Arkell, music by Harold Fraser-Simson and Ivor Novello (produced New York, 1922; London, 1924).
Whirled into Happiness, music by Robert Stolz, adaptation of a work by Robert Bodanzky and Bruno Hardt-Warden (produced Lon-

don, 1922).

Toni, with Douglas Furber, music by Hugo Hirsch (produced Hanley, Staffordshire, 1923; London, 1924).

Madame Pompadour, with Frederick Lonsdale, music by Leo Fall, adaptation of an Austrian play (produced London, 1923).   London, Ascherberg Hopwood and Crew, 1924.

Head over Heels (lyrics only, with Adrian Ross), book by Seymour Hicks, music by Harold Fraser-Simson (produced London, 1923).

The Buried Cable; or, Dirty Work at the Cross-Roads (produced London, 1924).   London, French, 1924.

Orange Blossom, adaptation of a French play (produced London, 1924).

Katja the Dancer, with Frederick Lonsdale, music by Jean Gilbert, lyrics by Graham, adaptation of a work by L. Jacobsohn and R. Osterreicher (produced Bradford, 1924; London, 1925; as *Katya,* produced New York, 1926).

The Grand Duchess, adaptation of a play by Alfred Savoir (produced London, 1925).

Clo-Clo, with Douglas Furber, music by Franz Lehár (produced Liverpool and London, 1925).

Betty in Mayfair (lyrics only), book by J. Hastings Turner, music by Harold Fraser-Simson, adaptation of the book *The Lilies of the Field* by Turner (produced London, 1925).   London, French, 1929.

Cleopatra (lyrics only), book by J. Hastings Turner, music by Oscar Straus (produced London, 1925).

Sky High, with Harold Atteridge, music by Robert Stolz and others (produced New York, 1925).

Riquette (lyrics only), book by Gertrude E. Jennings, music by Oscar Straus, adaptation of a play by Rudolf Schanzer and Ernest Welisch (produced Detroit and Glasgow, 1925).

Merely Molly (lyrics only), book by J. Hastings Turner, music by Herman Finck and Joseph Meyer (produced London, 1926).

The Blue Mazurka (lyrics only), book by Monckton Hoffe, music by Franz Lehár, adaptation of a play by Leo Stein and Bella Jenbach (produced London, 1927).

By Candle Light, adaptation of a play by Siegfried Geyer (produced Southsea, Hampshire, and London, 1928).   London, French, 1930.

Lady Mary (lyrics only), book by Frederick Lonsdale and J. Hastings Turner, music by Albert Sirmay (produced London, 1928).

Our Peg (lyrics only), book by Edward Knoblock, adaptation of the play *Masks and Faces* by Tom Taylor and Charles Reade.   London, French, 1929.

Hunter's Moon, adaptation of a play by Sophus Michaelis (produced London, 1929).

There's No Fool Like an Old Fool (produced London, 1929).

The Good Companions (lyrics only, with Frank Eyton), book by J.B. Priestley and Edward Knoblock, music by Richard Addinsell, adaptation of the novel by Priestley (produced London and New York, 1931).   London and New York, French, 1935.

White Horse Inn, music by Ralph Benatzky and Robert Stolz, adaptation of a play by Blumenthal and Kadelburg (produced London, 1931; New York, 1936).

The Land of Smiles, music by Franz Lehár, adaptation of a play by Ludwig Herzer and Fritz Lohner (produced London, 1931; as *Yours Is My Heart,* produced New York, 1946).

Lady-in-Waiting, adaptation of a play by Ottilio Orbok and Jacques Natanson (produced London, 1931).

Viktoria and Her Hussar, music by Paul Abraham, adaptation of a work by Alfred Grunwald and Fritz Lohner (produced London, 1931).   London, Fox, 1945.

Casanova, music by Johann Strauss, adaptation of a play by Hans Muller (produced London, 1932).

Doctor's Orders, adaptation of a play by Louis Verneuil (produced London, 1933).

Roulette, adaptation of a play by Laszlo Fodor (produced London, 1935).

Rise and Shine, with Desmond Carter, music by Robert Stolz, adaptation of a work by Arnold and Gilbert (produced London, 1936).

Verse

Ballads of the Boer War (as Coldstreamer).   London, Richards, 1902.

Fiscal Ballads.   London, Arnold, 1905.

More Misrepresentative Men.   New York, Fox Duffield, 1905.

Verse and Worse.   London, Arnold, 1905.

Misrepresentative Women and Other Verses.   London, Arnold, and New York, Duffield, 1906.

Familiar Faces.   London, Arnold, and New York, Duffield, 1907.

Deportmental Ditties and Other Verses.   London, Mills and Boon, and New York, Duffield, 1909.

Canned Classics and Other Verses.   London, Mills and Boon, 1911.

The Motley Muse: Rhymes for the Times.   London, Arnold, and New York, Longman, 1913.

Rhymes for Riper Years.   London, Mills and Boon, 1916.

The World We Laugh In: More Deportmental Ditties.   London, Methuen, 1924.

Strained Relations.   London, Methuen, 1926.

The World's Workers.   London, Methuen, 1928.

Adam's Apples.   London, Methuen, 1930.

The King's Horses (and the King's Men) (song), with Noel Gay.   New York, Feist, 1930.

Verse as Col. D. Streamer

Baby's Baedeker: An International Guide-Book.   New York, Russell, 1902.

Perverted Proverbs.   New York, Russell, 1903.

Misrepresentative Men.   New York, Fox Duffield, 1904; London, Gay and Bird, 1905; augmented edition, London, Gay and Hancock, 1910.

Other

A Group of Scottish Women.   London, Methuen, and New York, Duffield, 1908.

The Bolster Book: A Book for the Bedside.   London, Mills and Boon, and New York, Duffield, 1910.

The Mother of Parliaments.   London, Methuen, 1910; Boston, Little Brown, 1911.

The Perfect Gentleman: A Guide to Social Aspirants.   London, Arnold, and New York, Duffield, 1912.

Splendid Failures.   London, Arnold, and New York, Longman, 1913.

The Complete Sportsman.   London, Arnold, 1914.

(Selections).   London, Methuen, 1934.

*   *   *

For nearly 40 years Captain Harry Graham was an indefatigable composer of miscellaneous light verse, but the only products of his skilful pen that remain current are his *Ruthless Rhymes.* The rhymed preface to the first (1899) volume suggested that these were addressed "To children of maturer years/(From seventeen to ninety-nine)"; and urged "fond parents" to keep the volume far from the reach of children "of tender age (from two to eight)." Perhaps this advice should not be taken too seriously; but it does seem that the rhymes were meant originally for the adult sense of humour, and were only later appropriated by the young, presumably for the sake of their cheerful sadism. Typically a "ruthless rhyme" describes with relish some domestic calamity, preferably a violent death, and rounds off the account with some nonchalantly inadequate reflection.

> When Grandmamma fell off the boat
> And couldn't swim (and wouldn't float)
> Matilda just stood by and smiled.
> I almost could have slapped the child.

The victim may equally well be a juvenile as an adult, however, as in "Tender-heartedness":

> Billy, in one of his nice new sashes,
> Fell in the fire and was burnt to ashes.
> Now, although the room grows chilly,
> I haven't the heart to poke poor Billy.

In *More Ruthless Rhymes* the catastrophes are even more enterprisingly varied, and the rhyming is as deft and the phrasing as neatly witty as ever. W.H. Auden and John Garrett in *The Poet's Tongue* (1935) seem to have been the first to introduce Harry Graham into a poetry anthology intended for the young, but since then their example has been followed by a number of other editors. It would seem that, even in the bloodthirsty world of today, the engaging subtlety of Graham's wit maintains its appeal, even in competition with his cruder imitators.

Graham's prose fiction includes one volume, *Happy Families,* which he described as "A Story for the Young of All Ages." In this, three impeccably upper-class children, Alice and Martin and Timothy, in the guise of their detective agency, "Almartim's Limited," pursue in the park a suspicious character who turns out to be a duke and an old friend of their explorer-father. Taken off for the summer to the duke's delightful country estate they meet adventures which are genuinely dangerous as well as funny, and which lead to the capture of two burglars and a villainous "fence." The story appeals on two levels—to children as straightforward and amusing adventure, and to adults by its more sophisticated touches of characterisation and wit. It must be admitted that it has dated a good deal, however, partly at least because of its excessively elevated social setting in what one reviewer called "the governessed classes."

—Frank Whitehead

GRAHAM, Lorenz (Bell). American. Born in New Orleans, Louisiana, 27 January 1902. Educated at the University of Washington, Seattle, 1921; University of California, Los Angeles, 1923–24; Virginia Union University, Richmond, 1934–36, B.A. 1936; Columbia University, New York; New York University. Married Ruth Morris in 1929; four children. Teacher, Monrovia College, Liberia, 1924–29, and Richmond Adult Schools, Virginia, 1930–33; educational adviser, Civilian Conservation Corps, Virginia and Pennsylvania, 1936–42; housing manager, Newport News Housing Authority, Virginia, 1942–46; real estate salesman and building contractor, Long Island, New York, 1946–49; social worker, Queens Federation of Churches, New York, 1948–56; probation officer, Los Angeles County, California, 1957–67; Lecturer, California State University, Pomona, 1970–78. Recipient: Child Study Committee award, 1959; Martin Luther King award, 1975. Address: 1400 Niagara Avenue, Claremont, California 91711, U.S.A.

PUBLICATIONS FOR CHILDREN

Fiction

Tales of Momolu, illustrated by Letterio Calapai. New York, Reynal, 1946.
South Town. Chicago, Follett, 1958.
North Town. New York, Crowell, 1965.
I, Momolu, illustrated by John Biggers. New York, Crowell, 1966.
Whose Town? New York, Crowell, 1969.
Carolina Cracker. Boston, Houghton Mifflin, 1972.
Detention Center. Boston, Houghton Mifflin, 1972.
Stolen Car. Boston, Houghton Mifflin, 1972.
Runaway. Boston, Houghton Mifflin, 1972.
Song of the Boat, illustrated by Leo and Diane Dillon. New York, Crowell, 1975.
Return to South Town. New York, Crowell, 1976.

Other

How God Fix Jonah, illustrated by Letterio Calapai. New York, Reynal, 1946.
The Story of Jesus, illustrated by William Walsh. New York, Gilberton, 1955.
The Ten Commandments, illustrated by Norman Nodel. New York, Gilberton, 1956.
John Brown's Raid: A Picture History. New York, Scholastic, 1972.
Directions 3–4, with John Durham and Elsa Graser. Boston, Houghton Mifflin, 2 vols., 1972.
John Brown: A Cry for Freedom. New York, Crowell, 1980.

*

Manuscript Collection: Kerlan Collection, University of Minnesota, Minneapolis.

Lorenz Graham comments:

I started wanting to write while I was teaching in Africa. Then and there it became startlingly clear to me that there were no honest books about Africans for young readers. Later I realized that almost no decent books about black Americans were available. I am a black. My writings about Africans and Americans try to depict the characters as real people. While I write primarily for young readers I receive many interesting comments from adults. I believe my books have promoted understanding.

* * *

Lorenz Graham writes Bible stories and fiction distinguished by their contextual realism, which furthers his goal of promoting human understanding, especially interracial understanding.

Following his service in Liberia as a missionary, Graham published 21 Bible stories written in pidgin English in *How God Fix Jonah.* Since he heard these stories "sung" in Liberia, Graham wrote them as poems so they could be read aloud in their original rhythms. In an introduction he discusses the characteristics of Liberian English and the context in which the stories were told. This volume with its striking wood engravings by Letterio Calapai has long been out of print. In the 1970's five of the Bible stories from this collection were issued in new editions as picture books for younger children: *David He No Fear, Every Man Heart Lay Down, God Wash the World and Start Again, Hongry Catch the Foolish Boy,* and *A Road Down in the Sea.* Although there is a brief introduction to each book, the Liberian context of the stories and the nature of Liberian speech patterns and idioms is not explained as clearly as in *How God Fix*

Jonah.

Graham's two novels about Momolu also are based on his experiences in Liberia. They tell about the commonplace activities of an adolescent boy and his family in the Liberian hinterland, keeping an even balance between ethnographic description and action. These novels are unusual among stories written by Americans at the time in assuming a Liberian perspective throughout.

Graham's fiction is marked by its strong social message and its realistic description of social problems that result from lack of understanding between rural and urban people in Liberia and blacks and whites in the United States. His four novels, *South Town, North Town, Whose Town?* and *Return to South Town* provide a social history of interracial relations in the United States in the 1950's and 1960's. The novels focus on David Williams and his family as they live in South Town after World War II, move to North Town where they encounter new forms of prejudice and racism, and finally David's return to South Town to practice medicine and serve the black community. These novels depict in great detail how racism and prejudice in different times and places affect the lives of "Negroes." Prejudice is shown in all its dimensions: white against black, black against white, black against black, and white against white. However, there are always a few individuals who are exceptions to group prejudices and interact freely across real and imagined racial barriers. The stories are frankly realistic in depicting a wide range of interracial problems, but the hero is almost always able to solve the problems that he confronts, which reflects Graham's underlying belief in the ultimate solution of failures in human understanding.

All of Graham's fiction, his Bible stories, and his recent biography of John Brown are written to educate young readers. The importance of enduring human values is paramount in all of his writing.

—Nancy J. Schmidt

GRAHAME, Kenneth. British. Born in Edinburgh, 8 March 1859. Educated at St. Edward's School, Oxford, 1868–75. Married Elspeth Thomson in 1899; one son. Worked for Grahame Currie and Spens, parliamentary agent's office, London, 1875–79. From 1879 gentleman-clerk, and secretary, 1898–1907, Bank of England, London. Secretary of the New Shakespere Society, London, 1877–91. *Died 6 July 1932.*

PUBLICATIONS FOR CHILDREN

Fiction

The Golden Age.   London, Lane, and Chicago, Stone and Kimball, 1895.
Dream Days.   London and New York, Lane, 1898; revised edition, 1899.
The Wind in the Willows, illustrated by Graham Robertson.   London, Methuen, and New York, Scribner, 1908.
First Whisper of "The Wind in the Willows," edited by Elspeth Grahame.   London, Methuen, 1944; Philadelphia, Lippincott, 1945.

Other

My Dearest Mouse: "The Wind in the Willows" Letters.   London, Pavilion, 1988.

Editor, *Lullaby-Land: Songs of Childhood,* by Eugene Field, il-

lustrated by John Lawrence.   New York, Scribner, 1897; London, Lane, 1898.
Editor, *The Cambridge Book of Poetry for Children.*   London, Cambridge University Press, 2 vols., and New York, Putnam, 1916.

PUBLICATIONS FOR ADULTS

Short Stories

The Headswoman.   London and New York, Lane, 1898.

Other

Pagan Papers.   London, Elkin Mathews and Lane, 1893; Chicago, Stone and Kimball, 1894.
Fun o' the Fair.   London, Dent, 1929.
The Kenneth Grahame Day Book, edited by Margery Coleman.   London, Methuen, 1937.
Paths to the River Bank: The Origins of "The Wind in the Willows", edited by Peter Haining.   London, Souvenir Press, 1983.

*

Critical Studies: *Kenneth Grahame: Life, Letters, and Unpublished Work* by Patrick R. Chalmers, London, Methuen, 1933; *Kenneth Grahame 1859–1932: A Study of His Life, Work, and Times,* London, Murray, 1959, as *Kenneth Grahame: A Biography,* Cleveland, World, 1959, abridged as *Beyond the Wild Wood: The World of Kenneth Grahame,* Exeter, Devon, Webb and Bower, 1982, and New York, Facts on File, 1983, by Peter Green; *Kenneth Grahame* by Eleanor Graham, London, Bodley Head, and New York, Walck, 1963.

*   *   *

It was *The Golden Age,* presently followed by *Dream Days,* that "made" Kenneth Grahame's name. Indeed, so great was the success of these books, both in Britain and America, that *The Wind in the Willows* at first disappointed readers. Several publishers (including those who held the earlier books) had in fact turned down the manuscript. Publishing history is full of these wry mischances. Yet all three books have more in common than may at first appear. All have a seminal place in later fiction. And all derive so much from the accidents of their author's life that some relevant facts should first be set out here.

Grahame's childhood was one of uprooting and loss. He was born in Edinburgh in 1859, the third of four children; in his first few years the family lived in the Western Highlands, near Loch Fyne. This pleasant time was ended by the mother's death when Kenneth was five. The children were despatched to their maternal grandmother at Cookham Dene in Berkshire—a loved place that relives in Grahame's books—but three years later they were moved again. Meanwhile the advocate father, destroyed by the loss of his wife, resigned his post (as Sheriff-Substitute of Argyllshire), drifted to France, and died, an alcoholic, at Le Havre. The fates of the four young Grahames (presently three, for the oldest, Willie, died at 16) lay with unimaginative southern relatives; they inflicted their worst blow on Kenneth by refusing to let him go on to Oxford, though his record at school should have made this a natural step. Such luxuries were thought unsuitable, and a place was found for him in the Bank of England. He had a conformist streak, and rose in time to one of the Bank's three top positions. But the sense of deprivation remained. His other half-life, of intense dream-fantasy, was to channel itself, by various chances, into the books we know.

Grahame's first printed writings were lightweight period essays, ephemeral stuff, though fashionable at the time. But William Ernest Henley, editor of the *National Observer,* noticed one that was different: "The Olympians"; he urged Grahame to write more in this kind. Grahame did; and *The Golden Age* and *Dream Days* were the result. They are, in simplest terms, made up of events in the daily lives of five orphaned children, living in a country house with unloved relatives. Allies are mostly found among the servants, or the odd bachelor solitaries—an artist, maybe a doctor. But the adult and child worlds are distinct. The children live, with marvellous vividness, in the imagination, acting out each book they read, entering, as it were, each picture. (See "Its Walls Were As of Jasper.") One may note that when Edward the oldest goes away to school, the narrator stays behind, still in childhood. In life, Kenneth went off too. Wild Wood? Wide World? Not for Rat; not for Grahame, either.

Grahame was not by temperament an original, yet here he was an original indeed. Nobody yet had so fully pursued this sharp child's view of child and adult, seen with a child's exactness, set down with an adult's skill. The books would affect not only children's fiction (notably the Nesbit-style family story), but the whole child-cult for adults in the new century. Not widely read today, they yet will always be a brilliant find for perceptive readers.

The Wind in the Willows (whose influence can be seen in animal fantasies from Uttley to Adams), began as a series of episodes told to Grahame's 4-year-old son Alistair. Without this waiting listener the book as we know it would probably never have been written. The animal cast, which at first so much perplexed Grahame's adult readers, came naturally enough in a nursery narrative. Are they not creatures of fable and fairy tale? What else, after all? The child-theme of *The Golden Age* and *Dream Days* was, for Grahame, played out; all five children at the end of the tale were already moving towards the Olympian world. Yet animal comrades, neither old nor young, free both from childhood's rules and adult burdens (like undergraduates) exactly fitted the need. As it happens, Grahame had already given thought (expressed in his Introduction to Aesop and elsewhere) to the unjust human roles imposed on animals in didactic fables. Even so, like most major works of children's fiction, *The Wind in the Willows* is not so much a book for the young as a book for Grahame himself about himself, for the streak of childhood that stayed in him undissolved: an autobiography of the mind. Some episodes can be seen as wholly personal: "Wayfarers All," in which Rat is held by friends from the lure of bohemian wanderings, and is offered the consolation of turning the whole affair into poetry, is notably of this kind.

But the first reviews suggest the general perplexity. "For ourselves," the *Times* critic wrote, "we lay *The Wind in the Willows* reverently aside, and again, for the hundredth time, take up *The Golden Age.*" "Grown-up readers," this writer adds, "will find it monstrous and elusive." For *Punch* it was "a sort of irresponsible holiday story in which the chief characters are woodland animals, who are represented as enjoying most of the advantages of civilisation." Arnold Bennett took a bolder view. "The author may call his chief characters the Rat, the Mole, the Toad—they are human beings, and are meant to be nothing but human beings....The book is an urbane exercise in irony at the expense of the English human character and mankind. It is entirely successful."

Yet Grahame was not by intent an adult ironist. As narrative, the book is truly in key with a young child's mind, not least in the merging of outward fact with the inward fact of fantasy. Motor and train exist with mediaeval dungeon. The very size of the creatures varies easily with the scene. "The Toad was train-size; the train was Toad-size"—thus Grahame answered a query on this point. As a result, no pictures, even Shepard's, even Rackham's, are wholly satisfactory, though both are fine on the scenery. It might be worth pointing out that much that is characteristic in *The Wind in the Willows* is foreshadowed in the two earlier books—the camaraderie,

the food and feasts, the secret haunts, the obsession with ships (or boats) and water, the long days of summer, the pantheism, the woods under winter snow—and the literary ambiences. But in those earlier books the Wide World is always near. In *The Wind in the Willows* the carefree days are held. It is a book which (in Peter Green's apt comment) stops the clock. Its potent English pastoral dream—reflected too in so much Georgian poetry—remains unchanged. The earliest readers in 1908 and thereafter must have thought this permanence true of Edwardian life itself. History was soon to give the book a further asset—nostalgia, and nostalgia is one of the few commodities that do not decline with time.

And so, *The Wind in the Willows* has been for most of the century a prime best-seller and an unmistakeable landmark in child-literature. Few educated people grow up without meeting its characters, its phrases ("messing about in boats," for instance), its evocative woods and waters. Children mainly prefer the preposterous deeds of Toad (a character almost certainly evolved for the small-boy Alistair); adults more often remember Rat and Mole, in the early chapters especially. A newcomer may quite reasonably wonder what keeps the book in living currency. The style is far from simple; it abounds with absorbed quotations, parody, and pastiche. Its values are not only "middle-class" but almost feudal. Not a girl or woman can be seen except when about some needed chore. But the central fusion of fact and fantasy still drives through these feelings.

—Naomi Lewis

GRAMATKY, Hardie. American. Born in Dallas, Texas, 12 April 1907. Educated at Stanford University, California, 1926–28; Chouinard Art School, Los Angeles, 1928–30. Served as training film supervisor in the United States Air Force, 1942–45. Married Dorothea Cooke in 1932; one daughter. Head animator, Walt Disney Productions, Hollywood, 1930–36; artist and reporter, *Fortune* magazine, New York, 1937–39, and other magazines. Commissioned Air Force war artist, Vietnam, 1966. Secretary of the American Watercolor Society, 1946–48. Recipient: American Watercolor Society High Winds Medal, 1979. *Died 29 April 1979.*

PUBLICATIONS FOR CHILDREN (illustrated by the author)

Fiction

Little Toot. New York, Putnam, 1939; London, Dent, 1946.
Hercules: The Story of an Old-Fashioned Fire Engine. New York, Putnam, 1940; Kingswood, Surrey, World's Work, 1960.
Loopy. New York, Putnam, 1941; London, Dent, 1947.
Creeper's Jeep. New York, Putnam, 1948; Kingswood, Surrey, World's Work, 1960.
Sparky: The Story of a Little Trolley Car. New York, Putnam, 1952; Kingswood, Surrey, World's Work, 1959.
Homer and the Circus Train. New York, Putnam, 1957; Kingswood, Surrey, World's Work, 1960.
Bolivar. New York, Putnam, 1961; Kingswood, Surrey, World's Work, 1962.
Nikos and the Sea God. New York, Putnam, 1963; Kingswood, Surrey, World's Work, 1964.
Little Toot on the Thames. New York, Putnam, 1964; Kingswood, Surrey, World's Work, 1965.
Little Toot on the Grand Canal. New York, Putnam, 1968; Kingswood, Surrey, World's Work, 1969.
Happy's Christmas. New York, Putnam, 1970; Kingswood, Surrey,

World's Work, 1971.
Little Toot on the Mississippi. New York, Putnam, 1973;
Kingswood, Surrey, World's Work, 1974.
Little Toot Through the Golden Gate. New York, Putnam, 1975;
Kingswood, Surrey, World's Work, 1977.

*

Manuscript Collections: University of Oregon Library, Eugene; Kerlan Collection, University of Minnesota, Minneapolis; de Grummond Collection, University of Southern Mississippi, Hattiesburg.

Illustrator: *The Treasure Hunter* by Isabel Boyd Proudfit, 1939; *Skwee-Gee* by Darwin and Hildegarde Teilhat, 1940.

Hardie Gramatky commented:

(1978) I like to feel that my work is designed to reach out to children of the younger age group (ages 5 to 8) as a challenge to their potential imaginations. Through an exciting visual approach (paintings that I do in full color) I relate picture to story in a way that makes children love and enjoy the power of words.

Research for my books is actually done right on the spot, as it were. The background of the story is authentic, which every child seems to appreciate. Through picture and story the reader travels to far-off worlds that he may never have an opportunity to see.

This is a creative venture—working with young minds. From the amount of mail I receive I feel certain the experiment has worked.

* * *

Mention *Sparky: The Story of a Little Trolley Car* to anyone, child or adult, and you'll probably get a puzzled look. Say *Little Toot* and the response will be, in all likelihood, a smile and an instant nod of recognition. The trolley car is demonstrably first cousin to the famous tugboat in character and plot. But Hardie Gramatky, author-illustrator of both books and of several others, grew rich and famous with the story of the perky tug while his other works are comparatively unknown. *Little Toot* is now years old, and, along with its sequels, is as much in demand as ever.

Gramatky's style is attractive; his stories are carefully constructed, simply written but never condescending. He builds on locales familiar to him, on characters children can empathize with. A prime example is *Nikos and the Sea God,* about a modern Greek boy who becomes involved with the formidable Poseidon. The text is enlivened by Gramatky's use of Greek words, readily understood in context. The author also created *Homer and the Circus Train, Creeper's Jeep,* and other satisfying entertainments.

His popularity and assurance of lasting renown, however, rest on the cornerstone of his career, *Little Toot,* and its successors. What makes some books classics and others, which seem equally appealing, also-rans, is a question which all authors (and publishers) would love to have the answer to. Most critics and readers agree that the doughty tugboat grabs and keeps its large audience, generation after generation, because of Toot's innate qualities. Always faced with overwhelming odds, sneered at because of his lack of size and strength, Little Toot is nevertheless the soul of pluck, comparable to the fellow who loses battles but wins the war. Boys and girls who are also small exult in his victories. Children respond to a well-told, suspenseful story which keeps them turning the pages to find out what happens next. But, most of all, they like the assurance they get from discovering that, like their hero, they count too—little though they be. A fringe benefit of the Little Toot books (which parents and educators value) is that they give readers information about life in various parts of America, England, and Italy. Still, the magnet of the stories is Gramatky's skillful adaptation of a theme at least as old as

that familiar since Biblical time, the triumph of David over Goliath.

—Jean F. Mercier

———

GRAY, Elizabeth Janet. See **VINING, Elizabeth Gray.**

———

GRAY, Nicholas Stuart. British. Born in Scotland, 23 October 1922. Educated privately. Actor and stage director. Recipient: Scottish Arts Council award, 1979. *Died 17 March 1981.*

PUBLICATIONS FOR CHILDREN

Fiction

Over the Hills to Fabylon, illustrated by the author. London, Oxford University Press, 1954; New York, Hawthorn, 1970.
Down in the Cellar, illustrated by Edward Ardizzone. London, Dobson, 1961.
The Seventh Swan: An Adventure Story, illustrated by Joan Jefferson Farjeon. London, Dobson, 1962.
The Stone Cage, illustrated by the author. London, Dobson, 1963.
Grimbold's Other World, illustrated by Charles Keeping. London, Faber, 1963; New York, Meredith Press, 1968.
The Apple-Stone, illustrated by William Stobbs. London, Dobson, 1965; New York, Meredith Press, 1969.
Mainly in Moonlight, illustrated by Charles Keeping. London, Faber, 1965; New York, Meredith Press, 1967.
The Boys, illustrated by Robin Adler. London, Dobson, 1968.
The Further Adventures of Puss in Boats, illustrated by W.M. Hatch. London, Faber, 1971.
The Edge of Evening, illustrated by Charles Stewart. London, Faber, 1976.
The Wardens of the Weir, illustrated by Carolyn Dinan. London, Dobson, 1978.
A Wind from Nowhere. London, Faber, 1978.
The Garland of Filigree, illustrated by W.M. Hatch. London, Dobson, 1979.

Plays

The Haunted (produced London, 1948).
Beauty and the Beast, illustrated by Joan Jefferson Farjeon (produced London, 1950). London, Oxford University Press, 1951.
The Tinder-Box, adaptation of a story by Hans Christian Andersen, illustrated by Joan Jefferson Farjeon. London, Oxford University Press, 1951.
The Princess and the Swineherd, illustrated by Joan Jefferson Farjeon (produced London, 1952). London, Oxford University Press, 1952.
Rapunzel (puppet play; produced London, 1953).
The Hunters and the Henwife, illustrated by Joan Jefferson Farjeon. London, Oxford University Press, 1954.
The Marvellous Story of Puss in Boots, music by Ronnie Hill, illustrated by Joan Jefferson Farjeon (also director: produced London, 1954). London, Oxford University Press, 1955.
The Imperial Nightingale, adaptation of a story by Hans Christian

Andersen, illustrated by Joan Jefferson Farjeon (also director: produced London, 1956). London, Oxford University Press, 1957.

New Clothes for the Emperor, adaptation of a story by Hans Christian Andersen, illustrated by Joan Jefferson Farjeon (produced London, 1957). London, Oxford University Press, 1957.

The Other Cinderella, with Due Acknowledgements to All the Earlier Versions, illustrated by Joan Jefferson Farjeon (produced London, 1982). London, Oxford University Press, 1958.

The Seventh Swan, illustrated by Joan Jefferson Farjeon. London, Dobson, 1962.

The Wrong Side of the Moon, based on the story by the Grimm brothers and his own story *The Stone Cage* (produced Edinburgh, 1966; London, 1968).

Lights Up (produced London, 1967).

New Lamps for Old, illustrated by Joan Jefferson Farjeon (also director: produced Guildford, Surrey, 1968). London, Dobson, 1968.

Gawain and the Green Knight, illustrated by Victor Ambrus. London, Dobson, 1969.

PUBLICATIONS FOR ADULTS

Novel

Killer's Cookbook. London, Dobson, 1976.

*

Illustrator: *James and Macarthur* by Jenny Laird, 1951.

Theatrical Activities:
Director: **Plays**—*Beauty and the Beast,* London, 1953; *The Marvellous Story of Puss in Boots,* London, 1954; *The Imperial Nightingale,* London, 1956; *New Clothes for the Emperor,* London, 1963; *The Wrong Side of the Moon,* tour, 1967; *New Lamps for Old,* Guildford, Surrey, 1968; *The Shepherd's Play,* Gloucestershire, 1975.
Actor: **Plays**—Francis in *The Haunted,* London, 1948; understudied The Beast in *Beauty and the Beast,* London, 1951; Prince Etienne in *The Princess and the Swineherd,* London, 1952; Puss in *The Marvellous Story of Puss in Boots,* London and tours; Second Suspicious Character, London, 1956, and later Four Winds in *The Imperial Nightingale;* Piers in *New Clothes for the Emperor,* London, 1957; Tomlyn in *The Wrong Side of the Moon,* Edinburgh, 1966, London, 1968; Slave of the Lamp in *New Lamps for Old,* Guildford, Surrey, 1968; Iago in *Othello* by Shakespeare, Malvern, Worcestershire, 1969.

*   *   *

Nicholas Stuart Gray's writing sprang first from his work in the theatre. His plays, ostensibly for children, often a development of familiar fairy tales, have the range and subtlety to attract an adult audience as well. Beneath the sparkle and the gaiety there are profounder themes—the beauty and the kindness and the terror of Death in *The Imperial Nightingale,* the inward shadows of self-distrust and the loneliness of being different in *Gawain and the Green Knight.* However familiar the story, the events are always unexpected. This is the kind of material, sensitive and intelligent, that children most need.

Some of the stories appear both as plays and novels. One of the most satisfying is *The Stone Cage,* the story of Rapunzel told by Tomlyn, the witch's cat and half-unwilling, half-fascinated familiar.

A daring, impudent, and devious cat, with a wry sense of humour, he believes himself to hate everyone and trust no one. His fellow-familiar, Marshall, the ancient raven, is terrified of magic. Between them they save Rapunzel, but are punished by exile to the terrible far side of the moon. Yet when Mother Gotel is caught by her own black magic, Marshall and Tomlyn elect to stay with her in her desolation until she has learned to grow a human heart again. Under Tomlyn's racy, throw-away, ironic account of things runs always the current of deeper feeling, the tragedy and triumphs of human experience. Through the witch herself, vicious, treacherous, and cruel as she is, we become increasingly aware of pity for self-inflicted misery as much as for the griefs of those who love.

The novels with original plots, such as *Down in the Cellar, The Apple-Stone,* and *The Garland of Filigree* (with its tiny, engaging, and quite irresponsible dragon), give scope for the author's hilarious inventiveness, but are never merely funny. They are peopled by redoubtable but completely credible children, whose encounters with magic are interwoven with their normal lives, and who slowly learn the heavy responsibilities of its power. Their adventures—exciting, absurd, sad, or horrific—always enlarge their understanding and sympathy.

The books of short stories, *Mainly in Moonlight, The Edge of Evening,* and *A Wind from Nowhere,* exhibit the full range and versatility of Gray's writing. They have the wildly unpredictable humour, the sudden darknesses and shadows, the poise between the worlds of night and day, of magic and reality, that show their author's Highland origin. Their demons and hippogriffs, knights and mermaids, sad little witches and perplexed humans are funny, touching, and fascinating. So are the animals—dogs, cats, horses, goats—beautifully drawn by a writer who loves and respects them. Some of the stories haunt the heart for a long time afterwards—the tragedy of stupidity and misunderstanding in "The Star Beast" and its curiously inverted reflection in "The Blot on the Landscape" (both "space" stories of a very unusual kind), the nostalgic sadness of "The Golden Beasts" or "The Stranger." Beneath them all is his deep caring for people and the haunting sense that we dwell in a lost paradise.

The last story of *A Wind from Nowhere,* "Once Upon a Time There Was a Chance," is on this theme, and is developed into the most unusual of all his novels, *The Wardens of the Weir.* The Avatar of the short story, by whose error our world went awry, is given his second chance, with the help of a small group of children, an old carthorse, a dog, and two cats, to redeem his mistake, to save the lost things of this earth and give them a new beginning. Here too ordinary life with its comedy and heartbreak still goes on, but the "magic" is powerful and moving. It leaves the reader convinced, as the author is, of the infinite value of all living creatures.

Laughter, magic, courage, and caring are the stuff of all Gray's work. His book have the rare gift of enlarging the spirit.

—Margaret Greaves

_____

GREAVES, Margaret. British. Born in Birmingham, Warwickshire, 13 June 1914. Educated at Alice Ottley School, Worcester, 1927–33; St. Hugh's College, Oxford (scholar), 1933–38, B.A. (honours) in English 1936, B. Litt. 1938, M.A. 1944. Served in the British Women's Land Army, 1941–43. English teacher, High School, Lincoln, 1938–40, Priory School, Shrewsbury, 1940–41, and Pate's Grammar School, Cheltenham, 1943–46; Lecturer, 1946–60, and Principal Lecturer and Head of the English Department, 1960–70, St. Mary's College, Cheltenham. Address: 8 Greenways, Winchcombe, Cheltenham, Gloucestershire GL54 5LG, England.

PUBLICATIONS FOR CHILDREN

Fiction

Gallimaufry series (*The Snowman of Biddle, The Rainbow Sun, King Solomon and the Hoopoes, The Great Bell of Peking*), illustrated by Jill McDonald. London, Methuen, 4 vols., 1971; Glendale, California, Bowmar, 4 vols., 1975.
The Dagger and the Bird, illustrated by Jill McDonald. London, Methuen, 1971; New York, Harper, 1975.
The Grandmother Stone. London, Methuen, 1972; as *Stone of Terror*, London, Target, and New York, Harper, 1974.
Little Jacko and the Wolf People, illustrated by Jill McDonald. London, Methuen, 1973.
The Gryphon Quest. London, Methuen, 1974.
Curfew. London, Methuen, 1975.
The Night of the Goat, illustrated by Trevor Ridley. London, Abelard Schuman, 1976.
Nothing Ever Happens on Sundays, illustrated by Gareth Floyd. London, BBC Publications, 1976.
The Abbotsbury Ring, illustrated by Laszlo Acs. London, Methuen, 1979.
A Net to Catch the Wind, illustrated by Stephen Gammell. New York, Harper, 1979.
Cat's Magic, illustrated by Joanna Carey. London, Methuen, 1980; New York, Harper, 1981.
Charlie, Emma, and Alberic, illustrated by Eileen Browne. London, Methuen, 1980.
The Snake Whistle, illustrated by Gareth Floyd. London, BBC Publications, 1980.
Charlie, Emma, and the Dragon Family, illustrated by Eileen Browne. London, Methuen, 1982.
Charlie, Emma, and the School Dragon, illustrated by Eileen Browne. London, Methuen, 1984.
The Monster of Roundwater, illustrated by Michael Bragg. London, Methuen, 1984.
Little Bear and the Papagini Circus, illustrated by Francesca Crespi. London, Methuen, and New York, Dial Press, 1986.
Charlie, Emma, and Dragons to the Rescue, illustrated by Eileen Browne. London, Methuen, 1986.
Hetty Pegler, Half-Witch, illustrated by Derek Crowe. London, Methuen, 1987.
Charlie, Emma, and the Juggling Dragon. London, Methuen, 1989.

Play

Television Play: *A Star for My Son*, 1980.

Verse

Nicky's Knitting Granny and the Cat, illustrated by Alice Englander. London, Methuen, 1985.
The Mice of Nibbling Village, illustrated by Jane Pinkney. London, Malin, and New York, Dutton, 1986.

Other

English for Juniors series (*Your Turn Next, One World and Another, Gallery, Two at Number Twenty, What Am I?*), illustrated by Jill McDonald. London, Methuen, 5 vols., 1966–72; as *Gallery Wonders*, Glendale, California, Bowmar, 1975.
A Little Box of Witches (retellings; *The Witch Cat, Kate Crackernuts, The Witch's Servant, Mother Cuspen*), illustrated by Francesca Crespi. London, Methuen, and New York, Dial Press, 4 vols., 1985.

Fairy Tale series (retellings; *The Princess and the Pea, Lucky Hans, The Musicians of Bremen, Red Riding Hood*), illustrated by Annegart Fuchschuber, Michèle Lemieux, Renate Mörtl-Rangnick, and Eva Scherbarth. London, Methuen, 4 vols., 1985.
Once There Were No Pandas: A Chinese Legend, illustrated by Beverley Gooding. London, Methuen, and New York, Dutton, 1985.
A Little Box of Ballet Stories (retellings; *Petrushka, Firebird, Coppelia*), illustrated by Francesca Crespi. London, Methuen, and New York, Dial Press, 3 vols., 1986.
Goldilocks and the Three Bears (retelling), illustrated by Maria Claret. London, Methuen, 1987.
The Magic Flute: The Story of Mozart's Opera, illustrated by Francesca Crespi. London, Methuen, and New York, Greenwillow, 1989.

Editor, *Scrap-Box: Poems for Grown-Ups to Share with Children*, illustrated by Jill McDonald. London, Methuen, 1969.

PUBLICATIONS FOR ADULTS

Other

The Blazon of Honour: A Study in Renaissance Magnanimity. London, Methuen, and New York, Barnes and Noble, 1964.
Regency Patron: Sir George Beaumont. London, Methuen, 1966.

*

Margaret Greaves comments:

I have never outgrown the children's books that I loved. As I have grown older I have only added to the range and depth of my imaginative reading. So, when I write for children, I write also for myself. Because I have lived nearly always in the country I think I have a particular caring for natural things, a feeling for the past, and a predisposition towards folklore and magic. But above all I care about people; and whether my stories are those of "real life" or "fantasy" (what is the distinction?—they are only different ways of presenting such glimmers of truth as one is privileged to see), the core of my interest is in human relationships.

* * *

In *Little Jacko and the Wolf People* Margaret Greaves presents a "western." There are dangers and courage, friendship and cooperation, ritual, magic, and celebration, wolves and desperadoes—an exciting package in a story told with swift economy and but a few hundred words for the very young.

At the other end of the age range, in *Curfew*, she explores a profound philosophical problem. Set in the early 19th century, the story concerns a boy on the run from justice whose gullibility has led him into a state where false witness can be upheld against him. His struggles to survive involve him in petty thefts and deceit, and eventually lead him to become entangled with smuggling and murder. As the boy-hero searches for honest values in a world both perfidious and generous he finds that law and justice are not in themselves sufficient guides to conduct. Only in probing a deeper moral understanding, he learns, will resolution be found for the dilemmas he must face. The adolescent reader who is used to having his stories neatly tied up at the end with evil overcome and triumphant virtue rewarded will find this novel's refusal to offer cut and dried answers salutary and stimulating.

If Greaves has the courage to leave her heroes (and readers!) in uncertainty and nagging doubt it is because, enriched in self-knowledge, they emerge from adventures equipped to face a more complex world. Neither the heroes and heroines of *The Dagger and the Bird* nor of *The Grandmother Stone* are assured of living happily ever after. In the former their long-lost brother has yet to adjust to the family, to fit into the warmth and harsh reality of life at the smithy after the insubstantial and wishfulfilling faerie world. Like his brother and sister before him, he will have to learn to choose wisely between truth and show.

Greaves conjures up a world of faerie magic in *The Dagger and the Bird,* as also in *The Gryphon Quest,* through a richness of language drawing concrete images, a world both tangibly present and shiftingly insubstantial, whereas the magic of books as various as the lighthearted Charlie and Emma stories, *The Monster of Roundwater,* and the romping *Cat's Magic,* on the one hand, and the more profound *The Snake Whistle* and *The Abbotsbury Ring,* on the other, manifests itself in commonplace and thoroughly modern settings. Indeed in Abbotsbury it seems that magic is after all nothing special, it can be stumbled on: it is love that must be earned and freely offered, as Magnus finds in *The Snake Whistle* where he has to struggle to reject the corrupting facility of undeserved magical powers. In *The Grandmother Stone,* a novel likely to attract an older readership, the power of magic and its association with credulity and popular superstition are measured against courage and independence of mind. Greaves handles the themes of witchcraft, iconolatry, and bigotry in a story set in Sark about the time of the civil wars. Her heroes survive in displaying a clear-sighted faith in the worth of people. They emerge, not to blaring trumpets and popular acclaim, but to a sense of personal maturity. Still isolated, they are, if sadder, wiser in self-knowledge and with fewer illusions about others. A remarkable feature of this novel too is its handling of dawning sexuality. Awakening physical awareness is evoked with sensitivity and totally without prurience.

Few children's writers can have commanded the range, assurance, and depth of Margaret Greaves.

—Myles McDowell

GREEN, Roger (Gilbert) Lancelyn. British. Born in Norwich, Norfolk, 2 November 1918. Educated at Dane Court, Pyrford, Surrey; Liverpool College; Merton College, Oxford, 1937–42, B.A. 1940, B.Litt. and M.A. 1944. Married June Burdett in 1948; two sons and one daughter. Actor, Oxford and London, 1942–45; antiquarian bookseller, Oxford, 1943; deputy librarian, Merton College, Oxford, 1945–50; William Noble Research Fellow in English, 1950–52, and member of Council, 1964–70, University of Liverpool. Editor, *Kipling Journal,* London, 1957–79. Andrew Lang Lecturer, St. Andrews University, Scotland, 1968. Recipient: Mythopoeic Society award, 1975; Scout Association Chief Scout's Medal, 1976; Mystery Writers of America Edgar Allan Poe award, for non-fiction, 1984. D.Litt.: University of Liverpool, 1981. *Died 8 October 1987.*

PUBLICATIONS FOR CHILDREN

Fiction

The Wonderful Stranger: A Holiday Romance, illustrated by John Baynes. London, Methuen, 1950.
The Luck of the Lynns, illustrated by Sheila Macgregor. London, Methuen, 1952.
The Secret of Rusticoker, illustrated by Sheila Macgregor. London, Methuen, 1953.

The Theft of the Golden Cat, illustrated by Edward McGrath. London, Methuen, 1955.
Mystery at Mycenae: An Adventure Story of Ancient Greece, illustrated by Margery Gill. London, Bodley Head, 1957; New York, A.S. Barnes, 1959.
The Land Beyond the North, illustrated by Douglas Hall. London, Bodley Head, 1958; New York, Walck, 1959.
The Land of the Lord High Tiger, illustrated by John S. Goodall. London, Bell, 1958.
The Luck of Troy, illustrated by Margery Gill. London, Bodley Head, 1961.

Other

The Sleeping Beauty and Other Tales, illustrated by Rene Cloke. Leicester, Ward, 1947.
Beauty and the Beast, and Other Tales, illustrated by Rene Cloke. Leicester, Ward, 1948.
The Story of Lewis Carroll. London, Methuen, 1949; New York, H. Schuman, 1950.
King Arthur and His Knights of the Round Table, illustrated by Lotte Reiniger. London, Penguin, 1953.
The Adventures of Robin Hood, illustrated by Arthur Hall. London, Penguin, 1956.
Old Greek Fairy Tales, illustrated by Ernest H. Shepard. London, Bell, 1958; New York, Roy, 1969.
Tales of the Greek Heroes, illustrated by Betty Middleton-Sandford. London, Penguin, 1958.
The Tale of Troy: Retold from the Ancient Authors, illustrated by Betty Middleton-Sandford. London, Penguin, 1958.
Heroes of Greece and Troy (includes *Tales of the Greek Heroes* and *The Tale of Troy*), illustrated by Heather Copley and Christopher Chamberlain. London, Bodley Head, 1960; New York, Walck, 1961; revised edition, Bodley Head, 1973.
The Saga of Asgard: Retold from the Old Norse Poems and Tales, illustrated by Brian Wildsmith. London, Penguin, 1960; as *Myths of the Norsemen,* London, Bodley Head, 1962.
The True Book about Ancient Greece, illustrated by N.G. Wilson. London, Muller, 1960.
Ancient Greece, illustrated by Carol Barker. London, Weidenfeld and Nicolson, 1962; New York, Day, 1969.
Once, Long Ago: Folk and Fairy Tales of the World, illustrated by Vojtěch Kubašta. London, Golden Pleasure Books, 1962; as *Once upon a Time: Folk and Fairy Tales of the World,* New York, Golden Press, 1962; as *My Book of Favourite Fairy Tales,* London, Hamlyn, 1969.
Authors and Places: A Literary Pilgrimage, illustrated by John Bowers. London, Batsford, 1963; New York, Putnam, 1964.
Ancient Egypt, illustrated by Elizabeth Hammond. London, Weidenfeld and Nicolson, 1963; New York, Day, 1964.
Tales of the Greeks and Trojans, illustrated by Janet and Anne Grahame-Johnstone. London, Purnell, 1964.
Tales from Shakespeare (*The Comedies* and *Tragedies and Romances*), illustrated by Richard Beer. London, Gollancz, 2 vols., 1964–65; New York, Atheneum, 1965.
Tales the Muses Told: Ancient Greek Myths, illustrated by Shirley Hughes. London, Bodley Head, and New York, Walck, 1965.
A Book of Myths, illustrated by Joan Kiddell-Monroe. London, Dent, and New York, Dutton, 1965.
Myths from Many Lands, illustrated by Janet and Anne Grahame-Johnstone. London, Purnell, 1965.
Folk Tales of the World, illustrated by Janet and Anne Grahame-Johnstone. London, Purnell, and Boston, Ginn, 1966.
Sir Lancelot of the Lake, illustrated by Janet and Anne Grahame-Johnstone. London, Purnell, 1966.
Stories of Ancient Greece, illustrated by Doreen Roberts. London,

Hamlyn, 1967.

Tales of Ancient Egypt, illustrated by Heather Copley.   London, Bodley Head, 1967; New York, Walck, 1968.

Jason and the Golden Fleece, illustrated by Janet and Anne Grahame-Johnstone.   London, Purnell, 1968.

The Tale of Ancient Israel, illustrated by Charles Keeping.   London, Dent, and New York, Dutton, 1969.

The Tale of Thebes, illustrated by Jael Jordan.   London and New York, Cambridge University Press, 1977.

Editor, *Modern Fairy Stories,* illustrated by Ernest H. Shepard. London, Dent, and New York, Dutton, 1955.

Editor, *The Book of Nonsense,* illustrated by Charles Folkard.   London, Dent, and New York, Dutton, 1956.

Editor, *Fairy Stories,* by Mary Louisa Molesworth.   London, Harvill Press, 1957.

Editor, *Tales of Make-Believe,* illustrated by Harry Toothill.   London, Dent, and New York, Dutton, 1960.

Editor, *The Book of Verse for Children,* illustrated by Mary Shillabeer.   London, Dent, 1962.

Editor, *Ten Tales of Detection.*   London, Dent, and New York, Dutton, 1967.

Editor, *Stories and Poems,* by Rudyard Kipling.   London, Dent, 1970.

Editor, *Thirteen Uncanny Tales,* illustrated by Ray Ogden.   London, Dent, and New York, Dutton, 1970.

Editor, *The Hamish Hamilton Book of Dragons,* illustrated by Krystyna Turska.   London, Hamish Hamilton, 1970; as *A Cavalcade of Dragons,* New York, Walck, 1970.

Editor, *Alice's Adventures in Wonderland, and Through the Looking-Glass and What Alice Found There,* by Lewis Carroll, illustrated by John Tenniel.   London and New York, Oxford University Press, 1971.

Editor, *Tales of Terror and Fantasy: Ten Stories from "Tales of Mystery and Imagination,"* by Edgar Allan Poe, illustrated by Arthur Rackham.   London, Dent, 1971.

Editor, *Ten Tales of Adventure,* illustrated by Philip Gough.   London, Dent, 1972.

Editor, *The Hamish Hamilton Book of Magicians,* illustrated by Victor Ambrus.   London, Hamish Hamilton, 1973; as *A Cavalcade of Magicians,* New York, Walck, 1973; as *A Book of Magicians,* London, Penguin, 1977.

Editor, *Strange Adventures in Time,* illustrated by George Adamson. London, Dent, and New York, Dutton, 1974.

Editor, *The Hamish Hamilton Book of Other Worlds,* illustrated by Victor Ambrus.   London, Hamish Hamilton, 1976; as *The Beaver Book of Other Worlds,* London, Beaver, 1978.

PUBLICATIONS FOR ADULTS

Novel

From the World's End: A Fantasy.   Leicester, Ward, 1948; New York, Ballantine, 1971.

Verse

The Lost July and Other Poems.   London, Fortune Press, 1945.
The Singing Rose and Other Poems.   Leicester, Ward, 1947.

Other

Tellers of Tales.   Leicester, Ward, 1946; revised edition, 1953; revised edition, London, Ward, and New York, Watts, 1965;

revised edition, London, Kaye and Ward, 1969.

Andrew Lang: A Critical Biography with a Short Title Bibliography. Leicester, Ward, 1946.

Poulton-Lancelyn: The Story of an Ancestral Home.   Oxford, Oxonian Press, 1948.

A.E.W. Mason: The Adventures of a Story Teller.   London, Parrish, 1952.

Fifty Years of Peter Pan.   London, Davies, 1954.

Into Other Worlds: Space-Flight in Fiction from Lucian to Lewis. London, Abelard Schuman, 1957; New York, Arno Press, 1975.

Lewis Carroll.   London, Bodley Head, 1960; New York, Walck, 1962.

J.M. Barrie.   London, Bodley Head, 1960; New York, Walck, 1961.

Mrs. Molesworth.   London, Bodley Head, 1961; New York, Walck, 1964.

Andrew Lang.   London, Bodley Head, and New York, Walck, 1962.

The Lewis Carroll Handbook, Being a New Version of a Handbook of the Literature of the Rev. C.L. Dodgson.   London, Oxford University Press, 1962; revised edition, London, Dawson, and New York, Barnes and Noble, 1970.

C.S. Lewis.   London, Bodley Head, and New York, Walck, 1963; revised edition, in *Three Bodley Head Monographs,* Bodley Head, 1969.

Kipling and the Children.   London, Elek, 1965.

C.S. Lewis: A Biography, with Walter Hooper.   London, Collins, and New York, Harcourt Brace, 1974.

"Holmes, This Is Amazing": Essays in Unorthodox Research. Privately printed, 1975.

Editor, *The Diaries of Lewis Carroll.*   London, Cassell, 2 vols., 1953; New York, Oxford University Press, 1954.

Editor, *A Century of Humorous Verse 1850–1950.*   London, Dent, and New York, Dutton, 1959.

Editor, *The Readers' Guide to Rudyard Kipling's Work.*   Canterbury, Gibbs, 1961.

Editor, *Plays and Stories,* by J.M. Barrie.   London, Dent, and New York, Dutton, 1962.

Editor, *The Works of Lewis Carroll,* illustrated by John Tenniel. London, Hamlyn, 1965.

Editor, *Kipling: The Critical Heritage.*   London, Routledge, and New York, Barnes and Noble, 1971.

Editor, with Morton Cohen, *The Letters of Lewis Carroll.*   London, Macmillan, 2 vols., 1979.

Editor, *The Selected Letters of Lewis Carroll.*   New York, Pantheon, 1982.

Translator, *The Searching Satyrs,* by Sophocles.   Leicester, Ward, 1946.

Translator, *Two Satyr Plays: Euripides' Cyclops and Sophocles' Ichneutai.*   London, Penguin, 1957.

*

Theatrical Activities:
Actor: **Play**—Pirate Noodler in *Peter Pan* by J.M. Barrie, London and tour, 1942–43.

Roger Lancelyn Green commented:
(1978) My intention with my first four works of fiction was to write exciting adventure stories set against a background of the way of life on a country estate in the 1920's and 1930's—a way of life that had almost passed away even as I wrote. But the setting was too "out of date" and not yet sufficiently "period" to satisfy the critics. None of the four reached a second edition—and two more (the set) remain unpublished.

Meanwhile, however, I had begun retelling myths, legends, and fairy tales—with great success. And I set myself to give young readers as many of the great stories of the ancient world as I could—mainly of ancient Greece but also Egypt, the Middle East, Scandinavia, and our own national legends. That many of these have been reprinted almost annually show that I have at least made good a "felt want" now that Latin and Greek are so little taught.

Deep study of Greek legends and my great love for Greece and its literature led me to attempt to use Greek legends as the basis of fictional narratives—"historical romances" in which the history was that of the world of Homer: *Mystery at Mycenae,* a detective story with Odysseus as the detective; *The Land Beyond the North,* an adventure story of the Argonauts' return from Calchis with the Golden Fleece; and, the most successful, *The Luck of Troy,* a spy story told from the point of view of a Greek boy in Troy during the siege and fall.

The Land of the Lord High Tiger was a departure in the direction of the Carroll-Nesbit tradition written round my old "stuffed animals" and the stories I told them as a child. This is my own favourite (*The Luck of Troy* is my best)—but again the sequel remains unpublished.

*   *   *

Although Roger Lancelyn Green's main contribution to children's literature is his distinguished work as a compiler, editor, and reteller of tales, there are in his impressively long list of titles some eight books, all, with the exception of *The Luck of Troy* (1961), published in the 1950's (and all except the last out of print), that are works of fiction in a stricter sense. It is a pity that Green should have neglected this form of writing for so long, for in the three "classical" novels for older readers, *Mystery at Mycenae, The Land Beyond the North,* and *The Luck of Troy,* there is evidence of a developing skill in creating intelligent and imaginative novels.

The Land of the Lord High Tiger, a whimsical tale for younger children, is a hotchpotch fantasy which Roger and Priscilla enter through a picture of a tiger on the bedroom wall. They become a prince and princess, encountering more or less predictable pieces of pantomime machinery such as three wishes, lost slippers, giants, wizards, a robber captain memorably named Habbakuk Hak, magic carpets (eaten by Tiger Moths!), and last-minute rescues. Odd oaths ("Screwtape and Slogarithma") and tortured puns ("only school-girls and tidal-waves can serge on them") have a period charm, while the villains are too funny to be frightening.

Green is much more at home in ancient Greece where his inventive flair combines well with his deep knowledge and love of classical myth, legend, and literature. *Mystery at Mycenae,* the story of Helen of Troy's earlier abduction as a young girl, told in the style of a detective novel, is perhaps marred by excessive schoolmasterly explanation and lines of dialogue such as "It's all a beastly muddle," and "I hawk at higher game, ha-ha," while half way through the gaff is blown on the mystery. But the blend of classical authenticity with imaginative speculation is vindicated in the sequel, *The Luck of Troy,* which is, as it were, the inside story of the last year of the great siege as experienced by the 12-year-old Nicostratus, Helen's son by Menelaus, who had been taken as a baby to Troy by Paris along with his mother. The complexities of the narrative are skilfully and imaginatively handled in clear, unfussy prose, while questions of loyalty, courage, and civilised conduct are explored through the boy's awakening consciousness of the conflict between his Greek origin and his Trojan upbringing. With the decline of the classics in schools, this novel, together with *The Land Beyond the North,* which is an audacious but not too implausible story linking Jason's journey to the Hyperboreans with Daedalus and the building of Stonehenge, is an imaginative as well as an effective way for a young reader to

become acquainted with classical antiquity.

—Graham Hammond

———————

GREENE, Bette (née Evensky). American. Born in Memphis, Tennessee, 28 June 1934. Educated at the University of Alabama, University, 1952; Memphis State University, 1953–54; Columbia University, New York, 1955. Married Donald Sumner Greene in 1959; one daughter and one son. Reporter, Memphis *Commercial Appeal,* 1950–52, and United Press, Memphis bureau, 1953–54; information officer, American Red Cross, Memphis, 1958–59, and Boston State Psychiatric Hospital, 1959–61. Recipient: Society of Children's Writers Golden Kite award, 1973. Agent: Alfred Lowman, Authors and Artists Group, 14 East 60th Street, New York, New York 10022. Address: 338 Clinton Road, Brookline, Massachusetts 02146, U.S.A.

PUBLICATIONS FOR CHILDREN

Fiction

Summer of My German Soldier. New York, Dial Press, 1973; London, Hamish Hamilton, 1974.
Philip Hall Likes Me. I Reckon Maybe, illustrated by Charles Lilly. New York, Dial Press, 1974; London, Hamish Hamilton, 1976.
Morning Is a Long Time Coming. New York, Dial Press, and London, Hamish Hamilton, 1978.
Get On Out of Here, Philip Hall. New York, Dial Press, 1981; London, Hamish Hamilton, 1982.
Them That Glitter and Them That Don't. New York, Knopf, 1983.
I've Already Forgotten Your Name, Philip Hall! New York, Knopf, 1983.

*

Manuscript Collection: Kerlan Collection, University of Minnesota, Minneapolis.

Bette Greene comments:

I grew up in a small town in the Arkansas Delta (the very eye of the Bible Belt) during the war bond and pin-up picture days of World War II. My friends considered me the luckiest girl in town because, while sugar was being rationed, my parents owned a country store full of gum and candy. But, on the contrary, I considered myself the unluckiest, unhappiest girl in town because my religion (Jewish) was alien to my community, my friends and especially myself. I used to sneak into the tents of itinerant Protestant preachers the way a teenager today might sneak into an X-rated movie. And as the evangelist spoke with easy familiarity of the fires of Hell, I could feel its heat. So I "caught" religion as simply as others caught colds.

And it is from these roots—of childhood sights, smells, and memories—that I write.

*   *   *

Bette Greene's *Summer of My German Soldier,* like many other first novels, has freshness of approach and an intensity of focus and feeling. A first class work, which obviously draws upon the author's own 1940's Arkansas childhood, it is a most interesting, unusual, and powerful study of a 12-year-old girl who harbours an escaped German prisoner-of-war. Its theme is her peculiar alienation from family and community on the one hand, and her desperate need to give and receive love and acceptance on the other. The irony is that Patty Bergen, who is an isolated Jew in a small and conservative WASP town, has only an enemy soldier and a black housemaid to turn to for friendship—outsiders all. The portrayal of Patty's parents is savage: her self-centered mother and bitter, brutal, tyrannical father are presented (without explanation) as life-denying villains. The young German soldier seems an unlikely combination of everything admirable, although this idealised, romantic picture is one which reflects Patty's viewpoint most appropriately.

In a sequel, *Morning Is a Long Time Coming,* Patty, now 18, escapes from her hateful parents, and stifling town. In Paris she meets and lives with a young Frenchman. The book's climax comes in an attempt to make contact with the mother of the hapless German soldier—a clumsy, pathetic venture which at least frees Patty from her obsession with his memory.

A remarkable contrast to the emotional intensity and seriousness of these books is offered by *Philip Hall Likes Me. I Reckon Maybe* and *Get On Out of Here, Philip Hall.* These are bright, sunny books consisting of episodes from the green and pleasant childhood days of 11-year-old Beth Lambert, a vivacious, happy, intelligent high-achiever. The unifying theme in each book is Beth's affection for her friend and rival, classmate Philip Hall. These are relaxed "fun" books for younger readers, and offer innocence and optimism in writing which has economy, drive and directness, with especially polished and convincing dialogue.

—Walter McVitty

GREENE, Constance C(larke). American. Born in New York City, 27 October 1924. Educated at Marymount Academy, New York, graduated 1942; Skidmore College, Saratoga Springs, New York, 1942–44. Married Philip M. Greene in 1946; two sons and three daughters. Agent: Marilyn Marlow, Curtis Brown, 10 Astor Place, New York, New York 10003. Address: 21 North Main Street, East Hampton, New York 11937, U.S.A.

PUBLICATIONS FOR CHILDREN

Fiction

A Girl Called Al, illustrated by Byron Barton. New York, Viking Press, 1969.
Leo the Lioness. New York, Viking Press, 1970.
The Good-Luck Bogie Hat. New York, Viking Press, 1971.
The Unmaking of Rabbit. New York, Viking Press, 1972.
Isabelle the Itch, illustrated by Emily McCully. New York, Viking Press, 1973.
The Ears of Louis, illustrated by Nola Langner. New York, Viking Press, 1974.
I Know You, Al, illustrated by Byron Barton. New York, Viking Press, 1975; London, Kestrel, 1977.
Beat the Turtle Drum, illustrated by Donna Diamond. New York, Viking Press, 1976.
Getting Nowhere. New York, Viking Press, 1977.
I and Sproggy, illustrated by Emily McCully. New York, Viking Press, 1978.
Your Old Pal, Al. New York, Viking Press, 1979.
Dotty's Suitcase. New York, Viking Press, 1980.
Double-Dare O'Toole. New York, Viking Press, 1981.
Al(exandra) the Great. New York, Viking Press, 1982.
Ask Anybody. New York, Viking Press, 1983.

Isabelle Shows Her Stuff. New York, Viking Kestrel, 1984.
Star Shine. New York, Viking Kestrel, 1985.
Just Plain Al. New York, Viking Kestrel, 1986.
The Love Letters of J. Timothy Owen. New York, Harper, 1986.
Monday I Love You. New York, Harper, 1988.
Isabelle and Little Orphan Frannie. New York, Viking Kestrel, 1988.

PUBLICATIONS FOR ADULTS

Novel

Other Plans. New York, St. Martin's Press, 1985.

*

Constance C. Greene comments:

If I had to categorize my books for children, I would say they were contemporary and, hopefully, funny. Maybe even a bit joyous on occasion. Children are hard-nosed, resilient, and tough little creatures. They know that life isn't a bowl of cherries but they like to laugh, perhaps even more than adults. And I hope I provide some laughter for them. *Beat the Turtle Drum,* however, is about two sisters, one of whom dies. The title is taken from a musical play by Ian Serraillier. For a long time I had wanted to write about death, as I myself had a sister who died, and it was a difficult task; but I'm glad I did what I set out to do.

*   *   *

Warmth, vitality, and wit, three distinguishing marks in Constance C. Greene's novels, are particularly evident in her characterizations. Her ability to draw believable characters, identifiable to the boy or girl next door, is Greene's strength and accounts for her high popularity with young readers. These distinctive creations successfully carry her stories, and though the plots are usually slim and episodic, they are accomplished with finesse.

With a sharply observant eye, Greene firmly roots her young protagonists in reality and rounds them out with individualized, sometimes quirky personalities who spout casual, glib, and often amusing dialogue. The result is a range of lively characters such as Ben (*The Good-Luck Bogie Hat*), who sees himself as a second Humphrey Bogart and Timothy (*The Love Letters of J. Timothy Owen*), who cribs from published love letters to woo his lady love. Two others that immediately come to mind are Al, who brightly debuted in Greene's first book (*A Girl Called Al*) and who has continued to shine through four others, and Isabelle from *Isabelle the Itch,* a feisty character who is probably most remembered for the daily fights she arranges with her friend and opponent Herbie. Supporting characters are not slighted either as evidenced by Herbie, who delights in making neck boils from wads of chewing gum and Al's long suffering but ever-supportive friend, the nameless narrator of the Al books.

Perhaps the most interesting of Greene's inventions, however, are the elderly, somewhat eccentric friends who bolster the protagonists' confidence, provide emotional refuge, and occasionally disperse tidbits of wisdom. One need only remember Mrs. Beebe (*The Ears of Louis*) who cheats at poker; Mr. Richards (*A Girl Called Al*), who polishes his kitchen floor with cloths tied to his shoes; the sympathic teacher (*Monday I Love You*) who bolsters Gracie's confidence when she is tormented about her looks, and Mrs. Stern (*Isabelle the Itch*), who continually paints her house and who, in a recent book, announces that she might marry again—completely unsettling Isabelle.

The underlying theme in Greene's work is self-adjustment. Sometimes the problem may loom large in the beholder's eye but is nevertheless just a growing-up pain, such as Al's fears of attending her father's wedding or Timothy's lovesick adoration of unreachable Sophie. Other times Greene probes at a more serious level: Gracie's embarrassment about her size 38D breasts, Frannie's inability to read, or Al's awakened consciousness to homeless people. Regardless, the resolution is brought about slowly through the character's own realization of the problem and his or her ability to cope with it. All of Isabelle's coaching to help Guy be less of a goody-goody, for example, is for naught until he tackles the job himself.

Following a number of lighter, episodic books, Greene's first foray into more heavily plotted novels came in 1976 with *Beat the Turtle Drum.* In this story she explores the adjustment of a young girl to her sister's death and in doing so shows an ability to deepen character portrayals to create a more complex novel. While still using a series of episodes to propel the action, the author moves each situation inevitably forward—toward Joss's death—with the characters, though griefstricken, able to handle the tragedy. *Dotty's Suitcase* was Greene's second attempt; here she uses a 1930's Depression setting with a sustained plotline running through the story. It is one of her best books and serves as a milestone in the author's career.

Greene's successful and well-loved characters (Isabelle and Al) continue to appear, and their awareness of social issues, such as the homeless and illiterate, bring a texture to the books that shows growth in the writer and her characters and is meaningful for readers as well.

Now in her 20th year of writing, Greene continues to grow and though she hasn't yet reached her potential, her delivery of believable characters ensures an ongoing popularity. Readers gravitate toward the strong personalities, the flow of frankness, and the strains of humor that Greene so smoothly and effectively provides.

—Barbara Elleman

GREENFIELD, Eloise (née Little). American. Born in Parmele, North Carolina, 17 May 1929. Educated at Miner Teachers College, Washington, D.C., 1946–49. Married Robert J. Greenfield in 1950; one son and one daughter. Clerk-typist, 1949–56, and supervisory patent assistant, 1956–60, U.S. Patent Office, Washington, D.C.; staff member, Unemployment Compensation Board, Washington, D.C., 1963–64; secretary, case control technician, and administrative assistant, Washington, D.C., 1964–68; director of adult fiction, 1971–73, and of children's literature, 1973–74, District of Columbia Black Writers Workshop; writer-in-residence, District of Columbia Commission on the Arts, 1973, 1985–86. Recipient: National Council for the Social Studies Woodson award, 1974; Women's International League for Peace and Freedom Jane Addams award, 1976; American Library Association Coretta Scott King award, 1978. Agent: Maria Brown Associates, 412 West 154th Street, New York, New York 10034, U.S.A.

PUBLICATIONS FOR CHILDREN

Fiction

Bubbles.   Washington, D.C., Drum and Spear Press, 1972; as *Good News,* New York, Coward McCann, 1977.
Sister, illustrated by Moneta Barnett.   New York, Crowell, 1974.
She Come Bringing Me That Little Baby Girl, illustrated by John Steptoe.   Philadelphia, Lippincott, 1974.
Me and Nessie, illustrated by Moneta Barnett.   New York, Crowell, 1975.

First Pink Light, illustrated by Moneta Barnett.   New York, Crowell, 1976.
Africa Dream, illustrated by Carole Byard.   New York, Day, 1977.
Talk about a Family, illustrated by James Calvin.   Philadelphia, Lippincott, 1978.
I Can Do It by Myself, with Lessie Jones Little, illustrated by Carole Byard.   New York, Crowell, 1978.
Grandmama's Joy, illustrated by Carole Byard.   New York, Collins, 1980.
Darlene.   New York, Methuen, 1980.
Daydreamers, illustrated by Tom Feelings.   New York, Dial Press, 1981.
Grandpa's Face, illustrated by Floyd Cooper.   New York, Philomel, 1988.
Nathaniel Talking, illustrated by Jan Spivey Gilchrist.   New York, Writers and Readers, 1988.

Verse

Honey, I Love and Other Love Poems, illustrated by Diane and Leo Dillon.   New York, Crowell, 1978.
Under the Honey Tree, illustrated by Amos Ferguson.   New York, Harper, 1988.

Recording: *Honey, I Love,* Honey Productions, 1982.

Other

Rosa Parks, illustrated by Eric Marlow.   New York, Crowell, 1973.
Paul Robeson, illustrated by George Ford.   New York, Crowell, 1975.
Mary McLeod Bethune, illustrated by Jerry Pinkney.   New York, Crowell, 1977.
Childtimes: A Three-Generation Memoir, with Lessie Jones Little, illustrated by Jerry Pinkney.   New York, Crowell, 1979.
Alesia, with Alesia Revis, illustrated by George Ford, photographs by Sandra Turner Bond.   New York, Putnam, 1981.

*   *   *

The late 1960's and early 1970's saw the introduction of many black writers to mainstream children's publishing. Eloise Greenfield was one of them, and her works, all of which portray aspects of the black American experience, collectively carry a positive message to both the black and the white youngsters who read them. Greenfield clearly states her aims in her article "Something To Shout About" (*Horn Book,* December 1975): "I want to encourage children to develop positive attitudes toward themselves and their abilities, to love themselves. I want to present to children alternative methods for coping with the negative aspects of their lives and to inspire them to seek new ways of solving problems." These desires are clearly reflected in her work, which includes picture books, several biographies of important black heroes, poetry, two short novels, and a family memoir.

A strong sense of family is apparent in all Greenfield's fiction. No matter what the story level, there is much love. In *First Pink Light,* a picture book, young Tyree wants to stay up to greet his father who will be arriving at dawn. In *Talk about a Family,* a brief novel, a girl named Genny begins to adjust to her parent's separation by coming to realize that they still love her and she surely loves them. *Childtimes,* a memoir for older children, contains narratives by Greenfield, her mother, and her grandmother, all of whom recall childhoods shaped by differing eras but nurtured by warm family relationships.

Greenfield's wish to inspire and accent the positive is easily seen throughout her work. Two recent works, *Darlene* and *Alesia,* are particularly strong examples. Both are about disabled black youngsters, one of them real, the other fictional. Both books encourage the view that the disabled are not unable. The fact that Alesia, a 17-year-old who is struggling to walk again after a severely disabling accident, is a real person will have particular meaning to handicapped minority youngsters in need of a role model.

Her wish to provide black youngsters positive role models and inform them of their past is also carried through in her simple biographies, which present the figures of Mary McLeod Bethune, Rosa Parks, and Paul Robeson. These were, in a sense, ground-breaking books, for they presented strong black men and women little written about in a format easily accessible for younger readers. They were a significant contribution toward easing the dearth of black history material available for young readers.

The artistic success of Greenfield's work varies. Her weakness is a didacticism which flaws some of her more pointedly bibliotherapeutic works such as *Bubbles,* about a boy learning to read, or *Darlene,* whose protagonist manages to have fun despite being confined to a wheelchair. Her best writing involves the warm evocation of tender childhood moods and emotions. *First Pink Light* and *She Come Bringing Me That Little Baby Girl* exemplify this in picture books. The poems of *Honey, I Love* are lyrical and emotionally appealing. For example it's impossible not to be caught up in the snapping, evocative rhythms of "Way Down in the Music": "I get way down in the music/Down inside the music/I let it wake me/take me/Spin me around and make me/Uh-get down." *Talk about a Family* and *Sister,* two brief novels, are well-knit stories that achieve their purposes, though the messages in *Sister* are sometimes too strongly stated. Greenfield's most ambitious and mature work is *Childtimes,* her three-generational memoir. Its intimacy, pride, and reverence are compelling. It's a moving story that embodies all of its author's aims in a manner that qualifies as both art and living history.

—Denise Murcko Wilms

GREENWOOD, Ted (Edward Alister Greenwood). Australian. Born in Melbourne, Victoria, 4 December 1930. Educated at Balwyn Primary School, 1936–41; Mont Albert Central School, 1942–43; Melbourne Boys' High School, 1944; Camberwell High School, 1945–47; Melbourne Teachers' College, 1949–50, teaching diploma; Royal Melbourne Institute of Technology, 1954–59, Diploma of Art 1959. Married Florence Lorraine Peart in 1954; two sons and two daughters. Primary teacher, Melbourne, 1948–56; lecturer in art education, Melbourne Teachers' College, 1956–60, and Toorak Teachers' College, Melbourne, 1960–68. Deputy chairman, Australia Arts Council Community Arts Board, 1978–83. Recipient: Australian Children's Book Council Picture Book of the Year award, 1969; Churchill fellowship, 1972; Australian Literary fellowship, 1975; Visual Art Board award, 1976. Address: 50 Hilton Road, Ferny Creek, Victoria 3786, Australia.

PUBLICATIONS FOR CHILDREN

Fiction (illustrated by the author)

Obstreperous.   Sydney and London, Angus and Robertson, 1970.
Aelfred.   Sydney, Angus and Robertson, 1970; London, Angus and Robertson, 1971.
V.I.P.: Very Important Plant.   Sydney and London, Angus and Robertson, 1971.
Joseph and Lulu and the Prindiville House Pigeons.   Sydney and London, Angus and Robertson, 1972.
Terry's Brrrmmm GT.   Sydney, Angus and Robertson, 1974; London, Angus and Robertson, 1976.
The Pochetto Coat, illustrated by Ron Brooks.   Richmond, Victoria, Hutchinson, 1978; London, Hutchinson, 1980.
A Day in the Life of Curious Eddie.   London, Angus and Robertson, 1979.
Ginnie.   London, Kestrel, 1979.
The Boy Who Saw God, illustrated by Genevieve Rees.   Richmond, Victoria, Hutchinson, 1980; London, Penguin, 1983.
Everlasting Circle.   Richmond, Victoria, Hutchinson, 1981; London, Hutchinson, 1982.
Flora's Treasures.   London, Hutchinson, 1982.
Marley and Friends.   Richmond, Victoria, Hutchinson, 1983; London, Hutchinson, 1984.
Ship Rock.   Richmond, Victoria, and London, Hutchinson, 1985.

Other

Warts and All: A Book of Body Talk, with Shane Fennessy, illustrated by Elizabeth Honey.   Richmond, Victoria, and London, Hutchinson, 1984.
I Don't Want to Know, with Shane Fennessy.   Hawthorne, Victoria, Hutchinson, 1986.

*

Illustrator: *Sly Old Wardrobe,* 1968, and *The Glass Room,* 1970, both by Ivan Southall; *Children Everywhere,* 1970.

Ted Greenwood comments:
Whether working in the picture-book or longer prose forms, I remain interested in the episodic, the cyclical, the open-ended, rather than the rounded, defined experience.

*   *   *

Ted Greenwood became a picture-book artist by accident rather than intent. He happened to be painting a portrait of the children's author Ivan Southall, who had just been asked by his publisher to supply a picture-book text. He suggested that Greenwood be invited to illustrate it. ("I don't think he knew any other artist!" Greenwood says.) The result was *Sly Old Wardrobe.* Although it was Greenwood's first attempt at book illustration, it won the 1969 Australian Picture Book of the Year award and set him off on a new career which has seen him develop from being an illustrator to becoming a serious author in his own right.

His books are, like the man himself, original and unconventional. He works from principle rather than precedent, being more concerned with philosophies and ideas than trends and formulas. His picture books don't even look like those of other illustrators. He sometimes distorts the shape of the type-matter itself, to match the sense of the text, e.g. in *Joseph and Lulu and the Prindiville House Pigeons* it is sometimes elongated to match the high-rise city buildings, and in *Terry's Brrrmmm GT* it goes "downhill" to match the descent of the fragile billy cart in the "soap-box derby." His drawings are sometimes fractured or incomplete, leading off the page in order to make the reader anticipate what might be on the following page, as in *V.I.P.: Very Important Plant.*

His previous career as a schoolteacher perhaps explains the didacticism in his work, which, even in the picture books, sets out to challenge children by presenting them with abstract ideas, sometimes obscurely portrayed, so that the reader is forced to ask questions, being cajoled into making necessary connections, into sharing with the author-illustrator the experience of "creating" the book's idea and message with every reading.

Greenwood is fascinated by the continuity of natural life, especially its cyclic nature, and has produced a number of interesting picture books exploring this idea. In *V.I.P.,* for instance, his text deliberately avoids capital letters, even at the start, suggesting that things (in this case, plants) do not suddenly *begin,* appearing from nowhere. Nor, in the case of Australian eucalypts, with their capacity for self-renewal after devastating bushfires, is there an abrupt end. There is always hope—shown here by the sprouting of a leaf bud on an apparently dead tree: life goes on in its inevitable way. Even an ancient rock, as in *Ship Rock,* is being constantly eroded, forever changing and adding life and sustenance to its environment. The cycle is most explicitly presented in *Everlasting Circle,* which presents children with the wonder of the migratory flight of the shearwater (mutton-bird) in its awesome circuit of the vast Pacific basin, repeated endlessly, year after year.

Greenwood's early novels have a poignancy about them. *The Pochetto Coat* is a sort of wistful dialogue between an aging and jaded circus clown and a little girl, while the hero of *The Boy Who Saw God,* struggling to come to terms with a spiteful stepfather and an obsession with the Bible, imagines he has been commanded by God to sacrifice a real live sheep. Like the picture books, these novels challenge the reader, with their multiple layers of meaning, some too obscure for the average child to grasp, but always with a deep, underlying humanity in exploring the need for friendship, trust, and acceptance in our lives.

Greenwood's simplest and most enjoyable books are *Ginnie* and *Marley and Friends,* which consist of episodic, child-centred stories based on the author's observations of, and responses to, the behaviour of his youngest daughter. These stories are written with warmth and humour, the natural grace of the language making them excellent for reading aloud to young children.

More recently he has combined with a doctor friend, Shane Fennessy, to produce some non-fiction books designed to give children honest, value-free information about things that concern them. For instance, *Warts and All: A Book of Body Talk,* written in straightforward and sensibly uncensored language, discusses such things as smelly feet, bed-wetting, nose-bleeding, masturbation, and even farting!

In all his work, Greenwood shows a deep concern and respect for children, and a desire to give them the best of his careful craftsmanship, as both a writer and illustrator.

—Walter McVitty

GREY OWL (Washaquonasin). Pseudonym for Archibald Stansfeld Belaney. Canadian. Born in Hastings, Kent, England, 18 September 1888; emigrated to Canada, 1906. Educated at Hastings Grammar School. Served in the Montreal Regiment, Canadian Army, 1915–17. Married 1) Angele Eguena in 1910, one daughter and one son; 2) Constance Holmes in 1918 (divorced 1921); 3) Gertrude Bernard (Anahareo) in 1927, one daughter; 4) Yvonne Perrier in 1937. Clerk, Cheale Brothers timber merchants, Hastings, 1904–05; guide, trapper, mail carrier and fire ranger, Ontario, 1907–31; warden, Riding Mountain National Park, 1931, and Prince Albert National Park, 1931–38. Adopted blood brother, Ojibwa tribe, 1920. Lecturer and filmmaker; regular contributor, *Forest and Outdoors* magazine, Montreal, 1930–38. *Died 13 April 1938.*

PUBLICATIONS FOR CHILDREN

Fiction

The Adventures of Sajo and Her Beaver People, illustrated by the author. London, Lovat Dickson, 1935; as *Sajo and the Beaver People,* New York, Scribner, 1936.

PUBLICATIONS FOR ADULTS

Other

The Men of the Last Frontier. London, Country Life, 1931; New York, Scribner, 1932.
Pilgrims of the Wild (autobiography). London, Lovat Dickson, 1934; New York, Scribner, 1935.
Grey Owl and the Beaver, with Harper Cory. London and New York, Nelson, 1935.
Tales of an Empty Cabin. London, Lovat Dickson, and New York, Dodd Mead, 1936.
A Book of Grey Owl: Pages from the Writings of Wa-sha-quonasin, edited by E.E. Reynolds. London, Davies, 1938; as *Beavers* and *On the Trail,* London, Cambridge University Press, 2 vols., 1940.
Grey Owl's Farewell to the Children of the British Isles. London, Lovat Dickson, 1938.

*

Critical Studies: *Grey Owl and I: A New Autobiography* by Anahareo, London, Davies, 1972, as *Devil in Deerskins: My Life with Grey Owl,* Toronto, New Press, 1972; *Wilderness Man: The Strange Story of Grey Owl* by Lovat Dickson, London, Macmillan, 1973; *Grey Owl's Favorite Wilderness* by Allison Mitcham, Moonbeam, Ontario, Penumbra, 1981.

Theatrical Activities:
Director: **Films**—*The Little People,* 1930; *The Beaver Family,* 1931; *The Trail; Winter; Men Against the Snow,* 1936.

*   *   *

Grey Owl's work indicates a great respect and affection for the wilderness and its inhabitants. In an era when these aspects of life were too quickly disappearing in the face of rapid development, and the antagonism between wilderness and civilization stood out in stark contrast, he provided a sensitive yet factual assessment of nature and its place in our culture. Four books form the nucleus of his work: *The Men of the Last Frontier, Pilgrims of the Wild, Tales of an Empty Cabin,* and *The Adventures of Sajo and Her Beaver People.* The first three books can be appreciated by readers of all ages, the last by children from 8 to 11 years.

Nature, wilderness, animal life and man's interaction with them: Grey Owl was a keen observer and through his writing one can see what is beautiful and harmonious as well as what is savage and predatory in nature.

Although Grey Owl would discount his emphasis on man, he has provided some vivid portraits of the men who inhabit these wilderness areas: courageous, honest, tale-telling, respecting each other for what they do, not for who they are, and keeping to a strict code of conduct in their work. Their hardships and joys, their pleasures and observations on life are best recorded in *The Men of the Last Frontier* and *Tales of an Empty Cabin.* He also portrayed men who abused the wilderness: men who killed wantonly, disregarding season and any thought of replenishing a species or leaving half-skinned carcasses strewn along a trail.

More important to Grey Owl was his concern with wildlife, especially the beaver. In *Tales of an Empty Cabin* and *Pilgrims of the Wild* he vividly depicts his life of hunting and his gradual disenchantment with the instruments of death: the steel jaw trap, the use of poison, and the rifle. This disenchantment turned into positive action when he adopted two beaver kittens whose mother had been killed in an out-of-season trap. His observations on their antics, personalities, eating habits, and interaction with man and nature are delightful. The depth of this human-animal relationship provides a poignant touch.

Grey Owl combined all of his knowledge of animals and nature in his only children's story, *The Adventures of Sajo and Her Beaver People*. This combination created a realistic adventure story guaranteed to keep a child's attention to the conclusion. It is the tale of two Indian children whose father is forced to sell one of their two beaver kittens to pay a debt to a local trader. The plot develops when the children and their pet set out to find their little friend. They endure all sorts of hardships before they are finally reunited.

All of Grey Owl's works illustrate the true nature of the animal whether beaver, deer, or wolf. He writes of their positive points as well as of the suffering and cruelty these creatures must endure from predatory animals, natural disaster, and man. His work has made and, one hopes, will continue to make people aware of wildlife and conservation. The material, written in far less sophisticated a manner than most of today's readers would demand, is still appropriate.

—Dorothy D. Siles

GRICE, Frederick. British. Born in Durham, 21 June 1910. Educated at Johnston School, Durham, 1922–28; King's College, University of London (Brewer prize), 1928–31, B.A. (honours) in English; Hatfield College, Durham University, 1931–32, teaching diploma. Served in the Royal Air Force, 1941–46: Flight Lieutenant. Married Gwendoline Simpson in 1939; two daughters. Assistant master, A.J. Dawson School, County Durham, 1934–40; Head of the English Department, Worcester College of Further Education, 1946–72. Recipient: Children's Rights Workshop Other award, 1977. *Died 8 February 1983.*

PUBLICATIONS FOR CHILDREN

Fiction

Aidan and the Strollers, illustrated by William Stobbs. London, Cape, 1960; as *Aidan and the Strolling Players,* New York, Duell, 1961.
The Bonny Pit Laddie, illustrated by Brian Wildsmith. London, Oxford University Press, 1960; as *Out of the Mines: The Story of a Pit Boy,* New York, Watts, 1961.
The Moving Finger, illustrated by Joan Kiddell-Monroe. London, Oxford University Press, 1962; as *The Secret of the Libyan Caves,* New York, Watts, 1963.
A Severnside Story, illustrated by William Papas. London, Oxford University Press, 1964.
The Luckless Apple, illustrated by Ian Ribbons. London, Oxford University Press, 1966.
The Oak and the Ash, illustrated by Trevor Ridley. London, Oxford University Press, 1968.
The Courage of Andy Robson, illustrated by Victor Ambrus. London, Oxford University Press, 1969.
The Black Hand Gang, illustrated by Doreen Roberts. London, Oxford University Press, 1971.
Young Tom Sawbones, illustrated by Ian Ribbons. London, Oxford University Press, 1972.
Nine Days' Wonder, illustrated by Paul Ritchie. London, Oxford University Press, 1976.

Johnny-Head-in-Air. London, Oxford University Press, 1978.
Water Breaks Its Neck. Oxford, Oxford University Press, 1986.

Other

Folk Tales of the North Country Drawn from Northumberland and Durham. London, Nelson, 1944.
Folk Tales of the West Midlands, illustrated by N.J.P. Turnbull. London, Nelson, 1952.
Folk Tales of Lancashire, illustrated by N.J.P. Turnbull. London, Nelson, 1953.
Rebels and Fugitives, illustrated by William Stobbs. London, Batsford, 1963; New York, Norton, 1964.
A Northumberland Missionary, illustrated by Ralph Lavers. London, Oxford University Press, 1963.
Jimmy Lane and His Boat (reader), illustrated by Eileen Green. London, Oxford University Press, 1963; New York, Watts, 1968.
The Rescue, and The Poisoned Dog (reader), illustrated by Gwyneth Cole. London, Oxford University Press, 1963; New York, Watts, 1968.
Bill Thompson's Pigeon (reader), illustrated by Maureen Warren. London, Oxford University Press, 1963; New York, Watts, 1968.
The Lifeboat Haul (reader), illustrated by John Lawrence. London, Oxford University Press, 1965.
Dildrum, King of the Cats, and Other English Folk Stories, illustrated by Julia Ball. London, Oxford University Press, 1967; New York, Watts, 1968.
Tales and Beliefs (reader), illustrated by Gunvor Edwards. London, Nelson, 1974.

PUBLICATIONS FOR ADULTS

Verse

Night Poem and Other Pieces. Tunbridge Wells, Kent, Peter Russell, 1955.
The Faithful City. Privately printed, 1960.

Other

Francis Kilvert: Priest and Diarist. Hereford, Kilvert Society, 1975.
Francis Kilvert and His World. London, Caliban, 1982.

Editor, *A Kilvert Symposium.* Hereford, Kilvert Society, 1975.

*

Manuscript Collection: de Grummond Collection, University of Southern Mississippi, Hattiesburg.

Frederick Grice commented:
(1978) I was born in the North of England, within hearing distance of the bells of Durham Cathedral. My father worked in a small colliery a few miles out of Durham. I think I had the best of three worlds—the world of the pit village with its stories of strikes, evictions, lock-outs, and accidents; the world of the beautiful mediaeval city of Durham where I went to school; and the world of the austerely beautiful countryside that encircled the colliery village.

The first book I wrote was a simple collection of North Country legends and folk tales. I was interested in them because they seemed to embody the spirit of the land and the people that were to be the main theme of my writing—*The Bonny Pit Laddie, The Oak and the Ash, The Courage of Andy Robson, Nine Days' Wonder,* etc. The variety of my interests, and in particular my interest in literature (for the greater part of my working life I have been a college tutor) has prompted me to investigate other themes such as the fortunes of strolling players in the late 18th and early 19th centuries, the lives of railway navvies, etc., but I write best and most authentically about the North, and these are the stories to which children most eagerly respond.

*   *   *

At a time when working-class children's stories were rare, *The Bonny Pit Laddie,* set in Frederick Grice's native Durham, came as a welcome phenomenon, its subject matter handled with deep feeling and skilful craftsmanship. True, it did not depict the contemporary scene. Set back more than half a century, it had the nostalgia that is apt to creep into this author's fiction. Thus, *A Severnside Story* has jukeboxes and leather-jacketed motor-cyclists to denote the 1960's, but one feels that the boy-hero, and certainly the author, would have been more at home in the Worcester of Elgar's youth. That is really the atmosphere which is so sensitively and poetically evoked. Grice stuck to the locations he knew. Even in *The Moving Finger* he is utilising his North African service in World War II, but understandably this book has less intimate, affectionate feeling, and is more of a conventionally contrived adventure story. *Johnny-Head-in-Air,* by contrast, after a Saharan prologue, goes back to the Hurricane pilot's boyhood holiday in the quiet English countryside and the origins of his obsession with flying.

Grice's strengths and weaknesses are very clearly exemplified in *Aidan and the Strollers,* a delightful tale of travelling actors of 1825. Characters and atmosphere are splendidly handled—indeed, there is a prodigality of almost Dickensian characters passing all too briefly across the everchanging scene. Plot construction and the maintenance of tension are less successful. Time lapses of several weeks are cursorily bridged in a paragraph or two, leaving the reader with unanswered questions. The author has tried to pour a heady quart into a pint-pot, yet shortage of space does not deter him from introducing long Shakespearean quotations and charming but not altogether necessary descriptions of rural sights and sounds.

If Grice excelled in male characterization, he seemed curiously uninterested in depicting the other sex. The absence of women in the Saharan adventure is understandable, but in a theatrical story one would have expected the actresses to make their presence felt. Aidan and his friend Jeremy might appear to a modern child unbelievably blind to the girls they must have met. Possibly the author, already 50 when this book appeared, was following the tradition of his own childhood reading, when there were books for boys and books for girls, as rigidly separated as school cloakrooms.

In his posthumous book, *Water Breaks Its Neck,* Grice used as setting the Radnorshire hills to which he had been increasingly drawn by the enthusiasm for Kilvert which became a dominant interest in his final years. It is a simple but eventful story, narrated by a shepherd boy in 1872, and shows no sign of any failing in his sensitivity or vigour.

Grice was a literary storyteller of style and integrity. For the "gentle" reader—the more bookish, imaginative child—his work offers great satisfaction.

—Geoffrey Trease

GRIFFITH, Helen V(irginia). American. Born in Wilmington, Delaware, 31 October 1934. Educated at Henry C. Conrad High School, Woodcrest, Delaware, graduated 1952. Since 1976 secretary/treasurer, S.G. Williams and Brothers, Wilmington. Ad-

dress: 410 Country Club Drive, Wilmington, Delaware 19803, U.S.A.

PUBLICATIONS FOR CHILDREN

Fiction

Mine Will, Said John, illustrated by Muriel Batherman. New York, Greenwillow, 1980.
Alex and the Cat, illustrated by Joseph Low. New York, Greenwillow, 1982.
Alex Remembers, illustrated by Donald Carrick. New York, Greenwillow, 1983.
More Alex and the Cat, illustrated by Donald Carrick. New York, Greenwillow, 1983.
Foxy. New York, Greenwillow, 1984; London, MacRae, 1985.
Nata, illustrated by Nancy Tafuri. New York, Greenwillow, 1985; London, MacRae, 1986.
Georgia Music, illustrated by James Stevenson. New York, Greenwillow, 1986.
Grandaddy's Place, illustrated by James Stevenson. New York, Greenwillow, 1987.
Journal of a Teenage Genius. New York, Greenwillow, 1987.
Emily and the Enchanted Frog, illustrated by Susan Condie Lamb. New York, Greenwillow, 1989.

*

Helen V. Griffith comments:
The memory of a story can last a lifetime. I try to make the memory a pleasant one.

*   *   *

Helen V. Griffith emerged on the children's book scene in a way reminiscent of her prose: quiet, poetic, and subtly powerful. She continues to attain success in a variety of forms (picture books, short chapter books, read-alone stories, and books for intermediate readers). She experiments freely with narrative techniques to complement stories illuminating the necessity of interdependent relationships. A gentle humor and ardent respect for human integrity and frailty permeate all her works. Already accomplished, Griffith promises to be an exciting and engaging writer.

Mine Will, Said John, Griffith's first picture book, recounts John's insistent search for the perfect pet. The author effectively portrays John's emotions, from slight irritation to genuine joy, with few, simple words. Readers delight as the chorus "Mine does, said John" ends each episode with a new animal and finally crescendos in John's triumphant "Mine will" as he hugs his yearned-for puppy. Griffith's story takes on added charm in the understanding parent-child relationship; John and his parents share not only a mutual love but also mutual respect.

Griffith's funny stories of Alex the dog and his unlikely feline buddy appear in four books to date. As Alex grows from a puppy, their friendship deepens, and their adventures extend beyond the safe boundaries of their young owner's backyard. The cat delivers his advice in an utterly cat-like deadpan and quietly supports and educates child-like Alex. Griffith captures these anthropomorphic characters and their amusing antics in lively dialogue constructed from limited vocabulary.

Foxy, a novel for intermediate readers, again reveals Griffith's concern with connections, be they between animals, humans, or animals and humans. Preadolescent Jeff feels uncomfortable camping for the first time with his parents in the Florida Keys. One night he mistakenly identifies a ragged, abandoned, starving dog as a fox.

When he learns his error, he also recognizes both his bond to this outcast animal and his ability to nurture it. Griffith tenderly explores Jeff's loneliness and desire to belong as she simultaneously focusses on his friend's ambivalence toward Jeff. The chapters, which alternate point of view between three primary characters, highlight unique personal struggles. Unfortunately the novel's popularity could suffer from its introspective qualities and the gentleness uncharacteristic of boys' books.

Griffith shifts into outright comedy in the hilarious fantasy *Journal of a Teenage Genius*. Zack's plight as a misunderstood scientist is engagingly related in his self-conscious first-person diary entries. The consistency of the novel's construction allows readers insight into Zack's home life, love life, career ambitions, and self-assessments. His straightforward accounting and genuineness provide laughs, even guffaws, at the expense of the unassuming young scientist.

Griffith's gift of style, melodious flair with words, and talent in telling a compelling story about characters who are also sensitive, whole human beings mesh solidly in the companion picture books about Janetta and her grandfather. Although published secondly, *Grandaddy's Place* introduces Janetta and her mother as they visit Grandaddy on his Georgia farm. The book's shining success emanates from Janetta and her grandfather's integrity of character. A city girl, Janetta needs time, patience, and the strength of will to peacefully co-exist with noisy farm animals and outdoor creatures. Grandaddy's life experience instilled in him the gentility and kindness to embrace his granddaughter with both humor and seriousness.

Enriched by James Stevenson's delicate, lush illustrations, *Georgia Music* emphasizes the vital connection between generations. Physical frailty prevents Grandaddy from maintaining his Georgia farm, and brings him reluctantly to live with his daughter and granddaughter in Baltimore. His depression deepens as the days pass. After many futile attempts, his granddaughter finally reaches and frees him by sharing the very music he taught her to love. Griffith's decision not to name the characters, ambiguously referred to as "the girl" and "grandaddy," strikes a resonant chord. This book stands as Griffith's crowning achievement. Her characters convey the complexity and interdependency of human relationships. Her elegant prose reminiscently evokes Georgia as a time and place. Her words poetically capture the quiet essence of togetherness as she conducts the communal night chorus of birds singing, insects chirping, and humans breathing.

—Cathryn M. Mercier

———

GRIFFITHS, G(ordon) D(ouglas). British. Born in Wallasey, Cheshire, 19 July 1910. Educated at Wallasey Grammar School, 1920–27; St. Luke's College, Exeter, 1957–58. Served in the Reconnaissance Corps, and acting sergeant, Intelligence Corps, British Army, 1943–46. Married Edith Grace Chalmers Lane in 1948. Farmer prior to 1943; French, Latin, and Greek teacher, Devon preparatory schools and Exeter Cathedral School, 1959–60; publishers' reader. *Died in July 1973.*

PUBLICATIONS FOR CHILDREN

Fiction

Mattie: The Story of a Hedgehog, illustrated by Elsie Wrigley. Kingswood, Surrey, World's Work, 1967; New York, Delacorte Press, 1977.

Silver Blue: A Story of the Ponies That Run Free on Dartmoor, illustrated by Elsie Wrigley. Kingswood, Surrey, World's Work, 1970.
Abandoned. Kingswood, Surrey, World's Work, 1973; Chicago, Follett, 1974.

PUBLICATIONS FOR ADULTS

Other

History of Teignmouth, with E.G.C. Griffiths. Teignmouth, Devon, Brunswick Press, 1965.

* * *

Judged by quantity only, the output of G.D. Griffiths might seem slight: no more than three books, whose economy of writing makes each rather less in length than the average novel. But these three books place their author in the highest rank of their special genre, the animal narrative. (See also Roberts, Williamson, and others.) It is a scrupulous genre, needing both informed observation and the ability to record its findings. It does *not* include the (often bestselling) humorous records of an author's adventures as vet or zoo-keeper. Animals are rarely themes for comedy, especially those caught up in the human world. A central feature of the form—and Griffiths illustrates this particularly well—is that, while neither sentimental nor anthropomorphic, it rouses a sympathetic understanding through the explicit presentation of its facts.

All of Griffiths's books are set in the Dartmoor region of Devon, one of the last surviving "wild" areas in southern England. Each focusses on a particular animal, living in a natural habitat yet affected both for good and ill by human contact. The subject of *Mattie* is a hedgehog, one of a family born in an old neglected garden near the moor. Outside a textbook there can be few more exact accounts of the creature's looks, behaviour, cycle of life from birth to old age and death. Griffiths, though, is not writing a textbook but a work lit by creative imagination; its impact stays. Characteristically, he shows how inescapably his creature is linked with the larger world around, not only that of insects, plants, other woodland fauna, but of the human kind. One nameless human kicks and kills; another tries to mend the harm, puts out milk, or a grass-filled flowerpot for shelter. *Mattie* is a memorable little book, a classic of its kind.

Silver Blue is far more ambitious in plan, but also—no doubt for this reason—the least "popular" work of the three. As if in contrast to the minuscule scale of the hedgehog story, this ranges widely over the moor, and over the years of the 19th century—a time when a certain wild strain of Dartmoor pony appeared and vanished. Thus, the tale follows a line of creatures, not one individual member. Yet it has all the essential Griffiths qualities—the knowledge, the sense of place, the austere and moving distinction. A beautiful book, it deserves to be better known.

Abandoned, arguably the peak work of the three, has the particularity of *Mattie* and the wider range of *Silver Blue*. Here, the focus returns to the individual creature—in this case, a cat. At 12 weeks old it is thrown out of a car on to a lonely Dartmoor road, and, after further human rejections, learns to accept the life of the moor. The deep snows of winter, the drought of summer, a heath fire (started by campers), floods when the swollen river overflows, illegal gintraps, a fox hunt—all these the cat survives, though not without scars. Humans betray but humans are also rescuers. A watchman at the claypits tends her after the fire; an old "lifer" at the prison finds her half dead and frozen in the stables, and shelters her through the winter; an elderly couple very gradually win her confidence at the end. In all the books, but especially in *Abandoned,* the sense of the moorland seasons is Brontëan in its beauty and its vividness. At the same time, the reader is always kept aware—if only by an illuminating line or two—of the human lives that touch the creature's anxious world: now, say, a difficult husband back from sea; now a prison warder sharing his charges' isolation. This grasp of the total scene, animal, human, elemental, makes *Abandoned* more than a genre example; it is a small but distinguished novel in its own right.

—Naomi Lewis

GRIFFITHS, Helen. Also writes as Helen Santos. British and Spanish. Born in London, 8 May 1939. Educated at Balham and Tooting College of Commerce, London (Matthew Arnold Memorial prize), 1953–55. Married Pedro Santos de la Cal in 1959 (died 1973); three daughters. Cowgirl, Bedfordshire, 1956; secretary, Blackstock Engineering, Cockfosters, Hertfordshire, 1957–58; office worker, Selfridge's, 1959, and Oliver and Boyd, publishers, 1959–60, both London; teacher of English as a foreign language, Madrid, 1973–76. Address: 42 Newbridge Road, Bath, Avon, England.

PUBLICATIONS FOR CHILDREN

Fiction

Horse in the Clouds, illustrated by Edward Osmond. London, Hutchinson, 1957; New York, Holt Rinehart, 1958.
Wild and Free, illustrated by Edward Osmond. London, Hutchinson, 1958.
Moonlight, illustrated by Edward Osmond. London, Hutchinson, 1959.
Africano. London, Hutchinson, 1961.
The Wild Heart, illustrated by Victor Ambrus. London, Hutchinson, 1963; New York, Doubleday, 1964.
The Greyhound, illustrated by Victor Ambrus. London, Hutchinson, 1964; New York, Doubleday, 1966.
The Wild Horse of Santander, illustrated by Victor Ambrus. London, Hutchinson, 1966; New York, Doubleday, 1967.
León, illustrated by Victor Ambrus. London, Hutchinson, 1967; New York, Doubleday, 1968.
Stallion of the Sands, illustrated by Victor Ambrus. London, Hutchinson, 1968; New York, Lothrop, 1970.
Moshie Cat: The True Adventures of a Majorcan Kitten, illustrated by Shirley Hughes. London, Hutchinson, 1969; New York, Holiday House, 1970.
Patch, illustrated by Maurice Wilson. London, Hutchinson, 1970.
Federico, illustrated by Shirley Hughes. London, Hutchinson, 1971.
Russian Blue, illustrated by Victor Ambrus. London, Hutchinson, and New York, Holiday House, 1973.
Just a Dog, illustrated by Victor Ambrus. London, Hutchinson, 1974; New York, Holiday House, 1975.
Witch Fear, illustrated by Victor Ambrus. London, Hutchinson, 1975; as *The Mysterious Appearance of Agnes,* New York, Holiday House, 1975.
Pablo, illustrated by Victor Ambrus. London, Hutchinson, 1977; as *Running Wild,* New York, Holiday House, 1977.
The Kershaw Dogs, illustrated by Douglas Hall. London, Hutchinson, 1978; as *Grip: A Dog Story,* New York, Holiday House, 1978.
The Last Summer: Spain 1936, illustrated by Victor Ambrus. London, Hutchinson, and New York, Holiday House, 1979.
Blackface Stallion, illustrated by Victor Ambrus. London, Hutchinson, and New York, Holiday House, 1980.

Love Forever. London, Macmillan, 1981.
Dancing Horses. London, Hutchinson, 1981; New York, Holiday House, 1982.
Hari's Pigeon. London, Hutchinson, 1982.
Rafa's Dog. London, Hutchinson, and New York, Holiday House, 1983.
The Dog at the Window. London, Hutchinson, and New York, Holiday House, 1984.
Caleb's Lamb (as Helen Santos). London, Scripture Union, 1984.
If Only (as Helen Santos). London, Scripture Union, 1987.

Other

Jesus as Told by Mark: A Simple Retelling of the Gospel of Mark, illustrated by Jenny Kisler. London, Scripture Union, 1983.

PUBLICATIONS FOR ADULTS

Novel

The Dark Swallows. London, Hutchinson, 1966; New York, Knopf, 1967.

*

Helen Griffiths comments:

I had my first book published at an early age, and my first few titles are obviously immature. Their purpose, I think, was sheer self-entertainment together with encouragement from my publishers to continue.

The main theme behind all my work, which I have endeavoured to express from the beginning, is to show animals free from the sentimental light in which they are so often portrayed in fiction. I have not tried to write sad books, as I have been accused of doing. I have tried and continue trying to portray a section of life as I see and feel it to be.

Many of my later books have a Spanish background, and in these I have tried to portray the country and the people as they really are, not as foreigners so often imagine them to be. I have also attempted to express how Spaniards feel towards animals, not cruel but indifferent, an attitude often misunderstood outside the country. I would like to think that these books may help people to know a little more about Spain.

*   *   *

Helen Griffiths's first published book was written when she was a schoolgirl of 15 or 16. Though she has gained in depth and range in her many subsequent novels, her strong descriptive manner and her central kindling theme (the lot of animals—those especially linked with man—in a predatory human world) remain the same. In almost every book it is some rare child, briefly sharing the genius of the animal, who makes a link between creature and humankind. Though knowledgeable enough about her horses, dogs, and cats, she is probably more of a novelist than a naturalist writer and because of the key role given to children in her stories, she is aptly ranked as a children's novelist.

Her first few stories were about horses in the South American plains—free wild creatures, mostly doomed to be caught and "broken" or slaughtered for their skins. The note of violence and cruelty that must attend such themes may not have lessened their popularity with the young. But she occasionally shows a greater subtlety. Perhaps the two best of her horse novels are *The Wild Heart* and *The Wild Horse of Santander* (note the recurring adjective). The first of these tells of a mare born wild on the pampas; left motherless at four months and surviving only by theft, she grows up a natural loner, even among her kind. But she is coveted by traders and others for her supreme racing speed. At the end of a terrible hunt she finds strange sanctuary—in a church. A foundling boy, brought up by the village priest, has to solve the problem of how to give her both liberty and life. The second novel tells of an 8-year-old blind Spanish boy, languid and over-cosseted, who is "given" a new-born foal, born to a half-wild mare after an escapade. A deep alliance grows between the two young creatures, and presently, without either bit or bridle, the horse (which no one else is able to touch) will race along day after day with the blind boy on his back. (What most disturbs the adults is that the horse and not the human is master of the two.) This perfect trust is cracked when the boy leaves for an operation to restore his sight.

In more recent novels she has written of dogs and cats—chiefly in the Spanish setting that she herself knows well. They are, inevitably, grim and poignant stories, though most have consoling endings. *León* is one of the most complex and important of these books—a classic of dog fiction. A clever Spanish village boy, Hilario, has the chance of going to medical school, but has to leave his beloved mongrel sheep-dog with relatives. Caught in the Civil War, and badly wounded, he does not return for several years, while León—chained, starved, beaten, abused, abandoned—tastes the fate of most of his kind in a Latin country. It is the chance of Hilario's medical skill that at last reunites the two. In other novels, based on personal fact, a nameless human (in fact, the author herself) has an operative part in the tale, and ensures a happier end. *Just a Dog,* a vivid account of the life of mongrel strays in Madrid, is of this kind; *Moshie Cat* is another. Two characteristic tales—*The Greyhound* and *Russian Blue*—have a London setting.

Of all her books, *Witch Fear* seems most to diverge from the pattern of the rest, yet basically it is still of the Griffiths kind. This interesting tale describes the situation of what we might now call an autistic child in a superstitious European village several centuries ago—a condition in this case caused by shock: the frightful death of her mother, a herbal healer, as a witch. Unable to communicate in expected human fashion, this girl is in much the same unhappy position as an animal in the rough peasant setting—indeed, her only natural alliance is with a rescued cat. Though (since this is fiction) truth comes out and the girl is saved from death, the basic Griffiths point is sharply made.

If the note of her novels is often sombre, this is because of their truth to human behaviour, too often where the normal is the mindless, mean, and gross. Yet (with equal truth), the animals are always shown as uncorrupt, and this increases the poignancy of their lot. Sad to say—whether through a paucity of ideas or total surrender to the mores of her adopted home—she has devoted her recent book *Dancing Horses* to lauding the miserable business of bullfighting.

—Naomi Lewis

GRUELLE, Johnny (John Barton Gruelle). American. Born in Arcalo, Illinois, 25 December 1880. Educated at schools in Indianapolis. Married Myrtle Swann in 1900; one daughter and two sons. Cartoonist and illustrator for Indianapolis *Star* and Cleveland *Press* from mid-1890's; wrote Sunday comic strip Mr. Twee Deedle for New York *Herald,* 1910–16, and Brutus page for New York *Herald Tribune,* 1929–38. *Died 9 January 1938.*

PUBLICATIONS FOR CHILDREN (illustrated by the author)

Fiction

Mr. Twee Deedle. New York, Cupples and Leon, 1913.
Mr. Twee Deedle's Further Adventures. New York, Cupples and Leon, 1914.
The Travels of Timmy Toodles. Garden City, New York, Martin, 1916.
My Very Own Fairy Stories. Chicago, Volland, 1917; as *My Very Own Fairy Book,* London, Brentano's, 1923.
The Funny Little Book. Chicago, Donohue, 1917.
Raggedy Ann Stories. Chicago, Volland, 1918; London, Brentano's, 1923.
Little Sunny Stories. Joliet, Illinois, Volland, 1919.
Friendly Fairies. Chicago, Volland, 1919; London, Brentano's, 1923.
Raggedy Andy Stories: Introducing the Little Rag Brother of Raggedy Ann. Chicago, Volland, 1920; London, Collins, 1978.
The Little Brown Bear. Chicago, Volland, 1920.
Orphant Annie Story Book. Indianapolis, Bobbs Merrill, 1921.
Eddie Elephant. Chicago, Volland, 1921.
Johnny Mouse and the Wishing Stick. Indianapolis, Bobbs Merrill, 1922.
The Magical Land of Noom. Chicago, Volland, 1922.
Raggedy Ann and Andy and the Camel with the Wrinkled Knees. Chicago, Donohue, 1924; as *The Camel with the Wrinkled Knees,* Springfield, Massachusetts, McLoughlin, 1941; London, Hutchinson, 1942.
Raggedy Ann's Wishing Pebble. Joliet, Illinois, Volland, 1925.
Raggedy Ann's Alphabet Book. Joliet, Illinois, Volland, 1925.
The Paper Dragon: A Raggedy Ann Adventure. Joliet, Illinois, Volland, 1926.
Beloved Belindy. Chicago, Donohue, 1926.
Wooden Willie. Joliet, Illinois, Volland, 1927.
Raggedy Ann's Magical Wishes. Joliet, Illinois, Volland, 1928.
Raggedy Andy's Number Book. Chicago, Volland, n.d.
Marcella Stories. Chicago, Volland, 1929.
The Cheery Scarecrow. Chicago, Donohue, 1929.
Golden Book. Chicago, Donohue, 1929.
A Mother Goose Parade. Chicago, Donohue, 1929.
Raggedy Ann in the Deep Deep Woods. Joliet, Illinois, Volland, 1930.
Raggedy Ann's Sunny Songs, music by Will Woodin. Chicago, Volland, 1930.
Raggedy Ann in Cookie Land. New York, n.i., 1931.
Raggedy Ann's Lucky Pennies. Joliet, Illinois, Volland, 1932.
Raggedy Ann and the Left-Handed Safety Pin. Racine, Wisconsin, Whitman, 1935.
Raggedy Ann in the Golden Meadow. Racine, Wisconsin, Whitman, 1935.
Raggedy Ann's Joyful Songs, music by Charles Miller. New York, Miller Music, 1937.
Raggedy Ann in the Magic Book, illustrated by Worth Gruelle. New York, Gruelle, 1939.
Raggedy Ann and the Golden Butterfly. New York, Gruelle, 1940.
Raggedy Ann and the Hoppy Toad. Springfield, Massachusetts, McLoughlin, 1940.
Raggedy Ann and the Laughing Brook. Springfield, Massachusetts, McLoughlin, 1940; London, Hutchinson, 1942.
Raggedy Ann Helps Grandpa Hoppergrass. Springfield, Massachusetts, McLoughlin, 1940; London, Hutchinson, 1942.
Raggedy Ann in the Garden. Springfield, Massachusetts, McLoughlin, 1940.
Raggedy Andy Goes Sailing. Springfield, Massachusetts, McLoughlin, 1941; London, Hutchinson, 1942.

Raggedy Ann and Andy and the Nice Fat Policeman, illustrated by
Worth Gruelle.   New York, Gruelle, 1942.
Raggedy Ann and Betsy Bonnet String.   New York, Gruelle, 1943.
Raggedy Ann and Andy, illustrated by Julian Wehr.   Akron, Ohio,
Saalfield, 1944.
Raggedy Ann in the Snow White Castle, illustrated by Justin Gruelle.
New York, Gruelle, 1946.
Raggedy Ann and the Slippery Slide, illustrated by Ethel Hays.
Akron, Ohio, Saalfield, 1947.
Raggedy Ann at the End of the Rainbow, illustrated by Ethel Hays.
Akron, Ohio, Saalfield, 1947.
Raggedy Ann's Adventure, illustrated by Ethel Hays.   Akron, Ohio,
Saalfield, 1947.
Raggedy Ann's Mystery, illustrated by Ethel Hays.   Akron, Ohio,
Saalfield, 1947.
Raggedy Ann's Fairy Stories.   Chicago, Donohue, n.d.
Raggedy Ann's Marcella.   Chicago, Donohue, n.d.
Stories about Raggedy Ann to Read Aloud, illustrated by Rachel Taft
Dixon.   London, Spring Books, 1960.
Raggedy Ann and the Golden Ring, illustrated by Worth Gruelle.
Indianapolis, Bobbs Merrill, 1961.
Raggedy Ann and the Happy Meadow, illustrated by Worth Gruelle.
Indianapolis, Bobbs Merrill, 1961.
Raggedy Ann and the Hobby Horse, illustrated by Worth Gruelle.
Indianapolis, Bobbs Merrill, 1961; London, Collins, 1978 (?).
Raggedy Ann and the Wonderful Witch, illustrated by Worth Gruelle.
Indianapolis, Bobbs Merrill, 1961.
Raggedy Ann and Andy and the Kindly Ragman, illustrated by John
Hopper.   Indianapolis, Bobbs Merrill, 1975.
Raggedy Ann and Andy and the Witchie Kissabye, illustrated by John
Hopper.   Indianapolis, Bobbs Merrill, 1975.
More Raggedy Ann and Andy Stories, edited by Martin Williams,
illustrated by the author and Worth and Justin Gruelle.   In-
dianapolis, Bobbs Merrill, 1977.

*

Illustrator: *Grimm's Fairy Tales* translated by Margaret Hunt, 1914;
Rhymes for Kindly Children by Fairmont Snyder, 1916; *All about
Hansel and Gretel,* 1917; *All about Mother Goose,* 1918; *The All
about Story Book,* 1929; *The Bam Bam Clock* by J.P. McEvoy, 1936;
Rhymes for Kindly Children by Ethel Fairmont, 1937; *The
Old-Fashioned Raggedy Ann and Andy ABC Book* by Robert Kraus,
1981.

* * *

Like a number of other American writers for children—L. Frank
Baum and Thornton Waldo Burgess, for example—Johnny Gruelle
was a highly prolific early 20th-century writer. He was also the
reputed author of much material turned out in his name long after his
death. One result has been that Gruelle, like the others, has only just
begun to receive critical and scholarly attention. His major creation
was the fictional rag doll, Raggedy Ann, who, with the other dolls
and toy animals from Marcella's nursery, had a secret life of her own
when the "real for sure people," in Gruelle's child-like phrase, were
asleep or away from the house.
   Their around-the-house adventures filled the first volume in the
Raggedy Ann series, *Raggedy Ann Stories,* and eventually three
others, *Raggedy Andy Stories, Beloved Belindy,* and *Marcella
Stories.* They are the sort of tales that delight small children. Raggedy
Ann, carelessly left outdoors, is washed down a drainpipe and
eventually rescued. She is dripped on by a careless house-painter and
has to be given a new face and knitting-yarn hair. However, an
episode like "The Taffy Pull" in the *Raggedy Andy* collection has a
suspense that all ages can appreciate: the dolls stage an evening

invasion of the kitchen, make candy, make a mess, and manage to
clean up, escape to the nursery and exactly resume their former
positions before the family returns from an outing.
   In the best stories, however, the dolls enter Johnny Gruelle's very
personal (but very 20th-century American) version of fairyland, the
"deep, deep woods" behind Marcella's house, "full of elves, and
fairies, and everything." Beginning with *Raggedy Ann and Andy and
the Camel with the Wrinkled Knees* and *Raggedy Ann's Wishing
Pebble* they have charming, book-length adventures which feature
amiable creatures like the Snarlyboodle and the Snoopwiggy, more
traditional figures like witches and goblins (some of them helpful
and none of them very cruel), eccentric kings, handsome princes and
beautiful princesses, and magic spells which can be broken with the
answer to such riddles as, "Why does a snicker-snapper snap snickers
from snuckers?"—altogether an adventurous place where simple
"kindliness," in Gruelle's word, usually wins out in the end.
   In the best of these longer tales—and *Wooden Willie* and, above
all, *The Paper Dragon* should be added to the list—Gruelle reveals
unique qualities, for the stories move at the charming pace of a group
of children playing an improvisational adventure game among themselves. Gruelle's style, moreover, is whimsically child-like in its
playful vocabulary and its invented proper names, and its tumbling
cadences. Adopting the narrative manner and the style of children in
telling his stories for children—that is Johnny Gruelle's unique
contribution to their literature.

—Martin Williams

———

GUY, Rosa (Cuthbert).   American.   Born in Trinidad, West In-
dies, 1 September 1928; moved to the United States, 1932. Educated
at New York University. Married Warner Guy (died); one son.
Worked with the American Negro Theatre, New York, mid-1940's.
Founding president, Harlem Writers Guild. Recipient: Children's
Rights Workshop Other award, 1987. Agent: Ellen Levine Literary
Agency, 432 Park Avenue South, Suite 1205, New York, New York
10016, U.S.A.

PUBLICATIONS FOR CHILDREN

Fiction

Bird at My Window.   Philadelphia, Lippincott, and London,
Souvenir Press, 1966.
The Friends.   New York, Holt Rinehart, 1973; London, Gollancz,
1974.
Ruby.   New York, Viking Press, 1976; London, Gollancz, 1981.
Edith Jackson.   New York, Viking Press, 1978; London, Gollancz,
1979.
The Disappearance.   New York, Delacorte Press, 1979; London,
Gollancz, 1980.
Mirror of Her Own.   New York, Delacorte Press, 1981.
New Guys Around the Block.   New York, Delacorte Press, and
London, Gollancz, 1983.
Paris, Pee Wee, and Big Dog, illustrated by Caroline Binch.   New
York, Delacorte Press, and London, Gollancz, 1984.
And I Heard a Bird Sing.   New York, Delacorte Press, and London,
Gollancz, 1987.
The Ups and Downs of Carl Davis III.   New York, Delacorte Press,
1989.

Other

Translator, *Mother Crocodile,* by Birago Diop, illustrated by John

Steptoe. New York, Delacorte Press, 1981.

PUBLICATIONS FOR ADULTS

Novels

A Measure of Time. New York, Holt Rinehart, 1983; London, Virago Press, 1984.
My Love, My Love; or, The Peasant Girl. New York, Holt Rinehart, 1985; London, Virago Press, 1987.

Play

Venetian Blinds (produced New York, 1954).

Other

Editor, *Children of Longing.* New York, Bantam, 1970.

*

Critical Study: *Presenting Rosa Guy* by Jerrie Norris, Boston, Twayne, 1988.

*   *   *

Why is Rosa Guy not ranked among the foremost writers of juvenile fiction in America? Her insight into the human condition equals Katherine Paterson's. She has Ursula Le Guin's feel for textures of place and setting as well as Robert Cormier's ability to contemplate the unspeakable without flinching. Why then is she relatively unknown when African American writers of considerable though lesser ability such as Walter Dean Myers and Virginia Hamilton garner the awards and top the recommended lists? The root cause undoubtedly lies in a vision of black America which, over 20 years after Martin Luther King's assassination, is still too unsettling for white America to accept.

Two contradictory themes run through all of Guy's novels: love and survival. Love is a basic human need. A tough street kid such as Imamu Jones, the hero of *The Disappearance* and *New Guys Around the Block,* hungers for it as much as languid Ruby Cathy in *Ruby.* But survival on the mean streets of a ghetto precludes trust and vulnerability. In *The Friends* Edith Jackson allows herself the illusion of thinking of Phyllisia Cathy as her friend, and it nearly destroys her. Thus the dilemma facing Guy's heroes and heroines: they cannot survive without love, they may not survive with it.

Merely getting through the day is an heroic act for the children who inhabit these pages. Their environment is a moonscape of social disintegration. Drugs, poverty, and death form the realities of their lives. The child with one responsible parent is lucky. Fat, mouthy Big Dog in the delightful adventure *Paris, Pee Wee, and Big Dog* is an aristocrat among his peers because he has a father. The book ends with Paris sobbing into his mother's arms, "Moms, oh, Moms, why do you always have to go to work? I miss you…" In *The Disappearance* Imamu Jones has difficulty accepting the stable environment of the Aimsley household as real. In her best and bleakest book, a sequel to *The Disappearance* with the strangely innocuous title *New Guys Around the Block,* Guy depicts a zombie world of drug addicts inhabiting the shells of burnt-out buildings, coming out at night like rats to feed. A car accident on his street wakes Imamu Jones in the middle of the night. He rushes to his window to see a horrific vision of the zombies stripping the victims. Did it happen, or did he dream it? In the morning everything is gone, except the yellow chalk lines on the asphalt to mark where the bodies lay. Like Imamu, Guy swings wildly between rage and compassion. Why won't the police

do something to clear the streets of the drug pushers and addicts? Why is a psychopath like Iggy released from jail? Yet from the moment of his birth what chance does a person like Iggy have to become anything else? Does a society that allows children to grow up in such conditions have any right to judge them? The book ends on a note of disturbing moral ambiguity. Guy refuses to condemn even Olivette Larouche, Imamu's intriguing friend and an even more dangerous sociopath than Iggy. Imamu has no answers, except to save himself.

Guy's feelings for Harlem reflect Imamu's. Her heart is filled with what Harlem could be. She loves the people she depicts with such verve and color. Her ear is attuned to the rhythms of their conversations. She proclaims their courage; celebrates their joy; feels their weariness; mourns them when they fall into the pit of drugs and despair. But it isn't enough. Good doesn't win out. The brightest dreams cannot overcome when the larger society has written off the ghetto.

There is anger in Rosa Guy. And deep sorrow. Perhaps that accounts for her relative neglect. The mirror she holds up is too bright, and we don't like what we see.

—Eric A. Kimmel

———

HADER, Berta and Elmer. Americans. HADER, Berta (née Hoerner): Born in San Pedro, Coahuila, Mexico, in 1891. Educated at the University of Washington, Seattle, 1909–12; California School of Design, San Francisco, 1915–18. Married Elmer Hader in 1919; one son. Staff artist, San Francisco *Bulletin,* 1916–18. *Died 6 February 1976.* HADER, Elmer (Stanley): Born in Pajaro, California, 7 September 1889. Educated at the California School of Design, San Francisco, 1907–10; Julian Academy, Paris, 1912–14. Served in the Army Camouflage Corps during World War I. Worked as apprentice silversmith, surveyor's assistant, and locomotive fireman, 1906–10; vaudeville actor. *Died 7 September 1973.* Recipients: American Library Association Caldecott Medal, 1949.

PUBLICATIONS FOR CHILDREN (illustrated by the authors)

Fiction

Two Funny Clowns. New York, Coward McCann, 1929.
Lions and Tigers and Elephants Too, Being an Account of Polly Patchin's Trip to the Zoo. London and New York, Longman, 1930.
Under the Pig-Nut Tree. New York, Knopf, and London, Allen and Unwin, 2 vols., 1930–31.
The Farmer in the Dell. New York, Macmillan, 1931.
Tooky, The Story of a Seal Who Joined the Circus. New York and London, Longman, 1931.
Chuck-a-Luck and His Reindeer. Boston, Houghton Mifflin, 1933.
Spunky. New York, Macmillan, 1933.
Whiffy McMann. New York and London, Oxford University Press, 1933.
Midget and Bridget. New York, Macmillan, 1934.
Jamaica Johnny. New York, Macmillan, 1935.
Billy Butter. New York, Macmillan, 1936.
Tommy Thatcher Goes to Sea. New York, Macmillan, 1937.
Cricket, The Story of a Little Circus Pony. New York, Macmillan, 1938; Birmingham, Combridge, 1939.
Cock-a-Doodle Doo: The Story of a Little Red Rooster. New York, Macmillan, 1939.

The Cat and the Kitten.   New York, Macmillan, 1940.
Little Town.   New York, Macmillan, 1941.
The Story of Pancho and the Bull with the Crooked Tail.   New York, Macmillan, 1942; London, Hale, 1946.
The Mighty Hunter.   New York, Macmillan, 1943; London, Hale, 1947.
Rainbow's End.   New York, Macmillan, 1945.
The Skyrocket.   New York, Macmillan, 1946.
Big City.   New York, Macmillan, 1947.
The Big Snow.   New York, Macmillan, 1948.
Little Appaloosa.   New York, Macmillan, 1949.
Squirrely of Willow Hill.   New York, Macmillan, 1950.
Lost in the Zoo.   New York, Macmillan, 1951.
Little White Foot.   New York, Macmillan, 1952.
Wish on the Moon.   New York, Macmillan, 1954.
Home on the Range: Jeremiah Jones and His Friend Little Bear in the Far West.   New York and London, Macmillan, 1955.
The Runaways.   New York, Macmillan, 1956.
Ding Dong Bell, Pussy's in the Well.   New York, Macmillan, 1957.
Little Chip of Willow Hill.   New York, Macmillan, 1958.
Reindeer Trail.   New York, Macmillan, 1959.
Mister Billy's Gun.   New York, Macmillan, and London, Macmillan, 1960.
Quack Quack.   New York, Macmillan, 1961.
Little Antelope: An Indian for a Day.   New York, Macmillan, 1962.
Snow in the City.   New York, Macmillan, and London, Collier Macmillan, 1963.
Two Is Company, Three's a Crowd.   New York, Macmillan, and London, Collier Macmillan, 1965.

Verse

What'll You Do When You Grow Up???   New York and London, Longman, 1929.

Other

The Picture Book of Travel.   New York, Macmillan, 1928.
Picture Book of Mother Goose.   New York, Coward McCann, 1930.
Picture Book of the States.   New York, Harper, 1932.
Stop, Look, Listen.   New York, Longman, 1936.
Green and Gold: The Story of the Banana.   New York, Macmillan, 1936.
The Inside Story of the Hader Books.   New York, Macmillan, 1937.
The Little Stone House: A Story of Building a House in the Country.   New York, Macmillan, 1944.
The Friendly Phoebe.   New York, Macmillan, 1953.

*

Bibliography: by Edward Kemp, in *Imprint: Oregon* (Eugene), Spring-Fall 1977.

Manuscript Collections: University of Oregon Library, Eugene; May Massee Collection, Emporia State University, Kansas.

Illustrators: *The Ugly Duckling,* 1927; *Chicken Little,* 1927; *Wee Willie Winkie,* 1927; *Hansel and Gretel,* 1927; *Donald in Numberland* by Jean Murdoch Peedie, 1927; *The Little Red Hen,* 1928; *The Old Woman and the Crooked Sixpence,* 1928; *The Story of the Three Bears,* 1928; *The Wonderful Locomotive* by Cornelia Meigs, 1928; *The Story of Mr. Punch* by Octave Feuillet, 1929; *A Monkey Tale,* 1929, *Little Elephant,* 1930, *Baby Bear,* 1930, *Lion Cub,* 1931, *Humpy,* 1937, and *Stripey,* 1939, all by Hamilton Williamson; *Timothy and the Blue Cart* by Elinor Whitney, 1930; *Big Fellow at Work,* by Dorothy Baruch, 1930; *Sonny Elephant* by

Madge Bigham, 1930; *A Good Little Dog,* 1930, *Bingo Is My Name,* 1931, and *Here, Bingo!,* 1932, all by Anne Stoddard; *The Play-Book of Words* by Prescott Lecky, 1933; *Jimmy the Groceryman* by Jane Miller, 1934; *Everyday Fun,* 1935, and *Who Knows,* 1937, both by Julia Hahn; *The Smiths and Rusty,* 1936, and *Wings for the Smiths,* 1937, both by Alice Dalgliesh; *A Visit from St. Nicholas* by Clement C. Moore, 1937; *Marcos, A Mountain Boy of Mexico* by Melicent Lee, 1937; *The Farmer* by Henry B. Lent, 1937; *Banana Tree House* by Phillis Garrard, 1938; *Timothy Has Ideas* by Miriam E. Mason, 1943; *Mr. Peck's Pets* by Louise Hunting Seaman, 1947. Elmer Hader only: *Charm* by Mary Margaret McBride and Alexander Williams, 1927, and *How Dear to My Heart* by McBride, 1940; *Adventures of Theodore Roosevelt* by Edwin Emerson, 1928; *The Story of Water Supply,* 1929, and *The Story of Health,* 1931, both by Hope Holway; *The Story of Markets* by Ruth Orton Camp, 1929; *The Garden of the Lost Key* by Forrestine Hooker, 1929; *Down Ryton Water* by Eva Gaggin, 1941; *The Isle of Que* by Elsie Singmaster, 1948.

*   *   *

Berta and Elmer Hader, a husband and wife team, wrote and illustrated children's books from the 1920's through the 1960's. The upgrading of children's literature during the nearly five decades that the Haders were associated with children's books can be seen in their works. While some of their earlier works may be considered of dubious quality, their later books possess good literary style and careful coordination of pictures and text. There is variety in their books, though most of them are stories about animals. At a time when children's picture books contained anthropomorphic animals that were overly "cute," the Haders carefully created animals in all their animal dignity.

A common setting of books by the Haders is Willow Farm, which is sure to be the rural area where they lived in the little house they built themselves. The story of the building of this house is told in their picture book *The Little Stone House.* Willow Farm is the setting of *Squirrely of Willow Hill,* a story about Mr. and Mrs. McGinty who care for a squirrel, tame him and spoil him; but when spring comes, set him free in a park. Mr. and Mrs. McGinty and Willow Farm are revisited in *Little White Foot,* about the peaceful coexistence of a mouse family and a human family which results in the belling of the family cat to protect the lives of the mice.

The care and understanding of animal ways shown in both *Squirrely of Willow Farm* and *Little White Foot* are shown over and over again in the Haders' books. *Quack Quack* is a mallard duck aided for a time by people, but allowed to return to the wilds again. The skunk and the fawn, kept for a while by the retired carpenter in *Rainbow's End,* both return to their lives in the forest. A similar event occurs in *Cock-a-Doodle Doo* when Little Red, a baby chick hatched with ducks, finds his way back to the barnyard to live with his own kind.

The best known of the Haders' works is *The Big Snow,* which received the Caldecott Medal in 1949. It is a book that shows the careful detail that typifies many of their works. *The Big Snow* is an animal book. People appear in the illustrations only twice, and are important only because of their relationship with the animals. The story has three parts. The animals prepare for winter, there is a snowstorm, and animals and people cope with the results of the heavy snow. The many details of the book deserve attention. Bright blue endpapers show many designed snowflakes. On the page preceding the title page a wild goose, the late fall symbol, is shown flying into the book. The frontis-piece is a full color picture of a snow scene, a promise of the major intent of the book. Central to this picture are the many animals in it: deer, raccoons, skunks, squirrels, rabbits, a cardinal, and a blue jay. The title page itself is almost stark, reminiscent of a quiet heavy snowfall; it is decorated only with seven snowflakes. The back of the title page shows a man and a woman surrounded by snow, a small self portrait of the Haders, which is a trademark of a Hader book.

On the first page of the story, the geese return. These heralds of winter appear across the top of each page throughout the first half of the book guiding the reader's eye through the pages. The final appearance of the geese is a full-color page that is shared with no other animal. The geese at the top of each page have been witness to the preparation made for winter by a variety of animals. With their disappearance midway in the book, winter takes over. Snow starts to fall and the reader is witness to the simple drama of a tremendous snowfall.

The story tells of the effect of the snowfall, the shoveling out, and of an old couple who share food with animals whose survival is threatened by the heavy snow. The story ends on Ground Hog Day when the ground hog predicts six more weeks of winter in this uncomplicated and satisfying paragraph: "The ground hog was right. It was a long cold winter for the birds and the animals on the hill, but the little old man and the little old woman put out food for them until the warm spring came. And that was the end of the BIG SNOW."

In *Rainbow's End* the reader sees a reflection of the main character as he examines the injured birds the children bring him to be cared for: "Toby always felt sad for these feathered creatures that made his day happier with their pretty ways and their sweet songs." So it seems this genuine appreciation for the companionship of animal life permeates Berta and Elmer Hader's books. This care is expressed through the stories—animals characterize only themselves, behave according to their instincts, and are allowed to remain happily in natural surroundings with their own kind—and is displayed even more clearly in the illustrations, beautiful representations of animals in careful proportion showing each animal as it really is. Surely this is one of the Haders' greatest contributions to children's books.

—Mary J. Lickteig

HAGON, Priscilla. See **ALLAN, Mabel Esther.**

HAIG-BROWN, Roderick (Langmere). Canadian. Born in Lancing, Sussex, England, 21 February 1908; emigrated to Canada, 1926. Educated at Charterhouse, Godalming, Surrey. Served in the Canadian Army, 1939–45: Major. Married Ann Elmore in 1934; one son and three daughters. Worked as a logger, trapper, fisherman, and guide, Washington, U.S.A., 1926, and British Columbia, 1927–29; provincial magistrate and judge, Campbell River Children's and Family Court, British Columbia, 1942–75. Frequent broadcaster and moderator of television programs. Chancellor, University of Victoria, British Columbia, 1970–73. Recipient: Canadian Library Association Book of the Year Medal, 1947, 1964; Governor-General's citation, 1948; Crandell Conservation Trophy, 1955; Vicky Metcalf award, 1966. LL.D.: University of British Columbia, Vancouver, 1952. *Died 9 October 1976.*

PUBLICATIONS FOR CHILDREN

Fiction

Silver: The Life of an Atlantic Salmon, illustrated by J.P. Moreton. London, A. and C. Black, 1931.

Ki-yu: A Story of Panthers, illustrated by Kurt Wiese. Boston, Houghton Mifflin, 1934; as *Panther,* London, Cape, 1934.
Starbuck Valley Winter, illustrated by Charles De Feo. New York, Morrow, 1943; London, Collins, 1944.
Saltwater Summer. Toronto, Collins, and New York, Morrow, 1948; London, Collins, 1949.
Mounted Police Patrol. London, Collins, and New York, Morrow, 1954.
Fur and Gold, illustrated by Paul Duff. Toronto, Longman, 1962.
The Whale People, illustrated by Mary Weiler. London, Collins, 1962; New York, Morrow, 1963.
Alison's Fishing Birds, illustrated by Jim Rimmer. Vancouver, Colophon, 1980.

Other

Captain of the Discovery: The Story of Captain George Vancouver, illustrated by Robert Banks. Toronto and London, Macmillan, 1956.
The Farthest Shores, illustrated by Frank Newfeld. Toronto, Longman, 1960.

PUBLICATIONS FOR ADULTS

Novels

Pool and Rapid: The Story of a River, illustrated by C.F. Tunnicliffe. Toronto, McClelland and Stewart, and London, A. and C. Black, 1932.
Timber: A Novel of Pacific Coast Loggers. New York, Morrow, 1942; as *The Tall Trees Fall,* London, Collins, 1943.
On the Highest Hill. Toronto, Collins, and New York, Morrow, 1949; London, Collins, 1950.

Short Stories

Woods and River Tales, edited by Valerie Haig-Brown. Toronto, McClelland and Stewart, 1980.

Other

The Western Angler: An Account of Pacific Salmon and Western Trout in British Columbia. New York, Derrydale Press, 1939.
Return to the River: A Story of the Chinook Run. New York, Morrow, 1941; London, Collins, 1942.
A River Never Sleeps. Toronto, Collins, and New York, Morrow, 1946; London, Collins, 1948.
Measure of the Year. Toronto, Collins, and New York, Morrow, 1950.
Fisherman's Spring. Toronto, Collins, and New York, Morrow, 1951.
Spring Congregation Address 1952: Power and People. Vancouver, University of British Columbia, 1952.
Fisherman's Winter. New York, Morrow, 1954.
Divine Discontent: An Address to the Annual Assembly of Victoria College. Victoria, British Columbia, Victoria Daily Times, 1954.
The Case for the Preservation of Strathcona Park. Victoria, British Columbia, Daily Colonist, 1955.
Fabulous Fishing in Latin America.... New York, Pan American World Airways, 1956.
The Face of Canada, with others. Toronto, Clarke Irwin, 1959; London, Harrap, 1960.
Fisherman's Summer. Toronto, Collins, and New York, Morrow, 1959.

The Living Land: An Account of the Natural Resources of British Columbia. Toronto, Macmillan, and New York, Morrow, 1961.
The Pacific Northwest, with Stewart Holbrook and Nard Jones, edited by Anthony Netboy. New York, Doubleday, 1963.
A Primer of Fly Fishing. Toronto, Collins, and New York, Morrow, 1964.
Fisherman's Fall. Toronto, Collins, and New York, Morrow, 1964.
Canada's Pacific Salmon, revised edition. Ottawa, Queen's Printer, 1967.
The Canadians 1867–1967. Toronto, Macmillan, 1967.
The Salmon. Ottawa, Queen's Printer, 1974.
Bright Waters, Bright Fish: An Examination of Angling in Canada. Vancouver, Douglas and McIntyre, and Portland, Oregon, Timber Press, 1980.
The Master and His Fish, edited by Valerie Haig-Brown. Toronto, McClelland and Stewart, and Seattle, University of Washington Press, 1981.
Writings and Reflections: From the World of Roderick Haig-Brown, edited by Valerie Haig-Brown. Toronto, McClelland and Stewart, and Seattle, University of Washington Press, 1982.

*

Manuscript Collection: University of British Columbia Library, Vancouver.

Theatrical Activities:
Actor: **Films**—*Out of the North,* 1952; *Rural Magistrate.*

*   *   *

Before the "boom period" of the last two decades, Roderick Haig-Brown was an undisputed giant of Canadian children's literature. The two-time winner of the Canadian Library Association Medal had distinguished himself as a writer of animal stories, boys' adventures, history, biography, and a bildungsroman of pre-contact Native life. His works combined well-established genres, especially the animal and adventure story, with his deep knowledge and appreciation of the Canadian landscape and his respect for what he called "quiet heroes." His work as logger, fisherman, trapper, and guide sharpened his knowledge of nature and deepened his understanding of human nature; his lifelong love of nature provided inspiration and guides for his writing.

Four works illustrate his achievements in the different genres. *Ki-yu: A Story of Panthers* draws on detailed study of panthers; but, in the manner of the realistic animal story, he elevates his presentation of details to the level of symbol. Ki-yu, the most noble animal of the area, engages in heroic confrontation with the most dedicated hunter, one who respects and understands his prey. *Captain of the Discovery* combines historical facts with sensitive understanding of the challenges and responsibilities of leadership to present the life of George Vancouver, the 18th-century explorer who showed respect for his own men as well as the lands and people he encountered.

Starbuck Valley Winter describes the coming of age of teenager Don Morgan, who spends a winter trapping to earn money for a new fishing boat. While Haig-Brown draws on ideas of manly virtue found in boys' adventure novels, his presentations of Don's inner life and of his struggles and achievements in the rugged West Coast landscape are convincing and authentic, drawn as they are on the author's own experience and knowledge. *The Whale People* is also an initiation novel, this time about a Nootka Indian teenager who assumes the role of chief after the death of his father. As in his other books, Haig-Brown's research is impeccable. More significant, he succeeds in recreating the inner life of someone of another culture and time, capturing the hero's response to his physical, social, and, perhaps most important, spiritual environments.

Although some critics consider Haig-Brown's writing old-fashioned, using 19th- and early 20th- century forms and focussing mainly on heroic male figures, his books are important treatments of a significant aspect of the Canadian experience: the human encounter with the grandeur and danger of the natural environment.

—Jon C. Stott

————

HALAM, Ann. Pseudonym for Gwyneth A. Jones. British. Born in Manchester, Lancashire, 14 February 1952. Educated at the University of Sussex, Brighton, B.A. (honours) 1973. Married Peter Gwilliam in 1976; one son. Executive officer, Manpower Services Commission, Hove, Sussex, 1975–77. Lives in Brighton. Agent: Herta Ryder, c/o Toby Eady Associates, 7 Gledhow Gardens, London SW5 0BL, England.

PUBLICATIONS FOR CHILDREN

Fiction

Ally Ally, Aster. London, Allen and Unwin, 1981.
The Alder Tree. London, Allen and Unwin, 1982.
King Death's Garden. London, Orchard, 1986.
The Daymaker. London, Orchard, 1987.
Transformations. London, Orchard, 1988.

Fiction as Gwyneth A. Jones

Water in the Air. London, Macmillan, and New York, Macmillan, 1977.
The Influence of Ironwood. London, Macmillan, 1978.
The Exchange. London, Macmillan, 1979.
Dear Hill. London, Macmillan, 1980.
The Hidden Ones. London, Women's Press, 1988.

PUBLICATIONS FOR ADULTS

Novels as Gwyneth A. Jones

Divine Endurance. London, Allen and Unwin, 1984; New York, Arbor House, 1987.
Escape Plans. London, Allen and Unwin, 1986.
Kairos. London, Unwin Hyman, 1988.

*   *   *

That Ann Halam displayed immediately a high degree of professionalism is no surprise. She was already established, in her alter ego of Gwyneth A. Jones, as a most efficient writer of science fiction. Some hints of uncertainty in her handling of exotic elements in her first two books, Norse in *Ally Ally, Aster,* Gothic in *The Alder Tree,* may be traced not to immaturity but to inexperience in meeting the supposed needs of a youthful audience. Both books are imaginative, unconventional, disturbing, at times frightening.

Ally Ally, Aster came out of Halam's native North Country. In her third book, marking a big stride forward both structurally and imaginatively, she found a setting in her present home country. *King Death's Garden* is a story about Brighton in which the town, if not in its more familiar aspect, plays a leading role. It is also a story of abnormality in a (fairly) normal world. Maurice, the most unheroic hero, is a sickly and on the whole unattractive boy who seems to find some perverse satisfaction in the asthma and other "allergies" that set him apart from his peers. Having no friends and only an indifferent great aunt to look after him, he takes to spending his time in "King Death's Garden," the cemetery on to which his house joins. Here he forgets his disabilities and takes on a different, adventurous life shared with many ghosts, benign and sinister. The macabre elements in the story are nicely balanced by the glimpses of school life in which the lovely Pakistani Jasmin, whom Maurice adores hopelessly, and "Ghengis Khan," an appallingly active small girl, play important parts. Humour breaks out, not only in these scenes, but also in the character of Moth, a wayward spirit who haunts the graveyard.

After this strange and literally haunting story there seemed no obvious step forward for Halam. Instead she moved in a quite different direction. The linked novels *The Daymaker* and *Transformations* display an altogether higher level of creativity. The time is the future, how remote the reader is left to guess. Inland, the relatively organized area of the country, enjoys a rural economy offering a modest standard of living. Each small community has its covener, a woman trained to make the best of natural resources in the total absence of technology. In this she makes use of magic, in which her natural aptitude has been strengthened and directed by years of study at Hillen Coven. Machines of the past, which survive in remote places, are considered dangerously irrelevant by the coveners, and with violent hatred and fear by ordinary people. It is into this world that Zanne is born, a small, determined, obstinate girl and a prodigy in magic. She is an obvious choice for training at Hillen. There is one fatal flaw in her: she loves machines, their beauty, their efficiency, their potential for good. At a critical point in her training she takes a perilous journey, with another trainee for company, into the Outland in search of the Daymaker, a long-silenced power station which she hopes to bring back to life. The journey, with its hazards and wonders, is described with great power. Its crisis is most moving, the resolution intellectually and emotionally satisfying.

When the second story *Transformations* opens Zanne is older, but not much. She has been sent on a mission to put another "Maker" to death. The mission brings her to a remote community, Minith, in which the human rules promoted by Hillen Coven have been corrupted into puritanical dogma. Minith is dedicated to hard toil and little joy. A few exceptions to this rule lead Zanne to a grim explanation of the mystery. Minith lies under the influence of a Maker, and its leaking radioactivity is poisoning land and people. There are very serious implications underlying this exciting story of adventure, and story and message are powerfully reinforced by the vivid reality in which the scene and its people are drawn. There are some striking character studies, not least that of the indomitable little heroine.

Halam must be under the strongest pressure, inner and external, to follow the delightful Zanne along more of the dusty roads of Inland. It is to be hoped that she resists. Hers is too vital an art to be confined within the bounds of a series.

—Marcus Crouch

HALDANE, J(ohn) B(urdon) S(anderson). Indian. Born in Oxford, England, 5 November 1892; son of the scientist John Scott Haldane; brother of Naomi Mitchison, *q.v.*; moved to India, 1957; became citizen, 1961. Educated at Lynam's School, Oxford; Eton College, 1905–11; New College, Oxford, 1911–14, B.A. 1914, M.A. Served in the Black Watch in France, Iraq, and India, 1914–19:

Captain. Married 1) Charlotte Franken in 1926 (divorced 1945), one stepson; 2) Helen Spurway in 1945. Fellow of New College, 1919–22; Reader in Biochemistry, Cambridge University, 1923–33; geneticist, John Innes Horticultural Research Institution, London, 1927–36; Fullerian Professor of Physiology, Royal Institution, London, 1930–32; Professor of Genetics, 1933–36, and Weldon Professor of Biometry, 1936–57, University College, London; Research Professor, Indian Statistical Institute, Calcutta, 1957–61; worked for Council of Scientific and Industrial Research, Calcutta, 1961–62; Head of Genetics and Biometry, Government of Orissa, Bhubaneswar, 1962–64. President, Genetical Society, 1932–36; science correspondent, 1937–50, and chairman of the Editorial Board, 1940–50, *Daily Worker,* London (joined Communist Party, 1942; resigned, 1950). Recipient: Royal Society Darwin Medal, 1952; Royal Anthropological Institute Huxley Medal, 1956; Linnean Society Darwin-Wallace Medal, 1958; National Academy of Sciences Kimber Medal, 1961; Accademia dei Lincei Feltrinelli prize, 1961. D.Sc.: University of Groningen, 1946; Oxford University, 1961; Honorary Doctorate: University of Paris, 1949; LL.D.: University of Edinburgh, 1956. Honorary Fellow, New College, 1961. Corresponding member, Société de Biologie, 1928; Fellow, Royal Society, 1932; Chevalier, Legion of Honour, 1937; honorary member, Moscow Academy of Sciences, 1942; corresponding member, Deutsche Akademie der Wissenschaften, 1950, National Institute of Sciences of India, 1953, and Royal Danish Academy of Sciences, 1956. *Died 1 December 1964.*

PUBLICATIONS FOR CHILDREN

Fiction

My Friend Mr. Leakey, illustrated by Leonard Rosoman. London, Cresset Press, 1937; New York, Harper, 1938.

PUBLICATIONS FOR ADULTS

Novel

The Man with Two Memories. London, Merlin Press, 1976.

Other

Daedalus; or, Science and the Future: A Paper Read to the Heretics, Cambridge, on February 4th, 1923. London, Kegan Paul Trench Trubner, 1923; New York, Dutton, 1924.
Callinicus: A Defence of Chemical Warfare. London, Kegan Paul Trench Trubner, and New York, Dutton, 1925.
Animal Biology, with Julian Huxley. Oxford, Clarendon Press, 1927.
The Last Judgment: A Scientist's Vision of the Future of Man. New York and London, Harper, 1927.
Possible Worlds and Other Essays. London, Chatto and Windus, 1927; as *Possible Worlds and Other Papers,* New York, Harper, 1928.
Science and Ethics (lecture). London, C.A. Watts, 1928.
Enzymes. London, Longman, 1930; Cambridge, Massachusetts Institute of Technology Press, 1965.
Materialism (miscellany). London, Hodder and Stoughton, 1932.
The Causes of Evolution. London, Longman, and New York, Harper, 1932.
The Inequality of Man and Other Essays. London, Chatto and Windus, 1932; as *Science and Human Life,* New York, Harper, 1933.

Biology in Everyday Life, with John Randal Baker. London, Allen and Unwin, 1933.

Fact and Faith. London, C.A. Watts, 1934.

Human Biology and Politics. London, British Science Guild, 1934.

Science and the Supernatural: A Correspondence Between Harold Lunn and J.B.S. Haldane. London, Eyre and Spottiswoode, and New York, Sheed and Ward, 1935.

The Outlook of Science, edited by William Empson. London, Routledge, 1935.

Science and Well-Being, edited by William Empson. London, Routledge, 1935.

The Chemistry of the Individual (lecture). London, Oxford University Press, 1938.

The Marxist Philosophy. London, Birkbeck College, 1938.

A.R.P. [Air Raid Precautions]. London, Gollancz, 1938.

Heredity and Politics. London, Allen and Unwin, and New York, Norton, 1938.

How to Be Safe from Air Raids. London, Gollancz, 1938.

The Marxist Philosophy and the Sciences. London, Allen and Unwin, 1938; New York, Random House, 1939.

Science and Everyday Life. London, Lawrence and Wishart, 1939; New York, Macmillan, 1940.

Science and You. London, Fore Publications, 1939.

Keeping Cool and Other Essays. London, Chatto and Windus, 1940; as *Adventures of a Biologist,* New York, Harper, 1940.

Science in Peace and War. London, Lawrence and Wishart, 1940.

New Paths in Genetics. London, Allen and Unwin, 1941; New York, Harper, 1942.

Dialectical Materialism and Modern Science. London, Labour Monthly, 1942.

Why Professional Workers Should Be Communists. London, Communist Party, 1945.

A Banned Broadcast and Other Essays. London, Chatto and Windus, 1946.

Science Advances. London, Allen and Unwin, and New York, Macmillan, 1947.

What Is Life? New York, Boni and Gaer, 1947; London, Lindsay Drummond, 1949.

Is Evolution a Myth? A Debate Between Douglas Dewar, C. Merson Davies and J.B.S. Haldane. London, Paternoster Press, 1949.

Everything Has a History (essays). London, Allen and Unwin, 1951.

The Biochemistry of Genetics. London, Allen and Unwin, and New York, Macmillan, 1954.

The Argument from Animals to Men: An Examination of Its Validity for Anthropology (lecture). London, Royal Anthropological Institute, 1956.

Karl Pearson 1857–1957 (address). London, Biometrika Trustees, 1958.

The Unity and Diversity of Life (lecture). Delhi, Government of India Publications Division, 1958.

Science and Indian Culture. Calcutta, New Age Publishers, 1965.

Science and Life: Essays of a Rationalist. London, Pemberton-Barrie and Rockliff, 1968.

On Being the Right Size and Other Essays. Oxford, Oxford University Press, 1985.

Editor, *You and Heredity,* by Amram Scheinfeld and Morton D. Schweitzer. London, Chatto and Windus, 1939.

*

Critical Studies. *J.B.S.: The Life and Work of J.B.S. Haldane* by Ronald W. Clark, London, Hodder and Stoughton, 1968, New York, Coward McCann, 1969; *Haldane: The Life and Work of J.B.S. Haldane with Special Reference to India* by Krishna R. Dronamraju, Aberdeen, Aberdeen University Press, 1985.

* * *

It was a mathematician who wrote *Alice in Wonderland* a century ago. It was one of the greatest polymaths of our own time who wrote another of the best books for children ever published, *My Friend Mr. Leakey,* but who, unlike Lewis Carroll, left it at that. Perhaps in Carroll work and play were more sharply divided. All the zest and delight in the strangeness of the universe that illuminated J.B.S. Haldane's scientific research, all "the power to connect things in his mind in unexpected ways" noted in Sir Peter Medawar's preface to *J.B.S.* are at their height in this volume. The paperback edition is especially valuable for a preliminary paragraph in which the author's voice speaks as directly as it does in the narrative. "Professor Haldane has been used for experiments ever since he was three....Some of the things that happened to him are nearly as queer as the things that happen in this book. He thinks...science can be more exciting than magic...the nearest things he has to a dragon in his house are two she-newts, Flosshilda and Berenice....He is bald, weighs about 15 stone, and is fond of swimming." Children were still writing to him about the book in 1962, when he told one that "a green lizard 4 feet long" had trespassed into his Indian bathroom.

There are three minor stories in the volume: one about a man who gives rats biscuits containing powdered iron filings and then draws them by a powerful magnet into a pit, one about an anaconda fitted with status-symbolic golden teeth by his millionaire owner, and one about the naiad Miss Wandle with a magic shop in Wandsworth. All have startling freshness and ingenuity, but in the actual Mr. Leakey adventures invention tumbles over itself in glory. He is a real magician, a member of the International Congress of Sorcerers on the Brocken, and has his meals grilled by a small dragon (who wears asbestos boots when out of the fire) and served by an octopus. Strawberries are fetched from New Zealand by a jinn whose incautious colleagues get stomach ache from radio waves, find the lower air crowded with aeroplanes, and are pelted with shooting stars by angels if they fly too high. When Mr. Leakey gives a party he temporarily transforms his guests into human-sized versions of whatever they choose (a whimsical film star turned butterfly finds herself with goggly eyes and a proboscis). He travels on a magic carpet which "hovers stiffly" a foot above floors covered with books. He makes the author practise being invisible, which produces a (physiologically justified) "nasty giddy feeling." And so on. Nothing could be more characteristic of the man who wrote in his last years "the world is not only queerer than anyone has imagined but queerer than anyone *can* imagine."

—Renée Haynes

————

HALE, Kathleen. British. Born Broughton, Biggar, Lanarkshire, 24 May 1898. Educated at Manchester High School for Girls; Manchester School of Art; University College, Reading (scholar), 1916–18; Central School of Art, London; East Anglian School of Painting and Drawing. Married Douglas McClean in 1926 (died 1967); two sons. Artist: paintings exhibited at New English Arts Club, London Group, Grosvenor Galleries, Vermont Gallery, Warwick Public Library Gallery, Gallery Edward Harvane, New Grafton Gallery, Parkin Gallery; metal groups and pictures exhibited at Lefevre Galleries, Leicester Galleries, and Oxford Arts Centre; mural for Festival of Britain Schools Section, London, 1951; Orlando Ballet for Festival Gardens, London, 1951. Fellow, Society of Industrial Artists and Designers. O.B.E. (Officer, Order of the British

Empire), 1976. Address: Tod House, Forest Hill, Oxford, England.

PUBLICATIONS FOR CHILDREN (illustrated by the author)

Fiction

Orlando, The Marmalade Cat: A Camping Holiday. London, Country Life, and New York, Scribner, 1938.
Orlando's Evening Out. London, Penguin, 1941.
Orlando's Home Life. London, Penguin, 1942.
Orlando, The Marmalade Cat, Buys a Farm. London, Country Life, 1942.
Henrietta, The Faithful Hen. London and New York, Transatlantic Arts, 1943.
Orlando, The Marmalade Cat: His Silver Wedding. London, Country Life, 1944.
Orlando, The Marmalade Cat, Becomes a Doctor. London, Country Life, 1944.
Orlando's Invisible Pyjamas. London, Transatlantic Arts, 1947.
Orlando, The Marmalade Cat: A Trip Abroad. London, Country Life, 1949.
Orlando, The Marmalade Cat, Keeps a Dog. New York, Country Life, 1949.
Orlando, The Judge. London, Murray, 1950.
Orlando's Country Life: A Peep-Show Book. London, Chatto and Windus, 1950.
Puss-in-Boots: A Peep-Show Book. London, Chatto and Windus, 1951.
Orlando, The Marmalade Cat: A Seaside Holiday. London, Country Life, 1952.
Manda. London, Murray, 1952; New York, Coward McCann, 1953.
Orlando's Zoo. London, Murray, 1954.
Orlando, The Marmalade Cat: The Frisky Housewife. London, Country Life, 1956.
Orlando's Magic Carpet. London, Murray, 1958.
Orlando, The Marmalade Cat, Buys a Cottage. London, Country Life, 1963.
Orlando and the Three Graces. London, Murray, 1965.
Orlando, The Marmalade Cat, Goes to the Moon. London, Murray, 1968.
Orlando, The Marmalade Cat, and the Water Cats. London, Cape, 1972.
Henrietta's Magic Egg. London, Allen and Unwin, 1973.

*

Illustrator: *I Don't Mix Much with Fairies*, 1928, and *Plain Jane*, 1929, both by Mary R. Harrower; *Basil Seal Rides Again* by Evelyn Waugh, 1963.

Kathleen Hale comments:

I began writing my books for my own children. Then I wrote for children who were deprived of family love—especially those evacuated during the last war, torn from their parents and sent to sometimes unsympathetic homes. I've tried to keep the parent relationship, with love and understanding, alive for children who are denied it. I also wrote the books for *my own* rather cold childhood, thereby living out a warmth that was lacking when I was a child.

*   *   *

Kathleen Hale's numerous picture books about Orlando the Marmalade Cat provide an excellent example of the kind of book which is enjoyed most when it is read aloud to a child of the right age, and at the same time pored over with the fascinated alertness that brings to light new things to notice in the illustrations with every re-reading. For Orlando's adventures have come in books of varied shapes and sizes (including some very large ones); but invariably the text and the pictures have been carefully integrated so that the story-line carried by the words is echoed and often embellished by the richly inventive lithographs. As an instance of what the pictures can add to the words one might mention *Orlando's Evening Out,* where the "cots" in which the kittens are fast asleep are shown to be Master's slippers, while Master himself, with Orlando on one knee and Orlando's wife Grace on the other, is no more than a bald head hidden behind the *Daily Mews.* This story involves a visit to the circus in the course of which Orlando involuntarily becomes a star performer, and the orchestra ends up by playing "He's a Jolly Good Feline...." It will be seen that Kathleen Hale's verbal humour relies a good deal upon puns; sometimes these are not particularly good ones, but the word-play can at times be wittily original—Tinkle's coinage "Hot Wartle" must surely have passed into the accepted lingo of not a few families.

The humour hinges also on a complex interweaving of the humanised feline world of Orlando and his family and a richly eccentric human world. One of the very best of the stories is *Orlando's Invisible Pyjamas.* This starts with Orlando slipping out one snowy evening to take a dead mouse to the nightwatchman who is guarding a hole in the road (the kitten Tinkle sees him and says: "Hello Farver, you've grown a Mousetache!"); unfortunately Mr. Pusey, the nightwatchman, does not really appreciate Orlando's gift when it is deposited in his frying-pan alongside his sausages, and in the ensuing flurry Orlando's hind quarters are drenched with paraffin. The following day Tinkle finds an embarrassed Orlando hiding in the snowy pampas grass, "quite bald from the waist to the tip of his tail." His family smuggles him home camouflaged by a "Modesty Awning," and while the kittens and Mr. Pusey do their best to entertain him as he lies in bed, Grace knits him a pair of pyjamas which look just like real fur. Trouble comes only when he meets a dog and all his fur stands on end except his pyjamas—an incident entertainingly reinforced by the illustration. The later stories have tended to become increasingly fantastical and highly elaborated, but the series as a whole offers a wealth of enjoyment—ideal, one would say, for the intelligent six-year-old, but capable of being appreciated on some level at almost any age from four to eight.

—Frank Whitehead

———

HALL, Aylmer. Pseudonym for Norah Eleanor Lyle Hall, née Cummins. British. Born in Surrey, 24 April 1914. Educated at Clifton High School, Bristol, 1927–32; St. Hugh's College, Oxford, 1932–35, B.A. (honours) in modern languages 1935. Married Robert Aylmer Hall in 1938; one son and one daughter. Personal assistant to the Secretary, New Commonwealth Institute, London, 1936; assistant press librarian, Royal Institute of International Affairs, London, 1937–39; chief press librarian in Research Division, Ministry of Information, London, 1939–40. Agent: Winant Towers Ltd., 45–47 Clerkenwell Green, London ECIR 0HT. Address: 28 Burghley Road, London S.W. 19, England.

PUBLICATIONS FOR CHILDREN

Fiction

The Mystery of Torland Manor, illustrated by Nat Long. London,

Harrap, 1952.

The Admiral's Secret. London, Harrap, 1953.

The K.F. Conspiracy, illustrated by R.C.W. Meade. London, Harrap, 1955.

The Sword of Glendower, illustrated by Janet Duchesne. London, Methuen, 1960; as *The Search for Lancelot's Sword,* New York, Criterion, 1962.

The Devilish Plot, illustrated by John Hodder. London, Hart Davis, 1965.

The Tyrant King: A London Adventure. London, London Transport Board, 1967.

The Marked Man. London, Hart Davis, 1967.

Colonel Bull's Inheritance. London, Macmillan, 1968; New York, Meredith Press, 1969.

Beware of Moonlight. London, Macmillan, 1969; New York, Nelson, 1970.

The Minstrel Boy. London, Macmillan, 1970.

PUBLICATIONS FOR ADULTS

Other

Editor (as N. Hall), *The Chronology of the Second World War.* London, Royal Institute of International Affairs, 1947.

*

Aylmer Hall comments:

The first five books by "Aylmer Hall" were written at the instigation ct, and in collaboration with, my husband, as serial stories for our small son at his preparatory school. Later, when my husband's job became too demanding, I was a solo performer with a very good and helpful trainer. The last books, all set in Ireland, from which my family come, were inspired by our acquiring a country refuge in West Cork, but their historical setting has been very carefully prepared.

*   *   *   .

Aylmer Hall's earlier books have perhaps too "dated" a quality about them for the modern taste: the recent past of the immediately post-war years seems to belong to the Boys' Own era much more than to the present day. Intrepid public-schoolboys get mixed up in murky political criminality and the Great British Virtues prevail, while the settings, though strongly evoked, are redolent of much that has been popular schoolboy diet before.

For all that, Aylmer Hall is much more than just another writer in a tired tradition. In spite of the stereotyped upper-middle-class heroes with their public-school code there is a sensitively considered dimension of anxiety and self-doubt running through. Far from intrepid, in fact, her heroes are capable of almost numbing fear. If they succeed it is not without near-miss moments of failure.

Michael Mannering in *The Admiral's Secret,* tangling with sinister ex-Nazi opportunists, moves with trepidation and frequent lapses of that presence of mind so essential in your archetypal schoolboy hero. Later, in *The K.F. Conspiracy,* though older and more assured, when he finds himself in the thick of a mittel-European border war, the first elation quickly gives way to a sense of personal inadequacy, fear, and exhaustion.

The whole register of the recent past has an air of theatricality. This may be one reason why the more remote historical romances appear rather less mannered. In *Colonel Bull's Inheritance* Hall evokes the time and place of the West of Ireland in the 18th century in a tightly constructed plot in which the boy-hero finds himself caught in the crossfire of no less than four opposing parties. This is indeed a very workmanlike novel, for the complicated elements of

plot are cleverly mixed and balanced in a story that never for a moment loses its line and clarity. Where the earlier novels would tie themselves in knots but for the explanatory set speeches rather ingenuously introduced from time to time, in the later novels the dialogue springs naturally from character and incident and the plots unfold with subtle ease.

In the earlier books the commitment was to a generalised ethic: the heroes survived because of their fidelity to a code of conduct. Yet in working through their predicaments the code took on a deeply personal relevance. In her later books, however, codes and causes are shown to be as hollow as the strutting attitudes they beget. The only values to have any currency are those based on mutual love and respect. Sean Daly in *The Minstrel Boy* is surrounded by charismatic characters whose personal metals are found weakened under stress, while his own humbler creed stands the test of betrayal, starvation, and torture. The anchor of Sean's faith is his growing love for Margaret. Hall's concern now is with the inescapable personal dimension in moral decision.

—Myles McDowell

———

HALL, Lynn. American. Born in Lombard, Illinois, 9 November 1937. Educated at schools in Iowa. Married Dean Green in 1960 (divorced 1961). Secretary, Fort Worth, Texas, 1955–57; veterinarian's assistant, Des Moines, Iowa, 1957–66; copywriter, Ambro Advertising Agency, Des Moines, 1966–69. Since 1969 full-time writer. Recipient: Boston *Globe-Horn Book* award, 1981. Address: Touchwood, Route 2, Elkader, Iowa 52043, U.S.A.

PUBLICATIONS FOR CHILDREN

Fiction

The Shy Ones, illustrated by Greta Elgaard. Chicago, Follett, 1967.

The Secret of Stonehouse, illustrated by Joseph Cellini. Chicago, Follett, 1968.

Ride a Wild Dream, illustrated by George Roth. Chicago, Follett, 1969.

Too Near the Sun, illustrated by Stefan Martin. Chicago, Follett, 1970.

Gently Touch the Milkweed, illustrated by Rod Ruth. Chicago, Follett, 1970.

A Horse Called Dragon, illustrated by Joseph Cellini. Chicago, Follett, 1971; as *Wild Mustang,* New York, Scholastic, n.d.

Sticks and Stones, illustrated by Milton Glaser. Chicago, Follett, 1972.

The Famous Battle of Bravery Creek, illustrated by Herman Vestal. Champaign, Illinois, Garrard, 1972.

Dog Stories, illustrated by Joseph Cellini. Chicago, Follett, 1972.

The Siege of Silent Henry. Chicago, Follett, 1972.

Flash, Dog of Old Egypt, illustrated by Taylor Oughton. Champaign, Illinois, Garrard, 1973.

Barry, The Bravest St. Bernard, illustrated by Gil Cohen. Champaign, Illinois, Garrard, 1973.

Riff, Remember. Chicago, Follett, 1973.

To Catch a Tartar, illustrated by Joseph Cellini. Chicago, Follett, 1973.

Troublemaker, illustrated by Joseph Cellini. Chicago, Follett, 1974.

Bob, Watchdog of the River, illustrated by Taylor Oughton. Champaign, Illinois, Garrard, 1974.

Stray, illustrated by Joseph Cellini.   Chicago, Follett, 1974.

New Day for Dragon, illustrated by Joseph Cellini.   Chicago, Follett, 1975.

Captain, Canada's Flying Pony, illustrated by Tran Mawicke. Champaign, Illinois, Garrard, 1976.

Flowers of Anger, illustrated by Joseph Cellini.   Chicago, Follett, 1976.

Owney, The Traveling Dog, illustrated by Barbara Erikson.   Champaign, Illinois, Garrard, 1977.

Dragon Defiant, illustrated by Joseph Cellini.   Chicago, Follett, 1977.

Shadows, illustrated by Joseph Cellini.   Chicago, Follett, 1977.

The Mystery of Pony Hollow, illustrated by Ruth Sanderson.   Champaign, Illinois, Garrard, 1978.

The Mystery of the Lost and Found Hound, illustrated by Alan Daniel.   Champaign, Illinois, Garrard, 1979.

The Mystery of the Schoolhouse Dog, illustrated by William Hutchinson.   Champaign, Illinois, Garrard, 1979.

Dog of the Bondi Castle, illustrated by Michael Mariano.   Chicago, Follett, 1979.

The Whispered Horse.   Chicago, Follett, 1979.

The Leaving, illustrated by Lloyd Bloom.   New York, Scribner, 1980.

The Mystery of the Stubborn Old Man.   Champaign, Illinois, Garrard, 1980.

The Mystery of the Plum Park Pony, illustrated by Alan Daniel. Champaign, Illinois, Garrard, 1980.

Dragon's Delight.   Chicago, Follett, 1981.

The Haunting of the Green Bird, illustrated by David Cunningham. Chicago, Follett, 1981.

The Disappearing Grandad, illustrated by William Jefferson. Chicago, Follett, 1981.

The Mysterious Moortown Bridge, illustrated by Ruth Sanderson. Chicago, Follett, 1981.

The Ghost of the Great River Inn, illustrated by Allen Davis. Chicago, Follett, 1981.

The Horse Trader, illustrated by Ted Lewin.   New York, Scribner, 1981.

The Mystery of the Caramel Cat, illustrated by Ruth Sanderson. Champaign, Illinois, Garrard, 1981.

Danza!, illustrated by Sandra Rabinowitz.   New York, Scribner, 1981.

Half the Battle.   New York, Scribner, 1982.

Tin Can Tucker, illustrated by Ruth Sanderson.   New York, Scribner, 1982.

Megan's Mare.   New York, Scribner, 1983.

Denison's Daughter.   New York, Scribner, 1983.

The Mystery of Pony Hollow Panda, illustrated by William Hutchinson.   Champaign, Illinois, Garrard, 1983.

Uphill All the Way.   New York, Scribner, 1984.

The Boy in the Off-White Hat.   New York, Scribner, 1984.

The Something-Special Horse, illustrated by Sandra Rabinowitz. New York, Scribner, 1985.

The Giver.   New York, Scribner, 1985; London, Macmillan, 1987.

Just One Friend.   New York, Scribner, 1985.

Mrs. Portree's Pony.   New York, Scribner, 1986.

If Winter Comes.   New York, Scribner, 1986; London, Viking Kestrel, 1987.

Danger Dog.   New York, Scribner, 1986.

The Solitary.   New York, Scribner, 1986; London, Viking, 1988.

Letting Go.   New York, Scribner, 1987.

In Trouble Again, Zelda Hammersmith?, illustrated by Joe Yakovetic.   San Diego, Harcourt Brace, 1987.

Ride a Dark Horse.   New York, Morrow, 1987.

Flyaway.   New York, Scribner, 1987.

The Secret Life of Dagmar Schultz.   New York, Scribner, 1988.

Zelda Strikes Again!   San Diego, Harcourt Brace, 1988.

A Killing Freeze.   New York, Morrow, 1988.

Murder at the Spaniel Show.   New York, Scribner, 1988.

Where Have All the Tigers Gone?   New York, Scribner, 1988.

Dagmar Schultz and the Powers of Darkness.   New York, Scribner, 1989.

Other

Kids and Dog Shows.   Chicago, Follett, 1975.

Careers for Dog Lovers.   Chicago, Follett, 1978.

Tazo and Me, photographs by Jan Hall.   New York, Scribner, 1985.

*

Manuscript Collection: Kerlan Collection, University of Minnesota, Minneapolis.

Lynn Hall comments:

Since childhood, horses and dogs have been the central love of my life. I've tried to share this love with my readers, through my books.

*   *   *

Lynn Hall's early writing career focused on dog and horse stories. Later, however, she widened her horizons to develop stories that display her skills as a keen interpreter of young people who are making important discoveries about themselves or those around them.

Hall's earliest works are, for the most part, simple stories of courageous or otherwise memorable dog and horse protagonists. While many of these are flawed by contrived elements and excess sentimentality, some, such as *Riff, Remember,* about a Borzoi dog who tracks down the murderer of a boy who had befriended him, and *A Horse Called Dragon* (first of a four-book series), about a sturdy Mexican wild horse who becomes a founding sire of the Ponies of America breed, rise above such weakness to become above average examples of their genre.

Even when Hall turns to people-centered stories, animals are often nearby. Her easy mysteries, which frequently have a ghostly element running through them, often feature young girls whose involvement with a horse or dog is central to solving a conflict. In *The Mystery of Pony Hollow* Sarah is riding her newly acquired pony when she discovers an old cabin that holds a pony's restless ghost. In *The Mystery of the Caramel Cat,* which briefly harks back to a historical setting, a present-day child discovers a mysterious cat which she learns is a ghost restless over its betrayal of fugitives on the underground railroad.

Danza!, one of Hall's horse stories, is perhaps her finest blend of animal story and character study. Lyrical prose and careful development shape this memorable story of a Puerto Rican boy who comes to manhood as he watches the beloved colt he almost killed mature into a champion Paso Fino stallion. Hall's integration of plot, style, and characterization is consummate, and it isn't only horse story fans who will warm to her tale.

Hall's most mature work—and the best evidence of her growth as a writer—is found in her stories of adolescents in the process of hard-won self-understanding. Although animals are represented and sometimes important, the emphasis is decidedly upon people. The protagonists are diverse, but share a common introspective element. They are loners or are lonely, at odds with the shortcomings of themselves or those around them. As a result there is a persistent melancholy underlying much of Hall's fiction, as well as a strong sense of compassion and concern for others.

In *Sticks and Stones,* one of Hall's earliest young adult novels, she tackles the controversial topic of homosexuality. The story involves a boy named Tom Naylor who discovers that his friendship with a young man discharged from the Air Force on charges of homosexuality leads to a false assumption that he too is gay. Although the story has a somewhat abrupt finish, the depiction of the damage done by ignorance and prejudice is quite credible and will have its intended thought-provoking effect on readers.

The Leaving is one of the author's outstanding works. The setting is Iowa, and the protagonist is a girl named Roxanne who upon graduation decides to leave the farm she loves for a life in the city. While Roxanne's impending departure provides the story's surface structure, what emerges is an acute picture of a family whose physical togetherness is a thin cover for a loveless marriage and all of its repercussions.

Another excellent young adult story by Hall is *Just One Friend.* Hall has managed to create an eminently credible character in Dory Kjellings, an unattractive, mentally slow girl from a deprived, unresponsive family. Despite the many strikes against her, Dory still struggles to better herself and values school as the key to success and independence. But after three years in a special education setting, she finds the idea of being mainstreamed with other students terrifying.

Hall's willingness to take on controversial topics has had mixed success. *The Boy in the Off-White Hat* focuses on child sexual abuse. In it a 13-year-old girl named Skeeter learns that the little boy she babysits is being sexually molested by his mother's new boyfriend. In its effort to convey information about sexual abuse, the story becomes an overly expository case study, but it may prompt healthy discussion on ways to avoid the problems faced by the characters in the book.

The threat of nuclear attack hangs heavy over the characters in *If Winter Comes.* An international political confrontation makes a nuclear attack seem imminent. A suburban Chicago teenager and her boyfriend spend a weekend in terror that everything they experience may be the last time for them.

In a departure from heavy realism and somber self-searching, several of Hall's most recent works follow a humorous route. *The Secret Life of Dagmar Schultz* is a light comedy about a girl who invents a boyfriend and then must contend with an ever-growing web of lies. And two books about an impetuous heroine named Zelda Hammersmith target middle-grade readers for laughs. *In Trouble Again, Zelda Hammersmith?* and *Zelda Strikes Again!* present episodic stories that show the amusing and sometimes disastrous occurrences that befall a heroine who has a habit of leaping before she looks. Hall has not yet reached her stride as a writer of comedy. Some of her scenes are thoroughly amusing, while others strain and fall flat. But these books represent a stretch for Hall, and one must respect her efforts to strike out in a new direction.

Hall's prolific output in recent years has earned her a solid place in the children's book field, with her stories about young adults—and occasionally animals—emerging as her strongest suit.

—Denise Murcko Wilms

HALLARD, Peter. See **CATHERALL, Arthur.**

HAMILTON, Virginia (Esther). American. Born in Yellow Springs, Ohio, 12 March 1936. Educated at Antioch College, Yellow Springs, 1952–55, B.A. 1955; Ohio State University, Columbus,

1957–58; New School for Social Research, New York. Married Arnold Adoff, *q.v.,* in 1960; one daughter and one son. Whittall Lecturer, Library of Congress, Washington, D.C., 1975; Visiting Professor, Queens College, Flushing, New York, 1986–87. Recipient: Mystery Writers of America Edgar Allan Poe award, 1969; Boston *Globe-Horn Book* award, 1974, 1983, 1988; National Book award, 1975; American Library Association Newbery Medal, 1975, and Coretta Scott King award, 1983, 1986; Children's Rights Workshop Other award, 1986. Agent: Dorothy Markinko, McIntosh and Otis Inc., 310 Madison Avenue, New York, New York 10017. Address: Box 293, Yellow Springs, Ohio 45387, U.S.A.

PUBLICATIONS FOR CHILDREN

Fiction

Zeely, illustrated by Symeon Shimin.   New York, Macmillan, 1967.
The House of Dies Drear, illustrated by Eros Keith.   New York, Macmillan, 1968.
The Time-Ago Tales of Jahdu, illustrated by Nonny Hogrogian.   New York, Macmillan, 1969.
The Planet of Junior Brown.   New York, Macmillan, 1971; London, Gollancz, 1987.
Time-Ago Lost: More Tales of Jahdu, illustrated by Ray Prather.   New York, Macmillan, 1973.
M.C. Higgins, The Great.   New York, Macmillan, 1974; London, Hamish Hamilton, 1975.
Arilla Sun Down.   New York, Greenwillow, 1976; London, Hamish Hamilton, 1977.
Justice and Her Brothers.   New York, Greenwillow, 1978; London, Hamish Hamilton, 1979.
Dustland.   New York, Greenwillow, and London, MacRae, 1980.
Jahdu, illustrated by Jerry Pinkney.   New York, Greenwillow, 1980.
The Gathering.   New York, Greenwillow, and London, MacRae, 1981.
Sweet Whispers, Brother Rush.   New York, Philomel, 1982; London, Walker, 1987.
The Magical Adventures of Pretty Pearl.   New York, Harper, 1983.
Willie Bea and the Time the Martians Landed.   New York, Greenwillow, 1983.
A Little Love.   New York, Philomel, 1984; London, Gollancz, 1985.
Junius over Far.   New York, Harper, 1985.
A White Romance.   New York, Philomel, 1987; London, Gollancz, 1988.
The Mystery of Drear House.   New York, Greenwillow, 1987.

Other

W.E.B. Du Bois: A Biography.   New York, Crowell, 1972.
Paul Robeson: The Life and Times of a Free Black Man.   New York, Harper, 1974.
The People Could Fly: American Black Folk Tales, illustrated by Leo and Diane Dillon.   New York, Knopf, 1985; London, Walker, 1986.
Anthony Burns: The Defeat and Triumph of a Fugitive Slave.   New York, Knopf, 1988.
In the Beginning: Creation Stories from Around the World, illustrated by Barry Moser.   San Diego, Harcourt Brace, 1988.

Editor, *The Writings of W.E.B. Du Bois.*   New York, Crowell, 1975.

PUBLICATIONS FOR ADULTS

Other

Illusion and Reality (lecture).   Washington, D.C., Library of

Congress, 1976.

Editor, *Cambodians in Thailand: People on the Edge,* with Koula Hadjipanicolaou. Washington, D.C., U.S. Committee for Refugees, 1985.

*

Critical Study: *Virginia Hamilton: Ohio Explorer in the World of Imagination* by Marilyn F. Apseloff, Columbus, State Library of Ohio, 1979.

Virginia Hamilton comments:

The writing of books encompasses the whole of my life, although it isn't serious business for me in the sense that I need discuss it solemnly every moment. After all, writing has to be a part-time occupation. More than any other serious profession, it feeds and grows on living and living is what a writer must do full-time. Living full-time takes more energy and discipline than any writing I know of. It demands that one not let herself become uninvolved with life; or forget or fear to look at it.

The making of any fiction for me is foremost a self-viewing that becomes a force for life and living. The fiction becomes greater than the sum of fact, memory, and imagination that create it. At the last, it stands independent from the self and is often more mysterious than anything the writer of it may have experienced herself.

That is why I so often say that life is continuous, going in a circle. And everyone who is black who has lived and those now living have something to say to me and have something to do with the person I am. It must be that all people who have lived and those now living hold our common knowledge as humans and make us one people. That is why, although I generally write of the black experience, I place no restriction on whom or what kind of people I may write about. Writers must remain free to write as readers must have freedom of choice in order to read. Writing has to be fun for me, the writer, in the hopes that readers will respond to it with enthusiasm. Therein is an interchange of thought and feeling which has a way of bringing us together in communication.

*   *   *

Virginia Hamilton has heightened the standards for children's literature as few other authors have. She does not address children so much as she explores with them, sometimes ahead of them, the full possibilities of imagination. Even her farthest flung thoughts, however, are leashed to the craft of writing. There is clearly a hard-worked development from the first two books, which have some stiffness of language and incident, to later novels that weave fantastic characters and situations with credible assurance.

The early *Zeely* and *The House of Dies Drear* leave indelible flashing impressions—one of a six-and-a-half-foot swine shepherdess descended from African royalty and the other of an ancient, indomitable descendent of slaves who lives in a secret cavern and guards a treasure inherited from a wealthy abolitionist. The second book is better built but still does not fully break surface formality to the power underneath. Then, in *The Time-Ago Tales of Jahdu,* Hamilton frees her words into strong, rhythmic patterns that can follow her roving imagination.

The Planet of Junior Brown unites the graceful language of Jahdu with the sustained structure of imaginative fiction. The uncanny figure of Junior Brown—hugely fat, talented, and unhappy—revolves in his own troubled universe while strong, resourceful, street-wise Buddy swirls around him, caring. One has too much mother, the other none. Little by little their props fall. The two boys' peaceful haven, a concealed school closet in which the janitor has built a simulated solar system that lights up, is threatened and must be

dissembled. Their truancy is discovered. Junior's piano teacher slips from strangeness to madness, dragging Junior with her into disturbing hallucinations. Who can Buddy trust to help Junior in New York City? So many have already contributed to Junior's problems, and so many could seal his psychological doom in the guise of help. Coming to Junior's rescue, Buddy develops his own philosophy of leadership in the underground "planets" established by older homeless boys to take care of younger ones. At first he teaches, along with techniques of survival, "The highest law is to learn to live for yourself." By the end of the book Buddy has found a new trust. "We are together…because we have to learn to live for each other." Supporting such a resolution are richly realized characterizations and settings.

As *The Planet* is a city book, quick in pace, *M.C. Higgins, The Great* is a country book, with slow-gathering but inevitable power, natural imagery, and homemade music. M.C. Higgins is born of the hills and hardship. Every aspect of living requires enormous physical effort. But there are rewards: the knowledge of Sarah's Mountain, passed to the eldest son for generations; the abiding love of family. M.C. has passed all the land's tests of toughness but must face the outside threat of intruders upon the land—a stripminer's spoil heap that could bury his cabin any time, a music collector who takes his mother's voice on tapes in exchange for empty hints of help, a young stranger who tempts M.C.'s heart to follow her. The pictures and the relationships and the sounds that fit together here deepen in perspective with each reading. There is a sure direction that never slips into contrivance, an opening and closure of another world that one wants to visit—a unique place where six-fingered, red-haired blacks have made a vegetable farming commune stretched over with a rope web where children can climb and play. And they are as believable as the strength M.C. finds in himself, his family, his friends, his mountain.

Following these two touchstone titles, Hamilton experimented variously in both style and genre. *Arilla Sun Down,* about a black girl groping her way toward identity in a family that tugs strongly in different directions, is a first-person, present-tense narrative with a stream-of-consciousness flow. Impressionistic child language floats among half-buried images and snatches of adult conversation remembered piecemeal. The effect is vivid but sometimes amorphous, a problem that surfaces again later in the Justice science-fiction trilogy. These three books move from a realistic setting, which explains the mind control common to Justice, her twin brothers, and a friend, through their journey into a future wasteland peopled with bizarre creatures, to their final discovery of a utopian city which their combined powers help preserve. The concepts are intriguing but abstractly developed, and the situations are not always saved from confusion by the appearance of colorful fiction characters.

Sweet Whispers, Brother Rush is, on the other hand, one of Hamilton's most successful books. It ventures once again into new ways of exploring the human spirit—literally, in this case, since one of the three principal characters is a ghost. Brother Rush, who suffered painfully from porphyria and died in a car accident, has materialized during the final illness of his retarded 17-year-old nephew, Dabney, also porphyric. Rush first appears to Dab's sister Tree, the narrator. Tree enters Rush's time to look back at her own childhood and the earlier days of her mother, M'Vy, who abused Dab out of ignorance and frustration and who now struggles to make a living as a practical nurse away from home for weeks at a time. M'Vy has kept the children as best she can—alone, close, and completely unaware of their past. Dab's death ends that, bringing both shattering sorrow and revelation to 14-year-old Tree. The story is minutely and vividly detailed, with no jarring of continuity between scenes of present time and past. Each character takes shape from both current behavior and influential aspects of his or her background. This interplay of past and present is one of the most skillful aspects of the book; another is the emotional portraiture of several distinctive, empathetic individuals bared by crisis. The language is a blend of lilting black dialogue and the author's own peculiarly musical style.

The joining of the traditional and the innovative to make strong new literary structures is fundamental to all of Hamilton's work. Her award-winning books of folklore and mythology, *The People Could Fly: American Black Folk Tales* and *In the Beginning: Creation Stories from Around the World,* are evidence of an abiding interest that reveals itself in her fiction. *The Magical Adventures of Pretty Pearl* blends mythology and history with a god-child's wandering from Mount Kenya, where she lived with her brother John de Conquer, down through the world and woods of the American South, into hiding with black and Cherokee refugees, into the company of the giant hero John Henry himself. It is a sprawling work, memorable more for intense scenes than for any taut plot progression, but the story-within-story framework itself is ingeniously conceived. In *Anthony Burns: The Defeat and Triumph of a Fugitive Slave,* Hamilton has done a masterly job of melding historical fact with fictional characterization to the enhancement of both. She alternates between the tense courtroom scenes of a well-documented trial in which Burns is tried as a runaway slave and fictionalized recollections of his youth. Mystery is another convention that Hamilton uses unconventionally—in the Caribbean-set *Junius over Far,* for instance; in *Willie Bea and the Time the Martians Landed,* about a family affected by Orson Welles's famous broadcast on Halloween of 1938; and, more obviously, in *The Mystery of Drear House,* a somewhat clumsy sequel to *The House of Dies Drear.*

Not only in craft, but also in content, Hamilton is concerned with recharging old ways with new currents. *A Little Love,* a novel that dignifies the term teenage romance, casts four black characters so three-dimensionally that a reader will sense their presence almost physically. A slow, heavyset teenager with artistic hands and a flair for work in her food-service major at a vocational high school, Sheema becomes obsessed by the thought of finding her father, who left home the day her mother died in Sheema's childbirth. Sheema's boyfriend Forrest strongly supports her through difficult days at school and home, where the grandparents who have raised her seem to be deserting her now—her grandfather increasingly absent from home, her grandmother increasingly absentminded. The parallel relationships between the young people and the old are touchingly detailed as both couples find new closeness through Sheema's rite of passage, a trip south with Forrest to confront her father. This book reaffirms the strength of ordinary people who are figuratively and sometimes literally hungry for love. The attentive development, rhythmic narrative in black English, and vivid scenes extend Hamilton's range to romance. *A White Romance* portrays youngsters who, having neither tradition nor even family, attempt to create both through friendship and courtship—and sometimes illusory escape into drugs.

From romance to mystery, from short story to anthology to biography, from the realistic to the fantastic, Hamilton has crossed boundaries of time, space, style, and genre. Inventive minds cannot be confined. Of course, any writer so aesthetically ambitious risks uneven effects, but Hamilton's successes doubly repay our attention to her total body of work. There are symbols in each of Hamilton's books that could be discussed at length, but the importance of her writing rests on more than symbolism or sounding the black experience. She has taken artistic integrity as far as it will go, beyond thought of popular reading, but with much thought to communicating. This is a tradition which is accepted in adult literature and which must be accepted in children's literature if it is to be considered a true art form. With plenty of books that fit easily, there must be that occasional book that grows the mind a size larger.

—Betsy Hearne

HANSEN, Joyce. American. Born in New York City, 18 October 1942. Educated at Pace University, New York, B.A. in English 1972; New York University, M.A. in English Education 1978. Married to Matthew Nrelson. Since 1973 English teacher, New York; since 1987 Mentor, Empire State College, Brooklyn, New York. Address: c/o Walker and Co., 720 Fifth Avenue, New York, New York 10019, U.S.A.

PUBLICATIONS FOR CHILDREN

Fiction

The Gift-Giver. Boston, Houghton Mifflin, 1980.
Home Boy. Boston, Houghton Mifflin, 1982.
Which Way Freedom? New York, Walker, 1986.
Yellowbird and Me. Boston, Houghton Mifflin, 1986.
Out from This Place. New York, Walker, 1988.

*

Joyce Hansen comments:

I write realistic fiction about contemporary children. The setting for my three contemporary novels is New York City. I also write historical fiction for young people. My two historical novels—*Which Way Freedom?* and *Out from This Place*—are set during the American Civil War and Reconstruction.

* * *

Joyce Hansen has a gift for interweaving socio-political themes with problems of personality. In her novels about family vulnerability in American inner cities, she draws upon autobiographical material and her knowledge of West Indian immigrants in New York. *The Gift-Giver* and its sequel *Yellowbird and Me* are about youngsters in the Bronx; *Home Boy* alternates between a Caribbean setting and a chaotic urban environment. Hansen's two fictionalized treatments of the Civil War, *Which Way Freedom?* and *Out from This Place,* reflect the scholarly advances of revisionist historians.

Family dispersion is emphasized in the inner city stories—a diffusion of parents and children resulting from problems of poverty, substandard housing, and job insecurity. Ghetto schools come under particular scrutiny, although Hansen does not target the school as a unique social failure. She places the shortcomings of the school within the larger context of urban disintegration. This thematic content makes her stories issue-oriented in the sense that they are life-oriented; they do not gloss over the impact of public policies on the daily struggles of the urban poor.

Hansen is a creative storyteller who builds her cosmopolitan settings in ways that shed light on character motivation. She lets Doris, a 10-year-old, narrate *The Gift-Giver.* This strategy allows the author to reveal indirectly the child's resentment toward overprotective parents. Doris supplies clues that explain parental anxieties and the other personal and environmental conditions that disrupt family life. The novel's structure is episodic, but the author's unmistakable tie with her characters produces its own dramatic power.

Hansen counterbalances characterizations of Doris and her friend Amir. Major themes come into focus primarily through the actions of Amir, while a strong sense of verisimilitude is felt through her child narrator. Amir is a somewhat mysterious figure and serves as a symbol of Hansen's positive values: the importance of family, belief in self, a determination to progress and act responsibly. On the other hand Doris represents the immaturities of a normal 10-year-old. By placing her in the narrator role, Hansen keeps her astute observations of childhood in the foreground, and lets her idealism emerge symbolically and unobtrusively.

Home Boy juxtaposes Caribbean and New York settings and their impact upon a father-son relationship. The author uses a different technique in this narrative: fast cinematic intercuts from one time frame to another. This fracturing of time parallels the alienation of the central characters as their long-held American Dream is rapidly extinguished.

Early chapters set up the basic dimensions of the family's hardships in New York. A deeper character development occurs when Hansen backtracks to St. Cruz Island—to the boyish antics of young Marcus and his friends, the peace-making efforts of a grandmother, the foolishness of a well-meaning but thoroughly de-Africanized teacher. Details of setting are sometimes used to highlight frustration, as when Marcus and his father Rudy meet and a painful awkwardness engulfs them: "Rudy gulped down his beer and they let the television absorb their discomfort."

The two historical novels, *Which Way Freedom?* and *Out from This Place,* are organized around a group of epigraphs drawn from historical studies and documents. These quotations often foretell what the slave protagonists, Obidiah and Easter, will encounter as they experience the American Civil War. For example, a Northern general's actual statement to his Southern captives hints at the Northern betrayal of blacks that the fictional slaves will ultimately face: "Not only will we [the Union Army] abstain from all interferences with your slaves, but we will, with an iron hand, crush any attempt at insurrection on their part."

Besides using this documentary method of linking history and the inventions of fiction, Hansen constructs a plot that exposes the workings of the plantation system. She draws a convincing picture of how slaves had limited access to information and had to improvise accordingly. She reveals the necessity of ever-evolving and supportive slave networks.

Whether Hansen aims to evoke the life and times of a 20th-century Northern city or a 19th-century Southern plantation, she has such a firm grasp of regional and historical detail that she builds characterization spontaneously from that base. This combination of background knowledge and novelistic technique accounts for her success in reconstructing the realities of black experience.

—Donnarae MacCann

HARDCASTLE, Michael. Also writes as David Clark. British. Born in Huddersfield, Yorkshire, 6 February 1933. Educated at schools in Huddersfield. Served in the Royal Army Educational Corps, 1951–56. Newspaper reporter, 1956–59; literary editor, Bristol *Evening Post,* 1959–65; chief feature writer, Liverpool *Daily Post,* 1965–67. Since 1967 freelance writer. M.B.E. (Member, Order of the British Empire), 1988. Address: 17 Molescroft Park, Beverley, North Humberside HU17 7EB, England.

<small>PUBLICATIONS FOR CHILDREN</small>

Fiction

Soccer Is Also a Game. London, Heinemann, 1966; as *Soccer Comes First,* London, Dragon, 1971.
Redcap. London, Collins, 1967.
Shoot on Sight, London, Heinemann, 1967.
Aim for the Flag. London, Heinemann, 1967; Chicago, Follett, 1969.
The Chasing Game. London, Heinemann, 1968; revised edition, Southport, Lancashire, Hardcastle, 1976.

Goal, illustrated by James Hunt. London, Heinemann, 1969.
Dive to Danger, illustrated by Richard Kennedy. London, Benn, 1969.
Shilling a Mile, illustrated by Richard Kennedy. London, Benn, 1969; as *Walk for Us,* n.d.
Stop That Car!, illustrated by Richard Kennedy. London, Benn, 1970.
Reds and Blues, illustrated by Richard Kennedy. London, Benn, 1970.
The Hidden Enemy. London, Epworth Press, 1970; revised edition, as *Hidden Enemy,* Southport, Lancashire, Hardcastle, 1976.
Strike!, illustrated by Richard Kennedy. London, Benn, 1970.
Smashing!, illustrated by Richard Kennedy. London, Benn, 1970.
Don't Tell Me What to Do. London, Heinemann, 1970.
Come and Get Me, illustrated by Richard Kennedy. London, Benn, 1971.
Live in the Sky, illustrated by Richard Kennedy. London, Benn, 1971.
Shelter, illustrated by Richard Kennedy. London, Benn, 1971.
A Load of Trouble, illustrated by Richard Kennedy. London, Benn, 1971.
Blood Money, illustrated by Richard Kennedy. London, Benn, 1971.
It Wasn't Me, illustrated by Richard Kennedy. London, Benn, 1971.
In the Net, illustrated by Trevor Stubley. London, Methuen, 1971.
Playing Ball. London, Heinemann, 1972.
Goals in the Air. London, Heinemann, 1972.
Island Magic. London, Heinemann, 1973.
United!, illustrated by Trevor Stubley. London, Methuen, 1973.
Away from Home, illustrated by Trevor Stubley. London, Methuen, 1974.
Free Kick, illustrated by Trevor Stubley. London, Methuen, 1974.
The Demon Bowler. London, Heinemann, 1974.
The Big One. London, Nelson, 1974.
The Chase. London, Nelson, 1974.
On the Run. London, Nelson, 1974.
Heading for Goal. London, Nelson, 1974.
Contact series (*Last Across, The Match, Dead of Night, Road Race, A Hard Man, Catch, Day in the Country, The Long Drop*), illustrated by Gareth Floyd. London, Collins, 8 vols., 1974.
Flare Up. London, Nelson, 1975.
Get Lost. London, Nelson, 1975.
Money for Sale, illustrated by Fermin Rocker. London, Heinemann, 1975.
Life Underground, illustrated by Roger Harris. London, Heinemann, 1975.
Mark Fox series (*The First Goal, Breakaway, On the Ball, Shooting Star, Goal in Europe, Kick Off, Attack!*). London, Armada, 7 vols., 1976–82.
Where the Action Is. London, Heinemann, 1976.
The Saturday Horse, illustrated by Trevor Stubley. London, Methuen, 1977.
First Contact series (*Go and Find Him, River of Danger, The Great Bed Race, Night Raid*), illustrated by Maureen and Gordon Gray. London, Collins, 4 vols., 1977.
Strong Arm, illustrated by Gareth Floyd. London, Benn, 1977.
Fire on the Sea, illustrated by Gareth Floyd. London, Benn, 1977.
Holiday House, illustrated by Gareth Floyd. London, Benn, 1977.
Crash Car, illustrated by Gareth Floyd. London, Benn, 1977.
Soccer Special, illustrated by Paul Wright. London, Methuen, 1978.
Top of the League. London, Heinemann, 1979.
The Reporters (*Top Soccer, Top Fishing, Top Speed*). London, Harrap, 3 vols., 1979–81.
The Switch Horse, illustrated by Paul Wright. London, Methuen, 1980.

Go for Goal, illustrated by Ron Sandford. London, Benn, 1980.
Racing Bike, illustrated by Ron Sandford. London, Benn, 1980.
Snakerun, illustrated by Ron Sandford. London, Benn, 1980.
Hot Wheels, illustrated by Ron Sandford. London, Benn, 1980.
Behind the Goal. London, Pelham, 1980.
Half a Team, illustrated by Trevor Stubley. London, Methuen, 1980.
The Gigantic Hit. London, Pelham, 1982.
Roar to Victory, illustrated by Patrice Aitken. London, Methuen, 1982.
Fast from the Gate, illustrated by Patrice Aitken. London, Methuen, 1983.
Caught Out, illustrated by Trevor Parkin. London, Methuen, 1983.
Hooked! London, Longman, 1984.
The Team That Wouldn't Give In, illustrated by Trevor Parkin. London, Methuen, 1984.
Double Holiday, illustrated by Shirley Bellwood. London, Blackie, 1985.
Winning Rider. London, Methuen, 1985.
Tiger of the Track. London, Methuen, 1985.
The Shooters. London, Methuen, 1986.
James and the TV Star. London, Blackie, 1986.
No Defence. London, Deutsch, 1986.
One Kick. London, Faber, 1986.
Snookered! London, Blackie, 1987.
Mascot. London, Methuen, 1987.
Quake. London, Faber, 1988.
The Rival Games. London, Methuen, 1988.
The Magic Party, illustrated by Vanessa Julian-Ottie. London, Blackie, 1988.
Kickback. London, Faber, 1989.
The Green Machine. London, Methuen, 1989.

Fiction as David Clark (illustrated by Richard Kennedy)

Goalie. London, Benn, 1972.
Splash. London, Benn, 1972.
Run. London, Benn, 1973.
Top Spin. London, Benn, 1973.
Grab. London, Benn, 1974.
Winner. London, Benn, 1975.
Volley. London, Benn, 1975.
Roll Up. London, Benn, 1975.

*   *   *

Sporting fiction for young readers is still in its formative stages, and has not yet reached the point where individual writers may be acclaimed as masters of the genre. But Michael Hardcastle's football novels clearly demonstrate that he must be seriously regarded as a writer of children's fiction and not simply as a successful author of football stories. First with his Scorton Rovers novels following the fortunes of a Football League team winning promotion to the first Division, then in his Bank Vale United series about the local rivalries of a Sunday Junior League, and in the Mark Fox sequence, one football-daft lad's progress from school football to the twin towers of Wembley, he displays an uncanny understanding of what passes through the young footballer's mind and a true awareness of what really goes on in football on and off the field.

The First Goal introduces Mark, the youngest member of his school team, for whom "the next match in which he played was always the most important of his life." In *Breakaway* his career appears to falter, he is suspended from his school team, and then gets sent off the field in a youth league match. The news that he has been selected for the County Youth XI for a representative match in London (which forms the central narrative of *On the Ball*) sets him

back on course. Mark Fox is no stereotyped Roy of the Rovers hero; he is flesh and blood, no stranger to despair when the world seems against him.

In the Net, the first of the Bank Vale United series, presents an agonizing dilemma often confronting keen and enthusiastic soccer players, the shadow of the School Rugby XV looming over their Saturday afternoons. In *United!* the team goes through a bad patch and recruits a star forward who proves to be a troublemaker. Two of the regular stalwarts of the side have a hard time keeping the side together. *Away from Home,* in fact, concerns only three of the team invited to join an arduous Town Boys' three matches in five days tour. Each member of the party comes under scrutiny in turn, his character subjected to a deeper inspection than is usually the case in other books of the series where two or three players at the most can feature at all prominently.

If the rewards of sports fiction are tempting, the pitfalls awaiting authors who venture into this specialized field can be daunting. One false line of dialogue, one error in either description or situation, and the vital effect of the total reality is irretrievably lost. Hardcastle triumphantly surmounts these difficulties. Capturing the hard slog young footballers put into their training, their anxieties about fitness, team rivalries and jealousies, the iniquities of referees, the seemingly callous attitude of coaches and sportsmasters to potentially serious injuries, and the exhaustion of the dressing room, his stories are authentic and convincing to the last detail.

—Alan Edwin Day

———

HARDING, Lee (John). Australian. Born in Colac, Victoria, 17 February 1937. Educated in Australian primary schools. Married 1) Carla Bleeker in 1960 (divorced 1974), two sons and one daughter; 2) Irene Anne Pagram in 1982, one daughter. Freelance photographer, 1953–70. Recipient: Ditmar award, 1970, 1972; Alan Marshall award, 1978; Australian Children's Book of the Year award, 1980. Agent: Virginia Kidd, 538 East Hartford Street, Milford, Pennsylvania 18337, U.S.A.

PUBLICATIONS FOR CHILDREN

Fiction

The Fallen Spaceman, illustrated by Lee Walsh. Melbourne, Cassell, 1973; London, Cassell, 1975; revised edition, New York, Harper, 1980.
The Children of Atlantis, illustrated by Irene Pagram. Melbourne, Cassell, 1976.
The Frozen Sky, illustrated by Kristine Ammitzball. Melbourne, Cassell, 1976.
Return to Tomorrow, illustrated by Irene Pagram. Melbourne, Cassell, 1976.
The Weeping Sky Melbourne, Cassell, 1977.
Displaced Person. Melbourne, Hyland House, 1979; as *Misplaced Persons,* New York, Harper, 1979.
The Web of Time Melbourne, Cassell, 1979.
Waiting for the End of the World Melbourne, Hyland House, 1983.

PUBLICATIONS FOR ADULTS

Novels

A World of Shadows. London, Hale, 1975.
Future Sanctuary. Toronto, Laser, 1976.

CHILDREN'S WRITERS

Plays

Radio Plays: *Journey into Time* serial, 1978; *The Legend of New Earth* serial, 1979.

Other

Chained, photographs by John Bergland. Melbourne, Ron Smith, 1972.

Editor, *Beyond Tomorrow: An Anthology of Modern Science Fiction* Melbourne, Wren, 1976; abridged edition, London, New English Library, 1977.
Editor, *The Altered I: An Encounter with Science Fiction.* Melbourne, Norstrilia Press, 1976; revised edition, New York, Berkley, 1978.
Editor, *Rooms of Paradise* Melbourne, Quartet, 1978; New York, St. Martin's Press, 1979.

*   *   *

In all his novels for young people, Lee Harding has used the notion of worlds existing very much like our own and only differing in a few vital points as the basis of his plots. These differences tend to highlight aspects of human behaviour rather than, as in many other science-fiction stories, concentrating on technological curiosities. All the novels feature a hero, usually orphaned, who has to face a testing time. Most often the struggle is with his own character more than with external terrors. There is a recurring motif of future possibilities in Harding's novels, an appropriate theme for adolescent readers. Tied to this, and also appropriate for a writer of science fiction, is the idea that the future is not fixed but consists of infinite outcomes.

Harding brought a refreshing liveliness to the area of books for reluctant readers with his first four titles: *The Fallen Spaceman, The Children of Atlantis, The Frozen Sky,* and *Return to Tomorrow.* His first major novel for children, *The Weeping Sky,* takes up many of the themes evident in the readers. The setting is mediaeval Europe, but in the Crusades the enemy is from the North, the pope sits in Athens, and the people worship the "One True God" who had sent his only son to die on a wheel. Set against the power of the church are the Scientists, a group who have to work in secret for fear of persecution. Both groups regard the phenomenon of The Wall, a glass-like sheet seeming to hang in the air and weep, with awe. Beyond The Wall an apprentice Scientist finds another world, even more violent and repellent than the one he knows. *The Weeping Sky* is a tightly written and exciting novel which due to some unfortunate editing has not been available to as wide an audience as it might otherwise have attracted. In *The Web of Time* human ideas about time rather than concepts of the supernatural are examined in a fast-paced adventure story. This is the one novel that features technical wizardry, in this instance a time machine, but the machine is a mere backdrop to a further look at the idea of the co-existence of many worlds, in this case separated by time. Indeed the power of the mind is shown to be more effective than the machine in crossing the boundaries of time.

In Harding's best-known novel, *Displaced Person,* the hero Graeme comes to the conclusion that our world is manipulated by outside forces who adjust space and time as part of some great experiment. Graeme starts to feel out of touch with his everyday world, people look right through him, colour begins to ebb, and he finds himself alone in a grey world. Initially Graeme thinks his mind must be disturbed, but finally he concludes that he is actually displaced from his usual world, and finding two companions in the grey world confirms this view. However, for the reader the questions are left more open. Is Graeme's experience perhaps a manifestation

of alienation? Or perhaps the story is suggesting other worlds are within us and can be experienced with an adjustment to our perception. The puzzles about reality are part of the book's fascination. *Waiting for the End of the World* has a more conventional fictional setting in a nasty future when the population is kept under control with drugs, and those outside the cities roam the land in lawless gangs. As in his other novels Harding creates a suspenseful and exciting narrative, and again the theme of possibilities is central. In this novel the notion of another world, in this case a ghostly hoard from ancient European times, seems incongruous in an Australian setting, despite the European origins of the "dreamers." More valid and important to the ideas in the novel is the resolve of a group of three young people to strike out in a new direction with the hope of somehow changing the direction of their bloody world.

Harding uses the resources of science fiction to explore human failings, but despite Graeme's theories about outside control in *Displaced Person,* this author's compelling stories suggest a hopeful view of human resilience.

—Kerry White

———

HARNETT, Cynthia (Mary). British. Born in London, 22 June 1893. Educated at private schools; Chelsea School of Art, London; studied with the artist G. Vernon Stokes. Recipient: Library Association Carnegie Medal, 1952. *Died 25 October 1981.*

PUBLICATIONS FOR CHILDREN

Fiction

Velvet Masks, illustrated by G. Vernon Stokes. London, Medici Society, 1937.
The Pennymakers, with G. Vernon Stokes, illustrated by the authors. London, Eyre and Spottiswoode, 1937.
Junk, The Puppy, with G. Vernon Stokes, illustrated by the authors. London, Blackie, 1937.
Banjo, The Puppy, with G. Vernon Stokes, illustrated by the authors. London, Blackie, 1938.
To Be a Farmer's Boy, with G. Vernon Stokes, illustrated by the authors. London, Blackie, 1940.
Mudlarks, with G. Vernon Stokes, illustrated by the authors London, Collins, 1941.
Mountaineers, with G. Vernon Stokes, illustrated by the authors. London, Collins, 1941.
Ducks and Drakes, with G. Vernon Stokes, illustrated by the authors. London, Collins, 1942.
Bob-Tail Pup, with G. Vernon Stokes, illustrated by the authors. London, Collins, 1944.
Sand Hoppers, with G. Vernon Stokes, illustrated by the authors. London, Collins, 1946.
Two and a Bit, with G. Vernon Stokes, illustrated by the authors. London, Collins, 1948.
Follow My Leader, with G. Vernon Stokes, illustrated by the authors. London, Collins, 1949.
The Great House, illustrated by the author. London, Methuen, 1949; Cleveland, World, 1968.
Pets Limited, with G. Vernon Stokes, illustrated by the authors. London, Collins, 1950.
The Wool-Pack, illustrated by the author. London, Methuen, 1951; as *Nicholas and the Woolpack,* New York, Putnam, 1953; as *The Merchant's Mark,* Minneapolis, Lerner, 1984.
Ring Out, Bow Bells!, illustrated by the author. London, Methuen,

1953; as *The Drawbridge Gate,* New York, Putnam, 1954.
The Green Popinjay, illustrated by the author. Oxford, Blackwell, 1955.
Stars of Fortune, illustrated by the author. London, Methuen, and New York, Putnam, 1956.
The Load of Unicorn, illustrated by the author. London, Methuen, 1959; as *Caxton's Challenge,* Cleveland, World, 1960; as *The Cargo of Madalena,* Minneapolis, Lerner, 1984.
A Fifteenth Century Wool Merchant, illustrated by the author. London, Oxford University Press, 1962.
The Writing on the Hearth, illustrated by Gareth Floyd. London, Methuen, 1971; New York, Viking Press, 1973.

Other

David's New World: The Making of a Sportsman, with G. Vernon Stokes, illustrated by the authors. London, Country Life, 1937.
Getting to Know Dogs, illustrated by G. Vernon Stokes. London, Collins, 1947.
Monasteries and Monks, illustrated by Edward Osmond. London, Batsford, 1963.

Editor, *In Praise of Dogs: An Anthology in Prose and Verse,* illustrated by G. Vernon Stokes. London, Country Life, 1936.

*   *   *

After the publication of *The Writing on the Hearth* Cynthia Harnett announced that it was to be her last book. Since it took her 10 years to complete the research necessary before she would begin writing, and she was in her eighties then, one can see why. This is an indication of the meticulous way in which she prepared her historical novels. Every detail had to be accurate. It is important that the distance between Ewelme church and the manor house be correctly stated, for example, and one can check that it is. Many children use her story *The Wool-Pack* as a basis for projects, as enough of Burford village has remained recognisable from mediaeval days for them to pace out the hero's adventures on the actual ground.

Her books are not only enjoyable historical adventures but provide a vivid reconstruction of the period, and are often used by teachers as background material for lessons without spoiling the story. *Stars of Fortune* is the story of George Washington's English forebears. *Ring Out, Bow Bells!* tells of the real Dick Whittington (of pantomime fame) who was thrice Lord Mayor of London. In researching this book, the author explored bomb-blasted London at the end of World War II, using Stow's 16th-century street plans, and was able to discover the mediaeval foundations of many of the houses she describes in the story, including Whittington's own, from the ruins of which a black cat appeared to share her sandwiches!

The Lord of Unicorn is an exciting tale of the rivalry between early printers and the scriveners or handwriters, and incidentally the reader absorbs a good deal about Caxton and the printing trade. Yet nowhere does it seem like a lesson. Her books are storybooks first and foremost, with a wealth of corroborative detail. Illustrated by her own little line drawings interpolated into the text, her books appeal mainly to children between nine and 13.

—Ann G. Hay

———

HARRIS, Aurand. American. Born in Jamesport, Missouri, 4 July 1915. Educated at Jamesport public schools, 1920–32; University of Kansas City, 1932–36, A.B. 1936; Northwestern University, Evanston, Illinois, 1937–39, M.A. 1939; Columbia University, New York (John Golden prize, 1945), 1945–47. Auditorium teacher, Gary public schools, Indiana, 1939–41; Head of the Drama Department, William Woods College, Fulton, Missouri, 1942–45; drama teacher, Grace Church School, New York, 1946–77; drama teacher, Columbia University Teachers College, New York, summers 1958–63; playwright-in-residence, University of Florida, Tallahassee, 1972; drama teacher, Western Connecticut State College, Danbury, summer 1976; playwright-in-residence, University of Texas, Austin, 1976–84, University of Kansas, Lawrence, 1979, Young Audiences, Cleveland, autumns 1981–84, California State University, Northridge, 1982, Nebraska Theatre Caravan, Omaha, 1982, Indiana University-Purdue University, Indianapolis, 1985 and 1988, American School of Madrid, Spain, 1986, and New York University, New York, 1988. Associated with summer theatre in Cape May, New Jersey, 1946, Bennington, Vermont, 1947, Peaks Island, Maine, 1948, and Harwich, Massachusetts, 1963–82. Recipient: American Theatre Association Chorpenning Cup, 1967, 1986; National Endowment for the Arts grant, 1976. Fellow, American Theatre Association, 1985. Address: c/o Anchorage Press, Box 8067, New Orleans, Louisiana 70182, U.S.A.

PUBLICATIONS FOR CHILDREN

Plays

Pinocchio and the Fire-Eater (produced Gary, Indiana, 1940). New York, McGraw Hill, 1967.
Once upon a Clothesline (produced Fulton, Missouri, 1944). Boston, Baker, 1945.
The Doughnut Hole. New York, French, 1947.
The Moon Makes Three. New York, French, 1947.
Seven League Boots (produced Cleveland, 1947). Boston, Baker, 1948.
Circus Days (produced Seattle, 1948). New York, French, 1949; revised version, as *Circus in the Wind,* 1960.
Pinocchio and the Indians (produced Seattle, 1949). New York, French, 1949.
Simple Simon; or, Simon Big-Ears (produced Washington, D.C., 1952; Slough, Buckinghamshire, 1964). Anchorage, Kentucky, Children's Theatre Press, 1953.
Buffalo Bill (produced Seattle, 1953). Anchorage, Kentucky, Children's Theatre Press, 1954.
We Were Young That Year. New York, French, 1954.
The Plain Princess, adaptation of the book by Phyllis McGinley (produced Kalamazoo, Michigan, 1954). Anchorage, Kentucky, Children's Theatre Press, 1955.
The Flying Prince (produced Washington, D.C., 1965). New York, French, 1958; revised version (produced Fort Wayne, Indiana, 1984), New Orleans, Anchorage Press, 1985.
Junket (No Dogs Allowed), adaptation of the story by Anne H. White (produced Louisville, Kentucky, 1959). Anchorage, Kentucky, Children's Theatre Press, 1959.
The Brave Little Tailor (produced Charleston, West Virginia, 1960; London, 1966). Anchorage, Kentucky, Children's Theatre Press, 1961.
Pocahontas (produced Birmingham, Alabama, 1961). Anchorage, Kentucky, Children's Theatre Press, 1961.
Androcles and the Lion (produced New York, 1964; Sheffield, 1968). Anchorage, Kentucky, Children's Theatre Press, 1964.
Rags to Riches, adaptation of stories by Horatio Alger, music by Eva Franklin, lyrics by Harris and Franklin (produced Harwich, Massachusetts, 1965; Teddington, Middlesex, 1970). Anchorage, Kentucky, Anchorage Press, 1966.
A Doctor in Spite of Himself, adaptation of a play by Molière (produced New York, 1966). Anchorage, Kentucky, Anchorage Press, 1968.

The Comical Tragedy or Tragical Comedy of Punch and Judy, music by Glenn Mack (produced Atlanta, 1969). Anchorage, Kentucky, Anchorage Press, 1970.

Just So Stories, adaptation of the stories by Rudyard Kipling (produced Tallahassee, Florida, 1971). Anchorage, Kentucky, Anchorage Press, 1971.

Ming Lee and the Magic Tree. New York, French, 1971.

Steal Away Home, adaptation of work by Jane Kristof (produced Louisville, Kentucky, 1972). Anchorage, Kentucky, Anchorage Press, 1972.

Peck's Bad Boy, adaptation of the novel by George Wilbur Peck (produced Harwich, Massachusetts, 1973). Anchorage, Kentucky, Anchorage Press, 1974.

Robin Goodfellow (produced Harwich, Massachusetts, 1974). Anchorage, Kentucky, Anchorage Press, 1977.

Yankee Doodle (produced Austin, Texas, 1975). Anchorage, Kentucky, Anchorage Press, 1975.

Star Spangled Salute (produced Harwich, Massachusetts, 1975). Anchorage, Kentucky, Anchorage Press, 1975.

Six Plays for Children (includes *Androcles and the Lion, Rags to Riches, Punch and Judy, Steal Away Home, Peck's Bad Boy, Yankee Doodle*), edited by Coleman A. Jennings. Austin, University of Texas Press, 1977.

A Toby Show (produced Austin, Texas, 1978). New Orleans, Anchorage Press, 1978.

The Arkansaw Bear (produced Austin, Texas, 1980). New Orleans, Anchorage Press, 1980.

Treasure Island, adaptation of the novel by Robert Louis Stevenson (produced Northridge, California, 1982). New Orleans, Anchorage Press, 1983.

The Magician's Nephew, adaptation of the novel by C.S. Lewis (produced Austin, Texas, 1983). Chicago, Dramatic Publishing, 1984.

Ride a Blue Horse (produced Indianapolis, 1985). New Orleans, Anchorage Press, 1986.

Huck Finn's Story (produced Akron, Ohio, 1987). New Orleans, Anchorage Press, 1988.

Other

Editor, with Coleman A. Jennings, *Plays Children Love: A Treasury of Contemporary and Classic Plays for Children 1–2,* illustrated by Susan Swan and Lee Duran. New York, Doubleday, vol. 1, 1981; New York, St. Martin's Press, vol. 2, 1988.

PUBLICATIONS FOR ADULTS

Plays

Ladies of the Mop. Evanston, Illinois, Row Peterson, 1945.

Madam Ada. New York, French, 1948.

And Never Been Kissed, adaptation of the novel by Sylvia Dee. New York, French, 1950.

Fashion, adaptation of the play by Anna Cora Mowatt. Boston, Baker, 1981.

*

Manuscript Collection: University of Texas Library, Austin.

Critical Study: *The Dramatic Contributions of Aurand Harris to Children's Theatre in the United States* by Coleman A. Jennings, unpublished dissertation, New York University, 1974 (includes bibliography).

Theatrical Activities:

Director: **Play**—*Rags to Riches,* Shanghai, 1987 (first foreigner officially invited to direct a children's play in the People's Republic of China).

Aurand Harris comments:

I write for children because they and I like the same thing in theatre—a good story, interesting characters, excitement, fantasy, beauty, and fun. My plays are usually based on history, legend, myth, or children's classics, and are conceived and executed in a variety of styles ranging from *commedia dell'arte* to melodrama to poetic fantasy. Best of all, there is an increasing and receptive audience that lets you know when it is enjoying itself.

*   *   *

Aurand Harris, author of some 38 published plays for children, is America's most-produced children's theatre playwright. His plays, constantly produced since the late 1940's, have enormously enriched the literature of American children's theatre.

During the 10-year period from 1946 to 1955, Harris experimented with a variety of plays. He had been writing not only for audiences of children, but for teenagers and adults as well. Writing for children, however, provided Harris with opportunities which were unfettered by the naturalistic limitations usually expected by adult audiences. Because children are imaginative and willing to accept any theatrical form if it is honestly presented, he found great satisfaction in writing for them and since 1955 has written only for children and youth.

To write successful plays for children's theatre, an author must understand the youthful audience with the same thoroughness that he knows the techniques of playwriting. An audience comprised of children of various ages, representing many stages of maturity with widely differing interests and abilities to concentrate, presents an extra dimension of challenge to the playwright. Children are sensitive, perceptive, and quick to react overtly and honestly to whatever they see and hear. Harris's sensitivity to child audiences, his desire to create plays of high quality which adults perform for youth, and his thoroughly practical knowledge of all aspects of theatre have made him the respected professional playwright he is today.

Harris's children's plays are usually derived from fairy tales and legends, history, and other published writing. Harris has written some original plots, but creating new stories has obviously been of secondary interest to him. Of even greater importance is the way he has learned to shape the content. As his craftsmanship has steadily increased throughout his career, so has the range of maturity in the audience for whom he writes. In his late plays he has broadened his approach to include older youth, though he continues to command the attention of the younger audience members.

In writing each of his plays, Harris has recreated a dramatic form from the adult theatre with adjustments that make it suitable for a child audience. His selection of form, such as of *commedia dell'arte,* late-19th-century melodrama, comedy with sober overtones, dramatic chronicle, lighthearted farce, or musical revue is determined by the presence of intrinsic qualities which appeal to children.

Because the six elements of dramatic form, theme, plot, character, dialogue, song, and spectacle are so closely interdependent in Harris's plays, the works exhibit a vital theatricality to which young audiences respond. Each of his plays, unified and satisfactorily resolved, has a unique quality of its own. The most outstanding examples of this unified and unique playwriting are *Androcles and the Lion* and *The Arkansaw Bear.*

—Coleman A. Jennings

HARRIS, Christie (Lucy, née Irwin). Canadian. Born in Newark, New Jersey, United States, 21 November 1907. Educated at Provincial Normal School, Vancouver, teacher's certificate 1925. Married Thomas Arthur Harris in 1932; three sons and two daughters. Schoolteacher, British Columbia, 1925–32; freelance scriptwriter, Canadian Broadcasting Corporation, 1936–63; women's editor, *British Columbia News Weekly,* Abbotsford, 1951–57. Recipient: Canadian Library Association Book of the Year award, 1967, 1977; Vicky Metcalf award, 1973; Canada Council Children's Literature prize, 1981. Member, Order of Canada, 1981. Address: Suite 1604, Emerald Terrace, 2045 Nelson Street, Vancouver, British Columbia V6G IN8, Canada.

PUBLICATIONS FOR CHILDREN

Fiction

Cariboo Trail. Toronto and New York, Longman, 1957.
You Have to Draw the Line Somewhere, illustrated by Moira Johnston. Toronto, McClelland and Stewart, and New York, Atheneum, 1964.
West with the White Chiefs, illustrated by Walter Ferro. Toronto, McClelland and Stewart, and New York, Atheneum, 1965.
Raven's Cry, illustrated by Bill Reid. Toronto, McClelland and Stewart, and New York, Atheneum, 1966.
Confessions of a Toe-Hanger, illustrated by Moira Johnston. Toronto, McClelland and Stewart, and New York, Atheneum, 1967.
Forbidden Frontier, illustrated by E. Carey Kenney. Toronto, McClelland and Stewart, and New York, Atheneum, 1968.
Let X Be Excitement. Toronto, McClelland and Stewart, and New York, Atheneum, 1969.
Secret in the Stlalakum Wild, illustrated by Douglas Tait. Toronto, McClelland and Stewart, and New York, Atheneum, 1972.
Sky Man on the Totem Pole?, illustrated by Douglas Tait. Toronto, McClelland and Stewart, and New York, Atheneum, 1975.
The Mystery at the Edge of Two Worlds, illustrated by Lou Crockett. Toronto, McClelland and Stewart, and New York, Atheneum, 1978.

Other

Once upon a Totem (Indian legends), illustrated by John Frazer Mills. Toronto, McClelland and Stewart, and New York, Atheneum, 1963.
Figleafing Through History: The Dynamics of Dress, with and illustrated by Moira Johnston. Toronto, McClelland and Stewart, and New York, Atheneum, 1971.
Mule Lib, with Tom Harris, illustrated by Franklin Arbuckle. Toronto, McClelland and Stewart, 1972.
Once More upon a Totem (Indian legends), illustrated by Douglas Tait. Toronto, McClelland and Stewart, and New York, Atheneum, 1973.
Mouse Woman and the Vanished Princesses (Indian legends), illustrated by Douglas Tait. Toronto, McClelland and Stewart, and New York, Atheneum, 1976.
Mouse Woman and the Mischief-Makers (Indian legends), illustrated by Douglas Tait. Toronto, McClelland and Stewart, and New York, Atheneum, 1977; London, Macmillan, 1978.
Mouse Woman and the Muddleheads (Indian legends), illustrated by Douglas Tait. Toronto, McClelland and Stewart, and New York, Atheneum, 1979; London, Macmillan, 1980.
The Trouble with Princesses (Indian legends), illustrated by Douglas Tait. Toronto, McClelland and Stewart, and New York, Atheneum, 1980.

The Trouble with Adventurers (Indian legends), illustrated by Douglas Tait. Toronto, McClelland and Stewart, and New York, Atheneum, 1982.

*

Manuscript Collection: University of Calgary Library, Alberta.

Christie Harris comments:

My books have grown out of my own background. Three of my five children, after they were grown up, gave me their own case histories, which I wrote as fiction. My interest in the early Canadian west, combined with the fact that I lived on a homestead as a child, produced three junior historical novels. And my very great interest in the remarkable culture of our Northwest Coast Indians has led me to rewrite their legends into seven collections and to use other legends in a science fiction book. Indian lore has combined with new scientific findings about the sensitivity of plants to produce a fantasy.

This same interest led me to write *Raven's Cry,* a fictionalized history of our coast told from the Indian point of view. Although it won several awards as a *children's* book, *Raven's Cry* is used in universities as a study in culture contact.

My fashion-artist daughter's enthusiasm for the psychology of dress and the recent clothing revolution sparked our collaboration on *Figleafing Through History.* And my continuing family-orientation brought my husband in with his recollections of World War I and the incredible mule he fought with.

*   *   *

Christie Harris is one of the more prolific Canadian authors of books for children with some 20 books to her credit. Her output covers a number of genres—historical fiction, fictionalized biography, and retellings of Indian legends. Her most successful writing is in the area of Northwest Pacific Indian mythology. Harris is adept at taking the rich and varied material available and developing it into stories which retain the original flavor of the legends and also bear the distinctly original character of her own writing. *Once upon a Totem* is a collection of five tales based on the adventures of Indian ancestors and tales of mythical tribal heroes which were represented on the exquisitely carved and painted totem poles produced by these people. Each of Harris's retellings is prefaced by a brief description of the nature of the legend and the history behind it, a useful device which places the legends in their proper historical perspective. Her language with its dignified rhythms accurately reflects the nature of a proud, intelligent and highly creative people. The Mouse Woman books and *The Trouble with Princesses* are easily Harris's best books. In *Mouse Woman and the Vanished Princesses* the character of Mouse Woman is expertly delineated in six tales of princesses who were lured away from their tribes by spirits or "narnauks." Embodying many of the characteristics of a mouse as well as a human person, Mouse Woman's task is to give advice to the princesses and assist them to return safely to their tribes. Mouse Woman is amusingly and affectionately described; we are told that her fondness for bits of wool to be ravelled into mouse nests is one weakness of a "very, very proper little being." The six tales reflect the universality of human nature and, at the same time, give the reader a good idea of the peculiarities of Indian coastal life. The two other Mouse Woman books deal further with her helpful activities. The vigour and sophisticated wit of Northwest Coast mythology are here aptly brought to light.

The stories in *The Trouble with Princesses* are prefaced by brief introductions in which Harris notes how much Northwest Coast Indian princesses resemble their counterparts in European folklore. Although they dress in furs and live in cedar homes, they are royalty, and, like old world princesses, have terrifying adventures, brave great dangers and risk their lives for love. The adventures of Harris's regal and enterprising heroines are related with a discerning awareness of the oral tradition of folklore, and they are as intensely exciting as those of standard fairy tales.

Historical fiction is a genre in which Harris seems less comfortable. *Cariboo Trail, Raven's Cry, Forbidden Frontier,* and *West with the White Chiefs* deal with such events in British Columbia history as the Cariboo gold rush, the treatment of the Haida Indians by white fur traders, and a journey across the Rockies in 1863. In *Forbidden Frontier,* for example, the friendship that finally develops between the white girl, Megan, and the half-Indian girl, Alison, seems improbable in the light of Megan's betrayal of Alison's boyfriend. Although written with reasonable competence, generally Harris's historical fiction is not memorable.

Least successful are the fictionalized biographies of Harris's own children. *Confessions of a Toe-Hanger* follows the development of an enthusiastic girl in a large family through adolescence and early married life. Feeny zips through childhood wondering what to do with her life and finally discovers that all one has to do is "be oneself." Characterization is shallow—Feeny doesn't seem to go through an observable maturing process; rather, she seems suddenly to discover a basic truth on the last page of the book.

The Mystery at the Edge of Two Worlds, a straightforward adventure tale based on the history of Lucy Island, is marred by Harris's attempt to incorporate a Northwest Coast legend into the story. The inherent dignity of the mythology is belittled as a result. Harris is obviously not as comfortable with contemporary characters and situations as she is with her retellings of Indian tales. Lark, the heroine, is not realistically portrayed: she verbally overreacts in most situations and her dialogue does not ring true. The plot is adequate and sweeps the reader along, but Lark and her friends fail to come to life, unlike, for example, the Mouse Woman.

Secret in the Stlalakum Wild, a story set in the forests of British Columbia, is partly fantasy and partly an adventure story. The theme of conservation in nature is a bit overworked but does not detract from the fact that Harris has produced a very readable story based on Indian mythology and created an extremely likable heroine. It is evident that Harris's writing skills are most highly developed in dealing with Northwest Coast Indian mythology. Perhaps the restrained and dignified rhythms and cadences of the language of the original stories impose a necessary restraint on her creativity while allowing her to bring a fresh approach to the material.

—Fran Ashdown

HARRIS, Geraldine (Rachel). British. Born 17 October 1951. Educated at King's College, Cambridge, 1973–77, B.A. (honours) 1977, M.A. 1980; Wadham College, Oxford, 1977–84, D.Phil. in Egyptology 1985. Married Richard G.E. Pinch in 1978. Freelance Egyptologist and writer. Address: c/o Macmillan Publishers, 4 Little Essex Street, London WC2R 3LF, England.

<small>PUBLICATIONS FOR CHILDREN</small>

Fiction

White Cranes Castle, illustrated by Lisa Jensen. London, Macmillan, 1979.
Seven Citadels series:
   Prince of the Godborn. London, Macmillan, and New York, Greenwillow, 1982.

The Children of the Wind. London, Macmillan, and New York, Greenwillow, 1982.
The Dead Kingdom. London, Macmillan, and New York, Greenwillow, 1983.
The Seventh Gate. London, Macmillan, and New York, Greenwillow, 1983.

Other

Gods and Pharaohs from Egyptian Mythology, illustrated by John Sibbick and David O'Connor. London, Lowe, 1982; New York, Schocken, 1983.
The Junior Atlas of Ancient Egypt. London, Lionheart, 1989.

<small>PUBLICATIONS FOR ADULTS</small>

Other

New Kingdom Votive Offerings to Hathor. Oxford, Griffith Institute, 1989.

*

Geraldine Harris comments:

All my work draws inspiration from myth and legend. *White Cranes Castle* is based on Japanese myths, legends, and folklore but has an historical setting. The four books that make up the *Seven Citadels* quartet are set in an invented world but they have a classic quest theme and are influenced by the myths of many cultures. *Dancing Day* blends fantasy with science fiction by creating a futuristic society with a complex mythology as its basis.

*   *   *

At first sight there may seem little to connect an academic Egyptologist with a fantasy for younger children set in mediaeval Japan, and a major and very complex four-volume fantasy epic that appeals to adults as well as to older children. However on closer examination several important connections emerge, all crucial when considering the work of Geraldine Harris.

Both works of fiction are set in highly ordered, hierarchical societies that are in decline. In both, religion permeates the lives of all the participants. It is the failure to remember and observe divine commands that has brought about the decay of nation and inhabitant. In *White Cranes Castle* Akari finds his contemporaries abandoning the old ways in favour of new, more exciting ideas. Kerish-lo-Taan, hero of the *Seven Citadels* series, is a member of the ruling house of Galkis, descended from the god Zeldin—but most of the rest of the Imperial house have chosen to ignore their divine origin, and the responsibilities that brings, in pursuit of personal gain and the lust for power. It is knowledge of, and a willingness to adhere to divine commands, that bring about the spiritual growth enabling both heroes to succeed in their respective tasks—though this is accompanied by personal sacrifice of a high order.

White Cranes Castle tells how the unconsidered cousin, Akari, is able to rouse and converse with the eight-headed dragon, which has had to rise from its lake bed to bring the rain the country so badly needs. Within the confines of a short book there is already in *White Cranes Castle* evidence of the author's love of colour, and of her vivid imaginative powers.

In the much longer *Seven Citadels* these blossom: it is no mean feat to sustain the imaginative force required to invent and people the world of Zindar and to engage the reader in Kerish-lo-Taan's quest for the legendary saviour of Galkis. The saviour is imprisoned; it will take seven keys to unlock him. The keys are held by seven sorcerers—remarkably individual creations—each of whom must first be found and then persuaded to give up a key. Surrendering a key means surrendering immortality. The sorcerers allow Harris much scope for imagination, but it is in the creation of the hideous, cynical, acid-tongued Gidjabolgo, Kerish's companion for so much of the journey, that she has devised one of the most unusual and unexpectedly attractive characters in children's fantasy.

Harris studied many folklores before turning to postgraduate work in Egyptology, but it is from that little-known and exceptionally rich corpus of myth and legend that one may begin to pick up some of the threads she weaves so well. In *Gods and Pharaohs from Egyptian Mythology* one finds a strongly hierarchical society which did eventually decline, and in which the power and presence of the gods pervaded the whole of mortal life. Concern about death, and interest in life after death, is also a major preoccupation in Ancient Egypt. The story of the unconsidered mouse helping the mighty lion is Egyptian (though better known in its Greek form) and the boats that take souls to the Underworld in Ancient Egypt have a memorably terrifying parallel in *Seven Citadels*. Hubris is of course punishable in most religions. The themes of love and death that feature so largely in Harris's work make a refreshing change from the good-versus-evil, or light-against-dark, themes of many other stories. Her overall narrative drive and sheer imaginative power bring zest, resonance, and a strong individual flavour to her work. It will be exciting to see what this talented newcomer will produce next.

—Felicity Trotman

HARRIS, Mary K(athleen). British. Born in Harrow, Middlesex, 22 September 1905. Educated at Harrow County School for Girls, 1915–22. *Died in 1966.*

PUBLICATIONS FOR CHILDREN

Fiction

Gretel at St. Bride's, illustrated by Drake Brookshaw. London, Nelson, 1941.
The Wolf, illustrated by Kathleen Cooper. London, Sheed and Ward, 1946; revised edition, New York, Sheed and Ward, 1955.
The Niche over the Door. London, Sheed and Ward, 1948.
Henrietta at St. Hilary's. London, Staples Press, 1953.
Thomas, illustrated by Cliff Roberts. New York, Sheed and Ward, 1956.
A Safe Lodging, illustrated by Don Bolognese. New York, Sheed and Ward, 1957.
Emily and the Headmistress. London, Faber, 1958.
Seraphina, illustrated by Sheila Rose. London, Faber, 1960.
Penny's Way, illustrated by Sheila Rose. London, Faber, 1963.
The Bus Girls, illustrated by Eileen Green. London, Faber, and New York, Norton, 1965.
Jessica on Her Own, illustrated by Alison Prince. London, Faber, 1968.

Other

Elizabeth, illustrated by R.M. Sax. New York, Sheed and Ward, 1961.
Helena, illustrated by Michael Hampshire. New York, Sheed and Ward, 1964.

PUBLICATIONS FOR ADULTS

Novels

Fear at My Heart. London and New York, Sheed and Ward, 1951.
My Darling from the Lion's Mouth. London, Chatto and Windus, 1956; as *I Am Julie,* New York, Crowell, 1956.
Lucia Wilmot. London, Chatto and Windus, 1959.

*   *   *

Mary K. Harris had no illusions about childhood. Looking back on her own schooldays (she went to her secondary school in 1915), she recalled that "I found myself amongst a group of children who were consistently horrid to each other," but she realized later "that these hateful school children were only hateful in a mass, that, in their own secret, solitary selves they were as aghast at each other as I was." There's no doubt that, like many less intelligent people, she remained all her life obsessed by her schooldays, but she turned her obsession to splendid account and gave us some of the best school stories we have. Her writing career began slowly and her early work was mainly for Guide magazines and for Sheed and Ward, the Catholic publishers—she was a convert.

Her Faber books, to their advantage, have no special axes to grind but it is interesting to note that her early Catholic story, *The Wolf,* shows her talent much more clearly than her conventional early school stories, *Gretel at St. Bride's* and *Henrietta of St. Hilary's.* Gretel, however, is not a stock heroine. The solitary quality of childhood is seen in her in extreme form. The year is 1941 and she is a refugee from Nazi Germany whereas "all the girls at St. Bride's ever worried about was Saturday sweets and getting into the hockey eleven."

Harris's progression from the boarding schools of these early books and *Emily and the Headmistress,* via the grammar-school boarding hostel of *Seraphina* to the boarder-less grammar schools of *Penny's Way* and *The Bus Girls,* and eventually to the Secondary Modern of *Jessica on Her Own,* seems almost uncannily deliberate, as if Harris with each book was simply attempting to get nearer and nearer to a wider number of potential readers. In fact, her social situations are a lot more complex than this would suggest. Jessica, the first of her heroines to go to a Secondary Modern, is the daughter of a Cambridge graduate mother, a very different type from the mothers in the two previous books. After her not completely successful attempt at the Ruffles (cousins, perhaps, of Eve Garnett's Ruggles) in *Emily and the Headmistress,* Harris never seemed to put a foot wrong in her social nuances. But it is imaginative conviction that counts, of course, not social awareness. Harris's books are never manufactured to support a thesis, but she certainly wrote with purpose. She aimed to make ordinary life interesting and meaningful. She felt it important to help children to understand themselves and each other, to make them realize, as she herself had not realized until much later, that other children are also vulnerable.

Emily and the Headmistress rather stands alone. The typical Harris heroine is 12 or 13; Emily is only eight. But it was in this book that the author first achieved her individuality. It was followed by *Seraphina,* her only novel told in the first person, a marvellously imagined story, rich in detail, strong in plot. Harris had showed there could be a school story which did not suffer from conservatism, xenophobia, snobbery, the underrating of learning (the list is Orwell's).

Nothing Harris wrote was solemn; everything was entertaining. In her books she explored with amused understanding the different pressures on adolescent girls as they come to terms with life, with the conflicting demands of home and school, and the difficulties and rewards of friendship. She had an ability to create not just one or two characters in each book but a whole form, even the feeling of a whole school, of individuals. In her last book, *Jessica on Her Own,* she moved out of the pure school story. School and home were equally important.

—Ann Thwaite

————

HARRIS, Rosemary (Jeanne). British. Born in London, 20 February 1923. Educated at Thorneloe School, Weymouth; St. Martin's, Central, and Chelsea schools of art, London; Department of Technology, Courtauld Institute, London, 1950. Served in the Red Cross Nursing Auxiliary, Westminster Division, London, 1941–45. Picture restorer, 1949; reader, Metro-Goldwyn-Mayer, 1951–52; children's book reviewer, the *Times,* London, 1970–73. Recipient: Library Association Carnegie Medal, 1969; Arts Council grant, 1971. Lives in London. Agent: A.P. Watt Ltd., 20 John Street, London WC1N 2DR, England.

PUBLICATIONS FOR CHILDREN

Fiction

The Moon in the Cloud. London, Faber, 1968; New York, Macmillan, 1969.
The Shadow on the Sun. London, Faber, and New York, Macmillan, 1970.
The Seal-Singing. London, Faber, and New York, Macmillan, 1971.
The Bright and Morning Star. London, Faber, and New York, Macmillan, 1972.
The King's White Elephant, illustrated by Errol Le Cain. London, Faber, 1973.
The Flying Ship, illustrated by Errol Le Cain. London, Faber, 1975.
I Want to Be a Fish, illustrated by Jill Bennett. London, Kestrel, 1977.
A Quest for Orion. London, Faber, 1978.
Green Finger House, illustrated by Juan Wijngaard. London, Eel Pie, 1979.
Tower of the Stars. London, Faber, 1980.
The Enchanted Horse, illustrated by Pauline Baynes. London, Kestrel, 1981.
Janni's Stork, illustrated by Juan Wijngaard. London, Blackie, and New York, Harper, 1982.
Zed. London, Faber, 1982.
Summers of the Wild Rose. London, Faber, 1987.
Colm of the Islands, illustrated by Pauline Baynes. London, Walker, 1989.

Plays

Television Plays: *Peronik,* 1976; *The Unknown Enchantment,* 1982.

Other

The Child in the Bamboo Grove (legend), illustrated by Errol Le Cain. London, Faber, 1971; New York, Phillips, 1972.
The Lotus and the Grail: Legends from East to West, illustrated by Errol Le Cain. London, Faber, 1974; abridged edition, as *Sea Magic and Other Stories of Enchantment,* New York, Macmillan, 1974.
The Little Dog of Fo (legend), illustrated by Errol Le Cain. London, Faber, 1976.

Beauty and the Beast, illustrated by Errol Le Cain. London, Faber, 1979; New York, Doubleday, 1980.
Heidi (retelling), illustrated by Tomi Ungerer. London, Benn, 1983.

Editor, *Love and the Merry-Go-Round,* illustrated by Pauline Baynes. London, Hamish Hamilton, 1988.

PUBLICATIONS FOR ADULTS

Novels

The Summer-House. London, Hamish Hamilton, 1956.
Voyage to Cythera. London, Bodley Head, 1958.
Venus with Sparrows. London, Faber, 1961.
All My Enemies. London, Faber, 1967; New York, Simon and Schuster, 1973.
The Nice Girl's Story. London, Faber, 1968; as *Nor Evil Dreams,* New York, Simon and Schuster, 1974.
A Wicked Pack of Cards. London, Faber, 1969; New York, Walker, 1970.
The Double Snare. London, Faber, 1974; New York, Simon and Schuster, 1975.
Three Candles for the Dark. London, Faber, 1976.

*

Rosemary Harris comments:
I look on all my writings as very similar in essence. This doesn't, of course, apply to the same extent to picture books—but I hope I never give the impression of "writing down," only of simplifying or omitting subjects that wouldn't really be appropriate for young children.

*   *   *

Rosemary Harris makes nonsense of any distinction between adult and children's fiction. She writes only for her peers of any age.

The Egyptian trilogy begins lightheartedly, though it never shirks human evil. *The Moon in the Cloud* tells how Reuben, the musician and animal tamer, sets out for Kemi to obtain a pair of lions for Noah's ark and so to earn a passage for himself and his wife Thamar. He suffers dangers and distress, becomes chief musician to the young Pharaoh, Merenkere, and eventually achieves his mission in surprising ways, helped by his formidable cat, Cefalu. The two succeeding books, though witty and engaging as ever, grow increasingly sombre in theme. *The Shadow on the Sun* is the story of Merenkere's emerging greatness and of his love for Meri-Mekhmet. It is Reuben who rescues her when she is abducted by the evil Prince of Punt. *The Bright and Morning Star* probes the grief of Reuben and Thamar for their sick autistic son and that of Merenkere for his weak and treacherous heir, but is yet a celebration of human greatness and generosity. The pace never flags, but the excitement is generated as much by language as by action. Its vivid images and rhythms, brilliant and sometimes sinister, echo the sunlight and darkness of the characters, the contrasts of the empty desert, hollow and vast beneath the stars or the relentless day, and the sophisticated yet barbaric beauty of Kemi, or the stifling horror of the voodoo-haunted jungles of Punt. The animals are as delightfully individual as the human characters, yet always retaining their own animal nature. Their comments are often the vehicle of the story's delicate and sharp-edged irony.

In *The Seal-Singing* the author moves into the contemporary world, but her Scottish island is tainted by ancient witchcraft. She shows a sympathetic understanding of adolescents in her study of the young cousins, with their loves and jealousies and uncertainties, and a fascinating knowledge of the seals themselves. Rock and wind and sea are unforgettably present. The story is tense and exciting though lightly handled.

Harris also writes for younger children. *The Child in the Bamboo Grove* and *The Little Dog of Fo* are charming Chinese tales, while *The Enchanted Horse* transfers an English folktale to an Indian setting. *Janni's Stork* tells of a witty Dutch housewife and the boy she befriends.

In *A Quest for Orion* and *Tower of the Stars* she evokes a sombre vision of a world crumbling into ruin and slavery beneath a savage totalitarian tyranny. Tiny, isolated groups of young people resist and struggle to survive. The impression is wholly bleak; and the mixture of magic symbols, science fiction, and "alternative time" theories is not completely convincing. But the characters and their personal relationships are powerfully evoked.

In two of her most recent books she again breaks new ground. *Zed* is the tense and very moving story of an eight-year-old boy caught up as hostage in a terrorist attack. He recalls it eight years later, so that throughout the book the child's grief and disillusionment are set against the maturity and concern for others which is achieved through the experience. *Summers of the Wild Rose* is a compassionate story of first love between an English girl and a half-Jewish boy under the growing shadow of Nazi power—a tragic journey from innocence to experience. As in all her books, a faith in essential goodness balances her unflinching portrayal of the darkness that threatens it. These are compelling stories through which the reader can grow in understanding and widen experience.

—Margaret Greaves

HAUGAARD, Erik (Christian). Danish. Born in Copenhagen, 13 April 1923. Educated at Black Mountain College, North Carolina, 1941–42; New School for Social Research, New York, 1945–47. Served in the Royal Canadian Air Force, 1942–45: Flight Sergeant; King Christian X Medal (Denmark). Married 1) Myrna Seld in 1949 (died 1981), two children; 2) Masako Taira in 1986. Worked as farm laborer in Fyn, Denmark, 1938–40, and shepherd in Wyoming. Whittall Lecturer, Library of Congress, Washington, D.C., 1973. Recipient: Boston *Globe-Horn Book* award, 1967; Women's League for Peace and Freedom Jane Addams award, 1968; Danish Cultural Minister's award, 1970; Chapelbrook Foundation award, 1970; Japan Foundation fellowship, 1981; Children's Literature Association Phoenix award, 1988. Address: Toad Hall, The Quay, Ballydehob, County Cork, Ireland.

PUBLICATIONS FOR CHILDREN

Fiction

Hakon of Rogen's Saga, illustrated by Leo and Diane Dillon. Boston, Houghton Mifflin, 1963; as *Hakon's Saga,* London, Faber, 1964.
A Slave's Tale, illustrated by Leo and Diane Dillon. Boston, Houghton Mifflin, 1965; London, Gollancz, 1966.
Orphans of the Wind, illustrated by Milton Johnson. Boston, Houghton Mifflin, 1966; London, Gollancz, 1967.
The Little Fishes, illustrated by Milton Johnson. Boston, Houghton Mifflin, 1967; London, Gollancz, 1968.
The Rider and His Horse, illustrated by Leo and Diane Dillon. Boston, Houghton Mifflin, 1968; London, Gollancz, 1969.

The Untold Tale, illustrated by Leo and Diane Dillon. Boston, Houghton Mifflin, 1971.
A Messenger for Parliament. Boston, Houghton Mifflin, 1976.
Cromwell's Boy. Boston, Houghton Mifflin, 1978.
Chase Me, Catch Nobody! Boston, Houghton Mifflin, 1980; London, Granada, 1982.
Leif the Unlucky. Boston, Houghton Mifflin, 1982.
A Boy's Will, illustrated by Troy Howell. Boston, Houghton Mifflin, 1983.
The Samurai's Tale. Boston, Houghton Mifflin, 1984.
Prince Boghole, illustrated by Julie Downing. New York, Macmillan, 1987.
Princess Horrid. New York, Macmillan, 1989.

Other

Translator, *The Complete Fairy Tales and Stories of Hans Andersen.* New York, Doubleday, and London, Gollancz, 1974; shortened version, as *Hans Christian Andersen: His Classic Fairy Tales,* illustrated by Michael Foreman, London, Gollancz, 1976; New York, Doubleday, 1978.

PUBLICATIONS FOR ADULTS

Play

The Heroes (produced Antioch, Ohio, 1958).

Verse

25 Poems. Tappernöje, Denmark, Squire Press, 1957.

Other

Portrait of a Poet: Hans Christian Andersen and His Fairy Tales (lecture). Washington, D.C., Library of Congress, 1973.

*

Manuscript Collections: Kerlan Collection, University of Minnesota, Minneapolis; de Grummond Collection, University of Southern Mississippi, Hattiesburg.

Erik Haugaard comments:

I conceive of my fellow men as individuals: lonely figures trying to understand the dilemma they are born into. To live, to survive, is to me an heroic task but not necessarily a tragic one; victory is possible, at least on an individual level. The possibility of love and friendship exists; it is not a matter of chance but of choice. I cannot conceive of literature without this faith; the choiceless man going to his doom is but a silent brute, and he would not have left behind him the literature, art, and music of which we have a right to be justly proud.

*   *   *

Erik Haugaard is an author with a deep commitment. Gleaming through his artist's sense of time, place, and character is his belief in the human spirit and the dignity of mankind. He blends a wide variety of truths that underscore this belief.

In *Hakon of Rogen's Saga* Hakon tells his own story of love and hate, freedom and slavery, life and death. The novel rings forth in epic language that evokes a feeling of Viking times. *A Slave's Tale* continues the saga as Hakon sets forth from Norway to return Rark, a former slave, to his native Brittany. Helga, the slave girl of the first novel, is a stowaway. She recounts the starkly tragic tale with deep emotion. There is a delicate balance between the fate of the characters (even the minor ones) and the underlying message of the meaning of war.

Again, Haugaard interprets history and gives it deeper meaning in *Orphans of the Wind*, a tale of the sea and of the American Civil War. This is Jim's story as he sets sail as a deck boy from Bristol to the United States. Here is a master storyteller who impressively interweaves the denigrating effect of slavery and the grimness of war.

Guido, a 12-year-old orphan in Naples during World War II, is one of *The Little Fishes* who escapes from the degradation imposed by the Germans. With two other children, he makes his way to Cassino where he hopes to find freedom. A harrowing odyssey, the novel carries with it a forceful testament against war. The power of the human spirit permeates the book and radiates a passionate urge to survive. With equal forcefulness, Haugaard traces the search for self in *The Rider and His Horse*. The source is the writings of Josephus. The time is 72–73 A.D. when a group of Jews, the Zealots, are making a last hopeless stand against the Romans. 15-year-old David questions the meaning of everything around him and is caught up in the tragic episode. He emerges with an awareness of the moment of his experiences and a sense of identity.

The Untold Tale is a story of the war between Denmark and Sweden in the 17th century. *A Messenger for Parliament* presents another facet of war, the 17th-century English Civil War. Young Oliver's involvement in the brutal conflict is described with pace, and also with Haugaard's keen observation and interpretation of history.

16th-century feudal Japan comes alive in *The Samurai's Tale,* seen through the eyes of Taro, whose father has been murdered by the soldiers of the warlord. Lord Akiyama raises Taro as his son. His duties start in the kitchen and continue in the stable.

Finally he is trained in the Samurai tradition, following their rigid code. He responds to the deep sense of loyalty, the formal manners, the acceptance of Zen, and the love of poetry. Surrounded by turbulence, Taro adapts readily to his milieu. When Lord Akiyama is executed, Taro sets out to avenge his death. We are taken close to the Samurai lifestyle as Taro muses, creates poetry, acts when action is needed. Haugaard shares his knowledge of the period with a sense of authority which adds substance and texture to the highly adventurous story. He leaves the reader much to ponder over—psychologically and philosophically.

In *Prince Boghole*, an intriguing title, Desmond, King of Eire, sets out to find a husband for his daughter, Princess Orla, heir to his kingdom of Munster. When three suitors come to the kingdom, King Desmond plans to have a contest to select the best man of the three. Haugaard develops a solution that is not only ingenious but gratifying. The novel reveals another facet of the writer's creative power.

Throughout his earlier novels there is the steady beat of the senselessness of war and the evils of slavery. Haugaard captures language and speech patterns that admirably suit background and characters. Situations are often grim, events almost unbearable. With poetic prose Haugaard speaks out in a clear and unmistakable voice about the futility of war and the need for freedom and understanding. He accomplishes this without moralizing or weakening the power of the story.

In the more recent novels, the scope of his imagination and interests broadens, which seems to indicate that Haugaard is an ever-developing and powerful writer.

Recognition must also be given to Haugaard for his fresh and artful translation of *The Complete Fairy Tales and Stories of Hans Andersen*. His faithfulness to Andersen's language and spirit is a remarkable feat.

—Mae Durham Roger

HAWES, Charles Boardman. American. Born in Clifton Springs, New York, 24 January 1889. Educated at schools in Bangor, Maine; Bowdoin College, Brunswick, Maine, graduated 1911; Harvard University, Cambridge, Massachusetts (Longfellow fellow), 1911–12. Married Dorothea Cable in 1916; two sons. Taught at Harrisburg Academy, Pennsylvania, one year; staff member, *Youth's Companion*, Boston; associate editor, *Open Road*, Dayton, Ohio. Recipient: American Library Association Newbery Medal, 1924. *Died 15 July 1923.*

PUBLICATIONS FOR CHILDREN

Fiction

The Mutineers. Boston, Atlantic Monthly Press, 1920; London, Heinemann, 1923.
The Great Quest, illustrated by George Varian. Boston, Atlantic Monthly Press, 1921; London, Heinemann, 1922.
The Dark Frigate. Boston, Atlantic Monthly Press, 1923; London, Heinemann, 1924.

PUBLICATIONS FOR ADULTS

Other

Whaling, completed by Dorothea Hawes. New York, Doubleday, and London, Heinemann, 1924.
Gloucester, By Land and Sea: The Story of a New England Seacoast Town. Boston, Little Brown, 1928.

*   *   *

Charles Boardman Hawes's untimely death at 35 cut short a career that might have rivaled Robert Louis Stevenson's had it run its course. With the exception of two novels, *The Dark Frigate* and *The Mutineers,* Hawes's work is long out of print. Derivative and flawed as these two books are, they both reveal what an inspired storyteller Hawes at his best could be.

Except for the fact that *The Dark Frigate* and *The Mutineers* are set in different centuries, they could both be the same book. The lawful masters of the ship are murdered and the vessel taken over by pirates. But once the villains gain the upper hand, their luck deserts them. No longer can they do anything right. Eventually the heroes outwit them and regain the ship, leaving the evildoers to a richly deserved fate. If that sounds familiar it is because we have read that tale before: Stevenson's *Treasure Island.*

Hawes never was able to escape the shadow of that great book. His prose and narrative skill often approach the master's, but he is unable to sustain the performance over an entire novel. *The Mutineers* is the more successful of the two works, and one of the most gripping adventures ever written about the China clipper trade. *The Dark Frigate* is much more uneven. It begins too late, continues too long, and seems awash in an impossibly archaic dialect that owes far too much to Kingsley's *Westward, Ho!* Yet even this leaking, lumbering galleon of a book has its moments. Tom Jordan's takeover of *The Rose of Devon,* the murder of Captain Candle, and the fight with the Porcupine ketch are episodes of high adventure that can stand with the best.

The basic flaw of both *The Dark Frigate* and *The Mutineers* is their lack of a villain of the stature of Long John Silver. It is Silver, so charming, so menacing, who makes *Treasure Island* pulse with excitement. By contrast, Hawes's villains—Jordan, Falk, and Kipping—are weaklings and petty crooks. Hawes is much more successful with his minor characters. In the Fagin-like Jacob of *The Dark Frigate* we apparently have an anomaly: a Jewish pirate! The black cook of *The Mutineers* is shrewd and courageous, an original and admirable figure in spite of his minstrel show dialect. But even his roots may lie in a similar character in Kipling's *Captains Courageous*.

At the time of his death Charles Boardman Hawes was a second-rate writer trying to make up with detail what he lacked in originality. Nevertheless his work showed promise of great things to come. Had he been allowed to live longer, had he been less bookish, had he actually sailed before the mast himself like Jack London and Herman Melville, he might stand today as one of the great writers of the sea. As it is, he is not very far behind them.

—Eric A. Kimmel

HAYES, John F(rancis). Canadian. Born in Dryden, Ontario, 5 August 1904. Educated at the University of Toronto evening classes, 1930–45. Married Helen Eileen Casselman in 1927; two sons and one daughter. Writer, MacLean-Hunter Publishing Company, 1925–27, Consolidated Press, 1927–29, and Saturday Night Press, 1928, all Toronto; sales promotion writer, General Motors of Canada, Oshawa, Ontario, 1929–30; head of the Creative Department, 1930–34, and assistant sales manager, 1935, Brigdens Ltd., Toronto; sales promotion manager, Moffats Ltd., Weston, Ontario, 1937–40; executive assistant, 1940–45, sales manager, 1945–47, vice-president and general manager, 1947–50, vice-president and general manager of the Montreal Branch, 1950–56, and director and member of the Executive Committee, Southam Press Ltd., Toronto; managing director, Southam Printing Company, Toronto, 1956–60. Director, Toronto Graphic Arts Association. Recipient: Governor-General's award, 1952, 1954; Quebec Government Scientific and Literary award, 1955; Canadian Library Association Book of the Year Medal, 1959; Vicky Metcalf award, 1964. *Died in November 1980.*

PUBLICATIONS FOR CHILDREN (illustrated by Fred J. Finley)

Fiction

Buckskin Colonist. Toronto, Copp Clark, 1947; Oxford, Blackwell, 1948.
Treason at York. Toronto, Copp Clark, 1949.
A Land Divided. Toronto, Copp Clark, 1951; Philadelphia, Westminster Press, 1954.
Rebels Ride at Night. Toronto, Copp Clark, 1953.
Bugles in the Hills. Toronto, Copp Clark, 1955; Oxford, Blackwell, and New York, Messner, 1956.
The Dangerous Cove: A Story of Early Days in Newfoundland. Toronto, Copp Clark, 1957; New York, Messner, 1960.
Quest in the Cariboo. Toronto, Copp Clark, 1960.
Flaming Prairie: A Story of the Northwest Rebellion of 1885. Toronto, Copp Clark, 1965.
The Steel Ribbon. Toronto, Copp Clark, 1967.
The Nation Builders. Toronto, Copp Clark, 1968.
On Loyalist Trails: A Story about the United Empire Loyalists, illustrated by J. Merle Smith. Toronto, Copp Clark, 1971.

PUBLICATIONS FOR ADULTS

Other

The Renovation Business. Toronto, Crane, 1962.
Switzerland. Toronto, Air Canada, 1962.
The Challenge of Change: 50 Years 1912–1962. Toronto, Downtown Church Workers Association, 1962.

Into a Nation. Toronto, Canadian Council of Churches, 1966.
Wilderness Mission: The Story of Sainte-Marie-among-the-Hurons. Toronto, Ryerson Press, 1969.

*   *   *

The historical novels of John F. Hayes provide a near panorama, in fiction, of pre-20th-century Canadian history. The earliest setting is Newfoundland in 1676; the latest, the Prairies in 1885. Hayes dealt with most regions of Canada (the Maritimes, Ontario, the Prairies, British Columbia), omitting only the far north and, significantly, Quebec. And he tackled all major conflicts—again with one important exception involving Quebec: the Battle of the Plains of Abraham which resulted in the final fall of New France to the British. Why Hayes assiduously avoided Quebec subjects seems to be due to a reluctance to confront English-French antagonisms within Canada. Accordingly, another potentially divisive topic—the removal of the Acadians (*A Land Divided*)—is treated so as to defuse the historical situation of the long-lasting hostilities felt by the actual participants. Thus the expulsion is smoothed over with pro-British justifications; thus the cruelty of the eviction is minimized; and thus the Acadian co-hero, Pierre—though his family is expelled—even joins the English Navy. The reality was starker, and passions ran deeper, than Hayes allowed. Accordingly, though the novel certainly contains moments of excitement and various authentic details of the period, it nevertheless violates the spirit of the time.

Hayes's other historical novels treat the settlement of Newfoundland (*The Dangerous Cove*), the Loyalist emigration to Canada (*On Loyalist Trails*), the War of 1812 (*Treason at York*), the Selkirk settlers (*Buckskin Colonist*), the Mackenzie Rebellion (*Rebels Ride at Night*), the British Columbia gold rush (*Quest in the Cariboo*), the early days of the Mounties (*Bugles in the Hills*), the building of the Canadian Pacific Railway (*The Steel Ribbon*), and the Riel Rebellion (*Flaming Prairie*). In these books he was generally true to the reality of the times he treats, and the historical facts, though accurate and reasonably detailed, are usually not intrusions into the story but rather enrichments of it. The historical events are quite exciting in themselves, and this contributes to the total excitement and interest that the novels create.

Hayes's fiction typically locates a teen-age male hero plus a close friend in an exciting historical time or place. Soon the boys, for reasons often connected with their fathers, find themselves at the focal point between good and evil groups and, acting, prevent calamities from happening—or at least attenuate them. The main hero generally has a close relationship with his father, and the father's praise of his son's manly achievements is frequent. In various books (*The Dangerous Cove, A Land Divided*) the hero is even allowed the wish-fulfilment situation of rescuing his father from dangerous enemies. Further, where the hero's father is dead (*Rebels Ride at Night*), a substitute father soon steps forth to become the beneficiary of good deeds and the source of praise that boys desire. The father's (or substitute's) occupation is often important, incidentally, for the boy frequently follows in his footsteps. Action so satisfactory of boyhood dreams and male role expectations is one of the prominent elements in the books and one of the reasons that boys like them.

The defects in Hayes's fiction are sporadic, occurring to different degrees in different books, but fatal to none. These include the improbabilities of plot, repetitive action, weak concluding paragraphs, and dialogue which is acceptable but not inspired. His strength, besides historical authenticity, was the ability to create, notwithstanding defects, tales of excitement with which a boy can easily identify because they meet his psychological needs for adventure, manly behaviour, success, and parental praise.

—John Robert Sorfleet

HAYWOOD, Carolyn. American. Born in Philadelphia, Pennsylvania, 3 January 1898. Educated at High School for Girls and Normal School, both Philadelphia; Pennsylvania Academy of Fine Arts (Cresson traveling scholar), 1923–25. Teacher, Friends Central School, Philadelphia; assistant in the studio of Violet Oakley; portrait painter and mural artist. Address: 210 Lynnebrook Lane, Philadelphia, Pennsylvania 19118, U.S.A.

PUBLICATIONS FOR CHILDREN (illustrated by the author)

Fiction

When I Grow Up. Racine, Wisconsin, Whitman, 1931.
"B" Is for Betsy. New York, Harcourt Brace, 1939.
Two and Two Are Four. New York, Harcourt Brace, 1940.
Betsy and Billy. New York, Harcourt Brace, 1941.
Primrose Day. New York, Harcourt Brace, 1942.
Back to School with Betsy. New York, Harcourt Brace, 1943.
Here's a Penny. New York, Harcourt Brace, 1944.
Betsy and the Boys. New York, Harcourt Brace, 1945.
Penny and Peter. New York, Harcourt Brace, 1946.
Little Eddie. New York, Morrow, 1947.
Penny Goes to Camp. New York, Morrow, 1948.
Eddie and the Fire Engine. New York, Morrow, 1949.
Betsy's Little Star. New York, Morrow, 1950.
Eddie and Gardenia. New York, Morrow, 1951.
The Mixed-Up Twins. New York, Morrow, 1952.
Eddie's Pay Dirt. New York, Morrow, 1953.
Betsy and the Circus. New York, Morrow, 1954.
Eddie and His Big Deals. New York, Morrow, 1955.
Betsy's Busy Summer. New York, Morrow, 1956.
Eddie Makes Music. New York, Morrow, 1957.
Betsy's Winterhouse. New York, Morrow, 1958.
Eddie and Louella. New York, Morrow, 1959.
Annie Pat and Eddie. New York, Morrow, 1960.
Snowbound with Betsy. New York, Morrow, 1962.
Here Comes the Bus! New York, Morrow, 1963.
Eddie's Green Thumb. New York, Morrow, 1964.
Robert Rows the River. New York, Morrow, 1965.
Eddie the Dog Holder. New York, Morrow, 1966.
Betsy and Mr. Kilpatrick. New York, Morrow, 1967.
Ever-Ready Eddie. New York, Morrow, 1968.
Taffy and Melissa Molasses. New York, Morrow, 1969.
Eddie's Happenings. New York, Morrow, 1971.
A Christmas Fantasy, illustrated by Glenys and Victor Ambrus. New York, Morrow, 1972; Leicester, Brockhampton Press, 1973.
Away Went the Balloons. New York, Morrow, 1973.
"C" Is for Cupcake. New York, Morrow, 1974.
Eddie's Valuable Property. New York, Morrow, 1975.
A Valentine Fantasy, illustrated by Glenys and Victor Ambrus. New York, Morrow, 1976.
Betsy's Play School, illustrated by James Griffin. New York, Morrow, 1977.
Eddie's Menagerie, illustrated by Ingrid Fetz. New York, Morrow, 1978.
The King's Monster, illustrated by Victor Ambrus. New York, Morrow, 1980.
Halloween Treats, illustrated by Victoria de Larrea. New York, Morrow, 1981.
Santa Claus Forever!, illustrated by Glenys and Victor Ambrus. New York, Morrow, 1983; Oxford, Oxford University Press, 1986.
Happy Birthday from Carolyn Haywood, illustrated by Wendy Watson. New York, Morrow, 1984.
Summer Fun, illustrated by Julie Durrell. New York, Morrow, 1986.

How the Reindeer Saved Santa, illustrated by Victor Ambrus. New York, Morrow, 1986; Oxford, Oxford University Press, 1987.
Merry Christmas from Eddie. New York, Morrow, 1986.
Hello, Star, illustrated by Julie Durrell. New York, Morrow, 1987.

Other

Editor, *Make a Joyful Noise! Bible Verses for Children.* Philadelphia, Westminster Press, 1984.

*

Manuscript Collections: Free Library, Philadelphia; Kerlan Collection, University of Minnesota, Minneapolis; de Grummond Collection, University of Southern Mississippi, Hattiesburg.

Carolyn Haywood comments:
I write for children because I feel that they need to know what is going on in their world and they can best understand it through stories about their world.

*　　*　　*

Carolyn Haywood is a prolific writer of very popular books that appeal to children in the 7 to 10 age group. Since her first junior novel appeared many years ago, her recognition as one of the premier writers of mildly exciting adventure stories involving the typical concerns of normal, middle-class children has steadily grown.

The reasons for Haywood's immense success are numerous. One of these surely must be the attractive plots of her stories, centered on the day-by-day experiences of ordinary yet extremely vigorous, active, and dominant children. Haywood creates imaginative yet wholesome situations for these children to live through, often with problems to solve. These problem conditions, of little actual consequence except for the great deal of activity they allow her characters to perform, are typical of those found in children's lives. These are predicaments which the child reader easily recognizes as ones that could actually happen to him. They are situations spun through narrative plots much like those found in the typical social novel, that is, a telling out of ever-widening social arrangements rather than the depiction of well-developed representations of personality. As well, they use an episodic, short-story form of organization. The chapters of Haywood's books are so lightly threaded, one to the other, that each of them can be read almost by itself.

The main characters of Haywood's tales are idealized, unsophisticated, even stereotyped children. They are flat or "mythical" people who enter and leave the episodes in her stories with much of the same set of qualities. These fictional children, who seldom if ever pause to question their responses to the forces set against them, are nonetheless highly endearing to young readers. Furthermore, Haywood makes sure these readers understand fully the motives of her fictionalized subjects by describing them in direct and steadfast fashion. By this means her readers are left with little or nothing to infer about their personalities or motivations. This may seem defective writing, but it is a style that young children have repeatedly shown they prefer over an indirect or subtle development of character in books. It obviously was soon apparent to Haywood that these characters were so believable to her readers that she could successfully write a series on some of them. Thus Betsy and Eddie have emerged as main attractions in several of Haywood's different stories.

—Patrick Groff

HEADLEY, Elizabeth.   See CAVANNA, Betty.

HEDDERWICK, Mairi.   British.   Born in Gourock, Renfrewshire, Scotland, 2 May 1939. Educated at St. Columba's Girls School, Kilmacolm, Renfrewshire, until 1957; Edinburgh College of Art, 1957–61; Jordanhill College of Education, Glasgow, 1961–62. Divorced; one son and one daughter. Crofter and designer, Coll, Inner Hebrides, 10 years. Address: 15 Ardconnel Terrace, Inverness IV2 3HE, Scotland.

PUBLICATIONS FOR CHILDREN (illustrated by the author)

Fiction

Katie Morag Delivers the Mail.   London, Bodley Head, 1984; Boston, Little Brown, 1988.
Katie Morag and the Two Grandmothers.   London, Bodley Head, and Boston, Little Brown, 1985.
Katie Morag and the Tiresome Ted.   London, Bodley Head, and Boston, Little Brown, 1986.
Katie Morag and the Big Boy Cousins.   London, Bodley Head, and Boston, Little Brown, 1987.
Peedie Peebles' Summer or Winter Book.   London, Bodley Head, 1989; as *P.D. Peebles' Summer or Winter Book,* Boston, Little Brown, 1989.

PUBLICATIONS FOR ADULTS

Other

Views of Scotland.   Gartocharn, Dunbarton, Famedram, 1981.
An Eye on the Hebrides.   Edinburgh, Canongate, 1989.

*

Illustrator: *The Old Woman Who Lived in a Vinegar Bottle* by Rumer Godden, 1972; *Herself and Janet Reachfar,* 1975, *Janet Reachfar and the Kelpie,* 1976, and *Janet Reachfar and Chickabird,* 1978, all by Jane Duncan; *The Gift of the Tarns* by E.R. Taylor, 1977; *A Cat Called Rover; A Dog Called Smith* by Wendy Body, 1981; *Hamish and the Wee Witch,* 1986, and *Hamish and the Fairy Bairn,* 1989, both by Moira Miller; *Our Best Stories* edited by Anne Wood and Ann Pilling, 1986.

Mairi Hedderwick comments:

All my work comes from the hotch potch jumble of events and feelings that float around in my memory box. I am a totally subjective writer/illustrator/communicator. (I prefer the last description—must be the African Missionary Grandfather in me).

I can only write, draw, and talk about what I have experienced. The Katie Morag books are a pure nostalgia rerun of the young family-rearing island years in the Inner Hebrides of Scotland. Katie Morag is the late third child, my family long since grown up. Her bedroom is full of the toys and detritus that were my own children's. She wears my daughter's clothes. Grannie Island cooks on my Rayburn stove. Katie Morag's good moods and bad moods are all mine. As a mature(?) woman, I threw my old teddy bear into the sea—twice...

Peedie Peebles is the second menopausal child. With him I am trying to get away from the island but I see sea landscapes hovering in the background still.

*   *   *

Mairi Hedderwick depicts Scottish island life with affection and understanding, mercifully devoid of the sentimentality that so often afflicts similar locations. She herself was an island dweller in the 1960's when she became a classic "drop-out" from civilisation, running a small printing press with her family on the island of Coll in the Hebrides. She looks back to this time with nostalgia but no regrets, using her experiences as a background for her highly successful picture books.

Katie Morag Delivers the Mail was welcomed not only as a first-rate picture book for young children but for the arrival of a *Scottish* artist and writer—a rare being. Katie Morag is a resourceful small girl living in the post office on the island of Struay. The success of the illustrations lies in the minute details so beloved by children—the animals wreaking unseen havoc, the clutter of goods on the shelves of the shop, and the bustling, everyday life of a closeknit community. The storyline is a simple one. Sent to deliver five parcels, Katie Morag dawdles along the way, stops to paddle in a burn, and falls in. The parcel labels become illegible and are hastily delivered—to the wrong addresses. Only one reaches its correct destination at her redoubtable grannie's house who comes to the rescue by helping to sort out the muddle. Grannie plays a central role in all four Katie Morag books. She is depicted in dungarees, often with her head deep in the innards of a tractor. Hedderwick was surprised that the book was chosen as an example of a non-sexist picture book. With no crusading in mind, she had simply portrayed a woman doing her everyday tasks, a common occurrence on the island.

Katie Morag's Grannie Island is contrasted with her Grannie Mainland in *Katie Morag and the Two Grandmothers.* The fancy ways of Grannie Mainland with her hair rollers, powder, and paint come in handy when the prize sheep Alcina falls in the Boggy Loch just before the Annual Show.

But the most successful book is undoubtedly *Katie Morag and the Tiresome Ted,* which shows sibling rivalry at its worst. When a new baby appears, Katie Morag vents her wrath on her teddy bear, which is flung into the sea only to be washed ashore several times. The illustrations are splendid with the island's population of human and wildlife skilfully portrayed along with a dramatic storyline.

Hedderwick has since departed from Katie Morag with a small, "lift the flap" book, *Peedie Peebles' Summer or Winter Book.* The storyline is minimal, in a book suitable for the youngest child. Following the routine of a toddler in both summer and winter, the child can watch the antics of Peedie Peebles who is blissfully unaware of the disturbance to his long-suffering parents. The lavish details of the illustrations and the pleasure of investigating underneath the flap make this a particularly enjoyable book for sharing.

—Valerie Bierman

HEIDE, Florence Parry.   Has also written as Alex B. Allen; Jamie McDonald.   American.   Born in Pittsburgh, Pennsylvania, 27 February 1919. Educated at Ellis School, Pittsburgh, graduated 1935; Wilson College, Chambersburg, Pennsylvania; University of California, Los Angeles, B.A. 1939. Married Donald C. Heide in 1943; three sons and twin daughters. Worked for RKO, and in public relations and advertising, New York; former public relations director, Pittsburgh Playhouse. Litt.D.: Carthage College, Kenosha, Wisconsin, 1979. Agent: Marilyn Marlow, Curtis Brown, 10 Astor Place,

New York, New York 10003. Address: 6910 Third Avenue, Kenosha, Wisconsin 53140, U.S.A.

PUBLICATIONS FOR CHILDREN

Fiction

Benjamin Budge and Barnaby Ball, illustrated by Sally Mathews. New York, Four Winds Press, 1967.
Maximilian, with Sylvia W. Van Clief, illustrated by Ed Renfro. New York, Funk and Wagnalls, 1967.
The Day It Snowed in Summer, with Sylvia W. Van Clief, illustrated by Kenneth Longtemps. New York, Funk and Wagnalls, 1968.
How Big Am I?, with Sylvia W. Van Clief, illustrated by George Suyeoka. Chicago, Follett, 1968.
It Never Is Dark, with Sylvia W. Van Clief, illustrated by Don Almquist. Chicago, Follett, 1968.
Sebastian, with Sylvia W. Van Clief, illustrated by Betty Fraser. New York, Funk and Wagnalls, 1968.
That's What Friends Are For, with Sylvia W. Van Clief, illustrated by Brinton Turkle. New York, Four Winds Press, 1968.
Hannibal (as Jamie McDonald), with Anne and Walter Thiess, illustrated by Anne and Walter Thiess. New York, Funk and Wagnalls, 1968.
Maximilian Becomes Famous, illustrated by Ed Renfro. New York, Funk and Wagnalls, 1969.
The New Neighbor, with Sylvia W. Van Clief, illustrated by Jerry Warshaw. Chicago, Follett, 1970.
Alphabet Zoop, illustrated by Sally Mathews. New York, McCall, 1970.
Giants Are Very Brave People, illustrated by Charles Robinson. New York, Parents' Magazine Press, 1970.
The Little One, illustrated by Kenneth Longtemps. New York, Lion Press, 1970.
Sound of Sunshine, Sound of Rain, illustrated by Kenneth Longtemps. New York, Parents' Magazine Press, 1970.
Look! Look! A Story Book, illustrated by Carol Nicklaus. New York, McCall, 1971.
The Key, illustrated by Ati Forberg. New York, Atheneum, 1971.
The Shrinking of Treehorn, illustrated by Edward Gorey. New York, Holiday House, 1971; London, Kestrel, 1975.
Some Things Are Scary, illustrated by Robert Osborne. New York, Scholastic, 1971.
Who Needs Me?, illustrated by Sally Mathews. Minneapolis, Augsburg, 1971.
My Castle, illustrated by Symeon Shimin. New York, McGraw Hill, 1972.
The Mystery of the Missing Suitcase, with Sylvia W. Van Clief, illustrated by Seymour Fleishman. Chicago, Whitman, 1972.
The Mystery of the Silver Tag, with Sylvia W. Van Clief, illustrated by Seymour Fleishman. Chicago, Whitman, 1972.
The Hidden Box Mystery, with Sylvia W. Van Clief, illustrated by Seymour Fleishman. Chicago, Whitman, 1973.
Mystery at MacAdoo Zoo, with Sylvia W. Van Clief, illustrated by Seymour Fleishman. Chicago, Whitman, 1973.
Mystery of the Whispering Voice, with Sylvia W. Van Clief, illustrated by Seymour Fleishman. Chicago, Whitman, 1974.
Mystery of the Melting Snowman, with Roxanne Heide, illustrated by Seymour Fleishman. Chicago, Whitman, 1974.
Mystery of the Vanishing Visitor, with Roxanne Heide, illustrated by Seymour Fleishman. Chicago, Whitman, 1975.
Mystery of the Bewitched Bookmobile, with Roxanne Heide, illustrated by Seymour Fleishman. Chicago, Whitman, 1975.
When the Sad One Comes to Stay. Philadelphia, Lippincott, 1975.
Growing Anyway Up. Philadelphia, Lippincott, 1976.

Mystery of the Lonely Lantern, with Roxanne Heide, illustrated by Seymour Fleishman. Chicago, Whitman, 1976.
Mystery at Keyhole Carnival, with Roxanne Heide, illustrated by Seymour Fleishman. Chicago, Whitman, 1977.
Brillstone Break-In, with Roxanne Heide. Chicago, Whitman, 1977.
Mystery of the Midnight Message, with Roxanne Heide, illustrated by Seymour Fleishman. Chicago, Whitman, 1977.
Fables You Shouldn't Pay Any Attention To, with Sylvia W. Van Clief, illustrated by Victoria Chess. Philadelphia, Lippincott, 1978.
Banana Twist. New York, Holiday House, 1978.
Secret Dreamer, Secret Dreams. Philadelphia, Lippincott, 1978.
Fear at Brillstone, with Roxanne Heide. Chicago, Whitman, 1978.
Mystery at Southport Cinema, with Roxanne Heide, illustrated by Seymour Fleishman. Chicago, Whitman, 1978.
Face at the Brillstone Window, with Roxanne Heide. Chicago, Whitman, 1979.
Mystery of the Mummy's Mask, with Roxanne Heide, illustrated by Seymour Fleishman. Chicago, Whitman, 1979.
Body in the Brillstone Garage, with Roxanne Heide. Chicago, Whitman, 1980.
Mystery of the Forgotten Island, with Roxanne Heide, illustrated by Seymour Fleishman. Chicago, Whitman, 1980.
A Monster Is Coming! A Monster Is Coming!, with Roxanne Heide, illustrated by Rachi Farrow. New York, Watts, 1980.
Black Magic at Brillstone, with Roxanne Heide, illustrated by Joe Krush. Chicago, Whitman, 1981.
Treehorn's Treasure, illustrated by Edward Gorey. New York, Holiday House, 1981; London, Kestrel, 1983.
Time's Up!, illustrated by Marylin Hafner. New York, Holiday House, 1982.
The Problem with Pulcifer, illustrated by Judith Glasser. New York, Lippincott, 1982.
The Wendy Puzzle. New York, Holiday House, 1982.
Time Bomb at Brillstone, with Roxanne Heide, illustrated by Joe Krush. Chicago, Whitman, 1982.
Banana Blitz. New York, Holiday House, 1983.
Mystery on Danger Road, with Roxanne Heide, illustrated by Seymour Fleishman. Chicago, Whitman, 1983.
Treehorn's Wish, illustrated by Edward Gorey. New York, Holiday House, 1984; Oxford, Oxford University Press, 1986.
Time Flies!, illustrated by Marylin Hafner. New York, Holiday House, 1984.
Tales for the Perfect Child, illustrated by Victoria Chess. New York, Lothrop, 1985; London, Piccadilly Press, 1986.

Fiction (as Alex B. Allen, with Sylvia W. Van Clief)

Basketball Toss Up, illustrated by Kevin Royt. Chicago, Whitman, 1972.
No Place for Baseball, illustrated by Kevin Royt. Chicago, Whitman, 1973.
Danger on Broken Arrow Trail, illustrated by Michael Norman. Chicago, Whitman, 1974.
Fifth Down, illustrated by Dan Siculan. Chicago, Whitman, 1974.
The Tennis Menace, with David Heide, illustrated by Timothy Jones. Chicago, Whitman, 1975.

Verse (songs)

Songs to Sing about Things You Think About, music by Sylvia W. Van Clief, illustrated by Rosalie Schmidt. New York, Day, 1971.
Christmas Bells and Snowflakes, music by Sylvia W. Van Clief. New York, Southern Music, 1971.
Holidays! Holidays!, music by Sylvia W. Van Clief. New York, Southern Music, 1971.

Other

Lost! (textbook), with Roxanne Heide.   New York, Holt Rinehart, 1973.

I See America Smiling (textbook), with Roxanne Heide.   New York, Holt Rinehart, 1973.

No Roads for the Wind (textbook), with David Fisher Parry.   New York, Macmillan, 1974.

Who Can? (reader), with Sylvia W. Van Clief.   New York, Macmillan, 1974.

Lost and Found (reader), with Sylvia W. Van Clief.   New York, Macmillan, 1974.

Hats and Bears (reader), with Sylvia W. Van Clief.   New York, Macmillan, 1974.

Tell about Someone You Love (textbook), with Roxanne Heide.   New York, Macmillan, 1974.

God and Me, illustrated by Ted Smith.   St. Louis, Concordia, 1975.

You and Me, illustrated by Ted Smith.   St. Louis, Concordia, 1975.

Changes, illustrated by Kathy Counts.   St. Louis, Concordia, 1978.

I Love Every-People, with Roxanne Heide, illustrated by John Sandford.   St. Louis, Concordia, 1978.

Who Taught Me? Was It You, God?, illustrated by Terry Whittle.   St. Louis, Concordia, 1978.

By the Time You Count to Ten, illustrated by Pam Erickson.   St. Louis, Concordia, 1979.

*

Florence Parry Heide comments:

A late bloomer, I started to write only when my five children had started school. Since I'd never written before, I wasn't sure then (and am not sure yet) what I want most of all to write or what I am best at writing, so I keep trying a great variety: picture books, juvenile novels, mysteries; funny books, sad books—I love them all. There are so many ideas waiting out there, so many unwritten stories, so many characters yet to be invented, so many many words to spin. What an adventure!

*   *   *

Florence Parry Heide has drawn most sustained notice as author of the Treehorn books, drolleries enhanced by the witty drawings of Edward Gorey. As much for adults as children are her three spoofs on perfect and obnoxious children. Hilarity reigns in the two books about Jonah, as well as the two about Noah. Worthy of note are three stories for young adolescents in which Heide deftly fleshes out the character of the troubled, female protagonists. For reluctant readers Heide offers the action of 20 mysteries, each solved in 128 pages by the children of The Spotlight Detective Club or two teenagers of Brillstone Apartments. For young children Heide has authored two dozen fair-to-middling picture books including some for Lutheran publishing houses and some textbook readers. In two decades Heide has written about 75 books. Until her death Sylvia Van Clief was second author for nearly one-third of the titles. Then Heide's twin daughter Roxanne became collaborator for 15 of the mysteries and five other titles.

Diminutive in an adult-dominated setting, the deadly serious Treehorn believes he is becoming even smaller in *The Shrinking of Treehorn.* The various, unruffled responses of mother (as long as you don't do it at the table), father, friend, teacher (we don't shrink in this class), and principal to the shrinking of Treehorn endow the story with clichés that are cleverly twisted and generate the reader's empathy for his neglected feeling. The writing is scrupulously controlled; Heide adroitly unfolds the perplexing and preposterous circumstances with restraint and sobriety, and allows Treehorn himself to put an end to his unusual condition. The delectable, bridled humor is taken up in the pen and ink drawings.

In *Treehorn's Treasure* he is possessed of an even more fertile imagination, largely fed by a craving for comic books and the fantastic products of their ads, which money can buy. Father urges Treehorn to save his dollar allowance because "money doesn't grow on trees." Treehorn puts the dollar in an envelope already addressed to Instant Magic and tucks it in a tree. Before long he observes the leaves are changing to dollar bills, thus furnishing him the wherewithal to make his purchases. The reader readily accepts the fantasy while the unbelieving adults of Treehorn's universe consistently react obliquely. The engaging interplay of illustration and text augment meaning and refine the portrayal of the unique boy. Gorey's trenchant black-on-white drawings place lovable Treehorn on the latticework of an angular environment, except for the occasional balloons that convey the little fellow's wild imaginings.

One does not reveal the wish made before blowing out the candles on a birthday cake lest the wish not come true. In *Treehorn's Wish* the wish of the final page of text is not shared with the reader but a wry story is built around the three wishes granted to Treehorn by a genie of golden earrings and long robe who appears out of a puff of smoke from the jug Treehorn has found in the yard. Although at the beginning of the day Treehorn hopes his parents may lavish him with presents to make up for the past meager years, by breakfast he has reason to believe his father and mother are more concerned about matters other than his birthday. Treehorn's first wish assures he will have a birthday cake and the second, candles. Neglect and admonishments of the day are countered by Treehorn's effusive thoughts about ways to use his third wish. Gorey's sophisticated line drawings perfectly complement the bittersweet account of stoical Treehorn's unusual birthday. The final illustration, at once conclusive and provocative, shows Treehorn alone at the kitchen table blowing the candles of his cake; two empty chairs attend him.

The format of Heide's spoofs might suggest the books are for beginning readers but the titles should be read as warning labels. These tales are for the worldly wise of all ages, those ready for a dose of irreverence. *The Problem with Pulcifer* introduces a child who will not watch television. Parents and school personnel worry about the boy who prefers to read books and refuses to succumb to television addiction as everybody else in the book has. Seven short pieces in *Fables You Shouldn't Pay Any Attention To* and in *Tales for the Perfect Child* treat the flip side of moral sketches. Greedy Gretchen (the gluttonous fish in *Fables*), after displaying her disgusting eating habits at lunch, is satiated and doesn't go for the worm on the hook while the other fish, who have eaten daintily and are still hungry, meet their doom. *Tales* might have been subtitled Techniques to Get Your Own Way. Arthur prefers his comfortable old clothes but acquiesces to his mother's command to get dressed up for the visit to Aunt Eunice. Arthur dutifully puts on his finest clothes and then goes to the kitchen to pour himself a large glass of grape juice. The three books might not be appreciated by the perfect parents who try so hard but anyone ready to chuckle at some sprightly commentary on proper behavior will be amused by the tongue-in-cheek humor.

Jonah in *Banana Twist* applies for admission to a boarding school that promises a television set and refrigerator in every dorm room. Upon arrival in *Banana Blitz* Jonah finds his roommate to be none other than the antagonist of the earlier book, Goober. Zany antics and slapstick humor give one meaning to the common word of the titles, although bananas play their part in each book. Surely both Jonah and Goober are one-of-a-kind boys, even though one-dimensional. Similar in tone are the books about Noah, *Time's Up!* and *Time Flies!*. The son of an efficiency fanatic shares, in first person, his viewpoints about adjusting to a new neighborhood and a baby sister. The writing style is breezy; coincidence and misunderstanding advance the plots and bring about satisfying endings.

Keenly sensitive characterization and tight prose distinguish Heide's first-person narratives for emerging adolescents. The point of view, like an autobiographical monologue, is consistently of the girl protagonist, who introduces the audience to other characters in the dimensions she sees fit but also freely reveals to the reader her innermost feelings. The author provides a vivid and profound character study.

Sara (*When the Sad One Comes to Stay*) is ultimately confronted with the choice between her calculating, success-bent mother and the shabby, elderly neighborhood character who proffers warmth and friendship, recalling in Sara's mind the halcyon days before she was snatched from her easygoing father. Crazy Maisie, who staves off loneliness (the sad one) with aberrant behavior, loses out to mother, an inevitable denouement, realistic but vexing.

In *Growing Anyway Up* Florence shuns facing up to relationships with adults and classmates. Convinced that her thoughts and feelings are kept secret by not letting anyone look into her eyes, Florence veils herself behind peculiar ocular rituals and other distancing mannerisms. Exuberant Aunt Nina helps her become more forbearing of her taciturn mother and the lump who will be her stepfather.

Severely disturbed Caroline of *Secret Dreamer, Secret Dreams* cannot speak to anyone, not even her patient and loving father. Her delight in her dog gives promise of recovery but in the last sentence Caroline laments, "Brumm barks helplessly, his voice unintelligible as my own, his message and mine forever undelivered."

Heide skillfully handles the egocentric adolescent's testing and tasting of life, evolving alliances with parents and other adults, who usually represent contending values. The transitory solutions of early teen years, neither tidy nor assuredly optimistic, are used to fashion bothersome and provocative endings. Heide's particular strength lies in her delineation of character.

—Selma K. Richardson

HEINLEIN, Robert A(nson). American. Born in Butler, Missouri, 7 July 1907. Educated at Central High School, Kansas City, graduated 1924; University of Missouri, Columbia, 1924–25; United States Naval Academy, Annapolis, Maryland, B.S. 1929; University of California, Los Angeles, 1934–35. Served in the United States Navy, 1929 until retirement because of physical disability, 1934. Married 1) Leslyn McDonald (divorced); 2) Virginia Gerstenfeld in 1948. Owner, Shively and Sophie silver mines, Silver Plume, Colorado, 1934–35; worked in mining and real estate, 1936–39; civilian engineer, Philadelphia Navy Yard, 1942–45. Candidate for California State Assembly, 1938; Forrestal Lecturer, United States Naval Academy, 1973. Recipient: Hugo award, 1956, 1960, 1962, 1967; Grand Master Nebula award, 1974; *Locus* award, 1985. Guest of Honor, World Science Fiction Convention, 1941, 1961, 1976. L.H.D.: Eastern Michigan University, Ypsilanti, 1977. *Died 8 May 1988.*

PUBLICATIONS FOR CHILDREN

Fiction

Rocket Ship Galileo, illustrated by Thomas Voter. New York, Scribner, 1947; London, New English Library, 1971.
Space Cadet, illustrated by Clifford Geary. New York, Scribner, 1948; London, Gollancz, 1966.
Red Planet, illustrated by Clifford Geary. New York, Scribner, 1949; London, Gollancz, 1963.
Farmer in the Sky, illustrated by Clifford Geary. New York, Scribner, 1950; London, Gollancz, 1962.

Between Planets, illustrated by Clifford Geary. New York, Scribner, 1951; London, Gollancz, 1968.
The Rolling Stones, illustrated by Clifford Geary. New York, Scribner, 1952; as *Space Family Stone,* London, Gollancz, 1969.
Starman Jones, illustrated by Clifford Geary. New York, Scribner, 1953; London, Sidgwick and Jackson, 1954.
The Star Beast, illustrated by Clifford Geary. New York, Scribner, 1954; London, New English Library, 1971.
Tunnel in the Sky. New York, Scribner, 1955; London, Gollancz, 1965.
Time for the Stars. New York, Scribner, 1956; London, Gollancz, 1963.
Citizen of the Galaxy. New York, Scribner, 1957; London, Gollancz, 1969.
Have Space Suit—Will Travel. New York, Scribner, 1958; London, Gollancz, 1970.
Starship Troopers. New York, Putnam, 1959; London, New English Library, 1961.
Podkayne of Mars: Her Life and Times. New York, Putnam, 1963; London, New English Library, 1969.

PUBLICATIONS FOR ADULTS

Novels

Beyond This Horizon. Reading, Pennsylvania, Fantasy Press, 1948; London, Panther, 1967.
Sixth Column. New York, Gnome Press, 1949; as *The Day after Tomorrow,* New York, New American Library, 1951; London, Mayflower, 1962.
Waldo, and Magic Inc. New York, Doubleday, 1950; as *Waldo, Genius in Orbit,* New York, Avon, 1958.
The Puppet Masters. New York, Doubleday, 1951; London, Museum Press, 1953.
Double Star. New York, Doubleday, 1956; London, Joseph, 1958.
The Door into Summer. New York, Doubleday, 1957; London, Panther, 1960.
Methuselah's Children. New York, Gnome Press, 1958; London, Gollancz, 1963.
The Robert Heinlein Omnibus. London, Sidgwick and Jackson, 1958.
Stranger in a Strange Land. New York, Putnam, 1961; London, New English Library, 1965.
Glory Road. New York, Putnam, 1963; London, New English Library, 1965.
Farnham's Freehold. New York, Putnam, 1964; London, Dobson, 1965.
Three by Heinlein (includes *The Puppet Masters, Waldo, Magic Inc.*). New York, Doubleday, 1965; as *A Heinlein Triad,* London, Gollancz, 1966.
A Robert Heinlein Omnibus. London, Sidgwick and Jackson, 1966.
The Moon Is a Harsh Mistress. New York, Putnam, 1966; London, Dobson, 1967.
I Will Fear No Evil. New York, Putnam, 1970; London, New English Library, 1972.
Time Enough for Love: The Lives of Lazarus Long. New York, Putnam, 1973; London, New English Library, 1974.
The Number of the Beast. New York, Fawcett, and London, New English Library, 1980.
Friday. New York, Holt Rinehart, and London, New English Library, 1982.
Job: A Comedy of Justice. New York, Ballantine, and London, New English Library, 1984.
The Cat Who Walks Through Walls: A Comedy of Manners. New York, Putnam, 1985; London, New English Library, 1986.

To Sail Beyond the Sunset: The Life and Loves of Maureen Johnson. New York, Putnam, and London, Joseph, 1987.

Short Stories

The Man Who Sold the Moon. Chicago, Shasta, 1950; London, Sidgwick and Jackson, 1953.
Universe. New York, Dell, 1951.
The Green Hills of Earth. Chicago, Shasta, 1951; London, Sidgwick and Jackson, 1954.
Revolt in 2100. Chicago, Shasta, 1953; London, Digit, 1959.
Assignment in Eternity. Reading, Pennsylvania, Fantasy Press, 1953; London, Museum Press, 1955; abridged edition, as *Lost Legacy,* London, Digit, 1960.
The Menace from Earth. New York, Gnome Press, 1959; London, Dobson, 1966.
The Unpleasant Profession of Jonathan Hoag. New York, Gnome Press, 1959; London, Dobson, 1964; as *6 x H: Six Stories,* New York, Pyramid, 1961.
Orphans of the Sky. London, Gollancz, 1963; New York, Putnam, 1964.
The Worlds of Robert A. Heinlein. New York, Ace, 1966; London, New English Library, 1970.
The Past Through Tomorrow: Future History Stories. New York, Putnam, 1967; abridged edition, London, New English Library, 2 vols., 1977.
The Best of Robert Heinlein 1939–1959, edited by Angus Wells, London, Sidgwick and Jackson, 1973.
Destination Moon. Boston, Gregg Press, 1979.
Expanded Universe. New York, Grosset and Dunlap, 1980.

Plays

Screenplays: *Destination Moon,* with Rip Van Ronkel and James O'Hanlon, 1950; *Project Moonbase,* with Jack Seaman, 1953.

Television Plays: scripts for *Tom Corbett, Space Cadet* series, 1950's.

Other

The Discovery of the Future (address). Los Angeles, Novacious, 1941.
Of Worlds Beyond: The Science of Science-Fiction Writing, with others, edited by Lloyd Arthur Eshbach. Reading, Pennsylvania, Fantasy Press, 1947; London, Dobson, 1965.
The Science Fiction Novel, with others, edited by Basil Davenport. Chicago, Advent, 1959.
The Notebooks of Lazarus Long. New York, Putnam, 1978.

Editor, *Tomorrow, The Stars: A Science Fiction Anthology.* New York, Doubleday, 1952.

*

Bibliography: *Robert A. Heinlein: A Bibliography* by Mark Owings, Baltimore, Croatan House, 1973.

Manuscript Collection: University of California Library, Santa Cruz.

Critical Studies: *Seekers of Tomorrow* by Sam Moskowitz, Cleveland, World, 1966; *Heinlein in Dimension: A Critical Analysis* (includes bibliography) by Alexei Panshin, Chicago, Advent, 1968; *Robert A. Heinlein, Stranger in His Own Land,* San Bernardino, California, Borgo Press, 1976, and *The Classic Years of Robert A. Heinlein,* Borgo Press, 1977, both by George Edgar Slusser; *Robert A. Heinlein* edited by Martin H. Greenberg and Joseph D. Olander, New York, Taplinger, and Edinburgh, Harris, 1978; *Robert A. Heinlein: America as Science Fiction* by H. Bruce Franklin, New York, Oxford University Press, 1980, Oxford, Oxford University Press, 1981; *Yesterday or Tomorrow? The Work of Robert A. Heinlein* by R. Reginald, San Bernardino, California, Borgo Press, 1984.

*   *   *

Robert A. Heinlein's pioneering role in the development of juvenile science fiction has helped make him an acknowledged master of modern science fiction. Before 1947, children's science fiction was little more than Tom Swift adventures and comics featuring Buck Rogers and Flash Gordon. In 1947 Heinlein published *Rocket Ship Galileo,* clearly identifiable both as science fiction and as junior novel. Accepted favorably by readers and reviewers alike, the novel marked the first time mainstream children's literature recognized science fiction. Publication of subsequent science fiction, some by Heinlein himself and the rest by authors encouraged by his example, gained respectability for the genre as a valid subcategory of children's literature.

Rocket Ship Galileo is a story of several boys who fly to the moon in a home-made atomic-powered rocket. There they discover the ruins of an extant lunar civilization and destroy the base of some Nazis secretly planning World War III. Replete with exciting incident and gadgetry, *Rocket Ship Galileo* is also a novel in which teenagers, like many of the novel's putative readers, worry about their vocational goals, suffer parental misunderstandings, and seek to achieve a competence that instills pride. Another positive quality of the novel is its style: terse and colloquial, fast moving, and nicely balanced between scientific terminology and everyday speech.

The best of Heinlein's other juveniles follow this pattern: a skillful blending of science-fiction topics and young adult subjects. *Red Planet* narrates Jim Marlowe's adventures at school and with Willie, a ball-like animal that is actually a young Martian. Not as fast-paced as its predecessor, the novel still interests because it describes a society and the Martian biology Heinlein employs in the famous *Stranger in a Strange Land. Farmer in the Sky* weaves together futuristic agricultural techniques on Ganymede and Bill Lermer's indecision over whether to return to earth for additional schooling or to remain as a pioneer. Subplots concerning Bill's relationship with his parents and organizing boy scouting are also intended to appeal to youth. *Citizen of the Galaxy,* taking place in a future with conditions similar to the Roman Empire, explores various modes of structuring society and investigates several opposing economic theories. Anticipating Engdahl's characteristic emphasis, Heinlein, here, is more interested in explaining ideas than in narrating incidents.

Perhaps the most provocative of Heinlein's juveniles is *Tunnel in the Sky.* Rod Walker and his classmates participate in a test of survival techniques on an unknown planet. Unexpectedly lost and stranded, 15 teenagers band together. At the point where a genuine community has developed and children have even been born, the group is found and brought back to earth. Regardless of the maturity shown, most are required to revert to teenage roles. Especially illuminating is the novel's look at an adult society which recognizes only chronological age and sorts out and treats youth accordingly.

Although not all of Heinlein's juvenile science fiction comes up to the level of *Rocket Ship Galileo* and *Tunnel in the Sky,* his place in children's literature seems assured on both historical and literary grounds.

—Francis J. Molson

————

HENRY, Marguerite (née Breithaupt). American. Born in Milwaukee, Wisconsin, 13 April 1902. Educated at Riverside High School, Milwaukee; Milwaukee State Teachers College, two years. Married to Sidney Crocker Henry. Recipient: American Library Association Newbery Medal, 1949; Western Heritage award, 1967; University of Minnesota Kerlan award, 1975. Address: P.O. Box 385, Rancho Santa Fe, California 92067, U.S.A.

PUBLICATIONS FOR CHILDREN

Fiction

Auno and Tauno: A Story of Finland, illustrated by Gladys Blackwood. Chicago, Whitman, 1940.
Dilly Dally Sally, illustrated by Gladys Blackwood. Akron, Ohio, Saalfield, 1940.
Geraldine Belinda, illustrated by Gladys Blackwood. New York, Platt and Munk, 1942.
Their First Igloo on Baffin Island, with Barbara True, illustrated by Gladys Blackwood. Chicago, Whitman, 1943; London, Gifford, 1945.
A Boy and a Dog, illustrated by Diana Thorne and Ottilie Foy. Chicago, Wilcox and Follett, 1944.
Justin Morgan Had a Horse (stories), illustrated by Wesley Dennis. Chicago, Wilcox and Follett, 1945; revised edition, Chicago, Rand McNally, 1954.
The Little Fellow, illustrated by Diana Thorne. Philadelphia, Winston, 1945; revised edition, Chicago, Rand McNally, 1975.
Misty of Chincoteague, illustrated by Wesley Dennis. Chicago, Rand McNally, 1947; London, Collins, 1961.
Always Reddy, illustrated by Wesley Dennis. New York, McGraw Hill, 1947.
King of the Wind, illustrated by Wesley Dennis. Chicago, Rand McNally, 1948; London, Constable, 1957.
Little-or-Nothing from Nottingham, illustrated by Wesley Dennis. New York, McGraw Hill, 1949.
Sea Star: Orphan of Chincoteague, illustrated by Wesley Dennis. Chicago, Rand McNally, 1949; London, Collins, 1968.
Born to Trot, illustrated by Wesley Dennis. Chicago, Rand McNally, 1950; excerpts, as *One Man's Horse,* 1977.
Brighty of the Grand Canyon, illustrated by Wesley Dennis. Chicago, Rand McNally, 1953; London, Collins, 1970.
Cinnabar, The One O'Clock Fox, illustrated by Wesley Dennis. Chicago, Rand McNally, 1956.
Misty, The Wonder Pony, illustrated by Clare McKinley. Chicago, Rand McNally, 1956.
Black Gold, illustrated by Wesley Dennis. Chicago, Rand McNally, 1957.
Muley-Ears, Nobody's Dog, illustrated by Wesley Dennis. Chicago, Rand McNally, 1959.
Gaudenzia, Pride of the Palio, illustrated by Lynd Ward. Chicago, Rand McNally, 1960; London, Collins, 1971; as *The Wildest Horse Race in the World,* Rand McNally, 1976; as *Palio: The Wildest Horse Race in the World,* London, Fontana, 1976.
Five O'Clock Charlie, illustrated by Wesley Dennis. Chicago, Rand McNally, 1962; London, Collins, 1963.
Stormy, Misty's Foal, illustrated by Wesley Dennis. Chicago, Rand McNally, 1963; London, Collins, 1965.
White Stallion of Lipizza, illustrated by Wesley Dennis. Chicago, Rand McNally, 1964; London, Blackie, 1976.
Mustang, Wild Spirit of the West, illustrated by Robert Lougheed. Chicago, Rand McNally, 1966; London, Collins, 1968.
San Domingo, The Medicine Hat Stallion, illustrated by Robert Lougheed. Chicago, Rand McNally, 1972; London, Collins, 1975; as *Peter Lundy and the Medicine Hat Stallion,* Rand McNally, 1977.
Stories from Around the World. Chicago, Rand McNally, 1974.
Misty Treasury (omnibus). Chicago, Rand McNally, 1982.

Other

Alaska [Argentina, Brazil, Canada, Chile, Mexico, Panama, West Indies, Australia, The Bahamas, Bermuda, British Honduras, Dominican Republic, Hawaii, New Zealand, and *Virgin Islands] in Story and Pictures,* illustrated by Kurt Wiese. Chicago, Whitman, 16 vols., 1941–46.
Birds at Home, illustrated by Jacob Bates Abbott. Chicago, Donohue, 1942; revised edition, Northbrook, Illinois, Hubbard Press, 1972.
Robert Fulton, Boy Craftsman, illustrated by Lawrence Dresser. Indianapolis, Bobbs Merrill, 1945.
Benjamin West and His Cat Grimalkin, illustrated by Wesley Dennis. Indianapolis, Bobbs Merrill, 1947.
Album of Horses, illustrated by Wesley Dennis. Chicago, Rand McNally, 1951; shortened version, as *Portfolio of Horses,* 1952; as *Portfolio of Horse Paintings,* 1964.
Wagging Tails: An Album of Dogs, illustrated by Wesley Dennis. Chicago, Rand McNally, 1955; as *Album of Dogs,* 1970.
All about Horses, illustrated by Wesley Dennis. New York, Random House, 1962; London, W.H. Allen, 1963; revised edition, Chicago, Rand McNally, 1967.
Dear Readers and Riders. Chicago, Rand McNally, 1969.
A Pictorial Life of Misty, illustrated by Wesley Dennis. Chicago, Rand McNally, 1976.
Dear Marguerite Henry. Chicago, Rand McNally, 1978.
The Illustrated Marguerite Henry, illustrated by Wesley Dennis, Robert Lougheed, Lynd Ward, and Rich Rudich. Chicago, Rand McNally, 1980.
Our First Pony. Chicago, Rand McNally, 1984.

*

Manuscript Collection: Kerlan Collection, University of Minnesota, Minneapolis.

*   *   *

Mention horse stories to any young reader of the genre and the name Marguerite Henry is sure to enter the conversation. These readers are usually so passionate in their love for horses that they place few demands upon the literary quality of a book so long as it is about their favorite animal. Yet even among these readers, Henry's works are recognized as above and apart from the usual fare of animal adventure stories.

The quality that separates her from most writers of animal stories is her historical perspective. Her works are best appreciated if they are thought of and judged as historical romance, whether it be a fictional biography like *Benjamin West and His Cat Grimalkin,* or a fictional exploration of the events which historically trace the emergence of a particular breed of horse, as in *Justin Morgan Had a Horse* or *King of the Wind.*

It is partly because children do not come to her books thinking of them as historical works that they are so especially appealing. Teachers, and far too many writers, often ignore the needs of children, forgetting that if they are to be attracted to the study of history their interests must be aroused and their sympathies enlisted; and also forgetting that children want action, drama, adventure, and heroes. All of these can be found by children in the historical animal romances of Henry.

The use of the word "romance" here should not be interpreted as meaning trite and improbable, but rather to identify the romantic tradition for young readers sired so brilliantly by Stevenson. Although Will James's *Smoky* was based on the first-hand experience of a cowboy while Henry's stories are the result of painstaking research, both writers are in the same tradition. As writers of horse stories they demonstrate, first of all, a thorough knowledge of the breed depicted. The animals are objectively reported, and yet they are portrayed in such a way that their "character" is known and felt by humans, both within and outside the stories. The human characters, too, since most of them are actual people, are neither one-dimensional nor stereotyped.

However, it is the magical appeal of history—the merging of fact with imagination with legend—that gives the Henry books their trademark. Her stories are either implicitly or explicitly marked with prologues and epilogues, so that the web of history, the connection of things distant in time, place, person, and circumstance, reaches the consciousness of the young reader. The distant past touches the more recent past of the story time, which in turn touches the present and reaches out to the future of the reader's time.

The last paragraph of the epilogue in *Brighty* is a characteristic ending of a Henry book: "Especially on moonlit nights a shaggy little form can be seen flirting along the ledges, a thin swirl of dust rising behind him. Some say it is nothing but moonbeams caught up in a cloud. But the older guides swear it is trail dust out of the past, kicked up by Brighty himself, the roving spirit of the Grand Canyon— forever wild, forever free."

—James E. Higgins

* * *

HENTOFF, Nat(han Irving). American. Born in Boston, Massachusetts, 10 June 1925. Educated at Northeastern University, Boston, B.A. (summa cum laude) 1945; Harvard University, Cambridge, Massachusetts, 1946; the Sorbonne, Paris (Fulbright fellow), 1950. Married 1) Miriam Sargent in 1950 (divorced 1950); 2) Trudi Bernstein in 1954 (divorced 1959), two daughters; 3) Margot Goodman in 1959, two sons. Writer, producer, and announcer, WMEX Radio, Boston 1944–53; associate editor, *Down Beat* magazine, New York, 1953–57; co-founding editor, *Jazz Review,* 1959–60. Since 1958 staff writer and columnist, *Village Voice,* New York; since 1960 staff writer, the *New Yorker;* since 1984 columnist, Washington *Post.* Faculty member, New School for Social Research, New York, and New York University. Recipient: American Library Association Immroth Memorial award, 1983. Address: 25 Fifth Avenue, New York, New York 10003, U.S.A.

PUBLICATIONS FOR CHILDREN

Fiction

Jazz Country. New York, Harper, 1965.
I'm Really Dragged But Nothing Gets Me Down. New York, Simon and Schuster, 1968.
In the Country of Ourselves. New York, Simon and Schuster, 1971.
This School Is Driving Me Crazy. New York, Delacorte Press, 1976; London, Angus and Robertson, 1977.
Does This School Have Capital Punishment? New York, Delacorte Press, 1981; London, Angus and Robertson, 1982.
The Day They Came to Arrest the Book. New York, Delacorte Press, 1982; London, Angus and Robertson, 1985.

Other

Journey into Jazz, illustrated by David Stone Martin. New York, Coward McCann, 1968.
American Heroes: In and Out of School. New York, Delacorte Press, 1987.

PUBLICATIONS FOR ADULTS

Novels

Call the Keeper. New York, Viking Press, 1966; London, Secker and Warburg, 1967.
Onwards! New York, Simon and Schuster, 1968.
Blues for Charlie Darwin. New York, Morrow, 1982; London, Constable, 1983.
The Man from Internal Affairs. New York, Mysterious Press, 1985.

Other

Jazz Street, photographs by Dennis Stouk. London, Deutsch, 1960.
The Jazz Life. New York, Dial Press, 1961; London, Davies, 1962.
Peace Agitator: The Story of A.J. Muste. New York, Macmillan, 1963.
The New Equality. New York, Viking Press, 1964.
Our Children Are Dying. New York, Viking Press, 1966.
A Doctor among the Addicts. Chicago, Rand McNally, 1968.
A Political Life: The Education of John V. Lindsay. New York, Knopf, 1969.
State Secrets: Police Surveillance in America, with Paul Cowan and Nick Egleson. New York, Holt Rinehart, 1974.
Jazz Is. New York, Random House, 1976; London, W.H. Allen, 1978.
Does Anybody Give a Damn? On Education. New York, Knopf, 1977.
The First Freedom: A Tumultuous History of Free Speech in America. New York, Delacorte Press, 1980.
The 1984 Calendar: An American History, with Tim Keefe and Howard Levine. Lansing, Michigan, Point Blank Press, 1983.
Boston Boy (memoir). New York, Knopf, 1986.
John Cardinal O'Connor: At the Storm Center of a Changing American Catholic Church. New York, Scribner, 1988.

Editor, with Nat Shapiro, *Hear Me Talkin' to Ya: The Story of Jazz by the Men Who Made It.* New York, Rinehart, and London, Davies, 1955.
Editor, with Nat Shapiro, *The Jazz Makers.* New York, Rinehart, 1957; London, Davies, 1958.
Editor, with Albert J. McCarthy, *Jazz: New Perspectives on the History of Jazz.* New York, Rinehart, 1959; London, Cassell, 1960.
Editor, *The Essays of A.J. Muste.* Indianapolis, Bobbs Merrill, 1967.

*

Manuscript Collection: Boston University.

Nat Hentoff comments:
I like to write for children because, as a child, I so enjoyed books that were written for me. I hope I am continuing some of that kind of pleasure.
I also like to try to get children, and anyone else I write for, to think. And the very best way to do that is through telling stories about

people whose ideas, language, and actions sufficiently interest readers to compel them to think about what these characters are thinking, saying, and doing.

*   *   *

American teenage stories have traditionally been concerned with school fun, soda-fountain dating, keeping worn-out jalopies running, or persuading parents to consent to this or that unlikely scheme, much in the spirit of Booth Tarkington's *Seventeen* (1916). Fictional youngsters' social consciousness was bounded by the sports and comic pages of the local newspaper, if indeed it extended so far. But all that has changed: the young hero of *Seventeen* couldn't survive nowadays. Times are tougher than they used to be.

Nat Hentoff's youngsters of the 1970's and early 1980's are a troubled lot, faced with adult-sized problems not of their making; with decisions to make in their inexperienced adolescence which will, as they well know, affect them permanently. Just try telling them that these are "the happiest days of their lives."

Tom Curtis of *Jazz Country* cares for little in life but his trumpet. Jazz is his whole world—but his white skin shuts him out from the fellowship that means everything to him. The story of Tom's painful struggle for acceptance and excellence comes to no facile conclusion. He is still striving at story's end, but whether he will win his passport to Jazz Country he has yet to discover. In *I'm Really Dragged But Nothing Gets Me Down* Jeremy Wolf, a high-school senior, is faced with a watershed decision. Will he or will he not register for the draft on graduation? War drags on in Vietnam: failure to comply with the law may ruin his future and destroy his parents' hopes, and he desperately fears a possible jail sentence, but Jeremy's conscience insists that to register is to recognize the government's right to order him to kill. Outside influences, the arguments of family and friends, however painful, are as nothing to the conflict within. Jeremy's eventual unsatisfactory answer is no solution to his moral dilemma, and his pain remains. Perhaps life will anaesthetize his torment of conscience, but looking around him at the Establishment, he rather hopes it will not.

In the Country of Ourselves tells of an urban high school threatened with student revolution, over issues not entirely clear even to determined revolutionaries. Drug scares, two-way racism, and tough police tactics, exacerbated by the actions of a false friend to the student activists among the teaching staff, add to the complexity of the situation. To be either student or instructor in an American high school of the 1970's seems to have been a cruel and unusual punishment. Sam Davidson of *This School Is Driving Me Crazy* and *Does This School Have Capital Punishment?* certainly has his troubles, too, but is less haunted and rather more likeable and sympathetic than others of Hentoff's young heroes. Suspected (falsely) of conducting a shakedown operation in grade school, and of drug possession in high school, Sam keeps his cool, his courage, and his sense of humour.

These are the young Americans as Hentoff sees them, and his hard, sharp, "insider" style is exactly suited to theirs. In spite of all that life throws at them, these bright, tough, strong-willed kids keep on coming. Their language and their ways don't jibe with those of the older generation—but why should they? They're a lot older than *Seventeen*.

Hentoff's latest title has more of the flavour of an academic debate than of a work of fiction. *The Day They Came to Arrest the Book* is an examination of censorship in action. *Huck Finn* is on trial at George Mason High: those who would cleanse the school precincts of the perceived racism, sexism, and immorality of Twain's classic are met head-on by those defending freedom of speech (including that of Samuel Clemens), and the principle that a school is a place for the opening of minds, not for locking up books. Hentoff does his fair-minded best to give the censors a fair chance of making their case, but it's abundantly clear where his sympathies lie, and he is a most persuasive and valuable advocate.

—Joan McGrath

HERALD, Kathleen.   See **PEYTON, K.M.**

HEWARD, Constance.   British.   Born in 1884. *Died in 1968.*

PUBLICATIONS FOR CHILDREN

Fiction

Ameliaranne and the Green Umbrella, illustrated by S.B. Pearse. London, Harrap, and Philadelphia, Jacobs, 1920.
Cheery Tales [and *More Cheery Tales*] *for Little People.* London, S.P.C.K., 2 vols., 1920; New York, Macmillan, 2 vols., 1921.
The Twins and Tabiffa, illustrated by S.B. Pearse. London, Harrap, and Philadelphia, Jacobs, 1923.
Sunshiny Stories. London, Sheldon Press, 1924.
Grandpa and the Tiger, illustrated by Lilian Govey. London, Harrap, and Philadelphia, Jacobs, 1924.
The Story Book, edited by Isa M. Jackson. London, Collins, 1924.
Chappie and the Others, illustrated by Savile Lumley. London, Warne, 1926.
A Handful of Happiness, illustrated by Patience Arnold. London, Sheldon Press, 1926.
Kitty's Tea Party. London, Sheldon Press, 1926.
Mr. Pickles and the Party, illustrated by Anne Anderson. London, Warne, 1926.
Fairy Circle series (*Fairy* [*Gnome, Laughter, Story, Nonsense, Magic*] *Circle*). London, Collins, 6 vols., 1927.
Faithful Teddy. London, Sheldon Press, 1927.
The Fortune Finders. Leeds, E.J. Arnold, 1928.
An Eventful Holiday. Leeds, E.J. Arnold, 1928.
Ameliaranne Keeps Shop, illustrated by S.B. Pearse. London, Harrap, and Philadelphia, McKay, 1928.
A Tale of Two Mysteries. Leeds, E.J. Arnold, 1928.
Ameliaranne, Cinema Star, illustrated by S.B. Pearse. London, Harrap, 1929.
Ameliaranne and the Monkey, illustrated by S.B. Pearse. Philadelphia, McKay, 1929.
Rolf's First Earnings and Other Stories, illustrated by G. Robinson. London, Sheldon Press, 1929.
Tommy's Little Grains of Sand and Other Stories. London, Sheldon Press, 1930.
Benjy Comes. London, Wells Gardner, 1931.
Grandpa Nog and the Nimblies, illustrated by Muriel Gill. London, Harrap, and Philadelphia, McKay, 1937.
Billety Bill and the Big Brown Bear, illustrated by Muriel Gill. London, Harrap, and Philadelphia, McKay, 1937.
Ameliaranne at the Farm, illustrated by S.B. Pearse. London, Harrap, and Philadelphia, McKay, 1937.
Ameliaranne Gives a Christmas Party, illustrated by S.B. Pearse. London, Harrap, and Philadelphia, McKay, 1938.
Ameliaranne Camps Out, illustrated by S.B. Pearse. London,

Harrap, and Philadelphia, McKay, 1939.
Ameliaranne Keeps School, illustrated by S.B. Pearse. London, Harrap, and Philadelphia, McKay, 1940.
Ameliaranne Goes Touring, illustrated by S.B. Pearse. London, Harrap, and New York, McKay, 1941.
Chappie, illustrated by M.K. Mountain. London, Warne, 1945.
Dick in Command. Leeds, E.J. Arnold, 1950.
Bobby Budge from Nowhere. Leeds, E.J. Arnold, 1950.
Midnight, Our Pony, illustrated by C. Instrell. Leeds, E.J. Arnold, 1953.
Adventures [and *Further Adventures*] *of Christabel Jane and Chirpy*, illustrated by S.B. Pearse. London, Harrap, 2 vols., 1955.
Jonathan's Children, illustrated by Jane Paton. London, Harrap, 1963.
The House on the Edge of the Moor, illustrated by Edward Mortelmans. London, Harrap, 1968.

*   *   *

Constance Heward is best known for creating Ameliaranne, a helpful little girl related in spirit to Pollyanna, whose most striking features are her competence and her curl rags "which she wore from Friday night to Sunday morning."

Heward's career was a long one. The first picture book, *Ameliaranne and the Green Umbrella*, was published in 1920. It is also the simplest and best, introducing the heroine and her five little brothers and sisters, as well as their mother, Mrs. Stiggins, "who was poor and took in washing." Ameliaranne goes to the Squire's tea party while the rest of the family stay at home with a cold. Anxious that they should not miss out on all the good things, Ameliaranne hides her own tea cakes in her green umbrella, planning to smuggle them home. Miss Josephine, the Squire's strict sister, discovers the hoard; but all ends happily because the Squire soon realises Ameliaranne's unselfishness and he sends her home with cakes for everyone.

Although her last Ameliaranne book appeared in 1941, Heward continued to write for children until 1968, turning her hand to full-length adventure stories. These seem of less interest than her earlier books. Ameliaranne, in fact, took on a life apart from her creator. 12 additional Ameliaranne books were written by an assortment of authors. Continuity was preserved by using the same artist, S.B. Pearse, whose chubby, cheerful children, with their slightly vacant expressions, so brilliantly encapsulated the warm and cosy world of Ameliaranne.

In the hands of Eleanor Farjeon, Ameliaranne appears at her best—resourceful, engaging, and good natured, living in a safe and comfortable land next door to fantasy, where magic does not exactly exist, but where, all the same, the poor but pretty school mistress can have a beautiful new dress for the ball. At worst, the Ameliaranne imitators have merely copied the Heward style, emphasising what is static and priggish about the character. It is noticeable that Heward's own Ameliaranne becomes more wooden over the years. The spirited little girl who battles with Miss Josephine in *Green Umbrella* has become a collection of virtues by the final books.

Yet it is not difficult to see why she has always had readers. Heward was an extremely good storyteller, and she never allowed the action to flag. There is no bewildering uncertainty in her books; the world she creates is entirely under control and Ameliaranne is never at a loss. At best, this creates a sense of freshness and optimism. What is more, Ameliaranne's solutions to the various problems she encounters are simple, yet delightfully enterprising. She immediately recognises the thief who is pretending to be the shopkeeper's sailor son—because he does not roll from side to side as sailors do; and she hides the coins from the till for safety in a jar of pickled onions; the notes she wraps in her hair as curl papers.

Heward's books are easy to read. Her descriptions are well-worn but they are graphic, concrete, and so confidently used that they all contribute to the sense of friendly familiarity in her writing. Every child is apple-cheeked and no eye seems without a twinkle. The characters are stereotypes; but this makes them instantly recogniseable. "Oh, no! I wouldn't take it upon myself to be so bold," cries Mrs. Stiggins, and she continues to say the same thing at intervals throughout 20 books. On the other hand, Heward was undoubtedly writing for the undemanding 1920's. By today's tastes she is rather slavish in her support of a society where the rich man kept to his castle and the poor man stayed at his gate. Ameliaranne does not let us forget that she is the daughter of a washerwoman. "To think we've been hobnobbing with the gentry!" she cries in *Ameliaranne Camps Out*. You must know your place—and there is no room for complexity of thought or character. In *Grandpa and the Tiger*, a very curious early story, a tiger, whose only crime is that he has escaped and wandered into the hero's garden, is summarily shot and made into a rug.

Ameliaranne can appear almost banal in her simplicity; but she conveys an implicit assurance, and somewhere there is a world of security and order, where no disaster is so complete that common sense will not eventually triumph, to be rewarded by high tea and pink-iced cakes with cherries on top.

—Alison Sage

HEWETT, Anita. Also wrote as Anne Wellington. British. Born in Wellington, Somerset, 23 May 1918. Educated at the University of Exeter, 1936–39, teaching diploma, National Froebel Foundation, 1939. Served in the Women's Royal Air Force, 1940–45. Married Richard Duke in 1966. Primary school teacher, 1945–52; Principal, Shirley Hall School, Kingston Hill, Surrey, 1952–61; producer, Schools Broadcasting Department, BBC, London, 1962–70. *Died 13 March 1989.*

PUBLICATIONS FOR CHILDREN

Fiction

Elephant Big and Elephant Little, and Other Stories, illustrated by Charlotte Hough. London, Lane, 1955; New York, A.S. Barnes, 1960.
The Little Yellow Jungle Frogs and Other Stories, illustrated by Charlotte Hough. London, Lane, 1956; New York, A.S. Barnes, 1960.
Honey Mouse and Other Stories, illustrated by Margery Gill. London, Lane, 1957.
Think, Mr. Platypus, illustrated by Anne Marie Jauss. New York, Sterling, 1958.
Koala Bear's Walkabout, illustrated by Anne Marie Jauss. New York, Sterling, 1959.
The Laughing Bird, illustrated by Anne Marie Jauss. New York, Sterling, 1959.
A Hat for Rhinoceros and Other Stories, illustrated by Margery Gill. London, Bodley Head, 1959; New York, A.S. Barnes, 1960.
Piccolo, illustrated by Dick Hart. London, Bodley Head, 1960; New York, A.S. Barnes, 1961.
The Tale of the Turnip, illustrated by Margery Gill. London, Bodley Head, and New York, McGraw Hill, 1961.
The Little White Hen, illustrated by William Stobbs. London, Bodley Head, 1962; New York, McGraw Hill, 1963.
Piccolo and Maria, illustrated by Dick Hart. London, Bodley

Head, 1962.
The Elworthy Children, illustrated by Margery Gill. London, Bodley Head, 1963.
Dragon from the North, illustrated by Gioia Fiammenghi. London, McGraw Hill, 1965.
The Pebble Nest illustrated by Jennie Corbett. London, University of London Press, 1965.
The Bull Beneath the Walnut Tree and Other Stories, illustrated by Geraldine Spence. London, Bodley Head, 1966; New York, McGraw Hill, 1967.
Mrs. Mopple's Washing Line, illustrated by Robert Broomfield. London, Bodley Head, and New York, McGraw Hill, 1966.
Fire Engine Speedy, illustrated by Edward McLachlan. London, University of London Press, 1966.
Mr. Faksimily and the Tiger, illustrated by Robert Broomfield. London, Bodley Head, 1967; Chicago, Follett, 1969.
Animal Story Book, illustrated by Margery Gill and Charlotte Hough. London, Bodley Head, 1972.
Mr. Bingle's Apple Pie (as Anne Wellington), illustrated by Nita Sowter. London, Abelard Schuman, 1978.
Grandfather Gregory (as Anne Wellington), illustrated by Nita Sowter. London, Abelard Schuman, 1980.

Other (readers)

Clip the Crab's Adventure. Leeds, E.J. Arnold, 1950.
The Seven Proud Sisters and Other Stories, illustrated by M. Jarman. London, Ginn, 1952.
The Crocodile That Couldn't Swim, illustrated by C. Instrell. Leeds, E.J. Arnold, 1953.
Slink the Shadow. Leeds, E.J. Arnold, 1953.

* * *

Anita Hewett's background as a teacher is evident in her work. She wrote for the children she enjoyed teaching—the little ones, the eights and under. At one stage in her career she worked as a Schools Radio producer. Most of her stories are suitably short, to be read or told at one sitting. They almost always point a moral, unobtrusively and often humorously, but the educational content is there. They make ideal standbys for the classroom bookshelf.

The majority are animal fables in the Just-So tradition but lighter and tighter in texture. In the omnibus *Animal Story Book,* the stories are grouped geographically in four sections covering Africa, Australia, South America, and South-East Asia. They are informative as well as entertaining about wildlife. Most of them use the well-tried techniques of repetition and cumulative construction and, at times, these technical devices are in danger of becoming mechanical. But the style is always elegant and the pay-offs refreshingly unpredictable. In "The Leopard That Lost a Spot," for instance, Monkey teases Leopard by painting out one of his spots. When the rain washes it back, to the bewildered creature's relief, Monkey laughs and laughs till he falls out of his tree. "He did not fall on the soft leaves. Nor did he fall in the long grass. He fell where he deserved to fall—in the pot of yellow paint."

Hewett's picture books benefit from the contribution of distinguished artists. But the texts deserve the pictures. *Mr. Faksimily and the Tiger* is particularly successful—a charming, original tale about an intrepid photographer who goes into the jungle to snap Terrible Tiger. All he has for protection is his umbrella—but he uses it to good effect. Again, the end comes as a surprise and gives the story an unusual, satisfying twist.

Her two novels about Piccolo, an Italian urchin, and his donkey are different in kind. These are realistic stories—the first effortless, the second somewhat contrived. But both give an English child real insight into an unfamiliar lifestyle and, again, there is educational

value in the way Piccolo matures through his experiences. *The Elworthy Children,* another realistic story, also stands out from the main body of her work. With affectionate humour, Hewett describes the small adventures of a typical middle-class family. Five-year-old Polly and her older sister are the main characters and there is no doubt by the end of the book that the author understood the workings of a small child's mind.

—Joy Whitby

———

HIGHTOWER, Florence. American. Born in Boston, Massachusetts, 9 June 1916. Educated at Vassar College, Poughkeepsie, New York, A.B. 1937. Married James R. Hightower in 1940; four children. Lived in China, 1940–41, 1946–47. *Died 6 March 1981.*

PUBLICATIONS FOR CHILDREN

Fiction

Mrs. Wappinger's Secret, illustrated by Beth and Joe Krush. Boston, Houghton Mifflin, 1956; London, Lane, 1957.
The Ghost of Follonsbee's Folly, illustrated by Ati Forberg. Boston, Houghton Mifflin, 1958.
Dark Horse of Woodfield, illustrated by Joshua Tolford. Boston, Houghton Mifflin, 1962; London, Macdonald, 1964.
Fayerweather Forecast, illustrated by Joshua Tolford. Boston, Houghton Mifflin, 1967; London, Macdonald, 1968.
The Secret of the Crazy Quilt, illustrated by Beth and Joe Krush. Boston, Houghton Mifflin, 1972.
Dreamwold Castle. Boston, Houghton Mifflin, 1978.

*

Manuscript Collection: University of Wisconsin Library, Madison.

Florence Hightower commented:
(1978) I write novels in which I hope intelligent, reading children will find the same sustaining pleasure which intelligent, reading adults find in novels written for them. My novels deal with children in their relations with each other, their families, and their communities. My characters, like those in adult novels, are beset by problems and conflicts. Sometimes they can and do cope. Sometimes they can't or won't. Although I rely on a mechanical plot to bring my characters together in dramatic situations, I consider the unfolding of the plot of secondary importance to the unfolding of characters in their various relationships. The effectiveness of a novel, however, depends not on the intention of the author, but on the way he uses words. A story, well told, seems to grow and blossom as naturally and beautifully as a plant. A clumsily told story, though its intentions be of the best, never comes to life. It has been suggested to me by school teachers that I write stories using only words that are on lists which children of various ages are required in school to recognize. If I did this, my stories would be born dead. In writing each sentence, I use the best words I can think of and deploy them as skilfully as I know how. I always wish that my vocabulary were larger and my skill greater. Educators and other propagandists often expect writers for children to connive with them by sneaking doses of instruction, guidance, or uplift into their books. For a novelist, especially a children's novelist, to do this strikes me as stupid and degrading. He destroys the artistic integrity of his own work, lessens its impact, and perverts his true purpose in writing—which is to

reveal insights into the human condition in such a stirring, appealing, and moving way that he fires the imagination of his reader and inspires him to sharpen his own insights, challenges him to increase his knowledge, and persuades him to enlarge his sympathies by reading more novels, that he may grow up into a cultivated, discerning, novel-reading adult.

*   *   *

Perhaps it is because much of her writing reflected the activities of her own children and of the Maine island where they spent their vacations that Florence Hightower's stories have such lively and believable characters and such convincing settings. In her first book, *Mrs. Wappinger's Secret,* the action centers on an eccentric old woman who enlists the help of a young neighbor to help her find some treasure she believes is buried on her property, but the appeal lies not only in the plot but also in the insight into the likeable if often exasperating characters, especially in the depiction of Charlie's summer-weary father.

All of the Hightower books abound in humor, and in *Dark Horse of Woodfield* the author incorporates this through her distinctive characters yet manages to give a convincing picture of the Depression Era. In this story, as in others, there is a smooth blending of elements, of main plot and minor plots. The old, once-splendid house, Woodfield, is the setting for a warm family story, a horse story, and a love story, all nicely merged, and told with credible suspense. In *The Ghost of Follonsbee's Folly,* another vigorous family story, much of the appeal lies in the compatible union of odd and everyday events. Again, in *Fayerweather Forecast* the ebullient Fayerweather clan tolerates affectionately each member's idiosyncracies—and even uses them to advantage, as in the episode in which mother is working for a new school and employs the talents of her histrionic young daughter, who obligingly quavers a pitiful tale about how dreadfully antiquated the old school is. And yet, for all its buoyant humor, the story explores a mysterious murder. *The Secret of the Crazy Quilt* is a fast-paced, intricate story of rum-runners of the Prohibition Era, but the wit and humor of her style balance the grimness of the events, which are told in retrospect by two of the characters; here Hightower again proved adroit in weaving plot threads into a seamless whole.

—Zena Sutherland

HIGHWATER, Jamake. Tribal name: Piitai Sahkomaapii [Eagle Son]. Has also written as J Marks. American (Blackfeet Indian). Worked with San Francisco Contemporary Theatre, 1955–67; editor, Fodor Travel Guides, New York, 1970–75; Lecturer, New York University School of Continuing Education, 1980–85; Assistant Professor, Columbia University School of the Arts, 1983–86, and Graduate School of Architecture, since 1984; Guest Professor, University of Texas Health Science Center, Houston, 1985. Contributing editor, *Stereo Review,* New York, 1972–79; classical music editor, *SoHo Weekly News,* New York, 1975–79; columnist or contributor, *Indian Trader,* Billings, Montana, 1977–80, *New York Arts Journal,* 1978–84, *Native Arts/West,* Santa Fe, 1980–81, *Lone Star Review,* Dallas, 1981–83, *Christian Science Monitor,* Boston, and *Commonweal.* Host, *Indian America* program, WNET-TV, New York, 1982. Founding President, American Indian Community House, New York, 1976–78. Consultant, 1975–80, and since 1981 member of the Literature Panel, New York State Council on the Arts; since 1980 founding board member, Indian Arts Foundation, Albuquerque. Member of the Executive Board, PEN American Center, 1983–85, and Children's Literature Board, PEN, 1985–88. Since 1984 founding President, Native Land Foundation; since 1986 general director, Native Arts festival. Recipient: Women's International League for Peace and Freedom Jane Addams award, for non-fiction, 1979; Anisfield-Wolf award, 1980. D.F.A.: Minneapolis College of Art and Design, 1986. Agent: Alfred Hart, 419 East 57th Street, New York, New York 10022. Address: c/o The Native Land Foundation, P.O. Box 2026, Canal Street Station, New York, New York 10013, U.S.A.

PUBLICATIONS FOR CHILDREN

Fiction

Anpao: An American Indian Odyssey, illustrated by Fritz Scholder. Philadelphia, Lippincott, 1977.
The Sun, He Dies: The End of the Aztec World. New York, Lippincott, 1980.
Ghost Horse Cycle:
  Legend Days. New York, Harper, 1984.
  The Ceremony of Innocence. New York, Harper, 1985.
  I Wear the Morning Star. New York, Harper, 1986.
Eyes of Darkness. New York, Lothrop, 1985.

Verse

Moonsong Lullaby, photographs by Marcia Keegan. New York, Lothrop, 1981.

Other

Many Smokes. Many Moons: A Chronology of American Indian History Through Indian Art. Philadelphia, Lippincott, 1978.

Recording: *Anpao,* Folkways.

PUBLICATIONS FOR ADULTS

Novel

Journey to the Sky. New York, Crowell, 1978.

Other

Rock and Other Four Letter Words: Music by the Electric Generation (as J Marks). New York, Bantam, 1968.
Mick Jagger: The Singer Not the Song (as J Marks). New York, Curtis, 1973.
Fodor's Indian America: A Cultural and Travel Guide. New York, McKay, 1975; London, Hodder and Stoughton, 1976.
Song from the Earth: American Indian Painting. Boston, New York Graphic Society, 1976.
Ritual of the Wind: North American Indian Ceremonies, Music and Dances. New York, Viking Press, 1977; revised edition, New York, Van der Marck, 1984.
Dance: Rituals of Experience. New York, A and W, 1978.
Masterpieces of American Indian Painting. Santa Fe, Bell Editions, 2 vols., 1979–83.
The Sweet Grass Lives On: 50 Contemporary North American Indian Artists. New York, Crowell, 1980.
The Primal Mind: Vision and Reality in Indian America. New York, Harper, 1981.
Arts of the Indian Americas: Leaves from the Sacred Tree. New York, Harper, 1983.

Native Land: Sagas of the Indian Americas. Boston, Little Brown, 1986.
Shadow Show: An Autobiographical Insinuation. New York, Van der Marck, 1986.

Editor, *Words in the Blood: Contemporary Indian Writers of North and South America.* New York, New American Library, 1984.

Television Series (also narrator): *Native Land,* 1984, 1986.

*

Manuscript Collection: Native Land Foundation, New York.

Jamake Highwater comments:

I am an author who is Indian (not an Indian author), and as such I have spent my life attempting to transliterate into languages other than my own (Blackfeet) the essences of my cultural precepts which are fundamentally different from the conceptualizations of the dominant society. Happily my work seems to have significance both for Native Americans and non-Indians alike—which makes me believe that I have succeeded in producing a series of metaphors which bridge that great distance between peoples—a distance which consists not of space but of culture. I am equally trained in the culture of my own Indian people (the Blood Band of the Blackfeet Nation) and of the Western world; and it is this duplexity which gives me a strong motivation—since I discover in Western arts a ritual essence not unlike the mentality which is Indian. I have therefore used art to produce histories alternative to the Western chronicles which are, finally, but one way of looking at the past and one way of evaluating the events of the present.

*   *   *

Jamake Highwater is the author of several books, fiction and non-fiction, on Native American culture. *Anpao,* his best-known juvenile work, is a Native American *Alice in Wonderland.* Like Alice, it fits no category but its own. In *Anpao* characters suddenly appear, divide, change shape, vanish, and reappear like the Cheshire Cat. *Anpao* can be a bewildering book for it too rejects the logical, sequential patterns underlying the western concept of history. Where Carroll follows the byways of anti-logic and disorder down the rabbithole into Wonderland, Highwater takes his hero Anpao across a pre-Columbian landscape of the mind.

Anpao begins with a hero cut off from his past, from his people, from his beloved, and in the symbolic figure of his twin brother Oapna, from himself. Anpao's love for Ko-ko-mik-e-is, his search for his father, the Sun, and all his adventures become quests to restore what has been lost. Anpao's journey encompasses all planes. He moves through space and time, above the earth and below. There is no distinction between the physical world and the realm of dreams. Internal and external are one. Whatever can be imagined becomes real. Like a Zen koan, *Anpao* strives to break up the definitions by means of which the Western mind attempts to impose itself on the natural world.

In *Legend Days* and *The Ceremony of Innocence* Highwater takes the primal figure of Anpao and makes him a woman. Amana descends from the realm of myth into history. Rescued from the owls by the foxes, she becomes Memory, incorporating within herself the old songs and stories, the mythic soul of the Native American peoples. She is male and female, mother and warrior, hunter and nurturer, witness to the physical and spiritual extinction of the Plains tribes in the 19th century. Amana's own family disintegrates under the pressures from outside: poverty, intermarriage, alcoholism, false ideals, rejection of the old ways. No one wants to hear the old songs; no one believes the old stories. Sitko, Amana's grandson, is the only

hope for the future. Sitko will listen.

Sitko is Highwater. Both these books and those to come in this series can be considered efforts to define his personal history. In the figures of Jemima and Jaime, Highwater compassionately depicts how easily dreams go awry when people forget their roots. He also directs barbs at hypocritical Indians. Amana's being denied land on the Blackfoot reservation because there is no record of her on the tribal register is an ironic reflection of Highwater's own recent legal difficulties.

Many authors describe the details of the Native American's culture. Highwater is one of the few to open a window into his soul.

—Eric A. Kimmel

———

HILDICK, E(dmund) W(allace). British. Born in Bradford, Yorkshire, 29 December 1925. Educated at Wheelwright Grammar School, Dewsbury, Yorkshire, 1937–41; City of Leeds Training College, Yorkshire, 1948–50, teachers certificate. Served in the Royal Air Force, 1946–48. Married Doris Clayton in 1950. Junior assistant, Dewsbury Public Library, 1941–42; clerk, truck repair depot, Leeds, 1942–43; laboratory assistant, Admiralty Signals Establishment, Haslemere, Surrey, and Sowerby Bridge, Yorkshire, 1943–46; teacher, Dewsbury Secondary Modern School, 1950–54. Since 1954 self-employed writer. Visiting critic and associate editor, *Kenyon Review,* Kenyon College, Gambier, Ohio, 1966–67. Recipient: Tom-Gallon Trust award, for short story, 1957; Mystery Writers of America Edgar Allan Poe award, 1979. Address: c/o Coutts and Company Ltd., 440 The Strand, London WC2R 0QS, England.

PUBLICATIONS FOR CHILDREN

Fiction

Jim Starling, illustrated by Roger Payne. London, Chatto and Windus, 1958.
Jim Starling and the Agency, illustrated by Roger Payne. London, Chatto and Windus, 1958.
Jim Starling and the Colonel, illustrated by Roger Payne. London, Heinemann, 1960; New York, Doubleday, 1968.
Jim Starling's Holiday, illustrated by Roger Payne. London, Heinemann, 1960.
The Boy at the Window, illustrated by Ionicus. London, Chatto and Windus, 1960.
Jim Starling Takes Over, illustrated by Roger Payne. London, Blond, 1963; revised edition, London, New English Library, 1971.
Jim Starling and the Spotted Dog, illustrated by Roger Payne. London, Blond, 1963.
Jim Starling Goes to Town, illustrated by Roger Payne. London, Blond, 1963.
Meet Lemon Kelly, illustrated by Margery Gill. London, Cape, 1963; as *Lemon Kelly,* New York, Doubleday, 1968.
Birdy Jones. London, Faber, 1963; Harrisburg, Pennsylvania, Stackpole, 1969.
Mapper Mundy's Treasure Hunt, illustrated by John Cooper. London, Blond, 1963.
Lemon Kelly Digs Deep, illustrated by Margery Gill. London, Cape, 1964.
Louie's Lot. London, Faber, 1965; New York, David White, 1968.
The Questers, illustrated by Richard Rose. Leicester, Brockhampton Press, 1966; New York, Hawthorn, 1970.

Calling Questers Four, illustrated by Richard Rose. Leicester, Brockhampton Press, 1967.

The Questers and the Whispering Spy, illustrated by Richard Rose. Leicester, Brockhampton Press, 1967.

Lucky Les: The Adventures of a Cat of Five Tales, illustrated by Peter Barrett. London, Blond, 1967; revised edition, Leicester, Brockhampton Press, 1974.

Lemon Kelly and the Home-Made Boy, illustrated by Iris Schweitzer. London, Dobson, 1968.

Louie's S.O.S., illustrated by Iris Schweitzer. London, Pan, 1968; New York, Doubleday, 1970.

Birdy and the Group, illustrated by Richard Rose. London, Pan, 1968; Harrisburg, Pennsylvania, Stackpole, 1969.

Here Comes Parren, illustrated by Michael Heath. London, Macmillan, 1968; New York, World, 1972.

Back with Parren, illustrated by Michael Heath. London, Macmillan, 1968.

Birdy Swings North, illustrated by Richard Rose. London, Pan, 1969; Harrisburg, Pennsylvania, Stackpole, 1971.

Manhattan Is Missing illustrated by Jan Palmer. New York, Doubleday, 1969; London, Stacey, 1972.

Top Boy at Twisters Creek, illustrated by Oscar Liebman. New York, David White, 1969.

Birdy in Amsterdam, illustrated by Richard Rose. London, Pan, 1970; Harrisburg, Pennsylvania, Stackpole, 1971.

Ten Thousand Golden Cockerels, illustrated by Richard Rose. London, Evans, 1970.

The Dragon That Lived under Manhattan, illustrated by Harold Berson. New York, Crown, 1970.

The Secret Winners, illustrated by Gustave Nebel. New York, Crown, 1970.

The Secret Spenders, illustrated by Gustave Nebel. New York, Crown, 1971.

The Prisoners of Gridling Gap: A Report, With Expert Comments from Doctor Ranulf Quitch, illustrated by Paul Sagsoorian. New York, Doubleday, 1971; London, Stacey, 1973.

My Kid Sister, illustrated by Iris Schweitzer. New York, World, 1971; Leicester, Brockhampton Press, 1973.

The Doughnut Dropout, illustrated by Kiyo Komoda. New York, Doubleday, 1972.

Kids Commune, illustrated by Oscar Liebman. New York, David White, 1973.

The Active-Enzyme Lemon-Freshened Junior High School Witch, illustrated by Iris Schweitzer. New York, Doubleday, 1973.

The Nose Knows, illustrated by Unada Gliewe. New York, Grosset and Dunlap, 1973; London, Hodder and Stoughton, 1974.

Birdy Jones and the New York Heads. New York, Doubleday, 1974.

Dolls in Danger, illustrated by Val Biro. London, Hodder and Stoughton, 1974; as *Deadline for McGurk,* New York, Macmillan, 1975.

Louie's Snowstorm, illustrated by Iris Schweitzer. New York, Doubleday, 1974; London, Deutsch, 1975.

The Menaced Midget, illustrated by Val Biro. Leicester, Brockhampton Press, 1975.

The Case of the Condemned Cat, illustrated by Val Biro. London, Hodder and Stoughton, and New York, Macmillan, 1975.

Time Explorers Inc., illustrated by Nancy Ohanian. New York, Doubleday, 1976.

A Cat Called Amnesia, illustrated by Val Biro. New York, David White, 1976; London, Deutsch, 1977.

The Case of the Nervous Newsboy, illustrated by Val Biro. London, Hodder and Stoughton, and New York, Macmillan, 1976.

The Great Rabbit Robbery, illustrated by Val Biro. London, Hodder and Stoughton, 1976; as *The Great Rabbit Rip-Off,* New York, Macmillan, 1977.

The Top-Flight Fully-Automated Junior High School Girl Detective, illustrated by Iris Schweitzer. New York, Doubleday, 1977; as *The Top-Flight Fully-Automated Girl Detective,* London, Deutsch, 1979.

The Case of the Invisible Dog, illustrated by Lisl Weil. New York, Macmillan, and London, Hodder and Stoughton, 1977.

Louie's Ransom. New York, Knopf, 1978; London, Deutsch, 1979.

The Case of the Secret Scribbler, illustrated by Lisl Weil. New York, Macmillan, and London, Hodder and Stoughton, 1978.

The Case of the Phantom Frog, illustrated by Lisl Weil. New York, Macmillan, and London, Hodder and Stoughton, 1979.

The Case of the Treetop Treasure, illustrated by Lisl Weil. New York, Macmillan, and London, Hodder and Stoughton, 1980.

The Case of the Snowbound Spy, illustrated by Lisl Weil. New York, Macmillan, 1980.

The Case of the Bashful Bank Robber, illustrated by Lisl Weil. New York, Macmillan, 1981.

The Case of the Four Flying Fingers, illustrated by Lisl Weil. New York, Macmillan, 1981.

McGurk Gets Good and Mad, illustrated by Lisl Weil. New York, Macmillan, 1982.

The Case of the Felon's Fiddle, illustrated by Lisl Weil. New York, Macmillan, 1982.

The Case of the Slingshot Sniper, illustrated by Lisl Weil. New York, Macmillan, 1983.

The Ghost Squad Breaks Through. New York, Dutton, 1984.

The Ghost Squad Flies Concorde. New York, Dutton, 1985.

The Ghost Squad and the Halloween Conspiracy. New York, Dutton, 1985.

The Case of the Vanishing Ventriloquist, illustrated by Kathy Parkinson. New York, Macmillan, 1985.

The Ghost Squad and the Ghoul of Grünberg. New York, Dutton, 1986.

The Case of the Muttering Mummy, illustrated by Blanche Sims. New York, Macmillan, 1986.

The Ghost Squad and the Prowling Hermits. New York, Dutton, 1987.

The Case of the Wandering Weathervanes, illustrated by Denise Brunkus. New York, Macmillan, 1988.

The Ghost Squad and the Menace of the Malevs. New York, Dutton, 1988.

The Memory Tap. London, Macmillan, 1989.

Other

A Close Look at Newspapers [*Magazines and Comics, Television and Sound Broadcasting, Advertising*]. London, Faber, 4 vols., 1966–69.

Cokerheaton (storypack), illustrated by Roger Payne. London, Evans, 1971.

Rushbrook (storypack). London, Evans, 1971.

PUBLICATIONS FOR ADULTS as Wallace Hildick

Novels

Bed and Work. London, Faber, 1962.

A Town on the Never. London, Faber, 1963.

Lunch with Ashurbanipal. London, Faber, 1965.

Monte Carlo or Bust! (novelization of screenplay; as E.W. Hildick). London, Sphere, 1969; as *Those Daring Young Men in Their Jaunty Jalopies,* New York, Berkley, 1969.

Bracknell's Law. New York, Harper, 1975; London, Hamish Hamilton, 1976.

The Weirdown Experiment. New York, Harper, and London, Hamish Hamilton, 1976.

Vandals.   London, Hamish Hamilton, 1977.
The Loop.   London, Hamish Hamilton, 1977.

Other

Word for Word: A Study of Authors' Alterations, with Exercises.
   London, Faber, 1965; abridged edition, as *Word for Word: The Rewriting of Fiction,* New York, Norton, 1966.
Writing with Care: 200 Problems in the Use of English.   London,
   Weidenfeld and Nicolson, and New York, David White, 1967.
Thirteen Types of Narrative.   London, Macmillan, 1968; New York,
   Potter, 1970.
*Children and Fiction: A Critical Study in Depth of the Artistic and
   Psychological Factors Involved in Writing Fiction for and about
   Children.*   London, Evans, 1970; New York, World, 1971;
   revised edition, Evans, 1974.
Storypacks: A New Concept in English Teaching (as E.W. Hildick).
   London, Evans, 1971.
Only the Best: Six Qualities of Excellence.   New York, Potter, 1973.

                                   *

E.W. Hildick comments:

   In my fiction for children I have always been compelled to give
an accurate reflection of the contemporary background as I know it.
That is why the first half-dozen or so books are set in the industrial
working-class North of England, where I was brought up and worked
and taught until the mid-1950's. Then comes a batch (*Meet Lemon
Kelly,* the Questers books, and others) influenced by 7 years spent in
the New Town of Stevenage, near London. After that come the stories
with American settings (New York City, as in *Manhattan Is Missing,*
Ohio, and various Long Island and Connecticut suburbs). Such a
strong emphasis on the contemporary always courts the danger of
ephemerality—and to avoid this there must be some kind of
preservative; some acid or salt. Fortunately, my adolescent bent as
the Clown of the Class—so much the despair of my teachers at the
time—seems to have stood me in good stead as a writer, with the
humour, the slapstick, the occasional wit acting so effectively as a
preservative that many of my early books are still in print. About my
adult fiction in relation to the children's books, I've been interested
to note, when compiling the list, that there are often overlapping
themes and settings. Thus *Meet Lemon Kelly* was written around the
same time as *A Town on the Never* (both New Town books); *Lemon
Kelly Digs Deep* (a children's archeological quest) links with *Lunch
with Ashurbanipal* (British Museum background); while *Bracknell's
Law* and *Vandals* give rather sombre accounts of the vicissitudes of
British families living in the U.S., in contrast to the lighter shades of
my Anglo-U.S. children's books.

                           *   *   *

   E.W. Hildick has firm views about children and fiction and his
considerable output is aimed at putting his theory into practice. In
order to broaden the social background of children's books he
concentrates on working-class, or classless, characters and his
pioneering has paved the way for others. His intentions sometimes
dominate the story but generally he has created lively, humorous
plots, a style which is deceptively fluent, although deliberately
constructed for less able readers, and characterisation which is
sound, if not always deep. The books about Jim Starling and The
Questers demonstrate a new approach to the school story in which
school is shown as an integral part of the boys' lives, not a separate
way of life as in many pre-war stories. The Cement Street Secondary
Modern and its teachers will be familiar to many readers, and the
boys he writes about are recognisably those he hopes will read the
books. In *The Questers* he avoids the sentimentality inherent in the

theme by the pace and ingenuity of the plots in which the boys
attempt to involve their bed-ridden friend in their activities. Aimed
similarly at nine-to-12-year-olds, the series about Lemon Kelly is
action-packed with a minimum of narrative and shows the imagination and humour typical of his work. The exuberance of Hildick's
writing is especially noticeable in the stories about Louie, a highly
professional milkman with a trained band of schoolboy helpers who
overcome every hazard including rival milk companies, snowstorms,
and muggers to see that the milk gets through. The farcical situations
are anchored in reality by the down-to-earth Louie, and the short,
staccato sentences, particularly in *Louie's Lot,* stimulate an awareness of words, their meanings and shape. Two further groups of
stories are those about Birdy Jones and McGurk, for slightly older
and younger readers respectively. Keen observation of the contemporary world helps to make Birdy and his manager credible, but the
concept is farfetched and more obviously contrived to appeal to the
non-reading teenager. The McGurk books are an attempt to construct
a conventional detective mystery in a simple style around a trivial
incident such as whether the cat was guilty of catching and eating
the bird.

   Some of Hildick's more recent titles show the influence of the time
he has spent in America. In particular, the Ghost Squad books have
transatlantic settings, dialogue, and style. *The Ghost Squad Breaks
Through* is an original idea: the first of a series of adventure stories
centred around a gang of youngsters, four of whom are ghosts. They
continue to communicate with their two living friends by means of
a word processor, and Hildick creates the logic of the ghost world
and its interplay with the living with great ingenuity. The plots are
fast-moving and eventful and although there are flashes of humor
there is also menace and real danger for the squad. Like much of his
earlier output, the Ghost Squad books have no great literary quality
but they are professionally crafted and well designed for the non-
literary reader. It would be churlish not to be grateful for Hildick's
many books which offer action, humour, some believable characters,
and lively dialogue, and which are dedicated to the idea that reading
is fun.

                                                —Valerie Brinkley-Willsher

                        ————————

HILL, Douglas (Arthur).   Has also written as Martin Hillman.
Canadian.   Born in Brandon, Manitoba, 6 April 1935. Educated at
schools in Prince Albert, Saskatchewan; University of Saskatchewan, Saskatoon, 1952–57, B.A. (honours) in English 1957;
University of Toronto, 1957–59. Married Gail Robinson in 1958
(divorced 1978); one son. Series editor, Aldus Books, London,
1962–64. Since 1964 freelance writer. Literary editor, *Tribune,* London, 1971–84. Science fiction adviser, Rupert Hart-Davis, 1966–68,
Mayflower Books, 1969–71, J.M. Dent and Sons, 1972–74, and Pan
Books, 1974–80, all London. Recipient: Canada Council grant,
1966, 1969, 1970. Agent: Sheila Watson, Watson Little Ltd., Suite
8, 26 Charing Cross Road, London WC2H 0DG. Address: 3 Hillfield
Avenue, London N8 7DU, England.

PUBLICATIONS FOR CHILDREN

Fiction

Galactic Warlord.   London, Gollancz, 1979; New York, Atheneum,
   1980.
Deathwing over Veynaa.   London, Gollancz, 1980; New York,
   Atheneum, 1981.

Day of the Starwind. London, Gollancz, 1980; New York, Atheneum, 1981.

Planet of the Warlord. London, Gollancz, 1981; New York, Atheneum, 1982.

Young Legionary: The Earlier Adventures of Keill Randor. London, Gollancz, 1982; New York, Atheneum, 1983.

The Huntsman. London, Heinemann, and New York, Atheneum, 1982.

Have Your Own Extraterrestrial Adventure. London, Sparrow, 1983.

Warriors of the Wasteland. London, Heinemann, and New York, Atheneum, 1983.

Alien Citadel. London, Heinemann, and New York, Atheneum, 1984.

Exiles of ColSec. London, Gollancz, and New York, Atheneum, 1984.

The Caves of Klydor. London, Gollancz, 1984; New York, Atheneum, 1985.

The Moon Monsters, illustrated by Jeremy Ford. London, Heinemann, 1984.

ColSec Rebellion. London, Gollancz, and New York, Atheneum, 1985.

How Jennifer (and Speckle) Saved the Earth, illustrated by André Amstutz. London, Heinemann, 1986.

Blade of the Poisoner. London, Gollancz, and New York, McElderry, 1987.

Master of Fiends. London, Gollancz, 1987; New York, McElderry, 1988.

Goblin Party, illustrated by Paul Demayer. London, Gollancz, 1988.

Other

Coyote the Trickster: Legends of the North American Indians, with Gail Robinson, illustrated by Graham McCallum. London, Chatto and Windus, 1975; New York, Crane Russak, 1976.

The Exploits of Hercules, illustrated by Tom Barling. London, Pan, 1978.

Editor, *Alien Worlds.* London, Heinemann, 1981.
Editor, *Planetfall.* Oxford, Oxford University Press, 1986.

PUBLICATIONS FOR ADULTS

Other

The Supernatural, with Pat Williams. London, Aldus, 1965; New York, Hawthorn, 1966.

The Opening of the Canadian West. London, Heinemann, and New York, Day, 1967.

Magic and Superstition. London, Hamlyn, 1968.

John Keats. London, Morgan Grampian, 1968.

Regency London. London, Macdonald, 1969.

Fortune Telling. London, Hamlyn, 1970.

A Hundred Years of Georgian London. London, Macdonald, 1970; New York, Hastings House, 1971.

Return from the Dead. London, Macdonald, 1970; as *The History of Ghosts, Vampires, and Werewolves,* New York, Harrow, 1973.

Bridging a Continent (as Martin Hillman). London, Aldus, 1971; revised edition, London, Reader's Digest Association, 1978, 1979.

The Scots to Canada. London, Gentry, 1972.

The Comet. London, Wildwood, 1973.

Witchcraft, Magic, and the Supernatural, with others. London, Octopus, 1974.

The English to New England. London, Gentry, and New York, Potter, 1975.

Fortune Telling: A Guide to Reading the Future. London, Hamlyn, 1978.

The Illustrated "Faerie Queene" (retelling). New York and London, Newsweek, 1980.

Editor, *The Peasants' Revolt: A Collection of Contemporary Documents.* London, Jackdaw, 1966.

Editor, *Window on the Future.* London, Hart Davis, 1966.

Editor, *The Way of the Werewolf.* London, Panther, 1966.

Editor, *The Devil His Due.* London, Hart Davis, 1967; New York, Avon, 1969.

Editor, *Warlocks and Warriors.* London, Mayflower, 1971.

Editor, *Tribune 40.* London, Quartet, 1977.

Editor, *The Shape of Sex to Come.* London, Pan, 1978.

*

Douglas Hill comments:

Principally, and unashamedly, I now write science fiction and fantasy adventure for children. It does not pretend to be children's "literature," nor to aim at what a publisher has called the "literate tip of the iceberg." I know too well the social and cultural pressures that divert children, today, from reading. I also know that they cannot be brought from television and comics to complex and demanding "literature" in a single step. They must ascend a ladder—and I supply some of the rungs. To change the metaphor: if children's books were motorcars, I would make Minis—accessible, popular, and lively ways for everyone to acquire the motoring (reading) habit. If all cars were Rolls-Royces, only the privileged few would drive.

*   *   *

Douglas Hill's childhood interest in science fiction led to his later becoming a reviewer of that genre for a weekly newspaper in England, then to his editing science fiction anthologies, and finally to his writing in the genre. While Hill has edited and written numerous books for adult audiences, of those produced for children and young adults he is best known for three science fiction series for early adolescents: *Last Legionary, The Huntsman,* and *ColSec.* Each of these groupings of books shares several common characteristics. The central character is a heroic male who is of almost epic proportions, but all of the series have one or more strong female characters. The books in the three series are adventure-oriented and action-packed, but all of the series share a common theme which relates to mankind's desire for freedom from oppression and the need for good to fight actively against evil. Each book in a series can stand alone because the separate titles end at a concluding point in the series' episodic plots. As well, every book, after a series' initial volume, incorporates a recapitulation chapter.

Hill's first series, *Last Legionary,* consists of five books—really a quartet plus a prequel. *Galactic Warlord* introduces Keill Randor who comes from the planet Moros whose people are all trained from childhood to be superb warriors. While the Legions of Moros are for hire, their ethics will not allow them to be mercenaries for aggressors or would-be exploiters. The Warlord, the series' villain, realizing that Moros would oppose anyone seeking ultimate power, delivers a preemptive strike against them, and only Randor escapes immediate death from radiation. Later the Overseers, a group of leading intellectuals from the Inhabited Worlds, replace Randor's radiation-riddled skeleton with an organic alloy. Remembering his friend's dying words, "Avenge the murder of Moros," the bionic Legionary is easily convinced by the Overseers to seek out and destroy the Warlord, a quest that carries Randor and his winged alien companion Glr through the next three books: *Deathwing over Veynaa; Day of the*

Starwind; and *Planet of the Warlord*. In the quartet Hill had made passing references to Randor's childhood. Because children's questions kept calling for more details about Randor's growing up and training period, Hill wrote the prequel *Young Legionary: The Earlier Adventures of Keill Randor*, which consists of four linked stories.

Hill's next two series were both trilogies. *The Huntsman*, the first title in the series bearing the same name, presents a post-nuclear holocaust Earth whose inhabitants have reverted to a preindustrial society. The people are being kept at this primitive level of development by aliens called Slavers. When Finn Feral sets out to rescue his father and sister from the aliens, he discovers that not only are the Slavers using humans as workers, they are also carrying out a scientific breeding program to turn humans back into brute animals. For Feral the task in *Warriors of the Wasteland* and *Alien Citadel* then becomes one not just of rescuing his family but also of freeing humankind from Slaver bondage.

ColSec stands for Colonization Section, part of the totalitarian Organization that came to rule Earth after the "Virus Decades." When the Civil Defenders capture members of teenage gangs populating the wastes of the inner cities or the countryside, these "criminals" are not sent to prison but are exiled by being placed on ColSec spaceships programmed to land on wild, uninhabited planets. If the scards (discards) survive and colonize the planet, then the Organization exploits the new colony's resources. *Exiles of ColSec* introduces three boys and two girls, all teens, who have survived the crashlanding of a ColSec ship on the planet Klydor. Under the leadership of Cord MaKiy, the group's first task is simply to learn how to survive in a land where they cannot immediately differentiate between the harmful and the harmless. In *The Caves of Klydor* and *ColSec Rebellion* the five, having successfully adapted to their new environment, realize that true freedom on Klydor will never be possible as long as ColSec controls the colonies. With the help of Bren Lathan, once a space explorer but now a rebel leader, the five return to Earth to recruit freedom fighters from among the teenage gangs. Though the series concludes with the colonies having achieved independence, Earth remains under Organization control, but the idea of freedom has been introduced.

—David H. Jenkinson

HILL, Lorna (née Leatham). British. Born in Durham, 21 February 1902. Educated at Durham High School for Girls; Le-Manoir, Lausanne; University of Durham, B.A. 1926. Married V.R. Hill in 1928; one daughter. Address: Brockleside, Keswick, Cumbria CA12 5UP, England.

PUBLICATIONS FOR CHILDREN

Fiction

Marjorie & Co., illustrated by Gilbert Dunlop. London, Art and Educational, 1948.
Stolen Holiday, illustrated by Gilbert Dunlop. London, Art and Educational, 1948.
Border Peel, illustrated by Esmé Verity. London, Art and Educational, 1950.
A Dream of Sadler's Wells, illustrated by Eve Guthrie. London, Evans, 1950; New York, Holt, 1955.
Veronica at the Wells, illustrated by Eve Guthrie. London, Evans, 1951; as *Veronica at Sadler's Wells*, New York, Holt, 1955.
They Called Her Patience, illustrated by Gilbert Dunlop. London, Burke, 1951.
Masquerade at the Wells, illustrated by Eve Guthrie. London, Evans, 1952; as *Masquerade at the Ballet*, New York, Holt, 1957.
It Was All Through Patience, illustrated by Gilbert Dunlop. London, Burke, 1952.
No Castanets at the Wells, illustrated by Eve Guthrie. London, Evans, 1953; as *Castanets for Caroline*, New York, Holt, 1956.
Jane Leaves the Wells, illustrated by Eve Guthrie. London, Evans, 1953.
Castle in Northumbria, illustrated by Gilbert Dunlop. London, Burke, 1953.
Ella at the Wells, illustrated by Eve Guthrie. London, Evans, 1954.
Dancing Peel, illustrated by Esmé Verity. London, Nelson, 1954.
So Guy Came Too, illustrated by Joanna Curzon. London, Burke, 1954.
Return to the Wells, illustrated by Eve Guthrie. London, Evans, 1955.
Dancer's Luck, illustrated by Esmé Verity. London, Nelson, 1955.
The Five Shilling Holiday, illustrated by Joanna Curzon. London, Burke, 1955.
Rosanna Joins the Wells, illustrated by Eve Guthrie. London, Evans, 1956.
The Little Dancer, illustrated by Esmé Verity. London, Nelson, 1956; New York, Nelson, 1957.
Principal Role, illustrated by Esmé Verity. London, Evans, 1957.
Swan Feather, illustrated by Esmé Verity. London, Evans, 1958.
Dancer in the Wings, illustrated by Esmé Verity. London, Nelson, 1958.
Dress-Rehearsal, illustrated by Esmé Verity. London, Evans, 1959.
Back-Stage, illustrated by Esmé Verity. London, Evans, 1960.
Dancer in Danger, illustrated by Esmé Verity. London, Nelson, 1960.
The Vicarage Children, illustrated by Marcia Lane Foster. London, Evans, 1961.
Vicki in Venice, illustrated by Esmé Verity. London, Evans, 1962.
Dancer on Holiday, illustrated by Esmé Verity. London, Nelson, 1962.
No Medals for Guy, illustrated by Gilbert Dunlop. London, Nelson, 1962.
More About Mandy, illustrated by Ann Kent Robinson. London, Evans, 1963.
The Secret, illustrated by Esmé Verity. London, Evans, 1964.
The Vicarage Children in Skye, illustrated by Elizabeth Grant. London, Evans, 1966.

Other

La Sylphide: The Life of Marie Taglioni. London, Evans, 1967.

PUBLICATIONS FOR ADULTS

Novels

The Other Miss Perkin. London, Hale, 1978.
The Scent of Rosemary. London, Hale, 1978; New York, Pinnacle, 1980.

*

Lorna Hill comments:

My "pony" books, set in Northumberland where I lived for most of my life, were written for my daughter Vicki when she was small. Vicki became a dancer and trained at the Sadler's Wells Ballet School (now the Royal Ballet School), and this was how I obtained the background for my ballet books.

* * *

Lorna Hill's *A Dream of Sadler's Wells* set a pattern which she was to follow consistently through the 1950's and early 1960's. It is a wish-fulfilment story about Veronica Weston, a child dancer, recently orphaned, who is sent to live with some rich, snobbish relations in Northumberland. Here, besides riding and enjoying a romantic friendship with a boy musician, she secretly practices her dancing, until, in the end, she auditions for Sadler's Wells Ballet School and is accepted as a student. *A Dream of Sadler's Wells* was the first of a long series of inter-locking "Wells" novels, following Veronica's entirely predictable progress through the ballet school to starring roles at Covent Garden and marriage with the young musician, while at the same time widening out to include the dancing careers of other talented orphans, or daughters of Northumbrian county families.

In the early books Hill attempts to show something of the genuinely hard life of a ballet student—"groans, sighs and panting breath filled the studio"—but reality soon drowns in syrupy romance. Hill may assert that "a ballet school is full of heartache," but the heartache is of a most novelettish kind. Her heroines struggle with malicious guardians who refuse them dancing lessons, or jealous rivals who plot against them, but never with the technical demands of their art. They are clearly born to be ballerinas, with their strong, slender feet and huge dark eyes; and they acquire their perfect "line" as much by instinct as from their lessons. The only conflict they experience is between their careers and marriage to some devoted suitor, but a satisfactory, fairy-tale ending is invariably reached.

What made these books enormously popular was the glamour they offered, a decorous glamour which suited the unsophisticated teenagers of the 1950's, who could overlook the stereotyped, class-ridden characterization and repetitive plots. Hill presents a day-dream world of famous, beautiful, aristocratic people—occasionally contrasted with the vulgar lower classes—who inhabit Scottish castles and Northumbrian stately homes, who hunt and go to balls, wear Dior models, dance at Royal Gala performances before the Queen, receive proposals from Ruritanian monarchs, and subside into happy-ever-after marriages while still emotionally, if not actually, teenagers.

Among all the candy-floss romance, one book, *The Vicarage Children,* stands out. This is a realistic, everyday chronicle of a clergy family without wealth or talent, who find plenty to enjoy in spite of the limitations of life in their small Northumberland village. With her feet on the ground for once, Hill depicted genuine family situations, and showed that she could draw ordinary characters with warmth and humour.

—Angela Bull

HINTON, S(usan) E(loise). American. Born in Tulsa, Oklahoma, in 1950. Educated at the University of Tulsa, degree in education 1970. Married David Inhofe in 1970; one son. Recipient: *Media and Methods* award, 1975; American Library Association Newcott Caldeberry award, 1976 and Young Adult Services Division award, 1988. Lives in Tulsa. Address: c/o Delacorte Press, 1 Dag Hammarskjöld Plaza, New York, New York 10017, U.S.A.

PUBLICATIONS FOR CHILDREN

Fiction

The Outsiders. New York, Viking Press, 1967; London, Gollancz, 1970.

That Was Then, This Is Now. New York, Viking Press, and London, Gollancz, 1971.

Rumble Fish. New York, Delacorte Press, 1975; London, Gollancz, 1976.

Tex. New York, Delacorte Press, 1979; London, Gollancz, 1980.

Taming the Star Runner. New York, Delacorte Press, 1988.

Play

Screenplay: *Rumble Fish,* with Francis Ford Coppola, 1983.

*

Critical Study: *Presenting S.E. Hinton* by Jay Daly, Boston, Twayne, 1987.

* * *

The novels of S.E Hinton expose the poverty of many stories tailored for "reluctant readers." At their worst, such books are based on the fallacy that kids with problems want to read about Kids with Problems: Trouble down Gas Street, or Stabbings on the East Side, wherever your potential market is enduring its crises. Characterisation is often two-dimensional and even condescending. If they are to know their subjects with sympathy, adult authors need both the capacity and the opportunity to listen to urban teenagers; neither is easily acquired.

Hinton was 16 when she wrote her enormously popular *The Outsiders,* and it may well be her youthful perspective which gave an unusual immediacy to language, character, and setting. Her plots are distinguished from the formula stories by the mercurial, vulnerable, yet often courageous qualities of the protagonists. They frequently display an adolescent capacity for self-dramatisation which is particularly evident in exaggerated imitations of older boys. Ponyboy Curtis, the central character of *The Outsiders* (who reappears in a minor role in *That Was Then, This Is Now*), is convincing to young readers because, beneath the toughness necessary for survival, his needs are as various, his generosities as warm, his irrationalities as extreme, as those of a teenager from any social background. Much of the appeal of the two novels lies in the narrators' struggles to resolve the tension which they share with Hinton's audience, between public image and private feeling.

Hinton's plots are controlled with economy. The maelstrom of abrasive encounters may stretch credulity, but it was a platitude of the late 1960's that in some American cities the events of the streets beggared fiction. In *The Outsiders* gang rituals and class warfare, an accidental killing, a flight, lead to a poignant but just resolution. *That Was Then, This Is Now* explores the relationship between Bryon and his closest friend, his unofficially adopted brother, Mark. Events and impulses which neither can contain drive them against their wills into a hostility which culminates in Bryon turning Mark in to the police.

In *Rumble Fish* Hinton shifts her viewpoint from that of the thoughtful if confused narrators who are, she has implied, reflections of herself as a teenager. Rusty-James regrets the passing of the gang conflicts in which his idolised older brother, The Motorcycle Boy, excelled. He cannot understand the present disenchantment of his brother, for whom no relationship, no experience, offers meaning. The Motorcycle Boy's loss of innocence and hope is total, and a virtually suicidal death is inevitable. Rusty-James is left alone, without orientation. In *Rumble Fish* some of the author's limitations begin to be confirmed: there is a suggestion of repetition in the plot, for example, and physical descriptions tend to lean upon mechanical references to hair and eyes. Yet this is also the most ambitious of Hinton's novels, for her subject, Rusty-James, little understood by others or by himself, unable to make a pattern of the events and characters around him, represents an element of urban life which is at once pathetic and menacing.

Tex also depends upon the lines of tension strung between an admired older brother and an uncertain narrator. This time the setting is rural and the boys are thrust into uneasy closeness through the lengthy absences of their widower father on the rodeo circuit. As in the other novels, events and revelations move with an almost blatantly dramatic rapidity which compels attention. It is not surprising that Hollywood adapted *Tex* and most of Hinton's other novels for the cinema.

Hinton's most recent work, *Taming the Star Runner*, shares with its predecessors the "problem" male adolescent as protagonist. Travis is sent to stay with his uncle in Oklahoma as an alternative to a juvenile detention hall after he has attacked his stepfather. A tough city kid, he has a hard time fitting into his new life until he begins working at his uncle's horse ranch. There he gets to know Casey, an 18-year-old who runs the ranch's riding school and jumps professionally with her horse, the wild Star Runner. Not exactly a friendship, certainly not a romance, their relationship gives him back his street toughness, but channeled into a more constructive force. Casey tries to tame the Star Runner to jump because he *can* do it. The horse's unbridled (and therefore dangerous) talent parallels Travis's ability—the boy who tried to kill his stepfather can also write. By the end of the book he has in fact sold his first novel, and is beginning to get along with his uncle and peers. This comes at a high price: in the climax of his "taming" Travis and Casey witness the Star Runner's destruction in a lightning storm. While the symbolism in the book is mercifully not overdone, Hinton seems to have lost some of her authenticity of voice in portraying male adolescents. At times the contradiction between Travis's delinquency and his ability to write is too forced. Indeed, perhaps the most interesting issue in the novel, his writing talent, is treated offhandedly, without a proper exploration of his inspiration. That *any* teenager would be inspired and disciplined enough to write a publishable novel is unusual—though Hinton's own early work is proof that it can be done successfully. That process is well worth demystifying.

—Geoff Fox and George Walsh

HOBAN, Russell (Conwell). American. Born in Lansdale, Pennsylvania, 4 February 1925. Educated at Lansdale High School; Philadelphia Museum School of Industrial Art, 1941–43. Served in the United States Army Infantry, 1943–45: Bronze Star. Married 1) Lillian Aberman (i.e., the illustrator Lillian Hoban) in 1944 (divorced 1975), one son and three daughters; 2) Gundula Ahl in 1975, three sons. Magazine and advertising agency artist and illustrator; story board artist, Fletcher Smith Film Studio, New York, 1951; television art director, Batten Barton Durstine and Osborn, 1951–56, and J. Walter Thompson, 1956, both in New York; freelance illustrator, 1956–65; advertising copywriter, Doyle Dane Bernbach, New York, 1965–67. Since 1967 full-time writer; since 1969 has lived in London. Recipient: Christopher award, 1972; Whitbread award, 1974; Ditmar award (Australia), 1982; John W. Campbell Memorial award, 1982. Agent: David Higham Associates Ltd., 5–8 Lower John Street, London W1R 4HA, England.

PUBLICATIONS FOR CHILDREN

Fiction

Bedtime for Frances, illustrated by Garth Williams. New York,

Harper, 1960; London, Faber, 1963.
Herman the Loser, illustrated by Lillian Hoban. New York, Harper, 1961; Kingswood, Surrey, World's Work, 1972.
The Song in My Drum, illustrated by Lillian Hoban. New York, Harper, 1962.
London Men and English Men, illustrated by Lillian Hoban. New York, Harper, 1962.
Some Snow Said Hello, illustrated by Lillian Hoban. New York, Harper, 1963.
The Sorely Trying Day, illustrated by Lillian Hoban. New York, Harper, 1964; Kingswood, Surrey, World's Work, 1965.
A Baby Sister for Frances, illustrated by Lillian Hoban. New York, Harper, 1964; London, Faber, 1965.
Bread and Jam for Frances, illustrated by Lillian Hoban. New York, Harper, 1964; London, Faber, 1966.
Nothing to Do, illustrated by Lillian Hoban. New York, Harper, 1964.
Tom and the Two Handles, illustrated by Lillian Hoban. New York, Harper, 1965; Kingswood, Surrey, World's Work, 1969.
The Story of Hester Mouse Who Became a Writer, illustrated by Lillian Hoban. New York, Norton, 1965; Kingswood, Surrey, World's Work, 1969.
What Happened When Jack and Daisy Tried to Fool the Tooth Fairies. New York, Four Winds Press, 1965.
Henry and the Monstrous Din, illustrated by Lillian Hoban. New York, Harper, 1966; Kingswood, Surrey, World's Work, 1967.
The Little Brute Family, illustrated by Lillian Hoban. New York, Macmillan, 1966.
Save My Place, with Lillian Hoban, illustrated by Lillian Hoban. New York, Norton, 1967.
Charlie the Tramp, illustrated by Lillian Hoban. New York, Four Winds Press, 1967.
The Mouse and His Child, illustrated by Lillian Hoban. New York, Harper, 1967; London, Faber, 1969.
A Birthday for Frances, illustrated by Lillian Hoban. New York, Harper, 1968; London, Faber, 1970.
The Stone Doll of Sister Brute, illustrated by Lillian Hoban. New York, Macmillan, and London, Collier Macmillan, 1968.
Harvey's Hideout, illustrated by Lillian Hoban. New York, Parents' Magazine Press, 1969; London, Cape, 1973.
Best Friends for Frances, illustrated by Lillian Hoban. New York, Harper, 1969; London, Faber, 1971.
The Mole Family's Christmas, illustrated by Lillian Hoban. New York, Parents' Magazine Press, 1969; London, Cape, 1973.
Ugly Bird, illustrated by Lillian Hoban. New York, Macmillan, 1969.
A Bargain for Frances, illustrated by Lillian Hoban. New York, Harper, 1970; Kingswood, Surrey, World's Work, 1971.
Emmet Otter's Jug-Band Christmas, illustrated by Lillian Hoban. New York, Parents' Magazine Press, and Kingswood, Surrey, World's Work, 1971.
The Sea-Thing Child, illustrated by Brom Hoban. New York, Harper, and London, Gollancz, 1972.
Letitia Rabbit's String Song, illustrated by Mary Chalmers. New York, Coward McCann, 1973.
How Tom Beat Captain Najork and His Hired Sportsmen, illustrated by Quentin Blake. New York, Atheneum, and London, Cape, 1974.
Ten What? A Mystery Counting Book, illustrated by Sylvie Selig. London, Cape, 1974; New York, Scribner, 1975.
Dinner at Alberta's, illustrated by James Marshall. New York, Crowell, 1975; London, Cape, 1977.
Crocodile and Pierrot, with Sylvie Selig, illustrated by Selig. London, Cape, 1975; New York, Scribner, 1977.
A Near Thing for Captain Najork, illustrated by Quentin Blake. London, Cape, 1975; New York, Atheneum, 1976.

Arthur's New Power, illustrated by Byron Barton. New York, Crowell, 1978; London, Gollancz, 1980.

The Twenty-Elephant Restaurant, illustrated by Emily McCully. New York, Atheneum, 1978; London, Cape, 1980.

The Dancing Tigers, illustrated by David Gentleman. London, Cape, 1979.

La Corona and the Tin Frog, illustrated by Nicola Bayley. London, Cape, 1979.

Flat Cat, illustrated by Clive Scruton. London, Methuen, and New York, Philomel, 1980.

Ace Dragon Ltd., illustrated by Quentin Blake. London, Cape, 1980.

The Serpent Tower, illustrated by David Scott. London, Methuen, 1981.

The Great Fruit Gum Robbery, illustrated by Colin McNaughton. London, Methuen, 1981; as *The Great Gumdrop Robbery,* New York, Philomel, 1982.

They Came from Aargh!, illustrated by Colin McNaughton. London, Methuen, and New York, Philomel, 1981.

The Battle of Zormla, illustrated by Colin McNaughton. London, Methuen, and New York, Philomel, 1982.

The Flight of Bembel Rudzuk, illustrated by Colin McNaughton. London, Methuen, and New York, Philomel, 1982.

Ponders (Jim Frog, Big John Turkle, Charlie Meadows, Lavinia Bat), illustrated by Martin Baynton. London, Walker, and New York, Holt Rinehart, 4 vols., 1983–84.

The Rain Door, illustrated by Quentin Blake. London, Gollancz, 1986; New York, Crowell, 1987.

The Marzipan Pig. London, Cape, 1986; New York, Farrar Straus, 1987.

Verse

Goodnight, illustrated by Lillian Hoban. New York, Norton, 1966; Kingswood, Surrey, World's Work, 1969.

The Pedaling Man and Other Poems, illustrated by Lillian Hoban. New York, Norton, 1968; Kingswood, Surrey, World's Work, 1969.

Egg Thoughts and Other Frances Songs, illustrated by Lillian Hoban. New York, Harper, 1972; London, Faber, 1973.

Other

What Does It Do and How Does It Work? Power Shovel, Dump Truck, and Other Heavy Machines. New York, Harper, 1959.

The Atomic Submarine: A Practice Combat Patrol under the Sea. New York, Harper, 1960.

PUBLICATIONS FOR ADULTS

Novels

The Lion of Boaz-Jachin and Jachin-Boaz. London, Cape, and New York, Stein and Day, 1973.

Kleinzeit. London, Cape, and New York, Viking Press, 1974.

Turtle Diary. London, Cape, 1975; New York, Random House, 1976.

Riddley Walker. London, Cape, and New York, Summit, 1980.

Pilgermann. London, Cape, and New York, Summit, 1983.

The Medusa Frequency. London, Cape, and New York, Atlantic Monthly Press, 1987.

Plays

The Carrier Frequency, with Impact Theatre Co-operative

(produced London, 1984).

Riddley Walker, adaptation of his own novel (produced Manchester, 1986).

Television Play: *Come and Find Me,* 1980.

* * *

The virtues of Russell Hoban's picture books surely owe something to his early years as a television art director, copywriter, and free-lance illustrator. There are an elegance and wit about them, combined with the fairly unerring selection of apt illustrations (often by Lillian Hoban) which, one suspects, are the product of a talent and industry normally summed up by the word professionalism. And though these books, because of their repetitive sentence-structures and simplified vocabularies, are sometimes included in Reading Schemes, it is important to realise that many of them are more than that implies.

The best known is probably the series about Frances the Badger, who, with her father and mother, baby sister, and best friend Thelma, goes through the kinds of experiences that children between the ages of 4 and 7 enjoy reading about. The books are anthropomorphic, with the badgers wearing clothes, and talking and behaving like humans generally. But what is so captivating about them is the combination of witty observations and shrewd common sense. When Frances begins to feel that her mother is busier than usual because of the new baby, she decides to run away:

"Well," said Frances, "things are not very good here anymore. No clothes to wear. No raisins for the oatmeal. I think maybe I'll run away."

"Finish your breakfast," said Mother. "It is about time for the school bus."

"What time will dinner be tonight?" said Frances.

"Half past six," said Mother.

"Then I shall have plenty of time to run away after dinner," said Frances, and she kissed her mother goodbye and went to school.

The pattern of these stories is re-assuringly familiar and almost cosy at times, with the liberal middle-class badger parents exercising just the right degree of permissive control in dealing with Frances's problems, which are usually resolved happily. But occasionally the parents' patience wears thin, and Frances has to learn that some things have to be accepted for the way they are.

The combination of wit and elegance with something rather more formidable is also presented a shade less delicately in some of the other picture books, such as *The Stone Doll of Sister Brute,* for example. In *How Tom Beat Captain Najork and His Hired Sportsmen* (illustrated by Quentin Blake) Tom has a hilarious time outwitting his aunt Miss Fidget Wonkham-Strong and her efforts to subdue him. The very qualities of fooling around, which his aunt tries so hard to crush, prove just the thing to defeat Captain Najork at the games of Womble, Muck, and Sneedball, and so a deeply serious defence of natural joy is seen to underpin this whole delightful fantasy.

Similar use of fantasy, though of an increasingly sombre kind, dominates the longer stories which have begun to appear since *The Mouse and His Child* in the mid-1960's. Increasingly recognised as a modern children's classic, or a modern classic which uses the form of children's fiction, this picaresque story describes the adventures of a clockwork-toy mouse and his son after they have been rescued from a dustbin by a passing tramp. Their wanderings through a modern urban civilisation bring them close to disaster and failure many times. They meet a variety of toys and animals, including a prophetic Frog, an aristocratic toy Elephant and a philosophical Muskrat; they constantly need rewinding, and flounder for a time in a muddy lake. Above all, they are pursued by Manny Rat, a ruthless and ingenious predator, who can be viciously cruel, for example, to a broken down toy-donkey:

> "You're not well," said Manny Rat. "I can see that easily. What you need is a long rest." He picked up a heavy rock, lifted it high, and brought it down on the donkey's back, splitting him open like a walnut. "Put his works in the spare-parts can," said Manny Rat to Ralphie.

Increasingly, as this powerful, comic, and disturbing narrative develops, however, we become aware that the pilgrimage of the mouse and his child is centred upon three very human needs, the desire for a territory or home of their own, like the one they knew in the toyshop, their desire to become self-winding and independent, and finally their desire to know what is beyond "The Last Visible Dog" they see mentioned everywhere, and which comes to represent Infinity. Again the ending is deceptively ambiguous, for though the mouse and his child do find the apparent security of a renovated Dolls' House and are surrounded by their friends, they also learn that there is nothing "beyond the Last Visible Dog but us," and that no one is ever completely self-winding—"That's what friends are for." Even more ominously for some readers, however, is the fact that Manny Rat himself remains at large, if apparently reformed.

The violence and witty allusiveness found in *The Mouse and His Child,* including a theatre which parodies Beckett's work, for example, is not something which all children find palatable, and one suspects that, though its reputation will continue to grow, it will appeal to children of at least 12 and upwards. *The Sea-Thing Child* may be found even more oblique by young readers, for it has none of the narrative energy of *The Mouse and His Child,* dealing, as it does, with an animal washed up on the sea-shore and his conversations mainly with a fiddler-crab and an albatross. Even so, its themes, the need for absolute honesty with oneself and being true to one's own nature, in this case trying to make a bow for a violin if you are a fiddler-crab and going back to sea if you are a sea-bird, are absolutely central to Hoban's work. There is nothing "beyond the Last Visible Dog but us."

Equally the adult novels will probably prove too demanding for all but the most alert adolescent readers, though there are elements of wit and fantasy in them, especially *Kleinzeit* and *Turtle Diary,* which many will enjoy. Since the late 1970's, in fact, and the emergence of Hoban as a serious adult novelist, particularly with the publication of *Riddley Walker,* an amazing picture of the future relayed to us by an illiterate 12-year-old, it is tempting to suggest that Hoban has put most of his energy into his adult books. *Pilgermann,* ostensibly a historical novel set in the Middle East in the 11th century, and *The Medusa Frequency,* a contemporary novel about a writer of comic serials, engage with themes that will daunt all but the brightest teenager.

Among his children's books since 1975, *Arthur's New Power* and *Dinner at Alberta's* are very like a continuation of the Badger series, with stories about a crocodile family, while *The Twenty-Elephant Restaurant* is no more than a cheerful anecdote. *La Corona and the Tin Frog* and *The Marzipan Pig* contain some typically Hobanesque features, but, though a new vein of gentle domestic humour appears in *The Great Fruit Gum Robbery* and *They Came from Aargh!,* *A Near Thing for Captain Najork* and *The Rain Door* by contrast seem more laboured. A recent work, *Ponders,* a set of linked stories about the creatures who live near a pond, including a bat, a frog, and a heron, evokes an amusing, gentle, world, with a hint of melancholy that will fascinate some children, but may lack sufficient grip for others. Hoban is a remarkable writer, and whatever he publishes is bound to be of interest, but perhaps only *The Dancing Tigers* comes near the quality of his earlier children's stories, an apparently modest

picture book, but witty, powerful, and mythic, like an idiosyncratic mixture of Blake and Woody Allen.

—Dennis Butts

HODGES, C(yril) Walter. British. Born in Beckenham, Kent, 18 March 1909. Educated at Dulwich College, London, 1922–25; Goldsmiths' College School of Art, London, 1925–28. Served in the British Army, 1940–46. Married Greta Becker in 1936; two sons. Since 1929 stage and exhibition designer, mural painter, and freelance book, magazine, and advertisement illustrator. Designer of productions, Mermaid Theatre, 1951–52, 1964, and St. George's Theatre, 1976, London. Art director, Encyclopaedia Britannica Films, Chicago, 1959–61. Judith E. Wilson Lecturer, Cambridge University, 1974; Adjunct Professor of Theatre, Wayne State University, Detroit, 1980–83; visiting scholar, University of Maryland, College Park, 1983. Since 1979 design consultant and adviser for Globe Theatre Reconstruction Project. Has designed exhibitions for Lloyds and the U.K. Provident Institution, and murals for the Chartered Insurance Institute, 1934, and the U.K. Provident Institution, 1957. Individual show of Elizabethan theatre reconstructions and designs, Folger Shakespeare Library, Washington, D.C., 1988. Recipient: Library Association Kate Greenaway Medal, for illustration, 1965. D. Litt.: University of Sussex, Brighton, 1979. Agent: Laura Cecil, 17 Alwyne Villas, London N1 2HG. Address: 36 Southover High Street, Lewes, East Sussex BN7 1HX, England.

PUBLICATIONS FOR CHILDREN (illustrated by the author)

Fiction

Columbus Sails. London, Bell, and New York, Coward McCann, 1939.
The Flying House: A Story of High Adventure. London, Benn, 1947; as *Sky High: The Story of a House That Flew,* New York, Coward McCann, 1947.
The Namesake. London, Bell, and New York, Coward McCann, 1964.
The Marsh King. London, Bell, and New York, Coward McCann, 1967.
The Overland Launch. London, Bell, 1969; New York, Coward McCann, 1970.
Playhouse Tales. London, Bell, and New York, Coward McCann, 1974.
Plain Lane Christmas. London, Dent, and New York, Coward McCann, 1978.

Other

Shakespeare and the Players. London, Bell, and New York, Coward McCann, 1948.
Shakespeare's Theatre. London, Oxford University Press, and New York, Coward McCann, 1964.
The Norman Conquest. London, Oxford University Press, and New York, Coward McCann, 1966.
Magna Carta. London, Oxford University Press, and New York, Coward McCann, 1966.
The Spanish Armada. London, Oxford University Press, 1967; New York, Coward McCann, 1968.
The English Civil War. London, Oxford University Press, 1972; as *The Puritan Revolution,* New York, Coward McCann, 1972.

The Emperor's Elephant. London, Oxford University Press, 1975.
The Battlement Garden: Britain from the Wars of the Roses to the Age of Shakespeare. London, Deutsch, 1979; New York, Clarion, 1980.

PUBLICATIONS FOR ADULTS

Other

The Globe Restored: A Study of the Elizabethan Theatre. London, Benn, 1953; revised edition, London, Oxford University Press, and New York, Coward McCann, 1968.
The Globe Playhouse 1599–1613: A Conjectural Drawing. London, Benn, and New York, Coward McCann, 1959.
Shakespeare's Second Globe: The Missing Monument. London, Oxford University Press, 1973.

Editor, with Samuel Schoenbaum and Leonard Leone, *The Third Globe: Symposium for the Reconstruction of the Globe Playhouse.* Detroit, Wayne State University Press, 1981.

*

Manuscript Collection: Folger Shakespeare Library, Washington, D.C.

Illustrator: *King Richard's Land,* 1933, and *Mr. Sheridan's Umbrella,* 1935, both by L.A.G. Strong; *Treasures of English Verse* edited by Herbert Strang, 1934; *The Happy Mariners* by Gerald W. Bullet, 1935; *Plays in Verse and Mime* by Rosalind Vallance, 1935; *Know Ye Not Agincourt* by Leslie Barringer, 1936; *The Squirrel's Granary* by William Beach Thomas, 1936; *My Garden by the Sea* by Robert A. Foster-Melliar, 1936; *The Schoolboy King* by Mark Dallow, 1937; *Trixie (Stories of the Circus)* by Bob Barton and G. Ernest Thomas, 1937; *New Tales from Shakespeare,* 1938, *More New Tales from Shakespeare,* 1939, *New Tales from Malory,* 1939, and *New Tales of Troy,* 1940, all by G.B. Harrison; *A Book of Famous Pirates* by A.M. Smyth, 1940; *The Watchers* by A.E.W. Mason, 1940; *Mutiny in the Caribbean* by G.W. Keeton, 1940; *They Wanted Adventure* by Kenneth Macfarlane, 1940; *Sister of the Angels,* 1940, *Smoky-House,* 1940, *The Little White Horse,* 1946, and *Make Believe,* 1949, all by Elizabeth Goudge; *The Ship Aground,* 1940, and *Painted Ports,* 1948, both by C. Fox Smith; *They Raced for Treasure,* 1946, *Flight to Adventure,* 1947, *There's No Escape,* 1950, *Mountain Rescue,* 1955, and *The Silver Sword,* 1956, all by Ian Serraillier; *Adventures of Button and Mac* by Ursula Hourihane, 1946; *The Story of the Treasure Seekers,* 1947, *The New Treasure Seekers,* 1947, and *The Would-Be-Goods,* 1947, all by E. Nesbit; *The Swiss Family Robinson* by Johann David and Johann Rudolf Wyss, 1949; *Cocos Gold* by Ralph Hammond, 1950; *The Chronicles of Robin Hood,* 1950, *The Queen Elizabeth Story,* 1951, *The Armourer's House,* 1951, *Brother Dusty-Feet,* 1952, *The Eagle of the Ninth,* 1954, and *The Shield Ring,* 1956, all by Rosemary Sutcliff; *Redcap Runs Away* by Rhoda Power, 1952; *The Crown of Violet,* 1952, and *Bows Against the Barons,* revised edition, 1966, both by Geoffrey Trease; *Sea-Dogs and the Pilgrim Fathers* edited by John Hampdon, 1953; *Queen Elizabeth and the Spanish Armada* by Frances Winwar, 1954; *A Swarm in May,* 1955, *Chorister's Cake,* 1956, and *Cathedral Wednesday,* 1960, all by William Mayne; *Will Shakespeare and the Globe Theatre* by Anne Terry White, 1955; *The King's Snare* by Helen Lobdell, 1955; *The Adventures of Huckleberry Finn* and *The Adventures of Tom Sawyer,* both by Mark Twain, 1955; *Cold Hazard* by Richard Armstrong, 1956; *Ransom for a Knight* by Barbara Leonie Picard, 1956; *The Three Musketeers* by Dumas, 1957; *Once-upon-a-Time Storybook* by Rose Dobbs, 1958;

The Flight and Adventures of Charles II by Charles Norman, 1958; *The Kidnapping of Kensington* by Bruce Carter, 1958; *The Golden Stile* by Gwen Walker, 1958; *Castles and Kings* by Henry Treece, 1959; *Red Indian Folk and Fairy Tales* by Ruth Manning-Sanders, 1960; *The Siege and Fall of Troy* by Robert Graves, 1962; *Three Against London* by Rachel Varble, 1962; *Growing Up in the Thirteenth Century,* 1962, *The Story of the Crusades,* 1963, and *Growing Up with the Norman Conquest,* 1965, all by Alfred Duggan; *The Shoe Shop Bears,* 1963, and *Hannibal and the Bears,* 1965, both by Margaret J. Baker; *The Lion in the Gateway* by Mary Renault, 1964; *The Richleighs of Tantamount* by Barbara Willard, 1966; *The Complete Pelican Shakespeare* edited by Alfred Harbage, 1969; *The Nine Questions* by Edward Fenton, 1969; *The Rime of the Ancient Mariner* by Samuel Taylor Coleridge, 1971; *The Pied Piper of Hamelin* by Robert Browning, 1971; *The Sea-Beggar's Son* by F.N. Monjo, 1974; *Here Come the Clowns* by Lowell Swortzell, 1978; *The New Cambridge Shakespeare,* 12 vols., 1984–89; *The Boar's Head Playhouse,* 1986, and *Shakespeare's Playhouses,* 1987, both by Herbert Berry.

C. Walter Hodges comments:

It is a truth more or less universally acknowledged by those concerned with literature for children, that children ought not to be written down to. But is the opposite also true, that they ought not to be *written up from?* Surely not. Those who are nowadays called Children's Writers (and their illustrators) are adults, engaged as adults in highly-skilled creative, imaginative work; and children in their own imaginations are as near adult as need be for an intelligent readership. Many of the books that most attracted me and my friends when I was young were not specifically written as "children's books"; therefore today, though I write mostly for children, I do not bother extremely to make my books only suitable for them at their age. I like to make them also suitable for me at mine. Besides, I am quite sure that children of any age ought not to be given children's books that are not suitable for adults to read.

*   *   *

C. Walter Hodges's particular talent is for the making of novels out of historical events, always those which have a momentum and a grandeur of their own. He is a quiet author, using no tricks of technique, and obtruding his own personality scarcely at all. This method gives an extraordinary verisimilitude to his stories; the author's cunning and skill become invisible, and one is apparently reading "what really happened."

In *Columbus Sails,* Hodges's first full-length book, the story is told from three different viewpoints; that of a monk who knows about the difficulties that Columbus surmounted to get his expedition financed, that of a sailor who can relate the events of the voyage, and that of an Indian in Spain, who knows how it all ended. The diffusion of the narrative voice, and the fact that each narrator tells not really his own story—the narrators are barely characterised—but that of the voyage, establishes Hodges's predominant tone.

Alfred Daneleg, through whose eyes the early years of King Alfred are told in *The Namesake,* is a more rounded character, yet still functions largely as a clear-eyed narrator of the course of history. But the change from *Columbus Sails* is very great. In Alfred Hodges found a subject that set his imagination alight. The battles and shifts of fortune of those grim times, the iron hearts and wolf's hunger of the Danes, and the brave, thoughtful, capable, and loving young man who rescued England have inspired the writer, and shine for the reader. A moral as well as a physical struggle was waged by Alfred; and that gives a depth and subtlety to the story. *The Namesake* is a fine historical novel and probably Hodges's best book.

The Marsh King, a sequel to *The Namesake,* completes the tale of Alfred's early wars. The opening page tells us that the story has been garnered from two eye-witnesses, but much more is in the book than these two could probably have known, and once again we are looking at very transparent narrators. In effect this is straight narration, lacking the central consciousness of Alfred Daneleg in *The Namesake*. This is a fast moving, adventurous story, a tale of battles and treachery, but a certain resonance is missing, and it is not quite the equal of the earlier book.

In *The Overland Launch* Hodges found a more modern subject. This is the true, though incredible, story of the determination of a lifeboat coxswain to get his boat in the sea and launched on a rescue mission, even though it meant hauling it up and over a hill with the most notorious ascent and descent in the West Country, in the teeth of a terrible storm. The successful achievement of this impossible task gives Hodges an epic and thrilling subject. He catches very well the temper of West Country men, and the burr of their voices. A memorable book.

Playhouse Tales is a set of short stories all about actors and playwrights of Shakespeare's time, on which Hodges is an expert. Entirely at home in this period, not now very fashionable for historical writers, Hodges is in relaxed and humorous mood. We do not need his careful notes to tell us that many of the incidents are authentic; sunny, intricate and ornate, these tales feel right for the Elizabethan atmosphere.

Hodges is an admirable craftsman; his self-effacing manners as an author should not lead one to undervalue his skill.

—Jill Paton Walsh

HOFF, Syd(ney). American. Born in New York City, 4 September 1912. Educated at New York public schools; National Academy of Design. Married Dora Berman in 1937; two daughters. Daily cartoonist ("Laugh It Off"), King Features Syndicate, 1957–71. Lives in Miami Beach, Florida. Agent: Scott Meredith Literary Agency, 845 Third Avenue, New York, New York 10022, U.S.A.

PUBLICATIONS FOR CHILDREN (illustrated by the author)

Fiction

Muscles and Brains. New York, Dial Press, 1940.
Eight Little Artists. New York, Abelard Schuman, 1954.
Patty's Pet. New York, Abelard Schuman, 1955.
Danny and the Dinosaur. New York, Harper, 1958; Kingswood, Surrey, World's Work, 1969.
Sammy, The Seal. New York, Harper, 1959; Kingswood, Surrey, World's Work, 1960.
Julius. New York, Harper, 1959; Kingswood, Surrey, World's Work, 1960.
Ogluk, The Eskimo. New York, Holt Rinehart, 1960.
Where's Prancer? New York, Harper, 1960.
Oliver. New York, Harper, 1960; Kingswood, Surrey, World's Work, 1961.
Who Will Be My Friends? New York, Harper, 1960; Kingswood, Surrey, World's Work, 1964.
Little Chief. New York, Harper, 1961; Kingswood, Surrey, World's Work, 1962.
Albert the Albatross. New York, Harper, 1961; Kingswood, Surrey, World's Work, 1962.
Chester. New York, Harper, 1961; Kingswood, Surrey, World's Work, 1969.

Stanley. New York, Harper, 1962; Kingswood, Surrey, World's Work, 1963.
Grizzwold. New York, Harper, 1963; Kingswood, Surrey, World's Work, 1964.
Lengthy. New York, Putnam, 1964; Kingswood, Surrey, World's Work, 1965.
Mrs. Switch. New York, Putnam, 1967.
Irving and Me. New York, Harper, 1967.
Wanda's Wand. Norwalk, Connecticut, Gibson, 1968.
The Witch, The Cat, and the Baseball Bat. New York, Grosset and Dunlap, 1968.
Slithers. New York, Putnam, 1968.
Baseball Mouse. New York, Putnam, 1969.
Jeffrey at Camp. New York, Putnam, 1969.
Mahatma. New York, Putnam, 1969.
Roberto and the Bull. New York, McGraw Hill, 1969; Kingswood, Surrey, World's Work, 1971.
Herschel the Hero. New York, Putnam, 1969; Kingswood, Surrey, World's Work, 1971.
The Horse in Harry's Room. New York, Harper, 1970; Kingswood, Surrey, World's Work, 1971.
The Litter Knight. New York, McGraw Hill, 1970.
Palace Bug. New York, Putnam, 1970.
Siegfried, Dog of the Alps. New York, Grosset and Dunlap, 1970.
Wilfred the Lion. New York, Putnam, 1970.
The Mule Who Struck It Rich. Boston, Little Brown, 1971.
Thunderhoof. New York, Harper, 1971; Kingswood, Surrey, World's Work, 1972.
When Will It Snow?, illustrated by Mary Chalmers. New York, Harper, 1971.
Ida the Bareback Rider. New York, Putnam, 1972.
My Aunt Rosie. New York, Harper, 1972.
Pedro and the Bananas. New York, Putnam, 1972.
A Walk Past Ellen's House. New York, McGraw Hill, 1973; Kingswood, Surrey, World's Work, 1980.
Amy's Dinosaur. New York, Windmill, 1974.
Kip Van Wrinkle. New York, Putnam, 1974.
Katy's Kitty. New York, Windmill, 1975.
Pete's Pup. New York, Windmill, 1975.
Barkley. New York, Harper, 1975; Kingswood, Surrey, World's Work, 1976.
The Littlest Leaguer. New York, Windmill, 1976.
Walpole. New York, Harper, 1977; Kingswood, Surrey, World's Work, 1978.
Henrietta Lays Some Eggs. Champaign, Illinois, Garrard, 1977.
Henrietta, The Early Bird. Champaign, Illinois, Garrard, 1978.
Henrietta, Circus Star. Champaign, Illinois, Garrard, 1978.
Henrietta Goes to the Fair. Champaign, Illinois, Garrard, 1979.
Slugger Sal's Slump. New York, Windmill, 1979.
Santa's Moose. New York, Harper, 1979.
Nutty Noodles. New York, Scholastic, 1979.
Scarface Al and His Uncle Sam. New York, Coward McCann, 1980.
Henrietta's Halloween. Champaign, Illinois, Garrard, 1980.
Merry Christmas, Henrietta. Champaign, Illinois, Garrard, 1980.
Henrietta's Fourth of July. Champaign, Illinois, Garrard, 1981.
Soft Skull Sam. New York, Harcourt Brace, 1981.
Happy Birthday, Henrietta! Champaign, Illinois, Garrard, 1983.
Barney's Horse. New York, Harper, 1987.
Mrs. Brice's Mice. New York, Harper, 1988.

Plays

Giants and Other Plays for Kids (includes *Lion in the Zoo, Children on the Moon, The Family, Wild Flowers*). New York, Putnam, 1973.

Television Plays: *Tales of Hoff* series, 1947.

Other

Syd Hoff's Joke Book.   New York, Putnam, 1972.
Jokes to Enjoy, Draw, and Tell.   New York, Putnam, 1974; as *Sid Hoff Shows You How to Draw Cartoons,* New York, Scholastic, 1979.
Dinosaur Do's and Don't's.   New York, Windmill, 1975.
Gentleman Jim and the Great John L.   New York, Coward McCann, 1977; Kingswood, Surrey, World's Work, 1979.
Sid Hoff's Best Jokes Ever.   New York, Putnam, 1978.
Boss Tweed and the Man Who Drew Him (on Thomas Nast).   New York, Coward McCann, 1978.
Mighty Babe Ruth.   New York, Scholastic, 1980.
How to Draw Dinosaurs.   New York, Windmill, 1981.
The Man Who Loved Animals (on Henry Bergh).   New York, Coward McCann, 1982.
The Young Cartoonist: The ABC's of Cartooning.   New York, Farrar Straus, and Windlesham, Surrey, Springwood, 1983.
Syd Hoff's Animal Jokes.   New York, Lippincott, 1985.

PUBLICATIONS FOR ADULTS

Other

Military Secrets.   New York, Hillair, 1943.
Feeling No Pain: An Album of Cartoons.   New York, Dial Press, 1944.
Mom, I'm Home! (cartoons).   New York, Dutton, 1945.
Oops! Wrong Party (cartoons).   New York, Dutton, 1951.
It's Fun Learning Cartooning.   New York, Stravon, 1952.
Oops! Wrong Stateroom! (cartoons).   New York, Washburn, 1953.
Out of Gas! (cartoons).   New York, Washburn, 1954.
Okay—You Can Look Now! (cartoons).   New York, Duell, 1955.
The Better Hoff (cartoons).   New York, Holt Rinehart, 1961.
Upstream, Downstream, and Out of My Mind.   Indianapolis, Bobbs Merrill, 1961.
Twixt the Cup and the Lipton.   Indianapolis, Bobbs Merrill, 1962.
So This Is Matrimony (cartoons).   New York, Pocket Books, 1962.
Hunting, Anyone? (cartoons).   Indianapolis, Bobbs Merrill, 1963.
From Bed to Nurse; or, What a Way to Die (cartoons).   New York, Dell, 1963.
Learning to Cartoon.   New York, Stravon, 1966.
The Art of Cartooning.   New York, Stravon, 1973.
Editorial and Political Cartooning: From Earliest Times to the Present....   New York, Stravon, 1976.

*

Manuscript Collections: Kerlan Collection, University of Minnesota, Minneapolis; University of California, Los Angeles; de Grummond Collection, University of Southern Mississippi, Hattiesburg; Syracuse University, New York; Library of Congress, Washington, D.C.

Illustrator: *Parm Me* by Alex Kober, 1945; *Hello Muddah, Hello Fadduh!,* 1964, and *I Can't Dance!,* 1964, both by Allan Sherman; *I Should Have Stayed in Bed!,* 1965, *The Homework Caper,* 1966, and *The Rooftop Mystery,* 1968, all by Joan M. Lexau; *A Chanukah Fable for Christmas* by Jerome Coopersmith, 1969; *Henri Goes to the Mardi Gras* by Mildred Wright, 1971; *Donald and the Fish That Walked* by Edward R. Ricciuti, 1974; *The Snake That Couldn't Slither* by Peggy Bradbury, 1976; *The Boy Who Could Find Anything,* 1978, and *Bigfoot Makes a Movie,* 1979, both by Joan Lowery Nixon; *Arthur Gets What He Spills* by Louise Armstrong, 1979; *Play Ball with Roger the Dodger* by Al Campanis, 1980; *Don't Be My*

Valentine by Joan M. Lexau, 1985; *I Saw You in the Bathtub* edited by Alvin Schwartz, 1989.

*   *   *

At his best, Syd Hoff creates likable human and animal characters whose simple, often humorous exploits provide the beginning reader with an engaging stimulus to read the easily managed texts. The plots themselves are generally straightforward, dealing positively with concepts familiar to and easily grasped by early elementary audiences. Very often, an animal character will leave its normal environment to explore the larger world, returning home safely after a series of adventures (*Lengthy, Barkley, Slithers,* and *Danny and the Dinosaur,* for instance). During these escapades, humor is created by adult figures who respond to the animal as if it were human and usually in the way, and by children who welcome it as a delightful new playmate, offering acceptance when adults do not.

Another typical Hoff plot involves unlikely heroes in either human or animal form, such as Bernard in *Baseball Mouse,* who helps a human baseball team emerge victorious, and Harold in *The Littlest Leaguer,* who manages a home run after a whole season of benchsitting. A closely related theme is that of people who are "different" but eventually come to be appreciated, such as Stanley, a caveman who prefers painting to hunting, and the good witch Mrs. Switch. Even when reworking these basic themes with different characters but barely altered plots, Hoff generally manages the telling with such bright good humor that children continue to respond with delighted enthusiasm.

However, from an adult perspective, some of Hoff's work is marred by lapses that are not easily overlooked. There are some characters in the beginning readers who are not particularly likable, and whose exploits are not especially funny. Jeffrey Spink, who spends virtually his entire session of summer camp either eating or sleeping, is one of these; Bernard (*Baseball Mouse*), who ultimately saves the day by cheating for his team, is another. These occasional problems become more obvious in the full-length *Irving and Me,* in which the main character treats his only friend with puzzling insensitivity, and continually badgers his parents to buy him a dog. Artie's own remorse for his behavior is intended to make it more palatable and even humorous, but the humor falls flat, largely because he is an unappealing character. In fact, the only character in the novel who is at all endearing is the reformed town bully; the others are too realistic to be caricatures, but drawn too broadly to be acceptable on a realistic level. The humor that usually works in the shorter tales, partly because it is never examined too deeply, wears much too thin in this longer work.

More serious flaws are Hoff's reinforcement of ethnic prejudices and sexual stereotypes in this novel, and in some of the shorter works as well. *Little Chief,* for instance, is blatantly stereotypical in its portrayal of the main character; sexual stereotypes abound in "The Family," one of the plays in *Giants and Other Plays for Kids.* The treatment of characters does not seem to be deliberately unkind; nevertheless, Hoff's attitudes seem rather antiquated and insensitive.

Hoff's more recent work does not indicate much positive development as a children's writer. In *Barney's Horse* he abandons his standard formula of animals and children to pair an animal and an adult, but neither character is particularly interesting, and even its basic plot is unconvincing. Despite the flaws that become apparent in a close examination of Hoff's work, however, the humor and simplicity which combine in his most deserving stories will probably keep works such as *Danny and the Dinosaur, Amy's Dinosaur,* and *The Horse in Harry's Room* among the perennial favorites of children just beginning to read.

—Christine Doyle Francis

HOGARTH, Grace (Weston, née Allen). Has also written as Grace Allen; Amelia Gay; Allen Weston. American. Born in Newton, Massachusetts, 5 November 1905. Educated at Newton High School, 1919–23; University of California, Berkeley, 1923–24; Vassar College, Poughkeepsie, New York, 1924–27, B.A. 1927; Massachusetts School of Art, 1927–28; Yale University School of Fine Arts, New Haven, Connecticut, 1928–29; Columbia University, New York, 1935–36. Married 1) William David Hogarth in 1936 (died 1965), two children; 2) Philip L. Sayles in 1971 (divorced 1977). Staff artist, then children's books editor, Oxford University Press, New York and London, 1929–38, Chatto and Windus, London, 1938–39, and Houghton Mifflin, Boston, 1940–43; British representative for Houghton Mifflin, 1943–47, and other publishers, 1947–56, London; children's book editor, 1956–63, managing director, 1963–66, and chairman and managing director, 1966–72, Constable, later Longman Young Books, London. Editor, Lifetime Library, 1968–70. Governor, North London and Camden Schools for Girls, 1963–71; member of the Executive Committee, Association of Governing Bodies of Girls' Public Day School Trust, 1969–71. Address: 24 Nuffield Lodge, 22 Shepherds Hill, London N6 5AH, England.

PUBLICATIONS FOR CHILDREN

Fiction

Lucy's League (as Amelia Gay), illustrated by Nora S. Unwin. London, Hodder and Stoughton, 1950; as Grace Hogarth, New York, Harcourt Brace, 1951.
John's Journey (as Amelia Gay), illustrated by Nora S. Unwin. London, Hodder and Stoughton, 1952; as Grace Hogarth, New York, Harcourt Brace, 1952.
The Funny Guy, illustrated by Fritz Wegner. London, Hamish Hamilton, and New York, Harcourt Brace, 1955.
As a May Morning. New York, Harcourt Brace, and London, Hamish Hamilton, 1958.
A Sister for Helen, illustrated by Pat Marriott. London, Deutsch, 1976.

Other

Australia: The Island Continent, illustrated by Howard W. Willard. Boston, Houghton Mifflin, 1943.

PUBLICATIONS FOR ADULTS

Novels

This to Be Love (as Grace Allen). London, Cape, 1949.
The End of Summer. London, Cape, 1951.
Children of This World. London, Cape, 1953.
Murders for Sale (as Allen Weston, with Andre Norton). London, Hammond, 1954.

Other

Editor, with Caroline Hogarth, *American Cooking for English Kitchens.* London, Hamish Hamilton, 1957.
Editor, with Lee Kingman and Harriet Quimby, *Illustrators of Children's Books 1967–1976.* Boston, Horn Book, 1978.

*

Manuscript Collection: Vassar College Library, Poughkeepsie, New York.

Illustrator: *A Bible ABC*, 1943.

Grace Hogarth comments:

For nearly all of my working life I was an editor of children's books rather than a writer of them. I think it is always a temptation for editors to write because they are so constantly exposed to writing, but I confess that I found publishing books for children far easier than writing them.

My first job, after university and two years of art school, was as Staff Artist in the Oxford University Press in New York just before the depression. I survived this by illustrating and editing some of the books on the children's list and by designing jackets, laying out ads, etc. Although I am not an artist of much ability, I found this experience and training of the greatest help to me when I became a publisher of books for children.

My most successful children's books were *The Funny Guy* and *As a May Morning*, and I wrote both of them when my own children were the appropriate ages for them. There is nothing like a young audience for honest criticism and assistance!

*   *   *

Grace Hogarth has made a dual contribution to the field of children's books, both as an editor and an author. Her first job was as children's editor at the Oxford University Press in New York and then as children's editor for a number of publishing houses in Britain. In 1957 she started the children's list at Constable and discovered many distinguished authors and artists who are at the peak of their careers today. Although there have been talented editors in both Britain and the United States, Hogarth is unique in her experience in the field of children's books on both sides of the Atlantic. She has been of immense value in introducing important children's writers from one country to another. There has long been a tendency to feel that children must not be subjected to books which are "too foreign," and Hogarth has tried hard to change this attitude. In an article she wrote for the *Horn Book* in 1965 she says, "Editors on both sides of the Atlantic are apt to say 'American children would never understand this' or 'Whatever will English children make of these peculiar clothes?' What we tend to overlook is the obvious truth that children everywhere are keenly interested in, and ready to learn about, other children, and the odder the better."

Perhaps because she started her career as an art student her interest in book illustration has always been as keen as her insistence on quality in writing. She illustrated her own editions of *A Bible ABC* for the youngest readers.

The Funny Guy, perhaps the most popular of her children's books, takes place in America in 1900 and tells of the year when Helen Hamilton's mother goes into hospital and Helen acquires the nickname of "the funny guy" from her classmates at school. Through a subscription to *St. Nicholas* magazine Helen learns that writing is fun and can bring new friends. This book was followed by *As a May Morning*, a novel for older children which explored the pleasures and pains of leaving childhood for an alien adult world. Hogarth's writing is very much concerned with human relations and the importance of coming to terms with one another.

—Ann Bartholomew

———

HOLLAND, Isabelle. Has also written as Francesca Hunt. American. Born in Basel, Switzerland, 16 June 1920. Educated at private schools in England; University of Liverpool, 1938–40; Tulane University, New Orleans, B.A. in English 1942. Publicity director, Crown Publishers, New York, 1956–60, and Lippincott, publishers, Philadelphia, 1960–66; assistant to the publisher, *Harper's* magazine, New York, 1967–68; publicity director, Putnam's Sons, publishers, New York, 1968–69. Lives in New York City. Recipient: Church and Synagogue Library Association Ott award, 1983 (twice). Agent: Elaine Markson Literary Agency, 44 Greenwich Avenue, New York, New York, 10011, U.S.A.

PUBLICATIONS FOR CHILDREN

Fiction

Cecily. Philadelphia, Lippincott, 1967; London, Severn House, 1985.
Amanda's Choice. Philadelphia, Lippincott, 1970.
The Man Without a Face. Philadelphia, Lippincott, 1972.
The Mystery of Castle Renaldi (as Francesca Hunt). Middletown, Connecticut, Xerox, 1972.
Heads You Win, Tails I Lose. Philadelphia, Lippincott, 1973.
Journey for Three, illustrated by Charles Robinson. Middletown, Connecticut, Xerox, 1974; London, Macdonald and Jane's, 1978.
Of Love and Death and Other Journeys. Philadelphia, Lippincott, 1975; as *Ask No Questions,* London, Macdonald and Jane's, 1978.
Alan and the Animal Kingdom. Philadelphia, Lippincott, 1977; London, Macdonald and Jane's, 1979.
Hitchhike. Philadelphia, Lippincott, 1977.
Dinah and the Green Fat Kingdom. Philadelphia, Lippincott, 1978.
Now Is Not Too Late. New York, Lothrop, 1980.
Summer of My First Love. New York, Fawcett, 1981; London, Severn House, 1987.
A Horse Named Peaceable. New York, Lothrop, 1982.
Abbie's God Book, illustrated by James McLaughlin. Philadelphia, Westminster Press, 1982.
Perdita. Boston, Little Brown, 1983; London, Severn House, 1987.
God, Mrs. Muskrat, and Aunt Dot, illustrated by Beth and Joe Krush. Philadelphia, Westminster Press, 1983.
After the First Love. New York, Fawcett, 1983; London, Severn House, 1988.
The Empty House. New York, Lippincott, 1983; London, Severn House, 1985.
Kevin's Hat, illustrated by Leonard B. Lubin. New York, Lothrop, 1984.
Green Andrew Green, illustrated by Pat Steiner. Philadelphia, Westminster Press, 1984.
The Island. Boston, Little Brown, 1985; London, Severn House, 1986.
Jenny Kiss'd Me. New York, Fawcett, 1985; London, Severn House, 1986.
Henry and Grudge. New York, Walker, 1986.
Love and the Genetic Factor. New York, Fawcett, 1987.
The Christmas Cat, illustrated by Kathy Mitchell. New York, Golden, 1987.
Toby the Splendid. New York, Walker, 1987.
Thief. New York, Fawcett, 1989.
The Easter Donkey. New York, Golden, 1989.

PUBLICATIONS FOR ADULTS

Novels

Kilgaren. New York, Weybright and Talley, 1974; London, Collins, 1975.

Trelawny. New York, Weybright and Talley, 1974; as *Trelawny's Fell,* London, Collins, 1976.
Moncrieff. New York, Weybright and Talley, 1975; as *The Standish Place,* London, Collins, 1976.
Darcourt. New York, Weybright and Talley, 1976; London, Collins, 1977.
Grenelle. New York, Rawson, 1976; London, Collins, 1978.
The deMaury Papers. New York, Rawson, 1977; London, Collins, 1978.
Tower Abbey. New York, Rawson, 1978; London, Collins, 1979.
The Marchington Inheritance. New York, Rawson, 1979; London, Collins, 1980.
Counterpoint. New York, Rawson, 1980; London, Collins, 1981.
The Lost Madonna. New York, Rawson, 1981; London, Collins, 1982.
A Death at St. Anselm's. New York, Doubleday, 1984; London, Severn House, 1985.
Flight of the Archangel. New York, Doubleday, 1985; London, Severn House, 1986.
A Lover Scorned. New York, Doubleday, 1986; London, Severn House, 1987.
Bump in the Night. New York, Doubleday, 1988; London, Severn House, 1989.

*

Manuscript Collections: Kerlan Collection, University of Minnesota, Minneapolis; de Grummond Collection, University of Southern Mississippi, Hattiesburg.

Isabelle Holland comments:
   The Greek philosopher Heraclitus said "character is destiny." Some well-known contemporary writer—possibly the late Elizabeth Bowen—said "character is plot." In my books I write about what interests me most: the development of character, its growth of understanding of self, and its relationship to others. To me this is the basis of all stories, and I look upon myself primarily as a story teller.

*   *   *

   After a productive career in publishing, Isabelle Holland began writing for children in the late 1960's. Her first novel, *Cecily,* originally published for adults, appeared in 1967 and was praised for its lucid prose and convincing characterizations. It concerns the experiences of an unhappy 13-year-old girl in an English boarding school whose brilliant and beautiful teacher rejects her. Because the novel revealed exceptional insight into the young girl's psyche, Holland was asked to write for children, and *Amanda's Choice* was published in 1970. Since that time, Holland has written many fine books for children. She often treats controversial subjects—death, homosexuality, rape, the dangers of hitchhiking—but she avoids treating these topics with a didactic tone. Rather she skillfully embeds social, psychological, and moral messages within believable dramatic situations.
   A great many of Holland's protagonists are lonely, isolated children or young adults. Often these characters are struggling to survive in a painful family situation. In *Amanda's Choice* the central character is the daughter of a loving father and his selfish second wife. Amanda herself belongs to a tradition of obnoxious, misunderstood children in children's literature. When her conflicts become unbearable, she runs away and seeks her friend Manuel in New York City. Without family, friends, or resources, Amanda at last begins to accept her father's love. In *Dinah and the Green Fat Kingdom* Holland portrays a 12-year-old plagued with weight problems. She experiences intense conflicts with her slim attractive mother and her gifted older brother. Dinah finds relief in a secret

woodland bower, where she spins humorous fantasies about a clever nation of fat people. Eventually Dinah learns to manage her weight problem and also effects a reconciliation with her mother. Because of Holland's deft uses of detail, the novel is much more than a tract about how to solve the problems of juvenile obesity.

Several of Holland's books treat controversial topics with tact and psychological insight. *Hitchhike* depicts the dangers of hitchhiking. Angry at her father, Pat Mallory hitches rides first with a middle-aged man and later with four young men. In the second instance, she barely escapes gang rape. Although the book is well written, it is Holland's most didactic work. She handles taboo subjects much more skillfully in *The Man Without a Face* and *Perdita*. Charles Norstadt isolates himself in resentment from his older sister Gloria and his attractive unstable mother and finds comfort, like Salinger's Holden Caulfield, in his younger sister Meg and a tomcat. When he learns that Gloria will return home in the fall, Charles is desperate to enter boarding school and enlists the tutoring services of Justin McLeod, "the man without a face," a teacher who had been disfigured in an accident involving a student and alcohol. By the end of the summer, Charles has faced some disillusionments about his dead war hero father, grieved about the tomcat's sudden death, and experienced a homosexual encounter with Justin. Charles does gain some maturity and insight but not without immense pain.

At the time of its publication *The Man Without a Face* was highly controversial. Many parents objected to Holland's sympathetic treatment of the homosexual teacher. Holland presents Justin as a compassionate, caring, if flawed human being, not a monstrous child abuser.

With similar psychological perception and sympathy, Holland depicts the emotional struggles of a young girl, Perdita, who is found unconscious in a dry well after having been raped and beaten. Though she must summon all of her courage, Perdita manages to find the strength to heal.

Many critics claim that Holland's novel, *Of Love and Death and Other Journeys* is her masterpiece. In this realistic work the 15-year-old Meg has lived a fascinatingly unconventional life in Europe with her mother and latest stepfather. Her life changes painfully with her mother's surgery for cancer and her father's arrival. Meg must come to terms with losing her mother and also adapt to an entirely new way of life. In this fine novel Holland portrays death and grief compassionately but unsentimentally and displays remarkable skill in revealing the nuances of family conflict. Plot, setting, theme, and character are admirably integrated, and Holland creates believable dialogue among her witty, sophisticated characters.

In a difficult world Holland's characters are amazingly resourceful. They find unexpected ways to survive. Some characters turn to animals for comfort, as do Dinah in *The Green Fat Kingdom,* Alan in *Alan and the Animal Kingdom,* and Jessamy in *A Horse Named Peaceable.* Others find a stay against loneliness in creating imaginary friends. In *God, Mrs. Muskrat, and Aunt Dot* Rebecca Smith, an 11-year-old orphan, is lonely, imaginative, and verbal. She turns to her imaginary friend, Mrs. Muskrat, a kindly earthmother who freely gives her cookies, comfort, and love. Eventually Rebecca must reconcile her real and imaginary worlds. In *Abbie's God Book* a young character survives emotionally through expressing her religious beliefs.

Holland justly deserves her reputation as an accomplished novelist for children and young adults. She expresses in lucid prose the complexities of relationships, insists upon the need for young adults to accept responsibility for their lives, as well as the consequences of their actions, and celebrates the power of the human spirit to heal itself and to survive the most painful circumstances.

—Anita Moss

HOLLING, Holling C(lancy). American. Born in Holling Corners, Michigan, 2 August 1900. Educated at Leslie High School, Michigan, graduated 1917; Art Institute of Chicago, graduated 1923. Married Lucille Webster in 1925. Member of the Zoology Department, Chicago Museum of Natural History, 1923–26; taught on the New York University World Cruise, 1926–27. After 1927 freelance designer, advertising artist, and book illustrator. *Died 7 September 1973.*

PUBLICATIONS FOR CHILDREN

Fiction (illustrated by the author)

Little Big-Bye-and-Bye. Chicago, Volland, 1926.
Choo-Me-Choo, illustrated by Lucille Holling. Minneapolis, Buzza, 1928.
Rum-Tum-Tummy, The Elephant Who Ate. Akron, Ohio, Saalfield, 1928.
Claws of the Thunderbird: A Tale of Three Lost Indians. Chicago, Volland, 1928.
Rocky Billy: The Story of the Bounding Career of a Rocky Mountain Goat. New York, Macmillan, 1928.
The Twins Who Flew round the World. New York, Platt and Munk, 1931.
Little Buffalo Boy, illustrated by Holling C. and Lucille Holling. New York, Garden City Publishing Company, 1939.
Paddle-to-the-Sea. Boston, Houghton Mifflin, 1941; London, Collins, 1945.
Tree in the Trail. Boston, Houghton Mifflin, 1942; London, Collins, 1948.
Seabird, illustrated by Holling C. and Lucille Holling. Boston, Houghton Mifflin, 1948; London, Collins, 1960.
Minn of the Mississippi. Boston, Houghton Mifflin, 1951.
Pagoo, illustrated by Holling C. and Lucille Holling. Boston, Houghton Mifflin, 1957.

Other

New Mexico Made Easy, with Words of Modern Syllables. Chicago, Clancy, 1923.
The Book of Indians, illustrated by Holling C. and Lucille Holling. New York, Platt and Munk, 1935; London, Cassell, 1938.
The Book of Cowboys, illustrated by Holling C. and Lucille Holling. New York, Platt and Munk, 1936; London, Cassell, 1938.

PUBLICATIONS FOR ADULTS

Verse

Sun and Smoke: Verse and Woodcuts of New Mexico. Privately printed, 1923.

*

Manuscript Collection: University of Oregon Library, Eugene.

Illustrator: *Blot, The Little City Cat* by Phyllis Crawford, 1930; *The Road in Storyland* edited by Watty Piper, 1932, and *Children of Other Lands* by Piper, 1943.

* * *

A writer with the consummate gift of storytelling and the ability to teach through sharing remarkable bits and pieces of information,

Holling C. Holling moved from his companion collections *The Book of Indians* and *The Book of Cowboys* of the 1930's to a group of singular books which offer blendings of rare elements. He offered in these books "a unique vision of the country, each focusing first on the wild life Mr. Holling knew so well, but spreading wide into the works of men and the sweep of history."

The first of these geo-historical-fiction volumes, *Paddle-to-the-Sea,* is a tremendously original and arresting story with a mixture of imagination and a wealth of information employing techniques pioneered and perfected by Holling and his artist wife. The story follows the adventures of Paddle, carved into a miniature canoe by an Indian boy. Paddle comes to travel from "the hills above Lake Superior" across the Great Lakes, and eventually to France, encountering suspenseful situations of many kinds. The values of this story for today's readers are described fully in a penetrating analysis, "The Teaching of Paddle-to-the-Sea," by Terry Borten in *Learning* (January, 1977). He comments on the energy, simplicity, understanding, and appeal in the story, and the allowance Holling makes for the feelings of children. "What we teachers need is Holling's insight into the relationship between narrative action and factual information."

Holling's consuming interest in nature combined with history is further developed in *Tree in the Trail* which traced the beginnings (1610) of a cottonwood tree in the Great Plains to the ox yoke which "traveled with a tune" to the Santa Fe Trail. To Indians this lonely giant represented a peace-medicine tree; to other travelers a landmark until 1834 when lightning and wind struck it down. Blending anthropology and zoology with geography and history, the prose captures the excitement of both the historical setting, the old Southwest—together with the realia linked with its emergence. The authenticity stems from the author's personal saddle-horse contact with thousands of miles of plains, deserts, and mountains; he was able to transfer to the reader the sights, knowledge, and awe he absorbed.

In *Seabird* Holling told the intriguing story of an ivory gull carved by a young lad onto a whaling ship. Traveling on the family's vessels over four generations, this marvelous gull witnessed the enormous changes sailors and their ships experienced as they moved around the seas of the world into modern times. In *Minn of the Mississippi* a mud turtle travels from the head-waters of the great waterway along its colorful shores to the Gulf, bringing alive the people, their work, and evidences of early exploration. *Pagoo* is an experimental narrative about a hermit crab, drawn into a whirlwind of action described in vivid detail. He eventually returns to the "endless rocking rhythms of the sea." In each of these books Holling makes himself felt through his vibrant text and imagery.

—Clara O. Jackson

———

HOLMAN, Felice. American. Born in New York City, 24 October 1919. Educated at Syracuse University, New York, B.A. 1941. Married Herbert Valen in 1941; one daughter. Advertising copywriter, New York, 1944–50. Lives in Del Mar, California. Address: c/o Scribner's, 866 Third Avenue, New York, New York 10022, U.S.A.

PUBLICATIONS FOR CHILDREN

Fiction

Elizabeth, The Bird Watcher, illustrated by Erik Blegvad. New York, Macmillan, 1963.

Elizabeth the Treasure Hunter, illustrated by Erik Blegvad. New York, Macmillan, 1964.

Silently, The Cat, and Miss Theodosia, illustrated by Harvey Dinnerstein. New York, Macmillan, and London, Collier Macmillan, 1965.

The Witch on the Corner, illustrated by Arnold Lobel. New York, Norton, 1966; London, Lutterworth Press, 1967.

Victoria's Castle, illustrated by Lillian Hoban. New York, Norton, 1966.

Elizabeth and the Marsh Mystery, illustrated by Erik Blegvad. New York, Macmillan, 1966; London, Collier Macmillan, 1974.

Professor Diggins' Dragons, illustrated by Ib Ohlsson. New York, Macmillan, and London, Collier Macmillan, 1966.

The Cricket Winter, illustrated by Ralph Pinto. New York, Norton, 1967.

The Blackmail Machine, illustrated by Victoria de Larrea. New York, Macmillan, 1967; London, Collier Macmillan, 1968.

A Year to Grow, illustrated by Emily McCully. New York, Norton, 1968.

The Holiday Rat, and The Utmost Mouse, illustrated by Wallace Tripp. New York, Norton, 1969.

Solomon's Search, illustrated by Mischa Richter. New York, Grosset and Dunlap, 1970.

The Future of Hooper Toote, illustrated by Gahan Wilson. New York, Scribner, 1972.

The Escape of the Giant Hogstalk, illustrated by Ben Shecter. New York, Scribner, 1974; as *The Escape of the Giant Hogweed,* London, Abelard Schuman, 1978.

Slake's Limbo. New York, Scribner, 1974; London, Macmillan, 1980.

The Murderer. New York, Scribner, 1978.

The Wild Children. New York, Scribner, 1983.

Terrible Jane, illustrated by Irene Trivas. New York, Scribner, 1987.

Verse

At the Top of My Voice and Other Poems, illustrated by Edward Gorey. New York, Norton, 1970.

I Hear You Smiling and Other Poems, illustrated by Laszlo Kubinyi. New York, Scribner, 1973.

The Song in My Head and Other Poems, illustrated by Jim Spanfeller. New York, Scribner, 1985.

Other

The Drac: French Tales of Dragons and Demons, with Nanine Valen, illustrated by Stephen Walker. New York, Scribner, 1975.

*

Manuscript Collection: Kerlan Collection, University of Minnesota, Minneapolis.

Felice Holman comments:
I write about things that are based on life in the real world, but are separated from it by a scrim that takes the glare away.

* * *

In 1963 Felice Holman presented her first book for readers five to eight years old but clearly aimed at an audience of girls. *Elizabeth, The Bird Watcher* was a rather predictable novel—nice but unexceptional—about a child devoted to her feathered friends. A marauding squirrel helps himself to the food Elizabeth provides for the birds, a problem resolved to the satisfaction of all, including the squirrel. The book was followed by two more on the doings of Elizabeth and by a number of other books, all of which proved the author's increasing use of the imagination.

Since Holman is essentially a poet, it's not surprising that even her minor stories are enhanced by lyrical prose, striking imagery. Then in 1970 she published her first volume of verse for children. *At the Top of My Voice* was praised for originality, humor, and point. A wonderful way of introducing young people to the power of poetry, the poems are all based solidly on situations children understand. This book was followed by *I Hear You Smiling,* and selections from both volumes continue to show up in anthologies—evidence of popular appeal.

Holman's sense of fun inspired her to write *The Escape of the Giant Hogstalk.* The story is that rare jewel, convincing absurdity, with giggles interspersed with horse laughs all the way. Anthony Wilson-Brown, a trial to his "Wealthy Aristocratic Family"—he *will* fool around instead of attending to his lessons—is sent to the Caucasus ("an out-of-the-way place depending on where you happen to be, of course"). He finds a legendary plant, the Giant Hogstalk, and plants its seed back home at the Royal Botanic Gardens. Grown to immensity, the plant escapes and spreads havoc among the citizens and merriment among Holman's audience. The story has a nifty coda, suggesting further adventures of the Hogstalk.

Slake's Limbo, the novel of a 13-year-old boy (homeless, friendless, an experienced outcast) is a milestone. Universally praised, the story describes how Artemis Slake spends 121 days in a cave under Grand Central Station in New York, how he gets food, keeps warm, and evades officialdom. The book is not only a heartening saga; it's memorable for authenticity of details on the mysterious, subterranean world of an inner city. Holman gave an absorbing account of the research which is the firm foundation of *Slake's Limbo* in *Horn Book* (October 1976).

The Wild Children, set in the Russia of the early 1920's, is also a story about homelessness and the alternative worlds that develop in times of crisis. Holman's careful research is again in evidence in this historical novel about 12-year-old Alex, who finds a new family of sorts with the *bezprizorni,* or wild children, of the streets of Moscow. His own family members have been declared enemies of the state and taken away by the secret police. Told in a spare style, the story is both an exciting adventure story (the gang eventually escaping to Finland) and emotionally compelling.

Her passion for authenticity is also obvious in *The Drac: French Tales of Dragons and Demons.* With her collaborator, Nanine Valen, Holman investigated archives, journals, libraries, and private homes tracking down the genesis of legends about supernatural things that terrorized villages in France in ancient days. A versatile and gifted author-poet, Holman will certainly continue to be heard from.

—Jean F. Mercier

HOOVER, H(elen) M(ary). American. Born in Stark County, Ohio, 5 April 1935. Educated at Louisville High School; Mount Union College, Alliance, Ohio; Los Angeles School of Nursing. Agent: Russell and Volkening, 50 West 29th Street, New York, New York 10001. Address: 9405 Ulysses Court, Burke, Virginia 22015, U.S.A.

PUBLICATIONS FOR CHILDREN

Fiction

Children of Morrow.   New York, Four Winds Press, 1973; London,

Methuen, 1975.
The Lion's Cub.   New York, Four Winds Press, 1974.
Treasures of Morrow.   New York, Four Winds Press, 1976.
The Delikon.   New York, Viking Press, 1977; London, Methuen, 1978.
The Rains of Eridan.   New York, Viking Press, 1977; London, Methuen, 1978.
The Lost Star.   New York, Viking Press, 1979; London, Methuen, 1980.
Return to Earth.   New York, Viking Press, 1980; London, Methuen, 1981.
This Time of Darkness.   New York, Viking Press, 1980; London, Methuen, 1982.
Another Heaven, Another Earth.   New York, Viking Press, 1981; London, Methuen, 1983.
The Bell Tree.   New York, Viking Press, 1982.
The Shepherd Moon.   New York, Viking, and London, Methuen, 1984.
Orvis.   New York, Viking Kestrel, and London, Methuen, 1987.

Other

The Dawn Palace: The Story of Medea.   New York, Dutton, 1988.

*

Manuscript Collection: Kerlan Collection, University of Minnesota, Minneapolis.

Critical Study: *Science Fiction: The Mythos of a New Romance* by Janice Antczak, New York, Neal Schuman, 1985.

H.M. Hoover comments:

I started to read at four and have never stopped. As a child I read indiscriminately, juvenile or adult, junk or classic. Now, as a writer, remembering my own reading habits as a child, I know I can't possibly imagine another child's interests, or reading level, and try to satisfy them, but only hope that what pleases and interests me has the same appeal for other readers.

*   *   *

One attribute of good science fiction is that it operates on more than one level, presenting a rousing good adventure tale while stimulating consideration of more serious matters relating to science, technology, and social science. H. M. Hoover's works are a reflection of this attribute. In *The Shepherd Moon* the story line is of a privileged 13-year-old girl's discovery of a being from space who turns out to be from one of Earth's artificial satellite moons. This modified human tries to conquer Earth and is thwarted by Merry and her grandfather. The underlying message is an exploration of the uses of power and privilege and the consequences of overcrowding on Earth. This dual thrust is found in all of Hoover's science fiction.

Each of Hoover's books features a strong, young female protagonist. These youths are isolated in some way from their parents and in most of the books are preoccupied with self until they establish a growing relationship with an older mentor. Varina, a Delikon and a child at the age of 307, reveres Sidra, the t'kyna on a conquered Earth ruled by *The Delikon.* Karen is left an orphan in a mutiny and is befriended by Theo, a biologist. Together they unravel the many mysteries in *The Rains of Eridan.* Though there is a supportive adult, the youth is the main character and each is fully realized. These characters have qualities that make them special in some way, but each also behaves in the way a youth would, with the attendant fears, hurts, and joys.

A frequent criticism of science fiction is that it is all plot and no characterization. Hoover presents the reader with a strong plot, but her characters are as alive as the action. An exploration of emotions and interactions is an important element in each of her books and there is always the development of a caring relationship. One could even say that Hoover writes love stories, when one defines love in the terms of caring about another. Lian, a teenage astrophysicist who is on the planet Balthor with her parents to study a supernova, is rescued from a crash by the leader of an archeological expedition. She finds satisfaction and possibly a new career when her trust and caring for supposedly native creatures called lumpies leads to the discovery that these beings are sentient travelers from another planet and that the site of the excavation is actually a starship. These travelers from *The Lost Star* evolve before our eyes from endearing pets to intelligent beings, as we see them through Lian's perspective.

Hoover's books are replete with imagery and her skill in crafting phrases and sentences that create vivid mental representations is marvelous. Her interest in nature results in detailed descriptions of the landscape of any world she has created, including the Earth in future centuries. The reader never strains to enter those worlds because the land with its flora and fauna is so expressively presented. In *The Lost Star* we see the exotic creatures on Balthor through the eyes of humans on that planet who create analogies to creatures on Earth. The description is so much a part of the action that it does not become tedious. Indeed, it enhances the action of the story.

The concept of myth is a feature in many of Hoover's science-fiction books. Because she is writing of a future time, she enables the reader to see that much of the knowledge and behavior of today will be translated into myths centuries from now. The alert reader will make the connection to the myths we share today and realize that they were grounded in fact but have evolved into story over time. This interest in myth has led Hoover into a new direction—her latest book is *The Dawn Palace*, a novel of Medea and the calamities that befell her. Extensive research and an awareness of the cultural mores of the Greek world in the time of Medea have led Hoover to present an account that is more sympathetic to Medea than is typical. Using her talent for imagery and rich detail, Hoover allows the reader to be present in that world of long ago and to participate in the pain and frustration that Medea felt throughout her life. Young adults will relate to this finely crafted novel and will gain an appreciation for events in another time.

Whether traveling to the past or the future, Hoover carries her readers along by creating a vivid world that is immediately accessible and characters that the reader cares about. The adventurous plots provide satisfaction, and one looks forward to the next adventure.

—M. Jean Greenlaw

HOPE-SIMPSON, Jacynth (née Cureton). Also writes as Helen Dudley. British. Born in Birmingham, Warwickshire, 10 November 1930. Educated at King Edward VI High School, Birmingham; University of Lausanne, 1949; St. Hugh's College, Oxford, Dip. Ed. 1953, M.A. 1956. Married Dermot Hope-Simpson in 1955; one daughter. English teacher, Bournemouth School for Girls, 1953–54, and Croham Hurst School, Croydon, 1954–57; examiner, Oxford and Cambridge General Certificate of Education, 1957–58. Chairman, West Country Writers' Association, 1980–82. Address: Franchise Cottage, Newtown, Milborne Port, Sherborne, Dorset DT9 5BJ, England.

PUBLICATIONS FOR CHILDREN

Fiction

Anne, Young Swimmer. London, Constable, 1960.
The Stranger in the Train, illustrated by Prudence Seward. London, Hamish Hamilton, 1960.
Young Netball Player. London, Constable, 1961.
The Great Fire, illustrated by Pat Marriott. London, Hamish Hamilton, 1961; New York, Dutton, 1962.
Danger on the Line, illustrated by Janet Duchesne. London, Hamish Hamilton, 1962.
The Man Who Came Back. London, Hamish Hamilton, 1962.
The Ice Fair, illustrated by Pat Marriott. London, Hamish Hamilton, 1963.
The Ninepenny, illustrated by Janet Duchesne. London, Hamish Hamilton, 1964.
The Witches' Cave, illustrated by Janet Duchesne. London, Hamish Hamilton, 1964.
The Edge of the World, illustrated by Peter Warner. London, Hamish Hamilton, 1965; New York, Coward McCann, 1966.
The High Toby, illustrated by Lynette Hemmant. London, Hamish Hamilton, 1966.
Escape to the Castle, illustrated by Mary Russon. London, Hamish Hamilton, 1967.
The Unknown Island. London, Hamish Hamilton, 1968; New York, Coward McCann, 1969.
The Gunner's Boy. London, Heinemann, 1973.
Save Tarranmoor! London, Heinemann, 1974.
The Hijacked Hovercraft, illustrated by Jeroo Roy. London, Heinemann, 1975.
Black Madonna. London, Heinemann, 1976; Nashville, Nelson, 1977.
Vote for Victoria, illustrated by Jael Jordan. London, Heinemann, 1976.

Other

Basic Certificate English: A Revision Course in the Grammar and Structure of the English Language, with Answers. London, Hamish Hamilton, 1966.
They Sailed from Plymouth. London, Hamish Hamilton, 1970.
Elizabeth I. London, Hamish Hamilton, 1971.
Who Knows? Twelve Unsolved Mysteries. London, Heinemann, 1974; Nashville, Nelson, 1976.
Always on the Move, illustrated by Jolyne Knox. London, Heinemann, 1975.
The Making of the Machine Age. London, Heinemann, 1978.

Editor, *The Hamish Hamilton Book of Myths and Legends,* illustrated by Raymond Briggs. London, Hamish Hamilton, 1964; as *The Curse of the Dragon's Gold: European Myths and Legends,* New York, Doubleday, 1969.
Editor, *The Hamish Hamilton Book of Witches,* illustrated by Krystyna Turska. London, Hamish Hamilton, 1966; as *A Cavalcade of Witches,* New York, Walck, 1967; as *Covens and Cauldrons,* London, Beaver, 1977.
Editor, *Tales in School: An Anthology of Boarding-School Life,* illustrated by John Lawrence. London, Hamish Hamilton, 1971.

PUBLICATIONS FOR ADULTS

Novels

The Bishop of Kenelminster. London, Putnam, 1961.

The Bishop's Picture. London, Putnam, 1962.
The Unravish'd Bride. London, Putnam, 1963.
The Hooded Falcon (as Helen Dudley). London, Futura, 1979.
Island of Perfumes. London, Hale, 1985.
Cottage Dreams. London, Hale, 1985.

*

Jacynth Hope-Simpson comments:

I should like to feel that I write for a wide range of children, with enough incident and pace to attract the reluctant reader and with (one hopes) enough depth of content to appeal to more "bookish" readers. One of my basic beliefs is that while one may need to simplify both language and one's material in writing for children, one must never write down to them, I believe accuracy to be of the utmost importance, especially as so many ideas are formed at a surprisingly early age. On an imaginative level, I am particularly interested in places and the interaction between place and personality.

*   *   *

The earliest traditions of story telling for children were strongly moral and didactic in their intention; children were taken seriously because their instruction was a serious matter. Increasingly since the 1950's, this emphasis has changed to an attempt to evoke the nature of childhood itself as being of prime significance.

Jacynth Hope-Simpson's position is more consistent with the older tradition. She takes her subject matter from a wide range of incident and location, and its seriousness is represented more by a talent for realism, but this is of a kind that grows from mundane and continuous contact with children. In *Danger on the Line,* for example, the small crisis is prompted by Antony's discovery that Clare, the small daughter of the master in charge of the outdoor model steam railway, was upset because "A large piece of sharp black gravel was stuck in her left nostril." In the same way in the more ambitious *Escape to the Castle,* Vaclav's adventure begins on a hot night in his Prague attic when he becomes unendurably aware of being shut out from a larger life, an unwilling prisoner (not helped by his younger brother's preoccupation with squeezing his insect bites). He locates this larger life in the Castle where his delight in Mozart's music is challenged by a meeting with the composer weighed down by problems of his own. This theme possibly needs fuller treatment to realise its complexity; but the neat ordering of surprise—where stock stories involve improbable escapes from realistic castles, this escape is from cramping domesticity in search of an ideal in a castle—is characteristic of the author's unobtrusive originality. This originality is given fuller scope in *The Gunner's Boy.* Mark and Peter are the sons of a Dartmoor parson sent to stay with an aunt in Plymouth while their mother impatiently awaits the tardy arrival of the latest child in competition with the family cat which is similarly disadvantaged. Mark is bookish and Peter, the younger boy, is mad to go to sea. Peter runs away to join a Spanish expedition but hurts his leg on the way down to the harbour, and Mark, going to bring him back, is taken in his place and becomes the reluctant, and sensitive, narrator of the story. This, again, provides more than conventional battle scenes on *The Revenge* and hardships at sea, for Mark is taken on board the *San Pablo* after the battle and sees the humane side of the despised and hated Spaniards.

The characteristic qualities of these stories include: respect for the child reader which entails such authentic details as, in the London of *The Great Fire,* "The shop signs swung over their heads; a striped pole for the barber, a knee boot for the bootmaker"; a precise sense of place whether 17th-century London, the Prague of Mozart, or Drake's Plymouth and contemporary Finistère; and pre-eminently a strong sense of dramatic realism so that child adventures, of the past

and of today, are consistently related to an encircling and clearly defined adult world.

—Kenneth J. Sterck

———

HOUGH, (Helen) Charlotte (née Woodyatt). British. Born in Brockenhurst, Hampshire, 24 May 1924. Educated at Frensham Heights School, Farnham, Surrey. Served in the Women's Royal Naval Service. Married Richard Hough (i.e., Bruce Carter, *q.v.*) in 1943 (divorced 1980); four daughters. Agent: Curtis Brown, 162–168 Regent Street, London WIR 5TB. Address: 1-A Ivor Street, London NW1 9PL, England.

PUBLICATIONS FOR CHILDREN (illustrated by the author)

Fiction

Jim Tiger. London, Faber, 1956; Indianapolis, Bobbs Merrill, 1958.
Morton's Pony. London, Faber, 1957.
The Home-Makers. London, Hamish Hamilton, 1957.
The Hampshire Pig. London, Hamish Hamilton, 1958.
The Story of Mr. Pinks. London, Faber, 1958.
The Animal Game. London, Faber, 1959.
The Trackers. London, Hamish Hamilton, 1960.
Algernon. London, Faber, 1961; New York, A.S. Barnes, 1962.
Anna and Minnie. London, Faber, 1962.
Three Little Funny Ones. London, Hamish Hamilton, 1962.
The Owl in the Barn. London, Faber, 1964.
More Funny Ones. London, Faber, 1965.
Red Biddy and Other Stories. London, Faber, 1966; New York, Coward McCann, 1967.
Sir Frog and Other Stories. London, Faber, 1968.
Educating Flora and Other Stories. London, Faber, 1968.
Abdul the Awful (includes *Sir Frog and Other Stories* and *Educating Flora and Other Stories*). New York, McCall, 1970.
Queer Customer. London, Heinemann, 1972.
Wonky Donkey. London, Heinemann, 1975.
Bad Cat. London, Heinemann, 1975.
Pink Pig. London, Heinemann, 1975.
Charlotte Hough's Holiday Book. London, Heinemann, 1975; as *The Holiday Story Book,* London, Beaver, 1976.
The Mixture as Before. London, Heinemann, 1976.

Verse

A Bad Child's Book of Moral Verse. London, Faber, and New York, Walck, 1970.

Other

My Aunt's Alphabet, with Billy and Me (reader). London, Hamish Hamilton, 1969.
Verse and Various (miscellany). London, Dent, 1979.

PUBLICATIONS FOR ADULTS

Novel

The Bassington Murder. London, Elek, and New York, St. Martin's

Press, 1980.

*

Illustrator: *The House on the Moor*, 1948, *The Thirteenth Adventure*, 1949, *Steeple Folly*, 1950, *Castaway Camp*, 1951, and *The Barnstormers*, 1953, all by M.E. Atkinson; *The Adventures of Tommy* by Lillian Miozzi, 1950; *I Carried the Horn*, 1951, *Goodbye to Hounds*, 1952, and *Riders from Afar*, 1954, all by Christine Pullein-Thompson; *Land of Ponies* by Marjorie M. Oliver, 1951; *Barry's Exciting Year*, 1951, *Barry Gets His Wish*, 1952, and *Barry's Great Day*, 1954, all by A. Stephen Tring; *Two of Us* by Janet Branford, 1952; *Mystery at Winton's Park*, 1952, and *Hotel Doorway*, 1953, both by Lorna Lewis; *The Wonderful Farm* by Marcel Aymé, 1952; *Smoky Joe*, 1952, *Smoky Joe in Trouble*, 1953, and *Smoky Joe Goes to School*, 1956, all by Laurence Meynell; *Prince among Ponies* by Josephine Pullein-Thompson, 1952; *Five Proud Riders* by Ann Stafford, 1953; *The Sheepdog Adventure* by Ethelind Fearon, 1953; *The Enchanted Horse* by April Jaffé, 1953; *Peril on the Iron Road*, 1953, and *Gunpowder Tunnel*, 1955, both by Bruce Carter; *Black Beauty* by Anna Sewell, 1954; *Elephant Big and Elephant Little*, 1955, *The Little Yellow Jungle Frogs*, 1956, and *Animal Story Book*, 1972, all by Anita Hewett; *The Boy with the Green Thumb* by Barbara Euphan Todd, 1956; *The Flying Jacket* edited by Betty Willsher, 1964; *Time for a Story* edited by Eileen Colwell, 1967; *Galápagos* by Richard Hough, 1975; *What Katy Did* by Susan Coolidge.

*   *   *

Charlotte Hough is a writer of marked individuality and versatility, qualities not easily combined. She writes in both prose and verse, and for a wide age-span, ranging from the very small children to whom *Wonky Donkey* is meant to be read aloud, to the eleven-year-olds who want junior novels such as *Queer Customer*. Further—though this is not the place to attempt an assessment of her talents as an illustrator—it must be remarked that in some of her books, notably *Wonky Donkey,* her pictures are so integrated with her text that the latter (often no more than a single sentence or a single word per page) cannot be criticised in isolation.

Within the purely verbal context, however, it can be said that all her work, for whatever age, exhibits certain consistent features. There is always a great sense of fun, and infectious enthusiasm for words, a delight in juggling with them. This dexterity is naturally most marked in her use of rhyme and assonance. *A Bad Child's Book of Moral Verse* is not unworthy to stand on the shelf beside the Belloc volumes of an earlier day. But this same verbal dexterity is also a feature of her prose, which shows much of the same neatness and economy. Exuberance without waste of words is the paradox she contrives to achieve, so that the reader is whirled along.

These high spirits and robust good humour cannot obscure the fact that Hough is in the great moralist tradition of English children's literature. Whether writing of children or adults or of animals to whom human frailties are transferred—the conceited guinea-pig, Mr. Pinks, the maladroit Jim Tiger, or Morton's pony, the elderly and sagacious pony as reliable and protective as a grown-up—she makes her points with a light touch, so that the very weaknesses of her characters render them the more lovable.

Probably it is her shorter pieces—her animal stories and fairy tales making fresh use of old material, giant and goblin, mermaid and princess—that represent her most original contribution. At the same time, a junior novel such as *Queer Customer,* with its central theme of a boy's natural but unnecessary dread of an operation, must not be underrated. It displays another, more realistic side to her work, and her sympathetic depiction of the characters is full of insight and

humanity.

—Geoffrey Trease

———

HOUGH, Richard. See **CARTER, Bruce.**

———

HOUSTON, James A(rchibald). Canadian. Born in Toronto, Ontario, 12 June 1921. Educated at John Wanless Primary School, and Northern Vocational High School, both Toronto; Ontario College of Art, 1939–40; Ecole Grande Chaumière, Paris, 1947; Unichi Hiratsuka, Tokyo, 1958–59. Served in the Toronto Scottish Regiment, 1940–45. Married 1) Alma G. Bardon in 1950 (divorced 1966), two sons; 2) Alice Watson in 1967. Arctic adviser, Canadian Guild of Crafts, 1949–52; civil administrator, Canadian Government, West Baffin, Eastern Arctic, 1953–62. Associate director, 1962–72, and since 1972 master designer, Steuben Glass, New York. Artist: individual shows—Canadian Guild of Crafts, 1953, 1955, 1957; Robertson Galleries, Ottawa, 1953; Calgary Galleries, 1966; Canadiana Galleries, Edmonton, 1977; Yaneff Gallery, Toronto, 1983, 1986; Steuben Glass, 1987; represented in collections of Glenbow-Alberta Museum of Art, Montreal Museum of Fine Arts, National Gallery of Art, Ottawa. Recipient: Canadian Library Association Book of the Year Medal, 1966, 1968, 1980; American Indian and Eskimo Cultural Foundation award, 1966; Vicky Metcalf award, 1977, for short story, 1981; Inuit Kuavati award, 1979; Royal Canadian Academy of Art Citation of Merit award, 1987. D. Litt.: Carleton University, Ottawa, 1972; D.H.L.: Rhode Island College, Providence, 1975; D.F.A.: Rhode Island School of Design, Providence, 1979; D.D.L.: Dalhousie University, Halifax, Nova Scotia, 1987. Honorary Fellow, Ontario College of Art, and Fellow, Royal Society of Art, London, 1981. Officer, Order of Canada, 1972. Address: 24 Main Street, Stonington, Connecticut 06378, U.S.A.

Publications for Children (illustrated by the author)

Fiction

Tikta'liktak: An Eskimo Legend. Toronto, Longman, and New York, Harcourt Brace, 1965.
Eagle Mask: A West Coast Indian Tale. Toronto, Longman, and New York, Harcourt Brace, 1966.
The White Archer: An Eskimo Legend. Toronto, Longman, and New York, Harcourt Brace, 1967.
Akavak: An Eskimo Journey. Toronto, Longman, and New York, Harcourt Brace, 1968.
Wolf Run: A Caribou Eskimo Tale. Toronto, Longman, and New York, Harcourt Brace, 1971.
Ghost Paddle: A Northwest Coast Indian Tale. Toronto, Longman, and New York, Harcourt Brace, 1972.
Kiviok's Magic Journey: An Eskimo Legend. Toronto, Longman, and New York, Atheneum, 1973.
Frozen Fire: A Tale of Courage. Toronto, McClelland and Stewart, and New York, Atheneum, 1977; London, Penguin, 1979.
River Runners: A Tale of Hardship and Bravery. Toronto, McClelland and Stewart, and New York, Atheneum, 1979; London, Penguin, 1981.
Long Claws: An Arctic Adventure. Toronto, McClelland and

Stewart, and New York, Atheneum, 1981.

Black Diamonds: A Search for Arctic Treasure. Toronto, Mc-Clelland and Stewart, and New York, Atheneum, 1982.

Ice Swords: An Undersea Adventure. Toronto, McClelland and Stewart, and New York, Atheneum, 1985.

The Falcon Bow: An Arctic Legend. Toronto, McClelland and Stewart, and New York, McElderry, 1986.

Whiteout. Toronto, Key Porter, 1988.

Other

Editor, *Songs of the Dream People: Chants and Images from the Indians and Eskimos of North America.* Toronto, Longman, and New York, Atheneum, 1972.

PUBLICATIONS FOR ADULTS (illustrated by the author)

Novels

The White Dawn: An Eskimo Saga. Toronto, Longman, New York, Harcourt Brace, and London, Heinemann, 1971.

Ghost Fox. Toronto, McClelland and Stewart, New York, Harcourt Brace, and London, Collins, 1977.

Spirit Wrestler. Toronto, McClelland and Stewart, New York, Harcourt Brace, and London, Collins, 1980.

Eagle Song. Toronto, McClelland and Stewart, and New York, Harcourt Brace, 1983.

Plays

Screenplays: *The White Dawn,* 1973; *So Sings the Wolf,* 1976; *Kalvak,* 1976; *Art of the Arctic Whalemen,* 1978; *Legends of the Salmon People,* 1978.

Other

Eskimo Prints. Barre, Massachusetts, Barre Publishers, 1967.
Ojibwa Summer. Barre, Massachusetts, Barre Publishers, 1972.

*

Manuscript Collection: National Library of Canada, Ottawa.

Illustrator: *Shoot to Live,* 1944; *Nuki,* by Alma Houston, 1955; *Ayorama,* by Raymond de Coccola and Paul King, 1956; *Tuktut/Caribou,* 1957; *The Unicorn Was There,* by Elizabeth Pool, 1966; *The Private Journal of Captain G.F. Lyon of H.M.S. Hecla, During the Recent Voyage of Discovery under Captain Parry, 1821–1823* by George Francis Lyon, 1970; *First Came the Indians* by M.J. Wheeler, 1983.

James A. Houston comments:

In some ways children as we know them do not exist in the world of Eskimos and Northern Indians. Children to them are simply small adults in the process of growing, of reaching maturity. There are no children's stories there, only adult myths and legends and truths about life.

My stories are not really children's stories. They are simply northern stories that are suitable for both children and adults. I consider that my adult-length books are also suitable for children.

*   *   *

James A. Houston is best known for his discovery of Inuit (Eskimo) art and his stories about Inuit life. Less known are his tales based on the lives of Canadian Indians. At first he treated native

societies in a "pure" form, that is, as they were before the intrusion of European culture. More recently Houston has added modern settings pairing a white teenager with a native one.

Houston's pure Inuit novels generally emphasize the starkness of the environment, a boy hero's successful struggle for survival, and the concomitant attainment of some special insight, often spiritual or moral in nature, which helps to mark his entrance into manhood.

Tikta'liktak, the author's first book, tells the story of an Inuit boy faced with a struggle for survival in very hostile circumstances—adrift on an ice-floe, then isolated on a barren island—who proves his spiritual strength and physical resourcefulness in overcoming his difficulties. Though the ending is a bit anticlimatic, the tale is a good one. Similar is *Wolf Run,* the story of a starving boy who ventures into the barrens to hunt food for his family; after much agony he is saved by what, in a moment of insight, he believes to be the spirits of his grandparents in the guise of two helpful wolves. This novel, though containing much good writing, falters at the conclusion due to the unconvincing—at least for non-Inuit readers—*deus ex machina* denouement of the helpful wolves.

The same situation—a quest for food for a starving family—is presented in *Long Claws,* although here a starring role is held by a girl as well as a boy. Together Pitohok and his sister Upik cope with hunger, storms, fatigue, and a bear, receiving guidance from an owl at some crucial moments. The *deus ex machina* criticism is avoided, however, by alternative, more naturalistic, possible explanations for the owl's actions—e.g. its scratching away of some snow, which leads the children to a cache of trout below, may be attributed to hunger as well as to the supernatural.

Particularly reflective of conventional morality is *The White Archer,* which tells of an Inuit boy Kungo, whose parents are killed and whose sister is abducted by Indian raiders—who, in their turn, are reacting to the murder of an Indian by an Inuk. Kungo vows revenge and spends some years preparing for it, but by the time he has it at hand he doesn't take it. At the crucial moment he realizes that he has unconsciously learned the value of compassion from two old people who cared for him, and his act of self-restraint leads to eventual reunion with his sister and reconciliation with his former enemies. The morality is good, but unfortunately Kungo's change of heart is not entirely convincing: his passion for revenge is too easily dissipated. Similarly, in the sequel, *The Falcon Bow,* Kungo helps Indians and Inuit avoid another misunderstanding which could have led to war and instead brings both peoples closer together. However, the plot is not among Houston's best, and this tale of reconciliation and peace is most interesting to child (as opposed to adult) readers in its incidental "how to" passages: how to build an igloo, start a fire with a bow drill, construct and use a kayak, etc.

More satisfying is *Akavak.* Here the Inuit boy helps his dying grandfather fulfil a last wish: to travel over formidable mountains to visit his brother. Though the grandfather dies as the trip is completed, it is not without passing on much of himself and the secrets of the mountains to Akavak, who proves himself during the journey. The tale is stark and simple on the surface but very rich and emotionally rewarding underneath. The impact is achieved through understatement, as in Anglo-Saxon poetry. A slight criticism might be that more background could be provided. A different Inuit story is *Kiviok's Magic Journey.* An Arctic fairytale, it is both typical of its genre and enjoyable, though it lacks some of the harsh struggle characteristic of the other Inuit books.

Houston's pure Indian tales also mark the passage from boyhood to manhood, but they do not have the same focus on survival in a stark environment that the Inuit stories reveal. Man, not nature, provides the chief threat. The Indian books are connected through the character Hooits: in *Ghost Paddle* he is the brave youth who will marry a princess of the Eagle clan; in *Eagle Mask* he is the grandfather in the royal line in that same clan. *Eagle Mask,* written first, tells of the coming of age of Hooits' grandson, Skemshan.

Skemshan's transition from youth to man is marked by his merit in confronting a bear, in going whaling, in a minor encounter with raiders, and in receiving a spiritual message from a sacred eagle. Though the details of Indian life are interesting and certain events are exciting, the book's structure is weak; difficulties with point-of-view, transitions, and a plethora of minor episodes produce an unintegrated work. *Ghost Paddle,* written more recently, is better unified. In it Hooits himself makes the jump from boyhood to manhood by virtue of his courage and compassion during an attempt to reconcile the Eagle and Raven clans. He is successful without bloodshed, and the novel ends with a statement opposing the "killing winds of war," a sentiment similar to that of *The White Archer.*

In 1977 Houston shifted to 20th-century encounters, based in part on real events, between white and native teenagers. Typically the plots rapidly evolve into a "lost in the barrens" or "two against the wilderness" situation, with the white and Indian (*River Runners*) or Inuit (the *Frozen Fire* trilogy) boys faced with a struggle for survival. The adult world is not absent—instead, is able to be contacted or help out in a few situations—but the basic stories are tales of teenage testing, of hardship and courage, of struggle and success, of companionship, coming of age, and the overcoming of preconceived cultural biases. In the process, the white boys learn respect and affection for the northern environment and native ways, and the native boys learn some practical advantages of modern technology and education. *River Runners* and *Frozen Fire* are exciting books, and are significantly better than the latter's sequels, *Black Diamonds* and *Ice Swords,* which reveal less credibility in plot, less development in character, and less resonance in theme.

The best of these books, however, is the most recent, *Whiteout.* This contemporary tale of a rebellious urban teenager, sent by his mother to stay with an uncle in an isolated Arctic settlement, is a fine work about the maturation process: first love, acceptance of responsibility, building of character through challenges confronted and dangers overcome. The choice of a musically talented protagonist is inspired and credible: as Johnathan comes to appreciate the sharp flavour and harsh beauty of the North, and as he comes to recognize the needs of others as well as the demands of his own career and desires, he is able to translate his experience, through composition, into music, and in so doing his talent is confirmed and his final choice justified. Correspondingly, there is a maturity and focus to the writing that outdoes Houston's other white-native children's books and is comparable to his best adult fiction. *Whiteout* is a work that does not provide easy answers but instead asks the perennial, growth-oriented human questions; it is the kind of novel that can enlarge a child reader and his perspectives.

Overall, Houston's work conveys well the everyday life of the native peoples he portrays and the environmental reality of the regions in which they live. He is at his best in presenting the plight of protagonists struggling for survival: the inner conflict against one's own flagging will as well as the external conflict against the environment. In all cases, incidentally, Houston's illustrations enrich the novels.

—John Robert Sorfleet

HOWE, James. American. Born in Oneida, New York, 2 August 1946. Educated at Boston University, 1964–68, B.F.A 1968; Hunter College, New York, M.A. 1977. Married 1) Deborah Smith in 1969 (died 1978); 2) Betsy Imershein in 1981, one daughter. Freelance actor and director, 1971–75; literary agent, Lucy Kroll Agency, New York, 1976–81. Lives in Hastings-on-Hudson, New York. Agent: Amy Berkower, Writers House Inc., 21 West 26th Street, New York, New York 10010, U.S.A.

PUBLICATIONS FOR CHILDREN

Fiction

Bunnicula: A Rabbit Tale of Mystery, with Deborah Howe, illustrated by Alan Daniel. New York, Atheneum, 1979; London, Hodder and Stoughton, 1984.
Teddy Bear's Scrapbook, with Deborah Howe, illustrated by David S. Rose. New York, Atheneum, 1980.
Annie Joins the Circus, illustrated by Leonard Shortall. New York, Random House, 1982.
Howliday Inn, illustrated by Lynn Munsinger. New York, Atheneum, 1982; London, Dragon, 1987.
The Case of the Missing Mother, illustrated by William Cleaver. New York, Random House, 1983.
The Celery Stalks at Midnight, illustrated by Leslie Morrill. New York, Atheneum, 1983; London, Hodder and Stoughton, 1986.
A Night Without Stars. New York, Atheneum, 1983.
The Day the Teacher Went Bananas, illustrated by Lillian Hoban. New York, Dutton, 1984; London, Viking Kestrel, 1985.
How the Ewoks Saved the Trees, illustrated by Walter Helez. New York, Random House, 1984.
Morgan's Zoo, illustrated by Leslie Morrill. New York, Atheneum, 1984.
Mister Tinker in Oz, illustrated by David S. Rose. New York, Random House, 1985.
What Eric Knew. New York, Atheneum, 1985.
Eat Your Poison, Dear. New York, Atheneum, 1986.
A Love Note for Baby Piggy. New York, Marvel, 1986.
Stage Fright. New York, Atheneum, 1986.
There's a Monster under My Bed, illustrated by David S. Rose. New York, Atheneum, 1986.
I Wish I Were a Butterfly, illustrated by Ed Young. New York, Harcourt Brace, 1987.
Nighty-Nightmare, illustrated by Leslie Morrill. New York, Atheneum, 1987.
The Fright before Christmas, illustrated by Leslie Morrill. New York, Morrow, 1988.
Scared Silly, illustrated by Leslie Morrill. New York, Morrow, 1989.

Other

The Hospital Book, photographs by Mal Warshaw. New York, Crown, 1981.
The Muppet Guide to Magnificent Manners, illustrated by Peter Elwell. New York, Random House, 1984.
When You Go to Kindergarten, photographs by Betsy Imershein. New York, Knopf, 1986.
Babes in Toyland (retelling), illustrated by Allen Atkinson. New York, Harcourt Brace, 1986.
Carol Burnett: The Sound of Laughter. New York, Viking, 1987.
The Secret Garden (retelling), illustrated by Thomas B. Allen. New York, Random House, 1987.

*

James Howe comments:

As a writer for children, I have many responsibilities—the responsibility to give the reader well-crafted language that is appropriate for the story at hand, to use language that respects the reader's intelligence while stretching his or her appreciation of what language can do, to articulate what the child cannot, to give positive values in a world where values have been demeaned, to make demands on the reader's mind and spirit, to entertain, and to make the reader laugh. Humor is the most precious gift I can give to my reader, a reminder that the world is not such a terribly serious place. There is more than video games and drugs and nuclear threats; there is laughter—and there is hope. In the end, however, my primary responsibility as a writer is to the hidden child in the reader and in myself, and to the belief that—though we are years apart—when I open my mouth to speak, the child will understand. Because in that hidden part of ourselves, we are one.

* * *

James Howe has an outrageous funny bone that makes the reader laugh out loud while reading the adventures of Harold, Chester, Howie, Bunnicula, and the Monroe family. It is the delicious humor permeating Howe's stories that enables the reader to accept the various plots and storylines, which are based on the familiar Dracula story.

The first of these stories is *Bunnicula: A Rabbit Tale of Mystery*. The story is told by Harold, the Monroe family dog and details the peculiar events after the arrival of a tiny rabbit found in a local movie theater during a showing of *Dracula* and named Bunnicula. Chester, the observant and clever cat, is convinced of Bunnicula's nefarious antecedents and thus begins a romp through a series of hilarious adventures trying to prove Chester correct. Although the other animals in the story talk, Bunnicula does not speak. Howe sets up a series of situations which inevitably cause all kinds of complications. Howe has Chester reading books and doing reference work in his search for the truth about Bunnicula while Harold is a carefree dog who loves chocolate cupcakes with cream centers. By a series of inferences we come to the conclusion that Chester could be right, especially when the veggies turn white and the fang-like teeth of Bunnicula are noticed. At the same time we love Bunnicula who seems so misunderstood and our love is conveyed through Harold who becomes his protector.

Chateau Bow-Wow is the setting of *Howliday Inn* where Chester and Harold are boarded while their family is on vacation. Unusual things happen at the Chateau, and Chester convinces Harold that they must solve this terrifying mystery and even possible murder. The importance of Howard and Heather, the two dachshunds, is overlooked by all, including the criminal Harrison. All is solved by Chester and the Monroes gain a new member of their family.

In *The Celery Stalks at Midnight* Howe has created a madcap chase of Bunnicula whom Chester is convinced will turn the neighborhood gardens into a vast field of zombie vegetables. *Nighty-Nightmare* is the story of an overnight camping trip which includes the story of how Bunnicula came to be a vampire—according to Chester.

Howe's books are clever and filled with contemporary references that entertain. It is the sheer fun of following the suspicions of Chester while feeling comforted in Harold's calmness and developing a real concern for Bunnicula that captures a child reader.

—Jane Anne Hannigan

HOWES, Edith (Annie). New Zealander. Born in London, England, c. 1874. Educated at schools in Kaiapoi and Christchurch. Teacher, Wellington Girls' College; infant mistress, Gore Public School. Member, Royal Society of New Zealand. *Died in July 1954.*

PUBLICATIONS FOR CHILDREN

Fiction

The Sun's Babies, illustrated by Frank Watkins. London, Cassell, 1910.
Fairy Rings, illustrated by Frank Watkins. London, Cassell, 1911.
Rainbow Children, illustrated by Alice B. Woodward. London, Cassell, 1912.
Where Bell-Birds Chime. Christchurch, Whitcombe and Tombs, 1912.
The Cradle Ship, illustrated by Florence Mary Anderson. London, Cassell, 1916.
Wonderwings and Other Fairy Stories, illustrated by Alice Polson. Auckland, Whitcombe and Tombs, 1918.
Little Make-Believe, illustrated by Alice Polson. Auckland, Whitcombe and Tombs, 1919.
The Singing Fish, illustrated by Florence Mary Anderson. London, Cassell, 1921.
Snowdrop. Auckland, Whitcombe and Tombs, 1923.
The Dream Girl's Garden. London, Ward Lock, 1923.
The Enchanted Road, illustrated by Janet Smalley. New York, Morrow, 1927.
Silver Island, illustrated by Kathleen Coales. Auckland, Whitcombe and Tombs, and London, Oxford University Press, 1928.
Sandals of Pearl, illustrated by Audrey Chalmers. New York, Morrow, 1928; London, Dent, 1929.
The Golden Forest, illustrated by M. Lee Thompson. London, Dent, 1933.
Mrs. Kind Bush, illustrated by Anne Anderson. London, Cassell, 1933.
Riverside Family, illustrated by McGregor Williams. Auckland, Collins, 1944.

Other

Maoriland Fairy Tales. London, Ward Lock, 1913.
Whitcombe's Story Books (The Rainbow, The Poppy Seed, More Tales of Maori Magic, Drums of the Sea, The Lovely Lady and Other Stories, Lizzie Limpet and Other Stories, Willie Wagtail and Other Tales, Safe Going, Out of the Night, Young Pioneers). Auckland, Whitcombe and Tombs, 10 vols., 1923–34; *Drums of the Sea* published London, Burns Oates, 1939.
The Long Bright Land: Fairy Tales from Southern Seas, illustrated by Dorothy P. Lathrop. Boston, Little Brown, 1929.
The Great Experiment, illustrated by William Smith. London, Dent, 1932.

PUBLICATIONS FOR ADULTS

Other

Stewart Island. Christchurch, Whitcombe and Tombs, 1913.
Marlborough Sounds: The Waters of Restfulness. Auckland, Whitcombe and Tombs, 1919.
Tales Out of School. Auckland, Whitcombe and Tombs, 1919.
The World So Full. London, Cassell, 1922.

* * *

Edith Howes was a school teacher whose major interest was nature study, and a great many of her stories have the strongly didactic intention of informing children about New Zealand's bush, beach, and marine life.

Writing within the fashion of the period she delivered her messages through the medium of fantasy, and every variety of gossamer-winged fairy flits through the pages of her books. The most famous was *The Cradle Ship,* which ran into numerous editions and was translated into French, Italian, and Danish. Daringly advanced for the period it aimed to teach children "the facts of life" when twins who wanted to know where the new baby had come from were taken by their mother onto the Cradle Ship. On their voyage they saw every variety of animal with its young, beginning with insects and fish who abandoned their eggs, progressing to the more caring birds, marsupials, and mammals, until they finally understood that human babies "grow beneath their Mother's heart."

Edith Howes believed firmly in the power of knowledge and deplored the prevailing secrecy in sexual matters. In an adventure story for older readers, *The Golden Forest,* she left the reader in no doubt that a young man had died from venereal disease: "he wasted his youth, he depleted his vitality…there must be growth and maturity before the giving of cells." The speaker is the boy's father who concluded, "You are fortified, strengthened, cleansed by knowledge."

When liberated from the sentimental "Flower Fairy" syndrome, Howes wrote directly and well, as in the first really indigenous New Zealand adventure story, *Silver Island,* which has the Swiss Family Robinson theme of a family of children marooned on an off-shore island. *Riverside Family* gives a good picture of a country family of the period, and *Young Pioneers* is a well-researched story about early settlers. These are the books which still appeal; her fairy stories can only be regarded as interesting period pieces.

—Betty Gilderdale

HOWKER, Janni. British. Born in Nicosia, Cyprus, 6 July 1957. Educated at Kendal High School, Westmorland; Lancaster University, Lancashire, B.A. (honours) in independent studies, M.A. in creative writing. Married Mick North in 1988 (second marriage). Has worked as park attendant, research assistant, landlady, housemother for mentally handicapped children, Open University examiner, and assistant in hostel for the mentally ill. Since 1984 freelance writer. Recipient: International Reading Association award, 1985; Tom-Gallon Trust award, for short story, 1985; *Observer*-Rank Organisation prize, 1985; Whitbread award, 1985; Silver Pencil award (Netherlands), 1987; Maugham award, 1987. Address: c/o Julia MacRae Books, 87 Vauxhall Walk, London SE11 5HJ, England.

PUBLICATIONS FOR CHILDREN

Fiction

Badger on the Barge and Other Stories. London, MacRae, and New York, Greenwillow, 1984.
The Nature of the Beast. London, MacRae, and New York, Greenwillow, 1985.
Isaac Campion. London, MacRae, and New York, Greenwillow, 1986.

Plays

Screenplay: *The Nature of the Beast,* 1988.

Television Play: *Badger on the Barge,* from her own story, 1987.

*

Janni Howker comments:

I like stories, especially the stories that the people in north Lancashire tell each other about the events and feelings which are important in their lives. I like to look at maps of this area too, but I still find them difficult to read and I think this must be because my real interest lies in the folk who inhabit and *make* the landscape rather than in its geographical features. I would like to think of my stories as maps of the inner landscapes of my community—a place where all manner of strange, frightening, sad, funny, and bewildering things can happen.

*　　*　　*

Janni Howker was the most remarkable British writer of fiction for young people to emerge in the mid-1980's, a time when new talent was scarce. Her first book *Badger on the Barge* was highly acclaimed and won several awards; her second and third, *The Nature of the Beast* and *Isaac Campion,* swiftly consolidated her reputation. Though praise for these books was high, it was not excessive; they are of true quality.

Badger on the Barge is in no way apprentice work; the writer, though young and decidedly regional, was already very accomplished. The book consists of a group of five longish short stories, all of which are about relationships between young and old people. Helen in the title story befriends a crusty old woman who lives on a barge and is fighting for her independence; Liz in "The Topiary Garden" meets old Sally Beck who could only make a life for herself by pretending to be a boy. Jane in "The Egg-Man" glimpses through the crazy old man's grief for a long-dead wife the depth and vulnerability of love. Yet none of the stories is concerned only with the young-old relationship; each has also a sub-theme, interwoven with the main one and resolved with it. They are ingeniously organized and limpidly written, and at the same time subtle and perceptive. The most poignant and atmospheric is *Jakey,* in which an old boatman is about to die and his young friend Steven, dreaming, sees a dark shape following Jakey's boat: "a great grey shape, like a shark, swimming behind, slowly, secretly." It is Jakey's death.

In *The Nature of the Beast* Howker adapted her gift for the apt and sounding phrase to a first-person narration by a rough working-class boy. The setting is northern, on the edge of an industrial town; the Haverstock Beast—if it exists—prowls around, savaging farmers' stock and spreading fear among the people. Is the beast real or symbolic? The mill on which the town depended has closed; unemployment is also a beast that is ravaging the community. In the end it seems that a beast of anger and frustration is inside the boy himself: "I'm going to take over where the Beast left off," he says. Though there is warmth in the story, it is a chilling conclusion.

Isaac Campion has a similar setting to that of *The Nature of the Beast,* but set back in time to the limits of living memory, for Isaac is supposedly telling his story to the author, just before his death in 1984 at the age of 96. The year is 1901. Isaac's older brother has been killed as the result of a foolish dare from the son of his father's hated enemy; Isaac must leave school to work without pay for Father, a horse dealer and a harsh, violent man. On impulse Isaac frustrates Father's plan to take a hideous revenge. Immediately afterwards the steamboat carrying a cargo of Irish mares for Father is thought to have sunk in a storm. Father comes home drunk, defeated, apparently ruined, yet hard and bitter still. Later the steamer is seen to be safe, riding at anchor; but Isaac has had enough, and will be off to America by the end of summer.

This is a brief, emotionally intense novel, full of the passionate power of hatred and the close but often suffocating or infuriating relationships between members of a family. There is compassion too for the horses that "dragged the whole weight of work behind them…until they were done for, and sent to the knacker's, or buried in a ditch." It gives a gritty, wholly convincing picture of a bleak world of hard-driven people. "I know I can endure it," thinks Isaac. "I was put on the earth to endure it. But there must be more to living a life than this." The book is not in the end pessimistic, however. In Isaac himself—poor, ordinary lad though he is—the human spirit shines. There's nothing shining about Father, but even in him there is something heroic: a fierce determination to fight, survive, and win in grim surroundings.

Howker's first three books suggest that hers is a major talent, but the second and third could be said to belong to general as much as to young people's fiction, and it remains to be seen whether she will stay within the bounds of the children's list.

—John Rowe Townsend

HUGHES, Monica (née Ince). Canadian. Born in Liverpool, Lancashire, England, 3 November 1925; daughter of the mathematician E.L. Ince; became Canadian citizen, 1957. Educated at the Convent of the Holy Child Jesus, Harrogate, Yorkshire, graduated 1942; Edinburgh University, 1942–43. Served in the Women's Royal Naval Service, 1943–46. Married Glen Hughes in 1957; two daughters and two sons. Dress designer, London, 1948–49, and Bulawayo, Zimbabwe, 1950; bank clerk, Umtali, Zimbabwe, 1951; laboratory technician, National Research Council, Ottawa, 1952–57. Recipient: Vicky Metcalf award, 1981, 1983; Canada Council prize, 1982, 1983. Address: 13816–110A Avenue, Edmonton, Alberta T5M 2M9, Canada.

PUBLICATIONS FOR CHILDREN

Fiction

Gold-Fever Trail: A Klondike Adventure, illustrated by Patricia Peacock. Edmonton, Alberta, LeBel, 1974.
Crisis on Conshelf Ten. Toronto, Copp Clark, and London, Hamish Hamilton, 1975; New York, Atheneum, 1977.
Earthdark. London, Hamish Hamilton, 1977.
The Tomorrow City. London, Hamish Hamilton, 1978.
The Ghost Dance Caper. London, Hamish Hamilton, 1978.
Beyond the Dark River. London, Hamish Hamilton, 1979; New York, Atheneum, 1981.
The Keeper of the Isis Light. London, Hamish Hamilton, 1980; New York, Atheneum, 1981.
The Guardian of Isis. London, Hamish Hamilton, 1981; New York, Atheneum, 1982.
Hunter in the Dark. Toronto, Clarke Irwin, 1982; New York, Atheneum, 1983; London, MacRae, 1985.
Ring-Rise, Ring-Set. London, MacRae, and New York, Watts, 1982.
The Isis Pedlar. London, Hamish Hamilton, 1982; New York, Atheneum, 1983.
The Beckoning Lights, illustrated by Richard A. Conroy. Edmonton, Alberta, LeBel, 1982.
The Treasure of the Long Sault, illustrated by Richard A. Conroy. Edmonton, Alberta, LeBel, 1982.
Space Trap. Toronto, Groundwood, and London, MacRae, 1983; New York, Watts, 1984.
My Name Is Paula Popowich! Toronto, Lorimer, 1983.
Devil on My Back. London, MacRae, 1984; New York, Atheneum, 1985.
Sandwriter. London, MacRae, 1985; New York, Holt, 1988.
The Dream Catcher. London, MacRae, 1986; New York, Atheneum, 1987.

Blaine's Way. Toronto, Irwin, 1986; London, Severn House, 1988.
Log Jam. Toronto, Irwin, 1987; as *Spirit River,* London, Methuen, 1988.

*

Manuscript Collection: University of Calgary, Alberta.

Monica Hughes comments:
I write primarily science fiction because I find the world of "what if" the most exciting and challenging place to be in and to write about. It is also a very flexible medium through which to approach and, hopefully, to deal with the problems that young people are facing in today's society. I feel very strongly about our world, its ecological balance, and the even graver dangers that face us today, and these feelings are sometimes reflected in my work, as are my attitudes towards the aboriginal peoples—especially of the new world—whose culture and skills were so long despised by the European settlers and missionaries: only now are we becoming aware of the depth and complexity of their knowledge.

My plots derive from everyday life, from asking "what if?" and "what would happen then?," and from taking simple themes and working them out through the lives of my characters, whether in today's world or some future place and time.

*   *   *

Monica Hughes's earliest science-fiction adventure novels introduced her distinctive voice and unique preoccupations to a wide audience of enthusiastic young adults. All were (and in frequent reprints and translations worldwide remain) deservedly popular whether read superficially for their exciting heroics or more deeply for their insights into the psychologies of maturing adolescents and for their speculations about the complex interrelationships between culture, environment, and personality. As even her earliest novels demonstrated, however, the science-fiction genre was (and remains) merely a means to an end with Hughes: her tales are set in the future or on distant galaxies only when contemporary settings do not lend themselves to adequate exploration of her themes.

"Truth of character," Hughes insists, is the essence of all good literature, and her novels present a gallery of credible, contemporary adolescents struggling to transform themselves into responsible adults. Her protagonists have exciting adventures, but for the thoughtful reader, it is the maturing effects of the adventures on the central characters that is of most interest. Whether the novels are set in the past, present, or future, readers identify with her heroes and heroines because they are introduced realistically as typically thoughtless, complacent adolescents: most share their readers' 20th-century problems with parents, peers, and schooling. Plotting leads Hughes's characters to recognize an impending crisis (most frequently one with potentially devastating consequences for the entire society); the situation forces them to come to terms with themselves and with the society in which they live, to reevaluate their preconceptions and priorities, and so to mature sufficiently to accept the challenges they had previously assumed were adult problems. In other words, Hughes's adventures—no matter how intrinsically exciting in themselves—are also metaphors for whatever in life leads to socially responsible maturity.

Like her literal as well as literary ancestor Sir Thomas More, Hughes is a serious (albeit non-professional) anthropologist; as in his *Utopia,* her protagonists are moulded by the cultures in which they are reared but are then jolted into new perspectives on themselves and their environments through experiencing alternate ways of life. The science fiction novels depict hypothetical societies, of course, but all are either modeled on existing subcultures or extrapolated from recognizable aspects and tendencies of modern society.

In *Ring-Rise, Ring-Set*, for example, Liza is the product of an only slightly advanced version of ours which is depending on its technology to survive a forthcoming Ice Age; she irresponsibly leaves the safety of her enclosed City and survives by living with a migratory Inuit tribe. The culture and life depicted here (as in similarly structured novels) is based on Hughes's extensive research into today's Inuit culture. Liza is at first horrified by the life, but then comes to understand and appreciate it. Her perspective on both cultures leads her to see both the futility of attempting to fight the changing environment through science as well as the harsh realities mere survival entails when living in harmony with it. The climax of the novel centres on her attempt to find a viable alternative.

Beyond the Dark River is similar in structure, but is also a literary tour de force in point of view and modes of perception. Here two subcultures have survived the collapse of Western civilization thanks to their isolation from it. 15-year-old Hutterite Benjamin meets the 14-year-old Cree Indian Daughter-of-She-Who-Came-After as both search the ruins hoping to find solutions for problems that have arisen among their peoples. Both view and evaluate all they see in their cultures' terms. Thus the abandoned city they explore (clearly Edmonton) is literally "Gomorrah" to Benjamin: he tries unsuccessfully to explain to his companion that "God sent his judgment on the land and slew the evil-doers. And when that was done, He cleansed the vile city with flames." The Cree, however, do not perceive reality in terms of cause and effect: to the girl, the "Old Ones" who had built the "Place of the Dead" had simply lost their power and gone away. The two find the solutions to their cultures' problems from each other rather than in the ruins of the city; each returns home with modified perceptions and new optimism for the future.

Variations on these themes and structures are found in both Hughes's other science fiction and her realistic novels. *Crisis on Conshelf Ten* contrasts a restrictive, legalistic colonial society with its permissive, revolutionary counterpart: its protagonist comes to see that both are self-defeating. *Devil on My Back* and *The Dream Catcher* examine alternatives to a rigidly class-structured, technology-oriented society: the hero of the former experiences life in a culture modeled on North American Indian tribal life while the heroine of the latter, the product of an absolutely classless society which evolved through cultivation of psychic abilities and non-verbal communication, samples and evaluates all three. The *Isis* trilogy (appropriately set in a far distant, future galaxy) explores the responses of a teenage girl reared in isolation from human contact to the arrival of settlers on her planet.

Hughes's contemporary novels deal with similar themes. *The Ghost Dance Caper* focuses on the conflicts experienced by a city boy of mixed descent (father American Indian, mother white) attempting to reconcile his life in the city with his heritage—his grandfather remains on a reservation and permits him to experience vividly described traditional rituals. *Log Jam* centres on the culture shock experienced by two 1980's adolescents: Lenora suffers the effects of her mother's divorce and remarriage; she meets the Indian Isaac Manyfeathers who had been imprisoned because he could not adjust to city life. Both are able to come to terms with their personal lives as a result of their shared adventure. *Blaine's Way,* by contrast, is a realistic examination of a boy growing to manhood in rural Ontario through the Great Depression and early years of World War II.

Hunter in the Dark, however, remains Hughes's masterpiece. A lack in our culture is its focus: we provide none of the rituals or tests (common in "primitive" cultures) by which a physically mature adolescent can prove his maturity to himself. (The novel rejects sex as a solution.) Its protagonist is forced to confront his own mortality when he discovers that he has a probably fatal disease his parents have concealed from him. Determined to prove himself "adult" before it is too late, he undertakes a dangerous hunting expedition alone and, as in Faulkner's *The Bear,* comes of age in unexpected

ways. Adults will find themselves as impressed and moved by this work as younger readers are.

—Gerald J. Rubio

HUGHES, Richard (Arthur Warren). British. Born in Weybridge, Surrey, 19 April 1900. Educated at Charterhouse School, Godalming, Surrey; Oriel College, Oxford, 1919–22, B.A. 1922. Served in the British Army, 1918; in the Admiralty, London, 1940–45: O.B.E. (Officer, Order of the British Empire), 1946. Married Frances C.R. Bazley in 1932; five children. Co-founder and director, Portmadoc Players, Wales, 1922–25; vice-chairman, Welsh National Theatre, 1924–36; petty constable of Langharne, 1936; filmwriter, Ealing Studies, London, 1945–55; Gresham Professor of Rhetoric, Gresham College, University of London, 1955–56. Recipient: Femina Vie Heureuse prize, 1931; Arts Council award, 1961; Welsh Arts Council award, 1973. D.Litt.: University of Wales, Cardiff, 1956. Fellow, Royal Society of Literature, 1962. Honorary member, American Academy (Blashfield Foundation Address, 1969). *Died 28 April 1976.*

PUBLICATIONS FOR CHILDREN

Fiction

Burial, and The Dark Child (verse and story). Privately printed, 1930.
The Spider's Palace and Other Stories, illustrated by George Charlton. London, Chatto and Windus, 1931; New York, Harper, 1932.
Don't Blame Me! and Other Stories, illustrated by Fritz Eichenberg. London, Chatto and Windus, and New York, Harper, 1940.
Gertrude's Child, illustrated by Rick Schreiter. New York, Harlin Quist, 1966; London, W.H. Allen, 1967.
The Wonder-Dog: The Collected Children's Stories, illustrated by Antony Maitland. London, Chatto and Windus, and New York, Greenwillow, 1977.
Gertrude and the Mermaid, illustrated by Nicole Claveloux. New York, Harlin Quist, 1979.

PUBLICATIONS FOR ADULTS

Novels

A High Wind in Jamaica. London, Chatto and Windus, 1929; as *The Innocent Voyage,* New York, Harper, 1929.
In Hazard: A Sea Story. London, Chatto and Windus, and New York, Harper, 1938.
The Human Predicament:
   1. *The Fox in the Attic.* London, Chatto and Windus, and New York, Harper, 1961.
   2. *The Wooden Shepherdess.* London, Chatto and Windus, and New York, Harper, 1973.

Short Stories

A Moment of Time. London, Chatto and Windus, 1926.
In the Lap of Atlas: Stories of Morocco, edited by Richard Poole. London, Chatto and Windus, 1979.

Plays

The Sisters' Tragedy (produced Oxford and London, 1922). Oxford, Blackwell, 1922.
The Man Born to Be Hanged (produced Portmadoc, 1923; London, 1924). Included in *The Sisters' Tragedy and Three Other Plays*, 1924.
A Comedy of Good and Evil (produced London, 1924; as *Minnie and Mr. Williams*, produced New York, 1948). Included in *The Sisters' Tragedy and Three Other Plays*, 1924.
Danger (broadcast 1924). Included in *The Sisters' Tragedy and Three Other Plays*, 1924.
The Sisters' Tragedy and Three Other Plays (includes *The Man Born to Be Hanged, A Comedy of Good and Evil, Danger*). London, Heinemann, 1924; as *A Rabbit and a Leg: Collected Plays*, New York, Knopf, 1924; as *Plays*, London, Chatto and Windus, 1966.

Screenplays: *A Run for Your Money*, with others, 1949; *The Divided Heart*, with Jack Whittingham, 1954.

Radio Play: *Danger*, 1924.

Verse

Lines Written upon First Observing an Elephant Devoured by a Roc.... London, Golden Cockerel Press, 1922.
Gipsy-Night and Other Poems. London, Golden Cockerel Press, and Chicago, Ransom, 1922.
Ecstatic Ode on Vision. Privately printed, 1923.
Meditative Ode on Vision. Privately printed, 1923.
Confessio Juvenis: Collected Poems. London, Chatto and Windus, 1926.

Other

Richard Hughes: An Omnibus. New York, Harper, 1931.
The Administration of War Production, with J.D. Scott. London, Her Majesty's Stationery Office, 1955.
Fiction as Truth: Selected Literary Writings, edited by Richard Poole. Bridgend, Glamorgan, Poetry Wales Press, 1983; Chester Springs, Pennsylvania, Dufour, 1984.

Editor, with Robert Graves and Alan Porter, *Oxford Poetry 1921*. Oxford, Blackwell, 1921.
Editor, *Poems*, by John Skelton. London, Heinemann, 1924.

*

Critical Studies: *Richard Hughes* by Peter Thomas, Cardiff, University of Wales Press, 1973; *Richard Hughes: Author, Father* by Penelope Hughes, Gloucester, Sutton, 1984; *Richard Hughes, Novelist* by Richard Poole, Bridgend, Glamorgan, Poetry Wales Press, 1987.

*   *   *

Richard Hughes's understanding of the child mind is demonstrated most convincingly not in the small books which he wrote specifically for young readers, but in that remarkable novel on which his reputation was first based, *A High Wind in Jamaica*. Early in the story the children experience one of those minor earth-tremors which are commonplace in the tropics. They are told that it is an earthquake. At the end of the book, after tempest, piracy, and murder, they reach safety. What they remember most is that they have been in an earthquake. The precise nature of the protective sieve through which their experiences have been filtered remains unstated, but

anyone who works with children will recognize the authenticity of the author's observation.

The two volumes of short stories written for children are admittedly minor writing, trifles tossed off for particular occasions and not regarded seriously by the writer. This is not to say that he withholds part of his creative skills. Hughes was always a craftsman, with respect for his medium whatever the prospective audience. *The Spider's Palace* is a set of 20 stories written under stimulus of Hughes's friendship with Clough Williams-Ellis and his family, and the first tale—"Living in W'ales"—pays good-humoured tribute to the architect and his infectious enthusiasms. Similarly *Don't Blame Me!* is the result of the Second World War, when seven children from Merseyside arrived on the author's doorstep in North Wales. In the months before they drifted home he told them this baker's-dozen of stories.

Hughes has two favourite devices. One is the literal interpretation of a colloquial expression. In "The Elephant's Picnic" in the second and better volume, the elephant fills the saucepan with water and pops the kettle in it to boil. The kettle refuses to get tender, so the elephant unpacks his trunk and sleeps comfortably in his pyjamas, while the unfortunate kangaroo, who has no trunk and consequently no night-wear, stays awake and keeps the fire going. In the morning the kettle is "as tender as tender could be." The second device is the application of fairy-tale conventions to a contemporary scene. In the title story a young man buys a motor-bike which metamorphoses into a crocodile. The humour is consistently serious, with none of the posturing which many writers for adults adopt when entertaining the young. The stories are distinguished by a plain unadorned prose. For this reason, as well as for the fertile inventiveness of the narrative and the pervading humour, they have always been popular with those who tell stories aloud. They need to be told "just-so," but the effect is one of spontaneous creation.

—Marcus Crouch

———

HUGHES, Shirley. British. Born in Hoylake, Lancashire, 16 July 1929. Educated at West Kirby High School for Girls; Liverpool Art School; Ruskin School of Art, Oxford. Married John Vulliamy in 1952; two sons and one daughter. Freelance illustrator and writer. Currently, Visiting Tutor in Illustration, Ruskin School of Art, Oxford. Member of the Management Committee, Society of Authors, 1983–86. Since 1985 member of the Registrar's Advisory Committee for Public Lending Right. Recipient: Children's Rights Workshop Other award, 1976; Library Association Kate Greenaway Medal, 1977; Eleanor Farjeon award, 1984. Address: 63 Lansdowne Road, London W11 2LG, England.

PUBLICATIONS FOR CHILDREN (illustrated by the author)

Fiction

Lucy and Tom's Day. London, Gollancz, and New York, Scott, 1960.
The Trouble with Jack. London, Bodley Head, 1970.
Lucy and Tom Go to School. London, Gollancz, 1973.
Sally's Secret. London, Bodley Head, 1973.
Helpers. London, Bodley Head, 1975; as *George the Babysitter*, Englewood Cliffs, New Jersey, Prentice Hall, 1977.
Lucy and Tom at the Seaside. London, Gollancz, 1976.
Dogger. London, Bodley Head, 1977; as *David and Dog*, Englewood Cliffs, New Jersey, Prentice Hall, 1978.

It's Too Frightening for Me! London, Hodder and Stoughton, 1977; as *Haunted House,* Englewood Cliffs, New Jersey, Prentice Hall, 1978.

Moving Molly. London, Bodley Head, 1978; Englewood Cliffs, New Jersey, Prentice Hall, 1979.

Up and Up. London, Bodley Head, and Englewood Cliffs, New Jersey, Prentice Hall, 1979.

Here Comes Charlie Moon. London, Bodley Head, 1980; New York, Lothrop, 1986.

Lucy and Tom's Christmas. London, Gollancz, 1981; New York, Viking Kestrel, 1986.

Alfie Gets in First. London, Bodley Head, 1981; New York, Lothrop, 1982.

Alfie's Feet. London, Bodley Head, and New York, Lothrop, 1982.

Charlie Moon and the Big Bonanza Bust-up. London, Bodley Head, 1982.

Alfie Gives a Hand. London, Bodley Head, and New York, Lothrop, 1983.

An Evening at Alfie's. London, Bodley Head, and New York, Lothrop, 1984.

Lucy and Tom's ABC. London, Gollancz, 1984; New York, Viking Kestrel, 1986.

Chips and Jessie. London, Bodley Head, 1985; New York, Lothrop, 1986.

Nursery Collection (Bathwater's Hot, When We Went to the Park, Noisy, All Shapes and Sizes, Colours, Two Shoes New Shoes). London, Walker, and New York, Lothrop, 6 vols., 1985–86.

Another Helping of Chips. London, Bodley Head, 1986; New York, Lothrop, 1987.

Lucy and Tom's 123. London, Gollancz, and New York, Viking Kestrel, 1987.

The Big Alfie and Annie Rose Storybook. London, Bodley Head, 1988; New York, Lothrop, 1989.

Verse

Out and About. London, Walker, and New York, Lothrop, 1988.

Other

Editor, *Over the Moon: A Book of Sayings.* London, Faber, 1980.

*

Illustrator: *World's End Was Home* by Nan Chauncy, 1952; *Follow the Footprints,* 1953, *The World Upside Down,* 1954, and *The Toffee Join,* 1968, all by William Mayne; *All Through the Night* by Rachel Field, 1954; *The Bell Family,* 1954, *New Town,* 1960, and *The Painted Garden* revised edition, 1961, all by Noel Streatfeild; *The Journey of Johnny Rew* by Anne Mainwaring Barrett, 1954; *Mr. Punch's Cap* by Kathleen Fidler, 1956; *The Man of the House* by Allan Campbell McLean, 1956; *William and the Lorry,* 1956, and *The Merry-Go-Round,* 1963, both by Diana Ross; *Guns in the Wild,* 1956, *Katy at Home,* 1957, and *Katy at School,* 1959, all by Ian Serraillier; *Lost Lorrenden,* 1956, *Fiona on the Fourteenth Floor,* 1964, *The Sign of the Unicorn,* 1968, *The Wood Street Group,* 1970, *The Wood Street Secret,* 1970, *The Wood Street Rivals,* 1971, *The Wood Street Helpers,* 1973, and *Away from Wood Street,* 1976, all by Mabel Esther Allan; *Adventure on Rainbow Island,* 1957, *The Jade Green Cadillac,* 1958, *The Lost Tower Treasure,* 1960, *The Singing Strings,* 1961, and *Operation Smuggle,* 1964, all by Dorothy Clewes; *The Boy and the Donkey* by Diana Pullein-Thompson, 1958; *Rolling On,* 1960, *Mary Ann Goes to Hospital,* 1961, and *Cottage by the Lock,* 1962, all by Mary Cockett; *Flowering Spring* by Elfrida Vipont, 1960; *Fell Farm Campers* by Marjorie Lloyd, 1960; *The Bronze Chrysanthemum* by Sheena Porter, 1960; *Fairy Tales,* 1961,

and *More Fairy Tales,* 1970, both by Hans Christian Andersen; *Plain Jane,* 1961, *Place Mill,* 1962, and *A Stone in a Pool,* 1964, all by Barbara Softly; *Willy Is My Brother* by Peggy Parish, 1963; *Tales of Tigg's Farm,* 1963, *Meet Mary Kate,* 1963, *A Dream of Dragons,* 1965, *Satchkin Patchkin,* 1966, *Mary Kate and the Jumble Bear* [*School Bus*], 2 vols., 1967–70, *Mrs. Pinny and the Blowing Day* [*Sudden Snow, Salty Sea Day*], 3 vols., 1968–72, and *Mother Farthing's Luck,* 1971, all by Helen Morgan; *The Shinty Boys,* 1963, and *The New Tenants,* 1968, both by Margaret MacPherson; *Tim Rabbit's Dozen,* 1964, and *From Spring to Spring,* 1978, both by Alison Uttley; *Stories for Seven-Year-Olds* [*Six-Year-Olds, Five-Year-Olds, Under-Fives, Nine-Year-Olds*] and *More Stories for Seven-Year-Olds,* all edited by Sara and Stephen Corrin, 6 vols., 1964–79; *Roller Skates,* 1964, and *Lucinda's Year of Jubilo,* 1965, both by Ruth Sawyer; *The Cat and Mrs. Cary* by Doris Gates, 1964; *Stories from Grimm,* 1964; *Tales the Muses Told* by Roger Lancelyn Green, 1965; *The Twelve Dancing Princesses,* 1965; *Kate and the Family Tree,* 1965, *The Smallest Doll,* 1966, and *The Smallest Bridesmaid,* 1966, all by Margaret Storey; *The Faber Book of Nursery Stories* edited by Barbara Ireson, 1966; *The Witch's Daughter,* 1966, and *Squib,* 1971, both by Nina Bawden; *Little Bear's Pony,* 1966, and *Hazy Mountain,* 1975, both by Donald Bisset; *Wayland's Keep* by Angela Bull, 1966; *Porterhouse Major* by Margaret J. Baker, 1967; *Home and Away* by Ann Thwaite, 1967; *A Day on Big O,* 1968, *Rainbow Pavement,* 1970, and *Donkey Days,* 1977, all by Helen Cresswell; *My Naughty Little Sister* series by Dorothy Edwards, 9 vols., 1968–82; *A Crown for a Queen,* 1968, *The Toymaker's Daughter,* 1968, *Malkin's Mountain* revised edition, 1970, *The Three Toymakers* revised edition, 1970, and *Bog Woppit,* 1978, all by Ursula Moray Williams; *Flutes and Cymbals* edited by Leonard Clark, 1968; *The Bicycle Wheel,* 1969, *The Ruth Ainsworth Book,* 1970, *The Phantom Fisherboy,* 1974, *The Phantom Round-about,* 1977, and *The Pirate Ship and Other Stories,* 1980, all by Ruth Ainsworth; *Moshie Cat,* 1969, and *Federico,* 1971, both by Helen Griffiths; *Cinderella* by Charles Perrault, 1970; *Eight Days to Christmas,* 1970, and *Ginger,* 1972, both by Geraldine Kaye; *The Lost Angel* by Elizabeth Goudge, 1971; *The Smell of Privet* by Barbara Sleigh, 1971; *Burnish Me Bright* by Julia W. Cunningham, 1971; *The Little Broomstick* by Mary Stewart, 1971; *Dancing Day* by Robina Willson, 1971; *The Thirteen Days of Christmas* by Jenny Overton, 1972; *A House in the Square* by Joan G. Robinson, 1972; *The First* [*Second, Third*] *Margaret Mahy Story Book,* 3 vols., 1972–75; *Hospital Day* by Leila Berg, 1972; *Mother's Help* by Susan Dickinson, 1972; *The Hollywell Family* by Margaret Kornitzer, 1973; *The Gauntlet Fair* by Alison Farthing, 1974; *Jacko and Other Stories* by Jean Sutcliffe, 1974; *Miss Hendy's House* by Joan Drake, 1974; *Peter Pan and Wendy* retold by May Byron, 1976; *The Snake Crook* by Ruth Tomalin, 1976; *Make Hay While the Sun Shines* edited by Alison Abel, 1977; *A Throne for Sesame* by Helen Young, 1977; *Trouble with Dragons* by Oliver Selfridge, 1978; *The Snailman* by Brenda Sivers, 1978; *Pottle Pig* by Nancy Northcote, 1978; *Witchdust* by Mary Welfare, 1980; *A Cat's Tale* by Rikki Cate, 1982; *Five to Eight* by Dorothy Butler, 1985; *The Secret Garden* by Frances Hodgson Burnett, 1988.

Shirley Hughes comments:

Having worked for years as an interpretive illustrator in both colour and line, I approached the business of writing through wanting to design my own picture books. In conceiving a story, I tend to think in pictures rather than words, and the text develops out of these, like the captions to a silent film.

I feel that the words in a picture book should carry the bare bones of the narrative, constantly referring attention to the pictures where the richness and detail of the story lies. They should point up the humour and help to build up the visual climaxes, sometimes not by what they describe but what they leave for the reader to see for himself. But they must always sound well read aloud. When I began to write longer stories for an older age group I still put drawings on every page. They are paced with the narrative as a kind of counterpoint to the action of the plot.

My own books have grown out of real situations with which very small children can identify, perhaps even at an age before they can fully appreciate fairy tales. They are mostly set in a city background—my own part of London to be exact. The domestic details are very local and English, but I hope the themes are fairly universal.

* * *

Shirley Hughes thinks pictures in narratives and narratives in pictures. She is an artist storyteller whose work has so singularly matched the tales that others have told that only now, when she has joined the novelists in her own right, are we able to judge just how successfully she has made a stylistic unity of everything she has done.

She draws the world she sees, foregrounding people of all ages in every possible pose against a background that locates the characters in late 20th-century cities and towns, events and interactions. The events have a three-dimensionality that provokes from very young readers and teachers an immediate recognition. The details highlight something significant in the text, or else they give the text significance. It is no longer possible to think of Dorothy Edwards's *My Naughty Little Sister* without remembering Shirley Hughes's characterization of Bad Harry. He bears a family likeness to later scamps, Alfie and Charlie Moon. The street in Ruth Sawyer's New York in *Roller Skates* came nearer to British readers as the result of the drawings that made the reader see them, and Mary Stewart's *The Little Broomstick* gained concreteness from the illustrations which gave more movement to the story than the plot itself. Celebration pictures in poetry books and the illustrations of common sayings (*Make Hay While the Sun Shines*) are examples of local observation and fluent drawing skill. Storytelling with pictures is, when Shirley Hughes undertakes it, as likely to entertain children at a book fair as in anthologies like those of Sara and Stephen Corrin. Her drawings are narratives in their own right, not simply pictures to be seen through.

Before they can read, children create stories for what they see. In her own picture books Hughes presents layers of significance for adults who read to and with children. For those who come to a book for the first time Hughes makes a tale of what they know, and gives to their limited experience a universal significance that adults recognise, as in the Lucy and Tom books, which present everyone's idea of how things are or might be. Simple and everyday as their incidents are, compared with the more arcane and fantastic productions for young readers that graphic designers indulge in, Hughes joins Beatrix Potter and Maurice Sendak in giving children pictures that they remember. They see their own 20th-century decade in the pages and they smack their hands in appreciation.

Since *Helpers* and *Dogger*, the pictures and incidents have had extended significance. George the babysitter looks after children, with their help, of course, in a world where Mum has to go out for the day. Dogger is the solacing transitional object in a world that would be frightening without him. When George takes the children for sweets and to the "rec" in multicultural London, the book tells a tale about children and grown-ups beyond the narrative distilled from the pictures into the text. What isn't said but is clearly seen, is an important layer of Hughes's writing. The concrete nearness to the lives of her readers of everything that she draws makes her books specially significant of their time in that they reject a fictive past in favour of an actual present. Her character Alfie, a solid, knowing child, is typical of many. When he seems to have shut the door on himself, and the frantic adults alert everyone in the street, Alfie

calmly deals with the situation and "gets in first." In *Alfie Gives a Hand* he relinquishes his beloved security blanket in order to take the hand of an overwrought friend at a birthday party.

Hughes has also experimented with telling a story only with pictures. *Up and Up* is like a silent film or a TV story with the sound turned off, relying on the spectator to create the text. Hughes uses all the conventions that an artist has at her command (focus, point of view, relative size, framing) and calls on the way of looking that TV-nurtured children can use to understand pictures. The result is an imaginative fantasy, without dialogue or narrator, about a girl who, after eating an Easter egg (after all, birds come from eggs), discovers she could fly. Neither the neighbours nor the balloonist can bring her down to earth until she is ready. It is an artistic tour de force of visual imagery.

The obverse of this technique creates *It's Too Frightening for Me!*, *Here Comes Charlie Moon,* and *Charlie Moon and the Big Bonanza Bust-up*. Here Hughes takes on the role of a writer, with great skill, and shows how pictures interweave with a full text. Her success lies in her strong sense of the demotic—telling it like it is. The first Charlie Moon book is written in the historic present, so that the ribbon of drawing along the top of the page creates a unity with the "what happens next" of the tale, a comedy thriller of seaside escapades and foolery, created around Charlie's aunt's joke shop and the kinds of characters who were once seaside entertainers. The book bonanza of the second story lets Hughes draw Thames-side London, celebrate librarians who run book fairs, and put herself into the story as the lady illustrator who is altogether nicer than the TV personality who writes books yet despises children.

In the recent Chips and Jessie books Hughes combines text with pen-and-ink strip cartoons to relate the adventures of Chips and Jessie and their friends and families. While the text is relatively straightforward, the cartoons undercut and sometimes lampoon the story with witty dialogue and sarcastic asides from Albert and Barkis, Chips's cat and Jessie's dog. Although at times the page layout is a little busy, overall the combination is successful, and the humour infectious.

Hughes knows how an artist can tell stories to children who normally expect to see them flittering before their eyes. Part of the skill is to make young readers respond imaginatively to what they see. The rest, of course, is art that they can share with the artist.

—Margaret Meek

HUGHES, Ted (Edward James Hughes). British. Born in Mytholmroyd, Yorkshire, 17 August 1930. Educated at Mexborough Grammar School, Yorkshire; Pembroke College, Cambridge, 1951–54, B.A. in archaeology and anthropology 1954, M.A. 1959. Served in the Royal Air Force, 1948–50. Married 1) the poet Sylvia Plath in 1956 (died 1963), one daughter and one son; 2) Carol Orchard in 1970. Worked as a rose gardener, night watchman in a steelworks, zoo attendant, teacher, and reader for the Rank Organisation, in the 1950's; lived in the United States, 1957–59: taught at the University of Massachusetts, Amherst, 1957–58. Founding editor, with Daniel Weissbort, *Modern Poetry in Translation* magazine, London, 1964–71. Recipient: New York Poetry Center First Publication award, 1957; Guinness award, 1958; Guggenheim fellowship, 1959; Maugham award, 1960; Hawthornden prize, 1961; City of Florence International Poetry prize, 1969; Etna-Taormina prize, 1973; Queen's Gold Medal for Poetry, 1974; *Signal* Poetry award, 1979, 1983, 1985; Royal Society of Literature Heinemann award, 1980; *Guardian* award, 1985; Maschler award, 1985. Honorary Fellow, Pembroke College, Cambridge, 1986. O.B.E. (Officer, Order of the

British Empire), 1977. Poet Laureate, 1984. Lives in North Tawton, Devon. Address: c/o Faber and Faber Ltd., 3 Queen Square, London WC1N 3AU, England.

PUBLICATIONS FOR CHILDREN

Fiction

How the Whale Became, illustrated by George Adamson. London, Faber, 1963; New York, Atheneum, 1964.
The Iron Man: A Story in Five Nights, illustrated by George Adamson. London, Faber, 1968; as *The Iron Giant,* New York, Harper, 1968.
Ffangs the Vampire Bat and the Kiss of Truth, illustrated by Chris Riddell. London, Faber, 1986.
Tales of the Early World, illustrated by Andrew Davidson. London, Faber, 1988.

Plays

The Coming of the Kings (broadcast 1964; produced London, 1972). Included in *The Coming of the Kings and Other Plays,* 1970.
The Tiger's Bones (broadcast 1965). Included in *The Coming of the Kings and Other Plays,* 1970.
Beauty and the Beast (broadcast 1965; produced London, 1971). Included in *The Coming of the Kings and Other Plays,* 1970.
The Price of a Bride (broadcast 1966). Excerpt published in *Here, Now and Beyond,* edited by Nancy Coniston Martin, London, Oxford University Press, 1968.
The Demon of Adachigahara, music by Gordon Crosse (cantata; produced Shrewsbury, 1968). London, Oxford University Press, 1969.
Sean, The Fool, The Devil and the Cats (broadcast 1968; produced London, 1971). Included in *The Coming of the Kings and Other Plays,* 1970.
The Coming of the Kings and Other Plays (includes *The Tiger's Bones; Beauty and the Beast; Sean, The Fool, The Devil and The Cats*). London, Faber, 1970; augmented edition, as *The Tiger's Bones and Other Plays for Children* (includes *Orpheus*), New York, Viking Press, 1974.
Orpheus (broadcast 1971). Chicago, Dramatic Publishing Company, 1973.
The Pig Organ; or, Pork with Perfect Pitch, music by Richard Blackford (produced London, 1980).

Radio Plays: *The Coming of the Kings,* 1964; *The Tiger's Bones,* 1965; *Beauty and the Beast,* 1965; *The Price of a Bride,* 1966; *The Head of Gold,* 1967; *Sean, The Fool, The Devil and the Cats,* 1968; *Orpheus,* 1971.

Verse

Meet My Folks!, illustrated by George Adamson. London, Faber, 1961; Indianapolis, Bobbs Merrill, 1973; revised edition, Faber, 1987.
The Earth-Owl and Other Moon-People, illustrated by R.A. Brandt. London, Faber, 1963.
Nessie the Mannerless Monster, illustrated by Gerald Rose. London, Faber, 1964; as *Nessie the Monster,* Indianapolis, Bobbs Merrill, 1974.
Five Autumn Songs for Children's Voices, illustrated by Phillida Gili. Crediton, Devon, Gilbertson, 1969.
Autumn Song, illustrated by Nina Carroll. Kettering, Northamptonshire, Steane, 1971.
Spring, Summer, Autumn, Winter. London, Rainbow Press, 1974;

revised edition, as *Season Songs,* New York, Viking Press, 1975; London, Faber, 1976; revised edition, Faber, 1987.
Earth-Moon, illustrated by the author. London, Rainbow Press, 1976.
Moon-Whales and Other Moon Poems, illustrated by Leonard Baskin. New York, Viking Press, 1976; revised edition, as *Moon-Whales,* London, Faber, 1988.
Moon-Bells and Other Poems. London, Chatto and Windus, 1978.
Under the North Star, illustrated by Leonard Baskin. London, Faber, and New York, Viking Press, 1981.
What Is the Truth? A Farmyard Fable, illustrated by R.J. Lloyd. London, Faber, and New York, Harper, 1984.

Other

Poetry in the Making: An Anthology of Poems and Programmes from "Listening and Writing." London, Faber, 1967; abridged edition, as *Poetry Is,* New York, Doubleday, 1970.

Editor, with Seamus Heaney, *The Rattle Bag: An Anthology.* London, Faber, 1982.

PUBLICATIONS FOR ADULTS

Short Story

The Threshold. London, Steam Press, 1979.

Plays

The House of Aries (broadcast 1960). Published in *Audience* (Cambridge, Massachusetts), Spring 1961.
The Calm (produced Boston, 1961).
The Wound (broadcast 1962). Included in *Wodwo,* 1967; revised version (produced London, 1972).
Epithalamium (produced London, 1963).
The House of Donkeys (broadcast 1965). Published in *Living Language,* Autumn 1974.
Seneca's Oedipus (produced London, 1968; Los Angeles, 1973; New York, 1977). London, Faber, 1969; New York, Doubleday, 1972.
Orghast (produced Persepolis, 1971). Excerpt published in *Performance* (New York), December 1971.
Eat Crow. London, Rainbow Press, 1971.
The Story of Vasco, music by Gordon Crosse, adaptation of a play by Georges Schehadé (produced London, 1974). London, Oxford University Press, 1974.

Radio Plays: *The House of Aries,* 1960; *A Houseful of Women,* 1961; *The Wound,* 1962; *Difficulties of a Bridegroom,* 1963; *Dogs,* 1964; *The House of Donkeys,* 1965.

Verse

The Hawk in the Rain. London, Faber, and New York, Harper, 1957.
Pike. Northampton, Massachusetts, Gehenna Press, 1959.
Lupercal. London, Faber, and New York, Harper, 1960.
Selected Poems, with Thom Gunn. London, Faber, 1962.
The Burning of the Brothel. London, Turret, 1966.
Recklings. London, Turret, 1967.
Scapegoats and Rabies: A Poem in Five Parts. London, Poet and Printer, 1967.
Animal Poems. Crediton, Devon, Gilbertson, 1967.
Gravestones (6 broadsides), linocuts by Gavin Robbins. Exeter,

Devon, Exeter College of Art, 1967; as *Poems,* 1 vol., 1968.

I Said Goodbye to Earth. London, Turret, 1969.

A Crow Hymn. Frensham, Surrey, Sceptre Press, 1970.

The Martyrdom of Bishop Farrar. Crediton, Devon, Gilbertson, 1970.

A Few Crows. Exeter, Devon, Rougemont Press, 1970.

Four Crow Poems. Privately printed, 1970.

Crow: From the Life and Songs of the Crow. London, Faber, 1970; New York, Harper, 1971; revised edition, Faber, 1972.

Fighting for Jerusalem. Ashington, Northumberland, Mid-NAG, 1970.

Amulet. Privately printed, 1970.

Corgi Modern Poets in Focus 1, with others, edited by Dannie Abse. London, Corgi, 1971.

Crow Wakes. Woodford Green, Essex, Poet and Printer, 1971.

Poems, with Ruth Fainlight and Alan Sillitoe. London, Rainbow Press, 1971.

In the Little Girl's Angel Gaze. London, Steam Press, 1972.

Selected Poems 1957–1967. London, Faber, 1972; New York, Harper, 1973.

Prometheus on His Crag: 21 Poems. London, Rainbow Press, 1973.

The Interrogator: A Titled Vulturess. London, Scolar Press, 1975.

Cave Birds. London, Scolar Press, 1975; revised edition, as *Cave Birds: An Alchemical Cave Drama,* London, Faber, 1978; New York, Viking Press, 1979.

The New World, music by Gordon Crosse. London, Oxford University Press, 1975.

Eclipse. Knotting, Bedfordshire, Sceptre Press, 1976.

Gaudete. London, Faber, and New York, Harper, 1977.

Chiasmadon. Baltimore, Seluzicki, 1977.

Sunstruck. Knotting, Bedfordshire, Sceptre Press, 1977.

A Solstice. Knotting, Bedfordshire, Sceptre Press, 1978.

Orts. London, Rainbow Press, 1978.

Moortown Elegies. London, Rainbow Press, 1978.

Adam and the Sacred Nine. London, Rainbow Press, 1979.

Remains of Elmet: A Pennine Sequence, photographs by Fay Godwin. London, Rainbow Press, 1979; revised edition, London, Faber, and New York, Harper, 1979.

Night-Arrival of Sea-Trout, The Iron Wolf, Puma, Brooktrout, Pan, Woodpecker, Wolverine, Eagle, Mosquito, Tapir's Saga, Wolf-Watching, Mice Are Funny Little Creatures, Weasels at Work, Fly Inspects (broadsides). North Tawton, Devon, Morrigu Press, 1979–83.

Four Tales Told by an Idiot. Knotting, Bedfordshire, Sceptre Press, 1979.

In the Black Chapel (poster). London, Victoria and Albert Museum, 1979.

Moortown. London, Faber, 1979; New York, Harper, 1980.

Sky-Furnace, painting by Roger Vick. North Tawton, Devon, Caricia Fine Arts, 1981.

A Primer of Birds, illustrated by Leonard Baskin. Lurley, Devon, Gehenna Press, 1981.

Selected Poems 1957–1981. London, Faber, 1982; as *New Selected Poems,* New York, Harper, 1982.

River, photographs by Peter Keen. London, Faber, 1983; New York, Harper, 1984.

Flowers and Insects: Some Birds and a Pair of Spiders, illustrated by Leonard Baskin. London, Faber, and New York, Knopf, 1986.

The Cat and the Cuckoo. Winchester, Wykeham Press, 1988.

Recordings: *Poets Reading 5,* Jupiter, 1962; *The Poet Speaks 5,* Argo, 1965; *Crow,* Claddagh, 1973; *The Poetry and Voice of Ted Hughes,* Caedmon, 1977; *Selections from Crow and Wodwo,* Caedmon, 1979.

Other

Wodwo (miscellany). London, Faber, and New York, Harper, 1967.

Shakespeare's Poem (essay). London, Lexham Press, 1971.

Henry Williamson: A Tribute. London, Rainbow Press, 1979.

Editor, with Patricia Beer and Vernon Scannell, *New Poems 1962.* London, Hutchinson, 1962.

Editor, *Here Today.* London, Hutchinson, 1963.

Editor, with Thom Gunn, *Five American Poets.* London, Faber, 1963.

Editor, *Selected Poems,* by Keith Douglas. London, Faber, 1964; New York, Chilmark Press, 1965.

Editor, with Olwyn Hughes, *Ariel,* by Sylvia Plath. London, Faber, 1965; New York, Harper, 1966.

Editor, *A Choice of Emily Dickinson's Verse.* London, Faber, 1968.

Editor, *With Fairest Flowers While Summer Last: Poems from Shakespeare.* New York, Doubleday, 1971; as *A Choice of Shakespeare's Verse,* London, Faber, 1971.

Editor, *Crossing the Water,* by Sylvia Plath. London, Faber, and New York, Harper, 1971.

Editor, *Winter Trees,* by Sylvia Plath. London, Faber, 1971; New York, Harper, 1972.

Editor, and Translator with János Csokits, *Selected Poems,* by János Pilinszky. Manchester, Carcanet, 1976.

Editor, and Translator with Yehuda Amichai, *Amen,* by Amichai. New York, Harper, 1977; London, Oxford University Press, 1978.

Editor, *Johnny Panic and the Bible of Dreams, and Other Prose Writings,* by Sylvia Plath. London, Faber, 1977; augmented edition, Faber, and New York, Harper, 1979.

Editor, *New Poetry 6.* London, Hutchinson, 1980.

Editor, *The Collected Poems of Sylvia Plath.* London, Faber, and New York, Harper, 1981.

Editor, with Frances McCullough, *The Journals of Sylvia Plath.* New York, Dial Press, 1982.

Editor, with Seamus Heaney, *1980 Anthology: Arvon Foundation Poetry Competition.* Todmorden, Lancashire, Kilnhurst, 1982.

Editor, with Seamus Heaney, *The Rattle Bag: An Anthology.* London, Faber, 1982.

Editor, *Sylvia Plath's Selected Poems.* London, Faber, 1985.

Translator, with Assia Gutmann, *Selected Poems,* by Yehuda Amichai. London, Cape Goliard Press, 1968; expanded edition, as *Poems,* New York, Harper, 1969; London, Penguin, 1971.

Translator, with Yehuda Amichai, *Time,* by Amichai. New York, Harper, and London, Oxford University Press, 1979.

*

Bibliography: *Ted Hughes: A Bibliography 1946–1980* by Keith Sagar and Stephen Tabor, London, Mansell, 1983.

Critical Studies: *Ted Hughes,* London, Longman, 1972, and *The Art of Ted Hughes,* London, Cambridge University Press, 1975, revised edition, 1978, both by Keith Sagar, and *The Achievement of Ted Hughes* edited by Sagar, Manchester, Manchester University Press, and Athens, University of Georgia Press, 1983; *Thom Gunn and Ted Hughes* by Alan Bold, Edinburgh, Oliver and Boyd, 1976; *Sylvia Plath and Ted Hughes* by Margaret Dickie Uroff, Urbana, University of Illinois Press, 1979; *Ted Hughes: The Unaccommodated Universe, with Selected Critical Writings by Ted Hughes and Two Interviews* by Ekbert Faas, Santa Barbara, California, Black Sparrow Press, 1980; *Ted Hughes: A Critical Study* by Terry Gifford and Neil Roberts, London, Faber, 1981; *Myth in the Poetry of Ted Hughes: A Guide to the Poems* by Stuart Hirschberg, Portmarnock, County Dublin, Wolfhound Press, and Totowa, New Jersey, Barnes and

Noble, 1981; *Ted Hughes* by Thomas West, London, Methuen, 1985; *Ted Hughes* by Dennis Walder, Milton Keynes, Buckinghamshire, Open University Press, 1987.

*   *   *

Bearing in mind even the precedent of T.S. Eliot and *Old Possum,* few could have expected such an *éminence noir* of contemporary poetry as Ted Hughes to have followed the fierce poetic energy, the searingly realistic view of the battle between the forces of life and death contained in *The Hawk in the Rain* and *Lupercal,* with *Meet My Folks.*

But, particularly in a writer of Hughes's formidable power and accomplishment, there are more ways than one of conveying a conception of reality; and the significance should never be forgotten of Hughes's remark in *Poetry for You:* "Poets write poems to amuse themselves, partly." Occasionally, the touch in *Meet My Folks,* a bizarre verse gallery of imaginary family portraits, is uncertain. But there is more than a hint of things to come in Hughes's work for children: the frequent, unmistakeable buzz of imaginative shock:

> That Crack in the road looks harmless. My Father
>   knows it's not.
> The World may be breaking into two and starting at that
>   spot.

The Earth-Owl is an attempt, disturbingly and enrichingly successful, to detect and identify those secret creatures colonizing the worlds within us, inhabiting the thought-planets drifting somewhere beyond the rim of the mind, and from which perhaps our dreams arise. The often long and galumphing lines of verse sometimes drop to earth, winded; but the shorter, tauter poems are unremittingly effective and create for the reader a whole new area of imaginative experience.

Aimed at rather young children and couched mainly in lines that shamble and sprint in the manner of a pantomime horse, *Nessie the Mannerless Monster* springs to life the moment the creature rises in the loch and "smashes the water to mist." It is a joyful, life-enhancing fable, a form Hughes adopts with immensely increased authority and originality in the prose *How the Whale Became.* Equally effective as these creation-myth stories is *The Iron Man,* told in language as clear and strong as pebbles, and in which the boy Hogarth confronts the unknown with courage and a growing self-knowledge.

The story is weakened only by its somewhat predictable ending; but there can be no such reservation about *Season Songs.* These poems present an unforgettable vision: of winter's attack; of the oak as a railway station where one waits for spring ("Will it stop for you?"); of the newly born March calf plunging "to scatter his seething joy…to find himself himself." The hunted stag doubles back weeping as the huntsman pull aside "the camouflage of their terrible planet"; and the famous murder of Cock Robin is re-enacted as the death of summer, a tractor ("with my gear grinding glottle") voicing its own particular lament and promise.

The revised edition of *Moon-Whales* reprints poems from *The Earth-Owl* and *Moon-Bells* with a substantial body of new pieces, but the join of early with later work is indistinguishable, and the resonance of the poems is as profound and haunting as anything written by Hughes elsewhere. *Tales of the Early World,* a natural successor to the powerful fable *What is the Truth?,* also marks a return to the sphere of *How the Whale Became.* The 10 creation stories in *Tales of the Early World,* told in clear, undecorated prose and with an uncompromising fidelity to the realities of the world he represents, again reveal Hughes as arguably the finest living mythmaker in the English language. The collection ranks with *The Iron Man* as among his most striking prose achievements.

At the same time, nothing in the whole canon of Hughes's work so clearly illuminates the qualities of mystery and revelation at its core as the poetry of *Season Songs:* that celebration, in subtly balanced terms, of victor and vanquished, survivor and slain. Many children enter, vicariously, the world of writers of Hughes's stature through the work of other, perhaps lesser, poets. Such an approach is unnecessary here, and the good fortune is the adult's as well as the child's.

—Charles Causley

———

HULL, Katharine, and WHITLOCK, Pamela. British. **HULL, Katharine:** Born in London, 18 July 1921. Educated at St. Mary's Convent, Ascot, Berkshire; Lady Margaret Hall, Oxford. Served in the Women's Royal Air Force, 1941–45: Flying Officer. Married Paul Buxton in 1950 (divorced 1970); two sons and one daughter. *Died in November 1977.* **WHITLOCK, Pamela (Frances):** Born in Penang, Malaysia, 21 March 1920. Educated at St. Mary's Convent, Ascot, Berkshire, 1934–39. Served in the Women's Royal Air Force, 1941–45. Married John Bell in 1954; five daughters. Publicity assistant, Jonathan Cape, publishers, London, 1939–40; children's books editor, Collins, publishers, London, 1946–52, and founding editor, *Collins Magazine,* 1947–52; children's books editor, Oxford University Press, in the 1950's. *Died 3 June 1982.*

PUBLICATIONS FOR CHILDREN

Fiction (illustrated by Pamela Whitlock)

The Far-Distant Oxus. London, Cape, 1937; New York, Macmillan, 1938.
Escape to Persia. London, Cape, 1938; New York, Macmillan, 1939.
Oxus in Summer. London, Cape, 1939; New York, Macmillan, 1940.
Crowns. London, Cape, 1947.

Other by Pamela Whitlock

Editor, *All Day Long: An Anthology of Poetry for Children,* illustrated by Joan Hassall. London, Oxford University Press, 1954.
Editor, *The Open Book: A Collection of Stories, Essays, Poems, Songs and Music,* illustrated by Marcia Lane Foster. London, Collins, and New York, Kenedy, 1956.

*   *   *

The initial claim to fame of Katharine Hull and Pamela Whitlock arose from the fact that they were teenagers when their first book was written. That *The Far-Distant Oxus* is still read with enjoyment over 50 years later indicates that it had more than curiosity value. It is basically a holiday adventure story with all the elements loved by young readers: ponies, camping, and an absence of interfering adults. Readers identify with the exploits of the six children on Exmoor because they imagine they would enjoy this sort of self-directed holiday. It is full of incident, ranging from the trivial to the epic, but the difficulties they encounter are not ignored. The journey by raft down the "Oxus" to the sea, for instance is undertaken with never a thought of how they will get back against the current.

Although there are obvious parallels with writers like Arthur Ransome and M.E. Atkinson, there is nothing imitative about *The*

Far-Distant Oxus and its sequels. The authors had a direct, clear style, and the dialogue and continuous action, pared of unnecessary description, carry the reader through the now unfashionable length of the stories. There is, however, a certain amateurish quality in the writing. The characterisation is less detailed and deep than it might be and the children have a tendency to make speeches rather than to talk.

This is not true of the more mature *Crowns,* a later book not in the Oxus sequence. This is also wish-fulfilment of a kind in which four cousins invent a private kingdom where they can order things to suit their own natures: romantic, organising, impulsive, or solitary and contemplative. Through their imaginings they discover more about what they want in life and what they are. Their "real" lives—comfortable, middle-class, and monied—are sharply observed and their secret world vividly imagined.

—Valerie Brinkley-Willsher

HULME BEAMAN, S.G.   See **BEAMAN, S.G. Hulme.**

HUNT, Francesca.   See **HOLLAND, Isabelle.**

HUNT, Irene. American. Born in Newton, Illinois, 18 May 1907. Educated at the University of Illinois, Urbana, B.A. 1939; University of Minnesota, Minneapolis, M.A. 1946; University of Colorado, Boulder. French and English teacher, Oak Park public schools, Illinois, 1930–45; Instructor in Psychology, University of South Dakota, Vermillion, 1946–50; teacher, 1950–65, and director of Language Arts, 1965–69, Cicero public schools, Illinois. Recipient: American Library Association Newbery Medal, 1967. Address: 2591 Countryside Boulevard, Clearwater, Florida 33519, U.S.A.

PUBLICATIONS FOR CHILDREN

Fiction

Across Five Aprils.   Chicago, Follett, 1964; London, Bodley Head, 1965.
Up a Road Slowly.   Chicago, Follett, 1966; London, Macdonald, 1967.
Trail of Apple Blossoms, illustrated by Don Bolognese.   Chicago, Follett, 1968; London, Blackie, 1970.
No Promises in the Wind.   Chicago, Follett, 1970.
The Lottery Rose.   New York, Scribner, 1976.
William.   New York, Scribner, 1977.
Claws of a Young Century.   New York, Scribner, 1980.
The Everlasting Hills.   New York, Scribner, 1985.

*

Manuscript Collection: Kerlan Collection, University of Minnesota, Minneapolis.

*   *   *

With her first book, *Across Five Aprils,* Irene Hunt established herself as one of America's finest historical novelists. The story begins with the outbreak of the Civil War in April 1861 and ends in April 1865, shortly after the conflict has ended. Far from the actual battle scenes, the Creightons, on their farm in southern Illinois, feel the cruel impact of war, caught as they are between the North and South. The scope of the narrative is broad, yet details of family life are intimate. The telling is poetic, compassionate, and sometimes angry.

Up a Road Slowly, perhaps the author's best-known novel, tells of a girl's growing up. When the book was awarded the Newbery Medal in 1967, Hunt said in her acceptance speech:

> Often children are troubled and in a state of guilt. One can say to them, "You are not unique. There is in all of us only a thin veneer of civilization that separates us from the primitive." It is in books that one finds there are other cowards in the world, other youngsters who are ashamed of their environment, other people who have strange, dark thoughts, who have had experiences too ugly to admit. Julie, in *Up a Road Slowly,* is not set apart by virtue of her high-mindedness or moral values. But for a watchful family she might well have stepped into the same trouble in which some of her young readers may find themselves.…

Hunt's third book, *Trail of Apple Blossoms,* recreates the life and times of John Chapman, known as Johnny Appleseed. In the early 1800's this American folk hero traveled alone through the Ohio Valley, planting apple seeds and seedling trees as he went. *Trail of Apple Blossoms* is not a biography, but a historical novel, picturing Johnny Appleseed as he may have been—a heroic man with a reverence for life whose beneficent influence touched pioneer America.

No Promises in the Wind is a story of the United States in 1932, in the depths of the Great Depression. During this troubled time, bands of children took to the roads and roamed the country, eking out an existence as best they could. The book follows the adventures of two of these children, Josh Grondowski and his brother Joey, as they run away from their home in Chicago and wander south to Louisiana where they join a carnival. While the characterizations, particularly those of the brothers, are strong, the reader is likely to remember the story most for its realistic picture of the Depression in America.

The Lottery Rose begins with the grim story of George Burgess, a battered child. Misunderstood at school, brutally abused at home, he centers all his affection and hope on the rosebush he won in a lottery. Removed from his home and placed in a school for boys, he resists the kindness he is shown. It is only gradually, through the patience of teachers and his involvement in someone else's tragedy, that he begins to reach out to others. Hunt's novel is searching, poignant, and uncompromisingly honest.

William is a novel of contemporary life in the American Deep South. Two divided families are drawn together for the strength and understanding that one can give the other. The fact that one family is black and the other white is only incidental to the story, which deals with the crises that rise from the interwoven relationships of the characters. The young hero, growing from childhood to adolescence, learns the meaning of Heraclitus's words, "As all things flow, nothing abides. Into the same river one cannot step twice."

Claws of a Young Century spans the years from 1900 to 1918. The heroine, Ellen Archer, is dedicated to the struggle for women's rights in America. Separated from her husband, who travels the world as a foreign correspondent, she leads a life considered unconventional and strange for a woman of her generation. Many characters, some of them historic figures, appear against the backdrop of the Boer War, events leading up to World War I, and the war itself. It is a sweeping story of triumph and tragedy.

The Everlasting Hills is set in 1936 in the Colorado Rockies. The protagonist is Jeremy, a 12-year-old, mentally handicapped boy who lives with his father and sister Bethany. When Bethany falls in love Jeremy feels he can no longer depend on her and runs away, to live eventually with the old local hermit Ishmael. The book charts Jeremy's growth to a responsible teenager, primarily through the new, this time reciprocal and giving friendship with Ishmael. Their relationship and characters are delicately portrayed, and reveal some of Hunt's finest qualities.

—Clyde Robert Bulla

———

HUNT, Mabel Leigh. American. Born in Coatesville, Indiana, 1 November 1892. Educated at DePauw University, Greencastle, Indiana, 1910–12; Western Reserve University Library School, Cleveland, 1923–24. Children's and branch librarian, Indianapolis, 1926–38. *Died 3 September 1971.*

PUBLICATIONS FOR CHILDREN

Fiction

Lucinda, A Little Girl of 1860, illustrated by Cameron Wright. New York, Stokes, 1934.
The Boy Who Had No Birthday, illustrated by Cameron Wright. New York, Stokes, 1935.
Little Girl with Seven Names, illustrated by Grace Paull. New York, Stokes, 1936.
Susan, Beware!, illustrated by Mildred Boyle. New York, Stokes, 1937.
Benjie's Hat, illustrated by Grace Paull. New York, Stokes, 1938.
Little Grey Gown, illustrated by Ilse Bischoff. New York, Stokes, 1939.
Michel's Island, illustrated by Kate Seredy. New York, Stokes, 1940.
John of Pudding Lane, illustrated by Clotilde Funk. New York, Stokes, 1941.
Billy Button's Butter'd Biscuit, illustrated by Katherine Milhous. New York, Stokes, 1941; London, Standard Art Book Company, 1943.
Corn-Belt Billy, illustrated by Kurt Wiese. New York, Grosset and Dunlap, 1942.
Peter Piper's Pickled Peppers, illustrated by Katherine Milhous. New York, Stokes, 1942; London, Standard Art Book Company, 1943.
The Peddler's Clock, illustrated by Elizabeth Orton Jones. New York, Grosset and Dunlap, 1943.
Young Man of the House, illustrated by Louis Slobodkin. Philadelphia, Lippincott, 1944.
Sibby Botherbox, illustrated by Marjory Collison. Philadelphia, Lippincott, 1945.
Such a Kind World, illustrated by Edna Potter. New York, Grosset and Dunlap, 1947.
The Double Birthday Present, illustrated by Elinore Blaisdell. Philadelphia, Lippincott, 1947.
Matilda's Buttons, illustrated by Elinore Blaisdell. Philadelphia, Lippincott, 1948.
The Wonderful Baker, illustrated by Grace Paull. Philadelphia, Lippincott, 1950.
The 69th Grandchild, illustrated by Elinore Blaisdell. Philadel-

phia, Lippincott, 1951.
Ladycake Farm, illustrated by Clotilde Funk. Philadelphia, Lippincott, 1952.
Singing among Strangers, illustrated by Irene Gibian. Philadelphia, Lippincott, 1954.
Miss Jellytot's Visit, illustrated by Velma Ilsley. Philadelphia, Lippincott, 1955.
Stars for Cristy, illustrated by Velma Ilsley. Philadelphia, Lippincott, 1956; London, Blackie, 1958.
Cristy at Skippinghills, illustrated by Velma Ilsley. Philadelphia, Lippincott, 1958; London, Blackie, 1960.
Cupola House, illustrated by Nora S. Unwin. Philadelphia, Lippincott, 1961.
Johnny-Up and Johnny-Down, illustrated by Harold Berson. Philadelphia, Lippincott, 1962.
Beggar's Daughter. Philadelphia, Lippincott, 1963.

Other

"Have You See Tom Thumb?" (biography of Charles Sherwood Stratton), illustrated by Fritz Eichenberg. New York, Stokes, 1942.
Better Known as Johnny Appleseed, illustrated by James Daugherty. Philadelphia, Lippincott, 1950.
Tomorrow Will Be Bright (reader), illustrated by Tommy Shoemaker. Boston, Ginn, 1958.

*

Manuscript Collection: Kerlan Collection, University of Minnesota, Minneapolis.

*   *   *

An author whose books appeal chiefly to pre-teenage girls, Mabel Leigh Hunt drew on her Quaker upbringing for several of her stories. *Lucinda,* her first book, the story of an Indiana Quaker child during the Civil War, has been praised for its well-chiseled prose and for the author's power to evoke the feeling of the Indiana countryside. A second book about a Quaker child, *Little Girl with Seven Names* has retained its popularity, dealing as it does with a perennial childhood problem, the child who is teased in school because she is different. In Melissa-Louisa-Amanda-Miranda-Cynthia-Jane-Farlow's case, it is not her Quaker upbringing which brings her ridicule from her schoolmates, but her excessively long name. The ingenious way in which Melissa Louisa manages to rid herself of a couple of her forenames is the main thrust of the slim plot of this warm little book.

Miss Jellytot's Visit is the story of Kate O'Dea, who, after her mother has had a visitor, decides that she, too, wishes to be treated as a guest, and who, as Miss Jellytot, comes for a six-day "visit" to the O'Dea family. One of the first books to deal in a realistic, sympathetic way with a mother-child relationship, this gently humorous story still appeals to girls in the early grades.

Ladycake Farm, although it has been kept in print, has not fared as well as some of her other books at the hands of contemporary critics. One of the first books to attempt a realistic and sympathetic portrayal of blacks, it deals with a black family which buys a farm in a previously all-white area. Hard work and determination lead to the family's acceptance by their neighbors at the end of the story, but the father's advice to his children to smile in the face of insults has been felt by many reviewers to be degrading. In comparison with most current fiction for children about blacks, *Ladycake Farm* now seems dated; few children will read it with pleasure.

Hunt's juvenile biographies are characterized by meticulous research and a feeling for the kind of interesting detail which serves to make the period come alive for a young reader. Still in print, her

Better Known as Johnny Appleseed, the life of the legendary John Chapman, was a Newbery Honor Book in 1951. Also well and accurately written is *"Have You Seen Tom Thumb?,"* a biography of the midget Charles Sherwood Stratton.

—Margaret F. Maxwell

———

HUNT, Peter (Leonard). British. Born in Rugby, Warwickshire, 2 September 1945. Educated at the University College of Wales, Aberystwyth, 1963–67, B.A. in English 1966, M.A. 1969; University of Wales, Cardiff, Ph.D. 1981. Married Sarah Wilkinson in 1981; three daughters. Lecturer in English, University of Wales Institute of Science and Technology, Cardiff, 1968–87. Since 1988 Senior Lecturer in English, University of Wales, Cardiff. Visiting Professor, University of Michigan, Ann Arbor, 1977; Visiting Lecturer, Massachusetts Institute of Technology, Cambridge, 1982. From 1983 Principal Associate, John Kirkman Communication Consultancy. Fellow, Institute of Scientific and Technical Communicators. Recipient: Society for Technical Communication (U.S.A.) award, 1987. Address: West Sundial Cottage, Downend, Horsley, Stroud, Gloucestershire GL6 0PF, England.

PUBLICATIONS FOR CHILDREN

Fiction

The Maps of Time. London, MacRae, 1983.
A Step Off the Path. London, MacRae, 1985.
Backtrack. London, MacRae, 1986.
Sue and the Honey Machine, illustrated by Duncan Smith. London, MacRae, 1989.
Fay Cow and the Mystery of the Missing Milk, illustrated by Duncan Smith. London, MacRae, 1989.
Going Up. London, MacRae, 1989.

PUBLICATIONS FOR ADULTS

Other

Children's Book Research in Britain. Cardiff, University of Wales, 1977; revised edition, with Beth Humphries and Sarah Wilkinson, 1982.

Editor, *Further Approaches to Research in Children's Literature.* Cardiff, University of Wales, 1982.
Editor, *Bevis,* by Richard Jefferies. Oxford, Oxford University Press, 1989.
Editor, *Critical Approaches to Children's Literature.* London, Routledge, 1989.

*

Peter Hunt comments:

As a professional academic, and critic of children's books, I feel that children should be treated with the greatest respect: and so, my first three novels are consciously experimental—trying to push back the possibilities of narrative and of style. As such, they are a "difficult" read, but that perhaps is one way to challenge the sophistication of other media. My newer books try to reach a wider audience by making style and structure less complex, while refusing to compromise on viewpoint and content. I hope that my commitment to narrative theory and the intelligence of developing readers comes out in the books.

*　　*　　*

The transition from critic to writer is so tricky that it is not surprising so few have attempted it. One who has successfully transferred from being a writer on children's books to a writer of them is Peter Hunt. Well known for his series of essays on aspects of children's literature which appeared before his first novel was published, Hunt must be one of the few writers for young people to possess a Ph.D. in children's literature. His intellectually rigorous articles have been a regular feature of the journal *Signal.* Hunt's attitude towards children's books is illuminated by his three novels for young people and reinforces his belief that children's books benefit from experimentation.

The Maps of Time uses themes of fantasy, combines them with reality, and also comments on the art of telling stories. Four teenagers are on a camping holiday with Simon, a curate, and the younger, introverted Sam. Sam is a fascinating character whose personality emerges slowly in the slight glimpses the reader is given and whose full depth is hardly realised by the others in the party. His powers, recognised by the mysterious Harald, centre around a series of maps and a pencil Sam has bought in a secondhand bookshop in Hay on Wye. As the story emerges it is discovered that Sam can restore a part of the country to the last century by drawing around the map in pencil. This part of the narrative covers the main body of the book until a particularly climatic event occurs. Hunt then provides the reader with four different versions of subsequent events: one each from two of the teenagers which shows that the love affair that appears to have developed between them is in fact one-sided, one told through Sam's eyes, and one that could possibly have been the truth. The final chapter brings these threads together, only to end on a note of uncertainty. *The Maps of Time* is a skilfully constructed piece of writing, with subtle characterisation often developing through oblique glimpses of personality and some felicities of style; Sam, for instance, is introduced to the reader as "hot and sweating and four years behind the others."

A Step Off the Path is also experimental but in this case the attempt to be consistently clever seems to have overridden other considerations. A group of characters who might have stepped out of an Iris Murdoch novel (with names to match) is thrown together in a commune on the England-Wales border. While the four elder children—Seb, Perdy, Tim, and Anna—spend a camping weekend helping the last descendants of King Arthur's court escape over the border, fighting treachery both within and outside their ranks, Jo, Seb's sister, stays at home telling a remarkably similar story to the twins, Matt and Jassy. However, where does the reality start and the fiction end, the author asks, to the accompaniment of a series of quotations from the likes of D.H. Lawrence and Cyril Connolly and apposite comments from the novel's characters. Although the book contains some pleasing features (the Arthurian tribe is uncompromisingly realistic, Merlin being a particularly powerful creation), it fails mainly because it is too explicit and wordy. Hunt's first book benefitted as much by what was implied rather than stated: with some judicious pruning *A Step Off the Path* might have achieved the same powerful effect.

Nevertheless there is nothing too clever about *Backtrack,* Hunt's most recent novel. An almost straightforward exposition of detection, it loses none of its effect by being more simple. Rill and Jack, thrown together by accident, develop a fascinating love-hate relationship as they unravel another accident which happened 70 years previously and in which, by chance, both of their great uncles were involved. The plots they discover change so quickly that again it is difficult to distinguish between fact and fiction, a feature emphasised by the apparently contemporary references to the accident scattered through the book which equally could be genuine or fabricated. *Backtrack* gets to the same point as *A Step Off the Path*; however, it also successfully says what it wants to say and encompasses the fascinatingly quirky relationship between the two main protagonists.

Where does Hunt go now? Having produced three novels which experiment with form and time, does he want to say more on the subject or experiment with writing for a less sophisticated group, for instance? His writings have not often achieved easy popularity with either critics or children. There are some who would maintain that for this reason he would be wise not to pursue any experimentation. However, Hunt in his critic mode would be the first to say that children's tastes cannot be so easily assessed. There is a significant number of young people, not necessarily the most sophisticated or proficient readers, who would find these books both rewarding and beneficial.

—Keith Barker

HUNTER, Kristin (Elaine, née Eggleston). American. Born in Philadelphia, Pennsylvania, 12 September 1931. Educated at Charles Sumner School and Magnolia Public School, both Philadelphia; Haddon Heights High School, New Jersey, graduated 1947; University of Pennsylvania, Philadelphia, 1947–51, B.S. in education 1951. Married 1) Joseph Hunter in 1952 (divorced 1962); 2) John I. Lattany in 1968. Philadelphia columnist and feature writer, Pittsburgh *Courier*, 1946–52; teacher, Camden, New Jersey, 1951; copywriter, Lavenson Bureau of Advertising, Philadelphia, 1952–59; research assistant, School of Social Work, University of Pennsylvania, 1961–62; copywriter, Wermen and Schorr, Philadelphia, 1962–63; information officer, City of Philadelphia, 1963–64, 1965–66; director of health services, Temple University, Philadelphia, 1971–72; director, Walt Whitman Poetry Center, Camden, 1978–79. Lecturer in Creative Writing, 1972–79, Adjunct Professor of English, 1980–83, and since 1983 Senior Lecturer in English, University of Pennsylvania. Writer-in-residence, Emory University, Atlanta, 1979. Recipient: Fund for the Republic prize, for television documentary, 1955; Whitney fellowship, 1959; Bread Loaf Writers Conference De Voto fellowship, 1965; Sigma Delta Chi award, for reporting, 1968; National Council on Interracial Books for Children award, 1968; National Conference of Christians and Jews Brotherhood award, 1969; Christopher award, 1974; Drexel citation, 1981; New Jersey Council on the Arts fellowship, 1982, 1985; Pennsylvania Council on the Arts fellowship, 1983. Agent: Don Congdon Associates, 156 Fifth Avenue, Suite 625, New York, New York 10010. Address: 721 Warwick Road, Magnolia, New Jersey 08049, U.S.A.

PUBLICATIONS FOR CHILDREN

Fiction

The Soul-Brothers and Sister Lou. New York, Scribner, 1968; London, Macdonald, 1971.
Boss Cat, illustrated by Harold Franklin. New York, Scribner, 1971.
The Pool Table War. Boston, Houghton Mifflin, 1972.
Uncle Daniel and the Raccoon. Boston, Houghton Mifflin, 1972.
Guests in the Promised Land: Stories. New York, Scribner, 1973.
Lou in the Limelight. New York, Scribner, 1981.

PUBLICATIONS FOR ADULTS

Novels

God Bless the Child. New York, Scribner, 1964; London, Muller, 1965.
The Landlord. New York, Scribner, 1966; London, Pan, 1970.
The Survivors. New York, Scribner, 1975.
The Lakestown Rebellion. New York, Scribner, 1978.

Plays

The Double Edge (produced Philadelphia, 1965).

Television Play: *Minority of One,* 1956.

*   *   *

Kristin Hunter's considerable reputation is based on a small body of work. The novel *The Soul-Brothers and Sister Lou,* the short stories *Guests in the Promised Land,* and the short humorous tale *Boss Cat* are all set in the same environment, the overcrowded, poor, mainly black, urban ghettos of the East Coast. In *Sister Lou* a 14-year-old girl sees her friends on the street hassled by police, denied every opportunity—even her own family distrusts them. She sees her mother always afraid of the unknown, entrapped by her fear of need, holding back her son from any chance to make his own way. There are dirt, anger, ugliness, and fear in Hunter's ghetto—the police fatally shoot Lou's unarmed friend, mistaking his epilepsy for defiance. The novel reflects the 1960's. Afro-consciousness is emerging, anger is intensifying. But there is strong love in the families that struggle together and dance together. Sister Lou ends up with a successful rock group and money for college, an ending which has been attacked as contrived. It may be statistically unlikely, but it fits the mood of the book, the essentially undaunted optimism of the author whose unequivocal message is that the spark of life burns bright among the stereotyped disadvantaged. The stories in *Guests in the Promised Land* expand and reinforce this message. Time has moved on and drugs have moved onto the streets as yet another hazard for those growing up there. A stretch in prison teaches Junior the realities of being a small-time crook; Little David talks the King Kongs out of rumbling with the Kools; and Robert will not settle for being a guest in the promised land and reacts with violence and destruction at the white man's country club.

Children's books have generally ignored or romanticized ghetto life. Hunter's work is optimistic but not in any way idealized. Her vision is steely when it views cruelty or discrimination. Her books open a salutary window on this world for young people of other cultures and other backgrounds, but for those who know her world and live there, suddenly there is someone who not only understands, but tells it like it is.

—Brigitte Weeks

HUNTER, (Maureen) Mollie (née McVeigh). British. Born in Longniddry, East Lothian, 30 June 1922. Educated at Preston Lodge School, East Lothian. Married Thomas McIlwraith in 1940; two sons. May Hill Arbuthnot Lecturer, 1975. Recipient: Scottish Arts Council Literary award, 1972, 1977; Child Study Committee award, 1972; Library Association Carnegie Medal, 1975. Agent: A.M. Heath and Co. Ltd., 79 St. Martin's Lane, London WC2N 4AA, England; or, McIntosh and Otis Inc., 475 Fifth Avenue, New York,

New York 10017, U.S.A. Address: The Shieling, Milton, by Drumnadrochit, Inverness-shire IV3 6UA, Scotland.

PUBLICATIONS FOR CHILDREN

Fiction

Patrick Kentigern Keenan, illustrated by Charles Keeping. London, Blackie, 1963; as *The Smartest Man in Ireland,* New York, Funk and Wagnalls, 1965.
Hi Johnny, illustrated by Drake Brookshaw. London, Evans, 1963.
The Kelpie's Pearls, illustrated by Charles Keeping. London, Blackie, 1964; New York, Funk and Wagnalls, 1966.
The Spanish Letters, illustrated by Elizabeth Grant. London, Evans, 1964; New York, Funk and Wagnalls, 1967.
A Pistol in Greenyards, illustrated by Elizabeth Grant. London, Evans, 1965; New York, Funk and Wagnalls, 1968.
The Ghosts of Glencoe. London, Evans, 1966; New York, Funk and Wagnalls, 1969.
Thomas and the Warlock, illustrated by Charles Keeping. London, Blackie, and New York, Funk and Wagnalls, 1967.
The Ferlie, illustrated by Michal Morse. London, Blackie, and New York, Funk and Wagnalls, 1968.
The Bodach, illustrated by Gareth Floyd. London, Blackie, 1970; as *The Walking Stones,* New York, Harper, 1970.
The Lothian Run. New York, Funk and Wagnalls, 1970; London, Hamish Hamilton, 1971.
The 13th Member. New York, Harper, and London, Hamish Hamilton, 1971.
The Haunted Mountain, illustrated by Trevor Ridley. London, Hamish Hamilton, and New York, Harper, 1972.
A Sound of Chariots. New York, Harper, 1972; London, Hamish Hamilton, 1973.
The Stronghold. New York, Harper, and London, Hamish Hamilton, 1974.
A Stranger Came Ashore. London, Hamish Hamilton, and New York, Harper, 1975.
The Wicked One. London, Hamish Hamilton, and New York, Harper, 1977.
A Furl of Fairy Wind, illustrated by Stephen Gammell. New York, Harper, 1977.
The Third Eye. London, Hamish Hamilton, and New York, Harper, 1979.
You Never Knew Her as I Did! London, Hamish Hamilton, and New York, Harper, 1981.
The Knight of the Golden Plain, illustrated by Marc Simont. London, Hamish Hamilton, and New York, Harper, 1983.
The Dragonfly Years. London, Hamish Hamilton, 1983; as *Hold on to Love,* New York, Harper, 1984.
I'll Go My Own Way. London, Hamish Hamilton, 1985; as *Cat, Herself,* New York, Harper, 1986.
The Three-Day Enchantment, illustrated by Marc Simont. New York, Harper, 1985.
Escape from Loch Leven. Edinburgh, Canongate, 1987.
The Mermaid Summer. London, Hamish Hamilton, and New York, Harper, 1988.

Other

Flora MacDonald and Bonnie Prince Charlie. London, Methuen, 1987.

PUBLICATIONS FOR ADULTS

Plays

A Love-Song for My Lady (produced Inverness, 1961). London, Evans, 1961.
Stay for an Answer (produced Inverness, 1962). London, French, 1962.

Other

Talent Is Not Enough: Mollie Hunter on Writing for Children. New York, Harper, 1976.

*

Mollie Hunter comments:

I write for children because I like them as *people,* because I'm primarily a storyteller, and because the kind of tales I can spin for them are those that seem naturally to be suggested by a life-long exploration of my own country's folklore and history. The books that have resulted fall into three categories—fantasy for the younger reader, historical novels for those in their early teens, and "realistic" novels for young adults. The fantasies subscribe to the tradition of the orally transmitted folktale, in which the simplicity of the language is more apparent than real—in that it is this very quality which may sustain a high degree of poetic imagery, and which thus may be capable also of projecting deep and universal truths. In the historical novels, although the plots derive from the past of my own country, the themes again are still always those which apply universally, and in which the reader may therefore see his or her own emotions reflected. The latter is yet again the case with the "realistic" novels which deal with personal relationships set against a social tapestry of latter-day Scotland, but in which the setting is still incidental to the theme that carries the story's true significance. All three types of book, in effect, are simply varying facets of what I conceive to be the proper function of any writer—i.e., to entertain, and in the course of this to express something of one's own philosophy. To attempt this for young readers, I find, is a discipline as rewarding as it is exacting.

*   *   *

Mollie Hunter is one of Scotland's most important writers of fiction for older children and teenagers, and as a writer she moves with seeming ease from such a painstakingly reconstructed historical narrative (and by this I do not mean to suggest that the writing is ever turgid, laboured, or weighed down by the fruits of her research—that is never the case) as *Escape from Loch Leven,* a novel that recounts how Mary Queen of Scots, held in thrall at Loch Leven Castle, manages to escape with the assistance of a young page boy, Will Douglas, to her most recent published work, *The Mermaid Summer,* which sees her returning to her other principal preoccupation as an imaginative writer, how the forces of magic and folklore can suddenly impinge upon young, innocent lives. In *The Mermaid Summer* a fisherman learns to rue the day that he denied the existence of mermaids, and the revenge that the mermaid wreaks upon Eric Anderson extends to his grandchildren and, indeed, to all the male inhabitants of the village where they live. They are later obliged to listen to the warnings and advice of a sly old crone nicknamed "the Howdy," whom they fear almost as much as the mermaid herself. Only by paying heed to the old woman's words can they escape from the terrible fate that awaits them all.

What is perhaps most memorable about Hunter's work is the speed and economy of her writing. Like all good work, her novels capture the hearts and minds of her readers from the very first sentence—just enough is told of what is to come to whet one's appetite for the next sentence, and what is told is always spoken in a very particular voice, a voice peculiar to that novel alone, a voice that always sounds like the voice of a real person sitting next to you, whispering some matter of real concern into your ear. It is a very effective narrative technique, as in the opening of *Escape from Loch Leven*: "News of her has come at last from England; and it is the worst I ever dreaded to hear." Who is the "her" that is being spoken of? And why is the news so much to be dreaded? The fact is that we dearly wish to know, and we wish to know quickly—so we read on. The opening words of *The Mermaid Summer* are equally effective, but in a slightly different way: "About a hundred years ago, they say, there was a mermaid who ruled the cold, wild sea that washes around northern lands." That is a more impersonal voice, and the statement has a wide, generalising sweep because that is the kind of information the author needs to give us from the start before settling down to relate the particular, dire consequences of this baldly stated fact. But note the cunning use of the turn of phrase "they say." There is just a spice of mystery in that—something compellingly strange, as if, like Eric Anderson himself, it wouldn't be too surprising if we were to take the tale with a pinch of salt—just as Eric Anderson himself does, of course, with the most terrible and terrifying consequences. Hunter has written more than a dozen novels for young people, and each one has its own enthralling, captivating qualities. Most of all perhaps they have the quality of compulsive readability.

—Michael Glover

HUNTER, Norman (George Lorimer). British. Born in Sydenham, Kent, 23 November 1899. Educated at Beckenham County School, Kent. Served in the London Irish Rifles, and at Headquarters, 9th Division, 1918–19. Married Sylvia Mary Rangel in 1923; one son and two daughters. Chief copywriter, S.H. Benson Ltd., London, 1938–49, P.N. Barrett Company, Johannesburg, 1949–58, and Central Advertising Ltd., Johannesburg, 1958–70. Also a conjurer: has performed at Maskelyne's Theatre of Magic, St. George's Hall, London, and at the Little Theatre, London; Associate of the Inner Magic Circle. Address: 23 St. Olave's Close, Penton Road, Staines, Middlesex TW18 2LH, England.

PUBLICATIONS FOR CHILDREN

Fiction

The Bad Barons of Crashbania, illustrated by Eve Garnett. Oxford, Blackwell, 1932.
The Incredible Adventures of Professor Branestawm, illustrated by W. Heath Robinson. London, Lane, 1933.
Professor Branestawm's Treasure Hunt and Other Incredible Adventures, illustrated by James Arnold. London, Lane, 1937.
Larky Legends, illustrated by James Arnold. London, Lane, 1938; abridged edition, as *The Dribblesome Teapots and Other Incredible Stories*, London, Bodley Head, 1969.
Stories of Professor Branestawm, illustrated by W. Heath Robinson. Leeds, E.J. Arnold, 1939.
Jingle Tales. London, Warne, 1941.
The Peculiar Triumph of Professor Branestawm, illustrated by George Adamson. London, Bodley Head, 1970.
The Home-Made Dragon and Other Incredible Stories, illustrated by Fritz Wegner. London, Bodley Head, 1971.
Professor Branestawm Up the Pole, illustrated by George Adamson. London, Bodley Head, 1972.
The Frantic Phantom and Other Incredible Stories, illustrated by Geraldine Spence. London, Bodley Head, 1973.
Wizards Are a Nuisance, illustrated by Quentin Blake. London, BBC Publications, 1973.

Professor Branestawm's Great Revolution, illustrated by David Hughes. London, Bodley Head, 1974.
Dust-Up at the Royal Disco, illustrated by Fritz Wegner. London, Bodley Head, 1975.
Professor Branestawm 'round the Bend, illustrated by Derek Cousins. London, Bodley Head, 1977.
Count Bakwerdz on the Carpet, illustrated by Babette Cole. London, Bodley Head, 1979.
Professor Branestawm's Perilous Pudding, illustrated by Derek Cousins. London, Bodley Head, 1979.
Sneeze and Be Slain and Other Incredible Stories, illustrated by Babette Cole. London, Bodley Head, 1980.
The Best of Branestawm. London, Bodley Head, 1980.
Professor Branestawm and the Wild Letters, illustrated by Gerald Rose. London, Bodley Head, 1981.
Professor Branestawm's Pocket Motor Car, illustrated by Gerald Rose. London, Bodley Head, 1981.
Professor Branestawm's Building Bust-Up, illustrated by Gerald Rose. London, Bodley Head, 1982.
Professor Branestawm's Mouse War, illustrated by Gerald Rose. London, Bodley Head, 1982.
Professor Branestawm's Crunchy Crockery, illustrated by Gerald Rose. London, Bodley Head, 1983.
Professor Branestawm's Hair-Raising Idea, illustrated by Gerald Rose. London, Bodley Head, 1983.

Other

Puffin Book of Magic, illustrated by Jill McDonald. London, Penguin, 1968; as *Norman Hunter's Book of Magic*, London, Bodley Head, 1974; as *The Wizard Book of Magic*, New York, Sterling, 1978.
Professor Branestawm's Dictionary, illustrated by Derek Cousins. London, Bodley Head, 1973.
Professor Branestawm's Compendium of Conundrums, Riddles, Puzzles, Brain-Twisters, and Dotty Descriptions, illustrated by Derek Cousins. London, Bodley Head, 1975.
Professor Branestawm's Do-It-Yourself Handbook, illustrated by Jill McDonald. London, Bodley Head, 1976.
Vanishing Ladies and Other Magic, illustrated by Jill McDonald. London, Bodley Head, 1978.

PUBLICATIONS FOR ADULTS

Other

Simplified Conjuring for All: A Collection of New Tricks Needing No Special Skill or Apparatus, With Suitable Patter. London, Pearson, 1923.
Advertising Through the Press: A Guide to Press Publicity. London, Pitman, 1925.
New and Easy Magic: A Further Series of Novel Magical Experiments Needing No Special Skill or Apparatus for Their Performance, With Suitable Patter. London, Pearson, 1925.
Hey Presto: A Book of Effects for Conjurers, illustrated by Sid Lorraine. London, Bagshawe, 1931.
New Conjuring Without Skill. London, Lane, 1935.
Successful Conjuring for Amateurs, edited by F.J. Camm. London, Pearson, 1951; as *Successful Magic for Amateurs*, New York, Arco, 1952; revised edition, as *Successful Conjuring*, Arco, 1964.

*

Norman Hunter comments:
I write two kinds of children's books—well, three kinds if you

include my books on magic and how-to-do-it. I began by writing stories about funny kings and queens in which I took plots from traditional fairy tales and bent them out of shape a bit. These stories have now developed into a series of adventures of the King and Queen of Incrediblania. The other books deal with the adventures of Professor Branestawm, a highly learned gentleman who spends so much time knowing about extraordinary things he has no time to think of ordinary ones. He invents machines which eventually turn on him and has the kind of adventures an absentminded professor might well have, only a great deal more so. The magic overflows into the stories to some extent because I frequently visit libraries, schools, book exhibitions, and bookshops and do a little magic show in which some of the magic is tied up with Professor Branestawm and his inventions. I am sometimes asked what age children my books appeal to. I think the Incrediblania stories are appreciated by children from about seven or perhaps younger, while the Professor Branestawm stories are for slightly older ones, say from nine, but a lot depends on the children. As the books are funny I also have a number of adult readers and I find mums and dads are quite happy to read my stories to their children and sometimes sneak the books away from the children to read themselves, which I like very much.

*　　*　　*

Sheer high spirits and exuberant good humour are the hallmarks of Norman Hunter's popular comic stories. *The Incredible Adventures of Professor Branestawm* and its sequel, *Professor Branestawm's Treasure Hunt,* were first published in the 1930's and have retained their comic appeal for children ever since. Taking the stock figure of the eccentric, absentminded Professor, Hunter made an engagingly dotty and unworldly character of him, gave his two faithful companions—Colonel Dedshott of the Catapult Cavaliers, none too bright but a loyal friend, and the much-tried housekeeper Mrs. Flittersnoop, always on the point of going off to stay with sister Aggie until the latest trouble is over—and involved them in a series of crazy misadventures arising from the Professor's weird machines, which never, of course, perform in exactly the way intended.

Some of these earlier stories, though they are enjoyed by children as much as ever, show their age now, with their emphasis, for instance, on radio broadcasting and mention of the long defunct Children's Hour. But Hunter has kept his hero up with the times, and since his own retirement and return to England from South Africa has published further Professor Branestawm collections, where the Professor shows himself quite at home with television, supermarkets, and so on (even if he falls foul of the Way Ahead and Right Outside Group of Advanced Artists by agreeing with Mrs. Flittersnoop that her little nephew could do better. The irate Artists take their revenge on the Professor's painting machine, "loosening screws and inserting plastic spanners of very bad design into the works"). Perhaps the humour of these later collections is slightly too sophisticated, compared to that of their predecessors, to suit the taste of the modern child, but the appeal still lies in the delightfully farcical situations and the author's command of comic language, with many incidental touches such as the alarm clock which "sounded more like Robin Hood's wedding in technicolour than an alarm clock." This is a very English type of humour, including the timeless setting of the little town of Great Pagwell with its municipal bureaucracy.

Hunter's other stories have been comic fairy tales. This is a difficult genre to tackle; the dangers of coyness and whimsy lie in wait, but Hunter avoids them, again by the genial verve of his language; who could resist the King of Incrediblania's comment that he sees "a most second-hand-looking person" coming down the street, or the remark that "horses are deliberately unsuitable on battleships." These stories are well served by the pleasingly ornate illustrations of Fritz Wegner, as was Professor Branestawm first by

Heath Robinson and later by George Adamson.

—Anthea Bell

———

HUNTER BLAIR, Pauline. See **CLARKE, Pauline.**

———

HURWITZ, Johanna (née Frank). American. Born in New York City, 9 October 1937. Educated at Queens College, Flushing, New York, 1955–58, B.A. in English 1958; Columbia University, New York, 1958–59, M.L.S. 1959. Married Uri Levi Hurwitz in 1962; one daughter and one son. Children's librarian, New York Public Library, 1959–64; Lecturer in Children's Literature, Queens College, 1965–68; librarian, Calhoun School, 1968–75, and New Hyde Park school district, 1975–77, both New York. Since 1978 children's librarian, Great Neck Public Library, New York. Visiting storyteller, New York Public Library, 1964–67; teacher of writer's workshops in children's literature, Hofstra University, Hempstead, New York, 1981, 1986. Recipient: Swedish Institute grant, 1988. Address: 10 Spruce Place, Great Neck, New York, 11021, U.S.A.

PUBLICATIONS FOR CHILDREN

Fiction

Busybody Nora, illustrated by Susan Jeschke. New York, Morrow, 1976.
Nora and Mrs. Mind-Your-Own-Business, illustrated by Susan Jeschke. New York, Morrow, 1977.
The Law of Gravity, illustrated by Ingrid Fetz. New York, Morrow, 1978.
Much Ado about Aldo, illustrated by John Wallner. New York, Morrow, 1978.
Aldo Applesauce, illustrated by John Wallner. New York, Morrow, 1979.
New Neighbors for Nora, illustrated by Susan Jeschke. New York, Morrow, 1979.
Once I Was a Plum Tree, illustrated by Ingrid Fetz. New York, Morrow, 1980.
Superduper Teddy, illustrated by Susan Jeschke. New York, Morrow, 1980.
Aldo Ice Cream, illustrated by John Wallner. New York, Morrow, 1981.
Baseball Fever, illustrated by Ray Cruz. New York, Morrow, 1981.
The Rabbi's Girls, illustrated by Pamela Johnson. New York, Morrow, 1982.
Tough-Luck Karen, illustrated by Diane deGroat. New York, Morrow, 1982.
Rip-Roaring Russell, illustrated by Lillian Hoban. New York, Morrow, 1983.
DeDe Takes Charge!, illustrated by Diane deGroat. New York, Morrow, 1984.
The Hot and Cold Summer, illustrated by Gail Owens. New York, Morrow, 1984.
The Adventures of Ali Baba Bernstein, illustrated by Gain Owens. New York, Morrow, 1985.
Russell Rides Again, illustrated by Lillian Hoban. New York, Morrow, 1985.

Hurricane Elaine, illustrated by Diane deGroat. New York, Morrow, 1986.

Yellow Blue Jay, illustrated by Donald Carrick. New York, Morrow, 1986.

Class Clown, illustrated by Sheila Hamanaka. New York, Morrow, 1987.

Russell Sprouts, illustrated by Lillian Hoban. New York, Morrow, 1987.

The Cold and Hot Winter, illustrated by Carolyn Ewing. New York, Morrow, 1988.

Teacher's Pet, illustrated by Sheila Hamanaka. New York, Morrow, 1988.

Hurray for Ali Baba Bernstein, illustrated by Gail Owens. New York, Morrow, 1989.

Other

Anne Frank: Life in Hiding, illustrated by Vera Rosenberry. Philadelphia, Jewish Publication Society, 1988.

*

Manuscript Collection: Kerlan Collection, University of Minnesota, Minneapolis.

Johanna Hurwitz comments:

More than anything else, I hope children gain pleasure from my books. I do not write with deep messages or hidden meanings. If upon completion of my book, the reader is eager to read another (by me or by someone else too), then I know I have been successful.

* * *

After 20 years as a children's librarian, Johanna Hurwitz knows what children like to read; her considerable writing talent and gentle but accurate sense of humor have enabled her to translate this knowledge into a series of successful short novels for elementary school children. In the typical Hurwitz novel, the protagonist is a likable young child facing common difficulties of childhood: making friends in a new school, getting along with siblings at home, and trying to find a place to fit in, both at home and in school. The children are always resourceful and amusing, but never ridiculous; their major problem is usually resolved by book's end.

A Hurwitz novel is like a finely-focused close-up photograph; the main character is well-defined, but other characters remain mostly in the background, furthering the plot as it relates to the central figure. This is not to say that Hurwitz can only describe childhood from a single point of view; it is often the case that characters who make cameo appearances in one story come into full focus as central figures in later works. Occasionally even incidents that have been described in one novel are encountered from another point of view in another book, such as the class play about French history which turns up in both *Tough-Luck Karen* and *DeDe Takes Charge!*. Hurwitz is adept at depicting the world according to fourth-grader Aldo Sossi, but works equally well from the perspectives of his middle sister Karen, older sister Elaine, and his best friend DeDe. The technique of concentrating on one personality at a time allows Hurwitz to develop indepth character portrayals without burdening her novels with a complexity beyond the grasp of her intended audience.

Hurwitz's novels for early elementary school, those about Nora, her brother Teddy, and their friend Russell, make excellent beginning chapter books for reading aloud. Each chapter is self-contained while furthering a more general plot, which provides for the closure sought by children around the first-grade level. Humorous twists and gentle irony abound as Hurwitz explores common experiences such as the first day of kindergarten, experimentation with crude language, and children's birthday parties. Often the adults as well as the children are apt to learn a few things, as when Russell gives his parents a report card evaluating their child-rearing skills.

But Hurwitz is at her best in novels involving upper-elementary to junior high children. Three especially fine novels involving two nine-year-olds and a girl of 13 demonstrate that Hurwitz is able to deal powerfully and poignantly with the more complex problems of growth and self-discovery, without abandoning her trademark humor. In *Baseball Fever* Ezra Kaufman attempts to reconcile his own interests with his father's diametrically opposed expectations. Karen Sossi, the heroine of *Tough-Luck Karen,* is a 13-year-old whose normal adolescent difficulties are complicated by her position as a middle child between two academically superior siblings. Cricket Kaufman faces a bewildering shift in self-image when for the first time in her life she is not the undisputed top student in her class (*Teacher's Pet*). In all three novels the protagonists demonstrate identifiable growth between the opening and the conclusion. Their problems are serious, but the Hurwitz touch, from gentle irony to all-out hilarity, makes getting to the solutions a joy as well as a challenge.

The only Hurwitz novels that do not work well are those in which the protagonists encounter difficulties that are more extraordinary than universal. She errs in treating circumstances such as the death of a parent (*The Rabbi's Girls*) and divorce (*DeDe Takes Charge!*) with much the same serio-comic attitude she employs when Aldo has difficulty making friends in his new school. There are undeniably lighter moments in the most dreadful circumstances; however, glossing over the intense pain in these novels makes their happy resolutions finally unconvincing.

An unfortunate aspect of Hurwitz's work is the occasional lapse into ethnic stereotypes. In two of her best works she makes the poorest student in the class a Hispanic in one case, and an oriental refugee in the other. These negative references are especially puzzling since she so rarely alludes to ethnicity at all, other than in *The Rabbi's Girls,* in which the Levin family encounters the pain of discrimination. While serious in themselves, these misjudgments are not frequent in Hurwitz's work, and could easily be edited out of future editions of the novels. Most of the time Hurwitz provides her young readers with believable heroes and heroines facing the common but important crises of childhood, and treats them to much laughter on the way to convincing, attainable solutions of their problems.

—Christine Doyle Francis

———

HUTCHINS, Pat (née Goundry). British. Born in Catterick Camp, Yorkshire, 18 June 1942. Educated at Darlington School of Art, County Durham, 1958–60, intermediate certificate; Leeds College of Art, 1960–62, national diploma in illustration. Married Laurence Hutchins in 1966; two children. Assistant art director, J. Walter Thompson advertising agency, London, 1963–66; lived in New York, 1966–68. Recipient: Library Association Kate Greenaway Medal, 1975. Address: 75 Flask Walk, London NW3 1ET, England.

PUBLICATIONS FOR CHILDREN (illustrated by the author)

Fiction

Rosie's Walk. New York, Macmillan, and London, Bodley Head, 1968.

Tom and Sam. New York, Macmillan, 1968; London, Bodley Head, 1969.
The Surprise Party. New York, Macmillan, 1969; London, Bodley Head, 1970.
Clocks and More Clocks. New York, Macmillan, and London, Bodley Head, 1970.
Changes, Changes. New York, Macmillan, and London, Bodley Head, 1971.
Titch. New York, Macmillan, 1971; London, Bodley Head, 1972.
Good Night, Owl. New York, Macmillan, 1972; London, Bodley Head, 1973.
The Silver Christmas Tree. New York, Macmillan, and London, Bodley Head, 1974.
The House That Sailed Away, illustrated by Laurence Hutchins. New York, Greenwillow, 1975; London, Bodley Head, 1976.
Follow That Bus!, illustrated by Laurence Hutchins. New York, Greenwillow, and London, Bodley Head, 1977.
Happy Birthday, Sam. New York, Greenwillow, and London, Bodley Head, 1978.
The Best Train Set Ever. New York, Greenwillow, 1978; London, Bodley Head, 1979.
One-Eyed Jake. New York, Greenwillow, and London, Bodley Head, 1979.
The Mona Lisa Mystery, illustrated by Laurence Hutchins. New York, Greenwillow, and London, Bodley Head, 1981.
1 Hunter. New York, Greenwillow, and London, Bodley Head, 1982.
You'll Soon Grow into Them, Titch. New York, Greenwillow, and London, Bodley Head, 1983.
The Curse of the Egyptian Mummy, illustrated by Laurence Hutchins. New York, Greenwillow, and London, Bodley Head, 1983.
King Henry's Palace. New York, Greenwillow, and London, Bodley Head, 1983.
The Very Worst Monster. New York, Greenwillow, and London, Bodley Head, 1985.
The Doorbell Rang. New York, Greenwillow, and London, Bodley Head, 1986.
Where's the Baby? New York, Greenwillow, and London, Bodley Head, 1988.

Verse

The Wind Blew. New York, Macmillan, and London, Bodley Head, 1974.
Don't Forget the Bacon! New York, Greenwillow, and London, Bodley Head, 1976.
The Tale of Thomas Mead. New York, Greenwillow, and London, Bodley Head, 1980.

*   *   *

If Pat Hutchins had only produced one book—*Rosie's Walk*—she would nevertheless have earned her place in *Twentieth-Century Children's Writers.* Yet *Rosie's Walk* has a text of a mere 36 words. It is a picture book, of course, and its art work (which shows Rosie the hen going for a walk "across the yard, around the pond…past the mill…under the beehives" and getting home in time for dinner) is strong and attractive. But it is neither the 36 words on their own nor the art work on its own that would entitle Hutchins to her entry: it is the brilliant interplay of the two, the assured use of dramatic irony. For young children listening to the story of Rosie, walking, will never hear a mention of the fox who, they can see from the pictures, is one step behind her, always tripped up (whether accidentally or intentionally is Hutchins's secret) by the strutting hen.
A close second to *Rosie's Walk* is *Good Night, Owl,* where, again,

the text plays a large part in the book's success. Owl tries to sleep—but all day long the birds and animals in his tree wake him up, each with its own cry; but when at nightfall the tree quietens down at last, then it is owl's turn to screech. In *Titch* Hutchins uses her talent with combined word and picture to show dramatically how the youngest member of a family—only allowed the smallest and most boring of options by his elder brother and sister—has to be content with a mere seed when it comes to gardening. But he plants the seed—which grows and grows.…
In a sequel, *You'll Soon Grow into Them, Titch,* careful picture watchers will pick up clues pointing to the arrival of a new baby in the family, someone to whom Titch, hitherto the youngest, can assign *his* cast-off clothes. Recently Hutchins has experimented with a Monster family, in *The Very Worst Monster* and *Where's the Baby?.* The Monsters may be green-nosed, long-eared, and clawed but, especially Grandma who sings the praises of the Baby no matter what misdemeanours he has been up to, they are immensely human and lovable.
This author-artist, whose every picture book is a magnet for young listeners and readers, has also created three extraordinary picture books that enticingly explore the importance of learning to read (*The Tale of Thomas Mead* "who never, ever learned to read") and basic mathematics: *1 Hunter* is a witty counting book, and in *The Doorbell Rang* Ma's 12 cookies, made for Victoria and Sam, have to be shared by an ever-increasing number of children as the doorbell rings…and rings.
Hutchins is an excellent storyteller. As an artist she naturally first turned to the picture book as her medium. But, gloriously alive to family lore and to children's fantasies, she has since written four attractive stories for under nines, each illustrated by her husband, Laurence Hutchins. *The House That Sailed Away* is the most complete and best planned of these: readers willingly adopt the dotty Hutchins family who sail away inside their house in a flood and find themselves on a desert island—with pirates, and treasure, and Grandma! The school stories, *Follow That Bus!, The Mona Lisa Mystery,* and *The Curse of the Egyptian Mummy* are funny, too, but more complex and, because less personal, lacking just that touch of sharp idiosyncrasy that is the hall-mark of a true Hutchins.

—Elaine Moss

———

ISH-KISHOR, Sulamith. American. Born in London, England, in 1896. Educated at Hunter College, New York. Recipient: Jewish Book Council of America Charles and Bertie Schwartz award, 1964, 1972; Association of Jewish Libraries Sydney Taylor award, 1969. *Died 23 June 1977.*

PUBLICATIONS FOR CHILDREN

Fiction

The Heaven on the Sea and Other Stories, illustrated by Penina Ish-Kishor. New York, Bloch, 1924.
Little Potato and Other Stories, illustrated by J. Russack. New York, Board of Education, 1937.
How the Weatherman Came, illustrated by Rebecca Andrews. New York, Board of Education, 1938.
The Palace of Eagles and Other Stories, illustrated by Alice Horodisch. New York, Shoulson Press, 1948.
The Stranger Within the Gates and Other Stories, illustrated by Alice

Horodisch. New York, Shoulson Press, 1948.
A Boy of Old Prague, illustrated by Ben Shahn. New York, Pantheon, 1963; London, Chatto and Windus, 1966.
Our Eddie. New York, Pantheon, 1969.
Drusilla: A Novel of the Emperor Hadrian, illustrated by Thomas Morley. New York, Pantheon, 1970.
The Master of Miracle: A New Novel of the Golem, illustrated by Arnold Lobel. New York, Harper, 1971.

Other

The Bible Story. New York, United Synagogue of America, 1921.
The Children's Story of the Bible. New York, Educational Stationery House, 1930.
Children's History of Israel from the Creation to the Present Time. New York, Jordan, 3 vols., 1930–33.
Jews to Remember, illustrated by Kyra Markham. New York, Hebrew Publishing Company, 1941.
American Promise: A History of Jews in the New World, illustrated by Grace Hick. New York, Behrman House, 1947.
Friday Night Stories, 1, 2, and 4. New York, Women's League of the United Synagogue of America, 3 vols., 1949.
The Carpet of Solomon: A Hebrew Legend, illustrated by Uri Shulevitz. New York, Pantheon, 1966.
Pathways Through the Jewish Holidays, edited by Benjamin Efron. New York, Ktav, 1967.

PUBLICATIONS FOR ADULTS

Other

Magnificent Hadrian: A Biography. New York, Minton Balch, and London, Gollancz, 1935.
Everyman's History of the Jews. New York, Fell, 1948.
How Theodor Herzl Created the Jewish National Fund. New York, Jewish National Fund, 1960.
Blessed Is the Daughter, with Meyer Waxman and Jacob Sloan. New York, Shengold, 1960.

*   *   *

Sulamith Ish-Kishor's writing reveals substantial and sure knowledge of her subject matter. Her contribution lies especially in two novels and a legend.

Her book *A Boy of Old Prague* represents a difficult feat. Tomás, a Christian boy, is bound to a Jewish family. He takes with him insidious, evil tales he has heard about the Jews. As he experiences life in the Ghetto, and a pogrom, he is drawn to Jews and develops compassion and understanding. The plight of the Jews in the 16th century is so skillfully related that the reader gains insight into the injustices dealt to them throughout history. Without pyrotechnics, the author lets her story unfold, and it is her understatement that gives the novel a quiet but gripping power. Ish-Kishor not only interprets the past but also illuminates the present, a true mark of excellence.

Our Eddie offers another facet of Jewish life. The story of the Raphel family, first in England and then in New York, centers on Eddie and on the rest of the family. There is keen perception of Eddie as a human being, and as the son of a man who cannot bring himself to a realization of what society apart from his own vision is like. This is a tapestry of a particular kind of Jewish life, full of emotion, conflict, and contrast. The author's reminiscences are deeply moving, agonizing at times, with a masterful blending of story and style.

Ish-Kishor retells a brief but important Hebrew legend in *The*

Carpet of Solomon. Her love for the tale is evident as she describes Solomon's dream in which he goes to the end of the Earth by means of a magic carpet. His humbling experiences draw him closer to the wisdom for which he is known. The author creates an appropriate atmosphere and sets a dream-like mood. The underlying message is delivered with no sermonizing.

Her knowledge of Jewish history, mores, and legends is enhanced by an intensity of style appropriate for each book. She had the touch of the craftsman coupled with an artistic use of language.

—Mae Durham Roger

———

JACKSON, Jesse. American. Born in Columbus, Ohio, 1 January 1908. Educated at Ohio State University, Columbus, 1927–29. Married Ann Newman in 1938; one daughter. Worked in boys' camps and with private youth agencies, and as a juvenile probation officer; worked for the Bureau of Economic Research. From 1974 Lecturer, Appalachian State University, Boone, North Carolina. Recipient: MacDowell Colony fellowship; National Council for the Social Studies Woodson award, 1975. D. Litt.: Appalachian State University, 1982. *Died 14 April 1983.*

PUBLICATIONS FOR CHILDREN

Fiction

Call Me Charley, illustrated by Doris Spiegel. New York, Harper, 1945.
Anchor Man, illustrated by Doris Spiegel. New York, Harper, 1947.
Room for Randy, illustrated by Frank Nicholas. New York, Friendship Press, 1957.
Charley Starts from Scratch. New York, Harper, 1958.
Tessie, illustrated by Harold James. New York, Harper, 1968.
The Sickest Don't Always Die the Quickest. New York, Doubleday, 1971.
The Fourteenth Cadillac. New York, Doubleday, 1972.

Other

Black in America: A Fight for Freedom, with Elaine Landau. New York, Messner, 1973.
Make a Joyful Noise unto the Lord! The Life of Mahalia Jackson, Queen of Gospel Singers. New York, Crowell, 1974.

*   *   *

Jesse Jackson wrote of ordinary people and ordinary events with extraordinary skill. He wrote of communication breakdowns at the family breakfast table, of high heel shoes which are too tight to be comfortable but also too new to discard, of Halloween night dances with masks and musicians, of nurturing hope, and of recurrent despair. Jackson's fictional people are not heroes and heroines, they are everyday mothers, fathers, sisters, brothers, nurses, doctors, printers, librarians, domestics—persons to be found in all communities. His novels of teenagers depict the struggles of young blacks for dignity and for excellence among their own people and among their white contemporaries. Portraits of whites as well as of blacks show individuals in turmoil, with not entirely dissimilar goals and dreams, frustrations, and fears.

Call Me Charley, Jackson's first novel, is a forthright story of a young black who has come to a white neighborhood and finds himself unwelcome on the block and in the school. It is only with time and effort that he wins some respect and friendship and is able to participate in group activities. The book ends with Charley still making adjustments; there are no easy solutions.

Tessie is the story of a Harlem girl who wins a scholarship to a Fifth Avenue private school. It is hard for Tessie, her father, her mother, her brother, her old Harlem friends, and her new school friends to relate to her changed roles. Tessie learns that she cannot please all the people in her life all of the time, and that she has to please herself as well as others. The ending of this book shows the beginning of Tessie's adjustment to life in two worlds; but it is only a beginning and the future remains uncertain. This story also rings true.

Jackson was one of the most successful of black American writers focusing on the interrelationships, feelings, and values of persons of several cultures, several religious groups, and several classes. His stories are fast moving, and his characters come alive to express a multi-ethnic society, with both difficulties and rewards for those striving for equity within it.

—Mary Lystad

JAMES, Will(iam Roderick). Pseudonym for Joseph Ernest Nephtali Dufault. Canadian. Born in St. Nazaire de Acton, Quebec, 6 June 1892. Educated at a Catholic primary school, Montreal; California School of Fine Arts, San Francisco, 1919; Yale University School of Fine Art, New Haven, Connecticut, 1921. Served in the United States Army, 1918–19. Married Alice Conradt in 1920 (separated 1935). Worked as cowhand, rodeo rider, and stunt man for Thomas Ince Studio, Hollywood. Served a prison sentence for cattle rustling, 1915. Recipient: American Library Association Newbery Medal, 1927. *Died 3 September 1942.*

PUBLICATIONS FOR CHILDREN (illustrated by the author)

Fiction

Smoky the Cowhorse. New York, Scribner, 1926.
Sand. New York, Scribner, 1929.
Sun Up: Tales of the Cow Camps. New York, Scribner, 1931.
Big Enough. New York, Scribner, 1931.
Uncle Bill: A Tale of Two Kinds of Cowboy. New York, Scribner, 1932.
In the Saddle with Uncle Bill. New York, Scribner, 1935.
Young Cowboy. New York, Scribner, 1935.
Scorpion, A Good Bad Horse. New York, Scribner, 1936.
Look-See with Uncle Bill. New York, Scribner, 1938.
The Dark Horse. New York, Scribner, 1939.
My First Horse. New York, Scribner, 1940.
Horses I've Known. New York, Scribner, 1940.

Other

Cowboys North and South. New York, Scribner, 1924.
Drifting Cowboy. New York, Scribner, 1925.
Lone Cowboy: My Life Story. New York, Scribner, 1930.
Cowboy in the Making. New York, Scribner, 1937.
The Will James Cowboy Book, edited by Alice Dalgliesh. New York, Scribner, 1938.

PUBLICATIONS FOR ADULTS

Novels

The Three Mustangeers. New York, Scribner, 1933.
Home Ranch. New York, Scribner, 1935.
Flint Spears, Cowboy Rodeo Contestant. New York, Scribner, 1938.
The American Cowboy. New York, Scribner, 1942.

Short Stories

Book of Cowboy Stories. New York, Scribner, 1951; London, Phoenix House, 1952.

Other

Cow Country. New York and London, Scribner, 1927.
All in a Day's Riding. New York and London, Scribner, 1933.
Will James: The Spirit of the Cowboy (exhibition catalogue), edited by J.M. Neil. Lincoln, Nebraska, Nicolaysen Art Museum, 1985.

*

Critical Studies: *Will James, The Gilt Edged Cowboy* by Anthony A. Amaral, Los Angeles, Westernlore Press, 1967, revised edition, as *Will James: The Last Cowboy Legend,* Reno, University of Nevada Press, 1980; *Will James: The Life and Work of a Lone Cowboy* by William Gardner Bell, Flagstaff, Arizona, Northland Press, 1987.

Illustrator: *Wild Animal Homesteads* by Enos A. Mills, 1923; *Tombstone: An Iliad of the Southwest* by Walter Noble Burns, 1933.

*   *   *

The stories written by Will James, a cowboy himself, concern cowboys and horses, all that relates to the lives of cowboys and horses. *Smoky the Cowhorse* is James at his best. At one time controversial for its colloquial quality, James's style is the spoken language of the range-rider, or seems to be; its grammatical structures are convincingly those of idiomatic language. Despite the credible dialect of poorly educated cowhands, the stories are filled with fine stylistic elements. With visual imagery, James describes the cow country and its rugged terrain, the range and its prairie vastness. When James writes of horses, his language is equally vivid, for he recreates the squeak of saddle leather, the shaking of a corral as a pony hits the earth, the stirring of dust that looks like a "young cloud." The action of the horses, as they writhe, bucking and struggling, or plunge, gallop, or buck, is convincingly vivid. Since the publication of *Smoky* in 1926, attitudes toward treatment of animals have changed, of course. *Young Cowboy,* for example, seems brutal though accurate in its description of steer roping. Publication dates, however, alert the reader to the fact that the life and work of the cowboy, too, have changed. The stories, despite the expected limitations of subject matter, come alive when they describe the actions of the cow ponies.

Characterization is most convincing when James writes of horses, the "crethures" he loves so well. One horse is different from another, despite the similar natures of their lives. Perhaps James assumes more knowledge of the horse's thinking than a realistic story should, but James is not overwhelmingly sentimental. He confines himself largely to telling what Smoky, his most famous horse character, sees, rather than revealing Smoky's emotions. This reserve is necessary, helpful in making the horses convincing characters. Although James's stories do not have clear themes beyond the unifying idea that a cowboy's life is filled with hard work he loves, they explicitly detail pieces and parts of equipment as well as techniques for working with horses.

When James's stories focus on the cowboy rather than on the horse as central character, as in *Flint Spears* and *Uncle Bill,* for example, they lose some of their vitality. In recreating the routine, the training, the activities of cowboy life, James seems to make a typical cowboy of every character, rather than making a cowboy a believable human being.

James, his own illustrator, shows great skill in depicting horses in all attitudes and poses; his realistic pictures are alive with motion, and his horses seem alive with muscular vitality.

—Rebecca J. Lukens

———————

JARRELL, Randall. American. Born in Nashville, Tennessee, 6 May 1914. Educated at schools in California and Tennessee; Vanderbilt University, Nashville (editor, *Masquerader*), B.S. in psychology 1936 (Phi Beta Kappa), M.A. in English 1939. Served as a celestial navigation tower operator in the United States Army Air Corps, 1942–46. Married 1) Mackie Langham in 1940 (divorced); 2) Mary Eloise von Schrader in 1952, two stepdaughters. Instructor in English, Kenyon College, Gambier, Ohio, 1937–39, University of Texas, Austin, 1939–42, and Sarah Lawrence College, Bronxville, New York, 1946–47; Associate Professor, 1947–58, and Professor of English, 1958–65, Woman's College of the University of North Carolina (later University of North Carolina at Greensboro). Lecturer, Salzburg Seminar in American Civilization, 1948; Visiting Fellow in Creative Writing, Princeton University, New Jersey, 1951–52; Fellow, Indiana School of Letters, Bloomington, Summer 1952; Visiting Professor of English, University of Illinois, Urbana, 1953; Elliston Lecturer, University of Cincinnati, Ohio, 1958. Acting literary editor, the *Nation*, New York, 1946–47; poetry critic, *Partisan Review*, New Brunswick, New Jersey, 1949–53, and *Yale Review*, New Haven, Connecticut, 1955–57; member of the Editorial Board, *American Scholar*, Washington, D.C., 1957–65. Consultant in Poetry, Library of Congress, Washington, D.C., 1956–58. Recipient: *Southern Review* prize, 1936; Jeannette Sewell Davis prize, 1943, Levinson prize, 1948, and Oscar Blumenthal prize, 1951 (*Poetry*, Chicago); John Peale Bishop Memorial prize (*Sewanee Review*), 1946; Guggenheim fellowship, 1946; American Academy grant, 1951; National Book award, 1961; University of North Carolina Gardner award, 1962; American Association of University Women award, 1964; Ingram Merrill award, 1965. D.H.L.: Bard College, Annandale-on-Hudson, New York, 1962. Member, American Academy, 1961; Chancellor, Academy of American Poets, 1965. *Died 14 October 1965.*

PUBLICATIONS FOR CHILDREN

Fiction

The Gingerbread Rabbit, illustrated by Garth Williams. New York, Macmillan, and London, Collier Macmillan, 1964.
The Bat-Poet, illustrated by Maurice Sendak. New York, Macmillan, 1964; London, Kestrel, 1977.
The Animal Family, illustrated by Maurice Sendak. New York, Pantheon, 1965; London, Hart Davis, 1967.
Fly by Night, illustrated by Maurice Sendak. New York, Farrar Straus, 1976; London, Bodley Head, 1977.

Verse

A Bat Is Born, illustrated by John Schoenherr. New York, Doubleday, 1978.

Other

The Rabbit Catcher and Other Fairy Tales of Ludwig Bechstein. New York, Macmillan, and London, Macmillan, 1962.
The Golden Bird and Other Fairy Tales by the Brothers Grimm. New York, Macmillan, and London, Macmillan 1962.
Snow-White and the Seven Dwarfs: A Tale from the Brothers Grimm, illustrated by Nancy Ekholm Burkert. New York, Farrar Straus, 1972; London, Kestrel, 1974.
The Juniper Tree and Other Tales from Grimm, with Lore Segal, illustrated by Maurice Sendak. New York, Farrar Straus, 1973; London, Bodley Head, 1974.
The Fisherman and His Wife, illustrated by Margot Zemach. New York, Farrar Straus, 1980.

PUBLICATIONS FOR ADULTS

Novel

Pictures from an Institution: A Comedy. New York, Knopf, and London, Faber, 1954.

Play

The Three Sisters, adaptation of a play by Chekhov (produced New York, 1964; London, 1965). New York, Macmillan, 1969.

Verse

Five Young American Poets, with others. New York, New Directions, 1940.
Blood for a Stranger. New York, Harcourt Brace, 1942.
Little Friend, Little Friend. New York, Dial Press, 1945.
Losses. New York, Harcourt Brace, 1948.
The Seven-League Crutches. New York, Harcourt Brace, 1951.
Selected Poems. New York, Knopf, 1955; London, Faber, 1956.
Uncollected Poems. Privately printed, 1958.
The Woman at the Washington Zoo: Poems and Translations. New York, Atheneum, 1960.
Selected Poems. New York, Atheneum, 1964.
The Lost World: New Poems. New York, Macmillan, 1965; London, Eyre and Spottiswoode, 1966.
The Complete Poems. New York, Farrar Straus, 1969; London, Faber, 1971.
The Achievement of Randall Jarrell: A Comprehensive Selection of His Poems with a Critical Introduction, edited by Frederick J. Hoffman. Chicago, Scott Foresman, 1970.
Jerome: The Biography of a Poem. New York, Grossman, 1971.

Other

Poetry and the Age. New York, Knopf, 1953; London, Faber, 1955.
Poets, Critics, and Readers (address). Charlottesville, University Press of Virginia, 1959.
A Sad Heart at the Supermarket: Essays and Fables. New York, Atheneum, 1962; London, Eyre and Spottiswoode, 1965.
The Third Book of Criticism. New York, Farrar Straus, 1969; London, Faber, 1975.
Kipling, Auden & Co.: Essays and Reviews 1935–1964. New York, Farrar Straus, 1980; Manchester, Carcanet, 1981.

About Popular Culture. Winston-Salem, North Carolina, Palaemon Press, 1981.
Randall Jarrell's Letters: An Autobiographical and Literary Selection, edited by Mary Jarrell. Boston, Houghton Mifflin, 1985; London, Faber, 1986.

Editor, *The Anchor Book of Stories.* New York, Doubleday, 1958.
Editor, *The Best Short Stories of Rudyard Kipling.* New York, Hanover House, 1961; as *In the Vernacular: The English in India* and *The English in England,* New York, Doubleday, 2 vols., 1963.
Editor, *Six Russian Short Novels.* New York, Doubleday, 1963.

Translator, with Moses Hadas, *The Ghetto and the Jews of Rome,* by Ferdinand Gregorovius. New York, Schocken, 1948.
Translator, *Goethe's Faust, Part One.* New York, Farrar Straus, 1976; London, Faber, 1978.

*

Bibliography: "Randall Jarrell: A Bibliography of Criticism 1941–1981" by Jeffrey Meyers, in *Bulletin of Bibliography* (Boston), December 1982; *Randall Jarrell: A Descriptive Bibliography 1929–1983* by Stuart Wright, Charlottesville, University Press of Virginia, 1986.

Manuscript Collections: Walter Clinton Jackson Library, University of North Carolina, Chapel Hill; Berg Collection, New York Public Library.

Critical Studies: *Randall Jarrell 1914–1965* edited by Robert Lowell, Peter Taylor, and Robert Penn Warren, New York, Farrar Straus, 1967; *Randall Jarrell* by Karl Shapiro, Washington, D.C., Library of Congress, 1967; *The Poetry of Randall Jarrell* by Suzanne Ferguson, Baton Rouge, Louisiana State University Press, 1971, and *Critical Essays on Randall Jarrell* edited by Ferguson, Boston, Hall, 1983; *Randall Jarrell* by M.L. Rosenthal, Minneapolis, University of Minnesota Press, 1972; *Randall Jarrell* by Bernetta Quinn, Boston, Twayne, 1981; *Worlds and Lives: The Poetry of Randall Jarrell* by Charlotte H. Beck, New York, Associated Faculty Press, 1983; *Randall Jarrell's Children's Books,* La Jolla, California, Green Tiger Press, 1984, and *The Children's Books of Randall Jarrell,* Athens, University of Georgia Press, 1988, both by Jerry Griswold; "Randall Jarrell Issue" of *South Carolina Review* (Clemson), Fall 1984.

*   *   *

"The trouble isn't making poems," Randall Jarrell's little bat-poet bitterly says, "the trouble's finding somebody that will listen to them." Such an assertion, made by one of America's leading contemporary poets, gives rise to a series of speculations about Jarrell and his unique contribution to children's literature. For whereas reviewers hailed *The Animal Family,* the story of a lonely hunter who finds a mermaid, a bear, a lynx, and a boy who live together in understanding, it becomes apparent that joy and a happy ending are what make most readers comfortable.

In his first book, *The Gingerbread Rabbit,* Jarrell also devises a happily-ever-after. But here he was only wetting his feet. Elements of "The Gingerbread Boy" permeate this story for the very young; there is but one verse in the book, the call of the vegetable man hawking turnip-greens (published in another form as an adult poem) and yet one can find all the embryonic themes which were used in his subsequent books—innocence, loneliness, the search for a home and fulfillment, fear, love, and forebodings of death.

These themes recur on a more poetic level in *The Animal Family,* *The Bat-Poet,* and *Fly by Night,* and these books, one suspects, will stir and elicit a response now and in future years by the most sensitive adults and children. For the reaction of many reviewers and critics, among these (most amazingly!) other poets, often makes it painfully clear that the entire point of what Jarrell has so beautifully done is completely misunderstood. These critics fail to recognize that they are the pompous, egotistical mockingbirds of *The Bat-Poet* who listen only to their own songs and voices, who do not hear the little bat crying out in loneliness, with a need to be heard, loved, protected, and accepted for his individual contribution. The hunter and mermaid of *The Animal Family* and David of *Fly by Night* represent, among others, those with this same loneliness and search. The knowledge that they are different from others, that growth is painful and love hard-won takes a different turn in all three books; each character has his mentor, his own personality, and whether in human or animal form the fall from innocence is dealt with on various meaningful levels.

Jarrell drew from the animal world a symbolic level that deserves careful study. Is the owl of fear and possible death in *The Bat-Poet* any relation to the owl of security and mother-love of *Fly by Night*? The symbols are many, and Jarrell explored them through beautiful prose and magnificent poetry. It is quite possible, one feels, that the lack of formal poetry in *The Animal Family* makes it a less formidable, more comfortable story for some readers.

As in his adult poetry, Jarrell was laying bare his own emotions in his work for children, and never more so than in *The Bat-Poet* which is, to me, the most eloquent story ever written about the sensitivity and life of a poet, about pompous critics, or, indeed, what the making of poems is all about.

—Myra Cohn Livingston

JELLICOE, (Patricia) Ann. British. Born in Middlesbrough, Yorkshire, 15 July 1927. Educated at Polam Hall, Darlington, County Durham; Queen Margaret's, Castle Howard, Yorkshire; Central School of Speech and Drama, London (Elsie Fogarty prize, 1947), 1944–47. Married 1) C.E. Knight-Clarke in 1950 (marriage dissolved 1961); 2) Roger Mayne in 1962, one son and one daughter. Actress, stage manager, and director, in London and the provinces, 1947–51; founding director, Cockpit Theatre Club, London, 1952–54; lecturer and director, Central School of Speech and Drama, 1954–56; literary manager, Royal Court Theatre, London, 1973–75; founding director, 1979–85, and President, 1986, Colway Theatre Trust. O.B.E. (Officer, Order of the British Empire), 1984. Agent: Margaret Ramsay Ltd., 14-A Goodwin's Court, London WC2N 4LL, England.

PUBLICATIONS FOR CHILDREN

Plays

You'll Never Guess (also director: produced London, 1973). Included in *3 Jelliplays,* 1975.
Two Jelliplays: Clever Elsie, Smiling John, Silent Peter, and A Good Thing or a Bad Thing (also director: produced London, 1974). Included in *3 Jelliplays,* 1975.
3 Jelliplays. London, Faber, 1975.

PUBLICATIONS FOR ADULTS

Plays

Rosmersholm, adaptation of the play by Ibsen (also director:

produced London, 1952; revised version produced London, 1959). San Francisco, Chandler, 1960.

The Sport of My Mad Mother (also co-director: produced London, 1958). Published in *The Observer Plays*, London, Faber, 1958; revised version, London, Faber, 1964; with *The Knack*, New York, Dell, 1964.

The Lady from the Sea, adaptation of a play by Ibsen (produced London, 1961).

The Knack (produced Cambridge, 1961; also co-director: London, 1962; Boston, 1963; New York, 1964). London, Encore, and New York, French, 1962.

The Seagull, with Adriadne Nicolaeff, adaptation of a play by Chekhov (produced London, 1964).

Der Freischütz, translation of the libretto by Friedrich Kind, music by Weber (produced London, 1964).

Shelley; or, The Idealist (also director: produced London, 1965). London, Faber, and New York, Grove Press, 1966.

The Rising Generation (produced London, 1967). Published in *Playbill 2*, edited by Alan Durband, London, Hutchinson, 1969.

The Giveaway (produced Edinburgh, 1968; London, 1969). London, Faber, 1970.

Flora and the Bandits (also director: produced Dartington, Devon, 1976).

The Reckoning (also director: produced Lyme Regis, Dorset, 1978).

The Bargain (also director: produced Exeter, 1979).

The Tide (also director: produced Axminster, Devon, 1980).

The Western Women, music by Nick Brace, adaptation of a story by Fay Weldon (also co-director: produced Lyme Regis, Dorset, 1984).

Other

Some Unconscious Influences in the Theatre. London and New York, Cambridge University Press, 1967.
Devon: A Shell Guide, with Roger Mayne. London, Faber, 1975.
Community Plays: How to Put Them On. London, Methuen, 1987.

*

Theatrical Activities:
Director: **Plays**—*The Confederacy* by Vanbrugh, London, 1952; *The Frogs* by Aristophanes, London, 1952; *Miss Julie* by Strindberg, London, 1952; *Rosmersholm* by Ibsen, London, 1952; *Saint's Day* by John Whiting, London, 1953; *The Comedy of Errors*, London, 1953; *Olympia* by Ferenc Molnar, London, 1953; *The Sport of My Mad Mother* (co-director, with George Devine), London, 1958; *For Children* by Keith Johnstone, London, 1958; *The Knack* (co-director, with Keith Johnstone), London, 1962; *Skyvers* by Barry Reckord, London, 1963; *Shelley*, London, 1965; *You'll Never Guess*, London, 1973; *Two Jelliplays*, London, 1974; *A Worthy Guest* by Paul Bailey, London, 1974; *Six of the Best*, London, 1974; *Flora and the Bandits*, Dartington, Devon, 1976; *The Reckoning*, Lyme Regis, Dorset, 1978; *The Bargain*, Exeter, 1979; *The Tide*, Axminster, Devon, 1980; *The Poor Man's Friend* by Howard Barker, Bridport, Dorset, 1981; *The Garden* by Charles Wood, Sherborne, Dorset, 1982; *The Western Women* (co-director, with Chris Fog and Sally-Ann Lomax), Lyme Regis, Dorset, 1984; *Entertaining Strangers* by David Edgar, Dorchester, Dorset, 1985.

*   *   *

Ann Jellicoe's first play for children was *You'll Never Guess*, a superb version of the Rumpelstiltskin story. This was followed by *Clever Elsie*, *Smiling John*, *Silent Peter*, and *A Good Thing or a Bad*

Thing. These two plays demonstrate many of the aspects of the style which has made her adult plays so successful. In both plays a spare, realistic dialogue is used, and there is a sense of rhythm in the text which is particularly characteristic of her writing and requires careful attention in production. There is in neither play a hint of her using a special style for children, no fear of the whimsical patronising stuff children's plays are so often made of. She understands what will make children laugh or simply engage their attention.

In *Clever Elsie* she takes a traditional tale as the basis for her play. In fact several age old ideas are there, besides the tale of Elsie's overactive imagination projecting a series of future disasters, all of them based on misunderstandings. It is a play of ideas, and works well with the full age range under 11 years, but it especially appeals to infants who are quite capable of grasping the fact that the characters' simplicity and lack of logic lead them up the wrong path. The young audience is placed in a position of greater knowledge, but knowledge gained by the children using their own powers of logic, and this adds to their delight.

In *A Good Thing or a Bad Thing* the overall story or plot is of more importance—again a story using traditional elements. There are a queen, a princess in need of rescue, and a monster to threaten both her and the audience. Her rescuer, however, is not the traditional prince but a mere gardener's boy, whom we see living in very ordinary circumstances with his mother. The monster is quite imaginary—it is never seen, only heard—but in production there is not a child in the audience who fails to see it, claws and all, marching across the stage and dangerously near the front row! The tale is again a simple one but the conflicts presented are extremely powerful. The play is in fact essentially about power—the power of the mother, the ruler, the unknown and feared—which is why it evokes such a strong response from children.

This play differs from *Clever Elsie* in structure, in that Jellicoe leaves more room for direct contact with the audience and suggests areas where ad-libbing and consultation with the children is vital to the play. *Clever Elsie* has a much more contained, constructed feel to it, so that if played with *A Good Thing or a Bad Thing* the two nicely complement each other in style and make up an excellent programme.

Jellicoe, who has herself both acted and directed, leaves room in both plays for the actor and director to complete the production. Neither play requires elaborate settings or effects and can be played not only in theatres but on tour in schools very easily, the only vital technical requirements being a reasonable sound system.

—Joan Mills

———

JOHNS, W(illiam) E(arl). Also wrote as William Earle; Jon Early. British. Born in Bengeo, Hertfordshire, 5 February 1893. Educated at a school in Bengeo; Hertford Grammar School, 1905–07; articled to a Hertford surveyor, 1907–12. Married Maude Hunt in 1914 (died 1961), one son; lived with Doris May Leigh from 1924. Sanitary inspector, Swaffham, Norfolk, 1912–13. Served in the Norfolk Yeomanry, 1913–15, and in the Machine Gun Corps, in Egypt and Salonika, 1916–17; transferred to the Royal Flying Corps (later Royal Air Force), 1917, and served until 1927: shot down and captured in France, 1918; Flying Officer, 1920–27; lecturer, Air Defence Cadet Corps, later Air Training Corps, and writer for the Ministry of Defence, London, 1939–45. Aviation illustrator from 1927; founding editor, *Popular Flying*, 1932–39, and *Flying*, 1938–39, both London; columnist ("The Passing Show"), *My Garden* magazine, London, 1937–44, and for *Modern Boy*, *Pearson's*, *Boys' Own Paper*, and *Girls' Own Paper*. Died 21 June 1968.

PUBLICATIONS FOR CHILDREN

Fiction (Biggles series from 1945, and Worrals and Gimlet series all
    illustrated by Leslie Stead)

The Camels Are Coming. London, John Hamilton, 1932; as *Biggles, Pioneer Air Fighter,* London, Armada, 1982.
The Cruise of the Condor: A Biggles Story. London, John Hamilton, 1933.
Biggles of the Camel Squadron. London, John Hamilton, 1934.
Biggles Flies Again. London, John Hamilton, 1934.
Biggles Learns to Fly. London, Boys' Friend Library, 1935.
Biggles Flies East, illustrated by Howard Leigh and Alfred Sindall. London, Oxford University Press, 1935.
Biggles Hits the Trail, illustrated by Howard Leigh and Alfred Sindall. London, Oxford University Press, 1935.
Biggles in France. London, Boys' Friend Library, 1935.
The Black Peril: A Biggles Story. London, John Hamilton, 1935; as *Biggles Flies East* (not same as 1935 book), London, Boy's Friend Library, 1938.
Biggles in Africa, illustrated by Howard Leigh and Alfred Sindall. London, Oxford University Press, 1936.
Biggles & Co., illustrated by Howard Leigh and Alfred Sindall. London, Oxford University Press, 1936.
Biggles—Air Commodore, illustrated by Howard Leigh and Alfred Sindall. London, Oxford University Press, 1937.
Biggles Flies West, illustrated by Howard Leigh and Alfred Sindall. London, Oxford University Press, 1937.
Biggles Flies South, illustrated by Howard Leigh and Jack Nicolle. London, Oxford University Press, 1938.
Biggles Goes to War, illustrated by Howard Leigh and Martin Tyas. London, Oxford University Press, 1938.
Champion of the Main, illustrated by H. Gooderman. London, Oxford University Press, 1938.
Biggles Flies North, illustrated by Howard Leigh and Will Narraway. London, Oxford University Press, 1939.
Biggles in Spain, illustrated by Howard Leigh and J. Abbey. London, Oxford University Press, 1939.
The Rescue Flight: A Biggles Story, illustrated by Howard Leigh and Alfred Sindall. London, Oxford University Press, 1939.
Biggles in the Baltic, illustrated by Howard Leigh and Alfred Sindall. London, Oxford University Press, 1940.
Biggles in the South Seas, illustrated by Norman Howard. London, Oxford University Press, 1940.
Biggles—Secret Agent, illustrated by Howard Leigh and Alfred Sindall. London, Oxford University Press, 1940.
Worrals of the W.A.A.F. London, Lutterworth Press, 1941.
Spitfire Parade: Stories of Biggles in War-Time, illustrated by Ratcliffe Wilson. London, Oxford University Press, 1941.
Biggles Sees It Through, illustrated by Howard Leigh and Alfred Sindall. London, Oxford University Press, 1941.
Biggles Defies the Swastika, illustrated by Howard Leigh and Alfred Sindall. London, Oxford University Press, 1941.
Biggles in the Jungle, illustrated by Terence Cuneo. London, Oxford University Press, 1942.
Sinister Service, illustrated by Stuart Tresilian. London, Oxford University Press, 1942.
Biggles Sweeps the Desert, illustrated by Leslie Stead. London, Hodder and Stoughton, 1942.
Worrals Flies Again. London, Hodder and Stoughton, 1942.
Worrals Carries On. London, Lutterworth Press, 1942.
Worrals on the War-Path. London, Hodder and Stoughton, 1943.
Biggles—Charter Pilot, illustrated by Mendoza. London, Oxford University Press, 1943.
Biggles "Fails to Return", illustrated by Leslie Stead. London, Hodder and Stoughton, 1943.

Biggles in Borneo, illustrated by Stuart Tresilian. London, Oxford University Press, 1943.
King of the Commandos, illustrated by Leslie Stead. London, University of London Press, 1943.
Gimlet Goes Again. London, University of London Press, 1944.
Worrals Goes East. London, Hodder and Stoughton, 1944.
Biggles in the Orient. London, Hodder and Stoughton, 1945.
Worrals of the Islands: A Story of the War in the Pacific. London, Hodder and Stoughton, 1945.
Biggles Delivers the Goods. London, Hodder and Stoughton, 1946.
Gimlet Comes Home. London, University of London Press, 1946.
Sergeant Bigglesworth C.I.D. London, Hodder and Stoughton, 1947.
Comrades in Arms. London, Hodder and Stoughton, 1947.
Gimlet Mops Up. Leicester, Brockhampton Press, 1947.
Worrals in the Wilds. London, Hodder and Stoughton, 1947.
Biggles Hunts Big Game. London, Hodder and Stoughton, 1948.
Biggles' Second Case. London, Hodder and Stoughton, 1948.
Gimlet's Oriental Quest. Leicester, Brockhampton Press, 1948.
The Rustlers of Rattlesnake Valley. London, Nelson, 1948.
Worrals Down Under. London, Lutterworth Press, 1948.
Biggles Breaks the Silence. London, Hodder and Stoughton, 1949; as *Biggles in the Antarctic,* London, Armada, 1970.
Biggles Takes a Holiday. London, Hodder and Stoughton, 1949.
Gimlet Lends a Hand. Leicester, Brockhampton Press, 1949.
Worrals Goes Afoot. London, Lutterworth Press, 1949.
Worrals in the Wastelands. London, Lutterworth Press, 1949.
Worrals Investigates. London, Lutterworth Press, 1950.
Biggles Gets His Men. London, Hodder and Stoughton, 1950.
Gimlet Bores In. Leicester, Brockhampton Press, 1950.
Another Job for Biggles. London, Hodder and Stoughton, 1951.
Biggles Goes to School. London, Hodder and Stoughton, 1951.
Biggles Works It Out. London, Hodder and Stoughton, 1951.
Gimlet Off the Map. Leicester, Brockhampton Press, 1951.
Biggles—Air Detective. London, Latimer, 1952.
Biggles Follows On. London, Hodder and Stoughton, 1952.
Biggles Takes the Case. London, Hodder and Stoughton, 1952.
Gimlet Gets the Answer. Leicester, Brockhampton Press, 1952.
Biggles and the Black Raider. London, Hodder and Stoughton, 1953.
Biggles in the Blue. Leicester, Brockhampton Press, 1953.
Biggles in the Gobi. London, Hodder and Stoughton, 1953.
Biggles of the Special Air Police. London, Thames Publishing Company, 1953.
Biggles and the Pirate Treasure, and Other Biggles Adventures. Leicester, Brockhampton Press, 1954.
Biggles Cuts It Fine. London, Hodder and Stoughton, 1954.
Biggles, Foreign Legionnaire. London, Hodder and Stoughton, 1954.
Biggles, Pioneer Airfighter. London, Thames Publishing Company, 1954.
Gimlet Takes a Job. Leicester, Brockhampton Press, 1954.
Kings of Space, illustrated by Leslie Stead. London, Hodder and Stoughton, 1954.
Adventure Bound, illustrated by Douglas Relf. London, Nelson, 1955.
Biggles' Chinese Puzzle and Other Biggles Adventures. Leicester, Brockhampton Press, 1955.
Biggles in Australia. London, Hodder and Stoughton, 1955.
Return to Mars, illustrated by Leslie Stead. London, Hodder and Stoughton, 1955.
Biggles of 266. London, Thames Publishing Company, 1956.
Biggles Takes Charge. Leicester, Brockhampton Press, 1956.
No Rest for Biggles. London, Hodder and Stoughton, 1956.
Now to the Stars, illustrated by Leslie Stead. London, Hodder and

Stoughton, 1956.
Biggles Makes Ends Meet.   London, Hodder and Stoughton, 1957.
Adventure Unlimited, illustrated by Douglas Relf.   London, Nelson, 1957.
Biggles of the Interpol.   Leicester, Brockhampton Press, 1957.
Biggles on the Home Front.   London, Hodder and Stoughton, 1957.
To Outer Space, illustrated by Leslie Stead.   London, Hodder and Stoughton, 1957.
Biggles Buries a Hatchet.   Leicester, Brockhampton Press, 1958.
Biggles on Mystery Island.   London, Hodder and Stoughton, 1958.
Biggles Presses On.   Leicester, Brockhampton Press, 1958.
The Edge of Beyond, illustrated by Leslie Stead.   London, Hodder and Stoughton, 1958.
Biggles at World's End.   Leicester, Brockhampton Press, 1959.
Biggles' Combined Operation.   London, Hodder and Stoughton, 1959.
Biggles in Mexico.   Leicester, Brockhampton Press, 1959.
The Death Rays of Ardilla, illustrated by Leslie Stead.   London, Hodder and Stoughton, 1959.
Adventures of the Junior Detection Club.   London, Parrish, 1960.
Biggles and the Leopards of Zinn.   Leicester, Brockhampton Press, 1960.
Biggles Goes Home.   London, Hodder and Stoughton, 1960.
To Worlds Unknown, illustrated by Leslie Stead.   London, Hodder and Stoughton, 1960.
Where the Golden Eagle Soars, illustrated by Colin Gibson.   London, Hodder and Stoughton, 1960.
The Quest for the Perfect Planet, illustrated by Leslie Stead.   London, Hodder and Stoughton, 1961.
Biggles and the Missing Millionaire.   Leicester, Brockhampton Press, 1961.
Biggles and the Poor Rich Boy.   Leicester, Brockhampton Press, 1961.
Biggles Forms a Syndicate.   London, Hodder and Stoughton, 1961.
Biggles Goes Alone.   London, Hodder and Stoughton, 1962.
Biggles Sets a Trap.   London, Hodder and Stoughton, 1962.
Orchids for Biggles.   Leicester, Brockhampton Press, 1962.
Worlds of Wonder: More Adventures in Space, illustrated by Leslie Stead.   London, Hodder and Stoughton, 1962.
Biggles and the Plane That Disappeared.   London, Hodder and Stoughton, 1963.
Biggles Flies to Work.   London, Dean, 1963.
Biggles' Special Case.   Leicester, Brockhampton Press, 1963.
Biggles Takes a Hand.   London, Hodder and Stoughton, 1963.
Biggles Takes It Rough.   Leicester, Brockhampton Press, 1963.
The Man Who Vanished into Space.   London, Hodder and Stoughton, 1963.
Biggles and the Black Mask.   London, Hodder and Stoughton, 1964.
Biggles and the Lost Sovereigns.   Leicester, Brockhampton Press, 1964; as *Biggles and the Lost Treasure,* London, Knight, 1978.
Biggles Investigates and Other Stories of the Air Police.   Leicester, Brockhampton Press, 1965.
Biggles and the Blue Moon.   Leicester, Brockhampton Press, 1965.
Biggles and the Plot That Failed.   Leicester, Brockhampton Press, 1965.
Biggles Looks Back.   London, Hodder and Stoughton, 1965.
Biggles Scores a Bull.   London, Hodder and Stoughton, 1965.
Biggles in the Terai.   Leicester, Brockhampton Press, 1966.
Biggles and the Gun Runners.   Leicester, Brockhampton Press, 1966.
Biggles and the Penitent Thief.   Leicester, Brockhampton Press, 1967.
Biggles Sorts It Out.   Leicester, Brockhampton Press, 1967.
Biggles and the Dark Intruder.   London, Knight, 1967.
Biggles in the Underworld.   Leicester, Brockhampton Press, 1968.

The Boy Biggles.   London, Dean, 1968.
Biggles and the Deep Blue Sea.   Leicester, Brockhampton Press, 1968.
Biggles and the Little Green God.   Leicester, Brockhampton Press, 1969.
Biggles and the Noble Lord.   Leicester, Brockhampton Press, 1969.
Biggles Sees Too Much.   Leicester, Brockhampton Press, 1970.
Biggles of the Royal Flying Corps (selection), edited by Piers Williams.   Maidenhead, Berkshire, Purnell, 1978.

Other

Fighting Planes and Aces, illustrated by Howard Leigh.   London, John Hamilton, 1932.
The Modern Boy's Book of Pirates.   London, Amalgamated Press, 1939.
The Biggles Book of Heroes.   London, Parrish, 1959.
The Biggles Book of Treasure Hunting, illustrated by William Randell.   London, Parrish, 1962.

Editor, *The Modern Boy's Book of Aircraft.*   London, Amalgamated Press, 1931.

PUBLICATIONS FOR ADULTS

Novels

Mossyface (as William Earle).   London, Mellifont Press, 1932.
The Spy Flyers.   London, John Hamilton, 1933.
Sky High.   London, Newnes, 1936; revised edition, London, Latimer, 1951.
Steeley Flies Again.   London, Newnes, 1936; revised edition, London, Latimer, 1951.
Blue Blood Runs Red (as Jon Early).   London, Newnes, 1936.
Murder by Air.   London, Newnes, 1937; revised edition, London, Latimer, 1951.
The Murder at Castle Deeping.   London, John Hamilton, 1938; revised edition, London, Latimer, 1951.
Desert Night: A Romance.   London, John Hamilton, 1938.
Wings of Romance: A Steeley Adventure.   London, Newnes, 1939; revised edition, London, Latimer, 1951.
The Unknown Quantity.   London, John Hamilton, 1940.
No Motive for Murder.   London, Hodder and Stoughton, 1958; New York, Washburn, 1959.
The Man Who Lost His Way.   London, Macdonald, 1960.

Short Stories

The Raid.   London, John Hamilton, 1935.
Doctor Vane Answers the Call.   London, Latimer, 1950.
Short Sorties.   London, Latimer, 1953.
Sky Fever and Other Stories.   London, Latimer, 1953.

Plays

Radio Plays (with G.R. Ranier): *The Machine That Disappeared,* 1942; *The Charming Mrs. Nayther,* 1942.

Other

The Pictorial Flying Course, with Harry M. Schofield, illustrated by Johns.   London, John Hamilton, 1932.
The Air V.C.'s.   London, John Hamilton, 1935.
Some Milestones of Aviation.   London, John Hamilton, 1935.
The Passing Show: A Garden Diary by an Amateur Gardener.

London, My Garden, 1937.
No Surrender, with R.A. Kelly. London, Harrap, 1969.

Editor, *Wings: A Book of Flying Adventures.* London, John Hamilton, 1931.
Editor, *Thrilling Flights.* London, John Hamilton, 1935.

*

Critical Studies: *Biggles: The Authorised Biography* by John Pearson, London, Sidgwick and Jackson, 1979; *By Jove, Biggles: The Life of Captain W.E. Johns* by Peter Berresford Ellis and Piers Williams, London, W.H. Allen, 1981.

Illustrator: *Desert Wings* by Covington Clarke, 1931.

*   *   *

The emergence of flying stories in the closing years of the 19th century can be seen not only as an extension of the traditional adventure story, but as a response to the actual developments in aviation at that time. Early writers in the genre owed rather more to fantasy and invention than scientific knowledge, but by the time of World War I, writers such as P.F. Westerman began to produce more realistic stories.

W.E. Johns built upon this tradition. Unlike Westerman, Johns had actually seen a good deal of active service. Originally a soldier who had experienced trench warfare in Gallipoli, he transferred to the Royal Flying Corps in 1917, and was a member of the 55th Squadron involved in bombing raids on Germany. Shot down in 1918, he finished the war in a prison camp, but remained in the R.A.F. until 1927, obtaining further flying experience in India and Iraq.

In 1932 he published in the magazine *Popular Flying* "The White Fokker," his first story about Biggles, the pilot who would become his most enduring creation. "Biggles" is the nickname of James Bigglesworth, at this time a teenager but already a Flight Commander on active service in France during World War I. Members of Biggles's squadron are regularly being ambushed and killed by a German Fokker B. VII, but, though Biggles eventually manages to trap and to shoot down the German pilot, what Johns emphasises is not just the skill and courage of his hero, but the cruelty of war, including its psychological damage.

In these early stories, Biggles is no stereotyped hero but a patriotic, skilful, highly-strung young man, who several times comes close to tears, even hysteria, when comrades are lost. In the magazine stories, collected in such books as *The Camels Are Coming* and *Biggles of the Camel Squadron,* Johns successfully conveys how many flyers felt and behaved, with their mixture of idealism and apparent flippancy, in the days when the average life expectancy of a new pilot was sometimes estimated to be about three weeks.

The problem for Johns was where to go once he had exhausted his early war experiences. *The Cruise of the Condor* pointed the way, in a tale about the post-war adventures of Biggles and two of his wartime comrades, the Hon. Algernon Lacey and flight-sergeant Smyth, on a treasure-hunt in the wilds of Brazil. Later books show Johns adopting equally conventional plots, and with the addition to Biggles's team of 15-year-old Ginger Hebblethwaite, the stories tend to focus upon the group's attempts to solve mysteries. The narrative line becomes increasingly formulaic, as the group separate for their investigations, and one part of the group always has to rescue the other from its difficulties. Thus in *Biggles—Air Commodore,* for example, the characters set out to find out why merchant ships are being sunk in the Indian Ocean, but when the group separate to begin their search, Ginger and Algy crash in the jungle, and have to be rescued by Biggles, and later when Biggles and Ginger are lost on an island Algy has to return the compliment. Thus a device initially

used to create suspense soon became predictable and monotonous.

The outbreak of World War II enabled Johns to describe Biggles resuming active service in such books as *Biggles Defies the Swastika* and *Biggles in the Orient.* (He also wrote 11 books about a heroine Squadron Officer Joan Worralson, "Worrals" of the Women's Auxiliary Air Force, as well as a series about an army hero, "Gimlet" King of the Commandos.) After the war, Johns continued to narrate Biggles's career, usually as an officer in the Air Police, in such books as *Sergeant Bigglesworth C.I.D.* and *Biggles Works It Out.* From 1954 he also began to publish a series of science-fiction stories, beginning with *Kings of Space,* the first of 10 books about the adventures of Professor Brane and the crew of his spaceship.

Despite the science fiction, and the stories about Worrals and Gimlet, however, it is the books—102 all told—about Biggles upon which Johns's reputation rests. In 1964 indeed the first UNESCO Statistical Year Book reported that so many books about him had been published worldwide that Biggles was the most popular juvenile hero in the world. Yet these books are the subject of considerable controversy. Although Johns hoped that his flying-story adventures would teach his juvenile readers such virtues as courage, sportsmanship "according to the British idea," teamwork, and loyalty to the Empire, many critics have pointed to the presence of racism implicit in any defence of imperialism, and to the simple, stereotyped view of foreigners present in Johns's works.

As the plots in the later stories became more formulaic and predictable, and the language became increasingly littered with clichés, and as the character of Biggles himself became more tight-lipped and imperturbable, so Johns's attitude seems to have shifted from a differentiation between good and bad Germans in the early war stories to a derogatory treatment of most non-Europeans in the later books. In this respect Johns is partly the product of his time, of course, and it is pleasing to learn that in his last unfinished tale Biggles's successor was to have been an Indian. For these reasons, however, the major interest of most of Johns's books today is likely to be of a cultural or historical kind, but readers and commentators do him a disservice when they ignore the early stories.

—Dennis Butts

JOHNSON, Annabel and Edgar. Also write as A.E. Johnson. Americans. **JOHNSON, Annabel (née Jones):** Born in Kansas City, Missouri, 18 June 1921. Educated at William and Mary College, Williamsburg, Virginia, 1939–40; Art Students' League, New York. Married Edgar Johnson in 1949. **JOHNSON, Edgar (Raymond):** Born in Washoe, Montana, 24 October 1912. Educated at Billings Polytechnic Institute, Montana; Kansas City Art Institute; Alfred University, New York. Head of the Ceramics Department, Kansas City Art Institute, 1948–49. Recipients: Western Writers of America Spur award, 1967. Address: 2925 South Teller, Denver, Colorado 80227, U.S.A.

PUBLICATIONS FOR CHILDREN

Fiction

As a Speckled Bird (by Annabel Johnson alone). New York, Crowell, 1956; London, Hodder and Stoughton, 1958.
The Big Rock Candy. New York, Crowell, 1957.
The Black Symbol, illustrated by Brian Saunders. New York, Harper, 1959; Leicester, Brockhampton Press, 1960.
Torrie, illustrated by Pearl Falconer. New York, Harper, 1960;

Leicester, Brockhampton Press, 1961.
The Bearcat. New York, Harper, and London, Hamish Hamilton, 1960.
The Rescued Heart. New York, Harper, 1961.
The Secret Gift (as A.E. Johnson). New York, Doubleday, and London, Hodder and Stoughton, 1961.
Pickpocket Run. New York, Harper, 1961.
Wilderness Bride. New York, Harper, 1962.
A Golden Touch. New York, Harper, 1963.
The Grizzly, illustrated by Gilbert Riswold. New York, Harper, 1964; Bath, Chivers, 1973.
A Peculiar Magic, illustrated by Lynd Ward. Boston, Houghton Mifflin, 1965.
The Burning Glass. New York, Harper, 1966.
Count Me Gone. New York, Simon and Schuster, 1968.
A Blues I Can Whistle (as A.E. Johnson). New York, Four Winds Press, 1969.
The Last Knife. New York, Simon and Schuster, 1971.
Finders Keepers. New York, Four Winds Press, 1981.
An Alien Music. New York, Four Winds Press, 1982.
The Danger Quotient. New York, Harper, 1984.
Prisoner of Psi. New York, Atheneum, 1985.
A Memory of Dragons. New York, Atheneum, 1986.

*

Manuscript Collection: Kerlan Collection, University of Minnesota, Minneapolis.

Annabel and Edgar Johnson comment:

Books by Annabel and Edgar Johnson can be counted on to concern themselves with some aspect of life in the western United States, either past or present. Their historical novels have concerned such commonplace aspects of life in the mountain states as the gold rush, unionizing the coal mines, the westward trek across the Oregon and Mormon trails, and the early days of the fur trade, and yet reviewers have felt that these stories have immediacy and bearing upon the lives of young people today.

*   *   *

Annabel and Edgar Johnson's historically located stories are distinguished by a highly economical use of detail which, without any evident labouring to do so, brings home to us just what life must have been like on the American frontier in the 19th century. Even more impressive is the unobtrusive but wholesomely insistent moral concern which is discreetly embodied in the narrative texture itself: as the story unfolds we find ourselves sharing the young protagonist's discovery of the realities of human nature in other people and in himself or herself. In *Torrie* the 14-year-old heroine is unwillingly uprooted from her comfortable home in St. Louis to undertake a 2000 mile trek by ox-drawn wagon to California. As the hardships of the journey unroll, only slowly does she learn to value the qualities of leadership now revealed in her insignificant-looking schoolmaster father, the staunchness and selflessness of her mother, the love of her parents for each other and for herself and her brother. It is not till the climax of the journey, when she accidentally learns that the true purpose of her parents in undertaking their migration has been concern for her own health, that the full extent of her misconception of herself and her parents is made clear to her. The rigours of the dangerous and eventful journey have brought a new stature as well as a new self-knowledge to each member of the family; and we leave them established in a cabin in California, with the prospect of a new pioneering farming life ahead of them, and a securely founded love burgeoning between Torrie and Jess, the family's young hired teamster.

Torrie has a strong emotional appeal for girls of any age above about 12, whereas *The Black Symbol* is rather more of a boys' book, though not exclusively so. The central character is Barney, who runs away from his uncle to search for his gold-miner father, and joins a travelling medicine show run by the smooth-talking Dr. Cathcart. Dr. Cathcart and his assistant Hoke Wilson clearly owe something to "The King" and "The Duke" in *Huckleberry Finn,* and the core of the book is Barney's gradual discovery of the coldhearted sadistic ruthlessness of these two villains. The detailed trickery of the carnival is neatly worked into the plot, which involves two other members of the troupe, the frightened negro boy Billy, and the blind "Strong Man" Steve.

In their later fiction the Johnsons have moved increasingly towards the present day, and in their most recent novels into the future. In *Finders Keepers* two independent-minded teenagers struggle desperately to survive in the aftermath of a catastrophic explosion at a nuclear power plant near Denver; there is a graphic and disturbing depiction of panic and savagery among the city dwellers who swarm westward into mountainous country to escape the radioactive fall-out. In *An Alien Music* the ecological disaster is a manmade build-up of carbon dioxide in the atmosphere which heats the earth's surface to a point where it becomes uninhabitable. Jesse, a 15-year-old orphan girl with Indian blood, bluffs her way on to the NASA Sky-Lab which her brother has helped design to carry a select group of people to the planet Mars to form a human colony there. The excitements of the ensuing space voyage are exceptionally convincing, both in their technological aspects and in the treatment of human tensions within the crew. In particular Jesse's shifting and ambivalent relationship with the commander, Ben Hammond, brings into focus important questions concerning the nature of leadership, democracy, and self-discipline. *The Danger Quotient* starts in the year 2127 in an underground colony built as refuge from the nuclear holocaust, whence the young narrator journeys by means of a "time refractor" to Denver in 1981, 1945, and 1918 seeking insight into factors that could decide his own fate as well as that of his fellow-survivors. His contacts at these different dates with members of the same American family are interwoven with great ingenuity into a pattern adding an absorbing human dimension to the temporal jigsaw puzzle. Each of these three novels is told in the first person, in the authentic-sounding idiom of an American teenager yet with a linguistic flair which is able to encompass subtle moral and social issues.

Prisoner of Psi achieves similar effects through a slightly more complex narrative structure in which segments of third-person narrative are intercut with excerpts from the diary kept by Tris, the psychically gifted son of a noted television psychic who has been kidnapped, in 2000 A.D., by a ruthless terrorist organisation. The gripping story of his eventual rescue makes skilful use of E.S.P. paraphernalia and at the same time explores subtly and sensitively (not for the first time in the Johnsons' fiction) the topic of misunderstanding and conflict between parent and child. *A Memory of Dragons* is set in an unspecified future of world conflict and shortages, with an impending secession from the United States by its western states actively on the cards. Sought as an ally by both sides on account of his flair for inventing high-tech gadgetry, Paul Killian's involvement is complicated by an inchoate burden of personal guilt which he is able to exorcise only after a series of time-travel excursions into an ancestor's experiences of the earlier American Civil War. As with its immediate predecessors, the intricate and absorbing narrative is conveyed through a series of brief, enticingly readable cameos which are brilliantly orchestrated into a complex yet coherent whole.

—Frank Whitehead

JOHNSON, Crockett. Pseudonym for David Johnson Leisk. American.   Born in New York City, 20 October 1906. Educated at Cooper Union, New York, 1924; New York University, 1925. Married Ruth Krauss, *q.v.,* in 1940. Drew weekly panel "Little Man with the Eyes" for *Collier's,* 1938–41, and the syndicated comic strip "Barnaby," 1941–62, and panel "Barkis," 1955. *Died 11 July 1975.*

PUBLICATIONS FOR CHILDREN (illustrated by the author)

Fiction

Who's Upside Down?   New York, Scott, 1952; as *Upside Down,* Chicago, Whitman, 1969.
Harold and the Purple Crayon.   New York, Harper, 1955; London, Constable, 1957.
Is This You?, with Ruth Krauss.   New York, Scott, 1955; London, Pitman, 1966.
Harold's Fairy Tale: Further Adventures with the Purple Crayon. New York, Harper, 1956.
Harold's Trip to the Sky.   New York, Harper, 1957.
Terrible, Terrifying Toby.   New York, Harper, 1957.
Time for Spring.   New York, Harper, 1957.
The Blue Ribbon Puppies.   New York, Harper, 1958.
Harold at the North Pole: A Christmas Journey with the Purple Crayon.   New York, Harper, 1958.
Merry Go Round.   New York, Harper, 1958.
Ellen's Lion: Twelve Stories.   New York, Harper, 1959; Kingswood, Surrey, World's Work, 1964.
The Frowning Prince.   New York, Harper, 1959.
Harold's Circus.   New York, Harper, 1959.
Will Spring Be Early or Will Spring Be Late?   New York, Crowell, 1960.
A Picture for Harold's Room: A Purple Crayon Adventure.   New York, Harper, 1960; Kingswood, Surrey, World's Work, 1963.
Harold's ABC.   New York, Harper, 1963.
The Lion's Own Story: Eight New Stories about Ellen's Lion.   New York, Harper, 1963; Kingswood, Surrey, World's Work, 1964.
We Wonder What Will Walter Be When He Grows Up?   New York, Holt Rinehart, 1964; Kingswood, Surrey, World's Work, 1966.
Castles in the Sand, illustrated by Betty Fraser.   New York, Holt Rinehart, 1965; Kingswood, Surrey, World's Work, 1967.
Gordy and the Pirate, and the Circus Ringmaster, and the Knight, and the Major League Manager, and the Western Marshal, and the Astronaut, and a Remarkable Achievement.   New York, Putnam, 1965.
The Emperor's Gifts.   New York, Holt Rinehart, 1965; Kingswood, Surrey, World's Work, 1966.

PUBLICATIONS FOR ADULTS

Other

Barnaby.   New York, Holt, 1943.
Barnaby and Mr. O'Malley.   New York, Holt, 1944.
Barkis: Some Precise and Some Speculative Interpretations of the Meaning of a Dog's Bark at Certain Times and in Certain (Illustrated) Circumstances.   New York, Simon and Schuster, 1956.

*

Illustrator: *The Carrot Seed,* 1945, *How to Make an Earthquake,* 1954, and *The Happy Egg,* 1967, all by Ruth Krauss; *Story of Money* by Constance Foster, 1950; *Willie's Adventures* by Margaret Wise

Brown, 1954; *Mickey's Magnet* by Franklin and Branley, 1956; *The Little Fish That Got Away* by Bernardine Cook, 1957.

*   *   *

Crockett Johnson was the creator of *Barnaby,* a comic strip forever cherished in the memories of those who knew it. Mr. O'Malley, Barnaby's inefficient fairy godfather, is the key figure. Square and squat and hatted, Mr. O'Malley has inadequate wings, a cigar for a wand, and a lifetime membership in the Little Men's Chowder and Marching Society. He is badly miscast as a fairy godfather, and Barnaby spends most of his time extracting himself from the messes Mr. O'Malley gets both of them into.

Johnson wrote a number of children's books as well. These are blessed with the same clear drawings and pervasive humor as the *Barnaby* strip, though the humor is less adult. Johnson managed the delicate feat of writing whimsically for children without falling into sentimentality. *Harold and the Purple Crayon,* perhaps his most successful book for children, is a virtuoso performance. The simple, convincing pictures illustrate a gently humorous text about a little boy creating his own adventurous excursion into the world with his purple crayon. The firm purple line grows from page to page, making a moon, a road, an ocean, a picnic, and animals to eat the leftovers, a city full of windows (but not the right window), until Harold, always calm and in command, draws his own window, his own bed and his own covers to pull up, and so ends his expedition. *A Picture for Harold's Room,* an "I Can Read Book," is a little flatter, perhaps because of the restricted vocabulary; *Harold's ABC* may be slightly too intricate for its audience.

Ellen's Lion and *The Lion's Own Story* demonstrate Johnson's ability to keep a nice balance between imagination and reality. The two books are collections of very brief stories consisting of dialogues between Ellen (perhaps 5 years old) and her stuffed lion. Ellen leads an extremely busy and adventurous life being a knight, a mountain climber, a doctor, and planning to be a "lady fireman." She is sometimes aided, but reluctantly, by her lion, who never for a moment forgets that he is stuffed, has button eyes and no powers of locomotion. He is the realist, she the Walter Mitty; together they make two amusing books, very Crockett Johnson.

Another Walter Mitty character is Gordy, of *Gordy and the Pirate,* who encounters on the way home from school a pirate and several other romantic figures, all of whom invite him to the most tempting adventures. But Gordy remembers each time, just in time, that this is the day he promised to go straight home from school. And so, eventually, he does: "And, for Gordy, that was indeed a remarkable achievement." Unfortunately, the gentle irony of the story may well go over the heads of its intended readers.

And that, indeed, may be the principal problem with some of Johnson's stories. It is not that he was given to winking over the heads of children at the adults who might be reading the stories aloud. It is just that the perspective necessary to catch the joke may be a little beyond the child for whom the story is meant. Johnson always perceived the humor of the human ego, though kindly. Just as Mr. O'Malley's inflated self-esteem is the basis for much of the fun in *Barnaby,* so some of the humor in the two *Ellen* books and the main joke of *We Wonder What Will Walter Be When He Grows Up?* depends upon a recognition of egocentricity. But small children, who are themselves egocentric, may not see it. And some of the word play in *Walter*—the characterization of the mole as the "deepest thinker," the giraffe as the "highest thinker" and so forth—seems to rest upon an acquaintance with certain clichés which little children may not have.

—Anne Scott MacLeod

JONES, Diana Wynne. British. Born in London, 16 August 1934. Educated at Friends' School, Saffron Walden, Essex. 1946–53; St. Anne's College, Oxford, 1953–56, B.A. 1956. Married J.A. Burrow in 1956; three sons. Recipient: *Guardian* award, 1978. Agent: Laura Cecil, 17 Alwyne Villas, London N1 2HG. Address: 9 The Polygon, Clifton, Bristol BS8 4PW, England.

PUBLICATIONS FOR CHILDREN

Fiction

Wilkins' Tooth, illustrated by Julia Rodber. London, Macmillan, 1973; as *Witch's Business,* New York, Dutton, 1974.
The Ogre Downstairs. London, Macmillan, 1974; New York, Dutton, 1975.
Eight Days of Luke. London, Macmillan, 1975; New York, Greenwillow, 1988.
Cart and Cwidder. London, Macmillan, 1975; New York, Atheneum, 1977.
Dogsbody. London, Macmillan, 1975; New York, Greenwillow, 1977.
Power of Three. London, Macmillan, 1976; New York, Greenwillow, 1977.
Charmed Life. London, Macmillan, and New York, Greenwillow, 1977.
Drowned Ammet. London, Macmillan, 1977; New York, Atheneum, 1978.
Who Got Rid of Angus Flint?, illustrated by John Sewell. London, Evans, 1978.
The Spellcoats. London, Macmillan, and New York, Atheneum, 1979.
The Magicians of Caprona. London, Macmillan, and New York, Greenwillow, 1980.
The Four Grannies, illustrated by Thelma Lambert. London, Hamish Hamilton, 1980.
The Homeward Bounders. London, Macmillan, and New York, Greenwillow, 1981.
The Time of the Ghost. London, Macmillan, 1981.
Witch Week. London, Macmillan, and New York, Greenwillow, 1982.
Archer's Goon. London, Methuen, and New York, Greenwillow, 1984.
Warlock at the Wheel and Other Stories. London, Macmillan, and New York, Greenwillow, 1984.
Fire and Hemlock. New York, Greenwillow, 1984; London, Methuen, 1985.
Howl's Moving Castle. London, Methuen, and New York, Greenwillow, 1986.
A Tale of Time City. New York, Greenwillow, and London, Methuen, 1987.
The Lives of Christopher Chant. London, Methuen, and New York, Greenwillow, 1988.
Chair Person, illustrated by Glenys Ambrus. London, Hamish Hamilton, 1989.

Plays

The Batterpool Business (produced London, 1967).
The King's Things (produced London, 1969).
The Terrible Fisk Machine (produced London, 1970).

Other

The Skiver's Guide, illustrated by Chris Winn. London, Knight, 1984.

Editor, *Hidden Turnings: A Collection of Stories Through Time and Space.* London, Methuen, 1989.

PUBLICATIONS FOR ADULTS

Novel

Changeover. London, Macmillan, 1970.

*

Diana Wynne Jones comments:
Everything I have written so far has been fantasy, and a great deal of it comic. I want to provide exciting and amusing reading for children, and I should be bored myself if I did not. But I also try to use fantasy—just as one would use a metaphor—to say things about life. It seems to me that very complicated things can be said to children by these simple means, and appreciated by them. (In the same way, I think children can grasp difficult words if the sentence and story are lucid enough.) Each time I write a book I try to say something new, with the result that each book turns out differently from the ones before—which surprises, puzzles, and pleases me in about equal proportions.

*   *   *

The amazingly prolific (and high-quality) author Diana Wynne Jones is not far short of publishing her 20th full-length children's novel, in less than 20 years. Ever striving for originality, and remaining so far faithful to the genre of fantasy, in each book she employs a different supernatural theme and setting, for example, the traditional nasty old witch, legendary gods operating in the modern world, the enchanted animal, tiny fairy people living in secret, the unhappy ghost, fantasy wargaming, and time travel.

Children are her main characters, usually unhappy, unsettled children to whom magic comes first as an extra burden, and then, if they can master it, as a way of solving their personal crises. The common problems of child life—absent or hostile parents, quarrelsome siblings, and powerlessness against adult caprice—are solved by magic operated by a child who has achieved a new self-realisation on the road to maturity. In this way Jones follows the tradition of E. Nesbit, whose child characters often experience magical adventures while their family lives are disturbed.

In *The Ogre Downstairs,* her accomplished second novel, two families are "united" when the "ogre," father of two boys, marries a mother of three children. To make peace, stepfather gives each group a chemistry set. But the chemicals turn out to be magic, and as the children can't understand the Latin labels, and experiment blindly, endless disasters are caused and the children daren't explain to mother. When mother walks out in despair at the chaos at home, her children can only get her back by making friends with the other children and their hated stepfather.

Each book contains realistic family situations, and the business of living, not excluding death, is seriously analysed. The heroine of *Dogsbody* is Irish, with a father in prison: he escapes and is killed. The Little People in *Power of Three* are threatened with extinction when humans plan to flood their moor; they have also been engaged in a blood feud with a tribe of water spirits. Many of her main characters lose their parents one way or another, either by death or permanent separation, like Jamie in *The Homeward Bounders,* who takes 100 years to get back to his own world, by which time his family is dead.

In an article for the *Times Literary Supplement* (11 July 1975) Jones explained how children accept tragic elements in their reading, and how fantasy can help them: "tragedy is both close and frequent among children...Possibly what they love is the core of tragedy, modified by fantasy and its sting removed by laughter." She does indeed balance the serious side of her stories with generous helpings of humour, including slapstick pile-ups and recurring mis-understandings.

Two linked sequences of novels have developed out of her work, one comic and one heroic. The Chrestomanci cycle (*Charmed Life, The Magicians of Caprona, Witch Week, The Lives of Christopher Chant*) is set in a world where magic exists and is legalised. Chrestomanci is appointed by the government as chief enchanter and troubleshooter to prevent magic being used for evil purposes. In the first three novels he helps children discover their particular magical talent; the stories are told with plenty of humour, as the children's experiments with magic go wrong or turn into practical jokes. *The Lives of Christopher Chant* recapitulates the plot of *Charmed Life* in a more serious mode. Christopher, who will become the Chrestomanci of the first three books, is flattered by his dubious uncle Ralph into using his magic powers to travel to other worlds and bring back strange goods. Before he discovers Ralph's true wickedness he loses several of his nine lives.

Jones is also the creator of the secondary world of Dalemark, a feudal country rather like mediaeval Iceland, once ruled by a king but now divided into free North and tyrannised South. Here is scope for serious political commentary relevant to our own times, and Clennen spies for the North in *Cart and Cwidder*, and Mitt joins the underground revolutionaries in *Drowned Ammet*. The supernatural element in Dalemark is derived not so much from magical talent as from the gods of Dalemark, who bestow their favours on our heroes and heroines when they decide, however uncertain and ignorant of their potential, to dare their utmost in the service of Good against Evil.

The Spellcoats, set in Dalemark's legendary past, and one of Jones's best books, tells how the girl Tanaqui saves her people from a terrible enchanter by weaving two spellcoats that counteract his magic. The story is told by Tanaqui, and we observe how she gradually becomes more confident in her powers as she enlists the help of the local deities of river and landscape. In the brilliant, moving climax we are not even told whether she wins her struggle: her narrative ends as she sets out to use the second spellcoat, and a final note from a keeper of antiquities centuries later (contemporary with the other two Dalemark novels) describes the discovery of the two spellcoats in a marsh.

In the 1980's, responding to increasing enthusiasm from her adult readers, including many science-fiction addicts, Jones has maintained her original plotting and consciously written on two levels, so that although still published "for children" she deploys political and romantic elements to please adult readers, and has moved into the science-fiction genre. *Archer's Goon,* with its family of good and bad wizards controlling a town, is clearly a satire on local government (and was deliberately published in 1984). *A Tale of Time City* uses the science-fiction concept of a Time Patrol working to preserve historical events as we know them and defeat rogue time-travellers out to change history for greed. The setting, however, is Time City itself, an exotic place out of time which monitors all other epochs.

A new development, the fantasy romance for teenagers, has been very successful, producing two books considered among her best, *Fire and Hemlock* and *Howl's Moving Castle. Fire and Hemlock,* exceptionally long, recounts the story of a girl of today who fatefully meets a young man under the spell of the Faerie Queen. Over the nine years she knows him, their friendship develops, through her teenage crush and several years of separation when she is bewitched by the Queen herself, until she is old enough at 19 to meet him on equal terms—but it is Halloween and Tom's life and soul are forfeit to the demonic powers unless she can save him.

Howl's Moving Castle, set in a kind of Fairyland, is the love story of Howl, a young wizard, and the formerly lovely Sophie, who has been enchanted into the shape of an old woman. She becomes Howl's housekeeper, hoping to find out how to get her youth back, and a love-hate relationship develops between them as she tries to keep her identity secret. Rich in invention, this story is more carefully shaped than usual, for it must be admitted that Jones has not reached the wide readership in the United Kingdom that her dedication to quality and originality deserve primarily because of the rambling nature of her plotting, and the way she takes her readers' intelligence and previous reading experience in science-fiction and fantasy genres for granted; however, these are the features that continue to endear her to her admirers.

—Jessica Yates

JONES, Gwyneth A.   See HALAM, Ann.

JORDAN, June.   American.   Born in New York City, 9 July 1936. Educated at Midwood High School, Brooklyn, New York; Northfield School for Girls, Massachusetts, 1950–53; Barnard College, New York, 1953–55, 1956–57; University of Chicago, 1955–56. Married Michael Meyer in 1955 (divorced 1966); one son. Assistant to the producer of the film *The Cool World,* 1964; research associate, Mobilization for Youth Inc., New York, 1965–66; director, Voice of the Children, 1967–70; member of the English Department, City College, New York, 1967–70, 1972–75, and 1977–78, Connecticut College, New London, 1968, Sarah Lawrence College, Bronxville, New York, 1971–75, and Yale University, New Haven, Connecticut, 1974–75. Associate Professor, 1978–82, since 1982 Professor of English, and since 1986 director of the Poetry Center and the Creative Writing Program, State University of New York, Stony Brook. Poet-in-residence, Teachers and Writers Collaborative, New York, 1966–68, MacAlester College, St. Paul, Minnesota, 1980, Loft Mentor Series, Minneapolis, 1983, and Walt Whitman Birthplace, Huntington, New York, 1988; Reid Lecturer, Barnard College, 1976; Chancellor's Lecturer, University of California, Berkeley, 1986; playwright-in-residence, New Dramatists, New York, 1987–88. Member of the Executive Board, PEN American Center, 1980–84, Poets and Writers Inc. since 1979, American Writers Congress since 1981, Center for Constitutional Rights since 1984, and Authors Guild since 1986. Recipient: Rockefeller grant, 1969; American Academy in Rome Environmental Design prize, 1970; Creative Artists Public Service grant, 1978; Yaddo fellowship, 1979, 1980; National Endowment for the Arts fellowship, 1982; National Association of Black Journalists award, 1984; New York Foundation for the Arts fellowship, 1985; Massachusetts Council on the Arts award, 1985; MacDowell Colony fellowship, 1987. Address: Department of English, State University of New York, Stony Brook, New York 11790, U.S.A.

PUBLICATIONS FOR CHILDREN

Fiction

His Own Where—.   New York, Crowell, 1971.
New Life, New Room, illustrated by Ray Cruz.   New York, Crowell, 1975.
Kimako's Story, illustrated by Kay Burford.   Boston, Houghton Mifflin, 1981.

Verse

Who Look at Me?   New York, Crowell, 1969.

Other

Dry Victories.   New York, Holt Rinehart, 1972.
Fannie Lou Hamer (biography), illustrated by Albert Williams. New York, Crowell, 1972.

Editor, with Terri Bush, *The Voice of the Children.*   New York, Holt Rinehart, 1970.
Editor, *Soulscript: Afro-American Poetry.*   New York, Doubleday, 1970.

PUBLICATIONS FOR ADULTS

Plays

Freedom Now Suite, music by Adrienne B. Torf (produced New York, 1984).
The Break, music by Adrienne B. Torf (produced New York, 1984).
The Music of Poetry and the Poetry of Music, music by Adrienne B. Torf (produced Washington, D.C., and New York, 1984).
Bang Bang Über Alles, music by Adrienne B. Torf, lyrics by Jordan (produced Atlanta, 1986).

Verse

Some Changes.   New York, Dutton, 1971.
Poem: On Moral Leadership as a Political Dilemma (Watergate, 1973).   Detroit, Broadside Press, 1973.
New Days: Poems of Exile and Return.   New York, Emerson Hall, 1974.
Things That I Do in the Dark: Selected Poetry.   New York, Random House, 1977; revised edition, Boston, Beacon Press, 1981.
Passion: New Poems 1977–80.   Boston, Beacon Press, 1980.
Living Room.   New York, Thunder's Mouth Press, 1985.
Lyrical Campaigns: Selected Poems.   London, Virago Press, 1989.

Recordings: *Things That I Do in the Dark and Other Poems,* Spoken Arts, 1978; *For Somebody to Start Singing,* with Bernice Reagon, Black Box-Watershed, 1980.

Other

Civil Wars (essays).   Boston, Beacon Press, 1981.
On Call: New Political Essays 1981–1985.   Boston, South End Press, 1985.
Moving Towards Home: Political Essays.   London, Virago Press, 1989.

*

June Jordan comments:

Children/young people seem to me the most important, demanding readership for whom you can write. They are new lives in the world and, therefore, capable of perpetuating the society we now endure or of devising new, positive ways of being alive in humane fellowship. For this reason, I always undertake the writing of books for children as a political and moral opportunity to foster constructive social change.

*   *   *

June Jordan's reputation as a writer for children rests largely on her highly acclaimed novel *His Own Where—*. This is perfectly fitting—it is a masterpiece; Jordan captures the essence of black lives and language in just a few pages. This essence is love, and whether the love is selfish, romantic, benevolent, or materialistic Jordan shows it developing in and providing hope for 16-year-old Buddy and 14-year-old Angela. Buddy and Angela create their "own where" in a deserted cemetery, "a place for loving." Considerable critical attention has been given to the use of "black English" in this novel. In my opinion this style (which adds lyricism to the already exceptionally graceful prose) is secondary, but necessary, to the total effect. *His Own Where—*is more than a love story; it is also a commentary on the ability of black youths to survive in a society that is designed to destroy them: "Buddy leaning on the wall be thinking that the whole city of his people like a all-night emergency room. People mostly suffering, uncomfortable and waiting." But through Buddy and Angela we become aware that creativity and an instinct for survival will make it better: "Where can we go beside the cemetery.…What else is there?…It be like a big, open box…behind them there be a locked-up house where no one ever live.…They see how they would open it up, how they would live inside, what they would do with only the birds, the water and the skylight fallen blinding into it.…And so begins a new day of the new life in the cemetery. Jordan's other children's books reflect her concern for the future of children and for the total fulfillment of the black child. *Who Look at Me?* gives Jordan's vision of what it is like to "exist as Number Two…/If you deny it you should try/being Number Two." The book is extraordinary; it commands: "See me brown girl…/I am black alive and looking back at you."

These books are positive interpretations of and for black children; unfortunately they cannot work by their mere availability. They must be recommended and even (sometimes) pushed by teachers and others who recognize the strong feelings, meaningful images, and real truths that Jordan has revealed.

—Jacqueline Brown Woody

JUDAH, Aaron. British. Born in Bombay, India, 19 October 1923. Educated at Anglo-Indian schools, graduated 1941. Married in 1977; one son. Bridge-boy on a Cunard ship, 1943–44; draughtsman in a munitions factory, London, 1945. Qualified as a physiotherapist, 1949, and practicing physiotherapist in London, Norway, Israel, India, Australia, France, and Spain, 1949–72. From 1972 part-time physiotherapist, and freelance writer. Address: 6 Lower Denmark Road, Ashford, Kent TN23 1SU, England.

PUBLICATIONS FOR CHILDREN

Fiction

Tommy with the Hole in His Shoe, illustrated by Sheila Hawkins. London, Faber, 1957.
Tales of Teddy Bear, illustrated by Sheila Hawkins.   London, Faber, 1958.
The Adventures of Henrietta Hen, illustrated by Sheila Hawkins. London, Faber, 1958.
Miss Hare and Mr. Tortoise, illustrated by Sheila Hawkins.   London, Faber, 1959.
The Pot of Gold and Two Other Tales, illustrated by Mervyn Peake. London, Faber, 1959; New York, A.S. Barnes, 1960.

God and Mr. Sourpuss, illustrated by Richard Kennedy. London, Faber, 1959; New York, A.S. Barnes, 1960.

Basil Chimpy Isn't Bright, illustrated by Sheila Hawkins. London, Faber, 1959.

Henrietta in the Snow, illustrated by Sheila Hawkins. London, Faber, 1960.

Basil Chimpy's Comic Light, illustrated by Sheila Hawkins. London, Faber, 1960.

Anna Anaconda: The Swallowing Wonder, illustrated by John Howson. London, Faber, 1960.

Henrietta in Love, illustrated by Sheila Hawkins. London, Faber, 1961.

The Proud Duck, illustrated by the author. London, Faber, 1961.

The Elf's New House, illustrated by Sheila Hawkins. London, Faber, 1962.

Ex-King Max Forever!, illustrated by the author. London, Faber, 1963.

The Careless Cuckoos, illustrated by Sheila Hawkins. London, Faber, 1963.

The Fabulous Haircut, illustrated by the author. London, Faber, 1964.

On the Feast of Stephen, illustrated by Sheila Hawkins. London, Faber, 1965.

PUBLICATIONS FOR ADULTS

Novels

Clown of Bombay. London, Faber, 1963; New York, Dial Press, 1968.

Clown on Fire. London, Macdonald, 1965; New York, Dial Press, 1967.

Cobweb Pennant. London, Dent, 1968.

Lillian's Dam. London, Dent, 1970.

*

Aaron Judah comments:

My biggest hazard now is the opposition offered by television. I am writing some stories for my own son and using him as a kind of editor-cum-soundingboard. This is the first time I am writing for an actual child rather than for myself as a child, and something different is certainly appearing. My stories admittedly make very strong demands on the child's imagination. The reading process is the opposite of the stupefactive effect of daily TV. The contest is very unequal, but one presses on. The audience for the creative writer is shrinking but as long as a single mite is still listening, one writes.

*   *   *

Aaron Judah peoples his stories with childlike humans of all ages, and with animals. The animals inhabit both the real world of nature, where the chase and sudden death are part of the order of things, and also the anthropomorphic world in which they represent the vices and virtues. Foxes are cunning, camels haughty and selfish, monkeys irresponsible, while owls are learned, hedgehogs kindly, and pandas old and wise. Nothing very unusual in all this, of course, the very stuff of the best nursery stories in the tradition of Beatrix Potter and Alison Uttley. Again, like many a good storyteller before him, Judah tells a tale to point a moral without falling into moralising attitudes.

The nursery story is an over-constrained genre: all the more remarkable that this writer should have brought a freshness to it. His language is necessarily simple, direct, used with economy (though he'll stretch the young reader where precision demands it); his images are concrete, his tone often lyrical without being coy or

whimsical. There are drama, often heavily charged with emotion, rich humour, and inventive characterisation. No one who has met Mr. Makeshift Monkey in *Tommy with the Hole in His Shoe* or Anna Anaconda is likely easily to forget them.

The tone is central to the success of these tales. The words leap from the page demanding to be read aloud. He *shares* the experience of the stories with the young reader or listener. His voice is that of an enthralled observer excitedly and intimately drawing attention to the wonder he sees around him. Nor is he above admitting ignorance when the wonder runs beyond his grasp. We never know what fearsome presence caused the desperate Henrietta to scurry to the hollow oak (*The Adventures of Henrietta Hen*). We cannot tell, and Judah doesn't attempt to explain, what it was that God did to change Mr. Sourpuss, but we delight in that gentleman's joy at his new-found happiness.

Miss Hare and Mr. Tortoise brings together under one title all that is best in this writer's work. There are desperate fear, tenderness, humour, lyricism, harsh reality, and the celebration of wonder all artfully balanced in this exquisite love story, and what must surely be the gentlest, most reassuring low-key ending of any bedtime story ever written.

—Myles McDowell

———

JUSTER, Norton. American. Born in Brooklyn, New York, 2 June 1929. Educated at the University of Pennsylvania, Philadelphia, B. Arch. 1952; University of Liverpool (Fulbright scholar), 1952–53. Served in the United States Naval Reserve Civil Engineer Corps, 1954–57. Married Jeanne Ray in 1964. Architect, Juster and Gugliotta, New York, 1960–68; instructor in environmental design, Pratt Institute, New York, 1960–70. Since 1969 architect, Juster-Pope Associates, Shelburne Falls, Massachusetts, and since 1970 Professor of Design, Hampshire College, Amherst, Massachusetts. Recipient: Ford grant, 1960; George G. Stone Center for Children's Books award, 1971. Agent: Sterling Lord Literistic, 1 Madison Avenue, New York, New York 10010. Address: 259 Lincoln Avenue, Amherst, Massachusetts 01002, U.S.A.

PUBLICATIONS FOR CHILDREN

Fiction

The Phantom Tollbooth, illustrated by Jules Feiffer. New York, Epstein and Carroll, 1961; London, Collins, 1962.

The Dot and the Line: A Romance in Lower Mathematics. New York, Random House, 1963; London, Nelson, 1964.

Alberic the Wise and Other Journeys, illustrated by Domenico Gnoli. New York, Pantheon, 1965; London, Nelson, 1966.

Verse

Otter Nonsense, illustrated by Eric Carle. New York, Philomel, 1982; London, Faber, 1983.

As: A Surfeit of Similes, illustrated by David Small. New York, Morrow, 1989.

PUBLICATIONS FOR ADULTS

Other

Stark Naked: A Paranomastic Odyssey, illustrated by Arnold Roth. New York, Random House, 1969.

So Sweet to Labor: Rural Women in America 1865–1895. New York, Viking Press, 1979.

* * *

In Norton Juster's *The Phantom Tollbooth*, young Milo has become painfully bored with school: he regards "the process of seeking knowledge as the greatest waste of time of all." One afternoon when he dejectedly returns home from school, he discovers that a large package has mysteriously appeared in his room. The box contains a turnpike tollbooth and accompanying signs. Milo drives his pedal car past the tollbooth into the fantasy portion of the plot where enchantment, magic, and impossible events become believable.

In the fantasy realm beyond the magical tollbooth, Milo travels to the cities of Dictionopolis and Digitopolis where he encounters adventures, characters, and places that are allegories for the subjects he has studied in school. In both places, Milo encounters grotesque parodies of learning. In Dictionopolis, Milo learns from Faintly Macabre the Official Which that the problems in the Kingdom of Wisdom have resulted from the banishment of the Princesses Rhyme and Reason, who represent good sense, grace, and decorum. Their absence robs knowledge of human meaning and emotional significance. One story that Milo hears can serve as an example of this. Faintly tells Milo that, as the Official Which, she was given the task of "choosing which words were to be used for all occasions." At first she offered helpful guidelines such as "brevity is the soul of Wit." In the absence of Rhyme and Reason, however, the guide quickly became the tyrant. If brevity is good, miserliness of words is better. Soon the pronouncement "Silence is Golden" became law. Instead of enhancing communication, notions of effective language have led to silence.

Without Rhyme and Reason, the use of words and numbers can become mere games devoid of human meaning. This state of affairs directly parallels Milo's earlier disenchantment with schooling and shows how the fantasy world of *The Phantom Tollbooth* acts as a commentary on, indeed a corrective of, Milo's perceptions of his life in the actual world.

When Milo decides to set out on a quest to bring back the Princesses Rhyme and Reason from the Mountains of Ignorance, he is clearly also searching for his own identity in relationship to the subjects he studies in school. After many adventures he rescues the Princesses from the Castle in the Air. When he returns to his own room, having been away only an hour, he discovers that he has a new sense of the pleasures and beauties of the world around him. He appears to have achieved a strong identity that will not be depressed and overburdened by pressures in school. When the tollbooth disappears from his room, he regrets its loss but concludes that the real world around him provides more than ample adventure.

The Phantom Tollbooth owes much to *Alice's Adventures in Wonderland* in style and theme. As in *Alice,* the humor is developed through wordplay. Juster literalizes idioms, a device that children especially like, as seen in an episode where Milo jumps to a place call Conclusions. Puns are used throughout the book: at a banquet in Dictionopolis, for example, "rigamaroles," "ragamuffins," and "synonym buns" are served. Like Alice, Milo's growth in character is indicated by his assertion of identity against the restrictions of a foolish and sterile educational system, particularly as seen in his increasing ability to use language effectively. Unlike *Alice,* however, *The Phantom Tollbooth* is not obviously a dream fantasy but instead relies on the device of the magical tollbooth to create the structure of the fantasy world.

—William D. Anderson

KAHL, Virginia (Caroline). American. Born in Milwaukee, Wisconsin, 18 February 1919. Educated at Milwaukee-Downer College, 1936–40, B.A. 1940; University of Wisconsin, Madison, 1956–57, Master of Library Science 1957. Library assistant, Milwaukee Public Library, 1942–48; librarian, Berlin, and command librarian, Salzburg, United States Army, 1948–55; librarian, Madison public schools, Wisconsin, 1958–61; library director, Menomonee Falls Public Library, Wisconsin, 1961–68. Since 1970 librarian, Alexandria Library, Virginia. Member of the faculty, George Washington University Continuing Education for Women Center, Washington, D.C., 1970–80. Address: c/o Scribner's 866 Third Avenue, New York, New York 10022, U.S.A.

PUBLICATIONS FOR CHILDREN (illustrated by the author)

Fiction

Away Went Wolfgang! New York, Scribner, 1954.
Maxie. New York, Scribner, 1956.
Droopsi. New York, Scribner, 1958.
Here Is Henri!, with Edith Vacheron. New York, Scribner, 1959.
More about Henri!, with Edith Vacheron. New York, Scribner, 1961.
Giants, Indeed! New York, Scribner, 1974.
Whose Cat Is That? New York, Scribner, 1979.

Verse

The Duchess Bakes a Cake. New York, Scribner, 1955; London, Collins, 1977.
Plum Pudding for Christmas. New York, Scribner, 1956.
The Habits of Rabbits. New York, Scribner, 1957.
The Perfect Pancake. New York, Scribner, 1960.
The Baron's Booty. New York, Scribner, 1963.
How Do You Hide a Monster? New York, Scribner, 1971.
Gunhilde's Christmas Booke. New York, Scribner, 1972.
Gunhilde and the Hallowe'en Spell. New York, Scribner, 1975.
How Many Dragons Are Behind the Door? New York, Scribner, 1977.

*

Virginia Kahl comments:
My books will appeal, I hope, to those children who enjoy a simple fantasy and possess a sense of the ridiculous; they carry no message. I am old-fashioned enough to believe that picture books are to be enjoyed by young readers. I leave to others the job of introducing them to the seamy side of life. Early childhood, when books are introduced, should be a time of joy and gaiety. I want children to enjoy my stories, laugh at the pictures, and think back indulgently on my bumbling characters. Probably the single experience that has most influenced my writing was my sojourn in Austria. I was overwhelmed by the scenery and loved the people; and the city of Salzburg is always in the back of my mind when I write my books. As for my pictures, my first editor, Alice Dalgliesh, remarked that she had seldom seen such simple illustrations. Fortunately, they seem appropriate to the text.

* * *

Virginia Kahl is a humorist of the slapstick school. Her "Duchess" books are founded on exuberant exaggeration, the multiplication of some small incident until a mad chaos engulfs the dukedom. A hint of these madcap happenings comes with a mere mention of the Duchess's over-large family: "Madeleine, Gwendolyn, Jane and

Clothilde,/ Willibald, Genevieve, Maud and Mathilde…"—thirteen daughters altogether. This group is soon entangled in the Duchess's innocent-looking ventures, which somehow run riot while the Duke looks on helplessly.

Kahl's success as an entertainer is best seen in *The Duchess Bakes a Cake*—a fantasy which combines rowdy humour with serene rationality. When an over-supply of yeast sends a cake dough rising to heaven with the cook trapped on top, the crisis is resolved when the youngest Duchess child gets hungry. Then everyone simply eats enough of the dough to bring the Duchess down.

> "How lovely!" the Duchess said, "Come, let us sup."
> "I'll start eating down; you start eating up."

The winning combination in this book is apparently the clarity with which silliness and logic have been joined; the personality of the high-born, scatter-brained Duchess; the easily chanted refrain ("All I wanted to make/was a lovely light luscious delectable cake"); the unlabored rhyme and evenly accented rhythm of the verse (which help emphasize the narrative content rather than the form); and the unfamiliar words for small children to savor: pummel, catapult, minstrel, etc.

In *The Baron's Booty* and *The Habits of Rabbits* the plot lines are more familiar: kidnappers overwhelmed by the purely childlike behavior of children they've abducted, rabbits producing an over-population of ridiculous proportions. Yet these are ideal vehicles for the Duchess character and for employing a popular motif of folk-tales—the central role of the youngest family member.

Another memorable creation is a milk-cart dog (in *Away Went Wolfgang!*) who is so seized by the work ethic that he dashes over the cobblestone streets and spills the milk before it can be delivered. Working out his problem entails a surprise incident which turns the milk into another saleable product: butter. But Wolfgang's characterization—the portrayal of devotion and excess energy in a young dog—outshines other features in this tale.

Such high creativity has not been maintained in works like *Gunhilde's Christmas Booke* or *Maxie*. The former presents a predictable series of episodes in which Christmas customs are explained to non-Christians. The rhymed text provides a lighthearted dimension, but the narrative lacks liveliness as well as the usual Christmas ingredients: reverence or wonder. In the latter book the dachshund, Maxie, is allowed to be an explicit moralizer, and is consequently much less attractive than Wolfgang.

Kahl is a writer whose best works for preschool and kindergarten children should not be permitted to lapse into obscurity. The inspired imagination and good craftsmanship in the early books are not often surpassed; and although runaway cake batter is a motif in folk literature, the treatment applied by Kahl is entirely unprecedented. Her work as a whole offers readers a wealth of fresh images and personalities.

—Donnarae MacCann

KAMM, Josephine (Mary, née Hart). British. Born in London, 30 December 1905. Educated at Queen's College School, London, 1915–17; Parents National Educational School, Burgess Hill, Sussex, 1917–23; Triangle Secretarial College, London, 1923. Married George Emile Kamm in 1929 (died); one son. Shorthand typist, British Commonwealth Union, London, 1924–26; assistant secretary, Empire Industries Association, London, 1926–29; shorthand typist, then senior information officer, Ministry of Information,

London, 1939–46; senior information officer, Central Office of Information, London, 1946. Member of National Council, 1957–69, and Executive Committee, 1963–69, National Book League; member of Executive Committee, London Centre of PEN International, 1965–69; member of Committee of Management, Fawcett Library, London, 1967–75. Recipient: Jewish Book Council of America Isaac Siegel Memorial award, 1963. *Died 31 August 1989.*

PUBLICATIONS FOR CHILDREN

Fiction

He Went with Captain Cook, illustrated by G.S. Ronalds.   London, Harrap, 1952.
Janet Carr, Journalist.   London, Lane, 1953; revised edition, Leicester, Brockhampton Press, 1972.
Student Almoner.   London, Lane, 1955.
Return to Freedom, illustrated by William Stobbs.   London and New York, Abelard Schuman, 1962.
Out of Step, illustrated by Jillian Willett.   Leicester, Brockhampton Press, 1962.
Young Mother.   Leicester, Brockhampton Press, and New York, Duell, 1965.
No Strangers Here.   London, Constable, 1968.
First Job.   Leicester, Brockhampton Press, 1969.
Where Do We Go from Here?   Leicester, Brockhampton Press, 1972.
The Starting Point.   Leicester, Brockhampton Press, 1975.
Runaways.   London, Hodder and Stoughton, 1978.

Other

Abraham: A Biography, with Philip Cohen.   London, Union of Liberal and Progressive Synagogues, 1948.
They Served the People (biographies).   London, Lane, 1954.
Men Who Served Africa, illustrated by G.S. Ronalds.   London, Harrap, 1957.
Leaders of the People.   London and New York, Abelard Schuman, 1959.
The Story of Sir Moses Montefiore.   London, Vallentine Mitchell, 1960.
The Story of Mrs. Pankhurst, illustrated by Faith Jaques.   London, Methuen, 1961; as *The Story of Emmeline Pankhurst,* New York, Meredith Press, 1968.
Malaria Ross, illustrated by Anne Linton.   London, Methuen, 1963; New York, Criterion, 1964.
Malaya and Singapore, illustrated by W.B. White and A.W. Gatnell.   London, Longman, 1963.
A New Look at the Old Testament, illustrated by Gwyneth Cole.   London, Gollancz, 1965; as *Kings, Prophets, and History,* New York, McGraw Hill, 1966.
The Story of Fanny Burney, illustrated by Val Biro.   London, Methuen, 1966; New York, Meredith Press, 1967.
Joseph Paxton and the Crystal Palace, illustrated by Faith Jaques.   London, Methuen, 1967.
The Hebrew People: A History of the Jews from Biblical Times to the Present Day.   London, Gollancz, 1967; New York, McGraw Hill, 1968.
Explorers into Africa.   London, Gollancz, and New York, Crowell Collier, 1970.
The Slave Trade.   London, Evans, 1980.

Editor, *A Tale of Two Cities,* by Charles Dickens, illustrated by Barry Wilkinson.   London, Collins, 1973.

PUBLICATIONS FOR ADULTS

Novels

All Quiet at Home.   London, Longman, 1936.
Disorderly Caravan.   London, Harrap, 1938.
Nettles to My Head.   London, Duckworth, 1939.
Peace, Perfect Peace.   London, Duckworth, 1947.
Come, Draw This Curtain.   London, Duckworth, 1948.

Other

Progress Toward Self-Government in the British Colonies.   London, Fosh and Cross, 1945.
African Challenge: The Story of the British in Tropical Africa. London, Nelson, 1946.
Daughter of the Desert: The Story of Gertrude Bell.   London, Lane, 1956; as *Gertrude Bell, Daughter of the Desert,* New York, Vanguard Press, 1956.
How Different from Us: A Biography of Miss Buss and Miss Beale. London, Bodley Head, 1958.
Hope Deferred: Girls' Education in English History.   London, Methuen, 1965.
Rapiers and Battleaxes: The Women's Movement and Its Aftermath. London, Allen and Unwin, 1966.
Indicative Past: A Hundred Years of the Girls' Public Day School Trust.   London, Allen and Unwin, 1971.
John Stuart Mill in Love.   London, Gordon and Cremonesi, 1977.

*

Josephine Kamm comments:

I had hoped to write from the time I first contributed to my school magazine; but a full-time job followed by marriage delayed the plan until my only son started nursery school. I published three adult novels before the outbreak of war in 1939. Throughout the war I worked in the Ministry of Information, chiefly as a writer on Commonwealth affairs. My writing for children began in a haphazard fashion. I never thought seriously about it until I was invited to contribute *He Went with Captain Cook* to a series of novels on great explorers. I found the experience so enjoyable that I decided to continue. My wartime experience led me to concentrate from time to time on a nonfiction book about the Commonwealth for older children, but I remained equally interested in fiction. Historical and career novels were followed by novels on some of the problems which confront young people today, such as racial prejudice, illegitimacy, adoption, and early marriage. These books have been interspersed with non-fiction books for adults.

*   *   *

Josephine Kamm's first children's novels were commissioned to fulfil a clearly defined but limited function—to make useful information more palatable by supplying it in fictional form. Thus *Janet Carr, Journalist* gives us some idea how a woman's magazine is run, but the plot is feeble, and the characterisation stilted. *Student Almoner,* another of the Career Novels for Girls, is rather more successful, retaining our interest by its moderately perceptive portrayal of the student Barbara as shy and lacking confidence in her ability to complete her hospital training successfully, and so communicating some insight into the tasks undertaken by an almoner, and the qualities needed for them. The author's one historical novel, *Return to Freedom,* also carries a heavy information load (the little-known story of how Cromwell did his best to repeal the 400-year-old edict banishing all Jews), accompanied by a rather sparse leavening of fictional incident.

In her later books Kamm has moved into the "problem" novel, seeking to provide enlightened guidance for the teenager on the issues underlying such difficult (and fashionable) topics as race relations, pregnant schoolgirls, pupil power, adolescent crushes, too-early marriage, and so on. In every case the illustrative story is briskly and competently told, and the background to it filled out with painstaking detail; yet despite the good intentions the overwhelming impression is that of stock situations peopled with stereotyped characters whose psychology is rarely probed in any depth. On the credit side, the values underlying the author's rather pedestrian narrative are unfailingly worthy, decent, and humane. Moreover she clearly tries to avoid offering over-simplified solutions; thus at the end of *Out of Step* when 17-year-old Betty Fielding has learned that her brown-skinned Guyanese hero returns her love, we leave her also uncomfortably aware that her most difficult problems still lie ahead.

The deficiencies show up most obviously in *Where Do We Go from Here?* where, although the main theme is pupil power, so many different sixth-formers with different problems are drawn into the net that superficiality of treatment becomes inevitable.

The Starting Point has rather more to be said for it, at any rate in the portrayal of the young husband Dan whose immature dependence on his over-possessive mother nearly wrecks his marriage. However, the best of these novels is also the one that is most widely read, *Young Mother.* Here the depiction of the 16th-year-old schoolgirl's reactions to her pregnancy and to the birth of her illegitimate child does show, within limits, genuine insight, particularly in her unexpected discovery that she cannot bear to part with her baby, in her unsuccessful attempts (defeated by her own immaturity) to keep it and care for it, and in her ultimate acceptance that the best thing she can do for her child is to let it go to the highly suitable adoptive couple to whom it had earlier been promised. Even here, though, the reader gets at most only a very muted sense of what it really feels like to be pregnant and to give birth.

Kamm is, then, one of these writers whose work throws into sharp relief the question of how much weight should be attached to the adult's judgment of juvenile fiction. Is it not possible that what we regard as tired cliché may come to the inexperienced 15-year-old as revelation? Undoubtedly many adolescent girls do read Kamm's novels avidly; and perhaps for parent, teacher, or librarian they are best seen as potential stepping-stones to fiction which carries a higher charge of imaginative vitality.

—Frank Whitehead

KARIUKI, Elijah.   Kenyan.   Address: c/o Longman Kenya Ltd., P.O. Box 18033, Nairobi, Kenya.

PUBLICATIONS FOR CHILDREN

Fiction

The Sun's Daughter.   Nairobi, East African Publishing House, 1976.
Ziki, My Monkey Boy.   Nairobi, Longman, 1979.
A Car Named Safari.   Nairobi, Longman, 1981.
The Engine Puzzle.   Nairobi, Longman, 1981.
The Fire Puzzle.   Nairobi, Longman, 1981.
The Irrigation Puzzle.   Nairobi, Longman, 1981.
The Underground Water Puzzle.   Nairobi, Longman, 1981.
This Country Is My Country.   Nairobi, Longman, 1981.

*   *   *

Elijah Kariuki writes fiction based on folklore and contemporary life for Kenyan school children. His books have been published in series of supplementary school readers, and as a result his stories are didactic; but they also include events and adventures of interest to primary and secondary school children.

The Sun's Daughter is based on a common theme in East African folklore of a handsome young man, Magasi, who refuses to marry any local woman, including the chief's daughter, because he wants to marry the most beautiful woman of all, the sun's daughter Kasai. While travelling in search of Kasai he is captured by an ogre, who tricks him into choosing between marrying the ogre's cannibal daughter or death. Magasi chooses death, but is able to escape before he is killed. Eventually he finds Kasai and upon first meeting they know they are meant for each other, but Magasi must kill the ogre before they can marry. After the couple is married, their kingdoms are united under Magasi's rule, and there is peace and happiness for many years.

A Car Named Safari is about the repair of a 1949 car which the hero dreams of entering in the East African Safari auto race. Like Kariuki's stories in the Puzzlecrackers Series, this one includes adventure, technical knowledge, and cooperation in the achievement of a common goal. The 13-year-old hero and his friends are assisted by his cousin, an auto mechanic, in repairing the car. Although the car is too old to enter in the East African Safari, they plan to drive it to the site of the race. Because of a flat tire and engine trouble en route, they arrive in time to see only the last car, which crashes. They become heroes by taking the injured drivers to the hospital and a newspaper article is written about their car. The interest of the story is heightened by clearly delineated characters who include the hero's bossy younger brother, his proud and unfriendly "friend" Paul, and his feeble grandfather who cares only about his goats.

The stories in the Puzzlecrackers Series are about science, technology, and the importance of hard work. They are more explicitly didactic than *A Car Named Safari* in including diagrams that illustrate science principles discussed in the stories. As in Kariuki's other books, there also are black and white drawings of action from the stories. *The Engine Puzzle* is about car repair, in this case an old pickup truck. The child heroes learn about the history of the steam engine, and how the engine, battery, and other car parts work. They find learning all the information difficult, but are able to repair the truck and are rewarded by being able to ride in it.

The three boys who founded the Babanyeta Science Club are the core characters in all the stories in the Puzzlecrackers Series. In *The Fire Puzzle* they learn to make a biogas digester. Although they have difficulty believing that good will come of all the cow dung they collect, they successfully build and demonstrate a biogas digester and decide to build a gas factory to aid their community. Their success is a result of careful planning and hard work, as is the success of the heroes and heroines of the other stories in the series. In *The Irrigation Puzzle* a girl is admitted to the science club after overcoming sex prejudice because she is very good at science. The children join with informed adults in the Harambee spirit to acquire knowledge, plan the project, prepare the field, and build irrigation structures with community involvement. There is much excitement during the construction and a celebration when the irrigation system works. In *The Underground Water Puzzle* the children build a borehole in a village that has no water supply. They must learn about water underground and receive help from an engineer to achieve their goal.

Ziki, My Monkey Boy is about a boy's pet monkey as well as community development. Although the boy characters are not fond of monkeys because they steal maize that the boys must guard, and sometimes harm children, the hero rescues a monkey with a broken leg and cares for him with assistance from a veterinarian. Ziki, the monkey, learns to fetch cattle, harvest maize, scare animals from the farm, and shake hands. Thanks to him there is a record maize harvest, but Ziki runs off to the forest where he belongs. Although he becomes a maize thief, he never steals maize from the hero's farm. The cultural background of this story includes many facets of contemporary rural Kenyan life including seeing a film on deforestation, planting trees for a national project, doing chores at home and school, and making toys from wood.

Some of the same children appear as characters in *This Country Is My Country* as in *A Car Named Safari*. In this story the hero's grandfather tells about the Maasai in the good old days, and a "strange bachelor" tells stories about his experiences in World War II. The boy heroes engage in childhood rivalry, raise rabbits, care for a wounded crown bird, and assist with a community project to build a hospital. As in Kariuki's other fiction, the action is constructed around facets of contemporary life with which Kenyan children are familiar.

Kariuki is nearly unique among African children's writers in selecting science as a focus for fiction. He writes stories about a wide range of topics that both promote nationalism and entertain.

—Nancy J. Schmidt

KATZ, Welwyn (née Wilton). Canadian. Born in London, Ontario, 7 June 1948. Educated at the University of Western Ontario, London, 1966–69, B.S.C. (honours) in mathematics 1969; Althouse College of Education, London, 1969–70, diploma in education 1970. Married Albert N. Katz in 1973; one daughter. Mathematics teacher, London secondary schools, 1970–77. Recipient: International Children's Fiction Contest prize, 1987; Canada Council grant, 1981, 1983, 1985 (twice), 1988. Agent: Nancy Colbert, Colbert Agency Inc., 303 Davenport Road, Toronto, Ontario M5R 1K5. Address: 103 Windsor Avenue, London, Ontario N6C 1Z8, Canada.

PUBLICATIONS FOR CHILDREN

Fiction

The Prophecy of Tau Ridoo, illustrated by Michelle Desbarats. Edmonton, Alberta, Tree Frog Press, 1982.
Witchery Hill. Vancouver, Douglas and McIntyre, and New York, Atheneum, 1984; London, Angus and Robertson, 1988.
Sun God, Moon Witch. Vancouver, Douglas and McIntyre, 1986.
False Face. Vancouver, Douglas and McIntyre, 1987; New York, McElderry, 1988.
The Third Magic. Vancouver, Douglas and McIntyre, 1988; New York, McElderry, 1989.

*

Welwyn Katz comments:

I am particularly interested in the ancient legends that have been passed down for hundreds, even thousands of years. For these stories of past times to be kept alive from generation to generation, there must be something "true" about them, something of modern validity. What I try to do in my novels is enmesh the truths of legend with ordinary reality. I write books that, for the most part, are set on modern-day Earth, but I make ancient superstitions and legends parallel the ordinary realism of the plot. My characters resolve modern problems by brushing against the ancient.

*   *   *

The novels of Welwyn Katz all deal with some aspect of the supernatural or mythic. The characters are either physically transported to another realm where much of the action takes place, as in *The Prophecy of Tau Ridoo* and *The Third Magic,* or, as in *Witchery Hill, Sun God, Moon Witch,* and *False Face,* they are confronted by supernatural forces in ordinary and familiar surroundings. The plots generally revolve around the ancient conflict of good against evil—an evil that is either externalized and focused in a specific character or internalized within the main character, as he or she unknowingly falls under evil influences.

The *Prophecy of Tau Ridoo* is a fairly standard fantasy adventure in which the five Aubrey children are transported to the mysterious and dangerous world of Tau Ridoo. Separated and pursued by agents of the evil Red General, the children manage to survive with the help of the sorceress Cooky and her magic, and struggle to defeat the evil force that has kept Tau Ridoo in darkness for almost 700 years. The action is brisk and enlivened by touches of humor.

A dark and sinister tale, *Witchery Hill* brings 14-year-old Mike and his divorced journalist father to Guernsey for a prolonged stay with his father's friends, the St. George family. Outwardly all is happy and serene, but as Mike slowly befriends the rather sullen daughter Lisa, he becomes aware of hostile undercurrents. 13-year-old Lisa, a diabetic and deeply devoted to her father, reveals her suspicions that her beautiful stepmother is a practicing witch, engaged in a deadly struggle for control of the local coven.

As the action unfolds, Mike's unsatisfactory relationship with his father and his struggle to understand the psychic power of evil bring matters to a head in a climactic scene in which he is left alone to prevent a terrible sacrifice and destroy the ancient power that holds the coven together.

This theme continues in *Sun God, Moon Witch.* Dreading the thought of spending the summer with her cousin Patrick in a sleepy English village, Thorny McCabe quickly discovers that, far from being quiet and dull, the village is the center of a dramatic controversy over the ancient stone circle of Awen-Ur. All too soon she finds herself caught in a terrible struggle between a mysterious lady in white and the fiery local squire as the powers of light battle the forces of dark for control of the world.

Departing somewhat from this theme, *False Face* is set in present-day Canada and has as its protagonists two unhappy adolescents brought together in an uneasy alliance through their discovery of a rare pair of Iroquois false face masks belonging to an outcast medicine man. Troubled by the acrimonious divorce of her parents, 13-year-old Laney finds comfort in the small face mask she has found. 14-year-old Tom, half-Indian and determined to preserve his ethnic identity, is deeply resentful of Laney's casually ignorant attitude to the masks, which represent an important aspect of Indian culture. As the emotional conflicts with the adults in their lives grow, so does their understanding of the true and terrifying power of the masks.

The Third Magic returns to more familiar themes, drawing its inspiration from Arthurian legends. On a visit to England, 15-year-old Morgan Lefevre is mistaken for one of her ancestors and is summoned to the alien world of Nwm where she finds herself caught between the opposing forces of two magics.

Reminiscent in tone and theme to early Robert Westall, particularly *The Wind Eye* and *The Watch House,* Katz's books are compelling reading. She is a strong storyteller (though there are occasional touches of melodrama in her earlier books), and her characters are well drawn. She seems to be in tune with the adolescent psyche and is able to convey the painful confusions of that time of life in a succinct and sympathetic manner. She is harder on the adult characters who, if they are not the actual embodiment of evil, are somewhat remote and slow to understand or respond to the situations around them, almost as if life had deadened their feelings and perceptions.

Her strongest book, in my opinion, is *False Face,* which builds in emotional intensity until one reads at almost breathless pace. It is also the book that explores, in greater depth, the tendency for evil which exists in all of us and which, if not recognized and guarded, can so easily be released.

—Divna Todorovich

KAYE, Geraldine (née Hughesdon). British. Born in Watford, Hertfordshire, 14 January 1925. Educated at Felixstowe College, Suffolk, 1934–39; Watford Grammar School, 1939–42; London School of Economics, 1946–49, B.Sc. (honours) in economics 1949. Served in the Women's Royal Naval Service, 1943–46. Married Barrington Kaye in 1948 (divorced 1975); two daughters and one son. Scriptwriter, Malayan Film Unit, Malaya, 1951–52; teacher, Methodist Girls School, Paya Lebar, Singapore, 1952–54, and Mitford Colmer School, London, 1962–64. Recipient: Children's Rights Workshop Other award, 1985. Agent: A.M. Heath and Co. Ltd., 79 St. Martin's Lane, London WC2N 4AA. Address: 39 High Kingsdown, Bristol, Avon BS2 8EW, England.

PUBLICATIONS FOR CHILDREN

Fiction

The Boy Who Wanted to Go Fishing, illustrated by Peggy Fortnum. London, Methuen, 1960; as *Kassim Goes Fishing,* 1969.
Kwasi and the Parrot and Other Stories. London, Oxford University Press, 1961.
Kwasi Goes to Town, illustrated by Valerie Herbst. London and New York, Abelard Schuman, 1962.
Kofi and the Eagle, illustrated by Sheila Hawkins. London, Methuen, 1963.
Chik and the Bottle House, illustrated by Peggy Fortnum. London, Nelson, 1965.
The Raffle Pony, illustrated by Gareth Floyd. Leicester, Brockhampton Press, 1966.
Oh, Essie!, illustrated by Rosemary Honeybourne. London, Benn, 1966.
The Blue Rabbit, illustrated by Clyde Pearson. Leicester, Brockhampton Press, 1967.
Kassim and the Sea Monkey, illustrated by Gay Galsworthy. London, Longman, 1967.
Koto and the Lagoon, illustrated by Joanna Stubbs. London, Deutsch, 1967; New York, Funk and Wagnalls, 1969.
The Tail of the Siamese Cat, illustrated by Ferelith Eccles Williams. London and New York, Nelson, 1967.
The Sea Monkey, illustrated by Gay Galsworthy. London, Longman, and Cleveland, World, 1968.
Tawno, Gypsy Boy, illustrated by Gareth Floyd. Leicester, Brockhampton Press, 1968.
Runaway Boy, illustrated by Michal Morse. London, Heinemann, 1971.
Nowhere to Stop, illustrated by Gareth Floyd. Leicester, Brockhampton Press, 1972.
Marie Alone. London, Heinemann, 1973.
The Rotten Old Car, illustrated by Leslie Wood. Leicester, Brockhampton Press, 1973; Chicago, Children's Press, 1976.
Tim and the Red Indian Headdress, illustrated by Carolyn Dinan. Leicester, Brockhampton Press, 1973; Chicago, Children's Press, 1976.
The Yellow Pom-Pom Hat, illustrated by Margaret Palmer.

Leicester, Brockhampton Press, 1974; Chicago, Children's Press, 1976.
Goodbye, Ruby Red, illustrated by Robin Lawrie. Leicester, Brockhampton Press, 1974; Chicago, Children's Press, 1976.
Joanna All Alone, illustrated by Mary Dinsdale. Newton Abbot, Devon, David and Charles, 1974; Nashville, Nelson, 1975.
A Nail, A Stick, and a Lid, illustrated by Linda Birch. Leicester, Brockhampton Press, 1975; Chicago, Children's Press, 1976.
Billy-Boy, illustrated by Gareth Floyd. London, Hodder and Stoughton, 1975.
Children of the Turnpike, illustrated by Gareth Floyd. London, Hodder and Stoughton, 1976.
A Different Sort of Christmas, illustrated by Doreen Caldwell. London, Kaye and Ward, 1976.
Where Is Fred?, illustrated by Mike Cole. London, Knight, 1976; Chicago, Children's Press, 1977.
Penny Black. London, Heinemann, 1976.
Joey's Room. London, Macmillan, 1978.
King of the Knock-Down Gingers, illustrated by Glenys Ambrus. London, Hodder and Stoughton, 1979.
The Beautiful Take-Away Palace, illustrated by Glenys Ambrus. London, Kaye and Ward, 1980.
The Day after Yesterday, illustrated by Glenys Ambrus. London, Deutsch, 1981.
The Plum Tree Party, illustrated by Gabrielle Stoddart. London, Hodder and Stoughton, 1981.
Frangipani Summer. London, Macmillan, 1983.
The Sky-Blue Dragon, illustrated by Glenys Ambrus. London, Hodder and Stoughton, 1983.
The Donkey Strike, illustrated by Glenys Ambrus. London, Hodder and Stoughton, 1984.
Comfort Herself, illustrated by Jennifer Northway. London, Deutsch, 1984.
The Biggest Bonfire in the World, illustrated by Glenys Ambrus. London, Hodder and Stoughton, 1985.
The Call of the Wild Wood, illustrated by Abigail Pizer. London, Hodder and Stoughton, 1986.
The School Pool Gang, illustrated by Glenys Ambrus. London, Hodder and Stoughton, 1986.
A Breath of Fresh Air. London, Deutsch, 1987.
The Rabbit Minders, illustrated by Glenys Ambrus. London, Hodder and Stoughton, 1987.
Great Comfort. London, Deutsch, 1988.
The Donkey Christmas. London, Hodder and Stoughton, 1988.
Summer in Small Street, illustrated by Joanna Carey. London, Methuen, 1989.

Other (readers)

Tales for Malayan Children. Singapore, Donald Moore, 1956.
The Creek Near Kwarme's Village and Other Stories, illustrated by Lorna Paull. London, Oxford University Press, 1961.
Kwaku and the Bush Baby. London, Oxford University Press, 1961.
Kwaku Goes Shopping. London, Oxford University Press, 1961.
Susie and Sophie and Other Stories, illustrated by Gene Adams. London, Oxford University Press, 1961.
Nii-Ofrang and His Garden and Other Stories, illustrated by Lorna Paull. London, Oxford University Press, 1962.
Kwabena and the Leopard, illustrated by Elizabeth Vaughan. London, Oxford University Press, 1964.
Yaa Goes South, illustrated by Elizabeth Vaughan. London, Oxford University Press, 1967.
Bonfire Night, illustrated by George Adamson. London, Macmillan, 1968.
Eight Days to Christmas, illustrated by Shirley Hughes. London,

Macmillan, 1970.
In the Park, illustrated by Lynette Hemmant. London, Macmillan, 1970.
The Rainbow Shirt, illustrated by Lynette Hemmant. London, Macmillan, 1970.
Red Shoes. London, Oxford University Press, 1971.
Nowhere to Go. London, Oxford University Press, 1971.
The Tin Soldier. London, Oxford University Press, 1971.
Donkey Boy, illustrated by Prudence Seward. London, Oxford University Press, 1972.
Ginger, illustrated by Shirley Hughes. London, Macmillan, 1972.
The Children of the Brown Family, illustrated by Gavin Rowe. London, Oxford University Press, 1973.
A Mad Skipping Cat. London, Macmillan, 1974.
Scrap's Club. London, Macmillan, 1974.
To Catch a Thief, illustrated by Trevor Stubley. London, Oxford University Press, 1975.
Adventure [and *Another Adventure*] *in London,* illustrated by Mary Dinsdale. London, Oxford University Press, 2 vols., 1975–78.
Christmas Is a Baby, illustrated by Richard Butler. London, Macmillan, 1975.
Pegs and Flowers, illustrated by Richard Butler. London, Macmillan, 1975.
In Portobello Road, illustrated by Mary Dinsdale. London, Oxford University Press, 1976.
In the New Forest, illustrated by Trevor Stubley. London, Oxford University Press, 1976.
Week Out. London, Longman, 1978.
A Life of Her Own, illustrated by Anne Knight. London, Oxford University Press, 1978.
The Birthday Ball, illustrated by Lesley Smith. London, Macmillan, 1982.

*

Geraldine Kaye comments:
I write for the whole child age range but I have tended to write for older children and teenagers as my own children have grown up. I write quite a lot about children in different cultures and environments and I am especially interested in the child who is culturally an outsider: the Gypsy child or the child of mixed parentage. It also seems to me to be important to try to give recognition to the fact that we live in a very fluid, rapidly changing society in which there is no longer clear consensus on many issues of social behaviour.

*   *   *

It is no accident that makes Geraldine Kaye in demand at creative writing courses. Participants encounter no mystique, no sense of the weighty English literary tradition, no talk of inspiration and the Muse. Instead, they meet an unpretentious professional who makes no large claims for her work, someone ever willing to exercise her craft in a commissioned series title, yet no mere cipher but a writer of skill, individuality, and conviction.
The early stories, such as *The Boy Who Wanted to Go Fishing* and *Kofi and the Eagle,* make use of Kaye's knowledge of Malaya and Africa. Within the simple form of Methuen's Read Aloud series they contain a richness characteristic of the author. The background details are authentic, the plot lines clear and uncluttered, the observation precise, with a quiet wisdom imbuing the whole. Many later stories spring from Kaye's long interest in gypsies and the disadvantaged. *Runaway Boy,* for example, takes the adjustment of Danny Baker, on escape from an approved school, to life in the open and eventual adoption by a gypsy family, while *Billy-Boy* and *Nowhere to Stop* both explore the gap between gypsies and the communities in which they settle. More recent work shows a concern for children

adapting to new countries and new cultures, as in *The Day after Yesterday,* a moving story of a Chinese girl coming to terms with both life in England and a tragedy in her past, or *The Beautiful Take-Away Palace.*

Kaye's professionalism manifests itself in the range of her publications: a year's output might include a brief supplementary reader, a novel for teenagers with reading difficulties, and a full-length book. Inevitably quality does vary, but the results are always competent and readable—and usually much more. *Nowhere to Stop* is typical of Kaye's gifts: the social concern informs but never unbalances the story; the characters live on outside the pages; the style is accessible, the plot skilfully paced, and we are treated to warmth without sentimentality.

Recent outstanding work includes *A Breath of Fresh Air,* which recreates the horror of the slave trade, and *Comfort Herself,* the story of a girl's struggle to find her own path when torn between relations in England and Ghana. Both demonstrate the ability to center a story in a precise location with specific tensions and yet give its theme a universal quality. Kaye may not be likely to reach the ranks of Carnegie Medal winners but she is read, understood, and enjoyed by a wide audience, and leaves those readers with a sense of sympathies extended.

—Peggy Heeks

KEATS, Ezra Jack. American. Born in Brooklyn, New York, 11 March 1916. Educated at Thomas Jefferson High School, Brooklyn. Served in the United States Army Air Corps during World War II. Muralist for the Works Progress Administration in the 1930's, then freelance commercial artist; taught in the School of Visual Arts, New York, 1947–48, and Workshop School, New York, 1955–57. Recipient: American Library Association Caldecott Medal, 1963; Boston *Globe-Horn Book* award, for illustration, 1970; University of Southern Mississippi award, 1980. *Died 6 May 1983.*

PUBLICATIONS FOR CHILDREN (illustrated by the author)

Fiction

My Dog Is Lost, with Pat Cherr. New York, Crowell, 1960.
The Snowy Day. New York, Viking Press, 1962; London, Bodley Head, 1967.
Whistle for Willie. New York, Viking Press, 1964; London, Bodley Head, 1966.
Jennie's Hat. New York, Harper, 1966.
Peter's Chair. New York, Harper, 1967; London, Bodley Head, 1968.
A Letter to Amy. New York, Harper, 1968; London, Bodley Head, 1969.
Goggles! New York, Macmillan, 1969; London, Bodley Head, 1970.
Hi, Cat! New York, Macmillan, 1970; London, Bodley Head, 1971.
Apt. 3. New York, Macmillan, 1971; London, Hamish Hamilton, 1972.
Pet Show! New York, Macmillan, and London, Hamish Hamilton, 1972.
Psst! Doggie—. New York, Watts, 1973.
Skates! New York, Watts, 1973.
Dreams. New York, Macmillan, and London, Hamish Hamilton, 1974.

Kitten for a Day. New York, Watts, 1974.
Louie. New York, Greenwillow, 1975; London, Hamish Hamilton, 1976.
The Trip. New York, Greenwillow, and London, Hamish Hamilton, 1978.
Maggie and the Pirate. New York, Four Winds Press, 1979.
Louie's Search. New York, Four Winds Press, and London, Mac-Rae, 1980.
Regards to the Man in the Moon. New York, Four Winds Press, 1981; London, Macmillan, 1985.
Clementina's Cactus. New York, Viking Press, 1982; London, Methuen, 1983.

Other

John Henry: An American Legend. New York, Pantheon, 1965.

Editor, *Over in the Meadow* (verse). New York, Four Winds Press, 1971; London, Hamish Hamilton, 1973.

PUBLICATIONS FOR ADULTS

Other

Editor, *God Is in the Mountain* (quotations). New York, Holt Rinehart, 1966.
Editor, *Night* (quotations), photographs by Beverly Hall. New York, Atheneum, 1969.

*

Manuscript Collections: Gutman Library, Harvard University, Cambridge, Massachusetts; de Grummond Collection, University of Southern Mississippi, Hattiesburg.

Theatrical Activities:
Designer: **Play**—*The Trip,* music and lyrics by Stephen Schwartz, New York, 1983.

Illustrator: *Jubilant for Sure,* 1954, and *Sure Thing for Shep,* 1956, both by Elizabeth Lansing, 1956; *Chester* by Eleanor Clymer, 1954; *Wonder Tales of Dogs and Cats* by Florence Carpenter, 1955; *Mystery on the Isle of Skye* by Phyllis A. Whitney, 1955; *A Change of Climate,* 1956, and *The Tournament of the Lions,* 1960, both by Jay Williams, and *Danny Dunn and the Anti-Gravity Paint,* 1956, *Danny Dunn on a Desert Island,* 1957, *Danny Dunn and the Homework Machine,* 1958, and *Danny Dunn and the Weather Machine,* 1959, all by Williams and Raymond Abrashkin; *Three Young Kings* by George Albee, 1956; *Wee Joseph* by William MacKellar, 1957; *The Indians Knew* by Tillie S. Pine, 1957, and *The Pilgrims Knew,* 1957, *The Chinese Knew,* 1958, *The Eskimos Knew,* 1962, and *The Egyptians Knew,* 1964, all by Pine and Joseph Levine; *And Long Remember* by Dorothy Canfield Fisher, 1959; *Grasses* by Irmengarde Eberle, 1960; *Nihal of Ceylon* by Eleanor A. Murphey, 1960; *Desmond's First Case* by Herbert Best, 1961; *In the Night* by Paul Showers, 1961; *The Rice Bowl Pet* by Patricia Miles Martin, 1962; *What Good Is a Tale?* by Solveig P. Russell, 1962; *The Peterkin Papers* by Lucretia P. Hale, 1963; *Tia Maria's Garden* by Ann Nolan Clark, 1963; *The Flying Cow* by Ruth Collins, 1963; *Zoo, Where Are You?* by Ann McGovern, 1964; *Speedy Digs Downside Up* by Maxine Kumin, 1964; *In a Spring Garden* edited by Richard Lewis, 1965; *The Naughty Boy: A Poem* by John Keats, 1965; *How to Be a Nature Detective* by Millicent Selsam, 1966; *The Little Drummer Boy* by Katherine Kennicott Davis, Henry Onorati, and Harry Simeone, 1968; *In the Park* by Esther Hautzig, 1968; *Two*

Tickets to Freedom by Florence B. Freedman, 1971; *The King's Fountain* by Lloyd Alexander, 1971; *Penny Tunes and Princesses* by Myron Levoy, 1972.

Ezra Jack Keats commented:

(1978) My purpose in creating books for children is to share my experiences with them, ranging from the real world and feeling to fantasy. I hope children, whoever they may be, will discover that they are important, resourceful, and that they can have hope and self-esteem.

* * *

In his early books *The Snowy Day* and *Whistle for Willie* Ezra Jack Keats came forward with his own unmistakable style of illustration and text: the cut-out and gouache collage that gaily and vividly simplifies and stylises urban landscapes while the precise, almost scannable text, a separate statement for each page, concentrates the incidents of the stories—each a learning situation for under-fives—into easily memorable details.

All Keats's books combine the child's excitement at discovering new abilities and attitudes—like whistling (in *Whistle for Willie*), coping with ambivalent emotions (*Peter's Chair*), outwitting tougher and older kids (*Goggles*), or helping (a blind man in *Apt. 3*)—with a strong sense of the grim urban reality in which their little heroes Peter, Archie, Sam, and Louie grow up. Yet the New York street with its litter, its grimy building fronts, and graffiti-covered walls which always serves as a back-drop has the rich and lively atmosphere of home just as much as the interior of Peter, Sam, and Ben's apartment block where every inmate is known to the boys. Keats does not gloss over the stark urban reality. He presents it as the emotionally secure child would experience it, full of solid objects like traffic lights, trees, walls, and pavements to draw on and play around on. This environment is as tangible in the illustrations—which little fingers find irresistibly redrawable, particularly in *The Snowy Day* with its footprints, stickmarks, and "angels" made in the snow, its piling snow mountains and sparkling snow crystals—as in the text which laconically sets out the simple facts of inner and outer landscape in description and dialogue. Small things matter: found objects like sticks, cardboard boxes, pieces of chalk, goggles, cats, landmarks like look-out pipe and traffic light, the patient attention of grown-ups, friendship, planned and unplanned get-togethers like birthday parties (*A Letter to Amy*) and pet shows (*Pet Show*), or improvised street entertainment (*Hi, Cat!, The Trip*).

The world of these little books is at once open to discovery and quite secure, as exemplified in the wordless *Clementina's Cactus,* where Clementina's curiosity and delight in a flowering cactus are held just enough in check by her father to keep her from being hurt by its prickles. It is a world peopled with children, grown-ups, and animals which are ultimately friendly, though they may be scary at first. There the child becomes gently and gradually socialised, yet not without experiencing the normal, ambivalent feelings of pride at achieving and envy at others being better at something, of love for parents and friends and jealousy (for a newly arrived baby sister, for instance), of fear when bullied and triumph when successful through using wit, persistence, or courage. It revolves around the simple games of small children alone or in groups, and because it uses hardly any props except animals, it is universal, classless, and timeless.

There is some development and change in Keats's style from the first books to later work, particularly in the illustrations which have shifted the emphasis from witty cut-out collage to highly impressionistic shadow-play. Also, Keats increasingly tackles emotions on top of the sense-and-action experience of young children, for instance, in the Louie stories *The Trip* and *Louie's Search* where a lonely, uprooted, and fatherless boy overcomes his sense of isolation. He does this in the first with the help of an imaginative game of make-believe, a fantasy trip back to his old neighborhood friends, which gives him the strength to go out into the streets of his new neighborhood, dressed up, because it is Halloween, but confident that he will make new friends there. In the second he goes out into a strange and hostile world like the fairytale hero, not only in search of adventure, but also in search of a father, and he is again successful. But this time he has to pass a difficult test of courage first, because the man he eventually finds is fearsome and suspicious and has to be won round by a proof of Louie's man-to-man honesty. More than other Keats heroes Louie sets an example of how courage and imagination combine in the difficult task of growing up.

—Gertrud Mander

KEEPING, Charles (William James). British. Born in London, 22 September 1924. Educated at Frank Bryant School for Boys, Kennington, London; Regent Street Polytechnic School of Art, London, 1946–52, National Diploma in art and design. Served in the Royal Navy, 1942–46: telegraphist. Married Renate Meyer in 1952; three sons and one daughter. Printing trade apprentice, 1938; worked as an engineer and rent collector; Visiting Lecturer in Lithography, Regent Street Polytechnic School of Art, 1956–63; Visiting Lecturer in Lithography, Croydon College of Art and Design, Surrey, 1962–78; Visiting Lecturer in Printmaking, Camberwell School of Arts and Crafts, London, from 1979. Artist and book designer and illustrator. Member, Society of Industrial Artists. Recipient (for illustration): Library Association Kate Greenaway Medal, 1968, 1982; Victoria and Albert Museum Francis Williams Memorial prize, 1972, 1977; Bratislava Biennale Golden Apple award, 1975; Maschler award, 1987; W.H. Smith award, 1988. *Died 16 May 1988.*

PUBLICATIONS FOR CHILDREN (illustrated by the author)

Fiction

Black Dolly. Leicester, Brockhampton Press, 1966; as *Molly o' the Moors,* Cleveland, World, 1966.
Shaun and the Cart-Horse. London, Oxford University Press, and New York, Watts, 1966.
Charley, Charlotte, and the Golden Canary. London, Oxford University Press, and New York, Watts, 1967.
Alfie and the Ferry Boat. London, Oxford University Press, 1968; as *Alfie Finds the Other Side of the World,* New York, Watts, 1968.
Joseph's Yard. London, Oxford University Press, and New York, Watts, 1969.
Through the Window. London, Oxford University Press, and New York, Watts, 1970.
The Garden Shed. London, Oxford University Press, 1971.
The Spider's Web. London, Oxford University Press, 1972.
The Nanny Goat and the Fierce Dog. London, Abelard Schuman, 1973; New York, Phillips, 1974.
Richard. London, Oxford University Press, 1973.
The Railway Passage. London, Oxford University Press, 1974.
Wasteground Circus. London, Oxford University Press, 1975.
Inter-City. London, Oxford University Press, 1977.
Miss Emily and the Bird of Make-Believe. London, Hutchinson, 1978.
Willie's Fire-Engine. Oxford and New York, Oxford University Press, 1980.
Sammy Streetsinger. Oxford, Oxford University Press, 1984; New York, Oxford University Press, 1987.

Plays

Television Plays: *Joseph's Yard,* and *Through the Window,* both from his own stories, 1970.

Other

River. London, Oxford University Press, 1978.

Editor, *Tinker Tailor: Folk Songs.* Leicester, Brockhampton Press, 1968; Cleveland, World, 1969.
Editor, *Cockney Ding Dong.* London, Kestrel, 1975.
Editor, *Book of Classic Ghost Stories.* London, Blackie, 1986; New York, Bedrick, 1987.
Editor, *Classic Tales of the Macabre.* London, Blackie, and New York, Bedrick, 1987.

*

Illustrator: *Man Must Measure* by Ted Kavanagh, 1955; *Heute und Morgen 2* and *3* by Martha Freudenberger and Magda Kelber, 1956–57; *The Silver Branch,* 1957, *Warrior Scarlet,* 1958, *The Lantern Bearers,* 1959, *Knight's Fee,* 1960, *Dawn Wind,* 1961, *Beowulf,* 1961, *Heroes and History,* 1965, *The Mark of the Horse Lord,* 1965, *Dragon Slayer,* 1966, *The Capricorn Bracelet,* 1973, and *Blood Feud,* 1977, all by Rosemary Sutcliff; *Bridges,* 1958, *Roads,* 1959, *Canals,* 1961, *Ships,* 1962, *Railways,* 1964, *Wells,* 1965, *Dams,* 1966, and *Harbours and Docks,* 1967, all by John Stewart Murphy; *Merrily on High* by Guthrie Foote, 1959; *Riverbend Bricky,* 1960, and *Bricky and the Hobo,* 1964, both by Ira Nesdale; *Tales of Pirates and Castaways,* 1960, and *Tales of the West Country,* 1961, both by Kathleen Fidler; *The Queen of Trent* by Mitchell Dawson, 1961; *King Solomon's Mines* by Rider Haggard, 1961; *The Golden Age,* 1962, and *Dream Days,* 1962, both by Kenneth Grahame; *Lost John* by Barbara Leonie Picard, 1962; *Tipiti the Robin* by René Guillot, 1962; *The Shadow-Line, and Within the Tides* by Joseph Conrad, 1962; *Three Trumpets* by Ruth Chandler, 1962; *Harriet and the Cherry Pie* by Clare Compton, 1963; *The Latchkey Children* by Eric Allen, 1963; *Knights of the Golden Table,* 1963, and *The Treasure of Siegfried,* 1964, both by E.M. Almedingen; *Patrick Kentigern Keenan,* 1963, *The Kelpie's Pearls,* 1964, and *Thomas and the Warlock,* 1967, all by Mollie Hunter; *The Castle and the Harp* by Philip Rush, 1963; *Grimbold's Other World,* 1963, *Mainly in Moonlight,* 1965, *The Apple-Stone,* 1969, and *Over the Hills to Fabylon,* 1970, all by Nicholas Stuart Gray; *The Horned Helmet,* 1963, *The Children's Crusade,* 1964, *The Last of the Vikings,* 1964, *Splintered Sword,* 1965, *Swords from the North,* 1967, *The Dream-Time,* 1967, and *The Invaders,* 1972, all by Henry Treece; *The Moonstone* by Wilkie Collins, 1963; *They Told Mr. Hakluyt* edited by Frank Knight, 1964; *Whitsun Warpath* by Elizabeth Grove, 1964; *The Story of Egypt* by Jacoba Sporry, 1964; *Jenny,* 1964, *The Next-Doors,* 1964, and *Mrs. Jenny,* 1966, all by Joan Tate; *Wuthering Heights* by Emily Brontë, 1964; *The King's Contest,* 1964, *The Sky-Eater,* 1966, and *Poko and the Golden Demon,* 1968, all by James Holding; *The Rain Boat* by Lace Kendall, 1965; *Elidor* by Alan Garner, 1965; *Damien the Leper's Friend* by John Reginald Milsome, 1965; *Your English* by Denys Thompson and R.J. Harris, 1965; *King Horn,* 1965, and *The Wildman,* 1976, both by Kevin Crossley-Holland, and *Beowulf* translated by Crossley-Holland, 1982; *Bent Is the Bow,* 1965, and *The Red Towers of Granada,* 1966, both by Geoffrey Trease; *The Life of Our Lord* by Henry Daniel-Rops, 1965; *An Owl for His Birthday,* 1966, *The Haunted Mine,* 1968, *A Boy and His Bike,* 1976, and *The Story of Tod,* all by Richard Potts; *All Quiet on the Western Front* by Erich Maria Remarque, 1966; *Island of the Great Yellow Ox,* 1966, and *The Flight of the Doves,* 1968, both by Walter Macken; *Komantcia* by Harold

Keith, 1966; *Celtic Folk and Fairy Tales* by Eric and N.I.S. Protter, 1967; *With Books on Her Head* by Edna Walker Chandler, 1967; *Champion of Charlemagne* by Marie Butts, 1967; *Bach* by Frederic Westcott, 1967; *The Cold Flame* by James Reeves, 1967, and *An Anthology of Free Verse* edited by Reeves, 1968; *The Christmas Story,* 1968; *The Mixture as Before,* 1968, and *Of Human Bondage,* both by W. Somerset Maugham; *After Many a Summer,* 1969, and *Time Must Have a Stop,* 1969, both by Aldous Huxley; *The Tale of Ancient Israel* by Roger Lancelyn Green, 1969; *The Castle of Otranto* by Horace Walpole, 1969; *Mr. Britling Sees It Through* by H.G. Wells, 1969; *Knights, Beasts and Wonders* by Margaret J. Miller, 1969; *The Heroes* by Charles Kingsley, 1970; *The God Beneath the Sea,* 1970, and *The Golden Shadow,* 1973, both by Leon Garfield and Edward Blishen, and *The Wedding Ghost* by Garfield, 1985; *The Angry Valley* by Nigel Grimshaw, 1970; *Early Encounters* by John Watts, 1970; *Five Fables from France,* 1970, and *The Strange Feathery Beast,* 1973, both by Lee Cooper; *Ruined City,* 1970, and *On the Beach,* 1970, both by Nevil Shute; *The Poet's Tales* edited by William Cole, 1971; *The Idiot* by Feodor Dostoevsky, 1971; *Enjoy Reading!* by R.E. Rogerson, 1971; *The Valley of the Frost Giants* by Mary Francis Shura, 1971; *Wizards and Wampum* by Roger Squire, 1972; *The Twelve Labors of Hercules* by Robert Newman, 1972; *Flood Warning* by Paul Berna, 1972; *Weland, Smith of the Gods* by Ursula Synge, 1972; *I'll Tell You a Tale* by Ian Serraillier, 1973; *The Ghost Stories of M.R. James,* 1973; *Weirdies,* 1973, *Monsters, Monsters, Monsters,* 1974, and *Spectres, Spooks, and Shuddery Shades,* 1977, all by Helen Hoke; *When Darkness Comes* by Robert Swindells, 1973; *The Birds and Other Stories* by Lewis Jones, 1973; *The Magic Horns,* 1974, and *The Mermaid's Revenge and Other Stories,* 1979, both by Forbes Stuart; *The Little Book of Sylvanus* by David Kossoff, 1975; *Tower Blocks* by Marian Lines, 1975; *Terry on the Fence,* 1975, *A Kind of Wild Justice,* 1978, and *Break in the Sun,* 1980, all by Bernard Ashley; *About the Sleeping Beauty* by P.L. Travers, 1975; *Les Misérables* by Victor Hugo, 1976; *The Robbers* by Nina Bawden, 1979; *The Tale of Prince Igor* retold by Leonard Clark, 1979; *The Batsford Book of Stories in Verse for Children,* 1979, and *The Sun, Dancing,* 1982, both edited by Charles Causley, and *Jack the Treacle Eater and Other Poems* by Causley, 1987; *Breakback Alley* by Tony Drake, 1979; *Gods and Men* by John Bailey and others, 1981; *The Highwayman* by Alfred Noyes, 1981; *The Posthumous Papers of the Pickwick Club,* 1981, *Great Expectations,* 1981, *Our Mutual Friend,* 1982, *The Mystery of Edwin Drood,* 1982, *David Copperfield,* 1983, and *Hard Times,* 1983, all by Charles Dickens; *The Beginning of the Armadilloes,* 1982, and *Rikki-Tikki-Tavi and Other Animal Stories,* 1984, both by Rudyard Kipling; *Stumpy, Dr. Jekyll and Mr. Hyde, The Wrecker, New Arabian Nights,* and *More New Arabian Nights* all by Robert Louis Stevenson; *The Lady of Shalott,* 1986; *The Tale of Sir Gawain* retold by Neil Philip, 1987; *Black Beauty* by Anna Sewell, 1988; *Dracula* by Bram Stoker, 1988; *Frankenstein* by Mary Shelley, 1988.

Charles Keeping commented:

(1978) I suppose many of my picture books for children have grown out of something observed or overheard during my numerous long walks around London. A few relate directly to experiences from my own childhood. *The Spider's Web,* for example, came from early thoughts recalled from childhood, whereas *The Railway Passage* grew out of a conversation with a comparative stranger in a pub.

I like a picture book to be more than just entertaining or a collection of pretty pictures. It should present a variety of ideal and interesting situations to stimulate thought, but I *don't* like moral solutions.

*   *   *

Always a masterly illustrator of other people's words, Charles Keeping, like many of today's finest children's book artists, moved over to writing and illustrating his own books. While he was not in any way a born writer, although capable of the occasional telling phrase, it is certainly true that he was at his best as an artist when working to his own inspiration. Moreover he learned the trick of making his text a foil for the pictures and pared his words increasingly so as to convey more and more of his information visually, a technique used to great effect in *Richard,* the story of a day in the life of a London police horse, where no detail of stabling or grooming is omitted yet the text is reduced to hardly more than captions. In this way Keeping kept his flat, prosaic sentences simple for young readers and relied on his pictures to provide the imaginative stimulus they need.

Keeping's style changed much over the years but his world remained the same, the streets and yards of London's east end and the banks of London's river which he knew deeply, almost instinctively, and portrayed with a detailed and observant sympathy that makes his books a chronicle for adults as well as a pleasure for children. The bold swathes of colour he used in his cockney fairy tale *Charley, Charlotte, and the Golden Canary,* which won him the Kate Greenaway Medal, and the watery brilliance of *Alfie and the Ferry Boat*—in which a small boy crosses the Thames and discovers "the other side of the world"—gave way to a subtler use of line, but his work, although more delicate, lost nothing of its strength. It became, if anything, more formidable.

There was always a sombre element in Keeping's imagination, but in later years he could become truly frightening, using strange angles and foreshortenings to suggest the transformations that the mind can work on the physical world. The chicken, seen through the fence in *The Spider's Web,* is a crimson, glaring basilisk one moment, a harmless fowl the next. Perhaps his most savage work was in the tormented black, white, and sepia illustrations to Alfred Noyes's poem *The Highwayman,* the most curious, Keeping's own modern fable, *Sammy Streetsinger,* in which a not entirely successful story is redeemed by the manic intensity of his pictures. Fortunately Keeping's perception of things innocent or benevolent was equally acute and the last word may, after all, belong to the gentle melancholy that pervades his 1987 illustrations to *Black Beauty.*

How far, in his later work, Keeping can be called a creator of children's books may be questioned. He can be violent, gloomy, and difficult. He was undoubtedly one of the outstanding figures of his time.

—Anne Carter

———

KEITH, Harold (Verne). American. Born in Lambert, Oklahoma Territory, 8 April 1903. Educated at Lambert High School, graduated 1921; Northwestern State College, Alva, Oklahoma (Scroll scholarship, 1922), 1921–24; University of Oklahoma, Norman, B.A. in history 1929, M.A. 1938. Married Virginia Livingston in 1931; two children. Elementary school teacher, Amorita, Oklahoma, 1922–23; sports correspondent, *Daily Oklahoman,* Oklahoma City, Tulsa *World,* Oklahoma, Kansas City *Star,* Missouri, and Omaha *World-Herald,* Nebraska, 1922–29; assistant grain buyer, Red Star Milling Company, Hutchinson, Kansas, 1929–30; sports publicity director, University of Oklahoma, 1930–69. President, College Sports Information Directors, 1964–65. Set U.S. Masters national records for the two- and three-mile runs, 1973, and 10,000 meters run, 1974. Recipient: American Library Association Newbery Medal, 1958; Western Heritage award, 1975, 1979; Western Writers of America Spur award, 1975. Agent: Oscar Collier, Collier Associates, 280 Madison Avenue, New York, New York 10016. Address: 2318 Ravenwood, Route 3, Norman, Oklahoma 73071, U.S.A.

PUBLICATIONS FOR CHILDREN

Fiction

Shotgun Shaw: A Baseball Story, illustrated by Mabel Jones Woodbury.   New York, Crowell, 1949.
A Pair of Captains, illustrated by Mabel Jones Woodbury.   New York, Crowell, 1951.
Rifles for Watie.   New York, Crowell, 1957; London, Oxford University Press, 1960.
Komantcia.   New York, Crowell, 1965; London, Oxford University Press, 1966.
Brief Garland.   New York, Crowell, 1971.
The Runt of Rogers School.   Philadelphia, Lippincott, 1971.
Go Red, Go!, illustrated by Ned Glattauer.   Nashville, Nelson, 1972.
The Bluejay Boarders, illustrated by Harold Berson.   New York, Crowell, 1972.
Susy's Scoundrel, illustrated by John Schoenherr.   New York, Crowell, 1974.
The Obstinate Land.   New York, Crowell, 1977.

Other

Boys' Life of Will Rogers, illustrated by Karl S. Woerner.   New York, Crowell, 1937.

PUBLICATIONS FOR ADULTS

Other

Sports and Games.   New York, Crowell, 1941; revised edition, 1960.
Oklahoma Kickoff (on football).   Privately printed, 1948.
Forty-Seven Straight: The Bud Wilkinson Era at Oklahoma.   Norman, University of Oklahoma Press, 1984.

*

Manuscript Collections: Northwestern State College Library, Alva, Oklahoma; University of Oklahoma Library, Norman.

Harold Keith comments:
I like to write straight at the young people themselves. I like to use a variety of fields for background—Civil War in the west, Comanche Indians, regional sports history, baseball, football, boys' and girls' basketball, bluejays, coyotes, the Cherokee Strip land run of 1893—almost anything that will let me research an unfamiliar field and learn more about it. It would be very dull, I believe, to write two books about the same topic or the same sport.

Hundreds of boys and girls from all over the United States write letters to me telling me what they like or dislike about my books. This is very useful to a writer. I answer every letter I receive.

*   *   *

Harold Keith's first books for children reflected some of his own interests; *Boys' Life of Will Rogers* emanated from Keith's master's thesis on Rogers's father, and *Sports and Games,* a Junior Literary Guild selection, from his remarkable record as a competitive athlete. A prolific writer of short stories for boys' magazines, Keith also wrote several sports novels. In his Newbery acceptance speech he gave much credit for the acclaim he earned for *Rifles for Watie* to the skills he had learned at a school for writers, analyzing the elements of the book (contrast, characterization, a crucial decision) in relation to what had been taught in writing classes. The mechanics, however, are fortunately not obtrusive in the book itself, a story of the Civil War in which a young Union soldier is sent behind the Confederate lines to try to discover where Stand Watie, a Cherokee, is getting new rifles that had been intended for the Union Army. The book is a strong indictment of war, showing that there are tragedy and deprivation, as well as heroism, on both sides. The protagonist, Jeff, is captured by the Confederates and successfully pretends to be one of them, so that for a time he lives and works with his enemies—and so learns that they are young men much like himself. The change from a carefree youth who saw only one side of the issues of the war to a mature young man who could understand the viewpoint of the enemy gives the story depth of characterization. The historical details are accurate and vivid; the writing style has an easy narrative flow.

Although Keith has successfully used contemporary settings in some stories (*Susy's Scoundrel,* the story of an Amish child's pet coyote, or the story of wild pets, *The Bluejay Boarders*), he is at his best when writing about the past, for then his interest in history, especially that of the Civil War period, gives life to fiction. In *Komantcia,* based on the true story of a young Spaniard taken captive by the Comanches in 1865, Pedro adjusts to the native American culture and then embraces it; Keith makes the story completely convincing by incorporation of well-researched historical details.

—Zena Sutherland

KELLEHER, Victor (Michael Kitchener). British. Born in London, 19 July 1939. Educated at the University of Natal, Pietermaritzburg, B.A. in English 1962; University of St. Andrews, Fife, Dip. Ed. 1963; University of the Witwatersrand, Johannesburg, B.A. (honours) 1969; University of South Africa, Pretoria, M.A. 1970, D.Litt. et Phil. 1973. Married Alison Lyle in 1962; one son and one daughter. Junior Lecturer in English, University of the Witwatersrand, 1969; Lecturer, then Senior Lecturer, in English, University of South Africa, 1970–73; Lecturer in English, Massey University, Palmerston North, New Zealand, 1973–76. Senior Lecturer, 1976–84, and Associate Professor of English, 1984–87, University of New England, Armidale, New South Wales. Recipient: Patricia Hackett prize, for short story, 1978; Australia Council fellowship, 1982; Australian Children's Book of the Year award, 1983; Australian Science Fiction Achievement award, 1984. Address: 149 Wigram Road, Glebe, New South Wales 2037, Australia.

PUBLICATIONS FOR CHILDREN

Fiction

Forbidden Paths of Thual, illustrated by Antony Maitland. London, Kestrel, 1979.
The Hunting of Shadroth. London, Kestrel, 1981.
Master of the Grove. London, Kestrel, 1982.
Papio. London, Kestrel, 1984.
The Green Piper. Melbourne, Viking Kestrel, 1984; London, Viking Kestrel, 1985.
Taronga. Melbourne, Viking Kestrel, 1986; London, Hamish Hamilton, 1987.
The Makers. Melbourne, Viking Kestrel, 1987.
Baily's Bones. Melbourne, Viking Kestrel, 1988.

PUBLICATIONS FOR ADULTS

Novels

Voices from the River. London, Heinemann, 1979.

The Beast of Heaven. St. Lucia, University of Queensland Press, 1984.
Em's Story. St. Lucia, University of Queensland Press, 1988.

Short Stories

Africa and After. Brisbane, University of Queensland Press, 1983; as *The Traveller,* 1987.

*

Victor Kelleher comments:

I have no single aim in writing for children. I try to write exciting, adventurous stories because those are the kinds of stories I appreciated as a child; and, like many writers, I enjoy recapturing the feelings and responses of my childhood. But, equally, I am concerned with pursuing serious issues, and at this level I draw no great distinction between my work for children and my work for adults. I suppose one of the many advantages of writing for children is that it enables me to pursue certain ideas that the majority of adults simply don't take seriously. For example, I can explore the complex and, I believe, vital relationship between the human and the animal worlds without having to feel any sense of apology. Similarly, I'm free to express myself through the medium of story—an approach that is largely frowned on by critics of adult fiction.

*   *   *

Victor Kelleher's first three books belong to that order of fantasy in which the external hazardous journey symbolises an inner search for self-knowledge on the way to maturity. In each case the exploration is into the nature of power and its attendant dangers, acquisition of power being, after all, even at the simplest level, consequent upon the growth to adulthood.

In writing such stories Kelleher faces the problem of creating a coherent and consistent mythology, and conveying its essentials without overloading the book with informative detail. He succeeds best in *The Hunting of Shadroth,* where the central issue is the nature of violence. Although it is Kulok, the Clan's new young leader, who has unleashed this violent force, nevertheless Tal, whose role is to destroy Shadroth, its physical manifestation, shares the guilt for the monster's reappearance. This he realises only gradually, during his difficult journey with Lea, Kulok's eminently calm and rational sister, and the Feln, the great cat whose peaceful co-existence with the Clan is threatened by Kulok's violence. With their help, but ultimately through his own courage, resourcefulness, and growing maturity, Tal defeats Shadroth in a terrifying battle and restores Kulok to a sense of his wrongdoing. But although tempted then to retreat to the peace of the Grasslands and the Gentle Folk, Tal realises that his place is with his own Clan, sharing their strengths and weaknesses and the continuing struggle against the violence within them.

Forbidden Paths of Thual has a similar theme, but the outcome is less satisfying. Quen overcomes his own temptations towards cruelty and greed and defeats the ruthless, steely-eyed Mollag soldiers who are oppressing his people. But he then retreats to the peace and service of the forest, a personal solution which Tal had rightly denied himself. He also shatters into pieces the symbolic stone, the Eye of Desire, which had tempted him. But victory over greed for power is not to be achieved by fragmentation of desire, any more than by the fragmentation of knowledge that had occurred earlier.

Derin, hero of *Master of the Grove,* is not so much in danger from his own weaknesses as from the lies and half-truths told him by his allies as a means of deceiving and so defeating their common enemy. Though this is a device that leads to unnecessary confusions in the detail of the story, its implications could fruitfully be discussed by intelligent readers of 12 and over.

All three books could be read at a similar age solely for adventure. And if the details of the symbolic representation of psychological truths are strongly reminiscent at times of Le Guin's *Earthsea* trilogy, the action and suspense in each book is ingeniously varied, as each hero, with his distinctive animal helper, proceeds on his dangerous quest.

The Green Piper, a fantasy story on a simpler level, is a reworking of the legend of the Pied Piper of Hamelin, with the magical, enchanting dream piper promising relief from the woes of the world, replaced by an evil sci-fic monster whose aim is to use the captive rats and children for his own sinister purposes. It is an exciting, sometimes frightening story, skilfully worked out, but with little of the underlying themes of the earlier books—save perhaps in the final chilling suggestion that though the piper has been defeated this time, there may yet be a repeat performance in which he will succeed.

Papio and *Taronga* are set in real rather than imaginary locations. In *Papio* the Australian boy David and his black American friend, Jem, set out to release two baboons from a research station in Africa where they are being subjected to painful and eventually fatal medical research. Jem, like Lea in *The Hunting of Shadroth*, is the calm, rational character. She can perceive that David's drive to help the baboons is partly motivated by a need to resolve his personal problems. The ethics of a resort to violence is again an important element in the story, and the insight into the natural lives of the baboons in the African bush makes this a particularly appealing novel.

In *Taronga*, the animals at the centre of the story are in a Sydney Zoo. The time is post-holocaust, when although Australia has escaped direct devastation from the nuclear war it has not escaped the nuclear ethos—everyone for him- or herself in a bitter struggle for survival. Ben has in his favour an unusual ability to control animals by telepathic communication, but is deeply distressed to find himself repeatedly betraying their trust to save himself. Only one other person, the aboriginal girl Ellie, has preserved a humanity towards others in these chaotic and violent times. With her help Ben learns the old aboriginal wisdom that the earth must be shared with animals on a basis of equality, and that one must face and accept the evil both in oneself and in the past. The man/animal theme, central to this story as to the others, is symbolised here in Ben's equivocal and ambivalent relationship with the captive tiger Raja, whom he can at first only control through the exercise of power, but with whom in the end he establishes a truly reciprocal understanding.

In their very different ways all these books provide excellent, thoughtful, though sometimes taxing and disturbing reading.

—Winifred Whitehead

KELLOGG, Steven. American. Born in Norwalk, Connecticut, 26 October 1941. Educated at the Rhode Island School of Design, Providence, B.F.A. 1963; American University, Washington, D.C. Married Helen Hill in 1967; four stepdaughters and two stepsons. Instructor in etching, American University, 1966. Recipient: Silver Paintbrush award (Netherlands), 1974. Address: c/o William Morrow Inc., 105 Madison Avenue, New York, New York 10016, U.S.A.

PUBLICATIONS FOR CHILDREN (illustrated by the author)

Fiction

The Wicked Kings of Bloon. Englewood Cliffs, New Jersey,

Prentice Hall, 1970.
Can I Keep Him? New York, Dial Press, 1971.
The Mystery Beast of Ostergeest. New York, Dial Press, 1971; London, Warne, 1977.
The Orchard Cat. New York, Dial Press, 1972.
Won't Somebody Play with Me? New York, Dial Press, 1972; London, Warne, 1977.
The Island of the Skog. New York, Dial Press, 1973; London, Warne, 1977.
The Mystery of the Missing Red Mitten. New York, Dial Press, 1974; London, Bodley Head, 1980.
Much Bigger Than Martin. New York, Dial Press, 1976; London, Warne, 1977.
The Mysterious Tadpole. New York, Dial Press, 1977; London, Warne, 1979.
The Mystery of the Magic Green Ball. New York, Dial Press, 1978; London, Bodley Head, 1980.
Pinkerton, Behave! New York, Dial Press, 1979; London, Warne, 1981.
The Mystery of the Flying Orange Pumpkin. New York, Dial Press, 1980.
A Rose for Pinkerton. New York, Dial Press, 1981; London, Warne, 1982.
The Mystery of the Stolen Blue Paint. New York, Dial Press, 1982.
Tallyho, Pinkerton! New York, Dial Press, 1982; London, Hutchinson, 1983.
Ralph's Secret Weapon. New York, Dial Press, and London, Hutchinson, 1983.
Best Friends. New York, Dial Press, 1986; London, Hutchinson, 1988.
Aster Aardvark's Alphabet Adventures. New York, Morrow, 1987.
Prehistoric Pinkerton. New York, Dial Press, 1987.
If You Made a Million. New York, Morrow, 1989.

Other (retellings)

There Was an Old Woman. New York, Parents' Magazine Press, 1974; London, Warne, 1978.
Paul Bunyan. New York, Morrow, 1984.
Chicken Little. New York, Morrow, 1985; London, Hutchinson, 1987.
Pecos Bill. New York, Morrow, 1986.
Johnny Appleseed. New York, Morrow, 1988.

*

Illustrator: *Gwot! Horrible Funny Hairticklers* by George Mendoza, 1967; *Martha Matilda O'Toole* by James Copp, 1969; *Brave Johnny O'Hare* by Eleanor B. Heady, 1969; *The Rotten Book* by Mary Rodgers, 1969; *Matilda Who Told Lies and Was Burned to Death,* 1970, and *The Yak, The Python, The Frog,* 1975, both by Hilaire Belloc; *Mrs. Purdy's Children* by Ruth Loomis, 1970; *Granny and the Desperadoes* by Peggy Parish, 1970; *Mister Rogers' Songbook* by Fred Rogers, 1970; *Can't You Pretend?* by Miriam Young, 1970; *Here Comes Tagalong* by Anne Mallett, 1971; *Crabapple Night,* 1971, and *The Very Peculiar Tunnel,* 1972, both by Jan Wahl; *The Castles of the Two Brothers* by Aileen Friedman, 1972; *Abby* by Jeanette Franklin Caines, 1973; *Come Here, Cat* by Joan L. Nodset, 1973; *You Ought to See Herbert's House* by Doris Herold Lund, 1973; *Kisses and Fishes* by Liesel Moak Skorpen, 1974; *How the Witch Got Alf* by Cora Annett, 1975; *The Smartest Bear and His Brother Oliver,* 1975, *The Most Delicious Camping Trip Ever,* 1976, *Grouchy Uncle Otto,* 1977, and *Millicent the Magnificent,* 1978, all by Alice Bach; *The Great Christmas Kidnaping Caper* by Jean van Leeuwen, 1975; *The Boy Who Was Followed Home* by Margaret Mahy, 1975; *Yankee Doodle* by Edward Bangs, 1976; *Awful*

Alexander by Judith Chaote, 1976; *Gustav the Gourmet Giant* by Lou Anne Bigge Gaeddert, 1976; *Barney Bipple's Magic Dandelions* by Carol Chapman, 1977; *Appelard and Liverwurst*, 1978, and *Liverwurst Is Missing*, 1981, both by Mercer Mayer; *The Pickle Plan* by Marilyn Singer, 1978; *Jill the Pill* by Julia Castiglia, 1979; *There's an Elephant in the Garage* by Douglas Davis, 1979; *Molly Moves Out* by Susan Pearson, 1979; *Once, Said Darlene* by William Sleator, 1979; *Uproar on Hollercat Hill* by Jean Marzollo, 1980; *The Day Jimmy's Boa Ate the Wash*, 1980, and *Jimmy's Boa Bounces Back*, 1984, both by Trinka Noble; *A Change of Plans* by Alan Benjamin, 1982; *The Ten-Alarm Camp-Out* by Cathy Warren, 1983; *A: My Name Is Alice* by Jane Bayer, 1984; *How Much Is a Million?* by David M. Schwartz, 1985; *Iva Dunnit and the Big Wind* by Carol Purdy, 1985; *Leo, Zack, and Emmie Together Again*, and *Tom, Zack, and Emmie in Winter*, both by Amy Ehrlich, 1987.

* * *

Steven Kellogg's great Dane Pinkerton provides the most descriptive image of his work: a happy, sprawling romp. Kellogg's picture books can be roughly divided into those stories he writes himself and those he only illustrates. Unlike illustrators such as Maurice Sendak and Arnold Lobel, who have distinctive prose as well as illustrative styles, Kellogg's writing is so nondescript as to make it difficult to distinguish his own stories from those of others without first checking the title pages. There is, however, a distinctive "Kellogg-style" story. This usually features a simple episode getting rapidly out of hand, providing Kellogg with an opportunity to exhibit his talent for depicting crowds of hysterically happy humans and animals knocking into each other.

Kellogg is an enormously prolific illustrator. Few artists achieving his commercial success would bother illustrating the work of unknown and generally undistinguished writers. But Kellogg's need to keep working apparently outstrips his own ability to create new material. This might pose a problem for Sendak, but Kellogg's textual requirements are simple enough that any number of writers can keep him supplied.

Kellogg's style works. It can be successfully and endlessly applied to a variety of subjects ranging from the alphabet (*A: My Name Is Alice*) to American folklore (*Paul Bunyan*) to numerical concepts (*How Much Is a Million?*) as well as to any number of picture books (*Can I Keep Him?*, *The Day Jimmy's Boa Ate the Wash*, *The Island of the Skog*). Unlike Chris Van Allsburg or Paul O. Zelinsky, Kellogg is not one to experiment with new forms. He has found his niche.

Recent criticism of Kellogg has been savage. A review of *Johnny Appleseed* described his work as "blowsy...undisciplined..." While accurate in one sense, it must also be noted that it is precisely these overblown qualities that are the basis for Kellogg's appeal. Kellogg does manifest a compulsive need to fill up every inch of blank space. Unlike Peter Spier, Nancy Ekholm Burkert, and Maurice Sendak, artists who also incorporate a great deal of intricate detail in their illustrations, Kellogg's figures and objects jostle and collide. They seem charged with nervous energy, never sitting still. Everything on the page appears to be in frantic motion with no place for the eye to rest. This works well with light, slightly zany material such as *Chicken Little* and *A: My Name Is Alice*, or where unrestrained excess is the book's whole point (*Paul Bunyan*, *How Much Is a Million?*). It fails in *Johnny Appleseed*, where the theme of the gentle man living in harmony with his surroundings finds itself at odds with the frenetic illustrations.

Kellogg may not be one of the 20th century's great artists, but he deserves recognition as a genial, unpretentious illustrator whose distinctive manic style works effectively when matched with the right material.

—Eric A. Kimmel

———

KELLY, Eric (Philbrook). American. Born in Amesbury, Massachusetts, 16 March 1884. Educated at Dartmouth College, Hanover, New Hampshire, A.B. 1906, M.A. 1929. Married Katherine Collins Merrill in 1924. Staff member, Westfield *Times*, Massachusetts, 1906, Springfield *Union*, Massachusetts, 1906–11, *Hunterton Gazette*, High Bridge, New Jersey, 1912, Boston *Herald*, 1914–18, and Boston *Transcript*, summers 1922–24; Instructor in English, 1921–29, Professor of Journalism, 1929–54, and Emeritus Professor, 1954–60, Dartmouth College. Lecturer (Kosciuszko Foundation scholar), University of Krakow, Poland, 1925–26; member of mission to Mexico, Office of Foreign Relief and Rehabilitation Operations, 1943. Vice-President, Paderewski Commission; trustee, Kosciuszko Foundation. Recipient: American Library Association Newbery Medal, 1929; Kosciuszko Foundation Gold Medal, 1956. Chevalier, 1934, and Commander, 1945, Order Polonia Restituta. *Died 3 January 1960.*

PUBLICATIONS FOR CHILDREN

Fiction

The Trumpeter of Krakow, illustrated by Angela Pruszynska. New York, Macmillan, 1928; London, Chatto and Windus, 1968.
The Blacksmith of Vilno, illustrated by Angela Pruszynska. New York, Macmillan, 1930.
The Golden Star of Halich, illustrated by Angela Pruszynska. New York, Macmillan, 1931.
The Christmas Nightingale, illustrated by Marguerite de Angeli. New York, Macmillan, 1932.
Three Sides of Agiochook, illustrated by Le Roy Appleton. New York, Macmillan, 1935.
Treasure Mountain, illustrated by Raymond Lufkin. New York, Macmillan, 1937.
At the Sign of the Golden Compass, illustrated by Raymond Lufkin. New York, Macmillan, and Birmingham, Combridge, 1938.
In Clean Hay. Privately printed, 1940.
On the Staked Plain, illustrated by Harve Stein. New York, Macmillan, 1940.
From Star to Star, illustrated by Manning Lee. Philadelphia, Lippincott, 1944.
The Hand in the Picture, illustrated by Irena Lorentowicz. Philadelphia, Lippincott, 1947.
The Amazing Journey of David Ingram. Philadelphia, Lippincott, 1948.

Other

A Girl Who Would Be Queen: The Story and Diary of the Young Countess Krasinska, with Clara Hoffmanowa, illustrated by Vera Bock. Chicago, McClurg, 1939.
Polish Legends and Tales. New York, Polish Publication Society of America, 1971.

PUBLICATIONS FOR ADULTS

Other

The Hope of All the Poles in the World. Chicago, Polish Roman Catholic Union Archives and Museum, 1941.
The Land of the Polish People. New York, Stokes, 1943; revised edition, Philadelphia, Lippincott, 1952.

* * *

The larger body of Eric Kelly's creative writing results from his deep love and respect for a land, Poland, and a people not his own except by adoption. Although generally regarded as literature for younger readers, Kelly's fiction has been widely enjoyed by the reading public at large. Characterized by an unerring blend of good story-telling and Poland's colorful history, his fiction has brought to readers an appreciation for the cultural and intellectual history of Poland and the aspirations and ideals of a valiant and honorable people.

Kelly's intense appreciation for medieval art and architecture, his love of natural beauty, and his eye for detail found expression in a variety of Polish tales and legends. In his "By Order of the Queen," which first appeared in 1924 in *St. Nicholas*, Kelly describes Krakow as a city of gold—"yellow in dawn, gray in dusk, blue in the midday, but gold, gold, gold in the sweet hour of sunset." He is equally at ease with characterization. In "By Order of the Queen," for example, the buyers and sellers in the market place are seen in jocular, conversational mood; yet as though setting a stage and chiseling a special character for the engrossing and suspenseful story to follow, Kelly introduces early a woman flitting "from bargain-stall to bargain-stall, glancing within as if searching for someone." She is not an old woman, he says, "but there is that about her which tells of age in other terms than years." "By Order of the Queen" and other Eric Kelly stories which appeared in *St. Nicholas* in the mid-1920's are but earlier harbingers of his highly acclaimed trilogy—*The Trumpeter of Krakow*, *The Blacksmith of Vino*, and *The Golden Star of Halich*.

The best known and most representative of the trilogy is *The Trumpeter of Krakow* which won the Newbery Medal. The general setting of this unusual historical romance is the city of Krakow; the specific setting, the parish church of St. Mary the Virgin. This church with its gothic architecture, the royal castle on Wawel Hill, the old and renowned Krakow University, and city streets at night time provide a proper backdrop for a dramatic, swift-moving, action-packed story. The politics of Krakow's constant threat from invading Tartars or greedy Russian tsars during the 15th century provide warp and woof to Kelly's exciting literary canvas, while a rich historical tradition is continued in the hourly trumpeting of the Polish *Heynal* from a tower in St. Mary's. The young trumpeter Joseph Charnetski and his family, the wise and revered Professor Jan Kanty, alchemists, hypnotists, thieves, and ruffians provide suspenseful action in a drama told in rich, poetic prose. *The Trumpeter of Krakow* is analogous in some respects to Victor Hugo's *Notre-Dame de Paris*; assuredly it places Kelly among the most capable American creators of juvenile fiction of his own period or any other.

—Charity Chang

KEMP, Gene (née Rushton). British. Born in Wigginton, Staffordshire, 27 December 1926. Educated at Wigginton Church Primary School; Tamworth Girls' High School, Staffordshire; University of Exeter, Devon (exhibitioner), 1945–48, B.A. (honours) in English 1948. Married 1) Norman Pattison in 1949 (divorced 1958), one daughter; 2) Allan Kemp in 1958, one daughter and one son. Teacher, St. Sidwell's Combined Primary School, Exeter, 1963–79, and Rolle College, Exmouth, Devon, 1974–75. Since 1979 freelance writer. Recipient: Children's Rights Workshop Other award, 1977; Library Association Carnegie Medal, 1978. M.A.: University of Exeter, 1984. Agent: Gerald Pollinger, Laurence Pollinger Ltd., 18 Maddox Street, London W1R 0EU. Address: 6 West Avenue, Exeter, Devon EX4 4SD, England.

PUBLICATIONS FOR CHILDREN (books through 1981 illustrated by Carolyn Dinan)

Fiction

The Prime of Tamworth Pig. London, Faber, 1972.
Tamworth Pig Saves the Trees. London, Faber, 1973.
Tamworth Pig and the Litter. London, Faber, 1975.
Christmas with Tamworth Pig. London, Faber, 1977.
The Turbulent Term of Tyke Tiler. London, Faber, 1977.
Gowie Corby Plays Chicken (not illustrated). London, Faber, 1979.
Dog Days and Cat Naps (short stories). London, Faber, 1980.
The Clock Tower Ghost. London, Faber, 1981.
No Place Like. London, Faber, 1983.
Charlie Lewis Plays for Time, illustrated by Vanessa Julian-Ottie. London, Faber, 1984.
The Well, illustrated by Chantal Fouracre. London, Faber, 1984.
Jason Bodger and the Priory Ghost. London, Faber, 1985.
Mr. Magus Is Waiting for You, illustrated by Alan Baker. London, Faber, 1986.
Juniper: A Mystery, illustrated by Chloe Cheese. London, Faber, 1986.
Tamworth Pig Stories, illustrated by Carolyn Dinan. London, Faber, 1987.
Crocodile Dog, illustrated by Elizabeth Manson-Bahr. London, Heinemann, 1987.
I Can't Stand Losing. London, Faber, 1987.
Room with No Windows. London, Faber, 1989.

Other

Editor, *Ducks and Dragons: Poems for Children*, illustrated by Carolyn Dinan. London, Faber, 1980.

*

Gene Kemp comments:
 I seek to entertain—a little.

*   *   *

The broad appeal of Gene Kemp's stories is indicated by the fact that *The Turbulent Term of Tyke Tiler* was not only awarded the Library Association's Carnegie Medal but was also joint winner of the Other Award for 1977. This truly innovatory book gives new dimensions to the day-school story, and an authoritative boost to feminism. More convincingly than any other juvenile book it demolishes many accepted ideas about aspirational and experiential differences between boys and girls. The realization of this is all the more significant to the reader because it only becomes apparent after the tantalizing twist in the story's tail (when the 11-year-old "hero" turns out to be a heroine). The book is also a comically touching account of the friendship between bright-as-a-button Tyke and a dim but engaging boy. The exactly appropriate first person narrative is punctuated by consciously dire playground rhymes and jokes which sharpen its pacy succinctness.

Gowie Corby Plays Chicken, another book with a primary school setting, also deals with a rebellious leading character and an unusual friendship. It never quite rises to Tyke Tiler's literally shattering-rooftop heights, although it has similar style and exhilaration. The lively mood is sustained in Kemp's recent full-length story, *The Clock Tower Ghost*. Once again her main characters are not obviously those with whom readers might easily identify; spiteful, greedy, nine-year-old Amanda is simply awful, and the gloomy ghost that she discovers in her new home is hardly endearing. This is, in a sense, another book about an ill-assorted pair of friends. The bond that is reluctantly forged between girl and ghost brings about not only some anarchically entertaining situations but also the reform of Amanda, and, for the spirit, a long awaited release from his hundred years of haunting.

The Tamworth stories are more magical and innocent, though Thomas, the human hero who shares the honours with the socially crusading pig, is occasionally obstreperous. These tales for younger children combine domestic cosiness and questing outdoor themes, and strike echoes of Milne's Pooh stories. (There is even an inverted reference to these in the naming of the anti-hero Christopher Robin Baggs.) Thomas pursues his adventures in the company of a poetry-spouting rabbit and a mathematically inclined hedgehog—his two floppy toys who, like Pooh, and Piglet, are fully alive in the context of small-boy and animal rapport. Tamworth Pig, of course, is not only really alive but larger than life; his personality, like the ardour of his conservationist campaigns, is comically convincing.

Animals are also enlivening elements in *Dog Days and Cat Naps.* In this collection of short stories Kemp's crispness of style and feeling for the vivid rumbustiousness of primary school cultures are used to good effect. Events and relationships are acutely observed, and each story produces a strong measure of excitement and genuine surprise.

Kemp has produced two thought-provoking but incisively funny books for teenagers, *No Place Like* and *I Can't Stand Losing.* The first of these features a "no nukes" family which, noisy and voluble, hardly lives up to the "peace house" notice adorning its front door. Pete, the leading character who enters the new world of sixth form college life, finds himself in various rites of passage situations. In *I Can't Stand Losing* the serious issues addressed again include that of the nuclear threat. A family of "no-hopers" who draw strength from their toughly idealistic mum have to pull themselves up by their own bootstraps when she packs her case and declares she is off to Greenham Common. Whether Chernobyl, and the spread of AIDS, will ultimately change society is left as an open question.

Juniper is an outstanding addition to Kemp's stories for eight- to 12-year-olds. It is both a mystery and an adventure, and the unlikely heroine Juniper retains her resilience despite disadvantage: "…I only have half an arm and my father is a criminal. And my mother is…a bit loopy." Like *The Turbulent Term of Tyke Tiler, Juniper* focuses on a friendship between a girl and a boy (in this case from different races), but despite flashes of Kemp's characteristically spicy humour, it has a moving and haunting quality.

—Mary Cadogan

KENDALL, Carol (née Seeger). American. Born in Bucyrus, Ohio, 13 September 1917. Educated at Bucyrus High School, graduated 1935; Ohio University, Athens, 1935–39, A.B. 1939 (Phi Beta Kappa). Married Paul Murray Kendall in 1939 (died 1973); two daughters. Address: 928 Holiday Drive, Lawrence, Kansas 66044, U.S.A.

PUBLICATIONS FOR CHILDREN

Fiction

The Other Side of the Tunnel, illustrated by Lilian Buchanan. London, Lane, 1956; New York, Abelard Schuman, 1957.
The Gammage Cup, illustrated by Erik Blegvad. New York, Harcourt Brace, 1959; as *The Minnipins,* London, Dent, 1960.
The Big Splash, illustrated by Lilian Obligado. New York, Viking

Press, 1960.
The Whisper of Glocken, illustrated by Imero Gobbato. New York, Harcourt Brace, 1965; London, Bodley Head, 1967.
The Firelings. London, Bodley Head, 1981; New York, Atheneum, 1982.

Other

Sweet and Sour: Tales from China, with Yao-wen Li, illustrated by Shirley Felts. London, Bodley Head, 1978; New York, Seabury Press, 1979.
Haunting Tales from Japan. Lawrence, University of Kansas, 1985.
The Wedding of the Rat Family (Chinese folktale), illustrated by James Watts. New York, McElderry, 1988.

PUBLICATIONS FOR ADULTS

Novels

The Black Seven. New York, Harper, 1946; London, Lane, 1950.
The Baby-Snatcher. London, Lane, 1952.

*

Manuscript Collection: Ohio University Library, Athens.

Carol Kendall comments:

Fantasy is what I most enjoy writing. I like it for its agelessness and its simplicity, probably because I like to concentrate on ageless and simple themes: truth, honor, courage, goodness. I try for morality without mawkishness; fantasy seems to me the best means of achieving it.

*   *   *

The books of Carol Kendall are distinguished for their inventiveness and mixture of comic and serious content. In *The Gammage Cup* the author was interested in depicting stalwart, inner-directed people on the one hand, and on the other hand the pettiness and tyranny of conformists.

Literary fantasies offer the pleasure of looking in two different directions at once: toward an imaginary place and toward the world as we know it. *The Gammage Cup* provides this diverting interplay, as well as a theme which is particularly adaptable for children. For example, the oddities of the non-conforming protagonists can be treated playfully. Kendall's heroine, Muggles, has her own system of tidiness: "All was in perfect order…the way she liked it—the far-corner pile, the hearthstone pile, the under-the-table pile." And since the non-conformists are outnumbered by the rest of the Minnipin villagers, their underdog position allows for exciting encounters and conflicts.

A further necessity in fantasies is to develop a sense of solidity in imaginary realms. This entails descriptive skill and high ingenuity, notable qualities in the Kendall fantasies. The history and geography of the Minnipin valley, the system of government, the values, economy, forms of recreation—these all take shape without direct exposition. Most important, the language of the Minnipins reminds us of their world apart and at the same time its ties with the world the reader knows. Minnipins have merry-go-longs, bobble-boards, haggle-fetes, picklicks, kickety balls, wasso birds, soups with enriching huddlestone tansy. And because both *The Gammage Cup* and its sequel, *The Whisper of Glocken,* are wilderness survival tales, the books offer a double ethnology: the "civilized" Minnipin way of life and the survival tactics of the adventurers.

The Minnipins, after they patch up their internal political quarrel, cause the total extermination of the invading Mushroom army. Yet the Mushrooms have some human qualities, and, without their being developed as symbols of total evil, the Minnipin victory seems almost like a case of genocide. In *The Whisper of Glocken* this problem doesn't arise. The new Minnipin heroes are captured by members of the threatening Hulk society, but both groups escape each other in the end. This is in keeping with the theme: culture diversity is to be valued.

In *The Firelings* characters are typed as the proverbial village idiot, drunk, scold, stuffed shirt, and so on. But once the dangerous setting and political intrigue capture the reader's attention, this two-dimensionality isn't a drawback. The character of the total civilization dominates as the author explores cultural responses to natural disasters. A population of small people (Firelings) face extinction unless they abandon their superstitious reaction to the showers of ash that portend a volcanic eruption. The ease with which mob psychology leads to cruelty and injustice is the theme Kendall illumines through her meticulously imagined landscapes and dramatic conflicts.

Narratives which depend upon social commentary for their meaning and cohesiveness take the risk of becoming dated. Kendall's fantasies are sufficiently allegorical to avoid widespread rejection on this basis. She is an advocate of individual and collective fulfillment, yet she carefully avoids exhortations of any kind. As for her style, it has that graphic quality which heightens veracity and readability.

—Donnarae MacCann

KENNEDY, (Jerome) Richard. American. Born in Jefferson City, Missouri, 23 December 1932. Educated at Portland State University, Oregon, 1954–58, B.S. (honours) 1958; Oregon State University, Corvallis, 1964–65. Served in the United States Air Force, 1951–54: Staff Sergeant. Married Lillian Nance in 1960 (divorced 1974); two sons. Elementary school teacher, Harrisburg and Dayton, Oregon, 1968–69. Since 1974 custodian, Oregon State University Marine Science Center, Newport. Has also worked as bookseller, cab driver, woodcutter, and janitor. Address: 415 West Olive, Newport, Oregon 97365, U.S.A.

PUBLICATIONS FOR CHILDREN

Fiction

The Parrot and the Thief, illustrated by Marcia Sewall. Boston, Little Brown, 1974.
The Contests at Cowlick, illustrated by Marc Simont. Boston, Little Brown, 1975.
The Blue Stone, illustrated by Ronald Himler. New York, Holiday House, 1976.
Come Again in the Spring, illustrated by Marcia Sewall. New York, Harper, 1976.
The Porcelain Man, illustrated by Marcia Sewall. Boston, Little Brown, 1976; London, Hamish Hamilton, 1977.
Oliver Hyde's Dishcloth Concert, illustrated by Robert Andrew Parker. Boston, Little Brown, 1977.
The Dark Princess, illustrated by Donna Diamond. New York, Holiday House, 1978.
The Rise and Fall of Ben Gizzard, illustrated by Marcia Sewall. Boston, Little Brown, 1978.
The Leprechaun's Story, illustrated by Marcia Sewall. New York,

Dutton, 1979.
The Lost Kingdom of Karnica, illustrated by Uri Shulevitz. San Francisco, Sierra Club, 1979.
The Mouse God, illustrated by Stephen Harvard. Boston, Little Brown, 1979.
Inside My Feet: The Story of a Giant, illustrated by Ronald Himler. New York, Harper, 1979.
Crazy in Love, illustrated by Marcia Sewall. New York, Dutton, 1980.
Song of the Horse, illustrated by Marcia Sewall. New York, Dutton, 1981.
The Boxcar at the Center of the Universe, illustrated by Jeff Kronen. New York, Harper, 1982.
Amy's Eyes, illustrated by Richard Egielski. New York, Harper, 1985; London, MacRae, 1986.
Collected Stories, illustrated by Marcia Sewall. New York, Harper, 1987.

Verse

Delta Baby and Two Sea Songs, illustrated by Lydia Dabcovich and Charles Mikolaycak. Reading, Massachusetts, Addison Wesley, 1979.

* * *

Richard Kennedy's success as a storyteller lies in his fertile imagination, his ability to structure a narrative economically, his philosophical turn of mind, and his lucid, sometimes comical, style. He experiments with different fictional modes—a practice that perhaps contributes to the spontaneity that distinguishes his work.

The Blue Stone is an original fairytale based upon a riddle; *The Porcelain Man* is a simple magical tale reminiscent of a German *märchen*; *The Mouse God* is a whimsical satire in the tradition of Hans Andersen; *The Dark Princess* is a mystical romance after the manner of Laurence Housman fantasies; *Crazy in Love* is a folksy parable with rich symbolic overtones; *Song of the Horse* is a lyrical celebration of animal-child relationships; *The Boxcar at the Center of the Universe* is an initiation novel that experiments with framing devices and extravagant imagery; *Amy's Eyes* is a doll fantasy with layer upon layer of implicit commentary about identity formation, obsessive conduct, and the kind of bitterness that hardens into malice.

On rare occasions Kennedy's fanciful plots are too cumbersome to be credible. This flaw impairs *Inside My Feet* and, to a lesser degree, the initiation novel. In all his other works of fiction, form and content are well-integrated, the thematic materials are often profound, and the storylines are ingenious.

The Blue Stone illustrates Kennedy's ability to blend the simple and the sublime. The plot is too complicated to paraphrase, and yet it all boils down to a naive "nature" myth. In the end the reader sees how angels are made from bits of sky that fall to earth and are swallowed by swallows. But before this discovery there are dozens of twists in the story when men swallow the sky stone and become ducks, women swallow them and become hens, and poems turn pigs into bread loaves and loaves into pigs. To avoid narrative chaos, the author structures the story in tight relationship to a riddle.

Jack and Bertie are an archetypal peasant couple with a lively sense of wonder and a gift for unpretentious poetic speech. Jack finds the blue stone while he is "splashering about" in the creek and Bertie swallows it when the noonday soup is "starting to agitate." An astrologer, Zork, is one of several intriguing villains: "He had a long stork-like way about him, also a sharp nose and a scraggly little head that popped up through his red cape as if he had squeezed his head small by bearing down too hard on tiny schemes."

Kennedy's overall narrative style is as casual as the dialogue between the characters. This adds unity while also enabling the author to highlight such fragments of poetic description as the lines about "dark and careful cats" crouching in wonder.

Thematic benchmarks help the reader keep track of the complicated rules of magic. Warnings in the riddle about vengeance and anger make it easy for a child to follow the moral thread. The art of writing such a complex parable is to some extent the art of evoking a clearcut ethical system, and at the same time suggesting that there is a reservoir of unstated meaning just below the surface. In *The Blue Stone* Bertie's naive comments carry a wealth of implication: "The working of heaven," she says, "is enough to tire a person out completely."

Kennedy's powers as a lyrical and philosophical writer reach a new height in *Amy's Eyes*. And because he needs an intricate plot and cast of characters in order to share his world view, he makes considerable demands on his readers—demands upon their power of concentration, suspension of disbelief, and willingness to confront human enigmas. At the same time the author makes the whole fanciful journey easy. His narrative flows from one familiar epigraph to another, all drawn from Mother Goose. Plotlines such as loving a doll into life and grappling with gold-crazed pirates are already conventional in children's literature. Moreover, the intricate narrative strands are intelligibly woven together as Kennedy makes the most of other simple patterns: inversions (when dolls become people and people become dolls); superimpositions (when the most magnanimous character assumes traits of the most ruthless); contrasts, as when "The Golden Man" (Amy's beloved father) confronts "Goldnose" (a fiendish pirate). And always there is Kennedy the phrase maker. He completes his image of an abandoned lover with a deceptively simple dinner scene: "…Miss Quince glared at her plate and stabbed at every one of her peas individually, and chewed each to extinction with terrible method."

Kennedy's children's books cannot be defined as tales exclusively for the young. *Amy's Eyes* is the most multi-leveled and warrants the accolade bestowed by another eminent fantasy writer, Lloyd Alexander: "[It] sets a new high standard for all of us concerned with quality in literature.…"

—Donnarae MacCann

KENNEDY, X.J. Pseudonym for Joseph Charles Kennedy. American. Born in Dover, New Jersey, 21 August 1929. Educated at Seton Hall College, South Orange, New Jersey, B.Sc. 1950; Columbia University, New York, M.A. 1951; the Sorbonne, Paris, Cert. Litt. 1956. Served in the United States Navy, 1951–55. Married Dorothy Mintzlaff in 1962; one daughter and four sons. Teaching Fellow, 1956–60, and Instructor, 1960–62, University of Michigan, Ann Arbor; teacher, University of North Carolina, Greensboro, 1962–63; Assistant Professor, 1963–67, Associate Professor, 1967–73, and Professor of English, 1973–79, Tufts University, Medford, Massachusetts. Visiting Lecturer, Wellesley College, Massachusetts, 1964, and University of California, Irvine, 1966–67; Bruern Fellow in American Literature, University of Leeds, 1974–75. Poetry editor, *Paris Review,* Paris and New York, 1962–64; editor, with Dorothy M. Kennedy, *Counter/Measures* magazine, 1972–74. Recipient (for poetry): Hopwood award, 1959; Bread Loaf Writers Conference fellowship, 1960; Lamont Poetry Selection award, 1961; Bess Hokin prize (*Poetry,* Chicago), 1961; National Endowment for the Arts grant, 1967; Shelley Memorial award, 1970; Guggenheim fellowship, 1973; Los Angeles *Times* award, 1985. L.H.D.: Lawrence University, Appleton, Wisconsin, 1988. Agent: Curtis Brown, 10 Astor Place, New York, New York 10003. Address: 4 Fern Way,

Bedford, Massachusetts 01730, U.S.A.

PUBLICATIONS FOR CHILDREN

Fiction

The Owlstone Crown, illustrated by Michele Chessare. New York, Atheneum, 1983.

Verse

One Winter Night in August and Other Nonsense Jingles, illustrated by David McPhail. New York, Atheneum, 1975.
The Phantom Ice Cream Man: More Nonsense Jingles, illustrated by David McPhail. New York, Atheneum, 1979.
Did Adam Name the Vinegarroon?, illustrated by Heidi Johanna Selig. Boston, Godine, 1982.
The Forgetful Wishing-Well, illustrated by Monica Incisa. New York, Atheneum, 1985.
Brats, illustrated by James Watts. New York, Atheneum, 1986.
Ghastlies, Goops, and Pincushions: Nonsense Verse, illustrated by Ron Barrett. New York, McElderry, 1989.

Other

Editor, with Dorothy M. Kennedy, *Knock at a Star: A Child's Introduction to Poetry,* illustrated by Karen Ann Weinhaus. Boston, Little Brown, 1982.

PUBLICATIONS FOR ADULTS

Verse

Nude Descending a Staircase: Poems, Song, A Ballad. New York, Doubleday, 1961.
Growing into Love. New York, Doubleday, 1969.
Bulsh. Providence, Rhode Island, Burning Deck, 1970.
Breaking and Entering. London, Oxford University Press, 1972.
Emily Dickinson in Southern California. Boston, Godine, 1974.
Celebrations after the Death of John Brennan. Lincoln, Massachusetts, Penmaen Press, 1974.
Three Tenors, One Vehicle: A Book of Songs, with James E. Camp and Keith Waldrop. Columbia, Missouri, Open Places, 1975.
French Leave: Translations. Florence, Kentucky, Robert L. Barth, 1983.
Hangover Mass. Cincinnati, Bits Press, 1984.
Cross Ties: Selected Poems. Athens, University of Georgia Press, 1985.

Other

The Bedford Guide for College Writers (textbook), with Dorothy M. Kennedy. New York, St. Martin's Press, 1987.

Editor, with James E. Camp, *Mark Twain's Frontier.* New York, Holt Rinehart, 1963.
Editor, *An Introduction to Poetry* (textbook). Boston, Little Brown, 1966; revised edition, 1971, 1974, 1978, 1982, 1986.
Editor, with Keith Waldrop and James E. Camp, *Pegasus Descending: A Book of the Best Bad Verse.* New York, Macmillan, and London, Collier Macmillan, 1971.
Editor, *Messages: A Thematic Anthology of Poetry.* Boston, Little Brown, 1973.
Editor, *An Introduction to Fiction.* Boston, Little Brown, 1976;

revised edition, 1979, 1983, 1987.
Editor, *Literature: An Introduction to Fiction, Poetry, and Drama.* Boston, Little Brown, 1976; revised edition, 1979, 1983, 1987.
Editor, *The Tygers of Wrath: Poems of Hate, Anger, and Invective.* Athens, University of Georgia Press, 1981.
Editor, with Dorothy M. Kennedy, *The Bedford Reader.* Boston, Bedford, 1982; revised edition, New York, St. Martin's Press, 1985, 1988.
Editor, *This Body of Silk,* by Sue Ellen Thompson. Boston, Northeastern University Press, 1986.

*

X. J. Kennedy comments:

The titles of my books for children may give the impression that nonsense is all I care about. Oh, I care about nonsense fervently, but in poetry for children, nonsense isn't everything. And so, at least a part of each verse collection tries to deal with the world that children know; one collection, *The Forgetful Wishing-Well,* is more or less realistic throughout. In *The Owlstone Crown,* my favorite among my children's books and my only novel to date, this earth serves as point of departure for a fantastic other earth. The story's plot and characters owe something to *The Divine Comedy, Hamlet, Macbeth, The Wizard of Oz,* and Raymond Chandler's private eye fiction; and all that might be held against me, but so far, no one has seemed to mind.

*   *   *

One of the worlds of X.J. Kennedy lies just next door in a neighborhood where mothers keep pet pigs, play slide trombones, and bake inedible pies while fathers conjure up a good whirl for their entire families in a concrete mixer. Through their houses pass an assortment of odd aunts, uncles, and grandparents, as well as a monstrous mouse who crashes a birthday party. It is a heady place where the Tooth Fairy, fabric shrinkers, "a birthday cake so full of eggs/It cackles, clucks and scratches," are part of everyday living, where salami subs, gumball machines, staplers, and cough drops enjoy a life of their own. It is, most importantly, a world where children may exercise their own imaginations to create still more fun. "My mother's big green gravy boat/Once thought he was a navy boat./I poured him over my mashed potatoes/And out swam seven swift torpedoes./Torpedoes whizzed and whirred, and—WHAM!/One bumped smack into my hunk of ham…"

Kennedy's imagination overflows with absurdities. Spaghetti, he writes, makes very unusual shoelaces. In winter one can prepare "Snowflake Souffle" by stirring it with "two hind legs," baking it in an igloo and slicing it with a "rusty ice-skate." The Thrift-Rite Supermart provides enough frozen delicacies to whip up an "Instant Storm." A coat made of cocoa skin makes one feel "All warm and scummy."

His "far out family" includes a great-great-Grandma who sleeps in a treehouse, an Aunt Jill who insists that dill stalks will afford "sour puss" pickles "a few good tickles," and Cousin Carrée who serves—both literally and figuratively—"a good square meal" including ground round shaped into bricks with hamburger buns squeezed into squares. His "…uncle, General Doug MacDougal,/Sleeps nights inside a huge blue bugle" while "All four of my uncle Erics/Tear their hair and throw hysterics." In *Brats* Kennedy conjures up scores of annoying youngsters who are either victims or perpetrators of further hilarity. "At the laundromat Liz Meyer/Flung her brothers in the dryer./Round and round they've whizzed for years,/Not yet dry behind the ears."

In addition to zany family situations which include household pets, there are "Unheard-Of Birds and Couldn't-Be Beasts" as well as attic ghosts and a variety of "Cheerful Spirits." Dinosaurs fascinate Kennedy, as do creatures of the sea. In addition to a limerick

about a nervous sea captain from Cheesequake, there is a rousing story poem about Mackeral Mack and Halibut Hal. Kennedy's lines sing: "With walloping tails, the whales off Wales/Whack waves to wicked whitecaps…" In this, as in all of his work, Kennedy outshines mere versifiers with a superb use of rhyme, meter, onomatopoeia, alliteration, and delightful wordplay. "The cows that browse in pastures/Seem not at all surprised/That as they moo they mow the lawn/And their milk comes pasture-ized." Digested by a giant snail, Uncle Artemus McPhail remarks that he "finds this whole thing hardly moving." In his animal alphabet, *Did Adam Name the Vinegarroon?,* he writes of a tyrannosaur: "Yet tyrants, under Time's slow hand,/Must one day bow their necks./Now in museums—bones wired—stand/Tyrannosaurus wrecks." Kennedy's work is rich in simile and metaphor; "…bats drowse in houses' eaves/Like tents collapsed for storage," a mole "tunnels underneath your lawn/To shoulder up a wrinkle," and an iguana "demonstrates the signs/Of somewhat hasty wrapping."

While a good portion of Kennedy's early verse for children in *One Winter Night in August* and *The Phantom Ice Cream Man* appear as strictly nonsensical, there is, as in all excellent nonsense, a toehold on reality, a recognition of the human condition. Mothers may not buy "six paper swimming pools" or "backscratchers for a pig" but they do enjoy bargain sales. Mighty Mump cereal may not contain "sugar, corncobs, and dye" but televised it is "made up to look/simply ethereal." In a recent book of poetry, *The Forgetful Wishing Well,* lies Kennedy's other world of reality where sticky ice cream cones, forbidden TV watching, excuses to stay up late, reactions to ugly deer statues, and even a child's poignant sense of loss are explored. "I take my plastic rocket ship/To bed, now that I'm older./My wooly bear is packed away—/Why do the nights feel colder?" Humor remains keen, as in conversations between a crocus and artichoke, a truck and taxi. A schoolbus, window screen, fog, snow, and old stone mill are personified. But nonsense has been routed. One can see in "Roofscape" a skyscraper shadowing "A low-kneeling church," watch pigeons, traffic snarls and the world as it is. An unforgettable use of onomatopoeia occurs in "Rain into River" where "Rain into river/falling/tingles/one/at/a/time/the trout's/tin shingles." Kennedy's title poem, "To a Forgetful Wishing Well," sets the tone. "All summer long, your round stone eardrum held/Wishes I whispered down you. None came true./Didn't they make one ripple in your mind?/I even wished a silver pail for you."

Kennedy is at home in both worlds; to each he is making a significant contribution.

—Myra Cohn Livingston

———

KENNEMORE, Tim. British. Born in London, 2 February 1957. Address: c/o Faber and Faber, 3 Queen Square, London WC1N 3AU, England.

PUBLICATIONS FOR CHILDREN

Fiction

The Middle of the Sandwich. London, Faber, 1981.
The Fortunate Few. London, Faber, 1981; New York, Coward McCann, 1982.
Wall of Words. London, Faber, 1982.
Here Tomorrow, Gone Today (short stories). London, Faber, 1983.
Changing Times. London, Faber, 1984.

*   *   *

With only a handful of books to her credit, Tim Kennemore is making her mark on children's fiction. Her first full-length story, *The Middle of the Sandwich,* appeared in 1981, and underlined the fact that there was a resurgence of interest in the school story, even though the new wave in this genre represented a departure from the traditional boarding school sagas of the 1920's and 1930's. *The Middle of the Sandwich* has a day school setting and is concerned with disorientation at the upper junior level. It is a measure of Kennemore's skill that she brings a sense of freshness and discovery to this well-trodden scheme. As in all her books she is an acutely aware, detached observer, who harnesses both comedy and drama to good effect.

Helen, the heroine, has to spend a term at a village primary school; this term is sandwiched between her more permanent education at a private preparatory school and a London comprehensive, and at first everything and everyone seem hostile. There is some extremely perceptive use of the confines of school to heighten emotions and relationships, and the obedient, well-behaved Helen learns how to cope with her new situation by drawing on unexpected inner resources.

Helen turns out to be the most conformist of Kennemore's heroines. Her next, the 14-year-old Jodie Bell in *The Fortunate Few,* starts off with far more assertion and talent. She is a gymnast, whose adventures are set in a world of the future (which nevertheless is related closely to our own) in which gymnastics seems to have taken over from football as the most popular spectator sport. Although Jodie is believable as a character, the book is a merciless send-up of professional exploitation; journalists and publicity men are treated as trenchantly as are officials in sports promotion and big business circles. This book's sparkling satirical edge makes it appropriate for adult audiences as well as for children, and it seems that Kennemore's stories, which show a consistently developing maturity, are likely to appeal to a wide range of readers as they can be appreciated at various levels. *Wall of Words,* for example, is at one level a satisfying family saga; at another it represents black humour as biting as that of *The Fortunate Few* (her leading child characters have a morbid passion for embalming, spontaneous explosion, and other unsocial activities).

Here Tomorrow, Gone Today demonstrates her flair for the short story. Four of the tales in this collection have school settings; three are more concerned with family relationships. They encompass every shade of Kennemore's humour from mild irony to gulping satire. Her ability to convey naturalistic adolescent dialogue (bad jokes and all!) comes across robustly in these episodes which have as their theme the debunking of pompous adults and precocious teenagers. There are threads of feminism too, which are the more telling for being stumbled upon by the reader rather than rammed home. In "The Black Sheep," for example, the M.P. parent so bitterly resented by the weedy, depressive Russell turns out to be his mother and not his father: her agent, prime minister, and rival candidate are also firmly feminine.

There is nothing particularly new about Kennemore's plots and themes, but her treatment of these is always satisfyingly inventive.

—Mary Cadogan

KERR, James Lennox. See **DAWLISH, Peter.**

KERR, (Anne-)Judith. British. Born in Berlin, Germany, 14 June 1923; daughter of the writer Alfred Kerr; left Germany, 1933, moved to England, 1936, naturalized citizen, 1947. Educated at schools in Germany, Switzerland, France, and England; Central School of Art, London (scholar), 1945. Married the writer Nigel Kneale in 1954; one daughter and one son. Secretary, Red Cross, London, 1941–45; teacher and textile designer, 1946–53; reader, script editor, and script writer, BBC-TV, London, 1953–58. Lives in London. Address: c/o William Collins Ltd., 8 Grafton Street, London W1X 3LA, England.

PUBLICATIONS FOR CHILDREN (illustrated by the author)

Fiction

The Tiger Who Came to Tea. London, Collins, and New York, Coward McCann, 1968.
Mog the Forgetful Cat. London, Collins, 1970; New York, Parents' Magazine Press, 1972.
When Hitler Stole Pink Rabbit. London, Collins, 1971; New York, Coward McCann, 1972.
When Willy Went to the Wedding. London, Collins, 1972; New York, Parents' Magazine Press, 1973.
The Other Way Round (not illustrated). London, Collins, and New York, Coward McCann, 1975.
Mog's Christmas. London, Collins, and Cleveland, World, 1976.
A Small Person Far Away. London, Collins, 1978; New York, Coward McCann, 1979.
Mog and the Baby. London, Collins, 1980.
Mog in the Dark. London, Collins, 1983; New York, Larousse, 1984.
Mog and Me. London, Collins, 1984.
Mog's Family of Cats. London, Collins, 1985.
Mog's Amazing Birthday Caper. London, Collins, 1986.
Mog and Bunny. London, Collins, 1988; New York, Knopf, 1989.

*

Judith Kerr comments:

The picture books were for my children—in fact, a lot of the ideas came from my children in the first place, and also from my husband. They were the sort of ideas which amused us all. Mog is our cat. The novels also were written for my children, but deal with my own childhood as a refugee from Hitler, first in Switzerland and France, later in England during the war. It was so different from the way they grew up that I wanted them to know about it, and I wanted also to explain that it wasn't nearly as horrific as it sounded. Perhaps most of all it was a way of remembering my own parents, now long dead.

*   *   *

Judith Kerr's twin talents as writer and illustrator have been in quantitative balance in her popular picture books about Mog the cat, which were aimed, successfully, at the under-fives. With these she proved herself a thoroughly competent, professional, imaginative children's author—one among many. Real distinction, however, she achieved with her two autobiographical stories for young readers over ten which chart her exceptionally eventful childhood and adolescence as the daughter of a famous German Jewish writer and refugee from Nazi Germany. Together, *When Hitler Stole Pink Rabbit* and *The Other Way Round* tell Anna's (alias Judith's) 12-year odyssey that takes her to three countries (Switzerland, France, England) and makes her trilingual. It is a lively, detached, and objective narrative, helped by a distance of 30 years between event and writing down, a precise memory, a warm sense of humour, and profound insight into the growing self-awareness and world perception of child and teenager. Both books derive most of their interest from the interaction of outside political events with inside subjective experience of child and teenager, the first story the more poignantly so because little Anna is as yet incapable of grasping the momentous historical changes which force her universally respected father to leave his native country and end his brilliant career, thus changing their lives from wealthy middle-class to destitute stateless. Yet Kerr demonstrates convincingly how all that matters for the child is family togetherness and emotional security, while lack of money or settled home is of secondary importance. Both in Switzerland and France little Anna bravely takes everything in her stride: drastically reduced living conditions, changing playmates and teachers, lack of toys and money, even adjusting to a new language and being cut by Nazi Germans on holiday in their temporary Swiss home. Only a brief separation from her parents proves traumatic, because the warm understanding in a secure family is her be-all and end-all, natural squabbling and disappointments notwithstanding. Anna thus has as happy a childhood as any child growing up in much more sheltered circumstances.

The 18-year old Anna in *The Other Way Round*, however, is learning independence the hard way because of the conditions the war and her enemy-alien status put her into, and because she feels for her aging parents in their appallingly reduced existence. They live in a cheap London hotel full of Central European refugees, her father a German-language writer without work and her mother doing menial jobs—the tragedy of exile! Yet Anna succeeds and overcomes by asserting the importance of her own life (secretary during the day, art student in the evening) in spite of her deep concern for her parents. She experiences first love and loss of love, first success and failure, the reward and monotony of work, the stirrings of creativity. Set against the richly detailed backcloth of the war, the Blitz and the Battle of Britain, rationing, air raids, buzz bombs and finally victory, Kerr's story of Anna's successful transition from lost schoolgirl to self-possessed art student is a chronicle of an epoch as much as of the grim refugee life Anna and her family have to live while waiting for the war to end. Together, the two books give the young reader a bit of important contemporary history, as seen and experienced by somebody who went through it vulnerable, yet open-eyed. There is no better way for the young reader to be brought up both against recent history and the psychological implications such turbulent times had for those growing up in them.

—Gertrud Mander

KERR, M.E. Pseudonym for Marijane Meaker; has also written as Ann Aldrich; M.J. Meaker; Vin Packer. American. Born in Auburn, New York, 27 May 1927. Educated at the University of Missouri, Columbia, B.A. 1949. Clerk, E.P. Dutton, publishers, 1949–50. Recipient: *Media and Methods* award, 1975; Christopher award, 1979; Society of Children's Book Writers Golden Kite award, 1982. Agent: McIntosh and Otis Inc., 310 Madison Avenue, New York, New York 10017. Address: 12 Deep Six Drive, East Hampton, New York 11937, U.S.A.

PUBLICATIONS FOR CHILDREN

Fiction

Dinky Hocker Shoots Smack.   New York, Harper, 1972; London, Gollancz, 1973.
If I Love You, Am I Trapped Forever?   New York, Harper, 1973; London, Pan, 1986.
The Son of Someone Famous.   New York, Harper, 1974; London, Gollancz, 1975.
Is That You, Miss Blue?   New York, Harper, 1975.

Love Is a Missing Person.   New York, Harper, 1975.
I'll Love You When You're More Like Me.   New York, Harper, 1977.
Gentlehands.   New York, Harper, and London, Bodley Head, 1978.
Little Little.   New York, Harper, 1981.
What I Really Think of You.   New York, Harper, 1982.
<u>*Him*</u> *She Loves?*   New York, Harper, 1984.
I Stay Near You.   New York, Harper, 1985; London, Pan, 1986.
Night Kites.   New York, Harper, 1986.
Fell.   New York, Harper, 1987.
Fell Back.   New York, Harper, 1989.

Other

Me Me Me Me Me: Not a Novel (autobiography).   New York, Harper, 1983.

PUBLICATIONS FOR ADULTS

Novels as Vin Packer

Dark Intruder.   New York, Fawcett, 1952; London, Miller, 1958.
Spring Fire.   New York, Fawcett, 1952; London, Consul, 1966.
Look Back to Love.   New York, Fawcett, 1953; London, Miller, 1958.
Come Destroy Me.   New York, Fawcett, 1954; London, Digit, 1958.
Whisper His Sin.   New York, Fawcett, 1954; London, Miller, 1959.
The Thrill Kids.   New York, Fawcett, 1955.
Dark Don't Catch Me.   New York, Fawcett, 1956.
The Young and Violent.   New York, Fawcett, 1956.
Three-Day Terror.   New York, Fawcett, 1957.
The Evil Friendship.   New York, Fawcett, 1958.
5:45 to Suburbia.   New York, Fawcett, 1958; London, Miller, 1959.
The Twisted Ones.   New York, Fawcett, and London, Miller, 1959.
The Girl on the Best-Seller List.   New York, Fawcett, 1960; London, Muller, 1961.
The Damnation of Adam Blessing.   New York, Fawcett, 1960; London, Muller, 1962.
Carol, In a Thousand Cities (as Ann Aldrich).   New York, Fawcett, 1960.
Something in the Shadows.   New York, Fawcett, 1961; London, Muller, 1962.
Intimate Victims.   New York, Fawcett, 1962; London, Muller, 1963.
Alone at Night.   New York, Fawcett, 1963; London, Muller, 1964.
The Hare in March.   New York, New American Library, 1966; London, Mayflower, 1968.
Hometown (as M.J. Meaker).   New York, Doubleday, 1967.
Game of Survival (as Marijane Meaker).   New York, New American Library, 1968.
Don't Rely on Gemini.   New York, Delacorte Press, 1969; London, Macmillan, 1970.
Shockproof Sydney Skate (as Marijane Meaker).   Boston, Little Brown, 1972.

Other as Ann Aldrich

We Walk Alone.   New York, Fawcett, 1955.
We, Too, Must Love.   New York, Fawcett, 1958.
We Two Won't Last.   New York, Fawcett, 1963.
Sudden Endings (on suicide; as M.J. Meaker).   New York, Doubleday, 1964.
Take a Lesbian to Lunch.   New York, Macfadden, 1972.

*

Manuscript Collection: Kerlan Collection, University of Minnesota,

Minneapolis.

M.E. Kerr comments:
I write to entertain. I hope I do.

* * *

Romance, humor, and a fascination with the underdog are the hallmarks of M. E. Kerr's popular and highly respected writing for young adults. An expert manipulator of the conventions of the contemporary teen novel—troubled or vulnerable young protagonist, problematic parents, and an ironic stance towards reality—Kerr chronicles the self-absorption of adolescence with equal parts of sympathy and good-natured satire. Her sympathy with teen tunnel vision proceeds from the belief expressed in her 1983 autobiography, *Me Me Me Me Me: Not a Novel,* that "What's going on in the world is secondary to what's going on in high school, for in those vulnerable teen years high school *is* the world." At the same time, Kerr confesses that "whenever you find a little smart-mouth, tomboy kid in any of my books, you have found me from long ago...." Humor helps the smart-mouth character cope with her situation while it suggests to the young reader that high school is not forever; it will be "the world" for just a few years. In Kerr's hands, being a teenager is significant, but more importantly, it is survivable.

Kerr's focus on high school as the world should not, however, be taken to mean that her characters never leave the halls of their respective schools. Kerr takes her characters to their favorite teen hang-outs, locales which reverberate with multiple associations in the context of the other novels. Seven of the books are set in Seaville, New York, a plush resort town modeled after East Hampton, Long Island where Kerr now lives. Three other novels take place either in Kerr's old hometown of Auburn, rechristened "Cayuta," or in La Belle, another one-factory town in upstate New York. If the setting is Seaville, Sweet Mouth is the place to go for a coke, The Surf Club is the place to dance, snobs belong to The Hadgfield Club (a.k.a. The Hatefilled Club), and The Witherspoon Funeral Home is the last stop before burial for half the citizenry. A major character in one Seaville novel may reappear as a bit player in another. The three upstate New York novels are less identically referential but the institutions mentioned in their respective pages—a prison, an orphanage, and a high-priced recovery haven for alcoholics—evoke the same claustrophobia.

Despite Kerr's frequent returns to familiar settings, only *Fell,* her more recent Seaville novel, was conceived as one novel in a series of novels. The other Seaville books and the novels set in upstate New York do lend themselves to being read differently, however, than they might be if they did not overlap in some of their particulars. One clue to the reading they invite is suggested by the profession of a main character in *I'll Love You When You're More Like Me,* the second Seaville novel. Young Sabra St. Amour stars in a daytime soap opera named *Hometown,* and has a large and loyal following of teenage fans, as does Kerr. Each of her hometown locales provides a familiar and therefore inviting setting for her readers and allows her, like Fedora Foxe, the producer of *Hometown,* to introduce new plotlines and characters to retain fans' interest.

But just as the plotlines of soap operas are not really new, "new" being the equivalent of "topical and updated," so too are Kerr's plots timely, and in some cases, eccentric refurbishings of standard soap opera fare. Romance shares top billing with domestic/familial ruptures, and there are plenty of dark family secrets and life-threatening or even fatal illnesses and accidents. Kerr's characters are often familiar types as well, sometimes regrettably familiar in their perpetuation of negative images of young women. More important, however, are the many superbly realized characters who populate her books.

Some of the most interesting of these make their appearances outside of Kerr's standard hometown locales and plots. Dinky Hocker, of *Dinky Hocker Shoots Smack,* lives in Brooklyn Heights with her sensitive cousin Natalia, lawyer father and do-gooder mother, Helen Hocker. Grossly overweight, Dinky drugs herself with food, not heroin; the book takes its title from the graffiti Dinky paints as a public act of revenge to embarrass her mother the night of a community awards banquet honoring Mrs. Hocker's volunteer work with recovering drug addicts. At home, Mrs. Hocker has mistaken manipulation for loving concern. Supposedly for Dinky's own good, Helen has cut her off from her politically conservative fellow weight watcher P. John, the one friend who supports Dinky's dieting but whom Mrs. Hocker views as being little better than a fat fascist. Although P. John plays second lead to Tucker Woolf, whose romance with Dinky's cousin Natalia occupies much of the book, P. John is a real scene stealer when he reappears near the end of the novel as a slimmed-down liberal who has shed prejudices along with pounds.

Even more arresting are the characters who come to life in *Is That You, Miss Blue?*. Flanders Brown, uprooted by the break-up of her parents' marriage, has been sent to an Episcopalian boarding school in Virginia. On her own for the first time, she discovers who she is as she makes friends with several of the school's nonconformists and observes the self-serving exclusivity of many of her fellow students. The paradox of their exclusivity is their conformity to peer pressure and the standards set by class leaders such as sophisticated France Shipp. France helps engineer the dismissal of Miss Blue, an inspired science teacher whose equally inspired religious experiences strike the headmistress of this ostensibly religious school as incipient insanity. Flanders's attitude towards Miss Blue mirrors her own growing maturity as she moves from mocking Miss Blue to respect and empathy for her former teacher.

Kerr also takes up the subject of religious belief vs. religious hypocrisy in two later novels. *Little Little,* set in upstate New York, is narrated alternately by Little Little La Belle and Sydney Cinnamon, two young people whose friendship might become a romance once Little Little's fiancé runs off with another woman. Knox Lionel, Little Little's sometime fiancé, is better known as Little Lion, a popular evangelical preacher whose religion is pure show biz. All four characters (including the "other" woman) are dwarves, a fact which only heightens the novel's carnival atmosphere because here Kerr is too much the smart-mouth kid. The jokes and frenetic pace of the novel inadvertently work to deny Sydney and Little Little their humanity. Kerr is much more successful in persuading readers to see past labels and stereotypes in *What I Really Think of You.* This novel's two narrators, Opal Ringer and Jesse Pegler, learn to come to terms with their own spirituality and the social, economic, and religious complexities of being preacher's kids.

Preacher's kids are not the only Kerr adolescents whose fathers (or, as in the case of *Gentlehands,* grandfather) provoke identity crises. In *The Son of Someone Famous,* Adam Blessing finds himself more cursed than blessed by having a politically powerful father who is celebrated for his shuttle diplomacy. *Him She Loves?* features a professional comedian who revives his career by ridiculing his daughter's boyfriend on national television, while *If I Love You, Am I Trapped Forever?* portrays an absentee and alcoholic father who is still too much of a child himself to be a parent to his son. *Love Is a Missing Person* depicts a dad who favors one child over the other, with negative consequences for all involved. None of these dads is much of a role model, but that is just as well since the one father figure who invites emulation is the most problematic of all; he's the infamous "Gentlehands" of Auschwitz. Given these troubled family histories, it is no wonder that the protagonists of most of the novels run into problems in the romance department as well. Breaking up, rather than living happily ever after, is the order of the day.

Kerr's habitually ironic stance towards the possibilities of romance is modulated by brief moments of lyricism in two of her most recent fictions. Like many of her novels, *Night Kites* follows the romantic fortunes of its young male protagonist, but Erick Rudd's loving and losing Nicki Marr is less important than the fact that he loves and will soon lose his older brother. Pete has AIDS and has come home to spend his last months with his family. Kerr's presentation of Pete's story is multilayered, empathetic, and embedded within his family's reactions. Kerr provides no easy answers or consolations because there aren't any answers beyond a few all-important grace notes of understanding and love.

I Stay Near You, a story in three parts, also subscribes to the importance of moments of understanding and love, but this three-generation saga devotes the greater part of each of its interlocked narratives to detailing the unhappy consequences of the passionate emotions precipitated by a romantic misalliance in the summer of 1943. By the time the story reaches the present, love has become a ghost from summers past. Nevertheless, that's still a notch or two more romantic than the events which befall the eponymous hero of *Fell,* who discovers that his lover romanced him as part of a scheme to benefit the man she really loves. Not to worry, though. John Fell is resilient—and he'll be back in a sequel with another entertaining and witty Kerr story in tow.

—Janice Alberghene

KIMENYE, Barbara. Ugandan. Born in East Africa. Private secretary to the government of the Kabaka of Buganda; staff member, *Uganda Nation,* Kampala. Since 1974 social worker in London. Address: c/o Nelson, Nelson House, Mayfield Road, Walton-on-Thames, Surrey KT12 5PL, England.

PUBLICATIONS FOR CHILDREN

Fiction

The Smugglers, illustrated by Roger Payne. London, Nelson, 1966.
Moses, illustrated by Rena Fennessy. Nairobi, Oxford University Press, 1967.
Moses and Mildred, illustrated by Rena Fennessy. Nairobi, Oxford University Press, 1967.
Moses and the Kidnappers, illustrated by Rena Fennessy. Nairobi, Oxford University Press, 1968.
Moses in Trouble, illustrated by Rena Fennessy. Nairobi, Oxford University Press, 1968.
The Winged Adventure, illustrated by Terry Hirst. Nairobi, Oxford University Press, 1969.
Moses in a Muddle, illustrated by Rena Fennessy. Nairobi, Oxford University Press, 1970.
Moses and the Ghost, illustrated by Rena Fennessy. Nairobi, Oxford University Press, 1971.
Paulo's Strange Adventure, illustrated by Olga J. Heuser. Nairobi, Oxford University Press, 1971.
Moses on the Move, illustrated by Mara Onditi. Nairobi, Oxford University Press, 1972.
Sarah and the Boy. Nairobi, Oxford University Press, 1973.
Martha the Millipede, illustrated by Mara Onditi. Nairobi, Oxford University Press, 1973.
Moses and the Penpal, illustrated by Mara Onditi. Nairobi, Oxford University Press, 1973.
Moses the Camper, illustrated by Mara Onditi. Nairobi, Oxford University Press, 1973.
The Runaways, illustrated by Mara Onditi. Nairobi, Oxford University Press, 1973.

PUBLICATIONS FOR ADULTS

Novels

The Gemstone Affair. London, Nelson, 1978.
The Scoop. London, Nelson, 1978.

Short Stories

Kalasanda. Nairobi and London, Oxford University Press, 1965.
Kalasanda Revisited. Nairobi and London, Oxford University Press, 1966.

*   *   *

Barbara Kimenye has written a fantasy *Martha the Millipede* in which a discontented millipede learns the hard way that millipedes do not wear shoes. However, most of her books are boys' and girls' adventure books, the most successful being the delightful Moses series in which she has done for African children what Richmal Crompton did for English children through her famous William books. Like William, Moses is an engaging schoolboy whose well-intentioned actions regularly land him and his gang in trouble with the authorities. But, unlike William, Moses's activities are confined to his boarding school, which bears the pretentious name Mukibi's Educational Institute for the Sons of African Gentlemen, but which is really a shabby, money-making institution for throw-outs from reputable schools.

Kimenye makes a distinction between high-spirited boys like Moses and bad boys such as the bully Magara, and Wakweya, the crook masquerading as a schoolboy. In between is "Itchy Fingers" who "when approached nicely" would always return an article to the owner although he might "absent-mindedly pick it up later in the day." With her humorous style Kimenye manages to keep everything in proportion. The boys' escapades are narrated with indulgent amusement, most of them being simply unfortunate, not wicked. One such escapade is the collapse of the dormitory thatched roof over the heads of the Headmaster and his deputy while Moses is trying to retrieve his pet snake from the roof. On another occasion, the cooks go on strike and stingy Mukibi puts the boys on kitchen duty. Their efforts to provide the school with decent meals in spite of the almost empty store lands Moses in a prickly pineapple patch, and he also gets tossed by a cow during an illegal milking session at night. For his pains he is punished by the authorities.

The adventures of Moses and his friends are most exciting and sound so probable that the reader is drawn into the stories. This is why the books have been so successful. Kimenye's other adventure books are not as successful, especially those about girls, such as *Sarah and the Boy* and *The Winged Adventure. Paulo's Strange Adventure* is full of improbable action while *The Runaways* makes copious use of slang. *The Smugglers* reads like the script of a stereotypical Western film or television thriller. Kimenye is at her best when she writes stories with an authentic African background about real people whose trials and tribulations she portrays with human understanding.

—Mabel D. Segun

KING, (David) Clive. British. Born in Richmond, Surrey, 24 April 1924. Educated at King's School, Rochester, Kent, 1933–41; Downing College, Cambridge, 1941–43, 1946–48, B.A. in English 1948; School of Oriental and African Studies, University of London,

1966–67. Served in the Royal Naval Volunteer Reserve, 1943–46: Sub-Lieutenant. Married 1) Jane Tuke in 1949 (divorced 1974); 2) Penelope Timmins in 1974; one daughter and one son. Administrative officer, Amsterdam, 1948–50, student welfare officer, Belfast, 1950–51, Lecturer, Aleppo, Syria, 1951–54, Visiting Professor, Damascus, 1954–55, Lecturer and Director of Studies, Beirut, 1960–66, and education officer, Madras, 1971–73, all for the British Council; warden, East Sussex County Council, Rye, 1955–60; education adviser, East Pakistan Education Centre, Dacca 1967–71. Agent: Murray Pollinger, 4 Garrick Street, London WC2B 9BH, England.

PUBLICATIONS FOR CHILDREN

Fiction

Hamid of Aleppo, illustrated by Giovanetti. New York, Macmillan, 1958.

The Town That Went South, illustrated by Maurice Bartlett. New York, Macmillan, 1959; London, Penguin, 1961.

Stig of the Dump, illustrated by Edward Ardizzone. London, Penguin, 1963.

The Twenty Two Letters, illustrated by Richard Kennedy. London, Hamish Hamilton, 1966; New York, Coward McCann, 1967.

The Night the Water Came, illustrated by Mark Peppé. London, Longman, 1973; New York, Crowell, 1982.

Snakes and Snakes, illustrated by Richard Kennedy. London, Kestrel, 1975.

Me and My Million. London, Kestrel, 1976; London, Crowell, 1979.

The Devil's Cut, illustrated by Val Biro. London, Hodder and Stoughton, 1978.

Ninny's Boat, illustrated by Ian Newsham. London, Kestrel, 1980; New York, Macmillan, 1981.

The Sound of Propellers, illustrated by David Parkins. London, Viking Kestrel, 1986.

The Seashore People. London, Viking Kestrel, 1987.

Plays

Poles Apart (produced London, 1975).
The World of Light (produced London, 1976).
Get the Message (produced London, 1987).

Television Play: *Good Snakes, Bad Snakes,* 1977.

Other (readers; illustrated by Jacqueline Atkinson)

High Jacks, Low Jacks. London, Benn, 1976.
First Day Out. London, Benn, 1976.
Accident. London, Benn, 1976.
The Secret. London, Benn, 1976.
The Birds from Africa, illustrated by Diana Groves. London, Macdonald, and Morristown, New Jersey, Silver Burdett, 1980.

*

Clive King comments:

Each of the things which I have written has been inspired by a particular place which I have visited or lived in. The settings are always as authentic as possible, and they determine the action. Some of my stories have required a great deal of research, but I try not to let it show. I am interested in putting abstract facts into the simplest and clearest language. I write best when I have a specific reader or group of readers in mind, and now that I am a full-time writer I try

to keep in touch with children, preferably in informal circumstances.

*   *   *

The settings of Clive King's stories reflect his varied and nomadic career. *Stig of the Dump* belongs to his childhood in the Manor House at Ash in the Kentish Downland; *The Town That Went South* is a by-product of his spell of educational duty in Rye; his Middle East service produced *The Twenty Two Letters*; *Snakes and Snakes* came out of his stay in India; and so on. The books illustrate his restlessness, his search for new ideas. The same restlessness perhaps accounts for a lack of high finish in his work, as if he never had time to pursue his initial idea to its logical end.

Few writers have been so prolific in ideas. Standing on a high point in Rye, especially when mist hides the grassy levels below, one might well imagine oneself on board ship. So in *The Town That Went South* King imagines the ancient town breaking free from the land and drifting ever southwards. A most promising concept. The performance too is good in this early book. All the human characters are caricatures, whether they are citizens or people encountered on the long voyage to Antarctica, and they have absurd names—Captain Voicepipe, for example—to match. The story is held together and given a unifying purpose by the central figure of Gargoyle, a "surly, lazy cat" who alone stays with the floating town to its last chilly landfall.

The Town That Went South is, I think, a more consistent book than *Stig of the Dump,* although the latter has enjoyed wider popular acclaim. Here, too, the initial concept is brilliant. Take an old chalk pit into which the locals have been throwing their rubbish for years. The litter of 20th-century civilization could be the stuff of life for a man of the Stone Age. Stig, who lives in the pit, is most inventive and resourceful in making use of old tins, rubber tubes, and other discarded objects. The companionship between Stig and Barney, a modern boy who at eight is about the Stone Age stage of development, is handled beautifully. But once the original and potentially fruitful situation has been established the author seems to lose interest, and some of the subsequent episodes are manufactured and unconvincing.

So too with later books like *The Twenty Two Letters,* a story about the invention of the alphabet, a marvellous subject which turns heavy in the telling, and *The Night the Water Came,* in which a promising beginning, describing a tropical island struck by a cyclone, is not sustained. In *Me and My Million* King ventured into the field of comedy, or more properly knockabout farce, an area in which he was clearly not at ease.

Perhaps surprisingly, King is a writer who responds well to the discipline of the "easy reader." His early essays showed invention and confidence in working within the strict limitations of the genre. Much his best book of this kind is *The Devil's Cut* in which he shows, at the level of a small boy, the coming of the Canal Age. Here is an easy reading book which is also a chapter in social and industrial history.

King's restless search for new themes for his stories has been as much a source of weakness as of strength. He seems to dissipate his creative energy. Either of two of his later books might have been better if he had directed all his forces to it. *The Sound of Propellers* is his most probing study in character. The central figure is a Tamil Indian struggling to cope with life in an English public school. He is a subtle person rather wasted on an absurd story of espionage which belongs more to the "Reward" tradition of the 1920's than to a more sophisticated age. This was followed by *The Seashore People,* an extraordinary and in essence brilliant study of the origins of human life. Based on the premise that "all things come from the sea," the story explores the relationships between man and the rest of the animal kingdom in the remote past. It is a strange, quasi-poetic book in which moments of great beauty are eclipsed by much pedestrian writing.

Ninny's Boat is King's most ambitious novel, in scale and in breadth of concept. It is a historical novel of the Dark Ages. Ninny has been enslaved by a tribe of Angles. The land-hungry pagans are planning to sail west to find a new home, and Ninny, by superior intelligence and using the friendship of Offa, the young leader of the expedition, gets a place in the boat. He faces storm and the perils of a great sea-snake, sees action in Britain, and plays an involuntary part in King Arthur's last battle. When the story closes he is working alongside the heroic Offa, learning to live with Britons and half-Romans in the enterprise of creating a new land: "There's room for us all if we don't rock the boat." *Ninny's Boat* is a big story about great events and with big ideas behind it, but it is presented in human terms with life-sized people, and for all the seriousness of the central theme there is much humour springing from the personalities of Ninny and his sharp-tongued girlfriend Elfrida. This is King's best-made novel and, if it lacks the originality of *Stig*, his most consistent and convincing achievement.

—Marcus Crouch

KING-SMITH, Dick. British. Born in Bitton, Gloucestershire, 27 March 1922. Educated at Marlborough College, Wiltshire, 1936–40; University of Bristol, B.Ed. 1975. Served in the Grenadier Guards, 1941–46: Lieutenant; mentioned in despatches. Married Myrle England in 1943; two daughters and one son. Farmer in Gloucestershire, 1947–67; teacher, Farmborough Primary School, Bath, 1975–82. Since 1982 freelance writer. Recipient: *Guardian* award, 1984. Agent: A.P. Watt Ltd., 20 John Street, London WC1N 2DR. Address: Diamond's Cottage, Queen Charlton, near Keynsham, Avon BS18 2SJ, England.

PUBLICATIONS FOR CHILDREN

Fiction

The Fox Busters, illustrated by Jon Miller. London, Gollancz, 1978; New York, Delacorte Press, 1988.
Daggie Dogfoot, illustrated by Mary Rayner. London, Gollancz, 1980; as *Pigs Might Fly,* New York, Viking Press, 1982.
The Mouse Butcher, illustrated by Wendy Smith. London, Gollancz, 1981; New York, Viking Press, 1982.
Magnus Powermouse, illustrated by Mary Rayner. London, Gollancz, 1982; New York, Harper, 1984.
The Queen's Nose, illustrated by Jill Bennett. London, Gollancz, 1983; New York, Harper, 1985.
The Sheep-Pig, illustrated by Mary Rayner. London, Gollancz, 1983; as *Babe, The Gallant Pig,* New York, Crown, 1985.
Harry's Mad, illustrated by Jill Bennett. London, Gollancz, 1984; New York, Crown, 1987.
Lightning Fred, illustrated by Michael Bragg. London, Heinemann, 1985.
Saddlebottom, illustrated by Alice Englander. London, Gollancz, 1985.
H. Prince, illustrated by Martin Honeysett. London, Walker, 1986.
E.S.P., illustrated by Peter Wingham. London, Deutsch, 1986.
Farmer Bungle Forgets, illustrated by Martin Honeysett. London, Walker, 1986; New York, Atheneum, 1987.
Noah's Brother, illustrated by Ian Newsham. London, Gollancz, 1986.

Dumpling, illustrated by Jo Davies. London, Hamish Hamilton, 1986.
Yob, illustrated by Abigail Pizer. London, Heinemann, 1986.
Tumbleweed, illustrated by Ian Newsham. London, Gollancz, 1987.
The Hodgeheg, illustrated by Linda Birch. London, Hamish Hamilton, 1987.
Cuckoobush Farm, illustrated by Kazuko. London, Orchard, 1987; New York, Greenwillow, 1988.
Friends and Brothers, illustrated by Susan Hellard. London, Heinemann, 1987.
Martin's Mice, illustrated by Jez Alborough. London, Gollancz, 1988; New York, Crown, 1989.
George Speaks, illustrated by Judy Brown. London, Viking Kestrel, 1988.
The Jenius, illustrated by Peter Firmin. London, Gollancz, 1988.
Emily's Legs, illustrated by Katinka Kew. London, Macdonald, 1988.
Dodo Comes to Tumbledown Farm, illustrated by John Sharp. London, Heinemann, 1988.
The Toby Man, illustrated by Ian Newsham. London, Gollancz, 1989.
Alice and Flower and Foxianna. London, Heinemann, 1989.
Beware of the Bull! London, Heinemann, 1989.
Henry Pond Poet. London, Hodder and Stoughton, 1989.
Dodos Are Forever, illustrated by David Parkins. London, Viking Kestrel, 1989.

Other

Pets for Keeps, illustrated by Alan Saunders. London, Penguin, 1986.
Town Watch, illustrated by Catherine Bradbury. London, Penguin, 1987.
Country Watch: Animals to Look out for in the Countryside, illustrated by Catherine Bradbury. London, Penguin, 1987.
Water Watch, illustrated by Catherine Bradbury. London, Penguin, 1988.

*

Dick King-Smith comments:
I came late to writing, after a good long time farming. Later I taught young children (and have 10 grandchildren of my own), and it is their potential enjoyment of a story that makes writing one, for me, so enjoyable.

*   *   *

There are some adults known to dislike Dick King-Smith's jovial, almost hearty anthropomorphism, but most of us, and certainly children between about eight and 12 were beguiled from the start by his engagingly stylish view of animal family life. His most important quality, however, is an ability to tell a jolly good adventure story, to stack danger and adversity and terrible odds against an unlikely hero. Add humour and affection and the result is bound to be attractive.

Such a combination demands a tricky balance that he had not yet perfected in his first novel, *The Fox Busters.* The joke, not the plot or the characters, dominates the book, and the humour borders on the facetious, as well as being over-allusive for readers too young to catch all the underlying references and much of the verbal highjinks. But *Daggie Dogfoot* and *The Mouse Butcher* are both very satisfying: a single hero, whom we grow to love, fights desperately against a terrifying enemy in a genuinely exciting plot, while the style, dialogue, and characterisation remain light and playful. It's very skilful storytelling. Daggie is a piglet whose deformed feet, instead of leading him to the slaughterhouse, enable him to become a mighty swimmer and saviour of the farm, and to do a neat conversion job on a pigman whose only idea of a good pig is a cooked one. *The Mouse Butcher* is more self-consciously humanised—the community of cats mirrors, a little laboriously, the snobberies and prejudices of human society—but the tale of how the rough-and-ready Butcher wins the heart of the lovely Persian in the manor and defeats the outcast villain can scarcely fail. And by King-Smith's own best standards, *Magnus Powermouse*, although amusing and with moments of thrilling danger, lacks the framework of a solid, well-executed plot and compelling narrative power.

With *The Sheep-Pig* he succeeds in balancing in one story the strongest qualities of all the others, and it must be safe now to award it that (often overworked) encomium, "a modern classic." A piglet, won at a local fair by a sheep farmer, realises that the only sensible way to handle sheep is to speak politely to them, and not only saves the farmer's flock (and his own bacon) from rustlers but goes on to astound the whole world by winning the Sheep-Dog Trials on television. It is deftly constructed, the animal and human characters are marvellously defined in dialogue, the suspense remains strong and quite unbullied by the joke, and the style is so clean and economic that our hero wins through to a frenzy of cheers without a hint of soppiness. King-Smith's affection for the animal qualities of his characters, springing from the genuine knowledge of an ex-farmer, brings a needed warmth to the jokes and excitement—a warmth typified in the mother-baby relationship that recurs throughout his work and is both loving and funny.

A late starter and prodigiously productive, he has also proved impressively consistent, adding to his regular animal novels a range of stories for beginner readers (*The Hodgeheg* is particularly charming, with a nicely judged black edge to its humour) and picture-book texts, and branching out into novels with human protagonists. *Noah's Brother*, an alternative story of the Ark, has a dark, almost bitter side to the joke, and a moralistic tone that is atypically heavy, and *Tumbleweed*, a gentle medieval parody about a nervous knight, is a pleasant but unremarkable fantasy that turned out to appeal strongly to small boys. Much more successful are *The Queen's Nose*, in which Harmony learns the best way to handle the wishes bestowed on her by a magic 50p piece, and *Harry's Mad*, which allows Harry to share the limelight with Madison, a super-intelligent parrot, in a satisfying slapstick thriller. But popular reads though these are, cunningly plotted and romping fun, they lack that special sparkle and élan of the animal stories, which must surely come from deep within King-Smith's own feelings, and it is with them that his reputation remains, carving a benchmark against which other animal novels are now judged.

—Stephanie Nettell

KINGMAN, (Mary) Lee. American. Born in Reading, Massachusetts, 6 October 1919. Educated at Colby-Sawyer College, New London, New Hampshire, A.A. 1938; Smith College, Northampton, Massachusetts, B.A. 1940. Married Robert H. Natti in 1945; one daughter and one son. Worked for Boston Manufacturers Mutual Fire Insurance Company, 1940–42; assistant, 1943–44, and juvenile editor, 1944–46, Houghton Mifflin, publishers, Boston; member, Folly Cove Designers, Gloucester, Massachusetts, 1946–71. Book editor, poster and calendar designer, council member, 1964–70, and since 1970, director, *Horn Book,* Boston. Address: Lanesville Station, Box 7126, Gloucester, Massachusetts 01930, U.S.A.

PUBLICATIONS FOR CHILDREN

Fiction

Pierre Pidgeon, illustrated by Arnold E. Bare. Boston, Houghton Mifflin, 1943.
Ilenka, illustrated by Arnold E. Bare. Boston, Houghton Mifflin, 1945.
The Rocky Summer, illustrated by Barbara Cooney. Boston, Houghton Mifflin, 1948.
The Best Christmas, illustrated by Barbara Cooney. New York, Doubleday, 1949; London, Constable, 1958.
Philippe's Hill, illustrated by Hildegard Woodward. New York, Doubleday, 1950.
The Quarry Adventure, illustrated by Barbara Cooney. New York, Doubleday, 1951; as *Lauri's Surprising Summer*, London, Constable, 1957.
Kathy and the Mysterious Statue, illustrated by Jean MacDonald Porter. New York, Doubleday, 1953.
Peter's Long Walk, illustrated by Barbara Cooney. New York, Doubleday, 1953.
Mikko's Fortune, illustrated by Arnold E. Bare. New York, Farrar Straus, 1955.
The Magic Christmas Tree, illustrated by Bettina. New York, Farrar Straus, 1956; London, Oxford University Press, 1957.
The Village Band Mystery, illustrated by Erik Blegvad. New York, Doubleday, 1956.
Flivver, The Heroic Horse, illustrated by Erik Blegvad. New York, Doubleday, 1958.
Ginny's First Secret, illustrated by Hazel Hoecker. Newton, Massachusetts, Phillips, 1958.
House of the Blue Horse. New York, Doubleday, 1960.
The Saturday Gang, illustrated by Burt Silverman. New York, Doubleday, 1961.
Peter's Pony, illustrated by Fen Lasell. New York, Doubleday, 1963.
Sheep Ahoy!, illustrated by Lisl Weil. Boston, Houghton Mifflin, 1963.
Private Eyes: Adventures with the Saturday Gang, illustrated by Burt Silverman. New York, Doubleday, 1964.
The Year of the Raccoon. Boston, Houghton Mifflin, 1966.
The Secret Journey of the Silver Reindeer, illustrated by Lynd Ward. New York, Doubleday, 1968; Kingswood, Surrey, World's Work, 1970.
The Peter Pan Bag. Boston, Houghton Mifflin, 1970.
Georgina and the Dragon, illustrated by Leonard Shortall. Boston, Houghton Mifflin, 1972.
The Meeting Post: A Story of Lapland, illustrated by Des Asmussen. New York, Crowell, 1972; London, MacRae, 1985.
Escape from the Evil Prophecy, illustrated by Richard Cuffari. Boston, Houghton Mifflin, 1973.
Break a Leg, Betsy Maybe! Boston, Houghton Mifflin, 1976.
Head over Wheels. Boston, Houghton Mifflin, 1978; London, Hamish Hamilton, 1979.
The Refiner's Fire. Boston, Houghton Mifflin, 1981.
The Luck of the "Miss L." Boston, Houghton Mifflin, 1986.

PUBLICATIONS FOR ADULTS

Other

Editor, *Newbery and Caldecott Medal Books 1956–1965.* Boston, Horn Book, 1965.
Editor, *Newbery and Caldecott Medal Award Winners and Honor Books 1922–1968.* Boston, Horn Book, 1968.

Editor, with Joanna Foster and Ruth Giles Lontoft, *Illustrators of Children's Books 1957–1966.* Boston, Horn Book, 1968.

Editor, *Newbery and Caldecott Medal Books 1966–1975.* Boston, Horn Book, 1975.

Editor, *A Horn Book Calendar.* Boston, Horn Book, 1977.

Editor, *The Illustrator's Notebook.* Boston, Horn Book, 1978.

Editor, with Grace Hogarth and Harriet Quimby, *Illustrators of Children's Books 1967–1976* Boston, Horn Book, 1978.

Editor, *Newbery and Caldecott Medal Books 1976–1985.* Boston, Horn Book, 1986.

*

Manuscript Collections: Kerlan Collection, University of Minnesota, Minneapolis; de Grummond Collection, University of Southern Mississippi, Hattiesburg.

Lee Kingman comments:

In looking back over 43 years of writing for children and young adults, and over 28 published books, I find them for the most part to have been inspired by the ages and interests of my two children and their friends as they grew up. The subjects range from kindergarten concerns (*Peter's Long Walk*) to young adult relationships (*The Peter Pan Bag*) and family relationships (*The Refiner's Fire*); the styles range from legend-like (*The Secret Journey of the Silver Reindeer*) through humorous (*Georgina and the Dragon*) to realistic (*The Year of the Raccoon* and, more recently, *Head over Wheels*, which I wrote after my son became a quadriplegic in a car accident and I found there was a dearth of fiction dealing with how traumas affect not only the victim but family and friends). Some are mysteries; some have Icelandic, Lapp, and Finnish-American backgrounds, inspired by my husband's Finnish heritage. I have always wanted to explore new subjects, learn new things, and have tried, in writing about them, to be sensitive to the style best suited to the kind and length of the material, the potential age ranges of readers, and the subjects themselves.

My daughter, Susanna Natti, has become a recognized illustrator of children's books and Viking Penguin will publish our first collaboration of story and pictures, *Catch the Baby!*, in 1990.

*   *   *

Lee Kingman has claimed an uncharted territory, Lapland, for her own in children's literature. *The Meeting Post* replaces the northern aura of mystery with an informed and friendly familiarity. Readers of *The Secret Journey of the Silver Reindeer* may well be intrigued to further study of this distant land, traditional home of nomads now imprisoned by the arbitrary boundaries of a nationalism foreign to them. Distant in time as well as in locale, *Escape from the Evil Prophecy* is an adventure of the 11th century, an era of unrest in Iceland. Christianity struggles with paganism, and democratic ideals with anarchy and blood-feud. Her hero and heroine personify the generosity of youth, and the difficulties of commitment to social change in the face of established custom.

Closer to home, *The Peter Pan Bag* owes its success with adolescents to Kingman's empathy with their painful *rites de passage* in a culture that makes a difficult time still more difficult by leaving its boundaries undefined. Runaway Wendy, 17 years old, longs for freedom. A Boston hippie-haven proves intoxicatingly attractive, but offers no solution to her identity problem. Though some of the actualities of life in a hippie pad have been glossed over, Kingman understands youngsters insistent upon recognition of their status as adults while they live, like Peter Pan, in Never-Never Land. *Georgina and the Dragon* stars 10-year-old Georgie, whose name evidences disappointment at the birth of a fifth daughter to a sonless father. In this slight, cheerful, mildly feminist story, dauntless Georgie

demonstrates just what girls can do. In the critically acclaimed *The Year of the Raccoon* Joey, an ordinary, normal 15-year-old, is sandwiched between two brilliant brothers, under the shadow of a successful, unconsciously domineering father, who expects great things of all his family. Joey's love for Bertie, his only-partly-tame raccoon, precipitates crisis in a family that has maintained a precarious balance on the edge of catastrophe. *Head over Wheels* might have been a tragedy in other hands. Terry and Kerry are identical twins. No one can tell them apart—until Terry is crippled in a car accident. Now a quadriplegic, he must chart a new course for a life to be spent in a wheelchair, with the support of his family and especially of his twin. This is a most perceptive, often painfully moving story. Sara hardly knows her father, but suddenly must go to live with him—in a barn, no less! Understanding grows between them, as she learns to appreciate his talent and warmth, while discounting his excesses of temperament, in *The Refiner's Fire*.

Alec wins a loathed Cabbage Patch doll in a raffle, instead of the rowboat he longs for, and he feels that his luck is all of one kind: BAD. Then fate takes a hand, when an elderly neighbour who has rescued the prize rowboat from an ignominious fate as a petunia planter decides to let Alec do her rowing for her, and even to enter the coveted craft in the year-end races, in *The Luck of the "Miss L,"* a slight but pleasant summer entertainment.

Though Kingman's picture books and plays for juniors do not rank with her work for more mature readers, and her writings are sometimes slight and uneven, her peaks are very, very high.

—Joan McGrath

_____

KINSEY, Elizabeth.   See CLYMER, Eleanor.

_____

KIPLING, (Joseph) Rudyard.   British.   Born in Bombay, India, 30 December 1865, of English parents; moved to England, 1872. Educated at the United Services College, Westward Ho!, Devon, 1878–82. Married Caroline Starr Balestier in 1892; two daughters and one son. Assistant editor, *Civil and Military Gazette*, Lahore, 1882–87; assistant editor and overseas correspondent, *Pioneer*, Allahabad, 1887–89; full-time writer from 1889; lived in London, 1889–92, and Brattleboro, Vermont, 1892–96, then returned to England; settled in Burwash, Sussex, 1902. Rector, University of St. Andrews, 1922–25. Recipient: Nobel Prize for Literature, 1907; Royal Society of Literature Gold Medal, 1926. LL.D.: McGill University, Montreal, 1907; D. Litt.: University of Durham, 1907; Oxford University, 1907; Cambridge University, 1907; University of Edinburgh, 1920; the Sorbonne, Paris, 1921; University of Strasbourg, 1921; D. Phil.: University of Athens, 1924. Honorary Fellow, Magdalene College, Cambridge, 1932. Associate member, Académie des Sciences Morales et Politiques, 1933. Refused the Poet Laureateship, 1895, and the Order of Merit. *Died 18 January 1936.*

PUBLICATIONS FOR CHILDREN

Fiction

The Jungle Book, illustrated by J. Lockwood Kipling and others. London, Macmillan, and New York, Century, 1894.

The Second Jungle Book, illustrated by J. Lockwood Kipling. London, Macmillan, and New York, Century, 1895; revised edition, Macmillan, 1895.

"Captains Courageous" : A Story of the Grand Banks, illustrated by I.W. Taber. London, Macmillan, and New York, Century, 1897.

Stalky & Co. London, Macmillan, and New York, Doubleday, 1899; revised edition, as *The Complete Stalky & Co.,* Macmillan, 1929, Doubleday, 1930.

Kim, illustrated by J. Lockwood Kipling. New York, Doubleday, and London, Macmillan, 1901.

Just So Stories for Little Children, illustrated by the author. London, Macmillan, and New York, Doubleday, 1902.

Puck of Pook's Hill, illustrated by H.R. Millar. London, Macmillan, and New York, Doubleday, 1906.

Kipling Stories and Poems Every Child Should Know, edited by Mary E. Burt and W.T. Chapin, illustrated by Charles Livingston Bull and others. New York, Doubleday, 1909.

Rewards and Fairies, illustrated by Frank Craig. London, Macmillan, and New York, Doubleday, 1910.

Land and Sea Tales for Scouts and Guides. London, Macmillan, and New York, Doubleday, 1923.

Ham and the Porcupine. New York, Doubleday, 1935.

PUBLICATIONS FOR ADULTS

Novel

The Light That Failed. New York, United States Book Company, 1890; London, Macmillan, 1891.

Short Stories

Plain Tales from the Hills. Calcutta, Thacker Spink, 1888; New York, Lovell, and London, Macmillan, 1890.

Soldiers Three: A Collection of Stories. Allahabad, Wheeler, 1888; London, Sampson Low, 1890.

The Story of the Gadsbys: A Tale Without a Plot. Allahabad, Wheeler, 1888; London, Sampson Low, and New York, Lovell, 1890.

In Black and White. Allahabad, Wheeler, 1888; London, Sampson Low, 1890; with *Soldiers Three,* New York, Lovell, 1890.

Under the Deodars. Allahabad, Wheeler, 1888; revised edition, London, Sampson Low, 1890.

The Phantom 'Rickshaw and Other Tales. Allahabad, Wheeler, 1888; revised edition, London, Sampson Low, 1890.

Wee Willie Winkie and Other Child Stories. Allahabad, Wheeler, 1888; revised edition, London, Sampson Low, and Chicago, Rand McNally, 1890.

Soldiers Three, and Under the Deodars. New York, Lovell, 1890.

The Phantom 'Rickshaw, and Wee Willie Winkie. New York, Lovell, 1890.

The Courting of Dinah Shadd and Other Stories. New York, Harper, and London, Macmillan, 1890.

Indian Tales. New York, United States Book Company, 1890.

Mine Own People. New York, United States Book Company, 1891.

Life's Handicap, Being Stories from Mine Own People. New York and London, Macmillan, 1891.

The Naulahka: A Story of West and East, with Wolcott Balestier. London, Heinemann, and New York, Macmillan, 1892.

Many Inventions. London, Macmillan, and New York, Appleton, 1893.

Soldier Tales. London, Macmillan, 1896; as *Soldier Stories,* New York, Macmillan, 1896.

The Day's Work. New York, Doubleday, and London, Macmillan, 1898.

The Kipling Reader. London, Macmillan, 1900; revised edition, 1901; as *Selected Stories,* 1925.

Traffics and Discoveries. London, Macmillan, and New York, Doubleday, 1904.

Abaft the Funnel. New York, Dodge, 1909.

Actions and Reactions. London, Macmillan, and New York, Doubleday, 1909.

A Diversity of Creatures. London, Macmillan, and New York, Doubleday, 1917.

Selected Stories, edited by William Lyon Phelps. New York, Doubleday, 1921.

Land and Sea Tales. London, Macmillan, and New York, Doubleday, 1923.

Debits and Credits. London, Macmillan, and New York, Doubleday, 1926.

Selected Stories. London, Macmillan, 1929.

Thy Servant a Dog, Told by Boots. London, Macmillan, and New York, Doubleday, 1930; revised edition, as *Thy Servant a Dog and Other Dog Stories,* Macmillan, 1938.

Humorous Tales. London, Macmillan, and New York, Doubleday, 1931.

Animal Stories. London, Macmillan, 1932; New York, Doubleday, 1938.

Limits and Renewals. London, Macmillan, and New York, Doubleday, 1932.

All the Mowgli Stories. London, Macmillan, 1933; New York, Doubleday, 1936.

Collected Dog Stories. London, Macmillan, and New York, Doubleday, 1934.

More Selected Stories. London, Macmillan, 1940.

Twenty-One Tales. London, Reprint Society, 1946.

Ten Stories. London, Pan, 1947.

A Choice of Kipling's Prose, edited by W. Somerset Maugham. London, Macmillan, 1952; as *Maugham's Choice of Kipling's Best: Sixteen Stories,* New York, Doubleday, 1953.

A Treasury of Short Stories. New York, Bantam, 1957.

(Short Stories), edited by Edward Parone. New York, Dell, 1960.

Kipling Stories: Twenty-Eight Exciting Tales. New York, Platt and Munk, 1960.

The Best Short Stories, edited by Randall Jarrell. New York, Hanover House, 1961; as *In the Vernacular: The English in India* and *The English in England,* New York, Doubleday, 2 vols., 1963.

Famous Tales of India, edited by B.W. Shir-Cliff. New York, Ballantine, 1962.

Phantoms and Fantasies: 20 Tales. New York, Doubleday, 1965.

Short Stories, edited by Andrew Rutherford. London, Penguin, 1971.

Twenty-One Tales, edited by Tim Wilkinson. London, Folio Society, 1972.

Tales of East and West, edited by Bernard Bergonzi. Avon, Connecticut, Limited Editions Club, 1973.

Kipling's Kingdom: Twenty-Five of Rudyard Kipling's Best Indian Stories, Known and Unknown, edited by Charles Allen. London, Joseph, 1987.

Play

The Harbour Watch (produced London, 1913; revised version, as *Gow's Watch,* produced London, 1924).

Verse

Schoolboy Lyrics. Privately printed, 1881.

Echoes (published anonymously), with Alice Kipling. Privately printed, 1884.

Departmental Ditties and Other Verses. Lahore, Civil and Military

Gazette Press, 1886; revised edition, London, Thacker Spink, 1890.

Departmental Ditties, Barrack-Room Ballads, and Other Verse. New York, United States Book Company, 1890.

Barrack-Room Ballads and Other Verses. London, Methuen, 1892; as *Ballads and Barrack-Room Ballads,* New York, Macmillan, 1892.

The Seven Seas. New York, Appleton, and London, Methuen, 1896.

Recessional. Privately printed, 1897.

An Almanac of Twelve Sports, illustrated by William Nicholson. London Heinemann, and New York, Russell, 1898.

Poems, edited by Wallace Rice. Chicago, Star, 1899.

Recessional and Other Poems. Privately printed, 1899.

The Absent-Minded Beggar. Privately printed, 1899.

With Number Three, Surgical and Medical, and New Poems. Santiago, Chile, Hume, 1900.

Occasional Poems. Boston, Bartlett, 1900.

The Five Nations. London, Methuen, and New York, Doubleday, 1903.

The Muse among the Motors. New York, Doubleday, 1904.

Collected Verse. New York, Doubleday, 1907; London, Hodder and Stoughton, 1912.

A History of England (verse only), with C.R.L. Fletcher. London, Oxford University Press-Hodder and Stoughton, and New York, Doubleday, 1911; revised edition, 1930.

Songs from Books. New York, Doubleday, 1912; London, Macmillan, 1913.

Twenty Poems. London, Methuen, 1918.

The Years Between. London, Methuen, and New York, Doubleday, 1919.

Verse: Inclusive Edition 1885–1918. London, Hodder and Stoughton, 3 vols., and New York, Doubleday, 1 vol., 1919; revised edition, 1921, 1927, 1933.

A Kipling Anthology: Verse. London, Methuen, and New York, Doubleday, 1922.

Songs for Youth, from Collected Verse. London, Hodder and Stoughton, 1924; New York, Doubleday, 1925.

A Choice of Songs. London, Methuen, 1925.

Sea and Sussex. London, Macmillan, and New York, Doubleday, 1926.

St. Andrews, with Walter de la Mare. London, A. and C. Black, 1926.

Songs of the Sea. London, Macmillan, and New York, Doubleday, 1927.

Poems 1886–1929. London, Macmillan, 3 vols., 1929; New York, Doubleday, 3 vols., 1930.

Selected Poems. London, Methuen, 1931.

East of Suez, Being a Selection of Eastern Verses. London, Macmillan, 1931.

Sixty Poems. London, Hodder and Stoughton, 1939.

Verse: Definitive Edition. London, Hodder and Stoughton, and New York, Doubleday, 1940.

So Shall Ye Reap: Poems for These Days. London, Hodder and Stoughton, 1941.

A Choice of Kipling's Verse, edited by T.S. Eliot. London, Faber, 1941; New York, Scribner, 1943.

Sixty Poems. London, Hodder and Stoughton, 1957.

A Kipling Anthology, edited by W.G. Bebbington. London, Methuen, 1964.

The Complete Barrack-Room Ballads, edited by Charles Carrington. London, Methuen, 1973.

Kipling's English History: Poems, edited by Marghanita Laski. London, BBC Publications, 1974.

Kipling: A Selection, edited by James Cochrane. London, Penguin, 1977.

Early Verse by Rudyard Kipling 1879–1889: Unpublished, Uncollected, and Rarely Collected Poems, edited by Andrew Rutherford. Oxford, Clarendon Press, and New York, Oxford University Press, 1986.

Other

Quartette, with others. Lahore, Civil and Military Gazette Press, 1885.

The City of Dreadful Night and Other Sketches. Allahabad, Wheeler, 1890.

The City of Dreadful Night and Other Places. Allahabad, Wheeler, and London, Sampson Low, 1891.

The Smith Administration. Allahabad, Wheeler, 1891.

Letters of Marque. Allahabad, Wheeler, 1891; selections published London, Sampson Low, 1891.

American Notes, with *The Bottle Imp,* by Robert Louis Stevenson. New York, Ivers, 1891.

Out of India: Things I Saw, and Failed to See, in Certain Days and Nights at Jeypore and Elsewhere. New York, Dillingham, 1895.

The Kipling Birthday Book, edited by Joseph Finn. London, Macmillan, 1896; New York, Doubleday, 1899.

A Fleet in Being: Notes of Two Trips with the Channel Squadron. London and New York, Macmillan, 1898.

From to Sea to Sea: Letters of Travel. New York, Doubleday, 2 vols., 1899; as *From Sea to Sea and Other Sketches,* London, Macmillan, 2 vols., 1900.

Works (Swastika Edition). New York, Doubleday, Appleton, and Century, 15 vols., 1899.

Letters to the Family (Notes on a Recent Trip to Canada). Toronto, Macmillan, 1908.

The Kipling Reader (not same as 1900 collection of short stories). New York, Appleton, 1912.

The New Army (6 pamphlets). New York, Doubleday, 1914; as *The New Army in Training,* London, Macmillan, 1 vol., 1915.

France at War. London, Macmillan, and New York, Doubleday, 1915.

The Fringes of the Fleet. London, Macmillan, and New York, Doubleday, 1915.

Tales of "The Trade." Privately printed, 1916.

Sea Warfare. London, Macmillan, and New York, Doubleday, 1916.

The War in the Mountains. New York, Doubleday, 1917.

To Fighting Americans (speeches). Privately printed, 1918.

The Eyes of Asia. New York, Doubleday, 1918.

The Graves of the Fallen. London, Imperial War Graves Commission, 1919.

Letters of Travel (1892–1913). London, Macmillan, and New York, Doubleday, 1920.

A Kipling Anthology: Prose. London, Macmillan, and New York, Doubleday, 1922.

Works (Mandalay Edition). New York, Doubleday, 26 vols., 1925–26.

A Book of Words: Selections from Speeches and Addresses Delivered Between 1906 and 1927. London, Macmillan, and New York, Doubleday, 1928.

The One Volume Kipling. New York, Doubleday, 1928.

Souvenirs of France. London, Macmillan, 1933.

A Kipling Pageant. New York, Doubleday, 1935.

Something of Myself for My Friends Known and Unknown. London, Macmillan, and New York, Doubleday, 1937.

Complete Works (Sussex Edition). London, Macmillan, 35 vols., 1937–39; as *Collected Works* (Burwash Edition), New York, Doubleday, 28 vols., 1941 (includes revised versions of some previously published works).

A Kipling Treasury: Stories and Poems. London, Macmillan, 1940.

Kipling: A Selection of His Stories and Poems, edited by John Beecroft. New York, Doubleday, 2 vols., 1956.

The Kipling Sampler, edited by Alexander Greendale. New York, Fawcett, 1962.

Letters from Japan, edited by Donald Richie and Yoshimori Harashima. Tokyo, Kenkyusha, 1962.

Pearls from Kipling, edited by C. Donald Plomer. New Britain, Connecticut, Elihu Burritt Library, 1963.

Rudyard Kipling to Rider Haggard: The Record of a Friendship, edited by Morton Cohen. London, Hutchinson, 1965; Rutherford, New Jersey, Fairleigh Dickinson University Press, 1968.

The Best of Kipling. New York, Doubleday, 1968.

Stories and Poems, edited by Roger Lancelyn Green. London, Dent, 1970.

Kipling's Horace, edited by Charles Carrington. London, Methuen, 1978.

American Notes: Rudyard Kipling's West, edited by Arrell M. Gibson. Norman, University of Oklahoma Press, 1981.

The Portable Kipling, edited by Irving Howe. New York, Viking Press, 1982.

O Beloved Kids: Rudyard Kipling's Letters to His Children, edited by Elliot L. Gilbert. London, Weidenfeld and Nicolson, 1983; New York, Harcourt Brace, 1984.

Kipling's India: Uncollected Sketches 1884–1888, edited by Thomas Pinney. London, Macmillan, and New York, Schocken, 1986.

The Illustrated Kipling, edited by Neil Philip. London, Collins, 1987.

A Choice of Kipling's Prose, edited by Craig Raine. London, Faber, 1987.

Kipling's Japan, edited by Hugh Cortazzi and George Webb. London, Athlone Press, 1988.

Editor, *The Irish Guards in the Great War.* London, Macmillan, and New York, Doubleday, 2 vols., 1923.

*

Bibliography: *Rudyard Kipling: A Bibliographical Catalogue* by James McG. Stewart, edited by A. W. Keats, Toronto, Dalhousie University-University of Toronto Press, 1959, London, Oxford University Press, 1960; "Kipling: An Annotated Bibliography of Writings about Him" by H.E. Gerber and E. Lauterbach, in *English Fiction in Transition 3* (Tempe, Arizona), 1960, and *8,* 1965.

Manuscript Collections: Cornell University Library, Ithaca, New York; Library of Congress, Washington, D.C.; Houghton Library, Harvard University, Cambridge, Massachusetts; Pierpont Morgan Library, New York.

Critical Studies (selection): *Rudyard Kipling: His Life and Work* by Charles Carrington, London, Macmillan, 1955, revised edition, 1978, as *The Life of Rudyard Kipling,* New York, Doubleday, 1955; *Rudyard Kipling* by Rosemary Sutcliff, London, Bodley Head, 1960, New York, Walck, 1961; *The Readers' Guide to Rudyard Kipling's Work,* Canterbury, Gibbs, 1961, and *Kipling The Critical Heritage,* London, Routledge, and New York, Barnes and Noble, 1971, both edited by Roger Lancelyn Green, and *Kipling and the Children* by Green, London, Elek, 1965; *Kipling's Mind and Art* edited by Andrew Rutherford, Edinburgh, Oliver and Boyd, and Stanford, California, Stanford University Press, 1964; *Rudyard Kipling* by J.I.M. Stewart, London, Gollancz, and New York, Dodd Mead, 1966; *Rudyard Kipling: Realist and Fabulist* by Bonamy Dobrée, London and New York, Oxford University Press, 1967; *Kipling and His World* by Kingsley Amis, London, Thames and Hudson, 1975, New York, Scribner, 1976; *The Strange Ride of Rudyard Kipling: His Life and Works* by Angus Wilson, London, Secker and Warburg, 1977,

New York, Viking Press, 1978; *Rudyard Kipling* by Lord Birkenhead, London, Weidenfeld and Nicolson, 1978; *Rudyard Kipling* by James Harrison, Boston, Twayne, 1982; *Rudyard Kipling and the Fiction of Adolescence* by Robert F. Moss, New York, St. Martin's Press, and London, Macmillan, 1982; *Kipling: Interviews and Recollections* edited by Harold Orel, London, Macmillan, 2 vols., 1983, New York, Barnes and Noble, 2 vols., 1984; *A Kipling Companion* by Norman Page, London, Macmillan, 1984; *Kipling and Orientalism* by B.J. Moore-Gilbert, London, Croom Helm, 1986; *Kipling's Hidden Narratives* by Sandra Kemp, Oxford, Blackwell, 1988; *Rudyard Kipling* by Martin Seymour-Smith, London, Macdonald, 1989.

*   *   *

Looking back over his work a few months before he died, Rudyard Kipling wrote: "Since the tales had to be read by children, before people realised that they were meant for grown-ups,...I worked the material in three or four overlaid tints and textures, which might or might not reveal themselves according to the shifting light of sex, youth, and experience." He wrote this specifically of his last children's book, *Rewards and Fairies,* but it applies to some extent to all his children's books—and this makes it particularly difficult to write of him as a "children's author."

Kipling's approach to the writing of fiction was by way of meticulous fact, originally that of the first class journalistic reporter (a position which he held for seven years in India—before returning to London at the age of 23, to find himself famous within a few months). In the experimental stage towards the end of his time in India, when his first and some of his most famous stories were written, he was learning to put himself in the place of the various types about whom he was writing, to think their thoughts and to speak their language. It was a period in literary history when writing in dialect was a growing fashion, particularly prevalent in America, and Kipling with his amazingly retentive memory was able to become an expert in many dialects—Cockney, Yorkshire, and Irish for his *Soldiers Three,* native Indians for *In Black and White,* the general conversation of higher-class "Anglo-Indians" at Simla in many of the *Plain Tales*—and it was inevitable for one who loved children as he did from an early age, that he should attempt their forms of speech and thought in the four stories of the original *Wee Willie Winkie* volume at the end of 1888, before he left India.

The next stories which Kipling wrote with children as their intended first readers became *The Jungle Book* and *The Second Jungle Book*—several of which made their first appearance in the American children's magazine *St. Nicholas.* Of these stories the eight concerning Mowgli—the Indian boy who was brought up by the wolves and became the Master of the Jungle, until he returned to his own kind in the end—became immediately among the best loved stories with young readers and a children's classic by the end of the century. "His stories are not animal stories in the realistic sense; they are wonderful, beautiful fairy tales," wrote Ernest Thompson Seton, the great Canadian naturalist and writer of the life-stories of real animals. Many games of "make-believe" in fact and fiction took Mowgli for their hero and his jungle for their new Fairyland, and not twenty years after the publication of *The Jungle Books,* Baden-Powell made such make-believe still more real for small boys all over the world by basing his Wolf-cubs—the junior Boy Scouts—on them.

As was natural for a writer of Kipling's vivid imagination, as soon as he had children of his own he began to invent stories to tell to them. Many of these were never written down, but one series became the established favourite, a series of incantatory tales that had to be told again and again, always in the same words, always "just-so." The first three appeared in *St. Nicholas* at the end of 1897. There was then a gap until mid-1900. Josephine, "the daughter that was all to him," who appears as Taffimai, died in 1899 at the age of six; but after a break Kipling was able to write down the rest of the tales he had made for her, and probably added a few more—and *Just So Stories* was published in 1902. This, the most unusual of Kipling's books, is probably the most timeless and the most enduring of his tales for children. It should be read aloud to obtain its best effect, but is enjoyed in different ways at almost any age.

Between writing the first and last of the Just So stories, Kipling published three other books which appeal strongly to boy readers as well as, and perhaps in different ways from, the adults for whom they were intended. The least well known, "*Captains Courageous*," is a full-length sea-story set among the old fishing-fleets on the Grand Banks in the North Atlantic. The theme is one of Kipling's favorites, that of the "young cub" being "licked into shape"—as of Mowgli learning to become Master of the Jungle before returning to put his particular accomplishments at the service of his own kind. In this case Harvey Cheyne, the spoilt son of an American millionaire, falls overboard from a luxury liner and is picked up by a fishing boat and made to "work his keep" for several months before returning to his family, having by then indeed "suffered a sea-change."

The next book aims at the same goal, but in a highly debatable manner: "There came to me the idea of beginning some tracts or parables for the young," wrote Kipling. "These, for reasons honestly beyond my control, turned themselves into a series of tales called *Stalky & Co.*" This book has probably met with more contradictory criticism than any of his other works. To the adult reader it can be enjoyed again and again as one of the greatest works of humour in the language—or it can be detested and condemned as "an unpleasant book about unpleasant boys at an unpleasant school." With boys themselves, however, it has always been a favorite, is not likely to have led them into any new forms of mischief, and is certainly now too much of a "period piece" to seem anything but a hilarious collection of yarns about a type of academy almost as obsolete as a Dame School.

Kipling's other book about a boy hero is *Kim*, which is now being classed among the great British novels—by Indian and Pakistani critics and scholars as well as British and American. It is as much, or no more, a boy's book as *Huckleberry Finn* and is enjoyed or not at various ages as variously as Mark Twain's classic. Once again it follows the development of a small boy with exceptional chances and at first no sense of duty or obligation as he develops mentally and spiritually to fill the place in the world for which he is uniquely fitted. But in the process Kim, the little Irish orphan brought up more or less as a native Indian, passes through a series of absorbing adventures set against the most vivid and authentic literary picture we have of India as Kipling saw and knew it nearly a century ago.

None of these last three books was meant specifically for young readers: but after *Just So Stories,* written for "the vanished Josephine," Kipling realised that he had two other children fast growing up and just as desirous of tales, even if of a different kind. The family had by now settled in an early 17th-century manor house in a secluded corner of Sussex; this, and a performance of scenes from *A Midsummer Night's Dream* which the two put on for their parents, brought forth *Puck of Pook's Hill*. These tales, and those in the sequel, *Rewards and Fairies*, cover English history, largely as it impinged on their own neighbourhood, from the end of the Roman Occupation to the days of the Napoleonic Wars, and many of them have been acclaimed as among the best historical stories ever written. The historian G.M. Trevelyan, for example, wrote in 1953: "As a piece of historical imagination I know nothing in the world better than the story in *Puck* called 'The Joyous Venture'…I can see no fault in it, and many a merit." And next to this he set "Simple Simon" and "The Tree of Justice" in *Rewards and Fairies*.

As the stories were written for Kipling's own children, who appear in them as Dan and Una, it is only right that the second volume is more difficult than the first, to match their advance in age and

understanding. And they were the last books that Kipling wrote for children. "Dan" was killed in the First World War, and, though "Una" married, she had no children—so we can but regret that Kipling wrote no "Tales of a Grandfather," while giving thanks for those stories already written: some of the greatest and most enduring of their kind in whatever compartment of literature we choose to set them.

As Patrick Chalmers wrote: he was one of those who "give their heart's best only when they give to a child."

—Roger Lancelyn Green

———

KITT, Tamara. See de **REGNIERS, Beatrice Schenk.**

———

KJELGAARD, Jim (James Arthur Kjelgaard). American. Born in New York City, 6 December 1910. Educated at Syracuse University, New York, two years. Married Edna Dresen in 1939; one daughter. Recipient: Western Writers of America Spur award, 1958. *Died 12 July 1959.*

PUBLICATIONS FOR CHILDREN

Fiction

Forest Patrol, illustrated by Tony Palazzo. New York, Holiday House, 1941; London, Sampson Low, 1948.
Rebel Siege, illustrated by Charles Wilson. New York, Holiday House, 1943.
Big Red, illustrated by Bob Kuhn. New York, Holiday House, 1945; London, Carousel, 1980.
Buckskin Brigade, illustrated by Ralph Ray, Jr. New York, Holiday House, 1947.
Snow Dog, illustrated by Jacob Landau. New York, Holiday House, 1948.
Kalak of the Ice, illustrated by Bob Kuhn. New York, Holiday House, 1949.
A Nose for Trouble, illustrated by Collett. New York, Holiday House, 1949.
Wild Trek, illustrated by Faye. New York, Holiday House, 1950; London, Collins, 1964.
Chip, The Dam-Builder, illustrated by Ralph Ray, Jr. New York, Holiday House, 1950.
Irish Red, Son of Big Red, illustrated by Ames. New York, Holiday House, 1951; London, Collins, 1958.
Fire-Hunter, illustrated by Ralph Ray, Jr. New York, Holiday House, 1951.
Trailing Trouble. New York, Holiday House, 1952.
Outlaw Red, Son of Big Red, illustrated by Ames. New York, Holiday House, 1953.
The Spell of White Sturgeon, illustrated by Stephen Voorhies. New York, Dodd Mead, 1953.
Haunt Fox, illustrated by Glen Rounds. New York, Holiday House, 1954.
Cracker Barrel Trouble Shooter, illustrated by Albert Orbaan. New York, Dodd Mead, 1954.
Lion Hound, illustrated by Jacob Landau. New York, Holiday House, 1955; London, Collins, 1957.

The Lost Wagon, illustrated by Albert Orbann.   New York, Dodd Mead, 1955.

Desert Dog, illustrated by Sam Savitt.   New York, Holiday House, 1956.

Trading Jeff and His Dog.   New York, Dodd Mead, 1956.

Wolf Brother, illustrated by Charles Wilson.   New York, Holiday House, 1957; London, Collins, 1963.

Wildlife Cameraman, illustrated by Sam Savitt.   New York, Holiday House, 1957.

Double Challenge, illustrated by Chris Kenyon.   New York, Dodd Mead, 1957.

Swamp Cat, illustrated by Edward Shenton.   New York, Dodd Mead, 1957.

We Were There at the Oklahoma Land Run, illustrated by Chris Kenyon.   New York, Grosset and Dunlap, 1957.

Rescue Dog of High Pass, illustrated by Edward Shenton.   New York, Dodd Mead, 1958.

The Black Fawn, illustrated by Erk.   New York, Dodd Mead, 1958.

The Land Is Bright.   New York, Dodd Mead, 1958.

Hound Dog and Other Yarns, illustrated by Paul Brown.   New York, Dodd Mead, 1958.

Stormy, illustrated by Louis Darling.   New York, Holiday House, 1959; London, Collins, 1964.

Hi Jolly, illustrated by Kendall Rossi.   New York, Dodd Mead, 1959.

Boomerang Hunter, illustrated by W.T. Mars.   New York, Holiday House, 1960.

Ulysses and His Woodland Zoo, illustrated by Kendall Rossi.   New York, Dodd Mead, 1960.

The Duck-Footed Hound, illustrated by Marc Simont.   New York, Crowell, 1960.

My Father's Collie.   New York, Dodd Mead, 1961.

Tigre, illustrated by Everett Raymond Kinstler.   New York, Dodd Mead, 1961.

Hidden Trail, illustrated by Louis Darling.   New York, Holiday House, 1962.

Fawn in the Forest and Other Wild Animal Stories, illustrated by Sam Savitt.   New York, Dodd Mead, 1962.

Two Dogs and a Horse, illustrated by Sam Savitt.   New York, Dodd Mead, 1964.

Furious Moose of the Wilderness, illustrated by Mort Künstler.   New York, Dodd Mead, 1965.

Dave and His Dog Mulligan, illustrated by Sam Savitt.   New York, Dodd Mead, 1966.

Coyote Song, illustrated by Robert MacLean.   New York, Dodd Mead, 1969.

Other

The Explorations of Père Marquette, illustrated by Stephen Voorhies.   New York, Random House, 1951.

Coming of the Mormons, illustrated by Stephen Voorhies.   New York, Random House, 1953.

The Story of Geronimo, illustrated by Charles Wilson.   New York, Grosset and Dunlap, 1958.

Editor, *The Wild Horse Roundup: A Collection of Stories by Members of the Western Writers of America,* illustrated by Paul Brown.   New York, Dodd Mead, 1957.

Editor, *Hound Dogs and Others: A Collection of Stories by Members of the Western Writers of America,* illustrated by Paul Brown.   New York, Dodd Mead, 1958.

*

Manuscript Collection: Kerlan Collection, University of Minnesota, Minneapolis.

*   *   *

An engaging animal, a colorful person, and a distinctive habitat are the three ingredients Jim Kjelgaard incorporated into most of his many books for young people. Using a writing mode as simple as his own life-style, he based his books on his own experiences, travels, and investigation.

His most notable books are the series about the Irish setter, his favorite dog. Different temperaments are characterized in *Big Red, Irish Red, Son of Big Red,* and *Outlaw Red, Son of Big Red.* He himself hunted with Irish setters, but he had interest in other dogs, too. His impressive list of dog books includes such breeds as the greyhound in *Desert Dog,* the husky in *Snow Dog* and *Wild Trek,* the wildfowl retriever in *Stormy,* and the collie in *Double Challenge.* Intrigued with the St. Bernard, he found it necessary to inform himself using Alfred Richard Sennett's book *Across the Great St. Bernard* to take notes about a place he was unable to visit. He extended his scope to other creatures of the wild such as *Kalak of the Ice, The Black Fawn, Chip,* and *Haunt Fox* about a polar bear, a deer, a beaver, and his own favorite animal respectively. In a letter to Dr. Irvin Kerlan to whom the last book is dedicated, the author wrote, "When I was a youngster, away back in 1929, it was impossible to get any sort of job. I went into the hills with two fox hounds, and before the winter was over I had 13. Naturally I didn't make any money, but I doubt if I've since had half as much fun!…I like red foxes, I think, better than any other animal."

In most of his books there is a human being in addition to an animal. His debut, *Forest Patrol,* describes a boy yearning to become a forest ranger. The main character in *Swamp Cat* and *Stormy* is a boy, in *Snow Dog* it is a trapper. In *The Story of Geronimo* he interpreted both the Apache Indian renegade and his adversaries. *Rebel Siege* portrayed the struggle of loyalties of a group in the Carolinas in 1780, written and published in the context of World War II.

The wilderness, either contemporary or historical, is the setting for most of Kjelgaard's books. As a child he was drawn to the woods where he observed animal life in natural habitat. During his first year after high school he and a friend spent an entire winter season in the Pennsylvania forest hunting and fishing. *Buckskin Brigade,* one of the author's favorite books, portrays pioneer life on the frontier. "Story hunts have led me from the Atlantic to the Pacific and from the Arctic Circle to Mexico City," he wrote on the jacket of *Coyote Song.* "Stories, like gold, are where you find them—3,000 miles from home or on the doorstep." While living in Wisconsin he wrote *The Spell of White Sturgeon* and *The Explorations of Père Marquette,* both with local settings. Historical fiction, such as *The Lost Wagon* about the Oregon Trail and *Fire-Hunter* suggesting the life of a prehistoric man, were the result of research and an educated imagination.

Kjelgaard was well-known to bibliographers seeking books for the reluctant reader and for occupational counseling. He specialized in telling a good story with simplicity, and encouraged fellow-authors to provide better reading for youth. In a letter to Dr. Kerlan he mused, "As for me, I'm 43 and a very plain sort of person. By that I mean if I had a choice between attending a party at the Stork Club or going bass fishing, I'd go fishing." Reviewers praised him for his fine plots and action. Reviewing for the *Horn Book* (August 1962), Margaret Warren Brown stated, "Much more mysterious than the mystery in *Hidden Trail* (the disappearance of an elk herd) is the author's ability to fashion an absorbing story out of such unlikely materials as a youthful photographer, a Conservation Department, an Airedale, and the migration pattern of elks."

The author's brother, John, provided the model for the forest ranger in the books. A game warden's responsibilities are outlined

Trailing Trouble and *A Nose for Trouble,* the wildlife cameraman is portrayed in a book with that title, and a naturalist whose plane is forced to land in the remote Canadian wilderness is described in *Wild Trek.* An avid reader can follow Kjelgaard's books and life chronologically, observing that the camera is substituted for a gun in his later works.

—Karen Nelson Hoyle

———————

KLEIN, Norma. American. Born in New York City, 13 May 1938. Educated at the Dalton School, New York, 1941–51; Elizabeth Irwin High School, 1952–56; Cornell University, Ithaca, New York, 1956–57; Barnard College, New York, 1957–60, B.A. (cum laude) in Russian 1960 (Phi Beta Kappa); Columbia University, New York, 1960–63, M.A. in Slavic languages 1963. Married Erwin Fleissner in 1963; two daughters. *Died 25 April 1989.*

PUBLICATIONS FOR CHILDREN

Fiction

Mom, The Wolf Man, and Me. New York, Pantheon, 1972; London, Heinemann, 1986.
It's Not What You Expect. New York, Pantheon, 1973; London, Pan, 1986.
Girls Can Be Anything, illustrated by Roy Doty. New York, Dutton, 1973.
Taking Sides. New York, Pantheon, 1974.
If I Had My Way, illustrated by Ray Cruz. New York, Pantheon, 1974.
Dinosaur's Housewarming Party, illustrated by James Marshall. New York, Crown, 1974.
Naomi in the Middle, illustrated by Leigh Grant. New York, Dial Press, 1974.
Confessions of an Only Child, illustrated by Richard Cuffari. New York, Pantheon, 1974.
Sunshine (novelization of a TV play). New York, Holt Rinehart, 1975; London, Everest, 1976.
The Sunshine Years. New York, Dell, 1975; London, Macdonald, 1984.
What It's All About. New York, Dial Press, 1975.
Blue Trees, Red Sky, illustrated by Pat Grant Porter. New York, Pantheon, 1975.
Hiding. New York, Four Winds Press, 1976.
It's OK If You Don't Love Me. New York, Dial Press, 1977; London, Pan, 1987.
Tomboy. New York, Four Winds Press, 1978.
Love Is One of the Choices. New York, Dial Press, 1978; London, Futura, 1981.
Visiting Pamela, illustrated by Kay Chorao. New York, Dial Press, 1979.
A Honey of a Chimp. New York, Pantheon, 1980.
Breaking Up. New York, Pantheon, 1980; London, Pan, 1986.
Robbie and the Leap Year Blues. New York, Dial Press, 1981.
The Queen of the What Ifs. New York, Fawcett, 1982.
Beginners' Love. New York, Dial Press, 1982; London, Pan, 1986.
Bizou. New York, Viking Press, 1983.
Angel Face. New York, Viking, 1984; London, Pan, 1987.

Snapshots. New York, Dial Press, 1984.
Give and Take. New York, Viking, 1985.
Family Secrets. New York, Dial Press, 1985.
The Cheerleader. New York, Knopf, 1985.
Going Backwards. New York, Scholastic, 1986; London, Pan, 1987.
Older Men. New York, Dial Press, 1987; London, Women's Press, 1988.
My Life as a Body. New York, Knopf, 1987.
Now That I Know. New York, Bantam, 1988.
No More Saturday Nights. New York, Knopf, 1988.
Learning How to Fall. New York, Bantam, 1989.

Verse

A Train for Jane, illustrated by Miriam Schottland. Old Westbury, New York, Feminist Press, 1974.

Other

Baryshnikov's Nutcracker, photographs by Ken Regan and others. New York, Putnam, 1983.

PUBLICATIONS FOR ADULTS

Novels

Give Me One Good Reason. New York, Putnam, 1973.
Coming to Life. New York, Simon and Schuster, 1974.
Girls Turn Wives. New York, Simon and Schuster, 1976.
French Postcards (novelization of screenplay). New York, Fawcett, 1979; London, Coronet, 1980.
Domestic Arrangements. New York, Evans, 1981; London, Futura, 1982.
Wives and Other Women. New York, St. Martin's Press, 1982; London, Macdonald, 1983.
The Swap. New York, St. Martin's Press, 1983.
Lovers. New York, Viking, 1984; London, Piatkus, 1986.
American Dreams. New York, Dutton, 1987.
That's My Baby. New York, Viking, 1988.
The World as It Is. New York, Dutton, 1989.

Short Stories

Love and Other Euphemisms New York, Putnam, 1972.
Sextet in A Minor: A Novella and Thirteen Short Stories. New York, St. Martin's Press, 1983.

*

Manuscript Collection: Kerlan Collection, University of Minnesota, Minneapolis.

Critical Study: *Presenting Norma Klein* by Allene Stuart Phy, Boston, Twayne, 1988.

Norma Klein commented:
(1983) I've always loved New York which is the background for many of my novels. It seemed to me when I began writing books for kids that most teenage novels were set in the midwest or the suburbs. I wanted to portray the kind of teenager I was and the kind my kids were—bright, thoughtful, idealistic people, not cheerleaders or football stars. I've tried to write the kinds of books I would have liked to read while in high school or college, books with the

complexity of novels for adults, but with a teenage protagonist.

*   *   *

Norma Klein is a prolific American author who has written for children, young adults, and adults. While all her books have met with success, it is as a writer of children's and young adult fiction that Klein has enjoyed the greatest recognition, becoming as it were a superstar second only to Judy Blume when it comes to having a large coterie of loyal young readers. Klein, like Blume, writes with uncompromising frankness about issues that are of concern to contemporary youth: sex and sexism, single or gay parents, disintegrating families, pornography, feminism—all have been grist for Klein's mill. As a result, she shares another honor with Blume; Klein's books for young readers are second only to Blume's when it comes to censorship attempts in the United States, a fact of which Klein is quite proud.

Most of Klein's children's books were written in the mid to late 1970's. Her first picture book, *Girls Can Be Anything,* was an expression of her strong feminist sentiments. In it two kindergarteners talk about life roles. Adam has clearly learned all the sexual stereotypes about what girls do and what boys do even at his tender age. It is up to Marina to point out to him that girls *can* be anything, just as boys can, and that if Adam is very lucky he may even grow up to be the husband of a president of the United States! Klein's message was clear but the story is not didactic; very stereotypic illustrations did weaken its point a bit, however. *If I Had My Way* is a fantasy in which children take over things, at least in their dreams; all the ways that adults dominate children are assumed by the children, and the adults' obvious bewilderment at dealing with their own strictures is perhaps more amusing—and instructive—to adults than to young readers. In *Naomi in the Middle,* Bobo, age nine and her sister Naomi, seven, have to come to terms with the fact that a new baby is on the way, and what this will mean to their present comfortable situation. While children loved the book, some adults were appalled by the little girls' frank discussion of where babies come from and the language used, e.g. penis and vagina. Klein's next picture book, *Blue Trees, Red Sky,* deals with the importance of a meaningful job to many women. The latter raised some adult hackles with its mention of "making pee pee" and the use of "vagina" and "penis" again. In this, her last picture book, Klein describes the travails that five-year-old fussbudget/homebody Carrie suffers when her mother makes her leave the comfort of home to visit Pamela at her house.

While Klein was writing books for a very young audience she also produced several that were for older children: *Mom, The Wolf Man, and Me; Confessions of an Only Child; Tomboy; What It's All About; A Honey of a Chimp;* and *Robbie and the Leap Year Blues. Mom, The Wolf Man, and Me* was her first novel, and a breakthrough book for its time. Brett is the 11-year-old daughter of an unmarried mother; their relationship is warm and mutually respectful. Her mother, to the consternation of many critics, relishes her life, and Brett suffers not at all from her then highly unorthodox family situation. But into this tranquil situation comes a problem in the form of an unusual red-haired man with a wonderful Irish wolfhound called Norma. It becomes obvious early on that Brett's mother, Deborah, is not only interested in "The Wolf Man," as Brett has named him, but is considering marrying him. How Brett handles her jealousy and fears of the new relationship makes a warm, funny, and loving family story that many consider Klein's finest work to date, its controversial aspects notwithstanding. *Confessions* deals with the impact of a new baby on an only child; the baby's death, however, shows Toe, the young protagonist, that it just might have been possible for her to share her parents' affection all along. In its sequel, *Tomboy,* a new baby has taken the place of the one who died, but family problems such as Dad's loss of his job and the death of a beloved dog serve to remind the family of their earlier loss. In both books the strength of family love in the face of adversity is both clear and strong. *What It's All About* is another family story, this time dealing with a child of Jewish-American and Asian-American parents who, although divorced, are still loving and protective of young Bernadette. Another family saga, *A Honey of a Chimp,* is also an animal story made controversial by the introduction of Emily's kindly uncle, who just happens to be gay. *Robbie* is the story of a boy who must divide his time between living with his divorced parents, but again, even though the family is sundered, Robbie is loved and respected by his parents. All Klein's preteen fiction has endured precisely because she, again like Judy Blume, speaks to issues and concerns of young readers with wit, understanding, and compassion. In spite of their often controversial elements, the books' portrayals of the powerful ties that bind loving family members together are important and certainly crucial lessions for younger readers to consider.

Over the course of her career, Klein has written nearly two dozen novels for teenage readers, almost all of which are still in print and read avidly by this age group. Klein has said that her aim in writing young adult books is to present central characters who are "strong and interesting" in the face of the problems of growing up in American society; in this she has for the most part succeeded admirably, as her legion of loyal young adult readers attests. *It's Not What You Expect* is a good example of how she has managed to accomplish that aim. 14-year-old twins Oliver and Carla decide to capitalize on Oliver's gourmet cooking skills by opening a restaurant in a house the two are caring for over the summer, and serve one dinner each evening at a reasonable price. They involve family and friends, and the restaurant is a success from the beginning, to the delight of everyone involved. Family problems arise, however: Dad, in a "midlife crisis," decides to leave and go to New York City to write a novel, picking up a new girlfriend in the process. Mom must cope with Dad's absence but also with the amorous advances of a neighbor, while older brother Tom's girlfriend is found to be pregnant. The twins offer Tom the restaurant's proceeds to pay for Sara Lee's abortion, but he angrily refuses. Carla, a strong young woman, is at first angry and hurt by all this, but eventually begins to realize that life just isn't always "what you expect," and grows as a result of her new understanding. The family is eventually reunited, but at some cost—and some acquired maturity—to all.

It's OK If You Don't Love Me, another ground-breaking young adult book, is the story of Jody, an urbane liberated Jewish young woman from a liberal, divorced New York family, who meets Lyle, a straightlaced midwestern Roman Catholic who, orphaned by an accident, has come to New York to live with his sister and her family. They fall in love despite their differences, and Jody attempts the difficult task of seducing Lyle. However, when Jody betrays Lyle with her former boyfriend Whitney, Lyle is alienated and deeply hurt. The clash of values arising from their differing backgrounds is not strong enough to keep Jody and Lyle apart forever, however, and eventually they are reconciled. What made *It's OK* controversial to critics was its explicit and frank details about the young people's sexual activity; the book's publisher, in fact, went so far as to issue it as an adult book despite the fact that it was clearly written for teenagers, a not unusual occurrence with Klein's more explicit tales. In spite of this, the book remains one of Klein's most popular books among the young adult audience.

In the 1980's Klein began shifting from female protagonists in many of her young adult novels and writing from the viewpoint of young males. In *Snapshots,* for example, Sean and Marc, fine amateur photographers, take nude photographs of Marc's beautiful younger sister, not out of salaciousness but simply because Tiffany is an exquisite child who is a natural model. The boys get into trouble when the person developing the photos reports them to the district attorney, who accuses them of producing child pornography. In *Give and Take,* Spence, an 18-year-old naif, has to fend off the attentions of women who seek to seduce him. In *Beginners' Love* the protagonist is Joel, a virgin who has his first affair, and *Angel Face* features Jason, whose family is falling apart, and who is not doing too well in either his school life or his love life. Klein has said that she writes from the boy's viewpoint because she wishes "there were more good novels about teenage boys, particularly about what boys feel about girls, their families, schools, the future."

In all her books for young adults Klein seems to strike a note with her readers that few other authors for this age group do consistently. This is obvious because she writes about the things that concern young people, both boys and girls: sexuality, sex roles and sexual behavior, peer relations, and family ties. She is both frank and honest in her portrayals of teenage angst, and, like her friend Judy Blume, both respects and cares for her readers. Like Blume also, she leavens her message with wit and humor, and her readers have responded by keeping her near the top of their list of best-loved authors for nearly two decades.

—Audrey Eaglen

———

KLEIN, Robin (née McMaugh). Australian. Born in Kempsey, New South Wales, 28 February 1936. Educated at Kempsey Primary School, 1941–47, and Newcastle Girls High School, 1948–51, both New South Wales. Married Karl Klein in 1956 (divorced 1979); two sons and two daughters. Has worked as tea lady, bookshop assistant, nurse, copper enamelist, and aide at a school for disadvantaged children. Recipient: Australian Children's Book Council award, 1983; Australia Council fellowship, 1985. Agent: Tim Curnow, Curtis Brown (Australia) Ltd., P.O. Box 19, Paddington, New South Wales 2021, Australia.

PUBLICATIONS FOR CHILDREN

Fiction

Honoured Guest, illustrated by Margaret Power.   Melbourne, Macmillan, 1979.
Sprung!, illustrated by Margaret Power.   Willoughby, New South Wales, Rigby, 1982.
Thing, illustrated by Alison Lester.   Melbourne and Oxford, Oxford University Press, 1982.
Junk Castle, illustrated by Rolf Heimann.   Melbourne, New York, and Oxford, Oxford University Press, 1983.
Oodoolay, illustrated by Vivienne Goodman.   Flinders Park, South Australia, Era, 1983.
Penny Pollard's Diary, illustrated by Ann James.   Melbourne and Oxford, Oxford University Press, 1983.
People Might Hear You.   Melbourne and London, Penguin, 1983; New York, Viking Kestrel, 1987.
Brock and the Dragon, illustrated by Rodney McRae.   Rydalmere, New South Wales, Hodder and Stoughton, 1984.
Hating Alison Ashley.   Melbourne and London, Penguin, 1984; New York, Penguin, 1985.
Penny Pollard's Letters, illustrated by Ann James.   Melbourne and Oxford, Oxford University Press, 1984.
Ratbags and Rascals, illustrated by Alison Lester.   Melbourne, Dent, and Oxford, Oxford University Press, 1984.
Thalia the Failure, illustrated by Rhyll Plant.   Gosford, New South Wales, Ashton Scholastic, 1984.
Thingnapped!, illustrated by Alison Lester.   Melbourne and Oxford, Oxford University Press, 1984.
The Tomb Comb, illustrated by Heather Potter.   Melbourne, Oxford University Press, 1984.
Annabel's Ghost (stories).   Melbourne, Oxford University Press, 1985.
Good for Something (audio book).   Caulfield East, Victoria, Arnold, 1985.
Serve Him Right! (audio book).   Caulfield East, Victoria, Arnold, 1985.
You're on Your Own (audio book).   Caulfield East, Victoria, Arnold, 1985.
The Enemies, illustrated by Noela Young.   North Ryde, New South Wales, Angus and Robertson, 1985; as *Enemies,* New York, Dutton, 1989.
Halfway Across the Galaxy and Turn Left.   Melbourne and London, Viking Kestrel, 1985; New York, Viking, 1986.
Separate Places, illustrated by Anna Lacis.   Kenthurst, New South Wales, Kangaroo Press, 1985.
Boss of the Pool, illustrated by H. Panagopoulos.   Adelaide, Omnibus, 1986; London, Viking Kestrel, 1987.
Games..., illustrated by Melissa Webb.   Melbourne, Viking Kestrel, 1986.
Penny Pollard in Print, illustrated by Ann James.   Melbourne, Oxford University Press, 1986.
The Princess Who Hated It, illustrated by Marie Smith.   Adelaide, Omnibus, 1986.
Birk the Berserker, illustrated by Alison Lester.   Adelaide, Omnibus, 1987.
Get Lost, illustrated by June Joubert.   Melbourne, Macmillan, 1987.
I Shot an Arrow, illustrated by Geoff Hocking.   Melbourne, Viking Kestrel, 1987.
The Last Pirate, illustrated by Rick Armor.   Melbourne, Rigby, 1987.
The Lonely Hearts Club, with Max Dann.   Melbourne, Oxford University Press, 1987; New York, Oxford University Press, 1988.
Parker-Hamilton, illustrated by Gaston Vanzet.   Melbourne, Rigby, 1987.
Laurie Loved Me Best.   Melbourne and London, Viking Kestrel, 1988.
Penny Pollard's Passport, illustrated by Ann James.   Melbourne, Oxford University Press, 1988.
Against the Odds, illustrated by Bill Wood.   Melbourne and London, Viking Kestrel, 1989.

Verse

The Giraffe in Pepperell, illustrated by Gill Tomblin.   Rydalmere, New South Wales, Hodder and Stoughton, 1978.
Snakes and Ladders, illustrated by Ann James.   Melbourne, Dent, and Oxford, Oxford University Press, 1985.

Other

Christmas, illustrated by Kristen Hilliard.   Sydney, Methuen, 1987.
Crookbook, illustrated by Kristen Hilliard.   Sydney, Methuen, 1987.
Don't Tell Lucy (miscellany), illustrated by Kristen Hilliard.   Sydney, Methuen, 1987.
Dear Robin...: Letters to Robin Klein.   Sydney, Allen and Unwin, 1988.

*

Robin Klein comments:
    I have no particular aim in mind when writing for children, other than trying to include some positive attitudes. I think children

assimilate too much gloom from TV and newspapers as it is. I don't try to modify situations or vocabulary levels—it's insulting to underestimate young readers. Nor do I sit down and deliberately attempt to introduce humour into a book, but often it will develop along those lines even though the underlying themes are quite serious.

*   *   *

Robin Klein has made an enviable reputation within her relatively short career. Popular and prolific, she is also versatile. She is probably best known for the series that began with *Penny Pollard's Diary* in 1983. Part of the charm of the Penny Pollard books is the directness and humour with which their 10-year-old heroine presents herself, in diary form or in the letters of the later volumes. Penny sees the world as a place of absurd rules and restrictions; she has a low opinion of adults and is usually found pondering the strategies of non-cooperation. Her ambitions—to be a jockey or an ace reporter—conflict with an everyday life that requires her to behave nicely as a flower girl at a wedding or visit an old people's home. Although Klein does not allow moral lessons to be too obvious, the comic narratives end not in rebellion but in good-humoured acceptance. The latest in the series, *Penny Pollard's Passport,* suggests that the author is losing interest: the heroine's letters home to Australia from a tourist holiday in Britain lack the usual sparkle and are often merely informative. Klein has been exceptionally fortunate in her publisher and illustrator. All four of the Penny Pollard books are visually enticing, lavishly illustrated with sketches, photographs, maps, and other embellishments which add to the considerable pleasures of the texts.

Klein's comic sense is at its best in the fantasy of space travel *Halfway Across the Galaxy and Turn Left.* The viewpoint is that of a technologically sophisticated family forced to spend time on Earth. The serious-minded heroine struggles to conform in an Australian school. Her parents think of the whole excursion as a joke; only with great difficulty are they persuaded not to dazzle the earthlings with their superior powers, to steal from supermarkets or forge banknotes. The reversal of stereotypical roles in family life provides much of the comedy; the visitors know nothing of the conventions by which mothers cook, fathers go out to work, and children obey their elders.

In spite of the undeniable charm of Klein's comic writing, her finest novel is also her most sombre. *People Might Hear You* is the story of isolation and displacement. Frances, a resourceful 12-year-old, is suddenly removed from her familiar world when her aunt—who is also her sole relative—marries a member of an exclusive religious sect. The new house is in effect a prison: the sect wants no contamination from the outside world. The suspense with which Klein tells the story of the girl's escape is matched by the interest in the characters, making this a memorable novel.

Klein has also written a number of problem novels: readable but thin and oversimplified. *Boss of the Pool,* in which a discontented schoolgirl learns maturity and tolerance by teaching a retarded boy to swim, is no more than competent. *Separate Places,* the story of adaption to divorce and remarriage, is similarly predictable.

Her wide range and the sheer number of Klein's books make her something of a phenomenon. She can write for the very young as well as for the over-10s to whom most of her work is directed. Her most beguiling creation is the pet stegosaurus of *Thing* and its sequel *Thingnapped!.* Klein and artist Alison Lester combine in an unusually engaging narrative. The humour is unforced, the tone just right. There is no higher praise for this kind of fantasy than to say that the author knows exactly when to stop.

—Brenda Niall

———

KNIGHT, Eric (Mowbray). Also wrote as Richard Hallas. British. Born in Menston, Yorkshire, 10 April 1897; moved to the United States, 1912. Educated at Bewerly School, Yorkshire; Boston Museum of Fine Arts; New York Academy of Design. Served in Princess Patricia's Canadian Light Infantry during World War I; United States Army during World War II: Major; Legion of Merit. Married 1) Dorothy Noyes Hall in 1917, three daughters; 2) Jere Knight in 1932. Journalist: staff member of several Connecticut newspapers, Bronx *Home News,* and Philadelphia *Sun* and *Public Ledger,* until 1934; film writer in Hollywood. *Died* (killed in action) *15 January 1943.*

PUBLICATIONS FOR CHILDREN

Fiction

Lassie Come-Home, illustrated by Marguerite Kirmse. Philadelphia, Winston, 1940; London, Cassell, 1942.

PUBLICATIONS FOR ADULTS

Novels

Invitation to Life. New York, Greenberg, 1934; London, Cassell, 1936.
Song on Your Bugles. London, Boriswood, 1936; New York, Harper, 1937.
The Flying Yorkshireman: Novellas, with others. New York, Harper, 1938.
You Play the Black and the Red Comes Up. London, Cassell, 1938; as Richard Hallas, New York, McBride, 1938.
Now Pray We for Our Country. London, Cassell, 1940; as *The Happy Land,* New York, Harper, 1940; as *This Is the Land,* Leeds, Morley Baker, 1969.
This above All. London, Cassell, and New York, Harper, 1941.
Sam Small Flies Again. New York, Harper, 1942; London, Cassell, 1943; as *Sam Small, The Flying Yorkshireman,* London, Spearman, 1958.

Other

They Don't Want Swamps and Jungles (radio talk). Ottawa, Director of Public Information, 1942.
World of Plenty, with Paul Rotha. London, Nicholson and Watson, 1945.
The Dedicated Life of Rainer Maria Rilke. Shorne, Kent, Ridgeway House, 1949; New York, Haskell House, 1974.
Portrait of a Flying Yorkshireman: Letters from Eric Knight in the United States to Paul Rotha in England, edited by Rotha. London, Chapman and Hall, 1952.

*   *   *

Eric Knight is one of a number of ambitious authors, starting perhaps with R.D. Blackmore, who contributed quite substantially to various branches of literature but by the verdict of posterity are known largely as writers for children. Within a space of ten years Knight published seven volumes, mainly full-length adult novels, including one that was widely hailed at the time in Britain and America for its originality and boldness, and which is still not entirely forgotten. *This above All* is concerned with problems of conscience and conflict of loyalties under the pressures of war; though written with obvious sincerity, it would probably be too earnest and at times too morbid for most tastes nowadays. Knight's several Yorkshire comedies featuring the amazing Sam Small might be better candidates for revival, but without any doubt his reputation will rest essentially on the merits of *Lassie Come-Home.*

Lassie was published in 1940, but a version of it had previously appeared as a magazine story, and in the last 50 years it has constantly been translated, adapted for the media, and, in the United States, re-issued with new illustrations and varying degrees of simplification. The 1940 version, running to 240 pages and with drawings by the distinguished animal illustrator Marguerite Kirmse, has the best claims to be treated as the standard text. Reviewers appear to have regarded it as an adult novel, and there are certainly a number of passages, especially those dealing with memories of World War I or the process of law in a Scottish court-room, which would be unlikely to interest young children. However, the central story is very simple; the dog-heroine, though by no means humanized, is by far the most interesting character; and the author is most careful to give vice and virtue their due reward in each chapter. The likelihood is that Knight originally designed the story largely as a pot-boiler which would have the widest possible appeal to people of all ages who enjoy a good read and have no objection to a fairly liberal infusion of sentiment.

Nowadays *Lassie* is usually recommended for children of eight or nine upwards, and I would certainly expect most young readers to enjoy the story, perhaps also to take something of value from it. The author's surely genuine love of dogs and his sense of outrage at the sufferings of the unemployed are likely to make a strong impression on many, while his craftsmanship is generally good enough to avoid the worst pitfalls of didacticism. There is nothing better in the book than the contrasting of humanity and brutality in the chapters featuring Rowlie Palmer, the travelling potter.

All in all, *Lassie* has quite an honourable place in the long line of dog-centred stories accessible to children, a line stretching from *The Dog Crusoe* (Ballantyne) and *Owd Bob* (Ollivant) to *Old Yeller* (Gipson) and *A Dog So Small* (Pearce).

—Alasdair K.D. Campbell

KNIGHT, Frank (Francis Edgar Knight). Has also written as Cedric Salter. British. Born in London, 15 August 1905. Educated at Whitgift Middle School, Croydon, Surrey. Served in the Royal Air Force, 1939–45: navigation instructor. Married Elizabeth Mildred Avice Mather in 1933; two sons and two daughters. Apprentice, 1921–25, and successively Third, Second, and First Mate, 1926–30, Merchant Navy: certified Master Mariner, 1928, and Extra Master Mariner, 1929; worked for marine insurance and yacht broking firms, and as a freelance journalist, 1931–39, 1946–70. Lives in Sussex. Agent: A.M. Heath and Co. Ltd., 79 St. Martin's Lane, London WC2N 4AA, England.

PUBLICATIONS FOR CHILDREN

Fiction

The Albatross Comes Home, illustrated by A.R. Morley. London, Hollis and Carter, 1949.
Four in the Half-Deck, illustrated by S. Drigin. London, Nelson, 1950.
The Island of the Radiant Pearls, illustrated by Stephen Russ. London, Hollis and Carter, 1950.
The Golden Monkey, illustrated by John S. Goodall. London, Macmillan, and New York, St. Martin's Press, 1953.

Strangers in the Half-Deck, illustrated by Robert Johnston. London, Nelson, 1953.
Acting Third Mate, illustrated by Robert Johnston. London, Nelson, 1954.
Voyage to Bengal, illustrated by P.A. Jobson. London, Macmillan, and New York, St. Martin's Press, 1954.
Clippers to China, illustrated by P.A. Jobson. London, Macmillan, and New York, St. Martin's Press, 1955.
Mudlarks and Mysteries, illustrated by P.A. Jobson. London, Macmillan, and New York, St. Martin's Press, 1955.
Two Girls and a Boat (as Cedric Salter), illustrated by Victor Bertoglio. London, Blackie, 1956.
The Bluenose Pirate, illustrated by P.A. Jobson. London, Macmillan, and New York, St. Martin's Press, 1956.
Family on the Tide, illustrated by Geoffrey Whittam. London, Macmillan, and New York, St. Martin's Press, 1956.
Please Keep Off the Mud, illustrated by P.A. Jobson. London, Macmillan, and New York, St. Martin's Press, 1957.
The Partick Steamboat, illustrated by P.A. Jobson. London, Macmillan, 1958; New York, St. Martin's Press, 1959.
He Sailed with Blackbeard, illustrated by P.A. Jobson. London, Macmillan, and New York, St. Martin's Press, 1958.
The Sea Chest: Stories of Adventure at Sea. London, Collins, 1960; New York, Platt and Munk, 1964.
Shadows on the Mud, illustrated by P.A. Jobson. London, Macmillan, 1960; and New York, St. Martin's Press, 1961.
The Slaver's Apprentice, illustrated by P.A. Jobson. London, Macmillan, and New York, St. Martin's Press, 1961.
The Last of Lallow's, illustrated by William Stobbs. London, Macmillan, and New York, St. Martin's Press, 1961.
Clemency Draper, illustrated by William Stobbs. London, Macmillan, and New York, St. Martin's Press, 1963.
The Ship That Came Home, illustrated by Derek Smouthy. London, Benn, 1963.
Up, Sea Beggars!, illustrated by John Lawrence. London, Macdonald, 1964.
Remember Vera Cruz!, illustrated by John Lawrence. London, Macdonald, 1965; New York, Dial Press, 1966.
Kit Baxter's War, illustrated by John Lawrence. London, Macdonald, 1966.
Olaf's Sword, illustrated by Andrew Sier. London, Heinemann, 1969; New York, Watts, 1970.

Other

Captain Anson and the Treasure of Spain. London, Macmillan, and New York, St. Martin's Press, 1959.
The Young Drake, illustrated by Azpelicueta. London, Parrish, 1962; New York, Roy, 1963.
John Harrison, The Man Who Made Navigation Safe. London, Macmillan, and New York, St. Martin's Press, 1962.
The Young Columbus, illustrated by Azpelicueta. London, Parrish, and New York, Roy, 1963.
Stories of Famous Ships, illustrated by Will Nickless. Edinburgh, Oliver and Boyd, 1963; Philadelphia, Westminster Press, 1966.
Stories of Famous Sea Fights, illustrated by Will Nickless. Edinburgh, Oliver and Boyd, 1963; Philadelphia, Westminster Press, 1967.
Stories of Famous Explorers by Sea, illustrated by Will Nickless. Edinburgh, Oliver and Boyd, 1964; Philadelphia, Westminster Press, 1966.
The Young Captain Cook, illustrated by Joan Howell. London, Parrish, 1964; New York, Roy, 1966.
Stories of Famous Explorers by Land, illustrated by Will Nickless. Edinburgh, Oliver and Boyd, 1965; Philadelphia, Westminster Press, 1966.

Stories of Famous Sea Adventures, illustrated by Will Nickless. Edinburgh, Oliver and Boyd, 1966; Philadelphia, Westminster Press, 1967.

Prince of Cavaliers: The Story of the Life and Campaigns of Rupert of the Rhine, illustrated by John Lawrence. London, Macdonald, 1967.

Rebel Admiral: The Life and Exploits of Admiral Lord Cochrane, Tenth Earl of Dundonald, illustrated by John Lawrence. London, Macdonald, 1968.

The Hero (on Lord Nelson), illustrated by John Lawrence. London, Macdonald, 1969.

Russia Fights Japan, illustrated by Roger Phillips. London, Macdonald, 1969.

Ships Then and Now. London, Benn, 1969; New York, Crowell Collier, 1970.

That Rare Captain: Sir Francis Drake, illustrated by John Lawrence. London, Macdonald, 1970.

Christopher Columbus. London, Burns Oates, 1970.

The Dardanelles Campaign, illustrated by Douglas Phillips. London, Macdonald, 1970.

General-at-Sea: The Life of Admiral Robert Blake, illustrated by Douglas Phillips. London, Macdonald, 1971.

Ships. London, Benn, 1973.

True Stories of the Sea, illustrated by Victor Ambrus. London, Benn, 1973.

True Stories of Exploration, illustrated by Victor Ambrus. London, Benn, 1973.

The Clipper Ship. London, Collins, 1973.

True Stories of Spying, illustrated by Victor Ambrus. London, Benn, 1975.

The Golden Age of the Galleon. London, Collins, 1976.

Editor, *They Told Mr. Hakluyt* (from Hakluyt's *Voyages*), illustrated by Charles Keeping. London, Macmillan, and New York, St. Martin's Press, 1964.

Editor, *Captain Cook and the Voyage of the "Endeavour" 1768–1771.* London, Nelson, 1968.

PUBLICATIONS FOR ADULTS

Novels

The Sea's Fool. London, Ward Lock, 1960.

Captains of the Calabar. London, Ward Lock, 1961.

Pekoe Reef. London, Ward Lock, 1962.

Play

The Last Adventures (as Cedric Salter), with Derek Patmore. Istanbul, Ahmet Halik Kitaberi, 1941.

Other

A Beginner's Guide to the Sea (small boat manual). London, Macmillan, and New York, St. Martin's Press, 1955.

The Sea Story, Being a Guide to Nautical Reading from Ancient Times to the Close of the Sailing Ship Era. London, Macmillan, and New York, St. Martin's Press, 1958.

A Guide to Ocean Navigation. London, Macmillan, and New York, St. Martin's Press, 1959.

*

Frank Knight comments:

My two interests have always been the sea and history. My earliest attempts at fiction (*Four in the Half-Deck,* etc.) were derived largely from my own experience at sea and were designed to give boys who might be bitten by the sea-bug some idea of what the life was really like. Later I decided to go further back in time, and here I drew largely upon the reminiscences of old sailors I had known in my youth—their memories of the great days of sail. The result was a series of children's novels (*The Golden Monkey,* etc.) set in various periods of nautical history, early 18th to mid-19th centuries. Later still demand from publishers for more fact and less fiction led me into straight history, biography, etc.

*   *   *

Frank Knight is a prolific writer of adventure novels for older children, historical and modern, on land and sea. He deals with the confusion and brutality of war by means of fast-moving plots full of plausible coincidences. *Kit Baxter's War* plunges 12-year-old Kit into the English Civil War when he rows out to warn a neighbour's ship that the town has been captured by Royalists, and then is unable to get back to shore. His fortunes rise and fall with the fighting over the next three years; at one point he captains his father's old ship into Plymouth; at another he is press-ganged into the navy and is nearly killed at the siege of Lyme Regis. Only at the very end does he discover who murdered his father and solve the other mysteries.

Young Roger in *Remember Vera Cruz!* suffers the discomfort of sailing with John Hawkins in the slave trade, is imprisoned by the Spaniards in Mexico, almost sacrificed by the Mexicans, joins Francis Drake and returns wounded to Essex to rest before going to sea again. In *Up, Sea Beggars!* young John has an English father and a Dutch mother, so joins the 16th-century revolt of the Dutch against Spain. He fights, at first a little bewildered, then more confidently, on land and sea as the Dutch flood the low ground. He rescues a dying priest who is being beaten up by his own side, saves a mysterious Dutch girl, Madeleine, chases a scarred villain who keeps changing his name, is imprisoned and almost hanged by the Spaniards but survives and solves the riddle of Madeleine's true identity.

The Clipper series is concerned with adventure on the high seas in the days of the clipper sailing ships; *The Patrick Steamboat* with the first days of steam; *Captain Anson and the Treasure of Spain* goes back to the 18th century.

The Last of Lallow's has a young heroine, Margaret, the daughter of an English country squire overwhelmed by the English Civil War. *Clemency Draper* also has a heroine, an orphan of character who is not suppressed by the horrors of an 18th-century orphanage or overcome by the temper of her eccentric benefactor. This is a cheerful, almost rollicking story, treating the terrors of the lives of the poor in Dickensian fashion, as young Clemency minds the foundling baby left in the stage coach, helps in the village shop and with solving the mystery of the French refugee.

Please Keep Off the Mud, Family on the Tide, Mudlarks and Mysteries, and *Shadows on the Mud* are modern stories of a brother and sister and their sailing dinghy around Chichester Harbour, told in bright and breezy style. The problems are soon solved against a secure home background. There is much backchat between the children: "The young are born to be blamed," as Brenda remarks when they have turned all the Sailing Club's equipment upsidedown and some adult has thereby lost something. The same local characters appear in all four books, one of which, *Shadows on the Mud,* touches on the problems of boys in an Approved School.

—Margaret Campbell

KONIGSBURG, E(laine) L(obI). American. Born in New York
City, 10 February 1930. Educated at Farrell High School, Pennsylvania; Carnegie Institute of Technology (now Carnegie-Mellon
University) Pittsburgh, B.S. 1952; University of Pittsburgh, 1952–
54. Married David Konigsburg in 1952; two sons and one daughter.
Bookkeeper, Shenago Valley Provision Company, Sharon, Pennsylvania, 1947–48; science teacher, Bartram School, Jacksonville,
Florida, 1954–55, 1960–62. Recipient: American Library Association Newbery Medal, 1968. Lives in Jacksonville, Florida. Address:
c/o Atheneum Publishers, 866 Third Avenue, New York, New York
10022, U.S.A.

PUBLICATIONS FOR CHILDREN (illustrated by the author)

Fiction

Jennifer, Hecate, Macbeth, William McKinley, and Me, Elizabeth.
New York, Atheneum, 1967; as *Jennifer, Hecate, Macbeth and
Me,* London, Macmillan, 1968.
From the Mixed-Up Files of Mrs. Basil E. Frankweiler. New York,
Atheneum, 1967; London, Macmillan, 1969.
About the B'nai Bagels. New York, Atheneum, 1969.
(George). New York, Atheneum, 1970; as *Benjamin Dickinson
Carr and His (George),* London, Penguin, 1974.
Altogether, One at a Time, illustrated by Gail E. Haley and others.
New York, Atheneum, 1971.
A Proud Taste for Scarlet and Miniver. New York, Atheneum,
1973; London, Macmillan, 1974.
The Dragon in the Ghetto Caper. New York, Atheneum, 1974;
London, Macmillan, 1979.
The Second Mrs. Giaconda. New York, Atheneum, 1975; London,
Macmillan, 1976.
Father's Arcane Daughter. New York, Atheneum, 1976; London,
Macmillan, 1977.
Throwing Shadows (stories). New York, Atheneum, 1979.
Journey to an 800 Number. New York, Atheneum, 1982; as *Jour-
ney by First Class Camel,* London, Hamish Hamilton, 1983.
Up from Jericho Tel. New York, Atheneum, 1986.

Play

The Second Mrs. Giaconda, adaptation of her own novel (produced
Jacksonville, Florida, 1976).

* * *

E.L. Konigsburg is a patchy, unpredictable, and fascinating writer.
Her contribution to children's literature can be conservatively assessed as superior, and since she is amazingly inventive and prolific,
it is happily permissible to assume that there will be more very good
things to come.
She is probably best known for her Newbery Medal winner of
1968, *From the Mixed-Up Files of Mrs. Basil E. Frankweiler,* an
inspired piece of wish fulfillment. What youngster with spunk and
imagination hasn't dreamed of having the freedom of a great
museum: liberty to roam at will, *touching everything*; to sleep in the
antique fourposters, bathe in the reflecting pool, and, best of all,
collect the good-luck coins from the fountain? Claudia and Jamie
Kincaid do all this and more. Their well-ordered plan for running
away from home and setting up light housekeeping in New York's
Metropolitan Museum of Art is neatly successful; and they return
safely home in their own good time: a most satisfying adventure.
One would almost hesitate to recommend such an accurate and
enticing escape manual to young readers for fear of inspiring emulation, if the story did not so clearly reveal the discomfort and incon-

venience of camping out in the world of ancient art as well as its
satisfactions. Claudia and Jamie make a success of it, but they are a
convincingly special pair of people.
So are the heroines of *Jennifer, Hecate....* Jennifer is a self-
proclaimed grade-school witch who enlists the narrator, little
Elizabeth, as her apprentice. The half-pretence private world of the
two little girls is amusing and touching, and their characters are
beautifully contrasted. The developing friendship of two lonely city
children is drawn with strokes of feathery delicacy. Jennifer is black,
and Elizabeth white, but the irrelevance of this detail makes its point
more convincingly than any amount of pious sermonizing could do.
About the B'nai Bagels is less touching and amusing than her
earlier books. 12-year-old Mark is aghast when his mother becomes
manager of his Little League baseball team, but the family members
become closer and learn a lot about each other in a season of shared
sportsmanship and problem solving. Then comes *(George).* The title
is a thumbnail description of young Ben's personality; it is split in a
most companionable way. His invisible other self George lives
within Ben's body (in parenthesis, as it were). Ben sees for George,
and George remembers and interprets for Ben. They need each other.
Though most of the adults who have dealings with Ben see him as
neurotic, he gives the impression of doing very well indeed, at least
as long as he has George. *Altogether, One at a Time* is a collection
of four short stories, all having to do with compromise and the need
for coming to terms with reality. From these pithy little pieces it is
quite a leap to *A Proud Taste for Scarlet and Miniver,* a not too
successful historic fantasy based on the life and times of Queen
Eleanor of Aquitaine. The historic facts are accurate, but the flavour
is wrong. Unmistakably, this is a cast of 20th-century masqueraders
in medieval garb.
From the 12th century Konigsburg moves back to the present for
The Dragon in the Ghetto Caper in which a youngster from a closed,
privileged community makes contact with the realities of life outside
his small protected world. His first ventures take him into a black
ghetto where he becomes involved with the local numbers runner.
Andrew J. Chronister is too knowing and cynical for a sheltered
child; this story seems to have been written with one eye on the adult
reader. *The Second Mrs. Giaconda* is a story of Leonardo da Vinci,
as seen by his young servant, the disrespectful, impish Salai, a true
historic personage. Through this brilliant work of historic imagination, Leonardo, the Duke and Duchess of Milan, and the rapscallion
Salai become vividly real and alive.
Back again to the present: Caroline Carmichael was kidnapped 17
years ago. Suddenly a woman appears, claiming to be the missing
heiress. Her arrival upon the scene dramatically changes the lives of
Heidi and Winston, two children who must learn to accept a stranger
as their long-lost half-sister, but a surprise ending reveals the fact
that it is not after all Caroline (*Father's Arcane Daughter*). Another
collection, *Throwing Shadows,* introduces several boy heroes who
discover what it is that makes each of them special and unique; and
each one of them is a character given strength and vitality in the
compass of a few pages. In *Journey to an 800 Number* stuffy young
Bo has been raised as a complete snob by his social-climbing mother.
When, however, he is despatched to spend the period of her second
honeymoon with his father, an itinerant camel-keeper who works the
convention circuit selling rides, Bo meets some extremely fascinating characters, and learns a few startling facts about himself, some
pleasing, some not, in a very amusing and sometimes moving story
of a uniquely American way of life.
In *Up from Jericho Tel* Konigsburg evokes the shade of the late
theatrical great Tallulah Bankhead, as compelling a personality in
death as ever on stage, to send two children, Jeanmarie Troxell and
Malcolm Soo, on a posthumous detective mission. They are required
to bring peace to her restless spirit by discovering which of her
friends betrayed her trust by stealing her treasure, the Regina Stone.
Konigsburg is fitfully brilliant. When she is good, she is extraor-

dinarily so; when she is a wee bit off form, she is still better than most. Her next work will be as much of a surprise package as her first: but the name Konigsburg on the title page will ensure that it will be well worth reading.

—Joan McGrath

KRASILOVSKY, Phyllis (née Manning). American. Born in Brooklyn, New York, 28 August 1926. Educated at Brooklyn College, evenings 1944–47; Cornell University, Ithaca, New York, 1949–50. Married William Krasilovsky in 1948; three daughters and one son. Teacher of children's literature, Marymount College, Tarrytown, New York, 1969–70; creative writing teacher, Katonah Library, New York, 1970–72. Address: 1177 Hardscrabble Road, Chappaqua, New York, 10514, U.S.A.

PUBLICATIONS FOR CHILDREN

Fiction

The Man Who Didn't Wash His Dishes, illustrated by Barbara Cooney. New York, Doubleday, 1950; Kingswood, Surrey, World's Work, 1962.
The Very Little Girl, illustrated by Ninon MacKnight. New York, Doubleday, 1953; Kingswood, Surrey, World's Work, 1959.
The Cow Who Fell in the Canal, illustrated by Peter Spier. New York, Doubleday, 1957; Kingswood, Surrey, World's Work, 1958.
Scaredy Cat, illustrated by Ninon MacKnight. New York, Macmillan, 1959; Kingswood, Surrey, World's Work, 1961.
Benny's Flag, illustrated by W.T. Mars. Cleveland, World, 1960; Kingswood, Surrey, World's Work, 1961.
The Very Little Boy, illustrated by Ninon MacKnight. New York, Doubleday, 1962; Kingswood, Surrey, World's Work, 1963.
Susan Sometimes, illustrated by Abbi Giventer. New York, Macmillan, and London, Macmillan, 1962.
The Girl Who Was a Cowboy, illustrated by Cyndy Szekeres. New York, Doubleday, and Kingswood, Surrey, World's Work, 1965.
The Very Tall Little Girl, illustrated by Olivia Cole. New York, Doubleday, 1969; Kingswood, Surrey, World's Work, 1970.
The Shy Little Girl, illustrated by Trina Schart Hyman. Boston, Houghton Mifflin, 1970; Kingswood, Surrey, World's Work, 1971.
The Popular Girls Club, illustrated by Trina Schart Hyman. New York, Simon and Schuster, 1972; Kingswood, Surrey, World's Work, 1974.
L.C. Is the Greatest. Nashville, Nelson, 1975.
The Man Who Tried to Save Time, illustrated by Marcia Sewall. New York, Doubleday, 1979.
The Man Who Entered a Contest, illustrated by Yuri Salzman. New York, Doubleday, 1980.
The First Tulips in Holland, illustrated by S.D. Schindler. New York, Doubleday, 1982.
The Man Who Cooked for Himself, illustrated by Mamoru Funai. New York, Parents' Magazine Press, 1982.
The Happy Times Storybook, illustrated by Ruth Sanderson. New York, Golden Books, 1987.

*

Phyllis Krasilovsky comments:
I wrote my first book, *The Man Who Didn't Wash His Dishes,* for a four-year-old boy who was dying of cancer. I wrote it as a letter and was told by his mother that he had to hear it "seven times a day." Considering that he was in pain most of the time, I realized I had something there. I have always enjoyed writing books for children, and telling stories to children (I do a lot of speaking and lecturing), but I was not really proud of being a children's book writer until I had to research the field for a course I was invited to give on the history of children's literature at Marymount College. At that time I became overwhelmed with the glory and the scope as well as the value of it, and ever since have been most proud and have felt most like an artist because of the children's books. It is heartwarming to realize that one can open the door to the world of reading by a good story!

* * *

Phyllis Krasilovsky has so mastered the art of providing adventure in small rooms that it would in her case be a deservedly flattering observation to assert that she does indeed create tempests in teapots. In a manner at once picturesque and direct, she snatches excitement out of the ordinary: the growth of flowers; the baking of cakes; the munching of grass—all carry within them expansive delights which she shares with readers and listeners, for it is apparent that she intends to be listened to as well as read.

A tulip bulb (*The First Tulips in Holland*) becomes an improvised history, a romance, a social upheaval, and a character study, all in a matter of 20 pages of text, none of which exceeds a few dozen words. A leisurely intensity compacted within her style enables a great deal to happen without any feeling of being hurried along. The flowers that characterize the Dutch landscape have their roots in Persia and possess a Turkish name. One little seed an everywhere. Why not? The entrancing quality of the tulip has crossed every boundary. In celebration of their universal appeal, Krasilovsky invents the daughter of the mythical first importer of the bulbs drawing crowds to her window, engrossed as they are by the progress of the plants. A once drab landscape flowers with excitement and eventually blossoms forever, or so it seems.

Ordinary-looking seeds can produce dramatic changes. Jack of beanstalk fame exchanged his cow for a few of them, and he ascended the heavens, and after several epic ventures retired a wealthy man. Krasilovsky not only has her seeds, but also a cow (*The Cow Who Fell in the Canal*) who dreams of the world beyond the windmill and the attractive compact cheese farm for which she is the principal producer. From a benign world filled with kindly people (such as populate all of Krasilovsky's books) emerges a restlessness which could be explosive, though never destructive. The dissatisfactions of her characters, and the revolutions they produce, seldom prove unsettling, at least not in the long run. The minds of all her creations show themselves quite capable of assimilating novelty, of learning from their mistakes, and of living, if necessary, in renovated landscapes. Accidents are applauded, as it appears that the whole universe responds happily to the adventure.

The worst that transpires is a series of comic blunders, rectified without any noticeable penalty. One bachelor decides to become super-efficient in order to save time, but the effected changes, which include sleeping in his clothes, have intolerable consequences. He resumes his earlier life-style wiser and happier. Another man who never washes his dishes (but who still insists on using only clean utensils) drinks from vases and the soap dish, amusing postures to say the least. He runs out of space and out of dishes. The conclusion, simple enough, is that it's easier to clean each dish immediately after use. The lessons are always apparent, and probably learned without aid of the narrative. But the muscular prose which turns attention to each of the words, and the continual movement make for a pleasurable experience regardless of the predictability. The experience is worth repeating for the pleasure alone. As Auden says,

"Pleasure is by no means an infallible guide, but it is the least fallible."

Krasilovsky exploits some simple but efficient techniques in a successful search for variety. Using her trip to the Netherlands as a basis for at least two books, she allows a super-stuffed bovine (her job, which she fulfills with zeal, is to eat incessantly) to command the perspective. In *The Cow Who Fell in the Canal* it is Hendrika's desire to see the world beyond her own charming environs that converts her accidental plunge into the canal into an excursion by barge to the city. Here the spectator becomes the spectacle. Crowds gather to gaze on a cow who focusses her sights upon ships, draw bridges, and cobblestones. Pulled ashore, she sniffs bicycles as well as flowers, pleasuring particularly in munching the trimming of a green-ribboned straw hat. But the succession of accidents restores everything to a degree of normalcy. Having seen the world beyond, Hendrika is quite content to return to full-time eating, particularly since she now wears the straw hat. This domestic remnant of the strange places has become the stuff which makes the daily chewing of forage an ideal occupation. She may reflect and dream with a leisure filled with productive industry. And she sports the heady remnant of her trip to the city.

The formula is simple enough. The ordinary provokes a longing for something different. This desire for change in turn results in a happy return to the original condition. But the cycle is no mere retracing of the inevitable. A circle is not necessarily circular to those who traipse along the circumference. To reach the starting point means the completion of a journey, enlarged by experience and the imagination.

—Leonard R. Mendelsohn

KRAUS, Joanna Halpert. American. Born in Portland, Maine, 7 December 1937. Educated at Sarah Lawrence College, Bronxville, New York, 1955–59, A.B. 1959; Westfield College, University of London, 1957–58; University of California, Los Angeles, 1961–63, M.A. 1963; Columbia University, New York, 1967–72, Ed.D. 1972. Married Ted M. Kraus in 1966; one son. Associate director, Baltimore Children's Theatre, 1960–61; drama director, Strathmere School of the Arts, North Gower, Ontario, summers 1961–63; director of drama, New Rochelle Academy, New York, 1962–63; chairwoman, Children's Theatre Showcase, New York, 1963–65; assistant director, Clark Center for Performing Arts, New York, 1963–65; drama teacher, YM-YWHA, New York, 1965–70; Instructor, New York City Community College, 1966–69, Columbia University Teachers College, 1970–71, and State University of New York, Purchase, 1970–72; Lecturer, 1972–73, and Assistant Professor, 1973–79, New York State University College, New Paltz. Associate Professor of Children's Drama, 1979–85, since 1985 Professor of Theatre, and since 1981 coordinator, Arts for Children, State University of New York, Brockport. Recording secretary, Children's Theatre Association of America, 1982–84. Recipient: American Theatre Association Chorpenning Cup, 1971; Creative Artists Public Service grant, 1976. Agent: Patricia Hale Whitton, New Plays Inc., P.O. Box 273, Rowayton, Connecticut 06853. Address: Department of Theatre, State University of New York College, Brockport, New York 14420, U.S.A.

PUBLICATIONS FOR CHILDREN

Fiction

Seven Sound and Motion Stories. Rowayton, Connecticut, New Plays, 1971; revised edition, as *Sound and Motion Stories,* 1980.

Plays

The Ice Wolf (produced New York, 1964). Rowayton, Connecticut, New Plays, 1967.
Mean to Be Free (produced New York, 1968). Rowayton, Connecticut, New Plays, 1968.
Vasalisa (produced Davidson, North Carolina, 1972). Rowayton, Connecticut, New Plays, 1973.
Circus Home (produced Seattle, 1977). Rowayton, Connecticut, New Plays, 1979.
The Dragon Hammer (produced Rowayton, Connecticut, 1977). Included in *The Dragon Hammer, and The Tale of Oniroku,* 1978.
The Dragon Hammer, and The Tale of Oniroku: Two Plays from the Far East, illustrated by Marisabina Russo. Rowayton, Connecticut, New Plays, 1978.
Why Am I Invisible—Especially at Lunch? (Snapshots of Women in Academe), with others (produced Rochester, New York, 1982).
The Last Baron of Arizona (produced Tempe, Arizona, 1984). Tempe, Arizona, Pyracantha Press, 1985.
Kimchi Kid (produced New Brunswick, New Jersey, 1986). Rowayton, Connecticut, New Plays, 1988.
The Shaggy Dog Murder Trial (produced Rochester, New York, 1986). New Orleans, Anchorage Press, 1988.

Other

The Great American Train Ride: Using Creative Dramatics for a Multi-Disciplinary Classroom Project. Rowayton, Connecticut, New Plays, 1975.

Editor, with Vicki Lewin, *In My Mind/In Your Mind: Rochester Kids Write.* Brockport, State University of New York College at Brockport, 1982.

*

Theatrical Activities:
Director: **Plays**—*The Indian Captive,* New Paltz, New York, 1973; *A Christmas Carol,* Brockport, New York, 1979; *Tom Sawyer,* Brockport, 1980.

Joanna Halpert Kraus comments:
I believe that the real purpose of theatre for young people is to illuminate in an exciting way the concerns of children today, to bring greater understanding of both the commonplace and the extraordinary, and to illustrate the concept of alternative choices which exist in everyone's life.

A play, a story, a poem are all personal statements, wrung out of conviction, wrought with care.

I have always worked with concepts and themes that attracted me at the start, such as themes of prejudice and quests for freedom. Children's theatre should touch the spirit, ignite the imagination, and engage the intellect.

*   *   *

Joanna Halpert Kraus has made a considerable name for herself in the fields of children's theatre and creative dramatics, both as an educator and as a playwright. Her best known play, *The Ice Wolf,* is a lyric, provocative, and haunting story of an Eskimo village controlled, mind and body, by shamans and superstitions. A fair-haired child, Anatou, is born to parents who reject her because of village taboos, and the play is essentially a well-honed, undogmatic plea for sanity, humanity, mercy, justice, and compassion. The flow of language and action is at times exquisite, and the play, unlike many contemporary plays for children, has value, in Horatian terms, to educate and entertain both children and adults. This critical evaluation is true of all Kraus's works, especially a play entitled *Mean to Be Free* which is a re-telling of the story of Harriet Tubman and the Underground Railway. The play is accurate and well-researched, but the intensity of the drama goes beyond facts. Early in the play the following speech summarizes the intensity of action, feeling, and dialogue that underlie the entire play:

> But this freedom train is goin' a long way. And the road ain't easy. You've got to sleep by day, walk by night. And never let folks know you're about. Watch me. You'll learn to hide as well as I can. You gotta walk so quiet that there's not even a sound of your bare feet on the earth. When you sleep, you gotta be so quiet that there's not a sound of breathing. Not a cough or a sneeze. Once this train starts, ain't no turning back.

Another of Kraus's works is a three-act, technically involved play based on a legend of wonder about the evil Baba Yaga, the grandmother of all witches, and Vasalisa, the adventurous daughter of a fur merchant in 17th-century Russia. Vasalisa is a modification of Cinderella, Pandora, and Psyche, and she manages to thwart Baba Yaga's guile by truth and goodness, although the play is not dogmatic. *Vasalisa* is framed by an interesting use of prologue and epilogue that involve a Skomoroki or Russian troubadour-acting company, and the entire work is rich with balalaika music, song, dance, and many visual effects. What should be more apparent about Kraus's plays is that they are packed with action, visual effects, and highly believable spirited dialogue. This is perhaps nowhere more apparent than in the anthology *Seven Sound and Motion Stories* which includes "The Winner," based on the Aesop fable of the sun and the wind; "Chaunteecleer," a retelling of a Chaucerian tale; "The First Night of Sleep," based on the African myth about Ananse the Spider; three contemporary stories; and a science fiction tale entitled "Veritas." Also included is the one-act play "The Tale of Oniroku," a retelling of a Japanese fairy tale. Each of these tales is tight, detailed, and self-contained.

—Rachel Fordyce

KRAUS, Robert. Also writes as E.S. Silly; I.M. Tubby. American. Born in Milwaukee, Wisconsin, 21 June 1925. Attended Layton Art School, Milwaukee, 1942; Art Students' League, New York, 1945. Married Pamela Wong in 1946; two sons. Cartoonist and illustrator: work published in *Saturday Evening Post, Esquire,* and *New Yorker.* Founding President and publisher, Windmill Books, 1966–83; from 1972, founding President, Springfellow Books, New York. Address: c/o Greenwillow Books, 105 Madison Avenue, New York, New York 10016, U.S.A.

PUBLICATIONS FOR CHILDREN

Fiction

Junior, The Spoiled Cat, illustrated by the author. New York and London, Oxford University Press, 1955.
All the Mice Came, illustrated by the author. New York, Harper, 1955.
Ladybug, Ladybug!, illustrated by the author. New York, Harper, 1957.
I, Mouse, illustrated by the author. New York, Harper, 1958.
Mouse at Sea, illustrated by the author. New York, Harper, 1959.
The Littlest Rabbit, illustrated by the author. New York, Harper, 1961.
The Trouble with Spider, illustrated by the author. New York, Harper, 1962.
Miranda's Beautiful Dream, illustrated by the author. New York, Harper, 1964.
Penguin's Pal, illustrated by the author. New York, Harper, 1964.
The Bunny's Nutshell Library (The Silver Dandelion, Juniper, The First Robin, Springfellow's Parade), illustrated by the author. New York, Harper, 4 vols., 1965.
Amanda Remembers, illustrated by the author. New York, Harper, 1965.
My Son, The Mouse, illustrated by the author. New York, Harper, 1966.
The Little Giant, illustrated by the author. New York, Harper, 1967.
Unidentified Flying Elephant, illustrated by Whitney Darrow. New York, Windmill, 1968.
The Children Who Got Married, illustrated by Edna Eicke. New York, Windmill, 1969.
Hello, Hippopotamus, illustrated by the author. New York, Windmill, 1969.
Rumple Nose-Dimple and the Three Horrible Snaps, illustrated by Mischa Richter. New York, Windmill, 1969.
The Christmas Cookie Sprinkle Snitcher, illustrated by Virgil Partch. New York, Windmill, 1969.
How Spider Saved Christmas, illustrated by the author. New York, Windmill, 1970.
Daddy Long Ears, illustrated by the author. New York, Windmill, 1970.
Whose Mouse Are You?, illustrated by Jose Aruego. New York, Macmillan, 1970; London, Hamish Hamilton, 1971.
Bunya the Witch, illustrated by Mischa Richter. New York, Windmill, 1971.
The Tail Who Wagged the Dog, illustrated by the author. New York, Windmill, 1971.
Ludwig, The Dog Who Snored Symphonies, illustrated by Virgil Partch. New York, Windmill, 1971.
Pip Squeak, Mouse in Shining Armor, illustrated by Richard Oldden. New York, Windmill, 1971.
Lillian, Morgan, and Teddy, illustrated by Edna Eicke. New York, Windmill, 1971.
Leo the Late Bloomer, illustrated by Jose Aruego. New York, Windmill, 1971; London, Hamish Hamilton, 1972.
The Tree That Stayed Up until Next Christmas, illustrated by Edna Eicke. New York, Windmill, 1972.
Good Night, Little A.B.C., with N.M. Bodecker, illustrated by Bodecker. New York, Springfellow, 1972; London, Cape, 1974.
Good Night, Richard Rabbit, illustrated by N.M. Bodecker. New York, Springfellow, 1972; London, Cape, 1974.
Milton the Early Riser, illustrated by Jose Aruego and Ariane Dewey. New York, Windmill, 1972; London, Hamish Hamilton, 1974.
Big Brother. New York, Parents' Magazine Press, 1973.
How Spider Saved Halloween. New York, Parents' Magazine Press, 1973.
Pip Squeaks Through, illustrated by Richard Oldden. New York, Springfellow, 1973.
Poor Mister Splinterfitz!, illustrated by Robert Byrd. New York, Springfellow, 1973.
Herman the Helper, illustrated by Jose Aruego and Ariane Dewey. New York, Windmill, 1974; London, Kestrel, 1977.
Rebecca Hatpin, illustrated by Robert Byrd. New York, Windmill,

1974.

Owliver, illustrated by Jose Aruego and Ariane Dewey. New York, Windmill, 1974; London, Kestrel, 1976.

Pinchpenny Mouse, illustrated by Robert Byrd. New York, Windmill, 1974; London, Andersen Press, 1976.

The Night-Lite Story Book, illustrated by N.M. Bodecker. New York, Windmill, 1975.

I'm a Monkey, illustrated by Hilary Knight. New York, Windmill, 1975.

Three Friends, illustrated by Jose Aruego and Ariane Dewey. New York, Windmill, 1975; London, Kestrel, 1978.

The Gondolier of Venice, illustrated by Robert Byrd. New York, Windmill, 1976; London, Andersen Press, 1977.

Kittens for Nothing, illustrated by Diane Paterson. New York, Windmill, 1976.

Boris Bad Enough, illustrated by Jose Aruego and Ariane Dewey. New York, Windmill, 1976; London, Hardy, 1983.

The Good Mousekeeper, illustrated by Hilary Knight. New York, Windmill, 1977.

Noel the Coward, illustrated by Jose Aruego and Ariane Dewey. New York, Windmill, 1977.

Springfellow, illustrated by Sam Savitt. New York, Windmill, 1978.

The Detectives of London, with Bruce Kraus, illustrated by Robert Byrd. New York, Windmill, 1978; London, Andersen Press, 1979.

Another Mouse to Feed, illustrated by Jose Aruego and Ariane Dewey. New York, Windmill, 1980.

Mouse Work, illustrated by Jose Aruego and Ariane Dewey. New York, Windmill, 1980.

Animal Families. New York, Windmill, 1980.

Mert the Blurt, illustrated by Jose Aruego and Ariane Dewey. New York, Windmill, 1980.

Puppet Pal Books (*Herman the Helper Lends a Hand, Leo the Late Bloomer Bakes a Cake, Milton the Early Riser Takes a Trip, Owliver the Actor Takes a Bow*), illustrated by Jose Aruego and Ariane Dewey. New York, Windmill, 4 vols., 1981; London, Methuen, 4 vols., 1982.

The King's Trousers, illustrated by Fred Gwynne. New York, Windmill, 1981.

How Spider Saved Turkey, illustrated by the author. New York, Windmill, 1981.

Tubby Books (as I.M. Tubby; *I'm a Little Tugboat* [*Fish, Baby, House, Airplane, Choo-Choo*]), illustrated by the author. New York, Windmill, 6 vols., 1981–82.

Leo the Late Bloomer Takes a Bath, illustrated by Jose Aruego and Ariane Dewey. New York, Windmill, 1981.

Herman the Helper Cleans Up, illustrated by Jose Aruego and Ariane Dewey. New York, Windmill, 1981.

Squeaky Books (as E.S. Silly; *Squeaky, Squeaky's One Man Band*), illustrated by the author. New York, Windmill, 2 vols., 1982.

Springfellow's Parade. New York, Windmill, 1982.

Pudgy Car Board Books (*Bumpy the Car, Tony the Tow Truck, Freddy the Fire Engine*). New York, Grosset and Dunlap, 1985.

Mrs. Elmo of Elephant House, illustrated by the author. New York, Delacorte Press, 1986.

How Spider Saved Valentine's Day, illustrated by the author. New York, Scholastic, 1986.

Where Are You Going, Little Mouse?, illustrated by Jose Aruego and Ariane Dewey. New York, Greenwillow, and London, MacRae, 1986.

Come Out and Play, Little Mouse, illustrated by Jose Aruego and Ariane Dewey. New York, Greenwillow, and London, MacRae, 1987.

Babytown Board Books (*The Babytown Express, Meet the Babies, A Sunny Day in Babytown, Welcome to Babytown*), illustrated by the author. New York, Simon and Schuster, 4 vols., 1987.

Happy Plumpy Board Books (*Happy Farm* and *Happy City*). New York, Simon and Schuster, 2 vols., 1987.

The Hoodwinking of Mrs. Elmo, illustrated by the author. New York Delacorte Press, 1987.

Spider's First Day at School, illustrated by the author. New York, Scholastic, 1987.

How Spider Saved Easter, illustrated by the author. New York, Hastings House, 1988.

Spider's Hometown, illustrated by the author. New York, Scholastic, 1988.

Mummy Dearest Creepy Hollow Whoooooooodunnit Series (*Mummy Knows Best, Mummy Vanishes, Private Eyes Don't Blink, The Phantom of Creepy Hollow*), illustrated by the author. New York, Warner, 4 vols., 1988.

Creepy Hollow Ghostly Glowing Haunted House, illustrated by the author. New York, Warner, 1988.

Screamy Mimi, illustrated by Hilary Knight. New York, Simon and Schuster, 1988.

Phil the Ventriloquist, illustrated by the author. New York, Greenwillow, 1989.

Verse

Shaggy Fur Face, illustrated by Virgil Partch. New York, Windmill, 1971.

Good Night, Little One, illustrated by N.M. Bodecker. New York, Springfellow, 1972; London, Cape, 1974.

The Old-Fashioned Raggedy Ann and Andy ABC Book, edited by Pam Kraus, illustrated by Johnny Gruelle. New York, Windmill, 1981.

Other

Animal Etiquette, illustrated by Whitney Darrow. New York, Windmill, 1969.

Don't Talk to Strange Bears, illustrated by Edward Koren. New York, Windmill, 1969.

The Rabbit Brothers. New York, Anti-Defamation League of B'nai B'rith, 1969.

Vip's Mistake Book, illustrated by Virgil Partch. New York, Windmill, 1970.

Night-Lite Calendar 1976, 1979, 1980, illustrated by Hilary Knight. New York, Dutton, 3 vols., 1976–79.

Mickey Mouse Calendar 1977, 1980, illustrated by Walt Disney Studios. New York, Dutton, 2 vols., 1976–79.

See the Moon, illustrated by the author. New York, Windmill, 1980.

Box of Brownies (*The Brownies' ABC's* [*Joke Book, Song and Dance Book*], *You Can Count on Brownies*), with Pam Kraus, illustrated by Palmer Cox. New York, Windmill, 4 vols., 1980; London, Hamish Hamilton, 4 vols., 1981.

See the Christmas Lights, illustrated by Pam Kraus. New York, Windmill, 1981.

Editor, *Nanook of the North*, by Robert J. Flaherty. New York, Windmill, 1971.

Editor, *Reggie Jackson's Scrapbook.* New York, Windmill, 1978.

*

Manuscript Collection: Syracuse University, New York.

Illustrator: *Red Fox and the Hungry Tiger* by Paul Anderson, 1962; *Rabbit and Skunk and the Big Fight*, 1964, *Rabbit and Skunk and the Spooks*, 1967, and *Rabbit and Skunk and the Scary Rock*, 1970, all by Carla Stevens; *Animail* by Cleveland Amory, 1976.

Robert Kraus comments:

I am fortunate that parents and children like my books and enjoy my sense of humor. I resumed illustrating my own stories in 1983 when I gave up publishing Windmill Books. I now illustrate all of my own books since I was trained as an artist and enjoy writing/drawing. It is the only way for me to fully express my stories. I have many more books planned for author/illustrator Robert Kraus. God bless him!

*   *   *

There is a consistency about Robert Kraus's storybooks that is comforting. Picking up one of his new offerings is always like greeting an old friend.

Although there's a sprinkling of other furry beings and a human or two, mice populate most of his works, joining his rabbits, frogs, teddy bears, and most recently (and his professed favorites) spiders. Kraus has picked the more helpless creatures—those vulnerable and dependent on the kindness of others for their existence—with which children can so readily identify. And they always triumph in the most delightful and unexpected way. Unexpected—that's a key to a Kraus book. Just when you're sure you know the ending, he applies a mild surprise that can both reassure a child and knock a few pegs from beneath a blasé grown-up.

In *Another Mouse to Feed*, Mr. and Mrs. Mouse figure 30 children are quite enough. She's taken on an extra job as a rollerskating instructor and he's holding down three jobs, and they're always too tired to enjoy the children they have. Then Mouse Thirty One appears on their doorstep. The children rally and take on small after-school jobs and help around the house. In fact, the Mouse family gets so comfortable that Mr. and Mrs. Mouse are able to pursue only those careers they really want and enjoy the family, too. In an ever so gentle way we see that family cooperation gives everyone a little time to relax and enjoy life and each other. In *The Good Mousekeeper* it's a cat who loves mice, but as foster children, not as meals. She cares for them lovingly and teaches her neighbor, Mrs. Tabby, not to "covet her neighbor's mice." Kraus demonstrates the beauty of foster love. In *Where Are You Going, Little Mouse?* a mouse runs away from home in search of a "better" family, only to discover (while hacking through the jungle and crossing the desert by camel) that he misses his own family. Of course in the end they are reunited, with a new appreciation of love.

One of my favorites is not a mouse, though, but a technicolor creature, *Mert the Blurt,* who blurts out family business to the neighbors: Aunt Martha goes skinny dipping; Aunt Patti wears contact lenses. His family worries just what will become of Mert. But in that typical Kraus twist, Mert becomes a successful television newscaster, making his family so proud of him. Along the same lines, *Owliver* is continually pretending day and night, performing in the mode of Sir Laurence Olivier. His mother encourages his talent with acting lessons and praise. His father, preferring his son take up medicine or the law, gives his son appropriate toys. But Kraus has the last laugh on all of us with aspirations for our offspring when the young owl grows up to become a fireman.

Kraus's messages are abundantly clear in his "human tales," too. In *The King's Trousers* he pokes fun at our feelings about the powerful. Bud the royal window-washer spreads the news that the king puts his trousers on one leg at a time—just like the rest of them. His subjects were furious that the king was no better than they. The king switches to royal robes and the disgruntled subjects, satisfied that he's different from them, serve him loyally, from then on.

Whether he writes about people or animals, Kraus makes us see ourselves a little more clearly.

—Mary Blount Christian

———

KRAUSS, Ruth (Ida). American. Born in Baltimore, Maryland, 25 July 1911. Educated in public elementary schools; at Peabody Institute of Music, Baltimore; New School for Social Research, New York; Maryland Institute of Art, Baltimore; Parsons School of Art, New York, graduate. Married David Johnson Leisk (i.e., Crockett Johnson q.v.) in 1940 (died 1975). Address: c/o Scholastic Books, 730 Broadway, New York, New York 10003, U.S.A.

PUBLICATIONS FOR CHILDREN

Fiction

A Good Man and His Good Wife, illustrated by Ad Reinhardt. New York, Harper, 1944; revised edition, 1962.
The Carrot Seed, illustrated by Crockett Johnson. New York, Harper, 1945.
The Great Duffy, illustrated by Richter. New York, Harper, 1946.
The Growing Story, illustrated by Phyllis Rowand. New York, Harper, 1947.
Bears, illustrated by Phyllis Rowand. New York, Harper, 1948.
The Happy Day, illustrated by Marc Simont. New York, Harper, 1949.
The Big World and the Little House, illustrated by Marc Simont. New York, Schuman, 1949.
The Backward Day, illustrated by Marc Simont. New York, Harper, and London, Hamish Hamilton, 1950.
The Bundle Book, illustrated by Helen Stone. New York, Harper, 1951.
A Hole Is to Dig: A First Book of First Definitions, illustrated by Maurice Sendak. New York, Harper, 1952; London, Hamish Hamilton, 1963.
A Very Special House, illustrated by Maurice Sendak. New York, Harper, 1953.
I'll Be You and You Be Me, illustrated by Maurice Sendak. New York, Harper, 1954.
How to Make an Earthquake, illustrated by Crockett Johnson. New York, Harper, 1954.
Charlotte and the White Horse, illustrated by Maurice Sendak. New York, Harper, 1955; London, Bodley Head, 1977.
Is This You?, with Crockett Johnson, illustrated by Johnson. New York, Scott, 1955; London, Pitman, 1966.
I Want to Paint My Bathroom Blue, illustrated by Maurice Sendak. New York, Harper, 1956.
The Birthday Party, illustrated by Maurice Sendak. New York, Harper, 1957.
Monkey Day, illustrated by Phyllis Rowand. New York, Harper, 1957.
Somebody Else's Nut Tree and Other Tales from Children, illustrated by Maurice Sendak. New York, Harper, 1958.
A Moon or a Button, illustrated by Remy Charlip. New York, Harper, 1959.
Open House for Butterflies, illustrated by Maurice Sendak. New York, Harper, and London, Hamish Hamilton, 1960.
"Mama, I Wish I Was Snow" "Child, You'd Be Very Cold," illustrated by Ellen Raskin. New York, Atheneum, 1962.
Eye Nose Fingers Toes, illustrated by Elizabeth Schneider. New York, Harper, 1964.
The Little King, The Little Queen, The Little Monster, and Other Stories You Can Make Up Yourself, illustrated by the author. New York, Scholastic, 1966.
This Thumbprint: Words and Thumbprints, illustrated by the author. New York, Harper, 1967.
The Happy Egg, illustrated by Crockett Johnson. New York, Scholastic, 1967.
Little Boat Lighter Than a Cork, illustrated by Esther Gilman.

Westport, Connecticut, and New York, Magic Circle Press-Walker, 1976.
Minestrone: A Ruth Krauss Selection, illustrated by the author. New York, Greenwillow, 1981.
Big and Little, illustrated by Mary Szilagyi.   New York, Scholastic, 1987.

Verse

I Can Fly, illustrated by Mary Blair.   New York, Simon and Schuster, 1950.
A Bouquet of Littles, illustrated by Jane Flora.   New York, Harper, 1963.
What a Fine Day for..., music by Al Carmines, illustrated by Remy Charlip.   New York, Parents' Magazine Press, 1967.
I Write It, illustrated by Mary Chalmers.   New York, Harper, 1970.
Everything under a Mushroom, illustrated by Margot Tomes.   New York, Four Winds Press, 1974.
Somebody Spilled the Sky, illustrated by Eleanor Hazard.   New York, Greenwillow, 1979.

PUBLICATIONS FOR ADULTS

Poem-Plays

The Cantilever Rainbow.   New York, Pantheon, 1965.
There's a Little Ambiguity Over There among the Bluebells and Other Theatre Poems.   New York, Something Else Press, 1968.
If Only.   Eugene, Oregon, Toad Press, 1969.
Under Twenty.   Eugene, Oregon, Toad Press, 1970.
Love and the Invention of Punctuation.   Lenox, Massachusetts, Bookstore Press, 1973.
This Breast Gothic.   Lenox, Massachusetts, Bookstore Press, 1973.
If I Were Freedom (produced Annandale-on-Hudson, New York, 1976).
Re-examination of Freedom (produced Boston, 1976).   West Branch, Iowa, Toothpaste Press, 1981.
Under 13.   Lenox, Massachusetts, Bookstore Press, 1976.
When I Walk I Change the Earth.   Providence, Rhode Island, Burning Deck, 1978.
Small Black Lambs Wandering in the Red Poppies (produced New York, 1982).
Ambiguity 2nd (produced Boston, 1985).

Productions include *A Beautiful Day, There's a Little Ambiguity Over There among the Bluebells, Re-Examination of Freedom, Newsletter, The Cantilever Rainbow, In a Bull's Eye, Pineapple Play, Quartet, A Show, A Play—It's a Girl!, Onward, Duet* (or *Yellow Umbrella*), *Drunk Boat, If Only, This Breast,* many with music by Al Carmines, Bill Dixon, and Don Heckman, produced in New York, New Haven, Boston, and other places, since 1964.

*

Manuscript Collection: Dupont School, Wilmington, Delaware.

*   *   *

After a long silence, Ruth Krauss was heard from again in 1976 when she published a new picture book. *Little Boat Lighter Than a Cork* is almost as tiny as its title, a walnut-shell craft in which a baby sails on a fantasy voyage. The simple, unpunctuated text is a lyrical lullaby and would be greeted as exceptional had it come from anyone else. But since *Little Boat* is by Krauss, it must be noted that it isn't a patch on the marvels of innovation she is capable of. In only one

instance of the new text does she dart into an aside reminiscent of her classics. That's when the infant passenger says to the boat, "I will rock you for the small streams and big rivers and for dolphins..." and interrupts the litany with "...for a red apple popping out of the water or is it the sun."

Her faithful following who have found Krauss's books virtual magnets since the appearance of her first in 1944 must miss the mirthful surprises she had previously offered. Millions of readers treasure their well-worn copies of *A Hole Is to Dig: A First Book of First Definitions.* People lined up in book stores to invest in the fun that book offered during the 1950's. Kids (and the kids still alive in adults) felt the pleasant shock of recognition when they met Krauss, an author who knew what they did: of course a hole is to dig; eyebrows are to go over eyes, a face is so you can make faces, a package is to look inside, etc. Another of her welcome earlier productions was *The Carrot Seed,* still enthusiastically read and listened to in a musical adaptation on a recording. The hero is a boy who is the ultimate in passive resistance and inflexible faith. Everyone tells the lad that the carrot seed he plants won't come up. He answers not a word. He bides his time. He pulls the weeds which spring up around his plant and he waters it. For a long time, nothing happens. "And then, one day, a carrot came up. Just as the little boy knew it would."

With *I'll Be You and You Be Me, Somebody Else's Nut Tree and Other Tales,* and her other satisfying stories, Krauss conveys the viewpoint of a child, the awesome imagination of a little one who knows that anything is possible. One of her most pixieish books is *The Little King, The Little Queen, The Little Monster, and Other Stories You Can Make Up Yourself* in which the same things happen to three characters who are each granted a wish by a good fairy. The repetition of plot and sameness of language here are veritable meat for the readers' fantasy feasts. The dessert is the author's wind-up, a hint to her audience that they write their own tales, and her additional suggestions: "The Little Elephant," "The Little Egg," "The Little?"

Regardless of what she may or may not contribute to literature in the future, Krauss has already earned lasting fame with the creation of timeless works, clearly understood and valued by everyone who speaks the *lingua franca* of childhood.

—Jean F. Mercier

KRUMGOLD, Joseph (Quincy). American. Born in Jersey City, New Jersey, 9 April 1908. Educated at New York University, B.A. 1928. Married Helen Litwin in 1946; one son. Press agent, writer, and producer, MGM, Paramount, Columbia, Republic and RKO pictures, New York, Hollywood, and Paris, 1929–40; producer and director, Film Associates, New York, and Office of War Information, 1940–46; President in charge of production, Palestine Films, New York and Jerusalem, 1946–52; owner of Joseph Krumgold Productions, 1952–60; writer, director, and producer, CBS, NBC, National Educational Television, and Westinghouse television, New York, Rome, and Istanbul, 1960–70. Recipient: American Library Association Newbery Medal, 1954, 1960; film prizes at Venice, Edinburgh, and Prague festivals. *Died 10 July 1980.*

PUBLICATIONS FOR CHILDREN

Fiction

Sweeney's Adventures, illustrated by Tibor Gergely.   New York, Random House, 1942.

...and Now Miguel, illustrated by Jean Charlot. New York, Crowell, 1953.
Onion John, illustrated by Symeon Shimin. New York, Crowell, 1959; London, Lutterworth Press, 1964.
Henry 3, illustrated by Alvin Smith. New York, Atheneum, 1967.
The Most Terrible Turk, illustrated by Michael Hampshire. New York, Crowell, 1969.

PUBLICATIONS FOR ADULTS

Novel

Thanks to Murder. New York, Vanguard Press, and London, Gollancz, 1935.

Plays

Screenplays: *The Blackmailer*, with Lee Loeb and Harold Buchman, 1936; *Adventure in Manhattan*, with others, 1936; *Lady from Nowhere*, with others, 1936; *Lone Wolf Returns*, 1936; *Jim Hanvey—Detective*, with Olive Cooper, 1937; *Join the Marines*, with Olive Cooper and Karl Brown, 1937; *Speed to Burn* (contributor), 1938; *Lady Behave*, with Olive Cooper, 1938; *Main Street Lawyer*, 1939; *The Phantom Submarine*, 1940; *The Crooked Road*, with others, 1940; *Seven Miles from Alcatraz*, 1942; *Hidden Hunger* (documentary), 1942; *Magic Town*, with Robert Riskin, 1947; *Dream No More*, 1950; *And Now Miguel* (documentary), 1953; *Adventure in the Bronx; The Promise;* and others.

Other

Where Do We Grow from Here: An Essay on Children's Literature. New York, Atheneum, 1968.

Editor, *The Oxford Furnace 1741–1925* (local history). Belvidere, New Jersey, Warren County Historical Society, 1975.

*

Joseph Krumgold commented:

(1978) The three most widely read books,...*and Now Miguel, Onion John,* and *Henry 3,* deal with a similar theme. They are a trilogy devoted to the drama of confirmation, that turn of life when a child is acknowledged to be grown-up. Whether this happens through ritual or less formally, it's a two-way process. The child is examined by the adult for his maturity and understanding. And—less obviously—the community is examined, its wisdom and values are measured with all innocence by the child. It is this fresh insight, the test we're put to by our young, that determines the shape of these stories.

*   *   *

In his two best books for children, ...*and Now Miguel* and *Onion John,* Joseph Krumgold succeeds in directing the genre of realistic fiction for a young audience to the same purpose of exposition and exploration that identifies the best novels for adults.

...*and Now Miguel* explores the developing awareness of a Mexican boy who lives on a sheep farm and, through Miguel's consciousness, gives us the texture and design of such a life. Krumgold was also a professional film-maker and the subject of this widely acclaimed book evolved during a film-making trip when Krumgold had the opportunity to live among families like Miguel's. Working as a film-maker yielded not only subject matter, but also particular techniques. While Krumgold's writing is not really

"cinematic," he had an intensely visual sense for the telling detail which may well have evolved from his experience with the camera.

In some ways *Onion John* is a more unusual book, dealing, again through the consciousness of a young boy, with the way in which Onion John, an eccentric East European, part-hobo, part-wizard, interrelates with the highly conventional expectations of small-town Middle America. Onion John has lived happily for years in his tiny self-built house using candles as his only form of lighting and storing his vegetables in numerous bathtubs in his living room. The townspeople decide to build Onion John a "proper" house. No one realises that such a house embodies a mass of expectations about how everyday life is to be conducted and eventually Onion John, unable to accommodate himself to these narrow expectations, sadly takes to the road again. A story of this kind is unusual in a book for children and Krumgold sustains a moving narrative without dropping into sentimentality.

More alert readers are likely to find Krumgold's preoccupations excessively macho. He was, for example, almost exclusively concerned with father-son relationships and, rather laughably, in *Henry 3* manages to discover that the flabby businessmen are really heroes under the skin when faced with a hurricane, while he turns their wives into caricatures of weakness and greed, hysterical over the loss of their furs. In this respect he can be viewed as the inheritor of such early writers of the boys' adventure tale as R.M. Ballantyne and G.A. Henty who, like Krumgold, celebrate a bonding of boys and men on an exclusion of females.

Krumgold's contribution rests less on such preoccupations than on his development of sophisticated narrative techniques. Few writers for children use the first person narrative with comparable conviction or have a comparable sense of how that form of narrative may be employed as a lens for exploring the world surrounding the "I."

—Gillian Thomas

KUSKIN, Karla (née Seidman). Has also written as Nicholas Charles. American. Born in New York City, 17 July 1932. Educated at Elizabeth Irwin High School; Antioch College, Yellow Springs, Ohio, 1950–53; Yale University, New Haven, Connecticut, 1953–55, B.F.A. 1955. Married Charles Kuskin in 1955; one son and one daughter. Recipient: National Council of Teachers of English award, for verse, 1979; New York Academy of Sciences award, 1980. Agent: Harriet Wasserman, Russell and Volkening, 551 Fifth Avenue, New York, New York 10017. Address: 96 Joralemon Street, Brooklyn, New York 11201, U.S.A.

PUBLICATIONS FOR CHILDREN (illustrated by the author)

Fiction

Just Like Everyone Else. New York, Harper, 1959.
Which Horse Is William? New York, Harper, 1959.
The Walk the Mouse Girls Took. New York and London, Harper, 1967.
Watson, The Smartest Dog in the U.S.A. New York, Harper, 1968.
What Did You Bring Me? New York, Harper, 1973.
A Space Story, illustrated by Marc Simont. New York, Harper, 1978.
The Philharmonic Gets Dressed, illustrated by Marc Simont. New York, Harper, 1982.

The Dallas Titans Get Ready for Bed, illustrated by Marc Simont. New York, Harper, 1986.
Jerusalem, Shining Still, illustrated by David Frampton.   New York, Harper, 1987.

Verse

Roar and More.   New York, Harper, 1956.
James and the Rain.   New York, Harper, 1957; London, Lutterworth Press, 1960.
In the Middle of the Trees.   New York, Harper, 1958.
The Animals and the Ark.   New York, Harper, 1958; London, Lutterworth Press, 1961.
Square as a House.   New York, Harper, 1960.
The Bear Who Saw the Spring.   New York, Harper, 1961.
All Sizes of Noises.   New York, Harper, 1962.
How Do You Get from Here to There? (as Nicholas Charles).   New York, Macmillan, and London, Macmillan, 1962.
Alexander Soames: His Poems.   New York, Harper, 1962.
ABCDEFGHIJKLMNOPQRSTUVWXYZ.   New York, Harper, 1963.
The Rose on My Cake.   New York and London, Harper, 1964.
Sand and Snow.   New York, Harper, 1965.
Jane Anne June Spoon and Her Very Adventurous Trip to the Moon (as Nicholas Charles).   New York, Norton, 1966.
In the Flaky Frosty Morning.   New York, Harper, 1969.
Any Me I Want to Be.   New York and London, Harper, 1972.
Near the Window Tree: Poems and Notes.   New York, Harper, 1975.
A Boy Had a Mother Who Bought Him a Hat.   Boston, Houghton Mifflin, 1976.
Herbert Hated Being Small.   Boston, Houghton Mifflin, 1979.
Dogs and Dragons, Trees and Dreams.   New York, Harper, 1980.
Night Again.   Boston, Little Brown, 1981.
Something Sleeping in the Hall.   New York, Harper, 1985.

PUBLICATIONS FOR ADULTS

Plays

Screenplays: *What Do You Mean by Design?,* 1973; *An Electric Talking Picture,* 1973.

*

Illustrator: *Xingu* by Violette and John Viertel, 1959; *Who Woke the Sun?* by M.S. Seidman, 1960; *Sing for Joy* by Norman and Margaret Mealy, 1961; *The Dog That Lost His Family* by Jean Lee Latham and Bee Lewi, 1961; *Oh Ye Jigs and Juleps,* 1962, and *Credos and Quips,* 1964, both by Virginia Hudson; *Harrison Loved His Umbrella,* by Rhoda Levine, 1964; *Boris the Lopsided Bear* by Gladys Schmitt, 1966; *Look at Me* by Marguerita Rudolph, 1967; *Big Enough* by Sherry Kafka, 1970; *What Shall We Do, and Allee Galloo!* edited by Marie Winn and Allan Miller, 1970; *The Monkey and the Crocodile* by Ellen Babbit, 1984; *Stone Soup* by Marcia Brown, 1984; *The Monster Who Grew Small* by Joan Grant, 1984.

Narrator: *Poetry Explained* (film strip), 1980.

Karla Kuskin comments:
   The first book I wrote and illustrated for children I printed on a small motor-driven press when I was a graphic arts student at Yale University. That was *Roar and More* in which I used typography to represent animal noises. Since then my books have ranged from simple, rather humorous picture books for very young children to

books of poetry for somewhat older readers. I write from imagination and memories of my own childhood—what made me laugh, what I loved reading. I am particularly fond of reading and writing poetry and think that it is something young children turn to quite naturally if they are not frightened away by overemphasis on unfamiliar forms and subject matter. In all my books, I try both to communicate my own thoughts and moods to young readers and also to elicit a response from them.

*   *   *

   Since Karla Kuskin's first book, a participative poetry book entitled *Roar and More,* this talented author-illustrator has worked imaginatively and successfully with a number of literary genres, always for younger children. These have included an alphabet book (*ABCDEFGHIJKLMNOPQRSTUVWXYZ*), a fanciful animal tale (*Watson, The Smartest Dog in the U.S.A.*), a concept book (*Square as a House*), and a cumulative rhyming tale (*James and the Rain*), much in the tradition of Marjorie Flack. However, it is with her short verse that Kuskin has made her most memorable contribution to literature for children. Beginning with *In the Middle of the Trees,* we find an outpouring of short poems which are universally childlike in their concepts yet perfect in their artlessly simple language. Certain to appeal to a young child's own experience is

> I'm very good at climbing
> I nearly climbed a tree
> But just as I was almost up
> I sort of skinned my knee.

The sly humor of "Sweet Delilah," a cat so perfect that

> From miles around the people came
> To watch her winning ways
> And they had nought to say but good
> And nought to give but praise

amuses adult readers, while children laugh at the way Delilah routs a pack of hungry wolves with her "barking loud harroo—" her one flaw.
   A further book of short poems, *The Rose on My Cake,* sings of winter clothing, birthday parties, and days when nothing goes right. It also includes the delightfully nonsensical "Hughbert and the Glue" and a hauntingly lyrical poem, "Once," which tells of a mouse that was once a queen:

> The world turns.
> The sun burns.
> The moon goes down to dawn....

   Kuskin's unusually imaginative and deftly humorous gift for projecting herself into various objects, natural and mechanical, is demonstrated in this same volume with her "If I Were a..." in which she ruminates on the feelings of a bird, a fish, a larkspur, and a sandwich. She carries this idea into a later book, *Any Me I Want to Be,* a riddle book in which each of a number of objects, from trees to parrots to mittens to a computer, describes itself. The child is encouraged to imagine what it would be like to be a tiny ant, a complacent parrot, or a rooted tree, and then to go further in expressing his "If I Were..." ideas in verse of his own.
   Kuskin's most successful poems are those which capture the essence of childish experience; her ability to think herself into a child's skin she says is due to the fact that she draws for her inspiration on memories of her own childhood. That she has been able to distill these memories into simple yet lighthearted verses which at their best are evocatively perfect for her small themes is

Kuskin's lasting talent.

—Margaret F. Maxwell

———

KYLE, Elisabeth. Pseudonym for Agnes Mary Robertson Dunlop; also wrote as Jan Ralston. British. Born in Ayr, Scotland. Educated privately. *Died 23 February 1982.*

PUBLICATIONS FOR CHILDREN

Fiction

Visitors from England, illustrated by A. Mason Trotter. London, Davies, 1941.
Vanishing Island, illustrated by A. Mason Trotter. London, Davies, 1942; as *Disappearing Island,* Boston, Houghton Mifflin, 1944.
Behind the Waterfall, illustrated by A. Mason Trotter. London, Davies, 1943.
The Seven Sapphires, illustrated by Nora Lavrin. London, Davies, 1944; New York, Nelson, 1957.
Holly Hotel, illustrated by Nora Lavrin. London, Davies, 1945; Boston, Houghton Mifflin, 1947.
Lost Karin, illustrated by Nora Lavrin. London, Davies, 1947; Boston, Houghton Mifflin, 1948.
The Mirrors of Castle Doone, illustrated by Nora Lavrin. London, Davies, 1947; Boston, Houghton Mifflin, 1949.
West Wind, illustrated by Francis Gower. London, Davies, 1948; Boston, Houghton Mifflin, 1950.
The House on the Hill, illustrated by Francis Gower. London, Davies, 1949.
Mystery of the Good Adventure (as Jan Ralston), illustrated by A. Mason Trotter. New York, Dodd Mead, 1950.
The Provost's Jewel, illustrated by Joy Colesworthy. London, Davies, 1950; Boston, Houghton Mifflin, 1951.
The Lintowers, illustrated by Joy Colesworthy. London, Davies, 1951.
The Captain's House, illustrated by Joy Colesworthy. London, Davies, 1952; Boston, Houghton Mifflin, 1953.
The Reiver's Road, illustrated by A.H. Watson. London, Nelson, 1953; as *On Lennox Moor,* New York, Nelson, 1954.
The House of the Pelican, illustrated by Peggy Fortnum. London and New York, Nelson, 1954.
Caroline House, illustrated by Robert Hodgson. London, Nelson, 1955; as *Carolina House,* New York, Nelson, 1955.
Run to Earth, illustrated by Mary Shillabeer. London, Nelson, 1957.
The Money Cat, illustrated by Cecil Leslie. London, Hamish Hamilton, 1958.
Eagle's Nest, illustrated by Juliette Palmer. London and New York, Nelson, 1961.
The Stilt Walkers. London, Heinemann, 1972.
Through the Wall, illustrated by Philip Moon. London, Heinemann, 1973.
The Yellow Coach, illustrated by Alexy Pendle. London, Heinemann, 1976.
The Key of the Castle, illustrated by Joanna Troughton. London, Heinemann, 1976.

Other

Queen of Scots: The Story of Mary Stuart, illustrated by Robert

Hodgson. London, Nelson, 1957.
Maid of Orleans: The Story of Joan of Arc, illustrated by Robert Hodgson. London, Nelson, 1957.
Girl with a Lantern, illustrated by Douglas Relf. London, Evans, 1961; as *The Story of Grizel,* New York, Nelson, 1961.
Girl with an Easel, illustrated by Charles Mozley. London, Evans, 1962; as *Portrait of Lisette,* New York, Nelson, 1963.
Girl with a Pen: Charlotte Brontë, illustrated by Charles Mozley. London, Evans, 1963; New York, Holt Rinehart, 1964.
Girl with a Song: The Story of Jenny Lind, illustrated by Charles Mozley. London, Evans, 1964; as *The Swedish Nightingale,* New York, Holt Rinehart, 1965.
Victoria: The Story of a Great Queen, illustrated by Annette Macarthur-Onslow. London, Nelson, 1964.
Girl with a Destiny: The Story of Mary of Orange, illustrated by Charles Mozley. London, Evans, 1965; as *Princess of Orange,* New York, Holt Rinehart, 1966.
The Boy Who Asked for More: The Early Life of Charles Dickens. London, Evans, 1966; as *Great Ambitions,* New York, Holt Rinehart, 1968.
Duet: The Story of Clara and Robert Schumann. London, Evans, and New York, Holt Rinehart, 1968.
Song of the Waterfall: The Story of Edvard and Nina Grieg. London, Evans, and New York, Holt Rinehart, 1970.

PUBLICATIONS FOR ADULTS

Novels

The Begonia Bed. London, Constable, and Indianapolis, Bobbs Merrill, 1934.
Orangefield. London, Constable, and Indianapolis, Bobbs Merrill, 1938.
Broken Glass. London, Davies, 1940.
The White Lady. London, Davies, 1941.
But We Are Exiles. London, Davies, 1942.
The Pleasure Dome. London, Davies, 1943.
The Skaters' Waltz. London, Davies, 1944.
Carp Country. London, Davies, 1946.
Mally Lee. London, Davies, and New York, Doubleday, 1947.
A Man of Talent. London, Davies, 1950; as *A Little Fire,* New York, Appleton, 1950.
The Tontine Belle. London, Davies, 1951.
Conor Sands. London, Davies, 1952.
The Regent's Candlesticks. London, Davies, 1954.
The Other Miss Evans. London, Davies, 1958.
Return to the Alcazar. London, Davies, 1962.
Love Is for the Living. London, Davies, 1966; New York, Holt Rinehart, 1967.
High Season. London, Davies, 1968.
Queen's Evidence. London, Davies, 1969.
Mirror Dance. London, Davies, 1970; New York, Holt Rinehart, 1971.
The Scent of Danger. London, Davies, 1971; New York, Holt Rinehart, 1972.
The Silver Pineapple. London, Davies, 1972.
The Heron Tree. London, Davies, 1973.
Free as Air. London, Davies, 1974.
Down the Water. London, Davies, 1975.
All the Nice Girls. London, Davies, 1976.
The Burning Hill. London, Davies, 1977.
The Stark Inheritance. London, Davies, 1978.
A Summer Scandal. London, Davies, 1979.
The Deed Box. London, Hale, 1981.
Bridge of the Blind Man. London, Hale, 1983.

CHILDREN'S WRITERS

Play

The Singing Wood, with Alec Robertson (produced Glasgow, 1957).

Other

The Mirrors of Versailles. London, Constable, 1939.
Forgotten as a Dream. London, Davies, 1953.
A Stillness in the Air. London, Davies, 1956.
Oh Say, Can You See? London, Davies, 1959.

*

Manuscript Collection: National Library of Scotland, Edinburgh.

* * *

Elisabeth Kyle's many titles made no dramatic contribution to children's literature but provided interesting and exciting stories for young readers for 35 years. Her love of Scotland was a consistent feature, giving authentic atmosphere to such titles as *Caroline House, Run to Earth,* and *The House of the Pelican,* the last a mystery conveying the contrasting moods of Edinburgh. *Caroline House* is a sentimental story and now very dated in terms of clothes, customs, and attitudes, but the underlying theme concerning Caroline's ancestors, Tobacco Lords of Glasgow, is absorbing. Like *Run to Earth,* it is a tale of the miscarriage of justice, and in both books a reliance on coincidence and convenience is evident in the plot. Family relationships are well drawn in Kyle's stories and, despite some stereotyped characters, this is clearly demonstrated in *Eagle's Nest* where a mystery about a 10-year-old burglary is skilfully combined with a background of forestry and the breeding of a rare eagle.

Among more recent books, *The Stilt Walkers* is set in London during the Great Exhibition of 1851. Kyle's feeling for history enabled her to recreate the atmosphere in spite of a rather melodramatic plot and some superimposed historical detail, and she created suspense and tension in an essentially ephemeral tale. In *The Key of the Castle* she returned to Scotland for the story of a page boy who wants to rescue Mary Queen of Scots from Lochleven. She wrote comfortably for 8-to-10-year-olds.

The other main group of her writing consists of fictionalised biographies. She treated her subjects with sympathy, and the story presentation may catch the interest of young readers despite the dangers of over-glamourisation. The historical subjects seem more successful than the musical ones; in particular the romantic story of Grizel Hume intertwines with that of Mary of Orange. In *Girl with a Destiny* Mary's story is told up to her accession to the English throne with William in 1688, while *Girl with a Lantern* tells of Grizel Hume's early life in Scotland, her exile with her father to Holland, and their eventual return with William and Mary. In *Girl with a Pen* the author took some liberties with the chronology, but the details of the Brontës' family life and of Charlotte's early difficulties are accurately researched. The style is old-fashioned and not always subtle but it is an imaginative and interesting reconstruction for young readers. Kyle was an accomplished writer, and her early books were valuable in their time, but many of her novels are now dated and it is to be hoped that publishers will resist the temptation to reprint them unrevised.

—Valerie Brinkley-Willsher

LAMPLUGH, Lois. British. Born in Barnstaple, Devon, 9 June 1921. Educated privately; B.A. (honours), Open University, 1980.

Served in the Auxiliary Territorial Service, 1939–43. Married Lawrence Carlile Davis in 1955; one daughter and one son. Member of the editorial staff, Jonathan Cape Ltd., publishers, London, 1947–57. Agent: A.P. Watt Ltd., 20 John Street, London WC1N 2DL. Address: Springside, Bydown, Swimbridge, Devon EX32 0QB, England.

PUBLICATIONS FOR CHILDREN

Fiction

The Pigeongram Puzzle, illustrated by William Stobbs. London, Cape, 1955.
Nine Bright Shiners, illustrated by William Stobbs. London, Cape, 1955.
Vagabonds' Castle, illustrated by William Stobbs. London, Cape, 1957.
Rockets in the Dunes, illustrated by William Stobbs. London, Cape, 1958.
The Sixpenny Runner, illustrated by William Stobbs. London, Cape, 1960.
Midsummer Mountains, illustrated by William Stobbs. London, Cape, 1961.
The Rifle House Friends, illustrated by Richard Kennedy. London, Deutsch, 1965.
The Linhay on Hunter's Hill, illustrated by Laszlo Acs. London, Deutsch, 1966.
The Fur Princess and the Fir Prince, illustrated by Jocelyne Pache. London, Dent, 1969.
Mandog (adaptation of television serial). London, BBC Publications, 1972.
Sean's Leap. London, Deutsch, 1979.
The Winter Donkey. London, Deutsch, 1980.
Falcon's Tor. London, Deutsch, 1984.

Plays

Television Series: *Honeyhill,* 1967–70.

PUBLICATIONS FOR ADULTS

Verse

The Quarry Hare. Privately printed, 1976.

Other

The Stream Way (autobiography). London, Golden Galley Press, 1948.
Barnstaple: Town on the Taw. Chichester, Sussex, Phillimore, 1983.
A History of Ilfracombe. Chichester, Sussex, Phillimore, 1984.
Minehead and Dunster. Chichester, Sussex, Phillimore, 1987.

Television Documentary: *The Old Navigator,* 1967.

*

Manuscript Collection: de Grummond Collection, University of Southern Mississippi, Hattiesburg.

Lois Lamplugh comments:
Georgeham, in north Devon, where I grew up, was a village lived in or visited by a number of writers during the 1920's and 1930's.

The most noteworthy was Henry Williamson, who in fact rented a cottage belonging to my grandmother, and wrote most, if not all of *Tarka the Otter* there. As a result, I heard a good deal of talk of books and writing during those years, which undoubtedly encouraged my own interest in writing.

Perhaps the most noticeable aspect of my books—even one or two among the earlier ones that belong to the adventure story category—is their sense of place. Often this is some part of north Devon, although I've never used actual place names and have occasionally altered places for my purpose (the island in *Sean's Leap*, for instance, is a compound of Lundy, Skokholm, Skomer, and Tresco in the Scilly Isles). *The Rifle House Friends*, my own favourite among my books, is essentially a picture of Georgeham as it was in the late 1920's and early 1930's. The Cornish setting of *The Winter Donkey* is of great importance to the story, deriving from a four-year stay in Cornwall. *Vagabonds' Castle* was prompted by visits to Italy, and *Midsummer Mountains* by visits to France.

On the whole I prefer to write for older children, but the sequence of more than 300 very short (600-word) stories in the *Honeyhill* series, and the cat fantasy *The Fur Princess and the Fir Prince*, were written during the years when my own children were fairly small.

*   *   *

Lois Lamplugh writes mainly for older children about children their own age. She sees herself following in the Arthur Ransome tradition; but although her earliest books are ostensibly adventure stories, it is the faithful attention to the detail of everyday life which is the striking feature of her later writing. She has, perhaps, rather more in common with adult writers such as Alan Sillitoe ("The Loneliness of the Long Distance Runner") and the 1950's and 1960's preoccupations with self-examination and realism.

In *The Winter Donkey* Goldie, a young seaside donkey, spends the winter at the smallholding belonging to Matthew's grandfather. She soon becomes a favorite with the whole village; but Matthew becomes especially close to her and, when she runs away to have a foal, he brings her back to safety. This simple story, however, is hung around much broader issues. It is a very important year in Matthew's life; he is facing the eleven-plus exam with all its implications for change. Would he follow his remote elder brother Stephen to grammar school, or would he go to the local Secondary Modern with his friends? Would he eventually strike out into the wider world, (even "to England"), or would he stay in the little Cornish village where he and generations of his family had been born and brought up?

These are themes which recur throughout Lamplugh's writing: a small community, looking at the outside world with a mixture of indifference, wonder, and vague contempt. Matthew's uneasy awareness of both worlds coincides with his growing out of childhood into adolescence. He is pulled by loyalty to his family and friends, but, on the other hand, he is fascinated by new people and possibilities. These are ideas which are shown particularly clearly in *The Rifle House Friends*, perhaps Lamplugh's most compact and intense book. Tacker becomes friendly with the eccentric owner of the Rifle House, Miss Lumley. However, he will not admit to this because he is afraid of his village friends' ridicule. By the end of the book, he is sufficiently confident of his own identity to show open friendship for Sarah, the new occupant of the Rifle House, even though she, too, is an outsider.

The best of Lamplugh's work is about people and places she knows intimately. It is often set in the West Country where she was born and brought up. *Sean's Leap*, for example, describes how Sean, a boy in care, runs away from the Island of Brytherne; it was written after Lamplugh had worked in a special school herself. Sean's immediate attraction to the wild horses on Brytherne, who "are tame because they are free," foreshadows the success of his own treatment by the islanders.

Lamplugh concentrates on the interior life of her characters, and their complex and fragile emotions. The incidents in her heroes' lives (and her main characters *are* nearly all boys) are like a collection of cinematic stills, but until we can recognise themes and patterns, their personalities are strangely blurred by the abundance of careful detail. Furthermore we sense that these boys might well not read her books: although each has an intense imagination, they are not verbal, literary children at all. This contrasts sharply with the sophisticated, even adult fashion in which they are presented and somehow makes them seem quite remote. Tacker is described as taking part in the "rollicking games of the village children," but we do not feel part of this fun.

Lamplugh's most recent book, *Falcon's Tor*, returns to the earlier straightforward adventure story. Aidan is thrown from a horse and knocked unconscious, travels back in time, and awakes in 1915, a period he has been fascinated with. His struggle to get back to his own time and family (despite his interest in World War I) and discovery of his connection to the family in the past make for a rather predictable if satisfying read.

The Lamplugh style is not really that of a storyteller. She is much more of a weaver of themes and atmosphere. Her books are best remembered for their cameo-like descriptions and the nostalgic feelings that they can evoke. Probably best enjoyed by a contemplative child or even an adult, her books yield more on a second or even third reading.

—Alison Sage

————

LAMPMAN, Evelyn Sibley. Also wrote as Lynn Bronson. American. Born in Dallas, Oregon, 18 April 1907. Educated at Oregon State University, Corvallis, B.S. 1929. Married Herbert Sheldon Lampman in 1934 (died 1943); two daughters. Continuity writer, 1929–34, and continuity chief, 1937–45, Radio KEX, Portland, Oregon; educational director, Radio KGW, Portland, 1945–52. Recipient: Western Writers of America Spur award, 1968, 1971. *Died 13 June 1980.*

PUBLICATIONS FOR CHILDREN

Fiction

Crazy Creek, illustrated by Grace Paull. New York, Doubleday, 1948.
Treasure Mountain, illustrated by Richard Bennett. New York, Doubleday, 1949.
The Bounces of Cynthiann', illustrated by Grace Paull. New York, Doubleday, 1950; Kingswood, Surrey, World's Work, 1960.
Elder Brother, illustrated by Richard Bennett. New York, Doubleday, 1951.
Captain Apple's Ghost, illustrated by Ninon MacKnight. New York, Doubleday, 1952; London, Hodder and Stoughton, 1953.
Tree Wagon, illustrated by Robert Frankenberg. New York, Doubleday, 1953.
Witch Doctor's Son, illustrated by Richard Bennett. New York, Doubleday, 1954.
The Shy Stegosaurus of Cricket Creek, illustrated by Hubert Buel. New York, Doubleday, 1955.
Navaho Sister, illustrated by Paul Lantz. New York, Doubleday, 1956.
Rusty's Space Ship, illustrated by Bernard Krigstein. New York, Doubleday, 1957.

Rock Hounds, illustrated by Arnold Spilka.   New York, Doubleday, 1958.
Special Year, illustrated by Genia.   New York, Doubleday, 1959.
The City under the Back Steps, illustrated by Honoré Valintcourt.   New York, Doubleday, 1960; London, Faber, 1962.
Princess of Fort Vancouver, illustrated by Douglas Gorsline.   New York, Doubleday, 1962.
The Shy Stegosaurus at Indian Springs, illustrated by Paul Galdone.   New York, Doubleday, 1962.
Mrs. Updaisy, illustrated by Cyndy Szekeres.   New York, Doubleday, 1963.
Temple of the Sun, illustrated by Lili Réthi.   New York, Doubleday, 1964.
Wheels West, illustrated by Gil Walker.   New York, Doubleday, 1965.
The Tilted Sombrero, illustrated by Ray Cruz.   New York, Doubleday, 1966.
Half-Breed, illustrated by Ann Grifalconi.   New York, Doubleday, 1967.
The Bandit of Mok Hill, illustrated by Marvin Friedman.   New York, Doubleday, 1969.
Cayuse Courage.   New York, Harcourt Brace, 1970.
Once upon Little Big Horn, illustrated by John Gretzer.   New York, Crowell, 1971.
The Year of the Small Shadow.   New York, Harcourt Brace, 1971.
Go Up the Road, illustrated by Charles Robinson.   New York, Atheneum, 1972.
Rattlesnake Cave, illustrated by Pamela Johnson.   New York, Atheneum, 1974.
White Captives.   New York, Atheneum, 1975.
The Potlatch Family.   New York, Atheneum, 1976.
Bargain Bride.   New York, Atheneum, 1977.
Squaw Man's Son.   New York, Atheneum, 1978.
Three Knocks on the Wall.   New York, Atheneum, 1980.

Fiction as Lynn Bronson

Timberland Adventure.   Philadelphia, Lippincott, 1950.
Coyote Kid.   Philadelphia, Lippincott, 1951.
Rogue's Valley.   Philadelphia, Lippincott, 1952.
The Runaway.   Philadelphia, Lippincott, 1953.
Darcy's Harvest, illustrated by Paul Galdone.   New York, Doubleday, 1956.
Popular Girl.   New York, Doubleday, 1957.

*

Manuscript Collection: University of Oregon Library, Eugene.

*   *   *

Evelyn Sibley Lampman, writing at times under the pen name of Lynn Bronson, wrote biographies, historical fiction, contemporary novels, and stories that are variously humorous, fanciful, or adventure-filled. She was primarily known, however, for fiction that deals with members of minority groups, particularly the Native American.

Among Lampman's less serious books are *The Shy Stegosaurus at Indian Springs*, the story of two children who find a friendly dinosaur, and *Captain Apple's Ghost*, in which a ghost to returns his former home and helps preserve it as a children's museum. Neither tale is wholly credible, but both are lively and amusing, with affable fantasy characters. Also cheerful, if at times contrived, is one of her earliest books, *The Bounces of Cynthiann'*; the motherless Bounce children are taken in by the town of Cynthianna in a tale that stresses the close ties among the children and that gives a good picture of small town life.

Special Year, one of the few serious books that does not concern an ethnic minority, is a remarkably perceptive story about preadolescent girls, with credible familial and peer group relationships, and with a realistic treatment of the conflict between adult standards and peer group mores. In *Elder Brother* Lampman pictured the cultural conflict within a Chinese-American family with no sons who adopt a boy from China; even at the turn of the century the girls in the family rebel against the traditional concepts of feminine role held by their new brother. The problems of Mexican-American migrants are examined in *Go Up the Road*, a book in which the plot and characterization are less effective than the exposing of the demeaning quality of migrant life and the organized efforts to improve it.

Lampman's sympathy for Native Americans and her understanding of the persecution and cultural conflict they have suffered made her stories about them, whether historical or invented, her best books. Of the historical fiction, three outstanding books are *The Tilted Sombrero*, *Cayuse Courage*, and *White Captives*. The first is set at the beginning of the Mexican War of Independence and describes the first Indian revolt against Spanish rule, a movement led by a priest. The setting is colorful, the historical details authentic, and the plot filled with action, but it is the picture the book gives of a stratified society and a rebellion against oppression that has major impact. *Cayuse Courage* is the story of the Whitman massacre told from the viewpoint of a young Indian boy, a book that enables readers to see the reasons for an event usually seen from a viewpoint sympathetic to the white pioneers.

Lampman's objectivity in seeing both the white and the Indian point of view was particularly evident in *White Captives*, based on a report written by Olive Oatman, who was taken captive by an Apache raiding party that had killed most of the members of a Mormon wagon train. The story has pace and poignancy, but it is most notable for the strong and varied characterization of Apache and Mohave Indians.

Of her novels that are pure fiction, *Half-Breed*, set in the past, is the story of a boy at home neither with the local Indians who spurn him because he is has a white father nor the white people who reject him because his mother is a Crow. Lampman concentrated, in such stories, on Native American children who face conflicting ways of life; in books with contemporary settings, such as *Navaho Sister*, Sad Girl must adjust to the new ways she finds in a government school—but must learn to be more tolerant herself. Whether the protagonist is white, as in *Rattlesnake Cave*, and learns to respect the dignity of the Native American traditions, or—as in *The Year of the Small Shadow*—is an Indian child thrust into a white environment, Lampman emphasized the fact that the child, resilient and courageous, can cope with change, accepting new patterns while retaining appreciation for the old.

—Zena Sutherland

LANGTON, Jane (née Gillson). American.   Born in Boston, Massachusetts, 30 December 1922. Educated at Wellesley College, Massachusetts, 1940–42; University of Michigan, Ann Arbor, 1942–45, B.S. (Phi Beta Kappa), 1944, M.A. 1945; Radcliffe College, Cambridge, Massachusetts, 1945–46, 1947–48, M.A. 1948; Boston Museum School of Art, 1958–59. Married William Langton in 1943; three sons. Researcher, *Discovery* program, WGBH Television, Boston, 1955–56; taught children's literature, Simmons College, Boston, 1979–80, and suspense novel writing at the Radcliffe Seminars, 1981. Recipient: Nero Wolfe award, for adult fiction, 1984. Agent: Dorothy Markinko, McIntosh and Otis Inc., 310 Madison Avenue, New York, New York 10017. Address: 9 Baker Farm Road, Lincoln,

Massachusetts 01773, U.S.A.

PUBLICATIONS FOR CHILDREN

Fiction

The Majesty of Grace, illustrated by the author. New York, Harper, 1961; as *Her Majesty, Grace Jones*, 1974.
The Diamond in the Window, illustrated by Erik Blegvad. New York, Harper, 1962; London, Hamish Hamilton, 1969.
The Swing in the Summerhouse, illustrated by Erik Blegvad. New York, Harper, 1967; London, Hamish Hamilton, 1970.
The Astonishing Stereoscope, illustrated by Erik Blegvad. New York, Harper, 1971.
The Boyhood of Grace Jones, illustrated by Emily McCully. New York, Harper, 1972.
Paper Chains. New York, Harper, 1977.
The Fledgling. New York, Harper, 1980.
The Fragile Flag. New York, Harper, 1984.

Other

The Hedgehog Boy: A Latvian Folktale, illustrated by Ilse Plume. New York, Harper, 1985.

PUBLICATIONS FOR ADULTS

Novels

The Transcendental Murder. New York, Harper, 1964; as *The Minute Man Murder*, New York, Dell, 1976.
Dark Nantucket Noon. New York, Harper, 1975.
The Memorial Hall Murder. New York, Harper, 1978.
Natural Enemy. New Haven, Connecticut, Ticknor and Fields, 1982.
Emily Dickinson Is Dead. New York, St. Martin's Press, 1984.
Good and Dead. New York, St. Martin's Press, 1986; London, Penguin, 1987.
Murder at the Gardner. New York, St. Martin's Press, 1988.

*

Manuscript Collections: Kerlan Collection, University of Minnesota, Minneapolis; Boston University.

Jane Langton comments:

My own favorites are a series that begins with *The Diamond in the Window*. These books are set in a real house in the real town of Concord, Massachusetts, and I hope the children are like real children. But their Uncle Freddy is fantastical, and because of his devotion to Concord's local saints, Emerson and Thoreau, the children's adventures are fantastic too, and awash with transcendentalism.

* * *

Jane Langton has proven herself a competent writer of "Nesbitian" fantasy—but with an American flavor. Several features of E. Nesbit's distinctive blend of realism and fantasy can be distinguished in Langton's series involving the Hall family, *The Diamond in the Window, The Swing in the Summerhouse, The Astonishing Stereoscope*, and *The Fledgling*. One feature is the warm family and home background against which the plot develops. Like Nesbit's fictional

children, Eleanor, Edward, and Georgie are free to enjoy their escapades because Aunt Lily and Uncle Freddy are wrapped up in their own affairs or willing to give the children considerable freedom. Unlike Nesbit's adult characters, Langton's become entangled in some of the children's own adventures, especially the humorous ones. Another feature is the use of some magical object whereby the Hall children can shuttle back and forth between the real world and fantasy ones. Langton is careful, as Nesbit was, to account for the objects' power. In the first three books, Prince Krishna, Aunt Lily's friend and master magician, gives the children the objects as gifts for their amusement, but he stipulates the conditions under which the magic works; the children struggle, often humorously, to respect these conditions. In the fourth book the Goose Prince's gift of flying can be accepted and used by Georgie provided her yearning to fly is matched by her accepting the inevitability of her growing up.

Langton assumes, as Nesbit did, the intelligence and curiosity of her intended readers and never talks down to them or reiterates the obvious. This is best demonstrated by incorporating into her narratives many references to the history of Concord and the lives and ideas of Emerson and Thoreau. These allusions and what the author does with them contribute to the relatively high level of thought and imaginative appeal of the novels. Among other things, Langton explores in her fantasies the possibility of a living link between transcendentalism and present-day Concord. Moreover, she contrasts two different understandings of history and its uses, and the variations explain some of the humor and much of the seriousness in the novels. Uncle Freddy's earnestness and penchant for applying Emersonian principles to almost any situation may trip him up occasionally, and his financial naivety drives the family virtually bankrupt. Nevertheless, the Halls' genuine goodness does testify that Emersonian idealism can motivate and inspire. What transpires within the Hall home and Uncle Freddy's Concord College of Transcendentalist Knowledge, even if it is sometimes silly, reflects a more appropriate and valid relationship to Concord's past and its legacy than does the chamber of commerce mentality of Mr. Preek and Miss Prawn, Uncle Freddy's rivals, who see in history only a source of tourist dollars and look upon Uncle Freddy's idealism as a lamentable lack of Yankee practicality. Perhaps the many allusions to Concord and two of its most famous citizens may intimidate some youngsters, but for those who enjoy challenges the novels are a delight.

—Francis J. Molson

———

LATHAM, Jean Lee. Has also written as Janice Gard; Julian Lee. American. Born in Buckhannon, West Virginia, 19 April 1902. Educated at West Virginia Wesleyan College, Buckhannon, A.B. 1925; Ithaca College, New York, B.O.E. 1928; Cornell University, Ithaca, New York, M.A. 1930; West Virginia Institute of Technology, Montgomery, 1942. Served as a trainer of inspectors, United States War Department Signal Corps, 1943–45: Silver Wreath, 1944. Head of English Department, Upshur County High School, West Virginia, 1926–28; substitute teacher, West Virginia Wesleyan College, 1927; teacher in drama and education departments, Ithaca College, 1928–29; editor-in-chief, Dramatic Publishing Company, Chicago, 1930–36. Freelance writer, 1936–41, and since 1945. Director, workshop in juvenile writing, Indiana University Writers' Conference, Bloomington, 1959–60, and Writers' Conference in the Rocky Mountains, 1963. Recipient: American Library Association Newbery Medal, 1956. D.Litt.: West Virginia Wesleyan College, 1956. Address: 12 Phoenetia Avenue, Coral Gables, Florida 33134, U.S.A.

PUBLICATIONS FOR CHILDREN

Fiction

Carry On, Mr. Bowditch, illustrated by John Cosgrave. Boston, Houghton Mifflin, 1955.
This Dear-Bought Land, illustrated by Jacob Landau. New York, Harper, 1957.
The Dog That Lost His Family, with Bee Lewi, illustrated by Karla Kuskin. New York, Macmillan, 1961.
When Homer Honked, with Bee Lewi, illustrated by Cyndy Szekeres. New York, Macmillan, 1961.
The Cuckoo That Couldn't Count, with Bee Lewi, illustrated by Jacqueline Chwast. New York, Macmillan, 1961.
The Man Who Never Snoozed, with Bee Lewi, illustrated by Sheila Greenwald. New York, Macmillan, 1961.
The Frightened Hero: A Story of the Siege of Latham House, illustrated by Barbara Latham. Philadelphia, Chilton, 1965.
What Tabbit the Rabbit Found, illustrated by Bill Dugan. Champaign, Illinois, Garrard, 1974.

Plays

The Alien Note. Chicago, Dramatic Publishing Company, 1930.
The Christmas Party, adaptation of the story by Zona Gale. Chicago, Dramatic Publishing Company, 1930.
Crinoline and Candlelight. Chicago, Dramatic Publishing Company, 1931.
The Giant and the Biscuits. Chicago, Dramatic Publishing Company, 1934.
The Prince and the Patters. Chicago, Dramatic Publishing Company, 1934.
Tommy Tomorrow. Chicago, Dramatic Publishing Company, 1935.
And Then What Happened? Chicago, Dramatic Publishing Company, 1937.
All on Account of Kelly. Chicago, Dramatic Publishing Company, 1937.
Mickey the Mighty. Chicago, Dramatic Publishing Company, 1937.
The Ghost of Rhodes Manor. New York, Dramatists Play Service, 1939.
Nine Radio Plays (includes *With Eyes Turned West, Mac and the Black Cat, Stew for Six, For Mister Jim, Debt of Honor, Cupid on the Cuff, Voices, The Way of Shawn, Discipline by Dad*). Chicago, Dramatic Publishing Company, 1940.

Plays as Julian Lee

Another Washington. Chicago, Dramatic Publishing Company, 1931.
The Christmas Carol, adaptation of the story by Charles Dickens. Chicago, Dramatic Publishing Company, 1931.
A Fiancé for Fanny. Chicago, Dramatic Publishing Company, 1931.
I Will! I Won't! Chicago, Dramatic Publishing Company, 1931.
Keeping Kitty's Dates. Chicago, Dramatic Publishing Company, 1931.
Washington for All. Chicago, Dramatic Publishing Company, 1931.
Thanksgiving for All, with Genevieve and Elwyn Swarthout, adaptation of *The Pompion Pie* by Jane Tallman. Chicago, Dramatic Publishing Company, 1932.
Christmas for All. Chicago, Dramatic Publishing Company, 1932.
Just for Justin. Chicago, Dramatic Publishing Company, 1933.
Tiny Jim. Chicago, Dramatic Publishing Company, 1933.
The Children's Book, with Harriette Wilburr and Nellie Meader Linn.

Chicago, Dramatic Publishing Company, 1933.
Lincoln Yesterday and Today. Chicago, Dramatic Publishing Company, 1933.
He Landed from London. Chicago, Dramatic Publishing Company, 1935.
Christmas Programs for the Lower Grades, with Ann Clark. Chicago, Dramatic Publishing Company, 1937.
Thanksgiving Programs for the Lower Grades, with Ann Clark. Chicago, Dramatic Publishing Company, 1937.
Big Brother Barges In. Chicago, Dramatic Publishing Company, 1940.
The Ghost of Lone Cabin. Chicago, Dramatic Publishing Company, 1940.

Verse

Who Lives Here?, illustrated by Benton Mahan. Champaign, Illinois, Garrard, 1974.

Other

555 Pointers for Beginning Actors and Directors. Chicago, Dramatic Publishing Company, 1935.
The Story of Eli Whitney, illustrated by Fritz Kredel. New York, Aladdin, 1953.
Medals for Morse, Artist and Inventor, illustrated by Douglas Gorsline. New York, Aladdin, 1954.
Trail Blazer of the Seas, illustrated by Victor Mays. Boston, Houghton Mifflin, 1956.
Young Man in a Hurry: The Story of Cyrus W. Field, illustrated by Victor Mays. New York, Harper, 1958.
On Stage, Mr. Jefferson!, illustrated by Edward Shenton. New York, Harper, 1958.
Drake, The Man They Called a Pirate, illustrated by Frederick Chapman. New York, Harper, and London, Hamish Hamilton, 1960.
Samuel F.B. Morse, Artist-Inventor, illustrated by Jo Polseno. Champaign, Illinois, Garrard, 1961.
Aladdin, illustrated by Pablo Ramirez. Indianapolis, Bobbs Merrill, 1961.
Ali Baba, illustrated by Pablo Ramirez. Indianapolis, Bobbs Merrill, 1961.
Nutcracker, illustrated by José Correas. Indianapolis, Bobbs Merrill, 1961.
Puss in Boots, illustrated by Pablo Ramirez. Indianapolis, Bobbs Merrill, 1961.
The Magic Fishbone, illustrated by Pablo Ramirez. Indianapolis, Bobbs Merrill, 1961.
Jack the Giant Killer, illustrated by Pablo Ramirez. Indianapolis, Bobbs Merrill, 1961.
Hop o' My Thumb, illustrated by Arnalot. Indianapolis, Bobbs Merrill, 1961.
The Ugly Duckling, Goldilocks and the Three Bears, and The Little Red Hen, illustrated by José Correas and Pablo Ramirez. Indianapolis, Bobbs Merrill, 1962.
The Brave Little Tailor, Hansel and Gretel, and Jack and the Beanstalk, illustrated by Pablo Ramirez and José Correas. Indianapolis, Bobbs Merrill, 1962.
Man of the Monitor: The Story of John Ericsson, illustrated by Leonard Everett Fisher. New York, Harper, 1962.
Eli Whitney, Great Inventor, Illustrated by Cary. Champaign, Illinois, Garrard, 1963.
The Chagres: Power of the Panama Canal. Champaign, Illinois, Garrard, 1964.
Sam Houston, Hero of Texas. Champaign, Illinois, Garrard, and London, Harper, 1965.

Retreat to Glory: The Story of Sam Houston. New York, Harper, 1965.
George W. Goethals, Panama Canal Engineer, illustrated by Hamilton Greene. Champaign, Illinois, Garrard, 1965.
The Columbia, Powerhouse of North America. Champaign, Illinois, Garrard, 1967.
David Glasgow Farragut, Our First Admiral, illustrated by Paul Frame. Champaign, Illinois, Garrard, 1967.
Anchor's Aweigh: The Story of David Glasgow Farragut, illustrated by Eros Keith. New York, Harper, 1968.
Far Voyager: The Story of James Cook. New York, Harper, 1970.
Rachel Carson, Who Loved the Sea, illustrated by Victor Mays. Champaign, Illinois, Garrard, 1973.
Elizabeth Blackwell, Pioneer Woman Doctor, illustrated by Ethel Gold. Champaign, Illinois, Garrard, 1975.

Translator, *Wa O'Ka,* by Pablo Ramirez, illustrated by Ramirez. Indianapolis, Bobbs Merrill, 1961.

PUBLICATIONS FOR ADULTS

Plays

Thanks Awfully! Chicago, Dramatic Publishing Company, 1929.
Christopher's Orphans. Chicago, Dramatic Publishing Company, 1931.
A Sign unto You. Chicago, Dramatic Publishing Company, 1931.
Lady to See You. Chicago, Dramatic Publishing Company, 1931.
The Blue Teapot. Chicago, Dramatic Publishing Company, 1932.
Broadway Bound. Chicago, Dramatic Publishing Company, 1933.
Master of Solitaire (produced New York, 1936). Chicago, Dramatic Publishing Company, 1935.
The Bed of Petunias. Chicago, Dramatic Publishing Company, 1937.
Here She Comes! Chicago, Dramatic Publishing Company, 1937.
Just the Girl for Jimmy. Chicago, Dramatic Publishing Company, 1937.
Have a Heart! Chicago, Dramatic Publishing Company, 1937.
What Are You Going to Wear? Chicago, Dramatic Publishing Company, 1937.
Talk Is Cheap. Chicago, Dramatic Publishing Company, 1937.
Smile for the Lady! Chicago, Dramatic Publishing Company, 1937.
Well Met by Moonlight. Chicago, Dramatic Publishing Company, 1937.
They'll Never Look There! New York, Dramatists Play Service, 1939.
The Arms of the Law. Chicago, Dramatic Publishing Company, 1940.
Old Doc. Chicago, Dramatic Publishing Company, 1940.
Gray Bread. Evanston, Illinois, Row Peterson, 1941.
People Don't Change. Chicago, Dramatic Publishing Company, 1941.
Señor Freedom. Evanston, Illinois, Row Peterson, 1941.
Minus a Million. New York, Dramatists Play Service, 1941.
The House Without a Key, adaptation of the novel by Earl Derr Biggers. Chicago, Dramatic Publishing Company, 1942.
The Nightmare. New York, French, 1943.

Radio Plays: for *First Nighter, Grand Central Station* and *Skippy Hollywood Theatre* programs, 1930–41.

Plays as Janice Gard

Lookin' Lovely. Chicago, Dramatic Publishing Company, 1930.
Listen to Leon. Chicago, Dramatic Publishing Company, 1931.

Depend on Me. Chicago, Dramatic Publishing Company, 1932.

*

Manuscript Collection: Kerlan Collection, University of Minnesota, Minneapolis.

*   *   *

"Never double on the trail" is the motto Jean Lee Latham adheres to in producing poetry, drama, imaginative stories, retold classics, historical fiction, and biographies for children. Her reputation is based primarily on her more than 20 biographies. She has a keen sense for selection of character and compresses technical detail into a swift narrative style. As a teacher of creative writing herself, she respects the demands of the craft.

Her list of biographies includes books about Samuel Morse, Sam Houston, and David Glasgow Farragut. She follows a pattern occasionally of writing fictionalized biography such as *Medals for Morse* and reworking it for a younger audience as *Samuel F.B. Morse* for another publisher. In an earlier century she may have used a pseudonym, for most of her books have male heroes and appeal to the mechanically inclined. Exceptions are the biographies of a doctor, Elizabeth Blackwell, and naturalist Rachel Carson. "I chose men who had it 'rough' and yet still managed to achieve something worthwhile, despite overwhelming setbacks," she remarked in an interview.

Latham has the capacity to make an enormous amount of material palatable to the young reader. Her most notable book, and the one for which she won the Newbery Medal, *Carry On, Mr. Bowditch,* incorporates a myriad of details about astronomy and mathematics without destroying the flow of the narrative. Rather than detracting from the story line, the details add an authenticity to the story. In *Trail Blazer of the Seas* she used quotes from letters, sample charts, and figures to verify the text.

The construction of her stories is based on a sound understanding of the craft. When she moved to Florida, she sought solitude in which she could "take narrative writing apart and find out what made it tick." She is an exponent of the word by word, line by line building of a story. The author slashes substantial sections from her working manuscripts, apparent in her original work in the Kerlan Collection at the University of Minnesota. In a trailer lined with reference books, she wrote five books, including the Newbery Medal winner. By telling a good yarn with skill, Latham has introduced America's native and immigrant heroes to children throughout the world.

—Karen Nelson Hoyle

———

LATTIMORE, Eleanor (Frances). American. Born in Shanghai, China, 30 June 1904. Educated at California School of Arts and Crafts, Berkeley, 1920–22; Art Students' League, New York, 1924; Grand Central Art School, New York, 1927. Married Robert Armstrong Andrews in 1934 (died 1963); two sons. Freelance artist, 1925–30. Group shows: Doll and Richards Gallery, Boston, 1923; Anderson Gallery, New York, 1924; Gibbes Gallery, Charleston, South Carolina, 1939. *Died 12 May 1986.*

PUBLICATIONS FOR CHILDREN (illustrated by the author)

Fiction

Little Pear. New York, Harcourt Brace, 1931; London, Museum

Press, 1947.
Jerry and the Pusa. New York, Harcourt Brace, 1932.
The Seven Crowns. New York, Harcourt Brace, 1933.
Little Pear and His Friends. New York, Harcourt Brace, 1934.
The Lost Leopard. New York, Harcourt Brace, 1935.
The Clever Cat. New York, Harcourt Brace, 1936.
Junior, A Colored Boy of Charleston. New York, Harcourt Brace, 1938.
Jonny. New York, Harcourt Brace, 1939.
The Story of Lee Ling. New York, Harcourt Brace, 1940.
Storm on the Island. New York, Harcourt Brace, 1942.
The Questions of Li-fu. New York, Harcourt Brace, 1942.
Peachblossom. New York, Harcourt Brace, 1943.
First Grade. New York, Harcourt Brace, 1944.
Bayou Boy. New York, Morrow, 1946.
Jeremy's Isle. New York, Morrow, 1947.
Three Little Chinese Girls. New York, Morrow, 1948; London, Angus and Robertson, 1961.
Davy of the Everglades. New York, Morrow, 1949.
Deborah's White Winter. New York, Morrow, 1949.
Indigo Hill. New York, Morrow, 1950.
Christopher and His Turtle. New York, Morrow, 1950.
The Fig Tree. New York, Morrow, 1951.
Bells for a Chinese Donkey. New York, Morrow, 1951; London, Angus and Robertson, 1959.
Lively Victoria. New York, Morrow, 1952.
Wu, The Gatekeeper's Son. New York, Morrow, 1953; London, Angus and Robertson, 1963.
Jasper. New York, Morrow, 1953.
Holly in the Snow. New York, Morrow, 1954.
Diana in the China Shop. New York, Morrow, 1955.
Willow Tree Village. New York, Morrow, 1955; London, Angus and Robertson, 1961.
Molly in the Middle. New York, Morrow, 1956.
Little Pear and the Rabbits. New York, Morrow, 1956; London, Angus and Robertson, 1963.
The Monkey of Crofton. New York, Morrow, 1957.
The Journey of Ching Lai. New York, Morrow, 1957; London, Angus and Robertson, 1959.
Happiness for Kimi. New York, Morrow, 1958.
Fair Bay. New York, Morrow, 1958; London, Angus and Robertson, 1964.
The Fisherman's Son. New York, Morrow, 1959; London, Angus and Robertson, 1962.
The Youngest Artist. New York, Morrow, 1959.
Beachcomber Boy. New York, Morrow, 1960.
The Chinese Daughter. New York, Morrow, 1960; London, Angus and Robertson, 1962.
The Wonderful Glass House. New York, Morrow, 1961.
Cousin Melinda. New York, Morrow, 1961.
The Bittern's Nest. New York, Morrow, 1962; London, Angus and Robertson, 1964.
Laurie and Company. New York, Morrow, 1962.
Janetta's Magnet. New York, Morrow, 1963.
The Little Tumbler. New York, Morrow, 1963; London, Angus and Robertson, 1964.
Felicia. New York, Morrow, 1964; London, Angus and Robertson, 1965.
The Mexican Bird. New York, Morrow, 1965; London, Angus and Robertson, 1966.
The Bus Trip. New York, Morrow, 1965.
The Search for Christina. New York, Morrow, 1966.
The Two Helens. New York, Morrow, 1967.
Bird Song. New York, Morrow, 1968.
The Girl on the Deer. New York, Morrow, 1969.
The Three Firecrackers. New York, Morrow, 1970.

More about Little Pear. New York, Morrow, 1971.
A Smiling Face. New York, Morrow, 1973.
The Taming of Tiger. New York, Morrow, 1975.
Adam's Key, illustrated by Alan Tiegreen. New York, Morrow, 1976.
Proudfoot's Way, illustrated by Beatrice Darwin. New York, Morrow, 1978; as *Which Way, Black Cat?*, New York, Scholastic, 1980.

*

Manuscript Collections: Kerlan Collection, University of Minnesota, Minneapolis; de Grummond Collection, University of Southern Mississippi, Hattiesburg.

Illustrator: *Turkestan Reunion* by Eleanor Holgate Lattimore, 1934; *Picture Tales from the Chinese* by Berta Metzger, 1934; *Rainbow Bridge* by Florence Crannell Means, 1934; *All Around the City* by Esther Freivogel, 1938.

Eleanor Lattimore commented:

(1978) I don't know quite what to say about my books except that I enjoy writing and always have been interested in children. Since I draw as well as write, I "see" my characters as I write about them. The settings are real, the characters imaginary. My stories, with one exception, are realistic. The exception is *Felicia*, about a cat who assumes the form of a girl.

*   *   *

Eleanor Lattimore's first book, *Little Pear*, which introduced China to the young readers of the 1930's and 1940's, remains a classic, and is a prototype for her many books for children written during a half-century. She merged an episodic plot, a strong character, and a detailed Chinese setting to produce the delightful story, and the five-year-old hero is memorable enough to be listed in Margery Fisher's *Who's Who in Children's Books* (1975). Sequels were published decades apart, although in *Little Pear and His Friends* (1934) he is only one year older, and remains a youngster in *Little Pear and the Rabbits* (1956) and *More about Little Pear* (1971). The Chinese culture permeates the text so thoroughly that the story cannot be separated from the place. Clothing, food, games, and customs are integrated into the child's adventures. Published the same year as Pearl Buck's *The Good Earth*, *Little Pear* seems naive in contrast.

The plots of her books are predictable, conforming to a pattern of a search or problem resolved. *The Fig Tree* concludes with the finding of a missing cup in a miniature tea set, while *The Fisherman's Son* solves the mystery of a stolen yellow bird. *Storm on the Island* challenges the resourcefulness of a family during a hurricane and its aftermath. A more contemporary story, *The Taming of Tiger*, follows a boy moving from the inner city to a suburb. A diversion from her usual plot is *Jonny*, describing a two-year-old child's entire day.

Lattimore created other memorable characters. *Junior, A Colored Boy of Charleston* was an effective book when published in 1938, sympathetically portraying an enterprising child who earned money for the family. However, the book is long since out-of-print and is not mentioned in Augusta Baker's *The Black Experience in Children's Books* (1971) or Charlemae Rollins's *We Build Together* (1967). There is interaction between children of two cultures in *The Story of Lee Ling*, when the Chinese girl meets an American girl with "yellow hair like corn." *The Chinese Daughter* deals with a mixed racial adoption, while *Jerry and the Pusa* sees China from the point of view of an American child. Childlike competitiveness exists in *Beachcomber Boy* when Barry's shell-collecting territory on the Carolina coast is invaded by Floridians.

In addition to China, the United States and other countries provide the background for a number of books. South Carolina is the setting for *The Youngest Artist*, New Hampshire for *The Clever Cat*. Japan, Denmark, and England serve as the backdrops for *Happiness for Kimi, The Seven Crowns*, and *The Lost Leopard*, respectively. *Happiness for Kimi*, S.C. Gross wrote in the *New York Times* (2 February 1958), "opens a Japanese wing in the author's oriental gallery. It has the simplicity and truth of a proverb touched with humor."

Lattimore's success was based on her understanding of story, children, and locale. She had *Little Pear* so clearly in mind that she wrote it in one week, according to a letter to Dr. Irvin Kerlan. Writing for the reader with one or two years of experience, she usually selected characters which appeal to that age group. Each character has at least one distinguishing feature, such as the six-year-old in *Adam's Key*. His personality is molded by being the youngest of five children and the inheritor of hand-me-downs. As M.L. Becker wrote in a review, the author "has often shown her desire to bridge the gulf of interracial misunderstanding and her power to send across it filaments of good-will from one child to another."

—Karen Nelson Hoyle

LAWRENCE, Ann (Margaret). British. Born in Tring, Hertfordshire, 18 December 1942. Educated at Hemel Hempstead Grammar School; University of Southampton, 1961–64, B.A. (honours) in English 1964. Married Alan Smith in 1971. Worked for the British Trust for Ornithology, Tring, 1964–66; cook, Lundy Field Society, Summer 1965; teacher, Aylesbury, Buckinghamshire, 1966–71, and Tring, 1969–71. *Died in May 1987.*

PUBLICATIONS FOR CHILDREN

Fiction

Tom Ass; or, The Second Gift, illustrated by Ionicus. London, Macmillan, 1972; New York, Walck, 1973.
The Travels of Oggy, illustrated by Hans Helweg. London, Gollancz, 1973.
The Half-Brothers, illustrated by Ionicus. London, Macmillan, and New York, Walck, 1973.
The Conjuror's Box, illustrated by Brian Aldridge. London, Kestrel, 1974.
Mr. Robertson's Hundred Pounds, illustrated by Elisabeth Trimby. London, Kestrel, 1976.
Between the Forest and the Hills, illustrated by Chris Nolan. London, Kestrel, 1977.
Oggy at Home, illustrated by Hans Helweg. London, Gollancz, 1977.
The Good Little Devil, illustrated by Ionicus. London, Macmillan, 1978.
Oggy and the Holiday, illustrated by Hans Helweg. London, Gollancz, 1979.
Mr. Fox, illustrated by Antony Maitland. London, Macmillan, 1979.
The Hawk of May, illustrated by Shirley Felts. London, Macmillan, 1980.
Beyond the Firelight (stories), illustrated by Gail Lewton. London, Macmillan, 1983.
There and Back Again (stories), illustrated by Shirley Felts. Oxford, Oxford University Press, 1985.
Summer's End: Stories of Ghostly Lovers, illustrated by Robert Kettell. Oxford, Oxford University Press, 1987.

Other (retellings)

Merlin the Wizard, illustrated by Susan Hunter. London, Methuen, and Milwaukee, Raintree, 1986.
Tales from Perrault, illustrated by Tony James Chance. Oxford and New York, Oxford University Press, 1989.

*

Ann Lawrence commented:

(1978) I write stories which amuse me and which I hope may amuse other people. Generally in the process of getting written they generate ideas, which are worked out and demonstrated through the characters and the development of the plot, but again these are ideas which interest me, and *may* interest someone else, rather than didactic pills hiding inside a coating of fiction. I have not the least intention of offering the young any assistance with their social adjustments, beyond that which comes as a matter of course when one makes the imaginative effort of putting oneself in someone else's shoes. I should think that books are to the older child what play is to the younger: an opportunity to try out all the roles and situations life offers in the safety of one's own imagination. I feel that this is something achieved as readily through a fairytale as through the most earnest of social documents; I cannot see that it is necessary for the reader to be able to identify with the *setting* of a story, as long as he or she can identify with the characters. Indeed my feeling is that it is easier to handle one's own emotions objectively when they are distanced by an historical or fanciful setting. I presume that this has always been the function of folktales, myths, fables, and legends of all kinds, and this is the tradition of storytelling in which I should like to believe that I work. I believe that all honest art is experimental, in the sense that every piece of work poses a problem of some sort which has to be worked out in its making. One cannot impose one's own solution on it, but must follow patiently the logic of the work itself.

I am concerned beyond anything with the extraordinariness of the ordinary (and following from that, with the baffling matter-o'-factness of marvels *once they have actually happened*) and with the powerful, magical clarity of any particular present moment, as soon as one becomes conscious of its unique presentness, even though nothing much may be happening—because that is the moment when *anything* could happen. I am also fascinated by people talking and the odd, revealing things they do while they are talking. Consequently I find myself trying to cast everything I write in pictures or in scenes of dialogue, so that my people and places can as far as possible speak for themselves. I do not want to explain them, I want to *show* them to you, as I see them, and let you meet them directly. I think of each book as an object, having size and shape; but also in terms of musical form, with key, rhythm, and dynamics, when regarded as a continuum, and I am always aware of having in mind some visual style which I hope to recall. However, these, like my "diagrams" of plot, characters, and ideas, are only working drawings—I do not know whether it is of any use or interest to a reader to know about them, except perhaps for the purpose of knowing that a good deal of thought may go to make even the slightest of literature.

It is my opinion that any style of which one is aware while reading is probably bad.

*   *   *

The death of Ann Lawrence in 1987 has deprived the children's book world of a significant writer. If her books had a common theme, it was the variety of human nature. If she had an outstanding quality, it was her unobtrusive, but always appropriate, style and her skill with dialogue.

The main body of her writing falls into the fantasy or historical genres. All her work was influenced, in one way or another, by folktale and legend and has the strength and exuberance of many folktales. Her early fantasies such as *Tom Ass, The Half-Brothers*, and *The Conjuror's Box* display her wide-ranging themes comprising, as they do, the tribulations of an overconfident youngest son in 15th-century London; a sophisticated tale of Renaissance life in Europe; and a dramatic fantasy with some thoughts about the nature of time. It was perhaps with *The Good Little Devil* that she found her own voice, creating characters and plot of much greater originality. In this, a mischievous imp appears to some monks who assume responsibility for him and try to educate him with the choirboys. Thus tamed, the imp becomes so unhappy that a compassionate Brother is moved to release him, freeing the imp to teach some necessary lessons to the boys who had persecuted him.

Lawrence has a direct and timeless style that suits the unusual settings and other times about which she writes and helps to give credibility to the fantasy she creates.

Among her historical novels, *Mr. Robertson's Hundred Pounds* is a rich novel about a boy who travels to Europe in 1595 in pursuit of a thief. Although it deals with questions of loyalty, love, religious tolerance, artistic ambition, and political ideology, the exciting plot makes this a stimulating and gripping novel for the reader of 12 and older. *The Hawk of May* is a tale of Sir Gawain, tricked into a compromising situation in order to discredit King Arthur's court. He is given a year to solve a riddle and save his life, and there is a simple perfection in the solution to the riddle and the climax of the story. The book will appeal to teenagers and possibly adults as well, because of the philosophical undertones about behaviour, choice, and freedom. The Arthurian theme was continued for much younger readers, and perhaps less successfully, in *Merlin the Wizard*. Because this tells only those parts of King Arthur's story where Merlin is directly involved, it is somewhat fragmentary and episodic. Often the most interesting part is what happens *between* Merlin's appearances and the text is full of statements like, "From then on Merlin was seldom at court" or "Merlin disappeared about his own affairs."

In her later works Lawrence turned her skill to the short story form. *Beyond the Firelight* is a title in the Flying Carpets series of Macmillan which consists of folktales and fairytales rewritten to bridge the gap between picture books and longer stories. Skilfully written, but not written down, to combine a simplicity of style with the timeless quality of folktale, *Beyond the Firelight* tells four short tales of supernatural creatures invading ordinary life: the boggart who disrupts a farm and is finally—with great difficulty—evicted by the farmer; the three strange sisters who help a girl with an impossible task of spinning fleeces; the pathetic creature who is finally liberated from service to a young man by an act of kindness. *There and Back Again* is another collection of stories and is typical of her work in that she bases them on familiar fairytale characters but creates with them something original and with universal appeal.

One of her last published works, *Summer's End*, fittingly combines many strands of Lawrence's work and is told with the style, characterisation, and wit so characteristic of all her work. Subtitled *Stories of Ghostly Lovers*, the fantasy of the traditional tales is complemented by the down-to-earth presence of the innkeeper's three daughters to whom they are told. Lawrence's writing had a quiet, subtle excellence which may have failed to make the headlines or win awards but which was directed by her own strong vision. Many of her books were more truly original and thought-provoking than those of other better-known writers.

—Valerie Brinkley-Willsher

LAWRENCE, Louise. Pseudonym for Elizabeth Rhoda Holden. British. Born in Leatherhead, Surrey, 5 June 1943. Educated at Poplar Road Primary School, Leatherhead, 1948–54; Lydney Grammar School, Gloucestershire, 1955–60. Married twice; two daughters and one son. Assistant librarian, Gloucestershire County Library, 1961–63, and at Forest of Dean branches, 1969–71. Agent: A.M. Heath, 79 St. Martin's Lane, London WC2N 4AA. Address: 22 Church Road, Cinderford, Gloucestershire GL14 2EA, England.

PUBLICATIONS FOR CHILDREN

Fiction

Andra. London, Collins, 1971.
The Power of Stars. London, Collins, and New York, Harper, 1972.
The Wyndcliffe. London, Collins, 1974; New York, Harper, 1975.
Sing and Scatter Daisies. New York, Harper, 1977.
Star Lord. New York, Harper, 1978; London, Bodley Head, 1987.
Cat Call. New York, Harper, 1980.
The Earth Witch. New York, Harper, 1981; London, Collins, 1982.
Calling B for Butterfly. New York, Harper, 1982; London, Bodley Head, 1988.
The Dram Road. New York, Harper, 1983.
Children of the Dust. London, Bodley Head, and New York, Harper, 1985.
Moonwind. London, Bodley Head, and New York, Harper, 1986.
The Warriors of Taan. London, Bodley Head, 1986; New York, Harper, 1988.

*

Louise Lawrence comments:

I write for teenagers; the books contain fantasy elements in a realistic setting—a combination of ordinary human characters influenced by extraordinary forces. Each story also touches upon some wider contemporary issue, such as violence, religion, the role of women, life after death, the conflict of science and nature.

It is not the world we must change, but human situations. Hope lies with the young, so I write for them stories that question what is or project what may be, that are tentative examinations of powers that transcend mundane existence, that search for lost values, for meanings and understanding in an age where so much gets disregarded. I do not regard my books as achievements, just attempts—and attempts that will take me a lifetime.

*   *   *

While many writers of adult science fiction are women, it is less common to find one who specialises in this genre for teenagers. Louise Lawrence's protagonists are girls, but this does not mean that boys will be switched off from reading their adventures, since her heroines have young men closely associated with them. Her first leading lady, Andra, lives in a far-distant future time when authority is accepted unquestioningly and everyone is programmed into subservience. The 15-year-old girl undergoes a brain transplant from an organ deep-frozen two thousand years earlier in the turbulent 1980's. Recovering, she sees her world through the senses of the original owner of her new brain and rebels against the narrowness of her existence. She sets up a dissident youth group, desperate to free themselves, even by escape to another planet. In *The Power of Stars* we return to our own earth and times, with a heroine who suddenly finds herself possessed by a frightening compulsion to destroy by the use of mental energy. Several tragic accidents occur, and her two boyfriends despair of finding a cure.

Moonwind is perhaps her most powerful novel to date, dealing with the uncomfortable emotional relationship growing between a young earth boy at work in a moon colony and a native-born alien girl. The tension between the two is well handled, and the failure of adults to believe results in an unconventional ending—whether we regard it as happy depends on our point of view.

There is incipient romance in the stories—not too much to annoy younger readers intent on the adventure, but carefully interwoven into the plots to add an extra dimension to the relationship of the characters. Her young people are genuine, their language is right, and whether the story is set in our own countryside or some sterile Sub-City the plots are believable. The natural rebellion of young readers is sympathetically channelled and Lawrence does not pull her punches—no conventional happy endings here but a savage twist right on the last page leaps out to stun us.

—Ann G. Hay

LAWSON, Robert. American. Born in New York City, 4 October 1892. Educated at Montclair High School, New Jersey; New York School of Fine and Applied Art, 1911–14. Served in the American Expeditionary Forces, 40th Engineers Camouflage Section, during World War I. Married Marie Abrams in 1922 (died 1956). Freelance magazine illustrator, New York, 1914–17; commercial artist, 1919–30; from 1930 freelance book illustrator. Individual shows (etchings): New York, 1932, 1933. Recipient: Society of American Etchers John Taylor Arms prize, 1931; American Library Association Caldecott Medal, 1941, and Newbery Medal, 1945. Died 26 May 1957.

PUBLICATIONS FOR CHILDREN (illustrated by the author)

Fiction

Ben and Me.   Boston, Little Brown, 1939.
They Were Strong and Good.   New York, Viking Press, 1940.
I Discover Columbus.   Boston, Little Brown, 1941; London, Harrap, 1943.
Rabbit Hill.   New York, Viking Press, 1944; London, Harrap, 1947.
Mr. Wilmer.   Boston, Little Brown, 1945; London, Muller, 1946.
Mr. Twigg's Mistake.   Boston, Little Brown, 1947.
Robbut: A Tale of Tails.   New York, Viking Press, 1948; London, Heinemann, 1949.
The Fabulous Flight.   Boston, Little Brown, 1949.
Smeller Martin.   New York, Viking Press, 1950.
McWhinney's Jaunt.   Boston, Little Brown, 1951.
Edward, Hoppy and Joe.   New York, Knopf, 1952.
Mr. Revere and I.   Boston, Little Brown, 1953.
The Tough Winter.   New York, Viking Press, 1954.
Captain Kidd's Cat.   Boston, Little Brown, and London, Muller, 1956.
The Great Wheel.   New York, Viking Press, 1957; London, Angus and Robertson, 1967.

Other

Dick Whittington and His Cat.   New York, Limited Editions Club, 1949.

Editor, Just for Fun: A Collection of Stories and Verses.   Chicago, Rand McNally, 1940.
Editor, Watchwords of Liberty: A Pageant of American Quotations.

Boston, Little Brown, 1943.

PUBLICATIONS FOR ADULTS (illustrated by the author)

Other

Country Colic.   Boston, Little Brown, 1944.
At That Time (autobiographical).   New York, Viking Press, 1947; London, Heinemann, 1949.
Robert Lawson, Illustrator: A Selection of His Characteristic Illustrations, edited by Helen L. Jones.   Boston, Little Brown, 1972.

*

Manuscript Collections: Free Library, Philadelphia; May Massee Collection, Emporia State University, Kansas.

Illustrator: The Wonderful Adventures of Little Prince Toofat by George Randolph Chester, 1922; The Wee Men of Ballywooden, 1930, The Roving Lobster, 1931, and From the Horn of the Moon, 1931, all by Arthur Mason; The Unicorn with Silver Shoes by Ella Young, 1932; Peik by Barbara Ring, 1932; The Hurdy-Gurdy Man by Margery Williams Bianco, 1933; Haven's End by John P. Marquand, 1933; Treasure of the Isle of Mist by W.W. Tarn, 1934; Slim by William Wister Haines, 1934; The Golden Horseshoe by Elizabeth Coatsworth, 1935; Drums of Monmouth, 1935, and Miranda Is a Princess, 1937, both by Emma Gelders Sterne; The Story of Ferdinand, 1936, Wee Gillis, 1938, The Story of Simpson and Sampson, 1941, and Aesop's Fables, 1941, all by Munro Leaf; Seven Beads of Wampum by Elizabeth Gale, 1936; Betsy Ross and Francis Scott Key both by Helen Dixon Bates, 1936; Four and Twenty Blackbirds edited by Helen Dean Fish, 1937; The Prince and the Pauper by Mark Twain, 1937; The Story of Jesus for Young People by Walter Russell Bowie, 1937; Under the Tent of Sky, 1937, and Gaily We Parade, 1940, both edited by John E. Brewton; I Hear America Singing by Ruth Barnes, 1937; Wind of the Vikings by Maribelle Cormack, 1937; Swords and Statues by Clarence Stratton, 1937; Mr. Popper's Penguins by Richard and Florence Atwater, 1938; One Foot in Fairyland by Eleanor Farjeon, 1938; A Tale of Two Cities by Charles Dickens, 1938; Pilgrim's Progress by John Bunyan, 1939; Poo-Poo and the Dragons by C.S. Forester, 1942; Prince Prigio by Andrew Lang, 1942; The Crock of Gold by James Stephens, 1942; Adam of the Road by Elizabeth Janet Gray, 1942; The Little Woman Wanted Noise by Val Teal, 1943; The Shoelace Robin by William Hall, 1945; Greylock and the Robins by Tom Robinson, 1946; Mathematics for Success by Mary A. Potter, 1952.

* * *

The only individual to win both the Newbery and Caldecott Medals, author-illustrator Robert Lawson holds a unique position in the history of American literature for children. His works are significant not only because of the recognition they received, however, but also because they support the notion that art both reflects and informs the values of an era.

A successful commercial artist and etcher, Lawson became internationally known during the 1930's as an illustrator of children's books following his collaboration with Munro Leaf for The Story of Ferdinand in 1936. He assumed the dual role of author-illustrator in 1939 with the publication of Ben and Me, first of four comic fantasies in which loquacious pets revealed the foibles of their notable owners—Benjamin Franklin, Christopher Columbus, Captain Kidd, and Paul Revere.

Whether illustrating his own texts or the texts of others, his drawings, characterized by traditional composition and an emphasis on meticulous draftsmanship, had the narrative quality which Barbara Bader in *American Picturebooks from Noah's Ark to The Beast Within* (1976) identifies as a particularly American attribute. This narrative quality appears in the tales he wrote as a strong sense of story conveyed through the forms, personae, and techniques associated with American humor. The two elements—words and pictures—merge to create a particular vision of American ideals and the American national character.

The four historical fantasies, for example, employ the talking beast motif, a familiar folklore device, but adapted to a convention of American humor, the comic monologue delivered by an apparently insignificant character who would be expected to celebrate rather than ridicule his betters. Although this same motif is apparent in the Newbery Medal-winning *Rabbit Hill* as well as in *The Tough Winter* and *Edward, Hoppy and Joe*, these are primarily stories of animal communities in the tradition of *The Wind in the Willows*. Yet the characters are basically American personalities, revealed not through lengthy description but through descriptive dialogue, complemented by explicit illustrations.

More obviously reflective of mid-20th-century American values are the Caldecott Medal-winning *They Were Strong and Good*, a picture book biography of Lawson's ancestors, and *The Great Wheel*, a period romance celebrating the ideal of America as the land of opportunity. Concurrently with these tributes to American virtues, however, Lawson satirized such American institutions as merchandising and tourism in *Mr. Wilmer, Mr. Twigg's Mistake*, and *The Fabulous Flight*. Similarly, *McWhinney's Jaunt*, often compared to the stories of Baron Munchausen, could also be interpreted as a humorous warning to gullible consumers; yet it is essentially a tall tale, American in style and tone, dominated by the angular figure of the Yankee peddler in 20th-century disguise.

Undoubtedly Lawson's delineation of the homely virtues thought to be particularly American and his use of literary and visual techniques considered characteristic elements in the American cultural tradition contributed much to his popularity in the 1940's and 1950's. From a later perspective, it has been noted that his treatment of minorities failed to transcend the sociological clichés of his time. Indeed, few of his human characters have the multi-dimensional personalities of his more memorable animal creations. Essentially a fabulist, he reflected the attitudes of his own era and yet, in his historical fantasies, notably *Ben and Me*, he managed to present for children an iconoclastic version of the traditions from which many of those attitudes were derived.

—Mary Mehlman Burns

LEAF, (Wilbur) Munro. Also wrote as John Calvert; Mun. American. Born in Hamilton, Maryland, 4 December 1905. Educated at the University of Maryland, College Park, A.B. 1927; Harvard University, Cambridge, Massachusetts, M.A. 1931. Served in the United States Army, 1942–46: Major. Married Margaret Butler Pope in 1926; two sons. Teacher and coach, Belmont Hill School, Massachusetts, 1929–30; teacher, Montgomery School, Wynnewood, Pennsylvania, 1931; reader, Bobbs Merrill, publishers, Indianapolis, 1932; editor and director, Frederick A. Stokes Company, publishers, New York, 1932–39; columnist ("Watchbirds"), *Ladies' Home Journal*, 1938–60. *Died 21 December 1976.*

PUBLICATIONS FOR CHILDREN

Fiction

Lo, The Poor Indian (as Mun), illustrated by the author. New York, Leaf Mahony Seidel and Stokes, 1934.
Robert Francis Weatherbee, illustrated by the author. New York, Stokes, 1935; London, Chatto and Windus, 1936.
The Story of Ferdinand, illustrated by Robert Lawson. New York, Viking Press, 1936; London, Hamish Hamilton, 1937.
Noodle, illustrated by Ludwig Bemelmans. New York, Stokes, 1937; London, Hamish Hamilton, 1938.
Wee Gillis, illustrated by Robert Lawson. New York, Viking Press, and London, Hamish Hamilton, 1938.
John Henry Davis, illustrated by the author. New York, Stokes, 1940.
The Story of Simpson and Sampson, illustrated by Robert Lawson. New York, Viking Press, 1941; London, Warne, 1944.
Gordon the Goat, illustrated by the author. Philadelphia, Lippincott, 1944; London, Warne, 1947.
Gwendolyn the Goose (as John Calvert), illustrated by Garrett Price. New York, Random House, 1946.
Boo, Who Used to Be Scared of the Dark, illustrated by Frances Hunter. New York, Random House, 1948; as *Boo, The Boy Who Didn't Like the Dark*, London, Publicity Products, 1954.
Sam and the Superdroop, illustrated by the author. New York, Viking Press, 1948.
The Wishing Pool, illustrated by the author. Philadelphia, Lippincott, 1960.
Turnabout. Philadelphia, Lippincott, 1967.

Other (illustrated by the author)

Grammar Can Be Fun. New York, Stokes, 1934; London, Ward Lock, 1951.
Manners Can Be Fun. New York, Stokes, 1936; London, Hamish Hamilton, 1937; revised edition, Philadelphia, Lippincott, 1958.
Safety Can Be Fun. New York, Stokes, 1938; London, Ward Lock, 1951; revised edition, Philadelphia, Lippincott, 1961.
Listen, Little Girl, Before You Come to New York, illustrated by Dick Rose. New York, Stokes, 1938.
The Watchbirds: A Picture Book of Behavior. New York, Stokes, 1939; London, Warne, 1945.
Your Library and Some People You Don't Want in It. New York, Wilson, 1939.
Fair Play. New York, Stokes, 1939; London, Warne, 1959.
More Watchbirds. New York, Stokes, 1940.
Fly Away, Watchbird! New York, Stokes, 1941.
Aesop's Fables, illustrated by Robert Lawson. New York, Heritage Press, 1941.
A War-Time Handbook for Young Americans. Philadelphia, Stokes, 1942.
Health Can Be Fun. Philadelphia, Stokes, 1943; London, Warne, 1944.
3 and 30 Watchbirds. Philadelphia, Lippincott, 1944.
Let's Do Better. Philadelphia, Lippincott, 1945; London, Warne, 1947.
How to Behave and Why. Philadelphia, Lippincott, 1946.
Arithmetic [History, Geography, Reading, Science] Can Be Fun. Philadelphia, Lippincott, 5 vols., 1949–60; London, Ward Lock, 5 vols., 1951–60; revised edition of *Geography Can Be Fun*, Lippincott, 1962.
Lucky You. Philadelphia, Lippincott, 1955.
Three Promises to You. Philadelphia, Lippincott, 1957.
Being an American Can Be Fun. Philadelphia, Lippincott, 1964.
Who Cares? I Do. Philadelphia, Lippincott, 1971.

Metric Can Be Fun. Philadelphia, Lippincott, 1976.

PUBLICATIONS FOR ADULTS

Other

You and Psychiatry, with William C. Menninger. New York, Scribner, 1948.

*

Illustrator: *The Danger of Hiding Our Heads* by the Committee on the Present Danger, 1951.

* * *

Munro Leaf was the author and illustrator of many stories for children—but only two of them are popular today. Of his slighter, ephemeral materials, such as the various *Watchbirds*, there is little to be said other than that they were suited to the tenor of their times, and were widely read, thanks to the *Ladies' Home Journal*, of which they were a feature between 1938 and 1960. Most of his other children's titles were more or less didactic and forgettable: he had a good-natured but inexorable urge to preach, on manners, self-improvement, patriotism, conformity. Some of the subjects he illustrated for the…*Can Be Fun* group, such as *Manners, Metrics*, and *Safety*, neither are nor require to be *Fun*; they are merely necessary. But for all that, twice in his career, Leaf struck a vein of purest gold, and producing two indisputable classics of children's literature isn't after all a bad score.

First and best is the well-loved *The Story of Ferdinand*. Ferdinand first appears as a large-eyed calf, gentle, sweet-natured, rather a worry to his loving mother for his failure to make a place for himself among the bovine roughnecks huffing and chuffing about the pasture. Ferdinand will have none of it. He likes to sit just quietly, by himself, smelling the flowers under his favourite cork tree. Time passes. Ferdinand and the rest are now stout young stock, eligible to be selected by the scouts from Madrid for that supreme honour—the bullring! The other bulls are anxiously showing off, running, leaping, butting, and snorting. Not Ferdinand. Let those who wish seek fame and glory; he wants none of it. Alas, at the worst possible moment, Ferdinand is stung by a bee in a *very* sensitive spot, and his subsequent antics arouse the admiration of the scouts. Here, they think, is a *fighter*! He is chosen, taken away to the city, and soon comes the moment of truth. Ferdinand must face the fierce, if frightened, banderilleros, picadores, and last of all, the gallant matador. Ferdinand sees nothing, is conscious of nothing, but the flowers in the lovely senoritas' hair. As before, as always, he sits quietly to smell the flowers…and they have to take Ferdinand home again. We leave him, perfectly content, under his favourite cork tree, the perfect ending for the hero of one of the most charming of all animal stories.

Wee Gillis has not quite the same universal appeal, but is in its way irresistible in its quirky charm and good humour. Wee Gillis is a half-breed of sorts: his mother was Lowland Scots, his father Highland. He spends his time alternately herding cattle in the Lowlands and stalking stags in the Highlands; but when he comes to years of discretion, both sides of his family insist that he must decide, once and for always, whether he will be High or Low. Gillis is torn between the two sides of the raging family argument, and finally goes off to make his momentous decision. As he ponders, he encounters a dejected man, who has constructed the biggest bagpipes in all of Scotland, and now hasn't got enough wind to play them. Gillis has all the lung power of a lad who has called cattle home through the Lowland mist, and who had held his breath for long minutes while stalking the wary Highland stag. HE can blow the pipes, and he does.

His problem is solved. He will live just between the Highlands and the Lowlands, and he will be the most famous piper in all of Scotland. Would that all problems could be so happily solved.

—Joan McGrath

————

LEE, Dennis (Beynon). Canadian. Born in Toronto, Ontario, 31 August 1939. Educated at the University of Toronto, B.A. 1962, M.A. in English 1964. Married 1) Donna Youngblut in 1961 (divorced 1972), two daughters and one son; 2) Susan Ruth Perly in 1985. Full-time writer. Taught at Victoria College, University of Toronto, 1964–67, and Rochdale College, Toronto, 1967–69; artist-in-residence, Trent University, Peterborough, Ontario, 1975. Editor, House of Anansi Press, Toronto, 1967–72; consulting editor, Macmillan of Canada, publishers, Toronto, 1973–78; poetry consultant, McClelland and Stewart, publishers, Toronto, 1981–84. Songwriter, *Fraggle Rock* television programme, Canadian Broadcasting Corporation, 1982–86. Recipient: Governor-General's award, for verse, 1973; Canadian Library Association Book of the Year Medal, 1975, 1978; Ruth Schwartz award, 1978; Philips Information Systems prize, 1985; Vicky Metcalf award, 1986. Address: c/o The Colbert Agency, 303 Davenport Road, Toronto, Ontario M5R 1K5, Canada.

PUBLICATIONS FOR CHILDREN

Fiction

The Ordinary Bath, illustrated by Jon McKee. Toronto, McClelland and Stewart, 1979.

Verse

Wiggle to the Laundromat, illustrated by Charles Pachter. Toronto, New Press, 1970.
Alligator Pie, illustrated by Frank Newfeld. Toronto, Macmillan, 1974; Boston, Houghton Mifflin, 1975.
Nicholas Knock and Other People, illustrated by Frank Newfeld. Toronto, Macmillan, 1974; Boston, Houghton Mifflin, 1977.
Garbage Delight, illustrated by Frank Newfeld. Toronto, Macmillan, 1977; Boston, Houghton Mifflin, 1978.
Jelly Belly, illustrated by Juan Wijngaard. Toronto, Macmillan, and London, Blackie, 1983.
Lizzy's Lion, illustrated by Marie-Louise Gay. Toronto, Stoddart, and London, Hodder and Stoughton, 1984.
The Dennis Lee Big Book, illustrated by Barb Klunder. Toronto, Gage, 1985.

Recordings: *Alligator Pie and Other Poems*, music by Don Heckman, Caedmon, 1978; *Fraggle Rock*, music by Philip Balsam, Muppet Music, 1984.

PUBLICATIONS FOR ADULTS

Verse

Kingdom of Absence. Toronto, Anansi, 1967.
Civil Elegies. Toronto, Anansi, 1968.
Civil Elegies and Other Poems. Toronto, Anansi, 1972.
Not Abstract Harmonies But. Vancouver and San Francisco, Kanchenjunga, 1974.

The Death of Harold Ladoo. Vancouver and San Francisco, Kanchenjunga, 1976.
Miscellany. Privately printed, 1977.
The Gods. Vancouver and San Francisco, Kanchenjunga, 1978.
The Gods (collection). Toronto, McClelland and Stewart, 1979.
The Difficulty of Living on Other Planets: An Adult Entertainment. Toronto, Macmillan, 1987.

Other

Notes on Rochdale. Ottawa, Canadian Union of Students, 1967(?).
Savage Fields: An Essay in Literature and Cosmology. Toronto, Anansi, 1977.

Editor, with R.A. Charlesworth, *An Anthology of Verse.* Toronto, Oxford University Press, 1964.
Editor, with R.A. Charlesworth, *The Second Century Anthologies of Verse, Book 2.* Toronto, Oxford University Press, 1967.
Editor, with Howard Adelman, *The University Game.* Toronto, Anansi, 1968.
Editor, *T.O. Now: The Young Toronto Poets.* Toronto, Anansi, 1968.
Editor, *The New Canadian Poets 1970–85.* Toronto, McClelland and Stewart, 1985.

*

Manuscript Collection: Fisher Rare Book Room, University of Toronto.

Critical Study: *Task of Passion: Dennis Lee at Mid-Career*, edited by Donna Bennett, Russell Brown, and Karen Mulhallen, Toronto, Descant, 1982.

Dennis Lee comments:
I can sum up the concerns of my children's poetry in two words: "roots" and "play." Beyond that, it sinks or swims on its own merits.

*   *   *

The key to Dennis Lee's poetry, both juvenile and adult, is that he is Canadian. Lee's Canadianness has two main aspects: first, his awareness of Canada as a unique place, his homeland; second, his awareness of Canada's colonial status, from which she must be liberated. In his children's poetry, these two aspects have their equivalents in the concepts of "roots" and "play." The former means literature both rooted in a particular time and place, and also articulating to the reader his own roots. The latter means literature which, in Lee's words, tries "to reanimate repressed feelings," which is emotionally released, free and joyous, full of play.
It was in response to these impulses that Lee's children's verse was written. Explaining its genesis in the epilogue to *Alligator Pie*, he writes that, when reading *Mother Goose* to his children, he began to realize the distance between the nursery rhymes and contemporary Canadian reality: "The details of *Mother Goose*—the wassails and Dobbins and pipers and pence—had become exotic; children loved them, but they were no longer home ground." At the same time, Lee recognized that Canadians "are a colonial people; leaving aside the political and economic aspects of the thing for now, we have always been a colony of the imagination, first of England and France, latterly of the United States." Lee's answer was to liberate Canadian children from the colonial mentality by creating poems rooted in the things that are part of a Canadian child's inner and outer life. And in doing so he found himself becoming liberated, regaining the ability to play.
Lee has published several volumes of children's poetry. Nursery rhymes (for preschoolers) appear in *Alligator Pie*, which includes

poems playing with incantatory Canadian place names ("Tongue Twister," "Kahshe or Chicoutimi"), activity songs ("Bouncing Song," "Rattlesnake Skipping Song"), and short word-play poems ("Skyscraper," "Willoughby Wallaby Woo"). Such works contain much pure play; alliteration, onomatopoeia, rhyme, and rhythm are so strongly stressed that the words often function as music. A few poems in the latter half of the book are more for children of school-entering age; they are longer and often more serious, sensitively exploring the child's inner world ("The Special Person," "The Friend").
For the 7–10 age group, the poems in *Nicholas Knock and Other People* are most appropriate. Most of them are longer, more complex in thought, and sometimes deal with such specialized topics as the Spadina Expressway or the Mackenzie Rebellion of 1837 (both, incidentally, anti-authoritarian people's struggles). One prominent subject is the child's imaginative world ("Mister Hoobody," "The Thing"), sometimes under threat from the adult "real" world ("Nicholas Knock"). Other poems deal with the child's reaction to close relationships ("Going Up North," "With My Foot in My Mouth"); these pieces—while rooted in a sense of self—express affection clearly though indirectly. The kind of black humour that sets children chortling is also given effective expression ("Oilcan Harry"). Play, of course, has its place in all the poems; at times, as in the Ookpik poems, it even becomes the theme, a liberating force. Lee describes Ookpik as "another of the vital figures that challenge how we are. He's a dancer, an embodiment of pure lyricism: harmless, pointless, irrepressible… There are four Ookpik poems, and by the last one he has become a kind of totemic figure or tutelary god for the books. The theme of play and the theme of roots fuse in that poem, as they often do." Ookpik: the "tutelary god" for the books. How does the last Ookpik poem end? "Ookpik,/Ookpick/By your Grace,/Help us/Live in/Our own/Space." Lee's final word, then, is directed at the need for Canadians to inhabit—both physically and imaginatively—their own space, their country.
Garbage Delight, illustrated by Frank Newfeld, is very similar in design and content to the previous two books. Unfortunately, in spite of some fine individual poems, it does not achieve as high a standard, overall, as its predecessors. The poetry is more uneven in quality; the prospective audience falls into a wider, less coherent age range; and the humour, rhyme, and rhythm are sometimes more strained. Thematically, there is less reference to political events and greater focus on one's self, including the joys afforded by play and eating—activities which literally and symbolically assert one's own imagination and taste. Technically, parody ("The Big Blue Frog and the Dirty Flannel Dog") and spoonerism ("The Big Molice Pan and the Bertie Dumb") are more apparent. Particularly prominent are Newfeld-Lee "insider" jokes, such as the cartoon strip depicting the pair, the pictures of Lee accompanying "Goofus," etc. Unfortunately, sometimes Newfeld's pictures in this volume limit the full expression of the exuberant play that Lee's words suggest. Thus Lee's "Bloody Bill" is a gory, messy tale, not adequately depicted by Newfeld's staid, neat illustrations. Similarly, Lee's "Garbage Delight" tells of a jumbled, indescribable mixture of everything gooey, sweet, and delicious, not Newfeld's ordered assortment of conventional sweets.
Such discrepancies between illustration and text are eliminated in *The Ordinary Bath*. Here Jon McKee's illustrations superbly parallel the overflowing imaginative exuberance of Lee's playful protagonist, as the child's imagination transforms his ordinary bathtub world into an extraordinary one, peopled with colorful monsters—friendly and otherwise—that pour out of the tap and join in his play. Yet even while his imagination exults in glorious freedom, the child knows its expression must be reconciled with the demands of the real world—in this case his mother's requirements that the floor be kept dry and the bath end at a certain time. The resolution of this tension, through harmonious written and pictorial techniques, provides an artful balancing of the two worlds, depicting the limits

of play at the point where freedom becomes anarchy.

Lizzy's Lion is a much lesser book. In 14 quatrains superimposed on 14 double-page illustrations by Marie-Louise Gay, the narrative tells of a rotten robber who, attempting to purloin Lizzy's piggy bank, encounters her pet lion and becomes the lion's lunch. Unfortunately there is a lack of variation from picture to picture which, added to the skimpiness of the text, suggests that both author and illustrator stretched their material too far.

In 1983 Lee extended his poetic range to what he calls "foetus literature": poems written for babies and young preschoolers. In *Jelly Belly* the sound and rhythm of words are at least as marked as in *Alligator Pie*, though the more recent volume is less varied and invigorating overall. However, there are some excellent activity poems ("Three Tickles," "The Army Went A-Marching"), and witty word-play is evident ("There Was An Old Lady"). Juan Wijngaard's superb illustrations admirably complement and extend the text. Beautifully grotesque, free, imaginative, humorous: they are very appealing to children and add much to the book's continuity, resonance, and integrity.

For the other end of the age spectrum Lee has published *The Difficulty of Living on Other Planets*, subtitled *An Adult Entertainment*. Though this collection uses many of the rhymes and rhythms of his children's poetry, the tone is different: sometimes more overtly nostalgic, occasionally more mystical, and often more cynical and satirical. A few of the poems are revisions of ones in *Nicholas Knock*. The cat in "The Cat and the Wizard," for example, becomes a "She"—adding a sexual suggestiveness to her relationship with the wizard. In "Nicholas Knock" some stanzas are added, others removed—increasing the mystical element. However, the collection as a whole is neither as compelling as Lee's other adult books nor as captivating as his better illustrated children's ones.

Overall, Lee's work represents the best in children's poetry; it dances off the page and involves the reader in its world.

—John Robert Sorfleet

LEE, Julian.   See **LATHAM, Jean Lee.**

LEE, Mildred.   American.   Born in Blocton, Alabama, 19 February 1908. Educated at Cairo High School, Georgia; Tift College, Forsyth, Georgia, 1925–26; Troy Normal College, Alabama, 1927; Columbia University, New York, 1936; New York University; University of New Hampshire, Durham, 1944. Married 1) Edward Cannon Schimpff in 1929, one daughter and one son; 2) James Henry Scudder in 1947, one daughter. Recipient: Child Study Committee award, 1964. Address: c/o Clarion Books, 52 Vanderbilt Avenue, New York, New York 10017, U.S.A.

PUBLICATIONS FOR CHILDREN

Fiction

The Rock and the Willow.   New York, Lothrop, 1963; London, Oxford University Press, 1975.
Honor Sands.   New York, Lothrop, 1966.
The Skating Rink.   New York, Seabury Press, 1969; London, Abelard Schuman, 1972.
Fog.   New York, Seabury Press, 1972.
Sycamore Year.   New York, Lothrop, 1974.

The People Therein.   New York, Clarion, 1980.

PUBLICATIONS FOR ADULTS

Novel

The Invisible Sun.   Philadelphia, Westminster Press, 1946.

*

Manuscript Collections: University of Wyoming Library, Laramie; Kerlan Collection, University of Minnesota, Minneapolis.

Mildred Lee comments:

My books are really "novels for young people" rather than children's books in that they all deal with the agonies and ecstasies of growing up and are suitable for readers of middle school or teen age.

*   *   *

The rain started sometime in the night. Enie woke to hear its patter on the new tin roof Papa and the boys had put on two weeks ago. As he laid his tools away Papa had predicted darkly that likely there'd be a drought now to ruin his crops if he ever got the ground broken to put them in. He said the new roof was bad luck, but Mamma's jawing him about it all winter was enough to drive a man to anything.

That opening paragraph from Mildred Lee's novel *The Rock and the Willow* introduces the landscape, tone, and feeling that characterize her best work: the poverty-stricken American rural South in the 1930's and later, peopled with characters who either struggle to better their lot in life or resign themselves to apathy. In *The Rock and the Willow*, Enie, the teenage heroine, is determined to go away and get a college education despite all the pressures on her to remain at home. *The Skating Rink* features Tuck Faraday, whose severe stutter leads his peers to call him "Dummy," but who eventually asserts his individuality and worth by developing his flair for skating. Luke, the young hero of *Fog*, must adjust to the sudden, untimely death of the father he somehow always took for granted until it was too late. In *The People Therein*, Lee's one venture into historical fiction, Lanthy Farr is forced to mediate the conflict between Drew Thorndike, the Boston botanist who has won her heart, and her family and friends in the mountain community of Dewfall Gap, who are deeply suspicious of outsiders.

Strong on atmosphere and character detail, Lee is much less confident when it comes to plotting. If her protagonists are living in fairly comfortable circumstances and are not faced with any major obstacles, as is the case in *Honor Sands* and *Sycamore Year*, then her narratives tend to be a bit slack. Suspense and dramatic tension generally spring from the plight of her central characters rather than from a tightly constructed plot.

Even in her slighter stories, though, Lee's craftsmanship is always apparent. She is gifted with a keen ear for the rhythms and expressions of the southern vernacular which she employs to lend color and veracity to her dialogue. She also has a knack for building sensual word pictures of her settings and characters in their various seasons and moods. As contemporary American writers for young teenagers go, she probably makes more demands of her readers than most in terms of concentration and reading ability, but for those who stick with her books, she probably also offers richer rewards when it comes to understanding the workings of the human heart.

In an era when many fiction writers for young people have latched onto one controversial subject after another, Lee has quietly continued to offer honest, realistic portraits of unsensational situations. Valuable in themselves, her books can also serve to point interested young readers toward such outstanding adult interpreters of the American south as Carson McCullers, Flannery O'Connor, and Eudora Welty.

—James Cross Giblin

LEE, Tanith. British. Born in London, 19 September 1947. Educated at Prendergaste Grammar School; Catford Grammar School, London; and an art college. Recipient: August Derleth award, 1980; World Fantasy Convention award, 1983. Lives in Sidcup, Kent. Address: c/o Macmillan London Ltd., 4 Little Essex Street, London WC2R 3LF, England.

PUBLICATIONS FOR CHILDREN

Fiction

The Dragon Hoard, illustrated by Graham Oakley. London, Macmillan, and New York, Farrar Straus, 1971.
Princess Hynchatti and Some Other Surprises, illustrated by Helen Craig. London Macmillan, 1972; New York, Farrar Straus, 1973.
Animal Castle, illustrated by Helen Craig. London, Macmillan, and New York, Farrar Straus, 1972.
Companions on the Road. London, Macmillan, 1975.
The Winter Players. London, Macmillan, 1976.
Companions on the Road, and The Winter Players. New York, St. Martin's Press, 1977.
East of Midnight. London, Macmillan, 1977; New York, St. Martin's Press, 1978.
The Castle of Dark. London, Macmillan, 1978.
Shon the Taken. London, Macmillan, 1979.
Prince on a White Horse. London, Macmillan, 1982.

PUBLICATIONS FOR ADULTS

Novels

The Birthgrave. New York, DAW, 1975; London, Futura, 1977.
Don't Bite the Sun. New York, DAW, 1976.
The Storm Lord. New York, DAW, 1976; London, Futura, 1977.
Drinking Sapphire Wine. New York, DAW, 1977.
Volkhavaar. New York, DAW, 1977; London, Hamlyn, 1981.
Vazkor, Son of Vazkor. New York, DAW, 1978; as *Shadowfire*, London, Futura, 1979.
Quest for the White Witch. New York, DAW, 1978; London, Futura, 1979.
Night's Master. New York, DAW, 1978; London, Hamlyn, 1981.
Death's Master. New York, DAW, 1979; London, Hamlyn, 1982.
Drinking Sapphire Wine (includes *Don't Bite the Sun*). London, Hamlyn, 1979.
Electric Forest. New York, DAW, 1979.
Sabella; or, The Blood Stone. New York, DAW, 1980.
Kill the Dead. New York, DAW, 1980.
Day by Night. New York, DAW, 1980.
Delusion's Master. New York, DAW, 1981.
The Silver Metal Lover. New York, DAW, 1982; London, Unwin, 1986.

Sung in Shadow. New York, DAW, 1983.
Anackire. New York, DAW, 1983; London, Futura, 1985.
Days of Grass. New York, DAW, 1985.
Dark Castle, White Horse. New York, DAW, 1986.
Delirium's Mistress. New York, DAW, 1986.
Night's Sorceries. New York, DAW, 1987.
The White Serpent. New York, DAW, 1988.
Forests of the Night. London, Unwin Hyman, 1989.
A Heroine of the World. New York, DAW, 1989.

Short Stories

The Betrothed. Sidcup, Kent, Slughorn Press, 1968.
Cyrion. New York, DAW, 1982.
Red as Blood; or, Tales from the Sisters Grimmer. New York, DAW, 1983.
The Beautiful Biting Machine. New Castle, Virginia, Cheap Street, 1984.
Tamastara; or, The Indian Nights. New York, DAW, 1984.
The Gorgon and Other Beastly Tales. New York, DAW, 1985.
Dreams of Dark and Light: The Great Short Fiction of Tanith Lee. Sauk City, Wisconsin, Arkham House, 1986.
The Book of the Beast. London, Unwin, 1988.
The Book of the Damned. London, Unwin, 1988.
Women as Demons: The Male Perception of Women Through Space and Time. London, Women's Press, 1989.

Plays

Radio Plays: *Bitter Gate*, 1977; *Red Wine*, 1977; *Death Is King*, 1979; *The Silver Sky*, 1980.

Television Plays: *Sarcophagus*, 1980, and *Sand*, 1981 (both *Blake's Seven* series).

Other

Unsilent Night (miscellany). Cambridge, Massachusetts, NESFA Press, 1981.

*

Bibliography: by Mike Ashley, in *Fantasy Macabre 4* (London), 1983.

*   *   *

Princess Hynchatti's castle possesses contradictory aspects. Here the weather is fine and the rooms welcoming, there it hails, earthquakes abound, the unvisited apartments are infested with spiders. Something of this division pervades Tanith Lee's work. Her books separate into those of a sunny disposition for younger children and those exhibiting a harsh brilliant intensity for whom an adolescent audience is presumed.

In the second category, reconciliation of such dualities is frequently the theme. Although they lack characterisation these stories display a profound psychological complexity. The influences of Jung, Malory, and novelists like Hermann Hesse have been fully absorbed to endow the form of the best of them with the sinister perfection of the spider's web. In *East of Midnight* an escaping prehistoric slave encounters his double from an adjacent woman-led magic-orientated universe; the plot hinges on their attempts to live in each other's worlds. *Shon the Taken* presents similar preoccupations. Ingeniously viewed from the angle of an outcast Bronze Age tribesman, it is an historical parable in which barbaric outsiders have overcome an effete civilisation only to succumb themselves to the same process.

Shon's, and the reader's, insight that the "spirits" believed to be Death's agents are more sophisticated creatures like himself is a triumph. When the priestess in *The Winter Players* discovers that she is the originator of a cult over which she has uncomprehendingly presided, Lee handles the contradictions of time travel with similar verve: the girl and her lover break the cycle by returning to a revised version of the present where the cult never existed.

Successfully blending mediaeval and prehistoric elements, the author has created an apparition of the European landscape uniquely hers. Forests, lakes, mountains pass before the invariably fugitive hero's eyes, like pictures on an arras. "Sewing hills and clouds together," "more like a tapestry of Autumn than Autumn itself"; the scene is often described in terms of textiles. Such an effect is heightened as the weather, the time of day, the mood of a town fluctuates with bewildering rapidity. The village that was friendly will be hostile when the hero returns. The ruined castle will later be bustling with order. Sometimes, like the fog invoked in *The Castle of Dark*, these changes are caused by magical intervention. Yet if the books rely heavily, perhaps too heavily, on occult phenomena to maintain the action, they are also uncompromisingly realistic. Havor in *Companions on the Road* finds a soldier "tearing earrings off the ears of a cripple girl" and the slaves heading for the mines in *East of Midnight* pass through mediaeval squalor sufficient to deter the most hardened romantic. One encounters throughout these works an atmosphere of high-strung vigilance, as though an elemental power were driving their author. Sleeplessness is a pervasive motif; Lilune from *The Castle of Dark* must not sleep or her possessing demon will escape, the mineworkers must not sleep, Havor must stay awake or succumb to his pursuers. Although increasingly one finds a concern for the nature of evil, the prevailing message is that people have the power of gods if they know how to develop it. And if we see Lilune's fledgling ability to "call" someone who will release her from the twilight world of "Dark" as both an adolescent's yearning and increasing power to take wing, we can appreciate the relevance of these works to young adults.

All the stranger is it to move to the books for younger children. If those discussed lack humour, here the by now familiar world of witches and castles is subjected to prolonged coy irony. All tension is syphoned off by a mannered nonchalance which carries the hero, of say *Prince on a White Horse*, from one confrontation with the monstrous to another. Heroes would "rather not" chase dragons, they would "quite like" to seek their fortunes, and dragons only look frightening. The stories in *Princess Hynchatti and Some Other Surprises* contain splendid variations on tradition. Prince Chirrad disastrously transforms a real swan into a princess. Dahli goes to the ball in rags and finds her prince similarly attired. Another hero prefers the witch who fixes the trials for him to the princess on whose behalf he carries them out. These tales are well complemented by the drawings of Helen Craig, as is the picture book *Animal Castle*, where Prince Rimtheed impetuously turns his realm into a home of spoilt animals. As with *The Dragon Hoard*, plots frequently turn on the arrival of an unwanted relative. Here Aunt Maligna's spell which alters Prince Jasleth into a raven for one hour a day helps him to restore the fortune simultaneously lost when his sister, Goodness, is amusingly compelled to live up to her name.

Since the 1970's Lee appears to have moved on to adult writing, but what she has already achieved as a children's writer is considerable, and even the hardest of her books will repay the diligent reader.

—John Churcher

—

LEESON, Robert (Arthur). British. Born in Barnton, Cheshire, 31 March 1928. Educated at Sir John Deane's Grammar School (scholar), 1939–44; University of London, External B.A. (honours) 1972. Served in the British Army in the Middle East, 1946–48. Married Gunvor Hagen in 1954; one son and one daughter. Journalist on local newspapers and magazines, England and Europe, 1944–56; reporter, 1956–58, parliamentary correspondent, 1958–61, feature writer, 1961–69, literary editor, 1961–80, and children's editor, 1969–84, *Morning Star*, London. Chairman, Writers' Guild, 1985–86. Recipient: Eleanor Farjeon award, 1985. Address: 18 McKenzie Road, Broxbourne, Hertfordshire, England.

PUBLICATIONS FOR CHILDREN

Fiction

Beyond the Dragon Prow, illustrated by Ian Ribbons. London, Collins, 1973.
'Maroon Boy, illustrated by Michael Jackson. London, Collins, 1974.
The Third Class Genie. London, Collins, 1975.
Bess, illustrated by Christine Nolan. London, Collins, 1975.
The Demon Bike Rider, illustrated by Jim Russell. London, Collins, 1976.
The White Horse. London, Collins, 1977.
Challenge in the Dark, illustrated by Jim Russell. London, Collins, 1978.
Silver's Revenge. London, Collins, 1978; New York, Collins, 1979.
Harold and Bella, Jammy and Me. London, Fontana, 1980.
Grange Hill Rules, OK? London, Fontana, 1980.
Grange Hill Goes Wild. London, Fontana, 1980.
It's My Life. London, Collins, 1980.
Grange Hill for Sale. London, Fontana, 1981.
Grange Hill: Home and Away. London, Fontana, 1982.
Candy for King. London, Collins, 1983.
Forty Days of Tucker J. London, Fontana, 1983.
Genie on the Loose. London, Hamish Hamilton, 1984.
Wheel of Danger, illustrated by Antony Kerins. London, Collins, 1986.
The Reversible Giant, illustrated by Chris Smedley. London, A. and C. Black, 1986.
Time Rope series (*Time Rope, Three Against the World, At War with Tomorrow, The Metro Gangs Attack*). London, Longman, 4 vols., 1986.
Slambash Wangs of a Compo Gormer. London, Collins, 1987.
Never Kiss Frogs!, illustrated by David Simonds. London, Hamish Hamilton, 1988.
Hey Robin! London, A. and C. Black, 1989.
How Alice Saved Captain Miracle. London, Heinemann, 1989.
Jan Alone. London, Collins, 1989.

Play

The Third-Class Genie, adaptation of his own story (produced Leicester, 1987).

Other

The Cimaroons. London, Collins, 1978.
The People's Dream, illustrated by Ken Sprague. Manchester, Co-operative Union, 1982.
Mum and Dad's Big Business, illustrated by Ken Sprague. Manchester, Co-operative Union, 1982.

CHILDREN'S WRITERS

PUBLICATIONS FOR ADULTS as R.A. Leeson

Other

United We Stand: An Illustrated Account of Trade Union Emblems.
    Bath, Adams and Dart, 1971.
Strike: A Live History 1887–1971.   London, Allen and Unwin,
    1973.
Children's Books and Class Society: Past and Present.   London,
    Writers and Readers, 1977.
*Travelling Brothers: The Six Centuries' Road from Craft Fellowship
    to Trade Unionism.*   London, Allen and Unwin, 1979.
Reading and Righting.   London, Collins, 1985.

*

Robert Leeson comments:
    Two things please me above all about writing for young people.
One is the freedom with which I can move from genre to genre, as
the spirit moves: historical novel, school story, adventure, science
fiction, fantasy, or domestic comedy. The other is the freedom it gives
to meet and work with one's readers around the country in junior or
secondary schools, learning from their experience, helping what
hopefully will be another generation of writers. I want to be thought
of as a storyteller who seeks to entertain, but leaves the hearer or the
reader with something to mull over afterwards.

*   *   *

    Robert Leeson is one of the most versatile of contemporary
children's writers. His early work in the 1970's was prompted by the
view that all kinds of children's books had become varieties of
middle-class fantasy. He wrote his first historical novels, *Beyond the
Dragon Prow* and the *'Maroon Boy* trilogy, to recreate the lives of
ordinary working people, following in the footsteps of that other
social realist Geoffrey Trease.
    Leeson has never lost sight of his commitment to foregrounding
"ordinary" people, but he now does it through a wider range of
stories. After revitalising historical fiction, he turned his attention to
the school story. *The Third Class Genie* is about a very ordinary
schoolboy, Alec, who finds a wish-granting genie in a sealed beer
can. The adventures that follow established Leeson as a comic writer
with an ear for authentic classroom argot.
    This was to prove useful when he was commissioned to write
books to tie in with the very popular TV series about Grange Hill
comprehensive. Leeson accepted, on condition that he could write
original novels using the same characters, rather than routine
novelisations of episodes already shown. This resulted in four
Grange Hill books and a follow-up about Tucker Jenkins's life after
leaving school.
    The five Grange Hill books were published over a period of three
years in the early 1980's, a time which also saw Leeson tackling a
difficult subject in his teenage novel *It's My Life.* Jan, the heroine,
has to cope with her mother's disappearance and her own developing
sexuality at the same time. Through both strands of the story, she
comes to some hard-won conclusions about men's expectations of
women. This novel has always been immensely popular with teenage
girls and, after much urging from this readership, Leeson has written
a sequel, *Jan Alone,* and is working on a third book about the same
character.
    In 1985 Leeson was given the Eleanor Farjeon award for services
to children's literature, specifically for writing workshops with
children in schools and his fund-raising for the Third World Book
Fund to supply schools and libraries with books. But the award also
followed publication of his *Reading and Righting,* a critical survey
of the history of children's books and a defence of the need for social

criticism.
    The most autobiographical of all Leeson's fiction for older readers
is *Candy for King,* the story of a gentle giant whose principles first
run him foul of his employers, then of the Union. Later in the Army,
in the Middle East, his officers are divided as to whether Candy's
talent for disaster makes him a hero or a Red rebel.
    The mid 1980's brought another change in direction for Leeson,
with the publication of his *Time Rope* quartet of books. These are
science fiction—a Wellsian view of the future entered by three
contemporary teenagers from different social backgrounds. *Time
Rope* is hard-hitting and often horrific but still reveals a lot about the
nature of social institutions, class, and the role of women.
    When the science-fiction and the comic veins in Leeson's writing
ran together, they produced the full-blooded innovation of *Slambash
Wangs of a Compo Gormer.* As the title suggests, Leeson invented a
complete new language to underpin this story of a weakling boy who
lives out a rich inner life through his own fighting fantasies. The
trouble, and the fun, begins when we discover that the alien world
Arnold thinks he has created has an independent existence of its own.
This is Leeson's most ambitious book by far and a tour de force.
    Leeson is entering the 1990's with a new specialism—shorter
series fiction for juniors. There will also be sequels to *The Reversible
Giant* and *Never Kiss Frogs!*

—Mary Hoffman

LE FEUVRE, Amy.   Also wrote as Mary Thurston Dodge.
British.   Born in Blackheath, London. Wrote serials for *Sunday at
Home* and *Quiver* magazines, London. *Died 29 April 1929.*

PUBLICATIONS FOR CHILDREN

Fiction

Eric's Good News (published anonymously).   London, Religious
    Tract Society, 1894; Chicago, Revell, 1896.
Probable Sons (published anonymously).   London, Religious Tract
    Society, 1895; Chicago, Revell, 1897.
Teddy's Button! (published anonymously).   London, Religious
    Tract Society, and Chicago, Revell, 1896.
Dwell Deep; or, Hilda Thorne's Life Story.   London, Religious
    Tract Society, and Chicago, Revell, 1896.
On the Edge of a Moor (published anonymously).   London,
    Religious Tract Society, and Chicago, Revell, 1897.
Odd (published anonymously).   London, Religious Tract Society,
    1897; as *The Odd One,* Chicago, Revell, 1897.
A Puzzling Pair, illustrated by Eveline Lance.   London, Religious
    Tract Society, and Chicago, Revell, 1898.
His Big Opportunity, illustrated by Sydney Cowell.   London, Hod-
    der and Stoughton, and Chicago, Revell, 1898.
Bulbs and Blossoms, illustrated by Eveline Lance.   London,
    Religious Tract Society, and Chicago, Revell, 1898.
A Thoughtless Seven.   London, Religious Tract Society, and
    Chicago, Revell, 1898.
The Carved Cupboard.   London, Religious Tract Society, and New
    York, Dodd Mead, 1899.
Bunny's Friends.   London, Religious Tract Society, and Chicago,
    Revell, 1899.
What the Wind Did.   Chicago, Revell, 1899.
Roses, illustrated by Sydney Cowell.   London, Hodder and
    Stoughton, and New York, Ketcham, 1899.

Legend-Led. London, Religious Tract Society, and New York, Dodd Mead, 1899.

Brownie, illustrated by W.H.C. Groome. London, Hodder and Stoughton, and New York, American Tract Society, 1900.

Olive Tracy. London, Hodder and Stoughton, 1900; New York, Dodd Mead, 1901.

A Cherry Tree. London, Hodder and Stoughton, 1901; as *Cherry, The Cucumber That Bore Fruit*, Chicago, Revell, 1901.

Heather's Mistress. London, Religious Tract Society, and New York, Crowell, 1901.

A Daughter of the Sea. London, Hodder and Stoughton, and New York, Crowell, 1902.

Odd Made Even, illustrated by Harold Copping. London, Religious Tract Society, 1902.

The Making of a Woman. London, Hodder and Stoughton, 1903.

Two Tramps. London, Hodder and Stoughton, and Chicago, Revell, 1903.

Jill's Red Bag, illustrated by Alfred Pearse. London, Religious Tract Society, and Chicago, Revell, 1903.

His Little Daughter. London, Religious Tract Society, 1904.

A Little Maid. London, Religious Tract Society, 1904.

Bridget's Quarter Deck. London, Hodder and Stoughton, 1905.

The Buried Ring, illustrated by Gordon Browne. London, Hodder and Stoughton, 1905.

The Children's Morning Message, illustrated by Jenny Wylie. London, Hodder and Stoughton, 1905.

Christina and the Boys, illustrated by Gordon Browne. London, Hodder and Stoughton, 1906.

The Mender, illustrated by W. Rainey. London, Religious Tract Society, 1906.

Miss Lavender's Boy and Other Sketches. London, Religious Tract Society, 1906.

Robin's Heritage, illustrated by Gordon Browne. London, Hodder and Stoughton, 1907.

Number Twa! London, Religious Tract Society, 1907.

The Chateau by the Lake. London, Hodder and Stoughton, 1907.

A Bit of Rough Road, illustrated by Percy Tarrant. London, Religious Tract Society, 1908.

Me and Nobbles. London, Religious Tract Society, 1908.

Us, and Our Donkey, illustrated by W.H.C. Groome. London, Religious Tract Society, 1909.

A Country Corner. London, Cassell, 1909.

His Birthday: A Christmas Sketch, illustrated by Eveline Lance. London, Religious Tract Society, 1909.

Joyce and the Rambler. London, Hodder and Stoughton, 1910.

A Little Listener, illustrated by W.H.C. Groome. London, Religious Tract Society, 1910.

Us, and Our Empire, illustrated by W.H.C. Groome. London, Religious Tract Society, 1911.

Tested! Philadelphia, Heidelberg Press, 1911; London, Partridge, 1912.

Four Gates. London and New York, Cassell, 1912.

Laddie's Choice, illustrated by W.H.C. Groome. London, Religious Tract Society, 1912; as Mary Thurston Dodge, New York, Dodd Mead, 1912.

Some Builders. London, Cassell, 1913.

Her Husband's Property. London, Religious Tract Society, 1913.

Herself and Her Boy. London, Cassell, 1914.

Harebell's Friend. London, Religious Tract Society, 1914.

Daddy's Sword. London, Hodder and Stoughton, 1915.

Joan's Handful. London, Cassell, 1915.

Dudley Napier's Daughters. London, Morgan and Scott, 1916.

A Madcap Family; or, Sybil's Home. London, Partridge, 1916.

Us, and Our Charge. London, Religious Tract Society, 1916.

Tomina in Retreat. London, Religious Tract Society, 1917.

Joy Cometh in the Morning, illustrated by Harold Copping. London, Religious Tract Society, 1917.

Dreamikins. London, Religious Tract Society, 1918.

A Happy Woman. London, Religious Tract Society, 1918.

Terrie's Moorland Home. London, Morgan and Scott, 1918.

Little Miss Moth. London, Partridge, 1919.

The Chisel. London, Religious Tract Society, 1919.

The Discovery of Damaris. London, Religious Tract Society, 1920.

Martin and Margot, illustrated by Gordon Browne. London, Religious Tract Society, 1921.

Oliver and the Twins, illustrated by Gordon Browne. London, Religious Tract Society, 1922.

The Children of the Crescent, illustrated by Arthur Twiddle. London, Religious Tract Society, 1923.

The Little Discoverers, illustrated by M.D. Johnston. London and New York, Oxford University Press, 1924.

My Heart's in the Highlands. London, Ward Lock, 1924.

A Girl and Her Ways. London, Ward Lock, 1925.

Granny's Fairyland. London, Sheldon Press, 1925.

Noel's Christmas Tree. London, Ward Lock, 1926.

Three Little Girls. London, Shaw, 1926.

Andy Man: A Story of Two Simple Souls. London, Pickering and Inglis, 1927.

Jock's Inheritance. London, Ward Lock, 1927.

Cousins in Devon. London, Religious Tract Society, 1928.

Adrienne. London, Ward Lock, 1928.

Alick's Corner. London, Religious Tract Society, 1929.

Around a Sundial, and Dicky's Brother. London, Pickering and Inglis, 1929.

Her Kingdom: A Story of the Westmorland Fells. London, Ward Lock, 1929.

Under a Cloud. London, Ward Lock, 1930.

Rosebuds: Choice and Original Short Stories. London, Pickering and Inglis, 1931.

A Strange Courtship. London, Ward Lock, 1931.

Mimosa's Field. London, Lutterworth Press, 1953.

Other

The Most Wonderful Story in the World: A Life of Christ for Little Children. London, Hodder and Stoughton, and Chicago, Revell, 1922; as *Little Tots' Story of Jesus*, Revell, 1928.

Chats with Children; or, Pearls for Young People Strung from the Word of Truth. London, Pickering and Inglis, 1926.

Stories of the Lord Jesus, with Lettice Bell, illustrated by E.S. Hardy. London, Shaw, 1933.

* * *

Amy Le Feuvre was one of the Religious Tract Society's more prolific authors. Her popularity, which began in the 1890's, was maintained through the first three decades of this century, and her writing was typical of the new approach of the evangelical writers to the young reader. The stern style of the earlier 19th century was now completely outmoded. In *A Puzzling Pair* she wrote of the "hell-fire" and "day of wrath" type of preaching as something marvellously old-fashioned. The street arab story, which had been the standard type of Sunday leisure reading since the late 1860's, was overworked. The new hero of the evangelical story was the artless child who brought a gospel message of love to the adult. There was much emphasis on "the strong and steadfast faith of childhood." As one of her characters remarked, "They live so near to the throne of the Eternal One that they draw those with whom they live to do the same."

Like many of her contemporaries she was particularly fond of the "quaint" child, "old-fashioned," with delicate health, a type modelled upon Paul Dombey. With their innocent prattle these children melted the cold, stern hearts of elders who had too long been preoccupied with material things. Her most popular story in this style was *Probable Sons*, in which the fragile, curly-haired little Milly—whose mispronunciation of "prodigal sons" is responsible for the title—brings her Uncle Edward back to Christ.

In a more robust manner, she wrote tales of family life, specializing in the outwardly naughty child, the odd one out, whose motives are consistently misunderstood by the adults. She made it clear that, unlike her evangelical predecessors, she thought that absent-minded disobedience and imaginative naughtiness were attractive childish traits and could well go hand in hand with an understanding of heavenly things. This is the theme of *Teddy's Button!*, perhaps her best-known story; Teddy, whose passionate wish is to follow in his father's footsteps and be a soldier, is persuaded first to join Christ's army and fight the bad elements in his nature. The Lutterworth Press (successors to the Religious Tract Society) have kept some of Le Feuvre's tales in print and these are still used as gift books in mission schools abroad.

—Gillian Avery

LE GUIN, Ursula K(roeber). American. Born in Berkeley, California, 21 October 1929; daughter of the anthropologist Alfred L. Kroeber. Educated at Radcliffe College, Cambridge, Massachusetts, A. B. in French 1951 (Phi Beta Kappa); Columbia University, New York (Faculty fellow; Fulbright fellow, 1953), M.A. in romance languages 1952. Married Charles A. Le Guin in 1953; two daughters and one son. Instructor in French, Mercer University, Macon, Georgia, 1954, and University of Idaho, Moscow, 1956; department secretary, Emory University, Atlanta, 1955; taught writing workshops at Pacific University, Forest Grove, Oregon, 1971, University of Washington, Seattle, 1971–73, Portland State University, Oregon, 1974, 1977, 1979, in Melbourne, Australia, 1975, at the University of Reading, England, 1976, Indiana Writers Conference, Bloomington, 1978 and 1983, and University of California, San Diego, 1979. Recipient: Boston *Globe-Horn Book* award, 1969; Nebula award, 1969, 1974 (twice); Hugo award, 1970, 1973, 1974, 1975; National Book award, 1972; Jupiter award, 1974 (twice), 1976; Gandalf award, 1979; University of Oregon Distinguished Service award, 1981; *Locus* award (twice), 1983; Janet Kafka award, 1986; Prix Lectures-Jeunesse (France), 1987. Guest of Honor, World Science Fiction Convention, 1975. D.Litt.: Bucknell University, Lewisburg, Pennsylvania, 1978; Lawrence University, Appleton, Wisconsin 1979; D.H.L.: Lewis and Clark College, Portland, 1983; Occidental College, Los Angeles, 1985. Lives in Portland, Oregon. Agent: Virginia Kidd, 538 East Harford Street, Milford, Pennsylvania 18337, U.S.A.

PUBLICATIONS FOR CHILDREN

Fiction

Earthsea. London, Gollancz, 1977; as *The Earthsea Trilogy*, London, Penguin, 1979.
   A Wizard of Earthsea, illustrated by Ruth Robbins. Berkeley, California, Parnassus Press, 1968; London, Gollancz, 1971.
   The Tombs of Atuan, illustrated by Gail Garraty. New York, Atheneum, 1971; London, Gollancz, 1972.
   The Farthest Shore, illustrated by Gail Garraty. New York, Atheneum, 1972; London, Gollancz, 1973.
Very Far Away from Anywhere Else. New York, Atheneum, 1976;

as *A Very Long Way from Anywhere Else*, London, Gollancz, 1976.
Leese Webster, illustrated by James Brunsman. New York, Atheneum, 1979; London, Gollancz, 1981.
The Beginning Place. New York, Harper, 1980; as *Threshold*, London, Gollancz, 1980.
The Adventure of Cobbler's Rune, illustrated by Alicia Austin. New Castle, Virginia, Cheap Street, 1982.
Solomon Leviathan's Nine Hundred and Thirty-First Trip Around the World, illustrated by Alicia Austin. New Castle, Virginia, Cheap Street, 1983.
A Visit from Dr. Katz, illustrated by Ann Barrow. New York, Atheneum, 1988; as *Dr. Katz*, London, Collins, 1988.
Catwings, illustrated by J. Schindler. New York, Orchard, 1988.
Catwings Return, illustrated by J. Schindler. New York, Orchard, 1989.
Fire and Stone, illustrated by Laura Marshall. New York, Atheneum, 1989.

PUBLICATIONS FOR ADULTS

Novels

Rocannon's World. New York, Ace, 1966; London, Tandem, 1972.
Planet of Exile. New York, Ace, 1966; London, Tandem, 1972.
City of Illusions. New York, Ace, 1967; London, Gollancz, 1971.
The Left Hand of Darkness. New York, Ace, and London, Macdonald, 1969.
The Lathe of Heaven. New York, Scribner, 1971; London, Gollancz, 1972.
The Dispossessed: An Ambiguous Utopia. New York, Harper, and London, Gollancz, 1974.
The Word for World Is Forest. New York, Putnam, 1976; London, Gollancz, 1977.
Malafrena. New York, Putnam, 1979; London, Gollancz, 1980.
The Eye of the Heron. New York, Harper, and London, Gollancz, 1983.
Always Coming Home. New York, Harper, 1985; London, Gollancz, 1986.

Short Stories

The Wind's Twelve Quarters. New York, Harper, 1975; London, Gollancz, 1976.
The Water Is Wide. Portland, Oregon, Pendragon Press, 1976.
Orsinian Tales. New York, Harper, 1976; London, Gollancz, 1977.
The Compass Rose. New York, Harper, 1982; London, Gollancz, 1983.
The Visionary: The Life Story of Flicker of the Serpentine, with *Wonders Hidden*, by Scott Russell Sanders. Santa Barbara, California, Capra Press, 1984.
Buffalo Gals and Other Animal Presences. Santa Barbara, California, Capra Press, 1987.

Plays

No Use to Talk to Me, in *The Altered Eye*, edited by Lee Harding. Melbourne, Norstrilia Press, 1976; New York, Berkley, 1980.
King Dog (screenplay), with *Dostoevsky*, by Raymond Carver and Tess Gallagher. Santa Barbara, California, Capra Press, 1985.

Verse

Wild Angels. Santa Barbara, California, Capra Press, 1975.
Tillai and Tylissos, with Theodora K. Quinn. N.p., Red Bull Press, 1979.

Torrey Pines Reserve.   Northridge, California, Lord John Press, 1980.
Gwilan's Harp.   Northridge, California, Lord John Press, 1981.
Hard Words and Other Poems.   New York, Harper, 1981.
In the Red Zone.   Northridge, California, Lord John Press, 1983.
Wild Oats and Fireweed.   New York, Harper, 1988.

Other

From Elfland to Poughkeepsie (lecture).   Portland, Oregon, Pendragon Press, 1973.
Dreams Must Explain Themselves.   New York, Algol Press, 1975.
The Language of the Night: Essays on Fantasy and Science Fiction, edited by Susan Wood.   New York, Putnam, 1979.
Dancing at the Edge of the World: Thoughts on Words, Women, Places.   New York, Grove Press, and London, Gollancz, 1989.

Editor, *Nebula Award Stories 11*.   London, Gollancz, 1976; New York, Harper, 1977.
Editor, with Virginia Kidd, *Interfaces*.   New York, Ace, 1980.
Editor, with Virginia Kidd, *Edges*.   New York, Pocket Books, 1980.

Recordings: *The Ones Who Walk Away from Omelas*, Alternate World, 1976; *Gwilan's Harp and Intracom*, Caedmon, 1977; *The Earthsea Triology*, Colophone, 1981; *Music and Poetry of the Kesh*, Valley Productions, 1985; *Rigel Nine: An Audio Opera*, Charisma, 1985; *The Left Hand of Darkness*, Warner, 1985; *The Word for World Is Forest*, Book of the Road, 1986.

*

Bibliography: *Ursula K. Le Guin: A Primary and Secondary Bibliography* by Elizabeth Cummins Cogell, Boston, Hall, 1983.

Manuscript Collection: University of Oregon Library, Eugene.

Critical Studies: *The Farthest Shores of Ursula K. Le Guin* by George Edgar Slusser, San Bernardino, California, Borgo Press, 1976; "Ursula Le Guin Issue" of *Science-Fiction Studies* (Terre Haute, Indiana), March 1976; *Ursula Le Guin* by Joseph D. Olander and Martin H. Greenberg, New York, Taplinger, and Edinburgh, Harris, 1979; *Ursula K. Le Guin: Voyager to Inner Lands and to Outer Space* edited by Joseph W. De Bolt, Port Washington, New York, Kennikat Press, 1979; *Ursula K. Le Guin* by Barbara J. Bucknall, New York, Ungar, 1981; *Ursula K. Le Guin* by Charlotte Spivack, Boston, Twayne, 1984; *Approaches to the Fiction of Ursula K. Le Guin* by James Bittner, Ann Arbor, Michigan, UMI Research Press, and Epping, Essex, Bowker, 1984.

*   *   *

Ursula K. Le Guin's immense reputation as a fantasy writer for children is founded essentially on the Earthsea trilogy—*A Wizard of Earthsea, The Tombs of Atuan*, and *The Farthest Shore*. Few writers have received more critical attention, and though this is partly due to her work as an adult science-fiction writer of great repute, it is mainly a well-justified tribute to the qualities of the Earthsea books.

The hero of all three books is Ged, a young magician in the first book, in the height of his powers in the second, and as the aging Archmage in the third. Misusing his powers in the first book, *A Wizard of Earthsea*, he releases into the world a nameless shadow— an evil which he must then chase and battle with to the ends of the earth. When he finally finds and confronts it, it bears his own name. In the second volume, *The Tombs of Atuan*, while searching for the missing half of a talismanic ring, Ged is captured and entombed in an underground labyrinth by the young priestess Tenar, dedicated to

death. His own fate, and the fate of all the world, depend on his being able to persuade her to choose life, and reject the power of death. In the final volume, *The Farthest Shore*, he and his young companion, a future Great King, are pitched against an enemy whose evil-doing is sapping the power of all the magicians in the world, the power of hope and joy and ritual and craftsmanship among the people. To secure his own immortality the corrupt magician has made a hole in the barrier between life and death, and light and joy are flowing out through it.

No paraphrase of plot or setting can do justice to the profound originality of these books, which have been repeatedly imitated, and always far excel the imitation. In the first place although there are wizards and dragons, and other clear similarities to the medieval literary landscape used by Tolkien, among many others, the setting, an elaborate huge archipelago of varied islands, is wholly invented and fully circumstantial. It is full of magic, magic used for high and commonplace purposes alike, but the magic is never arbitrary, and instead of convincing the reader that Earthsea is unlike the real world, it breathes a contagious sense that the real world too is full of wonders. More profound yet is the nature of the adventures that befall the characters. Imaginary the perils may be, as the magical defence for dealing with them are, but the adventures are real; they are the moral dangers, the moral triumphs of the inner world, seen with a fierce clarity. No doubt the author's vision is suffused with Jungian psychology, but one has no need to be an adherent or even capable of recognising the archetypes to see how this narration, far from being escapist, turns the reader round to face him- or herself. The language and imagery are extremely beautiful: "My name, and yours, and the true name of the sun, or a spring of water, or an unborn child are all syllables of the great word that is very slowly spoken by the shining of the stars..." but the moral vision of the work is challengingly bleak and austere. "You thought as a boy that a mage is one who can do anything. And the truth is that as a man's real power grows and his knowledge widens, ever the way he can follow grows narrower; until at last he chooses nothing, but does only and wholly what he *must* do..."

The last thing one would have expected of the author of Earthsea was a realistic adolescent novel, such as *Very Far Away from Anywhere Else*. The two young protagonists, Natalie and Owen, are each highly individual—he wholly unable to be the car-loving, normal, tear-away son his parents yearn for, but instead desperate to study at a serious college; she a serious musician. Though he resists the pressure to conform to stereotype in other ways, Owen succumbs to it in his relationship with Natalie, and nearly ruins everything with an unwelcome attempt to transform their friendship into a sexual one. Le Guins admirers have objected to the didactic tone of this book, which is undoubtedly present, as it is in so many other adolescent novels. But the rage which is palpable in the book—alongside a lot of human tenderness—is not really against the corrupting pressure on the young to advance too quickly into their sexual adulthood; rather it is against all the pressures by which individuals in their glorious oddity and variety are crushed into a few standard shapes by a society that hates non-conformity. *Very Far Away from Anywhere Else* is not a masterpiece, but it is well done, and its theme has been respectfully received in, for example, *The Dispossessed*, one of Le Guin's works on the adult list.

With *The Beginning Place* Le Guin twisted together the Earthsea strand and the realist strand in her imagination. A kind of place-slip happens when Hugh crosses a stream on the edge of the dismal modern city where he lives; he enters a wilderness of forest and stream and mountain. It is inhabited by another modern teenager, Irene, and by an ancient people living simple lives. Then there is a dragon that turns everything foul and must be found and killed. Hugh plays Sigurd's part, and the two are released from the suffocating control of their parents to live in the real world, and rent an apartment together. There are multiple resonances in this book, of Oedipus as well as of Sigurd among many others, and the position of the fantasy geography as a land of the inner world, of the mind, is clearer than in Earthsea, though less compellingly beautiful.

More recently Le Guin has embarked on the very different art of picture books. *Leese Webster*, the tale of a talented spider, is perhaps too much a short story with pictures to be a good picture book, but with *A Visit from Dr. Katz* Le Guin finds her usual unerring touch. This is a simple grammatical joke—Dr. Katz is two cats, and they cheer and divert a little girl confined to bed until she falls asleep. A loving and tender domestic text is beautifully illustrated. The publication of *Solomon Leviathan's Nine Hundred and Thirty-First Trip Around the World* in 1988 illuminates Le Guin's turn to picture books. It was written when the author was only 20. A youthful and exuberant blend of Kipling and Dr. Dolittle, shot through with Carroll-like philosophical word-play—"'Impossible,' said the Boa constrictor. 'Of two things, one must be bluer.' 'Not of two bananas,' said the Giraffe"—it clearly shows the seeds of her later achievement, the shaping intelligence that makes her fantasies always seem like paradigms of reality rather than escapes from it, and the power to evoke a sweep of lands and seas and weather and teeming life as a setting for even a simple story. In view of this early work perhaps the turn Le Guin's talent is now taking, complete with the emergence of a sly sense of humour that was not apparent in the high seriousness of Earthsea, is less surprising. Her most recent work includes *Fire and Stone*, a folktale-like picture book about a dragon that eats stones, not people, and *Catwings* and *Catwings Return*, finely illustrated by S.D. Schindler, which chronicle the adventures of a family of cats born with wings. These are little books in that most difficult of all genres, the just-beyond-a-picture book for the youngest who can read for themselves. And few writers since Beatrix Potter have been able to do talking animals without silliness. But Le Guin knows a lot about cats, can confront unflinchingly the nature of hunting to eat, and, the wings once granted, everything else is naturalistic and probable. A wonderful astringency—"Few people know what fish think about injustice, or anything else"—balances the tenderness and charm.

It is hard to see how Le Guin could exceed the merit of her existing work; but also hard to put any limit on what might be expected from a writer of such variety, such force, and such psychological depth.

—Jill Paton Walsh

L'ENGLE, Madeleine. American. Born Madeleine L'Engle Camp in New York City, 29 November 1918. Educated at Smith College, Northampton, Massachusetts, A.B. (honors) 1941; New School for Social Research, New York, 1941–42; Columbia University, New York, 1960–61. Married Hugh Franklin in 1946 (died 1986); two daughters and one son. Worked in the theatre, New York, 1941–47; member of the faculty, University of Indiana, Bloomington, summers 1965–66, 1971; writer-in-residence, Ohio State University, Columbus, 1970, and University of Rochester, New York, 1972. Since 1960 teacher, St. Hilda's and St. Hugh's School, New York; since 1966 librarian, Cathedral of St. John the Divine, New York; since 1970 president, Crosswicks Ltd., New York; since 1976 Lecturer, Wheaton College, Illinois; since 1976 member, Board of Directors, Authors League Foundation; president, Authors Guild of America. Recipient: American Library Association Newbery Medal, 1963; University of Southern Mississippi award, 1978; Smith College Medal, 1980, and Sophie award, 1984; American Book award, for paperback, 1980; *Logos* award, for adult non-fiction, 1981; Catholic Library Association Regina Medal, 1984; National

Council of Teachers of English ALAN award, 1986. Agent: Robert Lescher, 67 Irving Place, New York, New York 10009. Address: Crosswicks, Goshen, Connecticut 06756, U.S.A.

PUBLICATIONS FOR CHILDREN

Fiction

The Small Rain (for adults). New York, Vanguard Press, 1945; London, Secker and Warburg, 1955; abridged edition (for children), as *Prelude*, New York, Vanguard Press, 1968; London, Gollancz, 1972.
And Both Were Young. New York, Lothrop, 1949.
Camilla Dickinson. New York, Simon and Schuster, 1951; London, Secker and Warburg, 1952; as *Camilla*, New York, Crowell, 1965.
Meet the Austins. New York, Vanguard Press, 1960; London, Collins, 1966.
The Time Trilogy. New York, Farrar Straus, 1979.
  A Wrinkle in Time. New York, Farrar Straus, 1962; London, Constable, 1963.
  A Wind in the Door. New York, Farrar Straus, 1973; London, Methuen, 1975.
  A Swiftly Tilting Planet. New York, Farrar Straus, 1978; London, Souvenir Press, 1980.
The Moon by Night. New York, Farrar Straus, 1963.
The Twenty-Four Days Before Christmas, illustrated by Inga. New York, Farrar Straus, 1964.
The Arm of the Starfish. New York, Farrar Straus, 1965.
The Young Unicorns. New York, Farrar Straus, 1968; London, Gollancz, 1969.
Dance in the Desert, illustrated by Symeon Shimin. New York, Farrar Straus, and London, Longman, 1969.
Dragons in the Waters. New York, Farrar Straus, 1976.
A Ring of Endless Light. New York, Farrar Straus, 1980.
The Anti-Muffins, illustrated by Gloria Ortiz. New York, Pilgrim Press, 1980.
The Sphinx at Dawn: Two Stories, illustrated by Vivian Berger. New York, Seabury Press, 1982.
A House Like a Lotus. New York, Farrar Straus, 1984.
Many Waters. New York, Farrar Straus, 1986.

Plays

18 Washington Square, South (produced Northampton, Massachusetts, 1940). Boston, Baker, 1944.
How Now Brown Cow, with Robert Hartung (produced New York, 1949).
The Journey with Jonah, illustrated by Leonard Everett Fisher (produced New York, 1970). New York, Farrar Straus, 1967.

Verse

Lines Scribbled on an Envelope and Other Poems. New York, Farrar Straus, 1969.

Other

Everyday Prayers, illustrated by Lucile Butel. New York, Morehouse Barlow, 1974.
Prayers for Sunday, illustrated by Lucile Butel. New York, Morehouse Barlow, 1974.
Ladder of Angels: Scenes from the Bible Illustrated by Children of the World. New York, Seabury Press, 1979.

PUBLICATIONS FOR ADULTS

Novels

Ilsa. New York, Vanguard Press, 1946.
A Winter's Love. Philadelphia, Lippincott, 1957.
The Love Letters. New York, Farrar Straus, 1966.
The Other Side of the Sun. New York, Farrar Straus, 1971; London, Eyre Methuen, 1972.
A Severed Wasp. New York, Farrar Straus, 1982; London, Faber, 1984.

Verse

Weather of the Heart. Wheaton, Illinois, Shaw, 1978.

Other (essays)

A Circle of Quiet. New York, Farrar Straus, 1972.
The Summer of the Great-Grandmother. New York, Farrar Straus, 1974.
The Irrational Season. New York, Seabury Press, 1977.
Walking on Water. Wheaton, Illinois, Shaw, 1980; Tring, Hertfordshire, Lion, 1982.
And It Was Good: Reflections on Beginnings. Wheaton, Illinois, Shaw, 1983.
Dare to Be Creative. Washington, D.C., Library of Congress, 1984.
Trailing Clouds of Glory: Spiritual Values in Children's Books. Philadelphia, Westminster Press, 1985.
A Stone for a Pillow. Wheaton, Illinois, Shaw, 1986.
Two-Part Invention: The Story of a Marriage. New York, Farrar Straus, 1988.

Editor, with William B. Green, *Spirit and Light: Essays in Historical Theology.* New York, Seabury Press, 1976.

*

Manuscript Collections: Wheaton College, Illinois; Kerlan Collection, University of Minnesota, Minneapolis; de Grummond Collection, University of Southern Mississippi, Hattiesburg.

Madeleine L'Engle comments:

When I am asked why I write at least half of my books for children, especially since my first books were for adults, I answer, truthfully, that when I have something to say which I think is going to be too difficult for adults, I write it in a book for children. Children are excited by new ideas; they have not yet closed the doors and windows of their imaginations. Provided the story is a good story, and makes them want to keep turning the pages, nothing is too difficult for children. Most of my children's novels at least border on fantasy, and the response from children in hundreds of letters keeps me constantly stimulated. It is the children themselves who help me to move on from one book to the next.

* * *

A Wrinkle in Time, awarded the Newbery Medal two decades ago, both continues to be read by youngsters and readily stands up under critical scrutiny. Madeleine L'Engle's finest novel is, first of all, a realistic family novel. The Murrys are a closely knit, affectionate, supportive, and intelligent family; and these qualities, instead of seeming incredible or, worse yet, tiresomely banal, are both plausible and attractive because they derive from the family's behavior and words. The Murrys' goodness, in particular, is not innate or miraculously accounted for, but earned through hard choice and the

pain of self-sacrifice. *A Wrinkle in Time* is also a serious novel that unabashedly investigates the nature of good and evil and points out how the decisions and actions of individuals contribute to or detract from, whether intended or not, society's moral and ethical well-being. Moreover, the ethical problems explored—the proper use of knowledge, the rights of the individual versus those of society, the various demands of love, and the possibility that evil exists absolutely—are real problems. The Christian ethos of the novel, furthermore, is more implied than explicitly stated and is not preached. In short, the novel is didactic but carries its moral and ethical weight gracefully.

Another feature of *A Wrinkle in Time* is that it is a young adult novel that honestly portrays its protagonists, Meg Murry and Calvin O'Keefe, in situations typical of many young people—anxiety over physical appearance, unsettled parental relationships, peer and sibling rivalries, and the search for identity. The novel does all this neither by pandering to the biases of the putative young readership nor by suggesting no possible amelioration of the several situations except the morally bankrupt and psychologically irresponsible one of looking inside one's unhappy self or outside to one's peers experiencing the same problem. The characterization and prominence of Meg, incidentally, are happy anticipations of the non-sexist female protagonist of today. Finally, because *A Wrinkle in Time* features a futuristic mode of space travel and speculates about possible life elsewhere in the universe, it is science fiction. As such, it is a historically important book since it is the first juvenile SF novel not only admitted into the mainstream of children's literature but also honored in a significant way—thus heralding juvenile SF's coming of age.

A Wrinkle in Time, as is often the case, did not spring full grown from the author's imagination. In *Meet the Austins* L'Engle anticipated the form and achievement of her masterpiece. The Austins are also a warmly affectionate and close family whose obvious goodness is offset by enough failings to make the family believable and likeable. Preadolescent Vicky Austin, the main character, is an obvious predecessor of Meg Murry. The Austins, it would appear, were so liked by their creator as well as by many readers that three subsequent novels narrate their further adventures. *The Moon by Night* is a low-keyed, relatively unexciting account of a cross-country vacation trek undertaken by the family. *The Young Unicorns* describes the Austins' unwilling involvement in a plot to ferment civil turmoil in New York City. More intricately plotted and more serious thematically than the previous Austin novels—and in these respects similar to *A Wrinkle in Time*—the novel lacks the stylistic verve, the range of allusions, and the deft and interesting characterization that makes the former superior fiction. *A Ring of Endless Light*, despite the conventional, sometimes tedious romantic entanglement given Vicky, movingly depicts the Austins' response to Grandfather's imminent death. Striking too is the exploration of current experimentation concerning ESP, in particular involving dolphins.

Three other novels deserve attention. In *The Arm of the Starfish* L'Engle altered her usual approach a bit. Instead of working outward from within the intimate family circle, she has her main character, Adam Eddington, earn his way into the O'Keefe family. Unfortunately, the rest of the plot resembles formula cloak and dagger, and the goodness of the O'Keefes is stock and unbelievable. *A Wind in the Door*, the immediate sequel to *A Wrinkle in Time*, suffers in comparison with its predecessor. Although the human characters are virtually the same, their ethical concern sufficiently weighty, the adventures suitably fantastic, e.g., travelling into the bloodstream of Charles Wallace, and the technology plausibly extrapolated, the mixture of these elements is too contrived and predictable, and, hence, lacks freshness and interest. Highly speculative and intensely earnest, *A Swiftly Tilting Planet*, another companion volume to *A Wrinkle in Time*, involves the Murrys' becoming caught up in a "last chance" effort to avoid nuclear catastrophe. In a heavily plotted story spanning many centuries and involving many characters, Charles Wallace, again the central character, and assisted by the unicorn, Gaudior, in a struggle with the Echthroi, time-travels into the past to find several "Might-Have-Been" situations, and by entering "Within" key individuals and making the morally right decisions, undoes history and averts disaster.

Even if L'Engle had not written *A Wrinkle in Time*, she would still be counted among the relatively few novelists who manage to entertain their young readers while honestly portraying some of the problems that vex them. When *A Wrinkle in Time* is added to her corpus, however, L'Engle must be ranked as one of the truly important writers of juvenile fiction in recent decades.

—Francis J. Molson

LENSKI, Lois (Lenore). American. Born in Springfield, Ohio, 14 October 1893. Educated at local schools in Anna, Ohio, and high school in Sidney, Ohio, graduated 1911; Ohio State University, Columbus, 1911–15, B.S. in education 1915; Art Students' League, New York, 1915–20; Westminster School of Art, London, 1920–21. Married the artist Arthur Covey in 1921 (died 1960); one son and two stepchildren. Freelance illustrator from 1920. Individual shows: Weyhe Gallery, New York, 1927 (oils); Ferargils Gallery, New York, 1932 (watercolors); group shows: Pennsylvania Water Color Show, 1922; New York Water Color Show; Detroit Art Institute. Recipient: American Library Association Newbery Medal, 1946; Child Study Committee award, 1948; Catholic Library Association Regina Medal, 1969; University of Southern Mississippi award, 1969. Litt.D.: Wartburg College, Waverly, Iowa, 1959; Capital University, Columbus, 1966; Southwestern College, Winfield, Kansas, 1968; D.H.L.: University of North Carolina Women's College, Greensboro, 1962. *Died 11 September 1974.*

PUBLICATIONS FOR CHILDREN (illustrated by the author)

Fiction

Skipping Village. New York, Stokes, 1927.
A Little Girl of Nineteen Hundred. New York, Stokes, 1928.
Two Brothers and Their Animal Friends. New York, Stokes, 1929.
Two Brothers and Their Baby Sister. New York, Stokes, 1930.
Spinach Boy. New York, Stokes, 1930.
Benny and His Penny. New York, Knopf, 1931.
Grandmother Tippytoe. New York, Stokes, 1931.
Arabella and Her Aunts. New York, Stokes, 1932.
Johnny Goes to the Fair. New York, Minton Balch, 1932.
The Little Family. New York, Doubleday, 1932.
Gooseberry Garden. New York, Harper, 1934.
The Little Auto. New York and London, Oxford University Press, 1934; as *The Baby Car*, London, Oxford University Press, 1937.
Surprise for Mother. New York, Stokes, 1934.
Sugarplum House. New York, Harper, 1935.
Little Baby Ann. New York and London, Oxford University Press, 1935.
The Easter Rabbit's Parade. New York and London, Oxford University Press, 1936.
Phebe Fairchild, Her Book. New York, Stokes, 1936.
The Little Sail Boat. New York, Oxford University Press, 1937; as *The Little Sailing Boat*, London, Oxford University Press, 1938.
A-Going to the Westward. New York, Stokes, 1937.
Bound Girl of Cobble Hill. New York, Stokes, 1938.

The Little Airplane. New York and London, Oxford University Press, 1938.
Ocean-Born Mary. New York, Stokes, 1939.
Blueberry Corners. New York, Stokes, 1940.
The Little Train. New York and London, Oxford University Press, 1940.
Indian Captive. New York, Stokes, 1941.
The Little Farm. New York and London, Oxford University Press, 1942.
Bayou Suzette. Philadelphia, Lippincott, 1943.
Davy's Day. New York and London, Oxford University Press, 1943.
Let's Play House. New York and London, Oxford University Press, 1944.
Puritan Adventure. Philadelphia, Lippincott, 1944.
Strawberry Girl. Philadelphia, Lippincott, 1945; London, Oxford University Press, 1951.
Blue Ridge Billy. Philadelphia, Lippincott, 1946.
The Little Fire Engine. New York, Oxford University Press, 1946; London, Oxford University Press, 1947.
Surprise for Davy. New York, Oxford University Press, 1947.
Judy's Journey. Philadelphia, Lippincott, 1947; London, Oxford University Press, 1955.
Mr. and Mrs. Noah. New York, Crowell, 1948.
Boom Town Boy. Philadelphia, Lippincott, 1948.
Cotton in My Sack. Philadelphia, Lippincott, 1949.
Cowboy Small. New York, Oxford University Press, 1949; London, Oxford University Press, 1957.
Texas Tomboy. Philadelphia, Lippincott, 1950.
Papa Small. New York, Oxford University Press, 1951; London, Oxford University Press, 1957.
Prairie School. Philadelphia, Lippincott, 1951; London, Oxford University Press, 1959.
Peanuts for Billy Ben. Philadelphia, Lippincott, 1952.
We Live in the South. Philadelphia, Lippincott, 1952.
Mama Hattie's Girl. Philadelphia, Lippincott, 1953.
Corn-Farm Boy. Philadelphia, Lippincott, 1954.
Project Boy. Philadelphia, Lippincott, 1954.
We Live in the City. Philadelphia, Lippincott, 1954.
San Francisco Boy. Philadelphia, Lippincott, 1955.
A Dog Came to School. New York and London, Oxford University Press, 1955.
Berries in the Scoop. Philadelphia, Lippincott, 1956.
Big Little Davy. New York and London, Oxford University Press, 1956.
Flood Friday. Philadelphia, Lippincott, 1956.
We Live by the River. Philadelphia, Lippincott, 1956.
Davy and His Dog. New York and London, Oxford University Press, 1957.
Houseboat Girl. Philadelphia, Lippincott, 1957.
Little Sioux Girl. Philadelphia, Lippincott, 1958.
Coal Camp Girl. Philadelphia, Lippincott, 1959.
We Live in the Country. Philadelphia, Lippincott, 1960; London, Oxford University Press, 1961.
Davy Goes Places. New York, Walck, 1961.
Policeman Small. New York, Walck, 1962.
We Live in the Southwest. Philadelphia, Lippincott, 1962.
Shoo-Fly Girl. Philadelphia, Lippincott, 1963.
We Live in the North. Philadelphia, Lippincott, 1965.
High-Rise Secret. Philadelphia, Lippincott, 1966.
Debbie and Her Grandma. New York, Walck, 1967; London, Oxford University Press, 1968.
To Be a Logger. Philadelphia, Lippincott, 1967.
Christmas Stories. Philadelphia, Lippincott, 1968.
Deer Valley Girl. Philadelphia, Lippincott, 1968.
Debbie and Her Family. New York, Walck, 1969.

Debbie Herself.   New York, Walck, 1969.
Debbie and Her Dolls.   New York, Walck, 1970.
Debbie Goes to Nursery School.   New York, Walck, 1970.
Debbie and Her Pets.   New York, Walck, 1971.

Plays

The Bean-Pickers: A Migrant Play, music by Clyde Robert Bulla. Washington, D.C., National Council of Churches, 1952.
A Change of Heart: A Migrant Play, music by Clyde Robert Bulla. Washington, D.C., National Council of Churches, 1952.
Strangers in a Strange Land: A Migrant Play, music by Clyde Robert Bulla.   Washington, D.C., National Council of Churches, 1952.

Verse

Alphabet People.   New York, Harper, 1928.
Animals for Me.   New York and London, Oxford University Press, 1941.
Forgetful Tommy.   Harwinton, Connecticut, Greenacres Press, 1943.
Spring Is Here.   New York and London, Oxford University Press, 1945.
Now It's Fall.   New York, Oxford University Press, 1948.
I Like Winter.   New York and London, Oxford University Press, 1950.
We Are Thy Children (hymns), music by Clyde Robert Bulla.   New York, Crowell, 1952.
On a Summer Day.   New York and London, Oxford University Press, 1953.
Songs of Mr. Small, music by Clyde Robert Bulla.   New York, Oxford University Press, 1954.
Songs of the City, music by Clyde Robert Bulla.   New York, Marks Music, 1956.
Up to Six, Book I, music by Clyde Robert Bulla.   New York, Hansen Music, 1956.
I Went for a Walk, music by Clyde Robert Bulla.   New York, Walck, 1958.
At Our House, music by Clyde Robert Bulla.   New York, Walck, 1959; Kingswood, Surrey, World's Work, 1964.
When I Grow Up, music by Clyde Robert Bulla.   New York, Walck, 1960.
The Life I Live: Collected Poems.   New York, Walck, 1965.
City Poems.   New York, Walck, 1971.
Sing a Song of People, illustrated by Giles Laroche.   Boston, Little Brown, 1987.

Other

The Wonder City: A Picture Book of New York.   New York, Coward McCann, 1929.
The Washington Picture Book.   New York, Coward McCann, 1930.
My Friend the Cow.   Chicago, National Dairy Council, 1946.
Ice Cream Is Good.   Chicago, National Dairy Council, 1948.
Living with Others.   Hartford, Connecticut Council of Churches, 1952.

Editor, *Jack Horner's Pie: A Book of Nursery Rhymes.*   New York, Harper, 1927; as *Lois Lenski's Mother Goose*, n.d.
Editor, *Susie Mariar* (folk rhyme).   New York and London, Oxford University Press, 1939.

PUBLICATIONS FOR ADULTS (illustrated by the author)

Verse

Florida, My Florida.   Tallahassee, Friends of the Florida State

University Library, 1971.

Other

Adventures in Understanding: Talks to Parents, Teachers, and Librarians, 1944–1966.   Tallahassee, Friends of the Florida State University Library, 1968.
Journey into Childhood: Autobiography of Lois Lenski.   Philadelphia, Lippincott, 1972.

*

Bibliography: by Esther G. Witcher, in *The Lois Lenski Collection in the University of Oklahoma Library*, Norman, University of Oklahoma Library and School of Library Science, 1963; *The Lois Lenski Collection in the Florida State University Library* by Nancy Bird, Tallahassee, Florida State University Press, 1966.

Manuscript Collections: University of Oklahoma Library, Norman; Florida State University Library, Tallahassee; Amos Memorial Library, Sidney, Ohio; Capital University Library, Columbus, Ohio; Illinois State University Library, Normal; Kerlan Collection, University of Minnesota, Minneapolis; State University of New York, Buffalo; Syracuse University, New York.

Illustrator: *Children's Frieze-Book*, 1918; *Dolls from the Land of Mother Goose*, 1918; *The Golden Age*, 1921, and *Dream Days*, 1922, both by Kenneth Grahame; *The Green-Faced Toad* by Vera B. Birch, 1921; *Cinderella*, 1922; *My ABC Book*, 1922; *The Peep-Show Man* by Padraic Colum, 1924; *The Monkey That Would Not Kill* by Henry Drummond, 1925; *Chimney Corner Stories*, 1925, *Chimney Corner Fairy Tales*, 1926, *Fireside Stories*, 1927, *Candle-Light Stories*, 1928, *Chimney Corner Poems*, 1930, and *Fireside Poems*, 1930, all edited by Veronica S. Hutchinson; *A Merry-Go-Round of Modern Tales*, 1927, *The Hat-Tub Tale*, 1928, and *Mr. Nip and Mr. Tuck*, 1930, all by Caroline D. Emerson; *A Book of Princess Stories*, 1927, *A Book of Enchantments*, 1928, and *There Were Giants*, 1929, all edited by Kathleen Adams and Frances Atchinson; *Prudence and Peter and Their Adventures with Pots and Pans* by Elizabeth Robins and Octavia Wilberforce, 1928; *Sing a Song of Sixpence*, 1930; *Mother Goose Rhymes*, 1930; *Little Rag Doll*, 1930, and *A Name for Obed*, 1941, both by Ethel C. Phillips; *The Twilight of Magic* by Hugh Lofting, 1930; *Rustam, Lion of Persia*, 1930, and *Odysseus, Sage of Greece*, 1931, both by Alan Lake Chidsey; *Jolly Rhymes of Mother Goose* edited by Watty Piper, 1932, and *The Little Engine That Could* retold by Piper, 1945; *Golden Tales of the Prairie States* [*the Far West, Canada, New England, the Southwest, the Old South*], all edited by May Becker, 6 vols., 1932–41; *A Scotch Circus* by Tom Powers, 1934; *Betsy-Tacy*, 1940, *Betsy-Tacy and Tib*, 1941, *Over the Big Hill*, 1942, and *Down Town*, 1943, all by Maud Hart Lovelace; *Twenty-Two Short Stories of America* edited by E.R. Mirrielees, 1937; *Edgar, The 7:58* by Phil Stong, 1938; *Once on Christmas* by Dorothy Thompson, 1938; *Mother Makes Christmas* by Cornelia Meigs, 1940; *Indigo Treasure* by Frances Rogers, 1941; *The First Thanksgiving* by Lena Barksdale, 1942; *A Letter to Popsey* by Mabel La Rue, 1942; *They Came from France* by Clara Ingram Judson, 1943; *Five and Ten* by Roberta Whitehead, 1943; *The Surprise Place* by Mary Graham Bonner, 1945; *The Donkey Cart* by Clyde Robert Bulla, 1946; *Pinocchio* adapted by Allen Chaffee, 1946; *Read-to-Me-Storybook* by the Child Study Association, 1947.

*   *   *

Lois Lenski was a prolific author of books for children for more than 40 years. Her work, much of it still in print, is aimed at children from preschool through the middle elementary school years.

Lenski's writing is best described as sober, realistic, and straightforward. Her prose is easy to read, convincing but not vivid, and generally quite humorless. Had she chosen to write music, it would surely have been plainsong.

Her books for very young children form one body of work by themselves. Serious, very simply written, rather flat-footed, they have had an abiding appeal for many small children who seem to find in them a satisfying exactness, a comfortable familiarity. Lenski has a sure eye for those adult occupations most visible and interesting to young children. She writes about Mr. Small as a policeman, train engineer, farmer, boat captain, and cowboy, giving brief glimpses of his duties in each role. (Interesting occupations are exclusively male in Lenski's world.) The methodical activities of Mr. Small in whatever guise may strike some adults (and some children) as dull, but it is clear that many children identify closely with Lenski's characters and that, for them, the orderly, informative text is an aid to imaginative participation in the adult world at a level they can comprehend.

The second major part of Lenski's work comprises the so-called historical and regional series. Both sets of stories are fiction, both share the plain narrative style, the realism and the simplicity that characterize the books for younger children. Of the two, the regional series is probably the better known.

These books, as their name implies, explore American life in various parts of the country. Here, as in her books for young children, Lenski's interest in the working world is apparent; how a family gets its living is an important theme. Lenski's research is sound; the background facts are authentic and dialect is accurate. More unusual, particularly for the 1940's and 1950's, is her focus on the poorer levels of American society. Sharecroppers are depicted in *Cotton in My Sack*, Florida "crackers" in *Strawberry Girl*, and the mountain people who scratch a bare living in the Appalachians in *Blue Ridge Billy*. In all of these, Lenski presents patterns of life often invisible in children's books. For the most part, she does so with neither condescension nor sentimentality. The haphazard financial habits of the sharecropper family in *Cotton in My Sack* are given honestly, and the makeshift household arrangements of migrant worker families described sympathetically but entirely without pathos in *Judy's Journey*. Nevertheless, Lenski's values are ultimately conventional, and her literary realism has clear limits. There are problems in her stories but no tragedies; her characters face many difficulties, but few without solution. Plots generally center around a mild (sometimes mildly improbable) success story. And success usually requires that her characters trade the hand-to-mouth ways of lower-class living for something closer to middle-class behavior. The values of industry, education, sobriety, and thrift always triumph.

At their best, as in *Strawberry Girl*, the regional stories blend local color, simple plot, and uncomplicated characterization into plausible if rather predictable wholes. When Lenski is less successful, as in *To Be a Logger*, the research seems undigested, and the book remains a conglomerate of fact and message rather than a story with a shape and life of its own.

The historical stories are generally more detailed than the regional books, appealing to a slightly older audience. Otherwise, their strengths and weaknesses parallel those of the regional stories; realism is their greatest attraction (they are based on the experiences of real people); lack of humor, pat plots and sometimes an over-abundance of incident and informative detail weaken them.

—Anne Scott MacLeod

———

LE SIEG, Theo. See **SEUSS, Dr.**

———

LESTER, Julius. American. Born in St. Louis, Missouri, 27 January 1939. Educated at Fisk University, Nashville, 1956–60, B.A. 1960. Married 1) Joan Steinau in 1962 (divorced 1970), one daughter and one son; 2) Alida Carolyn Fechner in 1979, one son and one stepdaughter. Musician and singer. Since 1971 Professor of Afro-American Studies, University of Massachusetts, Amherst. Associate editor, *Sing Out*, New York, 1964–69; contributing editor, *Broadside of New York*, 1964–70; director, Newport Folk Festival, Rhode Island, 1966–68; lecturer, New School for Social Research, New York, 1968–70; producer and host, WBAI radio, New York, 1968–75; host, *Free Time*, WNET-TV, New York, 1971–73. Address: Department of Afro-American Studies, University of Massachusetts, Amherst, Massachusetts 01003, U.S.A.

PUBLICATIONS FOR CHILDREN

Fiction

Long Journey Home: Stories from Black History. New York, Dial Press, 1972; London, Longman, 1973.
Two Love Stories. New York, Dial Press, 1972; London, Kestrel, 1974.
This Strange New Feeling (short stories). New York, Dial Press, 1982; as *A Taste of Freedom: Three Stories from Black History*, London, Longman, 1983.

Other (retellings)

Black Folktales, illustrated by Tom Feelings. New York, Baron, 1969.
The Knee-High Man and Other Tales, illustrated by Ralph Pinto. New York, Dial Press, 1972; London, Kestrel, 1974.
The Tales of Uncle Remus: The Adventures of Brer Rabbit, illustrated by Jerry Pinkney. New York, Dial Press, and London, Bodley Head, 1987.
More Tales of Uncle Remus, illustrated by Jerry Pinkney. New York, Dial Press, 1988.

Editor, with Mary Varela, *Our Folk Tales: High John, The Conqueror, and Other Afro-American Tales*, illustrated by Jennifer Lawson. Privately printed, 1967.
Editor, *To Be a Slave*, illustrated by Tom Feelings. New York, Dial Press, 1968; London, Longman, 1970.

PUBLICATIONS FOR ADULTS

Novel

Do Lord Remember Me. New York, Holt Rinehart, 1985; London, Dent, 1987.

Verse

The Mud of Vietnam: Photographs and Poems. New York, Folklore Press, 1967.
Who I Am. New York, Dial Press, 1974.

Other

The 12-String Guitar as Played by Leadbelly: An Instructional Manual, with Pete Seeger. New York, Oak, 1965.
The Angry Children of Malcolm X. Nashville, Southern Student Organizing Committee, 1966.
Look Out, Whitey! Black Power's Gon' Get Your Mama! New York,

Dial Press, 1968; London, Allison and Busby, 1970.
Search for the New Land: History as Subjective Experience. New York, Dial Press, 1969; London, Allison and Busby, 1971.
Revolutionary Notes. New York, Baron, 1969.
All Is Well (autobiography). New York, Morrow, 1976.
Love Song: Becoming a Jew. New York, Holt Rinehart, 1988.

Editor, with Mary Varela, *To Praise Our Bridges: An Autobiography*, by Fanny Lou Hamer. Jackson, Mississippi, KIPCO, 1967.
Editor, *Ain't No Ambulances for No Nigguhs Tonight*, by Stanley Couch. New York, Baron, 1969.
Editor, *The Seventh Son: The Thought and Writings of W.E.B. Du Bois.* New York, Random House, 2 vols., 1971.

*

Julius Lester comments:

I believe that history is the lives of people more than it is the recording of politics and wars. Thus, my work seeks to explore and illumine the lives of ordinary men and women, who are history.

*   *   *

The fiction of Julius Lester bristles with social protest and yet transcends its political implications. At his artistic best Lester weaves narrative action, setting, characterization, and several different versions of black English into a remarkably integrated unit. In "Basketball Game," the first of two novellas in *Two Love Stories*, Lester creates a memorable portrait of a liberal black minister's family. Because Reverend Anderson challenges racism wherever possible, he situates his family in an otherwise all-white neighborhood and exposes his 14-year-old son to his first interracial romance. When the color bar wrenches the couple apart, we understand why conscious and unconscious survival tactics are such an overriding part of the family's daily existence. The author has an exceptional eye for meaningful details. The father's daily costume is a spotless, well-pressed dress suit irrespective of what the day's chores include, and there is a touching image of Rev. Anderson clumsily joining his son as he shoots for baskets, "leaping into the air in his suit, vest, and tie."

Black Folktales demonstrates Lester's artistry in a different mode. The book offers a young reader the traditional folk contests between weak and strong, and also includes sly comments about the slave/slavemaster relationship and about tyranny in general. The real beauty of these tales is the subtlety with which social messages are disguised, and the way the vernacular prose helps convey a dimension of biting satire. A young adult reader should be well versed in the history of slavery and in the dismantling of Reconstruction in order to hear what these stories of butterflies, snakes, devils, and bigger-than-life heroes are really saying. The six folktales in *The Knee-High Man and Other Tales* are not in this class. They have not been embellished with Lester's wit, nor do they have the kind of suggestive undercurrents that make *Black Folktales* so richly symbolic.

Lester's third fictional mode is the brief historical sketch. In 1972 he wrote the first set of six in *Long Journey Home*; in 1982 the second set of three in *This Strange New Feeling*. "Satan on My Track" (in *Long Journey Home*) features an itinerant guitar player who moves from plantation to plantation during the post-bellum years and sees how slavery is, for all practical purposes, reinstated. With dishonest landowners and no genuine system of legal redress for blacks, the life of the sharecropper is an echo of ante-bellum deprivation and confinement. The story's simple narrative structure embodies this message effortlessly. On the other hand, "Louis," a story of the Underground Railroad, doesn't lend itself to the telescoping of a short fictional form, even though the core of Lester's narrative is

factual. The extensive amount of action seems artificial without depth of characterization to enrich it, or a more complex treatment of theme. The title story in the later collection, "This Strange New Feeling," is hampered by the same problem. Its narrative is too dependent on the wide-ranging programmatic elements Lester is trying to cover. In the second story, "Where the Sun Lives," the author skillfully translates an array of paradoxes and psychological pressures into realistic drama. A young slave woman ultimately finds herself back on the auction block despite a customarily humane master and a paragon of a common-law husband. Her husband, a free black, is by law prevented from entering into a legal marriage with the heroine, and her former white master cannot cope with his own hurt pride when the young slave rejects the role of mistress.

The writer of historical fiction has the difficult task of blending social and personal experience, making sure that there is sufficient complexity to represent faithfully an era. The environment of a southern black is full of risk, and this complicates the literary problem further; a faithful rendering of incident is potentially sensational and can easily ensnare the writer in melodrama. Lester invests journalistic facts with a deep and sometimes metaphoric level of significance. His stories can engage us as both parables and regional exposés.

—Donnarae MacCann

LEVIN, Betty (née Lowenthal). American. Born in New York City, 10 September 1927. Educated at National Cathedral School, Washington, D.C., 1941–44; Lincoln School, New York, 1944–45; University of Rochester, New York, A.B. (high honors) 1949 (Phi Beta Kappa); Radcliffe College, Cambridge, Massachusetts, M.A. 1951; Harvard School of Education, Cambridge, Massachusetts, A.M.T. 1951. Married Alvin Levin in 1947; three daughters. Research assistant, Museum of Fine Arts, Boston, 1951–52; part-time teaching fellow, Harvard Graduate School of Education, 1953; creative writing fellow, Radcliffe Institute, 1968–70; Massachusetts coordinator, McCarthy Historical Archive, 1969; Instructor, Pine Manor Open College, Chestnut Hill, Massachusetts, 1971–75, and Emmanuel College, Boston, 1975; feature writer, Minute Man Publications, Lexington, Massachusetts, 1972; Special Instructor in Children's Literature, 1975–77, and Adjunct Professor of Children's Literature, 1977–87, Simmons College, Boston. Member of the Faculty, Radcliffe Seminars. Member of the Steering Committee, Children's Literature New England. Also a sheep farmer. Agent: Dorothy Markinko, McIntosh and Otis Inc., 310 Madison Avenue, New York, New York 10017. Address: Old Winter Street, Lincoln, Massachusetts 01773, U.S.A.

PUBLICATIONS FOR CHILDREN

Fiction

The Zoo Conspiracy, illustrated by Marian Parry. New York, Hastings House, 1973.
The Sword of Culann. New York, Macmillan, 1973.
A Griffon's Nest. New York, Macmillan, 1975.
The Forespoken. New York, Macmillan, 1976.
Landfall. New York, Atheneum, 1979.
The Beast on the Brink, illustrated by Marian Parry. New York, Avon, 1980.
The Keeping-Room. New York, Greenwillow, 1981.
A Binding Spell. New York, Dutton, 1984.

Put on My Crown. New York, Dutton, 1985.
The Ice Bear. New York, Greenwillow, 1986; London, MacRae, 1987.
The Trouble with Gramary. New York, Greenwillow, 1988.

*

Manuscript Collection: Kerlan Collection, University of Minnesota, Minneapolis.

Betty Levin comments:

Most of my writing reflects my early and continuing interest in agriculture and animal husbandry and in history. Through fiction I keep discovering new patterns and connections in which people are grounded in the land (or sea) that supports all life and which children very often feel and recognize most keenly. The historical element is the vertical connection or ground, linking today's reading child with those who were children, too, but in another time or age. Having begun with fantasy, I am now beginning to explore other fictional ways of spinning my yarns and knitting my fictional patterns.

*   *   *

Betty Levin has written realistic novels and fantasies as well as works which combine both genres. In her time-travel trilogy consisting of *The Sword of Culann, A Griffon's Nest,* and *The Forespoken* she draws on a rich background of Celtic and Norse mythologies. In each of the three books an American girl, Claudia, is drawn back through time by means of an ancient sword hilt kept by an old recluse. In *The Sword of Culann* Claudia and her stepbrother Evan find themselves in ancient Ireland as witnesses to the struggle between the fierce Queen Medb and Cuchulain (the House of Culann). In *A Griffon's Nest* the pair are brought to the Orkney Islands during medieval times. In *The Forespoken* the historical setting is the 19th-century Orkney Islands and Claudia travels there alone in pursuit of a crow belonging to the recluse.

The contemporary setting in each of the books is an island off the coast of Maine. Levin is skillful in writing of the physical realities of both worlds, especially the cold, dampness, dirt, and hard physical labour. She is less successful in integrating the stories of the large, squabbling family in Maine with the historical journeys through time. In the first book the juxtaposition of the family trying survival camping in Maine while the two youngest children are shifting backward and forward in time seems awkward. In the two later books the contemporary setting becomes less important as more of the emphasis shifts to relationships in the historical period.

Levin's more recent work has moved between fantasy and realism with a greater emphasis upon the realistic elements. *A Binding Spell,* the story of a family transplanted from a comfortable suburban life to the harshness of rural Maine, is set firmly in the here-and-now although a strand of fantasy runs through it. Young Wren finds mysterious traces of a horse in the deserted barn and around the property. A growing friendship with a neighbor who has refused to leave his house ever since tractors displaced the horses that he had loved leads to a greater involvement with the Pedersen clan, the family's nearest neighbors. The contemporary problems of family alcoholism, the difficulty of making friends in a new school, and the threat of death on the roads are blended with the story of the ghost horse which only Wren and the recluse can see. The book ends with each problem nearing solution, although none disappear with unrealistic finality. Levin's characters are well-drawn and believable, but the magical elements are not closely integrated with the realistic story, which would have stood well on its own.

The Ice Bear takes place in the mythical medieval Kingdom of Thyrne where the people are being oppressed by an evil lord during the king's absence. This situation, similar to the background of the Robin Hood stories, is brought to life through the adventures of the boy Wat, who is forced to set off with a strange young girl and an ice bear cub after the girl's father and the cub's mother have been hanged by the townspeople. While the girl longs to return to her northern homeland, Wat hopes to take the bear to the king and receive a large reward. Wat's respect for the girl, Kaila, grows as they travel, and his understanding of loyalty and duty gradually change. The book ends when Wat meets the king, but the ending leaves room for a sequel, so perhaps this will grow into another trilogy. Unencumbered by a dual time perspective, the book brings its unusual setting to vivid life and is one of Levin's strongest stories so far.

The Trouble with Gramary deals with real life in modern-day Maine. Merkka's grandmother Gramary is considered an eccentric by many townspeople. Her welding business is viewed as creating an eyesore, and the metal sculptures she makes are dismissed with ridicule. By the time the book ends Merkka has come to terms with her grandmother's need for artistic and personal integrity. Although Gramary dominates the book, Merkka and the rest of the family are also strong and believable characters. This book marks a departure from Levin's earlier writings and it remains to be seen whether this versatile writer will continue to move toward realism.

Levin is not an easy writer. Many of her early books with their preoccupation with the impingement of the past on the present and with ecological concerns and mythological predictions make difficult demands—demands which few young readers can meet. More recent books rely less on background knowledge outside the world of the book itself, but the descriptions are dense and the situations and characters complex. Time and effort are required to move into the worlds that Levin creates. Readers who are willing to immerse themselves in the strange settings and to struggle to understand the significance of mysterious events will find themselves embarking on an enriching experience. Levin's work grows in strength and scope with each book published.

—Adele M. Fasick

———

LEVITIN, Sonia (née Wolff). Also writes as Sonia Wolff. American. Born in Berlin, Germany, 18 August 1934; brought to the United States, 1938. Educated at the University of California, Berkeley, 1952–54; University of Pennsylvania, Philadelphia, 1954–56, B.S. in education 1956; San Francisco State University, 1957–60. Married Lloyd Levitin in 1953; one son and one daughter. Elementary school teacher, Mill Valley, California, 1956–57; adult education teacher, Daly City, California, 1962–64, and Acalanes Adult Center, Lafayette, California, 1965–72; creative writing teacher, Palos Verdes Peninsula, California, 1973–76. Since 1978 teacher, Writers' Program, University of California at Los Angeles Extension. Founder, STEP adult education corporation. Recipient: Jewish Book Council of America award, 1971; Western Writers of America Spur award, 1979; National Jewish Book award, 1988; Association of Jewish Libraries Sydney Taylor award, 1988. Agent: Toni Mendez Inc., 141 East 56th Street, New York, New York 10022. Address: 9617 Oak Pass Road, Beverly Hills, California 90210, U.S.A.

PUBLICATIONS FOR CHILDREN

Fiction

Journey to America, illustrated by Charles Robinson. New York, Atheneum, 1970; London, Macmillan, 1987.

Rita the Weekend Rat, illustrated by Leonard Shortall.   New York, Atheneum, 1971.

Roanoke: A Novel of the Lost Colony, illustrated by John Gretzer. New York, Atheneum, 1973.

Who Owns the Moon?, illustrated by John Larrecq. Berkeley, California, Parnassus, 1973.

Jason and the Money Tree, illustrated by Pat Grant Porter.   New York, Harcourt Brace, 1974.

A Single Speckled Egg, illustrated by John Larrecq. Berkeley, California, Parnassus, 1975.

The Mark of Conte, illustrated by Bill Negron. New York, Atheneum, 1976.

Beyond Another Door.   New York, Atheneum, 1977.

The No-Return Trail.   New York, Harcourt Brace, 1978.

A Sound to Remember, illustrated by Gabriel Lisowski.   New York, Harcourt Brace, 1979.

Nobody Stole the Pie, illustrated by Fernando Krahn.   New York, Harcourt Brace, 1980.

The Fisherman and the Bird, illustrated by Francis Livingston. Boston, Houghton Mifflin, 1982.

All the Cats in the World, illustrated by Charles Robinson. New York, Harcourt Brace, 1982.

The Year of Sweet Senior Insanity.   New York, Atheneum, 1982.

Smile like a Plastic Daisy.   New York, Atheneum, 1984.

A Season of Unicorns.   New York, Atheneum, 1986.

The Return.   New York, Atheneum, 1987.

Incident at Loring Groves.   New York, Dial Press, 1988.

Silver Days.   New York, Atheneum, 1989.

PUBLICATIONS FOR ADULTS

Novels

Reigning Cats and Dogs.   New York, Atheneum, 1978.

What They Did to Miss Lily (as Sonia Wolff).   New York, Harper, 1981; London, New English Library, 1982.

*   *   *

Versatility is a hallmark of Sonia Levitin's work. Her ability to write historical as well as realistic fiction captures a wide range of readers. She is an author who unfolds a story carefully and with attention to the details that bring life and caring to characters.

Journey to America, based on Levitin's own life, is the story of the Platt family's escape from Nazi Germany in 1938, told from the perspective of Lisa Platt. The courage of each member of the family and their willingness to leave everything held dear to seek freedom and safety capture the reader's attention. Levitin uses language that binds the reader to the story and the fears of Lisa as they arrive in Switzerland on their way to America. It is the struggle in Switzerland that is so hard for the family as money and then mother's health disappear. The Werfel family helps and finally speeds the family on their way to America. The recent sequel *Silver Days* lacks the strength of the earlier work, but is still revealing of what it was like to come to America and struggle through the early days of learning English and conforming to different ways.

In the picture book *A Sound to Remember* Levitin tells the story of a slow, clumsy child, Jacov, whom the Rabbi selects for the special honor of "blowing the shofar [ram's horn]" on the Jewish high holy days. Rosh Hashanah comes and Jacov cannot produce the beautiful sound. It is the Rabbi who comes up with a marvelous solution for Yom Kippur despite the anger and shame heaped upon Jacov.

In *Beyond Another Door* Daria comes to grips with the frightening power of extrasensory perception. A nondescript object, a glass dish won at a fair, acts as the catalyst to call her grandma's spirit back to help her cope with this ability. Throughout the story her mother is frightened and tries to push her away from anything that encourages this talent without ever speaking of the problem or of the grandmother's reputation as a gifted psychic. Most of Daria's friends turn away from her in fear of weird happenings, but new ones like Rob and Man believe in her. Levitin makes the distinction, so important to the story, of knowing something and causing it, which is a burden that gifted people such as Daria carry. She makes a tremendous impact on the reader in having Daria say towards the end of the story: "I can't just accept things without asking questions. It wouldn't be logical. Some people go too far, believing everything without even thinking." But it is also Daria's decision to commit herself to her painting and at the same time to seek help from Rob's father who is a psychologist studying this phenomenon that brings the unfolding of this story to a fullness.

Levitin moves into historical fiction in *The No-Return Trail*, the story, based on fact, of Nancy Kelsey, a 17-year-old wife and mother who makes the journey from Kentucky to California in the Bidwell-Bartleson expedition of 1841. Nancy grows and changes a great deal as she moves with the wagon train across the land and struggles with her womanhood and her relationship to her husband. In *Roanoke: A Novel of the Lost Colony* 16-year-old William Wythers joins emigrants bound for Virginia. Levitin uses what little fact is known about the colony at Ronsoke as the backdrop for William's growth into manhood.

The Mark of Conte is a bizarre, humorous story of a computer glitch which gives Conte Mark two school schedules, one for himself and one for Mark Conte, and stirs his imagination to consider graduation in two years. The plight of a young man in this predicament is delicious reading.

A Season of Unicorns and *Incident at Loring Groves* are young adult books that offer insight into adolescent concerns. Inky the protagonist of the first gathers the strength to face her fears by changing herself, and Cassiday and Ken risk popularity and peer pressure to accept responsibility and report the murder of a classmate in the second story.

In *The Return* Desta, a young Ethiopian Jewish girl, struggles to make the long journey to join "Operation Moses," the secret Exodus of Ethiopian Jews to Israel. This powerful and haunting story of thirst, starvation, and death is grim in parts but lyrical in its portrayal of the power of the human spirit—a concern that permeates all of Levitin's work and gives her stories their clarity and richness.

—Jane Anne Hannigan

———————

LEVOY, Myron. American. Born in New York City, 30 January 1930. Educated at City College, New York, B.S. in chemical engineering 1952; Purdue University, West Lafayette, Indiana, M.S. in chemical engineering 1953. Married Beatrice Fleischer in 1952; one daughter and one son. Has worked as a chemical engineer; now a full-time writer. Recipient: Silver Pencil award (Netherlands), 1981; Children's Literature prize (Austria), 1981; Young Adult Literature prize (West Germany), 1982; Buxtehude Bulle award (West Germany), 1982. Lives in New Jersey. Agent: Susan Cohen, Writers House Inc., 21 West 26th Street, New York, New York 10010, U.S.A.

PUBLICATIONS FOR CHILDREN

Fiction

The Witch of Fourth Street and Other Stories, illustrated by Gabriel

Lisowski. New York, Harper, 1972.
Penny Tunes and Princesses, illustrated by Ezra Jack Keats. New York, Harper, 1972.
Alan and Naomi. New York, Harper, 1977; London, Bodley Head, 1979.
A Shadow like a Leopard. New York, Harper, 1981.
Three Friends. New York, Harper, 1984.
The Hanukkah of Great-Uncle Otto, illustrated by Donna Ruff. Philadelphia, Jewish Publication Society, 1984.
Pictures of Adam. New York, Harper, 1986; London, Bodley Head, 1987.
The Magic Hat of Mortimer Wintergreen. New York, Harper, 1988; London, Macmillan, 1989.

PUBLICATIONS FOR ADULTS

Novel

A Necktie in Greenwich Village. New York, Vanguard Press, 1968.

Plays

The Penthouse Perspective (produced Northport, New York, 1967).
Eli and Emily (produced New York, 1969).
The Sun Is a Red Dwarf (produced New York, 1969).
Sweet Tom (produced New York, 1969).
Footsteps (produced New York, 1970). New York, Breakthrough Press, 1971.
Smudge (produced New York, 1971).

*

Myron Levoy comments:
In my work for young adults, a central concern has been for the loners, the oddballs. They are often confronted with a critical decision: whether to go along with the crowd and lose their uniqueness, or stay true to their own strange selves. There are no easy solutions. Their stories tend to be open-ended, with further struggles ahead, to be met, one hopes, with new strength and insight. Ramon, in *A Shadow like a Leopard*, perhaps speaks for them all in his outburst near the close of the book: "They can all shout! I don't care. Nobody's gonna tell me what to do. Not him [his father]. Not Harpo. Not Glasser. Nobody. I'm gonna be me from inside. Yeah, I made up my mind."

*   *   *

During his career in chemical engineering Myron Levoy also followed his inclination toward the humanities in general, and creative writing in particular, ultimately abandoning scientific work for full-time writing. With the exception of his most recent novel—*The Magic Hat of Mortimer Wintergreen*, a not entirely successful picaresque story of two children traveling with an itinerant magician—Levoy's work for young people is comfortably set against his own personal backgrounds, either New York City or middle-class suburbia in New Jersey.

The Witch of Fourth Street, his first children's book, is a collection of short stories evoking the spirit and atmosphere of New York's teeming Lower East Side during the early years of this century. European immigrants—Catholic, Protestant, or Jewish—live together peaceably in delapidated tenements, standing fast against the common enemy of poverty and sharing hopes for the future of their children in a new land. One notes a captivating freshness and a decided ring of authenticity in the sometimes humorous, sometimes poignant stories, which show how effective unpretentious language can be.

Levoy's first novel shot him into immediate fame, for *Alan and Naomi* was deservedly honored in the United States and in The Netherlands, Germany, and Austria. In 1944 Alan Silverman is a normal 12-year-old growing up in New York, doing well in school but reserving his greatest enthusiasm for playing stickball with his friend Shaun Kelly. But living in his apartment house is Naomi Kirshenbaum, a severely disturbed young refugee from France, still suffering from the profound shock of witnessing her father's murder by the Gestapo several years before. Alan's generous-hearted parents urge the boy to spend some time with Naomi in the hope of restoring her to mental health. Initially he rebels, fearful that he will be dubbed a sissy for giving up his afternoons to the "crazy-acting" girl; later he is inspired to begin patiently to communicate with her through an old puppet, while she gradually responds with her doll, at the same time learning to trust and to love. But when a chance anti-Semitic taunt is directed at Alan and results in a street brawl, the book reaches a heart-wrenching conclusion as Naomi, seeing Alan's bloody face, once again retreats from sanity. Levoy tackles some difficult subjects—the repercussions of Nazi horrors and the concept of personal responsibility—and presents them through the heroic action of a schoolboy. And one observes the author's skillful portrayal of adolescence that would characterize his future novels.

A Shadow like a Leopard tells of a Puerto Rican teenager entangled in the web of violence, crime, and poverty of New York's street gangs—and of the unlikely friendship that develops between the boy and a bitter, lonely old man in a wheelchair, a highly cultivated artist now living on public welfare. Although there is verisimilitude in the sordid background and in the use of the argot of the streets, the story, despite the author's obvious compassion, never rises above the conventional characters and predictable plot.

Two other contemporary novels feature 14-year-olds in a middle-class suburban town; both are engagingly original and are written with wry humor and a keen ear for adolescent jargon. *Three Friends* explores the complex possibilities of friendship among a trio of teenagers. Joshua is a brilliant, obsessive chess player but painfully different and self-conscious with his peers. He is drawn to another nonconformist, his schoolmate Karen, a forthright, articulate supporter of the women's movement; and he also feels real affection for Karen's friend Lori, an artistic but immature girl whose confusion over her sexual ambivalence toward both Karen and Joshua complicates the developing intimacy between the other two and nearly results in tragedy. The lengthy descriptions of chess tournaments may seem heavy and arcane to some readers, but the story is attractively unconventional, and the emotions that tie the three characters together are unusually well defined and sympathetically portrayed.

Another interesting, spirited heroine appears in *Pictures of Adam*, a book that once again reflects Levoy's admitted concern "for the outsider, the loner." Scornful of her vapid, materialistic classmates, Lisa Daniels is a talented amateur photographer well provided with expensive equipment. She is intrigued, and often infuriated, by Adam Bates, who lives in a ramshackle cabin outside of town but retreats into a strange fantasy world in order to hide the physical and emotional scars of his abused childhood. Within the pair's stormy relationship lies a genuine caring for each other and, as in *Alan and Naomi*, the author again demonstrates his gift for convincing the reader of the healing power of love.

Myron Levoy's masterpiece is clearly *Alan and Naomi*, whose emotional impact is all the more impressive for the book's unassuming modesty. Whether Levoy will ever transcend, or even equal, its artless force remains to be seen.

—Ethel L. Heins

LEWIS, C(live) S(taples). Also wrote as Clive Hamilton; N. W. Clerk. British. Born in Belfast, Northern Ireland, 29 November 1898. Educated at Wynyard House, Watford, Hertfordshire, 1908–10; Campbell College, Belfast, 1910; Cherbourg School, Malvern, Worcestershire, 1911–13, and Malvern College, 1913–14; privately, in Great Bookham, Surrey, 1914–17; University College, Oxford (scholar; Chancellor's English Essay prize, 1921), 1917, 1919–23, B.A. (honours) 1922. Served in the Somerset Light Infantry, 1917–19: First Lieutenant. Married Joy Davidman Gresham in 1956 (died 1960); two stepsons. Philosophy Tutor, 1924, and Lecturer in English, 1924, University College, Oxford; Fellow and Tutor in English, Magdalen College, Oxford, 1925–54; Professor of Medieval and Renaissance English, Cambridge University, 1954–63. Lecturer, University College of North Wales, Bangor, 1941; Riddell Lecturer, University of Durham, 1943; Clark Lecturer, Cambridge University, 1944. Recipient: Gollancz prize, 1937; Library Association Carnegie Medal, 1957. D.D.: University of St. Andrews, Fife, 1946; Docteur-ès-Lettres, Laval University, Quebec, 1952; D. Litt.: University of Manchester, 1959; Hon. Dr.: University of Dijon, 1962; University of Lyon, 1963. Honorary Fellow, Magdalen College, Oxford, 1955; University College, Oxford, 1958; Magdalene College, Cambridge, 1963. Fellow, Royal Society of Literature, 1948; Fellow, British Academy, 1955. *Died 22 November 1963.*

PUBLICATIONS FOR CHILDREN (illustrated by Pauline Baynes)

Fiction

The Chronicles of Narnia:
  The Lion, The Witch, and the Wardrobe. London, Bles, and New York, Macmillan, 1950.
  Prince Caspian: The Return to Narnia. London, Bles, and New York, Macmillan, 1951.
  The Voyage of the "Dawn Treader." London, Bles, and New York, Macmillan, 1952.
  The Silver Chair. London, Bles, and New York, Macmillan, 1953.
  The Horse and His Boy. London, Bles, and New York, Macmillan, 1954.
  The Magician's Nephew. London, Lane, and New York, Macmillan, 1955.
  The Last Battle. London, Lane, and New York, Macmillan, 1956.

Other

Letters to Children, edited by Lyle W. Dorsett and Marjorie Lamp Mead. New York, Macmillan, and London, Collins, 1985.

PUBLICATIONS FOR ADULTS

Novels

Out of the Silent Planet. London, Lane, 1938; New York, Macmillan, 1943.
Perelandra. London, Lane, 1943; New York, Macmillan, 1944; as *Voyage to Venus,* London, Pan, 1953.
That Hideous Strength: A Modern Fairy-Tale for Grown-Ups. London, Lane, 1945; New York, Macmillan, 1946; abridged edition, as *The Tortured Planet,* New York, Avon, 1958.
Till We Have Faces: A Myth Retold. London, Bles, 1956; New York, Harcourt Brace, 1957.

Short Stories

Of Other Worlds: Essays and Stories, edited by Walter Hooper. London, Bles, 1966; New York, Harcourt Brace, 1967.
The Dark Tower and Other Stories, edited by Walter Hooper. London, Collins, and New York, Harcourt Brace, 1977.

Verse

Spirits in Bondage: A Cycle of Lyrics (as Clive Hamilton). London, Heinemann, 1919.
Dymer (as Clive Hamilton). London, Dent, and New York, Dutton, 1926.
Poems, edited by Walter Hooper. London, Bles, 1964; New York, Harcourt Brace, 1965.
Narrative Poems, edited by Walter Hooper. London, Bles, 1969; New York, Harcourt Brace, 1972.

Other

The Pilgrim's Regress: An Allegorical Apology for Christianity, Reason, and Romanticism. London, Dent, 1933; New York, Sheed and Ward, 1935; revised edition, London, Bles, 1943; Sheed and Ward, 1944.
The Allegory of Love: A Study in Medieval Tradition. Oxford, Clarendon Press, and New York, Oxford University Press, 1936.
Rehabilitations and Other Essays. London and New York, Oxford University Press, 1939.
The Personal Heresy: A Controversy, with E.M.W. Tillyard. London and New York, Oxford University Press, 1939.
The Problem of Pain. London, Bles, 1940; New York, Macmillan, 1944.
The Weight of Glory. London, S.P.C.K., 1942.
The Screwtape Letters. London, Bles, 1942; New York, Macmillan, 1943; revised edition, as *The Screwtape Letters and Screwtape Proposes a Toast,* Bles, 1961; Macmillan, 1962.
Broadcast Talks: Right and Wrong: A Clue to the Meaning of the Universe, and What Christians Believe. London, Bles, 1942; as *The Case for Christianity,* New York, Macmillan, 1943.
A Preface to "Paradise Lost" (lectures). London and New York, Oxford University Press, 1942; revised edition, 1960.
Christian Behaviour: A Further Series of Broadcast Talks. London, Bles, and New York, Macmillan, 1943.
The Abolition of Man; or, Reflections on Education with Special Reference to the Teaching of English in the Upper Forms of Schools. London, Oxford University Press, 1943; New York, Macmillan, 1947.
Beyond Personality: The Christian Idea of God. London, Bles, 1944; New York, Macmillan, 1945.
The Great Divorce: A Dream. London, Bles, and New York, Macmillan, 1946.
Miracles: A Preliminary Study. London, Bles, and New York, Macmillan, 1947.
Vivisection. London, Anti-Vivisection Society, and Boston, New England Anti-Vivisection Society, 1947(?).
Transposition and Other Addresses. London, Bles, 1949; as *The Weight of Glory and Other Addresses,* New York, Macmillan, 1949.
The Literary Impact of the Authorized Version (lecture). London, Athlone Press, 1950; Philadelphia, Fortress Press, 1963.
Mere Christianity. London, Bles, and New York, Macmillan, 1952.
Hero and Leander (lecture). London, Oxford University Press, 1952.
English Literature in the Sixteenth Century, Excluding Drama. Oxford, Clarendon Press, 1954.
De Descriptione Temporum (lecture). London, Cambridge Univer-

sity Press, 1955.

Surprised by Joy: The Shape of My Early Life. London, Bles, 1955; New York, Harcourt Brace, 1956.

Reflections on the Psalms. London, Bles, and New York, Harcourt Brace, 1958.

Shall We Lose God in Outer Space? London, S.P.C.K., 1959.

The Four Loves. London, Bles, and New York, Harcourt Brace, 1960.

The World's Last Night and Other Essays. New York, Harcourt Brace, 1960.

Studies in Words. London, Cambridge University Press, 1960; revised edition, 1967.

An Experiment in Criticism. London, Cambridge University Press, 1961.

A Grief Observed (as N.W. Clerk; autobiography). London, Faber, 1961; Greenwich, Connecticut, Seabury Press, 1963.

They Asked for a Paper: Papers and Addresses. London, Bles, 1962.

Beyond the Bright Blur (letters). New York, Harcourt Brace, 1963.

Letters to Malcolm, Chiefly on Prayer. London, Bles, and New York, Harcourt Brace, 1964.

The Discarded Image: An Introduction to Medieval and Renaissance Literature. London, Cambridge University Press, 1964.

Screwtape Proposes a Toast and Other Pieces. London, Fontana, 1965.

Letters, edited by W.H. Lewis. London, Bles, and New York, Harcourt Brace, 1966.

Studies in Medieval and Renaissance Literature, edited by Walter Hooper. London, Cambridge University Press, 1966.

Spenser's Images of Life, edited by Alastair Fowler. London, Cambridge University Press, 1967.

Christian Reflections, edited by Walter Hooper. London, Bles, and Grand Rapids, Michigan, Eerdmans, 1967.

Letters to an American Lady, edited by Clyde S. Kilby. Grand Rapids, Michigan, Eerdmans, 1967; London, Hodder and Stoughton, 1969.

Mark vs. Tristram: Correspondence Between C.S. Lewis and Owen Barfield, edited by Walter Hooper. Cambridge, Massachusetts, Lowell House Printers, 1967.

A Mind Awake: An Anthology of C.S. Lewis, edited by Clyde S. Kilby. London, Bles, 1968; New York, Harcourt Brace, 1969.

Selected Literary Essays, edited by Walter Hooper. London, Cambridge University Press, 1969.

God in the Dock: Essays on Theology and Ethics, edited by Walter Hooper. Grand Rapids, Michigan, Eerdmans, 1970; as *Undeceptions: Essays on Theology and Ethics*, London, Bles, 1971.

The Humanitarian Theory of Punishment. Abingdon, Berkshire, Marcham Books Press, 1972.

Fern-Seed and Elephants and Other Essays on Christianity, edited by Walter Hooper. London, Fontana, 1975.

The Joyful Christian: 127 Readings, edited by William Griffin. New York, Macmillan, 1977.

They Stand Together: The Letters of C.S. Lewis to Arthur Greeves 1914–1963, edited by Walter Hooper. London, Collins, and New York, Macmillan, 1979.

C.S. Lewis at the Breakfast Table and Other Reminiscences, edited by James T. Como. New York, Macmillan, 1979; London, Collins, 1980.

The Visionary Christian: 131 Readings, edited by Chad Walsh. New York, Macmillan, 1981.

On Stories and Other Essays on Literature, edited by Walter Hooper. New York, Harcourt Brace, 1982.

Of This and Other Worlds, edited by Walter Hooper. London, Collins, 1982.

The Cretaceous Perambulator, with Owen Barfield, edited by Walter Hooper. Oxford, C.S. Lewis Society, 1983.

The Business of Heaven: Daily Readings from C.S. Lewis, edited by Walter Hooper. London, Fount, and New York, Harcourt Brace, 1984.

Boxen: The Imaginary World of the Young C.S. Lewis, edited by Walter Hooper. London, Collins, and San Diego, Harcourt Brace, 1985.

Present Concerns, edited by Walter Hooper. London, Fount, and San Diego, Harcourt Brace, 1986.

Timeless at Heart: Essays on Theology, edited by Walter Hooper. London, Fount, 1987.

The Essential C.S. Lewis, edited by Lyle W. Dorsett. New York, Macmillan, 1988.

Letters: C.S. Lewis and D.G. Calabria, edited and translated by Martin Moynihan. London, Collins, 1989.

Editor, *George MacDonald: An Anthology.* London, Bles, 1946; New York, Macmillan, 1947.

Editor, *Arthurian Torso, Containing the Posthumous Fragment of "The Figure of Arthur,"* by Charles Williams. London, and New York, Oxford University Press, 1948.

*

Bibliography: "A Bibliography of the Writings of C.S. Lewis" by Walter Hooper, in *Light on C.S. Lewis* edited by Jocelyn Gibb, London, Bles, 1965; *C.S. Lewis: An Annotated Checklist of Writings about Him and His Works* by Joe R. Christopher and Joan K. Ostling, Kent, Ohio, Kent State University Press, 1974.

Manuscript Collections: Bodleian Library, Oxford; Wheaton College, Illinois.

Critical Studies (selection): *C.S. Lewis* by Roger Lancelyn Green, London, Bodley Head, and New York, Walck, 1963, revised edition, in *Three Bodley Head Monographs*, Bodley Head, 1969, *C.S. Lewis: A Biography* by Green and Walter Hooper, London, Collins, and New York, Harcourt Brace, 1974, revised edition, 1988, and *Past Watchful Dragons: The Narnian Chronicles of C.S. Lewis*, New York, Macmillan, 1979, and *Through Joy and Beyond: A Pictorial Biography of C.S. Lewis*, New York, Macmillan, 1982, both by Hooper; *Light on C.S. Lewis* edited by Jocelyn Gibb, London, Bles, 1965; *The Lion of Judah in Never-Never Land: The Theology of C.S. Lewis Expressed in His Fantasies for Children*, Grand Rapids, Michigan, Eerdmans, 1973, and *The C.S. Lewis Hoax*, Portland, Oregon, Multinomah, both by Kathryn Ann Lindskoog; *The Secret Country of C.S. Lewis* by Anne Arnott, London, Hodder and Stoughton, 1974, Grand Rapids, Michigan, Eerdmans, 1975; *The Longing for Form: Essays on the Fiction of C.S. Lewis* edited by Peter J. Schakel, Kent, Ohio, Kent State University Press, 1977, and *Reading with the Heart: The Way into Narnia* by Schakel, Grand Rapids, Michigan, Eerdmans, 1979; *The Inklings: C.S. Lewis, J.R.R. Tolkien, Charles Williams and Their Friends* by Humphrey Carpenter, London, Allen and Unwin, 1978, Boston, Houghton Mifflin, 1979; *The Literary Legacy of C.S. Lewis* by Chad Walsh, New York, Harcourt Brace, and London, Sheldon Press, 1979; *A Guide Through Narnia* by Martha C. Sammons, Wheaton, Illinois, Shaw, and London, Hodder and Stoughton, 1979; *Narnia Explored* by Paul A. Karkainen, Old Tappan, New Jersey, Revell, 1979; *Companion to Narnia* by Paul F. Ford, New York, Harper, 1980; *C.S. Lewis, Spinner of Tales: A Guide to His Fiction* by Evan K. Gibson, Grand Rapids, Michigan, Christian University Press, 1980; *C.S. Lewis* by Margaret Patterson Hannay, New York, Ungar, 1981; *C.S. Lewis: The Art of Enchantment* by Donald E. Glover, Athens, Ohio University Press, 1981; *C.S. Lewis* by Brian Murphy, Mercer Island, Washington, Starmont House, 1983; *The Politics of Fantasy: C.S. Lewis and J.R.R. Tolkien* by Lee D. Rossi, New York and Epping,

Essex, Bowker, 1984; *Clive Staples Lewis: The Drama of a Life* by William Griffin, New York, Harper, 1986; *C.S. Lewis: His Literary Achievement* by C.N. Manlove, London, Macmillan, 1987; *C.S. Lewis* by Joe R. Christopher, Boston, Twayne, 1987; *C.S. Lewis, Man of Letters: A Reading of His Fiction* by Thomas Howard, Worthing, Sussex, Churchman, 1987; *Jack: C.S. Lewis and His Times* by George Sayer, London, Macmillan, 1988; *C.S. Lewis and His World* by David Barratt, Grand Rapids, Michigan, Eerdmans, 1988.

*   *   *

Ever since the first of the seven Narnia books appeared in 1950, C.S. Lewis has been perhaps the best-liked post-war "quality" writer for children in Britain. This success is all the more interesting because, at the time of publishing, these books ran directly across a number of attitudes and taboos in children's fiction—and in certain ways do so still. They contain violence, pain, and death. Their tone is often admonitory; they are morally and theologically didactic. It would be wrong, of course, to think these all disadvantages. Indeed, it could be said that Lewis won his readers not only by his stunning scenes and plot situations and by his manner—a well-gauged air of intimate authority—but by a deliberate *using* of large taboos, religion and death in particular.

In the autobiographical *Surprised by Joy*, and elsewhere, Lewis has valuably charted the reading, tastes, and events of his early life that led to these children's stories. "I wrote," he declared characteristically, "the books I should have liked to read. That's always been my reason for writing…no rot about 'self-expression.'" He was the younger of two brothers, born and brought up in Northern Ireland. Motherless at nine, with a moody Welsh solicitor father, he was accustomed to an inventive, dreaming, bookish solitude. "I am a product of long corridors, empty sunlit rooms, upstair indoor silences, attics explored in solitude, distant noises of gurgling cisterns and pipes, and the noise of wind under the tiles. Also of endless books." Most in the house were adult novels and of no interest to the myth-loving young romantic. What *did* make a lasting impact were E. Nesbit's three "magic" novels, *The Story of the Amulet* in particular. "It first opened my eyes to antiquity, 'the dark backward and abysm of time.' I can still reread it with delight." Gulliver was another favourite. Andersen's *Snow Queen* and Grahame's *Dream Days* must have been read about this time. At 12 he was caught by the spell of "Northernness"—Norse myths, Rackham's illustrations to *The Ring*, Morris's *Sigurd the Volsung*. At 16, under a private tutor, W.T. Kirkpatrick, he raced into Homer. "Day after day and month after month we drove gloriously onward, tearing the whole *Achilleid* out of the *Iliad*…and then reading the *Odyssey* entire, till the music of the thing and the clear bitter brightness…had become part of me." A year or so later, by way of *Phantastes*, he discovered George MacDonald—a major experience. All these and many other early-read tales go to the making of Narnia. Of all the books, the first, *The Lion, The Witch, and the Wardrobe*, remains the favourite (or the best-remembered, which may be the same thing). There are good enough reasons for this. It is usually the first one to be read, and the gateway to the rest; it also contains one of the great moments in children's fiction (in an empty room of an old vast rambling country house a wardrobe leads to a snowy forest, faun and dwarf and witch). But it was also the key book from Lewis's view, the one where he first set out precisely (as much to himself as to his readers) the Christ-role of Aslan, who dies to save Edmund, on the Stone Table, and then rises again; the pilgrimage role (fallible, favoured, leading to brightness) of the human children; and something more: his personal view that pagan myth and Christian gospel are not inimical. In the final Narnian story centaurs, fauns, real animals, and fabulous creatures pass with humans through the golden gate.

"In a certain sense," wrote Lewis, "I have never actually 'made' a story…I see pictures. Some of these pictures have a common flavour…which groups them together. Keep quiet and watch and they will begin joining themselves up.… I have no idea whether this is the usual way of writing stories.… It is the only one I know; images always come first." Where there are gaps, he added, some conscious inventing must at last be done.

Images always come first—much of the impact of the Narnian tales must come from this.

In *Prince Caspian* the four Pevensie children, already met in the first book, are drawn back, by a magic horn, to the aid of Caspian, in danger of death from his evil uncle Miraz who has usurped the throne. Advised of this by his half-dwarf tutor, Dr. Cornelius, Caspian escapes and goes (with the human children) to rally supporters and to restore the land to its original honour. Among his followers are the Old People, centaurs, fauns, squirrels, ravens, "a small but genuine giant, Wimbleweather, of Deadman's Hill," even Silenus and Bacchus. ("I wouldn't have felt very safe with Bacchus and all his wild girls if we'd met them without Aslan," murmurs Susan. "I should think not," says Lucy.) In the culminating battle, Peter fights with style. He "swung to face Sopespian, slashed his legs from under him, and with the back-cut of the same stroke, walloped off his head." Lewis never fails in describing such expertise.

Though it has weaknesses (and the improbable Eustace Scrubb is the principal one), *The Voyage of the "Dawn Treader"* seems the most intoxicating (or, one might say, intoxicated) of the Narnian books. The abiding influence throughout is Homeric, clearly going back to young Lewis's "glorious" race through the *Odyssey*. Edmund, Lucy, and their unloved cousin Eustace Scrubb enter a picture (like the children in Grahame's *Dream Days*). It is of an ancient dragon-prowed vessel in towering waves—and there they are on board, with young King Caspian, carrying out his vow to search for the seven loyal lords whom Miraz despatched "to the unknown Eastern Seas, beyond the Lone Islands." Eustace becomes a dragon (but recovers and mends his ways); a Sea Serpent nearly crushes the boat in its coils; and they reach the edge of the World's End, and look into Aslan's country. Only one may step into it—Reepicheep, the Knightly Mouse: "For you," says the Lamb, "the door into Aslan's country is from your own world."

But as sheer fairytale, *The Silver Chair* should take top place of the seven. Jill and Eustace, wretched at school, call Aslan's name, and find themselves on the edge of what must be the highest cliff in all fiction. Eustace falls—but Aslan wafts him on his breath to "the west of the world," Jill follows, and the two are sent on a quest to find the lost Prince Rilian, heir to the old King of Narnia. Aslan gives four signs to Jill, which she must not forget. (She does.) A Marsh-Wiggle, Puddleglum (one of Lewis's best creations), joins the journey as guide, to the Bottom of the World, where Rilian, enslaved by a Witch Queen, sits bound in a silver chair. A superb and magical story.

The Horse and His Boy, which could seem at first glance a witty vivacious Arabian Nights pastiche, provides a new pair of human children. A fair-haired fisherman's boy in dark Calormen (in fact a foundling, cast ashore as an infant) escapes being sold into slavery and, helped by a Talking Horse called Bree (echoes of Gulliver?) and joined by a fearless runaway girl called Aravis, makes the long perilous journey to Narnia—dungeons, mountains, haunted deserts—where in fact his own identity lies. This is a first-class story and children like it well. Yet, though Aslan provides the *gravitas* (aid in crisis, admonition: three real claw-stripes for Aravis) it remains one of the lighter-weight books of the seven. The children in *The Magician's Nephew*, most Nesbit-like of the novels, live in late-Victorian London, when "Mr. Sherlock Holmes was still living in Baker Street and the Bastables were looking for treasure in the Lewisham Road"; they are Digory (father in India, mother ill) and Polly who lives next door. Uncle Andrew, who dabbles in magic, propels the two into the Other Place, where Narnia is soon (in this book, indeed) to be created. Unfortunately through inquisitiveness (or scientific interest) Digory releases Jadis, a beautiful evil witch, from a prison-ing spell; she returns with the pair to London (a riotous Nesbit episode) and (symbolically) inserts herself into the new-born Narnia. Aslan sends Digory forth to collect the magic apple whose tree may help to keep her power at bay. A cabdriver and his horse (echoes of MacDonald's *North Wind*) join the return to Narnia and are given high roles in the kingdom. More contrived ("invented") than some of the books, it is not among the best. Yet the facts about Narnia's making deserve attention.

The final book, *The Last Battle*, is a curious and disturbing work, fine in passages, yet overambitious for its scope. In the last days of Narnia an ape called Shift finds a lion-skin, wraps it about his simple donkey servant, Puzzle, and claims that Aslan has returned. Through this poor puppet he orders the cutting down of the forests; he makes commercial pacts with the evil Calormenes, and sells the Narnian creatures off to work in the mines. When young Tirian, "last of the Kings of Narnia," calls for aid to "the helpers beyond the world," Jill and Eustace appear (from a railway train) and help to gather forces for the battle on Stable Hill. This gripping and terrible confrontation provides one of Lewis's best set-pieces. Aslan appears at last; the vanquished seem the victors; the frightful stable, from which no one returns alive, seems a bright and sunlit garden for Aslan-followers. The children realize that they were killed in a railway accident; Narnia disintegrates; the sun is squeezed like an orange; as we have noted, friendly creatures from all the stories pass with the humans through the golden gates; a kind of Judgment Day. "I see," says Lucy thoughtfully, "This garden is like the Stable. It is far bigger inside than it was outside." They are in Narnia, fresh and green; they are in their English home. "The dream is ended; this is the morning," Aslan says. End of the world? or end of these children's lives? It is hard to say.

One need not be a philosopher or even an adult to note the illogic and crotchets in Lewis's work. As a boy he was deeply unhappy at conventional boarding schools. Yet, it is the "progressive" school which provokes his ire. (*Did* such schools use only surnames, favour bullying?) He had real fondness for animals (excepting the ape and the wolf) and accorded them a nobler place in his books than most writers with a strong sense of hierarchy (Kipling, for instance). To eat a Talking Animal in Narnia was not to be thought of. Yet the very word "vegetarian" lashes him into fury, and he imposes on the vegetarian Eustace (who would in life need courage to hold his views) such qualities as cowardliness, meanness, greed. A loner and a dreamer himself, he commends the military virtues.

Yet readers read only what they read, and Lewis's books are outstanding witness to this fact. Without heavy prompting, what child perceives the symbolism in, say, the Stone Table episode? Would the young Lewis himself have done so? But wardrobe and lamppost are firmly lodged in every reader's mind. For all his convert's zeal he leaves a reader not so much with a dose of theology as a sensation of noble deeds, far distances, the freedom of space and time, the sure division of right and wrong. Matter of myth; matter of fairytale.

—Naomi Lewis

LEWIS, Elizabeth Foreman. American. Born in Baltimore, Maryland, 24 May 1892. Educated at Tome School, 1906–09; Maryland Institute of Fine Arts, Baltimore, 1909–10; Bryant and Stratton Secretarial School, Baltimore, 1916–17; Bible Seminary of New York, 1917. Married John Abraham Lewis in 1921 (died 1934); one son. Assistant treasurer, Women's Foreign Missionary Society, Shanghai, 1917–18; teacher in district schools, Chungking, 1918–

19, and at Boys' Academy, Nanking, 1919–21. Recipient: American Library Association Newbery Medal, 1933. *Died 7 August 1958.*

PUBLICATIONS FOR CHILDREN

Fiction (illustrated by Kurt Wiese)

Young Fu of the Upper Yangtze. Philadelphia, Winston, 1932; London, Harrap, 1934.
Ho-ming, Girl of New China. Philadelphia, Winston, 1934; London, Harrap, 1935.
China Quest. Philadelphia, Winston, 1937; London, Harrap, 1938.
When the Typhoon Blows. Philadelphia, Winston, 1942; London, Harrap, 1944.
To Beat a Tiger, One Needs a Brother's Help, illustrated by John Huehnergarth. Philadelphia, Winston, 1956; London, Harrap, 1957.

PUBLICATIONS FOR ADULTS

Other

Portraits from a Chinese Scroll. Philadelphia, Winston, 1938; London, Harrap, 1939.
Test Tubes and Dragon Scales, with George C. Basil. Philadelphia, Winston, 1940.

* * *

Elizabeth Foreman Lewis grew up amid a closely knit family whose love of church and of books influenced her choice of careers. As a young woman she studied religious education and literature and was active in church and settlement activities. In 1917 she was sent to China by the Methodist Women's Board. After her return to the United States, Lewis used her experiences in China as a background for her writings, both juvenile and adult. She saw opportunities in the first cultural revolution while portraying problems people have at times of social change. Her heroes and heroines have hope and determination; they make good use of opportunities for social and geographic mobility.

Lewis's most important novel for children is *Young Fu of the Upper Yangtze*, which won the Newbery Medal for 1933. This is the story of a 13-year-old Chinese country boy who is brought by his widowed mother to the bustling city of Chungking and apprenticed to a skilled coppersmith. As he delivers his Master's wares Fu explores the large metropolis and finds everywhere the conflicts born of superstition and prejudice, of Civil War, of old and new ideas. Fu is not an idealized hero: he is brave and honest, but he also wastes his master's time and his own. The book contains many Confucian proverbs which are employed by adult characters to point out to Fu the folly of his ways: "Laziness never filled a rice bowl." "There is no merit worthy of boasting."

Others of Lewis's children's books are for older children. They too focus on individual response to social change. *Ho-ming, Girl of New China* is the story of a young girl who must free herself from primitive beliefs before she can begin a new education in public-health nursing. As a girl not encouraged to think for herself, she must meet family resistance while retaining family loyalties. *To Beat a Tiger, One Needs a Brother's Help* is about young boys from different social backgrounds living in Shanghai. They witness disease, star-vation, and violent death, and become close friends as they pull together for survival during the Japanese invasion of China.

Lewis stated that by the time illness forced her to return to America, China and her people had become a major concern in her life. In time she had to write about them, she had to convince a few readers of the inherent greatness of the Chinese, who overcame mass torture and killing, poverty and disease, determined to structure a better world. Lewis's books were well received in America and in Europe. Indeed, through her sympathetic character portrayal, her swift plots, and her compelling prose, she has affected many young readers for several decades.

—Mary Lystad

LEWIS, Hilda (Winifred). British. Born in London, in 1896. Married Michael Lewis; one son. Taught in London for a few years; lived many years in Nottingham. *Died in February 1974.*

PUBLICATIONS FOR CHILDREN

Fiction

The Ship That Flew. London, Oxford University Press, 1939; New York, Criterion, 1958.
The Gentle Falcon, illustrated by Evelyn Gibbs. London, Oxford University Press, 1952; New York, Criterion, 1957.
Here Comes Harry, illustrated by William Stobbs. London, Oxford University Press, and New York, Criterion, 1960.
Harold Was My King. London, Oxford University Press, 1968; New York, McKay, 1970.

PUBLICATIONS FOR ADULTS

Novels

Pegasus Yoked. London, Hurst and Blackett, 1933.
Madam Gold. London, Hurst and Blackett, 1933.
Full Circle. London, Hurst and Blackett, 1935.
Pelican Inn. London, Jarrolds, 1937.
Because I Must. London, Jarrolds, 1938.
Said Dr. Spendlove. London, Jarrolds, 1940.
Penny Lace. London, Jarrolds, 1942.
Imogen under Glass. London, Jarrolds, 1943.
Strange Story. London, Jarrolds, 1945; New York, Random House, 1947.
Gone to the Pictures. London, Jarrolds, 1946.
The Day Is Ours. London, Jarrolds, 1947.
More Glass Than Wall. London, Macdonald, 1950.
No Mate, No Comrade. London, Macdonald, 1951.
Enter a Player. London, Macdonald, 1952.
Wife to Henry V. London, Jarrolds, 1954; New York, Putnam, 1957.
The Witch and the Priest. London, Jarrolds, 1956; New York, McKay, 1970.
I, Jacqueline. London, Jarrolds, 1957.
Wife to Great Buckingham. London, Jarrolds, 1959; New York, Putnam, 1960.
Call Lady Purbeck. London, Hutchinson, 1961; New York, St. Martin's Press, 1962.
A Mortal Malice. London, Hutchinson, 1963.
Wife to Charles II. London, Hutchinson, 1965; as *Catherine*, New York, St. Martin's Press, 1966.
Wife to the Bastard. London, Hutchinson, 1966; New York, McKay, 1967.

Harlot Queen. London, Hutchinson, and New York, McKay, 1970.
I Am Mary Tudor. London, Hutchinson, 1971; New York, McKay, 1972.
Mary the Queen. London, Hutchinson, 1973.
Bloody Mary. London, Hutchinson, 1974.
Rose of England. London, Hutchinson, 1977.
Heart of a Rose. London, Hutchinson, 1978.

*   *   *

Out of Hilda Lewis's large output of historical novels, only four were written for children. All her books are meticulous in detail and recreation of period, and the characters full of life and colour.

In *Here Comes Harry* she gives a vivid portrait of English court life in the 15th century as she draws a parallel between the lives of Harry Rushden, 13-year-old apprentice goldsmith who really wants to be a knight fighting for his King, and the child King Henry VI, alone and surrounded by political intrigue. In *The Gentle Falcon* the tragic tale of the French child Princess Isabella who was married to Richard II is presented in a similar fashion as seen through the eyes of her namesake and lady in waiting, Isabella Clinton. *Harold Was My King* is introduced by Lewis herself thus: "My tale is told by Edmund, an English boy who loses everything through the coming of William. It is bound to be somewhat prejudiced but Edmund tries to be fair and to look beyond his own losses. In the end he comes to understand that harsh man, the Conqueror. One day you will, very likely, read the old Chronicles for yourself and make up your own mind." Lewis chose her historical interpretation of events and fashioned her account around them. The excellence of her narration inspires further reading and research, surely one of the prime intentions of historical fiction, and the best way to engender an interest.

Her classic book is the one for younger children, *The Ship That Flew*. It is a book to put alongside *Puck of Pook's Hill* and *Tom's Midnight Garden*. Peter paid all the money he had in the world—"and a bit over"—for a tiny wooden ship, not larger than six inches, that he found in the curious old shop. It is a magic ship that grows and grows until he and his brother and sisters can all sail in her—the ship that flew. But this vessel is no mere Tardis; given to Frey the norse god as a wedding present by Odin, it is only magic if one believes. While the children believe, it takes them to Asgard, to Runnymede, to the Nile, and many more places and events. They meet Chaucer, Horatius, Robin Hood, and countless others from the pageant of history. Each new scene and character is portrayed in great detail and atmosphere, and the contrasts in the various historical periods are vivid and startling. Although first published in 1939, the book itself has travelled through time and lives on as a model of its kind.

—Fiona Waters

LEXAU, Joan M. Also writes as Joan L. Nodset. American. Born in St. Paul, Minnesota. Educated at College of St. Thomas and College of St. Catherine, both St. Paul; New School for Social Research, New York. Has worked as a salesperson, waitress, library clerk, and office worker; editorial secretary, *Catholic Digest*, St. Paul, 1953–55; advertising production manager, *Glass Packer* magazine, New York, 1955–56; reporter, *Catholic News*, New York, 1956–57; correspondent, Religious News Service, New York, 1957; children's books production liaison, Harper and Row, publishers, New York, 1957–61. Recipient: Child Study Committee award, 1963. Address: c/o Harper and Row, 10 East 53rd Street, New York, New York 10022, U.S.A.

PUBLICATIONS FOR CHILDREN

Fiction

Olaf Reads, illustrated by Harvey Weiss. New York, Dial Press, 1961.

Cathy Is Company, illustrated by Aliki. New York, Dial Press, 1961.

Millicent's Ghost, illustrated by Ben Shecter. New York, Dial Press, 1962.

The Trouble with Terry, illustrated by Irene Murray. New York, Dial Press, 1962.

Olaf Is Late, illustrated by Harvey Weiss. New York, Dial Press, 1963.

That's Good, That's Bad, illustrated by Aliki. New York, Dial Press, 1963.

José's Christmas Secret, illustrated by Don Bolognese. New York, Dial Press, 1963; revised edition, as *The Christmas Secret*, New York, Scholastic, 1973.

Benjie, illustrated by Don Bolognese. New York, Dial Press, 1964.

Maria, illustrated by Ernest Crichlow. New York, Dial Press, 1964.

I Should Have Stayed in Bed!, illustrated by Syd Hoff. New York, Harper, 1965; Kingswood, Surrey, World's Work, 1966.

More Beautiful than Flowers, illustrated by Don Bolognese. Philadelphia, Lippincott, 1966.

The Homework Caper, illustrated by Syd Hoff. New York, Harper, 1966.

A Kite over Tenth Avenue, illustrated by Symeon Shimin. New York, Doubleday, 1967.

Finders Keepers, Losers Weepers, illustrated by Tomie de Paola. Philadelphia, Lippincott, 1967.

Every Day a Dragon, illustrated by Ben Shecter. New York, Harper, 1967.

Three Wishes for Abner, illustrated by Gloria Kamen. Boston, Ginn, 1967.

Striped Ice Cream!, illustrated by John Wilson. Philadelphia, Lippincott, 1968.

The Rooftop Mystery, illustrated by Syd Hoff. New York, Harper, 1968; Kingswood, Surrey, World's Work, 1969.

A House So Big, illustrated by Fritz Siebel. New York, Harper, 1968.

Archimedes Takes a Bath, illustrated by Salvatore Murdocca. New York, Crowell, 1969.

Benjie on His Own, illustrated by Don Bolognese. New York, Dial Press, 1970.

Me Day, illustrated by Robert Weaver. New York, Dial Press, 1971.

Emily and the Klunky Baby and the Next-Door Dog, illustrated by Martha Alexander. New York, Dial Press, 1972.

I'll Tell on You, illustrated by Gail Owens. New York, Dutton, 1976.

I Hate Red Rover, illustrated by Gail Owens. New York, Dutton, 1979.

The Poison Ivy Case, illustrated by Marylin Hafner. New York, Dial Press, 1983.

Strawberry Shortcake and Sad Mr. Sun, illustrated by Pat Sustendal. Beverly, Massachusetts, Parker, 1983.

Don't Be My Valentine, illustrated by Syd Hoff. New York, Harper, 1985.

The Dog Food Caper, illustrated by Marylin Hafner. New York, Dial Press, 1985; London, A. and C. Black, 1987.

Fiction as Joan L. Nodset

Who Took the Farmer's Hat?, illustrated by Fritz Siebel. New York, Harper, 1963.

Go Away, Dog, illustrated by Crosby Bonsall. New York, Harper, 1963.

Where Do You Go When You Run Away?, illustrated by Adriana Saviozzi. Indianapolis, Bobbs Merrill, 1964.

Come Here, Cat, illustrated by Steven Kellogg. New York, Harper, 1973.

Other (folktales)

Crocodile and Hen, illustrated by Joan Sandin. New York, Harper, 1969.

It All Began with a Drip, Drip, Drip..., illustrated by Joan Sandin. New York, McCall, 1970; Kingswood, Surrey, World's Work, 1972.

T for Tommy, illustrated by Janet Compere. Champaign, Illinois, Garrard, 1971.

That's Just Fine, and Who-o-o Did It?, illustrated by Dora Leder. Champaign, Illinois, Garrard, 1971.

The Tail of the Mouse, illustrated by Roberta Langman. Boston, Ginn, 1974.

The Spider Makes a Web, illustrated by Arabelle Wheatley. New York, Hastings House, 1979.

Jack and the Beanstalk, illustrated by Carol Nicklaus. New York, Random House, 1980.

Other

Come! Sit! Stay!, illustrated by Marsha Winborn. New York, Watts, 1984.

PUBLICATIONS FOR ADULTS

Other

Editor, *Convent Life: Roman Catholic Religious Orders for Women in North America*. New York, Dial Press, 1964.

*

Manuscript Collections: Kerlan Collection, University of Minnesota, Minneapolis; de Grummond Collection, University of Southern Mississippi, Hattiesburg.

Joan M. Lexau comments:

I like kids, have a lot of child friends and relatives, remember being a child, how it felt. I always wanted to write and was reintroduced to children's books while working at Harper and Row, so I write books for children. I do a lot of easy-to-read books because I remember vividly the explosive joy of being able to read my first real book (but nothing about the process of learning to read). I am now getting into high interest, low vocabulary books for older children who are having trouble reading.

*   *   *

The sweet side of harsh reality defines the sentiment and the setting of some of Joan M. Lexau's most effective endeavours. When the scene is Harlem she sketches the street gangs and the tenements, the precarious financial circumstances and the inevitable one-adult households. But such socially erosive factors never dominate. They are the foil which sets off her most telling theme—the triumph of the human spirit.

It is never an epic victory. Harlem must remain what it is, an all-too-often inescapable terrain, a cauldron forever seething and threatening to reduce solid humanity into a soft decomposing mass. But there are those who with sustained commitment to decency and ordered existence achieve a succession of modest accomplishments in the ongoing struggle against the forces of uncertainty and despair. Benjie and his grandmother are two such unlikely victors in a field of battle against unsmiling, often savage hordes who use the innocent as their prey. Granny and Benjie might occupy the fourth floor of some overcrowded apartment where hopelessness engulfs most of the inhabitants, but Granny maintains a homey sense of class which is manifest even in a picture-book presentation. The fourth floor with no elevator becomes a game not a burden as "they set off down the stairs and down the stairs and down the stairs...to the sidewalk" (*Benjie*). The sameness settles into a tradition instead of becoming a treadmill. They might share a bathroom with a virtual horde of faceless occupants of this compartment of last resort, but Granny has long since devised a lifestyle which mingles impeccable cleanliness and an unchanging routine with a wry humour that sprinkles joy into an environment which might have been expected to have dried out everything living. She scrubs and scrubs. Benjie's scuffed shoes are treated with a brown crayon. Such homely aesthetics underline the triumph of invention over poverty. Eventually the over-shy Benjie himself secures a momentary mastery over his fears in order to recover Granny's lost earring, one of her few legitimate treasures. With despair glaring down upon them, Granny and Benjie uncover a generous measure of self-reliance, a very real accomplishment whose monument too often remains hidden within the soul of the doer.

Striped Ice Cream! is a tender idyll of another single-parent black family. The importance of a proper proportion of dreams and reality spices a situation which could degenerate into a series of bland sentiments or a sociological horror story. Mama insists that in spite of financial woes the family does get by. Her son retorts, "Sure...nobody said we didn't. We were just dreaming." Mama, who like Granny knows that the blend of reality and ideals is crucial, replies, "no harm in that...as long as we know it's a dream and don't spend all our time in just dreaming." Overblown dreams had cost the family its father, as illusions led to shame and then desertion. But there are dreams which not only serve as incentive, but which, with a mite of ingenuity, can be wedded to reality. The economically deprived family does manage to get the longed-for striped ice cream for the youngest girl's birthday.

Rafer (*Me Day*) finds all the ordinary amenities of birthdays (cake, authority in selecting television shows, and exemption from chores) offset by the absence of his father who, unable to find employment, fled the face of failure. His father does make an unexpected if temporary appearance to spend the day with Rafer. It's only a day to be sure, but even the father who succumbed to conditions emerges with the reassuring words. "Look, your mother and me are divorced. Not you kids. No way! You and me are tight, buddy. Together like glue." To which Rafer replies "Don't go so fast, Daddy...I want it to be a long, long day." The artistry in prolonging substantial pleasantries—soundings of Emerson—make frequent appearances in any of number of Lexau's situations. They do not solve circumstances, but they do considerably more than make them tolerable.

Snatching jewels from ordinary places appears as an embedded theme within the wide variety of Lexau's topics. The philosopher Archimedes (*Archimedes Takes a Bath*) might be an elderly genius, but he is also the archetypical child. Preoccupied with his thoughts, he finds hygiene and personal appearance bothersome matters. His attendant, a young boy, finally coaxes him into a tub where the irrepressible philosopher uses the experience to deduce a means to figure out a principle of physics, and in the process solves a palace mystery. His bath, a confinement of sorts not unlike the Harlem tenement, yields unexpected insights. Ingenuity is the connection of a series of things known to produce the unusual. The childlike sense of discovery must be maintained in the adult behaviour if the flow of treasures is not to cease.

Even with her zany adventures there is the element of strange people supplying answers. The eccentric Miss Hepp who doesn't appear to know what she is doing (and probably doesn't) (*The Dog Food Caper*) shakes up things and a solution to the mystery emerges where stale probability had exhausted itself. No wonder she earned herself the title of witch.

Human ingenuity can arise from genius, from eccentricity, or from calm determination to remain decent. Its wisdom can drop from seeming failures in the not-so-funny comedy of humours. In the process of tracing its whereabouts, Lexau is an appealing guide. There are many answers, many sources, many unlikely sages. The quest continues along with her ever-expanding writings for the young of all ages.

—Leonard R. Mendelsohn

————

LIFTON, Betty Jean (née Kirschner). American. Born in New York City. Educated at Barnard College, New York, B.A. 1948. Married the writer Robert Jay Lifton in 1952; one son and one daughter. Agent: Berenice Hoffman Literary Agency, 215 West 75th Street, New York, New York 10023. Address: 300 Central Park West, New York, New York 10024, U.S.A.

PUBLICATIONS FOR CHILDREN

Fiction

Joji and the Dragon, illustrated by Eiichi Mitsui. New York, Morrow, 1957.
Mogo the Mynah, illustrated by Anne Scott. New York, Morrow, 1958.
Joji and the Fog, illustrated by Eiichi Mitsui. New York, Morrow, 1959.
Kap the Kappa, illustrated by Eiichi Mitsui. New York, Morrow, 1960.
The Dwarf Pine Tree, illustrated by Fuku Akino. New York, Atheneum, 1963.
Joji and the Amanojaku, illustrated by Eiichi Mitsui. New York, Norton, 1965.
The Cock and the Ghost Cat, illustrated by Fuku Akino. New York, Atheneum, 1965.
The Rice-Cake Rabbit, illustrated by Eiichi Mitsui. New York, Norton, 1966.
The Many Lives of Chio and Goro, illustrated by Yasuo Segawa. New York, Norton, 1966.
Taka-Chan and I: A Dog's Journey to Japan, by Runcible, photographs by Eikoh Hosoe. New York, Norton, 1967.
Kap and the Wicked Monkey, illustrated by Eiichi Mitsui. New York, Norton, 1968.
The Secret Seller, illustrated by Etienne Delessert. New York, Norton, 1968.
The One-Legged Ghost, illustrated by Fuku Akino. New York, Atheneum, 1968.
The Mud Snail Son, illustrated by Fuku Akino. New York, Atheneum, 1971.
The Silver Crane, illustrated by Laszlo Kubinyi. New York, Seabury Press, 1971.
Good Night, Orange Monster, illustrated by Cyndy Szekeres. New York, Atheneum, 1972.
Jaguar, My Twin, illustrated by Ann Leggett. New York, Atheneum, 1976.

I'm Still Me.   New York, Knopf, 1981.

Play

Kap the Kappa, adaptation of her own story, in *Contemporary Children's Theater*, edited by Lifton.   New York, Avon, 1974.

Other

A Dog's Guide to Tokyo, photographs by Eikoh Hosoe.   New York, Norton, 1969.
Children of Vietnam, with Thomas C. Fox.   New York, Atheneum, 1972.

Editor, *Contemporary Children's Theater*.   New York, Avon, 1974.

PUBLICATIONS FOR ADULTS

Play

Moon Walk, music and lyrics by the Open Window (produced New York, 1970).

Other

Return to Hiroshima, photographs by Eikoh Hosoe.   New York, Atheneum, 1970; revised edition, as *A Place Called Hiroshima*, New York and London, Kodansha, 1985.
Twice Born: Memoirs of an Adopted Daughter.   New York, McGraw Hill, 1975; London, Penguin, 1977.
Lost and Found: The Adoption Experience.   New York, Dial Press, 1979.
The King of Children: A Biography of Janusz Korczak.   New York, Farrar Straus, and London, Chatto and Windus, 1988.

*   *   *

Betty Jean Lifton's prolific work as a writer reflects the influence of sojourns in the Far East. In her children's fiction such oriental themes as non-violence and the eternal recurrence of nature are accompanied by a cavalcade of strange creatures chiefly drawn from (often moralistic) Japanese folktales.

Among the folk creatures is Joji, a peace-loving scarecrow befriended by the very crows he is supposed to frighten away from a farmer's rice field. In *Joji and the Dragon* Joji's master discards him for a hired dragon. The crows scare off their would-be conqueror, thus enabling Joji to be restored to his rightful position. Captured by a rice-paddy-terrorizing demon in *Joji and the Amanojaku* he is again rescued by his crow friends who intimidate his ferocious captor. Joji, a lively espouser of non-violence, is appealing to the very young.

Another protagonist is a Kappa, a legendary Japanese river elf with a monkey's face and a turtle's back. In *Kap the Kappa* the mischievous Kap leaves his river home to be adopted by a fisherman whose family disguise him as a boy. However, his incorrigible pranks disclose his identity to all, and, after realizing he cannot be a human, he returns to the river and his true parents. An inspired creation, Kap inhabits other stories as well as a play which evinces the author's considerable skill as a playwright for children.

A mountain demon in *The Dwarf Pine Tree* grants a tiny evergreen its wish to become a dwarf pine tree beautiful enough to cure an ailing princess. The tree patiently undergoes the necessary painful transformation, is discovered and brought to the princess whose health is restored, and then it passes away to become a tree spirit. This poignant work reflecting the gentle spirit of Buddha emerges as a minor masterpiece.

Animal characters also abound in Lifton's books. A loyal rooster in the suspenseful and touching *The Cock and the Ghost Cat* sacrifices himself to protect his master from a ghost cat bent on stealing the household's provisions. The man-size title character of *The Rice-Cake Rabbit* makes the best rice-cakes in Japan but aspires to be a samurai, a profession reserved for men. He is banished to the moon when he succeeds. This gently ironic yarn is among the author's best. In *The Many Lives of Chio and Goro* the trans-migrating souls of a farm couple pass through animal life back to human life with comic complications in a tale which the reader can appreciate on several levels.

Lifton's stories have an audience range of ages four to 10. They are characterized by humor, an economy of words, vivid characterizations, well-structured narratives drawn from Japanese folktales without diluting the cultural source, and handsomely imaginative and colorful brush and ink illustrations by such artists as Eiichi Mitsui and Fuku Akino. Her fiction's appeal for young children and its effectiveness in stimulating interest in oriental culture are unquestionable. These factors earn Lifton a position of prominence in juvenile literature as an imaginative, sensitive, and skillful story teller.

—Christian H. Moe

————

LILLINGTON, Kenneth (James).   British.   Born in London, 7 September 1916. Educated at St. Dunstan's College, London, 1927–35; Wandsworth Training College, London, 1948–49. Served in the Royal Army Pay Corps, 1941–43; Royal Corps of Signals, 1943–46. Married Dulcie E. Lock in 1942; two daughters and two sons. Advertising copywriter, Temple Press, London, 1938–39; teacher, Walton-on-Thames School for Boys, Surrey, 1949–56; lecturer in French and English, Brooklands Technical College, Weybridge, Surrey, 1956–81. Lives in Cranleigh, Surrey. Address: c/o Faber and Faber, 3 Queen Square, London WC1N 3AU, England.

PUBLICATIONS FOR CHILDREN

Fiction

Soapy and the Pharaoh's Curse, illustrated by Julia Faithful.   London, Heinemann, 1957.
Conjurer's Alibi.   London, Nelson, 1960.
The Secret Arrow, illustrated by Robert Hodgson.   London, Nelson, 1960.
A Man Called Hughes, illustrated by D.L. Mays.   London, Nelson, 1962.
Young Man of Morning.   London, Faber, 1979.
What Beckoning Ghost?   London, Faber, 1983.
Isabel's Double.   London, Faber, 1984.
Selkie.   London, Faber, 1985.
Full Moon.   London, Faber, 1986.
An Ash-Blonde Witch.   London, Faber, 1987.
The Hallowe'en Cat, illustrated by Gareth Floyd.   London, Faber, 1987.
Gabrielle, illustrated by Gareth Floyd.   London, Faber, 1988.
Jonah's Mirror.   London, Faber, 1988.
Josephine.   London, Faber, 1989.

Plays

Blue Murder, in *The Windmill Book of One-Act Plays*, edited by E.R.

Wood. London, Heinemann, 1960.

My Proud Beauty, in *The Second Windmill Book of One-Act Plays*, edited by E.R. Wood. London, Heinemann, 1963.

The Fourth Windmill Book of One-Act Plays (includes *Make Your Play, Bring Out Your Dead, I'll Ring for More Toast, Is Horror Your Neighbour?, A Villa on Venus, You Never Heard Such Unearthly Laughter, The Cinderella Story*). London, Heinemann, 1967.

The First Book of Classroom Plays (includes *The Case of the Golden Cockerel, Words Fail Me, The Cat Princess, Professor Tugnutt's Time Machine, The Perfect Customer, In Darkest Britain, The Christmas Spirit, The Stove, Skeleton Plays*). London, Hale, 1967.

The Second Book of Classroom Plays (includes *The Blackfeet and the Cree, The Knocking on the Wall, The Picts Drop In, Professor Tugnutt's Truth Gas, For Crying Out Loud, The Boy Next Door, Robin Hood and the Jester, End of Part One*). London, Hale, 1968.

Cantaloup Crescent, in *The Fifth Windmill Book of One-Act Plays*, edited by E.R. Wood. London, Heinemann, 1970.

Olaf and the Ogre, in *The Sixth Windmill Book of One-Act Plays*, edited by E.R. Wood. London, Heinemann, 1972.

The Seventh Windmill Book of One-Act Plays (includes *Mockery Hollow, The Avenging Phoenix, I Am a Dustbin, Postman's Knock, A Latin Lesson, The Devil's Grandson, The Adventures of Chastity Pewke, Come What May*). London, Heinemann, 1972.

There's an End of May, in *The Eighth Windmill Book of One-Act Plays*, edited by E.R. Wood. London, Heinemann, 1975.

Other (retellings)

The Mikado, music by Arthur Sullivan. London, Faber Music, 1988.

A Christmas Carol. London, Faber Music, 1988.

PUBLICATIONS FOR ADULTS

Other

Read and Understand: Famous Stories, with Paul Snowden and Hiroshi Tsuchiya. Tokyo, Kirihara Shoten, 1988.

Editor, *Nine Lives: An Anthology of Poetry and Prose Concerning Cats*. London, Deutsch, 1977.

Editor, *For Better for Worse*. London, Angus and Robertson, 1979.

*   *   *

Kenneth Lillington made a welcome return to the world of children's books in 1979 with a historical novel, *Young Man of Morning*, which sprang from his experience of teaching ancient history to 11-year-olds. Since then, however, he has written novels aimed mainly at a teenage audience. His books contain a good helping of the supernatural and usually have a strong romantic theme. His characters are often working out their feelings for a boyfriend or girlfriend, which makes the books particularly appealing to young people at a time in their lives when they, too, may be experiencing similar anxieties.

Whether the supernatural element is in the form of magic, ghosts, science fiction, or simply legend, the books are firmly rooted in reality. In *Selkie* this encompasses the problems related to unemployment, growing up, changing relationships, class consciousness, and superstition. Catherine, the heroine, moves with her parents to Cornwall following her father's redundancy, and has to leave her boyfriend, Clive. At first she resents the move but soon she gets involved with Joe, a young labourer who works on their house, and together they try to solve the mystery of the legend of the Selkie, or seal-girl, that is at the centre of the book. Lillington captures the emotions of an adolescent girl trying to deal with her feelings about two boys from very different backgrounds and with her mother's snobbish attitude to Joe. The book also presents a very realistic portrait of the effects of redundancy and unemployment on people, their families and friends, that is as relevant today as it was in 1935 when the book is set.

An Ash-Blonde Witch and *Jonah's Mirror* contain rather more of the supernatural than the natural. *An Ash-Blonde Witch* is set in the 22nd century, where there are pockets of the world that have not changed, called Conservation Areas. When Sophie and her father are sent to study one of these areas—Urstwhile—the effect is like stepping back in time. The scientific skills of psychological healing and levitation that are commonplace in Sophie's world are taken to be magic by the people of Urstwhile and she is branded a witch. On the other hand, emotions like love and jealousy are no longer felt outside Urstwhile and Sophie's punishment for interfering in a Conservation Area is to suffer these emotions. The balance between science fiction and fairytale or fable is nicely held, and the ending, in which the witch Dorcas is transported out of the old-fashioned Urstwhile because her skills are thought to be valuable to the more advanced society, provides a humorous twist.

In *Jonah's Mirror* the two main characters, Jonah Sprockett, a millionaire and chairman of Sprockett Electricals, and his partner and fiancée Miss Wingbone, "arguably the cleverest woman in the world," are caught up in an elaborate fantasy. As a result of an experiment with a magic mirror Jonah finds himself locked in the strange world of Sudonia, which is inhabited by fairytale princesses, mythical beasts, and marauding knights, and where he falls in love with the beautiful Princess Miranda. Jonah thinks he has spirited himself into a parallel universe, but Miss Wingbone's theory is that it is all a dream and therefore a figment of his imagination. This ingenious explanation is rather complex to follow at times, particularly when Miss Wingbone herself enters Sudonia, but it provides endless opportunities for some wonderful tongue-in-cheek humour.

What Beckoning Ghost?, *Full Moon*, and *Isabel's Double* all deal with ghosts or apparitions. In *Full Moon* Lillington creates an intricate web of relationships between twins, sisters, parent and child, boyfriend and girlfriend, old and young, living and dead, and through these explores the kind of tensions that exist in such very close relationships. Ghosts, dreams, and visions of the past all play a part in the solving of the mystery surrounding Great Aunt Alice's death and her sister Clara's possible involvement. *Isabel's Double* is about the apparition of Isabel that has haunted her since childhood and that starts to haunt Mike, who becomes her boyfriend. After some help from a psychiatrist, the *doppelgänger* is finally conquered in a chilling climax involving psychic powers, spirits, and a painting of Isabel. The books dealing with ghosts and apparitions are more disturbing than his others, perhaps because it is not as easy to dismiss such psychic phenomena as pure fantasy.

On a lighter note, Lillington has recently turned to writing for a younger age group. His first story, *The Hallowe'en Cat*, questions whether magic is real or simply in the mind and leaves the reader guessing. The second, *Gabrielle*, featuring the same characters, is a straightforward story about the problems posed by jealousy, the ending of which is suitably moralistic.

The prevalence of romantic themes and strong female characters in Lillington's books probably makes them more appealing to teenage girls than to boys. His books for younger readers, however, will be equally enjoyed by boys and girls.

—Fiona Lafferty

LINDSAY, Norman (Alfred William). Australian. Born in Creswick, Victoria, 22 February 1879. Educated at Creswick State School and Creswick Grammar School. Married 1) Kate Parkinson in 1900 (divorced 1920), three sons, including the writer Jack Lindsay; 2) Rose Soady in 1920, two daughters. Artist and freelance illustrator: for the *Hawklet* sporting paper, after 1896, and *Tocsin*, both in Melbourne; co-editor, the *Rambler*, Melbourne, 1899; joined Sydney *Bulletin* in 1901, and chief cartoonist until 1923, and 1932–58; associated with the *Lone Hand*, Melbourne, 1907–21, and Endeavour Press, Sydney, 1932–35. Individual shows: Sydney and Melbourne, 1909; Adelaide, 1924; London, 1925; Sydney, 1968; Newcastle, New South Wales, 1969; group show: Exhibition of Australian Art, London, 1923. *Died 21 November 1969.*

PUBLICATIONS FOR CHILDREN (illustrated by the author)

Fiction

The Magic Pudding, Being the Adventures of Bunyip Bluegum and His Friends Bill Barnacle and Sam Sawnoff. Sydney, Angus and Robertson, 1918; London, Hamish Hamilton, and New York, Farrar and Rinehart, 1936.
The Flyaway Highway. Sydney, Angus and Robertson, 1936.

Verse

Puddin' Poems, Being the Best of the Verse from "The Magic Pudding." Sydney, Angus and Robertson, 1977.

PUBLICATIONS FOR ADULTS

Fiction

A Curate in Bohemia. Sydney, Bookstall, 1913; London, Laurie, 1937.
Hyperborea: Two Fantastic Travel Essays. London, Fanfrolico Press, 1928.
Madam Life's Lovers: A Human Narrative Embodying a Philosophy of the Artist in Dialogue Form. London, Fanfrolico Press, 1929.
Redheap. London, Faber, 1930; as *Every Mother's Son*, New York, Cosmopolitan, 1930.
The Cautious Amorist. New York, Farrar and Rinehart, 1932; London, Laurie, 1934.
Miracles by Arrangement. London, Faber, 1932; as *Mr. Gresham and Olympus*, New York, Farrar and Rinehart, 1932.
Saturdee. Sydney, Endeavour Press, 1933; London, Laurie, 1936; New York, AMS Press, 1976.
Pan in the Parlour. New York, Farrar and Rinehart, 1933; London, Laurie, 1934.
Age of Consent. London, Laurie, and New York, Farrar and Rinehart, 1938.
The Cousin from Fiji. Sydney and London, Angus and Robertson, 1945; New York, Random House, 1946.
Halfway to Anywhere. Sydney, Angus and Robertson, 1947.
Dust or Polish? Sydney and London, Angus and Robertson, 1950.
Rooms and Houses: An Autobiographical Novel. Sydney and London, Ure Smith, 1968.

Other

Norman Lindsay's Book 1–2, edited by Harold Burston. Sydney, Bookstall, 1912–15.
The Pen Drawings of Norman Lindsay, edited by Sydney Ure Smith and Bertram Stevens. Sydney, Angus and Robertson, 1918.

Creative Effort: An Essay in Affirmation. Sydney, Art in Australia, 1920; revised edition, London, Palmer, 1924.
Pen Drawings. Sydney, McQuitty, 1924.
The Etchings of Norman Lindsay. London, Constable, 1927.
Norman Lindsay's Pen Drawings. Sydney, Art in Australia, 1931.
Norman Lindsay Water Colour Book: Eighteen Reproductions in Colour from Original Watercolours, with an Appreciation of the Medium. Sydney, Springwood Press, 1939; augmented edition, Sydney and London, Ure Smith, 1969.
Paintings in Oil.... Sydney, Shepherd Press, 1945.
Bohemians of the Bulletin. Sydney, Angus and Robertson, 1965.
The Scribblings of an Idle Mind. Melbourne, Lansdowne Press, 1966.
Norman Lindsay's Ship Models. Sydney, Angus and Robertson, 1966.
Selected Pen Drawings. Sydney, Angus and Robertson, 1968; New York, Bonanza, 1970.
Pencil Drawings. Sydney, Angus and Robertson, 1969.
My Mask, for What Little I Know of the Man Behind It: An Autobiography. Sydney and London, Angus and Robertson, 1970.
Two Hundred Etchings, edited by Douglas Stewart. Sydney, Angus and Robertson, 1973.
Pen Drawings. Sydney, Ure Smith, 1974.
Norman Lindsay's Cats, edited by Douglas Stewart. Melbourne, Macmillan, 1975; revised edition, Melbourne, Sun, 1983.
Siren and Satyr: The Personal Philosophy of Norman Lindsay. Melbourne, Sun, 1976.
Favourite Etchings. Sydney, Angus and Robertson, 1977; London, Angus and Robertson, 1978; as *Etchings*, London, Angus and Robertson, 1982.
Letters of Norman Lindsay, edited by R.G. Howarth and A.W. Barker. Sydney and London, Angus and Robertson, 1979.
Norman Lindsay's War Cartoons, edited by Peter Fullerton. Melbourne and London, Melbourne University Press, 1983.
The World of Norman Lindsay, edited by Lin Bloomfield. Melbourne, Sun, 1983.
The Comic Art of Norman Lindsay, edited by Keith Wingrove. Sydney, Angus and Robertson, 1987.

Editor, *The Golden Shanty: Short Stories*, by Edward Dyson. Sydney, Angus and Robertson, 1963.

*

Critical Studies: *Norman Lindsay*, Melbourne, Lansdowne Press, 1962, and *Norman Lindsay: The Embattled Olympian*, Melbourne and London, Oxford University Press, 1973, both by John Hetherington: *Norman Lindsay: His Books, Manuscripts, and Autograph Letters in the Library of, and Annotated by, Harry F. Chaplin*, Sydney, Wentworth Press, 1969; *Norman Lindsay: A Personal Record* by Douglas Stewart, Melbourne, Nelson, 1975; *Portrait of Pa* by Jane Lindsay, Sydney, Angus and Robertson, 1983; *Norman Lindsay: Impulse to Draw* by Lin Bloomfield, Sydney, Bay, 1984.

Illustrator: *Oblation* by A.G. Stephens, 1902; *This Is the Book of Our New Selection* by Arthur H. Davis, 1903; *Satyrs and Sunlight*, 1909 and 1928, *Colombine*, 1920, and *Idyllia*, 1922, all by Hugh McCrae; *Satyricon*, 1910, and *The Complete Works of Gaius Petronius*, 1927; *Songs of a Campaign*, 1917, and *The Isle of San*, 1919, both by Leon Gellert; *The Man from Snowy River*, 1920, and *The Animals Noah Forgot*, 1933, both by A.B. Paterson; *The Inns of Greece and Rome* by W.C. Firebaugh, 1923; *Fauns and Ladies*, 1923, *The Passionate Neatherd*, 1926, and *Faces and Places*, 1974, all by Jack Lindsay, *Lysistrata*, 1925, and *Women in Parliament*, 1929, both by Aristophanes, *Propertius in Love*, 1927, and *Homage to Sappho*,

1928, all translated by Jack Lindsay, and *Loving Mad Tom*, 1927, edited by Jack Lindsay; *Thief of the Moon*, 1924, *Cuckooz Contrey*, 1932, and *Five Bells*, 1939, all by Kenneth Slessor; *The Antichrist* by Nietzsche, 1928; *As It Was in the Beginning* by Dulcie Deamer, 1929; *A Defence of Women* by John Donne, 1930; *Our Earth* by Kenneth Mackenzie, 1937; *Elegy for an Airman*, 1940, *Sonnets to an Unknown Soldier*, 1941, *Ned Kelly*, 1946, *Shipwreck*, 1947, *Sun Orchids and Other Poems*, 1952, *Fisher's Ghost*, 1960, and *The Garden of Ships*, 1962, all by Douglas Stewart; *Great Expectations* by Dickens, 1947; *A Drum for Ben Boyd* by Francis Webb, 1948; *The Letters of Rachel Henning* edited by David Adams, 1952; *The Collected Verse of A.B. Paterson*, 1982.

*   *   *

In Norman Lindsay's *The Magic Pudding* an urbane young koala called Bunyip Bluegum leaves home because of nuisances created by his Uncle Wattleberry's whiskers. Nattily dressed in Edwardian leisure-wear, Bunyip soon discovers a disadvantage of genteel strolling:

> Observe my doleful plight.
> For here am I without a crumb
> To satisfy a raging tum—
> O what an oversight!

"As he was indulging in these melancholy reflections he came round a bend in the road, and discovered two people in the very act of having lunch. These people were none other than Bill Barnacle, the sailor, and his friend, Sam Sawnoff, the penguin bold."

These boisterous characters invite Bunyip to share their pudding, which has the advantages of being inexhaustible and as variable in kind and flavours as the eaters wish. It is also a larrikin called Albert, with sprinting ability when not being dined upon, and with unrefined speech to express contempt of all but hearty eaters:

> Eat away, chew away, munch and bolt and guzzle,
> Never leave the table till you're full up to the muzzle!

The rest of the story is a rollick of campfire feasts and roaring songs, interrupted by desperate attempts to recover Albert from puddin' thieves. These are mostly a "snooting, snouting" Possum and his accomplice, "a bulbous, boozy-looking Wombat," but there is also "a Judge who's been poisoned/By Puddin' and Port."

In these adventures Bill and Sam produce the necessary snout-bending pugilistics; Bunyip Bluegum supplies encouragement, inspirations, and tactics. The nonsense story is told in fluent colloquial prose, in uproarious verse, and in the vigorous drawings of Lindsay at the height of his great ability as an illustrator in black-and-white.

So much of the fun and fast movement depends on sound that children of nine or 10, unable to read well enough to appreciate the rollicking prose and verse, often fail to enjoy the book. Read aloud, however, it's an instant success. There seems no upward limit to its "reading age."

Lindsay is said to have written the book to back one of his multitudinous opinions: that children prefer food to fairies. It may seem that, although he rejected the phoney faerie of Victorian fiction, he accepted the talking-animal mode; but perhaps his animal characters are metaphors, rather than personifications. Certainly Lindsay, a life-long experimenter in crafts, became so involved in his essay at a book for children that the story has none of the humourless stiffness of so many first attempts. In fact, *The Magic Pudding* is the only Australian children's book that is indisputably a classic.

He tried again, in 1936, but *The Flyaway Highway* lacks the glorious spontaneity of *The Puddin'*. It depends on outdated ideas (the platitudinous themes of late-Victorian popular fiction) and on

dated slang. In spite of its vigorous pen-drawings, and the presence of "the bloke with cow's hooves" (who seems to be an irreverent response to Kenneth Grahame's Pan), it fails to satisfy either children or adults.

—Dennis Hall

————

LINE, David. Pseudonym for Lionel Davidson. British. Born in Hull, Yorkshire, 31 March 1922. Served in the Royal Naval Submarine Service, 1941–46. Married Fay Jacobs in 1949; two sons. Freelance magazine journalist and editor, 1946–59. Recipient: Crime Writers Association Gold Dagger, for adult fiction, 1961, 1967, 1979. Agent: Curtis Brown, 162–168 Regent Street, London W1R 5TB, England.

PUBLICATIONS FOR CHILDREN

Fiction

Soldier and Me. New York, Harper, 1965.
Run for Your Life. London, Cape, 1966.
Mike and Me. London, Cape, 1974.
Under Plum Lake (as Lionel Davidson). London, Cape, and New York, Knopf, 1980.
Screaming High. London, Cape, and Boston, Little Brown, 1985.

PUBLICATIONS FOR ADULTS as Lionel Davidson

Novels

The Night of Wenceslas. London, Gollancz, 1960; New York, Harper, 1961.
The Rose of Tibet. London, Gollancz, and New York, Harper, 1962.
A Long Way to Shiloh. London, Gollancz, 1966; as *The Menorah Men*, New York, Harper, 1966.
Making Good Again. London, Cape, and New York, Harper, 1968.
Smith's Gazelle. London, Cape, and New York, Knopf, 1971.
The Sun Chemist. London, Cape, and New York, Knopf, 1976.
The Chelsea Murders. London, Cape, 1978; as *Murder Games*, New York, Coward McCann, 1978.

*   *   *

"David Line" is the pseudonym of the novelist Lionel Davidson. He is an occasional writer for children—only five novels in 20 years—but a very popular and successful one, whose books are highly regarded by teachers as well as having a proven direct appeal to children. Writing as David Line, he has published four children's novels, all thrillers, and under his own name a fifth, the children's fantasy *Under Plum Lake*. Although the choice of name clearly signifies the author's own sense of a difference not just of genre but of seriousness, nevertheless there are points in common between all of the books which declare them clearly the same author's work.

The Line stories are deceptively simple both in narrative and language. In fact they belong to a scarce and valuable form of children's writing, the nature of which accounts for their popularity with educators as well as children themselves. They are taut, lean, strongly plotted thrillers, with fast-moving narratives filled with unrelenting excitement and suspense—a traditional "good read" in fact. The economy of narrative style matches the economy of unembellished action: terse sentences, short paragraphs, and concise chapters all make the stories easy to read quickly. But the books are also highly literate and intelligent; simplicity does not mean simplification, spareness and pace of language do not bring cliché, and familiar situations avoid hackneyed stereotype by their freshness of particular setting and meticulous accuracy of technical detail.

Two of the books, *Run for Your Life* and *Mike and Me*, involved the same main character, Jim Woolcott. *Run for Your Life* is like a junior version of John Buchan's *The Thirty-Nine Steps*, and Woolcott strongly resembles an English schoolboy equivalent of Buchan's Richard Hannay. Like Hannay, Woolcott comes into accidental possession of significant political information, and is unable to free himself of it by simply informing the authorities; like Hannay, he is quickly on the run, pursued by those who wish to silence him; like Hannay, he has enemies who can assume plausible disguises and official roles, and is exposed in a familiar British landscape which is suddenly dangerous and isolating; and his equivalent of Hannay's powerful friends come finally to his aid. Woolcott is in most respects a reluctant adventurer, a conformist figure who dislikes avoidable hassle, but when occasion demands he proves intelligent and resourceful, adaptable and plucky. And in his convincing first-person narrative he shows a shrewd, iconoclastic wit and humour which often cut the adult world to size.

Unlike Hannay, however, Jim Woolcott is not alone. In *Run for Your Life* his adventures are shared (indeed caused) by a less orthodox companion. The refugee Hungarian schoolboy "Soldier" is a likeable oddity with a gift for finding trouble. This is the pattern for the other books too. In *Mike and Me* the action is confined to Woolcott's home town, but again involves dangerous information, escape, and hot pursuit; and again Woolcott has an eccentric partner, his naive and trouble-prone cousin Mike. The same pattern recurs in a more intricate and ambitious story, *Screaming High*, where the bright but circumspect schoolboy Nick is led into hair-raising adventures by his friendship with a maverick and wonderfully gifted adolescent trumpet-player known as Ratbag. Nick, like Woolcott, is a model of unwilling courage and resource when crisis strikes.

In each book there is a serious political or social theme—the politics of emigré Hungarians in *Run for Your Life*, unscrupulous property developers in *Mike and Me*, international drug trafficking in *Screaming High*—but each time it is deftly understated, its seriousness indicated but not allowed to subvert the primacy of adventure.

Under Plum Lake also has an "ordinary" schoolboy hero, Barry Gordon, with an extraordinary partner, Dido, and in narrative style and method there is much in common with the other books. But the stakes are higher here. Barry's world of (not quite) accidental adventure is Egon, a parallel world beneath the seas, an enigmatic co-existent universe to which Dido has lured him. Egon is a kind of Utopia, an enormously advanced and civilised world of general happiness and transcendent youthfulness and play. It is an alternative evolutionary outcome, a vision of what our world could one day be, but in some ways it is also a place of transfigured and perpetual childhood. After Barry's visit all memory of Egon should be erased from his mind, but it isn't. Barry is explicitly left psychologically damaged, stranded between two worlds. And therein lies his peril. *Under Plum Lake* is a lyrical but disturbing book, capable of simple readings but multiple interpretation. At one level the two worlds stand for childhood and maturity. Egon may represent specific fantasy delights of childhood, delights which are real and true in their psychological time, but which we, like Barry, cannot for our peace afford to revisit or recall, once childhood is over.

—Peter Hollindale

_____

LINGARD, Joan (Amelia). British. Born in Edinburgh, Scotland. Educated at Bloomfield Collegiate School, Belfast; Moray House Training College, General Certificate of Education. Has three children. Schoolteacher, Midlothian, 1953–61. Full-time novelist and television scriptwriter. Since 1979 member of the Council, Scottish Arts Council. Recipient: Scottish Arts Council bursary, 1969; Buxtehude Bulle prize (West Germany), 1987. Agent: David Higham Associates, 5–8 Lower John Street, London W1R 4HA, England. Address: 72 Great King Street, Edinburgh EH3 6QU, Scotland.

PUBLICATIONS FOR CHILDREN

Fiction

The Twelfth Day of July. London, Hamish Hamilton, 1970; Nashville, Nelson, 1972.
Across the Barricades. London, Hamish Hamilton, 1972; Nashville, Nelson, 1973.
Into Exile. London, Hamish Hamilton, and Nashville, Nelson, 1973.
Frying as Usual, illustrated by Priscilla Clive. London, Hamish Hamilton, 1973.
Maggie series:
　The Clearance. London, Hamish Hamilton, and Nashville, Nelson, 1974.
　The Resettling. London, Hamish Hamilton, and Nashville, Nelson, 1975.
　The Pilgrimage. London, Hamish Hamilton, 1976; Nashville, Nelson, 1977.
　The Reunion. London, Hamish Hamilton, 1977; Nashville, Nelson, 1978.
A Proper Place. London, Hamish Hamilton, and Nashville, Nelson, 1975.
Hostages to Fortune. London, Hamish Hamilton, 1976; Nashville, Nelson, 1977.
Snake among the Sunflowers. London, Hamish Hamilton, and Nashville, Nelson, 1977.
The Gooseberry. London, Hamish Hamilton, 1978; as *Odd Girl Out*, New York, Elsevier Nelson, 1979.
The File on Fraulein Berg. London, MacRae, and New York, Elsevier Nelson, 1980.
Strangers in the House. London, Hamish Hamilton, 1981; New York, Dutton, 1983.
The Winter Visitor. London, Hamish Hamilton, 1983.
The Freedom Machine. London, Hamish Hamilton, 1986.
The Guilty Party. London, Hamish Hamilton, 1987.
Rags and Riches. London, Hamish Hamilton, 1988.

Plays

Television Series: *Maggie*, 1981, 1982.

PUBLICATIONS FOR ADULTS

Novels

Liam's Daughter. London, Hodder and Stoughton, 1963.
The Prevailing Wind. London, Hodder and Stoughton, 1964.
The Tide Comes In. London, Hodder and Stoughton, 1966.
The Headmaster. London, Hodder and Stoughton, 1967.
A Sort of Freedom. London, Hodder and Stoughton, 1969.
The Lord on Our Side. London, Hodder and Stoughton, 1970.
The Second Flowering of Emily Mountjoy. Edinburgh, Harris, 1979; New York, St. Martin's Press, 1980.
Greenyards. London, Hamish Hamilton, and New York, Putnam,

1981.
Sisters by Rite. London, Hamish Hamilton, and New York, St.
  Martin's Press, 1984.
Reasonable Doubts. London, Hamish Hamilton, 1986.
The Women's House. London, Hamish Hamilton, 1989.

Plays

Television Plays: *The Sandyford Place Mystery* and *A Kiss, A Fond
Embrace,* from the novel *Square Mile of Murder* by Jack House,
1980; *Her Mother's House,* 1982.

*

Joan Lingard comments:

I began to write for children after writing my sixth adult novel *The
Lord on Our Side,* set in Ulster from the 1940's to the 1960's. The
late Honor Arundel, fellow writer and close friend, suggested I write
a book about Belfast for children. At that time—1967—the current
troubles were just beginning to build up. On thinking about it, I
realised that I had a book more or less ready made in my head: the
character Josie from my adult novel was transmuted into Sadie, her
brother Billy to Tommy, and I created Kevin, the Catholic boy, as a
balance to Sadie and his sister Brede as a counterweight to Tommy.
Thus Sadie and Kevin were born, and *The Twelfth Day of July* was
on its way. In this and four subsequent books I followed them through
the passage from childhood to maturity, a maturity forced upon them
prematurely by the situation in Ulster, the differences in their
religions, their exile, and the continuing demands of their families.

As a relief almost, in order to get a respite from thinking about
Ulster and its troubles, I created Maggie, a Glasgow girl, who, unlike
Sadie, does not intend to follow the traditional female role of
becoming a wife and mother but wants to go to university, become
a social anthropologist and push out the boundaries of her life, an
ambition not understood, although tolerated, by her family. In the
course of four books beginning with *The Clearance* I explored her
development through that crucial stage in which she is questioning
previously held concepts and beliefs and trying to find out what she
does and does not want from life.

I am particularly interested in characters caught up in social change
with all its attendant problems and stresses; also in the relationships
within families, and which part of their inheritance young people
retain, and which part reject, or attempt to.

*   *   *

Joan Lingard is tough and uncompromising, also lively,
humorous, and unfailingly accessible. It is partly her honesty that
evokes, within a few opening pages of each novel, a sharply realised
world peopled by real, flawed humans. Be it sun-saturated France in
Snake among the Sunflowers, the wild seascape of *The Winter
Visitor,* or the more familiar city settings of Belfast and Edinburgh,
she swiftly transports her readers to her setting. There, her characters
are firmly located, and located equally solidly in their class and
culture. The limitations and strengths of the adults are wholly convincing, shaped by their backgrounds. Even the food eaten (a feature
of every book!) adds not only to the realism but also to our understanding of the characters.

These strengths in Lingard's writing serve to contextualise her
major theme: the prejudices that rend society and even lives. Her
quintet of books about Protestant Sadie and Catholic Kevin, living
in strife-torn Belfast in virtually identical back-to-back terraces but
in religiously segregated streets, came almost a decade after she had
begun writing novels for adults. Through the eyes of children, she
conveys to young readers the bitterness and murderous hatred of the
divided city. But the plots make no concessions to her new audience.

In arguably the best in the series, *Across the Barricades,* the kind
ex-teacher who courageously allows the adolescent couple to meet
is murdered, and the only way they can remain together is to flee
Ulster.

The three high-spirited Belfast girls who open *The File on
Fraulein Berg* in wartime Belfast collude mindlessly with the
prevailing anti-German prejudice, without a moment's thought that
Fraulein Berg might herself be a victim of Nazi ideology. A fast-
paced story, with a particularly hilarious account of an illicit shopping spree in Dublin, ends on a very sober note indeed. Anti-German
feeling is also at the heart of *Snake among the Sunflowers.* No one
better exposes prejudice without falling into the all-too-common trap
of merely expressing it: here is the Scots grandmother in *The Winter
Visitor,* epitomising cast-iron, implacable bigotry when she asks
Nick about his mother's mysterious lodger: "Which foot does he kick
with?"

Lingard is equally realistic about the life chances she allows her
characters. Sadie, though bright, lively, friendly, and of independent
mind and spirit, is no Cinderella. The acme of her career is as a
domestic cleaner, her palace a dilapidated border cottage. Maggie,
the heroine of Lingard's second series, is also working class, but lives
in Glasgow, not troubled Belfast. So when she sets her sights at a
university education, setting up a plumbing business for her father
and uncle, and rehousing her grandmother after a fire *en route,* she
succeeds, despite her parents' total lack of understanding. But she
pays a realistic price for these ambitions: she loses her "prince,"
middle-class James. The first-person narrative used in the *Maggie*
quartet is a good vehicle for the author's humor and also frames two
rich portraits of adult women through the eyes of an adolescent:
James's ever busy, interfering, and painstakingly virtuous mother,
and Maggie's own strong, stubborn granny. The attitudes and
prejudices of each are drawn with a light touch but great sureness.

Another recurring theme is the relative powerlessness of children
in relation to the actions of adults. *Strangers in the House* and *The
Gooseberry* are both about children whose parents remarry despite
their own deepest wishes. Calum is wrenched from the coast to a
cramped Edinburgh tenement and it is only his stepsister's even
greater distress that brings him out of his shell, and "gooseberry"
Ellie is equally uneasy in her stepfather's tiny bungalow. The adults
are caring and try to be understanding but are ultimately motivated
by their own emotional needs rather than those of their children, and
it is to this that the children have finally to adjust. The lively humour,
the realistic school and neighbourhood scenes, the incidental characters all keep the stories moving lightly, intriguingly, and with
seldom a false note.

Also explored is the world of childhood loyalties and friendships.
Time and again, children find that friends of long standing are
moving along a different path. Though a common experience of
childhood, these rifts are painful. For 10-year-old Mungo, escaping
on *The Freedom Machine* from his father's imprisonment, his old
friend Billy's taunts are a huge source of unhappiness that he cannot
even begin to face until he makes a new friend while on the run.
Lingard is simultaneously empathic and wise in her treatment of
childhood betrayals and realignments.

One comes to expect much from this author and while *Rags and
Riches* is disappointingly shallow, another recent book, *The Guilty
Party,* is a tour de force. A 17-year-old Belfast girl campaigns against
the proposed nuclear power plant in the English village in which she
and her mother now live. Here is a rich brew of excitement, perceptively drawn relationships, conflicts of interest, and another vibrant
heroine, fighting a cause of direct relevance to the future of all
Lingard's readers.

—Gillian Klein

LINKLATER, Eric (Robert Russell). British. Born in Dounby, Orkney, 8 March 1899. Educated at Aberdeen Grammar School; studied medicine, then English at the University of Aberdeen, M.A. 1925. Served as a private in the Black Watch, 1917–19; Major in the Royal Engineers, commanding the Royal Engineers Orkney Fortress, 1939–41; member of staff, Directorate of Public Relations, War Office, 1941–45; temporary Lieutenant-Colonel in Korea, 1951: Territorial Decoration. Married Marjorie MacIntyre in 1933; two sons and two daughters. Assistant editor, *Times of India*, Bombay, 1925–27; assistant to the Professor of English Literature, University of Aberdeen, 1927–28; Commonwealth Fellow, Cornell University, Ithaca, New York, and the University of California, Berkeley, 1928–30; full-time writer from 1930. Rector, University of Aberdeen, 1945–48; Deputy Lieutenant of Ross and Cromarty, Scotland, 1968–73. Recipient: Library Association Carnegie Medal, 1945. L.L.D.: University of Aberdeen, 1946. Fellow, Royal Society of Edinburgh, 1971. C.B.E. (Commander, Order of the British Empire), 1954. *Died 7 November 1974.*

PUBLICATIONS FOR CHILDREN

Fiction

The Wind on the Moon, illustrated by Nicolas Bentley. London and New York, Macmillan, 1944.
The Pirates in the Deep Green Sea, illustrated by William Reeves. London and New York, Macmillan, 1949.

Other

Karina with Love, photographs by Karl Werner Gullers. London, Macmillan, 1958.

PUBLICATIONS FOR ADULTS

Novels

White-Maa's Saga. London, Cape, and New York, Peter Smith, 1929.
Poet's Pub. London, Cape, 1929; New York, Cape and Smith, 1930.
Juan in America. London, Cape, and New York, Cape and Smith, 1931.
The Men of Ness: The Saga of Thorlief Coalbiter's Sons. London, Cape, 1932; New York, Farrar and Rinehart, 1933.
Magnus Merriman. London, Cape, and New York, Farrar and Rinehart, 1934.
Ripeness Is All. London, Cape, and New York, Farrar and Rinehart, 1935.
Juan in China. London, Cape, and New York, Farrar and Rinehart, 1937.
The Sailor's Holiday. London, Cape, 1937; New York, Farrar and Rinehart, 1938.
The Impregnable Women. London, Cape, and New York, Farrar and Rinehart, 1938.
Judas. London, Cape, and New York, Farrar and Rinehart, 1939.
Private Angelo. London, Cape, and New York, Macmillan, 1946.
A Spell for Old Bones. London, Cape, 1949; New York, Macmillan, 1950.
Mr. Byculla: A Story. London, Hart Davis, 1950; New York, Harcourt Brace, 1951.
Laxdale Hall. London, Cape, 1951; New York, Harcourt Brace, 1952.
The House of Gair. London, Cape, 1953; New York, Harcourt Brace, 1954.
The Faithful Ally. London, Cape, 1954; as *The Sultan and the Lady*, New York, Harcourt Brace, 1955.
The Dark of Summer. London, Cape, 1956; New York, Harcourt Brace, 1957.
Position at Noon. London, Cape, 1958; as *My Fathers and I*, New York, Harcourt Brace, 1959.
The Merry Muse. London, Cape, 1959; New York, Harcourt Brace, 1960.
Roll of Honour. London, Hart Davis, 1961.
Husband of Delilah. London, Macmillan, 1962; New York, Harcourt Brace, 1963.
A Man over Forty. London, Macmillan, and New York, St. Martin's Press, 1963.
A Terrible Freedom. London, Macmillan, 1966.

Short Stories

The Crusader's Key. London, White Owl Press, and New York, Knopf, 1933.
The Revolution. London, White Owl Press, 1934.
God Likes Them Plain. London, Cape, 1935.
Sealskin Trousers and Other Stories. London, Hart Davis, 1947.
A Sociable Plover and Other Stories and Conceits. London, Hart Davis, 1957.
The Stories of Eric Linklater. London, Macmillan, 1968; New York, Horizon Press, 1969.

Plays

The Devil's in the News (produced in the 1930's). London, Cape, 1934.
The Crisis in Heaven: An Elysian Comedy (produced Edinburgh and London, 1944). London, Macmillan, 1944; New York, Macmillan, 1945.
To Meet the MacGregors (produced Glasgow, 1946?). Included in *Two Comedies*, 1950.
Love in Albania (produced Glasgow, 1948; London, 1949). London, English Theatre Guild, 1950.
Two Comedies: Love in Albania and To Meet the MacGregors. London and New York, Macmillan, 1950.
The Mortimer Touch, adaptation of *The Alchemist* by Ben Jonson (as *The Atom Doctor*, produced Edinburgh, 1950; as *The Mortimer Touch*, produced London, 1952). London, French, 1952.
Breakspear in Gascony. London, Macmillan, and New York, St. Martin's Press, 1958.

Screenplay: *The Man Between*, with Harry Kurnitz, 1953.

Verse

Poobie. Edinburgh, Porpoise Press, 1925.
A Dragon Laughed and Other Poems. London, Cape, 1930.

Other

Ben Jonson and King James: Biography and Portrait. London, Cape, 1931; New York, Cape and Smith, 1932.
Mary, Queen of Scots. London, Davies, and New York, Appleton Century, 1933.
Robert the Bruce. London, Davies, and New York, Appleton Century, 1934.
The Lion and the Unicorn; or, What England Has Meant to Scotland. London, Routledge, 1935.
The Cornerstones: A Conversation in Elysium. London and New York, Macmillan, 1941.

The Defence of Calais. London, His Majesty's Stationery Office, 1941.

The Man on My Back: An Autobiography. London and New York, Macmillan, 1941.

The Northern Garrisons: The Defence of Iceland and the Faroe, Orkney and Shetland Islands. London, His Majesty's Stationery Office, and New York, Garden City Publishing Company, 1941.

The Raft, and Socrates Asks Why: Two Conversations. London, Macmillan, 1942; New York, Macmillan, 1943.

The Highland Division. London, His Majesty's Stationery Office, 1942.

The Great Ship, and Rabelais Replies: Two Conversations. London, Macmillan, 1944; New York, Macmillan, 1945.

The Art of Adventure (essays). London, Macmillan, 1947.

The Campaign in Italy. London, Her Majesty's Stationery Office, 1951.

Our Men in Korea. London, Her Majesty's Stationery Office, 1952.

A Year of Space: A Chapter in Autobiography. London, Macmillan, and New York, Harcourt Brace, 1953.

The Ultimate Viking (essays). London, Macmillan, 1955; New York, Harcourt Brace, 1956.

Edinburgh. London, Newnes, 1960; New York, Macmillan, 1961.

Gullers' Sweden, photographs by Karl Werner Gullers. Stockholm, Almqvist och Wiksell, 1964.

Orkney and Shetland: An Historical, Geographical, Social, and Scenic Survey. London, Hale, 1965.

The Prince in the Heather. London, Hodder and Stoughton, 1965; New York, Harcourt Brace, 1966.

The Conquest of England. London, Hodder and Stoughton, and New York, Doubleday, 1966.

The Survival of Scotland: A Review of Scottish History from Roman Times to the Present Day. London, Heinemann, and New York, Doubleday, 1968.

Scotland. London, Thames and Hudson, and New York, Viking Press, 1968.

The Secret Larder; or, How a Salmon Lives and Why He Dies. London, Macmillan, 1969.

The Royal House of Scotland. London, Macmillan, 1970; as *The Royal House,* New York, Doubleday, 1970.

Fanfare for a Tin Hat: A Third Essay in Autobiography. London, Macmillan, 1970.

The Music of the North. Aberdeen, Haddo House Choral Society, 1970.

The Corpse on Clapham Common: A Tale of Sixty Years Ago. London, Macmillan, 1971.

The Voyage of the "Challenger". London, Murray, and New York, Doubleday, 1972.

The Black Watch: The History of the Royal Highland Regiment, with Andro Linklater. London, Barrie and Jenkins, 1977.

Editor, *The Thistle and the Pen: An Anthology of Modern Scottish Writers.* London, Nelson, 1950.

Editor, *John Moore's England: A Selection from His Writings.* London, Collins, 1970.

*

Critical Study: *Eric Linklater: A Critical Biography* by Michael Parnell, London, Murray, 1985.

*   *   *

Eric Linklater told the story of the genesis of *The Wind on the Moon* in a letter to me which was subsequently included in *Chosen for Children,* the Library Association's book about the Carnegie Medal. Allowing for natural exuberance—he was always rather larger than life—this can be accepted as the true account of one man's approach to writing for children. It cannot be recommended as a method to aspiring writers, but every original creative mind is idiosyncratic.

The Wind on the Moon was an improvisation, born of the necessity to entertain a pair of demanding children. It belongs in fact to that important group of books, those devised for the private entertainment of individual children. Where it differs from *Alice* and *The Wind in the Willows* is that it was the work of a professional novelist, with whom it must be a rule of life that nothing goes to waste. Even as he spun the rich absurdities out of his mind, Linklater must have known that it must eventually become a book. Its extemporary origin is revealed in an episodic structure, but the episodes are linked and related expertly. *The Wind on the Moon* is a comic fantasy which plays with the idea of humans translated into animal form. One of these is the detective who longed to be able to see over walls; out of this urge came, very naturally, an elongation of neck which ended only in his becoming a giraffe. This and other strange happenings are highly diverting. However, the story was devised in wartime, and although it offered plenty of scope for humour the war was no joke and neither was Nazism. Suddenly the light-hearted and frivolous tale turns serious. The children who had frolicked so joyously as kangaroos become involved in a struggle against tyranny. They suffer hardship and extreme danger and their dearest friend dies. The transition from farce to tragedy is abrupt, but Linklater is too accomplished a writer to fail to make it convincing.

Linklater won a Carnegie Medal with *The Wind on the Moon.* The award amused him because he regarded his book as a trifle written for an occasion. The mastery of construction, the vividly realized adventures, the sharp portraiture and effervescent writing made it a book which transcends its origins.

When he returned later to writing for children Linklater's inspiration was lacking. *The Pirates in the Deep Green Sea* had some characteristic touches, particularly in the invention of grotesque characters, and the crazy story was told with a nautical heartiness. But it quite lacked the spontaneity and the underlying passion which made *The Wind on the Moon* outstanding among the children's books of the war years.

—Marcus Crouch

———

LIONNI, Leo (nard). American. Born in Amsterdam, Netherlands, 5 May 1910; emigrated to the United States, 1939; naturalized citizen, 1945. Educated at the University of Zurich, 1928–30; University of Genoa, Ph.D. in economics 1935. Married Nora Maffi in 1931; two sons. Freelance designer, 1930–39; art director, N.W. Ayer and Son Inc., Philadelphia, 1939–47; design director, Olivetti Corporation, New York, 1949–59; art director, *Fortune* magazine, New York, 1949–62; co-editor, *Print,* 1950's; editor, *Panorama,* Milan, 1964–65. Head of the Graphics Design Department, Parsons School of Design, New York, 1952–54. Individual shows: Worcester Museum, Massachusetts, 1958; Philadelphia Art Alliance, 1959; Naviglio, Milan, 1963; Obelisco, Rome, 1964; Galleria dell'Ariete, Milan, 1966; Galleria del Milione, Milan, 1972; Linea 70, Verona, 1973; Il Vicolo, Genoa, 1973; Baukunst Galerie, Cologne, 1974; Klingspor Museum, Offenbach, 1974; Galleria CIAK, Rome, 1975; group shows: Museum of Modern Art, New York, 1954; Bratislava Biennale, 1967; Venice Biennale, 1972. Recipient: National Society of Art Directors award, 1955; Architectural League Gold Medal, 1956; Bratislava Biennale Golden Apple, 1967; Teheran Film Festival award, 1970; Christopher award, 1970; George G. Stone Center for Children's Books award, 1976; American Institute of Graphic

Arts Gold Medal, 1984. Agent: Agenzia Letteraria Internazionale, Corso Matteotti 3, Milan, Italy. Address: Porcignano, 53017 Radda in Chianti, Siena, Italy.

PUBLICATIONS FOR CHILDREN (illustrated by the author)

Fiction

Little Blue and Little Yellow. New York, McDowell Obolensky, 1959; Leicester, Brockhampton Press, 1962.
Inch by Inch. New York, Obolensky, 1960; London, Dobson, 1967.
On My Beach There Are Many Pebbles. New York, Obolensky, 1961; London, Abelard Schuman, 1977.
Swimmy. New York, Pantheon, 1963.
Tico and the Golden Wings. New York, Pantheon, 1964.
Frederick. New York, Pantheon, 1967; London, Abelard Schuman, 1971.
The Alphabet Tree. New York, Pantheon, 1968.
The Biggest House in the World. New York, Pantheon, 1968; London, Andersen Press, 1978.
Alexander and the Wind-Up Mouse. New York, Pantheon, 1969; London, Abelard Schuman, 1971.
Fish Is Fish. New York, Pantheon, 1970; London, Abelard Schuman, 1972.
Theodore and the Talking Mushroom. New York, Pantheon, 1971; London, Abelard Schuman, 1972.
The Greentail Mouse. New York, Pantheon, 1973.
In the Rabbitgarden. New York, Pantheon, 1975; London, Abelard Schuman, 1976.
A Colour of His Own. London, Abelard Schuman, 1975; New York, Pantheon, 1976.
Pezzettino. New York, Pantheon, 1975; London, Andersen Press, 1977.
I Want to Stay Here! I Want to Go There! A Flea Story. New York, Pantheon, 1977; London, Andersen Press, 1978.
Geraldine, The Music Mouse. New York, Pantheon, and London, Andersen Press, 1979.
Let's Make Rabbits: A Fable. New York, Pantheon, and London, Andersen Press, 1982.
Cornelius. New York, Pantheon, and London, Andersen Press, 1983.
Frederick's Fables: A Leo Lionni Treasury. New York, Pantheon, 1985; as *Frederick's Tales*, London, Andersen Press, 1986.
It's Mine! New York, Knopf, and London, Andersen Press, 1986.
Nicolas, Where Have You Been? New York, Knopf, and London, Andersen Press, 1987.
Six Crows. New York, Knopf, 1988; London, Andersen Press, 1989.
Tillie and the Wall. New York, Knopf, 1989.

Other

Who? (wordless). New York, Pantheon, 1983.
What? (wordless). New York, Pantheon, 1983.
Where? (wordless). New York, Pantheon, 1983.
When? (wordless). New York, Pantheon, 1983.
Letters [Numbers, Colors, Words] to Talk About. New York, Pantheon, 4 vols., 1985.

PUBLICATIONS FOR ADULTS

Other

Design for the Printed Page. New York, Fortune Magazine, 1960.

Il Taccuino di Leo Lionni. Milan, Electa, 1972.
La Botanica Parallela. Milan, Adelphi, 1976; translated by Patrick Creagh, as *Parallel Botany*, New York, Knopf, 1977.

*

Illustrator: *Mouse Days Calendar 1981*, 1980; *Mouse Days: A Book of Seasons* by Hannah Solomon, 1981; *Come with Us* by Naomi Lewis, 1982.

Leo Lionni comments:

Making books for children occupies a place of prime importance in my endeavors as an artist exploring the possibilities of self-expression and communication. Here, too, are hiding places for private doubts and fantasies, and for private sensual (aesthetic) pleasures. But everything, content and form, has to be simple, explicit, and logical to the utmost. This is not only an exciting challenge but an extraordinary discipline.

I try, in fact, to reduce complex, so-called adult problems (alienation, search for identity, violence, love) to the most elementary verbal and visual structures in the hope that little by little my fables will stimulate creative interpretation on all age levels, and release questions and meanings that lie hidden in the words and pictures.

* * *

Leo Lionni is primarily an artist. He communicates through shape and colour. Because, one suspects, he does not often find a writer whose vision and message match his own, most of his glowingly colourful picture books have his own texts. Like most of the great picture-book makers—Beatrix Potter, Ardizzone, Sendak—he has made a virtue of this necessity, fashioning a literary style that is precisely matched to his images. There is a rare degree of unity in his books which greatly increases their impact on the reader. His texts are designed to be read aloud; they are accordingly rather longer than many picture-book makers (and publishers) would consider desirable, but the delicate balance between word and picture is carefully maintained. The amount of detail in each picture is calculated to occupy the child's attention just for the time that the adult reader takes to read the text aloud.

Lionni's stories are invariably brief. Each contains a single idea and message. In their conception they owe much to the ancient makers of fables; in execution they have all the artist's idiosyncratic viewpoint. *Frederick*, for example, is the reverse side of the Aesop fable the Ant and the Cricket. In Aesop the ant is brought low because he wasted the summer in idle singing. Lionni's Frederick is a mouse who sits around, observing and thinking while his friends and relations store up a harvest against the coming cold. When they rebuke him he claims that he is working, gathering sunrays and colours and words. Winter comes, and the mice tell tales and eat their stores. When the corn is "only a memory" they turn to Frederick, and he warms them with memories of sunlight, brings back the colours of summer, and comforts them with a poem evoking the moods of the seasons. They may still be hungry, but Frederick has helped them through the lean days.

If this seems a rather cosy picture of the real world, others of Lionni's stories are coloured with a tart wit. In *Theodore and the Talking Mushroom* another mouse fails to placate his friends. When Theodore discovers a mushroom that can talk (but only the single word "Quirp") he interprets this to his companions as "the mouse should be venerated above all other animals." The deception works, but not for long. Theodore loses his crown and his livelihood.

The message is usually more positive than this. *Swimmy* shows that unity can be strength: a school of small fish defeat their big enemy by sailing in convoy. In *Cornelius*, a very funny story about crocodiles, the moral—again one which would be acceptable to

Aesop—is that it is right to experiment and not put up with inborn physical limitations. Cornelius chooses to walk upright while his brothers and sisters are content to crawl. He takes instruction from a monkey and learns to stand on his head and hang from his tail. When he demonstrates these new achievements to the other crocodiles, their reaction is "So what!" As he walks away disappointed, he observes that they are all trying to emulate his skills. "Life on the riverbeach would never be the same again."

The moral in *The Alphabet Tree* may be for adults only, and none the worse for that. The leaves of the alphabet tree have each a letter. Their one enemy is the wind which may blow them away. The word-bug advises them to join together to make words, and with this added strength they resist the wind. The words however are set out haphazard, and this distresses a passing caterpillar. Following his guidance they form themselves into sentences. Finally they join up to say something *really* important: PEACE ON EARTH AND GOODWILL TOWARD ALL MEN. They climb on to the caterpillar's back, and he sets off. But where? "'To the President,' said the caterpillar."

Lionni's control of words is so sure that it may pass unnoticed. Matched with these strong, richly coloured, and always humorous designs, which gain much from their bold cut-paper technique, his stories speak clearly and irresistibly to adult and child alike.

—Marcus Crouch

LIPKIND, William. Also wrote as Will. American. Born in New York City, 17 December 1904. Educated at City College, New York, B.A. 1927; Columbia University Law School, New York, 1928, and Graduate School, 1934–37, Ph.D. in anthropology 1937. Served in England and Germany in the United States Office of War Information, 1944–46. Married Maria Cimino in 1937. Studied Carajá and Javahé Indians in Brazil, 1938–40; Research Associate in Anthropology, Columbia University, 1940–42; Assistant Professor of Anthropology, Ohio State University, Columbus, 1942–44; Adjunct Assistant Professor, New York University, 1948–70. *Died 2 October 1974.*

PUBLICATIONS FOR CHILDREN

Fiction as Will (illustrated by Nicolas Mordvinoff, as Nicolas)

The Two Reds. New York, Harcourt Brace, 1950.
Finders Keepers. New York, Harcourt Brace, 1951; Kingswood, Surrey, World's Work, 1964.
Even Steven. New York, Harcourt Brace, 1952.
The Christmas Bunny. New York, Harcourt Brace, 1953.
Circus Ruckus. New York, Harcourt Brace, 1954.
Chaga. New York, Harcourt Brace, 1955.
Perry the Imp. New York, Harcourt Brace, 1956.
Sleepyhead. New York, Harcourt Brace, 1957.
The Magic Feather Duster. New York, Harcourt Brace, 1958.
Four-Leaf Clover. New York, Harcourt Brace, 1959.
The Little Tiny Rooster. New York, Harcourt Brace, 1960.
Billy the Kid. New York, Harcourt Brace, 1961.
Russet and the Two Reds. New York, Harcourt Brace, 1962.
The Boy and the Forest. New York, Harcourt Brace, 1964.

Fiction as William Lipkind

Boy with a Harpoon, illustrated by Nicolas Mordvinoff. New York,

Harcourt Brace, 1952.
Boy of the Islands, illustrated by Nicolas Mordvinoff. New York, Harcourt Brace, 1954.
Professor Bull's Umbrella, illustrated by Georges Schreiber. New York, Viking Press, 1954.
Nubber Bear, illustrated by Roger Duvoisin. New York, Harcourt Brace, 1966; London, Faber, 1968.

Other

Days to Remember: An Almanac, illustrated by Jerome Snyder. New York, Obolensky, 1961.

PUBLICATIONS FOR ADULTS

Verse

Beginning Charm for the New Year. New York, Weekend Press, 1951.

Other

Winnebago Grammar. New York, Columbia University Press, 1945.

*

Manuscript Collection: Kerlan Collection, University of Minnesota, Minneapolis.

*   *   *

William Lipkind's reputation in children's literature was assured by the publication of *The Two Reds*, a runner-up for the Caldecott Medal in 1951, and *Finders Keepers*, the winner in 1952. The honor gained here by Nicolas Mordvinoff, the illustrator of these books, doubtless has reflected upon Lipkind, Mordvinoff's long-time collaborator. Although Mordvinoff's illustrations in their books overshadowed Lipkind's literary contributions to them, one should not dismiss his effect on their success. There seems little doubt that Lipkind well understood the conventions of writing for young children. One children's author, Robert Burch, has remarked that it was a course on writing for children taught by Lipkind that gave him a healthy respect for children's books.

In general, Lipkind used two kinds of narrative plots in his picture books. One is based on fables and other forms of traditional literature. The other takes a more modern approach. An example of the first kind is *Finders Keepers*. Here two dogs fight over a bone instead of sharing it (a common dilemma in fables). They find, however, that this attitude will end only in the loss of the bone. Hence, they agree not to be selfish (the moral of the tale). *Nubber Bear* also contains some of the major motifs of folk literature, e.g., the small person (bear) disobeying authority and journeying away from home on a quest (for honey) that turns out to be fraught with peril and punishment. This serious story falls below Lipkind's usually satisfactory offering, however, because his experiment in having Nubber speak in couplets dissolves into strained doggerel.

That Lipkind can be both serious and frolicsome is apparent. In *Even Steven* a runt of a horse, Steven, proves his merit by recapturing a herd of stolen horses. Thus, he gets "even" for the slight mistreatments he has suffered because of his size. *The Two Reds* is a madcap adventure, full of slapstick humor (as is *Professor Bull's Umbrella*), in which a red cat, who tried to steal a red-haired boy's fish, and the boy, find (through parallel adventures) that it is better to be friends than enemies.

The strength of Lipkind's writing is implied by these remarks. It lies for one thing in the kind of characters he chooses, the dialogue they speak, and in the understandable manner in which he describes adventure and creates humor. The weakest parts of his books (*Finders Keepers* is a notable exception) are his awkward plots. Too often Lipkind's plots turn and twist with melodramatic, even haphazard, effects, which makes for loose-jointed and irregular structures, hard to follow—and to believe. In *Professor Bull's Umbrella* the professor's lost umbrella blows around, to no determinable effect, then miraculously (and incredibly) lands back in his hand just as it starts to rain.

If Lipkind's stories for young children generally are little more than mediocre, no such negative criticism can justifiably be lodged against his longer works for older children. *Boy of the Islands*, for example, exemplifies Lipkind's ability to depict in an easy and natural yet compelling style a historical adventure in a culture far removed from his reader's experience. Lipkind creates here an entirely convincing, well-formed, honestly motivated story of the difficulties of growing up in a primitive society. *Boy of the Islands* proves the obvious paradox that Lipkind's greatest literary success was with his lesser-selling books.

—Patrick Groff

LIPPINCOTT, Joseph Wharton. American. Born in Philadelphia, Pennsylvania, 28 February 1887. Educated at the Wharton School of Finance, University of Pennsylvania, B.S. in economics 1908. Served in the United States Naval Reserve during World War I. Married 1) Elizabeth Schuyler Mills (died 1943), two sons and one daughter; 2) Virginia Jones Mathieson in 1945. Member of the staff, 1908–15, Vice President, 1915–16, President, 1926–48, and Chairman of the Board, 1948–58, J.B. Lippincott, publishers, Philadelphia. President, Frederick A. Stokes Company, publishers, New York; President, Hibernia Mine Railroad. Director, Free Library of Philadelphia. *Died 22 October 1976.*

PUBLICATIONS FOR CHILDREN

Fiction

Bun, A Wild Rabbit, illustrated by the author. Philadelphia, Penn, 1918; revised edition, Philadelphia, Lippincott, 1953.
Red Ben, The Fox of Oak Ridge, illustrated by the author. Philadelphia, Penn, 1919; London, Harrap, 1938; revised edition, as *Little Red, The Fox*, Philadelphia, Lippincott, 1953.
Gray Squirrel, illustrated by the author. Philadelphia, Penn, 1921; revised edition, Philadelphia, Lippincott, 1954.
Striped Coat, The Skunk, illustrated by the author. Philadelphia, Penn, 1922; revised edition, Philadelphia, Lippincott, 1954.
Persimmon Jim, The Possum, illustrated by the author. Philadelphia, Penn, 1924; revised edition, Philadelphia, Lippincott, 1955.
Long Horn, Leader of the Deer. Philadelphia, Penn, 1928; revised edition, Philadelphia, Lippincott, 1955.
The Wolf King, illustrated by Paul Bransom. Philadelphia, Penn, 1933; London, Harrap, 1934.
The Red Roan Pony, illustrated by Lynn Bogue Hunt. Philadelphia, Penn, 1934; London, Harrap, 1935; revised edition, Philadelphia, Lippincott, 1951.
Chisel-Tooth, The Beaver, illustrated by Roland V. Shutts. Philadelphia, Penn, and London, Harrap, 1936.
Wilderness Champion, illustrated by Paul Bransom. Philadelphia, Lippincott, 1944; London, Hutchinson, 1948.
Black Wings, The Unbeatable Crow, illustrated by Lynn Bogue Hunt. Philadelphia, Lippincott, 1947.
The Wahoo Bobcat, illustrated by Paul Bransom. Philadelphia, Lippincott, 1950.
The Phantom Deer, illustrated by Paul Bransom. Philadelphia, Lippincott, 1954; as *No Name the Deer*, London, Macmillan, 1956.
Old Bill, The Whooping Crane. Philadelphia, Lippincott, 1958.
Coyote, The Wonder Wolf, illustrated by Ed Dodd. Philadelphia, Lippincott, 1964.

Other

Naturecraft Creatures, with G.J. Roberts. Philadelphia, Lippincott, 1933.
Animal Neighbors of the Countryside, illustrated by Lynn Bogue Hunt. Philadelphia, Lippincott, 1938; London, Hutchinson, 1940.

*   *   *

Publisher by vocation and naturalist by avocation, Joseph Wharton Lippincott wrote animal stories that had exciting plots and outdoor settings, used at times by the author as vehicles to plead for conservation of wild land and wildlife. Indeed, most of the creatures in Lippincott's books are wild animals, and the popularity of these books has surely been attributable in part to the sympathetic affection of the writing, an affection that never degenerates into sentimentality, and in part to the accuracy of Lippincott's observations of animal behavior. He writes without anthropomorphism, yet invests his subjects with personality; his characterization of human beings is more variable, being at times effective and at other times rather wooden.

Typical of Lippincott's earlier writing is *Persimmon Jim, The Possum*, in which a wily old possum evades the irate farmers on whose poultry he has preyed; the writing style is simplified and the plot quite patterned. With *The Red Roan Pony* and *Black Wings, The Unbeatable Crow*, he sharpened both style and pace and developed situations and characters that were colorful but realistic. In *Wilderness Champion* and its companion story, *The Wolf King*, he uses a device perennially appealing to readers: the lost pet which becomes feral and which later is tamed again; here the red setter pup, lost and raised by a wolf, remains loyal to the wolf even when he has been happily living with his master. A more unusual story is *The Wahoo Bobcat*, which describes the friendship between a huge bobcat, struggling to survive in a changing environment, the Florida swampland, and a boy of nine who tries to help the animal to escape from hunters. The background is striking, the plea for conservation strong and the plot developed with dramatic flair.

Several of Lippincott's stories have been revised, and a large part of his output remains in print. Although some of his people have an old-fashioned flavor, the animal characters, accurately drawn, have a lasting appeal.

—Zena Sutherland

LIPSYTE, Robert (Michael). American. Born in New York City, 16 January 1938. Educated at Columbia University, New York, 1953–59, B.A. in English 1957, M.S. in journalism 1959. Served in the United States Army, 1961. Married Marjorie L. Rubin; two children. Sports columnist, New York *Times*, 1957–71; columnist,

New York *Post*, 1977; essayist, CBS News, 1982–86; correspondent, NBC News, 1986–88. Since 1989 host, *The Eleventh Hour*, television program, New York. Recipient: Child Study Committee award, 1968. Agent: Theron Raines, Raines and Raines, 71 Park Avenue, New York, New York 10016. Address: c/o Harper and Row, 10 East 53rd Street, New York, New York 10022, U.S.A.

PUBLICATIONS FOR CHILDREN

Fiction

The Contender. New York, Harper, 1967; London, Pan, 1969.
One Fat Summer. New York, Harper, 1977.
Summer Rules. New York, Harper, 1981.
The Summerboy. New York, Harper, 1982.
Jock and Jill. New York, Harper, 1982.

Other

Assignment: Sports. New York, Harper, 1970.
Free to Be Muhammad Ali. New York, Harper, 1978.

PUBLICATIONS FOR ADULTS

Novels

Something Going, with Steve Cady. New York, Dutton, 1973.
Liberty Two. New York, Simon and Schuster, 1974.

Plays

Screenplays: *That's the Way of the World* (*Shining Star*), 1975; *The Act*, 1982.

Other

Nigger, with Dick Gregory. New York, Dutton, 1964; London, Allen and Unwin, 1965.
The Masculine Mystique. New York, New American Library, 1966.
Sportsworld: An American Dreamland. Chicago, Quadrangle, 1975.

*   *   *

"To everything there is a season and a time for every purpose under heaven." Summer is *the* season for Robert Lipsyte's fictional alter ego, Bobby Marks, whose adolescent misadventures dominate three of the author's breezily funny novels for children set in the New York Catskill Mountains area—*One Fat Summer, Summer Rules,* and *The Summerboy.* Through the course of these first-person narratives, Bobby changes and grows—from a spoiled 200 pound 14-year-old whom kids call The Crisco Kid "because he's fat in the can" through a summer as a 16-year-old camp counselor and would-be lover. Finally, in *The Summerboy*, Bobby shows his true character; he sacrifices his cherished summer job folding laundry to help his fellow employees get even with an unscrupulous and womanizing boss.

One of the ways that Lipsyte overcame his own early teen fat summers of overeating and overreading was to dive into sports with a passion; his high school years were saturated with swimming, softball, track, and judo. When he graduated college, he welded his compulsive interest in sports with his love for writing and became a sports journalist. He has utilized his journalistic skills to write two very successful non-fiction sports books for children and young

teens: *Free to Be Muhammad Ali*, a biography of the famous boxer, and *Assignment: Sports*, a collection of colorfully written feature articles on athletes and sports.

Lipsyte's most recent novel for young readers, *Jock and Jill*, also deals with sports. The story contains implausible plot twists and turns, but Lipsyte's hero—a suburban high school star pitcher named Jack Ryder—and Jillian, the unpredictably likeable and stubborn girl whose camera he smashes into while chasing a foul pop-up, are so believably portrayed that they convince the more skeptical readers to take the plot plunges they do. Jillian involves Jack the Jock in a scheme to help poor and hungry New York City kids, and soon the Mayor and a Puerto Rican street gang get pulled into the story, Jack's reputation is threatened, and his baseball career is put in jeopardy. Though Jack falls down, he doesn't break his crown, but Jill definitely comes tumbling after.

Probably Lipsyte's best and most read novel still is his first published story, *The Contender*. It is about a young Harlem high school dropout named Alfred Brooks who fights against the pull of drugs and gangs, against his guilt of abandoning his best friend caught by police in a robbery of the store where Alfred works, and against the pervasive despair he feels as a prisoner in a place with no future. One day he wanders into Donatelli's gym (modeled on the boxing club that boxing manager Cus·D'Amato ran for many years in New York) and accepts the challenge that Donatelli throws at him: "Everyone wants to be a champion. That's not enough. You have to start by wanting to be a contender…It's the climbing that makes the man. Getting to the top is an extra reward." These words guide and strengthen Alfred in his darkest moments. He stands his ground not only against seasoned boxers but against heavy peer pressure to help rob the small grocery store where he works. And when Alfred faces the truth about himself that he is a good boxer but not a champion, he displays the grit of a contender: he stays three rounds in the ring with a champion fighter and wins Donatelli's respect. He also gains a new-found self-respect.

Lipsyte wrote *The Contender* in 1967, the same year that saw the publication of S.E. Hinton's groundbreaking realistic young adult novel *The Outsiders* and a year before the publishing of Paul Zindel's trendsetting novel for teenagers *The Pigman*. *The Contender* too is a trailblazer because it transformed the junior sports novel from an action-packed, inspirational story of sports heroics into a realistic, coming of age story with sports serving as a metaphor for the real action in the novel: coping with life. Although today Lipsyte's first novel seems too dependent on plot coincidences and too filled with stereotyped secondary characters, *The Contender* has set the stage for more sophisticated sports metaphor novels to be published for teenagers. Highly praised and widely read novels such as Bruce Brooks's *The Moves Make the Man* and Robert Lehrman's *Juggling* owe a great deal to Lipsyte's 1967 novel.

Alfred Brooks doesn't succeed at boxing, he succeeds with his life because he has learned to contend with courage and confidence. And Bobby Marks (alias Robert Lipsyte) has followed in his footsteps.

—Jack Forman

———

LITTLE, (Flora) Jean. Canadian. Born in Tainan, Formosa, now Taiwan, 2 January 1932. Educated at schools in Guelph, Ontario; Victoria College, University of Toronto, B.A. in English 1955; Institute of Special Education, Salt Lake City. Visiting Instructor, Florida State University, Tallahassee; specialist teacher, Beechwood School for Crippled Children, Guelph. Recipient: Canadian Children's Book award, 1961; Vicky Metcalf award, 1974; Canada Council prize, 1978; Children's Literature prize (West Germany),

1981; Canadian Library Association Book of the Year award, 1985; Ruth Schwartz award, 1985. Address: 198 Glasgow Street North, Guelph, Ontario, Canada.

PUBLICATIONS FOR CHILDREN

Fiction

Mine for Keeps, illustrated by Lewis Parker. Boston, Little Brown, 1962; London, Dent, 1964.
Home from Far, illustrated by Jerry Lazare. Boston, Little Brown, 1965.
Spring Begins in March, illustrated by Lewis Parker. Boston, Little Brown, 1966.
Take Wing, illustrated by Jerry Lazare. Boston, Little Brown, 1968.
One to Grow On, illustrated by Jerry Lazare. Boston, Little Brown, 1969.
Look Through My Window, illustrated by Joan Sandin. New York, Harper, 1970.
Kate. New York, Harper, 1971.
From Anna, illustrated by Joan Sandin. New York, Harper, 1972.
Stand in the Wind, illustrated by Emily McCully. New York, Harper, 1975.
Listen for the Singing. New York, Dutton, 1977.
Mama's Going to Buy You a Mockingbird. Markham, Ontario, Penguin, 1984; New York, Viking Kestrel, 1985.
Lost and Found, illustrated by Leoung O'Young. Markham, Ontario, Penguin, and New York, Viking Kestrel, 1985.
Different Dragons, illustrated by Laura Fernandez. Markham, Ontario, Penguin, and New York and London, Viking Kestrel, 1986.

Verse

It's a Wonderful World. Privately printed, 1947.
When the Pie Was Opened. Boston, Little Brown, 1968.
Hey World, Here I Am!, illustrated by Barbara Di Lella. Toronto, Kids Can Press, 1986; New York, Harper, 1989.

Other

Little by Little: A Writer's Education. Markham, Ontario, Viking, 1987.

*

Manuscript Collection: Kerlan Collection, University of Minnesota, Minneapolis.

*   *   *

Jean Little's novels use motifs which also frequent adult Canadian literature (e.g. the immigrant experience), but she focuses these through children's experiences. For instance, she writes of the difficulty of a child's finding his own place in a family, a school, or country; she shows that intolerance is rooted in fear which activates both the victim and the victimizer; and she demonstrates that when people enlarge their window on the world, they can liberate both their own and others' inner humanity. Blind herself since birth, Little writes about "sight" in its fullest sense: insight. Philosophically, her books are infused with a Christian humanism, but they are neither didactic nor sectarian. She excels in her ability to develop complexity in characters, to depict the nuances in both hostile and loving relationships, and to keep plot subordinate to character while yet maintaining an interesting storyline. Her award-winning books, widely translated, draw additional power from their successful jux-taposing of the worlds of the children and the adult.

Her first book, *Mine for Keeps*, depicts every child's fear of new situations. The child, a cerebral palsy victim, indeed suffers from the cruelty of children in a new school, but she is more victimized by her own fear of inadequacy. Only when she escapes from the prison of self-pity does she begin to develop the insight necessary for good peer relationships. In this book Little goes beyond the mere handicap to explore the universalities that it imposes: feelings of self-pity, loneliness, inadequacy, and jealousy.

Home from Far presents a family who adopts two children shortly after losing a child. The book, revealing the resentments and split loyalties felt by both the natural and the foster children, demonstrates a child's terror of rejection, the necessity of discipline, and the healing power of parental love. *Spring Begins in March*, one of the several novels set in the imaginary town of Riverside, Ontario, gives us new perspectives on two families presented earlier. The book focuses on a child whose disenchantment at school and at home is intensified when a cranky grandmother comes to live with them, pushing her out of her room. Meg, the child, eventually adapts, gaining compassion and better self-discipline. *Take Wing* uses the story of a family's difficulty in accepting a son's mental retardation to illustrate the dangers of overprotecting children. Again, children's fear of peer ridicule is depicted in conjunction with the gradual revelation of some causes of the hostility.

One to Grow On tells the story of a 12-year-old girl in a large family in "Riverside." Feeling lonely, unimportant, and unloved, she irritates her family by telling lies to get attention. After being victimized by another liar, the heroine's new perspectives enable her to grow beyond pettiness. *Look Through My Window* tells of yet another WASP Riverside family, a relaxed one with one happy child. This child is introduced to an introspective, angry Jewish girl from a tense and intellectual family. Juxtaposing the two lifestyles and personality types, Little shows how learning to look through another's window helps dispel prejudice and personal animosities. *Kate*, its sequel, explores the roles of religious and cultural heritage in one's psychological make-up. A story with many resonances, it recreates the loneliness of those who live in private internal places and shows that taking risks to expand can bring both happiness and disaster. The book's conclusion shows that while growth and change may occasion loss in friendships, there is always the consolation of the memory of a shared past. *Hey World, Here I Am!*, written 15 years later, is a book comprised of poetry and prose sketches by "Kate"; in the Preface, Little explains how a fictional character can take hold of an author's imagination and write through the author.

Stand in the Wind depicts the complicated relationships of various children within two families, one a busting Canadian family with normal squabbling siblings and the other a rather anxious American family in which each parent openly favors one child. The vividly characterized children come to terms with each other when they are left alone for a week in a northern cottage. *From Anna*, one of Little's most successful books, is the story of a German family who flees Nazi Germany to settle in Toronto. The visually handicapped heroine, Anna, is a slight misfit in a lively, fractious family. Cruelly teased by her talented, arrogant older brother, she nevertheless grows out of a withdrawn unhappiness into insight; in the sequel, *Listen for the Singing*, her older brother becomes kinder to her, making it possible for her to respond to his misery after he is blinded in an accident. *Mama's Going to Buy You a Mockingbird* shows how the illness and death of a much-adored father in a closely knit family causes the adolescent male protagonist to withdraw and strike out in anger; through interaction with another child who has experienced a different kind of loss—abandonment by a mother—he begins to heal. Little's subsequent books, *Lost and Found* and *Different Dragons*, are written for a younger audience. Both stories feature pets and show a child overcoming personal limitations through interaction with a dog.

In her award-winning and highly acclaimed fictionalized autobiography *Little by Little: A Writer's Education* Little depicts the stages of her own social, psychological, intellectual, and artistic development. This book is an extraordinary achievement. It is lively to read because of an anecdotal structure build on memorable events, but its artistic merits derive from the author's subtle handling of point of view and tone: its speaking voice benefits from the grown artist's insight into and acceptance of an actual child's full range of real feelings, including those which our culture conditions children to repress: anger, envy, jealousy, pride, fear. The dramatization of the child's behaviour, often far from model, combined with the skillful presentation of the understandable feelings that produced that behaviour, produces a highly humorous and moving book with a depth that makes it equally enjoyable for children and adults.

One important component in the success of Little's books is their psychological realism. She often depicts those times when an ordinary child feels temporarily isolated and frightened in a threatening world. The movement of her books is such that the child's window on humanity is enlarged, and with broader perspectives, the child always achieves greater self-knowledge and inner happiness.

—Mary Rubio

———

LIVELY, Penelope (Margaret, née Low). British. Born in Cairo, Egypt, 17 March 1933; came to England, 1945. Educated at a boarding school in Sussex, 1945–51; St. Anne's College, Oxford, B.A. (honours) in modern history 1956. Married Jack Lively in 1957; one daughter and one son. Has been presenter for BBC Radio program on children's literature; regular reviewer for newspapers and magazines in England. Fellow, Royal Society of Literature, 1985. Recipient: Library Association Carnegie Medal, 1974; Whitbread award, 1976; Southern Arts Association prize, for adult fiction, 1979; Arts Council National Book award, for adult fiction, 1980; Booker prize, for adult fiction, 1987. Agent: Murray Pollinger, 4 Garrick Street, London WC2E 9BH. Address: Duck End, Great Rollright, Chipping Norton, Oxfordshire OX7 5SB, England.

PUBLICATIONS FOR CHILDREN

Fiction

Astercote, illustrated by Antony Maitland.   London, Heinemann, 1970; New York, Dutton, 1971.
The Whispering Knights, illustrated by Gareth Floyd.   London, Heinemann, 1971; New York, Dutton, 1976.
The Wild Hunt of Hagworthy, illustrated by Juliet Mozley.   London, Heinemann, 1971; as *The Wild Hunt of the Ghost Hounds*, New York, Dutton, 1972.
The Driftway.   London, Heinemann, 1972; New York, Dutton, 1973.
The Ghost of Thomas Kempe, illustrated by Antony Maitland.   London, Heinemann, and New York, Dutton, 1973.
The House in Norham Gardens.   London, Heinemann, and New York, Dutton, 1974.
Going Back.   London, Heinemann, and New York, Dutton, 1975.
Boy Without a Name, illustrated by Ann Dalton.   London, Heinemann, and Berkeley, California, Parnassus Press, 1975.
A Stitch in Time.   London, Heinemann, and New York, Dutton, 1976.
The Stained Glass Window, illustrated by Michael Pollard.   London, Abelard Schuman, 1976.

Fanny's Sister, illustrated by John Lawrence.   London, Heinemann, 1976; New York, Dutton, 1980.
The Voyage of QV66, illustrated by Harold Jones.   London, Heinemann, 1978; New York, Dutton, 1979.
Fanny and the Monsters, illustrated by John Lawrence.   London, Heinemann, 1979.
Fanny and the Battle of Potter's Piece, illustrated by John Lawrence.   London, Heinemann, 1980.
The Revenge of Samuel Stokes.   London, Heinemann, and New York, Dutton, 1981.
Uninvited Ghosts and Other Stories, illustrated by John Lawrence.   London, Heinemann, 1984; New York, Dutton, 1985.
Dragon Trouble, illustrated by Valerie Littlewood.   London, Heinemann, 1984.
Debbie and the Little Devil, illustrated by Toni Goffe.   London, Heinemann, 1987.
A House Inside Out, illustrated by David Parkins.   London, Deutsch, 1987; New York, Dutton, 1988.

Play

Television Play: *Time Out of Mind*, 1976.

Other

The Presence of the Past: An Introduction to Landscape History.   London, Collins, 1976.

PUBLICATIONS FOR ADULTS

Novels

The Road to Lichfield.   London, Heinemann, 1977.
Treasures of Time.   London, Heinemann, and New York, Doubleday, 1979.
Judgement Day.   London, Heinemann, 1980; New York, Doubleday, 1981.
Next to Nature, Art.   London, Heinemann, 1982.
Perfect Happiness.   London, Heinemann, 1983; New York, Dial Press, 1984.
According to Mark.   London, Heinemann, 1984; New York, Beaufort, 1985.
Moon Tiger.   London, Deutsch, 1987; New York, Grove Press, 1988.
Passing On.   London, Deutsch, 1989.

Short Stories

Nothing Missing But the Samovar and Other Stories.   London, Heinemann, 1978.
Corruption and Other Stories.   London, Heinemann, 1984.
Pack of Cards: Stories 1978–86.   London, Heinemann, 1986; New York, Grove Press, 1989.

Plays

Television Plays: *Boy Dominic* series (3 episodes), 1974.

*

Penelope Lively comments:
    Most of my books for children reflect, in one way or another, my own interest in the workings of memory—whether personal or collective. They all seem to come out differently—memory fantastical, memory experimental, memory pastoral or historical or

comical—but somehow, so far, the theme has persisted. My only excursion into non-fiction has been a respectful tribute to the history of the English landscape which I have found such a powerful inspiration.

*   *   *

Penelope Lively's first novel was published in 1970. She rapidly established herself as one of the most interesting and rewarding of contemporary novelists for children. The books are very different, to such an extent indeed that children (who notoriously enjoy the "mixture as before") may be disappointed when they try one after enjoying another. To an adult one of the great pleasures of her work is her ability to create entirely fresh and individual books which are yet variations on the theme "we are what we have been." Lively's concern is with identity through historical continuity. She is particularly interested in place, in the English landscape (from which she was separated during her most formative years as a child in Egypt) and in houses: "A house is a preservative," she has written, "a record of the lives it has sheltered." Her recent *A House Inside Out* reminds children that houses shelter other creatures as well as the human families that live in them.

The first book, *Astercote*, reflected an obsession the writer had at the time with deserted medieval villages. Lively was rightly criticized for her failure to create living characters and convincing dialogue but the story was intriguing—and exciting. *The Whispering Knights* and *The Wild Hunt of Hagworthy* explore two recurrent themes in English folklore. *The Driftway* is probably her least successful novel as far as child readers are concerned, but there is a great deal in it to absorb anyone interested in Lively's view of life. In *The Driftway* she "wanted to use landscape as a channel for historical memory." She wrote about "a road, a perfectly ordinary road, the B4525 from Banbury to Northampton, but a road that is very ancient and seemed to lend itself perfectly to a double symbolism." This sounds a little pretentious and it should be made clear at once that Lively is never pretentious. She is not trying to convey to children an appreciation of their own past and throwing in a story to make the message more palatable. The stories are seamless garments. As one critic has put it: "The concern isn't added to the story; rather the story is written out of it....There are real children, changing in relation to their experiences. The novels are dense with life, with flux and growth."

The stories are good ones. Most accessible of all is the Carnegie Medal-winner *The Ghost of Thomas Kempe*. Lively says that in this book she was indulging a taste for ghosts. "It is a light-hearted affair on the whole, but concerned with the serious matter of a child's awaking to the concept of memory." In fact, the serious matter is absorbed wholly in the comedy. It was the first book in which the writer seemed completely relaxed and in charge of her material. A lot of the fun derives from unlikely conjunctions; the ghost of a Jacobean sorcerer loose in a world of cake mixes, phone boxes, and biros.

Clever and delightful as it is, *Thomas Kempe* is a minor book compared with its successor *The House in Norham Gardens*. This is primarily the story of a quiet winter in the life of Clare Mayfield, aged 14, who lives with her great-aunts in a house in North Oxford with relics of the past. They acquire a couple of tenants: Maureen, who works for an estate agent, and John, an anthropology student from Uganda. Clare and her friend, Liz, eat baked beans and do their Latin homework together; she goes to London with John for the day; a Norfolk cousin stays the night. She has a bit part in the school *Macbeth*, and, finally, she has a bicycle accident and breaks her arm. These are the small outward events—but in Clare's mind other things are going on. This is a book about time and continuity and the relationship between the things we possess and the people we are.

Clare's great-grandfather was an anthropologist. In the attic in the house in Norham Gardens she finds one of the tamburans or ceremonial shields which he brought back from New Guinea in 1905. She becomes obsessed by this shield and the tribe it belonged to, who had no word for love in their language, no knowledge of their past, whose dead stayed with them as spirits, represented by the shields. Clare dreams about these people and feels she must return the shield. But when she does, in the hospital sleep after her accident, she knows it is too late for them. New Guinea is transformed before her eyes: the thatched huts become concrete bungalows; it is "time for Music Roundup" on the transistor radio and too late for tamburans. Clare gives the shield to the Pitt Rivers Museum. The winter is over and she chooses for her aunt's birthday not something from the antique shop (though the woman assures her "It's fashionable having old things") but a copper beech which will flourish for two hundred years. It is time to look forward.

Everything in this subtle, rich, compelling story is part of the pattern but there is nothing forced about the pattern; it seems entirely natural. Clare (a thinking, listening girl) and her aunts (early graduates, still interested in Africa and art though not in gutters or new pence) are entirely convincing—people one is glad to get to know. Lively has certainly written more exciting books, but it is a considerable achievement to write so honestly about the long Sunday afternoons, the creeping clocks, the boredom of being 14, without ever being boring. Her relaxed, flexible style copes equally well with visits to the butcher and the brisk, useless doctor and with "the shadows of another world and another time."

Going Back is another considerable achievement. Again it is centred on a house, this time Medleycott, a house in Somerset, built at the turn of the century, with rose garden and tennis lawn, goldfish pond, stables, and kitchen gardens. There is a great deal of circumstantial detail: splendid descriptions of the natural world ("clenched by frost" or "filmy with mist, the trees waist deep in it floating") and the convincing wartime background of land-girls and spam fritters, ration books, conscientious objectors, Spitfires and Hurricanes in playground games, and the knitting of balaclava helmets. But the war is incidental. It creates the situation and reinforces the alienation between Jane and Edward and their insensitive blustering father, who ultimately sends Edward away to school and precipitates the climax of the story. The suffering is real enough to make the reader weep.

The story is for the most part quiet and slow, but not easy to read. Lively makes few concessions to a young reader. Her style is often elliptical and the vocabulary difficult (she prefers "benign and munificent" to "kind and generous"). There is no clear time scale. "In the head all springs are one spring," and characters come into focus only at particular moments, and sometimes not at all. But the tension of the narrative is beautifully sustained and it is never dull. We care passionately about what happens to Jane and Edward, especially Edward. Less is expected of Jane, the narrator, as she is a girl; the class and sexist attitudes of the time are clear and painful. We are never sure that what we remember is what actually happened, as Lively says, but no one reading *Going Back* could forget it.

Again in *A Stitch in Time*, which won the Whitbread award, a house is at the centre; a rented house in Lyme Regis. "Places," she writes, are "like clocks—full of all the time there's ever been in them, and all the people, and all the things that have happened, like the ammonites in the stones." The ammonite reference is not a casual one, because the place this time is Lyme Regis and fossils are, of course, part of the story.

Maria Foster, only child of quiet boring parents, is not, like Jane Austen's young people, "wild to see Lyme." In fact, she is decidedly lukewarm about their holiday destination. Indeed, in spite of an agreeable habit of talking to inanimate objects and hearing their replies, Maria is rather a lukewarm dull girl. The book is a little lukewarm and dull itself. It lacks the richness of *The House in*

Norham Gardens, the flow of *Going Back*, and the atmosphere of both of them. Children will, however, find it a much easier and more straightforward book. There is much to enjoy; the pleasure in knowing names (quercus ilex, grass vetchling, gryphaea), the contrasting families on either side of the holiday fence, the descriptions of days which might have been entirely different ones, and the reminder of days long past when a girl called Harriet had reluctantly stiched a sampler, with a swing which still creaks in the garden where there is no swing, and a dog which still barks in a house where there are no dogs.

Animals come into their own in Lively's most important children's book of more recent years, *The Voyage of QV66*, an original exploration of a time after the Second Flood when Man has been wiped off the face of the earth and evolution, in some sense, has to start all over again. The immediate concern is with Stanley, the monkey in the crew of QV66, journeying to London in a search for identity. This is a book which can be enjoyed at many different levels. In spite of the assertion in a 1982 *Guardian* feature that, with her success as a novelist for adults, Lively said farewell to children's books, there has been a steady stream of children's books published in the 1980's, as well as the slightly earlier Fanny stories in Heinemann's Long Ago Children series, brought together under the title *Fanny and the Monsters* to give a satisfying picture of life in one particular Victorian family with a strong girl character. There has also been *The Revenge of Samuel Stokes*, which begins splendidly: "You may well ask how a smell of roast venison could come out of Mrs. Thornton's washing machine...." The idea behind the book—of the physical impact of the past on a contemporary housing estate—is a good one; but one has to admit, for all one's continued admiration for Lively's wit and ingenuity, that she is not quite enough at home with the denizens of Charstock Estate to make the fantasy as convincing as its most comparable predecessor, the ever-popular *Ghost of Thomas Kempe*.

—Ann Thwaite

LIVINGSTON, Myra Cohn. American. Born in Omaha, Nebraska, 17 August 1926. Educated at Sarah Lawrence College, Bronxville, New York, 1945–48, B.A. 1948. Married Richard R. Livingston in 1952; two sons and one daughter. Professional French horn player, 1940–48 (studied music with Darius Milhaud, 1944); assistant editor, *Campus* magazine, Los Angeles, 1948–50; worked in public relations for movie and musical personalities, 1949–52; instructor in creative writing for children, Dallas Public Library, 1959–64; instructor, Los Angeles County Museum of Art, 1966–67, Beverly Hills Public Library, 1966–74, and University of California Elementary School, Los Angeles, 1972; instructor, 1966–71, and poet-in-residence, 1966–84, Beverly Hills Unified School District. Since 1972 Senior Extension Instructor, University of California, Los Angeles. Has lectured on poetry and conducted writing workshops throughout the United States since 1959. Member of the Editorial Board, *New Advocate*, Needham Heights, Massachusetts. Recipient: National Council of Teachers of English award, for verse, 1980; National Jewish Book award, 1986. Agent: McIntosh and Otis, 310 Madison Avenue, New York, New York 10017. Address: 9308 Readcrest Drive, Beverly Hills, California 90210, U.S.A.

PUBLICATIONS FOR CHILDREN

Fiction

I'm Hiding, illustrated by Erik Blegvad. New York, Harcourt

Brace, 1961.
See What I Found, illustrated by Erik Blegvad. New York, Harcourt Brace, 1962.
I Talk to Elephants!, photographs by Isabel Gordon. New York, Harcourt Brace, 1962.
I'm Not Me, illustrated by Erik Blegvad. New York, Harcourt Brace, 1963.
Happy Birthday, illustrated by Erik Blegvad. New York, Harcourt Brace, 1964.
I'm Waiting, illustrated by Erik Blegvad. New York, Harcourt Brace, 1966.
Come Away, illustrated by Irene Haas. New York, Atheneum, 1974.

Verse

Whispers and Other Poems, illustrated by Jacqueline Chwast. New York, Harcourt Brace, 1958.
Wide Awake and Other Poems, illustrated by Jacqueline Chwast. New York, Harcourt Brace, 1959.
The Moon and a Star and Other Poems, illustrated by Judith Shahn. New York, Harcourt Brace, 1965.
Old Mrs. Twindlytart and Other Rhymes, illustrated by Enrico Arno. New York, Harcourt Brace, 1967.
A Crazy Flight and Other Poems, illustrated by James Spanfeller. New York, Harcourt Brace, 1969.
The Malibu and Other Poems, illustrated by James Spanfeller. New York, Atheneum, 1974.
The Way Things Are and Other Poems, illustrated by Jenni Oliver. New York, Atheneum, 1974.
4-Way Stop and Other Poems, illustrated by James Spanfeller. New York, Atheneum, 1976.
A Lollygag of Limericks, illustrated by Joseph Low. New York, Atheneum, 1978.
O Sliver of Liver, Together with Other Triolets, Cinquains, Haiku, Verses, and a Dash of Poems, illustrated by Iris Van Rynbach. New York, Atheneum, 1979.
No Way of Knowing: Dallas Poems. New York, Atheneum, 1980.
A Circle of Seasons, illustrated by Leonard Everett Fisher. New York, Holiday House, 1982.
Sky Songs, illustrated by Leonard Everett Fisher. New York, Holiday House, 1984.
A Song I Sang to You, illustrated by Margot Tomes. New York, Harcourt Brace, 1984.
Monkey Puzzle and Other Poems, illustrated by Antonio Frasconi. New York, Atheneum, 1984.
Celebrations, illustrated by Leonard Everett Fisher. New York, Holiday House, 1985.
Worlds I Know and Other Poems, illustrated by Tim Arnold. New York, Atheneum, 1985.
Sea Songs, illustrated by Leonard Everett Fisher. New York, Holiday House, 1986.
Earth Songs, illustrated by Leonard Everett Fisher. New York, Holiday House, 1986.
Higgledy-Piggledy, illustrated by Peter Sis. New York, Macmillan, 1986.
Space Songs, illustrated by Leonard Everett Fisher. New York, Holiday House, 1988.
There Was a Place and Other Poems. New York, McElderry, 1988.
Up in the Air, illustrated by Leonard Everett Fisher. New York, Holiday House, 1989.

Other

Editor, *A Tune Beyond Us: A Collection of Poetry*, illustrated by James Spanfeller. New York, Harcourt Brace, 1968.
Editor, *Speak Roughly to Your Little Boy: A Collection of Parodies*

and Burlesques, illustrated by Joseph Low.   New York, Harcourt
   Brace, 1971.
Editor, *Listen, Children, Listen: An Anthology of Poems for the Very
   Young*, illustrated by Trina Schart Hyman.   New York, Harcourt
   Brace, 1972.
Editor, *What a Wonderful Bird the Frog Are: An Assortment of
   Humorous Poetry and Verse*.   New York, Harcourt Brace, 1973.
Editor, *Poems of Lewis Carroll*.   New York, Crowell, 1973.
Editor, *One Little Room, An Everywhere: Poems of Love*, illustrated
   by Antonio Frasconi.   New York, Atheneum, 1975.
Editor, *O Frabjous Day: Poetry for Holidays and Special Occasions*.
   New York, Atheneum, 1977.
Editor, *Callooh! Callay! Holiday Poems for Young Readers*, il-
   lustrated by Janet Stevens.   New York, Atheneum, 1978.
Editor, *Poems of Christmas*.   New York, Atheneum, 1980.
Editor, *Why Am I Grown So Cold? Poems of the Unknowable*.   New
   York, Atheneum, 1982.
Editor, *How Pleasant to Know Mr. Lear! Edward Lear's Selected
   Works*.   New York, Holiday House, 1982.
Editor, *Christmas Poems*, illustrated by Trina Schart Hyman.   New
   York, Holiday House, 1984.
Editor, *Easter Poems*, illustrated by John Wallner.   New York,
   Holiday House, 1985.
Editor, *A Learical Lexicon: A Magnificent Feast of Boshblobberbosh
   and Fun from the Works of Edward Lear*, illustrated by Joseph
   Low.   New York, Atheneum, 1985.
Editor, *Thanksgiving Poems*, illustrated by Stephen Gammell.
   New York, Holiday House, 1985.
Editor, *Poems for Jewish Holidays*, illustrated by Lloyd Bloom.
   New York, Holiday House, 1986.
Editor, *Valentine Poems*, illustrated by Patience Brewster.   New
   York, Holiday House, 1987.
Editor, *Cat Poems*, illustrated by Trina Schart Hyman.   New York,
   Holiday House, 1987; Oxford, Oxford University Press, 1989.
Editor, *New Year's Poems*, illustrated by Margot Tomes.   New York,
   Holiday House, 1987.
Editor, *I Like You, If You Like Me: Poems of Friendship*.   New York,
   McElderry, 1987.
Editor, with Norma Farber, *These Small Stones*.   New York, Harper,
   1987.
Editor, *Poems for Mothers*, illustrated by Deborah Kogan Ray.
   New York, Holiday House, 1988.
Editor, *Poems for Fathers*, illustrated by Robert Casilla.   New York,
   Holiday House, 1989.
Editor, *Dilly Dilly Piccalilli: Poems for the Very Young*, illustrated
   by Eileen Christelow.   New York, McElderry, 1989.

PUBLICATIONS FOR ADULTS

Other

*When You Are Alone/It Keeps You Capone: An Approach to Creative
   Writing with Children*.   New York, Atheneum, 1973.
A Tribute to Lloyd Alexander.   Philadelphia, Drexel Institute, 1976.
The Child as Poet: Myth or Reality?   Boston, Horn Book, 1984.

Editor, with Zena Sutherland, *The Scott Foresman Anthology of
   Children's Literature*.   Chicago, Scott Foresman, 1984.

*

Myra Cohn Livingston comments:
   A deep respect for the emotions, sensitivities, and thoughts of
young people as they differ from those of adults has always been of
importance to me. *Whispers and Other Poems*, written when I was
a college freshman, is a reflection of my own childhood, and

although my recent poetry encompasses a more contemporary view
of childhood, I feel I have never departed from the child I was; the
child I know best. I am not consciously aware of writing *for* children:
my poetry seems to be born of the genre of childhood. The thousands
of young people with whom I share poetry and to whom I teach
something of the writing of it reinforce, for me, the feeling that the
early years encompass a freshness and wonder that must be nurtured,
a curiosity and celebration of the simple things which each
succeeding generation discovers anew. As an anthologist I am
conscious of choosing those poems which speak to the young in a
diction and emotional climate to which they can relate—something
of the universal experience from poets of all ages and countries which
may serve as an insight toward the individual growth and
humanization of the reader.

*   *   *

   In the tradition of Robert Louis Stevenson, Myra Cohn Livingston
fills her poetry for children with the elements of a child's own world
and experience: babbling brooks, starry skies, elephants, crocodiles,
kangaroos, balloons, whispering, jumping, pretending, discovering,
growing up, feathers and acorns and rubber bands and daisies, fathers
and beaches and math class, bedtime and bubblegum are the subjects
of her earlier work; working mothers, stepmothers, death, and
divorce are (most unlike Stevenson) the more somber elements of
her later poems. How our children's lives and concerns have changed
since the 1950's!
   Like Stevenson, Livingston transforms the everyday into the
poetic through a skillful use of metre, rhyme, and imagery.
Onomatopoeia and alliteration may add to the poetic effect:

   Whispers
      tickle through your ear
      telling things you like to hear.

   Whispers
      are as soft as skin
      letting little words curl in.

   Whispers
      come so they can blow
      secrets others never know.

Some of her poetry is concrete verse:

   Cold that day
      we started down
         tobogganing
            the snowy ground
               held our breath
                  around a tree
                     and Shirley Ann
                        squeezed tight to me;
                     Laura yelled,
                  as we flew past
               one crazy kid,
                  his skis half-smashed,
   and Margie steered
      around a sled
         until
            until
               I felt my head
                  go spinning round
                  in sprays of snow

Livingston's recent collaboration with painter Leonard Everett

Fisher has resulted in songs to the earth, sea, and sky that are particularly compelling, as complex, imagistic free verse joins dramatic double-page spread paintings. On a deep blue page of moon, sea spray, and boulders, *Sea Songs* begins:

> Crashing on dark shores, drowning, pounding
> breaker swallows breaker. Tide follows
> tide. Lost in her midnight witchery
> moon watches, cresting tall waves, pushing
> through mist and blackness the cold waters.

> > Moon, you have worked long.
> > Now rest…

While Livingston's earlier verse is perhaps most effective when read aloud to small groups of young children (or, better, read by parent to child), her later poetry will stimulate the imaginations of older children.

Livingston has been an intelligent and discriminating anthologist of poetry for children as well. She has collected poems for very young children by such poets as A. A. Milne, Theodore Roèthke, and Christina Rossetti (*Listen, Children, Listen*); humorous verse by W. S. Gilbert, Edward Lear, Ogden Nash, Phyllis McGinley, Robert Frost, even Ezra Pound (*What a Wonderful Bird the Frog Are*); love poems by William Butler Yeats, E. E. Cummings, Emily Dickinson, and others (*One Little Room, An Everywhere*) and poems of friendship (*I Like You, If You Like Me*); Christmas poems, Thanksgiving poems, and poems for other holidays and special occasions. She is an admirer of the work of Lewis Carroll and Edward Lear, and has also edited collections of their work (*Poems of Lewis Carroll* and *How Pleasant to Know Mr. Lear!*).

—Marcia G. Fuchs

LOBEL, Anita (née Kempler). American. Born in Krakow, Poland, 3 June 1934; emigrated to the United States, 1952; became citizen, 1956. Educated at schools in Stockholm and New York City; Pratt Institute, Brooklyn, New York, B.F.A. 1955; Brooklyn Museum Art School. Married Arnold Lobel, *q.v.*, in 1955 (died 1987); one daughter and one son. Textile designer and freelance illustrator. Recipient: Boston *Globe-Horn Book* award, for illustration, 1982, 1984. Lives in Brooklyn. Address: c/o Greenwillow Books, 105 Madison Avenue, New York, New York 10016, U.S.A.

PUBLICATIONS FOR CHILDREN (illustrated by the author)

Fiction

Sven's Bridge. New York, Harper, 1965.
The Troll Music. New York, Harper, 1966.
Potatoes, Potatoes. New York, Harper, 1967; Kingswood, Surrey, World's Work, 1969.
The Seamstress of Salzburg. New York, Harper, 1970.
Under a Mushroom. New York, Harper, 1970; Kingswood, Surrey, World's Work, 1972.
A Birthday for the Princess. New York, Harper, 1973; Kingswood, Surrey, World's Work, 1975.

Other (folktales)

King Rooster, Queen Hen. New York, Greenwillow, 1975; Kingswood, Surrey, World's Work, 1977.
The Pancake. New York, Greenwillow, 1978; Kingswood, Surrey,

World's Work, 1979.
The Straw Maid. New York, Greenwillow, and London, MacRae, 1983.

*

Illustrator: *Cock-a-Doodle Doo! Cock-a-Doodle Dandy!* by Paul Kapp, 1966; *Puppy Summer* by Meindert De Jong, 1966; *The Wishing Penny and Other Stories*, 1967; *Indian Summer* by F.N. Monjo, 1968; *The Little Wooden Farmer* by Alice Dalgliesh, 1968; *The Wisest Man in the World*, 1968, and *How the Tsar Drinks Tea*, 1971, both by Benjamin Elkin; *Someone Small* by Barbara Borack, 1969; *The Uproar*, 1970, and *Little John*, 1972, both by Doris Orgel; *Three Rolls and One Doughnut* edited by Mirra Ginsburg, 1970; *Soldier, Soldier, Won't You Marry Me?* edited by John Langstaff, 1972; *One for the Price of Two* by Cynthia Jameson, 1972; *Clever Kate* by Elizabeth Shub, 1973; *Christmas Crafts* by Carolyn Meyer, 1974; *Peter Penny's Dance* by Janet Quin-Harkin, 1976; *How the Rooster Saved the Day*, 1977, *A Treeful of Pigs*, 1979, *On Market Street*, 1980, and *The Rose in My Garden*, 1984, all by Arnold Lobel; *Fanny's Sister* by Penelope Lively, 1980; *Singing Bee!*, 1982, as *Sing a Song of Sixpence!*, 1983, edited by Jane Hart; *The Night Before Christmas* by Clement C. Moore, 1984; *A New Coat for Anna* by Harriet Ziefert, 1986; *Once: A Lullaby* by B.P. Nichol, 1986.

Anita Lobel comments:
Writing and illustrating books for children is a form of drama for me. I approach the construction of a picture book as if it were a theatre piece to be performed, assigning dialogue, dressing the characters, and putting them into an appropriate setting. Some books take the form of zany farces (*King Rooster, Queen Hen*, and *The Pancake*) Others, like *Peter Penny's Dance*, are a bit like *Around the World in Eighty Days*, a sort of movie or musical. *The Seamstress of Salzburg* and *A Birthday for the Princess* are more like operettas. *On Market Street* was constructed like a series of solos in a ballet, held together by a prologue and epilogue, with an implied divertimento for a score.

*   *   *

Humor pervades much of Anita Lobel's work from her earliest picture book for children, *Sven's Bridge*, to *The Pancake*, a retelling of the Danish folktale in an easy-to-read form. In *Sven's Bridge*, for instance, humor is embodied in the foolish character of the king who first orders that Sven's bridge be destroyed when his ship cannot pass through and then rebuilt when his carriage falls into the river. In *Under a Mushroom* it is not so much the actions of a character but the nature of the minor characters themselves—the Glump, the Schnooze, the Gizzygonk, and Dizzydonk along with the group of Gleeps and other characters—which make the reader laugh, and in *The Seamstress of Salzburg* more minor characters—the Queen and the fine ladies of the court—are humorous in their wishes to outdo one another in fine apparel and in their unskilled attempts to sew dresses for the coming marriage of the prince and the seamstress. In all of these works, as well as in *King Rooster, Queen Hen*, another retelling of a Danish folktale, and *The Pancake*, Lobel accentuates her humorous characters and situations through her illustrations of the Gleeps' pointed heads and noses, the pinned together gowns of the ladies, and the dumbfounded expression on each animal's face as the pancake evades every attempt, but the last, to eat it.

Several of Lobel's works concern more serious issues. *Potatoes, Potatoes* focuses on the brutal nature of war and its contradictory glamor as well as on the major roles of a mother. The mother character of *Potatoes, Potatoes*, for example, not only serves to protect her sons from joining in the fighting for a number of years but also functions as a peacemaker when she reminds them, and the opposing armies they lead, of their former lives of contentment. A

Birthday for the Princess contains a similar depth. In this work the king and queen learn that material goods and strict instruction are not the best means by which to raise a child. Their daughter yearns for love and attention, but when her parents continually fail to show their affection and concern, she runs away with a young organ-grinder and his monkey to a land where they love one another and are happy together. Her parents never regain the princess that they have so foolishly lost.

Whatever their particular tone might be, all of Lobel's books are characterized by their settings of long ago and their happy endings. *The Troll Music*, for instance, is set in a time of traveling musicians and a mischievous fun-loving troll. Its story ends happily with the musicians placating the troll family with a cake and gifts, the troll removing his spell over the instruments, and the musicians playing more beautifully than ever. *The Seamstress of Salzburg* illustrates the same two qualities. Set in a past of royalty, promenades, and transportation by horseback, this tale recalls the traditional form of the folktale especially in its happy ending. Not only does the seamstress marry her prince, but the ladies of the court gain the pride that comes from sewing their own gowns.

With her predominant tone of humor, occasional serious themes, settings from the past, and endings which leave the reader satisfied, Lobel ably illustrates the meaning of a statement she made to *Publishers Weekly* in 1971: "It's nice to tell a tale that is pleasant for a child to read, be diverting and at the same time have some kind of substance to it." Her books are clearly informed by the pleasant, substantial spirit of which she speaks.

—Jacqueline L. Gmuca

———

LOBEL, Arnold (Stark). American. Born in Los Angeles, California, 22 May 1933. Educated at schools in Schenectady, New York; Pratt Institute, Brooklyn, New York, B.F.A. 1955. Married Anita Kempler (i.e., Anita Lobel, *q.v.*) in 1955; one daughter and one son. Worked in advertising, 1955–58. Recipient: Christopher award, 1972, 1977; George G. Stone Center for Children's Books award, 1978; American Library Association Caldecott Medal, 1981; University of South Mississippi award, 1985; Society of Children's Book Writers Golden Kite award, for illustration, 1988. *Died 4 December 1987.*

PUBLICATIONS FOR CHILDREN (illustrated by the author)

Fiction

A Zoo for Mister Muster. New York, Harper, 1962.
A Holiday for Mister Muster. New York, Harper, 1963.
Prince Bertram the Bad. New York, Harper, 1963; Kingswood, Surrey, World's Work, 1970.
Giant John. New York, Harper, 1964; Kingswood, Surrey, World's Work, 1965.
Lucille. New York, Harper, and Kingswood, Surrey, World's Work, 1964.
The Bears of the Air. New York, Harper, 1965; Kingswood, Surrey, World's Work, 1966.
The Great Blueness and Other Predicaments. New York, Harper, 1968; Kingswood, Surrey, World's Work, 1970.
Small Pig. New York, Harper, 1969; Kingswood, Surrey, World's Work, 1970.
Frog and Toad Are Friends. New York, Harper, 1970; Kingswood, Surrey, World's Work, 1971.
Mouse Tales. New York, Harper, 1972; Kingswood, Surrey, World's Work, 1973.
Frog and Toad Together. New York, Harper, 1972; Kingswood, Surrey, World's Work, 1973.
Owl at Home. New York, Harper, 1975; Kingswood, Surrey, World's Work, 1976.
Frog and Toad All Year. New York, Harper, 1976; Kingswood, Surrey, World's Work, 1977.
How the Rooster Saved the Day, illustrated by Anita Lobel. New York, Greenwillow, and London, Hamish Hamilton, 1977.
Mouse Soup. New York, Harper, 1977; Kingswood, Surrey, World's Work, 1978.
Grasshopper on the Road. New York, Harper, 1978; Kingswood, Surrey, World's Work, 1979.
A Treeful of Pigs, illustrated by Anita Lobel. New York, Greenwillow, 1979; London, MacRae, 1980.
Days with Frog and Toad. New York, Harper, 1979; Kingswood, Surrey, World's Work, 1980.
Frog and Toad Tales (collection). Kingswood, Surrey, World's Work, 1981.
Uncle Elephant. New York, Harper, 1981; Kingswood, Surrey, World's Work, 1982.
Ming Lo Moves the Mountain. New York, Greenwillow, and London, MacRae, 1982.

Verse

Martha, The Movie Mouse. New York, Harper, 1966; Kingswood, Surrey, World's Work, 1967.
The Ice-Cream Cone Coot and Other Rare Birds. New York, Parents' Magazine Press, 1971.
On the Day Peter Stuyvesant Sailed into Town. New York, Harper, 1971.
The Man Who Took the Indoors Out. New York, Harper, 1974; Kingswood, Surrey, World's Work, 1976.
The Book of Pigericks: Pig Limericks. New York, Harper, 1983; London, Cape, 1984.
The Rose in My Garden, illustrated by Anita Lobel. New York, Greenwillow, and London, MacRae, 1984.
Whiskers and Rhymes. New York, Greenwillow, 1985; London, MacRae, 1986.
The Turnaround Wind. New York, Harper, 1988.

Other

Fables. New York, Harper, and London, Cape, 1980.
On Market Street (alphabet book), illustrated by Anita Lobel. New York, Greenwillow, and London, Benn, 1981.
Frog and Toad Coloring Book. New York, Harper, 1981.
The Frog and Toad Pop-Up Book. New York, Harper, and London, Heinemann, 1986.

Editor, *Gregory Griggs and Other Nursery Rhyme People.* New York, Greenwillow, and London, Hamish Hamilton, 1978.

*

Manuscript Collection: Kerlan Collection, University of Minnesota, Minneapolis.

Illustrator: *Bibletime, Hebrew Dictionary, Holiday Dictionary*, all by Sol Scharfstein, 1958; *Red Tag Comes Back* by Fred Phleger, 1961; *Something Old, Something New* by Susan Oneacre Rhinehart, 1961; *Little Runner of the Longhouse* by Betty Baker, 1962; *Terry and the Caterpillars*, 1962, *Greg's Microscope*, 1963, *Let's Get Turtles*, 1965, and *Benny's Animals*, 1966, all by Millicent E. Selsam; *Let's Be Indians*, 1962, *Let's Be Early Settlers with Daniel Boone*, 1967, and *Dinosaur Time*, 1974, all by Peggy Parish; *The Secret Three*, 1963, and *Ants Are Fun*, 1968, both by Mildred Myrick; *The Quarreling Book*, 1963, and *Someday*, 1965, both by Charlotte Zolotow; *Red Fox and His Canoe*, 1964, *Oscar Otter*, 1966, *The Strange Disappearance of Arthur Cluck*, 1967, and *Sam the Minuteman*, 1969, all by Nathaniel Benchley; *Miss Suzy*, 1964, *Miss Suzy's Easter Surprise*, 1972, *Miss Suzy's Christmas*, 1973, and *Miss Suzy's Birthday*, 1974, all by Miriam Young; *Dudley Pippin* by Phil Ressner, 1965; *The Witch on the Corner* by Felice Holman, 1966; *The Magic Spectacles*, 1966, and *Junk Day on Juniper Street*, 1969, both by Lilian Moore; *The Star Thief* by Andrea Di Noto, 1967; *The Four Little Children Who Went round the World*, 1968, and *The New Vestments*, 1970, both by Edward Lear; *The Microscope* by Maxine Kumin, 1968; *The Comic Adventures of Old Mother Hubbard* by Sarah Catherine Martin, 1968; *The Terrible Tiger*, 1969, *Circus*, 1974, *Nightmares*, 1976, *The Mean Old Mean Hyena*, 1978, *The Headless Horseman Rides Tonight*, 1980, and *Tyrannosaurus Was a Beast*, 1988, all by Jack Prelutsky, and *The Random House Book of Poetry for Children* edited by Prelutsky, 1983; *I'll Fix Anthony* by Judith Viorst, 1969; *Tot Botot and His Little Flute* by Laura E. Cathon, 1970; *Hansel and Gretel* by the Grimm Brothers, 1971; *The Master of Miracle* by Sulamith Ish-Kishor, 1971; *Hildilid's Night* by Cheli Ryan, 1971; *Seahorse* by Robert A. Morris, 1972; *Good Ethan* by Paula Fox, 1973; *The Clay Pot Boy* by Cynthia Jameson, 1973; *As I Was Crossing Boston Common* by Norma Farber, 1975; *As Right as Right Can Be* by Anne K. Rose, 1976; *Merry, Merry Fibruary* by Doris Orgel, 1977; *Tales* [*More Tales*] *of Oliver Pig* by Jean Van Leeuwen, 2 vols., 1979–81; *The Tale of Meshka the Kvetch* by Carol Chapman, 1980; *A Three Hat Day* by Laura Geringer, 1985; *The Random House Book of Mother Goose*, 1986, as *Arnold Lobel's Book of Mother Goose*, 1987; *Bear All Year* [*Gets Dressed, Goes Shopping*], 3 vols., 1986, *Bear's Busy Morning*, 1986, and *Where's the Guinea Pig?* [*Turtle? Dog?, Cat?*], 4 vols., 1987, all by Harriet Ziefert; *The Devil and Mother Crump* by Valerie Scho Carey, 1987.

*   *   *

As a creator of picture books, Arnold Lobel's achievement has been enormous. Beginning in 1961 with his illustrations to Fred Phleger's *Red Tag Comes Back* and in 1962 with *A Zoo for Mister Muster*, the first work Lobel both wrote and illustrated, his 27-year career was launched. During that time Lobel was continually recognized for the quality of both his texts and illustrations. A number of his works have been included among the *New York Times* Best Illustrated Books and the Children's Book Showcase, while several have received the Christopher award and been named Caldecott Honor Books. In 1973 *Frog and Toad Together* was recognized with a Newbery Honor designation, and *Fables* was awarded the Caldecott Medal in 1981.

Undoubtedly Lobel's list of awards owes much to his memorable characters. Frog and Toad, Small Pig and Owl are readily identified with by both children and adults. Indeed, who can not see themselves in Owl, frightened of the mysterious bumps under his covers or in Toad, waiting every day for letters that never come until Frog, understanding his need, writes him a note? Clearly Lobel's characters live in the reader's memories well after the stories are told and the books put away for the next day or the next child. In Lobel's words, finely drawn characters "have a life outside of that book, so that when the child gets back to the book, he refreshes his memory, he reunites himself with it. But when he closes the book, they're still there. Those are the characters that live."

Not only are Lobel's characters memorable, but his works contain two other timeless qualities which have traditionally defined classic works of children's literature: humor and truth.

The first of these qualities takes many forms. There is the simple warmth that pervades the Christmas celebration of the two friends in *Frog and Toad All Year*; the humorous reaction to Ming Lo and his wife as they try to move their mountain and then believe that they have done so, in the literary folktale of *Ming Lo Moves the Mountain*; the absurdist nature of common objects like milk bottles and door keys as they assume the shape of birds in *The Ice-Cream Cone Coot and Other Rare Birds*; and the satirical points made in *Grasshopper on the Road* when the grasshopper meets the obsessive house- and world-cleaning fly and the three butterflies devoted to routine. Such diversity and depth of Lobel's humor underscore the importance of this quality in his work.

Universal truths abound as well. The farmer's wife in *Small Pig* discovers that she must respect, not deny, the living space of others— in this case, the favorite mudhole of Small Pig. And in *Fables*, a mouse finds out that continued perservance will end in attaining what was sought. But perhaps the greatest truth of Lobel's stories is the meaning of friendship. That theme resounds again and again in works such as *A Zoo for Mister Muster*, with its story of the animals' affection for the man who visits them each day and *On Market Street* where a boy journeys to the various vendors and buys "presents for a friend"—his beloved white cat.

Such truths emerge, Lobel told the audience during the 1983 Everychild conference, from his inner being. He found out early in his career that anticipating what children will want to read is not the answer. He needed to write, instead, "out of the middle of myself, to work out of the sadness and, of course, the joy." Sadness exists in Lobel's work as it does in *Uncle Elephant* when the main character suffers the loss of his father and mother who are missing at sea. But laughter and happiness ultimately prevail in the character of Uncle Elephant who cares for and amuses his nephew until the parents are found.

Through his work of more than a quarter of a century, Lobel explored the many dimensions of the picture book. He illustrated the words of others, complementing and interpreting, without overshadowing, their texts. As a writer, he created narrative and nonsense poetry, limericks, and nursery rhymes; wove literary folktales and fables; and formed animal fantasies, using and extending the conventions of the controlled vocabulary, easy-to-read genre.

In this diversity and through his memorable characters, humor, and truths, one final quality emerges: Lobel's ability to merge such timeless elements. Through both his stories and illustrations, Lobel created truly unified picture books for children.

—Jacqueline L. Gmuca

LOCKE, Elsie (Violet, née Farrelly). New Zealander. Born in Hamilton, 17 August 1912. Educated at Waiuku school, 1917-29; Auckland University, B.A. 1933. Married John Gibson Locke in 1941; two sons and two daughters. Secretary, Woman Today Society, and member of the editorial committee, *Woman Today* magazine, Wellington, 1937–39. Member of the National Committee, New Zealand Campaign for Nuclear Disarmament, 1956–65. Recipient: Katherine Mansfield award (*Landfall* magazine), for essay, 1958. D.D.L.: University of Canterbury, Christchurch, 1987. Address: 392 Oxford Terrace, Christchurch 1, New Zealand.

Publications for Children

Fiction

The Runaway Settlers, illustrated by Antony Maitland. Auckland, Blackwood and Janet Paul, and London, Cape, 1965; New York,

Dutton, 1966.

The End of the Harbour, illustrated by Katrina Mataira. Auckland, Blackwood and Janet Paul, and London, Cape, 1968.

Moko's Hideout, illustrated by Elisabeth Plumridge and Beatrice Foster-Barham. Christchurch, Whitcoulls, 1976.

The Boy with the Snowgrass Hair, with Ken Dawson, illustrated by Jean Oates. Christchurch, Whitcoulls, 1976.

Explorer Zach, illustrated by David Waddington. Christchurch, Pumpkin Press, 1978.

Journey under Warning. Auckland, Oxford University Press, 1983.

A Canoe in the Mist, illustrated by John Shelley. London, Cape 1984.

Other

A Land Without a Master. Wellington, Department of Education, 1962.

Viet-nam. Wellington, Department of Education, 1963.

Six Colonies in One Country, illustrated by Stephen Furlonger. Wellington, Department of Education, 1964.

Provincial Jigsaw Puzzle, illustrated by Stephen Furlonger. Wellington, Department of Education, 1965.

The Long Uphill Climb: New Zealand 1876–1891, illustrated by David A. Cowe. Wellington, Department of Education, 1966.

High Ground for a New Nation, illustrated by David A. Cowe. Wellington, Department of Education, 1967.

The Hopeful Peace and the Hopeful War, illustrated by David A. Cowe. Wellington, Department of Education, 1968.

Growing Points and Prickles: Life in New Zealand 1920–1960, illustrated by Cath Brown and R.E. Brockie. Christchurch, Whitcombe and Tombs, 1971.

It's the Same Old Earth, illustrated by Victor Ambrus. Wellington, Department of Education, 1973.

Maori King and British Queen (textbook), illustrated by Murray Grimsdale. Amersham, Buckinghamshire, Hulton, 1974.

Look under the Leaves (ecology), edited by David Young and David Ault, illustrated by David Waddington. Christchurch, Pumpkin Press, 1975.

Snow to Low Levels: Interaction in a Disaster. Christchurch, Whitcoulls, 1976.

Crayfishermen and the Sea: Interaction of Man and Environment. Christchurch, Whitcoulls, 1976.

A Land Without Taxes: New Zealand from 1800 to 1840. Wellington, Department of Education, 1979; revised edition, as *The Kauri and the Willow: How We Lived and Grew from 1801–1942*, Wellington, Government Printer, 1984.

Two Peoples, One Land: A History of Aotearoa/New Zealand, illustrated by Elisabeth Plumridge. Wellington, Government Printer, 1988.

PUBLICATIONS FOR ADULTS

Verse

The Time of the Child: A Sequence of Poems. Privately printed, 1954.

Other

The Shepherd and the Scullery-Maid. Christchurch, New Zealand Communist Party, 1950.

The Human Conveyor Belt. Christchurch, Caxton Press, 1968.

The Roots of the Clover: The Story of the Collett Sisters and Their Families. Privately printed, 1971.

Discovering the Morrisons (and the Smiths and the Wallaces): A Pioneer Family History. Privately printed, 1976.

The Gaoler (on Henry Monson). Palmerston North, Dunmore Press, 1978.

Student at the Gates (memoir). Christchurch, Whitcoulls, 1981.

Editor, *Gordon Watson, New Zealander–1912–1945: His Life and Writings*. Auckland, New Zealand Communist Party, 1949.

*

Manuscript Collections: Alexander Turnbull Library, Wellington; Canterbury Public Library, Christchurch.

Elsie Locke comments:

Although as a child I walked to school with serial stories writing themselves in my head, I did not settle down to being a writer until my own children were growing into their teens. By that time I was thoroughly hooked on children's books, and my own ideas were budding, and still keep budding from year to year. To me, writing a story for children is a way of sharing. Naturally I share those themes that stir my interest, imagination, sympathy, sense of fun, delight, and concern. History, nature, and peace get into my books because I am keen about these matters. My grandparents and great-grandparents were pioneers in the early days of New Zealand. Around the family fireside I listened to many adventurous tales and I think today's children might like to do the same. Whether my readers live in New Zealand and enjoy the familiar settings, or somewhere else and find the settings exotic, I am giving them a small piece of a big world whose glory is the great variety of places and peoples and languages and customs—not to mention all the other living things, the sky and land and the sea. My best-known work is *The Runaway Settlers*.

*   *   *

Elsie Locke imbues her children's historical novels with sincerity and fairness resulting from thorough research and from having learnt the Maori language in order to reflect more accurately the Maori viewpoint.

In her first novel, *The Runaway Settlers*, based on a real family, her characters in their struggle to survive make some mutually respectful and helpful contact with the Maori people. But her achievement here is in breathing life into a most remarkable pioneer woman and six lively children. In 1859, Mary Small escapes with her children from the drunken brutality of her husband, changes their name to Phipps, and finally reaches Lyttelton from Sydney. A series of incidents brings them to Governor's Bay where in time they establish themselves through hard work and determination. Yet how they sing! One son nearly perishes on the goldfields. Another contributes to the climax of the story when he goes with his mother on her amazing trek across the Southern Alps, driving 34 head of cattle for sale near Hokitika.

In the novels that follow Locke turns her attention to Maori-European relationships in friendship and war. The David-Jonathan friendship between David and Honatana is a binding symbol of hope through *The End of the Harbour*, set in the Waiuku district of 1860. Complex events, including broken promises by inefficient officials, drag settlers and Maoris into the troubles of the wars. The pity of it is that Potatau teaches "Let there be no evil between Maori and Pakeha." Yet greed and treachery add to the troubles. Land rights, today a prime political matter, and the difficulties of establishing justice and peace become central concerns.

A dispute over land rights also leads to the unfortunate Wairau Affray of 1843, subject of *Journey under Warning*. When Wakefield's Company, having bought land cheaply in Nelson, sends surveyors to the Wairau Plain, the Maoris gather their Te Rauparaha to protect the land that is still rightfully theirs. Although events are seen through the eyes of Gibby Banks, aged 15, who has to develop considerable skills and courage to survive the bloodshed, the character to make the strongest impression is Will Morrison, a Scot under Company orders, who experiences the crisis of the conflict. The passions, prejudices, and different points of view, including revenge, held by each group, are presented with sympathy, but the detailed complexity requires advanced readership.

A natural disaster, the eruption of Mount Tarawera in 1866, provides the crisis for *A Canoe in the Mist*. This highly dramatic novel clearly describes the settlement of Te Wairoa, the customs and dances of the Maori people, the beauty of the famous Pink and White Terraces, and the approaching doom, compelling the reader to believe in the waka wairua, the ghost canoe which predicts disaster. The central characters are two girls aged 11. Mattie is English, thus allowing an enlarged dimension of the world. The mixture of historical and fictional characters includes the girls' parents, uncouth tourists, the landlord Joe McRae, the schoolteacher, and Tuhoto the tohunga. They show varying degrees of courage and aroha through the long terror. Strong criticism is made by various characters of desecrating tourists and untrustworthy greedy pakehas. Perhaps the most telling moment of bi-cultural insensitivity comes when Tuhoto dies in a pakeha sanitorium after surviving four days of being buried under volcanic mud. "Pakeha ignorance had broken the tapu and killed him." In such ways in her novels, Locke has made an accumulation of statements about our needs in this country for greater understanding between races.

As well, her deeply-felt concern about environmental issues informs her shorter pieces, such as *It's the Same Old Earth* and *Look under the Leaves*, important poems and articles about ecology. Her short stories in *Moko's Hideout*, in a regrettably dismal production, are about an ugly-duckling-like paua finding his own beauty, a New Zealand gecko which is a unique baby-producing gecko, the godwits which migrate to Siberia, and two keas, "entertainers, thieves, and vandals," and birds of beauty. *Explorer Zach* is a longer short story with period details of the 1920's. Though Zach at eight is not always fully credible, his travels through the countryside with his dog Bruce are zestfully described.

Lastly, *The Boy with the Snowgrass Hair* is an episodic account of exploration in six parts linked by an interlude for planning the next trip. Tom, aged 14, recounts his adventures in mountains and river valleys with varying interesting companions. Inexperienced Lou, aged 14, is small in stature but grows in spirit. Above all, the reader is made aware of the power and beauty of this New Zealand mountain country.

—Diane Hebley

LOFTING, Hugh (John). American. Born in Maidenhead, Berkshire, 14 January 1886; emigrated to the United States, 1912; naturalized citizen. Educated at Mount St. Mary's College, Chesterfield, Derbyshire; Massachusetts Institute of Technology, Cambridge, 1904–05; London Polytechnic, 1906–07. Served in the Irish Guards in Flanders, 1916–17. Married 1) Flora W. Small in 1912 (died 1927), one son and one daughter; 2) Katherine Harrower-Peters in 1928 (died 1928); 3) Josephine Fricker in 1935, one son. Prospector and surveyor in Canada, 1908–09; civil engineer, Lagos Railway, West Africa, 1910–11, and United Railways, Havana, Cuba, 1912; worked for British Ministry of Information, New York, 1915. Recipient: American Library Association Newbery Medal, 1923. *Died 27 September 1947.*

PUBLICATIONS FOR CHILDREN (illustrated by the author)

Fiction

The Story of Dr. Dolittle, Being the History of His Peculiar Life and Astonishing Adventures in Foreign Parts. New York, Stokes, 1920; as *Doctor Dolittle*, London, Cape, 1922.
The Voyages of Dr. Dolittle. New York, Stokes, 1922; London, Cape, 1923.
Dr. Dolittle's Post Office. New York, Stokes, 1923; London, Cape, 1924.
The Story of Mrs. Tubbs. New York, Stokes, 1923; London, Cape, 1924.
Dr. Dolittle's Circus. New York, Stokes, 1924; London, Cape, 1925.
Dr. Dolittle's Zoo. New York, Stokes, 1925; London, Cape, 1926.
Dr. Dolittle's Caravan. New York, Stokes, 1926; London, Cape, 1927.
Dr. Dolittle's Garden. New York, Stokes, 1927; London, Cape, 1928.
Dr. Dolittle in the Moon. New York, Stokes, 1928; London, Cape, 1929.
Noisy Nora. New York, Stokes, and London, Cape, 1929.
The Twilight of Magic, illustrated by Lois Lenski. New York, Stokes, 1930; London, Cape, 1931.
Gub Gub's Book: An Encyclopedia of Food. New York, Stokes, and London, Cape, 1932.
Dr. Dolittle's Return. New York, Stokes, and London, Cape, 1933.
Tommy, Tilly and Mrs. Tubbs. New York, Stokes, 1936; London, Cape, 1937.
Dr. Dolittle and the Secret Lake. Philadelphia, Lippincott, 1948; London, Cape, 1949.
Dr. Dolittle and the Green Canary. Philadelphia, Lippincott, 1950; London, Cape, 1951.
Dr. Dolittle's Puddleby Adventures. Philadelphia, Lippincott, 1952; London, Cape, 1953.

Verse

Porridge Poetry: Cooked, Ornamented, and Served by Hugh Lofting. New York, Stokes, 1924; London, Cape, 1925.

Other

Dr. Dolittle's Birthday Book. New York, Stokes, 1935.

PUBLICATIONS FOR ADULTS

Verse

Victory for the Slain. London, Cape, 1942.

*

Critical Study: *Hugh Lofting* by Edward Blishen, in *Three Bodley Head Monographs*, London, Bodley Head, 1968.

*   *   *

The stubby, square-nosed Dr. Dolittle, animal doctor extraordinary from Puddleby-on-the-Marsh, is one of the most popular and enduring of children's heroes. The man who invented him, Hugh Lofting, imagined a figure whose innocence and common sense anchored the most fantastic of adventures firmly within the limits of credibility. For it is the essentially pedestrian nature of the Doctor's style—from his unperturbed expression to his plain language and practical solutions—that makes the whole lunatic world he inhabits possible.

Lofting was a young soldier serving in Flanders during World War I—and much concerned about the terrible conditions and fate of the Army horses—when he conceived of Dr. Dolittle, a doctor turned animal vet who, because he learns the languages of his patients, is able to enter worlds and adventures inconceivable to others.

Neither the fantasy nor the subject were wholly alien to Lofting's character. As a child he had kept a miniature zoo and wildlife museum in his mother's linen cupboard and had enjoyed making up stories for his brothers and sisters. After an education in a Jesuit school, Lofting worked for a time as an architect, then became a civil engineer and visited Canada, Africa, and the West Indies. These facts are important. Both the nature of his work and the places he saw provided him with a rich fund of material and settings for the Doctor's voyages—he had a keen eye for detail and an obvious love of travel.

The first Dr. Dolittle stories, written from the trenches in letters home, were intended to make his two small children laugh. Dr. Dolittle was at first a comic character, a man who got into muddles. Even his appearance, as illustrations in the margins of the letters showed, was a little ludicrous; a portly, ungainly man, wearing clothes that could have been smart and yet were somehow too big and quite inappropriate. It was only in later books, perhaps as Lofting himself became older and more disillusioned by the war, that the Doctor changes. His lightheartedness gives way to seriousness, and the compassionate side to his nature is constantly emphasised in accounts of his hatred of all aggression and bullying, his growing disapproval of hunting, ill-run zoos, and pet shops.

In the first of what were to be 12 separate books on the doctor's adventures, *The Story of Dr. Dolittle*, Dr. John Dolittle is simply an ordinary doctor, with human patients. The trouble is that he keeps so many animals as pets, appearing to prefer their company, that one by one his patients, irritated and alarmed by the other occupants of his house, forsake him. Even his sister Sarah, anxious about the dwindling income, leaves.

Finally his only remaining patient is Matthew Mugg, the Cat's-Meat-Man, who suggests that the doctor should start earning his living instead as an animal doctor. Polynesia, the doctor's wise and somewhat dictatorial parrot, offers to teach him the language of the animals, starting with the ABC of birds. Before long, Puddleby-on-the-Marsh is transformed by the presence of short-sighted cart horses in spectacles. Dr. Dolittle's success is assured. Because he can actually communicate with the animals, they can tell him what is wrong with them, rather than leaving the diagnosis up to guess-work.

Dr. Dolittle's first adventure takes him to the Land of the Monkeys in Africa to cure thousands of sick gorillas, orangoutans, chimpanzees, and marmosets. The grateful patients present him with a pushmi-pullyu, a shy animal with a head at each end who eats with one mouth and talks with another, and with a marked character of his own, like the Doctor's other friends. Chee-Chee, the monkey, is nervous, and Too-Too, the owl, wise. Dabdab is a practical duck who becomes the Doctor's housekeeper. Gub Gub the pig is very greedy, and as such the natural butt of Lofting's obvious love of puns, jokes, and comic situations. Later books introduce Dobbin the horse, Sophie the seal, and a strange and unfathomable moon cat called Iffy. There are dozens more.

The books are also something of an education. While subsequent adventures take the Doctor to ever more outlandish places—the Moon, the Secret Lake—Lofting nonetheless manages to provide a good deal of practical and detailed information about geography, vegetation, species of animal, and some history, for example, references to Wilberforce and the slave trade (approximately the period in which the stories are set).

Lofting's other books for children lack the magic of Dr. Dolittle.

The first of the Doctor's adventures was published, to immediate critical success, in New York in 1920. It was illustrated, as they all were, by the author's charming, somewhat dotty pen and ink drawings, which are quite as much part of the books as the stories themselves and in some ways even more memorable.

Recently Lofting has come in for attack for his use of words like "nigger" and "coon" and for his comical portrayal of the "savages" he encounters. These are uncharacteristic and thoughtless lapses in books that are otherwise so carefully designed. Recent editions of some of the books have been edited to remove offensive terminology and characterizations. Besides, these lapses should not be allowed to spoil the books' real worth: their innocence, the lack of all whimsy, and the fact that Lofting was a genuinely original writer with an unusually inventive mind and a great gift for adventure.

—Caroline Moorehead

———

LOVELACE, Maud Hart (Palmer). American. Born in Mankato, Minnesota, 25 April 1892. Educated at the University of Minnesota, Minneapolis, 1911–12. Married Delos W. Lovelace in 1917 (died 1967); one daughter. *Died 11 March 1980.*

PUBLICATIONS FOR CHILDREN

Fiction

Betsy-Tacy, illustrated by Lois Lenski. New York, Crowell, 1940.
Betsy-Tacy and Tib, illustrated by Lois Lenski. New York, Crowell, 1941.
Over the Big Hill, illustrated by Lois Lenski. New York, Crowell, 1942; as *Betsy and Tacy Go over the Big Hill*, 1961 (?).
Down Town, illustrated by Lois Lenski. New York, Crowell, 1943; as *Betsy and Tacy Go Down Town*, 1961.
Heaven to Betsy, illustrated by Vera Neville. New York, Crowell, 1945.
Betsy in Spite of Herself, illustrated by Vera Neville. New York, Crowell, 1946.
Betsy Was a Junior, illustrated by Vera Neville. New York, Crowell, 1947.
Betsy and Joe, illustrated by Vera Neville. New York, Crowell, 1948.
Carney's House Party, illustrated by Vera Neville. New York, Crowell, 1949.
The Tune Is in the Tree, illustrated by Eloise Wilkin. New York, Crowell, 1950.
Emily of Deep Valley, illustrated by Vera Neville. New York, Crowell, 1950.
The Trees Kneel at Christmas, illustrated by Gertrude Howe. New York, Crowell, 1950.
Betsy and the Great World, illustrated by Vera Neville. New York, Crowell, 1952.
Winona's Pony Cart, illustrated by Vera Neville. New York, Crowell, 1953.
Betsy's Wedding, illustrated by Vera Neville. New York, Crowell, 1955.
What Cabrillo Found, illustrated by Paul Galdone. New York, Crowell, 1958.
The Valentine Box, illustrated by Ingrid Fetz. New York, Crowell, 1966.

Other

The Golden Wedge: Indian Legends of South America, with Delos

W. Lovelace, illustrated by Charlotte Chase. New York, Crowell, 1942.

PUBLICATIONS FOR ADULTS

Novels

The Black Angels. New York, Day, 1926.
Early Candlelight. New York, Day, 1929.
Petticoat Court. New York, Day, 1930; London, Sampson Low, 1931.
The Charming Sally. New York, Day, 1932.
One Stayed at Welcome, with Delos W. Lovelace. New York, Day, 1934.
Gentlemen from England, with Delos W. Lovelace. New York, Macmillan, 1937.

*

Manuscript Collection: University of Oregon Library, Eugene.

*   *   *

Many authors turn to childhood memories for inspiration, but Maud Hart Lovelace knit her life and art into a particularly tight weave. Her main body of work, the 10 books that comprise the Betsy-Tacy series (plus three related titles), are recreations of the happy days she spent growing up in Mankato, Minnesota (here called Deep Valley), in the early 1900's. She did grow up in that small yellow cottage so familiar to her readers. Her father, like Betsy Ray's, owned a shoe store. And her sisters, fictionalized as Julia and Margaret, appear in the books as do many of her friends.

In *Betsy-Tacy* Betsy invites the painfully shy Tacy Kelly to her 5th birthday party. A misunderstanding distances them, but eventually the two become fast friends. In the second book, they are joined by Thelma Mueller, a fearless though not overly imaginative child. Now they are *Betsy-Tacy and Tib.* The next two books, *Over the Big Hill* and *Down Town,* find Betsy the acknowledged leader and with a burning desire to be a writer. She gets her friends involved in all sorts of schemes and plans redolent of the era: their first automobile ride, a furious fight with Julia and pals to see who will be Queen of Summer, and one memorable incident where the trio takes up the cause of a Syrian girl harassed by boys in the town. This theme of helping immigrants reappears in a later book, *Emily of Deep Valley,* in which Betsy's crowd is only mentioned peripherally.

Perhaps Lovelace's most popular books are the four that take place when Betsy and her Crowd are in high school. Anchored by yearly events and family traditions, Lovelace changes these familiar happenings in each book to enhance the particular story. These four volumes are filled with the concerns teenage girls have always had, boyfriends, school, self-doubts. Yet it is all wrapped in a cloak of nostalgia that recreates a simpler time, a happier place.

As a series, this one is particularly satisfying because it takes Betsy through her wedding to the young man the other books have foreshadowed as her true love. The readers, girls eight through 13 primarily, are taken with the completeness of it all. And while Lovelace is a believer in happy ever afters, she is a feminist as well; most of her characters succeed at lofty ambitions. Betsy becomes a writer, Julia an opera star, Carney finishes Vassar, and Tib finds a career in fashion design. That diminutive blond is particularly disdainful of men who prize her delicate looks rather than her accomplishments.

Librarians are familiar with mothers who loved this series as girls, now bringing their daughters in to meet their old friends. For friends are what the Ray family and entourage become to readers—warm,

comfortable, slipped on as easily as a favorite piece of clothing. Lovelace broke no new ground, reached no dazzling heights. She did something almost as difficult, she endured.

—Ilene L. Cooper

————

LOWRY, Lois (née Hammersberg). American. Born in Honolulu, Hawaii, 20 March 1937. Educated at Brown University, Providence, Rhode Island, 1954–56; University of Southern Maine, Portland, B.A. in English 1972. Married Donald Lowry in 1956 (divorced 1977); two daughters and two sons. Recipient: Boston *Globe-Horn Book* award, 1987; Child Study Committee award, 1987; Christopher award, 1988. Agent: Claire Smith, Harold Ober Associates, 40 East 49th Street, New York, New York 10017. Address: 34 Hancock Street, Boston, Massachusetts 02114, U.S.A.

PUBLICATIONS FOR CHILDREN

Fiction

A Summer to Die. Boston, Houghton Mifflin, 1977; London, Kestrel, 1979.
Find a Stranger, Say Goodbye. Boston, Houghton Mifflin, 1978; London, Kestrel, 1980.
Anastasia Krupnik. Boston, Houghton Mifflin, 1979; London, Fontana, 1986.
Autumn Street. Boston, Houghton Mifflin, 1980; as *The Woods at the End of Autumn Street,* London, Dent, 1987.
Anastasia Again! Boston, Houghton Mifflin, 1981; London, Fontana, 1986.
Anastasia at Your Service. Boston, Houghton Mifflin, 1982; London, Fontana, 1987.
The One Hundredth Thing About Caroline. Boston, Houghton Mifflin, 1983.
Taking Care of Terrific. Boston, Houghton Mifflin, 1983.
Anastasia, Ask Your Analyst. Boston, Houghton Mifflin, 1984.
Us and Uncle Fraud. Boston, Houghton Mifflin, 1984.
Anastasia on Her Own. Boston, Houghton Mifflin, 1985.
Switcharound. Boston, Houghton Mifflin, 1985.
Anastasia Has the Answers. Boston, Houghton Mifflin, 1986.
Anastasia's Chosen Career. Boston, Houghton Mifflin, 1987.
Rabble Starkey. Boston, Houghton Mifflin, 1987; as *The Road Ahead,* London, Dent, 1988.
All About Sam, illustrated by Diane deGroat. Boston, Houghton Mifflin, 1988.
Number the Stars. Boston, Houghton Mifflin, 1989.

PUBLICATIONS FOR ADULTS

Other

Black American Literature (textbook). Portland, Maine, Weston Walsh, 1973.
Literature of the American Revolution (textbook). Portland, Maine, Weston Walsh, 1974.
Values and the Family. Portland, Maine, Weston Walsh, 1977.
Here in Kennebunkport (photographs), text by Frederick H. Lewis. Brattleboro, Vermont, Durrell, 1978.

*

Manuscript Collection: Kerlan Collection, University of Minnesota, Minneapolis.

* * *

Lois Lowry's contemporary realistic fiction focuses on dilemmas of adolescence. Fascinated with "the general continuity of life, the beginnings and ends, transitions, people's adjustments to change," Lowry well depicts the many facets of American family life. Lowry's families, not all of them with two college-educated, upper middle-class parents and well-adjusted children, usually foster the love and respect that allow children to cope successfully with problems.

Best known for her Anastasia series, she has created a prototype for the American family: father Myron, Harvard English professor and published poet; mother Katherine, freelance artist and consultant; Anastasia and Sam, their precocious, independent children. Family life at its best comes alive with witty dialogue, believable characters, and important themes about children growing up with good values and attitudes. These novels about Anastasia's maturation from 10 to 13 include adolescents' typical concerns: humiliation and fear of failure in school, sibling rivalry, crushes on boys and teachers, unhappiness with names and even religion, a grandparent's death, the trauma of moving and making new friends, boredom, independence, money, peer pressure, puberty's raging hormones, and career decisions. Even little brother Sam is featured in a book (*All About Sam*). The way the Krupniks survive their problems—with good humor, imagination, and compassion—suggests a model for the ideal family.

Another close-knit family (with a college English professor father also) is depicted in Lowry's first novel, *A Summer to Die*, inspired by her sister's death. Narrated by 13-year-old Meg Chalmers, it recounts the year she loses her sister (15) to leukemia. Struggling with an "ugly duckling" complex, Meg resents her more popular, prettier sister; her parents' and friends' support enables her to resolve her guilt and realize as time goes on, "the jagged edges of sadness are softened by memories." She emerges from the family tragedy more self-confident about her own talents.

Another dark vision of childhood is *Autumn Street*, in which traumatic events follow six-year-old Elizabeth Lorimer's move with her mother into her grandparents' home while her father serves in World War II. Stories of Nazi and Japanese atrocities, her grandfather's stroke, two playmates' deaths (one, from a brutal murder; the other, from her neglect), and her father's being maimed in the war all end the child's innocence. Death also threatens family unity in *Us and Uncle Fraud* when 11-year-old Louise Cunningham almost loses her older brother. However, with the happy ending Lowry usually provides, Louise and her parents realize how very lucky they are to have each other. She even realizes that visiting Uncle Claude, who lives in his own dream-weaving fantasy world, has destroyed her naive trust that adults tell the truth.

Another variation of Lowry's central theme of the child in the family is seen in *Find a Stranger, Say Goodbye*, as adopted 17-year-old Natalie Armstrong searches for her biological parents after high school graduation. Having learned the truth, she leaves for college to study medicine, strengthened by the past, confident about the future. A different adventure in searching for self-identity is undertaken by Enid Crowley (14) in *Taking Care of Terrific*. While babysitting four-year-old Joshua (Tom Terrific, he prefers), Enid (Cynthia, she calls herself) explores the magical night world of Boston's Public Garden with her friends until the police arrest them. Family values gone awry are evident when parents fail to take an active interest in their children's lives.

In contrast, loving relationships thrive in several one-parent families portrayed by Lowry. In *Rabble Starkey* the protagonist (12) and her 26-year-old mother, Sweet Hosanna, move in with a family whose mother is institutionalized; they demonstrate the strength of their close bond by sharing their love with an extended family. Rather than dwelling on the obvious hardships of a poor, single parent, Lowry glorifies the remarkable family ties that make a success story against the odds: a love-struck Sweet Hosanna ran off to marry a stranger at 13 and returned to her West Virginia home a year later with baby Parable (Rabble); by the novel's end, Sweet Hosanna plans to attend college, promising a bright future for both. Another positive portrayal of single-parent families is *The One Hundredth Thing About Caroline* in which 11-year-old Caroline Tate's mother frequently praises her children's special qualities and provides for them despite a limited budget. In the sequel, *Switcharound*, Caroline and brother J.P. visit their remarried father, whom they have not seen in years. He expects Caroline not only to babysit six-month-old twins but also to share their room. Sister and brother resolve their feuding to collaborate on ways to survive their summer visit.

Lowry's fictional families are not perfect—they would not be realistic if they were—but they provide unconditional love and support when calamity strikes. While avoiding shocking "problem novels," Lowry does not shelter her adolescent readers from the real world. They can identify, laugh, and cry with these believable characters who grow wiser with each problem resolved. Thus, Lowry helps children answer their own baffling questions about self-identity and human relationships.

—Laura M. Zaidman

———

LUNN, Janet (Louise, née Swoboda). Canadian. Born in Dallas, Texas, United States, 28 December 1928; became Canadian citizen, 1963. Educated at a high school in Montclair, New Jersey, graduated 1946; Notre Dame Convent, Ottawa, 1947; Queen's University, Kingston, Ontario, 1947–50. Married Richard Lunn in 1950 (died); four sons and one daughter. Children's editor, Clarke Irwin, publishers, Toronto, 1972–75; children's book consultant, Ginn and Company, Scarborough, Ontario, 1968–78; writer-in-residence, Regina Public Library, Ontario, 1982–83. Since 1988 writer-in-residence, Kitchener Public Library, Ontario. Chairwoman, Writers Union of Canada, 1984–85. Recipient: Vicky Metcalf award, 1981; Canadian Library Association award, 1982, 1987. Agent: Lucinda-Vardey Agency, 297 Seaton Street, Toronto, Ontario M5A 2T6. Address: R.R. 2, Hillier, Ontario K0K 2J0, Canada.

PUBLICATIONS FOR CHILDREN

Fiction

Double Spell. Toronto, PMA Books, 1968; London, Heinemann, 1985; as *Twin Spell*, New York, Harper, 1969.
The Root Cellar. Toronto, Lester and Orpen Dennys, 1981; New York, Scribner, and London, Heinemann, 1983.
Shadow in Hawthorn Bay. Toronto, Lester and Orpen Dennys, and New York, Scribner, 1986; London, Walker, 1988.
Amos's Sweater. Toronto, Groundwood, 1988.
A Hundred Shining Candles. Toronto, Lester and Orpen Dennys, 1989.
Duck Cakes for Sale. Toronto, Groundwood, 1989.

Other

Larger Than Life (Canadian history), illustrated by Emma Hesse. Victoria, British Columbia, Press Porcépic, 1979.

The Twelve Dancing Princesses (retelling), illustrated by Laszlo Gal. Toronto, London, and New York, Methuen, 1979.

PUBLICATIONS FOR ADULTS

Other

The County, with Richard Lunn. N.p., Prince Edward County Council, 1967.

*

Janet Lunn comments:

Most of my stories are set in—or partly in—historical times. I like how events in one time are connected to events in other times and I sometimes wonder if time mightn't flow in more than one direction—like a reversing falls. So I write about that. In *Double Spell* the main character is two people, twins. One day they are walking past an antique store when they are drawn, as if by a magnet, to an old doll in the window. From this moment the doll leads them into a mystery, that can only be solved by understanding something that happened more than 100 years earlier.

The Root Cellar is about Rose who goes back in time. Through an old root cellar she finds herself in the time of the American Civil War. The friends she makes in the 19th century lead her into an adventure that helps her to understand a lot more about herself and the people she knows in her own 1980's time.

Shadow in Hawthorn Bay is an historical novel. There's no moving back and forth in time except that Mary Urquhart, the heroine, is a seer. She sees into the future, into the past and into the present distance. When she comes to Canada from the Highlands of Scotland because she hears her cousin call her, she sets in motion a very hard time for herself.

I am a grandmother now and have had a lifetime to watch time flow and to look for the patterns in it. Sometimes, though, I leave history alone and write a small funny story; I have written stories for two picture books. One is called *Amos's Sweater* and is about an old sheep who wants his wool back. The other is about an old woman who always seems to have more on her hands than she wants—and it's always her own fault. It's called *Duck Cakes for Sale*.

I can't leave history alone, though, and I am working on two books now. One is a history of Canada for children, the other is a new historical novel. It's related to both *The Root Cellar* and *Shadow in Hawthorn Bay*.

*   *   *

As a Canadian who was born and grew up as an American, Janet Lunn is very conscious of the potential confusion of identity experienced by border crossers. In her novels for young adults, she crosses not only national borders, but also time, age, and gender borders—appropriate for readers negotiating the shift from child to adult. All of Lunn's novels contain an element of the supernormal: time-shift (in *The Root Cellar*), and second sight (visions of the past in *Double Spell* and visions of the future in *Shadow in Hawthorn Bay*). But her fictions are always woven into geographically and historically accurate settings.

In *The Root Cellar* Rose—an orphan who looks like Anne of Green Gables but behaves like Mary from *The Secret Garden*—feels herself out of her own time and place. It is only when she "time-shifts" into the 1860's through the root cellar of her aunt's dilapidated house that she finds her own identity. Her journey into the past takes her first to the house as it was at the time of the American Civil War,

to Will whose family owned the house, and to Susan, who would eventually marry him. From there she goes with Susan from Prince Edward County in Ontario to Washington, D. C. to find Will who, in sympathy with his United Empire Loyalist roots, has gone to fight in the Civil War. The journey that Rose and Susan take, shown on a map at the front of the book, is geographically accurate—as is the time of the train they took from Oswego to New York City (Lunn held the train timetable for that date). The identity quest too is psychologically accurate: Rose finds the capacity to control her own destiny, and also finds her emotional connection with the place she lives and her adoptive family.

In *Double Spell* 12-year-old twins Jane and Elizabeth discover their family history through a mysterious connection they have with a doll they chance upon in a Toronto antique shop. Although they don't actually time-shift, they both suddenly begin to share atavistic, often vaguely frightening memories, of a time over 100 years earlier when the doll was new. The supernatural events counterpoint the finely observed details of Toronto past and present. And the genealogical table at the end of the book gives physical reality to the twins' psychic experiences.

Although *Shadow in Hawthorn Bay* is the most recent of Lunn's novels, it is set furthest back in time—1815. Instead of modern characters who find the past, this story is about Mairi, a pioneer girl who can see the future but is drawn to her past. She comes to Prince Edward County (where *The Root Cellar* is set and where Lunn lives) from Scotland, because she hears her cousin Duncan call. He had always been her twin, her shadow, her double; she has to go to him. But when she arrives, she finds him dead and his family gone back to Scotland. The story is a bizarre love triangle. Mairi is torn between her Canadian suitor's desire to marry her, and Duncan's desire—from beyond the grave—to drown her in Hawthorn Bay, as he drowned himself. Her quest involves coming to terms with herself, her relationship with Luke, her new home, Canada, and the double-edged gift of her two sights.

The gender and age borders that Lunn crosses in her novels are less marked than the temporal and spatial ones, but they are clearly visible. In *The Root Cellar* Rose manages to take a controlling role when she travels in the past partly because she crosses a gender line. Her androgynous 20th-century jeans and tee-shirt disguise her as a boy in the 19th century. The age boundary that usually inhibits children from recognizing that grown-ups, especially elderly ones, might once have been children, is crossed as well. The young Susan who goes with Rose on her journey turns up as a "shifted" old woman who appears to Rose in the 20th-century house. And it is Susan's grandmother, Mairi, who appears as a young girl in *Shadow in Hawthorn Bay*.

Although Lunn's novels, like many works of young adult fiction, are about the burning issue of an identity quest, what makes them different is her capacity to see identity as multiple, not as a single thing which can be sought and found. For the characters in her books, identity is about finding a way of integrating various parts of the individual—a redemptive, Jungian notion made visible.

—Lissa Paul

———

LYNCH, Patricia (Nora). Irish. Born in Cork, 7 June 1898. Educated at a convent school, and secular schools in Ireland, Scotland, England, and Belgium. Married Richard Michael Fox in 1922. Feature writer, *Christian Commonwealth*, Dublin, 1918–20. Recipient: Tailteann Festival Silver Medal, 1947. *Died 1 September 1972.*

PUBLICATIONS FOR CHILDREN

Fiction

The Green Dragon. London, Harrap, 1925.
The Cobbler's Apprentice, illustrated by M.R. Lamb. London, Shaylor, 1930.
The Turf-Cutter's Donkey, illustrated by Jack B. Yeats. London, Dent, 1934; New York, Dutton, 1935.
The Turf-Cutter's Donkey Goes Visiting, illustrated by George Altendorf. London, Dent, 1935; as *The Donkey Goes Visiting*, New York, Dutton, 1936.
King of the Tinkers, illustrated by Katherine C. Lloyd. London, Dent, and New York, Dutton, 1938.
The Turf-Cutter's Donkey Kicks Up His Heels, illustrated by Eileen Coghlan. New York, Dutton, 1939; London, Dent, 1952.
The Grey Goose of Kilnevin, illustrated by John Keating. London, Dent, 1939; New York, Dutton, 1940.
Fiddler's Quest, illustrated by Isobel Morton-Sale. London, Dent, 1941; New York, Dutton, 1943.
Long Ears: The Story of a Little Grey Donkey, illustrated by Joan Kiddell-Monroe. London, Dent, 1943.
Strangers at the Fair and Other Stories, illustrated by Eileen Coghlan. Dublin, Browne and Nolan, 1945; London, Penguin, 1949.
Lisheen at the Valley Farm and Other Stories, with Helen Staunton and Teresa Deevy. Dublin, Gayfield Press, 1945.
Brogeen of the Stepping Stones, illustrated by Alfred Kerr. London, Kerr Cross, 1947.
The Mad O'Haras, illustrated by Elizabeth Rivers. London, Dent, 1948; as *Grania of Castle O'Hara*, Boston, Page, 1952.
The Dark Sailor of Youghal, illustrated by Jerome Sullivan. London, Dent, 1951.
The Boy at the Swinging Lantern, illustrated by Joan Kiddell-Monroe. London, Dent, 1952.
Brogeen Follows the Magic Tune, illustrated by Peggy Fortnum. London, Burke, 1952; New York, Macmillan, 1968.
Delia Daly of Galloping Green, illustrated by Joan Kiddell-Monroe. London, Dent, 1953.
Brogeen and the Green Shoes, illustrated by Peggy Fortnum. London, Burke, 1953.
Brogeen and the Bronze Lizard, illustrated by Grace Golden. London, Burke, 1954; New York, Macmillan, 1970.
Orla of Burren, illustrated by Joan Kiddell-Monroe. London, Dent, 1954.
Tinker Boy, illustrated by Harry Kernoff. London, Dent, 1955.
Brogeen and the Princess of Sheen, illustrated by Christopher Brooker. London, Burke, 1955.
The Bookshop on the Quay, illustrated by Peggy Fortnum. London, Dent, 1956.
Brogeen and the Lost Castle, illustrated by Christopher Brooker. London, Burke, 1956.
Fiona Leaps the Bonfire, illustrated by Peggy Fortnum. London, Dent, 1957; as *Shane Comes to Dublin*, New York, Criterion, 1958.
Cobbler's Luck, illustrated by Christopher Brooker. London, Burke, 1957.
The Old Black Sea Chest: A Story of Bantry Bay, illustrated by Peggy Fortnum. London, Dent, 1958.
Brogeen and the Black Enchanter, illustrated by Christopher Brooker. London, Burke, 1958.
The Stone House at Kilgobbin, illustrated by Christopher Brooker. London, Burke, 1959.
Jinny the Changeling, illustrated by Peggy Fortnum. London, Dent, 1959.
The Runaways. Oxford, Blackwell, 1959.
Sally from Cork, illustrated by Elizabeth Grant. London, Dent, 1960.
The Lost Fisherman of Carrigmor, illustrated by Christopher Brooker. London, Burke, 1960.
Ryan's Fort, illustrated by Elizabeth Grant. London, Dent, 1961.
The Longest Way Round, illustrated by D.G. Valentine. London, Burke, 1961.
The Golden Caddy, illustrated by Juliette Palmer. London, Dent, 1962.
Brogeen and the Little Wind, illustrated by Beryl Sanders. London, Burke, 1962; New York, Roy, 1963.
The House by Lough Neagh, illustrated by Nina Ross. London, Dent, 1963.
Brogeen and the Red Fez, illustrated by Beryl Sanders. London, Burke, 1963.
Holiday at Rosquin, illustrated by Mary Shillabeer. London, Dent, 1964.
Guests at the Beech Tree, illustrated by Beryl Sanders. London, Burke, 1964.
The Twisted Key and Other Stories, illustrated by Joan Kiddell-Monroe. London, Harrap, 1964.
Mona of the Isle, illustrated by Mary Shillabeer. London, Dent, 1965.
Back of Beyond, illustrated by Susannah Holden. London, Dent, 1966.
The Kerry Caravan, illustrated by James Hunt. London, Dent, 1967.

Other

Knights of God: Stories of the Irish Saints, illustrated by Alfred Kerr. London, Hollis and Carter, 1945; Chicago, Regnery, 1955.
The Seventh Pig and Other Irish Fairy Tales, illustrated by Jerome Sullivan. London, Dent, 1950; revised edition, as *The Black Goat of Slievemore and Other Irish Tales*, 1959.
Tales of Irish Enchantment (legends), illustrated by Fergus O'Ryan. Dublin, Clonmore and Reynolds, and London, Burns Oates, 1952.

PUBLICATIONS FOR ADULTS

Other

A Story-Teller's Childhood (autobiography). London, Dent, 1947; New York, Norton, 1962.

*   *   *

Country gatherings like fairs and races and tinker encampments play a large part in Patricia Lynch's stories, and to the natural bustle and exuberance of these events and places a magic element is often added. At the fair in *The Turf-Cutter's Donkey*, Eileen and Seamus are followed around by a small man and a pig, and the children find that they can fly simply by jumping in the air. But Eileen's boots have been mended by a leprechaun, and this makes plausible the elaborate sequence of events that follows. In the Long Ears series, magic is unrestrained and owes a great deal to the type of Irish folktale that deals in talking animals and bewildering changes in settings and objects. Usually an odd collection of characters is brought together: a couple of children, a ballad singer, an apple woman, a leprechaun, tinker, changeling, or captain of a barge. Action is continuous and always directed towards the achievement of a moral resolution. The goal of the central characters is domestic cosiness, and often they are waifs and strays to make the point more telling.

Sheila, in *The Grey Goose of Kilnevin*, is sent on an errand to Bridgie Swallow, and at once a formal pattern is established: the ritualized quest, with tests and trials at every step. Sheila gets the three pounds of butter and much else besides; like all Lynch's heroines she is clever and spirited and always ready to share her few possessions with any strangers that she may meet along the road. A number of peculiar alliances result from the latter: a fox makes friends with the little grey goose, and a scarecrow provides a coat for the Ballad singer.

The fantasy is usually down-to-earth with a strong rough-and-tumble flavour; but sometimes the characters are taken right off the ground and swept into a mythological realm. This is not always successful. The author has made good use of the standard figures of Irish legend and myth: the wise woman of the mountain; the fool who recovers his wits; the Fianna, ancient warrior band; the salmon of knowledge; the Children of Lir who were changed into swans by a malicious stepmother; and so on. But Lynch has no sense of the numinous and sometimes the magical episodes have a picture postcard element when they aren't enlivened by sheer rumbustious humour.

Two excellent stories with no supernatural overtones appeared in the 1940's: *Fiddler's Quest* and *The Mad O'Haras*. Again, in each of these we have the movement towards emotional security. In the former, Ethne Cadogan, the fiddler of the title, comes to Ireland to search for her traditional home, Inniscoppal (the Island of Horses), and her itinerant grandfather. Unusually, the book has an urban setting, a courtyard in Dublin; it is also the only novel by Lynch to exploit the romantic aspect of Irish nationalism. Nial Desmond is a Republican on the run; at one point in the narrative Ethne and the Rafferty children drive a cartload of guns through an army barricade. Suspense is maintained admirably through a series of incidents that includes shooting and evacuation. The book has a kind of realism that is not found often in her work, and it is offset to good effect by the use of familiar stereotypes like the ballad singer and the story teller.

Ethne the fiddler is a talented child; like Grania in *The Mad O'Haras* she has plans for a career. Grania won't submit to convention, unlike her cousin Sally who longs to be a jockey but works as a hairdresser, a suitable girl's occupation. Lynch's heroines face up to opposition and overcome it. Grania means to be a painter, and wins a scholarship to a Dublin art school. First, however, she helps to solve the problems of her wild relatives in whom the ramshackle, devil-may-care quality of Irish life is embodied. The romantic O'Haras have tinker blood and live in a tumbledown castle. The perennial Irish theme of "bad blood" is indicated here, but naturally in the children's book context it is muted and easily resolved.

There is no complexity of situation or motive in Lynch's stories, and little attempt at character differentiation. The central characters are effectively interchangeable. The predominant virtue is kindness, and if its rewards are sometimes disproportionate this is acceptable in terms of the rigid fairytale structure. Even the straightforward children's novels have a simplified moral basis. The author went on producing alternate fantasy and family tales along the lines that she had laid down in the 1930's and early 1940's. In *Tinker Boy*, for instance, there is acknowledgement of the glamour of vagabond life; but the tinkers' apparent lawlessness is really an illusion. It was always easy to get the better of the dreadful King of the Tinkers with his spotted kerchief. When villainy is larger than life it ceases to be frightening and of course many of Lynch's books are for younger children who can relish without question the white pigs and mermaids and changelings and magic boots.

Jinny the Changeling employs familiar motifs: the four swans, the quest for a missing father, the swirling mists that are conjured up to mask queer goings-on. The Clerys are a poor but generous family whose fortunes begin to change when they find a baby in a clump of bushes. ("You're a dote of a Changeling," everyone says about Jinny.) As usual when she tries to be poetic about the supernatural Lynch descends into a kind of vulgarity: it is all pretty-pretty where

it should be delicate and ethereal. There is in fact a slight sense of dislocation in the stories that move from one plane to another: those that work best are completely magical or completely prosaic (though in later books like *Tinker Boy* the dreariness of small Irish towns is beginning to make itself felt).

Lynch's reputation rests on her assured evocations of fairground and bog and fairy rath, the racy outspoken quality of her dialogue, and her ability to amalgamate the traditional folktale with the present-day children's story.

—Patricia Craig

LYON, Elinor. British. Born in Guisborough, Yorkshire, 17 August 1921. Educated at Headington School, Oxford, 1934–38; St. George's School, Montreux, Switzerland, 1939; Lady Margaret Hall, Oxford, 1940–41. Served in the Women's Royal Naval Service, 1942–44. Married Peter Wright in 1944; two sons and two daughters. Address: Bron Meini, Harlech, Gwynedd, Wales.

<small>PUBLICATIONS FOR CHILDREN</small>

Fiction

Hilary's Island, illustrated by Eileen Soper and the author. London, Hodder and Stoughton, 1948; New York, Coward McCann, 1949.
Wishing Watergate, illustrated by the author. London, Hodder and Stoughton, and New York, Coward McCann, 1949.
The House in Hiding, illustrated by the author. London, Hodder and Stoughton, and New York, Coward McCann, 1950.
We Daren't Go A-Hunting, illustrated by the author. London, Hodder and Stoughton, 1951.
Run Away Home, illustrated by the author. London, Hodder and Stoughton, and New York, Viking Press, 1953.
Sea Treasure, illustrated by the author. London, Hodder and Stoughton, 1955.
Dragon Castle, illustrated by the author. London, Hodder and Stoughton, 1956.
Daughters of Aradale, illustrated by the author. London, Hodder and Stoughton, 1957; New York, White Lion, 1974.
The Golden Shore, illustrated by the author. London, Hodder and Stoughton, 1957.
Rider's Rock, illustrated by the author. London, Hodder and Stoughton, 1958; Chicago, Follett, 1968.
Cathie Runs Wild, illustrated by the author. London, Hodder and Stoughton, 1960; Chicago, Follett, 1968.
Carver's Journey, illustrated by the author. London, Hodder and Stoughton, 1962; as *The Secret of Hermit's Bay*, Chicago, Follett, 1967.
Green Grow the Rushes, illustrated by Graham Byfield. Leicester, Brockhampton Press, 1964; Chicago, Follett, 1967.
Echo Valley, illustrated by Mary Dinsdale. Leicester, Brockhampton Press, 1965; Chicago, Follett, 1967.
The Dream Hunters, illustrated by Mary Dinsdale. Leicester, Brockhampton Press, 1966; Chicago, Follett, 1967.
Strangers at the Door, illustrated by Mary Dinsdale. Leicester, Brockhampton Press, 1967; Chicago, Follett, 1969.
The Day That Got Lost, illustrated by Caroline Sharpe. Leicester, Brockhampton Press, 1968.
The Wishing Pool, illustrated by Mary Dinsdale. Leicester, Brockhampton Press, 1970; Nashville, Nelson, 1972.
The King of Grey Corrie, illustrated by Elizabeth Haines. Leicester,

Brockhampton Press, 1975.
The Floodmakers, illustrated by Elizabeth Haines.   London, Hodder and Stoughton, 1976.

*

Elinor Lyon comments:
   My books are adventure stories, mostly for the 10–12 age group, though the last four are for younger readers. As well as excitement and humour, I have tried to express deeper themes that arouse strong feelings in most children—justice, freedom, and compassion. The settings are mainly the wild parts of Scotland and Wales. *The Golden Shore* is about ancient Greece and is the only one with an element of fantasy.

*   *   *

   Within the holiday adventure genre, ranging from Arthur Ransome as its pioneer and outstanding exponent, to Blyton—and worse—we should give Elinor Lyon a fairly high place. Although her contribution has been overlooked in favour of David Severn, Malcolm Saville, and Monica Edwards, she was one of the 1940's and 1950's British writers who gave equal roles to girls, and portrayed sensitive boys, before the discovery of "sexism" in the 1970's.
   Although her characters are mainly middle-class, they are not rich, and despise ostentatious wealth. The plots are down-to-earth: no gangs of international crooks, and if the plot turns on a search for treasure, that "treasure" is more likely to be a family heirloom of sentimental value than a fabulous collection of jewels.
   Her children do run into danger, but are often usually physically prepared, by previous climbing, swimming, or rowing experience, and parental warnings are duly given for the readers' benefit. Her child characters are individuals, and after the initial tension between the local inhabitants of a holiday area and the holiday makers, the children band together to solve whatever mystery or treasure hunt is on offer.
   Lyon's holiday adventures fall into two main groups: self-contained stories set in the countryside or seaside of Great Britain, and a series about Ian and Sovra, brother and sister living on the west coast of Scotland.
   In the first category the most notable are *Wishing Watergate*, in which children follow clues to a sluice within the mountain where a stream's course was secretly turned; *Sea Treasure*, about three children who take up the hobby of making and sailing model boats in order to chart sea currents; *Dragon Castle*, set in Wales, about a lost, ruined castle and its rightful owner; and *Rider's Rock*, also set in Wales, about a village buried in the sand and the children who explore its cottages—and are trapped inside when a tidal wave surges over them.
   The Ian and Sovra saga is spread over eight full-length books and two shorter ones (*The King of Grey Corrie* and *The Floodmakers*) about Sovra's children, the last of Lyon's books to be published. Ian and Sovra's chief friend is Alastair, the young impoverished owner of Kindrachill, a Highland estate which includes mountain territory and sea coast. In *We Daren't Go A-Hunting* they track down a gang of incompetent deer poachers. In *Run Away Home* Lyon introduces Cathie Gunn, who runs away from her Birmingham orphanage in search of a babyhood memory of silver sand and shells, and discovers that she is a member of Alastair's family. *Daughters of Aradale* tells how Cathie, Sovra, and Ian recreate the flight of a Jacobite fugitive.
   Different again is *The Golden Shore*, where two cousins travel back in time to Ancient Greece, and discover the realities of life in a peasant village threatened by barbarian invasion. Apart from the time travel device Lyon never uses magical devices in her books, yet many of them have a kind of fantastic, spiritual quality which derives from

her use of fate, prophecy, and coincidence, and the Celtic historical and legendary background to many of her stories. With these qualities, and the lighthearted dialogue—particularly in delineating the character of Ian Kennedy and his habit of making irrelevant remarks about scientific oddities ("Did you know that crocodiles can't struggle with their eyes shut?")—Lyon's books were much loved among 1950's and 1960's library users, and deserved mass-market paperback editions rather more than some other writers of her period still in print today.

—Jessica Yates

———————

MACDONALD, Caroline.   New Zealander.   Born in Taranaki, 1 October 1948. Editor of teaching materials, Deakin University, Geelong, Australia, 1984–88. Recipient: New Zealand Literary Fund Choysa bursary, 1983; New Zealand Library Association Esther Glen Medal, 1984; New Zealand Children's Book of the Year award, 1985. Agent: Margaret Connolly, Curtis Brown, 27 Union Street, Paddington, New South Wales 2021, Australia. Address: P.O. Box 4189, Hamilton, New Zealand.

PUBLICATIONS FOR CHILDREN

Fiction

Elephant Rock.   Auckland, Hodder and Stoughton, 1984; London, Hodder and Stoughton, 1988.
Visitors, illustrated by Garry Meeson.   Auckland, Hodder and Stoughton, 1984; London, Hodder and Stoughton, 1988.
Yellow Boarding House.   Auckland, Oxford University Press, 1985.
Joseph's Boat, illustrated by Chris Gaskin.   Auckland, Hodder and Stoughton, 1988.
Earthgames, illustrated by Chris Johnson and Rowena Cory.   Melbourne, Rigby, 1988.
The Lake at the End of the World.   Auckland, Hodder and Stoughton, 1988; New York, Dial Press, 1989.

*

Caroline Macdonald comments:
   Future fiction, science fiction, the supernatural and the mystical are the thematic areas I'm interested in. I like to suggest there's a strange edge to be found in a mundane world. I enjoy forming characters who are for some reason removed from the usual processes of conditioning.

*   *   *

   Although Caroline Macdonald's novels and picture book texts have a wide range of subject matter and environments, they all demonstrate her preoccupation with young people who are in some way isolated. Their separation from normal peer groups renders them more sensitive to the unusual, be it visitors from outer space, time slips, or challenging circumstances. The child alone is inevitably more dependent on adults, and her multi-layered novels are sensitive explorations of parent-child relationships, which often suffer from a breakdown in communication.
   Her first book *Elephant Rock* daringly and uncompromisingly examines the situation of 12-year-old Ann whose mother is dying of cancer. The pitfalls inherent in such a scenario are deftly avoided

through the use of a time-slip device that enables Ann to relive her mother's youth and consequently understand and more readily accept the impending bereavement.

Kaye Webb once quoted a child who said of another novel, "I felt older after reading this." The same statement could apply to *Elephant Rock*: the reader will grow through experiencing it. Although inevitably sad, it is neither depressing nor sentimental as the spare economical prose is allowed to make its own impact.

Visitors is a counterpoint of differing cross-threads of communication. The "Visitors" are from Outer Space and have been trapped in this world for hundreds of years. Every attempt to escape has failed because they cannot find anyone to understand their messages. Finally they select Terry, a lonely boy, to help them. Terry is the classic poor little rich boy, given every luxury by his hard-working professional parents except their time and attention. He retreats into the world of the small screen and picks up pictures from the Visitors on video. He cannot understand their meaning until he is helped by Maryanne, a physically handicapped school friend who, because she herself can only communicate effectively through a word processor, has more insight into what the Visitors are trying to say and solves the puzzle. The Visitors' predicament thus highlights the human problems, and solving the one assists in easing the others. Not only is Maryanne revealed as an intelligent girl instead of an object of pity, but Terry's parents are alerted to his needs.

In addition to investing fantasy with a compelling life of its own, Macdonald demonstrates considerable scientific acumen as Maryanne and Terry have to work out various aspects of wavelengths and light refraction in order to free the Visitors.

There is a move away from fantasy in *Yellow Boarding House*, which is set in Australia where a New Zealand mother and her daughter Lyndsay are stranded in Melbourne with no money when the father fails to return from a trip to Queensland. The mother is forced to work in order to pay their way and Lyndsay, alone in a strange city, inadvertently becomes involved with a drug-smuggling gang. The mother-daughter relationship is astutely portrayed; the mother under stress still protectively treats Lyndsay like a child, while Lyndsay, emerging into adulthood, is resentful at not being given responsibility or taken into her mother's confidence.

A father and son feature in the long picture book *Joseph's Boat*. Here the isolation is through living on a small island, away from other children or any female influence. Joseph is motherless and his father, immersed in day-to-day farming, fails to realize that Joseph's pleas to accompany him on visits to the mainland stem from loneliness. It is not until Joseph takes a boat and is nearly lost at sea that communication is satisfactorily established with his father. Chris Gaskin's pictures are a particularly evocative accompaniment to this book.

Her latest novel *The Lake at the End of the World* is set in 2025 when the world has virtually been killed by pollution except for a lake and its environs in New Zealand. Unknown to one another two groups of people live near its shore, one a highly structured community who inhabit underground caves, the other a family consisting of father, mother, and daughter, Diana, who eke out a subsistence living above ground. The novel opens when teenage Hector from the community finds his way into the outside world and meets Diana. Their differing circumstances lead to widely divergent viewpoints but both have to cooperate when the formerly utopian underground community becomes a dystopia as its leadership degenerates into tyranny.

The book unobtrusively asks large questions about power, the direction of agricultural management, and industrial pollution. A potent contrast is drawn between the authoritarian but sheltered regime of the community and the family, vulnerable to the exigencies of weather, accident, and illness. Nevertheless, it is the family who retains the myth-making capacity, as they weave stories about the Lake that dominates their existence. In the technological environ-

ment of the caves, musical instruments lie idle and the voices of poets have been silenced.

—Betty Gilderdale

————

MacDONALD, Golden. See **BROWN, Margaret Wise**.

————

MacGIBBON, Jean (née Howard). British. Born in London, 25 January 1913. Educated at St. Leonard's School, St. Andrews, Scotland; Royal Academy of Dramatic Art, London. Married James MacGibbon in 1934; two sons and one daughter. Editorial director, MacGibbon and Kee, publishers, London, 1948–54. Recipient: Children's Rights Workshop Other award, 1975. Address: 8 Quay Street, Manningtree, Essex CO11 1AU, England.

PUBLICATIONS FOR CHILDREN

Fiction

Peter's Private Army, illustrated by Janet Duchesne. London, Hamish Hamilton, 1960.
Red Sail, White Sail, illustrated by Janet Duchesne. London, Hamish Hamilton, 1961.
The Red Sledge, illustrated by Janet Duchesne. London, Hamish Hamilton, 1962.
Pam Plays Doubles. London, Constable, 1962.
The View-Finder, illustrated by Janet Duchesne. London, Hamish Hamilton, 1963.
A Special Providence, illustrated by William Stobbs. London, Hamish Hamilton, 1964; New York, Coward McCann, 1965.
Liz. London, Hamish Hamilton, 1966; New York, Scribner, 1969.
Sandy in Hollow Tree House, illustrated by Janet Duchesne. London, Hamish Hamilton, 1967.
The Tall Ship, illustrated by Janet Duchesne. London, Hamish Hamilton, 1967.
The Great-Great Rescuers, illustrated by Janet Duchesne. London, Hamish Hamilton, 1967.
The Spy in Dolor Hugo. London, Heinemann, 1973.
Hal. London, Heinemann, 1974.
Jobs for the Girls. London, Heinemann, 1975.
After the Raft Race. London, Heinemann, 1976.
Three's Company. London, Chatto and Windus, 1978.

PUBLICATIONS FOR ADULTS

Novel

When the Weather's Changing (as Jean Howard). London, Putnam, 1945.

Other

I Meant to Marry Him: A Personal Memoir. London, Gollancz, 1984.

Translator, *Women of Islam*, by Assia Djébar. London, Deutsch,

1961.
Translator, *Girls of Paris*, by Nicole de Buron. London, Blond, 1962.

*

Jean MacGibbon comments:

(1978) After writing for adults for some 20 years, I began to write for children in 1959 at the suggestion of Richard Hough. Since then I have written exclusively for children of all ages. More recently my books for older children have attracted critical attention as exemplifying a new and more realistic trend in children's fiction. *Liz* was the first of these. *Hal* went further in this genre and was welcomed by librarians and educationists for breaking new ground in subject matter and treatment, specially of multi-racial groups in an urban setting. Since I left London the background of my books has changed. But adolescents everywhere have the same preoccupations and with the stimulus of a changed environment I look forward to writing further books on similar themes, specially for "reluctant" (not "backward") readers.

*   *   *

Jean MacGibbon has written successfully for the very young, but she excels in teenage stories, better expressed as novels for young adults, which mix the requisite outdoor adventures with inward psychological realism. The most notable are *The View-Finder*, *Hal*, and *Three's Company*. She has an alert eye for people, a vivid memory, a feeling for landscape with its colours, hideaways, tidal waters, the dreamy heat of a long summer afternoon, as well as a strong grip on the practical, describing with total conviction the workings of a ship, a tricky cliff climb, a new method of teaching a difficult, multi-racial class. A deep feeling for water and boats pervades many of her books, fusing well in the historical adventure, *A Special Providence*, a boy's view of *The Mayflower*, refreshingly irreverent towards the Pilgrim Fathers. MacGibbon's special merit is in her lack of sentimentality toward family life. She knows in her bones the darker relations between parents, and that the young too can have cravings of excess, mindless destruction, even murder, and that tragedy may occur at any age.

> "You don't have to mind," Milly said, "You mustn't mind too much. No one thinks it's your fault."
> Liz put the soup down. It made her feel sick. "You don't understand," she said. Looking queerly at Milly, "I enjoyed it."

These books finely convey the qualms, perplexities, frustrations, and growing sexual dilemmas of adolescence, "the shadows of disappointment that spoil moments of happiness." Readers can readily identify with Liz, mercurial, often confused, more complex than most fictional characters, a graphic example of the multitudinous processes of growing up. Most MacGibbon books expose conflicts: between adults, adults and the young, and among the young themselves, together with the uneasy isolation in which teenagers can live, needing to venture out, obstinately determined to stay in. A quiet domestic exchange can have the force of a bomb.

> "It's not just being *sea-sick*. I don't want to go." Mr. Mitchell shifted uncomfortably: "Better go, son. Miss a lot in life through not making an effort."
> Tension was building up, devious, subterranean, of which Chris' obduracy, his mother's will, were only outward expressions. Quietly, with reproachful intensity, she said: "You're *so* like your Dad."

Chris stared at his plate, filleting his fried dab with extreme care. His father could be heard masticating; with his little finger he hooked out a small cast of bones and flesh.

With a family, or a youth-gang, too often exists a mystery, something not quite right, not wholly explicable, vaguely menacing. Again and again a nerviness begins, not blatant or sensational, but underlying the games and explorings, the sailing and camping, the trailing of a war-time spy, the games on Hampstead Heath.

Finally, these books contain an awareness of contemporary issues recognizable to readers of all classes—Mods and Rockers, racial rivalries, dissension in classroom and common-room. They are prominent in *Hal*, set in a cosmopolitan and grim London of selfish or predatory adults, loneliness, struggling idealism and sexuality, harsh antagonisms and sudden, exciting communal enterprises—a school play, the creation of a playground from wasteland. These centre round the subtle relationships of a West Indian girl and a white boy. Here too, realism is foremost. For this author, happy endings may possibly occur, but they are not inevitable and cannot be forced.

—Peter Vansittart

———

MacGREGOR, Ellen. American. Born in Baltimore, Maryland, 15 May 1906. Educated at schools in Garfield and Kent, Washington; University of Washington, Seattle, B.S. in library science 1926; University of California, Berkeley, 1931. Children's librarian in Wyoming, California, Idaho, Florida, Oregon, and Hawaii; research librarian, International Harvester, Chicago. *Died 29 March 1954.*

PUBLICATIONS FOR CHILDREN

Fiction

Tommy and the Telephone, illustrated by Zabeth. Chicago, Whitman, 1947.
Miss Pickerell Goes to Mars, illustrated by Paul Galdone. New York, McGraw Hill, 1951; London, Blackie, 1957.
Miss Pickerell and the Geiger Counter, illustrated by Paul Galdone. New York, McGraw Hill, 1953; London, Blackie, 1958.
Miss Pickerell Goes Undersea, illustrated by Paul Galdone. New York, McGraw Hill, 1953; London, Blackie, 1959.
Miss Pickerell Goes to the Arctic, illustrated by Paul Galdone. New York, McGraw Hill, 1954; London, Blackie, 1960.
Theodore Turtle, illustrated by Paul Galdone. New York, McGraw Hill, 1955; London, Faber, 1956.
Mr. Ferguson of the Fire Department, illustrated by Paul Galdone. New York, McGraw Hill, 1956.
Mr. Pringle and Mr. Buttonhouse, illustrated by Paul Galdone. New York, McGraw Hill, 1957.
Miss Pickerell on the Moon, with Dora Pantell, illustrated by Charles Geer. New York, McGraw Hill, 1965.
Miss Pickerell Goes on a Dig, with Dora Pantell, illustrated by Charles Geer. New York, McGraw Hill, 1966.
Miss Pickerell Harvests the Sea, with Dora Pantell, illustrated by Charles Geer. New York, McGraw Hill, 1968.
Miss Pickerell and the Weather Satellite, with Dora Pantell, illustrated by Charles Geer. New York, McGraw Hill, 1971.
Miss Pickerell Meets Mr. H.U.M., with Dora Pantell, illustrated by Charles Geer. New York, McGraw Hill, 1974.
Miss Pickerell Takes the Bull by the Horns, with Dora Pantell, illustrated by Charles Geer. New York, McGraw Hill, 1976.

Miss Pickerell to the Earthquake Rescue, with Dora Pantell, illustrated by Charles Geer.   New York, McGraw Hill, 1977.
Miss Pickerell and the Supertanker, with Dora Pantell, illustrated by Charles Geer.   New York, McGraw Hill, 1978.
Miss Pickerell Tackles the Energy Crisis, with Dora Pantell, illustrated by Charles Geer.   New York, McGraw Hill, 1980.
Miss Pickerell on the Trail, with Dora Pantell, illustrated by Charles Geer.   New York, McGraw Hill, 1981.
Miss Pickerell and the Blue Whale, with Dora Pantell, illustrated by Charles Geer.   New York, McGraw Hill, 1982.

*   *   *

Good science fiction, like good nonsense or fantasy, must be firmly grounded in the world of reality, as Ellen MacGregor understood so well. A minor but genuine original in the field of science fiction for very young readers is her Miss Lavinia Pickerell, heroine of a series of slightly cockeyed scientific adventures.

Miss Pickerell is the last person you'd expect to find up in the air or down a mine shaft—until you become properly acquainted. She isn't quite the prim, spinsterly person her appearance suggests. True, she is angular and stiff, wears old-fashioned clothes and an outlandish hat: looks, indeed, like a model for New England Gothic. But she is full of fun, and always ready to try something new. She has a good memory for facts, and plenty of common sense, but is by no means an intimidating scientific genius. With her seven busy nieces and nephews, Miss Pickerell is a lot like everybody's favourite maiden aunt.

Miss Pickerell's first adventure took her to Mars—quite by mistake, as an inadvertent stowaway on a space ship. Naturally, once having arrived, Miss Pickerell made the best of her opportunity to add Martian red rocks to her famous collection. Which led indirectly to her *next* adventures, with a Geiger counter to test for radioactivity and later in an undersea search for a sunken ship containing her rock collection, lost at sea en route to an exhibition. No salvage company was going to claim *her* belongings. And so on, one adventure leading into another.

To Mars, to the Arctic, above the ground or below, Miss Pickerell is dauntless, intrepid, and eager. It's all good fun, but with a bonus. The scientific basis of each of the Miss Pickerell stories is scrupulously accurate. Although she was careful not to overburden her fragile plots with didactic passages explaining gravity, radiation, etc., MacGregor managed very skillfully to incorporate a good deal of information that a child reader could absorb almost without realizing it. With rare judgement, she gauged just how much to present to the 8–12 age group who are Miss Pickerell's audience. A clear picture in bold outline, rather than a mass of confusing and discouraging detail, is most apt to appeal to and instruct that active age group.

And such diverse information is provided! Simple but sound explanations of weightlessness in space travel, atomic energy and carbon 14 testing, nuclear-powered submarines and the continental shelf, the "bends" afflicting divers who surface too rapidly—there seems no end to it. Just as there is no end to the curiosity and enthusiasm of the young readers who love Miss Pickerell.

MacGregor herself completed only four of these well-loved books before her early death; but most fortunately for her eager young public she left boxes of notes and plans for further Miss Pickerell adventures. In the sympathetic hands of Dora Pantell, faithful to the spirit of the original works, Miss Pickerell continues to learn and to teach.

—Joan McGrath

* * *

MacINTYRE, Elisabeth. Australian. Born in Sydney, New South Wales, 1 November 1916. Educated at Sydney Church of England Girls Grammar School; Bowral High School; art student at East Sydney Technical College. Worked in the Land Army during World War II. Married John Roy Eldershaw in 1951; one daughter. Designer, Lever's Advertising Agency, Lintas, 1937–42; freelance artist and feature writer, the *Age*, Melbourne, Sydney *Sunday Telegraph, Australian Woman's Weekly*, and the New South Wales Education Department *School Magazine*; devised and illustrated television cartoons for the Australian Broadcasting Commission. Recipient: Australian Children's Book Council Picture Book of the Year award, 1965; Australian Literature Board fellowship, 1973–76; Australia-Japan Foundation fellowship, 1977. Address: 2/3 Pacific Street, Bronte, New South Wales 2024, Australia.

PUBLICATIONS FOR CHILDREN (illustrated by the author)

Fiction

Ambrose Kangaroo: A Story That Never Ends.   Sydney, Consolidated Press, 1941; New York, Scribner, 1942.
The Handsome Duckling.   Sydney, Dawfox, 1944.
The Black Lamb.   Sydney, Dawfox, 1944.
The Forgetful Elephant.   Sydney, Dawfox, 1944.
The Willing Donkey.   Sydney, Dawfox, 1944.
Ambrose Kangaroo Has a Busy Day.   Sydney, Consolidated Press, 1944.
Jane Likes Pictures.   New York, Scribner, and London, Collins, 1959.
Ambrose Kangaroo Goes to Town.   Sydney and London, Angus and Robertson, 1964.
Hugh's Zoo.   New York, Knopf, and London, Constable, 1964.
Ninji's Magic, illustrated by Mamoru Funai.   New York, Knopf, 1966; London, Angus and Robertson, 1967.
The Purple Mouse.   Nashville, Nelson, 1975.
It Looks Different When You Get There.   Sydney and London, Hodder and Stoughton, 1978.
Ambrose Kangaroo Delivers the Goods.   Sydney, Angus and Robertson, 1978.
A Wonderful Way to Learn the Language.   Sydney and London, Hodder and Stoughton, 1982.

Plays

Radio Serials: *The Riddle of Rum Jungle*, 1957; *The Kings of Corroboree Plains*, 1960.

Verse

Susan, Who Lives in Australia.   New York, Scribner, 1944; as *Katherine*, Sydney, Australasian Publishing Company, and London, Harrap, 1946; revised edition, Sydney and London, Angus and Robertson, 1958.
Mr. Koala Bear.   New York, Scribner, 1954; London, Angus and Robertson, 1966.
The Affable, Amiable Bulldozer Man.   New York, Knopf, 1965; London, Angus and Robertson, 1966.

Other

Willie's Woollies: The Story of Australian Wool.   Melbourne, Georgian House, 1951.

*

Manuscript Collections: Mitchell Library, Sydney; Lu Rees Collection, Canberra College of Advanced Education.

Illustrator: *Three Cheers for Piggy Grunter* by Noreen Shelley, 1959; *The Story House* by Ruth Fenner, 1960.

Elisabeth MacIntyre comments:

Simple and lighthearted as my books may be, they are a sincere attempt to say something I really believe in. A straight book about conservation might seem dull, but, as I see it, my *Affable, Amiable Bulldozer Man* sums up the whole subject painlessly. And a book about someone coping with a disability could be depressing; but I like to think that, in *The Purple Mouse*, it can still be a wryly amusing account of rising above problems that might seem insurmountable if the girl hadn't been too worried about other things to worry about them.

At first I wrote and illustrated picture books, using words sparingly. Now less interested in how things look, and more concerned in how they seem to *be*, I write full-length books, not so much for children, more for young adults—they seem to be becoming younger every year.

* * *

Elisabeth MacIntyre's reputation was made initially through her picture books, which she wrote and illustrated. Of these *Susan* (published in Australia and Britain as *Katherine*), a straightforward, amusing, uncomplicated description of a little girl "who lives in Australia/With her toys and her pets and her paraphernalia" has proved to have the most universal and lasting appeal. Two later picture books, *Hugh's Zoo* (a runner-up for the Australian Children's Book of the Year award) and *The Affable, Amiable Bulldozer Man* were produced during the 1960's, when public awareness of nature conservation was being very actively stirred; both have this "message" to put across, and neither has quite the same sense of gaiety and fun as *Katherine*. The author's first full-length novel (for the 8–11 age group) was *Ninji's Magic*, a well-coordinated story set in contemporary New Guinea. The theme, sensitively handled, is the reaction of a primitive, superstitious village community to the introduction of a school and the white man's education, exemplified in the clash, subsequently resolved, between the boy, Ninji, and his grandfather. The considerable background research behind this work is excellently assimilated.

In *The Purple Mouse* (for the 10–13 age group), the author tackles with empathy the problem of deafness, a subject with which she is personally familiar, and which she had wanted to write about for a long time. She shows how a teenage girl begins to overcome this handicap, and cope with the inevitable social problems it brings. The story is laced with a keen sense of humour—an ingredient so often missing from "social problem" novels.

More recently, MacIntyre has turned to the older teenage audience: *It Looks Different When You Get There* is concerned with a heroine who decides against an abortion for her illegitimate child. Again, the narrative is striking for its gentle humour and the heroine's own sense of the ridiculous, as well as the compassion with which the author develops this situation. This book demonstrates the most significant development of MacIntyre's skill.

—Barbara Ker Wilson

MACKAY, Claire (née Bacchus). Canadian. Born in Toronto, Ontario, 21 December 1930. Educated at Jarvis Collegiate Institute, graduated 1948; University of Toronto, 1948–52, B.A. (honours) in political science and economics 1952; University of British Columbia, Vancouver, 1968–69; University of Manitoba, Winnipeg, certificate in rehabilitation counselling 1971. Married Jackson F. Mackay in 1952; three sons. Library assistant, Polysar Corporation, Sarnia, Ontario, 1952–55; medical social worker, Wascana Hospital, Regina, Saskatchewan, 1969–71; research librarian, Steelworkers' Union, Toronto, 1972–78. Since 1978 freelance researcher and writer. Visiting writer, John Wanless School, Toronto, 1986, and Toronto libraries, 1987. Since 1986 consultant, Houghton Mifflin Canada. Member of Board of Directors, Children's Book Centre, Toronto, 1985–89. Recipient: Ontario Arts Council grant, 1980, 1983, 1984, 1985, 1986, 1989; Ruth Schwartz award, 1982; Vicky Metcalf award, for body of work, 1983, for short story, 1988. Address: 6 Frank Crescent, Toronto, Ontario M6G 3K5, Canada.

PUBLICATIONS FOR CHILDREN

Fiction

Mini-Bike Hero, illustrated by Merle Smith. Richmond Hill, Ontario, Scholastic, 1974.
Mini-Bike Racer, illustrated by Merle Smith. Richmond Hill, Ontario, Scholastic, 1976.
Exit Barney McGee, illustrated by David Simpson. Richmond Hill, Ontario, Scholastic, 1979.
One Proud Summer, with Marsha Hewitt. Toronto, Women's Educational Press, 1981.
Mini-Bike Rescue. Richmond Hill, Ontario, Scholastic, 1982.
The Minerva Program. Toronto, Lorimer, 1984; Oxford, Oxford University Press, 1987.

Other

Pay Cheques and Picket Lines: All About Unions in Canada. Toronto, Kids Can Press, 1987.

*

Claire Mackay comments:

I got into the field of children's writing almost by accident (the first novel was written for my son) and have continued because people (publishers and kids) keep asking me to write books. I have tried, I think, to be faithful to a pair of comments in my earliest letters from children: "I like your stories because you put all the adventures in at the right time"; and "You're on our side!"

* * *

In her six novels for young teenagers, Claire Mackay draws on her own experiences as a child growing up in an active and radical political family, as the mother of three boys, and as a social worker and counsellor. The joy of riding mini-bikes across the Canadian prairies, the dilemmas of relating to parents, and the traumas of discovering the economic forces of adult life are described in her stories with the realism of one who has been there as either teenager or adult.

Mackay's first novel, *Mini-Bike Hero*, reveals her considerable strengths as a writer for young adults. The 12-year-old hero Steve MacPherson must hide his new love of riding mini-bikes from his father, who is still grieving over the death of his own brother, killed years ago in a motorcycle accident. From a motorcycle shop owner, who had lost his son, Steve learns the skills of his new hobby, but must confront the moral dilemmas his secrecy creates. The book clearly delineates the character conflicts of the hero, joyfully describes the pleasures of riding, and adds just enough adventure to make it a thoroughly satisfying novel. Unfortunately, two sequels— *Mini-Bike Racer*, about the conflicts between Steve and his friend Kim, and *Mini-Bike Rescue*, the story of the adventures of the boys' friend Julie, sent to Ontario to learn to become more "lady-like"— rely too heavily on such plot thrillers as kidnapping by a bank robber and a motorcycle rescue from an attacking bear.

Set in the metropolis of Toronto, *Exit Barney McGee* and *The Minerva Program* focus on the inner struggles of two troubled young adolescents. In the former, Barney McGee runs away to Toronto to escape his mother's new husband and their new baby and to search for his father, who he discovers is a down-and-out alcoholic. In the latter, Minerva is at the point of raising her self-confidence by becoming a member of the school's computer club when she is accused of altering the grades of herself and her friends. In the struggle to prove her innocence, she also learns of the tensions and fears of her mother. In both books, the process of maturing involves not only facing the truth about oneself but also the real characters of one's parents.

Set in 1946 in an industrial town in Quebec, *One Proud Summer* (written with Marsha Hewitt) describes 13-year-old Lucille's growing involvement in a textile worker's strike. While the fears of the heroine and the intolerable conditions of the laborers are vividly described, the authors present the management and owners as stereotypes, with some characters becoming stage villains.

Although her plots are sometimes melodramatic, with events seeming contrived devices to increase reader excitement rather than to reveal and develop character, Mackay's books, in their clear and sympathetic portrayal of young teenage boys and girls facing the difficult choices involved in growing up, have justly earned a place as important Canadian novels about contemporary life.

—Jon C. Stott

MACKAY, Constance D'Arcy. American. Born in St. Paul, Minnesota. Educated at Boston University, 1903–04. Married Roland Holt in 1923 (died 1931). Director of Pageantry and Drama, War Camp Community Service, 1918–19. *Died 21 August 1966.*

PUBLICATIONS FOR CHILDREN

Plays

The Queen of Hearts (produced Boston, 1904).
The House of the Heart and Other Plays (includes *The Goose-herd and the Goblin, The Enchanted Garden, Nimble-Wit and Fingerkin, A Little Pilgrim's Progress, A Pageant of Hours, On Christmas Eve, The Elf Child, The Princess and the Pixies, The Christmas Guest*). New York, Holt, 1909.
The Silver Thread and Other Folk Plays (includes *The Forest Spring, The Foam Maiden, Troll Magic, The Three Wishes, A Brewing of Brains, Siegfried, The Snow Witch*). New York, Holt, 1910.
The Pageant of Patriotism (also director: produced Brooklyn, New York, 1911).
Patriotic Plays and Pageants for Young People (includes *Pageant of Patriots* [*Princess Pocahontas; George Washington's Fortune; Daniel Boone, Patriot; Benjamin Franklin, Journeyman; The Boston Tea Party; Abraham Lincoln, Rail Splitter*] and *The Hawthorne Pageant* [*Merrymount* and *In Witchcraft Days*]). New York, Holt, 1912.
The Pageant of Schenectady (also director: produced Schenectady,

New York, 1912). Schenectady, New York, Gazette Press, 1912.
The Historical Pageant of Portland, Maine, music by Will C. Macfarlane (also director: produced Portland, 1913). Portland, Southworth, 1913.
The Beau of Bath and Other One-Act Plays of Eighteenth-Century Life (includes *The Silver Lining, Ashes of Roses, Gretna Green, Counsel Retained, The Prince of Court Painters*). New York, Holt, 1915; London, Dent, 1924.
Plays of the Pioneers (includes *The Pioneers, The Fountain of Youth, May-Day, The Vanishing Race, The Passing of Hiawatha, Dame Greel o' Portland Town*). New York, Harper, 1915.
William of Stratford: Shakespeare's Tercentenary Pageant (produced Baltimore, 1916).
The Forest Princess and Other Masques (includes *The Gift of Time, A Masque of Conservation, The Masque of Pomona, A Masque of Christmas, The Sun Goddess*). New York, Holt, 1916.
Memorial Day Pageant. New York, Harper, 1916.
Pageant of Sunshine and Shadow (produced New York, 1916). Included in *Youth's Highway and Other Plays*, 1929.
Patriotic Christmas Pageant (produced San Francisco, 1918).
Victory Pageant (produced New York, 1918).
Franklin. New York, Holt, 1921.
America Triumphant: A Pageant of Patriotism. New York, Appleton, 1926.
Youth's Highway and Other Plays (includes *In the Days of Piers Ploughman, A Calendar of Joyful Saints, The Pageant of Sunshine and Shadow, The First Noël*). New York, Holt, 1929.
Midsummer Eve: An Outdoor Fantasy (in verse). New York and London, French, 1929.
Ladies of the White House. Boston, Baker, 1948.
A Day at Nottingham: A Festival at Which All the Playgrounds of a City Can Take Part. New York, National Recreational Association, 1952.

PUBLICATIONS FOR ADULTS

Other

Costumes and Scenery for Amateurs. New York, Holt, 1915; revised edition, 1932.
How to Produce Children's Plays. New York, Holt, 1915.
The Little Theatre in the United States. New York, Holt, 1917.
Patriotic Drama in Your Town: A Manual of Suggestions. New York, Holt, 1918.
Play Production in Churches and Sunday Schools. New York, Playground and Recreation Association of America, 1921.
Rural Drama Bibliography. New York, Playground and Recreation Association of America, n.d.

Editor, *Suggestions for the Dramatic Celebration of the 300th Anniversary of the Purchase of Manhattan, 1626–1926.* New York, Playground and Recreation Association of America, 1926.

*   *   *

Constance D'Arcy Mackay was a notable early advocate and writer of community and children's drama in the United States. Also a seasoned producer, she invariably accompanied her works with instructions for their production by community and school groups. Her productive writing career, extending from 1904 to 1952, encompassed a variety of dramatic forms from folk and history plays to pageant dramas and morality plays. Believing that youth yearns for the heroic and the wonderful, she peopled her dramas with leading characters who realize heroic and humane virtues by overcoming danger and difficulty.

Based on international folktales, *The Silver Thread and Other Folk Plays* presents seven durable dramas marked by quaint superstitions and homely truths. Typical is *The Foam Maiden*, a Celtic tale in which a fisherman boy suffers retribution from capturing a mermaid. Through the other well-wrought plays march Cornish goblins, Norwegian trolls, and other creatures to captivate the youthful spectator. The plays are masterfully filled with sprightly characters and situations.

Less durable dramatic types in the Mackay canon are the morality play and the masque. Both intermix allegorical and human figures, and accent a moral. Examples of the morality play are found in a collection of 10 short verse plays, *The House of the Heart and Other Plays*. Masques, which add the element of spectacle and the intent of outdoor production, appear in *The Forest Princess and Other Masques*. Representative of the short plays contained there is *A Masque of Conservation* in which forest spirits persuade a young land owner not to sell his forest to callous woodcutters. In both anthologies the plays are imaginatively written, even if somewhat locked into their own time.

Two collections of Mackay's pageant plays reveal another aspect of her writing. Although many of the short plays were originally conceived as episodes in historical pageants (a form which recreated events in a community's past for a particular occasion), they can stand independently. *Plays of the Pioneers* embraces plays ranging in subject from western pioneers and Indians to a patriotic New England tavern mistress of 1775. *Patriotic Plays and Pageants for Young People* offers short dramas focusing on the youth of American notables like Washington, Franklin, Lincoln, and Daniel Boone, and encompassing groups like the Pilgrims and Puritans. Generally well-structured, the dramas convincingly revivify historical periods and figures.

Exemplifying the author's best biography dramas are *Franklin*, a full-length play credibly showing its hero's development from printer's apprentice to statesman, and *The Beau of Bath and Other One-Act Plays of Eighteenth-Century Life*, a collection of six short verse plays set in England and treating such personages as Edmund Burke, the actresses Kitty Clive and Peg Woffington, and the author Fanny Burney. The high quality of the dialogue and the characterizations, and the vivid credibility of the period created in these plays are theatrical strengths.

Mackay's dramas display worthy content and literary quality, imaginative theatricality, and a respect for the intelligence of the young. That her dramas are not produced today does not diminish their worth and their historical influence. She stands tall as an early leader in her field.

—Christian H. Moe

MACKEN, Walter (Augustine). Irish. Born in Galway, 3 May 1915. Educated at Presentation Convent National School and Patrician Brothers' Secondary School, Galway. Married Margaret Mary Kenny in 1936; two sons. Member, Taibhdhearc, Gaelic-language theatre, Galway, 1932–36, and actor, manager, and producer, 1939–48; insurance salesman, London, 1937–38; actor, 1948–51, government representative on Board of Directors, and assistant manager and artistic adviser, 1965 (resigned 1966), Abbey Theatre, Dublin. Full-time writer and occasional actor, 1951–64. *Died 22 April 1967.*

PUBLICATIONS FOR CHILDREN

Fiction

Island of the Great Yellow Ox, illustrated by Charles Keeping.

London, Macmillan, and New York, Macmillan, 1966.
The Flight of the Doves. London, Macmillan, and New York, Macmillan, 1968.

Play

Television Play: *Island of the Great Yellow Ox*, from his own story, 1972.

PUBLICATIONS FOR ADULTS

Novels

Quench the Moon. London, Macmillan, and New York, Viking Press, 1948.
I Am Alone. London, Macmillan, 1949.
Rain on the Wind. London, Macmillan, 1950; New York, Macmillan, 1951.
The Bogman. London, Macmillan, and New York, Macmillan, 1952.
Sunset on the Window-Panes. London, Macmillan, 1954; New York, St. Martin's Press, 1955.
Sullivan. London, Macmillan, and New York, Macmillan, 1957.
Seek the Fair Land. London, Macmillan, and New York, Macmillan, 1959.
The Silent People. London, Macmillan, and New York, Macmillan, 1962.
The Scorching Wind. London, Macmillan, and New York, Macmillan, 1964.
Brown Lord of the Mountain. London, Macmillan, 1967; as *Lord of the Mountain: A Novel of Ireland*, New York, Macmillan, 1967.

Short Stories

The Green Hills and Other Stories. London, Macmillan, and New York, St. Martin's Press, 1956.
God Made Sunday and Other Stories. London, Macmillan, and New York, Macmillan, 1962.
The Coll Doll and Other Stories. Dublin, Gill and Macmillan, and London, Macmillan, 1969.

Plays

Mungo's Mansion: A Play of Galway Life (produced Dublin, 1946; as *Galway Handicap*, produced London, 1947). London, Macmillan, 1947.
Vacant Possession (produced London, 1954). London, Macmillan, 1948.
Home Is the Hero (produced Dublin, 1952; New York, 1954). London, Macmillan, 1953.
Twilight of a Warrior (produced Dublin, 1955). London, Macmillan, 1956.
Look in the Looking Glass (produced Dublin, 1958).
The Voices of Doolan (produced Dublin, 1960).
Recall the Years (produced Dublin, 1966).

*

Manuscript Collection: University Library, Wuppertal, West Germany.

*   *   *

Walter Macken wrote only two books for children, *Island of the Great Yellow Ox* and *The Flight of the Doves.* Both show resourceful, ingenious yet innocent children in danger from wicked adults.

In *Island of the Great Yellow Ox* four boys become marooned on an island where Agnes, an archaeologist, and her husband, the Captain, are engaged in an obsessive search for a golden idol. Since the children know too much, the adults try to eliminate them. To the boys, the malice of the villains is incomprehensible, although they do share something of the excitement of the search. The problems of the youngsters are practical rather than psychological, and the account of their predicament is vivid and convincing. From our point of view, the villains are indeed explained, but their internal and mutual conflicts are not well integrated with the action of the book. Agnes is warped by her obsession and she manipulates the Captain through his guilt about drinking. We understand, but the boys, with whom we are invited to identify, do not.

If the story, to some degree, remains fantastic, the island setting, a favourite one with Macken, is firmly authentic and the natural enemies, such as storms, are more terrifying than the villains.

The Flight of the Doves is the more serious and satisfying work. Finn and Derval Dove flee across Ireland from their cruel stepfather to seek Granny. The chase allows Macken to diversify both the locations and the characters. Being themselves outside the law, the children are helped by others similarly placed. Uncle Toby, who has law on his side, is an outright villain, but most characters are capable of surprising. Mickser, a criminal, is kind to the children; Powder, a tinker, would betray them. Michael, an off-duty policeman who functions as a good fairy, is prepared to tread a legal tightrope.

The themes emerge from the interplay of character. With Finn we learn that appearances deceive, that law and justice are not necessarily identical. Most importantly, Macken explores the relationship between the rationally plausible and the intuitive. Finn inspires instinctive trust. He has a natural goodness and responsibility that certain adults lack, but he is saved from authorial idealisation to some degree by his unawareness of it. Character, in this book, is more of a piece with the action and there are splendid dramatic scenes. The final confrontation is well worthy of an author who was also a playwright.

Macken was able to observe and create the child mentality, to construct exciting narrative and to deploy a language which is direct and honest but whose terseness restrains him from overindulging his sentimental optimism.

—A.W. England

MacLACHLAN, Patricia. American. Born in Cheyenne, Wyoming. Married Robert MacLachlan; two sons and one daughter. Has taught English and creative writing. Lives in Leeds, Massachusetts. Recipient: Society of Children's Book Writers Golden Kite award, 1980; American Library Association Newbery Medal, 1986. Address: c/o Harper and Row, 10 East 53rd Street, New York, New York 10022, U.S.A.

PUBLICATIONS FOR CHILDREN

Fiction

Through Grandpa's Eyes, illustrated by Deborah Ray.   New York, Harper, 1980.
Arthur, For the Very First Time, illustrated by Lloyd Bloom.   New York, Harper, 1980.
Moon, Stars, Frogs, and Friends, illustrated by Tomie de Paola.   New York, Pantheon, 1980.

Mama One, Mama Two, illustrated by Ruth Lercher Bornstein.   New York, Harper, 1982.
Cassie Binegar.   New York, Harper, 1982.
Tomorrow's Wizard, illustrated by Kathy Jacobi.   New York, Harper, 1982.
Seven Kisses in a Row, illustrated by Maria Pia Marrella.   New York, Harper, 1983.
Unclaimed Treasures.   New York, Harper, 1984.
Sarah, Plain and Tall.   New York, Harper, 1985; London, MacRae, 1986.
The Facts and Fictions of Minna Pratt.   New York, Harper, 1988.

*   *   *

All of Patricia MacLachlan's work so far has been directed to children—not to young adults—and it shows a fine mastery of the difficult art of writing for preadolescents without flippancy, patronizing, or sentimentality. MacLachlan was a wife and a mother before she became a writer; her books are markedly autobiographical, for she feels a close connection not only to her own childhood and that of her children but, through anecdote and memory, to her family's past. "Just what is the magic," she has asked, "the literature or the life from which it grows?"

As a writer she began modestly with picture-book texts; two of them might have been dismissed as therapeutic problem novels in miniature, were it not for their calm, straightforward narrative tone. *Through Grandpa's Eyes* tells of a little boy's experiences with his blind grandfather—a sensory revelation of the way the elderly man ingeniously and independently manages to live an active and satisfying life. In *Mama One, Mama Two* a little girl is taken by a kindly social worker to live with a loving foster mother while her own unhappy mother is sent "to a place where doctors and nurses could help her."

But more important books were on the way. With a deep awareness of the child's instinctive resistance to change and healthy self-centeredness, MacLachlan views children not in isolation but in their close, though sometimes stormy, relationships with nurturing adults. Her first novel, *Arthur, For the Very First Time*, is centered on an observant, introspective, yet entirely believable child; and *Cassie Binegar* intensifies MacLachlan's theme of rebelliousness, growth, and acceptance. Both books gave early evidence of the author's originality, compassionate and non-didactic approach, droll humor, and carefully chastened yet fluent style. Already evident too was her preoccupation with intergenerational affinities and her idiosyncratic, unconventional characters.

MacLachlan's stories, unified by her recurring themes and underlying convictions, belong mainly in the realm of realism. Only once has the author created a sustained work of fantasy—*Tomorrow's Wizard*—which recounts five magical tales about a cranky wizard, his cheerful young apprentice, and a good-natured talking horse. Exhibiting again MacLachlan's inventiveness, structural skill, and lyrical, witty prose, the book is pure delight.

In *Unclaimed Treasures*, her longest, most complex, and multi-layered novel, a passionate 11-year-old girl full of grandiose notions about life and love struggles to distinguish between the ordinary and the extraordinary. The ebullient story rests on artless craftsmanship and imagistic writing—a celebration of abiding love, human uniqueness, and, incidentally, of art and music. Among other memories, one finds unforgettable the recurring presence of a pair of happily determined elderly ladies, sitting in the garden playing two parts of a Beethoven trio.

Contained in *Arthur, For the Very First Time* was a hint of the story of the Newbery Medal winner *Sarah, Plain and Tall*, a spare, exquisite, diminutive novel. Into a yearning motherless pioneer family living on the prairie comes a strong, independent, vibrant woman from the coast of Maine. According to the author, the book grew out of what her mother used to call "the heroics of a common life." In its subtle unfolding the story takes on an uncommon crystalline clarity and displays two paradoxes of true art—silences that speak more eloquently than words, and a profound simplicity, which here sets forth the intricacies of human relationships.

Music and eccentricity of character become even more prominent in *The Facts and Fictions of Minna Pratt*. In a slapdash but caring household, Minna's father is a psychologist, and her bemused mother a children's book writer who never asks, like other mothers, "Did you pass your math test? What did you have for lunch?" but rather, "Do you ever think of love?" or "What is the quality of beauty?" No one is concerned that Minna's younger brother sings—in public— the newspaper headlines, or that his friend Emily plays baseball wearing enormous dangly rhinestone earrings "shaped like chandeliers." And Minna, playing her cello and longing only for a proper vibrato, finds a soulmate in the radiant Lucas, who has not only a fine, professional vibrato on the viola but also a well-hidden collection of frogs. Here MacLachlan wonderfully transmutes the ordinary into the extraordinary. And although the book is full of delicious madness and Mozart, it is also full of the clear-eyed honesty and deep wisdom that characterize her other stories about children teetering on the edge of growing up.

—Ethel L. Heins

———

MacPHERSON, Margaret (née McLean). British. Born in Colinton, Midlothian, 29 June 1908. Educated privately in Edinburgh; at Edinburgh University, 1926–29, M.A. Married Duncan MacPherson in 1929 (died 1971); seven sons. Member, Commission of Inquiry into Crofting, Inverness, 1951–54. Since 1960 honorary secretary, Skye Labour Party; since 1970 member, Highlands and Islands Development Council. Agent: David Fletcher, 57 John Street, Penicuik, Midlothian EH26 8AL. Address: Ardrannach, Torvaig, Portree, Isle of Skye, Scotland.

PUBLICATIONS FOR CHILDREN

Fiction

The Shinty Boys, illustrated by Shirley Hughes. London, Collins, and New York, Harcourt Brace, 1963.
The Rough Road, illustrated by Douglas Hall. London, Collins, 1965; New York, Harcourt Brace, 1966.
Ponies for Hire, illustrated by Sheila Rose. London, Collins, and New York, Harcourt Brace, 1967.
The New Tenants, illustrated by Shirley Hughes. London, Collins, and New York, Harcourt Brace, 1968.
The Battle of the Braes, illustrated by Gavin Rowe. London, Collins, 1972.
The Boy on the Roof, illustrated by Charles Front. London, Collins, 1974.

*

Margaret MacPherson comments:
I had always wanted to write a book. As a young girl I scribbled away but never had anything published. I married a crofter and was too busy rearing a large family of boys to do any writing. But I had not forgotten my ambition, and when the boys were well on their way to being grown up, I started to write once again.

*   *   *

Margaret MacPherson tells a galloping story, both in action and feeling. Wisely, she sticks to her own home ground, the Gaelic speaking and politically conscious—meaning, in the Highlands, history-conscious—Isle of Skye. The boy and girl characters are well and truly in the adult world of dealings and quarrels, deceits and jealousies, or equally passionate loyalties, over croft land, cattle beasts, houses, as well as rights and prejudices—though I doubt if MacPherson has ever plumbed the darkest depths of the Free Churches! The children are on the whole—and this is true to life—quite a lot nicer than the grownups, though no little angels, and they see just as clearly the astonishing beauty of the landscape or equally astonishing grimness.

MacPherson knows the detail of crofting life, the heavy weight of the peat creel, the dividing up of the small catch of fish, handling sheep at the dipping, cooking, milking, and folk crowding into the low rooms of the black houses: "We never opened windows. Fresh air was a thing to be kept outside." Much is done through conversation, and here the Gaelic grammar and idiom underlying English speech in the Highlands are beautifully done.

In *The Battle of the Braes*, based on real happenings, there is a delicate shift into the narrative of a completely Gaelic speaker of the turbulent 1880's, turned into English but giving a genuine insight into another culture with a somewhat different—dare one say better?—set of values. MacPherson could probably write an equally exciting, close-knit yarn with an English background, but if so her young readers would lose the feeling of having for a while lived somewhere else and having taken part in its vivid and active life. There are plenty of Skye stories to be told yet, and she is the one to tell them.

—Naomi Mitchison

———

MacVICAR, Angus. British. Born in Argyll, Scotland, 28 October 1908. Educated at Campbeltown Grammar School, 1920–26; Glasgow University, 1926–30, M.A. 1930. Served in the Royal Scots Fusiliers, 1940–45: Captain; mentioned in despatches. Married Jean Smith McKerral in 1936; one son. Reporter and assistant editor, Campbeltown *Courier*, 1931–33. Honorary Sheriff Substitute of Argyll, 1967. Litt.D.: Stirling University, 1988. Agent: A.M. Heath, 79 St. Martin's Lane, London WC2N 4AA, England. Address: Achnamara, Southend, Campbeltown, Argyll PA28 6RW, Scotland.

PUBLICATIONS FOR CHILDREN

Fiction

The Crocodile Men. London, Art and Educational, 1948.
The Black Wherry. London, Foley House Press, 1948.
Faraway Island, illustrated by Denis Alford. London, Foley House Press, 1949.
King Abbie's Adventure, illustrated by James Clark. London, Burke, 1950.
Stubby Sees It Through, illustrated by Lunt Roberts. London, Burke, 1950.
The Grey Pilot. London, Burke, 1951.
Tiger Mountain, illustrated by Jack Matthew. London, Burke, 1952.
The Lost Planet. London, Burke, 1953.
Return to the Lost Planet. London, Burke, 1954.
Dinny Smith Comes Home. London, Burke, 1955.
Secret of the Lost Planet. London, Burke, 1955.

The Atom Chasers. London, Burke, 1956.
The Atom Chasers in Tibet. London, Burke, 1957.
Satellite 7. London, Burke, 1958.
Red Fire on the Lost Planet. London, Burke, 1959.
Peril on the Lost Planet. London, Burke, 1960.
Space Agent from the Lost Planet. London, Burke, 1961.
Space Agent and the Isles of Fire. London, Burke, 1962; New York, Roy, 1963.
Kilpatrick, Special Reporter. London, Burke, 1963.
The High Cliffs of Kersivay, illustrated by Douglas Relf. London, Harrap, 1964.
Space Agent and the Ancient Peril. London, Burke, 1964.
Life-Boat—Green to White, illustrated by Paul Sharp. Leicester, Brockhampton Press, 1965.
The Kersivay Kraken, illustrated by Douglas Relf. London, Harrap, 1966.
The Cave of the Hammers, illustrated by Hilary Abrahams. London, Kaye and Ward, 1968.
Super Nova and the Rogue Satellite [*Frozen Man*]. Leicester, Brockhampton Press, 2 vols., 1969–70.

Plays

Radio Plays: has adapted 19 of his books into radio serials.

Television Plays: *The Lost Planet*, and *Return to the Lost Planet*, from his own stories.

Other

Let's Visit Scotland. London, Burke, 1966; revised edition, with John C. Caldwell, New York, Day, 1967.
Rescue Call: The Story of the Life-Boatmen. London, Kaye and Ward, 1967.

PUBLICATIONS FOR ADULTS

Novels

The Purple Rock. London, Stanley Paul, 1933.
Death by the Mistletoe. London, Stanley Paul, 1934.
The Screaming Gull. London, Stanley Paul, 1935.
The Temple Falls. London, Stanley Paul, 1935.
The Ten Green Brothers. London, Stanley Paul, 1936.
The Cavern. London, Stanley Paul, 1936.
Flowering Death. London, Stanley Paul, 1937.
The Crooked Finger. London, Stanley Paul, 1937.
Crime's Masquerader. London, Stanley Paul, 1938.
The Singing Spider. London, Stanley Paul, 1938.
11 for Danger. London, Stanley Paul, 1939.
Strangers from the Sea. London, Stanley Paul, 1939.
The Crouching Spy. London, Stanley Paul, 1941.
Commodore Norah. London, Pemberton, 1942.
Death on the Machar. London, Stanley Paul, 1947.
The Other Man. London, Pemberton, 1947.
Greybreak. London, Stanley Paul, 1947.
Fugitive's Road. London, Stanley Paul, 1949.
Escort to Adventure. London, Stanley Paul, 1952.
The Dancing Horse. London, Long, 1961.
The Killings on Kersivay. London, Long, 1962.
The Hammers of Fingal. London, Long, 1963.
The Grey Shepherds. London, Long, 1964.
Murder at the Open. London, Long, 1965.
The Canisbay Conspiracy. London, Long, 1966.
Night on the Killer Reef. London, Long, 1967.

Maniac. London, Long, 1969.
Duel in Glenfinnan. London, Long, 1969.
The Golden Venus Affair. London, Long, 1972.
The Painted Doll Affair. London, Long, 1973.

Plays

Minister's Monday. Galashiels, Selkirk, McQueen, 1957.
Final Proof. Glasgow, Brown and Ferguson, 1958.
Mercy Flight. Glasgow, Brown and Ferguson, 1959.
Storm Tide. Glasgow, Brown and Ferguson, 1960.
Under Suspicion. Glasgow, Brown and Ferguson, 1962.
Stranger at Christmas. Glasgow, Brown and Ferguson, 1964.

Radio Plays: *The Singing Spider, Strangers from the Sea, The Dancing Horse, The Hammers of Fingal, The Canisbay Conspiracy*, and *Night on Killer Reef*, from his own novels; *The Four Green Feathers; The Dragon Star; Murray of the Mercy Flight; The Glens of Glendale* series, 1954–59.

Television Series: *Confessions of a Minister's Son*, 1965–70.

Other

Salt in My Porridge: Confessions of a Minister's Son. London, Jarrolds, 1971.
Heather in My Ears: More Confessions of a Minister's Son. London, Hutchinson, 1974.
Rocks in My Scotch: Still More Confessions of a Minister's Son. London, Hutchinson, 1977.
Silver in My Sporran: Confessions of a Writing Man. London, Hutchinson, 1979.
Bees in My Bonnet. London, Hutchinson, 1982.
Golf in My Gallowses: Confessions of a Fairway Fanatic. London, Hutchinson, 1983.
Gremlins in My Garden: Confessions of a Harassed Horticulturalist. London, Hutchinson, 1985.
Capers in My Kirk: Confessions of a Would-Be Christian. London, Hutchinson, 1987.

*

Angus MacVicar comments:

I found myself with one talent—the ability to tell a story. For over half a century I have been trying hard to develop it.

*   *   *

Angus MacVicar's range is wide, including schoolboy stories, adventure tales, and science fiction. It is perhaps unfortunate that, in Britain at least, his books are out of print.

The Grey Pilot is based on a true story about Bonnie Prince Charlie's adventure after the Battle of Culloden but it is, as the author states, an adventure story, not an historical work, and the exciting part of the book is certainly the account of how Donald McLeod, the Grey Pilot, and his son Murdoch became involved in helping the Prince to escape. As in that book, so too in books like *Stubby Sees It Through* and *Kilpatrick, Special Reporter* the author is at his best when involved in fast-moving adventure with plenty of action and dialogue and with the characters only lightly sketched. The settings vary, Scotland frequently but sometimes abroad, but the approach is predictable—a group of characters, united in their love for adventure and mystery solving, lots of fast-moving action, plenty of dialogue, and a minimum of descriptive writing, all of which result in books which appeal to many children.

Oddly enough, it is in his science-fiction books that MacVicar produces his most descriptive writing both of scenery and human beings—"the red, pear-shaped fruit on the trees, growing upwards like fat candle-sticks, the salmon-pink rocks, sharp and unweathered like crystal, the green turf that was composed not of grass, but of fine spongy moss." It is almost as if his concentration on the scientific aspect of these books has sharpened his awareness of the countryside and its people. His characterisations are sharper, more clearly defined, and much better developed. These are the kind of people who *could* be going on rocket flights.

Since it is many years since the Lost Planet books were written and present-day children are now quite blasé about moon flights, it is remarkable that MacVicar's science-fiction books still have the power to interest and excite. Familiarity with count-downs does not prevent the reader becoming quite tense as the moment of blast-off approaches. Obviously the author enjoyed writing these books and the challenge they presented brought forth his best writing. Although science fiction is not my favourite theme, I find MacVicar's handling of the subject quite rivetting and much more powerful than his other stories. The books pulsate with action and the atmosphere crackles with tension.

MacVicar is not a sophisticated writer but he is a worthy successor to his Highland forebears, a storyteller who knows the essence of good storytelling.

—Margaret Walker

MAGORIAN, Michelle. British. Address: c/o Viking Kestrel, 27 Wrights Lane, London W8 5TZ, England.

PUBLICATIONS FOR CHILDREN

Fiction

Goodnight, Mister Tom.   London, Kestrel, and New York, Harper, 1981.
Back Home.   New York, Harper, 1984; London, Kestrel, 1985.

* * *

Michelle Magorian is concerned solely with people and their emotions. From them everything else flows—plot, style, themes, and ideas. Her novels reach out and embrace her young readers, enfolding them in a deep, welcoming armchair of a story, with no artfully polished gloss or awkward spikes of incomprehension. No other contemporary British writer has quite her ability to bring a lump to the throat or produce that wistfully satisfied sigh as a book closes.

Goodnight, Mister Tom, a first novel that gathered both literary awards and top sales, was reputed to have reduced hardened typesetters to tears with its tale of a pathetically cowed eight-year-old boy evacuated from London's East End in the first year of the war and billeted on a crusty old widower, and of the unexpected love and warmth of mutual dependence that comes to them both. The framework of plot is minimal: the child arrives, gradually settles into a near-idyllic rural scene, returns to the horrors of his old life when his mother demands it, and is rescued by the old man. What interests Magorian are the motives, emotions, and relationships of her characters, set into the (carefully researched) domestic detail of their daily lives. Willie Beech—a deliberately young "green" name, contrasted with the sturdy old countryman's "brown" Tom Oakley—has to work through his terror, insecurity, and, when his young, exuberantly alive friend is killed in an air raid, his grief, to emerge with a mature,

forward-looking confidence. Certain harrowing scenes, when Willie's mother, a guilt-ridden religious psychopath, is driven by an inner torment to savage brutality, seemed to some reviewers and parents strong meat for under-12s, but the gut response of children everywhere has proved Magorian's instinct to be right.

Back Home offers something of a mirror image of that first novel, but with less raw, uninhibited feelings. Another evacuee, a 12-year-old girl, returns to a grey, ration-book England after five years with a loving surrogate family in Vermont; she is homesick for a place she should not consider home, lonely and isolated, misinterpreting those around her and cruelly misunderstood by others. Not cowed like Willie, Rusty is a proud, tough little New World spirit clashing with a socially rigid and war-weary Old World. Rusty's mother, like Tom Oakley, has to learn a new love and a new self-image, and Rusty, like Willie, battles through bitter heartbreak and darkness into sunshine. Both books studiously capture the England of the 1940's—its authoritarianism, its class-consciousness, the new hope it gave girls and women to reach for personal fulfilment—but simply, through speech and character, never as abstract concepts.

Long but luxuriantly flowing and easy to read, Magorian's novels are the sort of books to curl up with in an old-fashioned way, whose characters, though never without subtlety, demand to be loved or hated before asking to be understood. They have a cathartic emotional appeal that is hugely satisfying.

—Stephanie Nettell

MAGUIRE, Gregory.   American.   Born in Albany, New York, 9 June 1954. Educated at the State University of New York, Albany, 1972–76, B.A. 1976; Simmons College, Boston, 1977–78, M.A. 1978. English teacher, Vincentian Elementary School, Albany, 1976–77; staff member, 1979–83, and Associate Director and Assistant Professor, 1983–87, Center for the Study of Children's Literature, Simmons College, Boston. Recipient: Bread Loaf Writers' Conference fellowship, 1978; Blue Mountain Center fellowship, 1986, 1987, 1988, 1989. Address: 4 Hubbard Street, Jamaica Plain, Massachusetts 02130, U.S.A.

PUBLICATIONS FOR CHILDREN

Fiction

The Lightning Time.   New York, Farrar Straus, 1978; London, Chatto and Windus, 1979.
The Daughter of the Moon.   New York, Farrar Straus, 1980.
Lights on the Lake.   New York, Farrar Straus, 1981.
The Dream Stealer.   New York, Harper, 1983.
I Feel Like the Morning Star.   New York, Harper, 1989.
The Peace and Quiet Diner, illustrated by David Perry.   New York, Parents' Magazine Press, 1989.

PUBLICATIONS FOR ADULTS

Other

Editor, with Barbara Harrison, *Innocence and Experience: Essays and Conversations on Children's Literature.*   New York, Lothrop, 1987.

*

Manuscript Collection: Kerlan Collection, University of Minnesota, Minneapolis.

Gregory Maguire comments:

While a number of my books are set in the Adirondack mountains of upstate New York, which is not far from where I was born and raised, I think that the magic of a particular geographical place is only part of the compulsion which sets me writing. The other part—to the extent I can identify it—is rooted in a fascination for the healing and prophetic power of both poetry and dreams. There are sections of each one of my books which were suggested by my own dreams; also, I often read poetry before sitting down to write—it helps magnify my sympathies and focus my intentions.

*   *   *

Gregory Maguire is a fantasy writer, whose early work uses the traditions of British fantasy writing for the young, in American settings. His first novel, *The Lightning Time*, is highly derivative, yet crisp and fresh in execution. It is suffused with a pantheistic sense of the sacredness of beautiful places, in this case a mountainside overlooking Canaan Lake, in New York State, where young Daniel Rider has been sent to stay with his grandmother. The story contains magic lightning, a walking stone lion from Europe talking beasts, an episode in which the hero and heroine change sizes and enter the burrow of "a small furry animal," a very well-worn and implausible story line—children and Grandma defeat wicked developer—and a surprise ending—Daniel's "cousin," his companion in adventure, is really an apparition from the past, his grandmother as a child—a motif which bears more than a passing resemblance to Philippa Pearce's *Tom's Midnight Garden*. For all its faults, *The Lightning Time* is full of promise and the author's evident delight in his material; Maguire is already well able technically and stylistically to achieve his effects.

Lights on the Lake, Maguire's third book, returns to Canaan Lake and Daniel Rider. Unhampered this time by stage villains imposed by the plot, the book offers the loving and witty evocation both of the landscape and the small-town community in which Daniel is now living, and the process of making friends and settling in. There is a strong fantasy element in the story, in which Daniel is drawn into the dreams of neighbours, and into danger on the frozen lake. In the heart of the story is a traumatized poet, Nikos Griskas, dumped on the doorstep of a retreat house in the village, and acting like a zombie. Nobody knows how to help Nikos. The answer lies in the strange lights that play uncannily on the lake and suspend time, freezing even leaf fall while they last.

Between these two titles came *The Daughter of the Moon*, set in an ugly street in Chicago, where Erikka makes friends with a bookshop owner and a boy from an orphanage. Her family life is crowded and desperately humdrum, and the bookshop is a refuge for her. When she annoys some customers (a wicked rich couple) the bookshop is threatened, and a plot concerning the theft and retheft of an autographed copy of Walt Whitman's poems is set in motion. Another thread of the story concerns a watercolour landscape, painted for her by her aunt, into which she can step, to be transported to Canaan Lake. This space-shift fantasy leads to the reuniting of the bookseller and his long lost sweetheart.

At this stage Maguire's scope seemed predictable; he was a charming writer, full of human warmth and exuberance, deeply attached to a single place, and a little liable to preciosity. Nobody could have expected *The Dream Stealer*. Robust, touching, funny, and profound, *The Dream Stealer* is the work of a writer finding his voice, and putting not a foot wrong. As in his earlier work he happily raids earlier literature for elements of the story, which makes liberal use of Russian folktale. As in his earlier work a wonderfully detailed, warm, and humorous picture of a little community, young and old,

bright and grumpy, emerges. And this time there is a powerful story line both magical—what does the terrible wolf want?—and realistic—how will the village survive the winter if the trains don't bring passengers to buy their goods, because the wolf is scaring everyone away? As well as the wit and skill of the narrator there is an underlying resonant meditation on the meaning of dreams, memory, and desire.

With *I Feel Like the Morning Star* Maguire has changed tack. Although it is set in the future, in a fallout shelter, it is the first of his books not to involve any element of fantasy in the plot. In a mode deeply unlike most science fiction, the interest of this book is entirely in the portrayal of character, this time of three teenagers, two boys and a girl, living in a community under stress. Their lives are regulated by a committee supposedly democratic, but actually getting above itself; those who ask questions are "treated" to silence them. The oppression is doubly sinister because the committee is probably well-meaning. Nobody knows what is happening above ground. Among the imprisoned is a one-time campaigning folk singer, who won't sing. In an extraordinary climax the singer sings at last, while the teenagers acting pied piper to a group of children escape pursuit and emerge above ground to find themselves gazing at a living tree. The whiff of whimsy and of implausibility that weakened Maguire's early work has entirely disappeared, and *I Feel Like the Morning Star* is powerful and authoritative; his belief in the central importance of dreams and of story-telling is now openly articulated.

Maguire's talents now look unpredictable: formidable and still developing.

—Jill Paton Walsh

———

MAHY, Margaret. New Zealander. Born in Whakatane, 21 March 1936. Educated at the University of Auckland, B.A. 1957, Diploma of Librarianship 1958. Has two daughters. Assistant librarian, Petone Public Library, 1958–59; librarian, School Library Service, Christchurch, 1967–76. Since 1976 children's librarian, Canterbury Public Library, Christchurch. Recipient: New Zealand Library Association Esther Glen award, 1970, 1973, 1983, 1985; New Zealand Literary Fund grant, 1975; British Library Association Carnegie Medal, 1983, 1985; *Observer* prize, 1987. Address: R.D.1, Lyttelton, New Zealand.

PUBLICATIONS FOR CHILDREN

Fiction

The Dragon of an Ordinary Family, illustrated by Helen Oxenbury. New York, Watts, and London, Heinemann, 1969.
A Lion in the Meadow, illustrated by Jenny Williams. New York, Watts, and London, Dent, 1969; augmented edition, as *A Lion in the Meadow and Five Other Favourites*, Dent, 1976.
Mrs. Discombobulous, illustrated by Jan Brychta. New York, Watts, and London, Dent, 1969.
Pillycock's Shop, illustrated by Carol Barker. New York, Watts, and London, Dobson, 1969.
The Procession, illustrated by Charles Mozley. New York, Watts, and London, Dent, 1969.
The Little Witch, illustrated by Charles Mozley. New York, Watts, and London, Dent, 1970.
Sailor Jack and the 20 Orphans, illustrated by Robert Bartelt. New York, Watts, and London, Dent, 1970.

The Princess and the Clown, illustrated by Carol Barker. New York, Watts, and London, Dobson, 1971.

The Boy with Two Shadows, illustrated by Jenny Williams. New York, Watts, and London, Dent, 1971.

The First [Second, Third] Margaret Mahy Story Book: Stories and Poems, illustrated by Shirley Hughes. London, Dent, 3 vols., 1972–75.

The Man Whose Mother Was a Pirate, illustrated by Brian Froud. London, Dent, 1972; New York, Atheneum, 1973.

The Railway Engine and the Hairy Brigands, illustrated by Brian Froud. London, Dent, 1973.

Rooms for Rent, illustrated by Jenny Williams. New York, Watts, 1974; as *Rooms to Let*, London, Dent, 1975.

The Witch in the Cherry Tree, illustrated by Jenny Williams. London, Dent, and New York, Parents' Magazine Press, 1974.

Clancy's Cabin, illustrated by Trevor Stubley. London, Dent, 1974.

The Rare Spotted Birthday Party, illustrated by Belinda Lyon. London, Watts, 1974.

Stepmother, illustrated by Terry Burton. London, Watts, 1974.

The Bus under the Leaves, illustrated by Margery Gill. London, Dent, 1975.

Ultra-Violet Catastrophe! or, The Unexpected Walk with Great-Uncle Magnus Pringle, illustrated by Brian Froud. London, Dent, and New York, Parents' Magazine Press, 1975.

The Great Millionaire Kidnap, illustrated by Jan Brychta. London, Dent, 1975.

The Boy Who Was Followed Home, illustrated by Steven Kellogg. New York, Watts, 1975; London, Dent, 1977.

Leaf Magic, illustrated by Jenny Williams. London, Dent, 1976; New York, Parents' Magazine Press, 1977.

The Wind Between the Stars, illustrated by Brian Froud. London, Dent, 1976.

David's Witch Doctor, illustrated by Jim Russell. London, Watts, 1976.

The Pirate Uncle, illustrated by Mary Dinsdale. London, Dent, 1977.

Nonstop Nonsense, illustrated by Quentin Blake. London, Dent, 1977; New York, McElderry, 1989.

The Great Piratical Rumbustification, and The Librarian and the Robbers, illustrated by Quentin Blake. London, Dent, 1978; Boston, Godine, 1986.

Raging Robots and Unruly Uncles, illustrated by Peter Stevenson. London, Dent, 1981.

The Haunting. London, Dent, 1982; New York, Atheneum, 1983.

The Great Chewing-Gum Rescue and Other Stories, illustrated by Jan Ormerod. London, Dent, 1982.

The Pirates' Mixed-Up Voyage, illustrated by Margaret Chamberlain. London, Dent, 1983.

The Changeover: A Supernatural Romance. London, Dent, and New York, Atheneum, 1984.

Leaf Magic and Five Other Favourites, illustrated by Margaret Chamberlain. London, Dent, 1984.

The Birthday Burglar, and A Very Wicked Headmistress, illustrated by Margaret Chamberlain. London, Dent, 1984; Boston, Godine, 1988.

Jam: A True Story, illustrated by Helen Craig. London, Dent, 1985; Boston, Atlantic Monthly Press, 1986.

The Catalogue of the Universe. London, Dent, 1985; New York, Atheneum, 1986.

The Downhill Crocodile Whizz and Other Stories, illustrated by Ian Newsham. London, Dent, 1986.

The Tricksters. London, Dent, 1986; New York, McElderry, 1987.

Aliens in the Family. London, Methuen, and New York, Scholastic, 1986.

Mahy Magic (short stories), illustrated by Shirley Hughes. London, Dent, 3 vols., 1986.

Memory. London, Dent, and New York, McElderry, 1987.

The Horrible Story and Others, illustrated by Shirley Hughes. London, Dent, 1987.

The Door in the Air and Other Stories, illustrated by Diana Catchpole. London, Dent, 1988.

The Blood and Thunder Adventure on Hurricane Peak, illustrated by Wendy Smith. London, Dent, 1989.

Plays

Television Scripts: *A Land Called Happy Woolly Valley; Once upon a Story; The Margaret Mahy Story Book Theatre.*

Verse

Seventeen Kings and Forty Two Elephants, illustrated by Charles Mozley. London, Dent, 1972; New York, Dial Press, 1987.

The Tin Can Band and Other Poems, illustrated by Honey de Lacey. London, Dent, 1989.

Other (readers)

Look under V, illustrated by Deirdre Gardiner. Wellington, Department of Education School Publications Branch, 1977.

The Crocodile's Christmas Sandals, illustrated by Deirdre Gardiner. Wellington, Department of Education School Publications Branch, 1982; as *The Crocodile's Christmas Thongs*, Melbourne, Nelson, 1985.

Story Chest Books (*Cooking Pot, Fast and Funny, Roly-Poly, Sing to the Moon, Tiddalik*), with Joy Cowley and June Melser, illustrated by Deirdre Gardiner, Lynette Vondruska, Jo Davies, Isabel Lowe, Annie Dickeson, Philip Webb, and others. Auckland, Shortland, and Leeds, Arnold Wheaton, 5 vols., 1982.

Shopping with a Crocodile. Wellington, Department of Education School Publications Branch, 1983.

Mrs. Bubble's Baby. Wellington, Department of Education School Publications Branch, 1983.

The Bubbling Crocodile, illustrated by Deirdre Gardiner. Wellington, Department of Education School Publications Branch, 1983.

A Crocodile in the Library [in the Garden], illustrated by Deirdre Gardiner. Wellington, Department of Education School Publications Branch, 2 vols., 1983–85.

Fantail, Fantail, illustrated by Bruce Phillips. Wellington, Department of Education School Publications Branch, 1984.

Going to the Beach, illustrated by Dick Frizzell. Wellington, Department of Education School Publications Branch, 1984.

The Dragon's Birthday, illustrated by Philip Webb. Auckland, Shortland, 1984.

Ups and Downs and Other Stories, illustrated by Philip Webb. Auckland, Shortland, 1984.

The Spider in the Shower, illustrated by Rodney McRae. Auckland, Shortland, 1984.

Wibble-Wobble and Other Stories. Auckland, Shortland, 1984.

The Great Grumbler and the Wonder Tree, illustrated by Diane Perham. Wellington, Department of Education School Publications Branch, 1984.

The Adventures of a Kite, illustrated by David Cowe. Auckland, Shortland, 1985; Leeds, Arnold Wheaton, 1986.

The Cake, illustrated by David Cowe. Auckland, Shortland, 1985; Leeds, Arnold Wheaton, 1986.

The Catten, illustrated by Jo Davies. Auckland, Shortland, 1985; Leeds, Arnold Wheaton, 1986.

Clever Hamburger, illustrated by Rodney McRae. Auckland, Shortland, 1985; Leeds, Arnold Wheaton, 1986.

The Earthquake, illustrated by Diane Perham. Auckland,

Shortland, 1985.

Out in the Big Wild World, illustrated by Rodney McRae. Auckland, Shortland, 1985.

Rain, illustrated by Elizabeth Fuller. Auckland, Shortland, 1985.

Sophie's Singing Mother, illustrated by Jo Davies. Auckland, Shortland, 1985; Leeds, Arnold Wheaton, 1986.

Beautiful Pig. Auckland, Shortland, 1986; Leeds, Arnold Wheaton, 1987.

A Very Happy Birthday, illustrated by Elizabeth Fuller. Auckland, Shortland, and Leeds, Arnold Wheaton, 1986.

The Funny Funny Clown Face, illustrated by Miranda Whitford. Auckland, Heinemann, 1986.

The Long Grass of Tumbledown Road. Auckland, Shortland, 1986; Leeds, Arnold Wheaton, 1987.

The Robber Pig and the Ginger Beer [*Green Eggs*], illustrated by Rodney McRae. Auckland, Shortland, 2 vols., 1986; Leeds, Arnold Wheaton, 2 vols., 1987.

Arguments, illustrated by Kelvin Hawley. Auckland, Shortland, 1986.

An Elephant in the House, illustrated by Elizabeth Fuller. Auckland, Shortland, 1986.

The Fight on the Hill, illustrated by Jan van der Voo. Auckland, Shortland, 1986; Leeds, Arnold Wheaton, 1987.

Jacko, The Junk Shop Man, illustrated by Jo Davies. Auckland, Shortland, 1986.

The Mouse Wedding, illustrated by Elizabeth Fuller. Auckland, Shortland, 1986.

Squeak in the Gate, illustrated by Jo Davies. Auckland, Shortland, 1986.

The Three Wishes, with others, illustrated by Rodney McRae and others. Auckland, Shortland, 1986.

The Man Who Enjoyed Grumbling, illustrated by Wendy Hodder. Auckland, Heinemann, 1986.

Muppy's Ball, illustrated by Jan van der Voo. Auckland, Heinemann, 1986.

Tinny Tiny Tinker, illustrated by David Cowe. Auckland, Shortland, 1986.

The Tree Doctor, illustrated by Wendy Hodder. Auckland, Heinemann, 1986.

Mr. Rooster's Dilemma, illustrated by Elizabeth Fuller. Auckland, Shortland, 1986; as *How Mr. Rooster Didn't Get Married*, Leeds, Arnold Wheaton, 1986.

Baby's Breakfast, illustrated by Madeline Beasley. Auckland, Heinemann, 1986.

Feeling Funny, illustrated by Rodney McRae. Auckland, Heinemann, 1986.

The Garden Party, illustrated by Rodney McRae. Auckland, Heinemann, 1986.

My Wonderful Aunt, illustrated by Deirdre Gardiner. Auckland, Heinemann, 4 vols., 1986.

The New House Villain, illustrated by Elizabeth Fuller. Auckland, Heinemann, 1986.

A Pet to the Vet, illustrated by Philip Webb. Auckland, Heinemann, 1986.

The Pop Group, illustrated by Rodney McRae. Auckland, Heinemann, 1986.

Tai Taylor and His Education [*and the Sweet Annie, Goes to School, Is Born*], illustrated by Nick Price. Auckland, Heinemann, 4 vols., 1986–87.

The Terrible Topsy-Turvy, Tissy-Tossy Tangle, illustrated by Vicki Smillie-McItoull. Auckland, Heinemann, 1986.

Trouble on the Bus, illustrated by Wendy Hodder. Auckland, Heinemann, 1986.

Mr. Rumfitt, illustrated by Nick Price. Auckland, Heinemann, 1987.

The Man Who Walked on His Hands, illustrated by Martin Bailey.

Auckland, Shortland, 1987.

Guinea Pig Grass, illustrated by Kelvin Hawley. Auckland, Shortland, 1987.

No Dinner for Sally, illustrated by John Tarlton. Auckland, Shortland, 1987.

The Girl Who Washed in Moonlight, illustrated by Robyn Belton. Auckland, Heinemann, 1987.

The Haunting of Miss Cardamon, illustrated by Korky Paul. Auckland, Heinemann, 1987.

Iris La Bonga and the Helpful Taxi Driver, illustrated by Vicki Smillie-McItoull. Auckland, Heinemann, 1987.

The Mad Puppet, illustrated by Jon Davis. Auckland, Heinemann, 1987.

As Luck Would Have It, illustrated by Deirdre Gardiner. Auckland, Shortland, 1988.

A Not-So-Quiet Evening, illustrated by Glenda Jones. Auckland, Shortland, 1988.

Sarah, The Bear and the Kangaroo, illustrated by Elizabeth Fuller. Auckland, Shortland, 1988.

PUBLICATIONS FOR ADULTS

Other

New Zealand: Yesterday and Today. London, Watts, 1975.

*

Manuscript Collection: J.M. Dent and Sons Ltd., London.

Margaret Mahy comments:

A child's attitude to reading depends on its exposure to books and language in its home from the earliest years. I have an almost fanatical belief in the importance of reading aloud to children, so many of my stories are written with this intention. I am constantly aware of the pictorial possibilities which, for instance, animals provide so abundantly. Children particularly love rhymes and rhythmic verse because they can join in the choruses. They can identify happily with the most extraordinary events if these are described with almost prosaic understatement and dry humour.

*   *   *

Margaret Mahy has proved to be an unusually versatile story teller. Although two Carnegie Medals have in recent years brought her renown as a writer of novels, she first made her mark as the author of picture-book texts and of simple narratives. Despite the different focuses required by these various genres, Mahy constantly employs unlikely situations to engage the attention of her readers—children or teenagers—and the resulting stories and novels combine elements of realism and fantasy inventively, exuberantly, and at times comically; they are almost always tinged with verbal richness.

Generally, Mahy's picture-book texts combine a commonplace down-to-earth situation with an intrusive element of the unbelievable or the unlikely to give the story a certain amount of narrative piquancy. In *The Boy Who Was Followed Home* a schoolboy is trailed one day by a single hippopotamus but on subsequent days by hippopotamuses who continue to increase dramatically in number. *A Lion in the Meadow* invokes an interesting relationship between the different kinds of thought processes of a boy and his mother. And in *The Boy with Two Shadows*, a witch choses a schoolboy to care for her shadow during her absence, causing him and his own shadow endless embarrassments until she rewards him handsomely for his trouble.

Mahy's comparatively short, simple tellings exhibit her characteristic method and naturally give her scope for amplification. These narratives begin simply, and quickly strike at the heart of the events. *The Rare Spotted Birthday Party*, which begins, "It was Mark's birthday in two days time but he was not happy about it," turns out to be the story of a birthday party for a group of boys all recovering from the measles—a situation with an obvious appeal of humor and ingenuity for the child mind. And in *Ultra-Violet Catastrophe* Mahy's way with words calls up humorous turns of expression. When Sally—against her will—is taken to visit Aunt Anne, "Sally could tell at once that she [Aunt Anne] had not improved. She was tiny, and terribly neat and clean. She looked more like a freshly dusted china ornament than any real person."

Two longer stories, published together as *The Birthday Burglar, and A Very Wicked Headmistress*, are full-blown examples of Mahy's zany sense of humor. "The Birthday Burglar" is riddled with alliteration and opens in a traditional story-telling manner; "On Barleycorn Island, in the middle of Vagabond Bay, there was an unusually beautiful house built of brick and in it lived a lonely boy called Bassington." The second of these two tales also begins auspiciously: "There was once a wicked headmistress called Miss Taffeta who ran a select school for girls." The reader, soon learning that Miss Taffeta had been an aerial trapeze artist, is immediately drawn into the absurdity of the outrageous events: "She thought nothing of being fired out of a cannon wearing a smile and a bikini and occasionally—when too much gunpowder was used—only a smile." Full of preposterous improbabilities, the narrative rides forward to a crashing end, devoid of all purpose but sheer entertainment.

Without entirely deserting picture-book and story texts, Mahy has since 1982 developed into a writer of full-fledged novels. Not only did *The Haunting* and *The Changeover* each receive a Carnegie Medal, but she went on to write three more novels that are individually significant—*The Catalogue of the Universe*, *The Tricksters*, and *Memory*.

In the two Carnegie Medal winners, Mahy exploited her customary feeling for possible interconnections between realism and fantasy. *The Haunting*, the story of a close-knit intergenerational family, centers on Barney, who believes he is being visited by the ghost of a supposedly long-dead relative; but it turns out that it is not he but his repressed and silent older sister who has inherited the family's genetic potential for extraordinary psychic experiences. *The Changeover*, set in 20th-century urban New Zealand, combines an unlikely set of circumstances—Laura's ambivalent feelings towards her divorced mother and her young brother Jacko's illness caused by the possession of an evil spirit.

In *The Catalogue of the Universe*, a realistic love story with no trace of the supernatural, Angela, born out of wedlock, seeks and finds—with unhappy results—her father and is ultimately consoled by the love of Tycho Potter, who is tremendously intellectual but lacking in self-confidence. Employing an elusive supernatural element in *The Tricksters*, Mahy tinges the Christmas vacation of the large Hamilton family at their seaside home with a touch of the uncanny when they are suddenly visited and as suddenly abandoned by three brothers claiming to be descendants of the original builder of the house.

It is noteworthy that Barney, the protagonist of *The Haunting*, is eight years old, while Laura Chant, the protagonist of *The Changeover*, is 14. As the novels succeed each other, the protagonists increase in age. Angela May in *The Catalogue of the Universe* is 18 years old; Ariadne, called Harry, in *The Tricksters*, is 17; and Jonny Dart in *Memory* is 19. And Mahy utilizes the subtle methods of the novelist to present the problems and experiences of teenagers who are aware of their sexuality and are at the same time increasingly concerned about the relationship between love and sex.

Made up of intricately woven plot strands and rich in verbal texture, the novels cannot be encapsulated in any single generalization, but a number of discernable elements are common to them all.

Although the stories are set in New Zealand, they evoke, on the whole, an international 20th-century ambiance in which divorced parents, single-parent families, and even Alzheimer's disease are part of the social fabric, along with shopping malls, television, portable radios, and wrecked cars. Yet in *Memory* there are references to the existence of Maori problems in the contemporary life of New Zealand. Frequently, the lives of individuals and families are invaded by supernatural and/or psychological manifestations—ghosts, witchcraft, illusive or elusive characters. Yet each novel deals with human destinies and is at the same time replete with humor, rich imagery, and emotional perception. In these novels the uncanny may assume variable forms—not only the ghost in *The Haunting*, the possession by an evil spirit in *The Changeover*, the unexplainable appearance and departure of the three brothers in *The Tricksters*, but also such matters as the influence of ancient Greek philosophers on the character Tycho Potter in *The Catalogue of the Universe* and the appearance of a boy from outer space in the science-fiction novel *Aliens in the Family*.

In her exuberant combinations of the extraordinary and the ordinary Mahy has skillfully combined plot strands in obligato form. In *The Changeover, The Catalogue of the Universe*, and *The Tricksters* the sexuality of the protagonists—always presented emotionally and perceptively but never physiologically—is only part of a larger family story in which character conflicts are generally resolved. But in *Memory*, where the uncanny consists essentially of psychological and physiological considerations, Mahy most successfully bonds her double-stranded story. Jonny Dart, unemployed and rebellious against society, suffers from a feeling of unsubstantiated guilt caused by the death of his sister when he was 14. Searching for her friend Bonny, who might reveal the truth to him, Jonny comes upon an old lady, Sophie West, suffering from Alzheimer's disease and helps her home. He begins to feel a need to aid and support her because of the unsavory conditions of her living quarters and becomes concerned about bringing order into her life. Jonny's flashbacks of past events and feelings are played against the absurdly outrageous yet genuinely pathetic statements of Sophie; and as the story moves to its denouement, not only is Sophie properly cared for but Jonny undergoes experiences that are cathartic and ultimately redemptive. In addition to having pared down her narrative complexities to a single strand, Mahy has employed language that overrides the possibility of unimaginative sordidness in her account of two kinds of mental distress.

Mahy's versatility as a story teller cannot be considered merely as a progression from the simple to the complex. Even in her picture-book texts and uncomplicated traditional narratives she worked with the basic elements that she continued to develop later in other ways: realism and fantasy, humor and a sensitivity to words—to what they do and what they mean. In her novels she has established the 20th-century world as it manifests itself in New Zealand; and, not surprisingly, this world seems little different from many other parts of the globe. But in choosing to write about contemporary situations involving families and young adults, she has mastered the oblique narrative methods of the novelist; and gracefully avoiding the tragic, she has attained success as a writer of what could certainly be considered high comedy tinged with fantasy.

—Paul Heins

MAJOR, Kevin (Gerald) Canadian. Born in Stephenville, Newfoundland, 12 September 1949. Educated at Memorial University of Newfoundland, St. John's, B.Sc. 1973. Married Anne Crawford in 1982; two sons. Teacher, Roberts Arm, Newfoundland,

1971–72, and Carbonear, Newfoundland, 1973; teacher of special education and biology, Eastport Central High School, 1974–76. Recipient: Ruth Schwartz award, 1978; Canada Council prize, 1979; Canadian Library Association Book of the Year award, 1979; Canadian Young Adult Book award, 1981. Lives in Newfoundland. Agent: Nancy Colbert, The Colbert Agency, 303 Davenport Road, Toronto, Ontario M5R 1K5, Canada.

PUBLICATIONS FOR CHILDREN

Fiction

Hold Fast. Toronto, Clarke Irwin, 1978; New York, Delacorte Press, 1980.
Far from Shore. Toronto, Clarke Irwin, 1980; New York, Delacorte Press, 1981.
Thirty-Six Exposures. New York, Delacorte Press, 1984.
Dear Bruce Springsteen. Toronto, Doubleday, 1987; New York, Delacorte Press, 1988; London, Viking Kestrel, 1989.
Blood Red Ochre. Toronto, Doubleday, and New York, Delacorte Press, 1989.

Other

Editor, *Doryloads* (anthology of Newfoundland literature and art). Portugal Cove, Newfoundland, Breakwater, 1974.

PUBLICATIONS FOR ADULTS

Other

Terra Nova National Park, with James A. Tuck. Ottawa, Parks Canada, 1983.

*

Kevin Major comments:

My first three books have all been set in Newfoundland, the part of North America where I was born and where I have lived almost all my life. I have attempted to show the unique character of the island—its landscape, speech patterns, humour—through stories about its young people and their families. On a broader level, the novels are stories about growing up. Many of the experiences that the teenage boys face in both novels (rebellion against authority, arising sexuality) are faced by young people growing up anywhere. The books, although of particular interest to young people, are enjoyed by adults as well, partly because of the frankness with which the characters are portrayed.

The fourth novel, *Dear Bruce Springsteen,* is set outside Newfoundland, but in the latest book I have again returned to the island, although this time the book is set partly in Newfoundland's past, at the time of the now extinct Beothuk Indians.

* * *

Kevin Major's first novel, *Hold Fast,* met immediate critical acclaim in Canada and received three national awards. Such a beginning could have lured many novice authors into repeating a successful formula. Stylistically, Major has departed markedly from *Hold Fast* in each of his three subsequent novels, and by doing so successfully he has become one of Canada's premier writers for adolescents.

Hold Fast begins and ends with death. When 14-year-old Michael's parents are accidentally killed, Michael and his brother

Brent, aged six, are separated. Brent remains with Aunt Flo and Grandfather while Michael moves to a city to live with his aunt and uncle and their two teenage children, Curtis and Marie. Curtis and Michael, who initially share few common interests, gradually discover mutual concerns, including a growing dislike for Curtis's dictatorial father. Michael's environment becomes increasingly unbearable, reaching crisis proportions following a school incident. Used to small-town friendliness, Michael finds himself taunted by the city in-crowd for his supposedly bumpkinish ways. The teasing eventually leads to Michael's accidentally giving one of the boys a concussion. Expelled from school, Michael is ordered by Uncle Ted to apologize to the victim. Unwilling to accept further injustices in this overly-controlled house, Michael runs away to his old home and, surprisingly, is joined by Curtis. Death, which separated the brothers, reunites them for Grandfather's death allows Michael to remain with Aunt Flo and Brent. Curtis returns to his father with no guarantee that the message inherent in his running away has been heard.

Far from Shore follows Chris, 15, over an 11-month period as his life and family disintegrate. Chris's father, unable to find work in Newfoundland, leaves the family to seek employment in Alberta. Without his father's influence, Chris's behavior deteriorates. He fails grade 10, and increased drinking causes him to lose his old friends. He replaces them with an older, tougher crowd. Following one drunken spree, Chris is charged with being involved in the vandalization of a local school. Given an opportunity to redeem himself, Chris displays poor judgment as a summer camp counsellor and almost kills a young camper. Sobered by the incident, Chris, at the book's conclusion, resumes his schooling while his father returns to seek work or to take the family to Alberta. The book's impact is enhanced by Major's multi-narrator technique involving five characters: Chris, his sister Jennifer, mother Lucy, father Gord, and Reverend Wheaton, the local minister.

Each of the 36 chapters in *Thirty-Six Exposures* serves as a snapshot revealing an aspect of the life of 17-year-old Lorne who is concluding grade 12 in Marten, Newfoundland. The final two months contain many endings and beginnings. When Lorne's friend Trevor is unjustly suspended from Mr. Ryan's history class, the normally shy Lorne leads a classroom strike and a school walkout until Trevor is reinstated. Beginnings include Lorne's not using his valedictory address as a vehicle of revenge against Ryan and a romance with Elaine wherein sex and love become confused. Endings involve not only school and changed relationships with parents, but Trevor's accidental death. Not wanting to find himself saying at age 65, "If only…," Lorne questions conforming to the pattern of further education, marriage, and local employment.

Dear Bruce Springsteen is the salutation of 51 letters that 14-year-old Terry Blanchard directs to the rock superstar over a seven-month period. While the letters treat many of Terry's egocentric problems—poor grades, girl anxieties, physique—the theme of a boy's trying to "find" his father runs through the unanswered correspondence. Abandoned by his father some six months before, Terry lives in an apartment with his working mother and younger sister. Despite Terry's father's leaving to play in a country music band, Terry defends him against his mother's criticisms. Home tensions increase when Terry buys a guitar and his mother fears his father's "dreamer" pattern is being repeated. The longest letter, a nine-pager, describes Terry's physical journey to seek out his father and their discovery of each other.

The strength of Major's writing derives from his uncompromisingly authentic portrayal of the male adolescent. Major's dialogue, sometimes criticized for its earthiness, accurately reflects adolescents' use of language which incorporates "throw-away-words" devoid of intrinsic meaning. Without engaging in exploitation, Major acknowledges the emergence and seeming omnipresence of adolescent sexuality. In one sense, Major is a regional writer for his novels' settings reflect his natal province, Newfoundland, and capture, in varying degrees, islander speech patterns, ways and concerns; yet Major's characters and their problems are recognizable to any North American reader.

—David H. Jenkinson

————

MANNING, Rosemary (Joy). Has also written as Sarah Davys; Mary Voyle. British. Born in Weymouth, Dorset, 9 December 1911. Educated at Royal Holloway College, University of London, 1930–33, B.A. in classics 1933. Worked as a shop assistant and secretary; from late 1930's teacher. Address: 20 Lyndhurst Gardens, London NW3 5NR, England.

PUBLICATIONS FOR CHILDREN

Fiction

Green Smoke, illustrated by Constance Marshall. London, Constable, and New York, Doubleday, 1957.
Dragon in Danger, illustrated by Constance Marshall. London, Constable, 1959; New York, Doubleday, 1960.
The Dragon's Quest, illustrated by Constance Marshall. London, Constable, 1961; New York, Doubleday, 1962.
Arripay, illustrated by Victor Ambrus. London, Constable, 1963; New York, Farrar Straus, 1964.
Boney Was a Warrior, illustrated by Lynette Hemmant. London, Hamish Hamilton, 1966.
The Rocking Horse, illustrated by Lynette Hemmant. London, Hamish Hamilton, 1970.
Dragon in the Harbour, illustrated by Peter Rush. London, Kestrel, 1980.

Other

Heraldry, illustrated by Janet Price. London, A. and C. Black, 1966.
Railways and Railwaymen. London, Kestrel, 1977.

Editor, *The Shepherd's Play, and Noah and the Flood: Two Miracle Plays*. Glasgow, Grant, 1955.
Editor, *A Grain of Sand: Poems*, by William Blake, illustrated by Blake. London, Bodley Head, 1967; New York, Watts, 1968.
Editor, *Great Expectations*, by Charles Dickens, illustrated by Gareth Floyd. London, Collins, 1970.

PUBLICATIONS FOR ADULTS

Novels

Remaining a Stranger (as Mary Voyle). London, Heinemann, 1953.
A Change of Direction (as Mary Voyle). London, Heinemann, 1955.
Look, Stranger. London, Cape, 1960; as *The Shape of Innocence*, New York, Doubleday, 1961.
The Chinese Garden. London, Cape, 1962; New York, Farrar Straus, 1963.
Man on a Tower. London, Cape, 1965.
Open the Door. London, Cape, 1983.

Other

From Holst to Britten: A Study of Modern Choral Music. London, Worker's Music Association, 1949.
A Time and a Time: An Autobiography (as Sarah Davys). London, Calder and Boyars, 1971; as Rosemary Manning, London, Boyars, 1986.
A Corridor of Mirrors (autobiography). London, Women's Press, 1987.

*

Rosemary Manning comments:

My first three children's books, all still in print, were written for Sue, the small daughter of a friend. Perhaps this gives them a personal quality which comes out in the relationship between the green Dragon and Sue. Now grown up, Sue does not figure in the fourth "dragon book," which is dedicated to my friends.

*   *   *

The puzzle for outsiders is to find the link between Rosemary Manning, the academic, business-like woman who has had considerable professional success outside writing, and the author of the bedtime stories of R. Dragon, 1,500 years old, with a weakness for almond buns.

The first three Dragon stories appeared between 1957 and 1961, dedicated to Susan Elisabeth Astle who may have been their inspiration. Certainly the books appear to have roots in a familiar landscape and a close relationship with a child listener. The opening of the first book, *Green Smoke*, establishes the associations very clearly: "This is a story about a girl called Susan, or Sue for short, who went for a seaside holiday to Constantine Bay in Cornwall." The immediate, unpretentious style is maintained. Not for Manning's readers the puzzle of sorting out detailed landscape instructions: "Just think of the rockiest rocks, the sandiest sand, the greenest sea and the bluest sky you can possibly imagine and you will have some idea of Constantine Bay."

Susan finds a dragon in a secret cove, a dragon with a fund of stories which he is willing to share—of Cornish giants and magical creatures and, especially, of King Arthur. The Arthurian theme is continued in *The Dragon's Quest*, where the dragon is missing, gone on a visit, but leaves Sue his account of his adventures at Arthur's court to keep her company. The technique is of stories within a story, a framework elaborated by Paul Biegel in *The King of the Copper Mountains*, and one could complain that it provides here neither the satisfaction of an old tale retold well nor the originality of new tales. *Dragon in Danger* changes the pattern, telling what happened when R. Dragon decided to visit Sue's home near London. The Dragon stories were out of print for many years until the Puffin editions of 1967–74, and in some ways they rate as period pieces, with their cosy background of Mummy and Daddy and workmen who say "Thank you kindly mum." Their strength is the intimate storytelling voice which immediately commands attention. R. Dragon reappeared in 1980 after a hibernation of some 20 years in a tale set in present-day Weymouth, *Dragon in the Harbour*, which retained the light touch and persuasive tone of the three early stories.

Endearing as the stories of Sue and R. Dragon are, Manning's most impressive children's book is *Arripay*, a story of Harry Paye, the 15th-century privateer who sailed the Dorset coast in the reign of Henry IV. In this novel, firmly founded on historical fact, Manning tackles a theme worthy of Rosemary Sutcliff. Against a precisely realised setting of Poole harbour is a robust tale of piracy, greed, and betrayal through which we follow Adam, a boy out of sorts with his family and neighbours, with no stomach for violence, nor yet the temperament for a monk's life, until he finds eventually a role which he can accept.

It is ironical that today *Arripay* is largely forgotten, lost in the anti-historical swing which followed the vogue for historical stories in the 1950's, while *Green Smoke* is in its fifth Puffin reprint. Thoughts on this paradox may well have inspired Manning's much-quoted article, "Whatever Happened to Onion John" (*The Times Literary Supplement*, 4 December 1969) but by now the fickleness of literary fashion is likely to be of only marginal interest to an author whose writing for children ceased as Susan Elisabeth Astle grew to adulthood.

—Peggy Heeks

MANNING-SANDERS, Ruth. British. Born in Swansea, Glamorgan, in 1888. Educated at schools in Sheffield and Manchester; Channing House boarding school, London; Manchester University. Married George Sanders (died 1952); one son and one daughter. Travelled for two years with Rosaire's Circus. Recipient: Blindman International Poetry prize, 1926. *Died 12 October 1988.*

PUBLICATIONS FOR CHILDREN

Fiction

Children by the Sea, illustrated by Mary Shepard. London, Collins, 1938; as *Adventure May Be Anywhere*, New York, Stokes, 1939.
Elephant. New York, Stokes, 1938; London, Collins, 1940.
Mystery at Penmarth, illustrated by Anne Bullen. London, Collins, 1940; New York, McBride, 1941.
Circus Book. London, Collins, 1947; as *The Circus*, New York, Chanticleer Press, 1948.
Circus Boy, illustrated by Annette Macarthur-Onslow. London, Oxford University Press, 1960.
The Smugglers, illustrated by William Stobbs. London, Oxford University Press, 1962.
The Crow's Nest, illustrated by Lynette Hemmant. London, Hamish Hamilton, 1965.
Slippery Shiney, illustrated by Constance Marshall. London, Hamish Hamilton, 1965.
The Extraordinary Margaret Catchpole. London, Heinemann, 1966.
The Magic Squid, illustrated by Eileen Armitage. London, Methuen, 1968.
The Spaniards Are Coming!, illustrated by Jacqueline Riszi. London, Heinemann, 1969; New York, Watts, 1970.
Ram and Goat, illustrated by Robin Jacques. London, Methuen, 1974.
Young Gabby Goose, illustrated by James Hodgson. London, Methuen, 1975.
Boastful Rabbit, illustrated by James Hodgson. London, Methuen, 1978.
Oh Really, Rabbit!, illustrated by James Hodgson. London, Methuen, 1980.
Hedgehog and Puppy Dog Tales. London, Methuen, 1982.

Other

Swan of Denmark: The Story of Hans Christian Andersen, illustrated by Astrid Walford. London, Heinemann, 1949; New York, McBride, 1950.
Peter and the Piskies: Cornish Folk and Fairy Tales, illustrated by

Raymond Briggs. London, Oxford University Press, 1958; New York, Roy, 1966.
Red Indian Folk and Fairy Tales, illustrated by C. Walter Hodges. London, Oxford University Press, 1960; New York, Roy, 1962.
Animal Stories, illustrated by Annette Macarthur-Onslow. London, Oxford University Press, 1961; New York, Roy, 1962.
A Book of Giants [*Dwarfs, Dragons, Witches, Wizards, Mermaids, Ghosts and Goblins, Princes and Princesses, Devils and Demons, Charms and Changelings, Ogres and Trolls, Sorcerers and Spells, Magic Animals, Monsters, Enchantments and Curses, Kings and Queens, Spooks and Spectres, Cats and Creatures, Heroes and Heroines, Marvels and Magic, Magic Adventures, Magic Horses*], illustrated by Robin Jacques. London, Methuen, 22 vols., 1962–84; New York, Dutton, 22 vols., 1964–84.
Damian and the Dragon: Modern Greek Folk-Tales, illustrated by William Papas. London, Oxford University Press, 1965; New York, Roy, 1966.
Stories from the English and Scottish Ballads, illustrated by Trevor Ridley. London, Heinemann, and New York, Dutton, 1968.
The Glass Man and the Golden Bird: Hungarian Folk and Fairy Tales, illustrated by Victor Ambrus. London, Oxford University Press, and New York, Roy, 1968.
Jonnikin and the Flying Basket: French Folk and Fairy Tales, illustrated by Victor Ambrus. London, Oxford University Press, and New York, Dutton, 1969.
Gianni and the Ogre, illustrated by William Stobbs. London, Methuen, 1970; New York, Dutton, 1971.
A Choice of Magic, illustrated by Robin Jacques. London, Methuen, and New York, Dutton, 1971.
The Three Witch Maidens, illustrated by William Stobbs. London, Methuen, 1972.
Tortoise Tales, illustrated by Donald Chaffin. London, Methuen, 1972; Nashville, Nelson, 1974.
Sir Green Hat and the Wizard, illustrated by William Stobbs. London, Methuen, 1974.
Grandad and the Magic Barrel, illustrated by Robin Jacques. London, Methuen, 1974.
Old Dog Sirko: A Ukrainian Tale, illustrated by Leon Shtainmets. London, Methuen, 1974.
Stumpy: A Russian Tale, illustrated by Leon Shtainmets. London, Methuen, 1974.
Fox Tales, illustrated by James Hodgson. London, Methuen, 1976.
Scottish Folk Tales, illustrated by William Stobbs. London, Methuen, 1976.
The Town Mouse and the Country Mouse: Aesop's Fable Retold, illustrated by Harold Jones. London, Angus and Robertson, 1977.
Robin Hood and Little John, illustrated by Jo Chesterman. London, Methuen, 1977.
Old Witch Boneyleg, illustrated by Kilmeny Niland. London, Angus and Robertson, 1978.
The Cock and the Fox, illustrated by Jenny Williams. London, Angus and Robertson, 1978.
Folk and Fairy Tales (collection), illustrated by Robin Jacques. London, Methuen, 1978.
The Haunted Castle, illustrated by Kilmeny Niland. London, Angus and Robertson, 1979.
Robin Hood and the Gold Arrow, illustrated by Jo Chesterman. London, Methuen, 1979.
Tales of Magic and Mystery, illustrated by Christopher Quaile. London, Methuen, 1985.

Editor, *A Bundle of Ballads*, illustrated by William Stobbs. London, Oxford University Press, 1959; Philadelphia, Lippincott, 1961.
Editor, *Birds, Beasts and Fishes* (poetry anthology), illustrated by

Rita Parsons. London, Oxford University Press, 1962.
Editor, *The Red King and the Witch: Gypsy Folk and Fairy Tales*,
   illustrated by Victor Ambrus. London, Oxford University Press,
   1964; New York, Roy, 1965.
Editor, *The Hamish Hamilton Book of Magical Beasts*, illustrated by
   Raymond Briggs. London, Hamish Hamilton, 1965; as *A Book
   of Magical Beasts*, New York, Nelson, 1970.
Editor, *Festivals*, illustrated by Raymond Briggs. London,
   Heinemann, 1972; New York, Dutton, 1973.
Editor, *A Cauldron of Witches*, illustrated by Scoular Anderson.
   London, Methuen, 1988.

PUBLICATIONS FOR ADULTS

Novels

The Twelve Saints. London, Christophers, 1925; New York, Clode,
   1926.
Selina Pennaluna. London, Christophers, 1927.
Waste Corner. London, Christophers, 1927; New York, Clode,
   1928.
Hucca's Moor. London, Faber, 1929.
The Crochet Woman. London, Faber, and New York, Coward
   McCann, 1930.
The Growing Trees. London, Faber, and New York, Morrow, 1931.
She Was Sophia. London, Cobden Sanderson, 1932.
Run Away. London, Cassell, 1934.
Mermaid's Mirror. London, Cassell, 1935.
The Girl Who Made an Angel. London, Cassell, 1936.
Luke's Circus. London, Collins, 1939; Boston, Little Brown, 1940.
Mr. Portal's Little Lions. London, Hale, 1952.
The Golden Ball. London, Hale, 1954.
Melissa. London, Hale, 1957.

Verse

The Pedlar and Other Poems. London, Selwyn and Blount, 1919.
Karn. Richmond, Surrey, Leonard and Virginia Woolf, 1922.
Pages from the History of Zachy Trenoy. London, Christophers,
   1923.
The City. London, Benn, and New York, Dial Press, 1927.

Other

The West of England. London, Batsford, 1949.
Seaside England. London, Batsford, 1951.
The River Dart. London, Westaway, 1951.
The English Circus. London, Laurie, 1952.

*   *   *

To note that Ruth Manning-Sanders, undoubtedly best-known for
her retellings of folktales from all over the world, also produced
original work may be misleading, since the successful handling of
folk material calls in itself for a high degree of creativity: a sympathy
for the traditional themes and a feeling for language which enabled
Manning-Sanders to present her tales in a vigorous style which is
neither old-fashioned nor anachronistically modernized. And it is
interesting to find folk themes cropping up time and again in those
stories she wrote which are not retellings of traditional material, and
which range from mystery adventure, through historical novels, to
simple but attractive stories for younger readers.
   Even *Mystery at Penmarth*, first published in 1940 and bearing
many of the hallmarks of a dated prewar genre with its ponies,
children's secret societies, comic servants, and Vicar, has stories of

historical Cornwall and accounts of Cornish customs woven into the
plot. Cornwall is again the setting for *The Smugglers*, a first-person
narrative by the local Squire's son Ned of smuggling at the period
when that activity seemed romantic; the revenue men are the villains
of the piece, and all ends well for Ned and his much admired hero,
the dashing smuggler Zach. It is the author's feeling for her Cornish
background that counts here.
   The ethics of smuggling are seen from a more sombre viewpoint
in *The Extraordinary Margaret Catchpole*, a novel based on the
real-life story of the Suffolk farm girl who took up, disastrously, with
a smuggler named William Laud, was twice condemned to death—
for horse-stealing and for escaping from prison—and finally
transported to Australia, where she made good. The social conditions
of hardship in which the agricultural poor of the late 18th-century
lived are well realized, and Margaret herself makes an attractive
heroine.
   However, perhaps the best of Manning-Sanders's historical novels
is *Circus Boy*, another first-person narrative, presenting the world of
the travelling showmen of Victorian times through the eyes of
Tommy Gough. With his father's circus he travels the English and
Irish countryside, and the family suffer a fairytale reversal of fortune
when they are engaged to perform at the Crystal Palace. There is
plenty of verve in this story; the background detail is excellent, and
the author enters into the spirit of circus life as lived by the artistes
themselves.
   For younger readers, *The Spaniards Are Coming!*, written as part
of the Long Ago Children series, follows the fortunes of Simon and
Beth, who are peripherally involved with the Spanish Armada: a
good introduction to the subject and the period. Two little stories for
young children just beyond the picture book and reading primer stage
are *The Magic Squid* and *The Crow's Nest*. Yet again it is interesting
that even in these simple stories with their modern settings—the
former in the Channel Islands, the latter in Scotland—the author
makes telling use of such traditional themes as the magical sea
creature, which must eventually be returned to its native element,
and the thieving-magpie motif. The adult reader will be reminded of
Manning-Sanders's feeling for traditional folk material and skill in
handling it, and the child reader of these books will be led on to her
fine collections of folktales and ballads.

—Anthea Bell

———

MARCHANT, Bessie. British. Born in Petham, Kent, 12
December 1862. Educated privately. Married Jabez Ambrose Comfort in 1889; one daughter. Lived in Charlbury, Oxfordshire. *Died
10 November 1941.*

PUBLICATIONS FOR CHILDREN

Fiction

The Old House by the Water. London, Religious Tract Society,
   1894.
In the Cradle of the North Wind. Edinburgh, Nimmo, 1896.
Weasel Tim. London, Culley, 1897.
Among the Torches of the Andes. Edinburgh, Nimmo, 1898; as *On
   the Track*, London, Sampson Low, 1924.
The Bonded Three, illustrated by William Rainey. London,
   Blackie, 1898.
Yuppie. London, Culley, 1898.
The Girl Captives, illustrated by William Rainey. London, Blackie,
   1899.

The Humbling of Mark Lester. London, Simpkin Marshall, 1899.

Winning His Way. London, Gall and Inglis, 1899.

The Rajah's Daughter; or, The Half-Moon Girl. London, Partridge, 1899; as *The Half-Moon Girl*, 1924.

Tell-Tale-Tit. London, Culley, 1899.

The Ghost of Rock Grange. London, S.P.C.K., 1900.

Held at Ransom. London, Blackie, 1900.

Cicely Frome, The Captain's Daughter. Edinburgh, Nimmo, 1900.

In the Toils of the Tribesmen. London, Gall and Inglis, 1900.

From the Scourge of the Tongue. London, Melrose, 1900.

Among Hostile Hordes. London, Gall and Inglis, 1901.

The Fun o' the Fair. London, Culley, 1901.

In Perilous Times. London, Gall and Inglis, 1901.

That Dreadful Boy! London, Culley, 1901.

Three Girls on a Ranch [*in Morocco, in Mexico*], illustrated by William Rainey. London, Blackie, 3 vols., 1901–11.

Tommy's Trek. London, Blackie, 1901.

The Bertrams of Ladywell, illustrated by John Jellicoe. London, Wells Gardner, 1902.

A Brave Little Cousin. London, S.P.C.K., 1902.

Fleckie. London, Blackie, 1902.

The House at Brambling Minster. London, S.P.C.K., 1902.

Leonard's Temptation. London, Culley, 1902.

The Secret of the Everglades. London, Blackie, 1902; New York, Mershon, 1915.

A Heroine of the Sea. London, Blackie, 1903.

Lost on the Saguenay. London, Collins, 1903.

The Owner of Rushcote. London, Culley, 1903.

The Captives of the Kaid. London, Collins, 1904.

Chupsie. London, Culley, 1904.

The Girls of Wakenside. London, Collins, 1904.

Hope's Tryst. London, Blackie, 1904.

Yew Tree Farm. London, S.P.C.K., 1904.

Caspar's Find. London, Culley, 1905.

A Daughter of the Ranges, illustrated by A.A. Dixon. London, Blackie, 1905.

The Debt of the Damerals. London, Clarke, 1905.

The Mysterious City, illustrated by W.S. Stacey. London, S.P.C.K., 1905.

The Queen of Shindy Flat, illustrated by Charles Sheldon. London, Wells Gardner, 1905.

Athabasca Bill. London, S.P.C.K., 1906.

A Girl of the Fortunate Isles, illustrated by Paul Hardy. London, Blackie, 1906.

Kenealy's Ride. London, Gall and Inglis, 1906.

Maisie's Discovery, illustrated by R. Tod. London, Collins, 1906.

Uncle Greg's Man Hunt. London, Culley, 1906.

Darling of Sandy Point, illustrated by Harold Piffard. London, S.P.C.K., 1907.

Juliette, The Mail Carrier, illustrated by R. Tod. London, Collins, 1907.

The Mystery of the Silver Run. London, Wells Gardner, 1907.

No Ordinary Girl, illustrated by Frances Ewan. London, Blackie, 1907; New York, Caldwell, 1911.

Sisters of Silver Creek, illustrated by Robert Hope. London, Blackie, 1907.

The Apple Lady, illustrated by G. Soper. London, Collins, 1908.

A Courageous Girl, illustrated by William Rainey. London, Blackie, 1908.

Daughters of the Dominion. London, Blackie, 1908.

Rolf the Rebel, illustrated by W.S. Stacey. London, S.P.C.K., 1908.

An Island Heroine, illustrated by W.H. Margetson. London, Collins, 1909.

Jenny's Adventure. London, Butcher, 1909.

The Adventures of Phyllis, illustrated by F. Whiting. London, Cassell, 1910.

The Black Cockatoo, illustrated by Lancelot Speed. London, Religious Tract Society, 1910.

A Countess from Canada, illustrated by Cyrus Cuneo. London, Blackie, 1910.

Greta's Domain, illustrated by William Rainey. London, Blackie, 1910.

Molly of One Tree Bend. London, Butcher, 1910.

The Deputy Boss, illustrated by Oscar Wilson. London, S.P.C.K., 1910.

The Ferry House Girls, illustrated by W.R.S. Stott. London, Blackie, 1911.

A Girl of Distinction, illustrated by William Rainey. London, Blackie, 1911.

Redwood Ranch, illustrated by Harold Piffard. London, S.P.C.K., 1911.

A Girl of the Northland, illustrated by N. Tenison. London, Hodder and Stoughton, 1912.

His Great Surrender, illustrated by Gordon Browne. London, S.P.C.K., 1912.

A Princess of Servia, illustrated by William Rainey. London, Blackie, 1912.

The Sibyl of St. Pierre, illustrated by William Rainey. London, Wells Gardner, 1912.

The Western Scout, illustrated by W.S. Stacey. London, S.P.C.K., 1912.

The Youngest Sister, illustrated by William Rainey. London, Blackie, 1912.

The Adventurous Seven, illustrated by W.R.S. Stott. London, Blackie, 1913.

The Heroine of the Ranch, illustrated by Cyrus Cuneo. London, Blackie, 1913.

Denver Wilson's Double, illustrated by W. Douglas Almond. London, Blackie, 1914.

Helen of the Black Mountain. London, Blackie, 1914.

The Loyalty of Hester Hope, illustrated by William Rainey. London, Blackie, 1914.

A Mysterious Inheritance. London, Blackie, 1914.

A Girl and a Caravan. London, Blackie, 1915.

Joyce Harrington's Trust. London, Blackie, 1915.

Molly Angel's Adventures. London, Blackie, 1915.

A Canadian Farm Mystery; or, Pam the Pioneer. London, Blackie, 1916.

A Girl Munition Worker. London, Blackie, 1916.

The Unknown Island. London, Blackie, 1916.

The Gold-Marked Charm. London, Blackie, 1917.

Lois in Charge; or, A Girl of Grit, illustrated by Cyrus Cuneo. London, Blackie, 1917.

A V.A.D. in Salonika. London, Blackie, 1917.

Cynthia Wins, illustrated by John E. Sutcliffe. London, Blackie, 1918.

A Dangerous Mission, illustrated by Wal Paget. London, Blackie, 1918.

Norah to the Rescue, illustrated by W.R.S. Stott. London, Blackie, 1919.

A Transport Girl in France. London, Blackie, 1919.

Sally Makes Good, illustrated by Leo Bates. London, Blackie, 1920.

The Girl of the Pampas. London, Blackie, 1921.

Island Born, illustrated by Leo Bates. London, Blackie, 1921.

The Mistress of Purity Gap. London, Cassell, 1921; New York, Funk and Wagnalls, 1922.

Harriet Goes a-Roaming. London, Blackie, 1922.

The Fortunes of Prue. London, Ward Lock, 1923.

Rachel Out West, illustrated by Henry Coller. London, Blackie, 1923.

A Bid for Safety. London, Ward Lock, 1924.

Diana Carries On.   London, Nelson, 1924.
The Most Popular Girl in the School.   London, Partridge, 1924.
Sylvia's Secret, illustrated by W.E. Wightman.   London, Blackie, 1924.
By Honour Bound.   London, Nelson, 1925.
Her Own Kin.   London, Blackie, 1925.
To Save Her School, illustrated by H.L. Bacon.   London, Partridge, 1925.
Delmayne's Adventures.   London, Collins, 1925.
Cousin Peter's Money.   London, Sheldon, 1926.
Di the Dauntless, illustrated by W.E. Wightman.   London, Blackie, 1926.
Millicent Gwent, Schoolgirl.   London, Warne, 1926.
Molly in the West, illustrated by F.E. Hiley.   London, Blackie, 1927.
The Two New Girls.   London, Warne, 1927.
Glenallan's Daughters.   London, Nelson, 1928.
Lucie's Luck, illustrated by F.E. Hiley.   London, Blackie, 1928.
The Bannister Twins, illustrated by E. Brier.   London, Nelson, 1929.
Hilda Holds On, illustrated by F.E. Hiley.   London, Blackie, 1929.
How Nell Scored.   London, Nelson, 1929.
Laurel the Leader.   London, Blackie, 1930.
Cuckoo of the Log Raft.   London, Newnes, 1931.
Two on Their Own, illustrated by F.E. Hiley.   London, Blackie, 1931.
The Homesteader Girl, illustrated by V. Cooley.   London, Nelson, 1932.
Jane Fills the Breach, illustrated by F.E. Hiley.   London, Blackie, 1932.
Silla the Seventh.   London, Newnes, 1932.
Deborah's Find, illustrated by Henry Coller.   London, Blackie, 1933.
The Courage of Katrine.   London, Warne, 1934.
Erica's Ranch.   London, Blackie, 1934.
Lesbia's Little Blunder.   London, Warne, 1934.
Hosea's Girl.   London, Hutchinson, 1934.
Anna of Tenterford, illustrated by F.E. Hiley.   London, Blackie, 1935.
Felicity's Fortune.   London, Blackie, 1936.
Nancy Afloat.   London, Nelson, 1936.
A Daughter of the Desert.   London, Blackie, 1937.
Miss Wilmer's Gang, illustrated by J.A. May.   London, Blackie, 1938.
Waifs of Woollamoo.   London, Warne, 1938.
A Girl Undaunted; or, The Honey Queen, illustrated by J.A. May.   London, Blackie, 1939.
Marta the Mainstay.   London, Blackie, 1940.
Two of a Kind.   London, Blackie, 1941.
The Triumphs of Three.   London, Blackie, 1942.

*   *   *

Bessie Marchant was important in the history of girls' adventure stories as one of the first writers to allow her female characters real adventure in settings from Canada to South Africa, Brazil to Borneo. The heroines meet many dangers but triumph through hard work and indomitable spirit. Typical is *Di the Dauntless* in which Di treks into the Moroccan desert to search for her father. She escapes from a band of Riffs, avoids being sold into slavery, and returns home safely, to be drawn into the arms of a handsome young pilot.

This introduces another common element. Despite the independence and intrepid natures of Marchant's heroines, domestic matters are very much part of their lives. After playing a prominent part in an undertaking involving diamond mines and bandits, the heroine of *Held at Ransom* is told, "But you can do so many things that no boy or man can ever manage, housekeeping and all that sort of work." Similarly one of the heroines of *Three Girls in Mexico* "had

come to her woman's kingdom of loving and being loved," and some now unfashionable advice is given to Hester in *The Loyalty of Hester Hope*: "There is a lot of nonsense talked in these days about the emancipation of women and that sort of thing…the only chance of married happiness is for man to be what his Maker intended he should be—the head of the house."

It is easy to laugh at synopses of Marchant's plots, but she upholds universal virtues. Her books are in the tradition of the happy family story with brothers and sisters bound together by mutual affection, exhibiting unselfishness, courage, self-sacrifice and cheerfulness. Barbara, in *The Triumphs of Three*, gives up the chance of a good post as a teacher to look after the elderly couple who had made sacrifices to give her a chance in life. *The Courage of Katrine* is full of pious comments, such as, "It was to his credit that he had mastered the temptation and held firmly to what he knew to be his duty."

The stories were also important in showing that brains and scientific ability were an asset for a girl. In *Di the Dauntless* two girls make a wireless receiver; Hester Dayrell in *The Rajah's Daughter* joins an expedition to Borneo in search of the missing Darwinian link; and many crises are averted by the heroines' abilities to speak the local language.

World War I gave many girls an opportunity to break out of domestic restrictions, and Marchant reflected this in *A Girl Munition Worker* in which the heroine, working in a cordite factory, defeats a spy. Although *Sally Makes Good* is set in post-war Tasmania, Sally's two sisters had been a departmental manager in a munition factory and a WAAS driver in France. Sally's skills are rather different—sweeping, dusting, cooking and washing—and her form of "making good" is to fall in love and marry before her accomplished but rather silly older sisters.

The plots are certainly implausible and marred by the colossal coincidences by which most of them are resolved. Typically, when Audrey comes to London, in *The Gold-Marked Charm*, the first person she meets is a man she had known long before in the Soudan; and in *The Loyalty of Hester Hope* there is a terrible inevitability when the Russian who is sent to help Hester run the farm turns out to be the long-lost father of a child who had earlier been taken into the household. However, the stories must have been a very liberating and escapist experience for young readers earlier this century. The struggles of the young heroines to survive and accomplish daring undertakings, the fast action, and the promise of domestic bliss to come would have carried them through the moralising and the improbabilities.

—Valerie Brinkley-Willsher

————

MARK, Jan(et Marjorie, née Brisland).   British.   Born in Welwyn, Hertfordshire, 22 June 1943. Educated at Ashford Grammar School, Kent, 1954–61; Canterbury College of Art, 1961–65, National Diploma in Design 1965. Married Neil Mark in 1969; one daughter and one son. Teacher, Southfields School, Gravesend, Kent, 1965–71. Writer-in-residence, Oxford Polytechnic, 1982–84. Recipient: Library Association Carnegie Medal, 1977, 1984; *Guardian* Special prize, 1981; *Observer*-Rank Organisation prize, 1982; Angel Literary award, 1983, for adult novel, 1987. Agent: Murray Pollinger, 4 Garrick Street, London WC2E 9BH. Address: 98 Howard Street, Oxford OX4 3BY, England.

PUBLICATIONS FOR CHILDREN

Fiction

Thunder and Lightnings, illustrated by Jim Russell.   London,

Kestrel, 1976; New York, Crowell, 1979.

Under the Autumn Garden, illustrated by Colin Twinn. London, Kestrel, 1977; New York, Crowell, 1979.

The Ennead. London, Kestrel, and New York, Crowell, 1978.

Divide and Rule. London, Kestrel, 1979; New York, Crowell, 1980.

The Short Voyage of the Albert Ross, illustrated by Gavin Rowe. London, Granada, 1980.

Nothing to Be Afraid Of (short stories), illustrated by David Parkins. London, Kestrel, 1980; New York, Harper, 1981.

Hairs in the Palm of the Hand (short stories), illustrated by Jan Ormerod. London, Kestrel, 1981; as *Bold as Brass*, London, Hutchinson, 1984.

The Long Distance Poet, illustrated by Steve Smallman. Cambridge, Dinosaur, 1982.

The Dead Letter Box, illustrated by Mary Rayner. London, Hamish Hamilton, 1982.

Aquarius. London, Kestrel, 1982; New York, Atheneum, 1984.

Feet and Other Stories, illustrated by Bert Kitchen. London, Kestrel, 1983.

Handles. London, Kestrel, 1983; New York, Atheneum, 1985.

Two Stories, illustrated by Clive King. Oxford, Inky Parrot Press, 1984.

Trouble Half-Way, illustrated by David Parkins. London, Viking Kestrel, 1985; New York, Atheneum, 1986.

At the Sign of the Dog and Rocket. London, Longman, 1985.

Fur, illustrated by Charlotte Voake. London, Walker, and New York, Harper, 1986.

Out of the Oven, illustrated by Antony Maitland. London, Viking Kestrel, 1986.

Frankie's Hat (short stories), illustrated by Quentin Blake. London, Viking Kestrel, 1986.

Fun, illustrated by Michael Foreman. London, Gollancz, 1987.

Dream House. London, Viking Kestrel, 1987.

Enough Is Too Much Already and Other Stories. London, Bodley Head, 1988.

The Twig Thing, illustrated by Sally Holmes. London, Viking, 1988.

Plays

Izzy (televised 1983). London, Longman, 1985.

Interference (televised 1986). London, Longman, 1987.

Captain Courage and the Rose Street Gang, with Stephen Cockett. London, Collins, 1987.

Television Plays: *Izzy*, 1983; *Interference*, 1986; *Handles*, from her own story, 1989.

PUBLICATIONS FOR ADULTS

Novel

Zeno Was Here. London, Cape, and New York, Farrar Straus, 1987.

*

Jan Mark comments:

I write about children because I like to have my characters in decent perspective, but I don't mind who reads the books. Some of them obviously appeal to younger children, others seem to have found an adult readership, and, in a way, this is a safeguard. Since I do not know my audience in advance, I cannot aim at it. I can only try to write as well as I am able and hope to find a sympathetic response in anyone, of any age, who reads what I have written. I write to meet the demands of myself as an adult, not those of the child I once was. Anyone who claims to know what children want is implying a homogeneity which does not exist. This is the language of mass advertising, which has no place in the writing of fiction, for children or for anyone else.

*   *   *

Jan Mark's first novel *Thunder and Lightnings* was published in 1976, winning both the Penguin/Guardian competition and the Carnegie Medal. Her output since then has been prolific and richly varied; her mastery of the techniques of fiction seems utterly secure from the picture book through to the adult novel.

Thunder and Lightnings is a book about friendship, haunted by the poignant realisation that "Everything go....Everything go that you like best. That never come back." Elegaic, bittersweet, the book is also warmly human. Its oblique approach to character and emotion, spare dialogue, and quiet plot are echoed in a number of later books: *Under the Autumn Garden, Handles* (also a Carnegie Medal winner). *Trouble Half-Way, At the Sign of the Dog and Rocket, Dream House.* Shorter fiction has mined the same vein: intimate, comic, sad, verbally precise. There is an affinity with William Mayne, whose influence gave her, she has said, "the courage to say exactly what you mean." This exactness in her work can take the reader's breath away, as in *Thunder and Lightnings* when Andrew registers the really shocking thing when Victor's mother hits him: "the silence of it."

The friendship of the bright newcomer Andrew and "thick" local Victor is immensely touching, and prefigures equally surefooted portraits in the later books. Mark's subtlety of apprehension and expression are modulated through close observation of speech patterns, body language, and human behavior alone and in groups. Her wicked sense of humour sparkles in the hilarious short story "William's Version" in the collection *Nothing to Be Afraid Of*, in which a preschool child gleefully demolishes his grandmother's nursery tale of the three little pigs, and "Time and the Hour" in *Hairs in the Palm of the Hand*, which is as flawlessly constructed as P.G. Wodehouse's "The Great Sermon Handicap." Her short stories rank with her best work. They include a number of brilliant studies of children in school, and are especially acute about the pains and pleasures of adolescence, in stories such as "I Was Adored Once Too" in *Feet*. The random verbal crossfire of the teenagers in *Enough Is Too Much Already*, besides being very funny, is the closest any writer has come to an accurate notation of adolescent banter.

Dream House, a story about emotional cross-currents in a group of children on the fringes of a manor house turned over to courses on the arts, is once again concerned chiefly with the nature and uses of friendship. It shows very clearly how human relationships can, without compassion, be reduced to a battle of wits between user and used. Manipulation and the abuse of friendship lie at the heart of her three fiercely-written metaphysical thrillers for older children, *The Ennead, Divide and Rule*, and *Aquarius*. The characters keep themselves close, secret; those who open themselves up are destroyed. Yet those who will not open in the end destroy themselves, like Viner in *Aquarius* who cannot admit or name the love he feels for the rain-king Morning Light. Viner arrives in a land where "friendship is a trade"; he thinks perhaps he can practice it as "a mystery." In a moment of aching tenderness he nearly succeeds: as he lies in the dark beside Morning Light, "A strand of hair trailed across his mouth, and he bit it, gently." His failure is a terrible one, and the way in which it is presented takes *Aquarius* across any meaningful barrier between children's and adult literature. Viner is set up as the book's hero, and then the reader is slowly alienated from him. This deliberate transgression of the implicit bond between writer and reader is even clearer in two searing short stories. "Childermas" and "Mr. and Mrs Johnson" (*Two Stories*), which chillingly deconstruct the material of children's fantasies: fairies at the bottom of the garden, dolls with independent characters and feelings.

Mark is a remarkably gifted writer who at her best—in, say, the story "It Wasn't Me" in *Frankie's Hat*—can invest the trivial details of life with resonant meaning. At the heart both of her writing in a naturalistic mode such as *Thunder and Lightnings* and in a symbolic one such as *Aquarius* is an unusual intellectual toughness which makes even her work for young children challenging, demanding, and rewarding.

—Neil Philip

MARKOOSIE (Patsauq). Canadian. Born in Port Harrison, Quebec, 19 June 1942. Educated at Port Harrison Elementary School and a high school in Yellowknife, Northwest Territories; earned commercial pilot's licence, and carpentry diploma. Married Zipporah Kudluk in 1961 (divorced 1974); one son and four daughters. Pilot, Atlas Aviation, Resolute, Northwest Territories, 1969–75; translator, Northern Quebec Innuit Association, Montreal and Port Harrison, 1975–76. Since 1976 manager of the Community Council, Inukjuak, Quebec; since 1978 administrator of Public Services, Government of Quebec. Agent: McGill-Queen's University Press, 855 Sherbrooke Street West, Montreal, Quebec H3A 2T7, Canada.

PUBLICATIONS FOR CHILDREN

Fiction

Harpoon of the Hunter, illustrated by Germaine Arnaktauyok. Montreal and London, McGill-Queen's University Press, 1970.

*

Markoosie comments:

Harpoon of the Hunter is an Eskimo story handed down from one generation to the next. It tells of a boy hunter who becomes a man through one episode in his life.

*　*　*

The publication of *Harpoon of the Hunter* was significant in the history of Canadian publishing since it marked the first appearance of an Eskimo fiction story published in English. After the tale was serialized in the Eskimo newsletter *Inuttituut*, Markoosie was urged to make an English translation in order to give the story the wide audience it deserved.

Markoosie writes of the difficult struggle for survival in an inhospitable environment and the courage and indomitable fortitude displayed by the inhabitants of a bleak, forbidding land. The story begins in a dramatic fashion as a small settlement is attacked during the night by a rabid polar bear. 16-year-old Kamik accompanies the small band of hunters who plan to track down and destroy this potential threat to the entire group. Their mission ends in tragedy and Kamik, the sole survivor of another attack by the now-wounded bear, is left to make his way home. He is found by searchers after suffering incredible hardships and all seems well as he and his tribe embark on a move to a larger settlement. During the move, his mother and future wife are killed and Kamik, bereft, chooses to end his life and find the peace of which his dying father had spoken.

Markoosie's spare, unembellished language gives the story the heightened impact of a Greek drama. The tragic tale has a fitting setting—the stark and silent landscape provides a contrast to the constant motion of the characters across it. The writing reminds one that the oral tradition is still very much a part of the Eskimo way of life. The story has the immediacy of the spoken word due to Markoosie's use of simple sentence structure and avoidance of descriptive passages. The writing is characterized, above all, by action. Something is continually happening or about to happen and the reader is led swiftly to the tale's conclusion. Tension is emphasized by the author's technique of shifting from one scene to another. The single-minded hatred of the wounded bear is juxtaposed effectively against the group of hunters whose hunger and inadequate weapons render them horribly vulnerable. Ooramik's dream of disaster provides an ominous hint of the death of the hunters.

Harpoon of the Hunter is a brilliantly successful portrayal of courage in the face of impossible odds.

—Fran Ashdown

MARSHALL, Edward. See **MARSHALL, James.**

MARSHALL, James (Edward). Also writes as Edward Marshall. American. Born in San Antonio, Texas, 10 October 1942. Educated at New England Conservatory of Music, Boston, 1960–61; Southern Connecticut State College, New Haven, B.A. in history 1967; Trinity College, Hartford, Connecticut, 1967–68. French and Spanish teacher, Cathedral High School, Boston, 1968–70. Since 1970 freelance writer and illustrator. Agent: Sheldon Fogelman, 10 East 40th Street, New York, New York 10016, U.S.A.

PUBLICATIONS FOR CHILDREN (illustrated by the author)

Fiction

George and Martha. Boston, Houghton Mifflin, 1972; London, Methuen, 1974.
What's the Matter with Carruthers? Boston, Houghton Mifflin, 1972.
Yummers! Boston, Houghton Mifflin, 1972; London, Methuen, 1974.
George and Martha Encore. Boston, Houghton Mifflin, 1973.
Miss Dog's Christmas Treat. Boston, Houghton Mifflin, 1973.
The Stupids Step Out, with Harry Allard. Boston, Houghton Mifflin, 1974; London, Methuen, 1976.
Willis. Boston, Houghton Mifflin, 1974.
The Guest. Boston, Houghton Mifflin, 1975.
Eugene. Boston, Houghton Mifflin, 1975.
Sing Out, Irene. Boston, Houghton Mifflin, 1975.
Snake, His Story. Boston, Houghton Mifflin, 1975.
Speedboat. Boston, Houghton Mifflin, 1976.
George and Martha Rise and Shine. Boston, Houghton Mifflin, 1976.
Miss Nelson Is Missing! [*Back, Has a Field Day*], with Harry Allard. Boston, Houghton Mifflin, 3 vols., 1977–85.
A Summer in the South. Boston, Houghton Mifflin, 1977; London, Evans, 1979.
The Stupids Have a Ball, with Harry Allard. Boston, Houghton Mifflin, 1978.
George and Martha One Fine Day. Boston, Houghton Mifflin,

1978; London, Kestrel, 1981.

Portly McSwine. Boston, Houghton Mifflin, 1979; London, Dent, 1981.

George and Martha, Tons of Fun. Boston, Houghton Mifflin, 1980.

The Stupids Die, with Harry Allard. Boston, Houghton Mifflin, 1981.

Taking Care of Carruthers. Boston, Houghton Mifflin, 1981; London, Bodley Head, 1983.

Rapscallion Jones. New York, Viking Press, 1983; London, Bodley Head, 1984.

George and Martha Back in Town. Boston, Houghton Mifflin, 1984.

The Cut-Ups. New York, Viking Kestrel, 1984; London, Bodley Head, 1985.

Wings: A Tale of Two Chickens. New York, Viking Kestrel, 1986; London, A. and C. Black, 1987.

Three Up a Tree. New York, Dial Press, and London, A. and C. Black, 1986.

Merry Christmas, Space Case. New York, Dial Press, 1986.

Yummers Too: The Second Course. Boston, Houghton Mifflin, 1986.

The Cut-Ups Cut Loose. New York, Viking Kestrel, 1987.

George and Martha Round and Round. Boston, Houghton Mifflin, 1988.

Fox on the Job. New York, Dial Press, 1988.

The Cut-Ups at Camp Custer. New York, Viking Kestrel, 1989.

Fiction as Edward Marshall

Troll Country. New York, Dial Press, 1980; London, Bodley Head, 1981.

Space Case. New York, Dial Press, 1980.

Three by the Sea. New York, Dial Press, 1981; London, Bodley Head, 1982.

Fox in Love. New York, Dial Press, 1982; London, Bodley Head, 1983.

Fox and His Friends. New York, Dial Press, and London, Bodley Head, 1982.

Fox at School. New York, Dial Press, 1983; London, Bodley Head, 1984.

Fox on Wheels. New York, Dial Press, 1983.

Fox All Week. New York, Dial Press, and London, Bodley Head, 1984.

Four on the Shore. New York, Dial Press, and London, A. and C. Black, 1985.

Other (retellings)

Mother Goose. New York, Farrar Straus, 1979.

Red Riding Hood. New York, Dial Press, 1987; as *Little Red Riding Hood*, London, Collins, 1987.

Goldilocks and the Three Bears. New York, Dial Press, 1988; as *Goldilocks*, London, Collins, 1988.

*

Manuscript Collections: Kerlan Collection, University of Minnesota, Minneapolis; University of Oregon Library, Eugene.

Illustrator: *Plink, Plink, Plink* by Byrd Baylor, 1971; *All the Way Home* by Lore Segal, 1973; *Dinosaur's Housewarming Party* by Norma Klein, 1974; *The Piggy in the Puddle* by Charlotte Pomerantz, 1974; *The Tutti-Frutti Case*, 1975, *It's So Nice to Have a Wolf Around the House*, 1977, *Bumps in the Night*, 1979, *I Will Not Go to Market Today*, 1979, and *There's a Party at Mona's Tonight*, 1981, all by Harry Allard; *The Frog Prince* retold by Edith Tarcov,

1974; *Mary Alice*, 1975, *Bonzini!*, 1976, *Nosey Mrs. Rat*, 1985, and *Mary Alice Returns*, 1986, all by Jeffrey Allen; *Dinner at Alberta's* by Russell Hoban, 1975; *Someone Is Talking about Hortense* by Laurette Murdock, 1975; *A Day with Whisker Wickles* by Cynthia Jameson, 1975; *The Boy Who Cried Wolf* by Freya Littledale, 1976; *Lazy Stories* retold by Diane Wolkstein, 1976; *Carrot Nose* by Jan Wahl, 1978; *MacGoose's Grocery* by Frank Asch, 1978; *How Beastly!* by Jane Yolen, 1980; *The Exploding Frog and Other Fables* retold by John McFarland, 1981; *Roger's Umbrella* by Daniel Pinkwater, 1982; *The Night Before Christmas* by Clement C. Moore, 1985; *Haunted House Jokes* by Louis Phillips, 1987; *Cinderella* retold by Barbara Karlin, 1989.

James Marshall comments:

I have literally hundreds of notebooks and sketchbooks, and I always carry one with me. My published books grow out of these.

*   *   *

James Marshall, the prolific author-illustrator of more than 40 books principally for very young children (grades 1–5) has illustrated nearly an equal number by others since his career began in 1971. His books use wit and humor to convey themes suitable for the young: respect, kindness, and friendship. His illustrations likewise mix bold colors and simple outlines with visual puns. An acknowledged debt to such different artists as Maurice Sendak and Edward Gorey shows in his work, to whom he has dedicated a book each. His stories often paradoxically link opposites: adult sophistication and novelty meld with the traditional format of stories for children. In story and illustration, he intends to give the reader, as he says, "two diverse elements that shouldn't go together, but when they do it clicks." His better stories do click for both parent and child.

The series of seven George and Martha books, the fifth of which was dedicated to Sendak, shows these qualities best. In these short vignettes, a pair of hippos, named after the protagonists of Edward Albee's *Who's Afraid of Virginia Woolf*, demonstrate their mutual affection, tolerance, and forgiveness of each other's foibles and failings. Each book consists of five very short and often linked stories, in which, for example, George looms over the refrigerators he's raiding, Martha incongruously walks a tightrope, the two take turns scaring each other, or Martha lends George the irritating cuckoo clock which he had bought for her present.

Another series which he has illustrated and written with Harry Allard chronicles the inane adventures of the Stupid family. These satirize the antics of the nuclear American family in the mass media of the 1950's and feature Stanley Q. Stupid, Mrs. Stupid, their children Buster and Petunia, dog Kitty, cat Xylophone, and assorted Stupid kin. These are calculated to amuse adults and children, though on different levels; for example, in *The Stupids Have a Ball*, the Stupids celebrate their children's failing report cards.

The popular series of Miss Nelson books also co-authored with Harry Allard deal with the adventures of grade-school children in relating to their sweet teacher Miss Nelson and her alter ego Miss Viola Swamp. In Marshall's own series about grade-school friends, Spider, Lolly, and Sam try to top each other's scary stories in *Three by the Sea*, *Four on the Shore*, and *Three Up a Tree*. Other books feature the cross bear Carruthers and his friends Emily Pig and Eugene Turtle. *What's the Matter with Carruthers?* and *Taking Care of Carruthers* emphasize mutual responsibility among these friends. Emily and Eugene appear also in *Yummers!* and the sequel *Yummers Too* gentle satires on Emily's frequent lapses from her diet. The newest series, six easy readers begun under the pen name of Edward Marshall, features Fox, named from Fassbinder's film, who is often outfoxed by his younger sister Louise or by fate. But this adolescent hero fumbles on to success. An adult version of this inept unfoxy hero bumbles his way through *Rapscallion Jones*.

Other books about diverse friendships include *Willis*, wherein Bird, Lobster, and Snake put on a show at the beach to buy sun glasses for their friend Willis the Alligator. In *The Guest* the unlikely friends are moose Mona and a snail, Maurice. *Speedboat* celebrates the unlikely friendship of the dog Jasper Raisintoast, an irresponsible adventurer, and his stay-at-home friend Tweedy Jones. In *Portly McSwine* a worrywart pig, despite his friends' reassurances, anticipates endlessly the misadventures possible at his party on National Snout Day. He even gets a swine flu shot. *Space Case* shows how people trivialize the extraordinary. A flying saucer found by Buddy McGee is just another gadget to his family; to those at school, an electronic calculator; and to those out on the streets at Halloween, just another kid in costume. In *Merry Christmas, Space Case* the flying saucer keeps its promise to return at Christmas despite being stopped for speeding and lingering at a science-fiction movie. It rescues Buddy from the rotten, rich Goober twins by turning them into snowmen. Similarly in *Troll Country* a little girl defeats the real trolls that her mother believes in but that her stolid father ignores. Marshall's books occasionally play with the format of the adult mystery story. In *Miss Dog's Christmas Treat* the reader is to find the missing box of candy. *A Summer in the South*, spoofing Agatha Christie, features detective Eleanor Owl, her assistant Mr. Paws (a cat), and various eccentrics such as Don Coyote, a reclusive hypochondriac, at an island's resort hotel where a stolen Egyptian treasure is retrieved. His illustrations grace similar spoofs such as Harry Allard's *Bumps in the Night*, which are clever imitations of Edward Gorey's sets and costumes for the New York production of *Dracula*.

Recently Marshall has illustrated or retold versions of classical children's stories, such as Edith Tarcov's *The Frog Prince*; John McFarland's *The Exploding Frog and Other Fables*, retold from Aesop; and Clement C. Moore's *The Night Before Christmas*. These have amusing touches in the unusual selections chosen or the illustrations; for example one line-up of characters in Marshall's own retelling of *Mother Goose* recalls a familar scene from TV's *Muppet Show*. But with his witty retelling and illustrations for *Red Riding Hood* and *Goldilocks and the Three Bears*, Marshall has gone further to make these familiar stories his own. Red Riding Hood's house is copied from the author's house in Connecticut, even to its number 93. Grannie, who lies in bed reading from a pile of books, is modeled after a neighbor and scholar of children's literature. The heroine is a brunette innocent who is misled by the courteous wolf in the forest. But at the end of the story, she has learned her lesson well and avoids a charming alligator who beckons to her with hat and cane in hand. In contrast, the little blond heroine of *Goldilocks and the Three Bears* is a pest, notorious among her neighbors. She reminds readers of the two bad boys in *The Cut-Ups* and *The Cut-Ups Cut Loose*. She deliberately ignores signs warning against the short cut through the forest. She breaks into the charming Victorian cottage (modeled after quaint 19th-century summer homes in a church campground near the author's Connecticut home) of the very civilized and courteous bears. She eats up or spills the porridge, breaks chairs, and beds, after replying to her own invitation "I don't mind if I do." She mistakes the brown fur in the cottage for signs of a kitty. She chooses the Baby Bear's toy-cluttered bed for sleep when she is "quite tuckered out." When the bears return, she jumps out the window and they hope never to see this rude interloper again. Both of these books have been acclaimed by reviewers and librarians for their fresh approaches to familiar stories. They demonstrate that Marshall has developed into a confident reteller of classic stories.

Marshall's own original stories, parodies, and retellings, along with their clever but simple illustrations, offer humor, wit, and occasionally sophistication. He takes the perennial concerns of young children and balances them against the greater virtues of that age—being infinitely forgiving, trusting, and loving, totally honest, eager to learn (even French in the case of George), and unfailingly

supportive of friends despite their obvious faults. Thus life in many of Marshall's stories, especially the George and Martha books, resolves itself through "mini-farces," artful stories told and illustrated in a seemingly artless style.

—Hugh T. Keenan

MARTIN, David. Has also written as Spinifex. British. Born Ludwig Detsinyi in Budapest, Hungary, 22 December 1915. Educated at schools in Germany. Served as a first-aid orderly in the International Brigade, Spain, 1937–38. Married Elizabeth Richenda Powell in 1941; one son. Worked for European Service, BBC, and the *Daily Express*, 1938–47, and literary editor, *Reynolds News*, 1945–47, all in London; foreign correspondent in India, 1948–49; Hindu Madras correspondent in Australia 1949–69. Writer-in-residence, Western Australian Institute of Technology, Bentley, 1981. Since 1973 member of the Council, Australian Society of Authors. Recipient: Australian Council Senior fellowship, 1973, 1975, 1979, 1981. A.M. (Member, Order of Australia), 1988. Agent: Curtis Brown (Australia), 86 William Street, Paddington, New South Wales 2021. Address: 28 Wood Street, Beechworth, Victoria 3747, Australia.

PUBLICATIONS FOR CHILDREN

Fiction

Hughie, illustrated by Ron Brooks.   Melbourne, Nelson, and New York, St. Martin's Press, 1971; London, Blackie, 1972.
Frank and Francesca.   Melbourne, Nelson, 1972; London, Blackie, 1973.
Gary, illustrated by Con Aslanis.   Melbourne, Cassell, 1972; London, Cassell, 1975.
The Chinese Boy.   Sydney, Hodder and Stoughton, and Leicester, Brockhampton Press, 1973.
The Cabby's Daughter.   Sydney, Hodder and Stoughton, and Leicester, Brockhampton Press, 1974.
Katie, with Richenda Martin, illustrated by Noela Young.   Sydney, Hodder and Stoughton, and Leicester, Brockhampton Press, 1974.
Mister P and His Remarkable Flight, illustrated by Astra Lacis. Sydney, Hodder and Stoughton, 1975; as *Mister P Street Pigeon*, London, Macdonald, 1988.
The Devilish Mystery of the Flying Mum.   Melbourne, Nelson, 1977.
The Mermaid Attack.   Collingwood, Victoria, Outback Press, 1978.
The Man in the Red Turban, illustrated by Genevieve Rees.   Richmond, Victoria, Hutchinson, 1978.
Peppino Says Goodbye.   Adelaide, Rigby, 1980.
Peppino Turns His Luck.   Adelaide, Rigby, and Leeds, Edward Arnold, 1982.
Peppino and the Tobacco War.   Adelaide, Rigby, 1984.
The Girl Who Didn't Know Kelly.   Richmond, Victoria, Hutchinson, 1985.
Clowning Sim, illustrated by Jan Martin.   Blackburn, Victoria, Collins Dove, 1988.

Verse

I Rhyme My Time: A Selection of Poems for Young People, illustrated by Robert Ingpen.   Milton, Queensland, Jacaranda Press, 1980.
The Kitten Who Wouldn't Purr, illustrated by Mark Payne.   Mel-

bourne, Macmillan, 1987; London, Macmillan, 1988.

Other

Fox on My Door (autobiography).   Blackburn, Victoria, Collins Dove, 1987.

PUBLICATIONS FOR ADULTS

Novels

Tiger Bay.   London, Martin and Reid, 1946.
The Stones of Bombay.   London, Wingate, 1949.
The Young Wife.   London, Macmillan, 1962.
The Hero of Too.   London, Cassell, 1965; as *The Hero of the Town*, New York, Morrow, 1965.
The King Between.   Melbourne and London, Cassell, 1966; as *The Littlest Neutral*, New York, Crown, 1966.
Where a Man Belongs.   Melbourne and London, Cassell, 1969.

Short Stories

The Shoes Men Walk In.   London, Pilot Press, 1946.
Foreigners.   Adelaide, Rigby, 1981.

Plays

The Shepherd and the Hunter (produced London, 1945).   London, Wingate, 1946.
The Young Wife (produced Melbourne, 1966).

Verse

Battlefields and Girls.   Glasgow, Maclellan, 1942.
Trident, with Hubert Nicholson and John Manifold.   London, Fore, 1944.
From Life: Selected Poems.   Sydney, Current, 1953.
Rob the Robber, His Life and Vindication (as Spinifex).   Melbourne, Waters, 1954.
Poems 1938–1958.   Sydney, Edwards and Shaw, 1958.
Spiegel the Cat: A Story-Poem.   Melbourne, Cheshire, 1961; London, Cassell, 1969; New York, Potter, 1971.
The Gift: Poems 1959–1965.   Brisbane, Jacaranda Press, 1966.
The Idealist.   Brisbane, Jacaranda Press, 1968.

Other

Psychological Effects of the "Western" Film, with F.E. Emery.   Melbourne, University of Melbourne Department of Visual Aids, 1957.
Television Tension Programmes.   Canberra, Australian Broadcasting Control Board, 1963.
On the Road to Sydney (travel).   Melbourne, Nelson, 1970.
I'll Take Australia, photographs by Georg Lindström.   Milton, Queensland, Jacaranda Press, 1978.
Armed Neutrality for Australia.   Blackburn, Victoria, Collins Dove, 1984.

Editor, *Rhyme and Reason: 34 Poems.*   London, Fore, 1944.
Editor, *New World, New Song: A Selection of Poems from the Left.*   Sydney, Current, 1955.

*

Manuscript Collection: National Library of Australia, Canberra.

David Martin comments:

I make no sharp distinction between writing for young readers and other readers. My "young novels" are often concerned with the struggle of outsiders (Australian aborigines, Chinese on the Australian goldfields, etc.). I came to young fiction fairly late in life, and don't intend to concentrate on it exclusively. I like writing for teenagers because they respond honestly to an honest story: they do not require attention-whipping novelty at any price. I write about girls with as much sincerity and pleasure as I do about boys.

*   *   *

David Martin, described by one critic as "the most improbable Australian writer who ever existed," has origins both European and Jewish. His contribution to Australian children's literature has thus been distinguished by a somewhat exotic quality. He has, understandably, chosen to espouse the cause of neglected minority groups in his adopted country, and has enriched its literature for the young in terms of content if not in style.

In his first children's book, *Hughie*, he took as his theme the plight of the Aborigines, ironically treated as aliens in their own country. In *The Chinese Boy* he showed how Chinese goldminers were persecuted during the goldrushes of the 1860's at Kiandra and Lambing Flat, in New South Wales. *The Man in the Red Turban* is the story of one of the conspicuous itinerant Indian hawkers who plied their wares in suspicious and conservative white rural Australia during the Great Depression of the 1930's. This book also reflects the author's repugnance towards capitalist exploitation of the working classes.

Martin can handle raw humour with gusto and is at his best in exploring the thoughts, fears, hopes, and preoccupations of children, rather than what they actually say. His particular themes are the value of love and the necessity for struggle, as exemplified in his best work, such as *The Cabby's Daughter*, set in the Victorian gold-mining town of Beechworth in 1902, or *Mister P and His Remarkable Flight*, which examines the same theme in the life of an "outsider" pigeon, rather than an alienated human—such as the famous bushranger outlaw, Ned Kelly, in *The Girl Who Didn't Know Kelly*. His Peppino books, for younger readers, about an immigrant boy's experiences in Italy and Australia, are also about the need to stand up for one's rights in the face of opposition, bullying, and conflict.

The didacticism in Martin's early novels for children seems heavy-handed today, as does their old-fashioned *Boy's Weekly* flavour, which relies on colourful and spectacular incident rather than strong characterisation or fully thought-out thematic treatment. His books are seldom totally satisfying because of this dichotomy; plot and propaganda do not grow naturally out of one another with any sense of unity. His habit of fragmenting families, sometimes by death (as in *The Cabby's Daughter* and *Frank and Francesca*) or desertion (the hero of *Clowning Sim* has a succession of foster parents) may at first seem a melodramatic device, but it reflects something of the state of the author's own childhood (he was raised by a stepmother in what was, to him, a foreign country).

Generally, Martin has been at his weakest in portraying major characters—his are mainly types. His minor characters, sometimes only glimpsed, are often more memorable than his improbable heroes or his dastardly villains. Sim, the boy who can't stop clowning (*Clowning Sim*) is probably his most rounded and interesting character.

In spite of his stylistic shortcomings and excesses, Martin is a writer of life, zest, and humour who shares strong personal emotions with his readers. In *Fox on My Door*, he also shares with them his reminiscences of an eventful life, and his thoughts (not at all morbid) about death—even down to the preparations he has carefully made for it! It is this kind of "improbability" which makes Martin unique among Australian writers for children.

—Walter McVitty

MARTIN, J(ohn) P(ercival). British. Born in Scarborough, Yorkshire, in 1880. Married Nancy Mann, two sons and two daughters; also a second marriage. Became Methodist minister in 1902: missionary in South Africa; chaplain during World War I, serving mainly in Palestine; minister, Timberscombe, Somerset, 1945–66. *Died in March 1966.*

PUBLICATIONS FOR CHILDREN (illustrated by Quentin Blake)

Fiction

Uncle. London, Cape, 1964; New York, Coward McCann, 1966.
Uncle Cleans Up. London, Cape, 1965; New York, Coward Mc-Cann, 1967.
Uncle and His Detective. London, Cape, 1966.
Uncle and the Treacle Trouble. London, Cape, 1967.
Uncle and Claudius the Camel. London, Cape, 1969.
Uncle and the Battle for Badgertown. London, Cape, 1973.

*   *   *

J.P. Martin's stories belong to the distinctively English tradition of high-spirited nonsensical fantasy, originated by Carroll and Lear in the mid-19th century and continued down to the present day by such writers as Lofting, Norman Hunter, and Roald Dahl. As a general rule nonsense is most effective if it is firmly anchored to known realities—with Carroll, for instance, there is the calm common sense of Alice herself, and with Lofting the down-to-earth setting of Puddleby-on-the-Marsh. At first sight Martin's stories are about as far from reality as one could possibly imagine. Their setting is an un-geographical never-never land inhabited by a bizarre population of animals, magicians, ghosts, and dwarfs, together with a sprinkling of incongruous human beings. The behavior of these characters is as extravagant and unfathomable as their names, of which Jellytussle, Noddy Ninety, and Alonzo Whitebeard are typical examples. At the level of pure entertainment the stories are quite likely to succeed with young children from ages six or seven upwards, although some may find the whole farrago just too bewildering, and some adults might be uneasy at the degree of violence and the apparent adulation of wealth and power.

But there is another level in these stories, certainly detectable by adults or perceptive teenagers. The dominant theme throughout each of the six volumes is the struggle for supremacy between the people of Homeward, led by the mighty elephant Uncle, and the gang of disreputable hooligans living nearby in the squalor of Badfort. Without any doubt the author, born in 1880 and ordained in 1902 as a Methodist minister, was thinking consciously or subconsciously of the "two nations" of Victorian England and the contrast between a great land-owner and his impoverished neighbours. In this respect there is a most obvious echo of *The Wind in the Willows*; but whereas Grahame invites his readers to sympathize exclusively with Badger and the River-bankers against the Wildwooders, Martin does seem to allow for the possibility of an alternative view. However great the apparent contrast between virtue and villainy in the warring factions, the persistent reader may well conclude at some stage that Uncle is really a pompous old autocrat, and in point of courage, ingenuity,

and spirited invective no match for his arch-enemy Beaver Hateman. The author was probably a thoughtful critic of society as well as a devout Christian—but he had the good sense totally to exclude direct preaching from his stories.

Each of Martin's six published books, including the three which were edited after his death, contain at least one or two episodes in his liveliest vein, and on balance there is little to choose between them. His reputation would probably be much higher if he had been persuaded to condense the whole rambling saga into just one volume. The first-published book should certainly be read first, but *Uncle and His Detective*, with its relatively coherent plot and such memorable characters as the master sleuth A.B. Fox and Leominster the lion butler, may well prove to be the favourite with many children.

—Alasdair K.D. Campbell

MARTIN, Patricia Miles. Also wrote as Jerry Lane; Miska Miles. American. Born in Cherokee, Kansas, 14 November 1899. Educated at East High School, Denver, graduated 1917; San Mateo College, California, 1965–66. Married Edward Richard Martin in 1942 (died 1979). Recipient: Christopher award, 1972. *Died 2 January 1986.*

PUBLICATIONS FOR CHILDREN

Fiction

Sylvester Jones and the Voice in the Forest, illustrated by Leonard Weisgard. New York, Lothrop, 1958.
The Pointed Brush, illustrated by Roger Duvoisin. New York, Lothrop, 1959; Kingswood, Surrey, World's Work, 1960.
Chandler Chipmunk's Flying Lesson and Other Stories, illustrated by Margo Locke. New York, Abingdon Press, 1960.
Happy Piper and the Goat, illustrated by Kurt Werth. New York, Lothrop, 1960.
The Little Brown Hen, illustrated by Harper Johnson. New York, Crowell, 1960.
Suzu and the Bride Doll, illustrated by Kazue Mizumura. Chicago, Rand McNally, 1960; Kingswood, Surrey, World's Work, 1964.
The Raccoon and Mrs. McGinnis, illustrated by Leonard Weisgard. New York, Putnam, 1961.
Benjie Goes into Business, illustrated by Paul Galdone. New York, Putnam, 1961.
Show and Tell, illustrated by Tom Hamil. New York, Putnam, 1962.
The Rice Bowl Pet, illustrated by Ezra Jack Keats. New York, Crowell, 1962.
The Lucky Little Porcupine, illustrated by Lee Smith. New York, Putnam, 1963.
The Birthday Present, illustrated by Margo Locke. Nashville, Abingdon Press, 1963.
Little Two and the Peach Tree, illustrated by Joan Berg. New York, Atheneum, 1963.
The Greedy One, illustrated by Kazue Mizumura. Chicago, Rand McNally, 1964; Kingswood, Surrey, World's Work, 1965.
No, No, Rosina, illustrated by Earl Thollander. New York, Putnam, 1964.
Calvin and the Cub Scouts, illustrated by Tom Hamil. New York, Putnam, 1964.
The Broomtail Bronc, illustrated by Margo Locke. Nashville, Abingdon Press, 1965.
Jump Frog Jump, illustrated by Earl Thollander. New York, Put-

nam, 1965.

The Bony Pony, illustrated by Glen Dines. New York, Putnam, 1965.

Rolling the Cheese, illustrated by Alton Raible. New York, Atheneum, 1966.

The Pumpkin Patch, illustrated by Tom Hamil. New York, Putnam, 1966.

Mrs. Crumble and Fire Engine No. 7, illustrated by Earl Thollander. New York, Putnam, 1966.

Friend of Miguel, illustrated by Genia. Chacago, Rand McNally, 1967.

Trina's Boxcar, illustrated by Robert Jefferson. Nashville, Abingdon Press, 1967; as *Trina*, New York, Scholastic, 1972.

Dolls from Cheyenne, illustrated by Don Almquist. New York, Putnam, 1967.

Woody's Big Trouble, illustrated by Paul Galdone. New York, Putnam, 1967.

A Long Ago Christmas, illustrated by Albert Orbaan. New York, Putnam, 1968.

Grandma's Gun, illustrated by Robert Corey. San Carlos, California, Golden Gate Books, 1968.

Kumi and the Pearl, illustrated by Tom Hamil. New York, Putnam, 1968.

One Special Dog, illustrated by John and Lucy Hawkinson. Chicago, Rand McNally, 1968.

The Dog and the Boat Boy, illustrated by Earl Thollander. New York, Putnam, 1969.

That Cat! 1-2-3, illustrated by Unada. New York, Putnam, 1970.

There Goes the Tiger!, illustrated by Tom Hamil. New York, Putnam, 1970.

Navajo Pet, illustrated by John Hamberger. New York, Putnam, 1971.

Be Brave, Charlie, illustrated by Bonnie Johnson. New York, Putnam, 1972.

Cat, illustrated by Jonathan Goell. Boston, Ginn, 1974.

Hide, illustrated by Jon McIntosh. Boston, Ginn, 1974.

How Can You Hide an Elephant?, illustrated by George Ulrich. Boston, Ginn, 1974.

In the Zoo (as Jerry Lane), illustrated by Blair Drawson. Boston, Ginn, 1974.

Run! (as Jerry Lane), illustrated by Joel Snyder. Boston, Ginn, 1974.

Fiction as Miska Miles

Kickapoo, illustrated by Wesley Dennis. Boston, Little Brown, 1961.

Dusty and the Fiddlers, illustrated by Erik Blegvad. Boston, Little Brown, 1962.

See a White Horse, illustrated by Wesley Dennis. Boston, Little Brown, 1963.

Pony in the Schoolhouse, illustrated by Erik Blegvad. Boston, Little Brown, 1964.

Mississippi Possum, illustrated by John Schoenherr. Boston, Little Brown, 1965.

Fox and the Fire, illustrated by John Schoenherr. Boston, Little Brown, 1966.

Teacher's Pet, illustrated by Fen Lasell. Boston, Little Brown, 1966.

The Pieces of Home, illustrated by Victor Ambrus. Boston, Little Brown, 1967.

Rabbit Garden, illustrated by John Schoenherr. Boston, Little Brown, 1967.

Uncle Fonzo's Ford, illustrated by Wendy Watson. Boston, Little Brown, 1968.

Nobody's Cat, illustrated by John Schoenherr. Boston, Little Brown, 1969.

Apricot ABC, illustrated by Peter Parnall. Boston, Little Brown, 1969.

Hoagie's Rifle-Gun, illustrated by John Schoenherr. Boston, Little Brown, 1970.

Eddie's Bear, illustrated by John Schoenherr. Boston, Little Brown, 1970.

Gertrude's Pocket, illustrated by Emily McCully. Boston, Little Brown, 1970.

Annie and the Old One, illustrated by Peter Parnall. Boston, Little Brown, 1971.

Wharf Rat, illustrated by John Schoenherr. Boston, Little Brown, 1972.

Somebody's Dog, illustrated by John Schoenherr. Boston, Little Brown, 1973.

Otter in the Cove, illustrated by John Schoenherr. Boston, Little Brown, 1974.

Tree House Town, illustrated by Emily McCully. Boston, Little Brown, 1974.

Swim, Little Duck, illustrated by Jim Arnosky. Boston, Little Brown, 1976.

Chicken Forgets, illustrated by Jim Arnosky. Boston, Little Brown, 1976.

Aaron's Door, illustrated by Alan Cober. Boston, Little Brown, 1977.

Small Rabbit, illustrated by Jim Arnosky. Boston, Little Brown, 1977.

Beaver Moon, illustrated by John Schoenherr. Boston, Little Brown, 1978.

Noisy Gander, illustrated by Leslie Morrill. New York, Dutton, 1978.

Mouse Six and the Happy Birthday, illustrated by Leslie Morrill. New York, Dutton, 1978.

Jenny's Cat, illustrated by Wendy Watson. New York, Dutton, 1979.

This Little Pig, illustrated by Leslie Morrill. New York, Dutton, 1980.

Horse and the Bad Morning, with Ted Clymer, illustrated by Leslie Morrill. New York, Dutton, 1982.

Plays

Two Plays about Foolish People (includes *An Invitation to Supper* and *Little Ugo and the Foolish Ones*), illustrated by Gabriel Lisowski. New York, Putnam, 1972.

Verse

Sing, Sailor, Sing, illustrated by Graham Booth. San Carlos, California, Golden Gate Books, 1966; Kingswood, Surrey, World's Work, 1968.

Other

John Fitzgerald Kennedy, illustrated by Paul Frame. New York, Putnam, 1964.

Abraham Lincoln, illustrated by Gustav Schrotter. New York, Putnam, 1964.

Pocahontas, illustrated by Portia Takakjian. New York, Putnam, 1964.

Daniel Boone, illustrated by Glen Dines. New York, Putnam, 1965.

Jefferson Davis, illustrated by Salem Tamer. New York, Putnam, 1966.

Andrew Jackson, illustrated by Salem Tamer. New York, Putnam, 1966.

John Marshall, illustrated by Salem Tamer. New York, Putnam,

1967.

Dolley Madison, illustrated by Unada.   New York, Putnam, 1967.

Jacqueline Kennedy Onassis, illustrated by Paul Frame.   New York, Putnam, 1969.

Zachary Taylor, illustrated by Tran Mawicke.   New York, Putnam, 1969.

The Dog Next Door and Other Stories (reader), with Theodore Clymer.   Boston, Ginn, 1969.

James Madison, illustrated by Richard Cuffari.   New York, Putnam, 1970.

Eskimos: People of Alaska, illustrated by Robert Frankenberg.   New York, Parents' Magazine Press, 1970.

Indians: The First Americans, illustrated by Robert Frankenberg.   New York, Parents' Magazine Press, 1970.

Thomas Alva Edison, illustrated by Fermin Rocker.   New York, Putnam, 1971.

Chicanos: Mexicans in the United States, illustrated by Robert Frankenberg.   New York, Parents' Magazine Press, 1971.

May I Come In? (reader), with Theodore Clymer.   Boston, Ginn, 1976.

*

Manuscript Collections: de Grummond Collection, University of Southern Mississippi, Hattiesburg; Kerlan Collection, University of Minnesota, Minneapolis.

Patricia Miles Martin commented:

(1978) It is my hope that through my books children will be interested in reading—not only my work—but in further reading. It is my intention to pass on to young people my own values and standards.

*   *   *

Patricia Miles Martin provided the young reader with an opportunity to expand his own horizon to include unusual animals, cultural pluralism, and famous people. She was a craftswoman, researching and writing with unusual respect for her subjects.

Flora and fauna interested the author since her debut, *Sylvester Jones and the Voice in the Forest.* She selected unlikely heroes such as those of *Mississippi Possum, The Lucky Little Porcupine,* and *Wharf Rat.* Even her alphabet book, *Apricot ABC,* is an ecological story following the web of life: "An *Apricot* tree grew knobbly and tall/Beside a rickety garden wall....it startled a *Bee.*" Martin's feelings for the earth and for life's stages are apparent in many books, but are epitomized in *Annie and the Old One.* Natural elements are depicted in other books. "The account of the blizzard and what came of it is refreshingly down to earth, with no heroics," reviewer Mary Dunham wrote of *Pony in the Schoolhouse* for the *Christian Science Monitor* (5 November 1964). Selma G. Lanes commented in *Book Week* (3 April 1966) that in *Fox and the Fire* "Both author and illustrator are naturalists at heart, and not a single false or anthropomorphic note is struck in this simple, straightforward tale of a fox's eye-view of a natural disaster and its aftermath." In a review of *Mississippi Possum,* Alice Dalgliesh wrote of the animal in the flood in *Saturday Review* (19 June 1965), "Simple, direct, well-written, this story succeeds in making the reader care about the little possum that lived in a hollow log and was afraid of people....Stories like this, written in a natural way, need all the recognition that is their due."

Animals manifest human child-like and parental behavior in recent books such as *Small Rabbit, Noisy Gander,* and *This Little Pig.* Rabbit parents warn their young one about dangerous hawk, fox, and humans, and humor arises from mistaken identities. Papa gander continually honks, but ultimately saves the farmyard creatures from

the peril of the coyote, while in the third title the runt of seven piglets becomes the leader. The spare plots in these books fail to measure up to those of her earlier books. In *Swim, Little Duck,* she had eloquently portrayed the coziness of the familiar, while offering real information about ducks, but *Beaver Moon,* based on a legend, is such a mixture of fact and fiction that it loses its strength.

Annie and the Old One deals with aging and death in an American Indian setting. *Aaron's Door* attempts to describe contemporary adoption, and the problems hostile Aaron has in accepting his new sister Debbie. There is a parallel between these two books—in the first a hedgehog stays in his den awaiting spring, and in the second Aaron locks himself in his room, and is eventually forced to emerge.

Martin rarely identifies cultures less familiar to the general reading audience as ethnically or racially different. It is only by implication or in the illustrations that the families in *Mississippi Possum* or *The Little Brown Hen* are black or that the heroine of *Teacher's Pet* is a migrant fruit picker in Colorado. The author opens the door on Japanese family life in *The Greedy One, Kumi and the Pearl,* and *Little Two and the Peach Tree,* and documents tribal American-Indian culture in *Navajo Pet* and *Annie and the Old One.*

Martin's non-fiction books are primarily in series and range historically from the Supreme Court Justice John Marshall to Jacqueline Kennedy Onassis. Typical are the "See and Read Beginning to Read Biographies" directed to youngsters grades two to four. Books about Chicano, Eskimo, and Indian cultures in what is now America are in A Stepping Stone Book series for youngsters.

Martin's skill as a poet is manifest in both verse and prose texts. *Sing, Sailor, Sing* opens, "In the year of fourteen-thirty two/There was a boy Bartholmeu/In Portugal/He lived in a time when no one knew/What was false and what was true/In Portugal."

Reviewers use words and phrases such as "heartwarming," "quiet beauty," and "gentle dignity" to describe Martin's texts. *Annie and the Old One* has been honored as a Newbery Honor Book, in addition to receiving other awards.

—Karen Nelson Hoyle

———

MASEFIELD, John (Edward). British. Born in Ledbury, Herefordshire, 1 June 1878. Educated at Warwick School, 1888–90; cadet on merchant training ship *Conway,* Liverpool, 1891–93. Served in the British Red Cross in France and Gallipoli, 1915; commissioned by British government to observe and write on Battle of the Somme, 1916–17. Married Constance de la Cherois Crommelin in 1903 (died 1960); one daughter and one son. Apprentice on White Star barque *Gilcruix* on trip to Chile, 1894; Sixth Officer, White Star mail ship *Adriatic,* 1895; bartender, Columbian Hotel, New York, 1895; worked at Alexander Smith carpet factory, Yonkers, New York, 1895–97; worked in City of London, 1897; clerk, Capital and Counties Bank, London, 1898–1901; art exhibition secretary, Wolverhampton, 1902; sub-editor, *Speaker* magazine, London, 1903; staff member, Manchester *Guardian,* 1904–05, and feature writer from 1907. Lectured in the United States, 1916 and 1918, and for the British Council in many European countries. President, Society of Authors, 1937–67; first President, National Book League; member, British Council Books and Periodicals Committee. Recipient (for poetry): Royal Society of Literature Polignac prize, 1912; Shakespeare prize (Hamburg), 1938; William Foyle prize, 1961; National Book League prize, 1964. D. Litt.: Yale University, New Haven, Connecticut, 1918; Harvard University, Cambridge, Massachusetts, 1918; Oxford University, 1922; Cambridge University, 1931; LL.D.: University of Aberdeen, 1922; Honorary degrees: universities of Glasgow, 1923, Manchester, 1923, Liverpool, 1930, St. Andrews, 1930, and Wales, 1932. Honorary member, American Academy, 1930; named Poet Laureate, 1930; Order of Merit, 1935; Royal Society of Literature Companion of Literature, 1961. *Died 12 May 1967.*

PUBLICATIONS FOR CHILDREN

Fiction

A Book of Discoveries, illustrated by Gordon Browne. London, Wells Gardner, and New York, Stokes, 1910.
Lost Endeavour. London, Nelson, 1910; New York, Macmillan, 1917.
Martin Hyde, The Duke's Messenger, illustrated by T.C. Dugdale. London, Wells Gardner, and Boston, Little Brown, 1910.
Jim Davis; or, The Captive of the Smugglers. London, Wells Gardner, 1911; New York, Stokes, 1912.
The Midnight Folk. London, Heinemann, and New York, Macmillan, 1927.
The Bird of Dawning; or, The Fortune of the Sea. London, Heinemann, and New York, Macmillan, 1933.
The Box of Delights; or, When the Wolves Were Running. London, Heinemann, and New York, Macmillan, 1935.
Dead Ned: The Autobiography of a Corpse.... London, Heinemann, and New York, Macmillan, 1938.
Live and Kicking Ned. London, Heinemann, and New York, Macmillan, 1939.

PUBLICATIONS FOR ADULTS

Novels

Captain Margaret: A Romance. London, Grant Richards, and Philadelphia, Lippincott, 1908.
Multitude and Solitude. London, Grant Richards, 1909; New York, Kennerley, 1910.
The Street of To-Day. London, Dent, and New York, Dutton, 1911.
Sard Harker. London, Heinemann, and New York, Macmillan, 1924.
Odtaa. London, Heinemann, and New York, Macmillan, 1926.
The Hawbucks. London, Heinemann, and New York, Macmillan, 1929.
The Taking of the Gry. London, Heinemann, and New York, Macmillan, 1934.
Victorious Troy!; or, "The Hurrying Angel." London, Heinemann, and New York, Macmillan, 1935.
Eggs and Baker; or, The Days of Trial. London, Heinemann, and New York, Macmillan, 1936.
The Square Peg; or, The Gun Fella. London, Heinemann, and New York, Macmillan, 1937.
Basilissa: A Tale of the Empress Theodora. London, Heinemann, and New York, Macmillan, 1940.
Conquer: A Tale of the Nika Rebellion in Byzantium. London, Heinemann, and New York, Macmillan, 1941.
Badon Parchments. London, Heinemann, 1947.

Short Stories

A Mainsail Haul. London, Elkin Mathews, 1905; revised edition, 1913; New York, Macmillan, 1913.
A Tarpaulin Muster. London, Grant Richards, 1907; New York, Dodge, 1908.

The Taking of Helen. London, Heinemann, and New York, Macmillan, 1923.

Plays

The Campden Wonder (produced London, 1907). Included in *The Tragedy of Nan and Other Plays*, 1909.
The Tragedy of Nan (produced London, 1908). Included in *The Tragedy of Nan and Other Plays*, 1909.
The Tragedy of Nan and Other Plays (includes *The Campden Wonder* and *Mrs. Harrison*). London, Grant Richards, and New York, Kennerley, 1909.
The Tragedy of Pompey the Great (produced London, 1910). London, Sidgwick and Jackson, and Boston, Little Brown, 1910; revised version (produced Manchester, 1914), Sidgwick and Jackson, and New York, Macmillan, 1914.
The Witch, adaptation of a play by Hans Wiers-Jenssen (produced Glasgow, 1910; London, 1911). New York, Brentano's, 1926; as *Anne Pedersdotter*, Boston, Little Brown, 1917.
Philip the King (produced Bristol and London, 1914). Included in *Philip the King and Other Poems*, 1914.
The Faithful (produced Birmingham, 1915; London and New York, 1919). London, Heinemann, and New York, Macmillan, 1915.
Good Friday: A Dramatic Poem (produced London, 1917). New York, Macmillan, 1915; as *Good Friday: A Play in Verse*, Letchworth, Hertfordshire, Garden City Press, 1916.
The Sweeps of Ninety-Eight (produced Birmingham, 1916). With *The Locked Chest*, Letchworth, Hertfordshire, Garden City Press, and New York, Macmillan, 1916.
The Locked Chest (produced London, 1920). With *The Sweeps of Ninety-Eight*, Letchworth, Hertfordshire, Garden City Press, and New York, Macmillan, 1916.
Esther, adaptation of the play by Racine (produced Wootton, Berkshire, 1921). London, Heinemann, and New York, Macmillan, 1922.
Berenice, adaptation of the play by Racine (produced Oxford, 1921). London, Heinemann, and New York, Macmillan, 1922.
Melloney Holtspur (produced London, 1923). London, Heinemann, and New York, Macmillan, 1922.
A King's Daughter: A Tragedy in Verse (produced Oxford, 1923; London, 1928). London, Heinemann, and New York, Macmillan, 1923.
Tristan and Isolt: A Play in Verse (produced Oxford, 1923; London, 1927). London, Heinemann, and New York, Macmillan, 1927.
The Trial of Jesus (produced London, 1926). London, Heinemann, and New York, Macmillan, 1925.
Verse and *Prose Plays.* New York, Macmillan, 2 vols., 1925.
The Coming of Christ (produced Oxford, 1928). London, Heinemann, and New York, Macmillan, 1928.
Easter: A Play for Singers. London, Heinemann, and New York, Macmillan, 1929.
End and Beginning. London, Heinemann, and New York, Macmillan, 1933.
A Play of Saint George. London, Heinemann, and New York, Macmillan, 1948.

Verse

Salt-Water Ballads. London, Grant Richards, 1902; New York, Macmillan, 1913.
Ballads. London, Elkin Mathews, 1903; revised edition, as *Ballads and Poems*, 1910.
The Everlasting Mercy. London, Sidgwick and Jackson, and Portland, Maine, Smith and Sale, 1911.
The Story of a Round-House and Other Poems. New York, Macmillan, 1912; revised edition, 1913.

The Widow in the Bye Street. London, Sidgwick and Jackson, 1912; with *The Everlasting Mercy*, New York, Macmillan, 1912.

Dauber. London, Heinemann, 1913; with *The Daffodil Fields*, New York, Macmillan, 1923.

The Daffodil Fields. London, Heinemann, and New York, Macmillan, 1913.

Philip the King and Other Poems. London, Heinemann, and New York, Macmillan, 1914.

Good Friday: A Dramatic Poem. New York, Macmillan, 1915.

Good Friday and Other Poems. New York, Macmillan, 1916.

Sonnets. New York, Macmillan, 1916.

Salt-Water Poems and Ballads. New York, Macmillan, 1916; revised edition, as *Poems*, 1929, 1935, 1953.

Sonnets and Poems. Letchworth, Hertfordshire, Garden City Press, 1916.

The Cold Cotswolds. Privately printed, 1917.

Poems of John Masefield, edited by Henry Seidel Canby and others. New York, Macmillan, 1917.

Lollingdon Downs and Other Poems. New York, Macmillan, and London, Heinemann, 1917.

Rosas. New York, Macmillan, 1918.

Reynard the Fox; or, The Ghost Heath Run. New York, Macmillan, and London, Heinemann, 1919.

Animula. London, Chiswick Press, 1920.

Enslaved. New York, Macmillan, 1920.

Enslaved and Other Poems. London, Heinemann, and New York, Macmillan, 1920.

Right Royal. New York, Macmillan, and London, Heinemann, 1920.

King Cole. London, Heinemann, and New York, Macmillan, 1921.

The Dream. London, Heinemann, and New York, Macmillan, 1922.

Selected Poems. London, Heinemann, 1922; New York, Macmillan, 1923; revised edition, 1938.

King Cole and Other Poems. London, Heinemann, 1923; as *King Cole, The Dream, and Other Poems*, New York, Macmillan, 1923.

The Dream and Other Poems. New York, Macmillan, 1923.

The Collected Poems of John Masefield. London, Heinemann, 1923; revised edition, 1932, 1938; as *Poems*, 1946.

Poems. New York, Macmillan, 2 vols., 1925.

Sonnets of Good Cheer to the Lena Ashwell Players.... London, Mendip Press, 1926.

Midsummer Night and Other Tales in Verse. London, Heinemann, and New York, Macmillan, 1928.

South and East. London, Medici Society, and New York, Macmillan, 1929.

The Wanderer of Liverpool (verse and prose). London, Heinemann, and New York, Macmillan, 1930.

Poems of the Wanderer: The Ending. Privately printed, 1930.

Minnie Maylow's Story and Other Tales and Scenes. London, Heinemann, and New York, Macmillan, 1931.

A Tale of Troy. London, Heinemann, and New York, Macmillan, 1932.

A Letter from Pontus and Other Verse. London, Heinemann, and New York, Macmillan, 1936.

Lines on the Tercentenary of Harvard University. New York, Macmillan, 1936; London, Heinemann, 1937.

The Country Scene in Poems and Pictures, illustrated by Edward Seago. London, Collins, 1936; New York, Collins, 1938.

Tribute to Ballet in Poems and Pictures, illustrated by Edward Seago. London, Collins, and New York, Macmillan, 1938.

Some Verses to Some Germans. London, Heinemann, and New York, Macmillan, 1939.

Shopping in Oxford. London, Heinemann, 1941.

Gautama the Enlightened and Other Verse. London, Heinemann, and New York, Macmillan, 1941.

Natalie Maisie and Pavilastukay: Two Tales in Verse. London, Heinemann, and New York, Macmillan, 1942.

A Generation Risen. London, Collins, 1942; New York, Macmillan, 1943.

Land Workers. London, Heinemann, 1942; New York, Macmillan, 1943.

Wonderings: Between One and Six Years. London, Heinemann, and New York, Macmillan, 1943.

Reynard the Fox...with Selected Sonnets and Lyrics. London, Heinemann, 1946.

On the Hill. London, Heinemann, and New York, Macmillan, 1949.

Selected Poems (new selection). London, Heinemann, and New York, Macmillan, 1950.

In Praise of Nurses. London, Heinemann, 1950.

Bluebells and Other Verse. London, Heinemann, and New York, Macmillan, 1961.

Old Raiger and Other Verse. London, Heinemann, 1964; New York, Macmillan, 1965.

In Glad Thanksgiving. London, Heinemann, and New York, Macmillan, 1967.

The Sea Poems. London, Heinemann, 1978.

Selected Poems, edited by John Betjeman. London, Heinemann, and New York, Macmillan, 1978.

Selected Poems, edited by Donald E. Stanford. Manchester, Carcanet, 1984.

Other

Sea Life in Nelson's Time. London, Methuen, 1905; New York, Macmillan, 1925.

On the Spanish Main; or, Some English Forays on the Isthmus of Darien.... London, Methuen, and New York, Macmillan, 1906.

Chronicles of the Pilgrim Fathers. London, Dent, and New York, Dutton, 1910.

My Faith in Woman Suffrage. London, Woman's Press, 1910.

William Shakespeare. London, Williams and Norgate, and New York, Holt, 1911; revised edition, London, Heinemann, and New York, Macmillan, 1954.

John M. Synge: A Few Personal Recollections.... Churchtown, Ireland, Cuala Press, and New York, Macmillan, 1915.

Gallipoli. London, Heinemann, and New York, Macmillan, 1916.

The Old Front Line; or, The Beginning of the Battle of the Somme. London, Heinemann, and New York, Macmillan, 1917.

The War and the Future. New York, Macmillan, 1918; as *St. George and the Dragon*, London, Heinemann, 1919.

The Poems and Plays of John Masefield. New York, Macmillan, 2 vols., 1918.

The Battle of the Somme. London, Heinemann, 1919.

John Ruskin. Privately printed, 1920.

The Taking of Helen and Other Prose Selections. New York, Macmillan, 1924; as *Recent Prose*, London, Heinemann, 1924; revised edition, Heinemann, 1932; Macmillan, 1933.

Shakespeare and Spiritual Life (lecture). London and New York, Oxford University Press, 1924.

With the Living Voice (lecture). London, Heinemann, and New York, Macmillan, 1925.

Oxford Recitations. New York, Macmillan, 1928.

Chaucer (lecture). Cambridge, University Press, and New York, Macmillan, 1931.

Poetry (lecture). London, Heinemann, 1931; New York, Macmillan, 1932.

The Conway: From Her Foundation to the Present Day. London, Heinemann, and New York, Macmillan, 1933; revised edition, Heinemann, 1953; Macmillan, 1954.

Collected Works (Wanderer Edition). London, Heinemann, 5 vols.,

1935–37.

Some Memories of W.B. Yeats (includes verse). Dublin, Cuala Press, and New York, Macmillan, 1940.

In the Mill (autobiography). London, Heinemann, and New York, Macmillan, 1941.

The Nine Days Wonder: The Operation Dynamo. London, Heinemann, and New York, Macmillan, 1941.

The Twenty Five Days. London, Heinemann, 1941.

I Want! I Want! London, National Book Council, 1944; New York, Macmillan, 1945.

New Chum (autobiography). London, Heinemann, 1944; New York, Macmillan, 1945.

A Macbeth Production. London, Heinemann, 1945; New York, Macmillan, 1946.

Thanks Before Going.... London, Heinemann, 1946; New York, Macmillan, 1947; revised edition, Heinemann, 1947.

A Book of Both Sorts: Selections from the Verse and Prose of John Masefield. London, Heinemann, 1947.

A Book of Prose Selections. London, Heinemann, and New York, Macmillan, 1950.

St. Katherine of Ledbury and Other Ledbury Papers. London, Heinemann, 1951.

So Long to Learn: Chapters of an Autobiography. London, Heinemann, and New York, Macmillan, 1952.

An Elizabethan Theatre in London. Privately printed, 1954.

The Story of Ossian. London, Heinemann, and New York, Macmillan, 1959.

Grace Before Ploughing: Fragments of Autobiography. London, Heinemann, and New York, Macmillan, 1966.

The Letters of John Masefield to Florence Lamont, edited by Corliss and Lansing Lamont. London, Macmillan, and New York, Columbia University Press, 1979.

Letters to Reyna, edited by William Buchan. London, Buchan and Enright, 1983.

Letters to Margaret Bridge, 1915–1919, edited by Donald E. Stanford. Manchester, Carcanet, 1984.

Letters from the Front 1915–17, edited by Peter Vansittart. London, Constable, 1984; New York, Watts, 1985.

Brangwen: The Poet and the Dancer (letters), edited by John Gregory. Lewes, Essex, Book Guild, 1988.

Editor, with Constance Masefield, *Lyrists of the Restoration....* London, Grant Richards, 1905; New York, Stokes, n.d.

Editor, *The Poems of Robert Herrick*. London, Grant Richards, 1906.

Editor, *Dampier's Voyages....* London, Grant Richards, 2 vols., 1906; New York, Dutton, 1907.

Editor, *A Sailor's Garland*. London, Methuen, and New York, Macmillan, 1906.

Editor, *The Lyrics of Ben Jonson, Beaumont, and Fletcher*. London, Grant Richards, 1906.

Editor, with Constance Masefield, *Essays, Moral and Polite 1660–1714*. London, Grant Richards, 1906; Freeport, New York, Books for Libraries Press, 1971.

Editor, *An English Prose Miscellany*. London, Methuen, 1907.

Editor, *Defoe* (selections). London, Bell, and New York, Macmillan, 1909.

Editor, *The Loyal Subject*, in *The Works of Beaumont and Fletcher*, edited by A.H. Bullen. London, Bell, 1910.

Editor, *My Favourite English Poems*. London, Heinemann, and New York, Macmillan, 1950.

Translator, *Polyxena's Speech from the Hecuba of Euripides*. New York, Macmillan, 1928.

*

Bibliography: *Bibliography of John Masefield* by C.H. Simmons, New York, Columbia University Press, 1930; London, Oxford University Press, 1931.

Manuscript Collections: Bodleian Library, Oxford; Humanities Research Center, University of Texas, Austin; Houghton Library, Harvard University, Cambridge, Massachusetts; Berg Collection, New York Public Library; Yale University Library, New Haven, Connecticut.

Critical Studies: *John Masefield* by L.A.G. Strong, London, Longman, 1952; *John Masefield* by Muriel Spark, London, Peter Nevill, 1953; *John Masefield* by Margery Fisher, London, Bodley Head, and New York, Walck, 1963; *Remembering John Masefield*, by Corliss Lamont, Rutherford, New Jersey, Fairleigh Dickinson University Press, 1971, London, Kaye and Ward, 1972; *John Masefield* by Sanford Sternlicht, Boston, Twayne, 1977; *John Masefield: A Life* by Constance Babington Smith, London, Oxford University Press, and New York, Macmillan, 1978.

*   *   *

John Masefield wrote few books specifically for children. Outstanding among them are the two classic fantasies, *The Midnight Folk* and its sequel *The Box of Delights*, which together form one of the finest and most original contributions to children's literature in recent times. Less original, but still fresh and exciting, are the two historical adventure stories, *Jim Davis* and *Martin Hyde*. There is also an early work, *A Book of Discoveries*, the story of two brothers exploring the landscape and natural history of their home surroundings, which has long been undeservedly out of print but challenges comparison with Richard Jefferies's *Bevis* (1882).

This group of books is distinguished, but forms only a small part of Masefield's prolific output. However, the canon of Masefield's work for children has recently been extended by enterprising publishers who have rightly questioned the initial classification of several other books as "adult fiction." *The Bird of Dawning*, a memorable sea story, has been published in a paperback edition for teenage readers; it is set in the 19th century at the time of the famous "tea races," when fast clipper ships vied with each other in carrying cargoes of tea from the Far East to London. In this story "Cruiser" Trewsbury, the very young second mate of the clipper *Blackgauntlet*, finds himself commanding the one ship's boat to escape her shipwreck. After a desperate struggle for bare survival in the boat, Cruiser and his few men find another clipper, *The Bird of Dawning*, drifting abandoned in the Atlantic, and sail her themselves to a daring victory in the tea race. It is a story, like so many of Masefield's, of disaster, long adversity, and triumph, achieved by the sheer tenacity and optimism of heroes who refuse to accept defeat. For Cruiser, a stoical and disciplined endurance of extreme danger merges with a sense of exhilaration, of more intense and heightened living. This is a central experience in Masefield's fiction, and one which has a particular appeal and value for young readers.

Extreme danger is also explored in *Dead Ned* and *Live and Kicking Ned*, two other novels which have been re-issued in children's paperback editions. They tell the story of Ned Mansell, a young apprentice surgeon in late 18th-century London. A victim of circumstantial evidence, Ned is wrongly accused of murder, convicted, imprisoned in Newgate, and hanged at Tyburn. But fate has reserved him for a life which seems often scarcely preferable to death. He is cut down and revived by his friends, only to be forced to flee the country as surgeon on a slaving ship. After his torments of injustice and despair, he lives to face yet greater perils in Africa. Ned Mansell lacks the disciplined and hopeful resolution of Cruiser Trewsbury, and it takes him much longer to recover a confident energy for life, but the dark excitement of the stories is once again an inspiriting testament to the human will to survive. These two compelling novels belong without question to children's literature, and bear a clear resemblance to the best work of Leon Garfield.

Another of Masefield's stories, the sad and richly atmospheric adventure story *Lost Endeavour*, has been commonly listed as a children's story and has always defied classification. Like several of Masefield's books, it is the story of a treasure hunt, starting with a kidnapping in England and going on to high adventure on the Spanish Main. Its action-filled, romantic quest and rapid twists of fortune make it a powerful children's story, but it is also a wistful and moving narrative of lost hopes, unfulfilled, elusive dreams, and tantalising glimpses of the unattainable. It asks of the reader a mature acceptance that things do not always turn out well, nor fortunate destinies fall to those who deserve them.

Masefield's historical adventures for children are charged with the same consciousness of the dark side of adventure, and the realistic ordeals which are a precondition of effective courage and resolute survival. In *Martin Hyde* the hero, caught up in the Monmouth rebellion against James II, quickly loses his early romantic notions of adventure and describes it as "a life of sordid unquiet, pursued without plan, like the life of an animal." Jim Davis, in the story named after him, is another accidental and unwilling recruit to the life of adventure and danger—this time as the captive accomplice of smugglers during the Napoleonic wars. Jim is often lonely, homesick, and afraid, and alertly sympathetic to the sufferings of others. Yet the honesty and realism of these stories neither subdue their excitement nor detract from the vigorous optimism of their effect.

The two great fantasies carry to its extreme the sense of solitude and danger as the pathway to a richer, more abundant life. Both books are treasure hunts: in *The Midnight Folk* the search is for the lost cathedral treasure of Santa Barbara, once entrusted to Kay Harker's great-grandfather, and in *The Box of Delights* for a magic box which gives entry to the past and the chance of finding the elixir of life. Good and evil fight for possession of the treasures. Young Kay Harker is a lonely child, yet his part in the struggle against evil opens up for him a vast empire of imagination, lit with richly varied experiences and peopled by a marvellous gallery of human and animal companions and enemies. In the end, truth and illusion, reality and imagination, are impossible to separate. The comic and the evil blend, the everyday and the exotic intermingle, to produce a matchless unity of laughter and fear, familiarity and wonder. The stories are a triumph of liberated imagination. But Kay in his unique world belongs with Masefield's other heroes in that special quality of innocent sturdiness and enterprise which no ill-fortune can totally subdue. Above all else, Masefield's fiction offers to children an enhanced, confident sense of life's possibilities.

—Peter Hollindale

MATHIS, Sharon Bell. American. Born in Atlantic City, New Jersey, 26 February 1937. Educated at Morgan State College, Baltimore, B.A. in sociology 1958; Catholic University, Washington, D.C., M. Sc. in library science 1975. Married Leroy F. Mathis in 1957 (divorced 1979); three daughters. Interviewer, District of Columbia Children's Hospital, 1958–59; teacher, Holy Redeemer Elementary School, 1960–65, Charles Hart Junior High School, 1965–72, and Stuart Junior High School, 1972–75, all in Washington, D.C.; librarian, Benning Elementary School, Washington, D.C., 1975–76. Since 1976 librarian Friendship Educational Center, Washington, D.C. Writer-in-residence, Howard University, Washington, D.C., 1972–73. Column editor ("Ebony Jrs. Speak!"), *Ebony Jr.* magazine, Chicago. Recipient: Council for Interracial Books for Children award, 1969; Bread Loaf Writers Conference grant, 1970; American Library Association Coretta Scott King award, 1974; MacDowell fellowship, 1978. Agent: Curtis Brown, 10 Astor Place, New York, New York 10003, U.S.A.

PUBLICATIONS FOR CHILDREN

Fiction

Brooklyn Story, illustrated by Charles Bible. New York, Hill and Wang, 1970.
Sidewalk Story, illustrated by Leo Carty. New York, Viking Press, 1971.
Teacup Full of Roses. New York, Viking Press, 1972.
Listen for the Fig Tree. New York, Viking Press, 1974.
The Hundred Penny Box, illustrated by Leo and Diane Dillon. New York, Viking Press, 1975.

Other

Ray Charles, illustrated by George Ford. New York, Crowell, 1973.
Cartwheels. New York, Scholastic, 1977.

*   *   *

Sharon Bell Mathis has proudly described her books as "salutes to black kids." Her recurring theme is the experience of being black: she talks about dignity, about blacks supporting each other, and about the preservation of black culture. Generally the dialogue in her books is a mild form of black English, natural-sounding and easy to read. Although Mathis has dipped into non-fiction, her best-known works are two books that are essentially short stories and two novels.

In *Sidewalk Story*, one of the briefer books, Mathis depicts a special friendship. Lilly Etta Allen is horrified one day to see her best friend's belongings being dumped on the sidewalk; the family has been evicted for not paying rent. At once Lilly Etta plans how she can help the Browns, but nothing works until her own unselfish action draws attention to the family's plight. Lilly Etta's disgusted rejoinder when things are not going her way ("Phooey!") echoes throughout this nicely plotted tale about being a friend. Mathis's shortest book is perhaps her most moving. *The Hundred Penny Box* is great-great Aunt Dew's most valued possession: the box contains one penny for each year of her life. Since Aunt Dew has come to live with them, John loves to count out the pennies while Aunt Dew recollects times and people long gone. John's mother, however, treats Aunt Dew like a child, and wants to substitute a mahogany chest for the large unsightly wooden box. John responds to Aunt Dew's need to keep her own box: "When I lose my hundred penny box, I lose me," she insists. This story is a sensitive portrayal of a young boy's love for an aged relative.

Teacup Full of Roses is probably Mathis's most popular book. The title phrase is used by the central character, Joe, to describe a wished-for place where trouble never comes. Plucky and streetsmart, Joe is confident of his own ability, but he worries about his brothers. Paul, the oldest and his mother's favorite, has recently returned from a drug rehabilitation program but is still addicted; Davey, the youngest, is bright and a skilled athlete, but naive. Steering clear of didacticism, Mathis shows how Paul's drug dependence brings tragedy to his family. Powerfully motivated characters, skillful foreshadowing, and a taut storyline make this book memorable reading.

The African celebration of Kwanza, which begins the day after Christmas, is the focal event in *Listen for the Fig Tree*. Muffin's father, a cab driver, was killed a year previously by two black youths on Christmas Day. Since then, Muffin (blind since the age of 10) has looked after her grieving, irresponsible mother. Muffin is eager to take part in this year's Kwanza Festival at the Black Museum, but Momma resents her intention to go to a party on the anniversary of her father's death. Mathis portrays Muffin as capable and self-sufficient, describing the methods she uses to perform tasks sighted people take for granted. Muffin can deal with her blindness, but her basic beliefs are shaken when she is nearly raped by a black assailant. The Kwanza Festival helps Muffin to have faith again in the concept of black unity.

—Karen Stang Hanley

MATTINGLEY, Christobel (Rosemary, née Shepley). Australian. Born in Adelaide, South Australia, 26 October 1931. Educated at Presbyterian Ladies College, Pymble, New South Wales, 1940–45; The Friends' School, Hobart, Tasmania, 1945–47; University of Tasmania, Hobart, 1948–51, B.A. (honours) 1951; Public Library of Victoria Training College, 1952, Certificate of Proficiency 1952. Married Cecil David Mattingley in 1953; one daughter and two sons. Librarian, Department of Immigration, Canberra, 1951, Latrobe Valley Libraries, Victoria, 1953, in England, 1954–55, Prince Alfred College, Adelaide, 1956–57, and St. Peter's Girls' School, Adelaide, 1966–70; acquisitions librarian, 1971, and reader services librarian, 1972, Wattle Park Teachers' College, Adelaide; reader services librarian, Murray Park College of Advanced Education, Adelaide, 1973–74. Presenter, *Children's Books to Enjoy* program (TV), 1973–74. Writer-in-residence, West Australian College of Advanced Education, Churchlands, 1982. Recipient: Australia Council fellowship, 1975, 1983; International Youth Library scholarship, 1976; Children's Book Council Junior Book of the Year award, 1982; National Parks and Wildlife Services award, 1983. Agent: A.P. Watt, 20 John Street, London WC1N 2DL, England. Address: 18 Allendale Grove, Stonyfell, South Australia 5066, Australia.

PUBLICATIONS FOR CHILDREN

Fiction

The Picnic Dog, illustrated by Carolyn Dinan. London, Hamish Hamilton, 1970.
The Windmill at Magpie Creek, illustrated by Gavin Rowe. Leicester, Brockhampton Press, 1971.
Worm Weather, illustrated by Carolyn Dinan. London, Hamish Hamilton, 1971.
Emu Kite, illustrated by Gavin Rowe. London, Hamish Hamilton, 1972.
Queen of the Wheat Castles, illustrated by Gavin Rowe. Leicester, Brockhampton Press, 1973.
The Battle of the Galah Trees, illustrated by Gareth Floyd. Leicester, Brockhampton Press, 1973.
Show and Tell, illustrated by Helen Sallis. Sydney, Hodder and Stoughton, and Leicester, Brockhampton Press, 1974.
Tiger's Milk, illustrated by Anne Ferguson. Sydney and London, Angus and Robertson, 1974.
The Surprise Mouse, illustrated by Carolyn Dinan. London, Hamish Hamilton, 1974.
Lizard Log, illustrated by Helen Sallis. Sydney, Hodder and Stoughton, 1975.
The Great Ballagundi Damper Bake, illustrated by Will Mahony.

Sydney and London, Angus and Robertson, 1975.
The Long Walk, illustrated by Helen Sallis. Melbourne, Nelson, 1976; London, Hamish Hamilton, 1977.
The Special Present, illustrated by Noela Young. Sydney, Collins, 1976; London, Collins, 1977.
New Patches for Old. London, Hodder and Stoughton, 1977.
The Big Swim, illustrated by Elizabeth Honey. Melbourne, Nelson, 1977; London, Hamish Hamilton, 1978.
Budgerigar Blue, illustrated by Tony Oliver. Sydney, Hodder and Stoughton, 1977; London, Hodder and Stroughton, 1978.
The Jetty, illustrated by Gavin Rowe. London, Hodder and Stoughton, 1978.
Black Dog, illustrated by Craig Smith. Sydney, Collins, 1979; London, Bodley Head, 1980.
Rummage, illustrated by Patricia Mullins. Sydney and London, Angus and Robertson, 1981.
Brave with Ben, illustrated by Elizabeth Honey. Melbourne, Nelson, 1982; London, Hamish Hamilton, 1983.
Lexl and the Lion Party, illustrated by Astra Lacis. Sydney, Hodder and Stroughton, 1982.
Duck Boy, illustrated by Patricia Mullins. Sydney and London, Angus and Robertson, 1983; New York, Atheneum, 1986.
Southerly Buster. Sydney and London, Hodder and Stoughton, 1983.
The Magic Saddle, illustrated by Patricia Mullins. Sydney, Hodder and Stoughton, 1983; London, Hodder and Stoughton, 1984.
The Angel with a Mouth-Organ, illustrated by Astra Lacis. Sydney and London, Hodder and Stoughton, 1984; New York, Holiday House, 1986.
Ghost Sitter, illustrated by Christina Brimage. London, Hardy, 1984.
The Miracle Tree, illustrated by Marianne Yamaguchi. Sydney, Hodder and Stoughton, and San Diego, Harcourt Brace, 1985.
McGruer and the Goat. Sydney and London, Angus and Robertson, 1987.

Plays

Television Writing: *The Long Walk*, from her own novel, 1978; *Do You See What I See? Women Artists of Australia*, 1981; *Come to the Party! Children's Libraries*, 1982; *Rummage*, from her own novel, 1983.

PUBLICATIONS FOR ADULTS

Other

Editor, *Survival in Our Own Land: Aboriginal Experience in South Australia since 1836*. Netley, South Australia, Wakefield Press, 1985.

*

Christobel Mattingley comments:
My memories of childhood are intense and vivid, and my development as a writer began at an early age. The power of words and the magic of books had already enthralled me before I started school, and by the age of eight I was reading widely, writing poetry, and making up stories and plays. I was always conscious of an affinity with nature and at nine was introduced to serious nature study by an enlightened teacher and began keeping copious diaries of careful observations. At 10 I had my first publishing acceptance, in a natural history magazine. My father's work as a civil engineer building dams and bridges in various parts of Australia made me aware of the need for harmony between man and nature and

intensified my love for wilderness areas. Experiencing childhood again with my own family acted as a catalyst for writing, and my stories have evolved as a combination of everyday events, places and personalities reinforcing my own emotion of childhood.

* * *

The style and content of Christobel Mattingley's writing has changed markedly since the publication of her first children's book in 1970. Her early work, which found a ready audience of younger readers, was in the Australian realist style of its period and was strongly influenced by the author's own childhood memories and observations of her own growing family at the time. The events in these books were always of the ordinary everyday kind, such as a kite-flying contest in *Emu Kite*, or a fancy-dress party in *Worm Weather*, and the problems were commonplace and believable. Cathy, in *Queen of the Wheat Castles*, tries to save the lives of unwanted kittens by finding owners for them. The under-sized Antony in *Tiger's Milk* just wants to grow bigger and stronger. (The book's solution is a recipe which any child can try at home.)

Some of these early books dwelt on the common fears of ordinary children. In *The Long Walk* Michael finds his bus trip to and from school an intimidating ordeal. Brad needs to come to terms with his fear of the sea in *The Jetty*, and Peter has to undergo his own ordeal by water in *The Big Swim*. In *Brave with Ben* the young hero has to overcome his fear of dense bushland, which he does with the help of a friendly dog. In one of Mattingley's earliest yet most successful books, *The Windmill at Magpie Creek*, Tim develops an aversion to heights, and to aggressive magpies. In each case, the solutions are natural and unforced.

In the adolescent novels *New Patches for Old* and *Southerly Buster*, conflict with peer groups and adults is an important issue.

A new phase in Mattingley's writing began in 1974, when she took her children to Europe for the first time. This resulted in a broadening of her work, and a corresponding move away from homely, domestic dramas in everyday Australian settings to much larger themes—and the introduction of fantasy—played out on an international stage. Subsequent travels abroad resulted in such books as *Rummage*, the story of a street-market junk dealer who learns the futility of denying his own nature in order to conform to the expectations of others. This English-flavoured story was inspired by a visit to London. An extended stay in Germany (including a period spent in residence in Munich, while attached to the International Youth Library) resulted in romantic wish-fulfilment fantasies set in that country. *Lexl and the Lion Party*, for instance, describes the delight of a young boy when his favourite carved stone lions, from the buildings and monuments in the city in which he lives, come to life one midnight. *The Angel with a Mouth-Organ* is a poignant story of the struggle of a closely-knit refugee family to stay together on their arduous flight from their unspecified European homeland during World War II. *The Miracle Tree* is also about people separated from their loved ones by war, this time in Japan. For 20 years Taro, a gardener, has hoped for a miracle which would see him united once more with his beautiful wife, missing since the atomic bomb blast in her city of Nagasaki. As in the other stories of this period, there is pathos and sentiment, and the wishes do come true. This story resulted from a visit the author made to Japan in 1981 to be with her daughter, who was living there as an exchange student. Similarly, *McGruer and the Goat*, a comic tale of a retired sea captain and his pet octopus, had its beginnings in a lecture tour of New Zealand. Travel has enriched the nature and scope of Mattingley's writing, adding to its emotional warmth and depth, as well as its variety.

—Walter McVitty

MAYNE, William (James Carter). Has also written as Martin Cobalt; Dynely James; Charles Molin. British. Born in Hull, Yorkshire, 16 March 1928. Educated at the Cathedral Choir School, Canterbury, 1937–42. Lecturer, Deakin University, Geelong, Victoria, 1976, 1977; Fellow in Creative Writing, Rolle College, Exmouth, Devon, 1979–80. Recipient: Library Association Carnegie Medal, 1958. Agent: David Higham Associates, 5–8 Lower John Street, London W1R 4HA, England.

PUBLICATIONS FOR CHILDREN

Fiction

Follow the Footprints, illustrated by Shirley Hughes. London, Oxford University Press, 1953.
The World Upside Down, illustrated by Shirley Hughes. London, Oxford University Press, 1954.
A Swarm in May, illustrated by C. Walter Hodges. London, Oxford University Press, 1955; Indianapolis, Bobbs Merrill, 1957.
The Member for the Marsh, illustrated by Lynton Lamb. London, Oxford University Press, 1956.
Choristers' Cake, illustrated by C. Walter Hodges. London, Oxford University Press, 1956; Indianapolis, Bobbs Merrill, 1958.
The Blue Boat, illustrated by Geraldine Spence. London, Oxford University Press, 1957; New York, Dutton, 1960.
A Grass Rope, illustrated by Lynton Lamb. London, Oxford University Press, 1957; New York, Dutton, 1962.
The Long Night, illustrated by D.J. Watkins-Pitchford. London, Blackwell, 1958.
Underground Alley, illustrated by Marcia Lane Foster. London, Oxford University Press, 1958; New York, Dutton, 1961.
The Gobbling Billy (as Dynely James, with Dick Caesar). London, Gollancz, and New York, Dutton, 1959; as William Mayne and Dick Caesar, Leicester, Brockhampton Press, 1969.
The Thumbstick, illustrated by Tessa Theobald. London, Oxford University Press, 1959.
Thirteen O'Clock, illustrated by D.J. Watkins-Pitchford. Oxford, Blackwell, 1960.
The Rolling Season, illustrated by Christopher Brooker. London, Oxford University Press, 1960.
Cathedral Wednesday, illustrated by C. Walter Hodges. London, Oxford University Press, 1960.
The Fishing Party, illustrated by Christopher Brooker. London, Hamish Hamilton, 1960.
Summer Visitors, illustrated by William Stobbs. London, Oxford University Press, 1961.
The Changeling, illustrated by Victor Ambrus. London, Oxford University Press, 1961; New York, Dutton, 1963.
The Glass Ball, illustrated by Janet Duchesne. London, Hamish Hamilton, 1961; New York, Dutton, 1962.
The Last Bus, illustrated by Margery Gill. London, Hamish Hamilton, 1962.
The Twelve Dancers, illustrated by Lynton Lamb. London, Hamish Hamilton, 1962.
The Man from the North Pole, illustrated by Prudence Seward. London, Hamish Hamilton, 1963.
On the Stepping Stones, illustrated by Prudence Seward. London, Hamish Hamilton, 1963.
Words and Music, illustrated by Lynton Lamb. London, Hamish Hamilton, 1963.
Plot Night, illustrated by Janet Duchesne. London, Hamish Hamilton, 1963; New York, Dutton, 1968.
A Parcel of Trees, illustrated by Margery Gill. London, Penguin, 1963.
Water Boatman, illustrated by Anne Linton. London, Hamish

Hamilton, 1964.

Whistling Rufus, illustrated by Raymond Briggs. London, Hamish Hamilton, 1964; New York, Dutton, 1965.

Sand, illustrated by Margery Gill. London, Hamish Hamilton, 1964; New York, Dutton, 1965.

A Day Without Wind, illustrated by Margery Gill. London, Hamish Hamilton, and New York, Dutton, 1964.

The Big Wheel and the Little Wheel, illustrated by Janet Duchesne. London, Hamish Hamilton, 1965.

Pig in the Middle, illustrated by Mary Russon. London, Hamish Hamilton, 1965; New York, Dutton, 1966.

No More School, illustrated by Peter Warner. London, Hamish Hamilton, 1965.

Dormouse Tales (*The Lost Thimble*, *The Steam Roller*, *The Picnic*, *The Football*, *The Tea Party*) (as Charles Molin), illustrated by Leslie Wood. London, Hamish Hamilton, 5 vols., 1966.

Earthfasts. London, Hamish Hamilton, 1966; New York, Dutton, 1967.

Rooftops, illustrated by Mary Russon. London, Hamish Hamilton, 1966.

The Old Zion, illustrated by Margery Gill. London, Hamish Hamilton, 1966; New York, Dutton, 1967.

The Battlefield, illustrated by Mary Russon. London, Hamish Hamilton, and New York, Dutton, 1967.

The Big Egg, illustrated by Margery Gill. London, Hamish Hamilton, 1967.

The Toffee Join, illustrated by Shirley Hughes. London, Hamish Hamilton, 1968.

Over the Hills and Far Away. London, Hamish Hamilton, 1968; as *The Hill Road*, New York, Dutton, 1969.

The Yellow Aeroplane, illustrated by Trevor Stubley. London, Hamish Hamilton, 1968; Nashville, Nelson, 1974.

The House on Fairmount, illustrated by Fritz Wegner. London, Hamish Hamilton, and New York, Dutton, 1968.

Ravensgill. London, Hamish Hamilton, and New York, Dutton, 1970.

Royal Harry. London, Hamish Hamilton, 1971; New York, Dutton, 1972.

A Game of Dark. London, Hamish Hamilton, and New York, Dutton, 1971.

The Incline. London, Hamish Hamilton, and New York, Dutton, 1972.

The Swallows (as Martin Cobalt). London, Heinemann, 1972; as *Pool of Swallows*, Nashville, Nelson, 1974.

Robin's Real Engine, illustrated by Mary Dinsdale. London, Hamish Hamilton, 1972.

Skiffy, illustrated by Nicholas Fisk. London, Hamish Hamilton, 1972.

The Jersey Shore. London, Hamish Hamilton, and New York, Dutton, 1973.

A Year and a Day, illustrated by Krystyna Turska. London, Hamish Hamilton, and New York, Dutton, 1976.

Party Pants, illustrated by Joanna Stubbs. London, Knight, 1977.

Max's Dream, illustrated by Laszlo Acs. London, Hamish Hamilton, and New York, Greenwillow, 1977.

IT. London, Hamish Hamilton, 1977; New York, Greenwillow, 1978.

While the Bells Ring, illustrated by Janet Rawlins. London, Hamish Hamilton, 1979.

Salt River Times, illustrated by Elizabeth Honey. Melbourne, Nelson, and London, Hamish Hamilton, 1980; New York, Greenwillow, 1981.

The Mouse and the Egg, illustrated by Krystyna Turska. London, MacRae, 1980; New York, Greenwillow, 1981.

The Patchwork Cat, illustrated by Nicola Bayley. London, Cape, and New York, Knopf, 1981.

All the King's Men. London, Cape, 1982; New York, Delacorte Press, 1988.

Winter Quarters. London, Cape, 1982.

Skiffy and the Twin Planets. London, Hamish Hamilton, 1982.

A Small Pudding for Wee Gowrie, illustrated by Martin Cottam. London, Macmillan, 1983.

The Mouldy, illustrated by Nicola Bayley. London, Cape, and New York, Knopf, 1983.

Hob Stories (*Red Book*, *Green Book*, *Yellow Book*, *Blue Book*), illustrated by Patrick Benson. London, Walker, and New York, Philomel, 4 vols., 1984.

Drift. London, Cape, 1985; New York, Delacorte Press, 1986.

Animal Library (*Come Come to My Corner*, *Corbie*, *Mousewing*, *Tibber*, *Barnabas Walks*, *Lamb Shenkin*, *A House in Town*, *Leapfrog*), illustrated by Kenneth Lilly, Peter Visscher, Martin Baynton, Jonathan Heale, Barbara Firth, and Sarah Fox-Davies. London, Walker, 8 vols., 1986–87; first 3 vols. published Englewood Cliffs, New Jersey, Prentice Hall, 1987.

Kelpie. London, Cape, 1987.

Gideon Ahoy! London, Viking Kestrel, 1987; New York, Delacorte Press, 1989.

Tiger's Railway, illustrated by Juan Wijngaard. London, Walker, 1987.

The Blemyahs, illustrated by Juan Wijngaard. London, Walker, 1987.

Other

Editor, with Eleanor Farjeon, *The Hamish Hamilton Book of Kings*, illustrated by Victor Ambrus. London, Hamish Hamilton, 1964; as *A Cavalcade of Kings*, New York, Walck, 1965.

Editor, with Eleanor Farjeon, *The Hamish Hamilton Book of Queens*, illustrated by Victor Ambrus. London, Hamish Hamilton, 1964; as *A Cavalcade of Queens*, New York, Walck, 1965.

Editor (as Charles Molin), *Ghosts, Spooks, Spectres*. London, Hamish Hamilton, 1967; New York, David White, 1968.

Editor, *The Hamish Hamilton Book of Heroes*, illustrated by Krystyna Turska. London, Hamish Hamilton, 1967; as *William Mayne's Book of Heroes*, New York, Dutton, 1968.

Editor, *The Hamish Hamilton Book of Giants*, illustrated by Raymond Briggs. London, Hamish Hamilton, 1968; as *William Mayne's Book of Giants*, New York, Dutton, 1969.

Editor, *Ghosts: An Anthology*. London, Hamish Hamilton, and New York, Nelson, 1971.

*

Composer: incidental music for *Holly from the Bongs* by Alan Garner, 1965.

*   *   *

William Mayne has some claim to be the most important modern English children's writer. Certainly no other author has had such a sustained output of such range, individuality, and distinction—but he is in many ways an unsatisfactory "major" figure.

Despite having produced close on 100 books for all ages and in most genres he is still thought to be more liked by critics than by children. His language, always quirky and alert, has been described as inaccessible or oversophisticated. Even his work for younger children, such as *Robin's Real Engine* or *No More School*, can be dense, and seems to undervalue narrative.

Unlike Alan Garner, Mayne's books rarely seem to touch upon deep or allusive themes, tending rather to emphasise the local and interpersonal, the ordinary rather than the dramatic. Even supernatural elements turn back into the personal (as in *IT*) or into the social landscape (*Earthfasts*). More recently, however, in books such as *Winter Quarters, Drift,* and *The Blemyahs*, it has become more obvious that the oblique linguistic surface of his texts disguise very subtle and far-reaching preoccupations.

Style, then, is the key to Mayne. As Peter Hollindale observed: "The style of a Mayne novel operates as a form of continuous subdued recoil against the narrative shape and impetus" and these stylistic tricks, of inversion, of shifting the grammatical categories of words, and of developing subtle rhythms from relatively simple sentence structures might be shown in this example from one of his best books, *Ravensgill*:

> They were bones. They were bones of a hand; and in the other loop lay the separated wrist bones of another hand, and the arms were beyond, and the skull, clean and round and grown to the floor with the settling water, and beyond the skull the backbone, the worn spoons of the pelvis, a broken thigh bone and its whole fellow, and the lower bones of the legs. In the manacled grasp of the skeleton, Bob saw a small thing that was gold but not a coin, and hung on a tiny failing fingerbone a ring; and these he took, for Grandma, and this was her husband.

That extract also shows Mayne's fidelity to the three-way contract between author, reader, and character. He rarely abstracts; he stays close to the perceptions of his protagonists—not only in terms of their understanding, but also in their modes of perception.

Mayne's first two books, although minor, showed his penchant for idiosyncratic dialogue, and for the creation of the elliptical and allusive intimate family dialect (best seen in books like *The Battlefield*). They also introduced his fascination for the arcane (surfacing as treasure hunts or local quests) and his genius for absorbing and transmitting regional differences.

With *A Swarm in May*, the first book in a quartet set around Canterbury Choir School, Mayne made a mature and original contribution to the moribund school story genre. *A Grass Rope*, set in his native Yorkshire, won the 1958 Carnegie Medal, and he continued through the 1960's with a series of striking regional books. His ear for dialect could be faulty on occasion (as with *The Twelve Dancers*), but the capacity to populate a landscape with real people rather than types is marvellously sustained in books like *The Rolling Season* (set in Wiltshire), or *Pig in the Middle* (set in an inner city), the stifling atmosphere of *Sand* (the northeast coast), or the neglected *A Parcel of Trees*.

Ravensgill, a contemporary feud story, is perhaps his best work from this period. The solid Yorkshire atmosphere is also strong in Mayne's first excursion into fantasy, *Earthfasts*. He has also used fantasy as psychological allegory, in the sombre *A Game of Dark*, in which Donald's struggle to cope with his dying father is paralleled by his fantasy life.

The 1970's saw Mayne extending his range from the ebullient Yorkshire extravaganza of *Royal Harry*, to *IT* which borders on self-parody, to the hypnotic *The Jersey Shore*. This stylistic tour de force is largely the reminiscences of an old man addressed to a small boy as they sit beside the sea in New Jersey—but it is also a subtle exploration of history, family, and race.

Perhaps Mayne's most impressive narrative achievement has been *Salt River Times*, a novel in the form of short stories set in urban Australia, and since then, he has ranged widely over age groupings and subjects. *Tiger's Railway* is a comedy set in Eastern Europe; *Winter Quarters* deals with contemporary Romanies; *Gideon Ahoy!*'s central character is mentally handicapped, and in *All the King's Men* and *The Blemyahs* he seems to be creating new dimensions of myth and original areas of folklore.

Mayne's influence on British children's literature has been pervasive. He has shown that the oblique, the subtle, the low-key, and

the allusive can reach children, and that a distinctive, unpatronising style can find a market. In his mild and witty way, he has expanded the capacities of children's books.

His status may remain ambiguous, because he has not been seen to produce a bestseller or an acknowledged masterpiece. But, as more critics turn to children's literature, Mayne's genius is being analysed and appreciated more and more, and his reputation seems likely to grow.

—Peter Hunt

MAZER, Norma Fox. American. Born in New York City, 15 May 1931. Educated at Antioch College, Yellow Springs, Ohio, 1949–50; Syracuse University, New York, 1957–59. Married the writer Harry Mazer in 1950; three daughters and one son. Has worked as a secretary at a radio station, punch press operator, and cashier. Recipient: Christopher award, 1976; Children's Literature prize (Germany), 1982; Mystery Writers of America Edgar Allan Poe award, 1982. Agent: Elaine Markson, 44 Greenwich Avenue, New York, New York 10012; or, Abner Stein, 10 Roland Gardens, London SW7 3PH, England. Address: Brown Gulf Road, Jamesville, New York 13078, U.S.A.

PUBLICATIONS FOR CHILDREN

Fiction

I, Trissy. New York, Delacorte Press, 1971.
A Figure of Speech. New York, Delacorte Press, 1973.
Saturday, The Twelfth of October. New York, Delacorte Press, 1975.
Dear Bill, Remember Me? and Other Stories. New York, Delacorte Press, 1976.
The Solid Gold Kid, with Harry Mazer. New York, Delacorte Press, 1977.
Up in Seth's Room. New York, Delacorte Press, 1979.
Mrs. Fish, Ape, and Me, The Dump Queen. New York, Dutton, 1980.
Taking Terri Mueller. New York, Avon, 1981; London, Methuen, 1988.
Summer Girls, Love Boys and Other Stories. New York, Delacorte Press, 1982.
When We First Met. New York, Four Winds Press, 1982.
Someone to Love. New York, Delacorte Press, 1983.
Supergirl (novelization of screenplay). New York, Warner, and London, Severn House, 1984.
Downtown. New York, Morrow, 1984.
Three Sisters. New York, Scholastic, 1986.
A, My Name Is Ami. New York, Scholastic, 1986; as *A for Ami*, London, Penguin, 1988.
B, My Name is Bunny. New York, Scholastic, 1987; as *A Name Like Bunny*, London, Penguin, 1988.
After the Rain. New York, Morrow, 1987; London, Macmillan, 1988.
Silver. New York, Morrow, 1988.
Heartbeat, with Harry Mazer. New York, Bantam, 1989.

Other

Editor, with Marjorie Lewis, *Waltzing on Water: Poetry by Women.*

New York, Delacorte Press, 1989.

*

Critical Study: *Presenting Norma Fox Mazer* by Sally Holmes Holtze, Boston, Twayne, 1987.

Norma Fox Mazer comments:

When I write, I want a story that captures the reader, keeps her/him turning the pages. I want to write the truth as well as I know it. The truth of lives interests me. The small details. The relationships of people. I'm particularly interested in the fate and lives of girls and women. If I have any "message" for my readers, it's for the need for courage, it's that life can be difficult and often is, but is also a bountiful blessing.

*   *   *

Norma Fox Mazer has written a number of highly acclaimed books for young adult readers. Her main characters are young people on the verge of adulthood, struggling with self-image and interest in the opposite sex. Some lead ordinary lives; some have to face enormous social problems, such as drunken driving, teenage sex, discrimination against the poor and handicapped, care of the frail elderly. Mazer's characters are not all admirable, but they are believable and provide insight into why people behave the way they do.

In *When We First Met*, Jenny Pennoyer falls in love with the son of the drunken driver who killed her older sister. Emotions of hatred, guilt, forgiveness, and caring are expressed. Relationships are complex, often explosive, and they ring true.

Up in Seth's Room is about an adolescent boy and girl who fall in love, with the boy demanding an active sexual relationship and the girl refusing because she wants to wait until she is older. Seth persists. "If at first you don't succeed…that's the male creed," he tells her. The girl Finn holds firm. And they find they can remain friends, good friends.

Mrs. Fish, Ape, and Me, The Dump Queen is about people who are on the fringe of society. Mrs. Fish is a middle-aged spinster cleaning woman; Ape is an older bachelor who runs the town dump; and Me, the dump queen, is an orphan adolescent, ridiculed by her peers and desperate for affection. Eventually these three come together as a family unit; they are not your stereotypical family, but they are a fully functioning one, providing love and comfort to one another.

After the Rain is a stunning portrait of two human beings, a grandfather and a granddaughter, who begin to take walks together every afternoon when the grandfather's health is not such that he can safely go out alone anymore. The grandfather grasps hold of each of his final days and the granddaughter learns to understand and admire him while also learning to understand herself and her passage to adulthood.

Mazer's descriptive ability is excellent. The reader is able to see vividly what her characters look like, what their physical environment consists of, and most importantly, how they feel about themselves and others.

—Mary Lystad

———

McCAFFREY, Anne (Inez). American. Born in Cambridge, Massachusetts, 1 April 1926. Educated at Stuart Hall, Staunton, Virginia; Montclair High School, New Jersey; Radcliffe College, Cambridge, Massachusetts, B.A. (cum laude) in Slavonic languages and literature 1947; studied meteorology at City of Dublin University. Married E. Wright Johnson in 1950 (divorced 1970); two sons and one daughter. Copywriter and layout designer, Liberty Music Shops, New York, 1948–50; copywriter, Helena Rubinstein, New York, 1950–52. Currently runs a thoroughbred horse stud farm in Ireland; since 1978 director, Dragonhold Ltd., and since 1979 director, Fin Film Productions. Has performed in and directed several operas and musical comedies in Wilmington and Greenville, Delaware. Secretary-Treasurer, Science Fiction Writers of America, 1968–70. Recipient: Hugo award, 1968, 1979; Nebula award, 1968; E.E. Smith award, 1976; Gandalf award, 1979; Balrog award, 1980. Agent: Virginia Kidd, 538 East Harford Street, Milford, Pennsylvania 18337, U.S.A. Address: Dragonhold, Kilquade, Greystones, County Wicklow, Ireland.

PUBLICATIONS FOR CHILDREN

Fiction

Dragonsong. New York, Atheneum, and London, Sidgwick and Jackson, 1976.
Dragonsinger. New York, Atheneum, and London, Sidgwick and Jackson, 1977.
Dragondrums. New York, Atheneum, and London, Sidgwick and Jackson, 1979.
The Harper Hall of Pern (omnibus). New York, Doubleday, 1979(?).

PUBLICATIONS FOR ADULTS

Novels

Restoree. New York, Ballantine, 1967; London, Rapp and Whiting, 1968.
Dragonflight. New York, Ballantine, 1968; London, Rapp and Whiting, 1969.
Decision at Doona. New York, Ballantine, 1969; London, Rapp and Whiting, 1970.
The Ship Who Sang. New York, Walker, 1969; London, Rapp and Whiting, 1971.
The Mark of Merlin. New York, Dell, 1971; London, Millington, 1977.
The Ring of Fear. New York, Dell, 1971; London, Millington, 1979.
Dragonquest. New York, Ballantine, 1971; London, Rapp and Whiting-Deutsch, 1973.
To Ride Pegasus. New York, Ballantine, 1973; London, Dent, 1974.
The Kilternan Legacy. New York, Dell, 1975; London, Millington, 1976.
Dinosaur Planet. London, Futura, 1977; New York, Ballantine, 1978.
The Dragonriders of Pern (omnibus). New York, Doubleday, 1978.
The White Dragon (Dragonrider). New York, Ballantine, 1978; London, Sidgwick and Jackson, 1979.
Crystal Singer. New York, Ballantine, and London, Severn House, 1982.
The Coelura. Columbia, Pennsylvania, Underwood Miller, 1983; with *Nerilka's Story*, London, Bantam, 1987.
Moreta, Dragonlady of Pern. New York, Ballantine, and London, Severn House, 1983.
Dinosaur Planet Survivors. New York, Ballantine, and London, Futura, 1984.

Stitch in Snow. Columbia, Pennsylvania, Underwood Miller, 1984.
Killashandra. New York, Ballantine, 1985; London, Bantam, 1986.
Nerilka's Story. New York, Ballantine, 1986; with *The Coelura*, London, Bantam, 1987.
Habit Is an Old Horse. Seattle, Dryad Press, 1986.
The Year of the Lucy. New York, Tor, 1986; London, Corgi, 1987.
The Lady. New York, Ballantine, 1987.
The Carradyne Touch. London, Macdonald, 1988.
Dragonsdawn. New York, Del Rey, 1988; London, Bantam, 1989.

Short Stories

A Time When. Cambridge, Massachusetts, NESFA Press, 1975.
Get Off the Unicorn. New York, Ballantine, 1977; London, Corgi, 1979.
The Worlds of Anne McCaffrey. London, Deutsch, 1981.

Other

Editor, *Alchemy and Academe: A Collection of Original Stories Concerning Themselves with Transmutations, Mental and Elemental, Alchemical and Academic.* New York, Doubleday, 1970.
Editor, *Cooking Out of This World.* New York, Ballantine, 1973.

*

Bibliography: *Leigh Brackett, Marion Zimmer Bradley, Anne McCaffrey: A Primary and Secondary Bibliography* by Rosemarie Arbur, Boston, Hall, 1982.

Manuscript Collections: Syracuse University, New York; Kerlan Collection, University of Minnesota, Minneapolis.

* * *

Pern is a futuristic fantasy world in which dragons bond with special humans in a lifelong relationship and wherein a history of a people is related extending throughout many novels. Pernian society is that artful combination of medieval lifestyle and an alternative world with telepathic capabilities between dragon and rider. The dragonriders and their dragons protect the people of Pern from the evil of Thread, a periodic micro-spore-like organism that destroys life, by burning the thread to extinction. All of the novels of Pern are interwoven so that a reader encounters many of the same characters and events as new episodes are added.

Anne McCaffrey wrote the Harper Hall trilogy as a segment of this history involving two young people, Menolly in *Dragonsong* and *Dragonsinger* and Piemur in *Dragondrums*. Although McCaffrey writes in a romantic mode, Menolly is not a typical female in a romance. She has heroic qualities but it is closer to what readers expect of a hero than a heroine. Menolly is a young girl gifted in music whose father perceives her as disobedient and possessing an inappropriate talent. She develops her sense of herself through mental and physical suffering and through joy in impressing (a term for dragon and fire-lizard bonding) nine fire lizards, caring for them, and keeping them a secret. Menolly wishes to be a harper where her talent for song writing and singing will be valued. She is not a character whose pride or ambition drive her but rather a naive, gentle, brave young woman who must share her music. But McCaffrey does not make this easy for Menolly. She must go through the apprenticeship rigors of Harper Hall training while battling peer pressures as well as the doubting and testing of the various masters. Masterharper Robinton provides direction and solace, as she struggles to reach her goals. McCaffrey delights in adding complexity to a plot,

and the fire lizards which accompany Menolly serve as such a literary device. They act as messengers on the one hand and as protectors of Menolly on the other. Although Menolly is portrayed as gentle, her strength is revealed in her determination to leave the Sea Hold of her father and live outside the protection of its walls.

Piemur is a young boy at Harper Hall who possesses a magnificent voice and all of the impudence that McCaffrey can portray. His pranks and potential are interwoven throughout Menolly's story, and it is Piemur who helps her in the care of the fire lizards. In *Dragondrums* Piemur loses his singing voice and is sent as an apprentice to the drum master. This cloaks his real work as a Harper Hall spy for Master Robinton. Pern stories are filled with plot and counter-plot as the omnipresence of Thread dominates the human fights and intrigues. Piemur has all of the inventiveness and humor of a skilled spy and manages to land on his feet in several trying situations. Of course, Piemur is also determined that he will impress a fire lizard at all costs, an aim that leads to his greatest trouble.

McCaffrey provides readers with details of a world and its society that is captivating and different. She describes the magnificence of the dragons with their telepathic abilities including an impression ceremony so that the reader is brought into this bonding process. At the same time she describes the small fire lizards who seem to resemble in part their larger friends. The relationship of the dragons and fire lizards is hinted at in these stories but the actual genetic altering that produced dragons from the fire lizards is only revealed in *Dragonsdawn*, a prequel to the rest of the Pern stories. In these stories the fire lizards are portrayed more as pets than as bonded companions, although Menolly's nine lizards will rush to defend her at any cost.

McCaffrey focuses in these three novels on the development of the crafts and guild halls with emphasis on the power of the Harpers, who transmit the cultural and historical record of the people of Pern and also monitor the political and social life to keep the people attuned to responsibility. Although danger is lethal on Pern when Thread falls, danger forms a secondary level of plot and counterplot as power struggles among various Weyrs and Holds take place in daily life.

—Jane Anne Hannigan

———

McCAUGHREAN, Geraldine (née Jones). British. Born in Enfield, Middlesex, 6 June 1951. Educated at Enfield County Grammar School for Girls, 1963–69; Southgate Technical College, Middlesex, 1969–70; Christ Church College of Education, Canterbury, Kent, 1973–77, B.Ed. (honours) 1977. Married John McCaughrean in 1988. Secretary, Thames Television, London, 1970–73; secretary, 1977, and sub-editor, 1978–79 and 1983–88, Marshall Cavendish, publishers, London; editorial assistant, Rothmans, Ware, Hertfordshire, 1980–82; editor, Banbury *Focus*, Oxfordshire, 1982. Recipient: Whitbread award, 1987; Library Association Carnegie Medal, 1989. Agent: Giles Gordon, Anthony Sheil Associates, 43 Doughty Street, London WC1N 2LF. Address: 3 Melton Drive, Didcot, Oxfordshire OX11 7JP, England.

PUBLICATIONS FOR CHILDREN

Fiction

Seaside Adventure, illustrated by Chrissie Wells. London, Hamlyn 1986.
Tell the Time, with Chrissie Wells, illustrated by Wells. London,

Hamlyn, 1986.

A Little Lower Than the Angels.   Oxford, Oxford University Press, 1987.

A Pack of Lies.   Oxford, Oxford University Press, 1988; New York, Oxford University Press, 1989.

Other (retellings)

1001 Arabian Nights, illustrated by Stephen Lavis.   Oxford, Oxford University Press, 1982.

The Canterbury Tales, illustrated by Victor Ambrus.   Oxford, Oxford University Press, 1984; Chicago, Rand McNally, 1985.

The Story of Noah.   Dorking, Surrey, Templar, 1987.

The Story of Christmas.   Dorking, Surrey, Templar, 1988.

Translator, *Who's That Knocking on My Door?*, by Michel Tilde.   Oxford, Oxford University Press, 1986.

PUBLICATIONS FOR ADULTS

Novel

The Maypole.   London, Secker and Warburg, 1989.

Other (textbooks) as Geraldine Jones

Adventure in New York.   London, Oxford University Press, 1979.

Raise the Titanic.   Oxford, Oxford University Press, 1980.

Modesty Blaise.   Oxford, Oxford University Press, 1981.

*

Geraldine McCaughrean comments:

Rich imagery, full-blooded adventure and characters of interest and depth characterize my books which tackle action, the exotic, the daring and the passionate rather than the domestic. They are commonly read aloud by teachers. Friendship, love, hate, and violence are frequent preoccupations, although there is plenty of humour too. I recommend them to older children with competent reading skills and vocabulary, or to be read aloud, as younger children could be put off by coming to the books too early.

*   *   *

Geraldine McCaughrean's experience as a reteller of tales—for instance her colloquial and lively version of *The Canterbury Tales*—shows in the economical narrative and vivid imagery of her novels.

Set in medieval England, *A Little Lower Than the Angels*, which won the Whitbread Children's Novel award in 1987, certainly evokes a Chaucerian world, with hoax miracles and morbid fears of the plague. Gabriel, a stonemason's apprentice ill-treated by his master, joins a travelling troupe of players. As he has never seen a play in his life, he is dazzled by the visual effects of the pageant, and in his wonderment finds it hard to tell the difference between illusion and reality. Garvey, the jolly-faced head of the troupe, plays God, and that's how Gabriel looks up to him, while he thinks of the sallow-faced Frenchman who plays Lucifer as the Devil-Man himself. With his fair curls and angelic features, Gabriel begins to believe in his own angelic status and power, particularly after Garvey hits on the idea of putting on miracle plays. As Gabriel's confusion slowly clears, he sees Garvey's lack of scruples and the Frenchman's fatherlike kindness.

A Little Lower Than the Angels conjures up powerful images which linger in the mind—Gabriel's eyeview of the crowd as he perches on his "cloud" in his peacock wings, the "reality" of heaven and hell, the plague-stricken villages and the terror-stricken people, desperate for a miracle. The medieval atmosphere is brilliantly recreated, and poetic language nicely balanced with down-to-earth, terse dialogue. If Gabriel at first seems unduly innocent for an 11-year-old, the context soon convinces, and the characters live off the page. The novel should be accessible to good readers of about 12, and also has considerable adult appeal.

Illusion and trickery also come into *A Pack of Lies*, a collection of 11 stories within a framework. A strange young man who calls himself MCC Berkshire turns up at the antique shop which Ailsa's mother can barely keep going, and offers to work without wages. He immediately displays astonishing virtuosity as a storyteller—telling a beguiling tale about the history of the item a customer is interested in, which almost every time induces the customer to part with his money. He tells a story of ham horror about a four poster bed to impress an American, a sad love story to a young couple interested in a Chinese willow pattern plate—the story is always appropriate, and MCC's range is extensive. "A pack of lies" for everyone, say Ailsa and her mother. The linking narrative is firmly rooted in everyday reality, but MCC's stories turn out to have more than an element of truth in them, while his own identity has much to do with the nature of fiction and the way characters so often take over from their creators. Ingeniously put together, *A Pack of Lies* is an enticing collection.

McCaughrean's powers of evocation and suggestion are considerable, and it will be interesting to see where they take her to next.

—Jennifer Taylor

———

McCAUGHREN, Tom. Irish. Born in Ballymena, County Antrim, Northern Ireland, 11 August 1936. Educated at Ballymena Technical High School, 1949–51; Millar's Academy, Ballymena, 1952–53. Married Frances Byrne in 1970; four daughters. Reporter, Dungannon *Courier and News*, County Tyrone, 1954, Ballymena *Weekly Telegraph* and Belfast *Telegraph*, 1954–55; reporter and defence correspondent, *Irish Times*, Dublin, 1955–68. Reporter, 1968–75, assistant news editor, 1975–76, and since 1977 security correspondent, RTE Radio and Television, Dublin. Recipient: Reading Association of Ireland Children's Book award, 1985; Irish Book award, 1987. Address: c/o The Children's Press, 90 Lower Baggot Street, Dublin 2, Ireland.

PUBLICATIONS FOR CHILDREN

Fiction

The Legend of the Golden Key, illustrated by Terry Myler.   Dublin, Children's Press, 1983.

The Legend of the Phantom Highwayman, illustrated by Terry Myler.   Dublin, Children's Press, 1983.

Run with the Wind, illustrated by Jeanette Dunne.   Dublin, Wolfhound Press, 1983.

The Legend of the Corrib King, illustrated by Terry Myler.   Dublin, Children's Press, 1984.

Run to Earth, illustrated by Jeanette Dunne.   Dublin, Wolfhound Press, 1984.

The Children of the Forge, illustrated by Terry Myler.   Dublin, Children's Press, 1985.

Run Swift, Run Free, illustrated by Jeanette Dunne.   Dublin,

Wolfhound Press, 1986.
The Silent Sea, illustrated by Terry Myler.   Dublin, Children's Press, 1987.

Other

The Peacemakers of Niemba.   Dublin, Browne and Nolan, 1966.

*

Tom McCaughren comments:

For many years a gap existed in Irish literature. For some reason children's fiction had virtually ceased to be produced. The few children's books that were being produced were being published elsewhere. It was for that reason that I began writing children's fiction. Other writers had also come to notice this lapse in our literary tradition, and in 1981, with the help of the Arts Council, the first children's books in many years began to appear. My first book, *The Legend of the Golden Key*, was published in 1983, and like several of those that were to follow, was an adventure story involving some aspect of our history or folklore. I had also noticed that while good wildlife fiction had been produced elsewhere, it had not appeared in Ireland. And so came my three books on the fox. With them, my books took on an international dimension, as editions have now appeared in other countries and other languages.

*   *   *

Since he began writing for children in 1983 Tom McCaughren has become one of the most popular and successful of Irish children's writers. His works can be divided into two separate categories, his adventure stories and his wildlife trilogy. His first book *The Legend of the Golden Key* and its sequels *The Legend of the Phantom Highwayman* and *The Legend of the Corrib King* are lively adventure stories which were published in a short uniform format. Despite this limitation, however, their contemporary portrayal of the traditional adventure story was a welcome addition to the Irish scene. A distinctive feature of these books is their affectionate sense of people and places. This helps to stimulate in children an interest in their local environment and folk tradition at a time when they are particularly receptive. The first two are set in McCaughren's home area of County Antrim and the third in the west of Ireland. *The Children of the Forge* is very much in the same style. Its slightly greater length allows more scope for a variety of themes to be introduced. An added international dimension to this story draws on McCaughren's experience in Lebanon as security correspondent for Irish television.

It was with the first volume of his wildlife trilogy *Run with the Wind* that McCaughren received serious critical attention. This book perfectly exemplifies the best of the genre. It is the story of a fox colony fighting for survival, told vividly and unsentimentally. The personalities of the individual foxes are carefully drawn, yet they remain true to their animal natures. The later volumes *Run to Earth* and *Run Swift, Run Free* further develop the characters and give us a picture of the animal world that is particularly detailed and fascinating. These books provide a thoughtful and thought-provoking picture of the environment. They are written in a style that flows easily and fluently; McCaughren never allows his detailed knowledge of and obvious commitment to the environment to overwhelm his story.

His latest book *The Silent Sea* is a return to the adventure story and is his most successful to date in this genre. In all of McCaughren's books the place and ambience are captured most skilfully, but in none is the landscape contemporary, and relevant and he introduces us to an engaging and well-drawn cast of characters. As increasing international recognition shows, McCaughren is develop-

ing as a skilful and confident writer.

—Sheila Flanagan

———

McCLOSKEY, (John) Robert.   American.   Born in Hamilton, Ohio, 15 September 1914. Educated at Vesper George Art School, Boston, 1932–34; National Academy of Design, New York (President's award, 1936), 1934–36; American Academy in Rome (fellow), 1939. Served in the United States Army Infantry, 1942–45: Sergeant. Married Margaret Durand, daughter of Ruth Sawyer, *q.v.*, in 1940; two daughters. Artist and illustrator: sculpted a bas relief in Hamilton, 1935, and painted a mural in Boston. Group shows: National Academy and Tiffany Foundation, both New York; Society of Independent Artists, Boston. Recipient: American Library Association Caldecott Medal, 1942, 1958; Catholic Library Association Regina Medal, 1974. D.Litt.: Miami University, Oxford, Ohio, 1964; Mount Holyoke College, South Hadley, Massachusetts, 1967. Address: Little Deer Isle, Maine 04650, U.S.A.

PUBLICATIONS FOR CHILDREN (illustrated by the author)

Fiction

Lentil.   New York, Viking Press, 1940.
Make Way for Ducklings.   New York, Viking Press, 1941; Oxford, Blackwell, 1944.
Homer Price.   New York, Viking Press, 1943; London, Penguin, 1976.
Blueberries for Sal.   New York, Viking Press, 1948; London, Angus and Robertson, 1967.
Centerburg Tales.   New York, Viking Press, 1951; abridged edition, as *More Homer Price*, New York, Scholastic, 1963.
One Morning in Maine.   New York, Viking Press, 1952; London, Penguin, 1976.
Time of Wonder.   New York, Viking Press, 1957; London, Penguin, 1977.
Burt Dow, Deep-Water Man.   New York, Viking Press, 1963.

*

Manuscript Collection: May Massee Collection, Emporia State University, Kansas.

Illustrator: *Yankee Doodle's Cousins* by Anne Burnett Malcolmson, 1941; *Tree Toad* by Robert Hobart Davis, 1942; *The Man Who Lost His Head* by Claire Huchet Bishop, 1942; *Trigger John's Son* by Tom Robinson, 1949; *Journey Cake, Ho!* by Ruth Sawyer, 1953; *Junket* by Anne H. White, 1955; *Henry Reed, Inc.*, 1955, *Henry Reed's Journey*, 1963, *Henry Reed's Baby-Sitting Service*, 1966, and *Henry Reed's Big Show*, 1970, all by Keith Robertson.

*   *   *

I once read a fifth-grade book report that ended with the sentence: "Robert McCloskey is a Yankee Doodle Dandy of a writer." And I thought then, and think now, that no other author for children over the past 50 years fits that description so well.

The fifth grader was writing about the book *Homer Price*, a story of a boy growing up in the small midwestern American town of McCloskey's boyhood 70 years ago. There is a lot of McCloskey in Homer, who loves to invent and tinker with all sorts of gadgets, and in *Lentil*, his other boy hero, who loves to play the harmonica. Like Twain's Tom Sawyer, McCloskey's boys have the knack of getting themselves into and out of fantastic adventures and misadventures. The incidents in these books are authentically shaped out of actual experience and touched with the gentle humor of a grown-up's remembrance. As McCloskey says of his work: "I have one foot resting on reality and the other foot planted firmly on a banana peel."

McCloskey's stories also have the distinct quality of the grand exaggeration and broad humor that one finds in the tall tales of traditional American folklore. The episode of the doughnut machine in *Homer Price* is as well-known to American children today as any of the adventures of folk characters like Paul Bunyan and Pecos Bill, and it would seem as much at home in a collection of American folklore as it would in an anthology of fiction. James Daugherty found McCloskey's "boy" books to be "America laughing at itself with a broad and genial humanity, without bitterness or sourness or sophistication." Through these books young readers today and in the future can be in touch with the folk America of their grandparents and great-grandparents.

McCloskey's picture books for younger children usually grow out of real incidents that have occurred in actual families, either his own, as in *One Morning in Maine, Blueberries for Sal*, and *Time of Wonder*, or that of Mr. and Mrs. Mallard in *Make Way for Ducklings*. These books have won great acclaim for the illustrations, but one should not overlook the writing. McCloskey, like Daugherty and Kate Seredy, was one of those illustrators who, at the urging of that remarkable children's editor May Massee, discovered that he had a talent for writing as well as for drawing. And he brought to that writing the same painstaking integrity that marks his illustration. As he says: "It's a good feeling to be able to put down a line and know that it's right."

In the picture books McCloskey usually employs a straightforward matter-of-fact style, except for *Time of Wonder*, which is more like a prose poem, uniquely written in second-person narrative. Though he admittedly "thinks in pictures," McCloskey's stories are always skillfully tuned for the ear, so that they are particularly suited for reading aloud. They are also especially suited for the young child because they are full of gentle wisdom and reassurance, while always focussing on what's right in the world.

In almost 50 years of writing and illustrating books for children McCloskey has not once produced anything that is not of the highest quality. To repeat my fifth-grade friend, he is indeed "a Yankee Doodle Dandy of a writer."

—James E. Higgins

McCORD, David (Thompson Watson). American. Born in New York City, 15 November 1897. Educated at Lincoln High School, Portland, Oregon, graduated 1917; Harvard University, Cambridge, Massachusetts, A.B. in physics 1921, A.M. in romance languages 1922. Served in the Field Artillery, United States Army, 1918: Second Lieutenant. Associate editor, 1923–25, and editor, 1940–46, *Harvard Alumni Bulletin*; member of the drama staff, Boston *Evening Transcript*, 1923–28. Executive director, Harvard Fund Council, 1925–63; Phi Beta Kappa Poet, Harvard University, 1938, Tufts College, Medford, Massachusetts, 1938 and 1978, College of William and Mary, Williamsburg, Virginia, 1950; Massachusetts Institute of Technology, Cambridge, 1973, and Colby College, Waterville, Maine, 1979; lecturer, Lowell Institute, Boston, 1950; staff member, Bread Loaf Writers Conference, Vermont, 1958, 1960, 1962, 1964; Instructor in Creative Writing, Harvard University, summers 1963, 1965, 1966; Visiting Professor, Framingham

State College, Massachusetts, 1974; councilor, Harvard Society of Advanced Study and Research, 1967–72; member, Overseers' Visiting Committee, Department of Astronomy, Harvard University. Painter: several individual shows of water colors. Honorary member, Phi Beta Kappa, 1938; honorary life associate, Dudley House, Harvard University; honorary member, Senior Common Room, Lowell House, Harvard University. Recipient: New England Poetry Club Golden Rose, 1941; William Rose Benét award, 1952; Guggenheim fellowship, 1954; American Academy grant, 1961; Sarah Josepha Hale award, 1962; Miriam Kallen award, 1976; National Council of Teachers of English award, for verse, 1977; Littauer Foundation grant, 1983; Harvard Medal, 1984. Litt.D.: Northeastern University, Boston, 1954; University of New Brunswick, Fredericton, 1963; Williams College, Williamstown, Massachusetts, 1971; Keene State College, New Hampshire, 1983; Skidmore College, Saratoga Springs, New York, 1986; LL.D.: Washington and Jefferson College, Washington, Pennsylvania, 1955; L.H.D.: Harvard University, 1956; Colby College, 1968; Framingham State College, 1975; Fitchburg State College, Massachusetts, 1986; Art.D.: New England College, Henniker, New Hampshire, 1956; Ed.D.: Suffolk University, Boston, 1979; D.C.L.: Simmons College, Boston, 1983. Fellow, American Academy of Arts and Sciences; Benjamin Franklin fellow, Royal Society of Arts, London. Address: Harvard Club of Boston, 374 Commonwealth Avenue, Boston, Massachusetts 02215, U.S.A.

PUBLICATIONS FOR CHILDREN

Verse

Far and Few, illustrated by Henry B. Kane. Boston, Little Brown, 1952.
Take Sky (single poem). Privately printed, 1961.
Take Sky (collection), illustrated by Henry B. Kane. Boston, Little Brown, 1962.
Books Fall Open (bookmark). New York, Children's Book Council, 1964.
All Day Long, illustrated by Henry B. Kane. Boston, Little Brown, 1966.
Every Time I Climb a Tree, illustrated by Marc Simont. Boston, Little Brown, 1967.
For Me to Say, illustrated by Henry B. Kane. Boston, Little Brown, 1970.
Mr. Bidery's Spidery Garden, illustrated by Henry B. Kane. London, Harrap, 1972.
Pen, Paper and Poem. New York, Holt Rinehart, 1973.
Away and Ago, illustrated by Leslie Morrill. Boston, Little Brown, 1974.
The Star in the Pail, illustrated by Marc Simont. Boston, Little Brown, 1975.
One at a Time: His Collected Poems for the Young, illustrated by Henry B. Kane. Boston, Little Brown, 1977.
Speak Up, illustrated by Marc Simont. Boston, Little Brown, 1980.
All Small, illustrated by Madelaine Gill Linden. Boston, Little Brown, 1986.

Recording: *The Pickety Fence and 51 Other Poems*, Pathways of Sound.

PUBLICATIONS FOR ADULTS

Short Story

The Camp at Lockjaw. New York, Doubleday, 1952.

Play

Alice in Botolphland. Boston, St. Botolph Club, 1932.

Verse (includes broadsheets)

Floodgate. Cambridge, Massachusetts, Washburn and Thomas, 1927.
Oxford Nearly Visited: A Fantasy. Cambridge, Massachusetts, Cygnet Press, 1929.
Fiftieth Anniversary Ode. Boston, St. Botolph Club, 1930.
Chocorua. Privately printed, 1932.
The Crows. New York, Scribner, 1934.
Bay Window Ballads. New York, Scribner, 1935.
The Stretch. Privately printed, 1937.
Twelve Verses from XII Night. Privately printed, 1938.
The Knowing. Privately printed, 1938.
Reflection in Blue. Privately printed, 1939.
And What's More. New York, Coward McCann, 1941.
The Legend of St. Botolph. Privately printed, 1942.
Christmas 1943. Privately printed, 1943.
On Occasion. Cambridge, Massachusetts, Harvard University Press, 1943.
Remembrance of Things Passed. Boston, Club of Odd Volumes, 1947.
Midway in This Middle Year of the Twentieth Century. Privately printed, 1950.
A Star by Day. New York, Doubleday, 1950.
Poet Always Next But One. Williamsburg, Virginia, College of William and Mary, 1951.
Blue Reflections on the Merchants Limited. Boston, Club of Odd Volumes, 1952.
The Old Bateau and Other Poems. Boston, Little Brown, 1953.
Ten Limericks. Privately printed, 1953.
Odds Without Ends. Boston, Little Brown, 1954.
By Swancote Pool. Privately printed, 1954.
Whereas to Mr. Franklin. Boston, Old South Association, 1954.
60 Lines for Three-Score Hatch. Boston, India Wharf Rats Club, 1957.
Sonnets to Baedecker. Meriden, Connecticut, Meriden Gravure Company, 1965.
In Memory of Sir Winston Churchill, 25 January 1965. Privately printed, 1965.
H.R.H. H.H.R. Privately printed, 1965.
Observation Tower. Boston, Club of Odd Volumes, 1966.
Roland Hayes. Privately printed, 1967.
Poem for the Occasion. Boston, Colonial Society of Massachusetts, 1970.
Spree Fever. Privately printed, 1970.
Thomas Dudley Cabot. Privately printed, 1972.
R.R.: Lines, Sharp as Serifs, on the By-Passing of His Ninetieth Birthday. Privately printed, 1973.
Sestina for the Queen. Boston, Bostonian Society, 1976.
The Children's World. Privately printed, 1979.

Other

Oddly Enough (essays). Cambridge, Massachusetts, Washburn and Thomas, 1926.
Stirabout (essays). Cambridge, Massachusetts, Washburn and Thomas, 1928.
H.T.P.: Portrait of a Critic (on Henry Taylor Parker). New York, Coward McCann, 1935.
Notes on the Harvard Tercentenary. Cambridge, Massachusetts, Harvard University Press, 1936.
An Acre for Education, Being Notes on the History of Radcliffe College. Cambridge, Massachusetts, Radcliffe College, 1938; revised edition, 1954, 1958, 1963.
About Boston: Sight, Sound, Flavor and Inflection, illustrated by the author. New York, Doubleday, 1948.
...as Built with Second Thoughts. Boston, Centennial Commission of the Boston Public Library, 1953.
The Related Man. Boston, American Academy of Arts and Sciences, 1953.
David McCord's Oregon. Boston, Massachusetts Historical Society, 1959.
On the Frontier of Understanding (address). Fredericton, University of New Brunswick, 1959.
The Language of Request: Fishing with a Barbless Hook (essays). Washington, D.C., American Alumni Council, 1961.
The Fabrick of Man: Fifty Years of the Peter Bent Brigham Hospital. Boston, Hospital Celebration Committee, 1963.
In Sight of Sever: Essays from Harvard. Cambridge, Massachusetts, Harvard University Press, 1963.
Art and Education (lecture), with David B. Little and Sinclair H. Hitchings. Boston, Boston Public Library, 1966.
Children and Poetry (lecture). Chicago, University of Chicago Press, 1966.
Notes from Four Cities 1927–1953. Worcester, Massachusetts, A.J. St. Onge, 1969.
Celebration: 1925–1975 (history of Harvard College Fund). Privately printed, 1975.

Editor, *Once and For All* (essays). New York, Coward McCann, 1929.
Editor, *What Cheer: An Anthology of American and British Humorous and Witty Verse.* New York, Coward McCann, 1945; as *The Pocket Book of Humorous Verse*, New York, Pocket Books, 1946; as *The Modern Treasury of Humorous Verse*, New York, Doubleday, 1951.
Editor, *Bibliotheca Medica: Physician for Tomorrow.* Boston, Harvard Medical School, 1966.
Editor, *New England Revisited*, by Arthur Griffin. Boston, Houghton Mifflin, 1966.
Editor, *Stow Wengenroth's New England.* Barre, Massachusetts, Barre Publishers, 1969.

*

Manuscript Collections: Boston Public Library; Houghton Library, Harvard University, Cambridge, Massachusetts; and other collections.

David McCord comments:

Giving a rather long talk to a group of children's librarians gathered at the University of Chicago a dozen years ago, I was forced to come to grips with myself over the natural question: Why does one write for children? The most generous and general answer, I suppose, is simply: Why not? But perhaps I had a special reason.

For me the small years, as Frank Kendon calls them, were never lonely, though I had neither brother nor sister nor much of anyone to play with. Childhood, and even most of my boyhood, marred by recurring malaria but not by the resulting large amount of solitude and freedom from school, left me with time to read, work with my hands, and raise chickens. I very early built and operated, with unmalarial fever, a licensed wireless telegraph station, not unaware that the dot-dash code itself is language of pure rhythm and a kind of haunting poetry in isolation. Above all, I soon became a countryman at heart: learned to look on the sky with as much affection as on the land; to walk in silence, listen, notice things and to explore with almost equal young delight the wonders of the backyard or the wilderness. That is literally true, for I began all this in Woodmere on Long Island, New York, adjacent to a poultry farm, and finished it out west beside the wild Rogue River on my uncle's ranch in Oregon: a slice of frontier life as yet unvanished, where a boy could pan for gold for pocket money, with little chance to spend it. Thrill enough it was to have it weighed out on the big brass scales of an old bank in a town about as old as 1849.

I read and was read to aloud. And into the far west I took remembrance of my Presbyterian grandmother Reed's lovely voice and the rhythm of the King James version of the Bible. My own reading wavered on another kind of scale between the Oz books, Dickens, Ralph Henry Barbour, Mark Twain, Jules Verne; Lear, Carroll, and Gilbert; W.W. Jacobs, Jack London, and such. I also read three equally indispensable magazines: *St. Nicholas*, Gernsback's *Modern Electrics*, and *The Reliable Poultry Journal*. By the time I was 10 I had read five or six books by the New Brunswick writer, Charles G.D. Roberts, from cover to cover. I still consider *Red Fox* one of the two greatest animal stories ever written. The other one for me—of course, years later—is *Tarka the Otter* by Henry Williamson. Another thing: because I was read aloud to when very young, I came to love the sound of words as well as the look of them on paper.

I began to write verse when I was 15, and verse for children when just out of Graduate School at Harvard. Now, some 400 poems-for-children later, I dare to offer one or two rules for the conduct of this seemingly simple but dangerously abstruse art.

First, just be a child before you grow up and let nothing interfere with the process. Write it all *out* of yourself and *for* yourself as you remember that weasel body with the eagle eyes. Next, never take the phrase "writing verse *for* children" seriously. If you write *for* them you are lost. Ask your brain's computer what you know about a child's mind and what goes on inside it. The answer is zero. What do they think of this calamitous new world which you don't even pretend to understand? They do not compare it with the past. It is the only world they know. Don't ever even pretend you are *looking* at the young; just make sure the young are *looking* at you. Make your readers believe you are letting them into your own dark life, into your own serene confusion, not you into theirs. Never talk down; and if for weeks at a time you have absolutely nothing to say, fight the uphill fight and do not say it.

*   *   *

David McCord has often been called an acrobat with language—an apt description of this poet whose verses are filled with surprising rhythm and sound effects and inventive rhyming twists, all done with acrobatic grace and playfulness. Typical of McCord, for instance, is the characterization of a little bat as not "flight able" (to rhyme with "gable"); and description of three flying geese as making a V "with two in the caboose and one in the/a-po-gee"; and a combination of poem and picture in which a dangling rope and long narrow line of print force the reader to read up the page about the grasshopper who is climbing up out of a well (all three poems in *Far and Few*).

A playful tone permeates almost all of the poems, whatever the subject matter, because exploration of the textures of language is so paramount an aim for this poet. Remembering this, one can still group the subjects loosely into five major categories: 1) poems about small creatures—a newt, bats, frogs, crickets, ants, and many others; 2) poems written in the first person about the thoughts and feelings of a child who is flying kites, fishing, eating, drawing pictures, skating, taking castor oil, going to the dentist, making a snowman, jumping in autumn leaves—all in the course of daily living indoors and out; 3) a few poems for or about children, written from the vantage point of an adult looking back; 4) poems primarily of language exploration and word play ("You *know* the word *cathedral*,/How about *Tetartohedral*?" from "The Look and Sound

of Words" in *For Me to Say*); 5) two groups of poems, in *Take Sky* and *For Me to Say*, demonstrating the writing of 10 verse-forms, beginning with couplet and ending with haiku.

It is interesting to note which poems—out of this array of more than 200—are most often reprinted by anthologists and writers of children's literature texts. My informal survey indicates that there are two top favorites, appearing over and over again: the chant about the pickety fence from "Five Chants" and "This Is My Rock" (both in *Far and Few*). The chant catches the pickety, lickety sounds and the quick, brittle rhythm of the childhood game of running along and clicking a stick on a fence. This is one of the simpler language-play poems, easy to read without stumbling on rhythm or syntax. "This Is My Rock" is also an easily read poem, but serious in tone and without word-play. In fact, it is one of the least typical of McCord's poems. In it a child simply speaks about a rock where he likes to sit and watch the sun and sky and the coming of the evening. Are these two poems first choices because of their simplicity and readability, as well as their charm?Children undoubtedly turn away from many of the more complex poems because of the language difficulties—unless, of course, an adult is helping with the interpretation. What, for instance, is an uninitiated child to make of the tricky algebra here (from "Exit *x*" in *For Me to Say*):

> If *vex*
> is *x*2,
> will equal one-no-three.

Also difficult are lines like these from the poem "O-U-G-H" in *All Day Long*: "Supposing *Though's* not tho, but more like *thoff*,/and *sough's sow's* not a pig that sows, but *soff*?"

McCord should be read aloud to young children who are just discovering him—read aloud by adults who enjoy the rhythms and won't trip up on the word-play. A good book to begin on is *Every Time I Climb a Tree*, a collection of 25 of the earlier poems, produced as a picture book with large bright water-color illustrations. Here are not only "This Is My Rock", the pickety fence poem, and the grasshopper poem mentioned earlier, but two short ones that show McCord at his best in the game of inventing rhymes: "Glowworm" with its rhyming "knowworm", "down belowworm", "slowworm", and "Helloworm!"; and "I Want You to Meet" in which "Lady-bug" is rhymed with "Sadiebug," "Mrs. Gradybug," "oldmaidybug," and "fraidybug." Also there are winter poems, food poems (one especially for lovers of bananas and cream), Halloween and Christmas poems, and of course the title poem about pleasures of climbing a tree (good for ants though not for pants). Almost all are just for fun and surprise and present little reading difficulty. Not strictly for fun are "This Is My Rock" and the five-line poem "Cocoon," perhaps even more moving for adults than for children, about the little caterpillar who has three good tries before it dies.

Another collection of earlier poems for the youngest readers is *The Star in the Pail*, this one also colorfully illustrated and presented as a picture book. Here, too, are easily read poems. Most readers, however, would probably vote for *Every Time I Climb a Tree*—so full of old favorites—if a choice had to be made between the two collections.

Though a great many of McCord's poems have been in print for over 40 years, few of them are what contemporary children might consider old-fashioned. True, there's the reference (in "The Trouble Was Simply That" in *For Me to Say*) to a boy's hat with its good crown and lining and brim. "*What*?" a boy today might wonder. And readers who are girls might wish there were more girls in the poems, and might even take offense at the attitude toward girls revealed in the lines "Little boys out for trout,/Little girls flumped about" (from "Dr. Klimwell's Fall" in *Take Sky*). But wit with words is for both girls and boys and does not go out of date. McCord's ingenious and crisp inventions will doubtless go on pleasing readers for years to come. Might as well expect Edward Lear to move into oblivion.

—Claudia Lewis

————

McGINLEY, Phyllis (Louise). American. Born in Ontario, Oregon, 21 March 1905. Educated at a school in Iliff, Colorado; Sacred Heart Academy, Ogden, Utah; Ogden High School; University of Utah, Salt Lake City, graduated 1927; University of Southern California, Los Angeles. Married Charles L. Hayden in 1937 (died 1972); two daughters. Schoolteacher in Utah, 1928, and New Rochelle, New York, 1929–34; worked for an advertising agency, New York, 1930's; staff writer, *Town and Country*, New York, 1937. Member, Advisory Board, *American Scholar*, Washington, D.C. Recipient (for verse): Christopher award, 1955; Poetry Society award, 1955; Catholic Writers Guild award, 1955; Edna St. Vincent Millay award, 1955; St. Catherine de Siena Medal, 1956; Catholic Institute of the Press award, 1960; Pulitzer Prize, 1961; Catholic Poetry Society Spirit Gold Medal, 1962; Laetare Medal, Notre Dame University, 1964; Campion award, 1967. D.Litt.: Wheaton College, Illinois, 1956; St. Mary's College, Notre Dame, Indiana, 1958; Marquette University, Milwaukee, 1960; Dartmouth College, Hanover, New Hampshire, 1961; Boston College, 1962; Wilson College, Chambersburg, Pennsylvania, 1964; Smith College, Northampton, Massachusetts, 1964; St. John's University, Jamaica, New York, 1964. Member, American Academy, 1955. *Died 22 February 1978.*

PUBLICATIONS FOR CHILDREN

Fiction

The Horse Who Lived Upstairs, illustrated by Helen Stone. Philadelphia, Lippincott, 1944.
The Plain Princess, illustrated by Helen Stone. Philadelphia, Lippincott, 1945.
A Name for Kitty, illustrated by Feodor Rojankovsky. New York, Simon and Schuster, 1948; London, Muller, 1950.
The Most Wonderful Doll in the World, illustrated by Helen Stone. Philadelphia, Lippincott, 1950.
The Horse Who Had His Picture in the Paper, illustrated by Helen Stone. Philadelphia, Lippincott, 1951.
Blunderbus, illustrated by William Wiesner. Philadelphia, Lippincott, 1951.
The Make-Believe Twins, illustrated by Roberta MacDonald. Philadelphia, Lippincott, 1953.
The B Book, illustrated by Robert Jones. New York, Crowell Collier, 1962; London, Collier Macmillan, 1968.

Plays

Walk the Plank! A Pirate Squall, music by Gladys Rich. New York, Schirmer, 1928.
Garden Magic: A Flower Fantasy, music by Gladys Rich. New York, Fischer, 1931.

Verse

All Around the Town, illustrated by Helen Stone. Philadelphia, Lippincott, 1948.
The Year Without a Santa Claus, illustrated by Kurt Werth. Philadelphia, Lippincott, 1957; Leicester, Brockhampton Press, 1960.
Lucy McLockett, illustrated by Helen Stone. Philadelphia, Lippincott, 1959; Leicester, Brockhampton Press, 1961.
Sugar and Spice: The ABC of Being a Girl, illustrated by Colleen Browning. New York, Watts, 1960.
Mince Pie and Mistletoe, illustrated by Harold Berson. Philadelphia, Lippincott, 1961.
Boys Are Awful, illustrated by Ati Forberg. New York, Watts, 1962.
How Mrs. Santa Claus Saved Christmas, illustrated by Kurt Werth. Philadelphia, Lippincott, 1963; Kingswood, Surrey, World's Work, 1964.
A Girl and Her Room, illustrated by Ati Forberg. New York, Watts, 1963.
Wonderful Time, illustrated by John Alcorn. Philadelphia, Lippincott, 1966.
A Wreath of Christmas Legends, illustrated by Leonard Weisgard. New York, Macmillan, 1967.

Other

Wonders and Surprises: A Collection of Poems. Philadelphia, Lippincott, 1968.

PUBLICATIONS FOR ADULTS

Plays

Small Wonder (revue), with others, music by Baldwin Bergersen and Albert Selden (produced New York, 1948).

Screenplay (English narration): *The Emperor's Nightingale*, 1951.

Verse

On the Contrary. New York, Doubleday, 1934.
One More Manhattan. New York, Harcourt Brace, 1937.
A Pocketful of Wry. New York, Duell, 1940; revised edition, New York, Grosset and Dunlap, 1959.
Husbands are Difficult; or, The Book of Oliver Ames. New York, Duell, 1941.
Stones from a Glass House: New Poems. New York, Viking Press, 1946.
A Short Walk from the Station. New York, Viking Press, 1951.
The Love Letters of Phyllis McGinley. New York, Viking Press, 1954; London, Dent, 1955.
Merry Christmas, Happy New Year. New York, Viking Press, 1958; London, Secker and Warburg, 1959.
Times Three: Selected Verse from Three Decades. New York, Viking Press, 1960; as *Times Three: Selected Verse from Three Decades with Seventy New Poems*, London, Secker and Warburg, 1961.
Christmas con and pro. Berkeley, California, Hart Press, 1971.
Confessions of a Reluctant Optimist, edited by Barbara Wells Price. Kansas City, Missouri, Hallmark Editions, 1973.

Other

The Province of the Heart (essays). New York, Viking Press, 1959; Kingswood, Surrey, World's Work, 1961.
Sixpence in Her Shoe (autobiography). New York, Macmillan, 1964; London, Dent, 1966.
Saint-Watching. New York, Viking Press, 1969; London, Collins, 1970.

*

Manuscript Collection: Syracuse University Library, New York.

Critical Study: *Phyllis McGinley* by Linda Welshimer Wagner, New York, Twayne, 1971.

* * *

Best known for her light verse for adults (which won her a Pulitzer Prize in 1961), Phyllis McGinley wrote outstanding and memorable fiction and poetry for children as well. Here, her light touch and tender heart are enhanced by moral lessons and happy endings: characters like Esmeralda, the "Plain Princess," live happily ever after, "or at least as happily as it possible in this mortal world."

McGinley's first book for children, *The Horse Who Lived Upstairs*, was inspired by a set of drawings of horses done by her friend Helen Stone, whose old-fashioned, lively, and realistic drawings grace many of McGinley's books for children. *The Horse Who Lived Upstairs* is about Joey, who lives in a fourth-floor stall in a big brick building in New York City and pulls a fruit and vegetable wagon for Mr. Polaski. But Joey is discontented. He wants to live in the country, "in a red barn with a weathervane," with a meadow where he can "run and kick up his heels." Then Mr. Polaski gets a truck, and Joey's dream comes true: he is sent to a farm. However, he soon discovers that he is no happier in the country. His barn is cold in winter and hot in summer; he must work pulling a plow from dawn to dusk; and he is lonely for his city friends: "I don't think I belong in the country after all....I am now more discontented than ever." When Mr. Polaski is unable to get new tires for his truck, he returns for Joey and brings him back home to the city. "How did you like the country?" Joey's New York friends ask. "The country is all right for country animals," he replies, "but I guess I am just a City horse at heart." Joey has learned his lesson, and is "never discontented again." (He even becomes quite a celebrity in *The Horse Who Had His Picture in the Paper*.)

The Plain Princess is a "once upon a time, in a distant kingdom" fairytale about eight-year-old princess Esmeralda, who has everything: golden hair, a fair complexion, excellent posture and grace, even golden braces for her teeth. Yet, she is plain. And, like some plain princesses, she's a snob. But when she learns to stop turning her nose up at the world, to be proud of the work of her own hands, and to be unselfish—her nose turns down, her mouth turns up, and her eyes start to glow. Now beautiful, in appearance as well as in character, she lives happily ever after (with the aforementioned proviso).

Dulcy, the six-going-on-seven heroine of *The Most Wonderful Doll in the World*, like equine Joey, finds it hard to be satisfied with "Things as They Are." She is always wishing "her fly-away hair could be ringlets or that she lived on a farm instead of a pretty village or that she were tall and slim instead of plump and rosy-round." She feels the same about her dolls, "always wishing things were a little different or a little better." When, one winter, Dulcy loses her new doll, Angela, in the snow, the plain little doll grows in Dulcy's imagination, far prettier than all her other dolls. Naturally, when Dulcy finds Angela in the Spring, she has a hard but important lesson to learn: "Everybody has a dream," said Dulcy's mother. "And sometimes people get mixed up about what is dream and what is real. That's how it happened with Angela. You remembered your dream of her."

All Around the Town is a clever alphabet book, in verse, of "the gay things/The stray things/That city children see," from aeroplanes (that "advertise/And write amusing messages/Across the city skies") to "a million winking Windows/When the dusk is coming down," "'Xcavations," and the city Zoo. *Lucy McLockett*, in pictures, prose, and verse, tells us about Lucy, a five-year-old, "plump/And curly/And good as gold" who loses a tooth, and then begins to lose other things—mittens, grocery lists, even herself in a large depart-

ment store—until Mr. Repairs screws her head on straight and she learns to *think*. *A Girl and Her Room* is a nostalgic look in verse at the stage of a girl's life as reflected in the changes in her bedroom: from a baby's room of crib, bottles, and talcum powder, to that of a teenager, with diaries, invitations to football games, and shoes with heels:

> Jump ropes, Mother Goose,
> All forgot.
> But the room remembered
> If she did not.
> And someday, maybe,
> After a bit,
> Another little girl
> May live in it.

Wonderful Time is about minutes, hours, night, day, sun, moon, the four seasons, and clocks.

McGinley's books for children are books to treasure, for a child's delight and an adult's pleasure.

—Marcia G. Fuchs

McGOUGH, Roger. British. Born in Liverpool, Lancashire, 9 November 1937. Educated at St. Mary's College, Crosby, Lancashire; Hull University, Yorkshire, B.A. in French and geography 1957, Cert. Ed. 1960. Married 1) Thelma Monaghan in 1970 (marriage dissolved 1980), two sons; 2) Hilary Clough in 1986, one son. Schoolteacher, Liverpool, 1960–64; lecturer, Liverpool College of Art, 1969–70; poetry fellow, University of Loughborough, Leicestershire, 1973–75. Formerly, member of the performing group The Scaffold. Free-lance writer and performer. Recipient: *Signal* award, 1984; BAFTA award, for television play, 1985. Agent: A.D. Peters, 5th Floor, The Chambers, Chelsea Harbour, Lots Road, London SW10 0XF, England.

PUBLICATIONS FOR CHILDREN

Fiction

The Great Smile Robbery, illustrated by Tony Blundell. London, Kestrel, 1982.
The Stowaways, illustrated by Tony Blundell. London, Viking Kestrel, 1986.

Plays

Wind in the Willows (lyrics only, with William Perry), book by Jane Iredale, music by Perry, adaptation of the story by Kenneth Grahame (produced Washington, D.C., 1984; New York, 1985).

Television Play: *Fast Forward*, 1986.

Verse

Mr. Noselighter, illustrated by André François. London, G. Whizzard, 1976.
You Tell Me, with Michael Rosen, illustrated by Sara Midda. London, Kestrel, 1979.
Sky in the Pie, illustrated by Satoshi Kitamura. London, Kestrel, 1983.

Nailing the Shadow, illustrated by Marketa Prachatická.   London, Viking Kestrel, 1987.
An Imaginary Menagerie, illustrated by Tony Blundell.   London, Viking Kestrel, 1988.

Other

Noah's Ark, illustrated by Ljiljana Rylands.   London, Dinosaur, 1986.

Editor, *Strictly Private: An Anthology of Poetry*, illustrated by Graham Dean.   London, Kestrel, 1981.
Editor, *The Kingfisher Book of Comic Verse*, illustrated by Caroline Holden.   London, Kingfisher, 1986.

PUBLICATIONS FOR ADULTS

Plays

Birds, Marriages and Deaths, with others (produced London, 1964).
The Chauffeur-Driven Rolls (produced Liverpool, 1966).
The Commission (produced Liverpool, 1967).
The Puny Little Life Show (produced London, 1969).   Published in *Open Space Plays*, edited by Charles Marowitz, London, Penguin, 1974.
Zones (produced Edinburgh, 1969).
Stuff (produced London, 1970).
P.C. Plod (produced London, 1971).
Wordplay (produced London, 1975).
Summer with Monika, music by Andy Roberts (produced London, 1978).
Watchwords (produced Nottingham, 1979).
Like Father, Like Son, Like (produced Nottingham, 1980).
Lifeswappers (produced Edinburgh and London, 1980).
All the Trimmings, music by Peter Brewis (produced London, 1980).
Golden Nights and Golden Days (produced on tour, 1980).
Behind the Lines (revue), with Brian Patten (produced London, 1982).
The Mouthtrap, with Brian Patten (produced Edinburgh and London, 1982).
A Matter of Chance, adaptation of a story by Nabokov (produced Edinburgh and London, 1988).

Screenplay: *Plod*, 1972.

Radio Plays: *Gruff: A TV Commercial*, 1977; *Walking the Dog*, 1981; *The Narrator*, 1985.

Television Plays: *The Lifeswappers*, 1976; *Kurt, B.P. Mungo, and Me*, 1983.

Verse

The Mersey Sound: Penguin Modern Poets 10, with Adrian Henri and Brian Patten.   London, Penguin, 1967; revised edition, 1974, 1983.
Frinck, A Life in the Day of, and Summer with Monika: Poems (novel and verse).   London, Joseph, and New York, Ballantine, 1967.
Watchwords.   London, Cape, 1969.
After the Merrymaking.   London, Cape, 1971.
Out of Sequence.   London, Turret, 1973.
Gig.   London, Cape, 1973.
Sporting Relations.   London, Eyre Methuen, 1974.
In the Glassroom.   London, Cape, 1976.
Summer with Monika, revised edition.   London, Deutsch, 1978.

Holiday on Death Row.   London, Cape, 1979.
Unlucky for Some.   London, Bernard Stone, 1980.
Waving at Trains.   London, Cape, 1982.
New Volume, with Adrian Henri and Brian Patten.   London, Penguin, 1983.
Crocodile Puddles.   London, Pyramid, 1984.
Melting into the Foreground.   London, Viking, 1986.

Recordings: *The Incredible New Liverpool Scene*, CBS, 1967; *McGough McGear*, Parlophone; "*Scaffold*" *Live at Queen Elizabeth Hall*, Parlophone; "*Scaffold*" *L. The P.*, Parlophone; *Grimms*, Island; *Fresh Liver*, Island; *Sleepers*, DJM; *McGough/Patten*, Argo; *Summer with Monika*, Island, 1978; *Gifted Wreckage*, with Brian Patten and Adrian Henri, Talking Tape, 1984; *Jelly Pie*, with Brian Patten, Puffin, 1987.

*

Manuscript Collection: University of Hull.

*   *   *

One of the most striking things about Roger McGough's poetry is the way it crosses the boundaries between writing for children and writing for adults. Many of his poems appear in both formats—for example, "First Day at School" and "The Lesson" from *In the Glassroom*, "The Lake" from *Holiday on Death Row*, and "The Identification" from *Gig*, are reprinted in the anthology for children *Strictly Private*; poems from *Melting into the Foreground* appear in *Nailing the Shadow*. This impressive talent for being genuinely accessible to two audiences, without condescension, is rooted in the key characteristics of his poetry.

He deals with everyday events, and in dealing with death, sex, violence, or politics, he almost always relates them to the personal. His humour and joking wordplay seem to be weapons used to keep a sense of proportion or to keep despair at bay.

McGough's appeal may begin with the "squib"—"I quite often confuse/My quees and my poos"—but even the apparent trivia need an intelligent response, as in *An Imaginary Menagerie*: "Ever see/a llama/harm a/fly?/Not their/Kharma/that's why." The poems very often combine the serious ending and the sharp poetic phrase which contrast with the casual surface:

> If violence is what you want
> Then this is the poem for you.
> 15 lines of action packed fury
> Starring, the Fist, the Boot,
> Even the Knife. No Guns.
> I do not have a licence
> For carrying guns in my poems.
> Nevertheless there is plenty of
> Screaming and swearing. Horrible.
> Blood soaks through the page
> Like an amazing image.
>
> But what is the point of a
> Poem about violence you ask?
> The answer, I hope, will not be
> Waiting outside to follow you home.

Many of his poems can therefore be read in strikingly different ways at different ages. His famous "The Lesson," in which a teacher bloodily massacres a class of "nooligans" can be taken as funny, moralistic, or horrific in fact or implication.

His books, then, are constantly inventive, and the tone seems, at least at first, to be light. Thus a collection such as *Sky in the Pie* may seem to contain a high proportion of the trivial, but very often the reader is caught by an ironic or tragic switch of tone. Take, for example, "The Pet," in which a little boy's mother constantly refuses to let him keep an animal:

I'm ten now
And big for my age
And I've just built
A wooden cage

For now I've a pet
To put inside
Something belonging
To someone who died

He keeps me company
When I feel sad
He's my pet slipper
And I call him 'Dad'.

Because the poems are personal and immediate, rather than abstract, they are accessible; because McGough has retained a child-like clarity of perception, and plays with words in the true exploratory sense of the word "play," he rarely writes poems for a disguised adult audience (as, for example, does A. A. Milne). The problems and jokes he deals with in his collections for children are problems and jokes at any age. Often the only difference in his adult collections is that the subject-matter turns to the problems and ironies of sex and age.

If anything, his manner has tended to become both more inventive on the surface, and more sombre in the subtext as he has aged, and this applies across the range of poetry written in any same period.

Of course, walking the tightrope as he does between the trivial and the profound, the comic and the tragic, there are failures. *An Imaginary Menagerie* may have been designed for older children, but not only is its format misleading, the verses seem to miss *any* audience because a good deal of knowledge is required to interpret the verses—but there is not enough "solid matter" to keep the attention of a reader with that amount of knowledge.

Of his two prose works, *The Great Smile Robbery* is the more inventive and ingenious, integrating Tony Blundell's illustrations very closely with the text. *The Stowaways*, a collection of conventional anecdotes about childhood, suffers from a rather too self-consciously friendly and casual tone, which his poems almost always escape.

McGough is a performance poet, a highly entertaining deliverer of his own verse, and so some of it is slightly thin on the page, without his presence. He is also, I think, greatly underestimated as a serious poet, perhaps because of the misleading surface texture of his poetry—but that is one of his great strengths for children coming to poetry, for his deadpan wit and relevance are widely appreciated.

—Peter Hunt

McGRAW, Eloise Jarvis. American. Born in Houston, Texas, 9 December 1915. Educated at Classen High School, Oklahoma City, graduated 1932; Principia College, Elsah, Illinois, B.A. in art 1937; University of Oklahoma, Norman, 1938; University of Colorado, Boulder, 1939; Museum Art School (now Pacific Northwest College of Art), Portland, Oregon, 1970–76. Married William Corbin McGraw in 1940; one son and one daughter. Instructor in Painting, Oklahoma City University, 1942–43; teacher, Lewis and Clark College, Portland, 1965–66, and Portland State University, summers,

1970–78. Recipient: Mystery Writers of America Edgar Allan Poe award, 1978. Agent: Emily Jacobson, Curtis Brown, 10 Astor Place, New York, New York 10003. Address: 1970 Indian Trail, Lake Oswego, Oregon 97034, U.S.A.

PUBLICATIONS FOR CHILDREN

Fiction

Sawdust in His Shoes. New York, Coward McCann, 1950.
Crown Fire. New York, Coward McCann, 1951.
Moccasin Trail. New York, Coward McCann, 1952.
Mara, Daughter of the Nile. New York, Coward McCann, 1953; London, Penguin, 1986.
The Golden Goblet. New York, Coward McCann, 1961; London, Methuen, 1964.
Merry Go Round in Oz, with Lauren Lynn McGraw, illustrated by Dick Martin. Chicago, Reilly and Lee, 1963.
Greensleeves. New York, Harcourt Brace, 1968.
Master Cornhill. New York, Atheneum, 1973; London, Penguin, 1987.
A Really Weird Summer. New York, Atheneum, 1977.
Joel and the Great Merlini, illustrated by Jim Arnosky. New York, Pantheon, 1979.
The Forbidden Fountain of Oz, with Lauren Lynn McGraw, illustrated by Dick Martin. N.p., International Wizard of Oz Club, 1980.
The Money Room. New York, Atheneum, 1981.
Hideaway. New York, Atheneum, 1983.
The Seventeenth Swap. New York, Atheneum, 1986; London, Viking Kestrel, 1988.
The Trouble with Jacob. New York, McElderry, and London, Viking Kestrel, 1988.

Play

Steady, Stephanie. Chicago, Dramatic Publishing Company, 1962.

PUBLICATIONS FOR ADULTS

Novel

Pharaoh. New York, Coward McCann, 1958.

Other

Techniques of Fiction Writing. Boston, The Writer, 1959.

*

Manuscript Collection: University of Oregon Library, Eugene.

Eloise Jarvis McGraw comments:

Five of my books have historical settings. Three of these, *Mara, Pharaoh,* and *The Golden Goblet,* are laid in ancient Egypt, the study of which was an almost obsessive hobby of mine for 25 years. One, *Moccasin Trail,* deals with the American west, specifically Oregon, in pioneer days (1845–46), and another, *Master Cornhill,* with the London of 1665–66, the years of the Great Plague and the Great Fire. I very much enjoy research, and also sharing the results of it with readers through the synthesis of fiction. My other books are set more or less specifically in the present day, though *A Really Weird Summer* was the first that could truly be called "contemporary." In this, and in other ways, it represented a step in a new direction for me.

My early books are built around dramatic action plots, though at the core of the story is always emotional development and an intellectual concept or theme of some sort. But with *Greensleeves* I began plotting in a different, less rigid way, and the "tone of voice" of the later books has altered accordingly. However, their chief emphasis, as in the earlier ones, is on character. I begin with a character, invariably.

My next book is a return to historical fiction (Bayeux Tapestry, England just after the Conquest) and I am currently so deep into research that yesterday I took a lesson in how to spin wool with a drop-spindle, just to see how it would feel.

I write about what passionately interests me at the time, I write as well and clearly as I can, and I am hard to please while writing and never really satisfied with the final result—though I make sure it is the best I am capable of producing at the moment. More than once a strong motive in my undertaking a certain book is my wish that someone had written a book about this so that I could read it. I believe I always, in the end, write for myself.

*   *   *

Although Eloise Jarvis McGraw wrote successful short stories for children before the publication of *Sawdust in His Shoes* in 1950, it is through her full-length books that she has gained her current prominence. Her first four books came within a period of four years and all were acclaimed.

McGraw's first and third novels, although quite different in character and tone, both deal with adjustment, a recurring theme in children's literature. The first, *Sawdust in His Shoes*, centers around the young hero's adjustment from circus life to farm life. The story moves forward with a swift-paced action in tune with the mettle of its characters. The characters are drawn by their creator with precision and understanding and their language is the racy, though rich, language of circus and farm. McGraw's third book, *Moccasin Trail*, deals with the difficult adjustment of a white youth who has spent much of his young life with the tribe of Crow Indians who adopted him after he was seriously injured by a fierce grizzly. As with McGraw's first book, this too is one with character emphasis. It is told with warmth and a perceptive understanding of the two-way adjustments necessary for the hero's acceptance of and acceptance by his own family.

Crown Fire, like her first and her third books, has a strong character emphasis and plenty of suspenseful, rapidly moving, dramatic action. The book's title is a logging term used to describe fire raging uncontrollably across tree tops. Although the story has colorful and authentic details about logging, the book's title is a symbol for the hero's temper, an explosive, uncontrollable "fire." Setting, action, pace, and style combine to make *Crown Fire* a considerable achievement.

As a departure from works influenced by her own childhood, McGraw successfully casts *Mara, Daughter of the Nile* in the Egypt of the Pharaohs. As its title suggests, this is a story with a heroine, not a hero. It is also less a book of character than of action, sometimes brutal action. Yet, like her earlier books, this one too has a lucid style with the ring of authenticity so characteristic of all McGraw's novels.

The Golden Goblet is also set in ancient Egypt. This is basically the story of Ranofer, a young Egyptian lad who longs to be a goldsmith like his father. For a long while it appears that Ranofer's ambition is forever to be thwarted by his wicked half-brother, Gebu, with whom Ranofer lives after their father's death. The climax of the drama is reached when Ranofer, with the help of two friends, unravels the mystery of a golden goblet by trapping his evil brother and the brother's equally evil accomplice in the tomb they are attempting to rob.

Like *The Golden Goblet*, some of McGraw's later works are characterized by strong elements of mystery and suspense, and, in some cases, also by intricately related themes of difficult adjustments, painful relationships, and extreme loneliness, an excellent example being *A Really Weird Summer*. In this contemporary story four children must adjust to an indefinite future and the almost certain likelihood of their parents' divorce. The Anderson children have been placed, temporarily, as paying guests of their great-aunt and uncle who live in a strange old inn in Reeves Ferry, Oregon. The situation is difficult for all four children, but especially for the two oldest— Nels, 12, and Stevie, 10. The story centers around Nels who, during most of the summer, finds escape in the secret make-believe world of his mind where he creates new relationships, almost obliterating the old. Nels's make-believe world provides an absorbing mystery, deftly handled by McGraw. Needless to say, Nels works himself through and beyond his severe stress over the separation of his parents and the uncertainty of the future; indeed, with the certainty of one who has arrived at great truth, Nels is finally able to tell Stevie with determination: "All us kids have got to *stay together*, that's the big thing....If we stick together, then whatever happens outside— whatever the grown-ups do—it won't matter so much. D'you see? We'll still be *us*."

Hideaway also concerns loneliness and the support children can give each other when the adult world is lacking. A teenage boy leaves home after his mother's remarriage and father's neglect, and decides to hide out in his grandparent's house, who he believes are on vacation. He breaks into the empty house, to discover his grandparents have moved and the new people living there are also away. He stays anyway, and befriends the girl being paid to keep an eye on the house. She too is from an unstable family situation, being passed from foster home to foster home. Their friendship helps them come to terms with their difficult circumstances.

McGraw is a gifted writer with a special knowledge and understanding of children. Her writing is many-faceted and finely honed; her literary trademarks are vivid characterization, suspenseful action, and intricate plots.

—Charity Chang

———————

McGREGOR, Iona. British. Born in Aldershot, Hampshire, 7 February 1929. Educated at Monmouth School for Girls; University of Bristol, B.A. (honours) 1950. Sub-editor, *Dictionary of the Older Scottish Tongue*, Edinburgh University Press, 1951–57; classics teacher, Simon Langton Girls' School, Canterbury, 1958–62, and Beaverwood School, Chislehurst, Kent, 1962–69. From 1969 classics teacher, St. George's School for Girls, Edinburgh. Address: 9 Saxe Coburg Street, Edinburgh EH3 5BN, Scotland.

PUBLICATIONS FOR CHILDREN

Fiction

An Edinburgh Reel.   London, Faber, 1968.
The Popinjay.   London, Faber, 1969.
The Burning Hill.   London, Faber, 1970.
The Tree of Liberty.   London, Faber, 1972.
The Snake and the Olive.   London, Faber, 1974.

Other

Edinburgh and the Eastern Lowlands: Lothian, Fife, and the Borders.   London, Faber, 1979.
Wallace and Bruce (textbook).   Edinburgh, Oliver and Boyd, 1986.

PUBLICATIONS FOR ADULTS

Novel

Death Wore a Diadem.   London, Women's Press, 1989.

Play

Radio Play: *A Kind of Glory*, 1971.

Other (study notes)

The Importance of Being Earnest.   London, Penguin, 1987.
The Adventures of Huckleberry Finn.   London, Penguin, 1988.

*

Iona McGregor comments:

As a writer I have always needed the stimulus of "history" to set an edge on my imagination, although by this I mean the minutiae of daily living and the impatience of new ideas rather than great events or the people who initiated them. Eastern Scotland, the background I most enjoy writing about, is visually still close to its past. I could say that in a very small way I am searching for lost time, since it is the effort to strip these scenes and places of modern accretions which brings my characters alive for me.

*   *   *

When reading Iona McGregor's books one is reminded of the drawings by Hogarth and Rowlandson—the scene is a mass of people. Her aim is to interpret these characters as flesh and blood realities, and she succeeds very well. She is at her best when dealing with her native Scotland, and her interest in history is the peg on which many of her stories are hung. However, she has to thank her training in the classics for her exactness in speech.

In *The Popinjay* we are immediately introduced to the central character, 16-year-old David Lindsay, the popinjay of the title. David is summoned from Bordeaux in 1546 by the Cardinal Archbishop Beaton to St. Andrews; his future looks rosy and his insolence is matched only by his dreams. However, soon all is changed, the Archbishop murdered, David a wounded fugitive—and it is at this point that McGregor really gets to grips with her characters. David begins to learn what life is like in the terror-stricken and plague-infested town, and his development to maturity through his involvement with the fishergirl, Elspeth, and Father Anthony from the Priory, shows evidence of the author's acute understanding of human nature. The whole story rings true and the reader is completely involved throughout.

No doubt it is because the author is so interested in the 18th century that she writes about it so confidently and convincingly, especially in her recreation of Edinburgh at this time. Her touch is so sensitive and the writing so vivid that the reader can almost smell the stench and hear the noises of the crowds and carriages in the Lawnmarket and Canongate. This is the setting which inspires McGregor to some of her finest writing, and *An Edinburgh Reel* is as lively as the dance itself. Christine's father, embittered by his experience as a prisoner after Culloden, returns to Edinburgh vowing vengeance on his unknown betrayer after the battle, whereas his daughter wants him to forgive and forget. The pages are scattered with fascinating characters—Lord Balmuir, the elderly judge, Lucky Robertson who owns the pie shop, Ewan McDonnell who tries to tempt Christine's father back into Jacobite plotting, and many more. McGregor blends them all into a colorful picture of Edinburgh life, pulsating with vigour and vitality. Everything in the book echoes the authenticity of her writing, the marvellous dialogue, the jostling crowds, the

personal hatreds and hopes, and the contrasting natures of the main protagonists. It is a glorious piece of writing, compulsive and exhilarating and a fine example of McGregor at her best.

—Margaret Walker

———

McKEE, David (John).   British. Freelance painter, illustrator, and cartoonist. Recipient: Children's Literature prize (West Germany), 1987. Address: c/o Andersen Press, 62–65 Chandos Place, London WC2N 4NW, England.

PUBLICATIONS FOR CHILDREN (illustrated by the author)

Fiction

Bronto's Wings.   London, Dobson, 1964.
Two Can Toucan.   London, Abelard Schuman, 1964; New York, Abelard Shuman, 1965.
Mr. Benn, Red Knight.   London, Dobson, 1967; New York, McGraw Hill, 1968.
Mark and the Monocycle.   London and New York, Abelard Shuman, 1968.
Elmer: The Story of a Patchwork Elephant.   London, Dobson, and New York, McGraw Hill, 1968; revised edition, London, Andersen Press, 1989.
123456789 Benn.   London, Dobson, and New York, McGraw Hill, 1970.
The Magician Who Lost His Magic.   London and New York, Abelard Schuman, 1970.
Six Men.   Montchaldorf, Switzerland, Nord-Sud Verlag, 1971; London, A. and C. Black, 1972.
Lord Rex, The Lion Who Wished.   London and New York, Abelard Schuman, 1973.
The Magician and the Sorcerer.   London, Abelard Schuman, and New York, Parents' Magazine Press, 1974; as *Melric and the Sorcerer*, London, Methuen, 1987.
The Day the Tide Went Out, and Out, and Out....   London, Abelard Schuman, 1975; New York, Abelard Schuman, 1976.
Elmer Again and Again.   London, Dobson, 1975.
The Magician and the Petnapping.   London, Abelard Schuman, and Boston, Houghton Mifflin, 1976.
Two Admirals.   London, Andersen Press, and Boston, Houghton Mifflin, 1977.
The Magician and the Balloon.   London, Abelard Schuman, 1978; New York, Bedrick, 1986.
Tusk Tusk.   London, Andersen Press, 1978; Woodbury, New York, Barron's, 1979.
The Magician and the Dragon.   London, Abelard Schuman, 1979; as *Melric and the Dragon*, London, Methuen, 1987.
Big Game Benn.   London, Dobson, 1979.
King Rollo and the Bread [*Birthday, New Shoes, Tree, Dishes, Balloons, Bath, King Frank, Search*].   London, Andersen Press, 9 vols., 1979–81; first 3 vols. published Boston, Little Brown, 1979; first 4 vols. published as *The Adventures of King Rollo*, New York, Penguin, 1 vol., 1986.
Big Top Benn.   London, Dobson, 1980.
Not Now, Bernard.   London, Andersen Press, 1980.
The Magician and Double Trouble, illustrated by David Hope. London, Abelard Schuman, 1981.
I Hate My Teddy Bear.   London, Andersen Press, 1982; New York, Clarion, 1984.

King Rollo's Playroom and Other Stories. London, Andersen Press, 1983.

The Hill and the Rock. London, Andersen Press, 1984; New York, Clarion, 1985.

King Rollo's Letter and Other Stories. London, Andersen Press, 1984.

Two Monsters. London, Andersen Press, 1985; New York, Bradbury Press, 1986.

King Rollo's Spring [Summer, Autumn, Winter]. London, Andersen Press, 4 vols., 1986.

The Sad Story of Veronica Who Played the Violin. London, Andersen Press, 1987.

The Magician's Apprentice. London, Blackie, 1987.

Snow Woman. London, Andersen Press, 1987; New York, Lothrop, 1988.

Who's a Clever Baby, Then? London, Andersen Press, 1988; New York, Lothrop, 1989.

The Magician and the King's Crown. London, Blackie, 1988.

Plays

Screenplay: *Greenback Hell,* 1974.

Television Plays: *Mr. Benn* series.

Other

Hans in Luck. London and New York, Abelard Schuman, 1967.

Mathematics Everywhere. London, Longman, 1969.

The Man Who Was Going to Mind the House: A Norwegian Folk-Tale. London, Abelard Schuman, 1972; New York, Abelard Schuman, 1973.

Mr. Benn Annual. London, Argus Press, 1972.

*

Illustrator: *The Poor Farmer and the Robber Knights* by Walter Kreye, 1969; *Hector's House Annual,* 1969–73; *Bertha the Tanker* by Liane Smith, 1969; *Vamos Amigos* by Heloise Lewis, 1971; *Mr. Drackle and His Dragons* by Elizabeth Hull Froman, 1971; *Joseph the Border Guard,* 1972, *Joachim the Dustman,* 1974, and *Joachim the Policeman,* 1975, all by Kurt Baumann; *Kids' London* by Elizabeth Holt, 1972; *Fire,* 1973, *The Day We Went to the Seaside,* 1973, and *What in the World,* 1979, all by David Mackay; *Piccolo Book of Parties and Party Games* by Deborah Manley, 1973; *The Follyfoot Pony Quiz Book* by Christine Pullein-Thompson, 1974; *Yan and the Gold Mountain Robbers,* 1974, and *Yan and the Firemonsters,* 1976, both by Sydney Paulden; *Cook for Your Kids!* by Merry Archard, 1975; *Fiery Frederica* by Christine Nöstlinger, 1975; *Helping* by Caroline Moorehead, 1975; *Tomfoolery,* 1975, *Witcracks,* 1975, and *A Twister of Twists, A Tangler of Tongues: Tongue Twisters,* 1976, all edited by Alvin Schwartz; *Okki-Tokki-Unga: Action Stories* edited by Beatrice Harrop, 1976, and *Harlequin* edited by Harrop and David Gadsby, 1981; *A Book of Elephants* edited by Katie Wales, 1977; *The King of Quizzical Island* by Gordon Snell, 1978; *Albert's World Tour* by Rosemary Weir, 1978; *Super Gran,* 1978, *Super Gran Rules, O.K.!,* 1981, *Super Gran Superstar,* 1982, *More Television Adventures of Super Gran,* 1984, *Super Gran on Holiday,* 1985, and *Super Gran at the Circus,* 1987, all by Forrest Wilson; *A Book of Pig Tales,* 1979, *A Book of Bears,* 1981, *A Book of Cats,* 1983, *Stories for a Prince,* 1983, and *A Book of Mice,* 1987, all edited by Rosemary Debnam; *Abracadabra Guitar!* by Hilary Bell, 1980; *Jeffy, The Burglar's Cat,* 1981, and *Spid,* 1985, both by Ursula Moray Williams; *Blue Bell Hill Games* edited by R.A. Smith, 1982; *The Speckled Panic,* 1982, *The Choking Peril,* 1985, and *Gary Who?,* 1988, all by Hazel Towson;

The Wizard of Oz, 1982, and *The Marvellous Land of Oz,* 1985, both by L. Frank Baum; *Game-Songs with Professor Dogg's Troupe* edited by Harriet Powell, 1983; *Paddington and the Knickerbocker Rainbow [at the Zoo, at the Fair, and the Marmalade Maze],* 4 vols., 1984–87, *Paddington's Painting Exhibition,* 1985, as *Paddington's Art Exhibition,* 1986, and *Paddington's Busy Day [Magical Christmas],* 2 vols., 1987–88, all by Michael Bond; *A Book of Dragons* edited by Joan Cass, 1985; *Hands On, Hands Off* by Christopher Schenk, 1986; *Something New for Bear to Do* by Shirley Isherwood, 1986; *Pudmuddle Jumps In: Poems* edited by Beverly Mathias and Jill Bennett, 1987; *The Scourge of the Dinner Ladies* by David Tinkler, 1987.

*   *   *

A seamless bond between illustrations and text characterises David McKee's picture books. Readers can also be certain that his books will be laced with both wit and humor. He employs a spectrum of styles from the lyrical, especially when animals are featured, to the semi-realistic, when children are the main focus, to the comic-strip, as in the King Rollo series or in *Two Monsters.* All are recognisably his work, direct and appealing to children. He is on their side.

Just as he calls on a variety of styles in his considerable output, so McKee returns to certain themes. Most obviously, he uses specific characters in whole series, King Rollo for one and Mr. Benn for another. King Rollo underpins the least demanding of his work— Rollo is no older than the early readers he addresses but, being a king, can do all the things that young children would like to do themselves like scaring grown-ups. There are even tiny books, such as *King Rollo and King Frank,* for tiny hands.

The Mr. Benn series moves beyond the nursery into a large and fantastic world. Mr. Benn is a meek sort of chap, but he has only to go to the costume shop and don another outfit to be transported into the appropriate place and time to become involved in a wild and wonderful adventure with dragons, perhaps, or elephants or even entire circuses. When all is satisfactorily resolved, he trots out of the shop attired once more in his dark suit and bowler hat, always with a souvenir of his expedition and the promise of more adventures in future. The series featuring Melric the Magician has a Camelot-style setting but the characters, including the hero, behave much like contemporary mortals, though helped with convenient powers.

McKee is closely in touch with young children and, in works that seek to help them explore ideas and values, he draws often on folktales and offers his own interpretations. *Two Can Toucan, Tusk Tusk,* and his early Elmer books all have echoes of traditional tales and address personal aspirations and conflict. The message of *Tusk Tusk* is in fact a dismal one, suggesting that so long as there is difference there must inevitably be conflict. White and black elephants fight to the death of all except the few pacifists, who slide off into the forests, from which emerge a generation later only grey elephants...but lately, the last line tells us "the little ears and the big ears have been giving each other strange looks." *Two Monsters* offers a happier resolution and an important lesson. The monsters fight so bitterly over whose view is correct that they demolish the intervening mountain—and learn that one sees things differently if one looks in different directions.

So (justly) confident is McKee of the unity between his two media that he occasionally pulls off a book in which the pictures say a good deal more than, and sometimes something quite different from, the line or so of text per page. In *Not Now, Bernard* the text speaks for Bernard's parents, always too busy doing things to give Bernard the attention he wants. But the pictures tell the story through a child's eyes and the reader is compelled to pay attention to the monster who gobbles Bernard up! Equally preoccupied are the parents in *Snow Woman,* though they do insist on the term "snowperson," while demonstrating non-sexist distribution of their own domestic tasks. The children, however, are not convinced nor is the matter satisfactorily resolved: when the snow couple disappear, the children decide to build a genderless snow bear.

The divergence of text and picture in *I Hate My Teddy Bear* is practically subversive. Parents are likely to find themselves out of control of reading the book as their preliterate children, instead of merely listening appreciatively, tell them the story from the bizarre activities in the pictures. Nothing could be more calculated to instill in young children a real love of books than enabling them to interpret and enjoy them for themselves, with sharing them as an optional extra.

—Gillian Klein

* * *

McKILLIP, Patricia (Anne). American. Born in Salem, Oregon, 29 February 1948. Educated at San Jose State University, B.A. 1971, M.A. in English 1973. Recipient: World Fantasy award, 1975. Agent: Howard Morhaim Literary Agency, 174 Fifth Avenue, Room 709, New York, New York 10010, U.S.A.

PUBLICATIONS FOR CHILDREN

Fiction

The House on Parchment Street, illustrated by Charles Robinson. New York, Atheneum, 1973.
The Throme of the Erril of Sherill, illustrated by Julie Noonan. New York, Atheneum, 1973.
The Forgotten Beasts of Eld. New York, Atheneum, 1974; London, Futura, 1987.
The Night Gift, illustrated by Kathy McKillip. New York, Atheneum, 1976.
Riddle of Stars. New York, Doubleday, 1979; as *The Chronicles of Morgan, Prince of Hed*, London, Sidgwick and Jackson, 1981.
   The Riddle Master of Hed. New York, Atheneum, 1976; London, Sidgwick and Jackson, 1979.
   Heir of Sea and Fire. New York, Atheneum, 1977; London, Sidgwick and Jackson, 1979.
   Harpist in the Wind. New York, Atheneum, and London, Sidgwick and Jackson, 1979.
Moon-Flash. New York, Atheneum, 1984.
The Moon and the Face. New York, Atheneum, 1985.
The Changeling Sea. New York, Atheneum, 1988.

PUBLICATIONS FOR ADULTS

Novel

Stepping from the Shadows. New York, Atheneum, 1982.
Fool's Run. New York, Warner, and London, Macdonald, 1987.

* * *

The body of Patricia McKillip's writing justifies Northrop Frye's classification of all literature into two categories—riddles and charms. Riddles ponder the mystery of all creation, searching out the identity of the homely needle and scrutinizing the meaning of life itself. Charms consider the means of effecting control over substance and circumstance. They are entrancing, but often self-deluding in that they hint at a superficial power employed by one with insuffi-

cient knowledge of self and situation. The wizardess in *The Forgotten Beasts of Eld* must relinquish her powers in return for self-discovery. There are charms enough in McKillip's many realms, but the overriding success in her fiction lies largely in her ability to exploit the splendor and efficacy of the riddle; the quest rather than the solution.

In her three-novel sequence *Riddle of Stars* the riddle proves the driving force which generates not only plots but also characters and settings. By the time an answer is forthcoming the revelation often appears self-evident because it was embedded in the fullness of a quest and not in any resolution. Questions are always more provocative than answers; the latter show finality, the former are forever energizing. Avenues, ingenuity of approaches, ongoing determination, perpetual inquiry—these manifestations of a fulfilled life are inevitably tied to the riddle. It is significant enough in and of itself that its very statement is worthy of a search. Raederle, princess of An, inquires of the pig woman what it is she is interested in. "The answer to a riddle." But what riddle? The response: "You'll see for yourself soon enough."

In a masterful early work, *The Throme of the Erril of Sherill*, the protagonist undertakes the seemingly hopeless task of finding something which he as well as everyone else acknowledges does not exist. A form of a riddle-provoking quest, the endeavour proves non-being is itself an idea which the resourceful can build upon. The throme, as it turns out, is in fact a poetic composition. The tale itself is dotted with suggestive words which require being so that they can be defined, "throme," "cnite," "erril," perhaps even the proper name Damsen. Cnite sounds like knight, erril like earl, Damsen like damsel. A slight phonemic shift is all that separates strangeness from familiarity, being from non-being. So small a gap suggests that the separation between fable and existence might be small enough that a modified utterance (a charm?) could turn every woman or man into an enchanter of sorts. It is at the very least the sort of intriguing suggestion that unites the reader and the writer.

The reader need not remain a stranger in these unusual realms. Excitement, the stuff of inquiry, enforces a readership into a wonderment similar to that experienced by the characters. Worlds where shape-changers are more important than heroes or wise men show that perceiving an inspired vision is an active role. The present, the participation, the perception are all more significant than who did what or what happens.

Wonderment and awareness are the real motifs. "There is no Throme, and if it does not exist, it is always just beyond my outstretched hand, just beyond my eyesight," which is almost the same as saying there is no reality outside the tale. Fantasy literature is not escape, but involvement; fable neither pastime nor heritage, but the lifeblood of the present as well as its animator, source, and reason.

It is hard not to identify with Kyreol in *Moon-Flash* as she explains her trip of discovery down the river "to see new worlds, or see the same world, and know that everything is new." Presumably every facet of her life has been pre-planned from her birth, including her activities, rituals, place of residence, and even her husband. She does not really object to the inevitability, but she strives to understand the meaning of existence within these perimeters. She concludes that perhaps there is no difference between the Riverworld and the world from which she fled. "The dreams change shapes, but the dreamer never changes," an apt reaction for the reader-participant in McKillip's world.

Connections and realization descend with a suddenness. The kindly priest in *The House on Parchment Street* observes "I never realized before how much a group of boys whistling sounds like Irish banshees wailing for the souls of the dead." Here the deeds of the dead are re-enacted. Parchment Street itself caves in, but its past proves permanent. Certainly the riddles are indelible, a reason for the enduring nature of the nursery rhymes with their perpetual celebration of politics, plague, fire, and death. All these catastrophes pass away, while the rhythm and rhyme of them remains forever intact as a riddle whose quest is never done.

Above all, there is a part for the reader and the reciter in this ongoing parade of creation and manifestation. The environments McKillip produces remain familiar in their very strangeness, as if the reader senses the imminent belonging. The riddle need not be solved, and even if it is, the involvement remains permanent.

—Leonard R. Mendelsohn

* * *

McKINLEY, (Jennifer Carolyn) Robin. American. Born in Warren, Ohio, 16 November 1952. Educated at Dickinson College, Carlisle, Pennsylvania, 1970–72; Bowdoin College, Brunswick, Maine, 1973–75, B.A. (summa cum laude) in English 1975. Editor and transcriber, Ward and Paul, Washington, D.C., 1972–73; research assistant, Research Associates, Brunswick, 1976–77; bookstore clerk, Maine, 1978; teacher and counselor in private secondary school, Natick, Massachusetts, 1978–79; editorial assistant, Little Brown, publishers, Boston, 1979–81; barn manager on horse farm, Massachusetts, 1981–82; clerk, Books of Wonder, New York, 1983; freelance editor, 1983–85. Recipient: American Library Association Newbery Medal, 1985. Lives in Maine and New York City. Agent: Merrilee Heifetz, Writers House Inc., 21 West 26th Street, New York, New York 10010, U.S.A.

PUBLICATIONS FOR CHILDREN

Fiction

The Door in the Hedge. New York, Greenwillow, 1981; London, MacRae, 1984.
The Blue Sword. New York, Greenwillow, 1982; London, MacRae, 1983.
The Hero and the Crown. New York, Greenwillow, and London, MacRae, 1985.
The Outlaws of Sherwood. New York, Greenwillow, 1988.

Other (retellings)

Beauty: A Retelling of the Story of Beauty and the Beast. New York, Harper, 1978; London, MacRae, 1983.
Tales from the Jungle Book. New York, Random House, 1985.
Black Beauty, illustrated by Susan Jeffers. New York, Random House, 1986; London, Hamish Hamilton, 1987.
The Light Princess, illustrated by Katie Thamer Treherne. San Diego, Harcourt Brace, 1988.

Editor, *Imaginary Lands.* New York, Greenwillow, 1985; London, MacRae, 1987.

* * *

In her Newbery Medal acceptance speech in 1985 Robin McKinley commented, "I can't remember a time when the stories I told myself weren't about shy, bumbling girls who turned out to be heroes."

In books of fairytales, legend, and fantasy, McKinley's Girls Who Do Things are intelligent, loyal, and courageous—eager and not afraid to cross the physical and psychological barriers that lie between them and the fulfillment of their destinies. They escape and

defy the limiting spheres to which they seem confined through sometimes extraordinary feats of prowess and endurance. McKinley's young inspirational heroines mature as they become aware of their hidden strengths and potential and begin to view the world around them with a "new clarity of perception."

Her novel *Beauty* is a retelling of "Beauty and the Beast." While keeping many of the traditional elements, McKinley brings a freshness and intensity to the story, told from the viewpoint of Beauty, the youngest of three sisters, who describes herself as a "thin, awkward, undersized" young girl who is ever conscious of the inappropriateness of her chosen sobriquet. Beauty, one of McKinley's determined and courageous heroines, changes during her enforced sojourn in the castle of the Beast from her tomboy image into a beautiful, mature young woman able to wear the silver dress of a princess, who begins to see—as she grows to feel trust and sympathy towards the Beast—with a "new depth or roundness." Beauty's love of books, her care and affection for her horse Greatheart, the warmth of her family relationships, and the story of her sisters' own romances are woven into and enrich this traditional tale whose symbolic import is enhanced by McKinley's treatment of theme.

There is adventure and romance in the fantasies *The Blue Sword* and *The Hero and the Crown*, set in the imaginary kingdom of Damar, each book relating the story of a "damalur-sol"—a "Lady Hero." In *The Blue Sword* Harry Crewe is kidnapped from the outermost post of the Homelanders by Corlath, King of the Hillfolk of Damar. Harry holds fast to her courage and gradually becomes aware of her inherited gift of "kelar"—the "Gift of Seeing." She is trained to ride and wield a sword in battle, earning a place as one of Corlath's elite Riders. Harry, a vivacious, forthright, and determined leader in combat and diplomacy is a worthy inheritor of the legendary sword, Gonturan, the sword of the flame-haired Lady Aerin, "Dragon-Killer."

Aerin, the protagonist in McKinley's Newbery Medal book *The Hero and the Crown*, is the daughter of the King of Damar and "the witchwoman," who wins her title as "swordbearer" in her father's court through fighting, with courage and intelligence, the dragons that plague the kingdom. Almost destroyed by the great dragon Maur, Aerin journeys to the valley of Luthe, an immortal "mage," who helps her journey both physically and spiritually so that she overcomes the "dragon" of despair, and comes to acknowledge her inner strength and power. In a striking passage, Aerin meets in an inner sanctuary Agsded, her uncle—the evil counterpart of herself—and wrests from him the "Hero's Crown," which holds the strength of Damar. Triumphant in battle against the Northerners who threaten Damar, she returns to her home to claim her rightful position as queen.

McKinley writes that landscape is important to her, and in *The Blue Sword* and *The Hero and the Crown*, the harsh sand and gritty winds of the desert, the stone City and the Damarian Hills of her imaginary kingdom Damar form an integral element of the story. McKinley's romantic narratives are richly descriptive. Whether describing the colorful, luxurious interior of a king's tent, a deathly combat against the scorching fire of a great dragon, or the warm breath and soft nose of a favorite horse, McKinley's attention to detail brings a vital quality and vividness to her text.

In *The Outlaws of Sherwood* McKinley's Robin Hood is an anxious, cautious, and somewhat enigmatic character, whose necessary escape after killing a fellow forester is seen by Lady Marian and the philosophizing Much as an opportunity to establish a rebel Saxon band deep within Sherwood Forest. A spirit of humorous "derring-do," romance, and high adventure is carried, rather, by other members of his band, while Lady Marian dons his mantle of decisive leadership. The disguised boy outlaw, Lady Cecily, is another of McKinley's spirited and courageous heroines—whose love for Little John adds a tender note. The story has both traditional and unique elements, and life in Sherwood Forest for the "green young outlaws" is vividly presented in a version which McKinley hopes is "historically unembarrassing."

McKinley's books challenge the reader to respond not only to inspirational role models who dare to "do things," but to share in stories that take the reader beyond the borders of their own lands, and which are written in a rich and stylistic prose.

—Hilary S. Crew

—————

McLEAN, Allan Campbell. British. Born in Walney Island, Lancashire, 18 November 1922. Educated at Walney Island Elementary School and Barrow-in-Furness Junior Technical School, Lancashire. Served in the Royal Air Force in North Africa, Sicily, and Italy, 1941–46. Married Margaret Elizabeth White in 1946; two sons and one daughter. Clerk, J.F. Dobson, accountants, Barrow-in-Furness, 1938–41. Recipient: Frederick Niven award, for fiction, 1962; Scottish Arts Council award, 1972. Agent: A.M. Heath, 79 St. Martin's Lane, London WC2N 4AA, England; or, Brandt and Brandt, 1501 Broadway, New York, New York 10036, U.S.A. Address: Anerley Cottage, 16 Kingsmills Road, Inverness IV2 3JS, Scotland.

PUBLICATIONS FOR CHILDREN

Fiction

The Hill of the Red Fox. London, Collins, 1955; New York, Dutton, 1956.
The Man of the House, illustrated by Shirley Hughes. London, Collins, 1956; *Storm over Skye*, New York, Harcourt Brace, 1957.
Master of Morgana. New York, Harcourt Brace, 1959; London, Collins, 1960.
Ribbon of Fire. London, Collins, and New York, Harcourt Brace, 1962.
A Sound of Trumpets. New York, Harcourt Brace, 1966; London, Collins, 1967.
The Year of the Stranger. London, Collins, 1971; New York, Walck, 1972.

PUBLICATIONS FOR ADULTS

Novels

The Carpet-Slipper Murder. London, Ward Lock, 1956; New York, Washburn, 1957.
Death on All Hallows. London, Ward Lock, and New York, Washburn, 1958.
Deadly Honeymoon. London, Ward Lock, 1958.
Murder by Invitation. London, Ward Lock, 1959.
Stand-In for Murder. London, Ward Lock, 1960.
The Islander. London, Collins, 1962; as *The Gates of Eden*, New York, Harcourt Brace, 1962.
The Glasshouse. New York, Harcourt Brace, 1968; London, Calder and Boyars, 1969.

Other

Explore the Highlands and Islands. Inverness, Highlands and Islands Development Board, 1972.
The Highlands and Islands of Scotland. London, Collins, 1976;

New York, Crown, 1977.

*

Allan Campbell McLean comments:

All my historical novels for young people—*Ribbon of Fire, A Sound of Trumpets, The Year of the Stranger*—are based upon actual historical happenings in the Isle of Skye. My aim has been to present the young reader with a picture of the 19th-century life in the Scottish Highlands that he or she would be unlikely to acquire from school textbooks.

* * *

To read Allan Campbell McLean's novels is to be transported straightway into the Highlands and islands of Scotland which provide the authentic background to his full-blooded adventure stories. He uses the main character as narrator, and this personal involvement adds realism and excitement to the tales. An Englishman who has lived many years in Scotland, McLean has a poet's ear for language, and his attention to the cadences and rhythms of the speech of the people results in truly authentic dialogue. His writing is frequently centered on social injustice and hardship, but this is historically true of the period and setting of his books and reinforces the impact of his writing.

Master of Morgana is probably the book least inspired by his social conscience, but it is a vehicle for powerfully dramatic descriptions of the lives of fishermen in Skye. Niall is seeking the man responsible for his brother's near fatal accident, and his adventures are gripping and exciting. Yet it is frequently the drama of the boy and his fellow fishermen struggling with the stormy sea which makes the greatest impression. Salmon fishing technique is minutely described, and the power of the sea in all its fury is fully equalled by the author's descriptive prose and skill in creating atmosphere. However, it is in *The Year of the Stranger* that McLean's writing reaches its height. A tale of injustice and harshness, it grips the reader from the very first sentence: "Something wet and cold hit me across the belly, jerking me awake...." Tension and excitement build up though interspersed with passages of poetic beauty, and soon the story becomes an allegory with visionary splendour breathtaking in its effect. Here is an ideal mixture of harshness and gentleness, excitement and peace, history and hope, all skillfully interwoven to produce a thought-provoking story.

McLean is a writer so attuned to his background and environment that his writing always rings true. Description and action are finely balanced to produce first-rate adventure stories which linger in the memory for a long time.

—Margaret Walker

—————

McNEILL, Janet. British. Born in Dublin, Ireland, 14 September 1907. Educated at Birkenhead School, Cheshire, 1914–24; St. Andrews University, Scotland, M.A. in classics 1929. Married Robert P. Alexander in 1933 (died 1973); three sons (one deceased) and one daughter. Secretary, Belfast *Telegraph*, 1930–33. Agent: A.P. Watt Ltd., 20 John Street, London WC1N 2DL. Address: St. Monica's, Cote Lane, Westbury-on-Trym, Bristol BS9 3UN, England.

PUBLICATIONS FOR CHILDREN

Fiction

My Friend Specs McCann, illustrated by Rowel Friers. London,

Faber, 1955.

A Pinch of Salt, illustrated by Rowel Friers. London, Faber, 1956.

A Light Dozen: Eleven More Stories, illustrated by Rowel Friers. London, Faber, 1957.

Specs Fortissimo, illustrated by Rowel Friers. London, Faber, 1958.

This Happy Morning, illustrated by Rowel Friers. London, Faber, 1959.

Special Occasions: Eleven More Stories, illustrated by Rowel Friers. London, Faber, 1960.

Various Specs, illustrated by Rowel Friers. London, Faber, 1961; New York, Nelson, 1971.

Try These for Size, illustrated by Rowel Friers. London, Faber, 1963.

The Giant's Birthday, illustrated by Walter Erhard. New York, Walck, 1964.

Tom's Tower, illustrated by Mary Russon. London, Faber, 1965; Boston, Little Brown, 1967.

The Mouse and the Mirage, illustrated by Walter Erhard. New York, Walck, 1966.

The Battle of St. George Without, illustrated by Mary Russon. London, Faber, and Boston, Little Brown, 1966.

I Didn't Invite You to My Party, illustrated by Jane Paton. London, Hamish Hamilton, 1967.

The Run-Around Robins, illustrated by Monica Brasier-Creagh. London, Hamish Hamilton, 1967.

Goodbye, Dove Square, illustrated by Mary Russon. London, Faber, and Boston, Little Brown, 1969.

Dragons, Come Home! and Other Stories, illustrated by John Lawrence. London, Hamish Hamilton, 1969.

Umbrella Thursday, illustrated by Carolyn Dinan. London, Hamish Hamilton, 1969.

Best Specs: His Most Remarkable Adventures, illustrated by Rowel Friers. London, Faber, 1970.

The Other People. Boston, Little Brown, 1970; London, Chatto and Windus, 1973.

The Youngest Kite, illustrated by Elizabeth Haines. London, Hamish Hamilton, 1970.

The Prisoner in the Park. London, Faber, and Boston, Little Brown, 1971.

Much Too Much Magic, illustrated by Carolyn Harrison. London, Hamish Hamilton, 1971.

A Helping Hand, illustrated by Jane Paton. London, Hamish Hamilton, 1971.

Wait for It and Other Stories. London, Faber, 1972.

A Monster Too Many, illustrated by Ingrid Fetz. Boston, Little Brown, 1972.

A Snow-Clean Pinny, illustrated by Krystyna Turska. London, Hamish Hamilton, 1973.

A Fairy Called Andy Perks, illustrated by John Lawrence. London, Hamish Hamilton, 1973.

We Three Kings. London, Faber, and Boston, Little Brown, 1974.

Ever After. London, Chatto and Windus, and Boston, Little Brown, 1975.

The Magic Lollipop, illustrated by Linda Birch. Leicester, Brockhampton Press, 1975; Chicago, Children's Press, 1976.

The Three Crowns of King Hullabaloo, illustrated by Mike Cole. Leicester, Brockhampton Press, 1975; Chicago, Children's Press, 1976.

Just Turn the Key and Other Stories, illustrated by Douglas Hall. London, Hamish Hamilton, 1976; as *Free Parking and Other Stories*, London, Beaver, 1978.

Plays

Finn and the Black Hag, music by Raymond Warren. London,

Novello, 1962.

Switch On—Switch Off and Other Plays (includes *Can I Help You?*, *There's a Man in That Tree*, *Clothes-Line*, *Three from Four Leaves One*, *Burning Topic*). London, Faber, 1968.

Graduation Ode, music by Raymond Warren (produced Belfast, 1968).

Other (readers)

It's Snowing Outside, illustrated by Carol Barker. London, Macmillan, 1968.

The Day They Lost Grandad, illustrated by Julius. London, Macmillan, 1968.

The Nest Spotters, illustrated by Geraldine Spence. London, Macmillan, 1972.

The Family Upstairs, illustrated by Trevor Stubley. London, Macmillan, 1973.

My Auntie, illustrated by George Him. London, Macmillan, 1975.

Go On, Then, illustrated by Terry Reid. London, Macmillan, 1975.

Growlings, illustrated by Richard Rose. London, Macmillan, 1975.

The Day Mum Came Home, illustrated by Prudence Seward. London, Macmillan, 1976.

Look Who's Here, illustrated by Gerald Rose. London, Macmillan, 1976.

The Hermit's Purple Shirts. London, Macmillan, 1976.

Billy Brewer Goes on Tour. London, Macmillan, 1976.

PUBLICATIONS FOR ADULTS

Novels

A Child in the House. London, Hodder and Stoughton, 1955.

Tea at Four O'Clock. London, Hodder and Stoughton, 1956.

The Other Side of the Wall. London, Hodder and Stoughton, 1956.

A Furnished Room. London, Hodder and Stoughton, 1958.

Search Party. London, Hodder and Stoughton, 1959.

As Strangers Here. London, Hodder and Stoughton, 1960.

The Early Harvest. London, Bles, 1962.

The Maiden Dinosaur. London, Bles, 1964; as *The Belfast Friends*, Boston, Houghton Mifflin, 1966.

Talk to Me. London, Bles, 1965.

The Small Widow. London, Bles, 1967; New York, Atheneum, 1968.

Plays

Gospel Truth. Belfast, Carter, 1951.

More than 20 radio plays.

*

Janet McNeill comments:

I began writing fantasy for children because an active and agile imagination is a great help to a child confronted by the facts of a largely materialistic world. I then found it possible, and interesting, to write of the children in this world and their reaction to it. I am always glad if I can make a child laugh and remember laughing.

* * *

Janet McNeill is a godsend equally to adults who advocate reading for enjoyment and to children who want to enjoy what they read. She has a special brand of quirky humour and lightness of touch, even when writing about intrinsically serious subjects. Few authors have such empathy with children, from the very young to confused adolescents.

In the books for younger readers—even in those tailored to the demands and format of a particular series—all the children show a perceptiveness typified by little Madge in *A Helping Hand*. Though led by naive logic to some odd conclusions about the characteristics of old age, she creates a satisfying relationship with the crotchety couple next door.

For preadolescents, there is the ludicrous world of Specs McCann and his friend Curly, the close-knit society of schoolboys, with their in-jokes and their extraordinary speech patterns. The hazards and misfortunes of being a growing boy in a world controlled by (to him) unpredictable and prejudiced adults have never been better portrayed. Likewise, Matt and his friends, in *The Battle of St. George Without*, are involved with eccentric yet believable adults. McNeill sees oddities of character with the child's eye, that perception which is so devastating in the classroom; yet the comic element sharpens perspective, especially when the largely make-believe gang-life of adolescents impinges on the adult world of real crime and danger.

The same characters, grown older, reappear in *Goodbye, Dove Square*, coping with typically urban stress and change. Rehoused in a high-rise flat, Matt looks back nostalgically to the warm untidy life when walls were thicker and people "took things the way they were." The environment is constricting and nasty, the gang is splitting up, Matt alone is still at school. Internal adjustments are difficult; his mates now enjoy enviable wealth and freedom; for them, displacement is alleviated by compensations which he cannot share. Everything exacerbates his feeling that there are many things he cannot understand, even about himself, much less about other people and their bewildering relationships.

Kate, in *The Other People*, also has problems of coming to terms with a new life. Her difficulty is more a matter of adjusting to a reality which proves entirely different from her rosy expectations. Like Matt, she finds a way of piecing together the complicated jigsaws of adult life. Each of them reaches some understanding of the separateness and of the individual importance of other people.

McNeill not only has her own distinctive way of writing "realistic" stories. She has a gift, too, for letting elements of fantasy creep into tales firmly set in the everyday world. The vivid evocation of school life in *Tom's Tower*, for example, slides convincingly into the realms of fancy. Many of her short stories, too, contain some twist of circumstance, some unexpected slant. Even the commonplace is never banal, and what *seems* quite ordinary turns out to be rather odd—not far-fetched, not forced, but perceived as more-than-ordinary by an author who makes a truth of the truism that some people can see more than meets the eye.

—Cecilia Gordon

MEADER, Stephen W(arren). American. Born in Providence, Rhode Island, 2 May 1892. Educated at Rochester High School; Moses Brown School, Providence; Haverford College, Pennsylvania, A.B. 1913. Married 1) Elizabeth White Hoyt in 1916 (died 1962), two sons and two daughters; 2) Patience R. Ludlam in 1963. Case worker, Children's Aid Society, Newark, New Jersey, 1913–14; secretary, Essex County Big Brother Movement, Newark, 1915; member of the publicity department, Reilly and Britton, publishers, Chicago, 1916; assistant editor, *Country Gentleman* magazine, Philadelphia, 1916–21; advertising writer, Holmes Press, Philadelphia, 1921–27; copy writer, 1927–57, and associate copy director, 1941–57, N.W. Ayer and Son, Philadelphia. *Died 18 July 1977.*

PUBLICATIONS FOR CHILDREN

Fiction

The Black Buccaneer, illustrated by the author. New York, Harcourt Brace, 1920.

Down the Big River, illustrated by the author. New York, Harcourt Brace, 1924.

Longshanks, illustrated by Edward Caswell. New York, Harcourt Brace, 1928.

Red Horse Hill, illustrated by Lee Townsend. New York, Harcourt Brace, 1930.

Away to Sea, illustrated by Clinton Balmer. New York, Harcourt Brace, 1931.

King of the Hills, illustrated by Lee Townsend. New York, Harcourt Brace, 1933.

Lumberjack, illustrated by Henry Pitz. New York, Harcourt Brace, 1934; London, Bell, 1955.

The Will to Win and Other Stories, illustrated by John Gincano. New York, Harcourt Brace, 1936.

Who Rides in the Dark?, illustrated by James MacDonald. New York, Harcourt Brace, 1937; Oxford, Blackwell, 1938.

T-Model Tommy, illustrated by Edward Shenton. New York, Harcourt Brace, 1938.

Boy with a Pack, illustrated by Edward Shenton. New York, Harcourt Brace, 1939.

Bat, The Story of a Bull Terrier, illustrated by Edward Shenton. New York, Harcourt Brace, 1939.

Clear for Action!, illustrated by Frank Beaudouin. New York, Harcourt Brace, 1940.

Blueberry Mountain, illustrated by Edward Shenton. New York, Harcourt Brace, 1941; London, Bell, 1960.

Shadow in the Pines, illustrated by Edward Shenton. New York, Harcourt Brace, 1942.

The Sea Snake, illustrated by Edward Shenton. New York, Harcourt Brace, 1943.

The Long Trains Roll, illustrated by Edward Shenton. New York, Harcourt Brace, 1944.

Skippy's Family, illustrated by Elizabeth Korn. New York, Harcourt Brace, 1945.

Jonathan Goes West, illustrated by Edward Shenton. New York, Harcourt Brace, 1946.

Behind the Ranges, illustrated by Edward Shenton. New York, Harcourt Brace, 1947.

River of the Wolves, illustrated by Edward Shenton. New York, Harcourt Brace, 1948.

Cedar's Boy, illustrated by Lee Townsend. New York, Harcourt Brace, 1949.

Whaler 'round the Horn, illustrated by Edward Shenton. New York, Harcourt Brace, 1950; London, Museum Press, 1953.

Bulldozer, illustrated by Edwin Schmidt. New York, Harcourt Brace, 1951.

The Fish Hawk's Nest, illustrated by Edward Shenton. New York, Harcourt Brace, 1952.

Sparkplug of the Hornets, illustrated by Don Sibley. New York, Harcourt Brace, 1953.

The Buckboard Stranger, illustrated by Paul Calle. New York, Harcourt Brace, 1954.

Guns for the Saratoga, illustrated by John Cosgrave. New York, Harcourt Brace, 1955.

Sabre Pilot, illustrated by John Polgreen. New York, Harcourt Brace, 1956.

Everglades Adventure, illustrated by Charles Beck. New York, Harcourt Brace, 1957.

The Commodore's Cup, illustrated by Don Sibley. New York, Harcourt Brace, 1958.

The Voyage of the Javelin, illustrated by John Cosgrave. New York, Harcourt Brace, 1959.
Wild Pony Island, illustrated by Charles Beck. New York, Harcourt Brace, 1959.
Buffalo and Beaver, illustrated by Charles Beck. New York, Harcourt Brace, 1960.
Snow on Blueberry Mountain, illustrated by Don Sibley. New York, Harcourt Brace, 1961.
Phantom of the Blockade, illustrated by Victor Mays. New York, Harcourt Brace, 1962.
The Muddy Road to Glory, illustrated by George Hughes. New York, Harcourt Brace, 1963.
Stranger on Big Hickory, illustrated by Don Lambo. New York, Harcourt Brace, 1964.
A Blow for Liberty, illustrated by Victor Mays. New York, Harcourt Brace, 1965.
Topsail Island Treasure, illustrated by Marbury Brown. New York, Harcourt Brace, 1966.
Keep 'em Rolling, illustrated by Al Savitt. New York, Harcourt Brace, 1967.
Lonesome End, illustrated by Ned Butterfield. New York, Harcourt Brace, 1968.
The Cape May Packet, illustrated by Robert Frankenberg. New York, Harcourt Brace, 1969.

Other

Trap Lines North. New York, Dodd Mead, and London, Harrap, 1936.

*   *   *

Stephen W. Meader lived his first 12 years in Providence, Rhode Island, where his father taught at a religious school. His family then moved to rural New Hampshire, where his father was a timber cutter. Two important childhood influences were books and the outdoor life near the timber camps. After college, doing social work with both the Children's Aid Society and the Big Brother Movement gave him particular knowledge of the interests and needs of boys.

An incredibly prolific author for almost 50 years, Meader was one of a number of writers who concentrated on adolescent and young adult male characters, their enterprises and their dreams. He wrote fast-moving and fast-reading mysteries, adventure and sports stories, and stories of young boys making the transition into adulthood. Among the more suspenseful of his mysteries are *Red Horse Hill*, a cracking story of a boy and his horses which focuses on a lost will; *Who Rides in the Dark?*, featuring a masked rider whose identity is finally solved by an orphaned stable boy; and *Shadow in the Pines*, about a young country boy, highly knowledgeable about his rural environment, who helps the FBI in rounding up a gang of saboteurs. These adolescent characters are spirited and curious, which indeed they need to be in order to meet the exciting challenges all around them.

Meader's adventure stories often revolve about American expansion and war. He is exceptionally able to interpret the culture of ethnic regions at times of American expansion. *Buffalo and Beaver* is a story of western adventure in the days of the mountain men. *Everglades Adventure* is a tale of action and suspense set in Fort Dallas, Florida. Meader is also skilled in his war stories, presenting fairly and accurately the arguments of all sides. *Guns for the Saratoga* is an authentic story of privateering during the Revolutionary War. *Phantom of the Blockade* concerns life aboard a Confederate blockade runner in the Civil War. *The Sea Snake* is about a Nazi agent on the North Carolina Coast during World War II. *Sabre Pilot* concerns a jet fighter pilot in the Korean War.

Meader's sports stories and his stories of early occupational

success concentrate on the needs of adolescents to excel and be independent. He wrote about a small high school basketball team and its uphill fight for the State championship (*Sparkplug of the Hornets*), sailing for the yacht club fleet (*The Commodore's Cup*), the story of a Maine boy who starts a contracting business with a reconditioned bulldozer (*Bulldozer*), and the story of two boys in the Pocono Mountains of Pennsylvania who discover that they can grow blueberries commercially (*Blueberry Mountain*).

Meader was successful in writing of young people facing problems of growing up, adapting to new environments, choosing careers, and achieving goals in spite of initial obstacles and setbacks. He did this with understanding of human needs, concern for human development, and unshakeable belief in American growth and opportunity.

—Mary Lystad

———

MEANS, Florence Crannell. American. Born in Baldwinsville, New York, 15 May 1891. Educated at Henry Read School of Art, Denver, 1910–12; Kansas City Baptist Theological Seminary, 1912; McPherson College, Kansas, summers 1922–29; University of Denver, 1923–24. Married Carleton Bell Means in 1912 (died 1973); one daughter. Freelance writer and lecturer from 1912. Recipient: Child Study Committee award, 1946. *Died 19 November 1980.*

PUBLICATIONS FOR CHILDREN

Fiction

Rafael and Consuelo, with Harriet Louise Fullen. New York, Friendship Press, 1929.
A Candle in the Mist, illustrated by Marguerite de Angeli. Boston, Houghton Mifflin, 1931.
Ranch and Ring, illustrated by Henry Peck. Boston, Houghton Mifflin, 1932.
Dusky Day, illustrated by Manning Lee. Boston, Houghton Mifflin, 1933.
A Bowlful of Stars, illustrated by Henry Pitz. Boston, Houghton Mifflin, 1934.
Rainbow Bridge, illustrated by Eleanor Lattimore. New York, Friendship Press, 1934.
Penny for Luck, illustrated by Paul Quinn. Boston, Houghton Mifflin, 1935.
Tangled Waters, illustrated by Herbert Morton Stoops. Boston, Houghton Mifflin, 1936.
The Singing Wood, illustrated by Manning Lee. Boston, Houghton Mifflin, 1937.
Shuttered Windows, illustrated by Armstrong Sperry. Boston, Houghton Mifflin, 1938.
Adella Mary in Old New Mexico, illustrated by Herbert Morton Stoops. Boston, Houghton Mifflin, 1939.
Across the Fruited Plain, illustrated by Janet Smalley. New York, Friendship Press, 1940.
At the End of Nowhere, illustrated by David Hendrickson. Boston, Houghton Mifflin, 1940.
Children of the Promise, illustrated by Janet Smalley. New York, Friendship Press, 1941.
Whispering Girl, illustrated by Oscar Howard. Boston, Houghton Mifflin, 1941.
Shadow over Wide Ruin, illustrated by Lorence Bjorklund. Boston, Houghton Mifflin, 1942.

Teresita of the Valley, illustrated by Nicholas Panesis. Boston, Houghton Mifflin, 1943.

Peter of the Mesa, illustrated by Janet Smalley. New York, Friendship Press, 1944.

The Moved-Outers, illustrated by Helen Blair. Boston, Houghton Mifflin, 1945.

Great Day in the Morning, illustrated by Helen Blair. Boston, Houghton Mifflin, 1946.

Assorted Sisters, illustrated by Helen Blair. Boston, Houghton Mifflin, 1947.

The House under the Hill, illustrated by Helen Blair. Boston, Houghton Mifflin, 1949.

The Silver Fleece, with Carl Means, illustrated by Edwin Schmidt. Philadelphia, Winston, 1950.

Hetty of the Grande Deluxe, illustrated by Helen Blair. Boston, Houghton Mifflin, 1951.

Alicia, illustrated by William Barss. Boston, Houghton Mifflin, 1953.

The Rains Will Come, illustrated by Fred Kabotie. Boston, Houghton Mifflin, 1954.

Knock at the Door, Emmy, illustrated by Paul Lantz. Boston, Houghton Mifflin, 1956.

Reach for a Star. Boston, Houghton Mifflin, 1957.

Borrowed Brother, illustrated by Dorothy Bayley Morse. Boston, Houghton Mifflin, 1958.

Emmy and the Blue Door, illustrated by Frank Nicholas. Boston, Houghton Mifflin, 1959.

But I Am Sara. Boston, Houghton Mifflin, 1961.

That Girl Andy. Boston, Houghton Mifflin, 1962.

Tolliver. Boston, Houghton Mifflin, 1963.

It Takes All Kinds. Boston, Houghton Mifflin, 1964.

Us Maltbys. Boston, Houghton Mifflin, 1966.

Our Cup Is Broken. Boston, Houghton Mifflin, 1969.

Smith Valley. Boston, Houghton Mifflin, 1973.

Other Stories: *Frankie and Willie May Go a Far Piece, All "Round Me Shinin'," Some California Poppies and How They Grew*, and others, published by the Baptist Board of Education, New York, in the 1940's.

Plays

Pepita's Adventure in Friendship. New York, Friendship Press, 1929.

Other plays: *The Black Tents: A Junior Play of Life among the Bedouins of Syria, Tara Finds the Door to Happiness*, and several missionary plays.

Other

Children of the Great Spirit: A Course on the American Indian, with Frances Somers Riggs. New York, Friendship Press, 1932.

Carvers' George: A Biography of George Washington Carver, illustrated by Harve Stein. Boston, Houghton Mifflin, 1952.

PUBLICATIONS FOR ADULTS

Other

Sagebrush Surgeon (biography of Clarence G. Salsbury). New York, Friendship Press, 1955.

Sunlight on the Hopi Mesas: The Story of Abigail E. Johnson. Philadelphia, Judson Press, 1960.

Pamphlets on American Indian tribes for the Baptist Missionary Society.

*

Manuscript Collection: University of Colorado Library, Boulder.

Florence Crannell Means commented:

(1978) Flossy Crannell, six years old, charted her future in staggering capitals: she would be a *great* writer, a *great* painter, a kindergartener, a missionary. My father was a Baptist clergyman in upstate New York and we lived in a sea of books. Our house was often enlivened by visitors of every kind and color, unusual at the end of the 19th century when the United States was both isolationist and isolated, before the airplane, the radio, the television. So it was not strange that I began to write—and sell—little stories about children of other kinds and colors, some of them illustrated by the author, since I had had some art school training. I got material from visiting and retired missionaries, from government reports on Indian work, and from the blessed public library. Finally, a Hopi Indian love story brought me a check that allowed me to visit the Hopi reservation.

I had been asked, two years earlier, to write *Rafael and Consuelo*, about Mexicans in the U.S. My first full-length book, *A Candle in the Mist*, was based on the pioneering of my maternal grandparents in 1872, but my emphasis became increasingly on the beauty and needs of our ethnic minorities. I went alone, except during my husband's vacations, to visit the Hopi and several other tribes—Navajo, Mono, Otomi, Crow. I visited the blacks of our tidal and Carolina low country, the beautiful old villages of the Spanish Americans in Colorado and New Mexico, California's oriental groups, even an unbelievable Chinese village ruled by rival tongs.

What I found was much beauty, much poverty, and grace and love—and far too often a great painful loneliness. So, with my husband's help, I did my best to bring what I saw to our children and young adults.

*   *   *

As more children's book departments were established in American publishing companies during the 1930's, a new need also grew: books for "young adults." One of the first writers to fill this need was Florence Crannell Means. Moreover, she went far beyond the "career" type of story which soon became popular to tackle difficult real-life situations with characters presented in depth. She was one of the first to write sympathetically about minority groups, articulating their struggle for dignity, security, and education—or just plain survival.

Her first stories, such as *A Candle in the Mist*, were in the pioneer genre. But though her plots may have been built out of typical frontier activities, her characters are not stereotyped. They have individuality and strength.

It was probably natural to follow pioneer stories with Indian stories; but Means did not write typical Indian stories. A Baptist minister's daughter, she grew up in a household where people of many nationalities and races were welcomed wholeheartedly; thus she developed sympathy and insight into the problems of minorities, with a special interest in Indians of the southwest. Among others, she portayed Navajos (*Tangled Waters*) and Hopis (*Whispering Girl*). She took time to observe people in their home territory before writing about them. She always put her characters first, bringing out their habits and problems as an integral part of their personalities and their stories.

This concern for human values accounts for the survivability of her stories. Although *Shuttered Windows* and *Great Day in the Morning* are now "period pieces" (blacks are called negroes, and their worlds are basically separate from whites'), the books are still valid as to story and character and valuable as social history. The same can be said of *The Moved-Outers* which dealt with *nisei* (American-born children of Japanese parents) in internment camps on the West Coast during World War II. Reading this now, one wonders if the young people could really have been so mild and cooperative with officials; but they were patriotic, as well as heart-broken; it is still a moving story—and it stands as an obvious yardstick for the change to the cynical outspokenness of today's young people.

In later books, Means presented with great honesty the discouragement and bitterness of a 20-year-old Hopi Indian girl (*Our Cup Is Broken*) and the unflattering selfishness in desperate times of some members of a young girl's family in Colorado in the early 1900's (*Smith Valley*). In other words, her multi-layered stories of all kinds of people are not goody-goody, missionary-inspirational; they are honest, realistic, and, always, interesting and well-written.

—Lee Kingman

MEIGS, Cornelia (Lynde). Also wrote as Adair Aldon. American. Born in Rock Island, Illinois, 6 December 1884. Educated at Bryn Mawr College, Pennsylvania, A.B. 1907. English teacher, St. Katherine's School, Davenport, Iowa, 1912–13; Instructor, Professor of English, and Professor Emeritus, Bryn Mawr College, 1932–50. Worked for United States War Department, Washington, D.C., 1942–45. Recipient: Drama League prize, 1915; American Library Association Newbery Medal, 1934; Women's International League for Peace and Freedom Jane Addams award, 1971. L.H.D.: Plano University, Texas, 1967. *Died 8 October 1973.*

PUBLICATIONS FOR CHILDREN

Fiction

The Kingdom of the Winding Road, illustrated by Frances White. New York, Macmillan, 1915.
Master Simon's Garden. New York, Macmillan, 1916.
The Pool of Stars. New York, Macmillan, 1919.
The Windy Hill. New York, Macmillan, 1921.
The New Moon, illustrated by Marguerite de Angeli. New York, Macmillan, 1924.
Rain on the Roof, illustrated by Edith Ballinger Price. New York, Macmillan, 1925.
The Trade Wind, illustrated by Henry Pitz. Boston, Little Brown, 1927; London, Hodder and Stoughton, 1928.
As the Crow Flies. New York, Macmillan, 1927.
Clearing Weather, illustrated by Frank Dobias. Boston, Little Brown, 1928.
The Wonderful Locomotive, illustrated by Berta and Elmer Hader. New York, Macmillan, 1928.
The Crooked Apple Tree, illustrated by Helen Mason Grose. Boston, Little Brown, 1929.
The Willow Whistle, illustrated by E. Boyd Smith. New York, Macmillan, 1931.
Swift Rivers, illustrated by Forrest Orr. Boston, Little Brown, 1932.
Wind in the Chimney, illustrated by Louise Mansfield. New York, Macmillan, 1934.
The Covered Bridge, illustrated by Marguerite de Angeli. New York, Macmillan, 1936.
Young Americans: How History Looked to Them While It Was in the Making. Boston, Ginn, 1936.
The Scarlet Oak, illustrated by Elizabeth Orton Jones. New York, Macmillan, 1938; Birmingham, Combridge, 1939.
Call of the Mountain, illustrated by James Daugherty. Boston, Little Brown, 1940.
Mother Makes Christmas, illustrated by Lois Lenski. New York, Grosset and Dunlap, 1940.
Vanished Island, illustrated by Dorothy Bayley. New York, Macmillan, 1941.
Mounted Messenger, illustrated by John Wonsetler. New York, Macmillan, 1943.
The Two Arrows. New York, Macmillan, 1949.
The Dutch Colt, illustrated by George and Doris Hauman. New York, Macmillan, 1952.
Fair Wind to Virginia, illustrated by John Wonsetler. New York, Macmillan, 1955.
Wild Geese Flying, illustrated by Charles Geer. New York, Macmillan, 1957.
Mystery at the Red House, illustrated by Robert Maclean. New York, Macmillan, 1961.

Fiction as Adair Aldon

The Island of Appledore, illustrated by W.B. King. New York, Macmillan, 1917.
The Pirate of Jasper Peak. New York, Macmillan, 1918.
At the Sign of the Two Heroes, illustrated by S. Gordon Smyth. New York, Century, 1920.
The Hill of Adventure, illustrated by J. Clinton Shepherd. New York, Century, 1922.

Plays

The Steadfast Princess. New York, Macmillan, 1916.
Helga and the White Peacock. New York, Macmillan, 1922.

Other

Invincible Louisa: The Story of the Author of "Little Women". Boston, Little Brown, 1933; as *The Story of Louisa Alcott*, London, Harrap, 1935.
Jane Addams: Pioneer for Social Justice: A Biography. Boston, Little Brown, 1970.

Editor, *Glimpses of Louisa: A Centennial Sampling of the Best Short Stories*, by Louisa May Alcott. Boston, Little Brown, 1968.

PUBLICATIONS FOR ADULTS

Novel

Railroad West. Boston, Little Brown, 1937.

Other

The Violent Men: A Study of Human Relations in the First American Congress. New York, Macmillan, 1949.
What Makes a College? A History of Bryn Mawr. New York, Macmillan, 1956.
Saint John's Church, Havre de Grace, Maryland, 1809–1959. Havre de Grace, Democratic Ledger, 1959.
The Great Design: Men and Events in the United Nations from 1945

to 1963.   Boston, Little Brown, 1963.
Louisa May Alcott and the American Family Story.   London, Bodley Head, 1970; New York, Walck, 1971.

Editor and part author, *A Critical History of Children's Literature.*   New York, Macmillan, 1953; revised edition, 1969; London, Collier Macmillan, 1969.

* * *

Although Cornelia Meigs, who also wrote under the pseudonym of Adair Aldon, is best remembered for her Newbery Medal biography of Louisa May Alcott, *Invincible Louisa*, and for her comprehensive, astute *A Critical History of Children's Literature* (revised in 1969), she also made a significant contribution in several genres to children's literature with historical fiction, mysteries, and drama. Her particular interest in the development of the United States was reflected in many books; her experiences of storytelling within the family circle were a source of her sense of narrative flow; her empathy for children was echoed repeatedly in stories in which they are faced with obstacles and rise to conquer their problems.

Meigs's first book for children, *The Kingdom of the Winding Road*, was published in 1915 but is now out of print, as are many of her other titles. Her second book, *Master Simon's Garden*, received wider critical acclaim; it is a strikingly effective message about intolerance: in a rigidly Puritan Massachusetts town, Master Simon is reviled for wasting time and space on a beautiful garden, an expression of his love and tolerance, but his legacy is appreciated by future generations. Her interest in the past is also evident in *The Willow Whistle*, a tale of pioneer life in the midwest; in *Wind in the Chimney*, in which two English children are instrumental in helping their widowed mother keep her new home in America just after the American Revolution; and in *The Covered Bridge*, set in Vermont in 1788, which has a strong sense of local history and the New England countryside.

Meigs's play *The Steadfast Princess* won the Drama League Prize in 1915, and her dramatic flair is repeatedly clear in such mystery stories as *Mystery at the Red House*, which has a plot that is exciting despite the book's slow pace. In this book, as well as in *The Dutch Colt* and *Wild Geese Flying*, young protagonists rise to the occasion and solve problems in an exciting but believable manner.

While Meigs seldom created memorable characters or drew her characters in depth, her plots are absorbing, her historical backgrounds authoritative but unobtrusive, and her themes—especially in historical fiction—strong. She wrote with perspective and polish. If all her writing is not great, many of her books have elements of greatness. Reviewing another author's book, she wrote, "No book can be said to have even the elements of greatness unless it can stand the task of recollection," and many of Meigs's stories can indeed stand that task.

—Zena Sutherland

———

MELWOOD, Mary. Pseudonym for Eileen Mary Lewis, née Hall. British. Born in Carlton-in-Lindrick, Nottinghamshire. Educated at Retford County High School for Girls, Nottinghamshire. Married Morris Lewis in 1939; two sons. Recipient: Arts Council award, 1964, 1966; *Observer*-Rank Organisation prize, 1982. Agent: Europa Books, 6 Park Street, Kemptown, Brighton, Sussex BN2 2BS; or Patricia Whitton, New Plays Inc., Box 273, Rowayton, Connecticut 06853, U.S.A. Address: 5 Hove Lodge Mansions, Hove Street, Hove, Sussex BN3 2TS, England.

PUBLICATIONS FOR CHILDREN

Fiction

Nettlewood.   London, Deutsch, 1974; New York, Seabury Press, 1975.
The Watcher Bee.   London, Deutsch, 1982.

Plays

The Tingalary Bird (produced London, 1964).   New York, New Plays, 1964.
Five Minutes to Morning (produced London, 1965).   New York, New Plays, 1966.
Masquerade (produced Nottingham, 1970).
The Small Blue Hoping Stone, music by Nancy Kelel (produced Detroit, 1976).

Radio Play: *It Isn't Enough*, 1957.

PUBLICATIONS FOR ADULTS

Novel

Reflections in Black Glass.   London, Deutsch, 1987.

* * *

Mary Melwood's first play, *The Tingalary Bird*, arrived in an unpromising world. For a form of entertainment that is so much appreciated there is remarkably little demand for children's theatre. Certainly there is none from its audience. A high percentage of children in England don't know what theatre is and those that do would surely not be capable of registering a protest were all children's theatre to disappear overnight. Such demand as exists is manufactured by a few adults working in the field or by the occasional parent looking for something to take the kids to as a change from the zoo. If children's theatre is at the mercy of this handful of adults, naturally its playwrights are too. *The Tingalary Bird* had a lot of surviving to do.

Since 1945 children's theatre had been dominated by small heroic touring companies taking their work into schools with desperately limited facilities. Inevitably they looked for small-cast plays with no technical requirements whatever. Writers had to provide this kind of play or not be performed at all. Circumstances created a very restricted art form which those who cared came to regard as the only thing children wanted. In the 1960's, when Theatre in Education got under way, custom-built plays were wanted and were frequently assembled by the companies themselves, thus cutting out the playwright entirely. Any playwright with ambitions to write a work for children with a quarter of the staging difficulties of *Peter Pan* was doomed. Children's theatre began to petrify. John Osborne had happened in adult theatre, but children's plays had scarcely put a toe out of the fairy ring.

By some miracle, Melwood, a teacher in Nottingham, knew none of this and blithely sent her play, with a small cast but with massive technical needs, to Caryl Jenner, who had the good sense to hire a theatre and put it on. The play was successful, the Arts Council of Great Britain granted it an award (the first ever for a kids' play), and children's theatre had taken a great leap forward.

As the curtain went up on a pleasant sailor singing an equally pleasant song, the audience in 1964 could not have the slightest idea that Melwood was going to ask seven-year-olds to examine with her the breakdown of a marriage.

An ancient couple living in a failed inn are terrified to discover a huge caged bird has arrived in their living room during a thunder storm. Through this electrifying visitor, Melwood looks at the causes of their shattered relationship. At first they seem very simple; plainly the old woman is nasty, plainly the old man is nice. A subtler conflict emerges as one realises that each character holds a different version of the truth; the old man sees the bird's eyes are golden, the old woman says they are green. Both are correct. The audience begins to see that each has driven the other into these extremes of their personalities and, since nobody leaves, a suspicion that each finds their bitter tussle necessary is confirmed by the old woman's line, of her husband, "I should have missed him if he'd got away."

All stormy night the battle goes on. By dawn the beautiful bird has gone, the old man is heartbroken and the old woman utterly routed. Her horde of gold has been revealed, her dusty doll's cradle, kept for a child she never had, is broken, the key to her bare food cupboard is in her husband's possession and, believe it or not, it has been funny lots of the time. The old woman throws down her broomstick, symbol of her authority, opts out of trying to keep the forest tidy, and goes to bed. But as she sneaks back to recover the doll occupant of the cradle one feels she is not so much defeated as diminished, and that this is all to the good. She is no longer frantically being clean enough and thrifty enough or selfish enough for two. The Tingalary Bird has set her husband free from her, but it has also set her free from having to compensate for the old man's delightful deficiencies. The relationship will never be reasonable but it has been reasoned. The audience leaves her wiser and well entertained.

Thereafter Melwood began to write specifically for Caryl Jenner's Unicorn company and particularly for Matyelok Gibbs, its artistic director, who created all Melwood's dashing unsentimentalised old ladies and for whom *The Small Blue Hoping Stone* was written.

Five Minutes to Morning is resolved by another "all nighter." Set in a ruined schoolroom, the play involves a boy who has recently inherited the property, and who resists his clear duty to allow Mrs. Venny, the old school teacher, to continue to occupy the premises. The second act reworks, in a dream sequence, the struggle within himself between enlightenment and chaos as represented by Mrs. Venny and Tom Skinch, the would-be buyer of the property. With this play Melwood is suggesting to her audience that the true excitement in our lives lies not in that furtively thrilling, brutal side of us but in the more dangerous area of our flights of fancy (at one point the schoolroom apparently takes off and flies) and, more sombrely, in learning. Not a fashionable theme.

To convey this theme, Melwood deliberately confuses vision with perception. Significantly, Jolyon, the boy, loses his spectacles at old Mrs. Venny's front door and doesn't get them back till the end of the play. From there on it is the schoolmarm's surprisingly racy and tart version of the world that he must adopt. During his nightmare he sometimes magnifies things to clarify the truth for himself. A vast squirrel cavorts with a football-size hazel nut, the cat is a sleek, affectionate giantess, but the wild white pony, a sort of fierce, living grail, is a reversal of itself and comes tamely to Mrs. Venny's door to be fed. Skinch, in the first act a belligerent landowner, turns total killer and becomes the Unruly Creature. Everything has a changed perspective so that Jolyon can understand and decide. He does—at five minutes to morning. He chooses Mrs. Venny while yet acknowledging that the tension and balance between the Venny and Skinch in him is his fundamental vitality.

In my experience, the danger of this play is that Skinch's naughty boy act and his very amusing flouting of authority in the early stages of the nightmare sequence so endears him to the children that they are inclined to see him as a sort of William grown up, not as the malignant destroyer of us all that Melwood intends. The play loses direction.

Still, Melwood remains a writer for children of the first order. My one regret is that she is English, though it has been left to America

to perform *The Small Blue Hoping Stone*. It is always an adventure to be involved in a Melwood production. I envy my colleagues across the water.

—Ursula M. Jones

MERRIAM, Eve. American. Born in Philadelphia, Pennsylvania, 19 July 1916. Educated at Cornell University, Ithaca, New York; University of Pennsylvania, Philadelphia, A.B. 1937; University of Wisconsin, Madison; Columbia University, New York. Has two sons. Copywriter, 1939–42; radio writer, 1942–46; moderator of weekly program on poetry, WQXR Radio, New York, 1942–46; columnist, *PM*, 1945; feature editor, *Deb* magazine, New York, 1946; fashion copy editor, *Glamour* magazine, New York, 1947–48; member of the field project staff, Bank Street College of Education, New York, 1958–60; teacher, City College, New York, 1966–69. Recipient: Yale Series of Younger Poets award, 1945; CBS-TV fellowship, 1959; Obie award, 1977; National Council of Teachers of English award, for verse, 1981. Agent: Marian Reiner, 71 Disbrow Lane, New Rochelle, New York 10804. Address: 101 West 12th Street, Apartment 4-R, New York, New York 10011, U.S.A.

PUBLICATIONS FOR CHILDREN

Fiction

What Can You Do with a Pocket?, illustrated by Harriet Sherman. New York, Knopf, 1964.
Do You Want to See Something?, illustrated by Abner Graboff. New York, Scholastic, 1965.
Small Fry, illustrated by Garry MacKenzie. New York, Knopf, 1965.
Miss Tibbett's Typewriter, illustrated by Rick Schreiter. New York, Knopf, 1966.
Andy All Year Round, illustrated by Margo Hoff. New York, Funk and Wagnalls, 1967.
Epaminondas, illustrated by Trina Schart Hyman. Chicago, Follett, 1968; London, Collins, 1969; as *That Noodle-Head Epaminondas*, New York, Scholastic, 1972.
Project 1-2-3, illustrated by Harriet Sherman. New York, McGraw Hill, 1971.
Boys and Girls, Girls and Boys, illustrated by Harriet Sherman. New York, Holt Rinehart, 1972.
Unhurry Harry, illustrated by Gail Owens. New York, Four Winds Press, 1978.
Good Night to Annie, illustrated by John Wallner. New York, Four Winds Press, 1980.
The Christmas Box, illustrated by David Small. New York, Morrow, 1985.
The Birthday Door, illustrated by Peter J. Thornton. New York, Morrow, 1986.
Where Is Everybody?, illustrated by Diane deGroat. New York, Simon and Schuster, 1989.

Verse

There Is No Rhyme for Silver, illustrated by Joseph Schindelman. New York, Atheneum, 1962.
Funny Town, illustrated by Evaline Ness. New York, Crowell

Collier, 1963.

It Doesn't Always Have to Rhyme, illustrated by Malcolm Spooner. New York, Atheneum, 1964.

Don't Think about a White Bear, illustrated by Murray Tinkelman. New York, Putnam, 1965.

Catch a Little Rhyme, illustrated by Imero Gobbato. New York, Atheneum, 1966.

Independent Voices, illustrated by Arvis Stewart. New York, Atheneum, 1968.

Finding a Poem, illustrated by Seymour Chwast. New York, Atheneum, 1970.

I Am a Man: Ode to Martin Luther King, Jr., illustrated by Suzanne Verrier. New York, Doubleday, 1971.

Out Loud, illustrated by Harriet Sherman. New York, Atheneum, 1973.

Rainbow Writing. New York, Atheneum, 1976.

The Birthday Cow, illustrated by Guy Michel. New York, Knopf, 1978.

A Word or Two with You: New Rhymes for Young Readers, illustrated by John Nez. New York, Atheneum, 1981.

If Only I Could Tell You: Poems for Young Lovers and Dreamers, illustrated by Donna Diamond. New York, Knopf, 1983.

Jamboree: Rhymes for All Times, illustrated by Walter Gaffney-Kessel. New York, Dell, 1984.

A Book of Wishes for You. Norwalk, Connecticut, Gibson, 1985.

Blackberry Ink, illustrated by Hans Wilhelm. New York, Morrow, 1985.

Fresh Paint, illustrated by David Frampton. New York, Macmillan, 1986.

A Sky Full of Poems. New York, Dell, 1986.

Halloween ABC, illustrated by Lane Smith. New York, Macmillan, and London, Macmillan, 1987.

You Be Good and I'll Be Night: Jump-on-the-Bed Poems, illustrated by Karen Lee Schmidt. New York, Morrow, 1988.

Chortles: New and Selected Wordplay Poems, illustrated by Sheila Hamanaka. New York, Morrow, 1989.

Other

The Real Book about Franklin D. Roosevelt, illustrated by Bette J. Davis. New York, Doubleday, 1952; London, Dobson, 1961.

The Real Book of Amazing Birds, illustrated by Paul Wenck. New York, Doubleday, 1952; London, Dobson, 1960.

The Voice of Liberty: The Story of Emma Lazarus. New York, Farrar Straus, 1959.

A Gaggle of Geese, illustrated by Paul Galdone. New York, Knopf, 1960.

Mommies at Work, illustrated by Beni Montresor. New York, Knopf, 1961.

What's in the Middle of a Riddle?, illustrated by Murray Tinkelman. New York, Collier, 1963.

The Story of Ben Franklin, illustrated by Brinton Turkle. New York, Scholastic, 1965.

Bam! Zam! Boom!: A Building Book, illustrated by William Lightfoot. New York, Walker, 1972.

Ab to Zogg: A Lexicon for Science-Fiction and Fantasy Readers, illustrated by Al Lorenz. New York, Atheneum, 1977.

Daddies at Work, illustrated by Eugenie Fernandez. New York, Simon and Schuster, 1989.

Editor, with Nancy Larrick, *Male and Female under 18: Frank Comments from Young People about Their Sex Roles Today*. New York, Discus Books, 1973.

Translator, *Christmas*, by Dick Bruna, illustrated by Bruna. New York, Doubleday, 1971.

Recordings: *Catch a Little Rhyme*, 1976; *Out Loud*, 1988.

PUBLICATIONS FOR ADULTS

Plays

Inner City, music by Helen Miller, adaptation of *The Inner City Mother Goose* by Merriam (produced New York, 1971).

Out of Our Fathers' House, with Paula Wagner and Jack Hofsiss, music by Ruth Crawford Seeger and others, adaptation of the book *Growing Up Female in America* edited by Merriam (produced New York, 1975). New York, French, 1975.

The Club (produced New York, 1976; London, 1978). New York, French, 1976.

At Her Age. New York, French, 1979.

Dialogue for Lovers: Sonnets of Shakespeare Arranged for Dramatic Presentation (produced New York, 1980). New York, French, 1981.

And I Ain't Finished Yet (produced New York, 1981).

Plagues for Our Time, music by Tom O'Horgan (produced New York, 1983).

Woman Alive: Conversation Against Death (libretto), music by Patsy Rogers (also director: produced New York, 1983).

Street Dreams, music by Helen Miller (produced New York, 1984).

Television Play: *We the Women*, 1975.

Verse

Family Circle. New Haven, Connecticut, Yale University Press, 1946.

Tomorrow Morning. New York, Twayne, 1953.

The Double Bed from the Feminine Side. New York, Cameron, 1958.

The Trouble with Love. New York, Macmillan, 1960.

Basics: An I-Can-Read Book for Grownups. New York, Macmillan, 1962.

The Inner City Mother Goose. New York, Simon and Schuster, 1969.

The Nixon Poems. New York, Atheneum, 1970.

A Husband's Notes about Her: Fictions. New York, Macmillan, 1976.

Other

Montgomery, Alabama, Money, Mississippi, and Other Places. New York, Cameron, 1956.

Emma Lazarus: Woman with a Torch. New York, Citadel Press, 1956.

Figleaf: The Business of Being in Fashion. Philadelphia, Lippincott, 1960.

After Nora Slammed the Door: American Women in the 1960's: The Unfinished Revolution. Cleveland, World, 1964.

Man and Woman: The Human Condition. Denver, Research Center on Woman, 1968.

Equality, Identity, and Complementarity: Changing Perspectives of Man and Woman, with others, edited by Robert H. Amundson. Denver, Research Center on Woman, 1968.

Editor, *Growing Up Female in America: Ten Lives*. New York, Doubleday, 1971.

*

Manuscript Collections: Kerlan Collection, University of

Minnesota, Minneapolis; de Grummond Collection, University of Southern Mississippi, Hattiesburg; Schlesinger Library, Radcliffe College, Cambridge, Massachusetts.

Theatrical Activities:
Director: *Out of Order* by Janet Neipris, New York, 1982; *Woman Alive: Conversation Against Death*, New York, 1983.

* * *

Eve Merriam's versatility is astounding. A keen observer of contemporary life, she brings to her poetry a fresh outlook on all phases of the modern world, its delights as well as absurdities. Agile and penetrating, she beguiles her readers with a variety of rhythms, rhymes, and forms attuned to the spirits of the young. Her craftsmanship is exemplary.

Merriam's themes range from the joy of words and word-play through a gamut of observations about contemporary life. Her concerns for humanity, ecology, and the quality of life often find expression in the part played by poetry itself with its possibilities for self-expression. What underlies all her writing is the art of asking the child-reader to extend horizons, develop sensibility, cultivate curiosity, and become aware of the creativity for both the individual and society. "I cannot speak until you come," says a poem, "Reader, reader, come with me."

For the child who accepts this invitation and enters into Merriam's work there will be the love of words and sounds for their own sake. In her poem "Having Words" she lists the things that the word *umbrage* is not, and tells her audience that "You'll have to find out for yourself what it is." She plays with the alphabet, numbers, punctuation, the points of the compass, and a myriad of other objects and ideas, always asking the reader to join in the fun. Yet she warns against mediocrity. A cliché, she explains, "is what we all say when we're too lazy to find another way." It is her unique talent that she is able to avoid didacticism by playing a dual role as poet and reader. Writing of *it* and *they*, she comments that *"They* just make it all up,/and we go along." By becoming part of the *we* she never points an accusing finger at the child.

She can be delightfully caustic, attacking television and its ridiculous commercials, the supermarket with its "banana detergent," "deodorant pie," plastic plants that "keep us germ-proof and dirt-free," "artificial lawns with real crab grasses," and the "cult" of bargain sales. "You can take away my mother,/you can take away my sister,/ but don't take away/my little transistor." Here again her pose is that of one with the reader. Often she uses personification. All of the things of the day make us hurry and deprive us of time to speak. Yet, "slowly, says the darkness,/you can talk to me."

Recent books, *Blackberry Ink* and *You Be Good and I'll Be Night: Jump-on-the-Bed Poems*, written for the very young, abound in joyous rhythms and repetitive phrases that appeal to the physical activity of young children. Similarly, *If Only I Could Tell You: Poems for Young Lovers and Dreamers* catches the yearnings, joys, and questions of first love. In *Fresh Paint* she once again invites readers to open their eyes to a world that contains not only junk mail, chemical tanks, and waste, but a new pencil, a new moon, and fresh paint that inspires the imagination to turn "whatever color I conjure when I close my eyes."

Some of her finest writing is about people whose "independent voices" have wrought meaningful changes in the world. Her poems about poetry itself are memorable. In "How to Eat a Poem" she advises the reader to "bite in...." The poem "is ready and ripe now, whenever you are." In "Reply to the Question: *How Can You Become a Poet*?" she suggests young writers observe the varying phases of the leaf in spring, summer, and autumn and then "in winter/when there is no leaf left/invent one."

Merriam's invitations to participate in both poetry and life are invitations that ring with anticipation and challenge. They are impossible to resist!

—Myra Cohn Livingston

———

MERRILL, Jean (Fairbanks). American. Born in Rochester, New York, 27 January 1923. Educated at Allegheny College, Meadville, Pennsylvania, B.A. in English 1944 (Phi Beta Kappa); Wellesley College, Massachusetts, M.A. 1945; University of Madras (Fulbright fellow), 1952–53. Assistant feature editor, 1945–46, and feature editor, 1946–49, *Scholastic* magazine, New York; associate editor, 1950–51, and editor, 1956–57, *Literary Cavalcade*, New York; associate editor, 1965–66, and consultant, 1969–71, Bank Street College of Education Publications Division, New York. Agent: Dorothy Markinko, McIntosh and Otis, 310 Madison Avenue, New York, New York 10017. Address: Angel's Ark, 29 South Main Street, Randolph, Vermont 05060, U.S.A.

PUBLICATIONS FOR CHILDREN

Fiction

Henry, The Hand-Painted Mouse, illustrated by Ronni Solbert. New York, Coward McCann, 1951.
The Woover, illustrated by Ronni Solbert. New York, Coward McCann, 1952.
Boxes, illustrated by Ronni Solbert. New York, Coward McCann, 1953.
The Tree House of Jimmy Domino, illustrated by Ronni Solbert. New York and London, Oxford University Press, 1955.
The Travels of Marco, illustrated by Ronni Solbert. New York, Knopf, 1956.
A Song for Gar, illustrated by Ronni Solbert. New York, McGraw Hill, 1957.
The Very Nice Things, illustrated by Ronni Solbert. New York, Harper, 1959.
Blue's Broken Heart, illustrated by Ronni Solbert. New York, McGraw Hill, 1960.
Tell about the Cowbarn, Daddy, illustrated by Lili Wronker. New York, Scott, 1963.
The Pushcart War, illustrated by Ronni Solbert. New York, Scott, 1964; London, Hamish Hamilton, 1973.
The Elephant Who Liked to Smash Small Cars, illustrated by Ronni Solbert. New York, Pantheon, 1967.
Red Riding, illustrated by Ronni Solbert. New York, Pantheon, 1968.
The Black Sheep, illustrated by Ronni Solbert. New York, Pantheon, 1969.
Mary, Come Running, illustrated by Ronni Solbert. New York, McCall, 1970.
Here I Come—Ready or Not!, illustrated by Frances Scott. Chicago, Whitman, 1970.
How Many Kids Are Hiding on My Block?, illustrated by Frances Scott. Chicago, Whitman, 1970.
Please, Don't Eat My Cabin, illustrated by Frances Scott. Chicago, Whitman, 1971.
The Second Greatest Clown in the World. Boston, Houghton Mifflin, 1971.
The Jackpot. Boston, Houghton Mifflin, 1971.
The Toothpaste Millionaire, illustrated by Jan Palmer. Boston, Houghton Mifflin, 1972.

Maria's House, illustrated by Frances Scott. New York, Atheneum, 1974.

Plays

Tightrope Act, in *Isn't That What Friends Are For?*, edited by Bank Street College of Education. Boston, Houghton Mifflin, 1972.
Mary Come Running (libretto), music by Gwyneth Walker (produced Randolph, Vermont, 1983).

Television Play: *The Claws in the Cat's Paw*, 1956.

Verse

Emily Emerson's Moon, illustrated by Ronni Solbert. Boston, Little Brown, 1960.

Other

Shan's Lucky Knife: A Burmese Folk Tale, illustrated by Ronni Solbert. New York, Scott, 1960; Kingswood, Surrey, World's Work, 1961.
The Superlative Horse: A Tale of Ancient China, illustrated by Ronni Solbert. New York, Scott, 1961.
High, Wide and Handsome and Their Three Tall Tales, illustrated by Ronni Solbert. New York, Scott, 1964.
The Bumper Sticker Book, illustrated by Frances Scott. Chicago, Whitman, 1973.

Editor, with Ronni Solbert, *A Few Flies and I* (haiku), by Issa Kobayashi, translated by R.H. Blyth and Nobuyuki Yuasa. New York, Pantheon, 1969.

*

Manuscript Collections: Rare Book Division, University of Wyoming Library, Laramie; de Grummond Collection, University of Southern Mississippi, Hattiesburg; Kerlan Collection, University of Minnesota, Minneapolis; Rutgers University, New Brunswick, New Jersey.

Jean Merrill comments:

As to my general motivation as a writer, I would say that it is to celebrate those aspects of the human experience that affirm the creative and life-reverencing instinct in man. To the extent that a writer for children occasionally glimpses himself, as does any adult directing his concern to children, I am conscious of more specific motivations, among them:
—to educate—in the sense of socializing the child in the direction of a constructive use of his potential;
—to entertain—to encourage the capacity for joy by enticing the free play of a child's curiosity, humor, and inventiveness;
—to liberate—by opening up the child to emotional as well as to intellectual experience.
Though I am referring to "the child" as if he were a receptacle, the child for whom one essentially writes is oneself, and at base writing is motivated by one's own need to resolve the enigma of life. I am always the imagined reader, as well as writer, of my books.
Writers for children are often asked whether they feel limitations on subject matter or theme in writing for children. I have never felt constrained in writing for children about anything that concerned me as an adult; what I perceive as touchstones of the human experience are as appropriate, indeed essential, to books for very young readers as to books for the literate 14-year-old.
One must obviously be selective of the language and metaphor that will most readily translate one's perceptions to children of

various ages, but this necessity is no more a limitation than trying to converse with adults of background or experience different from one's own. And finding the word or symbol that will translate my feeling into a form accessible to a child is to me the essential challenge of writing.
My interest in writing children's books may have derived from the impact certain books had on me as a child and a wish to recreate the quality of that experience. Certainly, one of the satisfactions of writing for children is the intensity of caring young readers lavish on the books they like.
It is often the books we read as children that stay with us the longest, whose titles, characters, plots, and emotional tone we never forget. Their significance with repeated readings is imprinted on memory until they are as much a part of the landscape that forever colors our perception and expectation of the world as the faces of our parents and the look and smell of the houses we grew up in.
Given this extra durability that may attach to what children read, whatever a writer feels may be worth communicating seems to me to be additionally worth communicating to children. And seems also to require of those of us who write for children that we be uncompromising enemies of the shoddy, meretricious, or sentimental in our work.

*   *   *

Jean Merrill has earned her solid reputation as a children's writer by the consistently fine quality of her books. Her themes and formats are varied. Her interest in the Far East has produced some fine books such as *High, Wide and Handsome, Shan's Lucky Knife*, and *The Superlative Horse*. Her picture books are clever, original, and appealing to young listeners. One good example of this genre is *The Elephant Who Liked to Smash Small Cars. Elephant* presents the conflicts between "doing your own thing" and harming others; it is also a story of growing up, of becoming aware of others' needs. While some adults worry about the violence—i.e., the elephant's delight in smashing small cars and the "tit-for-tat" treatment he receives—young children seem to be deeply satisfied both by the portrayal of Elephant's antisocial drives and the resolution of them.
Merrill writes equally effectively for older children. Though one of her earlier and most famous books, *The Pushcart War*, is identified as for children 9 to 12, it really is for ages 9 to 90. The humorous wisdom and courageous actions of the pushcart owners in resisting the onslaughts of the powerful trucking concerns appeal to adults as well as children.
The Pushcart War exemplifies a favorite theme of Merrill—the struggle of the small and weak against the strong and mighty. In a delightful book for older readers, *The Toothpaste Millionaire* (also shown on film as a television special), a young black boy, Rufus, invents an effective toothpaste from simple materials. As his product oversells the established brands by nearly 100%, the enraged manufacturers try to put him out of business. As in *The Pushcart War*, the big corporations meet their comeuppance, even though Rufus is already dreaming up new enterprises.
Merrill's humanistic concerns are evident in all her books. In *The Superlative Horse* merit doesn't depend on outward trappings but on inward ability. In *The Black Sheep*, a book for younger children, there is gentle insight into the worth of the "different" individual.
Merrill not only catches the flow and flavor of real children's language but structures it in such naturalistic speech that even poor readers become absorbed in her stories. She blends long and short sentences, sentence fragments, phrases, and dialogue so skillfully that it reads as "real talk written down"; and the young reader immediately identifies with the characters. She has mastered the subtle art of "immediacy"—the reader is there and the adventure is happening to him or her.
One last observation: Merrill is also intrigued by mathematics. Her

pleasure in this science often makes it more meaningful to the reader than most textbooks on the subject. Rufus can become a toothpaste millionaire because he can understand cost and profit; in *The Push-cart War* a professor carries percentage to its ultimate absurdity; in "The Seventeen Horses of Ali" (a story in *Discoveries: An Individualized Approach to Reading*), she presents a playful puzzle in fractions that might well awaken delight in mathematics.

A craftsman with words, a prolific and creative writer, a humorous mathematician, and a fine storyteller—Merrill is all these things; but above all, she is a tender but strong affirmer of human rights.

—Betty Boegehold

———

MEYNELL, Laurence (Walter). Also wrote as Valerie Baxter; Robert Eton; Geoffrey Ludlow; A. Stephen Tring. British. Born in Wolverhampton, Staffordshire, 9 August 1899. Educated at St. Edmund's College, Ware, Hertfordshire. Served in the Honourable Artillery Company during World War I; Royal Air Force, 1939–45: mentioned in despatches. Married 1) Shirley Ruth Darbyshire in 1932 (died 1955), one daughter; 2) Joan Belfrage in 1956 (died 1986). Articled pupil in a land agency, 1920's; worked as a schoolteacher and an estate agent. General editor, Men of the Counties series, Bodley Head, publishers, London, 1955–57; literary editor, *Time and Tide*, London, 1958–60. *Died 14 April 1989.*

PUBLICATIONS FOR CHILDREN

Fiction

Smoky Joe, illustrated by Charlotte Hough. London, Lane, 1952.
Smoky Joe in Trouble, illustrated by Charlotte Hough. London, Lane, 1953.
Policeman in the Family, illustrated by Neville Dear. London, Oxford University Press, 1953.
Under the Hollies, illustrated by Ian Ribbons. London, Oxford University Press, 1954.
Bridge under the Water, illustrated by John S. Goodall. London, Phoenix House, 1954; New York, Roy, 1957.
Animal Doctor, illustrated by Raymond Sheppard. London, Oxford University Press, 1956.
Smoky Joe Goes to School, illustrated by Charlotte Hough. London, Lane, 1956.
Sonia Back Stage. London, Chatto and Windus, 1957.
The Young Architect, illustrated by David Knight. London, Oxford University Press, 1958.
District Nurse Carter. London, Chatto and Windus, 1958.
Nurse Ross Takes Over. London, Hamish Hamilton, 1958.
The Hunted King. London, Bodley Head, 1959.
Nurse Ross Shows the Way. London, Hamish Hamilton, 1959.
Monica Anson, Travel Agent. London, Chatto and Windus, 1959.
Nurse Ross Saves the Day. London, Hamish Hamilton, 1960.
Bandaberry. London, Bodley Head, 1960.
Nurse Ross and the Doctor. London, Hamish Hamilton, 1962.
The Dancers in the Reeds. London, Hamish Hamilton, 1963.
Good Luck, Nurse Ross. London, Hamish Hamilton, 1963.
Scoop. London, Hamish Hamilton, 1964.
The Empty Saddle. London, Hamish Hamilton, 1965.
Break for Summer. London, Hamish Hamilton, 1965.
Shadow in the Sun. London, Hamish Hamilton, 1966.
The Suspect Scientist. London, Hamish Hamilton, 1966.
The Man in the Hut, illustrated by Tony Hart. London, Kaye and Ward, 1967.
Peter and the Picture Thief, illustrated by Tony Hart. London, Kaye and Ward, 1969.
Jimmy and the Election, illustrated by Tony Hart. London, Kaye and Ward, 1970.
Tony Trotter and the Kitten, illustrated by Peter Edwards. London, Kaye and Ward, 1971.
The Great Cup Tie, illustrated by Gareth Floyd. London, Kaye and Ward, 1974.

Fiction as A. Stephen Tring

The Old Gang, illustrated by John Camp. London, Oxford University Press, 1947.
Penny Dreadful, illustrated by T.R. Freeman. London, Oxford University Press, 1949.
The Cave by the Sea, illustrated by T.R. Freeman. London, Oxford University Press, 1950.
Barry's Exciting Year, illustrated by Charlotte Hough. London, Oxford University Press, 1951.
Barry Gets His Wish, illustrated by Charlotte Hough. London, Oxford University Press, 1952.
Young Master Carver: A Boy in the Reign of Edward III, illustrated by Alan Jessett. London, Phoenix House, 1952; New York, Roy, 1957.
Penny Triumphant, illustrated by T.R. Freeman. London, Oxford University Press, 1953.
Penny Penitent, illustrated by T.R. Freeman. London, Oxford University Press, 1953.
Barry's Great Day, illustrated by Charlotte Hough. London, Oxford University Press, 1954.
Penny Puzzled, illustrated by T.R. Freeman. London, Oxford University Press, 1955.
The Kite Man. Oxford, Blackwell, 1955.
Penny Dramatic, illustrated by T.R. Freeman. London, Oxford University Press, 1956.
Penny in Italy, illustrated by T.R. Freeman. London, Oxford University Press, 1957.
Frankie and the Green Umbrella, illustrated by Richard Kennedy. London, Hamish Hamilton, 1957.
Pictures for Sale, illustrated by Christopher Brooker. London, Hamish Hamilton, 1958.
Penny and the Pageant, illustrated by Kathleen Gell. London, Oxford University Press, 1959.
Peter's Busy Day, illustrated by Raymond Briggs. London, Hamish Hamilton, 1959.
Ted's Lucky Ball, illustrated by James Russell. London, Hamish Hamilton, 1961.
Penny Says Good-bye, illustrated by Kathleen Gell. London, Oxford University Press, 1961.
The Man with the Sack, illustrated by Peter Booth. London, Hamish Hamilton, 1963.
Chad, illustrated by Joseph Acheson. London, Hamish Hamilton, 1966.

Fiction as Valerie Baxter

Jane: Young Author. London, Lane, 1954.
Elizabeth: Young Policewoman. London, Lane, 1955.
Shirley: Young Bookseller. London, Lane, 1956.
Hester: Ship's Officer. London, Hamish Hamilton, 1957.

Other

Builder and Dreamer: A Life of Isambard Kingdom Brunel, illustrated by Lee Kenyon. London, Lane, 1952; revised edition,

as *Isambard Kingdom Brunel*, London, Newnes, 1955.
Rolls, Man of Speed: A Life of Charles Stewart Rolls. London, Lane, 1953; revised edition, as *The Hon. C.S. Rolls*, London, Newnes, 1955.
Great Men of Staffordshire. London, Lane, 1955.
The First Men to Fly: A Short History of Wilbur and Orville Wright. London, Laurie, 1955.
James Brindley: The Pioneer of Canals. London, Laurie, 1956.
Our Patron Saints, illustrated by John Turner. London, Acorn Press, 1957.
Thomas Telford: The Life Story of a Great Engineer, illustrated by Donald Forster. London, Lane, 1957.
Farm Animals, illustrated by Jennifer Miles. London, Ward, 1958.
Airmen on the Run: True Stories of Evasion and Escape by British Airmen of World War II, illustrated by Richard Kennedy. London, Odhams Press, 1963.
The Beginning of Words: How English Grew, with Colin Pickles. London, Blond, 1970; New York, Putnam, 1971.

PUBLICATIONS FOR ADULTS

Novels

Mockbeggar. London, Harrap, 1924; New York, Appleton, 1925.
Lois. London, Harrap, and New York, Appleton, 1927.
Bluefeather. London, Harrap, and New York, Appleton, 1928.
Death's Eye. London, Harrap, 1929; as *The Shadow and the Stone*, New York, Appleton, 1929.
Camouflage. London, Harrap, 1930; as *Mystery at Newton Ferry*, Philadelphia, Lippincott, 1930.
Asking for Trouble. London, Ward Lock, 1931.
Consummate Rose. London, Hutchinson, 1931.
Storm Against the Wall. London, Hutchinson, and Philadelphia, Lippincott, 1931.
The House on the Cliff. London, Hutchinson, and Philadelphia, Lippincott, 1932.
Paid in Full. London, Harrap, 1933; as *So Many Doors*, Philadelphia, Lippincott, 1933.
Watch the Wall. London, Harrap, 1933; as *The Gentlemen Go By*, Philadelphia, Lippincott, 1934.
Odds on Bluefeather. London, Harrap, 1934; Philadelphia, Lippincott, 1935.
Inside Out! or, Mad as a Hatter (as Geoffrey Ludlow). London, Harrap, 1934.
Third Time Unlucky! London, Harrap, 1935.
On the Night of the 18th.... London, Nicholson and Watson, and New York, Harper, 1936.
Women Had to Do It! (as Geoffrey Ludlow). London, Nicholson and Watson, 1936.
The Door in the Wall. London, Nicholson and Watson, and New York, Harper, 1937.
The House in the Hills. London, Nicholson and Watson, 1937; New York, Harper, 1938.
The Dandy. London, Nicholson and Watson, 1938.
The Hut. London, Nicholson and Watson, 1938.
His Aunt Came Late. London, Nicholson and Watson, 1939.
And Be a Villain. London, Nicholson and Watson, 1939.
The Creaking Chair. London, Collins, 1941.
The Dark Square. London, Collins, 1941.
Strange Landing. London, Collins, 1946.
The Evil Hour. London, Collins, 1947.
The Bright Face of Danger. London, Collins, 1948.
The Echo in the Cave. London, Collins, 1949.
The Lady on Platform One. London, Collins, 1950.
Party of Eight. London, Collins, 1950.

The Man No One Knew. London, Collins, 1951.
The Frightened Man. London, Collins, 1952.
Danger round the Corner. London, Collins, 1952.
Too Clever by Half. London, Collins, 1953.
Give Me the Knife. London, Collins, 1954.
Where Is She Now? London, Collins, 1955.
Saturday Out. London, Collins, 1956; New York, Walker, 1962.
The Sun Will Shine. London, Transworld, 1956.
The Breaking Point. London, Collins, 1957.
One Step from Murder. London, Collins, 1958.
The Abandoned Doll. London, Collins, 1960.
The House in Marsh Road. London, Collins, 1960.
The Pit in the Garden. London, Collins, 1961.
Moon over Ebury Square. London, Hale, 1962.
Virgin Luck. London, Collins, 1963; New York, Simon and Schuster, 1964.
Sleep of the Unjust. London, Collins, 1963.
More Deadly Than the Male. London, Collins, 1964.
Double Fault. London, Collins, 1965.
Die by the Book. London, Collins, 1966.
The Imperfect Aunt. London, Hale, 1966.
Week-end in the Scampi Belt. London, Hale, 1967.
The Mauve Front Door. London, Collins, 1967.
Death of a Philanderer. London, Collins, 1968; New York, Doubleday, 1969.
Of Malicious Intent. London, Collins, 1969.
The Shelter. London, Hale, 1970.
The Curious Crime of Miss Julia Blossom. London, Macmillan, 1970.
The End of the Long Hot Summer. London, Hale, 1972.
Death by Arrangement. London, Macmillan, and New York, McKay, 1972.
A Little Matter of Arson. London, Macmillan, 1972.
A View from the Terrace. London, Hale, 1972.
The Fatal Flaw. London, Macmillan, 1973; New York, Stein and Day, 1978.
The Thirteen Trumpeters. London, Macmillan, 1973; New York, Stein and Day, 1978.
The Fortunate Miss East. London, Hale, 1973; New York, Coward McCann, 1974.
The Woman in Number Five. London, Hale, 1974; as *Burlington Square*, New York, Coward McCann, 1975.
The Fairly Innocent Little Man. London, Macmillan, 1974; New York, Stein and Day, 1977.
The Footpath. London, Hale, 1975.
Don't Stop for Hooky Hefferman. London, Macmillan, 1975; New York, Stein and Day, 1977.
Hooky and the Crock of Gold. London, Macmillan, 1975.
The Lost Half Hour. London, Macmillan, 1976; New York, Stein and Day, 1977.
The Vision Splendid. London, Hale, 1976.
The Folly of Henrietta Dale. London, Hale, 1976.
The Little Kingdom. London, Hale, 1977.
Folly to Be Wise. London, Hale, 1977.
Hooky Gets the Wooden Spoon. London, Macmillan, and New York, Stein and Day, 1977.
Papersnake. London, Macmillan, 1978.
The Dangerous Year. London, Hale, 1978.
The Sisters. London, Hale, 1979.
Hooky and the Villainous Chauffeur. London, Macmillan, 1979.
The Lady Who Wasn't. London, Hale, 1980.
Hooky and the Prancing Horse. London, Macmillan, 1980.
Hooky Goes to Blazes. London, Macmillan, 1981.
Parasol in the Park. London, Hale, 1981.
The Blue Door. London, Hale, 1982.
The Secret of the Pit. London, Macmillan, 1982.

The Visitor. London, Hale, 1983.
Silver Guilt. London, Macmillan, 1983.
False Gods. London, Hale, 1984.
The Open Door. London, Macmillan, 1984.
Quenells. London, Hale, 1985.
Affair at Barwold. London, Macmillan, 1985.
Hooky Catches a Tartar. London, Macmillan, 1986.
The Abiding Thing. London, Hale, 1986.
The Rivals. London, Hale, 1987.
Hooky on Loan. London, Macmillan, 1987.
Hooky Hooked. London, Macmillan, 1988.

Novels as Robert Eton

The Pattern. London, Harrap, 1934.
The Dividing Air. London, Harrap, 1935.
The Bus Leaves for the Village. London, Nicholson and Watson, 1936.
Not in Our Stars. London, Nicholson and Watson, 1937.
The Journey. London, Nicholson and Watson, 1938.
Palace Pier. London, Nicholson and Watson, 1938.
The Legacy. London, Nicholson and Watson, 1939.
The Faithful Years. London, Nicholson and Watson, 1939.
The Corner of Paradise Place. London, Nicholson and Watson, 1940.
St. Lynn's Advertiser. London, Nicholson and Watson, 1947.
The Dragon at the Gate. London, Nicholson and Watson, 1949.

Play

Screenplay: *The Umbrella,* with H. Fowler Mear, 1933.

Verse

The Ballad of Pen Fields, with a Plan of the Battlefield. Privately printed, 1927.

Other

Bedfordshire. London, Hale, 1950.
Famous Cricket Grounds. London, Phoenix House, 1951.
"Plum" Warner. London, Phoenix House, 1951.
Exmoor. London, Hale, 1953.

*

Manuscript Collection: Mugar Memorial Library, Boston University.

*   *   *

A. Stephen Tring, better known as Laurence Meynell, deserves to be ranked with Geoffrey Trease and E.W. Hildick for his endeavours to introduce realism and vitality into stories for boys.

His first boy's school story, *The Old Gang,* follows traditional formulae although he abandons the prestigious boarding-school setting to deal with grammar school and secondary modern school rivalries. This racy novel is told in the first person by a member of "the old gang," Frank Dilmot. It is highly readable, packed with incident, with a strong emphasis on various sports and feuds, rivalries and pranks. Authenticity is reduced by the introduction of an incredible mystery, and unacceptable attitudes tend to prevail, but regardless of such faults *The Old Gang* remains in print with its lively, convincing dialogue, its quick humour, and its notable schoolboy trio, Frank, Joe, and Mickey.

In the three books about Barry Briggs, Tring breaks free from the accepted patterns of an earlier period to create a strong central character, whose hopes, fears, and fantasies are vividly presented to the reader in a highly realistic framework particularly of family life on a council housing estate. This series shows more originality and realism than *The Old Gang* and was unusual in the 1950's for its rounded portrayal of parents. In this series the mystery elements are more feasible than in some of Tring's other books, but the introduction of upper-class characters detracts from the otherwise excellent realism of this series.

The Penny series for girls is less memorable than either *The Old Gang* or the Barry series. *Penny Dreadful* shows a degree of originality and zest not maintained in later titles of the series. The young heroine and her family are reasonably well-drawn and plots are packed with action, but the fairly affluent background of the series has little relevance to the readership of a later period. As in *The Old Gang,* rather incredible mystery situations are introduced and unacceptable attitudes persist.

As an experienced writer of stories for both adults and for children Tring proved willing to use his expertise to cater for particular contemporary needs: no easy task. His success is partly due to his readable, sometimes deceptively easy style of writing, and also to his combination of action with realism. His most successful work in this area is without doubt the series of books about Barry Briggs.

—Anne W. Ellis

———

MILES, Miska. See **MARTIN, Patricia Miles.**

———

MILLER, Madge. American. Born in Pittsburgh, Pennsylvania, 31 May 1918. Educated at Chatham College, Pittsburgh, B.A. 1939; Case Western Reserve University, Cleveland, A.M. 1940. Married Howard R. Eulensstein in 1955; one son and one daughter. Teacher of English, French, and Spanish, Pittsburgh public schools, 1941–45; speech and drama teacher, Fillion Studios, Pittsburgh, 1946–49; playwright, Pittsburgh Children's Theatre, 1947–50; playwright-director, Knickerty-Knockerty Players, Pittsburgh, 1950–71. Recipient: American Theatre Association Chorpenning Cup, 1970. Agent: Anchorage Press, P.O. Box 8067, New Orleans, Louisiana 70182, U.S.A.

PUBLICATIONS FOR CHILDREN

Plays

The Land of the Dragon (produced Pittsburgh, 1945). Anchorage, Kentucky, Children's Theatre Press, 1946.
The Princess and the Swineherd (produced Pittsburgh, 1953). Chicago, Dramatic Publishing Company, 1946.
The Pied Piper of Hamelin (produced Pittsburgh, 1948). London, Dobson, 1948; Anchorage, Kentucky, Children's Theatre Press, 1951.
Hansel and Gretel (produced Pittsburgh, 1949). London, Dobson, 1949; Anchorage, Kentucky, Children's Theatre Press, 1951.
Pinocchio (produced Pittsburgh, 1950). Anchorage, Kentucky, Children's Theatre Press, 1954.
Puss in Boots (produced Pittsburgh, 1950). Anchorage, Kentucky, Children's Theatre Press, 1954.

Snow White and Rose Red (produced Pittsburgh, 1951).
Anchorage, Kentucky, Children's Theatre Press, 1954.
Robinson Crusoe, adaptation of the novel by Daniel Defoe
(produced Pittsburgh, 1951). Anchorage, Kentucky, Children's
Theatre Press, 1954.
Alice in Wonderland, adaptation of the story by Lewis Carroll
(produced Pittsburgh, 1951). Anchorage, Kentucky, Children's
Theatre Press, 1953.
The Emperor's Nightingale (produced Richmond, Virginia, 1962).
Anchorage, Kentucky, Children's Theatre Press, 1961.
The Unwicked Witch: An Unlikely Tale (produced Pittsburgh, 1964).
Anchorage, Kentucky, Children's Theatre Press, 1964.

Other plays: *Ali Baba, Beauty and the Beast, The Emperor's New
Clothes, The Little Mermaid, Merlin the Magician, The Red Shoes,
OPQRS, etc.*; and *The Elves and the Shoemaker, Hok Lee and the
Dwarfs, Princess Pocahontas, Rapunzel, The Sleeping Beauty,* and
St. George and the Dragon, all with Larry Villani.

*

Madge Miller comments:

I am an advocate of fantasy. The fairytales which make up the bulk
of my playwriting material are to me the best possible literary form
with which first to delight the child, then, when he is emotionally
ready, to help him experience a greater awareness of the inner
problems of human beings. He learns that he is not alone in his fears
and his confusions. He identifies with those on stage who fight
against great odds to win independence and "live happily." As a
subtle dividend he receives a valuable moral education which
suggests to him the advantage of right behavior. The universality and
timelessness of these age-old themes furnish his mind with valuable
inner resources to last a lifetime. I write to create a real world of
make-believe from which the child can gain a better understanding
of the sometimes unbelievable world of reality.

*   *   *

Madge Miller's plays for children were not written to be read as
literature; they were written to be performed before audiences of
children. Yet her original plays and adaptations have literary merit;
and they were tested many times by many different audiences before
they were finally published.

Theatrical elements in Miller's original works underscore the
collaborative nature of dramatic art. *The Unwicked Witch* opens with
a shadow puppet show as Hobble, Gobble, and Wobble play tag high
in the sky. This scene sets the tone of the play. The play ends when
the witches promise to reform, Grandfather finds his tune, Lucky
Luke gets his pot of gold, and Winona, the witches' unwicked ward,
finds her true and mortal self.

The three-dragon confrontation in *The Land of the Dragon* invites
the audience to accept one of the dragons as real and two others as
make-believe. The scene is fun for the audience and a challenge for
the costumer and director. The plot is a variation of girl meets boy,
girl loses boy, girl marries boy in a Chinese setting with many of the
conventions of oriental theatre.

In *OPQRS, etc.* the villain, a tyrant named Otto, decrees that the
alphabet is to begin with O, that everything in his land must be
painted orange, including the grass, and that everyone must eat only
orange-colored food. His wrongheaded oppression is so extreme and
so petty that it is laughable. The story is excellent, raising questions
which could challenge a university class. The litany of laws recited
several times seems overdone. And woe unto those set designers who
must work with so much orange.

Too often adaptations are dismissed by critics, but adapting the
stories of children for the stage is an art in itself. In *Hansel and Gretel*

Miller enhances the psychological issues explored in the original
story by adding a Forest Fairy and Trudi, a girl who had been changed
into a black cat by the Wicked Witch. In *Robinson Crusoe* the action
is stepped up by the addition of three cannibals and a talking parrot.
The actors who play the cannibals speak a Polynesian-like gibberish
and, therefore, depend on movement and gesture to communicate
with the audience. Two of the miller's sons have been cut from
Miller's version of *Puss in Boots.* Lise, added as a servant of the
treacherous Enchanter, provides the comedy in her deliberate misap-
prehension of her master's words. The Enchanter is outwitted, as
well, by Puss in a delightfully expanded magic show.

Characteristically, Miller defangs the frightening. The witch in
Hansel and Gretel is a doddering, myopic old fool. Her search
through a book of charms is a comic highlight of the play. The three
witches in *The Unwicked Witch* are more irksome than evil. Small
One the dragon in *The Land of the Dragon* is as gentle as a Saint
Bernard.

Miller's work will not suit those who like their children's theatre
to include lots of interaction between audience and player. Her work
is well-crafted theatre which is best set on a proscenium stage.

—Nels Juleus

MILNE, A(lan) A(lexander). British. Born in London, 18
January 1882. Educated at Westminster School, London (Queen's
scholar), 1893–1900; Trinity College, Cambridge (editor, *Granta,*
1902), 1900–03, B.A. (honours) in mathematics 1903. Served in the
Royal Warwickshire Regiment, 1914–18. Married Dorothy de
Sélincourt in 1913; one son, Christopher Robin Milne. Freelance
journalist, 1903–06; assistant editor, *Punch,* London, 1906–14. *Died
31 January 1956.*

PUBLICATIONS FOR CHILDREN

Fiction

Once on a Time, illustrated by H.M. Brock. London, Hodder and
Stoughton, 1917; New York, Putnam, 1922.
A Gallery of Children, illustrated by Saida. London, Stanley Paul,
and Philadelphia, McKay, 1925.
Winnie-the-Pooh, illustrated by Ernest Shepard. London,
Methuen, and New York, Dutton, 1926.
The House at Pooh Corner, illustrated by Ernest Shepard. London,
Methuen, and New York, Dutton, 1928.
Prince Rabbit, and the Princess Who Could Not Laugh, illustrated
by Mary Shepard. London, Ward, and New York, Dutton, 1966.

Plays

Make-Believe (includes *The Princess and the Woodcutter, Oliver's
Island, Father Christmas and the Hubbard Family*), music by
George Dorlay, lyrics by C.E. Burton (produced London, 1918).
Included in *Second Plays,* 1921.
The Man in the Bowler Hat: A Terribly Exciting Affair (produced
New York, 1924; London, 1925). London and New York,
French, 1923.
King Hilary and the Beggarman (produced London, 1926).
Toad of Toad Hall, music by H. Fraser-Simson, adaptation of the
story *The Wind in the Willows* by Kenneth Grahame (produced
Liverpool, 1929; London, 1930). London, Methuen, and New
York, Scribner, 1929.

The Ugly Duckling (for children). London, French, 1941; in *Twenty-Four Favorite One-Act Plays*, edited by Bennett Cerf and Van H. Cartmell, New York, Doubleday, 1958.

Verse (illustrated by Ernest Shepard)

When We Were Very Young. London, Methuen, and New York, Dutton, 1924.
Now We Are Six. London, Methuen, and New York, Dutton, 1927.

PUBLICATIONS FOR ADULTS

Novels

Lovers in London. London, Alston Rivers, 1905.
Mr. Pim. London, Hodder and Stoughton, 1921; New York, Doran, 1922; as *Mr. Pim Passes By*, London, Methuen, 1929.
The Red House Mystery. London, Methuen, and New York, Dutton, 1922.
Two People. London, Methuen, and New York, Dutton, 1931.
Four Days' Wonder. London, Methuen, and New York, Dutton, 1933.
One Year's Time. London, Methuen, 1942.
Chloe Marr. London, Methuen, and New York, Dutton, 1946.

Short Stories

The Secret and Other Stories. London, Methuen, and New York, Fountain Press, 1929.
Birthday Party and Other Stories. New York, Dutton, 1948; London, Methuen, 1949.
A Table near the Band and Other Stories. London, Methuen, and New York, Dutton, 1950.

Plays

Wurzel-Flummery (produced London, 1917). London and New York, French, 1922; revised version, in *First Plays*, 1919.
Belinda: An April Folly (produced London and New York, 1918). Included in *First Plays*, 1919.
The Boy Comes Home (produced London, 1918). Included in *First Plays*, 1919.
First Plays (includes *Wurzel-Flummery, The Lucky One, The Boy Comes Home, Belinda, The Red Feathers*). London, Chatto and Windus, and New York, Knopf, 1919.
The Red Feathers (produced Leeds, 1920; London, 1921). Included in *First Plays*, 1919.
The Lucky One (produced New York, 1922; Cambridge, 1923; London, 1924). Included in *First Plays*, 1919; as *Let's All Talk about Gerald* (produced London, 1928).
The Camberley Triangle (produced London, 1919). Included in *Second Plays*, 1921.
Mr. Pim Passes By (produced Manchester, 1919; London, 1920; New York, 1921). Included in *Second Plays*, 1921.
The Romantic Age (produced London, 1920; New York, 1922). Included in *Second Plays*, 1921.
The Stepmother (produced London, 1920). Included in *Second Plays*, 1921.
Second Plays (includes *Make-Believe, Mr. Pim Passes By, The Camberley Triangle, The Romantic Age, The Stepmother*). London, Chatto and Windus, 1921; New York, Knopf, 1922.
The Great Broxopp: Four Chapters in Her Life (produced New York, 1921; London, 1923). Included in *Three Plays*, 1922.
The Truth about Blayds (produced London, 1921; New York, 1922). Included in *Three Plays*, 1922.
The Dover Road (produced New York, 1921; London, 1922). Included in *Three Plays*, 1922.

Three Plays (includes *The Dover Road, The Truth about Blayds, The Great Broxopp*). New York, Putnam, 1922; London, Chatto and Windus, 1923.
Berlud, Unlimited (produced London and New York, 1922).
Success (produced London, 1923; as *Give Me Yesterday*, produced New York, 1931). London, Chatto and Windus, 1923; New York, French, 1924.
The Artist: A Duologue. London and New York, French, 1923.
To Have the Honour (produced London, 1924; as *To Meet the Prince*, produced New York, 1929). London and New York, French, 1925.
Ariadne; or, Business First (produced New York and London, 1925). London and New York, French, 1925.
Portrait of a Gentleman in Slippers: A Fairy Tale (produced Liverpool, 1926; London, 1927). London and New York, French, 1926.
Four Plays (includes *To Have the Honour, Ariadne, Portrait of a Gentleman in Slippers, Success*). London, Chatto and Windus, 1926.
Miss Marlow at Play (produced London, 1927; New York, 1940). London and New York, French, 1936.
The Ivory Door: A Legend (produced New York, 1927; London, 1929). New York, Putnam, 1928; London, Chatto and Windus, 1929.
The Fourth Wall: A Detective Story (produced London, 1928; as *The Perfect Alibi*, produced New York, 1928). New York, French, 1929; London, French, 1930.
Michael and Mary (produced New York, 1929; London, 1930). London, Chatto and Windus, 1930; New York, French, 1932.
They Don't Mean Any Harm (produced London and New York, 1932).
Four Plays (includes *Michael and Mary, To Meet the Prince, The Perfect Alibi, Portrait of a Gentleman in Slippers*). New York, Putnam, 1932.
Other People's Lives (produced London, 1932). London and New York, French, 1935.
More Plays (includes *The Ivory Door, The Fourth Wall, Other People's Lives*). London, Chatto and Windus, 1935.
Miss Elizabeth Bennet, adaptation of the novel *Pride and Prejudice* by Jane Austen (produced London, 1938). London, Chatto and Windus, 1936.
Sarah Simple (produced London, 1937; New York, 1940). London, French, 1939.
Gentleman Unknown (produced London, 1938).
Before the Flood. London and New York, French, 1951.

Screenplays: *The Bump*, 1920; *Five Pounds Reward*, 1920; *Bookworms*, 1920; *Twice Two*, 1920; *Birds of Prey* (*The Perfect Alibi*), with Basil Dean, 1930.

Verse

For the Luncheon Interval: Cricket and Other Verses. London, Methuen, and New York, Dutton, 1925.
Behind the Lines. London, Methuen, and New York, Dutton, 1940.
The Norman Church. London, Methuen, 1948.

Other

The Day's Play (*Punch* sketches). London, Methuen, 1910; New York, Dutton, 1925.
The Holiday Round (*Punch* sketches). London, Methuen, 1912; New York, Dutton, 1925.
Once a Week (*Punch* sketches). London, Methuen, 1914; New York, Dutton, 1925.

Happy Days (*Punch* sketches).   New York, Doran, 1915.
Not That It Matters.   London, Methuen, 1919; New York, Dutton, 1920.
If I May.   London, Methuen, 1920; New York, Dutton, 1921.
The Sunny Side.   London, Methuen, 1921; New York, Dutton, 1922.
(*Selected Works*).   London, Library Press, 7 vols., 1926.
The Ascent of Man.   London, Benn, and New York, Dutton, 1928.
By Way of Introduction.   London, Methuen, and New York, Dutton, 1929.
Those Were the Days: The Day's Play, The Holiday Round, Once a Week, The Sunny Side.   London, Methuen, and New York, Dutton, 1929.
When I Was Very Young (autobiography).   London, Methuen, and New York, Fountain Press, 1930.
A.A. Milne (selections).   London, Methuen, 1933.
Peace with Honour: An Enquiry into the War Convention.   London, Methuen, and New York, Dutton, 1934; revised edition, 1935.
It's Too Late Now: The Autobiography of a Writer.   London, Methuen, 1939; as *Autobiography*, New York, Dutton, 1939.
War with Honour.   London, Macmillan, 1940.
War Aims Unlimited.   London, Methuen, 1941.
Going Abroad?   London, Council for Education in World Citizenship, 1947.
Books for Children: A Reader's Guide.   London, Cambridge University Press, 1948.
Year In, Year Out.   London, Methuen, and New York, Dutton, 1952.

*

Bibliography: *A.A. Milne: A Handlist of His Writings for Children* by Brian Sibley, Chislehurst Common, Kent, Henry Pootle Press, 1976; *A.A. Milne: A Critical Bibliography* by Tori Haring-Smith, New York, Garland, 1982.

Manuscript Collection: Humanities Research Center, University of Texas, Austin.

Critical Studies: *A.A. Milne* by Thomas Burnett Swann, New York, Twayne, 1971; *The Enchanted Places* by Christopher Milne, London, Eyre Methuen, 1974, New York, Dutton, 1975; *The Pooh Perplex* by Frederick C. Crews, Milton Keynes, Buckinghamshire, Clark, 1979; *Winnie-the-Pooh, Capitalist Lackey?* by Simon Colverson, Andoversford, Gloucestershire, Whittington Press, n.d.; *The Tao of Pooh* by Benjamin Hoff, London, Methuen, 1982.

*   *   *

A.A. Milne was a successful writer and dramatist for many years before and after the publication of the children's books for which he is famous. Even in children's literature, the Christopher Robin stories and verses were not his only achievement; his other work included *Once on a Time*, a comic fantasy about the war between Euralia and Barodia, and *Toad of Toad Hall*, a play based on Kenneth Grahame's *The Wind in the Willows*. But Milne's reputation rests immovably on the four Christopher Robin books: two of stories, *Winnie-the-Pooh* and *The House at Pooh Corner*, and two of verses, *When We Were Very Young* and *Now We Are Six*.

All four were published in the space of five years, while Milne's son Christopher was a small boy. Clearly Christopher was the inspiration; and Pooh and Piglet, Tigger and Eeyore, Kanga and Roo were originally his toys. Mrs. Milne had already brought them to life and given them individual voices, said Milne in his autobiography, and the artist Ernest Shepard "drew them as one might say from the living model." It should be said, incidentally, that this is one of the few, exceptional cases—the Alice books are another—where the illustrator could claim to rank as co-creator. Christopher Robin,

Pooh, Piglet, and the rest are Shepard's characters as well as Milne's.

The setting of the stories that make up *Winnie-the-Pooh* and *The House at Pooh Corner* is the Hundred-Acre Wood: a happy, self-contained Arcadian world in which all animals are equal and none more equal than others, a reassuring world in which nobody will ever come to any harm. For the child reader or hearer, there is pleasant scope for condescension towards Pooh, the Bear of Very Little Brain, or towards Owl, whose wisdom and spelling fall so far short of his pretensions; whereas the child can identify contentedly with Christopher Robin, who always knows what to do, and to whom the animals go for help as if to an adult. The characters themselves are drawn with two or three simple strokes: Piglet is small, squeaky, and timid, Eeyore the donkey is gloomy, Tigger bouncy, Kanga maternal; and Pooh—admitted by the author to be the favourite among them all—is slow-witted, vain, greedy, and yet, in the way of teddy bears, extremely lovable. The incidents are not only funny but curiously memorable. Few adults who grew up on *Winnie-the-Pooh* can have forgotten Pooh dangling from a sky-blue balloon and pretending to be a cloud, or Pooh and Piglet trying to trap a Heffalump or tracking a Woozle round the spinney in the snow. The Expotition to the North Pole, the problem of What Tiggers Like to Eat, and the game of Pooh-sticks are lodged by now in what could almost be called the folk-memories of the 20th century.

One of the pleasures of these books is the way they move effortlessly into verse from time to time; Pooh is constantly singing a song or humming a hum. Milne was an extremely accomplished versifier. The two books of poems, *When We Were Very Young* and *Now We Are Six*, are notable for their ingenuity. Stanza forms and rhyme schemes are handled with such mastery that one hardly notices how intricate they often are. Milne was well aware of this: whatever else his verses lacked, he said, they were technically good.

Many of the verses are extremely funny: for example "The King's Breakfast" ("I do like a little bit of butter to my bread") or "The Little Black Hen" or "The Knight Whose Armour Didn't Squeak." Others are pitched precisely at the small child's eye level ("John had/Great big/Waterproof/Boots on" or "Halfway down the stairs/Is a stair/Where I sit./There isn't any/Other stair/quite like/It."). Charges of sentimentality have been levelled at Milne, especially over "Vespers" ("Little Boy kneels at the foot of the bed") but, interestingly, he himself said in a "preface to parents" that in his poems he had tried to indicate "the uncharming part of a child's nature: the egotism and the heartlessness"; and he pointed out that in "Vespers" it was not "God bless Mummy, because I love her so," but "God bless Mummy, I know that's right"; not "God bless Daddy because he buys me food and clothes," but "God bless Daddy, I quite forgot." Admittedly, when Milne goes on to say that "the truth about a child is also that, fresh from its bath, newly powdered and curled, it is a lovely thing, God wot," one is reminded that from a good deal of internal evidence it seems unlikely that he ever bathed the baby himself; and the world of Pooh and Christopher Robin is undoubtedly a comfortable, bourgeois, nanny-protected world. But then, that was the world in which, 60 years ago, Christopher Milne was a small boy.

The four books have one essential quality that makes children's books last; they appeal both to the child and to the adult who has pleasure in reading them aloud; indeed, they are never really outgrown. They have bubbling humour, easy and skilful craftsmanship, quick, light characterisation, and the much-maligned but genuine quality of charm.

—John Rowe Townsend

MINARIK, Else (Holmelund).   American.   Born in Denmark, 13 September 1920; emigrated to the United States, 1925. Educated at Queens College, New York. Married 1) Walter Minarik (died

1963), one daughter; 2) the journalist Homer Bigart in 1970. Reporter, *Daily Sentinel*, Rome, New York; teacher, Commack, Long Island, 1940's Address: c/o Greenwillow Books, 105 Madison Avenue, New York, New York 10016, U.S.A.

PUBLICATIONS FOR CHILDREN

Fiction

Little Bear, illustrated by Maurice Sendak. New York, Harper, 1957; Kingswood, Surrey, World's Work, 1965.
No Fighting, No Biting!, illustrated by Maurice Sendak. New York, Harper, 1958; Kingswood, Surrey, World's Work, 1969.
Father Bear Comes Home, illustrated by Maurice Sendak. New York, Harper, 1959; Kingswood, Surrey, World's Work, 1960.
Cat and Dog, illustrated by Fritz Siebel. New York, Harper, 1960; Kingswood, Surrey, World's Work, 1969.
Little Bear's Friend, illustrated by Maurice Sendak. New York, Harper, 1960; Kingswood, Surrey, World's Work, 1961.
Little Bear's Visit, illustrated by Maurice Sendak. New York, Harper, 1961; Kingswood, Surrey, World's Work, 1962.
Little Giant Girl and the Elf Boy, illustrated by Garth Williams. New York, Harper, 1963.
A Kiss for Little Bear, illustrated by Maurice Sendak. New York, Harper, 1968; Kingswood, Surrey, World's Work, 1969.
What If?, illustrated by Margaret Bloy Graham. New York, Greenwillow, 1987.
It's Spring!, illustrated by Margaret Bloy Graham. New York, Greenwillow, 1989.
Percy and the Five Houses, illustrated by James Stevenson. New York, Greenwillow, 1989.

Verse

The Winds That Come from Far Away and Other Poems, illustrated by Joan Berg. New York, Harper, 1964.

Other

Translator, *My Grandpa Is a Pirate*, by Jan Lööf. New York, Harper, 1968.

*   *   *

While recently she has written some charming picture books with a variety of characters, Else Minarik is still best-known for her series of books about Little Bear, an appealing cub who resembles a preschool child. Minarik's genius lies in her ability to create three-dimensional characters and humorous plots within the limits of a very simple text, accessible to beginning readers. In the Little Bear books, she focuses on the crucial concerns of young children: the tug and pull between the need for independence and taking risks and the need for reassurance and security; the interplay between the real world and the child's imaginary world; the need for acceptance and for friendship. Minarik's insight and emotional accuracy, coupled with her gentle humor, make these miniature stories rich and satisfying.

Little Bear is a thoroughly likeable character. He is imaginative, affectionate, and adventurous. He concocts fantasy games and tales, begs for stories, enjoys his friends and family. His world is secure and loving. He never ventures too far from home; his excursions are lighthearted. Play is his main occupation. No cares or responsibilities weigh him down.

In *Little Bear*, the first book in the series and the most satisfying because of the resolution, unity, and completeness of the stories,

Mother Bear is the stable, constant center of Little Bear's world. He ventures away from her to explore and play, but returns to her again and again for reassurance and affection. She never disappoints him, even in "Birthday Soup" when she arrives just in time with the cake. And she promises to be this dependable forever: "I never did forget your birthday, and I never will."

In *Father Bear Comes Home* Father Bear is less central to Little Bear's life, more exotic, but still gently accepting of Little Bear's imagination: "if you find a mermaid," said Father Bear, "ask her to picnic with us." Little Bear's world expands in *Little Bear's Friend*: "I climbed to a treetop and I saw the wide world." The first human character enters the series, a little girl named Emily. She becomes Little Bear's friend and joins the other animals in play. When Emily goes to school at the end of the book, Little Bear, left behind, cries. Once again, it is Mother Bear who gives comfort. "My goodness, Little Bear," she said. "You will be going to school, too, and you will learn to write. Then you can write to Emily." And so we learn that Little Bear is growing up.

Grandmother and Grandfather Bear are introduced in *Little Bear's Visit*, giving just the sort of wholehearted acceptance and love that grandparents are so good at. Little Bear "had some bread and jam, cake and cookies, milk and honey, and an apple. 'Have some more,' said Grandmother. 'Yes, thank you,' said Little Bear. 'I am not eating too much, am I?' 'Oh no, no!' said his grandmother." Both Grandmother and Grandfather tell stories, and the visit ends predictably with a sleeping Little Bear being carried home on his father's shoulder. It is no wonder that Little Bear decides to send Grandmother a present in *A Kiss for Little Bear*. He sends her a drawing and she sends him a kiss that gets passed from friend to friend before it finally reaches Little Bear. The story brings all the animals together for a festive celebration at the skunks' wedding.

The Little Bear books are notable for the graceful simplicity of the language, which avoids the choppy repetition characteristic of most books for beginning readers. And they are remarkable for their wealth of warmth, humor, and understanding. Although their format makes them accessible to new independent readers, it is the preschool child, hearing them read aloud, who will enjoy them most. They capture his world and highlight his concerns with clarity, insight, and love.

—Christine McDonnell

———————

MITCHELL, (Sibyl) Elyne (Keith, née Chauvel). British and Australian. Born in Melbourne, Victoria, 30 December 1913. Educated at St. Catherines, Melbourne. Married Thomas Walter Mitchell in 1935 (died 1984); two daughters and two sons (one deceased). Agent: Curtis Brown, 162–168 Regent Street, London W1R 5TB, England, or P.O. Box 19, Paddington, Sydney, New South Wales 2021. Address: Towong Hill, Corryong, Victoria 3707, Australia.

PUBLICATIONS FOR CHILDREN

Fiction

The Silver Brumby, illustrated by Ralph Thompson. London, Hutchinson, 1958; New York, Dutton, 1959.
Silver Brumby's Daughter, illustrated by Grace Huxtable. London, Hutchinson, 1960; as *The Snow Filly*, New York, Dutton, 1961.
Kingfisher Feather, illustrated by Grace Huxtable. London, Hutchinson, 1962.
Winged Skis, illustrated by Annette Macarthur-Onslow. London,

Hutchinson, 1964.

Silver Brumbies of the South, illustrated by Annette Macarthur-Onslow. London, Hutchinson, 1965.

Silver Brumby Kingdom, illustrated by Annette Macarthur-Onslow. London, Hutchinson, 1966.

Moon Filly, illustrated by Robert Hales. London, Hutchinson, 1968.

Jinki, Dingo of the Snows, illustrated by Michael Cole. London, Hutchinson, 1970.

Light Horse to Damascus, illustrated by Victor Ambrus. London, Hutchinson, 1971.

Silver Brumby Whirlwind, illustrated by Victor Ambrus. London, Hutchinson, 1973.

The Colt at Taparoo, illustrated by Victor Ambrus. Richmond, Victoria, Hutchinson, 1975; London, Hutchinson, 1976.

Son of the Whirlwind, illustrated by Victor Ambrus. Richmond, Victoria, and London, Hutchinson, 1976.

The Colt from Snowy River, illustrated by Victor Ambrus. Richmond, Victoria, Hutchinson, 1979; London, Hutchinson, 1980.

Snowy River Brumby, illustrated by Victor Ambrus. Richmond, Victoria, Hutchinson, 1980; London, Hutchinson, 1981.

Brumby Racer, illustrated by Victor Ambrus. Richmond, Victoria, Hutchinson, 1981; London, Hutchinson, 1982.

PUBLICATIONS FOR ADULTS

Novels

Flow River, Blow Wind. Sydney, Australasian Publishing Company, and London, Harrap, 1953.

Black Cockatoos Mean Snow. London, Hodder and Stoughton, 1956.

The Man from Snowy River (novelization of screenplay). Sydney and London, Angus and Robertson, 1982.

Discoverers of the Snowy Mountains (novelization of screenplay). Melbourne, Macmillan, 1985.

Other

Australia's Alps. Sydney and London, Angus and Robertson, 1942.

Speak to the Earth. Sydney and London, Angus and Robertson, 1945.

Soil and Civilization. Sydney and London, Angus and Robertson, 1946.

Images in Water. Sydney, Angus and Robertson, 1947.

Australian Treescape: A Photographic Study. Sydney, Ure Smith, 1950.

Light Horse: The Story of Australia's Mounted Troops. Melbourne and London, Macmillan, 1978.

The Snowy Mountains, photographs by Mike James. Adelaide, Rigby, 1980.

Chauvel Country: The Story of a Great Australian Pioneering Family. Melbourne, Macmillan, 1983.

A Vision of Snowy Mountains. Melbourne, Macmillan, 1988.

Editor, *Stories of Australian Horses.* South Yarra, Victoria, Currey O'Neil, 1983.

*

Elyne Mitchell comments:

The children's books simply grew out of the life we led. I had had six adult books published, and a growing family. The children were on Correspondence School work, which I had to teach. So *The Silver Brumby* was written for the eldest—something exciting about wild horses to introduce her to the mountain world which I loved so much. Very soon after it was written, the first road was built through the mountains, the Silver Brumby country. Some of the wilderness was no longer wilderness, but it was possible to take very young children skiing and walking, and the whole family grew to love the snow country. More Brumby stories were written, and a ski story for Harry, then a dingo story, and the story of World War I, in which the hero is a horse in my father's Light Horse, and more brumby stories.

*   *   *

In the Australian Alps where the Granite Tors of the Ramshead Range stretch between Mt. Kosciusko and the icy waters of the Crackenback River, the wind roars as it flattens the springy snowgrass, dark storms sweep across the skyline, and snow falls in silent flakes or comes in wild tremendous blizzards. In summer the gums and tussocks bow to the breezes and sunset turns every ridge and hill-top into gold and the valleys into "long fingers of blue shadow." This is the home country of Elyne Mitchell which she loves as passionately as she does her own horses and the wild horses who roam free. She writes lovingly of brumbies who move across the landscape together or alone, the colts who, run together and fight for a herd of their own as each young stallion establishes a claim to his own mares.

This is the country in which Bel Bel, the cream brumby mare, "gave birth to a colt foal, pale like herself or paler in a wild, black storm." So Thowra, the silver brumby, whose name means wind, born in the wind and as fleet as the wind, begins a long fight for supremacy over man and fellow beast. The initial story, *The Silver Brumby*, is written with a deeply lyrical feeling for the wild horses and the territory over which they roam, and was highly commended by the judges of the Australian Children's Book of the Year award in 1959, and the sequel, *Silver Brumby's Daughter*, was commended in 1961. *Winged Skis*, a mystery adventure set in the ski resorts of the Australian Alps, was highly commended in 1965.

Mitchell has been criticised in her own country for the anthropomorphism of her horses who, in the earlier stories, talk together in human terms. However, her brumby stories are widely read not only by children in Australia but have been translated into Spanish, German and Finnish, and are published both in Britain and the United States. They are strongly felt regional novels, connected as a series by the struggle for survival of each generation in freedom and dignity. There are savage and bloody battles between stallions, tender and loyal familial relationships between sire and progeny, the sexual pursuit of his mate by the male, and, in *Silver Brumby Whirlwind*, a mystical farewell and a sense of destiny fulfilled as Thowra bids farewell to his true friend Benni, the kangaroo. Then the whirlwind of the south encircles him, and he returns to his own country forever.

In the later Brumby books, which become a coda to the Silver Brumby saga, there is a strong sense of interaction between the humans from the homesteads of the Monaro and their horses. But always the primary human world is subsumed by the free-flowing secondary world of the silver brumby's progeny. The author's style now is less mannered than it was in the "middle" Brumby books and in *Jinki* where there is no circling dance of the brumbies to justify her elliptical use of language. *Light Horse to Damascus* is the story of a Queenslander, Dick Osborne, and his horse Karloo who with the Australian Light Horse beat their way across the desert to war and to Damascus. Literary techniques which succeeded when the author was writing from personal involvement are no longer valid. It is for her Silver Brumby that Mitchell will be remembered as a writer.

—H.M. Saxby

MITCHISON, Naomi (Margaret, née Haldane). British. Born in Edinburgh, 1 November 1897; daughter of the scientist John Scott Haldane; sister of J. B. S. Haldane, *q.v.* Educated at Lynam's School, Oxford; St. Anne's College, Oxford. Served as a volunteer nurse, 1915. Married G. R. Mitchison (who became Lord Mitchison, 1964) in 1916 (died 1970); three sons and two daughters. Labour candidate for Parliament, Scottish Universities constituency, 1935; member, Argyll County Council, 1945–66; member, Highland Panel, 1947–64, and Highlands and Islands Development Council, 1966–76. Tribal adviser, and Mmarona (Mother), to the Bakgatla of Botswana, 1963–89. D. Univ.: University of Stirling, Scotland, 1976; University of Dundee, Scotland, 1985; D. Litt.: University of Strathclyde, Glasgow, 1983. Honorary Fellow, St. Anne's College, 1980, and Wolfson College, 1983, both Oxford. Officer, French Academy, 1924. C. B. E. (Commander, Order of the British Empire), 1985. Address: Carradale House, Carradale, Campbeltown, Scotland.

PUBLICATIONS FOR CHILDREN

Fiction

The Hostages and Other Stories for Boys and Girls, illustrated by Logi Southby. London, Cape, 1930; New York, Harcourt Brace, 1931.
Boys and Girls and Gods. London, Watts, 1931.
The Big House. London, Faber, 1950.
Graeme and the Dragon, illustrated by Pauline Baynes. London, Faber, 1954.
The Land the Ravens Found, illustrated by Brian Allderidge. London, Collins, 1955.
Little Boxes, illustrated by Louise Annand. London, Faber, 1956.
The Far Harbour, illustrated by Martin Thomas. London, Collins, 1957.
Judy and Lakshmi, illustrated by Avinash Chandra. London, Collins, 1959.
The Rib of the Green Umbrella, illustrated by Edward Ardizzone. London, Collins, 1960.
The Fairy Who Couldn't Tell a Lie, illustrated by Jane Paton. London, Collins, 1963.
Henny and Crispies. Wellington, New Zealand, Department of Education, 1964.
Ketse and the Chief, illustrated by Christine Bloomer. London, Nelson, 1965; New York, Nelson, 1967.
Friends and Enemies, illustrated by Caroline Sassoon. London, Collins, 1966; New York, Day, 1968.
The Big Surprise. London, Kaye and Ward, 1967.
Don't Look Back, illustrated by Laszlo Acs. London, Kaye and Ward, 1969.
The Family at Ditlabeng, illustrated by Joanna Stubbs. London, Collins, 1969; New York, Farrar Straus, 1970.
Sun and Moon, illustrated by Barry Wilkinson. London, Bodley Head, 1970; Nashville, Nelson, 1973.
Sunrise Tomorrow. London, Collins, and New York, Farrar Straus, 1973.
The Danish Teapot, illustrated by Patricia Frost. London, Kaye and Ward, 1973.
Snake!, illustrated by Polly Loxton. London, Collins, 1976.
The Little Sister, with works by Ian Kirby and Keetla Masogo, illustrated by Angela Marrow. Cape Town, Oxford University Press, 1976.
The Wild Dogs, with works by Megan Biesele, illustrated by Polly Loxton. Cape Town, Oxford University Press, 1977.
The Brave Nurse and Other Stories, illustrated by Polly Loxton. Cape Town, Oxford University Press, 1977.
The Two Magicians, with Dick Mitchison, illustrated by Danuta Laskowska. London, Dobson, 1978.
The Vegetable War, illustrated by Polly Loxton. London, Hamish Hamilton, 1980.

Plays

Nix-Nought-Nothing: Four Plays for Children (includes *My Ain Sel'*, *Hobyah! Hobyah!*, *Elfen Hill*). London, Cape, 1928; New York, Harcourt Brace, 1929.
Kate Crackernuts: A Fairy Play. Oxford, Alden Press, 1931.
An End and a Beginning and Other Plays (includes *The City and the Citizens*, *For This Man Is a Roman*, *In the Time of Constantine*, *Wild Men Invade the Roman Empire*, *Charlemagne and His Court*, *The Thing That Is Plain*, *Cortez in Mexico*, *Akbar, But Still It Moves*, *The New Calendar*, *American Britons*). London, Constable, 1937; as *Historical Plays for Schools*, 2 vols., 1939.

Other

The Swan's Road (on the Vikings), illustrated by Leonard Huskinson. London, Naldrett Press, 1954.
The Young Alexander the Great, illustrated by Betty Middleton-Sandford. London, Parrish, 1960; New York, Roy, 1961.
Karensgaard: The Story of a Danish Farm. London, Collins, 1961.
The Young Alfred the Great, illustrated by Shirley Farrow. London, Parrish, 1962; New York, Roy, 1963.
Alexander the Great, illustrated by Rosemary Grimble. London, Longman, 1964.
A Mochudi Family, illustrated by Stephen John. Wellington, New Zealand, Department of Education, 1965.
Highland Holiday, photographs by John K. Wilkie. Wellington, New Zealand, Department of Education, 1967.
African Heroes, illustrated by William Stobbs. London, Bodley Head, 1968; New York, Farrar Straus, 1969.

Editor, *An Outline for Boys and Girls and Their Parents*. London, Gollancz, 1932.

PUBLICATIONS FOR ADULTS

Novels

The Conquered. London, Cape, and New York, Harcourt Brace, 1923.
Cloud Cuckoo Land. London, Cape, 1925; New York, Harcourt Brace, 1926.
The Corn King and the Spring Queen. London, Cape, and New York, Harcourt Brace, 1931; as *The Barbarian*, New York, Cameron, 1961.
The Powers of Light. London, Cape, and New York, Peter Smith, 1932.
Beyond This Limit. London, Cape, 1935.
We Have Been Warned. London, Constable, 1935; New York, Vanguard Press, 1936.
The Blood of the Martyrs. London, Constable, 1939; New York, McGraw Hill, 1948.
The Bull Calves. London, Cape, 1947.
Lobsters on the Agenda. London, Gollancz, 1952.
Travel Light. London, Faber, 1952.
To the Chapel Perilous. London, Allen and Unwin, 1955.
Behold Your King. London, Muller, 1957.
Memoirs of a Spacewoman. London, Gollancz, 1962.
When We Become Men. London, Collins, 1965.
Cleopatra's People. London, Heinemann, 1972.
Solution Three. London, Dobson, and New York, Warner, 1975.

Not by Bread Alone. London, Boyars, 1983.
Early in Orcadia. Glasgow, Drew, 1987.

Short Stories

When the Bough Breaks and Other Stories. London, Cape, and New York, Harcourt Brace, 1924.
Black Sparta: Greek Stories. London, Cape, and New York, Harcourt Brace, 1928.
Barbarian Stories. London, Cape, and New York, Harcourt Brace, 1929.
The Delicate Fire: Short Stories and Poems. London, Cape, and New York, Harcourt Brace, 1933.
The Fourth Pig: Stories and Verses. London, Constable, 1936.
Five Men and a Swan: Short Stories and Poems. London, Allen and Unwin, 1958.
Images of Africa. Edinburgh, Canongate, 1980.
What Do You Think Yourself? Scottish Short Stories. Edinburgh, Harris, 1982.
Beyond This Limit: Selected Shorter Fiction of Naomi Mitchison, edited by Isobel Murray. Edinburgh, Scottish Academic Press, 1986.

Plays

The Price of Freedom, with L. E. Gielgud (produced Cheltenham, 1949). London, Cape, 1931.
Full Fathom Five, with L.E. Gielgud (produced London, 1932).
As It Was in the Beginning, with L. E. Gielgud. London, Cape, 1939.
The Corn King, music by Brian Easdale, adaptation of the novel by Mitchison (produced London, 1950).
Spindrift, with Denis Macintosh (produced Glasgow, 1951). London, French, 1951.

Verse

The Laburnum Branch. London, Cape, 1926.
The Alban Goes Out. Harrow, Middlesex, Raven Press, 1939.
The Cleansing of the Knife and Other Poems. Edinburgh, Canongate, 1978.

Other

Anna Comnena. London, Howe, 1928.
Comments on Birth Control. London, Faber, 1930.
The Home and a Changing Civilisation. London, Lane, 1934.
Vienna Diary. London, Gollancz, and New York, Smith and Haas, 1934.
Socrates, with Richard Crossman. London, Hogarth Press, 1937; Harrisburg, Pennsylvania, Stackpole, 1938.
The Moral Basis of Politics. London, Constable, 1938; Port Washington, New York, Kennikat Press, 1971.
The Kingdom of Heaven. London, Heinemann, 1939.
Men and Herring: A Documentary, with Denis Macintosh. Edinburgh, Serif, 1949.
Other People's Worlds (travel). London, Secker and Warburg, 1958.
A Fishing Village on the Clyde, with G. W. L. Patterson. London, Oxford University Press, 1960.
Presenting Other People's Children. London, Hamlyn, 1961.
Return to the Fairy Hill (autobiography and sociology). London, Heinemann, and New York, Day, 1966.
The Africans: A History. London, Blond, 1970.
Small Talk: Memories of an Edwardian Childhood. London, Bodley Head, 1973.

A Life for Africa: The Story of Bram Fischer. London, Merlin Press, and Boston, Carrier Pigeon, 1973.
Oil for the Highlands? London, Fabian Society, 1974.
All Change Here: Girlhood and Marriage (autobiography). London, Bodley Head, 1975.
Sittlichkeit (lecture). London, Birkbeck College, 1975.
You May Well Ask: A Memoir 1920–1940. London, Gollancz, 1979.
Mucking Around: Five Continents over Fifty Years. London, Gollancz, 1981.
Margaret Cole 1893–1980. London, Fabian Society, 1982.
Among You, Taking Notes: The Wartime Diary of Naomi Mitchison 1939–1945, edited by Dorothy Sheridan. London, Gollancz, 1985.
Naomi Mitchison (autobiographical sketch). Edinburgh, Saltire Society, 1986.

Editor, *An Outline for Boys and Girls and Their Parents.* London, Gollancz, 1932.
Editor, with Robert Britton and George Kilgour, *Re-Educating Scotland.* Glasgow, Scoop, 1944.
Editor, *What the Human Race Is Up To.* London, Gollancz, 1962.

*

Manuscript Collections: National Library of Scotland, Edinburgh; University of Texas, Austin.

Naomi Mitchison comments:

I like writing for children because it means writing straight: not putting in clever bits or the kind of passage which is only there to impress and perhaps confuse the reader. Children are very critical and they want a good story. I think I am essentially a story teller, not an observer of manners or morals. I hope young people will get from my stories what I got from E. Nesbit's. I have been lucky to have a critical audience—children of my own and later grandchildren—who have kept me on my toes. I like reading my books aloud and they have been willing to listen and tell me, for instance, what I have left out and ought to have told the reader.

One big pleasure of writing children's books is that I need not be ashamed of having a happy ending, something I like increasingly as real life gets further away from it.

*   *   *

Naomi Mitchison's books have brought to many children in our epoch what feel like direct experiences of living at other times, in other places, and in alien cultures, among people with strange customs, clothes, festivals, beliefs, and assumptions about the world; people who yet remain vivid characters, with recognizable, sharable feelings—love, grief, homesickness, fear, anger, loyalty, and conflicts of loyalty.

Most of her stories are set in periods of deep collective changes, sudden or gradual, seen as they shape the lives of individuals and families. They may happen when great civilizations clash, or interact, or crossfertilize one another; or when industrial culture burns into some traditional way of life; or in the midst of modern war, when small groups lose their hostility to one another and unite against one great enemy, as in the enchanting *The Rib of the Green Umbrella,* whose hero is a boy in the Italian Resistance movement.

Among my own favourites is *The Hostages.* Though it contains brief historical sketches linking each tale with its predecessor along a thousand years, these stories are lively and concrete, untainted by the useful dreary hold-all abstractions of the textbook. And each story, wherever or whenever it takes place, has an extraordinarily vivid sensory quality. The details of landscapes, roads, houses, clothes, kitchens, all kinds of work are shown with a clarity which extends even to smells—of flowers or food or horses or sweaty crowds or blood. Such sensations, surviving through centuries of historical change, make every scene actual to the reader. So does Mitchison's quick awareness of moods and feelings and emotional reactions, whether in a tired young Etruscan boy captive made to walk, full of sadness and shame, along hot interminable streets in a Roman Triumph; in the chilly terror of a prehistoric girl child lost in British mountain mists near a sacred stone; in a modern misunderstanding between an English and an Indian schoolfriend (as in *Judy and Lakshmi*); or in the allegiances, divided between past wisdom and future change, of children growing up in Africa (where the author was in fact the adoptive mother of a Botswana tribe). Her own deep roots in Scottish history and folklore with its wizards and elves and nixies flowered as early as 1928 in *Nix-Nought-Nothing*, and underline her living understanding of such beliefs at any time.

Mitchison's work has not only given a great deal of enjoyment and opened many new horizons to readers and read-to; it has above all extended human sympathy to understand and to feel with and for "all sorts and conditions of men."

—Renée Haynes

MONJO, F(erdinand) N(icolas, III). American. Born in Stamford, Connecticut, 28 August 1924. Educated at Stamford High School; Columbia University, New York, B.A. 1946. Married Louise Elaine Lyczak in 1950; three sons and one daughter. Editor, Golden Books, Simon and Schuster, 1953–58, and American Heritage Junior Library, 1958–61, both New York; assistant director, Books for Boys and Girls, Harper and Row, New York, 1961–69; vice-president and editorial director, Books for Boys and Girls, Coward McCann and Geoghegan, New York, 1969–78. *Died 9 October 1978.*

PUBLICATIONS FOR CHILDREN

Fiction

Indian Summer, illustrated by Anita Lobel. New York, Harper, 1968; Kingswood, Surrey, World's Work, 1969.
The Drinking Gourd, illustrated by Fred Brenner. New York, Harper, 1970; Kingswood, Surrey, World's Work, 1971.
The One Bad Thing about Father, illustrated by Rocco Negri. New York, Harper, 1970.
Pirates in Panama, illustrated by Wallace Tripp. New York, Simon and Schuster, 1970.
The Jezebel Wolf, illustrated by John Schoenherr. New York, Simon and Schuster, 1971; London, Dent, 1973.
The Vicksburg Veteran, illustrated by Douglas Gorsline. New York, Simon and Schuster, 1971.
Slater's Mill, illustrated by Laszlo Kubinyi. New York, Simon and Schuster, 1972.
Rudi and the Distelfink, illustrated by George Kraus. New York, Windmill, 1972.
The Secret of the Sachem's Tree, illustrated by Margot Tomes. New York, Coward McCann, 1972.
Poor Richard in France, illustrated by Brinton Turkle. New York, Holt Rinehart, 1973.
Me and Willie and Pa, illustrated by Douglas Gorsline. New York, Simon and Schuster, 1973.
Grand Papa and Ellen Aroon, illustrated by Richard Cuffari. New York, Holt Rinehart, 1974.
The Sea-Beggar's Son, illustrated by C. Walter Hodges. New York,

Coward McCann, and London, Chatto and Windus, 1974.
King George's Head Was Made of Lead, illustrated by Margot Tomes. New York, Coward McCann, 1974.
Letters to Horseface, illustrated by Don Bolognese and Elaine Raphael. New York, Viking Press, 1975.
Gettysburg: Tad Lincoln's Story, illustrated by Douglas Gorsline. New York, Windmill, 1976.
Willie Jasper's Golden Eagle, illustrated by Douglas Gorsline. New York, Doubleday, 1976.
Zenas and the Shaving Mill, illustrated by Richard Cuffari. New York, Coward McCann, 1976.
The Porcelain Pagoda, illustrated by Richard Egielski. New York, Viking Press, 1976.
A Namesake for Nathan, illustrated by Eros Keith. New York, Coward McCann, 1977.
The House on Stink Alley: A Story about the Pilgrims in Holland, illustrated by Robert Quackenbush. New York, Holt Rinehart, 1977.
Prisoners of the Scrambling Dragon, illustrated by Arthur Geisert. New York, Holt Rinehart, 1980.

Other

Clarence and the Burglar, illustrated by Paul Galdone. New York, Coward McCann, 1973; Kingswood, Surrey, World's Work, 1975.

Translator, with Nina Ignatowicz, *The Crane*, by Reiner Zimnik illustrated by Zimnik. New York, Harper, 1970; London, Penguin, 1974.

*

Manuscript Collection: Kerlan Collection, University of Minnesota, Minneapolis.

*   *   *

F.N. Monjo's sense of history was people-centered. His historical books, novels, novelettes, easy-reading history books, and young biographies revolve around both the great and the near-great of the past. His own sense of family history was equally people-centered. He grew up surrounded by Americana in the stories his family told of his father's fur-merchant ancestors and his mother's plantation-bred forebears. Monjo determined his own writing course, having noted as an editor that "most of the fun of history lay in the details most children's books seemed to omit."

Monjo's ability to capture those detailed glimpses and transmit them to eager readers can be measured by the success of three of his many books: *The Drinking Gourd, Indian Summer*, and his extremely popular *Poor Richard in France*.

The Drinking Gourd is both fact and fiction in an easy-to-read format. Written in a straightforward, unadorned style, it is Monjo's second book, and it established both his reputation and the direction of his work. The story of an Underground Railway stop and the young minister's son who helps a family of black fugitives, the book appeals to both head and heart of the young reader. Monjo is not patronizing to either.

His first book, *Indian Summer*, was also well-received. But events in American publishing and the awareness of librarians have made the book a problem for Monjo. It is the story of a pioneer family and the mother and children who fight off an attack by cowardly marauding Indians. Monjo's talent for frill-less, direct storytelling was already very apparent in this story. But organizations like the Council on Interracial Books have been critical of the tale. And in her introduction to a selected bibliography, *American Indian Authors for Young Readers*, Mary Gloyne Byler escalated the attack. Monjo countered in a persuasive article in *School Library Journal* saying that an author has an obligation to inform himself on a topic but has the right to choose that topic and its point of view. Still, the controversy has not died.

In his National Book award nominee, *Poor Richard in France*, Monjo is at his unassailable best. Here his sense of humor—slightly impish and impious—can be plainly seen. In the five years between this book and his first, Monjo perfected his simple style. There is not a loose word or unnecessary phrase in the book, a charming anecdotal view of Franklin through his grandson's eyes. It is a technique Monjo used again and again in later books to great advantage. The use of the child narrator is a common juvenile book technique, but Monjo made the child's voice authentically his own. And his gimlet eye, slightly softened by the child's lens through which he peers, gives us a fresh and appealing look at any number of otherwise overworked periods of history.

Except for his friend and colleague Jean Fritz, Monjo had no peer in the writing of easy-reading history books.

—Jane Yolen

MONTGOMERY, L(ucy) M(aud). Canadian. Born in Clifton (now New London), Prince Edward Island, 30 November 1874. Educated at schools in Cavendish, Prince Edward Island, and Prince Albert, Saskatchewan; Prince of Wales College, Charlottetown, Prince Edward Island, teacher's certificate 1894, teacher's license 1895; Dalhousie College, Halifax, Nova Scotia, 1895–96. Married Ewan Macdonald in 1911; two sons. Schoolteacher, Bideford, 1894–95, 1896–97, and Lower Bedeque, 1897–98, both in Prince Edward Island; assistant postmistress, Cavendish, 1898–1911; staff member, Halifax *Echo*, 1901–02. Fellow, Royal Society of Arts, 1923. O.B.E. (Officer, Order of the British Empire), 1935. *Died 24 April 1942.*

PUBLICATIONS FOR CHILDREN

Fiction

Anne of Green Gables, illustrated by M.A. and W.A. Claus. Boston, Page, and London, Pitman, 1908.
Anne of Avonlea. Boston, Page, and London, Pitman, 1909.
Kilmeny of the Orchard, illustrated by George Gibbs. Boston, Page, and London, Pitman, 1910.
The Story Girl. Boston, Page, and London, Pitman, 1911.
Chronicles of Avonlea. Boston, Page, and London, Sampson Low, 1912.
The Golden Road. Boston, Page, 1913; London, Cassell, 1914.
Anne of the Island. Boston, Page, and London, Pitman, 1915.
Anne's House of Dreams. New York, Stokes, and London, Constable, 1917.
Rainbow Valley. Toronto, McClelland and Stewart, and New York, Stokes, 1919; London, Constable, 1920.
Further Chronicles of Avonlea..., illustrated by John Goss. Boston, Page, 1920; London, Harrap, 1953.
Rilla of Ingleside. Toronto, McClelland and Stewart, New York, Stokes, and London, Hodder and Stoughton, 1921.
Emily of New Moon. New York, Stokes, and London, Hodder and Stoughton, 1923.
Emily Climbs. New York, Stokes, and London, Hodder and Stoughton, 1925.
The Blue Castle. Toronto, McClelland and Stewart, New York, Stokes, and London, Hodder and Stoughton, 1926.
Emily's Quest. New York, Stokes, and London, Hodder and Stoughton, 1927.
Magic for Marigold. Toronto, McClelland and Stewart, New York, Stokes, and London, Hodder and Stoughton, 1929.
A Tangled Web. New York, Stokes, 1931; as *Aunt Becky Began It*, London, Hodder and Stoughton, 1931.
Pat of Silver Bush. New York, Stokes, and London, Hodder and Stoughton, 1933.
Mistress Pat: A Novel of Silver Bush. New York, Stokes, and London, Harrap, 1935.
Anne of Windy Poplars. New York, Stokes, 1936; as *Anne of Windy Willows*, London, Harrap, 1936.
Jane of Lantern Hill. Toronto, McClelland and Stewart, New York, Stokes, and London, Harrap, 1937.
Anne of Ingleside. New York, Stokes, and London, Harrap, 1939.
The Road to Yesterday. Toronto, McGraw Hill Ryerson, 1974; London, Angus and Robertson, 1975.
The Doctor's Sweetheart and Other Stories, edited by Catherine McLay. Toronto, McGraw Hill Ryerson, and London, Harrap, 1979.
Akin to Anne: Tales of Other Orphans, edited by Rea Wilmshurst. Toronto, McClelland and Stewart, 1988.

PUBLICATIONS FOR ADULTS

Verse

The Watchman and Other Poems. Toronto, McClelland and Stewart, 1916; New York, Stokes, 1917; London, Constable, 1920.
The Poetry of Lucy Maud Montgomery, edited by Kevin McCabe and John Ferns. Markham, Ontario, Fitzhenry and Whiteside, 1987.

Other

Courageous Women, with Marian Keith and Mabel Burns McKinley. Toronto, McClelland and Stewart, 1934.
The Green Gables Letters to Ephraim Weber 1905–1909, edited by Wilfrid Eggleston. Toronto, Ryerson Press, 1960.
The Alpine Path: The Story of My Career. Don Mills, Ontario, Fitzhenry and Whiteside, 1974.
My Dear Mr. M.: Letters to G.B. MacMillan, edited by Francis W.P. Bolger and Elizabeth R. Epperly. Toronto, McGraw Hill Ryerson, 1980.
Spirit of Place: L.M. Montgomery and Prince Edward Island, edited by Francis W. P. Bolger. Toronto, Oxford University Press, 1982.
The Selected Journals 1: 1889–1910 [2: 1910–1921], edited by Mary Rubio and Elizabeth Waterston. Toronto, Oxford University Press, 2 vols., 1985–87.

*

Critical Studies: *The Years Before "Anne"* by Francis W.P. Bolger, Charlottetown, Prince Edward Island Heritage Foundation, 1975; *The Wheel of Things: A Biography of L.M. Montgomery* by Mollie Gillen, Don Mills, Ontario, Fitzhenry and Whiteside, 1975, London, Harrap, 1976; *L.M. Montgomery: An Assessment* edited by John Robert Sorfleet, Guelph, Ontario, Canadian Children's Press, 1976; *L.M. Montgomery: A Preliminary Biography* by Ruth Weber Russell, Waterloo, Ontario, University of Waterloo Library, 1986.

*   *   *

At times, L.M. Montgomery's work challenges conventional

opinion about what makes a children's book. Is it a child or adolescent protagonist? Then what does one do with such books as *Anne's House of Dreams* and *Anne of Ingleside*, wherein Anne is a married mother with, eventually, five children? Is it comparatively innocuous subject matter? Then what does one do with the bitterness and jealousies evident in extended family relationships in many of the novels, or the marital hatred of Olivia and Peter Kirk in *Anne of Ingleside*, or the actual separation of the protagonist's parents in *Jane of Lantern Hill*—not to mention the frequent deaths of children and adults in the books? In fact, virtually all of Montgomery's fiction—including *The Blue Castle* and *A Tangled Web*, sometimes termed "adult" novels—is read and enjoyed by children and adolescents. This is because Montgomery deals with the psychological realities and conflicts of childhood and adolescence: need for an independent identity and for respect in an unjust and repressive world run by adults; flare-ups of hatred as well as love for family, relatives, and others; cross-sex hostility as well as affection; stirrings of passion versus fear of the changes it implies and inner perspectives it reveals; and so on. Indeed, a Freudian analysis of Montgomery's work, related to what we know of her inner life, could be at least as interesting—and revealing—as existing analyses of Lewis Carroll's *Alice in Wonderland*.

Her best-known book is *Anne of Green Gables*, first of a long series. This tale of an orphaned girl, sent by mistake to an elderly brother and sister who expect a boy, was enormously successful, and its heroine was termed by Mark Twain "the dearest, and most lovable child in fiction since the immortal Alice." The novel counterpoises child and adult perspectives, and this provides the basis for much of the novel's humour as well as some pathos. Anne is childhood spontaneity and imagination confronting adult conventionalism and dogmatism—both social and religious. Her words and actions effectively undermine the hypocrisy of the adult world and deflate its pretensions, while at the same time asserting the value of imaginative reality in a society which tends to deny it. And, while portraying Anne and the other characters—not to mention the land and the psychological relationships—realistically, Montgomery adds force to her depiction by drawing on the powers of fairytale archetype: the orphaned heroine coming to an unknown land, where she is involved in a case of mistaken identity, gains protectors, demonstrates her worth, defeats her enemies, and is finally reconciled with her Prince Charming, Gilbert Blythe.

Anne of Green Gables was followed by five other Anne books plus associated works such as *Rainbow Valley* and *Rilla of Ingleside* in which she appears. These later books show a considerable falling-away from the qualities of the first, as the original inspiration, a red-haired hoyden, inevitably growing up, encounters the more stringent social pressures and realities facing a young woman. Only *Anne of the Island*, which focuses on the exciting period of Anne's college years and her various courtships, comes anywhere near the readability of the first Anne book.

With *Emily of New Moon*, Montgomery initiated her second series. The Emily trilogy presents what might be called a "Portrait of the Artist" in the successive stages of girl, teenager, and young woman. As might be expected, these novels draw upon Montgomery's own childhood experiences even more extensively than her other books. The first novel reveals that, like Anne, Emily is an orphan, though her father's death is not antecedent to the book's beginning but occurs in the third chapter. Besides being a writer by nature and circumstance, Emily is notable for her "flashes" of mystical insight and moments of second sight. As for literary considerations, *Emily of New Moon*—like its sequels, *Emily Climbs* and *Emily's Quest*—competently relates symbolism, characterization, irony, and other stylistic concerns to a coherent and consistent exposition of theme and plot. In fact, except for a slightly over-rich effect in some of the passages representing Emily's thoughts, as a group this trilogy is better integrated and more satisfying than the Anne series.

Among Montgomery's later novels are *The Blue Castle* and *A Tangled Web*, appealing especially to adolescent girls. The former is clearly the better: except for some momentary falterings, it's a good, enjoyable book of its type—the identity crisis *cum* love story—which has a solid technical underpinning (e.g., the symbolism) as well. Reading it leads one to wonder—with reason, according to the Montgomery journals—about the state of Montgomery's own mind and marriage at the time. *A Tangled Web*, by contrast, has the defects its title implies; there are too many threads of plot and unbelievable situations, resulting in a not really satisfactory book.

In the fiction of Montgomery's final decade, two new protagonists are introduced. The first is Pat Gardiner—unusual in Montgomery's work because she has both parents living—who appears in *Pat of Silver Bush* and its sequel *Mistress Pat*. The earlier of the two is slightly the better. Its theme is the child's fear of change in the face of its inevitability. There are a few tear-jerking passages, and children might laugh at Judy Plum's Irish dialect when the novel is read aloud, but overall it is not a memorable book, perhaps because Pat is an Anne without spirit, an Emily without ability.

Montgomery's final heroine is Jane Stuart in *Jane of Lantern Hill*. Though with no outstanding talents, Jane has a hard core of selfhood which enables her to survive the bitter hostility of a tyrannical grandmother whose interference has maintained a ten-year marital separation between Jane's parents. Further, eventually Jane's self-directed actions enable her to become the instrument for her parents' reconciliation. This tale of tyranny, self-identity, and reunion is one that rewards psychological analysis. Also suggestive are the settings, rural Prince Edward Island and urban Toronto—the latter a notable innovation in Montgomery's novels. It's a book well worth a child's reading.

Overall, Montgomery's work is marked by a succession of unforgettable heroines seen against the backdrop of the beautiful Prince Edward Island landscape. Within them their isolated selves struggle to flourish against a set of outside pressures that urge conformity and denial of selfhood as the price of social acceptance. Yet they do not submit, and eventually their struggles are rewarded by their acceptance as them*selves*, not as mere specious semblances. And further, the outer Island landscape tends to operate in parallel to the heroines' inner lives, bringing comfort when needed, as it did for Montgomery herself. Indeed, in showing the importance of heroic inner struggle at the same time as stressing the outer physical landscape, Montgomery reveals herself to be operating within the mainstream of the Canadian literary tradition.

—John Robert Sorfleet

MONTGOMERY, Rutherford (George).   Also wrote as A.A. Avery; Al Avery; Everitt Proctor. American. Born in Straubville, North Dakota, 12 April 1894. Educated at schools in Velva, North Dakota; Colorado Agricultural College, Fort Collins; Western State College, Gunnison, Colorado; University of Nebraska, Lincoln. Served in the United States Army Air Corps, 1917–18: Sergeant. Married Eunice Opal Kirks in 1930; one son and two daughters. Teacher, Hot Springs Elementary School, Wyoming, 1915–17; teacher and principal, Delta County High Schools, Cedaredge, Colorado, 1921–24; principal, Montrose County Junior High School, Colorado, 1924–28; manager, Chamber of Commerce, 1928–32, and judge, Court of Records, 1932–37, Gunnison County, Colorado; state budget and efficiency commissioner, Denver, 1937–39; creative writing teacher, adult education classes, Los Gatos, California, 1955–57; writer, Walt Disney Studios, Burbank, California, 1958–62. Freelance writer, 1939–74; ghost writer for Dick Tracy series, 1941–46. Recipient: Western Writers of America Spur award, 1966. *Died 3 July 1985.*

PUBLICATIONS FOR CHILDREN

Fiction

Troopers Three, illustrated by Zhenya Gay. New York, Doubleday, 1932.

Broken Fang, illustrated by Lynn Bogue Hunt. Chicago, Donohue, 1935.

Carcajou, illustrated by L.D. Cram. Caldwell, Idaho, Caxton, 1936; Bristol, Arrowsmith, 1937.

Yellow Eyes, illustrated by L.D. Cram. Caldwell, Idaho, Caxton, 1937; London, Blackie, 1939.

Gray Wolf, illustrated by Jacob Bates Abbott. Boston, Houghton Mifflin, 1938; London, Hutchinson, 1939.

Timberline Tales, illustrated by Jacob Bates Abbott. Philadelphia, McKay, 1939; London, Hutchinson, 1951.

The Trail of the Buffalo, illustrated by Kurt Wiese. Boston, Houghton Mifflin, 1939.

Orphans of the Wild, illustrated by Janet Dean. Bristol, Arrowsmith, 1939.

Midnight, illustrated by Jacob Bates Abbott. New York, Holt, 1940; London, Hutchinson, 1944.

Stan Ball of the Rangers, illustrated by Jacob Bates Abbott. Philadelphia, McKay, 1941.

Ice Blink, illustrated by Rudolph Freund. New York, Holt, 1941; London, Hutchinson, 1949.

A Yankee Flier with the R.A.F. [*in the Far East, in North Africa, in the South Pacific, in Italy, over Berlin, in Normandy, on a Rescue Mission, under Secret Orders*] (as Al Avery), illustrated by Paul Laune and Clayton Knight. New York, Grosset and Dunlap, 9 vols., 1941–46.

Thumbs Up!, illustrated by E. Franklin Wittmack. Philadelphia, McKay, 1942; London, Hutchinson, 1943.

Hurricane Yank, illustrated by James Shimer. Philadelphia, McKay, 1942; London, Hutchinson, 1943.

Ghost Town Adventure, illustrated by Russell Sherman. New York, Holt, 1942.

Husky, Co-Pilot of the Pilgrim, illustrated by Jacob Landau. New York, Holt, 1942; London, Ward Lock, 1949.

Spike Kelly of the Commandos, illustrated by J.R. White. Racine, Wisconsin, Whitman, 1942.

Out of the Sun, illustrated by Clayton Knight. Philadelphia, McKay, 1943; London, Wells Gardner Darton, 1947.

War Wings, illustrated by Clayton Knight. Philadelphia, McKay, 1943; London, Wells Gardner Darton, 1948.

Trappers' Trail, illustrated by Harold Cressingham. New York, Holt, 1943; London, Hutchinson, 1948.

Warhawk Patrol, illustrated by Clayton Knight. Philadelphia, McKay, 1944; London, Wells Gardner Darton, 1948.

Big Brownie, illustrated by Jacob Landau. New York, Holt, 1944; London, Hutchinson, 1947.

Sea Raiders Ho!, illustrated by E. Franklin Wittmack. Philadelphia, McKay, 1945; London, Wells Gardner Darton, 1947.

Thunderboats Ho!, illustrated by E. Franklin Wittmack. Philadelphia, McKay, 1945; London, Wells Gardner Darton, 1948.

Rough Riders Ho!, illustrated by E. Franklin Wittmack. Philadelphia, McKay, 1946.

Blue Streak and Doctor Medusa, illustrated by Francis Kirn. Racine, Wisconsin, Whitman, 1946.

The Mystery of the Turquoise Frog, illustrated by Millard McGee. New York, Messner, 1946; London, Hutchinson, 1951.

Kildee House, illustrated by Barbara Cooney. New York, Doubleday, 1949; London, Faber, 1953.

The Mystery of Crystal Canyon, illustrated by Taylor Oughton. Philadelphia, Winston, 1951.

Hill Ranch, illustrated by Barbara Cooney. New York, Doubleday, 1951.

The Capture of the Golden Stallion, illustrated by George Giguere. Boston, Little Brown, 1951.

Wapiti, The Elk, illustrated by Gardell Christensen. Boston, Little Brown, 1952.

Mister Jim, illustrated by Paul Galdone. London, Faber, 1952; Cleveland, World, 1957.

McGonnigle's Lake, illustrated by Garry Mackenzie. New York, Doubleday, 1953; London, Faber, 1957.

White Mountaineer, illustrated by Gardell Christensen. Boston, Little Brown, 1953.

The Golden Stallion's Revenge, illustrated by George Giguere. Boston, Little Brown, 1953; London, Hodder and Stoughton, 1955.

The Golden Stallion to the Rescue, illustrated by George Giguere. Boston, Little Brown, 1954; London, Hodder and Stoughton, 1956.

Amikuk, illustrated by Marie Nonnast. Cleveland, World, 1955.

The Golden Stallion's Victory, illustrated by George Giguere. Boston, Little Brown, 1956; London, Hodder and Stoughton, 1957.

Claim Jumpers of Marble Canyon, illustrated by William Moyers. New York, Knopf, 1956.

Beaver Water, illustrated by Robert Doremus. Cleveland, World, 1956.

Mountain Man. Cleveland, World, 1957.

Jets Away! New York, Dodd Mead, 1957.

Tom Pittman, U.S.A.F., illustrated by Sam Kueskin. New York, Duell, 1957.

White Tail, illustrated by Marie Nonnast. Cleveland, World, 1958.

In Happy Hollow, illustrated by Harold Berson. New York, Doubleday, 1958.

The Silver Hills, illustrated by Robert Frankenberg. Cleveland, World, 1958.

Kent Barstow, Special Agent, illustrated by Sam Kueskin. New York, Duell, 1958.

The Golden Stallion and the Wolf Dog, illustrated by Percy Leason. Boston, Little Brown, and London, Hodder and Stoughton, 1958.

A Horse for Claudia and Dennis, with Natlee Kenoyer. New York, Duell, 1958.

Jet Navigator, Strategic Air Command, with Grover Heiman. New York, Duell, 1959.

The Golden Stallion's Adventure at Redstone, illustrated by Percy Leason. Boston, Little Brown, 1959; London, Hodder and Stoughton, 1960.

Tim's Mountain, illustrated by Julian de Miskey. Cleveland, World, 1959.

Missile Away. New York, Duell, 1959.

Mission Intruder, illustrated by Larry Lurin. New York, Duell, 1960.

The Odyssey of an Otter, illustrated by Hamilton Greene. New York, Golden Press, 1960; London, Purnell, 1962.

Weecha, The Raccoon, illustrated by Lawrence Tyler Dresser. New York, Golden Press, 1960; London, Purnell, 1962.

King of the Castle, illustrated by Russell Peterson. Cleveland, World, 1961.

Kent Barstow, Space Man, illustrated by Albert Orbaan. New York, Duell, 1961.

Klepty, illustrated by Polly Montgomery Hecathorn. New York, Duell, 1961.

Cougar, illustrated by Robert Magnusen. New York, Golden Press, 1961; London, Purnell, 1962.

El Blanco, illustrated by Gloria Stevens. New York, Golden Press,

1961.

The Capture of West Wind, illustrated by Albert Micale. New York, Duell, 1962.

Monte, The Bear Who Became a Celebrity, illustrated by Charles Geer. New York, Duell, 1962.

Kent Barstow and the Commando Flight, illustrated by George Wilson. New York, Duell, 1963.

Crazy Kill Range, illustrated by Lorence Bjorklund. Cleveland, World, 1963.

The Defiant Heart, illustrated by Paul Laune. New York, Duell, 1963.

McNulty's Holiday, illustrated by Charles Geer. New York, Duell, 1963.

Kent Barstow on a B-70 Mission. New York, Duell, 1964.

Kent Barstow Aboard the Dyna Soar, illustrated by George Wilson. New York, Duell, 1964.

Ghost Town Gold, illustrated by Lorence Bjorklund. Cleveland, World, 1965.

The Stubborn One, illustrated by Don Miller. New York, Duell, 1965.

Into the Groove. New York, Dodd Mead, 1966.

Thornbush Jungle, illustrated by Lorence Bjorklund. Cleveland, World, 1966.

A Kinkajou on the Town, illustrated by Lorence Bjorklund. Cleveland, World, 1967.

The Golden Stallion and the Mysterious Feud, illustrated by Albert Michini. Boston, Little Brown, 1967; Leicester, Brockhampton Press, 1970.

Corey's Sea Monster, illustrated by Harvey Kidder. Cleveland, World, 1969.

Pekan, The Shadow, illustrated by J.D. Nenninger. Caldwell, Idaho, Caxton, 1970.

Big Red, A Wild Stallion, illustrated by Pers Crowell. Caldwell, Idaho, Caxton, 1971.

Rufus, illustrated by J.D. Nenninger. Caldwell, Idaho, Caxton, 1973.

Fiction as Everitt Proctor

The Last Cruise of the "Jeanette". Philadelphia, Westminster Press, 1944.

Thar She Blows. Philadelphia, Westminster Press, 1945; London, Pictorial Art, 1947.

Men Against the Ice, illustrated by Isa Barnett. Philadelphia, Westminster Press, 1946.

Plays

Screenplays: *Killers of the High Country*, 1959; *The Hound That Thought He Was a Raccoon*, with Albert Aley, 1960; *Flash, The Teenage Otter*, with Albert Aley, 1961; *Sancho, The Homing Steer*, 1961; *Ida, The Off-Beat Eagle*, 1962; *El Blanco, The Legend of a White Stallion*, 1962.

Other

See Catch (reader), illustrated by Ralph Crosby Smith. Boston, Ginn, 1955.

The Golden Stallion Picture Book, illustrated by Al Brulé. New York, Grosset and Dunlap, 1962.

Snowman. New York, Duell, 1962.

The Living Wilderness, illustrated by Campbell Grant. New York, Torquil, 1964.

Dolphins as They Are. New York, Duell, 1966.

Editor, *A Saddlebag of Tales: A Collection of Stories by Members of the Western Writers of America*, illustrated by Sam Savitt. New York, Dodd Mead, 1959.

PUBLICATIONS FOR ADULTS

Novels

Call of the West. New York, Grosset and Dunlap, 1933.

Anything for a Quiet Life (as A.A. Avery). New York, Farrar and Rinehart, 1942.

Black Powder Empire. Boston, Little Brown, 1955; London, Ward Lock, 1957.

Posted Water. London, Ward Lock, 1959.

Sex Isn't Everything. New York, Torquil, 1961.

Smoky Trail. London, Ward Lock, 1967.

Other

High Country. New York, Derrydale Press, 1938.

*

Manuscript Collection: University of Oregon Library, Eugene.

* * *

Rutherford Montgomery was of the American west, and he wrote with love and perception of its landscape, animals, and people. Almost all his fiction for boys and girls mirrors the mountains, deserts, flora, and fauna through vivid descriptions, much as the adult western novels of Ernest Haycox, Luke Short, and Bill Gulick are known for the same colorful background in which to spin a good yarn.

Montgomery begins his stories with action, and then pauses to paint the setting for his reader, as in *The Golden Stallion and the Mysterious Feud*:

> The scene was familiar to Charlie, but it always made him pause. There was an immensity to the picture which made him feel small and not very important. The park lay like a green jewel enclosed in a circle of forest that rose and sloped upward over the foothills toward the steep ridges. The ridges angled on up to form peaks and rims of naked granite high above timberline, where banks of snow made patterns on the north slopes. The whole scene was etched against an incredibly blue sky. Here there was no roar of highway traffic, no gray haze of city smog. This was as it had been for a thousand years.

The Golden Stallion series, like successful series books by other writers, will find a place on library shelves for many years. Montgomery's plots are simple, with idyllic settings and stories well-paced, featuring a young hero and his Mexican-American friend, Pedro, working the western range, desert, and mountains. The stallion is described with more love, color, and strength than are Montgomery's human characters, perhaps indicating his own sense of values. This latter element may reflect his years in Hollywood with Walt Disney Studios.

The successful book often engenders a sequel or series, and Montgomery, craftsman and businessman, was very much aware of the engaging formula which needs only a bit of transplanting to flourish and provide fruit. *Kildee House* places a retired, simple man, Kildee, in a tiny home in the midst of a redwood forest where both animals with human character qualities and a boy and girl with less complex animal characteristics adopt Mr. Kildee. The boy represents greed, lack of respect for nature and others; the lonely girl needs love and understanding. Kildee ministers to the young people's needs and becomes overwhelmed by the complexities of caring for the adopted animal cohabitants of his tree house. *Kildee House* is a charming book, and Montgomery reused these story elements in writing *McGonnigle's Lake*, another formula story including two young people on motorbikes and an old loner, a prospector with a large menagerie of animals (burros, beavers, a marmot, a badger, and a snake). The simple tale of solving the elderly prospector's problems is set in the California coastal range, salted with gold and a Rocky Mountain flavor.

Claim Jumpers of Marble Canyon provides still another good adventure. It will not survive for its literary quality, but its good design with two boys aiding an old prospector uncle on a uranium search will endure. The three undergo the ravages of a sandstorm, desert thirst, snakes, a chase, and confrontation with claim jumpers. The western dialogue seems straight from Disney and television: "We'll tie this varmint so he can't follow us." Active verbs, simple sentences, quick dialogue, and good plotting sustain this story and almost all Montgomery's fiction, whether he writes of the American west, or the wild animals he knows well, or of early aviation from his military experiences in World War I.

As the bibliography indicates, Montgomery was prolific, and what will endure of his writing is that element he knew best—the American west with dramatic and occasionally stark landscape, its wild animals depicted with understanding and love or respect, its inhabitants—ranchers, miners, prospectors, hermits, and honest, hard-working youngsters. He adapted his writing to the contemporary reader by setting his young folks on motorbikes rather than horses, placing a Geiger counter in his/her hand rather than a pick axe, creating a sidekick who represents a minority group as well as a friend. These adjustments to rope in the wandering reader may detract from the lasting significance of Montgomery's work, but his books were not written for posterity. He created simple stories reflecting values embraced by parents and teachers. These stories do have a timeless quality because Montgomery set them against a timeless background.

—Edward Kemp

MOORE, Dorothea (Mary). British. Born in London in 1881. Educated at Godolphin School, Salisbury; Cheltenham Ladies College. Served in the Voluntary Aid Detachment, 1914. Actress on tour with the Alex Maclean Company, 1911–12. *Died 19 May 1933.*

PUBLICATIONS FOR CHILDREN

Fiction

Mistress Dorothy. London, National Society, 1902.
Evelyn. London, Nelson, 1904.
God's Bairn. London, Blackie, 1904; as *Marlowe of the Fens*, 1934.
Brown. London, Nisbet, 1905; New York, Eaton and Mains, 1907; as *Three Feet of Valour*, Nisbet, 1921.
Sydney Lisle, illustrated by Wal Paget. London, Partridge, 1905; Philadelphia, McKay, 1910; as *A Golden Dawn*, Partridge, 1925.
Jepthah's Lass. London, Partridge, 1907.
Elizabeth's Angel and Other Stories. London, National Society, 1907.
Knights of the Red Cross. London, Nelson, 1907.
Pamela's Hero, illustrated by A.A. Dixon. London, Blackie, 1907.

A Plucky School-Girl. London, Nisbet, 1908.
The Christmas Children. London, Partridge, 1909; as *The Children of the Marshes*, 1927.
The Luck of Ledge Point, illustrated by C. Horrell. London, Blackie, 1909.
A Lady of Mettle. London, Partridge, 1910.
The Making of Ursula. London, Partridge, 1910.
The Lucas Girls, illustrated by Tom Peddie. London, Partridge, 1911.
Under the Wolf's Fell. London, Partridge, 1911.
Nadia to the Rescue. London, Nisbet, 1912.
A Runaway Princess. London, Partridge, 1912.
Terry the Girl-Guide, illustrated by A.A. Dixon. London, Nisbet, 1912.
A Brave Little Royalist, illustrated by John Campbell. London, Nisbet, 1913.
Only a Girl! London, Partridge, 1913.
Rosemary the Rebel. London, Partridge, 1913.
Captain Nancy. London, Nisbet, 1914.
Cecily's Highwayman, illustrated by John Campbell. London, Nisbet, 1914.
Septima, Schoolgirl. London, Cassell, 1915.
Wanted, An English Girl: The Adventures of an English Schoolgirl in Germany. London, Partridge, 1916.
The New Girl. London, Nisbet, 1917.
The Head Girl's Sister. London, Nisbet, 1918.
Tam of Tiffany's. London, Partridge, 1918.
Her Schoolgirl Majesty. London, Partridge, 1918.
Head of the Lower School. London, Nisbet, 1919; New York, Putnam, 1920.
A Nest of Malignants. London, S.P.C.K., 1919; New York, Macmillan, 1920.
The Right Kind of Girl. London, Nisbet, 1920.
The New Prefect. London, Nisbet, 1921.
An Adventurous Schoolgirl, illustrated by Archibald Webb. London, Cassell, 1921; New York, Funk and Wagnalls, 1922.
Greta of the Guides. London, Partridge, 1921.
Guide Gilly, Adventurer. London, Nisbet, 1922.
The New Girl at Pen-y-Gant. London, Nisbet, 1922.
The Only Day-Girl. London, Nisbet, 1923.
A Young Pretender. London, Nisbet, 1924.
Fen's First Term. London, Cassell, 1924.
In the Reign of the Red Cap, illustrated by Archibald Webb. London, Sheldon Press, 1924.
Smuggler's Way, illustrated by H.M. Brock. London, Cassell, 1924.
A Rough Night. London, Partridge, 1925.
"Z" House. London, Nisbet, 1925.
My Lady Venturesome. London, Sheldon Press, 1926.
Perdita, Prisoner of War. London, Cassell, 1926.
A Schoolgirl Adventurer. London, A. and C. Black, 1927.
Tenth at Trinder's. London, Cassell, 1927.
Adventurers All!, illustrated by P. Walford. London, Partridge, 1927.
Brenda of Beech House. London, Nisbet, 1927.
Seraphine-Di Goes to School. London, Religious Tract Society, 1927.
Darry the Dauntless. London, Cassell, 1928.
A Rebel of the Third. London, Nisbet, 1929.
Adventurers Two. London, Sheldon Press, 1929.
The Wrenford Tradition. London, Nisbet, 1929.
Judy, Patrol Leader [Lends a Hand]. London, Collins, 2 vols., 1930–32.
Nicky of Nine Schools. London, Oxford University Press, 1932.
Sara to the Rescue. London, Nisbet, 1932.
At Friendship's Call. London, Oxford University Press, 1932.

Dick of the Day-Girls. London, Nisbet, 1933.
Queens for Choice. London, Oxford University Press, 1934.
Babs Goes to Court. London, Sheldon Press, 1936.
The Crooked Headstone. London, Pearson, 1939.

PUBLICATIONS FOR ADULTS

Novels

My Lady Bellamy. London, Nisbet, 1909.
When the Moon Is Green. London, Partridge, 1917.

Plays

My Lady Bellamy (produced Margate, Kent, and London, 1910).
The Grey Mask, with Alexander Maclean (produced Margate, Kent, 1912).
By the King's Leave, with Alexander Maclean (produced Margate, Kent, 1912).
Lilies and Lavender (produced London, 1929).

*   *   *

Like Bessie Marchant, Angela Brazil, and others who were writing at the start of the 20th century, Dorothea Moore endeavoured to produce a more robust type of fiction than the unexciting domestic stories that had hitherto been staple reading matter for girls. Her books were popular for almost four decades and her range was wide. She contributed poems, plays, and well-structured short stories to several children's magazines, including *Little Folks* and *The Girls' Own Paper,* and to *Blackie's,* the *Oxford,* and *British Girls'* annuals. The liveliness of her short stories, however, was not always conveyed in her novels which, particularly after the 1920's, sometimes lacked style and inventiveness.

Some of her school stories feature rebellious characters like the heroine of *Tenth at Trinder's,* who initially resist discipline and conformity but are nudged by staunch chums, admired prefects, and fearfully understanding headmistresses into acceptance of team-spiritedness and loyalty to the school. Moore makes strong use of the customary alarms and accidents of the genre (girls rescuing schoolmates from burning, drowning, or literal cliff-hanging, etc.). But she is at her best when describing lower key aspects of school life in a series of persuasive images of girls cycling to school in broad-brimmed felt hats and well-brushed blue serge gymslips, or changing into white frocks for "exuberantly cooked" suppers, and dutifully awaiting their turns on bathroom rotas, and so on. These vignettes not only convey the rhythms of school routines but a greater sense of period (the 1920's) than Moore managed to achieve in her historical stories. *Cecily's Highwayman, In the Reign of the Red Cap, The Luck of Ledge Point,* and several other of her historical novels lack this integral feeling for period, although, with plenty of peripheral excitement and atmosphere, they succeed at the romance level.

A Girl Guide Commissioner, Moore made her most significant contribution to girls' fiction with *Terry the Girl-Guide* in 1912. This was the first full-length guiding novel to be published, and its authentic re-creation of the pioneering mood set a pattern that other authors were to follow for some 30 years. Moore produced colourful variations on the theme in several stories of teenage princesses from vaguely Ruritanian backgrounds who were redeemed—either physically or psychologically—by contact with the idealism, resourcefulness, and grit of the typical British Girl Guide (*A Young Pretender, Brenda of Beech House,* etc.). By 1930, however, she seemed at last to have exhausted guiding as a story writing stimulus, and *Judy, Patrol Leader* is no more than a disappointing rehash of the in-

gredients that made her vigorous early books on the theme so memorable.

Many of Moore's heroines experience engaging flashes of wry self-awareness, but the main characteristic of her stories is that they have an overall charm that has ensured their long-lasting appeal to girls—and to women who now read them nostalgically.

—Mary Cadogan

———

MOORHEAD, Diana (née Kinns). New Zealander. Born in Horsell, Surrey, England, 28 May 1940. Educated at St. Mary's, Horsell, 1946–51; St. Catherine's, Bramley, Surrey, 1951–52; Waihi College, New Zealand, 1953–57; Auckland University (Lissie Rathbone scholar, 1958), 1958–60, B.A. in English 1961. Married Raymond John Moorhead in 1961; one son and one daughter. Sales assistant, Whitcombe and Tombs, booksellers, Auckland, 1961–62; play center supervisor, Swanson and Te Atatu, 1967–69; librarian, Massey High School, Auckland, 1969–80, and Kelston Boys High School, 1981–85; mobile librarian, Takapuna City, 1986–87. Since 1987 librarian-in-charge, Glenfield Public Library. Recipient: International Youth Library bursary, 1976, 1981. Address: 58 Yeovil Road, Te Atatu, Auckland 8, New Zealand.

PUBLICATIONS FOR CHILDREN

Fiction

In Search of Magic, illustrated by Keith Clark. Auckland and Leicester, Brockhampton Press, 1971.
The Green and the White, illustrated by Victor Ambrus. Leicester, Brockhampton Press, 1974.
Gull Man's Glory, illustrated by Sam Thompson. London, Hodder and Stoughton, 1976.

*

Manuscript Collection: International Youth Library, Schloss Blutenburg, Munich, West Germany.

Diana Moorhead comments:

Apart from *In Search of Magic* (an early work for younger readers), my books are fantasies for the 10–12 age group. I try to create an exact and inherently logical setting for each one, as background for the themes I am exploring; and in fact the setting is often in my mind long before the plot develops. I write partly for myself, but mostly to share with others the delight that fantasy has always given me.

*   *   *

Diana Moorhead's first book, *In Search of Magic,* while it gave some hint of her ability to produce a simple, well-rounded story for younger children, was unremarkable; her reputation as a children's novelist began with the appearance of the second book, *The Green and the White.*

Here, her capacity for telling a well-paced story with dexterity and economy is demonstrated beyond doubt. Jochim, the young king of Verdontis, is charged by his wizard to enter the northern mountains, home of the feared Shrinn, in search of the Luck Charm which alone can arrest the blight which is upon his kingdom. Ostensibly an adventure story, the tale has depths which explore human prejudice and superstitions. Before all else, it is an exploration of the power of good over evil, of intelligent persistence in the face of ignorance.

The characters are created precisely. A hint of sentimentality in the handling of the relationship between Jochim and his betrothed, Elise, does not mar the whole. The novel is clearly intended for the 9-to-11 age group for which subtlety of sexual relationship is irrelevant. In fact, Moorhead handled a sophisticated theme deftly, ensuring access at all stages of the book to children of this age group.

Gull Man's Glory predicts a world which, presumably recovering from nuclear devastation, has assumed a form dictated by the aridness of the land. A race of winged humans, accidentally produced before the catastrophe by irresponsible genetic experiment, now forms colonies of sea-birds on the cliffs, Flet, a young gull man who has been taught to read secretly by the Meddick, or wise man, becomes involved with Lorianne, ward of the Lord of Southmark (one of the small feudal kingdoms into which the land has been divided). Flet is a youth of spirit and intelligence whose dawning realisation that it is possible to question, added to his dangerous, if chivalrous decision to protect Lorianne from her uncle's plotting, leads him, by route of fast-moving adventures, to both an acceptance of his own difference and the vision of richer possibilities in life.

Again, direct, simple language is used skilfully, to create a place the reader can believe in and characters who live. The difficult parable form is used with apparent ease; the tale is credible, the issues real.

This ease—the natural ability to tell a story which flows—is Moorhead's chief strength. The fact that it brings her books within reach of the less intellectual child, while still providing depths of underlying significance, is fortuitously good, a characteristic regrettably rare in work of quality.

—Dorothy Butler

MORAY WILLIAMS, Ursula. British. Born in Petersfield, Hampshire, 19 April 1911. Educated privately and at schools in Annecy, France, and Winchester. Married Peter John in 1935 (died 1974); four sons. Agent: Curtis Brown Ltd., 162–168 Regent Street, London W1R 5TA. Address: Court Farm House, Beckford, near Tewkesbury, Gloucestershire, England.

PUBLICATIONS FOR CHILDREN

Fiction

Jean-Pierre, illustrated by the author. London, A. and C. Black, 1931.
The Pettabomination, illustrated by the author. London, Archer, 1933; revised edition, London, Lane, 1948.
Kelpie, The Gipsies' Pony, illustrated by the author and Barbara Moray Williams. London, Harrap, 1934; Philadelphia, Lippincott, 1935.
Anders and Marta, illustrated by the author. London, Harrap, 1935.
Adventures of Anne, illustrated by the author. London, Harrap, 1935.
The Twins and Their Ponies, illustrated by the author. London, Harrap, 1936.
Sandy-on-the-Shore, illustrated by the author. London, Harrap, 1936.
Tales for the Sixes and Sevens, illustrated by the author. London, Harrap, 1936.
Dumpling, illustrated by the author. London, Harrap, 1937.

Elaine of La Signe, illustrated by the author and Barbara Moray Williams. London, Harrap, 1937; as *Elaine of the Mountains*, Philadelphia, Lippincott, 1939.
Adventures of Boss and Dingbat, photographs by Peter John. London, Harrap, 1937.
Adventures of the Little Wooden Horse, illustrated by Joyce Lankester Brisley. London, Harrap, 1938; Philadelphia, Lippincott, 1939.
Adventures of Puffin, illustrated by Mary Shillabeer. London, Harrap, 1939.
Peter and the Wanderlust, illustrated by Jack Matthew. London, Harrap, 1939; Philadelphia, Lippincott, 1940; revised edition, as *Peter on the Road*, London, Hamish Hamilton, 1963.
Pretenders' Island, illustrated by Joyce Lankester Brisley. London, Harrap, 1940; New York, Knopf, 1942.
A Castle for John-Peter, illustrated by Eileen Soper. London, Harrap, 1941.
Gobbolino the Witch's Cat. London, Harrap, 1942.
The Good Little Christmas Tree, illustrated by the author. London, Harrap, 1943.
The Three Toymakers, illustrated by the author. London, Harrap, 1945; revised edition, London, Hamish Hamilton, 1970; New York, Nelson, 1971.
The House of Happiness, illustrated by the author. London, Harrap, 1946.
Malkin's Mountain, illustrated by the author. London, Harrap, 1948; revised edition, London, Hamish Hamilton, 1970; New York, Nelson, 1972.
The Story of Laughing Dandino, illustrated by the author. London, Harrap, 1948.
Jockin the Jester, illustrated by Barbara Moray Williams. London, Chatto and Windus, 1951; Nashville, Nelson, 1973.
The Binklebys at Home, illustrated by the author. London, Harrap, 1951.
The Binklebys on the Farm, illustrated by the author. London, Harrap, 1953.
The Secrets of the Wood, illustrated by the author. London, Harrap, 1955.
Grumpa, illustrated by the author. Leicester, Brockhampton Press, 1955.
Goodbody's Puppet Show, illustrated by the author. London, Hamish Hamilton, 1956.
Golden Horse with a Silver Tail, illustrated by the author. London, Hamish Hamilton, 1957.
Hobbie, illustrated by the author. Leicester, Brockhampton Press, 1958.
The Moonball, illustrated by the author. London, Hamish Hamilton, 1958; New York, Meredith Press, 1967.
The Noble Hawks. London, Hamish Hamilton, 1959; as *The Earl's Falconer*, New York, Morrow, 1961.
The Nine Lives of Island Mackenzie, illustrated by Edward Ardizzone. London, Chatto and Windus, 1959; as *Island Mackenzie*, New York, Morrow, 1960.
Beware of the Animal, illustrated by Jane Paton. London, Hamish Hamilton, 1964; New York, Dial Press, 1965.
Johnnie Tigerskin, illustrated by Diana Johns. London, Harrap, 1964; New York, Duell, 1966.
O for a Mouseless House!, illustrated by the author. London, Chatto and Windus, 1964.
High Adventure, illustrated by Prudence Seward. London, Nelson, 1965.
Cruise of the "Happy-Go-Gay," illustrated by Gunvor Edwards. London, Hamish Hamilton, 1967; New York, Meredith Press, 1968.
A Crown for a Queen, illustrated by Shirley Hughes. London, Hamish Hamilton, and New York, Meredith Press, 1968.

The Toymaker's Daughter, illustrated by Shirley Hughes.   London, Hamish Hamilton, 1968; New York, Meredith Press, 1969.

Mog, illustrated by Faith Jaques.   London, Allen and Unwin, 1969.

Boy in a Barn, illustrated by Terence Dalley.   London, Allen and Unwin, and New York, Nelson, 1970.

Johnnie Golightly and His Crocodile, illustrated by Faith Jaques.   London, Chatto Boyd and Oliver, 1970; New York, Harvey House, 1971.

Traffic Jam, illustrated by Robert Hales.   London, Chatto and Windus, 1971.

Man on a Steeple, illustrated by Mary Dinsdale.   London, Chatto and Windus, 1971.

Mrs. Townsend's Robber, illustrated by Gavin Rowe.   London, Chatto and Windus, 1971.

Out of the Shadows, illustrated by Gavin Rowe.   London, Chatto and Windus, 1971.

Castle Merlin.   London, Allen and Unwin, and Nashville, Nelson, 1972.

A Picnic with the Aunts, illustrated by Faith Jaques.   London, Chatto and Windus, 1972.

The Kidnapping of My Grandmother, illustrated by Mike Jackson.   London, Heinemann, 1972.

Tiger-Nanny, illustrated by Gunvor Edwards.   Leicester, Brockhampton Press, 1973; Nashville, Nelson, 1974.

Grandpapa's Folly and the Woodworm-Bookworm, illustrated by Faith Jaques.   London, Chatto and Windus, 1974.

The Line, illustrated by Barry Wilkinson.   London, Penguin, 1974.

No Ponies for Miss Pobjoy, illustrated by Pat Marriott.   London, Chatto and Windus, 1975; Nashville, Nelson, 1976.

Bogwoppit, illustrated by Shirley Hughes.   London, Hamish Hamilton, and Nashville, Nelson, 1978.

Jeffy, The Burglar's Cat, illustrated by David McKee.   London, Andersen Press, 1981.

Bellabelinda and the No-Good Angel, illustrated by Glenys Ambrus.   London, Chatto and Windus, 1982.

The Further Adventures of Gobbolino and the Little Wooden Horse, illustrated by Pauline Baynes.   London, Penguin, 1984.

Spid, illustrated by David McKee.   London, Andersen Press, 1985.

Grandma and the Ghowlies, illustrated by Susan Varley.   London, Andersen Press, 1986.

Paddy on the Island, illustrated by Tor Morisse.   London, Andersen Press, 1987.

Plays

The Autumn Sweepers and Other Plays (includes *Mother Josephine Bakes Bread*, *Forfeits*, *Tavi of Gold*, *The Organ Grinder: A Mime*, *A Sea Ballet*), illustrated by the author.   London, A. and C. Black, 1933.

The Good Little Christmas Tree, from her own story.   London, French, 1951.

The House of Happiness, from her own story.   London, French, 1951.

The Pettabomination, from her own story.   London, French, 1951.

Verse

Grandfather, illustrated by the author.   London, Allen and Unwin, 1933.

Other

For Brownies: Stories and Games for the Pack and Everybody Else, illustrated by the author.   London, Harrap, 1932.

More for Brownies, illustrated by the author.   London, Harrap, 1934.

Children's Parties, and Games for a Rainy Day.   London, Corgi, 1972.

*

Ursula Moray Williams comments:

I began to write in 1930 and *Jean-Pierre* was published in 1931. Of course I had written all my life, but this was my first published work, and there has been a steady flow ever since. I have only written childrens' books (not *for* children, but they seem to like them!).

We were read aloud to all our childhood, but I never read childrens' books now. I shall read them avidly when I have finished writing.

*   *   *

Ursula Moray Williams has written over 60 children's stories and plays, notable for the variety of their appeal to a range of ages from three to 13; and though some of the earlier stories may now seem old-fashioned, she continues to write with unabated zest. A good storyline, a simple and compelling lucidity of language, a firm though not overpowering moral attitude, and an irrepressible sense of fun are common to all her stories. Kindness, compassion, and concern for others are almost invariably set against selfish greed, heartlessness, trickery, and violence, a confrontation which is most explicit in three stories about a beautiful but heartless and often maliciously spiteful doll, Marta. *The Three Toymakers*, *Malkin's Mountain*, and *The Toymaker's Daughter* are set in a fantasy kingdom of peasants, mountain scenery and magic with a strong folklore element in the telling, though they are less astringent than the traditional folktale. Akin to these tales are *Adventures of the Little Wooden Horse* and *Gobbolino the Witch's Cat*. They share the fantasy folktale element, but the observation of the complexities of good and evil is sharper and less sentimental. As the stories are episodic they are well-suited to reading aloud in instalments to six or seven-year-olds, and the two main characters, the "quiet little horse" and the unhappy witch's cat, still have charm and sure appeal for children. In a pleasantly alarming and adventurous sequel, *The Further Adventures of Gobbolino and the Little Wooden Horse*, these two characters combine to rescue Gobbolino's wicked sister Sootica from the witch, demonstrating incidentally the values of a kind heart and faithfulness and that even witches deserve loyalty and compassion.

In a different, lighthearted, and amusing vein of fantasy are two picture books with an Edwardian flavour, the ingenious *Grandpapa's Folly and the Woodworm-Bookworm* and *A Picnic with the Aunts*; the absurdly lunatic *Johnnie Golightly and His Crocodile*; *Tiger-Nanny*, the story of a tiger-cub who loves children—to look after, not to eat; *The Kidnapping of My Grandmother*, a Parisian adventure with a Paul Berna flavour; and *Mog*, a zany story of two eccentric old ladies.

There is an impish delight in mischief in some more recent books for seven to 10-year-olds. In *Jeffy, The Burglar's Cat* Miss Amity's enjoyment of her criminal activities is almost too much for Jeffy's reforming zeal; in *Bogwoppit* there is no taming either the determined young heroine or the extraordinary marshy and mischievous bogwoppits she encounters; and though the work ethic triumphs in the girls' boarding-school story *No Ponies for Miss Pobjoy*, there is strong sympathy for the pony-mad rebels as well. The youngest ghowlie in *Grandma and the Ghowlies* is full of mischief too, a determinedly disruptive poltergeist, who sets everyone by the ears, but really only needs to be loved. This is a lively and amusing ghost story, with some touching little scenes as well as a variety of problems and trials for Grandma in her attempt to find new homes for the five waif-like ghostlings. In *Spid*, on the other hand, the eponymous spider-hero creates his own welcome, ingratiating himself so ingeniously and effectively even with spider-haters that in the end he has to assert his independence. He wants to live his own life, not be anyone's pet. *Bellabelinda and the No-Good Angel* tells how an unsuccessful guardian angel finally makes the grade with the help of three mischievous boys and a lollipop lady who claims descent from a witch; while *Paddy on the Island* is a quietly amusing little story of a boy who escapes from his overbearing family to a desert island, where he finds at first some of the peace he seeks, but also the adventures and the mixture of good and bad fortune a wishing stone can be expected to bring.

For older readers, *Boy in a Barn* is an adventure story with a mountain peasant background similar to that of the earlier fantasies, but set in postwar Europe; *The Noble Hawks* an historical story of a 14th-century yeoman's son who longs to be a falconer. *Castle Merlin* is a story of the present day, but exploiting the continuing popularity of time fantasies, and *The Line* is an imaginative story of a magical modern invention. There are some uncertainties in handling the more complex plots of these stories, and some stereotyping in the minor characters; but the main characters are seen to develop in self-awareness and maturity, and there are witty and satirical undertones to the writing which, while bearing affinity to the slyly wicked humour of the stories for younger children, add a further dimension to Moray Williams's story-telling. She is an inventive as well as a prolific writer, and in their different ways her books are well-written, pleasantly intriguing, and occasionally achieve a haunting power and a delightfully sharp and witty observation of the foibles of mankind.

—Winifred Whitehead

MOREY, Walt(er Nelson). American. Born in Hoquiam, Washington, 3 February 1907. Educated at Benkhe Walker Business College, 1927. Married 1) Rosalind Alice Ogden in 1934 (died 1977); 2) Peggy Kilburn in 1978. Construction worker, millworker, and theatre manager in Oregon and Washington, 1930's; burner foreman and superintendent, Kaiser Shipyards, Vancouver, Washington, 1940–45; deep-sea diver and fish trap inspector, Alaska, 1951; director, Oregon Nut Cooperative, Newberg, 1960–61. Since 1937 filbert farmer. Agent: Lenniger Literary Agency, 104 East 40th Street, New York, New York 10016. Address: 10830 S.W. Morey Lane, Wilsonville, Oregon 97070, U.S.A.

PUBLICATIONS FOR CHILDREN

Fiction

Gentle Ben, illustrated by John Schoenherr. New York, Dutton, 1965; London, Dent, 1966.
Home Is the North, illustrated by Robert Shore. New York, Dutton, 1967; London, Dent, 1968.
Kävik, The Wolf Dog, illustrated by Peter Parnall. New York, Dutton, 1968; London, Dent, 1969.
Angry Waters, illustrated by Richard Cuffari. New York, Dutton, 1969; London, Dent, 1970.
Gloomy Gus. New York, Dutton, 1970; as *The Bear at Friday Creek*, London, Dent, 1971.
Deep Trouble. New York, Dutton, 1971; London, Dent, 1972.
Scrub Dog of Alaska. New York, Dutton, 1971; London, Sidgwick and Jackson, 1975.
Canyon Winter. New York, Dutton, 1972; London, Dent, 1974.
Runaway Stallion. New York, Dutton, 1973.
Run Far, Run Fast. New York, Dutton, 1974.
Year of the Black Pony. New York, Dutton, 1976; London, Collins, 1977.
Sandy and the Rock Star. New York, Dutton, 1979.
The Lemon Meringue Dog. New York, Dutton, 1980.

Other

Operation Blue Bear. New York, Dutton, 1975.

PUBLICATIONS FOR ADULTS

Other

North to Danger, with Virgil Burford. New York, Day, 1954; revised edition, Caldwell, Idaho, Caxton, 1969.

*

Manuscript Collection: University of Oregon Library, Eugene.

*   *   *

Walt Morey is a writer in the Jack London tradition; many of his books are animals stories set in Alaska. Morey's Alaska is that of the 1950's, the years just before the territory achieved statehood, and he writes from his experience of living and working there, primarily in the occupations concerning salmon-fishing on which the economy of the area depended. Life in small settlements like Orca City is rough and tough; many of the people are as migrant as the salmon on their annual run, and while qualities such as courage and endurance are valued, ruthless exploitation is equally a condition of survival. The message of many of Morey's novels is a questioning of this situation; their formula is often that of an adolescent boy who is for some reason a "loner"; he befriends an animal whom he has to defend from adults who would use or kill it. These stories do not stay long on library shelves; their vivid descriptions of icy wastes combined with the warmth of their emotional tone make them popular reading.

Gentle Ben is still one of the best-loved. Ben, contrary to generally held opinions of the nature of bears, especially those soured by ill-treatment in captivity, becomes the pet of young Mark Andersen and is saved by him not only from the villagers of Orca City but also from big-game hunters from the outside world.

Home Is the North and *Kävik, The Wolf Dog* both have Malamute dogs as their animal heroes, and both contrast the land of the wild and free with civilisation as represented by Seattle, the port of embarkation for Alaska. In the first, the orphan Brad fights to stay and work on the fishing boats rather than join his aunt in Seattle, especially as this means giving up his dog, Mickie. In the second, Kävik survives ill treatment and privation in his attempts to make the long journey home to the north. The latter, perhaps because it centres on the animal's reactions rather than humans', is the better book; it is both moving and powerful.

In *Gloomy Gus* Eric Strong's pet bear is sold by his elders to a circus and filial loyalty leads him to accept this, much as he dislikes it. *Scrub Dog of Alaska* is another story of making good. Dave Martin, son of an Indian mother and a white father, has to stand up to the racist sneers of his father's relatives in the States. His dog Scrub develops from being the weakest of the litter to being the leader of the pack. *Canyon Winter* is an exciting survival story of a boy who is marooned by a plane crash in the Cascade Mountains over the winter. This experience and the influence of the old recluse who saves him make him, on his return to civilisation, a fierce conservationist.

In *Canyon Winter*, and in all his later books, Morey takes as his setting not the Alaska of his young maturity, but the Oregon of his childhood and retirement, which he describes vividly from memory and from research of earlier pioneer days. *Runaway Stallion* is his first book to have a horse as its main animal character in a story of a racehorse running wild until adopted by a boy on an isolated ranch. His best book in this genre, though, is *Year of the Black Pony*, which draws more deeply on autobiographical sources and which has a well-sustained climax in the boy hero's being carried home safely by his horse when lost in a Christmas blizzard. Morey's heroes are often boys and young men who achieve maturity by protecting animals against predatory adults; those in *Sandy and the Rock Star* and *The Lemon Meringue Dog* are contemporary youths, a pop singer and a young coastguard in "drug bust" programme.

Respect and concern for wild life and the wild places of the earth are Morey's themes; his message is the conservationist one of a proper balance between man and nature.

—Mary Croxson

MORGAN, Alison (Mary, née Raikes). British. Born in Bexley, Kent, 2 March 1930. Educated at St. Helen's School, Northwood, Middlesex, 1943–47; Somerville College, Oxford, 1949–52, B.A. (honours) 1952; University of London, 1952–53, Cert. Ed. 1953. Married John Morgan in 1960; two sons. Taught in secondary modern school, Malvern, Worcestershire, 1953–54, and in girls' grammar school, Newtown, Montgomery, 1954–59. Since 1964 Justice of the Peace. Recipient: Welsh Arts Council award, 1973. Agent: A.P. Watt Ltd., 20 John Street, London WC1N 2DL. Address: Talcoed, Llanafan, near Builth Wells, Powys, Wales.

PUBLICATIONS FOR CHILDREN

Fiction

Fish, illustrated by John Sergeant. London, Chatto and Windus, 1971; as *A Boy Called Fish*, New York, Harper, 1973.
Pete. London, Chatto and Windus, 1972; New York, Harper, 1973.
Ruth Crane. London, Chatto and Windus, 1973; New York, Harper, 1974.
The Raft, illustrated by Trevor Parkin. London, Abelard Schuman, 1974.
At Willie Tucker's Place, illustrated by Trevor Stubley. London, Chatto and Windus, 1975; Nashville, Nelson, 1976.
River Song, illustrated by John Schoenherr. New York, Harper, 1975; London, Chatto and Windus, 1976.
Leaving Home. London, Chatto and Windus, 1979; as *All Sorts of Prickles*, New York, Elsevier Nelson, 1979.
Paul's Kite, illustrated by Vanessa Julian-Ottie. London, Chatto and Windus, 1981; New York, Atheneum, 1982.
Christabel, illustrated by Mariella Jennings. London, MacRae, 1984.
Bright-Eye, illustrated by Vanessa Julian-Ottie. London, Viking Kestrel, 1984.
Staples for Amos, illustrated by Charles Front. London, MacRae, 1986.
The Eyes of the Blind. Oxford, Oxford University Press, 1986.
The Wild Morgans, illustrated by Liz Roberts. London, Viking Kestrel, 1988.

*

Alison Morgan comments:
Fish, Pete, Ruth Crane, and *At Willie Tucker's Place* form a quartet of stories set in a hypothetical mid-Wales with different children from the village community as major characters in each case. *The Raft* is a short story concerned with two boys, one disabled and the other afraid of water, who in the course of a dangerous adventure learn to understand something of each other's problems. *River Song* traces a year in the life of a group of riverside birds.

In *Leaving Home* and its sequel, *Paul's Kite*, although the main character has come from a mid-Wales setting similar to that of the earlier books, the stories concern his new life, first in a South Wales seaside town and later in London.

*   *   *

Alison Morgan's books fall into distinct categories but each shares common themes and a common attitude to life. Whether overtly or as an underlying issue, her novels are always concerned with children being tested, or testing themselves, and in the process learning about themselves or about other people.

She writes with an admirable lack of sentimentality and even in her shortest pre-novels she contrives to create a past and a future for her characters and a continuity for the countryside. Life is going on all around and the incident at the heart of each book is not plucked out and written as a self-contained episode. This strong feeling for the countryside and the community must come from Morgan's own view of life and yet she manages to write objectively, keeping herself out of the book and letting characters and events speak for themselves.

Her first group of novels is set in a small Welsh village. *Fish*, which immediately established her as a significant new writer for children, began a thread which was to run through many of her novels—that of the outsider who gradually gains acceptance. Three other books also chronicle events in LLanwern: *Pete, At Willie Tucker's Place*, and *Ruth Crane*, which is aimed at a slightly older reader and introduces an American teenager. Perhaps because of the dramatic nature of this story—Ruth's mother and sister are badly injured in a car accident which kills her father—and the older readership, it does not fit entirely happily into the group but it still raises some thought-provoking questions about outsiders and about changes imposed from without. Two later books, *Leaving Home* and *Paul's Kite*, also deal with the adjustments which have to be made when changes are imposed concerning, as they do, a boy sent from his home to live with relatives in London.

All of Morgan's stories show a deep awareness of the environment, particularly of the continuity of nature, and this is the subject matter of two of her books: *River Song*, which describes a year in the life of a colony of birds, and *Bright-Eye*. The latter is perhaps the more successful because of its format as a short story in the Kestrel Kites series aimed at early readers of seven-to-nine years who are not yet ready for the complexity of a full-length novel. The length is appropriate for what is essentially a small incident in which Amanda struggles to hatch and rear a wild duck when an egg is rescued from the plough by her father. The conservation theme is lightly handled and, despite offering a lot of information about wildlife, it never becomes a tract. Morgan's accurate ear for the rhythms of speech is evident in creating a warm family story, strong on domestic life, seeming to recreate real—if economical—speech and always told from a child's eye view.

Another relatively short book for the middle years is *Staples for Amos* which, in the same way that *Bright-Eye* tells a self-contained chapter from Amanda's life, describes an episode in a boy's life as he searches for the right sort of staples so that antagonistic Amos will mend the fence and stop the bullocks coming through. As so often in Morgan's work, this superficially self-contained incident touches on deeper themes, in this case racial prejudice. As well as a search for staples, it is a search for acceptance in the local community by the part West Indian boy and his mother.

The Eyes of the Blind is a totally different book, suitable for confident teenage readers. Benjamin (grandson of the prophet Isaiah) is caught up in an Assyrian seige and the novel tells the events of his flight to Jerusalem, initially in the convoy of women and children, largely in the company of Adad, blind son of the Assyrian general. It is a demanding read, full of detail, but the rewards are in proportion to the demands made on the reader. At the heart of the book are universal themes and personal relationships which are as relevant today as 2000 years ago. As in her other books, the two boys learn much about each other as they pass through dangers and stirring times together and, in this respect, it is not unlike a much shorter book, *The Raft*, where two boys facing danger together learn to appreciate something of what it is like to be the other—one disabled, one with a disabling fear of water.

—Valerie Brinkley-Willsher

————————

MORGAN, Helen (Gertrude Louise, née Axford). British. Born in Ilford, Essex, 11 April 1921. Educated at Barking Abbey Grammar School, Essex, 1932–37; Royal National College for the Blind, London, 1938–42. Married Tudor Meredydd Morgan in 1954; three daughters. Lives in Wales. Agent: Rosemary Bromley, Juvenilia Literary Agency, Avington Lodge, Avington, near Winchester, Hampshire SO21 1DB. Address: c/o Barclays Bank, Caverley Road, Tunbridge Wells, Kent, England.

PUBLICATIONS FOR CHILDREN

Fiction

The Little Old Lady: Four Stories, illustrated by Irene Hawkins. London, Faber, 1961.
Tales of Tigg's Farm, illustrated by Shirley Hughes. London, Faber, 1963.
Meet Mary Kate, illustrated by Shirley Hughes. London, Faber, 1963.
A Mouthful of Magic, illustrated by W.J. Gale. London, Harrap, 1963.
Two in the Garden [*in the House, on the Farm, by the Sea*], illustrated by Jillian Willett. Leicester, Brockhampton Press, 4 vols., 1964–67.
The Tailor and the Sailor and the Small Black Cat, illustrated by Michael Hoare. London, Nelson, 1964.
A Dream of Dragons and Other Tales, illustrated by Shirley Hughes. London, Faber, 1965.
Satchkin Patchkin, illustrated by Shirley Hughes. London, Faber, 1966; Philadelphia, Macrae Smith, 1970.
Mary Kate and the Jumble Bear and Other Stories, illustrated by Shirley Hughes. London, Faber, 1967.
Mrs. Pinny and the Blowing Day [*Sudden Snow, Salty Sea Day*], illustrated by Shirley Hughes. London, Faber, 3 vols., 1968–72.
Mary Kate and the School Bus and Other Stories, illustrated by Shirley Hughes. London, Faber, 1970; as *Mary Kate*, Nashville, Nelson, 1972.
Mother Farthing's Luck, illustrated by Shirley Hughes. London, Faber, 1971.
The Sketchbook Crime, illustrated by Jim Russell. Exeter, Wheaton, 1980.

*

Helen Morgan comments:

I write for children because I like children. I like to make them laugh and to stimulate their imaginations and to make them feel safe. Childhood doesn't last long. It ought to be happy.

* * *

To appraise the achievement of a gifted writer whose implied readers are always the very young is to seek out the ways in which the plot, theme, narrative, and form all combine to show something which is significant, precursory, and new.

Helen Morgan's work is often rooted in the homely and the accessible, the here-and-now of young childhood that criticism used misguidedly to call "realism." The Mary Kate tales and "Two" books slow down and turn into art the action, sounds, sights, feelings, of childhood. The universal experiences—birthdays, bonfires, losing a tooth, starting school—need space for reflection. Deceptively simple techniques of form like the length of chapters and the interplay of episodes help a storyteller who never seems to be in a hurry catch the quintessential *slowness* of childhood time.

Stories such as those about the indomitable washerwoman Mrs. Pinny link the rustic ordinary with the fabulous, so encouraging reading as venture and possibility. The passing of time is important in her stories: events often happen all in a day and can be held in the head. Her first pages tend to be crucial parts of the invitation. "It was a beautiful bright and blowing day—a windy, wonderful washing day. The clouds were splashes of frothy suds and the sun was a piece of yellow soap in the deep blue bowl of the sky." The young reader has the cohesion of theme, plot, image, and action.

Her original fairytales are miniature masterpieces. The stories of *Satchkin Patchkin*, the little green Magic Man, and Jasper Dark, the anti-hero of *Mother Farthing's Luck*, make folk worlds with their own music, motifs, and potentiality for both order and misrule.

In all Morgan's writing, there is a craftswoman's care for what language can achieve. We find a poetic resonance too rare in writing for the very young ("the fluttering, twittering, golden, glittering morning made her forget the Workday Wednesday") and at times ("Long, long ago, when days were slow and there was time for looking…") an extraordinary musicality.

—Colin Mills

————————

MORRIS, (Margaret) Jean. Also writes as Kenneth O'Hara. British. Born in Sevenoaks, Kent, 15 January 1924. Educated at Bromley High School, Kent; University of London, honours graduate. Has one daughter. Recipient: Arts Council bursary, for drama, 1955. Address: Flat 1, 56 Pevensey Road, Eastbourne, East Sussex, BN21 3HT, England.

PUBLICATIONS FOR CHILDREN

Fiction

The Path of the Dragons. London, Hutchinson, 1980.
Twist of Eight, illustrated by Jolyne Knox. London, Chatto and Windus, 1981.
The Donkey's Crusade. London, Bodley Head, 1983.
The Song under the Water. London, Bodley Head, 1985.
The Troy Game. London, Bodley Head, 1987.
The Paper Canoe. London, Bodley Head, 1988.

Play

The Spongees, in *Eight Plays 1*, edited by Malcolm Stuart Fellows. London, Cassell, 1965.

PUBLICATIONS FOR ADULTS

Novels

Man and Two Gods. London, Cassell, 1953; as *A Man and Two Gods*, New York, Viking Press, 1954.
Half of a Story. London, Cassell, 1957.
The Adversary. London, Cassell, 1959.
The Blackamoor's Urn. London, Cassell, 1962.
A Dream of Fair Children. London, Cassell, 1966.

Novels as Kenneth O'Hara

A View to a Death. London, Cassell, 1958.
Sleeping Dogs Lying. London, Cassell, 1960; New York, Macmillan, 1962.
Underhandover. London, Cassell, 1961; New York, Macmillan, 1963.
Double Cross Purposes. London, Cassell, 1962.
Unknown Man, Seen in Profile. London, Gollancz, 1967.
The Bird-Cage. London, Gollancz, 1968; New York, Random House, 1969.
The Company of St. George. London, Gollancz, 1972.
The Delta Knife. London, Gollancz, 1976.
The Ghost of Thomas Penry. London, Gollancz, 1977.
The Searchers of the Dead. London, Gollancz, 1979.
Nightmares' Nest. London, Gollancz, 1982.

Plays

Island of Gulls (produced Guildford, Surrey, 1956).
Anne of Cleves (televised 1970). Published in *The Six Wives of Henry VIII*, edited by J.C. Trewin, London, Elek, 1972.

Radio Plays: *Safety of the City*, 1961; *The Heretic*, 1962; *Sonata Form of Words*, 1962; *Royal Hunt and Storm*, 1963; *The Mislaid Cause*, 1964; *The Singing Bird*, 1964; *Explosions*, 1965; *Travelling in Winter*, 1971; *The Road to Oxford*, 1976.

Television Play: *Anne of Cleves*, 1970.

Other

The Monarchs of England. New York, Charterhouse, 1975.

Translator, with Radost Pridham, *The Peach Thief and Other Bulgarian Stories*. London, Cassell, 1968.

*   *   *

Jean Morris is, quite possibly, the most interesting fantasy writer of the past 10 years or so. Her use of magic is so reasoned and practical, so basic to life as she presents it, that it seems natural rather than supernatural—something which she may owe to Ursula K. Le Guin (*Earthsea* trilogy). This is not cancelled out by episodes of powerful eeriness, nor by the fact that her animals use human language occasionally, but they do so sparingly, and they speak sense.
The Path of the Dragons is by far the most complex and demanding of her novels. If you know nothing at all about old Greek and

northern myths, if you have never heard of Atlantis, you will lose much of its point. Her views though are not conventional, nor do they taste of the schoolroom. Her Atlantids (inhabitants of Atlantis) are exceptionally gifted: they have computers, air-transport, radio communication; they can also read thoughts. They have no servants, they eat no meat, and they usefully carry their skills—toned down to local level—to needy tribes elsewhere. But can this advanced society last? The assigned dragon-roads in the sky are disturbed. Vast, sage, and splendid, "the most intelligent life-form known to the Atlantids," may also owe a little to Le Guin. The tale will take in much before the island finally vanishes. A gross fellow, Heracles, with a club and a dead lion's skin, sad and stinking, over his shoulder, comes to reconnoitre. The Hyperion/Apollo story (not in the least like Keats's version) is played out. Atlas's burden is both of knowledge and of ignorance. Ideas abound. The dialogue entertains. All these things keep a laden but remarkable vessel buoyant and afloat.
Twist of Eight contains eight tales, each casting a fresh glance at certain legendary stereotypes (Cinderella, Perseus, True Thomas). This is easily the most accessible of Morris's books, even to quite young children; its ideas have wit and sense for anyone. The most original story is about a conscientious horse who, hired for a brief ride, refuses to take part in the Andromeda exploit. He sees no reason why he should prefer princesses to sea-monsters. "If the princess were rescued," he asks, "would the sea-monster have anything *else* to eat?"
Newcomers to Morris should start with *The Donkey's Crusade* which shows her individual quality at its best. Thomas, 15, a novice in an Antioch monastery but by birth and teaching (and desire) a "traveller" or guide, is summoned by the Abbot to conduct a certain Brother James to the distant East, on a wild quixotic mission to the legendary Prester John. (Did he not once offer help in rescuing the Holy City from the infidel?) They are joined by a Frankish flute-playing urchin Aubery—but the wisest member is the fourth, a sage and sometimes cynical donkey, who carries the loads, speaks human language (only when he must), and is perhaps the conscience of the band. As a traveller's tale, the book stands up to anything in that genre for detail, landscape, characters, wonders. As a quest tale alone it should endure, a notable reminder that the search is rather more than the finding.
The Troy Game, another striking Morris original, is again a quest. Brannock, younger son of a king (chief king of a group of seven smallish kingdoms), is sent on a journey by the Merlin-like Mennor. "There is far more to this errand than knowing every path in the Seven Kingdoms...I need you to go to a place to which there is no path: to go to the hall of my Order." Few people have ever seen this hall. Mennor gives the boy a golden brooch, worn and scratched, but engraved with lines that are in fact the paths of the old troy maze, long overgrown with grass and brambles in the grounds. Heading as directed into the eastern wild, Brannock very soon loses his fine horse, his scarlet tunic, and his arrogance (but not his dog, Goldeneye), and acquires a companion, his girl cousin Eilian. She (and her cat) will be indispensable on the long and teasing journey, with its terrors, joys, and marvels. A time comes when the only hope is to summon the Wild Hunt, and to do this you must give all—perhaps lose all. A tremendous episode; the Hunt does not select its victims. Magic is not imposed on this thrilling book; it is intrinsic.
Water is the prevailing element of *The Song under the Water*. It works Jem's father's mill. Jem himself loves to swim, in secret, in the forest pools. It can be a danger, when floods invade the village. The villagers speak with dread of the ominous Water Horse. And it holds the strange water-boy Thorn, who becomes Jem's friend, and seems perhaps a reflection of himself. Thorn, he finds, has a link with the great chateau, where the mysterious Lady Esclairemont lives in solitude. And the water draws all the characters together when, as the floods rise, the Lady opens her doors to the villagers. The book

has some fine passages as well as plenty of Morris expertise. But the plot runs obscurely, and the magic isn't wholly absorbed; as a sum of the parts it is probably the least successful of her books.

The Paper Canoe, on the other hand, her latest book to date, and the only one with contemporary people and setting, is commended to all Morris-followers. It has its oddities, its journey too; but in place of the supernatural, we find ourselves in in a powerful daydream. The girl Carly ("a pale resentful shrimp of a girl") has a holiday job in a garden centre with two older boys: Jonathan, handsome, bossy, and humourless, and Raff, a kindly country boy from a long line of Hardyan skilled farmworkers. All three are awaiting exam results, and Carly, clever enough in many things, is the most troubled. Her father's recent death (which brought the family back from Kenya to dull and rainy England) hasn't broken his domination. Will she have failed him in the geography papers—*his* special subject, not hers? Absorbed in Mary Kingsley's *Travels in West Africa*, she starts on a vivid daydream journey down a great African river, leading, she believes, to the sea. The interlinking of the girl's two lives during this week of waiting is most skilfully done; every (literate) teenager should give a recognising nod.

Morris is always an entertaining writer, witty and quotable. Her serious underlying ideas are usually voiced, thought, or discussed by the characters themselves. Her books are not widely popular, but they are a young (or older) connoisseur's discovery, and they gain more and more with each rereading. This can be said of very few works of junior fiction today.

—Naomi Lewis

MOWAT, Farley (McGill). Canadian. Born in Belleville, Ontario, 12 May 1921. Educated at public schools in Trenton, Belleville, Windsor, Richmond Hill, and Toronto, Ontario, and Saskatoon, Saskatchewan; University of Toronto, B.A. 1949. Served in the Canadian Army Infantry and Intelligence Corps, 1940–46: Captain. Married 1) Frances Thornhill in 1947, two sons; 2) Claire Angel Wheeler in 1965. Freelance writer. Recipient: University of Western Ontario President's Medal, for short story, 1952; Anisfield-Wolf award, for non-fiction, 1954; Governor-General's award, 1957; Canadian Library Association award, 1958; National Association of Independent Schools award, 1963; Canadian Centennial Medal, 1967; Leacock Medal, 1970; Vicky Metcalf award, 1970; Queen's Silver Jubilee Medal, 1978. D.Litt.: Laurentian University, Sudbury, Ontario, 1970; University of Victoria, British Columbia, 1982; Lakehead University, Thunder Bay, Ontario, 1986; LL.D.: University of Toronto, 1973; University of Lethbridge, Alberta, 1973; University of Prince Edward Island, Charlottetown, 1979. Officer, Order of Canada, 1981. Agent: Herta Ryder, c/o Toby Eady Associates, 7 Gledhow Gardens, London SW5 0BL, England. Address: c/o McClelland and Stewart Ltd., 481 University Avenue, Suite 900, Toronto, Ontario M5G 2E9, Canada.

PUBLICATIONS FOR CHILDREN

Fiction

Lost in the Barrens, illustrated by Charles Geer. Boston, Little Brown, 1956; London, Macmillan, 1957.
The Black Joke, illustrated by D. Johnson. Toronto, McClelland and Stewart, 1962; Boston, Little Brown, 1963; London, Macmillan, 1964.

The Curse of the Viking Grave, illustrated by Charles Geer. Boston, Little Brown, 1966; London, Pan, 1979.

Other

Owls in the Family, illustrated by Robert Frankenberg. Boston, Little Brown, 1961; London, Macmillan, 1963.

PUBLICATIONS FOR ADULTS

Short Stories

The Snow Walker. Toronto, McClelland and Stewart, 1975; Boston, Little Brown, 1976; London, Heinemann, 1978.

Plays

Television Scripts: *Sea Fare* (*Telescope* series), 1964; *Diary of a Boy on Vacation*, 1964; and others.

Other

People of the Deer (on the Ihalmiut Eskimos). Boston, Little Brown, and London, Joseph, 1952; revised edition, Toronto, McClelland and Stewart, 1975.
The Regiment (on the Hastings and Prince Edward Regiment). Toronto, McClelland and Stewart, 1955.
The Dog Who Wouldn't Be. Boston, Little Brown, 1957; London, Joseph, 1958.
The Grey Seas Under. Boston, Little Brown, 1958; London, Joseph, 1959.
The Desperate People (on the Ihalmiut Eskimos). Boston, Little Brown, 1959; London, Joseph, 1960; revised edition, Toronto, McClelland and Stewart, 1976.
The Serpent's Coil (on salvaging ships). Toronto, McClelland and Stewart, 1961; Boston, Little Brown, and London, Joseph, 1962.
Never Cry Wolf. Toronto, McClelland and Stewart, and Boston, Little Brown, 1963; London, Secker and Warburg, 1964.
Westviking: The Ancient Norse in Greenland and North America. Boston, Little Brown, 1965; London, Secker and Warburg, 1966.
Canada North. Boston, Little Brown, 1967; revised edition, as *Canada North Now: The Great Betrayal*, Toronto, McClelland and Stewart, 1976; as *The Great Betrayal*, Little Brown, 1976.
This Rock Within the Sea: A Heritage Lost (on Newfoundland), photographs by John de Visser. Boston, Little Brown, 1968.
The Boat Who Wouldn't Float. Toronto, McClelland and Stewart, 1969; Boston, Little Brown, and London, Heinemann, 1970.
Sibir: My Discovery of Siberia. Toronto, McClelland and Stewart, 1970; as *The Siberians*, Boston, Little Brown, 1971; London, Heinemann, 1972.
A Whale for the Killing. Toronto, McClelland and Stewart, and Boston, Little Brown, 1972; London, Heinemann, 1973.
Wake of the Great Sealers. Boston, Little Brown, 1973.
And No Birds Sang (war memoirs). Toronto, McClelland and Stewart, 1979; Boston, Little Brown, and London, Cassell, 1980.
The World of Farley Mowat: A Selection, edited by Peter Davison. Boston, Little Brown, 1980.
Sea of Slaughter. Toronto, McClelland and Stewart, and Boston, Atlantic Monthly Press, 1984; London, Bantam, 1986.
My Discovery of America. Toronto, McClelland and Stewart, and Boston, Atlantic Monthly Press, 1985.
Virunga: The Passion of Dian Fossey. Toronto, McClelland and Stewart, 1987; as *Woman in the Mists: The Story of Dian Fossey and the Mountain Gorillas of Africa*, New York, Warner, 1987;

London, Macdonald, 1988.

Editor, *Coppermine Journey: An Account of Great Adventure*, by
Samuel Hearne. Toronto, McClelland and Stewart, and Boston,
Little Brown, 1958.
Editor, *The Top of the World*:
1. *Ordeal by Ice*. Toronto, McClelland and Stewart, 1960; Boston, Little Brown, and London, Joseph, 1961.
2. *The Polar Passion: The Quest for the North Pole, with Selections
from Arctic Journals*. Toronto, McClelland and Stewart,
1967; Boston, Little Brown, 1968.
3. *Tundra: Selections from the Great Accounts of Arctic Land
Voyages*. Toronto, McClelland and Stewart, 1973.

*

Manuscript Collection: McMaster University, Hamilton, Ontario.

Critical Study: *Farley Mowat* by Alex Lucas, Toronto, McClelland
and Stewart, 1976.

Farley Mowat comments:

I am a simple fellow and I like simple things. Particularly do I like
natural things, and this includes people who live natural lives
(Eskimos, fishermen, northern Indians, seamen under sail, etc.).
These are the kind of people I have always chosen to write
about—people who are attuned to the natural world and who feel
competent and at home with natural existence. High civilisations
such as those of cities scare me since they inevitably lead their
populations into holocausts.
The whole purpose of my writing has been to try and stir people's
conscience in relation to the enormous destruction we are visiting on
the rest of animate creation and the planet on which we all live.

*   *   *

The initial scene in *The Curse of the Viking Grave* furnishes a
compendium of themes, images, and ideas which dominate all of
Farley Mowat's writing. In a sparsely furnished cabin-schoolhouse,
a craggy-faced trapper, former Orkney Islander long transplanted in
the Canadian north, instructs his charges by relating tales of early
Scandinavian expeditions to the New World. The student population,
three young boys, is instantly recognizable as a microcosm of the
family of man, the roll comprising the trapper's own orphaned
nephew, a Cree Indian, and a half-Eskimo. Together they
demonstrate heterogeneity, individuality, and brotherhood. Along
with their teacher, they rehearse a virtual Arctic catechism, one which
might be formulated to read that, from the time of the Vikings on,
the north is everyone's destination, or should be, that a harsh climate
masks what is in fact an outpost utopia, and that privation is only an
attitude away from becoming revealed as the virtue of simplicity.
The vast landscape enforces notions of unity, of man with man, and
of man with nature. The Eskimo, for example, view the deer not as
a commodity to be reaped, but as a self-sacrificing brother who lays
down his life to secure the survival of an ice-land compatriot.
The Arctic itself is no mere arena housing perpetual spectacle of
self-discovery and survival. Far from being a designated backdrop,
the landscape, Arctic or otherwise, becomes the most telling dimension in Mowat's fiction, so much so that it substantially reduces the
significance of such conventionally dominant literary components
as plot and character to subordinate status. His characters function
less as configurations of individuals than as mouthpieces for tundra,
prairie, or isolated fishing village, while his plots prove primarily to
be conveyances for involving readers with settings too long silenced
by popular stereotypes. *The Black Joke*, a sea adventure, seems more
intent upon animating sleepy French islands a few miles off the coast

of Newfoundland than in supplying any historical extravaganza. *Lost
in the Barrens* appears more concerned with the locale than with the
young heroes contending within it. A young boy flees, northward of
course, to escape the unspeakable fate of being schooled in the
debilitating south. The barrens, it might seem, provide difficulties
precisely because they are a place of promise. Their native population, Eskimos, presumed by the principal characters to be vicious
xenophobics, turn out to be warm and generous hosts, reflecting a
land which, despite name and reputation, is neither savage nor
desolate.
Mowat's fiction, no less than his book-length treatises on behalf
of birds, wolves, and whales, promotes the notion of the brotherhood
of all creation, although such kinship cannot always be equated with
convenient living arrangements. His recollections of two untameable
owls (*Owls in the Family*) whose irrepressible wilderness ways force
the family into many a comic posture, and the touching sometimes
farcical mannerisms of a pet (*The Dog Who Wouldn't Be*) who
persists in a determination to be human, suggest ultimate barriers to
unity. But distinctiveness of habit need not imply distance. Man and
beast bring out the best in each other. Mowat, the man with a cause,
reaches out towards all creatures, including his audience, invoking
an emotional chord which bestirs at least vicarious residence in the
barrens, Regina, or the Miquelon Islands.

—Leonard R. Mendelsohn

MUKERJI, Dhan Gopal. Indian. Born near Calcutta, 6 July
1890; emigrated to the United States, 1910. Educated at Indian
schools; Hindu priest-initiate, 1904–06; University of Calcutta,
1908; Tokyo University, 1909; University of California, Berkeley,
1910–13; Stanford University, California, Ph. B. 1914. Married
Ethel Ray Dugan in 1918; one son. Lecturer. Lived in New Milford,
Connecticut. Recipient: American Library Association Newbery
Medal, 1928. *Died (suicide) 14 July 1936.*

PUBLICATIONS FOR CHILDREN

Fiction

Kari the Elephant, illustrated by J.E. Allen. New York, Dutton,
1922; London, Dent, 1923.
Jungle Beasts and Men, illustrated by J.E. Allen. New York, Dut-
ton, 1923; London, Dent, 1924.
Hari the Jungle Lad, illustrated by Morgan Stinemetz. New York,
Dutton, 1924.
Gay-Neck: The Story of a Pigeon, illustrated by Boris Artzybasheff.
New York, Dutton, 1927; London, Dent, 1928.
Ghond the Hunter, illustrated by Boris Artzybasheff. New York,
Dutton, 1928; London, Dent, 1929.
The Chief of the Herd, illustrated by Mahlon Blaine. New York,
Dutton, and London, Dent, 1929.
Bunny, Hound and Clown, illustrated by Kurt Wiese. New York,
Dutton, 1931.
The Master Monkey, illustrated by Florence Weber. New York,
Dutton, 1932.
Fierce-Face: The Story of a Tiger, illustrated by Dorothy P. Lathrop.
New York, Dutton, 1936.

Other

Hindu Fables for Little Children, illustrated by Kurt Wiese. New

York, Dutton, 1929.
Rama, The Hero of India: Valmiki's "Ramayana" Done into a Short English Version, illustrated by Edgar Parin d'Aulaire. New York, Dutton, 1930; London, Dent, 1931.

PUBLICATIONS FOR ADULTS

Novel

The Secret Listeners of the East. New York, Dutton, 1926.

Plays

Chintamini: A Symbolic Drama, with Mary Carolyn Davies, adaptation of a play by Girish C. Ghose. Boston, Badger, 1914.
Layla-Majnu. San Francisco, Paul Elder, 1916.
The Judgment of Indra, in *Drama*, edited by A.D. Dickinson. New York, Doubleday, 1922; in *Fifty One-Act Plays*, edited by Constance M. Martin, London, Gollancz, 1934.

Verse

Rajani: Songs of the Night. San Francisco, Paul Elder, 1916.
Sandhya: Songs of Twilight. San Francisco, Paul Elder, 1917.

Other

Caste and Outcast (autobiography). New York, Dutton, and London, Dent, 1923.
My Brother's Face. New York, Dutton, 1924; London, Butterworth, 1925.
The Face of Silence (on Ramakrishna). New York, Dutton, 1926; London, Wassenaar, 1973.
A Son of Mother India Answers. New York, Dutton, 1928.
Visit India with Me. New York, Dutton, 1929.
Devotional Passages from the Hindu Bible. New York, Dutton, 1929.
Disillusioned India. New York, Dutton, 1930.
Daily Meditation; or, The Practice of Repose. New York, Dutton, 1933.
The Path of Prayer. New York, Dutton, 1934.

Editor and Translator, *The Song of God: Translation of the Bhagavad-Gita.* New York, Dutton, 1931; London, Dent, 1932.

*   *   *

Dhan Gopal Mukerji wrote the kind of books for children first made popular by Ernest Thompson Seton, stories of wildlife in which the landscape plays almost as important a part as the animals and birds whose lives are described. "Grey Owl" is another writer in the same genre, and was Mukerji's contemporary.

For the most part his books are anecdotal, a stringing together of incidents from his boyhood in Northern India. For example, in *Ghond the Hunter* Ghond describes village life and ceremonies, recalls journeys to Agra, Delhi, and Kashmir, and tells stories of various animals he had befriended—a mongoose, a pet panther. *Kari the Elephant* and *Jungle Beasts and Men* consist of similar assorted incidents.

The Chief of the Herd is in the classic animal-story mould. It tells the life of Sirdar the elephant, leader of the herd: election as leader, a mate, a son, a forest fire, a flood. The book is packed with interesting observations on animal lore. Mukerji writes in a clear prose which occasionally topples over into lushness—"heavy kine

throbbing with fat draw their silken flanks through the grain fields"—but which is in the main vivid and lively in its evocation of the Indian scene.

His prize-winning book *Gay-Neck* lacks the narrative power of a Kipling or a Henry Williamson, but must have had for its readers the charm of an exotic setting and the excitement of patriotic sentiment. Gay-Neck the pigeon is trained by his young master in Calcutta, travels to the Himalayas, and is then loaned during the 1914–18 War to the Indian army. He carries vital messages across the trenches from behind enemy lines, survives his ordeal, and is returned, wounded and frightened, to his beloved master in India where the healing powers of the Lama in the Himalayan monastery set him once more at peace and give him courage to fly again.

Mukerji's creatures are not credited with as much human sentiment as Kipling's in *The Jungle Book*. It is illuminating to contrast the two: the outsider Englishman's exotic Jungle with its animals each addressing each other in a curious stylised biblical language, each animal strongly characterised as an individual but nevertheless obeying the Law of the Jungle, an invention of Kipling's, older of course than man-made laws but still an evolved code with, one cannot help but suspect, affinities with English law; and the native-born Mukerji's more accurately observed jungle where the animals when they speak utter a plainer prose but where the natural world fits into a divine scheme of things, where "you cannot destroy one species of animal without upsetting the balance of life. Life is a whole. There is no escape from this." These words were written in 1929. Mukerji, with a view of life arising out of the same oriental philosophy that, however diluted, produced the hippie trail to Katmandu, foresaw dangers which the west is only now choosing to recognise.

—Mary Rayner

———

MUN. See **LEAF, Munro.**

———

MUNSCH, Robert. Canadian. Born in Pittsburgh, Pennsylvania, 11 June 1945; became Canadian citizen, 1983. Educated at Fordham University, Bronx, New York, 1965–69, B.A. in history 1969; Boston University, 1969–70, M.A. in anthropology 1971; Tufts University, Medford, Massachusetts, 1971–72, M.Ed. in child studies 1973; studied for the Jesuit priesthood for 7 years. Married Ann Beeler in 1973; two daughters and one son. Teacher, Bay Area Childcare, Coos Bay, Oregon, 1973–75. Head Teacher, Family Studies Laboratory Preschool, 1975–84, Assistant Professor, 1980–84, and since 1984 Adjunct Professor of Family Studies and children's writer-in-residence, University of Guelph, Ontario. Professional storyteller. Recipient: Ruth Schwartz award, 1985; Juno award, for recording, 1985. Address: c/o Writers Union, 24 Ryerson Avenue, Toronto, Ontario M5T 2P3, Canada.

PUBLICATIONS FOR CHILDREN

Fiction

Mud Puddle, illustrated by Sami Suomalainen. Toronto, Annick Press, 1979.

The Dark, illustrated by Sami Suomalainen. Toronto, Annick Press, 1979.
The Paper Bag Princess, illustrated by Michael Martchenko. Toronto, Annick Press, 1980; London, Hippo, 1982.
Jonathan Cleaned Up, Then He Heard a Sound, illustrated by Michael Martchenko. Toronto, Annick Press, 1981.
The Boy in the Drawer, illustrated by Michael Martchenko. Toronto, Annick Press, 1982.
Murmel, Murmel, Murmel, illustrated by Michael Martchenko. Toronto, Annick Press, 1982.
Angela's Airplane, illustrated by Michael Martchenko. Toronto, Annick Press, 1983.
David's Father, illustrated by Michael Martchenko. Toronto, Annick Press, 1983.
The Fire Station, illustrated by Michael Martchenko. Toronto, Annick Press, 1983.
Mortimer, illustrated by Michael Martchenko. Toronto, Annick Press, 1983; Oxford, Oxford University Press, 1985.
Millicent and the Wind, illustrated by Suzanne Duranceau. Toronto, Annick Press, 1984.
Thomas's Snowsuit, illustrated by Michael Martchenko. Toronto, Annick Press, 1985.
50 Below Zero, illustrated by Michael Martchenko. Toronto, Annick Press, 1985.
Love You Forever, illustrated by Sheila McGraw. Scarborough, Ontario, Firefly, 1986.
I Have to Go!, illustrated by Michael Martchenko. Toronto, Annick Press, 1987.
Moira's Birthday, illustrated by Michael Martchenko. Toronto, Annick Press, 1987.
A Promise Is a Promise, illustrated by Vladyana Krykorka. Toronto, Annick Press, 1988.
Pigs, illustrated by Michael Martchenko. Toronto, Annick Press, 1989.

Recordings: *Munsch: Favourite Stories*, Kids' Records, 1983; *Murmel, Murmel, Munsch: More Outrageous Stories*, Kids' Records, 1985; *Love You Forever*, Kids' Records, 1987.

*

Robert Munsch comments:
My stories all develop through storytelling to groups of children. My goal when I make them up is to keep an audience happy.

*   *   *

Robert Munsch, who is Canada's best-selling author of picture books, is a story teller who performs for large audiences in concert halls. His earliest books grew from story-telling sessions with preschoolers in the University of Guelph's Child Studies laboratory school, and his books' popularity with children draws from his continuing method of composition—telling and retelling stories to children hundreds of times before enshrining the stories in print. His books, which have been translated into nine languages, have also appeared in sound recording and animated film format. Between 1979, when his first book appeared, and 1988, his books have sold over three million copies.

As pure entertainment, a Munsch story often begins with an ordinary child, going about his daily business, who suddenly finds himself in a situation of disorder or chaos. The forces responsible for the upset are variously presented as fantastic, mythic, or melodramatic, though these forces are invariably drawn from the child's ordinary world, one in which dirt, fears, stubbornness, or childish enthusiasms can bring upset into the orderly adult world. Speaking from the child's viewpoint, the narrative persona heightens

the ordinary into a zany situation which, through exaggeration, becomes humorous. In the end, order is usually restored—frequently by the child itself—but a moral is never drawn. In fact, the adults who were upset by the disorder are sometimes made to look comical through one of Munsch's puckish lines.

In stories like *Mud Puddle, Jonathan Cleaned Up, Then He Heard a Sound*, and *The Boy in the Drawer*, the child protagonist does not consciously get dirty or create the mess: an outside force is responsible. However, the child must cope with the consequences. In *Mud Puddle*, for instance, little Jule Ann, freshly scrubbed and put in the back yard by her mother, stands helpless as a mud puddle jumps all over her. After various repetitions of this situation, Jule throws soap and water on the mud puddle who then runs away. In *Jonathan Cleaned Up* a little boy who is left in a clean living room watches as the wall opens and a subway of people appear and disappear, leaving the room in disarray. Held guilty for the mess, Jonathan finds the mayor and gets the subway rerouted. In *The Boy in the Drawer* a little girl finds untidiness in her room being created by a "bad boy" who lives in her drawer, but she quells his destructive tendencies by being kind to him. Munsch shows a subtle understanding of how little children feel when they find themselves in messes which they did not intend to create; on a psychological level, these stories undoubtedly mirror a child's natural desire to displace guilt onto a "bad" force outside itself, and then restore equilibrium to a cross parent, without losing face, by dispelling its anarchic "double."

Another grouping of stories depicts children creating mayhem in the adult world by ordinary ornery behaviour. Mortimer (*Mortimer*) sings his naughty song when he doesn't want to go to sleep; Thomas (*Thomas's Snowsuit*) doesn't want to put on his snowsuit before playing in the snow; and Andrew (*I Have to Go!*) refuses to "go pee" before getting into the car for a long trip. In each case the comedy results from Munsch's hammed-up depiction of how a small determined child can disrupt the adult world. Just when the adults think they have re-established order, there is usually a comic denouement. Another story in this vein, *Moira's Birthday*, is a comic account of what happens when a little girl's birthday invitation list gets out of hand.

One of Munsch's earliest successes was *The Paper Bag Princess*, a story which reverses the situation in Andersen's *The Little Swineherd* (where the princess is too superficial to realize the value of the prince's gifts when he is dressed like a swineherd). The little girl in Munsch's feminist tale uses her wits against the dragon's strength, saving the prince who has been carried away, only to be told by the rescued prince that her singed dress looks a "mess." Adding an "adult hook," Munsch concludes, "They didn't get married after all." This book has sold over 600,000 copies in its first eight years.

In the phenomenally successful *Love You Forever*, Munsch has written a book which appeals equally to children, mothers, and grandmothers—but for totally different reasons. The storyline is simple: a baby is born, grows up, has his own child, and loves it as well as the aged mother who looked after him. Children respond to the repetitions and ludicrous situations (like seeing a mother rock a grown-up man), whereas adults respond to the message that cycles of love cement family ties, remaining constant amid the change and loss in human life. This book has sold over 600,000 copies in its first two years.

Munsch's small picture books are as simple as fables, but they have no overt moral, despite the fact that the stories operate within a reassuring cultural framework, showing that children (even girls) can exert control over their environment; that fear can create its own demons; that neatness and order are approved by parents; that tolerance and understanding of others' differences are desirable; and that love is the single most abiding force in human life. Munsch's presentation of anarchy and use of taboo words ("go pee") sometimes draw negative responses from adults, but children merely delight in

Munsch's zany exaggerations, his skill as a storyteller, and his ability to dramatize a child's way of feeling.

—Mary Rubio

MURPHY, Jill (Frances). British. Born in London, 5 July 1949. Educated at Chelsea, Croydon, and Camberwell schools of art. Worked in a children's home for four years, and as a nanny for one year. Freelance writer and illustrator. Recipient: *Parents* Best Books for Babies award, 1987. Lives in Cornwall. Agent: A.P. Watt Ltd., 20 John Street, London WC1N 2DL, England.

PUBLICATIONS FOR CHILDREN (illustrated by the author)

Fiction

The Worst Witch. London, Allison and Busby, 1974; New York, Schocken, 1980.
The Worst Witch Strikes Again. London, Allison and Busby, and New York, Schocken, 1980.
Peace at Last. London, Macmillan, and New York, Dial Press, 1980.
A Bad Spell for the Worst Witch. London, Kestrel, 1982.
On the Way Home. London, Macmillan, 1982.
Whatever Next! London, Macmillan, 1983; as *What Next, Baby Bear!*, New York, Dial Press, 1984.
Five Minutes' Peace. London, Walker, and New York, Putnam, 1986.
All in One Piece. London, Walker, and New York, Putnam, 1987.
Peace at Last—In Miniature! London, Macmillan, 1987.
Worlds Apart. London, Walker, 1988.

*

Illustrator: *The Duke Who Had Too Many Giraffes* by Fiona Macdonald, 1977; *The Witch in Our Attic* by Brian Ball, 1979.

Jill Murphy comments:
I have always drawn since I can remember, and written stories from an early age (four to be exact): the two skills were automatically linked. I still feel more comfortable in the company of children, so it's natural I should like to write about things they appreciate.

*   *   *

Jill Murphy has a particular talent for writing stories that appeal to children who have learned the basic skill of reading, and want something bright and enticing to make them enjoy books thenceforward—an art more difficult than it might seem.

Her stories about Mildred Hubble, the worst witch, take themes relevant to all children—school, pets, friends, magic, getting into trouble—and by placing them in a school for witches she can allow herself a degree of exaggeration and funny invention which makes them immensely attractive.

Some of the same ability to understand what children like can be seen in her latest novel, *Worlds Apart*, which must represent every 10-year-old girl's dream. Susan Hunter finds that her long-lost father is a famous TV star: she tracks him down and there's a reconciliation between her parents so they may all live happily ever after. Adults will see some important unanswered questions in this book, but children will read it with unalloyed pleasure.

Murphy's lively style as a writer is matched by her ability as an artist. In a succession of popular picture books her glowing colour and attention to domestic detail have produced highly attractive pictures. These accompany texts in which contemporary situations that will be recognised by every family are handled with humour and affection. Using animal characters for the most part, she again allows herself the scope for pleasant exaggeration. How one sympathises with Father Bear in *Peace at Last*—and with Mrs. Large in *Five Minutes' Peace*! Yet one also understands exactly the need for the young elephants to be with their mother—and the visual joke which concludes *All in One Piece* (a further adventure of the Large family) will appeal to parents and children alike.

Murphy knows and gets on well with children, and perhaps that is the secret of her greatest strength—her accessibility. She reaches out to the reader, parent or child, and draws that reader straight into the book. That's a talent that many would envy enormously, and which must place her work high in the ranks of books children actually enjoy.

—Felicity Trotman

MURPHY, Shirley Rousseau. American. Born in Oakland, California, 20 May 1928. Educated at the California School of Fine Arts (now San Francisco Art Institute), 1947–51, A.A. in fine art and commercial art 1951. Married Patrick J. Murphy in 1951. Packaging designer, Sam Kweller, Los Angeles, 1952–53; interior decorator, Bullock's Department Store, Los Angeles, 1953–55; teacher of mosaics, San Bernardino Valley College, California, 1953–61; documents assistant, Canal Zone Library Museum, Panama, 1964–67. Painter and sculptor. Individual shows: Jack Carr Gallery, South Pasadena, California, 1957; San Bernardino Valley College, and Whittier Art Association, California, both 1958; Ojai Valley Art Center, California, and Ash Grove Gallery, Los Angeles, both 1959; Cherry Gallery, San Bernardino, and Light House Gallery, Hermosa Beach, California, both 1960; Richmond Museum, California, 1963. Since 1963 freelance writer. Agent: Elaine Markson Agency, 44 Greenwich Avenue, New York, New York 10011. Address: Route 1, Box 59J, Grandview Lake, Jasper, Georgia 30143, U.S.A

PUBLICATIONS FOR CHILDREN

Fiction

The Sand Ponies, illustrated by Erika Weihs. New York, Viking Press, 1967.
White Ghost Summer, illustrated by Barbara McGee. New York, Viking Press, 1967.
Elmo Doolan and the Search for the Golden Mouse, illustrated by Fritz Kredel. New York, Viking Press, 1970.
Carlos Charles, with Patrick Murphy. New York, Viking Press, 1971.
Poor Jenny, Bright as a Penny. New York, Viking Press, 1974.
The Grass Tower, illustrated by Charles Robinson. New York, Atheneum, 1976.
The Ring of Fire. New York, Atheneum, 1977.
Silver Woven in My Hair, illustrated by Alan Tiegreen. New York, Atheneum, 1977; London, Macdonald and Jane's, 1978.
The Flight of the Fox, illustrated by Don Sibley. New York, Atheneum, 1978.
The Pig Who Could Conjure the Wind, illustrated by Mark Lefkowitz. New York, Atheneum, 1978.

Soonie and the Dragon, illustrated by Susan Vaeth. New York, Atheneum, 1979.
The Wolf Bell. New York, Atheneum, 1979.
The Castle of Hape. New York, Atheneum, 1980.
Caves of Fire and Ice. New York, Atheneum, 1980.
Mrs. Tortino's Return to the Sun, with Patrick Murphy, illustrated by Susan Russo. New York, Lothrop, 1980.
The Joining of the Stone. New York, Atheneum, 1981.
Tattie's River Journey, illustrated by Tomie de Paola. New York, Dial Press, and London, Methuen, 1983.
Valentine for a Dragon, illustrated by Kay Chorao. New York, Atheneum, 1984.
Nightpool. New York, Harper, 1985.
The Ivory Lyre. New York, Harper, 1987.
The Dragonbards. New York, Harper, 1988.
Medallion of the Black Hound, with Welsh Suggs. New York, Harper, 1989.

*

Manuscript Collection: de Grummond Collection, University of Southern Mississippi, Hattiesburg.

Shirley Rousseau Murphy comments:

I grew up in California, riding the horses my father trained. My mother was an artist, and after high school I attended the same art school where she had gone. I have worked as a commercial artist and as an interior decorator. For many years I painted, and did welded metal sculpture. I exhibited my work on the west coast, sometimes in Mexico, and once in Panama. When I was 33 we moved to the Panama Canal Zone. There I worked in the Canal Zone library processing books and helping with the library museum. And I knew by then that I wanted to write. I stopped painting, stopped welding, and bought a typewriter. I've never regretted it, it is exactly what I love doing.

I find that ideas emerge slowly, from deep places in the mind. They form into story slowly. At first each idea is a separate shadow moving out from a tangle of images. My job is to discover the meaning that wants to make itself clear, and to help it form into story. The most pleasurable part of writing, for me, is after the first draft, when I revise and rewrite. In the revisions one can make characters come even more alive, give greater depth to the scenes, and find the full meaning of the story.

We live beside a lake now, and my best time for thinking about story is while swimming. Our Weimaraner is a great swimmer; we have races. He will be in a book one day. I will never stop writing; it is not so much a profession as it is a way of life, a way of seeing life.

*   *   *

Shirley Rousseau Murphy's carefully chosen words create images of the most magnificent animals who combine intelligence and wisdom in a caring manner. She is a painter working with the medium of words, addressing age-old concerns. Although she has drawn from folklore for some of her novels, she is primarily a modern fantasy writer.

Several of her novels trace their roots from traditional literature but with an added twist. In *Soonie and the Dragon* Soonie develops clever solutions to problems by using her common sense as the key. She saves three princesses by imitating their talents and sees through the plight of the three-headed griffin finally to gain Dan Long as her suitor. In *Valentine for a Dragon* the young demon suffers in his love of the magnificent dragon Fervicent. Each gift he offers fails to kindle a response in her, but often because it is the wrong kind of gift—a paper valentine card that turns to ashes or fudge that turns to cocoa.

But when the dragon uses her fire to save the town party and the demon gives her a special gift of color tones for the fire the two are happily united. In *Silver Woven in My Hair* Murphy weaves a number of Cinderella stories taken from an 1893 collection into the main fabric of another Cinderella story. Thursey the protagonist paints and writes the tales in secret and comes to love the young goatherd Gillie, in reality the young prince.

The Flight of the Fox is a soaring novel that places two unlikely characters together, Rory the kangaroo rat and Crispin the lemming. Charlie Gribble is the human observer and helper when permitted. "The Fox" is a model airplane found on a dump and reconstructed by Rory, Crispin, and Charlie while under the observation of starlings who overrun and plague the town. Murphy captures the behavior and characteristics of each animal and also the chattering and gossip-like movement of the starlings. One is reminded of Hoban's *The Mouse and His Child* with this mixture of the technological and the natural.

In five books Murphy created the land of Ere, but it is in *The Joining of the Stone* that the final resolution of the conflict between good and evil is revealed. Lobon must bring about the joining of the rune stone to save Ere, but he has a more demanding goal, to kill the dragon-man Dracvadrig who had killed his father. Although Murphy permits both Lobon and Meaths, a seer, to be flawed, this does not detract from the resolution of the plot.

Har Dragonbards fantasy triology begins with *Nightpool* in which Tebriel, the king's son, is injured and nursed to health by a colony of talking otters. Thus begins the battle for good in the world of Tirror in which dragons and their singing bards seek each other out as the means to halt the evil of the unliving that has invaded the world in the person of Quazelzeg, master of monstrous hordes. Teb finds Seastrider, his singing dragon, and the mission is begun. In *The Ivory Lyre* and finally in *The Dragonbards* the conflict is resolved. Murphy has a wondrous ability to describe animals with such beauty and sensitivity that the reader is forced to believe in their intelligence and their contribution to the good.

—Jane Anne Hannigan

———

MYERS, Walter Dean. Has also written as Walter M. Myers. American. Born in Martinsburg, West Virginia, 12 August 1937. Educated at Empire State College, New York. Served in the United States Army, 1955–58. Married Constance Brendel in 1973 (second marriage); one daughter and one son from previous marriage. Employment supervisor, New York State Department of Labor, Brooklyn, 1966–69; senior editor, Bobbs Merrill, publishers, New York, 1970–77; part-time teacher of creative writing and Black history, New York, 1974–75. Has also worked as a mail clerk, office messenger, and factory interviewer. Since 1977 freelance writer. Recipient: American Library Association Coretta Scott King award, 1980, 1985, 1989; National Endowment of the Arts grant, 1982, 1989; MacDowell fellowship, 1988. Address: 2543 Kennedy Boulevard, Jersey City, New Jersey 07304, U.S.A.

PUBLICATIONS FOR CHILDREN

Fiction

Where Does the Day Go? (as Walter M. Myers), illustrated by Leo Carty. New York, Parents' Magazine Press, 1969.
The Dancers, illustrated by Anne Rockwell. New York, Parents' Magazine Press, 1972.
The Dragon Takes a Wife, illustrated by Ann Grifalconi. In-

dianapolis, Bobbs Merrill, 1972.

Fly, Jimmy, Fly!, illustrated by Moneta Barnett. New York, Putnam, 1974.

Fast Sam, Cool Clyde, and Stuff. New York, Viking Press, 1975.

Brainstorm, photographs by Chuck Freeman. New York and London, Watts, 1977.

Mojo and the Russians. New York, Viking Press, 1977.

Victory for Jamie, illustrated by Norm Walker. New York, Scholastic, 1977.

It Ain't All for Nothin'. New York, Viking Press, 1978.

The Young Landlords. New York, Viking Press, 1979.

The Black Pearl and the Ghost, illustrated by Robert Quackenbush. New York, Viking Press, 1980.

The Golden Serpent, illustrated by Alice and Martin Provensen. New York, Viking Press, 1980; London, MacRae, 1981.

Hoops. New York, Delacorte Press, 1981.

The Legend of Tarik. New York, Viking Press, 1981.

Won't Know Till I Get There. New York, Viking Press, 1982.

The Nicholas Factor. New York, Viking Press, 1983.

Tales of a Dead King. New York, Morrow, 1983.

Motown and Didi: A Love Story. New York, Viking Kestrel, 1984.

Mr. Monkey and the Gotcha Bird, illustrated by Leslie Morrill. New York, Delacorte Press, 1984.

The Outside Shot. New York, Delacorte Press, 1984.

Adventure in Granada. New York, Viking Kestrel, 1985.

The Hidden Shrine. New York, Viking Kestrel, 1985.

Duel in the Desert. New York, Viking Kestrel, 1986.

Ambush in the Amazon. New York, Penguin, 1986.

Crystal. New York, Viking Kestrel, 1987.

Shadow of the Red Moon. New York, Harper, 1987.

Sweet Illusions. New York, Teachers and Writers Collaborative, 1987.

Fallen Angels. New York, Scholastic, 1988.

Me, Mop, and the Moondance Kid, illustrated by Rodney Pate. New York, Delacorte Press, 1988.

Scorpions. New York, Harper, 1988.

Other

The World of Work: A Guide to Choosing a Career. Indianapolis, Bobbs Merrill, 1975.

Social Welfare: A First Book. New York, Watts, 1976.

*

Walter Dean Myers comments:

When I was a child books were my secret friends. I never had to explain to them why I couldn't speak as clearly as the other children, or that I felt badly about not having money for things that other kids seemed to have, or that I wasn't very good at making human friends. Now that I'm grown books are still my friends, but the secret's out.

* * *

Harlem permeates Walter Dean Myers's novels for children and teenagers, even the stories set in places very remote from New York. In *Fallen Angels*, for example, Myers writes about the Vietnam War and a black 17-year-old recruit named Richie Perry who enlists because he can't afford college and because he wants to get out of the crime-ridden Harlem neighborhood where he grew up. Although the agony and the tragedy of the war take place in the Vietnam hinterlands, Richie's thoughts are often in Harlem and with his family and friends there. When he is one of the few in his unit who survives his tour of duty, he can't wait to return to the place from where he fled.

The animals in *Mr. Monkey and the Gotcha Bird*, a children's

picture book that Myers adapted from African and Carribean folktales, talk in a rhythmic parody of black English that owes more to Myers's growing up in Harlem than to any linguistic affinity with Africa or Central America.

Myers remembers from his own childhood many positive experiences (such as reading from the newspaper to his mother while she did housework and getting his first typewriter from his father), but he doesn't look through rose-colored glasses when he writes about the dangerous and deadend reality of Harlem—the gangs (such as he depicts in *Scorpions*), drugs, school dropouts, broken families, crime, and pervasive hopelessness. In *Motown and Didi*, the author's most adult novel, Myers creates two products of the Harlem tragedy—Didi, a girl stymied in her attempt to enter college because of a brother who eventually drugs himself to death and a mother who has a nervous breakdown, and Motown, a homeless, likeable loner. What these two young people do to survive demonstrates how Myers uses the harsh realities of Harlem to provide a proving ground in which his characters mature. Didi and Motown employ their streetsmarts to overcome their environment and develop an ethical code, a capacity to love, and a commitment to help others.

In *Hoops*, 17-year-old Lonnie Jackson plays basketball to earn his ticket out of Harlem. His troubled but wise coach tells him, "You got to learn to use your talent and you got to cover yourself." When he and his coach are offered large sums of money to shave points off a game, Lonnie is forced to draw on his sense of right and wrong as well as his athletic skills. The next year, to pay off an athletic scholarship he won to go to college, Lonnie helps an autistic child relate to the outside world, and in this sequel to *Hoops* (entitled *The Outside Shot*) he again fights off an attempted basketball fix.

Myers transforms the world of Harlem abandoned apartments into a business opportunity for the five bright, enterprising teenage heroes of *The Young Landlords*, and he provides four of them with the challenge of exonerating the fifth member of the group who has been accused of stealing. This scenario of Harlem neighborhood buddies extricating themselves from a crisis brought on by youthful irresponsibility and exuberance is repeated in three of his other novels—*Mojo and the Russians*, *Fast Sam, Cool Clyde, and Stuff*, and *Won't Know Till I Get There*. There is a certain sameness to these lighthearted, relatively innocent adventures, but they provide preteenage readers with good evidence that kids are kids, even in Harlem.

The author's repertoire of stories also includes two science fiction/fantasy novels whose spiritual roots can be traced to Myers's Harlem experiences. *The Legend of Tarik* is ostensibly about a young knight in medieval North Africa who was orphaned early in life because of a genocidal attack on his people by a warrior-tyrant named El Muerte (The Death). In this mixture of Don Quixote and The Lone Ranger, Tarik seems like a medieval Motown who—inspired by love for a woman and by vengeance for crimes against his loved ones—fights an uphill battle against Evil (in the person of El Muerte). Almost too late does Tarik realize the dehumanizing effect that even killing for good reasons can have. And, in a somewhat implausible and wooden novel called *The Nicholas Factor*, Myers tackles the issue of elitist, secret societies that depend on willing, unthinking followers—a characteristic common both to racist groups like the Ku Klux Klan and inner city youth gangs.

Myers has opened up a part of America that once was closed to young readers. He has at once illuminated the hopelessness of black urban life and pointed a way it can be overcome—and at the same time has helped narrow the gap between black and white youth.

—Jack Forman

MYERS, Walter M. See **MYERS, Walter Dean.**

––––––––––

NAUGHTON, Bill (William John Francis Naughton). British. Born in Ballyhaunis, County Mayo, Ireland, 12 June 1910; grew up in Lancashire, England. Educated at St. Peter and St. Paul School, Bolton, Lancashire. Civil Defence driver in London during World War II. Married to Ernestine Pirolt. Has worked as a lorry driver, weaver, and coal-bagger. Recipient: Screenwriters Guild award, 1967, 1968; Italia prize, for radio play, 1974; Children's Rights Workshop Other award, 1978. Address: Kempis, Orrisdale Road, Ballasalla, Isle of Man, United Kingdom.

PUBLICATIONS FOR CHILDREN

Fiction

Pony Boy. London, Pilot Press, 1946.
The Goalkeeper's Revenge and Other Stories, illustrated by Dick De Wilde. London, Harrap, 1961.
The Goalkeeper's Revenge, and Spit Nolan, illustrated by Trevor Stubley. London, Macmillan, 1974.
A Dog Called Nelson, illustrated by Charles Mozley. London, Dent, 1976.
My Pal Spadger, illustrated by Charles Mozley. London, Dent, 1977.

PUBLICATIONS FOR ADULTS

Novels

Rafe Granite. London, Pilot Press, 1947.
One Small Boy. London, MacGibbon and Kee, 1957.
Alfie. London, MacGibbon and Kee, and New York, Ballantine, 1966.
Alfie, Darling. London, MacGibbon and Kee, 1970; New York, Simon and Schuster, 1971.

Short Stories

Late Night on Watling Street and Other Stories. London, Mac-Gibbon and Kee, 1959; New York, Ballantine, 1966.
The Bees Have Stopped Working and Other Stories. Exeter, Wheaton, 1976.

Plays

My Flesh, My Blood (broadcast 1957). London, French, 1959; revised version, as *Spring and Port Wine* (produced Birmingham, 1964; London, 1965; as *Keep It in the Family*, produced New York, 1967), London, French, 1967.
She'll Make Trouble (broadcast 1958). Published in *Worth a Hearing: A Collection of Radio Plays*, edited by Alfred Bradley, London, Blackie, 1967.
June Evening (broadcast 1958; produced Birmingham, 1966). London, French, 1973.
All in Good Time (as *Honeymoon Postponed*, televised 1961; as *All in Good Time*, produced London, 1963; New York, 1965). London, French, 1964.
Alfie (as *Alfie Elkins and His Little Life*, broadcast 1962; as *Alfie*, produced London, 1963; New York, 1964). London, French, 1964.
He Was Gone When We Got There, music by Leonard Salzedo (produced London, 1966).
Annie and Fanny (produced Bolton, Lancashire, 1967).
Lighthearted Intercourse (produced Liverpool, 1971).

Screenplays: *Alfie*, 1966; *The Family Way*, with Roy Boulting and Jeffrey Dell, 1966; *Spring and Port Wine*, 1970.

Radio Plays: *Timothy*, 1956; *My Flesh, My Blood*, 1957; *She'll Make Trouble*, 1958; *June Evening*, 1958; *Late Night on Watling Street*, 1959; *The Long Carry*, 1959; *Seeing a Beauty Queen Home*, 1960; *On the Run*, 1960; *Wigan to Rome*, 1960; *'30–'60*, 1960; *Jackie Crowe*, 1962; *Alfie Elkins and His Little Life*, 1962; *November Day*, 1963; *The Mystery*, 1973; *A Special Occasion*, 1982.

Television Plays: *Nathaniel Titlark* series, 1957; *Starr and Company* series 1958; *Yorky* series, with Allan Prior, 1960–61; *Looking for Frankie*, 1961; *Honeymoon Postponed*, 1961; *Somewhere for the Night*, 1962; *It's Your Move*, 1967.

Other

A Roof over Your Head (autobiography). London, Pilot Press, 1945.
On the Pig's Back: An Autobiographical Excursion. Oxford and New York, Oxford University Press, 1987.
Saintly Billy: A Catholic Boyhood. Oxford, Oxford University Press, 1988.

*   *   *

Bill Naughton is not so much a children's writer as a writer about childhood and young manhood whose books appeal greatly to young as well as adult readers.

Naughton was largely self-educated in public libraries during the depression years. His first book, *A Roof over Your Head*, was written while he was working as a Civil Defence driver in wartime London. It takes the form of a series of autobiographical sketches which do not follow on chronologically and which end in an unsatisfactory, tailing-off way. However, this book, despite its clumsy construction and occasionally uncertain style, already demonstrates Naughton's power as a writer and chronicler of life in the working class industrial Lancashire of the 1930's. Naughton's ear for dialogue and ironic humour are already in evidence. But, above all, the intensity of feeling that Naughton evokes in writing about poverty and hardship and their effect on the family, and in writing about love between man and woman, parent and child, are conveyed with a rawness in this first book that has become his hallmark, albeit somewhat overlaid with nostalgia in his recent, more polished writings.

Closest in form to *A Roof over Your Head*, *One Small Boy* takes the form of a novel yet it is clearly based on Naughton's own life. Events are seen from the point of view of the boy Michael, who starts life in Ireland and then moves to an industrial town in the north of England with his family (Bolton?). The reader follows Michael's *rites de passage* through school days (often very funny), relationships with parents and friends, and later on with girls. Irish dialect words, colloquialisms, and regionalisms lend Naughton's dialogue a precise and robust sense of place.

Pony Boy and *Alfie* are novels set mainly in London. *Pony Boy* tells of the adventures of two boys, Corky and Ginger, who have just left school. *Alfie*, Naughton's most well-known novel, was first written as a radio play (*Alfie Elkins and His Little Life*) and was also made into a film. It relates, with much situation comedy, the amorous adventures of a young man with a succession of girl friends, only to find that a crucial success is to elude him. As in all Naughton's writing, the world depicted is a male-dominated one in which female characters are seen only in relation to the hero, which gives a rather dated feel to these books.

Naughton's collections of short stories—*Late Night on Watling Street*, *The Goalkeeper's Revenge*, and *My Pal Spadger*—are in the main "street corner" stories (i.e., they treat the interactions and adventures of the groups of boys who gathered on street corners in the days before radio and television). Other stories are set in particular work places. As always, Naughton's exact detail of northern community and working life lends credibility and interest to his writing. Economy and clarity of construction combine with humour and sensitivity in the best of these stories, which appear simple and direct and yet imply much about people and situations.

At the center of the stage, always, in Naughton's work is the everyday life of the ordinary working-class youth, presented in its complexity, with depth, feeling, and sincerity. Naughton's influence in putting working-class characters on the literary map has been considerable, for children's books and for books written for adults. As Naughton himself says: "I write mostly about the life I have known."

—Rosemary Stones

NAYLOR, Phyllis Reynolds. American. Born in Anderson, Indiana, 4 January 1933. Educated at Joliet Junior College, Illinois, 1951–53, diploma 1953; American University, Washington, D.C., 1959–63, B.A. in psychology 1963. Married Rex V. Naylor in 1960 (second marriage); two sons. Clinical secretary, Billings Hospital, Chicago, 1953–56; teacher in elementary schools, Hazelcrest, Illinois, 1956; assistant executive secretary, Montgomery County Education Association, Rockville, Maryland, 1958–59; editorial assistant, National Education Association *NEA Journal*, Washington, D.C., 1959–60. Since 1960 freelance writer. Recipient: Society of Children's Book Writers Golden Kite award, 1978; Child Study Committee award, 1983; Mystery Writers of America Edgar Allan Poe award, 1985; National Endowment for the Arts fellowship, 1987; Society of School Librarians International Book award, 1988. Agent: Bill Reiss, John Hawkins and Associates, Suite 1600, 71 West 23rd Street, New York, New York 10010. Address: 9910 Holmhurst Road, Bethesda, Maryland 20817, U.S.A.

PUBLICATIONS FOR CHILDREN

Fiction

The Galloping Goat and Other Stories, illustrated by Robert Jefferson. Nashville, Abingdon Press, 1965.
Grasshoppers in the Soup, illustrated by Elsa Bailey. Philadelphia, Fortress Press, 1965.
Jennifer Jean, The Cross-Eyed Queen, illustrated by Harold K. Lamson. Minneapolis, Lerner, 1967.
Knee-Deep in Ice Cream and Other Stories, illustrated by Johanna Sperl. Philadelphia, Fortress Press, 1967.
The New Schoolmaster, illustrated by Mamoru Funai. Morristown, New Jersey, Silver Burdett, 1967.
A New Year's Surprise, illustrated by Jack Endewett. Morristown, New Jersey, Silver Burdett, 1967.
To Shake a Shadow, illustrated by Gloria Kamen. Nashville, Abingdon Press, 1967.
What the Gulls Were Singing, illustrated by Jack Smith. Chicago, Follett, 1967.

When Rivers Meet, illustrated by Allan Eitzen. New York, Friendship Press, 1968.
Dark Side of the Moon, illustrated by Joseph Papin. Philadelphia, Fortress Press, 1969.
Meet Murdock, illustrated by Gioia Fiammenghi. Chicago, Follett, 1969.
The Private and Other Stories, illustrated by Elsa Bailey. Philadelphia, Fortress Press, 1969.
To Make a Wee Moon, illustrated by Beth and Jo Krush. Chicago, Follett, 1969.
Making It Happen, illustrated by Joe De Velasco. Chicago, Follett, 1970.
Ships in the Night, illustrated by Otto Reinhardt. Philadelphia, Fortress Press, 1970.
Wrestle the Mountain, illustrated by Paul Giovanopoulos. Chicago, Follett, 1971.
No Easy Circle, illustrated by Lou Aronson. Chicago, Follett, 1972.
To Walk the Sky Path, illustrated by Jack Endewett. Chicago, Follett, 1973.
Witch's Sister, illustrated by Gail Owens. New York, Atheneum, 1975.
Walking Through the Dark, illustrated by James and Ruth McCrea. New York, Atheneum, 1976.
Witch Water, illustrated by Gail Owens. New York, Atheneum, 1977; London, W.H. Allen, 1979.
The Witch Herself, illustrated by Gail Owens. New York, Atheneum, 1978; London, W.H. Allen, 1979.
How Lazy Can You Get?, illustrated by Alan Daniel. New York, Atheneum, 1979; London, Hamish Hamilton, 1980.
Change in the Wind. Minneapolis, Augsburg Press, 1980.
Eddie, Incorporated, illustrated by Blanche Sims. New York, Atheneum, 1980.
Shadows on the Wall, illustrated by Ruth Sanderson. New York, Atheneum, 1980.
All Because I'm Older, illustrated by Leslie Morrill. New York, Atheneum, 1981.
Faces in the Water, illustrated by Ruth Sanderson. New York, Atheneum, 1981.
Footprints at the Window, illustrated by Ruth Sanderson. New York, Atheneum 1981.
The Boy with the Helium Head, illustrated by Kay Chorao. New York, Atheneum, 1982.
Never Born a Hero. Minneapolis, Augsburg Press, 1982.
A String of Chances, illustrated by Ruth Sanderson. New York, Atheneum, 1982.
The Mad Gasser of Bessledorf Street, illustrated by Andrew Rhodes. New York, Atheneum, 1983.
The Solomon System, illustrated by Ronald Himler. New York, Atheneum, 1983.
A Triangle Has Four Sides. Minneapolis, Augsburg Press, 1983.
Night Cry, illustrated by Ruth Sanderson. New York, Atheneum, 1984.
Old Sadie and the Christmas Bear, illustrated by Patricia Montgomery Newton. New York, Atheneum, 1984.
The Agony of Alice, illustrated by Blanche Sims. New York, Atheneum, 1985.
The Dark of the Tunnel, illustrated by Ronald Himler. New York, Atheneum, 1985.
The Bodies in the Bessledorf Hotel, illustrated by Gail Owens. New York, Atheneum, 1986.
The Keeper, illustrated by Ronald Himler. New York, Atheneum, 1986.
The Baby, The Bed, and the Rose, illustrated by Mary Szilagyi. New York, Clarion, 1987.
Beetles, Lightly Toasted, illustrated by Melodye Rosales. New

York, Atheneum, 1987.
The Year of the Gopher, illustrated by John Steven Gurney.   New
   York, Atheneum, 1987.
Maudie in the Middle, with Lura Schield Reynolds, illustrated by
   Judith Gwyn Brown.   New York, Atheneum, 1988.
One of the Third Grade Thonkers, illustrated by Walter Gaffney-Kes-
   sell.   New York, Atheneum, 1988.
Alice in Rapture, Sort Of, illustrated by Blanche Sims.   New York,
   Atheneum, 1989.
Keeping a Christmas Secret, illustrated by Lena Shiffman.   New
   York, Atheneum, 1989.

Other

How to Find Your Wonderful Someone.   Philadelphia, Fortress
   Press, 1972.
An Amish Family, illustrated by George Armstrong.   Chicago,
   O'Hara, 1974.
Getting Along in Your Family, illustrated by Rick Cooley.   Nash-
   ville, Abingdon Press, 1976.
How I Came to Be a Writer, illustrated by Lou Carbone.   New York,
   Atheneum, 1978.
Getting Along with Your Friends, illustrated by Rick Cooley.   Nash-
   ville, Abingdon Press, 1980.
Getting Along with Your Teachers, illustrated by Rick Cooley.
   Nashville, Abingdon Press, 1981.

PUBLICATIONS FOR ADULTS

Novels

Revelations.   New York, St. Martin's Press, 1979; London, Sphere,
   1981.
Unexpected Pleasures.   New York, Putnam, 1986.

Other

*Crazy Love: An Autobiographical Account of Marriage and Mad-
   ness*.   New York, Morrow, 1977.
In Small Doses (essays).   New York, Atheneum, 1979.
The Craft of Writing the Novel.   Boston, The Writer, 1989.

*

Manuscript Collections: Kerlan Collection, University of
Minnesota, Minneapolis; de Grummond Collection, University of
Southern Mississippi, Hattiesburg.

Phyllis Reynolds Naylor comments:

As soon as I finish writing a mystery, I want to do a humorous
book, a realistic novel, or an adventure story. Because life is like
that—exciting, boring, scary, thrilling, wonderful, terrible, and
always changing from day to day. When there is a crisis in my novels,
I am working out problems on paper where they aren't quite so
threatening, deciding how and even whether I could cope. My
characters are old and young, wealthy and poor, uneducated and
privileged because I want to experience everything. And the only
way I know how to do this is to become the people in my books.

*   *   *

   Phyllis Reynolds Naylor is a prolific, versatile writer of books for
widely divergent audiences ranging from preschoolers to adults. She
writes well in a variety of forms and styles, including comic adventure stories, philosophical time-travel fantasies, realistic novels

about adolescents maturing, dark problem novels, and various kinds
of non-fiction.

   Naylor has a talent for humorous invention. In stories such as *The
Bodies in the Bessledorf Hotel* and *Beetles, Lightly Toasted* she
creates funny predicaments that appeal to children's sense of humor.
Sometimes this humor becomes routine or merely silly, but often it
contains threads of genuine anxiety or uncertainty that lead to deeper
insights.

   The York Trilogy, a fantasy series consisting of *Shadows on the
Wall*, *Faces in the Water*, and *Footprints at the Window*, won acclaim
for its convincing characterizations, complex and intriguing plot, and
challenging philosophical explorations. In these novels the central
character Dan Roberts confronts difficulties in 4th- and 14th-century
England as well as in 20th-century Pennsylvania. Hereditary disease,
war, plague, and the nature of chance are some of the themes treated.

   In her realistic novels about adolescents, Naylor reveals the
growth and dilemmas of authentically drawn young people. In *A
String of Chances*, one of her best, 16-year-old Evie experiences a
summer away from home, living with a cousin and the cousin's
husband, who are expecting a baby. She has her first serious romance,
gains insights into her family's patterns of behavior, and struggles
with her longstanding dislike of a boy who is living at her parents'
home for the summer. Evie's father is a country preacher, and she
confronts her own religious doubts and questions, especially when
the beloved baby Joshua suddenly dies. What might easily have
become trite and stereotypical is not at all so: Evie's father is loving
and genuine and has a sense of humor; the baby's death and the
consequent grief of all involved are presented with truthfulness and
depth; and Evie emerges stronger and wiser but without easy resolutions to her religious questions or to her difficulties in romance. The
milieu of small-town life is aptly brought to life, and even the minor
characters are intriguing and vital.

   The Year of the Gopher is narrated by 17-year-old George
Richards, whose well-to-do suburban Minneapolis family suffers
from performance expectations that have ruled family behavior for
three generations. George revolts against these expectations by
refusing to go to college (his lawyer father would prefer that he go
to an Ivy League school as he himself did) and chooses to find
blue-collar work instead, at least for a year. Naylor draws the world
of George's teenage peers with observant, accurate detail. George's
first sexual relationship, his relationship with his siblings, and his
maturing realizations about life are all presented without clichés or
sensationalism.

   Some of Naylor's books might accurately be described as problem
novels, since a difficult social or psychological issue forms the
central theme of these works. *The Keeper*, which deals with the
recognition and consequences of mental illness in a boy's father, is
an example of such a novel. But Naylor's approach to the problems
treated in these novels is not narrow or didactic. The characters are
shown struggling with painful realities of life in ways that do not set
them apart from other human beings, though their situations may be
unusually complex or hard to bear.

   In such books as *An Amish Family* and *Maudie in the Middle* (the
latter co-authored with Lura Schield Reynolds, the writer's mother),
Naylor weaves together factual information with fictional elements.
It is noteworthy how thoroughly Naylor imbues all of her work—not
only the non-fiction or semi-autobiographical fiction—with the particularity of place, family, and ethnic culture.

   Naylor's work is distinguished by her skill at diversity. From
comedy to tragedy, from books for younger children to books for
older young adults, in novels with rural settings or urban landscapes,
from fantasy to realism, she reveals a fine sense of the unexpected
difficulties and rewards of life. Her characters have depth, individuality, and complexity, and Naylor has the power to make them
matter to us. She treats her characters with an admirable mixture of
sympathy and critical insight. Symptomatic of Naylor's vision is her

willingness to present religious, ethical, and psychological issues without a hidden—or, for that matter, obvious—agenda, but simply with honesty and sensitivity.

—John D. Stahl

NEEDHAM, (Amy) Violet. British. Born in London, 5 June 1876. Educated at home. *Died 8 June 1967.*

PUBLICATIONS FOR CHILDREN

Fiction

The Black Riders, illustrated by Anne Bullen. London, Collins, 1939.
The Emerald Crown, illustrated by Anne Bullen. London, Collins, 1940.
The Stormy Petrel, illustrated by Joyce Bruce. London, Collins, 1942.
The Horn of Merlyns, illustrated by Joyce Bruce. London, Collins, 1943.
The Woods of Windri, illustrated by Joyce Bruce. London, Collins, 1944.
The House of the Paladin, illustrated by Joyce Bruce. London, Collins, 1945.
The Changeling of Monte Lucio, illustrated by Joyce Bruce. London, Collins, 1946.
The Bell of the Four Evangelists, illustrated by Joyce Bruce. London, Collins, 1947.
The Boy in Red, illustrated by Joyce Bruce. London, Collins, 1948.
The Betrayer, illustrated by Joyce Bruce. London, Collins, 1950.
Pandora of Parrham Royal, illustrated by Joyce Bruce. London, Collins, 1951.
The Avenue, illustrated by Joyce Bruce. London, Collins, 1952.
How Many Miles to Babylon?, illustrated by Joyce Bruce. London, Collins, 1953.
Adventures at Hampton Court, illustrated by Will Nickless. London, Lutterworth Press, 1954.
Richard and the Golden Horse Shoe, illustrated by Joyce Bruce. London, Collins, 1954.
The Great House of Estraville, illustrated by Joyce Bruce. London, Collins, 1955.
The Secret of the White Peacock, illustrated by Joyce Bruce. London, Collins, 1956.
The Red Rose of Ruvina, illustrated by Richard Kennedy. London, Collins, 1957.
Adventures at Windsor Castle, illustrated by David Walsh. London, Lutterworth Press, 1957.

*   *   *

Violet Needham's first book, *The Black Riders*, was published in 1939, at a time when the action of most books for children revolved around ponies, dormitories, and secret passages. She avoided all the conventions of the genre by setting many of her own books in an imaginary European Empire and its satellite kingdoms and principalities. Yet, despite their Ruritanian background, Needham's novels are refreshingly free of the jangling of spurs and the clashing of sabres. Her heroes may sometimes be kings—boy-kings, in fact—but the regal trappings are always subordinate to the development of plot and character, and the royal heroes are recognisable and convincing children who, by virtue of the setting and their rank, can be

subjected to dangers which would seem excessive in more realistic circumstances. Few children, even in the more lurid adventure stories, can be subjected to assassination attempts or slow poisoning without some suspension of the reader's belief, but high drama of this kind is acceptable in a setting of acknowledged romantic fantasy.

Above all, though, Needham was concerned with character. Her heroes may be kings but they are often reluctant ones. *The Emerald Crown* is set in the kingdom of Flavonia, which is ruled by a usurper. The people hope for the return of a legendary lost heir who will restore the most legitimate line to the throne, but in the end the true king turns out to be an English schoolboy who doesn't want to be "a rotten little king of a rotten little country." He overcomes his reluctance eventually but his struggle is typical of those confronting Needham's heroes. They must all face unbearable decisions, and choose between the call of duty and their own wills, or between loyalty to their country and loyalty to their friends. In *The Stormy Petrel*, young Carol becomes Emperor after the sudden death of his grandfather and is totally unprepared for the threatened revolution and assassination attempts which accompany his accession. Dick, "The Stormy Petrel" and hero of many of the books, must, in *The Betrayer*, decide between loyalty to his emperor and country, and his devotion to a friend who threatens the security of both.

Not all Needham's books were concerned with political intrigue in fictitious kingdoms. She wrote four conventional stories with English settings, among them *The Bell of the Four Evangelists* and *The Horn of Merlyns*, which centred on the finding of long-lost treasure, the ending of family feuds, and similar stock ingredients of children's books of the period. Her finest work, though, is to be found in her historical novels, especially *The Woods of Windri* and *The Changeling of Monte Lucio*, absorbing linked adventure stories which take place in imaginary countries, and *The Boy in Red*, a richly detailed novel set in the Netherlands during the revolt against the Spanish. In this book, and her only other straightforward historical story, *The Avenue*, Needham drew upon the family background of her Dutch mother for inspiration.

Needham holds a unique position among British writers for children. Apart from one or two isolated examples, no other writer has attempted to create the same brand of romantic adventure. She was in her sixties when her first book was published (*The Black Riders* had been written 20 years before and rejected by publishers as being too difficult for children) and perhaps this may explain why her style and themes were so different from those of other writers of the period. Whatever the reason, her books enjoyed enormous popularity and are still regarded with fanatical devotion by those adults who enjoyed her work when they were young.

—Lance Salway

NEEDLE, Jan. British. Born in Holybourne, Hampshire, 8 February 1943. Educated at Church Street School, Portsmouth, Hampshire, 1947–54; Portsmouth Grammar School, 1954–60; University of Manchester, 1968–72, B.A. (honours) in drama 1972. Reporter, Portsmouth *Evening News*, 1960–64; reporter and sub-editor, *Daily Herald and Sun*, London, 1964–68. Agent: David Higham Associates, 5–8 Lower John Street, London W1R 4HA; or Rochelle Stevens and Company, 15–17 Islington High Street, London N1 1LQ, England.

PUBLICATIONS FOR CHILDREN

Fiction

Albeson and the Germans. London, Deutsch, 1977.

My Mate Shofiq. London, Deutsch, 1978.
A Fine Boy for Killing. London, Deutsch, 1979.
The Size Spies, illustrated by Roy Bentley. London, Deutsch, 1979.
Rottenteeth, illustrated by Roy Bentley. London, Deutsch, 1980.
The Bee Rustlers, illustrated by Paul Wright. London, Collins, 1980.
A Sense of Shame and Other Stories. London, Deutsch, 1980.
Wild Wood, illustrated by William Rushton. London, Deutsch, 1981.
Losers Weepers, illustrated by Jane Bottomley. London, Methuen, 1981.
Another Fine Mess, illustrated by Roy Bentley. London, Deutsch, 1981.
Piggy in the Middle. London, Deutsch, 1982.
Going Out (novelization of television series). London, Fontana, 1983.
A Pitiful Place (short stories). London, Deutsch, 1984.
Tucker's Luck (novelization of television series). London, Fontana, 1984.
Great Days at Grange Hill (novelization of television series). London, Deutsch, 1984.
A Game of Soldiers (novelization of his own television series). London, Armada, 1985.
Behind the Bike Sheds (novelization of his own television series). London, Methuen, 1985.
Tucker in Control (novelization of television series). London, Deutsch, 1985.
Wagstaffe the Wind-Up Boy, illustrated by Roy Bentley. London, Deutsch, 1987.
Uncle in the Attic, illustrated by Robert Bartelt. London, Heinemann, 1988.
Skeleton at School, illustrated by Robert Bartelt. London, Heinemann, 1988.
In the Doghouse, illustrated by Robert Bartelt. London, Heinemann, 1988.
The Sleeping Party, illustrated by Robert Bartelt. London, Heinemann, 1988.
The Thief (novelization of his own television series). London, Hamish Hamilton, 1989.

Plays

The Rebels of Gaslight Street. London, Collins, 1986.

Television Plays: *A Game of Soldiers* series, 1983; *Behind the Bike Sheds* series, 1985; *Bogeymen* (*Dramarama* series), 1988; *The Thief,* 1988.

PUBLICATIONS FOR ADULTS

Plays

Radio Plays: *Paulo Baby,* 1972; *A Place of Execution,* 1974; *Celebration for a Million Deaths,* 1976; *The Incendiarist,* with Lawrence McDermott, 1978; *Men of Violence,* 1979; *Thanks for Nothing,* 1979; *Certain Souvenirs,* 1980.

Television Plays: *Truckers* series, 1987; *Soft Soap,* 1987.

Other

Brecht, with Peter Thomson. Oxford, Blackwell, and Chicago, University of Chicago Press, 1981.

*   *   *

Jan Needle's writing for children resists easy categorisation by age, group, or genre. He has written, for example, a very funny and inventive picture book about a rascally pirate called *Rottenteeth* and created for it the wettest hero imaginable, Everett Dymme, who is nagged incessantly by the princess whose hand he eventually wins. At the other end of the scale, and for a very much older reader, there is his bleak historical novel *A Fine Boy for Killing.* In many respects this is his most ambitious book, dealing as it does with the daily life of pressed men and boys in the navy during the Napoleonic Wars. It is unsparing in its presentation of the complete incomprehension by the officer class of the men whose lives they brutalised. It ought to be very well-known.

He is much better-known for *My Mate Shofiq* and *A Sense of Shame,* which aim at a presentation of the way in which the lives of young people reflect the issues current in our society. They are full of good intention and "relevant"—*My Mate Shofiq* presents the growing friendship of a young English boy for the Pakistani boy in his class at school. There are some telling moments as the English boy's (and the reader's) awareness is expanded, but the lives we are presented with remain, it seems to me, the vehicle for an idea. There is nothing to match the unsentimental sympathy which can encompass even the brutal captain in *A Fine Boy for Killing.*

Perhaps the best place to start is with his first novel, *Albeson and the Germans,* which is intended for slightly younger readers but again has a contemporary setting. This is much less issue-laden and much more inconsequential (in the best sense), and so the full confusion of the central character and the attraction and revulsion he feels for his "friend," the sinister older boy, is more fully developed. The book also has the most straightforwardly exciting climax I have read for a long time.

In a quite different vein, though for much the same age group, is the completely zany *The Size Spies. Wild Wood* is much more interesting; it was put quickly into paperback—something which doesn't always happen to Needle's books. In *Wild Wood* we have the world turned upside down, at least as far as *The Wind in the Willows* is concerned. It is a careful, thoughtful, and very funny book in which history is rewritten and the heroes turn out not to be the aristocratic grotesque like Toad but the labouring poor on the fringes of his domain driven finally into rebellion by his self-opinionated carelessness. I can't think of anything more relevant to our present condition than that.

In recent years Needle has shifted to writing for television and adapting popular television series into novels. *Tucker's Luck* and *Tucker in Control,* for instance, recreate the misadventures of teenage boys whose lives revolve around girls, drink, and the dole office. Other novelizations like *Behind the Bike Sheds* and *Great Days at Grange Hill* are chronicles of school life. Fast and infuriatingly flip (just like teenagers), these lightweight books undoubtedly sell well to the age group they document, but they leave no mark. It is hoped that Needle won't abandon entirely the kind of writing he proved so adept at with *A Fine Boy for Killing.*

—Eric Hadley and George Walsh

———————

NESBIT, E(dith). Also wrote as E. Bland; Fabian Bland. British. Born in London, 15 August 1858. Educated at an Ursuline convent in Dinan, France, 1869, and at schools in Germany and Brighton. Married 1) the writer Hubert Bland in 1880 (died 1914), two sons, one daughter, one adopted daughter, and one adopted son; 2) Thomas Terry Tucker in 1917. Journalist, elocutionist, greeting cards decorator; poetry critic, *Athenaeum* magazine, London, 1890's; co-editor, *Neolith* magazine, London, 1907–08; general editor, Children's Bookcase series, Oxford University Press and Hodder and Stoughton, 1908–11. Founding member, 1884, and member of the Pamphlet Committee, Fabian Society. Granted a Civil List pension, 1915. *Died 4 May 1924.*

PUBLICATIONS FOR CHILDREN

Fiction

Listen Long and Listen Well, with others. London, Tuck, 1893.
Sunny Tales for Snowy Days, with others. London, Tuck, 1893.
Told by Sunbeams and Me, with others. London, Tuck, 1893.
Fur and Feathers: Tales for All Weathers, with others. London, Tuck, 1894.
Lads and Lassies, with others. London, Tuck, 1894.
Tales That Are True, for Brown Eyes and Blue, with others, edited by Edric Vredenburg, illustrated by M. Goodman. London, Tuck, 1894.
Tales to Delight from Morning till Night, with others, edited by Edric Vredenburg, illustrated by M. Goodman. London, Tuck, 1894.
Hours in Many Lands: Stories and Poems, with others, edited by Edric Vredenburg, illustrated by Frances Brundage. London, Tuck, 1894.
Doggy Tales, illustrated by Lucy Kemp-Welch. London, Ward, 1895.
Pussy Tales, illustrated by Lucy Kemp-Welch. London, Ward, 1895.
Tales of the Clock, illustrated by Helen Jackson. London, Tuck, 1895.
Dulcie's Lantern and Other Stories, with Theo Gift and Mrs. Worthington Bliss. London, Griffith Farran, 1895.
Treasures from Storyland, with others. London, Tuck, 1895.
Tales Told in Twilight: A Volume of Very Short Stories. London, Nister, 1897.
Dog Tales, and Other Tales, with A. Guest and Emily R. Watson, edited by Edric Vredenburg, illustrated by R.K. Mounsey. London, Tuck, 1898.
Pussy and Doggy Tales, illustrated by Lucy Kemp-Welch. London, Dent, 1899; New York, Dutton, 1900.
The Story of the Treasure Seekers, Being the Adventures of the Bastable Children in Search of a Fortune, illustrated by Gordon Browne and Lewis Baumer. London, Unwin, and New York, Stokes, 1899.
The Book of Dragons, illustrated by H.R. Millar. London and New York, Harper, 1900.
Nine Unlikely Tales for Children, illustrated by H.R. Millar and Claude Shepperson. London, Unwin, and New York, Dutton, 1901.
The Wouldbegoods, Being the Further Adventures of the Treasure Seekers, illustrated by Arthur H. Buckland and John Hassell. London, Unwin, 1901; New York, Harper, 1902.
Five Children and It, illustrated by H.R. Millar. London, Unwin, 1902; New York, Dodd Mead, 1905.
The Revolt of the Toys and What Comes of Quarrelling, illustrated by Ambrose Dudley. London, Nister, and New York, Dutton, 1902.
Playtime Stories. London, Tuck, 1903.
The Rainbow Queen and Other Stories. London, Tuck, 1903.
The Phoenix and the Carpet, illustrated by H.R. Millar. London, Newnes, and New York, Macmillan, 1904.
The Story of the Five Rebellious Dolls. London, Nister, 1904.
The New Treasure Seekers, illustrated by Gordon Browne and Lewis Baumer. London, Unwin, and New York, Stokes, 1904.
Cat Tales, with Rosamund Bland, illustrated by Isabel Watkin. London, Nister, and New York, Dutton, 1904.

Pug Peter: King of Mouseland, Marquis of Barkshire, D.O.G., P.C. 1906, Knight of the Order of the Gold Dog Collar, Author of Doggerel Lays and Days..., illustrated by Harry Rountree. Leeds, Alf Cooke, 1905.
Oswald Bastable and Others, illustrated by C.E. Brock and H.R. Millar. London, Wells Gardner, 1905; New York, Coward McCann, 1960.
The Story of the Amulet, illustrated by H.R. Millar. London, Unwin, 1906; New York, Dutton, 1907.
The Railway Children, illustrated by C.E. Brock. London, Wells Gardner, and New York, Macmillan, 1906.
The Enchanted Castle, illustrated by H.R. Millar. London, Unwin, 1907; New York, Harper, 1908.
The House of Arden, illustrated by H.R. Millar. London, Unwin, 1908; New York, Dutton, 1909.
Harding's Luck, illustrated by H.R. Millar. London, Hodder and Stoughton, 1909; New York, Stokes, 1910.
The Magic City, illustrated by H.R. Millar. London, Macmillan, 1910; New York, Coward McCann, 1958.
The Wonderful Garden; or The Three C's, illustrated by H.R. Millar. London, Macmillan, 1911; New York, Coward McCann, 1935.
The Magic World, illustrated by H.R. Millar and Spencer Pryse. London and New York, Macmillan, 1912.
Wet Magic, illustrated by H.R. Millar. London, Laurie, 1913; New York, Coward McCann, 1937.
Our New Story Book, with others, illustrated by Elsie Wood and Louis Wain. London, Nister, and New York, Dutton, 1913.
The New World Literary Series, Book Two, edited by Henry Cecil Wyld. London, Collins, 1921.
Five of Us—And Madeline, edited by Mrs. Clifford Sharp, illustrated by Nora S. Unwin. London, Unwin, 1925; New York, Adelphi, 1926.
Fairy Stories, edited by Naomi Lewis, illustrated by Brian Robb. London, Benn, 1977.

Plays

Cinderella (produced London, 1892). London, Sidgwick and Jackson, 1909.
The Magician's Heart (produced London, 1907).

Verse

Songs of Two Seasons, illustrated by J. MacIntyre. London, Tuck, 1890.
The Voyage of Columbus, 1492: The Discovery of America, illustrated by Will and Frances Brundage. London, Tuck, 1892.
Our Friends and All about Them. London, Tuck, 1893.
As Happy as a King, illustrated by S. Rosamund Praeger. London, Ward, 1896.
Dinna Forget, with G.C. Bingham. London, Nister, 1897; New York, Dutton, 1898.
To Wish You Every Joy. London, Tuck, 1901.

Other

The Children's Shakespeare, edited by Edric Vredenburg, illustrated by Frances Brundage. London, Tuck, 1897; Philadelphia, Altemus, 1900.
Royal Children of English History, illustrated by Frances Brundage. London, Tuck, 1897.
Twenty Beautiful Stories from Shakespeare: A Home Study Course, edited by E.T. Roe, illustrated by Max Bihn. Chicago, Hertel and Jenkins, 1907.
The Old Nursery Stories, illustrated by W.H. Margetson. London, Oxford University Press-Hodder and Stoughton, 1908.

My Sea-Side Book, with George Manville Fenn. London, Nister, and New York, Dutton, 1911.
Children's Stories from Shakespeare, with *When Shakespeare Was a Boy*, by F.J. Furnivall. Philadelphia, McKay, 1912.
Children's Stories from English History, with Doris Ashley, edited by Edric Vredenburg, illustrated by John H. Bacon and Howard Davie. London, Tuck, 1914.
Long Ago When I Was Young, illustrated by Edward Ardizzone. London, Whiting and Wheaton, and New York, Watts, 1966.

Editor, with Robert Ellice Mack, *Spring* [*Summer, Autumn, Winter*] *Songs and Sketches*. London, Griffith Farran, and New York, Dutton, 4 vols., 1886.
Editor, with Robert Ellice Mack, *Eventide Songs and Sketches*. London, Griffith Farran, 1887; as *Night Songs and Sketches*, New York, Dutton, 1887.
Editor, with Robert Ellice Mack, *Morning Songs and Sketches*. London, Griffith Farran, 1887; as *Noon Songs and Sketches*, New York, Dutton, 1887.
Editor, with Robert Ellice Mack, *Lilies and Heartsease: Songs and Sketches*. New York, Dutton, 1888(?).
Editor, *The Girl's Own Birthday Book*. London, Drane, 1894.
Editor, *Poet's Whispers: A Birthday Book*. London, Drane, 1895.
Editor, *A Book of Dogs, Being a Discourse on Them, with Many Tales and Wonders...*, illustrated by Winifred Austin. London, Dent, and New York, Dutton, 1898.
Editor, *Winter-Snow*, illustrated by H. Bellingham Smith. New York, Dutton, 1898(?).

PUBLICATIONS FOR ADULTS

Novels

The Prophet's Mantle (as Fabian Bland, with Hubert Bland). London, Drane, 1885; Chicago, Belford Clarke, 1889.
The Secret of the Kyriels. London, Hurst and Blackett, and Philadelphia, Lippincott, 1899.
The Red House. London, Methuen, and New York, Harper, 1902.
The Incomplete Amorist. London, Constable, and New York, Doubleday, 1906.
Daphne in Fitzroy Street. London, George Allen, and New York, Doubleday, 1909.
Salome and the Head: A Modern Melodrama. London, Alston Rivers, 1909; as *The House with No Address*, New York, Doubleday, 1909.
Dormant. London, Methuen, 1911; as *Rose Royal*, New York, Dodd Mead, 1912.
The Incredible Honeymoon. New York, Harper, 1916; London, Hutchinson, 1921.
The Lark. London, Hutchinson, 1922.

Short Stories

Something Wrong. London, Innes, 1893.
Grim Tales. London, Innes, 1893.
The Butler in Bohemia, with Oswald Barron. London, Drane, 1894.
In Homespun. London, Lane, and Boston, Roberts, 1896.
Thirteen Ways Home. London, Treherne, 1901.
The Literary Sense. London, Methuen, and New York, Macmillan, 1903.
Man and Maid. London, Unwin, 1906.
These Little Ones. London, George Allen, 1909.
Fear. London, Stanley Paul, 1910.
To the Adventurous. London, Hutchinson, 1923.
Tales of Terror, edited by Hugh Lamb. London, Methuen, 1983.

In the Dark: Tales of Terror, edited by Hugh Lamb. Wellingborough, Northamptonshire, Thorsons, 1988.

Plays

A Family Novelette, with Oswald Barron (produced London, 1894).
The King's Highway (produced London, 1905).
The Philandrist; or, The Lady Fortune-Teller, with Dorothea Deakin (produced London, 1905).
Unexceptionable References (produced London, 1912).

Verse

Lays and Legends. London and New York, Longman, 2 vols., 1886–92.
The Lily and the Cross. London, Griffith Farran, and New York, Dutton, 1887.
The Star of Bethlehem. London, Nister, 1887.
Leaves of Life. London and New York, Longman, 1888.
The Better Part and Other Poems. London, Drane, 1888.
Easter-Tide: Poems, with Caris Brooke. London, Drane, and New York, Dutton, 1888.
The Time of Roses, with Caris Brooke and others. London, Drane, 1888.
By Land and Sea. London, Drane, 1888.
Landscape and Song. London, Drane, and New York, Dutton, 1888.
The Message of the Dove: An Easter Poem. London, Drane, and New York, Dutton, 1888.
The Lilies Round the Cross: An Easter Memorial, with Helen J. Wood. London, Nister, and New York, Dutton, 1889.
Corals and Sea Songs. London, Nister, 1889.
Life's Sunny Side, with others. London, Nister, 1890.
Sweet Lavender. London, Nister, 1892.
Flowers I Bring and Songs I Sing (as E. Bland), with H.M. Burnside and A. Scanes. London, Tuck, 1893.
Holly and Mistletoe: A Book of Christmas Verse, with Norman Gale and Richard Le Gallienne. London, Ward, 1895.
A Pomander of Verse. London, Lane, and Chicago, McClurg, 1895.
Rose Leaves. London, Nister, 1895.
Songs of Love and Empire. London, Constable, 1898.
The Rainbow and the Rose. London and New York, Longman, 1905.
Ballads and Lyrics of Socialism 1883–1908. London, Fabian Society, 1908.
Jesus in London: A Poem. London, Fifield, 1908.
Ballads and Verses of the Spiritual Life. London, Elkin Mathews, 1911.
Garden Poems. London, Collins, 1912.
Many Voices. London, Hutchinson, 1922.

Other

Wings and the Child; or, The Building of Magic Cities. London, Hodder and Stoughton, and New York, Doran, 1913.

Editor, *Battle Songs*. London, Max Goschen, 1914.
Editor, *Essays*, by Hubert Bland. London, Max Goschen, 1914.

*

Critical Studies: *E. Nesbit: A Biography* by Doris Langley Moore, London, Benn, 1933, revised edition, Philadelphia, Chilton, 1966, Benn, 1967; *Magic and the Magician: E. Nesbit and Her Children's Books* by Noel Streatfield, London, Benn, and New York, Abelard Schuman, 1958; *E. Nesbit* by Anthea Bell, London, Bodley Head,

1960, New York, Walck, 1964; *A Woman of Passion: The Life of E. Nesbit* by Julia Briggs, London, Hutchinson, 1987.

*   *   *

E. Nesbit was one of those writers who do not perceive when they have found their level, and repine for the career they think they should have had in some other field of literature. She believed in herself primarily as a poet, but her quite numerous books of verse are now wholly neglected while the tales she wrote for children "to keep the house going" are recognized as little masterpieces of ingenuity and humour.

They fall into two categories, those based on magic and fantasy as in fairy tales from time immemorial, and those which are realistic and credible comedies of juvenile behaviour. To the first group belongs the trilogy which comprises *Five Children and It, The Phoenix and the Carpet*, and *The Story of the Amulet*. The major works in the second group also form a trilogy, *The Story of the Treasure Seekers, The Wouldbegoods*, and *The New Treasure Seekers*. Each volume can be read independently of the others. It is hard to choose between the two genres, in both of which, though imitated, Nesbit remains inimitable.

The protagonists, whether the plot hinges on magic or the adventures and misadventures of the human child, are usually families of what was then average size—four or five—with parents who are often got out of the way by absence abroad or some other simple expedient for leaving the children to their own world. Since they are differentiated by age as well as character, young readers can identify either with the eldest, aged about 11 to 14, or the little ones from six upwards. The smallest may be an infant. With no trace of priggishness, the elder ones, whether girls or boys, feel protective responsibility towards the others. Nesbit has little interest in school life and her *dramatis personae* seldom appear in situations where conformity and discipline are admired. Their virtues are courage, kindliness, a high sense of honour, and good manners, on which she lays particular stress.

Unlike most of her Victorian predecessors, she never intrudes religion, there are no pious death-bed scenes, no conversions or serious repentances. Wrongdoers are assigned only minor parts. "She was not a nice woman, and I am glad to say that she goes out of this story almost at once"—such is her typical way of dismissing a necessary but dislikable instrument of the story in *Harding's Luck*. Except when they can be given amusing roles, of which fortunately she creates many, her grown-ups tend to be somewhat sentimentalized.

The children's background is in general a rather hard-up section of the middle class. There is little pocket money, and treats that have to be paid for are scarce. Nesbit was an active pioneering socialist and a founder member of the Fabian Society, but she was able to combine its tenets, not very consistently, with unashamed imperialism and conventional, though unobtrusive, patriotism. In this respect her children are as truly Edwardian as the clothes they wear in the delightful illustrations, chiefly by H.R. Millar.

Although she occasionally touches with sympathy on the overworked and underprivileged, she does not allow political creeds to shape her narratives, and indeed she is more inclined to idealize the pre-industrial past than to look forward to a progressive future. The hero of *Harding's Luck*, a sequel to *The House of Arden*, is a crippled boy from the slums of Deptford. She describes both him and his squalid home with down-to-earth conviction, for she knew the living conditions of the poor through the charities she organized, but she provides him with aristocratic ancestors and noble aspirations, nor, when she has her youthful audience in view, does she recommend any subversion of the existing social order. She took a pride in not preaching at children and never writing down to them. Her prose, lucid and unpretentious but not oversimplified, lends itself perfectly to being read aloud.

The authors who influenced her most were probably Dickens, to whom she was devoted, though, in her youth, he had been decidedly out of fashion, Rudyard Kipling, and F. Anstey. The last-named certainly inspired the turn her imagination took when she depicted normal, everyday people caught up in amazing supernatural situations. Like him, she dealt with such manifestations humorously and avoided—at least in stories for juveniles—anything that might be frightening. Her magical creatures, the Psammead, the Phoenix, and the Mouldiwarp, are all endearing personalities in their own right. When she introduced historic scenes or distant lands, she took considerable trouble over the correctness of local colour but always with a light touch and a knack for singling out features entertaining to a child.

After her comic sense, perhaps Nesbit's greatest strength is her keen memory for the details which catch the eyes and ears of childhood, and which somehow she contrives to bring copiously into every tale without in the least slowing up her answers to the eager question: "What happens next?"

—Doris Langley Moore

NESS, Evaline (née Michelow). American. Born in Union City, Ohio, 24 April 1911. Educated at Ball State Teachers College, Muncie, Indiana, 1931–32; Chicago Art Institute, 1933–35; Corcoran School of Art, Washington, D.C., 1943–45; Art Students' League, New York, 1947; Accademia di Belle Arti, Rome, 1951–52. Married 1) the law enforcement officer Eliot Ness in 1938 (divorced 1946); 2) Arnold Bayard in 1959. Teacher of children's art classes, Corcoran School of Art, 1945–46, and Parsons School of Design, New York, 1959–60; fashion illustrator, Saks Fifth Avenue, New York, and magazine illustrator, 1946–49. From 1959 freelance illustrator. Recipient: American Library Association Caldecott Medal, 1967. *Died 12 August 1986.*

PUBLICATIONS FOR CHILDREN (illustrated by the author)

Fiction

A Gift for Sula Sula. New York, Scribner, 1963.
Josefina February. New York, Scribner, 1963; London, Chatto Boyd and Oliver, 1970.
Exactly Alike. New York, Scribner, 1964; Edinburgh, Oliver and Boyd, 1968.
Pavo and the Princess. New York, Scribner, 1964.
A Double Discovery. New York, Scribner, 1965.
Sam, Bangs, and Moonshine. New York, Holt Rinehart, 1966; London, Bodley Head, 1967.
The Girl and the Goatherd; or, This and That and Thus and So. New York, Dutton, 1970.
Do You Have the Time, Lydia? New York, Dutton, 1971; London, Bodley Head, 1972.
Yeck Eck. New York, Dutton, 1974.
Marcella's Guardian Angel. New York, Holiday House, 1979.
Fierce the Lion. New York, Holiday House, 1980.

Other

Long, Broad, and Quickeye. New York, Scribner, 1969; London, Chatto Boyd and Oliver, 1971.
An American Colonial Paper House: To Cut Out and Color. New

York, Scribner, 1975.
This Is a Paper Palace: To Cut Out and Color. New York, Scribner, 1976.
Four Rooms from the Metropolitan Museum of Art: To Cut Out and Color. New York, Scribner, 1977.
A Victorian Paper House: To Cut Out and Color. New York, Scribner, 1978.
A Shaker Paper House: To Cut Out and Color. New York, Scribner, 1979.

Editor, *Amelia Mixed the Mustard and Other Poems* (anthology). New York, Scribner, 1975.

*

Manuscript Collection: Kerlan Collection, University of Minnesota, Minneapolis.

Illustrator: *The Story of Ophelia* by Mary J. Gibbons, 1954; *The Bridge* by Charlton Ogburn, Jr., 1957; *The Sherwood Ring* by Elizabeth Pope, 1958; *Lonely Maria*, 1960, and *The Princess and the Lion*, 1963, both by Elizabeth Coatsworth; *Ondine* by Maurice Osborne, 1960; *Listen—The Birds* by Mary Britton Miller, 1961; *Across from Indian Shore* by Barbara Robinson, 1962; *Where Did Josie Go?*, 1962, *Some Cheese for Charles*, 1963, *Josie and the Snow*, 1964, *Josie's Buttercup*, 1967, and *Too Many Crackers*, 1971, all by Helen Buckley; *Thistle and Thyme*, 1962, and *A Scottish Songbook*, 1969, both edited by Sorche Nic Leodhas, and *All in a Morning Early*, 1963, and *Kellyburn Braes*, 1968, both by Nic Leodhas; *Macaroon*, 1962, and *Candle Tales*, 1968, both by Julia W. Cunningham; *Funny Town* by Eve Merriam, 1963; *A Pocketful of Cricket* by Rebecca Caudill, 1964; *Coll and His White Pig*, 1965, and *The Truthful Harp*, 1967, both by Lloyd Alexander; *Favorite Fairy Tales Told in Italy* edited by Virginia Haviland, 1965; *Tom Tit Tot: An English Folk Tale*, 1965, and *Mr. Miacca: An English Folk Tale*, 1967, both edited by Joseph Jacobs; *Pierino and the Bell* by Sylvia Cassedy, 1966; *Some of the Days of Everett Anderson*, 1970, *Everett Anderson's Christmas Coming*, 1971, and *Don't You Remember?*, 1973, all by Lucille Clifton; *Joey and the Birthday Present*, 1971, and *The Wizard's Tears*, 1975, both by Maxine Kumin and Anne Sexton, and *What Color Is Caesar?*, by Kumin, 1978; *Old Mother Hubbard and Her Dog* by Sarah Catherine Martin, 1972; *The Woman of the Wood* by Algernon Black, 1973; *The Steamroller* by Margaret Wise Brown, 1974; *The Lives of My Cat Alfred* by Nathan Zimelman, 1976; *The Warmint* by Walter de la Mare, 1976; *The Devil's Bridge* by Charles Scribner, Jr., 1978; *The Hand-Me-Down Doll* by Steven Kroll, 1983.

*   *   *

Evaline Ness was, in my opinion, the most brilliant and original illustrator of children's books in America in recent times. But she also wrote as well as illustrated several books, created books on doll houses, and assembled a collection of children's poetry called *Amelia Mixed the Mustard and Other Poems.*

Each of her own books is for younger children, and each is an excellent example of that category. Like another writer-illustrator, Maurice Sendak, who is usually billed above her (but not by me), her texts are as carefully conceived as is her artwork; and both are blended into so satisfactory a whole that it's difficult to consider them separately.

Take *Yeck Eck*, for example. It begins, "This small person, Tana Jones, had everything she wanted except the thing she wanted most, A BABY." As the humorous fantasy unfolds, a friend with numerous younger siblings donates a baby to Tana (which she promptly names Agift). Agift cries, "Yeck, Eck!"—words interpreted by Tana to

mean, "Take me!" As more and more babies are donated to her, the text spills over onto the bibs and dresses and walls—the words become part of the art. But even dream wishes end, when the babies prefer an adult caregiver to Tana. Now hearing their burbling cries, Tana sadly asks herself, "What does Yeck-Eck mean?" And herself answers, "Only a baby knows."

If the art and text interweave here to create a charming whole, what of the message? In the age of Women's Lib, how did Ness dare to create a heroine who wants to play with babies rather than paints, skates, or trucks? (Shh! Many children still agree with Tana!) The answer is, Ness never cut her cloth—or her stories—to fit the fad of the moment; but, on the other hand, she was often in advance of the current trend. In a book called *The Girl and the Goatherd*, written before the Women's Movement gained public notice, a girl seeks the traditional gift of beauty. But before she receives that desired beauty, she wins the love of the Goatherd who likes her as she is; and beauty, once attained, proves worthless. A crotchety, stubborn heroine who comes to comprehend the superficial value of physical perfection? An unlikely theme for those days!

Or consider *Do You Have the Time, Lydia?* A hectic activist, Lydia races from one non-traditional interest to another. Yet, unlike that of the present crop of feminist writers, the activism here is only the background of the story, which focuses rather on Lydia's inability to finish a job and her insensitivity to her younger brother. Though the story's theme is a universal one of changing values, the background images may well linger longer in young readers' memories than the more strident messages received from some feminist presses.

All Ness's protagonists are girls except one—the boy in her illustrations to the scary English folktale, *Mr. Miacca.* And each girl is a unique creation both in character and in the problems she faces; perhaps, considering the interchangeability of more prolific authors' characters, in Ness's case, less is more. And not only do the girls assume a three-dimensional reality, the adults too, when present, are unique individuals. The only three families shown are single-parent families. The girl in *Exactly Alike* lives with younger twin brothers and a mother constantly busy with sewing to sustain the family. The girl must take care of the naughty, teasing twins, a job that would tax an adult's patience. But she learns to cope with the situation by persistence and initiative. In *Yeck Eck* Tana lives with a father who drives a taxicab; Josefina, in *Josefina February*, lives with a poor farmer uncle; and in Ness's most famous book, *Sam, Bangs, and Moonshine* (a Caldecott Medal winner), the young Samantha, called Sam, lives with a fisherman father.

Sam has "the reckless habit of lying." Or, as her father implores her, "Talk real, not moonshine....Moonshine is flummadiddle. Real is the opposite." Sam's mother is dead—but not to Sam. In the "moonshine" she spins to her cat Bangs, to her friend Thomas, and to herself, she sees her mother as a mermaid. Then she sends Thomas on a quest for an imaginary kangaroo which has gone to live with her mermaid mother in a seacave; and she ignores her conscience, which speaks through Bangs, of the dangers of the incoming tide. Bangs goes after Thomas, and both seem lost when a sudden storm hits the coast.

At this point, a dedicated feminist might have Sam involved in the active rescue work; but here Ness gives Sam the harder job—that of waiting alone with her suffering. And in that suffering (which all of us sometimes endure), Sam finally recognizes that "real" is Thomas, is Bangs, is no mother. But her perceptive father reassures her that "there is good moonshine and bad moonshine—it's just important to know the difference." And Sam, like Josefina February, is able to make a hard choice to help a friend.

Ness's words speak for themselves; their poetry, their clarity, their honesty well match her subtle but straightforward portraits of children. Unlike the present trend of presenting "ugly" children under the guise of reality, Ness gave us, in both words and pictures, children as they really are—beautiful, straight, and honest, involved in the pleasures and problems of life.

—Betty Boegehold

NEVILLE, Emily Cheney. American. Born in Manchester, Connecticut, 28 December 1919. Educated at Oxford School, 1931–36; Bryn Mawr College, Pennsylvania, A.B. 1940; Albany Law School, New York, J.D. 1976; admitted to the New York bar, 1977. Married Glenn T. Neville in 1948 (died 1965); three daughters and two sons. Office worker 1940–41, and feature writer, 1941–44, New York *Daily Mirror*. Currently in private law practice. Recipient: American Library Association Newbery Medal, 1964; Women's International League for Peace and Freedom Jane Addams award, 1966. Address: Keene Valley, New York 12943, U.S.A.

PUBLICATIONS FOR CHILDREN

Fiction

It's Like This, Cat, illustrated by Emil Weiss.   New York, Harper, 1963; London, Angus and Robertson, 1969.
Berries Goodman.   New York, Harper, 1965; London, Angus and Robertson, 1970.
The Seventeenth Street Gang, illustrated by Emily McCully.   New York, Harper, 1966.
Traveler from a Small Kingdom, illustrated by George Mocniak.   New York, Harper, 1968.
Fogarty.   New York, Harper, 1969.
Garden of Broken Glass.   New York, Delacorte Press, 1975.
The Bridge, illustrated by Ronald Himler.   New York, Harper, 1988.

*

Manuscript Collection: Kerlan Collection, University of Minnesota, Minneapolis.

Emily Cheney Neville comments:

I enjoy writing conversation and dialogue, and having characters show themselves by what they say. Therefore the characters are somewhat fragmentary and do not have clearly narrated roles or purposes. No heavy messages. You can show a reader how you think people talk or act, but the child reader can draw his or her own conclusions. I like my books to be a bit funny.

*   *   *

Emily Cheney Neville is the author of several books for children, the most notable of which, *It's Like This, Cat* (awarded the Newbery Medal), is worthy of attention for its honest rendering of the scenes and sounds of New York City, the natural language of its teenage hero, Dave Mitchell, and the telling of some events not for the squeamish.

It's Like This, Cat is a far cry from the saccharine stories which flooded the children's book market for years about blonde white children who always lived in the suburbs, in pleasant houses, with idyllically married parents—stories which left those children whose circumstances were less rosy feeling deprived. Writers like Neville realize that children face many problems and well-designed books can help them clarify and meet their troubles. *It's Like This, Cat* does all this and more.

For one thing, Dave Mitchell's language "feels right." He says,

"My pop is full of hot air," or "It must be lousy to be in the city without any family or friends," or "Why do I have a nut for a friend?" Is this literature for children? Yes, when juxtaposed against the realistic slang-filled speech, we can find the hero describing his day at Coney Island like this: "I kick off my shoes and stand with my feet in the ice water and the sun hot on my chest. Looking out at the horizon with its few ships and some sea gulls and planes overhead, I think: It's mine, all mine, I could go anywhere in the world. I could. Maybe I will." What freedom, what daydreams are conveyed and how natural for a city boy to feel such sensations away from buildings and cement! The words are simple, yet given brightness by contrast. And there is depth, too—the probing of a child's innermost thoughts. These short quotes are only a glimpse of the art with which Neville has crafted this story. New York's skyscrapers, back alleys, parks, and zoos are a backdrop for the hero's adventures and difficulties. We suffer with him in his father's lack of understanding, sympathize with him when a kitten is thoughtlessly killed, and enjoy his conversations with the tom cat that fills a void in his life.

Today's teenager may find some of the expressions dated but the events discussed are recurrent, always new. Dave Mitchell's world, like F. Scott Fitzgerald's, is a moment of historical time. Parts of it such as Fulton Fish Market have vanished forever, but it is fun to step back and walk through places which cannot be seen again or to find their reality in books even though you have never known the originals.

It's Like This, Cat is satisfying on several levels—it is a good story, well told, and it has something important to say about life. Such qualifications make any book literature and this one has a special niche in children's stories.

—Carolyn T. Kingston

NEWELL, Crosby.   See BONSALL, Crosby.

NEWMAN, Robert (Howard). American. Born in New York City, 3 June 1909. Educated at the Ethical Culture School, New York; Brown University, Providence, Rhode Island, 1927–28. Served in the Office of War Information, New York, 1942–44: Chief, Radio Outpost Division. Married Dorothy Crayder in 1936; one daughter. Radio writer, 1936–42: created *City Hospital* series. *Died 7 December 1988.*

PUBLICATIONS FOR CHILDREN

Fiction

The Boy Who Could Fly, illustrated by Paul Sagsoorian.   New York, Atheneum, 1967; London, Hutchinson, 1968.
Merlin's Mistake, illustrated by Richard Lebenson.   New York, Atheneum, 1970; London, Hutchinson, 1971.
The Testing of Tertius, illustrated by Richard Cuffari.   New York, Atheneum, 1973; London, Hutchinson, 1974.
The Shattered Stone, illustrated by John Gretzer.   New York, Atheneum, 1975; London, Hutchinson, 1976.
Night Spell, illustrated by Peter Burchard.   New York, Atheneum, 1977.

The Case of the Baker Street Irregular, illustrated by David Stone. New York, Atheneum, 1978; as *A Puzzle for Sherlock Holmes*, London, Hutchinson, 1979.
The Case of the Vanishing Corpse, illustrated by David Stone. New York, Atheneum, 1980; London, Hutchinson, 1981.
The Case of the Somerville Secret, illustrated by David Stone. New York, Atheneum, 1981.
The Case of the Threatened King, illustrated by David Stone. New York, Atheneum, 1982.
The Case of the Etruscan Treasure. New York, Atheneum, 1983.
The Case of the Frightened Friend. New York, Atheneum, 1984.
The Case of the Murdered Players. New York, Atheneum, 1985.
The Case of the Indian Curse. New York, Atheneum, 1986.
The Case of the Watching Boy. New York, Atheneum, 1987.

Other

The Japanese: People of the Three Treasures, illustrated by Mamoru Funai. New York, Atheneum, 1964.
Grettir the Strong, illustrated by John Gretzer. New York, Crowell, 1968.
The Twelve Labors of Hercules, illustrated by Charles Keeping. New York, Crowell, 1972; London, Hutchinson, 1973.

PUBLICATIONS FOR ADULTS

Novels

Identity Unknown. Chicago, Ziff Davis, 1945.
The Enchanter. Boston, Houghton Mifflin, 1962.
Corbie. New York, Harcourt Brace, 1966; London, Hutchinson, 1967.

Plays

Radio Series: *Inner Sanctum Mysteries*, 1938–42; *Adventures of the Thin Man*, 1939; *Big Sister*, 1945–52.

Television Series: *City Hospital*, 1950–52; *Search for Tomorrow*, 1968–70; *Another World*, 1970–72; *Return to Peyton Place*, 1973–74.

*

Manuscript Collection: Mugar Memorial Library, Boston University.

*   *   *

Robert Newman was an author for whom the classics had great appeal. *The Twelve Labors of Hercules* is an excellent introduction to the Greek legends, and his "sequels" to the Sherlock Holmes stories (starting with *The Case of the Baker Street Irregular*) make good reading. However, his particular appeal for children is to be found in his three books about the world of Arthurian legend (*Merlin's Mistake*, *The Testing of Tertius*, and *The Shattered Stone*). He has a strong feel for the period, but does not regard it as sacrosanct, since he is able to poke gentle fun at its style. The very concept of *Merlin's Mistake* is comic. At the birth of Tertius, his godfather Merlin endows him with the gift of all possible knowledge. However, since the wizard was already under the spell of the enchantress Nimue, his intentions got muddled and Tertius was blessed with all *future* knowledge, but not even the simple ability to cure warts. In his teens the boy sets off on a quest to remedy this defect, and is joined by Brian, in search of knightly adventures.

Various odd characters attach themselves to the travellers and Tertius's knowledge proves useful when he circumvents fire and steel by using a burning-glass to light a fire, and gets the goldsmith to grind lenses to make spectacles and a telescope. To get them out of a tight spot he "invents" gunpowder, incurring the wrath of Nimue for upsetting history, but as he finds her using a computer to aid her witchery she cannot really complain. In the second book Tertius, at last apprenticed to Merlin, calls again on Brian, now happily married, to join him in France to help defend Europe from the Mongol hordes. There is a superb mix of ancient and modern when Tertius calls up the Tank Corps and a fighter squadron to help defeat the Tartars.

Newman's language is splendidly varied, and the tongue of High Chivalry, where "varlets" and "paynims" abound, is given an affectionate parody, which can only be done successfully by someone who really cares for what he mocks. Children appreciate good "tongue-in-cheek" humour, and that they will get in plenty here.

His last books continued with the detective/mystery theme, and are less successful than the mediaeval "spoofs." Too many other books of this type are on the market already, and he did not seem to have been able to transfer his zany humour and mastery of language.

—Ann G. Hay

———

NICHOLS, Ruth (Joanne). Canadian. Born in Toronto, Ontario, 4 March 1948. Educated at the University of British Columbia, Vancouver, B.A. (honours) 1969; McMaster University, Hamilton, Ontario (Woodrow Wilson fellow) M.A. 1972, Ph.D. 1977. Married William Norman Houston in 1974. Lecturer, Carleton University, Ottawa, 1974. Recipient: Canada Council Fellowship, 1972, 1973, 1974; Canadian Library Association award, 1973. Lives in Toronto. Agent: Nancy Colbert, The Colbert Agency, 303 Davenport Road, Toronto, Ontario M5R 1K5. Address: c/o Gage Educational Publishing Company, 164 Commander Boulevard, Agincourt, Ontario M1S 3C7, Canada.

PUBLICATIONS FOR CHILDREN

Fiction

A Walk Out of the World, illustrated by Trina Schart Hyman. Toronto, Longman, and New York, Harcourt Brace, 1969.
The Marrow of the World, illustrated by Trina Schart Hyman. Toronto, Macmillan, and New York, Atheneum, 1972.
Song of the Pearl. Toronto, Macmillan, and New York, Atheneum, 1976.
The Left-Handed Spirit. Toronto, Macmillan, and New York, Atheneum, 1978.

PUBLICATIONS FOR ADULTS

Novel

Ceremony of Innocence. London, Faber, 1969.

Other

Framework for Reading, with Joan Dean. London, Evans, 1974.

*

Manuscript Collection: Mills Memorial Library, McMaster University, Hamilton, Ontario.

Ruth Nichols comments:

The process of my development can be followed in print since my earliest published book, *A Walk Out of the World*, was published when I was 21, and other books have followed at regular intervals. Most of these are fantasy. I believe fantasy provides a valid and important means of examining the human passions and the nature of our relationship to reality.

* * *

For its readers fantasy embodies the will's ability to transcend the known. But the rationale for that metaphysical act must be expressed in a time-tested formula that leads the way through the labyrinths of fantasy to a satisfying conclusion. If the body cannot follow the mind in its passage through eons of time past, time to come, and worlds in space, the compensation for this lack lies in the reality of words to say that it can be done.

In her autobiographical novel, *Ceremony of Innocence*, Ruth Nichols traces her precocious contact with her memory of eternity: she professes a metaphysical contact that gives her stories the roots of reality and the limbs of fantasy. Her almost total recall of childhood encounters and conversations allows her to develop her plot on several planes, one of which is the intuitive. This novel seems to state the apologia for her familiarity with the psychic world.

Nichols writes about what she knows, the first principle of convincing composition. She begins her two fantasies for children in places known to her: in Ontario's Georgian Bay cottage country in *The Marrow of the World*; *A Walk Out of the World* is into a Vancouver park out of a crowded apartment house. But she intuits so much more than the given physical settings that place her books in Canada. She is first of this world, then of another, a remembered one in which her second self finds a friendly ambience to range metaphysically.

She understands the majesty of ritual, and she initiates her heroes in ritual. She tells the reader too that there is a way that things are done, and that way has an almost fateful logic. Her disciplined pen hews to the moral line as good vanquishes evil; she is quite sure what good is. The other-worldly characters are all her own wishes come true—they do as she bids, even in the delicious pursuit of evil. For it is never in question, the ending. The way however must be strewn with pitfalls so that the good can be fully and finally appreciated. But even it has a bitter sweetness. This world must be borne yet a space, while the untranscended life measures out its days on earth. Then the promised second walk out of the world for Tobit and Judith will be the last one. In *The Marrow of the World* Philip and Linda carry tangible marks of their time travel; their promised gift they will carry even during their terrestrial life.

These chosen earthlings feel emotion and sensations like pain, but they intuit more than they understand of their roles through the uncharted forests of fantasy. They only know they must be good people. Judith and Tobit are more sympathetic characters than Philip and Linda in *The Marrow*; they are not so remote from the readers' longing for the impossible. In *The Marrow* the author has perfected the stylization of her quest fantasy and the characters are altogether more decisive, colder. And their readers fear the shadows more, and do not trust the author as totally.

Nichols wrote *A Walk Out of the World* when she was 18, and won the Canadian Association of Children's Librarians' Bronze Medal for the best book of the year in 1972 for *The Marrow of the World*. These first works are exemplars of style; she learned the rudiments early. Now only the elements will be expanded as she matures, and she may yet develop into Canada's very best fantasist.

—Irma McDonough Milnes

———

NICHOLSON, (Sir) William (Newzam Prior). British. Born in Newark-on-Trent, Nottinghamshire, 5 February 1872. Educated at Magnus Grammar School, Newark; Hubert von Herkomer's art school, Bushey, Hertfordshire, two years; Académie Julian, Paris. Married 1) Mabel Pryde in 1893, three sons, including the painter Ben Nicholson, and one daughter; 2) Edith Phillips in 1919, one daughter. Artist: collaborated with James Pryde on posters as the "Beggarstaff Brothers"; also stage designer. Knighted, 1936. *Died 16 May 1949.*

PUBLICATIONS FOR CHILDREN (illustrated by the author)

Fiction

Clever Bill. London, Heinemann, and New York, Doubleday, 1926.
The Pirate Twins. London, Faber, and New York, Coward Mc-Cann, 1929.

Other

An Alphabet. London, Heinemann, and New York, Russell, 1898.

PUBLICATIONS FOR ADULTS

Other

Characters of Romance (lithographs). London, Heinemann, and New York, Russell, 1900.
Twelve Portraits. London, Heinemann, and New York, Russell, 2 vols., 1900–02.
The Book of Blokes. London, Faber, 1929.
William Nicholson (illustrations). London, Penguin, 1948.

*

Illustrator: *An Almanac of Twelve Sports* by Rudyard Kipling, 1898; *London Types* by William Ernest Henley, 1898; *The Square Book of Animals* by Arthur Waugh, 1899; *The Velveteen Rabbit* by Margery Williams Bianco, 1922; *The Hour of Magic*, 1922, *True Travellers*, 1923, and *Moss and Feather*, 1928, all by W. H. Davies; *Polly* by John Gay, 1923; *Memoirs of a Fox-Hunting Man* by Siegfried Sassoon, 1929.

Critical Studies: *William Nicholson* by Marguerite Steen, London, Collins, 1943; *William Nicholson* by Lillian Browse, London, Hart Davis, 1956; *William Nicholson, Drawings and Prints* (exhibition catalogue) by Duncan Robinson, London, Arts Council, 1980.

* * *

As artist only, William Nicholson would not qualify for the present book—though his illustrations for Margery Bianco's *The Velveteen Rabbit* still make that story memorable. But as artist-author of two distinguished picture books for the very young, *Clever Bill* and *The Pirate Twins*, he holds an unquestioned place. Quite apart from the technical interest of the art itself, both books show an absolute ease and mastery in the linking of text and pictures; each little drama speeds along with a blithe assurance, and the turns and twists engage us to the end. In *Clever Bill* the little girl Mary is invited to visit her Aunt (we are shown the actual letter of reply); she excitedly plans what to take—then forgets to pack her favourite doll, the soldier bandsman Bill. BUT "he ran/and he ran/and he ran/and he ran so fast that/he was just in time to meet her train at Dover./'Clever Bill!'" (So run the last six pages.) A perfect story.

Better than a summary, though, is a text itself in full. *The Pirate Twins* runs thus: "One evening on the sands/Mary found/the Pirate Twins./She took them Home/and bathed them/and fed them/on this/and that/and the other./She taught them how to dress/what the S stands for/where to find Jamaica/and the Milky Way/how to dance/and how to play" [one is shown clashing cymbals, the other with bagpipes] "but they didn't care/they bit their nails and sucked their thumbs,/put things into the cat's milk,/played dominoes in bed. UNTIL/one fine day/they left a note and/stole a boat/and sailed away/to sea/but they never forgot their Home/and always came back/in time for/Mary's birthday." The note—see back a few pages—says: "Dear Mary, we have gone for ever. Don't worry. Back soon. Love form B and A/xxxx."

These picture books belong to a later period than Nicholson's striking poster work with James Pryde (as "the Beggarstaff Brothers") and his series of coloured woodcuts which Whistler persuaded the publisher Heinemann to commission at the turn of the century. But they retain the flavour of this earlier work in their bold and jaunty line, clear light colours, and exciting masses of black. The interwoven pictures and words are as fresh and current today as when the books were first devised for Nicholson's young daughter over 60 years ago.

—Naomi Lewis

NICOLL, Helen. British. Born in Natland, Westmorland, 10 October 1937. Educated at schools in Bristol; Dartington Hall, Devon; Froebel Education Institute, London. Married Robert Kime in 1970; one daughter and one son. Producer of children's programmes, BBC television, 1967–71; editor, *The Egg* magazine, 1977–79. Since 1983 producer, Cover to Cover Cassettes, Wiltshire. Lives in Wiltshire. Address: c/o Heinemann Ltd., Michelin House, 81 Fulham Road, London SW3 6RB, England.

PUBLICATIONS FOR CHILDREN

Fiction (illustrated by Jan Pienkowski)

Meg and Mog. London, Heinemann, 1972; New York, Atheneum, 1973.
Meg's Eggs. London, Heinemann, 1972; New York, Atheneum, 1973.
Meg at Sea. London, Heinemann, 1973; New York, Harvey House, 1976.
Meg on the Moon. London, Heinemann, 1973; New York, Harvey House, 1976.
Meg's Car. London, Heinemann, 1975.
Meg's Castle. London, Heinemann, 1975.
Meg's Veg. London, Heinemann, 1976.
Mog's Mumps. London, Heinemann, 1976; New York, Penguin, 1982.
Quest for the Gloop: The Exploits of Murfy and PHIX. London,
Heinemann, 1980.
Mog at the Zoo. London, Heinemann, 1982; New York, Penguin, 1984.
Mog in the Fog. London, Heinemann, 1984.
Owl at School. London, Heinemann, 1984; New York, Penguin, 1985.
Mog's Box. London, Heinemann, 1987.

Other

Editor, *Poems for Seven Year Olds and Under*, illustrated by Michael Foreman. London, Kestrel, 1983.

*   *   *

The simple but richly coloured line drawings of Jan Pienkowski have blended with Helen Nicoll's brief sharp text to give the Meg and Mog books the impact of good strip cartoons. The principal characters, the witch Meg, her cat Mog, and their familiar Owl are clearly figures from the dark moonlit side of life; but the author has, as it were, transferred their scene of action to the common daylight. Indeed, written at a level suitable for the very young, the stories are actually an artless and effective example of situation comedy. When the trio make their excursion into outer space in *Meg on the Moon*, or in *Meg's Castle* into the mediaeval world, such a trip is not so much the product of a naturally fantastic order as a diversion sought out to alleviate the tedium of suburban isolation. Other characters are rare and, curiously, nearly always faceless, their features masked by space helmet or a knight's visor or, in *Meg at Sea* behind helicopter glass. While Meg retains the cauldron, the flying besom, the tattered widow's weeds, and conical hat—the full uniform and equipment of any properly accredited witch—her magic is only shakily controlled and applied with some misgivings. Nor can a beneficial outcome be predicted with much confidence. The broiling sun conjured up to aid the crops in *Meg's Veg* and the wind invoked to speed the becalmed ship in *Meg at Sea* both overfulfil their magical contract to produce respectively drought and storm. The eggs summoned as a teatime treat are enormous and inedible; in the night they hatch dinosaurs (*Meg's Eggs*). The same spell which releases Mog from captivity in *Mog at the Zoo* imprisons Meg herself.

To young children uncertain of their own powers and the power of household implements, Meg's hit-or-miss spells must be particularly compelling. As it imitates life's habit of presenting desired ends in undesirable form Meg's magic displays an effortless didactic charm. However it is notable that in a real crisis the heroine will as often and more unerringly choose a practical solution. After self-inflicted witchcraft has marooned Meg and her entourage on a tiny island (*Meg at Sea*), she reveals the attributes of an accomplished Girl Guide, first employing a magnifying glass to make fire and then her cape to telegraph SOS smoke signals in morse code. It is resourcefulness of this kind, combined with Meg's skill at piloting spaceships and growing vegetables, which has presumably placed these books on lists of those recommended as showing women in a more positive and active light. Certainly these brief and amusing stories abound in practical detail. In *Mog in the Fog* a sherpa offers Mog a cup of tea with butter in it. Within its limits *Meg's Veg* is a faultless gardening manual. But as the series progresses something of the aura of Tony Hancock's weary home life in Railway Cuttings gathers itself about the domestic threesome; a slight depression insinuates itself as the extravagance of moon jaunts gives way to the more rueful and mundane humour of *Mog's Mumps*.

In the very latest tales Meg shows some concern to exercise more properly her responsibility as the head of a one-parent family. Owl is lovingly packed off to school with a lunch box to learn soaring and swooping with the other owls (*Owl at School*). When Mog puts in his trade union claim for a lunch box too in *Mog's Box*, a spell quickly delivers one the size of a suitcase; with a characteristic sting in the tail it contains nothing more nourishing than a caterpillar.

With the first eight stories coming thick and fast between 1972 and 1976, then just four more appearing from 1982 until the present, it seems Nicoll has waning or only intermittent interest in these delightful characters. In other hands one can imagine them syndicated in comic strips all around the globe. Nor, perhaps more wisely, has *Quest for the Gloop*, a confusing science-fantasy farrago in which a little green man and his robot complete a successful intergalactic search for the life-saving Gloop, been followed by a sequel.

—John Churcher

NIMMO, Jenny. British. Born in Windsor, Berkshire, 15 January 1944. Educated at private boarding schools, 1950–60. Married David Wynn Millward in 1974; two daughters and one son. Actress and assistant stage manager, Theatre Southeast, Sussex and Kent, 1960–63; governess, Amalfi, Italy, 1963; photographic researcher, 1964–66, assistant floor manager, 1966–68 and 1971–74, and director and writer of children's programs, 1970, all BBC Television, London. Since 1975 full-time writer. Recipient: Smarties prize, 1986; Welsh Arts Council Tir na n'Og award, 1987. Agent: Murray Pollinger, 4 Garrick Street, London WC2E 9BH, England. Address: Henllan Mill, Llangynyw, Welshpool, Powys SY21 9EN, Wales.

PUBLICATIONS FOR CHILDREN

Fiction

The Bronze Trumpeter, illustrated by Caroline Scrace. London, Angus and Robertson, 1975.
Tatty Apple, illustrated by Priscilla Lamont. London, Methuen, 1984.
The Snow Spider, illustrated by Joanna Carey. London, Methuen, 1986; New York, Dutton, 1987.
Emlyn's Moon, illustrated by Joanna Carey. London, Methuen, 1987; as *Orchard of the Crescent Moon*, New York, Dutton, 1989.
The Red Secret, illustrated by Maureen Bradley. London, Hamish Hamilton, 1989.
The Chestnut Soldier. London, Methuen, 1989.

*

Jenny Nimmo comments:

I live and work in a rural community in Wales where my three bilingual children are growing into an old but vigorous culture. Here place names hark back to legend and it seems to me that the past is still part of the rhythm of everyday life. My books are concerned with the very real problem of growing children, and most of them are set in a landscape which is undeniably magical; they are described as fantasies.

*   *   *

Writers who live in Wales have a special responsibility as well as rare opportunities, both of which come from the ageless tradition of mysticism, magic, and quirky humour natural to the Celtic world. Richly imaginative, and possibly explosive, material lies all around on the hills, in the huddled stone cottages, in the playground and the butcher's shop. Here is the source of Jenny Nimmo's highly in-dividual books.

For a writer of such potential Nimmo's debut was modest in scale. Her first notable book was *Tatty Apple*, 90-odd pages of large print in Methuen's Read Aloud series. Into this pint pot she poured, with all the exuberance of the beginner, a gallon or two of sparkling ideas. The scene is her own Mid Wales, the central character Owen-Owen, a small boy of indomitable spirit and high humour. Owen-Owen wants to have a ride on the little railway that carries tourists and local shoppers down the valley to Welshpool. He is too young to go alone, Mam is too busy, and sister Elin, who has been before, remembers too well the pain of the bumpy ride. Owen-Owen bribes Elin with a little hen, got from irascible Mr. Evans, and while he is at Mr. Evans's farm he finds Tatty Apple, a green rabbit. Tatty Apple is magical. Nimmo holds the magic firmly in check, and allows most of the action, which is lively and very amusing, to come out of the characters and their situation.

Joyous as the book is, it did not prepare the reader for what was to follow. *The Snow Spider*, although still governed by the physical limitations of publication in a series, is a big book in its theme and its implications. Every Welsh writer must come under the influence of *The Mabinogion*, that extraordinary mixture of mediaeval romances, hero tales, Arthurian legends, and wry humour which is the foundation stone of Welsh literature. The theme of *The Snow Spider* comes directly from that book. Gwyn, at nine, is a reluctant magician. His scatty Nain has hailed him as the reincarnation of Math, Lord of Gwynedd, and given him a most unpromising collection of junk as his birthday present. With these to hand Gwyn sets out to solve the mystery of Bethan, the sister who disappeared from the mountain. His quest brings him many marvellous experiences, some of them dangerous, for among the forces ranged against him is the spirit of Efnisien, the most inexplicably malignant figure in the mediaeval saga. Gwyn's task has to be performed while he continues with his normal life of school and farm and his on/off relationships with his neighbours. Nimmo brings off her complicated story with much skill, blending the wonderful and the ordinary with a sure hand and maintaining the right atmosphere with some unobtrusively lovely descriptions of landscape and (a basic element in the Welsh scene) weather.

The setting and some of the characters of *The Snow Spider* are carried over into *Emlyn's Moon*, another story of magic and of personal and family dilemmas. This time the focus is on Nia, a member of the numerous Lloyd family who are Gwyn's neighbours. The Lloyd farm has foundered, and Mr. Lloyd and his brood move to the town where he runs the butcher's shop. Nia ("Nia-can't-do-nothing" to her insensitive family) suffers at home and school from a sense of inadequacy, from which she is rescued by Emlyn and his artist father (who have troubles enough of their own). Gwyn's magic plays a part too. There are deeper implications in this story, and Nimmo explores them confidently. Again the writing is sensitive and evocative, and the eloquence is always at the service of the story. Nia in her plight is a touching figure and her salvation is something to be taken very seriously, but the book is also full of humour and sharply drawn portraits.

Nimmo is a living example of the basic formula for success in an author: write what you know. She works in big ideas on a small canvas, which she fills with the figures of her own rural community. Magic or no magic, hers is a real world, viewed with a keen and understanding eye and with rich appreciation of its fun and its folly. It is early days to predict her future development, but from the evidence of three fairly small books it is safe to say that Nimmo will delight a steadily widening audience for a long time.

——Marcus Crouch

NIXON, Joan Lowery. American. Born in Los Angeles, California, 3 February 1927. Educated at the University of Southern California, Los Angeles, 1944–47, B.A. in journalism 1947; California State College, 1948–49, elementary teaching credential. Married Hershell H. Nixon in 1949; three daughters and one son. Elementary school teacher, Los Angeles, 1947–50; creative writing instructor, Midland College, Texas, 1971, and University of Houston, 1974–78. Member of the Board of Directors, Society of Children's Book Writers, Los Angeles, 1976–79. Recipient: Mystery Writers of America Edgar Allan Poe award, 1980, 1981, 1987; Western Writers of America Golden Spur award, 1988. Agent: Amy Berkower, Writers House Inc., 21 West 26th Street, New York, New York 10010. Address: 10215 Cedar Creek Drive, Houston, Texas 77042, U.S.A.

PUBLICATIONS FOR CHILDREN

Fiction

Mystery of Hurricane Castle, illustrated by Velma Ilsley. New York, Criterion, 1964.

Mystery of the Grinning Idol, illustrated by Alvin Smith. New York, Criterion, 1965.

Mystery of the Hidden Cockatoo, illustrated by Richard Lewis. New York, Criterion, 1966.

Mystery of the Haunted Woods, illustrated by Theresa Brudi. New York, Criterion, 1967.

Mystery of the Secret Stowaway, illustrated by Joan Drescher. New York, Criterion, 1968.

Delbert, The Plainclothes Detective, illustrated by Philip Smith. New York, Criterion, 1971.

The Alligator under the Bed, illustrated by Jan Hughes. New York, Putnam, 1974.

The Mysterious Red Tape Gang, illustrated by Joan Sandin. New York, Putnam, 1974.

The Secret Box Mystery, illustrated by Leigh Grant. New York, Putnam, 1974.

The Mysterious Prowler, illustrated by Berthe Amoss. New York, Harcourt Brace, 1976.

The Boy Who Could Find Anything, illustrated by Syd Hoff. New York, Harcourt Brace, 1978.

Danger in Dinosaur Valley, illustrated by Marc Simont. New York, Putnam, 1978.

Muffie Mouse and the Busy Birthday, illustrated by Geoffrey Hayes. New York, Seabury Press, 1978.

Bigfoot Makes a Move, illustrated by Syd Hoff. New York, Putnam, 1979.

The Kidnapping of Christina Lattimore. New York, Harcourt Brace, 1979.

The New Year's [*Valentine, Halloween, April Fool, Happy Birthday, Thanksgiving, Christmas Eve, Easter*] *Mystery*, illustrated by Jim Cummins. Chicago, Whitman, 8 vols., 1979–81.

Gloria Chipmunk, Star!, illustrated by Diane Dawson. Boston, Houghton Mifflin, 1980.

Casey and the Great Idea, illustrated by Amy Rowen. New York, Dutton, 1980.

If You Say So, Claude, illustrated by Lorinda Bryan Cauley. New York, Warne, 1980.

The Seance. New York, Harcourt Brace, 1980; London, Granada, 1983.

Kidnapped on Astarr, illustrated by Paul Frame. Champaign, Illinois, Garrard, 1981.

Mysterious Queen of Magic, illustrated by Paul Frame. Champaign, Illinois, Garrard, 1981.

Mystery Dolls from Planet Urd, illustrated by Paul Frame. Cham-

paign, Illinois, Garrard, 1981.

The Spectre. New York, Delacorte Press, 1982; London, Granada, 1983.

Days of Fear, photographs by Joan Menschenfreund. New York, Dutton, 1983.

The Gift, illustrated by Andrew Glass. New York, Macmillan, 1983.

A Deadly Game of Magic. New York, Harcourt Brace, 1983; London, Corgi, 1988.

Magnolia's Mixed-Up Magic, illustrated by Linda Bucholtz-Ross. New York, Putnam, 1983.

The Ghosts of Now. New York, Delacorte Press, 1984; London, Corgi, 1987.

The House on Hackman's Hill. New York, Scholastic, 1985.

Maggie, Too. San Diego, Harcourt Brace, 1985.

The Stalker. New York, Delacorte Press, 1985; London, Corgi, 1987.

And Maggie Makes Three. San Diego, Harcourt Brace, 1986.

Beats Me, Claude, illustrated by Tracey Campbell Pearson. New York and London, Viking Kestrel, 1986.

The Other Side of Dark. New York, Delacorte Press, 1986; London, Hodder and Stoughton, 1988.

The Dark and Deadly Pool. New York, Delacorte Press, 1987.

A Family Apart. New York, Bantam, 1987.

Fat Chance, Claude, illustrated by Tracey Campbell Pearson. New York, Viking Kestrel, 1987.

Haunted Island. New York, Scholastic, 1987.

Maggie Forevermore. San Diego, Harcourt Brace, 1987.

Caught in the Act. New York, Bantam, 1988.

In the Face of Danger. New York, Bantam, 1988.

Secret, Silent Screams. New York, Delacorte Press, 1988.

Island of Dangerous Dreams. New York, Dell, 1989.

A Place to Belong. New York, Bantam, 1989.

You Bet Your Britches, Claude, illustrated by Tracey Campbell Pearson. New York, Viking Kestrel, 1989.

Star Baby. New York, Bantam, 1989.

Whispers from the Dead. New York, Delacorte Press, 1989.

Other

Five Loaves and Two Fishes, illustrated by Aline Cunningham. St. Louis, Concordia, 1976.

Who Is My Neighbor?, illustrated by Aline Cunningham. St. Louis, Concordia, 1976.

Oil and Gas: From Fossils to Fuels, with Hershell H. Nixon, illustrated by Jean Day Zallinger. New York, Harcourt Brace, 1977.

The Son Who Came Home Again, illustrated by Aline Cunningham. St. Louis, Concordia, 1977.

Volcanoes: Nature's Fireworks, with Hershell H. Nixon. New York, Dodd Mead, 1978.

When God Listens, illustrated by James McIlrath. Huntington, Indiana, Our Sunday Visitor, 1978.

When God Speaks, illustrated by James McIlrath. Huntington, Indiana, Our Sunday Visitor, 1978.

The Butterfly Tree, illustrated by James McIlrath. Huntington, Indiana, Our Sunday Visitor, 1979.

Before You Were Born, illustrated by James McIlrath. Huntington, Indiana, Our Sunday Visitor, 1980.

Glaciers: Nature's Frozen Rivers, with Hershell H. Nixon. New York, Dodd Mead, 1980.

Earthquakes: Nature in Motion, with Hershell H. Nixon. New York, Dodd Mead, 1981.

Land under the Sea, with Hershell H. Nixon. New York, Dodd Mead, 1985.

If You Were a Writer, illustrated by Bruce Degen. New York, Four

Winds Press, 1988.

PUBLICATIONS FOR ADULTS

Other

Writing Mysteries for Young People.   Boston, The Writer, 1977.
The Grandmother's Book.   Nashville, Abingdon Press, 1979.

*

Joan Lowery Nixon comments:

I began writing for children when my two eldest daughters asked me to. They said, "Write a book, and make it a mystery, and put us in it." To please them I did, and I enjoyed it so much I've written for children of all ages ever since. I suppose one reason I like to write for young people is that I am still strongly in touch with my own childhood. The problems of today are different now, but the emotions—the joys and pains and fears and embarrassments and longings—remain the same. Also I sincerely like young people as friends, and I enjoy reading many of the good books they like to read.

*   *   *

Joan Lowery Nixon has written many books for children at elementary, junior high school, and high school levels. She is best known for her fast-paced, ingenious mystery stories. At the beginner reader level the mysteries are suspenseful as well as good fun. *The Secret Box Mystery* is about Michael John and the box he brings to school for his science project. The box gurgles, hisses, and makes a cooing sound. What is it? An elf owl. Nixon has a number of other delightful First-Read Alone Mysteries such as *The Christmas Eve Mystery, The Easter Mystery*, and *The Halloween Mystery*. She also has a number of inventive Space Detective Books for upper elementary grades: *Kidnapped on Astarr, Mystery Dolls from Planet Urd*.

Her mysteries for older children are psychological thrillers, involving complicated characterizations and plots and demanding the reader's participation in solving the crimes. Two of these books, *The Kidnapping of Christina Lattimore*, and *The Seance*, won the coveted Edgar Allan Poe award. In the former, Christina and a young reporter set out to prove her innocence when her kidnappers claim that she was an accomplice to their crime. In the latter, what begins as a game, with Lauren and five other girls gathered in a candlelight circle, develops into murder of the participants; soon it will be Lauren's turn.

A Deadly Game of Magic concerns Lisa and her friends, caught in a violent storm which leaves them stranded by an old deserted house, strewn with odd tricks and gadgets, the paraphernalia for a practiced magician. Lisa has always dreamed of being a magician; now her life depends on it.

The Spectre is about nine-year-old Julie, an abused child, and the friend she makes in the hospital, 17-year-old Dina, a victim of Hodgkins disease. Julie and Dina share feelings of fear and despair, but eventually their support of each other allows them hope.

Nixon also writes funny, rolicking books about people, their predicaments, and their relationships. *Beats Me, Claude* is about a happy couple who live in a quiet cabin in the rolling hills of Texas. Shirley attempts to make an apple pie for Claude and ends up using the pie both to capture escaped criminals who show up at her door and to cajole Claude into adopting two deserving orphans.

Nixon's skillful writing and boundless imagination make young readers want to read on, to find out what surprises wait on the next page and discover if their solutions to her never-ending puzzles are correct ones. She is also a writer of warmth, understanding young people's concerns and questions about self and life, as well as their

need for excitement.

—Mary Lystad

———

NODSET, Joan L.   See **LEXAU, Joan M.**

———

NORMAN, Lilith. Australian. Born in Sydney, New South Wales, 27 November 1927. Educated at Sydney Girls' High School, 1940–44. Library assistant, Newtown Library, Sydney, 1947–49; telephonist, Bonnington Hotel, London, 1950–51; sales assistant, Angus and Robertson Books, Sydney, 1952–53; nurse, Balmain District Hospital, Sydney, 1953–56; library assistant, 1956–58, research officer, 1958–66, and children's librarian, 1966–70, Sydney Public Library; assistant editor, 1970–76, and editor, 1976–78, New South Wales Department of Education *School Magazine*. Since 1978 freelance writer. Recipient: Queen's Silver Jubilee Medal, 1977. Agent: Curtis Brown (Australia), P.O. Box 19, Paddington, New South Wales 2021, Australia.

PUBLICATIONS FOR CHILDREN

Fiction

Climb a Lonely Hill.   London, Collins, 1970; New York, Walck, 1972.
The Shape of Three.   London, Collins, 1971; New York, Walck, 1972.
The Flame Takers.   Sydney and London, Collins, 1973.
A Dream of Seas, illustrated by Edwina Bell.   Sydney and London, Collins, 1978.
My Simple Little Brother, illustrated by David Rae.   Sydney and London, Collins, 1979.
The Laurel & Hardy Kids.   Sydney, Random House, 1989.

Plays

Television Play: in *Catch Kandy* series, 1973.

Short plays published in *School Magazine*, Sydney.

Other

Mocking-Bird Man (reader), illustrated by Astra Lacis.   Sydney and London, Hodder and Stoughton, 1977.

PUBLICATIONS FOR ADULTS

Other

The City of Sydney: Official Guide.   Sydney, City Council, 1959.
Facts about Sydney.   Sydney, City Council, 1959.
Asia: A Select Reading List.   Sydney, City Council, 1959.
Some Notes on the Early Land Grants at Potts Point.   Sydney, City Council, 1959.
A History of the City of Sydney Public Library.   Sydney, City Council, 1960.
Notes on the Glebe.   Sydney, City Council, 1960.
Historical Notes on Paddington.   Sydney, City Council, 1961.
Historical Notes on Newtown.   Sydney, City Council, 1962.

The Brown and Yellow: Sydney Girls' High School 1883–1983.
Melbourne, Oxford University Press, 1983.

*

Lilith Norman comments:

I managed to avoid becoming a writer for quite a long time, mainly, I think, because it seemed like very hard work for a very speculative result. It wasn't until I started working as a children's librarian that I realised *these* were the books I wanted to write. I was lucky, for as well as being perhaps the most rewarding and personal form of writing, it was also one of the most disciplined. And I believe discipline is the forgotten word of our times. Discipline in writing, to me, means honing your style, your rhythm, and, most of all, your own thinking, till everything has a true sharp edge, as precise and delicate as a craftsman's tool. I like to write about ordinary children trying to cope, for I believe that most of us can cope with whatever is thrown at us, *if we really have to*—otherwise we'd all be living in caves still. I've written about realistic situations in *Climb a Lonely Hill* and *The Shape of Three*, but I've written fantasy in *The Flame Takers*. And there's the rub! Having put a tentative toe in the great ocean of fantasy, everything else seems flat and commonplace. I want to swim and dive in that ocean, I want it to become my home, I don't know if I can, but I shall have to try, with, perhaps, occasional forays back to land for relaxation.

*   *   *

If there is any theme common to Lilith Norman's very diverse books, it is the effect of environment on character. Her children are products of their backgrounds, which are quite different in every novel.

In *Climb a Lonely Hill* there is an almost totally deprived home where the mother's early death caused the father to squander what little money he had on drink. Jack, his teenage son, reacts to this by being conformist and reluctant to make decisions, whereas Susan, his daughter, is sharp and resourceful beyond her years. Yet when the children have to survive in the harsh outback after a car crash which kills their uncle, it is Jack who has to take command because Susan's foot is injured, and in the fight against heat, dust, thirst, and flies he finally learns initiative and with it self-respect.

The exploration of heredity and environment is central to *The Shape of Three*. Here fraternal twins Shane and Greg Herbert accidentally meet Bruce Cunningham, who is the exact replica of Greg. Subsequent investigation reveals that they were all born in Sydney on the same night but a hospital emergency had caused the babies to be muddled. Greg and Bruce are the true identical twins and Shane is the Cunningham. The climax of the story comes when the children are restored to their rightful families and bewildered Bruce finds himself in the hurly-burly of a large warm Roman Catholic lower-middle class home, whereas the bereft Shane has to adjust to being the only child of a wealthy Protestant estate-agent father and neurotic perfectionist mother. The convincing contrast drawn between the Herbert and Cunningham households highlights the poignancy of Bruce and Shane's dilemmas as they struggle not only with uprooting but with vague feelings of hereditary kinship for their new-found relatives.

The background of *The Flame Takers* is different again, and there is another original theme—that of the sudden and inexplicable dying of talent. Here not only professional actor parents but also their musical son suddenly lose their inspirational flame and become bourgeois and materialistic. These changes are somehow connected with a sadistic schoolmaster and a fat chess-playing German, but no real explanation is given, and the book's strengths lie less in plot than in the exploration of yet another type of family and of central Sydney rather than the suburbs of the previous novel.

A Dream of Seas is a totally different type of fantasy in which Norman sees legendary selkie—seal people—folklore in terms of the present-day Sydney surf-riding scene. A boy—whose real name is never given and who is known only by his nickname of "Seasick"—feels drawn towards the sea, in which his father had drowned. In his daydreams seals and surfies are indistinguishable and when he himself gets a surfboard he paddles out to sea, feeling free of his mother who has re-married and is expecting another child. Throughout the book there are flashes to a young shadow seal and its mother which echo the relationship between the boy and his mother, until the final pages when the boy and the shadow seal become one and a child cries, "Look, Mum. Look at the sea!"

There could hardly be a stronger contrast than between this book and *My Simple Little Brother*, humorously written in the first-person Australian vernacular by the elder brother of five-year-old Fieldsy. Fieldsy's problem is that he takes metaphorical sayings literally and each chapter is a separate episode of his interpretation of such sayings as "turning the tables," "the wrong end of the stick," or "throwing the baby away with the bath water."

Norman has shown courage and originality in tackling unusual subjects. She has a keen ear for Australian speech patterns and dialogue. She is an astute observer and whether depicting people or places she accurately portrays the diversity of an emerging nation in a time-worn continent.

—Betty Gilderdale

———

NORTH, Andrew. See **NORTON, Andre.**

———

NORTH, Sterling. American. Born near Edgerton, Wisconsin, 4 November 1906. Educated at the University of Chicago, A.B. 1929. Married Gladys Buchanan in 1927; one son and one daughter. Reporter, 1929–31, and literary editor, 1932–43, Chicago *Daily News*; literary editor, New York *Post*, 1943–49, and New York *World Telegram and Sun*, 1949–56; founding editor, North Star Books, Houghton Mifflin, publishers, Boston, 1957–64. *Died 21 December 1974.*

PUBLICATIONS FOR CHILDREN

Fiction

The Five Little Bears, illustrated by Clarence Biers and Hazel Frazee. Chicago, Rand McNally, 1935; London, Shaw, 1940.
The Zipper ABC Book, illustrated by Keith Ward. Chicago, Rand McNally, 1937.
Greased Lightning, illustrated by Kurt Wiese. Philadelphia, Winston, 1940.
Midnight and Jeremiah, illustrated by Kurt Wiese. Philadelphia, Winston, 1943.
The Birthday of Little Jesus, illustrated by Valenti Angelo. New York, Grosset and Dunlap, 1952; Manchester, World Distributors, 1953.
Son of the Lamp-Maker: The Story of a Boy Who Knew Jesus, illustrated by Manning Lee. Chicago, Rand McNally, 1956.
Rascal: A Memoir of a Better Era, illustrated by John Schoenherr. New York, Dutton, 1963; as *Rascal: The True Story of a Pet*

Raccoon, London, Hodder and Stoughton, 1963; abridged edition, as *Little Rascal*, New York, Dutton, 1965; Leicester, Brockhampton Press, 1966.
The Wolfling, illustrated by John Schoenherr. New York, Dutton, 1969; London, Heinemann, 1970.

Other

Abe Lincoln: Log Cabin to White House, illustrated by Lee Ames. New York, Random House, 1956.
George Washington, Frontier Colonel, illustrated by Lee Ames. New York, Random House, 1957.
Young Thomas Edison, illustrated by William Barss. Boston, Houghton Mifflin, 1958.
Thoreau of Walden Pond, illustrated by Harve Stein. Boston, Houghton Mifflin, 1959.
Captured by the Mohawks and Other Adventures of Radisson, illustrated by Victor Mays. Boston, Houghton Mifflin, 1960.
Mark Twain and the River, illustrated by Victor Mays. Boston, Houghton Mifflin, 1961.
The First Steamboat on the Mississippi, illustrated by Victor Mays. Boston, Houghton Mifflin, 1962.

PUBLICATIONS FOR ADULTS

Novels

Midsummer Madness. New York, Grosset and Dunlap, 1933.
Tiger. Chicago, Reilly and Lee, 1933.
Plowing on Sunday. New York, Macmillan, 1934.
Night Outlasts the Whippoorwill. New York, Macmillan, 1936; London, Cobden Sanderson, 1937.
Seven Against the Years. New York, Macmillan, 1939.
So Dear to My Heart. New York, Doubleday, 1947; London, Odhams Press, 1949.
Reunion on the Wabash. New York, Doubleday, 1952.

Verse

(*Poems*). Chicago, University of Chicago Press, 1925.

Other

The Pedro Gorino: The Adventures of a Negro Sea-Captain in Africa, with Harry Dean. Boston, Houghton Mifflin, 1929; as *Umbala*, London, Harrap, 1929.
The Writings of Mazo De La Roche. Boston, Little Brown, n.d.
Being a Literary Map of These United States Depicting a Renaissance No Less Astonishing Than That of Periclean Athens or Elizabethan London, with Gladys North, map by Frederic J. Donseif. New York, Putnam, 1942.
Hurry Spring! New York, Dutton, 1966.
Raccoons Are the Brightest People. New York, Dutton, 1966; as *The Raccoons of My Life*, London, Hodder and Stoughton, 1967.

Editor, with Carl Kroch, *So Red the Nose; or, Breath in the Afternoon: Literary Cocktails* (recipes). New York, Farrar and Rinehart, 1935.
Editor, with C.B. Boutell, *Speak of the Devil: An Anthology of the Appearances of the Devil in the Literature of the Western World*. New York, Doubleday, 1945.

*

Manuscript Collection: Boston University Library.

*   *   *

Exceptional children's books are often by authors who do not customarily write for young audiences. Sterling North's *Rascal* and *The Wolfling* are prime examples. The latter touches upon the hardships of frontier life, but stresses its pleasures, especially the pleasures of companioning with a creature who is part wolf, part dog. This well-crafted "documentary novel" is as idyllic in tone as the author's masterpiece, *Rascal*, but less complex in its overall texture. *Rascal* is a pastoral drama about a child and a raccoon; but, more important, the surface plot is a means for picturing a region, an era, and an unusual family. The simplified edition, *Little Rascal*, is too attenuated to be anything more than a mundane memoir.

The narration of *Rascal* is a shrewd mixture of child and adult points of view. A raccoon kit is captured by two Wisconsin boys during World War I. Both the diction and action convey the perspective of childhood as Sterling warns his friend, "You'll get a licking when you get home," and Oscar puts up a bold front: "Ishkabibble, I should worry!" When Sterling describes his Saint Bernard, time has subtly shifted and we see an adult perspective and prose style: "Wowser never started a fight, but after being challenged, badgered, and insulted, he eventually would turn his worried face and great sad eyes upon his tormenter, and more in sorrow than in anger, grab the intruder by the scruff of the neck, and toss·him into the gutter." The parallel between human and animal offspring has symbolic as well as dramatic importance. Sterling is indulged by his father to the point where he can build his 18-foot canoe in the living room; Rascal is pampered as a baby would be pampered (dining with the adults, sharing Sterling's bed). In adulthood, Rascal leaves his human family to find a mate, while the boy faces a more demanding kind of maturity—even the subordination of his own desires for the sake of others. The reader feels the simultaneous sadness and triumph in growing up when Sterling is able to say finally: "Do as you please, my little Raccoon; it's your life."

The language of the novel underpins the symbolic comparisons. Animals are personified (as when Wowser has a "worried face") and, conversely, the boy is depicted as very close to the animal world. Sterling's deceased mother schooled him as a naturalist, and the meticulous training of pets helps the child deal with his bereavement. Characterization is developed through surface action and in deeper ways. The protagonist puzzles over his mother's death, but the reader is able to fill out the family portraits with information that the boy is not himself conscious of. For example, we learn that his father removed himself from the premises when each of his four children were born. Sterling doesn't see this as a clue to his father's overall personality, but the reader relates this information to the scenes in which Sterling is left alone with his pet. Indirectly we see the father's compulsion to withdraw from his parental role. The pressures on the father are not stated explicitly. The general cultural setting suggests what they might be: a war that sends one son to the trenches; a burgeoning industrialization that places commerce at the hub of existence; a rigidly conformist tendency in some neighbors and family members.

The textural complexity in *Rascal* is developed through a mixture of modes—a blend of the realistic, romantic, and local color traditions. Countervailing moods enrich the story because it is both a celebration and a lamentation. After evoking the bliss of childhood freedom, North subtly separates the naive realm of nature from the enigmatic realm of human history. By the time Sterling and Rascal are separated in a literal sense, the reader has enjoyed the thematic depth and psychological veracity which make a novel memorable.

—Donnarae MacCann

NORTON, Andre (Alice Mary Norton). Also writes as Andrew North; Allen Weston. American. Born in Cleveland, Ohio, 17 February 1912. Educated at Western Reserve University, Cleveland, 1930–32. Children's librarian, Cleveland Public Library, 1932–50; special librarian, Library of Congress, Washington, D.C., during World War II; editor, Gnome Press, New York, 1950–58. Recipient: Grand Master of Fantasy award, 1977; Gandalf award, 1977; Fritz Leiber award, 1983; Lensman award, 1983, 1987; Grand Master Nebula award 1983; Jules Verne award, 1984; Daedalus award, 1986. Address: 1600 Spruce Avenue, Winter Park, Florida 32789, U.S.A.

PUBLICATIONS FOR CHILDREN

Fiction

The Prince Commands, illustrated by Kate Seredy. New York, Appleton Century, 1934.
Ralestone Luck, illustrated by James Reid. New York, Appleton Century, 1938.
Follow the Drum. New York, Penn, 1942.
The Sword Is Drawn, illustrated by Duncan Coburn. Boston, Houghton Mifflin, 1944; London, Oxford University Press, 1946.
Scarface, illustrated by Lorence Bjorklund. New York, Harcourt Brace, 1948; London, Methuen, 1950.
Sword in Sheath, illustrated by Lorence Bjorklund. New York, Harcourt Brace, 1949; as *Island of the Lost*, London, Staples Press, 1953.
Star Man's Son, 2250 A.D., illustrated by Nicolas Mordvinoff. New York, Harcourt Brace, 1952; London, Staples Press, 1953; as *Daybreak, 2250 A.D.*, New York, Ace, 1954.
Star Rangers. New York, Harcourt Brace, 1953; London, Gollancz, 1968; as *The Last Planet*, New York, Ace, 1955.
At Swords' Point. New York, Harcourt Brace, 1954.
The Stars Are Ours! Cleveland, World, 1954.
Yankee Privateer, illustrated by Leonard Vosburgh. Cleveland, World, 1955.
Star Guard. New York, Harcourt Brace, 1955; London, Gollancz, 1969.
The Crossroads of Time. New York, Ace, 1956; London, Gollancz, 1967.
Stand to Horse. New York, Harcourt Brace, 1956.
Sea Siege. New York, Harcourt Brace, 1957.
Star Born. Cleveland, World, 1957; London, Gollancz, 1973.
Star Gate. New York, Harcourt Brace, 1958; London, Gollancz, 1970.
The Time Traders. Cleveland, World, 1958.
The Beast Master. New York, Harcourt Brace, 1959; London, Gollancz, 1966.
Galactic Derelict. Cleveland, World, 1959.
Storm over Warlock. Cleveland, World, 1960.
The Sioux Spaceman. New York, Ace, 1960; London, Hale, 1976.
Shadow Hawk. New York, Harcourt Brace, 1960; London, Gollancz, 1971.
Ride Proud, Rebel! Cleveland, World, 1961.
Catseye. New York, Harcourt Brace, 1961; London, Gollancz, 1962.
The Defiant Agents. Cleveland, World, 1962.
Lord of Thunder. New York, Harcourt Brace, 1962; London, Gollancz, 1966.
Rebel Spurs. Cleveland, World, 1962.
Key Out of Time. Cleveland, World, 1963.
Judgment on Janus. New York, Harcourt Brace, 1963; London, Gollancz, 1964.
Ordeal in Otherwhere. Cleveland, World, 1964.

Night of Masks. New York, Harcourt Brace, 1964; London, Gollancz, 1965.
The X Factor. New York, Harcourt Brace, 1965; London, Gollancz, 1967.
Quest Crosstime. New York, Viking Press, 1965; as *Crosstime Agent*, London, Gollancz, 1975.
Steel Magic, illustrated by Robin Jacques. Cleveland, World, 1965; London, Hamish Hamilton, 1967; as *Gray Magic*, New York, Scholastic, 1967.
Moon of Three Rings. New York, Viking Press, 1966; London, Longman, 1969.
Victory on Janus. New York, Harcourt Brace, 1966; London, Gollancz, 1967.
Octagon Magic, illustrated by Mac Conner. Cleveland, World, 1967; London, Hamish Hamilton, 1968.
Operation Time Search. New York, Harcourt Brace, 1967.
Dark Piper. New York, Harcourt Brace, 1968; London, Gollancz, 1969.
Fur Magic, illustrated by John Kaufmann. Cleveland, World, 1968; London, Hamish Hamilton, 1969.
The Zero Stone. New York, Viking Press, 1968; London, Gollancz, 1974.
Postmarked the Stars. New York, Harcourt Brace, 1969; London, Gollancz, 1971.
Uncharted Stars. New York, Viking Press, 1969; London, Gollancz, 1974.
Dread Companion. New York, Harcourt Brace, 1970; London, Gollancz, 1972.
Ice Crown. New York, Viking Press, 1970; London, Longman, 1971.
Android at Arms. New York, Harcourt Brace, 1971; London, Gollancz, 1972.
Exiles of the Stars. New York, Viking Press, 1971; London, Longman, 1972.
The Crystal Gryphon. New York, Atheneum, 1972; London, Gollancz, 1973.
Dragon Magic, illustrated by Robin Jacques. New York, Crowell, 1972.
Breed to Come. New York, Viking Press, 1972; London, Longman, 1973.
Forerunner Foray. New York, Viking Press, 1973; London, Longman, 1974.
Here Abide Monsters. New York, Atheneum, 1973.
The Jargoon Pard. New York, Atheneum, 1974; London, Gollancz, 1975.
Lavender-Green Magic, illustrated by Judith Gwyn Brown. New York, Crowell, 1974.
Iron Cage. New York, Viking Press, 1974; London, Kestrel, 1975.
Outside, illustrated by Bernard Colonna. New York, Walker, 1975; London, Blackie, 1976.
The Day of the Ness, with Michael Gilbert, illustrated by Gilbert. New York, Walker, 1975.
Knave of Dreams. New York, Viking Press, 1975; London, Kestrel, 1976.
No Night Without Stars. New York, Atheneum, 1975; London, Gollancz, 1976.
Red Hart Magic, illustrated by Donna Diamond. New York, Crowell, 1976; London, Hamish Hamilton, 1977.
Wraiths of Time. New York, Atheneum, 1976; London, Gollancz, 1977.
Star Ka'at, with Dorothy Madlee, illustrated by Bernard Colonna. New York, Walker, 1976; London, Blackie, 1977.
The Opal-Eyed Fan. New York, Dutton, 1977.
Trey of Swords (short stories). New York, Grosset and Dunlap, 1977; London, Star, 1979.
Star Ka'at World, with Dorothy Madlee, illustrated by Jean Jenkins.

New York, Walker, 1978.
Quag Keep. New York, Atheneum, 1978.
Seven Spells to Sunday, with Phyllis Miller. New York, Atheneum, 1979.
Star Ka'ats and the Plant People, with Dorothy Madlee, illustrated by Jean Jenkins. New York, Walker, 1979.
Voorloper, illustrated by Alicia Austin. New York, Ace, 1980.
Star Ka'ats and the Winged Warriors, with Dorothy Madlee, illustrated by Jean Jenkins. New York, Walker, 1981.
Gryphon in Glory. New York, Atheneum, 1981.
Ten Mile Treasure. New York, Pocket Books, 1981.
House of Shadows, with Phyllis Miller. New York, Atheneum, 1984.
Ride the Green Dragon, with Phyllis Miller. New York, Atheneum, 1985.

Fiction as Andrew North

Sargasso of Space. New York, Gnome Press, 1955; as Andre Norton, London, Gollancz, 1970.
Plague Ship. New York, Gnome Press, 1956; as Andre Norton, London, Gollancz, 1971.
Voodoo Planet. New York, Ace, 1959.

Other

Rogue Reynard, illustrated by Laura Bannon. Boston, Houghton Mifflin, 1947.
Huon of the Horn, illustrated by Joe Krush. New York, Harcourt Brace, 1951.
Bertie and May, with Bertha Stenn Norton, illustrated by Fermin Rocker. New York, World, 1969; London, Hamish Hamilton, 1971.

Editor, with Ernestine Donaldy, *Gates to Tomorrow: An Introduction to Science Fiction.* New York, Atheneum, 1973.
Editor, *Small Shadows Creep: Ghost Children.* New York, Dutton, 1974; London Chatto and Windus, 1976.

PUBLICATIONS FOR ADULTS

Novels

Murder for Sale (as Allen Weston, with Grace Hogarth). London, Hammond, 1954.
Secret of the Lost Race. New York, Ace, 1959; as *Wolfshead,* London, Hale, 1977.
Star Hunter. New York, Ace, 1961.
Eye of the Monster. New York, Ace, 1962.
Witch World. New York, Ace, 1963; London, Tandem, 1970.
Web of the Witch World. New York, Ace, 1964; London, Tandem, 1970.
Three Against the Witch World. New York, Ace, 1965; London, Tandem, 1970.
Year of the Unicorn. New York, Ace, 1965; London, Tandem, 1970.
Warlock of the Witch World. New York, Ace, 1967; London, Tandem, 1970.
Sorceress of the Witch World. New York, Ace, 1968; London, Tandem, 1970.
Merlin's Mirror. New York, DAW, 1975; London, Sidgwick and Jackson, 1976.
The White Jade Fox. New York, Dutton, 1975; London, W.H.

Allen, 1976.
Velvet Shadows. New York, Fawcett, 1977.
Yurth Burden. New York, DAW, 1978.
Zarsthor's Bane. New York, Ace, 1978; London, Dobson, 1981.
Snow Shadow. New York, Fawcett, 1979.
Iron Butterflies. New York, Fawcett, 1980.
Horn Crown. New York, DAW, 1981.
Forerunner. New York, Tor, 1981.
Moon Called. New York, Simon and Schuster, 1982.
Caroline, with Enid Cushing. New York, Pinnacle, 1982.
'Ware Hawk. New York, Atheneum, 1983.
Wheel of Stars. New York, Simon and Schuster, 1983.
Stand and Deliver. New York, Dell, 1984.
Gryphon's Eyrie, with A.C. Crispin. New York, Tor, 1984.
Were-Wrath. New Castle, Virginia, Cheap Street, 1984.
Forerunner: The Second Venture. New York, Tor, 1985.
Flight in Yiktor. New York, Tor, 1986; London, Methuen, 1988.
The Gate of the Cat. New York, Ace, 1987.
Serpent's Tooth. Privately printed, 1988.
Imperial Lady. New York, Tor, 1989.

Short Stories

High Sorcery. New York, Ace, 1970.
Garan the Eternal. Alhambra, California, Fantasy, 1972.
Spell of the Witch World. New York, DAW, 1972; London, Prior, 1977.
The Many Worlds of Andre Norton, edited by Roger Elwood. Radnor, Pennsylvania, Chilton, 1974; as *The Book of Andre Norton,* New York, DAW, 1975.
Perilous Dreams. New York, DAW, 1976.
Lore of the Witch World. New York, DAW, 1980.

Other

Editor, *Bullard of the Space Patrol,* by Malcolm Jameson. Cleveland, World, 1951.
Editor, *Space Service.* Cleveland, World, 1953.
Editor, *Space Pioneers.* Cleveland, World, 1954.
Editor, *Space Police.* Cleveland, World, 1956.
Editor, *Baleful Beasts and Eerie Creatures.* Chicago, Rand McNally, 1976.
Editor, with Robert Adams, *Magic in Ithkar.* New York, Tor, 2 vols., 1985.
Editor, *Tales of Witch World.* New York, Tor, 2 vols., 1987–88.
Editor, *Four from the Witch World.* New York, Tor, 1989.
Editor, with Martin H. Greenberg, *Catfantastic.* New York, DAW, 1989.

*

Bibliography: *Andre Norton: A Primary and Secondary Bibliography* by Roger C. Schlobin, Boston, Hall, 1980.

Manuscript Collections: Andre Norton Ltd., Winter Park, Florida; George Arents Research Library, Syracuse University, New York.

Andre Norton comments:

I enjoy writing imaginative fiction and always have. I began writing historical, adventure, and spy stories, since at that time book-length science fiction or fantasy was not acceptable. I do a great deal of research for each book and over the years I've collected a large reference library. It is pleasing when a book of mine interests a reader and causes him or her to want to know more about some particular point I have mentioned. I consider sci-fi and fantasy excellent stretchers of anyone's imagination and keys to speculation which may lead to unusual discoveries.

* * *

The science-fiction novels of Andre Norton are remarkable for their fast action and evocation of strange places, and can make an important contribution to the development of wonder and imagination in young adolescent boys, whose reading of fiction can too easily be confined to brutal violence in a seedy modern underworld. Not that girls do not read them: girls are often included among the protagonists, and in some stories play the main part, notably in *Ice Crown* and *Dread Companion*. Basically Norton writes straightforward adventure stories in which the conflict is between Good and Evil, and the qualities of courage, endurance, friendship, unselfishness, loyalty, and resourcefulness are assumed in the heroes and heroines, as are complete freedom from callousness and vindictiveness. Some of the novels are conventional science fiction, as *Sargasso of Space*, *Plague Ship*, and *Postmarked the Stars*, in all of which Dave Thorsen pursues his occupation of Galactic trader; many, such as *Catseye* and *The Beast Master*, relate adventures on distant planets between men and strange aborigines at some time in the future; while a few, such as *Steel Magic*, *Fur Magic* and *Dread Companion*, deal in outright magic.

The most common initial situations are migration to new planets caused by world destruction, or exploratory missions to undeveloped worlds by members of communities which are highly developed technologically. In either case there is a mingling of medieval and future technologies: stunners and blasters with bows and arrows, flitters with animal-drawn vehicles; and more likely than not powerful machines, left behind by now-vanished Forerunners, will be discovered and become the focus of the plot. Almost always atmosphere, climate, and topographical features will be similar to what can be found on earth, and it is this, perhaps more than any other factor, which marks the work as science fantasy rather than science fiction, so far as distinction can be made.

Norton is greatly interested in animals, and radiation-mutated animals, capable of telepathic communication with man, and helping him, are very common, as in *Catseye* and *The Beast Master*. In *Breed to Come* cat mutants are the main characters, and rival man, whereas in *Iron Cage* bear mutants, though not technologically advanced, are the moral superiors of man. In *Steel Magic*, *Fur Magic*, and *The Jargoon Pard* human beings are for a while turned into animals, and the resulting physical sensations well imagined. Labyrinthine underground passages are commonly encountered, and it is here in particular that Norton displays brilliance in the evocation of lurking menace. As when dealing with imagined technology she shows considerable art in promoting suspension of disbelief by what she leaves unsaid.

Doubt of identity and parallel worlds in time are two familiar SF themes she uses. In *Android at Arms* Andras, fighting to regain his kingdom, is uncertain until the end of the story whether he is, indeed, Andras, or a humanoid counterfeit. In *The Crossroads of Time* and *Quest Crosstime* a kind of cross-time Interpol provides extremely fast action. In *Knave of Dreams*, one of her best novels, the two themes are combined, for Ramsay Kimble awakens in a world of which he has dreamed, inhabiting the body of a young prince, who, the focal point of warring factions, has just died.

Entirely in the world of magic are *Fur Magic*, which takes Cory into mythological worlds of the North American Indian, *Steel Magic*, a bizarre but successful incursion into the Arthurian world of Merlin, and *Dread Companion*, probably her most remarkable achievement, in which Kilda penetrates a kind of Gaelic mythology world of illusion, perpetually shifting and changing.

There are two books of a quite different kind, though both successful: *Bertie and May*, which describes the lives of two young girls in the Ohio countryside of the 1880's, and *Shadow Hawk*, a historical

novel of Ancient Egypt.

For the most part Norton's style is unobtrusively effective, but pseudo-archaisms do intrude occasionally, as in the Janus books, while experiments in construction are not wholly successful in *Iron Cage* and *The Crystal Gryphon*.

—Norman Culpan

———

NORTON, Mary (née Pearson). British. Born in London, 10 December 1903. Educated at St. Margaret's Convent, East Grinstead, Sussex. Married 1) Robert C. Norton in 1926, two daughters and two sons; 2) Lionel Bonsey in 1970. Actress, Old Vic Theatre Company, London, 1925–26; lived in Portugal, 1926–39; worked for the BBC, 1940, and the British Purchasing Company, New York, 1941; from 1942 actress in London. Recipient: Library Association Carnegie Medal, 1953. Address: The Old Rectory, Kilcoe, Aughadown, Ballydehob, West Cork, Ireland.

PUBLICATIONS FOR CHILDREN

Fiction

The Magic Bed-Knob; or, How to Become a Witch in Ten Easy Lessons, illustrated by Waldo Peirce. New York, Hyperion Press, 1943.
The Magic Bed-Knob, illustrated by Joan Kiddell-Monroe. London, Dent, 1945.
Bonfires and Broomsticks, illustrated by Mary Adshead. London, Dent, 1947.
The Borrowers, illustrated by Diana Stanley. London, Dent, 1952; New York, Harcourt Brace, 1953.
The Borrowers Afield, illustrated by Diana Stanley. London, Dent, and New York, Harcourt Brace, 1955.
Bedknob and Broomstick (revised versions of *The Magic Bed-Knob* and *Bonfires and Broomsticks*), illustrated by Erik Blegvad. London, Dent, and New York, Harcourt Brace, 1957.
The Borrowers Afloat, illustrated by Diana Stanley. London, Dent, and New York, Harcourt Brace, 1959.
The Borrowers Aloft, illustrated by Diana Stanley. London, Dent, and New York, Harcourt Brace, 1961.
Poor Stainless, illustrated by Diana Stanley. London, Dent, and New York, Harcourt Brace, 1971.
Are All the Giants Dead?, illustrated by Brian Froud. London, Dent, and New York, Harcourt Brace, 1975.
The Borrowers Avenged, illustrated by Pauline Baynes. London, Kestrel, and New York, Harcourt Brace, 1982.

* * *

With the Borrowers Mary Norton created a powerful mythology, which she clad in such circumstantial detail that these creatures now seem always to have been part of English folklore. This minuscule race, entirely dependent upon human beings whom they suppose to have been created for their benefit—"Human beans are *for* borrowers—like bread's for butter"—are not fairies; they are earthly, practical material beings, who live by "borrowing" the morsels that careless humans leave around. "They thought," says the old woman who tells the child Kate their story, "that human beings were just invented to do the dirty work—great slaves put there for them to use. At least, that's what they told each other. But my brother said that, underneath, he thought they were frightened. It was because they were frightened, he thought, that they had grown so small. Each generation had become smaller and smaller, and more and more hidden." By the time Kate hears their story they have vanished forever.

Pod, Homily and Arrietty, Uncle Hendreary, Aunt Lupy, the cousins Timmis and Eggletina—their very names are borrowed, and oddly changed in the borrowing. They echo human follies and delusions (though Norton achieves her object without Swiftian savagery), and ultimately, in their never-ending quest for permanency, the human predicament. "I only wanted her to know we were *safe*," Arrietty says of her human friend at the end of *The Borrowers Avenged*. "Peagreen looked back at her. He was smiling his quizzical, one-sided smile. 'Are we?' he said gently. 'Are we? Ever?'"

Adults may read the five books as a parable of the human condition or of the wanderings of the homeless and stateless of this century; children, while probably recognizing their poignance, read them for the excellence of the stories, and for the marvellous ingenuity of the practical detail, for a world observed from the height of six inches. We never see the Borrowers achieve the stability for which they crave. At the end of *The Borrowers* they are driven out from their home under the kitchen floorboards in the big old house by all the terror that humans can devise—gas, dogs, ferrets—and are last seen fleeing through the fields. *The Borrowers Afield* takes up the story of their flight, describes their life in the open air with the winter closing in on them as they vainly look for Borrower relations to give them shelter. In *The Borrowers Afloat* they have to leave the gamekeeper's cottage where they have taken refuge because the house is to be shut up, and without its occupants they would starve. Escaping by a drain they voyage downstream in an old kettle looking again for shelter. In *The Borrowers Aloft* they have settled in a model village but are wrenched away by greedy humans who observe them moving among the village's plaster residents, and hope to make a fortune out of putting them on show. They escape by means of a balloon contrived out of the materials they find in their attic-prison, but though they make their way home to Little Fordham they know that there is no longer safety there, that once more they must set out on their quest. 21 years after this last was written *The Borrowers Avenged* takes up their story at the moment when they are leaving their village. They find a new resting-place behind a grate in the nearby Old Rectory. But the reader knows, as do the Borrowers, that it cannot last.

The characters of the three Borrowers, the parents Pod and Homily, their daughter Arrietty, 13 at the beginning of the saga, nearly 17 when it ends, are subtly drawn: Pod the bread-winner, sturdy, brave, dependable, but limited in his outlook by lack of learning and a profound conservatism; Homily the home-maker, anxiously genteel, looking on with shocked horror, tinged with no little envy, at such Borrower families as the Overmantels with their wild and worldly ways, terrified of the world beyond the floorboards; and Arrietty, the questing spirit, who, though loyal and affectionate, has aspirations and longings that her scandalized parents find unnatural, longings for the blue sky, and open air, and space where she can climb and run, and, even more dangerous, an urge to talk to, and even befriend, human beings. She wants to tell her father, but in his view and that of her mother it was still a disgrace, almost a tragedy, to be "seen"; to them it meant broken homes, wearisome treks across unexplored country, and the labour of building anew. "No good never really came to no one from any human bean," says Pod roundly, though it is typical of the humour of the books that in *The Borrowers* he does show himself regularly to bed-ridden Aunt Sophy who drinks a decanter of Fine Old Pale Madeira every night and after the first three glasses never believes in anything she sees.

This sort of humour also pervades *Bedknob and Broomstick*, the story of Miss Price, that excellent English gentlewoman who is also an amateur witch but rather undecided about the ethics of what she is doing, and *Are All the Giants Dead?*, a fantasy about the hereafter

of fairytale characters, both entertaining stories but without the depth of the Borrower books.

—Gillian Avery

NWAPA, Flora (Florence Nwanzuruahu Nkiru Nwapa). Nigerian. Born in Ogutu, East Central State, 18 January 1931. Educated at Archdeacon Crowther's Memorial Girls' School, Elelenwa, 1945–48; Church Missionary Society Girls' School, Lagos, 1949–50; Queen's College, Lagos, 1951; University College, Ibadan, 1953–57; University of Edinburgh, 1957–58, B.A. (London) 1957, Dip. Ed. (Edinburgh) 1958. Married Gogo Nwakuche in 1967; three children. Woman education officer, Calabar, 1958; teacher, Queen's School, Enugu, 1959–62; assistant registrar (public relations), University of Lagos, 1962–67; commissioner and member of the Executive Council, East Central State, 1970–75: with ministries of Health and Social Welfare; Lands, Survey, and Urban Development; and Establishments. Since 1978 managing director, Tana Press Ltd. and Flora Nwapa and Company, Enugu. Agent: David Bolt Associates, 12 Heath Drive, Send, Surrey GU23 7EP, England. Address: Tana Press Ltd., 2-A Menkiti Lane, Ogui, Enugu, Nigeria.

PUBLICATIONS FOR CHILDREN

Fiction

Emeka, Driver's Guard, illustrated by Roslyn Isaacs. London, University of London Press, 1972.
Mammywater, illustrated by Obiora Udechukwu. Enugu, Tana Press, 1979.
Journey to Space, illustrated by Chinwe Orieke. Enugu, Tana Press, 1980.
The Miracle Kittens, illustrated by Emeka Onwudinjo. Enugu, Tana Press, 1980.
The Adventures of Deke, illustrated by Obiora Udechukwu. Enugu, Tana Press, 1980.

Other

My Tana Colouring Book, illustrated by P.S.C. Igboanugo. Enugu, Tana Press, 1979.
My Animal Number Book, illustrated by Emeka Onwudinjo. Enugu, Tana Press, 1981.

PUBLICATIONS FOR ADULTS

Novels

Efuru. London, Heinemann, 1966.
Idu. London, Heinemann, 1970.
Never Again. Enugu, Nwamife, 1974.
One Is Enough. Enugu, Tana Press, 1982.
Women Are Different. Enugu, Tana Press, 1986.

Short Stories

This Is Lagos and Other Stories. Enugu, Nwankwo Ifejika, 1971.
Wives at War and Other Stories. Enugu, Tana Press, 1980.

Verse

Cassava Song and Rice Song. Enugu, Tana Press, 1986.

* * *

Flora Nwapa began her literary career by writing stories for young girls. These stories were never published, but were developed into the novels about Nigerian women for which she has earned an international reputation as a fiction writer. Following the Nigerian Civil War, Nwapa resumed writing stories for children and founded a publishing company devoted to producing literature for children. As a publisher she has encouraged the writing of easy books for new readers and commissioned Nigerian artists to create picture books with Nigerian content that will teach Nigerian children to read and count.

Emeka, Driver's Guard, the first of Nwapa's children's books, appeared in the Modern English Readers Series. Like all stories in this series, it is didactic and moralistic. It educates children about the duties of a driver's guard and emphasizes the value of attending school and succeeding at academic studies. The plot about childhood hardships includes themes common to stories about orphans written by authors from all parts of the world. As in most African fiction published in Europe, the illustrations do not depict the Nigerian setting of the story.

All of Nwapa's other children's stories have been published in Nigeria. They incorporate, without explanation, facets of eastern Nigerian culture, including folklore, which are familiar to Nigerian children and include drawings by Nigerian artists that are integral to telling the stories.

Most of Nwapa's stories are in the Read It Yourself Series. As is characteristic of stories for new readers, Nwapa's are very simple and sometimes are little more than superficial Nigerian adaptations of common western types. *The Miracle Kittens* is such a story in which a cat and her kittens rid a house of rats after diverse human attempts all fail. It is the illustrations more than the words that give this story its Nigerian content. *Journey to Space*, in contrast, is a fantasy which incorporates elements of folklore about two Nigerian children who are carried by a lift through the roof of their apartment to the sky, where they meet a talking dog and fairies from the moon. Although the children never reach their goal, the moon, they enjoy their adventures in space before the fairies return them to their apartment and warn them not to play in the lift in the future.

Mammywater is Nwapa's only children's book in which the creative powers so evident in her adult fiction are fully utilized. The story is based on oral traditions about Mammy Water that are widely known in southern Nigeria and Cameroon. Like the female deities in Nwapa's novels, Mammy Water is a deity who resides in a lake. The story includes common themes about such deities: Mammywater takes humans to live with her, changes herself into many different forms, and has a home famous for its riches at the bottom of a lake. The fast-moving story told primarily in dialogue by two Nigerian children has a moral, too—humility is a valuable human characteristic.

As both a writer and publisher Nwapa is helping the development of Nigerian children's literature.

—Nancy J. Schmidt

NYE, Robert. British. Born in London, 15 March 1939. Educated at Dormans Land, Sussex; Hamlet Court, Westcliff, Essex; Southend High School, Essex. Married 1) Judith Pratt in 1959

(divorced 1967), three sons; 2) Aileen Campbell in 1968, one daughter, one stepdaughter, and one stepson. Since 1961 freelance writer: since 1967 poetry editor, the *Scotsman*; since 1971 poetry critic, *The Times*. Writer-in-residence, University of Edinburgh, 1976–77. Recipient: Eric Gregory award, 1963; Scottish Arts Council bursary, 1970, 1973, and publication award, 1970, 1976; James Kennaway Memorial award, 1970; *Guardian* Fiction prize, 1976; Hawthornden prize, 1977. Fellow, Royal Society of Literature, 1977. Agent: Anthony Sheil Associates, 43 Doughty Street, London WC1N 2LF, England; or, Wallace and Sheil Inc., 177 East 70th Street, New York, New York 10021, U.S.A. Address: 2 Westbury Crescent, Wilton, Cork, Ireland.

PUBLICATIONS FOR CHILDREN

Fiction

Taliesin, illustrated by Sheila Hawkins. London, Faber, 1966; New York, Hill and Wang, 1967.
Wishing Gold, illustrated by Helen Craig. London, Macmillan, 1970; New York, Hill and Wang, 1971.
Poor Pumpkin, illustrated by Derek Collard. London, Macmillan, 1971; as *The Mathematical Princess and Other Stories*, New York, Hill and Wang, 1972.
Out of the World and Back Again, illustrated by Joanna Troughton. London, Collins, 1977; as *Out of This World and Back Again*, Indianapolis, Bobbs Merrill, 1978.
The Bird of the Golden Land, illustrated by Krystyna Turska. London, Hamish Hamilton, 1980.
Harry Pay the Pirate. London, Hamish Hamilton, 1981.
Three Tales (includes *Beowulf, Wishing Gold, Taliesin*). London, Hamish Hamilton, 1983.

Other (retellings)

March Has Horse's Ears, illustrated by Sheila Hawkins. London, Faber, 1966; New York, Hill and Wang, 1967.
Bee Hunter: Adventures of Beowulf, illustrated by Aileen Campbell. London, Faber, 1968; as *Beowulf: A New Telling*, New York, Hill and Wang, 1968; as *Beowulf, The Bee Hunter*, Faber, 1972.
Cricket: Three Stories, illustrated by Shelley Freshman. Indianapolis, Bobbs Merrill, 1975; as *Once upon Three Times*, London, Benn, 1978.

PUBLICATIONS FOR ADULTS

Novels

Doubtfire. London, Calder and Boyars, and New York, Hill and Wang, 1968.
Falstaff. London, Hamish Hamilton, and Boston, Little Brown, 1976.
Merlin. London, Hamish Hamilton, 1978; New York, Putnam, 1979.
Faust. London, Hamish Hamilton, 1980; New York, Putnam, 1981.
The Voyage of the Destiny. London, Hamish Hamilton, and New York, Putnam, 1982.

Short Stories

Tales I Told My Mother. London, Calder and Boyars, 1969; New York, Hill and Wang, 1970.
Penguin Modern Stories 6, with others. London, Penguin, 1970.

The Facts of Life and Other Fictions. London, Hamish Hamilton, 1983.

Plays

Sawney Bean, with William Watson (produced Edinburgh, 1969; London, 1972; New York, 1982). London, Calder and Boyars, 1970.
Sisters (broadcast, 1969; produced Edinburgh, 1973). Included in *Penthesilea, Fugue, and Sisters*, 1975.
Penthesilea, adaptation of the play by Heinrich von Kleist (broadcast, 1971; produced London, 1983). Included in *Penthesilea, Fugue, and Sisters*, 1975.
The Seven Deadly Sins: A Mask, music by James Douglas (produced Stirling and Edinburgh, 1973). Rushden, Northamptonshire, Omphalos Press, 1974.
Mr. Poe (produced Edinburgh and London, 1974).
Penthesilea, Fugue, and Sisters. London, Calder and Boyars, 1975.

Radio Plays: *Sisters*, 1969; *A Bloody Stupit Hole*, 1970; *Reynolds, Reynolds*, 1971; *Penthesilea*, 1971; *The Devil's Jig*, with Humphrey Searle, from a work by Thomas Mann, 1980.

Verse

Juvenilia 1. Northwood, Middlesex, Scorpion Press, 1961.
Juvenilia 2. Lowestoft, Suffolk, Scorpion Press, 1963.
Darker Ends. London, Calder and Boyars, and New York, Hill and Wang, 1969.
Agnus Dei. Rushden, Northamptonshire, Sceptre Press, 1973.
Two Prayers. Richmond, Surrey, Keepsake Press, 1974.
Five Dreams. Rushden, Northamptonshire, Sceptre Press, 1974.
Divisions on a Ground. Manchester, Carcanet, 1976.

Other

Editor, *A Choice of Sir Walter Ralegh's Verse.* London, Faber, 1972.
Editor, *William Barnes: A Selection of His Poems.* Cheadle, Cheshire, Carcanet, 1972.
Editor, *A Choice of Swinburne's Verse.* London, Faber, 1973.
Editor, *The Faber Book of Sonnets.* London, Faber, 1976; as *A Book of Sonnets*, New York, Oxford University Press, 1976.
Editor, *The English Sermon 1750–1850.* Manchester, Carcanet, 1976.
Editor, *PEN New Poetry.* London, Quartet, 1986.

*

Manuscript Collections: University of Texas, Austin; National Library of Scotland, Edinburgh; University of Edinburgh; Colgate University, Hamilton, New York.

*   *   *

Robert Nye is a Rabelaisian storyteller of reckless heroes, feckless kings, vampire-ridden fens, and headless horses. Widows play chess with blackbirds, a king grows horse's ears, failed suitors get beheaded. Enormous respect for the possibilities of words pervades his work. Imagery is simple but vivid, conveying the joys of climbing, sailing, dreaming, loving, becoming a hare, used with sufficient demands to make the reader think imaginatively, yet drawn from quotidian life. "Even the light had a brief look about it, as though it were a trespasser." A boy sees a buzzard, high, "like a full-stop scratched on the sun." Details, funny, preposterous, homely, are

incessantly invented but the plot, so essential to the young, is carefully preserved. Jack will get Jill, the riddles be answered, the youngest son with treasure, true poets outmatch bad poets. Nevertheless, by a small twist of narrative, unexpected line of dialogue, old heroes are given more humanity, more realism, most notably in *Bee Hunter* and *March Has Horse's Ears*. Magic has its place, but is generally kept in its place by elementary human needs. Splendour is shot through with earthiness. The villainous Unferth "began gnawing at his finger nails. They tasted of dirt and where he had been poking at his boil. Unferth hated the taste of himself, but he had to have it." Such figures relate to recognisable loneliness, unpopularity, the humour and tensions of family and communal life, the casual feelings that may accompany the most grandiose exploits. Panting from slaying the dragon, Beowulf develops toothache; the great poet Taliesin shows sly, schoolboy mischief. A dragon may have legitimate grievance, a villain or monster have pathos, a golden warrior reveal flaws. The rhythms, adroit repetitions, the unusual words carefully planted, make these stories excellent for reading aloud. *Wishing Gold* perfectly confirms this.

—Peter Vansittart

———

OAKLEY, Graham. British. Born in Shrewsbury, Shropshire, 27 August 1929. Educated at a grammar school; Warrington Art School, Lancashire, 1950. Scenic artist in various repertory companies, 1950–55, and at Royal Opera House, London, 1955–57; staff member, Crawford Advertising Agency, 1960–62; designer, BBC Television, London, 1962–77. Since 1977 freelance writer and illustrator. Address: c/o Macmillan Children's Books, 4 Little Essex Street, London WC2R 3LF, England.

PUBLICATIONS FOR CHILDREN (illustrated by the author)

Fiction

The Church Mouse. London, Macmillan, and New York, Atheneum, 1972.
The Church Cat Abroad. London, Macmillan, and New York, Atheneum, 1973.
The Church Mice and the Moon. London, Macmillan, and New York, Atheneum, 1974.
The Church Mice Spread Their Wings. London, Macmillan, 1975; New York, Atheneum, 1976.
The Church Mice Adrift. London, Macmillan, 1976; New York, Atheneum, 1977.
The Church Mice at Bay. London, Macmillan, 1978; New York, Atheneum, 1979.
Magical Changes. London, Macmillan, 1979; New York, Atheneum, 1980.
The Church Mice at Christmas. London, Macmillan, and New York, Atheneum, 1980.
Hetty and Harriet. London, Macmillan, 1981; New York, Atheneum, 1982.
The Church Mice in Action. London, Macmillan, 1982; New York, Atheneum, 1983.
Henry's Quest. London, Macmillan, and New York, Atheneum, 1986.
The Diary of a Church Mouse. London, Macmillan, 1986; New York, Atheneum, 1987.
The Church Mice Chronicles. London, Macmillan, 1986.

*

Illustrator: *Monsters and Marlinspikes* by Hugh Popham, 1958; *Kidnapped* by Robert Louis Stevenson, 1960; *Discovering the Bible* by David Scott Daniell, 1961; *The King of the Golden River* by John Ruskin, 1961; *White Horizons* by Charles Kervern, 1962; *The Three Feathers*, 1963, *Skillywidden*, 1965, and *The Bird-Catcher and the Crow-Peri*, 1968, all by Mollie Clarke; *The White Dragon*, 1963, and *Jack of Dover*, 1966, both by Richard Garnett; *Grandmother's Footsteps* by Patricia Ledward, 1966; *Stories Told round the World* by Taya Zinkin, 1968; *The Ancient World* by Robert Ogilvie, 1969; *The Water Wheel* by Brian Read, 1970; *The Dragon Hoard* by Tanith Lee, 1971; *The Two Sisters* by Elizabeth MacDonald, 1975.

* * *

Graham Oakley belongs to the growing band of author/artists whose books are conceived as a single entity, words and pictures sharing the burden of the story. Unusually for one who is an artist first and a writer second, he does not make the mistake of simply trying to get away with as few words as possible, regardless of their quality. Such deceptive simplicity is as difficult to carry off successfully as anything a writer can be asked to do. Instead, Oakley writes as he draws, with a wealth of incidental detail and asides. Pictures and text are used equally to embellish and advance the tale he has to tell, his one guiding principle being never to repeat the identical joke in both media.

Except for one excursion into total wordlessness with *Magical Changes*, where the pages are divided horizontally on the time-honoured principle of "heads, bodies, and legs," to produce a set of fantastic variations on the original pictures, he has remained faithful to the setting and characters introduced in his first book, *The Church Mouse*. Arthur, the mouse of the title, inhabits a splendid church, filled with Victorian gothic ornament. "Sampson, the church cat, had listened to so many sermons about the meek being blessed and everybody really being brothers that he had grown quite frighteningly meek and treated Arthur just like a brother." But, though in no danger, Arthur is lonely and tired of a diet of choirboys' sweets. He solves this problem by persuading the vicar to let him bring in the rest of the town's mice, with a promise that the mice will keep the church tidy in return for a weekly ration of cheese. Their ensuring adventures range from trapping a burglar (Sampson helps the mice tie his shoelaces together and roll him in the carpet) to sabotaging the Wortlethorpe Municipal Moon Programme (*The Church Mice and the Moon*) and getting rid of an undesirable curate (*The Church Mice at Bay*). Inevitably in a series of this kind, not all the books reach the consistently high standard of the first. Some of the plots strain credulity too far. *The Church Cat Abroad* even sees Sampson and two of the mice marooned on a desert island. But in every case the narrative and pictures combine to give the books an enjoyable satirical edge, appreciated by adults as well as children. The scientists of WOMUMP are horrified when their television screen apparently reveals an archangel with a trumpet on the way to the moon—really a tombstone glimpsed overhead as Sampson and the mice tow the rescued astronauts back to the vestry—and delighted when the moon itself seems actually to be made of cheese. Festive television screens, in *The Church Mice at Christmas*, show nothing but violence. A captured burglar reclines at ease in his cell, being fed tea and Christmas cake by a paper-hatted copper. All these details, adding richness and interest to the main story, are an integral part of Oakley's distinctive style and help to give his books a more long-lasting appeal than the general run of picture books.

—Anne Carter

O'BRIEN, Robert C. Pseudonym for Robert Leslie Conly. American. Born in Brooklyn, New York, 11 January 1918. Educated at schools in Amityville, Long Island, New York; Williams College, Williamstown, Massachusetts, 1935–37; Juilliard School of Music, New York; Columbia University, New York; University of Rochester, New York, B.A. in English 1940. Married Sally McCaslin in 1943; one son and three daughters. Worked in an advertising agency, 1940; researcher and writer, *Newsweek* magazine, New York, 1941–44; reporter, *Times-Herald*, 1944–46, and *Pathfinder* magazine, 1946–51, both Washington, D.C.; staff member, rising to senior assistant editor, *National Geographic* magazine, Washington, D.C., 1951–73. Recipient: American Library Association Newbery Medal, 1972; Mystery Writers of America Edgar Allan Poe award, 1976. *Died 5 March 1973.*

PUBLICATIONS FOR CHILDREN

Fiction

The Silver Crown, illustrated by Dale Payson. New York, Atheneum, 1968; London, Gollancz, 1973.
Mrs. Frisby and the Rats of Nimh, illustrated by Zena Bernstein. New York, Atheneum, 1971; London, Gollancz, 1972.
Z for Zachariah. New York, Atheneum, and London, Gollancz, 1975.

PUBLICATIONS FOR ADULTS

Novel

A Report from Group 17. New York, Atheneum, 1972; London, Gollancz, 1973.

*

Manuscript Collection: Kerlan Collection, University of Minnesota, Minneapolis.

* * *

Robert C. O'Brien was a serious writer; that is to say, he dealt with important moral themes in some depth. He was, like C.S. Lewis, a notable example of a sophisticated writer who found the flexible conventions of children's fiction a convenient medium for exploring his own ideas.

Only his second novel, *Mrs. Frisby and the Rats of Nimh*, has achieved wide popularity as well as critical acclaim. At the level of children's animal story it describes the heroic efforts of a mother fieldmouse to save her invalid child from imminent death from the farmer's plough. In the course of her struggle, she gets involved with a colony of hyper-intelligent rats who have escaped from a research laboratory. These rats are confronting the questions that face industrial man and clearly obsess O'Brien: whether to use technological expertise to create a competitive mechanised society that exploits and eventually destroys its environment or whether to opt for a civilisation that respects the individual and natural resources. These were hackneyed topics among dissident American youth of the early 1970's, but O'Brien's use of talking rats who are testing out the options for themselves provides a fresh new focus; the problems somehow appear clearer and more real in the context of an animal story than they ever could in a conventional "human" novel. O'Brien's inoffensive didacticism is carried easily by a most moving and original narrative.

His earlier novel, *The Silver Crown*, is again about a civilisation, this time our own, threatened by exploitation and destruction. An evil power, oddly derived from the 5th-century St. Jerome, is about to infiltrate society first with muggings, race riots, and arson and eventually through the control of everybody's minds. O'Brien seems to have a firm belief in the notion of Evil as the source of man's troubles. His third children's book, *Z for Zachariah*, takes us to the stage when our civilisation *has* destroyed itself through a nuclear holocaust; a 16-year-old girl survivor records her macabre experiences in the form of a daily diary that reminds one of a French New Wave novel.

O'Brien's output was slender and uneven, but characterised by remarkable inventiveness, dramatic power, and a clear narrative style that enabled complex ideas to be felt as well as understood.

—Aidan Warlow

O'CONNOR, Patrick. See **WIBBERLEY, Leonard**.

ODAGA, Asenath (Bole). Kenyan. Born in Rarieda, 5 July 1938. Educated at Ngiya Girls School, 1950–52; Alliance Girls High School, Kikuyu, 1953–54; Kikuyu Teacher Training College, 1955–56; University of Nairobi, 1971–74, B.A. (honours) in literature 1974, Dip. Ed. 1974, M.A. 1981. Married James Charles Odaga in 1958; five children. Tutor, Church Missionary Society Teacher Training College, Ngiya, 1957–58; teacher, Butere Girls School, 1959–60; headmistress, Nyakach Girls School, 1961–63; assistant secretary, Kenya Dairy Board, Nairobi, 1965–67; secretary, Kenya Library Services, Nairobi, 1968; advertising assistant, *East African Standard* newspaper and Kerr Downey and Selby Safaris, both Nairobi, 1969–70; assistant director of the curriculum development programme, Christian Churches Educational Association, Nairobi, 1974–75; research fellow, Institute of African Studies, University of Nairobi, 1976–81. Since 1982 freelance writer. Founding member and Secretary General, Writers Association of Kenya; since 1988 chairman, Children's Literature Association of Kenya. Address: P.O. Box 1743, Kisumu, Kenya.

PUBLICATIONS FOR CHILDREN

Fiction

Jande's Ambition, illustrated by Adrienne Moore. Nairobi, East African Publishing House, 1966.
The Secret of the Monkey Rock, illustrated by William Agutu. London, Nelson, 1966.
The Diamond Ring, illustrated by Adrienne Moore. Nairobi, East African Publishing House, 1967.
The Angry Flames, illustrated by Adrienne Moore. Nairobi, East African Publishing House, 1968.
Sweets and Sugar Cane (short stories), illustrated by Beryl Moore. Nairobi, East African Publishing House, 1969.
The Villager's Son, illustrated by Shyam Varma. London, Heinemann, 1971.
Kip on the Farm, illustrated by Beryl Moore. Nairobi, East African Publishing House, 1972.
Kip at the Coast, illustrated by Gay Galsworthy. London, Evans, 1977.
Kip Goes to the City, illustrated by Gay Galsworthy. London, Evans, 1977.

The Shade Changes. Kisumu, Lake, 1984.
The Storm, illustrated by Njoroge. Kisumu, Lake, 1986.
The Rag Ball, illustrated by Jos Odaga. Kisumu, Lake, 1987.
Munde Goes to the Market, illustrated by Peter Odaga. Kisumu, Lake, 1987.
Munde and His Friends, illustrated by Peter Odaga. Kisumu, Lake, 1987.
The Silver Cup, illustrated by Peter Odaga. Kisumu, Lake, 1988.

Other (in Luo language)

Poko Nyar Mugumba (Poko Mugumba's Daughter), illustrated by Sophia Ojienda. Nairobi, Foundation, 1978.
Ange ok Tel (Regret Never Comes First), illustrated by Joe Odaga. Kisumu, Lake, 1982.
Sigendini gi Timbe Luo Moko (Stories and Some Customs of the Luo), illustrated by Alice Odaga. Kisumu, Lake, 1982.
Ogilo Nungo Piny Kirom. Nairobi, Heinemann, 1983.

Other (folktales)

The Hare's Blanket and Other Tales, illustrated by Adrienne Moore. Nairobi, East African Publishing House, 1967.
Thu Tinda: Stories from Kenya. Nairobi, Uzima Press, 1980.
The Two Friends, illustrated by Barrack Omondi. Nairobi, Bookwise, 1981.
Kenyan Folk Tales, illustrated by Margaret Humphries. Caithness, Scotland, Humphries, 1981.

Editor, with David Kirui and David Crippen, *God, Myself, and Others*. Nairobi, Evangel, 1976.

PUBLICATIONS FOR ADULTS

Novels

Between the Years. Kisumu, Lake, 1987.
A Bridge in Time. Kisumu, Lake, 1987.
Riana. Kisumu, Lake, 1988.

Short Stories

A Reed on the Roof, Block Ten, With Other Stories. Kisumu, Lake, 1982.

Plays (in Luo language)

Miaha (The Bride) (produced Nairobi, 1981).
Simbi Nyaima (The Sunken Village) (produced Kisumu, 1982). Kisumu, Lake, 1983.

Other

Nyathini Koa e Nyuolne Nyaka Higni Adek (in Luo: Your Child from Birth to Age Three). Nairobi, Evangel, 1976.
Oral Literature: A School Certificate Course, with A. Bole Odaga and S. Kichamu Akivaga. Nairobi, Heinemann, 1982.
Yesterday's Today: The Study of Oral Literature. Kisumu, Lake, 1984.
Literature for Children and Young People in Kenya. Nairobi, Kenya Literature Bureau, 1985.
Luo-English, English-Luo Dictionary. Kisumu, Lake, 1987.

*

Asenath Odaga comments:

My writing is for members of my society: adults and children. It is about their daily experiences and involvement with life. The bits and pieces that fit into the stream of their existence and make their life whole are interesting to read about, and it is from these bits that I try to create realistic and objective work.

For children, apart from writing about what they are familiar and can identify with, I collect stories that were told and still are told orally among the various peoples of Kenya. These oral narratives are interesting and entertaining, but they are also educative and instructive. They embody the wisdom and philosophy of our ancestors which are our children's heritage, a heritage to which children should have access through the written word, since it is no longer possible to follow the traditional methods of telling and preserving that heritage.

*   *   *

Asenath Odaga is a prominent Kenyan children's writer and publisher of materials in English and Luo. She believes that Kenyan children should start their education by reading literature about "the close and familiar things forming their lives." Her fiction for younger children focuses on children's daily activities at home or school and especially on oral traditions, many of which she has collected, whereas her young adult fiction concentrates on urban settings, social issues, and value conflicts that are commonplace in Africa in the 1980's.

Several of Odaga's children's books focus on Kenyan oral traditions. *Yesterday's Today* includes a broad selection of oral literature (tales, proverbs, riddles, tongue twisters, and songs) that Odaga collected throughout Kenya. This volume, intended for older children and the general public, is illustrated with photographs and includes exercises to increase the reader's understanding of oral literature. *The Hare's Blanket and Other Tales*, written for younger children, includes four rabbit trickster tales which are simple summaries of the original tales told largely in dialogue. In contrast, *Thu Tinda* includes fictionalized folktales that incorporate songs, extensive dialogue, and a patterned ending, retold for older children. Odaga has used her imagination in "modernizing" these tales. Odaga also writes adventure stories. Some, like *The Diamond Ring*, blend oral traditions with experiences from contemporary life. When the hero, a herd boy, goes to visit his grandfather, he obtains a protective charm from Black Wizard and a magic song from his mother. On his journey the hero encounters dwarves, giants, snakes, and dangerous animals, and passes through a town that has cars, lorries, and houses similar to those he is familiar with, but the people speak a strange language and hold him prisoner. He escapes from all dangers through wit, cunning, protective charms, and his magic song. The hero wonders if he has been dreaming, but his grandfather confirms that the strange people are Kande, and tells him about their activities in the old days.

Other adventure stories, especially those for young adults, focus on contemporary urban life, but incorporate traditional customs and lifestyles. *The Shade Changes*, for example, is a detective story set in Mombasa, about a marriage of convenience of a young woman to an older man who is her father's business partner, in which the bride is kidnapped and her father's house is robbed of wealth gained illegally. The characters are motivated by conflicting sets of values that focus on "traditional" family values and contemporary urban values of wealth and status which are familiar to young adults in Africa. Like all Odaga's fiction, this story has lessons to teach, but it is not explicitly didactic. It is a well-crafted adventure story. Most of Odaga's fiction written for younger children *is* explicitly didactic. The short stories collected in *Sweets and Sugar Cane* and the series of Kip books are educational stories that describe such adventures as helping on the farm, going to market, molding clay figures,

playing games, and taking trips to Nairobi by car or train. *Jande's Ambition* is an autobiographical schoolgirl story that describes the life of a western Kenyan girl from early childhood until she enrolls in teacher training college. Experiences familiar to Kenyan and other African school-children such as difficulty earning school fees, failing exams, and conflict between family responsibilities and attending school are included in this fast-moving story told largely in dialogue.

Odaga writes a wide variety of literature for children of all ages. The popularity of her books in Kenya reflects her skill at creating interesting and exciting stories based on people, places, events, and traditions with which they are familiar.

—Nancy J. Schmidt

———

O'DELL, Scott. American. Born in Los Angeles, California, 23 May 1898. Educated at Occidental College, Los Angeles, 1919; University of Wisconsin, Madison, 1920; Stanford University, California, 1920–21; University of Rome, 1925. Served in the United States Air Force during World War II. Film cameraman, 1920's; book editor of a Los Angeles newspaper, 1940's. Established Scott O'Dell award for historical fiction, 1981. Recipient: American Library Association Newbery Medal, 1961; Children's Literature prize (West Germany), 1963, 1968; Hans Christian Andersen International Medal, 1972; University of Southern Mississippi award, 1976; Catholic Library Association Regina Medal, 1978; O'Dell award, 1987. Lives in New York State. Agent: McIntosh and Otis, 310 Madison Avenue, New York, New York 10017. Address: c/o Houghton Mifflin, 2 Park Street, Boston, Massachusetts 02108, U.S.A.

PUBLICATIONS FOR CHILDREN

Fiction

Island of the Blue Dolphins. Boston, Houghton Mifflin, 1960; London, Constable, 1961.
The King's Fifth, illustrated by Samuel Bryant. Boston, Houghton Mifflin, 1966; London, Constable, 1967.
The Black Pearl, illustrated by Milton Johnson. Boston, Houghton Mifflin, 1967; London, Longman, 1968.
The Dark Canoe, illustrated by Milton Johnson. Boston, Houghton Mifflin, 1968; London, Longman, 1969.
Journey to Jericho, illustrated by Leonard Weisgard. Boston, Houghton Mifflin, 1969.
Sing Down the Moon. Boston, Houghton Mifflin, 1970; London, Hamish Hamilton, 1972.
The Treasure of Topo-el-Bampo, illustrated by Lynd Ward. Boston, Houghton Mifflin, 1972.
Child of Fire. Boston, Houghton Mifflin, 1974.
The Hawk That Dare Not Hunt by Day. Boston, Houghton Mifflin, 1975.
The 290. Boston, Houghton Mifflin, 1976; London, Oxford University Press, 1977.
Zia, illustrated by Ted Lewin. Boston, Houghton Mifflin, 1976; London, Oxford University Press, 1977.
Carlota. Boston, Houghton Mifflin, 1977; as *The Daughter of Don Saturnino*, London, Oxford University Press, 1979.
Kathleen, Please Come Home. Boston, Houghton Mifflin, 1978.
The Captive. Boston, Houghton Mifflin, 1979.
Sarah Bishop. Boston, Houghton Mifflin, 1980.
The Feathered Serpent. Boston, Houghton Mifflin, 1981.

The Spanish Smile.   Boston, Houghton Mifflin, 1982.
The Amethyst Ring.   Boston, Houghton Mifflin, 1983.
The Castle in the Sea.   Boston, Houghton Mifflin, 1983.
Alexandra.   Boston, Houghton Mifflin, 1984.
The Road to Damietta.   Boston, Houghton Mifflin, 1985.
Streams to the River, River to the Sea.   Boston, Houghton Mifflin, 1986.
The Serpent Never Sleeps: A Novel of Jamestown and Pocahontas.   Boston, Houghton Mifflin, 1987.
Black Star, Bright Dawn.   Boston, Houghton Mifflin, 1988.

Other

The Cruise of the Arctic Star, illustrated by Samuel Bryant.   Boston, Houghton Mifflin, 1973.

PUBLICATIONS FOR ADULTS

Novels

Woman of Spain.   Boston, Houghton Mifflin, 1934.
Hill of the Hawk.   Indianapolis, Bobbs Merrill, 1947; London, Corgi, 1955.
The Sea Is Red.   New York, Holt Rinehart, 1958.

Other

Representative Photoplays Analyzed.   Hollywood, Palmer Institute of Authorship, 1924.
Man Alone, with William Doyle.   Indianapolis, Bobbs Merrill, 1953; as *Lifer*, London, Longman, 1954.
Country of the Sun: Southern California: An Informal History and Guide.   New York, Crowell, 1957.
The Psychology of Children's Art, with Rhoda Kellogg.   San Diego, California, Communications Research Machines Associates, 1967.

*

Manuscript Collection: University of Oregon Library, Eugene.

*   *   *

It's a pity if any adult reader who loves historical adventure stories of the first rank misses the works of Scott O'Dell merely because they are labeled as "juveniles." It has only been in recent years, with explicit depiction of sex and violence, that much of the adult fare in the genre, which has its roots in the works of Scott and Dumas, has become unsuitable for younger readers. If O'Dell were writing 40 to 50 years ago he would undoubtedly have been in the company of such writers as C.S. Forester, Nordhoff and Hall, and Kenneth Roberts; and a generation or two before that with Stevenson, Henty, Marryat, Dana, and Jack London. These writers had broad appeal, but perhaps their most enthusiastic audience consisted of readers between the ages of 12 and 16. O'Dell, after a long and successful career as a journalist, historian, and writer for adults, found that audience with the publication of *Island of the Blue Dolphins*.

When O'Dell speaks of himself as a practitioner in the field of children's literature he uses the term "writer of books that children read," rather than "writer of children's books." Indeed, O'Dell's strength as a writer for children is best explained by the fact that he does not write directly for them. As he says: "Books of mine which are classified officially as books written for children, were not written for children. Instead, and in a very real sense, they were written for myself. There is about them, however, one distinction

which I feel is important to this form of literature: they were written consistently in the emotional area that children share with adults." O'Dell also recognizes that the young reader "has the ability, which in adults is either eroded or entirely lost, to identify himself with the characters of a story." So rather than write with a child audience in mind, O'Dell aesthetically disciplines himself by selecting a young person to narrate his tales. Indeed, he is a master of first-person narrative, which in itself is not only the unifying and coherent influence which heightens the truth and significance of his stories, but also the element which assimilates into the tales all of the author's research, personal knowledge, and experience, without a single trace of pedantic or didactic intrusion.

O'Dell is, in a very real way, a different person each time he tells a story. This gives each of his books an individual quality that is uniquely suited for its natural and cultural setting. The cadence of the narrative voice, the metaphorical symbols, and the limiting perimeters of the narrator's scope, all unite to produce a story that is plausible and consistent, and poetically satisfying as well.

Karana, the Indian girl of *Island of the Blue Dolphins*, begins her story: "I remember the day the Aleut ship came to our island. At first it seemed like a small shell afloat in the sea. Then it grew longer and was a gull with folded wings." In contrast, Bright Morning in *Sing Down the Moon* tells a Navajo story in the natural rhythms and allusions of Navajo speech. "The day the waters came was a wonderful day. I heard the first sounds of their coming while I lay awake in the night. At first it was a whisper, like a wind among the dry stalks of our cornfield. After a while it was a sound like the feet of warriors' dancing. Then it was a roar that shook the earth."

O'Dell's stories are vivid in locale and authentic in historical background and detail. Several of them, like *The Black Pearl* and *The Dark Canoe*, are set in the coastal region of southern California, a setting with which he is very familiar; while others, such as *The King's Fifth*, are set further inland around the canyon country of southwestern United States. In a trilogy of grand scope (*The Captive, The Feathered Serpent*, and *The Amethyst Ring*) O'Dell captures the history, lore, and landscape of New Spain during the time of the bloody conquest of the Aztecs and their emperor, Montezuma, by Hernando Cortez.

In his most recent historical novels, O'Dell has returned to the story element for which he is best-known by so many young readers: an adventurous female protagonist and first-person narrator. These later works are of varied sophistication. *The Road to Damietta* is not a conventional historical novel. It is the story of the transformation of Francis Bernardone from a bon vivant to the ascetic saint of Assisi, as narrated by an aristocratic young woman who is madly in love with him. *The Serpent Never Sleeps: A Novel of Jamestown and Pocahontas* is seen through the eyes of Serena Lynn, a tempestuous young heroine. It is in *Streams to the River, River to the Sea* that O'Dell returns again to the simple straightforward narration that made *Island of the Blue Dolphins* such a memorable work. In this book the remarkable young Shoshone girl Sacagawea gives her own account of her extraordinary adventures with the Lewis and Clark expedition. The verisimilitude of this historical novel brings Sacagawea to life in a manner that no biographic work has been able to achieve. It is O'Dell at his very best—and that is high praise indeed.

—James E. Higgins

O'FAOLAIN, Eileen (née Gould). Irish. Born in Cork in 1902. Educated at University College, Cork. Married the writer Sean O'Faolain in 1928; one daughter (the writer Julia O'Faolain) and one son. *Died in 1988.*

PUBLICATIONS FOR CHILDREN

Fiction

The Little Black Hen, illustrated by Trefor Jones.   London, Oxford
   University Press, and New York, Random House, 1940; as *The
   Fairy Hen*, Dublin, Parkside Press, 1945.
The King of the Cats, illustrated by Nano Reid.   Dublin, Talbot
   Press, 1941; New York, Morrow, 1942.
Miss Pennyfeather and the Pooka, illustrated by Nora McGuinness.
   Dublin, Browne and Nolan, 1942; New York, Random House,
   1946.
The Children of Crooked Castle.   Dublin, Browne and Nolan, 1945.
May Eve in Fairyland.   Dublin, Parkside Press, 1945.
Miss Pennyfeather in the Springtime, illustrated by Muriel Brandt.
   Dublin, Browne and Nolan, 1946.
The Shadowy Man, illustrated by Phoebe Llewellyn Smith.   Lon-
   don, Longman, 1949.
The White Rabbit's Road, illustrated by Phoebe Llewellyn Smith.
   London, Longman, 1950.
High Sang the Sword, illustrated by Brian Wildsmith.   London,
   Oxford University Press, 1959.

Other (retellings)

Irish Sagas and Folk-Tales, illustrated by Joan Kiddell-Monroe.
   London, Oxford University Press, and New York, Walck, 1954.
Children of the Salmon and Other Irish Folktales, illustrated by Trina
   Schart Hyman.   London, Longman, and Boston, Little Brown,
   1965.

*   *   *

Eileen O'Faolain's output is almost entirely in the realms of
fairytale, fantasy, and retellings of old sagas and myths from Irish
folklore. It is not a large output, but in the context of Irish children's
literature it is significant. It spans several decades and provided
during World War II and the immediate post-war period in Ireland a
literature which spoke to children in a familiar language and showed
them that adventure and fairy are only just around the corner. Like
some of the very best of children's stories, they were written with a
specific child in mind—Julia, the author's daughter. All of her stories
have an element of fantasy and in every instance the fantasy and
magic are wrought through the animal world. Enchanted animals are
the link between the real world and that of fairy—hens, cats, dogs,
donkeys, and foals are the key to a magic world, a world which even
they fear and respect. Even in the Miss Pennyfeather stories, which
revolve around an eccentric old lady living by the River Lee in Cork,
animals are important and can act and speak as humans some of the
time. Like Patricia Lynch, by whom she was overshadowed,
O'Faolain was attuned to the rhythms and lore of the old storytellers.
She recounted how the core of the story of *The Little Black Hen*, long
a firm favourite with her readers, was given to her by an old shanchie
or storyteller. He was in conversation with the author one day and
pointing to distant hills commented, "The fairies are in a bad way
this long time. The Queen is dead. Ah, but that Cliona was always a
bad queen." From this chance comment came the story of Cossey
Darg who is captured by Cliona and made to work in the royal
kitchens beneath the fairy fort, and of the children Julie and Garret
who set about rescuing her and the other bewitched creatures. By the
end of the story all that remains from the fairy world is the little mob
cap which in her excitement the little hen forgets to remove. Finding
it the old woman Biddy comments: "They believe it now. But later
on, when they grow up, they won't believe it. I'll keep this little cap
to show them, then—and they will know that it all really happened,
and that it wasn't just one of old Biddy's silly fairy-stories after all,
but the true story of Cossey Darg and the Queen of the Muskerry
fairies." She has that little cap to this very day.

—Pat Donlon

———

O'HARA, Mary (Mary O'Hara Alsop).   American.   Born in Cape
May Point, New Jersey, 10 July 1885. Educated at Packer Institute,
Brooklyn, New York. Married 1) Kent K. Parrot in 1905 (divorced
1922), one daughter and one son; 2) Helge Sture-Vasa in 1922
(divorced 1947). Writer and composer. *Died 15 October 1980.*

PUBLICATIONS FOR CHILDREN

Fiction

My Friend Flicka.   Philadelphia, Lippincott, 1941; London, Eyre
   and Spottiswoode, 1943.
Thunderhead.   Philadelphia, Lippincott, 1943; London, Eyre and
   Spottiswoode, 1945.
Green Grass of Wyoming.   Philadelphia, Lippincott, 1946; London,
   Eyre and Spottiswoode, 1947.
The Catch Colt (fictionalization of her stage play).   London,
   Methuen, 1979.

Play

The Catch Colt, music by O'Hara (produced Washington D.C.).
   New York, Dramatists Play Service, 1964.

PUBLICATIONS FOR ADULTS

Novels

The Son of Adam Wingate.   New York, McKay, and London, Eyre
   and Spottiswoode, 1952.
Wyoming Summer.   New York, Doubleday, 1963.

Plays

Screenplays: *The Last Card*, with Molly Parro, 1921; *Life's Darn
Funny*, with Arthur Ripley, 1921; *There Are No Villains*, 1921; *Turn
to the Right*, with June Mathis, 1922; *The Prisoner of Zenda*, 1922;
Peg o' My Heart, 1922; *The Age of Desire*, with Lenore Coffee and
Dixie Willson, 1923; *Merry-Go-Round*, with Finis Fox and Harvey
Gates, 1923; *The Woman on the Jury*, 1924; *Braveheart*, 1925; *The
Home Maker*, 1925; *The Honeymoon Express*, 1926; *Frames*, 1927;
Perch of the Devil, 1927.

Other

Let Us Say Grace (as Mary Sture-Vasa).   Boston, Christopher,
   1930.
Novel-in-the-Making.   New York, McKay, 1954.
A Musical in the Making.   Chevy Chase, Maryland, Markane
   Publishing, 1966.
Flicka's Friend: The Autobiography of Mary O'Hara.   New York,
   Putnam, 1982.

*

Music: *Esperan*, 1943; *May God Keep You*, 1946; *Wyoming Suite*, 1946; *Windharp*; and other works for piano.

*   *   *

Mary O'Hara's reputation as a children's author rests upon her trilogy of American ranch life, *My Friend Flicka, Thunderhead*, and *Green Grass of Wyoming*. Based on the author's experiences as a Wyoming rancher, the novels record seven years in the life of Ken McLaughlin, the younger son of Rob McLaughlin, a West Point graduate who has left the Army to raise thoroughbred horses, and his wife, Nell, an artistic Bryn Mawr graduate. The three books are unified by their account of Ken's recurring clashes with his strong-willed father, the boy's gradual maturing and reconciliation with Rob, and the adult McLaughlins' long-standing financial troubles at their Goose Bar Ranch.

The works are closely linked. *My Friend Flicka* introduces the McLaughlin family, establishes their financial straits, and relates 10-year-old Ken's efforts to tame his colt, Flicka, a descendant of a wild white range stallion, the Albino. *Thunderhead* resumes the narrative two years later, telling of the birth and training of Flicka's first foal, a white colt resembling the Albino. The story of Ken's two-year-long opposition to his father's determination to geld the fractious Thunderhead is intensified by a growing estrangement between Rob and Nell; the tensions, however, are eased by the family's achieving a degree of financial security and by Nell's pregnancy. *Green Grass of Wyoming*, the most traditionally constructed of the books, tells two stories: that of Rob McLaughlin's grudging but eventual acceptance of Thunderhead as the Goose Bar stud and that of the developing romance between 17-year-old Ken and the grand-niece of a wealthy horse-breeder.

Although working within the conventions of the realistic animal story, O'Hara avoids the usual pitfalls of the genre. She does not blink at the biological facts of life, but she sets reproduction and the transmission of genetic types at the heart of the novels. Nor does she gloss over the occasional conflicts of family life. She makes the subtle antagonisms between Rob and Nell and the quarrels between the day-dreaming Ken and the determined Rob as much a part of the books as the genuine love that all three share. She deals, in fact, with all of the facets of life, from the impact of climate and space to that of politics and economics, making the works accounts of believably fallible persons who are trying, at considerable cost to themselves, to live the life of their dreams.

—Fred Erisman

———

OKORO, Anezi. Nigerian. Born in Arondizuogu, 17 May 1929. Educated at the Methodist College, Uzuakoli, 1941–45; Dennis Memorial Grammar School, Onitsha, 1946–47; University College, Ibadan, 1948–52; University of Bristol, England, 1953–56, M.B., Ch.B. 1956; University of Edinburgh, F.R.C.P. 1977. Married Eseohe Olumese; five children. House surgeon, University College Hospital, Ibadan, 1956–57; medical officer, 1957–64, and consultant dermatologist, 1965–66, Ministry of Health, Lagos; Associate Lecturer, College of Medicine, University of Lagos, 1964–66; consultant dermatologist, Ministry of Health, Enugu, 1966–74; Senior Lecturer, 1967–74, Reader, 1974–75, and since 1975 Professor of Medicine, University of Nigeria, Nsukka. Director, Nigerian National Petroleum Corporation, Lagos, 1977–81. Visiting Professor, Medical College of Georgia, Augusta, 1987, and University of Minnesota, Minneapolis, 1988. Since 1986 President, African Association for Dermatology. Address: Skin Clinic, University of Nigeria Teaching Hospital, P.M.B. 01129, Enugu, Nigeria.

PUBLICATIONS FOR CHILDREN

Fiction

The Village School, illustrated by Frances Effiong. Lagos, African Universities Press, 1966.
The Village Headmaster, illustrated by Frances Effiong. Ibadan, African Universities Press, 1967.
Febechi down the Niger, illustrated by Monica Eloji. Enugu, Nwamife, 1971.
Febechi in Cave Adventure, illustrated by Emma Okoro. Enugu, Nwamife, 1971.
One Week One Trouble, illustrated by Charles Ohu. Ibadan, African Universities Press, 1973.
Dr. Amadi's Postings, illustrated by the author. Benin City, Ethiope, 1975.
Education Is Great, illustrated by Emma Okereke. Enugu, Fourth Dimension, 1986.
Double Trouble. Lagos, African Universities Press, 1989.
Je Je Kule. Enugu, Fourth Dimension, 1989.

Play

Television Play: *I Do*, 1988.

PUBLICATIONS FOR ADULTS

Other

Pictorial Handbook of Common Skin Diseases. London, Macmillan, 1981.

*

Anezi Okoro comments:

My books, aimed at children 10–14 years, are simple stories, spiced with innocent but hair-raising adventure. They lack the more popular twists of blatant violence and rampant sex. The setting is African, but some of the characters are widely travelled. The heroes, heroines, and villains are irrepressible and young.

*   *   *

Set in the colonial period in the Nigerian village, Amanzu, Anezi Okoro's *The Village School* is one particular school, the Central School. In addition, *The Village School* depicts a very rigid and somewhat hostile school system and its effect on African children. The village primary school comes alive from the moment the roll is called in the morning to the moment when the end of term brings an exciting change—going for holiday. In *The Village School* Mr. Offor the headmaster and his staff believe strongly that the cane for whipping pupils is a very important part of the teaching method, and use the young children as laborers on their farms and in their various household chores. The iron discipline of Mr. Offor and his staff creates distance between the school authority and the African pupils. When Mr. Offor is transfered to another school the adult community is sad but quite a good number of the African children do not feel the same—"Why waste goodwill on an old man who bullied everybody?" This cold relationship between staff and pupils gives way to a warm and cordial one with the arrival of Mr. Mozie who does not believe in caning just for the fun of it. The adventures in these two books essentially deal with rumors about the coming and arrival of a new headmaster, a boy getting lost, and a variety of pranks Nigerian pupils play in school. School life routines, various weekend activities, and Amanzu community activities provide the background for the adventures.

The thrust of *Febechi down the Niger* and *Febechi in Cave Adventure* is one of the adventures of young Febechi. In *Double Trouble*, living up to his nickname, "Willie in Trouble," Wilson Tagboe steals out of school one night to be initiated into a secret cult. But this adventure leads him into far more serious trouble than he had ever imagined. *One Week One Trouble* is about Wilson Tagboe's various problems in adjusting to high school life.

In all Okoro's works for children, beside the series of adventures that sustain reading zest, especially among Nigerian children, there are elements of didacticism: school rules to be followed, obedience to authority (the prefects, teachers, and headmaster), regular study habits, and work in the school garden. Not strong in technique, Okoro's works are generally shorter than African young adult and adult literary works. Because of their brevity, these fictional works—mainly adventure stories—can be completed and in most cases understood in less time, giving the primary school pupil a positive feeling of achievement. With due regard to the emotional and intellectual development of the Nigerian child, the action in Okoro's works moves in a simple chronological manner. He does not use complex sentences or sophisticated literary allusions because children are not yet mature enough to grapple with these concepts. These works do not proclaim any complex psychological theme or philosophical position. Yet for all their simplicity and apparent transparency, they offer a logical starting point in literary education for Nigerian school children.

—Osayimwense Osa

OLDFIELD, Pamela. British. Born in London, in 1931. Has one son and one daughter. Has worked as a teacher and secretary. Lives in Kent. Address: c/o Blackie Children's Books, 7 Leicester Place, London WC2H 7BP, England.

PUBLICATIONS FOR CHILDREN

Fiction

Melanie Brown Goes to School, illustrated by Carolyn Dinan. London, Faber, 1970.
Melanie Brown Climbs a Tree, illustrated by Carolyn Dinan. London, Faber, 1972.
The Adventures of Sarah and Theodore Bodgitt. Leicester, Brockhampton Press, 1974.
The Halloween Pumpkin, illustrated by Ferelith Eccles Williams. London, Hodder and Stoughton, 1974; Chicago, Children's Press, 1976.
Melanie Brown and the Jar of Sweets, illustrated by Carolyn Dinan. London, Faber, 1974.
Simon's Extra Gran, illustrated by Derek Lucas. London, Knight, 1974; Chicago, Children's Press, 1976.
A Witch in the Summer House, illustrated by Susan Hunter. London, Hodder and Stoughton, 1976.
The Terribly Plain Princess and Other Stories, illustrated by Glenys Ambrus. London, Hodder and Stoughton, 1977.
The Adventures of the Gumby Gang, illustrated by Lesley Smith. London, Blackie, 1978.
The Gumby Gang Again, illustrated by Lesley Smith. London, Blackie, 1978.
Katy and Dom, illustrated by Jane Paton. Brighton, Angus and Robertson, 1978.
Children of the Plague, illustrated by Janet Duchesne. London, Hamish Hamilton, 1979.
More About the Grumby Gang, illustrated by Lesley Smith. London, Blackie, 1979.
The Princess Well-I-May, illustrated by Glenys Ambrus. London, Hodder and Stoughton, 1979.
The Gumby Gang Strikes Again, illustrated by Lesley Smith. London, Blackie, 1980.
The Rising of the Wain, illustrated by Thelma Lambert. London, Abelard, 1980.
The Riverside Cat, illustrated by Charlotte Voake. London, Hamish Hamilton, 1980.
Cloppity, illustrated by Linda Birch. London, Hamish Hamilton, 1981.
The Willerbys and the Burglar [*Haunted Mill, Old Castle, Sad Clown, Bank Robbers, Mystery Man*], illustrated by Shirley Bellwood. London, Blackie, 6 vols., 1981–84.
Parkin's Storm, illustrated by Peter Westcott. London, Abelard, 1982.
The Gumby Gang on Holiday, illustrated by Lesley Smith. London, Blackie, 1983.
Tommy Dobbie and the Witch-Next-Door, illustrated by Glenys Ambrus. London, Hodder and Stoughton, 1983.
Ghost Stories, illustrated by Gavin Rowe. London, Blackie, 1984.
Barnaby and Bell and the Birthday Cake, illustrated by Jenny Williams. London, Piccadilly, 1985.
Barnaby and Bell and the Lost Button, illustrated by Jenny Williams. London, Piccadilly, 1985.
The Christmas Ghost, illustrated by Vanessa Julian-Ottie. London, Blackie, 1985.
Ginger's Nine Lives, illustrated by Linda Birch. London, Blackie, 1986.
The Return of the Gumby Gang, illustrated by Kate Rogers. London, Blackie, 1986.
Toby and the Donkey, illustrated by Linda Birch. London, Methuen, 1986.
The Ghosts of Bellering Oast, illustrated by Vanessa Julian-Ottie. London, Blackie, 1987.
Spine Chillers, illustrated by Colin Robinson. London, Blackie, 1987.
Sam, Sue and Cinderella, illustrated by Jenny Williams. London, Methuen, 1989.
Bomb Alert. London, Armada, 1989.
Secret Persuader. London, Armada, 1989.

Other

Stories from Ancient Greece (retellings), illustrated by Nick Harris. London, Kingfisher, 1988.

Editor, *Helter-Skelter: Stories for Six-Year-Olds*, illustrated by Linda Birch. London, Blackie, 1983.
Editor, *Hurdy Gurdy*, illustrated by Linda Birch. London, Blackie, 1984; as *Merry-Go-Round: Stories for Seven-Year-Olds*, Sevenoaks, Kent, Knight, 1985.
Editor, *Roller Coaster*, illustrated by Linda Birch. London, Blackie, 1986.

PUBLICATIONS FOR ADULTS

Novels

The Heron Saga:
The Rich Earth. London, Futura, 1980.

This Ravished Land. London, Futura, 1980.
After the Storm. London, Futura, 1981.
White Water. London, Futura, 1982.
Green Harvest. London, Century Hutchinson, 1983.
Summer Song. London, Century Hutchinson, 1984.
Golden Tally. London, Century Hutchinson, 1985.
The Gooding Girl. London, Century Hutchinson, 1985.
The Stationmaster's Daughter. London, Century Hutchinson, 1986.
Lily Golightly. London, Century Hutchinson, 1987.
Turn of the Tide. London, Century Hutchinson, 1988.
A Dutiful Wife. London, Joseph, 1989.

*   *   *

Pamela Oldfield is a prolific writer for young children who manages to maintain a remarkably consistent standard. Her assured knowledge of the primary school age group for which she writes leads to confident handling of her always appropriate themes. Her style is unobtrusive, suited to her subjects and comfortably within the abilities of her intended readers. She provides ephemerally absorbing entertainment to hook young children on to the idea of books for enjoyment—essential carbohydrate in the reading diet.

Her earliest books, about Melanie Brown, were cosy stories for four- to six-year-olds full of small domestic preoccupations and ideal for reading aloud. More recent titles show the same skill in appealing to preschool children and leading them on to an enjoyment of longer texts. The Barnaby and Bell stories are small dramas concerning a rag doll and a teddy, while in *Tommy Dobbie and the Witch-Next-Door* Oldfield takes the familiar situation of the small child who cannot get his mother's attention. On a very small canvas she skillfully contrasts the domesticity of the setting with the farcical appearance of an elephant, a tiger, and a pig (conjured up by a helpful neighbourhood witch) until the boy finally gains his mother's attention when he appears as a mouse. This is a fantasy which most small children would recognize as true to life in one sense, hilariously fantastic in others.

When young readers are gaining in confidence and beginning to read voraciously, there is something to be said for books in a series that provide a familiar framework for the development of reading skills. The series of mysteries in which the Willerbys feature provides such a framework, as do the books about the Gumby Gang. In these, three children, hindered by four-and-a-half-year-old Bet and Buster the dog, plan excitements and good deeds (which always turn out wrong) with all the paraphernalia of passwords and secret meeting places. They are not memorable stories but they are well-crafted and appeal to six- to eight-year-olds.

The Halloween Pumpkin is another lively story for younger readers in which a pumpkin face originally made to scare witches frightens almost everyone else until it is finally dispatched by a pig. Also for six- to eight-year-olds is *Children of the Plague*, a rare foray for Oldfield into the straightforward historical setting. This is quite a strong story about an undaunted small girl who is left to fend for herself as members of her family die in the plague of 1665—or are unavoidably elsewhere. It gives a good flavour of the period within its brief framework.

For older readers of eight to 11, Oldfield writes undemandingly of ghosts and witches. They offer no real threat; no deep emotions are stirred but she creates good, exciting or amusing tales, well-plotted with believable main characters. Secondary characters like Miss Timms, the librarian in *A Witch in the Summer House*, are frequently caricatured and there are stereotyped situations: absent parents, absentminded uncles. It is, however, easy to see the attractions for the young reader of stories in which 10-year-olds cope single-handedly with time-travelling witches or misplaced ghosts. In *A Witch in the Summer House* Emma inadvertently "summons" a

witch across four centuries and has trouble in finding the dismissing spell to return her to her own time. Meanwhile the witch causes mild chaos to village life. In *The Ghosts of Bellering Oast* twins Cathy and Paul get involved in a present-day mystery connected with a tragedy in the past. The resolution comes through cooperation between the twins and two perky ghosts who missed their chance to leave this world when they died and must now wait for another opportunity. Finally both old and new mysteries are resolved, although not before another near-tragedy occurs. In *Ghost Stories* Oldfield writes about ghosts who are, on the whole, gentle and helpful in their interaction with children. It is perhaps the fact that her stories are told sympathetically from the child's point of view that both stops the ghosts and witches from appearing threatening and accounts for the book's appeal with younger readers.

Oldfield writes with an easy prose style, an ear for dialogue, and minimum description. There is also accurate observation of children and their relationships with adults (even when the adults are largely absent). The plot is all important but many of her stories are thought-provoking for those who look beneath the surface.

—Valerie Brinkley-Willsher

———

OLLIVANT, Alfred. British. Born in 1874. Educated at Rugby School, Warwickshire; Royal Military Academy, Woolwich, London, graduated 1893; commissioned officer in Royal Artillery; resigned because of injury, 1895. Married Hilda Wigram in 1914; one daughter. *Died 19 January 1927.*

PUBLICATIONS FOR CHILDREN

Fiction

Owd Bob, The Grey Dog of Kenmuir. London, Methuen, 1898; as *Bob, Son of Battle,* New York, Doubleday, 1898.
Redcoat Captain, illustrated by Graham Robertson. London, Murray, and New York, Macmillan, 1907.

PUBLICATIONS FOR ADULTS

Novels

Danny. New York, Doubleday, 1902; London, Murray, 1903.
The Gentleman. London, Murray, and New York, Macmillan, 1908.
The Taming of John Blunt. London, Methuen, and New York, Doubleday, 1911.
The Royal Road, Being the Story of the Life, Death, and Resurrection of Edward Hankey of London. London, Methuen, and New York, Doubleday, 1912.
Boy Woodburn. London, Jenkins, and New York, Doubleday, 1918.
Two Men. London, Allen and Unwin, and New York, Doubleday, 1919.
One Woman. London, Allen and Unwin, 1921; New York, Doubleday, 1922.
Old For-Ever. London, Allen and Unwin, 1922; New York, Doubleday, 1923.
Devil Dare. London, Heinemann, 1923; New York, Doubleday, 1924.
Boxer and Beauty. London, Heinemann, and New York,

Doubleday, 1924.
To-morrow. London, Alston Rivers, and New York, Doubleday, 1927.

Short Stories

The Brown Mare and Other Studies of England under the Cloud. London, Allen and Unwin, and New York, Knopf, 1916.

Other

The Next Step: An Essay on the Missing Policeman. London, Allen and Unwin, 1919; Philadelphia, Jacobs, 1920.

* * *

Alfred Ollivant was the son of a colonel and grandson of a bishop, and in all probability would never have thought of applying his literary talents but for a riding accident which ended his military career almost before it had begun. As it turned out he achieved considerable success as the author of more than a dozen widely assorted novels, among them a blood-and-thunder Napoleonic romance, a cautionary tale of a Londoner's gradual descent to ruin, and a family saga set in his native Sussex. One story, *Redcoat Captain*, was intended for children but has long since passed into oblivion; another, his first attempt, and no doubt intended for the widest audience he could reach, is now generally read in a slightly abridged edition and as such is regarded as a classic dog story for older children.

Owd Bob, always known in America as *Bob, Son of Battle*, in fact stands rather apart from other stories in the canine genre, first, because the dog-characters complement rather than over-shadow the humans; and second, because behind the fairly conventional and often blood-drenched episodes of men and dogs in action, the author was trying to convey something about the sources of joy and sorrow in life and about the balance of good and evil in an imperfect world. In other words he was setting his sights at the level of an epic.

In essence *Owd Bob* is the story of a prolonged rivalry between two farmers in the Cumbrian dales, culminating each year in the prestigious sheep-dog trials, and finally transformed by the loser into a self-destroying feud. The author's lack of writing experience at the time does reveal itself through a tendency to repetitiveness in the long chain of events described and in a certain air of anti-climax in the closing chapters, after the sheep-killing mystery has been solved. There are too many pretentious phrases, like "the red eye of the morning peered aghast over the shoulder of the dyke," and perhaps too much use of a difficult Cumbrian dialect. Nevertheless, for all its faults *Owd Bob* passes the crucial test of haunting the memory long after one has read it. The two principal dogs have their moments, but the author's real triumph lies in the situation and character of his Shylockian anti-hero, Adam M'Adam. Driven to near-madness by the hostility of a closed community and his own misfortunes, M'Adam like Shylock inspires revulsion and sympathy in about equal measures. This portrayal of a sturdy outsider overwhelmed by circumstances is as relevant for today's readers as it was for those of an earlier era.

—Alasdair K.D. Campbell

ONEAL, Zibby (Elizabeth Oneal, née Bisgard). American. Born in Omaha, Nebraska, 17 March 1934. Educated at Stanford University, California, 1952–54; University of Michigan, Ann Arbor, 1966–68, B.A. Married Robert M. Oneal in 1955; one daughter and one son. Since 1971 Lecturer in English, University of Michigan. Recipient: Christopher award, 1982; Boston *Globe-Horn Book* award, 1985. Agent: Marilyn Marlow, Curtis Brown, 10 Astor Place, New York, New York 10003. Address: 501 Onondage Street, Ann Arbor, Michigan 48104, U.S.A.

PUBLICATIONS FOR CHILDREN

Fiction

War Work, illustrated by George Porter. New York, Viking Press, 1971.
The Improbable Adventures of Marvelous O'Hara Soapstone, illustrated by Paul Galdone. New York, Viking Press, 1972.
Turtle and Snail, illustrated by Margot Tomes. Philadelphia, Lippincott, 1979.
The Language of Goldfish. New York, Viking Press, 1980; London, Gollancz, 1987.
A Formal Feeling. New York, Viking Press, 1982; London, Gollancz, 1983.
In Summer Light. New York, Viking, 1985; London, Gollancz, 1986.
Maude and Walter, illustrated by Maxie Chambliss. New York, Lippincott, 1985.

Other

Grandma Moses: Painter of Rural America, illustrated by Donna Ruff. New York, Viking, 1986.

*

Manuscript Collection: Kerlan Collection, University of Minnesota, Minneapolis.

Zibby Oneal comments:
I am especially interested in adolescent characters and, though I have written books for and about younger children, in recent years I have concentrated on books in which adolescents are central characters. I think my interest originates in what I perceive as the inherent drama of adolescence. So much is being experienced for the first time in these years, so much is being learned. Adolescents are on the brink of becoming what they will be as adults and their problems and perplexities are a rich source for fiction. How a young person negotiates this brief passage between childhood and the adult world is a subject that I find of continuing interest.

* * *

Zibby Oneal is most noted for her three young adult novels, *The Language of Goldfish, A Formal Feeling* which was named a Best Book of the Year by the *New York Times* and won a Christopher award, and *In Summer Light* which won the Boston *Globe-Horn Book* award. Though each book is a distinct entity, there are common threads—elements that are obviously important to the author. There is a female protagonist in each book, whose angst takes different shapes but whose struggle to find who she is and what her place in the world will be is the focus of the book. Art plays a major role in two of the books, and images of color, line, and shape are replete in all three of the books. Though there is the expected misconnection between the protagonist and the adults in her life, each has a supportive sibling who ameliorates the sense of isolation. Oneal also makes use of the flashback technique in each book, which gives the reader a context for the conflict. Each book is one of intense conflict, though there is a coolness of style that permeates; the reader watches as if at a play, and applauds the resolution.

For Carrie in *The Language of Goldfish*, growing up is very hard, and she fights the changes that are happening to her body and her emotions. Carrie seems to be a puzzle piece that got in the wrong box; she just can't seem to fit in anywhere. Carrie and her sister had enjoyed a secret language they used with the goldfish in the pond in their yard, which becomes a symbol of all the things of childhood that Carrie wants to remain the same. Carrie wants nothing to change while her sister Moira is eagerly accepting her maturity and considers the secret language to be a thing of the past. The powerful internal struggle causes Carrie to experience anxiety attacks and she attempts suicide. *The Language of Goldfish* reflects the trauma of growing up that many young adults face. The feeling of being on the outside, of having no one to talk to who understands the sense of isolation and the fear is paramount in the book. The use of rich metaphor in descriptive passages and short sentences in dialogue heightens the sensation of personal isolation within a vibrant world. The only device that doesn't work is the image of the island in the middle of the goldfish pond. It plays a central role as the metaphor for Carrie's anguish, yet the image keeps slipping and is not fully recognized.

Emily Dickinson wrote "After great pain, a formal feeling comes—," which is the metaphor for Oneal's second novel. Anne is home from boarding school, still trying to come to terms with the sudden death of her mother the year before and now the unexpected remarriage of her father. She runs to forget and as the book progresses it becomes obvious that she has repressed a great many incidents of her relationship with her mother as well as the attendant emotions. Oneal maintains the formal feeling in images such as Anne perceiving everyone as being on the other side of a glass pane, and in the repetition of the feeling that to lose control was the worst thing you could do. Oneal makes excellent use of detail and creates suspense by using small incidents to build to the climax. This is a powerful novel that probes human emotions with insight and elegant style.

In Summer Light is a modern rendition of the fairytale Sleeping Beauty. Kate is a young woman forced by a bout of mononucleosis (glandular fever) to spend her summer at the island home of her parents. Kate is hedged about by the thorny conflict with her artist father and her lack of understanding of her mother. Kate finally wins release when a visiting graduate student, there to catalog her father's work, enables her to accept the decision she has made to resume her painting. Oneal once again uses the elements of conflict with a parent, a sense of separateness, the need to be liked, and the need to please. She again makes use of the image of an island, and color flows throughout the story. A warmth in this book is reflected in the hot summer setting as well as in the relationships of the characters.

Oneal has carved a niche for herself in the world of the young adult novel. Though her books are about the travails of adolescents, they are written with elegance and style and will transcend the merely popular offerings that come with monotonous regularity from so many authors of this genre.

—M. Jean Greenlaw

O'NEILL, Judith (née Lyall).   Australian.   Born in Melbourne, Victoria, 30 June 1930. Educated at Mildura High School, Victoria, 1942–47; University of Melbourne (Derham prize, 1950; Rotary Foundation fellowship, 1952), 1948–52, B.A. (honours) in English 1951, M.A. in English 1952; University of London (Story-Miller prize, 1953), 1952–53, postgraduate certificate in education 1953. Married John Cochrane O'Neill in 1954; three daughters. Tutor in English, University of Melbourne, 1954–56 and 1960–62; tutor,

Open University, Cambridge, England, 1971–72; English teacher, St. Mary's School, Cambridge, 1973–82. Agent: A.P. Watt Ltd., 20 John Street, London WC1N 2DL, England. Address: 9 Lonsdale Terrace, Edinburgh EH3 9HN, Scotland.

PUBLICATIONS FOR CHILDREN

Fiction

Jess and the River Kids.   London, Hamish Hamilton, 1984.
Stringybark Summer, illustrated by Valerie Littlewood.   London, Hamish Hamilton, 1985.
Deepwater.   London, Hamish Hamilton, 1987.
The Message.   London, Hamish Hamilton, 1989.

Other

Martin Luther.   London, Cambridge University Press, 1975; Minneapolis, Lerner, 1979.
Transported to Van Diemen's Land: The Story of Two Convicts. London and New York, Cambridge University Press, 1977.

PUBLICATIONS FOR ADULTS

Other

Editor, *Critics on Keats*.   London, Allen and Unwin, 1967; Coral Gables, Florida, University of Miami Press, 1968.
Editor, *Critics on Charlotte and Emily Brontë*.   London, Allen and Unwin, and Coral Gables, Florida, University of Miami Press, 1968.
Editor, *Critics on Pope*.   London, Allen and Unwin, and Coral Gables, Florida, University of Miami Press, 1968.
Editor, *Critics on Jane Austen*.   London, Allen and Unwin, and Coral Gables, Florida, University of Miami Press, 1969.
Editor, *Critics on Marlowe*.   London, Allen and Unwin, 1969; Coral Gables, Florida, University of Miami Press, 1970.
Editor, *Critics on Blake*.   London, Allen and Unwin, and Coral Gables, Florida, University of Miami Press, 1970.

*

Judith O'Neill comments:

As I am an Australian, living in exile in Britain now for 25 years, it is not surprising that my stories are all set in Australia and all in the past. I like to take an isolated community—a river-town in 1943, a sawmilling settlement in the bush in 1908, a farming valley in 1914, a strange sect in a remote house in 1945— and to tell a story as it is seen through the eyes of a girl or a boy aged between 12 and 14 years. I begin with the place itself—always one I know and love well from my own childhood—and I move from the place to the central character and to the story. I hope my stories will help my readers to enter imaginatively into a world quite different from their own. I hope my books will make my readers laugh and cry.

*   *   *

Judith O'Neill's first novel *Jess and the River Kids*, set during World War II, demonstrates her skill as a storyteller and her ability to evoke the atmosphere of an Australian setting without this ever overwhelming the narrative. Jess impatiently waits for the sermon to end: "It was the last Sunday in January—hot and dry. The Minister's sad, Scottish voice droned on and on in the heat. He was praying for all the people in the world and Jess knew it was going to take him a very long time." Her Sundays are spent down by the river, painting or reading. On this particular Sunday she meets two young boys, Kenny and Snowy, and the eccentric Old Lizzie. The three are neighbours on two houseboats and an unlikely friendship develops. Jess is fascinated by Old Lizzie's tales of her childhood back in the Old Country, in Northumbria. As in all of her novels, the underlying theme is friendship and relationships particularly with regard to the fickleness of adolescent attachments. The simple storyline with somewhat predictable plot was followed by a second more complex novel, *Stringybark Summer*, which is again set in a small community, but this time at the turn of the century. Relationships again play a major role, as does the skilful portrayal of the daily life in a small logging community. In these immaculately researched novels, the reader learns much of the work of the community, and in *Stringybark Summer* the dangers and hard work involved in logging are graphically described. The central character, Sophie, is sent to live with her aunt and uncle and several cousins while her mother awaits the birth of her second child. From her well-ordered life on the farm, Sophie reluctantly tries to adjust to life in the bush, made more complicated by the presence of her boisterous cousins. Gradually she comes to enjoy her new life and watches the work of this community—men working at the mill, the shoeing of the great horses at the forge, and the skill of the loggers felling the great mountain ashes. Another strand of the story lies in Sophie's fear of horses, a fear that overwhelms her on her first meeting with the huge grey horse Clinker. Gradually overcoming her terror, the girl develops a warm friendship with the horse. The novel is filled with small happenings—the disappearance of her little cousin, the extraordinary Christmas celebrated in the billiard shed—but rushes to a major climax with the collapse of the bridge when the first steam engine crosses.

By far the most accomplished of O'Neill's books is *Deepwater*, a mature, many-layered account dealing with the prejudices of a small community during World War I. In the previous books, characters are somewhat idealistically described—they are either good or bad. In *Deepwater* the central theme is the same—an independent young girl growing up in a close family in a small township. "When the war started—the Great War as we used to call it—my brother Laurie was the first in our Valley to join up. Plenty of boys went into the army after him but he was the first. I think he was glad to get away. The Valley can seem like a prison if you've never been out of it." 14-year-old Char's life then changes forever. Having to leave school, she takes her brother's place on the farm. Other changes come too. With the "Schoolie" at the war, the replacement turns out to be a surprising substitute—a young woman. Miss Playfair's misplaced patriotism sets alight nationalistic feelings among the townsfolk with their suspicions being directed against their neighbours with a German name, the Henschkes.

The search into Miss Playfair's ancestors led O'Neill into research of her own. She describes her astonishing discoveries in *Transported to Van Diemen's Land*, a short illustrated account of the early settlers. In particular, it tells the story of William Lyall and Ann Ross, both transported from England for petty theft some 150 years ago. They married and founded the author's family, and their story was handed down through their relatives, often romantically embellished on the way! O'Neill was able to separate fact from fiction and thus discover the truth of her background.

—Valerie Bierman

ORGEL, Doris (née Adelberg). American. Born in Vienna, Austria, 15 August 1929; emigrated to the United States, 1940. Educated at Radcliffe College, Cambridge, Massachusetts, 1946–48; Barnard College, New York, B.A. (cum laude) 1950 (Phi Beta Kappa). Married Shelley Orgel in 1949; two sons and one daughter. Worked for magazine and book publishers, 1950–55; taught writing workshops, Bridgeport University and Fairfield University, both Connecticut; frequent contributor, *Cricket Magazine*; children's book reviewer, New York *Times*. Recipient: Child Study Committee award, 1978; Association of Jewish Libraries Sydney Taylor award, 1979. Lives in New York City. Agent: Writers House Inc., 21 West 26th Street, New York, New York 10010, U.S.A.

PUBLICATIONS FOR CHILDREN

Fiction

Sarah's Room, illustrated by Maurice Sendak.   New York, Harper, 1963; London, Bodley Head, 1972.
Cindy's Snowdrops, illustrated by Ati Forberg.   New York, Knopf, 1966; London, Hamish Hamilton, 1967.
Cindy's Sad and Happy Tree, illustrated by Ati Forberg.   New York, Knopf, 1967.
In a Forgotten Place, illustrated by James McMullan.   New York, Knopf, 1967.
Whose Turtle?, illustrated by Martha Alexander.   Cleveland, World, 1968.
On the Sand Dune, illustrated by Leonard Weisgard.   New York, Harper, 1968.
Phoebe and the Prince, illustrated by Erik Blegvad.   New York, Putnam, 1969.
Merry, Rose, and Christmas-Tree June, illustrated by Edward Gorey.   New York, Knopf, 1969.
Next Door to Xanadu, illustrated by Dale Payson.   New York, Harper, 1969; as *Next-Door Neighbors*, 1979.
The Uproar, illustrated by Anita Lobel.   New York, McGraw Hill, 1970.
The Mulberry Music, illustrated by Dale Payson.   New York, Harper, 1971.
Bartholomew, We Love You!, illustrated by Pat Grant Porter.   New York, Knopf, 1973.
A Certain Magic.   New York, Dial Press, 1976.
The Devil in Vienna.   New York, Dial Press, 1978; London, Simon and Schuster, 1989.
Risking Love.   New York, Dial Press, 1985.
My War with Mrs. Galloway, illustrated by Carol Newsom.   New York, Viking Kestrel, 1985.
Whiskers Once and Always, illustrated by Carol Newsom.   New York, Viking Kestrel, 1986.
Midnight Soup and a Witch's Hat, illustrated by Carol Newsom.   New York, Viking Kestrel, 1987.
Starring Becky Suslow, illustrated by Carol Newsom.   New York, Viking Kestrel, 1989.
Crack in the Heart.   New York, Fawcett, 1989.

Verse

Grandma's Holidays (as Doris Adelberg), illustrated by Paul Kennedy.   New York, Dial Press, 1963.
Lizzie's Twins (as Doris Adelberg), illustrated by N.M. Bodecker.   New York, Dial Press, 1964.
The Good-byes of Magnus Marmalade, illustrated by Erik Blegvad.   New York, Putnam, 1966.
Merry, Merry Fibruary, illustrated by Arnold Lobel.   New York, Parents' Magazine Press, 1977.

Other (retellings)

The Tale of Gockel, Hinkel, and Gackeliah, illustrated by Maurice

Sendak.   New York, Random House 1961.
Schoolmaster Whackwell's Wonderful Sons: A Fairy Tale, illustrated by Maurice Sendak.   New York, Random House, 1962.
The Heart of Stone: A Fairy Tale, illustrated by David Levine.   New York, Macmillan, and London, Collier Macmillan, 1964.
The Story of Lohengrin, The Knight of the Swan, illustrated by Herbert Danska.   New York, Putnam, 1966.
A Monkey's Uncle, illustrated by Mitchell Miller.   New York, Farrar Straus, 1969.
Baron Munchausen: Fifteen Truly Tall Tales, illustrated by Willi Baum.   Reading, Massachusetts, Addison Wesley, 1971.
The Child from Far Away, illustrated by Michael Eagle.   Reading, Massachusetts, Addison Wesley, 1971.
Little John, illustrated by Anita Lobel.   New York, Farrar Straus, 1972.
Godfather Cat and Mousie, illustrated by Ann Schweninger.   New York, Macmillan, 1986.

Translator, *Dwarf-Long-Nose*, by Wilhelm Hauff, illustrated by Maurice Sendak.   New York, Random House, 1960; London, Bodley Head, 1979.
Translator, *The Enchanted Drum*, by Walter Grieder, illustrated by Grieder.   New York, Parents' Magazine Press, 1969.
Translator, *The Grandma in the Apple Tree*, by Mira Lobe, illustrated by Judith Gwyn Brown.   New York, McGraw Hill, 1970.

*

Manuscript Collection: Kerlan Collection, University of Minnesota, Minneapolis.

*   *   *

The trajectory of Doris Orgel's career as a writer for children is intimately bound up with her personal history as an Austrian Jewish refugee who escaped with her family when Hitler annexed Austria, and who was subsequently educated in America. Her earliest work for children was in translating and retelling German fairytales: particularly *Dwarf-Long-Nose* by Wilhelm Hauff, and Clemens Brentano's *The Tale of Gockel, Hinkel, and Gackeliah*, skillfully translated and retold in English. Hauff's masterful literary fairytale is recreated, in Orgel's translation, in clean and lucid prose, and appealingly illustrated by Maurice Sendak.

These translations and retellings were soon followed by stories of children experiencing loss (in *Cindy's Sad and Happy Tree*, the cutting down of a favorite elm) and of connections between the generations (in *The Mulberry Music*, the ties 11-year-old Libby feels for her Grandma Liza). These sensitively written stories provide symbolic expression for the sense of loss and yearning for attachment that accompanies the experience of exile.

Other of Orgel's books are playful explorations of verbal and imaginative nonsense. In *Merry, Merry Fibruary*, for example, Orgel explores whimsical humor through rollicking nonsense rhymes. *Phoebe and the Prince* similarly plays with language and ideas in absurd and comic ways.

With *A Certain Magic*, Orgel began to address the legacy of mid 20th-century events in Europe. Through the symbols of a magical emerald and a special doll, the device of a wartime journal kept by the refugee girl Gertrude Ehrenteil, and the affectionate, inquisitive friendship of 11-year-old Jenny for her Aunt Trudl (the Gertrude of the journal), Orgel recreates, in an interesting synthesis, a contemporary American child's realization of what an Austrian child's awareness of Hitler's threat was like in 1938. The distance between Jenny's comparatively innocent life and Trudl's dislocated, threatened existence is bridged with honesty and imagination.

In *The Devil in Vienna* Orgel transforms her own experience into powerful fiction most directly and completely. In this much-acclaimed novel, partially told through letters between Inge Dornenwald, who is Jewish, and Lieselotte Vessely, who is Catholic, the period of the Austrian *Anschluss* is vividly recreated, not only in its political but also in its cultural and mundane personal details. The friendship of Inge and Lieselotte undergoes severe testing, but it endures. It is a dramatic and moving story, complex, realistic, and suspenseful. The novel effectively shows the links between personal and political values under the pressures of a totalitarian movement. *The Devil in Vienna* is a major achievement, and a book of considerable significance for children's literature in the 20th century.

Finally, Orgel has written novels for younger and older children that are set entirely in the contemporary American milieu. *My War with Mrs. Galloway* and *Whiskers Once and Always*, related books, show Rebecca, starting at age seven, in her daily adventures with her cat, her mother, who is divorced, her babysitters, and friends. With touches of whimsical humor, these books convey a convincing and appealing sense of a sturdy modern urban child's life and growth. In *Risking Love* Dinah Moskowitz, Barnard student, tells the story of her self-discovery and evolution through therapy. Her humor and defensiveness, her experience of sexuality and romance, her fear—rooted in her parents' divorce—that love is not lasting, and the exploratory digressions of psychotherapy are absorbingly created.

Orgel is a skillful writer who has bridged her European origins and American experience with insight and imagination, creating a legacy of historical awareness, humor, and shared humanity through children's literature.

—John D. Stahl

ORMONDROYD, Edward.   American.   Born in Wilkinsburg, Pennsylvania, 8 October 1925. Educated at the University of California, Berkeley, A.B. 1951 (Phi Beta Kappa), M.L.S. 1958. Served in the United States Naval Reserve, 1943–45. Married to Joan Ormondroyd; four stepchildren and three children from previous marriage. Has worked as merchant seaman, bookstore clerk, paper factory machine operator; technical services librarian, Finger Lakes Library System, Ithaca, New York. Address: R.D. 2, Newfield, New York 14867, U.S.A.

PUBLICATIONS FOR CHILDREN

Fiction

David and the Phoenix, illustrated by Joan Raysor.   Chicago, Follett, 1957.
The Tale of Alain, illustrated by Robert Frankenberg.   Chicago, Follett, 1960.
Time at the Top, illustrated by Peggie Bach.   Berkeley, California, Parnassus Press, 1963; London, Heinemann, 1976.
Theodore, illustrated by John Larrecq.   Berkeley, California, Parnassus Press, 1966.
Michael, The Upstairs Dog, illustrated by Cyndy Szekeres.   New York, Dial Press, 1967.
Broderick, illustrated by John Larrecq.   Berkeley, California, Parnassus Press, 1969.
Theodore's Rival, illustrated by John Larrecq.   Berkeley, California, Parnassus Press, 1971.
Castaways on Long Ago, illustrated by Ruth Robbins.   Berkeley, California, Parnassus Press, 1973.
Imagination Greene, illustrated by John Lewis.   Berkeley, Califor-

nia, Parnassus Press, 1973.

All in Good Time, illustrated by Ruth Robbins. Berkeley, California, Parnassus Press, 1975.

Johnny Castleseed, illustrated by Diana Thewlis. Boston, Houghton Mifflin, 1985.

Verse

Jonathan Frederick Aloysius Brown, illustrated by Suzi Spector. San Carlos, California, Golden Gate Books, 1964.

*

Edward Ormondroyd comments:

The child I once was, and still am, somewhere, loved certain kinds of books. I try to write those kinds of books to please him. I am delighted when I succeed in beguiling not only him, and myself, but other children as well.

* * *

Edward Ormondroyd is best known for his contribution to the genre of time-travel fiction. His novels with the most lasting appeal, *Time at the Top* and its sequel, *All in Good Time*, approach the subject in a unique and intriguing way by employing an unusual and sophisticated narrative style. In both, Ormondroyd makes himself a character who supplies needed information from another time period and therefore helps to advance the plot. In the first book young Susan Shaw, seeking solitude after a particularly trying day, wants to escape to the seventh floor of her apartment building to admire the view but "The elevator kept on going." Susan has been delivered into the Victorian household of the Walker family, whose home had been in the same location 100 years earlier. Susan quickly becomes involved in a plot to rescue Victoria and Robert Walker's mother from an evil man who marries widows and subsequently absconds with their money. Most time-travel novels for young people conclude with the main character returning to the book's original time period or setting in possession of increased insights into global or personal problems, but Ormondroyd's Susan, who has become enamored of the sights and fragrances of the previous century, resolves to use the last of her three trips in the elevator to return once again to 1881 with her father in tow; she is sure a marriage between Mr. Shaw and Mrs. Walker will result and she will subsequently be able to stay with her new friends in their time. In *All in Good Time* Susan, with the help of the Walker children, succeeds in the final defeat of the villainous Mr. Sweeney and the joyous pairing of the two adults.

In his novels Ormondroyd creates characters that are believable and then places them in incredible situations that defy reality; he judiciously offers fragments of evidence—an old photograph, a diary, newspapers—that mount until young readers must ask the question: "Did this really happen?" These books, replete with mystery, adventure, slapstick, and intrigue, are fun to read yet challenging because of the time-shift possibilities.

Ormondroyd has additionally turned his talents to the field of picture books and, at various times during his career, has produced books which appeal to a younger audience. *Theodore* is "...an old experienced bear, comfortably smudgy..." who is sometimes forgotten by his owner Lucy; he is philosophical about her carelessness because "...she understands bears." After the stuffed bear accidently suffers the indignity and discomfort of a tumble in the washing machine and dryer and is then jolted out of the wagon on his trip home, he is discovered by Lucy who does not recognize him in his "...shiny and golden and fluffy..." new fur. Some dogs and cats and a boy with a sticky taffy sucker help Theodore to return to his comfortable rumpled old self. Theodore's reunion with Lucy is heartwarming and reinforces his faith in Lucy as someone with a

perception of what makes stuffed bears happy. In *Theodore's Rival* Theodore feels displaced by one of Lucy's new birthday presents, a musical panda. "Not—not another—bear? It can't be! *I'm* the bear in this family!" Theodore's jealous response strikes a familiar chord with children who feel threatened by a sibling or a new child in the classroom. When panda Benjamin disappears in the supermarket, Theodore seizes the opportunity to engineer his rescue which delights Lucy and reinforces his perception that Lucy truly understands bears "And pandas too, of course." Theodore's relationship with Lucy echoes the reality of a parent-child relationship and children are reassured by the forgive-and-forget attitude demonstrated by both Lucy and her stuffed bear. In *Broderick* an extremely literate mouse with a burning ambition to make his mark in the world becomes the most accomplished and renowned surfer in mouse history. Using elements of humor and adventure, Ormondroyd again offers children a book they can take to heart. Ormondroyd's most recent picture book, *Johnny Castleseed*, leaves behind the fantasy of his previous books and breaks new ground for the author. A father and son, during their visit to a California beach, build an elaborate sand castle using only their hands. Their glorious creation inspires many other families to try their hands at sand castle construction and sand castles soon sprout along the beach in much the same way that Johnny Appleseed's trees germinated because of his seed planting efforts. The instructions for making the sand castle are delivered by Evan's father in such a straightforward and concise way that they could actually be used on the beach as a simple manual.

Ormondroyd approaches themes and subjects that interest young people, such as time travel, activities at the beach, and teddy bears, in an original and direct fashion. His books are never precious or coy but speak in a clear and childlike voice to young readers. It is for this no-nonsense approach to writing for children that he is most appreciated.

—Ellen G. Fader

———

O'SHEA, Pat (née Shiels). Irish. Born in Galway, 22 January 1931. Educated at Presentation Convent, 1935–44, and Convent of Mercy, 1945–47, both Galway. Married J.J. O'Shea in 1953 (separated); one son. Recipient: British Arts Council drama bursary, 1967. Lives in Manchester. Address: c/o Oxford University Press, Walton Street, Oxford OX2 6DP, England.

PUBLICATIONS FOR CHILDREN

Fiction

The Hounds of the Morrigan, illustrated by Stephen Lavis. Oxford, Oxford University Press, 1985; New York, Holiday House, 1986.

Other

Finn MacCool and the Small Men of Deeds (retelling), illustrated by Stephen Lavis. Oxford, Oxford University Press, and New York, Holiday House, 1987.

*

Pat O'Shea comments:

The Hounds of the Morrigan, although set in the present, is built on the scaffolding of Irish mythology. It is a comic fantasy in which two children, Pidge and Brigit, are asked to go on a quest—by the

Irish God, the Dagda—to recover a blood-stained pebble and prevent it falling into the hands of the Morrigan, the goddess of death and destruction. Their journey is epic and during it they meet and are helped by many diverse characters: an earwig who thinks he's Napoleon, a comic watchfrog named Puddeneen Whelan, a wise fox named Cooroo, and many others including the hero Cuchulain, Gods in various guises, and a Garda (police) sergeant who plays a key role. As a backdrop I drew on my knowledge of the countryside and folk customs that I absorbed as a child during summer holidays at Cregmore and Kilbannon in County Galway. I grew up knowing a good deal of the mythology from fireside stories and my school primers. Further mythological background material I garnered from books collected over the years and from the reference section in Manchester Central Library.

The second book *Finn MacCool and the Small Men of Deeds* is much smaller in scale—a humorous retelling of an Irish folktale in my own style. Every Seanachie (traditional storyteller) in Ireland has his or her own interpretation of tales from the common treasure chest. So in the story I was simply following the old tradition, using up-to-date language and contemporary attitudes here and there, as people have always done in the intervening centuries since the stories were first conceived.

In this story, Finn, assisted by eight small men with special and individual talents, solves the mystery of who is stealing the children of the King of the Giants and restores the children to a grateful Daddy!

*   *   *

It is rare that an author emerges with a first novel with such style and assurance as did Pat O'Shea. *The Hounds of the Morrigan* is the fruit of 10 year's labour and is a richly woven fabric of fantasy in a definite Celtic pattern.

The book has a huge cast of characters, human, fairy, and animal. The basic theme of the book is of Pidge and his sister Brigit's somewhat unwilling journey and quest that ultimately conquers the evil Morrigan and dispels the powers of Olc Glas, the snake who wants to bring destruction to the world.

As fantasy it obeys all the rules, creating a world that is solid, safe, and believable. Pidge and Brigit are the channels and instigators of the fantasy and are themselves caught up and perplexed by the rapidly changing landscapes they pass on their quest. The borders between reality and fantasy are smudged but, as one of the wise ones explains: "You are still in Ireland, but you are in Faery too. Here it is like, and it is unlike, the same and not the same...Our frontiers are made of mists and dreams and tender waters: thresholds are crossed from time to time...the two worlds go hand in hand." With great skill and deftness O'Shea takes us on a complex journey with as many twists and loops and devices as a piece of Celtic interlace border on an old book. Indeed, it is not surprising that it is one such old manuscript, discovered by Pidge in a Galway bookshop, that is the key which unlocks the old magic of the Morrigan and her pack of hounds. Brigit must surely be speaking for every reader when she confesses "I like being afraid, but not too much."

The twists and turns of the plot, with many breath-holding Hitchcock-like moments of suspense and fear keep the reader turning the pages of this generous novel. With great assurance the author handles the moments of genuine fear and provides light relief in the ground-level world of frogs, spiders, and ear-wigs, all of whom speak their own highly idiosyncratic, colourful, and infectious language. The local cadences and use of words are well observed, being distinctly Irish without any trace of the "Shure-and-begorrah" brogue so beloved of writers in the 1940's and 1950's. Everyone speaks with his or her own precise language—so that the iron weathervane utters a type of Newspeak Bureaucratic: "Dear sir, or madam, business as unusual. Insomuch as, heretofore and not-

withstanding, please excuse brevity of reply. Yours cordially." This is the first major work of fantasy since Patricia Lynch which harnesses the wealth of Celtic myth and legend and creates from it a credible and exciting narrative of universal appeal.

The same humour and inventiveness is used with success in the retelling of the traditional story of Finn in *Finn MacCool and the Small Men of Deeds*.

—Pat Donlon

OVERTON, Jenny (Margaret Mary). British. Born in Cranleigh, Surrey, 22 January 1942. Educated at Guildford County Grammar School, Surrey, 1953–60; Girton College, Cambridge, 1961–64, B.A. (honours) 1964, M.A. 1966. Appeals secretary, 1965–66, and Principal's private secretary, 1966–67, Newnham College, Cambridge; assistant editor, Aluminium Federation, London, 1967–69; editor, Macmillan, publishers, Basingstoke, Hampshire, 1969–71; from 1971 editor, Lutterworth Press, Guildford, Surrey. Address: c/o J.F. Overton, Crest Hill, Peaslake, Guildford, Surrey, England.

PUBLICATIONS FOR CHILDREN

Fiction

Creed Country. London, Faber, 1969; New York, Macmillan, 1970.
The Thirteen Days of Christmas, illustrated by Shirley Hughes. London, Faber, 1972; Nashville, Nelson, 1974.
The Nightwatch Winter. London, Faber, 1973.
The Ship from Simnel Street. London, Faber, and New York, Greenwillow, 1986.

*   *   *

With a small output of work to date, Jenny Overton has established herself as an original and gifted novelist. Her skill lies in capturing the many-sided experience of family life, often spanning an age range from mid childhood to early adult independence. The forced co-existence of touchy, competitive, and vulnerable young people, each at his or her own uniquely stressful stage of growth, each with individual doubts, problems, and ambitions, formed the background to all of her first three books, though in other respects *The Thirteen Days of Christmas* seemed an unlikely product of the same imagination as *Creed Country* and its sequel *The Nightwatch Winter*.

The Thirteen Days of Christmas is a comic fantasy, enjoyed by children across a wide age range. Its subject is a crazily improbable version of the carol "The Twelve Days of Christmas." The carol is interpreted literally, with truly awesome implications for the sheer number of presents cast upon the besieged heroine. At the centre of the fantasy is a highly practical domestic situation—the desire of two young boys to marry off their elder sister, whose household accomplishments unfortunately exclude the gift of cookery, to an ardent lover who is so rich that the defect will not matter. The story is imaginatively conceived and wittily told.

Overton's most recent book, *The Ship from Simnel Street*, shares much in imaginative conception with *The Thirteen Days of Christmas*. Again a familiar song, in this case the folk song "Polly Oliver," supplies the basis for a fanciful extravaganza rooted in the affections of family life, the practicalities of food and baking, and the calendar of festival, which marks out the year. Polly Oliver is a baker's daughter in a southern English naval town in the early 19th century, and she runs away to join her soldier lover who is fighting in the Peninsular War. While Polly's father vainly searches Portugal to find her, her mother conceives the idea of sending off a mammoth load of cakes to the army there, quite literally enough to feed a regiment. The vast and wonderful baking that ensues, just like the spate of presents in the earlier book, combines warm and extravagant comedy with a serious point about family life and loyalty.

Overton's eye and ear for family drama, as shown in these straightforward tales, are also at work in the more complex and and realistic situations of *Creed Country* and *The Nightwatch Winter*, novels of some difficulty which require an older, more sophisticated reader. In these books the humour works in counterpoint against the explosive emotional tensions of adolescence. In *Creed Country*, for example, evidence of Sarah's first emotional entanglement is the subject of banter and mockery in her crowded family circle, and we are made aware how funny it is to adolescents who are callously uninvolved; but the story also brings out fully her embarrassment, uncertainty, and pain.

Other elements are common to all four novels: a remarkable (and very rare) ability to communicate the wonder and the communal delight of music; an often playful and sardonic but nonetheless serious concern with religious belief and observance; and a sense of cycle, change, and festival, both in the seasonal landscape and in human society, with all its periodic rituals of school and home. *Creed Country* and *The Nightwatch Winter* are, in part, stories of tension and crisis, but their distinction lies especially in their humour and psychological insight, in their rich sense of place and history, and in the highly professional control of demanding and intricate plots.

—Peter Hollindale

———————

OWEN, (John) Gareth. British. Born in Ainsdale, Lancashire, 15 March 1936. Educated at Merchant Taylors' School, Crosby, Lancashire, 1949–52; Bretton Hall College of Education, Bretton, Yorkshire, 1958–60, certificate in education (University of Leeds); Goldsmiths' College, University of London, 1960–61. Divorced. Teacher, Downshall Secondary Modern School, Ilford, Essex, 1961–65; Lecturer and Senior Lecturer, Bordesley College of Education, Birmingham, 1965–82. Owner and manager of independent record company, 1976–83. Recipient: *Signal* award, for poetry, 1986. Agent: Rogers Coleridge and White, 20 Powis Mews, London W11 1JN, England.

PUBLICATIONS FOR CHILDREN

Fiction

The Final Test, illustrated by Paul Wright. London, Gollancz, 1985.
The Man with Eyes like Windows. London, Collins, 1987.
Douglas the Drummer, illustrated by Paul Dowling. London, Fontana, 1989.
Ruby and the Dragon, illustrated by Bob Wilson. London, Fontana, 1989.
Saving Grace. London, Collins, 1989.

Plays

Mr. Chips and the Silver Chicken (pantomime; produced Birmingham, 1977).

Alice in Dreamsville (musical; produced Birmingham, 1979).
Voices, in *Drama 1*, edited by John Foster. London, Macmillan, 1987.
Don't Look Down, in *Drama 2*, edited by John Foster. London, Macmillan, 1987.

Verse

Salford Road, illustrated by Mike Hurlow. Privately printed, 1976.
Song of the City, illustrated by Jonathan Hills. London, Fontana, 1985.
Bright Lights Blaze Out, with Alan Bold and Julie O'Callaghan. Oxford, Oxford University Press, 1986.

PUBLICATIONS FOR ADULTS

Plays

Wedding Breakfast (produced Birmingham, 1972).
A Play Called George (produced Birmingham, 1973).
Margaret Born (produced Birmingham, 1973; New York, 1982).
The Confessions of Jon-Jack Crusoe (also director: produced Edinburgh, 1973).
Penalty (produced Birmingham, 1975).
Traveller (produced Birmingham, 1975).
Mandog (produced Birmingham, 1975; New York, 1978).
Rumpus (musical; produced Birmingham, 1976).
Double Exposure (produced Birmingham, 1976).
In and Out the Windows (produced Birmingham, 1976).
Widowmaker (produced Birmingham, 1977).
Silver Chicken (produced Birmingham, 1977).
Salford Road, music by Richard Isen (produced New York and Edinburgh, 1979).
The Ladder Gag (produced Edinburgh and London, 1980).
The House of Mr. Vanzetti (produced Birmingham, 1982).

Verse

Nineteen Fragments. Birmingham, Birmingham Arts Lab Press, 1974.

*

Gareth Owen comments:

My novels and poems aren't children's books but are about childhood. I try to see the world through the mind of the child that once was me but I use the skill and experience of an adult to try to make the vision significant, interesting or funny. I suppose I'm a romantic about the real and the commonplace. I write so that things won't pass away entirely. I'm shoring up a dyke against Time. Always too, in the further recesses of my mind, I have a hope that there's another soul out there who will say, "That's how it was for me." Writing is much more to do with memory and recognition than with mere invention.

*   *   *

The reception given to *Song of the City* in 1985, its imaginative presentation, and its prestigious Signal award, confirmed Gareth Owen's status as a nationally known poet. It is undoubtedly one of the richest collections of poetry for children to appear in the 1980's.

Owen's work had long been favored by anthologists and teachers. In his adopted home area of Birmingham, his performances of poetry for children and adults had been valued. The enterprising re-issue in 1988 of *Salford Road* enables us to see samples of his early published work. "Our School," "The Fight," and "Winter Days" use simple, though not simplistic, forms to shape everyday observations, memories, and reflections. "Ping Pong," from 1971, shows a sense of adventure in a form that was to be nurtured in later work. "Denis Law" is a superbly evocative chant on a theme which was to become dominant in his work. Sporting skill is celebrated in a way that combines hero worship, a passion for expertise, and the demotic voice of a community:

> He's a whiplash when he's in control,
> He can swivel like an eel,
> And twist and sprint in such a way
> It makes defences reel.

Other high points of the *Salford Road* collection are the title poem, an affectionate and generous picture of felt-life within a Lancashire town. In its verve and rhythm, "Street Boy," from 1974, predates the energetic and diverse voices who were to come later, such as Michael Rosen and John Agard:

> Just you read my name, man,
> Writ for all to see.
> The walls is red with stories
> The streets is filled with me.

Song of the City displays to the full Owen's resourcefulness, energy, and range as a poet. From the parodic "Owl and the Astronaut," through the audacity of "Typewriting Class," to the humane and breathtakingly spare, musical title poem, it paints on the kind of broad canvas that few poets at work for children could match. "Miss Creedle Teaches Creative Writing" shows the hand of a writer who has learned what he knows about children, literacy, and language the hard way:

> Does the music carry you away like a river?
> What is the name of the river? Can you smell it?
> Foetid is an exciting adjective.

There's a healthy pinpricking of all who would make children's experience twee or over-precious in that poem, as there is in "Real Life" and "Drama Lesson" (in *Salford Road*). Again, the poems about sport catch the essential thrill of spectatorship. The poems on space are technically adroit. His reflections are always rooted in realism, and he conveys well the value of community in forming children's consciousness. Owen's ability to reflect upon his own youth, in a poem like "Salcombe, 1948" (*Song of the City*), is fresh-voiced and vigorous, without the tendency within his generation to lapse into Larkinian self-regard.

Two recent novels for older readers show tantalising glimpses of what could emerge from this ever-surprising writer. In *The Final Test* he explores without any hint of self-consciousness the relationship of two adolescent boys, one of whom has a crippling terminal illness. Again he uses sport (cricket) as an image for both their aspirations and their camaraderie. *The Man with Eyes like Windows* is a lucid, sometimes unsettling account of the ways in which adults, as always, try to sanitise and manage adolescent fears and anxieties. When a boy goes out to seek his errant Dad, a "roadie" with a popular singer, the cultural references are vividly drawn. Owen has the courage not to tie up the loose ends of lives, or of the novel.

—Colin Mills

OXENHAM, Elsie J. Pseudonym for Elsie Jeanette Dunkerley. British. Born in Southport, Lancashire. Daughter of William Arthur Dunkerley, i.e., the writer John Oxenham. *Died 9 January 1960.*

PUBLICATIONS FOR CHILDREN

Fiction

Goblin Island, illustrated by T. Heath Robinson. London, Collins, 1907.
A Princess in Tatters. London, Collins, 1908.
The Conquest of Christina, illustrated by G.B. Foyster. London, Collins, 1909.
The Girl Who Wouldn't Make Friends. London, Nelson, 1909.
Mistress Nanciebel, illustrated by James Durden. London, Hodder and Stoughton, 1909.
A Holiday Queen, illustrated by E.A. Overnell. London, Collins, 1910.
Rosaly's New School, illustrated by T.J. Overnell. Edinburgh, Chambers, 1913.
Girls of the Hamlet Club. Edinburgh, Chambers, 1914.
Schoolgirls and Scouts, illustrated by A.A. Dixon. London, Collins, 1914.
At School with the Roundheads, illustrated by H.C. Earnshaw. Edinburgh, Chambers, 1915.
Finding Her Family. London, S.P.C.K., 1915.
The Tuck-Shop Girl. Edinburgh, Chambers, 1916.
A School Camp Fire. Edinburgh, Chambers, 1917.
The School of Ups and Downs, illustrated by H.C. Earnshaw. Edinburgh, Chambers, 1918.
A Go-Ahead Schoolgirl, illustrated by H.C. Earnshaw. Edinburgh, Chambers, 1919.
Expelled from School, illustrated by Victor Prout. London, Collins, 1919.
The Abbey Girls, illustrated by A.A. Dixon. London, Collins, 1920.
The School Torment, illustrated by H.C. Earnshaw. Edinburgh, Chambers, 1920.
The Twins of Castle Charming. London, Swarthmore Press, 1920.
The Girls of the Abbey School, illustrated by Elsie Wood. London, Collins, 1921.
The Two Form-Captains, illustrated by Percy Tarrant. Edinburgh, Chambers, 1921.
The Abbey Girls Go Back to School, illustrated by Elsie Wood. London, Collins, 1922.
The Captain of the Fifth, illustrated by Percy Tarrant. Edinburgh, Chambers, 1922.
Patience Joan, Outsider. London, Cassell, 1922; New York, Funk and Wagnalls, 1923.
The Junior Captain. Edinburgh, Chambers, 1923.
The New Abbey Girls, illustrated by Elsie Wood. Edinburgh, Chambers, 1923.
The Abbey Girls Again. London, Collins, 1924.
The Girls of Gwynfa. London and New York, Warne, 1924.
The School Without a Name, illustrated by Nina K. Brisley. Edinburgh, Chambers, 1924.
"Tickles"; or, The School That Was Different. London, Partridge, 1924.
The Testing of the Torment, illustrated by P.B. Hickling. London, Cassell, 1925.
Ven at Gregory's, illustrated by Nina K. Brisley. Edinburgh, Chambers, 1925.
The Abbey Girls in Town, illustrated by Rosa Petherick. London, Collins, 1926.
The Camp Fire Torment, illustrated by Nina Browne. Edinburgh, Chambers, 1926.
Queen of the Abbey Girls, illustrated by E.J. Kealey. London,

Collins, 1926.

The Troubles of Tazy, illustrated by Percy Tarrant. Edinburgh, Chambers, 1926.

Jen of the Abbey School, illustrated by F. Meyerheim. London, Collins, 1927.

Patience and Her Problems, illustrated by Molly Benatar. Edinburgh, Chambers, 1927.

Peggy Makes Good!, illustrated by H.L. Bacon. London, Partridge, 1927.

The Abbey Girls Win Through. London, Collins, 1928.

The Abbey School. London, Collins, 1928.

The Crisis in Camp Keema, illustrated by Percy Tarrant. Edinburgh, Chambers, 1928.

Deb at School, illustrated by Nina K. Brisley. Edinburgh, Chambers, 1929.

The Girls of Rocklands School. London, Collins, 1929.

The Abbey Girls at Home, illustrated by I. Burns. London, Collins, 1930.

The Abbey Girls Play Up. London, Collins, 1930.

Dorothy's Dilemma, illustrated by Nina K. Brisley. Edinburgh, Chambers, 1930.

The Second Term at Rocklands. London, Collins, 1930.

The Abbey Girls on Trial. London, Collins, 1931.

Deb of Sea House, illustrated by Nina K. Brisley. Edinburgh, Chambers, 1931.

The Third Term at Rocklands. London, Collins, 1931.

Biddy's Secret. Edinburgh, Chambers, 1932.

The Camp Mystery. London, Collins, 1932.

The Girls of Squirrel House. London, Collins, 1932.

The Reformation of Jinty. Edinburgh, Chambers, 1933.

Rosamund's Victory. London, Harrap, 1933.

The Call of the Abbey School. London, Collins, 1934.

Jinty's Patrol. London, Newnes, 1934.

Maidlin to the Rescue, illustrated by R. Cloke. Edinburgh, Chambers, 1934.

Joy's New Adventure. Edinburgh, Chambers, 1935.

Peggy and the Brotherhood. London, Religious Tract Society, 1936.

Rosamund's Tuck-Shop. London, Religious Tract Society, 1937.

Sylvia of Sarn. London and New York, Warne, 1937.

Damaris at Dorothy's. London, Sheldon Press, 1937.

Maidlin Bears the Torch. London, Religious Tract Society, 1937.

Schooldays at the Abbey. London, Collins, 1938.

Rosamund's Castle. London, Religious Tract Society, 1938.

Secrets of the Abbey, illustrated by Heade. London, Collins, 1939.

Stowaways in the Abbey. London, Collins, 1940.

Damaris Dances. London, Oxford University Press, 1940.

Patch and a Pawn. London and New York, Warne, 1940.

Adventure for Two, illustrated by Margaret Horder. London, Oxford University Press, 1941.

Jandy Mac Comes Back. London, Collins, 1941.

Pernel Wins, illustrated by Margaret Horder. London, Muller, 1942.

Maid of the Abbey, illustrated by Heade. London, Collins, 1943.

Elsa Puts Things Right, illustrated by Margaret Horder. London, Muller, 1944.

Two Joans at the Abbey, illustrated by Margaret Horder. London, Collins, 1945.

Daring Doranne. London, Muller, 1945.

An Abbey Champion, illustrated by Margaret Horder. London, Muller, 1946.

Robins in the Abbey. London, Collins, 1947.

The Secrets of Vairy, illustrated by Margaret Horder. London, Muller, 1947.

Margery Meets the Roses. London, Lutterworth Press, 1947.

A Fiddler for the Abbey, illustrated by Margaret Horder. London,

Muller, 1948.

Guardians of the Abbey, illustrated by Margaret Horder. London, Muller, 1950.

Schoolgirl Jen at the Abbey. London, Collins, 1950.

Selma at the Abbey. London, Collins, 1952.

Rachel in the Abbey, illustrated by M.D. Neilson. London, Muller, 1952.

A Dancer from the Abbey. London, Collins, 1953.

The Song of the Abbey. London, Collins, 1954.

The Girls at Wood End. London, Blackie, 1957.

Tomboys at the Abbey. London, Collins, 1957.

Two Queens at the Abbey. London, Collins, 1959.

Strangers at the Abbey. London, Collins, 1963.

* * *

Elsie J. Oxenham wrote 90 books for girls. She has sometimes been described as a writer of school stories, but few of her books come strictly within this category. They cover a wide range of themes and embody a seriousness and a depth of characterization that are unusual in the genre.

Like Angela Brazil, Dorita Fairlie Bruce, and Elinor M. Brent-Dyer, Oxenham wrote numerous short stories for girls' magazines as well as full-length books, providing an accurate picture of the life of many British middle-class girls in the 1920's and 1930's. By the 1940's her stories had an old-fashioned flavour; some readers, however, found this—and the books' religious overtones—intriguing.

The author was a Guardian in the Camp Fire Association, an organization which never achieved the same popularity in England as in America. It is featured in several of her books. Oxenham also wrote about the Girl Guide Movement, for which she judged several folk dance contests. The theme of her *Peggy and the Brotherhood* is the conflicting appeal of these two organizations. Oxenham presents both groups sympathetically, the Camp Fire standing "for beauty and poetry" and Guiding representing "bigness" and, of course, practicality.

Many of Oxenham's books are grouped into series. The Abbey series is the largest (approximately 40 books) and the most addictive. It combines several attractive elements. There is a romanticized sense of history, expressed through an ancient Abbey. This forms a picturesque background for the folk dancing and other activities of the Hamlet Club, which is the linking factor of the series. The Club is founded initially to bring together the girls of Miss Macey's school who live in isolated hamlets, and also to counterbalance the snobbish influence of the school's sophisticated "Townies." The Hamlet Club stresses the "other meaning" of Hamlet—"To be or not to be"—which Oxenham interprets as an exhortation to sacrifice one's own interests for others.

For young readers the Hamlet Club's main appeal was probably its adoption of the May Queen rituals which involved a lot of dressing up and colourful symbolism. Oxenham apparently derived these from the May Day ceremony instituted by John Ruskin in 1881 at Whitelands Training College in London. Frequent descriptions of country dancing reflect the author's interest in the work of the English Folk Dance and Song Society, some of whose leading lights (including Cecil Sharp) are portrayed in the Abbey books.

The series is permeated by Oxenham's feeling for the countryside: this creates a mellow mood but is not overdone. (There are suggestions of mud as well as glowing sunshine in the beechwoods, of perspiration as well as prettification in the folk dance sequences.) Oxenham's ability to combine realism with romance has indelibly impressed her characters—and the values which they represent—on the minds of readers. Many adults still enthusiastically collect her books.

—Mary Cadogan

PALMER, C(yril) Everard. Canadian. Born in Kendal, Jamaica, 15 October 1930. Educated at Mico Training College, Jamaica, teaching diploma 1955; Lakehead University, Thunder Bay, Ontario, B.A. 1973. From 1971 teacher, Red Rock, Ontario. Address: c/o Scholastic Publications, 123 Newkirk Road, Richmond Hill, Ontario L4C 3G5, Canada.

PUBLICATIONS FOR CHILDREN (illustrated by Laszlo Acs)

Fiction

The Cloud with the Silver Lining. London, Deutsch, 1966; New York, Pantheon, 1967.
Big Doc Bitteroot. London, Deutsch, 1968; Indianapolis, Bobbs Merrill, 1971.
The Sun Salutes You. London, Deutsch, 1970; Indianapolis, Bobbs Merrill, 1971.
The Hummingbird People. London, Deutsch, 1971.
A Cow Called Boy, illustrated by Charles Gaines. Indianapolis, Bobbs Merrill, 1972; London, Deutsch, 1973.
The Wooing of Beppo Tate. London, Deutsch, 1972.
Baba and Mr. Big, illustrated by Lorenzo Lynch. Indianapolis, Bobbs Merrill, 1972; London, Deutsch, 1974.
My Father, Sun-Sun Johnson. London, Deutsch, 1974.
A Dog Called Houdini, illustrated by Maurice Wilson. London, Deutsch, 1978.
Beppo Tate and Roy Penner; The Runaway Marriage Brokers: Two Stories. London, Deutsch, 1980.
Houdini, Come Home, illustrated by Gavin Rowe. London, Deutsch, 1981.

PUBLICATIONS FOR ADULTS

Novel

A Broken Vessel. Kingston, Jamaica, Pioneer Press, 1960.

*   *   *

The Jamaican village of Kendal is the setting for C. Everard Palmer's rich studies of West Indian life. Of his early work he has written, "These books are intended to revive for adults fast-disappearing or totally extinct aspects of Jamaican life and for children creating them because they have missed them." Kendal, Palmer's own birthplace, is remote in place as well as time: it is 130 miles from Kingston and 4 miles up the hill road from the coastal hamlet of Green Island. It is rural and largely self-sufficient: it is easy to see from these books why a West Indian calls his village "my community." The rise and fall of reputations, the feuds and the power struggles provide the plot dynamics, and each story culminates in a set-piece—a hurricane, a fire, a trial, or some village festivity which re-affirms the bonds of the community. The stories have strong characterisation, racing narratives, and abundant and colourful detail. Palmer has a vivid and exuberant humour and a highly individual style; he makes full use of dialect. Except to West Indian readers, who will appreciate these novels as literature of their heritage, the setting may appear strange and exotic. But their ambience, the world of the village, is universal.

The Cloud with the Silver Lining is a warm and gentle story of two boys who keep the family smallholding going when the breadwinner, their grandfather, is immobilized by an accident. *Big Doc Bitteroot* contains Palmer's most memorable character, Kelso Crane. He is a larger-than-life itinerant quack doctor who dazzles the unsophisticated villagers until one of his cures goes wrong and he is brought

to trial. *The Sun Salutes You* again treats of village politics when Mike Johnson challenges Matt Southern's control not only of the trucking business but also of the villagers' lives. While Matt corrupts the police to stay in power, Mike enlists the aid of superstition in the person of a Pocomanian prophetess, Shepherdess Annie. *The Hummingbird People* tells of rival villages' plans to celebrate the return from war of three airmen. The "jollifying" of their plans and counterplans has the book humming with exuberance. *The Wooing of Beppo Tate* is a comedy of courtship between Mr. Tate and Mrs. Belmont and between the latter's daughter, Daphne, and the former's adopted son, Beppo. Beppo has enough trouble in his new role without falling in love. But all ends happily in this successful story for older children. *A Cow Called Boy* is a simple anecdotal tale of Josh whose pet calf follows him to school and causes chaos in the classroom. The enforced sale of Boy which results involves the whole village. *Baba and Mr. Big* tells of the kinship between an old man and a hawk. It is Jim Anderson, a newcomer, who brings them together, for capturing the hawk is the price of his initiation into the village gang; but in the process he learns new values.

My Father, Sun-Sun Johnson is Palmer's best book so far and is again for older readers. Rami Johnson takes his father's side when his parents part and his mother marries Jake, a man with a driving need for success. But Sun-Sun Johnson and his son too have their success in rebuilding their lives and conquering adversity.

Apart from *Beppo Tate and Roy Penner*, Palmer's latest work reflects not the West Indies of his youth but the Canada of his present home. In two animal stories for younger readers, *A Dog Called Houdini* and *Houdini, Come Home*, the setting is the Arctic north rather than the tropical south. But the warmth, humour, and insight into the pressures of life in small communities, which are the characteristic features of Palmer's work, are still to be found.

—Mary Croxson

———

PARDOE, M(argot Mary). British. Born in London, 7 August 1902. Educated privately; at Abbots Hill, Hemel Hempstead, Hertfordshire; Mademoiselle Fontaine's finishing school, Neuilly, France; studied music and singing in London and Paris. Married John Francis Swift in 1934; one son. Proprietor, Crossacres Hotel, Selworthy, Somerset, 1937–47. Address: c/o P.L.P. Swift, Church Farm House, Weston Colville, Cambridge CB1 5PE, England.

PUBLICATIONS FOR CHILDREN

Fiction

The Far Island, illustrated by R.M. Turvey. London, Routledge, 1936.
Four Plus Bunkle, illustrated by J.D. Evans. London, Routledge, 1939.
Bunkle Began It [Butts In, Bought It, Breaks Away, and Belinda, Baffles Them, Went for Six, Gets Busy], illustrated by Julie Neild. London, Routledge, 8 vols., 1942–51.
The Ghost Boat, with Howard Biggs, illustrated by Webster Murray. London, Hodder and Stoughton, 1951.
Bunkle's Brainwave, illustrated by Mary Smith. London, Routledge, 1952.
Bunkle Scents a Clue, illustrated by Pamela Kemp. London, Routledge, 1953.
The Boat Seekers, illustrated by B. Kay. London, Hodder and Stoughton, 1953.

Charles Arriving, illustrated by Leslie Atkinson.   London, Routledge, 1954.
The Dutch Boat, illustrated by Leslie Atkinson.   London, Hodder and Stoughton, 1955.
May Madrigal, illustrated by Leslie Atkinson.   London, Routledge, 1955.
Argle's Mist, illustrated by Leslie Atkinson.   London, Routledge, 1956; as *Curtain of Mist*, New York, Funk and Wagnalls, 1957.
The Nameless Boat, illustrated by Leslie Atkinson.   London, Hodder and Stoughton, 1957.
Argle's Causeway, illustrated by Leslie Atkinson.   London, Routledge, 1958.
Argle's Oracle, illustrated by Audrey Fawley.   London, Routledge, 1959.
The Greek Boat Mystery.   London, Hodder and Stoughton, 1960.
Bunkle Brings It Off, illustrated by Audrey Fawley.   London, Routledge, 1961.

*   *   *

Although M. Pardoe wrote other adventure stories and time fantasies, it is the series of books about Bunkle which made her such a popular writer during the 1940's and 1950's, and which are still remembered with affection. Bunkle is the nickname given to young Billy de Salis by his elder brother and sister because, as they say, he talks "a lot of bunk." And it is Bunkle's skill at talking his way out of dangerous situations which carries him breathlessly through a succession of adventures, beginning in 1939 with *Four Plus Bunkle*. This book tells how he and his brother and sister, while on holiday in France, are entrusted with the task of delivering a secret document into the hands of the British Secret Service. Later adventures involve the de Salis children with German spies in Devon, black marketeers in Hampshire, and Communist kidnappers in the Pyrenees, but, although the plots may be melodramatic, Pardoe's stories were far superior to similar adventure stories of the period. Unlike other writers of the time, she placed her characters very firmly in the real world. Bunkle may go to school at Winchester and have a father in the Secret Service, but, like other children, he has to endure the wartime discomforts of rationing, the blackout, and bombing. The de Salis family may take tea at Gunter's but the cream in the cakes is mock, and they are well aware that their way of life is under threat. "When this war ends," muses Mrs. de Salis in *Bunkle Butts In*, "I don't think that any of us are going to be able to go back to the sort of life we used to lead." It is this awareness of wider issues which lifts Pardoe's stories out of the conventional holiday-adventure rut.

The Bunkle books are also distinguished by realistic observation of character. While the children in comparable books remain marooned in an ageless limbo, the de Salis family mature and develop as the series progresses. Bunkle is 10 years old in *Four Plus Bunkle*, his first adventure. By the time the series ends, he is 17, and his elder sister is married and has a child. And, unlike other children's book heroes of the period, the de Salises have an existence below the waist. "What are we to do?" asks Bunkle's sister in *Four Plus Bunkle*, as she and her brothers emerge from a hiding place in a small French town, desperate to relieve themselves. "Why didn't we think of this? It's another of the things we didn't think of. How *do* they manage in books?"

It is realistic detail like this, coupled with exact description of place, which make the Bunkle books so memorable. The settings of the stories range from the French Riviera, the Pyrenees, and Switzerland to Guernsey, The Orkneys, and Chichester Harbour, but, in each case, the landscape is accurately observed, and the various journeys of the de Salis family can be followed on a map. In the later books, the geographical precision can become tedious, and the plots of *Bunkle Baffles Them* and *Bunkle Scents a Clue* sink almost without trace beneath thick blankets of inconsequential local colour. The

earlier books, though, are rich in atmospheric description, and one remembers them not so much for their plots as for their settings: the dismal out-of-season seaside resort in war time that is the background for *Bunkle Began It*, the marshy coastal creeks of *Bunkle Butts In*, the rain-sodden second-rate riverside hotel in *Bunkle Breaks Away*, perhaps the best book in the series. Few authors of the time conveyed so subtly and yet so vividly the gloom and austerity of wartime and post-war Britain.

Despite Pardoe's skill at evocative description—or possibly because of it—the Bunkle books remain period pieces. The upper-middle-class milieu and the dated dialogue are out of step with today's taste, and political and scientific changes have blunted the relevance of the plots. Yet the books are well worth reading, if only for the character of Bunkle himself. Lively, resourceful, insolent, clever, exasperating—he is a memorable creation, and Pardoe deserves credit for investing a familiar fictional formula with such an engaging hero.

—Lance Salway

———

PARISH, Peggy (Margaret Cecile Parish).   American.   Born in Manning, South Carolina, 14 July 1927.   Educated at the University of South Carolina, Columbia, B.A. in English 1948; Peabody College (now Vanderbilt University), Nashville, 1950.   Teacher in Kentucky and Oklahoma, and at Dalton School, New York, 1948–67.   *Died 19 November 1988.*

PUBLICATIONS FOR CHILDREN

Fiction

Good Hunting, Little Indian, illustrated by Leonard Weisgard.   New York, Scott, 1962.
Willy Is My Brother, illustrated by Shirley Hughes.   New York, Scott, and London, Gollancz, 1963.
Amelia Bedelia, illustrated by Fritz Siebel.   New York, Harper, 1963; Kingswood, Surrey, World's Work, 1964.
Thank You, Amelia Bedelia, illustrated by Fritz Siebel.   New York, Harper, 1964; Kingswood, Surrey, World's Work, 1965.
Amelia Bedelia and the Surprise Shower, illustrated by Fritz Siebel.   New York, Harper, 1966; Kingswood, Surrey, World's Work, 1967.
Key to the Treasure, illustrated by Paul Frame.   New York, Macmillan, 1966.
Clues in the Woods, illustrated by Paul Frame.   New York, Macmillan, and London, Collier Macmillan, 1968.
Little Indian, illustrated by John E. Johnson.   New York, Simon and Schuster, 1968.
A Beastly Circus, illustrated by Peter Parnall.   New York, Simon and Schuster, 1969.
Granny and the Indians, illustrated by Brinton Turkle.   New York, Macmillan, 1969.
Jumper Goes to School, illustrated by Cyndy Szekeres.   New York, Simon and Schuster, 1969.
Granny and the Desperadoes, illustrated by Steven Kellogg.   New York, Macmillan, 1970.
Ootah's Lucky Day, illustrated by Mamoru Funai.   New York, Harper, 1970; Kingswood, Surrey, World's Work, 1971.
Snapping Turtle's All-Wrong Day, illustrated by John E. Johnson.   New York, Simon and Schuster, 1970.
Come Back, Amelia Bedelia, illustrated by Wallace Tripp.   New

York, Harper, 1971; Kingswood, Surrey, World's Work, 1973.

Haunted House, illustrated by Paul Frame. New York, Macmillan, and London, Collier Macmillan, 1971.

Granny, The Baby, and the Big Gray Thing, illustrated by Lynn Sweat. New York, Macmillan, 1972; Kingswood, Surrey, World's Work, 1973.

Play Ball, Amelia Bedelia, illustrated by Wallace Tripp. New York, Harper, 1972; Kingswood, Surrey, World's Work, 1973.

Too Many Rabbits, illustrated by Leonard Kessler. New York, Macmillan, 1974; Kingswood, Surrey, World's Work, 1975.

Pirate Island Adventure, illustrated by Paul Frame. New York, Macmillan, 1975.

Good Work, Amelia Bedelia, illustrated by Lynn Sweat. New York, Greenwillow, 1976; Kingswood, Surrey, World's Work, 1977.

Teach Us, Amelia Bedelia, illustrated by Lynn Sweat. New York, Greenwillow, 1977; Kingswood, Surrey, World's Work, 1978.

Hermit Dan, illustrated by Paul Frame. New York, Macmillan, 1977.

Zed and the Monsters, illustrated by Paul Galdone. New York, Doubleday, 1979; Kingswood, Surrey, World's Work, 1980.

Be Ready at Eight, illustrated by Leonard Kessler. New York, Macmillan, 1979.

Amelia Bedelia Helps Out, illustrated by Lynn Sweat. New York, Greenwillow, 1979; Kingswood, Surrey, World's Work, 1981.

Amelia Bedelia and the Baby, illustrated by Lynn Sweat. New York, Greenwillow, 1981.

No More Monsters for Me!, illustrated by Marc Simont. New York, Harper, 1981.

Mr. Adams's Mistake, illustrated by Gail Owen. New York, Macmillan, 1982; London, Macmillan, 1983.

The Cats' Burglar, illustrated by Lynn Sweat. New York, Greenwillow, 1983.

Amelia Bedelia Goes Camping, illustrated by Lynn Sweat. New York, Greenwillow, 1985.

Merry Christmas, Amelia Bedelia, illustrated by Lynn Sweat. New York, Greenwillow, 1986.

The Ghosts of Cougar Island. New York, Dell, 1986.

Amelia Bedelia's Family Album, illustrated by Lynn Sweat. New York, Greenwillow, 1988.

Scruffy, illustrated by Kelly Oechsli. New York, Harper, 1988.

Good Hunting, Blue Sky, illustrated by James Watts. New York, Harper, 1988.

Other

My Golden Book of Manners, illustrated by Richard Scarry. New York, Golden Press, 1962; London, Golden Pleasure Books, 1963.

Let's Be Indians, illustrated by Arnold Lobel. New York, Harper, 1962.

The Story of Grains: Wheat, Corn, and Rice, with W.W. Crowder, illustrated by William Moyers. New York, Grosset and Dunlap, 1965.

Let's Be Early Settlers with Daniel Boone, illustrated by Arnold Lobel. New York, Harper, 1967.

Costumes to Make, illustrated by Lynn Sweat. New York, Macmillan, 1970; London, Collier Macmillan, 1971.

Sheet Magic: Games, Toys and Gifts from Old Sheets, illustrated by Lynn Sweat. New York, Macmillan, and London, Collier Macmillan, 1971.

Dinosaur Time, illustrated by Arnold Lobel. New York, Harper, 1974; Kingswood, Surrey, World's Work, 1975.

December Decorations: A Holiday How-To Book, illustrated by Barbara Wolff. New York, Macmillan, 1975.

Let's Celebrate: Holiday Decorations You Can Make, illustrated by Lynn Sweat. New York, Greenwillow, 1976.

Mind Your Manners!, illustrated by Marylin Hafner. New York, Greenwillow, 1978.

Beginning Mobiles, illustrated by Lynn Sweat. New York, Macmillan, 1979.

I Can—Can You? (readers), illustrated by Marylin Hafner. New York, Greenwillow, 4 vols., 1980; as *See and Do Book Bag*, London, MacRae, 4 vols., 1980.

*

Manuscript Collection: Kerlan Collection, University of Minnesota, Minneapolis.

* * *

Peggy Parish had the formula for combining humor and word-play in a way that fulfills a child's need for the obvious. She wrote several successful series of which Amelia Bedelia is best-known. Introduced in *Amelia Bedelia*, the character amazes her audience with ridiculous episodes. Amelia Bedelia is quite literal in her interpretation of everyday events. Her first day as the maid for the Rogers family, she dusts with dusting powder, draws the drapes by sketching, and dresses the chicken in trousers and socks. Her delicious lemon meringue pie rescues her from dismissal. In *Amelia Bedelia and the Surprise Shower* she and Cousin Alcolu help throw a bridal shower complete with gifts and garden hose. Following her dismissal, in *Come Back, Amelia Bedelia* she pounds the pavement looking for a job while leaving havoc in her wake. Her outrageous interpretation of baseball terminology in *Play Ball, Amelia Bedelia* runs the gamut from stealing bases to running home. Her predicaments are obvious enough to allow early readers the enjoyment of a play on words.

Granny and the Indians introduces another unique and likable character. Alone with a gun that doesn't shoot, Granny Guntry proves competent in dealing with Indians, desperadoes, and wolves. Granny's a nice, sweet, tough, and independent old lady who wants things done her way. Her casual brushes with danger are just close enough to be exciting. The action never ceases until things are settled to her liking.

The mystery series involving Jed, Liza, and Bill Roberts are longer but provide enough action to maintain interest and enjoyment. The children always manage to keep the adults in suspense while unraveling the mysteries. Grandpa Roberts provides the initial clues for two of the mysteries that involve word scrambles, secret codes, and picture clues. Though easy to read, deciphering the clues becomes absorbing and draws the reader into the intrigue.

In contrast to her other work, Parish's stories about Little Indian are stereotypical. The lack of names for the characters in *Good Hunting, Little Indian* is offensive. Many readers today will be insulted by the implication that all Indians are called "Little Indian" while earning a name.

Parish showed great skill in combining an ever-popular subject, monsters, with an easy reader format. *No More Monsters for Me!* and *Zed and the Monsters* provide humorous and involving situations with a flowing text—the dynamics for enjoyable stories.

—Martha J. Fick

———

PARK, (Rosina) Ruth (Lucia). Australian. Born in Auckland, New Zealand. Educated at St. Benedict's College; University of Auckland. Married the writer D'Arcy Niland in 1942 (died 1967); five children. Proofreader and editor of children's page, Auckland *Star*; editor of children's page, *Zealandia*, Auckland; welfare worker in Auckland. Recipient: Sydney *Morning Herald* prize, for novel,

1948; Miles Franklin award, for novel, 1978; Australian Children's Book Council Book of the Year award, 1981; Premier's award, 1981; Boston *Globe-Horn Book* award, 1982. Lives in Sydney. Agent: Curtis Brown, P.O. Box 19, Paddington, New South Wales 2021, Australia.

PUBLICATIONS FOR CHILDREN

Fiction

The Hole in the Hill, illustrated by Jennifer Murray.   Sydney, Ure Smith, 1961; London, Macmillan, 1962; as *Secret of the Maori Cave*, New York, Doubleday, 1964.
The Ship's Cat, illustrated by Richard Kennedy.   London, Macmillan, and New York, St. Martin's Press, 1961.
Uncle Matt's Mountain, illustrated by Laurence Broderick.   London, Macmillan, and New York, St. Martin's Press, 1962.
The Road to Christmas, illustrated by Noela Young.   London, Macmillan, and New York, St. Martin's Press, 1962.
The Road under the Sea, illustrated by Jennifer Murray.   Sydney, Ure Smith, 1962; London, Macmillan, 1963; New York, Doubleday, 1966.
The Muddle-Headed Wombat, illustrated by Noela Young.   Sydney, Educational Press, 1962; London, Angus and Robertson, 1963.
The Shaky Island, illustrated by Iris Millington.   London, Constable, and New York, McKay, 1962.
The Muddle-Headed Wombat on Holiday, illustrated by Noela Young.   Sydney, Educational Press, and London, Angus and Robertson, 1964.
Airlift for Grandee, illustrated by Sheila Hawkins.   London, Macmillan, and New York, St. Martin's Press, 1964.
The Muddle-Headed Wombat in the Treetops, illustrated by Noela Young.   Sydney, Educational Press, and London, Angus and Robertson, 1965.
The Muddle-Headed Wombat at School, illustrated by Noela Young.   Sydney, Educational Press, and London, Angus and Robertson, 1966.
The Muddle-Headed Wombat in the Snow, illustrated by Noela Young.   Sydney, Educational Press, and London, Angus and Robertson, 1966.
Ring for the Sorcerer, illustrated by William Stobbs.   Sydney, Horwitz Martin, 1967.
The Sixpenny Island, illustrated by David Cox.   Sydney, Ure Smith, and London, Macmillan, 1968; as *Ten-Cent Island*, New York, Doubleday, 1968.
The Muddle-Headed Wombat on a Rainy Day, illustrated by Noela Young.   Sydney, Educational Press, 1969; London, Angus and Robertson, 1970.
The Runaway Bus, illustrated by Peter Tierney.   Sydney, Hodder and Stoughton, 1969.
Nuki and the Sea Serpent: A Maori Story, illustrated by Zelma Blakely.   London, Longman, 1969.
The Muddle-Headed Wombat in the Springtime, illustrated by Noela Young.   Sydney, Educational Press, and London, Angus and Robertson, 1970.
The Muddle-Headed Wombat on the River, illustrated by Noela Young.   Sydney, Educational Press, and London, Angus and Robertson, 1971.
The Muddle-Headed Wombat and the Bush Band, illustrated by Noela Young.   Sydney, Angus and Robertson, 1973.
Callie's Castle, illustrated by Kilmeny Niland.   Sydney and London, Angus and Robertson, 1974.
The Gigantic Balloon, illustrated by Kilmeny and Deborah Niland.   Sydney, Collins, 1975; London, Collins, and New York, Parents' Magazine Press, 1976.

The Muddle-Headed Wombat and the Invention, illustrated by Noela Young.   London, Angus and Robertson, 1975.
The Muddle-Headed Wombat on Clean-Up Day, illustrated by Noela Young.   Sydney and London, Angus and Robertson, 1976.
Come Danger, Come Darkness.   Sydney and London, Hodder and Stoughton, 1978.
The Adventures of the Muddle-Headed Wombat, illustrated by Noela Young.   Sydney, Angus and Robertson, 1979; London, Angus and Robertson, 1980.
When the Wind Changed, illustrated by Deborah Niland.   Sydney, Collins, 1980; New York, Coward McCann, 1981.
Playing Beatie Bow.   Melbourne, Nelson, 1980; London, Kestrel, 1981; New York, Atheneum, 1982.
The Muddle-Headed Wombat Is Very Bad, illustrated by Noela Young.   Sydney, Angus and Robertson, 1981.
The Muddle-Headed Wombat Stays at Home, illustrated by Noela Young.   Sydney, Angus and Robertson, 1982.
The Big Brass Key, illustrated by Noela Young.   Sydney, Hodder and Stoughton, 1983.
My Sister Sif.   Ringwood, Victoria, Viking Kestrel, 1986; London, Viking Kestrel, 1987.
Callie's Family, illustrated by Kilmeny Niland.   Sydney, Angus and Robertson, 1988; London, Angus and Robertson, 1989.
James, illustrated by Deborah Niland.   Ringwood, Victoria, Viking O'Neil, 1988.

Plays

The Uninvited Guest.   Sydney and London, Angus and Robertson, 1948.

Radio Plays: *The Muddle-Headed Wombat* series.

Verse

Roger Bandy, illustrated by Deborah and Kilmeny Niland.   Adelaide, Rigby, 1977.

Other

Merchant Campbell, illustrated by Edwina Bell.   Sydney, Collins, 1976.

PUBLICATIONS FOR ADULTS

Novels

The Harp in the South.   Sydney, Angus and Robertson, London, Joseph, and Boston, Houghton Mifflin, 1948.
Poor Man's Orange.   Sydney, Angus and Robertson, 1949; London, Joseph, 1950; as *12½ Plymouth Street*, Boston, Houghton Mifflin, 1951.
The Witch's Thorn.   Sydney, Angus and Robertson, 1951; London, Joseph, and Boston, Houghton Mifflin, 1952.
A Power of Roses.   Sydney, Angus and Robertson, and London, Joseph, 1953.
Pink Flannel.   Sydney, Angus and Robertson, 1955; as *Dear Hearts and Gentle People*, Ringwood, Victoria, Penguin, 1981.
One-a-Pecker, Two-a-Pecker.   Sydney, Angus and Robertson, 1957; London, Joseph, 1958; as *Frost and the Fire*, Boston Houghton Mifflin, 1958; London, Pan, 1962.
The Good-Looking Women.   Sydney, Angus and Robertson, 1961; London, Joseph, 1962.
Serpent's Delight.   New York, Doubleday, 1962.
Swords and Crowns and Rings.   Melbourne, Nelson, 1977; Lon-

don, Joseph, and New York, St. Martin's Press, 1978.
Missus. Melbourne, Nelson, and London, Joseph, 1985; New York, St. Martin's Press, 1987.

Plays

The Harp in the South, with Leslie Rees, adaptation of the novel by Park (broadcast 1949). Montmorency, Victoria, Yackandandah, 1987.

Radio Play: *The Harp in the South*, with Leslie Rees, 1949.

Television Play: *No Decision*, with D'Arcy Niland, 1964.

Other

The Drums Go Bang (autobiographical), with D'Arcy Niland. Sydney, Angus and Robertson, 1956.
The Companion Guide to Sydney. Sydney and London, Collins, 1973; New York, Scribner, 1976.
Norfolk Island and Lord Howe Island. Dover Heights, New South Wales, Serendip, 1982.
The Sydney We Love, with Cedric Emanuel. Melbourne, Nelson, 1983.
The Tasmania We Love, with Cedric Emanuel. Melbourne, Nelson, 1987.

*   *   *

When Ruth Park created the Muddle-Headed Wombat for a radio programme, she introduced Australian children to a delightful and endearing character whose adventures are related in a popular and timeless series of books for younger children, with satisfyingly complementary illustrations. A lively sense of logical nonsense and a gift for zany dialogue are perhaps the outstanding ingredients of these stories. Park, in fact, belongs to that select body of writers who have successfully conceived a "cult" figure within children's literature. And, for Australian children, there is a special delight in the Muddle-Headed Wombat because he is a "dinkum Aussie," a home-bred creature to place alongside the imported bears, elephants, and woodland creatures in books that originate overseas.

A gifted adult novelist and a distinguished journalist, Park is perhaps the most unassuming and least pretentious of Australia's writers for the young. In *Callie's Castle* (runner-up for the Australian Book of the Year award, 1975) she turned to a new form of fiction, for young teenagers. Set in Sydney, this is a gentle, understated story about a girl, growing up, who longs for solitude within her family circle. The author brings to Callie's story the same perception and eye for detail as she shows in her occasional short stories for young readers (for example, "The Freedom of the City," in the anthology *The Cool Man*) and in her regular adult articles for newspapers and journals.

She has made an interesting observation on her attitude towards creating a character. She writes: "I don't portray real children in stories; I create a fictional child very much as a gipsy makes a blanket…a rag here, a tuft of wool there. I pick up a habit of speech, a mannerism, a colour of eye…and try to make somebody real out of the bits. I don't always succeed but I do find it a joyful business trying."

In *Come Danger, Come Darkness* Park used the vivid historical background of Norfolk Island, where she lived for several years, for the tale of Otter, nephew of the Commandant of the penal colony, who becomes involved in the escape of a convict. But it is *Playing Beatie Bow* (Australian Book of the Year, 1981) which displays her most subtle and memorable writing for children, in the story of a present-day Sydney child who is able to slip through time into the early days of the Colony.

—Barbara Ker Wilson

PARKER, Richard. British. Born in Stanmore, Middlesex, 15 February 1915. Educated at Kingsbury County Training College, London. Served in the British Army during World War II. Married Kathleen Hook in 1939; five children. Library assistant, Maidstone Public Library, Kent, 1934–36; secretary to Rupert Croft-Cooke, 1937–38; reporter, *Kent Messenger*; primary school teacher for many years. Address: 36 Central Parade, Herne Bay, Kent, England.

PUBLICATIONS FOR CHILDREN

Fiction

Escape from the Zoo, illustrated by Val Biro. London, Sylvan Press, 1945.
A Camel from the Desert, illustrated by Val Biro. London, Sylvan Press, 1947.
The Penguin Goes Home, illustrated by Val Biro. London, Chatto and Windus, 1951.
A Moor of Spain: The Story of a Rogue, illustrated by John Harwood. London, Penguin, 1953.
The Three Pebbles, illustrated by Prudence Seward. London, Collins, 1954; New York, McKay, 1956.
The Sword of Ganelon. London, Collins, 1957; New York, McKay, 1958.
Lion at Large, illustrated by Paul Hogarth. Leicester, Brockhampton Press, 1959; New York, Nelson, 1961; as *Midnight Beast*, New York, Scholastic, n.d.
More Snakes than Ladders, illustrated by Jillian Willett. Leicester, Brockhampton Press, 1960; as *Almost Lost*, New York, Nelson, 1962.
New Home South, illustrated by Prudence Seward. Leicester, Brockhampton Press, 1961; as *Voyage to Tasmania*, Indianapolis, Bobbs Merrill, 1961.
A Valley Full of Pipers, illustrated by Richard Kennedy. London, Gollancz, 1962; Indianapolis, Bobbs Merrill, 1963.
The House That Guilda Drew, illustrated by Prudence Seward. Leicester, Brockhampton Press, 1963; Indianapolis, Bobbs Merrill, 1964.
The Boy Who Wasn't Lonely, illustrated by Prudence Seward. Leicester, Brockhampton Press, 1964; Indianapolis, Bobbs Merrill, 1965.
Perversity of Pipers, illustrated by Richard Kennedy. London, Gollancz, and Princeton, New Jersey, Van Nostrand, 1964.
Private Beach, illustrated by Victor Ambrus. London, Harrap, 1964; New York, Duell, 1965.
Second-Hand Family, illustrated by Gareth Floyd. Leicester, Brockhampton Press, 1965; Indianapolis, Bobbs Merrill, 1966.
M for Mischief, illustrated by Juan Ballesta. London, Constable, 1965; New York, Duell, 1966.
The Punch Back Gang, illustrated by John Plant. London, Harrap, 1966; as *New in the Neighborhood*, New York, Duell, 1966.
One White Mouse, illustrated by Rene Hummerstone. Leicester, Brockhampton Press, 1966; as *No House for a Mouse*, Chicago, Follett, 1968.
The Hendon Fungus. London, Gollancz, 1967; New York, Meredith Press, 1968.
A Sheltering Tree. New York, Meredith Press, 1969; London, Gollancz, 1970.
Spell Seven, illustrated by Trevor Ridley. London, Longman, and

New York, Nelson, 1971.

The Old Powder Line. London, Gollancz, and New York, Nelson, 1971.

Paul and Etta, illustrated by Gavin Rowe. Leicester, Brockhampton Press, 1972; Nashville, Nelson, 1973.

Frank's Fire. London, Macmillan, 1972.

John Morris's Mermaid. London, Macmillan, 1972.

Not at Home. London, Macmillan, 1972.

One Green Bottle, illustrated by Michael Jackson. London, Heinemann, 1973.

A Time to Choose. London, Hutchinson, 1973; New York, Harper, 1974.

He Is Your Brother, illustrated by Gareth Floyd. Leicester, Brockhampton Press, 1974; Nashville, Nelson, 1976.

Snatched, illustrated by Peter Kesteven. Newton Abbot, Devon, David and Charles, 1974; as *Three by Mistake*, Nashville, Nelson, 1974.

Beyond the Back Gate, illustrated by Peter Dennis. London, Abelard Schuman, 1975.

Boy into Action, illustrated by Trevor Parkin. London, Abelard Schuman, 1975.

The Fire Curse, illustrated by Trevor Stubley. London, Heinemann, 1975.

Hugo Takes Off, illustrated by Trevor Stubley. London, Hodder and Stoughton, 1976; as *The Runaway*, Nashville, Nelson, 1977.

Quarter Boy. London, Heinemann, and Nashville, Nelson, 1976.

In and Out the Window. London, Hutchinson, 1976.

Plays

Six Plays for Boys (includes *The New Football Boots, The Rabbit Hutch, The Wish, The Medicine Man, The Raft, No Excitement*). London, Methuen, 1951.

Seven Plays for Boys (includes *The Rehearsal, The Hut, The Waxworks, Lazy Jack, The Dilemma, A Message to the Kite, The Coconut Shy*). London, Methuen, 1953.

Other (readers)

Brother Turgar and the Vikings, illustrated by Joan Milroy. London, Ginn, 1959.

The Kidnapped Crusaders, illustrated by Richard Kennedy. London, Ginn, 1959.

The Green Highwayman, illustrated by Richard Kennedy. London, Ginn, 1960.

Goodbye to the Bush, illustrated by Kenneth Brown. London, Ginn, 1963.

Lost in a Shop, illustrated by Carol Barker. London, Macmillan, 1968.

Me and My Boots, illustrated by George Adamson. London, Macmillan, 1968.

Keeping Time, illustrated by Jane Hickson. London, Heinemann, 1973.

Digging for Treasure, illustrated by Trevor Stubley. London, Benn, 1976.

Flood, illustrated by Trevor Stubley. London, Benn, 1976.

Sausages on the Shore, illustrated by Trevor Stubley. London, Benn, 1976.

The Sunday Papers, illustrated by Trevor Stubley. London, Benn, 1976.

PUBLICATIONS FOR ADULTS

Novels

Only Some Had Guns. London, Collins, 1952.

The Gingerbread Man. London, Collins, 1953; New York, Scribner, 1954.

A Kind of Misfortune. London, Collins, 1954; New York, Scribner, 1955.

Draughts in the Sun. London, Collins, 1955.

Harm Intended. New York, Scribner, 1956; London, Secker and Warburg, 1957.

Fiddler's Place. London, Davies, 1961.

Boy on a Chain. London, Davies, 1964; as *Killer*, New York, Doubleday, 1964.

*

Richard Parker comments:

I began writing for children when I became a teacher, and to begin with the stories were largely a by-product. They were written to give enjoyment to or to help some particular group of children, sometimes technically and sometimes emotionally. Some stories were written for individuals, some for the class I happened to be teaching at the time. After two years (1959–61) in the Australian education system, however, I became less interested in education and more concerned with writing as a profession. Nowadays I find myself writing a story because it seems a good one and presents interesting problems, and worry far less about who will read it.

*   *   *

Over-zealous pigeon-holing of writers and writing for the young often ceases to be useful when appreciation of the prolific and dedicated like Richard Parker is supplanted by a genre approach which makes "boys adventure" (or "the teenage novel") do for all. His books are mainly for adolescents, or slightly younger readers; most of his protagonists are boys. But the thematic underpinning of his work is the reader's pleasure in a tale well-structured and narrated.

An astute awareness of a readership which likes to be drawn in early, and carried by plots with pace and tailored episodes, informs all his work. Central characters are often lonely, insecure, uncertain, in between: recently orphaned and bound for a foreign country in *New Home South*; rootless, nomadic in *The House That Guilda Drew*; fostered unlovingly in *Second-Hand Family*. The pitfalls of over-dramatising or voyeurism are always avoided. The adults are often well-meaning but unhelpful. Parker's strong storylines make his readers secure enough to face the potentially trying such as the pressures brought upon children by an autistic sibling (and an insensitive father) in *He Is Your Brother*. His dialogue is vivid, especially when family tensions are below the surface of domestic small talk. The uneasy conversations between the moody girl and her unwelcome foster-brother in *Paul and Etta*, the half-understood bickering of unhappy parents in *Hugo Takes Off* often foster in his teenage readers a new kind of reading—to discern atmosphere and relationships. Parker can deal unobtrusively with the often-fraught hinterland between childhood and young adulthood.

He never uses fictional devices for mere effect, always for a refining of plot and ideas. The clever time-shift in *The Old Powder Line* reveals to the young that the old were once young, too. A loss of memory at a pop festival enables the young hero in *In and Out the Window* to see himself and his surroundings afresh. Books which range widely in geographical and historical contexts still keep the story in the foreground so that, invited in, the young gain a sense of place and period. The vivid Australian backcloth of the Pipers books adds vigour and a rough edge to plots and characters. The absorbing portrayal of the Anglo-Saxon boy's quest in *The Sword of Ganelon* and the superb smuggling story set in 19th-century Kent—*A Sheltering Tree*—display a genuine talent for coherent historical writing. In recent writing, Parker has shown a willingness to tackle contemporary themes without being ingratiating or trendy. There is in all his work a concern for technique which is solid, but never dull, a respect for the young which is not overbearing.

—Colin Mills

—————

PARRISH, Anne. American. Born in Colorado Springs, Colorado, 12 November 1888. Educated at Misses Ferris's School and San Luis School, Colorado Springs; Misses Hebb's School, Claymont, Delaware; Philadelphia School of Design. Married 1) Charles Albert Corliss in 1915 (died 1936); 2) Josiah Titzell in 1938 (died 1943). Recipient: Harper prize, 1925. *Died 5 September 1957.*

PUBLICATIONS FOR CHILDREN

Fiction

Knee-High to a Grasshopper, with Dillwyn Parrish, illustrated by the authors. New York, Macmillan, 1923.
The Dream Coach, with Dillwyn Parrish, illustrated by the authors. New York, Macmillan, 1924.
The Story of Appleby Capple, illustrated by the author. New York, Harper, 1950.

Verse

Floating Island, illustrated by the author. New York, Harper, and London, Benn, 1930.

PUBLICATIONS FOR ADULTS

Novels

A Pocketful of Poses. New York, Doran, and London, Hodder and Stoughton, 1923.
Semi-Attached. New York, Doran, 1924; London, Brentano's, 1926.
The Perennial Bachelor. New York, Harper, 1925; London, Heinemann, 1926.
To-morrow Morning. New York, Harper, and London, Heinemann, 1927.
All Kneeling. New York, Harper, 1928; London, Benn, 1929.
The Methodist Faun. New York, Harper, 1929; London, Benn, 1930.
Loads of Love. New York, Harper, and London, Benn, 1932.
Sea Level. New York, Harper, and London, Hamish Hamilton, 1934.
Golden Wedding. New York, Harper, and London, Hamish Hamilton, 1936.
Mr. Despondency's Daughter. New York, Harper, and London, Hamish Hamilton, 1938.
Pray for Tomorrow. New York, Harper, 1941.
Poor Child. New York, Harper, 1945; London, Heinemann, 1947.
A Clouded Star. New York, Harper, 1948; London, Heinemann, 1949.
And Have Not Love. New York, Harper, 1954; as *And Have Not Charity*, London, Hutchinson, 1955.
The Lucky One. New York, Harper, 1958.

Short Stories

Lustres. New York, Doran, 1924.

*   *   *

Anne Parrish, born into a family of painters, took naturally to a deep appreciation of people and of nature. She and her brother created fantasy stories and games about both during their childhood, and later collaborated as authors/illustrators of several children's books where fantasy, mystery, and adventure are paramount.

Parrish became well-known for her adult novels, some of which were bestsellers. As an author of books for children, she is best remembered for *Floating Island* and *The Story of Appleby Capple*. Both of these books are dream-like and witty, expressing very human emotions in non-human disguises. *Floating Island*, told in verse, is one of a number of books about dolls and other toys popular in the early part of this century. It was the author's favorite of her books. The doll family—consisting of Mr. and Mrs. Doll, William Doll, Annabel Doll, Baby Doll, and Dinah the Cook—live in a proper doll house in a proper toy store. When they are bought by a devoted uncle and shipped across the seas to his niece, they, fortunately or unfortunately, are shipwrecked and find themselves on a tropical island. The family members are scattered on the island, and each has to react alone to unknown beauty and unknown terror. Their reactions to the special wonders of ferns and sea shells and wild blossoms, and to the special threats of crabs and monkeys and large birds, are told strictly through the eyes of small dolls, some of whom are unbendable. The Dolls make very intelligent use of their stay on the island and they enjoy its surprises; but all except Dinah ultimately leave it for a proper existence again. The book is imaginative and wistful and gentle, but somewhat outdated in its stereotypical approach to family life and to sex and racial differences. *The Story of Appleby Capple* grew out of a letter game the author and her brother invented as children. It indicates the author's awareness of the delight children receive from playing with unusual, multicolored, and splendid words.

Parrish once said that "for pure joy there is nothing like working on a book for children." Her joy is communicated in these works, with their combination of reverence for nature and understanding of human foibles.

—Mary Lystad

—————

PATCHETT, Mary Elwyn (Osborne). Has also written as David Bruce. Australian. Born in Sydney, New South Wales, 2 December 1897. Educated at New England Girls' School, Armidale; Church of England Girls' Grammar School, Sydney. Married Stanser Patchett (died); one son and one daughter (deceased). Journalist, *Sun* group of newspapers, Sydney, 1926–31, then freelance writer in England and Europe; ran beauty salon in London; lived in the Caribbean in the 1930's, and in London from 1946. Lives in Reading. Address: c/o Abelard Schuman, 7 Leicester Place, London WC2H 7BP, England.

PUBLICATIONS FOR CHILDREN

Fiction

Ajax, The Warrior, illustrated by Eric Tansley. London, Lutterworth Press, 1953; as *Ajax, Golden Dog of the Australian Bush*,

Indianapolis, Bobbs Merrill, 1953.
Kidnappers of Space. London, Lutterworth Press, 1953; as *Space Captives of the Golden Men*, Indianapolis, Bobbs Merrill, 1953.
The Lee Twins, Beauty Students. London, Lane, 1953.
Tam the Untamed, illustrated by Joan Kiddell-Monroe. London, Lutterworth Press, 1954; Indianapolis, Bobbs Merrill, 1955.
Lost on Venus. London, Lutterworth Press, 1954; as *Flight to the Misty Planet*, Indianapolis, Bobbs Merrill, 1956.
Evening Star, illustrated by Olga Lehmann. London, Lutterworth Press, 1954.
Adam Troy, Astroman. London, Lutterworth Press, 1954.
"Your Call, Miss Gaynor," illustrated by Bill Martin. London, Lutterworth Press, 1955.
Treasure of the Reef, illustrated by Joan Kiddell-Monroe. London, Lutterworth Press, 1955; as *The Great Barrier Reef*, Indianapolis, Bobbs Merrill, 1958.
Undersea Treasure Hunters, illustrated by Joan Kiddell-Monroe. London, Lutterworth Press, 1955; as *The Chance of Treasure*, Indianapolis, Bobbs Merrill, 1957.
Send for Johnny Danger. London, Lutterworth Press, 1956; New York, McGraw Hill, 1958.
Return to the Reef, illustrated by Joan Kiddell-Monroe. London, Lutterworth Press, 1956.
Sally's Zoo, illustrated by Pat Marriott. London, Hamish Hamilton, 1957.
Outback Adventure, illustrated by Joan Kiddell-Monroe. London, Lutterworth Press, 1957.
Caribbean Adventurers, illustrated by William Stobbs. London, Lutterworth Press, 1957.
The Mysterious Pool, illustrated by Pat Marriott. London, Hamish Hamilton, 1958.
The Brumby, illustrated by Juliet McLeod. London, Lutterworth Press, 1958; as *Brumby, The Wild White Stallion*, Indianapolis, Bobbs Merrill, 1959.
The Call of the Bush, illustrated by Brian Wildsmith. London, Lutterworth Press, 1959.
The Quest of Ati Manu, illustrated by Stuart Tresilian. London, Lutterworth Press, 1960; Indianapolis, Bobbs Merrill, 1962.
Warrimoo, illustrated by Roger Payne. Leicester, Brockhampton Press, 1961; Indianapolis, Bobbs Merrill, 1963.
Come Home, Brumby, illustrated by Stuart Tresilian. London, Lutterworth Press, 1961; as *Brumby, Come Home*, Indianapolis, Bobbs Merrill, 1962.
The End of the Outlaws, illustrated by Roger Payne. London, Lutterworth Press, 1961; Indianapolis, Bobbs Merrill, 1963.
Dangerous Assignment, illustrated by Roger Payne. Leicester, Brockhampton Press, 1962; Indianapolis, Bobbs Merrill, 1964.
The Golden Wolf, illustrated by Roger Payne. London, Lutterworth Press, 1962; Indianapolis, Bobbs Merrill, 1965.
Circus Brumby, illustrated by Stuart Tresilian. London, Lutterworth Press, 1963.
The Venus Project, illustrated by Roger Payne. Leicester, Brockhampton Press, 1963.
Ajax and the Haunted Mountain, illustrated by Roger Payne. London, Lutterworth Press, 1963; Indianapolis, Bobbs Merrill, 1966.
Tiger in the Dark, illustrated by Roger Payne. Leicester, Brockhampton Press, 1964; New York, Duell, 1966.
Ajax and the Drovers, illustrated by Roger Payne. London, Lutterworth Press, 1964.
Stranger in the Herd, illustrated by Stuart Tresilian. London, Lutterworth Press, 1964; New York, Duell, 1966.
The White Dingo, illustrated by Peter Kesteven. London, Lutterworth Press, 1965.
Brumby Foal, illustrated by Victor Ambrus. London, Lutterworth Press, 1965.
Summer on Wild Horse Island, illustrated by Roger Payne.

Leicester, Brockhampton Press, 1965; New York, Meredith Press, 1967.
The Terror of Manooka, illustrated by Roger Payne. London, Lutterworth Press, 1966.
Summer on Boomerang Beach, illustrated by Roger Payne. Leicester, Brockhampton Press, 1967.
Festival of Jewels, illustrated by Roger Payne. Leicester, Brockhampton Press, 1968.
Farm Beneath the Sea, illustrated by H. Johns. London, Harrap, 1969.
Quarter Horse Boy, illustrated by Roger Payne. London, Harrap, 1970.
The Long Ride, illustrated by Michael Charlton. London, Lutterworth Press, 1970.
Rebel Brumby, illustrated by Roger Payne. Guildford, Surrey, Lutterworth Press, 1972.
Roar of the Lion, illustrated by Douglas Phillips. Guildford, Surrey, Lutterworth Press, 1973.
Hunting Cat. London, Abelard Schuman, 1976.

PUBLICATIONS FOR ADULTS

Novels

Wild Brother. London, Collins, 1954.
Cry of the Heart. London, Collins, 1956; New York, Abelard Schuman, 1957.
The Saffron Woman. London, Heinemann, 1958.
Brit. London, Hodder and Stoughton, 1961.
In a Wilderness. London, Hodder and Stoughton, 1962; as *Dingo*, New York, Doubleday, 1963.
The Last Warrior. London, Hodder and Stoughton, 1965; New York, Doubleday, 1966.

Other

The Proud Eagles. London, Heinemann, 1960; Cleveland, World, 1961.
A Budgie Called Fred. London, Barker, 1964.
Bird of Jove (as David Bruce). New York, Putnam, 1971.

*

Mary Elwyn Patchett comments:
    All my books, for adults and for children, concern my main interests—animals, falconry, undersea exploration, interplanetary flight, history—and almost all are factual adventure. The animals concerned range from a great Berkut eagle from Central Asia to a small hunting cat from Trinidad. I often use Australian background and animals, and I work on accuracy.
    If I had another life to live it would be spent with animals; not to tame them, or to sentimentalize over them, nor to make them replicas of myself or improve their love-lives, but simply to understand them and, if I could, to compensate a little for the hideous things which man has done, and is doing, to them.
    I don't think I write especially for children, with the exception of a few books for small children. I just think of an idea and write the book in the best way I can.

*   *   *

    Though some of her early books are on other subjects, Mary Elwyn Patchett's main theme, and her best, is animal life. She makes an attempt to understand the natures of animals as themselves and not merely as adjuncts to human life. This sympathy, together with her concern for their often threatened lives and her intimate knowledge of their surroundings, gives her books vision and vigour. The movement and freedom of her writing, the independence of her characters, and their ability to deal with the unexpected and dangerous, could well be the inheritance from an Australian birth and an upbringing in the bush.

Her best book by most counts is *Tiger in the Dark*, a quest in the Australian interior for the supposedly extinct Australian marsupial tiger-wolf. A blind Aboriginal child serves as guide. *Roar of the Lion*, an African story, is about a boy's struggle to come to terms with the inevitable separation from his pet lioness cub when, at maturity, she must return to her life in the wild. In the Brumbies books, a series about wild horses in Australia, Joey Muhan tries, against great odds, to protect the brumbies from hunters and to build up a herd in a place where they can live in safety. The Ajax books describe the life of a girl on a cattle station in the Australian outback. *Quarter Horse Boy*, also a story of the outback, is about an Aboriginal boy's skill with horses and his affectionate adoption by the human family for whom he works.

Other books include *Farm Beneath the Sea*, which combines science fiction with facts about marine life and some evocative descriptions. The Dexter family, having undergone a lung operation to make them breathe like fish, descend a hundred feet below the surface of the Pacific among the "incredible blaze of multicolored corals. They looked almost lush in the way flowers do. The small fishey-life swarmed about them like bees around spring flowers." Here they live and set up an experimental attempt to farm the sea bed. A friendly dolphin helps. *Summer on Wild Horse Island* is, again, set beside the Great Barrier Reef among the sharks and barracudas.

—Nancy Shepherdson

PATERSON, Katherine (née Womeldorf). American. Born in Qing Jiang, China, 31 October 1932; came to the United States, 1940. Educated at King College, Bristol, Tennessee, 1950–54, A.B. (summa cum laude) 1954; Presbyterian School of Christian Education, Richmond, Virginia, 1955–57, M.A. 1957; Kobe School of the Japanese Language, Japan, 1957–59; Union Theological Seminary, New York, 1961–62, M.R.E. 1962. Married John Barstow Paterson in 1962; two sons and two adopted daughters. Teacher, Lovettsville Elementary School, Virginia, 1954–55; missionary, Presbyterian Church Board of World Missions, Shikoku Island, Japan, 1957–61; master of Sacred Studies and English, Pennington School for Boys, New Jersey, 1963–65. Recipient: National Book award, 1977, 1979; American Library Association Newbery Medal, 1978, 1981; Christopher award, 1979; University of Southern Mississippi award, 1983; University of Minnesota Kerlan award, 1983; Catholic Library Association Regina Medal, 1988. Litt.D.: King College, 1978; Saint Mary-of-the-Woods College, Indiana, 1981; University of Maryland, College Park, 1982; Washington and Lee University, Lexington, Virginia, 1982; D.H.L.: Otterbein College, Westerville, Ohio, 1980; Shenandoah College, Winchester, Virginia, 1986. Lives in Barre, Vermont. Address: c/o E.P. Dutton, 2 Park Avenue, New York, New York 10016, U.S.A.

PUBLICATIONS FOR CHILDREN

Fiction

The Sign of the Chrysanthemum, illustrated by Peter Landa.   New York, Crowell, 1973; London, Kestrel, 1975.

Of Nightingales That Weep, illustrated by Haru Wells.   New York, Crowell, 1974; London, Kestrel, 1976.
The Master Puppeteer, illustrated by Haru Wells.   New York, Crowell, 1975.
Bridge to Terabithia, illustrated by Donna Diamond.   New York, Crowell, 1977; London, Gollancz, 1978.
The Great Gilly Hopkins.   New York, Crowell, 1978; London, Gollancz, 1979.
Angels and Other Strangers: Family Christmas Stories.   New York, Crowell, 1979; as *Star of Night*, London, Gollancz, 1980.
Jacob Have I Loved.   New York, Crowell, 1980; London, Gollancz, 1981.
Rebels of the Heavenly Kingdom.   New York, Dutton, and London, Gollancz, 1983.
Come Sing, Jimmy Jo.   New York, Dutton, 1985; London, Gollancz, 1986.
Park's Quest.   New York, Dutton, 1988; London, Gollancz, 1989.

Other

Who Am I?, illustrated by David Stone.   Richmond, C.L.C. Press, 1966.
To Make Men Free: Learning Center Box.   Richmond, John Knox Press, 1973.
Justice for All People.   New York, Friendship Press, 1973.
Consider the Lilies: Plants of the Bible, with John Paterson, illustrated by Anne Ophelia Dowden.   New York, Crowell, 1986.

Translator, *The Crane Wife*, by Sumiko Yagawa, illustrated by Suekichi Akaba.   New York, Morrow, 1981.
Translator, *The Tongue-Cut Sparrow* (Japanese folktale), retold by Momoko Ishii, illustrated by Suekichi Akaba.   New York, Dutton, 1987.

PUBLICATIONS FOR ADULTS

Other

Gates of Excellence: On Reading and Writing Books for Children. New York, Elsevier Nelson, 1981.
The Spying Heart: More Thoughts on Reading and Writing Books for Children.   New York, Dutton, 1989.

*

Manuscript Collection: Kerlan Collection, University of Minnesota, Minneapolis.

Katherine Paterson comments:

My aim as a writer is to engage young readers in the life of a story that came out of me, but which is not mine, but ours. I don't just want my readers' time or attention, I want their lives. I want their senses, imagination, intellect, emotions, and all the experiences they have known breathing life into the words upon the page. I hope to do my part so well that young readers will delight to join me as co-authors.

* * *

The quest for the father—or the mother—is a recurrent theme and structural pattern in the novels of Katherine Paterson. Whether it is paramount or subordinate in any given story, whether its object is living or dead, a known presence or a fantasy, that quest infuses Paterson's stories with a metaphysical meaning, reflective of her values as well as providing her work with a principle of unity. A particular family, however impaired, provides a framework that anchors each novel in reality, simultaneously enabling meaning to transcend the limitations of historical time and cultural locale. In Paterson's fictions the bruised or broken family and the search for the father become milieu and metaphor for the archetypal heroic quest, the end of which, according to Joseph Campbell's theory of the monomyth, is that moment of spiritual enlightenment when the hero attains "transpersonal centeredness," that is, when he or she penetrates to the source of life, rises above the individual self, and achieves atonement (at-one-ment) with the universal will, a ubiquitous power out of which all things rise. Because the quest is an archetypal pattern, and because Paterson is adroit at fusing several levels of story, her novels are powerful dramas, never overtly didactic or sectarian, both eliciting and restraining heart-felt emotion.

The quest for the father is most overt in Paterson's first and latest novels, *The Sign of the Chrysanthemum* and *Park's Quest*. The protagonists of both books—the orphaned Muna in 12th-century Heiankyo (the Japanese for "City of Eternal Peace"), and the semi-orphaned Parkington Waddell Broughton V in post-Vietnam Washington, D.C.—deliberately set out to find their biological fathers of whom they know almost nothing. Through a painful passage each come to know a spiritual father-guide and protector, the sword maker Fukuji and Uncle Frank respectively.

The Master Puppeteer depicts two heroes, Jiro and Kinshi, who, though they know their biological fathers, struggle to reconcile in those parents, Hanji the puppet maker and Yoshida the puppeteer, their cruel, destructive facets with their humane, benificent qualities. *Bridge to Terabithia* subsumes the quest for the father in the theme of friendship that conquers death. Nonetheless, the parents of both Jesse Aarons and Leslie Burke and the relationships between them and their children are intrinsic to the story, and the revelation of the heretofore abstracted Mr. Aarons as a sympathetic guide and protector provides an image of a universal power who cares that children die and that others cannot comprehend why. Gilly Hopkins in *The Great Gilly Hopkins* has to surrender the vision of her biological mother as a true parent and to recognize "god" and "home" in the huge-lapped Maime Trotter, who loves the child as she is. Having achieved union with this mother-goddess, Gilly is able to return to the real world of her biological grandmother and, like Park and Louise, to give and accept love.

The dissolution of the families of both protagonists of *Rebels of the Heavenly Kingdom* calls forth Mei Lin and Wang Lee on their journeys. Mei Lin's father is the archetypal ogre who figuratively chews her up by selling her to the army for the soldiers' pleasure. Wang Lee's father is weak, can do nothing but stand by, helpless to prevent his son's enslavement. Finally, after the betrayal and slaughter of a war of zealotry, Mei Lin and Wang Lee marry, their union symbolizing that they have beheld the face of the Father, that is, they have attained a glimpse of a world united in justice and peace. Their vision is practically translated through their subsequent cultivation of the land and the raising of their male and female children as equals, both acts of healing of the "great angry wound[s] upon the flesh of the earth."

In *Of Nightingales That Weep* and *Come Sing, Jimmy Jo* the protagonists' search for the father is more involved, complicated in the former by the incorporation of a father figure and a bridegroom into the same character, and in the latter by the exigency of the protagonist's choice between his biological father and the stepfather who has raised him. In the Japanese historical romance, when the dwarf Goro marries Takiko's widowed mother, he invades the child's idyllic relationship with her mother and the memory of her hero father. For several turbulent years Takiko regards Goro, in turn, as misshapen monster, tolerable stepfather and mentor, then ogre-father whom she can neither conquer nor conciliate. Ultimately recognizing the "little god" in Goro, she realizes he is her love and heartsease. Thus, for Takiko, discovery of the father is one with finding a husband and becoming a mother. When James Johnson's quest in

Come Sing, Jimmy Jo discloses that the gentle Jerry Lee is not his biological father, the boy feels betrayed, abandoned. After James has courageously disavowed the cowardly, opportunistic Flem Keeser, he comes face to face with the mother-goddess figure, in this novel Grandma, who has come to take him to his family. James's decision to acknowledge Jerry Lee as his real father reflects his atonement (repentance for his self centeredness) and his at-one-ment with the father.

Setting serves many functions in the novels. The specific time in history and the actual geographical location, carefully researched and finely detailed, incite the protagonists' dreams and influence the kinds of persons they become. The famine of 1783–87 has reduced the populace of Osaka to bestial scavengers plundering and burning their city in *The Master Puppeteer*. The movement back and forth, in and out of the streets of Osaka and the disciplined world of the Hanaza, the theater compound, provides the novel with a structural framework, creates and controls the dramatic and emotional tension, and incorporates a major theme, that life and art reflect each other. *Bridge to Terabithia*, set in contemporary America, is more immediately about place—those special places that entice children into secret realms where they become kings and queens and heroic defenders against giants of evil—but the specific places are not so fully depicted as the Japanese city and country-scapes.

Setting also engenders major images and symbols knit smoothly into the pattern of each novel. The binding images of a novel often become symbols of the main characters and their relationships, as do fire and the sword in *The Sign of the Chrysanthemum*, the potter's clay and the koto Takiko plays in *Of Nightingales That Weep*, the songs the Johnson Family perform solo or in harmony in *Come Sing, Jimmy Jo*, and the coconut shell from which Park, Thanh, and the Grandfather drink the water in the springhouse in *Park's Quest*.

A significant source of additional images and symbols is literary allusion, a particularly distinctive characteristic of Paterson's narrative technique which serves also as a structural and thematic device. Allusions connect the stories of her humble characters with similar stories of more eminent figures and thus extend meaning beyond the individual toward the universal. Each of Paterson's nine novels is couched within references to other literary works—fairytales, Japanese and Biblical myth, heroic epic; poetry, drama, song lyrics. For the author, committed to both Christianity and to honest, unblinking confrontation of contemporary reality, literary allusion is particularly useful, for it permits the disclosure of authorial values without narrative commentary, an attribute appealing to a writer whose style is characteristically lean and who eschews didacticism in favor of the imaginative and emotional power of story.

In *Of Nightingales That Weep*, the epigraph from a No play suggests the archetypal theme that human love partakes of the divine in its power to transform the bestial into the beautiful. The novel affirms the verity of the epigraph, which states that the meeting of human hearts can change a "fragile dream of joy/Into the lasting love of waking life!" Subsequent novels are less romantic, more ironic, perhaps none more complex than *Jacob Have I Loved*, in which the controlling referents are the traditional Appalachian carol "I Wonder as I Wander" and the biblical account of God's preference for an apparently undeserving but favored younger twin. The meaning of the myth is explored, finally ironically overturned in its literal sense, and only ambiguously reaffirmed by an ending in which allusion and Paterson's fiction coalesce swiftly and brilliantly. In *Come Sing, Jimmy Jo* the song lyrics, which comprise the dominant allusions including "Keep on the Sunny Side," "Wayfaring Stranger," and "Will the Circle Be Unbroken?," are clues to the tensions and theme of the story: people are sojourners on earth, scourged by life's disjunctions, but journeying to a state of unity and bliss. The two paramount sources of allusion in *The Great Gilly Hopkins* are fairytales, including Tolkien's trilogy, and Wordsworth's "Intimations of Immortality." Both function primarily to accentuate the development of the protagonist and to articulate an age-old theme of the reconciliation of separate and isolated entities in an eternal synthesis.

More than any of its forerunners, *Park's Quest*, whose basic story pattern and theme are reminiscent of *The Great Gilly Hopkins*, seems more consciously shaped by its dominant referent, the exploits of the Arthurian Round Table, particularly Parzival's quest for the Holy Grail. In a final deft allusion to the Grail story, Paterson accomplishes what she does so often at the end of her stories. She draws together various levels of story, disparate images and themes, in a final consummate image so that fictional elements overlap, intertwine, and subtly take on the ambience of one another. Beyond this, the allusion with which each of Paterson's novels closes becomes an objective correlative of the protagonists' assent to the fundamental truth of the earlier literary work, despite the continual challenging and undercutting of that truth through out their fictions. Paterson's novels invariably end with such an allusion in scenes that symbolically reveal that their heroes, in beholding the face of the Father, have attained a glimpse of the source and meaning of life and have become ripe to understand, in Campbell's words, "how the sickening and insane tragedies of this vast and ruthless cosmos are completely validated in the majesty of Being."

Paterson's imagination has obviously been shaped by literature, notably by mythology and the Bible. It is natural, then, that her original and provocative stories reflect archetypal patterns amplified by meanings accrued to them in subsequent literary classics. For, as Campbell again reminds us, mythological figures that come down to us are "controlled and intended statements of certain spiritual principles." Paterson's finely crafted characters are some of the thousand faces of the archetypal hero.

—M. Sarah Smedman

PATON WALSH, Jill (Gillian Paton Walsh, née Bliss). British. Born in London, 29 April 1937. Educated at St. Michael's Convent, North Finchley, London, 1943–55; St. Anne's College, Oxford, 1955–59, Dip. Ed. 1959, M.A. (honours) in English. Married Antony Edmund Paton Walsh in 1961; one son and two daughters. English teacher, Enfield Girls Grammar School, Middlesex, 1959–62; Whittall Lecturer, Library of Congress, Washington, D.C., 1978. Visiting Faculty Member, Center for the Study of Children's Literature, Simmons College, Boston, 1978–86. Founder, with John Rowe Townsend, *q.v.*, Green Bay Publishers, 1986. Recipient: Whitbread award, 1974; Boston *Globe-Horn Book* award, 1976; Arts Council Creative Writing fellowship, 1976; Smarties prize, 1985. Address: 72 Water Lane, Histon, Cambridge CB4 4LR, England.

PUBLICATIONS FOR CHILDREN

Fiction

Hengest's Tale, illustrated by Janet Margrie. London, Macmillan, and New York, St. Martin's Press, 1966.
The Dolphin Crossing. London, Macmillan, and New York, St. Martin's Press, 1967.
Fireweed. London, Macmillan, 1969; New York, Farrar Straus, 1970.
Goldengrove. London, Macmillan, and New York, Farrar Straus, 1972.
Toolmaker, illustrated by Jeroo Roy. London, Heinemann, 1973; New York, Seabury Press, 1974.

The Dawnstone, illustrated by Mary Dinsdale. London, Hamish Hamilton, 1973.
The Emperor's Winding Sheet. London, Macmillan, and New York, Farrar Straus, 1974.
The Butty Boy, illustrated by Juliette Palmer. London, Macmillan, 1975; as *The Huffler*, New York, Farrar Straus, 1975.
Unleaving. London, Macmillan, and New York, Farrar Straus, 1976.
Children of the Fox. New York, Farrar Straus, 1978.
   Crossing to Salamis, illustrated by David Smee. London, Heinemann, 1977.
   The Walls of Athens, illustrated by David Smee. London, Heinemann, 1977.
   Persian Gold, illustrated by David Smee. London, Heinemann, 1978.
A Chance Child. London, Macmillan, and New York, Farrar Straus, 1978.
The Green Book, illustrated by Joanna Stubbs. London, Macmillan, 1981; New York, Farrar Straus, 1982.
Babylon, illustrated by Jenny Northway. London, Deutsch, 1982.
A Parcel of Patterns. London, Kestrel, and New York, Farrar Straus, 1983.
Lost and Found, illustrated by Mary Rayner. London, Deutsch, 1984.
Gaffer Samson's Luck, illustrated by Brock Cole. New York, Farrar Straus, 1984; London, Viking Kestrel, 1985.
Torch. London, Viking Kestrel, 1987; New York, Farrar Straus, 1988.
Birdy and the Ghosties, illustrated by Alan Marks. London, Macdonald, 1989.

Other

Wordhoard: Anglo-Saxon Stories, with Kevin Crossley-Holland. London, Macmillan, and New York, Farrar Straus, 1969.
The Island Sunrise: Prehistoric Britain. London, Deutsch, 1975; New York, Seabury Press, 1976.

PUBLICATIONS FOR ADULTS

Novels

Farewell, Great King. London, Macmillan, and New York, Coward McCann, 1972.
Lapsing. London, Weidenfeld and Nicolson, 1986; New York, St. Martin's Press, 1987.
A School for Lovers. London, Weidenfeld and Nicolson, 1989.

Short Stories

Five Tides. Cambridge, Green Bay, 1986.

*

Manuscript Collection: Kerlan Collection, University of Minnesota, Minneapolis.

Jill Paton Walsh comments:
I am a children's writer predominantly because of my personal tastes as a reader. I like plot—dreams of action—and I like simple methods of narration. My governing principle has always been to make whatever I am writing as plain and accessible as possible, not only to appeal to young readers, but to make my work as far as I can the sort of thing I like. My preferred subjects lie predominantly in

that large area of experience that children and adults have in common, though latterly, and as my own children grow older, I have begun to explore more adult material. The technical challenge of making adult statements that are transparent enough for children holds an inexhaustible challenge, however, so that although I may write more adult fiction, I never expect to cease working also for children.

* * *

For a writer of the highest quality (and it would not be appropriate to put her into any lower category) Jill Paton Walsh has been prolific. Her work also shows great diversity of subject and mood. Her dominant characteristic is integrity. When inspiration fails, one suspects, she stops writing. From her earliest books she shows a fierce pride in her craft and a deep respect for her readers.

After what one would hesitantly call a tentative start in *Hengest's Tale*, written soon after she gave up full-time teaching and bearing some marks of the classroom, she quickly found a characteristic style in two stories of World War II, *The Dolphin Crossing* about the evacuation from Dunkirk, and *Fireweed* about the London Blitz. In each she examined a major event of history through the reactions of two young people whose own lives and relationships are profoundly affected by their experiences.

Her instinct for a time of "The Breaking of Nations" led Paton Walsh to the most important of her early historical novels, *The Emperor's Winding Sheet*. The scene is Constantinople in the last days of the Byzantine Empire. Again the action is viewed through the eyes of a youth, an English boy who, by means which are in no way contrived, turns up in the city as it hardens itself for the siege. The Greeks call him Vrethiki because he is their "lucky find," and adopt him as a mascot whose presence will be a guarantee of success. Vrethiki accepts his role unwillingly, but in the days of the siege his timidity fades and his judgment of the heroes and cowards who make up the Emperor's forces becomes sounder. In the end he lays aside his English origins and finds that he too has a part to play in the final tragedy. There is no room for partisanship in the story. Greek and Turk are alike in having ideals; the clash of those different ideals brings disaster and destruction. Instead of identifying good and bad the reader discovers that nothing is simple.

A strong sense of time runs through Paton Walsh's work. It lies at the heart of two non-historical novels which are, for some readers, the most personal and moving of all her books. *Goldengrove* and *Unleaving* are linked novels separated by a number of years, in publication and in their action. Goldengrove is a house on the coast of Cornwall. It belongs to Gran, and every year Madge and Paul spend their summers there. This summer is different. Madge is conscious of her maturing body. Playing with Paul on the beach has, for her at least, developed some emotional undertones. Then there is Ralph, the blind scholar who is staying in Gran's cottage. Madge reads to him, uncomprehendingly from *Seven Types of Ambiguity*, happily from *Alice*, with acute distress from *Paradise Lost*. She has always assumed that one day she will marry Paul, but when she discovers that there is an unsurmountable obstacle to this, she turns to Ralph and is rejected. The bitterness turns to physical illness, from which she recovers to an acceptance that "some things were too late to put right." The story ends on this quiet note.

When the story begins again in *Unleaving* Madge is older, preparing for Oxford, and Gran is dead. The old lady has left Goldengrove to her, and the house is let to a reading party from the university. With her instinct for helping lame dogs Madge becomes involved with one of the students, who is finding it especially painful to make the transition from boy to man. As another student says shrewdly: "Madge doesn't need it [to think]. Her feelings lead her right." And in a way so it proves. In parallel with the main narrative there are strands of another story in which an unidentified Gran delights in

and learns from her grandchildren. Only in the last pages is it made clear that this is Madge 60 years on, in old age finding the key to the meaning of her life.

Whether these two books are children's books is a matter for (largely unprofitable) debate. They are beyond question books of the highest excellence in which the process of growing up is explored with fine sensitivity and in which, to a degree rare in this writer's work, the reader becomes deeply involved. The passage of time has not changed my initial opinion that in these books Paton Walsh's highest achievement is to be found.

She returned to more characteristic themes in a trilogy of historical novels, beginning with *Crossing to Salamis*, in which she examines the Greek contribution to civilisation. In a way this is also the theme of a very different story, *Torch*. This powerful and disturbing novel is set in a post-nuclear world. Industrial civilization has long ago been destroyed. The story opens in a village ruled by convention and half-understood traditions. Two young people, Cal and Dio, are about to enter into a marriage of their parents' convenience (it will amalgamate two pieces of land), and they must go to the ruined temple to seek the blessing of the Guardian. The Guardian is dying. He makes a reluctant Dio his heir, and dies before he can give the young man anything but the most inadequate instructions about his duties. Dio does as he has been told, finds an ancient torch and lights it from the rays of the sun. Then the couple, supported by a few friends, begin a journey through the mountains. By now the reader, in the wisdom of hindsight, has discovered that the scene is Greece, and that Cal and Dio (their full classical names are not hard to guess) have charge of the Olympic torch. Their task is to find places where the Olympic ideals are still honoured. Ceremonial Games are not lacking, in Corfu, North Africa and Provence, but the ideal has been submerged in ritual, crude population control, or the ultimate professionalism (in which the athletes have become pampered slaves). The torch flickers and dies. Then, when at last the travellers reach a depopulated and ruined Britain and run along the beach in a sudden excess of joy, the torch blazes again. The story is told with great power, its details are remarkably consistent, the conclusions are—against all the odds—curiously heartening.

This most astonishing piece of quasi-historical writing can be contrasted with *A Parcel of Patterns*, a story that adheres rigidly to historical fact. This is the story of Eyam, the Derbyshire village which, when the Plague struck in 1665, accepted voluntary isolation in order to check the spread of the disease to happier communities. The events have been fully documented and they are presented here with the minimum of invention. Virtually all the characters have real names, and it was the writer's task to clothe their long-dead bones with living flesh. An eyewitness, the young girl Mal Percival, a survivor, tells the story artlessly and movingly, varying the record of tragedy with moments of tenderness as well as greed and heartlessness. The story is heroic, but the actors are no heroes, just vulnerable humans in an intolerable dilemma.

Paton Walsh has always been the despair of those who like to put their authors into tidy packages. Among these stories of great events and crises of history comes *Gaffer Samson's Luck*, the story of a small boy in a small village, coping with problems which, by external standards, are trivial enough. James goes to live in a Fenland village which is all sky, flat fields, and brimming drains. Being neither "village" nor "estate" he has no part to play in local affairs. His only friend (unwanted) is another outcast, Angey who is "caravan" and scruffy. Then there is Gaffer Samson, an old man terminally ill, who helps James to see beauty and interest in the flat land. In hunting for Gaffer's "luck," a lost talisman, James learns to read the landscape and to find means to come to terms with the village. The simple story is told with rare beauty of style and with deep understanding. There are no heroes or villains, just a small community looked at affectionately and with candour. This is the slightest of Paton Walsh's books but by no means the least important. This is a writer who never wastes her rare talents, but who brings to each book the same professionalism, wisdom, and regard both for her craft and her public.

—Marcus Crouch

———

PATTEN, Brian. British. Born in Liverpool, Lancashire, 7 February 1946. Educated at Sefton Park Secondary School, Liverpool. Formerly reporter, *Bootle Times*, and editor, *Underdog*, both Liverpool. Regents Lecturer, University of California, San Diego, 1985. Recipient: Eric Gregory award, 1967; Arts Council grant, 1969; Mystery Writers of America special award, 1976. Agent: Anthony Sheil Associates Ltd., 43 Doughty Street, London WC1N 2LF. Address: c/o Penguin Books, 27 Wrights Lane, London W8 5TZ, England.

PUBLICATIONS FOR CHILDREN

Fiction

The Elephant and the Flower: Almost-Fables, illustrated by Meg Rutherford. London, Allen and Unwin, 1970.
Manchild. London, Covent Garden Press, 1973.
Two Stories. London, Covent Garden Press, 1973.
Mr. Moon's Last Case, illustrated by Mary Moore. London, Allen and Unwin, 1975; New York, Scribner, 1976.
Emma's Doll, illustrated by Mary Moore. London, Allen and Unwin, 1976.
Jimmy Tag-Along, illustrated by David Mostyn. London, Viking Kestrel, 1988.

Plays

The Pig and the Junkle (produced Nottingham, 1975; London, 1977).
The Sly Cormorant (produced London, 1977).
The Ghosts of Riddle Me Heights (produced Birmingham, 1980).
Gargling with Jelly, adaptation of his own poems (produced Hull, 1988).

Radio Play: *The Hypnotic Island*, 1977.

Television Plays: *The Man Who Hated Children*, 1978; *Mr. Moon's Last Case*, from his own story, 1983.

Verse

The Sly Cormorant and the Fishes: New Adaptations into Poetry of the Aesop Fables, illustrated by Errol Le Cain. London, Kestrel, 1977.
Gargling with Jelly, illustrated by David Martyn. London, Viking Kestrel, 1985.

Other

Jumping Mouse (American Indian tale), illustrated by Mary Moore. London, Allen and Unwin, 1972.

Editor, *Gangsters, Ghosts, and Dragonflies: A Book of Story Poems*, illustrated by Terry Oakes. London, Allen and Unwin, 1981.

PUBLICATIONS FOR ADULTS

Plays

Behind the Lines (revue), with Roger McGough (produced London, 1982).
The Mouthtrap, with Roger McGough (produced Edinburgh and London, 1982).

Radio Play: *Blind Love*, 1983.

Verse

Portraits. Privately printed, 1962.
The Mersey Sound: Penguin Modern Poets 10, with Adrian Henri and Roger McGough. London, Penguin, 1967; revised edition, 1974, 1983.
Little Johnny's Confession. London, Allen and Unwin, 1967; New York, Hill and Wang, 1968.
Atomic Adam. London, Fulham Gallery, 1967.
Notes to the Hurrying Man: Poems Winter '66-Summer '68. London, Allen and Unwin, and New York, Hill and Wang, 1969.
The Homecoming. London, Turret, 1969.
The Irrelevant Song. Frensham, Surrey, Sceptre Press, 1970.
Little Johnny's Foolish Invention: A Poem (bilingual edition), translated by Robert Sanesi. Milan, M'Arte, 1970.
Walking Out: The Early Poems of Brian Patten. Leicester, Transican, 1970.
At Four O'Clock in the Morning. Frensham, Surrey, Sceptre Press, 1971.
The Irrelevant Song and Other Poems. London, Allen and Unwin, 1971; revised edition, 1975.
When You Wake Tomorrow. London, Turret, 1971.
And Sometimes It Happens. London, Steam Press, 1972.
The Eminent Professors and the Nature of Poetry as Enacted Out by Members of the Poetry Seminar One Rainy Evening. London, Poem-of-the-Month Club, 1972.
Double Image, with Michael Baldwin and John Fairfax. London, Longman, 1972.
The Unreliable Nightingale. London, Rota, 1973.
Vanishing Trick. London, Allen and Unwin, 1976.
Grave Gossip. London, Allen and Unwin, 1979.
Love Poems. London, Allen and Unwin, 1981.
New Volume, with Adrian Henri and Roger McGough. London, Penguin, 1983.
Storm Damage. London, Unwin Hyman, 1988.

Recordings: *Selections from Little Johnny's Confession and Notes to the Hurrying Man and New Poems*, Caedmon, 1969; *Vanishing Trick*, Tangent, 1976; *The Sly Cormorant*, Argo, 1977; *Gifted Wreckage*, with Roger McGough and Adrian Henri, Talking Tape, 1984; *Jelly Pie*, with Roger McGough, Puffin, 1987.

Other

Editor, with Pat Krett, *The House That Jack Built: Poems for Shelter*. London, Allen and Unwin, 1973.
Editor, *Clare's Countryside: Natural History Poetry and Prose*, by John Clare. London, Heinemann, 1981.

*   *   *

Much of Brian Patten's verse is as accessible to children as to adults. The gentle tone, the air of approachability, the delicacy of his imagination are all contributory factors. So is the hard underlying muscle of thought and organisation contained in his best work:

something his art conceals by a deceptive and casual-seeming simplicity of manner.

Often, he presents a childlike, but never childish, view of town and city life. As with a child, the eye is not always entirely innocent. He gazes, with unwavering curiosity, at the minutiae of existence, and at its complexities and clichés. He reveals a sensibility profoundly aware of ever-present possibility of the magical and the miraculous, as well as of the granite-hard realities. He is a poet very much of his age, and writes in unintimidating present-day terms: important means, certainly, by which a child might first begin to recognize the poetry of the everyday and the apparently commonplace.

Each of his published books of "adult" verse yields something for the child. *Notes to the Hurrying Man* for example, includes the now celebrated fable "You'd Better Believe Him":

> Discovered an old rocking-horse in Woolworth's,
> He tried to feed it but without much luck
> So he stroked it, had a long conversation about
> The trees it came from, the attics it had visited.

There is the allegorical love-song that is at the same time the surface-story of a small dragon found nesting among the coal in a wood-shed:

> If you believed in it I would come
> hurrying to your house to let you share my wonder,
> but I want instead to see
> if you yourself will pass this way.

There are also such less-anthologised but equally effective pieces as "Bombscare," "Mr. Jones Takes Over," "The Necessary Slaughter." These are all undiluted poems, beautifully calculated, informed—even in their darkest moments—with courage and hope. Patten, uncompromisingly, goes all out for the poem, not the audience: and the rest follows. The publication of a selection, primarily for children, of his "adult" poems seems overdue.

The Elephant and the Flower, prose "almost-fables" for younger children, is more ambitious in scope: a mixture of sober realism and wild fancy on the alluring subject of the possible existence of parallel worlds. But as a prose writer Patten is at his best with the shorter piece. His retelling of a Plains Indian creation-myth, *Jumping Mouse*, is a small masterpiece: an authoritative realization of the complicated theme of the interrelationship of all earthly creatures. It has a compassionate simplicity, an inevitability of movement, and—particularly towards the close—a nobility of voice, and marks a creative writer unusually well-attuned to the imaginative needs of the child. Once received and absorbed, Patten's best work is something incapable of ever being entirely lost or discarded.

—Charles Causley

PAULSEN, Gary. American. Born in Minneapolis, Minnesota, 17 May 1939. Educated at Bemidji State University, Minnesota, 1957–58; University of Colorado, Boulder, 1976. Served in the United States Army, 1959–62. Married Ruth Ellen Wright in 1971 (second marriage); one son. Has worked as a teacher, electronics field engineer, actor, director, farmer, rancher, truck driver, trapper, professional archer, singer, and sailor. Lives in Becida, Minnesota. Agent: Jonathan Lazear, 430 First Avenue North, Suite 416, Minneapolis, Minnesota 55401, U.S.A.

PUBLICATIONS FOR CHILDREN

Fiction

Mr. Tucket, illustrated by Noel Sickles. New York, Funk and Wagnalls, 1969.
The C.B. Radio Caper, illustrated by John Asquith. Milwaukee, Raintree, 1977.
The Curse of the Cobra, illustrated by John Asquith. Milwaukee, Raintree, 1977.
The Foxman. Nashville, Nelson, 1977.
The Golden Stick, illustrated by Jerry Scott. Milwaukee, Raintree, 1977.
Tiltawhirl John. Nashville, Nelson, 1977.
Winterkill. Nashville, Nelson, and London, Abelard, 1977.
The Green Recruit, with Ray Peekner. Independence, Missouri, Independence Press, 1978.
Hope and a Hatchet. Nashville, Nelson, 1978.
The Night the White Deer Died. Nashville, Nelson, 1978.
The Spitball Gang. New York, Elsevier, 1980.
Dancing Carl. Scarsdale, New York, Bradbury Press, 1983.
Popcorn Days and Buttermilk Nights. New York, Dutton, 1983.
Tracker. New York, Bradbury Press, 1984.
Dogsong. New York, Bradbury Press, 1985.
Sentries. New York, Bradbury Press, 1986.
The Crossing. New York, Orchard, 1987.
Hatchett. New York, Bradbury Press, 1987; as *Hatchet*, London, Macmillan, 1989.
The Island. New York, Orchard, 1988.
The Voyage of the Frog. New York, Orchard, 1989.
The Winter Stories. New York, Orchard, 1989.

Other

Dribbling, Shooting, and Scoring Sometimes, photographs by Heinz Kluetmeier. Milwaukee, Raintree, 1976.
The Grass Eaters, illustrated by Kathy Goff. Milwaukee, Raintree, 1976.
Martin Luther King, The Man Who Climbed the Mountain, with Dan Theis. Milwaukee, Raintree, 1976.
The Small Ones, illustrated by Kathy Goff. Milwaukee, Raintree, 1976.
Careers in an Airport, photographs by Robert Nye. Milwaukee, Raintree, 1977.
Hitting, Pitching, and Running Maybe, photographs by Heinz Kluetmeier. Milwaukee, Raintree, 1977.
Riding, Roping, and Bulldogging—Almost, photographs by Heinz Kluetmeier. Milwaukee, Raintree, 1977.
Tackling, Running, and Kicking—Now and Again, photographs by Heinz Kluetmeier. Milwaukee, Raintree, 1977.
Forehanding and—Backhanding If You're Lucky, photographs by Heinz Kluetmeier. Chicago, Children's Press, 1978.
Hiking and Backpacking, with John Morris, illustrated by Ruth Wright. New York, Messner, 1978.
Running, Jumping, and Throwing—If You Can, photographs by Heinz Kluetmeier. Chicago, Children's Press, 1978.
Canoeing, Kayaking, and Rafting, with John Morris, illustrated by John Peterson and Jack Storholm. New York, Messner, 1979.
Downhill, Hotdogging, and Cross-Country—If the Snow Isn't Sticky, photographs by Heinz Kluetmeier and Willis Wood. Milwaukee, Raintree, 1979.
Facing Off, Checking, and Goaltending—Perhaps, photographs by Heinz Kluetmeier and Melchior DiGiacomo. Milwaukee, Raintree, 1979.
Going Very Fast in a Circle—If You Don't Run Out of Gas, photographs by Heinz Kluetmeier and Bob D'Olivo. Mil-

waukee, Raintree, 1979.

Launching, Floating High, and Landing—If Your Pilot Light Doesn't Go Out, photographs by Heinz Kluetmeier. Milwaukee, Raintree, 1979.

Pummeling, Falling, and Getting Up—Sometimes, photographs by Heinz Kluetmeier and Joe DiMaggio. Milwaukee, Raintree, 1979.

Track, Enduro, and Motocross—Unless You Fall Over, photographs by Heinz Kluetmeier. Milwaukee, Raintree, 1979.

Athletics, with Roger Barrett, photographs by Heinz Kluetmeier. Milwaukee, Macdonald, 1980.

Ice Hockey, with Roger Barrett, photographs by Heinz Kluetmeier and Melchior DiGiacomo. Milwaukee, Macdonald, 1980.

Motor-cycling, with Roger Barrett, photographs by Heinz Kluetmeier and others. Milwaukee, Macdonald, 1980.

Motor Racing, with Roger Barrett, photographs by Heinz Kluetmeier and Bob D'Olivo. Milwaukee, Macdonald, 1980.

Skiing, with Roger Barrett, photographs by Heinz Kluetmeier and Willis Wood. Milwaukee, Macdonald, 1980.

Tennis, with Roger Barrett, photographs by Heinz Kluetmeier. Milwaukee, Macdonald, 1980.

TV and Movie Animals, with Art Browne, Jr. New York, Messner, 1980.

Sailing, From Jibs to Jibing, illustrated by Ruth Wright Paulsen. New York, Messner, 1981.

PUBLICATIONS FOR ADULTS

Novels

The Death Specialists. New York, Major, 1976.
The Implosion Effect. New York, Major, 1976.
C.B. Jockey. New York, Major, 1977.
The Sweeper. New York, Raven, 1980.
Meteorite-Track 291. New York, Pinnacle, 1981.
Survival Guide. New York, Pinnacle, 1981.
Compkill. New York, Pinnacle, 1981.
Clutterkill. New York, Raven, 1981.
The Meatgrinder. New York, Raven, 1984.
Murphy. New York, Walker, and London, Hale, 1987.
Murphy's Gold. New York, Walker, 1988.
Night Rituals. New York, Fine, 1989.
The Madonna Stories. Minneapolis, Van Vliet, 1989.

Plays

Communications (produced New Mexico, 1974).
Together-Apart (produced Denver, 1976).

Other

The Special War, with Raymond Friday Locke. Los Angeles, Sirkay, 1966.
Some Birds Don't Fly. Chicago, Rand McNally, 1968.
The Building a New, Buying an Old, Remodeling a Used, Comprehensive Home and Shelter How-to-Do-It Book. Englewood Cliffs, New Jersey, Prentice Hall, 1976.
Farm: A History and Celebration of the American Farmer. Englewood Cliffs, New Jersey, Prentice Hall, 1977.
Successful Home Repair. Farmington, Michigan, Structures, 1978.
Money-Saving Home Repair Guide. Milwaukee, Ideals, 1981.

*   *   *

Gary Paulsen's recent books for early teens are all in a sense

survival stories. Some deal, in traditional fashion, with boys alone in the wilderness, living off the land. But Paulsen is also concerned for the survival of the human mind and spirit in a world of death and total war, and a civilization empty of meaning or compassion. His stories, though grim and sometimes brutally explicit, are ultimately hopeful. His young people do find help, from the old, from their own inner resources, or from a retreat from civilization into the natural world.

Paulsen writes in short, simple, highly charged sentences, and sentence fragments; rhythm and repetition often give his style the effect of poetry. ("It was as if she had been waiting for him, waiting for John, standing in the moonlight against the snow, waiting for him.") His books have the same tense, compressed quality; some seem more like short stories than novels, and this as well as style and rugged action links Paulsen with the Hemingway tradition. The most innovative in form, *Sentries*, intersperses the stories of four contemporary young people with accounts of three men left mentally and physically destroyed by the last three American wars. There is no explicit connection between the stories; in combination, however, they suggest that the four young people are "sentries" whose awakened perceptions and ability to love may help guard us from the next, and final war.

Paulsen's writing is strongly emotional; it is less their individuality than their intensity of feeling that keeps his characters alive. Given a naturally dramatic situation to work from, he can achieve real power; he is less successful with the events of ordinary life. In *Dancing Carl*, where he attempts to show how one strange, broken man can affect the lives of two small-town boys, he insists too much on the significance of the episode, and the effect is sentimental—an adult's nostalgic view of childhood. *The Crossing*, on the other hand, which also deals with the relationship between a boy and a broken war veteran, is a story that asks its own questions. Manny Bustos is a Mexican street boy, scrambling to stay alive and aware that unless he can somehow cross the border into the United States, he will sooner or later be captured and sold into prostitution. Sergeant Robert Locke is an alcoholic, drinking himself brain-dead in Mexican bars to forget Vietnam. Their meeting, their strange friendship, and what comes of it carry their own weight of meaning and feeling, with no need for comment or emphasis from the author.

Paulsen lives in Minnesota and has driven his own dog-team in the Iditarod, the 1049-mile race across Alaska. Much of his work has a distinctly northern flavor; in two Newbery Honor Books—*Dogsong* and *Hatchett*—boys come of age by learning to survive in northern wilderness. Russel, the Eskimo protagonist of *Dogsong*, feels a growing dissatisfaction with his people's modern ways and sets himself to learn bow hunting and dog driving from old Oogruk. In his long journey by dog-sled, he dreams himself back in time, a hunter of mammoths who drives a team of wolves. He becomes a part of his dogs and they part of him, and from all this grows the song that is for him alone—the "Dogsong" that ends the book. In *Dogsong* Paulsen conveys vividly both the practical reality and the spiritual quality of the far North.

Unlike Russel, 13-year-old Brian of *Hatchett* has no wise teacher or ancient cultural tradition to draw upon when his plane goes down in the forests of Canada, leaving only him alive. He is a child of our culture, and his ignorance of the natural world is abysmal. He does not even know what to call the plants and animals he sees; it is an effective touch that the omniscient narrator does not name them either, leaving the reader equally helpless. Brian's inability to come to grips mentally with his situation, his muddled thinking and lack of any useful skills make him one of the least qualified and most convincing Robinson Crusoes in literature. Yet he does learn eventually to find food, to make fire, to shoot with a bow, even to see the beauty around him. By the time he is rescued, Brian is permanently changed; he is far more observant and thoughtful, and knows what is really important in his life.

Both Russel and Brian survive not by "conquering" nature, but by becoming part of it. And both, in becoming part of it, become more aware and more truly themselves. They don't simply survive—they grow.

—Suzanne Rahn

PEACOCKE, Isabel Maud. New Zealander. Born in Auckland, in 1881. Educated privately. Married George Edward Cluett. Teacher, Dilworth School, Auckland, 10 years. Freelance writer and broadcaster: regular contributor to *New Zealand Herald*, Auckland. Founding member, later president, New Zealand Penwomen's Club. *Died in October 1973.*

PUBLICATIONS FOR CHILDREN

Fiction

My Friend Phil, illustrated by Margaret Tarrant. London, Ward Lock, and Chicago, Rand McNally, 1915.
Dicky, Knight-Errant, illustrated by Harold Copping. London, Ward Lock, 1916; New York, McBride, 1917.
Patricia-Pat. London, Ward Lock, 1917.
Robin of the Round House. London, Ward Lock, 1918.
The Misdoings of Micky and Mac. London, Ward Lock, 1919.
Piccaninnies, illustrated by Trevor Lloyd. Auckland, Whitcombe and Tombs, 1920.
The Sand Babies, illustrated by Trevor Lloyd. Auckland, Whitcombe and Tombs, 1921.
The Sand Playmates. Auckland, Whitcombe and Tombs, 1921.
Teenywiggles, illustrated by Gwyneth Richardson. Auckland, Whitcombe and Tombs, 1921.
Ginger. London, Ward Lock, 1921.
Quicksilver, illustrated by Harold Copping. London, Ward Lock, 1922.
The Adopted Family. London, Ward Lock, 1923.
Little Bit o' Sunshine. London, Ward Lock, 1924.
His Kid Brother. London, Ward Lock, 1926.
Brenda and the Babes. London, Ward Lock, 1927.
When I Was Seven. London, Ward Lock, 1927.
Tatters. London, Ward Lock, 1928.
The Runaway Princes. London, Ward Lock, 1929.
Haunted Island. London, Ward Lock, 1930.
The Dwarf of Dark Mountain. London, Ward Lock, 1931.
The Cruise of the Crazy Jane. London, Ward Lock, 1932.
The Guardians of Tony. London, Ward Lock, 1933.
Cathleen with a "C." London, Ward Lock, 1934.
Marjolaine. London, Ward Lock, 1935.
The Good Intentions of Angela. London, Ward Lock, 1937.
Lizbett Anne. London, Ward Lock, 1939.

Verse

Songs of the Happy Isles. Christchurch, Whitcombe and Tombs, 1910.
The Bonny Book of Humorous Verse, illustrated by Trevor Lloyd. Auckland, Whitcombe and Tombs, 2 vols., 1920.

Other

David Copperfield's Youth (based on the novel by Dickens). Auck-land, Whitcombe and Tombs, 1905(?).
The Boy Heroes of France (based on a novel by G.A. Henty). Auckland, Whitcombe and Tombs, 1921.

PUBLICATIONS FOR ADULTS

Novels

Cinderella's Suitors. London, Ward Lock, 1918.
The Guardian. London, Ward Lock, 1920.
Figs from Thistles. London, Ward Lock, 1921.
The House at Journey's End. London, Ward Lock, 1925.
Waif's Progress (as Isabel M. Cluett). London, Hodder and Stoughton, 1929.
April, May, June. London, Ward Lock, 1943.
Shadow Valley. London, Ward Lock, 1945.
London Called Them. London, Ward Lock, 1946.
Halcyon's Family. London, Ward Lock, 1947.
Deadly Nightshade. London, Ward Lock, 1948.
Rich Man's Ridge. London, Ward Lock, 1949.
Concerning the Marlows. London, Ward Lock, 1950.
No More Tears. London, Ward Lock, 1951.
The Little Tree. London, Ward Lock, 1952.
The Uncertain Lover. London, Ward Lock, 1953.
Incompatibles in Love. London, Ward Lock, 1955.
Change Partners. London, Ward Lock, 1955.

Other

Butterfingers; or, Green Fingers Gone Wrong: A Book for Disgruntled Gardeners. Wellington, Reed, 1945.

* * *

Isabel Maud Peacocke was one of New Zealand's most prolific writers. In addition to her adult novels she wrote over 20 full-length children's novels, two smaller fantasy stories, shortened versions of the classics for the popular Whitcombe's Story books, and numerous plays, poems, and newspaper articles. The quality of her children's books is variable—perhaps the best were written between *The Misdoings of Micky and Mac* (1919), in which she largely shed the sentimental style of her earlier novels, and 1928, after which many of the plots became repetitive.

Although she was the first teacher at the Anglican Dilworth School, which was established for boys from disadvantaged backgrounds, Peacocke made no attempt to use her experiences there as inspiration for the popular school stories of the period. Few of her books depict interaction between children; she was almost totally preoccupied with relationships between adult and child. In general her adults behave irresponsibly. A number of her books revolve round the problems of guardianship; others have parents who blatantly place their own interests before those of their child. *Little Bit o' Sunshine* and *His Kid Brother* show fathers who are on the wrong side of the law, but there are mothers, such as the singer in *The Adopted Family* and the writer in *Brenda and the Babes*, who abandon their children in pursuit of their art.

The overall message of her novels is that adults ought to know better. Her children, by contrast, are high-spirited but well-intentioned. Unlike those of their elders, their misdemeanours stem from unselfish motives coupled with inexperience of adult reactions. The twin heroes of *The Misdoings of Micky and Mac*, for instance, in a munificent gesture fill their uncle's room and pockets with beans in varying stages of preservation having taken literally his statement that he could not marry because he "hadn't the beans."

Living as she did in an affluent part of Auckland, she often shows the effects of snobbery. The main theme in *Quicksilver* and *Marjolaine* is the difficulty of association between children of differing social backgrounds, coming not from the children themselves but from the well-to-do parents. She also uses the opportunities presented to contrast differing types of education, clearly preferring the liberal to the authoritarian.

Undoubtedly her experience as a teacher ensured that her child characters were well-observed, but the view is an adult one: these are books for older sisters amused to see the gaucheries of the younger ones. Only in *The Cruise of the Crazy Jane* and *Cathleen with a "C"* does she give a convincing child's eye view through the first person narration of Cathleen.

The strengths of her books lie in their humour, their well-managed plots, and their strong sense of place. She is the only New Zealand writer to date to set a body of work in Auckland—the city which shelters one third of the entire population of the country. Not only the city centre but the different suburbs, the sea shore, and the flanking hills spring to life under her pen to provide a much needed local setting for the New Zealand reader.

—Betty Gilderdale

PEARCE, (Ann) Philippa. British. Born in Great Shelford, Cambridgeshire. Educated at Perse Girls' School, Cambridge, 1929–39; Girton College, Cambridge, B.A. (honours) in English and history 1942, M.A. Married Martin Christie in 1963 (died 1965); one daughter. Civil servant, 1942–45; scriptwriter and producer, 1945–58, and freelance producer, 1960–62, BBC Radio, London; assistant editor, Educational Department, Clarendon Press, Oxford, 1958–60; children's editor, André Deutsch Ltd., publishers, London, 1960–67. Freelance reviewer and lecturer. Recipient: Library Association Carnegie Medal, 1959; Whitbread award, 1978. Agent: Laura Cecil, 17 Alwyne Villas, London N1 2HG, England.

PUBLICATIONS FOR CHILDREN

Fiction

Minnow on the Say, illustrated by Edward Ardizzone. London, Oxford University Press, 1955; as *The Minnow Leads to Treasure*, Cleveland, World, 1958.
Tom's Midnight Garden, illustrated by Susan Einzig. London, Oxford University Press, and Philadelphia, Lippincott, 1958.
Still Jim and Silent Jim. Oxford, Blackwell, 1960.
Mrs. Cockle's Cat, illustrated by Antony Maitland. London, Constable, 1961; Philadelphia, Lippincott, 1962.
A Dog So Small, illustrated by Antony Maitland. London, Constable, 1962; Philadelphia, Lippincott, 1963.
The Strange Sunflower, illustrated by Kathleen Williams. London, Nelson, 1966.
The Children of the House, with Brian Fairfax-Lucy, illustrated by John Sergeant. London, Longman, and Philadelphia, Lippincott, 1968; as *The Children of Charlecote*, London, Gollancz, 1989.
The Elm Street Lot, illustrated by Mina Martinez. London, BBC Publications, 1969; augmented edition, London, Kestrel, 1979.
The Squirrel Wife, illustrated by Derek Collard. London, Longman, 1971; New York, Crowell, 1972.
What the Neighbours Did and Other Stories, illustrated by Faith Jaques. London, Longman, 1972; New York, Crowell, 1973.
The Shadow-Cage and Other Tales of the Supernatural, illustrated

by Janet Archer. London, Kestrel, and New York, Crowell, 1977.
The Battle of Bubble and Squeak, illustrated by Alan Baker. London, Deutsch, 1978.
The Way to Sattin Shore, illustrated by Charlotte Voake. London, Kestrel, and New York, Greenwillow, 1983.
Lion at School and Other Stories, illustrated by Caroline Sharpe. London, Viking Kestrel, 1985; New York, Greenwillow, 1986.
Who's Afraid and Other Strange Stories, illustrated by Peter Melnyczuk. London, Viking Kestrel, 1986; New York, Greenwillow, 1987.
Emily's Own Elephant, illustrated by John Lawrence. London, MacRae, 1987; New York, Greenwillow, 1988.
The Tooth Ball, illustrated by Helen Ganly. London, Deutsch, 1987.
Freddy, illustrated by David Armitage. London, Deutsch, 1988.
Old Belle's Summer Holiday, illustrated by William Geldart. London, Deutsch, 1989.

Other

Beauty and the Beast, illustrated by Alan Barrett. London, Longman, and New York, Crowell, 1972.
Wings of Courage (adaptation), by George Sand, illustrated by Hilary Abrahams. London, Kestrel, 1982.

Editor, *Stories from Hans Christian Andersen*, illustrated by Pauline Baynes. London, Collins, 1972.

*   *   *

Philippa Pearce began to write in her mid-thirties, when she was convalescing after tuberculosis, and her mind went back to the countryside in which she had spent her childhood. Her father was a flour-miller at Great Shelford, Cambridgeshire, and the family was brought up in the mill-house, whose garden ran down to the river. She and her sister and brothers swam and fished in the Cam, and had an old canoe on it. The first result of these recollections was *Minnow on the Say*, a repainting of her childhood scene in the form of an adventure story of the type then fashionable—two boys (of somewhat different social classes), a canoe on the river, and a treasure-hunt whose outcome changes the life of one of the boys. The book now seems rather conventional and contrived, but at the time it was widely praised for its freshness. In retrospect, one may see that it gave Pearce great confidence in the handling of landscape. The waterside setting of Great Barley (Great Shelford) is lovingly recreated, and Pearce was to draw on the same landscape, with its surrounding fens and market towns, in subsequent books—to the extent that she creates a country of the mind, an invented world that is richer with meaning than the "real" East Anglia.

Minnow on the Say was a runner-up for the Carnegie Medal. Pearce's next book, *Tom's Midnight Garden*, won that medal. It would have been outrageous if it hadn't; the book is one of the finest pieces of writing for children produced since World War II, a classic in the front rank of children's literature. The setting is the same imaginary part of East Anglia; Tom, bored and lonely, is staying with a childless aunt and uncle in a flat which is part of what was once a fine country house. Unable to sleep because of the rich food his doting aunt forces on him, he finds that at night the house—or, more precisely, the garden—reverts to its former existence; and in the garden he meets Hatty, one of the Victorian children who once lived there. Night after night he and Hatty play their games and talk together, and Tom becomes deeply involved with her. But—and this is what lifts the book above ordinary fantasy—time is not standing still in this night-existence. Hatty is growing up, all too fast, and Tom cannot come to terms with this. The book's ending is both painful and exhilarating; its achievement is to combine a richly imaginative story with the profoundly serious "message" that children *must* grow up. *Tom's Midnight Garden* is, in fact, a reply to *Peter Pan*.

No author would be likely to write a better book than this, and Pearce hasn't. *A Dog So Small* consolidated her reputation, with its delicately constructed account of Ben Blewitt (a child as bored and lonely as Tom) and his fantasy-companion, "a dog so small you could see it only with your eyes shut." The book recapitulated the theme (found in both *Minnow on the Say* and *Tom's Midnight Garden*) of the relationship between childhood and old age, and showed how the solitary child's creation of a fantasy world can be both enriching and destructive. Following the writing of it, Pearce went into a somewhat fallow period in her career, producing the texts for a few unremarkable picture books, and collaborating with Major Sir Brian Fairfax-Lucy on *The Children of the House*, a novel about four children growing up in a great house before World War I (she rewrote his original text, which had been intended for adults). Not until 1969 did she produce another major book of her own. This was *The Elm Street Lot*, a collection of short stories about a working-class street and its children. *What the Neighbours Did and Other Stories* is in the same vein: a set of short stories about children's everyday experiences, as perceived through their own eyes. After this there was a five-year gap until *The Shadow-Cage and Other Tales of the Supernatural*, a set of children's ghost stories. Then in 1978 came Pearce's first full-length novel since *A Dog So Small*: *The Battle of Bubble and Squeak*, which describes a family's squabbles over a pair of gerbils. The style of writing in these later books is restrained, with a careful avoidance of melodrama, much in the manner of William Mayne. Pearce has been praised because, as one reviewer put it, she has "deliberately dispensed with all the usual props of children's fiction and has limited herself to the severest realism."

After another five-year gap Pearce began publishing a steady stream of books, including two collections of short stories, some quirky picture books, and the acclaimed *The Way to Sattin Shore*. With the latter she has returned to her earlier form of telling an emotionally powerful and satisfying story, at the same time retaining the clear, restrained style of the later books. The story focuses on 10-year-old Kate, who lives with her mother, grandmother, and brothers, and whose father presumably was drowned on the day Kate was born. The mystery surrounding his death unfolds gradually, and the mounting tension is skilfully reflected in Kate's relationships with her brothers and grandmother. The plot twists to a gripping conclusion, and reveals Pearce once again as a first-rate writer.

—Humphrey Carpenter and George Walsh

PEASE, Howard. American. Born in Stockton, California, 6 September 1894. Educated at Stanford University, California, A.B. 1923. Served in the American Expeditionary Forces at Base Hospital 3, France, 1918–19. Married 1) Pauline Nott in 1927 (died), one son; 2) Rossie Ferrier in 1956. Merchant seaman, early 1920's; teacher in public and private schools, California, 1924–25, 1928–34; Instructor in English, Vassar College, Poughkeepsie, New York, 1926–27. Recipient: Child Study Committee award, 1947. *Died 14 April 1974.*

PUBLICATIONS FOR CHILDREN

Fiction

The Tattooed Man, illustrated by Mahlon Blaine. New York, Doubleday, and London, Heinemann, 1926.

The Jinx Ship, illustrated by Mahlon Blaine. New York, Doubleday, and London, Heinemann, 1927.

Shanghai Passage, illustrated by Paul Forster. New York, Doubleday, 1929.

The Gypsy Caravan, illustrated by Harrie Wood. New York, Doubleday, 1930.

Secret Cargo, illustrated by Paul Forster. New York, Doubleday, 1931.

The Ship Without a Crew. New York, Doubleday, 1934.

Wind in the Rigging. New York, Doubleday, 1935.

Hurricane Weather. New York, Doubleday, 1936.

Foghorns, illustrated by Anton Otto Fischer. New York, Doubleday, 1937.

Captain Binnacle, illustrated by Charles E. Pont. New York, Dodd Mead, 1938; London, Harrap, 1939.

Jungle River, illustrated by Armstrong Sperry. New York, Doubleday, 1938.

Highroad to Adventure, illustrated by Frank Dobias. New York, Doubleday, 1939.

Long Wharf. New York, Doubleday, 1939.

The Black Tanker. New York, Doubleday, 1941.

Night Boat and Other Tod Moran Mysteries. New York, Doubleday, 1942.

Thunderbolt House, illustrated by Armstrong Sperry. New York, Doubleday, 1944.

Heart of Danger. New York, Doubleday, 1946.

Bound for Singapore. New York, Doubleday, 1948.

The Dark Adventure. New York, Doubleday, 1950.

Captain of the "Araby." New York, Doubleday, 1953.

Shipwreck. New York, Doubleday, 1957.

Mystery on Telegraph Hill. New York, Doubleday, 1961.

*   *   *

Howard Pease's World War I service in France as well as his merchant marine experience in the Pacific provided him with first hand experiences with adventure. He translated a love of travel and fascination with intrigue into over 20 mysteries featuring, and aimed at, young men. Pease's plots are predictable only in terms of their surprise turns; his characters are persons with real feelings and real abilities at solving curious human problems.

The Tod Moran mysteries consist of over a dozen titles, from *The Tattooed Man* (1926) to *Mystery on Telegraph Hill* (1961). Tod Moran, Third Mate, has an enviable career on trading vessels which go across the Pacific as far as Manila and Hong Kong. Tod is a young lad who keeps his cool in the face of typhoons and earthquakes, murder and deception in faraway places. Even on a simple overnight vacation voyage out of San Francisco Bay, though, he finds strange events to pique his interest and stir him into action for the cause of social order.

Typical of Pease's sea tales is *Secret Cargo*, a story about Larry Mathews, a poor boy who sets off to earn his own living somehow. He ships out from New Orleans on an old trading vessel bound for the South Seas. There is a death on board which Larry believes is not accidental; he then goes about solving the mystery of what was actually a murder. *Jungle River* features Don Carter who travels into the New Guinea jungle in search of his father, lost in an airplane accident.

Pease's writing is swift and concise. His characters, whether from industrial United States or primitive jungle societies, are carefully drawn, and interactions between peoples of different cultures—such as American plantation owners and Philippine laborers, American soldiers and Japanese captors—show understanding of human groups and human needs. The author was at ease writing about major North and South American ports and cities and a wide variety of

Pacific Islands under colonial rules. He carried into the 20th century the American boy's dreams of independence and opportunity, which are satisfied primarily in unusual places doing unusual things, all for the cause of human justice. Fantasy, yes. Capital fantasy.

—Mary Lystad

PECK, Richard (Wayne). American. Born in Decatur, Illinois, 5 April 1934. Educated at De Pauw University, Greencastle, Indiana, 1952–56, B.A. 1956; University of Exeter, Devon, 1954–55; Southern Illinois University, Carbondale, M.A. 1959; Washington University, St. Louis, 1960–61. Served in the United States Army in Germany, 1956–58. Instructor, Southern Illinois University, Carbondale, 1958–60; high school English teacher, Northbrook, Illinois, 1961–63; textbook editor, Scott Foresman, Chicago, 1963–65; Instructor in English and Education, Hunter College and Hunter High School, New York, 1965–71; assistant director, Council for Basic Education, Washington, D.C., 1969–70. Recipient: Mystery Writers of America Edgar Allan Poe award, 1977. Agent: Sheldon Fogelman, 155 East 72nd Street, New York, New York, 10021, U.S.A.

PUBLICATIONS FOR CHILDREN

Fiction

Don't Look and It Won't Hurt. New York, Holt Rinehart, 1972.
Dreamland Lake. New York, Holt Rinehart, 1973.
Through a Brief Darkness. New York, Viking Press, 1973; London, Collins, 1976.
Representing Super Doll. New York, Viking Press, 1974.
The Ghost Belonged to Me. New York, Viking Press, 1975; London, Collins, 1977.
Are You in the House Alone? New York, Viking Press, 1976; London, Pan, 1986.
Monster Night at Grandma's House, illustrated by Don Freeman. New York, Viking Press, 1977.
Ghosts I Have Been. New York, Viking Press, 1977.
Father Figure. New York, Viking Press, 1978.
Secrets of the Shopping Mall. New York, Delacorte Press, 1979.
Close Enough to Touch. New York, Delacorte Press, 1981.
The Dreadful Future of Blossom Culp. New York, Delacorte Press, 1983.
Remembering the Good Times. New York, Delacorte Press, 1985.
Blossom Culp and the Sleep of Death. New York, Delacorte Press, 1986.
Princess Ashley. New York, Delacorte Press, 1987.
Those Summer Girls I Never Met. New York, Delacorte Press, 1988.

Other

The Creative Word 2, with Stephen N. Judy. New York, Random House, 1973.

Editor, *Urban Studies: A Research Paper Casebook.* New York, Random House, 1974.
Editor, *Transitions: A Literary Paper Casebook.* New York, Random House, 1974.
Editor, *Pictures That Storm Inside My Head* (poetry anthology). New York, Avon, 1976.

PUBLICATIONS FOR ADULTS

Novels

Amanda/Miranda. New York, Viking Press, and London, Gollancz, 1980.
New York Time. New York, Delacorte Press, and London, Gollancz, 1981.
This Family of Women. New York, Delacorte Press, and London, Gollancz, 1983.

Other

A Consumer's Guide to Educational Innovations, with Mortimer Smith and George Weber. Washington, D.C., Council for Basic Education, 1972.

Editor, with Ned E. Hoopes, *Edge of Awareness: Twenty-Five Contemporary Essays.* New York, Dell, 1966.
Editor, *Sounds and Silences: Poetry for Now.* New York, Delacorte Press, 1970.
Editor, *Mindscapes: Poems for the Real World.* New York, Delacorte Press, 1971.
Editor, *Leap into Reality: Essays for Now.* New York, Dell, 1973.

*

Richard Peck comments:

The focus of my books is to introduce younger adolescents to the reading of fiction and contemporary poetry. Though the themes of my novels are meant to be serious reflections of adolescents' concerns, I try to write in forms popular with them: comedy, melodrama, wish-fulfillment, the supernatural, and mystery.

*   *   *

Richard Peck has said, "A young adult novel is the chronicle of one step in a young character's climb to maturity. It can be comic, tragic, and often faltering, but it is always a step up." Peck's interest in adolescents and his understanding of those steps which they must climb is shown through books whose themes touch young people closely—friendship, loneliness, relationships with peers and with family. His work shows a concern that young people find a sense of belonging, and that they should not feel alone at times when they must cope with problems that threaten to overwhelm them: the death of a friend or parent, rape, an unwanted pregnancy. At the same time, Peck's protagonists are adolescents who are, or come to be, independent of the crowd, who learn to be responsible and to have respect for self and others.

He writes *for* the adolescent knowing that they also enjoy humor, the supernatural, and the melodramatic as well as contemporary realistic novels. He extends their horizons by including in his books protagonists who venture from home on journeys of independence, and characters (sometimes ghosts) who have connections with the past. In his books adolescents meet a wealth of diverse characters ranging from perceptive and witty elderly people to love-sick teachers. Peck is adept at sketching a character in a few lines. Many of his secondary characters are parents: a father scarred by his experience of Vietnam, an overbearing snobby mother pushing her daughter toward being a "Super Doll," parents who have opted out from the lives of their teenagers, and parents who are often themselves alone, and who try single-handedly to understand and support their teenagers.

Peck writes sensitively about the emotions of boys and their relationships. When in *Father Figure* Jim Atwater's mother commits suicide, Jim is left fending off feelings of guilt, and describes his pent-eelings and following events in a glib tone, as if from a long dista Left in the care of an elderly, sympathetic, though emotionally int grandmother, Jim takes responsibility for his younger broth However, when it is arranged that he and Byron join their fathe finds that his buried resentment at his father's leaving the fami ght years before causes him to feel anger and jealousy over the b that grows between Byron and their father.

Fa and son relationships are prominent in several of Peck's nove *Remembering the Good Times* Buck adjusts to his parents' divo nd makes the decision to live with his father; their easy-goin ng relationship is contrasted to the distant relationship betw Trav and his parents. Remembering how the close frieno grew between himself, Trav, and Kate, all from very differ backgrounds, Buck in his narrative leads up to Trav's suicidrav, driven by an inner despair, withdraws from his friends and pts, and not until it is too late do his friends realize the depth of hi hdrawal, and the signals he was giving out to them. Peck offer: easy solution to the problem of teenage suicide. It is a probl he implies, that concerns everyone. The novel is a story of teena olation, a lack of communication, and the loss of roots, but it als out love and friendship and moving forward with hope.

In se *Enough to Touch* Matt's father is understanding and suppe when Matt is overwhelmed by grief on the death of his girlfr Dory. It is Margaret, a girl who is not afraid to be different who lly helps Matt free himself from self-pity. Peck writes sensiy about Matt's emotions and growing love for Margaret.

In ater vein, Peck provides humor in the plight of 16-year-old Drew hose *Summer Girls I Never Met*. It is not with delight that Drew ks forward to a Baltic cruise with his sister Steph—a 14-ydd "pain"—and their unknown grandmother, when his plans included a driving licence and "maybe even girls." Their grancher, "the Sweetheart of Swingtime" who is on the cruise for hst performance, is another of Peck's singular, clear-eyed elderlaracters who seem to understand young people intuitively. But Dis perceptive too, and is able to gauge the changes in Steph and lelf that summer as they grow to love and respect their grancher, to learn bittersweet truths about their grandmother and familationships and the reason for their grandmother's invitation.

Hu and the supernatural are deliciously blended in Peck's four Bloss Culp books, whose setting is Bluff City, U.S.A., 1913 and 1914. incomparable, spunky Blossom Culp who carefully distingui herself from the popular, beautiful, and wealthy people aroun r and who goes by rules of her own is first seen through the eyf Alexander Armsworth in *The Ghost Belonged to Me*. Alexa, always seemingly reluctant to spend company either with ghost with Blossom, is nonetheless irresistibly caught up with the g ith the skinniest legs ever seen, who lives in a two-room dwell just "over the streetcar tracks" from the Armsworths' substa home. Alexander's "receptiveness" to the spirit world invol im with the ghost of young Inez Dumaine who lies buried on the nsworth property.

The velopment of Blossom's "gift" in *Ghosts I Have Been* involv oth Blossom and Alexander in a series of adventures into the suatural world of haunts in both the latter title and the other Bloss Culp books. Peck's ghosts however are not blurred spectral being t distinct individuals, examples of his deftly drawn character aits. In solving their problems, Alexander and Blossom travel aces far from Bluff City both in the present and in the past.

Bla is one of several strong, adolescent female characters in Peck' els. The author portrays intelligent, resourceful girls, who are w g and able to make their own decisions and take on respo ities, sometimes for others. In *Don't Look and It Won't Hurt* (, the dependable middle sister, takes on the responsibility of vis her sister who is waiting for the birth of her baby, and persu her give the baby up. Carol in effect takes her parents'

place in showing love and care to both her sisters.

Gail in *Are You in the House Alone?* also has a painful decision to make when she is raped by the disturbed son of a prominent family in town—whether to stand up in a courtroom and risk losing and feeling "raped" again, in a situation where the law protects the offender and not the victim. Although Gail does not testify, she is strong enough not to run away from the problem and thinks clearly through her options, realizing her own responsibility and that of others in protecting others.

In *Representing Super Doll* Peck contrasts the independent Verna, the warmth and love of her family, and her mother's knowledge that Verna must "learn to make [her] own way," with Darlene who, manipulated and exploited by her mother, is made into a "Teen Super Doll."

Relationships between mothers and daughters are a common theme in many of Peck's books. In *Princess Ashley* Chelsea distances herself from her mother as much as possible until a tragic event brings her to value her mother's work as a guidance counselor. It is also a novel about peer pressure and friendship, as Chelsea works out her own values.

Peck writes with understanding about the emotions and relationships of adolescents. Using humor, a variety of well-drawn characters, and his knowledge of what young people like to read, Peck creates entertaining books that appeal to both sexes.

—Hilary S. Crew

PECK, Robert Newton. American. Born in Vermont, 17 February 1928. Educated at Rollins College, Winter Park, Florida, B.A. 1953. Served in the 88th Infantry Division, United States Army, 1945–47. Married Dorothy Houston in 1958; one son and one daughter. Formerly, lumberjack, paper mill worker, hog killer; advertising executive. Since 1978 director, Rollins College Writers Conference. Writer of songs and television commercials and jingles. Recipient: *Media and Methods* award, 1975. Address: 500 Sweetwater Club Circle, Longwood, Florida 32779, U.S.A.

PUBLICATIONS FOR CHILDREN

Fiction

A Day No Pigs Would Die. New York, Knopf, 1972; London, Hutchinson, 1973.
Millie's Boy. New York, Knopf, 1973.
Soup, illustrated by Charles Gehm. New York, Knopf, 1974.
Soup and Me, illustrated by Charles Lilly. New York, Knopf, 1975.
Wild Cat, illustrated by Hal Frenck. New York, Holiday House, 1975.
I Am the King of Kazoo, illustrated by William Bryan Park. New York, Knopf, 1976.
Rabbits and Redcoats, illustrated by Laura Lydecker. New York, Walker, 1976.
Hamilton, illustrated by Laura Lydecker. Boston, Little Brown, 1976.
Hang for Treason. New York, Doubleday, 1976.
Last Sunday, illustrated by Ben Stahl. New York, Doubleday, 1977.
Trig, illustrated by Pamela Johnson. Boston, Little Brown, 1977.
Patooie, illustrated by Ted Lewin. New York, Knopf, 1977.
Soup for President, illustrated by Ted Lewin. New York, Knopf, 1978.
Trig Sees Red, illustrated by Pamela Johnson. Boston, Little

Brown, 1978.

Basket Case. New York, Doubleday, 1979.

Hub, illustrated by Ted Lewin. New York, Knopf, 1979.

Mr. Little, illustrated by Ben Stahl. New York, Doubleday, 1979.

Clunie. New York, Knopf, 1979.

Soup's Drum, illustrated by Charles Robinson. New York, Knopf, 1980.

Trig Goes Ape, illustrated by Pamela Johnson. Boston, Little Brown, 1980.

Soup on Wheels, illustrated by Charles Robinson. New York, Knopf, 1981.

Kirk's Law. New York, Doubleday, 1981.

Justice Lion. Boston, Little Brown, 1981.

Trig or Treat, illustrated by Pamela Johnson. Boston, Little Brown, 1982.

Banjo, illustrated by Andrew Glass. New York, Knopf, 1982.

Soup in the Saddle, illustrated by Charles Robinson. New York, Knopf, 1983.

Soup's Goat, illustrated by Charles Robinson. New York, Knopf, 1984.

Dukes. Englewood, Florida, Pineapple Press, 1984.

Soup on Ice, illustrated by Charles Robinson. New York, Knopf, 1985.

Jo Silver. Englewood, Florida, Pineapple Press, 1985.

Spanish Hoof. New York, Knopf, 1985.

Soup on Fire, illustrated by Charles Robinson. New York, Delacorte Press, 1987.

Soup's Uncle, illustrated by Charles Robinson. New York, Delacorte Press, 1988.

Arly. New York, Walker, 1989.

Soup's Hoop, illustrated by Charles Robinson. New York, Delacorte Press, 1989.

Play

King of Kazoo, music and lyrics by Peck, illustrated by William Bryan Park. New York, Knopf, 1976.

Verse

Bee Tree and Other Stuff, illustrated by Laura Lydecker. New York, Walker, 1975.

Other

Path of Hunters: Animal Struggle in a Meadow, illustrated by Betty Fraser. New York, Knopf, 1973; London, Macdonald and Jane's, 1974.

PUBLICATIONS FOR ADULTS

Novels

The Happy Sadist. New York, Doubleday, 1962.

Fawn. Boston, Little Brown, 1975.

The King's Iron. Boston, Little Brown, 1977.

Eagle Fur. New York, Knopf, 1978.

The Seminole Seed. Englewood, Florida, Pineapple Press, 1983.

Hallapoosa. New York, Walker, 1988.

The Horse Hunters. New York, Random House, 1988.

Other

Secrets of Successful Fiction. Cincinnati, Writer's Digest, 1980.

Fiction Is Folks: How to Create Unforgettable Characters.

Cincinnati, Writer's Digest, 1983.

My Vermont. Englewood, Florida, Peck Press, 2 vols., 1987.

*

Robert Newton Peck comments:

I want kids to know that pork chops are not made by DuPout of soybeans. Pigs are killed because man is a predator; all of ire is predatory…even a carrot.

In my books, authority figures (parents, teachers, etc.) are ng and kind and respected by the kids in the story…as Soup I revered Miss Kelly.

*   *   *

Robert Newton Peck is a talented and prolific writer)se success seems to be undermining his craftsmanship. His firnd unquestionably best, book is *A Day No Pigs Would Di* his episodic, autobiographical novel of a crucial year in a Vermorm boy's life is wrapped firmly around the central theme of the ron-ship between father and son. The language of the book is collal, the tone is warm and often humorous, yet the story deals whe fundamentals of life and death, growth and change, love and In his 13th year, Rob Peck acquires and loses his first pet, a pigch proves barren and must be slaughtered, since a Vermont farm aed for no such luxury as an entirely useless animal, however bed. In the same year, Rob also comes to understand better the fa he loves, and loses him, too, to death. The two strands of stare wound together skillfully; the apparently casual structure of tbok builds to a strong climax.

Peck has returned to the father-son theme in several subent books (*Fawn, Hang for Treason, Millie's Boy*). All of the noare basically tragic, all are punctuated with episodes of violence, ally described in savage detail. With each of his serious novels, act, Peck's preoccupation with physical violence looms larger, so does a certain immaturity of attitude. *Hang for Treason* ifair example. This novel of early Revolutionary days in Vermhas strengths: a good sense of place, a few strong characterizatiand some powerful scenes—like the hanging at Fort Ticonderoghat stay in the mind. Yet the book as a whole is marred by graus, detailed descriptions of extreme violence, and by the adcent lasciviousness of Peck's treatment of sexuality. The colloquiyle, which worked well in *Pigs*, is pushed beyond reasonable ls in *Treason.* In an effort to create the sense of 18th-century rural ch, Peck has taken to using nouns as verbs (to "fist" a man, to l" a cow), an affectation that palls quickly.

Some of Peck's work descends to plain bad. *Clunie*, the ı of a retarded girl, her tormenters, and her lone defender, is ally simplistic. The book raises troubling, complex questicbut provides only sentimental answers. *Kirk's Law* is contrived, ow, and wholly unbelievable, made more annoying by an artificyle and the author's straining after significance.

A more recent story, *Spanish Hoof*, is dedicated to "the hark-ing woman of America, who, often without a husband, raiab-bages, calves, and children." The major protagonists are moand daughter. Like *Pigs* this short novel is set in the depressiothe 1930's and takes as its theme a child's passage from the depnce of childhood to the responsibilities of adult life. The atmosphere is gentler than in any of Peck's father-son novels, but the shas little of the emotional impact of *Pigs*. Peck divides his cters neatly into good and bad, and again succumbs to the tempn to provide sentimental solutions to hard problems.

Peck also writes some light-hearted, humorous books fang children. Of these, the most successful are the Soup storietich are cheerful, funny reminiscences, somewhat embroide no doubt, of Peck's boyhood adventures with his friend Soup. Tare by now quite a few Soup books, all of which follow a similar pattern. Most children enjoy them very much, though an adult may tire of the arch elaboration of style.

Those who admired *Pigs* have often been disappointed by Peck's work since that strong beginning. Nevertheless, we look with interest at each new title by this erratic author, hoping that he will sometime match the achievement of that first powerful, moving story.

—Anne Scott MacLeod

———

PEET, Bill (William Bartlett Peet). American. Born in Grandview, Indiana, 29 January 1915. Educated at John Herron Art Institute, Indianapolis, 1933–37. Married Margaret Brunst in 1937; two sons. Writer-illustrator, Walt Disney Studio, Hollywood, 1937–64. Recipient: George C. Stone Center for Children's Books award, 1985. Address: 11478 Laurelcrest Road, Studio City, California 91604, U.S.A.

PUBLICATIONS FOR CHILDREN (illustrated by the author)

Fiction

Goliath II. New York, Golden Press, 1959.
Chester the Worldly Pig. Boston, Houghton Mifflin, 1965; London, Deutsch, 1985.
Farewell to Shady Glade. Boston, Houghton Mifflin, 1966; London, Deutsch, 1967.
Capyboppy. Boston, Houghton Mifflin, 1966; London, Deutsch, 1969.
Buford the Little Bighorn. Boston, Houghton Mifflin, 1967; London, Deutsch, 1968.
Jennifer and Josephine. Boston, Houghton Mifflin, 1967; London, Deutsch, 1970.
Fly Homer Fly. Boston, Houghton Mifflin, 1969; London, Deutsch, 1974.
The Whingdingdilly. Boston, Houghton Mifflin, and London, Deutsch, 1970.
The Wump World. Boston, Houghton Mifflin, 1970; London, Deutsch, 1976.
How Droofus the Dragon Lost His Head. Boston, Houghton Mifflin, 1971; London, Deutsch, 1972.
The Ant and the Elephant. Boston, Houghton Mifflin, 1970; London, Deutsch, 1975.
The Spooky Tail of Prewitt Peacock. Boston, Houghton Mifflin, 1972; London, Deutsch, 1978.
Merle the High Flying Squirrel. Boston, Houghton Mifflin, 1974; London, Deutsch, 1978.
Cyrus the Unsinkable Sea Serpent. Boston, Houghton Mifflin, 1975; London, Deutsch, 1977.
The Gnats of Knotty Pine. Boston, Houghton Mifflin, 1975; London, Deutsch, 1977.
Big Bad Bruce. Boston, Houghton Mifflin, 1977; London, Deutsch, 1979.
Eli. Boston, Houghton Mifflin, 1978; London, Deutsch, 1980.
Cowardly Clyde. Boston, Houghton Mifflin, 1979; London, Deutsch, 1980.
Encore for Eleanor. Boston, Houghton Mifflin, 1981; London, Deutsch, 1982.
Pamela Camel. Boston, Houghton Mifflin, 1984; London, Deutsch, 1985.
Jethro and Joel Were a Troll. Boston, Houghton Mifflin, 1987.

Plays

Screenplays (with others): *Pinocchio,* 1940; *Dumbo,* 1941; *Fantasia,* 1941; *Song of the South,* 1946; *Cinderella,* 1950; *Alice in Wonderland,* 1951; *Peter Pan,* 1953; *Sleeping Beauty,* 1959; *One Hundred and One Dalmatians,* 1961; *The Sword in the Stone,* 1963; and short subjects.

Verse

Hubert's Hair-Raising Adventure. Boston, Houghton Mifflin, 1959; London, Deutsch, 1960.
Huge Harold. Boston, Houghton Mifflin, 1961; London, Deutsch, 1964.
Smokey. Boston, Houghton Mifflin, 1962; London, Deutsch, 1964.
The Pinkish Purplish Bluish Egg. Boston, Houghton Mifflin, 1963; London, Deutsch, 1967.
Randy's Dandy Lions. Boston, Houghton Mifflin, 1964.
Ella. Boston, Houghton Mifflin, 1964; London, Deutsch, 1966.
Kermit the Hermit. Boston, Houghton Mifflin, 1965; London, Deutsch, 1967.
The Caboose Who Got Loose. Boston, Houghton Mifflin, 1971; London, Deutsch, 1974.
Countdown to Christmas. San Carlos, California, Golden Gate Books, 1972.
The Luckiest One of All. Boston, Houghton Mifflin, 1982; London, Deutsch, 1983.
No Such Things. Boston, Houghton Mifflin, 1983.
The Kweeks of Kookatumdee. Boston, Houghton Mifflin, 1985; London, Deutsch, 1986.
Zella, Zack, and Zodiac. Boston, Houghton Mifflin, 1986; London, Deutsch, 1987.

Other

An Autobiography. Boston, Houghton Mifflin, 1989.

*

Bill Peet comments:

Many years ago I illustrated the works of others, but found it to be frustrating. In writing my own stories I am able to choose the subject matter, the things I enjoy drawing, which is far more satisfactory, and far more creative. I am not an author who illustrates, but an illustrator who writes. Such freedom is a luxury after working for over 27 years at the Disney Studio where so many cooks can spoil the broth.

Of all the responses in letters from the kids, their comments about the humor in my books please me most—"Your books are funny and make us laugh." Reading should be fun for the young ones (and for everyone).

*   *   *

Bill Peet's widely read picture books for young children have an exotic patina of fantasy and realistic detail with simple but imaginatively sympathetic illustrations by the author. Although the majority of Peet's texts are in prose, he uses a number of poetic devices to enhance his text, namely alliteration, assonance, consonance, and internal rhyme. Also, the texts have a balance and poise that are characteristic of the work of an author who gives attention to rhythm and the crystallizing properties of good versification, even though he is writing in prose. While his play of words and sounds may be a bit saccharine for an adult audience, children love it; and while many children forget titles of stories that have been read to them, because of Peet's repetition of sound few forget *Kermit the Hermit, The Whingdingdilly, Huge Harold,* or *The Caboose Who Got Loose.*

Peet's characters are equally memorable because they all have a peculiarity or singularity that takes them off the level of stereotypes. Droofus, in *How Droofus the Dragon Lost His Head*, is a grass-eating dragon, not just a kind and good one. Scamp, the dog in *The Whingdingdilly*, wants to be a horse, but "Not just any horse. Scamp wanted to be a great horse like Palomar the giant Percheron who lived on the farm just across the road." Zack is an abandoned ostrich chick who gets a zebra foster mother. The structural pattern of most of Peet's works is consistent. The main character is introduced, there is enough exposition to set the scene before conflict is introduced, and then follows a straightforward, lively, and suspense-filled narration. The climax comes swiftly and the resolution is satisfying. Typical emotions are fear and anticipation coupled with gratification at the end of the story.

Peet's illustrations fit very well with his texts. There is a slight sense of exaggeration and elongation, even awkwardness or gawkiness in the characters that is charming rather than demeaning. Perhaps the most appealing quality in the pictures of main characters, however, is their eyes and mouths, both of which are highly expressive and not without a sense of irony, perspective, and introspection. Peet's stories for children are eminently readable, and the pictures are strong enough to stand on their own.

—Rachel Fordyce

PERKINS, Lucy Fitch. American. Born in Maples, Indiana, 12 July 1865. Educated at Old Union School, Kalamazoo, Michigan; Kalamazoo High School, 1879–83; Museum of Fine Arts School, Boston, 1883–86. Married Dwight Heald Perkins in 1891; one daughter and one son. Illustrator, Prang Educational Company, Boston, 1886, and Chicago, 1893–1903; teacher, Pratt Institute School of Fine Arts, Brooklyn, 1887–91. *Died 18 March 1937.*

PUBLICATIONS FOR CHILDREN (illustrated by the author)

Fiction

The Dutch Twins. Boston, Houghton Mifflin, and London, Constable, 1911.
The Japanese Twins. Boston, Houghton Mifflin, 1912; London, Constable, 1913.
The Irish Twins. Boston, Houghton Mifflin, 1913; London, Cape, 1922.
The Eskimo Twins. Boston, Houghton Mifflin, 1914; London, Cape, 1922.
The Mexican Twins. Boston, Houghton Mifflin, 1915; London, Cape, 1955.
The Cave Twins. Boston, Houghton Mifflin, 1916; London, Cape, 1922.
The Belgian Twins. Boston, Houghton Mifflin, 1917; London, Cape, 1940.
The French Twins. Boston, Houghton Mifflin, 1918; London, Cape, 1939.
The Spartan Twins. Boston, Houghton Mifflin, 1918; London, Cape, 1936.
Cornelia: The Story of a Benevolent Despot. Boston, Houghton Mifflin, 1919.
The Scotch Twins. Boston, Houghton Mifflin, 1919; London, Cape, 1922.
The Italian Twins. Boston, Houghton Mifflin, 1920; London, Cape, 1952.
The Puritan Twins. Boston, Houghton Mifflin, 1921; London, Cape, 1955.
The Swiss Twins. Boston, Houghton Mifflin, 1922; London, Cape, 1936.
The Filipino Twins. Boston, Houghton Mifflin, 1923; London, Cape, 1949.
The Colonial Twins of Virginia. Boston, Houghton Mifflin, 1924; London, Cape, 1949.
The American Twins of 1812. Boston, Houghton Mifflin, 1925; London, Cape, 1951.
The American Twins of the Revolution. Boston, Houghton Mifflin, 1926; London, Cape, 1943.
Mr. Chick, His Travels and Adventures. Boston, Houghton Mifflin, 1926.
The Pioneer Twins. Boston, Houghton Mifflin, 1927; London, Cape, 1943.
The Farm Twins. Boston, Houghton Mifflin, 1928.
Kit and Kat: More Adventures of the Dutch Twins. Boston, Houghton Mifflin, 1929.
The Indian Twins. Boston, Houghton Mifflin, 1930; London, Cape, 1938.
The Pickaninny Twins. Boston, Houghton Mifflin, 1931.
The Norwegian Twins. Boston, Houghton Mifflin, 1933; London, Cape, 1936.
The Spanish Twins. Boston, Houghton Mifflin, 1934; London, Cape, 1952.
The Chinese Twins. Boston, Houghton Mifflin, 1935; London, Cape, 1936.
The Dutch Twins and Little Brother, completed by Eleanor Ellis Perkins. Boston, Houghton Mifflin, 1938.

Verse

The Goose Girl: A Mother's Lap-Book of Rhymes and Pictures. Chicago, McClurg, 1906.

Other

Aesop's Fables. New York, Stokes, and London, Harrap, 1908.
The Dutch Twins Primer. Boston, Houghton Mifflin, 1917.

Editor, *Robin Hood: His Deeds and Adventures as Recounted in the Old English Ballads.* New York, Stokes, and London, Jack, 1906.
Editor, *The Twenty Best Fairy Tales by Hans Andersen, Grimm, and Miss Mulock.* New York, Stokes, and London, Harrap, 1907.
Editor, *A Midsummer-Night's Dream for Young People*, based on the play by Shakespeare. New York, Stokes, and London, Harrap, 1907.

PUBLICATIONS FOR ADULTS

Other

A Book of Joys: The Story of a New England Summer. Chicago, McClurg, 1907.

*

Manuscript Collection: Free Library, Philadelphia.

Illustrator: *A Wonder Book* by Nathaniel Hawthorne, 1908; *Stories of the Pilgrims* by Margaret Blanche Pumphrey, 1912; *Little Pioneers* by Maude Warren, 1916; *News from No-Town* by Eleanor Ellis Perkins, 1919; *The Children's Year Book* edited by Maud

Summers, 1923; *The Fairyland Reader* by Edgar Dubs Shimer, 1935; *Mother Goose Book*; *The Enchanted Peacock and Other Stories* by Julia Brown.

* * *

Lucy Fitch Perkins drew inspiration from two experiences: a visit to Ellis Island in New York where she saw the polyglot oppressed people who were immigrating to the United States in the 1920's, and a visit to a Chicago school where she marveled at what the teachers were accomplishing with children of 27 different nationalities. Her fame as a writer for children rests upon her Twins series for ages 8 to 10. The series began with *The Dutch Twins* in 1911 and soon included many more. An early comment on these titles by Bertha E. Mahony and Elinor Whitney in their book *Realms of Gold* (1929) read: "Each book tells of the doings of children in various countries with truth, simplicity, and genuine skill in holding the interest of young readers....The fact that Mrs. Perkins has been able to maintain freshness and life in so long a series is worthy of appreciation."

Perkins later added several stories with American historical backgrounds (for example, *The American Twins of 1812* and *The Colonial Twins of Virginia*) and had published 24 Twins books by the time of her death at age 72. Their enduring vitality and usefulness are proven by the fact that ten or more of them have been reissued for today's youngsters. Although a few critics have felt that the Twins books tended to stereotype nationalities and to "emphasize differences," is that bad? They serve to crystallize children's ideas of how other people live and to show what values immigrant children have contributed to American life. The author's goal was to foster just such cross-cultural understanding.

—Norma R. Fryatt

PETERSHAM, Maud and Miska. Americans. **PETERSHAM, Maud (Sylvia, née Fuller):** Born in Kingston, New York, 5 August 1889. Educated at Vassar College, Poughkeepsie, New York, graduated 1912; New York School of Fine and Applied Arts. Married Miska Petersham in 1917; one son. Worked for International Art Service, New York. *Died 29 November 1971.* **PETERSHAM, Miska:** Born Mikaly Petrezselyem in Törökszentmiklós, Hungary, 20 September 1888; emigrated to England, 1911, and to the United States, 1912. Educated at the Royal Academy of Art, Budapest. Commercial artist; worked for International Art Service, New York. *Died 15 May 1960.* Recipients: American Library Association Caldecott Medal, 1946.

PUBLICATIONS FOR CHILDREN (illustrated by the authors)

Fiction

Miki. New York, Doubleday, 1929.
The Ark of Father Noah and Mother Noah. New York, Doubleday, 1930.
Auntie and Celia Jane and Miki. New York, Doubleday, 1932.
Get-a-Way, and Háry János. New York, Viking Press, 1933; London, Lovat Dickson, 1935.
Miki and Mary: Their Search for Treasure. New York, Viking Press, 1934; London, Lovat Dickson, 1935.
My Very First Book. New York, Macmillan, 1948.
The Box with Red Wheels. New York, Macmillan, 1949; London, Macmillan, 1958.
The Circus Baby. New York, Macmillan, 1950; London, Macmillan, 1958.

Off to Bed: Seven Stories for Wide-Awakes. New York, Macmillan, 1954.
The Boy Who Had No Heart. New York, Macmillan, 1955.
The Peppernuts. New York, Macmillan, and London, Macmillan, 1958.

Other

The Story Book of Clothes [*Food, Houses, Things We Use, Transportation, Earth's Treasures, Gold, Iron and Steel, Oil, Ships, Trains, Wheels, Coal, Aircraft, Foods from the Field, Rice, Sugar, Wheat, Corn, Cotton, Rayon, Silk, Things We Wear, Wool*]. Philadelphia, Winston, 24 vols., 1933–39; *Coal, Iron and Steel, Oil, Houses, Food, Clothes, Gold, Transportation, Wheels, Aircraft, Ships, Trains*, London, Dent, 12 vols., 1936–38; *Cotton, Rayon, Rice, Wheat, Wool, Corn*, London, Wells Gardner Darton, 6 vols., 1947–48.
David. Philadelphia, Winston, and London, Dent, 1938.
Joseph and His Brothers. Philadelphia, Winston, and London, Dent, 1938.
Moses. Philadelphia, Winston, and London, Dent, 1938.
Ruth. Philadelphia, Winston, and London, Dent, 1938.
An American ABC. New York, Macmillan, 1941.
America's Stamps: The Story of One Hundred Years of United States Postage Stamps. New York, Macmillan, 1947.
The Story of the Presidents of the United States of America. New York, Macmillan, 1953; revised edition, 1966.
The Silver Mace: A Story of Williamsburg. New York, Macmillan, 1956.

*

Manuscript Collections: May Massee Collection, Emporia State University, Kansas; University of Oregon Library, Eugene; Kerlan Collection, University of Minnesota, Minneapolis.

Illustrators: *The Cambridge Book of Poetry for Children* (illustrated by Maud alone) edited by Kenneth Grahame, 1916; *Everyday Classics: Primer—Second Reader* by Franklin T. Baker and Ashley H. Thorndike, 1917; *A Child's Own Book of Verse* edited by Ada Maria Skinner and Frances Wickes, 3 vols., 1917; *Fil and Filippa* by John Stuart Thomson, 1917; *Guld the Cavern King* by Mary L.B. Branch, 1918; *History Stories for Primary Grades*, 1919, and *History Stories*, 1925, both by John Wayland; *Tales of Enchantment from Spain* by Elsie S. Eells, 1920; *Enchanted Forest* by William Bowen, 1920; *Children of Ancient Britain* by Louise Lamprey, 1921; *Twenty-Four Unusual Stories for Boys and Girls* edited by Anna Cogswell Tyler, 1921; *The Broom Fairies* by Ethel May Gate, 1922; *Rootabaga Stories*, 1922, and *Rootabaga Pigeons*, 1923, both by Carl Sandburg; *Tales from Shakespeare* by Charles and Mary Lamb, 1923; *Under the Story Tree*, 1923, *The F-U-N Book*, 1923, *In Animal Land*, 1924, *Billy Bang Book*, 1927, *Little Indians*, 1930, and *Zip the Toy Mule and Other Stories*, 1932, all by Mabel La Rue; *The Language Garden*, 1924, and *Number Friends*, 1927, both by Inez M. Howard and others; *The Poppy Seed Cakes* by Margery Clark, 1924; *Marquette Readers*, 1924; *Nursery Friends from France*, 1925, and *Tales Told in Holland*, 1926, both by Olive B. Miller; *The Pathway to Reading* by Bessie Coleman and others, 1925; *Little Ugly Face* by Florence Coolidge, 1925; *Philippine National Literature Book Two* by Harriet Fansler and Isidoro Panlasigui, 1925; *The Easy Book*, 1926, and *The Picnic Book*, 1934, both by Jean Y. Ayer, and *Everyday Stories* by Ayer and others, 1929; *Children of the Mountain Eagle*, 1927, *Pran of Albania*, 1929, and *Young Trajan*, 1931, all by Elizabeth Cleveland Miller; *Where Was Bobby?* by Marguerite Clément, 1928; *Everyday Canadian Primer*, 1928; *Pleasant*

Pathways, 1928; *Winding Roads*, 1928, *Faraway Hills*, 1929, and *Heights and Highways*, 1929, all edited by Wilhelmina Harper and A.J. Hamilton; *The Magic Doll of Roumania* by Marie, Queen of Romania, 1929; *New Trails*, 1930, and *Beckoning Road, Rich Cargoes, Treasure Trove*, and *Wings of Adventure*, 4 vols., 1931, all edited by S. V. Rowland, W.D. Lewis, and E.J. Marshall; *The Christ Child*, 1931; *Martin the Goose Boy*, 1932, and *The Four and Lena*, 1938, both by Marie Barringer; *Heidi* by Johanna Spyri, 1932; *Pinocchio* by Carlo Collodi, 1932; *Albanian Wonder Tales* by Post Wheeler, 1936; *Susannah the Pioneer Cow*, 1941, and *Miss Posy Longlegs*, 1955, both by Miriam Evangeline Mason; *A Little Book of Prayers* by Emilie Johnson, 1941; *Jesus' Story*, 1942; *Literature* edited by E.A. Cross and Elizabeth Lehr, 7 vols., 1943–48; *The Rooster Crows: A Book of American Rhymes and Jingles*, 1945; *Told under the Christmas Tree*, 1948; *A Bird in the Hand: Sayings from Poor Richard's Almanack* by Benjamin Franklin, 1951; *Rip van Winkle, and The Legend of Sleepy Hollow* by Washington Irving, 1951; *In Clean Hay* by Eric Kelly, 1953; *The Shepherd Psalm* (illustrated by Maud alone), 1962.

*   *

"I don't think any American can appreciate this country as I do," Miska Petersham stated during his acceptance speech for the Caldecott Medal in 1946. This remark was properly directed towards adults, for what did it matter to a child poring over the books of the Petershams in the 1920's, 1930's, and even today that Miska came from Hungary and Maud was born in the United States?

Yet, the adventures of *Miki* and his trip to Hungary—climbing into a feather pillow bed, dancing to gypsy music, warming himself against a white clay stove, listening to shepherds' tales of warriors who raced across the Milky Way, watching Sari, the goose, dressed in strudel dough—this was the magic, the touchstone to another world that the Petershams' own backgrounds made possible. So it was with *Miki and Mary*—children boarding a ship to visit distant lands—as well as a seemingly forgotten book, *Auntie*. There were children like Celia Jane, Flossie, and Trailing Arbutus in America's multi-racial world, with stern Puritan figures like Grandfather and Auntie, the schoolteacher: the Petershams mixed a sense of haunting mystery about adults with touches of levity—the magic table and a schoolroom scene bordering on hilarity.

The child, it seems to me, is not concerned with who writes the text or illustrates any given book, but rather that both words and pictures enrich as a whole. It was the Petershams' talent that their backgrounds and interests spurred them to bridge many worlds, places and themes, whether illustrating the story of *The Christ Child*, which reflected the deeply religious aspect of their being, or using Benjamin Franklin's wisdom as the text for *A Bird in the Hand*, or satisfying a young reader's curiosity for facts in their Story Books of Things We Use.

Their love for animals is omnipresent in all of their books, yet dominant in such as *Off to Bed* or *The Circus Baby*. The animals in *Miki* and *Auntie*, however, seem more credible that in the later books where they often become almost cartoon-like and a bit too precious. *The Rooster Crows: A Book of American Rhymes and Jingles* (a questionable subtitle, for many of the verses originated in England) brings together many elements of the Petershams' art, yet seems less successful to me than their earlier books, where their own sense of story, of broadening worlds with an appropriate dash of dignity, discovery, and humor, prevails.

Certainly in dozens of books Miska Petersham showed his appreciation for America and Maud her religious background in a blending which showed respect for other cultures and races, with a regard for the child who wished his facts to be presented with visual accompaniment. Although the Petersham texts may appear to be somewhat simplistic today, it is well to remember that their concern

for multi-ethnic and racial consciousness made its first appearance in book form in 1929, many years before other authors and illustrators took into account this important aspect of books for the young reader.

—Myra Cohn Livingston

———

PETRY, Ann (Lane). American. Born in Old Saybrook, Connecticut, 12 October 1908. Educated at Connecticut College of Pharmacy (now University of Connecticut School of Pharmacy), 1928–31, Ph.G. 1931; Columbia University, New York, 1943–44. Married George D. Petry in 1938; one daughter. Pharmacist, James Pharmacy, Old Saybrook and Old Lyme, Connecticut, 1931–38; writer and reporter, *Amsterdam News*, New York, 1938–41; women's editor, *People's Voice*, New York, 1941–44; Visiting Professor of English, University of Hawaii, Honolulu, 1974–75. Secretary, Authors League of America, 1960. Recipient: Houghton Mifflin Literary fellowship, 1946; National Endowment for the Arts grant, 1977. D.Litt.: Suffolk University, Boston, 1983; University of Connecticut, Storrs, 1988. Agent: Russell and Volkening Inc., 50 West 29th Street, New York, New York 10001. Address: 113 Old Boston Post Road, Old Saybrook, Connecticut 06475, U.S.A.

PUBLICATIONS FOR CHILDREN

Fiction

The Drugstore Cat, illustrated by Susanne Suba. New York, Crowell, 1949.
Harriet Tubman, Conductor on the Underground Railroad. New York, Crowell, 1955; as *The Girl Called Moses: The Story of Harriet Tubman*, London, Methuen, 1960.
Tituba of Salem Village. New York, Crowell, 1964.

Other

Legends of the Saints, illustrated by Anne Rockwell. New York, Crowell, 1970.

PUBLICATIONS FOR ADULTS

Novels

The Street. Boston, Houghton Mifflin, 1946; London, Joseph, 1947.
Country Place. Boston, Houghton Mifflin, 1947; London, Joseph, 1948.
The Narrows. Boston, Houghton Mifflin, 1953; London, Gollancz, 1954.

Short Stories

Miss Muriel and Other Stories. Boston, Houghton Mifflin, 1971.

*

Manuscript Collection: Mugar Memorial Library, Boston University.

Critical Studies: *Black on White: A Critical Study of Writing by American Negroes* by David Littlejohn, New York, Grossman, 1966; *Interviews with Black Writers* edited by John O'Brien, New York, Liveright, 1973.

Ann Petry comments:

Because I was born black and female, I write about survivors (especially when I write for children): a bad-tempered little cat (*The Drugstore Cat*); a slave indicted for witchcraft (*Tituba of Salem Village*); a runaway slave who risks her life in order to guide other slaves to the North and freedom (*Harriet Tubman*); men and women persecuted for their religious beliefs (*Legends of the Saints*).

*   *   *

Besides novels and stories for adults, acknowledged for their "finely controlled narrative skill," Ann Petry has written works of fiction and history in a different vein for children and young people. *The Drugstore Cat* is an everyday story with a pleasing charm. Of greater impact and reflective of the author's deep-seated interest in adding to both the accuracy and adequacy of the history of slavery in the United States is her magnificently drawn *Harriet Tubman, Conductor on the Underground Railroad*. In reconstructing her subject's life she "in delicate and evocative words which carry an underlying sturdiness and dignity...makes Harriet Tubman into a living figure and recreates in vivid scenes an era of struggle, hardship, and unshakable faith."

We follow this legendary Moses (born in Tidewater, Maryland, and influenced by the rebel Denmark Vesey) as she "walked, ran, hid, coaxed, cajoled, and prayed until some 300 of her people had been delivered into freedom." The structure of this fictionalized biography serves to maintain and heighten interest: to each chapter the author appends a summary of related events of the time, revealing the larger picture, the historical backdrop which lends further associations, perspective, and weight to the story. The description of the plantation where Harriet spent most of her formative years, the drastically different life patterns of the whites and blacks, the conversational exchanges, the family involvements: all spring to life. In the outdoor world which she finally reaches Harriet is overcome by the "hard-bought thing" freedom represents. "There was such glory over everything, the sun came like gold through the trees, and over the field, and I felt like I was in heaven."

Tituba of Salem Village focuses on a black woman slave, originally from Bridgewater, Barbados, who is one of the accused during the height of the witchcraft hysteria. The reconstruction of the several settings, the characterization of Tituba's harsh master, a "wrathful" and "impatient" man, and other members of his family, her husband John Indian, together with the pictures of the uneasy times and the surrounding atmosphere as it enveloped both children and adults, draw a reader to share intimately the mounting tension and irrationality. "They're catchin' witches in Salem Village just like they was chickens on a roost." Tituba emerges full-bodied and magnificent.

In great contrast, both in theme and telling, is *Legends of the Saints*, which reveals her storytelling powers in still different ways. This "wise and gentle book" presents glimpses of ten holy people from many lands and follows their experiences with simple dignity. Covered are: Christopher, Genesius, George, Blaise, Catherine of Alexandria, Nicholas, Francis of Assisi, Joan of Arc, Thomas More, and Martin de Porres, the Black barber-surgeon of Peru. The author captures the flavor of their times and touches their heroism. The style is direct and strong; simple sentences predominate, and the emphasis is on description and conversation. This little volume can be for its

readers a first step to wishing for more information about these individuals and the countries from which they came.

—Clara O. Jackson

————

PEYTON, K.M. Pseudonym for Kathleen Wendy Peyton; has also written as Kathleen Herald. British. Born in Birmingham, Warwickshire, 2 August 1929. Educated at Wimbledon High School; Manchester Art School, Art Teacher's Diploma 1951. Married Michael Peyton in 1950; two daughters. Art teacher, Northampton High School, 1953–55. Recipient: Library Association Carnegie Medal, 1970; *Guardian* award, 1970. Address: Rookery Cottage, North Fambridge Chelmsford, Essex CM3 6LP, England.

PUBLICATIONS FOR CHILDREN

Fiction

North to Adventure.   London, Collins, 1958; New York, Platt and Munk, 1965.
Stormcock Meets Trouble.   London, Collins, 1961.
The Hard Way Home, illustrated by R.A. Branton.   London, Collins, 1962; as *Sing a Song of Ambush*, New York, Platt and Munk, 1964.
Windfall, illustrated by Victor Ambrus.   London, Oxford University Press, 1962; as *Sea Fever*, Cleveland, World, 1963.
Brownsea Silver.   London, Collins, 1964.
The Maplin Bird, illustrated by Victor Ambrus.   London, Oxford University Press, 1964; Cleveland, World, 1965.
The Plan for Birdsmarsh, illustrated by Victor Ambrus.   London, Oxford University Press, 1965; Cleveland, World, 1966.
Thunder in the Sky, illustrated by Victor Ambrus.   London, Oxford University Press, 1966; Cleveland, World, 1967.
Flambards.   London, Oxford University Press, 1978.
   Flambards, illustrated by Victor Ambrus.   London, Oxford University Press, 1967; Cleveland, World, 1968.
   The Edge of the Cloud, illustrated by Victor Ambrus.   London, Oxford University Press, 1969; New York, World, 1970.
   Flambards in Summer, illustrated by Victor Ambrus.   London, Oxford University Press, 1969; New York, World, 1970.
Fly-by-Night, illustrated by the author.   London, Oxford University Press, 1968; Cleveland, World, 1969.
Pennington's Seventeenth Summer, illustrated by the author.   London, Oxford University Press, 1970; as *Pennington's Last Term*, New York, Crowell, 1971.
The Beethoven Medal, illustrated by the author.   London, Oxford University Press, 1971; New York, Crowell, 1972.
A Pattern of Roses, illustrated by the author.   London, Oxford University Press, 1972; New York, Crowell, 1973.
Pennington's Heir, illustrated by the author.   London, Oxford University Press, 1973; New York, Crowell, 1974.
The Team, illustrated by the author.   London, Oxford University Press, 1975; New York, Crowell, 1976.
The Right-Hand Man, illustrated by Victor Ambrus.   London, Oxford University Press, 1977; New York, Oxford University Press, 1979.
Prove Yourself a Hero.   London, Oxford University Press, 1977; New York, Collins World, 1978.
A Midsummer Night's Death.   London, Oxford University Press, 1978; New York, Collins, 1979.
Marion's Angels, illustrated by Robert Micklewright.   London and New York, Oxford University Press, 1979; as *Falling Angel*,

London, Methuen, 1983.

Flambards Divided. Oxford, Oxford University Press, 1981; New York, Philomel, 1982.

Dear Fred. London, Bodley Head, and New York, Philomel, 1981.

Going Home, illustrated by Chris Molan. Oxford, Oxford University Press, and New York, Philomel, 1982.

Who, Sir? Me, Sir? Oxford and New York, Oxford University Press, 1983.

Free Rein. New York, Philomel, 1983; as *The Last Ditch,* Oxford, Oxford University Press, 1984.

Froggett's Revenge, illustrated by Lesley Smith. Oxford, Oxford University Press, 1985.

Plain Jack, illustrated by the author. London, Hamish Hamilton, 1988.

Downhill All the Way. Oxford, Oxford University Press, 1988.

Skylark, illustrated by Liz Roberts. Oxford, Oxford University Press, 1989.

Darkling. London, Corgi, 1989.

Fiction as Kathleen Herald

Sabre, The Horse from the Sea, illustrated by Lionel Edwards. London, A. and C. Black, 1948; New York, Macmillan, 1963.

The Mandrake, illustrated by Lionel Edwards. London, A. and C. Black, 1949.

Crab the Roan, illustrated by Peter Biegel. London, A. and C. Black, 1953.

PUBLICATIONS FOR ADULTS

Novel

The Sound of Distant Cheering. London, Bodley Head, 1986.

*   *   *

As a suburban schoolgirl, Kathleen Herald longed to own a pony. It was a hopeless obsession. So at the age of nine, to cure her frustration, she began to write about horses. Her first story was published when she was only 15. Instead of going to university as her parents and teachers expected, she chose art school and later eloped with a fellow student. This independence of mind—following gut instincts and braving opposition to achieve what matters most at the time—is a recurrent theme in her novels. Ruth Hollis in *Fly-by-Night* is the dogged little girl K.M. Peyton once was—mad about horses. 13 years later, writing about her hero Fred Archer, she identifies with the extraordinary self-discipline of this legendary jockey who would starve fanatically to reduce weight for some crucial race and committed suicide at the height of his career, on the anniversary of his young wife's death. Four days after publishing *Dear Fred* Peyton had a serious riding accident in which she damaged her spine. She had to lie on her back for six weeks but was riding again within five months. It takes one indomitable spirit to appreciate the driving motivations of another.

After her marriage, Peyton collaborated with her husband. They contributed articles and stories for newspapers and were paid by the week to keep their readers hooked with cliff-hangers. The M in her pen name stands for Michael and her husband remains a powerful background influence both as inspiration and critic. In 1958 *North to Adventure,* one of their serials for *The Scout Magazine,* was published as a complete novel. It is worth noting that Peyton continues to write as easily for both sexes—some of her best characters are male like Uncle Russell, Will, Mark, and Dick in *Flambards.* If her obsession is horses, her husband's is boats. Though she says she writes books "to get away from boats and horses—and once away I

do get carried away!"—she has continued to explore both themes throughout her writing. *Windfall,* a story about fishing under sail, was the first book she wrote because she wanted to and not primarily for bread-and-butter. It established her as a serious novelist in her own right. From the 1960's onwards, Peyton developed steadily on her own to become one of Britain's leading children's writers, recognised internationally.

The way people begin their careers is often a clue to their later development. Art school gave her "the best of all training in observation." She still likes to illustrate her own stories where possible and regards the paintbrush as far superior to the pen. Her descriptive writing is exceptionally vivid. Her gift for invoking atmosphere puts you inside the skin of her characters so that you seem to see, hear, and even smell the places they inhabit. Many of her settings must be unfamiliar to her readers—the exclusive Pony Club world of *The Team* (a sequel to *Fly-by-Night*) and the bleak Essex coast along which the Maplin Bird sailed so dangerously. But her own knowledge gives the illusion of direct experience. And where she herself is breaking new ground, her research is so thorough that she achieves the same effect. If you want to learn about the competitive, fruity life of a Georgian coachman, read *The Right-Hand Man. The Edge of the Cloud* offers an insight into the oily reality that lay behind the glamour of early flying.

Peyton is unashamedly a romantic and has an exceptional gift for narrative. Very occasionally, as in *A Midsummer Night's Death,* her writing becomes overcharged with emotion. But her pot-boilers as well as the prestigious groups of associated novels for which she has won critical acclaim demonstrate her ability to create memorable characters. She has written with particular sympathy about adolescence. *A Pattern of Roses,* a delicate, subtle ghost story, contrasts two boys' struggle for identity at different periods of time. Tom is the product of that under-privileged rural society that preceded the Great War; Tim is suffering from the material affluence but spiritual poverty of our own day. *Marion's Angels,* a postscript to the Pennington trilogy, explores the raw innocence of first love.

In the 1980's, after an almost exclusive commitment to teenage writing, Peyton began to experiment with books for younger and older readers: *Going Home* and *Who, Sir? Me, Sir?* for eight-year-olds and *The Sound of Distant Cheering* for adults. Alongside, she continues to cater for her traditional fans: *Darkling* is a teenage love story set in racing. It is unfortunate that there are such rigid demarcation lines between the marketing of books for adults and books for children. Contemporary novelists like Peyton, whose writing bridges that gap, do not automatically reach their full potential readership. But film-makers have always recognised that an audience for fiction can span a wide age-range. It is no accident that since 1979 when *Flambards* was converted into a popular television serial, Peyton's work has been regarded as a rich source of adaptable material. Such exposure has in turn given her novels a new lease of life and deservedly brought her writing to the attention of a much wider public.

—Joy Whitby

————

PHIPSON, Joan (Margaret). Australian. Born in Warrawee, New South Wales, 16 November 1912. Educated at Frensham School, Mittagong, New South Wales. Married Colin Hardinge Fitzhardinge in 1944; one daughter and one son. Secretary, London, 1935–37; librarian, Frensham School, 1937–39; copywriter, Radio 2-GB, Sydney, 1939–41; telegraphist, Women's Auxiliary Australian Air Force, 1941–44. Recipient: Australian Children's Book award, 1953; Australian Children's Book Council Book of the

Year award, 1963; Australian Authors' award, 1975. Agent: A.P. Watt Ltd., 20 John Street, London WC1N 2DL, England. Address: Wongalong, Mandurama, New South Wales 2792, Australia.

PUBLICATIONS FOR CHILDREN

Fiction

Good Luck to the Rider, illustrated by Margaret Horder. Sydney and London, Angus and Robertson, 1953; New York, Harcourt Brace, 1968.
Six and Silver, illustrated by Margaret Horder. Sydney and London, Angus and Robertson, 1954; New York, Harcourt Brace, 1971.
It Happened One Summer, illustrated by Margaret Horder. Sydney, Angus and Robertson, 1957; London, Hamish Hamilton, 1964.
The Boundary Riders, illustrated by Margaret Horder. Sydney, Angus and Robertson, and London, Constable, 1962; New York, Harcourt Brace, 1963.
The Family Conspiracy, illustrated by Margaret Horder. Sydney, Angus and Robertson, and London, Constable, 1962; New York, Harcourt Brace, 1964.
Threat to the Barkers, illustrated by Margaret Horder. Sydney, Angus and Robertson, and London, Constable, 1963; New York, Harcourt Brace, 1965.
Birkin, illustrated by Margaret Horder. Melbourne, Lothian, and London, Constable, 1965; New York, Harcourt Brace, 1966.
A Lamb in the Family, illustrated by Lynette Hemmant. London, Hamish Hamilton, 1966.
The Crew of the "Merlin," illustrated by Janet Duchesne. Sydney, Angus and Robertson, and London, Constable, 1966; as *Cross Currents*, New York, Harcourt Brace, 1967.
Peter and Butch. Melbourne and London, Longman, and New York, Harcourt Brace, 1969.
The Haunted Night. Melbourne, Macmillan, and New York, Harcourt Brace, 1970.
Bass and Billy Martin, illustrated by Ron Brooks. Melbourne and London, Macmillan, 1972.
The Way Home. London, Macmillan, and New York, Atheneum, 1973.
Polly's Tiger, illustrated by Gavin Rowe. London, Hamish Hamilton, 1973; New York, Dutton, 1974.
Helping Horse. London, Macmillan, 1974; as *Horse with Eight Hands*, New York, Atheneum, 1974.
The Cats. London, Macmillan, and New York, Atheneum, 1976.
Hide till Daytime, illustrated by Mary Dinsdale. London, Hamish Hamilton, 1977.
Fly into Danger. New York, Atheneum, 1977; as *The Bird Smugglers*, Sydney, Methuen, 1979; London, Methuen, 1980.
Keep Calm. London, Macmillan, 1978; as *When the City Stopped*, New York, Atheneum, 1978.
No Escape. London, Macmillan, 1979; as *Fly Free*, New York, Atheneum, 1979.
Mr. Pringle and the Prince, illustrated by Michael Charlton. London, Hamish Hamilton, 1979.
A Tide Flowing. Sydney and London, Methuen, and New York, Atheneum, 1981.
The Watcher in the Garden. Sydney, Methuen, and New York, Atheneum, 1982; London, Methuen, 1983.
Beryl the Rainmaker, illustrated by Laszlo Acs. London, Hamish Hamilton, 1984.
The Grannie Season, illustrated by Sally Holmes. London, Hamish Hamilton, 1985.
Dinko. Sydney, Methuen, 1985.
Hit and Run. New York, Atheneum, 1985; London, Methuen,

1986.
Bianca. London, Viking Kestrel, and New York, McElderry, 1988.

Other

Christmas in the Sun, illustrated by Margaret Horder. Sydney and London, Angus and Robertson, 1951.
Bennelong, illustrated by Walter Stackpool. Sydney and London, Collins, 1975.

*

Manuscript Collection: Lu Rees Archives Collection, Canberra College of Advanced Education.

Joan Phipson comments:

I began to write for children almost by accident. The fact that I had reasonable success and enjoyed this branch of writing persuaded me to continue. I have become more and more interested, finding more and more scope for imaginative writing in this field, and would not now wish for any other. I find I enjoy the discipline of simple statements—the clarity of thought and expression necessary—and the obligation to be humble. The enthusiasm of children is genuine and heart-warming, if transitory, and the fact that each child grows up and away forces the writer to meet the demands of on-coming generations.

*   *   *

Joan Phipson began writing for children in a long-established tradition of stories of pleasant rural holiday adventures in the Australian bush, but has since moved towards tense dramas of personal conflict and social trauma. No children's books are more recognisably Australian than hers. Each is a personal response to a country with which she is so closely identified, yet each is universal in its essential concerns. She seems especially interested in the contrast between the values inherent in urban and country life, and is concerned to show what she regards as the superiority, in almost a moral sense, of the latter. Hence, there is an implied didacticism in most of her work.

A favourite Phipson theme is the need of the individual for acceptance. In *Peter and Butch*, or *The Boundary Riders*, a young child gives undue admiration to others—people who are older, wealthier, urbane, handsome. Phipson then places the contrasting characters in a situation of crisis, allowing the lowly gradually to assume leadership through their natural affinity with the earth, which proves to be more productive, constructive, and dependable than the superficial veneer of acquired learning embodied in their slick city cousins. In books such as *A Lamb in the Family, Polly's Tiger*, or *It Happened One Summer* acceptance of others comes simply as a result of the protagonist taking some sort of initiative to resolve a situation of conflict or distress. Yet the psychological depth is always seriously plumbed, whether simply in *Polly's Tiger*, where a girl copes with her feelings of alienation, or in *Peter and Butch*, in which a boy struggles with conflicting self-images.

A more recent development retains the innocence/experience thematic paradox yet sets it in a nightmare landscape of a timeless Australia in which three children explore their interrelationships and the whole ethos of this ancient land in the company of a sort of pantheistic spirit. Where *The Boundary Riders* took a literary cliché and, with directness and flair, infused it with contemporary thematic seriousness, *The Way Home* is unique in its concept and its depth of meaning.

Phipson has become a master of sustained suspense. She stretches her familiar themes to almost unbearable limits of tension in books such as *The Cats*, in which some hoodlums kidnap two brothers but become the prey of feral cats, or *No Escape*, which is quite claustrophobic in its depiction of two boys trapped like animals. Her most moving book is probably *A Tide Flowing*, which relentlessly examines the trauma of a young boy who has the burden of being the only witness at his mother's suicide. This is a full-scale psychological study of rejection.

Her scale can be large, as in *Keep Calm*, which examines the breakdown of a large city during a general strike, or during and after a nuclear holocaust, as in *Dinko*, an ambitious novel which, like *The Way Home*, tries to fuse elements of fantasy and realism. Her focus can be compact and concentrated, as in *No Escape*. She sometimes writes as a serious publicist for environmental conservation, as in *Fly into Danger*, yet can produce light-hearted comedies such as *Hide till Daytime* (two children spend the night locked in a large department store), *Mr. Pringle and the Prince*, or *The Grannie Season*, a story about a cricketing grandmother, for younger readers. She has even successfully attempted historical fiction, in *Bass and Billy Martin* (about Australian coastal exploration). Phipson is a prolific writer, of high quality, and with an extraordinary range and versality.

—Walter McVitty

PICARD, Barbara Leonie. British. Born in Richmond, Surrey, 4 December 1917. Educated at St. Katharine's School, Wantage, Berkshire, 1930–34. Address: c/o Oxford University Press, Walton Street, Oxford OX2 6DP, England.

PUBLICATIONS FOR CHILDREN

Fiction

The Mermaid and the Simpleton, illustrated by Philip Gough. London, Oxford University Press, 1949; New York, Criterion, 1970.
The Faun and the Woodcutter's Daughter, illustrated by Charles Stewart. London, Oxford University Press, 1951; New York, Criterion, 1964.
The Lady of the Linden Tree, illustrated by Charles Stewart. London, Oxford University Press, 1954; New York, Criterion, 1962.
Ransom for a Knight, illustrated by C. Walter Hodges. London, Oxford University Press, 1956; New York, Walck, 1967.
Lost John, illustrated by Charles Keeping. London, Oxford University Press, 1962; New York, Criterion, 1963.
The Goldfinch Garden: Seven Tales, illustrated by Anne Linton. London, Harrap, 1963; New York, Criterion, 1965.
One Is One, illustrated by Victor Ambrus. London, Oxford University Press, 1965; New York, Holt Rinehart, 1966.
The Young Pretenders, illustrated by Victor Ambrus. London, Ward, and New York, Criterion, 1966.
Twice Seven Tales, illustrated by Victor Ambrus. London, Kaye and Ward, 1968.

Other

The Odyssey of Homer, illustrated by Joan Kiddell-Monroe. London, Oxford University Press, and New York, Walck, 1952.
Tales of the Norse Gods and Heroes, illustrated by Joan Kiddell-Monroe. London, Oxford University Press, 1953.
French Legends, Tales, and Fairy Stories, illustrated by Joan Kiddell-Monroe. London, Oxford University Press, and New York, Walck, 1955.

Stories of King Arthur and His Knights, illustrated by Roy Morgan. London, Oxford University Press, 1955; New York, Walck, 1966.
German Hero-Sagas and Folk-Tales, illustrated by Joan Kiddell-Monroe. London, Oxford University Press, and New York, Walck, 1958.
The Iliad of Homer, illustrated by Joan Kiddell-Monroe. London, Oxford University Press, and New York, Walck, 1960.
The Story of Rama and Sita, illustrated by Charles Stewart. London, Harrap, 1960.
Tales of the British People, illustrated by Eric Fraser. London, Ward, and New York, Criterion, 1961.
The Tower and the Traitors (history), illustrated by William Stobbs. London, Batsford, and New York, Putnam, 1961.
Hero-Tales from the British Isles, illustrated by Gay Galsworthy. London, Ward, and New York, Criterion, 1963.
Celtic Tales: Legends of Tall Warriors and Old Enchantments, illustrated by Gay Galsworthy. London, Ward, 1964; New York, Criterion, 1965.
The Story of the Pandavas, Retold from the Mahabharata, illustrated by Charles Stewart. London, Dobson, 1968.
William Tell and His Son, from a translation by Bettina Hürlimann, illustrated by Paul Nussbaumer. London, Sadler, 1969.
Three Ancient Kings: Gilgamesh, Hrolf Kraki, Conary, illustrated by Philip Gough. London, Kaye and Ward, and New York, Warne, 1972.
Tales of Ancient Persia, Retold from the Shah-Nama of Firdausi, illustrated by Victor Ambrus. London, Oxford University Press, 1972; New York, Walck, 1973.

Editor, *Encyclopaedia of Myths and Legends of All Nations*, revised edition. London, Ward, 1962.

*

Barbara Leonie Picard comments:
From very early years I had intended to be a writer—but I came to be a children's writer by accident. My first books were original fairy stories told in the traditional vein, and were written entirely for my own amusement. When they were published, their success encouraged my publishers to persuade me to continue writing for young people on the subjects which held most interest for me: mythology, legends, and folklore. I have also written several historical novels for older children and teenagers on themes which attracted me. I never write any book unless it is to please myself.

*   *   *

Not surprisingly, because of her experience as a reteller of old tales, Barbara Leonie Picard's original writing lies in the two fields of the invented fairy story and the historical novel.

The collections of fairytales—*The Mermaid and the Simpleton*, *The Faun and the Woodcutter's Daughter*, and *Twice Seven Tales* (which includes *The Lady of the Linden Tree*)—derive from the main traditions of Europe and the East, but courtly romance preponderates. The motifs of the true folktale are often used but generally the themes are more orderly. The setting of court or castle is less idealized, with considerable descriptive detail, the product of research rather than the peasant's imagination. Maidens, except when enchanted, are always good and beautiful, and heroes, whether peasant or king, are deserving of whatever good fortune they gain. Moral virtues are always stressed, though trickery is permitted when it is the only way of overcoming evil. Some stories, in the Andersen tradition, lack a happy ending.

The historical novels are fine pieces of writing, considerably longer than the average children's book. *Ransom for a Knight* has a single-strand plot, but the determined little Alys and the not-very-bright Hugh, the serf's child, come through as satisfactory characters. All shades of mediaeval society are included: the baronial hall, the rich merchant's house, the peasant's hovel with its fleas. Alys's childish eagerness wins over most of the people she meets, and kind and unkind hearts are found among the wealthy and the poor, the honest and the dishonest, the Scots and the English. *Lost John* is an absorbing story of conflicting loyalties. Fighting is for killing, not for the exercise of knightly arts: the outlaws with whom John throws in his lot are not romantic Robin Hood figures. Too often, as in real life, motives are misunderstood and the wrong reactions follow. The ending may sound contrived, but does not seem so.

In *One Is One* Stephen fulfills all his ambitions, but is the cost worth it? The sensitive, artistic boy, rejected by his family, learns three times to love, in each case to lose its object through death. In its stress on knightly combat the book owes much to Picard's own retelling of Malory. Sir Pagan is too idealised to be real, yet this is how Stephen sees him. Through the three tragedies Stephen learns where his own future lies and that his prayers were after all answered. The "great house" setting of *The Young Pretenders* is attractive. The depiction of the main characters is remarkably acute. The theme is unusual—a rogue masquerading as a fleeing Jacobite to save his life. The children are never found out, but the story ends rather sadly because life goes on just as it did before Seumas came into it. Historical details are worked in effortlessly and understandably and never obtrude as they did just occasionally in *Ransom for a Knight*.

—Margaret M. Tye

PIERCE, Meredith Ann. American. Born in Seattle, Washington, 5 July 1958. Educated at the University of Florida, Gainesville, 1975–80, B.A. in liberal arts 1978, M.A. in English 1980. Teaching assistant, Office of Instructional Resources, 1978, and Department of English, 1978–80, University of Florida; bookseller, Bookland, 1981, and Waldenbooks, 1981–87, both Gainesville. Since 1987 library assistant, Alachua County library district, Gainesville. Recipient: *Scholastic Magazine* prize, 1973; International Reading Association award, 1983; Bread Loaf Writers Conference Broughton fellowship, 1984. Address: 703 N.W. 19th Street, Gainesville, Florida 32603, U.S.A.

PUBLICATIONS FOR CHILDREN

Fiction

The Darkangel. Boston, Little Brown, 1982; London, Collins, 1983.
A Gathering of Gargoyles. Boston, Little Brown, 1984.
Birth of the Firebringer. New York, Four Winds Press, and London, Macmillan, 1985.
The Woman Who Loved Reindeer. Boston, Atlantic Monthly Press, 1985; London, Hodder and Stoughton, 1987.
Where the Wild Geese Go, illustrated by Jamichael Henterly. New York, Dutton, 1988.
The Pearl of the Soul of the World. Boston, Little Brown, 1989.

*

Meredith Ann Pierce comments:
Drawing on mythology and folklore, fairytales and dreams, I write fantasy stories for both young readers and adults. My goal is to transport the reader into a world which is quite different from our own and yet is, at the same time, comprehensible. In making sense of that world, I try to make sense of ours. The fantasist's art is a kind of communal dreaming, through which writer and reader share experiences rich and strange.

* * *

The works of Meredith Ann Pierce reflect the wellspring of myth, magic, and religion that have influenced her and have taken new form in her interpretation. The well-read adolescent or adult can revel in both the story that Pierce tells and the search for connections to other stories in the body of fantasy literature.

The Darkangel and *A Gathering of Gargoyles* are the first two books of a proposed trilogy. Aeriel, the slave become heroine, had her beginning in a description of a patient's dream in Jung's autobiography. This stimulus become story is also influenced by the tales of Beauty and the Beast and Psyche and Eros. The resulting image, however, is Pierce's own. The books are a rich tapestry of love, devotion, faith, and courage, and like a tapestry the weaving moves slowly but inexorably to its full realization. These are not quick reads for the casual reader, but are books to be savored and pondered over. Aeriel seeks to avenge her mistress who has been captured by a vampire and in the process first becomes his slave and then his savior. In her need to free Irrylath from his haunted past, Aeriel follows a quest to find the missing lons who can become the steeds for Irrylath's brothers in the battle to free the land from the hold of the White Witch and her six vampire sons. The staunch love that Aeriel extends to the creatures and beings with whom she comes in contact holds the key to the success of her mission. This is a powerfully written and complex tale and one can only hope that the third book will be forthcoming.

When Caribou is 13 her sister-in-law foists a bastard child onto her to raise. As the child grows, it is obvious that he is not completely human, indeed he is a trangl who can take both human and stag form. Caribou becomes *The Woman Who Loved Reindeer*, though he is incapable of feeling human emotion until the end of the story. The elements of sacrifice, love, and devotion take many forms as Caribou becomes a leader and savior of her people as well as a woman who desires one she cannot have. There is a mythic quality to the story that is reminiscent of the tales of the Laplanders, though the setting is a two-mooned world. Pierce has told an adventurous tale, but at times the action seems overwrought.

It is obvious that Pierce is steeped in the mythology of our world, even when she chooses to create new worlds. The main characters in *Birth of the Firebringer* are unicorns who have been driven from their land by vicious wyverns and who inhabit a place that is threatened by deadly gryphons. The unicorns await a savior, the firebringer, who will lead them back to their promised land. This is a tale of high adventure and of coming-of-age, and the first in a proposed trilogy. Though it is a tale of good and evil, Pierce allows the reader to see that both good and evil are dependent on the perception of the viewer. As in life, there are no easy answers.

One of Pierce's latest books is a picture book of a child who falls into a fever state and strives to go *Where the Wild Geese Go*. As in most dreams, the storyline takes twists and turns that are hard to decipher and leaves the reader with much to puzzle out.

Pierce is a compelling storyteller, making use of the classic mythology that we respond to and placing it within a new context. When she is at her best, the tales are rich and evocative, stirring the reader to question as well as absorb. There are times, however, when her telling becomes too intricate, and the reader loses the thread of the tapestry.

—M. Jean Greenlaw

PILGRIM, Anne. See **ALLAN, Mabel Esther.**

PILLING, Ann. Also writes as Ann Cheetham. British. Born in Warrington, Lancashire, 17 October 1944. Educated at King's College, University of London, 1964–69, B.A. (honours) 1967, M.Phil. in English 1971. Married Joe Pilling in 1968; two sons. Has taught English in secondary schools. Publications officer, Federation of Children's Book Groups, 1978–81. Recipient: *Guardian* award, 1986. Agent: Gina Pollinger, 4 Garrick Street, London WC2E 9BH. Address: 57 St. John Street, Oxford OX1 2LQ, England.

PUBLICATIONS FOR CHILDREN

Fiction

The Year of the Worm, illustrated by Ian Newsham. London, Viking Kestrel, 1984.
Henry's Leg, illustrated by Rowan Clifford. London, Viking Kestrel, 1985.
The Friday Parcel, illustrated by Robert Bartelt. London, Blackie, 1986.
No Guns, No Oranges, illustrated by Jolyne Knox. London, Heinemann, 1986.
The Big Pink. London, Viking Kestrel, 1987.
The Beast in the Basement, illustrated by Jolyne Knox. London, Heinemann, 1988.
Dustbin Charlie, illustrated by Jean Baylis. London, Viking Kestrel, 1988.
On the Lion's Side. London, Heinemann, 1988.
Stan. London, Viking Kestrel, 1988.
The Big Biscuit, illustrated by Linda Birch. London, Hodder and Stoughton, 1989.
The Jungle Sale, illustrated by Robert Bartelt. London, Blackie, 1989.
Our Kid. London, Viking Kestrel, 1989.

Fiction as Ann Cheetham

Black Harvest. London, Collins, 1983.
The Beggar's Curse. London, Collins, 1984.
The Witch of Lagg. London, Collins, 1986.
The Pit. London, Collins, 1987.

Other

Editor, with Anne Wood, *Our Best Stories*, illustrated by Mairi Hedderwick. London, Hodder and Stoughton, 1986.

*

Ann Pilling comments:

Although I have written for younger children, and have enjoyed doing so, I regard myself as a children's novelist; and although when writing for children one's scope is limited in some ways, it is a mistake ever to talk down to them, or to think they deserve less than the best (poor style, flabby plot construction, two-dimensional characters).

I have two "hats". As Ann Cheetham I have written a quartet of ghost stories, sometimes called the *Black Harvest* series. These are ambitious, semi-fantastic stories involving children of the 1980's who are swept back into the past, to solve some kind of mystery. For each I did a considerable amount of research, e.g. *Black Harvest* deals with the Irish potato famine of the 1840's, *The Pit* is about the London Plague of 1665. I regard them as my most powerful books.

As Ann Pilling I have written a collection (all different) of much lighter, contemporary novels, set mainly in the north of England where I was brought up, though *On the Lion's Side* is set in Wales. Whatever my subject I have always aimed to tell a story well, and to fill my canvas with living, breathing human beings. Adults enjoy my books, which is a compliment. They are valued for their humour, their authenticity and in some cases (*Stan*) for their breathless pace.

As a Christian I believe in hope. Even in the ghost stories there is a peaceful, if not always totally happy, resolution of events. I feel we have been dogged too long in the world of children's literature by "the problem novel." Whatever misfortunes my characters suffer—and they are many—courage, hope, and cheerfulness shine through, I trust. I feel I can write no other way. If a child is deprived of hope, and of what D. H. Lawrence called "the wonder of life" then he is deprived of everything that makes living worthwhile.

*   *   *

Ann Pilling made her reputation with three lively novels centring on children who are quite unlike the conventional heroes of juvenile fiction. *The Year of the Worm*, possibly echoing Desmond Coke's earlier school story *The Worm*, concerns Peter Wrigley, an under-sized, nervous, and unpopular boy, tormented by other children and misunderstood by teachers. Henry Hooper in *Henry's Leg* is a compulsive hoarder who haunts dustbins to fill his attic with junk, including the plastic leg he finds outside a dress shop. Angela Collis-Browne in *The Big Pink* has to contend with her name, her awkward self-consciousness, and her weight problem on being transferred to a boarding school that is very unlike the Chalet School. The name of her dormitory, the Big Pink, is soon applied to the unhappy Angela herself.

These characters are placed in odd or embarrassing situations. Peter, with his secret chest-expanders, longs to be a hero but only makes himself ridiculous. Henry tries to make money by collecting recently dead hedgehogs to sell to the local polytechnic. Angela breaks the floor by trampolining on her bed and nearly pops out of her dress when performing on stage. However, the total effect of the novels is more conventional because, despite the turns of the plot, the outcome is rarely in doubt. The Worm at last does become a hero, saving the life of an injured companion on a hostelling trip and gaining an award for bravery. Henry survives the attention of local crooks, wins a reward, and sees his junk, including the leg, transformed into sculpture. Angela excels at music, gains recognition, and is awarded a special prize, the Silver Fish.

The scenes at home and school carry conviction, and Pilling writes with warmth and understanding. She handles relationships perceptively, showing how young people come to terms with themselves and others. Re-evaluation of the three boys in *The Year of the Worm* is partly achieved by seeing them through the eyes of the plump, intelligent Millicent. Henry's mixture of love and irritation for his incompetent mother is a more important element of his story than the conventional narrative about the crooks, and it is appropriate that the real happy ending is the return of his father, who had previously departed with a new girlfriend. Angela learns to come to terms with the feared Auntie Pat, the cool, progressive head of the school. Her crush on the teenage Seb Barrington-Ward and her support for an eccentric English teacher are delicately handled.

Pilling's recent books, *Stan* and *On the Lion's Side*, are more straightforward thrillers in which gripping events (the escape, the hunt for treasure) are presented in a dangerous contemporary setting. The backgrounds are meticulously realised: the risky hitchhiking, the demolition sites, and the terrorist hideout in *Stan*, the lonely cottage and the disused mineshaft of *On the Lion's Side*. Stan, a large

14-year-old, plans to escape from the last of a series of unsatisfactory foster homes to join his elder brother in Ireland. In a rather contrived though exciting opening, a packet of drugs gets hidden in his rucksack and he realises that a dangerous criminal is pursuing him. The two come face to face on the Irish ferry, when Stan flings the rucksack and the drugs into the sea. In Belfast he is plunged into a quite separate series of adventures with a terrorist gang, escaping from an ambush and explosion, crossing the border in a gun battle, being saved by members of a religious order, and eventually welcomed on the farm with his brother though "nothing was as he'd planned." Pilling presents the violence and the squalor vividly, but there is perhaps almost too much action in the book, as though it has been written with one eye on eventual screening. Stan is continually being threatened, abused, and injured. Ultimately, however, what remains in the mind are not the events but the unexpected kindnesses and decency of the ordinary people who help the boy on his way. Pilling's grasp of human characteristics and her quirky humour seem at present her strongest qualities.

—Robert Protherough

—————

PINKWATER, Daniel Manus. Also writes as Manus Pinkwater. American. Born in Memphis, Tennessee, 15 November 1941. Educated at Bard College, Annandale-on-Hudson, New York, B.A. 1964. Married Jill Schutz in 1969. Art instructor, Children's Aid Society, 1967–69, Lower West Side Visual Arts Center, 1969, and Henry Street Settlement, 1969, all New York, and Bonnie Brae Farm for Boys, Millington, New Jersey, 1969; assistant project director, Inner City Summer Arts Program, Hoboken, New Jersey, 1970. Regular commentator, *All Things Considered*, National Public Radio. Agent: Susan Cohen, Writers House Inc., 21 West 26th Street, New York, New York 10010, U.S.A.

PUBLICATIONS FOR CHILDREN (illustrated by the author)

Fiction

Wizard Crystal. New York, Dodd Mead, 1973.
Magic Camera. New York, Dodd Mead, 1974.
Lizard Music. New York, Dodd Mead, 1976.
The Big Orange Splot. New York, Hastings House, 1977.
The Blue Thing. Englewood Cliffs, New Jersey, Prentice Hall, 1977.
Fat Men from Space. New York, Dodd Mead, 1977.
The Hoboken Chicken Emergency. Englewood Cliffs, New Jersey, Prentice Hall, 1977.
The Last Guru. New York, Dodd Mead, 1978.
Alan Mendelsohn: The Boy from Mars. New York, Dutton, 1979.
Pickle Creature. New York, Four Winds Press, 1979.
Return of the Moose. New York, Dodd Mead, 1979.
Yobgorble, Mystery Monster of Lake Ontario. New York, Clarion, 1979.
Java Jack, with Luqman Keele. New York, Crowell, 1980.
The Magic Moscow. New York, Four Winds Press, 1980.
The Wuggie Norple Story, illustrated by Tomie de Paola. New York, Four Winds Press, 1980.
Attila the Pun. New York, Four Winds Press, 1981.
Tooth-Gnasher Superflash. New York, Four Winds Press, 1981.
The Worms of Kukumlima. New York, Dutton, 1981.
Roger's Umbrella, illustrated by James Marshall. New York, Dutton, 1982.

Slaves of Spiegel. New York, Four Winds Press, 1982.
The Snarkout Boys and the Avocado of Death. New York, Lothrop, 1982.
Young Adult Novel. New York, Crowell, 1982.
I Was a Second Grade Werewolf. New York, Dutton, 1983.
Devil in the Drain. New York, Dutton, 1984.
Ducks! Boston, Little Brown, 1984.
The Snarkout Boys and the Baconburg Horror. New York, Lothrop, 1984.
The Frankenbagel Monster. New York, Dutton, 1986.
The Moosepire. Boston, Little Brown, 1986.
The Muffin Fiend. New York, Lothrop, 1986.
Aunt Lulu. New York, Macmillan, 1988.
Guys from Space. New York, Macmillan, 1989.
Uncle Melvin. New York, Macmillan, 1989.

Fiction as Manus Pinkwater

The Terrible Roar. New York, Knopf, 1970.
Bear's Picture. New York, Holt Rinehart, 1972.
Fat Elliot and the Gorilla. New York, Four Winds Press, 1974.
Blue Moose. New York, Dodd Mead, 1975; London, Blackie, 1977.
Three Big Hogs. New York, Seabury Press, 1975.
Wingman. New York, Dodd Mead, 1975.
Around Fred's Bed, illustrated by Robert Mertens. Englewood Cliffs, New Jersey, Prentice Hall, 1976.

Other

Superpuppy: How to Choose, Raise, and Train the Best Possible Dog for You, with Jill Pinkwater. New York, Seabury Press, 1977.

*

Daniel Manus Pinkwater comments:
    Children are, in many ways, better readers than adults. They are less likely to be influenced by trivial or extrinsic details in their choices; and if they like a book they may read it many times. Also, some of them appear to be interested in the same things I am.

* * *

    If Daniel Manus Pinkwater were not so funny, so fond of word-play, and so prolific, he would probably receive much greater recognition from adults as an important children's book author. Adults welcome humor as entertainment, but rarely give it serious consideration. Pinkwater's child readers, on the other hand, know a good book when they see it, especially if it is one by Daniel Manus Pinkwater, a.k.a. Daniel M. Pinkwater, D. Manus Pinkwater, Manus Pinkwater, Daniel Pinkwater, and Honest Dan'l Pinkwater. The author's books are as various and overlapping as the names he is known by; Pinkwater has written and illustrated picture books for both very young and slightly older children, written slim novellas and full-length novels for still older readers, and published a young adult novel called *Young Adult Novel.*
    No matter which audience he addresses, Pinkwater deflates pretensions, sometimes with anarchic glee. While his works are often called fantasies or science fiction, he is less interested in the creation of a separate secondary world or alternate universe (as in *Alan Mendelsohn: The Boy from Mars*, or *The Worms of Kukumlima*) than he is in the eruption of the fantastic into everyday reality. A talking blue moose walks into Mr. Breton's restaurant on the edge of the deep woods, and while this arrival changes Mr. Breton's life considerably, the rules governing everyday reality stay much the same aside from such suspensions as the temporary transformation of the

kitchen floor into a spring meadow (*Blue Moose*) or the discovery of a railroad boxcar which operates as a time machine (*The Moosepire*).

Both types of fantasy celebrate eccentricity and the pursuit of hobbies ranging from familiar avocations like collecting comic books—a hobby shared by many of Pinkwater's protagonists—to highly improbable pastimes. One of the more recent examples of the latter appears in *Aunt Lulu* where the title character drives a dog sled team in New Jersey in the summer. The dogs, as well as their driver, are equipped with pink sunglasses. Aunt Lulu's unconventional behavior links her to dozens of other Pinkwater heroes and heroines who stand out from the crowd by virtue of their idiosyncracies, but some of these other characters are unhappy with their status as eccentrics or outsiders. At the same time, Pinkwater himself always sympathizes with the outsider; quirks or oddities prove to be useful talents by the conclusion of any given story.

Pinkwater's first picture book, *The Terrible Roar*, is a case in point. Much to his dismay, a baby lion discovers that his terrible roar makes all the objects and creatures in his environment disappear one by one until he is left utterly alone. Desolate, he roars again and is transported to the place where everything and everybody roared away have gone. The tidiness and comfort of the denouement are matched by illustrations in bright flat colors. The roar itself is depicted as smaller and smaller circles or solid disks of color laid atop each other so that their bottom edges almost touch. The image effectively suggests the roar's echoes as well as the idea of disappearance; the ever smaller circles seem to regress into infinity. Although Pinkwater's subsequent picture books are no match for the sophisticated simplicity and wit of this book's graphic design, their more overtly humorous contents are well-served by his line drawings in black and white and by the bold hues of his illustrations done with marking pens. For instance, when the protagonist of *Ducks!* tells his mother that he's met a large talking duck, her deadpan assertion that ducks usually lie is complemented by the comic incongruity of her half-maternal, half-punk persona; this Mom has spiked yellow hair tipped with green.

Her appearance is reminiscent of that of "Rat" Bentley Saunders, a fiercely independent young woman who is featured along with Winston Bongo and Walter Galt in both *The Snarkout Boys and the Avocado of Death* and in *The Snarkout Boys and the Baconburg Horror*. Like most of Pinkwater's full-length fiction and his novellas for intermediate and older readers, the Snarkout books' antic energy is fueled by punning allusions and references to other books (some of them Pinkwater titles), to icons of both popular and high culture, and to food. It is par for the course to find James Dean, *The Sorrows of Young Werewolf*, and a giant avocado capable of being modified into a thought-wave producing "Alligatron" all within the covers of the same book.

While Pinkwater's hyperbolic imagination has produced a number of other truly funny adventure/detective/fantasy stories such as *The Worms of Kukumlima, Yobgorble, Mystery Monster of Lake Ontario*, and *The Muffin Fiend*, he is at his best perhaps when his wit is tempered by his compassion for his characters' vulnerabilities. *Lizard Music, Alan Mendelsohn: The Boy from Mars*, and *Wingman* (a book which is not a comedy) all present intelligent and perceptive protagonists whose anxieties are resolved or made less threatening as a result of their fantastic adventures. By turns satiric and serious, Pinkwater's imagination is utopian at heart.

—Janice M. Alberghene

PINKWATER, Manus. See **PINKWATER, Daniel Manus.**

PLOWMAN, Stephanie. British. Born 28 December 1922. Educated at the University of London, B.A. (honours) in history 1944; graduate study, 1948–50, Ph.D. Married A.R. Hamilton-Dee (died 1957). Has taught in England, South Africa, and Ghana; Gulbenkian Research fellow, Lucy Cavendish College, Cambridge, 1969–72. Address: c/o Bodley Head, 32 Bedford Square, London WC1B 3SG, England.

PUBLICATIONS FOR CHILDREN

Fiction

Sixteen Sail in Aboukir Bay, illustrated by Richard Kennedy. London, Methuen, 1956.
To Spare the Conquered. London, Methuen, 1960.
The Road to Sardis. London, Bodley Head, 1965; Boston, Houghton Mifflin, 1966.
Three Lives for the Czar. London, Bodley Head, 1969; Boston, Houghton Mifflin, 1970.
My Kingdom for a Grave. London, Bodley Head, 1970; Boston, Houghton Mifflin, 1971.
A Time to Be Born and a Time to Die. London, Bodley Head, 1975.
The Leaping Song. London, Bodley Head, 1976.

Other

Nelson, illustrated by Richard Kennedy. London, Methuen, 1955.

PUBLICATIONS FOR ADULTS

Play

Radio Play: *The Royal Exiles*, 1953.

*

Stephanie Plowman comments:
The gestation period of my becoming a writer of historical fiction began when, as a 16-year-old, I was required to write an essay criticising the policy of Napoleon after 1807. The sheer lunacy of this made me start working out privately why I wanted to go on learning history—certainly not to be able to pontificate on the "mistakes" made by the greatest military intelligence of modern times when I myself possibly couldn't run a village post office. To learn people, then? What it was like to live during certain happenings? To make the past present?

Nowadays there are two stages. An age or incident takes possession, and the obsessive reading begins. And in the course of this, a sentence, or even a few words, call a character into being, i.e., a young officer who rode with his squadron from Novgorod in a futile attempt to save the Tsar, a single title among the list of books left by the Imperial children at Ekaterinburg. After this the manuscript writes itself.

* * *

The distinction between adult and children's literature is fine enough to encourage many people, including some of the most notable of writers of children's books, to believe that the distinction does not exist. Certainly it is difficult to think of Stephanie Plowman except as a novelist whose appeal is to a certain kind of reader, not to readers of a certain age. Her blend of passion and scholarship is so rare and precious that adults and children who are able to meet its demands are richer for the experience.

Plowman's major books fall into groups, those of classical Greece and those dealing with the last days of Imperial Russia. The latter are perhaps the more successful, but both groups show the same qualities of historical irony and personal involvement. It is the essence of these stories that they deal with historical figures, even though the central characters are invented. Seeing the real people through fictional eyes somehow gives them a sharper reality. There is a good example of this in *The Road to Sardis* where, at the lowest point of Athens's degradation, the hero sees a stranger examining the dismantled Long Walls with a professional eye. This is Thucydides, balancing despair at the destruction of his city against a historian's concern to prove the theory that Themistocles had built the walls in haste. There are equally telling portraits of Euripides and Socrates and a brilliant hostile thumb-nail sketch of Xenophon.

The Road to Sardis is mainly the story of the war between Athens and Sparta and the decline of democracy. Plowman showed Athens in her glory in *The Leaping Song*, which begins with Marathon and ends with Salamis when the Persian fleet was destroyed in the narrow seas. This is a more mature work, particularly in the control of narrative (which is occasionally difficult to follow in the earlier book), but the blend of fiction and history is similar and as effective.

Between the two Greek stories Plowman studied the Russian Revolution and wrote the novels *Three Lives for the Czar* and *My Kingdom for a Grave*. In these a young Russo-Scotsman witnesses the decline and fall of the Romanov dynasty and the outbreak of revolution. Alexei Hamilton is committed by traditional loyalty and personal affection to the Russian royal family, but neither blinds him to the fatal weakness which has doomed them. These are deeply moving novels, in which major research has been completely digested so that, although the writer's authority is never in question, the story is nearer to Greek tragedy than to modern history. The reader, with the narrator, is the helpless witness of world-shaking events. One hesitates, so near the time of publication, to prophesy classic status, but here, if anywhere in modern children's literature, one is in the presence of greatness.

—Marcus Crouch

POLAND, Marguerite. South African. Born in Johannesburg, Transvaal, 3 April 1950. Educated at Rhodes University, Grahamstown, 1968–70, B.A.; Stellenbosch University, Cape Province, 1971, honours degree in African languages; Natal University, Durban, 1976, M.A. Married Martin Oosthuizen in 1973; two daughters. Assistant, South African Museum, Cape Town, 1972; research assistant, Institute for Social Research, Natal University, 1973–75. Recipient: Percy Fitzpatrick award, 1979, 1984. Agent: Felicity Bryan, 2-A North Parade, Banbury Road, Oxford OX2 6PE, England. Address: 54 Ronalds Road, Kloof 3610, Durban, Natal, South Africa.

PUBLICATIONS FOR CHILDREN

Fiction

The Mantis and the Moon: Stories for the Children of Africa,

illustrated by Leigh Voigt.   Johannesburg, Ravan Press, 1979.
Nqalu, The Mouse with No Whiskers, illustrated by Cora Coetzee. Cape Town, Tafelberg, 1979.
Once at KwaFubesi, illustrated by Leigh Voigt.   Johannesburg, Ravan Press, 1981.
The Bush Shrike.   Johannesburg, Ravan Press, 1982.
The Fiery-Necked Nightjar: A Christmas Story, illustrated by Leigh Voigt.   Johannesburg, Ravan Press, 1983.
The Wood-Ash Stars, illustrated by Shanne Altshuler.   Cape Town, Philip, 1983.
Marcus and the Boxing Gloves [Go-Kart], illustrated by Cora Coetzee.   Cape Town, Tafelberg, 2 vols., 1984–88.
Shadow of the Wild Hare, illustrated by Leigh Voigt.   Cape Town, Philip, 1986.
The Small Clay Bull, illustrated by Shanne Altshuler.   Cape Town, Philip, 1986.

PUBLICATIONS FOR ADULTS

Novel

Train to Doringbult.   London, Bodley Head, 1987.

*

Manuscript Collections: Killie Campbell Africana Library, Durban; National English Literary Museum, Grahamstown.

Marguerite Poland comments:
When I was a child there were very few books available which were set in South Africa, none which gave a sense of "belonging." I have tried to rectify this lack. I was fortunate to have had the opportunity to study African folklore and various African languages. From these studies I developed an abiding interest in the African folk tradition. However, I do *not* reproduce folktales in any way but create original stories which draw inspiration from this rich tradition. I hope to raise both social and environmental issues. I write primarily to entertain, but hope too to give children insights into the complex past and present of my fascinating but tragic country. I hope, in some small way, to encourage children to hold dear that which is good and beautiful from the past but to aspire to a society that is just and equal for all.

*   *   *

Marguerite Poland's animal stories are highly regarded in South Africa but as yet little known elsewhere. Some have European forerunners, but most have been influenced by various African traditions in storytelling. All are notable for a lucid style and an acute and detailed observation of the natural life of the East Cape countryside where she once lived.

Nqalu, The Mouse with No Whiskers, is a finely illustrated story of a journey of self-discovery which bears comparison with Brian Patten's creation myth, *Jumping Mouse*—though on the simpler level of a charming moral tale extolling the virtues of modesty and courage.

Like Kipling's *Just So Stories*, the brief title story of *The Mantis and the Moon* is a *pourquoi* tale. The mantis tries to capture the moon in its journey across the sky, and is briefly blinded for his audacity, but he obtains the forgiveness he prays for. This is why his descendants still pray to the moon. The next and longer story is quite different in style and appeal. Ntini, a small otter, is swept away with his grandfather in the flood that follows when men have dammed the river. But his adventures are those of any wilful, mischievous small boy, who is nevertheless desperately in need of the assistance of the various small creatures (including a mouse and an owl) who rescue him from his enemies and reunite him with his grandfather. This variety of type and complexity of story within the same volume is refreshing but can also be disconcerting. Fortunately most of these tales can be read and enjoyed at different levels of understanding, at any age from eight upwards.

This is certainly true of "The Windflower" in *Once at KwaFubesi*. Lwembu the brown jumping spider is lured from her quiet country home to the town, where she lives on a squalid overcrowded rubbish heap, the prey of marauders and *tsotsis* like the big Zindlavini spiders, or the cockroaches, the Maphela. This can be read straightforwardly as an adventure story but it can also be read as a satirical story of the unhealthy and danger-ridden existence in South African black townships. In the same volume, "Sidenge's Potion," a trickster story in the vein of the Brer Rabbit or Anansi folktales, is comparatively sophisticated at all levels in its working out of the spring hare's complex attempts to become a "whistling diviner."

Other books contain traditional-type stories of the lives of Southern African peoples: San, Xhosa, Tsonga, and Zulu. *The Wood-Ash Stars* and *The Small Clay Bull* each contain four such lively tales incorporating folk beliefs, and telling of the adventures of children or the concerns of older people as they herd their animals, hunt, encounter hyenas, long for a child, or escape from the guns of the first white settlers.

There are also stories of white children. Round the simple activities of a 10-year-old country boy Poland has created two pleasant little books, of particular interest and value to South African youngsters, but typical of children's interests anywhere. In *Marcus and the Boxing Gloves* Marcus dreams of defeating the school bully and becoming champion, but learns that keeping promises is more important than winning fame. In *Marcus and the Go-Kart* he has adventures in town with new friends.

Shadow of the Wild Hare is a story for slightly older readers. Rosie frees a riverine rabbit which the Xhosa trapper is using as bait to catch jackals. Through her concern for this rare wild creature she learns to value both its individuality and need for freedom and the trapper's knowledge and wisdom.

There is evident respect and affection in most of these stories for African folklore and family life, but save for the bleak portrait of black townships already mentioned, there is little direct reference in them to racial inequalities within South Africa. *The Bush Shrike*, however, is a delicate and poignant teenage novel which reveals anew Poland's skill in conveying character and situation, but contains in addition an implicit protest against racial prejudice. 14-year-old Anna becomes interested in the storeman's son, Josh, a lonely, aloof boy. Together they explore the countryside, observing the wildlife for the nature records Josh is keeping. But their developing friendship comes to an abrupt end when Anna's parents discover that Josh has coloured blood and promptly send their daughter away to boarding school. Uneasy relationships under apartheid are also explored in a searching adult novel, *Train to Doringbult*. Here one is reminded of Doris Lessing's Rhodesian stories of black and white children growing up together in harmony and friendship, until the relationship changes inevitably into the distant one of master and servant.

Though readers outside South Africa may have some initial trouble with vernacular names of people, vegetation, and animals (the striking accompanying illustrations are often helpful here), and with the scattering of words and phrases from Afrikaans, Xhosa, Zulu, and other African languages, Poland's books are varied and interesting and deserve a wider audience.

—Winifred Whitehead

POLLAND, Madeleine A(ngela, née Cahill). Also writes as Frances Adrian. British. Born in Kinsale, County Cork, Ireland, 31 May 1918. Educated at Hitchin Girls' Grammar School, Hertfordshire, 1929–37. Served in the Women's Auxiliary Air Force, 1942–45. Married Arthur Joseph Polland in 1946; one daughter and one son. Assistant librarian, Letchworth Public Library, Hertfordshire, 1939–42 and 1945–46. Agent: Hilary Rubinstein, A.P. Watt Ltd., 20 John Street, London WC1N 2DL, England. Address: Edificio Hercules 406, Avenida Gamonal, Arroyo de la Miel, Malaga, Spain.

PUBLICATIONS FOR CHILDREN

Fiction

Children of the Red King, illustrated by Annette Macarthur-Onslow. London, Constable, 1960; New York, Holt Rinehart, 1961.
The Town Across the Water, illustrated by Brian Wildsmith. London, Constable, 1961; New York, Holt Rinehart, 1963.
Beorn the Proud, illustrated by William Stobbs. London, Constable, 1961; New York, Holt Rinehart, 1962.
Fingal's Quest, illustrated by W.T. Mars. New York, Doubleday, and London, Burns Oates, 1961.
The White Twilight, illustrated by William Stobbs. London, Constable, 1962; New York, Holt Rinehart, 1965.
Chuiraquimba and the Black Robes, illustrated by Juan Carlos Barberis. New York, Doubleday, and London, Burns Oates, 1962.
City of the Golden House, illustrated by Leo Summers. New York, Doubleday, 1963; Kingswood, Surrey, World's Work, 1964.
The Queen's Blessing, illustrated by William Stobbs. London, Constable, 1963; New York, Holt Rinehart, 1964.
Flame over Tara, illustrated by Omar Davis. New York, Doubleday, 1964; Kingswood, Surrey, World's Work, 1965.
Mission to Cathay, illustrated by Peter Landa. New York, Doubleday, 1965; Kingswood, Surrey, World's Work, 1966.
Queen Without Crown, illustrated by William Stobbs. London, Constable, 1965; New York, Holt Rinehart, 1966.
Deirdre, illustrated by Sean Morrison. New York, Doubleday, and Kingswood, Surrey, World's Work, 1967.
To Tell My People, illustrated by John Holder. London, Hutchinson, and New York, Holt Rinehart, 1968.
Stranger in the Hills, illustrated by Victor Ambrus. New York, Doubleday, 1968; London, Hutchinson, 1969.
To Kill a King, illustrated by John Holder. London, Hutchinson, 1970; New York, Holt Rinehart, 1971.
Alhambra, illustrated by Mary Frances Gaaze. New York, Doubleday, 1970; London, Hutchinson, 1971.
A Family Affair, illustrated by Trevor Stubley. London, Hutchinson, 1971.
Daughter to Poseidon, illustrated by John Holder. London, Hutchinson, 1972; as *Daughter of the Sea*, New York, Doubleday, 1972.
Prince of the Double Axe, illustrated by Gareth Floyd. London, Abelard Schuman, 1976.

PUBLICATIONS FOR ADULTS

Novels

Thicker than Water. New York, Holt Rinehart, 1965; London, Hutchinson, 1967.
The Little Spot of Bother. London, Hutchinson, 1967; as *Minutes of a Murder*, New York, Holt Rinehart, 1967.

Random Army. London, Hutchinson, 1969; as *Shattered Summer*, New York, Doubleday, 1970.
Package to Spain. London, Hutchinson, and New York, Walker, 1971.
Double Shadow (as Frances Adrian). New York, Fawcett, and London, Macdonald and Jane's, 1977.
Sabrina. New York, Delacorte Press, and London, Collins, 1979.
All Their Kingdoms. New York, Delacorte Press, and London, Collins, 1981.
The Heart Speaks Many Ways. New York, Delacorte Press, and London, Collins, 1982.
No Price Too High. New York, Delacorte Press, 1984; London, Piatkus, 1985.
As It Was in the Beginning. London, Piatkus, 1987.

*

Manuscript Collection: Mugar Memorial Library, Boston University.

Madeleine A. Polland comments:

(1978) Almost without exception my books for children may be said to be the product of my own intense consciousness of the reality of history, and the reality of historical figures as people. It has always been my idea to try to portray events in which children become involved in the dramatic past. And it is, of course, infinitely more plausible to create dramatic adventures for children in past centuries, when it was perfectly possible for them to be abandoned with the need to look after themselves. Except in times of war, which television presents in all its heartbreaking contemporary detail (leaving no imagination necessary), children's lives at the present tend to run on more scheduled lines, leaving adventure to the days of history.

(1983) I would add that if I have forsaken the children for the moment, it is with a preoccupation with people of all times and all ages. Although I would admit to a sneaking affection for the period of *Sabrina*—1912 onwards.

*   *   *

Madeleine A. Polland is noted for her impressive list of historical novels with backgrounds as various as her own native Ireland, China, Viking Denmark, Norman England, mediaeval Scotland, Moorish Spain, and ancient Crete. However, two recent books are contemporary, and one is a mixture of ancient and modern. If we take her books published in the 1970's as representative of her skill in writing for young people, we may conclude that she offers, whether historical or contemporary, a cultivated and thickly textured species of adolescent romantic fiction. These books illustrate what Frank Eyre may have had in mind when he included Polland in a small group of modern children's writers who "have produced books that in a less demanding age would have been outstanding."

Although the narrative of *To Kill a King* hinges on a Saxon plot to assassinate William the Conqueror, the main interest lies in the love of Merca and Edward which blossoms during the dangers of their flight to Scotland. Edward's love "saves" Merca from the contemplative life towards which her misery following her parents' slaughter by the Normans has led her. In *Alhambra* the dramatic conflict is supplied by the young Juanito's longing for Princess Nahid despite his fiercely patriotic rejection of the Moors with whom he has lived since early childhood. In *A Family Affair*, it is true, the incipient teenage romantic attachment of Alex, the English girl, to Christian, the Danish boy, during the annual family holiday in Copenhagen, is muted to allow more prominence to the improbable mystery thriller involving eccentric aunts and inept thefts from picture galleries. But young love is the principal theme in *Daughter*

to *Poseidon*, both in the contemporary framework story of Saran's dependence upon the love of Miklos, the Greek student, in assuaging her grief and feelings of guilt over her parents' death in a car crash, and also in the parallel though much bulkier historical narrative in which Saran is rescued from the sea by Mikolai, the Cretan youth who with Saran's resolute support saves Knossos from infiltration by the Hellenes. The interweaving of these two levels is imaginatively done, as is the exciting build-up to the earthquake and the overthrow of Paradocles.

Polland's historical researchers may seldom provide more than a vivid romanticised background to the drama she unfolds, and her plots on occasion may slip into the implausible. In her concern to convey emotion and describe mental states she may at times prolong the agony at the expense of narrative pace and indulge in slightly inflated prose, often marked by a trick of repeating names or other words, as in "she would be safer, safer against the threat of war" and "Saran felt the soft, soft touch of the fine linen on her legs." But she portrays her characters in bitter conflict, cruel dilemmas; they suffer pain and permanent injury on the road to self-knowledge. To the older reader who has not yet fully entered the world of adult fiction she may well provide a not inconsiderable bridge.

—Graham Hammond

———

POLLOCK, Mary. See **BLYTON, Enid.**

———

POOLE, (Jane Penelope) Josephine (née Cumpston). British. Born in London, 12 February 1933. Educated at Fyling Hall School, Cumberland, 1941–45; Queensgate School, London, 1945–50. Married 1) Timothy Ruscombe Poole in 1956, four daughters; 2) Vincent John Hawker Helyar in 1975, one daughter and one son. Solicitor's secretary, London, 1951–54; secretary, BBC Features Department, London, 1954–56. Agent: A.P. Watt Ltd., 20 John Street, London WC1N 2DL. Address: Poundisford Lodge, Poundisford, Taunton, Somerset, England.

PUBLICATIONS FOR CHILDREN

Fiction

A Dream in the House, illustrated by Peggy Fortnum. London, Hutchinson, 1961.
Moon Eyes. London, Hutchinson, 1965; Boston, Little Brown, 1967.
Catch as Catch Can. London, Hutchinson, 1969; New York, Harper, 1970.
Billy Buck. London, Hutchinson, 1972; as *The Visitor*, New York, Harper, 1972.
Touch and Go. London, Hutchinson, and New York, Harper, 1976.
The Open Grave, illustrated by Tony Kerins. London, Benn, 1979.
The Forbidden Room, illustrated by Tony Kerins. London, Benn, 1979.
Hannah Chance. London, Hutchinson, 1980.
Diamond Jack. London, Methuen, 1983.
Three for Luck, illustrated by Barrie Thorpe. London, Hutchinson, 1985.
Wildlife Tales, illustrated by Douglas Hall. London, Hutchinson,

1986.
The Loving Ghosts. London, Hutchinson, 1988.

Plays

Caractacus, music by Michael Dyer (produced 1986).

Television Plays: *The Inheritance* (*Shadows* series), 1976; *Ring a Rosie*, 1982; *With Love, Belinda*, 1982; *The Animal Lover*, 1982; *Three in the Wild: Fox, Buzzard, Dartmoor Pony*, 1984.

Other

When Fishes Flew: A Selection of Legends and Old Wives' Tales from the West Country, illustrated by Barbara Swiderska. London, Benn, 1978; as *Kings, Ghosts, and Highwaymen*, London, Carousel, 1981.
Golden Classics (*Puss in Boots, The Sleeping Beauty*), illustrated by Edmund Morin. London, Hutchinson, 2 vols., 1988.

PUBLICATIONS FOR ADULTS

Novels

The Lilywhite Boys. London, Hart Davis, 1968.
Yokeham. London, Murray, 1970.

Short Stories

West Country Tales (based on television plays), with others. Exeter, Webb and Bower, 1981.

Plays

Television Plays: *The Harbourer* (*Country Tales* series), 1975; *The Sabbatical, The Breakdown*, and *Miss Constantine* (*West Country Tales* series), 1981.

Other

The Country Diary Companion. Exeter, Webb and Bower, 1984.

*

Josephine Poole comments:
   I enjoy writing for children. I hope this makes the books enjoyable.

*   *   *

   Josephine Poole is a writer specialising in mystery: supernatural, in *Moon Eyes*, criminal, in *Catch as Catch Can*, and, all-pervadingly, in everything she does, the mystifying nature of life itself. She has a talent for building tension out of small details and creating menace in an apparently normal, friendly scene. In her handling of *la chasse humaine* she rivals Geoffrey Household, with whom she has much in common. The scene in *Touch and Go*, probably her most accomplished work to date, in which the heroine is hunted by unknown attackers round unfamiliar farm buildings in the dark and fog, is a masterpiece of its kind.
   The story of *Touch and Go*, racy, outrageous, and just plausible enough to suspend disbelief, is characteristic Poole country. Teenage Emily and her with-it, intellectual mother—Poole also has a knack of brief, astringent pen portraits as merciless as they are funny—have booked for a "farmhouse" holiday in Devon. On the way they crash the car and Emily, recovering overnight in hospital, stumbles on the

first clue in a sequence which leads her, with the help of her friend, Charles, to a gang of terrorists planning an explosion in the local naval college. The narrative ranges between the creepily sinister and the downright hilarious: the dialogue is crisp and realistic. In addition, there is the added ingredient which lifts Poole's writing a long way above the common. This is her treatment of her characters, and it is a thread which runs consistently through all her books. It sustains the occasional weaknesses of plot and gives an added depth to what would otherwise be no more than light entertainment. Emily is plump and unsophisticated for her age, the heroine of *Moon Eyes* imaginative but intellectually idle, yet both are intensely real, and, witches and smugglers notwithstanding, so are the worlds in which they live. This psychological element is carried even further in *Hannah Chance*. Here the heroine is actually an adult, a youngish schoolteacher, emotionally undeveloped, living with her clergyman father. Nor is her life made easier by her unfortunate name of Miss Chance. When a fellow-teacher disappears, she is badgered by a teenage boy into following up his conviction that the man has been murdered. But the real interest of the book lies less in the slightly contrived twists of the plot than in the growing relationship between the two: the retiring, self-critical woman and the intelligent, determined boy whose apparent confidence hides an equal need for reassurance. It is typical of Poole's way of thought that in both cases it is not years but intensity of living which brings maturity.
   In the past few years Poole has broadened her range further. While still writing mysteries for younger readers (*Three for Luck*) she has also begun writing young adult mysteries such as *Diamond Jack* and *The Loving Ghosts*, where romance takes a more prominent place beside mystery. She has also tried her hand at carefully researched short stories about animals in *Wildlife Tales*.

—Anne Carter

———

PORTER, Eleanor H(odgman). Also wrote as Eleanor Stuart. American. Born in Littleton, New Hampshire, 19 December 1868. Educated at the New England Conservatory of Music, Boston. Married John L. Porter in 1892. Choir and concert singer, then teacher; full-time writer from 1901. *Died 21 May 1920.*

PUBLICATIONS FOR CHILDREN

Fiction

Cross Currents, illustrated by William Stecher. Boston, Wilde, 1907; London, Harrap, 1928.
The Turn of the Tide, illustrated by Frank Merrill. Boston, Wilde, 1908; London, Harrap, 1928.
The Sunbridge Girls at Six Star Ranch (as Eleanor Stuart), illustrated by Frank Murch. Boston, Page, 1913; as *Six Star Ranch*, Page, and London, Stanley Paul, 1916.
Pollyanna, illustrated by Stockton Mulford. Boston, Page, and London, Pitman, 1913.
Pollyanna Grows Up, illustrated by H. Weston Taylor. Boston, Page, and London, Pitman, 1915.

PUBLICATIONS FOR ADULTS

Novels

The Story of Marco. Cincinnati, Jennings and Graham, 1911; Lon-

don, Stanley Paul, 1920.
Miss Billy. Boston, Page, 1911; London, Stanley Paul, 1914.
Miss Billy's Decision. Boston, Page, 1912; London, Stanley Paul, 1915.
Miss Billy—Married. Boston, Page, 1914; London, Stanley Paul, 1915.
Just David. Boston, Houghton Mifflin, and London, Constable, 1916.
The Road to Understanding. Boston, Houghton Mifflin, and London, Constable, 1917.
Oh, Money! Money! Boston, Houghton Mifflin, and London, Constable, 1918.
Dawn. Boston, Houghton Mifflin, 1919; as *Keith's Dark Tower*, London, Constable, 1919.
Mary Marie. Boston, Houghton Mifflin, and London, Constable, 1920.
Sister Sue. Boston, Houghton Mifflin, and London, Constable, 1921.

Short Stories

The Tangled Threads. Boston, Houghton Mifflin, 1919.
Across the Years. Boston, Houghton Mifflin, 1919.
The Tie That Binds. Boston, Houghton Mifflin, 1919.
Money, Love, and Kate, Together with The Story of a Nickel. New York, Doran, 1923; London, Hodder and Stoughton, 1924.
Hustler Joe and Other Stories. New York, Doran, 1924.
Little Pardner and Other Stories. New York, Doran, 1926; London, Hodder and Stoughton, 1927.
Just Mother and Other Stories. New York, Doran, 1927.
The Fortunate Mary. New York, Doubleday, 1928.

*   *   *

"Pollyanna" has achieved dictionary status as a word to describe a person of excessive optimism, and certainly Eleanor H. Porter's original Pollyanna is the doyenne of the storybook children who spread light and gladness wherever they go. This was a genre much favored by writers in the three decades before the First World War, and grew out of the evangelical story on which most of them would have been reared and their parents before them, the story of the child who spoke heavenly truths and converted its hard-hearted elders and wayward contemporaries. After Little Lord Fauntleroy (1886), whom Pollyanna much resembles, this genre became secularized; Pollyanna and her kind tame the crabby and melt the hearts of the obdurate by no heavenly message, merely by their own buoyant spirits. "For long years I have been a cross, crabbed, unlovable, unloved old man....Then one day, like one of the prisms that you love so well, little girl, you danced into my life, and flecked my dreary old world with dashes of the purple and gold and scarlet of your own bright cheeriness."

In *Pollyanna* the orphaned heroine arrives at the house of an aunt who doesn't want her, brings warmth into that cold heart, and reunites her with the lover she dismissed 15 years before, thaws the icy John Pendleton, shows a despairing minister the way he must tread, brings gladness to invalids and widows, cements marriages, finds homes for the homeless, whether puppies, kittens, or boys. Asked what the secret is Dr. Ames says: "As far as I can find out it is an overwhelming, unquenchable gladness for everything that has happened or is going to happen." Pollyanna herself calls it the "just being glad" game, and tells the story of how when she had asked for a doll for Christmas the good ladies who took an interest in her father and his parish sent crutches instead, and her father instructed her that she must be glad because she didn't need them. In *Pollyanna Grows Up* her story is continued, now in a city setting, where her influence is even more potent than before. Urging her to write about her

experiences, a contemporary says: "The instrument that you play on, Pollyanna, will be the great heart of the world; and to me that seems the most wonderful instrument of all....Under your touch, if you are skilful, it will respond with smiles or tears as you will." It was no doubt Porter's deep conviction that she herself was playing on the great heart of the world that made *Pollyanna* so successful.

—Gillian Avery

————

PORTER, Gene Stratton (Geneva Grace Stratton Porter). American. Born in Wabash County, Indiana, 17 August 1863. Attended public schools. Married Charles Darwin Porter in 1886; one daughter. Regular contributor, *McCall's Magazine*; photographic editor, *Recreation* magazine; member of the natural history department, *Outing* magazine; natural history photography specialist, *Photographic Times Annual Almanac*, four years. Founded Gene Stratton Porter Productions film company, 1922. *Died 6 December 1924.*

PUBLICATIONS FOR CHILDREN

Fiction

Freckles, illustrated by E. Stetson Crawford. New York, Doubleday, 1904; London, Murray, 1905.
A Girl of the Limberlost, illustrated by Wladyslaw T. Benda. New York, Doubleday, 1909; London, Hodder and Stoughton, 1911.
The Magic Garden, illustrated by Lee Thayer. New York, Doubleday, and London, Hutchinson, 1927.

Play

Screenplay: *A Girl of the Limberlost*, 1924.

Verse

Morning Face, illustrated by the author. New York, Doubleday, and London, Murray, 1916.

PUBLICATIONS FOR ADULTS

Novels

The Song of the Cardinal: A Love Story. Indianapolis, Bobbs Merrill, 1903; London, Hodder and Stoughton, 1913.
At the Foot of the Rainbow. New York, Outing Publishing Company, 1907; London, Hodder and Stoughton, 1913.
The Harvester. New York, Doubleday, and London, Hodder and Stoughton, 1911.
Laddie: A True-Blue Story. New York, Doubleday, and London, Murray, 1913.
Michael O'Halloran. New York, Doubleday, and London, Murray, 1915.
A Daughter of the Land. New York, Doubleday, and London, Murray, 1918.
Her Father's Daughter. New York, Doubleday, and London, Murray, 1921.
The White Flag. New York, Doubleday, and London, Murray, 1923.
The Keeper of the Bees. New York, Doubleday, and London,

Hutchinson, 1925.

Verse

The Fire Bird. New York, Doubleday, and London, Murray, 1922.
Jesus of the Emerald. New York, Doubleday, and London, Murray, 1923.

Other

What I Have Done with Birds: Character Studies of Native American Birds. Indianapolis, Bobbs Merrill, 1907; revised edition, New York, Doubleday, 1917; as *Friends in Feathers*, London, Curtis Brown, 1917.
Birds of the Bible. Cincinnati, Jennings and Graham, 1909; London, Hodder and Stoughton, 1910.
Music of the Wild, illustrated by the author. Cincinnati, Jennings and Graham, and London, Hodder and Stoughton, 1910.
Moths of the Limberlost, illustrated by the author. New York, Doubleday, 1912; London, Hodder and Stoughton, 1913.
After the Flood. Indianapolis, Bobbs Merrill, 1912.
Birds of the Limberlost. New York, Doubleday, 1914.
Homing with the Birds. New York, Doubleday, and London, Murray, 1919.
Wings. New York, Doubleday, 1923.
Tales You Won't Believe (natural history). New York, Doubleday, and London, Heinemann, 1925.
Let Us Highly Resolve (essays). New York, Doubleday, and London, Heinemann, 1927.

*

Critical Studies: *The Lady of the Limberlost: The Life and Letters of Gene Stratton Porter* by Jeanette Porter Meehan, New York, Doubleday, 1928, as *Life and Letters of Gene Stratton Porter*, London, Hutchinson, 1928; *Gene Stratton Porter* by Bernard F. Richards, Boston, Twayne, 1980.

*   *   *

Although Gene Stratton Porter's novels might now be called old-fashioned, they have several timeless qualities. Porter was a naturalist and a resident of the Limberlost area of northern Indiana; her motive was first of all to interest readers in the world of nature. Her books are filled with description of birds and moths particularly. The focal significance of the lives of some of her characters is the wilderness in which Elnora Comstock, the Bird Woman, and Freckles, in her best known books, *A Girl of the Limberlost* and *Freckles*, observe and collect, make notes and entice converts to nature study.

Characters like Elnora Comstock and Freckles seem perhaps to contemporary readers incredibly dedicated to the Golden Rule; they behave in an idealized manner, their anger shortlived and responding to reason, their selfishness recognized and yielding to love. Surprisingly, however, many of these characters are memorable, most significantly those who, like McLean the lumber boss in *Freckles*, live close to a natural environment. The city dwellers are more flat and therefore less believable, but Porter makes even them transcend their sinful natures for late conversions to goodness.

Two themes seem apparent in Porter's writing: first, a thematic reverence for nature and a Christian mystic's appreciation for a world that God has made perfect; and second, her optimism about human behavior and its perfectability. This latter theme is particularly evident in *A Girl of the Limberlost* wherein Elnora earns her way through high school by hunting rare moths. Her emergence in radiant maturity is echoed by her mother's change from sour to sweet.

Porter's nonfiction about birds and moths is accompanied by her own photographic illustrations, painstakingly filmed and meticulously accurate in color effects. In her fiction Porter's word pictures are equally carefully painted; her words clothe in natural detail the romantic stories of love that wins despite hardship and of vicious hatred that turns to incredible generosity. Sentimental as they seem to readers of today, and called both "saccharine" and "appealing" by her contemporaries, Porter's novels had great readership during the early years of the century.

—Rebecca J. Lukens

———

PORTER, Sheena. British. Born in Melton Mowbray, Leicestershire, 19 September 1935. Educated at King Edward VII Grammar School, Melton Mowbray, 1947–54; Loughborough College School of Librarianship, Leicestershire, 1955–56. Married Patrick Lane in 1966; two daughters. Library assistant, Leicester City Library, 1954–57; regional children's librarian, Nottinghamshire County Library, 1957–60; editorial assistant, Oxford University Press, London, 1960–61; regional children's librarian, Shropshire County Library, 1961–62. Recipient: Library Association Carnegie Medal, 1965. Address: 57 Gravel Hill, Ludlow, Shropshire, England.

P<small>UBLICATIONS FOR</small> C<small>HILDREN</small>

Fiction

The Bronze Chrysanthemum, illustrated by Shirley Hughes. London, Oxford University Press, 1961; Princeton, New Jersey, Van Nostrand, 1965.
Hills and Hollows, illustrated by Victor Ambrus. London, Oxford University Press, 1962.
Jacob's Ladder, illustrated by Victor Ambrus. London, Oxford University Press, 1963.
Nordy Bank, illustrated by Annette Macarthur-Onslow. London, Oxford University Press, 1964; New York, Roy, 1967.
The Knockers, illustrated by Gareth Floyd. London, Oxford University Press, 1965.
Deerfold, illustrated by Victor Ambrus. London, Oxford University Press, 1966.
The Scapegoat, illustrated by Doreen Roberts. London, Oxford University Press, 1968.
The Valley of Carreg-Wen, illustrated by Doreen Roberts. London, Oxford University Press, 1971.
The Hospital, illustrated by Robin Jacques. London, Oxford University Press, 1973.

*   *   *

Sheena Porter's stories are those of an author with impressive skills and a deep sense of history. She received the Carnegie Medal for *Nordy Bank*, a haunting holiday adventure story set in Shropshire. In this book, Bron, the main character, is not gifted with heroine-like qualities, but is shy, quiet, and introverted. In the course of the story she becomes difficult, aggressive, and withdrawn under the influence of the historic atmosphere pervading Nordy Bank. This strong awareness of place and past is subtly blended with down-to-earth factual detail of the minutiae of camping: a combination which enables different types of reader to enjoy this book at various levels. Porter adds to a sound setting peopled with convincing characters the intense drama of an escaped Alsatian dog. Bron successfully captures the dog, and in winning his confidence regains her own.

The reader shares Bron's anguish over the fate of Griff, a deaf army dog in need of retraining, but the climax of the book is reached with the choice which Bron has to make: a decision which involves conflicting loyalties and which is finally made for her by her parents.

Nordy Bank has qualities of other books by Porter: the authentic, identifiable background; the evolution of the leading character; relationships with parents and friends; convincing detail of family life and its various ramifications. *The Bronze Chrysanthemum* showed considerable potential, and this was fulfilled with *Jacob's Ladder* and *Nordy Bank*. Unlike many writers Porter has not been content to find a successful formula and slavishly repeat it. Her plots are remarkable for their wide range of location and of theme. By the late 1960's an increasing number of writers tended to deal with contemporary problems: a trend now in danger of being carried to extremes. Porter is perhaps marginally less successful in her novels on such themes, but she handles the serious problem of mental illness with acute sensitivity in *The Hospital*, environmental problems with awareness in *The Valley of Carreg-Wen*, and the timeless stepmother problem with understanding in *The Scapegoat*.

Porter, more than many contemporary writers for children, covers widely different themes. She wrote initially with the deliberate intention of providing a bridge between the easy adventure story and the more demanding material of writers like Lucy Boston and William Mayne, but she has developed as a distinguished writer for children in her own right. Children's literature is the richer for her contribution.

—Anne W. Ellis

POTTER, (Helen) Beatrix. British. Born in London, 28 July 1866. Educated privately. Married William Heelis in 1913. Settled in Sawrey, Lancashire as a farmer and sheep-breeder. Chairman, Herdwick Breeders' Association. Artist: Drawings Exhibition, Victoria and Albert Museum, London, 1972; National Book League, London, 1976; Abbott Hall Art Gallery, Kendal, Cumbria, 1983; Tate Gallery, London, 1987; Pierpont Morgan Library, New York, 1988. *Died 22 December 1943.*

PUBLICATIONS FOR CHILDREN (illustrated by the author)

Fiction

The Tale of Peter Rabbit. Privately printed, 1900; revised edition, London and New York, Warne, 1902.
The Tailor of Gloucester. Privately printed, 1902; revised edition, London and New York, Warne, 1903; as *The Tailor of Gloucester from the Original Manuscript*, 1969.
The Tale of Squirrel Nutkin. London and New York, Warne, 1903.
The Tale of Benjamin Bunny. London and New York, Warne, 1904.
The Tale of Two Bad Mice. London and New York, Warne, 1904.
The Tale of Mrs. Tiggy-Winkle. London and New York, Warne, 1905.
The Pie and the Patty-Pan. London and New York, Warne, 1905.
The Tale of Mr. Jeremy Fisher. London and New York, Warne, 1906.
The Story of a Fierce Bad Rabbit. London and New York, Warne, 1906.
The Story of Miss Moppet. London and New York, Warne, 1906.
The Tale of Tom Kitten. London and New York, Warne, 1907.
The Tale of Jemima Puddle-Duck. London and New York, Warne, 1908.

The Roly-Poly Pudding. London and New York, Warne, 1908; as *The Tale of Samuel Whiskers; or, The Roly-Poly Pudding*, London, Warne, 1926.
The Tale of the Flopsy Bunnies. London and New York, Warne, 1909.
Ginger and Pickles. London and New York, Warne, 1909.
The Tale of Mrs. Tittlemouse. London and New York, Warne, 1910.
The Tale of Timmy Tiptoes. London and New York, Warne, 1911.
The Tale of Mr. Tod. London and New York, Warne, 1912.
The Tale of Pigling Bland. London and New York, Warne, 1913.
The Tale of Johnny Town-Mouse. London and New York, Warne, 1918.
The Fairy Caravan. London, privately printed, and Philadelphia, McKay, 1929.
The Tale of Little Pig Robinson. Philadelphia, McKay, and London, Warne, 1930.
Sister Anne, illustrated by Katharine Sturges. Philadelphia, McKay, 1932.
Wag-by-Wall. London, Warne, and Boston, Horn Book, 1944.
The Tale of the Faithful Dove, illustrated by Marie Angel. London, Warne, 1955; New York, Warne, 1956.
The Sly Old Cat. London and New York, Warne, 1971.
The Tale of Tuppenny, illustrated by Marie Angel. London and New York, Warne, 1973.

Verse

Appley Dapply's Nursery Rhymes. London and New York, Warne, 1917.
Cecily Parsley's Nursery Rhymes. London and New York, Warne, 1922.
Beatrix Potter's Nursery Rhyme Book. London and New York, Warne, 1984.

Other

Peter Rabbit's Painting Book. London and New York, Warne, 1911.
Tom Kitten's Painting Book. London and New York, Warne, 1917.
Jemima Puddle-Duck's Painting Book. London and New York, Warne, 1925.
Peter Rabbit's Almanac for 1929. London and New York, Warne, 1928.
Yours Affectionately, Peter Rabbit: Miniature Letters by Beatrix Potter, edited by Anne Emerson. London and New York, Warne, 1983.

PUBLICATIONS FOR ADULTS

Other

The Art of Beatrix Potter: Direct Reproductions of Beatrix Potter's Preliminary Studies and Finished Drawings, Also Examples of Her Original Manuscript, edited by Leslie Linder and W.A. Herring. London and New York, Warne, 1955; revised edition, 1972.
The Journal of Beatrix Potter from 1881 to 1897, Transcribed from Her Code Writing by Leslie Linder. London and New York, Warne, 1966.
Letters to Children. Cambridge, Massachusetts, Harvard College Library Department of Printing and Graphic Arts, 1967.
Beatrix Potter's Birthday Book, edited by Enid Linder. London and New York, Warne, 1974.
Dear Ivy, Dear June: Letters from Beatrix Potter, edited by Margaret Crawford Maloney. Toronto, Other Press, 1977.

Beatrix Potter's Americans: Selected Letters, edited by Jane Crowell Morse.   Boston, Horn Book, 1981; London, Warne, 1982.

*

Bibliography: *A History of the Writings of Beatrix Potter, Including Unpublished Work* by Leslie Linder, London and New York, Warne, 1971.

Manuscript Collections: Leslie Linder Bequest (includes watercolours and sketches), National Book League, London; Free Library, Philadelphia.

Critical Studies: *The Tale of Beatrix Potter: A Biography*, London and New York, Warne, 1946, revised edition, 1968, 1985, and *The Magic Years of Beatrix Potter*, London and New York, Warne, 1978, both by Margaret Lane; *Beatrix Potter* by Marcus Crouch, London, Bodley Head, 1960, New York, Walck, 1961; *The History of "The Tale of Peter Rabbit,"* London and New York, Warne, 1976; *Cousin Beatie: A Memory of Beatrix Potter* by Ulla Hyde Parker, London, Warne, 1981; *Beatrix Potter in Scotland* by Deborah Rolland, London, Warne, 1981; *The Art of Beatrix Potter 1866–1943* (exhibition catalogue), Kendal, Cumbria, Abbot Hall Art Gallery, 1983; *Beatrix Potter: The Victoria and Albert Collection Catalogue* edited by Anne S. Hobbs and Joyce Irene Whalley, London, Victoria and Albert Museum, 1985, New York, Warne, 1986; *Beatrix Potter: Artist, Storyteller and Countrywoman*, London and New York, Warne, 1986, and *That Naughty Rabbit: Beatrix Potter and Peter Rabbit* London and New York, Warne, 1987, both by Judy Taylor; *The Real World of Beatrix Potter* by Elizabeth M. Battrick, Norwich, Jarrold, 1986; *Beatrix Potter* by Ruth MacDonald, Boston, Twayne, 1986; *Beatrix Potter* by Elizabeth Buchan, London, Hamish Hamilton, 1987; *Beatrix Potter 1866–1943: The Artist and Her World* by Judy Taylor, Joyce Irene Whalley, Anne Hobbs, and Elizabeth M. Battrick, London, Warne, 1987, New York, Warne, 1988; *Beatrix Potter's Derwentwater* by Wynne Bartlett and Joyce Irene Whalley, London, Warne, 1988.

Illustrator: *A Happy Pair* by F.E. Weatherley, 1893(?); *Comical Customers*, 1894(?); *Wayside and Woodland Fungi* by W.P.K. Findlay, 1967.

*   *   *

Beatrix Potter's tales for children are remarkable in that few of them include any children—or indeed any humans at all. Other writers for children had of course used animals as the main protagonists of their stories, and indeed by the time that Potter started writing at the beginning of the 20th century, the tradition of the animal story was well-established. But most stories were quite obviously about humans in animal form, with human attitudes and behaviour—a genre that goes back to Aesop. What particularly distinguished Potter's work was that her animals were primarily animals, in a world where the human was intrusive and unnecessary. Her natural history drawings are the key to her later work, for from a child she had shown great interest in the natural world, and had recorded it as she saw it, from the hesitant flower sketches of her childhood to the competent microscopic drawings of her late teens. She studied her own pet rabbit meticulously, and likewise the other creatures that aroused her interest: spiders, flies, ducks, mice. She made many scientifically accurate drawings, including a remarkable series of fungi, which astonish those who only know her from her Peter Rabbit books. She also had a great feeling for place, and her interest in landscape was heightened by a further interest in photography, a pursuit which she shared with her father on many a countryside photographic expedition. All this made her a careful and precise recorder of the natural scene and the little creatures that inhabit it.

With such a background she could have developed into a good artist and illustrator, but would not necessarily have become a good writer. However, it is quite obvious that for Potter the word and the picture were complementary. We can see this from the fact that some of the famous stories originated in pictorial letters, sent earlier in her life to children of her acquaintance. For she saw even as she wrote, and the picture and the tale made a coherent whole. Only later in life, when the imaginative faculty was weakening did she attempt to write round her pictures, while the fragmentary scraps of original writing not allied to illustrations show how bereft of inspiration she became when the cohesion of the word and its visual counterpart were lacking. Her drawings were made originally for her own pleasure, but she wasted nothing. She borrowed back the picture letters she had originally sent to the Moore children and reworked them to make her books; she remembered the story she had been told about an old tailor in Gloucester; even the mice that sat down to spin did so on chairs she had seen in her grandmother's house. She could see, both in her mind's eye and with her pencil, so accurately that readers who know the stories well can go about the countryside she knew and loved and say "That is in *Peter Rabbit*," or "That is the path in *Tom Kitten*." In the same way, the staff of the Textile Department in the Victoria and Albert Museum, London, were able to recognize the 18th-century costumes which she drew there many years before for use in *The Tailor of Gloucester*.

Nevertheless, out of these remembered incidents and re-used sketches, Potter created a whole new world of characters who are as alive today as they were more than 80 years ago, when Peter Rabbit first appeared. For many of us, Jemima Puddleduck, Mrs. Tiggy-Winkle, and Jeremy Fisher have personalities that transcend time and place, and how much, we may wonder, have the Potter tales affected the attitude to mice and rabbits of several generations of children! For the adult, faced with repeated requests for re-reading a favourite tale, it is also important that the language in which Potter chose to write her children's books was both simple and direct, with no attempt to write down to the young listener—indeed her use of the word "soporific" in *The Flopsy Bunnies* is notorious. As a result, her stories are as easy to read aloud as to listen to.

Potter was always very concerned about the actual appearance of her books, the text as much as the illustrations. She herself occasionally altered the amount of text appearing on the printed page, moving a word or two overleaf if she felt it would produce the page appearance that she desired. The format of the Peter Rabbit books was quite distinctive at the time when they made their first appearance, and in spite of changes in the style of children's books during the century, they remain much the same as when they were first published. An attempt to issue *The Pie and the Patty Pan* and *The Roly-Poly Pudding* in a larger format was not a success and they too eventually conformed to the established pattern of a size which fits so comfortably into small hands. The length of the stories too is right for the young child, being fairly short, with simple uncrowded events which can be understood by the very youngest listener.

If is difficult to sum up the reason for the popularity which Potter has enjoyed for more than three-quarters of a century—a popularity which shows no sign of diminishing in any of the many countries where her works have been published. Moreover, as recent exhibitions of her works have shown, she appeals equally to all ages, if for varying reasons, and has become something of a cult on both sides of the Atlantic. Undoubtedly part of the attraction must lie in the aptness of her illustrations to the text, and the perfection of the art work itself. But in the end the stories must stand or fall by the writing, and there is no doubt that as a storyteller she was able to create a complete world in which the characters go about their normal daily life, and into which we are allowed merely a brief peep. They inhabit a twilight world between reality and imagination, in which the very young child can also share. But for those long past their childhood she offers a gallery of characters whose personalities are so fixed in our minds that Benjamin Bunny, Squirrel Nutkin, and the rest exist forever in the timeless countryside of her own beloved Lakeland.

—Joyce Irene Whalley

POWER, Rhoda (Dolores le Poer). British. Born in Altrincham, Cheshire, in 1890. Educated at Oxford High School for Girls, 1903–09; Girton College, Cambridge, 1909–12. Director of Children's Broadcasting, BBC Radio, London, 1920's and 1930's. *Died 9 March 1957.*

PUBLICATIONS FOR CHILDREN

Fiction

Boys and Girls of History, with Eileen Power. London, Cambridge University Press, 1926; New York, Macmillan, 1927; revised edition, London, Dobson, 1968; New York, Roy, 1970.
More Boys and Girls of History, with Eileen Power. London, Cambridge University Press, and New York, Macmillan, 1928.
Ten Minute Tales and Dialogue Stories, illustrated by Gwen White. London, Evans, 1943.
Here and There Stories, illustrated by Phyllis Bray. London, Evans, 1945.
Redcap Runs Away, illustrated by C. Walter Hodges. London, Cape, 1952; Boston, Houghton Mifflin, 1953.
We Were There, illustrated by Charl. London, Allen and Unwin, 1955.
We Too Were There: More Stories from History, illustrated by Charl. London, Allen and Unwin, 1956.
From the Fury of the Norsemen and Other Stories, illustrated by Pauline Baynes. Boston, Houghton Mifflin, 1957.

Other

Union Jack Saints: Legends, with others. London, Constable, 1920.
Twenty Centuries of Travel: A Simple Survey of British History, with Eileen Power. London, Pitman, 1926.
Cities and Their Stories: An Introduction to the Study of European History, with Eileen Power. London, A. and C. Black, and Boston, Houghton Mifflin, 1927.
The Age of Discovery from Marco Polo to Henry Hudson. London and New York, Putnam, 1927.
How It Happened: Myths and Folktales, illustrated by Agnes Miller Parker. Cambridge, University Press, 1930; Boston, Houghton Mifflin, 1936.
Richard the Lionheart and the Third Crusade, edited by Eileen Power. London and New York, Putnam, 1931.
Stories from Everywhere, illustrated by Nina K. Brisley. London, Evans, and New York, Macmillan, 1931; as *The Big Book of Stories from Many Lands*, New York, Watts, 1970.
Great People of the Past (Ancient Times, A.D. 600–1600, Modern Times). London, Cambridge University Press, 3 vols., 1932; New York, Macmillan, 1 vol., 1933.
The Kingsway Histories for Juniors (From Early Days to Norman Times, Norman Times and the Middle Ages, The Peasants' Revolt to James I, From James I to Modern Times), illustrated by E. Hamilton Thompson. London, Evans, 4 vols., 1937–38.

PUBLICATIONS FOR ADULTS

Other

Under Cossack and Bolshevik. London, Methuen, 1919; as *Under the Bolshevik Reign of Terror*, New York, McBride, 1919.

*   *   *

In the 1930's intelligent school librarians and parents were always on the look-out for a new book by Rhoda Power. She could give young readers an interest in history which would last and take them on to serious study. Her *Boys and Girls of History*, written in collaboration with her sister, Eileen, the historian, were outstanding of their kind. They were halfway between fiction and solid history. She told her stories of these boys and girls through minor characters mostly, unless there happened to be a very well-documented child, like, for example, the young Mary Queen of Scots. On the whole they are the stories of apprentices, of children on the outskirts of some great event: the Bristol lad or the Burmese child attaching himself first to the extraordinary stranger Ralph Fitch, first Englishman to visit Burma, but deserting him for the greater honour of tending a white elephant.

By today's standards these are long stories with no talking down or easy vocabulary, but they are compulsive reading for anyone interested in the past and must have helped many a history teacher as well as her pupils. They range the world with endpaper maps showing the voyages; and they are packed with authentic detail described so vividly that they are never boring. In the voyage to the Bermudas in 1609 everyone is bailing the ships after a storm: "The richer ones looking strangely bedraggled for the colours in their silk doublets were running and the stuffing in their bombasted britches was so clogged with water that it smelt of wet hay." This I think gives a taste of her writing. When I collaborated with her in a BBC series she always knew exactly where I could get the right reference; she would never let me guess! Her *How It Happened* ranged the world of folklore (and has outstanding illustrations by Agnes Miller Parker), and here equally there is no talking down. She never sets herself above her child audience but expects them to be her equals. This was her strength.

—Naomi Mitchison

POWLING, Chris. British. Born in London, 16 February 1943. Educated at Bromley Grammar School, Kent; St. Catherine's College, Oxford, M.A. 1965; King's College, University of London, postgraduate certificate in education 1966; Royal Academy of Music, diploma in speech and drama 1968; Institute of Education, London, advanced diploma in education, 1970; University of Sussex, Brighton, M.A. 1984. Married Janet Smith in 1966; two daughters. Primary school teacher, 1966–75, and head teacher, 1975–85, London. Since 1985 Senior Lecturer in English, King Alfred's College, Winchester. Since 1976 occasional contributor and presenter, BBC Radio 4. Address: The Old Chapel, Easton, Near Winchester, Hampshire SO21 1EG, England.

PUBLICATIONS FOR CHILDREN

Fiction

Daredevils or Scaredycats, illustrated by Frank Rodgers. London,

Abelard, 1979.

Mog and the Rectifier, illustrated by Stephen Lavis. London, Abelard, 1980.

The Mustang Machine. London, Abelard, 1981.

Uncle Neptune. London, Abelard, 1982.

The Conker as Hard as a Diamond, illustrated by Jon Riley. London, Viking Kestrel, 1984.

Stuntkid, illustrated by Stephen Lavis. London, Blackie, 1985.

The Phantom Carwash, illustrated by Jean Baylis. London, Heinemann, 1986.

Fingers Crossed, illustrated by Jean Baylis. London, Blackie, 1987.

Flyaway Frankie, illustrated by Robert Bartelt. London, Blackie, 1987.

Bella's Dragon, illustrated by Robert Bartelt. London, Blackie, 1988.

Hiccup Harry, illustrated by Scoular Anderson. London, A. and C. Black, 1988.

Hoppity-Gap, illustrated by Maureen Bradley. London, Hamish Hamilton, 1988.

Ziggy and the Ice Ogre, illustrated by Peter Furmin. London, Heinemann, 1988.

Harry's Party, illustrated by Scoular Anderson. London, A. and C. Black, 1989.

Other

Roald Dahl, illustrated by Stephen Gulbis. London, Hamish Hamilton, 1983.

*

Chris Powling comments:

There are two kinds of bad faith for a children's author. One is to write "down" to the child reader; the other is to write "up" for the adult critic. I try very hard to avoid both errors in my books—and to remember always that children's books belong to *children* not to the adult who writes them or mediates them.

For me what matters most in my work is plot, humour, and a narrating voice as close as the text allows to that of a storyteller improvising out loud about his/her characters. If I can also capture something of the freshness, enthusiasm, and ruthless honesty of children at their best, so much the better. Children see the world from the viewpoint of someone who hasn't lived very long…and it's not a bad viewpoint. Certainly none of us becomes so wise we can afford to dispense with sheer astonishment at existence and what it entails. This is why writing for children seems to me to be just as serious as writing for adults—and a lot more fun.

*   *   *

Chris Powling's storytelling talent, his experience as a teacher, and his work as a broadcaster on both children's books and the wider cultural scene seem to invest his work so far with novelty and a genuine awareness of how contemporary children talk, interact, and read.

Each of his stories has a distinctive and immediate narrative voice that draws readers in, establishing a bond with the author and helping them along in their reading of what is often their first independent text. First pages are an important part of the invitation. In *Mog and the Rectifier* there is a letter from the first-person narrator. At the outset of *The Conker as Hard as a Diamond*, the reader is left in no doubt that the business of reading is an essentially collaborative enterprise: "It's rather a strange story. To tell you the truth I'm not sure I believe it myself—and I'm telling it. Let's hope you're better at believing things than I am." Children's voices are adeptly caught in his writing. He is in touch with their lore and language and trusts their banter, arguments, and conversations to drive the plots along.

Powling's stories for junior school children have no hint of moralising or didacticism, but challenging ideas, often concerning personal choices, rumble within the tales. In *Daredevils or Scaredycats*, nine short stories are linked by interplaying characters and the decisions they have to make about risk-taking and the pushing out of the boundaries of the sensible and the safe. Innovation is still too rare in writing for the age group, and Powling is not afraid to celebrate the diversity of actions, attitudes, lifestyles, and motives. "Jesus Wants Me for a Comrade," one of the stories, is a perfect example of a tale for readers of around 10 that presents potentially difficult notions—about pluralism and conflicting beliefs—within an accessible and very funny plot based on a Sunday school. In *Mog and the Rectifier* a well-trodden theme, gang loyalty versus personal aspiration, is invigorated within a pointedly contemporary fable about income tax evasion. In Mog, as in Red and Ellie in *Hoppity-Gap*, there is an assertive girl character at the center of the action: again, still too rare a feature of writing for the age group.

There is a strong sense of context, both geographical and cultural, in Powling's work. The children's patch of South London in *Mog and the Rectifier*, "a vast open-air memory bank with a traffic problem," counterpoints the variety of characters and the fast-moving plot. Part of the particularity of the everyday experience of the inner-city children Powling knows and writes of is the evidence of the past in the present that they see around them. For instance, the Cutty Sark plays an important part in the acting out of the power games between the gangs in *Mog and the Rectifier*. The action within both *The Phantom Carwash* and *Hoppity-Gap* is staged on desolate wasteground. Powling knows the secret places, the arches of railway bridges and graveyards, where city children enact their dramas and fantasies out of sight of the grown-ups.

Children's play and imaginings are the stuff of his stories for younger readers. Alpesh's annual competition at school, rich with linguistic fun around conkering, wheelies, and snicker-snackers, is extended to a superpowers' clash that becomes extraterrestrial. Lenny, in *The Phantom Carwash*, wishes for a very special Christmas present from a Santa Claus he does not quite believe in. In the carwash, "with giant spiders turning head over heels," and in Ziggy's ice-cream fountains, Powling finds precise images of our times for the ways in which the fantastic and the magical always lurk just beneath the commonplace.

Powling weaves new ways of telling into his texts so that jokes, notices, letters, and television broadcasts are shown as modes that writers have in their power. Significantly, his biography of Roald Dahl skilfully achieves the difficult task of showing children how writing grows out of lived experience. He makes plain his own regard for craftsmanship, while generously sharing an insider's account of the skill with those who might be the next generation of writers.

—Colin Mills

———

PRAEGER, (Sophia) Rosamond. Early works published as Sophia Rosamond Praeger. Irish. Born in Holywood, County Down, in 1867. Educated at the Belfast School of Art; Slade School of Fine Art, London. Sculptress. Honorary member, Royal Hibernian Academy, 1927; President, Ulster Academy of Arts (now Royal Ulster Academy), 1941–43. M.A.: Queen's University, Belfast. M.B.E. (Member, Order of the British Empire), 1939. *Died in 1954.*

PUBLICATIONS FOR CHILDREN (illustrated by the author)

Fiction

The Adventures of the Three Bold Babes. London, Longman, 1897.

Further Doings of the Three Bold Babes. London, Longman, 1898.
The Tale of the Little Twin Dragons. London, Macmillan, 1900.
How They Went to School. London, Blackie, 1903.
How They Went to the Seaside. London, Blackie, 1909.
How They Came Back from School. London, Blackie, 1911.
Wee Tony: A Day in His Life. London, Blackie, 1913.
Billy's Garden Plot. London, Blackie, 1918.
To School and Back, with Angusine Macgregor. London, Blackie, 1928.
The Young Stamp-Collectors. Limavady, County Londonderry, Portmoon Press, 1985.

Verse

A Visit to Babyland. London, Ward, 1896.
The Fearful Land of Forgets. London, Blackie, 1921.
Old Fashioned Verses and Sketches. Dundalk, Dundalgan Press, 1947.

Other

The Child's Picture Grammar. London, Allen, 1900.

* * *

Rosamond Praeger is better-known as a sculptress than as a children's author, yet her output of children's books is both original and significant. Handsome, large-format picture books for younger children make up the core of her work. As with most author-artists the books are a composite blend of words and image so that it becomes impossible to discuss one without comment on the other. All the books are intended for younger children and treat of the everyday world of such a young child at the turn of the century.

The author's work divides into realistic tales of everyday events in a small child's life and works of fantasy also featuring young children. Of the former "Me (Baby Writes a Book)" is a good example: it really could be subtitled "diary of a young child from aged six months to two years." It is a miniature social history of life in Edwardian England, with its full complement of personalities: nurses, nannies, housemaids, gardening boys, lots and lots of sisters and brothers, aunties and cousins, and even the by then essential chimney sweep also makes an appearance. The child leads us through the day-to-day activities of the house as they revolve around her and we also get a glimpse of seasonal activities with seaside holidays and winter snowmen and Christmas and birthday celebrations as highpoints in a secure and loving world.

The world of the everyday and the ordinary is again treated with great simplicity and to great effect in a trio of books about Hal and Kitty—*How They Went to School, How They Came Back from School,* and *How They Went to the Seaside.*

But Praeger's quirky sense of humour comes to the fore in the works of fantasy, in particular in *The Tale of the Little Twin Dragons, The Adventures of the Three Bold Babes,* and *Further Doings of the Three Bold Babes. The Tale of the Little Twin Dragons* is full of zany people: a Merman who is so infuriated by people's lack of belief in his existence that he reaps his revenge by turning all disbelievers into babies, for his baby garden. Eventually his baby garden comprises three men of science, a governess who taught 67 subjects, and a little girl who had passed her school examinations with honours in every branch. By the end of the saga all the enchanted babies have reverted to their normal size, and the little dragons Dragonet and Dragonetta are rewarded with knighthoods for their pains.

To fully appreciate a Praeger book the reader has to be well-versed in the lore and conventions of the traditional fairytale. The "Bold Bad Babes" books depend on an understanding of the role of dragons, knights, princesses, ogres, monsters, and giants for the

humour and the magic to work. The bold babes in question, Honoria, Hector, and Alisandre, are totally unperturbed by any of the strange creatures and they stomp their way through adventures and misadventures with complete equilibrium. The stories borrow something in style from the accumulative folktale: "These are the three bold babes reproving the dragon for his evil ways till he repents and promises to become a Vegetarian" is followed by another full-page illustration with the caption: "This is the dragon planting cabbages and watering them with his tears." The word "bold" in Hiberno-English has the meaning "naughty" rather than "brave" and both the meanings are implicit in the personality of the three babes in question.

Very much an author-illustrator of her period, Praeger could dazzle at times with the breathtaking originality of her concepts—the image of the Sea Serpent twisting himself into a Tubular Tunnel so that the Babes can cross the sea is a futuristic image in itself.

—Pat Donlon

———

PRELUTSKY, Jack. American. Born in Brooklyn, New York, 8 September 1940. Educated at High School of Music and Art, New York; Hunter College, New York. Married. Has worked as store assistant, cab driver, bus boy, photographer, furniture mover, potter, folksinger, and actor. Lives in Albuquerque, New Mexico. Address: c/o Greenwillow Books, 105 Madison Avenue, New York, New York 10016, U.S.A.

PUBLICATIONS FOR CHILDREN

Verse

A Gopher in the Garden and Other Animal Poems, illustrated by Robert Leydenfrost. New York, Macmillan, 1967.
Lazy Blackbird and Other Verses, illustrated by Janosch. New York, Macmillan, 1969.
Three Saxon Nobles and Other Verses, illustrated by Eva Rubin. New York, Macmillan, 1969.
The Terrible Tiger, illustrated by Arnold Lobel. New York, Macmillan, 1969; London, Bodley Head, 1975.
Toucans Two and Other Poems, illustrated by Jose Aruego. New York, Macmillan, 1970; as *Zoo Doings,* London, Hamish Hamilton, 1971.
Circus, illustrated by Arnold Lobel. New York, Macmillan, 1974; London, Hamish Hamilton, 1975.
The Pack Rat's Day and Other Poems, illustrated by Margaret Bloy Graham. New York, Macmillan, 1974.
Nightmares: Poems to Trouble Your Sleep, illustrated by Arnold Lobel. New York, Greenwillow, 1976; London, A. and C. Black, 1978.
It's Halloween [*Christmas, Thanksgiving*], illustrated by Marylin Hafner. New York, Greenwillow, 3 vols., 1977–82; *It's Halloween* published Kingswood, Surrey, World's Work, 1978.
The Snopp on the Sidewalk and Other Poems, illustrated by Byron Barton. New York, Greenwillow, 1977.
The Mean Old Mean Hyena, illustrated by Arnold Lobel. New York, Greenwillow, 1978.
The Queen of Eene, illustrated by Victoria Chess. New York, Greenwillow, 1978.
The Headless Horseman Rides Tonight: More Poems to Trouble Your Sleep, illustrated by Arnold Lobel. New York, Greenwillow,

1980; London, A. and C. Black, 1984.

Rainy Rainy Saturday, illustrated by Marylin Hafner. New York, Greenwillow, 1980.

Rolling Harvey Down the Hill, illustrated by Victoria Chess. New York, Greenwillow, 1980.

The Sheriff of Rottenshot, illustrated by Victoria Chess. New York, Greenwillow, 1982.

Kermit's Garden of Verses, illustrated by Brucy McNally. New York, Random House, 1982.

The Baby Uggs Are Hatching, illustrated by James Stevenson. New York, Greenwillow, 1982.

Zoo Doings: Animal Poems (includes *A Gopher in the Garden, Toucans Two*, and *The Pack Rat's Day*), illustrated by Paul O. Zelinsky. New York, Greenwillow, 1983.

It's Valentine's Day, illustrated by Yossi Abolafia. New York, Greenwillow, 1983.

It's Snowing! It's Snowing!, illustrated by Jeanne Titherington. New York, Greenwillow, 1984.

What I Did Last Summer, illustrated by Yossi Abolafia. New York, Greenwillow, 1984.

The New Kid on the Block, illustrated by James Stevenson. New York, Greenwillow, 1984; London, Heinemann, 1986.

My Parents Think I'm Sleeping, illustrated by Yossi Abolafia. New York, Greenwillow, 1985.

Ride a Purple Pelican, illustrated by Garth Williams. New York, Greenwillow, 1986.

Tyrannosaurus Was a Beast, illustrated by Arnold Lobel. New York, Greenwillow, 1988.

Other

Editor, *The Random House Book of Poetry for Children*, illustrated by Arnold Lobel. New York, Random House, 1983; as *The Walker Book of Poetry for Children*, London, Walker, 1984.

Editor, *Read-Aloud Rhymes for the Very Young*, illustrated by Marc Brown. New York, Knopf, 1986.

Translator, *The Mountain Bounder* by Heinrich Hoffman-Donner. New York, Macmillan, 1967.

Translator, *The Bad Bear*, by Rudolf Neumann, illustrated by Eva Rubin. New York, Macmillan, 1967.

Translator, *No End of Nonsense: Humorous Verses*, illustrated by Wilfried Blecher. New York, Macmillan, 1968; London, Abelard Schuman, 1970.

Translator, *The Wild Baby* [*Goes to Sea, Gets a Puppy*], by Barbro Lindgren, illustrated by Eva Eriksson. New York, Greenwillow, 3 vols., 1981–88.

Translator, *Brave Little Pete of Geranium Street*, by Rose and Samuel Lagercrantz, illustrated by Eva Eriksson. New York, Greenwillow, 1986.

*   *   *

The work of Jack Prelutsky lies outside the province of classical light verse, which stresses wit, decorum, and elegance. The broader limits of contemporary light verse include word-play and earthly humor, but even here his work eludes the category. What links him to the genre is his use of traditional form, a keen ear for lively rhythm, and a penchant for rollicking alliteration.

Prelutsky's verse is set apart by a fascination with the aberrations of human physiology and behavior, a taste for the macabre, and a curious delight in the gross and baser side of human nature. This is felt in his almost obsessive concern with gluttony and obesity, a greed that goes beyond familiar foods and dwells on a never-ending variety of non-edibles. Gretchen's pot contains "A lizard's gizzard, lightly mashed,/an ogre's backbone, slightly mashed." The wozzit eats

clothes, Herbert Glerbett eats 50 pounds of lemon sherbet and turns into "a thing that is a ghastly green,/a thing the world has never seen,/a puddle thing, a gooey pile/of something strange that does not smile." Pies made of nuts and bolts, of shoe polish and candied eyeballs are typical staples. Pumberly Pott's niece devours his automobile piece by piece. Many of Prelutsky's characters eat each other, the flonster, floober, flummie, and flakker, the frummick and frelly. Others squash each other by sheer force of overweight.

While all of this might be construed, by some, as nonsense, there is an element in the verse that goes beyond nonsense, for the reader is often threatened directly. The grobbles, It, lurpp, and preternatural creatures, Prelutsky warns, may also eat you. In *Nightmares: Poems to Trouble Your Sleep* and *The Headless Horseman Rides Tonight* a catalog of supernatural beings wallow in blood and death. The bogeyman will "crumple your bones in his bogey embrace," and the ghoul, having eaten other boys and girls, waits outside school "perhaps for you."

Here are echoes of the German school, of *Struwwelpeter* with cautionary tales to frighten, things that exist physically to attack beyond the limits of the page. *Rolling Harvey Down the Hill* is another instance of the darker side of human nature. Harvey is nasty, selfish, a cheat and braggart, a "tub of lard," a sadist who ties up his friends and, although he is rolled down the hill for punishment, the reader has learned that boys who dress neatly and "dumb" girls are outside of Harvey's accepted circle.

As an anthologist, editor of *The Random House Book of Poetry for Children* and *Read-Aloud Rhymes for the Very Young*, Prelutsky opts for the instant guffaw of earthy humor, bypassing the more serious kinds of poetry. His obvious belief in verse as quick, easily assimilated entertainment carries over to his most recent writing, *Ride a Purple Pelican, What I Did Last Summer, It's Valentine's Day*, and *It's Snowing! It's Snowing! The New Kid on the Block* furthers his view of women as addled, greedy, poorly mannered, thieving, sneaky, and mean. He writes of a snoring father, a mother who makes "Willy wail," his own ugly, stupid dog, and continues to dwell on satisfaction through food and/or neulogistic creatures such as Snillies, Yubbazubbles, Underwater Wibbles, Gloopy Gloppers, and a host of others. In his latest book, *Tyrannosaurus Was a Beast*, Prelutsky is at his best, capitalizing on the eating habits and nasty nature of beasts and adding his own witty asides.

Prelutsky has some lighter moments with word-play. In *The Sheriff of Rottenshot* there is a bicycling centipede who "merits medals,/working all those centipedals" and an ocelot who likes to "toss a lot" and "fuss a lot." As a craftsman Prelutsky knows the power of the anapestic line, alliteration, and the fun of making up foolish names and unusual creatures.

For readers who feel that physical force, gluttony, and a dose of fear are funny, Prelutsky will serve well. But for those of differing sensibility, other light verse may hold more appeal.

—Myra Cohn Livingston

———

PRICE, Evadne. Also wrote as Helen Zenna Smith. British. Born at sea, in 1896. Educated in West Maitland, New South Wales, and in Belgium. Worked for the Air Ministry during World War I. Married 1) C.A. Fletcher (died); 2) Kenneth A. Attiwill in 1929. Actress from 1906. Columnist, *Sunday Chronicle* and *Sunday Graphic*; feature writer, *Daily Sketch*; war correspondent, the *People*, 1943–45; astrology columnist, *She* magazine, and *Vogue Australia*, Sydney. Recipient: Severigne prize (France), for adult novel. *Died 17 April 1985.*

PUBLICATIONS FOR CHILDREN

Fiction

Just Jane. London, John Hamilton, 1928.
Meet Jane. London, Marriott, 1930.
Enter—Jane. London, Newnes, 1932.
Jane the Fourth. London, Hale, 1937.
Jane the Sleuth. London, Hale, 1939.
Jane the Unlucky, illustrated by Frank R. Grey. London, Hale, 1939.
Jane the Popular. London, Hale, 1939.
Jane the Patient. London, Hale, 1940.
Jane Gets Busy. London, Hale, 1940.
Jane at War. London, Hale, 1947.
Jane and Co. (omnibus), edited by Mary Cadogan. London, Macmillan, 1985.

PUBLICATIONS FOR ADULTS

Novels

Diary of a Red-Haired Girl. London, Long, 1932.
The Haunted Light. London, Long, 1933.
Strip Girl. London, Hurst and Blackett, 1934.
Probationer! London, Hurst and Blackett, 1934.
Society Girl. London, Harrap, 1935.
Red for Danger! London, Long, 1936.
Glamour Girl. London, Harrap, 1937.
The Dishonoured Wife. London, Jenkins, 1951.
Escape to Marriage. London, Jenkins, 1952.
My Pretty Sister. London, Jenkins, 1952.
Her Stolen Life. London, Milestone, 1954.
What the Heart Says. London, Hale, 1956.
The Love Trap. London, Hale, 1958.
Air Hostess in Love. London, Gresham, 1962.

Novels as Helen Zenna Smith

Not So Quiet...: Stepdaughters of War. London, Marriott, 1930; as *Stepdaughters of War*, New York, Dutton, 1930.
Women of the Aftermath. London, Long, 1931; as *One Woman's Freedom*, New York, Longman, 1932.
Shadow Women. London, Long, 1932.
Luxury Ladies. London, Long, 1933.
They Lived with Me. London, Long, 1934.

Plays

The Phantom Light, with Joan Roy-Byford (as *The Haunted Light*, produced London, 1928; as *The Phantom Light*, produced London, 1937). London, French, 1949.
Red for Danger (produced Richmond, Surrey, 1938).
Big Ben, with Ruby Miller (produced Malvern, Worcestershire, 1939).
Once a Crook, with Kenneth Attiwill (produced London, 1940). London, French, 1943.
Who Killed My Sister?, with Kenneth Attiwill (produced London, 1942).
Three Wives Called Roland, with Kenneth Attiwill (produced London, 1943).
Through the Door (also director: produced London, 1946).
What Lies Beyond (also director: produced Margate, Kent, 1948).
Cabin for Three, with Kenneth Attiwill (produced Southsea, Hampshire, 1949).
Blonde for Danger (produced London, 1949).
Wanted on Voyage, with Kenneth Attiwill (produced Wimbledon, 1949).

Screenplays: *Wolf's Clothing*, with Brock Williams, 1936; *When the Poppies Bloom Again*, with Herbert Ayres, 1937; *Merry Comes to Town*, with Brock Williams, 1937; *Silver Top*, with Gerald Elliott and Dorothy Greenhill, 1938; *Lightning Conductor*, with J. Jefferson Farjeon and Ivor McLaren, 1938; *Not Wanted on Voyage*, with others, 1957.

Other

She Stargazes (on astrology). London, Ebury Press, 1965.

*

Theatrical Activities:
Director: **Plays**—*Through the Door*, London, 1946; *What Lies Beyond*, Margate, Kent, 1948.
Actress: **Plays**—in *Peter Pan* by J.M. Barrie, Sydney, 1906; Nang Ping in *Mr. Wu* by H.M. Vernon and Harold Owen, tour 1914; toured in South Africa, and in *Oh, I Say* and *Within the Law*, 1915; Suzee in *Five Nights*, tour, 1919; Liliha in *The Bird of Paradise*, London, 1919, 1922; Sua-See in *The Dragon*, London, 1920; Tessie Kearns in *Merton of the Movies* by George S. Kaufman and Marc Connelly, London, 1923; Princess Angelica in *The Rose and the Ring*, London, 1923.

* * *

Evadne Price's series for children, the 10 Jane books (1928–47), was written as part of a long and varied career which ranged from actress to astrologer. I find it very curious that there is no extended analysis of Jane, and that she should have been called a literary curiosity like Fanny Hill! Jane is a mid-20th-century version of that motif in literature, "the little monster," the naughty child, which is at least as old as classical Greek mime. Her more immediate literary ancestor, however, may be sought for in the "pickles" and "scamps" of the nurseries of children's fiction of the 1880's onward, whose main characteristics are high-spiritedness and kind hearts, untainted by any element of malice, exemplifying that post-Dickensian vision of the child in literature as the embodiment of "original innocence" rather than original sin.

Price has categorically denied that the adventures of Jane were in any way modelled upon those of Richmal Crompton's William, of whom she said she had never heard until a critic had taken for granted that such was the case. This would serve as a warning against over-hasty ascriptions of influence. However, the comparison is almost an inevitable one, since the Jane books are contemporary with the William series, which continued to be written and to be in print many decades after the last Jane book had been published. The similarities are obvious. The high-spirited middle-class child, leader of a small group of cohorts, the background of English village or suburban life, the setting up of an opposition between the "natural," naughty child on the one hand, the whited sepulchre on the other, the stock adult characters in the background (stern fathers, angular spinsters, comic servants, the local aristocracy), and the short, episodic narrative pieces, whose nature allows for neither aging nor development, the child characters merely being repeatedly put through their paces, are common to both. The basic pattern is to display again and again the havoc wrought by the group of children in the midst of such adult activities as love-affairs, amateur theatricals, public meetings and fetes, sometimes during the trials of civilian life during the Second World War. Both authors attempted to write "full-length" novels about their characters as well as collections of short stories, but these are in the nature of occasional experiments only.

Too much, however, can be made of the Jane/William affinity. It is to be hoped that one day Price's individual qualities will be recognized in their own right, without external reference. She seems to me radically original in a number of ways. First, historically, Jane is among the first female leader of boys in children's literature, providing a positive, active female model for the readers. Second, Price's depiction of adults in books for children is "subversive": the manipulations and adsurdities of Jane's mother, the will-to-power of her grandparents, and the tone of sensible camaraderie between narrative voice and reader are rare in fiction for children even today. Third, despite occasional lapses into very 19th-century sentimentality in the stories, the strategy for survival advocated by Vilet the Cockney cook ("Lay low, Miss Jane love, and don't 'arp") is not a version of "suffer and be still," but commonsensical in a way both comforting and refreshing. Finally, Price's sophisticated parody of and literary reference to various narrative styles, modes, and conventions, and her use of cacorthography, in badly-spelt letter-narratives ostensibly by the child-protagonist herself, reveal the artistry with which these books are constructed. It is a great pity that copies of them are so rare.

—Sanjay Sircar

PRICE, Susan. British. Born in Round's Green, Staffordshire, 8 July 1955. Educated at Tividale Comprehensive School. Shop assistant, Co-operative Society Grocery, Dudley, Worcestershire, 1972–74; guide, Open Air Black Country Museum, 1979; writer-in-residence, North Riding College of Education, Scarborough, 1980, and Worcester Central Library, 1986. Recipient: Children's Rights Workshop Other award, 1975; Library Association Carnegie Medal, 1988. Agent: Michael Thomas, A.M. Heath, 79 St. Martin's Lane, London WC2N 4AA. Address: c/o Faber and Faber Ltd., 3 Queen Square, London WC1N 3AU, England.

PUBLICATIONS FOR CHILDREN

Fiction

The Devil's Piper. London, Faber, 1973; New York, Greenwillow, 1976.
Twopence a Tub. London, Faber, 1975.
Sticks and Stones. London, Faber, 1976.
Home from Home. London, Faber, 1977.
Christopher Uptake. London, Faber, 1981.
In a Nutshell, illustrated by Alison Price. London, Faber, 1983.
From Where I Stand. London, Faber, 1984.
Ghosts at Large, illustrated by Alison Price. London, Faber, 1984.
Odin's Monster, illustrated by Patrick Lynch. London, A. and C. Black, 1986.
The Ghost Drum. London, Faber, and New York, Farrar Straus, 1987.
Ghostly Tales. Loughborough, Leicestershire, Ladybird, 1987.
Here Lies Price. London, Faber, 1987.
The Bone Dog. London, Scholastic, 1988.
Master Thomas Katt. London, A. and C. Black, 1988.
Miss Sanders. London, Ladybird, 1988.
Crack-a-Story. London, Faber, 1989.

Other

The Carpenter and Other Stories (retellings). London, Faber, 1981.

*

Susan Price comments:

The more I write, the less I feel I want to make any "personal statement." I write for money; it's my living. I try to do my job as well as I can. That's all.

*   *   *

Susan Price is an instinctive writer with the ability to get inside her characters and make their stories real and immediate whether they are in fantasy, historical, or contemporary settings.

The Devil's Piper was written when she was only 16 and showed the confidence and originality which have developed in subsequent books. It is an exciting story with lively dialogue and convincing characters which give solidity to the enchanted world into which an evil-tempered leprechaun leads the four children.

Her second novel was very different. In *Twopence a Tub* she turned from fantasy to the very real problems facing the miners who were involved in the disastrous pit strike in Dudley in 1851. Her considerable achievement in recreating this situation was recognized by the Children's Rights Workshop which named *Twopence a Tub* winner of the Other award. Price draws on family records and memories to help her recreate the squalid poverty of the miners' lives, their spirit, and their brutality, and contrasts this with the affluence of the pit owners. Lesser writers might have been trapped into manufacturing a happy ending, but Price does not shirk the bitterness and frustration when the miners are forced to return to work accepting a reduction in their wages.

A number of Price's early books deal with similar theme of the struggles of a teenage boy to shake off the constraints of his home background or environment. 16-year-old Graeme, in *Sticks and Stones*, struggles to direct his own life despite the well-meaning but unimaginative care of his parents. In *Home from Home* Paul forms a close relationship with an elderly lady who provides a warmth and interest in him which is lacking in his own charmless home. In a very different book, *Christopher Uptake*, the central character is also a young man who wants only to be left in peace to get on with his own life. Set in Elizabethan England, it presents a chilling picture of religious tolerance and persecution, loyalty and betrayal, but Christopher's dilemma could be applied to any contemporary conflict and will speak directly to the thoughtful teenager.

In her more recent books Price has largely turned from realism to stories of ghosts and other fantasy themes. The exception is *From Where I Stand* which deals with the very real problems of racism and bullying in an urban school. Maybe because the theme is so important, this book is a little less successful as a novel but it is a deeply felt statement on an issue of real concern in the lives of many young people.

Like all the best writers of fantasy, Price plots her novels and short stories with great logic and confident story-telling. Frequently she has a strong vein of humour, as in *In a Nutshell* where she contrives to write a moral parable which is funny. Two tiny beings (in the Thumbelina and Tom Thumb tradition) come into the world and, after a great struggle to be reunited, become "humans" and healers. Ghosts feature in *Ghosts at Large* and *Here Lies Price*, both of which contain stories of very varied moods: moving and macabre, frightening and funny. Much of her success lies in her down-to-earth style and her skill in describing the details and creating the atmosphere which make the supernatural nature of her stories so believable, whether she is writing of a scary headless boggart or of Fearless Mary who sets herself up for life in her dealings with ghosts.

Perhaps Price's major achievement recently has been her Carnegie Medal-winning novel *The Ghost Drum* which tells an exotic tale of the stunting imprisonment of a young Czarevich and the training of a witch's apprentice. Her confident, economic style is fitted to the folktale basis of the story and she manages to adapt her style to each changing mood of the story. Her descriptions, though spare, bring each scene vividly to life ("the cold is so fierce the frost can be heard crackling and snapping as it travels through the air"). Each word works hard for its place in the narrative but, although it is so well-crafted, the story—like much of her recent work—lacks the passion evident in her early writing.

—Valerie Brinkley-Willsher

PRICE, Willard. American. Born in Peterborough, Ontario, Canada, 28 July 1887; moved to the United States, 1901. Educated at Western Reserve University, Cleveland, B.A. 1909; New York School of Philanthropy, 1911–12; Columbia University, New York, M.A. 1914. Married 1) Eugenia Reeve in 1914 (died 1929), one son; 2) Mary Selden in 1932. Member of the editorial staff, the *Survey*, New York, 1912–13; editorial secretary, Methodist Episcopal Church Board of Foreign Missions, 1915–19; editor, *World Outlook*, New York, 1915–20. Traveled on many expeditions for the National Geographic Society and the American Museum of Natural History, 1920–67. Litt.D.: Columbia University, 1930. *Died 14 October 1983.*

PUBLICATIONS FOR CHILDREN

Fiction

Amazon Adventure, illustrated by Georg Hartmann. New York, Day, 1949; London, Cape, 1951.
South Sea Adventure. New York, Day, and London, Cape, 1952.
Underwater Adventure. New York, Day, 1954; London, Cape, 1955.
Volcano Adventure. New York, Day, and London, Cape, 1956.
Whale Adventure. New York, Day, and London, Cape, 1960.
African Adventure. New York, Day, and London, Cape, 1963.
Elephant Adventure. New York, Day, and London, Cape, 1964.
Safari Adventure. New York, Day, and London, Cape, 1966.
Lion Adventure. New York, Day, and London, Cape, 1967.
Gorilla Adventure. New York, Day, and London, Cape, 1969.
Diving Adventure. New York, Day, and London, Cape, 1970.
Cannibal Adventure, illustrated by Pat Marriott. London, Cape, 1972; New York, Day, 1973.
Tiger Adventure, illustrated by Pat Marriott. London, Cape, 1979.
Arctic Adventure, illustrated by Pat Marriott. London, Cape, 1980.

Other

My Own Life of Adventure: Travels in 148 Lands. London, Cape, 1982.

PUBLICATIONS FOR ADULTS

Novel

Barbarian. New York, Day, 1941; London, Heinemann, 1942.

Other

Ancient Peoples at New Tasks. New York, Missionary Education Movement, 1918.
The Negro Around the World. New York, Doran, 1925.
The South Sea Adventure: Through Japan's Equatorial Empire. Tokyo, Hokuseido Press, 1936; as *Pacific Adventure*, New York, Reynal, 1936; as *Rip Tide in the South Seas*, London, Heinemann, 1936.
Japan's New Horizons. Tokyo, Hokuseido Press, 1938; as *Children of the Rising Sun*, New York, Reynal, 1938; as *Where Are You Going Japan?*, London, Heinemann, 1938; as *Japan Reaches Out*, Sydney, Angus and Robertson, 1938.
Japan Rides the Tiger. New York, Day, 1942.
Japan's Islands of Mystery. New York, Day, and London, Heinemann, 1944.
Japan and the Son of Heaven. New York, Duell, 1945; as *The Son of Heaven: The Problem of the Mikado*, London, Heinemann, 1945.
Key to Japan. New York, Day, and London, Heinemann, 1946.
Roving South: Rio Grande to Patagonia. New York, Day, 1948; as *Tropic Adventure*, London, Heinemann, 1949.
I Cannot Rest from Travel: An Autobiography of Adventure in Seventy Lands. New York, Day, and London, Heinemann, 1951.
The Amazing Amazon. New York, Day, and London, Heinemann, 1952.
Journey by Junk: Japan after MacArthur. New York, Day, 1953; London, Heinemann, 1954.
Adventures in Paradise: Tahiti and Beyond. New York, Day, 1955; London, Heinemann, 1956.
Roaming Britain: 8000 Miles Through England, Scotland, and Wales. New York, Day, 1958; as *Innocents in Britain*, London, Heinemann, 1958.
Incredible Africa. London, Heinemann, 1961; New York, Day, 1962.
The Amazing Mississippi. London, Heinemann, 1962; New York, Day, 1963.
Rivers I Have Known. New York, Day, 1965.
America's Paradise Lost. New York, Day, 1966.
Odd Way round the World. New York, Day, 1969.
The Japanese Miracle and Peril. New York, Day, and London, Heinemann, 1971.

Editor, *The Voice and the Book.* New York, American Bible Society, 1926.

*

Manuscript Collection: Syracuse University Library, New York.

Willard Price commented:

(1983) My aim in writing the "Adventure" series for young people was to lead them to read by making reading exciting and full of adventure. At the same time I want to inspire an interest in wild animals and their behavior. Judging from the letters I receive from boys and girls around the world, I believe I have helped open to them the worlds of books and natural history.

* * *

Willard Price's highly improbable adventures of Hal and Roger Hunt have all the ingredients of Superman except the boys wear safari suits and save animals rather than humans.

In the first of the adventures, *Amazon Adventure*, the framework is set for all the following books. John Hunt had "studied and collected animals for twenty years, supplying zoos, circuses and museums," and was planning a trip to South America accompanied by his sons, Hal and Roger. "No man could want better pals on a jungle journey. Hal, finished with school and about to go to college was as tall and strong as his father. Roger did not run to length, but he was alert and wiry, and brave enough." Hal and Roger, at 19 and 15, never seem to age and so remain conveniently popular with the widest age range of readers possible. Equally, there is never any real development in the two characters, Hal steady and almost a man, Roger endowed with great courage but not much common sense. The plot is always simple, a search for whatever kind of animal is required, but well endowed with feats of endurance and dramatic episodes, and the pages quite crammed with factual detail on the animals which the boys appear ever to have at their encyclopaedic finger tips. They also possess a remarkable facility for picking up scientific and technical detail relevant to the current project, and are therefore able to take on board ballooning, underwater diving or diamond mining without any hesitation or pause for training. Most of all they do have an extraordinary amount of luck. In *Gorilla Adventure* they survive between them a charge by an infuriated gorilla, fire in their cabin and a fight with their local guide, an attack by a mamba and then a spitting cobra, a 20-foot fall followed by a fight with a black leopard—all the while managing to collect 22 animals for their father, to find enough diamonds to maintain an ailing bush hospital, and to capture a python and a gorilla together with one rope.

The exploits may be fiction, but the facts and settings could only have come from real life; Price's tales are based on his own tumultuous and action-packed life. The detail in these adventure books is all accurate and undoubtedly has an enormous appeal to his wide following. Nothing gets in the way of the narration, of the boys' exploits and the constant stream of information—no time is wasted on philosophizing or theorizing, all is action and very successful.

—Fiona Waters

* * *

PRINCE, Alison. British. Born in Beckenham, Kent, 26 March 1931. Educated at Beckenham Grammar School, Kent, 1940–48; Slade School of Fine Art, London, 1948–51, diploma in fine art; Goldsmiths' College, University of London, 1953–54, art teachers' certificate. Married Goronwy Siriol Parry in 1957 (separated); one daughter and two sons. Head of art department, Elliott Comprehensive School, London, 1954–58. Fellow in creative writing, Jordanhill College of Education, Glasgow, 1988. Address: Burnfoot House, Whiting Bay, Isle of Arran KA27 8QL, Scotland.

PUBLICATIONS FOR CHILDREN

Fiction

The House on the Common, illustrated by the author. London, Methuen, 1969; New York, Farrar Straus, 1970.
The Red Alfa, illustrated by the author. London, Methuen, 1971; as *The Red Jaguar*, New York, Atheneum, 1972.
Ben's Fish, with Chris Connor, illustrated by Connor. London, Benn, 1972.
The Doubting Kind. London, Methuen, 1975; New York, Morrow, 1977.
The Night I Sold My Boots. London, Heinemann, 1979.
The Turkey's Nest. London, Methuen, 1979; New York, Morrow, 1980; as *Willow Farm*, New York, Ace, 1980.
Haunted Children (stories), illustrated by Michael Bragg. London,

Methuen, 1982.
Mill Green on Fire. London, Armada, 1982.
Mill Green on Stage. London, Armada, 1982.
The Sinister Airfield, illustrated by Edward Mortelmans. London, Methuen, 1982; New York, Morrow, 1983.
Goodbye Summer. London, Methuen, 1983.
Night Landings, illustrated by Edward Mortelmans. London, Methuen, 1983; New York, Morrow, 1984.
A Spy at Mill Green. London, Armada, 1983.
The Ghost Within (stories). London, Methuen, 1984.
Hands Off Mill Green! London, Armada, 1984.
The Others. London, Methuen, 1984.
Scramble!, illustrated by Anne Knight. London, Methuen, 1984.
Rock On, Mill Green. London, Armada, 1985.
A Job for Merv, illustrated by David Higham. London, Deutsch, 1986.
Nick's October. London, Methuen, 1986.
The Type One Super Robot, illustrated by the author. London, Deutsch, 1986; New York, Four Winds Press, 1988.
How's Business, illustrated by the author. London, Deutsch, 1987; New York, Four Winds Press, 1988.
The Blue Moon Day, illustrated by the author. London, Deutsch, 1988.
A Haunting Refrain (stories). London, Methuen, 1988.

Plays

Television Plays: *Joe* series, 1968–71; *War Stories*, 1970; *Trumpton*, 1970; scripts for *Watch with Mother* series.

Other (illustrated by the author)

Whosaurus? Dinosaurus!, with Jane Hickson. London, Studio Vista, 1975.
Who Wants Pets? London, Methuen, 1988.

PUBLICATIONS FOR ADULTS

Play

Radio Play: *Ellie Bagg's Account*, 1984.

Other

The Good Pets Guide. London, Armada, 1981.

*

Illustrator: *Don't Panic!*, 1975, *Keeping Time*, 1976, and *Get Well Soon*, 1978, all by Audrey Coppard; *Hello to Ponies*, 1979, and *Hello to Riding*, 1980, both by Jane Allen and Mary Danby.

Alison Prince comments:
Childhood seems to me to hold the key to the whole of a person's life, being the time when awareness is most acute, and most free from the pressures of convention which overlay it in later years. For this reason, children are the most vital section of the community to write for, and I would like to think my books supply interest for them throughout their growing years, right into their adult life. In the future, I very much want to write for the adult market, to provide a further continuity, for we are all at heart no more than grownup children, and we never lose our dreams.

* * *

Alison Prince is a writer of great versatility whose career began by writing for a BBC Television series for the under-fives. Her subsequent books have covered every age group from the youngest child's picture story book to sophisticated teenage novels.

A genre in which she has had considerable success is that of the short story—in particular, forays into the supernatural and fantasy world. *The Ghost Within* contains some macabre characters who seem to have been crafted with a malevolent delight! One example is "The Fire Escape" which contains Victorian melodrama linked to the modern-day taste for horror. Moving into a London house after a cottage in Lincolnshire, Lindsay's room is at the top of the house, the sash windows overlooking the rooftops and with a door out to the fire escape. Tension and fear builds up in the room: "The voice was close behind him, chiding and intimate. Lindsay jumped around. The room was empty. 'Who is it?' he whispered." The terrible secrets are gradually revealed through the old woman found lying in the street with her face charred and burned, and through the other occupant of the room, young William—who had died many years ago! It is a truly classic ghost story among seven other similarly chilling tales.

A Haunting Refrain also has a supernatural theme, only these stories are devoid of horror and have a more gentle flavour. Music links the present to the past and recalls events which intrude on the present. The reader is left to ponder the consequences, as in "Josef's Carol," a poignant story of a lonely boy and his imaginary friend whose lives, both real and imaginary, are linked to a sad, white-haired old man, locked in his silent world.

Prince's teenage novels are perhaps the most acutely observed—language, sexuality, and unconventional lifestyles are accurately and perceptively described. The dialogue is honest, forthright, and often humorous, and controversial subjects such as pregnancy are handled in a sympathetic and straightforward manner. *Goodbye Summer* and the sequel *Nick's October* charts the unpredictable, stormy, yet loving relationship between Nick and Sasha, whose families do little to encourage the liaison. The books highlight the uncertainty and insecurity of young people and explore their fears of the responsibility of marriage and work, and their relationships with friends and parents. They also portray the pressures of parental manipulation, in Sasha and Nick's case a menopausal mother and alcoholic father. But these are not heavyhanded lessons in teenage morality; they are written with a warmth and humour that make them refreshingly realistic.

Prince's most interesting book, however, is *How's Business*—an unusual novel in that it was written with the active participation of 21 seven- to 11-year-olds in a Lincolnshire primary school. The children suggested the storyline, developed the characters, and involved the whole community in their project. Set in war-time England, the plot is conventional enough, about a London evacuee sent to live in the Fens who is determined to return to London at the earliest opportunity. But the story totally absorbs the reader as the character of young How Grainger comes to life along with the other children and adults in the Fenland village. The war-time atmosphere is successfully created by its authors who were born many years after that time. Their imaginations have no doubt been fuelled by other books and films about this time and they have captured the pleasures and hardships in a surprisingly accurate way. To weld so many young and inexperienced young writers together and produce such an excellent product is a great accomplishment on Prince's part.

—Valerie Bierman

PROCTOR, Everitt. See **MONTGOMERY, Rutherford**.

PUDNEY, John (Sleigh). British. Born in Langley, Buckinghamshire, 19 January 1909. Educated at Gresham's School, Holt, Norfolk. Served in the Royal Air Force, 1940–45. Married 1) Crystal Herbert in 1934 (divorced 1955); 2) Monica Forbes Curtis in 1955, three children. Producer and writer, BBC, London, 1934–37; correspondent, *News Chronicle*, London, 1937–41; book critic, *Daily Express*, London, 1947–48; literary editor, *News Review*, London, 1948–50; director, Evans Brothers, publishers, London, 1950–53, and Putnam, publishers, London, 1953–63. Recipient: C.P. Robertson Memorial Trophy, 1965. *Died 10 November 1977.*

PUBLICATIONS FOR CHILDREN

Fiction

Saturday [*Sunday, Monday, Tuesday, Wednesday, Thursday, Friday*] *Adventure*, illustrated by Ley Kenyon and Douglas Relf. London, Lane, 2 vols., 1950–51, and Evans, 5 vols., 1952–56.
The Grandfather Clock, illustrated by Peggy Beetles. London, Hamish Hamilton, 1957.
Crossing the Road, illustrated by Janet and Anne Grahame-Johnstone. London, Hamish Hamilton, 1958.
Spring [*Summer, Autumn, Winter*] *Adventure*, illustrated by Douglas Relf. London, Evans, 4 vols., 1961–65.
The Hartwarp Light Railway [*Dump, Balloon, Circus, Bakehouse, Explosion, Jets*], illustrated by Ferelith Eccles Williams. London, Hamish Hamilton, 7 vols., 1962–67.
Tunnel to the Sky, illustrated by Christine Marsh. London, Hamish Hamilton, 1965.

Other

Six Great Aviators. London, Hamish Hamilton, 1955.

PUBLICATIONS FOR ADULTS

Novels

Jacobson's Ladder. London, Longman, 1938.
Estuary: A Romance. London, Longman, 1947.
Shuffley Wanderers: An Entertainment. London, Lane, 1948.
The Accomplice. London, Lane, 1950.
Hero of a Summer's Day. London, Lane, 1951.
The Net. London, Joseph, 1952.
A Ring for Luck. London, Joseph, 1953.
Trespass in the Sun. London, Joseph, 1957.
Thin Air. London, Joseph, 1961.
The Long Time Growing Up: A Romance. London, Dent, 1971.

Short Stories

And Lastly the Fireworks. London, Boriswood, 1935.
Uncle Arthur and Other Stories. London, Longman, 1939.
It Breathed Down My Neck: A Selection of Stories. London, Lane, 1946; as *Edna's Fruit Hat and Other Stories*, New York, Harper, 1947.
The Europeans: Fourteen Tales of a Continent. London, Lane, 1948.

Plays

The Little Giant (produced London, 1972).
Ted (televised, 1972; produced Leatherhead, Surrey, 1974).

Screenplays: *Conflict of Wings*, with Don Sharp, 1954; *The Blue Peter(Navy Heroes)*, with Don Sharp, 1955; *Fuss over Feathers*, 1955.

Television Play: *Ted*, 1972.

Verse

Spring Encounter. London, Methuen, 1933.
Open the Sky. London, Boriswood, 1934; New York, Doubleday, 1935.
Dispersal Point and Other Air Poems. London, Lane, 1942.
Beyond This Disregard. London, Lane, 1943.
South of Forty. London, Lane, 1943.
Almanack of Hope: Sonnets. London, Lane, 1944.
Ten Summers: Poems 1933–1943. London, Lane, 1944.
Flight above Cloud. New York, Harper, 1944.
Selected Poems. London, Lane, 1946.
Selected Poems. London, Lane, 1947.
Low Life: Verses. London, Lane, 1947.
Commemorations. London, Lane, 1948.
Sixpenny Songs. London, Lane, 1953.
Collected Poems. London, Putnam, 1957.
The Trampoline. London, Joseph, 1959.
Spill Out: Poems and Ballads. London, Dent, 1967.
Spandrels: Poems and Ballads. London, Dent, 1969.
Take This Orange: Poems and Ballads. London, Dent, 1971.
Selected Poems 1967–1973. London, Dent, 1973.
For Johnny: Poems of World War Two. London, Shepheard Walwyn, 1976.
Living in a One-Sided House. London, Shepheard Walwyn, 1976.

Other

The Green Grass Grew All Round. London, Lane, 1942.
Who Only England Know: Log of a War-time Journey of Unintentional Discovery of Fellow-Countrymen. London, Lane, 1943.
World Still There: Impressions of Various Parts of the World in Wartime. London, Hollis and Carter, 1945.
Music on the South Bank: An Appreciation of the Royal Festival Hall. London, Parrish, 1951.
His Majesty George VI: A Study. London, Hutchinson, 1952.
The Queen's People. London, Harvill Press, 1953.
The Thomas Cook Story. London, Joseph, 1953.
The Smallest Room: A History of Lavatories. London, Joseph, 1954; New York, Hastings House, 1955; revised edition, as *The Smallest Room: With an Annexe*, Joseph, 1959.
The Seven Skies: A Study of B.O.A.C. and its Forerunners since 1919. London, Putnam, 1959.
Home and Away: An Autobiographical Gambit. London, Joseph, 1960.
A Pride of Unicorns: Richard and David Atcherley of the R.A.F. London, Oldbourne, 1960.
Bristol Fashion: Some Accounts of the Earlier Days of Bristol Aviation. London, Putnam, 1960.
The Camel Fighter. London, Hamish Hamilton, 1964.
The Golden Age of Steam. London, Hamish Hamilton, 1967.
Suez: De Lesseps' Canal. London, Dent, 1968; New York, Praeger, 1969.
A Draught of Contentment: The Story of the Courage Group. London, New English Library, 1971.

Crossing London's River: The Bridges, Ferries, and Tunnels Crossing the Thames Tideway in London. London, Dent, 1972.
Brunel and His World. London, Thames and Hudson, 1974.
London's Docks. London, Thames and Hudson, 1975.
Lewis Carroll and His World. London, Thames and Hudson, and New York, Scribner, 1976.
Thank Goodness for Cake (memoirs). London, Joseph, 1978.
John Wesley and His World. London, Thames and Hudson, 1978; New York, Scribner, 1979.

Editor, with Henry Treece, *Air Force Poetry.* London, Lane, 1944.
Editor, *Laboratory of the Air: An Account of the Royal Aircraft Establishment of the Ministry of Supply, Farnborough.* London, Central Office of Information, 1948.
Editor, *Pick of Today's Short Stories.* London, Odhams Press, Putnam, and Eyre and Spottiswoode, 13 vols., 1949–63.
Editor, *Popular Poetry.* London, News of the World, 1953.
Editor, *The Book of Leisure.* London, Odhams Press, 1957.
Editor, *The Harp Book of Toasts.* London, Harp Lager, 1963.
Editor, *The Batsford Colour Book of London.* London, Batsford, 1965; New Rochelle, New York, Soccer Associates, 1966.
Editor, *Flight and Flying.* London, Hamish Hamilton, and New York, David White, 1968.

*

Manuscript Collection: University of Texas, Austin.

* * *

"All that a boy's book should be." "A crowded and exciting yarn." The reviewers greeted John Pudney's Fred and I stories enthusiastically in the 1950's and 1960's when they first appeared. Writing in the first person, Pudney presented the two boys, presumably in their early teens, at boarding school and on their holidays with Uncle George. He lives his life either at Fort X, doing mysterious research, or else receiving urgent calls and dashing off on top secret jobs. These are very hush-hush, but the boys always get involved. Uncle explodes with wrath over their mistakes, but invariably needs them to rescue him.

They are a resourceful outdoor couple, good at swimming, climbing, and boating; one has an interest in languages, one in history. Their attitude to girls is summed up by the comment on Lulu in *Summer Adventure*: "We found her quite a good sort, as girls go."

The books are called after the days of the week and season of the year. Each adventure begins quickly and dangerously; the pace keeps up to the safe ending. The backgrounds vary. *Tuesday Adventure* opens with the writer "I" taking a photograph of Fred on a mountain train in Norway, but Fred fiddles with a lever just before the camera clicks. The truck instantly plunges off down the track into the dark heart of a mountain where it sinks. There they find the stranger who behaved so suspiciously on the boat coming over from Newcastle and the story is away.

In *Friday Adventure*, while fiddling with a television set, they get an unexplained extra channel. After an embarrassing time in the toy department of a large London store—the boys blush easily—they get locked in a cupboard which precipitates them down into the bowels of the shop where strange drugged figures are at work and the man they saw on TV appears. This is considered the most dangerous episode of them all, during which Uncle George is kidnapped.

There are always a few laughs. The comic relief in *Summer Adventure* is provided by a goat that eats some of Uncle's papers and has to be taken by boat to France where a gang of smugglers threaten to kill it. Other stories are located on the Thames and in Malta: anywhere can, in no time at all, be converted into a setting in which international crooks can operate.

The Hartwarp series are equally full of action of a different kind, designed for a younger age group. The stories are shorter, the perils are milder. Hartwarp is a very accident-prone village with characters like Charley, Olly Took, and the Gaffer. By mistake the signal box may be blown up, but it lands safely in the village pond, as everything always ends happily. Even making cakes and delivering them becomes hazardous when Olly Took takes over the bakehouse. His self-raising flour causes the inhabitants to float in the air, but that makes the village so famous it appears on television and everybody is delighted.

—Margaret Campbell

PULLEIN-THOMPSON, Christine. Has also written as Christine Keir. British. Born in Wimbledon, Surrey, 1 October 1930; daughter of the writer Joanna Cannan, *q.v.*; twin sister of Diana Pullein-Thompson, *q.v.*, and sister of Josephine Pullein-Thompson, *q.v.*, and the writer Denis Cannan. Educated at Wychwood School, Oxford. Married Julian Popescu in 1954; two sons and two daughters. Director, Grove Riding Schools, Oxfordshire, 1945–55. Agent: Jennifer Luithlen Agency, 88 Holmfield Road, Leicester LE2 1SB. Address: The Old Parsonage, Mellis, Eye, Suffolk IP23 8EE, England.

PUBLICATIONS FOR CHILDREN

Fiction

It Began with Picotee, with Diana and Josephine Pullein-Thompson, illustrated by Rosemary Robinson. London, A. and C. Black, 1946.
We Rode to the Sea, illustrated by Mil Brown. London, Collins, 1948.
We Hunted Hounds, illustrated by Marcia Lane Foster. London, Collins, 1949.
I Carried the Horn, illustrated by Charlotte Hough. London, Collins, 1951.
Goodbye to Hounds, illustrated by Charlotte Hough. London, Collins, 1952.
Riders from Afar, illustrated by Charlotte Hough. London, Collins, 1954.
Phantom Horse, illustrated by Sheila Rose. London, Collins, 1955.
A Day to Go Hunting, illustrated by Sheila Rose. London, Collins, 1956.
The First Rosette, illustrated by Sheila Rose. London, Burke, 1956.
Stolen Ponies, illustrated by Sheila Rose. London, Collins, 1957.
The Impossible Horse (as Christine Keir), illustrated by Maurice Tulloch. London, Evans, 1957.
The Second Mount, illustrated by Sheila Rose. London, Burke, 1957.
Three to Ride, illustrated by Sheila Rose. London, Burke, 1958.
The Lost Pony, illustrated by Sheila Rose. London, Burke, 1959.
Ride by Night, illustrated by Sheila Rose. London, Collins, 1960.
The Horse Sale, illustrated by Sheila Rose. London, Collins, 1960.
Giles and the Elephant [*Greyhound, Canal*], illustrated by Dorothy Clark. London, Burke, 3 vols., 1960–62.
For Want of a Saddle, illustrated by Anne Bullen. London, Burke, 1960.
The Empty Field, illustrated by Anne Bullen. London, Burke, 1961.
The Open Gate, illustrated by Barbara Crocker. London, Burke, 1962.
Bandits in the Hills, illustrated by Janet Duchesne. London, Hamish Hamilton, 1962.
The Gipsy Children, illustrated by Janet Duchesne. London, Hamish Hamilton, 1962.
The Doping Affair, illustrated by Enid Ash. London, Burke, 1963; as *The Pony Dopers*, London, Atlantic, 1968.
Homeless Katie, illustrated by Prudence Seward. London, Hamish Hamilton, 1964.
No-One at Home, illustrated by C.R. Evans. London, Hamish Hamilton, 1964.
The Eastmans in Brittany, illustrated by Dorothy Clark. London, Burke, 1964.
Granny Comes to Stay, illustrated by Christine Marsh. London, Hamish Hamilton, 1964.
The Eastmans Move House, illustrated by Susan Broadley. London, Burke, 1965.
The Boys from the Café, illustrated by Mary Russon. London, Hamish Hamilton, 1965.
The Eastmans Find a Boy, illustrated by Joan Calvert. London, Burke, 1966.
The Stolen Car, illustrated by Elizabeth Grant. London, Hamish Hamilton, 1966.
The Lost Cow, illustrated by Lynette Hemmant. London, Hamish Hamilton, 1966.
A Day to Remember, illustrated by Lynette Hemmant. London, Hamish Hamilton, 1966.
Little Black Pony, illustrated by Lynette Hemmant. London, Hamish Hamilton, 1967.
Robbers in the Night, illustrated by Andrew Sier. London, Hamish Hamilton, 1967.
Room to Let, illustrated by Lynette Hemmant. London, Hamish Hamilton, 1968.
Dog in a Pram, illustrated by Prudence Seward. London, Hamish Hamilton, 1969.
Nigel Eats His Words, illustrated by Dorothy Clark. London, Burke, 1969.
Phantom Horse Comes Home [*Goes to Ireland, in Danger, Goes to Scotland*]. London, Armada, 4 vols., 1970–81.
Riders on the March. London, Armada, 1970.
They Rode to Victory. London, Armada, 1970.
I Rode a Winner. London, Armada, 1973; New York, Scholastic, 1978.
Black Beauty's Clan, with Diana and Josephine Pullein-Thompson. Leicester, Brockhampton Press, 1975.
Mystery [*Strange Riders, Prince, Secrets*] *at Black Pony Inn*, illustrated by Gareth Floyd. London, Pan, 4 vols., 1976–78.
Pony Patrol [*Fights Back, SOS, and the Mystery Horse*]. London, Dragon, 4 vols., 1977–80.
Black Beauty's Family, with Diana and Josephine Pullein-Thompson, illustrated by Elisabeth Grant. London, Hodder and Stoughton, 1978; New York, McGraw Hill, 1980.
Father Unknown. London, Dobson, 1982.
Black Beauty's Family 2, with Diana and Josephine Pullein-Thompson. London, Hamlyn Beaver, 1982.
Ponies in the Park, illustrated by Tony Morris. London, Beaver, 1982.
Ponies in the Forest. London, Beaver, 1983.
Ponies in the Blizzard. London, Beaver, 1984.
Wait for Me, Phantom Horse. London, Severn House, 1985.
A Home for Jessie, illustrated by Sheila Ratcliffe. Aylesbury, Buckinghamshire, Goodchild, 1986.
Stay at Home Ben, illustrated by Kate Rodgers. London, Hamish Hamilton, 1987.
Please Save Jessie, illustrated by Sheila Ratcliffe. Aylesbury, Buckinghamshire, Goodchild, 1987.

The Big Storm, illustrated by Lesley Smith. London, Hodder and Stoughton, 1988.
The Road Through the Hills, illustrated by Gavin Rowe. London, Hodder and Stoughton, 1988.

Other

The Follyfoot Pony Quiz Book, illustrated by David McKee. London, Pan, 1974.
A Pony to Love, illustrated by Claude Kailer and others. London, Pan, 1975.
Good Riding, illustrated by Christine Bousfield. London, Armada, 1975.
Riding for Fun, illustrated by Christine Bousfield. London, Armada, 1976.
Improve Your Riding, illustrated by Christine Bousfield. London, Armada, 1979.
Riding (as Christine Keir), illustrated by Glenn Steward. London, Granada, 1983.

Editor, *A Pony [Second Pony] Scrap Book*. London, Pan, 2 vols., 1972–73.
Editor, *Christine Pullein-Thompson's Book of Pony Stories*, illustrated by Gareth Floyd. London, Pan, 1975.
Editor, *The Second Book of Pony Stories*, illustrated by Ron Stenberg. London, Pan, 1977.
Editor, *Pony Parade*. London, Dragon, 1978.

*

Christine Pullein-Thompson comments:

I have written books since I was in my teens—all are for children varying from ages five to 16. Most concern ponies but more than 20 are for younger children without a pony to be seen. They are easy to read and, I hope, exciting.

*   *   *

Christine Pullein-Thompson has been writing children's pony stories for nearly 40 years, and her books demonstrate a consistency and professionalism not always found in children's books. She has had so many books published it would be astonishing if they were great works of literature, and indeed they are not. They do deserve, though, to be recognized for what they are, lightweight entertainment and escapism for children of 9–12 years. Particularly those who are pony-mad.

Her story line is usually strong, if sometimes rather farfetched. She can hold back the climax while developing the plot with considerable skill, and places her young heroes and heroines in quite inventive situations. *Phantom Horse* is a good example of this, and *Ride by Night* produces unexpected and dramatic complications with Romanian dissidents on the west coast of Scotland when they are least expected. Some of her more recent books, *Pony Patrol* and *Ponies in the Park*, for instance, show that her books have continued to be up-to-date with contemporary comments, terminology, and situations.

It is easy to pick holes in the writing, for she falls back on several standard phrases to get a quick effect. "I was so happy I felt like singing" is one, and whenever hunting is involved "a glorious burst of music" crops up far too often. But if the style is rather slapdash, it is also readable, and the dialogue is good.

She has also written several books for younger children in the Antelope and Reindeer series which demonstrate thoughtful, more careful writing and considerable powers of observation and understanding of human situations. Two of her information books, *Good Riding* and *Riding for Fun*, are excellent, well planned and imagina-

tive, offering useful information—like how to run a gymkhana and tips on hunting and cubbing or riding alone—not easily found in other pony books.

Christine Pullein-Thompson clearly writes for children, without one eye on the reviewer, and she has been rewarded by steady sales and continuity in print which few authors can match. To my mind there should be a place in children's bookshelves for quick undemanding reads, and adults should not dismiss these books as easily as they do, giving a child an all-too-often guilty feeling for enjoying what has been written simply to be enjoyed.

—Linda Yeatman

———

PULLEIN-THOMPSON, Diana. British. Born in Wimbledon, Surrey, 1 October 1930; daughter of the writer Joanna Cannan, *q.v.*; twin sister of Christine Pullein-Thompson, *q.v.*, and sister of Josephine Pullein-Thompson, *q.v.*, and the writer Denis Cannan. Educated at Wychwood School, Oxford. Married the museum director Dennis Farr in 1959; one son and one daughter. Staff member, Rosica Colin Ltd., literary agency, London, 1950–52; editorial assistant, Faith Press, London, 1958–59; director, Grove Riding Schools, Oxfordshire, 15 years. Address: 35 Esmond Road, London W4 1JG, England.

PUBLICATIONS FOR CHILDREN

Fiction

It Began with Picotee, with Christine and Josephine Pullein-Thompson, illustrated by Rosemary Robinson. London, A. and C. Black, 1946.
I Wanted a Pony, illustrated by Anne Bullen. London, Collins, 1946.
Three Ponies and Shannan, illustrated by Anne Bullen. London, Collins, 1947.
The Pennyfields. London, Collins, 1949.
A Pony to School, illustrated by Anne Bullen. London, Collins, 1950.
A Pony for Sale, illustrated by Sheila Rose. London, Collins, 1951.
Janet Must Ride, illustrated by Mary Gernat. London, Collins, 1953.
Horses at Home, and Friends Must Part, illustrated by Sheila Rose. London, Collins, 1954.
Riding with the Lyntons, illustrated by Sheila Rose. London, Collins, 1956.
The Boy and the Donkey, illustrated by Shirley Hughes. London, Collins, and New York, Criterion, 1958; as *The Donkey Race*, London, Armada, 1970.
The Secret Dog, illustrated by Geraldine Spence. London, Collins, 1959.
The Hidden River, illustrated by Sheila Rose. London, Hamish Hamilton, 1960.
The Boy Who Came to Stay, illustrated by Alan Breese. London, Faith Press, 1960.
The Battle of Clapham Common. London, Parrish, 1962.
Bindi Must Go, illustrated by Sheila Rose. London, Harrap, 1962.
Hermit's Horse. London, Armada, 1974.
Black Beauty's Clan, with Christine and Josephine Pullein-Thompson. Leicester, Brockhampton Press, 1975.
Ponies in the Valley. London, Collins, 1976.
Black Beauty's Family, with Christine and Josephine Pullein-Thompson, illustrated by Elisabeth Grant. London, Hodder and

Stoughton, 1978; New York, McGraw Hill, 1980.
Ponies on the Trail. London, Armada, 1978.
Ponies in Peril. London, Armada, 1979.
Cassidy in Danger. London, Dent, 1979.
Only a Pony. London, Armada, 1980.
A Foal for Candy. London, Sparrow, 1981.
The Pony Seekers. London, Sparrow, 1981.
Black Beauty's Family 2, with Christine and Josephine Pullein-Thompson. London, Hamlyn Beaver, 1982.
A Pony Found. London, Sparrow, 1983.

Other

Riding for Children. London, Foyle, 1957.

Editor, *True Horse and Pony Stories.* London, Armada, 1976.

PUBLICATIONS FOR ADULTS as Diana Farr

Novel

Choosing. London, Bodley Head, 1988.

Other

Gilbert Cannan: A Georgian Prodigy. London, Chatto and Windus, 1978.
Five at 10: Prime Ministers' Consorts since 1957. London, Deutsch, 1985.

*

Diana Pullein-Thompson comments:

My children's stories are written specifically for young people, not for book-buying parents or literary critics. The most favourably reviewed sell the least well. My first book, *I Wanted a Pony*, is probably my most popular work; yet much of it seems to me now over-dramatised and trivial. My own favourites are *Cassidy in Danger* and *Ponies in Peril*. Because the financial rewards of writing are so poor and there are always bills to be paid I tend to write too much and too often. The most encouraging remark ever made to me by a fan is, "I love your books so much that I keep them on a shelf by my pillow."

*   *   *

Diana Pullein-Thompson is a better writer than the pony book image she is associated with would lead most people to expect. Whether this has worked for or against her readers and more or fewer children have read her books because of the "pony tag" is hard to assess. But for those who have read her books, whatever the reason, the story tends to live on for a while after it has been finished, as is the way with all good books. This is because she really writes about people, and people situations, not just about ponies and riding situations. Her child characters are plausible, there are always plenty of ways to identify with the main character, and the emotional complications are graphically drawn.

Her first solo book, *I Wanted a Pony*, was written when, as she puts it, she was nearly a child herself, and her observations on grown-ups and family situations are shrewd. The commentary by the unhappy heroine on her cousins and on the horsey world they all live in is both perceptive and amusing. This, coupled with a good story told in an artless, almost naive style, makes the book memorable. It has been read by two generations of children and is still in demand.

After such a good start it might have been hard to go on, but she

has continued to develop with great effect the human and emotional situations in her books. *Riding with the Lyntons* and *Three Ponies and Shannan* are two examples where the children in the stories are involved with ponies and riding, but it is the personal misfortunes of the children that carry the reader along. *Friends Must Part* is a story many will warm to as it tells of a foolish disagreement between two great friends and their ensuing quarrel, painful to all, quite senseless and described so well. She is also able to convey the really nasty side of the horsey world, which so many children, tentative riders or outsiders, have witnessed or experienced, yet not often articulated.

Pullein-Thompson has not confined her writing to pony books. She has written for a religious publisher (*The Boy Who Came to Stay*), and several stories are set in London, which she knows as well as the horse world. *The Boy and the Donkey* is a good example of an urban story with its lonely child in a rundown street, gang warfare, and the unpredictability of town life. It is a well-written, touching book. *The Hidden River* and *The Secret Dog* are other examples of her sympathy with the loner, the child in a town, and the child whose world presents problems he can't contain.

Her contributions to the *Black Beauty* series, which she and her sisters wrote as sequels to Anna Sewell's *Black Beauty*, are imaginative and poignant. Black Princess, one of her creations, even found herself in France at the front during World War I.

Cassidy in Danger, one of Pullein-Thompson's more recent books, is perhaps her best. There is a pony in the story, but the heart of the matter is a girl whose upbringing has been so unsettled she has never learnt to read. As the story unfolds one warms not only to all the characters in the book, but to the author too for highlighting what can be a nightmare to so many children and conveying the problem in a sympathetic light to those who can read.

Some of the books appear dated now, for they are full of details (sums of money, social comments, children's slang, clothes, etc.) which have changed with the times. Her own suggestion that in reprints the date the book was written should be inserted in the opening sentence is a good one, for if a reader knows they are reading about 1956 or 1947 they are more prepared for the period slant—indeed, it can add interest to the story.

None of Diana Pullein-Thompson's books can be called profound, but they are perceptive and entertaining, and offer a genuinely good read to a young reader.

—Linda Yeatman

———

PULLEIN-THOMPSON, Josephine (Mary Wedderburn). Has also written as Josephine Mann. British. Born in Wimbledon, Surrey; daughter of the writer Joanna Cannan, *q.v.*; sister of Christine and Diana Pullein-Thompson, *qq.v.*, and the writer Denis Cannan. Educated at Wychwood School, Oxford. Since 1976 general secretary, PEN English Centre. M.B.E. (Member, Order of the British Empire), 1984. Address: 16 Knivet Road, London SW6 1JH, England.

PUBLICATIONS FOR CHILDREN

Fiction

It Began with Picotee, with Christine and Diana Pullein-Thompson, illustrated by Rosemary Robinson. London, A. and C. Black, 1946.
Six Ponies, illustrated by Anne Bullen. London, Collins, 1946.
I Had Two Ponies, illustrated by Anne Bullen. London, Collins, 1947.

Plenty of Ponies, illustrated by Anne Bullen. London, Collins, 1949.

Pony Club Team, illustrated by Sheila Rose. London, Collins, 1950.

The Radney Riding Club, illustrated by Sheila Rose. London, Collins, 1951.

Prince among Ponies, illustrated by Charlotte Hough. London, Collins, 1952.

One Day Event, illustrated by Sheila Rose. London, Collins, 1954.

Show Jumping Secret, illustrated by Sheila Rose. London, Collins, 1955.

Patrick's Pony, illustrated by Geoffrey Whittam. Leicester, Brockhampton Press, 1957.

Pony Club Camp, illustrated by Sheila Rose. London, Collins, 1957.

The Trick Jumpers, illustrated by Sheila Rose. London, Collins, 1958.

All Change, illustrated by Sheila Rose. London, Benn, 1961; as *The Hidden Horse*, London, Armada, 1982.

Race Horse Holiday. London, Armada, 1971.

Black Beauty's Clan, with Christine and Diana Pullein-Thompson. Leicester, Brockhampton Press, 1975.

Star-Riders of the Moor, illustrated by Elisabeth Grant. London, Hodder and Stoughton, 1976.

Black Beauty's Family, with Christine and Diana Pullein-Thompson, illustrated by Elisabeth Grant. London, Hodder and Stoughton, 1978; New York, McGraw Hill, 1980.

Fear Treks the Moor. London, Hodder and Stoughton, 1979.

Ride to the Rescue, illustrated by Elisabeth Grant. London, Hodder and Stoughton, 1979.

Ghost Horse on the Moor, illustrated by Eric Rowe. London, Hodder and Stoughton, 1980.

The No-Good Pony. London, Sparrow, 1981.

Treasure on the Moor, illustrated by Jon Davis. London, Hodder and Stoughton, 1982.

The Prize Pony. London, Sparrow, 1982.

The Hidden Horse, illustrated by Sheila Rose. London, Armada, 1982.

Black Beauty's Family 2, with Christine and Diana Pullein-Thompson. London, Hamlyn Beaver, 1982.

Pony Club Cup. London, Armada, 1983.

Save the Ponies! London, Sparrow, 1983.

Mystery on the Moor, illustrated by Chris Rothero. London, Hodder and Stoughton, 1984.

Pony Club Challenge. London, Fontana, 1984.

Pony Club Trek. London, Armada, 1985.

Suspicion Stalks the Moor, illustrated by Glenn Steward. London, Hodder and Stoughton, 1986.

Other

How Horses Are Trained. London, Routledge, 1961.

Ponies in Colour, photographs by Nicholas Meyjes. London, Batsford, and New York, Viking Press, 1962.

Learn to Ride Well. London, Routledge, 1966.

Ride Better and Better. London, Blackie, 1974.

Editor, *Horses and Their Owners*. London, Nelson, 1970.
Editor, *Proud Riders: Horse and Pony Stories*. Leicester, Brockhampton Press, 1973.

PUBLICATIONS FOR ADULTS

Novels

Gin and Murder. London, Hammond, 1959.

They Died in the Spring. London, Hammond, 1960.
Murder Strikes Pink. London, Hammond, 1963.
A Place with Two Faces (as Josephine Mann). London, Coronet, 1972; New York, Pocket Books, 1974.

*   *   *

Pony-mad readers make one basic demand. Their favourite writers must share with them an idealization of everything equine, believe that the clatter of hooves is the world's sweetest music, the smell of a stable more intoxicating than the finest perfume, and the possession of a pony the highest state of bliss. No writer has fulfilled these demands more satisfactorily than Josephine Pullein-Thompson. Every story she has written reveals her single-minded passion for horses. What makes her a dominant figure in the field of pony books, however, is that mere adoration is never enough for her. She writes with the serious purpose of turning her readers into better horsemen.

For her mother, Joanna Cannan, the ability to ride was something one scrambled into among the other delights of country life; her heroines learn horsemanship from their mistakes. By contrast Josephine's approach was much more professional. Her experiences as a riding instructor and Pony Club worker persuaded her that standards of riding needed to be raised, and she set about using the pony story, with its well-tried themes of struggle and achievement, as a vehicle for instruction. All her early books, from *Six Ponies* to *One Day Event*, show groups of children, or individuals, mastering the skills of horsemanship through various pony-centered events; and her readers are encouraged to identify with the most dedicated and persevering characters, as they school their ponies and improve their riding. Passages of direct technical instruction are boldly included, perhaps as advice given at a Pony Club rally; but these—acceptable, in any case to pony devotees—are made palatable to the general reader by the vitality of the style.

This brisk, cheerful style is one of Josephine Pullein-Thompson's assets. Her books are consistently readable. The Pullein-Thompsons were said to derive their dialogue from conversations they overheard among their riding school pupils, and Josephine's books are full of lively, realistic dialogue, swinging from grumbles to raptures, jokes to quarrels. Her characters, human and equine, are drawn on fairly basic and simple lines, but she handles her large casts with humour and ease.

In the 1960's Josephine Pullein-Thompson wrote mostly for adults, and when she returned to children's books in the 1970's she unfortunately plunged into a world of kidnappers, drug-smugglers, and horse thieves to which she was not suited. At the same time she used her considerable historical knowledge in her contributions to the tales of Black Beauty's imaginary descendants, in which she collaborated with her sisters. Her material is interesting, but comparison reveals the flatness of these modern versions beside the passion of the original Black Beauty.

In the 1980's she again took up the straightforward instructional story, and *The Prize Pony*, with its sympathetic treatment of an inexperienced young rider trying to manage a difficult pony, reaches the high levels of her first books. It offers the blend of clear advice and skilful story-telling that remains her distinctive contribution to the pony book.

—Angela Bull

PYE, Virginia (Frances Kennedy). British. Born in London, 27 October 1901; sister of the writer Margaret Kennedy. Educated privately. Married Sir David Pye in 1926; one daughter and two sons.

Address: Cuttmill Cottage, Shackleford, near Godalming, Surrey GU8 6BJ, England.

PUBLICATIONS FOR CHILDREN (illustrated by Richard Kennedy)

Fiction

Red-Letter Holiday, illustrated by Gwen Raverat. London, Faber, 1940.
Snow Bird. London, Faber, 1941.
Primrose Polly. London, Faber, 1942.
Half-Term Holiday. London, Faber, 1943.
The Prices Return. London, Faber, 1946.
The Stolen Jewels. London, Faber, 1948.
Johanna and the Prices. London, Faber, 1951.
Holiday Exchange. London, Faber, 1953.

PUBLICATIONS FOR ADULTS

Short Stories

St. Martin's Summer. London, Heinemann, 1930.

*

Virginia Pye comments:

I wrote my children's books during and after World War II. They have, therefore, the background of war time and post-war England and in this sense they are dated. I reread them recently and thought them even funnier than when I wrote them. The application for translation into German was made because "they give such a true picture for English family life." I believe this aspect is entirely undated and the relationship and interplay between the four children and their adult contacts is as true now as it was then and was in the books of E. Nesbit.

I am enchanted by most of the drawings by my cousin Richard Kennedy, particularly the small expressive ones which recapture perfectly the humour of a situation (for example, each child's rosy vision of the prospective return to London after the war in *The Prices Return*).

The Prices Return is my favourite. *Half-Term Holiday* is hilarious, but dated. *The Stolen Jewels* was written at the request of a children's librarian and was intended to be a carrot for slow readers; it didn't really come off. *Red-Letter Holiday* has a splendid ending and would make an excellent television episode. *Johanna and the Prices* (short stories) would make a nice paperback for a long journey or measles: very popular. *Primrose Polly* has a goodish, rather romantic, plot. *Snow Bird* and *Holiday Exchange* are, I think, averagely entertaining reading.

* * *

Virginia Pye's books were published between 1940 and 1953, and it is hard to believe that the modern holiday adventure story, inspired by Ransome's *Swallows and Amazons*, was only ten years old when the first of them, *Red-Letter Holiday*, was published. By 1940 the holiday adventure formula was in danger of being abused and stereotyped, but Pye, while using the conventions of the formula, provided a refreshing element of humour. Published during what was, for children's books, a rather bleak period because of wartime shortages and restrictions, it is not surprising that the Pye books were warmly welcomed by children's librarians and are uniformly praised in articles and conference papers of the period. What is surprising is that the books have been allowed to go out of print, particularly as

they are hardly dated by internal references.

Pye's most striking gifts are for portrayal of character and humour. Most of the books are concerned with the holiday adventures of the Price family—Susan, Tom, and Alan with the occasional involvement of their friend Johanna Allard. These four children come over as very real personalities. Alan, the youngest, is inclined to act without thinking, which sometimes involves the family in unexpected situations, as when he decides to improve on the idea of running a tea garden by displaying a notice "licensed to sell wines, spirits and tobacco" (*Red-Letter Holiday*), or, on a grander scale, to arrange with his Swiss pen-friend that their families should exchange houses (*Holiday Exchange*). However, when he is rendered *hors de combat* in *Primrose Polly*, Tom and Susan become involved in adventures without his help. Tom, though competent, is far from being the know-all elder brother, while Susan is well ahead of her time (except that she wears a skirt instead of jeans) in that she does not automatically assume the female role of feeding, and generally ministering to the wants of, her brothers. Johanna is even more unconventional, providing an outside catalyst for those adventures in which she features. Introduced to the Price family (*Red-Letter Holiday*) through a photograph which shows her wearing a white dress and playing a violin, she seems determined to give the lie to this image. Having acquired a black eye and a cut lip before setting out for Cornwall to join the Prices, she manages to lose the train en route and consequently arrives later then expected. She is also ready with the original suggestion which turns the action in a new direction.

The plot of *Red-Letter Holiday* was also well ahead of its time in that the central incident is concerned with finding the skeleton of a prehistoric monster—the kind of theme which was to become popular twenty years later. This book, like the other Pye stories, is packed with incident and moves quickly from one unlikely situation to another; but the succession of events is made credible by the observed detail of life around and the attention paid to the minor figures.

The characters, their conversations, and the humour stay in the mind long after the details of the adventures are forgotten.

—Sheila G. Ray

———

RAE, Gwynedd. British. Born in London, 23 July 1892. Educated at Manor House School, Brondesbury, London, 1907–09; Villa St. George's School, Paris, 1909–10. Served in the Voluntary Aid Detachment during World War I. Social worker. *Died 14 November 1977.*

PUBLICATIONS FOR CHILDREN (illustrated by Irene Williamson)

Fiction

Mostly Mary, illustrated by Harry Rountree. London, Mathews and Marrot, 1930; New York, Morrow, 1931.
All Mary, illustrated by Harry Rountree. London, Mathews and Marrot, 1931.
Mary Plain in Town. London, Cobden Sanderson, 1935.
Mary Plain on Holiday. London, Cobden Sanderson, 1937.
Mary Plain in Trouble. London, Routledge, 1940.
Mary Plain in War-Time. London, Routledge, 1942; as *Mary Plain Lends a Paw*, 1949.
Mary Plain's Big Adventure. London, Routledge, 1944.
Mary Plain Home Again. London, Routledge, 1949.
Mary Plain to the Rescue. London, Routledge, 1950.

Mary Plain and the Twins. London, Routledge, 1952.
Mary Plain Goes Bob-a-Jobbing. London, Routledge, 1954.
Mary Plain Goes to America. London, Routledge, 1957.
Mary Plain, V.I.P. London, Routledge, 1961.
Mary Plain's Whodunit. London, Routledge, 1965.

PUBLICATIONS FOR ADULTS

Novels

And Timothy Too. London, Blackie, 1934.
Leap Year Born. London, Blackie, 1935.

* * *

The continuing popularity of Gwynedd Rae's Mary Plain, "an unusual first-class bear from the bear-pits at Berne," is shown by the publication in 1976 of an omnibus edition of four of the early stories. Although she has never achieved the fame of other bears such as Paddington or Winnie-the-Pooh, Mary has always had her admirers among several generations of readers.

The books were given early publicity by broadcast readings in the BBC Radio programme *Children's Hour*, but there are also qualities inherent in the books which have ensured their lasting popularity: the warm, appealing character of the bear cub, the fun for children in decoding Mary's pictographic writing, and the humour which, without ever being unkind, often arises because the reader is cleverer than Mary. The animals, of course, are anthropomorphic, but children recognise the cub's behavior as that of a naughty small girl who can enjoy mischief denied to the young reader. The other bears also have their own natures: fussy, ineffectual Friska, greedy Bunch, and revered Big Wool.

Many of the stories were topical and some, such as those set in wartime, may now seem dated to adults but perhaps historical to the child. The domestic incidents are usually more successful than the wilder fantasies, such as Mary's starring role in a Hollywood film, but the universal nature of the young bear's behavior gives her something to say to each generation. Although superficially the stories are suitable for very young children, the skills needed to read the quite long texts and to appreciate the jokes make the book most suitable for 8 to 10-year-olds.

—Valerie Brinkley-Willsher

RANSOME, Arthur (Michell). British. Born in Leeds, Yorkshire, 18 January 1884. Educated at Old College, Windermere, 1893–97; Rugby College, Warwickshire, 1897–1901; Yorkshire College (now Leeds University), 1901. Married 1) Ivy Walker in 1909 (divorced 1924), one daughter; 2) Evgenia Shelepin in 1924. Office boy, Grant Richards, publishers, London, 1901–02; assistant, Unicorn Press, London, 1902–03; freelance writer, ghost writer, and publishers reader, after 1903; assistant editor, *Temple Bar* magazine, London, 1905–06; moved to Russia in 1913; correspondent, *Daily News*, 1915–19, and the *Observer*, 1917–19; correspondent in the Soviet Union, 1919–24, Egypt, 1924–25, 1929–30, and China, 1926–27; correspondent, 1921–29, and columnist, 1925–28, Manchester *Guardian*. Recipient: Library Association Carnegie Medal, 1937. Litt.D.: University of Leeds, 1952; M.A.: University of Durham. C.B.E. (Commander, Order of the British Empire), 1953. *Died 3 June 1967.*

PUBLICATIONS FOR CHILDREN

Fiction

Swallows and Amazons, illustrated by Helene Carter. London, Cape, 1930; Philadelphia, Lippincott, 1931.
Swallowdale, illustrated by Clifford Webb. London, Cape, 1931; Philadelphia, Lippincott, 1932.
Peter Duck, illustrated by the author. London, Cape, 1932; Philadelphia, Lippincott, 1933.
Winter Holiday, illustrated by the author. London, Cape, 1933; Philadelphia, Lippincott, 1934.
Coot Club, illustrated by the author and Helene Carter. London, Cape, 1934; Philadelphia, Lippincott, 1935.
Pigeon Post, illustrated by the author. London, Cape, 1936; Philadelphia, Lippincott, 1937.
We Didn't Mean to Go to Sea, illustrated by the author. London, Cape, 1937; New York, Macmillan, 1938.
Secret Water, illustrated by the author. London, Cape, 1939; New York, Macmillan, 1940.
The Big Six, illustrated by the author. London, Cape, 1940; New York, Macmillan, 1941.
Missee Lee, illustrated by the author. London, Cape, 1941; New York, Macmillan, 1942.
The Picts and the Martyrs; or, Not Welcome at All, illustrated by the author. London, Cape, and New York, Macmillan, 1943.
Great Northern? London, Cape, 1947; New York, Macmillan, 1948.
Coots in the North and Other Stories, edited by Hugh Brogan. London, Cape, 1988.

Verse

Aladdin and His Wonderful Lamp, illustrated by Mackenzie. London, Nisbet, 1919; New York, Brentano's 1920.

Other

The Imp and the Elf and the Ogre. London, Nisbet, 1910.
The Child's Book of the Seasons. London, Treherne, 1906.
The Things in Our Garden. London, Treherne, 1906.
Pond and Stream. London, Treherne, 1906.
Highways and Byways in Fairyland. London, Alston Rivers, 1906; New York, McBride, 1909.
Old Peter's Russian Tales, illustrated by Dmitri Mitrokhin. London, Jack, 1916; New York, Stokes, 1917.
The Soldier and Death: A Russian Folk Tale Told in English. London, Wilson, 1920; New York, Huebsch, 1922.
The War of the Birds and the Beasts and Other Russian Tales, edited by Hugh Brogan, illustrated by Faith Jaques. London, Cape, 1984.

PUBLICATIONS FOR ADULTS

Novel

The Elixir of Life. London, Methuen, 1915.

Short Stories

The Hoofmarks of the Faun. London, Secker, 1911.

Other

The ABC of Physical Culture. London, Henry Drane, 1904.
The Souls of the Streets and Other Little Papers. London, Brown

Langham, 1904.
The Stone Lady, Ten Little Papers, and Two Mad Stories. London, Brown Langham, 1905.
Bohemia in London. London, Chapman and Hall, and New York, Dodd Mead, 1907.
A History of Story-Telling: Studies in the Development of Narrative. London, Jack, 1909; New York, Stokes, 1910.
Edgar Allan Poe: A Critical Study. London, Secker, and New York, Kennerley, 1910.
Oscar Wilde: A Critical Study. London, Secker, 1912; New York, Kennerley, 1913.
Portraits and Speculations. London, Macmillan, 1913.
Radek and Ransome on Russia, Being Arthur Ransome's "Open Letter to America" with a New Preface by Karl Radek. New York, Socialist Publication Society, 1918.
Six Weeks in Russia in 1919. London, Allen and Unwin, 1919; as *Russia in 1919*, New York, Huebsch, 1919.
The Crisis in Russia. London, Allen and Unwin, and New York, Huebsch, 1921.
Racundra's First Cruise. London, Allen and Unwin, and New York, Huebsch, 1923.
The Chinese Puzzle. London, Allen and Unwin, 1927.
Rod and Line: Essays, Together with Aksakov on Fishing. London, Cape, 1929.
Fishing. Cambridge, University Press, 1955.
Mainly about Fishing. London, A. and C. Black, 1959.
The Autobiography of Arthur Ransome, edited by Rupert Hart-Davis. London, Cape, 1976.

Editor, *The World's Story Tellers.* London, Jack, and New York, Dutton, 12 vols., 1908–09.
Editor, *The Book of Friendship* [and *Love*]: *Essays, Poems, Maxims, and Prose Passages.* London, Jack, 2 vols., 1909–10; New York, Stokes, 2 vols., 1910–11.

Translator, *A Night in the Luxembourg*, by Rémy de Gourmont. London, Stephen Swift, 1912.
Translator, *A Week*, by Y.N. Libedinsky. London, Allen and Unwin, 1923.

*

Manuscript Collection: Brotherton Collection, Leeds.

Critical Studies: *Arthur Ransome* by Hugh Shelley, London, Bodley Head, 1960, New York, Walck, 1964; *The Life of Arthur Ransome* by Hugh Brogan, London, Cape, 1984; *Arthur Ransome and Captain Flint's Trunk* by Christina Hardyment, London, Cape, 1984; *Arthur Ransome's Lakeland: A Quest for the Real "Swallow and Amazons" Country* by Roger Wardale, Clapham, Yorkshire, Dalesman, 1986.

Illustrator: his own books *Swallowdale*, 1938, and *Swallows and Amazons*, 1938.

*   *   *

"It always rained on that day, both indoors and out of doors," wrote Arthur Ransome in his autobiography, recalling the mournful ending of the summer holidays, the return to Leeds from the farm in the Lakes where, until his father died when Arthur was 13, the Ransome family settled themselves for the Long Vacation. "The rain would stream down the window outside, and we with our noses pressed to the glass were blinded by our tears."

Besides this holiday everything else in his childhood was shadowy, it seemed, and when he came, late in life, to write his children's books it was only the holidays that he chose to record, recalling the intensity of delight of the sight of the lakeside farm at last, the ritual dipping of the hand in the water to prove that one had indeed "come home," the greeting of the familiar faces, all to find a place in the books: the kind farmer's daughter (a Swainson there, as she was in real life) who darned threadbare knickerbockers "in situ," the charcoal burners in the woods, the woodcutters, the friendly postman.

Of his 12 books for children only five concern the Lakes, but for most readers this is the background with which they identify Ransome. In *Coot Club, Secret Water, The Big Six*, and *Great Northern?*, the Norfolk Broads and Hebridean scenery is real enough, but one senses that for the author it has not the magic that sent him, during his bohemian years in London, hurrying to Euston whenever he could scrape together the fare to the north.

When the Swallows and Amazons sail Lake Windermere we are in landscape with all the elements that a child most wants, a lake like an inland sea, with islands in it where nobody goes, hills, streams, woods, places to light your own fires without interference. One can wander on the fells all day and meet nothing more than a crag-fast sheep. The natives churn up and down the lakes in their steamers in the distance, but they have no real existence in the children's minds. The characters exist in their holidays only; we are told nothing else of them and nothing else matters. It would be a betrayal to try to imagine them at school; they move for us in their own world where they are Authority. In so far as adult authority—their parents—exists, they co-operate, but their parents tacitly admit their children's holiday supremacy, and make no demands that the children cannot recognize as valid. When unjust authority descends in the shape of great-aunt, then children and mother and uncle are united in silent resistance. It is a dream-world thought up by a writer who still remembered with resentment how inadequate he had been throughout his school career, slow, stupid, pitifully short-sighted, the butt of both masters and boys.

Perfectly Ransome recaptures the child's deep absorption in himself and his doings, and succeeds in conveying the intense importance and excitement of day-to-day details when one is fending for oneself. He can recall it minutely, so that he can describe the ascent of a tree foothold by foothold, naming the branches that call for particular care. Success blended with occasional failure. Certainly the children manipulate their camps and their boats with serene efficiency; when they set out to divine water they find it; they can build a hut that does not fall down; their signalling systems work, their homing pigeons really do carry messages to reassure the grownups. But now and then even these children are fallible; the *Swallow* is wrecked and all the ecstatic holiday happiness temporarily with it: "it was if the summer itself had been the cargo of the little ship and had gone with her to the bottom of the lake."

The children themselves are a blend of fantasy and reality. Captain Nancy, bold and swashbuckling and defiant, could have no existence outside a story, but the Walker family are all aspects of the author himself. Roger, "ship's boy," is the child Arthur, enthusiastic, unthinking, confident that his elders will sort everything out; Titty, a rather older Arthur, fanciful, a worrier, but often the unexpected victor; John, the calm and business-like captain whom Arthur would have liked to have been, the boy whose commands are unquestioningly obeyed (as no elder brother's ever are). Susan, the brisk school matron, stands alone, Arthur Ransome's concession to the mothers of the 1930's anxious for the dry feet, clean teeth, and proper bedtime of their young. No one quarrels with Susan's dictatorial fussiness; to quarrel would be undignified. Ransome has given to his child characters a dignity and a stature that real children would dearly like to possess; it is one of the elements of his eternal appeal.

—Gillian Avery

RASKIN, Ellen. American. Born in Milwaukee, Wisconsin, 13 March 1928. Educated at the University of Wisconsin, Madison, 1945–49. Married Dennis Flanagan in 1966; one daughter by a previous marriage. From 1954 freelance artist and designer, New York: group shows—50 Years of Graphic Arts in America, 1966; Biennale of Illustrations, Bratislava, 1969; Biennale of Applied Graphic Art, Brno, 1972; Contemporary American Illustrators of Children's Books, toured U.S.A., 1974–75. Recipient: Boston *Globe-Horn Book* award, 1978; American Library Association Newbery Medal, 1979. *Died 8 August 1984.*

PUBLICATIONS FOR CHILDREN (illustrated by the author)

Fiction

Nothing Ever Happens on My Block. New York, Atheneum, 1966.
Spectacles. New York, Atheneum, 1968.
Ghost in a Four-Room Apartment. New York, Atheneum, 1969.
And It Rained. New York, Atheneum, 1969.
A & The; or, William T.C. Baumgarten Comes to Town. New York, Atheneum, 1970.
The Mysterious Disappearance of Leon (I Mean Noel). New York, Dutton, 1971.
The World's Greatest Freak Show. New York, Atheneum, 1971.
Franklin Stein. New York, Atheneum, 1972.
Moe Q. McGlutch, He Smoked Too Much. New York, Parents' Magazine Press, 1973.
Moose, Goose, and Little Nobody. New York, Parents' Magazine Press, 1974.
Figgs and Phantoms. New York, Dutton, 1974.
The Tattooed Potato and Other Clues. New York, Dutton, 1975; London, Macmillan, 1976.
Twenty-Two, Twenty-Three. New York, Atheneum, 1976.
The Westing Game. New York, Dutton, 1978; London, Macmillan, 1979.

Verse

Silly Songs and Sad. New York, Crowell, 1967.
Who, Said Sue, Said Whoo? New York, Atheneum, 1973.

*

Manuscript Collections: Milwaukee Public Library, Wisconsin; Kerlan Collection, University of Minnesota, Minneapolis; Children's Co-operative Book Center, University of Wisconsin, Madison.

Illustrator: *Happy Christmas* edited by Claire Huchet Bishop, 1956; *A Child's Christmas in Wales* by Dylan Thomas, 1959; *"Mama, I Wish I Was Snow" "Child, You'd Be Very Cold"* by Ruth Krauss, 1962; *We Dickinsons*, 1965, and *We Alcotts*, 1968, both by Aileen Fisher and Olive Rabe; *Poems of Edgar Allan Poe*, 1965; *The King of Men* by Olivia Coolidge, 1966; *Songs of Innocence* by William Blake, 2 vols., 1966; *The Jewish Sabbath* by Molly Cone, 1966; *The Paths of Poetry* edited by Louis Untermeyer, 1966; *D.H. Lawrence: Poems* edited by William Cole, 1967; *Ellen Grae*, 1967, and *Lady Ellen Grae*, 1968, both by Vera and Bill Cleaver; *Poems* by Robert Herrick, edited by Winfield Townley Scott, 1967; *Probability, The Science of Chance*, 1967, *This Is 4*, 1967, *Symmetry*, 1968, *Three and the Shape of Three*, 1969, *Circles and Curves*, 1969, and *A Question of Accuracy*, 1969, all by Arthur Razzell and K.G. Watts; *Books* by Susan Bartlett, 1968; *Inatuk's Friend* by Suzanne Stark Morrow, 1968; *A Paper Zoo!* by Renée Weiss, 1968; *Piping Down the Valleys Wild* edited by Nancy Larrick, 1968; *Come Along!* by

Rebecca Caudill, 1969; *Shrieks at Midnight* edited by Sara and John E. Brewton, 1969; *Goblin Market* by Christina Rossetti, 1970; *Elidor* by Alan Garner, 1970.

Ellen Raskin commented:

(1978) The only difference between words and pictures is that words describe verbal ideas, pictures delineate graphic ideas. In books they serve the same function: to tell a story. No matter what story I tell, my message is the same: books can be fun. Through words and pictures and the design of the book itself I try to create a world of surprises, waiting to be discovered by the child who opens the cover and turns the pages of my book.

* * *

Ellen Raskin was an artist of versatility and charm who specialized in verbal and visual puzzles. Her best work is linked to the concept of vision. Raskin saw vision as a multi-faceted faculty. Two of her best-known picture books focus on the differences between seeing and not-seeing. Iris Fogel, the nearsighted little girl in *Spectacles*, needs glasses because she cannot properly identify the people and objects in front of her. But is that a failing? What Iris thinks she sees is far more interesting than what is actually there. Do Iris's new glasses really help her see better? Maintaining too sharp a focus on reality may limit one's ability to explore and imagine other alternatives. At the end of the book Iris gets her glasses, but it is also obvious that she has no qualms about taking them off—"You see, everything looks like I suppose it's supposed to look…except for that red rhinoceros with a tulip in its ear."

Nothing Ever Happens on My Block deals with Chester Filbert, a boy with the opposite problem. Chester is blind to the events going on around him. As he sits on the curb loudly bemoaning the fact that nothing ever happens on his block a robbery is foiled; a house catches fire; a parachutist lands; a cat has kittens; an armored car breaks open and scatters 50-dollar bills all over the street. But Chester sees none of this. Having convinced himself that nothing exciting ever happens, he cannot see it when it does occur. Raskin clearly prefers the Iris Fogels of the world to the Chester Filberts. Glasses can correct myopia; nothing can correct the lack of imagination.

With this in mind, Raskin's move from picture books to mysteries can be regarded as a logical progression, although it may not have appeared so in 1971 when *The Mysterious Disappearance of Leon (I Mean Noel)* was published. Raskin, in fact, had found her element in the sense that the mystery novel can be seen as an indepth study of the problem of vision. One of the conventions of mystery writing is that all the necessary clues are present from the beginning. The challenge to the reader lies in distinguishing what is significant from what is not, avoiding false conclusions, and being able to fit the pieces together in the correct order to arrive at the solution.

Figgs and Phantoms, The Mysterious Disappearance of Leon (I Mean Noel), The Tattooed Potato and Other Clues, Twenty-Two, Twenty-Three, and *The Westing Game* are all excursions down a garden path strewn with unusual and often downright bizarre characters. *The Westing Game*, winner of the 1979 Newbery Medal, is the most intricate and successful of the four. Samuel J. Westing, the fabulously wealthy paper manufacturer, is dead. His 16 heirs—all residents of an exclusive Chicago apartment house—are paired (mismatched is a better word), given 10 thousand dollars and an envelope containing a clue consisting of four words written individually on cut squares of paper toweling. The words may go together in any order, or in no order at all. No pair has the same clue, nor is any pair obliged to share its clues with the others—though it is definitely in each one's interest to know what clues the others are holding. If any player drops out, his partner must leave the game too and return the 10 thousand dollars. The pair that solves the puzzle—the Westing Game—wins the entire estate. The scene is thus set for intrigue, skullduggery, and not a few mysterious disappearances and "accidents." And a question: is the corpse found lying on Samuel J. Westing's bed really that of Samuel J. Westing? And was he murdered?

Raskin's work is not without flaws. A fussy preciousness mars her less successful picture books and at time creeps into her novels. Her delightfully exotic characters can hardly be taken seriously as human beings. However, mysteries are seldom read for characterization. They are, as Graham Greene aptly put it, "entertainments." In that regard Raskin excelled. As both writer and illustrator she was always witty, always charming, and never failed to entertain.

—Eric A. Kimmel

RAWLINGS, Marjorie Kinnan. American. Born in Washington, D.C., 8 August 1896. Educated at Western High School, Washington, D.C.; University of Wisconsin, Madison, 1914–18, B.A. 1918 (Phi Beta Kappa). Married 1) Charles Rawlings in 1919 (divorced 1933); 2) Norton Sanford Baskin in 1941. Editor, YWCA National Board, New York, 1918–19; assistant service editor, *Home Sector* magazine, 1919; staff member, Louisville *Courier Journal*, Kentucky, and Rochester *Journal*, Rochester, New York, 1920–28; syndicated verse writer ("Songs of a Housewife"), United Features, 1926–28; fulltime writer in Florida from 1928. Recipient: O. Henry award, 1933; Pulitzer Prize, 1939. LL.D.: Rollins College, Winter Park, Florida, 1939; L.H.D.: University of Florida, Gainesville, 1941. Member, American Academy, 1939. *Died 14 December 1953.*

PUBLICATIONS FOR CHILDREN

Fiction

The Yearling, illustrated by Edward Shenton. New York, Scribner, and London, Heinemann, 1938.
The Secret River, illustrated by Leonard Weisgard. New York, Scribner, 1955.

PUBLICATIONS FOR ADULTS

Novels

South Moon Under. New York, Scribner, and London, Faber, 1933.
Golden Apples. New York, Scribner, 1935; London, Heinemann, 1939.
Jacob's Ladder. Coral Gables, Florida, University of Miami Press, 1950.
The Sojourner. New York, Scribner, and London, Heinemann, 1953.

Short Stories

When the Whippoorwill—. New York, Scribner, and London, Heinemann, 1940.

Other

Cross Creek. New York, Scribner, and London, Heinemann, 1942.
Cross Creek Cookery. New York, Scribner, 1942; as *The Marjorie Kinnan Rawlings Cookbook*, London, Hammond, 1961.
The Marjorie Kinnan Rawlings Reader, edited by Julia Scribner

Bigham. New York, Scribner, 1956.
Selected Letters, edited by Gordon E. Bigelow and Laura V. Monti. Gainesville, University Presses of Florida, 1983.

*

Manuscript Collection: University of Florida Libraries, Gainesville.

Critical Studies: *Frontier Eden: The Literary Career of Marjorie Kinnan Rawlings* by Gordon E. Bigelow, Gainesville, University of Florida Press, 1966; *Marjorie Kinnan Rawlings* by Samuel I. Bellman, New York, Twayne, 1974; *Marjorie Kinnan Rawlings: Sojourner at Cross Creek* by Elizabeth Silverthorne, New York, Viking, 1988.

*   *   *

Marjorie Kinnan Rawlings is a regional writer. Her work is inhabited by the simple people and natural settings of the Florida backwoods which she adopted as her home. Often paramount in her novels is the struggle against the vicissitudes of an uncertain existence by the poor white—the Florida cracker—commonly epitomized in an archetypical young protagonist with frontier virtues. Her first three major novels and much of her short fiction hold marked appeal for adolescent as well as adult readers.

South Moon Under depicts the difficulties of the hunter scratching out a living as a moonshiner in the Florida scrub country. The novel combines vividly descriptive scenes of rural existence with strong characterizations and an eventful plot. *Golden Apples* recounts the efforts of an orphaned and impoverished brother and sister to survive in late 19th-century northern Florida. They "squat" on the estate of an exiled and embittered young Englishman whom they patiently regenerate. The resourceful protagonist is a more convincing figure than the vaguely sketched Englishman in this flawed but dramatically forceful novel. In the novella *Jacob's Ladder* a rootless and destitute young cracker couple encounters adversities in luckless attempts to wrest a living from a bounteous but treacherous environment. The pair's deep mutual reliance and indomitable spirit are a poignant and emotionally powerful testament.

The author's internationally acclaimed novel *The Yearling* represents her finest achievement. The hero is 12-year-old Jody Baxter, who lives with his parents in the Florida hammock country of the 1870's. As his marginally existing family undergoes severe setbacks, Jody tames a fawn which becomes his forest-roaming companion. When, however, his pet cannot be restrained from eating the precious crops, it must be killed. The anguished boy feels betrayed by his father and severs their close relationship. Eventually they are reconciled. Tragedy has made a man of him. Throughout the story weave such themes as man's need to belong to the land which, in turn, belongs to those who lovingly cultivate it, and the inevitability of unfair and unexpected betrayal by man and nature. Rawlings's compellingly truthful portrait of a boy and his tender relationship is universally appealing. Her striking description of nature's elemental forces and the simple but significant events in the lives of people close to the land enrich an absorbingly ingenuous story. This distinguished novel stands as a classic of adult and children's literature.

Intended primarily for young children is the posthumously published story *The Secret River*. Its heroine is a little girl who on her own helps her empty-handed father by finding in the forest a fish-filled secret river. After sharing her catch with forest animals, she returns home with enough fish to restore her father's modest prosperity which, consequently, restores that of his neighbors. When she looks for the river again it has vanished, since the need for it has gone. Charmingly illustrated, this woodland idyll with simple story and message offers enchantment for the small child.

Rawlings is a pastoral writer of percipience and power all of whose stories—besides her memorable *The Yearling*—can be enjoyed by young people.

—Christian H. Moe

RAY, Mary (Eva Pedder). British. Born in Rugby, Warwickshire, 14 March 1932. Educated at Rugby High School, 1937–50; College of Arts and Crafts, Birmingham, 1950–52; College of the Ascension, Birmingham, 1952–57, London Diploma of Social Studies and Cambridge Certificate of Religious Knowledge; University of Kent, Canterbury, 1988. Parish worker, Sheffield Diocese, 1958–61; assistant matron, Warwickshire County Council Old People's Homes, Solihull, 1961–62; civil servant, Export Credits Guarantee Department, Birmingham, 1962–64, 1965–78; staff member, Amphenol Ltd., Whitstable from 1980; doctor's receptionist. Address: 2 Harcourt Drive, Canterbury, Kent CT2 8DP, England.

PUBLICATIONS FOR CHILDREN

Fiction

The Voice of Apollo, illustrated by John Cooper. London, Cape, 1964; New York, Farrar Straus, 1965.
The Eastern Beacon, illustrated by Janet Duchesne. London, Cape, 1965; New York, Farrar Straus, 1966.
Standing Lions, illustrated by Janet Duchesne. London, Faber, 1968; New York, Meredith Press, 1969.
Spring Tide, illustrated by Janet Duchesne. London, Faber, 1969.
Shout Against the Wind, illustrated by Peter Branfield. London, Faber, 1970.
A Tent for the Sun. London, Faber, 1971.
The Ides of April. London, Faber, 1974; New York, Farrar Straus, 1975.
Sword Sleep. London, Faber, 1975.
Beyond the Desert Gate. London, Faber, 1977.
Song of Thunder. London, Faber, 1978.
Rain from the West. London, Faber, 1980.
The Windows of Elissa. London, Faber, 1982.
The Golden Bees, illustrated by Lynda Gray. London, Faber, 1984.

Plays

The Mary Rose, music by Sydney Sagar (produced Rugby, 1983).
Dragons and Dinosaurs, music by Sydney Sagar (produced Cheltenham, 1985).
The Dolphin Boy, music by Sydney Sagar (produced Cheltenham, 1985).

Other

Living in Earliest Greece, illustrated by Peter Branfield. London, Faber, 1969.

*

Mary Ray comments:

After a gap since my early teens (when I had produced very horrific historical fiction and poetry), I began to write again quite suddenly in my late twenties when a friend told me that she had started a book and I could think of no good reason why I shouldn't too. It seemed obvious to me that I should write for children, as I was still very much under the influence of books that I had read as a child, and also that the books should have a classical setting. Since about the age of 6 I had never felt any strangeness or distance about what I had learned of the people of Greece and Rome and of earlier civilisations; I was at home in the period in the way that some people are at home in a place or a country. I started with Roman Britain, because I knew what the places looked like, and for me it is important that the three strands of the actual geographical first-hand knowledge, historical research, and imagination should all be as strong as I can make them. After I was able to go to Greece regularly I particularly enjoyed writing about people who lived there. I became fascinated by what was the same for me—smells and weather and mountains and ants—and what was quite different because the way that earlier people thought and the things they expected and accepted were different—slavery, pain, and the worship of different gods.

Looking back I can see that certain themes are usually important in my books. Creative people have a habit of turning up as characters, because making things, from jam to fine art, is very important to me, and my creative people often have to fight to be able to practice their skills as one does in real life. I also enjoy writing about the very old and the very young, which is a hangover from working in residential homes for mothers and babies and the old when I was a social science student. I am also obsessed by a theme very common in children's books—how and when you become able to come to terms with what life brings. I suppose this is because to children's writers their own childhood is still very alive. We remember what it hurt to learn, what we had to fight for and what we had to accept; the characters in our books follow where we went, or go the way we wish we had gone.

*   *   *

The historical novels of Mary Ray bear witness to a passionate interest in early western civilisation, as manifested in ancient Greece, Rome, and Britain, especially at times of turbulence and cultural change such as the birth of Christianity. Concepts which might be thought too complex for children's reading are bravely tackled by this committed writer who often hints at far more that she can express within the confines of a children's book.

Her attitude to the classical world is ambivalent. Although she is attracted to—even obsessed with—ancient culture, as shown in her detailed, loving descriptions of the landscape and the daily life, there are terrible drawbacks. Life is rigidly stratified and many of her characters are poor, enslaved, condemned to drudgery or forced marriage. Women are especially powerless. Although Roman civilisation is a highly organised creation, it needs Christian philosophy to perfect it.

Ray has written of the Mycenean period in *Standing Lions* and *Shout Against the Wind*. In the former she uses the theories of Robert Graves and others about the Mother Goddess and the annual sacrifice of the King in a tale of invasion and court intrigue. *Shout Against the Wind* is about refugees from the Dorian invasions, a group of people of different social class who sink these differences to make a new life.

Religion is an important element in her work, and all her main characters feel the need to communicate with some external power, to find the right god and make the right offering. She has written a cycle of novels about the early days of Christianity when it was a secret underground cult. The first book, *A Tent for the Sun*, about St. Paul's visits to Corinth, makes one feel the excitement and complete surrender of the soul demanded by the new faith.

Two stories about Camillus and the slave Hylas continue the theme of conversation to Christianity. In *The Ides of April*, set in Rome, Hylas is suspected of murder and Camillus helps him to freedom. Hylas is sheltered by a secret Christian, and it is suggested that Christ's power has brought the truth to light. In *Sword Sleep*, set in

Athens, their friendship has become closer and more romantic. Hylas is now a Christian, and the unhappy boy Flavius, befriended by them both, makes a third in their emotional bond. Themes which inspired Mary Renault are also dear to Ray: in her earlier books, Mycenean Greece and the cult of the Mother Goddess, and now the Athenian setting with its flashbacks to the wars of Alexander, and intense male friendships which could be described as quasi-love affairs.

The fourth book, *Beyond the Desert Gate*, takes Hylas to Palestine during the Jewish revolt against Roman rule. The quintet concludes with *Rain from the West*, when Camillus, Hylas, and Flavius are reunited in Roman Britain, and Hylas eventually marries Pyrrha (a character from *A Tent for the Sun*, who has travelled to Britain from Corinth).

Apart from this linked sequence, Ray has continued to write novels set in the turbulent times of the ancient world. *Song of Thunder* is about the eruption of Santorini in 1450 B.C., *The Golden Bees* about the peaceful time on Crete just prior to that eruption, and *The Windows of Elissa* about the siege of Carthage in 310 B.C. Her characters continue to be faced with life-and-death decisions, at the mercy of others who fear, and need to propitiate, capricious deities. Elissa's sister Sophi is threatened with sacrifice to Baal to save Carthage from destruction. There is no doubt about the evil side of human nature presented by Ray, just as true today as in the ancient world. Against this evil, her characters bravely uphold their faith in a greater force for good.

Having specialised in a particular theme and period, and chosen a formal, metaphoric style of writing, has inevitably endeared her to critics rather than the majority of children, but her Roman Empire sequence is still to be regarded as an important achievement in the field of the historical novel for children.

—Jessica Yates

RAYNER, Mary (Yoma, née Grigson). British. Born in Mandalay, Burma, 30 December 1933. Educated at Nazareth Convent, Ootacamund, India, 1943–45; St. Swithun's School, Winchester, 1945–51; University of St. Andrews, Fife, 1952–56, M.A. (honours) in English 1956. Married 1) E.H. Rayner in 1960 (divorced 1982), one daughter and two sons; 2) A.C.T. Hawksley in 1985. Editorial and production assistant, Hammond Hammond, publishers, London; copywriter, Longmans Green, publishers, London, 1959–62. Freelance writer and illustrator. Lives in Wiltshire. Agent: Laura Cecil, 17 Alwyne Villas, London N1 2HG, England.

PUBLICATIONS FOR CHILDREN (illustrated by the author)

Fiction

The Witch-Finder. London, Macmillan, 1975; New York, Morrow, 1976.
Mr. and Mrs. Pig's Evening Out. London, Macmillan, and New York, Atheneum, 1976.
Garth Pig and the Icecream Lady. London, Macmillan, and New York, Atheneum, 1977.
The Rain Cloud. London, Macmillan, and New York, Atheneum, 1980.
Mrs. Pig's Bulk Buy. London, Macmillan, and New York, Atheneum, 1981.
Crocodarling. London, Collins, 1985; New York, Bradbury Press, 1986.
Mrs. Pig Gets Cross and Other Stories. London, Collins, 1986; New York, Dutton, 1987.
Reilly. London, Gollancz, 1987.

Oh Paul! London, Heinemann, 1988.
Marathon and Steve. New York, Dutton, 1989.

*

Illustrator: *Harry* by Daphne Ghose, 1973; *The White Rabbit* by Stella Nowell, 1975; *Because of Blunder*, 1977, *Cass the Brave*, 1978, and *Silver's Day*, 1980, all by Griselda Gifford; *Dog Detective Ranjha* by Partap Sharma, 1978; *The Boggart* by Emma Tennant, 1980; *Daggie Dogfoot*, 1980, *Magnus Powermouse*, 1982, and *The Sheep-Pig*, 1983, all by Dick King-Smith; *The Dead Letter Box* by Jan Mark, 1982; *Mr. Weller's Long March* by Anthea Colbert, 1983; *Lost and Found* by Jill Paton Walsh, 1984; *Thank You for the Tadpole* by Pat Thomson, 1987.

*   *   *

The emergence of significant author-artists like Mary Rayner in the 1970's stimulated a refined critical appreciation. Their particular contribution to children's literature requires an evaluative language which can accommodate both the craft of the story teller-shower and the literary possibilities available to the young.

In her picture books about the Pig family, narrative patterns as old as story-telling in which terror is resolved, greed receives its deserts, and the elements harmonise with the world are firmly located within a contemporary universe of babysitters, supermarket trips, bunk beds, and ice-cream vans. Her pictures of Garth and his siblings, life-abundant and characterful, evoke bustle and *esprit de corps* in a way that lets the young reader in on the games, rhyme chanting, TV viewing, bathtime frolics, and bedtime exhaustion. Wryly humanised through movement, expression, gesture, and dress, the piglets enable children to be onlookers, revelling in both the fun and the form of early childhood.

The integration of the visual and the verbal makes available to the young particular kinds of pleasure and competence that school reading lessons too often leave out. Varying tones of colour in *The Rain Cloud* show changing weather and landscape while also shifting the pace of the plot. Children see the rites of passage being played out during the early days in school by looking at the ways the protagonists draw their pictures (and fight over the toys) in *Crocodarling*. Children look at Rayner's pictures to build up an expectation of what will happen next: an important thing to do in the suspense-laden stories of *Mr. and Mrs. Pig's Evening Out* and *Garth Pig and the Icecream Lady*. There is a sophisticated enjoyment which even her youngest readers gain from the gap between pictures and text: what's left unsaid when Mrs. Pig innocently welcomes the new babysitter (a Mrs. Wolf) or when Mr. Pig, left to mind the children, settles down obliviously with his newspaper (*The New Porker*). The artistry that combines pathos and irony with laughter, an oral tradition with witty realism, is a constant challenge to long-held notions of the picture book as mere preparation for "real" literary experience.

Rayner's work for older readers has established her as a versatile talent. *Oh Paul!*, for six-to-nine year olds, is saved from what could be a formulaic story in the "little boy who cannot get it right" mould by the writer's ability to catch the essence of a community within a short narrative span. Her ear for classroom talk is particularly acute. Similarly, in *Reilly*, readers of 10 and over are treated to sharply contemporary social observation as a stray cat observes the foibles and petty jealousies, based on subtle social differentiations within his adopted territory. Chilling motives echo off ordinary domestic events in *The Witch-Finder*, where strange, sometimes unspeakable, fears are folded within a simple-seeming surface story for young adolescents.

—Colin Mills

REANEY, James (Crerar). Canadian. Born in South Easthope, Ontario, 1 September 1926. Educated at Elmhurst Public School, Easthope Township, Perth County; Central Collegiate Vocational Institute, Stratford, Ontario, 1939–44; University College, Toronto (Epstein award, 1948), B.A. 1948, M.A. 1949, graduate study, 1956–58, Ph.D. in English 1958. Married Colleen Thibaudeau in 1951; two sons (one deceased) and one daughter. Member of the English Department, University of Manitoba, Winnipeg, 1949–56. Since 1960 Professor of English, Middlesex College, University of Western Ontario, London. Founding editor, *Alphabet* magazine, London, 1960–71. Active in little theatre groups in Winnipeg and London: founder, Listeners Workshop, London, 1966. Recipient: Governor-General's award, for poetry 1950, 1959, for drama, 1963; President's Medal, University of Western Ontario, 1955, 1958; Massey award, 1960; Chalmers award, 1975, 1976. D.Litt.: Carleton University, Ottawa, 1975. Officer, Order of Canada, 1975; Fellow, Royal Society of Canada, 1978. Agent: Sybil Hutchinson, 409 Ramsden Place, 50 Hillsboro Avenue, Toronto, Ontario M5R 1S8. Address: Department of English, University of Western Ontario, London, Ontario N6A 3K7, Canada.

PUBLICATIONS FOR CHILDREN

Fiction

The Boy with an "R" in His Hand, illustrated by Leo Rampen. Toronto, Macmillan, 1965.
Take the Big Picture. Erin, Ontario, Porcupine's Quill, 1986.

Plays

Names and Nicknames (produced Winnipeg, 1963). Rowayton, Connecticut, New Plays for Children, 1969.
Aladdin and the Magic Lamp, Apple Butter, Little Red Riding Hood (puppet plays; also director: produced London, Ontario, 1965). *Apple Butter* included in *Apple Butter and Other Plays*, 1973.
Let's Make a Carol, music by Alfred Kunz. Waterloo, Ontario, Waterloo Music, 1965.
Ignoramus (produced London, Ontario, 1966). Included in *Apple Butter and Other Plays*, 1973.
Colours in the Dark (produced Stratford, Ontario, 1967). Vancouver and Toronto, Talonbooks-Macmillan, 1970.
Geography Match (produced London, 1967). Included in *Apple Butter and Other Plays*, 1973.
All the Bees and All the Keys, music by John Beckwith (produced Toronto, 1972). Erin, Ontario, Press Porcépic, 1976.
Apple Butter and Other Plays for Children. Vancouver, Talonbooks, 1973.
At the Big Carwash (puppet play; produced Armstrong, British Columbia, 1979).

PUBLICATIONS FOR ADULTS

Plays

Night-Blooming Cereus music by John Beckwith (broadcast 1959; produced Toronto, 1960). Included in *The Killdeer and Other Plays*, 1962.
The Killdeer (produced Toronto, 1960; Glasgow, 1965). Included in *The Killdeer and Other Plays*, 1962; revised version (produced Vancouver, 1970), in *Masks of Childhood*, 1972.
One-Man Masque (also director: produced Toronto, 1960). Included in *The Killdeer and Other Plays*, 1962.
The Easter Egg (produced Hamilton, Ontario, 1962). Included in

Masks of Childhood, 1972.
The Killdeer and Other Plays. Toronto, Macmillan, 1962.
The Sun and the Moon (produced London, Ontario, 1965). Included in *The Killdeer and Other Plays*, 1962.
Listen to the Wind (also director: produced London, Ontario, 1966). Vancouver, Talonbooks, 1972.
The Canada Tree (produced Morrison Island, Ontario, 1967).
Three Desks (produced London, Ontario, 1967). Included in *Masks of Childhood*, 1972.
Don't Sell Mr. Aesop (produced London, Ontario, 1968).
Genesis (also director: produced London, Ontario, 1968).
Masque, with Ron Cameron (produced Toronto, 1972). Toronto, Simon and Pierre, 1974.
Masks of Childhood, edited by Brian Parker. Toronto, New Press, 1972.
The Donnellys: A Trilogy. Erin, Ontario, Press Porcépic, 1983.
  1. *Sticks and Stones* (produced Toronto, 1973). Erin, Ontario, Press Porcépic, 1975.
  2. *The St. Nicholas Hotel* (produced Toronto, 1974). Erin, Ontario, Press Porcépic, 1976.
  3. *Handcuffs* (produced Toronto, 1975). Erin, Ontario, Press Porcépic, 1977.
Baldoon, with C.H. Gervais (produced Toronto, 1976). Erin, Ontario, Porcupine's Quill, 1976.
The Dismissal; or, Twisted Beards and Tangled Whiskers (produced Toronto, 1977). Erin, Ontario, Press Porcépic, 1979.
The Death and Execution of Frank Halloway; or, The First Act of John Richardson's Wacousta (produced Timmins, Ontario, 1977). Published in *Jubilee 4* (Wingham, Ontario), 1978; complete version, as *Wacousta!* (produced Toronto, 1978), Erin, Ontario, Press Porcépic, 1979.
King Whistle! (produced Stratford, Ontario, 1979). Published in *Brick 8* (Ilderton, Ontario), Winter 1980.
Antler River (produced London, Ontario, 1980).
Gyroscope (produced Toronto, 1981). Toronto, Playwrights, 1983.
The Shivaree (opera), music by John Beckwith (produced Toronto, 1982).
I the Parade (produced Waterloo, Ontario, 1982).
The Canadian Brothers, from a novel by John Richardson (produced Calgary, 1983). Published in *Major Plays of the Canadian Theatre 1934–1984*, edited by Richard Perkyns, Toronto, Irwin, 1984.

Radio Plays: *Night-Blooming Cereus*, 1959; *Wednesday's Child*, 1962; *Canada Dash, Canada Dot* (3 parts), music by John Beckwith, 1965–67.

Verse

The Red Heart. Toronto, McClelland and Stewart, 1949.
A Suit of Nettles. Toronto, Macmillan, 1958.
Twelve Letters to a Small Town. Toronto, Ryerson Press, 1962.
The Dance of Death at London, Ontario. London, Ontario, Alphabet, 1963.
Poems, edited by Germaine Warkentin. Toronto, New Press, 1972.
Selected Shorter [and *Longer*] *Poems*, edited by Germaine Warkentin. Erin, Ontario, Press Porcépic, 2 vols., 1975–76.
Imprecations: The Art of Swearing. Windsor, Ontario, Black Moss Press, 1984.

Other

14 Barrels from Sea to Sea. Erin, Ontario, Press Porcépic, 1977.

*

Manuscript Collections: University of Toronto; Toronto Public Library.

Critical Studies: *James Reaney* by Alvin A. Lee, New York, Twayne, 1968; *James Reaney* by Ross G. Woodman, Toronto, McClelland and Stewart, 1971; *4 Canadian Playwrights* by Mavor Moore, Toronto, Holt Rinehart, 1973; *James Reaney* by J. Stewart Reaney, Agincourt, Ontario, Gage, 1977; *Profiles in Canadian Drama: James Reaney*, Wolfeboro, New Hampshire, Longwood, 1982; *Approaches to the Work of James Reaney* edited by Stan Dragland, Downsview, Ontario, ECW Press, 1983.

Theatrical Activities:
Director: **Plays**—*One-Man Masque*, Toronto, 1960; *Aladdin and the Magic Lamp*, *Apple Butter*, and *Little Red Riding Hood*, London, Ontario, 1965; *Listen to the Wind*, London, Ontario, 1966; *Genesis*, London, Ontario, 1968.
Actor: **Plays**—in *One-Man Masque* and *Night-Blooming Cereus*, Toronto, 1960.

James Reaney comments:

All my writings for children have resulted from such sources as requests by schools and children themselves or their parents in the form of school and library boards. The four plays (in *Apple Butter and Other Plays*) can be seen as my *Schulwerk* (Carl Orff) with a complete coverage of needs for preschool to late high school. What are these needs? Metaphors and mythology and regional versions of same in large, rich doses. The format derives from Peking Opera, children's games, and the *way* children put on plays. The aim is verbal magic, physical joy, and mental fireworks.

* * *

James Reaney's work reflects an unashamed Canadian identity that he communicates with conviction. He has said that a Canadian literary statement is as important as those of other and older nations. His own contribution is far from narrowly provincial, however. What's more, his uncommonly informed intellect allows his creative imagination to range intimately, allusively in the larger world.

In *The Boy with an "R" in His Hand* his approach provokes readers to take sides in the 1826 type-riot in William Lyon Mackenzie's printing office. He compels them to ask why the Tories hated Mackenzie, why there was a riot, why young Alex helped to exonerate Rebecca who had been unjustly branded as a robber. Reaney's clear understanding leads readers to a discovery of the operative historical and psychological processes—and history comes alive for them through each character's role. The initial worldly innocence of two young orphan brothers soon departs when events influence their allegiances, one to Mackenzie's, the other to their Tory uncle's side. Children can grasp the larger events through what happens to these boys. The novel's design is dramatic and anticipates Reaney's ultimate choice of drama as his favorite mode. Each chapter is a complete scene, and the whole divides easily into three acts.

In *Apple Butter* he presents the format for four plays, one of them for marionettes. He encourages the players and the audience to try on the formats and alter them to their own dimensions. The audiences are every bit as important as the players, as the playwright, as the plays. It is quite clear that people (on and off stage) are at Reaney's centre stage, and it is how people interact, react, and trans-act that concerns him always. Reaney actually provides the format for play in the sense of children's amusement through play—play on words and feelings, play on sounds and actions—that is, play within a play that also moves within a loose dramatic framework to a climax of fun.

Reaney says that *Geography Match* is "a shamelessly patriotic play and should be played recklessly and with all the stops pulled out." This kind of stage direction surely leads to the extravagances that communicate pure enjoyment to and from players and audience cumulatively. Each performance could be a new and different experience.

John Beckwith has composed musical accompaniments for Reaney's "Great Lakes Suite," six poems, and *All the Bees and All the Keys*, a fable. Reaney's inventions are natural springboards for Beckwith's ingenious embellishments. Their creative impulses harmonize playfully. Children can enjoy Reaney through the added musical dimension, although unaccompanied readings of both works are pure pleasure too.

Reaney displays his competence in works for children with the same creative involvement that he accords his work for older audiences.

—Irma McDonough Milnes

REES, David (Bartlett). British. Born in London, 18 May 1936. Educated at King's College School, Wimbledon, 1946–54; Queens' College, Cambridge, 1955–58, B.A. 1958, M.A. 1961. Married Jenny Lee Watkins in 1966; two sons. Lived in France, 1958–59; schoolmaster, Wilson's Grammar School, London, 1960–65; Head of the Department of English, Vyners School, Ickenham, Middlesex, 1965–68; Lecturer, 1968–73, and Senior Lecturer 1973–78, St. Luke's College, Exeter, Devon; Lecturer in Education, University of Exeter, 1978–84. Lived in the United States, 1982–83. Recipient: Library Association Carnegie Medal, 1979; Children's Rights Workshop Other award, 1980. Address: 69 Regent Street, Exeter, Devon EX2 9EG, England.

PUBLICATIONS FOR CHILDREN

Fiction

Storm Surge, illustrated by Trevor Stubley.   Guildford, Surrey, Lutterworth Press, 1975.
Quintin's Man.   London, Dobson, 1976; New York, Elsevier Nelson, 1979.
The Missing German.   London, Dobson, 1976.
Landslip, illustrated by Gavin Rowe.   London, Hamish Hamilton, 1977.
The Spectrum.   London, Dobson, 1977.
The Ferryman.   London, Dobson, 1977.
Risks.   London, Heinemann, 1977; Nashville, Nelson, 1978.
The Exeter Blitz.   London, Hamish Hamilton, 1978; New York, Elsevier Nelson, 1980.
The House That Moved, illustrated by Laszlo Acs.   London, Hamish Hamilton, 1978.
In the Tent.   London, Dobson, 1979; Boston, Alyson, 1985.
Silence.   London, Dobson, 1979; New York, Elsevier Nelson, 1981.
The Green Bough of Liberty.   London, Dobson, 1979.
The Lighthouse.   London, Dobson, 1980.
The Night Before Christmas Eve, illustrated by Peter Kesteven.   Exeter, Wheaton, 1980.
Miss Duffy Is Still with Us.   London, Dobson, 1980.
A Beacon for the Romans, illustrated by Peter Kesteven.   Exeter, Wheaton, 1981.
Holly, Mud and Whisky, illustrated by David Grosvenor.   London, Dobson, 1981.
The Milkman's on His Way.   London, Gay Men's Press, 1982.

The Mysterious Rattle, illustrated by Maureen Bradley. London,
Hamish Hamilton, 1982.
Waves. London, Longman, 1983.
The Burglar, illustrated by Ursula Sieger. Leeds, Arnold Wheaton,
1986.
Friends and Neighbours, illustrated by Clare Herroneau. Leeds,
Arnold Wheaton, 1986.
The Flying Island. London, Third House, 1988.

PUBLICATIONS FOR ADULTS

Novels

The Estuary. London, Gay Men's Press, 1983.
Out of the Winter Gardens. London, Olive Press, 1984.
A Better Class of Blond. London, Olive Press, 1985.
Watershed. Stamford, Connecticut, Knights Press, 1986.
The Hunger. London, Gay Men's Press, 1986.
Twos and Threes. London, Third House, 1987.
The Wrong Apple. Stamford, Connecticut, Knights Press, 1988.
Quince. London, Third House, 1988.
The Colour of His Hair. London, Third House, 1989.

Short Stories

Islands. Stamford, Connecticut, Knights Press, 1985.
Flux. London, Third House, 1988.

Other

*The Marble in the Water: Essays on Contemporary Writers of Fiction
for Children and Young People*. Boston, Horn Book, 1980.
*Painted Desert, Green Shade: Essays on Contemporary Writers for
Children and Young Adults*. Boston, Horn Book, 1984.

Editor, with Peter Robins, *Oranges and Lemons: Stories by Gay
Men*. London, Third House, 1987.

*

Manuscript Collection: School of Education Library, University of
Exeter.

David Rees comments:

Although I don't write much in a directly autobiographical way in
my books for children and teenagers, I find the material comes from
rearranging the patterns of my own childhood and adolescence. But
I've said everything I have to say about the teenage years; my most
recent books are for adults. These are more directly autobiographical
and current work in progress is in fact a full-length autobiography.

*   *   *

David Rees's first book, *Storm Surge*, was runner-up for the
Guardian award; in 1979 he took the Carnegie Medal with *The
Exeter Blitz*, and in 1980 the Other award for *The Green Bough of
Liberty*. These successes perhaps exemplify his virtues and vices as
a writer.

He has an unexceptional journeyman prose style, combined with
a good eye for subject matter that is relevant (coping with adolescence, sexuality, death) or intriguing and naturalistic (historical
incidents, disasters natural and man-made); he is clearly concerned
with the emotional, educational, and narrative needs of his audience.
On the other hand, he tends towards the ready-made in language and
character ("it made his head spin…"), his plots can be contrived (this

is particularly true of *The Exeter Blitz*, where history is moved around
for the sake of the story), with *The House That Moved* perhaps
over-local.

Rees's early work is notable for considerable energy, and some
uncertainty about the limits of the children's book. *Storm Surge*,
about floods on the east coast of England, has impressive atmosphere
and action, successfully confronts death and early marriage, although few characters are fully developed. *The Spectrum* is a rich
mixture of sexuality and superstition, centred on an historically
documented Devon poltergeist, and shows clearly Rees's juxtaposition of the sensual and the prescriptive. *The Exeter Blitz* is possibly
the least distinguished of his books, using continual abstraction
which allows little involvement with character; more impressive is
the low-keyed *Landslip*, a more controlled story of minor upheavals
in 19th-century East Anglia.

The status of *The Milkman's on His Way* as a children's book will
doubtless remain questionable, but it is probably Rees's best work.
It is a very explicit, and often painfully moving, account of
homosexual adolescence (which he had touched on in *Quintin's Man*
and *In the Tent*). Although it has the faults of the evangelical—
stridency of tone and the intrusion of scarcely disguised text-book
information—its commitment and certainty of purpose produce a
fluidity and involvement which outweigh the occasional
melodramatic contrivance.

Rees's collection of critical pieces on children's books, *The
Marble in the Water*, was disappointingly uneven in critical stance
and tone. Both as writer and critic he seems unsure of his methods
and medium, while remaining adventurous in his ideas for children's
books.

—Peter Hunt

———

REES, (George) Leslie (Clarence). Australian. Born in Perth,
Western Australia, 28 December 1905. Educated at Perth Modern
School; University of Western Australia, Nedlands (editor, *Black
Swan*), 1924–29, B.A.; University College, London University,
1930. Married Coralie Clarke in 1931 (died 1972); two daughters.
Drama critic, *Era*, London, 1931–35; co-founder, 1937, and
honorary chairman, 1938–63, Playwrights Advisory Board, Sydney;
federal play editor, 1937–57, and deputy director of drama, 1957–66,
Australian Broadcasting Commission. Writer-in-residence, Mt.
Lawley College of Advanced Education, Perth, 1975, and Curtin
University, Perth, 1988. President, Sydney Centre of International
PEN, 1967–75. Recipient: Australian Children's Book award, 1946;
Townsville Foundation Literature award, 1978. A.M. (Member,
Order of Australia), 1981. Address: 4/5 The Esplanade, Balmoral
Beach, New South Wales 2088, Australia.

PUBLICATIONS FOR CHILDREN

Fiction

Digit Dick on the Great Barrier Reef [*and the Tasmanian Devil, in
Black Swan Land, and the Lost Opals, and the Magic Jabiru, and
the Zoo Plot*], illustrated by Walter Cunningham, Latif Hutchings,
and others. Sydney, Sands, 4 vols., 1942–57, Ure Smith, 1 vol.,
1979, Angus and Robertson, 1 vol., 1982.
The Story of Shy the Platypus, illustrated by Walter Cunningham.
Sydney, Sands, 1944; London, Angus and Robertson, 1958.
Gecko, The Lizard Who Lost His Tail, illustrated by Walter Cunningham. Sydney, Sands, 1944; London, Angus and Robertson,

1958.

The Story of Karrawingi the Emu, illustrated by Walter Cunningham. Sydney, Sands, 1946.

The Story of Sarli the Barrier Reef Turtle, illustrated by Walter Cunningham. Sydney, Sands, 1947.

Mates of the Kurlalong, illustrated by Alfred Wood. Sydney, Sands, 1948.

The Story of Shadow the Rock Wallaby, illustrated by Walter Cunningham. Sydney, Sands, 1948.

Bluecap and Bimbi, The Blue Wrens, illustrated by Walter Cunningham. Sydney, Trinity House, 1948.

The Story of Kurri Kurri the Kookaburra, illustrated by Margaret Senior. Sydney, Sands, 1950; London, Angus and Robertson, 1958.

Quokka Island, illustrated by Arthur Horowicz. London, Collins, 1951.

The Story of Aroora the Red Kangaroo, illustrated by John Singleton. Sydney, Sands, 1952.

Two-Thumbs: The Story of a Koala, illustrated by Margaret Senior. Sydney, Sands, 1953.

Danger Patrol. Sydney and London, Collins, 1954.

The Story of Koonaworra the Black Swan, illustrated by Margaret Senior. Sydney, Sands, 1957; London, Angus and Robertson, 1959.

The Story of Wy-Lah the Cockatoo, illustrated by Walter Cunningham. Sydney, Sands, and London, Angus and Robertson, 1960.

The Story of Russ the Australian Tree Kangaroo, illustrated by Walter Cunningham. Sydney, Sands, 1964.

Boy Lost on Tropic Coast, illustrated by Frank Beck. Sydney, Ure Smith, 1968.

Mokee the White Possum, illustrated by Tony Oliver. Sydney, Hamlyn, 1973.

Panic in the Cattle Country. Adelaide, Rigby, 1974.

Billa the Wombat Who Had a Bad Dream, illustrated by Penny Walton. Sydney, Child, 1988.

Other

A Treasury of Australian Nature Stories. Sydney, Ure Smith, 1974.

PUBLICATIONS FOR ADULTS

Novel

Here's to Shane. Sydney, Wentworth, 1977.

Plays

Sub-Editor's Room (televised 1956), in *Best Australian One-Act Plays*, edited by William Moore and T. Inglis Moore. Sydney, Angus and Robertson, 1937.

Mother's Day, in *Six Australian One-Act Plays*. Sydney, Mulga, 1944.

The Harp in the South, with Ruth Park, adaptation of the novel by Park (broadcast 1949). Montmorency, Victoria, Yackandandah, 1987.

Radio Plays: *Lalor of Eureka*, 1938; *The Harp in the South*, with Ruth Park, 1949.

Television Play: *Sub-Editor's Room*, 1956.

Other

Towards an Australian Drama. Sydney and London, Angus and Robertson, 1953.

Spinifex Walkabout: Hitch-Hiking in Remote North Australia, with Coralie Rees. Sydney, Australasian Publishing Company, and London, Harrap, 1953.

Westward from Cocos: Indian Ocean Travels, with Coralie Rees. Sydney, Australasian Publishing Company, and London, Harrap, 1956.

Coasts of Cape York: Travels Around Australia's Pearl-Tipped Peninsula, with Coralie Rees. Sydney, Angus and Robertson, 1960.

People of the Big Sky Country, with Coralie Rees. Sydney, Ure Smith, 1970.

A History of Australian Drama:

The Making of Australian Drama: A Historical and Critical Survey from the 1830's to the Late 1960's. Sydney, Angus and Robertson, 1973; revised edition, 1978; London, Angus and Robertson, 1979.

Australian Drama in the 1970's: A Historical and Critical Survey. Sydney, Angus and Robertson, 1978; London, Angus and Robertson, 1979; revised edition, as *The History of Australian Drama 1970–85*, Sydney and London, Angus and Robertson, 1987.

Hold Fast to Dreams: Fifty Years in Theatre, Radio, Television, and Books. Sydney, Alternative Publishing Co-operative, 1982.

Editor, *Australian Radio Plays*. Sydney, Angus and Robertson, 1946.

Editor, *Modern Short Plays*. Sydney and London, Angus and Robertson, 1951.

Editor, *Mask and Microphone: Plays*. Sydney, Angus and Robertson, 1963.

*

Manuscript Collections: Mitchell Library, Sydney; University of Western Australia, Nedlands.

Leslie Rees comments:

I think children like exploring, recognising, discovering; they like adventure, meeting strange and interesting people, animals, and birds, they like laughing, play-acting, narrow escapes; but in the long run feeling secure with someone and something to put their faith in. I like these things too, because there's still a child and still a boy in me. I also like sharing with children the fun and excitement I've had in travelling and getting to know Australian creatures of the wild, and reaching unusual Australian places. And with this emphasis and this incentive I go to work finding a method and an idiom that will catch the interest of the young. I am gratified to find that some of my books have reached child audiences in most English-speaking countries, and in some non-English-speaking countries, with especially large audiences in Russia.

* * *

The contribution of Leslie Rees to Australian children's literature has been threefold: the development of fantasy for young readers; a loving concern for the wildlife of his country; and the keeping alive of the fast-moving adventure story for boys.

Digit Dick, an Australian Tom Thumb, has the universal appeal of diminutive creatures as well as an engaging personality of his own. In that Digit Dick's adventures take him to the Great Barrier Reef and other remote areas of the continent, Rees introduces his readers to an exotic landscape which he peoples with strangely exciting but authentic sea and bush creatures. Inseparable from the Digit Dick stories are the somewhat cartoon-like illustrations of Walter Cunningham which elaborate the author's wordplay and verbal exaggeration. But it was with *Mates of the Kurlalong* that Rees made his most significant contribution to the development of nonsense fantasy in Australia. Here he is less didactic than in his other stories for young children, and he exploits an hilarious central situation in which the hero "not exactly a wombat although he looked like one" and "not exactly a boy although he always behaved like one" commandeers a Sydney Harbour ferry. With an animal crew from Taronga Park Zoo a gloriously fantastic day of freedom begins, to end in a glorification of the endlessly possible adventures of uninhibited childhood.

It is in his series of Nature Tales, also faithfully and beautifully illustrated by Walter Cunningham, from *The Story of Shy the Platypus* through *The Story of Karrawingi the Emu*, the first recipient of the Australian Children's Book of the Year Award, to *Mokee the White Possum*, that Rees has made his most serious contribution to writing for children. Each story is a carefully detailed and authentic study of wildlife in which the title character moves inevitably and dramatically through his cycle of life. The writing is clearer, cleaner, and less wordy than in the Digit Dick stories. Developing readers easily identify with the struggle to survive and to maintain an ordained life-style of Shy the platypus, who "with the consciousness of motherhood upon her" turns from her cherished pool to the dark entrances of her tunnel under the surface of the earth. There is ready sympathy, too, for Karrawingi, the emu, who races through the bush at midnight, proclaiming his fatherhood—of eighteen oval eggs.

Rees has also written full-blooded, tense adventure stories for older boys such as *Danger Patrol*, based on a young Patrol Officer's adventures in a still primitive New Guinea and *Panic in the Cattle Country*, which explores the mystery of cattle in the Outback slaughtered and left with huge tearing wounds, by persons or creatures unknown. Rees's fascination with a geologically ancient continent, its aboriginal inhabitants and the white men who live in its remote vastness, its wildlife and the sweep of its rugged scenery, gives a peculiarly Australian flavour to a yarn belonging firmly in the tradition of the robust boys' adventure story.

—H. M. Saxby

REEVES, James. Pseudonym for John Morris Reeves. British. Born in London, 1 July 1909; brother of Joyce Gard, *q.v.* Educated at Stowe School, Buckinghamshire; Cambridge University, M.A. (honours) in English 1931. Married Mary Phillips in 1936 (died 1966); one son and two daughters. Taught in schools and colleges of education, 1933–52; from 1951 general editor, Poetry Bookshelf series, William Heinemann Ltd., London; from 1960 general editor, Unicorn Books, London. Fellow, Royal Society of Literature. *Died 1 May 1978.*

PUBLICATIONS FOR CHILDREN

Fiction

Pigeons and Princesses, illustrated by Edward Ardizzone. London, Heinemann, 1956.
Mulbridge Manor, illustrated by Geraldine Spence. London, Heinemann, 1958.
Titus in Trouble, illustrated by Edward Ardizzone. London, Bodley Head, 1959; New York, Walck, 1960.
Sailor Rumbelow and Britannia, illustrated by Edward Ardizzone. London, Heinemann, 1962.
Sailor Rumbelow and Other Stories (includes *Pigeons and Princesses* and *Sailor Rumbelow and Britannia*), illustrated by Edward Ardizzone. New York, Dutton, 1962.
The Strange Light, illustrated by Lynton Lamb. London, Heinemann, 1964; Chicago, Rand McNally, 1966.
The Pillar-Box Thieves, illustrated by Dick Hart. London, Nelson, 1965.
Rhyming Will, illustrated by Edward Ardizzone. London, Hamish Hamilton, 1967; New York, McGraw Hill, 1968.
Mr. Horrox and the Gratch, illustrated by Quentin Blake. London, Abelard Schuman, 1969.
The Path of Gold, illustrated by Krystyna Turska. London, Hamish Hamilton, 1972.
The Lion That Flew, illustrated by Edward Ardizzone. London, Chatto and Windus, 1974.
The Clever Mouse, illustrated by Barbara Swiderska. London, Chatto and Windus, 1976.
Eggtime Stories, illustrated by Colin McNaughton. London, Blackie, 1978.
The James Reeves Storybook, illustrated by Edward Ardizzone. London, Heinemann, 1978; as *The Gnome Factory and Other Stories*, London, Penguin, 1986.
A Prince in Danger, illustrated by Gareth Floyd. London, Kaye and Ward, 1979.

Plays

Mulcaster Market: Three Plays for Young People (includes *Mulcaster Market, The Pedlar's Dream, The Stolen Boy*), illustrated by Dudley Cutler. London, Heinemann, 1951; as *The Peddler's Dream and Other Plays*, New York, Dutton, 1963.
The King Who Took Sunshine. London, Heinemann, 1954.
A Health to John Patch: A Ballad Operatta. London, Boosey, 1957.

Verse

The Wandering Moon, illustrated by Evadne Rowan. London, Heinemann, 1950; New York, Dutton, 1960.
The Blackbird in the Lilac: Verses, illustrated by Edward Ardizzone. London, Oxford University Press, 1952; New York, Dutton, 1959.
A Puffin Quartet of Poets, with others, edited by Eleanor Graham, illustrated by Diana Bloomfield. London, Penguin, 1958.
Prefabulous Animiles, illustrated by Edward Ardizzone. London, Heinemann, 1957; New York, Dutton, 1960.
Ragged Robin, illustrated by Jane Paton. London, Heinemann, and New York, Dutton, 1961.
Hurdy-Gurdy: Selected Poems for Children, illustrated by Edward Ardizzone. London, Heinemann, 1961.
The Story of Jackie Thimble, illustrated by Edward Ardizzone. New York, Dutton, 1964; London, Chatto and Windus, 1965.
Complete Poems for Children, illustrated by Edward Ardizzone. London, Heinemann, 1973.
More Prefabulous Animiles, illustrated by Edward Ardizzone. London, Heinemann, 1975.

Other

English Fables and Fairy Stories, Retold, illustrated by Joan Kiddell-Monroe. London, Oxford University Press, 1954; New York, Walck, 1966(?).
Exploits of Don Quixote, Retold, illustrated by Edward Ardizzone. London, Blackie, 1959; New York, Walck, 1960.

Fables from Aesop, Retold, illustrated by Maurice Wilson.   London, Blackie, 1961; New York, Walck, 1962.

Three Tall Tales, Chosen from Traditional Sources, illustrated by Edward Ardizzone.   London and New York, Abelard Schuman, 1964.

The Road to a Kingdom: Stories from the Old and New Testaments, illustrated by Richard Kennedy.   London, Heinemann, 1965.

The Secret Shoemakers and Other Stories, illustrated by Edward Ardizzone.   London and New York, Abelard Schuman, 1966.

The Cold Flame, Based on a Tale from the Collection of the Brothers Grimm, illustrated by Charles Keeping.   London, Hamish Hamilton, 1967; New York, Meredith Press, 1969.

The Trojan Horse, illustrated by Krystyna Turska.   London, Hamish Hamilton, 1968; New York, Watts, 1969.

Heroes and Monsters: Legends of Ancient Greece Retold, illustrated by Sarah Nechamkin:
  1. *Gods and Voyagers*.   London, Blackie, 1969; New York, Two Continents, 1978.
  2. *Islands and Palaces*.   London, Blackie, 1971; as *Giants and Warriors*, Blackie, 1977; New York, Two Continents, 1978.

The Angel and the Donkey, illustrated by Edward Ardizzone.   London, Hamish Hamilton, 1969; New York, McGraw Hill, 1970.

Maildun the Voyager, illustrated by John Lawrence.   London, Hamish Hamilton, 1971; New York, Walck, 1972.

How the Moon Began, illustrated by Edward Ardizzone.   London, Abelard Schuman, 1971.

The Forbidden Forest and Other Stories, illustrated by Raymond Briggs.   London, Heinemann, 1973.

The Voyage of Odysseus: Homer's Odyssey Retold.   London, Blackie, 1973.

Two Greedy Bears (Persian folktale), illustrated by Gareth Floyd.   London, Hamish Hamilton, 1974.

Quest and Conquest: Pilgrim's Progress Retold, illustrated by Joanna Troughton.   London, Blackie, 1976.

Snow-White and Rose-Red, illustrated by Jenny Rodwell.   London, Andersen Press, 1979.

Editor, *Orpheus: A Junior Anthology of English Poetry*.   London, Heinemann, 2 vols., 1949–50.

Editor, *Heinemann Junior Poetry Books*.   London, Heinemann, 4 vols., 1954.

Editor, *The Merry-Go-Round: A Collection of Rhymes and Poems for Children*, illustrated by John Mackay.   London, Heinemann, 1955.

Editor, *A Golden Land: Stories, Poems, Songs New and Old*, illustrated by Gillian Conway and others.   London, Constable, and New York, Hastings House, 1958.

Editor, *A First Bible: An Abridgement for Young Readers*, illustrated by Geoffrey Fraser.   London, Heinemann, 1962.

Editor, *The Christmas Book*, illustrated by Raymond Briggs.   London, Heinemann, and New York, Dutton, 1968.

Editor, *One's None: Old Rhymes for New Tongues*, illustrated by Bernadette Watts.   London, Heinemann, 1968; New York, Watts, 1969.

Editor, *The Springtime Book: A Collection of Prose and Poetry*, illustrated by Colin McNaughton.   London, Heinemann, 1976.

Editor, *The Autumn Book: A Collection of Prose and Poetry*, illustrated by Colin McNaughton.   London, Heinemann, 1977.

Translator, *Primrose and the Winter Witch*, by Frantisek Hrubín, illustrated by Jirí Trnka.   London, Hamlyn, 1964.

Translator, *The Golden Cockerel and Other Stories*, by Alexander Pushkin, illustrated by Ján Lebis.   London, Dent, and New York, Watts, 1969.

Translator, *The Shadow of the Hawk and Other Stories*, by Marie de France, illustrated by Anne Dalton.   London, Collins, 1975; New York, Seabury Press, 1977.

PUBLICATIONS FOR ADULTS

Play

A.D. One: A Masque for Christmas.   Privately printed, 1974.

Verse

The Natural Need.   Deyá, Mallorca, Seizin Press, and London, Constable, 1935.

The Imprisoned Sea.   London, Editions Poetry London, 1949.

XIII Poems.   Privately printed, 1950.

The Password and Other Poems.   London, Heinemann, 1952.

The Talking Skull.   London, Heinemann, 1958.

Collected Poems 1929–1959.   London, Heinemann, 1960.

The Questioning Tiger.   London, Heinemann, 1964.

Selected Poems.   London, Allison and Busby, 1967; revised edition, 1977.

Subsong.   London, Heinemann, 1969.

Poems and Paraphrases.   London, Heinemann, 1972.

Collected Poems 1929–1974.   London, Heinemann, 1974.

Arcadian Ballads, illustrated by Edward Ardizzone.   Andoversford, Gloucestershire, Whittington Press, 1977.

The Closed Door.   Sidcot, Somerset, Gruffyground Press, and Brookston, Indiana, Twinrocker, 1977.

Other

Man Friday: A Primer of English Composition and Grammar.   London, Heinemann, 1953.

The Critical Sense: Practical Criticism of Prose and Poetry.   London, Heinemann, 1956.

Teaching Poetry: Poetry in Class Five to Fifteen.   London, Heinemann, 1958.

A Short History of English Poetry 1340–1940.   London, Heinemann, 1961; New York, Dutton, 1962.

Understanding Poetry.   London, Heinemann, 1965; New York, Barnes and Noble, 1968.

Commitment to Poetry.   London, Heinemann, and New York, Barnes and Noble, 1969.

Inside Poetry, with Martin Seymour-Smith.   London, Heinemann, and New York, Barnes and Noble, 1970.

How to Write Poems for Children.   London, Heinemann, 1971.

The Reputation and Writings of Alexander Pope.   London, Heinemann, and New York, Barnes and Noble, 1976.

The Writer's Approach to the Ballad.   London, Harrap, 1976.

Editor, with Denys Thompson, *The Quality of Education: Methods and Purposes in the Secondary Curriculum*.   London, Muller, 1947.

Editor, *The Poets' World: An Anthology of English Poetry*.   London, Heinemann, 1948; revised edition, as *The Modern Poets' World*, 1957.

Editor, *The Writer's Way: An Anthology of English Prose*.   London, Christophers, 1948.

Editor, with Norman Culpan, *Dialogue and Drama*.   London, Heinemann, 1950; Boston, Plays Inc., 1968.

Editor, *Selected Poems*, by D. H. Lawrence.   London, Heinemann, 1951.

Editor, *The Speaking Oak: English Poetry and Prose: A Selection*.   London, Heinemann, 1951.

Editor, *Selected Poems*, by John Donne.   London, Heinemann, 1952; New York, Macmillan, 1958.

Editor, *The Bible in Brief: Selections from the Text of the Authorised*

Version of 1611. London, Wingate, 1954; as *The Holy Bible in Brief*, New York, Messner, 1954.

Editor, *Selected Poems*, by John Clare. London, Heinemann, 1954; New York, Macmillan, 1957.

Editor, *Gulliver's Travels: The First Three Parts*. London, Heinemann, 1955.

Editor, *Selected Poems*, by Gerard Manley Hopkins. London, Heinemann, 1956; New York, Macmillan, 1957.

Editor, *Selected Poems*, by Robert Browning. London, Heinemann, 1956; New York, Macmillan, 1957.

Editor, *The Idiom of the People: English Traditional Verse from the Manuscripts of Cecil J. Sharp*. London, Heinemann, and New York, Macmillan, 1958.

Editor, *Selected Poems of Emily Dickinson*. London, Heinemann, 1959; New York, Barnes and Noble, 1966.

Editor, *Selected Poems*, by Samuel Taylor Coleridge. London, Heinemann, 1959.

Editor, *The Personal Vision....* London, Poetry Book Supplement, 1959.

Editor, *The Rhyming River: An Anthology of Verse*. London, Heinemann, 4 vols., 1959.

Editor, with William Vincent Aughterson, *Over the Ranges*. Melbourne, Heinemann, 1959.

Editor, *The Everlasting Circle: English Traditional Verse*. London, Heinemann, and New York, Macmillan, 1960.

Editor, with Desmond Flower, *The War 1939–1945*. London, Cassell, 1960; as *The Taste of Courage*, New York, Harper, 1960.

Editor, *The Unicorn Leacock*, by Stephen Leacock. London, Heinemann, 1960.

Editor, *Great English Essays*. London, Cassell, 1961.

Editor, *Selected Poetry and Prose of Robert Graves*. London, Hutchinson, 1961.

Editor, *Georgian Poetry*. London, Penguin, 1962.

Editor, *Gulliver's Travels: Parts I–IV*. London, Heinemann, 1964.

Editor, *The Cassell Book of English Poetry*. London, Cassell, and New York, Harper, 1965.

Editor, *Selected Poems*, by Jonathan Swift. London, Heinemann, and New York, Barnes and Noble, 1967.

Editor, with Martin Seymour-Smith, *A New Canon of English Poetry*. London, Heinemann, and New York, Barnes and Noble, 1967.

Editor, *An Anthology of Free Verse*. Oxford, Blackwell, 1968.

Editor, *The Reader's Bible*. London, Tandem, 1968.

Editor, *The Sayings of Dr. Johnson*. London, Baker, 1968.

Editor, with Seán Haldane, *Homage to Trumbull Stickney: Poems*. London, Heinemann, 1968.

Editor, *Poets and Their Critics 3: Arnold to Auden*. London, Hutchinson, 1969.

Editor, with Martin Seymour-Smith, *The Poems of Andrew Marvell*. London, Heinemann, and New York, Barnes and Noble, 1969.

Editor, *Chaucer: Lyric and Allegory*. London, Heinemann, 1970.

Editor, *A Vein of Mockery: Twentieth-Century Verse Satire*. London, Heinemann, 1973.

Editor, *Selected Poems*, by Thomas Gray. London, Heinemann, 1973; as *The Complete English Poems of Thomas Gray*, New York, Barnes and Noble, 1973.

Editor, *Five Late Romantic Poets*. London, Heinemann, 1974.

Editor, with Martin Seymour-Smith, *Selected Poems of Walt Whitman*. London, Heinemann, 1976.

Editor, with Robert Gittings, *Selected Poems of Thomas Hardy*. London, Heinemann, 1981.

*   *   *

"We must always provide poetry in such a way that it creates and nourishes a continuing craving for poetry and does not kill it by making poetry seem something childish," said James Reeves once at a conference, condemning cosy and sloppy verse and praising nursery rhymes and Walter de la Mare. He succeeded in keeping that advice in mind in his own poems, of which the humorous ones are most often quoted, like "Cows" from *The Blackbird in the Lilac*:

> Half the time they munched the grass, and all the time
>   they lay
> Down in the water-meadows, the lazy month of May
> A-chewing
> A-chewing
> To pass the hours away
> "Nice weather," said the brown cow
> "Ah," said the white.
> "Grass is very tasty
> Grass is all right."

All of the poems are short with a dancing rhythm and plenty of nonsense. They catch a mood quickly and lightly, like these examples from *The Wandering Moon*:

> So grim and gloomy
> Are the caves beneath the sea
> Oh, rare but roomy
> And bare and boomy
> Those soft sea caverns be.

or

> Waiting, waiting, waiting
> For the party to begin
> Waiting, waiting, waiting
> For the laughter and the din.
> Waiting, waiting, waiting
> With hair just so
> And clothes trim and tidy
> From topknot to toe.

or

> Slowly the hands move round the clock,
> Slowly the dew dies on the dock.
> Slow is the snail—but slowest of all
> The green moss spreads on the old brick wall.

When the poet turned to stories for younger children, he created unusual characters and backgrounds, like sailor Rumbelow, the little figure on the ship in a bottle, who loved Britannia in the glass ball, or Foo the clumsy Chinese potter, as well as the more usual royal families with Queens who bake cakes and Kings who hunt. Human failings, particularly pomposity or bad temper, are suitably mocked; kindness always wins in the end. Magic appears now and again, as in "The Old Woman and the Four Noises," in which friendly elves reassure the old country woman that they cause the noises in her cottage: "Don't be afraid...you cannot see me but I live in your front door and I bring you luck. Every time the door is opened or closed, I squeak just to remind you I am here." "What an odd thing," said the old woman, "I never knew before that there was such a thing as a door elf that squeaked, but now I come to think about it, I see no reason why there shouldn't be."

The Strange Light is a longer fantasy about a small girl who discovers, on the other side of a hedge in a field of sunshine, all the characters who are waiting for writers to use them in their books, an ingenious idea. Their faces take on a strange purple glow when an author is thinking of them. This fades when he changes his mind or becomes brighter when they are summoned to go off into a story.

One unattractive boy, who is never chosen, leads a revolt, but the heroine rushes back through the hedge to her uncle, who then writes a story about him and his gang, so all is well.

Mulbridge Manor is also set in the English country in summer but has a longer plot for older readers. A group of village children, led by the doctor's son, befriend an eccentric old lady at the Manor, help find a will, and defeat a criminal. Events move swiftly and unexpectedly, and, as in the short stories, virtue is rewarded with a happy ending, but fate plays some funny tricks on the way. The background and the characters are all briefly introduced; no words are wasted: "Mulcaster…was a sleepy place at the best of times…the bells in the cathedral tower dropped four notes on the silent air, almost apologetically, as if sorry to disturb the city in its sleep." The children enter at once on their bicycles, each with a characteristic gesture.

Reeves, besides writing his own very original verse and fiction, retold old fairy stories, Aesop's Fables, and the Bible. In *Sailor Rumbelow* he included the folk tales Rapunzel and Simple Jack, adding some spirited touches; in *The Forbidden Forest and Other Stories* he rescued ten of the lesser known of the Grimm brothers' collection. His short crisp sentences get swiftly to the point; none of the characters bandies words or minces matters.

When Reeves tackled *Exploits of Don Quixote*, he kept closer to the original Spanish text than do most English versions and obviously enjoyed the humour. In his introduction he wrote: "Knight and squire represent two sides of human nature—the desire to lead and the desire to serve, the need for a spiritual aim and the need for material well-being; the balance between madness and commonsense, illusion and reality, courage and prudence."

Perhaps Reeves welcomed Cervantes's creations as fitting companions to some of his own. But the last words on his talent must come from one of his poems:

> The sea is a hungry dog
> Giant and grey
> He rolls on the beach all day.
> With his clashing teeth and shaggy jaws
> Hour upon hour he gnaws
> The rumbling, tumbling stones,
> And "Bones, bones, bones, bones,"
> The giant sea-dog moans,
> Licking his greasy paws.
>
> But on quiet days in May or June
> When even the grasses on the dune
> Play no more their reedy tune,
> With his head between his paws
> He lies on the sandy shores
> So quiet, so quiet, he scarcely snores.

—Margaret Campbell

REID, Meta Mayne. British. Born in Woodlesford, Yorkshire, 23 January 1905. Educated at Leeds Girls' High School; Manchester University, 1924–27, B.A. (honours) in English. Married E. Mayne Reid in 1935; two sons. Chairwoman, Belfast PEN, 1960–61; President, Irish PEN, Dublin, 1970–72. Recipient: Listowel Festival Trophy, for verse, 1974. Address: 5 Millvale Court, Hillsborough BT26 6HR, Northern Ireland.

PUBLICATIONS FOR CHILDREN

Fiction

Phelim and the Creatures, illustrated by Sydney Passmore. London, Chatto and Windus, 1952.
Carrigmore Castle, illustrated by Richard Kennedy. London, Faber, 1954.
All Because of Dawks, illustrated by Geoffrey Whittam. London, Macmillan, and New York, St. Martin's Press, 1955.
Dawks Does It Again, illustrated by Geoffrey Whittam. London, Macmillan, and New York, St. Martin's Press, 1956.
Tiffany and the Swallow Rhyme, illustrated by Richard Kennedy. London, Faber, 1956.
The Cuckoo at Coolnean, illustrated by Richard Kennedy. London, Faber, 1956.
Dawks on Robbers' Mountain, illustrated by Geoffrey Whittam. London, Macmillan, and New York, St. Martin's Press, 1957.
Strangers in Carrigmore, illustrated by Richard Kennedy. London, Faber, 1958.
Dawks and the Duchess. London, Macmillan, 1958.
The McNeills at Rathcapple, illustrated by Brian Wildsmith. London, Faber, 1959.
Storm on Kildoney, illustrated by Geoffrey Whittam. London, Macmillan, and New York, St. Martin's Press, 1961.
Sandy and the Hollow Book, illustrated by Richard Kennedy. London, Faber, 1961.
The Tobermillin Oracle, illustrated by Richard Kennedy. London, Faber, 1962.
With Angus in the Forest, illustrated by Zelma Blakely. London, Faber, 1963.
The Tinkers' Summer, illustrated by Peggy Fortnum. London, Faber, 1965.
The Silver Fighting Cocks. London, Faber, 1966.
The House at Spaniard's Bay. London, Faber, 1967.
The Glen Beyond the Door. London, Faber, 1968.
The Two Rebels. London, Faber, 1969.
Beyond the Wide World's End, illustrated by Antony Maitland. Guildford, Surrey, Lutterworth Press, 1972.
The Plotters of Pollnashee, illustrated by Gareth Floyd. Guildford, Surrey, Lutterworth Press, 1973.
Snowbound by the Whitewater, illustrated by Peter Dennis. London, Abelard Schuman, 1975.
The Noguls and the Horse, illustrated by Tony Morris. London, Abelard Schuman, 1976.
A Dog Called Scampi, illustrated by John Laing. London, Abelard Schuman, 1980.

PUBLICATIONS FOR ADULTS

Novels

The Land Is Dear. London, Melrose, 1936.
Far-off Fields Are Green. London, Melrose, 1937.

Verse

No Ivory Tower. Walton-on-Thames, Surrey, Outposts, 1974.

*

Manuscript Collection: de Grummond Collection, University of Southern Mississippi, Hattiesburg.

Meta Mayne Reid comments:
    Although all the literary tradition is on my husband's side of the family I have written since I was very young. I am fortunate in being able to write any time and any place—at the station, on the bus, with my back to the TV set, among family talk. Poetry, perhaps, gives the

greatest pleasure, but writing for children aged 8 to 12 is a kind of poetry. It must transfix the moment, heighten the sense of wonder, and all the time allow the narrative to leap ahead on the backs of firmly drawn characters. I have written straightforward adventure stories, but I prefer fantasy or history as they present the challenge of making a new world.

My tales move on an Irish country background, and, since my family has lived in Northern Ireland for centuries, much of my detail springs from family stories. To be happy I must write something every day, which accounts for the 400–500 letters I send every year, most of them based on daily minutiae—a rich source of material since both fantasy and history demand practical foundations. My own favourites are *With Angus in the Forest* (Viking period) and *The Silver Fighting Cocks* (Napoleonic period).

* * *

Meta Mayne Reid's fiction is set in Ulster, usually in Down or Derry, and the books fall roughly into two categories: the straightforward historical novel and the present-day story with a basis of fantasy. Of the two, the former is the more successful. The time-traveling, magical, or symbolical formula usually produces an element of contrivance: the parallel episodes aren't always successfully integrated. Sometimes the author simply goes too far: the children turned into animals, for instance, in the Carrigmore series, are not convincing.

The House at Spaniard's Bay is one modern story that doesn't rely too heavily on the supernatural. A lively tale of illicit distilling, adolescent ambition, and infatuation, it has one exotic character—the tinker Judith—to embody the fey Irish quality that distinguishes the books. But the author can't resist introducing a figure from the past—the mythical Gráinne—who makes a rather theatrical appearance in a mountain cave. In *The Glen Beyond the Door* past and present are interwined in an episodic, unsatisfactory way.

A recent story for 10–12 year-olds, *The Noguls and the Horse*, uses the topical theme of terrorist bombing to show how a child can come to terms with her shaken sense of personal security. But Reid is at her best when she writes about the Planter community of the years between 1798 and 1810. The industry of the Scottish Presbyterian settlers in Ulster is posited as an alternative to the traditional fecklessness of the native Irish hill farmer. But the author is well aware of the potent romantic aspects of dispossession and insurrection. *The Two Rebels* gives an excellent account of the aftermath of the '98 Rebellion, when the countryside was swarming with soldiers and men on the run. The rebels of the title are typical insurgents: a young Presbyterian farmer and a liberal Protestant aristocrat.

Red-coats and revenue officers are the blustering authoritarian figures outwitted incessantly by resourceful children. The historical context gives point and vigour to the unoriginal themes, and domestic detail adds credibility. Complex social and racial distinctions are simplified effectively. The heroine is usually a well-adjusted but naturally exuberant girl who has been allowed to run wild: Priscilla McCurdy, for instance (in *The Silver Fighting Cocks*) thinks sadly that "she must stop pretending that she was a boy, and Jamie her dear brother, and be a demure young miss, learning how to be good wife in five years' time or so." Her friend Jamie is Catholic, and therefore in a lower social class: in *The Plotters of Pollnashee* the 11-year-old farmer's daughter is befriended by a gentleman's son—the point being made about natural affinities is still valid.

In *Beyond the Wide World's End* a couple of ragamuffins set off on a quest for emotional security—and find it, though there is a twist in the end. The year is 1810 and the author's research as usual has been meticulous.

Ulster has an intricate and sometimes romantic history that seems to offer enormous scope for the children's novelist—but so far Reid has been the only author to exploit it.

—Patricia Craig

———

REID BANKS, Lynne. See **BANKS, Lynne Reid.**

———

REY, H.A. and Margret. Americans. **REY, H.A.**: Also wrote as Uncle Gus. Born Hans Augusto Reyersbach in Hamburg, Germany, 16 September 1898; emigrated to the United States, 1940; became citizen, 1946. Educated at the University of Munich, 1919–20; University of Hamburg, 1920–23. Served in the German Infantry and Medical Corps, France and Russia, 1916–19. Married Margret Waldstein in 1935. Salesman for import firm, Rio de Janeiro, 1924–36. Freelance writer and illustrator in Paris, 1936–40, New York, 1940–63, and from 1963 in Cambridge, Massachusetts: taught astronomy at Cambridge Center for Adult Education. *Died 26 August 1977.* **REY, Margret (Elisabeth, née Waldstein)**: Born in Hamburg, Germany, in May 1906; emigrated to the United States, 1940; became citizen, 1946. Educated at Bauhaus, Dessau, 1927; Dusseldorf Academy of Art, 1928–29; University of Munich, 1930–31. Reporter and advertising copywriter, Berlin, 1928–29; photographer in London, Hamburg, and Brazil, 1930–35. Individual shows (watercolors): Berlin, 1929–34. Freelance writer in Paris, 1936–40, New York, 1940–63, and since 1963 in Cambridge, Massachusetts; from 1979 Professor of Creative Writing, Brandeis University, Waltham, Massachusetts. Agent: A.P. Watt Ltd., 20 John Street, London WC1N 2DL, England. Address: 14 Hilliard Street, Cambridge, Massachusetts 02138, U.S.A.

PUBLICATIONS FOR CHILDREN (illustrated by H.A. Rey)

Fiction

How the Flying Fishes Came into Being. London, Chatto and Windus, 1938.
Raffy and the Nine Monkeys. London, Chatto and Windus, 1939; as *Cecily G. and the Nine Monkeys*, Boston, Houghton Mifflin, 1942.
How Do You Get There? Boston, Houghton Mifflin, 1941; London, Folding Books, 1951.
Curious George. Boston, Houghton Mifflin, 1941; as *Zozo*, London, Chatto and Windus, 1942.
Elizabite: The Adventures of a Carnivorous Plant. New York, Harper, 1942; London, Chatto and Windus, 1964.
Tommy Helps, Too. Boston, Houghton Mifflin, 1943.
Curious George Takes a Job [*Rides a Bike, Gets a Medal, Flies a Kite, Learns the Alphabet, Goes to the Hospital*]. Boston, Houghton Mifflin, 6 vols., 1947–66; as *Zozo Takes a Job* [*Rides a Bike, Gets a Medal, Flies a Kite, Learns the Alphabet, Goes to the Hospital*], London, Chatto and Windus, 6 vols., 1954–67.

Fiction by Margret Rey

Pretzel. New York, Harper, 1944; London, Folding Books, 1950.
Spotty. New York, Harper, 1945; London, Folding Books, 1950.
Pretzel and the Puppies. New York, Harper, 1946.
Billy's Picture. New York, Harper, 1948; London, Chatto and

Windus, 1964.

Verse

Anybody at Home?   London, Chatto and Windus, 1939; Boston, Houghton Mifflin, 1943.
Tit for Tat.   New York, Harper, 1942.
Where's My Baby?.   Boston, Houghton Mifflin, 1943; London, Folding Books, 1950.
Feed the Animals.   Boston, Houghton Mifflin, 1944; London, Folding Books, 1950.
See the Circus.   Boston, Houghton Mifflin, and London, Chatto and Windus, 1956.

Other by H.A. Rey

Zebrology (drawings).   London, Chatto and Windus, 1937.
Aerodrome for Scissors and Paint.   London, Chatto and Windus, 1939.
Au Clair de la Lune and Other French Nursery Songs.   New York, Greystone Press, 1941.
Look for the Letters: A Hide-and-Seek Alphabet.   New York, Harper, 1945.
Mary Had a Little Lamb, with Margret Rey.   London, Penguin, 1951.
Find the Constellations.   Boston, Houghton Mifflin, 1954; revised edition, 1976.

Editor, *Humpty Dumpty and Other Mother Goose Songs.*   New York, Harper, 1943.

Other by H.A. Rey (as Uncle Gus)

Farm.   Boston, Houghton Mifflin, 1942.
Circus.   Boston, Houghton Mifflin, 1942; London, Folding Books, 1950.
Christmas Manger.   Boston, Houghton Mifflin, 1942.

Other by Margret Rey

Editor, with Alan J. Shalleck, *Curious George and the Dump Truck* [*Goes to the Circus, Goes Sledding, Goes Fishing, Goes to a Costume Party, Plays Baseball, Visits a Police Station, Walks the Pets, Goes to the Aquarium, and the Pizza, at the Fire Station, Goes Hiking, Visits the Zoo, at the Ballet, at the Airport, at the Laundromat*] (adapted from the *Curious George* film series). Boston, Houghton Mifflin, 16 vols., 1984–87.

PUBLICATIONS FOR ADULTS by H.A. Rey

Other

The Stars: A New Way to See Them.   Boston, Houghton Mifflin, 1952; as *A New Way to See the Stars*, London, Hamlyn, 1966; revised edition, Houghton Mifflin, 1967; as *The Stars*, London, Chatto and Windus, 1975.

*

Illustrator (H.A. Rey): *The Polite Penguin*, 1941, and *Don't Frighten the Lion!*, 1942, both by Margaret Wise Brown; *Katy No-Pocket* by Emmy Payne, 1944; *The Park Book* by Charlotte Zolotow, 1944; *We Three Kings and Other Christmas Carols*, 1944; *Egbert and His Marvellous Adventures* by Paul T. Gilbert, 1944; *The Daytime Lamp*

and Other Poems by Christian Morgenstern, 1973.

*   *   *

It matters little that the names Margret and H.A. Rey are practically unknown among the kindergarten set; what does matter is that their fictional offspring, Curious George, or Zozo in Great Britain, is instantaneously recognized and applauded by millions of children throughout the world. George, the curious little monkey, first saw light of day in the early 1940's when the world was wracked by war, and he immediately gained superstar status in the picture book world, maintaining it to this day.

It is easy, perhaps, for a critic to pass glibly over books like *Curious George* and its sequels when he is considering classic works in the field of children's literature. Such a critic might feel that there is an abyss between the comic strip and "the book," and that his job is to point out those elements which basically separate the two. For there is no denying that the Reys' work has strong links with the traditional comic strip, but therein one finds not only its energy and unique attraction to young children, but also the very subtle craftsmanship of its creators. (Yes *subtle*—for the best practitioners in broad physical humor achieve their effects in a seemingly effortless fashion.)

Since *Curious George* consistently heads the popularity list of what children themselves call "funny books," it is worth our attention to see if we can identify those components in *George* which help it maintain that high rank. As already mentioned, much of the humor in the *George* books is found in physical situations. This is the slapstick humor to be found not only in the comic strips and cartoon films, but in the traditional tall tales as well, and in the films of such comic greats as Chaplin. The humor is the same: a comic character steps into an everyday, ordinary situation and the world immediately turns topsy-turvy. The difference is that George is a child character who gets involved in the everyday incidents in which children often find themselves.

George is always simply introduced on the opening page (as in *Curious George Goes to the Hospital*):

> This is George.
> He lived with his friend, the man with the yellow hat.
> He was a good little monkey, but he was always curious.
> Today George was curious about the big box on the man's desk.

The child audience half knows and half waits to be surprised by the mischief and hilarity that will follow. It is indeed a simple story formula, but one that demands a writer (in this case a team) with a gifted sense of childlike humor and an endless inventiveness.

One last point about these books that adults should not miss. From children's responses to the *George* books it is evident that the man with the yellow hat is the kind of grownup that they most admire and respect. They constantly look for his yellow hat in the crowd, especially when George is center stage and up to his ears in trouble. They know that though he never intrudes, George's grownup friend is always there when he's needed.

—James E. Higgins

———

RICE, Alice (Caldwell) Hegan. American.   Born in Shelbyville, Kentucky, 11 January 1870. Educated at private schools. Married Cale Young Rice in 1902. Co-founder, Cabbage Patch Settlement House, Louisville, Kentucky. D. Litt.: Rollins College, Winter Park,

Florida, 1928; University of Louisville, 1937. *Died 10 February 1942.*

PUBLICATIONS FOR CHILDREN

Fiction

Mrs. Wiggs of the Cabbage Patch (as Alice Caldwell Hegan). New York, Century, 1901; London, Hodder and Stoughton, 1902.
Lovey Mary. New York, Century, and London, Hodder and Stoughton, 1903.
Captain June, illustrated by C.D. Weldon. New York, Century, and London, Hodder and Stoughton, 1907.

PUBLICATIONS FOR ADULTS

Novels

Sandy. New York, Century, and London, Hodder and Stoughton, 1905.
Mr. Opp. New York, Century, and London, Hodder and Stoughton, 1909.
A Romance of Billy-Goat Hill. New York, Century, and London, Hodder and Stoughton, 1912.
The Honorable Percival. New York, Century, and London, Hodder and Stoughton, 1914.
Calvary Alley. New York, Century, and London, Hodder and Stoughton, 1917.
Quin. New York, Century, and London, Hodder and Stoughton, 1921.
The Buffer. New York, Century, and London, Hodder and Stroughton, 1929.
Mr. Pete & Co. New York, Appleton Century, and London, Hodder and Stoughton, 1933.
The Lark Legacy. New York, Appleton Century, and London, Hodder and Stoughton, 1935.
Our Ernie. New York, Appleton Century, and London, Hodder and Stoughton, 1939.

Short Stories

Miss Mink's Soldier and Other Stories. New York, Century, and London, Hodder and Stoughton, 1918.
Turn About Tales, with Cale Young Rice. New York, Century, and London, Hodder and Stoughton, 1920.
Winners and Losers, with Cale Young Rice. New York, Century, and London, Hodder and Stoughton, 1925.
Passionate Follies: Alternate Tales, with Cale Young Rice. New York, Appleton Century, and London, Hodder and Stoughton, 1936.

Other

On Being Clinnicked: A Bit of a Talk over the Alley Fence. Franklin, Ohio, Eldridge, 1931.
My Pillow Book. New York, Appleton Century, 1937.
The Inky Way (autobiography). New York, Appleton Century, 1940.
Happiness Road. New York, Appleton Century, 1942.

* * *

Alice Hegan Rice is remembered now as the creator of Mrs. Wiggs, the purveyor of homespun philosophy: "The way to git

cheerful is to smile when you feel bad, to think about somebody else's headache when yer own is 'most bustin', to keep on believin' the sun is a-shinin' when the clouds is thick enough to cut." *Mrs. Wiggs of the Cabbage Patch* is an example of a book which has not so much been taken over by children as passed down to them. It was aimed originally at adult readers, and contains, as well as its account of the Wiggs family, their ups and downs and the way they cope with misfortune (from which no doubt the prosperous reader was expected to derive salutary lessons), the sub-plot of a chequered romance between their two benefactors. The Wiggs family is indeed poor, and Alice Hegan Rice, while allowing them to be "quaint"—addicts always recall how the girls Asia, Australia, and Europena have their pigtails ironed, five plaits to each head before they go for a wonderful first visit to the theatre—does not attempt to gloss over or prettify the desperate straits in which they find themselves when the rent can't be paid, the children cry with hunger, and the eldest boy, the bread-winner, dies from cold and lack of food. The book ends on a modest note of happiness with the lovers' quarrel sorted out and two of the children with settled jobs, but the author provides no fairy tale solution for the problems of the Mrs. Wiggses of this world. We meet her again in *Lovey Mary* where a little girl runs away from an orphanage with the small boy whom she tends and finds refuge with Mrs. Wiggs ("There ain't no hole so deep can't somebody pull you out"). With the large-hearted generosity with which readers by now identify her, Mrs. Wiggs takes them in and shelters them, and not only Mary and Tommy but Tommy's real mother too.

Captain June, the book which Rice wrote specifically for children, a story of a little American boy's stay in Japan, lacks the warmth and the interest of the stories of the Cabbage Patch.

—Gillian Avery

———

RICHARDS, Frank. Pseudonym for Charles Harold St. John Hamilton. British. Born in Ealing, Middlesex, 8 August 1876. Educated at schools in Ealing and Chiswick, including Thorn House School, Ealing. Song writer, with Percy Harrison. Freelance journalist, and staff member, as Martin Clifford, for *Pluck*, 1906, and *The Gem*, 1907–39; as Frank Richards, for *The Magnet*, 1908–40; as Owen Conquest and Ralph Redway, for *Boys' Friend*, from 1915; as Hilda Richards, for *School Friend*, and *The Magnet*, 1919–40; as Charles Hamilton, for *Modern Boy*, from 1928. Also contributed to *The Popular, Empire Library, Schoolboys' Own Library, Boys' Friend Library, The Marvel, Dreadnought, Boys' Journal, Boys' Herald, Vanguard Library*, and *The Nugget Library. Died 24 December 1961.*

PUBLICATIONS FOR CHILDREN

Fiction

Schoolboy series (*The Secret of the School, The Black Sheep of Sparshott, First Man In, Looking after Lamb, The Hero of Sparshott, Pluck Will Tell*). London, Merrett, 6 vols., 1946.
Billy Bunter of Greyfriars School, illustrated by R.J. Macdonald. London, Skilton, 1947.
Mascot Schoolboy series (*Top Study at Topham, Bunny Binks on the War-Path, The Dandy of Topham, Sent to Coventry*). London, John Matthew, 4 vols., 1947.
Billy Bunter's Barring-Out, illustrated by R.J. Macdonald. London, Skilton, 1948.
Billy Bunter's Banknote. London, Skilton, 1948.

Billy Bunter in Brazil. London, Skilton, 1949.
Billy Bunter's Christmas Party, illustrated by R.J. Macdonald. London, Skilton, 1949.
Billy Bunter among the Cannibals, illustrated by R.J. Macdonald. London, Skilton, 1950.
Billy Bunter's Benefit, illustrated by R.J. Macdonald. London, Skilton, 1950.
Jack of All Trades. London, Mandeville, 1950.
Billy Bunter Butts In, illustrated by R.J. Macdonald. London, Skilton, 1951.
Billy Bunter's Postal Order, illustrated by R.J. Macdonald. London, Skilton, 1951.
The Rivals of Rookwood School (as Owen Conquest). London, Mandeville, 1951.
Billy Bunter and the Blue Mauritius, illustrated by R.J. Macdonald. London, Skilton, 1952.
Billy Bunter's Beanfeast, illustrated by R.J. Macdonald. London, Cassell, 1952.
Billy Bunter's Brain-Wave, illustrated by R.J. Macdonald. London, Cassell, 1953.
Billy Bunter's First Case, illustrated by R.J. Macdonald. London, Cassell, 1953.
Billy Bunter the Bold, illustrated by R.J. Macdonald. London, Cassell, 1954.
Bunter Does His Best, illustrated by R.J. Macdonald. London, Cassell, 1954.
The Lone Texan. London, Atlantic, 1954.
Backing Up Billy Bunter, illustrated by C.H. Chapman. London, Cassell, 1955.
Billy Bunter's Double, illustrated by R.J. Macdonald. London, Cassell, 1955.
The Banishing of Billy Bunter, illustrated by C.H. Chapman. London, Cassell, 1956.
Lord Billy Bunter. London, Cassell, 1956.
Billy Bunter Afloat, illustrated by C.H. Chapman. London, Cassell, 1957.
Billy Bunter's Bolt, illustrated by C.H. Chapman. London, Cassell, 1957.
Billy Bunter the Hiker, illustrated by C.H. Chapman. London, Cassell, 1958.
Billy Bunter's Bargain, illustrated by C.H. Chapman. London, Cassell, 1958.
Bunter Comes for Christmas, illustrated by C.H. Chapman. London, Cassell, 1959.
Bunter Out of Bounds, illustrated by C.H. Chapman. London, Cassell, 1959.
Bunter Keeps It Dark, illustrated by C.H. Chapman. London, Cassell, 1960.
Bunter the Bad Lad. London, Cassell, 1960.
Billy Bunter at Butlin's, illustrated by C.H. Chapman. London, Cassell, 1961.
Billy Bunter's Treasure-Hunt, illustrated by C.H. Chapman. London, Cassell, 1961.
Bunter the Ventriloquist, illustrated by C.H. Chapman. London, Cassell, 1961.
Billy Bunter's Bodyguard, illustrated by C.H. Chapman. London, Cassell, 1962.
Bunter the Caravanner, illustrated by C.H. Chapman. London, Cassell, 1962.
Just Like Bunter, illustrated by C.H. Chapman. London, Cassell, 1963.
Big Chief Bunter, illustrated by C.H. Chapman. London, Cassell, 1963.
Bunter the Stowaway, illustrated by C.H. Chapman. London, Cassell, 1964.
Thanks to Bunter, illustrated by C.H. Chapman. London, Cassell, 1964.

Bunter and the Phantom of the Towers. London, Armada, 1965.
Bunter the Racketeer. London, Armada, 1965.
Bunter the Sportsman, illustrated by C.H. Chapman. London, Cassell, 1965.
Bunter the Tough Guy of Greyfriars. London, Armada, 1965.
Bunter's Holiday Cruise. London, Armada, 1965.
Bunter's Last Fling, illustrated by C.H. Chapman. London, Cassell, 1965.
Billy Bunter and the Man from South America. London, Hamlyn, 1967.
Billy Bunter and the School Rebellion. London, Hamlyn, 1967.
Billy Bunter and the Secret Enemy. London, Hamlyn, 1967.
Billy Bunter's Big Top. London, Hamlyn, 1967.
Billy Bunter and the Bank Robber. London, Hamlyn, 1968.
Billy Bunter, Sportsman. London, Hamlyn, 1968.
Billy Bunter and the Crooked Captain. London, Hamlyn, 1968.
Billy Bunter's Convict. London, Hamlyn, 1968.
Yarooh! A Feast of Frank Richards, edited by Gyles Brandreth. London, Eyre Methuen, 1976.
A New Anthology from the Works of Charles Hamilton, edited by John Wernham. Maidstone, Kent, Museum Press, 1977.

Fiction as Hilda Richards

Headland House series (*Winifred on the Warpath, The Girls of Headland House, Under Becky's Thumb*). London, Merrett, 3 vols., 1946.
Mascot Schoolgirl series (*Pamela of St. Olive's, The Stranded Schoolgirls, The Jape of the Term*). London, John Matthew, 3 vols., 1947.
Bessie Bunter of Cliff House School, illustrated by R.J. Macdonald. London, Skilton, 1949.

Fiction as Martin Clifford

The Secret of the Study. London, Mandeville, 1949.
Tom Merry and Co. of St. Jim's. London, Mandeville, 1949.
Rallying round Gussy. London, Mandeville, 1950.
The Scapegrace of St. Jim's. London, Mandeville, 1951.
Talbot's Secret. London, Mandeville, 1951.
Gold Hawk series (*Tom Merry's Secret, Tom Merry's Rival, The Man from the Past, Who Ragged Railton?, Skimpole's Snapshot, Trouble for Trimble, D'Arcy in Danger, D'Arcy on the Warpath, D'Arcy's Disappearance, D'Arcy the Reformer, D'Arcy's Day Off*). London, Hamilton, 11 vols., 1952.
A Strange Secret. Maidstone, Kent, Old Boys Book Club, 1968.

Other

Tom Merry's Own (annual; as Martin Clifford and Frank Richards). London, Mandeville, 4 vols., 1952–55.
Billy Bunter's Own (annual). London, Mandeville, 7 vols., 1953–59; London, Oxonhoath, 1 vol., 1960.

PUBLICATIONS FOR ADULTS

Play

Radio Play: *Plus ça Change; or, The 8:45 from Surbiton*, 1945.

Verse as Charles Hamilton

On the Ball! (song). Canvey Island, Essex, Woodford, 1908.

Other

The Autobiography of Frank Richards. London, Skilton, 1952.

*

Critical Studies: *The Charles Hamilton Companion* by John Wernham, Mary Cadogan, Eric Fayne, and Roger Jenkins, Maidstone, Kent, Museum Press, 7 vols., 1972–84; *The World of Frank Richards* by W.O.G. Lofts and Derek J. Adley, London, Baker, 1975; "Across Six Reigns" by Mary Cadogan and Patricia Craig, in *Howard Baker Greyfriars Annual,* 1978; *Greyfriars for Grown-Ups* by Lawrence Sutton, London, Howard Baker Press, 1980; *Frank Richards: The Chap Behind the Chums* by Mary Cadogan, London, Viking, 1988.

*   *   *

According to published statistics Charles Hamilton is the most prolific writer in the English language. He produced over 72 million words of published fiction, the equivalent of 2,000 novels. Under his 20 or so pen names he created many characters who have remained popular for decades with successive generations of readers. At least one of these seems likely to attain literary immortality; the name of Billy Bunter, the "Fat Owl" of the Greyfriars Remove, has become part of the language, synonymous with gluttonous obesity.

Hamilton is best remembered as Frank Richards for his stories of Greyfriars School in *The Magnet,* and as Martin Clifford writing of St. Jim's in *Pluck* and *The Gem.* For a fairly long period as well as producing 20,000 words each week for both *The Magnet* and *The Gem* he also as Owen Conquest wrote regular 5,000-word stories of Rookwood School for *Boys' Friend.* He was the original Hilda Richards, creating Cliff House School and Bessie Bunter for *School Friend.* Apart from school stories Hamilton's output included tales of romance, travel, the Wild West, detection, and adventure. He created over 100 fictional schools and new examples of his work are still coming to light.

Hamilton's school stories were addictive from the beginning though the quality of his writing improved over a period of 20 years, reaching a climax of style and presentation in the early 1930's. He perfected a fairly elaborate structure of interlocking episodes and plots, held together by an inner logic and consistency. Like some other children's authors (E. Nesbit, Richmal Crompton, etc.) Hamilton has more than a merely nostalgic appeal for many adults. The stories that are savoured uncritically by children can be appreciated by older readers for their technical accomplishment.

George Orwell's essay on boys' weeklies in the March 1940 issue of *Horizon* criticised the Frank Richards stories on both literary and sociological grounds. The essay contained several errors of fact, including Orwell's statement that the main body of the stories could not represent the output of one man. He conceded that Bunter was "a really first-rate character" but condemned the stories as tautological, artificial, facetiously padded, chauvinistic, and out of date. He also dismissed Richards's style as trite and easily imitated. Orwell here showed less discernment than many bright schoolboy readers of the 1920's and 1930's who wrote indignantly to *The Magnet's* editor, when substitute authors were used, to demand stories from "the real Frank Richards." In fact Hamilton's style is a highly individual blend of cosiness, satirical comment, and classical allusion that is deceptively difficult to analyse or imitate.

Orwell's major criticism, however, was that the stories were likely to persuade working-class boys to accept the established social structure of society. He condemned what he called the unreal and glamorized atmosphere of Hamilton's public schools and the gulf between this and the quality of life experienced by proletarian boys who enjoyed *The Magnet* and *The Gem.* Of course, if Orwell's

sociological assessments were accepted as valid literary criticism, the writers of fairy stories, thrillers, and fantasy fiction could equally be indicted for creating worlds removed from the limited "reality" known to readers from underprivileged homes.

Hamilton's spirited reply to these criticisms was published in the next issue of *Horizon.* He wrote that Orwell's idea of realism would destroy rather than edify the working-class readers about whom the critic showed so much concern: "Mr. Orwell would have told him that he is a shabby little blighter, his father an ill-used serf, his world a dirty, muddled, rotten sort of show!" Hamilton commented that he preferred to inject humour and warmth into his young readers' lives, on the assumption that "Happiness is the best preparation for adult misery if misery must come!"

A contrasting view from Orwell's of the influence of *The Magnet* and *The Gem* is expressed by Professor Robert Roberts in *The Classic Slum* (1971), his survey of Salford life in the early part of this century. According to Roberts, Hamilton's work "set ideals and standards. These our own tutors, religious and secular, had signally failed to do. In the final estimate it may well be found that Frank Richards during the first quarter of the twentieth century had more influence on the mind and outlook of young working-class England than any other single person, not excluding Baden-Powell."

Although Hamilton is celebrated for his manly and wholesome heroes like Harry Wharton and Bob Cherry, he is often at his most skilful with adolescent characters of a complex disposition, who flout adult authority and ideals of esprit de corps. Typical examples of these "outsiders" are the cynical and fastidious Cardew of St. Jim's, or Vernon-Smith, the flamboyant but resolute "Bounder" of Greyfriars. Hamilton's ironic humour counterbalances melodrama, contrivance, and repetition in his stories. Like P.G. Wodehouse, he could use a hackneyed or high-flown phrase and give it a comic, sophisticated flavour. There is also, of course, plenty of crude comedy—Bunter's perpetual tuck-pilfering, the whoopings and "yaroohs," the ghastly gurgles of masters struggling under the soot and glue of schoolboys' booby traps. However there is an overall subtlety of approach that has not always been acknowledged by critics. Hamilton is unsurpassed as a school story writer and remains the most resilient contributor to this minor but intriguing branch of English fiction.

After *The Magnet* ended Hamilton wrote a series of 38 hard-cover Greyfriars books (*Billy Bunter of Greyfriars School,* etc.), numerous annuals (*Billy Bunter's Own, Tom Merry's Own*), and paperbacks. Greyfriars School was featured in a series of BBC television programmes and Christmas plays in London's West End. Since 1969 Howard Baker has been regularly republishing Hamilton's boys' paper stories in facsimile editions. These have proved so popular that now over three-quarters of the 1,683 original stories from *The Magnet* have been reprinted, as well as many stories from *The Gem* and the annuals.

—Mary Cadogan

———

RICHARDS, Hilda. See **RICHARDS, Frank.**

———

RICHARDS, Laura E(lizabeth). American. Born in Boston, Massachusetts, 27 February 1850; daughter of the poet Julia Ward Howe and the educator Samuel Gridley Howe. Attended Miss Caroline Wilby's School, Boston. Married Henry Richards in 1871;

five daughters and two sons. Lived in Gardiner, Maine, after 1876. Associated with District Nurse Association and the National Child Labor Committee; founder, 1895, and president for 26 years, Woman's Philanthropic Union. Founded and with her husband ran Camp Merryweather (boys' summer camp), Lake Cobbosseecontee, 1900–30; president, Maine Consumers League, 1905–11. Recipient: Pulitzer prize, for biography, 1915. D.H.L.: University of Maine, Orono, 1936. *Died 14 January 1943.*

PUBLICATIONS FOR CHILDREN

Fiction

Five Mice in a Mouse-Trap, by the Man in the Moon, Done in Vernacular, from the Lunacular, illustrated by Kate Greenaway and others.   Boston, Estes, 1880.
Little Tyrant.   Boston, Estes, 1880.
Our Baby's Favorite.   Boston, Estes, 1881.
The Joyous Story of Toto, illustrated by E.H. Garrett.   Boston, Roberts, 1885; London, Blackie, 1886.
Toto's Merry Winter.   Boston, Roberts, 1887.
Queen Hildegarde.   Boston, Estes, and London, Gay and Bird, 1889.
Hildegarde's Holiday.   Boston, Estes, and London, Gay and Bird, 1891.
Captain January.   Boston, Estes, and London, Gay and Bird, 1891.
Hildegarde's Home.   Boston, Estes, 1892.
Melody.   Boston, Estes, 1893; London, Gay and Bird, 1895.
Marie.   Boston, Estes, 1894.
Narcissa; or, The Road to Rome, and In Verona: Two Tales.   Boston, Estes, 1894.
Nautilus.   Boston, Estes, 1895.
Five Minute Stories, illustrated by A.R. Whelan and Etheldred Barry.   Boston, Estes, 1895; London, Allenson, 1906.
Hildegarde's Neighbors.   Boston, Estes, 1895.
Jim of Hellas; or, In Durance Vile, and Bethesda Pool.   Boston, Estes, 1895.
Isla Heron, illustrated by Frank Merrill.   Boston, Estes, 1896.
"Some Say," and Neighbors in Cyrus.   Boston, Estes, 1896.
Three Margarets, illustrated by Etheldred Barry.   Boston, Estes, 1897.
Hildegarde's Harvest.   Boston, Estes, 1897.
Rosin the Beau.   Boston, Estes, 1898.
Margaret Montfort, illustrated by Etheldred Barry.   Boston, Estes, 1898.
Peggy, illustrated by Etheldred Barry.   Boston, Estes, 1899.
Quicksilver Sue, illustrated by W.D. Stevens.   New York, Century, 1899.
Chop-Chin and the Golden Dragon.   Boston, Little Brown, 1899.
The Golden-Breasted Koo-Too.   Boston, Little Brown, 1899.
Rita, illustrated by Etheldred Barry.   Boston, Estes, 1900.
Fernley House, illustrated by Etheldred Barry.   Boston, Estes, 1901.
The Green Satin Gown, illustrated by Etheldred Barry.   Boston, Estes, 1903.
More Five-Minute Stories, illustrated by Wallace Goldsmith.   Boston, Estes, 1903.
The Golden Windows: A Book of Fables for Young and Old.   Boston, Little Brown, 1903; London, Allenson, 1904.
The Merryweathers, illustrated by Julia Ward Richards.   Boston, Estes, 1904.
The Armstrongs, illustrated by Julia Ward Richards.   Boston, Estes, 1905.
The Silver Crown: Another Book of Fables.   Boston, Little Brown, and London, Allenson, 1906.
The Pig Brother and Other Fables and Stories.   Boston, Little Brown, 1908.
A Happy Little Time.   Boston, Estes, 1910.
The Naughty Comet and Other Fables and Stories.   London, Allenson, 1910; revised edition, 1925.
The Little Master.   Boston, Estes, 1913; as *Our Little Feudal Cousin of Long Ago,* Boston, Page, 1922.
Three Minute Stories, illustrated by Josephine Bruce.   Boston, Page, 1914.
Honor Bright, illustrated by Frank Merrill.   Boston, Page, 1920.
Honor Bright's New Adventure, illustrated by Elizabeth Withington.   Boston, Page, 1925.
Star Bright: A Sequel to Captain January, illustrated by Frank Merrill.   Boston, Page, 1927.
Harry in England, illustrated by Reginald Birch.   New York, Appleton Century, 1937.

Plays

The Pig Brother Play-Book (includes *The Pig Brother; The Shadow; For You and Me; The Useful Coal; The Sailor Man; The Cooky; Oh, Dear!; "Go" and "Come"; Child's Play; The Naughty Comet; The Tangled Skein; The Cake; Hokey Pokey; About Angels; The Great Feast; The Wheat-Field*).   Boston, Little Brown, 1915.
Fairy Operattas (includes *Cinderella, The Babes in the Wood, Beauty and the Beast, Bluebeard, The Three Bears, Good King Arthur, Puss in Boots, The Sleeping Beauty*), illustrated by Mary Robertson Bassett.   Boston, Little Brown, 1916.

Verse

Sketches and Scraps, illustrated by Henry Richards.   Boston, Estes, 1881.
Tell-Tale from Hill and Dale, illustrated by A. Hochstein.   Troy, New York, Nims, 1886.
Kasper Kroak's Kaleidoscope, with Henry Baldwin, illustrated by A. Hochstein.   Troy, New York, Nims, 1886.
In My Nursery.   Boston, Roberts, 1890.
Sundown Songs.   Boston, Little Brown, 1899.
The Hurdy-Gurdy.   Boston, Estes, 1902.
The Piccolo.   Boston, Estes, 1906.
Jolly Jingles.   Boston, Estes, 1912.
Tirra Lirra: Rhymes Old and New, illustrated by Marguerite Davis.   Boston, Little Brown, 1932; London, Harrap, 1933.
Merry-Go-Round: New Rhymes and Old, illustrated by Winifred Lefferts.   New York, Appleton Century, 1935.
I Have a Song to Sing to You, illustrated by Reginald Birch.   New York, Appleton Century, 1938.
Drawings by Kate Greenaway, Verses by Laura E. Richards from the Ladies' Home Journal 1895 and 1896, edited by Lucile Rasmussen.   Berkeley, California, Rasmussen Press, 1974.

Other

The Old Fairy Tales (*Beauty and the Beast* and *Hop o' My Thumb*), illustrated by Gordon Browne.   Boston, Roberts, and London, Blackie, 2 vols., 1886.
When I Was Your Age (autobiography).   Boston, Estes, 1894.
Snow-White; or, The House in the Wood.   Boston, Estes, 1900.
Florence Nightingale, The Angel of the Crimea.   New York, Appleton, 1909.
Two Noble Lives: Samuel Gridley Howe, Julia Ward Howe.   Boston, Estes, 1911.
Elizabeth Fry, The Angel of the Prisons.   New York, Appleton, 1916.
Abigail Adams and Her Times.   New York, Appleton, 1917.

Joan of Arc. New York, Appleton, 1919.
Laura Bridgman: The Story of an Opened Door. New York, Appleton, 1928.

Editor, *Baby's Rhyme [Story] Book.* Boston, Estes, 2 vols., 1878–79.
Editor, *Four Feet, Two Feet, and No Feet; or, Furry and Feathery Pets and How They Live.* Boston, Estes, 1885.

PUBLICATIONS FOR ADULTS

Novels

Love and Rocks. Boston, Estes, 1898.
Geoffrey Strong. Boston, Estes, 1901; London, Simpkin, 1912.
Mrs. Tree. Boston, Estes, 1902; London, Simpkin, 1912.
Mrs. Tree's Will. Boston, Estes, 1905.
Grandmother: The Story of a Life That Never Was Lived. Boston, Estes, 1907.
The Wooing of Calvin Parks. Boston, Estes, 1908.
"Up to Calvin's." Boston, Estes, 1910.
On Board the Mary Sands. Boston, Estes, 1911.
Miss Jimmy. Boston, Estes, 1913.
Pippin, A Wandering Flame. New York, Appleton, 1917.
A Daughter of Jehu. New York, Appleton, 1918.
In Blessed Cyrus. New York, Appleton, 1921.
The Squire. New York, Appleton, 1923.

Short Stories

For Tommy and Other Stories. Boston, Estes, 1900.

Plays

Seven Oriental Operettas (includes *A Royal Wooing, Abou Hassan the Wag, The Forty Thieves, Pretty Perilla, Aladdin, The Enchanted Birds, The Statue Prince*). Boston, Baker, 1924.
Acting Charades. Boston, Baker, 1924.

Verse

To Arms! Songs of the Great War. Boston, Page, 1918.
The Hottentot and Other Ditties, music by Twining Lynes. New York, Schirmer, 1939.

Other

Glimpses of the French Court: Sketches from French History. Boston, Estes, 1893.
Julia Ward Howe, 1819–1910, with Maud Howe Elliott. Boston, Houghton Mifflin, 2 vols., 1915.
Stepping Westward (autobiography). New York, Appleton, 1931.
Samuel Gridley Howe. New York, Appleton Century, 1935.
E.A.R. (on Edwin Arlington Robinson). Cambridge, Massachusetts, Harvard University Press, 1936.
"Please." Privately printed, 1936.
What Shall the Children Read? New York, Appleton Century, 1939.
Laura E. Richards and Gardiner (collection). Augusta, Maine, Gannett, 1940.

Editor, *Letters and Journals of Samuel Gridley Howe.* Boston, Estes, 2 vols., 1906–09; London, Lane, 2 vols., 1907–09.
Editor, *The Walk with God,* by Julia Ward Howe. New York, Dutton, 1919.

*

Manuscript Collections: Colby College Library, Waterville, Maine; Gardiner Public Library, Maine.

* * *

Laura E. Richards was a successful writer of both prose and poetry for children during the "golden age" of children's literature in the late 19th and early 20th centuries. Her work was widely published, but she is probably best remembered for her association with the famous *St. Nicholas* magazine, in which many of her verses appeared.

Except for a very few reprint editions, Richards's prose works for children are unavailable today. She wrote a number of biographies, mostly of women (Abigail Adams, Florence Nightingale, Elizabeth I, and others) using the semi-fictional approach common to most biographies for children of the time. Though she strengthened her accounts with excerpts from diaries, letters, and journals, Richards also greatly oversimplified both the characters of her subjects and the historical context of their lives. This, together with an old-fashioned style, has dated the biographies, and they are unlikely to be revived. The same must be said for such fiction as the Queen Hildegarde and Three Margarets series, both very popular in their time but now of interest mainly as period pieces.

It is in fact only her verse that has kept Richards's name alive in the field of children's literature. *Tirra Lirra* is included in most library poetry collections for children. The dominant mood of the verses in *Tirra Lirra* is cheerful and humorous. Lightheartedness was generally characteristic of the author, though some of Richards's verse published in *St. Nicholas* before the turn of the century reflected the sentimental attitudes of that period.

On the whole, however, Richards was a good deal less sentimental in her approach to children and poetry than were many of her contemporaries. Indeed, a slight acidity, surely welcome in the customarily earnest atmosphere of the late 19th century, often flavors her work. The wicked mockingbird whose practical joke caused the frog of Okefenokee to break his lovely green neck does not get off scot-free: "I'm happy to say/He was drowned the next day/In the waters of Okefenokee." Similarly, the aged cook dispatches without a quaver of remorse one of the seven little tigers who propose to eat him. No high-minded conclusions are ever drawn; Richards was not inclined to moralize.

Technically, Richards was a competent and facile versifier. She used a variety of rhyme schemes, mostly strong, unsubtle tetrameters, ballad forms, and limericks, though she never handled them with the intricacy of interest that, say, A.A. Milne could produce at his best. (On the other hand, she was never as far away from a child's point of view as Milne at his nostalgic worst.) She was fond—perhaps overfond—of nonsense words and repetition, certainly reflecting the influence of Edward Lear and Lewis Carroll. And while her made-up words were neither as witty as Carroll's nor as unselfconscious as Lear's, such inventions as the wigglewasticus and the ichthyosnortoryx gave her poems a nice sense of freedom. "Eletelephony," undoubtedly her best-known nonsense poem, is a truly funny play on tangled words, and "An elderly lady named Mackintosh/[who] set out to ride in a hackintosh" anticipates Ogden Nash.

Richards deserves her niche in children's literature. If she was never highly original, still she was humorous, irreverent, and pleasant to the ear. Unlike her prose, her verse is surprisingly undated.

—Anne Scott MacLeod

RIDGE, Antonia (Florence). British. Born in Amsterdam, Netherlands, 7 October 1895. Educated at schools in the Netherlands and England. Married James Henry Ridge in 1926; one daughter and one son. Writer and freelance broadcaster. Recipient: Writer's Guild award, for radio play, 1969. *Died in June 1981.*

PUBLICATIONS FOR CHILDREN

Fiction

The Handy Elephant and Other Stories, illustrated by A.E. Kennedy. London, Faber, 1946.
Rom-Bom-Bom and Other Stories, illustrated by A.E. Kennedy. London, Faber, 1946.
Hurrah for Muggins and Other Stories, illustrated by Francis Gower. London, Faber, 1947.
Endless and Co., illustrated by A.E. Kennedy. London, Faber, 1948.
Galloping Fred, illustrated by A.E. Kennedy. London, Faber, 1950.
Leave It to Brooks!, illustrated by Nora S. Unwin. London, National Magazine Company, 1950.
Jan and His Clogs, illustrated by Barbara C. Freeman. London, Faber, 1951; New York, Roy, 1952.
Stories from France (*The Market, The Station, The Village, The Farm, The Mountain, The Seaside*). Leicester, Brockhampton Press, 6 vols., 1956–57.
The Little Red Pony, with Mies Bouhuys, illustrated by Dick De Wilde. London, Harrap, 1960; Indianapolis, Bobbs Merrill, 1962.
Hurrah for a Dutch Birthday, with Mies Bouhuys, illustrated by Jillian Willett. London, Faber, 1964.
Melodia: A Story from Holland, with Mies Bouhuys, illustrated by Leslie Wood. London, Faber, 1969.

Plays

Puppet Plays for Children (includes *Spring Magic, Melodious Mixture, The Tropical Island, Blue Beans, A Cure for Lions, All Aboard the "Bookworm Bell"*), illustrated by Barbara C. Freeman. London, Faber, 1953.
Six Radio Plays (includes *Under the Monkey-Bread Tree, Hare and the Field of Millet, Three Mice for the Abbot, Emhammed of the Red Slippers, The Legend of Saint Basil, Saint Martha and the Tarasque of Tarascon*). Leeds, E.J. Arnold, 1954.
The Poppenkast; or, How Jan Klaassen Cured the Sick King. London, Faber, 1958; as *How Jan Klaassen Cured the King*, 1969.

Other

Jan Klaassen Cures the King: An Old Dutch Story, illustrated by Barbara C. Freeman. London, Faber, 1952.
Never Run from the Lion and Another Story (Algerian folk-tales), illustrated by Barbara C. Freeman. London, Faber, 1958; New York, Walck, 1959.

Translator, Père Castor Books (*Singing Bird House, Three Little Goats, The Moon Game, My Son Scamp, The Sun Box, Three Little Pigs, Me and My Master, The Good Friends, The Story of a Mouse, Little Goat Goes to Market, The Three Little Cats, The Breadcrumbs, The Animals Who Went Looking for Summer, A Rabbit Story, A Dog's Life, The Story of a Baby Lion Who Wasn't Hungry, Some Strange Animals, Come On, Neddy!, Snowball, Kathy's New Dress, The Old Grey Mare and the Little White Hen*), illustrated by Albertine Deletaille, Gerda Muller, and Lucile Butel. London, Harrap, 21 vols., 1960–70.

Translator, *Mission Underground*, by Norbert Casteret, illustrated by H. Johns. London, Harrap, 1968.

PUBLICATIONS FOR ADULTS

Novels

Family Album. London, Faber, and New York, Harper, 1952.
Cousin Jan. London, Faber, 1954.
Grandma Went to Russia. London, Faber, 1959.
The Thirteenth Child. London, Faber, 1962; as *The Royal Pawn*, New York, Appleton Century Crofts, 1963.
The Man Who Painted Roses: The Story of Pierre-Joseph Redouté. London, Faber, 1974.

Short Stories

By Special Request. London, Faber, 1958.

Plays

Radio Plays: *Maria Lafarge*, with Edith Saunders, 1968; *The Little French Clock*, 1969; *Au Clair de la Lune*, 1970; *Gentleman's Agreement*, 1972; and others.

Other

For Love of a Rose. London, Faber, 1965.

Editor, *A String of Beads*, by Dorothy McCall. London, Faber, 1960.

* * *

Antonia Ridge was one of the best short story writers that we had. To quote one reviewer—"she knows how to turn a tale well—as juicy as pippins in autumn." Her output was prolific, and in the children's field alone she was the author of many broadcast scripts as well as amusing and entertaining volumes of short stories such as *Rom-Bom-Bom, Hurrah for Muggins, Endless and Co.*, and *Galloping Fred*. These stories feature the animal characters with which she is associated—Fred the donkey, Muggins the dog, and Endless who is of course a Manx cat. A different kind of tale appears in *Never Run from the Lion*, which consists of two traditional folk-tales based on the theme of courage, admirable choices for reading aloud.

Much of Ridge's work revealed her Dutch inheritance. This is particularly so in the case of her best-known play, *The Poppenkast; or, How Jan Klaassen Cured the Sick King*, adapted from an old Dutch puppet play.

During the 1960's Ridge collaborated with the Dutch author Mies Bouhuys in producing a picture book illustrating the stress laid in Dutch family life on a child's birthday, called appropriately enough *Hurrah for a Dutch Birthday*. Bouhuys was also her co-author in the writing of *Melodia*, the story of a Dutch street organ. The scene is well set, the Dutch landscape with its dykes and windmills. Grandpa Brack, who owns Melodia, is a great favorite with the local children, but he and his wife are always hoping to visit their own six grandchildren in faraway America. The fairytale theme of the rich American visitor who makes it possible for this to happen is a well-worn one but very satisfying in the context of this story. The text is slightly marred, however, by a conversational style, wholly suitable for reading aloud, which becomes condescending in print.

Although Ridge was particularly good when writing for very young children—the English text to the Père Castor series of young picture books proves this—it is also true to say that her stories for adults, such as *The Thirteenth Child* and *Family Album*, are much enjoyed by older children. Their values are very sound, and they can be heartily recommended.

—Berna C. Clark

RIEU, E(mile) V(ictor). British. Born in London, 10 February 1887. Educated at St. Paul's School, London; Balliol College, Oxford, 1906–08. Served in the 105th Mahratta Light Infantry, 1918: 2nd Lieutenant; served in the Home Guard, 1943: Major. Married Nelly Lewis in 1914; two sons and two daughters. Manager, Oxford University Press, Bombay, 1912–19; educational manager, 1923–33, managing director, 1933–36, and adviser from 1936, Methuen, publishers, London; editor, Penguin Classics series, 1944–64. Member, Committee for New Translation of the Bible, from 1951. Recipient: Royal Society of Literature Benson Medal, 1968. D. Litt.: University of Leeds, 1949. Fellow, Royal Society of Literature (vice-president, 1958). C.B.E. (Commander, Order of the British Empire), 1953. *Died 11 May 1972.*

PUBLICATIONS FOR CHILDREN

Verse

Cuckoo Calling: A Book of Verse for Youthful People, illustrated by Violet M. Guy. London, Methuen, 1933.
A Puffin Quartet of Poets, with others, edited by Eleanor Graham, illustrated by Diana Bloomfield. London, Penguin, 1958.
The Flattered Flying Fish and Other Poems, illustrated by Ernest Shepard. London, Methuen, and New York, Dutton, 1962.

PUBLICATIONS FOR ADULTS

Verse

The Tryst and Other Poems. London, Oxford University Press, 1917.

Other

The Logic of Christian Faith. Goring, Berkshire, Layman, 1954.

Editor, with H.C. Bradley, *Letters de mon Moulin*, by Alphonse Daudet. London, Oxford University Press, 1912.
Editor, *The Prisoner of Zenda* (abridgement), by Anthony Hope. London, Frowde, 1915.
Editor, *A Book of Latin Poetry, from Ennius to Hadrian.* London, Methuen, 1925; 4th edition, New York, St. Martin's Press, 1953.
Editor, *Essays [More Essays] by Modern Masters.* London, Methuen, 2 vols., 1926–34.
Editor, with Peter Wait, *Modern Masters of Wit and Laughter.* London, Methuen, 1938.

Translator, *The Odyssey*, by Homer. London, Penguin, 1946.
Translator, *The Pastoral Poems*, by Virgil. London, Penguin, 1949.
Translator, *The Iliad*, by Homer. London, Penguin, 1950.
Translator, *The Four Gospels.* London, Penguin, 1952.
Translator, *The Voyage of Argo*, by Apollonius of Rhodes. London, Penguin, 1959.
Translator, *The Word: A Synthesis of the Four Gospels.* London,

Faith Press, 1965.

*   *   *

Before 1958 E.V. Rieu was known to the general public, if at all, as the editor of Penguin Classics and as the highly successful and idiosyncratic translator of Homer and Virgil. A very intelligent and humorous writer with a flexible turn of mind, one might have thought, but one who was essentially "adult." His book of verse *Cuckoo Calling* (1933) should have corrected this picture, but this book made little impact on readers. In 1958 Eleanor Graham included Rieu as one of her *Puffin Quartet of Poets.* She knew him professionally through her connections with Penguin Books and with Methuen (Rieu had been at one time managing director of the latter), and had been privileged to penetrate the facade of the business man and academic to the very private person who wrote verses for his own satisfaction. The *Quartet* set him in the company of his peers, his older contemporary Eleanor Farjeon and the much younger Reeves and Serraillier. Since then his poems have appeared from time to time in anthologies, but he has remained a secret, enigmatic figure.

The 29 poems selected by Eleanor Graham give an accurate impression of the range and quality of Rieu's work. He may play with fantastic ideas, but he is not a maker of fantasy worlds. For him the real world is fantasy enough, and his favourite method is to take an ordinary situation, turn it this way and that, upside-down if need be, and find in it some paradox or absurdity which will illuminate its ordinariness. Even the rhymes about such exotic creatures as flying-fish and hippopotami are gentle reflexions on human weaknesses. Mostly the objective is fun, but not the robust loud laugh, rather the inward glow that comes from a point suddenly taken or a truth revealed. He is a master of tenderness too, with sympathy wide enough to embrace the widowed mouse and the insomniac tortoise as well as the more obviously appealing domestic tabby. There is anguish in "The Lost Cat" and an elegiac resignation in "Cat's Funeral." All his verse is strongly formal. He is a craftsman who loves to polish and prune. So successfully does he cut out the inessential that some of his lapidary verses are briefer than their titles!

Rieu came nearest to giving away his secret in a most self-revealing poem called "The Paint Box." The poet urges the painter to paint "somebody utterly new." The dialogue continues:

> "I have painted the cook and a camel in blue
> And a panther in purple." "You painted them true.
>
> Now mix me a colour that nobody knows,
> And paint me a country where nobody goes.
> And put in it people a little like you,
> Watching a unicorn drinking the dew."

—Marcus Crouch

ROBERTS, (Sir) Charles G(eorge) D(ouglas). Canadian. Born in Douglas, New Brunswick, 10 January 1860. Educated at the Collegiate School, Fredericton, New Brunswick, 1874–76; University of New Brunswick, Fredericton (Douglas Medal in Latin and Greek; Alumni Gold Medal for Latin Essay), 1876–81, B.A. (honours) in mental and moral science and political economy 1879, M.A. 1881. Served in the British Army, 1914–15: Captain; transferred to the Canadian Army, 1916: Major; subsequently worked with Lord Beaverbrook in the Canadian War Records Office, London. Married 1) Mary Isabel Fenety in 1880 (died 1930), three sons and one daughter; 2) Joan Montgomery in 1943. Headmaster, Chatham Grammar School, New Brunswick, 1879–81, and York Street School, Fredericton, 1881–83; editor, *This Week*, Toronto, 1883–84; Professor of English and French, 1885–88, and Professor of English and Economics, 1888–95, King's College, Windsor, Nova Scotia; associate editor, *Illustrated American*, New York, 1897–98; co-editor, Nineteenth Century series, 1900–05; lived in England, 1911–25. Recipient: Lorne Pierce Medal, 1926. LL.D.: University of New Brunswick, 1906. Fellow, 1890, and president of Section 2, 1933, Royal Society of Canada; fellow, Royal Society of Literature, 1892; member, American Academy, 1898. Knighted, 1935. *Died 26 November 1943.*

PUBLICATIONS FOR CHILDREN

Fiction

The Raid from Beauséjour, and How the Carter Boys Lifted the Mortgage: Two Stories of Acadie. New York, Hunt and Eaton, 1894; *The Raid from Beauséjour* published as *The Young Acadian*, Boston, Page, 1907.
Reube Dare's Shad Boat: A Tale of the Tide Country. New York, Hunt and Eaton, 1895; as *The Cruise of the Yacht "Dido" : A Tale of the Tide Country*, Boston, Page, 1906.
Around the Campfire, illustrated by Charles Copeland. New York, Crowell, 1896; London, Harrap, 1906.
Earth's Enigmas: A Book of Animal and Nature Life, illustrated by Charles Livingston Bull. Boston, Lamson Wolffe, 1896; revised edition, Boston, Page, 1903; London, Duckworth, 1904.
The Kindred of the Wild: A Book of Animal Life, illustrated by Charles Livingston Bull. Boston, Page, 1902; London, Duckworth, 1903.
The Watchers of the Trails: A Book of Animal Life, illustrated by Charles Livingston Bull. Boston, Page, and London, Duckworth, 1904.
Red Fox: The Story of His Adventurous Career in the Ringwaak Wilds, and of His Final Triumph over the Enemies of His Kind, illustrated by Charles Livingston Bull. Boston, Page, and London, Duckworth, 1905.
The Haunters of the Silences: A Book of Animal Life, illustrated by Charles Livingston Bull. Boston, Page, and London, Duckworth, 1907.
In the Deep of the Snow, illustrated by Denman Fink. New York, Crowell, 1907.
The House in the Water: A Book of Animal Life, illustrated by Charles Livingston Bull and Frank Vining Smith. Boston, Page, 1908; London, Ward Lock, 1909.
The Backwoodsmen. New York, Macmillan, and London, Ward Lock, 1909.
Kings in Exile, illustrated by Paul Bransom and Charles Livingston Bull. London, Ward Lock, 1909; New York, Macmillan, 1910.
Neighbours Unknown, illustrated by Paul Bransom. London, Ward Lock, 1910; New York, Macmillan, 1911.
More Kindred of the Wild, illustrated by Paul Bransom. London, Ward Lock, and New York, Macmillan, 1911.
Babes of the Wild, illustrated by Warwick Reynolds. London and New York, Cassell, 1912; as *Children of the Wild*, New York, Macmillan, 1913.
The Feet of the Furtive, illustrated by Paul Bransom. London, Ward Lock, 1912; New York, Macmillan, 1913.
Hoof and Claw, illustrated by Paul Bransom. London, Ward Lock, 1913; New York, Macmillan, 1914.
The Secret Trails, illustrated by Paul Bransom and Warwick Reynolds. New York, Macmillan, and London, Ward Lock,

1916.
The Ledge on Bald Face, illustrated by Paul Bransom. London, Ward Lock, 1918; as *Jim: The Story of a Backwoods Police Dog*, New York, Macmillan, 1919.
Wisdom of the Wilderness. London, Dent, and New York, Dutton, 1922.
They Who Walk in the Wild, illustrated by Charles Livingston Bull. New York, Macmillan, 1924; as *They That Walk in the Wild*, London, Dent, 1924.
Eyes of the Wilderness, illustrated by Dorothy Burroughes. New York, Macmillan, and London, Dent, 1933.
Further Animal Stories. London, Dent, 1935.
Thirteen Bears, edited by Ethel Hume Bennett, illustrated by John A. Hall. Toronto, Ryerson Press, 1947.
Forest Folk, edited by Ethel Hume Bennett, illustrated by John A. Hall. Toronto, Ryerson Press, 1949.
King of Beasts and Other Stories, edited by Joseph Gold. Toronto, Ryerson Press, 1967.
Eyes of the Wilderness and Other Stories: A New Collection, illustrated by Brian Carter. London, Dent, 1980.
The Lure of the Wild: The Last Three Animal Stories, edited by John C. Adams. Ottawa, Borealis, 1980.

Other

A History of Canada for High Schools and Academies. Boston, Lamson Wolffe, 1897; London, Kegan Paul, 1898.

PUBLICATIONS FOR ADULTS

Fiction

The Forge in the Forest, Being the Narrative of the Acadian Ranger, Jean de Mer. Boston, Lamson Wolffe, 1896.
A Sister to Evangeline, Being the Story of Yvonne de Lamourie. Boston, Lamson Wolffe, 1898; London, Lane, 1900; as *Lovers in Acadie*, London, Dent, 1924.
The Heart of the Ancient Wood. New York, Silver Burdett, 1900; London, Methuen, 1902.
Barbara Ladd. Boston, Page, and London, Constable, 1902.
The Prisoner of Mademoiselle: A Love Story. Boston, Page, and London, Constable 1904.
The Heart That Knows. Boston, Page, and London, Duckworth, 1906.
A Balkan Prince. London, Everett, 1913.

Short Stories

By the Marshes of Minas. New York, Silver Burdett, 1900.
The Red Oxen of Bonval. New York, Dodd Mead, 1908.
Cock Crow. New York, Federal Printers, 1913.
In the Morning of Time. London, Hutchinson, and New York, Stokes, 1919.
The Last Barrier and Other Stories. Toronto, McClelland and Stewart, 1958.

Verse

Orion and Other Poems. Philadelphia, Lippincott, 1880.
Later Poems. Privately printed, 1881.
Later Poems. Fredericton, Crockett, 1882.
In Divers Tones. Boston, Lothrop, 1886.
Autotochthon. Privately printed, 1889.
Ave: An Ode for the Centenary of the Birth of Percy Bysshe Shelley, 4th August, 1792. Toronto, Williamson, 1892.

Songs of the Common Day, and Ave: An Ode for the Shelley Centenary. London, Longman, 1893.

The Book of the Native. Toronto, Copp Clark, and Boston, Lamson Wolffe, 1896.

New York Nocturnes and Other Poems. Boston, Lamson Wolffe, 1898.

Poems. New York, Silver Burdett, 1901; London, Constable, 1903.

The Book of the Rose. Boston, Page, 1903; London, R. Brimley Johnson, 1904.

Poems. Boston, Page, 1907.

New Poems. London, Constable, 1919.

The Sweet o' the Year and Other Poems. Toronto, Ryerson Press, 1925.

The Vagrant of Time. Toronto, Ryerson Press, 1927; revised edition, 1927.

Be Quiet Wind; Unsaid. Privately printed, 1929.

The Iceberg and Other Poems. Toronto, Ryerson Press, 1934.

Selected Poems. Toronto, Ryerson Press, 1936.

Twilight over Shaugamauk and Three Other Poems. Toronto, Ryerson Press, 1937.

Canada Speaks of Britain and Other Poems of the War. Toronto, Ryerson Press, 1941.

Selected Poems, edited by Desmond Pacey. Toronto, Ryerson Press, 1956.

Poets of the Confederation, with others, edited by Malcolm Mackenzie Ross. Toronto, McClelland and Stewart, 1960.

The Collected Poems of Charles G.D. Roberts, edited by Desmond Pacey and Graham Adams. Wolfville, Nova Scotia, Wombat Press, 1985.

Other

The Canadian Guide-Book: The Tourist's and Sportsman's Guide to Eastern Canada and Newfoundland. New York, Appleton, 1891; London, Heinemann, 1892.

The Land of Evangeline and the Gateways Thither...for Sportsman and Tourist. Kentville, Nova Scotia, Dominion Atlantic Railway Company, 1894.

Discoveries and Explorations in the Century (nineteenth century series). London, Chambers, 1903; Philadelphia, Linscott, 1904.

Canada in Flanders, vol. 3. London, Hodder and Stoughton, 1918.

Selected Poetry and Critical Prose, edited by W.J. Keith. Toronto, University of Toronto Press, 1974.

Editor, *Poems of Wild Life.* London, Scott, 1888.

Editor, *Northland Lyrics*, by William Carman Roberts, Theodore Roberts, and Elizabeth Roberts Macdonald. Boston, Small Maynard, 1899.

Editor, *Shelley's Adonais and Alastor.* Boston, Silver Burdett, 1902.

Editor, with Arthur L. Tunnell, *A Standard Dictionary of Canadian Biography: The Canadian Who Was Who.* Toronto, Trans-Canada Press, 2 vols., 1934–38.

Editor, with Arthur L. Tunnell, *The Canadian Who's Who*, vols. II and III. Toronto, Trans-Canada Press, 1936–39.

Editor, *Flying Colours: An Anthology.* Toronto, Ryerson Press, 1942.

Translator, *The Canadians of Old*, by Philippe Aubert de Gaspé. New York, Appleton, 1890; as *Cameron of Lochiel*, Boston, Page, 1905.

*

Critical Studies: *Sir Charles G.D. Roberts: A Biography* by Elsie M. Pomeroy, Toronto, Ryerson Press, 1943; *Charles G.D. Roberts* by W.J. Keith, Toronto, Copp Clark, 1969; *The Proceedings of the Charles G.D. Roberts Symposium*, Sackville, New Brunswick, Mount Allison University, 1984; *Sir Charles God Damn: The Life of Charles G.D. Roberts* by John Coldwell Adams, Toronto, University of Toronto Press, 1986.

*   *   *

Charles G.D. Roberts, one of the first three Canadians to be knighted (1935), probably received that honor because he was well known as a poet, possibly even deserving the title "father of Canadian poetry." In *Ten Canadian Poets* Desmond Pacey analyzes the achievement of Roberts solely as a poet, critically and with skill. But he makes no more than a passing note of what to me and to thousands of Roberts's readers at the end of the old century and the first of this was inescapable: Roberts stood head and shoulders above his few North American contemporaries, such as Ernest Thompson Seton, as a nature writer who made the wild animals, birds, fish, and even dragonflies of back-woods New Brunswick come alive on the printed page. He despised any anthropomorphic approach: fox was fox, lynx lynx, porcupine porcupine, bear bear, eagle eagle, grouse grouse, owl owl, a wise old trout a wise old trout. No nicknames; no concealing of nature's cruelty, the disaster of sub-zero weather or forest fire. He wrote the prose of a poet: color in his words, economy in style, drama in his action, rhythm in the wilderness life of hunter and hunted. Beyond all this, what set Roberts's stories apart was his unwavering respect for the dignity of life—the dignity of death—among these creatures of the wild.

Of his dozen books which gathered these stories together five or six stand out: *Red Fox* (a novel), *The Kindred of the Wild, The Watchers of the Trails, The Haunters of the Silences, The Feet of the Furtive, Kings in Exile.* The masterpiece is *Red Fox*, surely the one wild animal story in English to stand beside Henry Williamson's *Tarka the Otter* (the gem of them all) and Jack London's *The Call of the Wild.* But there is a purity about *Red Fox*, a spareness, a kind of breathlessness, isolation from human creatures, which it alone possesses. Are these books for children? They are for all ages, just as much as *The Wind in the Willows, The Jungle Books*, Hudson's *Far Away and Long Ago*, Sally Carrighar's *One Day on Beetle Rock*, H.M. Tomlinson's *The Brown Owl.*

Roberts was fortunate in his two illustrators: Charles Livingston Bull and Paul Bransom, and fortunate in his typographers too. The original books were (and remain) works of art to look at, a delight to handle. Could any child who has never paddled a canoe, camped in the wilderness, worn snowshoes, seen a raccoon fishing in a stream, or watched a dragonfly emerge from her private cellophane on a rock in the sun by a river fail to be enchanted by one of these books alone? I doubt it.

Let me close by saying that three years on my uncle's ranch in the old frontier by the wild Rogue River in Oregon when I was 12 to 15 gave me a chance to verify some of the things I had read about earlier in *Red Fox* and the other books. Two short stories in *The Watchers of the Trails*—"The Little Wolf of the Pool" (about the larva of the dragonfly) and "The Little Wolf of the Air" (about the dragonfly itself)—have a timeless pure magic in their fascination for young readers; they bring the wilderness to one's back door. They have the very look of everlastingness.

Years later, when I began to write poems for children I, too, was fortunate in my illustrator. For the naturalist-artist Henry B. Kane had read Roberts when *he* was a boy. *Red Fox* had made me wish to try to become a writer. The illustrations by Charles Livingston Bull had made Kane wish to become an artist.

—David McCord

ROBERTS, Elizabeth Madox. American. Born in Perryville, Kentucky, 30 October 1881. Educated at Covington Institute, Springfield, Kentucky; Covington High School, Kentucky, 1896–1900; attended State College of Kentucky (now University of Kentucky), Lexington, 1900–01, 1916; University of Chicago (McLaughlin prize; Fiske prize, 1921), 1917–21, Ph.B. in English, 1921 (Phi Beta Kappa). Private tutor and teacher in public schools, Springfield, 1901–10. Recipient: O. Henry award, 1930. L.H.D.: Russell Sage College, Troy, New York, 1933. Member, American Academy, 1940. *Died 13 March 1941.*

PUBLICATIONS FOR CHILDREN

Verse

Under the Tree. New York, Huebsch, 1922; London, Cape, 1928; revised edition, New York, Viking Press, 1930.

PUBLICATIONS FOR ADULTS

Novels

The Time of Man. New York, Viking Press, 1926; London, Cape, 1927.
My Heart and My Flesh. New York, Viking Press, 1927; London, Cape, 1928.
Jingling in the Wind. New York, Viking Press, 1928; London, Cape, 1929.
The Great Meadow. New York, Viking Press, and London, Cape, 1930.
A Buried Treasure. New York, Viking Press, 1931; London, Cape, 1932.
He Sent Forth a Raven. New York, Viking Press, and London, Cape, 1935.
Black Is My Truelove's Hair. New York, Viking Press, 1938; London, Hale, 1939.

Short Stories

The Haunted Mirror. New York, Viking Press, 1932; London, Cape, 1933.
Not by Strange Gods. New York, Viking Press, 1941.

Verse

In the Great Steep's Garden. Colorado Springs, Gowdy Simmons, 1915.
Song in the Meadow. New York, Viking Press, 1940.

*

Manuscript Collection: Library of Congress, Washington, D.C.

Critical Studies: *Elizabeth Madox Roberts: A Personal Note* by Glenway Wescott, New York, Viking Press, 1930; *Elizabeth Madox Roberts: An Appraisal* by J. Donald Adams and others, New York, Viking Press, 1938; *Elizabeth Madox Roberts, American Novelist* by Harry Modean Campbell and Ruel E. Foster, Norman, University of Oklahoma Press, 1956; *Herald to Chaos: The Novels of Elizabeth Madox Roberts* by Earl Rovit, Lexington, University Press of Kentucky, 1960; *Elizabeth Madox Roberts* by Frederick P.W. McDowell, New York, Twayne, 1963 (includes bibliography).

*   *   *

Elizabeth Madox Roberts, Kentucky-born novelist and poet who died in 1941, is best remembered for two of her several distinguished novels: *The Time of Man* (1926) and *The Great Meadow* (1930). In 1940 she published an uneven book of poems called *Song in the Meadow*. But way back in 1922 she had already produced her one undoubted masterpiece: a gentle, quiet book of verse for children, called very gently and quietly *Under the Tree*. It was revised and reissued in 1930 with enchanting illustrations by F.D. Bedford. Any discussion of her merit as a writer for children centers entirely on this collection, even though three or four of the poems included in the early part of *Song in the Meadow* sound like worthy echoes from the 1922 volume. And very clear as well as worthy echoes too.

So what does one say of this undiminished book, until recently still in print in hard cover? For Roberts, without question, remains absolutely unique in the field of verse for children. To me she is the only poet, man or woman, writing in the English language who possessed and consistently used the undisguised, uninterrupted voice of childhood. Excepting Emily Dickinson, not Blake, nor Lear, Carroll, Stevenson, Eugene Field, Christina Rossetti, Laura E. Richards, Eleanor Farjeon, Milne, Eve Merriam, Norma Farber, Marchette Chute, Aileen Fisher, Myra Cohn Livingston, Reeves, or Serraillier—no one who wrote or writes poems for children commanded or commands, as she did, not only the vocabulary but the attitude and voice-inflection of a small girl lost in wonder:

> A little light is going by,
> Is going up to see the sky,
> A little light with wings.
>
> I never could have thought of it,
> To have a little bug all lit
> And made to go on wings.

She was born to notice things and actions. The world implied, and she was already to infer. When her small brother Clarence begins his country school days, what does she do?

> We climb up on the fence and gate
> And watch until he's small and dim,
> Far up the street, and he looks back
> To see if we keep on watching him.

The average post-Georgian poet, I think, would have said, "To see if we keep watching him," omitting the "on." But not a child; not Roberts; not a poet of her special genius. Could the Greek and Latin poets with their gifts for onomatopoeia manage to describe the unexisting *sound* of a silent vanishing dirt Kentucky road as she does here?

> The road was going on and on
> Beyond to reach some other place....

Or look back into all the brook poetry you can think of, including Tennyson and Robert Frost, and try to match the flawless order of these first three lines of the fourth and last stanza of "The Branch," so settled in their utter calm that in the fourth line not one syllable and certainly not the magic of the perfect adjective "rough" will escape you:

> And where it is smooth there is moss on a stone,
> And where it is shallow and almost dry
> The rocks are broken and hot in the sun,
> And a rough little water goes hurrying by.

Two other things. In the total assembly of poems about Christmas, save for Thomas Hardy's "The Oxen," I can think of none to equal

Roberts's "Christmas Morning"—her wondrous imaginary visit to Bethlehem. Length forbids quoting all 10 stanzas. Here is the last one:

> While Mary put the blankets back
> The gentle talk would soon begin.
> And when I'd tiptoe softly out
> I'd meet the wise men going in.

Twice in the course of the 59 poems in *Under the Tree* there appears a certain small boy named with a certain not-quite-hidden tone of secret admiration. He's not called Tiny Tim or Huckleberry Finn or Christopher Robin. He has the far more romantic handle of Joe B. Kirk. Through many rereadings of this book I have often wondered about him: did he live to grow up? and what has he done with his life? His one big moment in the poems is in (or at) "The Picnic" when Miss Kate-Marie, the Sunday school teacher, kisses all the children. How marvellous, how real, how visible is Joe B. Kirk's reaction:

> She kissed us all and Joe B. Kirk;
> But Joe B. didn't mind a bit.
> He walked around and swung his arms
> And seemed to be very glad of it.

Among my personal desert island books I include a copy of *Under the Tree* to go with *The Wind in the Willows*.

—David McCord

ROBERTSON, Keith (Carlton). Also writes as Carlton Keith. American. Born in Dows, Iowa, 9 May 1914. Educated at the United States Naval Academy, Annapolis, Maryland, B.S. 1937. Served in the United States Navy: radioman on a battleship, 1930–33; officer, on destroyers, 1941–45; Captain, United States Naval Reserve. Married Elisabeth Hexter in 1946; two daughters and one son. Refrigeration engineer, 1937–41; worked for a publisher, 1945–47; free-lance writer, 1947–58 and since 1968. Lives in Hopewell, New Jersey. Address: c/o Viking Kestrel, 40 West 23rd Street, New York, New York 10010, U.S.A.

PUBLICATIONS FOR CHILDREN

Fiction

Ticktock and Jim, illustrated by Wesley Dennis. Philadelphia, Winston, 1948; as *Watch for a Pony*, London, Heinemann, 1949.
Ticktock and Jim, Deputy Sheriffs, illustrated by Everett Stahl. Philadelphia, Winston, 1949.
The Dog Next Door, illustrated by Morgan Dennis. New York, Viking Press, 1950.
The Missing Brother, illustrated by Rafaello Busoni. New York, Viking Press, 1950; London, Faber, 1952.
The Lonesome Sorrel, illustrated by Taylor Oughton. Philadelphia, Winston, 1952.
The Mystery of Burnt Hill, illustrated by Rafaello Busoni. New York, Viking Press, 1952.
Mascot of the Melroy, illustrated by Jack Weaver. New York, Viking Press, 1953.
Outlaws of the Sourland, illustrated by Isami Kashiwagi. New York, Viking Press, 1953.

Three Stuffed Owls, illustrated by Jack Weaver. New York, Viking Press, 1954.
Ice to India, illustrated by Jack Weaver. New York, Viking Press, 1955.
The Phantom Rider, illustrated by Jack Weaver. New York, Viking Press, 1955.
The Pilgrim Goose, illustrated by Erick Berry. New York, Viking Press, 1956.
The Pinto Deer, illustrated by Isami Kashiwagi. New York, Viking Press, 1956.
The Crow and the Castle, illustrated by Robert Grenier. New York, Viking Press, 1957.
Henry Reed Inc., illustrated by Robert McCloskey. New York, Viking Press, 1958.
If Wishes Were Horses, illustrated by Paul Kennedy. New York, Harper, 1958.
Henry Reed's Journey [*Baby-Sitting Service, Big Show*], illustrated by Robert McCloskey. New York, Viking Press, 3 vols., 1963–70.
The Year of the Jeep, illustrated by W.T. Mars. New York, Viking Press, 1968.
The Money Machine, illustrated by George Porter. New York, Viking Press, 1969.
In Search of a Sandhill Crane, illustrated by Richard Cuffari. New York, Viking Press, 1973.
Tales of Myrtle the Turtle, illustrated by Peter Parnall. New York, Viking Press, 1974.
Henry Reed's Think Tank. New York, Viking Kestrel, 1986.

Other

The Wreck of the Saginaw, illustrated by Jack Weaver. New York, Viking Press, 1954.
The Navy: From Civilian to Sailor, illustrated by Charles Geer. New York, Viking Press, 1958.
New Jersey. New York, Coward McCann, 1969.

PUBLICATIONS FOR ADULTS as Carlton Keith

Novels

The Diamond-Studded Typewriter. New York, Macmillan, 1958; London, Heinemann, 1960; as *A Gem of a Murder*, New York, Dell, 1959.
Missing, Presumed Dead. New York, Doubleday, 1961.
Rich Uncle. New York, Doubleday, 1963; London, Hale, 1965.
The Hiding Place. New York, Doubleday, 1965; London, Hale, 1966.
The Crayfish Dinner. New York, Doubleday, 1966; as *The Elusive Epicure*, London, Hale, 1968.
A Taste of Sangria. New York, Doubleday, 1968; as *The Missing Book-Keeper*, London, Hale, 1969.

*

Manuscript Collection: May Massee Collection, Emporia State University, Kansas.

*   *   *

Keith Robertson's boys are the natural descendants of Tom Sawyer and Penrod: bright, ambitious, inquisitive, and inventive; never still for a moment; often in hot water but safely out again before there is serious cause for alarm. They are boys who never grow up, just as Tom Sawyer remains a boy forever. Not in the magical sense of Peter Pan's Never Never Land agelessness, but simply because boyishness is their very essence.

Henry Reed always has some enterprises on hand; his world is divided between those who understand the necessity of rabbit-keeping and running small businesses having to do with earthworm culture, babysitting, or rodeo organization, and those of the older generation or even unsympathetic young people who object to such undertakings on trumped-up adult grounds such as trespass and game laws. All the Henry Reed books hang on some plot peg such as a babysitting agency (whose clients can only be described as fiendish), or a cross-country motor trip; but they are usually episodic and rambling; one harmless complication follows another, with never a dull moment spent on the boring business of life as most of us live it. No one could wish that Henry's sunny existence should change in any particular; he's such a contented young man it does one's heart good to meet him even in print.

Robertson's alternate heroes, the young Carson Street Detectives Neil and Swede, are, like Henry Reed, model American boys of about 1950 vintage, clean-cut, wholesome, bright young fellows with short haircuts who would do credit to any senior Boy Scout Troop. It is a restful pleasure to encounter these uncomplicated kids, after struggling through various tomes dealing with the tortured life and psyche of the typical mixed-up young hero of today's often harrowing fiction for children.

Henry, Neil, and Swede are not milksops; they encounter more adventures in a chapter than most of us do in a lifetime: but they are untroubled by problems beyond their power to solve. Their temporary difficulties may be complex in the extreme, but they *always* come out all right in the end: Mom is usually busy whipping up a batch of pies, and Dad has never yet failed to come through in a pinch. This is the mythical middle-America upon which nostalgia for a golden past is built. Home was never like this—but how nice if it had been! No wonder young readers enjoy the adventures of Henry Reed and the Carson Street Detectives. They leave you feeling that it isn't such a bad old world after all. An uncommonly pleasant sensation.

—Joan McGrath

ROBINSON, Joan (Mary) G(ale, née Thomas). Also wrote as Joan Gale Thomas. British. Born in Gerrard's Cross, Buckinghamshire, in 1910. Educated privately, and at Chelsea Illustrators' Studio, London. Married Richard Gavin Robinson in 1941 (second marriage); two daughters. *Died 20 August 1988.*

PUBLICATIONS FOR CHILDREN (illustrated by the author)

Fiction

My Book about Christmas (as Joan Gale Thomas). London, Mowbray, 1946; New York, Morehouse, 1947.
My Garden Book (as Joan Gale Thomas). London, Mowbray, 1947.
Debbie Robbie's Day Nursery. London, University of London Press, 1950.
Susie at Home. London, Harrap, 1953.
Teddy Robinson. London, Harrap, 1953.
More about Teddy Robinson. London, Harrap, 1954.
Teddy Robinson's Book. London, Harrap, 1955.
Dear Teddy Robinson. London, Harrap, 1956.
Mary-Mary. London, Harrap, 1957.
Teddy Robinson Himself. London, Harrap, 1957.

More Mary-Mary. London, Harrap, 1958.
Another Teddy Robinson. London, Harrap, 1960.
Madam Mary-Mary. London, Harrap, 1960.
Keeping Up with Teddy Robinson. London, Harrap, 1964.
Mary-Mary Stories (from *Mary-Mary, More Mary-Mary, Madam Mary-Mary*). London, Harrap, 1965; New York, Coward McCann, 1968.
When Marnie Was There, illustrated by Peggy Fortnum. London, Collins, 1967; New York, Coward McCann, 1968.
Charley, illustrated by Prudence Seward. London, Collins, 1969; New York, Coward McCann, 1970.
The House in the Square, illustrated by Shirley Hughes. London, Collins, 1972.
The Summer Surprise, illustrated by Glenys Ambrus. London, Collins, 1977.
Meg and Maxie. London, Gollancz, 1978; as *The Dark House of the Sea Witch,* New York, Coward McCann, 1979; as *The Sea Witch,* London, Beaver, 1981.

Verse as Joan Gale Thomas

A Stands for Angel. London, Mowbray, 1939; as *A Is for Angel,* New York, Lothrop, 1953.
Our Father. London, Mowbray, 1940; New York, Lothrop, 1952.
If Jesus Came to My House. London, Mowbray, 1941; New York, Lothrop, 1951.
God of All Things. London, Mowbray, 1948.
One Little Baby. London, Mowbray, 1950; New York, Lothrop, 1956.
Little Angels. London, Mowbray, 1951.
The Happy Year. London, Mowbray, 1953.
If I'd Been Born in Bethlehem. London, Mowbray, 1953; New York, Lothrop, 1954.
I Ask a Blessing. London, Mowbray, 1955.
Where Is God? London, Mowbray, 1957; New York, Lothrop, 1959.
The Christmas Angel. London, Mowbray, 1961.
Seven Days. London, Mowbray, 1964.

Other

Monsieur Charbon, défense de fumer (reader), with Gale Young, illustrated by Dick Robinson. London, Harrap, 1962.

*

Illustrator: *Tales of Betsy-May* by Enid Blyton, 1940; *The Dip Bucket,* 1941, *Lift Up the Latch,* 1942, *When the Fire Burns Blue,* 1944, and *Shadows on the Stairs,* 1946, all by Dorothy Ann Lovell; *Beryl's Wonderful Week* by Madeleine Collier, 1944; *Janey,* 1953, and *Janey and Her Friends,* 1953, both by Irene Pearl; *Jonathan on the Farm,* 1954, and *Jonathan and Felicity,* 1955, both by Mary Cockett; *The House under the Tree,* 1954, and *The House in Hyde Park,* 1956, both by Jennifer Ford; *The Carol Book,* 1959.

Joan G. Robinson commented:
(1978) I write slowly and laboriously, always hoping to achieve that final "spontaneity and simplicity" that I remember once being credited with in some review. I try to write from a child's-eye-view without going down on all fours; to entertain not only the child but, in stories for younger children, the patient adult reading aloud—but never at the child's expense.

The Joan Gale Thomas books stemmed from originally designing Christmas cards for Mowbrays, and then as material to illustrate.

The longer books for older children came as a welcome escape from the strict discipline of vocabulary and subject matter which governs the earlier books. These longer books were also an opportunity to write about the loner, the odd one out, the not-so-jolly—though not entirely without humour, I hope. This writing, too, proved to have its own discipline.

*   *   *

Joan G. Robinson wrote many well-crafted tales for the very young, including the Teddy Robinson and the slightly more sophisticated Mary-Mary series. Teddy Robinson the Bear, humorous, with make-believe but no magic, must have entered much family folklore. Nevertheless, her three novels for older children, *When Marnie Was There*, *Charley*, and *The House in the Square*, really established her serious reputation.

All these books are realised through a lonely, sensitive girl in a strange place, the loner, non-joiner, reticent and perforce ungiving, who "spoils everything," wanting both too little and too much, painfully enduring the dreamy poetry of growing up. One gets a direct feel of the child's day, the moments of wanting to be injured and misunderstood, the vindictive retorts stored up for defence, the puzzled resentment when only others get invited to the party, the expectation of disappointment. There is a sense of firelit rooms with a single mute figure in the dark outside, or a solitary mysterious human shadow at a high window. But also the joys of sudden acceptance in a big, cheerful family or of unexpected intimacies with a stranger, glamorous, strangely sympathetic, who may become the legendary, exclusive "best friend." Happiness exists, even if too often beyond reach. Life and people are exciting but unreliable. Robinson's careful observation often contains a drop of fantasy, a hint of fairy-tale glimmering among solid adventure, practical problems, the quarrels and thoughtlessness. Sudden betrayals can crack the world. An adopted child is shocked to discover that foster-parents are paid to love, that generous friendly adults can cheat and lie. The novels have strong awareness of place: wide Norfolk landscapes where creeks and marshes lie silent but alive, and a windmill is uncannily stark against the sky; and a London of tall soundless houses, empty gardens, statues that sometimes seem to breathe.

—Peter Vansittart

ROCKWELL, Anne (née Foote). American. Born in Memphis, Tennessee, 8 February 1934. Educated at the Sculpture Center, New York, 3 years; Pratt Institute, Brooklyn. Married Harlow Rockwell in 1955 (died); two daughters and one son. Member of production department, Silver Burdett, publishers, Morristown, New Jersey, 1952; secretary, Young and Rubicam, advertising, New York, 1953; assistant recreation leader, Goldwater Memorial Hospital, New York, 1954–56. Address: P.O. Box 379, Old Greenwich, Connecticut 06870, U.S.A.

PUBLICATIONS FOR CHILDREN (illustrated by the author)

Fiction

Paul and Arthur Search for an Egg. New York, Doubleday, 1964.
Gypsy Girl's Best Shoes. New York, Parents' Magazine Press, 1966.
Sally's Caterpillar, illustrated by Harlow Rockwell. New York, Parents' Magazine Press, 1966.
Molly's Woodland Garden. New York, Doubleday, 1971.

Paul and Arthur and the Little Explorer. New York, Parents' Magazine Press, 1972.
Thruway, with Harlow Rockwell. New York, Macmillan, 1972.
The Awful Mess. New York, Parents' Magazine Press, 1973.
Gift for a Gift. New York, Parents' Magazine Press, 1974.
The Gollywhopper Egg. New York, Macmillan, 1974; Kingswood, Surrey, World's Work, 1977.
The Story Snail. New York, Macmillan, 1974; Kingswood, Surrey, World's Work, 1977.
Big Boss. New York, Macmillan, 1975; Kingswood, Surrey, World's Work, 1977.
No More Work. New York, Greenwillow, 1976; Kingswood, Surrey, World's Work, 1978.
Albert B. Cub and Zebra: An Alphabet Storybook. New York, Crowell, 1977.
A Bear, A Bobcat, and Three Ghosts. New York, Macmillan, 1977.
Buster and the Bogeyman. New York, Four Winds Press, 1978.
Gogo's Car Breaks Down. New York, Doubleday, 1978.
Gogo's Pay Day. New York, Doubleday, 1978.
Timothy Todd's Good Things Are Gone. New York, Macmillan, 1978.
Willy Runs Away. New York, Dutton, 1978.
Blackout, with Harlow Rockwell. New York, Macmillan, 1979.
The Bump in the Night. New York, Greenwillow, 1979; London, Hamish Hamilton, 1983.
Henry the Cat and the Big Sneeze. New York, Greenwillow, 1980.
Honk Honk! New York, Dutton, 1980.
Out to Sea, with Harlow Rockwell. New York, Macmillan, 1980.
Walking Shoes. New York, Doubleday, 1980.
Happy Birthday to Me, with Harlow Rockwell. New York, Macmillan, 1981.
My Barber, with Harlow Rockwell. New York, Macmillan, 1981.
I Play in My Room, with Harlow Rockwell. New York, Macmillan, 1981.
Thump! Thump! Thump! New York, Dutton, 1981.
Big Bad Goat. New York, Dutton, 1982.
Can I Help? with Harlow Rockwell. New York, Macmillan, 1982.
How My Garden Grew, with Harlow Rockwell. New York, Macmillan, 1982.
I Love My Pets, with Harlow Rockwell. New York, Macmillan, 1982.
Sick in Bed, with Harlow Rockwell. New York, Macmillan, 1982.
The Night We Slept Outside, with Harlow Rockwell. New York, Macmillan, 1983.
My Backyard, with Harlow Rockwell. New York, Macmillan, 1984.
Our Garage Sale, with Harlow Rockwell. New York, Greenwillow, 1984.
When I Go Visiting, with Harlow Rockwell. New York, Macmillan, 1984.
First Comes Spring. New York, Crowell, 1985.
In Our House. New York, Crowell, 1985; London, Heinemann, 1986.
My Babysitter. New York, Crowell, 1985.
At Night. New York, Crowell, 1986.
At the Playground. New York, Crowell, 1986.
In the Morning. New York, Crowell, 1986.
In the Rain. New York, Crowell, 1986.
Come to Town. New York, Crowell, 1987.
Handy Hank Will Fix It. New York, Holt Rinehart, 1988.
Hugo at the Window. New York, Macmillan, and London, Macmillan, 1988.
Things to Play With. New York, Macmillan, 1988.
My Spring Robin, illustrated by Harlow Rockwell and Lizzy Rockwell. New York, Macmillan, 1989.
On Our Vacation. New York, Dutton, 1989.

Other

Filippo's Dome.   New York, Atheneum, 1967; London, Macmillan, 1968.
Glass, Stones and Crown: The Abbé Suger and the Building of St. Denis.   New York, Atheneum, and London, Macmillan, 1968.
The Good Llama.   Cleveland, World, 1968.
The Stolen Necklace: A Picture Story from India.   Cleveland, World, 1968.
Temple on a Hill: The Building of the Parthenon.   New York, Atheneum, 1968.
The Wonderful Eggs of Furicchia (retelling).   Cleveland, World, 1969.
Olly's Polliwogs, with Harlow Rockwell.   New York, Doubleday, 1970.
When the Drum Sang: An African Folktale.   New York, Parents' Magazine Press, 1970.
The Monkey's Whiskers: A Brazilian Folktale.   New York, Parents' Magazine Press, 1971.
Paintbrush and Peacepipe: The Story of George Catlin.   New York, Atheneum, 1971.
The Toolbox, with Harlow Rockwell.   New York, Macmillan, 1971.
Tuhurahura and the Whale (Maori legend).   New York, Parents' Magazine Press, 1971.
What Bobolino Knew (retelling).   New York, McCall, 1971.
The Dancing Stars: An Iroquois Legend.   New York, Crowell, 1972.
Machines.   New York, Macmillan, 1972.
Toad, with Harlow Rockwell.   New York, Doubleday, 1972.
The Boy Who Drew Sheep.   New York, Atheneum, 1973.
Games (and How to Play Them).   New York, Crowell, 1973.
Head to Toe, with Harlow Rockwell.   New York, Doubleday, 1973.
The Wolf Who Had a Wonderful Dream: A French Folktale.   New York, Crowell, 1973.
Befana: A Christmas Story (retelling).   New York, Atheneum, 1974.
Poor Goose: A French Folktale.   New York, Crowell, 1976.
I Like the Library.   New York, Dutton, 1977.
The Girl with a Donkey Tail.   New York, Dutton, 1979.
The Old Woman and Her Pig, and 10 Other Stories (retelling).   New York, Crowell, 1979.
The Supermarket, with Harlow Rockwell.   New York, Macmillan, 1979.
Up a Tall Tree, illustrated by Jim Arnosky.   New York, Doubleday, 1981.
When We Grow Up.   New York, Dutton, 1981.
Boats.   New York, Dutton, 1982; London, Hamish Hamilton, 1983.
Cars.   New York, Dutton, and London, Hamish Hamilton, 1984.
Nice and Clean, with Harlow Rockwell.   New York, Macmillan, 1984.
Trucks.   New York, Dutton, and London, Hamish Hamilton, 1984.
The Emergency Room, with Harlow Rockwell.   New York, Macmillan, 1985; as *Going to Casualty*, London, Hamish Hamilton, 1987.
Planes.   New York, Dutton, and London, Hamish Hamilton, 1985.
Big Wheels.   New York, Dutton, and London, Hamish Hamilton, 1986.
Fire Engines.   New York, Dutton, and London, Viking Kestrel, 1986.
Things That Go.   New York, Dutton, and London, Hamish Hamilton, 1986.
At the Beach, with Harlow Rockwell.   New York, Macmillan, and London, Macmillan, 1987.
Bear Child's Book of Hours.   New York, Crowell, 1987.
Bikes.   New York, Dutton, and London, Viking Kestrel, 1987.
The First Snowfall, with Harlow Rockwell.   New York, Macmillan, 1987.

Puss in Boots and Other Stories.   New York, Macmillan, 1988.
Trains.   New York, Dutton, 1988.

Editor, *Savez-Vous Planter les Choux? and Other French Songs.*   Cleveland, World, 1962; London, Hamish Hamilton, 1972.
Editor, *The Three Bears and 15 Other Stories.*   New York, Crowell, 1975; London, Hamish Hamilton, 1976.

*

Manuscript Collection: Kerlan Collection, University of Minnesota, Minneapolis.

Illustrator: *Eric and the Little Canal Boat* by Lillian Bason, 1967; *The Three Visitors*, 1967, *The Glass Valentine*, 1968, and *A Gift for Tolum*, 1972, all by Marjorie Hopkins; *The Minstrel and the Mountain* by Jane Yolen, 1967; *Mexicali Soup* by Kathryn Hitte, 1970; *Munachar and Munachar*, 1970, and *Master of All Masters*, 1972, both by Joseph Jacobs; *Legends of the Saints* by Ann Petry, 1970; *What Happens to a Hamburger* by Paul Showers, 1970; *The Dancers* by Walter Dean Myers, 1972; *Cunningham's Rooster* by Barbara Brenner, 1975; *Never Hit a Porcupine* by Barbara Williams, 1977; *Bing Bong Bang and Fiddle Dee Dee* by Gerda Mantinband, 1979; *The Stubborn Old Women* by Clyde Robert Bulla, 1980; *Gray Goose and Gander and Other Mother Goose Rhymes*, 1980; *The Turtle and the Two Ducks* by Patricia Plante, 1981; *The Emperor's New Clothes* by Hans Christian Andersen, 1982; *Toot! Toot!* by Steven Kroll, 1983.

Anne Rockwell comments:

My books are for the youngest of children. I loved, and still love, young children's picture books. I feel fortunate to have retained a sense of how young children see the world which enables me to do books for them. My own children reinforced this way of seeing in me so that I can focus on what most small children notice. I see that they are visually very alert and that illustrations can communicate where words are still difficult. In pictures they *see* everything.

*   *   *

In her 25 years of writing books for children, Anne Rockwell has directed her efforts toward a progressively younger audience. Having concentrated in earlier works on scientific and historical books for school-aged children, and on retellings of folktales from all over the world, she has more recently used her talents to create picture books and even board books for very young children. Yet she maintains in her creative work the best aspects of the earlier books: her interest in and talent for the telling of folktales, and a simplicity within diversity in her "true" stories which both satisfies and stimulates young readers.

Rockwell's books for beginning readers capture the flavor of the folktale so well, one easily forgets these are controlled-vocabulary stories. Two of the best of them are *The Story Snail* and *Big Boss*. In the former, a young boy sets out on a journey which is initiated by his encounter with a story-telling snail. He must use his wits and considerable determination to discover that what he most seeks is within him already. The language is simple but captivating; Rockwell even creates a magic word ("Fuzzbuzzoncetherewas") which becomes the hero's version of "Once upon a time."

In *Big Boss* a frog manages to outwit both a tiger and a fox who seek to eat him, and eventually becomes a most unlikely ruler of the forest. Again a seemingly powerless creature uses his imagination and determination, this time to triumph over more powerful adversaries. The clarity and brightness of Rockwell's illustrations is mirrored by that same clarity in her use of language. The folktale convention of word repetition lends itself well to the language limits of the controlled reader. When used by Rockwell, even controlled language has an imaginative, lilting quality.

Rockwell displays her knack for uncomplicated but interesting text in her books for preschool children as well. Sometimes teaming with husband Harlow, sometimes independently, she brings before children a wide range of experiences, always beginning with something common to most children and moving out from it. *Trucks*, for instance, starts with animal children playing with toy trucks, then moves beyond the toy trucks to describe a variety of other trucks and their functions. In the opening of *Planes*, two people stand outside, watching a plane fly overhead; again the child reader is provided with an almost universal experience as a point of departure for the rest of the book. Whether or not the child has ever seen a plane close up or has had the experience of flying, common ground has been provided as a starting point. In both books, Rockwell uses the effective technique of returning to the original scene at the end, which provides a satisfying closure.

In her books for slightly older preschoolers, Rockwell immediately engages children's interest with the adoption of a first-person point of view, in which the narrator is a young child moving through an experience described in great detail. Whether the experience is totally familiar to most children (*Sick in Bed, The Supermarket*), or possibly less familiar (*Our Garage Sale*, or *When I Go Visiting*, which details a boy's overnight stay with his grandparents), there is a basis of familiarity produced by the first-person perspective, which encourages the reader to follow along into possibly less familiar but always varied and interesting territory.

Two Rockwell books which could be enjoyed by children up to first-grade level are also worthy of note. *When We Grow Up* features members of a class talking about their ambitions for the future. It is refreshing in its non-sexist attitudes and jobs which include the typical and the more unusual as well. Her *First Comes Spring* follows Bear Child through all the seasons—ending, as she so often does, where she begins, and depicting a great variety of activities for each season. Unlike many books of this type which overwhelm young senses with too many images, Rockwell's text and illustrations give an overall view, then break the larger view into its smaller components. Again, the featured activities include some that are very familiar, some less common. Both of these books are interesting in themselves and also useful for stimulating thought beyond the confines of the specific texts.

From the realistic world of children's everyday experiences to the more imaginative world of the folktale, Rockwell's fine talent lies in her ability to endow her imaginary stories with realistic detail, and her realistic stories with enough variety to capture interest and stimulate imagination. In both types of stories, she combines surface simplicity with underlying diversity to create eminently worthwhile works for young children.

—Christine Doyle Francis

RODGERS, Mary. American. Born in New York City, 11 January 1931; daughter of the composer Richard Rodgers. Educated at Brearley School, New York, graduated 1948; Mannes College of Music, New York, 1943–48; Wellesley College, Massachusetts, 1948–51. Married 1) Julian B. Beaty, Jr., in 1951 (divorced 1957), one son and two daughters; 2) Henry Guettel in 1961, two sons. Script editor and assistant to the producer, New York Philharmonic Young People's Concerts, CBS-TV, 1957–71; script writer, Hunter College Little Orchestra Society, New York, 1958–59; columnist ("Of Two Minds"), with Dorothy Rodgers, *McCalls* magazine, New York, 1971–78. Composer and lyricist. Recipient: Christopher

award, 1973, 1975. Agent: Flora Roberts Inc., 157 West 57 Street, New York, New York 10019. Address: 91 Central Park West, New York, New York 10023, U.S.A.

PUBLICATIONS FOR CHILDREN

Fiction

The Rotten Book, illustrated by Steven Kellogg. New York, Harper, 1969.
Freaky Friday. New York, Harper, 1972; London, Hamish Hamilton, 1973.
A Billion for Boris. New York, Harper, 1974; London, Hamish Hamilton, 1975.
Summer Switch. New York, Harper, 1982; London, Hamish Hamilton, 1983.

Plays

Davy Jones' Locker (for marionettes; music and lyrics only), book by Arthur Birnkrant and Waldo Salt (produced New York, 1959).
Three to Make Music, music by Linda Rodgers Melnick, lyrics by Rodgers (produced New York, 1959).
Pinocchio (for marionettes), music by Rodgers, lyrics by Sheldon Harnick (produced New York, 1973).

Screenplays: *Freaky Friday*, 1977; *The Devil and Max Devlin*, with Jimmy Sangster, 1980.

PUBLICATIONS FOR ADULTS

Other

A Word to the Wives, with Dorothy Rodgers. New York, Knopf, 1970.

*

Manuscript Collection: Kerlan Collection, University of Minnesota, Minneapolis.

Music: **Plays**—*Once upon a Mattress* by Jay Thompson, Marshall Barer, and Dean Fuller, 1958; *Hot Spot* by Jack Weinstock and Willie Gilbert, 1963; *Young Mark Twain*, 1964; *The Mad Show* by Larry Siegel and Stan Hart, 1966; **Television**—*Mary Martin Spectacular*, 1959; *Feathertop*, 1961.

* * *

Humor is a scarce but precious commodity in contemporary technological society. Mary Rodgers breathes laughter into the situations, the characters, and the language of her books.

A child's imagination runs rampant in *The Rotten Book*, as Simon thinks of ways of being naughty. Fantasy is superimposed on a realistic background in *Freaky Friday* and its sequel, *A Billion for Boris*. Annabel Andrews awakens to find she has the body of her mother, while the ordinary events of life transpire. She witnesses the washing machine overflowing, and she mistakenly identifies her boyfriend Boris's mother as a cleaning lady, but she also participates in the parent-teacher conference in which she herself is discussed. Near tragedy is averted in *A Billion for Boris* when the television set projects tomorrow's news: the soup suspected of botulism can be destroyed, and people are persuaded to divert their plans.

The characters themselves are hilarious. Boris's eccentric artist mother has no organizational or financial skills, and he has balanced her checkbook since his ninth year. The participants in the school conference are caricatures of every child's teacher. Teenage Virginia has "theatrical aspirations, and correct grammar." Language and dialogue are wrought for their entertaining qualities. Even the dedication of the third book gives insight into the author's humor—"to my small sons, Adam and Alec, without whom I was finally able to finish it." According to the critic Betsy Wade, the author "appears to have a sharp ear for the particular tone adults use on children." Yet when the parents disagree about camp and a raincoat for Annabel, they use contemporary sophisticated adult expressions. The latter two books are narrated in the first person by 13 and then 14-year-old Annabel Andrews, and parentheses are used generously for asides directed to the reader.

Jane Langton noted in her review of *Freaky Friday* that "the pages rush by, right now in 1972, and it might all be happening in the apartment next door." The very incidents and phrases which make the books so specific will unfortunately also date them. Teenage pranks go in and out of fashion, and burning kleenex in the toilet is now passé. The telephone ad "let your fingers do the walking" and reference to the noted criminal lawyer, F. Lee Bailey, will fall dead on the ears of the next reading generation. Even now "hi-fi" has been replaced by "tapes" and the "hoover" is rarely used in America to refer to the vacuum cleaner. Slang such as "zing one of those carts" and alluding to the "monthly excuse" will contribute to the eventual demise of the books except as representative of an era.

Nevertheless, the books are very popular. Alix Nelson, in the *New York Times Book Review* (24 November 1974), noted that *A Billion for Boris* "assumes an urban and sophisticated frame of reference on the part of the reader, and it evokes so much New York City local color (from the Village to 125th Street by way of Central Park West, Lord & Taylor, and a walk-up on West 53rd) that it really is the perfect New York City book."

Mary Rodgers is the daughter of Richard Rodgers, and has composed children's musicals such as *Davy Jones' Locker, Young Mark Twain,* and *Pinocchio.*

—Karen Nelson Hoyle

RODMAN, Maia. See **WOJCIECHOWSKA, Maia.**

ROOSE-EVANS, James. British. Born in London, 11 November 1927. Educated at St. Benet's Hall, Oxford, B.A. 1952, M.A. 1957. Served in the Royal Army Educational Corps, 1947–49. Artistic director, Maddermarket Theatre, Norwich, 1954–55; member of the faculty, Juilliard School of Music, New York, 1955–56; staff member, Royal Academy of Dramatic Art, London, 1957–62; founding director, Hampstead Theatre Club, London, 1959–69. Since 1969 founding director, Stage Two Theatre Workshop, London. Since 1974 founder and chairman, Bleddfa Trust-Centre for Caring and the Arts in Mid Wales. Since 1981 ordained priest. Columnist, *Woman* magazine, London, 1986–88. Children's book reviewer for *Financial Times* and *Hampstead and Highgate Express.* Recipient: British Theatre Association award, 1983. Lives in London. Agent: David Higham Associates, 5–8 Lower John Street, London W1R 4HA, England.

PUBLICATIONS FOR CHILDREN (illustrated by Brian Robb)

Fiction

The Adventures of Odd and Elsewhere. London, Deutsch, 1971.
The Secret of the Seven Bright Shiners. London, Deutsch, 1972.
Odd and the Great Bear. London, Deutsch, 1973.
Elsewhere and the Gathering of the Clowns. London, Deutsch, 1974.
The Return of the Great Bear. London, Deutsch, 1975; as *Odd to the Rescue,* London, Magnet, 1983.
The Secret of Tippity-Witchit. London, Deutsch, 1975.
The Lost Treasure of Wales. London, Deutsch, 1977.

PUBLICATIONS FOR ADULTS

Plays

Cider with Rosie, with Sam Langdon, adaptation of the book by Laurie Lee (also director: produced London, 1963; revised version, produced Cheltenham, 1982).
The Little Clay Cart, adaptation of a work by Henry Wells (produced London, 1964). London, Elek, 1965.
Oedipus Now, adaptation of the translation by E.F. Watling of the play by Sophocles (also director: produced London, 1972).
84 Charing Cross Road, adaptation of the book by Helene Hanff (also director: produced Salisbury and London, 1981; New York, 1982).
Re: Joyce, with Maureen Lipman, music and lyrics by Richard Addinsell and Joyce Grenfell (produced Farnham, Surrey, and London, 1988).

Radio Documentaries: *The Female Messiah,* 1975; *Acrobats of God,* 1976; *The Third Adam,* from a book by Jerzy Peterkiewicz, 1977; *Your Isadora,* 1977; *Topsy and Ted* (play), 1977; *A Well Conducted Theatre,* 1981; *The Country of the Pointed Firs,* 1981; *Lady Managers,* 1982; *A Well Governed Stage,* 1983; *The Story of My Life* (on Augustus Hare), 1987.

Other

Directing a Play: James Roose-Evans on the Art of Directing and Acting. London, Studio Vista, and New York, Theatre Arts, 1968.
Experimental Theatre from Stanislavsky to Today. London, Studio Vista, and New York, Universe, 1970; revised edition, 1973; revised edition, as *Experimental Theatre from Stanislavsky to Peter Brook,* London, Routledge, and New York, Universe, 1984; revised edition, Routledge, 1989.
London Theatre: From the Globe to the National. London, Phaidon Press, and New York, Dutton, 1977.
Inner Journey, Outer Journey: Finding a Spiritual Centre in Everyday Life. London, Rider, 1987.

Editor, *Darling Ma: Letters of Joyce Grenfell.* London, Hodder and Stoughton, 1988.
Editor, *The Time of My Life: The Wartime Journals of Joyce Grenfell.* London, Hodder and Stoughton, 1989.

*

Theatrical Activities:
Director: **Plays**—most of his own plays, and plays at the Maddermarket Theatre, Norwich, 1954–55, and the Belgrade Theatre, Coventry, 1957–59; *Nothing to Declare,* on tour, 1959; Pitlochry

Festival (6 plays), 1960; *The Dumb Waiter* by Harold Pinter, London, 1960; *Under Milk Wood* by Dylan Thomas, London, 1961, 1973; at the Hampstead Theatre Club, London: *The Seagull* by Chekhov, 1962, *In at the Kill* by Frederick Bradnum, *Private Lives* by Noël Coward, *The Square* by Marguerite Duras, and *The Singing Dolphin* by Beverley Cross, 1963, *The Cloud* and *The Tower* by Barry Bermange, *The Corn Is Green* by Emlyn Williams, and *He Who Gets Slapped* by Leonid Andreyev, 1964, *Hippolytus* by Andrew Sinclair from a book by Dylan Thomas, *Flashing into the Dark*, and *Letters from an Eastern Front*, 1966, *Country Dance* by James Kennaway, *The Happy Apple* by Jack Pulman, *Nathan and Tabileth*, and *Oldenberg* by Barry Bermange, and *The Two Character Play* by Tennessee Williams, 1967, *Spitting Image* by Colin Spencer, 1968; *An Ideal Husband* by Wilde, London, 1965; *Chester Mystery Plays*, Chester, 1973; *The Taming of the Shrew*, London, 1974; *A Streetcar Named Desire* by Tennessee Williams, South Africa tour, *The Vortex* and *Fallen Angels*, both by Noël Coward, 1975; *Romeo and Juliet*, London, 1976; *An Inspector Calls* by J.B. Priestley, London, 1978; *Mate!* by C. Scott Forbes, London, 1978; *Donkeys' Years* by Michael Frayn and *Private Lives* by Coward, tour; *A Personal Affair* by Ian Curteis, London, 1982; *The Seven Year Itch* by George Axelrod, London, 1985; *Now We Are Sixty* by Giles Brandreth and Julian Slade, Cambridge, 1986; *The Best of Friends* by Hugh Whitemore, London, 1987.

*   *   *

The seven Odd and Elsewhere stories are conceived by James Roose-Evans as a single saga, though they can all be read separately. During their adventures Odd, the teddy-bear, and Elsewhere, the toy clown, achieve a sense of their own identity, an understanding of responsibility, and a purpose in life; in short, they begin to grow up. But as this process involves some muscular adventure, a good deal of humour, and a constant awareness of the joy of discovery—the reader may learn about, among other things, the National Trust, butterflies, Grimaldi, beekeeping, and even a few words of Welsh—there is little danger of solemnity overwhelming the narrative. This is not to say that there are no serious moments; the Great Bear and the King of the Clowns, the respective mentors of Odd and Elsewhere, have much to teach, but the author manages to avoid a patronizing tone, even when the occasional "moral" creeps in.

Roose-Evans has spent much of his working life in the theatre, and he is especially good at describing the excitement and anguish of public performance, a constant theme. Circuses and Arthurian myth, liberally modified, have provided inspiration for his stories—all of which are set in Fenton House, Hampstead, and Wales—but the main thread is the traditional one of the defeat of Evil by Good. The methods, though, are often unusual. Butterflies, birds, and bees, at different times, all play a crucial part in rescuing the heroes and their friends, and this reflects the general delight in Nature that informs the books.

The small bear and his friend begin as toys (Odd even loses an arm which is repaired in the first book), but they progress to being a real bear and a real clown and are sometimes indistinguishable from small boys who bleed when cut and experience shock, humiliation, and triumph. To an adult this may seem a fault, but Roose-Evans claims the device is a deliberate reflection of the way children identify with their toys.

Despite a few other infelicities—the out-of-place grotesquerie of Mr. Goodman and Arbuthnot on their first appearance, the killing off of enemies without regret, and the almost invariable consigning of females to kitchens—these books have a pace and inventiveness, a feeling for language, and an appreciation of lovable eccentricity that will make them delightful companions to generations of children.

Incidentally, Roose-Evans is well served by his illustrator, Brian Robb, who captures the tone exactly.

—Heather Neill

———————

ROSEN, Michael (Wayne). British. Born in Harrow, Middlesex, 7 May 1946. Educated at Harrow Weald County School, 1957–62; Watford Grammar School, Hertfordshire, 1962–64; Middlesex Hospital Medical School, London, 1964–65; Wadham College, Oxford, 1965–69, B.A. (honours) in English 1969. Married 1) Susanna Steele; 2) Geraldine Clark; five children. Freelance writer and broadcaster: created *Everybody Here* series, Channel 4 Television, London, 1982–83. Recipient: *Sunday Times*-National Union of Students Drama Festival award, 1968; Greater London Arts Association C. Day Lewis fellowship, 1976; *Signal* Poetry award, 1982; Children's Rights Workshop Other award, 1983. Agent: Peters Fraser and Dunlop, Fifth Floor, The Chambers, Chelsea Harbour, Lots Road, London SW10 0XF. Address: 49 Parkholme Road, London E8 3AQ, England.

PUBLICATIONS FOR CHILDREN

Fiction

Once There Was a King Who Promised He Would Never Chop Anyone's Head Off, illustrated by Kathy Henderson. London, Deutsch, 1976.
The Bakerloo Flea, illustrated by Quentin Blake. London, Longman, 1979.
Nasty!, illustrated by Amanda Macphail. London, Longman, 1982; revised edition, London, Penguin, 1984.
Hairy Tales and Nursery Crimes, illustrated by Alan Baker. London, Deutsch, 1985.
You're Thinking about Doughnuts, illustrated by Tony Pinchuck. London, Deutsch, 1987.
The Horribles (stories), illustrated by John Watson. London, Walker, 1988.
Norma and the Washing Machine, illustrated by David Higham. London, Deutsch, 1988.
The Class Two Monster, illustrated by Maggie Ling. London, Heinemann, 1989.

Verse

Mind Your Own Business, illustrated by Quentin Blake. London, Deutsch, and New York, Phillips, 1974.
Wouldn't You Like to Know, illustrated by Quentin Blake. London, Deutsch, 1977; revised edition, London, Penguin, 1981.
You Tell Me, with Roger McGough, illustrated by Sara Midda. London, Kestrel, 1979.
You Can't Catch Me!, illustrated by Quentin Blake. London, Deutsch, 1981.
Quick, Let's Get Out of Here, illustrated by Quentin Blake. London, Deutsch, 1983.
Bloody L.I.A.R.S., illustrated by Alan Gilbey. Privately printed, 1984.
Don't Put Mustard in the Custard, illustrated by Quentin Blake. London, Deutsch, 1985.
When Did You Last Wash Your Feet?, illustrated by Tony Pinchuck. London, Deutsch, 1986.
The Hypnotiser, illustrated by Andrew Tiffen. London, Deutsch, 1988.

We're Going on a Bear Hunt, illustrated by Helen Oxenbury. London, Walker, 1989.

Other

I See a Voice (on poetry). London, Thames Television-Hutchinson, 1981.
A Cat and Mouse Story (retelling), illustrated by William Rushton. London, Deutsch, 1982.
How to Get Out of the Bath and Other Problems, illustrated by Graham Round. London, Scholastic, 1984.
Scrapbooks (*Smelly Jelly Smelly Fish, Under the Bed, Hard-Boiled Legs, Spollyollydiddilytiddlyitis*), illustrated by Quentin Blake. London, Walker, 4 vols., 1986–87; first 3 vols. published Englewood Cliffs, New Jersey, Prentice Hall, 1986–87; last vol. published as *Down at the Doctor's*, New York, Simon and Schuster, 1987.
Silly Stories (jokes), illustrated by Mik Brown. London, Kingfisher, 1988.
The Wicked Tricks of Till Owlyglass (retellings), illustrated by Fritz Wegner. London, Walker, 1989.

Editor, *Everybody Here* (miscellany). London, Bodley Head, 1982.
Editor, *Inky Pinky Ponky: Children's Playground Rhymes*, with Susanna Steele, illustrated by Dan Jones. London, Granada, 1982.
Editor, with David Jackson, *Speaking to You*. London, Macmillan, 1984.
Editor, with Joan Griffiths, *That'd Be Telling*. Cambridge, Cambridge University Press, 1985.
Editor, *The Kingfisher Book of Children's Poetry*. London, Kingfisher, 1985.
Editor, *A Spider Bought a Bicycle and Other Poems*, illustrated by Inga Moore. London, Kingfisher, 1986.
Editor, *The Kingfisher Book of Funny Stories*, illustrated by Tony Blundell. London, Kingfisher, 1988.

PUBLICATIONS FOR ADULTS

Plays

Backbone (produced Oxford, 1967; London, 1968). London, Faber, 1968.
Stewed Figs (produced Durham, 1968).

Radio Play: *Regis Debray*, 1971.

Other

Did I Hear You Write? London, Deutsch, 1989.

*

Michael Rosen comments:

Mostly I write about myself. This is potentially very boring, but I try to make sure it isn't by meeting children in schools and libraries, and informally. I try to discover where my experiences overlap with theirs. Some people are worried about whether what I write is "poetry." If they are worried, let them call it something else, e.g., "stuff."

*   *   *

Michael Rosen is a poet and chronicler of urban fairy stories. His range includes playground chants, rap, blank verse autobiography, and reworked versions of nursery rhymes. He can engage toddlers and sixth-form students with equal facility. One might fairly nominate him as the poet laureate of post-war youth. There is indeed a hint of Betjeman about his ruminations on a West London childhood and at Pinner station, where Rosen waited for his "Mum" and contemplated "the big dark benches" their literary paths cross. Instead of Joan Hunter Dunn we have "Lizzie, I'm afraid of saying I think you're great…the teachers call you tomboy."

Now coarse, now sensitive; the author's treatment of wasps neatly exemplifies both modes. In *Wouldn't You Like to Know* pity is invoked first for a hooked fish whose "last moment is a ride in the sky" and then for a wasp doomed to extinction in a sealed jar. In the stories *Nasty!* wasps again feature, but now as vehicles of urban horror. With *You're Thinking about Doughnuts* and poems on pizza-eating by train or on scoffing cake from the fridge, we find a recurring preoccupation with food. There is a fantasy about mad meals like fried cork, a description of a family blow-out at the Hollywood Cafe. His son Joe suffers a nightmare of having his food removed. And most memorable, there is the garlic omelette which the author ate the night before a wedding. It is notable that in *Mind Your Own Business* it is "his brother who got married in a Wimpy Bar" but when a prose version appears in *That'd Be Telling* (an anthology Rosen edited with Joan Griffiths) the garlic has been transferred to blight his cousin's wedding. Such recycling of old material somehow adds to the charm. There is always room at the foot of the page for another chorus of "Down behind the dustbin I met a dog called Sid." The books are great tubs, from which items, pleasant or unpleasant, familiar or disconcerting, may be hauled, examined, and returned. There are old jokes like the one about the man with a banana in his ear. Friends like Harrybo come and go. Memories of the author's school days are interspersed with squibs about his own children. As though the darts which wounded him then were still in his back, the humiliations and compensations of childhood, bouncing on settees, sticking a toe up the cold tap, coming home to an empty house, or the restrictions of communal outings are lovingly recapitulated. As a younger one himself, Rosen is particularly acute on relations between brothers. "Watch" in *Quick, Let's Get Out of Here* and the competition to receive the most post in *Wouldn't You Like to Know* are comic gems. There are snapshots of his grandparents' Hackney, and of today's Hackney, to which he has returned, to rail against the racism he sees in the park. As a Jew, Rosen has experienced it firsthand; at school they threw "…a penny on the floor to see if I'd pick it up." Not only is nothing forgotten, each nugget of memory, even where deceit is later revealed, retains its original lustre. Thus the playground conman who "hypnotised Trevor" with a conker and the invisible bar Mike's brother kept over his bed are now immortalised in the collections. In *Quick, Let's Get Out of Here* the author visits a clearing house for "Lost things"—"I spread out on the floor all those things that I had lost and I've now got back again, and that makes me very happy." This might be a coda for the entire canon. In these collections seamlessly interwoven with Quentin Blake's drawings there are poems as well attuned to their young readers as any ever written.

More recently Rosen has tended to differentiate his writing either for the very young or for near school-leavers. The series including *Hard-Boiled Legs* and *Under the Bed* are scrapbooks on themes like bedtime or going to the doctor's. Despite their brevity, not always to be disparaged, they do not fail to find their mark. *When Did You Last Wash Your Feet?* is a much more ambitious project geared towards teenagers. Showing the influence of Raymond Briggs, it contains something to annoy or enchant the adult on every page. Acne is lovingly dwelt on, there are portraits of unsavoury teachers, and a recollection of the Pinner Village Stompers's only gig. The pages are festooned with cartoons and enlivened with simplistic, if well-meaning, propaganda against sexism, racism, and the class system. Diverging further, *Hairy Tales and Nursery Crimes* introduce with "Pushing books" (Puss in Boots) and "The Fried Pepper of Hamelin" clever exercises in surrealism. In *Don't Put Mustard in the Custard* we find verse on video and digital watches—authentic modern rhymes. And in *Nasty!* stories of giant fleas roaming the underground and mice committing hara-kiri reveal Rosen to be a prose writer of engaging dash.

—John Churcher

———

ROSS, Diana. British Born in Valletta, Malta, 8 July 1910. Educated at Kensington High School, London; Girton College, Cambridge, B.A. (honours) in history 1931; Central School of Art, London, 1932–34. Married Antony Denney in 1939 (divorced 1948); twin daughters and one son. Art teacher, 1930–34. Address: Minster House, Shaw, Melksham, Wiltshire, England.

PUBLICATIONS FOR CHILDREN

Fiction

The Story of the Beetle Who Lived Alone, illustrated by Margaret Kaye. London, Faber, 1941.
Uncle Anty's Album, with Antony Denney. London, Faber, 1942.
The Golden Hen and Other Stories, illustrated by Gri. London, Faber, 1942.
The Little Red Engine Gets a Name, illustrated by George Lewitt-Him. London, Faber, 1942.
The Wild Cherry, illustrated by Gri. London, Faber, 1943.
Nursery Tales, illustrated by Nancy Innes. London, Faber, 1944.
The Story of the Little Red Engine, illustrated by Leslie Wood. London, Faber, 1945.
The Story of Louisa, illustrated by Margaret Kaye. London, Penguin, 1945.
The Little Red Engine Goes to Market [*Goes to Town, Goes Travelling, and the Rocket, Goes Home, Goes to Be Mended, and the Taddlecombe Outing, Goes Carolling*], illustrated by Leslie Wood. London, Faber, 8 vols., 1946–71.
Whoo, Whoo, The Wind Blew, illustrated by Leslie Wood. London, Faber, 1946.
The Tooter and Other Nursery Tales, illustrated by Irene Hawkins. London, Faber, 1951.
The Enormous Apple Pie and Other Miss Pussy Tales, illustrated by Peggy Fortnum. London, Lutterworth Press, 1951.
Ebenezer the Big Balloon, illustrated by Leslie Wood. London, Faber, 1952.
The Bridal Gown and Other Stories, illustrated by Gri. London, Faber, 1952.
The Bran Tub, illustrated by Gri. London, Lutterworth Press, 1954.
William and the Lorry, illustrated by Shirley Hughes. London, Faber, 1956.
Child of Air, illustrated by Gri. London, Lutterworth Press, 1957.
The Dreadful Boy, illustrated by Prudence Seward. London, Hamish Hamilton, 1959.
The Merry-Go-Round, illustrated by Shirley Hughes. London, Lutterworth Press, 1963.
Old Perisher, illustrated by Edward Ardizzone. London, Faber, 1965.
Nothing to Do, illustrated by Constance Marshall. London, Hamish Hamilton, 1966.
I Love My Love with an A: Where Is He?, illustrated by Leslie Wood. London, Faber, 1972.

Other

The World at Work (*Getting You Things, Making You Things*). London, Country Life, 2 vols., 1939.

*

Diana Ross comments:
I always told stories from early childhood to my brother and sister. I began to write down my stories when I was teaching—to start the class off, I read my stories then they read theirs. The Red Engine series began as a goodnight story for my nephew John Scott who lived in a house above a railway cutting on a branch line. Most of the nursery tale and "true" type of story were based on incidents from family life. The ones I have most enjoyed writing have been the fairy stories written for myself—and most of all the Miss Pussy and old Jackanapes stories. Gri—who illustrated some of my books when I could persuade publishers of his merits—was in fact my cat who would sit on top of my drawings as I worked on them.

*   *   *

Diana Ross writes two kinds of stories: nursery tales for very young children and magical tales for anyone who enjoys the fiction of fairyland. She has produced both kinds concurrently over a period spanning more than 40 years. Her writing draws inspiration from knowledge and love of country matters. It also owes much to her artistic training—as Gri she illustrated many of her own books. Pleasure in her family circle is a third, formative influence.

When she was a child, Ross told stories to her brother and sister. Later, as teacher, mother, aunt, and grandmother, she went on telling them. And this first-hand awareness of small children *listening* to stories like *Whoo, Whoo, The Wind Blew*, shaped her style. Her nursery tales make constant use of repetition, alliteration, and the cumulative tricks that delight small children. She does not waste words. At the same time, there is a great deal of accurately observed detail—the kind that educates as well as entertains. *Ebenezer the Big Balloon* is a good example. It was no accident that BBC producers seized on her work. The 1950's was a time of expansion in children's radio and television, and Ross was a pioneer contributor.

She helped to develop a new kind of nursery realism—what she herself calls coat-and-gumboot stories about ordinary children doing ordinary things, like 4-year-old Johnny in "The Tooter." She was also one of the first to explore a new kind of hero. As anthropomorphic as Pooh and Piglet, the Little Red Engine was no longer a privileged middle-class, cuddly toy. He was a worker serving the whole community, in tune with the classless, mechanised society of post-war England. It is worth noting here that the first Little Red Engine story was published four years before W.V. Awdry's first railway book came into print.

The Miss Pussy stories are her most interesting fairytales, written as much for her own pleasure as to entertain her readers. The language and unusual use of the present tense is often very sophisticated. Miss Pussy is a feline Miss Matty in another *Cranford*. Old Tom Cat is her Captain Brown. But in their village there is an adversary—Jackanapes. And magic is an everyday occurrence. There is much quiet wisdom buried in these romantic tales. Ross writes mockingly but you sense her underlying compassion. She understands human frailty and even makes it appear endearing. In a moment of stress, Miss Pussy considers her ambivalent feelings for Jackanapes, lying sick and sorry for himself in his sleazy lodgings. "Perhaps," she thinks, "in the pattern of our lives we need the bad as much as the good. There is no sun without shadow, and I am as much in debt to Jackanapes for the tricks he has played upon me as perhaps I am to another for the good they have done me." Not to everybody's taste, but rare meat for a connoisseur.

—Joy Whitby

———

ROSS, Tony. British. Born in London, 10 August 1938. Educated at the Liverpool Regional College of Art, 1958–61. Married 1) Carol Dawn D'Arcy in 1961 (divorced); 2) Joan Lillian Spokes in 1971 (divorced); 3) Zoë Ash in 1979, one son and two daughters. Graphic designer, Littlewoods, Liverpool, 1961–62, and Smith Kline and French Pharmaceuticals, Welwyn Garden City, Hertfordshire, 1962–64; art director, Brunnings Advertising, Manchester, 1964–65; lecturer in illustration, Manchester Polytechnic, 1965–86. Recipient: Silver Pencil award (Netherlands) (twice); Silver Paintbrush award (Netherlands) (twice); Children's Literature prize (Germany). Address: Rivendell House, Kerswell, Cullompton, Devon EX15 2EW, England.

PUBLICATIONS FOR CHILDREN (illustrated by the author)

Fiction

Tales from Mr. Toffy's Circus (Big Ethel, Blodwen, Bop, Mr. Toffy, Samuel, Tiger Harry). London, Fabbri, 6 vols., 1973.
Hugo and the Man Who Stole Colours. London, Andersen Press, and Chicago, Follett, 1977.
Hugo and the Wicked Winter. London, Sidgwick and Jackson, 1977.
Norman and Flop Meet the Toy Bandit. London, Thurman, 1977.
Hugo and Oddsock. London, Andersen Press, 1978; Windermere, Florida, Rourke, 1982.
The Greedy Little Cobbler. London, Andersen Press, 1979; Woodbury, New York, Barrons, 1980.
The True Story of Mother Goose and Her Son Jack. London, Andersen Press, 1979; Windermere, Florida, Rourke, 1982.
Hugo and the Ministry of Holidays. London, Andersen Press, 1980; as *Hugo and the Bureau of Holidays*, Windermere, Florida, Rourke, 1982.
Naughty Nigel. London, Andersen Press, 1982; as *Naughty Nicky*, New York, Holt Rinehart, 1983.
Jack the Giantkiller. London, Andersen Press, 1983.
I'm Coming to Get You. London, Andersen Press, and New York, Dial Press, 1984.
Towser and the Terrible Thing [Water Rats, Sadie's Birthday, Haunted House, Funny Face, Magic Apple]. London, Andersen Press, 6 vols., 1984–85; first 3 vols. published New York, Pantheon, 1984.
Lazy Jack. London, Andersen Press, 1985; New York, Dial Press, 1986.
I Want My Potty. London, Andersen Press, and New York, Kane Miller, 1986.
Oscar Got the Blame. London, Andersen Press, 1987; New York, Dial Press, 1988.
Super Dooper Jezebel. London, Andersen Press, and New York, Farrar Straus, 1988.
I Want a Cat. London, Andersen Press, 1988; New York, Farrar Straus, 1989.

Plays

Television Plays: *What's in a Name, King of All the Birds, Oscar Buys the Biscuits, Muddy Milly, Spacemare* (all *Time for a Story* series), 1985–86; *Towser* series.

Other (retellings)

Goldilocks and the Three Bears. London, Andersen Press, 1976.
The Pied Piper of Hamelin. London, Andersen Press, 1977; New York, Lothrop, 1978.
Little Red Riding Hood. London, Andersen Press, 1978; New York,

Doubleday, 1979.
Jack and the Beanstalk. London, Andersen Press, 1980; New York, Delacorte Press, 1981.
Puss in Boots. London, Andersen Press, and New York, Delacorte Press, 1981.
The Enchanted Pig. London, Andersen Press, 1982; New York, Bedrick, 1983.
The Three Pigs. London, Andersen Press, and New York, Pantheon, 1983.
Jack the Giantkiller. London, Andersen Press, 1983.
The Boy Who Cried Wolf. London, Andersen Press, and New York, Dial Press, 1985.
Foxy Fables. London, Andersen Press, and New York, Kane Miller, 1986.
Stone Soup. London, Andersen Press, and New York, Dial Press, 1987.
Hansel and Gretel. London, Andersen Press, 1989.

*

Illustrator: *Did I Ever Tell You* series by Iris Grender, 6 vols., 1978–85; *Mr. Bowser* series, 9 vols., 1979–87, and *Chaos Comes to Chivvy Chase*, 1988, all by Philip Curtis; *Whizz Bang: Two Monkey Tales* by Patricia Gray and David Mackay, 1979; *The Charge of the Mouse Brigade*, 1979, and *The Tale of Admiral Mouse*, 1981, both by Bernard Stone; *Hare and Badger Go to Town* by Naomi Lewis, 1981; *The Methuen Book of Strange Tales*, 1981, and *The Methuen Book of Sinister Stories*, 1982, both edited by Jean Russell; *Clement Aplati* by Jeff Brown, 1982; *Kaspar and the Iron Poodle* by J.K. Hooper, 1982; *The Reluctant Vampire*, 1982, and *The Vampire's Revenge*, 1983, both by Eric Morecambe; *Le Plaisir des Mots* by Georges Jean, 1982; *Le Livre des Marins* by Dominique Duviard, 1983; *Le Livre de la Peinture* by Adrian Sington, 1983; *Paper Flags and Penny Ices*, 1984, and *Hanky-Panky*, 1986, both by Roger Collinson; *Marmalade Jim and the Fox* by Alan Sillitoe, 1984; *The Shrieking Face*, 1984, *Terrible Tuesday*, 1985, and *Pilkie's Progress*, 1986, all by Hazel Townson; *The End of the Tale and Other Stories* by W.J. Corbett, 1985; *Limericks* by Michael Palin, 1985; *William*, 1986, and *Just William*, 1987, both by Richmal Crompton; *Alfonso Bonzo* by Andrew Davies, 1986; *The Phantom Lollipop Lady*, 1986, and *Rhinestone Rhino*, 1989, both by Adrian Henri; *Jenna and the Troublemaker*, 1986, *The Trouble with Harry*, 1987, and *Anyone Seen Harry Lately?*, 1988, all by Hiawyn Oram; *The Treasure Sock* by Pat Thompson, 1986; *The King Bird* by A.H. Benjamin, 1987; *Dangleboots* by Dennis Hamley, 1987; *Open Door: Bill's Old Banger and Other Stories* by Elizabeth Lawrence, 1987; *Wesley and the Dinosaurs* by David Mackay, 1987; *Dixie's Demon*, 1987, *Wolf Pie*, 1987, and *Dr. Monsoon Taggert's Amazing Finishing Academy*, 1989, all by Andrew Matthews; *Meanwhile Back at the Ranch* by Trinka Noble, 1987; *Playschool Book of Songs*, 1987; *La Grande Bretagne*, 1987; *Fantastic Mr. Fox* by Roald Dahl, 1988; *The Whipping Boy* by Sid Fleischman, 1988; *The Fantora Family Files* by Adèle Geras, 1988; *The Clever Potato* by Vernon Scannell, 1988; *The Knight Who Was Afraid of the Dark* by Barbara Shook Hazen, 1989; *Earthlets, As Explained by Professor Xargle* by Jeanne Willis, 1989.

Tony Ross comments:

My main, and original interest in illustrating children's books, both in colour and black and white, gives way slightly to an interest in the words. I am happy to leave teaching to the teachers and philosophy to the philosophers, both of which abound in children's books. I try to entertain. Most of my aims and ambitions are private ones, and are better staying that way.

Trying to understand children, though, is proving to be a fascinating and enlightening experience.

The motivation, of course, is the enjoyment a pen and a sheet of blank paper brings—certainly to me, every time, hopefully to others.

*   *   *

Tony Ross is a prolific writer-illustrator, who has created a succession of memorable protagonists, from Hugo the Mouse, who meets interesting characters on his strange adventures, Naughty Nigel, a boy who deliberately mishears everything said to him, Towser the dog, whose admirable qualities include kindness and generosity, to Super Dooper Jezebel, the model child who gets snapped up by a crocodile. Ross is equally well-known for his updating of traditional folk- and fairytales in picture-book format, which cast a powerful charm upon children, parents, and teachers alike.

As for the first group, Ross successfully identifies the concerns and fantasy life of children. For example, how may a child reconcile the Santa story with the strong possibility, or certainty, that it is Mother or Father who fills the Christmas stocking? In *Hugo and the Ministry of Holidays* Ross offers a gratifying solution to the puzzle; his over-worked Santas enlist the aid of parents to resolve the delivery problems. Again, who is to say whether an imaginary friend conceived to act as a substitute for oneself in every awkward situation is any less "real" than one of flesh and blood, as in *Oscar Got the Blame*? Ross also touches the adult nerve; we all recognise the single-mindedness of Jessy in *I Want a Cat*, who takes her campaign to the extremes of wearing a cat suit and behaving in a feline manner; her parents finally capitulate whereupon she declares she hates cats and wants a dog; in their turn children have no difficulty in identifying with Jessy's wiles, and her fantasy of actually being the object of her own desires. A darker tale, *I'm Coming to Get You*, addresses a child's fear of the unknown, externally projected as a monster, and with a witty twist shows how easily and naturally fear is reduced and squashed in daylight.

Ross's literary tale-telling favours a deadpan humour and aims to establish intimacy with the reader. His visual style varies considerably, but whatever he does, he always displays a strong sense of page design, and a masterly control of his media. Deceptively sketchy at times, his pen romps along, in the tradition of English narrative illustration. However whiskery fine, feathery light, frothy, bold, or meticulously incised, the line has unquenchable vitality. Ross varies the medium to enhance the tone of the text. Watercolour might be lightly applied, in dip and skimming washes upon rapidly executed drawings as in *I Want My Potty*, a tale in which time is of essence. Jessy's story is pictured in crayon scribble as physically determined and full of purpose as the child herself. The magical world of *Hugo and the Man Who Stole Colours* is made more mysterious by shadowy cross hatching, which settles the images on the page.

Ross is an outstanding colourist. In his comic rural folktale world uninhibited colour floats across the skies—sharp lemon, sandy pinks, and melting conjunctions of unlikely green, cerulean, and rose. Though Ross uses a wide palette he often organises a painting in a limited range of close hues to create a particular mood, as in *Puss in Boots*, when he denotes Puss stopping the king's coach, and exemplifies the animal's nerves of steel by picturing it all in controlled cool hues of blue and grey. Witty visual metaphors reward close readings. Goldilocks stumps into her story in her oversize track shoes, about to "put her foot in it" almost continuously. Puss has his wild gold eyes set upon a fortune, and Lazy Jack is too idle to take his hands out of his pockets. Ross's cast is of generally genial grotesques. The most pleasant are only rarely sentimental, and the most loathsome are too bizarre to evoke any real horror. However stylised the figures, their poses are full of conviction, and there are little stories to be made from the details of appearance of even minor characters.

Ross's excellence as an artist is easy to demonstrate; his role as an interpreter of traditional tales is much more difficult to assess. There is no doubt that his pictorial interpretation always interlocks successfully with his own texts, but the relationship of his own text and the established one gives rise to very complex questions: how a writer may strike a sound balance between retelling and remaining true to the established text, or indeed, if he should attempt to do so. Ross does not take a radical line, but like many other retellers and civilisers of tales, he seems unaware of the nature of the deeper content. This does not matter when the updating is confined to surface details, as in *Goldilocks and the Three Bears*, or *Puss in Boots*, but surely it matters very much when he tinkers with so many elements that he actually affects the prime burden, diminishing what it offers in traditional terms without compensating by adding new positive content. Ross's updating of *The Enchanted Pig* is the perfect example of how easy it is to be dazzled by his richly inventive illustration, yet his interpretation reduces the spirit of what is one of the most moving tributes to the powers of human endurance and love in the fairytale canon. *The Three Pigs* also suffers a change of emphasis as Ross brings his version to a close in misplaced irony. His sad, isolated surviving pig is certainly not a more satisfying model for a child to behold than the robust victor of the established text. Ross is not so much a gifted interpreter of the tales, as a gifted interpreter of his own versions, and in general, new tales or old, an adroit, manipulative, and often inspired maker of aesthetically rewarding picture books.

—Jane Doonan

_____

ROUGHSEY, Dick (tribal name: Goobalathaldin). Australian. Born on Langunarnji Island, Gulf of Carpentaria, Queensland, in 1924. Educated at Mornington Island Mission School. Married Elsie Roughsey; six children. Stockman at Gregory Downs, Lorraine, and other cattle stations, Northern Territory, 1943–50; deckhand on the coastal ship *Cora*, early 1950's; yardman, Karumba lodge, 1962–63. From 1962 freelance artist: individual shows of bark paintings at Cairns School of Arts, Queensland, 1962, and galleries in Brisbane and Canberra. From 1973 Chairman, Aboriginal Arts Board. Recipient: Australian Children's Book Council Picture Book of the Year award, 1976, 1979; Weickhardt award, 1976. *Died 20 October 1985*.

PUBLICATIONS FOR CHILDREN (illustrated by the author)

Fiction

The Giant Devil Dingo. Sydney and London, Collins, 1973; New York, Macmillan, 1975.
The Rainbow Serpent. Sydney and London, Collins, 1975.
The Quinkins, with Percy Trezise. Sydney and London, Collins, 1978.
Banana Bird and the Snake Men, with Percy Trezise. Sydney, Collins, 1980.
Turramulli the Giant Quinkin, with Percy Trezise. Sydney, Collins, 1982.
The Magic Firesticks, with Percy Trezise. Sydney, Collins, 1983.
Gidja, with Percy Trezise. Sydney, Collins, 1984.
The Flying Fox Warriors, with Percy Trezise. Sydney, Collins, 1985.

PUBLICATIONS FOR ADULTS

Other

Moon and Rainbow: The Autobiography of an Aboriginal. Sydney,

Reed, 1971.

*

Illustrator (as Goobalathaldin Roughsey): *The Turkey and the Emu* by Labamu Roughsey, 1978.

*   *   *

Dick Roughsey was a full-blood Australian Aborigine, an elder of the Lardil tribe. His tribal name was Goobalathaldin, which meant "rough seas," hence his adopted English surname. He was making tree-bark pictures in the traditional Aboriginal way when in 1962 he met Percy Trezise, a retired pilot, who encouraged him to adapt his bark paintings using techniques more appropriate to European landscape painting. His first children's picture books—the first published works written and illustrated by an Australian Aboriginal—resulted from this friendship. Through his unique and arresting picture-book versions of Aboriginal myths, Roughsey offered the world something of the directness, dignity, and rhythms of the language of his people, the stark strength, boldness, and colour of their art, and something of their spiritual and practical affinity with the timeless land itself.

Gradually Trezise began sharing in the making of these books: "We first wrote a description of each scene, then I did the landscapes and Dick added the figures." Both men were dedicated to preserving aspects of the disappearing traditional aboriginal culture, feeling that the picture-book medium would bring these ancient myths to a universal audience through visual images that would create lasting impressions.

The Rainbow Serpent is one of the basic creation myths, central to traditional Aboriginal beliefs. *The Quinkins* are ancient spirit people of the Yalangi tribe. Some were "small, fat-bellied creatures, with large ugly heads, long teeth and claws." This Cape York story is about a Quinkin attempt to steal two children and how it was foiled by rival Quinkins. *The Giant Devil Dingo* tells of the evil Eelgin, the grasshopper woman who taught Gaiya, the giant dingo, to hunt and kill men for food. Eventually the dingo is ambushed and killed and from his bones the medicine man makes two small dingoes to be man's friend and helper. *Banana Bird and the Snake Men* illustrates an Olculla clan myth which explains the creation of a desert plateau and five particular rivers in Cape York, and subsequently the five clans of the Snake-language people.

All these books contain simple texts which have the quiet ring of authenticity, while the bold paintings are most impressive, powerful, and striking visual images. Each represents a splendid opportunity to help bridge cultures and promote understanding.

Since Roughsey's death, Percy Trezise has continued to produce books in the same spirit as the first attempts by his talented colleague.

—Walter McVitty

———

ROUNDS, Glen (Harold). American. Born near Wall, South Dakota, 4 April 1906. Educated at Kansas City Art Institute, 1926–27; Art Students' League, New York, 1930–31. Served in the United States Army Coast Artillery and Infantry, 1942–45: Staff Sergeant. Married 1) Mary Lucas in 1928 (divorced 1937); 2) Margaret Olmsted in 1938 (died 1968); one son. Worked as cowboy, baker, sign painter, textile designer; full-time writer since 1936. Recipient: American Association of University Women award, 1961, 1967, 1969, 1981; University of Minnesota Kerlan award, 1980. Address: Box 763, Southern Pines, North Carolina 28387, U.S.A.

PUBLICATIONS FOR CHILDREN (illustrated by the author)

Fiction

Lumbercamp.   New York, Holiday House, 1937; as *The Whistle Punk of Camp 15,* 1959.
Pay Dirt.   New York, Holiday House, 1938.
The Blind Colt.   New York, Holiday House, 1941.
Whitey's First Round-Up.   New York, Grosset and Dunlap, 1942.
Whitey's Sunday Horse.   New York, Grosset and Dunlap, 1943.
Whitey Looks for a Job.   New York, Grosset and Dunlap, 1944.
Whitey and Jinglebob.   New York, Grosset and Dunlap, 1946.
Stolen Pony.   New York, Holiday House, 1948; revised edition, 1969.
Whitey and the Rustlers.   New York, Holiday House, 1951.
Hunted Horses.   New York, Holiday House, 1951.
Whitey and the Blizzard.   New York, Holiday House, 1952.
Buffalo Harvest.   New York, Holiday House, 1952.
Lone Muskrat.   New York, Holiday House, 1953.
Whitey Takes a Trip.   New York, Holiday House, 1954.
Whitey Ropes and Rides.   New York, Holiday House, 1956.
Whitey and the Wild Horse.   New York, Holiday House, 1958.
Wild Orphan.   New York, Holiday House, 1961.
Whitey and the Colt-Killer.   New York, Holiday House, 1962.
Whitey's New Saddle.   New York, Holiday House, 1963.
The Snake Tree.   Cleveland, World, 1966.
Once We Had a Horse.   New York, Holiday House, 1971.
The Day the Circus Came to Lone Tree.   New York, Holiday House, 1973.
Mr. Yowder and the Lion Roar Capsules.   New York, Holiday House, 1976.
Mr. Yowder and the Steamboat.   New York, Holiday House, 1977.
Mr. Yowder and the Giant Bull Snake.   New York, Holiday House, 1978.
Blind Outlaw.   New York, Holiday House, 1980.
Mr. Yowder, The Peripatetic Sign Painter (omnibus).   New York, Holiday House, 1980.
Mr. Yowder and the Train Robbers.   New York, Holiday House, 1981.
Wild Appaloosa.   New York, Holiday House, 1983.
Mr. Yowder and the Windwagon.   New York, Holiday House, 1983.
The Morning the Sun Refused to Rise: An Original Paul Bunyan Tale.   New York, Holiday House, 1984.
Washday on Noah's Ark.   New York, Holiday House, 1985.

Plays

Radio Scripts: *School of the Air,* 1938–39.

Other

Ol' Paul, The Mighty Logger.   New York, Holiday House, 1936; revised edition, 1949, 1976.
Rodeo: Bulls, Broncs, and Buckaroos.   New York, Holiday House, 1949.
Swamp Life: An Almanac.   Englewood Cliffs, New Jersey, Prentice Hall, 1957.
Wildlife at Your Doorstep: An Illustrated Almanac.   Englewood Cliffs, New Jersey, Prentice Hall, 1958.
Beaver Business: An Almanac.   Englewood Cliffs, New Jersey, Prentice Hall, 1960.
Rain in the Woods and Other Small Matters.   Cleveland, World, 1964.
The Treeless Plains.   New York, Holiday House, 1967.
The Prairie Schooners.   New York, Holiday House, 1968.
Wild Horses of the Red Desert.   New York, Holiday House, 1969.

The Cowboy Trade.   New York, Holiday House, 1972.
The Beaver: How He Works.   New York, Holiday House, 1976.
Old MacDonald Had a Farm (retelling).   New York, Holiday House, 1989.

Editor, *Trail Drive*, from *Log of a Cowboy*, by Andy Adams.   New York, Holiday House, 1965; London, Whiting and Wheaton, 1966.
Editor, *Mountain Men*, by George F. Ruxton.   New York, Holiday House, 1966.
Editor, *The Boll Weevil*.   San Carlos, California, Golden Gate Books, 1967.
Editor, *Casey Jones*.   San Carlos, California, Golden Gate Books, 1968.
Editor, *The Strawberry Roan*.   San Carlos, California, Golden Gate Books, 1970.
Editor, *Sweet Betsy from Pike*.   Chicago, Children's Press, 1973.

*

Manuscript Collection: Kerlan Collection, University of Minnesota, Minneapolis.

Illustrator: *Flipper, A Sea-Lion* by Irma S. Black, 1940; *Tall Tale America* by Walter Blair, 1944; *"E" Company* by Frank O'Rourke, 1945; *Tatoosh* by Martha Hardy, 1947; *Uncle Swithin's Inventions* by Wheaton P. Webb, 1947; *Aesop's Fables*, 1949; *We Always Lie to Strangers*, 1951, *Who Blowed Up the Church House?*, 1952, *The Devil's Pretty Daughter*, 1955, *The Talking Turtle*, 1957, and *Sticks in the Knapsack*, 1958, all by Vance Randolph; *Grass, Our Greatest Crop* by Sarah J. Riedman, 1952; *Haunt Fox* by Jim Kjelgaard, 1954; *Those Glorious Mornings* by Paul Hyde Bonner, 1954; *Fire-Fly* by Paul M. Sears, 1956; *In the Arms of the Mountain* by Elizabeth Seeman, 1961; *A Wild Goose Tale*, 1961, *Dan and the Miranda*, 1962, *Big Blue Island*, 1964, *Mike's Toads*, 1970, *Squash Pie*, 1976, and *Down in the Boondocks*, 1977, all by Wilson Gage; *The Crocodile's Mouth*, 1966, and *American Tall Tale Animals*, 1968, both by Adrien Stoutenburg; *Billy Boy* edited by Richard Chase, 1966; *How the People Sang the Mountains Up* by Maria Leach, 1967; *Lucky Ladybugs*, 1968, *Tarantula, The Giant Spider*, 1972, and *Praying Mantis*, 1978, all by Gladys Conklin; *Contrary Jenkins* by Rebecca Caudill and James Ayars, 1969; *Folklore of the Great West* by John Greenway, 1969; *Ballads of the Great West* by Austin and Alta Fife, 1970; *Go Find Hanka!* by Alexander L. Crosby, 1970; *Farmer Hoo and the Baboons* by Ida Chittum, 1971; *A Twister of Twists, A Tangler of Tongues*, 1972, *Witcracks*, 1973, *Cross Your Fingers, Spit in Your Hat*, 1974, and *Kickle Snifters*, 1976, all edited by Alvin Schwartz, and *Tomfoolery*, 1973, and *Whoppers, Tall Tales, and Other Lies*, 1975, both by Schwartz; *I'm Going on a Bear Hunt* by Sandra S. Sivulich, 1973; *Jennie Jenkins* by Mark Taylor, 1975; *Three Fools and a Horse* by Betty Baker, 1975; *Lizard Lying in the Sun*, 1975, *The Happy Dromedary*, 1977, *Little Black Bear Goes for a Walk*, 1977, and *Elephant and Friends*, 1978, all by Berniece Freschet; *Tony, Granny, and George*, 1976, and *The Saving of P.S.*, 1977, both by Robbie Branscum; *Halfway Up the Mountain* by Theo E. Gilchrist, 1978; *The Lucky Man* by Mary Blount Christian, 1979; *Hush Up!*, 1980, *Shenandoah Noah*, 1985, and *Hanna's Hog*, 1988, all by Jim Aylesworth; *The Amazing Voyage of the New Orleans* by Judith St. George, 1980; *Uncle Lemon's Spring* by Jane Yolen, 1981; *The Old Woman and the Willy Nilly Man*, 1987, and *The Old Woman and the Jar of Umms*, 1989, both by Jill Wright; *Wild Pill Hickok and Other Old West Riddles* by David A. Adler, 1988; *Charlie Drives the Stage* by Eric A. Kimmel, 1989.

* * *

Glen Rounds specializes in subject matter with which he is completely acquainted, and expresses himself distinctively and authoritatively. For a number of years, the author "drifted" around the country, and did a great many jobs. His book *Pay Dirt* tells of mining; *Lumbercamp* focuses on lumbering, and several books depict the life of a cowboy. *The Cowboy Trade*, in contrast to glamorous versions of life in the west, is authentic, based in part on his childhood.

Rounds's realistic books are invariably set in two regions—the plains, particularly a ranch near Ekalaka, Montana, and near Southern Pines, North Carolina. His 11 Whitey books are reminiscent of his relationship with the cowboys on his father's ranch. *The Treeless Plains* is based on homesteaders' memories and his return to the territory as an adult. Even his single book about the American Indian, *Buffalo Harvest*, limits itself to the tribe in his area.

Rounds describes wildlife with sensitivity, and an authenticity based on hours spent at an abandoned farm and a swamp in North Carolina. *Wild Orphan* is a documentary of the first year of a beaver kit whose parents fell prey to traps; *Lone Muskrat* follows an aging animal. *Rain in the Woods and Other Small Matters* is more ecological, describing inter-relationships of flora and fauna.

While most of his books are realistic, the tall tales of his first book, *Ol' Paul*, come from Rounds's imagination, for the Paul Bunyan character was a device created for a lumber company's advertising campaign. The author is a good listener, and weaves anecdotes in his humorous books such as *The Day the Circus Came to Lone Tree* and *Mr. Yowder and the Lion Roar Capsules*.

Mr. Xenon Zebulon Yowder, "the World's Bestest and Fastest Sign Painter," covering the territory of Missouri, Kansas, Texas, and the Dakotas, is Rounds's lasting contribution to tall-tale characters. *Mr. Yowder, The Peripatetic Sign Painter* incorporates three tales published earlier, but with a more appropriate format for child readers. This "chapter book" surpasses the picture book usually associated with youngsters too young to assimilate the droll details, such as policemen "blowing their whistles and looking in rule books," which abound. The mangy lion, the sign-painter who "talked snake," and the pilot and captain who forsook card playing are unforgettable. At the conclusion of each tale, Rounds notes the disappearance of characters from that particular territory.

Rounds writes succinctly and effectively. Like a cowboy who must minimize his motions to save energy, the author is a master at economy of words. *Wild Horses of the Red Desert* opens with the sentence, "The Desert is a barren land of high rocky ridges and dusty sagebrush flats, where men seldom go." He uses the vernacular in the dialogue of his characters. Whitey wanted the "purtiest" colt on the ranch for his "Sunday" horse. In *Lumbercamp*, a paragraph in the chapter "Whiffler" reads, "Right away a gangling swamper by the name of Shikepoke spoke up. 'Reckon thet's a Sidehill Whiffler, Bub,' he said. 'They's quite a lot of 'em round right now. Yuh wanta be on the lookout for 'em.'" His robust folk humor is evident in the tall tales, but also in the dialogue of the characters. Because his books have a simple and direct approach, they are read by 7 to 10-year-old children, while adolescents needing "high interest low vocabulary" books also read them. Reviewers inevitably remind the adult that Rounds's ecology books such as *The Snake Tree* and books about the west should not be relegated only to the child's shelf.

—Karen Nelson Hoyle

———

RUBINSTEIN, Gillian (née Hanson).   British.   Born in Potten End, Hertfordshire, 29 August 1942. Educated at Queen Anne's, Caversham, Berkshire, 1954–60; Lady Margaret Hall, Oxford, 1961–64, B.A. and M.A. (honours) in modern languages; Stockwell

CHILDREN'S WRITERS

College, University of London, postgraduate diploma in education 1973. Married Philip Rubinstein in 1973 (second marriage); one son and two daughters. Research assistant, London School of Economics, 1964–65; administrative officer, Greater London Council, 1965–66; editor, Tom Stacey, publishers, London, 1969–72. Has also worked as a cook, cleaner, script assessor, part-time editor, journalist, and film critic. Moved to Australia in 1973. Recipient: Australian Children's Literature Peace prize, 1987; Australian National Children's Book award, 1988; Australian Council Literature Arts Board fellowship, 1988, and Australian Council performing arts grant, 1989. Agent: Caroline Lurie, Australian Literary Management, 2-A Armstrong Street, Middle Park, Victoria 3206. Address: 29 Seaview Road, Lynton, South Australia 5062, Australia.

PUBLICATIONS FOR CHILDREN

Fiction

Space Demons.   Adelaide, Omnibus, 1986; New York, Dial Press, 1988.
Answers to Brut.   Adelaide, Omnibus, 1988.
Beyond the Labyrinth.   Melbourne, Hyland House, 1988.
Melanie and the Night Animal.   Adelaide, Omnibus, 1988.

Other

Editor, *After Dark.*   Adelaide, Omnibus, 1988.
Editor, *Before Dawn.*   Adelaide, Omnibus, 1988.

*

Gillian Rubinstein comments:

I use a lot of material from my own childhood, and the rage I felt as a child is a great source of energy for me. I also watch children today closely. Three very nice ones live with me, ages 9 to 15, and they are a wonderful source of background—vocabulary, fashions, likes and dislikes and so on, though I never use them directly in stories. I write about 4 drafts of everything, and work on a word processor, which I find suits my type of writing very well, as I can type almost as fast as I can think, and the words kind of flow out onto the screen. I tend to have too many ideas—comes from a lifetime of reading and thinking about things—but I can't bear to leave any out, so my work tends to be very "dense," with lots of different themes interwoven, and things happening on many different levels. I keep ideas jotted down in a book or on pieces of paper or simply in my head, and look at them every now and then to see if they are ready to be turned into something yet. I like trying all sorts of different forms from very short picture book texts to complex novels. Every idea has its ideal shape and form and my job is to bring it into being to the best of my ability. I feel a great sense of responsibility and loyalty towards my ideas, as if I am their servant.

*   *   *

On the surface Gillian Rubinstein's first novel *Space Demons* is very much of the 1980's, not only in its idiom, but in its ingenious use of a computer game for its central dramatic situation. Its real concerns, however, are traditional: the uneasy relationships between parents and children, the stresses of school life, and preadolescent struggles towards self-knowledge. The three main characters are presented with skill and subtlety. The consciously charming, manipulative Andrew, only child of rich parents, has nothing in common with the violent, streetwise Mario, nor with Elaine, a forlorn victim of her father's restlessness. They come together through Andrew's need to find adversaries capable of matching him in his

challenging new computer game. The game, whose intricacies Andrew has to learn for himself, demands that the player "respond to hate"; the release of a player's destructive or self-destructive energies sweeps him out of the human world and into the game itself. At first exhilarating, but ultimately frightening, the Space Demons game is a means of exploring character. The more the children succeed in the terms set for them, the more they alienate themselves from families and friendships and from themselves. The final risk is to be lost forever, to disappear into the computer. The children finally discover that they can win only by choosing to lose; only by renouncing hatred of the self or of each other can they find the way out.

There is an impressive narrative skill in Rubinstein's dramatization of the clash between love and hate, between human ties and the abstract power of the computer program. It may be read simply as a thriller, but the moral questions give it substance as well as psychological interest.

Answers to Brut, less ambitious than *Space Demons* and written for younger readers, also shows Rubinstein's ability to sketch diverse family groupings and to show children in crisis. The Brut of the title is a bull terrier, owned by timid Caspian, stolen by envious Kel, and sold by Kel's opportunist father. The boys—enemies by temperament—must cooperate in order to save the dog from its brutal new owners. The happy ending dodges the problem of Brut's innate, innocent destructiveness which at times seems to be central to the story.

Beyond the Labyrinth, like *Space Demons,* is fantasy which owes its persuasiveness to the author's firm grasp of the everyday world. Set in an Australian coastal town, it celebrates the beauty of the natural world and assesses man's achievements. A visitor from the future—an alien androgynous being encountered on the beach by three children—brings into question all their assumptions about civilization on this planet. As in *Space Demons* Rubinstein's interest in human individuality and family relations gives warmth and humour to what might otherwise be an abstract moral fable. There is no easy satire at the expense of 20th-century man. Thus, when it is time for the visitor to return to her/his own time, the children are divided. One wants to leave the family in which he feels a misfit: oppressed by the fear of a nuclear disaster, he has never been able to find meaning in his comfortable middle-class existence. His brother, an amiable extrovert, feels no tug towards an alternative culture. For the girl, Victoria, the choice is painful. Rubinstein has written two endings for her novel. She invites her readers to throw the dice, and read the version chance provides. Most readers will read both. The second—privileged by its having the final pages of the text—is the more optimistic in terms of 20th-century man. "Live as if you will die tomorrow. Garden as if you will live forever" is the text Victoria chooses as she turns back to the everyday world.

Serious but never gloomy, at home with ideas but never arid, Rubinstein's two major novels achieve distinction within a demanding genre. In their imaginative range and the clarity and ease with which their intricate plots are worked out, *Space Demons* and *Beyond the Labyrinth* indicate a strong and developing talent.

—Brenda Niall

RUSH, Philip. British. Born in Palmers Green, London, 24 February 1908. Educated at Southgate Grammar School; London School of Economics. Married Geraldine Gould in 1931; one son and two daughters. Local government officer, East Ham, London, 1930–63; chief inspector of weights and measures, East Ham, 1963–65, and Borough of Bexley, London, 1965–68. Agent: John Johnson,

45–47 Clerkenwell Green, London EC1R 0HT. Address: 45 Castle Street, Canterbury, Kent CT1 2PY, England.

PUBLICATIONS FOR CHILDREN

Fiction

He Sailed with Dampier, illustrated by Richard Ogle. London, Boardman, 1947.
A Cage of Falcons, illustrated by Serena Chance. London, Collins, 1954.
Queen's Treason, illustrated by F. Partridge. London, Collins, 1955.
The Minstrel Knight, illustrated by Martin Thomas. London, Collins, 1955; Indianapolis, Bobbs Merrill, 1956.
King of the Castle, illustrated by Martin Thomas. London, Collins, 1956.
Red Man's Country, illustrated by Brian Keogh. London, Collins, 1957.
My Brother Lambert, illustrated by David Walsh. London, Phoenix House, and New York, Roy, 1957.
He Went with Dampier, illustrated by P.A. Jobson. London, Harrap, 1957; New York, Roy, 1958.
He Went with Franklin, illustrated by Anthony Douthwaite. London, Harrap, 1960.
Apprentice at Arms, illustrated by Christopher Brooker. London, Collins, 1960.
The Castle and the Harp, illustrated by Charles Keeping. London, Collins, 1963; New York, McGraw Hill, 1964.
Frost Fair, illustrated by Philip Gough. London, Collins, 1965; New York, Roy, 1967.
That Fool of a Priest and Other Tales of Early Canterbury, illustrated by David Knight. Oxford, Pergamon Press, 1970.
A Face of Stone, illustrated by David Harris. Leicester, Brockhampton Press, 1973.
Guns for the Armada, illustrated by Sheila Bewley. London, Hodder and Stoughton, 1975.
Death to the Strangers!, illustrated by Val Biro. London, Hodder and Stoughton, 1977.

Other

Great Men of Sussex, illustrated by Peter Rush. London, Lane, 1956.
Strange People: The Later Hanoverians 1760–1837, illustrated by Peter Rush. London, Hutchinson, 1958.
More Strange People: The Early Hanoverians 1714–1760, illustrated by Peter Rush. London, Hutchinson, 1958.
London's Wonderful Bridge, illustrated by Nancy Sayer. London, Harrap, 1959.
Strange Stuarts 1603–1714, illustrated by Peter Rush. London, Hutchinson, 1959.
How Roads Have Grown, illustrated by Caroline Norton. London, Routledge, 1960.
The Young Shelley, illustrated by Anne Linton. London, Parrish, 1961; New York, Roy, 1962.
Weights and Measures, with John A. O'Keefe. London, Methuen, 1962; New York, Roy, 1964.
The Book of Duels, illustrated by Peter Rush. London, Harrap, 1964.

PUBLICATIONS FOR ADULTS

Novels

Rogue's Lute. London, Dakers, 1944.

Mary Read, Buccaneer. London, Boardman, 1945.
Freedom Is the Man. London, Dakers, 1946.
Crispin's Apprentice. London, Dakers, 1948.
Pierce Allard. London, Hale, 1981.
Quayle. London, Hale, 1982.

*

Philip Rush comments:
The past has always fascinated me and my published work has always been historical.

*   *   *

Most of Philip Rush's stories are set in the middle ages, often in the area round Canterbury, and all centre on a particular historical event or character, generally seen through the eyes of a young person. An author's note identifies sources and separates fiction from fact, though Rush's attitude, particularly where social class is involved in conflict, is often ambivalent. Historical details are given plentifully and generally palatably.

Red Man's Country (which could have been called "He Went with Captain John Smith"), *He Went with Dampier*, and *He Went with Franklin* are successful pieces of formula writing. *He Went with Franklin*, which has no invented young hero, reads like a particularly gripping travel book rather than a novel. Always the characters are clearly differentiated, and racial prejudice (towards Indians and Eskimos) is shown to be misguided. *The Young Shelley* and *My Brother Lambert* present equally convincing and psychologically accurate portraits.

Other stories are more variable. In *Apprentice at Arms* and *The Castle and the Harp* fact reads like fiction, and *Frost Fair* is totally unconvincing. *King of the Castle* and *A Face of Stone* are both accounts of the Wat Tyler rebellion, the later book showing a real improvement of quality; Adam, the apprentice stonemason, is a likelier character than the callous and unattractive Sylvester.

The worst violence—the murder of the garrison of Bedford Castle in *The Castle and the Harp*—is shown off-stage, but in general battle and killing are plentiful. Hardship, particularly in the *He Went with*…stories, is related unflinchingly, and young readers are given an unglamourised picture. The same is also true of mediaeval life in the one book of short stories, *That Fool of a Priest*.

Philosophical and religious topics are dealt with openly—in the Tudor stories *Apprentice at Arms* and *Guns for the Armada* and in *The Minstrel Knight*, a retelling of an Anglo-Norman family history poem. Often, as in *Queen's Treason* and *A Face of Stone*, discussion of religious topics is a prominent feature.

Happy endings prevail because there are books for children, but where fortunate chance does not intervene there is always a slight melancholy.

—Margaret M. Tye

———

RUTHIN, Margaret. See CATHERALL, Arthur.

———

RYLANT, Cynthia. American. Born in Hopewell, Virginia, 6 June 1954. Educated at the University of Charleston, West Virginia, 1973–75, B.A. in English 1975; Marshall University, Huntington,

West Virginia, 1975–76, M.A. in English 1976; Kent State University, Kent, Ohio, 1980–81, M.L.S. 1981. Has one son. Address: P.O. Box 5031, Kent, Ohio 44240, U.S.A.

PUBLICATIONS FOR CHILDREN

Fiction

When I Was Young in the Mountains, illustrated by Diane Goode. New York, Dutton, 1982.
Miss Maggie, illustrated by Thomas di Grazia. New York, Dutton, 1983.
This Year's Garden, illustrated by Mary Szilagyi. New York, Bradbury Press, 1984.
A Blue-Eyed Daisy. New York, Bradbury Press, 1985.
The Relatives Came, illustrated by Stephen Gammell. New York, Bradbury Press, 1985.
Every Living Thing (stories). New York, Bradbury Press, 1985.
A Fine White Dust. New York, Bradbury Press, 1986.
Night in the Country, illustrated by Mary Szilagyi. New York, Bradbury Press, 1986.
Birthday Presents, illustrated by Sucie Stevenson. New York, Orchard, 1987.
Children of Christmas (stories), illustrated by Stephen Schindler. New York, Orchard, 1987; as *Silver Packages and Other Stories*, London, Orchard, 1987.
All I See, illustrated by Peter Catalonotto. New York, Orchard, 1988.
A Kindness. New York, Orchard, 1989.
Mr. Grigg's Work, illustrated by Julie Downing. New York, Orchard, 1989.

Verse

Waiting to Waltz: A Childhood, illustrated by Stephen Gammell. New York, Bradbury Press, 1984.

Other (readers)

Henry and Mudge [*in Puddle Trouble, in the Green Time, under the Yellow Moon, in the Sparkle Days, and the Forever Sea, Get the Cold Shivers*] illustrated by Sucie Stevenson. New York, Bradbury Press, 7 vols., 1987–89; first vol. published London, Gollancz, 1989.
But I'll Be Back Again: An Album. New York, Orchard, 1989.

*

Manuscript Collection: Special Collections, Kent State University, Ohio.

Cynthia Rylant comments:

Most of my books are based on my childhood in southern West Virginia with its rural Appalachian coal-mining towns and townsfolk influencing both the tone and theme of my work. Writers who have influenced me most are James Agee and William Maxwell. When I write I try to center down gut-level and put words to *feelings* rather than toward descriptive or action-filled passages. It is the interior I'm most interested in, and the poetry of the simple things.

*   *   *

Cynthia Rylant's work for children ranges from the picture book to poetry, from short stories to novels. Through this range, what one remembers is her use of language, bringing settings and characters to life.

Through the imagery of her language, setting becomes memorable as it does in the picture book story, *Night in the Country*. Using very few words, Rylant has us listen to the sweep of owl wings, the clink of dog chains and the unexpected "pump" of one apple hitting the ground. Not only the outside carries night sounds; the inside does as well with "the groans and thumps and squeaks that houses make when they are trying, like you, to sleep." Style extolled setting from Rylant's very first work, *When I Was Young in the Mountains*. Recognized as a Notable Children's Book for Young Readers by the American Library Association, this work captures the tenor of a young girl's life in the West Virginia mountains: the smell of cornbread, beans, and okra; the coolness of the swimming hole; the power of baptism; and the loving warmth of summer evenings when beans are shelled, pencils are sharpened by pocketknife, and stars sparkle. Because of Rylant's lyrical use of language, we come to know why the main character never dreamed of a world beyond the mountains when she was young. There, love, adventure, and security wrapped her close.

Characters are just as strongly evoked by Rylant's use of dialect and figurative language. *A Blue-Eyed Daisy*, an episodic novel for the middle-school child, has the sound of a story told out loud, a story relayed in a mountain dialect which ably reflects its main character Ellie. Through the third-person limited narrative, Ellie's everyday life as well as her fears and yearnings in the year before she turns 12 are revealed. Like every child, Ellie wants her father's love and is willing almost to shoot a beautiful doe to gain his admiration. She yearns for a valentine on Valentine's Day as well as a bedroom of her own, and worries about whether she will become an epileptic after seeing a classmate overcome with a seizure at school. Ellie is a well-drawn character, one the reader clearly identifies with and cares about.

Just as strongly depicted, this time through a first-person narrative, is Pete in Rylant's second novel for the middle-school child, *A Fine White Dust*. This work begins and ends with a symbol—broken pieces of a ceramic cross. Through much of the book, those pieces objectify Pete's disillusionment with religion, for he has been deserted by the evangelist preacher for whom he had left his own family and friends. However, by the end of the story Pete realizes that the pieces can be thrown away; he is ready for a new understanding of God. Applauded by reviewers for its focus on intense religious feelings, *A Fine White Dust* was named a Newbery Honor Book for 1987.

Distinctive to Rylant's work are her depictions of adult characters. Ellie's father is prominent in *A Blue-Eyed Daisy*. Like other coal miners, Oakey Farley used to drink, "to scare away the coming week," but with his accident in a slate fall and his inability to work, he begins to drink through the week as well. The novel traces Oakey's healing process, furthered by Ellie's love and Bullet, the hunting beagle he brings home one day.

Parents are not the only adult characters presented in a fully drawn manner. Rylant has become well-known for her portrayal of the elderly, especially those who are isolated and alone. Her second collection of short stories, *Children of Christmas*, is replete with portraits of the Christmas tree man who only experiences warmth and caring as families come to buy their trees before Christmas; of Philip's grandfather who sorely misses his wife; and of homeless Mae who stumbles into a library and finds enchantment and awe in the children's books which surround her. Unifying this collection of short stories is Rylant's perception that no matter how isolated and lonely one is, Christmas is a time of connection, of love and warmth, for all.

Theme unifies her other collections as well. In *Waiting to Waltz: A Childhood*, 30 poems trace Rylant's process of growing up in the small town of Beaver, West Virginia. The later poems in this work focus on the author's developing sexual awareness, her yearning to grow up as quickly as possible, and her experiences in the world outside her hometown. Pervading *Every Living Thing*, Rylant's first collection of short stories, is the empathy, comfort, and growth which result when child or adult befriends an animal.

Strongly unified works with fully delineated characters and setting describe Rylant's work to date. During the 1980's Rylant has emerged as a significant picture book author and writer for the middle-school child, especially recognized for her memorable language.

—Jacqueline L. Gmuca

SACHS, Marilyn (née Stickle). American. Born in New York City, 18 December 1927. Educated at Hunter College, New York, B.A. 1949; Columbia University, New York, M.S. in library science 1952. Married Morris Sachs in 1947; one daughter and one son. Librarian, Brooklyn Public Library, 1949–60, and San Francisco Public Library, 1961–67. Recipient: Association of Jewish Libraries Sydney Taylor award, 1983; Christopher award, 1986. Address: 733 31st Avenue, San Francisco, California 94121, U.S.A.

PUBLICATIONS FOR CHILDREN

Fiction

Amy Moves In, illustrated by Judith Gwyn Brown. New York, Doubleday, 1964.
Laura's Luck, illustrated by Ib Ohlsson. New York, Doubleday, 1965.
Amy and Laura, illustrated by Tracy Sugarman. New York, Doubleday, 1966.
Veronica Ganz, illustrated by Louis Glanzman. New York, Doubleday, 1968; London, Macdonald, 1969.
Peter and Veronica, illustrated by Louis Glanzman. New York, Doubleday, 1969; London, Macdonald, 1970.
Marv, illustrated by Louis Glanzman. New York, Doubleday, 1970.
The Bears' House, illustrated by Louis Glanzman. New York, Doubleday, 1971.
The Truth about Mary Rose, illustrated by Louis Glanzman. New York, Doubleday, and London, Macdonald, 1973.
A Pocket Full of Seeds, illustrated by Ben Stahl. New York, Doubleday, 1973; London, Macdonald and Jane's, 1978.
Matt's Mitt, illustrated by Hilary Knight. New York, Doubleday, 1975.
Dorrie's Book, illustrated by Anne Sachs. New York, Doubleday, 1975; London, Macdonald and Jane's, 1976.
A December Tale. New York, Doubleday, 1976.
A Secret Friend. New York, Doubleday, 1978; London, Corgi, 1988.
A Summer's Lease. New York, Dutton, 1979.
Bus Ride, illustrated by Amy Rowen. New York, Dutton, 1980.
Class Pictures. New York, Dutton, 1980.
Fleet-Footed Florence, illustrated by Charles Robinson. New York, Doubleday, 1981.
Hello...Wrong Number, illustrated by Pamela Johnson. New York, Dutton, 1981.
Call Me Ruth. New York, Doubleday, 1982.
Beach Towels, illustrated by Jim Spence. New York, Dutton, 1982.

Fourteen. New York, Dutton, 1983.
The Fat Girl. New York, Dutton, 1984; Oxford, Oxford University Press, 1985.
Thunderbird, illustrated by Jim Spence. New York, Dutton, 1985.
Underdog. New York, Doubleday, 1985; Oxford, Oxford University Press, 1987.
Baby Sister, New York, Dutton, 1986; Oxford, Oxford University Press, 1987.
Almost Fifteen. New York, Dutton, 1987; Oxford, Oxford University Press, 1988.
Fran Ellen's House. New York, Dutton, 1987.
Matt's Mitt, and Fleet-Footed Florence, illustrated by Charles Robinson. New York, Dutton, 1989.

Play

Reading Between the Lines (produced New York, 1971). New York, Children's Book Council, 1971.

*

Manuscript Collection: Kerlan Collection, University of Minnesota, Minneapolis.

Marilyn Sachs comments:

All my life, as a child and now as an adult, books have remained one of the more dependable pleasures. Friends come and go, days are not always sunny, and chocolate often gives me rashes. Whenever something hurts I have always been able to pick up a book and forget my troubles. I like to feel my books may be doing just this for children looking for comfort and pleasure.

*   *   *

Few authors can have demonstrated a steadier pattern of growth than that of Marilyn Sachs. Her earliest published work consisted of fairly run-of-the-mill stories of the trials and tribulations of pleasant and unremarkable preadolescents heroines; but from the background of one such title, *Amy and Laura*, a really formidable character emerges, to star in a story of her own. *Veronica Ganz*, the school bully, is big, mean, and friendless. Everyone is afraid of her, until smart-aleck shrimp Peter challenges her reign of terror, giving her a beating (with, of course, the help of two friends). Veronica can hardly believe it has happened; nor, when he stops to consider what he has done, can Peter. Once past this unusual ice-breaker, and the problems of bigness and smallness which have seemed so all-important, they become fast friends. Another kind of prejudice becomes a problem when it is time for Peter's bar mitzvah, and he insists that non-Jewish Veronica attend the ceremony. In the storm that follows, both youngsters learn just how much their friendship means to both of them.

The Truth about Mary Rose, set a generation later, tells of Veronica's daughter, whose life is haunted by the legend of her child-aunt, killed long ago in an apartment fire. The namesake Mary Rose must learn to let the past bury its dead. This story troubles child readers, not only with its tragic theme, but with the shock of finding their beloved Veronica suddenly a grown woman ("but she's *my* age...").

Perhaps too powerful for young readers is *The Bears' House*. Little Fran Ellen lives in horrible squalor: mother, deserted by father, has suffered a complete breakdown and lies helplessly weeping in her filthy bedroom, oblivious of her childrens' misery. They, meanwhile, try to conceal the situation, afraid that they will be separated or placed in an institution. Fran Ellen's refuge is a doll's house, inhabited by a family of bears. In imagination she escapes into their tiny perfect world, where she is loved and wanted. Her real and fantasy lives are on a collision course.

Fran Ellen's House, written years later, takes up the story of the disturbed family after the mother has undergone therapy and is once again attempting to cope with life, and with the children now returned to her care. They are happy to be together again, but they, and the bears' house, have suffered over the years spent apart. Baby Flora cannot resign herself to parting from her adoptive parents, the only "real" family she has; and Fran Ellen no longer finds refuge or solace in the bears' house. She has moved on, though with wistful backward glances: it is little sister Felice's house now.

Another serious work, *A Pocket Full of Seeds*, is a family tragedy in a broader sense and on a wider canvas. Nicole Nieman, swept into the Holocaust of World War II, develops from a jaunty, unreflective child into a courageous teenager who must face the rest of her life without her lost, beloved family, but will carry them forever in her heart. In *Call Me Ruth*, fictionalized social history, a poor but brave Russian immigrant garment worker in turn-of-the-century New York grows from a timid "greenhorn" into a dauntless union organizer, in the stirring recreation of a time and a way of life well worth remembering.

Others of Sachs's books have lighter subjects, and are in the main intended for a younger readership. *Dorrie's Book* is a child's own account of her transformation from spoiled only child to big sister, thanks to a set of triplets and a double adoption. *Fourteen* tells of the plight of a child whose author-mother persists in using her unwilling daughter as subject matter; *Class Pictures* of two girls growing and changing, and of their friendship, stretched but still strong. *Almost Fifteen* has a heroine forced to accept responsibility because her parents are unwilling (or unable) to do so; *Underdog* is the story of an almost frantic search for a lost dog—the only link to an orphaned youngster's recollected happiness. *The Fat Girl* is a reversal of the familiar Pygmalion theme, in which the young man who stirs Ellen's interest in her appearance is devoted to her only as long as she remains obese: as she gains confidence and loses weight, he distances himself. Now the problem is his, not hers.

Some of Sachs's work is in a different vein, the "Hi-Lo", high interest, controlled vocabulary titles so desperately needed to encourage weaker readers who are past the beginner-book stage, but need undemanding, attractive fare that will not insult their intelligence. Books like *Bus Ride* (dialogue only), and *Thunderbird*, about two kids getting acquainted in a library setting, fill the need admirably.

As well as her junior and young adult titles, Sachs has produced two picture-book baseball fantasies, *Matt's Mitt* and *Fleet-Footed Florence*, for younger readers. Her many fans are happily confident that there will be more good things to come.

—Joan McGrath

———

SALKEY, (Felix) Andrew (Alexander). Jamaican. Born in Colon, Panama, 30 January 1928. Educated at St. George's College, Kingston, Jamaica; Munro College, St. Elizabeth, Jamaica; University of London (Thomas Helmore Poetry prize, 1955), B.A. in English 1955. Married Patricia Verden in 1957; two sons. English teacher in a London comprehensive school, 1957–59; interviewer and scriptwriter, BBC External Services (Radio), London, 1952–76. Since 1976 Professor of Creative Writing, Hampshire College, Amherst, Massachusetts. Recipient: Guggenheim fellowship, 1960; Casa de las Américas Poetry prize, 1979. Address: Flat 8, Windsor Court, Moscow Road, London W.2, England; or, Department of English, Hampshire College, Amherst, Massachusetts 01002, U.S.A.

PUBLICATIONS FOR CHILDREN

Fiction

Hurricane, illustrated by William Papas.   London, Oxford University Press, 1964; New York, Oxford University Press, 1979.
Earthquake, illustrated by William Papas.   London, Oxford University Press, 1965; New York, Roy, 1969.
Drought, illustrated by William Papas.   London, Oxford University Press, 1966.
Riot, illustrated by William Papas.   London, Oxford University Press, 1967.
Jonah Simpson, illustrated by Gerry Craig.   London, Oxford University Press, 1969; New York, Roy, 1970.
Joey Tyson.   London, Bogle L'Ouverture, 1974.
The River That Disappeared.   London, Bogle L'Ouverture, 1980.
Danny Jones.   London, Bogle L'Ouverture, 1980.
The One: The Story of How the People of Guyana Avenge the Murder of Their Pasero with Help from Brother Anancy and Sister Buxton.   London, Bogle L'Ouverture, 1985.

Other

The Shark Hunters (reader), illustrated by Peter Kesteven.   London, Nelson, 1966.

Editor, *Caribbean Prose: An Anthology for Secondary Schools*.   London, Evans, 1967.

PUBLICATIONS FOR ADULTS

Novels

A Quality of Violence.   London, Hutchinson, 1959.
Escape to an Autumn Pavement.   London, Hutchinson, 1960.
The Late Emancipation of Jerry Stover.   London, Hutchinson, 1968.
The Adventures of Catullus Kelly.   London, Hutchinson, 1969.
Come Home, Malcolm Heartland.   London, Hutchinson, 1976.

Short Stories

Anancy's Score.   London, Bogle L'Ouverture, 1973.

Verse

Jamaica.   London, Hutchinson, 1973.
Land.   London, Readers and Writers, 1976.
In the Hills Where Her Dreams Live: Poems for Chile 1973–1978.   Havana, Casa de las Américas, 1979; Sausalito, California, Black Scholar Press, 1981.
Away.   London, Allison and Busby, 1980.

Other

Havana Journal.   London, Penguin, 1971.
Georgetown Journal: A Caribbean Writer's Journey from London via Port of Spain to Georgetown, Guyana, 1970.   London, New Beacon, 1972.

Editor, *West Indian Stories*.   London, Faber, 1960.
Editor, *Stories from the Caribbean*.   London, Elek, 1965; as *Island Voices: Stories from the West Indies*, New York, Liveright, 1970.
Editor, Caribbean Section, *Young Commonwealth Poets '65*.   London, Heinemann, 1965.

Editor, *Breaklight: An Anthology of Caribbean Poetry.*   London, Hamish Hamilton, 1971; as *Breaklight: The Poetry of the Caribbean*, New York, Doubleday, 1972.

Editor, with others, *Savacou 3–4.*   Kingston, Jamaica, and London, Caribbean Artists Movement, 2 vols., 1972.

Editor, *Caribbean Essays.*   London, Evans, 1973.

Editor, *Writing in Cuba since the Revolution: An Anthology.*   London, Bogle L'Ouverture, 1977.

Editor, *Caribbean Folk Tales and Legends.*   London, Bogle L'Ouverture, 1980.

*

Theatrical Activities:
Actor: **Film**—*Reggae* (narrator), 1978.

*   *   *

A particular interest in Andrew Salkey's writing lies in the way he presents West Indian tradition and culture to English readers. In no way does he compromise this to make it "easy" for reading but seems to assume, quite rightly, that what his readers miss through particular language they will gain through context. The value of this writing in an increasingly multi-racial society will be obvious.

The main body of his work—*Drought, Earthquake, Hurricane*, and, to some extent, *Riot* and *The Shark Hunters*—is concerned with natural disaster and its effect on the group of people concerned. These stories are told very much through the eyes and viewpoints of the children involved. These children are far more realistic, believable characters than the adults whose behaviour is unfairly stereotyped, at least to adult ears. It is easy to understand why children identify with the children of the stories as they attempt to understand, participate in, and overcome the difficulties with which they are surrounded. They have thoughts and fears which sometimes have to be kept from adults but which can be shared with children. It is because of this, and because of the predictability of the plots, that I would classify the author as a writer for juveniles—with nothing derogatory intended in that. As can be expected from the titles the plots have an intrinsic excitement which Salkey sustains well—helped by subdividing the chapters into short sections. However, in this group of works it is the events themselves, and not their effects on characters, which seem to dominate.

Jonah Simpson is different. It is a far more complex story involving the hero in the history and legend of Port Royal and weaving his fantasies into what turns out to be a modern adventure situation. This story has compelling threads of intrigue and mystery which transform ordinary events in the boy's life and force him to go deeper and deeper into the puzzle which increasingly seems to surround him. In Uncle Leonard, Samuel Palmer, and the castaway the author has built his strongest adult characters while Jonah himself grows throughout the story. This is the best of Salkey's work.

—Alan M. Lynskey

———

SANTOS, Helen.   See **GRIFFITHS, Helen**.

———

SARGENT, Pamela.   American.   Born in Ithaca, New York, 20 March 1948. Educated at the State University of New York, Bing-

hamton, B.A. in philosophy 1968, M.A. 1970. Model and sales clerk, Monigsbaum's, 1965–66, factory worker, Endicott Coil Company, 1966, and sales clerk, Towne Distributors, 1966, all Albany, New York; typist, Harpur College Library, Binghamton, 1966–67; office worker and receptionist, Webster Paper Company, Albany, 1969; teaching assistant in philosophy, State University of New York, Binghamton, 1969–71. Since 1971 freelance writer and editor. Agent: Joseph Elder Agency, 150 West 87th Street, Apartment 6-D, New York, New York 10024. Address: Box 486, Johnson City, New York 13790, U.S.A.

PUBLICATIONS FOR CHILDREN

Fiction

Watchstar.   New York, Pocket Books, 1980.
Earthseed.   New York, Harper, 1983; London, Collins, 1984.
Eye of the Comet.   New York, Harper, 1984.
Homesmind.   New York, Harper, 1984.
Alien Child.   New York, Harper, 1988.

PUBLICATIONS FOR ADULTS

Novels

Cloned Lives.   New York, Fawcett, 1976; London, Fontana, 1981.
The Sudden Star.   New York, Fawcett, 1979; as *The White Death*, London, Fontana, 1980.
The Golden Space.   New York, Simon and Schuster, 1982.
The Alien Upstairs.   New York, Doubleday, 1983.
Venus of Dreams.   New York, Bantam, 1986.
The Shore of Women.   New York, Crown, 1986; London, Chatto and Windus, 1987.
Venus of Shadows.   New York, Doubleday, 1988.

Short Stories

Starshadows.   New York, Ace, 1977.
The Best of Pamela Sargent.   Chicago, Academy, 1987.

Other

Editor, *Women of Wonder: Science Fiction Stories by Women about Women.*   New York, Random House, 1975; London, Penguin, 1978.

Editor, *More Women of Wonder: Science Fiction Novelettes by Women about Women.*   New York, Random House, 1976; London, Penguin, 1979.

Editor, *Bio-Futures: Science Fiction Stories about Biological Metamorphosis.*   New York, Random House, 1976.

Editor, *The New Women of Wonder: Recent Science Fiction Stories by Women about Women.*   New York, Random House, 1978.

Editor, with Ian Watson, *Afterlives: Stories about Life after Death.*   New York, Random House, 1986.

*

Manuscript Collection: David Paskow Science Fiction Collection, Temple University, Philadelphia.

*   *   *

Pamela Sargent's work has done much to enhance and advance the role of women in science fiction. As an editor she has compiled three volumes, *Women of Wonder*, *More Women of Wonder*, and *The New Women of Wonder*. In the introductory essays to these volumes, Sargent addresses the position of women in science fiction. The collections bring together examples of short fiction of the genre by women.

In her own fiction, both for adults and children, Sargent has created exemplary and exciting female characters who engage her readers. Adult readers find her works like *Venus of Dreams* and *The Shore of Women* to be entertaining and thought-provoking. Sargent brings these same strengths to her novels for young readers. In her introduction to *Women of Wonder* Sargent states: "Science-fiction novels for young adults and children can also offer role models for younger readers. This has happened often enough in the past for boys…There is no reason why this cannot be true for girls as well…"

Sargent's Earthminds trilogy begins with *Watchstar*. On a transformed Earth, Daiya belongs to a society of telepaths, but she must undergo her right of passage to join the mind Net of her village. The ordeal would not be an easy one; there were those who died in their quest and joined the Merged Ones. Daiya's journey takes on an added dimension when a glowing object falls from the sky. Rather than alerting the village Net, she decides to explore alone. She finds an alien spacecraft and a young man. Reiho, the alien, is without telepathic powers, but he is connected to Homesmind, a cybernetic intelligence of his world, by an implant. The nature of Daiya's quest changes as she comes to learn more about Reiho, his world, and her own. What she learns makes her unable to rejoin the people of her village, and she accepts Reiho's invitation to visit his comet world. Daiya's powers of mind are lost to her in the comet world. She learns of the beauties and problems of that world, but does not feel at home there and returns to her village. She is rejected by the villagers, even by the young man she loved, for she has changed and become something new. When the comet world tries to connect with the village, there is fear and resentment and the villagers attack the aliens Etey and Reiho. Daiya's mother gives birth to a nontelepathic child, a solitary; but Daiya quickly gives her to Etey to take to the comet world, rather than see her killed. Daiya lives as an outcast of her village, but Homesmind promises to watch over her.

Eye of the Comet continues the saga with Lydee, the solitary sister Daiya rescued from infanticide. Once more Sargent creates a strong female character who must face a test. Lydee journeys to Earth where she was born to be a link between it and the comet world. Lydee is shocked by the primitive life on Earth and finds the ways of Earth's people alien to her. Unlike the action that marked Daiya's quest, Lydee's conflict is more philosophical and psychological. Sargent allows her character to become a sounding board for discussion of questions of death and afterlife, the existence of the soul, and powers of the mind. Lydee meets Daiya, Reiho, and other characters from *Watchstar*; but although the cast of characters has grown and the settings are familiar to readers of the first novel, *Eye of the Comet* can stand alone as the story of a girl caught in the clash of two cultures and searching for identity and love.

Homesmind concludes the trilogy and Sargent continues the story of conflict between telepathic earthlings and the comet dwellers whose advanced technology allows them to link minds. Anra, the Earthborn heroine, lacks the gift of telepathy and must use Homesmind technology to enter the Net of her people. Again Sargent explores the philosophical questions raised in the trilogy's previous volumes, as she tells of the conditions of life on Earth and the comet world. Once more, it is a young female character who must deal with portentous events, such as alien invasion and the dissolution of her society.

Sargent explores space colonization in *Earthseed*. A cybernetic spaceship carries genetic material for breeding Earth children through the universe. As the ship nears a habitable planet, the children are readied for the project. Zoheret, with all her adolescent insecurities and fears, must leave the ship and face an ordeal for

survival with her peers. A complex examination of the motives for colonization provides part of the novel's conflict, and Sargent again focuses on the developing strengths of a young female character who finds herself in a rite of passage.

Sargent develops some of the same themes in *Alien Child*. Nita believes she is the only human being left on Earth as she lives her life in the Kwalung-Ibarra Institute with her alien guardian Llipel. Nita's quest for knowledge of her origin leads to her discovery of Sven, a boy raised in the same fashion by Llare, Llipel's companion. Nita and Sven leave the protection of the Institute to take up a quest to search for other human survivors. In a journey filled with hardship and wonder, they learn they are the only humans left on Earth. Llipel and Llare are waiting for them at the end of the quest with a visitor from space. Raen is a human, one of those who left Earth in its decaying days, fearful of war, to wander the universe. Those in space have changed and adapted, linking minds telepathically. Nita and Sven are not like them. Yet, Nita and Sven are not alone; there are more embryos to revive in the "cold room." Nita and Sven will be their guardians until they can take their places on Earth or with Raen and his people in space.

Sargent's stories are filled with science-fiction themes of space colonization, telepathy, aliens, and an Earth transformed. She provides the excitement of good storytelling and the intellectual speculations of quality science fiction. Sargent consistently provides strong female characters involved in arduous quest journeys who are the role models she stated girls needed to find in science fiction. Her work contributes to the demise of the stereotype of women in the world of science fiction.

—Janice Antczak

SAUER, Julia (Lina). American. Born in Rochester, New York, in 1891. Educated at the University of Rochester; New York State Library School, Albany. Head of children's department, Rochester Public Library, 1921–58. *Died 26 June 1983.*

PUBLICATIONS FOR CHILDREN

Fiction

Fog Magic. New York, Viking Press, 1943; London, Woodfield, 1960.
The Light at Tern Rock, illustrated by Georges Schreiber. New York, Viking Press, 1951.
Mike's House, illustrated by Don Freeman. New York, Viking Press, 1954.

Other

Editor, *Radio Roads to Reading: Library Book Talks Broadcast to Girls and Boys*. New York, Wilson, 1939.

*

Manuscript Collection: Kerlan Collection, University of Minnesota, Minneapolis.

*   *   *

In Julia Sauer's picture book for young people, *Mike's House*, as well as in her books for older children, *Fog Magic* and *The Light at*

Tern Rock, she shows a love of nature, place, and people. Sauer is meticulous in her handling of nature, in particular its less enjoyable aspects, such as blizzards and dense fogs. She is sensitive to place (for instance North Mountain in Nova Scotia, the setting for *Fog Magic*), providing details about a town or a building or a room which make them vividly three-dimensional. And most of all she cares about people, their inner fantasies and their outer behavior. The coexistence of fantasy and reality, especially among her child characters, is seen most clearly in *Fog Magic*. In this book Sauer states that most of us live in two worlds, our real world and the one we build for ourselves out of the books we read, the heroes we admire, the things we hope to do. This book's heroine, 11-year-old Greta, lives in a modern world on one side of the mountain, but is obsessed with another world, a lost fishing village on the other side of the mountain. The story goes back and forth from the real present to the conjured-up past, pointing out the thin line between a person's reality and his fantasy, and the need for an acceptance of the two.

Mike's House, a book for much younger children, is also concerned with human needs and dreams, and, importantly, human interdependence. Four-year-old Robert sees the public library as a second home, and a fictional character as his best friend. He does not wish to share this best friend with others, but as others reach out to help him, he is finally able to respond to them.

Sauer's understanding of human nature and human development comes through clearly in her works. She has an excellent command of words and imagery. Her style, though, is didactic, and her message is labored by today's standards. Nevertheless, her obvious caring for nature, place, and especially people contributes to her continued appeal.

—Mary Lystad

SAVILLE, (Leonard) Malcolm. British. Born in Hastings, Sussex, 21 February 1901. Educated at Richmond Hill School, Surrey, and other private schools. Married Dorothy May McCoy in 1926; two sons and two daughters. Member of the publicity department, Cassell and Company, publishers, London, 1920–22; member of the publicity department, and sales promotion manager, Amalgamated Press, London, 1922–36; sales promotion manager, 1936–40, and editor of "Sunny Stories" series and of general books, 1955–66, George Newnes, London; associate editor, *My Garden* magazine, London and Guildford, Surrey, 1947–52; publicity and feature writer, Kemsley Newspapers, London, 1952–55. *Died 30 June 1982.*

PUBLICATIONS FOR CHILDREN

Fiction

Mystery at Witchend, illustrated by G.E. Breary. London, Newnes, 1943; as *Spy in the Hills*, New York, Farrar and Rinehart, 1945.
Seven White Gates, illustrated by Bertram Prance. London, Newnes, 1944.
The Gay Dolphin Adventure. London, Newnes, 1945.
Trouble at Townsend. London, Transatlantic Arts, 1945.
The Secret of Grey Walls. London, Newnes, 1947.
The Riddle of the Painted Box, illustrated by Lunt Roberts. London, Transatlantic Arts, 1947.
Redshank's Warning, illustrated by Lunt Roberts. London, Lutterworth Press, 1948.
Two Fair Plaits, illustrated by Lunt Roberts. London, Lutterworth Press, 1948.

Lone Pine Five, illustrated by Bertram Prance. London, Newnes, 1949.
Strangers at Snowfell, illustrated by Wynne. London, Lutterworth Press, 1949.
The Master of Maryknoll, illustrated by Alice Bush. London, Evans, 1950.
The Sign of the Alpine Rose, illustrated by Wynne. London, Lutterworth Press, 1950.
The Flying Fish Adventure, illustrated by Lunt Roberts. London, Murray, 1950.
All Summer Through, illustrated by Joan Kiddell-Monroe. London, Hodder and Stoughton, 1951.
The Elusive Grasshopper, illustrated by Bertram Prance. London, Newnes, 1951.
The Buckinghams at Ravenswyke, illustrated by Alice Bush. London, Evans, 1952.
The Luck of Sallowby, illustrated by Tilden Reeves. London, Lutterworth Press, 1952.
The Ambermere Treasure, illustrated by Marcia Lane Foster. London, Lutterworth Press, 1953; as *The Secret of the Ambermere Treasure*, New York, Criterion, 1967.
Christmas at Nettleford, illustrated by Joan Kiddell-Monroe. London, Hodder and Stoughton, 1953.
The Secret of the Hidden Pool, illustrated by Lunt Roberts. London, Murray, 1953.
The Neglected Mountain, illustrated by Bertram Prance. London, Newnes, 1953.
Spring Comes to Nettleford, illustrated by Joan Kiddell-Monroe. London, Hodder and Stoughton, 1954.
The Long Passage, illustrated by Alice Bush. London, Evans, 1954.
Susan, Bill and the Ivy-Clad Oak [*Wolf-Dog, Golden Clock, Vanishing Boy, Dark Stranger, "Saucy Kate," Bright Star Circus, Pirates Bold*], illustrated by Ernest Shepard and T.R. Freeman. London, Nelson, 8 vols., 1954–61.
Saucers over the Moor, illustrated by Bertram Prance. London, Newnes, 1955.
Where the Bus Stopped. Oxford, Blackwell, 1955.
The Secret of Buzzard Scar, illustrated by Joan Kiddell-Monroe. London, Hodder and Stoughton, 1955.
Young Johnnie Bimbo, illustrated by Lunt Roberts. London, Murray, 1956.
Wings over Witchend. London, Newnes, 1956.
Lone Pine London. London, Newnes, 1957.
Treasure at the Mill, illustrated by Harry Pettit. London, Newnes, 1957.
The Fourth Key, illustrated by Lunt Roberts. London, Murray, 1957.
The Secret of the Gorge. London, Newnes, 1958.
Mystery Mine. London, Newnes, 1959.
Four-and-Twenty Blackbirds, illustrated by Lilian Buchanan. London, Newnes, 1959; as *The Secret of Galleybird Pit*, London, Armada, 1968.
Sea Witch Comes Home. London, Newnes, 1960.
Not Scarlet But Gold, illustrated by A.R. Whitear. London, Newnes, 1962.
A Palace for the Buckinghams, illustrated by Alice Bush. London, Evans, 1963.
Three Towers in Tuscany. London, Heinemann, 1963.
The Purple Valley. London, Heinemann, 1964.
Treasure at Amorys, illustrated by T.R. Freeman. London, Newnes, 1964.
Dark Danger. London, Heinemann, 1965.
White Fire. London, Heinemann, 1966.
The Thin Grey Man, illustrated by Desmond Knight. London, Macmillan, and New York, St. Martin's Press, 1966.

Man with Three Fingers, illustrated by Michael Whittlesea. London, Newnes, 1966.
Strange Story. London, Mowbray, 1967.
Power of Three. London, Heinemann, 1968.
Rye Royal. London, Collins, 1969.
Strangers at Witchend. London, Collins, 1970.
The Dagger and the Flame. London, Heinemann, 1970.
The Secret of Villa Rosa. London, Collins, 1971.
Where's My Girl? London, Collins, 1972.
Diamond in the Sky. London, Collins, 1974.
Marston, Master Spy. London, Heinemann, 1978.
Home to Witchend. London, Armada, 1978.

Other

Country Scrap Book. London, National Magazine Company, 1944; revised edition, London, Gramol, 1945.
Open-Air Scrap Book. London, Gramol, 1945.
Seaside Scrap Book. London, Gramol, 1946.
Jane's Country Year, illustrated by Bernard Bowerman. London, Newnes, 1946.
Adventure of the Life-Boat Service. London, Macdonald, 1950.
Coronation Gift Book. London, Daily Graphic-Pitkins, 1952.
King of Kings (life of Christ). London, Nelson, 1958; revised edition, Berkhamsted, Hertfordshire, Lion, 1975; Huntingdon, Indiana, Our Sunday Visitor, 1977.
Small Creatures, illustrated by John Kenney. London, Ward, 1959.
Country Book. London, Cassell, 1961.
Seaside Book. London, Cassell, 1962.
Come to London [*Cornwall, Devon, Somerset*]. London, Heinemann, 1 vol., Benn, 3 vols., 1967–70.
Eat What You Grow, illustrated by Robert Micklewright. London, Carousel, 1975.
Portrait of Rye, illustrated by Michael Renton. East Grinstead, Sussex, Goulden, 1976.
The Countryside Quiz Book, illustrated by Robert Micklewright. London, Carousel, 1978.
Wonder Why Book of Exploring a Wood, illustrated by Elsie Wrigley. London, Corgi, 1978.
Wonder Why Book of Exploring the Seashore, illustrated by Jenny Heath. London, Corgi, 1979.
Wonder Why Book of Wild Flowers Through the Year. London, Corgi, 1980.
The Seashore Quiz, illustrated by Robert Micklewright. London, Carousel, 1981.

Editor, *Words for All Seasons*, illustrated by Elsie and Paul Wrigley. Guildford, Surrey, Lutterworth Press, 1979.

*   *   *

Malcolm Saville's nearly 40-year-long career, the profusion of his books and their best-selling status, and the formulaic structures of his stories prompt obvious comparisons with Enid Blyton. To say this is not to place his name—or hers—upon the list of condemned authors. Like Blyton's, and like the necessarily candy-tasting, cyclamate-coloured, insubstantial works of recipe writers whose ageless children are set in sundrenched stables and impossible Swiss unfinishing schools of an endless summer holiday, his faithful bands of chums repeat the unkillable, splendid rituals of secret oaths, perfect campsites, night stalking, kidnapped twins, and mysterious watches with torches and binoculars on cliff edges at the very mid of night.

Much to be said for such delights; so much, that perhaps we may say that without them—without creaking Elizabethan Inns, lone pines and fog on the Stiperstones, without the landscapes of the

English late Romantic movement (Housman, Kipling)—children cannot be said to have entered the culture, any more than they can if they know no old songs nor fairy stories. And besides, Saville had something upright and manly to him: *his* beautiful tomboy is quietly and unwittingly in love with his excellent public school hero (*Lone Pine Five*); his working class evacuee has plenty of stomach and is patronized by nobody (*Seven White Gates*); his spectacled swot really does have an intellectual life of his own (*The Gay Dolphin Adventure*); his pert twins show the telepathic briskness of response and shrewdness of observation which make the state of twinhood so classically wantable (*Wings over Witchend*).

And Saville *was* willing to explore new territory. In the 1960's he began to tackle the difficult task of catering for the 13-plus age group with his seven books (starting with *Three Towers in Tuscany*) about Marston Baines, a Secret Service agent. These never achieved the success of the Lone Pine series, and their excitement has to some extent been eclipsed by the currently popular hard-hitting espionage thrillers, but they do offer sufficient action and romance to attract young teenage readers and older children.

Above all, Saville had and conveyed a powerful, at times sweeping feeling for the lovely, singular landscapes around Ludlow and Rye, forever unspoiled and unvisited by the Sunshine Club, strongly mysterious, varied, rich, solitary. His safe, careful, decent stories are the honest reading equivalent of the best of the Betty Box movies, and I for one would be sorry to see them disappear.

—Fred Inglis

———

SAWYER, Ruth. American. Born in Boston, Massachusetts, 5 August 1880. Educated at Mrs. Brackett's School, New York, 1887; Garland Kindergarten Normal School, graduated 1900; Columbia University, New York, B.S. 1904. Married Albert C. Durand in 1911; one son and one daughter. Helped organize kindergartens in Cuba, 1900; correspondent in Ireland for New York *Sun*, 1905, 1907; from 1908 professional storyteller and lecturer. Lived in Spain, 1931–32. Recipient: American Library Association Newbery Medal, 1937, and Laura Ingalls Wilder award, 1965; Catholic Library Association Regina Medal, 1965. *Died 3 June 1970.*

PUBLICATIONS FOR CHILDREN

Fiction

The Tale of the Enchanted Bunnies. New York, Harper, 1923.
Toño Antonio, illustrated by F. Luis Mora. New York, Viking Press, 1934.
Roller Skates, illustrated by Valenti Angelo. New York, Viking Press, 1936; London, Bodley Head, 1964.
The Year of Jubilo, illustrated by Edward Shenton. New York, Viking Press, 1940; as *Lucinda's Year of Jubilo*, London, Bodley Head, 1965.
The Least One, illustrated by Leo Politi. New York, Viking Press, 1941.
The Christmas Anna Angel, illustrated by Kate Seredy. New York, Viking Press, 1944; London, Cassell, 1948.
Old Con and Patrick, illustrated by Cathal O'Toole. New York, Viking Press, 1946.
The Little Red Horse, illustrated by Jay Hyde Barnum. New York, Viking Press, 1950.
Maggie Rose, Her Birthday Christmas, illustrated by Maurice Sen-

dak. New York, Harper, 1952.

The Gold of Bernardino. Privately printed, 1952.

A Cottage for Betsy, illustrated by Vera Bock. New York, Harper, 1954.

The Enchanted Schoolhouse, illustrated by Hugh Troy. New York, Viking Press, 1956; Leicester, Brockhampton Press, 1958.

The Year of the Christmas Dragon, illustrated by Hugh Troy. New York, Viking Press, 1960.

Daddles: The Story of a Plain Hound-Dog, illustrated by Robert Frankenberg. Boston, Little Brown, 1964.

Verse

A Child's Year-Book, illustrated by the author. New York, Harper, 1917.

Other

This Way to Christmas. New York, Harper, 1916; revised edition, 1967.

Picture Tales from Spain, illustrated by Carlos Sanchez. New York, Stokes, 1936.

The Long Christmas, illustrated by Valenti Angelo. New York, Viking Press, 1941; London, Bodley Head, 1964.

This Is the Christmas: A Serbian Folk Tale. Boston, Horn Book, 1945.

Journey Cake, Ho!, illustrated by Robert McCloskey. New York, Viking Press, 1953.

Dietrich of Berne and the Dwarf-King Laurin: Hero Tales of the Austrian Tirol, with Emmy Mollès, illustrated by Frederick Chapman. New York, Viking Press, 1963.

Joy to the World: Christmas Legends, illustrated by Trina Schart Hyman. Boston, Little Brown, 1966.

My Spain: A Story-Teller's Year of Collecting. New York, Viking Press, 1967.

Recording: *Ruth Sawyer, Storyteller*, 1965.

PUBLICATIONS FOR ADULTS

Novels

The Primrose Ring. New York, Harper, 1915.

Seven Miles to Arden. New York, Harper, 1916.

Herself, Himself, and Myself: A Romance. New York, Harper, 1917.

Leerie. New York, Harper, 1920.

The Silver Sixpence. New York, Harper, 1921.

Gladiola Murphy. New York, Harper, 1923.

Four Ducks on a Pond. New York, Harper, 1928.

Folkhouse: The Autobiography of a Home. New York, Appleton, 1932.

The Luck of the Road. New York, Appleton Century, 1934.

Gallant: The Story of Storm Veblen. New York, Appleton Century, 1936.

Short Stories

Doctor Danny. New York, Harper, 1918.

Plays

The Sidhe of Ben-Mor: An Irish Folk Play. Boston, Badger, 1910.

The Awakening (produced New York, 1918).

Other

The Way of the Storyteller. New York, Viking Press, 1942; London, Harrap, 1944; revised edition, Viking Press, 1962; London, Penguin, 1976.

How to Tell a Story. Chicago, Compton, 1962.

*

Manuscript Collection: College of Sainte Catherine Library, St. Paul, Minnesota.

Critical Study: *Ruth Sawyer* by Virginia Haviland, London, Bodley Head, and New York, Walck, 1965.

*   *   *

For most of her adult life a storyteller with consummate gifts—whose tales both oral and written could be characterized as living folk-art—Ruth Sawyer received both the Laura Ingalls Wilder and the Regina Medals for her numerous distinguished contributions to children's literature. Something of her strong positive personality and her unlimited creative power are conveyed by Virginia Haviland in her delightfully intimate and revealing monograph, *Ruth Sawyer*. In one characterization, Haviland says of her: "Sentences flowed full and colorful, projected in the still rich and vibrant voice—one more revelation of the teller's oral gifts. She was ever the story-teller, 'the way' shining through everything she had to say."

The procession of Sawyer's work had several emphases: stories she drew from her remembered childhood, legends and tales she collected from several countries, including some she visited for extended periods, e.g. Cuba, Ireland, Spain (the setting for *Toño Antonio* and *Picture Tales from Spain*), and finally works related to the festival of Christmas which she used as both a strong spiritual symbol and the focus for warm human ingathering.

Drawn from the recollections of her growing years is *Roller Skates*, Newbery Medal winner, featuring a 10-year-old tomboy, Lucinda Wyman, in an 1890 New York City setting. We see Lucinda's "higgledly-piggledy" life during a tremendous year of growth and learning. Its sequel, *The Year of Jubilo*, follows Lucinda after her father's death when she and her family resettle in their summer cottage in Maine. In this volume are more "impetuosities, brutal honesties, crudities" and examples of "cock-sure independence." Especially noteworthy are the letters written by Lucinda to those left behind in New York.

The author's rich and loving humor and her warmth—together with her appreciation of the richness of commonality as well as the festival quality in Christmas—is reflected in *This Way to Christmas*, real stories told to a lonesome boy stranded in northern New York. *The Long Christmas* contains Christmas legends and carols from around the world, together with a song of Saint Stephen with music. *The Christmas Anna Angel* follows the preparations of a Hungarian family during World War II for a bare Christmas, but the young heroine is resolute in her belief that her angel will provide cake for their tree. *This Is the Christmas*, a Serbian folktale, is told by a Serbian grandmother and features a blind boy shepherd who pipes to a carol. *Maggie Rose, Her Birthday Christmas* follows the daughter of an impoverished family in Maine who tries to raise some money so that her family can enjoy a birthday Christmas party. *The Year of the Christmas Dragon*, also set in Maine, presents a charming story, contrasting the long ago ancient times with "the time called now" and offering a wonderful spring promise. Referred to as "woven magic," *Joy to the World: Christmas Legends* contains a group of legends from ancient Arabia, Serbia, and Spain, as well as Christmas carols.

Journey Cake, Ho! is a lovely version of the old folktale. *The*

Enchanted Schoolhouse is the story of a young immigrant from Ireland. Eager to carry a bit of his beloved country with him, he captures "a wee fairyman" and conceals him in a teapot all the way to "Maine, USA where the two of them turned Lobster Cove topsy-turvy." Something of the relationship emerges in the fairyman's plea: "Laddy, laddy, let me loose. This is no country to be coming to. All the wizards in the world must have made it." The hero tales *Dietrich of Berne and the Dwarf-King Laurin* are drawn from the mountain people of the Austrian Tyrol. In life the hero Dietrich becomes Theodoric the Great, on whose shield the Red Lion rested. *My Spain: A Story-Teller's Year of Collecting* can be enjoyed by young people as well as adults for its picture of Spain and the charming adventures and people Sawyer encountered there.

Sawyer's composite work is "gloriously alive; all the warmth and delightful chuckliness of her personality flood through the stories she tells....She writes as a jongleur might speak, in a fashion much more intense and exalted and heightened than is usual." Her long and productive life and the treasured writing she left behind provide multiple and richly varied examples of "the way of the storyteller." As Sawyer remembered her Irish nurse Johanna's influence on her, she herself succeeded in handling words so that they "join hands and dance, making a fairy ring that completely encircled" her readers.

—Clara O. Jackson

SCANNELL, Vernon. British. Born in Spilsby, Lincolnshire, 23 January 1922. Educated at Queen's Park School, Aylesbury, Buckinghamshire; University of Leeds, Yorkshire, 1946–47. Served in the Gordon Highlanders, 1941–45. Married Josephine Higson in 1954; two daughters and three sons. Professional boxer, 1945–46; English teacher, Hazelwood School, Limpsfield, Surrey, 1955–62. Since 1962 freelance writer and broadcaster. Resident poet, village of Berinsfield, Oxfordshire, 1978; visiting poet, Shrewsbury School, Shropshire, 1978–79, and King's School, Canterbury, 1979. Recipient (for poetry): Heinemann award, 1961; Arts Council grant, 1967, 1970; Cholmondeley award, 1974; Southern Arts Writers fellowship, 1975; Society of Authors travelling scholarship, 1987. Fellow, Royal Society of Literature, 1960. Granted Civil List pension, 1981. Address: 51 North Street, Otley, West Yorkshire LS21 1AH, England.

PUBLICATIONS FOR CHILDREN

Fiction

The Dangerous Ones. Oxford, Pergamon Press, 1970.
A Lonely Game. Exeter, Wheaton, 1979.

Verse

Mastering the Craft. Oxford, Pergamon Press, 1970.
The Apple-Raid and Other Poems. London, Chatto and Windus, 1974.
Catch the Light, with Gregory Harrison and Laurence Smith. Oxford, Oxford University Press, 1982; New York, Oxford University Press, 1983.
The Clever Potato, illustrated by Tony Ross. London, Hutchinson, 1988.

PUBLICATIONS FOR ADULTS

Novels

The Fight. London, Peter Nevill, 1953.

The Wound and the Scar. London, Peter Nevill, 1953.
The Big Chance. London, Long, 1960.
The Shadowed Place. London, Long, 1961.
The Face of the Enemy. London, Putnam, 1961.
The Dividing Night. London, Putnam, 1962.
The Big Time. London, Longman, 1965.
Ring of Truth. London, Robson, 1983.

Plays

Radio Plays: *A Man's Game*, 1962; *A Door with One Eye*, 1963; *The Cancelling Dark*, music by Christopher Whelen, 1965.

Verse

Graves and Resurrections. London, Fortune Press, 1948.
A Mortal Pitch. London, Villiers, 1957.
The Masks of Love. London, Putnam, 1960.
A Sense of Danger. London, Putnam, 1962.
Walking Wounded. London, Eyre and Spottiswoode, 1965.
Epithets of War: Poems 1965–1969. London, Eyre and Spottiswoode, 1969.
Pergamon Poets 8, with Jon Silkin, edited by Dennis Butts. Oxford, Pergamon Press, 1970.
Selected Poems. London, Allison and Busby, 1971.
Company of Women. Frensham, Surrey, Sceptre Press, 1971.
Corgi Modern Poets in Focus 4, with others, edited by Jeremy Robson. London, Corgi, 1971.
Incident at West Bay. Richmond, Surrey, Keepsake Press, 1972.
The Winter Man: New Poems. London, Allison and Busby, 1973.
Meeting in Manchester. Rushden, Northamptonshire, Sceptre Press, 1974.
The Loving Game. London, Robson, 1975.
An Ilkley Quintet. Privately printed, 1975(?).
A Morden Tower Reading 1, with Alexis Lykiard. Newcastle upon Tyne, Morden Tower, 1976.
New and Collected Poems 1950–1980. London, Robson, 1980.
Winterlude. London, Robson, 1982.
Funeral Games and Other Poems. London, Robson, 1987.
Soldiering On: Poems of Military Life. London, Robson, 1989.

Other

Edward Thomas. London, Longman, 1963.
The Tiger and the Rose: An Autobiography. London, Hamish Hamilton, 1971.
Three Poets, Two Children, with Dannie Abse and Leonard Clark, edited by Desmond Badham-Thornhill. Gloucester, Thornhill Press, 1975.
Not Without Glory: Poets of the Second World War. London, Woburn Press, 1976.
A Proper Gentleman. London, Robson, 1977.
How to Enjoy Poetry. Loughton, Essex, Piatkus, 1983.
How to Enjoy Novels. London, Piatkus, 1984.
Argument of Kings: An Autobiography. London, Robson, 1987.

Editor, with Patricia Beer and Ted Hughes, *New Poems 1962*. London, Hutchinson, 1962.
Editor, *Your Attention Please: An Anthology from the Open University Poets.* Winchester, Hampshire, Hesperus, 1983.
Editor, *Sporting Literature.* Oxford, Oxford University Press, 1987.

*

Manuscript Collection: British Library, London.

Vernon Scannell comments:

I strongly agree with W.H. Auden who said that while there are some good poems which are only for adults because they presuppose adult experience in their readers, there are no good poems which are only for children. In other words I hope that none of my children's poems condescends or patronizes the young reader and that each one would give pleasure to a reader of any age.

*　　*　　*

The range of Vernon Scannell's talents—whether exemplified in his life or his art—is wide and consistently impressive. He has been a boxer, amateur and professional, a soldier with the Gordon Highlanders, serving in France and the Middle East during World War II, and has also worked in the fairground. As far as his literary career is concerned, he is perhaps best-known for his many collections of poetry for adults; he has also published an autobiography and written criticism and plays for the radio. His work for children includes two novels and several collections of verse.

One of Scannell's most remarkable qualities as a poet for children, and it is one which he has himself identified as being of prime importance in his own criticism, is an ability not merely to describe an action, a mood, an experience, but to enter into it through the medium of his writing, which means that when the reader comes into contact with it, the experience of reading is remarkably similar to actually participating in that which is described. It is a poetry of direct presentation, a poetry of happenings, a poetry that does not merely concern itself with the abstract reportage of events, but gets to the living roots of the events themselves. Something about the physical quality of the language impresses itself upon us, and perhaps this relates directly to the fact that Scannell has been in his life as much a man of action as one of reflection—the qualities that Yeats thought were antagonistic to each other, eternally irreconcilable.

Scannell's poetry for children uses a wide range of subject matter and a variety of techniques. He seems to be very much at home in a balladic stanza. Consider, for example, "The Ballad of Wee Duncan and Red John," in which a young boy, Wee Duncan Bain, is assisted back to his home in the thick of a raging storm by a stranger who proves to be, we are left in no doubt, the wraith of his father, who was himself lost in a storm off the Isle of Wight. There is a surging strength and a vividness in the simplicity of this ballad, a perfect matching of striding metre and clear, bold words, that leaves us in no doubt that the poet is very much at ease in this particular country of the mind. But his talents seem to suit other clothes just as well. The fascinating poem "Junk," for example, might be described as the barebones of a science-fiction novel set in verse. A father and his son peer into a shop window crowded with strange relics from the past, including primitive machines that were once operated manually, the skins of extinct animals that were once worn as clothes, and something "shaped/ Like an oblong box, its lifted lid/ Showed no interior but solid stuff/ In slender layers…" The poem beautifully points up the essential strangeness of so much that we take for granted in our lives, and helps children to perceive things anew as they come to grips with the meaning of the poem—something that happens slowly, but all the more profoundly precisely because of that fact. The strange object is, of course, a book…

—Michael Glover

———

SCARRY, Richard (McClure). American. Born in Boston, Massachusetts, 5 June 1919. Educated at the Boston Museum School of Fine Arts, 1939–42, 1969–71. Served in the United States Army in North Africa and the Mediterranean, 1942–46: Captain. Married Patricia Murphy in 1948; one son. Freelance artist and writer, New York, 1946–49, Connecticut, 1949–68, and Switzerland since 1968. Recipient: Mystery Writers of America Edgar Allan Poe Special award, 1976. Address: Schwyzerhus, 3780 Gstaad, Switzerland.

PUBLICATIONS FOR CHILDREN (illustrated by the author)

Fiction

The Great Big Car and Truck Book. New York, Simon and Schuster, 1951.
Rabbit and His Friends. New York, Simon and Schuster, 1953; London, Muller, 1954.
Naughty Bunny. New York, Golden Press, and London, Muller, 1959.
Tinker and Tanker. New York, Doubleday, 1960; London, Hamlyn, 1969.
Tinker and Tanker Out West. New York, Doubleday, 1961; London, Hamlyn, 1969.
Tinker and Tanker and Their Space Ship. New York, Doubleday, 1961; as *Tinker and Tanker Journey to Tootletown and Build a Spaceship*, New York, Golden Press, 1978.
Tinker and Tanker and the Pirates. New York, Doubleday, 1961.
Tinker and Tanker, Knights of the Round Table. New York, Doubleday, 1963; London, Hamlyn, 1969.
Tinker and Tanker in Africa. New York, Doubleday, 1963; London, Hamlyn, 1969.
Best Word Book Ever. New York, Golden Press, 1963; London, Hamlyn, 1964; revised edition, Golden Press, 1980; as *A Scarry Wordbook*, Hamlyn, 1979.
Polite Elephant. New York, Golden Press, 1964.
Is This the House of Mistress Mouse? New York, Golden Press, 1964.
Feed the Hippo His ABC's. New York, Golden Press, 1964.
Teeny Tiny Tales. New York, Golden Press, 1965; London, Hamlyn, 1970.
The Santa Claus Book. New York, Golden Press, 1965.
The Bunny Book. New York, Golden Press, 1965; London, Golden Pleasure Books, 1966.
Busy Busy World. New York, Golden Press, 1965; London, Hamlyn, 1966.
Egg in the Hole Book. New York, Golden Press, 1967.
Best Storybook Ever. New York, Golden Press, 1968; London, Hamlyn, 1969.
The Early Bird. New York, Random House, 1968; London, Collins, 1970.
The Great Pie Robbery. New York, Random House, and London, Collins, 1969.
The Supermarket Mystery. New York, Random House, and London, Collins, 1969.
Great Big Schoolhouse. New York, Random House, and London, Collins, 1969.
Great Big Air Book. New York, Random House, and London, Collins, 1971.
Best Stories Ever. New York, Golden Press, 1971.
Funniest Storybook Ever. New York, Random House, and London, Collins, 1972; selections, as *Little Bedtime Book* and *Mr. Fixit*, Random House and Collins, 2 vols., 1978.
Nicky Goes to the Doctor. New York, Golden Press, and London, Hamlyn, 1972.
Silly Stories. New York, Golden Press, 1973; London, Hamlyn, 1974.
Babykins and His Family. New York, Golden Press, 1973; London, Hamlyn, 1974.

Great Steamboat Mystery. New York, Random House, 1975; London, Collins, 1976.

Favorite Storybook. New York, Random House, and London, Collins, 1976.

Busy Town, Busy People. New York, Random House, and London, Collins, 1976.

Storytime. London, Collins, 1976; New York, Random House, 1978.

Lowly Worm Story Book. New York, Random House, 1977; London, Collins, 1979.

Busy, Busy Word Book. New York, Random House, 1977; as *Little Word Book*, 1978.

Postman Pig and His Busy Neighbors. New York, Random House, 1978; London, Fontana, 1979.

Toy Book. New York, Random House, 1978; London, Collins, 1979.

Bedtime Stories. New York, Random House, 1978.

Tinker and Tanker Tales of Pirates and Knights. New York, Golden Press, 1979.

To Market, To Market. New York, Golden Press, 1979.

Holiday Book. London, Collins, 1979.

Work and Play Book. London, Collins, 1979.

Mix or Match Storybook. New York, Random House, 1979; London, Collins, 1980.

Best First Book Ever. New York, Random House, 1979; London, Collins, 1980; revised edition as *Board Books* (*Colours, My House,* and *Things I Do*), London, Collins, 3 vols., 1982.

Huckle's Book. New York, Random House, and London, Collins, 1979.

Peasant Pig and the Terrible Dragon. New York, Random House, 1980; London, Collins, 1981.

Christmas Mice. New York, Golden Press, 1981.

Best Christmas Book Ever. New York, Random House, and London, Collins, 1981.

Busy Houses. New York, Random House, 1981; London, Collins, 1982.

Four Busy Word Books. New York, Random House, 1982.

The Best Mistake Ever! and Other Stories. New York, Random House, 1984; London, Collins, 1985.

Best Bumper Book Ever. London, Collins, 1984.

Biggest Word Book Ever! New York, Random House, 1985; London, Hamlyn, 1986.

Big and Little. Racine, Wisconsin, Golden Press, 1986.

My First Word Book. New York, Random House, 1986.

Best Music Book Ever. London, Hamlyn, 1987.

Things That Go. New York, Golden Press, 1987.

Things to Love. New York, Golden Press, 1987.

Busy Workers. New York, Golden Press, 1987.

Splish Splash Sounds. New York, Golden Press, 1988.

Best Two-Minute Stories Ever! New York, Golden Press, 1989.

Verse

The Hickory Dickory Clock Book. New York, Doubleday, 1961.

Other

Nursery Tales. New York, Simon and Schuster, 1958.

Manners. New York, Golden Press, 1962.

What Animals Do. New York, Golden Press, 1963.

A Tinker and Tanker Coloring Book. New York, Doubleday, 1963.

The Rooster Struts. New York, Golden Press, 1963; as *The Golden Happy Book of Animals,* 1964; as *Animals,* London, Hamlyn, 1964.

Animal Mother Goose. New York, Golden Press, 1964; London, Hamlyn, 1965.

Best Nursery Rhymes Ever. New York, Golden Press, 1964; London, Hamlyn, 1971.

Storybook Dictionary. New York, Golden Press, 1966.

Planes. New York, Golden Press, 1967.

Trains. New York, Golden Press, 1967; with *Cars,* London, Golden Pleasure Books, 1969.

Boats. New York, Golden Press, 1967; with *Planes,* London, Hamlyn, 1969.

Cars. New York, Golden Press, 1967.

What Do People Do All Day? New York, Random House, 1968; London, Collins, 1969.

What Animals Do. New York, Golden Press, 1968.

ABC Word Book. New York, Random House, 1971; London, Collins, 1972.

Look and Learn Library (*Best Stories Ever, Fun with Words, Going Places, Things to Know*). New York, Golden Press, 4 vols., 1971; last vol. published, London, Collins, 1976.

Hop Aboard, Here We Go! New York, Golden Press, and London, Hamlyn, 1972.

Find Your ABC's. New York, Random House, 1973.

Please and Thank You Book. New York, Random House, and London, Collins, 1973.

Best Rainy Day Book Ever. New York, Random House, 1974; London, Hamlyn, 1975.

European Word Book. London, Hamlyn, 1974.

Cars and Trucks and Things That Go. New York, Golden Press, and London, Collins, 1974.

Animal Nursery Tales. New York, Golden Press, and London, Collins, 1975.

Best Counting Book Ever. New York, Random House, 1975; London, Collins, 1976.

Busiest People Ever. New York, Random House, 1976; London, Collins, 1977.

Look-Look Books (*All Day Long, All Year Long, In My Town, Learn to Count, About Animals, At Work, My House, On the Farm, On Vacation* [*On Holiday*], *Short and Tall*). New York, Golden Press, 10 vols., 1976; London, Hamlyn, 10 vols., 1977.

Early Words. New York, Random House, 1976; London, Collins, 1977.

Color Book. New York, Random House, 1976; London, Collins, 1977.

Laugh and Learn Library. New York, Random House, and London, Collins, 4 vols., 1976.

Picture Dictionary. London, Collins, 1976.

Teeny Tiny ABC. New York, Golden Press, and London, Hamlyn, 1976.

Little ABC. New York, Random House, and London, Collins, 1976.

Learn to Count. New York, Golden Press, 1976.

Best Make-It Book Ever. New York, Random House, 1977; London, Collins, 1978.

Busy-Busy Counting Book. London, Collins, 1977; as *Little Counting Book,* New York, Random House, 1978.

Stories to Color. New York, Random House, 1978; London, Collins, 1979.

Little Word Book. New York, Random House, 1978.

Punch-Out Toy Book. New York, Random House, 1978.

Things to Learn. New York, Golden Press, 1978.

Little ABC. New York, Random House, 1978.

Lowly Worm Sniffy [*Word, Coloring, Car and Truck, Bath*] *Book.* New York, Random House, 5 vols., 1978–84; 1 vol. published as *Words,* London, Collins, 1982.

Busytown Pop-Up Book. New York, Random House, 1979; London, Collins, 1980.

Can You Count. London, Collins, 1979.

Lowly Worm Things on Wheels [*Where Does It Come From?, Tell-Time*] *Book.* London, Collins, 3 vols., 1979; New York, Random

House, 3 vols., 1980.
Busytown Shape Book. London, Collins, 1982.
Sticker Books (On Holiday, At School, I Can Count to Eleven). London, Collins, 3 vols., 1982.
Pig Will and Pig Won't: A Book of Manners. New York, Random House, and London, Collins, 1984.
Busy Fun and Learn Book. Racine, Wisconsin, Golden Press, 1984; London, Hamlyn, 1987.
Best Workbooks Ever! (*Fun with Letters* [*Words, Reading, Sounds*]). New York, Random House, 4 vols., 1986.
Best Workbooks Ever! (*Fun with Numbers*). New York, Random House, 3 vols., 1986.
Going Places on the Water [*in the Air, in the Car, with Goldbug*]. London, Collins, 4 vols., 1987.
Lowly Worm's Schoolbag (*Words, Colors, ABC's, Numbers*). New York, Random House, 4 vols., 1987.
Getting Ready for School [*Writing, Numbers, Reading*]. New York, Random House, 4 vols., 1987.
Activity Book. London, Collins, 1988.
Welcome to Scarrytown. London, Hamlyn, 1989.
Best Puzzle Word Book Ever. London, Hamlyn, 1989.

Editor, *Fables*, by Jean de La Fontaine. New York, Doubleday, 1963.

*

Illustrator: *The Boss of the Barnyard* by Joan Hubbard, 1949; *Two Little Miners* by Margaret Wise Brown and Edith Thacher Hurd, 1949, and *Little Indian* by Brown, 1954; *Let's Go Fishing*, 1949, *Mouse's House*, 1949, *Duck and His Friends*, 1949, *Brave Cowboy Bill*, 1950, and *The Party Pig*, 1954, all by Kathryn and Byron Jackson, and *The Animals' Merry Christmas*, 1950, *Here Comes the Parade*, 1951, *The New Golden Almanac*, 1952, and *The Golden Bedtime Book*, 1955, all by Kathryn Jackson, and *My Nursery Tale Book*, 1961, by Jackson and Patsy Scarry; *Little Benny Wanted a Pony* by Oliver Barrett, 1950; *The Animals of Farmer Jones* by Leah Gale, 1953; *Danny Beaver's Secret*, 1953, *Pierre Bear*, 1954, *The Bunny Book*, 1955, and *Just For Fun*, 1960, all by Patricia Scarry; *Smokey the Bear* by Jane Werner, 1955; *My First Golden Dictionary* by Mary Reed and Edith Osswald, 1956; *My Golden Book of Manners* by Peggy Parish, 1962; *Tommy Visits the Doctor* by Jean Seligman and Levine Milton, 1962; *Nonsense Alphabet* by Edward Lear, 1962; *I Am a Bunny* by Ole Risom, 1963; *Rudolph the Red-Nosed Reindeer* by Barbara Shook Hazen, 1964; *The Golden Book of 365 Stories*, 1966; *Best Mother Goose Ever*, 1970; *Mother Goose*, 1972; *With the Animals*, 1975 (as *Meet the Animals*, 1982), *All Day Long*, 1975 (as *My Day*, 1984), *My House*, 1975, and *On Holiday*, n.d., all by J.D. Bevington; *Chipmunk's ABC* by Roberta Miller, 1976; *The Gingerbread Man*, 1981; *Little Red Riding Hood*, 1981; *Old Mother Hubbard*, 1983; *This Little Pig Went to Market*, 1983; *One, Two, Buckle My Shoe*, 1983; *Little Miss Muffet*, 1983.

* * *

Richard Scarry's literary output enjoys a huge following among today's children. Part of his success may be attributed to the fact that his works are closely related in style to the medium of film or television in their emphasis on action. *What Do People Do All Day?*, a typical Scarry title, contains pages crammed with drawings depicting everyday activities in minute detail. The accompanying text is usually limited to a description of the particular action taking place. Occasionally, flip comments give the straightforward explanations an added dimension. Scarry's characters are both human and animal. In many cases animal figures intended to represent people and human figures are used in the same drawing, a technique which provides

humor (e.g., a schoolbus loaded with owl pupils) and interest. The illustrations tend to have an air of cosiness and cuteness due to Scarry's use of rounded angles and a perspective which makes the characters appear to be operating in a miniature setting. All the characters smile, even in such unlikely situations as the fire brigade rescue in *Hop Aboard, Here We Go!*

Scarry's books are usually lacking in plot—rather they are a cumulation of bits of information in various spheres of knowledge. A typical Scarry title, *Great Big Schoolhouse*, contains a series of some 20 two–three page vignettes centred on the theme of school activities. The author details in chronological order the events and activities in which school children are apt to be involved. The text is very like the dialogue one would expect to find in an educational television program—questions are asked, admonitions are made (with regard to dangerous objects, for example), and comments are made on the behaviour of the illustrated characters. Humor is often derived from a straightforward comment juxtaposed against a ridiculous drawing.

Like Dr. Seuss, Scarry has hit on a formula for success which he uses repeatedly. His books with their endearing characters have a certain charm. However, in exchange for commercial success he has probably forfeited any real creative development as an artist and as a writer.

—Fran Ashdown

———

SCHAEFER, Jack (Warner). American. Born in Cleveland, Ohio, 19 November 1907. Educated at Oberlin College, Ohio, A.B. in English 1929; Columbia University, New York, 1929–30. Married 1) Eugenia Hammond Ives in 1931 (divorced 1948), three sons and one daughter; 2) Louise Wilhide Deans in 1949, three stepchildren. Reporter, United Press, New Haven, Connecticut, 1930–31; assistant director of education, Connecticut State Reformatory, Cheshire, 1931–38; associate editor, 1932–39, and editor, 1939–42, New Haven *Journal-Courier*; editorial writer, Baltimore *Sun*, 1942–44; associate editor, Norfolk *Virginian-Pilot*, 1944–48; associate, Lindsay Advertising Company, 1949. Editor and publisher, *Theatre News*, 1935–40, *The Movies*, 1939–41, and *Shoreliner*, 1949, all New Haven. Recipient: Western Literature Association Distinguished Achievement award, 1975. Agent: Harold Matson, 276 Fifth Avenue, New York, New York 10001. Address: 554 East Coronado Road, Santa Fe, New Mexico 87501, U.S.A.

PUBLICATIONS FOR CHILDREN

Fiction

Shane. Boston, Houghton Mifflin, 1949; London, Deutsch, 1954; edited by James C. Work, Lincoln, University of Nebraska Press, 1984.
First Blood. Boston, Houghton Mifflin, 1953; London, Deutsch, 1954.
The Canyon. Boston, Houghton Mifflin, 1953; augmented edition, as *The Canyon and Other Stories*, London, Deutsch, 1955.
Old Ramon, illustrated by Harold West. Boston, Houghton Mifflin, 1960; London, Deutsch, 1962.
The Plainsmen, illustrated by Lorence Bjorklund. Boston, Houghton Mifflin, 1963.
Stubby Pringle's Christmas, illustrated by Lorence Bjorklund.

Boston, Houghton Mifflin, 1964.
Mavericks, illustrated by Lorence Bjorklund. Boston, Houghton Mifflin, 1967; London, Deutsch, 1968.

Other

New Mexico. New York, Coward McCann, 1967.

PUBLICATIONS FOR ADULTS

Novels

The Pioneers. Boston, Houghton Mifflin, 1954; London, Deutsch, 1957.
Company of Cowards. Boston, Houghton Mifflin, 1957; London, Deutsch, 1958.
Monte Walsh. Boston, Houghton Mifflin, 1963; London, Deutsch, 1965.
The Short Novels of Jack Schaefer. Boston, Houghton Mifflin, 1967.

Short Stories

The Big Range. Boston, Houghton Mifflin, 1953; London, Deutsch, 1955.
The Kean Land and Other Stories. Boston, Houghton Mifflin, 1959; London, Deutsch, 1960.
Tales from the West. London, Hamish Hamilton, 1961.
Incident on the Trail. London, Corgi, 1962.
Collected Stories. Boston, Houghton Mifflin, 1966.
Jack Schaefer and the American West: Eight Stories, edited by C.E.J. Smith. London, Longman, 1978.
Conversations with a Pocket Gopher and Other Outspoken Neighbors. Santa Barbara, California, Capra Press, 1978.
The Collected Short Stories of Jack Schaefer. New York, Arbor House, 1985.

Other

The Great Endurance Horse Race: 600 Miles on a Single Mount, 1908, from Evanston, Wyoming, to Denver. Santa Fe, New Mexico, Stagecoach Press, 1963.
Heroes Without Glory: Some Goodmen of the Old West. Boston, Houghton Mifflin, 1965; London, Deutsch, 1966.
Adolphe Francis Alphonse Bandelier. Santa Fe, New Mexico, Press of the Territorian, 1966.
Hal West: Western Gallery. Santa Fe, Museum of New Mexico Press, 1971.
An American Bestiary. Boston, Houghton Mifflin, 1975.

Editor, *Out West: An Anthology of Stories.* Boston, Houghton Mifflin, 1955; London, Deutsch, 1959.

*

Manuscript Collection: Western History Research Center, University of Wyoming, Laramie.

Critical Study: *Jack Schaefer* by Gerald W. Haslam, Boise, Idaho, Boise State University, 1975.

Jack Schaefer comments:
   I have never deliberately and consciously written stories for children. I do not believe anyone should do so—except a writer aiming at youngsters just learning to read. I have always written my stories for people, for readers, regardless of age, doing the best job I could in each instance according to the tune and the tone and the possibilities of the material I was using. None of my books is solely for children—or solely for adults. My mail through the years has shown that the books have done what I hoped they would do: attracted readers of all ages.

*   *   *

   Jack Schaefer's fiction-writing career began in 1949 with *Shane*, an understated tale of a gunman's involvement with a homesteading family in Wyoming, told from the point of view of their son. It ended in 1967 with *Mavericks*, the movingly evocative reminiscences of Old Jake Hanlon, a dying cowboy lost in his memories of the long-extinct American west. These two books typify Schaefer's writings for many readers; they are the terminal points of a group of works uniformly concerned with the theme of growing up and stressing the responsibility that comes with experience and maturity.
   Shane, although not originally written for a youthful audience, has grown increasingly popular with young readers. Its story is simple, its point clear. The book's first-person narration gives immediacy to the emotional tensions between Shane and the Starrett family. Young Bob Starrett, the narrator, is torn between his admiration for Shane and his love for his parents, and gradually learns of the complex responsibilities of adulthood. And Shane himself, a reformed gunfighter who reluctantly resumes his violent craft to preserve the stable lives of Joe and Marion Starrett, is a poignant, dignified personification of the responsible individual.
   Old Ramon continues the theme of growing up. As Ramon, an aged Mexican sheepherder, leads his patron's son through a summer's work in the pastures, the boy comes to see that independence and responsibility go hand-in-hand, and the truly mature person is the one who accepts them both. Less substantial is *Stubby Pringle's Christmas*, a tall tale about a cowpoke who substitutes for Santa Claus. Even this slight work, however, reveals Schaefer's view of responsibility, for Pringle gives up a night's festivities to make gifts for a penniless family.
   Mavericks is the ultimate extension of Schaefer's recurring theme. Jake Hanlon, recalling his 70-odd years as ranch-hand and cowboy, discovers that he has contributed to the destruction of the west that he loves. He sees at last the cost of progress, and is sickened by his vision. The responsible person, Schaefer implies, must see what Jake sees: that actions have consequences, and that modern comforts come at the expense of a cruder but more vital world. Maturity, therefore, means accepting one's responsibilities to the world, the environment, and one's self. Schaefer heeds his own advice; since 1967 he has devoted himself to writing of mankind's effect upon the western environment and its inhabitants.

—Fred Erisman

SCHLEE, Ann (née Cumming). British. Born in Greenwich, Connecticut, United States, 26 May 1934. Educated at Downe House; Somerville College, Oxford, 1953–56, B.A. 1956. Married D.N.R. Schlee in 1957; three daughters and one son. Recipient: *Guardian* award, 1980. Agent: Rogers Coleridge and White Ltd., 20 Powis Mews, London W11 1JN. Address: Qalvey, Upper Basildon, near Reading, Berkshire RG8 8LU, England.

PUBLICATIONS FOR CHILDREN

Fiction

The Strangers, illustrated by Pat Marriott. London, Macmillan,

1971; New York, Atheneum, 1972.

The Consul's Daughter. London, Macmillan, and New York, Atheneum, 1972.

The Guns of Darkness. London, Macmillan, 1973; New York, Atheneum, 1974.

Ask Me No Questions. London, Macmillan, 1976; New York, Holt Rinehart, 1982.

Desert Drum, illustrated by John Sewell. London, Heinemann, 1977.

The Vandal. London, Macmillan, 1979; New York, Crown, 1981.

PUBLICATIONS FOR ADULTS

Novels

Rhine Journey. London, Macmillan, 1980; New York, Holt Rinehart, 1981.

The Proprietor. London, Macmillan, and New York, Holt Rinehart, 1983.

Laing. London, Macmillan, 1987.

* * *

Ann Schlee has a rare gift. She writes with such fluency and clarity that nothing stands between the reader and the scenes she is inventing, it is like looking through clear glass. This is true style; there is no straining after original imagery which can so often work like a bead curtain, fragmenting the vision with carefully turned lumps of "beautiful writing."

Her first four books are historical novels for older children, each taking as its point of departure a little-known incident in English history. *The Strangers* is an adventure story culminating in the capture of the island of Tresco in the Scillies by the Parliamentary fleet in 1651, but it is also the story of a child face to face with strangers from a world completely new to her. *The Consul's Daughter* relies less on the trappings of a conventional children's adventure story (secret cave, coded inscription) and explores more obliquely the emotional maturing of a young girl involved in the seige of Algiers in 1816. The girl's jealousy of her father's young wife and new baby, her tentative relationship with one of the young officers on board the naval frigate in which they escape, her friendship with the ship's surgeon are all delicately and accurately drawn. Above all the stifling shuttered heat of Algiers and then the life at sea are brilliantly conveyed, and there is a fine battle scene. Suddenly you know what it must have felt like to be a young officer trained for fighting and at last within sight of the enemy; Trafalgar is over, Nelson dead, and you are desperately anxious not to have missed your last chance of action.

The Guns of Darkness is a more ambitious novel with a much wider sweep of narrative, taking as its theme the fall of the Emperor Theodore of Abyssinia. The story is told through the eyes of Louisa, whose older sister has married one of the Swiss missionaries who are forced by the Emperor to make the cannons with which he hopes to save his kingdom. There is something of a failure with the central character. Louisa is too impassive. With an Abyssinian mother and an English father she could be expected to suffer some conflict of loyalties and confusion of identities when her people are at war with the English, but this is not fully explored. No such criticism can be levelled at *Ask Me No Questions*. Here the conflicting demands made on a child having for the first time to make her own moral decisions in a terrifying situation are superbly developed. Laura, sent to stay with unsympathetic relatives to escape the cholera, becomes aware that the building next door houses hundreds of children in a state of squalor, starvation, and disease. It is a book that disturbs and distresses, but of all her children's novels this is the one that continues to

haunt the imagination long after it has been put down, a quality it shares with her later fine adult novels.

Desert Drum is a short story set in the Sudan, but with *The Vandal* Schlee broke new ground. This is a fantasy set in the not-very-distant future, in which her hero Paul dares to question the repressive urban society in which he has been brought up, and is banished by the authorities to a life of rural labour. It is always harder to write convincingly of a future society than of the past because so many details have to hang together; and for me this award-winning novel, though powerfully written, did not come off because I was not wholly convinced by the setting.

—Mary Rayner

————

SCHLEIN, Miriam. Has also written as Lavinia Stanhope. American. Born in New York City. Educated at Brooklyn College, New York. Has one daughter and one son. Address: 19 East 95th Street, New York, New York 10028, U.S.A.

PUBLICATIONS FOR CHILDREN

Fiction

A Day at the Playground, illustrated by Eloise Wilkin. New York, Simon and Schuster, 1951.

Tony's Pony, illustrated by Van Kaufman. New York, Simon and Schuster, 1952.

Go with the Sun, illustrated by Symeon Shimin. New York, Scott, 1952.

The Four Little Foxes, illustrated by Luis Quintanilla. New York, Scott, 1953.

When Will the World Be Mine?, illustrated by Jean Charlot. New York, Scott, 1953.

Elephant Herd, illustrated by Symeon Shimin. New York, Scott, 1954; Kingswood, Surrey, World's Work, 1967.

Oomi, The New Hunter, illustrated by George Mason. New York, Abelard Schuman, 1955; London, Abelard Schuman, 1958.

Little Red Nose, illustrated by Roger Duvoisin. New York and London, Abelard Schuman, 1955.

Puppy's House, illustrated by Katherine Evans. Chicago, Whitman, 1955; Edinburgh, Chambers, 1969.

Big Talk, illustrated by Harvey Weiss. New York, Scott, 1955.

Lazy Day, illustrated by Harvey Weiss. New York, Scott, 1955.

Henry's Ride, illustrated by Vane Earle. Nashville, Abingdon Press, 1956.

Deer in the Snow, illustrated by Leonard Kessler. New York and London, Abelard Schuman, 1956.

Something for Now, Something for Later, illustrated by Leonard Kessler. New York, Harper, 1956.

Little Rabbit, The High Jumper, illustrated by Theresa Sherman. New York, Scott, 1957.

Amazing Mr. Pelgrew, illustrated by Harvey Weiss. New York and London, Abelard Schuman, 1957.

A Bunny, A Bird, A Funny Cat, illustrated by Harvey Weiss. London and New York, Abelard Schuman, 1957.

Here Comes Night, illustrated by Harvey Weiss. Chicago, Whitman, 1957; Edinburgh, Chambers, 1967.

The Big Cheese, illustrated by Joseph Low. New York, Scott, 1958; London, Hamish Hamilton, 1965.

The Bumblebee's Secret, illustrated by Harvey Weiss. New York and London, Abelard Schuman, 1958.

Home, The Tale of a Mouse, illustrated by E. Harper Johnson. New York, Abelard Schuman, 1958.

Herman McGregor's World, illustrated by Harvey Weiss. Chicago, Whitman, 1958; Kingswood, Surrey, World's Work, 1972.

The Raggle Taggle Fellow, illustrated by Harvey Weiss. New York and London, Abelard Schuman, 1959.

Little Dog Little, illustrated by Hertha Depper. New York, Abelard Schuman, 1959.

The Fisherman's Day, illustrated by Harvey Weiss. Chicago, Whitman, 1959.

The Sun, The Wind, The Sea, and the Rain, illustrated by Joe Lasker. New York and London, Abelard Schuman, 1960.

Laurie's New Brother, illustrated by Elizabeth Donald. New York and London, Abelard Schuman, 1961.

Amuny, Boy of Old Egypt, illustrated by Thea Dupays. New York and London, Abelard Schuman, 1961.

The Pile of Junk, illustrated by Harvey Weiss. New York and London, Abelard Schuman, 1962.

Snow Time, illustrated by Joe Lasker. Chicago, Whitman, 1962; Edinburgh, Chambers, 1966.

The Snake in the Carpool, illustrated by N.M. Bodecker. New York and London, Abelard Schuman, 1963.

The Way Mothers Are, illustrated by Joe Lasker. Chicago, Whitman, 1963.

Who?, illustrated by Harvey Weiss. New York, Walck, 1963.

The Big Green Thing, illustrated by Elizabeth Dauber. New York, Grosset and Dunlap, 1963; London, Muller, 1968.

Big Lion, Little Lion, illustrated by Joe Lasker. Chicago, Whitman, 1964; Edinburgh, Chambers, 1966.

Billy, The Littlest One, illustrated by Lucy Hawkinson. Chicago, Whitman, 1966; Edinburgh, Chambers, 1969.

The Best Place, illustrated by Erica Merkling. Chicago, Whitman, 1968.

My House, illustrated by Joe Lasker. Chicago, Whitman, 1971.

The Rabbit's World, illustrated by Peter Parnall. New York, Four Winds Press, 1973.

The Girl Who Would Rather Climb Trees, illustrated by Judith Gwyn Brown. New York, Harcourt Brace, 1975.

Bobo the Troublemaker, illustrated by Ray Cruz. New York, Four Winds Press, 1976.

Other

Shapes, illustrated by Sam Berman. New York, Scott, 1952.

Fast Is Not a Ladybug: A Book about Fast and Slow Things. New York, Scott, 1953; as *Fast Is Not a Ladybird*, Kingswood, Surrey, World's Work, 1961.

Heavy Is a Hippopotamus, illustrated by Leonard Kessler. New York, Scott, 1954.

The Sun Looks Down, illustrated by Abner Graboff. New York, Abelard Schuman, 1954; London, Abelard Schuman, 1958.

How Do You Travel?, illustrated by Paul Galdone. Nashville, Abingdon Press, 1954.

It's about Time, illustrated by Leonard Kessler. New York, Scott, 1955.

City Boy, Country Boy, illustrated by Katherine Evans. Chicago, Children's Press, 1955.

Kittens, Cubs, and Babies, illustrated by Jean Charlot. New York, Scott, 1959.

My Family, illustrated by Harvey Weiss. New York, Abelard Schuman, 1960; London, Abelard Schuman, 1964.

Moon-Months and Sun-Days, illustrated by Shelly Sacks. New York, Scott, 1972.

Juju-Sheep and the Python's Moonstone, and Other Moon Stories from Different Times and Different Places, illustrated by Joe Lasker. Chicago, Whitman, 1973.

What's Wrong with Being a Skunk?, illustrated by Ray Cruz. New York, Four Winds Press, 1974.

Metric: The Modern Way to Measure, illustrated by Jan Pyk. New York, Harcourt Brace, 1975.

Careers in a Department Store (as Lavinia Stanhope), photographs by Robert L. Miller. Milwaukee, Raintree Editions, 1976.

Giraffe, The Silent Giant, illustrated by Betty Fraser. New York, Four Winds Press, 1976.

I Hate It, illustrated by Judith Gwyn Brown. Chicago, Whitman, 1978.

On the Track of the Mystery Animal: The Story of the Discovery of the Okapi, illustrated by Ruth Sanderson. New York, Four Winds Press, 1978.

I, Tut: The Boy Who Became Pharaoh, illustrated by Erik Hilgerdt. New York, Four Winds Press, 1979.

Snake Fights, Rabbit Fights, and More: A Book about Animal Fighting, illustrated by Sue Thompson. New York, Crown, 1979.

Antarctica, The Great White Continent. New York, Hastings House, 1980.

Lucky Porcupine!, illustrated by Martha Weston. New York, Four Winds Press, 1980.

Billions of Bats, illustrated by Walter Kessell. New York, Lippincott, 1982.

Rosh Hashanah and Yom Kippur, illustrated by Erika Weihs. New York, Behrman House, 1983.

Hanukkah, illustrated by Katherine Kahn. New York, Behrman House, 1983.

Shavuot, illustrated by Erika Weihs. New York, Behrman House, 1983.

Shabbat, illustrated by Amy Blake. New York, Behrman House, 1983.

Prayers and Blessings, illustrated by Amye Rosenberg. New York, Behrman House, 1983.

Passover, illustrated by Katherine Kahn. New York, Behrman House, 1983.

Sukkot and Simhat Torah, illustrated by Amye Rosenberg. New York, Behrman House, 1983.

Purim, illustrated by Ruth Heller. New York, Behrman House, 1983.

Project Panda Watch, illustrated by Robert Shetterly. New York, Atheneum, 1984.

What the Elephant Was: Strange Prehistoric Elephants. New York, Atheneum, 1985.

The Dangerous Life of the Sea Horse, illustrated by Gwen Cole. New York, Atheneum, 1986.

Big Talk. Chicago, Whitman, 1988.

*   *   *

Those who write for adults, or even for older children, can safely make certain assumptions about the understanding and abilities of their chosen audiences. Those who, like Miriam Schlein, write for beginning readers, can take very little for granted. Their little people are just setting out on the reader's voyage, and for this reason, their writer's responsibility is an especially heavy and exacting one. It is at this crucial time that lifelong readers and lovers of literature are so often made (and perhaps, who can tell, sometimes are lost as well). So much depends upon the materials offered them. If those first unsteady steps carry the reader into a land of enchantment and rich welcome, the chances are that he or she will return soon and frequently.

As Schlein so well understands, it is not merely a question of a small reading vocabulary that may impede that first important reading experience; a great part of the difficulty lies in the complex matter of grasping *concepts*. Here, though not only here, Schlein is an extremely important and influential writer for the beginner, for she has made the difficult explication of concepts for the beginning reader her province. Such deceptively simple works as *Fast Is Not a Lady Bug* and *Shapes* provide some basis for the understanding of intangibles, so baffling to readers who can readily grasp the meanings of words that lend themselves to concrete illustration.

Schlein's especial talent lies in her ability to explain while entertaining. Hers are works of charm and simplicity that have stood the tests of time and of many more or less successful attempts at emulation, none of which so far have surpassed her impressive achievement, for she is represented in most well-equipped libraries for young people, as well as in many classrooms and school science and supplementary reading collections. At a more advanced level of readership, her studies of animals and their distinctive behavior patterns have proved a treasure trove to young naturalists. From the giraffe to the humble skunk (as she so rightly points out, there is nothing wrong with being a skunk, but a lot wrong with human judgmental attitudes about skunkishness), her interest and enthusiasm for her subjects, and her passionate conservationism, shine through her words.

Though most of Schlein's books are truly "slim volumes," placed side by side they would fill a very wide shelf indeed—possibly the most important shelf in any library, for she is the welcoming lady holding open a door for the very youngest, most impressionable, arguably most important reader to enter.

—Joan McGrath

SCOTT, Ann. See **FRITZ, Jean.**

SCOTT, Bill (William Neville Scott). Australian. Born in Bundaberg, Queensland, 4 October 1923. Educated at Caboolture State Primary School. Served in the Royal Australian Navy, 1942–46. Married Mavis Richards in 1949; one son. Bookseller, publisher, and editor, 1950's and 1960's; now a full-time writer. Recipient: Mary Gilmore award, 1964; Australian Council fellowship, 1977, 1980, 1981. Address: 157 Pratten Street, Warwick, Queensland 4370, Australia.

PUBLICATIONS FOR CHILDREN

Fiction (illustrated by A.M. Hicks)

Boori. Melbourne and New York, Oxford University Press, 1978; London, Abelard Schuman, 1979.
Darkness under the Hills. Melbourne, Oxford, and New York, Oxford University Press, 1980.
Shadows among the Leaves. Melbourne and London, Heinemann, 1984.
Many Kinds of Magic (short stories), illustrated by Lisa Herriman. Melbourne, Penguin, 1988.

Verse

Following the Gold, illustrated by Kerry Argent. Adelaide, Omnibus, 1989.

Other

Editor, *Reading 360* series (*The Blooming Queensland Side, On the Shores of Botany Bay, The Golden West, Bound for South Australia, Upon Van Diemen's Land, The Victorian Bunyip, Australian Childhoods, Call of the Sea, From Nearby Lands, Going Bush, Success!, A Thousand Miles Away, Big Towns Little Towns, Ghosts Ghouls and Scary Things, Mirrors, Moments to Remember, The Play's the Thing, Then and Now, Tales of the Territory*). Melbourne, Longman Cheshire, 19 vols., 1981–84.

PUBLICATIONS FOR ADULTS (earlier books as W.N. Scott)

Short Stories

Some People. Brisbane, Jacaranda Press, 1968.
My Uncle Arch and Other People. Adelaide, Rigby, 1977.

Verse

Brother and Brother. Brisbane, Jacaranda Press, 1972.

Other

Focus on Judith Wright. Brisbane, University of Queensland Press, 1967.
Portrait of Brisbane, paintings by Cedric Emanuel. Adelaide, Rigby, 1976.
Tough in the Old Days (autobiography). Adelaide, Rigby, 1979.
Ned Kelly after a Century of Acrimony, with John Meredith. Sydney, Lansdowne Press, 1980.
Australian Bushrangers. Sydney, Child and Henry, 1983.
The Long and the Short and the Tall: A Collection of Australian Yarns. Sydney, Western Plains, 1985.
Brisbane Sketchbook. Brisbane, Herron, 1988.

Editor, *The Continual Singing: An Anthology of World Poetry.* Brisbane, Jacaranda Press, 1973.
Editor, *The Complete Book of Australian Folklore.* Sydney, Ure Smith, 1976.
Editor, *Bushranger Ballads.* Sydney, Ure Smith, 1976.
Editor, *The Second Penguin Australian Songbook.* Melbourne, Penguin Australia, 1980.
Editor, *Impressions on a Continent: A Collection of Australian Short Stories.* Melbourne, Heinemann, 1983.
Editor, *Penguin Book of Australian Humorous Verse.* Melbourne, Penguin, 1984.

*

Bill Scott comments:

Much of my writing has been concerned with Australian social history, and especially with the recording, documentation, and publication of Australian folklore. More recently I have been much more active in the field of writing for children though continuing to publish articles on aspects of folklore both in books and in national and international journals. Most of my writing for children reflects this interest in tradition and fantasy.

*   *   *

In *Boori* and its sequel, *Darkness under the Hills,* Bill Scott pays tribute to the spiritual dimensions of the post-Dreamtime life of Australian Aborigines. Essential to the narrative is the bond of the Land, a strict code of inter-personal and inter-tribal relationships, and, in particular, the demands of the Law which says that a man is responsible for what he does, not what he intends to do. Transgression of the Law demands atonement to restore harmony and balance to the individual and to Nature.

Boori was not born as other men but was created at the bidding of Ganba, chief among the tribes of spirits, by Old Budgerie, wise Counsellor of the People. It was Budgerie who taught Boori the skills of a warrior and Law-giver and the secrets of the Eagle-hawk skin. For Boori is a Goundir, a man of magical powers, who has his own spirit friend, Jaree, who lives in a small leather bag around his neck, a kind of alter-ego who sometimes acts as Boori's spiritual scout. The flashes of humour in Scott's book come from the friendly but sometimes testy, even astringent, bantering of Boori and his Jaree.

Both novels concern the working out of Boori's destiny as a Messenger. But first he has to bring into his friendship and service the big yellow dog, Dingo, spirit chief among the dingo people whose ability to change into the human shape of the warrior aids Boori as he pursues the heroic tasks of subduing the great water spirit, the Melong, and, in the second book, the totally evil Rakasha who broods as a blight over the Land. In the course of his odyssey Boori weaves spells, makes magic—even sending out his spirit from his body—and invokes the aid of the local spirits of the Land of his labours. He defeats a wily old magician; helps Perentie, the lizard spirit, regain opals stolen by the Puk-wudgies of the desert; and wrests from a malicious ghost, Cooran, a magic and deadly pointing bone before releasing the shade to the eternal campfires. There are moments of warmth as Boori establishes loving relationships with warriors whom he defeats and then befriends, and occasional deep psychological insights such as when Boori causes the perfumes, smells, sounds, and tastes Cooran had known as a man to pass before the inner eye of the greedy, grey ghost. Deftly woven into the framework of the narrative are fragments of Aboriginal legend (why the crow is black; the origin of the Milky Way), song, and dance-dramas.

Scott writes in an heroic style in keeping with his theme and evokes the Land, the Law, and the People in lyric and measured prose. At his best he creates terrifying images of horrific evil and apocalyptic battles.

Shadows among the Leaves is a children's story in a minor key in which the Shadows are formless Aboriginal Old Things or spirits, which have the force of an invisible storm, and which work to destroy those who would desecrate their jungle environment for personal gain.

In a note to *Boori* and in his glossaries the author acknowledges some of his sources claiming that, "Boori's story derives largely from Aboriginal myth and custom." He states, too, that he gives local names and traditions a wider geographical application. He has also voiced his belief that the same animating spirits are extant in all folklores and that puk-wudgies, for example, equate to the dwarves of western myth. Thus there is in Scott's writing an insistent and intrusive sense of other traditions breaking through the fabric of Aboriginal culture. The Christian sign of the cross is implicitly coupled with the Aboriginal sign of the rainbow. Water sirens, crystal balls, a warrior pinned to the earth by Lilliputian creatures may well be universal archetypes. But in Scott's second book, particularly, the use of such literary symbols along with proper names from eastern mythology reinforces an uneasy feeling that there is, in literature, a thin line dividing the secondary worlds of high fantasy from those composite societies derived from an eclectic use of folklore.

—H.M. Saxby

SEBESTYEN, Ouida (née Dockery). American. Born in Vernon, Texas, 13 February 1924. Married Adam Sebestyen in 1960; one son. Recipient: International Reading Association award, 1980; American Book award, for paperback, 1982; Silver Pencil award (Netherlands), 1984. Address: 115 South 36th Street, Boulder, Colorado 80303, U.S.A.

PUBLICATIONS FOR CHILDREN

Fiction

Words by Heart. Boston, Little Brown, 1979; London, Hamish Hamilton, 1987.
Far from Home. Boston, Little Brown, 1980.
IOU's. Boston, Little Brown, 1982.
On Fire. New York, Atlantic Monthly Press, 1985.
The Girl in the Box. Boston, Little Brown, 1988; London, Hamish Hamilton, 1989.

*

Manuscript Collections: Kerlan Collection, University of Minnesota, Minneapolis; de Grummond Collection, University of Southern Mississippi, Hattiesburg.

Ouida Sebestyen comments:
The American West—bleak and harsh but bursting with beauty and drama—has been my home and inspiration as well as the setting of my novels. I write about young people within families, about loving, forgiving and striking balances. I feel that young readers deserve not only an honest depiction of life, but also a hint—perhaps the hope—of how it might be. Although my characters are often poor, or victims of their time or circumstance, they are able to find more strength and goodness in themselves than they knew they had.

* * *

Ouida Sebestyen's first novel, *Words by Heart*, won numerous awards including the International Reading Association's Children's Book award given to a promising new writer. Sebestyen was 55 at the time, but she had been writing since she was 18. She was a new writer only in the sense of being published. The promise is being fulfilled as Sebestyen has produced five thought-provoking novels.

Sebestyen's novels are about family and love, but there is no easy love in any of her works. She writes of people struggling to understand and accept each other and about families trying to be. *Words by Heart* introduces Lena, a young black girl living in Texas in the early 20th century. Lena has aspirations to succeed and her father tells her at one point, "I want you not to know your place." But it seems that everyone in the community is striving to put the black family in a place of subservience. Papa accepts many slights and Lena struggles with her need for love and acceptance from her father and her anger at his forgiveness of others. The ultimate act of forgiveness comes when Papa saves the life of the boy who mortally wounds him, and asks Lena to forgive him as well. Lena acquiesces, but wonders who will come to fill her Papa's place in her life. The book is rich with detail and both major and minor characters are fully fleshed out. Each is seen with fears and hopes and the actions they use to mask their emotions. Just as one works up a real sense of spite toward a character, Sebestyen reveals an insight that makes the reader reassess. The strength of the book is in the careful rendering of character as well as the poignant storyline.

On Fire is the sequel to *Words by Heart*, though it is Sebestyen's fourth novel and her least successful one. Tater Haney is the boy who killed Lena's father and this book picks up the Haney family after they have fled their home in Texas. The book is very disjointed by trying simultaneously to explore the exploitation of mine workers in Colorado, the corruption of the leaders trying to form a union, and the emotions of various Haneys as well as a young woman that Sammy Haney hooks up with. There is little focus to the novel and one never gets emotionally involved as one does with *Words by Heart*.

A shabby boarding house and its emotionally wounded inhabitants provide a potent setting for an evocative novel about the tangled web of responsibilities and passions that underlies most human response. Each of the characters is *Far from Home* in the sense that each is lost and trying to make meaning out of a less than perfect life. Sebestyen allows the reader to see the loneliness and near despair of each character, but at the same time the hope that comes when people respond to each other and allow others to touch their lives. There are no easy answers and no happy ending, but the book is filled with the possibilities that hope brings.

None of Sebestyen's families is conventional and *IOU's* family consists of Annie who is a single parent estranged from her father and determined to live life her way, and her 13-year-old son Stowe, who is stoical about their straitened circumstances but laments to himself that everything he wants belongs to someone else or is used. At one point, Annie tells Stowe that they have become pinched from hoarding little bits of money, but most especially from hoarding themselves. The novel is about enduring and reaching out and building bridges between those who have lost each other. As in most of her books, Sebestyen's characters are as real as the people you know.

The Girl in the Box is stylistically very different from Sebestyen's earlier works. Told through diary entries and notes, it is written from the voice of a teenage girl who has been kidnapped and thrown in a cellar of some kind by an unknown assailant. There is food and water in the room, but no light. Jackie uses the typewriter and paper that was in her backpack to record her fears and emotions, question who the assailant might be, and write letters reassuring her parents and notes crying for help that she shoves through a crack in the door and that fall on uncaring ground. This is a frightening book, depicting a senseless crime with no motive and an ending that implies Jackie's death. It is at the same time a story of courage and resilience.

Sebestyen's works are provocative and thoughtful. They eschew the typical plot of the young adult novel and probe the inner recesses of human emotion. It took time for Sebestyen to find her voice, but it rings clearly today.

—M. Jean Greenlaw

SEED, Jenny (Cecile Eugenie Seed, née Booysen). South African. Born in Cape Town, 18 May 1930. Educated at Ellerslie High School, Cape Town. Married Robert Edward Seed in 1953; one daughter and three sons. Worked in Roads Department and Town Planning Department, Pietermaritzburg, early 1950's. Recipient: M.E.R. award (South Africa), 1987. Address: 10 Pioneer Crescent, Northdene, Natal 4093, South Africa.

PUBLICATIONS FOR CHILDREN

Fiction

The Dancing Mule, illustrated by Joan Sirr. London, Nelson, 1964.
The Always-late Train, illustrated by Pieter de Weerdt. Parow, South Africa, Nasionale Boekhandel, 1965.

Small House, Big Garden, illustrated by Lynette Hemmant. London, Hamish Hamilton, 1965.
Peter the Gardener, illustrated by Mary Russon. London, Hamish Hamilton, 1966.
Tombi's Song, illustrated by Dugald MacDougall. London, Hamish Hamilton, 1966; Chicago, Rand McNally, 1968; as *Ntombi's Song*, Johannesburg, Ravan Press, 1988.
To the Rescue, illustrated by Constance Marshall. London, Hamish Hamilton, 1966.
Stop Those Children!, illustrated by Mary Russon. London, Hamish Hamilton, 1966.
Timothy and Tinker, illustrated by Lynette Hemmant. London, Hamish Hamilton, 1967.
The River Man, illustrated by Dugald MacDougall. London, Hamish Hamilton, 1968.
The Voice of the Great Elephant, illustrated by Trevor Stubley. London, Hamish Hamilton, 1968; New York, Pantheon, 1969.
Canvas City, illustrated by Lynette Hemmant. London, Hamish Hamilton, 1968.
The Prince of the Bay, illustrated by Trevor Stubley. London, Hamish Hamilton, 1970; as *Vengeance of the Zulu King*, New York, Pantheon, 1970.
The Great Thirst, illustrated by Trevor Stubley. London, Hamish Hamilton, 1971; Scarsdale, New York, Bradbury Press, 1973.
The Red Dust Soldiers, illustrated by Andrew Sier. London, Heinemann, 1972.
The Broken Spear, illustrated by Trevor Stubley. London, Hamish Hamilton, 1972.
Warriors on the Hills, illustrated by Pat Ludlow. London, Abelard Schuman, 1975.
The Unknown Land, illustrated by Jael Jordan. London, Heinemann, 1976.
Strangers in the Land, illustrated by Trevor Stubley. London, Hamish Hamilton, 1976.
The Year One, illustrated by Susan Sansome. London, Hamish Hamilton, 1980.
The Policeman's Button, illustrated by Joy Pritchard. Cape Town, Human and Rousseau, 1981.
Gold Dust, illustrated by Bill le Fever. London, Hamish Hamilton, 1982.
The New Fire, illustrated by Mario Sickle. Cape Town, Human and Rousseau, 1983.
The 59 Cats, illustrated by Alida Carpenter. Pretoria, Daan Retief, 1983.
The Shell, illustrated by Ann Walton. Pretoria, Daan Retief, 1983.
The Sad Cat, illustrated by Marlize Groenewald. Pretoria, Daan Retief, 1984.
The Karoo Hen, illustrated by A. Venter. Pretoria, Daan Retief, 1984.
The Disappearing Rabbit, illustrated by Ann Walton. Pretoria, Daan Retief, 1984.
Big Boy's Work, illustrated by Paula Collins. Pretoria, Daan Retief, 1984.
The Spy Hill, illustrated by Nelda Vermaak. Cape Town, Human and Rousseau, 1984.
The Lost Prince, illustrated by Ann Walton. Pretoria, Daan Retief, 1985.
Day of the Dragon, illustrated by Paula Collins. Pretoria, Daan Retief, 1985.
Bouncy Lizzie, illustrated by Esther Boshoff. Pretoria, Daan Retief, 1985.
The Strange Blackbird, illustrated by Hettie Saaiman. Pretoria, Daan Retief, 1986.
The Far-Away Valley, illustrated by Joan Rankin. Pretoria, Daan Retief, 1987.
The Christmas Bells, illustrated by Hettie Saaiman. Pretoria, Daan

Retief, 1987.

Place among the Stones, illustrated by Helmut Starcke. Cape Town, Tafelberg, 1987.

The Station-Master's Hen, illustrated by Elizabeth de Villiers. Cape Town, Human and Rousseau, 1987.

The Corner Cat, illustrated by Elizabeth de Villiers. Cape Town, Human and Rousseau, 1987.

Hurry, Hurry, Sibusiso, illustrated by Cornelia Holm. Pretoria, Daan Retief, 1988.

Other

Kulumi the Brave: A Zulu Tale, illustrated by Trevor Stubley. London, Hamish Hamilton, and New York, World, 1970.

The Sly Green Lizard (Zulu folktale), illustrated by Graham Humphreys. London, Hamish Hamilton, 1973.

The Bushman's Dream: African Tales of the Creation, illustrated by Bernard Brett. London, Hamish Hamilton, 1974; Scarsdale, New York, Bradbury Press, 1975.

*

Jenny Seed comments:

My mother was a wonderful teller of tales, especially bedtime stories, and my father was a writer whose hand-written manuscripts filled the cupboards of his bedroom. Bearing these two facts in mind, it is not surprising that from an early age I too had a great desire to work with words, and that later, after my marriage when I began to try to write in earnest, my inclination was towards stories for children.

In some ways any writing career must be like a snowball rolling down a hill, gathering momentum and increasing in size the further it goes. Soon short snippets for the children's pages in newspapers and magazines lengthened out into small novels for younger readers, and as the books grew I found myself wanting not only an exciting plot but a deeper and more meaningful theme as well. I was aware of the tremendous influence an author of children's books may have on a young and impressionable mind, and I gave much thought and soul searching in an attempt to find answers that were at once simple enough for the reader and yet as honest as I could make them. Later when I turned to historical novels for the early teens this seeking became more accentuated. Though I did not realize it at the time my novels were probably an expression of my own need to find the reality of God.

It has been said that history is His Story. For me this was true. The more I delved into and became absorbed in the shattering and dramatic events of African history, the more I came to see that all was not just meaningless chaos. Behind the human triumphs and tragedies there was a great hand holding all together with unswerving purpose and uncompromising truth. For me personally the searching came to an end in 1974 when I became a Christian. For my books, the quest continues, but with a difference. I seem now to be able to write from a firmer standpoint, not so much blindly seeking after what is unknown, but rather reaching forward into a new country which is somehow already known.

*   *   *

Jenny Seed writes primarily historical fiction focusing on South African whites and secondarily folklore and fiction about South African blacks and stories for younger readers. In introductions or prefaces to most of her historical fiction she provides information about the setting and sources she used as background for the story. The historical sources include diaries, letters, and documents written by European explorers, traders, miners, missionaries, and government officials.

Seed's historical fiction for younger children is usually set in the 19th century in a specific historical context, but the action of the story focuses on a child's adventure. For example, *The Year One* takes place in Natal in 1850 when a British family arrives with a group of settlers, who are left impoverished by a dishonest settlement organizer. The action focuses on the family's struggle to survive, the heroine's fear of the strange new surroundings, and the rescue of her baby sister from an enraged monkey. *The Policeman's Button* also takes place in Natal, in 1890 when wars between Pondo clans were a threat to the farmers. The 10-year-old hero admires the Natal Mounted Police who come to protect the farmers and their property. He endangers his own life and that of others when he sneaks out at night to see what the police are doing, but is rescued by them. After the police have negotiated peace and left the area, the hero has a policeman's button, given to him by one of the police, to remind him of his experience. Several stories focus on mining, including *Gold Dust* about a young girl who works hard with her family during the Transvaal gold rush of 1874 and bravely rescues a miner who is ill with malaria during a storm, and *Canvas City*, about a family's attempt to become rich during the 1866 diamond "fever" at New Rush, which eventually became Kimberley, and their being cheated by their mining foreman. Both stories focus on the physical hardships of mining life and the importance of family solidarity in overcoming hardships.

Most of Seed's fiction for older children also is set in the 19th century. It incorporates real historical characters and details of historical events as presented in the sources used to create the background. Seed's attitude toward South African history is stated in the introduction to *The Broken Spear*. The fall of the Zulu kings at the hands of the Boer Trekkers is viewed as part of a larger conflict between "savages" and "civilization" and the wars that occurred as part of a worldwide conflict in which "primitive weapons" were pitted against firearms. She contrasts the "despotism" of Dingane the Zulu leader with the "enormous courage and determination" of the Boers. There is no mention of the Zulu perspective of defending their land, cattle, and people against encroachment by uncompromising foreigners.

The Broken Spear is about the Boer Trek of the 1830's, while *Strangers in the Land* is about British settlement in the Cape in the 1830's. Both stories present the physical hardships of travel and settlement in considerable detail and religion as an important factor enabling perseverance against forces of man and nature. Although *The Prince of the Bay* is told by an African boy in 1824 when Henry Fynn and other whites went to open up trade with the Zulu, the use of Fynn's diaries as a source leads to Eurocentric, negative descriptions of the Zulu. The real hero of the story is the white man who protects the narrator and other Africans from the treachery of their own people. The hero of *The Great Thirst*, which takes place in the 1830's in South West Africa (Namibia), is also an African boy who is confused by his contacts with Europeans and the behavior of Jonker Afrikaner, a real historical person condemned for his "bad" deeds. This adventure story about African warriors and the triumph of Christianity provides primarily negative depictions of Africans because of the focus on Jonker Afrikaner from a Eurocentric perspective. Although there are statements sympathetic to African perspectives in some of Seed's historical fiction, especially in the fiction for older children, these positive statements are overshadowed by negative stereotypes taken from the historical sources she used.

Some of Seed's fiction written for younger children, such as *Tombi's Song*, is more empathetic toward African characters. Tombi, a six-year-old Zulu girl who must walk to market through a forest, is fearful of a monster who lives there. When she jumps out of the way of a bus, she spills sugar she bought at the market, but is able to earn money to replace it by singing and dancing for visitors, and bravely returns home through the forest. *Kulumi the Brave* is based on oral literature. The hero, the son of a Zulu chief who fears he will take his kingdom, proves his bravery by defeating monsters and gets to marry the girl of his choice by tricking an ogress who is holding her captive.

Seed is skilled at writing stories that appeal to children of different ages. The popularity of her stories is evident from many of them being reprinted and reissued in new editions in England and America, as well as in South Africa.

—Nancy J. Schmidt

SEFTON, Catherine. See **WADDELL, Martin.**

SEGUN, Mabel D(orothy, née Aig-Imoukhuede). Nigerian. Born in Ondo, 18 February 1930. Educated at St. David's School, Akure, 1939–41; C.M.S. Girls' School, Lagos, 1942–47; University College, Ibadan, 1949–53. Married 1) Olujimi Jolaoso in 1951 (divorced); 2) Oludotun Segun in 1960 (divorced), two sons and one daughter. Teacher, St. Anne's School, Ibadan, 1953, and Methodist Girls' School, Lagos, 1954; education officer, Edo College, Benin City, 1954–55, and Government Teacher Training College, Abraka, 1955; teacher, Ahmadiyya Grammar School, Ibadan, 1956; education officer, Government Teacher Training College, Ibadan, 1957; teacher, Ibadan Boys' High School, 1958–59; editor, *Hansard*, Western Nigeria Legislature, Ibadan, 1959–61; information officer, Western Nigeria Ministry of Information, Ibadan, 1961–63; copywriter, Lintas Ltd., Lagos, 1964; trainee editor, Silver Burdett, publishers, Morristown, New Jersey, 1965, and Harper and Row, publishers, New York, 1966; editor, *Modern Woman*, Lagos, 1965–67, and Franklin Book Programmes, Lagos, 1967; education officer, 1967–68, and head, 1969–70, Federal Ministry of Education Broadcasting Unit, Lagos; head, Department of English and Social Studies, 1971–73 and 1974–79, and acting vice-principal, 1978–79, National Technical Teachers College, Lagos; deputy permanent delegate of Nigeria to Unesco, Federal Ministry of External Affairs, Paris, 1979–81; chief federal inspector of education, Federal Ministry of Education, Lagos, 1981–82. Since 1982 senior research fellow, Institute of African Studies, University of Ibadan. Executive secretary, Nigerian Book Development Council, Lagos, 1974–76. Since 1978 president, Children's Literature Association of Nigeria, Ibadan; since 1984 consultant, African Children's Literature Programme, Nairobi; since 1986 contributing editor, *Education Guardian 2*, Lagos. Recipient: Nigerian National Festival of the Arts Literature prize, 1953, 1954. Address: Institute of African Studies, University of Ibadan, Ibadan, Nigeria.

PUBLICATIONS FOR CHILDREN

Fiction

Youth Day Parade. Ibadan, Daystar Press, 1983.
Olu and the Broken Statue, illustrated by Olu Byron. Ibadan, New Horn Press, 1985.

Other

My Father's Daughter (autobiography), illustrated by Prue Theobalds. Lagos, African Universities Press, 1965.
My Mother's Daughter (autobiography), illustrated by Olu Byron. Ibadan, African Universities Press, 1987.

Editor, with Neville Grant, *Under the Mango Tree* (verse), illustrated by Maureen and Gordon Gray. Lagos, Longman, 2 vols., 1980.

PUBLICATIONS FOR ADULTS

Verse

Conflict and Other Poems. Ibadan, New Horn Press, 1986.

Other

Friends, Nigerians, Countrymen (essays). Oxford, Oxford University Press, 1977; as *Sorry No Vacancy*, Ibadan, University Press, 1985.
Ping Pong: Twenty-Five Years of Table Tennis. Ibadan, Daystar Press, 1989.

Editor, *Illustrating for Children.* Ibadan, Children's Literature Association of Nigeria, 1988.

*

Mabel D. Segun comments:

For decades, as a result of colonisation, Nigerian children have had to read imported books which were completely alien to their culture. As a result some of them are beginning to lose their personal identity and seem to be unaware of those African traditional values which held the society together. In my books I try to emphasise the importance of these values in a transitional society such as is depicted in *My Father's Daughter* or in a modern setting as in *Youth Day Parade. Olu and the Broken Statue* features a valuable artefact whose preservation represents a dilemma to three children. In the two volumes of *Under the Mango Tree*, African folktales have been turned into verse and translations made of traditional children's poems and folktale refrains.

*   *   *

In children's literature Mabel D. Segun is at her best in autobiography. Her autobiographical reader for children *My Father's Daughter* deals with the narrator's growth in a rural village and her interaction with her father, the village pastor and disciplinarian who eventually dominates her world view. When her father dies at the end of the novel the narrator is only eight, but her emerging personality has been strongly influenced by her strong kind clergyman father: "If father left us poor in money he did not leave us poor in the things which matter most in life. He taught us to sympathize with others, to place no premium on money, to be humble in office, and above all to lead useful lives." His death essentially brings about a sudden change of fortune in the narrator's life as she and her two brothers are sent from the cozy parsonage to live with a paternal uncle—"a journey into the unknown." *My Mother's Daughter*, the sequel to *My Father's Daughter* published 22 years later, essentially narrates the change of fortune in the narrator's life—separation from her mother, living with all sorts of relations and friends in circumstances quite different from what she was used to at the parsonage. Her life in a monogamous home in the parsonage gives way to life in a polygamous home of her uncle, with all the social problems associated with an African polygamous home—jealousy, suspicion, and unhealthy rivalry among the wives and among their offspring.

Both books are set during the colonial period, back when Nigerian schools celebrated the British Empire Day on May 24, and describe some events associated with World War II—especially British propaganda against Hitler as enemy of the God-fearing British nation, and enlistment of some Nigerians as part of the British empire to fight in faraway places like Burma and India. The language of these autobiographical works is quite simple and straightforward, avoiding abstract allusions.

My Father's Daughter and *My Mother's Daughter* are one story of a Nigerian woman who looks back on the joys, fears, trials, tribulations, and sorrows of her childhood and early adolescent days with an implicit depth of gratitude to her widowed mother to whom she feels overwhelmingly indebted for struggling to put her on the path of success. Written with childlike honesty and simplicity, alloyed with the maturity of the author's present adult disposition, this autobiography is interwoven with reflections on the cultural and social life in parts of Western Nigeria during colonial days.

Leaving looking back at her childhood days, Segun concentrates on present-day children's activities in Nigeria in *Youth Day Parade* and *Olu and the Broken Statue*. *Youth Day Parade* deals with a group of Zuma primary school children led by Tunde toward success—putting on a super performance on the parade day. Having been directed to lead the youth day parade by the headmaster, Tunde after some initial fear of the onerous task, pools his resources in organization, making do with what is available locally and whipping up enthusiasm in his school mates. This short story demonstrates that the virtues of unity, patriotism, and determination are indispensable in any worthwhile achievement. The selection of the characters names, Tunde (Yoruba), Audu (Hausa), Ekpo (Efik), Chike Wachukwu (Igbo), is deliberately meant to reflect the ethnic plurality of Nigeria, and subtly to indicate that setting aside ethnic differences for a cause especially in a multi-ethnic country like Nigeria will always produce positive results.

This use of diverse names to reflect the country's ethnic plurality is also apparent in *Olu and the Broken Statue*: Olu (Yoruba), Aigbe (Edo), and Ikem (Igbo) are friends from three ethnic groups. In order to raise funds to purchase new musical instruments for the school band, the headmaster ask the students to go out into the community to work for money. The prize for the group with the largest money collection is a silver cup. The various groups work and there are inter-team rivalries and inter-team cooperation. When Olu and his friends find a broken bronze statue they think of selling it for money rather than giving it to the national museum. Their sense of patriotism however comes to the fore and they do take it to the museum. In appreciation of their patriotism, the director of the museum makes a donation of 500 naira in addition to their own collection of 302 naira. The combined total of 802 naira wins them the first prize. The didactic thrust of this novel is patriotism. At a time when Nigeria's ancient artifacts are sold for exorbitant sums of money, Olu's group's decision to send their rare find to the museum is unique and is what Segun wants other children to emulate. Their major interest is not to have money from the sale of the broken statue but to help in their small way to preserve the ancient artifacts and cultural heritage of their nation.

Segun and Neville Grant have edited a two-volume collection of poems, *Under the Mango Tree*. The books essentially present a stimulating new course in reading and studying poetry at primary school level. Some old favourite songs and poems are included but the major emphasis is on new material related to the experience of children in Africa.

Segun's works for children are meant to teach Nigerian children acceptable Nigerian ways of life. In terms of accessibility, Segun's literary works for children do not pose much difficulty for African readers because quite a significant proportion of the content is rooted in the socio-cultural milieu of African children.

—Osayimwense Osa

SELDEN, George. Pseudonym for George Selden Thompson. American. Born in Hartford, Connecticut, 14 May 1929. Educated at Loomis School, 1943–47; Yale University, New Haven, Connecticut, B.A. 1951; University of Rome (Fulbright Fellow), 1951. Recipient: Christopher award, 1970. Lives in New York City. Address: c/o Farrar Straus and Giroux Inc., 19 Union Square West, New York, New York 10003, U.S.A.

PUBLICATIONS FOR CHILDREN

Fiction

The Dog That Could Swim under Water, illustrated by Morgan Dennis. New York, Viking Press, 1956.
The Garden under the Sea, illustrated by Garry MacKenzie. New York, Viking Press, 1957; as *Oscar Lobster's Fair Exchange*, New York, Harper, 1966.
The Cricket in Times Square, illustrated by Garth Williams. New York, Farrar Straus, 1960; London, Dent, 1961.
I See What I See!, illustrated by Robert Galster. New York, Farrar Straus, 1962.
The Mice, The Monks, and the Christmas Tree, illustrated by Jan Balet. New York, Macmillan, and London, Collier Macmillan, 1963.
Sparrow Socks, illustrated by Peter Lippman. New York, Harper, 1965.
The Dunkard, illustrated by Peter Lippman. New York, Harper, 1968.
Tucker's Countryside, illustrated by Garth Williams. New York, Farrar Straus, 1969; London, Dent, 1971.
The Genie of Sutton Place. New York, Farrar Straus, 1973.
Harry Cat's Pet Puppy, illustrated by Garth Williams. New York, Farrar Straus, 1974; London, Dent, 1978.
Chester Cricket's Pigeon Ride, illustrated by Garth Williams. New York, Farrar Straus, 1981.
Irma and Jerry, illustrated by Leslie Morrill. New York, Avon, 1982.
Chester Cricket's New Home, illustrated by Garth Williams. New York, Farrar Straus, and London, Dent, 1983.
Harry Kitten and Tucker Mouse, illustrated by Garth Williams. New York, Farrar Straus, 1986.
The Old Meadow, illustrated by Garth Williams. New York, Farrar Straus, 1987.

Plays

The Children's Story, adaptation of the work by James Clavell. New York, Dramatists Play Service, 1966.

Television Play: *The Genie of Sutton Place*.

Other

Heinrich Schliemann, Discoverer of Buried Treasure, illustrated by Lorence Bjorklund. New York, Macmillan, and London, Collier Macmillan, 1964.
Sir Arthur Evans, Discoverer of Knossos, illustrated by Lee Ames. New York, Macmillan, and London, Collier Macmillan, 1964.

*   *   *

George Selden's interest in archaeology and anthropology—aesthetic as well as historical confirmation of society—finds its place in his fiction for children as well as in his books on the archaeologists Heinrich Schliemann and Arthur Evans. Selden's best-known character Chester Cricket (*The Cricket in Times Square*), in a manner of thinking, is himself a type of cultural anthropologist. By chance he alights in a culture and environment quite foreign if not downright antithetical to his being. It does not take him long, however, to achieve intense interest and concern for the civilization he happened upon. He plumbs the excavations upon which the modern epic known as Manhattan arose. Chester views the subway system less as a means of travel than as a cultural phenomenon. It does bring diverse peoples together, and is a social and economic medium. More specifically it is a means of support for a family of Italian immigrants who eke out a precarious living from a newsstand where Chester is to make his erstwhile home. The newsstand also furnishes the element of the aesthetic as the Italian vendor, even faced with financial ruin, persists in stocking a sophisticated music periodical—an act which he knows to be of questionable commercial value, but which serves as a statement of a commitment to the arts. After all, without the arts not only the newsstand, but civilization itself is likely to fold.

The cricket becomes adopted as a pet, although some unintended misdemeanors threaten his imminent expulsion. Later he becomes an omen of good fortune, then the connective factor between the animal and human realms. Finally he himself becomes an artist and in this role brings about the salvation of the family. Even as his cultural and economic utility becomes increasingly pronounced, he remains, like the anthropologist, an outsider to the society he serves and observes. It is inevitable that he must return to his own indigenous realm.

Through the agency of Chester Selden has connected art and commerce, the natural and the artificial, the city and the country, the animal and the human. It is no wonder that this seemingly frail creature became too valuable to relinquish. Accordingly, Chester resurfaces in a number of sequels. In one he tours Manhattan on the back of a pigeon, gaining for himself and the reader a bird's-eye view of the metropolis. But it is back in his native environs (*Chester Cricket's New Home*) that the connectives between urban and rural life become most pronounced. The stump which is Chester's residence is described as if it were a mid-city penthouse. It is a place with a view, several of them in point of fact. To the front there is water, to the rear a footpath where he can watch the humans undertake their strolls. But his lease upon this idyllic spot soon lapses when a corpulent woman rests her rump upon the rotted stump and it collapses. The quest to find a new home brings him in touch with the rest of the pastoral dwellers. Even so, Chester's search has much in common with that of the frantic urbanite looking for a place to hang his hat.

Communication between all forms of life reverberates throughout Selden's works. *The Garden under the Sea*, an early book, is an underwater idyll, although much of the exchange is with the mortals above. *The Genie of Sutton Place* experiments with changing forms, and the unexpected discourse between the disparate parties is both suggestive and funny. The young protagonist's pet dog rescued from the pound re-enters the home from which he had been banished transformed into one of human kind. He has the body of a man, and he can talk, but his mind is still that of a dog. His canine manners produce some comic postures. The gift of speech notwithstanding, he is enormously gratified by the prospect of an imminent return to dogdom. Communication is wondrous, transformation horrendous, at least on a long-term basis.

For all his charm, Chester Cricket's most enduring stance is that of the impresario who heightens the roles of others and brings them into appreciative contact with each other. Even his brief stint as an operatic tenor, and hence an object of veneration and wonderment, never causes him to relinquish his position as the one who connects forms of nature. Those who expect another Disney-style Jiminy Cricket, that vaudevillian replacement of Carlo Collodi's tauntingly somber embodiment of conscience, will be disappointed for a mo-

ment. Then they will be elated upon discovering a more essential if less endearing figure. Selden's world has many characters, a number of them intriguing in their own way. But his manner is similar to that of Chester, to bring together the forms and the figures in active discourse and interchange with each other—and not to isolate them with idiosyncrasy.

—Leonard R. Mendelsohn

SENDAK, Maurice (Bernard). American. Born in Brooklyn, New York, 10 June 1928. Educated at Lafayette High School, New York (cartoonist, *Lafayette News*), graduated 1946; Art Students' League, New York, 1949–51. Illustrator of the *Mutt and Jeff* comic strip, All American Comics, New York, 1944–45; worked for Timely Service window display firm, New York, 1946–48, and in window display department of F.A.O. Schwarz, New York, 1948–51. Since 1951 freelance illustrator and writer. Instructor in Children's Literature, Yale University, New Haven, Connecticut, 1974–75; Instructor, Parsons School of Design, New York, 1974–79. Individual shows: Gallery of Visual Arts, New York, 1964; Rosenbach Foundation, Philadelphia, 1970, 1975; Trinity College, Hartford, Connecticut, 1972; Galerie Daniel Keel, Zurich, 1974; Ashmolean Museum, Oxford, 1975; American Cultural Center, Paris, 1978. Recipient: American Library Association Caldecott Medal, 1964, and Laura Ingalls Wilder award, 1983; Hans Christian Andersen International Medal, 1970; University of Southern Mississippi award, 1981; Boston *Globe-Horn Book* award, 1981; American Book award, 1982. L.H.D.: Boston University, 1977; D.F.A.: Princeton University, New Jersey, 1984. Honorary Royal Designer for Industry, Royal Society of Arts (London), 1986. Address: 200 Chestnut Hill Road, Ridgefield, Connecticut 06877, U.S.A.

PUBLICATIONS FOR CHILDREN (illustrated by the author)

Fiction

Kenny's Window. New York, Harper, 1956.
Very Far Away. New York, Harper, 1957; Kingswood, Surrey, World's Work, 1959.
The Sign on Rosie's Door. New York, Harper, 1960; London, Bodley Head, 1969.
Where the Wild Things Are. New York, Harper, 1963; London, Bodley Head, 1967.
Higglety Pigglety Pop! or, There Must Be More to Life. New York, Harper, 1967; London, Bodley Head, 1969.
In the Night Kitchen. New York, Harper, 1970; London, Bodley Head, 1971.
Outside over There. New York, Harper, and London, Bodley Head, 1981.

Plays

Really Rosie, adaptation of his own stories *The Sign on Rosie's Door* and *Nutshell Library* (televised, 1975). New York, Harper, 1975; revised version, music by Carole King (produced London and Washington, D.C., 1978; New York, 1980), New York, French, 1985.
Where the Wild Things Are, adaptation of his own story, music by Oliver Knussen (produced Brussels, 1980; London, 1984).

Television Play: *Really Rosie*, 1975.

Verse

The Nutshell Library (Alligators All Around, Chicken Soup with Rice, One Was Johnny, Pierre: A Cautionary Tale). New York, Harper, 4 vols., 1962; London, Collins, 4 vols., 1964.
Seven Little Monsters. New York, Harper, 1976; London, Bodley Head, 1977.

Other

The Acrobat. Privately printed, 1959.
The Magician: A Counting Book. Philadelphia, Rosenbach Foundation, 1971.
Pictures. New York, Harper, 1971; London, Bodley Head, 1972.
Some Swell Pup; or, Are You Sure You Want a Dog?, with Matthew Margolis. New York, Farrar Straus, and London, Bodley Head, 1976.

PUBLICATIONS FOR ADULTS

Other

Fantasy Sketches. Philadelphia, Rosenbach Foundation, 1970.
Questions to an Artist Who Is Also an Author: A Conversation Between Virginia Haviland and Maurice Sendak. Washington, D.C., Library of Congress, 1972.
A Conversation with Maurice Sendak, by Jeffrey Jon Smith. Elmhurst, Illinois, Smith, 1975.
Collection of Books, Posters and Original Drawings. New York, Schiller, 1984.
Posters. New York, Crown, 1986; London, Bodley Head, 1987.
Caldecott and Co.: Notes on Books and Pictures. New York, Farrar Straus, 1988; London, Reinhardt, 1989.

*

Manuscript Collection: Rosenbach Foundation, Philadelphia.

Critical Studies: *Catalogue for an Exhibition of Pictures by Maurice Sendak at the Ashmolean Museum, Oxford, December 16-February 29, 1975–76* edited by Brian Alderson, London, Bodley Head, 1975; *The Art of Maurice Sendak* by Selma G. Lanes, New York, Abrams, 1980, London, Bodley Head, 1981.

Theatrical Activities:
Director: **Television**—*Really Rosie*, 1975.
Designer: **Opera**—*The Magic Flute*, Houston, 1980; *Where the Wild Things Are*, Brussels, 1980, and London, 1984; *The Cunning Little Vixen*, New York, 1981; *L'Amour des Trois Oranges*, Glyndebourne, Sussex, 1982; *L'enfant et les Sortilèges*, Glyndbourne, Sussex, 1987.

Illustrator: *Atomics for the Millions* by M.C. Eidinoff and others, 1947; *The Wonderful Farm*, 1951, and *The Magic Pictures*, 1954, both by Marcel Aymé; *Good Shabbos, Everybody!* by Robert Garvey, 1951; *A Hole Is to Dig*, 1952, *A Very Special House*, 1953, *I'll Be You and You Be Me*, 1954, *Charlotte and the White Horse*, 1955, *I Want to Paint My Bathroom Blue*, 1956, *The Birthday Party*, 1957, *Somebody Else's Nut Tree*, 1958, and *Open House for Butterflies*, 1960, all by Ruth Krauss; *Maggie Rose* by Ruth Sawyer, 1952; *The Giant Story*, 1953, and *What Can You Do with a Shoe?*, 1955, both by Beatrice Schenk de Regniers; *Shadrach*, 1953, *Hurry Home, Candy*, 1953, *The Wheel on the School*, 1954, *The Little Cow and the Turtle*, 1955, *The House of Sixty Fathers*, 1956, *Along Came a Dog*, 1958, and *The Singing Hill*, 1962, all by Meindert De Jong;

The Tin Fiddle by Edward Tripp, 1954; *Mrs. Piggle-Wiggle's Farm* by Betty MacDonald, 1954; *Happy Hanukah, Everybody* by Hyman and Alice Chanover, 1955; *Seven Little Stories on Big Subjects* by Gladys Baker Bond, 1955; *The Singing Family of the Cumberlands* by Jean Ritchie, 1955; *The Happy Rain*, 1956, and *Circus Girl*, 1957, both by Jack Sendak; *Little Bear*, 1957, *No Fighting, No Biting!*, 1958, *Father Bear Comes Home*, 1959, *Little Bear's Friend*, 1960, *Little Bear's Visit*, 1961, and *A Kiss for Little Bear*, 1968, all by Else Minarik; *What Do You Say, Dear?*, 1958, and *What Do You Do, Dear?*, 1961, both by Sesyle Joslin; *Seven Tales* by Hans Christian Andersen, 1959; *The Moon Jumpers*, 1959, and *Let's Be Enemies*, 1961, both by Janice Udry; *Dwarf Long-Nose*, 1960, *The Tale of Gockel, Hinkel, and Gackeliah*, 1961, and *Schoolmaster Whackwell's Wonderful Sons*, 1962, all translated by Doris Orgel, and *Sarah's Room*, by Orgel, 1962; *The Big Green Book* by Robert Graves, 1962; *Mr. Rabbit and the Lovely Present* by Charlotte Zolotow, 1962; *She Loves Me, She Loves Me Not!* by Robert Keeshan, 1963; *The Griffin and the Minor Canon*, 1963, and *The Bee-Man of Orn*, 1964, both by Frank R. Stockton; *Nikolenka's Childhood* by Leo Tolstoy, 1963; *How Little Lori Visited Times Square* by Amos Vogel, 1963; *Pleasant Fieldmouse* by Jan Wahl, 1964; *The Bat-Poet*, 1964, *The Animal Family*, 1965, and *Fly by Night*, 1976, all by Randall Jarrell; *Hector Protector, and As I Went over the Water: Two Nursery Rhymes*, 1965; *Lullabies and Night Songs* edited by William Engvick, 1965; *Zlateh the Goat* by Isaac Bashevis Singer, 1966; *Poems from William Blake's Songs of Innocence*, 1967; *The Golden Key*, 1967, and *The Light Princess*, 1969, both by George MacDonald; *King Grisly-Beard*, 1973, and *The Juniper Tree and Other Tales*, 1973, by the Grimm Brothers; *Fortunia* by Marie Catherine Aulnoy, 1974; *The Love for Three Oranges: The Glyndebourne Version* by Frank Corsaro, 1984; *You Can't Get There from Here* by Ogden Nash, 1984; *The Nutcracker* by E.T.A. Hoffmann, 1984; *The Cunning Little Vixen* by Rudolf Tesnohlidek, 1985; *In Grandpa's House* by Philip Sendak, 1985; *Dear Mili* by Wilhelm Grimm, 1988.

Animator: *Seven Monsters* and *Bumble-Ardy* (*Sesame Street* television series), 1970.

*   *   *

During his distinguished career in children's books, Maurice Sendak has provided richly varied pictures for more than 80 works. Of this number, 11 have been stories that the artist himself has written. As might be expected, these works provide telling insights into those qualities of head and heart that have helped to make Sendak an international figure, possibly the pre-eminent children's picture-book practitioner of our time.

Sendak is often credited with being the first author-artist to deal openly with the feelings of young children. Of his own particular gifts, he has said, "If I have an unusual talent, it's not that I draw particularly better, or write particularly better, than other people. I've never fooled myself about that. Rather, it's that I remember things other people don't recall: the sounds and feelings and images—the emotional quality—of particular moments in childhood." Certainly each of Sendak's own stories is characterized by a loving observation of, and familiarity with, the ways of real children. He has also said, "To me, illustrating means having a passionate affair with the words," and this intensity of approach goes far toward explaining his uncanny ability to make palpable the emotional reality in which his tales take place.

The first book that Sendak wrote as well as illustrated, *Kenny's Window*, was published when the artist was 27 and already an established illustrator of such innovative works as Ruth Krauss's *A Hole Is to Dig*. An overly long and diffuse tale about an imaginative child eager to discover more about the world beyond his front door,

Kenny's Window constitutes a treasure trove of the themes, characters, and psychological excursions that would become the core of Sendak's mature work.

Undergoing psychoanalysis at the time, Sendak had become increasingly aware of the wellsprings in childhood of our deepest fears and desires. He had also just finished reading *One Little Boy*, a clinical study of a disturbed child by the psychologist Dorothy Baruch. To these influences he attributes the discovery of his prototypical child hero and the subject that has engaged his talent and sensibility from that moment on: children who, in his own words, "are held back by life and, one way or other, manage miraculously to find release from their troubles." More introspective than any of his future heroes, Kenny escapes into dreams and fantasy to discover significant—occasionally even painful—truths about his own life.

In his next book, *Very Far Away*, Sendak tells a modest, affecting story about small Martin, who must come to terms with a new and painful home truth: his mother is so busy caring for a new baby that she has no time for him when he most craves her attention. Martin opts to run off "very far away," which, in Sendakian terms, is "many times around the block and two cellar windows from the corner." There Martin and three new friends—a bird, a horse, and a cat—live together very happily "for an hour and a half." (Clearly the author knew how children reckon endless stretches of time and distance.) At story's end, a less sulky Martin returns home in the hope that his mother may now be free to answer at least a few of his questions.

The Sign on Rosie's Door finds a more exuberant and confident author lovingly recreating the Brooklyn of his own 1930's childhood. His irrepressible Rosie, based on a real-life child Sendak once spent months observing from his Brooklyn apartment window, is a heroine capable of carrying her less imaginative cronies aloft on flights of therapeutic fancy. In this way they can happily pass summer days otherwise filled with "nothing to do."

Sendak's next work was his perennially popular, *The Nutshell Library*, a medley of four miniature volumes: a reptilian alphabet, *Alligators All Around*; a rhymed romp through the months of the year, *Chicken Soup with Rice*; a forward-and-backwards counting book, *One Was Johnny*; and a contemporary cautionary tale done with wit and irresistible charm, *Pierre* ("The moral of Pierre is: CARE!"). Revealing the author at his most fanciful, this quartet has been referred to by one critic as a young listener's "Compleat Companion into literacy," and shows just how much a gifted writer could expand upon conventional themes.

With the work that won him the Caldecott Medal, *Where the Wild Things Are*, Sendak felt himself at "the end of a long apprenticeship in children's books." The story represented the culmination of his attempts to portray a child mastering "the uncontrollable and frightening aspects of his life" through the help of fantasy. Unlike Sendak's earlier protagonists, who tended to use fantasy and daydreams as escapes from real-world emotional confrontations, the intrepid Max has a temper-tantrum when his mother calls him "Wild Thing!" He then goes off to tame Wild Things of his own imagining, and returns home purged, even victorious—since the supper he didn't expect to get is waiting for him at his bedside. Though countless librarians and educators worried about the book's frightening aspects for young children—raw rage and monstrous fantasy figures—the work was an immediate success. Children seemed to find solace in a hero who could be angry with his mother and triumph over his own rage.

In the Night Kitchen is a less accessible, more personal picture-book fantasy. Beginning with another angry hero, Mickey, who has been rudely awakened by things that go bump in the night, Sendak conjures up a dream sequence about three look-alike bakers who pursue their culinary art while most children are fast asleep. If there are Freudian undertones to this work celebrating the sensual joys of early childhood, most young listeners are entranced by the trio of cooks, dead ringers for the movie comedian Oliver Hardy, and their

mysterious incantation: "MILK IN THE BATTER! MILK IN THE BATTER! WE BAKE CAKE! AND NOTHING'S THE MATTER!"

The intriguing and decidedly American fairytale *Higglety Pigglety Pop! or, There Must Be More to Life* begins where traditional fairytales leave off, at "And they lived happily ever after." Jennie, the story's dog heroine, has everything—a loving master, two windows from which to enjoy the view, two pillows (one for upstairs, one for down), and two eating bowls. Yet, she announces at the fantasy's start: "I am discontented. There must be more to life than having everything." The voracious Jennie, who looms so large in this most personal and mystifying Sendak tale, is no garden-variety fictional heroine. In real life, she was for 15 years the author's beloved pet Sealyham. When he was working on *Higglety*, Jennie was failing and his own mother was dying; Sendak felt disquieting intimations of mortality, and he wanted to immortalize Jennie, perhaps himself as well, in "the World Mother Goose Theatre." Many of Sendak's admirers feel that this is his most ambitious and poetic work. Certainly, it is the one tale in which the words have as much resonance and power as the pictures.

Sendak's third volume in the picture-book trilogy that began with *Wild Things* and was followed by *Night Kitchen*, is *Outside over There*, a beautiful work pictorially and the most arcane in terms of story. Its beginnings were in *The Juniper Tree*, a two-volume selection of tales from the Brothers Grimm that Sendak illustrated. One of the Grimm tales, "The Goblins," dealt with the substitution of a changeling for a real child, and the ambiguities of this situation so intrigued Sendak that he made a goblin kidnapping the central drama of the final picture book in his self-styled trilogy. The companion volumes are *Wild Things* and *Night Kitchen*, and what links them in the author's mind is that "they are all variations on a single theme: an examination of how children master various feelings—anger, boredom, fear, frustration, jealousy, to name a few—and manage to come to grips with the realities of their lives." Ida, the heroine of *Outside over There*, is the pluckiest of all Sendak's protagonists. She has a depressed and withdrawn mother, an absent father whom she misses desperately, and a young sibling to care for. Woven into this dark tale are elements of Sendak's own childhood: the birth of the Dionne quintuplets, the kidnapping of the Lindbergh baby. Though Ida ultimately triumphs over her burdens, the victory is only partial. Somehow the richness of Sendak's illustrations is not matched by a sufficiently dramatic story.

Though Sendak's detractors frequently claim his subject matter is too strong for his young audience, the author prides himself on never trying to shield children from harsh truths: "Children are willing to deal with many dubious subjects that parents think they shouldn't know about," he says. "Children are small courageous people who deal every day with a multitude of problems, just as adults do....What they yearn for most is a bit of truth somewhere."

In keeping with this willingness to tackle major themes honestly in his books for children, Sendak's latest illustrations are for a recently discovered fairytale by Wilhelm Grimm called *Dear Mili*. Its subject, the death of a child during a war, is handled with the most lyrical and heartbreakingly beautiful pictures of the artist's career. He manages to be true both to Grimm's words and to the grim truths of the Holocaust, which cast a pall on his own 1930's childhood.

—Selma G. Lanes

SEREDY, Kate. American. Born in Budapest, Hungary, 10 November 1899; emigrated to the United States, 1922. Educated at Academy of Arts, Budapest, art teacher's diploma. Served as a nurse during World War I. Ran a children's bookstore, 1933–34; owned a farm near Montgomery, New York, 1936-mid 1950's. Commercial artist and freelance illustrator. Recipient: American Library Association Newbery Medal, 1938. *Died 7 March 1975.*

PUBLICATIONS FOR CHILDREN (illustrated by the author)

Fiction

The Good Master. New York, Viking Press, 1935; London, Harrap, 1937.
Listening. New York, Viking Press, 1936.
The Singing Tree. New York, Viking Press, 1939; London, Harrap, 1940.
A Tree for Peter. New York, Viking Press, 1941.
The Open Gate. New York, Viking Press, 1943; London, Harrap, 1947.
The Chestry Oak. New York, Viking Press, 1948; London, Harrap, 1957.
Gypsy. New York, Viking Press, 1951; London, Harrap, 1952.
Philomena. New York, Viking Press, 1955; London, Harrap, 1957.
The Tenement Tree. New York, Viking Press, 1959; London, Harrap, 1960.
A Brand-New Uncle. New York, Viking Press, 1961.
Lazy Tinka. New York, Viking Press, 1962; London, Harrap, 1964.

Other

The White Stag. New York, Viking Press, 1937; London, Harrap, 1938.

Translator, *Who Is Johnny?*, by Leopold Gedö, illustrated by Gedö. New York, Viking Press, 1939.

*

Manuscript Collections: May Massee Collection, Emporia State University, Kansas; University of Oregon Library, Eugene.

Illustrator: *The Prince Commands* by Andre Norton, 1934; *Broken Son* by Sonia Daugherty, 1934; *The Selfish Giant*, 1935, and *The Gunniwolf*, 1936, both edited by Wilhelmina Harper; *Caddie Woodlawn*, 1935, and *Mademoiselle Misfortune*, 1936, both by Carol Ryrie Brink; *With Harp and Lute*, 1935, *The Oldest Story*, 1943, and *A Candle Burns for France*, 1946, all by Blanche Thompson, and *Bible Children*, 1937, edited by Thompson; *Winterbound* by Margery Williams Bianco, 1936; *Smiling Hill Farm*, 1937, and *A House for Ten*, 1949, both by Miriam Mason; *An Ear for Uncle Emil* by E.R. Gaggin, 1939; *Michel's Island* by Mabel Leigh Hunt, 1940; *The Christmas Anna Angel* by Ruth Sawyer, 1944; *Living Together at Home and at School* by Prudence Cutright and others, 1944; *Fun at the Playground* by Bernice Osler Frissell and Mary Louise Friebele, 1946; *The Wonderful Year* by Nancy Barnes, 1946; *Hoot-Owl* by Mabel La Rue, 1946; *Adopted Jane*, 1947, *Mary Montgomery, Rebel*, 1948, and *Pilgrim Kate*, 1949, all by Helen Daringer; *Little Vic* by Doris Gates, 1951; *Finnegan II* by Carolyn Sherwin Bailey, 1953; *A Dog Named Penny* by Clyde Robert Bulla, 1955.

* * *

Kate Seredy first made her mark as a writer in 1935 when May Massee, the children's editor at Doubleday, suggested that she write a book about her childhood in Hungary. Seredy did just that, and *The Good Master* was the result. Not only did May Massee become one of the outstanding children's book editors of her time, but Seredy

went on to win the Newbery Medal in 1938 for *The White Stag* and to make many distinguished contributions to the field of children's literature.

The Good Master is set on a farm on the great Hungarian plains, the home of the "good master," his son Jancsi, and Jancsi's turbulent cousin Kate. Since Seredy spent most of her summers on the plains, she is able to describe vividly the people and customs of Hungary. Harvest festivals, household crafts, and even the local cooking add colour to the warm family story. Seredy's first training was as an artist, and she contributed sensitive and detailed illustrations to all her own and to other people's books. Her stories depict the human situation, the hopes and beliefs of mankind. *The Good Master* was followed by *The Singing Tree* which tells about the effects of war on the "good master's" household. The Magyar legends she heard as a child inspired *The White Stag* and, though it was a prize-winning book, many people regard *The Good Master* as her best book.

Seredy is one of the first children's writers to have dealt with the problems of the alien. *The Singing Tree* tells of the life of Russian prisoners in Hungary during the war, as well as German refugee children who arrive to be restored to health. In *The Chestry Oak* a homeless little boy from Hungary is sent to America where he struggles to become part of that country. Although the hero is young the ideas are adult and explore the ways in which children are affected by the tragedy of war.

Although Seredy was Hungarian by birth and upbringing, she wrote English prose with no trace of foreign idiom. Her books explore values and characteristics familiar to us all, but freshly interesting against an unfamiliar background. In being both author and artist she gave her books an authenticity which is rare.

—Ann Bartholomew

———

SERRAILLIER, Ian (Lucien). British. Born in London, 24 September 1912. Educated at Brighton College, 1926–30; St. Edmund Hall, Oxford, 1931–35, M.A. 1935. Married Anne Margaret Rogers in 1944; three daughters and one son. Schoolmaster, Wycliffe College, Stonehouse, Gloucestershire, 1936–39, Dudley Grammar School, Worcestershire, 1940–46, and Midhurst Grammar School, Sussex, 1946–61. Since 1950 founder and general editor, with Anne Serraillier, New Windmill series (more than 330 books), Heinemann Educational Books, Oxford. Address: c/o Heinemann Educational Books Ltd., Halley Court, Jordan Hill, Oxford OX2 8EJ, England.

PUBLICATIONS FOR CHILDREN

Fiction

They Raced for Treasure, illustrated by C. Walter Hodges. London, Cape, 1946; abridged edition, as *Treasure Ahead*, London, Heinemann, 1954.
Flight to Adventure, illustrated by C. Walter Hodges. London, Cape, 1947; abridged edition, as *Mountain Rescue*, London, Heinemann, 1955.
Captain Bounsaboard and the Pirates, illustrated by Michael Bartlett and Arline Braybrooke. London, Cape, 1949.
There's No Escape, illustrated by C. Walter Hodges. London, Cape, 1950; New York, Scholastic, 1973.
Making Good, illustrated by Vera Jarman. London, Heinemann, 1955.
The Silver Sword, illustrated by C. Walter Hodges. London, Cape, 1956; New York, Criterion, 1959; as *Escape from Warsaw*, New

York, Scholastic, 1963.

The Cave of Death, illustrated by Stuart Tresilian. London, Heinemann, 1965.

Fight for Freedom, illustrated by John S. Goodall. London, Heinemann, 1965.

Plays (in verse)

The Midnight Thief, music by Richard Rodney Bennett, illustrated by Tellosa. London, BBC Publications, 1963.

Ahmet the Woodseller, music by Gordon Crosse, illustrated by John Griffiths. London, BBC Publications, 1965.

The Turtle Drum, music by Malcolm Arnold, illustrated by Charles Pickard. London, BBC Publications, 1967.

A Pride of Lions, music by Phyllis Tate (produced Nottingham, 1970). London, Oxford University Press, 1971.

Verse

The Weaver Birds, illustrated by the author. London, Macmillan, 1944; New York, Macmillan, 1945.

Thomas and the Sparrow, illustrated by Mark Severin. London, Oxford University Press, 1946.

The Tale of the Monster Horse, illustrated by Mark Severin. London, Oxford University Press, 1950.

The Ballad of Kon-Tiki and Other Verses, illustrated by Mark Severin. London, Oxford University Press, 1952.

Belinda and the Swans, illustrated by Pat Marriott. London, Cape, 1952.

Everest Climbed, illustrated by Leonard Rosoman. London, Oxford University Press, 1955.

A Puffin Quartet of Poets, with others, edited by Eleanor Graham, illustrated by Diana Bloomfield. London, Penguin, 1958.

Poems and Pictures. London, Heinemann, 1958.

The Windmill Book of Ballads, illustrated by Mark Severin and Leonard Rosoman. London, Heinemann, 1962.

Happily Ever After, illustrated by Brian Wildsmith. London, Oxford University Press, 1963.

The Challenge of the Green Knight, illustrated by Victor Ambrus. London, Oxford University Press, 1966; New York, Walck, 1967.

Robin in the Greenwood, illustrated by Victor Ambrus. London, Oxford University Press, 1967; New York, Walck, 1968.

Robin and His Merry Men, illustrated by Victor Ambrus. London, Oxford University Press, 1969; New York, Walck, 1970.

The Ballad of St. Simeon, illustrated by Simon Stern. London, Kaye and Ward, and New York, Watts, 1970.

The Tale of Three Landlubbers, illustrated by Raymond Briggs. London, Hamish Hamilton, 1970; New York, Coward McCann, 1971.

The Bishop and the Devil, illustrated by Simon Stern. London, Kaye and Ward, and New York, Warne, 1971.

Marko's Wedding, illustrated by Victor Ambrus. London, Deutsch, 1972.

Suppose You Met a Witch, illustrated by Ed Emberley. Boston, Little Brown, 1973.

I'll Tell You a Tale: A Collection of Poems and Ballads, illustrated by Charles Keeping and Renate Meyer. London, Longman, 1973; revised edition, London, Kestrel, 1976.

The Robin and the Wren, illustrated by Fritz Wegner. London, Kestrel, 1974.

How Happily She Laughs and Other Poems. London, Longman, 1976.

Other

Jungle Adventure (based on story by R.M. Ballantyne), illustrated

by Vera Jarman. London, Heinemann, 1953.

The Adventures of Dick Varley (based on story by R.M. Ballantyne), illustrated by Vera Jarman. London, Heinemann, 1954.

Beowulf the Warrior (in verse), illustrated by Mark Severin. London, Oxford University Press, 1954; New York, Walck, 1961.

Guns in the Wild (based on story by R.M. Ballantyne), illustrated by Shirley Hughes. London, Heinemann, 1956.

Katy at Home (based on story by Susan Coolidge), illustrated by Shirley Hughes. London, Heinemann, 1957.

Katy at School (based on story by Susan Coolidge), illustrated by Shirley Hughes. London, Heinemann, 1959.

The Ivory Horn: Retold from the Song of Roland, illustrated by William Stobbs. London, Oxford University Press, 1960.

The Gorgon's Head: The Story of Perseus, illustrated by William Stobbs. London, Oxford University Press, 1961; New York, Walck, 1962.

The Way of Danger: The Story of Theseus, illustrated by William Stobbs. London, Oxford University Press, 1962; New York, Walck, 1963.

The Clashing Rocks: The Story of Jason, illustrated by William Stobbs. London, Oxford University Press, 1963; New York, Walck, 1963.

The Enchanted Island: Stories from Shakespeare, illustrated by Peter Farmer. London, Oxford University Press, and New York, Walck, 1964; abridged edition, as *Murder at Dunsinane*, New York, Scholastic, 1967.

A Fall from the Sky: The Story of Daedalus, illustrated by William Stobbs. London, Nelson, and New York, Walck, 1966.

Chaucer and His World. London, Lutterworth Press, 1967; New York, Walck, 1968.

Havelok the Dane, illustrated by Elaine Raphael. New York, Walck, 1967; as *Havelok the Warrior*, London, Hamish Hamilton, 1968.

Heracles the Strong, illustrated by Rocco Negri. New York, Walck, 1970; London, Hamish Hamilton, 1971.

Have You Got Your Ticket? (reader), illustrated by Douglas Hall. London, Longman 1972.

The Franklin's Tale, Retold, illustrated by Philip Gough. London, Kaye and Ward, and New York, Warne, 1972.

Pop Festival (reader), illustrated by Douglas Hall. London, Longman, 1973.

The Sun Goes Free (reader). London, Longman, 1977.

The Road to Canterbury (tales from Chaucer retold), illustrated by John Lawrence. London, Kestrel, 1979.

Editor, with Ronald Ridout, *Wide Horizon Reading Scheme*. London, Heinemann, 4 vols., 1953–55.

Translator, with Anne Serraillier, *Florina and the Wild Bird*, by Selina Chönz, illustrated by Alois Carigiet. London, Oxford University Press, 1952.

PUBLICATIONS FOR ADULTS

Verse

Three New Poets, with Roy McFadden and Alex Comfort. Billericay, Essex, Grey Walls Press, 1942.

Other

All Change at Singleton: For Charlton, Goodwood, East and West Dean (local history). London, Phillimore, 1979.

Goodwood Country in Old Photographs, with Richard Pailthorpe.

Gloucester, Sutton, 1987.

*

Ian Serraillier comments:

I cannot remember a time when I did not want to become a writer. I was always practising, even while I was still at school, where we were brought up on Latin and Greek and hardly any English. I would not recommend this old-fashioned educational diet now. But it gave me an excellent formal training and a sound discipline in language structure, particularly verse technique. Oddly enough it was not English verse that we were made to write at school, but Latin and Greek verse, correctly conforming to all the rules even if the result was not impressive poetry. Since those early days I have not tried to write in any language but English.

* * *

Ian Serraillier's great strength is above all as a teller of tales. In his retellings, his verse and his fiction, it is his skill as a storyteller that is most in evidence. He knows exactly how to sustain the tension of a story and hold his readers, what to leave out and what to dwell on, and it is this which makes his versions of the ancient legends—of Heracles, Jason, or Theseus, of Beowulf or Sir Gawain—so effective. There are a simple strength and vigour in his writing, an enjoyment of physical skills and courage, and a fine narrative sense which makes the old stories work marvelously well for the average child who might not otherwise approach them.

His stories, prose and verse, read well aloud. He obviously composes with the spoken word in mind. All his writing appeals strongly to boys, if it is permissible these days to say so, and is enjoyable from, say, the age of eight.

He has put together several anthologies which include rewritten ballads and the like as well as his own verse. Though the force of the originals is sometimes weakened, he makes the old poems once more accessible to those who would be put off by archaic or dialect words. His own best verse is quirky and original, as in this "Tickle Rhyme":

> "Who's that tickling my back?" said the wall.
> "Me," said a small
> Caterpillar. "I'm learning
> To crawl."

As far as his original fiction goes, he has written one very fine story based on fact (*The Silver Sword*) and several rather unremarkable adventure stories. For example, *There's No Escape* is a war story set in a fictitious country in the Alps. The hero is dropped by parachute to rescue a missing scientist. England is at war with a fictitious enemy who bears a close resemblance to the German villains of cliché. It is perhaps unfair to quote at almost 40 years' remove, but to present-day readers the cliché verges at times on the comic. Even his middle-aged central European scientist talks like a British public schoolboy: "Well, Peter, we cannot remain here for ever. We must—how do you say—face the music alone now." There are a skillful build-up of excitement and a fine chase over the mountains, but such books cannot really compete with the good adult thrillers which are also available to this age group.

The Silver Sword is another matter. It is a fine achievement. The story is based on true events and is beautifully fitted to Serraillier's talent. It is the tale of the wanderings of a family of Polish children across war-torn Europe in search of their father and mother; it has a happy ending, for the three children are finally reunited with their parents in Switzerland, and Jan, the child who never finds anyone belonging to him, stays with them. The locale and the enemy do not have to be invented, and the simple matter-of-fact style in which the story is told makes it the more convincing and moving. Furthermore

this is not a simple goodies-versus-baddies tale. Not every German is portrayed as unsympathetic, and there is food for thought in the effect of wartime morality upon Jan, the boy who has joined the Balicki children in their quest and who has turned himself in order to survive into a brilliant and convincing liar.

—Mary Rayner

———

SETON, Ernest (Evan) Thompson. American. Born in South Shields, County Durham, England, 14 August 1860; emigrated to Canada, 1866; became United States citizen, 1931. Educated at Elizabeth Street and Victoria Street schools and Collegiate High School, Toronto; Ontario College of Art, Toronto, 1877–79; Royal Academy School of Painting and Sculpture, London, 1881; Art Students' League, New York, 1884; Académie Julian, Paris, 1891. Married 1) Grace Gallatin in 1896 (divorced 1935), one daughter, the writer Anya Seton; 2) Julia Moss Buttree in 1935, one adopted daughter. Artist for Wilhelms and Betzig, lithographic publishers, New York, 1883–84; illustrator for *The Century Dictionary*, New York, 1885–86; resort manager, Lake Ontario, 1887–90; Manitoba government naturalist after 1892. Freelance illustrator, naturalist, and lecturer. Founder of the Woodcraft Indians, later the Woodcraft League, 1902; chairman of the founding committee, 1910, and chief scout, 1910–15, Boy Scouts of America; founding president, Seton Institute, Santa Fe, New Mexico, 1930–46. Recipient (for naturalist illustrations): Camp-Fire Gold Medal, 1909; Société d'Acclimatation de France Medal, 1918; National Institute of Science Elliott Gold Medal, 1927; John Burroughs Medal, 1928; David Girou Medal, 1930. Associate, Royal Canadian Academy of Art; member, American Academy. *Died 23 October 1946.*

PUBLICATIONS FOR CHILDREN (illustrated by the author)

Fiction

Wild Animals I Have Known, Being the Personal Histories of Lobo, Silverspot, Raggylug, Bingo, The Springfield Fox, The Pacing Mustang, Wully, and Redruff. London, Nutt, 1898; New York, Scribner, 1899.
The Trail of the Sandhill Stag. New York, Scribner, and London, Nutt, 1899.
Raggylug the Cottontail Rabbit and Other Animal Stories. London, Nutt, 1900.
The Biography of a Grizzly. New York, Century, and London, Hodder and Stoughton, 1900.
Lives of the Hunted. New York, Scribner, 1901; London, Nutt, 1902.
Two Little Savages. Montreal, Montreal News Company, and New York, Doubleday, 1903; London, Grant Richards, 1904.
Monarch, The Big Bear of Tallac. New York, Scribner, 1904; London, Constable, 1905.
Animal Heroes, Being the Histories of a Cat, a Dog, a Pigeon, a Lynx, Two Wolves, and a Reindeer. New York, Scribner, 1905; London, Constable, 1906.
Woodmyth and Fable. Toronto, Briggs, and New York, Century, 1905.
The Natural History of the Ten Commandments. New York, Scribner, 1907; as *The Ten Commandments in the Animal World*, New York, Doubleday, 1923.
The Biography of a Silver-Fox; or, Domino Reynard of Goldur Town. New York, Century, and London, Constable, 1909.

Rolf in the Woods. New York, Doubleday, and London, Constable, 1911.

Wild Animals at Home. Toronto, Briggs, New York, Doubleday, and London, Hodder and Stoughton, 1913.

The White Reindeer, Arnaux, and The Boy and the Lynx. London, Constable, 1915.

The Slum Cat, Snap, and The Winnipeg Wolf. London, Constable, 1915.

Wild Animal Ways. New York, Doubleday, and London, Hodder and Stoughton, 1916.

The Preacher of Cedar Mountain: A Tale of the Open Country. New York, Doubleday, and London, Hodder and Stoughton, 1917.

Woodland Tales. New York, Doubleday, and London, Hodder and Stoughton, 1921.

Bannertail: The Story of a Gray Squirrel. New York, Scribner, 1922; London, Hodder and Stoughton, 1923.

Katug the Snow Child. Oxford, Blackwell, 1929.

Krag, The Kootenay Ram and Other Animal Stories. London, University of London Press, 1929.

Johnny Bear, Lobo, and Other Stories. New York, Scribner, 1935.

Great Historic Animals: Mainly about Wolves. New York, Scribner, 1937; as *Mainly about Wolves,* London, Methuen, 1937.

The Biography of an Arctic Fox. New York, Appleton Century, 1937.

Trail and Camp-Fire Stories, edited by Julia M. Seton. New York, Appleton Century, 1940.

Santana, The Hero Dog of France. Los Angeles, Phoenix Press, 1945.

Play

The Wild Animal Play for Children. New York, Doubleday, and London, Nutt, 1900.

Other

How to Play Indian. Philadelphia, Curtis, 1903; as *The Red Book; or, How to Play Indian,* privately printed, 1904.

The Birch-Bark Roll of the Woodcraft Indians. New York, Doubleday, 1906.

Boy Scouts of America: A Handbook of Woodcraft, Scouting, and Life-Craft. New York, Doubleday, 1910.

The Book of Woodcraft and Indian Lore. New York, Doubleday, and London, Constable, 1912.

The Forester's Manual: or, The Forest Trees of Eastern North America. New York, Doubleday, 1912.

Woodcraft Boys, Woodcraft Girls. New York, Edgar, 1915.

Sign Talk: A Universal Signal Code. New York, Doubleday, and London, Curtis Brown, 1918.

Editor, *The Animal Story Book.* Boston, Hall and Locke, 1902 (?).

Editor, *Famous Animal Stories: Animal Myths, Fables, Fairy Tales, and Stories of Real Animals.* New York, Brentano's, 1932; London, Lane, 1933.

PUBLICATIONS FOR ADULTS (illustrated by the author)

Other

A List of Animals of Manitoba. Toronto, Oxford University Press, 1886.

The Birds of Manitoba. Washington, D.C., United States National Museum, 1891.

Studies in the Art Anatomy of Animals. London and New York, Macmillan, 1896.

The National Zoo at Washington. Washington, D.C., Smithsonian Institution, 1901.

Pictures of Wild Animals. New York, Scribner, 1901.

Bird Portraits, text by Ralph Hoffman. Boston, Ginn, 1901.

Life-Histories of Northern Animals: An Account of the Mammals of Manitoba. New York, Scribner, 2 vols., 1909; London, Constable, 2 vols., 1910.

The War Dance and the Fire-Fly Dance. New York, Doubleday, 1910.

The Arctic Prairies: A Canoe Journey of 2000 Miles in Search of the Caribou, Being the Account of a Voyage to the Region North of Aylmer Lake.... New York, Scribner, 1911; London, Constable, 1912.

Lives of Game Animals: An Account of Those Land Animals in America North of the Mexican Border Which Are Considered "Game".... New York, Doubleday, and London, Hodder and Stoughton, 4 vols., 1925–28.

Animals Worth Knowing. New York, Doubleday, 1934.

The Buffalo Wind. Santa Fe, Seton Village Press, 1938.

Trail of an Artist-Naturalist: The Autobiography of Ernest Thompson Seton. New York, Scribner, 1940; London, Hodder and Stoughton, 1951.

The Best of Ernest Thompson Seton, edited by W. Kay Robinson. London, Hodder and Stoughton, 1949.

Ernest Thompson Seton's America: Selections from the Writings of the Artist-Naturalist, edited by Farida A. Wiley. New York, Devin Adair, 1954.

Animal Tracks and Hunter Signs, with Julia M. Seton. New York, Doubleday, 1958; London, Ward, 1959.

By a Thousand Fires: Nature Notes and Extracts from the Life and Unpublished Journals, edited by Julia M. Seton. New York, Doubleday, 1967.

The Worlds of Ernest Thompson Seton, edited by John G. Samson. New York, Knopf, 1976.

The Best of Ernest Thomson Seton, edited by Richard Adams. London, Fontana, 1982.

Editor, with Julia M. Seton, *The Gospel of the Redman: An Indian Bible.* New York, Doubleday, 1936; London, Methuen, 1937.

*

Manuscript Collections: Ernest Thompson Seton Memorial Library and Museum, Cimarron, New Mexico; Academy of American Arts and Letters Library, New York.

Critical Studies: *Ernest Thompson Seton, Naturalist* by Shannon and Warren Garst, New York, Messner, 1959; *Ernest Thompson Seton: Man in Nature* by John H. Wadland, Salem, New Hampshire, Ayer, 1978; *Black Wolf: The Biography of Ernest Thompson Seton* by Betty Keller, Vancouver, Douglas and McIntyre, 1984, Topsfield, Massachusetts, Salem House, 1985; *The Chief: Ernest Thompson Seton and the Changing West* by H. Allen Anderson, College Station, Texas A and M University Press, 1986.

Illustrator: *Bird-Life* by F. M. Chapman, 1887; *Four-Footed Americans* by Mabel Wright, 1898; *First Across the Continent* by Noah Brooks, 1901; *The Rhythm of the Redman* by Julia Buttree, 1930; *The Indian Costume Book* by Julia M. Seton, 1938.

*   *   *

The writings of Ernest Thompson Seton display the savvy of first-hand experience and the fascination of first time enterprise. His autobiography, *Trail of an Artist-Naturalist,* published when he was 80, reflects the same excited agony of discovery found in his first book, *Wild Animals I Have Known*. Even though his works abound in precise detail and acute observation derived from unrelenting study (a number of his books, including *Life-Histories of Northern Animals*, are essentially well-decorated catalogues of the fauna of a particular region), his controlled ebullience and knowing naivety demonstrate that Seton is legitimately within the ranks of writers for children.

His characters, arising from naturalists' notations, become distinct and appealing individuals. Lobo, now subject of a Walt Disney feature, appears in *Wild Animals I Have Known* as a stylized portrait of a predator. Rejecting the usual inclination of the leader to assemble an expansive pack, this singular wolf heads a select marauding band of but five lupines, each pre-eminent in some respect of size, agility, instinct, or aesthetics. The adventure-laden tale alternates between a wolf's and artist's eye view, and succeeds in ennobling predation decades prior to any ecologist's outcry. Lobo's uncanny capacity for rejecting poisoned segments of an animal carcass, his apparent appetite for practical jests, and his strongly suggested love of beauty fail to romanticize him out of belief. Ultimately the noble pack is violently exterminated, an end which Seton observed was the way of nature and thus inseparable from her beauties.

While Seton's description never strays from the facts of nature, the subjects of his narratives are invariably distinct and individual. To know nature is never to generalize but "to know one creature from his fellow." Accordingly the life story of a crow from *Wild Animals* includes on the same page the precise musical notation for specified signals in crow communication and a description of the hero Silverspot's predilection for toying with a carefully concealed collection of clam shells, white pebbles, bits of tin, and an old china cup. Wahb, solitary subject of *The Biography of a Grizzly*, likewise is at once typical and unique. The biggest grizzly in the park, he reputedly "knows more about plants and roots than a whole college of botanists." Such almost endearing respect for this savage hunter parallels Seton's approach to cruelty and violence. An incident in which a callous hunter cuts down a mother and three cubs, leaving Wahb an orphan and a loner throughout life, is presented without moralizing, though Seton with supple understatement concludes the narration with "That is why the post office is called Four-Bears. The Colonel seemed pleased with what he had done; indeed he told of it himself." *Lives of the Hunted*, comprising eight indelible biographies of preyed-upon creatures, also conveys compassion for wildlife without intrusive sentimentality. Death, sudden and cruel, is inevitable, but then so is the will to thrive.

While a significant number of Seton's books have been expropriated for children, not infrequently he writes explicitly for them. In 1900 he adapted *Wild Animals* into *The Wild Animal Play for Children*, a drama which contains "an alternate reading for very young children," with staging, music, costumes, and other dramatic effects carefully detailed by the author. The style, even of the simplified version, appears more suited for Jacobean masque than childhood recitation, but the conception provides ample scope for impersonation of woodland inhabitants, wildmen, and even of angels. His attention to children is by no means casual. He founded the Woodcraft League, served as its chief, and was author, editor, and illustrator of its guidebook. *The Birch-Bark Roll* is a compendium of outdoor life and lore. *Woodland Tales*, among others, is specifically addressed to a younger audience, while *Rolf in the Woods*, an elaborate series of adventures of a boy scout, a dog, and an Indian, is dedicated to the Boy Scouts of America.

His classic composition, *Two Little Savages*, is a thinly veiled autobiography of his youthful years which were stamped by an ingenuously impassioned determination to live as an Indian. With a companion, Yan, the youthful naturalist embarks upon an often awkward return to aborigine ways. The book is replete with moments touching and comic, and ideals deflated and irrepressible, but the young hero learns from a sequence of false starts and ends up

assembling a hard-earned but substantial accumulation of primitive lifestyles.

Seton's principal concern, however, continued to be the animals themselves. A second grizzly became the study for biography in *Monarch, The Big Bear of Tallac*. Unlike the earlier tale of Wahb, *Monarch* shows the interaction of human and animal becoming more conspicuous and less opposed. Seton's animal characters, posed against a natural landscape and confronting circumstances conforming to the environs, retain a lively caricature quite surpassing the dull personifications which dominate and denude animal denizens of many a children's book. His hallmark, individualized realistic fantasy, is applied to domestic creatures as well. *Animal Heroes* contains a low-keyed odyssey of a slum cat who prevails in a world designed and denigrated by man. Another chapter chronicles a game though smallish homing pigeon whose legendary perseverence is finally cut short by an eyrie of peregrines. The human figures become progressively more prominent, interacting with lynxes, bull terriers, and jack rabbits. Mankind even in its youth is cruel, but it can learn compassion. Seton's involvements seem to stress that repeated experience heartens rather than hardens the soul.

—Leonard R. Mendelsohn

SEUSS, Dr. Pseudonym for Theodor Seuss Geisel; also writes as Theo Le Sieg; Rosetta Stone. American. Born in Springfield, Massachusetts, 2 March 1904. Educated at schools in Springfield; Dartmouth College, Hanover, New Hampshire (editor, *Jack-o-Lantern*), A.B. 1925; Lincoln College, Oxford, 1925–26. Served in the United States Army Signal Corps and Information and Education Division, 1943–46: Lieutenant-Colonel; Legion of Merit. Married 1) Helen Marion Palmer in 1927 (died 1967); 2) Audrey Stone Dimond in 1968. Freelance magazine humorist and cartoonist from 1927; advertising illustrator, Standard Oil Company of New Jersey, 1928–41, and for Ford Motor Company; editorial cartoonist, *PM* magazine, New York, 1940–42; publicist, War Production Board, 1940–42; correspondent, *Life* magazine, Japan, 1954. Since 1957 founding president and editor-in-chief, Beginner Books, Random House Inc., New York. Individual shows: San Diego Fine Arts Museum, 1950; Dartmouth College, 1975; Toledo Museum of Art, Ohio, 1975; La Jolla Museum of Contemporary Arts, 1976. Recipient: Oscar, for documentary, 1946, 1947, for animated cartoon, 1951; Peabody award, for television cartoon, 1971 (twice); Zagreb International Cartoon Festival award, 1972; Emmy award, for television, 1977, 1982; American Library Association Laura Ingalls Wilder award, 1980; Catholic Library Association Regina Medal, 1982; Pulitzer Prize special citation, 1984. L.H.D.: Dartmouth College, 1956; American International College, Springfield, Massachusetts, 1968; Lake Forest College, Illinois, 1977; Brown University, Providence, Rhode Island, 1987; D. Litt.: Whittier College, California, 1980; John F. Kennedy University, 1983; University of Hartford, Connecticut, 1986; D.F.A.: Princeton University, New Jersey, 1985. Lives in La Jolla, California. Address: c/o Random House, 201 East 50th Street, New York, New York 10022, U.S.A.

PUBLICATIONS FOR CHILDREN

Plays

Screenplay: *Gerald McBoing-Boing* (cartoon), 1951.

Television Plays (animated cartoons): *How the Grinch Stole Christmas*, 1966; *Horton Hears a Who*, 1970; *The Cat in the Hat*, 1971; *The Lorax; Dr. Seuss on the Loose*, 1973; *Hoober Bloob Highway*, 1975; *Halloween Is Grinch Night; Pontoffel Pock Where Are You*, 1980; *The Grinch Grinches the Cat in the Hat*.

Verse (illustrated by the author)

And to Think That I Saw It on Mulberry Street. New York, Vanguard Press, 1937; London, Country Life, 1939.
The 500 Hats of Bartholomew Cubbins. New York, Vanguard Press, 1938; London, Oxford University Press, 1940.
The King's Stilts. New York, Random House, 1939; London, Hamish Hamilton, 1942.
Horton Hatches the Egg. New York, Random House, 1940; London, Hamish Hamilton, 1942.
McElligot's Pool. New York, Random House, 1947; London, Collins, 1975.
Thidwick, The Big-Hearted Moose. New York, Random House, 1948; London, Collins, 1968.
Bartholomew and the Oobleck. New York, Random House, 1949.
If I Ran the Zoo. New York, Random House, 1950.
Scrambled Eggs Super! New York, Random House, 1953; in *Dr. Seuss Storybook*, London, Collins, 1979.
Horton Hears a Who! New York, Random House, 1954; London, Collins, 1976.
On Beyond Zebra. New York, Random House, 1955.
If I Ran the Circus. New York, Random House, 1956; London, Collins, 1969.
The Cat in the Hat. New York, Random House, 1957; London, Hutchinson, 1958.
How the Grinch Stole Christmas. New York, Random House, 1957.
The Cat in the Hat Comes Back! New York, Random House, 1958; London, Collins, 1961.
Yertle the Turtle and Other Stories. New York, Random House, 1958; London, Collins, 1963.
Happy Birthday to You! New York, Random House, 1959.
One Fish, Two Fish, Red Fish, Blue Fish. New York, Random House, 1960; London, Collins, 1962.
Green Eggs and Ham. New York, Random House, 1960; London, Collins, 1962.
The Sneetches and Other Stories. New York, Random House, 1961; London, Collins, 1965.
Sleep Book. New York, Random House, 1962; London, Collins, 1964.
Hop on Pop. New York, Random House, 1963; London, Collins, 1964.
ABC. New York, Random House, 1963; London, Collins, 1964.
Fox in Socks. New York, Random House, 1965; London, Collins, 1966.
I Had Trouble in Getting to Solla Sollew. New York, Random House, 1965; London, Collins, 1967.
The Foot Book. New York, Random House, 1968; London, Collins, 1969.
I Can Lick 30 Tigers Today and Other Stories. New York, Random House, 1969; London, Collins, 1970.
Mr. Brown Can Moo! Can You? New York, Random House, 1970; London, Collins, 1971.
The Lorax. New York, Random House, 1971; London, Collins, 1972.
Marvin K. Mooney, Will You Please Go Now? New York, Random House, 1972; London, Collins, 1973.
Did I Ever Tell You How Lucky You Are? New York, Random House, 1973; London, Collins, 1974.
The Shape of Me and Other Stuff. New York, Random House, 1973; London, Collins, 1974.
There's a Wocket in My Pocket! New York, Random House, 1974; London, Collins, 1975.
Great Day for Up!, illustrated by Quentin Blake. New York, Random House, 1974; London, Collins, 1975.
Oh, The Thinks You Can Think. New York, Random House, 1975; London, Collins, 1976.
Because a Little Bug Went Ka-Choo! (as Rosetta Stone), with Michael Frith. New York, Random House, 1975.
Hooper Humperdink...? Not Him!, illustrated by Charles Martin. New York, Random House, 1976; London, Collins, 1977.
Oh Say Can You Say? New York, Random House, 1979; London, Collins, 1980.
Hunches in Bunches. New York, Random House, 1982.
The Butter Battle Book. New York, Random House, and London, Collins, 1984.
I Am Not Going to Get Up Today!, illustrated by James Stevenson. New York, Random House, 1987; London, Collins, 1988.

Verse as Theo Le Sieg

Ten Apples Up on Top!, illustrated by Roy McKie. New York, Random House, 1961; London, Collins, 1963.
I Wish That I Had Duck Feet, illustrated by B. Tobey. New York, Random House, 1965; London, Collins, 1967.
Come Over to My House, illustrated by Richard Erdoes. New York, Random House, 1966; London, Collins, 1967.
The Eye Book, illustrated by Roy McKie. New York, Random House, 1968; London, Collins, 1969.
In a People House, illustrated by Roy McKie. New York, Random House, 1972; London, Collins, 1973.
The Many Mice of Mr. Brice, illustrated by Roy McKie. New York, Random House, 1973; London, Collins, 1974.
Wacky Wednesday, illustrated by George Booth. New York, Random House, 1974; London, Collins, 1975.
Would You Rather Be a Bullfrog?, illustrated by Roy McKie. New York, Random House, 1975; London, Collins, 1976.
Please Try to Remember the First of October, illustrated by Arthur Cumings. New York, Random House, 1977; London, Collins, 1978.
Maybe You Should Fly a Jet! Maybe You Should Be a Vet!, illustrated by Michael Smollin. New York, Random House, 1980; London, Collins, 1981.
The Tooth Book, illustrated by Roy McKie. New York, Random House, 1981.

Other (illustrated by the author)

The Cat in the Hat Dictionary, by the Cat Himself, with Philip D. Eastman. New York, Random House, 1964.
The Cat in the Hat Songbook. New York, Random House, 1967.
My Book about Me—By Me, Myself. I Wrote It! I Drew It!, illustrated by Roy McKie. New York, Random House, 1969.
I Can Draw It Myself. New York, Random House, 1970.
I Can Write—By Me, Myself (as Theo Le Sieg). New York, Random House, 1971.
The Cat's Quizzer. New York, Random House, 1976; London, Collins, 1977.
I Can Read with My Eyes Shut! New York, Random House, 1978; London, Collins, 1979.

PUBLICATIONS FOR ADULTS

Short Story

The Seven Lady Godivas. New York, Random House, 1939.

CHILDREN'S WRITERS

Plays (as Theodor S. Geisel)

Screenplays: *Your Job in Germany* (*Hitler Lives*), 1946; *Design for Death*, with Helen Palmer Geisel, 1947; *The 5000 Fingers of Dr. T.*, with Allan Scott, 1953.

Other

Signs of Civilization! (as Seuss). La Jolla, California, La Jolla Town Council, 1956.
Lost World Revisited: A Forward-Looking Backward Glance. New York, Award Books, 1967.
You're Only Old Once. New York, Random House, 1986.

*

Manuscript Collection: Special Collections, University of California Library, Los Angeles.

Critical Study: *Dr. Seuss from Then to Now: A Catalogue of the Retrospective Exhibition* by Mary Stofflet, New York, Random House, 1986.

Illustrator: *Boners* and *More Boners*, both 1931.

*   *   *

A whole library of entertaining books has been created by Theodor Geisel, commonly known as Dr. Seuss. Fanciful invention characterizes all the stories, yet there is variety. *How the Grinch Stole Christmas* is a seasonal book, *Sleep Book* is a bedtime story, and *Fox in Socks* is a collection of such tongue twisters as "Through three cheese trees three free fleas flew." *The Sneetches, The Lorax*, and *Horton Hears a Who!* are moral tales, and *The 500 Hats of Bartholomew Cubbins* resembles a folktale. Seuss also varies his style with the use of verse, prose, limited and unlimited vocabularies.

The Cat in the Hat (with 223 words) and *Green Eggs and Ham* (with 50) represent the beginning of a relatively new genre: publications designed not as textbooks intended to increase skill, but as a form of pleasurable literature for beginners. In 1957 Seuss introduced the beguiling "cat in the hat" and demonstrated a remarkably high standard of readability in books the first grader could be expected to read independently.

In his earliest children's book, *And to Think That I Saw It on Mulberry Street*, Seuss established the pattern for books which consist of loosely joined imaginative scenes. Being constructed as daydreams, they lack a dynamic progression; but each scene is an ingenious improvisation that highlights the author's interest in word play. Narratives of this sort include *McElligot's Pool, Scrambled Eggs Super!, Sleep Book, If I Ran the Circus, If I Ran the Zoo*, and *On Beyond Zebra*.

Seuss's passion for words is exuberant but not reckless. In *If I Ran the Circus* he describes trapeze artists with a blend of grammatical logic and foolishness: "My Zoom-a-Zoop Troupe from West Upper Ben-Deezing/Who never quite know, while they zoop and they zoom,/Whether which will catch what one, or who will catch whom/Or if who will catch which by the what and just where,/Or just when and just how in which part of the air!"

Inventing new eccentrics is one of Seuss's most singular achievements, and the pages of the daydream books are crowded with odd creatures. One eats hot pebbles in order to blow smoke from his ears. Another bites his over-long tail before bedtime, and the sensation wakes him up exactly eight hours later.

In the *Sleep Book*, everyday experiences are intermixed with the fantastic, producing that reminder of home which the very young find satisfying. "Sleep thoughts/Are spreading/Throughout the whole land./The time for night-brushing of teeth is at hand./Up at Herk-Heimer Falls, where the great river rushes/And crashes down crags in great gargling gushes,/The Herk-Heimer Sisters are using their brushes./Those falls are just grand for tooth-brushing beneath/If you happen to be up that way with your teeth."

Seuss sustains a nice balance between characterization, incident, and thematic concerns in his folkloristic tales. *The 500 Hats of Bartholomew Cubbins* includes a peasant hero, an unscrupulous duke, and a magic hat. A key feature is the logic underlying the dramatic encounter of the hero with a king and an official executioner. With spooked hats reproducing themselves, the protagonist cannot obey the protocol—"hats off to the king"—nor remove his hat to be beheaded (a rule in the Royal Executioner's book). These bureaucratic realities anchor the story to human experience, while at the same time the magic is unrestrained. Stylistically, the many parallel phrases and happenings add decorative and structural strength.

Among the themes in the moral tales we find such problems as greed, racial prejudice, environmental irresponsibility, and disdain for the small and weak. The unflaggingly heroic elephant in *Horton Hears a Who!* finds a speck of dust which turns out to be a very small person—a "Who." Since Who voices are audible to elephant ears exclusively, the whole jungle is full of non-believers. A point about innate human worth is presented as the mob tries to crush a microscopic Who community.

The Butter Battle Book repeats Seuss's concerns about intolerance while adding a theme of great import: the arms race. And on a subtler level, he satirizes aggressive nationalism. A difference of opinion about the "proper" way to handle buttered bread leads to war. Seuss mocks the variation in manners that leads to expanding arsenals, and adds a jibe at behaviors that excite nationalistic fervor. He includes marching bands, fancy uniforms, and war-mongering slogans. Most insidious is the acculturation of the young: "But we Yooks, as you know,/when we breakfast or sup,/spread our bread," Grandpa said,/"with the butter side *up*." In accordance with historical realities, this arms race narrative is left open-ended.

Dr. Seuss is a well-disciplined nonsense poet. Since his work is alive with wit, rhythm, fanciful characters, and substantial themes, it is not surprising that his name has become a household word. Sometimes he draws upon the well-tested forms, motifs, and exaggerations of tall tales. But the full secret of his childlike humor is hard to determine. Ultimately it must derive from a deeply intuitive grasp of the child's perspective and free spirit.

—Donnarae MacCann

———

SEVERN, David. Pseudonym for David Storr Unwin. British. Born in London, 3 December 1918; son of the publisher Sir Stanley Unwin. Educated at Abbotsholme School, Derbyshire, 1933–36. Married Bridget Mary Herbert in 1945; twin daughter and son. Editorial assistant, League of Nations Secretariat, Geneva, 1938; worked for Unwin Brothers, printers, Woking, Surrey, 1939, and Basil Blackwell, booksellers, Oxford, 1940; member of the production department, George Allen and Unwin, publishers, London, 1941–43. Address: Garden Flat, 31 Belsize Park, London N.W.3, England.

PUBLICATIONS FOR CHILDREN

Fiction

Rick Afire!, illustrated by Joan Kiddell-Monroe. London, Lane,

1942.

A Cabin for Crusoe, illustrated by Joan Kiddell-Monroe. London, Lane, 1943; Boston, Houghton Mifflin, 1946.

Waggon for Five, illustrated by Joan Kiddell-Monroe. London, Lane, 1944; Boston, Houghton Mifflin, 1947.

Hermit in the Hills, illustrated by Joan Kiddell-Monroe. London, Lane, 1945.

Forest Holiday, illustrated by Joan Kiddell-Monroe. London, Lane, 1946.

Ponies and Poachers, illustrated by Joan Kiddell-Monroe. London, Lane, 1947.

Bill Badger and the Pine Martens [*Bathing Pool, Buried Treasure*], illustrated by Geoffrey Higham. London, Lane, 3 vols., 1947–50.

Wily Fox and the Baby Show [*Christmas Party, Missing Fireworks*], illustrated by Geoffrey Higham. London, Lane, 3 vols., 1947–50.

The Cruise of the "Maiden Castle," illustrated by Joan Kiddell-Monroe. London, Lane, 1948; New York, Macmillan, 1949.

Treasure for Three, illustrated by Joan Kiddell-Monroe. London, Lane, 1949; New York, Macmillan, 1950.

Dream Gold, illustrated by A.K. Lee. London, Lane, 1949; New York, Viking Press, 1952.

Crazy Castle, illustrated by Joan Kiddell-Monroe. London, Lane, 1951; New York, Macmillan, 1952.

Burglars and Bandicoots, illustrated by Joan Kiddell-Monroe. London, Lane, 1952.

Drumbeats!, illustrated by Richard Kennedy. London, Lane, 1953.

Blaze of Broadfurrow Farm, illustrated by Kiff and Wilmore. London, Lane, 1955.

Walnut Tree Meadow, illustrated by Kiff and Wilmore. London, Lane, 1955.

The Future Took Us, illustrated by Jillian Richards. London, Lane, 1958.

The Green-Eyed Gryphon, illustrated by Prudence Seward. London, Hamish Hamilton, 1958.

Foxy-Boy, illustrated by Lynton Lamb. London, Bodley Head, 1959; as *The Wild Valley*, New York, Dutton, 1963.

Three at the Sea, illustrated by Margery Gill. London, Bodley Head, 1959.

Jeff Dickson, Cowhand, illustrated by Patrick Williams. London, Cape, 1963.

Clouds over the Alberhorn. London, Hamish Hamilton, 1963.

A Dog for a Day, illustrated by Joseph Acheson. London, Hamish Hamilton, 1965.

The Girl in the Grove. London, Allen and Unwin, and New York, Harper, 1974.

The Wishing Bone, illustrated by Shirley Felts. London, Allen and Unwin, 1977.

Other

My Foreign Correspondent Through Africa, illustrated by Peter White. London, Meiklejohn, 1951.

PUBLICATIONS FOR ADULTS as David Unwin

Novels

The Governor's Wife. London, Joseph, 1954; New York, Dutton, 1955.

A View of the Heath. London, Joseph, 1956.

Other

Fifty Years with Father. London, Allen and Unwin, 1982.

*

David Severn comments:

The series of straightforward adventure stories, with which I made my name in the 1940's, provided entertainment in their time, but I would choose to be remembered not for them but for a handful of off-beat works: *Dream Gold, Drumbeats!, Foxy-Boy*, and *The Girl in the Grove*. I feel that my fantasies are the most interesting—and certainly the most original—of all my books.

* * *

David Severn has published children's books in a space of nearly 40 years, and in that time his style and the kind of book he writes have changed as he and his life have developed.

His early books, which established him as a writer, are all domestic adventures about four children and Crusoe (a young writer) on a farm in southern England. They reflect the low-key life so many people lived during and just after the war, when a day out with sandwiches or a trip to the local town in the pony cart could turn into an adventure. *Rick Afire!* was the first of this series and it set the pace for the others, notably *A Cabin for Crusoe*, which includes some good gypsy-lore and insight into their way of life, and *Forest Holiday*. All are told in a straightforward enjoyable style with the enthusiasm of a writer in his early twenties who has a touch of the boy scout about him. They are dated now, but when they were published they had a freshness and directness which appealed strongly to young readers.

Since then Severn has turned to writing books with some supernatural element in them. *Dream Gold* is about two boys who share an identical dream which takes them to the Pacific Islands where they are caught up in a tale of piracy and treasure, and *Drumbeats!* uses the medium of an African drum to transport children from a progressive co-educational school in England into an ill-fated expedition in Africa 30 years earlier. The technique is good, but the writing is at times rather heavy. A storm is coming, for instance, and he says, "But even as we watched, the clouds expanded, sprouting new buttresses, lifting visibly into the summer's sky." *The Future Took Us* is an adventure story of two boys who are taken into the future. Here the book carries more conviction because, as in *Dream Gold*, the main character is a boy, and Severn seems to be more at ease when writing about the emotions and reactions of his own sex. This point is confirmed by *The Girl in the Grove* where the heroine is a teenage girl. Although the story of an unhappy ghost and the modern adults is carefully constructed, the emotional turmoil of the girl is overwritten and the book lacks impact. It is not really a children's book.

Foxy-Boy, on the other hand, is a fantasy for younger children which holds their attention. A lonely little girl befriends a wild boy who has been brought up by foxes, and despite the total improbability the book reads well. The secret of his success here is that it is for younger children and has less emotion loaded in. Severn's latest book, *The Wishing Bone*, is one of his best. He is writing again for a younger age group where he has scored successes in the past, not only with *Foxy-Boy* but with his Bill Badger stories and his Antelope books, notably *The Green-Eyed Gryphon*, where again a magic talisman changes children's lives. In *The Wishing Bone* some children get caught in a life-sized fort which grew from a toy fort built by one of them, and the ensuing adventures are not only well told, but the humour behind the complications of "only one wish per person" and the mis-wishes is good. The characters are all well portrayed, and the magic element is used successfully. This book has the freshness and fun that his earlier stories had, although the children in *The Wishing Bone* are far more sophisticated than the children of the Crusoe adventure stories.

Severn's imagination and fascination with magical powers have been potent forces in his children's books, but his best books derive from his ability to tell a good story rather than from his introduction of the supernatural. His prose and his dialogue are not outstanding, but his descriptions of the countryside are, and most important of all, he can capture the mood and the exuberance of children.

—Linda Yeatman

———

SEWELL, Helen (Moore). American. Born in Mare Island, California, 27 June 1896. Educated at Packer Institute; Pratt Institute Art School, New York. Studied with the painter Archipenko. Freelance illustrator. *Died 24 February 1957.*

PUBLICATIONS FOR CHILDREN (illustrated by the author)

Fiction

A Head for Happy. New York, Macmillan, 1931.
Blue Barns. New York, Macmillan, 1933; London, Woodfield, 1955.
Ming and Mehitable. New York, Macmillan, 1936.
Peggy and the Pony. New York and London, Oxford University Press, 1937.
Jimmy and Jemima. New York, Macmillan, 1940.
Peggy and the Pup. New York and London, Oxford University Press, 1941.
Birthdays for Robin. New York, Macmillan, 1943; London, Hale, 1947.
Belinda the Mouse. New York and London, Oxford University Press, 1944.
Three Tall Tales, with Elena Eleska. New York, Macmillan, 1947.

Other

ABC for Everyday. New York, Macmillan, 1930.

Editor, *Words to the Wise: A Book of Proverbs.* New York, Dodd Mead, 1932.

*

Manuscript Collection: May Massee Collection, Emporia State University, Kansas.

Illustrator: *The Cruise of the Little Dipper* by Susanne Langer, 1924; *Menagerie* by Mary Britton Miller, 1928; *Sally Gabble and the Fairies* by Miriam S. Potter, 1929; *Mr. Hermit Crab* by Mimsey Rhys, 1929; *A Round of Carols* by Thomas Noble, 1929; *Building a House in Sweden* by Marjorie Cautley, 1931; *The Dreamkeeper and Other Poems* by Langston Hughes, 1932; *The Christmas Tree in the Woods* by Susan Smith, 1932; *Little House in the Big Woods*, 1932, *Farmer Boy*, 1933; *Little House on the Prairie*, 1935, *On the Banks of Plum Creek*, 1937, *By the Shores of Silver Lake*, 1939, *The Long Winter*, 1940, and *Little Town on the Prairie*, 1941, all by Laura Ingalls Wilder; *Broomstick and Snowflake* by Johan Falkberget, 1933; *Where is Adelaide?*, 1933, and *Ann Frances*, 1935, both by Eliza Orne White; *A First Bible*, 1934; *Cinderella*, 1934; *Away Goes*

Sally, 1934, *Five Bushel Farm*, 1939, *The Fair American*, 1940, *The White Horse*, 1942, *The Big Green Umbrella*, 1944, and *The Wonderful Day*, 1946, all by Elizabeth Coatsworth; *Bluebonnets for Lucinda*, 1934, and *Tagalong Tooloo*, 1941, both by Frances Clarke Sayers; *Peter and Gretchen of Old Nuremberg* by Viola May Jones, 1935; *Pinocchio* by Carlo Collodi, 1935; *Ten Saints* by Eleanor Farjeon, 1936; *Old John* by Máirín Cregan, 1936; *The Magic Hill and Other Stories*, 1937, and *The Princess and the Apple Tree and Other Stories*, 1937, both by A.A. Milne; *Baby Island* by Carol Ryrie Brink, 1937; *Jane Eyre* by Charlotte Brontë, 1938; *The Young Brontës* by Mary Louise Jarden, 1938; *Pride and Prejudice*, 1940, and *Sense and Sensibility*, 1957, both by Jane Austen; *The Blue-Eyed Lady* by Ferenc Molnar, 1942; *Book of Myths* by Thomas Bulfinch, 1942; *Christmas Magic* by James S. Tippett, 1944; *A Bee in Her Bonnet* by Eva Kristoffersen, 1944; *Boat Children of Canton* by Marion B. Ward, 1944; *Once There Was a Little Boy* by Dorothy Kunhardt, 1946; *The Brave Bantam* by Louise Seaman, 1946; *Azor*, 1948, *Azor and the Haddock*, 1949, and *Azor and the Blue-Eyed Cow*, 1951, all by Maude Cowley; *Secrets and Surprises* by Irmengarde Eberle, 1951; *Mrs. McThing* by Mary Chase, 1952; *The Bears on Hemlock Mountain*, 1952, and *The Thanksgiving Story*, 1954, both by Alice Dalgliesh; *Poems* by Emily Dickinson, 1952; *The Colonel's Squad*, 1952, *In the Beginning*, 1954, and *The Three Kings of Saba*, 1955, all by Alf Evers; *Grimm's Tales*, 1954.

* * *

Helen Sewell's contributions to children's literature have invariably been favorably commented on by her critics. It is virtually impossible, therefore, to discover a serious discussion of children's books that does not deal with her offerings on positive terms. This well-deserved high regard, which places Sewell in the upper echelon of the field of children's books, has come about, however, because of her illustrations for these books rather than for her efforts as a writer. In the latter half of her career, from roughly the mid-1940's onward, Sewell gave up almost entirely the writing of picture books. She concentrated on illustrations, to become one of the most honored of her profession, and very famous writers for children vied for her services as the illustrator of their texts. She remains, as well, one of the most adaptable. She revealed in one instance how she used the attractions children find in comic books to her advantage (in *Three Tall Tales* she imitated as nearly as possible the layout for the words as they are used in comics).

Far less familiar, even to the critics of children's literature, are the writings she did for children in the first half of her career. These books have never received the honors nor the attention of her illustrations. And rightly so, one must admit, since while the language of the studiously abbreviated picture books which Sewell both wrote and illustrated is by and large thoughtfully pleasant, clear in the way it relates concepts, and even at times amusing, it is not distinguished in either the themes or in their dramatic effects.

All of her early books are now obscure and out of print (with the exception of *Blue Barns*). *A Head for Happy* is told with few words, indeed. In fact, some of its pictures are given no explanation at all. The words Sewell uses are there to punctuate a story line of three little sisters who make a doll and then go around the world searching for a proper head to fit its body. *Blue Barns* is an amusing, gentle, and true story of a farm, a funny gander, and some wild geese. It is a small picture book, for beginning readers, whose brief text prohibits any remarkable literary effect by its author. The slight plot of *Ming and Mehitable* (a "closet drama," as one critic called it) illustrated another theme which would concern only a very young child. Here the heroine's dog runs away after being pestered by being dressed up in baby clothes. Since after a search its master can find no animal so friendly, she promises the dog freedom from such minor mistreatment if he will return. *Peggy and the Pony* likewise is a story of a preoccupation only a young child would appreciate, the unrequited wish for a pony. After a number of frustrations the girl in this tale does get her request. These quiet stories, very feminine in tone, have few psychological involvements.

But Sewell's attempts at rather more complicated plots of an obviously greater psychological nature, as in *Jimmy and Jemima* and in *Belinda the Mouse*, do little to advance her reputation as a distinctive writer. The ordinary language found here fails for that purpose. As noted, it was at about this point in her life that Sewell probably wisely decided to limit her work almost entirely to the illustration of works of writers more talented than she. It is important to note, as well, that the girlish stories of this outstanding illustrator, but rather ordinary writer, happily have lost little of their original attractiveness by the passage of time. They can still be enjoyed by today's children.

—Patrick Groff

SHANNON, Monica. American. Born in Belleville, Ontario, Canada; moved to the United States as an infant. Educated at schools in Seattle and Idaho; Bachelor of Library Science from school in California. Married. Worked in the Los Angeles Public Library, 1916–25. Recipient: American Library Association Newbery Medal, 1935. *Died 13 August 1965.*

PUBLICATIONS FOR CHILDREN

Fiction

California Fairy Tales, illustrated by C.E. Millard. New York, Doubleday, and London, Heinemann, 1926.
Eyes for the Dark, illustrated by C.E. Millard. New York, Doubleday, 1928; as *More Tales from California*, 1935.
Tawnymore, illustrated by Jean Charlot. New York, Doubleday, 1931.
Dobry, illustrated by Atanas Katchamakoff. New York, Viking Press, 1934; London Harrap, 1936.

Verse

Goose Grass Rhymes, illustrated by Neva Kanaga Brown. New York, Doubleday, 1930.

PUBLICATIONS FOR ADULTS

Other

Editor, *California in Print*. Los Angeles, Los Angeles Public Library, 1919.

*   *   *

Monica Shannon wrote five children's books—*California Fairy Tales, Eyes for the Dark, Goose Grass Rhymes, Tawnymore,* and *Dobry.* The first two are books of artistic fairytales; the third, a book of light-hearted verse; the fourth, a pirate story of a half-breed boy; and the fifth, the story of a Bulgarian peasant boy with aspirations to become a great artist.

Collectively Shannon's books attest to her intense appreciation of nature and environment; her respect for human, plant, and animal

life; and her regard for the cultural traditions in her own family background and that of others. Traces of Shannon's pleasant childhood spent in the mountains of Montana and California are evident in *Tawnymore, Dobry,* and the fairytales. From the Bulgarian immigrants who worked on her father's ranch young Monica learned about Bulgarian customs and folkways, and from the extensive mountain ranch lands over which she roamed freely during her childhood, she learned about animals, plants, and other natural life. Her keen eye for observing nature and the environment around her and her penchant for descriptive, colorful, and figurative language are clearly at work in all her writings. In "It's Going to Rain" from *Goose Grass Rhymes,* for example, Shannon describes in pictorial words and with poetic ease sun and shade playing tag, winds running races, and linen dancing on the clothes-lines. In "The Tree Toad," with equal ease, the poet shows readers a neat creature "with tidy rubbers on his feet," a creature who knows nothing but embarrassment. She knows the toad is embarrassed because "his color comes, his color goes." And as to the lowly caterpillar, Shannon is of the opinion that "he giggles, as he wiggles, across a hairy leaf."

The delightful tales published in *California Fairy Tales* and *Eyes for the Dark* are numerous and varied—an amalgamation of Spain, America, Ireland, and Fairyland itself. The tales begin with such interest-capturing openers as "Now it is true that three old witch women did live under a Judas tree, right where two parts of Kaweah River ran together like jabbering gossips" or "Now, once upon a time, when the Elder Berries were very young Berries and the Sierra Nevada Mountains were still down under the Pacific Ocean, a certain Pigwidgeon lived alongside the sea." Tales beginning in such a fashion lend themselves well to oral telling and/or reading, and it is not surprising that a number of them have been recorded.

Dobry, by far the most widely known of Shannon's works, is the inspiring story of a young Bulgarian peasant boy who determines to be a great sculptor; many of the incidents are based on the experiences of Atanas Katchamakoff, the Bulgarian-born sculptor who provided the illustrations for the book. Dobry lives with his mother, Roda, and his grandfather in a peaceful Bulgarian village. Dobry's father has been killed in war, and the mother's only ambition for her son is that "he be learning to take his father's place in the fields one day." Being too hard-working and practical-minded herself to understand her son's artistic bent, Roda is prone to remind Dobry that the big peasant he will grow up to be will have no time for picture making. But Dobry's grandfather, whose personal philosophy is that people should wish to be different rather than alike, gently coaxes Roda to an understanding that her son must be allowed to develop in directions other than those she has dreamed. It is this development that constitutes the narrative of the book, through which readers learn not only about Dobry but also about Bulgarian village life and the stability and strength of people who live close to the soil. The major characters in *Dobry* are strong and well-delineated, Grandfather being one of the chief among them. He is something of a homespun philosopher and storyteller, admired not only by his grandson but by everyone. Several of Grandfather's tales, such as the "Poplar Tree Story" and "The Story of Hadutzi-Dare" are cleverly interwoven into the fabric of *Dobry.* The pages which reveal the artistic, as well as the physical, development of Dobry are filled with colorful descriptions and imagery.

Although Shannon's literary works for children were all published between 1926 and 1934, the fact that three of them, *Dobry, California Fairy Tales,* and *More Tales from California* (originally *Eyes for the Dark*), still remain in print attests to their literary quality and universality of appeal.

—Charity Chang

SHARMAT, Marjorie Weinman. Also writes as Wendy Andrews. American. Born in Portland, Maine, 12 November 1928. Educated at Lasell Junior College, Auburndale, Massachusetts, 1946–47; Westbrook Junior College, Portland, 1947–48, graduated 1948. Married Mitchell B. Sharmat in 1957; two sons. Member of the circulation staff, Yale University Library, 1951–54, and Yale Law Library, 1954–55, New Haven, Connecticut. Agent: Harold Ober Associates, 40 East 49th Street, New York, New York 10017. Address: 8801 East Calle Plaza, Tucson, Arizona 85715, U.S.A.

PUBLICATIONS FOR CHILDREN

Fiction

Rex, illustrated by Emily McCully. New York, Harper, 1967.
Goodnight Andrew Goodnight Craig, illustrated by Mary Chalmers. New York, Harper, 1969.
Gladys Told Me to Meet Her Here, illustrated by Edward Frascino. New York, Harper, 1970.
A Hot Thirsty Day, illustrated by Rosemary Wells. New York, Macmillan, and London, Collier Macmillan, 1971.
51 Sycamore Lane, illustrated by Lisl Weil. New York, Macmillan, and London, Collier Macmillan, 1971; as *The Spy in the Neighborhood*, New York, Collier, 1974.
Getting Something on Maggie Marmelstein, illustrated by Ben Shecter. New York, Harper, 1971; London, Abelard Schuman, 1974.
A Visit with Rosalind, illustrated by Lisl Weil. New York, Macmillan, 1972.
Nate the Great, illustrated by Marc Simont. New York, Coward McCann, 1972; Kingswood, Surrey, World's Work, 1974.
Sophie and Gussie, illustrated by Lillian Hoban. New York, Macmillan, 1973; Kingswood, Surrey, World's Work, 1974.
Morris Brookside, A Dog, illustrated by Ronald Himler. New York, Holiday House, 1973.
Morris Brookside Is Missing, illustrated by Ronald Himler. New York, Holiday House, 1974.
Nate the Great Goes Undercover, illustrated by Marc Simont. New York, Coward McCann, 1974.
I Want Mama, illustrated by Emily McCully. New York, Harper, 1974.
Walter the Wolf, illustrated by Kelly Oechsli. New York, Holiday House, 1975.
I'm Not Oscar's Friend Anymore, illustrated by Tony DeLuna. New York, Dutton, 1975.
Nate the Great and the Lost List, illustrated by Marc Simont. New York, Coward McCann, 1975; Kingswood, Surrey, World's Work, 1977.
Burton and Dudley, illustrated by Barbara Cooney. New York, Holiday House, 1975.
Maggie Marmelstein for President, illustrated by Ben Shecter. New York, Harper, 1975.
The Lancelot Closes at Five, illustrated by Lisl Weil. New York, Macmillan, 1976.
The Trip and Other Sophie and Gussie Stories, illustrated by Lillian Hoban. New York, Macmillan, 1976; Kingswood, Surrey, World's Work, 1978.
Edgemont, illustrated by Cyndy Szekeres. New York, Coward McCann, 1976.
Mooch the Messy, illustrated by Ben Shecter. New York, Harper, 1976; Kingswood, Surrey, World's Work, 1978.
I'm Terrific, illustrated by Kay Chorao. New York, Holiday House, 1976.
I Don't Care, illustrated by Lillian Hoban. New York, Macmillan, 1977.
Nate the Great and the Phony Clue, illustrated by Marc Simont.

New York, Coward McCann, 1977; Kingswood, Surrey, World's Work, 1979.
A Big Fat Enormous Lie, illustrated by David McPhail. New York, Dutton, 1978.
Mitchell Is Moving, illustrated by Jose Aruego and Ariane Dewey. New York, Macmillan, 1978.
Thornton the Worrier, illustrated by Kay Chorao. New York, Holiday House, 1978.
Nate the Great and the Sticky Case, illustrated by Marc Simon. New York, Coward McCann, 1978.
Uncle Boris and Maude, illustrated by Sammis McLean. New York, Doubleday, 1979.
Mooch the Messy Meets Prudence the Neat, illustrated by Ben Shecter. New York, Coward McCann, 1979; Kingswood, Surrey, World's Work, 1980.
I Am Not a Pest, with Mitchell Sharmat, illustrated by Diane Dawson. New York, Dutton, 1979.
The 329th Friend, illustrated by Cyndy Szekeres. New York, Four Winds Press, 1979.
Scarlet Monster Lives Here, illustrated by Dennis Kendrick. New York, Harper, 1979.
Mr. Jameson and Mr. Phillips, illustrated by Bruce Degen. New York, Harper, 1979.
The Trolls of Twelfth Street, illustrated by Ben Shecter. New York, Coward McCann, 1979.
Octavia Told Me a Secret, illustrated by Roseanne Litzinger. New York, Four Winds Press, 1979.
Griselda's New Year, illustrated by Norman Chartier. New York, Macmillan, 1979.
Say Hello, Vanessa, illustrated by Lillian Hoban. New York, Holiday House, 1979.
Little Devil Gets Sick, illustrated by Marylin Hafner. New York, Doubleday, 1980.
What Are We Going to Do about Andrew?, illustrated by Ray Cruz. New York, Macmillan, 1980.
Sometimes Mama and Papa Fight, illustrated by Kay Chorao. New York, Harper, 1980.
Taking Care of Melvin, illustrated by Victoria Chess. New York, Holiday House, 1980.
The Day I Was Born, with Mitchell Sharmat, illustrated by Diane Dawson. New York, Dutton, 1980.
Grumley the Grouch, illustrated by Kay Chorao. New York, Holiday House, 1980.
Gila Monsters Meet You at the Airport, illustrated by Byron Barton. New York, Macmillan, 1980.
Twitchell the Wishful, illustrated by Janet Stevens. New York, Holiday House, 1981.
Nate the Great and the Missing Key, illustrated by Marc Simont. New York, Coward McCann, 1981.
Chasing after Annie, illustrated by Marc Simont. New York, Harper, 1981.
Lucretia the Unbearable, illustrated by Janet Stevens. New York, Holiday House, 1981.
Rollo and Juliet, Forever!, illustrated by Marylin Hafner. New York, Doubleday, 1981.
The Best Valentine in the World, illustrated by Lillian Obligado. New York, Holiday House, 1982.
Two Ghosts on a Beach, illustrated by Nola Langner. New York, Harper, 1982.
Nate the Great and the Snowy Trail, illustrated by Marc Simont. New York, Coward McCann, 1982.
Mysteriously Yours, Maggie Marmelstein, illustrated by Ben Shecter. New York, Harper, 1982.
Square Pegs. New York, Dell, 1982.
I Saw Him First. New York, Delacorte Press, 1983.
How to Meet a Gorgeous Guy. New York, Delacorte Press, 1983.

Frizzy the Fearful, illustrated by John Wallner.   New York, Holiday House, 1983.

Rich Mitch, illustrated by Loretta Lustig.   New York, Morrow, 1983.

Sasha the Silly, illustrated by Janet Stevens.   New York, Holiday House, 1984.

Bartholomew the Bossy, illustrated by Normand Chartier.   New York, Macmillan, 1984.

How to Meet a Gorgeous Girl.   New York, Delacorte Press, 1984.

The Story of Bentley Beaver, illustrated by Lillian Hoban.   New York, Harper, 1984; Kingswood, Surrey, World's Work, 1986.

He Noticed I'm Alive...And Other Hopeful Signs.   New York, Delacorte Press, 1984.

My Mother Never Listens to Me.   Chicago, Whitman, 1984.

Attila the Angry, illustrated by Lillian Hoban.   New York, Holiday House, 1985.

Two Guys Noticed Me...And Other Miracles.   New York, Delacorte Press, 1985.

Nate the Great and the Fishy Prize, illustrated by Marc Simont.   New York, Coward McCann, 1985.

How to Have a Gorgeous Wedding.   New York, Dell, 1985.

Get Rich Mitch!, illustrated by Loretta Lustig.   New York, Morrow, 1985.

One Terrific Thanksgiving, illustrated Lilian Obigado.   New York, Holiday House, 1985.

The Son of the Slime That Ate Cleveland, illustrated by Rodney Pate.   New York, Dell, 1985.

Who's Afraid of Ernestine?, illustrated by Maxie Chambliss.   New York, Coward McCann, 1986.

Nate the Great Stalks Stupidweed, illustrated by Marc Simont.   New York, Coward McCann, 1986.

Sorority Sisters series (*For Members Only; Snobs, Beware; I Think I'm Falling in Love; Fighting over Me; Nobody Knows How Scared I Am; Here Comes Mr. Right; Getting Closer; I'm Going to Get Your Boyfriend*).   New York, Dell, 8 vols., 1986–87.

Hooray for Mother's Day! [*Father's Day!*], illustrated by John Wallner.   New York, Holiday House, 2 vols., 1986–87.

Helga High-Up, illustrated by David Neuhaus.   New York, Scholastic, 1987.

Nate the Great and the Boring Beach Bag, illustrated by Marc Simont.   New York, Coward McCann, 1987.

Go to Sleep, Nicholas Joe, illustrated by John Himmelman.   New York, Harper, 1988.

Nate the Great Goes down in the Dumps, illustrated by Marc Simont.   New York, Putnam, 1989.

The Pizza Monster, with Mitchell Sharmat, illustrated by Denise Bruncus.   New York, Delacorte Press, 1989.

Fiction as Wendy Andrews

Vacation Fever.   New York, Putnam, 1984.

Supergirl Storybook (novelization of screenplay).   New York, Putnam, 1984.

Are We There Yet?   New York, Putnam, 1985.

Other

The Sign, illustrated by Pat Wong.   Boston, Houghton Mifflin, 1981.

Surprises (reader), with Mitchell Sharmat.   New York, Holt Rinehart, 1989.

Treasures (reader), with Mitchell Sharmat.   New York, Holt Rinehart, 1989.

Kingdoms (reader), with Mitchell Sharmat.   New York, Holt Rinehart, 1989.

*

Manuscript Collections: Maine Women Writers Collection, Westbrook College, Portland, Maine; de Grummond Collection, University of Southern Mississippi, Hattiesburg.

Marjorie Weinman Sharmat comments:

I write picture books, easy readers, novels for children, and, recently, novels for young adults. I have a resident pest in my head and that's why I'm a writer. This pest is never satisfied and constantly furnishes me with new ideas and nags me to get them on paper. I like to write funny books because I think that life is basically a serious business and needs a humorous counterbalance.

*   *   *

A prolific author of books for younger children, Marjorie Weinman Sharmat writes successfully for three age groups. Her first book, *Rex*, is a drolly imaginative tale of a small boy who has decided to be a dog and who is willing to bring the man next door his newspaper and slippers in his teeth to prove it. The gentle humor of her first story for preschoolers foreshadowed some of Sharmat's strongest features: a real originality in story concept and the ability to work within the constraints of a simplified vocabulary list in a fresh and original manner. *Nate the Great*, a tale with echoes of James Bond's Secret Agent 007, tells of a nine-year-old detective, Nate, who can solve any case, provided he is properly primed with pancakes, from finding a lost cat to unearthing a purloined picture, but who is glad as he walks off into the rain at the end of the book that he has taken his mother's advice and worn his rubbers.

Children who like the humor of *Nate the Great* also enjoy *Walter the Wolf*, a slyly humorous tale of a perfect young wolf who after years of practicing his violin, writing poetry, and never biting anybody decides to go into the biting business professionally. After his first "victim" bites him back, he decides that, although he is through trying to be perfect, biting is probably not the best way to make a living. Written with deadpan humor not at all dampened by the controlled vocabulary is *What Are We Going to Do about Andrew?*, a tale of a versatile lad whose parents find his ability to turn himself into a hippopotamus, and to fly, disconcerting. The book's unexpected ending will delight the child who feels that his parents do not appreciate his real worth.

Representative of another literary genre exploited successfully in several of Sharmat's books for young children is her *I'm Not Oscar's Friend Anymore*. In this juvenile stream-of-consciousness concept book, Oscar's "former friend" thinks of all his reasons for being mad at Oscar and thinks how sad Oscar must be feeling now that he has just lost his best friend. He finally decides he will do Oscar a big favor and make up. Sharmat's attempt to recreate the thought process of a young child is handled with charm and wit and has the ring of truth about it. For children in the middle grades, three books about Maggie Marmelstein, an urban sixth grader and her sometime friend Thad Smith, tell in a light-hearted and realistic manner the trials of being a sub-teenager.

Sharmat's novels for young adults include the ongoing *Sorority Sisters* series. These fast-paced well plotted short novels are characterized by Sharmat's humor and witty dialogue. However, although Sharmat writes successfully for both children and young adults, she is at her best when she is writing for the youngest children. The droll humor and the subtle charm of the best of her little books set them off as minor classics for preschoolers.

—Margaret F. Maxwell

SHARP, Margery. British. Born in 1905. Educated at Streatham Hill High School, London; Bedford College, University of London, B.A. (honours) in French. Married Major Geoffrey Castle in 1938. Army education lecturer in World War II. Lives in London. Address: c/o Heinemann Ltd., 81 Fulham Road, London SW3 6RB, England.

PUBLICATIONS FOR CHILDREN

Fiction

The Rescuers, illustrated by Judith Brook. London, Collins, and Boston, Little Brown, 1959.
Miss Bianca, illustrated by Garth Williams. London, Collins, and Boston, Little Brown, 1962.
The Turret, illustrated by Garth Williams. Boston, Little Brown, 1963; London, Collins, 1964.
Lost at the Fair, illustrated by Rosalind Fry. Boston, Little Brown, 1965; London, Heinemann, 1967.
Miss Bianca in the Salt Mines, illustrated by Garth Williams. London, Heinemann, and Boston, Little Brown, 1966.
Miss Bianca in the Orient, illustrated by Erik Blegvad. London, Heinemann, and Boston, Little Brown, 1970.
Miss Bianca in the Antarctic, illustrated by Erik Blegvad. London, Heinemann, 1970; Boston, Little Brown, 1971.
Miss Bianca and the Bridesmaid, illustrated by Erik Blegvad. London, Heinemann, and Boston, Little Brown, 1972.
The Magical Cockatoo, illustrated by Faith Jaques. London, Heinemann, 1974.
The Children Next Door, illustrated by Hilary Abrahams. London, Heinemann, 1974.
Bernard the Brave, illustrated by Faith Jaques. London, Heinemann, 1976; Boston, Little Brown, 1977.
Bernard into Battle, illustrated by Leslie Morrill. London, Heinemann, and Boston, Little Brown, 1979.

Other

Mélisande, illustrated by Roy McKie. London, Collins, and Boston, Little Brown, 1960.

PUBLICATIONS FOR ADULTS

Novels

Rhododendron Pie. London, Chatto and Windus, and New York, Appleton, 1930.
Fanfare for Tin Trumpets. London, Barker, 1932; New York, Putnam, 1933.
The Nymph and the Nobleman. London, Barker, 1932.
The Flowering Thorn. London, Barker, 1933; New York, Putnam, 1934.
Sophy Cassmajor. London, Barker, and New York, Putnam, 1934.
Four Gardens. London, Barker, and New York, Putnam, 1935.
The Nutmeg Tree. London, Barker, and Boston, Little Brown, 1937.
Harlequin House. London, Collins, and Boston, Little Brown, 1939.
The Stone of Chastity. London, Collins, and Boston, Little Brown, 1940.
Three Companion Pieces: Sophy Cassmajor, The Tigress on the Hearth, and The Nymph and the Nobleman. Boston, Little Brown, 1941; *The Tigress on the Hearth* published separately, London, Collins, 1955.
Cluny Brown. London, Collins, and Boston, Little Brown, 1944.

Britannia Mews. London, Collins, and Boston, Little Brown, 1946.
The Foolish Gentlewoman. London, Collins, and Boston, Little Brown, 1948.
Lise Lillywhite. London, Collins, and Boston, Little Brown, 1951.
The Gipsy in the Parlour. London, Collins, 1953; Boston, Little Brown, 1954.
The Eye of Love. London, Collins, and Boston, Little Brown, 1957; as *Martha and the Eye of Love*, London, New English Library, 1969.
Something Light. London, Collins, 1960; Boston, Little Brown, 1961.
Martha in Paris. London, Collins, 1962; Boston, Little Brown, 1963.
Martha, Eric, and George. London, Collins, and Boston, Little Brown, 1964.
The Sun in Scorpio. London, Heinemann, and Boston, Little Brown, 1965.
In Pious Memory. Boston, Little Brown, 1967; London, Heinemann, 1968.
Rosa. London, Heinemann, 1969; Boston, Little Brown, 1970.
The Innocents. London, Heinemann, 1971; Boston, Little Brown, 1972.
The Faithful Servants. London, Heinemann, and Boston, Little Brown, 1975.
Summer Visits. London, Heinemann, 1977; Boston, Little Brown, 1978.

Short Stories

The Lost Chapel Picnic and Other Stories. London, Heinemann, and Boston, Little Brown, 1973.

Plays

Meeting at Night (produced London, 1934).
Lady in Waiting, adaptation of her novel *The Nutmeg Tree* (produced New York, 1940; as *The Nutmeg Tree*, produced London, 1941). New York, French, 1941.
The Foolish Gentlewoman, adaptation of her own novel (produced London, 1949). London, French, 1950.

Television Play: *The Birdcage Room*, 1954.

*

Manuscript Collection: Houghton Library, Harvard University, Cambridge, Massachusetts.

* * *

Margery Sharp, as a children's writer, is primarily the creator of Miss Bianca. When, in *The Magical Cockatoo*, she abandons this enchanting mouse for the adventures of a little Victorian girl, her work seems thinner. Although the book has Sharp's usual wit and some entertaining social satire, Lally's adventures are mostly too trivial to arouse much suspense or sympathy. But the Miss Bianca series is caviare for any age—a sophisticated taste, addictive to those who acquire it.

The first of them, *The Rescuers*, is still for many readers the most delightful of all. It is here we first see the Mouse Prisoners' Aid Society in action, when Miss Bianca, the white mouse from the Embassy (later the Society's President), sets out with the plebeian Bernard and the nautical Norwegian mouse Nils, to rescue a poet from the Black Castle. Their horrific encounters with the warder's cat arouse real suspense and excitement.

In the later stories we are often reminded of the minute size of the mice, but in other respects they are more anthropomorphic than rodent. The characters remain unchanged, except that the low-born Bernard's devotion to Miss Bianca, originally rather touching, becomes imperceptibly a satirical absurdity. But Sharp's inventiveness is inexhaustible. Miss Bianca finds herself in the most dramatic and exciting situations, whether freezing in Antarctic wastes, lost in a salt-mine, exploring the main drain of the Embassy, or playing the harp to a cruel Ranee whose attendants are all too frequently condemned to be trampled to death by elephants. Her hairbreadth escapes from these dangers are as wittily contrived as they are unexpected. Bernard's mackintosh is inflated as a raft and wafted by cheerful gangs of juvenile delinquent bats; Miss Bianca captivates an elephant; they encounter a group of marble angels in a crypt, dispossessed from an old churchyard but consoling themselves with a rendering of "All Things Bright and Beautiful"—naturally in the manner of "a perfectly trained ladies-voice choir" with harp accompaniment.

Much of the humour derives from ironic contrast—the elegant sophistication of Miss Bianca's life and surroundings, mouse though she is, or her aristocratic culture set against Bernard's worthy but innocently vulgar tastes.

Only a child who reads well can fully enjoy these books, for their subtlest appeal is that of language itself, a delight in words and the rhythm of words for their own sake, a pleasure in a consciously mannered and elaborate diction akin to the pleasures of social ceremony, and the satirist's pleasure in impish and unexpected bathos:

> "What traces could there be but of blood upon these bricks, from the child's tender, bare feet? If only she had her bedroom slippers!" sighed Miss Bianca. "To be unshod makes for one danger more."
> "You mean she might pick up athlete's foot?" suggested Bernard sympathetically.

These are books for the connoisseur, and blessedly have no design at all upon the reader except that of entertainment.

—Margaret Greaves

SHERRY, Sylvia. British. Born in Newcastle-upon-Tyne, Northumberland. Educated at Heaton High School, and Kenton Lodge College of Education, both Newcastle; King's College, University of Durham (Spence Watson prize), B.A. in English. Married to Norman Sherry. Assistant mistress, Primary School and Girls' High School, and Lecturer, College of Education, 1955–60, all Newcastle; lived in Singapore, 1960–64. Agent: Jonathan Clowes Ltd., 22 Prince Albert Road, London NW1 7ST. Address: 6 Gillison Close, Melling, near Carnforth, Lancashire LA6 2AD, England.

PUBLICATIONS FOR CHILDREN

Fiction

Street of the Small Night Market. London, Cape, 1966; as *Secret of the Jade Pavilion*, Philadelphia, Lippincott, 1967.
Frog in a Coconut Shell. London, Cape, and Philadelphia, Lippincott, 1968.
A Pair of Jesus-Boots. London, Cape, 1969; as *The Liverpool Cats*, Philadelphia, Lippincott, 1969.

The Loss of the "Night Wind." London, Cape, 1970; as *The Haven Screamers*, Philadelphia, Lippincott, 1970.
A Snake in the Old Hut. London, Cape, 1972; Nashville, Nelson, 1973.
Dark River, Dark Mountain. London, Cape, 1975.
Mat, The Little Monkey, illustrated by Janusz Grabianski. London, Dent, and New York, Crane Russak, 1977.
A Pair of Desert-Wellies. London, Cape, 1985.
Rocky and the Ratman. London, Cape, 1988.

Plays

Television Plays: *Little Pig*, 1976; *It's Our Turn* series, 1977.

PUBLICATIONS FOR ADULTS

Novels

Girl in a Blue Shawl. London, Hamish Hamilton, 1978.
South of Red River. London, Hamish Hamilton, 1981.

*

Sylvia Sherry comments:
A novel for me begins with a place—a village, town, or particular area—and I do a lot of work finding out about the place and the people who live there. I hope to find the people I will write about in that setting. For example, Ah Wong, hero of my first novel, derived from a boy I saw working at a food stall in a street in Singapore at midnight. He was about 12 and was walking along the street tapping two pieces of bamboo together to tell people the noodle dish his stall made was ready. I hope also that the story will come out of the setting and will be an adventure that could happen only there. *The Loss of the "Night Wind"* was based on the loss of an actual fishing boat off the Northumberland coast. I like to travel and so my novels have a variety of settings. My aim is to create authentic characters in an authentic setting with an adventure plot. However, my three novels about Rocky O'Rourke, all set in Liverpool, have been the most popular of my children's fiction, and I hope this is because of their authenticity and adventure and their reflection of the true Liverpool atmosphere.

*   *   *

The consistent strength of Sylvia Sherry's novels from 1965 to 1988 has been the evocation of a distinctive place and period, whether it be contemporary Liverpool, the Lancashire moors in 1940, or a Malaysian coastal village at the time of the post-war Indonesian incursions. In all the full-length novels—which have tended to become more complex over the years—the central character is an enterprising boy aged 12 to 15, who overcomes some daunting peril by luck, courage, or blundering recklessness. The other characters are mainly adults, often hostile or unsympathetic to the hero, and rarely displaying any of the exemplary qualities which used to be normal in writings for children. Sherry does show considerable skill in building up tension gradually through perhaps nine or 10 short chapters while setting the scene, but her denouements and endings are apt to be disappointing.

Three of Sherry's nine books for children seem to require little comment. One, *Mat, The Little Monkey*, is a collection of picture stories for six to eight-year-olds. Two others, *The Loss of the "Night Wind"* and *Dark River, Dark Mountain*, may be described as good average mystery stories with strong local colour. The former has an interesting background of fishing boats and birdwatching in the Lindisfarne area, and the early development of its plot is both plausible and intriguing; but the explanation depends too much on an unlikely conspiracy of silence and an even stranger suppression of evidence by the hero and his friend. *Dark River, Dark Mountain* is more consistently credible, with the atmosphere of suspicion and spy-fever in a remote community after Dunkirk ringing absolutely true. The characters however are particularly unlikeable and the ending is likely to leave many readers dissatisfied.

At present Sherry is certainly best-known for her three Liverpool-based stories, *A Pair of Jesus-Boots*, televised in the 1970's, and the two sequels which have followed it after a lapse of 16 years. The first story introduces 13-year-old Rocky O'Rourke and his ill-assorted gang of friends, together with his far from idyllic family; his mother comes across as a dim-witted slut, his brother is a boastful, cowardly rogue while his small stepsister is severely disturbed and almost speechless. The use of an undiluted Liverpudlian dialect by all the characters presents another possible stumbling block, yet the story has enough pace and vivacity to keep one reading. The ending is hopeful, with Rocky rewarded for heroism and showing signs of a wiser outlook. Surprisingly, when we meet him again in *A Pair of Desert-Wellies* and *Rocky and the Ratman*, he is as reckless as ever, apparently dedicated to shoplifting and triumphing over real villains more through luck and impulsive courage than by taking thought. Perhaps the author feels that Liverpool itself, like Rocky, is an incorrigible case.

Sherry has been rightly acclaimed for her skill in portraying an English inner-city milieu through teenage eyes, but her success in applying the same technique to overseas settings has perhaps been undervalued. Her first two books, set in Singapore and Malaysia respectively, have conventional plots and predictable happy endings, but they also do full justice to her remarkable grasp of a community's social mechanisms and changing lifestyles. This facility is equally impressive in Sherry's later novel *A Snake in the Old Hut*, which in my opinion is also her finest achievement in the way of a gripping and stimulating narrative. The place this time is Kenya and the theme that of divided loyalties, treachery, and vengeance in a climate of violence. Among adventure stories which both inform the reader and invite him to think about moral issues, this little-known novel will stand comparison with the best.

—Alasdair K.D. Campbell

SHOTWELL, Louisa R(ossiter). American. Born in Chicago, Illinois, 1 May 1902. Educated at Wellesley College, Massachusetts, B.A. 1924; Stanford University, California, M.A. 1928. Formerly high school English teacher and college dean of women. Address: c/o Viking Penguin Inc., 40 West 23rd Street, New York, New York 10010, U.S.A.

PUBLICATIONS FOR CHILDREN

Fiction

Roosevelt Grady, illustrated by Peter Burchard. Cleveland, World, 1963; London, Bodley Head, 1966.
Adam Bookout, illustrated by W.T. Mars. New York, Viking Press, 1967.
Magdalena, illustrated by Lilian Obligado. New York, Viking Press, 1971.

Other

Beyond the Sugar Cane Field: UNICEF in Asia. Cleveland, World, 1964.

PUBLICATIONS FOR ADULTS

Play

The Dark Valley. New York, Friendship Press, 1964.

Other

This Is the Indian American [*Your Neighbor, the Migrant*]. New York, Friendship Press, 3 vols., 1955–58.
The Harvesters: Story of the Migrant People. New York, Doubleday, 1961.

Editor, with Elsie C. Pickhard, *Every Tribe and Tongue.* New York, Friendship Press, 1960.

*

Manuscript Collection: University of Wyoming, Laramie.

*   *   *

Louisa R. Shotwell is a good, dependable writer of readable books for children: her stories concern boys and girls of today, kids with problems to face and solve. Adam Bookout, for example, must realize and accept the fact that his parents have been killed in a plane crash. He has been unable to face the disaster, has fantasized that his parents are really still alive and will one day unexpectedly return, till at last, unable to remain in the neighborhood so haunted by his memories, he runs away from the aunties who are his guardians, to confront reality in the mixed milieu of the big city. It's a smoothly written book, with all ends neatly tied at its close.

Similarly with *Magdalena*. A Puerto Rican girl living in Brooklyn, Magdalena has problems in assimilation. Her long, lustrous black braids are a source of pride to her old-country grandmother and a misery to Magdalena. She doesn't want to look prim and old-fashioned beside the girls in her school; she longs for a short, smart, smooth haircut. But when she is tempted into a hairdresser's shop, and confronts her Nani with neatly clipped hair, the old woman is sure she has been bewitched and sets about exorcising her. A rather slight plot, smoothly handled, with a colorful and eccentric cast of characters and a neatly satisfactory happy ending.

But *Roosevelt Grady* falls into another category altogether. Roosevelt too is a boy with a problem, but his story is a special event in children's literature. This is a great book, and not only for child readers. Roosevelt's family are itinerant fruit pickers in the southwestern U.S.A., which means that they never stay more than a few weeks in any one place, for they must follow the crops to make a scanty living. Schooling becomes a very patchy business under these conditions—a few weeks here, a few weeks there. Roosevelt has been taught all about "taking away from" three or four times, but he never seems to get past that boring lesson to the one he longs for, the one that will teach him "putting into."

Roosevelt and his mother share a secret dream, of settling down to stay in one place, of Roosevelt and Sister going to a regular school, of little brother Matthew having the treatment that will perhaps cure his lameness, of baby Princess Anne growing up in a proper house with real curtains. In a bravely good-spirited story that is never consciously pathetic but often deeply moving, Roosevelt and his friend Manowar, a nameless waif, do all that two small boys can do to alter the Grady family's way of life.

This story too has at least a temporary happy ending: the longed-for home is a derelict bus, but to Roosevelt it is a dream come true. This is a story of dauntless courage, the ordinary, everyday kind that all too often passes unnoticed.

—Joan McGrath

———————

SILVERSTEIN, Shel(by). Also writes as Uncle Shelby. American. Born in Chicago, Illinois, in 1932. Served in the United States forces, Japan and Korea, 1950's. Divorced; one daughter. Former correspondent for *Pacific Stars and Stripes*. Free-lance cartoonist and writer for *Playboy*, Chicago, since 1956, and other magazines; also composer and song writer. Recipient: George C. Stone Center for Children's Books award, 1984 (twice). Address: c/o Harper and Row, 10 East 53rd Street, New York, New York 10022, U.S.A.

PUBLICATIONS FOR CHILDREN (illustrated by the author)

Fiction

Uncle Shelby's ABZ Book: A Primer for Tender Young Minds. New York, Simon and Schuster, 1961.
Uncle Shelby's Story of Lafcadio, The Lion Who Shot Back. New York, Harper, 1963.
Who Wants a Cheap Rhinoceros? (as Uncle Shelby). New York, Macmillan, 1964; revised edition, 1983; London, Cape, 1988.
The Giving Tree. New York, Harper, 1964; London, Cape, 1987.
The Missing Piece. New York, Harper, 1976.
The Missing Piece Meets the Big O. New York, Harper, 1981.

Verse

Uncle Shelby's A Giraffe and a Half. New York, Harper, 1964; as *A Giraffe and a Half*, London, Cape, 1988.
Uncle Shelby's Zoo: Don't Bump the Glump! New York, Simon and Schuster, and London, W.H. Allen, 1964.
Where the Sidewalk Ends: The Poems and Drawings of Shel Silverstein. New York, Harper, 1974; London, Cape, 1984.
A Light in the Attic: Poems and Drawings. New York, Harper, 1981; London, Cape, 1982.

Recording: *Where the Sidewalk Ends*, Columbia, 1984.

PUBLICATIONS FOR ADULTS

Plays

Gorilla (also director: produced Chicago, 1983).
Wild Life (includes *I'm Good to My Doggies, Chicken Suit Optional, The Lady or the Tiger Show*; produced New York, 1983).
Remember Crazy Zelda? (produced New York, 1984).
The Happy Hour (produced New York, 1985).
The Crate (produced New York, 1985).
One Tennis Shoe (produced New York, 1985).
Wash and Dry (produced New York, 1986).
Little Feet (produced New York, 1986).
Things Change (screenplay), with David Mamet. New York, Grove Press, 1988.

Screenplay: *Things Change*, with David Mamet, 1988.

Other (drawings)

Now Here's My Plan: A Book of Futilities. New York, Simon and Schuster, 1960.
Playboy's Teevee Jeebies. Chicago, Playboy Press, 1963.
More Playboy Teevee Jeebies. Chicago, Playboy Press, 1965.
Different Dances. New York, Harper, 1979.

*

Theatrical Activities:
Director: **Play**—*Gorilla*, Chicago, 1983.
Actor: **Film**—*Who Is Harry Kellerman and Why Is He Saying Those Terrible Things about Me?*, 1971.

*   *   *

It is easy to dismiss Shel Silverstein as a facile versifier with the knack of combining just the right amount of sentiment and impudence to assure mass appeal, but that would not be doing him justice. Literary merit aside, Silverstein, like Dr. Seuss and Judy Blume, is a force to be reckoned with. He can be weirdly idiosyncratic and even blatantly commercial. Yet the oddities among his collected works should not be allowed to mask a body of solid achievement in the form of three books well on their way to becoming classics: *The Giving Tree, Where the Sidewalk Ends*, and *A Light in the Attic*.

The Giving Tree is a deceptively simple parable about a tree that gives all it has to the little boy it loves. The text is as spare as Silverstein's drawings, which call to mind the cerebral cartoons of Jules Feiffer. In the end the tree is a stump and the boy an embittered old man. Critical interpretations are contradictory, telling more about the reader than the book. Ministers have read it from the pulpit as an allegory of Christian self-sacrifice; feminists have denounced it as advocating the exploitation of women. Uncle Shelby's only comment is that it is a story about a tree and a boy. One suspects him laughing in his beard.

No discussion of children's poetry can ignore *Where the Sidewalk Ends* and *A Light in the Attic*. For better or worse, the monumental success of these two books has transformed the way poetry is taught in American schools. What was once pretty and safe has now become wicked and nasty. Silverstein has spawned a host of imitators, most notably Jack Prelutsky. Jim Trelease, with Silverstein in mind, maintains that the first requirement of children's verse is that it be funny. Myra Cohn Livingston and other critics have protested against the crudity, violence, and mediocre writing currently passing itself off as children's poetry. However the worst of this is usually the work of imitators rather than of Silverstein himself.

Silverstein is by no stretch of the imagination a great poet. His verse reflects his background as a country songwriter. Plodding meters carry his rhymes and couplets. He alternates between naughtiness and sentimentality. He finds his best imagery in the garbage can: "Sarah Cynthia Sylvia Stout Would Not Take the Garbage Out." Nothing in Silverstein's work compares to the originality, lyric sense, and genuine feeling of Karla Kuskin, Valerie Worth, Myra Cohn Livingston, and Eve Merriam. Even so, it is hard to say whether this is the best Silverstein can do or if he is keeping a canny eye on his audience. His poems read like those a fourth grader would write in the back of his notebook when the teacher's eye was turned. That may be precisely their appeal.

Whatever his literary shortcomings, by convincing millions of children that poetry is neither difficult nor threatening, Silverstein has earned himself an honorable place among the great names in writing for children.

—Eric A. Kimmel

SINGER, Isaac Bashevis. American. Born Icek-Hersz Zynger in Leoncin, Poland, 14 July 1904; emigrated to the United States, 1935; became citizen, 1943. Educated at religious primary schools in Radzymin and, from 1908, Warsaw, and schools in Bilgorny, 1917–20; Tachkemoni Rabbinical Seminary, Warsaw, 1921–22. Married Alma Haimann in 1940; one son from earlier marriage. Proofreader and translator, *Literarishe Bleter*, Warsaw, 1923–33; associate editor, *Globus*, Warsaw, 1933–35; journalist, *Vorwärts* (*Jewish Daily Forward*) Yiddish newspaper, New York, from 1935. Founder, *Svivah* literary magazine. Recipient: Louis Lamed prize, 1950, 1956; American Academy grant, 1959; Daroff Memorial award, 1963; Foreign Book prize (France), 1965; two National Endowment for the Arts grants, 1966; Bancarella prize (Italy), 1968; Brandeis University Creative Arts award, 1969; National Book award, 1970, and for fiction, 1974; Association of Jewish Libraries Sydney Taylor award, 1971; Nobel Prize for Literature, 1978; Kenneth Smilen Present Tense award, 1980. D.H.L.: Hebrew Union College, Los Angeles, 1963; D.Lit.: Colgate University, Hamilton, New York, 1972; D.Litt.: Texas Christian University, Fort Worth, 1972; Ph.D.: Hebrew University, Jerusalem, 1973; Litt.D.: Bard College, Annandale-on-Hudson, New York, 1974; Long Island University, Greenvale, New York, 1979. Member, American Academy, 1965; American Academy of Arts and Sciences, 1969; Jewish Academy of Arts and Sciences; Polish Institute of Arts and Sciences. Address: 209 West 86th Street, New York, New York 10024, U.S.A.

PUBLICATIONS FOR CHILDREN (translated by the author and Elizabeth Shub)

Fiction

Zlateh the Goat and Other Stories, illustrated by Maurice Sendak. New York, Harper, 1966; London, Longman, 1970.
Mazel and Shlimazel; or, The Milk of a Lioness, illustrated by Margot Zemach. New York, Farrar Straus, 1967; London, Cape, 1979.
The Fearsome Inn, illustrated by Nonny Hogrogian. New York, Scribner, 1967; London, Collins, 1970.
When Shlemiel Went to Warsaw and Other Stories, translated by Channah Kleinerman-Goldstein and others, illustrated by Margot Zemach. New York, Farrar Straus, 1968; London, Longman, 1974.
Joseph and Koza; or, The Sacrifice to the Vistula, illustrated by Symeon Shimin. New York, Farrar Straus, 1970; London, Hamish Hamilton, 1984.
Alone in the Wild Forest, illustrated by Margot Zemach. New York, Farrar Straus, 1971; Edinburgh, Canongate, 1980.
The Topsy-Turvy Emperor of China, illustrated by William Pène du Bois. New York, Harper, 1971.
The Fools of Chelm and Their History, illustrated by Uri Shulevitz. New York, Farrar Straus, 1973.
A Tale of Three Wishes, illustrated by Irene Lieblich. New York, Farrar Straus, 1976.
Naftali the Storyteller and His Horse, Sus, and Other Stories, translated by the author and others, illustrated by Margot Zemach. New York, Farrar Straus, 1976; London, Oxford University Press, 1977.
The Power of Light: Eight Stories for Hanukkah, illustrated by Irene Lieblich. New York, Farrar Straus, 1980; London, Robson, 1983.
The Golem, illustrated by Uri Shulevitz. New York, Farrar Straus, 1982; London, Deutsch, 1983.
Stories for Children. New York, Farrar Straus, 1984.

Other

A Day of Pleasure: Stories of a Boy Growing Up in Warsaw (autobiographical), translated by Channah Kleinerman-Goldstein and others, photographs by Roman Vishniac. New York, Farrar Straus, 1969; London, MacRae, 1980.
Elijah the Slave: A Hebrew Legend Retold, illustrated by Antonio Frasconi. New York, Farrar Straus, 1970.
The Wicked City, illustrated by Leonard Everett Fisher. New York, Farrar Straus, 1972.
Why Noah Chose the Dove, illustrated by Eric Carle. New York, Farrar Straus, 1974.

PUBLICATIONS FOR ADULTS

Novels

The Family Moskat, translated by A.H. Gross. New York, Knopf, 1950; London, Secker and Warburg, 1966.
Satan in Goray, translated by Jacob Sloan. New York, Farrar Straus, 1955; London, Owen, 1958.
The Magician of Lublin, translated by Elaine Gottlieb and Joseph Singer. New York, Farrar Straus, 1960; London, Secker and Warburg, 1961.
The Slave, translated by the author and Cecil Hemley. New York, Farrar Straus, 1962; London, Secker and Warburg, 1963.
The Manor, translated by Elaine Gottlieb and Joseph Singer. New York, Farrar Straus, 1967; London, Secker and Warburg, 1968.
The Estate, translated by Joseph Singer, Elaine Gottlieb, and Elizabeth Shub. New York, Farrar Straus, 1969; London, Cape, 1970.
Enemies: A Love Story, translated by Aliza Shevrin and Elizabeth Shub. New York, Farrar Straus, and London, Cape, 1972.
Shosha, translated by Joseph Singer. New York, Farrar Straus, 1978; London, Cape, 1979.
Reaches of Heaven. New York, Farrar Straus, 1980; London, Faber, 1982.
The Penitent. New York, Farrar Straus, 1983; London, Cape, 1984.
King of the Fields. New York, Farrar Straus, 1988; London, Cape, 1989.

Short Stories

Gimpel the Fool and Other Stories, translated by Saul Bellow and others. New York, Farrar Straus, 1957; London, Owen, 1958.
The Spinoza of Market Street and Other Stories, translated by Elaine Gottlieb and others. New York, Farrar Straus, 1961; London, Secker and Warburg, 1962.
Short Friday and Other Stories, translated by Ruth Whitman and others. New York, Farrar Straus, 1964; London, Secker and Warburg, 1967.
Selected Short Stories, edited by Irving Howe. New York, Modern Library, 1966.
The Séance and Other Stories, translated by Ruth Whitman and others. New York, Farrar Straus, 1968; London, Cape, 1970.
A Friend of Kafka and Other Stories, translated by the author and others. New York, Farrar Straus, 1970; London, Cape, 1972.

A Crown of Feathers and Other Stories, translated by the author and others. New York, Farrar Straus, 1973; London, Cape, 1974.
Passions and Other Stories. New York, Farrar Straus, 1975; London, Cape, 1976.
Old Love. New York, Farrar Straus, 1979; London, Cape, 1980.
The Collected Stories. New York, Farrar Straus, and London, Cape, 1982.
The Image and Other Stories. New York, Farrar Straus, 1985; London, Cape, 1986.
Gifts. Philadelphia, Jewish Publication Society, 1985.
The Death of Methuselah and Other Stories. New York, Farrar Straus, and London, Cape, 1988.

Plays

The Mirror (produced New Haven, Connecticut, 1973).
Shlemiel the First (produced New Haven, Connecticut, 1974).
Yentl, The Yeshiva Boy, with Leah Napolin, adaptation of a story by Singer (produced New York, 1974). New York, French, 1979.
Teibele and Her Demon, with Eve Friedman (produced Minneapolis, 1978; New York, 1979). New York and London, French, 1984.

Other

In My Father's Court (autobiography), translated by Channah Kleinerman-Goldstein and others. New York, Farrar Straus, 1966; London, Secker and Warburg, 1967.
An Isaac Bashevis Singer Reader. New York, Farrar Straus, 1971.
The Hasidim: Paintings, Drawings, and Etchings, with Ira Moskowitz. New York, Crown, 1973.
Love and Exile: The Early Years: A Memoir. New York, Doubleday, 1984; London, Cape, 1985.
A Little Boy in Search of God: Mysticism in a Personal Light, illustrated by Ira Moskowitz. New York, Doubleday, 1976.
A Young Man in Search of Love, translated by Joseph Singer. New York, Doubleday, 1978.
Lost in America, translated by Joseph Singer. New York, Doubleday, 1981.
Nobel Lecture. New York, Farrar Straus, and London, Cape, 1979.
Isaac Bashevis Singer on Literature and Life: An Interview, with Paul Rosenblatt and Gene Koppel. Tucson, University of Arizona Press, 1979.
The Meaning of Freedom. West Point, New York, United States Military Academy, 1981.
My Personal Conception of Religion. Lafayette, University of Southwestern Louisiana Press, 1982.
One Day of Happiness. New York, Red Ozier Press, 1982.
Conversations with Isaac Bashevis Singer, with Richard Burgin. New York, Doubleday, 1985.

Editor, with Elaine Gottlieb, *Prism 2*. New York, Twayne, 1965.

Translator, *Pan*, by Knut Hamsun. Vilna, Kletzkian, 1928.
Translator, *Di Vogler* (The Vagabonds), by Knut Hamsun. Vilna, Kletzkian, 1928.
Translator, *In Opgrunt Fun Tayve* (In Passion's Abyss), by Gabriele D'Annunzio. Warsaw, Goldfarb, 1929.
Translator, *Mete Trap* (Mette Trap), by Karin Michäelis. Warsaw, Goldfarb, 1929.
Translator, *Roman Rolan* (Romain Rolland), by Stefan Zweig. Warsaw, Bikher, 1929.
Translator, *Viktorya* (Victoria), by Knut Hamsun. Vilna, Kletzkian, 1929.
Translator, *Oyfn Mayrev-Front Keyn Nayes* (All Quiet on the Western Front), by Erich Maria Remarque. Vilna, Kletzkian, 1930.

Translator, *Der Tsoyberbarg* (The Magic Mountain), by Thomas Mann. Vilna, Kletzkian, 4 vols., 1930.
Translator, *Der Veg oyf Tsurik* (The Road Back), by Erich Maria Remarque. Vilna, Kletzkian, 1931.
Translator, *Araber: Folkstimlekhe Geshikhtn* (Arabs: Stories of the People), by Moshe Smilansky. Warsaw, Farn Folk, 1932.
Translator, *Fun Moskve biz Yerusholayim* (From Moscow to Jerusalem), by Leon S. Glaser. New York, Jankowitz, 1938.

*

Bibliography: by Bonnie Jean M. Christensen, in *Bulletin of Bibliography 26* (Boston), January–March, 1969; *A Bibliography of Isaac Bashevis Singer 1924–1949* by David Neal Miller, Bern, Switzerland and New York, Lang, 1983.

Manuscript Collection: Butler Library, Columbia University, New York.

Critical Studies (selection): *Isaac Bashevis Singer and the Eternal Past* by Irving Buchen, New York, New York University Press, 1968; *The Achievement of Isaac Bashevis Singer* edited by Marcia Allentuck, Carbondale, Southern Illinois University Press, 1969; *Critical Views of Isaac Bashevis Singer* edited by Irving Malin, New York, New York University Press, 1969, and *Isaac Bashevis Singer* by Malin, New York, Ungar, 1972; *Isaac Bashevis Singer* by Ben Siegel, Minneapolis, University of Minnesota Press, 1969; *Isaac Bashevis Singer and His Art* by Askel Schiotz, New York, Harper, 1970; *Isaac Bashevis Singer, The Magician of West 86th Street* by Paul Kresh, New York, Dial Press, 1979; *The Brothers Singer* by Clive Sinclair, London, Allison and Busby, 1983; *Fear of Fiction: Narrative Strategies in the Works of Isaac Bashevis Singer* by David Neal Miller, Albany, State University of New York Press, 1985, and *Recovering the Canon: Essays on Isaac Bashevis Singer* edited by Miller, Leiden, Brill, 1986; *From Exile to Redemption: The Fiction of Isaac Bashevis Singer* by Grace Farrell Lee, Carbondale, Southern Illinois University Press, 1987; *Understanding Isaac Bashevis Singer* by Lawrence S. Friedman, Columbia, South Carolina University Press, 1988.

*   *   *

The observation is frequently made that all great authors somehow stand apart. Few modern writers embody that assertion as completely as Isaac Bashevis Singer who, among numerous other honors, has been awarded the National Book award and the Nobel Prize for Literature. Yet an outsider he remains: a Jew among Gentiles; a European in America; an old man living in a world that glorifies youth. In a scientific age he admits to believing in ghosts and demons. He writes in a nearly dead language for an audience that cannot read his work except in translation. And he writes for children, for whom kabbalistic mysteries, tales of wonder rabbis who lived in Poland two hundred years ago, and the musings of refugee littérateurs are as remote as the fertility rites of Hottentots. Why? Because, as Singer himself explains, "they still believe in God, the family, angels, devils, witches, goblins…and other obsolete stuff. They don't expect their beloved writer to redeem humanity. Young as they are, they know that it is not in his power. Only the adults have such childish illusions."

Singer may not believe in the power of writers to change the world, but, as one reared in the Hasidic tradition, he firmly believes in the power of stories, and in the ability of children to understand the most profound ideas if presented to them in the form of a tale. This intense respect for the child's ability to understand marks the best of Singer's juvenile work, just as it marks the work of Andersen, Carroll, Lewis, and Grahame. In fact a comparison with Singer's adult work frequently reveals the same themes—and often the same stories—written once for an audience of adults and, in a slightly different way, for an audience of children. The picture book *Joseph and Koza* deals with a Jewish goldsmith among Slavic pagans who falls in love and rescues a pagan girl. Similar situations, though of course treated at much greater length and with greater depth, form the plots of two adult novels, *The Slave* and *King of the Fields*. Kabbalistic speculations about reincarnation, demons, and the Messiah are major elements in Singer's writing and are as important in appreciating juvenile works such as *The Fearsome Inn, Mazel and Shlimazel*, and *Alone in the Wild Forest* as they are in understanding such adult writings as *Satan in Goray, The Spinoza of Market Street*, and *Gimpel the Fool*. Finally, *A Day of Pleasure* is simply a smaller, selected edition of Singer's adult autobiography *In My Father's Court*.

Equally important to any consideration of Singer's work is understanding where his roots as a writer lie. They run through the Yiddish masters I.L. Peretz and Sholem Aleichem to the great Russian writers of the 19th century who inspired them: Gogol, Dostoevsky, Chekhov, and Tolstoy. These influences shape the patterns of *Zlateh the Goat* and Singer's subsequent story collections down to his most recent, *The Power of Light*. Rollicking tales of the fools of Chelm rub elbows with stories of ghosts and demons. And then there are those like "Zlateh the Goat," "Menashe and Rachel," and "Naftali the Storyteller and His Horse, Sus," where nothing actually happens, but whose smells and textures are so rich they might have been wafted from the Cherry Orchard.

The inspired fabric of Singer's writing brings out the best in the artists chosen to illustrate it. Margot Zemach's rough figures capture the humor and sighs of ghetto folk. Irene Lieblich's paintings for *The Power of Light* are a shining tapestry of color. The stories in *Zlateh the Goat* reveal a warmth in Maurice Sendak that seems lacking in most of his recent major work. But it is in Singer's most recent book, *The Golem*, with pictures by Uri Shulevitz, that artist and writer capture the soul of a story.

The legend of the Golem is at least five hundred years old, and various elements of it can be traced all the way back to the time of the Talmud. The story appeared in several novelized treatments in the late 19th and early 20th centuries. H. Leivick's play, *The Golem*, is one of the masterpieces of the Yiddish theater. In the tale which has emerged from these varied traditional, romantic, and impressionistic elements, Rabbi Judah Leib of Prague is commanded by God to fashion a figure of a man from clay and bring it to life. This creature, the Golem, of enormous strength and size but of no intelligence whatsoever, saves the Jewish community from destruction. But the Golem lingers beyond his time; his powers are inadvertently misused and he becomes a rampaging menace that must somehow be confronted and laid to rest. Singer's version incorporates all the familiar elements of this powerful story: the ritual murder accusation; the Golem as Sorceror's apprentice; his love-lust for a lovely girl; his mindless pain in being alive and his fear of death. One idea, however, is new. The Emperor's decision to draft the Golem into his army makes it imperative for Rabbi Leib to end the creature's life. A Golem running wild in the streets is menacing enough, but a Golem accoutered with weapons of war and taught to fight in the service of an earthly monarch is an image of overwhelming horror. Singer does not elaborate, but the modern implications are not hard to see. Our world has its own Golem—nuclear energy—which men of science brought out of the earth to serve the forces of good in a time of danger. Now we are faced with an arsenal of Golems, all out of control, subject to no authority but the whims of generals, dictators, and politicians. To lay his Golem to rest Rabbi Leib must erase the holy name on its forehead. Will we be rid of our own Golems so easily? Shulevitz's mindless Golem in his gay landesknecht's costume capering goggle-eyed through the somber streets of the ghetto is as much a symbol of our age as Picasso's Guernica.

The greatest children's writers are great writers by any standard:

Defoe, Carroll, Stevenson, Twain. The 20th century will add no more than a handful of names to that number. One of them, however, will surely be that of Isaac Bashevis Singer.

—Eric A. Kimmel

———

SLEATOR, William (Warner, III). American. Born in Havre de Grace, Maryland, 13 February 1945. Educated at Harvard University, Cambridge, Massachusetts, 1963–67, B.A. in English 1967. Accompanist for ballet classes, Royal Ballet School, London, 1967–68; rehearsal pianist, Boston Ballet Company, 1974–83. Agent: Sheldon Fogelman, 10 East 40th Street, New York, New York 10016. Address: 77 Worcester Street, Boston, Massachusetts 02118, U.S.A.

PUBLICATIONS FOR CHILDREN

Fiction

Blackbriar, illustrated by Blair Lent. New York, Dutton, 1972.
Run. New York, Dutton, 1973.
House of Stairs. New York, Dutton, 1974; London, Macdonald, 1988.
Among the Dolls, illustrated by Trina Schart Hyman. New York, Dutton, 1975.
Into the Dream, illustrated by Ruth Sanderson. New York, Dutton, 1979.
Once, Said Darlene, illustrated by Steven Kellogg. New York, Dutton, 1979.
The Green Futures of Tycho. New York, Dutton, 1981; London, Macdonald, 1988.
That's Silly, illustrated by Lawrence DiFiori. New York, Dutton, 1981.
Fingers. New York, Atheneum, 1983.
Interstellar Pig. New York, Dutton, 1984; London, Hodder and Stoughton, 1987.
Singularity. New York, Dutton, 1985; London, Macdonald, 1988.
The Boy Who Reversed Himself. New York, Dutton, 1986; London, Macdonald, 1988.
The Duplicate. New York, Dutton, 1988.
Strange Attractors. New York, Dutton, 1989.

Other

The Angry Moon (retelling), illustrated by Blair Lent. Boston, Little Brown, 1970.

Incidental Music, for film: *Why the Sun and Moon Live in the Sky*, 1972.

PUBLICATIONS FOR ADULTS

Other

Take Charge: A Personal Guide to Behavior Modification, with William H. Redd. New York, Random House, 1976.

*

William Sleator comments:
I try to write books with realistic characters, settings and

situations—and then introduce weirdness in such a way that the reader will find it absolutely convincing. I have found that the best way for me to do this—and to make it as believable as possible—is to use science. Not only is science the ultimate reality; it is also true that actual scientific facts are as peculiar as anything I could dream up. It is true that gravity slows down time, and that time almost stops in the vicinity of a black hole. It is true that the pathway to chaos, in many different areas, follows similar patterns, and is governed by beautiful and sinister entities known as strange attractors. By making use of such real scientific facts in my plots, I try to create stories that are magical and fantastic, but might also really be possible some day.

* * *

William Sleator belongs to a new generation of science-fiction writers. In the 1940's and 1950's most science fiction was highly technological, its outlook essentially optimistic and pro-authority; its protagonists were clean-cut, responsible young men of action who knew how to follow orders. Sleator is distinctly contemporary in his de-emphasis on technology and distrust of authority. His protagonists are bored, resentful, ungracious, unprepared. His stories take place not in a distant future or faraway star system, but in the here and now; typically, some scientific anomaly erupts into the life of a very ordinary teenager, forces him into thought and action, and leaves him finally on better terms with his family and himself.

Sleator worked his way gradually into the genre. The early *Black-briar* and *Among the Dolls* are rather commonplace occult fantasy; his first venture into science fiction, *House of Stairs*, employs primarily psychological rather than scientific concepts. Four young people of widely differing personalities find themselves trapped in a giant maze consisting entirely of stairs. They come to realize that they are being used as experimental animals, trained by a food-dispensing machine to exhibit ever more bizarre and horrible behavior. What makes people change and what changes their attitudes toward others is a preoccupation of Sleator's that clearly lies behind his most powerful and frightening story.

Most of Sleator's recent books are inspired by scientific concepts that he finds intriguing—*Into the Dream* (one of the few fine science fiction stories written for 8 to 10-year-olds) plays with ESP and telekinesis, *The Green Futures of Tycho* with time travel, *Singularity* with other properties of time, *The Boy Who Reversed Himself* with universes of more than three dimensions, *The Duplicate* with cloning. Sleator's grasp of science is that of a fascinated layman rather than a professional and his handling of it (for example, of black holes in *Singularity*) is sometimes inaccurate. But this, though it may bother some readers, has little effect on his qualities as a storyteller—strong underlying logic, gripping suspense, and a protagonist who develops under pressure. An interest in family relationships is also characteristic of his work; the theme of sibling rivalry and its reconciliation is central in *Fingers, Singularity*, and *The Green Futures of Tycho*.

In Sleator's hands even a science-fiction formula can be regenerated. One of his best stories, *Interstellar Pig*, is based on the old premise of hostile aliens who take on human disguise. Expecting a dull vacation at the shore, Barney is eager to make friends with the attractive and sophisticated trio who move into the cottage next door, and flattered to join in their favorite pastime, a space fantasy combat game called Interstellar Pig. Only little by little does he learn that Joe, Manny, and Zena are members of three separate alien races, all battling for the Pig—that the "game" is only too real—and that once he has joined it, the fate of his own planet may be at stake. Unadventurous and immature, Barney makes an unlikely hero, and he is never more than one jump ahead of disaster. Yet he finds in himself surprising resources of courage and intelligence, even the supreme human quality of compassion.

He does not save the world; it makes an effective final twist that

the world was never in real danger after all. In Sleator's best work, there are no spectacular rewards for heroes like Barney, only the discovery of what was there all along—the beauty of the night sky, a brother's affection, the untapped potential in oneself.

—Suzanne Rahn

SLEIGH, Barbara (de Riemer). British. Born in Acock's Green, Worcestershire, 9 January 1906. Educated at St. Catherine's School, Bramley, Surrey; West Bromwich School of Art, Birmingham, 1922–25; Clapham High School Art Teacher's Training College, London, 1925–28, Art Teacher's Diploma. Married David Davis in 1935; one son and two daughters. Art teacher, Smethwick High School, Staffordshire, 1927–29; Lecturer, Goldsmiths' Teacher Training College, London, 1929–32; assistant, *Children's Hour* program, BBC Radio, London, 1932–35. Freelance broadcaster and radio writer from 1935. *Died 13 February 1982.*

PUBLICATIONS FOR CHILDREN

Fiction

Carbonel, illustrated by V.H. Drummond. London, Parrish, 1955; Indianapolis, Bobbs Merrill, 1957.
Patchwork Quilt, illustrated by Mary Shillabeer. London, Parrish, 1956.
The Singing Wreath and Other Stories, illustrated by Julia Comper. London, Parrish, 1957.
The Seven Days, illustrated by Susan Einzig. London, Parrish, 1958; New York, Meredith Press, 1968.
The Kingdom of Carbonel, illustrated by D.M. Leonard. London, Parrish, 1959; Indianapolis, Bobbs Merrill, 1960.
No One Must Know, illustrated by Jillian Willett. London, Collins, 1962; Indianapolis, Bobbs Merrill, 1963.
Jessamy, illustrated by Philip Gough. London, Collins, and Indianapolis, Bobbs Merrill, 1967.
Pen, Penny, Tuppence, illustrated by Meg Stevens. London, Hamish Hamilton, 1968.
The Snowball, illustrated by Patricia Drew. Leicester, Brockhampton Press, 1969.
West of Widdershins: A Gallimaufry of Stories Brewed in Her Own Cauldron, illustrated by Victor Ambrus. London, Collins, 1971; as *Stirabout Stories*, Indianapolis, Bobbs Merrill, 1971.
Ninety-Nine Dragons, illustrated by Gunvor Edwards. Leicester, Brockhampton Press, 1974.
Charlie Chumbles, illustrated by Frank Franus. London, Knight, 1977.
Grimblegraw and the Wuthering Witch, illustrated by Glenys Ambrus. London, Hodder and Stoughton, 1978; revised edition, London, Penguin, 1979.
Carbonel and Calidor, illustrated by Charles Front. London, Kestrel, 1978.

Other

North of Nowhere: Stories and Legends from Many Lands, illustrated by Victor Ambrus. London, Collins, 1964; New York, Coward McCann, 1966.
Funny Peculiar: An Anthology, illustrated by Jennie Garratt. Newton Abbot, Devon, David and Charles, 1975.
Winged Magic: Legends and Stories from Many Lands Concerning

Things That Fly, illustrated by John Patience.   London, Hodder and Stoughton, 1979.

Editor, *Broomsticks and Beasticles: Stories and Verse about Witches and Strange Creatures*, illustrated by John Patience.   London, Hodder and Stoughton, 1981.
Editor, *The Wind in the Willows*, by Kenneth Grahame, illustrated by Philip Mendoza.   London, Hodder and Stoughton, 1983.

Numerous radio plays.

PUBLICATIONS FOR ADULTS

Other

The Smell of Privet (autobiography).   London, Hutchinson, 1971.

*

Barbara Sleigh commented:
   (1978) I largely write fantasy, but, I hope, of a down-to-earth kind, avoiding mere whimsy. I feel strongly this leads young readers to wider horizons, and later to imaginative adult reading.

*   *   *

   Like many talented and versatile writers, Barbara Sleigh suffered the irritating injustice of being associated too exclusively with one outstanding creation, in her case *Carbonel*, a splendid and brilliantly observed character. But with all due respect to Carbonel (emphatically a cat demanding respect) Sleigh as a writer stands for a good deal more.
   She produced her first book only after a long apprenticeship as a storyteller for the BBC during the best years of sound radio, in which the word was all-important, before television destroyed the famous daily *Children's Hour* with an alternative making less mental demand. She learned what demands *could* safely be made on a child in subject matter and vocabulary, if the storyteller knew his job. That she knew hers is demonstrated not only in *Carbonel* and its sequels— the last, *Carbonel and Calidor*, 23 years later, displaying an undiminished fertility of fancy—but in her numerous other volumes.
   These vary from short story collections, such as *West of Widdershins*, and an anthology, *Broomsticks and Beasticles*, in which her own verses and folktale retellings are joined with similar pieces from other hands, to full-length books like *Jessamy*, in which a favourite old theme—the child who slips back in time, 1914 in this case—is developed with originality. Her personal attitude to magic and fantasy is stated in a brief introduction to *West of Widdershins*, a book which exemplifies her deft verbal economy and prodigality of ingenious ideas. One of its stories, "Miss Peabody," set in a prosaic school classroom, illustrates her preference for rooting these fantasies firmly in everyday life. Humour runs strongly through all her work. *Ninety-Nine Dragons* is especially full of it, and, though the good-natured, rather than fearsome, dragon has become almost a stereotype in children's fiction, Sleigh revealed once more her flair for giving a new brightness to whatever material she handled.
   In what has proved to be, with Mary Norton, Alan Garner, and many others, something of a golden age of fantasy, Sleigh earned a high place.

—Geoffrey Trease

SLOBODKIN, Louis.   American.   Born in Albany, New York, 19 February 1903. Educated at Beaux Arts Institute of Design, New York, 1918–23. Married Florence Gersh in 1927; two sons. Sculptor in studios in U.S.A. and France, 1931–35; Head of the Sculpture Department, Master Institute of United Arts, Roerich Museum, New York, 1934–37; Instructor in Sculpture, Art League, New York, 1935–36; Head of Sculpture Division, New York City Art Project, 1941–42. Awarded commissions and executed sculptures, reliefs, and statues for buildings in New York, Washington, D.C., Johnstown, Pennsylvania, and North Adams, Massachusetts, 1935–39. Numerous museum exhibitions. Member of the Board of Directors, Sculptors Guild, 1939–41; president, National Sculpture Society American Group, 1940–42; chairman, American Institute of Graphic Arts Artists Committee, 1946. Recipient: American Library Association Caldecott Medal, for illustration, 1944. *Died 8 May 1975.*

PUBLICATIONS FOR CHILDREN (illustrated by the author)

Fiction

The Friendly Animals.   New York, Vanguard Press, 1944.
Clear the Track for Michael's Magic Train.   New York, Macmillan, 1945.
The Adventures of Arab.   New York, Macmillan, 1946.
Hustle and Bustle.   New York, Macmillan, 1948.
Bixxy and the Secret Message.   New York, Macmillan, 1949.
Mr. Mushroom.   New York, Macmillan, 1950.
Dinny and Danny.   New York, Macmillan, 1951.
The Space Ship under the Apple Tree.   New York, Macmillan, 1952.
Circus, April 1st.   New York, Macmillan, 1953.
The Horse with High-Heeled Shoes.   New York, Vanguard Press, 1954.
Mr. Petersand's Cats and Kittens.   New York, Macmillan, 1954.
The Amiable Giant.   New York, Macmillan, 1955; London, Macmillan, 1958.
The Little Mermaid Who Could Not Sing.   New York, Macmillan, 1956.
Melvin the Moose Child.   New York, Macmillan, 1957; London, Macmillan, 1958.
The Space Ship Returns to the Apple Tree.   New York and London, Macmillan, 1958.
The Wide-Awake Owl.   New York, Macmillan, 1958.
Trick or Treat.   New York and London, Macmillan, 1959.
Gogo, The French Sea Gull.   New York, Macmillan, 1960.
A Good Place to Hide.   New York, Macmillan, 1961.
Picco, The Sad Italian Pony.   New York, Vanguard Press, 1961.
The Three-Seated Space Ship.   New York, Macmillan, 1962.
The Late Cuckoo.   New York, Vanguard Press, 1962.
Luigi and the Long-Nosed Soldier.   New York, Macmillan, and London, Collier Macmillan, 1963.
Moon Blossom and the Golden Penny.   New York, Vanguard Press, 1963.
The Polka-Dot Goat.   New York, Macmillan, and London, Collier Macmillan, 1964.
Colette and the Princess.   New York, Dutton, 1965.
Yasu and the Strangers.   New York, Macmillan, and London, Collier Macmillan, 1965.
Round Trip Space Ship.   New York, Macmillan, and London, Collier Macmillan, 1968.
The Space Ship in the Park.   New York, Macmillan, and London, Collier Macmillan, 1972.
Wilbur the Warrior.   New York, Vanguard Press, 1972.

Verse

Magic Michael.   New York, Macmillan, 1944.

The Seaweed Hat. New York, Macmillan, 1947.
Our Friendly Friends. New York, Vanguard Press, 1951.
Millions and Millions and Millions! New York, Vanguard Press, 1955.
One Is Good But Two Are Better. New York, Vanguard Press, 1956.
Nomi and the Lovely Animals. New York, Vanguard Press, 1960.
Up High and Down Low. New York, Macmillan, 1960.

Other

Thank You—You're Welcome. New York, Vanguard Press, 1957.
The First Book of Drawing. New York, Watts, 1958.
Excuse Me! Certainly! New York, Vanguard Press, 1959.
Read about the Policeman [*Postman, Busman, Fireman*]. New York, Watts, 4 vols., 1966–67.

PUBLICATIONS FOR ADULTS

Other

Fo'castle Waltz. New York, Vanguard Press, 1945.
Sculpture: Principles and Practice. Cleveland, World, 1949.

*

Manuscript Collection: University of Oregon Library, Eugene.

Illustrator: *The Moffats*, 1941, *The Middle Moffat*, 1942, *Rufus M*, 1943, *The Sun and the Wind and Mr. Todd*, 1943, *The Hundred Dresses*, 1944, and *Ginger Pye*, 1951, all by Eleanor Estes; *Many Moons* by James Thurber, 1943; *Peter the Great*, 1943, *Garibaldi*, 1944, and *Lenin*, 1945, all by Nina Baker; *Young Man of the House* by Mabel Leigh Hunt, 1944; *Russia and America* by Delia Goetz, 1945; *Robin Hood* by J. Walker McSpadden, 1946; *The Adventures of Tom Sawyer* by Mark Twain, 1946; *Jonathan and the Rainbow*, 1948, and *The King and the Noble Blacksmith*, 1950, both by Jacob Blanck; *Gertie and the Horse Who Thought and Thought* by Margarite Glendinning, 1951; *Red Head* by Edward Eager, 1951; *The Magic Fishbone* by Charles Dickens, 1953; *The Alhambra* by Washington Irving, 1953; *Evie and the Wonderful Kangaroo*, 1955, and *Evie and Cooky*, 1957, both by Irmengarde Eberle; *Pysen*, 1955, *The Saucepan Journey*, 1955, and *Little O*, 1957, all by Edith Unnerstad; *Shoes Fit for a King* by Helen E. Bill, 1956; *Love and Knishes*, 1956, and *Mazel Tov Y'all*, 1968, both by Sara Kasdan; *The Warm-Hearted Polar Bear* by Robert Murphy, 1957; *Upside Down Town* by F. Amerson Andrews, 1958; *Too Many Mittens*, 1958, *The Cowboy Twins*, 1960, *Io Sono/I Am*, 1962, *Mr. Papadilly and Willy*, 1964, and *Sarah Somebody*, 1969, all by Florence Slobodkin; *Martin's Dinosaur* by Reda Davis, 1959; *Clean Clarence*, 1959, and *Marshmallow Ghost*, 1960, both by Priscilla and Otto Friedrich; *Mr. Spindles and the Spiders* by Andrew Packard, 1961; *The Lovely Culpeppers* by Martha Uppington, 1963.

*   *   *

Louis Slobodkin was a prolific children's book author and illustrator who began to publish in the 1940's. He is best known for books which he both wrote and illustrated, though his illustrations for James Thurber's *Many Moons* and the work he did with his wife Florence should be noted.

Slobodkin's picture books are representative of a broad range of types within a category. The early picture books are faintly didactic, the emphasis being on an instructive lesson (*Dinny and Danny*) or an implied moral (*Magic Michael*). The use of the picture book as *exemplum*, however, is played down, and the illustrations do not accentuate the moral aspect of his works. Slobodkin also wrote obviously and intentionally didactic works, such as the courtesy books *Thank You—You're Welcome* and *Excuse Me! Certainly!*, as well as a "Read About" series on busmen, postmen, firemen, and policemen. This series contains narrative histories of the various professions accompanied by episodic vignettes related to a child's perception of the profession. Slobodkin's primary text for children who are interested in learning to illustrate is held in high repute by teachers of art, and the illustrations for Florence Slobodkin's dual language text *Io Sono/I Am* enhance the instructive level of the work.

Slobodkin is also noted for a series of juvenile fiction books on the themes of space travel, space inhabitants, and a child's imaginative relationship with his world and other-worldliness. Representative titles are *The Space Ship under the Apple Tree*, *The Space Ship in the Park*, and *The Three-Seated Space Ship*. Most of these works are centered on a peripatetic hero called Eddie and his friend from the planet Martinea.

Slobodkin's illustrations are very simple and functional—rarely more than suggestive of the actions discussed in the text. Yet the fact that Slobodkin was a sculptor obviously influenced his illustrating; movement, tension, and the dynamics of living figures read clearly through his illustration. Slobodkin's role as illustrator reached an apex in Eleanor Estes's stories about the Moffats and James Thurber's *Many Moons*, for which he received the Caldecott Medal.

—Rachel Fordyce

———

SLOBODKINA, Esphyr. American. Born in Siberia, Russia, 22 September 1908; emigrated to the United States, 1928; became citizen, 1935. Educated at a Russian high school, Harbin, Manchuria; National Academy of Design, New York. Married 1) Ilya Bolotowsky in 1933 (divorced 1936); 2) William L. Urquhart in 1960 (died 1963). President, Art Development Co., New York, 1945–68; assistant export manager, CBS/Hytron, Denver and New York, 1948–57. Since 1976 president, Urquhart-Slobodkina Inc. Recipient: two Yaddo fellowships; three MacDowell fellowships. Address: 309 Southwest 8th Street, Hallandale, Florida 33009, U.S.A.

PUBLICATIONS FOR CHILDREN (illustrated by the author)

Fiction

Caps for Sale. New York, Scott, 1940; Kingswood, Surrey, World's Work, 1959.
The Wonderful Feast. New York, Lothrop, 1955.
Little Dog Lost, Little Dog Found. New York, Abelard Schuman, 1956.
The Clock. New York and London, Abelard Schuman, 1956.
The Little Dinghy. New York and London, Abelard Schuman, 1958.
Behind the Dark Window Shade. New York, Lothrop, 1958.
Billie, illustrated by Meg Wohlberg. New York, Lothrop, 1959.
Pinky and the Petunias. New York, Abelard Schuman, 1959; London, Abelard Schuman, 1962.
Moving Day for the Middlemans. New York and London, Abelard Schuman, 1960.
Jack and Jim. New York and London, Abelard Schuman, 1961.
The Long Island Ducklings. New York, Lantern Press, 1961.
Boris and His Balalaika, illustrated by Vladimir Bobri. New York and London, Abelard Schuman, 1964.

Pezzo the Peddler and the Circus Elephant [*and the Thirteen Silly Thieves*]. New York and London, Abelard Schuman, 2 vols., 1967–70.
The Flame, The Breeze, and the Shadow. Chicago, Rand McNally, 1969.
Billy, The Condominium Cat. Reading, Massachusetts, Addison Wesley, 1980.
A Portable Library of Slobodkina Children's Books. Hallandale, Florida, Urquhart Slobodkina, 1988.

Play

Caps for Sale, music and lyrics by Tamara Schildkraut, adaptation of the book by Slobodkina. Hallandale, Florida, Urquhart Slobodkina, 1981.

PUBLICATIONS FOR ADULTS

Other

Notes for a Biographer. Great Neck, New York, Urquhart Slobodkina, 3 vols., 1976–85.
American Abstract Artists: Its Publications, Catalogs, and Membership. Great Neck, New York, Urquhart Slobodkina, 2 vols., 1976–80.
Ilya Bolotowsky: Letters and Drawings 1930–47. Hallandale, Florida, Urquhart Slobodkina, n.d.

*

Illustrator: *The Little Fireman*, 1938, *The Little Farmer*, 1948, *The Little Cowboy*, 1949, and *Sleepy ABC*, 1953, all by Margaret Wise Brown; *Hiding Places* by Louise Woodcock, 1943.

*   *   *

In her picture books Esphyr Slobodkina often uses for her purposes the "functions," as they are called, that appear in traditional folk literature. Slobodkina, born in old Russia, practices her dependency on this aged genre by relying on these old tales for the general structures of many of her stories. She borrows the essentials found in their accumulative plot schemes, their repetitive actions, and their mounting sense of suspense. Then she combines all these factors with a reduced form of language that very young children can comprehend. The resultant product proves to have a merit that exceeds the praise that she has received for this work. Her picture books do have a distinctive integrity that is hers alone, although her work is sometimes confused (in name only) with that of the more highly successful Louis Slobodkin.

Slobodkina's most distinguished effort, without any doubt, has been *Caps for Sale*. The sales of this book testify that it is among the most popular of any of its kind written so far. Reported to have sold over a million copies, it easily has found its place on the all-time best seller list. Young children are smitten by this uncomplicated yet intriguing tale of a simple cap seller, who after a disappointing day takes a rest under a tree. As soon as he dozes off, however, a band of monkeys descends and steals his caps. No amount of scolding on his part can get them back, he later finds. When he shakes his fist the monkeys merely return the gesture. Finally, in total exasperation he throws his own cap to the ground, and lo, so do all the monkeys—which nicely ends the story.

None of Slobodkina's later picture books have reached this exceptional level of success. This does not mean they are lacking in merit, however. On the contrary, some of her books for the very young are near-perfect examples of the cumulative tale, a format fancied by many picture-book writers, many of whom do not carry it off as well as she does. *The Wonderful Feast* is a prime example of Slobodkina's success with this "house-that-Jack-built" type of story. Here a farmer gives his horse some feed. Then, in order, a goat ate what the horse left; a hen what the goat left; a mouse what the hen left; and an ant ate the very last grain. All thought it a "wonderful feast." Highly simplistic stories of this nature need illustrations of notable excellence. Since Slobodkina is an artist of undoubted ability (her abstract art has been given much praise) she is able to infuse the simple words of her cumulative tales with a vigor far beyond that which they inherently contain. Instead of the art work in her books overshadowing their literary content, it magnifies and focuses it.

This arrangement seems to work the best (see *The Clock*), however, when Slobodkina stays with the very short text required for the cumulative story. In some of her longer displays of verbal text her limited ability to sustain a satisfactory fictional drama is apparent. In her *Pezzo the Peddler* books, for example, she tries to concoct spin-offs of *Caps for Sale*. Here a cap peddler loses and retrieves his caps in various ways. Even Slobodkina's use of many short sentences, a great deal of dialogue, and explicit descriptions cannot overcome the repetitive plots, which are simply too weak to sustain these books. On the other hand, Slobodkina has demonstrated, as in *Boris and His Balalaika*, that when she depends on her imagination rather than her past success she is fully able to write admirable longer plots.

—Patrick Groff

SLOTE, Alfred. Also writes as A.H. Garnet. American. Has worked as an educational television producer, journalist, and teacher. Lives in Ann Arbor, Michigan. Address: c/o Lippincott, 10 East 53rd Street, New York, New York 10022, U.S.A.

PUBLICATIONS FOR CHILDREN

Fiction

The Princess Who Wouldn't Talk, illustrated by Ursula Arndt. Indianapolis, Bobbs Merrill, 1964; Kingswood, Surrey, World's Work, 1966.
Stranger on the Ball Club. Philadelphia, Lippincott, 1970.
Jake. Philadelphia, Lippincott, 1971.
The Biggest Victory. Philadelphia, Lippincott, 1972.
My Father, The Coach. Philadelphia, Lippincott, 1972.
Hang Tough, Paul Mather. Philadelphia, Lippincott, 1973.
Tony and Me. Philadelphia, Lippincott, 1974.
Matt Gargan's Boy. Philadelphia, Lippincott, 1975.
My Robot Buddy, illustrated by Joel Schick. Philadelphia, Lippincott, 1975.
The Hot Shot, photographs by William LaCrosse. New York, Watts, 1977.
My Trip to Alpha I, illustrated by Harold Berson. New York, Lippincott, 1978.
Love and Tennis. New York, Macmillan, 1979.
The Devil Rides with Me and Other Fantastic Stories. New York, Methuen, 1980.
C.O.L.A.R.: A Tale of Outer Space, illustrated by Anthony Kramer. New York, Lippincott, 1981.
Clone Catcher, illustrated by Elizabeth Slote. New York, Lippincott, 1982.
Rabbit Ears. New York, Lippincott, 1982.
Omega Station, illustrated by Anthony Kramer. New York, Lippin-

cott, 1983.
The Trouble on Janus.   New York, Lippincott, 1985.
Moving In.   New York, Lippincott, 1988.
A Friend Like That.   New York, Lippincott, 1988.
Make-Believe Ballplayer, illustrated by Tom Newsom.   New York, Lippincott, 1989.

Other

The Moon in Fact and Fancy, illustrated by John Kaufmann. Cleveland, World, 1967; revised edition, 1971.
Air in Fact and Fancy, illustrated by Dan Dickas.   Cleveland, World, 1968.

PUBLICATIONS FOR ADULTS

Novels

Denham Proper.   New York, Putnam, 1953.
Lazarus in Vienna.   New York, McGraw Hill, 1956.
Strangers and Comrades.   New York, Simon and Schuster, 1964; London, W.H. Allen, 1965.

Novels as A.H. Garnet

The Santa Claus Killer, with Garnet Garrison.   New Haven, Connecticut, Ticknor and Fields, 1981; London, Gollancz, 1982.
Maze, with Garnet Garrison.   New Haven, Connecticut, Ticknor and Fields, 1982; London, Gollancz, 1983.

Short Stories

Preparation for Retirement, with Woodrow W. Hunter.   Ann Arbor, University of Michigan Press, 1968.

Other

Termination: The Closing at Baker Plant.   Indianapolis, Bobbs Merrill, 1969.

*   *   *

The books of Alfred Slote, appropriate for children ages seven to 12, are mainly sports fiction and science fiction. Characteristics of Slote's books are action-filled plots centered around male characters.

Baseball is the topic of most of the sports books. The books deal with two common themes: developing team work and becoming the winning team. But they are unlike typical sports books because they include plot elements outside the realm of sports and provide a view that keeps sports in perspective.

In *Stranger on the Ball Club*, central character Tim Foster is the new kid in town. In addition to adjusting to that status, he is also adjusting to the death of his mother. Tim finds a baseball mitt and keeps it, even though it is marked with a boy's name. The reader gets involved in the tangled web of stealing, lying, and trying to make things right again. Complicated plots unfold in other baseball stories. In *Jake* an orphan boy must deal with living with an uncle whose only interest is music. In *Hang Tough, Paul Mather* a 12-year-old pitcher faces an incurable blood disease.

The father-son relationship is the major focus of two of Slote's baseball books. In *My Father, The Coach*, Ezell Corkins is embarrassed by the bungling efforts his father makes at coaching his team. Ezell is ashamed of his father: his job, his clothes, his forgetfulness, and his demeanor. In the course of a season, Ezell has time to reassess his feelings for his father and confirms his love for him. Danny

Gargan in *Matt Gargan's Boy* has a very different situation. His father, a major league player, is divorced from his mother. Danny must deal with his father's expectations of him, as well as the father's absence.

Through all the sports action, these books manage to keep sports in perspective. In *Stranger on the Ball Club*, Tim Foster's dad speaks for many of the characters in other books as well: "Tim, I'm happy you made the team, happy you're making friends and liking it here. You don't have to be a baseball player as far as I'm concerned. Playing ball is fun, but there are more important things in life." We are frequently reminded of this: sports are fun and exciting and enrich life, but they are not life itself; only part of it.

The science-fiction stories differ in theme. Here the characters become involved in battles of good and evil and learn to appreciate both human qualities and the beauty of the earth. Of the six future-oriented science-fiction books, four are centered around Jack Jameson and his look-alike robot Danny One. In the first story, *My Robot Buddy*, Jack is given Danny as a birthday present. Together, they foil a "robot-napper"'s attempt to steal Danny. In subsequent adventures, Jack and Danny come to sympathize with the rights of robots programmed only to work in *C.O.L.A.R.* They later risk their own safety to save Earth from Dr. Drago who is intent on blowing up the world in *Omega Station*, and uncover the plot of a would-be deceiver about to overtake the throne on a faraway planet in *The Trouble on Janus.*

All of the stories about Jack Jameson put young people in charge of their adventures as they do in the two other science-fiction adventures. In *My Trip to Alpha I* the hero thwarts a plot to trap his Aunt Katherine forever in her look-alike "dummy" while her fortune is stolen. And, in *Clone Catcher*, Arthur Dunn helps people understand the rights of clones who had been created only to be used as "spare parts" in the master's body.

A secondary theme in these books is an appreciation of the treasures of the earth. Jack asks in *My Robot Buddy* if his robot could be programmed for happiness and is told "No...I'm afraid you have to be born a human being to be able to feel happiness for free: a nice day, a pretty sunset, a birdcall...important things like this, people get just being alive."

In two recent novels Slote departs from sports fiction and science-fiction topics. Father-child relationships are explored in *Moving In*, a story about 11-year-old Robby, his sister Peggy, and their recently widowed father. Fearing his father is becoming interested in a female business associate, Robby hopes to interfere by ruining their business. In a sequel, *A Friend Like That*, Robby becomes worried about future romances of his father. In the end the plot is resolved through improved father-son communication.

Considering the works of Slote, it is apparent the questions that he is asking: What makes up the relationship of father and son? What are a father's expectations? How can a son live up to them? Slote continues to develop plots to explore to these questions.

—Mary J. Lickteig

————

SMITH, C(icely) Fox.   British.   Born in Manchester, Lancashire, in 1882. *Died 8 April 1954.*

PUBLICATIONS FOR CHILDREN

Fiction

Three Girls in a Boat, with Madge Smith.   London, Oxford University Press, 1938.

The Ship Aground, illustrated by C. Walter Hodges. London and New York, Oxford University Press, 1940.

Painted Ports, illustrated by C. Walter Hodges. London and New York, Oxford University Press, 1948.

Knave-Go-By, illustrated by Ian Ribbons. London, Oxford University Press, 1951.

Seldom Seen, with Madge Smith, illustrated by Peggy Fortnum. London, Oxford University Press, 1954.

The Valiant Sailor, illustrated by Neville Dear. London, Oxford University Press, 1955; New York, Criterion, 1957.

Other

True Tales of the Sea, illustrated by Rowland Hilder. London, Oxford University Press, 1932.

All the Other Children: A Book of Young Creatures. London, Methuen, 1933.

PUBLICATIONS FOR ADULTS

Novels

The City of Hope. London, Sidgwick and Jackson, 1914.
Singing Sands. London, Hodder and Stoughton, 1918.
Peregrine in Love. London, Hodder and Stoughton, 1920.
Peacock Pride, with Madge Smith. London, Muller, 1934.

Short Stories

Tales of the Clipper Ships. London, Methuen, and Boston, Houghton Mifflin, 1926.

Verse

Songs of Greater Britain and Other Poems. London, Simpkin, 1899.
The Foremost Trail. London, Sampson Low, 1899.
Wings of the Morning. London, Mathews, 1904.
Lancashire Hunting Songs and Other Moorland Lays. Manchester, Cornish, 1909.
Sailor Town: Sea Songs and Ballads. London, Mathews, 1914; New York, Doran, 1919.
Songs in Sail and Other Chantys. London, Mathews, 1914.
The Naval Crown: Ballads and Songs of the War. London, Mathews, 1915.
Small Craft. London, Mathews, 1917.
Small Craft: Sailor Ballads and Chantys. New York, Doran, 1919.
Songs and Chanties 1914–1916. London, Mathews, 1919.
Rhymes of the Red Ensign. London, Hodder and Stoughton, 1919.
Ships and Folks. London, Mathews, 1920.
Rovings: Sea Songs and Ballads. London, Mathews, 1921.
Sea Songs and Ballads 1917–1922. London, Methuen, 1923; Boston, Houghton Mifflin, 1924.
Full Sail: More Sea Songs and Ballads. London, Methuen, and Boston, Houghton Mifflin, 1926.
Sailor's Delight. London, Methuen, 1931.

Other

Fighting Men. London, Mathews, 1916.
Sailor Town Days. London, Methuen, and Boston, Houghton Mifflin, 1923.
A Book of Famous Ships. London, Methuen, and Boston, Houghton Mifflin, 1924.

The Return of the "Cutty Sark." London, Methuen, 1924; Boston, Lauriat, 1925.
Ship Alley: More Sailor Town Days. London, Methuen, and Boston, Houghton Mifflin, 1925.
Ancient Mariners: Some Salt Water Yesterdays. London, Methuen, 1928.
There Was a Ship: Chapters from the History of Sail. London, Methuen, 1929; Hartford, Connecticut, Mitchell, 1930.
Sail Ho! Windjammer Sketches Alow and Aloft. London, Hopkinson, and New York, Payson, 1931.
The Thames. London, Methuen, 1931.
Ocean Racers. London, Philip Allan, 1931; New York, McBride, 1932.
Anchor Lane. London, Methuen, 1933.
All the Way Round: Sea Roads to Africa. London, Joseph, 1938.
The Story of Grace Darling. London, Oxford University Press, 1940.
The Voyage of the Trevessa's Boats. London, Oxford University Press, 1940.
Thames Side Yesterdays. Leigh-on-Sea, Essex, Lewis, 1945.
Here and There in England with the Painter Brangwyn. Leigh-on-Sea, Essex, Lewis, 1945.
Country Days and Country Ways: Trudging Afoot in England. Leigh-on-Sea, Essex, Lewis, 1947.
Ship Models. London, Country Life, 1951.

Editor, *A Book of Shanties*. London, Methuen, and Boston, Houghton Mifflin, 1927.
Editor, *A Sea Chest: An Anthology of Ships and Sailormen*. London, Methuen, and Boston, Houghton Mifflin, 1927.
Editor, *The Man Before the Mast, Being the Story of Twenty Years Afloat*, by George Sorrell. London, Methuen, 1928.
Editor, *Adventures and Peril, Being Extracts from the "Mariners Chronicle" and Other Sources....* London, Joseph, 1936; New York, Dodge, 1937.

*   *   *

The literary career of C. Fox Smith must be almost unique, since she turned to children's books only after some 40 years of varied authorship, most of which was concerned with either the English countryside or maritime history. Convincing background detail of land or sea is indeed an outstanding feature of all Smith's children's books, which also have the virtue of being continuously exciting and adventurous in the old-fashioned manner of Stevenson or Rider Haggard. As regards character and plot, these books are somewhat variable in quality. Usually the story is told by a teenage boy who has nothing particular about him except courage and endurance; the villains and eccentrics, however, are often quite lively, and just occasionally there are insights into the complexity of human behaviour and relationships. The style of plotting ranges from a barely perceptible framework to an intriguing tightly woven mystery, but always tending to rely too much on gigantic coincidences.

Smith is now chiefly known for three fairly similar historical sea-adventures. *The Ship Aground* is a straightforward tale of piracy and hidden treasure, quite exciting but rarely memorable. Its sequel, *Painted Ports*, is more of a chronicle than a standard adventure story, some of its episodes being quite light-hearted and some exceedingly grim. The author is at her very best in describing the Castle of Comfort island, where the young hero finds a gang of escaped convicts practising a reign of terror. *The Valiant Sailor*, published posthumously, is distinctly more ambitious than the other two. Here one of the principal characters, the narrator's father, is sensitively portrayed as the victim of his own conscience, and there are opportunities for the discerning reader to become aware of some universal moral issues and dilemmas.

Smith's remaining children's novels are land-based and set mainly in Devon. *Seldom Seen* was written with Madge Smith, and is concerned with farming in the immediate post-war era. Although infused with plenty of authentic detail and a good measure of tension in the later stages, it lacks the spark of inspiration needed to make a lasting impression. *Knave-Go-By*, on the other hand, is an historical novel with qualities which put it very near the highest class. As well as presenting an entirely convincing picture of various levels of society in the early 19th century, it includes a skilfully unravelled mystery and a host of colourful characters, including a fine comic creation in Professor Abracadabra. This is a book of the fairly rare sort that can be offered to either the studious or the impatient reader, with good hopes of satisfying both equally.

—Alasdair K.D. Campbell

SMITH, Dodie (Dorothy Gladys Smith). Has also written as C. L. Anthony; Charles Henry Percy. British. Born in Whitefield, Lancashire, 3 May 1896. Attended Whalley Range High School, Manchester; St. Paul's Girls' School, London; studied acting at Royal Academy of Dramatic Art, London, 1914–15. Married Alec Macbeth Beesley in 1939 (died 1987). Actress, 1915–22; buyer, Heal and Son, London, 1923–32; then full-time writer. Address: The Barretts, Finchingfield, Essex, England.

PUBLICATIONS FOR CHILDREN (illustrated by Janet and Anne Grahame-Johnstone)

Fiction

The Hundred and One Dalmatians. London, Heinemann, 1956; New York, Viking Press, 1957.
The Starlight Barking: More about the Hundred and One Dalmatians. London, Heinemann, and New York, Simon and Schuster, 1967.
The Midnight Kittens. London, W.H. Allen, 1978.

PUBLICATIONS FOR ADULTS

Novels

I Capture the Castle. Boston, Little Brown, 1948; London, Heinemann, 1949.
The New Moon with the Old. London, Heinemann, and Boston, Little Brown, 1963.
The Town in Bloom. London, Heinemann, and Boston, Little Brown, 1965.
It Ends with Revelations. London, Heinemann, and Boston, Little Brown, 1967.
A Tale of Two Families. London, Heinemann, and New York, Walker, 1970.
The Girl from the Candle-Lit Bath. London, W. H. Allen, 1978.

Plays

Call It a Day (produced Glasgow and London, 1935; New York, 1936). London, Gollancz, and New York, French, 1936.
Bonnet over the Windmill (also co-director: produced Leeds and London, 1937). London, Heinemann, 1937.

Dear Octopus (also co-director: produced Newcastle upon Tyne and London, 1938; New York, 1939). London, Heinemann, 1938; New York, French, 1939.
Lovers and Friends (produced New York, 1943). New York, French, 1947.
Letter from Paris, adaptation of the novel *The Reverberator* by Henry James (produced Brighton and London, 1952). London, Heinemann, 1954.
I Capture the Castle, adaptation of her own novel (produced Blackpool and London, 1954). London, Heinemann, 1955.
These People, Those Books (produced Leeds, 1958).
Amateur Means Lover (produced Liverpool, 1961). London, French, 1962.

Plays as C.L. Anthony

British Talent (produced London, 1923).
Autumn Crocus (produced London, 1931; New York, 1932). London, Gollancz, 1931; New York, French, 1933.
Service (produced London, 1932). London, Gollancz, 1932.
Touch Wood (produced London, 1934). London, Gollancz, 1934; New York, French, 1935.

Screenplays: *Schoolgirl Rebels* (as Charles Henry Percy), 1915; *The Uninvited*, with Frank Partos, 1944; *Darling, How Could You!*, with Lesser Samuels, 1951.

Other (autobiography)

Look Back with Love: A Manchester Childhood. London, Heinemann, 1974.
Look Back with Mixed Feelings. London, W.H. Allen, 1978.
Look Back with Astonishment. London, W.H. Allen, 1979.
Look Back with Gratitude. London, Muller Blond and White, 1985.

*

Theatrical Activities:
Director: **Plays**—*Bonnet over the Windmill* (co-director, with Murray Macdonald), London, 1937; *Dear Octopus* (co-director, with Glen Byam Shaw), Newcastle upon Tyne and London, 1938.
Actress: **Plays**—in the sketch *Playgoers* by Pinero, London, 1915; *Kitty Grey* by J.S. Piggott and *Mr. Wu* by H.M. Vernon and Harold Owen, toured, 1915; *Ye Gods* by Stephen Robert and Eric Hudson, and *Jane and Niobe*, 1916–17; *When Knights Were Bold* by Charles Marlowe, London, 1917; in music-hall sketches, in the Portsmouth Repertory Company, and in a concert party in Dieppe, 1918; Claudine in *Telling the Tale*, 1919–20; *French Leave* by Reginald Berkeley, 1921; *The Shewing Up of Blanco Posnet* and *You Never Can Tell* by Shaw, London, 1921; Ann in *The Pigeon* by Galsworthy, London and Zurich, 1922.

* * *

Dodie Smith is an interesting example of a writer whose continuing popularity to some extent defies the theorists. Her characters and attitudes are noticeably "upper class" for today, while her particular brand of fantasy has been overtaken by the more drastic imaginings of writers like Joan Aiken and Roald Dahl. Even her anthropomorphism is a more sentimental sort than the conscientiously scientific animal behaviour depicted in *Watership Down*. Nevertheless, *The Hundred and One Dalmations* and its sequel, *The Starlight Barking*, are still read and loved by children of all ages in a way not to be altogether explained by the fact of a Hollywood film.

I Capture the Castle, the book which made Smith's name as a

In *Last Was Lloyd* 12-year-old Lloyd Albert, a mother-ridden and overweight sixth grader, is last in everything, especially school sports. As a result he is a bully and a glutton. Lloyd first picks on and then befriends another bright outsider, Ancil. She leads him into changing his behavior and establishing his independence from his overprotective mother.

The First Hard Times takes up where *Last Was Lloyd* left off. Ancil Witherspoon has to adjust to her mother's remarriage to Harvey Hutton and the family's subsequent move to the coastal Georgia town of Hanover. She clings to a futile hope that her real father Alexander will return though he has been reported missing-in-action for 11 years. Her change from anger and grief to an acceptance of the new marriage is deftly handled.

Moonshadow of Cherry Mountain marked quite a departure from Smith's other books in setting and main character. It is set in the North Carolina mountains where she has a simple A-frame summer cabin. Moonshadow, a Labrador retriever, belongs to Greg, the 15-year-old son of school teachers Grant and Peg Riley. While the dog has to learn to adjust his territorial boundaries as the mountain lands are developed, the people also must adjust their boundaries as families with different values move in. Greg has to adjust to the Rileys' adoption of a daughter who is allergic to and frightened of his beloved dog.

Laura Upside-Down attempts to explore deeply religious intolerance and family conflicts. The central character Laura Catherine ("Cat") is happiest seeing the world upside down, hanging from a large tree. The novel deals with her attempts to see religious and family matters right side up. Her own family is agnostic. Her 10-year-old girl friends Zipporah Greengold and Anna Banner come from respectively an orthodox Jewish family and a fundamentalist Christian one. As the girls research the origins of Halloween, Thanksgiving, Hanukkah, and Christmas in preparing seasonal parties, they learn tolerance for each other's views. Unfortunately the messages and didacticism of the novel reduce the girls to researchers rather than doers.

Much simpler and more believable is *Return to Bitter Creek*. 12-year-old Lacey Bittner, her mother Ann Campbell Bittner, and David Habib, her mother's Iranian born lover of three years and a crafts blacksmith, return to the tiny mountain community of Bitter (i.e. Bittner) Creek, North Carolina, where Ann grew up, where Lacey was born illegitimately, and from whence Ann fled from when Lacey was two. An offer of a job for David at the local Craft School brings the threesome to Bitter Creek. Though it is another book about cultural, moral, and family differences, these concerns are embodied in the actions of the characters, who, major and minor, are strong and convincing. Smith's earlier books have been occasionally faulted for being too episodic, too crowded with peripheral details or plots. This book has a nice unity; the final chapter echoes by title and action the opening.

Karate Dancer features Smith's kind of paradoxical hero. 14-year-old Troy Matthews, a karate enthusiast, is disappointed and resentful that his mother and father are not interested in his growing karate skills, and in return tries to scorn their interests in music and photography. He envies other boys who do manly activities with their fathers. As the story develops, Troy and his family learn to meet each other halfway in their interests, while recognizing their differences. A romantic interest in Liesl Trunzo leads Troy to become her partner in the ballet *Coppelia*. His conflict with three karate students from a rival studio and his demonstration of karate skills to children with muscular distrophy at a summer camp contribute to his re-definition of masculinity. Smith alludes skillfully to the developing sexuality of Troy and Liesl. Too often young adult novels, such as the popular ones by S. E. Hinton, assume their characters are numb or neuter from the waist down.

One of the most original current writers of young adult novels, Smith continues to surprise readers by the variety and depth of her books. Her latest manuscript marks another such departure, for rather than being wholly realistic, *Voyages* contains a great deal of fantasy. In it a girl who has been held hostage is recovering in a hospital. A teacher introduces her to Norse mythology, especially the adventures of Freyr and his marvelous folding boat Skidbladnir. Suddenly that boat appears and takes her to that violent mythical Norse world. Her adventures help her to cope with her own trauma.

Throughout her varied books, Smith excels in describing the exterior details and the inner life of all of her protagonists, whether nine or 17, male or female, by writing assuredly and honestly about problems and situations that her readers confront. Consequently she is highly respected by both readers and critics of modern young adult novels.

—Hugh T. Keenan

SMITH, Emma. British. Born in Newquay, Cornwall, 21 August 1923. Married R.L. Stewart-Jones in 1951 (died 1957); one son and one daughter. Recipient: Atlantic award, 1947; Rhys Memorial prize, 1949; James Tait Black Memorial prize, 1950. Agent: Curtis Brown, 162–168 Regent Street, London W1R 5TB, England.

PUBLICATIONS FOR CHILDREN

Fiction

Emily: The Story of a Traveller, illustrated by Katherine Wigglesworth. London, Nelson, 1959; as *Emily: The Travelling Guinea Pig*, New York, McDowell Obolensky, 1959.
Out of Hand, illustrated by Antony Maitland. London, Macmillan, 1963; New York, Harcourt Brace, 1964.
Emily's Voyage, illustrated by Margaret Gordon. London, Macmillan, and New York, Harcourt Brace, 1966.
No Way of Telling. London, Bodley Head, and New York, Atheneum, 1972.

PUBLICATIONS FOR ADULTS

Novels

Maidens' Trip. London, Putnam, 1948.
The Far Cry. London, MacGibbon and Kee, 1949; New York, Random House, 1950.
The Opportunity of a Lifetime. London, Hamish Hamilton, 1978; New York, Doubleday, 1980.

Other

Village Children: A Soviet Experience. Moscow, Progress, 1982.

* * *

Emma Smith is an all too occasional writer for children. There is a shortage of family adventure stories in which the emphasis is firmly on good plotting, well-organised narrative structure, compulsive pace, tension, and excitement, but in which the author also respects the intelligence of young readers and does not try to oversimplify the disconcerting muddle of emotions that children have to cope with or the inevitable rifts of understanding between child and adult.

novelist, has now, in the way of many adult novels of the previous generation, come to fit comfortably into the halfway house we think of as adolescent reading, but the one for which she will be remembered is a story written for children. *The Hundred and One Dalmations*, for all its whimsicality, has genuine charm, as well as the never-failing fascination of a quest. Pongo and Missis Pongo, bravely turning their backs on the comforts of Regents Park, set out to rescue their 15 kidnapped puppies from the clutches of wicked Cruella de Vil and her furrier husband. They face fearful hardships, meet with unexpected friendship, help, and kindness, and discover unsuspected resources in themselves which bring them back home wiser and stronger dogs than they set out. The book has faults. Coincidence is stretched to its limits, too many of the characters are stereotypes, the humour is often arch, and the relationships of the dogs to their human "pets" coy to the point of nausea. But it is also funny, warmhearted, inventive, and touching. There is much stress on the doggy virtues of loyalty, courage, tenacity, and cheerfulness in adversity, as well as the more human ones of kindness, intelligence, and initiative. Even the villains have a kind of innocence too seldom evident in more up-to-date fables.

Innocence is perhaps Smith's most notable characteristic as a writer: not the innocence of ignorance but the kind which stems from simple, uncompromising views of right and wrong. In *The Midnight Kittens*, which deals with the loving difficulties of a pair of orphaned twins and their guardian grandmother, the story hinges on the troubles born of compromising with the truth. It may well be just this reassuring sense of certainty which is at the root of her appeal to children.

—Anne Carter

SMITH, Doris Buchanan. American. Born in Washington, D.C., 1 June 1934. Educated at South Georgia College, Douglas. Married R. Caroll Smith in 1954 (divorced 1977); four sons and one daughter. Recipient: Child Study Committee award, 1973; Bread Loaf Writers Conference fellowship, 1975. Lives in North Carolina and Georgia. Address: c/o Viking Penguin Inc., 40 West 23rd Street, New York, New York 10010, U.S.A.

PUBLICATIONS FOR CHILDREN

Fiction

A Taste of Blackberries, illustrated by Charles Robinson. New York, Crowell, 1973; London, Heinemann, 1975.
Kick a Stone Home. New York, Crowell, 1974.
Tough Chauncey, illustrated by Michael Eagle. New York, Morrow, 1974.
Kelly's Creek, illustrated by Alan Tiegreen. New York, Crowell, 1975.
Up and Over. New York, Morrow, 1976.
Dreams and Drummers. New York, Crowell, 1978.
Salted Lemons. New York, Four Winds Press, 1980.
Last Was Lloyd. New York, Viking Kestrel, 1981.
Moonshadow of Cherry Mountain. New York, Four Winds Press, 1982.
The First Hard Times. New York, Viking Kestrel, 1983.
Laura Upside-Down. New York, Viking Kestrel, 1984.
Return to Bitter Creek. New York, Viking Kestrel, 1986.
Karate Dancer. New York, Putnam, 1987.

Voyages. New York, Viking Kestrel, 1989.

*   *   *

Doris Buchanan Smith's 13 novels, principally for young adult readers, describe older children's daily lives, feelings, and problems with skill, sensitivity, and honesty. Often her books have broken new ground in realistic treatments of death, divorce, obesity, juvenile delinquency, unwed mothers, dyslexia, sexual drives, foster and step parents, and child abuse. But they seldom focus on these problems. The author begins with a character and then, as she has said, the character has problems because people do in real life. Nor do her books settle for neat solutions. Just as in life, some problems can not be solved but must be adjusted to or lived with.

Certainly Smith's experience in raising five of her own and over a score of foster children contributed to her insights into the nature of older children and their families. Her first published book *A Taste of Blackberries* brought critical success and recognition of her sensitivity to the internal life of a child. Dealing directly with the death of a child's playmate, it broke a taboo of 20th-century American children's fiction. It focuses on the guilt and loss of the unnamed narrator whose best friend Jamie, "a show-off and a clown," dies from an allergic reaction to a bee sting.

Her next books, *Kick a Stone Home* and *Tough Chauncey*, deal with alienation from family and friends, but their main characters are very different. The protagonist of *Kick a Stone Home*, Sara Jane Chambers, a 15-year-old Atlanta girl, faces only adjusting to her parents' divorce and moving to a new neighborhood. But Chauncey, a 13-year-old poor white, is illiterate, delinquent, belligerent, and disobedient to both parental and school authorities. He is beaten by his religiously fundamentalist grandfather and frequently abandoned by his immature mother, who drifts through life with a low-paying job and a series of rather worthless husbands and lovers. After Jack Levitt, a black boy from another broken home and his "best friend," frames him for the theft of a bike, he seriously injures himself attempting to hitch a ride on a freight train. He soon realizes that a foster home promises him more of a chance than does his family. It is a powerful story, well told.

Kelly's Creek deals with the social and educational problems of the dyslexia of nine-year-old Kelly O'Brian. His friendship with a college student who comes to do research in the tidal creek behind their coastal Georgia home leads Kelly to develop confidence and an interest in learning which leads to success in biology class, and a better relationship to his parents and older brother. This simply written book with sparse yet significant biological details was followed by *Up and Over*, which seemed to crowd in everything remarkable about the 1960's: streaking, student protests, drug addiction, racial tension, teenage marriages or pregnancy, over-rigorous parenting, and main-streaming of the handicapped. In the much simpler, much less traumatic story *Dreams and Drummers* 14-year-old Stephanie Stone's only problem is that she fails to agonize over the ordinary teenage woes of studies and dates.

Salted Lemons marked a return to more weighty issues. Set in the Atlanta of 1943 and drawing on details of Smith's youth, the book tells how 10-year-old Darby Bannister finds herself ostracized as a Yankee from Washington, D.C. and as a hick living just inside the county line who cannot attend the city school. The novel focuses on the paradoxes of prejudice, alienation, and friendship, nicely symbolized by the salted lemons that Darby learns to share with Yoko, a Japanese-American girl whose family is subsequently interred in Florida during the World War II spy hysteria. Religious extremes are represented by Darby's father's agnosticism; her mother's conventional Methodism; the fundamentalism of Fancy Potter, a poor white girl and Darby's friend; and the millenarianism of Jeannine, another friend whose family rents Yoko's empty house. These people teach Darby the importance of tolerance.

Smith has written two novels of exceptional quality in which this balance of attention is sustained with great professional skill.

Out of Hand is a "post-Ransome" story of holiday adventure. A family of lively children are sent to spend their summer at the primitive but delightful country farmhouse where their elderly Cousin Polly lives alone. The first part of the book is an idyllic celebration of the perfect open-air holiday. When Cousin Polly breaks her ankle, however, the idyll is spoilt by the intrusion of two strait-laced spinster cousins, who set out to impose a cheerless and deadening order. The rest of the novel traces a mounting feud between the children and the interlopers. As the narrative heart of the story this is always exciting and often funny, and it culminates in satisfying "victory." Yet it is also a maturing experience for the children, who come to feel a surprised compassion for their enemy and recognise that problems and motives are less simple than they seem. Children's feelings and attitudes are fairly balanced against those of the adults, and awkward conflicts of loyalty are not evaded. The book is a fine, zestful adventure story with an ending which, though reassuring, is not simplistic.

A midwinter blizzard in the Welsh hills is the focus of Smith's thriller, *No Way of Telling*. Basically the plot is both hackneyed and improbable, a melodrama of pursuers and pursued, romantic heroism and lethal villainy. What sets the book apart is the situation summarised in its title. The girl Amy lives with her elderly grandmother in an isolated, snowbound cottage. The two of them are swept up into this violent winter of murderous conflict, knowing that good and evil are at war around them, but with no way of knowing which is which. The claustrophobic nightmare of their predicament is excellently rendered, and so is Amy's brave, resourceful answer to the dangerous truth. The vivid realism of the setting, and the sensitive observation of the central relationship between child and grandmother, give depth, conviction, and originality to this exciting story.

For small children, *Emily's Voyage* is deservedly popular. Emily is a guinea pig with a practical nature, respectable habits, and a fondness for tea. Her addiction to travel is the pretext for an incongruous comic adventure, expertly told with the directness and economy, warmth and sensitivity that also characterise Smith's distinguished and underestimated work for older readers.

—Peter Hollindale

SMITH, Vian (Crocker). British. Born in Totnes, Devon, 2 February 1920. Educated at King Edward VI Grammar School, Totnes. Served in the British Army, 1939–46. Married Susan Spark in 1942; three sons and two daughters. Actor in a touring repertory company; freelance journalist until 1950; feature and news editor of south Devon newspapers, 1950–63; full-time writer, 1963–69. *Died 9 December 1969.*

PUBLICATIONS FOR CHILDREN

Fiction

Martin Rides the Moor, illustrated by Peter Forster. London, Constable, 1964; New York, Doubleday, 1965.
The Horses of Petrock. London, Constable, 1965.
King Sam, illustrated by Peter Forster. London, Constable, 1966; as *Tall and Proud*, New York, Doubleday, 1966.
A Second Chance. New York, Doubleday, 1966.
Come Down the Mountain. London, Constable, and New York, Doubleday, 1967.
The Lord Mayor's Show. London, Longman, 1968; New York, Doubleday, 1969.
Moon in the River, illustrated by Anthony Colbert. London, Longman, 1969.

Plays

Radio Plays: *When Sam Was King*, from his novel *King Sam*, 1967; *Come Down the Mountain*, from his own novel, 1969.

Other

Vian Smith's Parade of Horses, illustrated by Michael Charlton. London, Longman, 1970; as *Horses in the Green Valley*, New York, Doubleday, 1971.

PUBLICATIONS FOR ADULTS

Novels

Song of the Unsung. London, Hodder and Stoughton, 1945.
Candles to the Dawn. London, Hodder and Stoughton, 1946.
Hungry Waters. London, Hodder and Stoughton, 1947.
The Hand of the Wind. London, Hodder and Stoughton, 1948.
Holiday for Laughter. London, Hodder and Stoughton, 1949.
So Many Worlds. London, Hodder and Stoughton, 1950.
Stars in the Morning. London, Hodder and Stoughton, 1950.
Press Gang. London, Davies, 1961.
Question Mark. London, Davies, 1961; as *Pride of the Moor*, New York, Doubleday, 1962.
Genesis Down. London, Davies, 1962; New York, Doubleday, 1963.
Green Heart. New York, Doubleday, 1964.
The First Thunder. New York, Doubleday, 1965; London, Davies, 1966.
The Wind Blows Free. London, Davies, and New York, Doubleday, 1968.
The Minstrel Boy. London, Davies, and New York, Doubleday, 1970.

Plays

Radio Plays: *Press Gang*, from his own novel, 1964; *Room for the Family*, 1964; *The White Stallion*, 1964; *Green Heart*, from his own novel, 1964; *The Boy Who Made It*, 1965; *Sunday Morning on the Hill*, 1965; *Inherit the Earth*, 1966; *Three O'Clock on the Sixteenth*, 1967.

Television Plays: *Giants on Saturday*, 1965; *The First Thunder*, from his own novel, 1967.

Other

Dartmouth: Official Guide. Dartmouth, Devon, Dartmouth Corporation, 1958 (and later editions).
Portrait of Dartmoor. London, Hale, 1966.
A Horse Named Freddie. London, Stanley Paul, 1967.
Point-to-Point. London, Stanley Paul, 1968.
The Grand National: A History of the World's Greatest Steeplechase. London, Stanley Paul, 1969; Cranbury, New Jersey, A.S. Barnes, 1970.

*

Manuscript Collection: Boston University.

*   *   *

Vian Smith's love of, and faith in, horses is the recurrent theme of his books for young people. His creation of characters, and the relationship between members of a family and their friends, are always thoughtfully drawn and display a deep knowledge of human behaviour. In none of his stories is this more revealed than in his splendid tale of a young boy who became deaf, and whose father buys him a Dartmoor pony to help him recover from the shock of the deafness, and to give him an added interest in life. In this story, *Martin Rides the Moor*, the fierce independence of the boy, the patient skill of his friend Jane, and his little sturdy pony are prime factors in the boy's recovery. At one stage, the pony escapes and joins the herd, is badly mauled by jealous mares, and even bites Martin. Then it is Jane who realises that most of the trouble stems from the fact that the Dartmoor pony is in foal. Later in the story, Martin gets lost on the moor, and accidentally finds himself in a bog, but the pony knows how to get herself and her rider safely home.

Similarly, in *King Sam* we have a story of a young girl who contracts polio. Her doctor puts up a tremendous fight for her life, insisting on regular painful exercises. Her mother indulges her, but her father sees that the doctor is right, and after considerable effort manages to buy her a pony so that the goal of one day riding King Sam may induce her to make more effort to walk. Because of her love for the pony, the goal is achieved.

In *Come Down the Mountain* young Brenda Carter is worried about a horse left in the grounds of a local empty property having to fend for himself. The horse has feet that have become diseased due to neglect. The Bassett family, in whose grounds the horse was left, are not good landowners, so that if Brenda's father stirs things up regarding the horse, it may prove awkward because his father-in-law is a Bassett tenant. However, he decides to help Brenda get attention for the horse, and in the end all is well.

Moon in the River is a totally different story of an ancient tribe on Dartmoor, and the young lad who wanted to tame a mare instead of killing her for meat. Again the tender side of looking after a horse is uppermost. In fact, though Smith's knowledge of the human race was profound, his knowledge of horses was even greater.

—Berna C. Clark

SMITH, William Jay. American. Born in Winnfield, Louisiana, 22 April 1918. Educated at Blow School, St. Louis, 1924–31; Cleveland High School, 1931–35; Washington University, St. Louis, 1935–41, B.A. 1939, M.A. in French 1941; Institut de Touraine, Tours, France, 1938; Columbia University, New York, 1946–47; Wadham College, Oxford (Rhodes Scholar), 1947–48; University of Florence, 1948–50. Served in the United States Naval Reserve, 1941–45: Lieutenant. Married 1) the poet Barbara Howes in 1947 (divorced 1965), two sons; 2) Sonja Haussmann in 1966, one stepson. Assistant in French, Washington University, 1939–41; Instructor in English and French, 1946–47, and Visiting Professor of Writing, School of the Arts, and Acting Chairman, Writing Division, 1973–75, Columbia University; Instructor in English, 1951, and poet-in-residence and Lecturer in English, 1959–64, 1966–67, Williams College, Williamstown, Massachusetts. Writer-in-residence, 1965–66, Professor of English, 1967–68 and 1970–80, and since 1980 Professor Emeritus, Hollins College, Virginia. Consultant in Poetry, 1968–70, and Honorary Consultant, 1970–76, Library of Congress, Washington, D.C.; Lecturer, Salzburg Seminar in American Studies, 1974; Fulbright Lecturer, Moscow State University, 1981; poet-in-residence, Cathedral of St. John the Divine, New York, 1986–89. Poetry reviewer, *Harper's*, New York, 1962–66; editorial consultant, Grove Press, New York, 1968–70. Democratic Member, Vermont House of Representatives, 1960–62. Recipient: Young Poets prize, 1945, and Union League Civic and Arts Foundation prize, 1964 (*Poetry*, Chicago); Alumni citation, Washington University, 1963; Ford fellowship, for drama, 1964; Henry Bellamann Major award, 1970; Loines award, 1972; National Endowment for the Arts grant, 1972; National Endowment for the Humanities grant, 1975; Gold Medal of Labor (Hungary), 1978; New England Poetry Club Golden Rose, 1980; Ingram Merrill Foundation grant, 1982. D.Litt.: New England College, Henniker, New Hampshire, 1973. Member, 1975, and vice-president for literature, 1986–89, American Academy. Agent: Marilyn Marlow, Curtis Brown, 10 Astor Place, New York, New York 10003. Address: 1675 York Avenue, Apartment 20-K, New York, New York 10128, U.S.A.

PUBLICATIONS FOR CHILDREN

Verse

Laughing Time, illustrated by Juliet Kepes. Boston, Little Brown, 1955; London, Faber, 1956.
Boy Blue's Book of Beasts, illustrated by Juliet Kepes. Boston, Little Brown, 1957.
Puptents and Pebbles: A Nonsense ABC, illustrated by Juliet Kepes. Boston, Little Brown, 1959; London, Faber, 1960.
Typewriter Town, illustrated by the author. New York, Dutton, 1960.
What Did I See?, illustrated by Don Almquist. New York, Crowell Collier, 1962.
My Little Book of Big and Little (Little Dimity, Big Gumbo, Big and Little), illustrated by Don Bolognese. Riverside, New Jersey, Rutledge, 3 vols., 1963.
Ho for a Hat!, illustrated by Ivan Chermayeff. Boston, Little Brown, 1964; revised edition, 1989.
If I Had a Boat, illustrated by Don Bolognese. New York, Macmillan, 1966; Kingswood, Surrey, World's Work, 1967.
Mr. Smith and Other Nonsense, illustrated by Don Bolognese. New York, Delacorte Press, 1968.
Around My Room and Other Poems, illustrated by Don Madden. New York, Lancelot Press, 1969.
Grandmother Ostrich and Other Poems, illustrated by Don Madden. New York, Lancelot Press, 1969.

Other

Editor, with Louise Bogan, *The Golden Journey: Poems for Young People*, illustrated by Fritz Kredel. Chicago, Reilly and Lee, 1965; London, Evans, 1967.
Editor, *Poems from France*, illustrated by Roger Duvoisin. New York, Crowell, 1967.
Editor, *Poems from Italy*, illustrated by Elaine Raphael. New York, Crowell, 1972.
Editor, *A Green Place: Modern Poems*, illustrated by Jacques Hnizdovsky. New York, Delacorte Press, 1982.

Translator, *Children of the Forest*, by Elsa Beskow, illustrated by Beskow. New York, Delacorte Press, 1970.
Translator, *The Pirate Book*, by Lennart Hellsing, illustrated by Poul Ströyer. New York, Delacorte Press, and London, Benn, 1972.
Translator, with Max Hayward, *The Telephone*, by Kornei Chukovsky, illustrated by Blair Lent. New York, Delacorte Press, 1977.

PUBLICATIONS FOR ADULTS

Play

The Straw Market, music by the author (produced Washington, D.C., 1965; New York, 1969).

Verse

Poems.   New York, Banyan Press, 1947.
Celebration at Dark.   London, Hamish Hamilton, and New York, Farrar Straus, 1950.
Typewriter Birds.   New York, Caliban Press, 1954.
The Bead Curtain: Calligrams.   Privately printed, 1957.
Poems 1947–1957.   Boston, Little Brown, 1957.
Two Poems.   Pownal, Vermont, Mason Hill Press, 1959.
Prince Souvanna Phouma: An Exchange Between Richard Wilbur and William Jay Smith.   Williamstown, Massachusetts, Chapel Press, 1963.
The Tin Can and Other Poems.   New York, Delacorte Press, 1966.
New and Selected Poems.   New York, Delacorte Press, 1970.
A Rose for Katherine Anne Porter.   New York, Albondocani Press, 1970.
At Delphi: For Allen Tate on His Seventy-Fifth Birthday, 19 November 1974.   Williamstown, Massachusetts, Chapel Press, 1974.
Venice in the Fog.   Greensboro, North Carolina, Unicorn Press, 1975.
Verses on the Times, with Richard Wilbur.   New York, Gutenberg Press, 1978.
Journey to the Dead Sea: A Poem.   Omaha, Abattoir, 1979.
The Tall Poets.   Winston-Salem, North Carolina, Palaemon Press, 1979.
The Traveler's Tree: New and Selected Poems.   New York, Persea, 1980; Manchester, Carcanet, 1981.
Collected Translations: Italian, French, Spanish, Portuguese.   St. Paul, Minnesota, New Rivers Press, 1985.
The Tin Can.   Roslyn, New York, Stone House Press, 1988.
Journey to the Interior.   Roslyn, New York, Stone House Press, 1988.
Plain Talk: Epitaphs, Satires, Nonsense, Occasional, Concrete and Quotidian Poems.   New York, Center for Book Arts, 1988.

Christmas Card Poems (with Barbara Howes): *Lachrymae Christi and In the Old Country*, 1948; *Poems: The Homecoming and The Piazza*, 1949; *Two French Poems: The Roses of Saadi and Five Minute Watercolor*, 1950—all privately printed.

Other

The Spectra Hoax (criticism).   Middletown, Connecticut, Wesleyan University Press, 1961.
Children and Poetry: A Selective Annotated Bibliography, with Virginia Haviland.   Washington, D.C., Library of Congress, 1969; revised edition, 1979.
Louise Bogan: A Woman's Words.   Washington, D.C., Library of Congress, 1972.
The Streaks of the Tulip: Selected Criticism.   New York, Delacorte Press, 1972.
Army Brat: A Memoir.   New York, Persea, 1980; London, Penguin, 1982.

Editor and Translator, *Selected Writings of Jules Laforgue.*   New York, Grove Press, 1956.
Editor, *Herrick.*   New York, Dell, 1962.

Editor, *Light Verse and Satires*, by Witter Bynner.   New York, Farrar Straus, and London, Faber, 1978.
Editor, with Emanuel Brasil, *Brazilian Poetry 1950–1980.*   Middletown, Connecticut, Wesleyan University Press, 1983; London, Harper, 1984.
Editor, with J.S. Holmes, *Dutch Interior: Post-War Poetry of the Netherlands and Flanders.*   New York, Columbia University Press, 1984.
Editor, with Dana Gioia, *Poems from Italy.*   St. Paul, Minnesota, New Rivers Press, 1985.
Editor, with F.D. Reeve, *An Arrow in the Wall: Selected Poetry and Prose of Andrei Voznesensky.*   New York, Holt, and London, Secker and Warburg, 1987.

Translator, *Scirroco*, by Romualdo Romano.   New York, Farrar Straus, 1951.
Translator, *Poems of a Multimillionaire*, by Valéry Larbaud.   New York, Bonaccio and Saul, 1955.
Translator, *Two Plays by Charles Bertin: Christopher Columbus and Don Juan.*   Minneapolis, University of Minnesota Press, 1970.
Translator, with Leif Sjöberg, *Agadir*, by Artur Lundkvist.   Pittsburgh, International Poetry Forum, 1979.
Translator, with Ingvar Schousboe, *The Pact: My Friendship with Isak Dinesen*, by Thorkild Bjørnvig.   Baton Rouge, Louisiana State University Press, 1983.
Translator, *Moral Tales*, by Jules Laforgue.   New York, New Directions, 1985; London, Picador, 1987.
Translator, with Leif Sjöberg, *Wild Bouquet: Nature Poems*, by Henry Martinson.   Kansas City, Missouri, Bookmark Press, 1985.
Translator, with Edwin Morgan and others, *Eternal Moment: Selected Poems*, by Sandor Weöres.   St. Paul, Minnesota, New Rivers Press, and London, Anvil Press, 1988.
Translator, with Sonja Haussmann Smith, *The Madman and the Medusa*, by Tchicaya U Tam'Si.   Charlottesville, Virginia, University Press of Virginia, 1989.

*

Manuscript Collection: Washington University, St. Louis.

*   *   *

William Jay Smith represents an unusual phenomenon, that of a serious poet for adults trying to be funny—for children. It is understandable, then, that when this prize-winning poet showed a colleague his first attempts he was greeted with hoots of surprise bordering on reproach. This does not mean that Smith went into this new venture half-cocked, however. Smith was also a critic of poetry, and had given much thought as to what poetry should be and do. Smith's contributions to children's literature, therefore, present a rare opportunity to find out if a writer's work lives up to his expectations. There is a further interest, since Smith tells us that writing children's poems has given him the chance to explore themes he developed in his works for adults.

In Smith's books of poetry for children it can be seen, first, that his writing does fulfill to a large extent one of his major goals, to "risk everything and play for the highest stakes." It is clear that Smith's books of poetry for children offer many cleverly written bits of infectious nonsense on a wide range of topics. From page to page there is no telling what Smith will do next.

Second, most of Smith's poems for children reflect the technical soundness of good adult poetry, a standard which Smith has set for poems for the young. In general, his rhymes are usually bright and strong, his topics are the kind with appeal for children, and his figures of speech are far from clichés, yet well within the intellectual grasp of his readers (e.g. "Toaster": "a silver-scaled Dragon with Jaws of flaming red"). In Smith's collections of adult poetry he has been praised for "much leaving out, and stern self-correction." While there are bewildering exceptions to this seen in his poems for children, by and large they do reflect his studious effort. While some of his lines diminish into simple chatter, often of a playground variety (e.g. "Over and under/Over and under/Crack the whip/And hear it thunder"), and while Smith reverts at times to practical matters (e.g. in his poem "Dictionary"), his offerings to children usually aim to explore and try out new things and to maintain a sense of poesy.

Another goal Smith has set for poetry is that variety is everything. His poems for children certainly do explore a wide range of unexpected topics. The exasperation one often feels in reading conventional anthologies of poetry for children, with their seemingly endless items on nature and goodness ("sentimental drivel," Smith calls them), never applies to Smith. His heterogeneous offerings are a buffer against this. This exemption is also partly achieved from a fulfillment of another of his precepts for poetry, that it should be humorous. The chuckles abound in his books, almost on every page.

Finally, it is also true that in general Smith gets to his poem-making for children with "directness and élan—and without fuss," as he has said it should be done. His poems are playfully graphic, full of imagery, and song-like. This aspect of his writing is enhanced by his intensive use of verbs and nouns to carry the impact of what he says. Smith's direct approach to his task is also shown by his lack of pretension and condescension: he is obviously excited about experimenting with language for children, and the excitement shows.

—Patrick Groff

SMUCKER, Barbara Claassen. American: Canadian Landed Immigrant. Born in Newton, Kansas, 1 September 1915. Educated at Bethel College, North Newton, Kansas, 1932–33; Kansas State University, Manhattan, 1933–36, B.S. in journalism 1936; Rosary College Library School, River Forest, Illinois, 1963–65; University of Waterloo, Ontario, 1975–77. Married Donovan E. Smucker in 1939; two sons and one daughter. Teacher of journalism and English, Harper High School, Kansas, 1937–38; reporter, Newton *Evening Kansan*, 1939–41; teacher, Ferry Hall School, Lake Forest, Illinois, 1960–63; bookseller, Lake Forest Bookstore, 1963–67; children's librarian, Kitchener Public Library, Ontario, 1969–77; head librarian, 1977–82, and since 1982 Senior Fellow, Renison College, University of Waterloo. Recipient: Ruth Schwartz award, 1980; Canada Council prize, 1980; Kansas State University Distinguished Service award, 1980; Vicky Metcalf award, 1988. Litt.D.: University of Waterloo, 1986. Honorary Fellow, Renison College, 1982. Address: 57 McDougall Road, Waterloo, Ontario N2L 2W4, Canada.

PUBLICATIONS FOR CHILDREN

Fiction

Henry's Red Sea, illustrated by Allan Eitzen. Scottdale, Pennsylvania, Herald Press, 1955.
Cherokee Run, illustrated by Allan Eitzen. Scottdale, Pennsylvania, Herald Press, 1957.
Wigwam in the City, illustrated by Gil Miret. New York, Dutton, 1966; as *Susan*, New York, Scholastic, 1972.
Underground to Canada, illustrated by Tom McNeely. Toronto, Clarke Irwin, 1977; London, Penguin, 1978; as *Runaway to Freedom*, New York, Harper, 1977.
Days of Terror, illustrated by Kim La Fave. Toronto, Clarke Irwin, and Scottdale, Pennsylvania, Herald Press, 1979; London, Penguin, 1981.
Amish Adventure. Toronto, Irwin, and Scottdale, Pennsylvania, Herald Press, 1983; London, Penguin, 1984.
White Mist. Toronto, Irwin, 1985.
Jacob's Little Giant. Markham, Ontario, Penguin, 1987; New York, Viking Kestrel, 1988.
Jumbo. Toronto, Doubleday, 1989.

PUBLICATIONS FOR ADULTS

Play

The Abiding Place (oratorio), music by Ester Wiebe (produced Strasbourg, France, 1984). Winnipeg, Manitoba, Canadian Mennonite College, 1984.

*

Manuscript Collection: Kerlan Collection, University of Minnesota, Minneapolis.

Barbara Claassen Smucker comments:
Ideas for my books come in many ways. When they come it is with a pinch of magic, a drop of inspiration, and a great deal of excitement. I write for young people because I like their fresh response, buoyant enthusiasm, and honest frankness. I like my story heroes to have difficult goals to win and to strive for values that are the very best in our society.

*   *   *

Barbara Claassen Smucker's books treat issues with contemporary relevance within the framework of well-researched fiction based on specific historic events. Her books, informed by a compassionate understanding of human nature borne of her own Mennonite heritage, frequently show two ideologies or cultures in conflict with each other. The focus on the child's bruising encounters within this larger context allows for a satisfying resolution of the particular situation while giving the child reader insight into the causes of human fallability or social injustice in a contemporary world. Her books to date have dealt with political oppression, religious intolerance, cultural clashes, and the destruction of natural resources.

Two of her books deal with the Mennonites. *Henry's Red Sea*, an early account of their exodus from Europe, primarily conveys information about this religious sect. *Days of Terror*, her later treatment of the same narrative field, has much greater scope and psychological depth; it depicts the mass migration of Mennonites from the Russian Ukraine to Canada and the United States, and it records, through the eyes of a 10-year-old boy, the injustice suffered by the peaceful and hard-working Mennonites during the terror imposed by anarchy and famine during the 1917 Russian Revolution. *Underground to Canada* presents a much different kind of victimization, that of 19th-century American blacks. The heroine, a courageous young black girl, makes her way to Ontario, Canada through the "underground railway," seeking freedom and the promise of a happier life. *Wigwam in the City* portrays the cultural differences and social disharmony between American Indians and whites when the family of a young Indian girl moves from the reservation to Chicago so her father can find work. Though the events and psychological twists occasionally seem forced, the story has a true cultural basis. *White Mist*, a later book which treats Indian-white relations within the larger framework of current concerns over the death of forests because of acid rain, is a skillfully handled time-fantasy. *Jacob's Little Giant*, a book for younger children, continues the theme of the natural environment by focusing on a little boy's attachment to a giant Canada goose family that is recolonized on his father's farm by the Department of Natural Resources. *Amish Adventure* is a compelling and complex story of the encounter between two groups in contemporary Canadian society—the predominant empire-building Scots-Canadian and the minority Canadian-Amish who eschew modernization, maintaining 19th-century farming and living practices. Written from the perspective of a 12-year-old Scottish-Canadian boy who was riding in a speeding car that crashed into a horse and buggy on a country road, the story treats the boy's attempts to counter-act the ensuing devastation. Like Smucker's other books, this one gives indepth treatment to psychological, generational, and cultural forces which cause human intolerance and conflict.

—Mary Rubio

SNEDEKER, Caroline Dale (née Owen). Also wrote as Caroline Dale Owen. American. Born in New Harmony, Indiana, 23 March 1871. Educated at College of Music, Cincinnati. Married Charles Henry Snedeker in 1903 (died). Concert pianist and composer, early 1900's. *Died 22 January 1956.*

PUBLICATIONS FOR CHILDREN

Fiction

The Coward of Thermopylae. New York, Doubleday, 1911; as *The Spartan*, Doubleday, 1912; London, Hodder and Stoughton, 1913.
The Perilous Seat. New York, Doubleday, and London, Methuen, 1923.
Theras and His Town, illustrated by Mary Haring. New York, Doubleday, and London, Heinemann, 1924.
Downright Dencey, illustrated by Maginel Wright Barney. New York, Doubleday, and London, Heinemann, 1927.
The Beckoning Road, illustrated by Manning Lee. New York, Doubleday, 1929.
The Forgotten Daughter, illustrated by Dorothy P. Lathrop. New York, Doubleday, 1933.
Uncharted Ways, illustrated by Manning Lee. New York, Doubleday, 1935.
The White Isle, illustrated by Fritz Kredel. New York, Doubleday, 1940.
Luke's Quest, illustrated by Nora S. Unwin. New York, Doubleday, 1947.
A Triumph for Flavius, illustrated by Cedric Rogers. New York, Lothrop, 1955.
Lysis Goes to the Play, illustrated by Reisie Lonette. New York, Lothrop, 1962.

Other

The Black Arrowhead: Legends of Long Island, illustrated by Manning Lee. New York, Doubleday, 1929.

PUBLICATIONS FOR ADULTS

Novel

Seth Way (as Caroline Dale Owen). Boston, Houghton Mifflin, 1917.

Other

The Town of the Fearless (on New Harmony, Indiana). New York, Doubleday, 1931.

*   *   *

Many of the details of Caroline Dale Snedeker's life are important in a discussion of her writing, for her work was much influenced by certain people and places. Her birthplace, New Harmony, Indiana, had been founded as an ideal Utopian community by her great-grandfather, Robert Owen. From her grandmother she heard stories about the town's early days, and she used this narrative material in three of her books. Her family was a cultivated one, much interested in art, literature, and music. In her autobiographical essays she spoke of nine Italian paintings of Greek gods and goddesses which hung in her house when she was a child, and she pointed out their influence on her later work: "These same gods and goddesses…peopled my childish world and have never gone away. I have truly felt that to write about ancient Greece is a privilege."

It was Caroline's husband, the dean of St. Paul's Cathedral in Cincinnati and an excellent critic and teacher, who encouraged her to write. With his help she embarked upon a study of the classics, which provided her with the background of her first novel and of several of her subsequent ones. *The Coward of Thermopylae* did not achieve the recognition it deserved until it was reissued in a format more appealing to young readers under a new title, *The Spartan*. Not for several years did she write another novel; but *The Perilous Seat* enjoyed the same wide popularity as its predecessor. Snedeker traveled abroad—to Greece and Italy and to England, where her experiences in Cornwall and Devon brought her the keen interest in early Christianity in Britain which is evident in *The White Isle*; her account of a first-century church service "has been noted and cited as a reliable description."

A visit to Nantucket gave the author the inspiration for *Downright Dencey*, written while she was grief-stricken over the death of her husband. The novel, which remained in print for over half a century, recreates the unique atmosphere of the island in the early 19th century; its chief character is an impulsive, warmhearted Quaker girl. Beautifully written with an intensity of feeling, the book has been an enduring source of reading pleasure.

For many years Snedeker's books were avidly read by young people—and older ones as well. Her careful, scholarly research gave her work vividness and authenticity; and her integration of historical fact with highly imaginative plots as well as her sympathetic handling of characters added great vitality.

—Ethel L. Heins

SNYDER, Zilpha Keatley. American. Born in Lemoore, California, 11 May 1927. Educated at Whittier College, California, 1944–48, B.A. 1948; University of California, Berkeley, summers 1958–60. Married Larry A. Snyder in 1950; one daughter and two sons. Elementary school teacher, California, New York, Washington, D.C., and Alaska, 1948–62. Recipient: Christopher award, 1971, 1972; George G. Stone Center for Children's Books award, 1973. Address: 52 Miller Avenue, Mill Valley, California 94941, U.S.A.

PUBLICATIONS FOR CHILDREN

Fiction

Season of Ponies, illustrated by Alton Raible. New York,

Atheneum, 1964.

The Velvet Room, illustrated by Alton Raible. New York, Atheneum, 1965.

Black and Blue Magic, illustrated by Gene Holtan. New York, Atheneum, 1966.

The Egypt Game, illustrated by Alton Raible. New York, Atheneum, 1967.

Eyes in the Fishbowl, illustrated by Alton Raible. New York, Atheneum, 1968.

The Changeling, illustrated by Alton Raible. New York, Atheneum, 1970; Guildford, Surrey, Lutterworth Press, 1976.

The Headless Cupid, illustrated by Alton Raible. New York, Atheneum, 1971; Guildford, Surrey, Lutterworth Press, 1973.

The Witches of Worm, illustrated by Alton Raible. New York, Atheneum, 1972.

The Princess and the Giants, illustrated by Beatrice Darwin. New York, Atheneum, 1973.

The Truth about Stone Hollow, illustrated by Alton Raible. New York, Atheneum, 1974; as *The Ghosts of Stone Hollow*, Guildford, Surrey, Lutterworth Press, 1978.

Below the Root, illustrated by Alton Raible. New York, Atheneum, 1975.

And All Between, illustrated by Alton Raible. New York, Atheneum, 1976.

Until the Celebration, illustrated by Alton Raible. New York, Atheneum, 1977.

The Famous Stanley Kidnapping Case, illustrated by Alton Raible. New York, Atheneum, 1979.

A Fabulous Creature. New York, Atheneum, 1981.

Come On, Patsy, illustrated by Margot Zemach. New York, Atheneum, 1982.

The Birds of Summer. New York, Atheneum, 1983.

Blair's Nightmare. New York, Atheneum, 1984.

The Changing Maze, illustrated by Charles Mikolaycak. New York, Macmillan, 1985.

And Condors Danced. New York, Delacorte Press, 1987; London, Macmillan, 1989.

Squeak Saves the Day and Other Tooley Tales, illustrated by Leslie Morrill. New York, Delacorte Press, 1988.

Janie's Private Eyes. New York, Delacorte Press, 1989.

Verse

Today Is Saturday, photographs by John Arms. New York, Atheneum, 1969.

PUBLICATIONS FOR ADULTS

Novel

Heirs of Darkness. New York, Atheneum, 1978; London, Magnum, 1980.

*

Manuscript Collection: Kerlan Collection, University of Minnesota, Minneapolis.

Zilpha Keatley Snyder comments:

I am a fiction writer with a decided list towards the fantastical. Like most writers I write for the joy of it, to exorcise old ghosts, and because I can't seem to stop, but I am also aware of a very personal motivation. I write as a legitimate means of indulging in an apparently inborn vice—the tendency to make things up. I write for middle-aged children (9–14) because they are magical people.

*   *   *

The most outstanding characteristic of Zilpha Keatley Snyder's work is her sensitivity to, respect for, and appreciation of children. She seems to be attuned to the process of growing up, a process in which the imaginative young people Snyder writes about move freely between the everyday world adults know and the fanciful worlds children create to nourish the growth of their own minds and spirits. Although many of her characters read fantasy, they do not enter into someone else's fantasy world; they create their own worlds, often in groups through role playing or creative play. Sometimes an individual character, such as Robin in *The Velvet Room*, will enter into a very private world which walls her off from the harsh realities of the world outside; but even then that world is used not just to hide but to gather strength, to learn to be more or different or better than one has been before. Snyder capitalizes on the creative acts of the child without demeaning them. In addition, her novels possess a distinct charm and energy that carry readers into a story with the help of detailed descriptions and familiar characteristics.

The Stanley children are the main characters in four of Snyder's books, and each child in the family is notable for specific gifts and talents. Readers are introduced to the family in *The Headless Cupid* and Amanda immediately captures interest with her bizarre costume and her crow which she says is her "Familiar." Although Amanda is a stepsister to the Stanley children, she develops a strong and growing relationship with the younger half-siblings. The author respects young readers enough to have her characters, in this case the Stanley children, both accept and participate in Amanda's role playing while seeing through it as the means their stepsister uses to cope with her parents' divorce and her mother's remarriage. Even Amanda seems to be aware of what she is doing. In *The Famous Stanley Kidnapping Case*, it is Amanda's boastful tongue that causes the trouble but the united effort of all the children rescues them when they are captured by Red Mask and his gang. Snyder draws upon Blair's wild imagination to develop the story of *Blair's Nightmare* in which he seeks to bend the family's "no pets" rule but almost causes a tragedy in the process. In *Janie's Private Eyes*, the latest of the Stanley family novels, neighborhood pets are suddenly missing. A Vietnamese family is blamed; and Janie, with the aid of her family and Thuy and Huy Tran, seeks to solve this mystery and find the missing dogs with the aid of her newly formed detective agency.

Another group of books is Snyder's Greensky trilogy—*Below the Root*, *And All Between*, and *Until the Celebration*. Together these works create a richly detailed fanciful world beneath the cities above ground. Those that live in Greensky are often tempted to eat the wissenberries which make them drowsy, but here too the classic battles between good and evil are fought.

The Egypt Game is probably one of this author's most popular novels, and certainly one of her best. The Egypt game is an elaborate game played in a secret "temple" and filled with ritualistic gestures. Through his observations of the game, an old professor takes a new interest in life and ultimately saves the children from unexpected danger. Although there is no special note taken of the fact, the players are a mixed group racially and ethnically which was at the time of publication (1967) still somewhat rare in American books for children. Readers already know and care about April, Melanie, and Elizabeth as people before necessarily realizing that they are respectively caucasian, black, and Chinese.

Snyder has said that *The Witches of Worm* grew from her reading of historical accounts of the Salem witch trials and from observations of the strange personality of a kitten in the family. In this story Jessica brings home a skinny, ugly-looking kitten called Worm, although she never liked cats. Soon she begins doing mean things she would never do on her own, and realizes that Worm is really a witch's cat who has cast a spell on her. One of the strengths of this story is the fine line that divides the imagination of this lonely child who has been deserted by her father from the world of the supernatural.

Many of the young girls in Snyder's stories are lonely, either actually deserted by parents or left to their own devices for other reasons. Pamela in *Season of Ponies*, Snyder's first book, is unhappy because her father left her at Oak Farm with two stern old aunts for the summer. With the aid of an amulet her father gave her, however, Pamela meets a strange young man who appears out of the mist surrounded by horses and playing his flute. *The Changeling* is told in retrospect by a high school sophomore who reflects on the effect Ivy Carson, the eccentric dancer daughter of a large, troublesome family, had on Martha's own blossoming from a very shy young girl to an aspiring actress. Summer McIntyre of *The Birds of Summer* has no father and her mother doesn't seem to be able to take responsibility for herself let alone her two daughters, so 16-year-old Summer has to be responsible for the three of them. In this book it is as much the mother as the daughter who seems to be walking the fine line between reality and fantasy in the process of growing up. Summer does imagine a caring father and writes letters to him which she keeps in a box, but basically she is a very level-headed young woman dealing with serious problems created by the mother who should have been caring for her.

Carly in *And Condors Danced* feels that she is invisible most of the time. Her mother is ill and her father for the most part stern and indifferent, so she escapes to the mountains or to her Aunt Mehitabel's where she is freer to indulge her imagination. But reality intrudes on her spirited imaginative adventures and she has to cope with many real-life tragedies in this story set on a California ranch at the turn of the century. Robin of *The Velvet Room* separates herself from pressing family problems by "wandering off," both literally and figuratively. The velvet room of the title is the library of a deserted old house where Robin goes to read and dream about another life.

Black and Blue Magic, Eyes in the Fishbowl, and *A Fabulous Creature* all have young male protagonists. Harry Houdini Marco is almost 12 when he helps an old man on a city bus and is rewarded with magical wings. This is one of Snyder's funniest novels when the magic of the wings is juxtaposed with the problems of everyday life of a rather clumsy child, resulting in the "black and blue" of the title. Dion in *Eyes in the Fishbowl* gets involved in strange, perhaps supernatural events in a large, realistically described department store. In *A Fabulous Creature* James Fielding's "Don Juan Project," a plan to make him irresistible to girls, has to be carried out at an isolated resort where his parents take him for the summer.

Squeak Saves the Day and Other Tooley Tales is a collection of seven stories for younger readers featuring the Tooley family, very small creatures who live in a miniature world threatened by humans whom they call Stompers. These are short, very humorous stories of pure fantasy unlike most of Snyder's books for older children which exist in that fragile and magical space between reality and fantasy.

In most of her books, Snyder's characters are very real and believable young people who just happen to have a touch of magic. The real essence of child-life in her novels is in their creative lives, in the mysteries of that which is not quite known—or even knowable. This life of the imagination, played out slightly off center stage, helps characters cope effectively with the concerns of everyday existence.

—Kay E. Vandergrift

SOBOL, Donald J. American. Born in New York City, 4 October 1924. Educated at Fieldston School, New York, 1942; Oberlin College, Ohio, B.A. 1948; New School for Social Research, New York, 1949–51. Served in the United States Army Corps of En-

gineers, 1943–46. Married Rose Tiplitz in 1955; one daughter and three sons (one deceased). Reporter, New York *Sun*, 1948, and *Long Island Daily Press*, New York, 1949–51; buyer, R.H. Macy's, New York, 1953–54. Wrote "Two-Minute Mystery" syndicated newspaper series, 1959–68. Recipient: Mystery Writers of America Edgar Allan Poe award, 1975. Lives in Miami. Agent: McIntosh and Otis Inc., 310 Madison Avenue, New York, New York 10017, U.S.A.

PUBLICATIONS FOR CHILDREN

Fiction

The Double Quest, illustrated by Lili Réthi. New York, Watts, 1957.
The Lost Dispatch, illustrated by Anthony Palumbo. New York, Watts, 1958.
Encyclopedia Brown, Boy Detective, [and the Case of the Secret Pitch, Finds the Clues, Gets His Man, Solves Them All, Keeps the Peace, Saves the Day, Tracks Them Down, Shows the Way, Takes the Case, Lends a Hand, and the Case of the Dead Eagles, and the Case of the Midnight Visitor, Carries On, Sets the Pace, and the Case of the Mysterious Handprints, and the Case of the Treasure Hunt], illustrated by Leonard Shortall, Lillian Bradi, Ib Ohlsson, and Gail Owens. New York and Nashville, Nelson, 13 vols., 1963–77; New York, Four Winds Press, 2 vols., 1980–81; New York, Morrow, 2 vols., 1985–88; 6 vols. published London, Hamish Hamilton, 1980.
Secret Agents Four, illustrated by Leonard Shortall. New York, Four Winds Press, 1967.
Two-Minute Mysteries [*More* and *Still More Two-Minute Mysteries*]. New York, Scholastic, 3 vols., 1967–75.
Greta the Strong, illustrated by Trina Schart Hyman. Chicago, Follett, 1970.
Milton, The Model A, illustrated by Joan Drescher. Irvington-on-Hudson, New York, Harvey House, 1971.
Angie's First Case, illustrated by Gail Owens. New York, Four Winds Press, 1981.
Encyclopedia Brown (omnibus), illustrated by Leonard Shortall. London, Angus and Robertson, 1983.
Encyclopedia Brown Takes the Cake!, with Glenn Andrews, illustrated by Ib Ohlsson. New York, Four Winds Press, 1983.
The Amazing Power of Ashur Fine. New York, Macmillan, 1986.

Other

The First Book of Medieval Man, illustrated by Lili Réthi. New York, Watts, 1959; revised edition, as *The First Book of Medieval Britain*, London, Mayflower, 1960.
Two Flags Flying (biographies of Civil War leaders), illustrated by Jerry Robinson. New York, Platt and Munk, 1960.
The Wright Brothers at Kitty Hawk, illustrated by Stuart Mackenzie. New York, Nelson, 1961.
The First Book of the Barbarian Invaders, A.D. 375–511, illustrated by W. Kirtman Plummer. New York, Watts, 1962; London, Ward, 1963.
The First Book of Stocks and Bonds, with Rose Sobol. New York, Watts, 1963.
Lock, Stock, and Barrel (biographies of American Revolutionary War leaders), illustrated by Edward J. Smith. Philadelphia, Westminster Press, 1965.
The Amazons of Greek Mythology. South Brunswick, New Jersey, A.S. Barnes, and London, Yoseloff, 1972.
True Sea Adventures. Nashville, Nelson, 1975.
Disaster. New York, Pocket Books, 1979.
Encyclopedia Brown's [Second, Third] Record Book of Weird and

Wonderful Facts, illustrated by Sal Murdocca and Bruce Degen. New York, Delacorte Press, 3 vols., 1979–85.

Encyclopedia Brown's Book of Wacky Crimes [*Spies, Sports, Animals, Cars, Outdoors*], illustrated by Ted Enik. New York, Lodestar, 1 vol., 1982; New York, Morrow, 5 vols., 1984–87.

Editor, *A Civil War Sampler*, illustrated by Henry S. Gillette. New York, Watts, 1961.
Editor, *An American Revolutionary War Reader*. New York, Watts, 1964.
Editor, *The Strongest Man in the World*, illustrated by Cliff Schule. Philadelphia, Westminster Press, 1967.
Editor, *The Best Animal Stories of Science Fiction and Fantasy*. New York, Warne, 1979.

*

Manuscript Collection: Kerlan Collection, University of Minnesota, Minneapolis.

Donald J. Sobol comments:
I have tried to write the kinds of books I wanted to read when I was a boy but could not find.

* * *

Donald J. Sobol's Encyclopedia Brown series is well loved by middle-grade readers. Each book contains 10 mysteries, all solved by the boy detective, Encyclopedia Brown, son of the Chief of Police. The reader is also able to solve the mysteries; solutions are printed in the back of each book. The books are simply written in short, clear sentences. Each chapter is self-contained and quite brief. No time is wasted on description or character development. Idaville, Encyclopedia's home town, is a thinly sketched Anywhere, U.S.A. The people in Idaville are all two-dimensional, and easily divided into good guys and bad guys. This simplicity, brevity, and clarity are all a boon to the reluctant or shaky reader.

Complexity in writing style is not Sobol's intent, nor is it required for the success of these books. Although the stories are simply written, they are clever and fresh, and seldom obvious or easy to solve. The twist comes in the thinking, not in the vocabulary or the sentence structure. Each mystery is unpredictable and cannot be solved with the same techniques or logic that solve other cases. Sometimes we are looking at motive, sometimes at contradiction, sometimes at physical evidence. The logic and the type of clues are always changing. What is required to solve these is careful, meticulous reading. The hesitant, painstaking reader is rewarded. He has a distinct advantage over the skimmer. The tortoise wins the race.

In addition to the clever twists in the clues, these mysteries are funny in a goofy, childlike way that matches the simple writing style. They are loaded with puns and funny phrases. They also contain eccentric characters and outrageous situations which alternate with everyday events: the ordinary and the extraordinary mix.

In a sense these are formula books; the design of each is the same. This standardized structure might give the hesitant reader a sense of familiarity and therefore, confidence. But these books are not formula stories in their plot and logic. The uniformity in design is coupled with originality in thinking.

The key to Encyclopedia Brown's enormous popularity is enjoyment. The books are easy to read and fun to solve. They star a child who is the smartest person in town. And, as if that wasn't satisfying enough, the children who read and solve these prove that they are just as smart as Encyclopedia Brown himself.

—Christine McDonnell

SOFTLY, Barbara (née Frewin). British. Born in Ewell, Surrey, 12 March 1924. Educated at Nonsuch County Grammar School, Cheam, Surrey, 1938–42; Froebel Teachers Training College, London, 1942–44. Married Alan Softly in 1951. English and history teacher, Manor House School, Little Bookham, Surrey, 1944–55. Address: Bundels, Ridgway, Sidbury, Devon EX10 0SF, England.

PUBLICATIONS FOR CHILDREN

Fiction

Plain Jane, illustrated by Shirley Hughes. London, Macmillan, 1961; New York, St. Martin's Press, 1962.
Place Mill, illustrated by Shirley Hughes. London, Macmillan, and New York, St. Martin's Press, 1962.
A Stone in a Pool, illustrated by Shirley Hughes. London, Macmillan, and New York, St. Martin's Press, 1964.
Ponder and William [*on Holiday, at Home, at the Weekend*], illustrated by Diana John. London, Penguin, 2 vols., and London, Longman, 2 vols., 1966–74.
Hippo, Potta and Muss, illustrated by Tony Veale. London, Chatto Boyd and Oliver, 1969; New York, Harvey House, 1970.
A Lemon-Yellow Elephant Called Trunk, illustrated by Tony Veale. London, Chatto Boyd and Oliver, and New York, Harvey House, 1971.
Geranium, illustrated by Margaret Wetherbee. London, Hutchinson, 1972.

Other

Magic People, illustrated by Gunvor Edwards. Edinburgh, Oliver and Boyd, 1966; New York, Holt Rinehart, 1967.
More Magic People, illustrated by Gunvor Edwards. London, Chatto Boyd and Oliver, 1969; as *Magic People Around the World*, New York, Holt Rinehart, 1970.

PUBLICATIONS FOR ADULTS

Other

The Queens of England. Newton Abbot, Devon, David and Charles, and New York, Stein and Day, 1976.

*

Barbara Softly comments:
At seven years old I wanted to be a poet, but on visiting Westminster Abbey and seeing where poets were buried, I decided against it and to write stories instead! Historical novels were scribbled, written properly, and published after I finished teaching. Ponder the panda pyjama-case followed in stories originally written for a small nephew. Now, with a large garden and five cats, there seems only time for short stories, articles, and visits to local schools and libraries taking Ponder with me to meet the young children in person.

* * *

Barbara Softly is perhaps best loved for her Ponder and William stories. William's cousin Winifred has a panda pyjama-case which she lends him whenever he comes to stay. He calls it Ponder and it talks to him, making interesting things happen, though grown-ups might see them as very ordinary, such as making jelly and using the garden hose. One of the major attractions of these tales is the way that Ponder, the "imaginary friend" of so many solitary children, gives William a viewpoint on the adult world. All the things they do together and find so absorbing are the very things we take for granted, or find annoying. We see a power cut and the need to use candles as an irritant whereas Ponder makes William see it as a thrill. They are ideal stories for reading aloud to the very young, and, more than most bedtime tales, can be enjoyed by the parental reader; Ponder opens for us a window into the child's world and gives us ideas of experiences we might not otherwise have thought of sharing.

Softly's other books for the young, such as *Magic People*, also maintain the wonderment and delight of the world in which the young child finds himself. For older children her love of history comes to the fore, particularly in her very sensitive collection of biographies *The Queens of England*. Whether they are dynamic leaders, loving wives and mothers, tragically misguided, or just shadowy, nebulous figures eclipsed by dominant husbands, these women are brought to life and we see them as real people, playing their part in shaping the affairs of the country, and surely the best way of getting children hooked on history is to offer them someone with whom to empathise. Here they are spoiled for choice. Every girl reader should find someone here whose personality attracts, of whose life and times she would like to find out more: a great tribute to any writer.

—Ann G. Hay

SORENSEN, Virginia (née Eggertsen). American. Born in Provo, Utah, 17 February 1912. Educated at Brigham Young University, Provo, A.B. 1934; Stanford University, California. Married 1) Frederick C. Sorensen in 1933 (divorced), one daughter and one son; 2) the writer Alec Waugh in 1969 (died 1981). Writer-in-residence, State University of Oklahoma, Edmond, 1966–67. Recipient: Guggenheim fellowship, 1946, 1954; Child Study Committee award, 1956; American Library Association Newbery Medal, 1957. Fellow, Phi Beta Kappa. Agent: Curtis Brown, 10 Astor Place, New York, New York 10003. Address: 2521 Old Kanuga Road, Hendersonville, North Carolina 28739, U.S.A.

PUBLICATIONS FOR CHILDREN

Fiction

Curious Missie, illustrated by Marilyn Miller.   New York, Harcourt Brace, 1953.
The House Next Door: Utah 1896, illustrated by Lili Cassel.   New York, Scribner, 1954.
Plain Girl, illustrated by Charles Geer.   New York, Harcourt Brace, 1955.
Miracles on Maple Hill, illustrated by Beth and Joe Krush.   New York, Harcourt Brace, 1956; Leicester, Brockhampton Press, 1967.
Lotte's Locket, illustrated by Fermin Rocker.   New York, Harcourt Brace, 1964.
Around the Corner, illustrated by Robert Weaver.   New York, Harcourt Brace, 1971.
Friends of the Road.   New York, Atheneum, 1978.

PUBLICATIONS FOR ADULTS

Novels

A Little Lower Than the Angels.   New York, Knopf, 1942.

On This Star.   New York, Reynal, 1946.
The Neighbors.   New York, Reynal, 1947.
The Evening and the Morning.   New York, Harcourt Brace, 1949.
The Proper Gods.   New York, Harcourt Brace, 1951.
Many Heavens.   New York, Harcourt Brace, 1954.
Kingdom Come.   New York, Harcourt Brace, 1960.
The Man with the Key.   New York, Harcourt Brace, 1974.

Short Stories

Where Nothing Is Long Ago: Memories of a Mormon Childhood.   New York, Harcourt Brace, 1963.

*

Manuscript Collections: Special Collections, Boston University Library; Kerlan Collection, University of Minnesota, Minneapolis.

Critical Study: *Virginia Sorensen* by L.L. and Sylvia B. Lee, Boise, Idaho, Boise State University, 1978.

*   *   *

Virginia Sorensen's strong sense of family wins a warm response from her readers, and her best-loved work, the Newbery Medal-winning *Miracles on Maple Hill*, most successfully brings to life a family and a community. Father has returned at last from the war to a family that never gave up hope, but the time he has spent in prison camp has changed him. The whole family becomes tense and uneasy with Father's tension. Little things—voices, noises, small frustrations—cause trouble. Mother becomes convinced that the cure can be found in the country, at Grandmother's old place in Maple Hill. Father is not optimistic—the whole idea of retreat to the country strikes him as far-fetched and simplistic—but, unwillingly, he agrees: and the miracles begin. They are the simple miracles of nature, of healing and growth: but they seem miraculous indeed to city children. When at last trouble comes, as it will do even in Maple Hill, can the city family, so new to country ways and work, save the precious crop? Predictably enough they can and do, but the story is surprisingly suspenseful. Throughout, there is the warm strength of caring—for family, for neighbours, for the lonely old hermit living nearby among his goats. The message that people matter is one that bears repeating and remembering.

Plain Girl shares the same warmth, with even more respect for old country traditions. Esther is the only daughter in a family of Plain People—the Amish. Esther feels sadly like an only child, for her brother Daniel has flouted the strict ways of the People and gone off to see the world. He has cut his hair, wears buttons on his clothes—even drives a car! Esther is shocked but at the same time curious. When the time comes for her to go to school as the law dictates, she becomes friends with a little girl who is the very opposite of Plain, who wears pink frilly dresses and ribbons in her hair. Esther longs to try these pretty, different unPlain garments, to trade clothes with her friend Mary. But Daniel's return, saddened by his contact with the world and eager to be Plain once more, teaches her the value of her Amish ways.

In *Lotte's Locket* Danish Lotte is the eighth in her family to bear her historic name. When war-widowed mother marries an American, Lotte is torn between love of her "Mor" and devotion to her homeland: but the locket, a precious family heirloom, allows her to carry a little of her Danish heritage over the seas to her new home in America. In *Around the Corner* Junie (short for Junior) is forbidden to go where the "hillbillys" have moved into a condemned shack: but after curiosity lures him there, neighbourliness keeps bringing him back to visit the friendly family from West Virginia; and good things begin to happen.

Not as winning as others of her works, *Friends of the Road* is the sentimental story of two girls whose parents are in the foreign service, and who meet in Morocco. Though parted by circumstances, they keep their friendship alive through their letters.Sorensen's books are filled with a wholesome philosophy of love and caring. They are mild, even quaint, in contrast with the hard-hitting, no-holds-barred children's literature so prevalent today, but it will be a sad world when there is no place left in it for gentle kindliness.

—Joan McGrath

SOUTHALL, Ivan (Francis). Australian. Born in Canterbury, Victoria, 8 June 1921. Educated at Chatham State School; Mont Albert Central School; Box Hill Grammar School. Served in the Australian Army, 1941, and the Royal Australian Air Force, 1942–46: Distinguished Flying Cross. Married 1) Joyce Blackburn in 1945 (marriage dissolved), one son and three daughters; 2) Susan Stanton in 1976. Engraver, Melbourne *Herald and Weekly Times*, 1936–41, 1947. Gertrude Clarke Whittall Lecturer, Library of Congress, Washington, D.C., 1973; May Hill Arbuthnot Lecturer, University of Washington, Seattle, 1974; writer-in-residence, Macquarie University, Sydney, 1978. Foundation president, Knoxbrooke Training Centre for the Handicapped, Victoria. Recipient: Australian Children's Book Council Book of the Year award, 1966, 1968, 1969 (for picture book), 1971, 1976; British Library Association Carnegie Medal, 1972; Australian Writers award, 1974. Member, Order of Australia, 1981. Address: P.O. Box 25, Healesville, Victoria 3777, Australia.

PUBLICATIONS FOR CHILDREN

Fiction

Meet Simon Black, illustrated by Frank Norton. Sydney and London, Angus and Robertson, 1950.
Simon Black in Peril [*in Space, in Coastal Command, in China, and the Spaceman, in the Antarctic, Takes Over, at Sea*], illustrated by I. Maher and Wal Stackpool. Sydney and London, Angus and Robertson, 8 vols., 1951–62.
Hills End. Sydney and London, Angus and Robertson, 1962; New York, St. Martin's Press, 1963.
Ash Road, illustrated by Clem Seale. Sydney, Angus and Robertson, 1965; London, Angus and Robertson, and New York, St. Martin's Press, 1966.
The Fox Hole, illustrated by Ian Ribbons. Sydney, Hicks Smith, London, Methuen, and New York, St. Martin's Press, 1967.
To the Wild Sky, illustrated by Jennifer Tuckwell. Sydney and London, Angus and Robertson, and New York, St. Martin's Press, 1967.
Sly Old Wardrobe, illustrated by Ted Greenwood. Melbourne, Cheshire, and London, Angus and Robertson, 1968; New York, St. Martin's Press, 1969.
Let the Balloon Go, illustrated by Ian Ribbons. Sydney, Hicks Smith, London, Methuen, and New York, St. Martin's Press, 1968.
Finn's Folly. Sydney and London, Angus and Robertson, and New York, St. Martin's Press, 1969.
Chinaman's Reef Is Ours. Sydney and London, Angus and Robertson, and New York, St. Martin's Press, 1970.
Bread and Honey. Sydney and London, Angus and Robertson, 1970; as *Walk a Mile and Get Nowhere*, Englewood Cliffs, New Jersey, Bradbury Press, 1970.
Josh. Sydney and London, Angus and Robertson, 1971; New York, Macmillan, 1972.
Over the Top, illustrated by Ian Ribbons. Sydney, Hicks Smith, and London, Methuen, 1972; as *Benson Boy*, New York, Macmillan, 1973.
Head in the Clouds, illustrated by Richard Kennedy. Sydney and London, Angus and Robertson, 1972; New York, Macmillan, 1973.
Matt and Jo. Sydney, Angus and Robertson, and New York, Macmillan, 1973; London, Angus and Robertson, 1974.
What about Tomorrow? Sydney and London, Angus and Robertson, and New York, Macmillan, 1977.
King of the Sticks. Sydney, Collins, London, Methuen, and New York, Greenwillow, 1979.
The Golden Goose. London, Methuen, and New York, Greenwillow, 1981.
The Long Night Watch. London, Methuen, 1983; New York, Farrar Straus, 1984.
A City Out of Sight. Sydney, Angus and Robertson, 1984; London, Angus and Robertson, 1985.
Christmas in the Tree. Sydney, Hodder and Stoughton, 1985.
Rachel. Sydney and London, Angus and Robertson, and New York, Farrar Straus, 1986.
Blackbird. New York, Farrar Straus, 1988.

Play

Screenplay: *Let the Balloon Go*, with others, 1976.

Other

Journey into Mystery: A Story of the Explorers Burke and Wills, illustrated by Robin Goodall. Melbourne, Lansdowne Press, 1961.
Rockets in the Desert: The Story of Woomera. Sydney, Angus and Robertson, 1964; London, Angus and Robertson, 1965.
Lawrence Hargrave. Melbourne, Oxford University Press, 1964.
Indonesian Journey. Melbourne, Lansdowne Press, 1965; London, Newnes, and Boston, Ginn, 1966.
The Sword of Esau: Bible Stories Retold, illustrated by Joan Kiddell-Monroe. Sydney, Angus and Robertson, 1967; New York, St. Martin's Press, 1968.
The Curse of Cain: Bible Stories Retold, illustrated by Joan Kiddell-Monroe. Sydney, Angus and Robertson, and New York, St. Martin's Press, 1968.
Bushfire!, illustrated by Julie Mattox. Sydney, Angus and Robertson, 1968.
Seventeen Seconds. Sydney, Hodder and Stoughton, 1973; Leicester, Brockhampton Press, and New York, Macmillan, 1974.
Fly West. London, Angus and Robertson, 1974; New York, Macmillan, 1975.

PUBLICATIONS FOR ADULTS

Novels

Third Pilot. Sydney, Horwitz, 1958.
Flight to Gibraltar. Sydney, Horwitz, 1958; as *Terror Flight*, 1962.
Mediterranean Black. Sydney, Horwitz, 1959.
Sortie in Cyrenaica. Sydney, Horwitz, 1959.
Mission to Greece. Sydney, Horwitz, 1959.
Atlantic Pursuit. Sydney, Horwitz, 1960.

Short Stories

Out of the Dawn: Three Short Stories.   Privately printed, 1942.

Other

The Weaver from Meltham (biography of Godfrey Hirst).   Melbourne, Whitcombe and Tombs, 1950.
They Shall Not Pass Unseen.   Sydney, Angus and Robertson, 1956.
The Story of the Hermitage: The First Fifty Years of the Geelong Church of England Girls' Grammar School.   Melbourne, Cheshire, 1956.
A Tale of Box Hill: Day of the Forest.   Box Hill, Victoria, Box Hill City Council, 1957.
Bluey Truscott: Squadron Leader Keith William Truscott, R.A.A.F., D.F.C. and Bar.   Sydney, Angus and Robertson, 1958.
Softly Tread the Brave: A Triumph over Terror, Devilry, and Death by Mine Disposal Officers John Stuart Mould and Hugh Randal Syme.   Sydney, Angus and Robertson, 1960.
Woomera.   Sydney, Angus and Robertson, 1962.
Parson on the Track: Bush Brothers in the Australian Outback.   Melbourne, Lansdowne Press, 1962.
Indonesia Face to Face.   Melbourne, Lansdowne Press, 1964; London, Angus and Robertson, 1965.
A Journey of Discovery: On Writing for Children.   London, Kestrel, 1975; New York, Macmillan, 1976.

Editor, *The Challenge—Is the Church Obsolete? An Australian Response to the Challenge of Modern Society* (essays).   Melbourne, Lansdowne Press, 1966.

*

Manuscript Collections: National Library of Australia, Canberra; Lu Rees Archives, Canberra.

Ivan Southall comments:

In my books for children I see my own growth as a writer. It is my basic philosophy to regard the person who reads my work, whether the person be child or adult, as my emotional and intellectual equal. This means I make few, if any, concessions to the age of the reader. The reader must come to me. I cannot go to the reader. Yet, in my books for children, I have striven to identify (in the full sense of the term) with the emotional and physical state of being a young person, or experiencing life (or those areas of life about which I have written), with the emotional intensity of a young person. I believe I have had more to say in this particular way than in any other. It has been a writing experience, over a number of years, of some excitement, and some adventure, and some fulfilment.

*   *   *

Ivan Southall is the best-known and most discussed Australian children's writer of the 1960's and 1970's. His present reputation is as an author of unusual power and fierce, sometimes harsh integrity: one who makes no concessions for the sake of easy popularity. Yet all through the 1950's, before producing any of the work on which this reputation is founded, Southall had been turning out approximately a book a year of a very different kind about the adventures of Squadron Leader Simon Black of the Royal Australian Air Force.

Simon—wrote his creator in an article in the *Horn Book* in June 1968—"possessed in incredible measure virtue, honour, righteous anger, courage and inventiveness. Every incredible difficulty he cheerfully overcame with dignity, grandeur, and a very stiff upper lip." Southall grew tired of him, and found his limitations frustrating.

In 1960 he decided he was not going to write for children any more. Then, looking at his own children and their friends, he began to suspect that in their lives, "interacting one upon the other at an unknown depth...lay an unlimited source of raw material." And he wrote a further book, *Hills End* which, with its successor *Ash Road*, was to be the start of a different professional and personal life.

Both books confront groups of children and young people with catastrophes—flood in *Hills End*, fire in *Ash Road*—which they are ill-equipped to cope with. They muddle through precariously, with intermittent courage and resourcefulness. But also at times with silliness, squabbling, and confusion. Stiff upper lips are notably absent. These are real children, behaving as children might be expected to behave in such emergencies.

Southall's next three full-length novels dealt with somewhat similar, and in two cases even more harrowing, situations. In *To the Wild Sky* half a dozen youngsters from a crashed aircraft are stranded on a remote coast with little food and no water. The story describes their struggle to survive, but does not carry it through to its logical conclusion (death or rescue). The reader is not told what happens to them. Southall did not plan to write a sequel, and resisted heavy pressure to satisfy his readers' curiosity; but after 18 years he relented. We learn from *A City Out of Sight* that in spite of all perils, and the tensions and cross-purposes among themselves, the young people managed to win through. This belated happy ending was undoubtedly welcome to many, but it was possible to wonder whether it was artistically right: a door that had been intentionally left open was closed. In *Finn's Folly* three adults are killed in a road crash, a hillside is littered with drums of deadly cyanide, a mentally retarded boy is perilously at large, and a teenage couple talk love in the wreckage beside the body of the girl's father. The disaster in *Chinaman's Reef Is Ours* is manmade rather than natural: the assault of a mining company on a not-quite-abandoned ghost town which it intends to demolish in order to start mining again.

In all these books, characters are shown at the end of their tethers; the viewpoint moves around among several people; the technique is somewhat like that of a chess game in which the pieces are moved independently and yet combined in an overall strategy. By 1970 it had begun to seem that this was Southall's established formula. However, his full-length novels after *Chinaman's Reef* showed a clear change of direction exploring in growing depth the inner experience of a central main character.

With hindsight it can be seen that the way ahead had been indicated in a short book called *Let the Balloon Go*, published in 1968. This tells how a spastic boy, determined to be "a boy like any other boy," climbs to the top of an 80-foot tree, then faces the problem of getting down. It is a dizzyingly tense story, yet its true action takes place inside one boy's mind; and this is essentially true of three succeeding major novels.

In *Bread and Honey* the day is Anzac Day, when Australians commemorate their part in two world wars. Michael, aged 13, misses seeing the great parade in his town, encounters a strange girl of nine who lives in an imaginative world of her own, and in her company meets the local bully and thrashes the bully's henchman. Summarized in such terms it seems a slight story; but a great deal is happening inside Michael. He is worrying away at various problems of conduct and values: among them the ethics of meeting violence with violence (and on a bigger scale the glory and horror of war); the struggle between literal-minded and imaginative, conventional and spontaneous. Above all—an increasingly recurrent Southall theme—he is coming through an ordeal which is in some sense an initiation into manhood.

Josh, with which Southall won the Carnegie Medal, is an absorbing and disturbing story. Josh, a highly-strung, poetry-writing 14-year-old from the city, goes to remote Ryan's Creek, where members of his family were once leading citizens, and becomes highly unpopular with the local youngsters, from whom he suffers psychological and physical violence. Josh wins through to some kind of respect, and perhaps brings Ryan's Creek a useful catharsis. But at the end he will not be reconciled with the locals; he sets off to walk back to the city, on his own. It is the only way he can remain himself. The point of view is from right inside the tortured Josh, whose stream of consciousness is effectively, painfully presented.

In *What about Tomorrow?* there is again a profound sense of identification of the author with his central character. Sam, a 14-year-old boy in 1931, has crashed his bike and lost eight shillings' worth of newspapers he is delivering: an economic disaster that drives him into running away from home. Most of the book describes his journeyings over the next few days, during which he has encounters with several adults (mostly helpful) and falls in love with three girls in rapid succession. As with *Bread and Honey* and *Josh*, the experience is essentially that of growing up; but *What about Tomorrow?* also looks ahead to Sam's maturity; for the question is not only of growing up, but also of what one is growing up towards. What Sam is growing up towards is death in war. Forward flashes interspersed at intervals with the narrative show him as captain of a seaplane in World War II, flying to meet his fate. There is a preoccupation with fear, courage, the achievement of manhood through ordeal, and the nature of war and glory that is characteristic of Southall, as is the fierce and searching light he directs on human nature.

The Long Night Watch showed Southall still able to surprise and disturb. Early in World War II the members of SWORD (the Society for World Order under Divine Rule), a chosen elite led by an elderly and eccentric Brigadier, embark from Australia for a Pacific island to await the coming of their heroes, the Saviours of Light. Among a group of five young people whose actions and interactions are central to the story, two boys of 16 have to keep watch for this event—but when the awaited light comes, it signals the arrival of Japanese attackers, who rapidly take over. It's the end of SWORD. We don't know what happened to its members, but the author leaves room for a wild surmise: could it be that, in some sense, this elite was saved after all?

Southall has never hesitated to puzzle or challenge his readers or to present them with harrowing situations; sometimes it has seemed as if he were testing them, to see how much agony they could take. Yet his books are widely read; clearly there are youngsters who can accept what he offers and who find the experience rewarding.

—John Rowe Townsend

SPEARE, Elizabeth George. American. Born in Melrose, Massachusetts, 21 November 1908. Educated at Smith College, Northampton, Massachusetts, 1926–27; Boston University, A.B. 1930, M.A. 1932. Married Alden Speare in 1936; one son and one daughter. English teacher, high schools in Rockland, Massachusetts, 1932–35, and Auburn, Massachusetts, 1935–36. Recipient: American Library Association Newbery Medal, 1959, 1962, and Laura Ingalls Wilder award, 1989; Child Study Committee award, 1983; Scott O'Dell award, 1984; Christopher award, 1984. Address: 48 Bibbins Road, Easton, Connecticut 06612, U.S.A.

PUBLICATIONS FOR CHILDREN

Fiction

Calico Captive, illustrated by W.T. Mars. Boston, Houghton Mifflin, 1957; London, Gollancz, 1963.

The Witch of Blackbird Pond. Boston, Houghton Mifflin, 1958; London, Gollancz, 1960.
The Bronze Bow. Boston, Houghton Mifflin, 1961; London, Gollancz, 1962.
The Sign of the Beaver. Boston, Houghton Mifflin, 1983; London, Gollancz, 1984.

Other

Life in Colonial America. New York, Random House, 1963.

PUBLICATIONS FOR ADULTS

Novel

The Prospering. Boston, Houghton Mifflin, and London, Gollancz, 1967.

Other

Child Life in New England 1790–1840. Sturbridge, Massachusetts, Old Sturbridge Village, 1961.

*

Manuscript Collection: Mugar Memorial Library, Boston University.

*   *   *

Elizabeth George Speare's historical fiction represents an interesting historiographical as well as literary progression. Her early work in *Calico Captive* shows a young author struggling to do justice to an exciting incident, and to make good use of historical sources. From either a historical or a literary standpoint, this is not Speare's best work. There is no attempt to put this incident—the capture of a white girl and her family by Indians—in historical perspective. Granted, a young girl facing kidnap and an uncertain future is unlikely to view the Indians with much sympathy, but Speare does not develop another character in the story who could do so. Historiographically, of course, this represents a blindness to Native American perspectives not uncommon in that era. But Speare's return to Indian/white relations in her most recent Newbery Honor Book, *The Sign of the Beaver*, shows a more mature author at work. *The Sign of the Beaver* is a much more compelling tale of an encounter between Matt, the son of white settlers in the Maine territory, and Attean, a young Indian boy with a host of reasons to dislike and distrust whites. Speare creates a situation in which both boys must work together: Matt, to survive; Attean to learn to read. While there is still some stereotypical rendering of Indian English, this is a more balanced book than *Calico Captive*. In addition, characterization is richer, and the reader comes to understand better the dilemma of the Indians as they face white encroachment into Maine. By the time Matt must decide whether to wait for his family's return and risk being abandoned to a New England winter, or join Attean and his people on the trek west, the choice is real. Matt has been happy living with Attean's people and he and Attean have become true friends. By building sympathy for the Native American as well as white characters, Speare also reflects the changing historiography of the European settlement of the Americas.

Speare's two Newbery Medal books, *The Bronze Bow* and *The Witch of Blackbird Pond*, are equally interesting in their approach to religious persecution. While *The Witch of Blackbird Pond* has been criticized as sexist for marrying off each of the main female characters, and for recreating *Little Women*'s Beth and Jo in the characters of Mercy and Kit, this is a well-told tale that juxtaposes the bleak intolerance of life in New England with the freedom and spiritedness of Kit's earlier years in Barbados. Kit is a feisty character who befriends an old Quaker woman, and ends up accused of witchcraft. The story is allowed to play itself out to a satisfying conclusion, and though the tale touches on religious beliefs, it is not sanctimonious. The same cannot be said for *The Bronze Bow*, a story that appears to recommend acquiescence as a Christian response to persecution. *The Bronze Bow* often struggles between being a Sunday School lesson and surviving as a novel. The storyline, in which a young Jewish rebel learns to forgive his enemies after meeting Jesus, is neither original nor particularly compelling. There is insufficient story development to help the reader understand that Daniel gives up more than his anger against the Roman killers of his parents and usurpers of his homeland when he follows Jesus. He also breaks from the religious traditions passed on to him by the parents whose deaths he seeks to avenge. As in *Calico Captive*, Speare fails to recognize perspectives that could lift her story above a simple morality tale. Fortunately, however, Speare is an author who has grown in her work. *The Witch of Blackbird Pond* and *The Sign of the Beaver* are well-written from both historical and literary perspectives, and also have a degree of child appeal that ensure a continued readership for Speare's work.

—Linda S. Levstik

SPENCE, Eleanor (Rachel, née Kelly). Australian. Born in Sydney, New South Wales, 21 October 1928. Educated at Erina Primary School, 1935–40; Gosford High School, 1941–45; Sydney University, 1946–48, B.A. Married John A. Spence in 1952; two sons and one daughter. Teacher, Methodist Ladies' College, Burwood, New South Wales, 1949; librarian, Commonwealth Public Service Board, 1950–52; children's librarian, Coventry City Libraries, Coventry, England, 1953–54. Teacher's aide, 1974–75, and since 1976 teacher, Autistic Children's School, Sydney. Recipient: Australian Children's Book Council Book of the Year award, 1964, 1977; Australian Literature Board fellowship, 1980. Address: 85 Rickard Road, Empire Bay, New South Wales 2256, Australia.

PUBLICATIONS FOR CHILDREN

Fiction

Patterson's Track, illustrated by Alison Forbes. Melbourne, Oxford University Press, 1958; London, Angus and Robertson, 1959.
The Summer in Between, illustrated by Marcia Lane Foster. London, Oxford University Press, 1959.
Lillipilly Hill, illustrated by Susan Einzig. London, Oxford University Press, 1960; New York, Roy, 1963.
The Green Laurel, illustrated by Geraldine Spence. London, Oxford University Press, 1963; New York, Roy, 1965.
The Year of the Currawong, illustrated by Gareth Floyd. London, Oxford University Press, and New York, Roy, 1965.
The Switherby Pilgrims, illustrated by Corinna Gray. London, Oxford University Press, and New York, Roy, 1967.
Jamberoo Road, illustrated by Doreen Roberts. London, Oxford University Press, and New York, Roy, 1969.
The Nothing-Place, illustrated by Geraldine Spence. London, Oxford University Press, 1972; New York, Harper, 1973.
Time to Go Home, illustrated by Fermin Rocker. London, Oxford University Press, 1973.

The Travels of Hermann, illustrated by Noela Young. Sydney, Collins, 1973.
The October Child, illustrated by Malcolm Green. London, Oxford University Press, 1976; as *The Devil Hole*, New York, Lothrop, 1977.
A Candle for Saint Antony. London, Oxford University Press, 1977; New York, Oxford University Press, 1979.
The Seventh Pebble, illustrated by Sisca Verwoert. Melbourne and London, Oxford University Press, 1980.
The Left Overs. Sydney, Methuen, 1982; London, Methuen, 1983.
Me and Jeshua. Melbourne, Dove, 1984.
Miranda Going Home. Melbourne, Dove, 1985.
Mary and Frances. Melbourne, Dove, 1986.
Deezle Boy. Melbourne, Dove, 1987.

Other

A Schoolmaster, illustrated by Jane Walker. Melbourne, Oxford University Press, 1969.
A Cedar-Cutter, illustrated by Barbara Taylor. Melbourne, Oxford University Press, 1971.

PUBLICATIONS FOR ADULTS

Other

Another October Child: Recollections of Eleanor Spence. Melbourne, Dove, 1988.

*

Eleanor Spence comments:
With the exception of *The Travels of Hermann* my novels have generally been for readers from age 11 to young teens. All have Australian backgrounds and many of the experiences described were similar to episodes in my own (rural) childhood. In my later stories I have turned more to modern city life as background, and have twice used handicapped children as central characters—a deaf boy in *The Nothing-Place* and an autistic boy in *The October Child*.

* * *

Eleanor Spence is a pioneer among those writers who in the last 30 years have established a children's literature which is distinctively Australian in style and ethos. Her novels are distinguished by well-realised settings, sensitive characterisation, and quiet humour. Two themes are recurrent. One is the universal theme of self-examination during the early years of adolescence: "She was dimly aware of mysteries ahead, of problems not to be neatly solved like the sums in her arithmetic book, of a whole world of experience—in brief she had her first glimpse of growing up" (*The Green Laurel*). The other is a particular interest in Australian heritage from colonial settlement to post-war immigration: "He was beginning now to find fascination in the history of his own country, and of this history men like the Swagman were an essential element" (*The Year of the Currawong*).

Both themes are to be found in *Patterson's Track*. 13-year-old Karen is interested in Convict Cove and its association with a 19th-century runaway. In retracing with a group of friends and her brothers the path of the convict she learns as much about herself as about the mystery. *The Summer in Between* has the same setting (all Spence's novels are about Sydney and its environs). Faith Melville writes a play about Victorian settlers at her home at Booralee for her friends to act, and again self-discovery results. *Lillipilly Hill* is a historical novel; Victorian restraints upon the behavior of young ladies are defied by Harriet Wilmot in her adjustment to the rural community in New South Wales to which the family have emigrated. *The Green Laurel*, Spence's most highly regarded novel, is about the need for roots. This is shown in the character of the heroine, Lesley Somerville, from a fairground family, in her choice of architecture as a career and in her attempts to make a community of their new home in the immigrants' suburb of Blackbutt Hill. *The Year of the Currawong* takes as its centre of interest a disused silver mine on which the interests of the Kendall family converge when they move from the city to the isolated village of Currawong.

The Switherby Pilgrims and its sequel *Jamberoo Road* are popular Australian historical novels. In the 1840's, Miss Arabella Braithwaite, a figure reminiscent of the redoubtable Mrs. Caroline Chisholm, emigrates from Switherby in Yorkshire to Illawarra in New South Wales. She takes with her an assortment of destitute children to which she adds an aboriginal orphan, Cammy. With the help of their convict servant Ebenezer, they wrest a living out of virgin soil. The sequel gives the further histories of the children, especially Cassie Brown, who rejects the prosperous Edward Marlow of Falls Farm, Jamberoo, for Ebenezer.

There are new directions in the novels that follow. Boys rather than girls are the chief characters and social concern replaces the historical theme. *Time to Go Home* is a relaxed and humorous teenage novel about the competing claims of sport and work and home and school. But Rowan Price also takes time to coach a team of younger children in a poor neighborhood. The other two novels are about handicapped boys. Glen Calder, in *The Nothing-Place*, is struggling with deafness as a result of illness, as well as with the boredom of living in the vast anonymous suburb to which the family has moved. Keith Mariner, in *The October Child*, has an autistic younger brother, and the effects of this on the whole family are depicted with frankness and sensitivity.

Adolescent friendships tested against local social mores and a wider cultural context provide the theme for *A Candle for Saint Antony* and *The Seventh Pebble*. In the first, Justin is drawn to a refugee boy, Rudi, who represents European culture and a warmth of relationship which is feared by his family to be homosexual. Rachel, in *The Seventh Pebble*, is herself a Jewish refugee, but in this story, set in the Depression, her family has been assimilated into small-town Australia. Her friendship with a girl of an Irish labouring family also meets with disapproval. In these novels, friendship with an outsider is a means for the hero or heroine of self-definition and self-development. Adolescence, like post-colonial experience, is a melding of past experience and future potentiality.

The Left Overs is reminiscent of 19th-century children's fiction in its theme and sentiment. 11-year-old Drew strives to keep the family together in the face of circumstances which threaten disintegration. But this is not the 19th but the 20th century; Drew's appeal is made through television and the "family" are a group of children in care, children with multiple social and physical handicaps. The triumph of the story is that Drew's appeal restores them singly to their families. It is a touching and unusual tale.

—Mary Croxson

SPERRY, Armstrong. American. Born in New Haven, Connecticut, 7 November 1897. Educated at Yale School of Fine Arts, New Haven, 1918; Art Students' League, New York, 1919–21; Académie Colarossis, Paris, 1922. Served in the United States Navy, 1917. Married Margaret Mitchell in 1930; one son and one daughter. Assistant ethnologist, *Kaimiloa* expedition to the South Pacific, 1925–26; commercial artist and illustrator. Recipient: American Library Association Newbery Medal, 1941. *Died 28 April 1976.*

PUBLICATIONS FOR CHILDREN (illustrated by the author)

Fiction

One Day with Manu. Philadelphia, Winston, 1933.
One Day with Jambi in Sumatra. Philadelphia, Winston, 1934.
One Day with Tuktu, An Eskimo Boy. Philadelphia, Winston, 1935.
All Sail Set. Philadelphia, Winston, 1935; London, Lane, 1946.
Wagons Westward: The Old Trail to Santa Fe. Philadelphia, Winston, 1936; London, Lane, 1948.
Little Eagle, A Navajo Boy. Philadelphia, Winston, 1938.
Lost Lagoon. New York, Doubleday, 1939; London, Lane, 1943.
Call It Courage. New York, Macmillan, 1940; as *The Boy Who Was Afraid*, London, Lane, 1942.
Coconut, The Wonder Tree. New York, Macmillan, 1942; London, Lane, 1946.
Bamboo, The Grass Tree. New York, Macmillan, 1942; London, Lane, 1946.
No Brighter Glory. New York, Macmillan, 1942; London, Hutchinson, 1944.
Storm Canvas. Philadelphia, Winston, 1944.
Hull-Down for Action. New York, Doubleday, 1945; London, Lane, 1948.
The Rain Forest. New York, Macmillan, 1947; London, Lane, 1950.
Danger to Windward. Philadelphia, Winston, 1947; London, Lane, 1952.
Black Falcon. Philadelphia, Winston, 1949.
River of the West, illustrated by Henry Pitz. Philadelphia, Winston, 1952; London, Lane, 1954.
Thunder Country. New York, Macmillan, 1952; London, Lane, 1953.
Frozen Fire. New York, Doubleday, 1956; London, Lane, 1957.
South of Cape Horn. Philadelphia, Winston, 1958.

Other

The Voyages of Christopher Columbus. New York, Random House, 1950.
John Paul Jones, Fighting Sailor. New York, Random House, 1953.
Pacific Islands Speaking. New York, Macmillan, 1955.
Captain Cook Explores the South Seas. New York, Random House, 1955; revised edition, as *All about Captain Cook*, London, W.H. Allen, 1960.
All about the Arctic and Antarctic. New York, Random House, 1957.
All about the Jungle. New York, Random House, 1959; London, W.H. Allen, 1960.
The Amazon, River Sea of Brazil. Champaign, Illinois, Garrard, 1961; London, Muller, 1962.
Great River, Wide Land: The Rio Grande Through History. New York, Macmillan, and London, Collier Macmillan, 1967.

Editor, *Story Parade: A Collection of Modern Stories for Boys and Girls.* Philadelphia, Winston, 5 vols., 1938–42.

*

Illustrator: *Stars to Steer By*, 1934, and *House Afire!*, 1941, both by Helen T. Follett; *Shuttered Windows* by Florence Crannell Means, 1938; *Jungle River*, 1938, and *Thunderbolt House*, 1944, both by Howard Pease; *Boat Builder* by Clara Ingram Judson, 1940; *Teri Taro from Bora Bora* by William S. Stone, 1940; *Two Children of Brazil* by Rosa Brown, 1940; *Nicholas Arnold, Toolmaker* by Marion Hansing, 1941; *Winabojo, Master of Life* by James Clyde Bowman,

1941; *Dogie Boy* by Edith Heal, 1943; *Clipper Ship Men* by Alexander Laing, 1944; *Courage over the Andes* by Frederic Kummer, 1944; *Sky Highways* by Trevor Lloyd, 1945; *Story of Hiawatha* edited by Allen Chaffee, 1951.

* * *

Two of Armstrong Sperry's interests shaped the course of his writings for children. As an ethnologist in the South Pacific, he developed a deep and abiding interest in the life and culture of the island peoples. His service in the U.S. Navy gave an added dimension to his love of the sea and things nautical. Together, these two loves, plus his talent as an artist, gave shape and direction to his work.

His early works, such as the tales of Manu, Jambi, and Tuktu, are unlikely to be found in library collections of today, in an era rendered more sensitive to the feelings of minority cultures and racial pride than the 1930's. Coloured as they were by the prevailing attitudes of his day, Sperry's ethnological works for young readers would by critics of today be stigmatized as condescending in their approach: it is all too easy to lose the historical perspective that would credit him with enlightenment and objectivity, given their date of publication. A similar change of perspective has effectively ended the usefulness of such later titles as *Lost Lagoon* and *Hull-Down for Action*. They partake of the fierce emotions of World War II, specifically of the highly charged Pearl Harbor era, and naturally enough reflect the rage and rancour of that unhappy time. As with any "boys' book" produced in wartime, stereotypes of the antagonists as unredeemed villains are predictably two-dimensional.

Where Sperry shone, and continues to shine, and where he earned a place in the galaxy of notable children's writers, is with the timeless tale, in particular, with *Call It Courage*. It is the story of a Polynesian youth, Mafatu, a child of the sea people who fears the sea. As a tiny child, just old enough to remember, he suffered the loss of his mother in a hurricane at sea, and was rescued barely alive after the ordeal. Now, when the young men of the island are eager for the challenge of the deep, Mafatu hangs back, busying himself with net mending. He is pitied and despised by his people, and is the despair of his father, the chief. At last life becomes unendurable to Mafatu. He determines to face that which he fears—and if he must die, it will at least be a man's death. In a frail outrigger canoe, Mafatu sets out to find his fate, accompanied only by a dog, and without the knowledge or consent of his people. There follows a gripping account of adventure and survival with a veritable boyish Robinson Crusoe, alone on a remote island that is sometimes visited by a terrifying cannibal tribe. Of course Mafatu returns at last to his people in glorious triumph. His father, who had mourned him as dead, now sees his son wearing a necklace of boar's teeth, and carrying a spear, a man's weapon he has earned and now deserves. It is a tremendously satisfying story—the epic struggle of child-man against the elements, yet written well within the grasp of young readers not yet ready for full-length adult stories of survival. It is written unaffectedly, yet in the language of myth and legend.

Sperry's own illustrations admirably support the simple power of his heroic theme. Sperry's ethnological materials have come to honourable retirement, and his style of sentimental fictionalized biography is no longer much admired, but Sperry's achievement in *Call It Courage* ensures his continued presence in the best of children's collections.

—Joan McGrath

———

SPYKMAN, E(lizabeth) C(hoate). American. Born in South-

boro, Massachusetts, 17 July 1896. Educated at Westover School, Middlebury, Connecticut, graduated 1914. Married Nicholas John Spykman in 1931 (died 1943); two daughters. *Died 7 August 1965.*

PUBLICATIONS FOR CHILDREN

Fiction

A Lemon and a Star.   New York, Harcourt Brace, 1955; London, Macmillan, 1956.
The Wild Angel.   New York, Harcourt Brace, 1957; London, Macmillan, 1958.
Terrible, Horrible Edie.   New York, Harcourt Brace, 1960; London, Macmillan, 1961.
Edie on the Warpath.   New York, Harcourt Brace, 1966; London, Macmillan, 1967.

PUBLICATIONS FOR ADULTS

Other

Westover.   Middlebury, Connecticut, Westover School, 1959.

* * *

E.C. Spykman's four novels—the turn-of-the-century saga of the Cares family of Summerton, Massachusetts—are one of the treasures of children's literature. The four younger Cares, Ted, Jane, Hubert, and Edie, are independent, argumentative, and intelligent. They live in a comfortably well-off world of servants, sailboats, summers by the sea, and exciting new motor cars. Reminiscent of E. Nesbit's Bastable children, they spend most of their time plotting adventures and figuring out ways to circumvent the unreasonable rules and regulations of the adult world.

Though all four children are vivid and highly individualistic characters, Edie, the youngest, emerges as Spykman's most finely drawn portrait. In the first book—*A Lemon and a Star*—10-year-old Jane is the central figure while 5-year-old Edie is merely an annoying younger sibling. But in the course of the next three books, Edie moves to center stage. Impetuous, self reliant, always on the lookout for adventure, Edie Cares is one of the most spirited heroines ever to live between the covers of a children's book. She lops off her long hair and rides with the boys in a sheep round-up. She plots to capture an imagined kidnapper. She marches with the suffragettes. Yet throughout she maintains an inner tenderness and sensitivity which marks her as a fully developed—though not fully grown—human being, rather than a sterotypical "tomboy" character.

The great achievement of Spykman was this ability to create full and utterly believable characters, while at the same time presenting a richly evocative picture of the time and place in which they lived. With no sense of nostalgia, she presents in equal portions the joys and the sorrows of being young. The books live, for both children and adults, because they remain consistently true to the child's perception of the world. A concern for fairness and justice is ever present, but adult moralizing is absent. Humor, lightheartedness, and moments of tenderness make reading the books a delight. An underlying recognition of the fact that, in spite of the fun, growing up is a serious business, makes the memory of them linger long after the covers are closed.

—Susan Meyers

———

STEELE, Mary Q(uintard, née Govan). Also writes as Wilson Gage. American. Born in Chattanooga, Tennessee, 8 May 1922. Educated at the University of Chattanooga, B.S. 1943. Married William O. Steele, q.v., in 1943 (died 1979); two daughters and one son. Address: 329 Crestway Drive, Chattanooga, Tennessee 37411, U.S.A.

PUBLICATIONS FOR CHILDREN

Fiction

Journey Outside, illustrated by Rocco Negri.   New York, Viking Press, 1969; London, Macmillan, 1970.
The First of the Penguins, illustrated by Susan Jeffers.   New York, Macmillan, 1973; London, Macmillan, 1974.
Because of the Sand Witches There, illustrated by Paul Galdone. New York, Greenwillow, 1975; London, Macmillan, 1976.
The Eye in the Forest, with William O. Steele.   New York, Dutton, 1975.
The True Men.   New York, Greenwillow, 1976.
The Owl's Kiss: Three Stories.   New York, Greenwillow, 1978.
Wish, Come True, illustrated by Muriel Batherman.   New York, Greenwillow, 1979.
The Life (and Death) of Sarah Elizabeth Harwood.   New York, Greenwillow, 1980.

Fiction as Wilson Gage

The Secret of the Indian Mound, illustrated by Mary Stevens. Cleveland, World, 1958.
The Secret of the Crossbone Hill, illustrated by Mary Stevens. Cleveland, World, 1959.
The Secret of the Fiery Gorge, illustrated by Mary Stevens. Cleveland, World, 1960.
A Wild Goose Tale, illustrated by Glen Rounds.   Cleveland, World, 1961.
Dan and the Miranda, illustrated by Glen Rounds.   Cleveland, World, 1962.
Miss Osborne-the-Mop, illustrated by Paul Galdone.   Cleveland, World, 1963.
Big Blue Island, illustrated by Glen Rounds.   Cleveland, World, 1964.
The Ghost of Five Owl Farm, illustrated by Paul Galdone. Cleveland, World, 1966; London, Faber, 1967.
Mike's Toads, illustrated by Glen Rounds.   New York, World, 1970.
Squash Pie, illustrated by Glen Rounds.   New York, Greenwillow, 1976.
Down in the Boondocks, illustrated by Glen Rounds.   New York, Greenwillow, 1977.
Mrs. Gaddy and the Ghost, illustrated by Marylin Hafner.   New York, Greenwillow, 1979; London, Bodley Head, 1981.
Cully Cully and the Bear, illustrated by James Stevenson.   New York, Greenwillow, and London, Bodley Head, 1983.
The Crow and Mrs. Gaddy, illustrated by Marylin Hafner.   New York, Greenwillow, and London, Bodley Head, 1984.
Mrs. Gaddy and the Fast-Growing Vine, illustrated by Marylin Hafner.   New York, Greenwillow, 1985; London, Bodley Head, 1986.

Verse

Anna's Summer Songs [*Garden Songs*], illustrated by Lena Anderson.   New York, Greenwillow, 2 vols., 1988–89.

Other

Editor, *The Fifth Day* (poetry anthology), illustrated by Janina Domanska.   New York, Greenwillow, 1978.

PUBLICATIONS FOR ADULTS

Other

The Living Year: An Almanac for My Survivors (essays).   New York, Viking Press, 1972.

*

Manuscript Collection: Kerlan Collection, University of Minnesota, Minneapolis.

Mary Q. Steele comments:
My primary interest is in natural history, and especially birds. And the puzzle of humanity's place in the scheme of things follows as the night the day, and I suppose this is what I am talking about in my books, however light-hearted they may be. Which sounds a little pompous and I pray forgiveness.
I would hope my books would be enjoyed; I like to think the books make readers laugh. But I would hope too for the occasional reader who closes one of my books and ever after looks at the world of living things with some small measure of my own sense of astonishment and gratitude.

*   *   *

Mary Q. Steele is most noted for her Newbery Honor Book *Journey Outside* and for her enormously popular *Miss Osborne-the-Mop*. However, Steele has written a variety of children's books from simple stories for younger children such as *Mike's Toads*, to more complex considerations of death and suicide in *The Life (and Death) of Sarah Elizabeth Harwood*. The most common theme in Steele's books is an appreciation for nature. In *Mike's Toads* a young boy learns that taking small creatures out of their natural environment is not a good idea; in *The Life (and Death) of Sarah Elizabeth Harwood* one of the characters rescues and revives insects, and in *Dan and the Miranda* spiders cause humorous problems for a young scientist. While the natural history in these books is interesting and sometimes amusing, it does not always compensate for rather dated dialogue and unexciting storylines. In *Mike's Toad*, for instance, Mike's tendency to volunteer other people without asking their permission happens so frequently in the first few pages of the book that by the time the toads are introduced the story has become silly and predictable. It is hard to feel sympathy for a character who persists in an activity that invariably gets him into pointless trouble—or for parents who continue to bail him out.
It is Steele's second theme that has made stories such as *Miss Osborne-the-Mop* so popular. In these books Steele combines a child's eye view of magic and witchcraft with childlike wackiness. Not all of these books have been critically successful but they have been very popular with children who are just moving into "chapter" books. These stories are just strange and silly enough to be really appealing and to keep young readers reading.
A third theme in Steele's work has been an interest in placing characters in situations that require them to come to terms with some of the difficulties of living. In *The Life (and Death) of Sarah Elizabeth Harwood* a young girl contemplates suicide. Sarah lives in what her father describes as an eccentric family. Her brother calculates the nutritional levels of every food that he consumes, her sister traps herself in a tree while trying to study the sleeping habits

of birds, and her mother celebrates the rebirth of a plant by screaming to raise the dead. Not surprisingly, Sarah feels out of place, and unable to do anything right. After she misplaces a valuable album belonging to a friend, she becomes increasingly distraught. Her initial conclusion that suicide is her only way out is thwarted, and a visit to her aging grandmother helps Sarah gain some perspective on her problems. In *Wish, Come True*, two children enliven a three-week visit to Great Aunt's "small, rather dark, old-fashioned" apartment by learning to make their own entertainment—with a little magic. *Big Blue Island* takes a similar theme—a move from Detroit to an island on a Tennessee river—and traces a boy's growing self-reliance and appreciation for his unusual uncle.

The most interesting of Steele's books, however, is *Journey Outside*. In this short novel, Steele's attention to the environment is linked with an adolescent's quest for something more than the life that his people accept. Dilar of the Raft People has been raised on a string of rafts continuously moving along an underground river, searching for a "Better Place." Convinced that his people merely travel in circles, Dilar jumps off his family's raft, clambers through a cleft in the rock face, and discovers a world of "day" and "green." As Dilar searches the new world he has found, Steele builds an allegory in which common assumptions about how people "should" live are questioned. Is it better to store up for the future, or live for the moment? Dilar's search for wisdom leads him inevitably to himself. He decides to bring his people up into the world again. *Journey Outside* is fascinating on several levels, and could be read as a simple fantasy-adventure story, as well as an allegory. As with other award-winning books, however, this book probably has less child-appeal than Steele's lighter, more straightforward stories.

—Linda S. Levstik

STEELE, William O(wen). American. Born in Franklin, Tennessee, 22 December 1917. Educated at Cumberland University, Lebanon, Tennessee, 1936–40, B.A. 1940; University of Chattanooga, Tennessee, 1951. Served in the United States Army Air Corps during World War II. Married Mary Quintard Govan (i.e., Mary Q. Steele, *q.v.*) in 1943; two daughters and one son. Recipient: Women's International League for Peace and Freedom Jane Addams award, 1958. *Died 25 June 1979.*

PUBLICATIONS FOR CHILDREN

Fiction

The Golden Root, illustrated by Fritz Kredel. New York, Aladdin, 1951.
The Buffalo Knife, illustrated by Paul Galdone. New York, Harcourt Brace, 1952.
Over-Mountain Boy, illustrated by Fritz Kredel. New York, Aladdin, 1952.
Wilderness Journey, illustrated by Paul Galdone. New York, Harcourt Brace, 1953.
Winter Danger, illustrated by Paul Galdone. New York, Harcourt Brace, 1954; London, Macmillan, 1963.
Tomahawks and Trouble, illustrated by Paul Galdone. New York, Harcourt Brace, 1955.
We Were There on the Oregon Trail, illustrated by Jo Polseno. New York, Grosset and Dunlap, 1955.
David Crockett's Earthquake, illustrated by Nicolas. New York, Harcourt Brace, 1956.

We Were There with the Pony Express, illustrated by Frank Vaughn. New York, Grosset and Dunlap, 1956.
The Lone Hunt, illustrated by Paul Galdone. New York, Harcourt Brace, 1956; London, Macmillan, 1957.
Flaming Arrows, illustrated by Paul Galdone. New York, Harcourt Brace, 1957; London, Macmillan, 1958.
Daniel Boone's Echo, illustrated by Nicolas. New York, Harcourt Brace, 1957.
The Perilous Road, illustrated by Paul Galdone. New York, Harcourt Brace, 1958; London, Macmillan, 1960.
Andy Jackson's Water Well, illustrated by Michael Ramus. New York, Harcourt Brace, 1959.
The Far Frontier, illustrated by Paul Galdone. New York, Harcourt Brace, 1959; London, Macmillan, 1960.
The Spooky Thing, illustrated by Paul Coker. New York, Harcourt Brace, 1960.
The Year of the Bloody Sevens, illustrated by Charles Beck. New York, Harcourt Brace, 1963.
Wayah of the Real People, illustrated by Isa Barnett. Williamsburg, Virginia, Colonial Williamsburg Inc., 1964.
The No-Name Man of the Mountain, illustrated by Jack Davis. New York, Harcourt Brace, 1964.
Trail Through Danger, illustrated by Charles Beck. New York, Harcourt Brace, 1965.
Tomahawk Border, illustrated by Vernon Wooten. Williamsburg, Virginia, Colonial Williamsburg Inc., 1966.
Hound Dog Zip to the Rescue, illustrated by Mimi Korach. Champaign, Illinois, Garrard, 1970.
Triple Trouble for Hound Dog Zip, illustrated by Mimi Korach. Champaign, Illinois, Garrard, 1972.
John's Secret Treasure, illustrated by R. Dennis. New York, Macmillan, 1975.
The Eye in the Forest, with Mary Q. Steele. New York, Dutton, 1975.
The Man with the Silver Eyes. New York, Harcourt Brace, 1976.
The War Party, illustrated by Lorinda Bryan Cauley. New York, Harcourt Brace, 1978.
The Magic Amulet. New York, Harcourt Brace, 1979.

Other

John Sevier, Pioneer Boy, illustrated by Sandra James. Indianapolis, Bobbs Merrill, 1953.
The Story of Daniel Boone, illustrated by Warren Baumgartner. New York, Grosset and Dunlap, 1953; London, Muller, 1957.
Francis Marion: Young Swamp Fox, illustrated by Dick Gringhuis. Indianapolis, Bobbs Merrill, 1954.
The Story of Leif Ericson, illustrated by Pranas Lapé. New York, Grosset and Dunlap, 1954; London, Sampson Low, 1960.
De Soto: Child of the Sun, illustrated by Lorence Bjorklund. New York, Aladdin, 1956.
Westward Adventure: The True Stories of Six Pioneers. New York, Harcourt Brace, 1962.
The Old Wilderness Road: An American Journey. New York, Harcourt Brace, 1968.
The Wilderness Tattoo: A Narrative of Juan Ortiz. New York, Harcourt Brace, 1972.
Henry Woodward of Carolina: Surgeon, Trader, Indian Chief, illustrated by Hoyt Simmons. Columbia, South Carolina, Sandlapper Press, 1972.
The Cherokee Crown of Tannassy. Winston-Salem, North Carolina, Blair, 1977.
Talking Bones: Secrets of Indian Burial Mounds, illustrated by Carlos Llerena-Aguirre. New York, Harper, 1978.

*

Manuscript Collections: Kerlan Collection, University of Minnesota, Minneapolis; Special Collections, John Brister Library, Memphis State University, Tennessee.

William O. Steele commented:

(1978) My fiction for the 8 to 12-year-old reader has mostly been concerned with pioneer and Indian struggles in the southeastern U.S. during the 18th century when the red and white cultures clashed at the cutting edge of the frontier. I try always to see the past as it was, to put into books, not 20th-century characters with a fake pioneer dress of split cow hide, but 18th-century boys and men with buckskin shirts rubbing against their shoulder blades, and the smell of sweat and woodsmoke around them, and their bellies only half-full of dried deer meat and gritty ashcakes. What I am trying to get over to my readers is not events but people who make the events. History textbooks can give a reader the high spots—but it takes more than textbooks to give you the heart-squeezed hopelessness and fear that sounds of Indian warwhoops can cause.

In my books I try to give a true picture of what the unspoiled frontier country was like when it began to be settled, of the dangers and hardships and rewards of settling it. Above all I try to convey something of the real essence of the times, something of the restless, tough-bodied, forward-looking pioneer who pushes further and further into the wilderness. And I try to accomplish this in as entertaining a fashion as I can.

In the 1950's and 1960's I could write historical fiction from the white pioneer's viewpoint and not be criticised as slighting the Indian's side. Now in the 1970's I would not want to write that kind of book and probably would find no publisher if I did on account of today's ethnic sensitivity. In the future, so as to not waste a quarter of a century of research on the frontier period, I may switch to the Indian viewpoint in his struggles against the whites on the frontier. I would prefer, however, to go back in time to the fascinating prehistoric Indian groups of eastern America. It will be a challenge, but it seems to be a wide open field.

*   *   *

William O. Steele wrote what used to be confidently called "boys' books." Vigorous novels of pioneering, wilderness travel, and Indian fighting, written for readers of the middle years but strong enough for "reluctant readers" of 12 to 14, are his main stock in trade. Steele provides for maximum reader involvement: the major protagonist is always a young boy of 10 to 12 who is portrayed as staunch and resourceful, but never unrealistically brave or infallible. Most stories are set in the Tennessee wilderness during the pioneering period of American history, a background all but guaranteeing adventure.

The overarching theme of the novels usually involves a step by the young protagonist toward maturity; in the course of his adventures, he learns something important about himself and about life. In *Flaming Arrows* young Chad Rabun learns tolerance of others; in *The Buffalo Knife* Andy gains confidence in his own courage. At the very least, the outlook of the young hero is expanded: the Indian boy in *Wayah of the Real People* discards some of his superstitious fear of whites, as does Talatu in *The Man with the Silver Eyes*. But Steele never allows such themes to interfere with his central purpose, which is to tell a fast-moving, exciting story. In some books, indeed, the growing-and-learning motif is nearly smothered under an avalanche of physical adventure. In more thoughtful novels, like *Winter Danger* and *The Man with the Silver Eyes*, the elements are better balanced.

Characterization in Steele's stories centers on the young protagonist and is fairly simple. The boys are meant to be typical; one can be distinguished from the other mainly by the particular fear with which he comes to terms in the story. Adults, especially parents, are usually stock figures, brave, kind, supportive, but generalized. There are occasional exceptions: Caje's father, in *Winter Danger*, is

a footloose "woodsy" whose character is briefly but sharply sketched; Camp Green, the Daniel Boone-like "Long Hunter" and Mr. Rhea, the dolorous trader, both of *Wilderness Journey*, are memorable.

After the mid 1960's, Steele from time to time shifted the viewpoint in his stories, giving Indian-white encounters from the Indian's side. *Wayah of the Real People* shows white society in the Williamsburg of 1752 through the eyes of a young Cherokee boy sent to Brafferton Hall for a year of schooling. Adventure is minor, but the point of view is fresh. *The Man with the Silver Eyes*, a far more somber story of an Indian boy who discovers that he is half-white, acknowledges the inherent tragedy in the clash of cultures. Though its climax is overly theatrical, this book is a welcome departure from the simplistic view of Indian-as-enemy that prevails in most of Steele's early books.

Steele's novels are credible in period detail, lively in incident, and colorful with vernacular speech. They are sometimes glib and unconvincing at any deeper level; character change is often accomplished with unrealistic ease, and incidents of physical peril and violence frequently seem contrived or gratuitous.

Steele also wrote several tall tales drawn from Tennessee mountain lore. *Andy Jackson's Water Well*, *The No-Name Man of the Mountain*, and several other short books tell exaggerated tales with proper deadpan style and expressive local language. The language and humor of these tales are richer and livelier than those of the adventure fiction, but for young readers, they lack the strong narrative power and the sense of identification provided by the adventure novels.

—Anne Scott MacLeod

———

STEIG, William. American. Born in New York City, 14 November 1907. Educated at City College, New York, 1923–25; National Academy of Design, New York, 1925–29. Married 1) Elizabeth Mead in 1936 (divorced), one daughter and one son; 2) Karl Homestead in 1950 (divorced 1963), one daughter; 3) Stephanie Healey in 1964 (divorced 1966); 4) Jeanne Doron in 1969. Since 1930, freelance humorous artist. Individual shows: Downtown Gallery, New York, 1939; Smith College, Northampton, Massachusetts, 1940. Recipient: American Library Association Caldecott Medal, 1970; Christopher award, 1973; American Book award, for picture book, 1983. Address: R.F.D. 1, Box 416, Kent, Connecticut 06757, U.S.A.

PUBLICATIONS FOR CHILDREN (illustrated by the author)

Fiction

Roland, The Minstrel Pig. New York, Windmill, 1968; London, Hamish Hamilton, 1974.
Sylvester and the Magic Pebble. New York, Windmill, 1969; London, Abelard Schuman, 1972.
The Bad Island. New York, Windmill, 1969; revised edition, as *Rotten Island*, New York, Godine, 1984, London, Viking Kestrel, 1986.
Amos and Boris. New York, Farrar Straus, 1971; London, Hamish Hamilton, 1972.
Dominic. New York, Farrar Straus, 1972; London, Hamish Hamilton, 1973.
The Real Thief. New York, Farrar Straus, 1973; London, Hamish Hamilton, 1974.

Farmer Palmer's Wagon Ride. New York, Farrar Straus, 1974; London, Hamish Hamilton, 1975.

Abel's Island. New York, Farrar Straus, 1976; London, Hamish Hamilton, 1977.

The Amazing Bone. New York, Farrar Straus, 1976; London, Hamish Hamilton, 1978.

Caleb and Kate. New York, Farrar Straus, 1977; London, Hamish Hamilton, 1980.

Tiffky Doofky. New York, Farrar Straus, 1978; London, Hamish Hamilton, 1980.

Gorky Rises. New York, Farrar Straus, 1980; London, Gollancz, 1989.

Doctor De Soto. New York, Farrar Straus, 1982; London, Andersen Press, 1983.

Yellow and Pink. New York, Farrar Straus, 1984; London, Gollancz, 1986.

Solomon the Rusty Nail. New York, Farrar Straus, 1985; London, Gollancz, 1987.

Brave Irene. New York, Farrar Straus, 1986; London, Gollancz, 1988.

The Zabajaba Jungle. New York, Farrar Straus, 1987.

Spinky Sulks. New York, Farrar Straus, 1988.

Verse

An Eye for Elephants. New York, Windmill, 1970.

Other

C D B! New York, Windmill, 1968.
The Bad Speller (reader). New York, Windmill, 1970.
C D C? New York, Farrar Straus, 1984.

PUBLICATIONS FOR ADULTS

Other (drawings)

Man about Town. New York, Long and Smith, 1932.
About People: A Book of Symbolical Drawings. New York, Random House, 1939.
The Lonely Ones. New York, Duell, 1942.
All Embarrassed. New York, Duell, 1944.
Small Fry (*New Yorker* cartoons). New York, Duell, 1944; London, Phoenix House, 1947.
Persistent Faces. New York, Duell, 1945.
Till Death Do Us Part: Some Ballet Notes on Marriage. New York, Duell, 1947.
The Agony in the Kindergarten. New York, Duell, 1950.
The Rejected Lovers. New York, Knopf, 1951.
Dreams of Glory and Other Drawings. New York, Knopf, 1953.
The Steig Album. New York, Duell, 1953.
Continuous Performance (cartoons). New York, Duell, 1963.
Male/Female. New York, Farrar Straus, 1971.
Drawings. New York, Farrar Straus, 1979; London, Faber, 1980.
Ruminations. New York, Farrar Straus, 1984.

*

Illustrator: *How to Become Extinct* by Will Cuppy, 1941; *Mr. Blandings Builds His Dream House* by Eric Hodgins, 1947; *Listen Little Man! A Document from the Archives of the Orgone Institute* by William Reich, 1948; *Giggle Box* edited by Phyllis R. Fenner, 1950; *Consider the Lemming* by Jeanne Steig, 1988.

*   *   *

In 1968 when William Steig published his first children's book, *Roland, The Minstrel Pig,* he was 61 and had already enjoyed a successful career beginning in 1930 when he became a cartoonist and cover designer for the *New Yorker.* Since the publication of his first children's book, Steig has continued to make significant contributions to American children's literature with such distinguished picture books as *Sylvester and the Magic Pebble,* his two award-winning novels *Dominic* and *Abel's Island,* his readers *C D B!, C D C?,* and *The Bad Speller,* and a book of children's verse, *An Eye for Elephants.*

Steig's books feature such themes as the lost child who is saved from evil and reunited with the family; the hero whose quest includes time for friendship, community, art, and music, as well as weapons; a beneficent and deeply romantic conception of the natural world; such resonant archetypes as initiation, death, and rebirth, and magical transformations. Steig's themes are rendered in elegant, sometimes self-consciously literary language. The presiding voice in these works is urbane and witty, yet never condescending; rather it invites the young reader to participate in this humorous, sophisticated view of the world. Steig's books often reflect his childhood reading of *Grimms' Fairy Tales,* "Hansel and Gretel," *Pinocchio, Tales of King Arthur,* the Katzenjammer Kids, and his love of Charlie Chaplin films. For example, Steig's marvelous character Sylvester Duncan, the wondrous donkey who is turned into stone when he uses a magic pebble to escape from a hungry lion, reminds the reader of Pinocchio; as Pinocchio is locked into the wooden body of a puppet and yearns to be a real boy, so Sylvester, physically and spiritually paralyzed in the rock, longs for speech, for mobility, family, and community. In *The Amazing Bone* Steig draws upon the Grimms' story of fratricide in "The Singing Bone." Steig's amazing bone acts as a protective magical talisman for the innocent and vulnerable child, Pearl the pig.

In *Roland, The Minstrel Pig* Steig introduced many motifs and structural devices which have recurred in his work during the last 20 years: the use of droll anthropomorphized animals; the quest as a structural device; the celebration of art, nature, and community; and a felicitous mixture of art styles (primarily cartoon and impressionism). With full color cartoon illustrations, Steig introduces his readers to Roland, a pig who enjoys a safe and civilized community in which he plays his lute and sings for the gratified entertainment of his friends. In this innocent pastoral place dogs, cats, a cow, goat, monkey, goose, deer, bear, and even a parrot dance in harmonious delight. Eventually Roland's friends convince him that his talent deserves a wider audience. On his journey to find fame Roland confronts loneliness for the first time. More seriously, he encounters evil in the form of the scheming fox, Sebastion, who plans to eat him at an opportune moment. Sebastion nearly succeeds, but the King hears Roland singing and saves him to become the royal minstrel. Thus, Roland achieves the fame for which he longed, while the villainous fox is thrown into a dungeon to live the rest of his days "on nothing but stale bread with sour grapes and water."

While Roland finds happiness in a new home, many of Steig's childlike animal characters return home to celebrate a joyous reunion with their families. Among the most notable of these circular journeys are *Sylvester and the Magic Pebble, The Amazing Bone,* and the novel-length survival story *Abel's Island.*

Sylvester and the Magic Pebble justly deserves its wide recognition as one of the most distinguished works in contemporary American picture books. The opening scene shows Sylvester at home with his parents, happy and secure. Soon thereafter Sylvester finds a magic pebble and accidentally transforms himself into a rock to escape a ferocious lion. Mr. and Mrs. Donkey search everywhere and finally seek help from their local police (controversially depicted as rather befuddled pigs). The police and indeed the entire community turn out to search for the lost Sylvester but fail to locate him because he looks and smells like a rock instead of Sylvester. While Sylvester's parents grieve for their missing son, he undergoes a deathlike sleep as summer turns to autumn, and autumn yields to the isolation and frozen waste of winter. With spring's rebirth, Mr. and Mrs. Duncan try to revive their spirits by going on a picnic amid flowering trees, lush grass, and a profusion of impressionistic flowers. Luckily they use the rock that is Sylvester for a table. Mr. Duncan spies the shiny red pebble and places it on the rock, just as Sylvester exclaims, "I wish I were my real self again!" Instantly the Duncans are reunited amid the scattered picnic. The final illustration shows Sylvester at home curled securely between his parents on a rounded cozy sofa.

In this picture book Steig addresses children's fears of separation from their parents, as well as their fears and terrors and even wishes for radical transformations. He also reveals the power of nature as a healing force and introduces magic as a significant element.

In *The Amazing Bone* Steig portrays an innocent young female pig, Pearl, who dawdles in the woods after school and finds a talking bone, which first saves her from a band of robbers but fails to dupe a clever fox. The fox takes Pearl home to roast for dinner. As the fox tosses a salad and sharpens his cutlery, the bone begins to utter magic words that transform the fox into a tiny mouse-sized creature. Pearl and the bone go home to rejoicing parents.

Steig's two longer fantasies for children, *Abel's Island* and *Dominic*, also feature feisty animal characters as heroes. Abel, an Edwardian mouse in a velvet smoking jacket, is washed away in a storm as he gallantly tries to retrieve his wife's handkerchief. He takes shelter at last on an island, where he learns to fight for survival. Not only does he learn to survive physically; he also learns to create art and to appreciate nature in all of its moods. When he finally returns to his wife, Abel is much more resourceful than the mama's boy who had been washed away a year earlier. *Abel's Island* is a delightful addition to the long tradition of *Robinsonades* which appeared in the aftermath of *Robinson Crusoe*. Abel manages to maintain his elegant and civilized manners even as he must struggle against overwhelming odds to survive.

Dominic, the redoubtable dog hero, in the fantasy of the same title, finds himself discontent with existence and departs on the road to adventure. In this fantasy Steig delights in gentle parody of the heroic tradition. Unlike King Arthur, who receives his sword from the Lady in the Lake, Dominic receives his speare from a catfish in the pond. He also enjoys interludes in his heroic quest when he plays his piccolo and feels his romantic spirit resonate in tune with the rhythms of the universe. Dominic saves several victims of the evil Doomsday Gang along the way, undergoes a death and rebirth or spiritual transformation in the woods, and eventually awakes his own sleeping beauteous dog in a palace amid exquisite gardens. The two continue their adventures together. *Dominic* is a beautifully crafted, highly lyrical wish fulfillment fantasy. Yet Steig's humorous drawings and delicately satirical prose counter what would otherwise be a hopelessly sentimental story.

Many of Steig's picture books incorporate wish-fulfillment childhood fantasies. An adventurous frog in *Gorky Rises* concocts a magical potion enabling him to soar to the stars, break free of adult constraints, and yet return home safely with concrete and indisputable proof that his adventures have actually happened. In *Doctor De Soto* a mouse dentist outwits the crafty fox who poses as a patient. In *Solomon the Rusty Nail* Steig again features the theme of transformation and the child's concern with identity. When Solomon the rabbit wishes, he can transform himself into a rusty nail. Eventually this trick saves him from a hungry cat but backfires when the cat nails him into the house, where he is trapped in the wood. Later, he is released when the house burns, and Solomon becomes himself again and runs home to ecstatic parents. Change, though terrifying, Steig seems to imply, is finally a good and beneficent thing.

Most of Steig's children's picture books feature charming animal characters. With *Caleb and Kate* Steig uses human beings as central characters. Caleb, a carpenter, and Kate, a weaver, love each other, but "not every single minute." A marital spat sends Caleb into the

woods where an evil witch, Yedida, changes him into a dog, who then consoles and protects Kate in her grief. Eventually the evil spell is broken, and the couple are reunited. Steig's odd little book *Yellow and Pink* appears to be an allegory about the artist's relationship to his creations. Two small wooden figures, one yellow and one pink, explore the great philosophical issues, "Who am I?" and "Where did I come from?" Their ontological deliberations are interrupted when the artist checks to see whether their paint is dry. In *Brave Irene* Steig reveals the virtues of loyalty and friendship.

Steig is quite simply one of America's finest artists. His witty humorous books celebrate the powers of imagination, art, language, and nature. His comic works are deeply humane and appeal to children and adult critics alike. He has created enduring gifts for the world's children and has reminded all of his readers that laughter helps us to survive.

—Anita Moss

STEPTOE, John (Lewis). American. Born in Brooklyn, New York, 14 September 1950. Educated at the New York School of Art and Design, 1964–67. Married Stephanie Douglas in 1969; one daughter and one son. Freelance illustrator; teacher, Brooklyn Museum School, Summer 1970. Recipient: Society of Illustrators Gold Medal, 1970; American Library Association Newcott award, 1976, and Coretta Scott King award, 1982, for illustration, 1988; Boston *Globe-Horn Book* award, 1987. *Died 28 August 1989.*

PUBLICATIONS FOR CHILDREN (illustrated by the author)

Fiction

Stevie. New York, Harper, 1969; London, Longman, 1970.
Uptown. New York, Harper, 1970.
Train Ride. New York, Harper, 1971.
Birthday. New York, Holt Rinehart, 1972.
My Special Best Words. New York, Viking Press, 1974.
Marcia. New York, Viking Press, 1976.
Daddy Is a Monster...Sometimes. Philadelphia, Lippincott, 1980.
Jeffrey Bear Cleans Up His Act. New York, Lothrop, 1983.
Baby Says. New York, Lothrop, 1988.

Other (retellings)

The Story of Jumping Mouse. New York, Lothrop, 1984.
Mufaro's Beautiful Daughters: An African Tale. New York, Lothrop, 1987; London, Hamish Hamilton, 1988.

*

Illustrator: *All Us Come Cross the Water* by Lucille Clifton, 1973; *She Come Bringing Me That Little Baby Girl* by Eloise Greenfield, 1974; *Mother Crocodile* translated by Rosa Guy, 1981; *OUTside/INside Poems*, 1981, and *All the Colors of the Race*, 1982, both by Arnold Adoff; *Roses* by Barbara Cohen, 1984.

* * *

John Steptoe, a black writer who wrote and illustrated *Stevie* when he was only 17, filled his early books with the children and neighborhoods of his own life. Except for the idealized community in

Birthday, these neighborhoods are ghettoes, but Steptoe's pictures of them, suggesting Rouault in their shapes and colors, are glowing, and his children are coping well with their lives.

Uptown and *Train Ride* are sketches from life, with the grammar and vocabulary of urban black children, usually understandable to any reader. In *Uptown*, however, the words used by the two boys as they talk about the clothing they like—playboys, beavers, bad silks—could baffle the uninitiated.

Stevie has remained the most popular of these early books. Its situation is universal—the jealousy and annoyance of a boy of seven or eight—Robert—whose mother helps out a neighbor by taking in her little son for a few weeks. This could happen to a black or white family and the language is colloquial in a way that is hard to identify as strictly "black." What happens to Robert in the end has universality, too. After all the irritation has been expressed, positive feelings find their way in. Stevie is missed when he is gone.

In *Birthday*, *My Special Best Words*, and *Marcia*, Steptoe changes the scene. *Birthday* details the celebration of a black boy's eighth birthday in an imagined rural community where the warm spirit of cooperation and intimacy becomes the main point of the story. In *My Special Best Words* Steptoe writes a book for the young about three-year-old Bweela and her year-old brother, Javaka, who lived alone with their father. Bweela tells in black baby talk—not always easily read aloud—about the events of daily life, including attempts to toilet-train Javaka. The scenes are intimate, honest, and loving. In *Marcia* Steptoe moves up into teenage territory, writing a gentle love story with a sex problem at the center. Here, too, the language is the natural speech of the black characters, the tone is hopeful—so hopeful, in fact, that the story rises in the end toward an almost declamatory pitch.

Recently Steptoe has moved in new directions with his two large picture books that are retellings of old legends. *The Story of Jumping Mouse*, based on a Native American legend, tells of the courageous small mouse who successfully makes a journey to "the far-off land" though giving away her sight and sense of smell to others more in need. The pictures here are a new departure also—abundant nature scenes in muted black and white. *Mufaro's Beautiful Daughters*, on the other hand, is painted in glowing colors and takes the reader to the Africa of the ancient Zimbabwe region. Based on an African folktale, it tells of two daughters, one of whom is greedy and jealous, and the other kind to all. Of course it is the kind one who becomes the wife of the king.

Also unlike Steptoe's early work are two recent short picture books. In *Jeffrey Bear Cleans Up His Act*, Jeffrey (a humanized bear) is bored with school and the visiting speaker on garbage, and daydreams about how he would manage the class. In *Baby Says*, a short picture book for the very young with few words and large pictures, a toddler in a playpen tries to get the attention of an older brother. The relationship between these two small black children is a warm one, and the clear, bright pictures reflect the mood.

—Claudia Lewis

———

STEVENSON, James. American. Born in New York City, 11 July 1929. Educated at Yale University, New Haven, Connecticut, B.A. 1951. Served in the United States Marine Corps, 1951–53. Married Jane Walker in 1953; five sons and four daughters. Reporter, *Life* magazine, New York, 1955. Since 1956 artist and writer, the *New Yorker* magazine. Recipient: New York *Times* Best Illustrated Book award, 1980; Christopher award, 1983. Agent: Liz Darhansoff, 1220 Park Avenue, New York, New York 10128, U.S.A.

PUBLICATIONS FOR CHILDREN (illustrated by the author)

Fiction

Walker, The Witch, and the Striped Flying Saucer. Boston, Little Brown, 1969.
The Bear Who Had No Place to Go. New York, Harper, 1972.
Here Comes Herb's Hurricane! New York, Harper, 1973.
Could Be Worse! New York, Greenwillow, 1977.
Wilfred the Rat. New York, Greenwillow, 1977.
Help! Yelled Maxwell, with Edwina Stevenson. New York, Greenwillow, 1978.
The Sea View Hotel. New York, Greenwillow, 1978; London, Gollancz, 1979.
Winston, Newton, Elton, and Ed. New York, Greenwillow, 1978.
The Worst Person in the World. New York, Greenwillow, and London, Kestrel, 1978.
Fast Friends: Two Stories. New York, Greenwillow, 1979.
Monty. New York, Greenwillow, and London, Gollancz, 1979.
Clams Can't Sing. New York, Greenwillow, 1980.
Howard. New York, Greenwillow, 1980; London, Gollancz, 1981.
That Terrible Halloween Night. New York, Greenwillow, 1980.
The Night after Christmas. New York, Greenwillow, 1981; London, Gollancz, 1982.
The Wish Card Ran Out! New York, Greenwillow, 1981.
Oliver, Clarence, and Violet. New York, Greenwillow, 1982.
We Can't Sleep. New York, Greenwillow, 1982.
Barbara's Birthday. New York, Greenwillow, and London, Bodley Head, 1983.
Grandpa's Great City Tour. New York, Greenwillow, 1983.
The Great Big Especially Beautiful Easter Egg. New York, Greenwillow, and London, Gollancz, 1983.
What's under My Bed? New York, Greenwillow, 1983; London, Gollancz, 1984.
Worse than Willy! New York, Greenwillow, 1984; London, Gollancz, 1985.
Yuck! New York, Greenwillow, 1984; London, Gollancz, 1985.
Are We Almost There? New York, Greenwillow, 1985.
Emma. New York, Greenwillow, 1985; London, Gollancz, 1986.
That Dreadful Day. New York, Greenwillow, 1985.
Fried Feathers for Thanksgiving. New York, Greenwillow, 1986.
No Friends. New York, Greenwillow, 1986; London, Gollancz, 1987.
There's Nothing to Do! New York, Greenwillow, and London, Gollancz, 1986.
When I Was Nine. New York, Greenwillow, 1986.
Higher on the Door. New York, Greenwillow, 1987.
Happy Valentine's Day, Emma! New York, Greenwillow, 1987.
No Need for Monty. New York, Greenwillow, 1987.
Will You Please Feed Our Cat? New York, Greenwillow, and London, Gollancz, 1987.
The Supreme Souvenir Factory. New York, Greenwillow, 1988.
We Hate Rain! New York, Greenwillow, 1988.
The Worst Person in the World at Crab Beach. New York Greenwillow, 1988.
Oh No, It's Waylon's Birthday! New York, Greenwillow, 1989.

PUBLICATIONS FOR ADULTS

Novels

Do Yourself a Favor, Kid. New York, Macmillan, 1962.
The Summer Houses. New York, Macmillan, 1963.
Sometimes, But Not Always. Boston, Little Brown, 1967.
Cool Jack and the Beanstalk (comic strip novel). New York,

Penguin, 1976.

Other

Sorry, Lady—This Beach is Private! (cartoons). New York, Macmillan, 1963.
Something Marvelous Is About to Happen. New York, Harper, 1971.
Let's Boogie! (cartoons). New York, Dodd Mead, 1978.
Uptown Local, Downtown Express. New York, Viking Press, 1983.

*

Illustrator: *Weekend Guests* by William Zinsser, 1963; *If I Owned a Candy Factory* by James Walker Stevenson, 1968; *Tony and the Toll Collector* by Eric Stevenson, 1969; *Tony's Hard Work Day* by Alan Arkin, 1972; *Alec's Sand Castle* by Lavinia Ross, 1972; *Good Old James* by John Donovan, 1975; *What's a Father For?* by Sara D. Gilbert, 1975; *Jack the Bum and the Haunted House*, 1977, *Jack the Bum and the Halloween Handout*, 1977, and *Jack the Bum and the UFO*, 1978, all by Janet Schulman; *Say It!*, 1980, and *I Know a Lady*, 1984, both by Charlotte Zolotow; *The Baby Uggs Are Hatching*, 1982, and *The New Kid on the Block*, 1984, both by Jack Prelutsky; *How Do You Get a Horse Out of the Bathtub?*, 1983, *263 Brain Busters*, 1985, and *How Do You Lift a Walrus with One Hand?*, 1988, all by Louis Phillips; *Cully Cully and the Bear* by Wilson Gage, 1983; *Otto Is Different* by Franz Brandenberg, 1985; *Georgia Music*, 1986, and *Grandaddy's Place*, 1987, both by Helen V. Griffith; *I Am Not Going to Get up Today!* by Dr. Seuss, 1987; *Percy and the Five Houses* by Else Minarik, 1989.

* * *

James Stevenson's picture books, of which he is both artist and word provider (they are generally set out cartoon fashion) are among the most engaging in this field. His witty *New Yorker* cartoons are a pleasure to adults, but he also exactly aims at very young readers. Clearly he believes in his characters, his situations, so why should not we? Under the tireless invention, the zany logic, and the nice sense of story—the endings are particularly satisfying—a tiny moral note is usually lurking, not stuck on but intrinsic. Children like that too. Take *Monty*, one of his earliest books. Every day Monty the alligator ferries Arthur, Doris, and Tom over the stream to school and back in the afternoon. (They are, as it happens, rabbit, duck, and frog, but that is the idiom.) But the cheeky three are not very grateful; indeed, they are quite rude at times. One morning Monty declares that he is on vacation. The three try to devise other means of crossing the water, all ludicrously unsuccessful, until they realise how much old Monty is needed. The moment they voice this, Monty appears. "I thought you were on vacation," says one. "I am, but sometimes when I am on vacation I take a day off." In *Howard*, another vintage piece, a young wild duck gets left behind in the city when the others fly south for the winter. With newfound friends (a frog, a mouse) and after various mishaps, he (and they) find shelter in a derelict theatre. Other creatures join the community, visit museums, and produce their own plays and concerts—really, a well-spent winter. When spring arrives, and Howard's "group" returns, he says goodbye. But is it to the birds or to his friends? Ah, that's the clever bit.

Stevenson is again seen at his best in the moving yet hilarious *Clams Can't Sing*. Here, the seashore creatures are planning a gala festival: singing, dancing, reciting. Only the clams aren't asked to perform; for what can clams do? What indeed? The two little clams devise an extraordinary contribution to the show. (We too can see it in detail.) Yes, everyone can do something.

In *Yuck!* and *Happy Valentine's Day, Emma!* Stevenson, still in high form, offers a modish witch theme. Two wonderfully disgusting old sorceresses ("Stencheroo, Dolores!" cries one as she stirs her noxious brew) throw scorn at good little Emma, a witchlet who can't manage spells but has a nice nature and plenty of animal friends. With their help she deceives the awful pair into thinking that she has a spell or two up her sleeve. And everyone gets the right valentine.

In his most recent books a grandfather tells a boy and girl how he and his infant brother Wainie dealt long ago with the problems that are occupying the children now. The titles may suggest the themes—*No Friends* (they have moved to a new neighborhood), *There's Nothing to Do!*, *Worse than Willy!* (coping with a new baby brother), *Will You Please Feed Our Cat?*—but not the mad range of events that grandfather plucks out of his resourceful head with wildly euphoric Stevenson pictures to match.

Stevenson is a prolific worker—possibly too prolific (not all of his published works have crossed the Atlantic), but at his best he is very hard to match.

—Naomi Lewis

———

STEWART, A(gnes) C(harlotte). British. Born in Liverpool, Lancashire, 9 March. Educated privately. Married to Robert Frederick Stewart; one daughter. Recipient: Scottish Arts Council award, 1977. Address: Knowetop, Corsock, Castle Douglas, Kirkcudbrightshire DG7 3EB, Scotland.

PUBLICATIONS FOR CHILDREN

Fiction

The Boat in the Reeds, illustrated by Christopher Brooker. London, Blackie, 1960; Englewood Cliffs, New Jersey, Bradbury Press, 1970.
Falcon's Crag. London, Blackie, 1969.
The Quarry Line Mystery. London, Faber, 1971; Nashville, Nelson, 1973.
Elizabeth's Tower. London, Faber, and New York, Phillips, 1972.
Dark Dove. New York, Phillips, 1974; London, Macmillan, 1975.
Ossian House. London, Blackie, 1974; New York, Phillips, 1976.
Beyond the Boundary. London, Blackie, 1976.
Silas and Con. London, Blackie, and New York, Atheneum, 1977.
Brother Raimon Returns. London, Blackie, 1978.
Biddy Grant of Craigengill. London, Blackie, 1979.

PUBLICATIONS FOR ADULTS

Novel

Wandering Star. London, Hale, 1981.

*

A.C. Stewart comments:

I find it very difficult to write about my books: for any author so much of what goes into his books is unconscious and so when one comes to analyse them they are full of surprises. My chief concern is to tell a good story that will entertain; this is, I believe, what writing novels is about. Into my stories is bound to go much of what I believe in and care about, but if at the same time any form of advice to children gets in it is because it is part of the story and belongs in it—not as a lecture to the reader. I never meant to write for children but it has come about that way and now I find a greater interest and satisfaction in doing so than when writing for adults.

* * *

In A.C. Stewart's novels the narrative is much less significant than the setting. Place and character are fully and sensitively evoked as the narrative unfolds, at times almost somnolently. These are books about enduring human values rooted in the spirits of time and place, and to absorb these values her young heroes and heroines must learn to own with the heart. There are adventures to be sure, and gripping ones at that, told with arresting skill, but they rest less on the meeting of adversaries than on human struggle against the vicissitudes of nature in lonely and remote places.

Ian eventually sails the Shearwater of *The Boat in the Reeds*, and indeed sails it close to disaster over the bar. But this is no ordinary tale of courage at sea. He has earned his right to sail the boat in rebuilding it with loving care. The sailing is almost incidental to the owning, and the reader will remember the child pouring his heart and imagination into the derelict dinghy long after he forgets the near-fatal sailing. Similarly, a few adventures befall John in *Ossian House* as he roams his grandfather's lands, but as the slow tale unfolds the boy becomes a part of the continuity of the world of fells and glens, linking past, present, and foreseeable future in his growing love for his heritage. In *Dark Dove* Margaret draws strength from her roots in the Highlands, turning always to home exactly as her pigeons return to the loft.

If setting and the slow unfolding of character are central concerns of Stewart's novels, a distinguishing and recurring theme is the child-adult relationship. Each of her books brings a child and an adult together in mutual respect. And it is a remarkable quality of her writing that, though the child's perceptions are consistently at the centre, the principal grown-up characters are sensitively and fully adult. Child and adult complement each other while each remains true to his own station. There is nothing either patronizing or whimsical here. Adults are totally uncondescending; children are never precociously wise. Elizabeth leans on the crippled Lawrence in *Elizabeth's Tower* even as he draws strength from her mixture of practical good sense and child-like dependence. In each novel a similar relationship is developed; John and Duncan the shepherd in *Ossian House*; Margaret and Callum, the local laird, in *Dark Dove*; Ian and Tim the idler in *The Boat in the Reeds*. In *Brother Raimon Returns* Major Carpenter's affection for Alice is as generous as it is genuine while he and Michael share a wary antagonism of mutual respect.

It is in *Falcon's Crag* and its belated sequel, *Biddy Grant of Craigengill*, that Stewart's recurring concern with place and character and relationships is expressed at its most profound. Biddy grows to understand her Uncle Neil and Great Uncle Dermot as through her growing love for Craigengill she becomes attuned to the spirit of the place and its morose history. In these most absorbing of Stewart's novels she expresses perhaps most deeply what her other excellent novels have sought to clarify, that human values, like life, are found in the living, and are assayed as much in the heart as in the head.

—Myles McDowell

———

STOLZ, Mary (née Slattery). American. Born in Boston, Massachusetts, 24 March 1920. Educated at Birch Wathen School, New York; Columbia University, New York, 1936–38; Katherine Gibbs School, New York. Married 1) Stanley Stolz in 1940 (divorced 1956), one son; 2) Thomas C. Jaleski in 1965. Worked at R.H. Macy's, New York, and as secretary at Columbia University Teachers College. Recipient: Child Study Committee award, 1954; George G. Stone Center for Children's Books award, 1982. Agent: Roslyn Targ Literary Agency, 105 West 13th Street, New York, New York 10011. Address: P.O. Box 82, Longboat Key, Florida 34228, U.S.A.

PUBLICATIONS FOR CHILDREN

Fiction

To Tell Your Love. New York, Harper, 1950.
The Organdy Cupcakes. New York, Harper, 1951.
The Sea Gulls Woke Me. New York, Harper, 1951.
The Leftover Elf, illustrated by Peggy Bacon. New York, Harper, 1952.
In a Mirror. New York, Harper, 1953.
Ready or Not. New York, Harper, 1953; London, Heinemann, 1966.
Pray Love, Remember. New York, Harper, 1954.
Two by Two. Boston, Houghton Mifflin, 1954; London, Hodder and Stoughton, 1955; revised version, as *A Love, or a Season*, New York, Harper, 1964.
Rosemary. New York, Harper, 1955.
Hospital Zone. New York, Harper, 1956.
The Day and the Way We Met. New York, Harper, 1956.
Good-by My Shadow. New York, Harper, 1957; London, Penguin, 1964.
Because of Madeline. New York, Harper, 1957.
And Love Replied. New York, Harper, 1958.
Second Nature. New York, Harper, 1958.
Emmett's Pig, illustrated by Garth Williams. New York, Harper, 1959; Kingswood, Surrey, World's Work, 1963.
Some Merry-Go-Round Music. New York, Harper, 1959.
The Beautiful Friend and Other Stories. New York, Harper, 1960.
A Dog on Barkham Street, illustrated by Leonard Shortall. New York, Harper, 1960.
Belling the Tiger, illustrated by Beni Montresor. New York, Harper, 1961.
Wait for Me, Michael. New York, Harper, 1961.
The Great Rebellion, illustrated by Beni Montresor. New York, Harper, 1961.
Frédou, illustrated by Tomi Ungerer. New York, Harper, 1962.
Pigeon Flight, illustrated by Murray Tinkelman. New York, Harper, 1962.
Siri, The Conquistador, illustrated by Beni Montresor. New York, Harper, 1963.
The Bully of Barkham Street, illustrated by Leonard Shortall. New York, Harper, 1963.
Who Wants Music on Monday? New York, Harper, 1963.
The Mystery of the Woods, illustrated by Uri Shulevitz. New York, Harper, 1964.
The Noonday Friends, illustrated by Louis Glanzman. New York, Harper, 1965.
Maximilian's World, illustrated by Uri Shulevitz. New York, Harper, 1966.
A Wonderful, Terrible Time, illustrated by Louis Glanzman. New York, Harper, 1967.
Say Something, illustrated by Edward Frascino. New York, Harper, 1968.
The Dragons of the Queen, illustrated by Edward Frascino. New York, Harper, 1969.
The Story of a Singular Hen and Her Peculiar Children, illustrated by Edward Frascino. New York, Harper, 1969.
Juan, illustrated by Louis Glanzman. New York, Harper, 1970.
By the Highway Home. New York, Harper, 1971.

Leap Before You Look. New York, Harper, 1972.
Lands End, illustrated by Dennis Hermanson. New York, Harper, 1973.
The Edge of Next Year. New York, Harper, 1974.
Cat in the Mirror. New York, Harper, 1975.
Ferris Wheel. New York, Harper, 1977.
Cider Days. New York, Harper, 1978.
Go and Catch a Flying Fish. New York, Harper, 1979.
What Time of Night Is It? New York, Harper, 1981.
Cat Walk, illustrated by Erik Blegvad. New York, Harper, 1983; London, Armada, 1985.
Quentin Corn, illustrated by Pamela Johnson. Boston, Godine, 1985.
The Explorer of Barkham Street, illustrated by Emily Arnold McCully. New York, Harper, 1985.
Ivy Larkin. San Diego, Harcourt Brace, 1986.
The Cuckoo Clock, illustrated by Pamela Johnson. Boston, Godine, 1987.
The Scarecrows and Their Child, illustrated by Amy Schwartz. New York, Harper, 1987.
Storm in the Night, illustrated by Pat Cummings. New York, Harper, 1988.
Zekmet, The Stone Carver, illustrated by Deborah Nourse Lattimore. San Diego, Harcourt Brace, 1988.
Pangur Ban. New York, Harper, 1988.

Other

Night of Ghosts and Hermits: Nocturnal Life on the Seashore, illustrated by Susan Gallagher. San Diego, Harcourt Brace, 1985.

PUBLICATIONS FOR ADULTS

Novel

Truth and Consequence. New York, Harper, 1953.

*

Manuscript Collection: Kerlan Collection, University of Minnesota, Minneapolis.

Mary Stolz comments:

All children's book writers are asked why they don't write for adults. I have never formulated an answer satisfactory to a questioner. I don't attempt to formulate one for myself beyond the fact that I want to write for children, and the older I get the more I tend to do what I want to do. Long ago I wrote an adult book that was pleasantly received. From time to time I write short stories or articles for adults. But what I do best and most happily is write for children. I don't think it's easier than writing for adults. I don't think it's more difficult. It's different. The difference pleases me, so this is the part of the forest I remain in.

*   *   *

The birthday of a five-year-old near the end of *The Noonday Friends* comprises many of the compelling features identifying the singular experience of reading Mary Stolz. The circumstances leading to this most ordinary of special days are of little consequence, if not downright irrelevant. The moment, the present tense with an abundant awareness all its own, is of supreme importance to the author. Instead of being a component in a sequence of events, the treatment of the moment at hand is so enchanting that the past is reduced to little more than a genial anecdote, the future to an era that can wait. The plot remains a subdued entity alongside the primal enjoyment of the written word when it extends the immediacy of experience into the realm of the reader.

This birthday party is no mere day to remember, it is a model of a creative manner of cultivating a moment, inducing its singular properties with a radiance that seems too simple to contain the magic that it does. First of all the presents, tendered by a family and a friend who cannot afford store-bought products to a child who has yet to learn the stale grace of uttering, "It's the thought that counts." The babysitter offers a large box filled with cellophaned trinkets, decals, and cards culled from endless cereal boxes. "I also had my sisters…saving their cereal surprises too." Full marks, author and character, for originality in dreaming up an extensive no-cost childhood wonderland. But such simple gifts are a stock-in-trade frequency in reading Stolz. The presents continue. The elder sister offers a self-made book, a creation of many hours with each state of the United States on a separate page in a different color, a continuation of a babysitting activity that spontaneously emerged into a loving involvement that delighted both of them. The gift parallels the intriguing interaction between Stolz and her readers. As an author she is not principally a storyteller, but a molder of atmospheres in which she and her readers share enchanted moments constructed out of desire and the imagination. Even when they fade, they leave a legacy of enhanced self-understanding likely to evoke a personal era of good feeling.

A third offering, from financially strapped parents (the father an unemployed artist) is a ticket from an impromptu created family tourist bureau including an itinerary of an escorted walk through Greenwich Village after bedtime, "reasonable requests granted; bearer entitled to fifteen cents worth of refreshments." Such gifts of the Magi are founded not upon self-sacrifice, but on continuation and extension of relationships that reveal the magic of the ordinary. It would be good enough to eradicate the time for going to bed, but to glimpse as well what transpires during a period for reasons of age forbidden to behold, provides a realization of the mysteries which are ordinarily overlooked. But it is not Stolz's nature to overlook the underused by-products of existence.

No one acquainted with the more than 40 (and counting) of her books would accuse her of canonizing sentimentality. Quite the contrary. The dilemmas arise largely from the painful consciousness of loss, uncertainty, and the attendant frustration of not being understood. Polly (*Cider Days*) finds herself a continent apart from Kate, who for almost all her conscious life has been her inseparable friend and sole confidant. Life after Kate is not simply lonely, it is directionless and disillusioning. Kate's long delayed letter only confirms Polly's object demotion to a casual and very occasional correspondent. The solution to such self-debasement will come in a style satisfying, if already anticipated from the manner of the author. A new friend is already before her, and the friendship has begun to flower, if only Polly's self-imposed period of mourning did not provoke a sardonic assessment of a young girl who has much to offer and whose need of a friend has provoked a state of quiet desperation.

Again and again, it is the receptivity to the special qualities afforded by even the most ordinary of moments that enchants and elevates. Friendship itself is created by sensitive sharing of successive experiences, each of them rendered more than they are when enhanced by a companion who wishes to share them.

But Stolz does not preach. She doesn't have to. Her style makes the experience of the present of far grander importance than any solution rendered by happy conclusions. One of her more recent books, *Cat Walk*, sparkles with captivating celebrations of experiences, some heart-rending, others little more than ordinary activity, as a little girl's persistent practice of dressing a submissive barn kitten in doll's clothes and taking him for a walk in her small carriage. The volume is vintage Stolz. Among the more sparkling passages are the conversations among the animals, most of them former rejects as pets, who have become fortunately housed in a most unconventional home where compassion is accompanied by an intelligent approach to living.

The inner feelings speak for themselves, not in any confessional style, but in an honest and articulate manner of confronting thoughts that might ordinarily seem too difficult to extricate. Such challenges Stolz took on in her early books as *The Bully of Barkham Street*, now virtually a childhood classic. The subplots are as intriguing as the main storyline. The respectable housewife and mother has a younger brother who is committed to being a wanderer, and is now a hobo of several years standing. He is, however, non-belligerent and takes no stand against society at large. He proves an efficient listener and a provider of kindly counsel to his young nephew, the all-too-frequent victim of the bully next door. But the uncle does disappear on the sudden without goodbye or explanation. The agony of a loss which could be taken as betrayal is sensitively conveyed.

The sequel, *A Dog on Barkham Street*, defies odds which dictate that sequels are little more than warmed-over reappearances of characters and circumstances which have outworn their usefulness. Here the bully has his day of understanding. He is no force of evil, but an antagonist forced into the role through which he futilely sought to blanch the unrelenting agony of his existence. Mercifully there is no psychologizing. In its place is a remarkable capacity for articulating a point of view in a manner so simple and so comprehensive that it reduces probing analysis to something of a comic bore.

The prospect of reading through the Stolz canon provides little short of a capital justification of the art of living, a knowledge achieved less by what one learns than by the train of delights that attend each page. And while the plot seems less significant than the situation, many of the books are virtually indelible in the memory. Ask anyone who has read *The Bully of Barkham Street* within the past decade. Chances are they will recount the circumstances even if they cannot recall the author or the names of the characters. To be less famous than one's books is an achievement to be envied.

—Leonard R. Mendelsohn

STONE, Rosetta. See **SEUSS, Dr.**

STONG, Phil(ip Duffield). American. Born in Keosauqua, Iowa, 27 January 1899. Educated at Drake University, Des Moines, Iowa, A.B. 1919, 1924–25; Columbia University, New York, 1920–21; University of Kansas, Lawrence, 1923–24. Married Virginia Maude Swain in 1925. High school athletic director and journalism teacher, Iowa, 1919–23; editorial writer, Des Moines *Register*, 1923–25; wire editor, Associated Press, New York, 1925–26; copy editor, North American Newspaper Alliance, 1926–27; correspondent, *Liberty* magazine, New York, 1928, *Editor and Publisher*, New York, 1929, and New York *World*, 1929–31; screenwriter in Hollywood, 1932. Fellow, American Geological Society. Litt.D.: Parsons College, Fairfield, Iowa, 1939; LL.D.: Drake University, 1947. *Died 26 April 1957.*

PUBLICATIONS FOR CHILDREN (illustrated by Kurt Wiese)

Fiction

Farm Boy. New York, Doubleday, 1934.

Honk, The Moose. New York, Dodd Mead, 1935; London, Harrap, 1936.
No-Sitch, The Hound. New York, Dodd Mead, 1936; London, Harrap, 1937.
High Water. New York, Dodd Mead, 1937.
Edgar, The 7:58, illustrated by Lois Lenski. New York, Farrar and Rinehart, 1938.
Young Settler. New York, Dodd Mead, 1938.
Cowhand Goes to Town. New York, Dodd Mead, 1939.
The Hired Man's Elephant, illustrated by Doris Lee. New York, Dodd Mead, 1939.
Captain Kidd's Cow. New York, Dodd Mead, 1941.
Way Down Cellar. New York, Dodd Mead, 1942.
Missouri Canary. New York, Dodd Mead, 1943.
Censored, The Goat. New York, Dodd Mead, 1945.
Positive Pete! New York, Dodd Mead, 1947.
The Prince and the Porker. New York, Dodd Mead, 1950.
Hirum, The Hillbilly. New York, Dodd Mead, 1951.
Mississippi Pilot. New York, Doubleday, 1954.
A Beast Called an Elephant. New York, Dodd Mead, 1955.
Mike: The Story of a Young Circus Acrobat. New York, Dodd Mead, 1957.
Phil Stong's Big Book (omnibus). New York, Dodd Mead, 1961.

PUBLICATIONS FOR ADULTS

Novels

State Fair. New York, Century, and London, Barker, 1932.
Stranger's Return. New York, Harcourt Brace, and London, Barker, 1933.
Village Tale. New York, Harcourt Brace, and London, Barker, 1934.
Week-end. New York, Harcourt Brace, 1935.
The Farmer in the Dell. New York, Harcourt Brace, 1935.
Career. New York, Harcourt Brace, and London, Barker, 1936.
The Rebellion of Lennie Barlow. New York, Farrar and Rinehart, 1937.
Buckskin Breeches. New York, Farrar and Rinehart, and London, Barker, 1937.
Ivanhoe Keeler. New York, Farrar and Rinehart, 1939; London, Cassell, 1941.
The Long Lane. New York, Farrar and Rinehart, 1939.
The Princess. New York, Farrar and Rinehart, 1941.
The Iron Mountain. New York, Farrar and Rinehart, 1942.
One Destiny. New York, Reynal, 1942.
Jessamy John. New York, Doubleday, 1947.
Forty Pounds of Gold. New York, Doubleday, 1951.
Return in August. New York, Doubleday, 1953; London, Barker, 1954.
Blizzard. New York, Doubleday, 1955; London, Hodder and Stoughton, 1956.
The Adventures of "Horse" Barsby. New York, Doubleday, 1956.

Other

Shake 'em Up! A Practical Handbook of Polite Drinking, with Virginia Elliott. New York, Brewer and Warren, 1930.
County Fair. New York, Stackpole, 1938.
Horses and Americans. New York, Stokes, 1939.
If School Keeps. New York, Stokes, 1940.
Hawkeyes: A Biography of the State of Iowa. New York, Dodd Mead, 1940.
Marta of Muscovy: The Fabulous Life of Russia's First Empress. New York, Doubleday, 1945.

Gold in Them Hills, Being an Irreverent History of the Great 1849 Gold Rush. New York, Doubleday, 1947.

Editor, *The Other Worlds.* New York, Wilfred Funk, 1941; as *Modern Stories of Mystery and Imagination*, Garden City, New York, Garden City Publishing Company, 1942.

*

Manuscript Collection: University of Iowa libraries, Iowa City.

*   *   *

Phil Stong's emergence into children's literature was the rare example of a highly successful writer for adults who decided that writing for children was necessary to remind himself that directness, simplicity, and suspense are the critical ingredients of all good narrative writing. Stong was also convinced that the writer's roots must be the sources for his literary production. Born and raised in rural Iowa, Stong based all his better books on animals and the incidents of his youth.

The most famous of his books for children, *Honk, The Moose* (a runner-up for the 1936 Newbery Medal), remained in print until the mid 1980's. For a children's book to have this kind of staying power means it contains the ageless qualities that are associated with children's classics. *Honk* is a strongly masculine story in which boys joyfully indulge (traditionally, girls have read what boys like). Its slow-paced story allows Stong the space to flesh out his characters and to give marvelous descriptions of the northern midwest setting. It concerns some boys who one snowy winter find a hungry but decidedly friendly moose ensconced in their livery stable. Their failed attempts to dislodge Honk—and the attempts of the father, the police, the mayor and even the city council—provides Stong's reader with many humorously incongruent scenes. While this plot of a moose happy in his refuge is slight, Stong makes up for this with natural yet energetic dialogue, some of the best in children's literature. Included here are interesting and revealing comments on Finnish ethnolinguistics and culture which give the book a tone of studied authenticity.

Stong continued his powerful writing, on the level of *Honk*, for several years. Then, for some inexplicable reason, in the later years of his writing for children Stong seemed progressively to forget the formula that made such heralded accomplishments of his earlier books.

An example of his decline is *The Prince and the Porker*. This book evolves around the fantasy of a pig and a show horse, the best of friends, who carry on private conversations. The idea of a horse who cannot win prizes unless accompanied by a pig is too small a one to sustain even this slim volume, however, and its highly repetitive plot and its indecisive dialogue would thoroughly bore the modern child. It is punishing to observe here how the very standards Stong set for writers of children's books are so badly violated. The decline of Stong's capacity to concoct stories children appreciate is further evident in *Hirum, The Hillbilly* and in *A Beast Called an Elephant*. Both of these books lack adventure. Instead, they involve slow-moving, drably explanatory plots. Their stilted dialogue is matched by their failed attempts at humor and their lack of suspense. Worst of all, they do not center around children. As a whole, then, they contain nothing with which today's children can identify. (The copy of *A Beast Called an Elephant* I read for this review had not been checked out of a large library for 20 years!).

Stong did recover somewhat, from what was obviously the low point in his career, with *Mike: The Story of a Young Circus Acrobat*, which does have elements of adventure and suspense. But by and large it is true that the longer Stong wrote the lesser became his accomplishments. It is significant that an anthology of Stong's stories, *Phil Stong's Big Book*, issued in 1961, contains three of the first four stories he wrote for children.

—Patrick Groff

———

STOREY, Margaret. British. Born in London, 27 June 1926. Educated at Sutton High School, Surrey; Samuel King's School, Alston, Cumbria; St. Paul's Girls' School, London; Girton College, Cambridge, B.A. (honours) in English 1948, M.A. 1953. Private tutor, 1956–59; English teacher, Miss Ironside's School, London, 1959–69; senior teacher, Vale School, London, 1969–72; senior English teacher, The Study, Wimbledon, 1972–77, and Putney Park School, London, 1977. Agent: Curtis Brown, 162–168 Regent Street, London W1R 5TB, England.

PUBLICATIONS FOR CHILDREN

Fiction

Kate and the Family Tree, illustrated by Shirley Hughes. London, Bodley Head, 1965; as *The Family Tree*, Nashville, Nelson, 1973.
Pauline. London, Faber, 1965; New York, Doubleday, 1967.
The Smallest Doll, illustrated by Shirley Hughes. London, Faber, 1966.
The Smallest Bridesmaid, illustrated by Shirley Hughes. London, Faber, 1966.
Timothy and Two Witches, illustrated by Charles Stewart. London, Faber, 1966; New York, Dell, 1973.
The Stone Sorcerer, illustrated by Charles Stewart. London, Faber, 1967; as *The Stone Wizard*, 1979.
The Dragon's Sister, and Timothy Travels, illustrated by Charles Stewart. London, Faber, 1967; New York, Dell, 1974.
A Quarrel of Witches, illustrated by Doreen Roberts. London, Faber, 1970.
The Mollyday Holiday, illustrated by Janina Ede. London, Faber, 1971.
The Sleeping Witch, illustrated by Janina Ede. London, Faber, 1971.
Wrong Gear. London, Faber, 1973.
Keep Running. London, Faber, 1974; as *Ask Me No Questions*, New York, Dutton, 1975.
A War of Wizards, illustrated by Janina Ede. London, Faber, 1976.
The Double Wizard, illustrated by June Jackson. London, Faber, 1979.
Goodbye, Nanny Gray, with Jill Staynes. London, Bodley Head, 1987.
A Knife at the Opera, with Jill Staynes. London, Bodley Head, 1988.

*

Margaret Storey comments:

I write because I like writing; it's communicating ideas that interests me. No one in my books is a portrait of anyone I know, but places are often real ones. I have an acute recall of much of my childhood, a memory of frustrations, triumphs, failure to be understood, pleasures, and friends.

*   *   *

Margaret Storey began by writing for younger children. She has a great enthusiasm for wizardry and magic, and tales like *The Stone Sorcerer* and, most recently, *The Double Wizard*, show this clearly. She carefully defuses situations that could become frightening to the young reader, though a cleverly measured frisson of fear is allowed to creep up the spine, just enough to be enjoyable.

Her collections of tales about witches and magic, such as *The Dragon's Sister* and *A Quarrel of Witches*, balance excitement and humour. *The Smallest Bridesmaid* and *The Mollyday Holiday* are true-to-life stories of a little girl's joy when at last she is chosen to be a bridesmaid and, in the second story, when she goes on her long-awaited holiday. The drawings by Shirley Hughes are delightful. Most children will find something with which to identify in these stories of events which, at their age, are redletter days.

Her later books are for older girls, and invite them to identify with real-life situations which may be troubling them. *Pauline* is the story of a recently orphaned girl growing up with unsympathetic foster-parents who disapprove of her new friends. Storey does not talk down to her readers, nor does she resort to glib solutions to the problems she poses. The adolescent girl reading her books has to put something of herself into the situation.

In *Wrong Gear* a child of divorced parents is torn between loves and loyalties. She runs away from her father and his new wife to her mother, who is unable to take her in. Unexpected help comes from school, and she learns to grow up more happily. *Keep Running* is also a case of divided loyalty. A kidnapped girl builds up a complex relationship with her captor. While wanting to escape, she feels that because he has given her parole she owes him something and does not want to cause him trouble.

Since most teenagers at times feel torn between "want" and "ought," these books by an author who views their problems with sympathetic insight may well have a cathartic effect and prove helpful.

—Ann G. Hay

STORR, Catherine (née Cole). Has also written as Irene Adler; Helen Lourie. British. Born in London, 21 July 1913. Educated at St. Paul's Girls' School, London; Newnham College, Cambridge, 1932–36, 1939–41, B.A. (honours) in English 1935; West London Hospital, 1941–44, qualified medical practitioner 1944; Licensee, Royal College of Physicians; Member, Royal College of Surgeons. Married 1) the writer and psychiatrist Anthony Storr in 1942, three daughters; 2) Thomas Balogh in 1970. Assistant psychiatrist, West London Hospital, 1948–50; senior hospital medical officer, Department of Psychological Medicine, Middlesex Hospital, London, 1950–62; assistant editor, Penguin Books Ltd., London, 1966–70. Agent: A.D. Peters Ltd., 5th Floor, The Chambers, Chelsea Harbour, Lots Road, London SW10 0XF. Address: 12 Frognal Gardens, Flat 5, London NW3 6UX, England.

PUBLICATIONS FOR CHILDREN

Fiction

Ingeborg and Ruthy. London, Harrap, 1940.
Clever Polly and Other Stories, illustrated by Dorothy Craigie. London, Faber, 1952.
Stories for Jane, illustrated by Peggy Jeremy. London, Faber, 1952.
Clever Polly and the Stupid Wolf, illustrated by Marjorie-Ann Watts. London, Faber, 1955.
Polly, The Giant's Bride, illustrated by Marjorie-Ann Watts. London, Faber, 1956.

The Adventures of Polly and the Wolf, illustrated by Marjorie-Ann Watts. London, Faber, 1957; Philadelphia, Macrae Smith, 1970.
Marianne Dreams, illustrated by Marjorie-Ann Watts. London, Faber, 1958; as *The Magic Drawing Pencil*, New York, A.S. Barnes, 1960; revised edition, as *Marianne Dreams*, London, Penguin, 1964.
Marianne and Mark, illustrated by Marjorie-Ann Watts. London, Faber, 1960.
Lucy, illustrated by Dick Hart. London, Bodley Head, 1961; Englewood Cliffs, New Jersey, Prentice Hall, 1968.
Lucy Runs Away, illustrated by Dick Hart. London, Bodley Head, 1962; Englewood Cliffs, New Jersey, Prentice Hall, 1969.
Robin, illustrated by Peggy Fortnum. London, Faber, 1962; as *The Freedom of the Seas*, New York, Duell, 1965.
The Catchpole Story. London, Faber, 1965.
Rufus, illustrated by Peggy Fortnum. London, Faber, and Boston, Gambit, 1969.
Puss and Cat, illustrated by Carolyn Dinan. London, Faber, 1969.
Thursday. London, Faber, 1971; New York, Harper, 1972.
Kate and the Island, illustrated by Gareth Floyd. London, Faber, 1972.
The Painter and the Fish, illustrated by Alan Howard. London, Faber, 1975.
The Chinese Egg. London, Faber, and New York, McGraw Hill, 1975.
The Story of the Terrible Scar, illustrated by Gerald Rose. London, Faber, 1976.
Who's Bill? London, Macmillan, 1976.
Hugo and His Grandma, illustrated by Nita Sowter. Cambridge, Dinosaur, 1977.
Hugo and His Grandma's Washing Day, illustrated by Nita Sowter. Cambridge, Dinosaur, 1978.
Winter's End. London, Macmillan, 1978; New York, Harper, 1979.
Tales of Polly and the Hungry Wolf, illustrated by Jill Bennett. London, Faber, 1980.
Vicky. London, Faber, 1981.
The Bugbear, illustrated by Elaine McGregor Turney. London, Hamish Hamilton, 1981.
It Couldn't Happen to Me. Cambridge, Dinosaur, 1982.
February Yowler, illustrated by Gareth Floyd. London, Faber, 1982.
The Castle Boy. London, Faber, 1983.
Two's Company. London, Hardy, 1984.
It Shouldn't Happen to a Frog. London, Macmillan, 1984.
Wagga Storybooks (*Enter Wagga, Lost and Found Wagga, Wagga's Magic Ears, Watchdog Wagga*), illustrated by Colin Caket. London, Hamlyn, 4 vols., 1984.
Cold Marble and Other Ghost Stories. London, Faber, 1985.
The Underground Conspiracy. London, Faber, 1987.
The Boy and the Swan, illustrated by Laszlo Acs. London, Deutsch, 1987.
Not Too Young and Other Stories, with Griselda Gifford and Jill Kent. London, Macmillan, 1987.
Mrs. Circumference. London, Deutsch, 1989.
Daljit and the Unqualified Wizard. London, Heinemann, 1989.

Plays

Flax into Gold: The Story of Rumpelstiltskin (libretto), music by Hugo Cole. London, Chappell, 1964.

Television Plays: *Starting Out* series, 1973–78.

Other

Pebble (reader). London, Macmillan, 1979.

Pen Friends (reader), illustrated by Charles Front.   London, Macmillan, 1980.

People of the Bible series (*Noah and His Ark, Joseph and His Brothers, The Birth of Jesus, Jesus Begins His Work, Adam and Eve, Jonah and the Whale, The Prodigal Son, Miracles by the Sea, Moses of the Bulrushes, Joseph the Dreamteller, The First Easter, The Good Samaritan, Abraham and Isaac, Moses and the Plagues of Egypt, David and Goliath, St. Peter and St. Paul, Jesus and John the Baptist, Joseph the Long Lost Brother, Moses Leads His People, The Trials of Daniel, King David, Sampson and Delilah, Ruth's Story, Jesus the Healer*).   London, Watts, and Milwaukee, Raintree, 24 vols., 1982–86.

Feasts and Festivals, illustrated by Jenny Rhodes.   London, Hardy, 1983.

Great Tales from Long Ago (*Robin Hood, Hiawatha, The Pied Piper of Hamelin, Rip Van Winkle, Joan of Arc, King Midas and His Gold, King Arthur's Sword, Odysseus and the Enchanters, Theseus and the Minotaur, Dick Whittington, Androcles and the Lion, The Wooden Horse, Richard the Lionheart*).   London, Methuen, 13 vols., 1984–87; Milwaukee, Raintree, 12 vols., 1984–89; *The Wooden Horse* published as *The Trojan Horse*, Milwaukee, Raintree, 1985.

Easy Piano Picture Books (*Swan Lake, The Nutcracker, The Sleeping Beauty, Hansel and Gretel*), first vol. with Dianne Jackson.   London, Faber, 4 vols., 1987–89.

Let's Read Together series (*A Fast Move, Find the Specs, Grandpa's Birthday, Gran Builds a House*), illustrated by Toni Goffe.   London, Macdonald, 4 vols., 1987; Morristown, New Jersey, Silver Burdett, 3 vols., 1987; last vol. published as *Building a House*, Morristown, New Jersey, Silver Burdett, 1987.

Competitions and Ponies.   London, Macmillan, 1987.

PUBLICATIONS FOR ADULTS

Novels

A Question of Abortion (as Helen Lourie).   London, Bodley Head, 1962.

Freud for the Jung; or, Three Hundred and Sixty Six Hours on the Couch (as Irene Adler).   London, Cresset Press, 1963.

The Merciful Jew.   London, Barrie and Rockliff, 1968.

Black God, White God.   London, Barrie and Jenkins, 1972.

Unnatural Fathers.   London, Quartet, 1976.

Short Stories

Tales from the Psychiatrist's Couch.   London, Quartet, 1977.

Play

Radio Play: *Bevil*, 1984.

Other

Cook's Quick Reference: Essential Information on Cards.   London, Penguin, 1971.

Growing Up: A Practical Guide to Adolescence for Parents and Children.   London, Arrow, 1975.

Editor, *On Children's Literature*, by Isabelle Jan.   London, Allen Lane, 1973; New York, Schocken, 1974.

*

Manuscript Collection: Kerlan Collection, University of Minnesota Minneapolis.

Catherine Storr comments:

I am a compulsive writer and a natural storyteller, which is why I'm better and more successful at writing for children, who want a story above everything else, than I am at writing fiction for adults. I'm mainly interested in the area of the different faces of reality; hence the preoccupation with the possibilities of explaining events in more than one way—the "scientific" and "magical" explanations. I'm often classed as a writer of fantasy, but I prefer to think that I write in a sort of symbolic language which is no more obscure or pompous than that of folk or fairy stories.

I write for myself, only secondarily for a particular child, and then only if the child happens to want something I want to write. I consider writing to be for me a kind of auto-psycho-therapy, for which I'm fortunate enough to get paid by other people's attention and money as well as by what it does for me.

*   *   *

With any novelists, the fact of their profession is incidental: relevant, certainly, but not the main thing. Catherine Storr is widely known by the adults who buy her books approvingly to be a psychologist, and indeed there are details in her books which come from psychological interests, together with larger structures—the systematic duality of her stories, for instance, such that appearance and reality for the heroines run in clear and separate parallel throughout the narrative—which are surely the product of the analytic psychologist's frame of mind. Far more to the point, however, are the richly human characteristics of an unusually modest writer—modest in that one has constantly the sense that these books are lightly and easily written. The modesty belies great gifts: with greater ambitions, Storr could surely write as brilliantly and beautifully as the very best of children's novelists—do something as good as Philippa Pearce's *Tom's Midnight Garden*, say, or Joan Aiken's *The Whispering Mountain*. As it is, these bold, direct, continent tales are most stylishly directed to a few particular points of attention which are filled in with greater detail while the surrounding narrative moves briskly and briefly to the conclusion.

The duality I mentioned comes out most straightforwardly in the excellent Polly books. She takes the deeply traditional—if you like, Freudian-traditional—big bad wolf of fairy tale and makes him, in a rich, comic implausibility, into the inept, relentlessly stupid marauder of clever Polly's amiable suburban life. Persistent, gullible, dim, unfailingly goofy, the wolf pads round Chislehurst or Altrincham or Sutton Coldfield or wherever Polly lives, and—always promising to do his wolfish duty and gobble her up—is always outwitted by Polly's serene and patronizingly imperturbable good sense. One's only objection might be that Storr anaesthetizes the terrors which fairy tales embody so conveniently in any old big, bad, black omnivore rather too comfortably. Terrors still do walk abroad, after all, and if you don't call them "wolf," what name can they have? But little girls, it may be replied, have plenty to be frightened of, and it can only be exhilarating and strengthening to follow an example of such calm and affectionate (the heroine is often sorry for her wolf) resolution and adequacy as Polly.

The Polly books perfectly fit a congruence of tone, vocabulary, structure of sentiment and suspense to that of a normally impressionable little girl of, say, 7 years old. The Lucy books move at the same gentle but variously paced walk. To adapt a phrase, these stories walk like a child; they show a child's variety of attention, now closely focussed, now darting on to tell you what happens next, now coming comfortably to a close. The Lucy books would be an excellent first experience of reading a whole novel, but while making that rather limp developmental point of praise, I would also emphasize their warm sympathy, their recognisability, their loving faithfulness to the facts of a 7 or 8 year old's way of making up fictions in her head. The first Lucy book is perhaps a touch weaker than *Lucy Runs Away*. The duality here is between the real, tomboy, Lucy, who very believably wants nothing better than to *be* a boy, and her own lived fiction, Lew the detective. The brief little tale in which Lucy stows away in a robber's furniture van and effects the thieves' capture may even be found by a child to be less touching and to my mind certainly less real than the sequel in which the heroine carries out her threat to run away from her fantasy life into the real world, sounds the alarm to save a swimmer in trouble, and, sometimes frightened, sometimes tired, always indomitable, comes safely home. The best of this endearing, graceful tale, as it is of *Rufus*, is the delicate registration of railway journey and seaside, the sense Storr has of child's eye clarity of vision and child's pace which never fails her. I think it is best put by saying that hers are stories *told to listeners*, rather than novels written for readers.

This is true of the books written in a more major key, *Thursday* and the Marianne books, which mark the point at which the adult reader finds her enjoying larger and more demanding themes. A thriller like *The Catchpole Story* is thoroughly well done—a reworking of *Lucy* perhaps—where the moral interest is largely focussed on the interplay of 13-year-old girl and 7-year-old brother, and the way in which his perfectly spontaneous cheerfulness and tearfulness require her to maintain a grown-up courage and steadiness which she can, in a scarey adventure, only just manage. But the significance of neither novel lies in characterization, but rather in the truths to be learned about and from a reality which appears to be merely fantastic. In *Marianne Dreams* Marianne's long convalescence is the opportunity for entering the intense and vivid world of the dream house in which she constructs a model of the process of convalescence itself, and constructs it moreover on behalf of the invalid boy Mark, and in the face of the threats of death and destruction themselves. So the story is a metaphor for nursing, itself the noblest symbol in our pictures of femininity: of altruism, patience, gentleness—and gentleness, as the novel makes clear, is in no way incompatible with a tough insistence on self-determination. I think it is her best book, although the sequel moves into an altogether larger and more populated world and is the longest of Storr's novels. It is good of course, but shrewd rather than fine, gingerly rather than delicate about adolescent love and softness. *Marianne Dreams* has gravity and power (for all that it overworks suspense), and it correctly interweaves the psyche and morality.

None of these books is thin; each, like their heroines and heroes, is small and solid, and if Storr is an occasional rather than a dedicated writer, a good storyteller rather than an artist, and wholesome rather than really creative, her gifts and qualities are strong, humorous, motherly, and indispensable. This is not to sell her cheaply. *Marianne Dreams* is unquestionably a classic; with *Tom's Midnight Garden* and Gillian Avery's *The Warden's Niece* it may be taken to have initiated the remarkable flowering of children's novels we enjoyed in Britain for the twenty years after their publication. Polly and her Wolf are, by the same token, by now unshakeably settled in the galaxies of the primary school heavens: there are very few assemblies or storytimes in which they are not regularly acclaimed. Storr, in a way surprising but admirable in a clinical analyst, makes heroism out of great good sense and the kind of greatness and goodness only made possible by a sense of humour.

—Fred Inglis

———

STRANG, Herbert. Pseudonym for George Herbert Ely and C. James L'Estrange. British. **ELY, George Herbert:** Born in London in 1866. Married Margaret Ashworth. Worked for Oxford University Press from 1920. *Died 17 September 1958.* **L'ESTRANGE, C. James:** Born in London in 1867. Married Maude L'Estrange. Worked for Oxford University Press from 1920. *Died 8 January 1947.* Both writers edited, with others, many books and annuals as Mrs. Herbert Strang.

PUBLICATIONS FOR CHILDREN

Fiction

Tom Burnaby. London, Blackie, 1904; as *Young Tom Burnaby*, New York, Street and Smith, n.d.
Boys of the Light Brigade, illustrated by William Rainey. London, Blackie, 1904; as *The Light Brigade in Spain*, New York, Putnam, 1904.
Kobo, illustrated by William Rainey. London, Blackie, 1904; New York, Putnam, 1905.
Brown of Moukden, illustrated by William Rainey. London, Blackie, 1905; New York, Putnam, 1906; as *Jack Brown, The Hero*, New York, Street and Smith, n.d.; as *Jack Brown in China*, London, Oxford University Press, 1923.
The Adventures of Harry Rochester, illustrated by William Rainey. London, Blackie, and New York, Putnam, 1905.
Jack Hardy, illustrated by William Rainey. London, Hodder and Stoughton, 1906; Indianapolis, Bobbs Merrill, 1907.
One of Clive's Heroes, illustrated by William Rainey. London, Hodder and Stoughton, 1906; as *In Clive's Command*, Indianapolis, Bobbs Merrill, 1906.
Samba, illustrated by William Rainey. London, Hodder and Stoughton, 1906; as *Fighting on the Congo*, Indianapolis, Bobbs Merrill, 1906.
Rob the Ranger, illustrated by W.H. Margetson. London, Hodder and Stoughton, and Indianapolis, Bobbs Merrill, 1907.
With Drake on the Spanish Main, illustrated by Archibald Webb. London, Hodder and Stoughton, 1907; as *On the Spanish Main*, Indianapolis, Bobbs Merrill, 1909.
King of the Air, illustrated by W.E. Webster. London, Hodder and Stoughton, and Indianapolis, Bobbs Merrill, 1907.
On the Trail of the Arabs, illustrated by Charles Sheldon. Indianapolis, Bobbs Merrill, 1907.
Herbert Strang's Historical Series (*With Marlborough to Malplaquet*, *With the Black Prince*, *A Mariner of England*, *One of Rupert's Horse*, and *Lion-Heart*, all with Richard Stead; *Claud the Archer* and *In the New Forest*, both with John Aston; *Roger the Scout* and *For the White Rose*, both with George Lawrence). London, Hodder and Stoughton, 9 vols., 1907–12.
Humphrey Bold. London, Hodder and Stoughton, 1908; Indianapolis, Bobbs Merrill, 1909.
Barclay of the Guides, illustrated by H.W. Koekkoek. London, Hodder and Stoughton, 1908; New York, Doran, 1909.
Lord of the Seas, illustrated by C. Fleming Williams. London, Hodder and Stoughton, 1908; New York, Doran, 1910.
Palm Tree Island, illustrated by Archibald Webb and Alan Wright. London, Hodder and Stoughton, 1909; New York, Doran, 1910.
Settlers and Scouts, illustrated by T.C. Dugdale. London, Hodder and Stoughton, 1909; New York, Doran, 1910.
Swift and Sure. London, Hodder and Stoughton, 1909; New York, Doran, 1910.
The Cruise of the Gyro-Car, illustrated by A.C. Michael. London, Hodder and Stoughton, 1910.
The Adventures of Dick Trevanion, illustrated by William Rainey. London, Hodder and Stoughton, 1910.
Round the World in Seven Days, illustrated by A.C. Michael. London, Hodder and Stoughton, and New York, Doran, 1910.

The Flying Boat, illustrated by T.C. Dugdale. London, Hodder and Stoughton, 1911.

The Air Scout, illustrated by W.R.S. Stott. London, Hodder and Stoughton, 1911.

The Motor Scout, illustrated by Cyrus Cuneo. London, Hodder and Stoughton, 1912.

The Air Patrol, illustrated by Cyrus Cuneo. London, Hodder and Stoughton, 1912.

Cerdic the Saxon, with L.L. Weedon. London, Hodder and Stoughton, 1913.

A Little Norman Maid. London, Hodder and Stoughton, 1913; New York, Doran, n.d.

Sultan Jim, Empire Builder. London, Hodder and Stoughton, 1913.

A Gentleman-at-Arms. London, Hodder and Stoughton, 1914.

A Hero of Liège. London, Hodder and Stoughton, 1914.

Fighting with French. London, Hodder and Stoughton, 1915.

The Boy Who Would Not Learn. London, Oxford University Press, 1915; New York, Oxford University Press, 1921.

The Silver Shot. London, Oxford University Press, 1915; New York, Oxford University Press, 1921.

In Trafalgar's Bay. London, Oxford University Press, 1915; New York, Oxford University Press, 1921.

Burton of the Flying Corps. London, Hodder and Stoughton, 1916.

Frank Forester. London, Hodder and Stoughton, 1916.

The Old Man of the Mountain, illustrated by René Bull. London, Hodder and Stoughton, 1916.

Through the Enemy's Lines, illustrated by H.E. Elcock. London, Hodder and Stoughton, 1916.

Carry On!, illustrated by H.E. Elcock and H. Evison. London, Hodder and Stoughton, 1917.

With Haig on the Somme. London, Oxford University Press, 1917.

Steady, Boys, Steady. London, Hodder and Stoughton, 1917.

The Long Trail. London, Oxford University Press, 1918.

Tom Willoughby's Scouts. London, Oxford University Press, 1919.

The Blue Raider. London, Oxford University Press, 1919.

Bright Ideas, illustrated by C.E. Brock. London, Oxford University Press, 1920.

No Man's Island, illustrated by C.E. Brock. London, Oxford University Press, 1921.

The Cave in the Hills. London, Oxford University Press, 1922.

Bastable Cove. London, Oxford University Press, 1922.

Winning His Name, illustrated by C.E. Brock. London, Oxford University Press, 1922.

Honour First, illustrated by W.E. Wightman. London, Oxford University Press, 1923.

True as Steel, illustrated by C.E. Brock. London, Oxford University Press, 1923.

A Thousand Miles an Hour. London, Oxford University Press, 1924.

The Heir of a Hundred Kings. London, Oxford University Press, 1924.

Young Jack. London, Oxford University Press, 1924.

Martin of Old London. London, Oxford University Press, 1925.

Olwyn's Secret. London, Oxford University Press, 1925.

Dan Bolton's Discovery. London, Oxford University Press, 1926.

Strang's Penny Books (*Three Boys at the Fair, Kitty's Kitten, The Cinema Dog, Bill Sawyer's V.C., The Game of Brownies, Jenny's Ark, Baa-Baa and the Wide World, Tom Leaves School, The Mischief-Making Magpie, A Ride with Robin Hood, Pete's Elephant, Ten Pounds Reward, Adolf's Dog, The Adventures of a Penny Stamp, Don't Be Too Sure, Jack and Jocko, The Princess and the Robbers, The Christmas Fairy, The Seven Sons, The Red Candle, The Miller's Daughter, The Grey Goose Feathers, The Birthday Present, There Was a Little Pig, The Magic Smoke, The Children of the Ferry, Sugar Candy Town, Little Mr. Pixie, The Little Sea Horse, The Little Blue-Grey Hare*). London, Oxford

University Press, 30 vols., 1926–27.

Lost in London. London, Oxford University Press, 1927.

The River Pirates. London, Oxford University Press, 1927.

The Riders. London, Oxford University Press, 1928.

On London River. London, Oxford University Press, 1929.

Ships and Their Story: Scouting Stories. London, Oxford University Press, 1931.

Dickon of the Chase. London, Oxford University Press, 1931.

A Servant of John Company. London, Oxford University Press, 1932.

Other

The Boyhood of the King. London, Hodder and Stoughton, 1911.

Our Great Adventure. London, Hodder and Stoughton, 1913; New York, Oxford University Press, 1921.

The British Army [Navy] in War. London, Hodder and Stoughton, 2 vols., 1916.

The Empire in Arms. London, Hodder and Stoughton, 1916.

Great Britain and the War. London, Hodder and Stoughton, 1916; revised edition, 1918.

The Story of Daniel [Joseph]. London, Oxford University Press, 2 vols., 1927.

The Splendid Book for Boys. London, Oxford University Press, 1931.

Editor, *Herbert Strang's Annual*. London, Hodder and Stoughton, 10 vols., 1908–17, and London, Oxford University Press, 9 vols., 1918–26; continued as *The Oxford Annual for Boys*, Oxford University Press, 15 vols., 1927–41.

Editor, *Herbert Strang's Library*. London, Hodder and Stoughton and Oxford University Press, 56 vols., 1909–39.

Editor, *The Boys' Holiday [Story] Book*. London, Hodder and Stoughton, 2 vols., 1910.

Editor, *The Romance of the World*. London, Hodder and Stoughton, 23 vols., 1910–15.

Editor, *By Land and Sea*. London, Hodder and Stoughton, 1911.

Editor, *In School and Camp*. London, Hodder and Stoughton, 1911.

Editor, *The Red [Green, Blue, Brown, Purple, Orange, Scarlet] Book for Boys*. London, Hodder and Stoughton and Oxford University Press, 7 vols., 1911–20.

Editor, *Stirring Tales*. London, Hodder and Stoughton, 1911.

Editor, *Treasure Trove*. London, Hodder and Stoughton, 1911.

Editor, *Daring Deeds*. London, Hodder and Stoughton, 1912.

Editor, *Peril and Adventure*. London, Hodder and Stoughton, 1912.

Editor, *The Red Book of British Battles [the War]*. London, Hodder and Stoughton, 2 vols., 1914–15.

Editor, *The Blue Book of British Naval Battles [the War]*. London, Hodder and Stoughton, 2 vols., 1914–16.

Editor, *Herbert Strang's Book of Adventure Stories*. London, Hodder and Stoughton, 1914.

Editor, *Herbert Strang's Readers*. London, Hodder and Stoughton, 76 vols., 1914–41.

Editor, *This Year's Book for Boys*. New York, Doran, 1914.

Editor, *The Children's Hour*. London, Hodder and Stoughton, 6 vols., 1915.

Editor, *Little Talks about Birds and Beasts*. London, Hodder and Stoughton, 1915.

Editor, *The Battle and the Breeze*. London, Hodder and Stoughton, 1915.

Editor, *For the Flag*. London, Hodder and Stoughton, 1915.

Editor, *Shoulder to Shoulder*. London, Hodder and Stoughton, 1915.

Editor, *The Boys' Treasury*. London, Hodder and Stoughton, 1915.

Editor, *The Bugle Call.*   London, Hodder and Stoughton, 1915.
Editor, *Play the Game.*   London, Hodder and Stoughton, 1915.
Editor, *Hearts of Oak.*   London, Hodder and Stoughton, 1915.
Editor, *Ready, Aye Ready!*   London, Hodder and Stoughton, 1915.
Editor, *Great Battles of the British Army.*   London, Hodder and Stoughton, 1915.
Editor, *Every Boy's Book of the War.*   New York, Doran, 1916.
Editor, *With Our Brave Allies* [the British Army, the British Navy].   London, Hodder and Stoughton, 3 vols., 1916.
Editor, *Our Allies and Enemies.*   London, Hodder and Stoughton, 1916.
Editor, *The War at Sea* [on Land].   London, Hodder and Stoughton, 2 vols., 1916.
Editor, *The Clarion Call.*   London, Hodder and Stoughton, 1917.
Editor, *Fall In!*   London, Hodder and Stoughton, 1917.
Editor, *Fife and Drum.*   London, Hodder and Stoughton, 1917.
Editor, *The Oxford Annual for Scouts.*   London, Oxford University Press, 5 vols., 1919–23.
Editor, *The Red Book for Scouts.*   London, Oxford University Press, 1921.
Editor, *The Golden Book for Boys.*   London, Oxford University Press, 1922.
Editor, *The Big Books.*   London, Oxford University Press, 10 vols., 1923–29.
Editor, with Mrs. Herbert Strang, *The Great Books.*   London, Oxford University Press, 10 vols., 1925–30.
Editor, *One Hundred Poems for Boys* [Children, Girls].   London, Oxford University Press, 3 vols., 1925.
Editor, *Half Holiday Tales.*   London, Oxford University Press, 1926.
Editor, *Fifty Poems for Infants.*   London, Oxford University Press, 1927.
Editor, *Little Books of the Bible.*   London, Oxford University Press, 12 vols., 1927–36.
Editor, *Stories from the Bible.*   London, Oxford University Press, 6 vols., 1927.
Editor, with Mrs. Herbert Strang, *The Grand Books.*   London, Oxford University Press, 3 vols., 1928.
Editor, *Two Hundred Poems for Boys and Girls.*   London, Oxford University Press, 1928.
Editor, *The Happy Readers.*   London, Oxford University Press, 6 vols., 1929.
Editor, *Stories for the Class-Room.*   London, Oxford University Press, 6 vols., 1930.
Editor, *Scouting Stories.*   London, Oxford University Press, 1931.
Editor, with Mrs. Herbert Strang, *The Golden Story Books.*   London, Oxford University Press, 10 vols., 1931–36.
Editor, with Mrs. Herbert Strang, *The Golden Treasure Book for Boys.*   London, Oxford University Press, 1931.
Editor, *Toddles Own Book.*   London, Oxford University Press, 1931.
Editor, *A Treasury of English Prose for Schools.*   London, Oxford University Press, 1932.
Editor, *The Bright Books for Boys.*   London, Oxford University Press, 4 vols., 1933–36.
Editor, *The New Blue* [Buff] *Book for Boys.*   London, Oxford University Press, 2 vols., 1934.
Editor, *The New Red Book for Scouts.*   London, Oxford University Press, 1935.
Editor, *The Rainbow Readers.*   London, Oxford University Press, 16 vols., 1936.
Editor, *The Giant Book for Boys.*   London, Oxford University Press, 2 vols., 1937–38.
Editor, *The Happy Days Series*, by John Anderson.   London, Oxford University Press, 2 vols., 1937.
Editor, *The Picture Story Books*, by John Anderson.   London, Ox-

ford University Press, 15 vols., 1937–39.
Editor, *Round the World Series*, by John Anderson.   London, Oxford University Press, 5 vols., 1937–39.
Editor, *Gateway to Adventure* [Romance]: *Fifteen Stories for Boys* [Girls].   London, Oxford University Press, 2 vols., 1938.
Editor, *Jolly Days for Boys.*   London, Oxford University Press, 1939.
Editor, *Stories for Boys.*   London, Oxford University Press, 1940.

Other by George Herbert Ely

History of England from 1603 to the Present Time.   London, Blackie, 1896.

Editor, with others, *Blackie's Junior School Shakespeare.*   London, Blackie, 1893.

PUBLICATIONS FOR ADULTS

Other by C. James L'Estrange

Familiar London.   London, Nister, 1890.

Other by George Herbert Ely

Translator, *Songs of Béranger.*   London, Blackie, 1899.
Translator, *The Women of the Renaissance: A Study of Feminism*, by René de Maulde-la-Clavière.   London, Swan Sonnenschein, 1900.
Translator, *The Art of Life*, by René de Maulde-la-Clavière.   London, Swan Sonnenschein, 1902.
Translator, *Saint Cajetan*, by René de Maulde-la-Clavière.   London, Duckworth, 1902.

*   *   *

Herbert Strang, a synthetic name derived from two collaborators, George Herbert Ely and James L'Estrange, was one of those authors regarded in the early years of the 20th century as the likely successor to G.A. Henty as the master of boys' adventure stories. Nor is this view surprising, for Strang's first publisher, Blackie, had been Henty's, and many of Strang's titles, such as *With Drake on the Spanish Main* or *One of Clive's Heroes* almost echo those of the popular Victorian's. Like Henty, furthermore, Strang was able and willing to turn his hand to many different kinds of work, and in addition to producing over 50 full-length tales was responsible for School Readers, for retellings of Biblical stories, for editing a famous *Annual* for many years as well as anthologies of poetry and prose, and also collaborated with various scholars on a *Historical Series* with such titles as *One of Rupert's Horse.*

Most of the full-length tales follow a predictable pattern, where a young hero, usually in a foreign setting, encounters an immediate crisis, such as a shipwreck or a minor skirmish, from which he escapes only to become engaged in a more urgent mission, to gather secret information in *Barclay of the Guides*, or to warn of a threatened ambush in *Tom Burnaby*, but which in the performance involves the hero in even graver matters, the Indian Mutiny, the Slave Trade, the '45 Rebellion, to give three examples. Needless to say, the hero acquits himself valiantly and is ultimately rewarded with material success.

Strang's execution of this kind of formulaic plot is very limited, however. The heroes are endowed with little individuality, and other characters, especially foreigners, are treated as predictable stereotypes. The geographical backgrounds, sometimes attributed to the travels of L'Estrange, have a kind of vitality, especially the

African Congo in *Tom Burnaby*, but the historical background is often only peripheral, and has little of Henty's thorough, if dull, documentation, even in the *Historical Series*.

Like Westerman, Strang made some attempts to update his material, and in addition to his historical stories and tales of contemporary adventure in exotic parts, wrote several books about World War I, though works such as *With Haig on the Somme* are embarrassing to read now because of their overall lack of taste as well as depth. More interesting are a series of books in which Strang uses pseudo-scientific inventions as the background for his heroes' adventures, somewhat in the manner of Jules Verne.

King of the Air, for example, tells the story of young Tom Dorrell who designs and builds a strange airship, shaped like a bird but power-fuelled, which, because of its extraordinary capacity to hover, and to land vertically, is able not only to rescue sailors from drowning, but also to land on the flat roof of a Moroccan Kasbah and rescue a British diplomat, held hostage by rebel tribesmen! There is some attempt at comedy in the portrayal of Tom's rich eccentric patron, and a cowardly German salesman, Herr Schwab, but the book also reveals a disturbing anti-semitism. If Strang's books survive, it is likely to be because of the curiosity-value of their technology than because of their literary values.

—Dennis Butts

STRANGER, Joyce. Pseudonym for Joyce Muriel Wilson, née Judson. British. Born in Forest Gate, London, 26 May. Educated at County School for Girls, Dartford, Kent; University College, London, B.Sc. 1942. Married Kenneth B. Wilson in 1944; two sons and one daughter. Research chemist, Imperial Chemical Industries, Manchester, 1942–46. Lecturer and writer on dog training. Lives in Anglesey, Wales. Agent: Aitken and Stone, 29 Fernshaw Road, London SW10 0TG, England.

PUBLICATIONS FOR CHILDREN

Fiction

Wild Cat Island, illustrated by Joe Acheson. London, Methuen, 1961.
Circus All Alone, illustrated by Sheila Rose. London, Harrap, 1965.
Jason—Nobody's Dog, illustrated by Douglas Phillips. London, Dent, 1970.
The Honeywell Badger, illustrated by Douglas Phillips. London, Dent, 1972.
Paddy Joe. London, Collins, 1973.
The Hare at Dark Hollow, illustrated by Charles Pickard. London, Dent, 1973.
Trouble for Paddy Joe. London, Collins, 1973.
The Secret Herds: Animal Stories, illustrated by Douglas Reay. London, Dent, 1974.
Paddy Joe at Deep Hollow Farm. London, Collins, 1975.
The Fox at Drummer's Darkness, illustrated by William Geldart. London, Dent, 1976; New York, Farrar Straus, 1977.
The Wild Ponies, illustrated by Robert Rothero. London, Kaye and Ward, 1976.
Paddy Joe and Thomson's Folly. London, Pelham, 1979.
The Curse of Seal Valley. London, Dent, 1979.
Vet on Call. London, Carousel, 1981.
Double Trouble. London, Carousel, 1981.

Vet Riding High. London, Carousel, 1982.
No More Horses. London, Carousel, 1982.
Dial V.E.T. London, Carousel, 1982.
Marooned! London, Kaye and Ward, 1982.
The Hound of Darkness. London, Dent, 1983.
Shadows in the Dark. London, Kaye and Ward, 1984.
The Family at Fools' Farm. London, Dent, 1985.
Spy, The No-Good Pup. London, Dent, 1989.

Verse

Joyce Stranger's Book of Hanák's Animals, illustrated by Mirko Hanák. London, Dent, 1976.

PUBLICATIONS FOR ADULTS

Novels

The Running Foxes. London, Hammond, 1965; New York, Viking Press, 1966.
Breed of Giants. London, Hammond, 1966; New York, Viking Press, 1967.
Rex. London, Harvill Press, 1967; New York, Viking Press, 1968.
Casey. London, Harvill Press, 1968; as *Born to Trouble*, New York, Viking Press, 1968.
Rusty. London, Harvill Press, 1969; as *The Wind on the Dragon*, New York, Viking Press, 1969.
One for Sorrow. London, Corgi, 1969.
Zara. London, Harvill Press, and New York, Viking Press, 1970.
Chia, The Wildcat. London, Harvill Press, 1971.
Lakeland Vet. London, Harvill Press, and New York, Viking Press, 1972.
Walk a Lonely Road. London, Harvill Press, 1973.
Never Count Apples. London, Harvill Press, 1974.
Never Tell a Secret. London, Harvill Press, 1975.
Flash. London, Harvill Press, 1976.
Khazan, The Horse That Came Out of the Sea. London, Harvill Press, 1977.
A Walk in the Dark. London, Joseph, 1978.
The January Queen. London, Joseph, 1979.
The Stallion. London, Joseph, 1981.
Josse. London, Joseph, 1983.
The Hounds of Hades. London, Joseph, 1985.

Short Stories

A Dog Called Gelert and Other Stories. London, Corgi, 1973.
The Monastery Cat and Other Stories. London, Corgi, 1982.

Other

Kym: The True Story of a Siamese Cat. London, Joseph, 1976; New York, Coward McCann, 1977.
Two's Company. London, Joseph, 1977.
Three's a Pack. London, Joseph, 1980.
All about Your Pet Puppy. London, Pelham, 1980.
How to Own a Sensible Dog. London, Corgi, 1981.
Two for Joy. London, Joseph, 1982.
Stranger Than Fiction: The Biography of Elspeth Bryce-Smith. London, Joseph, 1984.
A Dog in a Million. London, Joseph, 1984.
Dog Days. London, Joseph, 1986.
Double or Quit. London, Joseph, 1987.

*

Manuscript Collection: Boston University.

Joyce Stranger comments:

I trained as a biologist. I have always spent my spare time watching animals, as I specialised in animal behaviour. Many books, especially those for children, are inaccurate, or sentimentalise or humanise the animal. Animals exist in their own right, live in worlds which impinge on ours but in no way are similar to ours. I try to show how (as far as a human can) animals live in a world that is real to *them*. In my adult books I am portraying country life in a state of change—the old ways and the little farms, the country sports that over-civilised urban people may end forever—to our great loss, as human and animal need to co-exist for balance, sanity, and to improve the quality of life. Man in an urban surrounding is doomed to increasing lack of mental stability. Those who retain the link with nature remain balanced—even the presence of a dog in the house restores proportion, if the dog is studied. No one is a hero or a great man to his dog—it speedily removes delusions of grandeur. The human-animal partnership is vital to all of us—but too many of us have lost the knowledge of this.

Too many believe the human is above the animals. We are animals. We experience pain, fear, panic; the expression in the eyes of a mouse with her young is that of a mother with her child. The reaction to danger is the same. We need to marvel at the intricacies of creation, the immense variety in the animal world, and we need to fight for the right to inherit wildlife in variety and not to reduce the marvels of creation to human tidiness and concrete prisons away from sun and trees and flowers. Suburban gardens and the cult of the family pet show men's needs—yet how many children's writers are aware of the tremendous bond between a boy who cares about animals and his dog, or the girl and her horse (and not on pony club levels)?

Training people to train their dogs reveals an enormous gap in understanding animals. Many failed relationships are due to the human partner believing the animal thinks on human terms. My five Carousel books are intended as part educational, in that they are aimed at trying to show in a light readable way, to people who would not read non-fiction, just how an animal's mind does work. When an animal is understood, the ensuing partnership is far more rewarding to both partners, in a way that most people would not understand as they have never experienced the total trust and obedience of an animal that works with them as opposed to being dependent on them. This is the theme of many of my books; for many people, an animal can provide a harmony lacking in day-to-day relationships with people; the animal asks little and gives all the time. I train people to train their dogs and understand them.

* * *

Joyce Stranger's work has a wide appeal. Many of her adult novels, especially those which are about animals, are enjoyed by children too. She has a knack with storylines which is hard to define. Indeed, how define the qualities which make a bestseller? *The Running Foxes*, which first established her reputation, was a best-seller, and many of her other novels share the same simplicity of outline and the same sympathetic insight into animal nature. A favourite theme is friendship between a person and an animal—no new theme, granted, but nevertheless given lively renewal in many of her books: *Jason—Nobody's Dog*, the Paddy Joe books, *Walk a Lonely Road*, and her latest children's novel, *Spy, The No-Good Pup*.

Stranger is keenly aware of the destructiveness of humankind. This defines a moral sense that runs through all her work. It sometimes means that a rather depressing tone pervades the story when the human protagonists feel guilty and remorseful. *The Honeywell Badger*, for instance, is about a boy and girl who are so keen to have a badger for a pet they pay a poacher for one and learn too late what problems they have brought upon themselves and the poor animal.

In *Trouble for Paddy Joe* the boy has neglected the training of his young Alsatian, Storm. Consequently the dog, ignoring Paddy Joe's call, wanders off and gets lost in a Scottish wilderness. Everything that happens during the boy's long search for the dog makes a convincing and interesting narrative—the finding of an old diary confirming a legend, the exploring of the island, the storm, and the solitary boat trip—but the reader is all this time in the company of Paddy Joe who is no coward but desperately sad, lonely, and guilty; his thoughtless launching of the boat in which he nearly dies from exposure is like a beckoning to death.

With *The Hare at Dark Hollow*, on the other hand, we can enjoy watching an animal's intelligence and resilience as it adapts to a series of changes in its habitat. In the rich area of "animal biography" in English literature this is a book of real distinction. It tells a year in the life of a young hare entirely from the animal's point of view. The reader learns that Dark Hollow is to be developed as building land. We see the emigration or destruction of wildlife, the chain reaction in a habitat once busy with small creatures, the new fears and dangers for survivors. The ending, a happy one, is also true: hares find refuge from human hunters and other predators on the grassy expanses of airfields. The tension, always present in Stranger's books, between animals' right to live and mankind's careless destructiveness provides a current of controlled feeling and mounting suspense throughout the book.

In *The Fox at Drummer's Darkness* Stranger found artistic form and expression which resolve the conflicting elements in her talent. It is an extraordinary achievement, transcending all the problems that dogged her earlier efforts to relate man and beast in one literary frame. Conceived, it seems, in one daemonic impulse of creation, it has something of the epic, something of the ballad. Its few human characters are simple, unchanging figures like statues; the constantly recurring themes of burning drought, ghostly army, threat of industrial poison, give the book a structural rhythm that works inexorably towards its climax. The farmer projects all his primitive fears upon the fox, the senile huntsman lives a fantasy of hunts that never will be, and Johnny Toosmall, nightwatchman at the factory, befriends the starving, scavenging animal. But it is the animal, the fox itself, who is at the centre, alive in every detail, its intelligence and endurance stretched to the utmost and described with loving insight and understanding.

> Men were asleep. The glowing street lamps showed nothing but the fox's shadow, growing eerily long, shrinking uncannily, fading, and re-appearing on the opposite side of him, worrying him. He was used to sun shadow and moon shadow, predictable as dusk and starset, but he had never seen ranked lamps before, nor watched the change as he ran between them.
>
> At first, as the shadow flashed along the ground, he froze, watching the unnerving shape freeze with him. Then, as he ran, it began to play again, first large, then small, a fleeting silent darkness glued to his paws by a magic that he never understood.
>
> A cat sped in front of him, turned, horrified, and swiftly slashed his face in quick daring. It knew the free ways better than he, so that it leaped, lightning fast, over a wall and vanished under a garden shed…

We find the same poetic style in the short pieces she has written for Hanák's animals. She has been refining this vivid, flowing language all her professional life.

—Gwen Marsh

STREATFEILD, (Mary) Noel. Also wrote as Susan Scarlett. British. Born in Amberley, Sussex, 24 December 1895. Educated at schools in St. Leonard's on Sea, Sussex; Laleham School, Eastbourne, Sussex; Academy of Dramatic Art, London. Actress in England, South Africa, and Australia, 1920's; joined Women's Voluntary Services in 1939. Recipient: Library Association Carnegie Medal, 1939. O.B.E. (Officer, Order of the British Empire), 1983. *Died 11 September 1986.*

PUBLICATIONS FOR CHILDREN

Fiction

Ballet Shoes, illustrated by Ruth Gervis.   London, Dent, 1936; New York, Random House, 1937.
Tennis Shoes, illustrated by D.L. Mays.   London, Dent, 1937; New York, Random House, 1938.
The Circus Is Coming, illustrated by Steven Spurrier.   London, Dent, 1938; revised edition, 1948, 1960; as *Circus Shoes*, New York, Random House, 1939.
Dennis the Dragon, illustrated by Ruth Gervis.   London, Dent, 1939.
The House in Cornwall, illustrated by D.L. Mays.   London, Dent, 1940; as *The Secret of the Lodge*, New York, Random House, 1940.
The Children of Primrose Lane, illustrated by Marcia Lane Foster.   London, Dent, 1941; as *The Stranger in Primrose Lane*, New York, Random House, 1941.
Harlequinade, illustrated by Clarke Hutton.   London, Chatto and Windus, 1943.
Curtain Up, illustrated by D.L. Mays.   London, Dent, 1944; as *Theater Shoes; or, Other People's Shoes*, New York, Random House, 1945.
Party Frock, illustrated by Anna Zinkeisen.   London, Collins, 1946; as *Party Shoes*, New York, Random House, 1947.
The Painted Garden, illustrated by Ley Kenyon.   London, Collins, 1949; revised edition, London, Penguin, 1961; as *Movie Shoes*, New York, Random House, 1949.
Osbert, illustrated by Susanne Suba.   Chicago, Rand McNally, 1950.
The Theater Cat, illustrated by Susanne Suba.   Chicago, Rand McNally, 1951.
White Boots, illustrated by Milein Cosman.   London, Collins, 1951; as *Skating Shoes*, New York, Random House, 1951.
The Fearless Treasure, illustrated by Dorothy Braby.   London, Joseph, 1952.
The Bell Family, illustrated by Shirley Hughes.   London, Collins, 1954; as *Family Shoes*, New York, Random House, 1954.
The Grey Family, illustrated by Pat Marriott.   London, Hamish Hamilton, 1956.
Wintle's Wonders, illustrated by Richard Kennedy.   London, Collins, 1957; as *Dancing Shoes*, New York, Random House, 1958.
Bertram, illustrated by Margery Gill.   London, Hamish Hamilton, 1959.
New Town, illustrated by Shirley Hughes.   London, Collins, 1960; as *New Shoes*, New York, Random House, 1960.
Apple Bough, illustrated by Margery Gill.   London, Collins, 1962; as *Traveling Shoes*, New York, Random House, 1962.
Lisa Goes to Russia, illustrated by Geraldine Spence.   London, Collins, 1963.
The Children on the Top Floor, illustrated by Jillian Willett.   London, Collins, 1964; New York, Random House, 1965.
Let's Go Coaching, illustrated by Peter Warner.   London, Hamish Hamilton, 1965.
The Growing Summer, illustrated by Edward Ardizzone.   London,

Collins, 1966; as *The Magic Summer*, New York, Random House, 1967.
Old Chairs to Mend, illustrated by Barry Wilkinson.   London, Hamish Hamilton, 1966.
Caldicott Place, illustrated by Betty Maxey.   London, Collins, 1967; as *The Family at Caldicott Place*, New York, Random House, 1968.
Gemma, illustrated by Betty Maxey.   London, Armada, 1968.
Gemma and Sisters, illustrated by Betty Maxey.   London, Armada, 1968.
The Barrow Lane Gang.   London, BBC Publications, 1968.
Gemma Alone.   London, Armada, 1969.
Goodbye Gemma.   London, Armada, 1969.
Thursday's Child, illustrated by Peggy Fortnum.   London, Collins, and New York, Random House, 1970.
Ballet Shoes for Anna, illustrated by Mary Dinsdale.   London, Collins, 1972.
When the Siren Wailed, illustrated by Margery Gill.   London, Collins, 1974; New York, Random House, 1977.
Far to Go, illustrated by Charles Mozley.   London, Collins, 1976.
Meet the Maitlands, illustrated by Antony Maitland.   London, W.H. Allen, 1978.
The Maitlands: All Change at Cuckly Place, illustrated by Antony Maitland.   London, W.H. Allen, 1979.

Plays

The Children's Matinee, illustrated by Ruth Gervis (includes *The Fourum, Me-ow, Olympus, The Princess and the Pea, The Cat, The Lily, Gentlemen of the Road, The Thirteenth Fairy*).   London, Heinemann, 1934.

Radio Plays: *The Bell Family* series, 1949–51; *New Town* series; *Kick Off*, 1973, and others.

Other

The Picture Show of Britain, illustrated by Ursula Koering.   Drexel Hill, Pennsylvania, Bell, 1951.
The First Book of Ballet.   New York, Watts, 1953; revised edition, London, Ward, 1963.
The First Book of England, illustrated by Gioia Fiammenghi.   New York, Watts, 1958; revised edition, London, Ward, 1963.
Queen Victoria, illustrated by Robert Frankenberg.   New York, Random House, 1958; London, W.H. Allen, 1961.
The Royal Ballet School.   London, Collins, 1959.
Ballet Annual.   London, Collins, 1959.
The January [February, March, April, May, June, July, August, September, October, November, December] Baby.   London, Barker, 12 vols., 1959.
Look at the Circus, illustrated by Constance Marshall.   London, Hamish Hamilton, 1960.
The Thames: London's River.   Champaign, Illinois, Garrard, 1964; London, Muller, 1966.
Enjoying Opera, illustrated by Hilary Abrahams.   London, Dobson, 1966; as *The First Book of the Opera*, New York, Watts, 1966.
Before Confirmation.   London, Heinemann, 1967.
The First Book of Shoes, illustrated by Jacqueline Tomes.   New York, Watts, 1967; London, Watts, 1971.
Red Riding Hood, illustrated by Svend Otto S.   London, Benn, 1970.
The Boy Pharaoh, Tutankhamen.   London, Joseph, 1972.
A Young Person's Guide to Ballet, illustrated by Georgette Borbier.   London and New York, Warne, 1975.

Editor, *The Years of Grace* (essays).   London, Evans, 1950; revised

sister, Ruth Gervis, have left them firmly imprinted in her readers' imaginations.

Two other books of equal brilliance followed quickly. The first, *Tennis Shoes*, was Streatfeild's favourite, for its heroine, Nicky, was something of a self-portrait. The story contrasts two sisters—Susan, pretty and popular, apparently an ideal heroine, and Nicky, difficult, uncooperative, and conceited. Yet by an extraordinary reversal of the usual standards in children's books, it is Nicky who proves to be the tennis star, while Susan is left on the sidelines. Geniuses, Streatfeild suggests, will inevitably be misfits, and a temperamental law unto themselves. Among her many portraits of child stars, none is more convincing than Nicky.

The Circus Is Coming, which won the Carnegie Medal, is probably her most outstanding book. Once again she took immense risks with her characters, and pulled them off. The plot concerns two orphan children who run away to the circus where their uncle works. The circus is shown as a tough world, in which the highest standards are expected, and the overprotected children find adjustment extremely taxing. All their pretensions are ruthlessly exposed, from Santa's violin playing to Peter's spurious gentlemanliness. The trials inflicted on them may seem excessively hard to some child readers, but the book is written with great integrity and reaches a completely satisfying solution.

Between 1939 and 1946 Streatfeild was too much occupied with war work and with adult novels to spend much time on her children's books. *The House in Cornwall* and *The Children of Primrose Lane* are run-of-the-mill adventure stories. *Curtain Up*, her most detailed look at the serious theatre, lacks proper organization, and is rather shapeless. Much the best of her war books is *Party Frock*, an original story and a splendid piece of craftsmanship. Streatfeild chose the difficult subject of a village pageant, and handled both its development and her huge cast with astonishing ease.

For 20 years after the war Streatfeild was the leading figure in the British children's book world. She lectured on children's books, reviewed them, campaigned against trashy "juveniles" and horror comics, and appeared in the first children's television book programmes. Her output, in fiction and non-fiction, was enormous, and if no single book quite reached the standard of her pre-war trio, her level remained high. *White Boots*, with its skating heroine, Lalla, who finally has the courage to say "I can't do it"; *The Growing Summer*, a celebration of the magic of Ireland, a country she knew and loved; and *Thursday's Child*, the story of an Edwardian orphan of invincible determination, are perhaps the best known; but her tales of the Bell family, originally written for radio; *The Fearless Treasure*, a social history of England worked into a fantasy framework; *Apple Bough*, with its gentle Victorian overtones; and the brilliantly written *The Boy Pharaoh, Tutankhamen*, also give some idea of her great range and versatility. In later years she complained that reviewers took her for granted, as a "national monument," but this was a tribute to her prestige and her immense sales.

Streatfeild's talent was to present life as dramatic and colourful, without resorting to artificial adventures; to draw lively, convincing characters; and to write in a flowing, easy style, laced with humour, that was immediately acceptable to children. Her stories are valuable as paths, luring inexperienced readers pleasantly onward into the world of books.

—Angela Bull

STRONG, L(eonard) A(lfred) G(eorge). British. Born in Plymouth, Devon, 8 March 1896. Educated at Brighton College, Sussex; Wadham College, Oxford (open classical scholar), 1915–16, 1919–20, B.A. 1920, M.A. Married Sylvia Brinton in 1926; one son.

Assistant master, Summer Fields School, Oxford, 1917, 1920–30; full-time writer from 1930; series editor for the publishers Gollancz, Nelson, and Blackwell, 1930's; visiting tutor, Central School of Speech and Drama, London; director, Methuen, publishers, London, 1938–58. Recipient: James Tait Black Memorial prize, 1946. Member, Irish Academy of Letters; Fellow, Royal Society of Literature. *Died 17 August 1958.*

PUBLICATIONS FOR CHILDREN

Fiction

Patricia Comes Home, illustrated by Ruth Cobb. Oxford, Blackwell, 1929.
The Old Argo, illustrated by Ruth Cobb. Oxford, Blackwell, 1931.
King Richard's Land, illustrated by C. Walter Hodges. London, Dent, 1933; New York, Knopf, 1934.
Fortnight South of Skye. Oxford, Blackwell, 1934; New York, Loring and Mussey, 1935.
The Westward Rock, illustrated by L.R. Brightwell. Oxford, Blackwell, 1934.
Mr. Sheridan's Umbrella, illustrated by C. Walter Hodges. London and New York, Nelson, 1935.
The Fifth of November, illustrated by Jack Matthew. London, Dent, 1937.
Odd Man In, illustrated by P. Lefroy. London, Pitman, 1938.
They Went to the Island, illustrated by Rowland Hilder. London, Dent, 1940.
Wrong Foot Foremost. London, Pitman, 1940.
House in Disorder. London, Lutterworth Press, 1941.
Sink or Swim. London, Lutterworth Press, 1945.

Verse

Amelia, Ye Aged Sowe, illustrated by Moubray Leigh. Oxford, Blackwell, 1932.

Other

Henry of Agincourt, illustrated by Jack Matthew. London and New York, Nelson, 1937.
The Man Who Asked Questions: The Story of Socrates, illustrated by Katharine Tozer. London and New York, Nelson, 1937.
English for Pleasure (broadcasts). London, Methuen, 1941.
Instructions to Young Writers. London, Museum Press, and New Rochelle, New York, Sportshelf, 1958.

PUBLICATIONS FOR ADULTS

Novels

Dewer Rides. London, Gollancz, and New York, Boni, 1929.
The Jealous Ghost. London, Gollancz, and New York, Knopf, 1930.
The Garden. London, Gollancz, and New York, Knopf, 1931.
The Brothers. London, Gollancz, and New York, Knopf, 1932.
Sea Wall. London, Gollancz, and New York, Knopf, 1933.
Corporal Tune. London, Gollancz, and New York, Knopf, 1934.
The Seven Arms. London, Gollancz, and New York, Knopf, 1935.
The Last Enemy. London, Gollancz, and New York, Knopf, 1936.
The Swift Shadow. London, Gollancz, 1937; as *Laughter in the West*, New York, Knopf, 1937.
The Open Sky. London, Gollancz, and New York, Macmillan, 1939.

CHILDREN'S WRITERS

The Bay. London, Gollancz, 1941; Philadelphia, Lippincott, 1942.
Slocombe Dies. London, Collins, 1942.
The Unpractised Heart. London, Gollancz, 1942.
All Fall Down. London, Collins, and New York, Doubleday, 1944.
The Director. London, Methuen, 1944.
Othello's Occupation. London, Collins, 1945; as *Murder Plays an Ugly Scene*, New York, Doubleday, 1945.
Trevannion. London, Methuen, 1948.
Which I Never: A Police Diversion. London, Collins, 1950; New York, Macmillan, 1952.
The Hill of Howth. London, Methuen, 1953.
Deliverance. London, Methuen, 1955.
Light above the Lake. London, Methuen, 1958.
Treason in the Egg: A Further Police Diversion. London, Collins, 1958.

Short Stories

Doyle's Rock and Other Stories. Oxford, Blackwell, 1925.
The English Captain and Other Stories. London, Gollancz, 1929; New York, Knopf, 1931.
The Big Man. London, Jackson, 1931.
Don Juan and the Wheelbarrow, and Other Stories. London, Gollancz, 1932; New York, Knopf, 1933.
Tuesday Afternoon and Other Stories. London, Gollancz, 1935.
Two Stories. London, Corvinus Press, 1936.
The Nice Cup o' Tea. London, Favil Press, 1938.
Evening Piece. Privately printed, 1939.
Sun on the Water and Other Stories. London, Gollancz, 1940.
Travellers: Thirty-One Selected Short Stories. London, Methuen, 1945.
The Doll. Leeds, Salamander Press, 1946.
Darling Tom and Other Stories. London, Methuen, 1952.

Plays

The Absentee. London, Methuen, 1939.
Trial and Error. London, Methuen, 1939.
The Director, adaptation of his own novel (produced Dublin, 1951).
Sea Winds, with Norah Lloyd (produced Farnham, Surrey, 1954).
It's Not Very Nice. London, Deane, and Boston, Baker, 1954.

Screenplays: *The Brothers,* with others, 1947; *Mr. Perrin and Mr. Traill,* with T.J. Morrison, 1948; *Tonight's the Night,* with Michael Pertwee and Jack Davies, 1954.

Verse

Dallington Rhymes. Oxford, Holywell Press, 1919.
Twice Four. Oxford, Holywell Press, 1921.
Dublin Days. Oxford, Blackwell, 1921; New York, Boni and Liveright, 1923.
Says the Muse to Me, Says She. Oxford, Holywell Press, 1922.
Eight Poems. Oxford, Holywell Press, 1923.
The Lowery Road. Oxford, Blackwell, 1923; New York, Boni and Liveright, 1924.
Seven Verses: Christmas 1924. Oxford, Holywell Press, 1924.
Seven Verses: Christmas 1925. Oxford, Holywell Press, 1925.
Difficult Love. Oxford, Blackwell, 1927.
At Glenan Cross: A Sequence. Oxford, Blackwell, 1928.
Northern Light. London, Gollancz, 1930.
Christmas 1930. Oxford, Holywell Press, 1930.
Selected Poems. London, Hamish Hamilton, 1931; New York, Knopf, 1932.
March Evening and Other Verses. London, Favil Press, 1932.
Call to the Swan. London, Hamish Hamilton, 1936.

Low's Company: Fifty Portraits, with Helen Spalding. London, Methuen, 1952.
The Magnolia Tree. Privately printed, 1953.
The Body's Imperfection: The Collected Poems. London, Methuen, 1957.

Other

Common Sense about Poetry. London, Gollancz, 1931; New York, Knopf, 1932.
A Defence of Ignorance (essay). New York, House of Books, 1932.
A Letter to W.B. Yeats. London, Hogarth Press, 1932.
Life in English Literature: An Introduction for Beginners, with Monica Redlich. London, Gollancz, 3 vols., 1932; edited by Russell Thomas, Boston, Little Brown, 3 vols., 1934; as *Outline of English Literature,* Gollancz, 1932.
The Hansom Cab and the Pigeons, Being Random Reflections upon the Silver Jubilee of King George V. London, Golden Cockerel Press, 1935.
Common Sense about Drama. London, Nelson, and New York, Knopf, 1937.
The Minstrel Boy: A Portrait of Tom Moore. London, Hodder and Stoughton, and New York, Knopf, 1937.
Shake Hands and Come Out Fighting (on boxing). London, Chapman and Hall, 1938.
John McCormack: The Story of a Singer. London, Methuen, and New York, Macmillan, 1941.
John Millington Synge. London, Allen and Unwin, 1941.
An Informal English Grammar. London, Methuen, 1943.
Authorship. London, Ross, 1944.
A Tongue in Your Head. London, Pitman, 1945.
Light Through the Cloud. London, Friends Book Centre, 1946.
The Art of the Short Story (lecture). London, Royal Society of Literature, 1947.
Maud Cherrill. London, Parrish, 1949; New York, Chanticleer Press, 1951.
The Sacred River: An Approach to James Joyce. London, Methuen, 1949; New York, Pellegrini and Cudahy, 1951.
John Masefield. London and New York, Longman, 1952.
Personal Remarks (essays). London, Nevill, 1953; New York, Liveright, 1954.
The Writer's Trade. London, Methuen, 1953.
The Story of Sugar. London, Weidenfeld and Nicolson, 1954.
Dr. Quicksilver 1660–1742: The Life and Times of Thomas Dover M.D. London, Melrose, 1955.
Flying Angel: The Story of the Missions to Seamen. London, Methuen, 1956.
The Rolling Road: The Story of Travel on the Roads of Britain. London, Hutchinson, 1956.
A Brewer's Progress 1757–1957: A Survey of Charrington's Brewery. Privately printed, 1957.
Courtauld Thomson: A Memoir. Privately printed, 1958.
Green Memory (autobiography). London, Methuen, 1961.

Editor, *Eighty Poems: An Anthology.* Oxford, Blackwell, 1924; as *By Haunted Stream: An Anthology of Modern English Poets,* New York, Appleton, 1924.
Editor, *The Best Poems of 1923* to *1927.* London, Bird, 5 vols., 1924–28; Boston, Small Maynard, 2 vols., 1924, and New York, Dodd Mead, 3 vols., 1925–28.
Editor, *Beginnings* (anthology of autobiographical essays). London, Nelson, 1935.
Editor, with C. Day Lewis, *A New Anthology of Modern Verse 1920–1940.* London, Methuen, 1941.
Editor, *English Domestic Life During the Last 200 Years: An Anthology Selected from the Novelists.* London, Allen and Unwin,

1942.
Editor, *Sixteen Portraits of People Whose Houses Have Been Preserved by the National Trust.* London, Naldrett Press, 1951.
Editor, *Fred Bason's Second Diary.* London, Wingate, 1952.
Editor, *Lorna Doone*, by R.D. Blackmore. London, Collins, 1958.

*   *   *

L.A.G. Strong's contribution to juvenile literature has been undeservedly, if understandably, obscured by his wider reputation as novelist and short story writer, poet, critic, and publisher. That he took children's fiction seriously is indicated not only by his own writing in that field but also by his pioneering efforts, as editor of Basil Blackwell's series Tales of Action in the late 1930's, to enlist first-class authors for the then-despised adventure-story and to demonstrate that excitement and literary quality were not incompatible.

Besides story-biographies of Socrates and Henry V, he himself produced a handful of junior novels, and such was his versatility that even in this genre there were hardly two that could be exactly classified together. Three were historical, but whereas *King Richard's Land* treated a great event, the Peasants' Revolt of 1381, *Mr. Sheridan's Umbrella* was pure invention, a light period piece set in Regency Brighton. *The Fifth of November*, though again dominated by an actual historical episode, was varied by the device (less hackneyed in 1937 than since) of allowing a modern child to travel back in time. All three books had one thing in common, a conscientiously researched background brought to life by a sensitive and dynamic imagination.

The modern books were even more difficult. *Wrong Foot Foremost* was a school story, fairly described by John Rowe Townsend as "the last flowering of the Talbot Baines Reed tradition." Nostalgic it may have been—Strong's well-filled life included 10 years as a schoolmaster—but it had a theme, the problem of merging two schools, which has since acquired a new relevance. *Odd Man In* dealt with the adventures of a young police detective. *Fortnight South of Skye*, an exciting tale of yachting in Scottish waters, was an early example of the "holiday adventure" written before Arthur Ransome had fully established that popular mode.

Strong occupies an intermediate position, part traditionalist, part innovator. He took a fresh and deeper look at history. He treated death and violence with honesty which, though less unusual now, at the time brought the accusation of producing "unsuitable material." On the other hand, he belongs to an age when there were still mainly "books for boys" and "books for girls," clearly distinguished. He wrote the former kind, and though many girls must have read them, their lack of feminine interest seems a regrettable deficiency today.

—Geoffrey Trease

————————

STUCLEY, Elizabeth (Florence). British. Born in Devon, 9 February 1906. Educated at St. James's School, West Malvern, Worcestershire, 1914–21; London School of Economics, 1933–35. Volunteer driver for French Army during World War II: mentioned in despatches, 1939. Married J.G.L. Northmore in 1955. Headmistress, St. Cuthbert's School, Bathampton, 1960–64; social worker. *Died 26 July 1974.*

PUBLICATIONS FOR CHILDREN

Fiction

Star in the Hand. London, Collins, 1946.

The Pennyfeather Family: A Family Chronicle with Suitable Morals. London, Nicholson and Watson, 1947.
The Secret Pony, illustrated by Richard Kennedy. London, Faber, 1950.
Magnolia Buildings, illustrated by Dick Hart. London, Bodley Head, 1960; as *Family Walk-Up*, New York, Watts, 1961.
Springfield Home, illustrated by Charles Mozley. London, Bodley Head, 1961; as *The Contrary Orphans*, New York, Watts, 1962.
Miss Georgie's Gang. London and New York, Abelard Schuman, 1970.

Other

Pollycon: A Book for the Young Economist, illustrated by Hugh Chesterman. Oxford, Blackwell, 1933.

PUBLICATIONS FOR ADULTS

Novels

The House Will Come Down. London, Duckworth, 1938.
Louisa. London, Duckworth, 1939.
Trip No Further. London, Sampson Low, 1946.
To End the Storm. London, Hutchinson, 1957.

Play

The Promised Land (produced Bideford, Devon, 1951).

Other

The Village Organizer (autobiography). London, Methuen, 1935.
Hebridean Journey with Johnson and Boswell. London, Christopher Johnson, 1956.
Teddy Boys' Picnic (miscellany). London, Blond, 1958.
Life Is for the Living: The Erratic Life of Elizabeth Stucley. London, Blond, 1959.

*   *   *

Elizabeth Stucley is in many ways a homely writer. Her books have the same appeal as Eve Garnett's *The Family from One End Street*, though brought nearer to our times, being set in the early 1960's. They share the same gentle, period charm where there is no real violence and nothing really out of the ordinary actually happens. They are essentially *safe* stories, and will be enjoyed by those children who still read the adventures of the Ruggles family.

The children in *Magnolia Buildings* are part of a large family. They are busily engaged in mundane preoccupations like the school play, gang squabbles, mother's going into hospital, and examinations (many modern children will not appreciate the trauma of the eleven-plus!). There are lots of sub-plots but no mainstream linking, only the importance of the family unit.

This is contrasted in *Springfield Home*, where the *need* for a family is vital. Gipsy Carlotta is put into a children's home when her ailing grandmother can no longer care for her, and she rebels constantly against the constraints and restrictions of her newly ordered life. Used to almost total freedom, she cannot fit in with the house-parents and other children. This is not what she wants from life. Another misfit in the home is a quiet, withdrawn boy who is desperate for the security of a home of his own and a real family. The two children are cleverly contrasted in the way they both opt out of the "establishment," but in the end they get on well together and share in the predictably happy ending.

The child who is most likely to read these books with pleasure is the slightly older girl who retreats into easy, safe reading which demands little of her; more adventurous children will probably find them boring.

—Ann G. Hay

SUDBERY, Rodie (née Tutton). British. Born in Chelmsford, Essex, 2 April 1943. Educated at Girton College, Cambridge, B.A. in mathematics 1964. Married Anthony Sudbery in 1964; two daughters. Address: 5 Heslington Croft, Fulford, York YO1 4NB, England.

PUBLICATIONS FOR CHILDREN

Fiction

The House in the Wood. London, Deutsch, 1968; as *A Sound of Crying,* New York, McCall, 1970.
Cowls. London, Deutsch, 1969.
Rich and Famous and Bad. London, Deutsch, 1970.
The Pigsleg. London, Deutsch, 1971.
Warts and All. London, Deutsch, 1972.
A Curious Place. London, Deutsch, 1973.
Inside the Walls, illustrated by Sally Long. London, Deutsch, 1973.
Ducks and Drakes. London, Deutsch, 1975.
Lightning Cliff, illustrated by Sally Long. London, Deutsch, 1975.
The Silk and the Skin. London, Deutsch, 1976.
Long Way Round, illustrated by Sally Long. London, Deutsch, 1977.
Somewhere Else. London, Deutsch, 1978.
A Tunnel with Problems. London, Deutsch, 1979.
The Village Secret. London, Deutsch, 1980.
Night Music. London, Gollancz, 1983.
Grandmother's Footsteps, illustrated by Vanessa Julian-Ottie. London, Hamish Hamilton, 1984.

*   *   *

Rodie Sudbery's novels are all based in family life and her outstanding skill is to explore the relationships among children and between children and adults without letting the adult's perception creep into the story. She has the ability to get under the skins of the children she writes about and enable the reader to feel what the characters are feeling. Rarely are the children in real danger (*Lightning Cliff* is perhaps an exception), nor are they underprivileged at home, and yet the problems and dilemmas they encounter are nonetheless real, and many young readers would identify with, and find comfort in, the situations.

Among her books for older readers are the five about the Devenish family. Polly is 12 in the first book *The House in the Wood* which, as well as being Sudbery's first published book, was a rare excursion for her into fantasy. The interaction of the past and the present are interestingly handled. The series continues with *Cowls* (a haunted house mystery), *Rich and Famous and Bad, Warts and All,* and *Ducks and Drakes,* in which Polly Devenish is an undergraduate. Sudbery is less successful in describing adolescent relationships than those of younger children but the series as a whole is both interesting and readable, with a refreshingly varied approach in each book.

Long Way Round stands out among her stories for 8–10-year-olds. Typically, the plot centers on a single situation of the sort which can seem trivial to an adult but overwhelming to a child. Simon and

Jeremy resent having to take a new girl with them on their journey to school but in the end, after some unobtrusive manipulation by their teacher, the three become friends. It is not every adult who can empathise with children as Sudbery seems to. Celia's abject misery at having to eat her packed lunch in Miss Jane's kitchen is tangible, as is her shy inability to admit that she made a mistake in getting off the school bus at the wrong stop. This skill at getting inside the children's heads and transmitting their thoughts and feelings makes her books full of relevance for young readers. *Inside the Walls* is another ordinary everyday story but her understanding of children lifts it above the ordinary. She makes natural use of dialogue, leaning on it heavily to carry her plots along and recreating accurately the direct and economical speech of young children talking among themselves. In *Lightning Cliff* her understanding of the dilemmas of childhood again lifts an unexceptional adventure story into something with more substance and quality which opens up questions of behaviour and morality.

In Cressida, the central character of *The Pigsleg,* Sudbery has created a powerful and dominating leader of a gang of children—all the offspring of university dons. As usual, she writes about the world which she knows which could lead her to be accused of writing cosily about middle-class children from privileged, or at least comfortable, backgrounds. There is, however, nothing cosy about the outcome of the dares in which Cressida's gang indulge. When things begin to get out of hand, the adults are finally involved and Cressida is cut down to size. It is part of Sudbery's success that she contrives to make Cressida an attractive character despite her unhealthy domination over the others and also to weave a very complex but clear picture of the relationships between four families.

Sudbery's most recent title is a contribution to the Antelope series which is aimed broadly at 6–8-year-olds who are just ready to enjoy a full-length story. The constraints of writing to a specific brief seem to have restricted her natural freedom to write the story she wants to write. Although her writing is as good as ever and her dialogue largely carries the story of *Grandmother's Footsteps* along in the children's words, there are none of the more subtle undertones which lift her other books above the level of the mundane and there is a feeling about it of unconcluded business. Nevertheless, young readers will enjoy the story about three children trying—not always successfully—to ensure that their grandmother's visit goes well, and perhaps it is unfair to ask more of a book for this age group than that it should be read with enjoyment.

—Valerie Brinkley-Willsher

SUDDABY, (William) Donald. Also wrote as Alan Griff. British. Born in Leeds, Yorkshire, in 1900. Educated at Manchester Cathedral School. Married twice; had children. Journalist, broadcaster, and freelance writer. *Died 17 March 1964.*

PUBLICATIONS FOR CHILDREN

Fiction

Lost Men in the Grass (as Alan Griff), illustrated by Eric Newton. London, Oxford University Press, 1940.
Masterless Swords: Variations on a Theme. London, Laurie, 1947.
New Tales of Robin Hood, illustrated by T. Heath Robinson. London, Blackie, 1950.
The Star Raiders, illustrated by Carl Haworth. London, Oxford University Press, 1950.

The Death of Metal, illustrated by William Stobbs. London, Oxford University Press, 1952.

Merry Jack Jugg, Highwayman, illustrated by Jack Matthew. London, Blackie, 1954.

Village Fanfare; or, The Man from the Future, illustrated by F.R. Exell. London, Oxford University Press, 1954.

The Moon of Snowshoes, illustrated by Leonard Rosoman. London, Oxford University Press, 1956.

Prisoners of Saturn, illustrated by Harold Jones. London, Lane, 1957.

Fresh News from Sherwood, illustrated by William Stobbs. London, Bodley Head, 1959; New York, A.S. Barnes, 1961.

Crowned with Wild Olive, illustrated by William Stobbs. London, Collins, 1961.

Tower of Babel. London, Collins, 1962.

A Bell in the Forest. London, University of London Press, 1964.

Robin Hood's Master Stroke. London, Blackie, 1965.

PUBLICATIONS FOR ADULTS

Short Story

Scarlet-Dragon: A Little Chinese Phantasy. Privately printed, 1923.

*   *   *

Donald Suddaby was that rare being, a distinguished writer of science fiction and fantasy for children. His literary roots lay in Verne and Wells, and his contemporaries included John Wyndham and John Christopher. But they all wrote adult fantasy (though much of it was read also by young readers), whereas Suddaby wrote his tales specifically for children, though they could be (and were) enjoyed too by appreciative adults.

Suddaby wrote only 14 books in 25 years and every one is well worth reading. His first book, *Lost Men in the Grass*, is an exciting imaginative fantasy about three men reduced to the size of ants, and their battles against insects, animals, and birds. It was a remarkable tour-de-force but, unfortunately, tended to be overlooked by reviewers due to the timing of its publication. After a 10-year gap came a regular series of remarkable books of many kinds, involving space-journeys to Venus and Saturn, mysterious and sinister visitors to Earth from other worlds, Robin Hood tales, historical adventures, and stories set in Biblical and mythological times. Outstanding, perhaps, were *The Death of Metal*, a sobering story about the effect of the disintegration of all metals upon people's everyday lives, and *Village Fanfare*, which dealt with the arrival of a strange visitor (or an army of identical visitors) to a sleepy Edwardian Shropshire village and the remarkable results which followed.

One of the most unusual talents in the field of children's literature, Suddaby brought a poet's sweep and descriptive power to his writing, allied to originality and humour.

—Brian Doyle

SUTCLIFF, Rosemary. British. Born in West Clanden, Surrey, 14 December 1920. Educated at Bideford School of Art, Devon. Member, Royal Society of Miniature Painters. Recipient: Library Association Carnegie Medal, 1960; Boston *Globe-Horn Book* award, 1972; Children's Rights Workshop Other award, 1978; Catholic Library Association Phoenix award, 1985. O.B.E. (Officer, Order of the British Empire), 1975. Fellow, Royal Society of Literature, 1982. Address: Swallowshaw, Walberton, Arundel, West Sussex BN18 0PQ, England.

PUBLICATIONS FOR CHILDREN

Fiction

The Armourer's House, illustrated by C. Walter Hodges. London and New York, Oxford University Press, 1951.

Brother Dusty-Feet, illustrated by C. Walter Hodges. London, Oxford University Press, 1952.

Simon, illustrated by Richard Kennedy. London, Oxford University Press, 1953.

The Eagle of the Ninth, illustrated by C. Walter Hodges. London, Oxford University Press, 1954; New York, Walck, 1961.

Outcast, illustrated by Richard Kennedy. London, Oxford University Press, and New York, Walck, 1955.

The Shield Ring, illustrated by C. Walter Hodges. London, Oxford University Press, 1956; New York, Walck, 1962.

The Silver Branch, illustrated by Charles Keeping. London, Oxford University Press, 1957; New York, Walck, 1959.

Warrior Scarlet, illustrated by Charles Keeping. London, Oxford University Press, and New York, Walck, 1958.

The Lantern Bearers, illustrated by Charles Keeping. London, Oxford University Press, and New York, Walck, 1959.

The Bridge-Builders. Oxford, Blackwell, 1959.

Knight's Fee, illustrated by Charles Keeping. London, Oxford University Press, and New York, Walck, 1960.

Dawn Wind, illustrated by Charles Keeping. London, Oxford University Press, 1961; New York, Walck, 1962.

The Mark of the Horse Lord, illustrated by Charles Keeping. London, Oxford University Press, 1965.

The Chief's Daughter, illustrated by Victor Ambrus. London, Hamish Hamilton, 1967.

A Circlet of Oak Leaves, illustrated by Victor Ambrus. London, Hamish Hamilton, 1968.

The Witch's Brat, illustrated by Robert Micklewright. London, Oxford University Press, and New York, Walck, 1970.

The Truce of the Games, illustrated by Victor Ambrus. London, Hamish Hamilton, 1971.

Heather, Oak, and Olive: Three Stories (includes *The Chief's Daughter, A Circle of Oak Leaves, A Crown of Wild Olive*), illustrated by Victor Ambrus. New York, Dutton, 1972.

The Capricorn Bracelet, illustrated by Charles Keeping. London, Oxford University Press, and New York, Walck, 1973.

The Changeling, illustrated by Victor Ambrus. London, Hamish Hamilton, 1974.

We Lived in Drumfyvie, with Margaret Lyford-Pike. London, Blackie, 1975.

Blood Feud, illustrated by Charles Keeping. London, Oxford University Press, and New York, Dutton, 1977.

Shifting Sands, illustrated by Laszlo Acs. London, Hamish Hamilton, 1977.

Sun Horse, Moon Horse, illustrated by Shirley Felts. London, Bodley Head, 1977; New York, Dutton, 1978.

Song for a Dark Queen. London, Pelham, 1978; New York, Crowell, 1979.

Frontier Wolf. London, Oxford University Press, 1980; New York, Dutton, 1981.

Eagle's Egg, illustrated by Victor Ambrus. London, Hamish Hamilton, 1981.

Bonnie Dundee. London, Bodley Head, 1983; New York, Dutton, 1984.

The Roundabout Horse, illustrated by Alan Marks. London, Hamish Hamilton, 1986.
Flame-Coloured Taffeta. Oxford, Oxford University Press, and New York, Farrar Straus, 1986.
A Little Dog Like You, illustrated by June Johnson. London, Orchard, 1987.
Little Hound Found, illustrated by Jo Davies. London, Hamish Hamilton, 1989.

Other

The Chronicles of Robin Hood, illustrated by C. Walter Hodges. London, Oxford University Press, 1950; New York, Oxford University Press, 1978.
The Queen Elizabeth Story, illustrated by C. Walter Hodges. London, Oxford University Press, 1950.
Houses and History, illustrated by William Stobbs. London, Batsford, 1960.
Beowulf, illustrated by Charles Keeping. London, Bodley Head, 1961; New York, Dutton, 1962; as *Dragon Slayer*, London, Penguin, 1966.
The Hound of Ulster (Cuchulain Saga), illustrated by Victor Ambrus. London, Bodley Head, and New York, Dutton, 1963.
A Saxon Settler, illustrated by John Lawrence. London, Oxford University Press, 1965.
Heroes and History, illustrated by Charles Keeping. London, Batsford, and New York, Putnam, 1965.
The High Deeds of Finn Mac Cool, illustrated by Michael Charlton. London, Bodley Head, and New York, Dutton, 1967.
Tristan and Iseult, illustrated by Victor Ambrus. London, Bodley Head, and New York, Dutton, 1971.
The Light Beyond the Forest: The Quest for the Holy Grail, illustrated by Shirley Felts. London, Bodley Head, 1979; New York, Dutton, 1980.
The Sword and the Circle: King Arthur and the Knights of the Round Table, illustrated by Shirley Felts. London, Bodley Head, and New York, Dutton, 1981.
The Road to Camlann: The Death of King Arthur, illustrated by Shirley Felts. London, Bodley Head, 1981; New York, Dutton, 1982.

Editor, with Monica Dickens, *Is Anyone There?* (on the Samaritans). London, Penguin, 1978.

PUBLICATIONS FOR ADULTS

Novels

Lady in Waiting. London, Hodder and Stoughton, 1956; New York, Coward McCann, 1957.
The Rider of the White Horse. London, Hodder and Stoughton, 1959; as *Rider on a White Horse*, New York, Coward McCann, 1959.
Sword at Sunset. London, Hodder and Stoughton, 1963; New York, Coward McCann, 1964.
The Flowers of Adonis. London, Hodder and Stoughton, 1969; New York, Coward McCann, 1970.
Blood and Sand. London, Hodder and Stoughton, 1987.

Plays

Mary Bedell (produced Chichester, 1986).

Screenplay: *Ghost Story*, with Stephen Weeks, 1975.

Other

Rudyard Kipling. London, Bodley Head, 1960; New York, Walck, 1961.
Blue Remembered Hills: A Recollection. London, Bodley Head, 1983; New York, Morrow, 1984.

*

Manuscript Collection: Kerlan Collection, University of Minnesota, Minneapolis.

Critical Study: *Rosemary Sutcliff* by Margaret Meek, London, Bodley Head, and New York, Walck, 1962.

*   *   *

In Rosemary Sutcliff's hands the children's historical novel has gained passion, insight, and depth. She makes demands of her readers, but that is right, for the best of her books are as satisfying also to the most discerning adult. Her main themes could be termed the continuity of history and the contiguity of peoples—the Light and the Dark, Pict and Scot, Roman and Briton, Briton and Saxon, Saxon and Norman. She is concerned with recreating history itself more than events and with interpreting the movements and relationships of peoples. She seems to have an instinctive communion with the past, and while she had suffered since childhood from a severely restricting arthritic condition, it is as though her very lack of mobility has given her an intensity of concentration which enables her to see and describe details that hardly occur to other writers. Her sense of place, and her feelings for the land and those who work it, add extra dimensions; and her command and understanding of military tactics and the very feeling of battle are not far short of astonishing.

Even with hindsight it is hard to find in her four earliest books the writer she has become. The dialogue tends to be archaic—she solved this problem magnificently later; and the stories have an idyllic cosiness about them, at times almost mawkishness. These are period pieces, but they contain hints of ancient rituals lost in folklore, such as she has since recreated particularly in her Roman-British novels. *Brother Dusty-Feet* has another recurrent *leitmotiv*, the rejected orphan. In fact, however, better introductions for children to her work are the much later Antelope books for younger readers. *Simon* is unusual in presenting the Civil War from both sides. There is much historical background which has to be explained, but pointers to future works are the problems presented by divided loyalties, the determination that life shall continue despite political or military upheavals, and the motivation of characters loyal to their convictions.

The Eagle of the Ninth has a situation and setting more to Sutcliff's liking. This is the first novel of a sequence, the others being *The Silver Branch*, *The Lantern Bearers*, and *Frontier Wolf*. An actual and a symbolic link between them emphasises the view that history is continuous: a main character in all four belongs to the same Roman family, and in each appears a signet ring passed on from father to son; it also features in *Dawn Wind* and *The Shield Ring*. In *The Eagle of the Ninth* Marcus Aquila, invalided out of the army, searches for clues to the fate of his father's legion which had marched out into the mists of northern Britain, and disappeared. Primarily an adventure story, culminating in a splendid chase, the book is distinguished also by its presentation of the meeting of two worlds, Roman and British, and in its atmosphere—ancient rituals; Hadrian's Wall as a living, vital, sprawling community—and terrain—bracken, heather, mist, furze, and rain.

Beric, in *Outcast*, is an archetypal Sutcliff hero. A Roman orphan, rescued from shipwreck, he is rejected by the British tribe that fostered him, becomes a slave in Rome, and, later, returns to Britain, and to freedom. This is an episodic novel, depending to some extent on coincidence, but with powerful sequences, notably when Beric serves as a galley-slave. For *The Shield Ring* she created a community of Vikings in the Lake District withstanding for years Norman attempts to eliminate them, until their fateful last stand. The feeling of place is nowhere bettered, but the action shifts awkwardly from person to person, possibly because the main character is female.

In *Warrior Scarlet* the copper and scarlet of the Golden People, worshippers of the sun, contrast strongly with the mysteries of the earth itself and the Little Dark People, who still live on, but as outcasts. This is not just a superb reconstruction of a people, a period, and an actual part of the South Downs, founded on meticulous research and prodigious powers of imagination, but also a sensitive and convincing account of a boy finding himself and ultimately his adult place in life. *Knight's Fee* and *Dawn Wind* are primarily about bringing peoples together. In the former the bickering of William II's barons highlights the need to unite Norman and Saxon; in the latter it is once again light and dark, Saxon and native Briton. In each book a boy has to make his own way in life to survive. Owain, in *Dawn Wind*, is perhaps Sutcliff's most interesting hero, in that his progress from being a boy who has lost his whole world depends largely on his own determination and effort, and he is faced on the way with several agonising choices.

The Mark of the Horse Lord is arguably her finest novel, for adults or children. Certainly it is a book of supreme assurance and maturity of style, construction, and content. The action is almost continuous, covering just two years, and from the tremendous opening sequence in the gladiatorial ring, climax follows climax. Phaedrus, a freed gladiator, agrees to impersonate the Lord of the Horse People. His insecure hold on his leadership, his strange but utterly plausible relationship with his ritual wife, and the struggle and differences of outlook between the Horse People and their neighbours, the Caledones, are staged against rites and dark mysteries, marvellously evoked and described. And in the last stark paragraph, which provides a totally unexpected ending, Phaedrus becomes what he really is, a tragic hero in the epic mould.

The pattern of history of the time and the reach of the tentacles of Rome, even in the throes of destruction, are clearly revealed in *The Silver Branch*. Two cousins desert from the Roman Army to support the cause of Carausius, murdered Emperor of Britain, against the usurper Allectus. In fact they fight for their beliefs rather than for Rome, and for the retention of some element of peaceful coexistence among peoples; and the eagle of the lost Ninth Legion reappears as a symbol now of unity. This is basically an adventure story, but *The Lantern Bearers* is more a slice of history, studded also with human conflicts and emotions. "We have been here four hundred years," says his commandant to the decurion Aquila, "and in three days we shall be gone." But Aquila, whose roots and family are in Britain, chooses to turn his back on Rome, and stays. Saxons kill his father and abduct his sister Flavia. Left to die, he is taken by a Jutish band to their homeland as a thrall. The community, Aquila among them, emigrate to Britain, and he finds his sister, now married to a Saxon. But she will not leave her husband, a choice Aquila understands only later when his own wife of political convenience sticks by him. He joins the cause of Ambrosius against Vortigern and Hengest, only to meet his own nephew in the height of battle. This is a book with excellent characterisation, whose main theme is the restoration of order out of chaos.

Between 1965 and 1977 Sutcliff published no major work for older children, but with *Blood Feud* she entered the lists again, taking as her background the Viking excursions to the Black Sea and their support of the emperor Basil II of Byzantium. A feud links the historical incidents and motivates the characters in this finely wrought story with a moving and satisfying conclusion. The Vikings themselves, and their humour and loyalties, are splendidly recaptured, particularly in the dialogue. After her earliest books, it has been

one of Sutcliff's most distinctive attributes that she makes her characters talk in ways that sound completely in period and in tune with a situation by the introduction of subtle changes to the order and rhythm of modern speech.

Sun Horse, Moon Horse belongs properly to the period shortly after the writing of *The Mark of the Horse Lord*, though it was not published until much later. Short, almost poetic, its story is woven around the making in the early Iron Age of the great White Horse in the chalk hillside near Uffington. *Song for a Dark Queen* is about the life and campaigns of Boudicca. The language is simpler than usual and its effect is heightened by the way colours are picked out for special emphasis, but the historian appears to overshadow the novelist, and the author seems partially hamstrung by the need to introduce satisfactory motivation to fit the historical facts.

With *Frontier Wolf* she returned triumphantly to her Roman-British sequence, some 60 years after the events of *The Silver Branch*. If the youthful Centurion Alexios Aquila is less convincing than some of her other heroes, his predicaments are fully believable, and the plot races and grips with heart-stopping twists. Particularly good also is the sense, at times almost the scent, of place, and the amazing detail of army life, conditions, and ritual. Latterly, however, though the will and the enthusiasm for writing have persisted, the imaginative energy has been less in evidence. Sutcliff's lifelong preoccupation with the romantic story surfaces in *Bonnie Dundee*, a portrait of the 17th-century Scottish Royalist, John Graham of Claverhouse, seen through the eyes of a young artist. *Flame-Coloured Taffeta*, an 18th-century adventure story based on the smuggling trade, is less substantial but more of one piece.

—Antony Kamm

SUTTON, Eve(lyn Mary, née Breakell). New Zealander. Born in Preston, Lancashire, England, 14 September 1906; emigrated to New Zealand, 1949; became citizen, 1955. Educated at the Park School, Preston, 1917–24; Goldsmiths' College, University of London, 1925–27, teachers' training diploma. Married Alfred Sutton in 1931; two sons. Primary school teacher, Deepdale, Lancashire, 1927–31. Recipient: New Zealand Library Association Esther Glen award, 1975. Agent: Ray Richards Agency, P.O. Box 31240, Milford, Auckland 9. Address: 84 Kohimarama Road, Flat 1, Auckland 5, New Zealand.

PUBLICATIONS FOR CHILDREN

Fiction

Green Gold, illustrated by Paul Wright. London, Hamish Hamilton, 1976.
Tuppenny Brown, illustrated by Paul Wright. London, Hamish Hamilton, 1977.
Johnny Sweep, illustrated by Paul Wright. London, Hamish Hamilton, 1977.
Moa Hunter, illustrated by Bernard Brett. London, Hamish Hamilton, 1978.
Skip for the Huntaway, illustrated by Ernest Papps. Wellington, Price Milburn, 1983.
Surgeon's Boy. Wellington, Mallinson Rendel, 1983; Barnstaple, Devon, Spindlewood, 1984.
Kidnapped by Blackbirders, illustrated by Fiona Kelly. Wellington, Mallinson Rendel, and Barnstaple, Devon, Spindlewood, 1984.

Valley of Heavenly Gold, illustrated by Doss. Wellington, Mallinson Rendel, 1987.

Verse

My Cat Likes to Hide in Boxes, illustrated by Lynley Dodd. London, Hamish Hamilton, 1973; New York, Parents' Magazine Press, 1974.

*

Eve Sutton comments:

My first venture into the field of children's literature, the picture book *My Cat Likes to Hide in Boxes*, came as the result of an amiable conversation with my cousin Lynley Dodd—"Wouldn't it be fun to do a book together?" But I like the actual writing and plotting, so it seemed natural to turn to books for older children. The early New Zealand scene has interested me ever since we came here and makes a natural background for my stories.

*   *   *

Eve Sutton's preferred field is a problematical one; that which caters, simultaneously, for able readers of seven and over, and slower readers of 11 and 12. Its requirements are exacting. The principal character must fall within the upper age group and yet be accessible to the sympathies of the younger, a limiting consideration by which few writers would care to be bound. Emotional exploration of character is virtually prohibited, the resultant hero usually emerging as a somewhat vacuous personality, independent and resourceful on the one hand, but inclined to excessive virtue on the other. But there are advantages; intelligent seven-year-olds are likely to be bored by stories about their peers, who are all too likely to be bound by the very constraints of overprotected family life which they themselves find so irksome. And less able 12-year-olds, if they can be reached, provide a ready ear for stories which are exciting, uncomplicated, and simply told.

Sutton contrives to avoid the pitfalls, while capitalising on the advantages. Certainly not one of her three youthful heroes, each obliged to make his own way alone in the wild young colony that was New Zealand in the mid-19th century, lacks individuality. Her use of the first person contributes to this success. Adam, Tuppenny, and Johnny emerge, in their different ways, as real boys, credible products of the backgrounds from which they have been plucked in England, and exposed to a bombardment of new impressions on the other side of the world. The story, in each case, is engrossing.

The apparent simplicity of the text of these short novels conceals, to some extent, Sutton's capacity for establishing place and character, and for managing a pace which is both swift enough to ensure interest and deliberate enough to avoid confusion. A surprising amount of detail is included: the horrors of the outward voyage, the brash jauntiness of the early colony, the rigours of breaking in virgin land for farming, the thrilling yet sickening experience of whaling, the backbreaking toil of gum-digging—and through it all, the pervasive sense of hope, of beginning, of man's willingness to risk death and face hardship in search of freedom.

Sutton's only book for very young children, *My Cat Likes to Hide in Boxes*, reveals a facility with language, rhythm, and rhyme, and a sure feeling for the nonsense-humour of early childhood. Its competence is undoubted; but the author's real aptitude—and preference—seems to be in books for older children.

—Dorothy Butler

SWINDELLS, Robert (Edward). British. Born in Bradford, Yorkshire, 20 March 1939. Educated at Huddersfield Polytechnic, Yorkshire, 1969–72, teaching certificate 1972; University of Bradford, Yorkshire, 1986–87, M.A. in peace studies 1987. Served in the Royal Air Force, 1957–60. Married Brenda Swindells in 1980 (second marriage); two daughters (from first marriage). Copyholder, 1954–57, and advertising clerk, 1960–67, Bradford *Telegraph and Argus*; engineer, Hepworth and Grandage, Bradford, 1967–69; elementary school teacher, Bradford, 1972–77; part-time teacher, 1977–80. Recipient: Children's Rights Workshop Other award, 1984. Agent: J. Luithcen, 88 Holmfield Road, Leicester. Address: 3 Upwood Park, Black Moor Road, Oxenhope, Keighley, West Yorkshire BD22 9SS, England.

PUBLICATIONS FOR CHILDREN

Fiction

When Darkness Comes. Leicester, Brockhampton Press, 1973; New York, Morrow, 1975.
A Candle in the Night. Newton Abbot, Devon, David and Charles, 1974; as *A Candle in the Dark*, Sevenoaks, Kent, Knight, 1983.
Voyage to Valhalla. London, Hodder and Stoughton, 1976.
The Ice-Palace, illustrated by June Jackson. London, Hamish Hamilton, 1977.
The Very Special Baby. London, Hodder and Stoughton, 1977; Englewood Cliffs, New Jersey, Prentice Hall, 1978.
Dragons Live Forever. London, Hodder and Stoughton, and Englewood Cliffs, New Jersey, Prentice Hall, 1978.
The Moonpath and Other Stories. Exeter, Wheaton, 1979; Minneapolis, Carolrhoda, 1983.
Norah's Ark. Exeter, Wheaton, 1979.
Norah's Shark. Exeter, Wheaton, 1979.
The Weather-Clerk, illustrated by Petula Stone. London, Hodder and Stoughton, 1979.
Ghost Ship to Ganymede, illustrated by Jeff Burns. Exeter, Wheaton, 1980.
Norah and the Whale, illustrated by Avril Haynes. Exeter, Wheaton, 1981.
Norah to the Rescue, illustrated by Avril Haynes. Exeter, Wheaton, 1981.
World Eater. London, Hodder and Stoughton, 1981.
The Wheaton Book of Science Fiction Stories, illustrated by Gary Long. Exeter, Wheaton, 1982.
Brother in the Land. Oxford, Oxford University Press, 1984; New York, Holiday House, 1985.
The Thousand Eyes of Night. London, Hodder and Stoughton, 1985.
The Ghost Messengers. London, Hodder and Stoughton, 1986.
Staying Up. Oxford, Oxford University Press, 1986.
Mavis Davis. Oxford, Oxford University Press, 1988.
The Postbox Mystery, illustrated by Kate Rogers. London, Hodder and Stoughton, 1988.
A Serpent's Tooth. London, Hamish Hamilton, 1988; New York, Holiday House, 1989.

Other

Translator, *Alfie* series (*Alfie and His Secret Friend; Who'll Save Alfie Atkins?; Alfie and the Monster; You're a Sly One, Alfie Atkins!*), by Gunilla Bergström. Exeter, Wheaton, 4 vols., 1979.

*

Robert Swindells comments:

I write fiction for young people in all age groups—novels, short stories, picture-book scripts, stories in verse. I write principally to entertain, but with the hope that my work might help children discover the joy of books and of reading. I am dedicated to the idea that we are all responsible for one another, and that we ought to conduct ourselves accordingly, doing no harm to any being. My work reflects this belief, insofar as I can cause it to do so.

* * *

"Slaves do not have boats," Caspar the Fisherman tells Nick, whose pauper parents have sold him into bondage, "But sometimes at night, in the full of the moon, there is a way for them if they believe and are brave" (The Moonpath). One way and another this perception is at the moral heart of most of Robert Swindells's books, as much in the infant level Norah and the Whale as in Voyage to Valhalla or A Serpent's Tooth which are suitable for the middle years of the secondary school. His young heroes and heroines are caught up in circumstances which will test their constancy to the utmost. It may be in a cause, such as the conditions of children in 19th-century coal mines, described with telling detail in A Candle in the Night; it may be in an oppressive responsibility such as that which 11-year-old Orville carries in World Eater or the infant Ali in The Very Special Baby; it may lie in the burdens of a relationship (A Serpent's Tooth, The Ice-Palace, When Darkness Comes) or in pursuit of an ideal (Voyage to Valhalla). In Brother in the Land Danny struggles against diminishing hope to preserve a memory of human civilization itself in a doomed world contaminated by nuclear fall-out.

Often the child will face acute dangers, and Swindells has the trick of creating terrifying tensions, both physical and psychological, especially in the earlier books. In later work the pressures come as much from within, a product of the child's awareness of a moral predicament, as from an opposing force. If Orville is instrumental in saving the Earth from the jaws of a space monster he must contend equally with daily bullying and name calling even though he knows these could be swept away if only he were to break faith and boast of his exploits.

In the first novel, When Darkness Comes, the child hero Morg faces up to the murderous Gawl, later to winter cold and starvation, and finally to an invading and well-armed tribe, yet remains steadfast to the ideal of the unity of his clan and the responsibilities of caring leadership. Life and conditions in a post-holocaust neo-stone age society are convincingly portrayed, yet the novel is somewhat over-written, the descriptive passages heavy with detail. Swindells follows with A Candle in the Night and here the style is tense and economical and highly effective in creating a world of pursuing dangers and grim, unremitting cruelty. In later novels the language becomes sparse, racy, often edgy—very much the child's voice as well as the child's eye at the centre.

These two earliest historical novels apart, Swindells's characters inhabit a real and familiar world. The setting is frequently Yorkshire and the issues are of the present age. There is a refreshing confidence that the child reader is capable of having a point of view on, say, strained marital relationships, the manipulation of public opinion by press and government, or the environmental responsibilities of big business, even on super power politics or the consequences of a nuclear war. Most importantly, if Swindells does not seek to protect the young reader from the awesome knowledge that heroes sometimes die in pursuit of their ideals (A Candle in the Night and Voyage to Valhalla) he offers at the same time a sense of moral balance. Daft Alice tells Lucy in A Serpent's Tooth, "It's good to believe in something...to know who you are...But you mustn't let it become the only thing in your life." Only against the grim vision of Brother in the Land does Daft Alice's advice appear inadequate, but then, in this impressive and unrelenting novel the collapse of moral order is balanced by Danny's growing awareness of sexual love.

Swindells offers few cosy endings. He respects the maturity of his young readers and offers them compelling and sometimes profound imaginative experiences in language which is both potent and easily accessible.

—Myles McDowell

SYME, (Neville) Ronald. Irish. Born in Lancashire, England, 13 March 1910. Educated at Durham School, 1924–26; Collegiate School, Wanganui, New Zealand, 1926–29. Served in the British Army Intelligence Corps, 1940–45: Major. Married Marama Amoa in 1960; one daughter. Cadet and officer, 1930–34, and gunner, 1939–40, British Merchant Service; reporter and foreign correspondent, 1934–39; assistant editor, John Westhouse and Peter Lunn Ltd., publishers, London, 1946–48; public relations officer, British Road Federation, London, 1948–50. Since 1979 public relations officer and parliamentary correspondent, Cook Islands Government. Address: P.O. Box 95, Rarotonga, Cook Islands.

PUBLICATIONS FOR CHILDREN

Fiction

That Must Be Julian, illustrated by William Stobbs. London, Lunn, 1947.
Julian's River War, illustrated by John Harris. London, Heinemann, 1949.
Ben of the Barrier, illustrated by J. Nicholson. London, Evans, 1949.
The Settlers of Carriacou. London, Hodder and Stoughton, 1953.
Gipsy Michael, illustrated by William Stobbs. London, Hodder and Stoughton, 1954.
They Came to an Island, illustrated by William Stobbs. London, Hodder and Stoughton, 1955.
Isle of Revolt, illustrated by William Stobbs. London, Hodder and Stoughton, 1956.
Ice Fighter, illustrated by William Stobbs. London, Hodder and Stoughton, 1956.
The Amateur Company. London, Hodder and Stoughton, 1957.
The Great Canoe. London, Hodder and Stoughton, 1957.
The Forest Fighters, illustrated by William Stobbs. London, Hodder and Stoughton, 1958.
River of No Return, illustrated by William Stobbs. London, Hodder and Stoughton, 1958.
The Spaniards Came at Dawn, illustrated by William Stobbs. London, Hodder and Stoughton, 1959.
Thunder Knoll, illustrated by William Stobbs. London, Hodder and Stoughton, 1960.
The Buccaneer Explorer, illustrated by William Stobbs. London, Hodder and Stoughton, 1960.
The Mountainy Men, illustrated by Richard Payne. London, Hodder and Stoughton, 1961.
Coast of Danger, illustrated by Richard Payne. London, Hodder and Stoughton, 1961.
Nose-Cap Astray, illustrated by Roger Payne. London, Hodder and Stoughton, 1962.
Two Passengers for Spanish Fork, illustrated by Brian Keogh. London, Hodder and Stoughton, 1963.
Switch Points at Kamlin, illustrated by Brian Keogh. London, Hodder and Stoughton, 1964.

The Dunes and the Diamonds, illustrated by Brian Keogh. London, Hodder and Stoughton, 1964.
The Missing Witness. London, Hodder and Stoughton, 1965.
The Saving of the Fair East Wind, illustrated by A.R. Whitear. London, Dent, 1967.

Other (illustrated by William Stobbs)

Full Fathom Five (not illustrated). London, Lunn, 1946.
Hakluyt's Sea Stories. London, Heinemann, 1948.
Bay of the North: The Story of Pierre Radisson, illustrated by Ralph Ray. New York, Morrow, 1950; London, Hodder and Stoughton, 1951.
Cortes of Mexico. New York, Morrow, 1951; as *Cortez, Conqueror of Mexico*, London, Hodder and Stoughton, 1952.
I, Mungo Park [*Captain Anson, Gordon of Khartoum*]. London, Burke, 3 vols., 1951–53.
Champlain of the St. Lawrence. New York, Morrow, 1952; London, Hodder and Stoughton, 1953.
Columbus, Finder of the New World. New York, Morrow, 1952.
The Story of Britain's Highways (not illustrated). London, Pitman, 1952.
La Salle of the Mississippi. New York, Morrow, and London, Hodder and Stoughton, 1953.
Magellan, First Around the World. New York, Morrow, 1953.
John Smith of Virginia. New York, Morrow, and London, Hodder and Stoughton, 1954.
Henry Hudson. New York, Morrow, 1955; as *Hudson of the Bay*, London, Hodder and Stoughton, 1955.
Balboa, Finder of the Pacific. New York, Morrow, 1956.
De Soto, Finder of the Mississippi. New York, Morrow, 1957.
The Man Who Discovered the Amazon (on Pizarro). New York, Morrow, 1958.
Cartier, Finder of the St. Lawrence. New York, Morrow, 1958.
On Foot to the Arctic: The Story of Samuel Hearne. New York, Morrow, 1959; as *Trail to the North*, London, Hodder and Stoughton, 1959.
Vasco Da Gama, Sailor Towards the Sunrise. New York, Morrow, 1959.
Captain Cook, Pacific Explorer. New York, Morrow, 1960.
Francis Drake, Sailor of the Unknown Seas. New York, Morrow, 1961.
First Man to Cross America: The Story of Cabeza de Vaca. New York, Morrow, 1961.
Walter Raleigh. New York, Morrow, 1962.
The Young Nelson, illustrated by Susan Groom and Trevor Parkin. London, Parrish, 1962; New York, Roy, 1963.
African Traveler: The Story of Mary Kingsley, illustrated by Jacqueline Tomes. New York, Morrow, 1962.
Francisco Pizarro, Finder of Peru. New York, Morrow, 1963.
Invaders and Invasions. London, Batsford, 1964; New York, Norton, 1965.
Nigerian Pioneer: The Story of Mary Slessor, illustrated by Jacqueline Tomes. New York, Morrow, 1964.
Alexander Mackenzie, Canadian Explorer. New York, Morrow, 1964.
Sir Henry Morgan, Buccaneer. New York, Morrow, 1965.
Francisco Coronado and the Seven Cities of Gold. New York, Morrow, 1965.
Quesada of Colombia. New York, Morrow, 1966.
William Penn, Founder of Pennsylvania. New York, Morrow, 1966.
Garibaldi, The Man Who Made a Nation. New York, Morrow, 1967.
Bolivar, The Liberator. New York, Morrow, 1968.
Captain John Paul Jones, America's Fighting Seaman. New York, Morrow, 1968.
Amerigo Vespucci, Scientist and Sailor. New York, Morrow, 1969.
Frontenac of New France. New York, Morrow, 1969.
Benedict Arnold, Traitor of the Revolution. New York, Morrow, 1970.
Vancouver, Explorer of the Pacific Coast. New York, Morrow, 1970.
Toussaint, The Black Liberator. New York, Morrow, 1971.
Zapata, Mexican Rebel. New York, Morrow, 1971.
John Cabot and His Son Sebastian. New York, Morrow, 1972.
Juarez, The Founder of Modern Mexico, illustrated by Richard Cuffari. New York, Morrow, 1972.
Verrazano, Explorer of the Atlantic Coast. New York, Morrow, 1973.
Fur Trader of the North: The Story of Pierre de la Verendrye, illustrated by Richard Cuffari. New York, Morrow, 1973.
John Charles Frémont, The Last American Explorer, illustrated by Richard Cuffari. New York, Morrow, 1974.
Marquette and Joliet, Voyagers on the Mississippi. New York, Morrow, 1974.
Geronimo, The Fighting Apache, illustrated by Ben Stahl. New York, Morrow, 1975.
Osceola, Seminole Leader, illustrated by Ben Stahl. New York, Morrow, 1976.

PUBLICATIONS FOR ADULTS

Other

The Story of British Roads. London, British Road Federation, 1951.
The Windward Islands (*Frontiers of the Caribbean, Islands of the Sun, A Schooner Voyage in the West Indies*), photographs by the author. London, Pitman, 3 vols., 1953.
The Story of New Zealand (*We Dip into the Past, Life in New Zealand Today, A Tour of New Zealand*). London, Pitman, 3 vols., 1954.
The Cook Islands (*The Coming of Man, Life in the Islands Today, A Tour of the Islands*). London, Pitman, 3 vols., 1955.
The Travels of Captain Cook, photographs by Werner Forman. New York, McGraw Hill, 1971; London, Joseph, 1972.
Isles of the Frigate Bird (autobiographical). London, Joseph, 1975.
The Lagoon Is Lonely Now (autobiographical). Wellington, Millwood Press, 1979.

*   *   *

Ronald Syme is best known for his exciting adventure stories for boys, moving at a fast pace and set in exotic settings in remote parts of the globe—although when the mood takes him, he is clearly capable of investing his plots with serious themes. *The Amateur Company*, for example, tells how Joe and Uncle Ben develop the natural resources of the island of Arorangi in the South Seas. When they depart, leaving behind them the destruction of a simple but tranquil and contented Arcadian community, both of them are troubled by some nagging doubts as to the lasting benefits of the changes arriving in the wake of their alien energy and technical know-how. And in *They Came to an Island* the same theme of the impact of an alien culture upon a primitive people is again discernible in the incident-packed story of mutiny and shipwreck, exploration and treasure hunting, but it is never obtrusive; the reader is not distracted.

If Syme has a fault it is the continuous piling up of climax upon climax. No sooner is one stirring episode out of the way than another is looming up; there is no time for reflection, and the story jerks along, breathless and impatient. But who would deny the inventiveness that allows the author this luxury? Nobody, certainly, has ever heard his readers complain.

The South Seas is often the locale of Syme's fiction: *Nose-Cap Astray*, the recovery of a space rocket by two boys, white and native, and *The Saving of the Fair East Wind*, the salvaging of an overloaded and abandoned cargo vessel, both feature the entertaining Prince Oro of Manapoa. But Syme is equally at home in the Caribbean of the 18th century. *Isle of Revolt* concerns a negro revolt against the English planters, and is seen through the eyes of Bill Holdsworth, the 15-year-old son of a planter, and his cousin Harry fresh out from England, while *The Settlers of Carriacou* relates the struggles of a small band of English colonists against powerful French attacks on the tiny island of Dominica. Another English cousin pops up in *Julian's River War*, in which Julian is a young Australian inventor who, with his assistant Snoddy, his sister Jannine, Percival Pomeroy the English cousin, and Uncle Eric, becomes involved in all sorts of mechanical contrivances, notably a car that sprouts wings and flies. At its own level this is a delightful book although the cast is really no more than a collection of stock characters.

But Syme no doubt realised that young readers welcome easily recognizable characters and situations. At this stage reading should essentially be full of fun and excitement, and these Syme provides in plenty.

—Alan Edwin Day

SYMONDS, John. British. Born in 1914. Address: c/oPindar Press, 66 Lyncroft Gardens, London NW6 1JY, England.

PUBLICATIONS FOR CHILDREN

Fiction

William Waste, illustrated by André François. London, Sampson Low, 1947.
The Magic Currant Bun, illustrated by André François. Philadelphia, Lippincott, 1952; London, Faber, 1953.
Travellers Three, illustrated by André François. Philadelphia, Lippincott, 1953.
The Isle of Cats, with Gerard Hoffnung. London, Laurie, 1955; revised edition, London, Scolar Press, 1979.
Away to the Moon, illustrated by Pamela Bianco. Philadelphia, Lippincott, 1956.
Lottie, illustrated by Edward Ardizzone. London, Lane, 1957.
Elfrida and the Pig, illustrated by Edward Ardizzone. London, Harrap, 1959; New York, Watts, 1960.
Dapple Grey: The Story of a Rocking-Horse, illustrated by James Boswell. London, Harrap, 1962.
The Story George Told Me, illustrated by André François. London, Harrap, 1963; New York, Pantheon, 1964.
Tom and Tabby, illustrated by André François. New York, Universe, 1964.
Grodge-Cat and the Window Cleaner, illustrated by André François. New York, Pantheon, 1965.
The Stuffed Dog, illustrated by Edward Ardizzone. London, Dent, 1967.
Harold: The Story of a Friendship, illustrated by Pauline Baynes. London, Dent, 1973.

PUBLICATIONS FOR ADULTS

Novels

The Lady in the Tower. London, Chapman and Hall, 1951.
The Bright Blue Sky. London, Chapman and Hall, 1956.
A Girl among Poets. London, Chapman and Hall, 1957.
The Only Thing That Matters. London, Unicorn Press, 1960; New York, Horizon Press, 1961.
Bezill. London, Unicorn Press, 1962.
Light over Water. London, Unicorn Press, 1963.
With a View on the Palace. London, Baker, 1966.
The Hurt Runner. London, Baker, 1968; New York, Day, 1969.
Prophecy and Parasites. London, Duckworth, 1973; New York, Braziller, 1975.
The Shaven Head. London, Duckworth, 1974.
Letters from England. London, Duckworth, 1975.
The Child: Prologue to an Earthquake. London, Duckworth, 1976.
The Guardian of the Threshold. London, Pindar Press, 1980.
Zélide. London, Pindar Press, 1984.
Sidony. London, Pindar Press, 1987.

Short Story

A Christmas Story. North Walsham, Norfolk, Warren House Press, 1977.

Plays

Sheila (produced London, 1953).
The Bicycle Play, and The Winter Forest. London, Duckworth, 1976.
The Bicycle Play (collection). London, Pindar Press, 1981.
The Lunatic Asylum Is on Fire!; Zilpah. London, Pindar Press, 1982.
The Revolutionary. London, Pindar Press, 1984.
The Soldier and the Werewolf. London, Pindar Press, 1985.
The Wall. London, Pindar Press, 1986.
The Great Happiness. London, Pindar Press, 1987.

Radio Play: *The Other House*, 1963.

Television Play: *I, Having Dreamt, Awake*, 1961.

Other

The Great Beast: The Life of Aleister Crowley. London, Rider, 1951; New York, Roy, 1952; revised edition, London, Macdonald, 1971.
The Magic of Aleister Crowley. London, Muller, 1958.
Madame Blavatsky, Medium and Magician. London, Odhams Press, 1959; as *The Lady with the Magic Eyes*, New York, Yoseloff, 1960; as *In the Astral Light*, London, Panther, 1965.
Thomas Brown and the Angels: A Study in Enthusiasm. London, Hutchinson, 1961.
Conversations with Gerald (on G.B.F. Hamilton). London, Duckworth, 1974.

Editor, with Kenneth Grant, *The Confessions of Aleister Crowley: An Autohagiography*, abridged edition. London, Cape, 1969; New York, Bantam, 1971; revised edition, London, Routledge, 1979.
Editor, with Kenneth Grant, *The Magical Record of Beast 666: The Diaries of Aleister Crowley 1914–1920.* London, Duckworth, 1972.
Editor, with Kenneth Grant, *Magick*, by Aleister Crowley. London,

Routledge, 1973.
Editor, with Kenneth Grant, *White Stains*, by Aleister Crowley. London, Duckworth, 1973.
Editor, with Kenneth Grant, *The Complete Astrological Writings of Aleister Crowley*. London, Duckworth, 1974.
Editor, with Kenneth Grant, *Moonchild*, by Aleister Crowley. London, Sphere, 1974.
Editor, with Kenneth Grant, *Magical and Philosophical Commentaries on the Book of the Law*, by Aleister Crowley. Montreal, 93 Publishing, 1974.

*   *   *

John Symonds's fantasies are shorter than most novels for older children, and his stories move quickly: they can be enjoyed by anyone over the age of about seven. Toys speak and have problems; children or playthings from the past meet children from this century and create a mutual understanding. *Lottie* is about the adventures of a doll and a dog in the 18th century; *Dapple Grey* is about a rocking horse trying to find his way home. The tone is always cheerful, often witty, and the endings satisfactory.

In *The Stuffed Dog* two modern schoolgirls, exploring an attic full of a miscellaneous collection of things bought at auction sales, discover a ventriloquist's doll a hundred years old. She tells the girls how the ventriloquist bullied her—so she stole his voice and ran away to hide in a box and fell asleep, but she is now repentant and wants to return his voice. The girls give her tea and take her to see the ventriloquist's house, where the doll is horrified to see that his dog has been stuffed. In the churchyard they find the grave with a carved headstone reading: "Poor Gerald is no more. Died dumb October 25, 1867." So they know it is all true. The doll asks to be returned to the box, where she lies looking so beautiful and peaceful.

This slightly eerie tale is told in a matter-of-fact way. The doll over tea remarks: "They're all dead, dead, dead," then fetches a deep sigh and says: "Please may I have another slice of cake?" The description of the tea table is original: "a gorgeous green cake raising its head proudly and a plate of bread and butter which crouched low with envy." The modern children have quite an adventure in the attic: the trunk that houses the doll's box is so large that one of them falls inside; she discovers a telescope through which she can see "pancakes and what looked like the prow of a ship painted pink. Gosh! It was Daisy's nose and the pancakes were her freckles and what appeared to be great white rocks were her teeth."

Harold is a story of a friendship between 20th-century Octavius, an only child, and an 18th-century ghost. Octavius's parents are always busy; he is left on his own. During their holiday in a house by the sea he meets a very old lady, Agnes Golightly, who has always lived in the attic and only comes down at night. She introduces him to Harold, who was killed falling off the church tower while looking at the gargoyles. Harold's punishment is that he must wander around until he can spend a week playing with another boy, so he and Octavius enjoy exploring a shipwreck together, and Octavius is tremendously happy at having helped him. Agnes Golightly's observations on all the inhabitants of the house provide the humour. The descriptions are all short but effective: "And the sea. It was as blue as the nose of a frozen child."

—Margaret Campbell

———

SYMONS, (Dorothy) Geraldine. Has also written as Georgina Groves. British. Born in Newera Eliya, Ceylon, 13 August 1909. Educated at Godolphin School, Salisbury, Wiltshire, 1920–27.

Served with the Red Cross, 1939–42, and the Voluntary Aid Detachment, 1943–46. Has worked for the BBC, the YWCA, and as a secretary, waitress, chambermaid, cook, and historic house guide, 1950–69. Address: 4 de Vaux Place, Salisbury, Wiltshire, England.

PUBLICATIONS FOR CHILDREN

Fiction

Minnie the Minnow, illustrated by the author. Ewell, Surrey, Tally Ho Books, n.d.
The Rose Window, illustrated by F.R. Exell. London, Heinemann, 1964; New York, Duell, 1966.
Morning Glory (as Georgina Groves), illustrated by Carol Barker. London, Whiting and Wheaton, 1966.
The Quarantine Child, illustrated by F.R. Exell. London, Heinemann, 1966.
The Workhouse Child, illustrated by Alexy Pendle. London, Macmillan, 1969; New York, Macmillan, 1971.
Miss Rivers and Miss Bridges, illustrated by Alexy Pendle. London, Macmillan, 1971; New York, Macmillan, 1972.
Mademoiselle, illustrated by Alexy Pendle. London, Macmillan, 1973.
Now and Then. London, Faber, 1977; as *Crocuses Were Over, Hitler Was Dead*, Philadelphia, Lippincott, 1978.
Second Cousins, Once Removed. London, Macmillan, 1978.

PUBLICATIONS FOR ADULTS

Novels

All Souls. London and New York, Longman, 1950.
French Windows. London and New York, Longman, 1952.
The Suckling. London, Macmillan, 1969.

Other

Children in the Close (autobiography). London, Batsford, 1959.

*   *   *

Geraldine Symons has written several books for children, five in a sequence that covers the years 1909–14. In these the central characters are Pansy and Atalanta, a complementary pair whose exploits are chronicled with rationality and gusto. Pansy on her own is less impressive, as *The Rose Window* shows; she is a conventional heroine without the formidable presence of Atalanta to set her off.

Atalanta is a triumph of characterization. She is stolid, logical, and down-to-earth without being in the least bit priggish. She is well-informed, rather blasé in manner and slapdash in appearance, and speaks with the gruff precision of a bored don. Pansy is more impressionable and frivolous: the combination of the two girls is enough to spark off the alarming or amusing events that the novels relate. In *The Workhouse Child* Pansy flees from the terrible matron of an orphanage and is forced to take refuge on the bloody floor of a butcher's shop. After a rather exciting afternoon, she finds Atalanta sitting calmly "on a molehill by a gorse bush reading *The Wide Wide World*." She goes on reading.

Miss Rivers and Miss Bridges, in the book of that title, are Atalanta and Pansy disguised as a couple of middle-aged suffragettes. This is the most remarkable and effective novel of the series: its surface humour doesn't detract in the least from the seriousness of the theme. It was published in 1971; it took roughly 60 years for the suffragette movement to get sympathetic treatment in children's literature. "If the Government persists in its pigheaded policy, I have no intention of stopping at a brick," Atalanta states. In fact she jumps off Westminister Bridge, and the two schoolgirls are later detained briefly in a prison cell. "Gross inefficiency" Atalanta concludes, after looking around. She becomes interested in prison reform.

In *Mademoiselle* the friends are staying in Paris just before the outbreak of war. *Mademoiselle* is really *fräulein*, a German spy who has walked into a diplomatic trap. In fact the whole spy genre is subtly parodied in this book. A faint mocking detachment is evident in the dedication ("To all patriotic sleuths"), but *Mademoiselle* is also an excellent adventure story. The precision of its detail raises the farcical moments to high comedy. And it has Atalanta to keep it firmly based on the ground. "Don't be so melodramatic and silly," she tells Pansy repressively.

The heroine of *Now and Then* is called Jassy, and she is one of those uncanny fictional children who can step into another era. She has only to walk down the garden to find herself back in 1940, digging a grave for two dogs that have been killed by enemy action or helping to apprehend a German pilot in a wood. The book is in a lower key than the Pansy and Atalanta stories; but it is none the less a distinguished addition to "time-travelling" fiction.

—Patricia Craig

TALBOT, Ethel. British.

PUBLICATIONS FOR CHILDREN

Fiction

Billy the Scout and His Day of Adventures, illustrated by Harold Earnshaw. London, Nelson, 1918.
The School on the Moor, illustrated by Noel Harrold. London, Cassell, 1919.
The Cosy-Comfy Book, illustrated by Anne Anderson. London, Collins, 1920.
Peggy's Last Term, illustrated by C.E. Brock. London, Nelson, 1920.
Farmyard Fun, illustrated by M. Morris. London, Collins, 1922.
Holiday Chums. London, Sheldon Press, 1923.
The Island Camp. London, Sheldon Press, 1923.
The Adventures of Woodeny and Other Stories, with Harold Avery and Ada Holman. London, Nelson, 1923.
Neighbours at School. London, Nelson, 1923.
The New Girl at the Priory. London, Ward Lock, 1923.
The Sport of the School, illustrated by J.R. Burgess. London, Chambers, 1923.
Two on an Island and Other Stories. London, Nelson, 1923.
Betty at St. Benedick's [*Holds the Reins*]. London, Nelson, 2 vols., 1924–29.
Billy at St. Bede's. London, Nelson, 1924.
The Bravest Girl in the School. London, Cassell, 1924.
The Luck of the School, illustrated by Molly Benatar. London, Chambers, 1924.
Sally at School. London, Nelson, 1924.
Scout Island. London, Nelson, 1924.
While Mother Was Away. London, Sheldon Press, 1924.
The Best of All Schools. London, Jarrolds, 1924.
Between Two Terms. London, Ward Lock, 1925.
Fellow Fags, illustrated by P. Walford. London, Sheldon Press, 1925.

The Girls of the Rookery School. London, Nelson, 1925.
Patricia, Prefect. London, Nelson, 1925.
The Stranger in the Train and Other Stories, illustrated by R.H. Brock. London, Sheldon Press, 1925.
That Wild Australian School-girl. London, South, 1925.
An Unexpected Schoolgirl. London, Cassell, 1925.
Bringing Back the Frasers and Other Stories. London, Nelson, 1926.
The Camp in the Wood. London, Epworth Press, 1926.
Jane and the Beanstalks, illustrated by R.B. Ogle. London, Pearson, 1926.
Little Black Tumgo's Tale and Other Stories. London, Epworth Press, 1926.
The Luckiest Girl at St. Chad's. London, Jarrolds, 1926.
The Magic Island. London, Children's Companion, 1926.
Rags: The Pranks of a Little Doggie. London, Epworth Press, 1926.
The School of None-Go-By, illustrated by Margaret Forbes. London, Ward Lock, 1926.
Aunt Mary. London, Sheldon Press, 1927.
Bunch at Boarding-School, illustrated by T. Heath Robinson. London, Warne, 1927.
The Family Next Door. London, Sheldon Press, 1927.
Jan at Island School, illustrated by E. Brier. London, Nelson, 1927.
Jill, Lone Guide, illustrated by R.B. Ogle. London, Pearson, 1927.
Just the Girl for St. Jude's. London, Cassell, 1927.
Let's Pretend Tales. London, Epworth Press, 1927.
Priscilla the Prefect. London, Sheldon Press, 1927.
Twenty-Six Ethel Talbot Tales for Girls, illustrated by R.H. Stone. London, Religious Tract Society, 1927.
Listening-in and Other Stories for Girls, with others. London, Nelson, 1927.
Adventures of Skurry the Scout. London, Epworth Press, 1928.
At School with Morag. London, Warne, 1928.
Baby Animals, illustrated by A.E. Kennedy. London, Nelson, 1928.
Brownies at St. Bride's. London, Warne, 1928.
Carol's Second Term, illustrated by W.B. Hamilton. London, Nelson, 1928.
The Half-and-Half Schoolgirl, illustrated by R.F.C. Waudby. London, Nelson, 1928.
Ranger Rose. London, Nelson, 1928.
Schoolgirl Rose. London, Cassell, 1928.
The New Centre-Forward, illustrated by R.H. Brock. London, Collins, 1929; as *Meta, The New Girl; Meta, Centre-Forward*; and *Meta's Last Term*, 3 vols., 1930–31.
The Peppercorn Patrol. London, Cassell, 1929.
Ranger Jo. London, Pearson, 1929.
Rhona Runs Away. London, Pilgrim Press, 1929.
Skipper & Co. London, Warne, 1929.
The Smiths of Silver Lane, illustrated by R.F.C. Waudby. London, Nelson, 1929.
Billy of the Wolf Cubs and Other "Good Turn" Tales. London, Epworth Press, 1930.
Jean's Two Schools, illustrated by E. Brier. London, Nelson, 1930.
Meggy at St. Monica's. London, Ward Lock, 1930.
Nancy, New Girl, and The Girl Who Was Different. London, Warne, 1930.
The Mystery of the Manor. London, Sheldon Press, 1930.
Little Books (*How Golly Grew Good, The Story of Little Bo-Peep, The Story of Mother Hubbard and the Silver Sixpence, The Adventure of Mary Contrary, The Adventures of Noah and Poll in Fairyland, The Ark Animal Scouts*). London, Religious Tract Society, 6 vols., 1931.
Brownies All! London, Warne, 1931.
The Foolish Phillimores. London, Nelson, 1931.
"Good Turn Tales" for Wolf Cubs. London, Epworth Press, 1931.

Anne of Queen Anne's. London, Warne, 1932.
The Brownie Pack and Other Good Turn Tales. London, Epworth Press, 1932.
Dearly Bought. London, Leng, 1932.
A Girl Die-Hard. London, Thomson, 1932.
Phoebe of the Fourth. London, Nelson, 1932.
Red Caps at School. London, Sheldon Press, 1932.
Anne-on-Her-Own. London, Ward Lock, 1933.
Fairy Tales for Brownie Folk. London, Epworth Press, 1933.
Paul and Pam: The Twins' Holiday Adventure. London, Warne, 1933.
Surprise Island. London, Blackie, 1933.
The Upper Hand. London, Leng, 1933.
Betty and the Brownies. London, Warne, 1934.
The Middletons Make Good. London, Nelson, 1934.
Mascot of the School. London, Hutchinson, 1934.
Brownie Island. London, Warne, 1935.
Fifty-Two Thrilling Stories for Girls, illustrated by Glossop. London, Hutchinson, 1935.
The Girls of the Big House. London, Nelson, 1935.
Pioneer Pat. London, Ward Lock, 1935.
Pluck at St. Cyprian's. London, Pilgrim Press, 1935.
Schoolgirl by Chance. London, Hutchinson, 1935.
Sea Rangers All. London, Warne, 1935.
Old House. London, Nelson, 1936.
Sea Rangers' Holiday. London, Warne, 1937.
Diana the Daring. London, Ward Lock, 1938.
Guide's Luck. London, Pearson, 1938.
Nesta on Her Own, illustrated by J.R. Burgess. London, Nelson, 1938.
Rangers and Strangers and Other Stories. London, Nelson, 1938.
Sadie Sees It Through. London, Ward Lock, 1939.
Terry's Only Term, illustrated by F.G. Moorson. London, Blackie, 1939.
The Warringtons in War-Time. London, Nelson, 1940.
Gerda Gets There. London, Ward Lock, 1940.
Jane Steps Out. London, Ward Lock, 1948.

Verse

London Windows. London, Swift, 1912.
Baby Fluff. London, Oxford University Press, 1921.

Other

The Story Natural History. London, Nelson, 1919; New York, Nelson, 1920.
My Picture Book of the Circus. London, Ward Lock, 1930.

*   *   *

For most of the 1920's and 1930's Ethel Talbot was remarkably prolific as a writer of juvenile poetry and prose. She covered a wide range of themes and skilfully adapted her style for different age groups. As E. Talbot she wrote several school and adventure stories for boys in *Chums, Little Folks*, and the *Boy's Own Paper*, but she is best known for her full-length school and Girl Guide novels for girls.

Her achievements are somewhat overshadowed by more celebrated writers of the period (Brazil, Bruce, etc.) and she never succeeded in creating characters who became as popular as theirs. Nevertheless, she wrote with similar zest and, at times, rather more imagination. Many of Talbot's stories are spiced with touches of magic and fantasy that are associated with symbolic places or objectives, like the old, protective tower in *Carol's Second Term* and the shepherdess tapestry that dominates the school hall in *Patricia,*

Prefect. She is possibly the only "schoolgirl" author who managed successfully to combine the disparate themes of down-to-earth school routines and elusive woodland magic ("The Girl Who Found the Fairies" in *Little Folks*, 1919).

In keeping with the traditions of the genre her heroines are usually "blade straight," "gamey," "comradey," and passionately concerned with *esprit de corps* and the honour of their schools. (The greatest compliment one Talbot girl can "gulp" out to another in her more emotional moments is "You're Chads!" or "You're Cyprians!") However, Talbot also considers the problems of the talented, artistic individualist forced by the confines of school life into prolonged uncongenial associations with ordinary or "philistine" girls. With more frankness than other school-story writers, too, in *Patricia, Prefect* she explores in depth the even trickier subject of a really intense relationship between a senior and a junior girl.

Her Girl Guide stories contain the expected excitements and demonstrations of adolescent pluck—spy-spotting while picking sphagnum moss on the moors during World War I, for example, in "Luck" (*British Girls' Annual*, 1919). But as well as conveying the expansive spirit of the early days of the movement, she produced some entertaining vignettes of over-enthusiastic tenderfoots whose approach to the business of Guiding was bizarrely removed from that of Baden-Powell.

Despite her versatility and occasionally challenging approach, Talbot is now remembered mainly for her conventional school stories about energetic chums who enjoy experiencing "the extreme joy of aching muscles after a topping afternoon's hockey," and who wholesomely follow this up by dancing foxtrots and Charlestons to gramophone accompaniments in the gym!

—Mary Cadogan

———————

TARKINGTON, (Newton) Booth. American. Born in Indianapolis, Indiana, 29 July 1869. Educated at Phillips Exeter Academy, New Hampshire; Purdue University, Lafayette, Indiana, 1888–89; Princeton University, New Jersey, 1891–93. Married 1) Laurel Louisa Fletcher in 1902 (divorced 1911), one daughter; 2) Susannah Robinson in 1912. Writer from 1893; also an artist: illustrated *Character Sketches* by James Whitcomb Riley and other works; member of the Indiana House of Representatives, 1902–03. Recipient: Pulitzer prize, 1919, 1922; American Academy Gold Medal, 1933, and Howells Medal, 1945; Roosevelt Distinguished Service Medal, 1942. A.M.: Princeton University, 1899; Litt.D.: Princeton University, 1918; De Pauw University, Greencastle, Indiana, 1923; Columbia University, New York, 1924; L.H.D.: Purdue University, 1939. Member, American Academy. *Died 19 May 1946.*

PUBLICATIONS FOR CHILDREN

Fiction

Penrod: His Complete Story. New York, Doubleday, 1931.
  Penrod. New York, Doubleday, and London, Hodder and Stoughton, 1914.
  Penrod and Sam. New York, Doubleday, 1916; London, Hodder and Stoughton, 1917.
  Penrod Jashber. New York, Doubleday, and London, Heinemann, 1929.
Seventeen. New York, Harper, and London, Hodder and Stoughton, 1916.

Play

The Ghost Story (produced 1922). Boston, Baker, 1922.

PUBLICATIONS FOR ADULTS

Novels

The Gentleman from Indiana. New York, Doubleday, 1899; London, Richards, 1900.

Monsieur Beaucaire. New York, McClure Phillips, 1900; London, Murray, 1901.

The Two Vanrevels. New York, McClure Phillips, and London, Richards, 1902.

Cherry. New York, Harper, 1903.

The Beautiful Lady. New York, McClure Phillips, and London, Murray, 1905.

The Conquest of Canaan. New York, Harper, 1905; London, Hodder and Stoughton, 1917.

His Own People. New York, Doubleday, and London, Murray, 1907.

The Guest of Quesnay. New York, McClure Phillips, and London, Heinemann, 1908.

Beasley's Christmas Party. New York, Harper, 1909.

The Flirt. New York, Doubleday, and London, Hodder and Stoughton, 1913.

Growth. New York, Doubleday, and London, Heinemann, 1927.

  The Turmoil. New York, Harper, 1914; London, Hodder and Stoughton, 1915.

  The Magnificent Ambersons. New York, Doubleday, and London, Hodder and Stoughton, 1918.

  The Midlander. New York, Doubleday, 1923; London, Heinemann, 1924.

Ramsey Milholland. New York, and London, Hodder and Stoughton, Doubleday, 1919.

Alice Adams. New York, Doubleday, and London, Hodder and Stoughton, 1921.

Gentle Julia. New York, Doubleday, and London, Hodder and Stoughton, 1922.

Women. New York, Doubleday, and London, Heinemann, 1925.

The Plutocrat. New York, Doubleday, and London, Heinemann, 1927.

Claire Ambler. New York, Doubleday, and London, Heinemann, 1928.

Young Mrs. Greeley. New York, Doubleday, and London, Heinemann, 1929.

Mirthful Haven. New York, Doubleday, and London, Heinemann, 1930.

Mary's Neck. New York, Doubleday, and London, Heinemann, 1932.

Wanton Mally. New York, Doubleday, 1932; London, Heinemann, 1933.

Presenting Lily Mars. New York, Doubleday, 1933; London, Heinemann, 1934.

Little Orvie. New York, Doubleday, 1934; London, Heinemann, 1935.

Mr. White, The Red Barn, Hell, and Bridewater. New York, Doubleday, 1935; London, Heinemann, 1937.

The Lorenzo Bunch. New York, Doubleday, and London, Heinemann, 1936.

Rumbin Galleries. New York, Doubleday, 1937; London, Heinemann, 1938.

The Heritage of Hatcher Ide. New York, Doubleday, and London, Heinemann, 1941.

The Fighting Littles. New York, Doubleday, 1941; London, Heinemann, 1942.

Kate Fennigate. New York, Doubleday, 1943; London, Hammond, 1946.

Image of Josephine. New York, Doubleday, 1945; London, Hammond, 1948.

The Show Piece (unfinished). New York, Doubleday, 1947; London, Hammond, 1951.

Three Selected Short Novels (includes *Walterson, Uncertain Molly Collicut,* and *Rennie Peddigoe*). New York, Doubleday, 1947.

Short Stories

In the Arena: Stories of Political Life. New York, McClure Phillips, and London, Murray, 1905.

The Spring Concert. New York, Ridgeway, 1910.

Harlequin and Columbine and Other Stories. New York, Doubleday, 1918; London, Heinemann, 1923.

The Fascinating Stranger and Other Stories. New York, Doubleday, and London, Brown, 1923.

Selections from Booth Tarkington's Stories, edited by Lilian Holmes Strack. Boston, Baker, 1926.

Plays

The Guardian, with Harry Leon Wilson. Privately printed, 1907; as *The Man from Home* (produced Chicago, 1907; New York, 1908), New York, Harper, 1908; revised edition, New York and London, French, 1934.

Cameo Kirby, with Harry Leon Wilson (produced New York, 1908).

Foreign Exchange, with Harry Leon Wilson (produced New York, 1909).

If I Had Money, with Harry Leon Wilson (produced New York, 1909); as *Getting a Polish* (produced New York, 1909).

Springtime (produced New York, 1909).

Your Humble Servant, with Harry Leon Wilson (produced New York, 1910). New York, Rosenfield, 1910.

Beauty and the Jacobin: An Interlude of the French Revolution (produced 1912). New York and London, Harper, 1912.

The Man on Horseback (produced 1912).

The Ohio Lady, with Julian Street. Privately printed, 1916; as *The Country Cousin* (produced New York, 1917), New York and London, French, 1921.

Mister Antonio (produced New York, 1916). New York, French, 1925; London, French, 1935.

Up from Nowhere, with Harry Leon Wilson (produced New York, 1919).

Clarence (produced New York, 1919). New York and London, French, 1921.

The Gibson Upright, with Harry Leon Wilson (produced Indianapolis, 1919). New York, Doubleday, 1919.

Poldekin (produced New York, 1920).

The Wren (produced Boston and New York, 1921). New York and London, French, 1922.

The Intimate Strangers (produced Washington, D.C. and New York, 1921). New York and London, French, 1921.

Rose Briar (produced New York, 1922).

The Trysting Place (produced 1923). New York and London, French, 1923.

Tweedles, with Harry Leon Wilson (as *Bristol Glass,* produced Cleveland, 1923; as *Tweedles,* produced New York, 1923). New York and London, French, 1924.

Magnolia (produced New York, 1923).

Bimbo, The Pirate (produced 1926). New York, French, 1924.

The Travelers (produced 1927). New York and London, French, 1927.

Station YYYY (produced 1927). New York, French, 1927.

How's Your Health?, with Harry Leon Wilson (produced New York, 1929).   New York and London, French, 1930.
Colonel Satan (produced New York, 1931).
The Help Each Other Club (produced 1933).   New York, Appleton, 1934.
Lady Hamilton and Her Nelson (produced 1945).   New York, House of Books, 1945.

Screenplays: *Edgar and the Teacher's Pet*, 1920; *Edgar's Hamlet*, 1920; *Edgar's Little Saw*, 1920; *Edgar, The Explorer*, 1921; *Get Rich Quick Edgar*, 1921; *Pied Piper Malone*, with Tom Geraghty, 1924; *The Man Who Found Himself*, with Tom Geraghty, 1925.

Radio Plays: *Maud and Cousin Bill* series, 1932–33 (75 episodes).

Other

The Works of Booth Tarkington (Autograph Edition).   New York, Doubleday, 27 vols., 1918–32.
The Works of Booth Tarkington (Seaweed Edition).   New York, Doubleday, 27 vols., 1922–32.
The Collector's Whatnot, with Hugh Kahler and Kenneth Roberts. Boston, Houghton Mifflin, 1923.
Looking Forward and Others (essays).   New York, Doubleday, and London, Heinemann, 1926.
The World Does Move (reminiscences).   New York, Doubleday, 1928; London, Heinemann, 1929.
Some Old Portraits: A Book about Art and Human Beings.   New York, Doubleday, 1939.
As I Seem to Me (essays).   Philadelphia, Curtis, 1941.
Your Amiable Uncle: Letters to His Nephews.   Indianapolis, Bobbs Merrill, 1949.
On Plays, Playwrights, and Playgoers: Selections from the Letters of Booth Tarkington to George C. Tyler and John Peter Toohey 1918–1925, edited by Alan S. Downer.   Princeton, Princeton University Library, 1959.

*

Bibliography: *A Bibliography of Booth Tarkington* by Dorothy Ritter Russo and Thelma L. Sullivan, Indianapolis, Indiana Historical Society, 1949, supplement in *Princeton University Library Chronicle 16*, 1955.

Critical Studies: *Booth Tarkington: Gentleman from Indiana* by James Woodress, Philadelphia, Lippincott, 1955; *Booth Tarkington* by Keith J. Fennimore, New York, Twayne, 1974; *My Amiable Uncle: Recollections about Booth Tarkington* by Susanah Mayberry, West Lafayette, Indiana, Purdue University Press, 1983.

Illustrator: *Antiquamania* by Kenneth Roberts, 1928.

*   *   *

Booth Tarkington's *Penrod* stories must be of particular interest to English readers in that they appear to be the inspiration for Richmal Crompton's William. Though Crompton always denied reading them the similarities are surely too close to be accidental. Both Penrod and William feel that the adult cards are hopelessly stacked against them; their story is the farcical havoc that boys can cause while intending to do good. "This is a boy's lot: anything he does, anything whatever, may afterwards turn out to have been a crime—he never knows." There is the same interruption to the elder sister's courtship, the same bribery by suitors: "The serious poetry of all languages has omitted the little brother; and yet he is one of the great trials of love—the immemorial burden of courtship" says the author in *Penrod*, amplifying this in *Seventeen* with: "During the glamours of early love, if there be a creature more deadly than the little brother of a budding woman, that creature is the little sister of a budding man."

Many of the characters are parallel, the good boy, for instance—Georgie Bassett in the Penrod books; designed to be a minister, always clean, devoted to his mother; though whereas William has three supporting Outlaws, Penrod has only Sam. There are whole episodes that are similar, such as the debacle of the children's pageant into which both are pressed by well-meaning ladies. And the hearts of both boys turn to melting ice cream when confronted by violet eyes and amber curls—this was habitual with American Bad Boys from Tom Sawyer on, but almost the first time the young English male had been shown so susceptible. *Penrod* indeed ends on this note, on the eve of the boy's 12th birthday, when as he sits on the garden fence in the setting sun, there is a gleam of amber curls, a tremulous laugh, and footsteps retreating: "in the grass, between Duke's forepaws, there lay a white note…'Your my Bow.'"

Penrod and its sequel *Penrod and Sam* come towards the end of the American celebration of Bad Boyhood which began in 1870 with Thomas Bailey Aldrich's account of his youthful exploits in Portsmouth, New Hampshire. All the writers who looked back with such nostalgia to a vanished golden age seem agreed that the optimum age was 12. As Tarkington put it: "A boy just 12 is like a Frenchman just elected to the Academy. Distinction and honor wait upon him.…11 is not quite satisfactory; it is only an approach…13 is embarrassed by the beginnings of a new colthood. But 12 is the top of boyhood." But whereas the chronicle of William Brown is all farce, *Penrod* and *Penrod and Sam* swing between farce and autobiography, sandwiched with a certain amount of sentimentality. There is in addition some shrewd observation: "There is no boredom (not even an invalid's) comparable to that of a boy who has nothing to do." And Tarkington can combine a richly comic account of the mayhem initiated by Penrod and his cronies at a children's party with insight into what caused it: "Underneath the surface, nearly all children's parties contain a group of outlaws who wait only for a leader to hoist the black flag. The group consists mainly of boys too shy to be at ease with the girls, but who wish to distinguish themselves in some way; and there are others, ordinarily well behaved, whom the mere actuality of a party makes drunken."

Seventeen shows how Penrod might have turned out in adolescence, only the subject is William Sylvanus Baxter, no longer in command of events but being tripped up by them as he courts Miss Pratt and suffers the agonies of first love. To outside observers he is pathetic and irritating, but "to himself he is sometimes exalted to almost divine heights." As funny, but sadder than *Penrod*, it has the same insight into how it feels to be young.

—Gillian Avery

———

TATE, Joan.   British.   Born in Tonbridge, Kent, 23 September 1922.   Married; two daughters and one son.   Freelance writer, translator, and publishers reader.   Address: 7 College Hill, Shrewsbury, Shropshire SY1 1LZ, England.

PUBLICATIONS FOR CHILDREN

Fiction

Jenny, illustrated by Charles Keeping.   London, Heinemann, 1964.
The Crane, illustrated by Richard Wilson.   London, Heinemann,

1964.

The Rabbit Boy, illustrated by Hugh Marshall. London, Heinemann, 1964.

Coal Hoppy, illustrated by J. Yunge-Bateman. London, Heinemann, 1964.

The Next-Doors, illustrated by Charles Keeping. London, Heinemann, 1964; New York, Scholastic, 1976.

The Silver Grill, illustrated by Hugh Marshall. London, Heinemann, 1964; New York, Scholastic, 1976.

Picture Charlie, illustrated by Laszlo Acs. London, Heinemann, 1964.

Lucy, illustrated by Richard Willson. London, Heinemann, 1964.

The Tree, illustrated by George Tuckwell. London, Heinemann, 1966; as *Tina and David*, Nashville, Nelson, 1973.

The Holiday, illustrated by Leo Walmsley. London, Heinemann, 1966.

Tad, illustrated by Leo Walmsley. London, Heinemann, 1966.

Bill, illustrated by George Tuckwell. London, Heinemann, 1966.

Mrs. Jenny, illustrated by Charles Keeping. London, Heinemann, 1966.

Bits and Pieces, illustrated by Quentin Blake. London, Heinemann, 1967.

The New House. Stockholm, Almqvist & Wiksell, 1967; London, Pelham, 1976.

The Soap Box Car. Stockholm, Almqvist & Wiksell, 1967.

The Old Car. Stockholm, Almqvist & Wiksell, 1967.

The Great Birds. Stockholm, Almqvist & Wiksell, 1967; London, Blackie, 1976.

The Train. Stockholm, Almqvist & Wiksell, 1967.

Polly. Stockholm, Almqvist & Wiksell, 1967; London, Cassell, 1976.

The Circus and Other Stories, illustrated by Timothy Jacques. London, Heinemann, 1967.

Letters to Chris, illustrated by Mary Russon. London, Heinemann, 1967.

Wild Martin, and The Crow, illustrated by Richard Kennedy. London, Heinemann, 1967.

Luke's Garden, illustrated by Quentin Blake. London, Heinemann, 1967; revised edition, London, Longman, 1976.

Sam and Me. London, Macmillan, 1968; New York, Coward McCann, 1969.

Out of the Sun. London, Heinemann, 1969.

Whizz Kid. London, Macmillan, 1969; as *Not the Usual Kind of Girl*, New York, Scholastic, 1974.

The Letter. Stockholm, Almqvist & Wiksell, 1969.

Puddle's Tiger. Stockholm, Almqvist & Wiksell, 1969.

The Caravan. Stockholm, Almqvist & Wiksell, 1969.

Edward and the Uncles. Stockholm, Almqvist & Wiksell, 1969.

The Secret. Stockholm, Almqvist & Wiksell, 1969.

Varieties:
1. *The Ball, The Lollipop Man, The Nest*, illustrated by Mary Dinsdale, John Dyke, and Prudence Seward. London, Macmillan, 1969.
2. *The Cheapjack Man, The Gobblydock, The Treehouse*, illustrated by Richard Rose, Jenny Williams, and Mary Dinsdale. London, Macmillan, 1969.

Clipper. London, Macmillan, 1969; as *Ring on My Finger*, 1971; New York, Scholastic, 1976.

The Long Road Home. London, Heinemann, 1971.

Gramp, illustrated by Robert Geary. London, Chatto Boyd and Oliver, 1971; revised edition, London, Pelham, 1979.

Wild Boy, illustrated by Trevor Stubley. London, Chatto Boyd and Oliver, 1972; New York, Harper, 1973.

Wump Day, illustrated by John Storey. London, Heinemann, 1972.

Ben and Annie, illustrated by Mary Dinsdale. Leicester, Brockhampton Press, 1973; New York, Doubleday, 1974.

Dad's Camel, illustrated by Margaret Power. London, Heinemann, 1973.

Jock and the Rock Cakes, illustrated by Carolyn Dinan. Leicester, Brockhampton Press, 1973; Chicago, Children's Press, 1976.

Grandpa and My Sister Bee, illustrated by Leslie Wood. Leicester, Brockhampton Press, 1973; Chicago, Children's Press, 1976.

Taxi! Paderborn, Schöningh, 1973.

Night Out. Stockholm, Almqvist & Wiksell, 1973.

The Match. Stockholm, Almqvist & Wiksell, 1973.

Dinah. Stockholm, Almqvist & Wiksell, 1973.

Journal for One. Stockholm, Almqvist & Wiksell, 1973.

The Man Who Rang the Bell. Stockholm, Almqvist & Wiksell, 1973.

Ginger Mick. London, Heinemann, 1974; revised edition, London, Longman, 1975.

The Runners, illustrated by Douglas Phillips. Newton Abbot, Devon, David and Charles, 1974; revised edition, London, Longman, 1977.

Dirty Dan. Stockholm, Almqvist & Wiksell, 1974.

Sandy's Trumpet. Stockholm, Almqvist & Wiksell, 1974.

Zena. Stockholm, Almqvist & Wiksell, 1974.

The Thinking Box. Stockholm, Almqvist & Wiksell, 1974.

The House That Jack Built. London, Pelham, 1976.

Crow and the Brown Boy, illustrated by Gay Galsworthy. London, Cassell, 1976.

Polly and the Barrow Boy, illustrated by Gay Galsworthy. London, Cassell, 1976.

Billoggs, illustrated by Trevor Stubley. London, Pelham, 1976.

You Can't Explain Everything. London, Longman, 1976.

See You and Other Stories. London, Longman, 1977.

See How They Run. London, Pelham, 1978.

Cat Country. Godalming, Surrey, Ram, 1979.

Turn Again, Whittington. London, Pelham, 1980.

Luke's Garden, and Gramp: Two Short Novels. New York, Harper, 1981.

Jumping Jo the Joker, illustrated by Maggie Dawson. London, Macmillan, 1984.

Other

Going Up. Stockholm, Almqvist & Wiksell, 3 vols., 1969–74.

Your Town, illustrated by Virginia Smith. Newton Abbot, Devon, David and Charles, 1972.

How Do You Do? Paderborn, Schöningh, 3 vols., 1973–76.

The Living River, illustrated by David Harris. London, Dent, 1974.

Your Dog, illustrated by Babette Cole. London, Pelham, 1975.

Disco Books (*Big Fish, Tom's Trip, The Day I Got the Sack, Girl in the Window, Supermarket, Gren, Day Off, Moped*), illustrated by Gay Galsworthy, Jill Cox, and George Craig. London, Cassell, 8 vols., 1975.

On Your Own 1–2. Exeter, Devon, Wheaton, 2 vols., 1977–78.

Club Books (*The Jimjob, The Totter Man, Trip to Liverpool, New Shoes*), illustrated by George Craig and Jill Cox. London, Cassell, 4 vols., 1981.

The Fox and the Stork and Other Fables (retellings from Aesop), illustrated by Svend Otto S. London, Pelham, 1985.

The Donkey and the Dog (retelling from Aesop), illustrated by Svend Otto S. London, Pelham, 1987.

Twenty Tales of Aesop, illustrated by Svend Otto S. London, Pelham, 1987.

Avalanche!, illustrated by Svend Otto S. London, Pelham, 1987.

Translator of more than 70 books for children by Gunnel Beckman, Astrid Lindgren, Svend Otto S., Gun and Ingvar Björk, Irmelin Sandman Lilius, and others; also translator of over 60 books for adults by Maj Sjöwall and Per Wahlöö, Maria Lang, Elisabeth

Söderström, Carl Nylander, Thomas Dinesen, and others.

*

Manuscript Collection: Kerlan Collection, University of Minnesota, Minneapolis.

* * *

There are many children who for various reasons cannot or do not wish to read, and it is for this group that Joan Tate writes the majority of her books. Not all these children have actual reading problems, but many are bored by the majority of books they see. Tate writes books like *Whizz Kid*, short, topical, full of snappy dialogue, and with a plot that is relevant and interesting to teenagers. These are the books which many reluctant readers will pick up; they are designed to be read by the 12–16 age group, but have an actual reading age of 9–10 years. The vivid stories have a simple vocabulary, an easy style, and are set in a working-class area with teenage motor mechanics, shop assistants (*The Rabbit Boy*), and nurses (*Letters to Chris*) as their main characters.

The everyday problems of urban living are tackled in a straightforward way which can capture the imagination of both boys and girls: the young marrieds in *Sam and Me*; the problem neighbours in *The Next-Doors*; the young West Indian couple in *Mrs. Jenny* coping with housing difficulties and the strange winter cold. The majority of these books have attractive, often dramatic covers designed to catch the eye. The type is big and bold, well-spaced but still looking like the good long read to be found in other paperbacks for teenagers. It is this physical attractiveness and boldness which help to popularise the books among teenage readers.

Wild Boy, first published as a short story in *Wild Martin, and The Crow*, has a strong storyline. After Will finds a wild boy living on the Yorkshire Moors above his home, the reader is intrigued enough to read on to find out what happens. There are never too many characters in her books to confuse the plot and the reader always feels drawn to identify with the hero and heroine. The expanded version has a deeper plot and more finely drawn characters than the short story.

Tate has also written a number of books for younger children; *Grandpa and My Sister Bee* and *Jock and the Rock Cakes* are examples of her simple picture stories with domestic settings and realistic dialogue for the 5–7-year-olds. In books such as *The New House* and *Billoggs* the author uses everyday settings but allows her characters more flights of fancy, more imagination than some stories. In *Billoggs* the old tramp decides that the scrap car will make an ideal home without realising that Susan, George, and Ester have used it as a base for their adventures.

Tate is a prolific writer who has specialised in that very difficult area, of writing for a specific audience rather than children at large. She has reached out to those young people who are not by instinct readers. She has also used the environment as a theme; *The Living River* is a leisurely and attractive look at the River Severn with a strong conservation message.

—Jean Russell

TAYLOR, Mildred D. American. Born in Jackson, Mississippi, in 1943. Educated at schools in Toledo, Ohio; University of Toledo, graduate; University of Colorado School of Journalism, Boulder, M.A. English and history teacher with the Peace Corps in Ethiopia, two years, then Peace Corps recruiter in the United States; study skills co-ordinator, University of Colorado Black Education Program, two years; office worker, Los Angeles. Recipient: American Library Association Newbery Medal, 1977, and Coretta Scott King award, 1982, 1988; Buxtehude Bulle prize (Germany), 1985; Boston *Globe-Horn Book* award, 1988; Children's Book Council award, 1988. Address: c/o Dial Press, 1 Dag Hammarskjold Plaza, New York, New York 10017, U.S.A.

PUBLICATIONS FOR CHILDREN

Fiction

Song of the Trees, illustrated by Jerry Pinkney. New York, Dial Press, 1975.
Roll of Thunder, Hear My Cry. New York, Dial Press, 1976; London, Gollancz, 1977.
Let the Circle Be Unbroken. New York, Dial Press, 1981; London, Gollancz, 1982.
The Gold Cadillac, illustrated by Michael Hays. New York, Dial Press, 1987.
The Friendship, illustrated by Max Ginsburg. New York, Dial Press, 1987; London, Gollancz, 1989.

* * *

Upon examining the works of Mildred D. Taylor, one cannot fail to be inspired by her unusually cohesive and consistent approach to historical writing for young people. For each of her five works to date Taylor has chosen an autobiographical base upon which to create stories of amazing power and spiritual ethos. Black experience of the 1930's through 1950 provides the framework for the stories. Taylor has selected various episodes both from her personal experience and from the stories related to her by her father, a powerful role model throughout her life. The stories offer a moving and honest perspective on the perils and the joys of black family life, primarily in Mississippi. The strength of the black family as a unit is emphasized as is the successful potential for confronting and dealing with adversity, when one has the spiritual resources of the family upon which to call. Taylor's works would be welcome at any point in time, but particularly so during a period when the problems and/or dissolution of minority family life are stressed in the media. Taylor communicates a natural and fluid style throughout her works. The storylines are clear-cut, easy to follow but never simplistic. The reader is always left to muse and indeed wonder at human action, inaction, and the far-reaching effects these factors may have upon the lives of others.

The Logan family, consisting of David, Mary, Caroline (Big Ma), and the children Stacey, Cassie, Christopher-John, and Little Man are first introduced in the story *Song of the Trees*, a short novel. The basic story, told from Cassie's perspective, involves the threat to land owned by the Logan family posed by an unscrupulous white neighbor who wishes to exploit their property by cutting down and selling the trees. The land, passed down from David Logan's father, is symbolic of the fortitude and strength of the family. The conflict is a spiritual as well as physical one. The image of the trees and the land are dominant and almost mystical, almost placing the work within the category of a romance. Even before Cassie, the major protagonist, sights the men illegally marking the trees to be cut, she notes that the "song of the trees" (the sound made by the wind blowing through the branches), has stopped and senses that something is amiss. It is the return of Mr. Logan from his railroad job in Louisiana that halts the progress of the evil plan. Damage has been done, but total desecration has been avoided. The family has been shaken but strengthened through the experience.

Cassie Logan also figures prominently in *Roll of Thunder, Hear My Cry, Let the Circle Be Unbroken*, and *The Friendship*. All three stories are told from Cassie's perspective, a young woman whose feisty spirit becomes fully developed during the course of the works. Cassie is an innocent with a far-seeing vision, questioning what others of her time fear to question. Knowingly and unknowingly, she risks both the futility and the danger of confrontation. Cassie is often shocked by what she learns, but in the true Logan tradition refuses to let her spirit be dominated or crushed.

Roll of Thunder, Hear My Cry traces the incidents in the lives of the Logan family over the period of about a year. The family continues its struggle to maintain balance and dignity in the face of southern racism. Educational inequities are laid bare, and the terrifying visits of the night riders, who descend upon defenseless blacks, become a reality. The prosecution of the misguided teenager T.J. for a crime perpetrated by whites also shakes the family, but serves to bind them to each other even more tightly.

Let the Circle Be Unbroken is the powerful sequel in which Cassie continues the story of her family and its attempts to cope with the inequities of southern justice. A foreshadowing of civil rights initiatives is seen in the actions of Mrs. Lee Annie who at the age of 65 decides she is going to register to vote, a dangerous aspiration in the Mississippi of the 1930's.

The Gold Cadillac departs from the relation of the lives of the Logan family and introduces a new family and a new era—the period of 1950. 'Lois is the narrator of the story about a family of four who encounter the realities of racism when they travel from Ohio to Mississippi to visit relatives—in a new gold cadillac. Again, the protagonist begins as an innocent who must adjust to the injustices of contemporary society, but who does so with the support of a loving family.

Taylor's most recent work to date, *The Friendship*, returns to the lives of the Logan family. This story focuses upon the events of one day in the life of the Logan children who witness an incident in the local country store. Mr. Tom Bee, a neighbor who has appeared earlier in *Let the Circle Be Unbroken*, confronts John Wallace, owner of the country store, in a test of wills. Tom Bee insists upon calling John Wallace by his first name, an "offense" not tolerated by white society of the 1930's. Bee is shot by Wallace for this "infraction," but in a scene filled with pathos and courage, he crawls away from the store still refusing to acquiesce to the store owner's demands. This is a drama within a drama; an incident involving Little Man in which he is insulted and threatened by Wallace's sons foreshadows the viciousness of the scene which follows. The reader is shown that the honesty of childhood and old age are treated with callous indifference by those who are steeped in racist philosophy. Yet the reader triumphs in the pride of both characters and (despite battles lost on the surface) in their continued strength.

While Taylor's literary material calls upon the injustices of the past for a significant part of the narration the stories are so well-written and told that they are cohesive narratives rather than a catalogue of injustices. Strong women play positive roles in these stories. The nobility of Big Ma (David Logan's mother) and Mary Logan (his wife) are a legacy that is passed down to Cassie Logan (daughter), also a strong young woman in her own right.

Taylor has included portraits of white characters (Jeremy Simms and Mr. Jamison) which show that there were some individuals who were mindful of the injustices done to the black populace. While these characters are unable to correct all situations for all people, they play their own role in the stories in their attempts to right wrongs. They are Taylor's hopeful response to her call for humanity.

A poetic vision, the art of the storyteller, and the ability to recreate the past in a thoroughly convincing manner distinguish Taylor's work. She has provided us with important vignettes from an unforgettable era, which stand as classics in the genre of American

historical fiction for children.

—Karen Patricia Smith

TAYLOR, Sydney (née Brenner). American. Born in New York City, 31 October 1904. Educated at New York University. Married Ralph Taylor in 1925; one daughter. Actress, Lenox Hill Players, New York, 1925–29; dancer, Martha Graham Dance Company, New York, 1930–35; instructor in dance and dramatics, Cejwin Camps, Port Jervis, New York, from 1942. Recipient: Jewish Book Council of America Isaac Siegel Memorial award, 1952; Association of Jewish Libraries award, 1979. *Died 12 February 1978.*

PUBLICATIONS FOR CHILDREN

Fiction

All-of-a-Kind Family, illustrated by Helen John. Chicago, Wilcox and Follett, 1951; London, Blackie, 1961.
More All-of-a-Kind Family, illustrated by Mary Stevens. Chicago, Follett, 1954; London, Blackie, 1967.
All-of-a-Kind Family Uptown, illustrated by Mary Stevens. Chicago, Follett, 1958.
Mr. Barney's Beard, illustrated by Charles Geer. Chicago, Follett, 1961.
Now That You Are Eight, illustrated by Ingrid Fetz. New York, Association Press, 1963.
A Papa Like Every One Else, illustrated by George Porter. Chicago, Follett, 1966.
The Dog Who Came to Dinner, illustrated by John E. Johnson. Chicago, Follett, 1966.
All-of-a-Kind Family Downtown, illustrated by Beth and Joe Krush. Chicago, Follett, 1972.
Ella of All-of-a-Kind Family, illustrated by Gail Owens. New York, Dutton, 1978.
Danny Loves a Holiday, illustrated by Gail Owens. New York, Dutton, 1980.

Author, director, and choreographer of many plays for children's camps.

*

Manuscript Collection: Kerlan Collection, University of Minnesota, Minneapolis.

*   *   *

An amateur writer, Sydney Taylor initially told the story of her own childhood in an orthodox Jewish family to her daughter at bedtime. Her books are purposeful, and despite soaring moments of brilliance, lack the careful development of plot, character, setting, and style.

The intent of the series books is to describe a family in New York City at the turn of the century, and to instill an attitude of pride in the reader. *All-of-a-Kind Family* introduces the reader to six siblings and to Jewish customs and holidays. The author writes knowingly, as she was herself the Sarah in the stories. Stimulated by letters from readers, she wrote chronologically about the blossoming family; the series covers five years, but was published over a period of 21 years. Taylor also wrote two beginning-to-read books with vocabularies of

150 words, *Mr. Barney's Beard* and *The Dog Who Came to Dinner*.

Taylor's method of creating plot is episodic: Mama places 12 buttons around the room for the child to find while dusting, or Henny charges her friends a penny each to see the baby bathed. Connections between the books are limited, as the author did not originally plan to write a series. There is some foreshadowing, though, as in *All-of-a-Kind Family* when Charlie finds his long lost love, the library lady whom the children already know. Bachelor Uncle Hiram marries the woman who rescued the little brother in *More All-of-a-Kind Family*.

Characters mature chronologically rather than by inner growth. The five sisters and brother, born at the close of the first book, father, mother, uncle and aunt have stable characteristics, and change little. Henrietta is consistently mischievous, and is reprimanded at school as well as at home. In *All-of-a-Kind Family Uptown*, Ella does state, "guess this is what growing up really means, Grace. Standing on your own two feet and being your own mountain." Aunt Lena becomes morose after falling victim to polio, but returns to her cheerful self following a single lecture from Mama.

The specific setting of the books is well handled. New York's east side, uptown, downtown, and the beach are the areas in which the children move, and the junk shop, library, market, and school are sketched in detail. References to the Fourth of July, settlement houses, and knitting for the Red Cross support the uniqueness of place and time, and there are constant examples of Jewish foods in the home: "Teiglech are fried balls of dough soaked in honey" and gefilte fish on Friday are important on the menu.

Anecdotes are expanded into entire chapters, and are spiced with humor. When Henny wore her sister's dress without permission and spilled tea on it, she dyed the entire garment in tea. Yiddish words and the word order of immigrants are interspersed throughout the text: "Schlumper (untidy one)" and "get away from the sink already." Mama states adages, like "do your work with good will and it'll get done twice as fast" or "there's nothing like keeping busy to help a person over a bad time." The point-of-view is inconsistent, as the narrator may relate the thoughts of one person, such as the library lady, but not another, such as Charlie. Taylor keeps the story moving swiftly in the All-of-a-Kind series, but uses the cumulative tale pattern in *Mr. Barney's Beard*.

Taylor's All-of-a-Kind Family books have remained in print in the United States since their initial publication. They have been compared to Margaret Sidney's *The Five Little Peppers* and Herman Wouk's *City Boy*. The author has endeared herself to librarians by providing stories in which the library is a focal point, while at the same time introducing children to an ethnic group in a pluralistic society.

—Karen Nelson Hoyle

TAYLOR, Theodore (Langhans). American. Born in Statesville, North Carolina, 23 June 1921. Educated at Cradock High School, Virginia; Fork Union Military Academy, Virginia, 1939–40; United States Merchant Marine Academy, Kings Point, New York, 1942–43. Served in the United States Merchant Marine, 1945–46, and Navy, 1950–55: Lieutenant. Married 1) Gweneth Ann Goodwin in 1946 (divorced 1977), two sons and one daughter; 2) Flora Gray Schoenleber in 1981. Sports editor, Portsmouth *Star*, Virginia, 1941–42, and Bluefield *News*, West Virginia, 1946–47; sports writer, NBC radio, New York, 1942; assistant director of public relations, New York University, 1947–48; director of public relations, YMCA schools and colleges, New York, 1948–50; reporter, Orlando *Sentinel*, Florida, 1949–50; publicist, Paramount Pictures, Hollywood, 1955–56; story editor, 1955–56, and associate producer, 1956–61,

Perlberg-Seaton Productions, Hollywood; freelance press agent for Hollywood studios, 1961–68. Producer and director of documentary films. Recipient: Women's International League for Peace and Freedom Jane Addams award, 1970; Western Writers of America Spur award, 1977; George G. Stone Center for Children's Books award, 1980. Agent: A. Watkins Inc., 150 East 35th Street, New York, New York 10016. Address: 1856 Catalina Street, Laguna Beach, California 92651, U.S.A.

PUBLICATIONS FOR CHILDREN

Fiction

The Cay. New York, Doubleday, 1969; London, Bodley Head, 1970.
The Children's War. New York, Doubleday, 1971.
The Maldonado Miracle. New York, Doubleday, 1973.
Teetoncey, illustrated by Richard Cuffari. New York, Doubleday, 1974.
Teetoncey and Ben O'Neal, illustrated by Richard Cuffari. New York, Doubleday, 1975.
The Odyssey of Ben O'Neal, illustrated by Richard Cuffari. New York, Doubleday, 1977.
The Trouble with Tuck. New York, Doubleday, 1981.
Sweet Friday Island. New York, Scholastic, 1984.
Walking Up a Rainbow. New York, Delacorte Press, 1986.
The Hostage, illustrated by Thomas McKeveny. New York, Delacorte Press, 1987.
Sniper. San Diego, Harcourt Brace, 1989.

Play

Television Play: *Sunshine, The Whale*, 1974.

Other

People Who Make Movies. New York, Doubleday, 1967.
Air Raid—Pearl Harbor!, illustrated by W.T. Mars. New York, Crowell, 1971.
Rebellion Town: Williamsburg 1776, illustrated by Richard Cuffari. New York, Crowell, 1973.
Battle in the Arctic Seas: The Story of Convoy PQ17, illustrated by Robert Andrew Parker. New York, Crowell, 1976.
A Shepherd Watches, A Shepherd Sings, with Louis Irigaray. New York, Doubleday, 1977.
The Battle off Midway Island, illustrated by Andrew Gloss. New York, Avon, 1981.
H.M.S. Hood vs. Bismarck: The Battleship Battle. New York, Avon, 1982.
Battle in the English Channel. New York, Avon, 1983.
Rocket Island. New York, Avon, 1985.

PUBLICATIONS FOR ADULTS

Novels

The Stalker. New York, Fine, 1987.
Monocolo. New York, Fine, 1989.

Plays

Screenplays: *Night Without End*, 1959; *Showdown*, 1973; 17 documentaries.

Television Play: *Tom Threepersons*, 1964.

Other

The Magnificent Mitscher.   New York, Norton, 1954.
Fire on the Beaches.   New York, Norton, 1958.
The Body Trade.   New York, Fawcett, 1968.
Special Unit Senator: An Investigation of the Assassination of Senator Robert F. Kennedy, with Robert A. Houghton.   New York, Random House, 1970.
The Amazing World of Kreskin, with Kreskin.   New York, Random House, 1973.
Jule: The Story of Composer Jule Styne.   New York, Random House, 1979.
The Cats of Shambala, with Tippi Hedren.   New York, Simon and Schuster, 1985; London, Century Hutchinson, 1986.

*

Manuscript Collection: Kerlan Collection, University of Minnesota, Minneapolis.

Theodore Taylor comments:
I don't approach a book for children any differently than I do a work for adults. I write the story as I see it and feel it. Above all, I try very hard not to "write down" to the younger reader. I'm more at home dealing with adventure. I prefer action simply because it is fun to write and hopefully offers the reading enjoyment which, to me, writing is all about.

*   *   *

Theodore Taylor was brought up in the American south; the Carolinas form the background of his Hatteras trilogy of historical children's books *Teetoncey, Teetoncey and Ben O'Neal*, and *The Odyssey of Ben O'Neal*. The earlier part of his career was spent in the navy and included service in World War II, the period in which he set *The Cay* and *The Children's War*. He has since worked in the film industry in California, which provides the locale of *The Maldonado Miracle*. As a writer, Taylor began with books for adults. It was only in 1967 that he began writing for children with *People Who Make Movies*.

Taylor's stories are adventure and survival tales. His hero is usually a 12-year-old boy living in a remote area whose values and attitudes are challenged by an incursion of the unfamiliar. In *The Cay* Philip, a white Virginian boy, is shipwrecked on an uninhabited Caribbean island with an elderly black sailor as the only other survivor. Dory, in *The Children's War*, lives on an Alaskan island which is occupied by the Japanese. Jose, in *The Maldonado Miracle*, is a Mexican wetback who becomes involved in an event which is regarded as miraculous by the superstitious peasantry. Only in the Hatteras trilogy do we see the hero grow up; Ben matures in his friendship with a shipwrecked English girl, Teetoncey, and marries her in the final pages of the third book.

The Cay, Taylor's first story for children, is his best-known work; it was widely acclaimed on its publication and has since been made into a successful film. However, it has since attracted hostile criticism from some American critics, such as Albert Schwartz, who calls it "an adventure story for white colonialists—however enlightened—to add to their racist mythology." It is seen as giving an exclusively white perspective on the black experience and as showing black people in a servile situation. Such criticism overrides literary considerations—William H. Armstrong's *Sounder* and Paula Fox's *The Slave Dancer*, which incurred similar criticism, were Newbery Medal winners; it also ignores the fact that all three books are historical stories. Each age re-interprets the myth of *Robinson*

Crusoe as an image of the human condition and *The Cay* is certainly a more hopeful image than *Lord of the Flies*. But the criticism levelled against it is deeply felt, and is a reminder that children's literature cannot afford to be unaware of cultural trends and the sensitivity of minorities.

—Mary Croxson

———

TAYLOR, William.   New Zealander. Born in Wellington, 11 October 1938. Divorced; two sons. Schoolteacher in New Zealand, 1960–84; principal, Ohakune School, 1978–84. Since 1984 full-time writer. Mayor of Ohakune, 1980–88. Address: 96 Clyde Street, Ohakune, New Zealand.

PUBLICATIONS FOR CHILDREN

Fiction

Pack Up Pick Up and Off.   Petone, Price Milburn, 1981.
My Summer of the Lions.   Auckland, Reed Methuen, 1986.
Shooting Through.   Auckland, Reed Methuen, 1986.
Break a Leg!   Auckland, Reed Methuen, 1987; London, Penguin, 1989.
Possum Perkins.   Auckland, Ashton Scholastic, 1987; as *Paradise Lane*, London, Century Hutchinson, and New York, Scholastic, 1987.
The Worst Soccer Team Ever!   Auckland, Reed Methuen, 1987; London, Penguin, 1989.
Making Big Bucks.   Auckland, Reed Methuen, 1987.
The Kidnap of Jessie Parker.   Auckland, Heinemann Reed, 1989.
I Hate My Brother Maxwell Potter.   Auckland, Heinemann Reed, 1989.
Agnes the Sheep.   Auckland, Ashton Scholastic, 1989.

Other

The Third Day (reader), illustrated by Nan Reid.   Wellington, Department of Education, 1982.

PUBLICATIONS FOR ADULTS

Novels

Episode.   London, Hale, 1970.
The Mask of the Clown.   London, Hale, 1970.
The Plekhov Place.   London, Hale, 1971.
Pieces in a Jigsaw.   London, Hale, 1972.
The Persimmon Tree.   London, Hale, 1972.
The Chrysalis.   London, Hale, 1974.

Other

Burnt Carrots Don't Have Legs.   Palmerston, Dunmore Press, 1976.

*

William Taylor comments:
I write fiction for young people—11–15 years. While reflective of

New Zealand, my work has a "universality" that appears to make it increasingly popular overseas, with publication in the U.K., U.S. and a number of European translations.

My work ranges from the humorous to the serious—and most points in-between. I imagine my prime aim is to tell a story and, secondly, to tell it as well as I can.

*   *   *

Because William Taylor has served an apprenticeship in writing adult fiction he brings a professionalism and an ability to to slice deeply and quickly into the heart of things. Since, also, he has taught enthusiastically in primary and intermediate schools and has served as a principal, he brings a wide knowledge of children from many different backgrounds. He shows a keen sympathy for them, especially for those suffering hurt, deprivation, or harassment because of poverty, race, sex, or prejudice.

Taylor's knowledge of New Zealand children is immediately obvious. The boys and girls of his dramas show great energy whether they are pursuing their sport or evading the law, running away, searching for the wrong-doer, putting on a play, organising a soccer team, or "making big bucks."

All the various types are there, individualised. 13-year-old Marty Smith attempts to come to terms with his grief at the sudden death of his mother by petty theft with his reluctant friend, the Samoan boy Ioane. Rosie Perkins is saved from the hopelessness of her family life by the warmth of the Geraghty family. The escaping boys in *Shooting Through* find the respite they need and the encouragement to make a new start from their experience with a Maori family in the remote mountain area of the North Island. The gang who dominate the pages of the trilogy beginning with *The Worst Soccer Team Ever!* humorously clown their way through their experiences of very early adolescence at the Greenhill Intermediate School.

There is a marked difference in tone and subject matter between the first four novels and the Greenhill trilogy. In the former the author captures the sense of place very exactly and the characters find their salvation amid a network of conflicting forces. The rabbiter's family in *Pack Up Pick Up and Off* finds itself vulnerable to the condescension and suspicion of rigid landowning settlement. The one-teacher school is at the centre, its children, activities, and workings beautifully observed.

In *Shooting Through* the desolation of the ghost town symbolises the wretchedness of the boys' lives. In this story and in the other two of this group, *My Summer of the Lions* and *Possum Perkins*, animals play an important role in the healing process. The two lions Felix and Felicity are a constant delight in this story.

Soccer matches, school plays, and the business of making money for the holidays are the chief motivating forces of the trilogy. The children, mostly preadolescents, are slangy, at times earthy, curious, cheeky but always cheerful. They handle their teachers and parents and parents' friends with good-natured casualness, grumbling when they have to do their jobs, trying to avoid work, but generally showing respect and concern for parents and teachers. Not only do the child characters show vitality and liveliness such as the redoubtable Lavender and Griller, so also do the adult characters.

Taylor's novels skim along, the narrative carried by the speed and vigour of the dialogue which is idiomatic and individualised. At the start of a match we hear, "'We're gonna waste ya,' says one. 'We're gonna waste ya,' said another. 'Can't wait,' and he grinned evilly." Tom Colman, Lavender Gibson, and their gang may be harum-scarum at times, they may not be angels, and because they are yet children there is an innocence even when they are headstrong. The trauma of adolescence is just around the corner.

Taylor has demonstrated his power of imagination in constructing such an exuberant world. When he broadens his scope to encompass other genres, possibly for age groups both younger and older than

that of 11–14, he could call on his many gifts as a writer to entertain and continue to enrich New Zealand writing in the deepest way.

—Tom Fitzgibbon

———

TERHUNE, Albert Payson. American. Born in Newark, New Jersey, 21 December 1872; son of the writer Mary Virginia Terhune (pseudonym: Marion Harland). Educated at Columbia University, New York, A.B. 1893. Married 1) Lorraine Marguerite Bryson in 1898 (died), one daughter; 2) Anice Morris Stockton. Journalist, New York *Evening World*, 1894–1916; freelance writer from 1916. Park commissioner, State of New Jersey, from 1925. Recipient: Columbia University Medal of Excellence, 1933. *Died 18 February 1942.*

PUBLICATIONS FOR CHILDREN

Fiction

Lad, A Dog. New York, Dutton, 1919; London, Dent, 1920.
Bruce. New York, Dutton, 1920.
Buff, A Collie and Other Dog Stories. New York, Doran, and London, Hodder and Stoughton, 1921.
Further Adventures of Lad. New York, Doran, 1922; London, Hodder and Stoughton, 1923; as *Dog Stories Every Child Should Know*, New York, Doubleday, 1941.
His Dog. New York, Dutton, and London, Dent, 1922.
Lochinvar Luck. New York, Doran, 1923; London, Hodder and Stoughton, 1924.
Treve. New York, Doran, and London, Hodder and Stoughton, 1924.
The Heart of a Dog, illustrated by Marguerite Kirmse. New York, Doran, 1924; London, Hodder and Stoughton, 1925.
Wolf. New York, Doran, 1925; London, Hodder and Stoughton, 1926.
My Friend the Dog, illustrated by Marguerite Kirmse. New York, Harper, 1926; London, Hutchinson, 1927.
Treasure. New York, Harper, 1926; London, Hutchinson, 1927; as *The Faith of a Collie*, New York, Grosset and Dunlap, 1949.
Gray Dawn. New York, Harper, 1927; London, Hutchinson, 1928.
The Luck of the Laird. New York, Harper, 1927; London, Hutchinson, 1929; as *A Highland Collie*, New York, Grosset and Dunlap, 1950.
Lad of Sunnybank. New York, Harper, 1929; London, Chapman and Hall, 1930.
A Dog Named Chips. New York, Harper, 1931; London, Chapman and Hall, 1932.
The Way of a Dog, Being Further Adventures of Gray Dawn and Some Others. New York, Harper, 1932; London, Chapman and Hall, 1933.
The Critter and Other Dogs. New York, Harper, 1936.
The Terhune Omnibus, edited by Max J. Herzberg, photographs by Margaret Bourke-White. New York, Harper, 1937; as *The Best-Loved Dog Stories*, New York, Grosset and Dunlap, 1954.
Grudge Mountain. New York, Harper, 1939; as *The Mystery of Grudge Mountain*, London, Chapman and Hall, 1939; as *Dog of the High Sierras*, New York, Grosset and Dunlap, 1951.
Loot! New York, Harper, 1940; as *Collie to the Rescue*, New York, Grosset and Dunlap, 1952.

Other

The Dog Book, illustrated by Diana Thorne. Akron, Ohio, Saalfield, 1932.
Real Tales of Real Dogs, illustrated by Diana Thorne. Akron, Ohio, Saalfield, 1935.
True Dog Stories, illustrated by Diana Thorne. Akron, Ohio, Saalfield, 1936.
A Book of Famous Dogs, illustrated by Robert Dickey. New York, Doubleday, 1937.
Dogs, illustrated by Kurt Wiese. Akron, Ohio, Saalfield, 1940.

PUBLICATIONS FOR ADULTS

Novels

Dr. Dale: A Story Without a Moral, with Marion Harland. New York, Dodd Mead, 1900.
Caleb Conover, Railroader. New York, Authors and Newspapers Association, and London, Cassell, 1907.
The New Mayor (novelization of play). New York, Ogilvie, 1908.
The Fighter. New York, Lovell, 1910; London, Methuen, 1919.
The Woman (novelization of play). Indianapolis, Bobbs Merrill, 1912.
Dad (3 chapters by Sinclair Lewis). New York, Watts, 1914; London, Methuen, 1920.
The Story of Damon and Pythias (novelization of screenplay). New York, Grosset and Dunlap, 1915.
The Years of the Locust. New York, Shores, 1917.
Dollars and Cents. New York, Shores, 1917.
Fortune. New York, Doubleday, 1918.
The Man in the Dark. New York, Dutton, 1921.
Black Gold. New York, Doran, and London, Hodder and Stoughton, 1922.
Black Caesar's Clan. New York, Doran, 1922; London, Hodder and Stoughton, 1924.
The Amateur Inn. New York, Doran, 1923; London, Hodder and Stoughton, 1924.
The Pest. New York, Dutton, 1923.
The Tiger's Claw. New York, Doran, 1924; London, Hodder and Stoughton, 1925.
Najib. New York, Doran, 1925; London, Hodder and Stoughton, 1926.
The Runaway Bag. New York, Doran, 1925.
Blundell's Last Guest. New York, Chelsea House, 1927.
Water! New York, Harper, 1928; London, Hutchinson, 1929.
The Secret of Sea-Dream House. New York, Harper, and London, Butterworth, 1929.
Letters of Marque. New York, Harper, 1934.
Unseen! New York, Harper, 1937.

Short Stories

Columbia Stories. New York, Dillingham, 1897.

Plays

Nero, with William C. de Mille (produced 1904).
Around the World in Thirty Days; or, The Greatest Trip Ever Made. New York, Street and Smith, 1914.
Black Wings. New York, Allen, 1928.

Screenplays: *The Night of the Pub*, 1920; *The Lotus Eater*, with Marion Fairfax, 1921; *Grand Larceny*, with Bess Meredyth and Charles Kenyon, 1922.

Verse

Bumps. New York, Harper, 1927.

Other

Syria from the Saddle. New York, Silver Burdett, 1896.
The World's Great Events. New York, Dodd Mead, 1908.
Superwoman. New York, Moffat, 1916; as *Famous Hussies of History*, Cleveland, World, 1943.
Wonder Women in History. London, Cassell, 1918.
Now That I'm Fifty (autobiography). New York, Doran, 1924.
To the Best of My Memory (autobiography). New York, Harper, 1930.
Proving Nothing. New York, Harper, 1930.
The Son of God. New York, Harper, 1932.
The Book of Sunnybank, photographs by Margaret Bourke-White. New York, Harper, 1934; as *Sunnybank, Home of Lad*, New York, Grosset and Dunlap, 1953.
Across the Line, edited by Anice Terhune. New York, Dryden Press, 1945.

*

Manuscript Collections: Library of Congress, Washington, D.C.; Central Connecticut State College, New Britain; Columbia University, New York.

*   *   *

Albert Payson Terhune was a prolific writer of popular literature in a number of different fields. He spent over 20 years as an editor and feature and sports writer on the New York *Evening World*. Outside his newspaper work, he wrote voluminously as well, producing travel accounts, fiction, popular history, and verse.

Though Terhune was not by intention a "children's writer," his most enduring popularity rests on his famous dog stories, which found a wide, if not an exclusive, audience among young readers. *Lad, A Dog* was published in 1919. Its immediate popularity inspired a second dog story, *Bruce*, which was in turn followed by *Buff, A Collie, Further Adventures of Lad*, and others at the rate of about one a year until 1937.

They were all quite successful, and all very much alike. The protagonist in each case is a collie—Terhune bred collies for years—whose adventures are the basis for a loosely gathered series of episodes that make up the book. These canine heroes (Terhune sometimes even calls Lad "the hero dog") embody the author's ideas of high personal virtue: they are brave, loyal, loving, understanding, honorable, and unfailingly obedient to The Law as laid down by The Master. Moreover, they feel every human emotion, including romantic love; Terhune's portrayal of animals is entirely sentimental and anthropomorphic. The analogy between the animal ("brute," as Terhune terms it) and the human world extends to the social order. Terhune makes constant reference to the differences between thoroughbreds and curs, with equally constant comment on the parallels with human behavior.

Terhune's popularity has dimmed over the past 25 years or so; only a few of his books remain in print, mostly the dog stories. Though he had the newspaperman's knack for making his work readable, much of it is by today's standards stilted in language, repetitious in plot, and sentimental in outlook. While it is not inconceivable that some young readers might still enjoy Terhune's dog stories, more naturalistic writing about animals, like Kjelgaard's or Gipson's, has proved to have better staying power.

—Anne Scott MacLeod

————

THIELE, Colin (Milton). Australian. Born in Eudunda, South Australia, 16 November 1920. Educated at Adelaide Teachers College, South Australia, 1937–38; University of Adelaide, B.A. 1941, Dip.Ed. 1947, Dip.T. Served in the Royal Australian Air Force, 1942–45. Married Rhonda Gill in 1945; two daughters. Teacher, Port Lincoln High School, South Australia, 1946–55, and Brighton High School, 1956; Lecturer, 1957–62, Senior Lecturer in English, 1962–63, Vice Principal, 1964, and Principal, 1965–72, Wattle Park Teachers College, Adelaide; Director, Murray Park College of Advanced Education, 1973; Principal, Wattle Park Teachers Centre, 1973–81. Formerly national book reviewer, Australian Broadcasting Commission; Commonwealth Literary Fund Lecturer in Australian Literature. Member, 1964–68, and since 1969 fellow, Australian College of Education; since 1967 council member, and president, 1987–89, Australian Society of Authors. Recipient: W.J. Miles Memorial prize, for poetry, 1944; Commonwealth Jubilee prize, for radio play, 1951; Fulbright scholarship, 1959; Grace Leven prize, for poetry, 1961; Commonwealth Literary Fund fellowship, 1967; Children's Literature prize (Austria), 1979, 1986; Australian Children's Book Council Book of the Year award, 1982; Silver Pencil award (Netherlands), 1986. Companion, Order of Australia, 1977. Address: 24 Woodhouse Crescent, Wattle Park, South Australia 5066, Australia.

PUBLICATIONS FOR CHILDREN

Fiction

The Sun on the Stubble. Adelaide, Rigby, 1961; London, White Lion, 1974.
Storm Boy, illustrated by John Baily. Adelaide, Rigby, 1963; London, Angus and Robertson, 1964; Chicago, Rand McNally, 1966.
February Dragon. Adelaide, Rigby, 1965; London, Angus and Robertson, 1966; New York, Harper, 1976.
The Rim of the Morning: Six Stories. Adelaide, Rigby, 1966; as *Storm Boy and Other Stories*, 1986.
Mrs. Munch and Puffing Billy, illustrated by Nyorie Bungey. Adelaide, Rigby, 1967.
Yellow-Jacket Jock, illustrated by Clifton Pugh. Melbourne, Cheshire, 1969.
Blue Fin, illustrated by Roger Haldane. Adelaide, Rigby, 1969; New York, Harper, 1974; London, Collins, 1976.
Flash Flood, illustrated by Jean Elder. Adelaide, Rigby, 1970.
Flip-Flop and the Tiger Snake, illustrated by Jean Elder. Adelaide, Rigby, 1970.
The Fire in the Stone. Adelaide, Rigby, 1973; New York, Harper, 1974; London, Penguin, 1981.
Albatross Two. Adelaide, Rigby, 1974; London, Collins, 1975; as *Fight Against Albatross Two*, New York, Harper, 1976.
Magpie Island, illustrated by Roger Haldane. Adelaide, Rigby, 1974; London, Collins, 1975.
Uncle Gustav's Ghosts. Adelaide, Rigby, 1974.
The Hammerhead Light. Adelaide, Rigby, 1976; New York, Harper, 1977.
The Shadow on the Hills. Adelaide, Rigby, 1977; New York, Harper, 1978.

The Skunks, illustrated by Mary Milton. Adelaide, Rigby, 1977.
Chadwick's Chimney, illustrated by Robert Ingpen. Sydney, Methuen, 1979; London, Methuen, 1980.
River Murray Mary, illustrated by Robert Ingpen. Adelaide, Rigby, 1979.
Ballander Boy, photographs by David Simpson. Adelaide, Rigby, 1979.
Tanya and Trixie, photographs by David Simpson. Adelaide, Rigby, 1980.
The Best of Colin Thiele. Adelaide, Rigby, 1980.
Little Tom Little, photographs by David Simpson. Adelaide, Rigby, 1981.
The Valley Between. Adelaide, Rigby, 1981.
The Undercover Secret. Adelaide, Rigby, 1982.
Patch Comes Home. Melbourne, Rigby, 1982.
Pinquo, illustrated by Mary Milton. Melbourne, Rigby, 1983.
Potch Goes Down the Drain. Melbourne, Rigby, 1984.
Pitch the Pony. Melbourne, Rigby, 1984.
Coorong Captive. Melbourne, Rigby, 1985.
Seashores and Shadows. Glebe, New South Wales, McVitty, 1985; as *Shadow Shark*, New York, Harper, 1988; as *Sharks in the Shadows*, London, Dent, 1988.
Farmer Schulz's Ducks. Glebe, New South Wales, McVitty, 1986; New York, Harper, 1988.
Skipton's Landing; and River Murray Mary, illustrated by Robert Ingpen. Adelaide, Rigby, 1986.
Shatterbelt. Glebe, New South Wales, McVitty, 1987.
Jodie's Journey. Glebe, New South Wales, McVitty, 1988.
Klontarf. Melbourne, Rigby, 1988.
Stories Short and Tall. Melbourne, Rigby, 1988.

Verse

Gloop the Gloomy Bunyip, illustrated by John Baily. Brisbane, Jacaranda Press, 1962; revised version, in *Gloop the Bunyip*, 1970.
Gloop the Bunyip, illustrated by Helen Sallis. Adelaide, Rigby, 1970.
Songs for My Thongs, illustrated by Sandy Burrows. Adelaide, Rigby, 1982.

Other

The State of Our State. Adelaide, Rigby, 1952.
Looking at Poetry. London, Longman, 1960.

Editor, with Greg Branson, *One-Act Plays for Secondary Schools.* Adelaide, Rigby, 3 vols., 1962–64; revised edition, as *Setting the Stage* and *The Living Stage*, 2 vols., 1969–70.
Editor, with Greg Branson, *Beginners, Please.* Adelaide, Rigby, 1964.
Editor, with Greg Branson, *Plays for Young Players.* Adelaide, Rigby, 1970.

PUBLICATIONS FOR ADULTS

Novels

Labourers in the Vineyard. Adelaide, Rigby, and London, Hale, 1970.
The Seed's Inheritance. Adelaide, Lutheran Publishing, 1986.

Plays

Burke and Wills (broadcast 1949). Included in *Selected Verse (1940–1970)*, 1970.

Radio Plays: *Burke and Wills*, 1949; *Edge of Ice*, 1951; *The Shark Fishers*, 1953; *Edward John Eyre*, 1962.

Verse

Progress to Denial.   Adelaide, Jindyworobak, 1945.
Splinters and Shards.   Adelaide, Jindyworobak, 1945.
The Golden Lightning.   Adelaide, Jindyworobak, 1951.
Man in a Landscape.   Adelaide, Rigby, 1960.
In Charcoal and Conté.   Adelaide, Rigby, 1966.
Selected Verse (1940–1970).   Adelaide, Rigby, 1970.

Other

Barossa Valley Sketchbook.   Adelaide, Rigby, 1968.
Heysen of Hahndorf (biography).   Adelaide, Rigby, 1968; revised edition, 1974.
Coorong, photographs by Mike McKelvey.   Adelaide, Rigby, and London, Hale, 1972.
Range Without Man: The North Flinders, photographs by Mike McKelvey.   Adelaide, Rigby, 1974.
The Little Desert, photographs by Jocelyn Burt.   Adelaide, Rigby, 1975.
Grains of Mustard Seed (on state education).   Adelaide, South Australia Education Department, 1975.
Heysen's Early Hahndorf.   Adelaide, Rigby, 1976.
The Bight.   Adelaide, Rigby, 1976.
Lincoln's Place.   Adelaide, Rigby, 1978.
Maneater Man: The Story of Alf Dean, The World's Greatest Shark Hunter.   Adelaide, Rigby, 1979.
The Adelaide Story.   Nambour, Peacock, 1982.
Writing for Children: A Personal View (lecture).   Dromkeen, Victoria, Oldmeadow, 1983.
South Australia Revisited.   Adelaide, Rigby, 1986.
Something to Crow About.   N.p., Commonwealth, 1986.
Coorong.   Adelaide, Wakefield Press, 1986.
A Welcome to Water.   Adelaide, Wakefield Press, 1986.
Ranger's Territory: The Story of Frank Woerle.   Sydney, Angus and Robertson, 1987.

Editor, *Jindyworobak Anthology.*   Adelaide, Jindyworobak, 1953.
Editor, with Ian Mudie, *Australian Poets Speak.*   Adelaide, Rigby, 1961.
Editor, *Favourite Australian Stories.*   Adelaide, Rigby, 1963.
Editor, *Handbook to Favourite Australian Stories.*   Adelaide, Rigby, 1964.

*

Colin Thiele comments:

I have always believed that writers for children are educators whether they intend to be or not. I also believe that writers are greatly influenced by their own lives—by the sights, sounds, smells, and tastes of their childhood, by the cities, hills, valleys, and rivers they knew, by the customs, character, and speech of the people they grew up with. These convictions have certainly influenced my own writing for children. They led me to concentrate on the regions and people I really know, and so almost all of my books have been set in South Australia.

One of the functions of literature for a reader of any age is the revelation of mankind to man—to comment on the variousness of the human condition, to heighten his awareness of the miraculous diversity of life. But the writer for young people has a different, perhaps a far greater, responsibility: he must lead his young followers with what humanity and compassion he can compass to travel a

worthwhile road to adulthood, avoiding brutality on the one hand and sentimentality on the other.

Whether he sets his story within the horizons of a family of potato growers or fishermen or gold miners or city businessmen does not matter in the least. For the edges of life may be as blunt or as sharp there as anywhere else. Love and bitterness, stupidity, excitement, envy and gratitude—the enjoyment and understanding of one's fellow man and of the earth and all its creatures—these may be dealt with as tellingly in Sleepy Hollow as in the most cosmopolitan crossroads of the world. Illumination is in the individual rather than the mass; the universal lies in the heart of man, not in any facade of streets, or hills, or houses.

*   *   *

Colin Thiele is among Australia's most versatile and best-known writers. His children's fiction, chiefly directed to the adolescent reader, favors isolated South Australian locales from the Coorong to the Outback where man makes his living from sea or land and where youth gains stature when confronting elemental forces. Themes persistently stress tenacity and courage and man's need to conserve nature's balance.

Heading the list of Thiele's fine novels of the sea is *Blue Fin*, in which a fisherman's bungling son redeems himself by saving the family's boat from a tornado-swept sea. Colorful accounts of tuna fishing interknit the exciting story. Offering an equally taut adventure, *Seashores and Shadows* focuses on a boy who with his young female cousin experiences a near-catastrophic shark hunt and, following a boat explosion, narrowly survives on a remote island with the girl's injured father until rescued. Other stories with similar settings are no less interesting. *Storm Boy*'s title character lives on the Coorong with his beachcomber father and makes a pet of a pelican later callously killed by hunters. In *The Hammerhead Light* an adolescent girl and a homeless old man rescue a storm-tossed ship by resourcefully reactivating an abandoned lighthouse's beacon. In *Albatross Two* a boy and his sister are caught in a conflict between a fishing community and oil-drillers whose offshore rig's explosion causes sealife-threatening pollution.

Other novels encompass a range of inland settings. *February Dragon* depicts the near-devastation of a scrub country family by a carelessly caused brushfire. *River Murray Mary* traces the economic and physical hardships of a 1920's grape-growing family. Trapped boys narrowly escaping from a sinkhole furnish the climactic action of *Chadwick's Chimney*. In *The Fire in the Stone* a resourceful Outback youth digs out precious opals from an old mine and hunts down an opal thief. South Australia's farming district is the milieu of both *The Sun on the Stubble*, a humorously nostalgic view of a rural youth's exploits evoking the Australian-German farm family's special character and customs, and *The Shadow on the Hills*, which recounts an Australian Tom Sawyer's lively adventures in surmounting comic mishaps and sparing an elderly hermit from injustice.

In addition to his admirably diversified short stories gathered in such collections as *The Rim of the Morning* and *Stories Short and Tall*, Thiele has written a number of successful books—increasing his output in the 1980's—for the preadolescent reader. *Pinquo* is the moving tale of a penguin, raised when injured as a chick by a girl and her brother, who returns to save a coastal town's inhabitants by alerting them to an earthquake-generated tidal wave before it strikes and who later loses its life when an oil slick from a storm-damaged tanker decimates half of the penguin colony. *Farmer Schulz's Ducks* relates the untiring efforts of a farmer to protect his ducks when crossing a busy road for a daily swim in the river; he finally succeeds with an underground pipe. Other representative books in the category are *Gloop the Bunyip*, about an antipodean folklore beastie whose frightening reputation is threatened when settlers invade his haunts; *Mrs. Munch and Puffing Billy* in which a child braves a flood to aid an ailing sister, and *Magpie Island* treating a bird's lonely exile on an island. All the above tales are accompanied by handsome illustrations.

Thiele is a masterful storyteller. International in appeal, his work is enriched by full-bodied characters, humor, regional color, and illuminating descriptions of endeavors from fishing and farming to opal mining and oil-drilling. Committed to man's better understanding of nature, Thiele is persuasive without being pontifical, informative without being pedantic, and never forgetful to spin a good yarn.

—Christian H. Moe

THOMAS, Joan Gale. See **ROBINSON, Joan G.**

THURBER, James (Grover). American. Born in Columbus, Ohio, 8 December 1894. Educated at Ohio State University, Columbus, 1913–14, 1915–18. Married 1) Althea Adams in 1922 (divorced 1935), one daughter; 2) Helen Wismer in 1935. Code clerk, American Embassy, Paris, 1918–20; reporter, Columbus *Dispatch*, 1920–24, Paris edition of Chicago *Tribune*, 1925–26, and New York *Evening Post*, 1926–27; editor, 1927, writer, 1927–38, then freelance contributor, *New Yorker*; also an illustrator from 1929: several individual shows. Litt.D.: Kenyon College, Gambier, Ohio, 1950; Yale University, New Haven, Connecticut, 1953; L.H.D.: Williams College, Williamstown, Massachusetts, 1951. *Died 2 November 1961.*

PUBLICATIONS FOR CHILDREN

Fiction

Many Moons, illustrated by Louis Slobodkin. New York, Harcourt Brace, 1943; London, Hamish Hamilton, 1945.
The Great Quillow, illustrated by Doris Lee. New York, Harcourt Brace, 1944.
The White Deer, illustrated by the author and Don Freeman. New York, Harcourt Brace, 1945; London, Hamish Hamilton, 1946.
The 13 Clocks, illustrated by Marc Simont. New York, Simon and Schuster, 1950; London, Hamish Hamilton, 1951.
The Wonderful O, illustrated by Marc Simont. New York, Simon and Schuster, and London, Hamish Hamilton, 1955.

PUBLICATIONS FOR ADULTS

Short Stories and Sketches (illustrated by the author)

The Owl in the Attic and Other Perplexities. New York, Harper, 1931.
The Seal in the Bedroom and Other Predicaments. New York, Harper, 1932.
My Life and Hard Times. New York, Harper, 1933.
The Middle-Aged Man on the Flying Trapeze: A Collection of Short Pieces. New York, Harper, and London, Hamish Hamilton, 1935.
Let Your Mind Alone! and Other More or Less Inspirational Pieces. New York, Harper, and London, Hamish Hamilton, 1937.

Cream of Thurber.... London, Hamish Hamilton, 1939.
The Last Flower: A Parable in Pictures. New York, Harper, and London, Hamish Hamilton, 1939.
Fables for Our Time and Famous Poems Illustrated. New York, Harper, and London, Hamish Hamilton, 1940.
My World—and Welcome to It. New York, Harcourt Brace, and London, Hamish Hamilton, 1942.
Men, Women, and Dogs: A Book of Drawings. New York, Harcourt Brace, 1943; London, Hamish Hamilton, 1945.
The Thurber Carnival. New York, Harper, and London, Hamish Hamilton, 1945.
The Beast in Me, and Other Animals: A New Collection of Pieces and Drawings about Human Beings and Less Alarming Creatures. New York, Harcourt Brace, 1948; London, Hamish Hamilton, 1949.
The Thurber Album: A New Collection of Pieces about People. New York, Simon and Schuster, and London, Hamish Hamilton, 1952.
Thurber Country: A New Collection of Pieces about Males and Females, Mainly of Our Own Species. New York, Simon and Schuster, and London, Hamish Hamilton, 1953.
Thurber's Dogs: A Collection of the Master's Dogs, Written and Drawn, Real and Imaginary, Living and Long Ago. New York, Simon and Schuster, and London, Hamish Hamilton, 1955.
A Thurber Garland. London, Hamish Hamilton, 1955.
Further Fables for Our Time. New York, Simon and Schuster, and London, Hamish Hamilton, 1956.
Alarms and Diversions. New York, Harper, and London, Hamish Hamilton, 1957.
Lanterns and Lances. New York, Harper, and London, Hamish Hamilton, 1961.
Credos and Curios. New York, Harper, and London, Hamish Hamilton, 1962.
Vintage Thurber: A Collection...of the Best Writings and Drawings of James Thurber. London, Hamish Hamilton, 2 vols., 1963.
Thurber and Company. New York, Harper, 1966; London, Hamish Hamilton, 1967.
92 Stories. New York, Avenel, 1985.
The Works of James Thurber (selected stories). New York, Longmeadow Press, 1986.

Plays

The Male Animal, with Elliott Nugent (produced New York, 1940; London, 1949). New York, Random House, 1940; London, Hamish Hamilton, 1950.
A Thurber Carnival, adaptation of his own stories (produced Columbus and New York, 1960). New York, French, 1962.

Wrote the books for the following college musical comedies: *Oh My! Omar*, with Hayward M. Anderson, 1921; *Psychomania*, 1922; *Many Moons*, 1922; *A Twin Fix*, with Hayward M. Anderson, 1923; *The Cat and the Riddle*, 1924; *Nightingale*, 1924; *Tell Me Not*, 1924.

Other

Is Sex Necessary? or, Why You Feel the Way You Do, with E.B. White. New York, Harper, 1929; London, Heinemann, 1930.
Thurber on Humor. Columbus, Martha Kinney Cooper Ohioana Library Association, 1953.
The Years with Ross. Boston, Little Brown, and London, Hamish Hamilton, 1959.
Selected Letters, edited by Helen Thurber and Edward Weeks. Boston, Little Brown, 1981; London, Hamish Hamilton, 1982.

*

Bibliographies: *James Thurber: A Bibliography* by Edwin T. Bowden, Columbus, Ohio State University Press, 1968; *James Thurber: An Annotated Bibliography of Criticism* by Sarah Eleanora Toombs, New York, Garland, 1987.

Manuscript Collection: Ohio State University Library, Columbus.

Critical Studies: *James Thurber* by Robert E. Morsberger, New York, Twayne, 1964; *The Art of James Thurber* by Richard C. Tobias, Athens, Ohio University Press, 1969; *James Thurber, His Masquerades: A Critical Study* by Stephen A. Black, The Hague, Mouton, 1970; *The Clocks of Columbus: The Literary Career of James Thurber* by Charles S. Holmes, New York, Atheneum, and London, Secker and Warburg, 1973, and *Thurber: A Collection of Critical Essays* edited by Holmes, Englewood Cliffs, New Jersey, Prentice Hall, 1974; *Thurber: A Biography* by Burton Bernstein, New York, Dodd Mead, and London, Gollancz, 1975; *Thurber's Anatomy of Confusion* by Catherine McGehee Kenney, Hamden, Connecticut, Shoe String Press, 1984; *James Thurber* by Robert Emmet Long, New York, Ungar, 1988.

Illustrator: *No Nice Girl Swears* by Alice Leone Moates, 1933; *Her Foot Is on the Brass Rail* by Don Marquis, 1935; *How to Raise a Dog…* by James R. Kinney and Ann Honeycutt, 1938; *Men Can Take It* by Elizabeth Hawes, 1939; *In a Word* by Margaret Samuels, 1939.

*　　*　　*

James Thurber, an American original in humor, satire, nonsense, drawing, and patently a wild tyrannothesaurus type when on the hunt for words, slipped into the field of children's literature by the back front gate, like a cat "walking on velvet"—an expression of his own. By 1943 he was well established through the *New Yorker*: (a) in prose; (b) in his childlike drawings of dominant women, dominated men, and semisomnolent dogs; and (c) apart from the *New Yorker*, for such wry pieces of psychological foolery as "The Secret Life of Walter Mitty" and "The Night the Bed Fell." In that year, without any warning, *Many Moons* appeared: a very slight but delicately enchanting fairytale involving royalty and an itemized royal retinue in the royal peck order of a Lord High Chamberlain, Royal Wizard, Royal Mathematician, Court Jester, and Royal Goldsmith. The King's daughter had fallen ill and wanted the moon. It takes but half an hour to tell you how she got it.

Many Moons was followed by *The Great Quillow*, designed perhaps for a somewhat older group, if one stops to consider its plot and the generous play of its language. And then, though surely *not* aimed just at children, came a trinity: *The White Deer, The 13 Clocks,* and *The Wonderful O*. Call them fairytales, or parodies of fairytales or pseudo fables; they are, it seems to me, entirely suitable for all readers between 9 and 99 who have imagination and a true sense of the ridiculous. The anatomy of these five books is interchangeable: impossible tasks, indomitable courage, improbable solutions, appropriate wizardry, and nothing so serious or warped as not to be funny.

The Great Quillow, a first-rate tale in concept and execution, offers an outsized giant, instead of a king, who plumps himself down on the edge of a village and not in it. To get rid of him and his crippling daily demands for food and entertainment is the problem facing the village council—tailor, butcher, candymaker, blacksmith, baker, candlemaker, lamplighter, cobbler, carpenter, and locksmith; plus the toymaker, not of the council, but the David of the story, with a mind more useful than a slingshot, and a blueprint of action which only a Thurber could have given him.

The White Deer follows the old fairytale prescription of tasks set by a princess, and three princes (rated A, D minus, and E) to

accomplish them. *The 13 Clocks*, by all odds the one masterpiece of the quintet, was written in Bermuda instead of whatever it was that Thurber went there to write; delightfully complex, dexterously sinister, mathematically proportional, *The Wonderful O* is all about disappointed pirates on the Island of Ooreo who set about removing the o's from all words that contain them. An attenuated tale, as if the life work of an oölogist (lgist) were reduced t chas befre yur eyes r rbs.

Auden once said he would test a prospective poet by asking if he (or she) likes to make lists of things. No need to ask this of Thurber who comes across with endless lists so curious they would have delighted Lear, Carroll, Rabelais, and Herman Melville. He loves to ring vowel changes—Rango, Rengo, Ringo, Rongo, Rungo, for example—in dozens of concatenations livelier than the catalogues of ships and whales. And at times he outdoes even L. Frank Baum in nonsense names, words, and phrases: Mok-Mok, Tocko, Duff of the Dolorous Doom, Thag, Wag, Gag; Prince Jorn, Hunder, St. Nillin's Day; Lobo, Bolo, Olob, Obol; Woddly; Golux, Zorn of Zorna, Xingu, the Todal who gleeped; puppybabble, whupple, thrug; "I'll slit you from your guggle to your zatch"; a blob of glup.

Another conspicuous hallmark of Thurber the fairytale teller is an increasing use, in the last three of these books, of rhyme *written as prose*, swimming like the scum on cocoa: "'I like the taste of wine,' he said, 'the feel of leather. I'll ride or drink your father down in any weather.'" You will find this going on more lyrically in E.B. White's *Stuart Little*, published in the same year as Thurber's *The White Deer*. White writes (as in straight prose): "She comes from fields once tall with wheat, from pastures deep in fern and thistle; she comes from vales of meadowsweet, and she loves to whistle." Not a new trick, but Thurber makes much of it. Perhaps too much of it: "'A bell of triumph, or a knell?' 'Time,' the old man said, 'will tell.'"

But his own best trick is a solitary one in that marvelous book *The 13 Clocks*: a couple of limericks done in an inverted style original, I think, with him:

> There was an old coddle so molly,
> He talked in a glot that was poly,
> His gaws were so gew
> That his laps became dew,
> And he ate only pops that were lolly.

Two of these books—*The 13 Clocks* and *The Wonderful O*—are illustrated in color by Marc Simont, winner of the 1957 Caldecott Medal. This reader considers Simont's work in *The 13 Clocks* his absolute masterpiece, inseparable from the text as Tenniel's from *Alice*.

—David McCord

———

THWAITE, Ann (Barbara, née Harrop). British. Born in London, 4 October 1932. Educated at Marsden Collegiate School, Wellington, New Zealand, 1942–45; Queen Elizabeth's Girls' Grammar School, Barnet, Hertfordshire, 1945–51; St. Hilda's College, Oxford, B.A. 1955, M.A. 1959. Married the writer Anthony Thwaite in 1955; four daughters. Lecturer, 1956–57, and Visiting Professor, 1985–86, Tokyo Women's University; publishers reader, 1958–65. Regular reviewer for *Times Literary Supplement*, London, and other publications, 1963–84; since 1974 member of the Editorial Board, *Cricket* magazine, La Salle, Illinois. Recipient: Duff Cooper Memorial prize, for non-fiction, 1986. Agent: Michael Shaw, Curtis Brown, 162–168 Regent Street, London W1R 5TB. Address: The Mill House, Low Tharston, Norfolk NR15 2YN, England.

PUBLICATIONS FOR CHILDREN

Fiction

The House in Turner Square, illustrated by Robin Jacques. London, Constable, 1960; New York, Harcourt Brace, 1961.
A Seaside Holiday for Jane and Toby, illustrated by Janet Martin. London, Constable, 1962.
Toby Stays with Jane, illustrated by Janet Martin. London, Constable, 1962.
Jane and Toby Start School, illustrated by Janet Martin. London, Constable, 1965.
Toby Moves House, illustrated by Janet Martin. London, Constable, 1965.
Home and Away, illustrated by Shirley Hughes. Leicester, Brockhampton Press, 1967; as *The Holiday Map*, Chicago, Follett, 1969.
The Travelling Tooth, illustrated by George Thompson. Leicester, Brockhampton Press, 1968.
The Day with the Duke, illustrated by George Him. Leicester, Brockhampton Press, and New York, World, 1969.
The Camelthorn Papers. London, Macmillan, 1969.
The Only Treasure, illustrated by Glenys Ambrus. Leicester, Brockhampton Press, 1970.
The Poor Pigeon, illustrated by Glenys Ambrus. Leicester, Brockhampton Press, 1974; Chicago, Children's Press, 1976.
Rose in the River, illustrated by John Dyke. Leicester, Brockhampton Press, 1974; Chicago, Children's Press, 1976.
Horrible Boy, illustrated by Glenys Ambrus. Leicester, Brockhampton Press, 1975; Chicago, Children's Press, 1976.
The Chatterbox, illustrated by Glenys Ambrus. London, Deutsch, 1978.
Tracks, illustrated by Gavin Rowe. London, Methuen, 1978.
A Piece of Parkin: A True Story from the Autobiography of Frances Hodgson Burnett, illustrated by Glenys Ambrus. London, Deutsch, 1980.
Pennies for the Dog, illustrated by Margery Gill. London, Deutsch, 1985.
Gilbert and the Birthday Cake, illustrated by Jack Harvey. London, Hutchinson, 1986.
Amy and the Night-Time Visits, illustrated by J.C. Skinner. London, Deutsch, 1987.

Other

The Young Traveller in Japan. London, Phoenix House, 1958.

Editor, *Allsorts 1–7*. London, Macmillan, 5 vols., 1969–72, and Methuen, 2 vols., 1974–75.
Editor, *All Sorts of Poems*. London, Angus and Robertson, 1978.

PUBLICATIONS FOR ADULTS

Other

Waiting for the Party: The Life of Frances Hodgson Burnett 1849–1924. London, Secker and Warburg, and New York, Scribner, 1974.
Edmund Gosse: A Literary Landscape 1849–1928. London, Secker and Warburg, and Chicago, University of Chicago Press, 1984.

Editor, *My Oxford*. London, Robson, 1977; with *My Cambridge*, edited by Ronald Hayman, New York, Taplinger, 1979.

*

Ann Thwaite comments:

My work over 25 years has been almost entirely devoted to children's books—reviewing, editing, talking about them, writing them. My main interests have been in bringing good reading and children together, and in preserving in fictional form my own experiences of children and places. My interest in children's writers of the past led me to spend four years writing a definitive biography of Frances Hodgson Burnett, and this book has taken me at last outside the field of children's books. I have now written a full-scale biography of Edmund Gosse, but I am still involved in many different ways with children's reading. My biography of A.A. Milne will be published in 1990.

*   *   *

What marks Ann Thwaite's work—her own and the selections for the *Allsorts* anthologies—is her acute understanding of contemporary sensibilities. Her eye unerringly selects the stories of daily life that are the stuff of fiction. Her ear is tuned to the rhythms of everyday speech, and to the finer diction of contemporary poetry.

From her picture books to her junior novels, Thwaite chooses stories that apparently play within conventional forms of children's literature but ultimately subvert them. *The Chatterbox*, a picture book, is a "cautionary tale for teachers" as Thwaite says—rather than the more usual caution for children. The story is about the virtue of talking in a primary school, rather than the virtue of silence.

Both *The Only Treasure* and *The Camelthorn Papers*, for older children, look like they ought to be conventional adventure stories of the kind that take in everything from *Treasure Island* to *The Famous Five*. But they're not. *The Only Treasure*, set in Jersey, does include the requisite map, notes on caves, and a mysterious warning to "Watch out for the only treasure." The heroine, Anna, does set out on what she imagines is a storybook adventure. She also thinks that the elegant Felicity, daughter of the local hotel owners, can help her. Instead it is Felicity who puts Anna in danger, and who is the "only treasure" of the warning.

The Camelthorn Papers, set in Libya, chronicles the adventures of English sisters Kate and Jessica and their half-English, half-Egyptian friend Gamal. It too begins as an apparently traditional adventure. Kate promises grocer Derek Lister, father of her best friend in England, that she will try to find the metal box of poems and journals he buried near Benghazi, under a camelthorn tree, just before he was taken prisoner during World War II. Kate, like Anna, does not find the treasure she was looking for. Instead she finds a story of loss: Derek Lister's lost youth and lost opportunity to be a poet; and the graves of the lost young men from England, Europe, and the Middle East who lie dead in the cemeteries. But there are other signs of loss in the story. There are, for example, snatches of poetry about loss from Philip Larkin and Wilfred Owen. In one remarkable scene the children come upon a young man who appears to be drowned. Kate gives him artificial respiration. In a garden-variety children's story the man is supposed to revive. In *The Camelthorn Papers* he doesn't. So by the time Kate finds Derek Lister's tin box under the camelthorn tree, the fact that the papers have crumbled to dust is not unexpected. The story Thwaite tells is not one of happily-ever-after fairytales, but a contemporary story of choices and possibilities, coded in the refrain that runs through the book: "He who does not keep moving is lost."

In her fiction Thwaite's ear for contemporary language often appears in the way she captures uncomfortable exchanges between parents and children. In *The Camelthorn Papers* it is in Kate's embarrassment at the banality of her mother's conversation. In *Tracks* Julie finds herself in the awkward position of arriving just as Ross is having an argument with his father about clothes. Ross, a typical teenager, wants to wear a comfortably tattered tee-shirt for a hike on the mountain. His father tells him to "go and change immediately"—a standard response. Thwaite's skill in the weaving of plot and language is evident in the story: proper mountain-climbing clothes become an integral part of the plot of the novel when Ross suffers from hypothermia.

It is inappropriate to close without mentioning *Allsorts*, an annual anthology of poems, stories, puzzles, and the like (in the tradition of the sort popular in the 19th century) she edited between 1969 and 1975. Thwaite commissioned new material for the anthologies; and each one is a tribute to the excellence of her literary taste. Children who received her *Allsorts* annuals were exposed very early to the likes of Vernon Scannell, X. J. Kennedy, Roy Fuller, Philip Larkin, Anthony Thwaite, Stevie Smith, Ted Hughes, James Fenton, Dannie Abse, Ian Serraillier, and Charles Causley. The list goes on, but it certainly includes most of the finest poets of our time, some of whom were chosen just as they were beginning to establish their reputations. What better introduction, for children (or grown-ups for that matter) to pleasures of contemporary literature?

—Lissa Paul

TITUS, Eve. Has also written as Nancy Lord. American. Born in New York City, 16 July 1922. Educated at New York University. Divorced; one son. Professional pianist. Agent: McIntosh and Otis Inc., 310 Madison Avenue, New York, New York 10017, U.S.A.

PUBLICATIONS FOR CHILDREN

Fiction (illustrated by Paul Galdone)

Anatole. New York, McGraw Hill, 1956; London, Lane, 1957.
Anatole and the Cat. New York, McGraw Hill, 1957; London, Lane, 1958.
Basil of Baker Street. New York, McGraw Hill, 1958.
My Dog and I (as Nancy Lord). New York, McGraw Hill, 1958.
Anatole and the Robot. New York, McGraw Hill, 1960; London, Bodley Head, 1961.
Anatole over Paris. New York, McGraw Hill, 1961; London, Bodley Head, 1962.
The Mouse and the Lion, illustrated by Leonard Weisgard. New York, Parents' Magazine Press, 1962.
Basil and the Lost Colony. New York, McGraw Hill, 1964; London, Hodder and Stoughton, 1975.
Anatole and the Poodle. New York, McGraw Hill, 1965; London, Bodley Head, 1966.
Anatole and the Piano. New York, McGraw Hill, 1966; London, Bodley Head, 1967.
Anatole and the Thirty Thieves. New York, McGraw Hill, and London, Bodley Head, 1969.
Mr. Shaw's Shipshape Shoeshop, illustrated by Larry Ross. New York, Parents' Magazine Press, 1970.
Anatole and the Toyshop. New York, McGraw Hill, 1970.
Basil and the Pygmy Cats. New York, McGraw Hill, 1971; London, Hodder and Stoughton, 1977.
Why the Wind God Wept, illustrated by James Barkley. New York, Doubleday, 1972.
Anatole in Italy. New York, McGraw Hill, 1973; London, Bodley Head, 1974.
Basil in Mexico. New York, McGraw Hill, 1976.
Anatole and the Pied Piper. New York, McGraw Hill, 1979.
Basil in the Wild West. New York, McGraw Hill, 1981.

Other

The Two Stonecutters, illustrated by Yoko Mitsuhashi. New York, Doubleday, 1967.

*

Manuscript Collection: Case Collection, Wayne State University, Detroit.

* * *

Eve Titus is known primarily for her Anatole and Basil books, but she has written several individual stories for magazines and in book form. The series stories maintain a high standard in plot and style, and have the precision and rhythm expected of a musician.

Anatole was her first published book, and has remained the most prominent. Anatole is a French mouse whose occupation is cheese tasting for M'sieu Duval. Either the cheese factory or Anatole's family is threatened in a different manner in each book, and the mouse *magnifique* comes to the rescue. The specific character or situation is obvious from the title. The belling of the cat is the classical theme used for the second story, while the robot Cheezak provides the challenge in the third book. The next six books deal with his family stranded on the Eiffel tower, the kidnapping of the model poodle Juliette, the salvaging of pearls from a grand piano, the foiling of thieves, the rescuing of his family from the clutches of a toyshop owner, and his visit to a cheese factory in Italy. *Anatole and the Toyshop* is the most dramatic, for the proprietor forces his six youngsters to ride their bicycles around the window display continually to attract an audience of shoppers.

The swiftly moving stories are sprinkled with French phrases and words. Repetition is used in introducing Anatole's wife Doucette, and their children, Paul, Paulette, Claude, Claudette, Georges, and Georgette. The three suspects in the Great Cheese Robbery are Baptiste the Baker, Blanchard the Barber, and Bernard the Bookseller. Titus uses rhythmical phrasing ("Concerning cheese, the world agrees a mouse's nose is better than a policeman's") and her sense of humor is revealed both in the situations and in the language, such as "And be quiet as mice!"

While Anatole is French, Basil is British and the books about him are written in the style of Arthur Conan Doyle's *Sherlock Holmes*. Basil lives at Baker Street, Number 221-B and solves mysteries with his doctor companion, David Q. Dawson. Plots, characters, and language have parallels with the Sherlockian canon. The introductory paragraphs tantalize, digress, and then proceed to the basic story. Conclusions invariably point to another adventure, as in *Basil and the Pygmy Cats* where there is reference to a Mexican adventure, and in *Basil and the Lost Colony* a mysterious note arrives. In the latter book, the detective and companion visit Tellmice, in which the inhabitants are unaware that Switzerland has regained her freedom in 1291. "Relda" the mouse opera star is introduced in the book, while Professor Ratigan, leader of the mouse underworld, captures the adventures in *Basil and the Pygmy Cats*.

The language used alludes to both mice and to Holmes. "Pawhand" and "shortpaw" refer to writing, while "Mouseland Yard" and "Mousemoor Prison" are locations, and after a heroic episode Basil is elected to lifetime membership in the Royal Academy of Mousology. In Holmesian tradition, Basil uses his deductive powers, wears a Persian robe, plays the violin, and enjoys Mrs. Judson's cheese soufflé. There is even the identification, "'Basil of Baker Street, I presume?'" Inconsistencies are rare, but Basil's pipe is described as being both "berrywood" and "meerwood" in *Basil of Baker Street*.

Titus has written other stories, but they don't have the inventiveness of those about Anatole and Basil. *My Dog and I*, written under the pseudonym Nancy Lord, is a slight picture book. *The Two Stonecutters* is a free adaptation from the Japanese, and too elaborate for a folktale. There is only a reference to the historic meeting in *The*

Mouse and the Lion, a "Reading Readiness book" in which the lion visits the world of people and the mouse has almost no role. *Mr. Shaw's Shipshape Shoeshop* has rhythm and a strong plot, but is too long. The Anatole and Basil books far outweigh the others in impact and popularity. The two characters are important enough to be represented by entries in Margery Fisher's *Who's Who in Children's Books*. Since the audience reading Basil books is considerably younger than those reading the Sherlock Holmes books, they may be seen as preparation for the Victorian detective rather than as a pastiche.

—Karen Nelson Hoyle

TODD, Barbara Euphan. Also wrote as Barbara Bower; Euphan. British. Born in Arksey, Yorkshire, 9 January 1890 (?). Educated at St. Catherine's School, Bramley, Surrey. Served in the Voluntary Aid Detachment, 1914–18. Married John Graham Bower in 1932 (died 1940). Regular contributor to *Punch*, London. *Died 2 February 1976.*

PUBLICATIONS FOR CHILDREN

Fiction

The 'normous Saturday Fairy Book, with Marjory Royce and Moira Meighn. London, Stanley Paul, 1924.
The 'normous Sunday Story Book, with Marjory Royce and Moira Meighn. London, Stanley Paul, 1925.
The Very Good Walkers, with Marjory Royce, illustrated by H.R. Millar. London, Methuen, 1925.
Mr. Blossom's Shop. London, Nelson, 1929.
Happy Cottage, with Marjory Royce. London, Collins, 1930.
South Country Secrets (as Euphan), with Klaxon. London, Burns Oates, 1935.
The Touchstone, with Klaxon. London, Burns Oates, 1935.
Worzel Gummidge; or, The Scarecrow of Scatterbrook, illustrated by Elizabeth Alldridge. London, Burns Oates, 1936.
Worzel Gummidge Again, illustrated by Elizabeth Alldridge. London, Burns Oates, 1937.
The Mystery Train. London, University of London Press, 1937.
The Splendid Picnic. London, University of London Press, 1937.
More about Worzel Gummidge. London, Burns Oates, 1938.
Mr. Dock's Garden, illustrated by Ruth Westcott. Leeds, E.J. Arnold, 1939.
Gertrude the Greedy Goose, illustrated by Benjamin Rabier. London, Muller, 1939.
The House That Ran Behind, with Esther Boumphrey. London, Muller, 1943.
Worzel Gummidge, The Scarecrow of Scatterbrook Farm (from *Worzel Gummidge; or, The Scarecrow of Scatterbrook* and *Worzel Gummidge Again*), illustrated by Ursula Koering. New York, Putnam, 1947.
Worzel Gummidge and Saucy Nancy, illustrated by Will Nickless. London, Hollis and Carter, 1947.
Worzel Gummidge Takes a Holiday, illustrated by Will Nickless. London, Hollis and Carter, 1949.
Aloysius Let Loose, with Klaxon, illustrated by A.E. Batchelor. London, Collins, 1950.
Earthy Mangold and Worzel Gummidge, illustrated by Jill Crockford. London, Hollis and Carter, 1954.
Worzel Gummidge and the Railway Scarecrows, illustrated by Jill

Crockford. London, Evans, 1955.
Worzel Gummidge at the Circus, illustrated by Jill Crockford. London, Evans, 1956.
The Boy with the Green Thumb, illustrated by Charlotte Hough. London, Hamish Hamilton, 1956.
The Wizard and the Unicorn, illustrated by Prudence Seward. London, Hamish Hamilton, 1957.
Worzel Gummidge and the Treasure Ship, illustrated by Jill Crockford. London, Evans, 1958.
The Shop Around the Corner, illustrated by Olive Coughlan. London, Hamish Hamilton, 1959.
Detective Worzel Gummidge, illustrated by Jill Crockford. London, Evans, 1963.
The Shop by the Sea, illustrated by Sarah Garland. London, Hamish Hamilton, 1966.
The Clock Shop, illustrated by Jill Crockford. Kingswood, Surrey, World's Work, 1967.
The Shop on Wheels, illustrated by Jill Crockford. Kingswood, Surrey, World's Work, 1968.
The Box in the Attic, illustrated by Lynette Hemmant. Kingswood, Surrey, World's Work, 1970.
The Wand from France, illustrated by Lynette Hemmant. Kingswood, Surrey, World's Work, 1972.

Plays

The Frog Prince, with Mabel Constanduros. London, French, 1956.
The Sleeping Beauty, with Mabel Constanduros. London, French, 1956.

Verse

Hither and Thither. London, Harrap, 1927.
The Seventh Daughter (as Euphan). London, Burns Oates, 1935.

Other

Stories of the Coronations (as Euphan), with Klaxon. London, Burns Oates, 1937.

PUBLICATIONS FOR ADULTS

Novel

Miss Ranskill Comes Home (as Barbara Bower). London, Chapman and Hall, and New York, Putnam, 1946.

*   *   *

The fame of Barbara Euphan Todd will rest on the stories which feature Worzel Gummidge and his fellow scarecrows. Typically, in *Worzel Gummidge; or, The Scarecrow of Scatterbrook*, John and Susan, aged 10 and 12, spend holidays at Scatterbrook Farm where they have hilarious and singularly credible adventures protecting the nature and escapades of these walking, talking scarecrows from discovery by adults. These stories are for sharing, and are excellent for reading aloud to children of eight or nine in chapters sufficiently self-contained to make satisfactory reading units. The dialogue of the scarecrows, such as "'Tain't disgustin'" will present problems to some children who try to read the stories for themselves, but there is a strong incentive to succeed.

The older people, especially the patronising though well-meaning Mrs. Bloomsbury-Barton, tend to be caricatures of "not-understanding" adults. But they are merely foils: the scarecrows themselves are strongly individualised and have real life breathed into them. Chief among these is Worzel Gummidge himself, with his turnip head, broomstick arms, and bottle-straw boots; he is full of professional pride, unpredictable, and almost always irritatingly right. Earthy Mangold is not very bright, and is professionally most inept, but she "allus tries to be comfortin'"; it is typical of her that she shoos away the hens so that the sparrows may get the grain, and that she cannot think of her hedgerow origin without aching once more to shelter the nests of the small birds and feel their wings flutter among her boughs. Little Upsidaisy, made from a milking stool, isn't very bright either, but she is always cheerful, while valetudinarian Hannah Harrow suffers from a variety of extraordinary complaints, from the "damping off" to "the mice"—for which complaint she is advised by her friends to swallow a mousetrap.

In all these stories, the excitement lies in the adventures, and the fun in the dialogue, especially in the scarecrows' irrefutable logic from quaint premises. Here is Gummidge's justification for his threat to wish that all human beings were turned into earwigs: "Nobody wouldn't think as grass could turn into milk, but it does," argued Gummidge. "And humans is more the shape o' earwigs than grass is the shape o'milk. Stands to reason."

The stories without Gummidge in the title have no scarecrows in them, and so lack their author's most magic touch, though they are mostly about magic: for instance, Fred has a Green Thumb, which brings to life a donkey cut in a hedge and causes a red hot poker plant to set fire to a sweet shop, while candytuft becomes real candy to replace lost sweets. These books, also, are good for reading aloud in convenient chapter units, and are easier than the Gummidge books for younger children to read for themselves.

—Norman Culpan

TODD, H(erbert) E(atton). British. Born in London, 22 February 1908. Educated at Christ's Hospital, Horsham, Sussex, 1919–25. Served in the Royal Air Force, 1940–45: Squadron Leader. Married Bertha Joyce Hughes in 1932 (died 1968); three sons. Clerk, Houlder Brothers Ltd., London, 1925–27, and British Foreign and Colonial Corporation, London, 1927–29; hosiery buyer, Bourne and Hollingsworth Ltd., London, 1929–31; salesman, 1931–47, and director and sales manager, 1947–69, F.G. Wigley and Company Ltd., London. From 1946 broadcaster and lecturer. *Died 25 February 1988.*

PUBLICATIONS FOR CHILDREN (books prior to 1976 illustrated by Lilian Buchanan)

Fiction

Bobby Brewster and the Winkers' Club, illustrated by Bryan Ward. Leicester, Ward, 1949.
Bobby Brewster. Leicester, Brockhampton Press, 1954.
Bobby Brewster—Bus Conductor. Leicester, Brockhampton Press, 1954.
Bobby Brewster's Shadow. Leicester, Brockhampton Press, 1956.
Bobby Brewster's Bicycle. Leicester, Brockhampton Press, 1957.
Bobby Brewster's Camera. Leicester, Brockhampton Press, 1959.
Bobby Brewster's Wallpaper. Leicester, Brockhampton Press, 1961.
Bobby Brewster's Conker. Leicester, Brockhampton Press, 1963.
Bobby Brewster—Detective. Leicester, Brockhampton Press, 1964.

Bobby Brewster's Potato. Leicester, Brockhampton Press, 1964.
Bobby Brewster and the Ghost. Leicester, Brockhampton Press, 1966.
Bobby Brewster's Kite. Leicester, Brockhampton Press, 1967.
Bobby Brewster's Scarecrow. Leicester, Brockhampton Press, 1968.
Bobby Brewster's Torch. Leicester, Brockhampton Press, 1969.
Bobby Brewster's Balloon Race. Leicester, Brockhampton Press, 1970.
Bobby Brewster's First Magic. Leicester, Brockhampton Press, 1970.
Bobby Brewster's Typewriter. Leicester, Brockhampton Press, 1971.
Bobby Brewster's Bee. Leicester, Brockhampton Press, 1972.
Bobby Brewster's Wishbone. Leicester, Brockhampton Press, 1974.
The Sick Cow, illustrated by Val Biro. Leicester, Brockhampton Press, 1974; Chicago, Children's Press, 1976.
Bobby Brewster's First Fun. Leicester, Brockhampton Press, 1974.
Bobby Brewster's Bookmark. London, Hodder and Stoughton, 1975.
George the Fire Engine, illustrated by Val Biro. London, Hodder and Stoughton, 1976; Chicago, Children's Press, 1978.
Changing of the Guard, illustrated by Val Biro. London, Hodder and Stoughton, 1978.
The Very, Very Long Dog, illustrated by Val Biro. London, Carousel, 1978.
The Roundabout Horse, illustrated by Val Biro. London, Hodder and Stoughton, 1978.
Here Comes Wordman!, illustrated by Val Biro. London, Carousel, 1979.
Bobby Brewster's Tea-Leaves, illustrated by David Barnett. London, Hodder and Stoughton, 1979.
King of Beasts, illustrated by Val Biro. London, Hodder and Stoughton, 1979.
The Big Sneeze, illustrated by Val Biro. London, Hodder and Stoughton, 1980.
Jungle Silver, illustrated by Val Biro. London, Hodder and Stoughton, 1981.
The Dial-a-Story Book, illustrated by Val Biro. London, Penguin, 1981.
Bobby Brewster's Lamp Post, illustrated by Lilian Buchanan. London, Hodder and Stoughton, 1982.
Changing of the Guard; Wallpaper Holiday, illustrated by Lilian Buchanan. London, Penguin, 1982.
The Tiger Who Couldn't Be Bothered, illustrated by Val Biro. London, Hodder and Stoughton, 1984.
Bobby Brewster's Hiccups, illustrated by Lilian Buchanan. London, Hodder and Stoughton, 1985.
Bobby Brewster's Old Van, illustrated by David Barnett. London, Hodder and Stoughton, 1986.
Bobby Brewster and the Magic Handyman, illustrated by David Barnett. London, Hodder and Stoughton, 1987.
The Sleeping Policeman, illustrated by Val Biro. London, Hodder and Stoughton, 1988.
Bobby Brewster's Jigsaw Puzzle, illustrated by Val Biro. London, Hodder and Stoughton, 1988.

Other

The Crawly Crawly Caterpillar, illustrated by Val Biro. London, Carousel, 1981.
The Tiny, Tiny Tadpole, illustrated by Val Biro. London, Carousel, 1982.
The Scruffy Scruffy Dog, illustrated by Val Biro. London, Hodder and Stoughton, 1983.

CHILDREN'S WRITERS

The Clever Clever Cats, illustrated by Val Biro. London, Hodder and Stoughton, 1985.
The Silly Silly Ghost, illustrated by Val Biro. London, Hodder and Stoughton, 1987.

*

Manuscript Collection: de Grummond Collection, University of Southern Mississippi, Hattiesburg.

Incidental Music: *Blackbird Pie* (play), 1956, and *The Circus King*, both by Capel Annand.

H.E. Todd commented:

(1978) All my stories are about Bobby Brewster, a small boy with a round face, blue eyes, and a nose like a button. He is part of me, part of my sons, and part of all the girls as well as boys to whom I tell stories. He is nearly 9 years old now—35 years ago he was three-and-a-half. That is when I started telling stories about him to my one son at the time, and since then I have told stories about him to thousands of children of all ages, races, creeds, colours all over the world, live, and also on radio and television.

I do not claim to write stories of great literary merit, or to teach a lesson or point a moral. I write and tell stories simply for fun. And my stories are written in exactly the same language as I tell them, for *telling* stories was my first joy and I was only persuaded to write them because people seemed to enjoy hearing them.

* * *

While H.E. Todd's stories are not necessarily in the mainstream of modern children's literature, his influence on children's reading has been profound. Even before his retirement from business he had become an assiduous and regular public storyteller of magnetic appeal, with a vast repertoire of tales of magic and other oddities in the life of his boy character Bobby Brewster. Bobby himself, and his parents, friends, teachers, and relations, are primarily vehicles round and by means of whom the magic takes effect. What is so good about the stories is that they are founded on everyday situations and everyday things—a wristwatch, pyjamas, parties, school, trying to get to sleep, domestic animals, a piece of chalk, musical instruments. Many of the situations are really funny. The stories have witty touches of detail, and they are told in public with the professional expertise, timing, and verve of many years' practice. A typical piece of Todd nonsense which yet has the ring of logic about it concerns Bobby's clothes hanging on the line which are objecting to not being worn to a party. So he finds out what occasions each prefers, and makes a list, including, "Pants don't mind what parties they go to because they can't see anyway. They prefer to hang on the line."

However, to speak well and to write well require different techniques. Some of the stories in the books have suffered in transition because they have not fully been translated into the medium of the printed word: asides which are acceptable in public become self-conscious in print. And though many of the situations have actually been suggested by children, the vein of profitable imagination and skilful working out of a plot is sometimes thin. Certainly the books of what one might call the middle period are the best, notably *Bobby Brewster and the Ghost* and *Bobby Brewster's Typewriter*.

—Antony Kamm

TOLKIEN, J(ohn) R(onald) R(euel). British. Born in Bloem-fontein, South Africa, 3 January 1892; came to England, 1895. Educated at King Edward's School, Birmingham, 1900–02, 1903–11; St. Philip's School, Birmingham, 1902–03; Exeter College, Oxford (open classical exhibitioner; Skeat prize, 1914), 1911–15, B.A. (honours), 1915, M.A. 1919. Served in the Lancashire Fusiliers, 1915–18: Lieutenant. Married Edith Mary Bratt in 1916 (died 1971); three sons and one daughter. Assistant, Oxford English Dictionary, 1919–20; Reader in English, 1920–23, and Professor of the English Language, 1924–25, University of Leeds, Yorkshire. At Oxford University: Rawlinson and Bosworth Professor of Anglo-Saxon, 1925–45; Fellow, Pembroke College, 1926–45; Leverhulme Research Fellow, 1934–36; Merton Professor of English Language and Literature, 1945–59; Honorary Fellow, Exeter College, 1963; Emeritus Fellow, Merton College. Andrew Lang Lecturer, University of St. Andrews, Fife, 1939; W.P. Ker Lecturer, University of Glasgow, 1953. Artist: individual show: Ashmolean Museum, Oxford, 1977. Recipient: International Fantasy award, 1957; Royal Society of Literature Benson Medal, 1966; Foreign Book prize (France), 1973; World Science Fiction Convention Gandalf award, 1974; Hugo award, 1978. D.Litt.: University College, Dublin, 1954; University of Nottingham, 1970; Oxford University, 1972; Dr. en Phil et Lettres: Liège, 1954; honorary degree: University of Edinburgh, 1973. Fellow, Royal Society of Literature, 1957. C.B.E. (Commander, Order of the British Empire), 1972. *Died 2 September 1973.*

PUBLICATIONS FOR CHILDREN

Fiction

The Hobbit; or, There and Back Again, illustrated by the author. London, Allen and Unwin, 1937; Boston, Houghton Mifflin, 1938; revised edition, 1951; revised edition, 1966; *The Annotated Hobbit*, edited by Douglas A. Anderson, London, Unwin Hyman, and Boston, Houghton Mifflin, 1989.
Farmer Giles of Ham, illustrated by Pauline Baynes. London, Allen and Unwin, 1949; Boston, Houghton Mifflin, 1950.
Smith of Wootton Major, illustrated by Pauline Baynes. London, Allen and Unwin, and Boston, Houghton Mifflin, 1967.
The Father Christmas Letters, edited by Baillie Tolkien, illustrated by the author. London, Allen and Unwin, and Boston, Houghton Mifflin, 1976.
Mr. Bliss, illustrated by the author. London, Allen and Unwin, 1982.

Verse

The Adventures of Tom Bombadil and Other Verses from the Red Book, illustrated by Pauline Baynes. London, Allen and Unwin, 1962; Boston, Houghton Mifflin, 1963.
Bilbo's Last Song, illustrated by Pauline Baynes. London, Allen and Unwin, and Boston, Houghton Mifflin, 1974.

PUBLICATIONS FOR ADULTS

Novels

The Lord of the Rings:
  The Fellowship of the Ring. London, Allen and Unwin, and Boston, Houghton Mifflin, 1954; revised edition, Allen and Unwin, 1966; Houghton Mifflin, 1967.
  The Two Towers. London, Allen and Unwin, 1954; Boston, Houghton Mifflin, 1955; revised edition, Allen and Unwin, 1966; Houghton Mifflin, 1967.

The Return of the King. London, Allen and Unwin, 1955; Boston, Houghton Mifflin, 1956; revised edition, Allen and Unwin, 1966; Houghton Mifflin, 1967.
The Silmarillion, edited by Christopher Tolkien. London, Allen and Unwin, and Boston, Houghton Mifflin, 1977.

Short Stories

Unfinished Tales of Númenór and Middle-Earth, edited by Christopher Tolkien. London, Allen and Unwin, and Boston, Houghton Mifflin, 1980.

Play

The Homecoming of Beorhtnoth Beorhthelm's Son (broadcast, 1954). Included in *The Tolkien Reader*, 1966; in *Tree and Leaf, Smith of Wootton Major, The Homecoming of Beorhtnoth Beorhthelm's Son*, 1975.

Radio Play: *The Homecoming of Beorhtnoth Beorhthelm's Son*, 1954.

Verse

Songs for the Philologists, with others. Privately printed, 1936.
The Road Goes Ever On: A Song Cycle, music by Donald Swann. Boston, Houghton Mifflin, 1967; London, Allen and Unwin, 1968; revised edition, Houghton Mifflin, 1978.
Poems and Stories. London, Allen and Unwin, 1980.

Other

A Middle English Vocabulary. Oxford, Clarendon Press, and New York, Oxford University Press, 1922.
Beowulf: The Monsters and the Critics. London, Oxford University Press, 1937.
Tree and Leaf (includes short story "Leaf by Niggle" and essay "On Fairy-Stories"). London, Allen and Unwin, 1964; Boston, Houghton Mifflin, 1965; revised edition, London, Unwin Hyman, 1988.
The Tolkien Reader. New York, Ballantine, 1966.
Tree and Leaf, Smith of Wootton Major, The Homecoming of Beorhtnoth Beorhthelm's Son. London, Allen and Unwin, 1975.
Pictures. London, Allen and Unwin, and Boston, Houghton Mifflin, 1979.
The Letters of J.R.R. Tolkien, edited by Humphrey Carpenter. London, Allen and Unwin, and Boston, Houghton Mifflin, 1981.
Finn and Hengest: The Fragment and the Episode, edited by Alan Bliss. London, Allen and Unwin, and Boston, Houghton Mifflin, 1983.
The Monsters and the Critics and Other Essays, edited by Christopher Tolkien. London, Allen and Unwin, 1983; Boston, Houghton Mifflin, 1984.
The History of Middle-Earth, edited by Christopher Tolkien:
The Book of Lost Tales 1–2. London, Allen and Unwin, 2 vols., 1983–84; Boston, Houghton Mifflin, 2 vols., 1984.
The Lays of Beleriand. London, Allen and Unwin, and Boston, Houghton Mifflin, 1985.
The Shaping of Middle-Earth. London, Allen and Unwin, and Boston, Houghton Mifflin, 1986.
The Lost Road and Other Writings. London, Unwin Hyman, and Boston, Houghton Mifflin, 1987.
The Return of the Shadow. London, Unwin Hyman, 1988; Boston, Houghton Mifflin, 1989.

Editor, with E. V. Gordon, *Sir Gawain and the Green Knight.* Oxford, Clarendon Press, and New York, Oxford University Press, 1925.
Editor, *Ancrene Wisse.* London, Oxford University Press, 1962; New York, Oxford University Press, 1963.

Translator, *Sir Gawain and the Green Knight, Pearl, and Sir Orfeo*, edited by Christopher Tolkien. London, Allen and Unwin, and Boston, Houghton Mifflin, 1975.
Translator, *The Old English Exodus*, edited by Joan Turville-Petre. Oxford, Clarendon Press, 1981.

*

Bibliography: *Tolkien Criticism: An Annotated Checklist* by Richard C. West, Kent, Ohio, Kent State University Press, 1970; revised edition, 1981.

Manuscript Collections: Wade Collection, Wheaton College, Illinois; Marquette University, Milwaukee.

Critical Studies (selection): *Master of Middle-Earth: The Fiction of J.R.R. Tolkien* by Paul Kocher, Boston, Houghton Mifflin, 1972, London, Thames and Hudson, 1973; *Tolkien's World*, London, Thames and Hudson, and Boston, Houghton Mifflin, 1974, and *Tolkien and the Silmarils*, Thames and Hudson, 1981, both by Randel Helms; *J.R.R. Tolkien: A Biography* (includes bibliography) by Humphrey Carpenter, London, Allen and Unwin, and Boston, Houghton Mifflin, 1977; *The Mythology of Middle-Earth* by Ruth S. Noel, London, Thames and Hudson, and Boston, Houghton Mifflin, 1977; *The Complete Guide to Middle-Earth* by Robert Foster, London, Allen and Unwin, and New York, Ballantine, 1978; *Tolkien's Art: A Mythology for England* by Jane C. Nitzche, London, Macmillan, 1979; *Tolkien: New Critical Perspectives* edited by Neil D. Isaacs and Rose A. Zimbardo, Lexington, University Press of Kentucky, 1981; *The Road to Middle-Earth* by T.A. Shippey, London, Allen and Unwin, 1982, Boston, Houghton Mifflin, 1983; *J.R.R. Tolkien: This Far Land* edited by Robert Giddings, London, Vision, 1983; *The Song of Middle-Earth: J.R.R. Tolkien's Themes, Symbols, and Myths* by David Harvey, London, Allen and Unwin, 1985.

*   *   *

The fantasy world of J.R.R. Tolkien, scholar and professor of mediaeval literature, had its base in stories he told to himself during his adolescence, which he elaborated during World War I into the saga of *The Silmarillion*, the love story of a beautiful Elf-woman and a mortal man. The story gave substance to a language he had invented—Elvish—and was inspired by his own love affair with his future wife. *The Silmarillion* remained unpublished until 1977, but other stories about his imaginary world of Middle-earth became world-famous. Although Tolkien's Middle-earth is based on our world, a new geography of mountain ranges and coastlines has been superimposed. In this essay I will deal with the Middle-earth fantasies *The Hobbit* and *The Lord of the Rings* (a work, probably, for adults, but one which is certainly enjoyed by many children) and the minor children's stories *Farmer Giles of Ham, Smith of Wootton Major*, "Leaf by Niggle," *The Father Christmas Letters*, and *Mr. Bliss*.

In the traditional English way his first published story came about as a family tale told to his children in the 1930's. The word "hobbit" swam into his head, and soon he had invented the genus of hole-dwelling manikins, 3–4 feet high, domesticated yet tough, idealised versions of the Olde English countryman. Published in 1937, *The Hobbit* was an extraordinary book for its time. The mood of children's books was realistic and anti-magical; critics and teachers demanded books about working-class urban life and thought magic was babyish. The fact that attitudes have changed so much over the years is due in no small measure to Tolkien. His readers, enjoying his books so much, had to justify themselves, and inspired by his own essay "On Fairy-Stories" found good reasons for reading fairy-tales in anthropological theories of human development. The human psyche, according to Jung, needed the emotional nourishment of tales of Quest, Victory of the Youngest Son, Defeat of the Dragon, if it was ever to mature. Primitive tribes knew this instinctively—modern man needed to relearn it.

The Hobbit is a comic and tragic tale, rich in magical adventure. Characters like the cantankerous old wizard Gandalf, the dragon Smaug, evil Gollum, and the 13 dwarves are all famous now. Bilbo, the Hobbit, undergoes great trials to discover courage and maturity. Although the climax is a terrible battle the moral crux of the book comes earlier. Thorin, the chief dwarf, owes his treasure to the hero who slew the dragon, but refuses to give him any reward, although he and his fellow Lake-men are made homeless when the dragon dies. Thorin fails the test, but Bilbo redeems him by giving the men an ancestral treasure of the dwarves to help their bargaining. One can only marvel at the imagination which created the sequence of exciting adventures in which elements from Norse and Teutonic myth have been blended—trolls, elves, giant spiders, a were-bear, dragon, wild wolves, and goblins all appear.

A sequel to *The Hobbit* was demanded, and for years Tolkien laboured to fit this story into the framework of Middle-earth history he had begun with *The Silmarillion*. To continue the story of the magic ring of invisibility which Bilbo "stole" from Gollum, Tolkien would have to start thousands of years after *The Silmarillion* takes place. The main characters would still be elves and men, and they would fight Sauron, servant of Morgoth who stole the silmarils of the earlier book. But he now had his hobbits as well, as comic commentary on the epic situation, and so his theme could be, as with *The Hobbit*, the triumph of weak over strong.

The Lord of the Rings tells how Frodo, Bilbo's nephew, inherits Bilbo's magic invisible ring, and with it a great burden. The ring can make its owner Ruler of the World (as in Wagner's Ring Cycle) and so it must be destroyed before Sauron, Lord of the Rings, who made it, can find it again. Frodo has to make the long and desperately dangerous journey to Sauron's country, Mordor, to throw the Ring into the Cracks of Doom.

Once more we marvel at the author's imagination, as the narrative is sustained through three long volumes. New adventures, heroes, and horrors meet us in every chapter. After volume 1 the fellowship of the Ring divides and we follow the fortunes of three separate groups. We encounter terrors like the Mines of Moria, Shelob the Spider, and the invisible Black Riders; beauty in Goldberry the River's daughter, Lórien the hidden forest; and fight the battles of Helm's Deep and the Pelennor Fields.

With a book so strong in plot, other elements must be weaker. There is no subtle characterisation: just good and evil, white and black. Moral choices are easily perceived, though not so easily made for all that: Boromir, for instance, makes the wrong choice, though basically a good man, and both Gollum and Saruman have a chance to repent. One cannot criticise Tolkien, however, for keeping to the laws of his genre and failing to give us the complex character-analysis of the 20th-century novel. In a prose epic modelled on fairytale many characters are unrounded because they are essentially archetypal. And so we have Aragorn the Hero, Arwen the Princess, Éowyn the Amazon, Galadriel the Enchantress, and Gandalf the Wizard.

In an epic where good must eventually triumph, fate and luck often work on the side of Good, and Tolkien occasionally hints that a Power is influencing events, though the characters still have the free will to take or reject these opportunities. So coincidence is frequently used: rescues happen in the nick of time, people meet by chance—yet those in tune with higher powers, such as Gandalf and Tom Bombadil, question whether chance is really the right word, if a Higher Power is at work.

Tolkien's epic style is often a stumbling-block to his critics. *The Lord of the Rings* is far from completely epic in diction, but when the hobbits' conversation and jokes are informal enough, but when Heroes talk with Elves and Wizards, antique style is used in which the language derives from Old English. "Verily," said Gandalf, "...that way lies our hope, where sits our greatest fear. Doom hangs still on a thread." The society of the horse-riders of Rohan is deliberately modeled on Anglo-Saxon culture, and their poetry, which Tolkien quotes, paraphrases Old English verse. However, while some critics complain of hackneyed clichés, others welcome the historical insight the style affords, especially teachers who have found Tolkien a great inspiration to students to return to the original sagas and epics. Certainly where children are concerned, *The Lord of the Rings* is a book which opens the door to adult literature. (It can be read by good readers from the age of eight upwards.)

Tolkien's minor works also became bestsellers. There was *Farmer Giles of Ham*, about a dragon less successful than Smaug, which also gave the supposed origins of the Oxfordshire villages of Thame and Worminghall. Two shorter stories, *Smith of Wootton Major* and "Leaf by Niggle," are really parables about Tolkien at the end of his career, the former about giving up trips to fairyland and the latter about facing death with his work unfinished. For *The Silmarillion*, the first child of his imagination, was still unpublished, pestering from fans continually interrupted him, and since *The Lord of the Rings* was published there had been many inconsistencies to correct.

The first fictional work to be published since his death was *The Father Christmas Letters* written yearly to his children in the guise of Father Christmas. Illustrated by the author, they are destined to become a children's classic. Father Christmas is helped, and hindered, by accident-prone Polar Bear, a new kind of comic character for Tolkien.

Mr. Bliss reproduces the manuscript of an unpublished story Tolkien wrote and illustrated for his children in the early 1930's; in its modern publication a printed text has been provided on facing pages, although Tolkien's graceful handwriting is still legible. It is a pretty silly story about a silly man who has adventures with his new car, and has some affinities with Beatrix Potter's work, as well as looking forward to the Shire of the hobbits in its portrayal of a Cotswold village at the turn of the century.

Tolkien left so many unpublished drafts of his Middle-earth tales that his son Christopher has continued to sort and transcribe them, with the possibility of working right through until the end of *The Lord of the Rings*. The first five volumes of *The History of Middle-earth* deal with early versions of *The Silmarillion*, which began as *The Book of Lost Tales* in 1917, when Tolkien was convalescing after the battle of the Somme. Volume 3, *The Lays of Beleriand*, contains poetic versions of two of the tales, and is probably the most accessible of these five books. With volume 6, *The Return of the Shadow*, Christopher began to transcribe early versions of *The Lord of the Rings*, and therefore this book is of absorbing interest to any lover of *The Fellowship of the Ring*. In first draft it appears to be much more of a "children's book," with its hero Bingo and the mysterious Trotter, and its informal, slangy dialogue; and one gradually notes, as chapters are redrafted, its evolution towards epic quality, taking on a more formal literary style and doom-laden theme.

Critics have argued since Edmund Wilson's criticism in 1956 about whether *The Lord of the Rings* is a great book. *The Lord of the Rings* has also inspired many children's and adult authors to write heroic fantasy, especially in trilogy form. Children's authors who have acknowledged a debt to Tolkien include Lloyd Alexander, C.S. Lewis, and Susan Cooper; others who feel they must react against his influence include Alan Garner, Robert Westall, and Ursula Le Guin. Adult fantasy authors modelling themselves partly on Tolkien, and partly on the American "pulp" magazine tradition of "sword-and-sorcery," seem to be proliferating even more now than in the years of the Tolkien cult (1965–75), and the Tolkien influence also lies behind the popular computer games set in fantasy worlds, and Fighting Fantasy programmed adventure books.

The Tolkien cult itself has passed through its phase of intense growth and publicity, to be revived among small groups of readers whenever they discover a common interest in Tolkien's world. As a classic of world literature *The Lord of the Rings* will bear out Stanley Unwin's prophecy and be read for years to come.

—Jessica Yates

———

TOMALIN, Ruth. Has also written as Ruth Leaver. British. Born in Piltown, County Kilkenny, Ireland. Educated at Chichester High School, Sussex; King's College, University of London, Diploma of Journalism 1939. Served in the Women's Land Army, 1941–42. Married 1) Vernon Leaver in 1942 (divorced), one son; 2) William N. Ross in 1971. Reporter for newspapers in Hampshire, Sussex, Dorset, and Hertfordshire, 1942–61. Since 1961 part-time press reporter, London Magistrates' Courts and Crown Courts. Address: c/o Barclays Bank, 15 Langham Place, London, W.1, England.

PUBLICATIONS FOR CHILDREN

Fiction

Green Ink (as Ruth Leaver).   London, Harrap, 1951.
The Sound of Pens (as Ruth Leaver), illustrated by Betty Ladler.   London, Blackie, 1955.
The Daffodil Bird, illustrated by Brian Wildsmith.   London, Faber, 1959; New York, A.S. Barnes, 1960.
The Sea Mice, illustrated by Sheila Rose.   London, Faber, 1962.
A Green Wishbone, illustrated by Gavin Rowe.   London, Faber, 1975.
A Stranger Thing, illustrated by Robin Jacques.   London, Faber, 1975.
The Snake Crook, illustrated by Shirley Hughes.   London, Faber, 1976.
Gone Away.   London, Faber, 1979.
Little Nasty, illustrated by Sue Scullard.   London, Faber, 1985.
A Summer Ghost.   London, Faber, 1986.
Another Day.   London, Faber, 1988.

PUBLICATIONS FOR ADULTS

Novels

All Souls.   London, Faber, 1952.
The Garden House.   London, Faber, 1964.
The Spring House.   London, Faber, 1968.
Away to the West.   London, Faber, 1972.
Long Since.   London, Faber, 1989.

Verse

Threnody for Dormice.   London, Fortune Press, 1947.
Deer's Cry.   London, Fortune Press, 1952.

Other

The Day of the Rose: Essays and Portraits.   London, Fortune Press, 1947.
W.H. Hudson (short biography).   London, Witherby, and New York, Philosophical Library, 1954.
W.H. Hudson (biography).   London, Faber, 1982.

Editor, *Best Country Stories*.   London, Faber, 1969.

*

Ruth Tomalin comments:

Most of my stories are about people and things of the English countryside. All are set in places well known to me at different times, ranging from a copse full of wild life (*The Daffodil Bird*) to Broadcasting House, London (*The Sea Mice*); and from a glass "watch-house" in a nature reserve (*A Stranger Thing*) to a reporters' room on a provincial evening paper (*Green Ink*).

*   *   *

Ruth Tomalin's work falls into two distinct categories. There are a number of short novels for children of 9 to 10, the best of which are *A Stranger Thing* and *A Summer Ghost*. There is also a group of novels concerned with the childhood and youth of Ralph Oliver and latterly his young cousin Rowan—*The Garden House, The Spring House*, and *Away to the West*; these are longer and far more demanding works, so difficult to classify that in the judgment of some critics they are adult novels and cannot be regarded as children's books at all.

Certainly the Ralph Oliver novels are far beyond the comprehension of the small children who will enjoy *The Sea Mice, The Daffodil Bird*, or *A Stranger Thing*. *The Garden House*, with its subtle vision of early childhood, is thematically recondite for adolescent readers and best regarded as an adult novel. But *The Spring House* and *Away to the West* are admirable stories for the right teenage reader, though their appeal is highly specialised. Unless readers share Tomalin's intimate knowledge and love of wildlife, her care for the English countryside, and her concern for the impact of humanity on landscape and fauna alike, the novels cannot be understood at their deepest imaginative level. But for those who do share these affections and concerns, they have much to offer. They are also, after all, about young people growing up—the problems of choosing a career, of coping with uncomprehending parents, of living through the anguish of first love. These are important themes in the novels, treated with sympathy, tact, and humour, and with acute, uncondescending insight.

The stories for younger readers are essentially miniatures—very brief and sharply focused, characteristically preoccupied with the private, often secret world of a single child. Although the range of plots and settings is quite wide, the best and most typical of the stories involve intimate meetings between children and wild creatures, and delicate suggestions of magic and ghostliness. A deceptive simplicity of narrative allows subtle exploration of the clandestine childhood territory between fear and wonder, and the most successful stories contrive to place children in situations of enforced solitude, where apprehension and nervous self-reliance prove to be the starting point for magical discovery.

The formula is a fragile one, and *Another Day* is an instance of a book which breaks it. This story engages with the themes of a full-length children's novel within the narrow compass of the short book. One half of the plot realistically traces Francie's effort to cope with the isolating effects of sudden promotion in her school in 1934, and her struggles with the jealousy, ostracism, and resentment of her peers. The other half is a ghost story, in which with the aid of a magic Celtic whistle Francie summons a "ghost from the future," who is finally identified as her grandson-to-be. *Another Day* attempts to be school story, pony story, ghost story, and even historical novel within a hundred pages, and not surprisingly emerges as cryptic and sketchy.

This is a rare technical misjudgement on the part of a writer who is usually in immaculate control of her chosen medium. In the short novels precision of setting is all-important. The settings can be urban and public (even Broadcasting House, in *The Sea Mice*) but transformed to privacy by the secret life of a child. More commonly they are rural and secluded, and offer shelter to fugitive children escaping from an uncongenial world; the most memorable of such sanctuaries are the wintry gazebo in *A Stranger Thing* and the haunted beech wood in *A Summer Ghost*. The beech wood in this excellent story stands for many of Tomalin's locales: it is "haunted" by the presence of a long-dead girl who loved it, but also by a family of red squirrels, newly released by modern naturalists to repopulate their former "haunts."

Solitary days in secret places, encounters and friendships between child and animals, nuances of the supernatural, combine in these stories to give strength and nurture to vulnerable children. The real-life, natural world assumes its own magic in these books. They are the product of a richly sensitive imagination and an infectious zest for the sheer diversity of life.

—Peter Hollindale

TOURTEL, Mary (née Caldwell). British. Born in Canterbury, Kent, in 1874. Educated at Canterbury Art School. Married Herbert Bird Tourtel (died 1931). Aviator. Wrote and illustrated Rupert serial for *Daily Express*, London, 1920–35. *Died 15 March 1948.*

PUBLICATIONS FOR CHILDREN (illustrated by the author)

Fiction

A Horse Book. London, Richards, 1901; New York, Stokes, 1902.
The Three Little Foxes. London, Richards, 1903.
The Adventures of Rupert the Little Lost Bear. London, Nelson, 1921.
The Little Bear and the Fairy Child. London, Nelson, 1921.
Margot the Midget; The Little Bear's Christmas. London, Nelson, 1922.
The Little Bear and the Ogres. London, Nelson, 1922.
Rupert Little Bear's Adventures:
  1. *Rupert and the Magic Toy Man, Rupert and the Princess, Rupert at School, Rupert and the Old Miser.* London, Sampson Low, 1924.
  2. *Rupert and the Magic Key, Rupert and the Brigands, Rupert and Reynard Fox, Rupert in Dreamland.* London, Sampson Low, 1924.
  3. *Rupert and the Robber Wolf, Rupert and the Dragon, Rupert and the Snowman, Rupert at the Seaside.* London, Sampson Low, 1925.
Rupert and the Enchanted Princess. London, Sampson Low, 1928.
Rupert and the Black Dwarf. London, Sampson Low, 1928.
Rupert and His Pet Monkey. London, Sampson Low, 1928.
Rupert and His Friend Margot; Rupert, Margot and the Fairies. London, Sampson Low, 1928.
Rupert in the Wood of Mystery. London, Sampson Low, 1929.
Further Adventures of Rupert and His Pet Monkey; Rupert and the Stolen Apples. London, Sampson Low, 1929.
Rupert and the Three Robbers. London, Sampson Low, 1929.
Rupert, The Knight and the Lady; Rupert and the Wise Goat's Birthday Cake. London, Sampson Low, 1929.

Rupert and the Circus Clown. London, Sampson Low, 1929.
Rupert and the Magic Hat. London, Sampson Low, 1929.
Daily Express Children's Annual. London, Lane Publications, 5 vols., 1930–34.
Rupert and the Little Prince. London, Sampson Low, 1930.
Rupert and King Pippin. London, Sampson Low, 1930.
Rupert and the Wilful Princess. London, Sampson Low, 1930.
Rupert's Mysterious Flight. London, Sampson Low, 1930.
Rupert in Trouble Again; Rupert and the Fancy Dress Party. London, Sampson Low, 1930.
Rupert and the Wooden Soldiers; Rupert's Christmas Adventure. London, Sampson Low, 1930.
Rupert and the Old Man of the Sea. London, Sampson Low, 1931.
Rupert and Algy at Hawthorne Farm. London, Sampson Low, 1931.
Monster Rupert. London, Sampson Low, 7 vols., 1931–50.
Rupert and the Magic Whistle. London, Sampson Low, 1931.
Rupert Gets Stolen. London, Sampson Low, 1931.
Rupert and the Wonderful Boots. London, Sampson Low, 1931.
Rupert and the Christmas Tree Fairies; Rupert and Bill Badger's Picnic Party. London, Sampson Low, 1931.
Rupert and His Pet Monkey Again; Beppo Back with Rupert. London, Sampson Low, 1932.
Rupert's Latest Adventure. London, Sampson Low, 1932.
Rupert and Prince Humpty-Dumpty. London, Sampson Low, 1932.
Rupert's Holiday Adventure; Rupert's Message to Father Christmas; Rupert's New Year's Eve Party. London, Sampson Low, 1932.
Rupert's Christmas Tree; Rupert's Picnic Party. London, Sampson Low, 1932.
Rupert, The Witch, and Tabitha. London, Sampson Low, 1933.
Rupert Goes Hiking. London, Sampson Low, 1933.
Rupert and Willy Wispe. London, Sampson Low, 1933.
Rupert, Margot and the Bandits. London, Sampson Low, 1933.
Rupert and Bill Keep Shop; Rupert's Christmas Thrills. London, Sampson Low, 1933.
Rupert and Algernon; Rupert and the White Dove. London, Sampson Low, 1934.
Rupert and Dapple. London, Sampson Low, 1934.
Rupert and Bill's Aeroplane Adventure. London, Sampson Low, 1934.
Rupert and the Magician's Umbrella. London, Sampson Low, 1934.
Rupert and Bill and the Pirates. London, Sampson Low, 1935.
Rupert at the Seaside; Rupert and Bingo. London, Sampson Low, 1935.
Rupert Gets Captured; Rupert and the Snow Babe's Christmas. London, Sampson Low, 1935.
Rupert, The Manikin and the Black Knight. London, Sampson Low, 1935.
Rupert and the Greedy Princess. London, Sampson Low, 1935.
Rupert and Bill's Seaside Holiday; Rupert and the Twin's Birthday Cake. London, Sampson Low, 1936.
Rupert and Edward and the Circus. London, Sampson Low, 1936.
The Rupert Story Book. London, Sampson Low, 1938.
Rupert Little Bear: More Stories. London, Sampson Low, 1939.
Rupert Again. London, Sampson Low, 1940.
The First [Second, Third] "St. Michael" Book of Rupert Favourites. Maidenhead, Berkshire, Purnell, 3 vols., 1978–79.

Verse

Humpty Dumpty Book of Nursery Rhymes, Told in Pictures. London, Treherne, 1902.

*

Bibliography: *The Rupert Index: A Bibliography of Rupert Bear* by W.O.G. Lofts and Derek J. Adley, privately printed, n.d.

Critical Study: *Rupert: A Bear's Life* by George Perry, London, Pavilion, 1985.

Illustrator: *The Rabbit Book*, 1904.

*   *   *

Mary Tourtel began to write and illustrate children's stories in the late 1890's, and proved herself an extremely competent animal illustrator early in her career. The flowering of this combined writing and illustrating skill, however, came with her creation of Rupert Bear in 1920. It seems likely that Rupert's existence was sparked off by another anthropomorphic animal character; the *Daily Mail* had launched Charles Folkard's Teddy Tail in 1915, and the strip that featured him quickly became immensely popular. The editor of the *Daily Express* wanted his paper to develop an equally appealing children's series, so Tourtel, who was married to an *Express* sub-editor, produced Rupert. (He was her third attempt at an animal hero for the *Daily Express*; she had experimented previously with two other series in this newspaper.)

She hit upon exactly the right formula with Rupert and his friends Bill Badger, Algy Pug, Edward Trunk, and Podgy Pig, who were addictive from the beginning. Tourtel enhanced the atmosphere of her simple, slightly static drawings by writing quatrain texts whose rhymes and rhythms were uncertain but intriguing. (The celebrated rhyming couplets came later in Alfred Bestall's time.) In her very first Rupert story, *The Little Lost Bear*, Tourtel gave full rein to her preoccupation with magic, and mystical quests. The pattern for the early Tourtel stories was one of Rupert shaking off parental restraints at the beginning of each episode but returning to cosy domestic serenity at the end. In between, not so much seeking adventure as stumbling upon it, he would suddenly discover weird castles and caves that seemed to spring up like mushrooms or mirages in the meadows near his home. He was often called upon to outwit ogres, dragons, and wicked dwarfs, or to rescue a Princess from the clutches of some malevolent witch. He often suffered capture and imprisonment, but of course always managed ingeniously to escape.

Rupert is the perpetual innocent abroad who never learns from his dramatic experiences; he remains astoundingly trusting even when, as the saga develops, he becomes more of a hero figure, setting out deliberately to right injustices, or to make symbolic questing journeys. Tourtel's stories abound in Arthurian echoes; one of her most popular characters, for example, is the Wise Old Goat, a magical Merlin-like recluse. There are also resonances from the stories of Grimm and Perrault.

The fairytale mood is emphasized by Rupert's mania for becoming airborne. Tourtel was an enthusiastic aviatrix. With her husband she had flown on a record-breaking Handley-Page trip from London to Belgium as early as 1919. She once commented that she liked "seeing the land as the birds saw it," and she happily foisted her passion for flight onto her furry hero. Rupert flies in an airship in the first Tourtel adventure; subsequently he has only to look at a laundry basket to find himself being transported through the skies on it, and Tourtel also air-lifts him by means of magic shoes, balloons, giant birds, umbrellas, and, of course, conventional aeroplanes. (In 1980, Rupert travelled by flying saucer; Bestall continued the astral traditions and, like Tourtel, was often extremely inventive about Rupert's modes of flying.)

Tourtel wrote and drew the strips in the *Daily Express* from 1920 to the middle of 1935. During this time many Rupert books were published, some made up from reprints of her newspaper strips and some from new, specially written stories. She had eventually to give up creating Rupert adventures because of failing eyesight. Alfred

Bestall, a cartoonist and book illustrator, then took on the series. He remained Rupert's regular writer and artist in the newspaper and the annuals until 1965. He then retired from producing the daily strips, although he still contributed one or two items to the annuals.

When Bestall assumed responsibility for the stories in 1935, he kept the regular Tourtel characters, but gave Rupert several new and colourful associates. He continued the balladic style but created a fresher, more relaxed mood than the slightly Gothic atmosphere built up by Tourtel. Bestall rounded out Rupert's village, Nutwood, and its environs, and gave these a sense of reality. He also injected more depth and definition into the mythical foreign parts, frost-palaces and sun-drenched islands that have attracted Rupert like a magnet now for over 60 years.

Bestall was instructed by the editor of the Rupert series to play down magic of the murkier variety. He did so, but introduced new fantasy elements into the stories by means of simplistic science fiction, in which several "boffins" helped Rupert to foil baddies by the use of technically advanced apparatus. Bestall also made Rupert into something of a detective; in the later stories he tends to give his energies to unravelling the clues of strange mysteries rather than to overcoming giants or monsters.

Bestall was the main contributor to the Rupert annuals (these are now, like the *Daily Express* strips, produced by a team). Their sales of well over 34 million copies have produced a world record for children's annuals. The saga has an apparent and satisfying changelessness, but Bestall actually carried out a certain amount of updating in deference to new social attitudes. He managed to do this without sacrificing any of the enchantment built up by Tourtel which still hangs over the strips and stories. Rupert has outlived many other comics and story-book animal heroes, and for decades now he has not only been a children's favourite but a cult figure for many adults.

—Mary Cadogan

———

TOWNSEND, John Rowe. British. Born in Leeds, Yorkshire, 10 May 1922. Educated at Leeds Grammar School, 1933–40; Emmanuel College, Cambridge, 1947–49, B.A. 1949, M.A. 1954. Served in the Royal Air Force, 1942–46: Flight Sergeant. Married Vera Lancaster in 1948 (died 1973); two daughters and one son. Reporter, *Yorkshire Post*, Leeds, 1946, and *Evening Standard*, London, 1949; sub-editor, 1949–53, and art editor, 1953–55, Manchester *Guardian*, and editor, *Guardian Weekly*, 1955–69; part-time children's books editor, *Guardian*, Manchester and London, 1969–78. Visiting Lecturer, University of Pennsylvania, Philadelphia, 1965, and University of Washington, Seattle, 1969, 1971; May Hill Arbuthnot Lecturer, Atlanta, 1971; Anne Carroll Moore Lecturer, New York Public Library, 1971; Whittall Lecturer, Library of Congress, Washington, D.C., 1976; member of the faculty, Simmons College, Boston, summers 1978, 1980, 1982. Recipient: Boston *Globe-Horn Book* award, 1970; English PEN award, 1970; Mystery Writers of America Edgar Allan Poe award, 1971; Christopher award, 1982. Address: 72 Water Lane, Histon, Cambridge CB4 4LR, England.

PUBLICATIONS FOR CHILDREN

Fiction

Gumble's Yard, illustrated by Dick Hart. London, Hutchinson, 1961; as *Trouble in the Jungle*, Philadelphia, Lippincott, 1969.

Hell's Edge. London, Hutchinson, 1963; New York, Lothrop, 1969.
Widdershins Crescent. London, Hutchinson, 1965; as *Goodbye to the Jungle,* Philadelphia, Lippincott, 1967; as *Goodbye to Gumble's Yard,* London, Penguin, 1981.
The Hallersage Sound. London, Hutchinson, 1966.
Pirate's Island, illustrated by Douglas Hall. London, Oxford University Press, and Philadelphia, Lippincott, 1968.
The Intruder, illustrated by Graham Humphreys. London, Oxford University Press, 1969; Philadelphia, Lippincott, 1970.
Goodnight, Prof, Love, illustrated by Peter Farmer. London, Oxford University Press, 1970; as *Goodnight, Prof, Dear,* Philadelphia, Lippincott, 1971.
The Summer People, illustrated by Robert Micklewright. London, Oxford University Press, and Philadelphia, Lippincott, 1972.
A Wish for Wings, illustrated by Philip Gough. London, Heinemann, 1972.
Forest of the Night. London, Oxford University Press, 1974; Philadelphia, Lippincott, 1975.
Noah's Castle. London, Oxford University Press, 1975; Philadelphia, Lippincott, 1976.
Top of the World, illustrated by Nikki Jones. London, Oxford University Press, 1976; Philadelphia, Lippincott, 1977.
The Xanadu Manuscript, illustrated by Paul Ritchie. London, Oxford University Press, 1977; as *The Visitors,* Philadelphia, Lippincott, 1977.
King Creature, Come. Oxford, Oxford University Press, 1980; as *The Creatures,* New York, Lippincott, 1980.
The Islanders. Oxford, Oxford University Press, and New York, Lippincott, 1981.
Clever Dick. Oxford, Oxford University Press, 1982.
A Foreign Affair. London, Kestrel, 1982; as *Kate and the Revolution,* New York, Lippincott, 1983.
Dan Alone. London, Kestrel, and New York, Lippincott, 1983.
Gone to the Dogs, illustrated by Andy Bylo. Oxford, Oxford University Press, 1984.
Cloudy-Bright. London, Viking Kestrel, and New York, Lippincott, 1984.
Tom Tiddler's Ground, illustrated by Mark Peppé. London, Viking Kestrel, 1985; New York, Lippincott, 1986.
The Persuading Stick. London, Viking Kestrel, 1986; New York, Lothrop, 1987.
Downstream. New York, Lippincott, 1987; London, Walker, 1988.
Rob's Place. London, Viking Kestrel, 1987; New York, Lothrop, 1988.
The Golden Journey. London, Viking Kestrel, and New York, Lippincott, 1989.
The Fortunate Isles. New York, Harper, 1989.

Other

Editor, *Modern Poetry: A Selection.* London, Oxford University Press, 1971; Philadelphia, Lippincott, 1974.

PUBLICATIONS FOR ADULTS

Other

Written for Children: An Outline of English Children's Literature. London, J. Garnet Miller, 1965; New York, Lothrop, 1967; revised edition, London, Kestrel, 1974; Philadelphia, Lippincott, 1975; revised edition, London, Kestrel, and New York, Harper 1983; revised edition, London, Penguin, 1987; New York, Harper, 1988.
A Sense of Story: Essays on Contemporary Writers for Children. London, Longman, and Philadelphia, Lippincott, 1971; revised edition, as *A Sounding of Storytellers: New and Revised Essays on Contemporary Writers for Children,* London, Kestrel, and New York, Lippincott, 1979.
25 Years of British Children's Books. London, National Book League, 1977.

*

Manuscript Collections: Kerlan Collection, University of Minnesota, Minneapolis; International Youth Library, Munich.

John Rowe Townsend comments:
   I wear two hats in connection with children's books: as a writer of them and as a writer about them.
   In the former capacity I began my career in the early 1960's with a sense that books dealing with the rougher side of real life, and with the problems and joys of growing up in contemporary society, were far too scarce in Britain. Hence *Gumble's Yard, Hell's Edge,* and *Widdershins Crescent.* Later, the feeling that these gaps were now being adequately filled, together with the continual urge to do something different, led me to broaden my fictional scope. I might try anything now.
   Under my other hat I have for some years written about children's books for various publications. I have also produced an historical survey of children's literature (*Written for Children*) and two sets of essays on contemporary children's writers (*A Sense of Story* and *A Sounding of Storytellers*). I tend to discuss children's books as literature rather than as influences in social, educational, or psychological development—but I hasten to add that literary criticism does not have to be narrowly aesthetic; it can and should take account of many aspects of a book. One thing I am certain of is that a good book for children must be a good book, period.

*   *   *

   A sense of story is not simply the title of John Rowe Townsend's survey of children's fiction, it is a statement of the unrelenting quest of an author who restlessly explores the variety of ways in which a tale unfolds. The remarkable and varied output of this storyteller shows few of the rough edges which might be anticipated among the creations of a tireless experimenter. Townsend's seemingly endless search for new means of manipulating a theme provides pleasant passage for readers, whether they are simply settled into an easychair evening, or are themselves engaged in a voyage of discovery of the ways and means of plotting and narration.
   Sometimes Townsend uncovers compelling variations in what might appear a tiresome theme. A submissive young girl finds that an ordinary-looking stick conveys to her the ability to bring others into conformity with her own will. A Midas touch, to be sure, but one which proves dissatisfying rather than disastrous. It becomes clear that only the power within the person, not that conveyed by a persuading stick, can provide the social fulfillment she seeks. Townsend's protagonists often are led to recognise that there are few objectives equal to self-understanding. But this formula from *The Persuading Stick* is far too facile to define the scope of Townsend's other endeavours. It does show that escape from intolerable circumstances, the uncovering of a mystery, the conquest of a personal flaw are all considerably less compelling than enhanced comprehension of the self. Discovery rather than corrective serves as a means by which Townsend unites the audience with the endeavours of the principals of the story.
   The telling of tales is a perpetual process of creation. Crafting sagas for presentation is most uncannily akin to shaping destiny. Townsend's experimentation in the telling of tales quite naturally leads to questions concerning the purpose of human existence. Like the bards of old, he provides material for insight, but declines to

impose answers. Such questions are engagingly considered in *King Creature, Come*, where genetic control has led to two distinct classes of humankind. The lesser, the creatures, are easily recognised as humanity as we know it. As indiscriminate breeders, however, their numbers have increased beyond their usefulness, and they are now largely deprived of the opportunity for education, advancement, and employment. The story is viewed largely through the eyes of the elect, although these quasi-narrators are sympathetic to such undisciplined creature-like pursuits as love and loyalty. Selective breeding also has weakened the master race's capacity to resist diseases. They can undertake inter-planetary travel, but a neighborhood a block away could prove lethal. The imperfections found in the creatures ultimately prove to be qualities essential to a delight in living. By contrast, the refinements of the elect make them more efficient and more capable, but less apprehensive of pleasure. Curiously, their advancement in intellect has somehow obliterated their sense of the aesthetic. As a storyteller, Townsend resists the temptation to preach, but the considerations laid before the reader extend the tale far beyond any resolution of the plot.

Tracing Townsend's technique is in itself a fascinating venture. He deals with the future by placing it alongside the present, featuring, for example, a romance between a gifted young physicist and a girl from the 21st century who has, as part of an experiment, been allowed to travel back in time. The complications of linking two of like sensibility prove insurmountable because they are products of two distinct eras. What happens to destiny when it becomes possible to mate with those of another era? Townsend appears determined to perplex his listeners (a designation perhaps more accurate than "reader," as the experience of pursuing his books is apt to be as auditory as it is visual). The disturbances derive from concerns which are likely to affect the outlook of the audience, concerns which appear certain to outlive memory of the plot. Certainly he is a master of suspense, but issues of destiny, belief, and other cosmic concerns intermingle with the all-too-human pleasures of an afternoon boat ride on the river. The story becomes a personal involvement interlaced with tempting strands of unanswered philosophic matters.

But Townsend is not all epic. *Top of the World* is not the Himalayas, but a decidedly uninviting high-rise complex where two caretaker parents eke out a livelihood as they endure the threats and other unpleasantries of the administrator—a modern-day troll whose very existence is an ongoing source of terror. Here Townsend demonstrates that a story need not depend on mystery, and that escapades are not merely devices of escape, but an effective means of uniting characters, forcing them into a harmonic union in spite of distinctly separate intentions. Almost every book contributes new material toward a comprehensive study of narrative techniques.

His characters, the principal ones at least, are usually adolescents, beings in a state of becoming within a society in a state of decay. *The Islanders* takes place in a settlement fashioned out of an alliance of mutineers and a native population. A compelling combination at one time, but now the social structure has ceased to be dynamic, and all newcomers are considered intruders. The adolescents prove a restless force, generating the change which keeps a social system alive. Narrative, it would appear, is more than an artistic device—it is a life force that keeps conditions from becoming static and decadent. Storytellers and adolescents have much in common, which is probably why fairytales, the most enduring of all narratives, are chiefly peopled by adolescents.

A storyteller resembles the maker of patchwork quilts, taking odds and ends, disparate shapes and unmatched colours and patterns and weaving them into a useful and fully artistic pattern. Townsend repeatedly shows how all sorts of sights and sounds, elements of past and present and a variety of perspectives can be linked with engaging results. Decadent Manchester neighborhoods resurface as the humble cottage of the fairytale. But it is the protagonist's altered perspective along with incredible energy that produces the resultant

changes.

Throughout the opus, Townsend's characters are more likely to be forces rather than memorable personalities. His latest work, *The Golden Journey*, however, represents a change. Here the characters become compelling creations in their own right, and in a way maintain an existence which appears as important as the plot itself. Eleni, the central figure, is a mystery—even to herself. At the outset of the work she appears almost without definition. By face and figure she could be taken for a boy as well as a girl. As a result she is able to maintain a position on a fishing boat, an occupation from which females were rigorously (and superstitiously) excluded. Her sole distinctive feature is her blue eyes, a unique quality on the island. Out of this nondescript entity emerges a defined character. The book is studded with some compelling characterizations, like the ageing priest who is the sole interpreter of divine messages, but who is now principally a dipsomaniac in search of handouts.

While there are characters who are memorable in themselves, they by no means obscure the opulence of the narrative. The imaginary isles furnish wonderment and mystery, cruelty and cunning. *The Golden Journey* is a curious juncture in Townsend's production. It would be a tempting enterprise to speculate what will come next in his opus. It is safe to suggest that it will be a jewel of another cut.

—Leonard R. Mendelsohn

TOZER, Katharine. British. Born c. 1905.

PUBLICATIONS FOR CHILDREN (illustrated by the author)

Fiction

The Wanderings of Mumfie. London, Murray, 1935.
Here Comes Mumfie. London, Murray, 1936.
Mumfie the Admiral. London, Murray, 1937.
Mumfie's Magic Box. London, Murray, 1938.
Mumfie's Uncle Samuel. London, Murray, 1939.
Noah: The Story of Another Ark. London, Murray, 1940.
Adventures of Alfie. London, Murray, 1941.
Mumfie Marches On. London, Murray, 1942.
Mumfie's Picture Book, edited by Eiluned Lewis. London, Murray, 1947.

*

Illustrator: *Paladins in Spain* by Eleanor Farjeon, 1937; *The Man Who Asked Questions* by L.A.G. Strong, 1937; *The Chinese Children Next Door* by Pearl S. Buck, 1943.

*   *   *

Margery Fisher has remarked that "stories about toys give children a wonderful chance to be naughty by proxy," and one might add that they also give plenty of scope for earnest authors to lecture and warn by proxy. Certainly the great majority of stories in this genre which survive from the hundred years or so up to World War II are unashamedly didactic and immovably rooted in conventional middle-class morality, Masefield's *The Midnight Folk* and its sequel being among the very few exceptions. Writing at the very end of this period, Katharine Tozer can hardly be said to have shown particular originality or any ability to break the mould of racial, social, and professional stereotypes. Her central characters, Mumfie the toy

CHILDREN'S WRITERS

elephant and his companion Scarecrow, always have a certain charm and in the later stories are effectively developed with contrasting personalities, but their assortment of friends or enemies from the nursery and fairyland are generally no better than stylized puppets. In the first book there is a deplorable scene in which the golliwog Jack Gingerbread is needlessly humiliated; and even in the jollier atmosphere of *Mumfie the Admiral*, the author's attitude towards Alabama the negro cook, whose reward at the end is to receive the "Illustrious Order of the Sit in the Sun and eat Melons," is crudely patronizing.

Assuredly, then, the secret of Tozer's success is not to be found in character-drawing, nor indeed in her plot construction, for by adult standards her central situations are generally of the tritest, and developed without the slightest hint of subtlety. Nevertheless her Mumfie books have been regularly reprinted and otherwise publicised during the last 40 years—and for several perfectly good reasons. First, she was able to apply most expertly the principle of "never a dull moment," with a new heading at the top of every page of text to indicate the unbroken run of action; second, she had obviously identified the sort of things that small children really enjoy around their own homes, such as climbing trees or gorging themselves at tea-parties, and made sure that these activities were well to the fore in her fictional settings; third, she did show a real imaginative power, which even mature readers can appreciate, in describing such things as Night's icefloored palace in *Mumfie's Magic Box*, or the climbing of the giant's mountain in *Mumfie's Uncle Samuel*; and last, but by no means least, as a talented artist she was able to illustrate almost every single incident with an appropriate full-page or inset drawing.

Tozer wrote eight stories in all, including one about an American boy called Noah and one about an animated puppet. Only the first five Mumfie books have survived, but a reading of them suggests that she was improving her technique all the time. *Magic Box* is perhaps the most imaginative and *Uncle Samuel* the best constructed and most entertaining.

—Alasdair K.D. Campbell

TRAVERS, P(amela) L(yndon). British. Born in Queensland, Australia, in 1906. Educated privately. Journalist, actress, and dancer, 1920's; regular contributor to the *Irish Statesman*, Dublin, 1920's and 1930's; worked for the British Ministry of Information in the United States during World War II. Writer-in-residence, Radcliffe College, Cambridge, Massachusetts, 1965–66; Smith College, Northampton, Massachusetts, 1966–67; Scripps College, Claremont, California, 1970. Recipient: Focus award, 1985. D.H.: Chatham College, Pittsburgh, 1978. O.B.E. (Officer, Order of the British Empire), 1977. Lives in London. Agent: David Higham Associates Ltd., 5–8 Lower John Street, London W1R 4HA. Address: c/o William Collins Sons Ltd., 8 Grafton Street, London W1X 3LA, England.

PUBLICATIONS FOR CHILDREN

Fiction

Mary Poppins, illustrated by Mary Shepard. London, Howe, and New York, Reynal, 1934; revised edition, New York, Harcourt Brace, 1981.
Mary Poppins Comes Back, illustrated by Mary Shepard. London, Dickson and Thompson, and New York, Reynal, 1935.

Happy Ever After, illustrated by Mary Shepard. Privately printed, 1940.
I Go by Sea, I Go by Land, illustrated by Gertrude Hermes. London, Davies, and New York, Harper, 1941.
Mary Poppins Opens the Door, illustrated by Mary Shepard and Agnes Sims. New York, Reynal, 1943; London, Davies, 1944.
Mary Poppins in the Park, illustrated by Mary Shepard. London, Davies, and New York, Harcourt Brace, 1952.
The Fox at the Manger, illustrated by Thomas Bewick. New York, Norton, 1962; London, Collins, 1963.
Mary Poppins from A to Z, illustrated by Mary Shepard. New York, Harcourt Brace, 1962; London, Collins, 1963.
Friend Monkey. New York, Harcourt Brace, 1971; London, Collins, 1972.
Mary Poppins in Cherry Tree Lane, illustrated by Mary Shepard. London, Collins, and New York, Delacorte Press, 1982.
Mary Poppins and the House Next Door, illustrated by Mary Shepard. New York, Delacorte Press, 1989.

Other

About the Sleeping Beauty, illustrated by Charles Keeping. New York, McGraw Hill, 1975; London, Collins, 1977.
Mary Poppins in the Kitchen: A Cookery Book with a Story, with Maurice Moore-Betty, illustrated by Mary Shepard. New York, Harcourt Brace, 1975; London, Collins, 1977.
Two Pairs of Shoes (folktales), illustrated by Leo and Diane Dillon. New York, Viking Press, 1980.

PUBLICATIONS FOR ADULTS

Other

Moscow Excursion. London, Dickson and Thompson, and New York, Reynal, 1935.
Aunt Sass. Privately printed, 1941.
Ah Wong. Privately printed, 1943.
Johnny Delaney. Privately printed, 1944.
In Search of the Hero: The Continuing Relevance of Myth and Fairy Tale (lecture). Claremont, California, Scripps College, 1970.
George Ivanovitch Gurdjieff. Toronto, Traditional Studies Press, 1973.
What the Bee Knows: Reflections on Myth, Symbol and Story. Wellingborough, Northamptonshire, Thorsons, 1989.

Translator, with Ruth Lewinnek, *The Way of Transformation: Daily Life as a Spiritual Exercise*, by Karlfried Dürckheim Montmartin. London, Allen and Unwin, 1971.

*

Critical Study: *Mary Poppins and Myth* by Staffan Bergsten, Stockholm, Almqvist & Wiksell, 1978.

P.L. Travers comments:
I have always said that I don't think I write for children specially. After all, my early writing was mostly poetry and I imagine that *Mary Poppins* stems from that. I am not a great one for seeking personal publicity and agree with C.S. Lewis when he says, in a letter, "There is only one creator and we merely mix the elements He gives us."

*   *   *

Before Mary Poppins—that most intriguing of English nannies—blew into children's fiction on an east wind in 1934 her author's reputation as a poet and dramatic critic had already been established. P.L. Travers's ability to combine poetic insight with a feeling for dramatic situation brought a balance and an inner intensity to her stories.

Mary Poppins is a many-faceted character. Superficially she seems the prim, archetypal nannie, reading "Everything a Lady Should Know" and exuding a competent aura of boot polish and Sunlight Soap. She crackles, however, not only with starch but with an elemental and challenging magic: the startlingly blue eyes of her Dutch Doll face can see "over the rim of the world" as well as into the minds of her charges. The children of the Banks family find that in Mary's company their fantasy exploits often find exciting expression. Magical adventures might arise at any moment from commonplace circumstances. For instance, Mary Poppins can casually pick up a plum painted on the pavement by a street artist and take a bite from it. Travers firmly believes that in children's stories an ordinary environment is an essential background for magic. "To climb or to fly you need a solid basis from which to take off; otherwise everything becomes too fey."

Certainly there is nothing sentimental or amorphous about Mary Poppins. She can be imaginative or sternly practical as occasion demands. Her actions often have a catalytic effect. The magic which she brings into the lives of the Banks children sharpens their understanding of themselves and reality: it is exuberant but not escapist. Unlike many other fictional immortals Mary never makes "happily ever after" promises. She implies that the only security is an ability to accept constant change; the temporary nature of her own presence in the Banks household is stressed by the fact of her sleeping on a camp bed. Her ever present parrot-headed umbrella and capacious carpet bag too are reminders that she is always ready to travel at a moment's notice.

The original Mary Poppins in 1934 was quickly followed by Mary Poppins Comes Back. Mary Poppins Opens the Door was intended as the last of the series. In its final pages Mary leaves the Banks family forever, although "the gifts she had brought would remain...." However in response to readers' demands a further volume, Mary Poppins in the Park, was produced in 1952, but its action takes place during the visits of Mary Poppins that were chronicled in the three previous books. This is true too of Mary Poppins in the Kitchen, published as recently as 1975. Mary becomes temporary cook for the Banks family and teaches the children to prepare attractive meals. The book consists of a story and some recipes for each day of the week.

The series was written over several years—but always firmly set against a background of nursery cosiness common to many English homes in the 1930's. (In the Walt Disney film there was a transposition to the Edwardian period but a similar atmosphere was conveyed.) Yet there is about the Mary Poppins stories something of the timeless appeal of the classic fairy tales.

In 1982, after a gap of 30 years, Travers produced another novel in the Mary Poppins saga. Like its predecessors, Mary Poppins in Cherry Tree Lane works on several levels. It can be read simply as a description of a huge, midsummer's eve romp spiced by plenty of zany happenings; but the serious mystical quality that found subtle expression in the earlier books is now stronger and more persuasive than ever.

A companion volume to Mary Poppins in Cherry Tree Lane came in 1989 with Mary Poppins and the House Next Door. Again the catalytic magic of the Banks family's nannie has suffered no toning down, and the author's inventiveness is still evident (notably in the episode dealing with the children's visit to the Man in the Moon). A brown and beautiful boy from the South Seas, temporarily residing in Cherry Tree Lane, is perhaps a little too golden to be true, but Mary Poppins and the other regular characters are conveyed with Travers's customary flair.

There are no magical overtones in I Go by Sea, I Go by Land. This account of two English children's wartime evacuation to the U.S.A. catches the atmosphere of the period—a grim acceptance of the "backs to the wall" situation coupled with a dogged optimism. For Sabrina and James there are also the excitement and apprehension of the U-boat-menaced sea trip to America, and a new life far away from home and parents. Their responses to change and challenge make lively reading. The wonders of the World's Fair and the Statue of Liberty possibly impress them less than the sophistication of American children—like their hostess's daughter who has permanently waved hair; or the satisfaction of having constant supplies of Coca-Cola, sweet corn, and out-of-season strawberries: "You can't wonder that the Americans are proud of their country." But underlying all the new discoveries and fulfilments is the fear about what might be happening to their parents left behind in England, exposed to the Blitz and the threat of invasion. Travers does not gloss over the severely disrupting effect on many young people of this wartime break-up of family life; but, as in the Mary Poppins books, her fictional children are nudged by circumstances into an acceptance of their responsibilities and an ability to cope with difficulties.

In The Fox at the Manger and Friend Monkey Travers brings together her interest in mythology and religion and her appreciation of nature. In her stories animals are more likely to be wild than domestic, as she considers that the latter have often been debased and made sycophantic by man. It is characteristic of her unsentimental attitude towards animals that the fox who joins the domesticated animals at the manger should give the Christ-child the rather surprising gift of his cunning—and that the child appreciates this above all the other gifts which are showered upon him.

In Friend Monkey the animal hero is equally robust. He is based upon Hanuman, the monkey lord of Hindu mythology, and his engaging efforts to help the human family who have adopted him usually result in chaos. Like most of Travers's stories this book implies that life cannot be tied up into neat packages. Monkey gives his friends no resting place, no panaceas. He opens their eyes frequently to deeper and more challenging aspects of life.

About the Sleeping Beauty is a re-telling of a traditional story. This suggests that fairyland "intersects our mortal world at every point and at every second. The two of them together make one web woven fine." The literal and symbolic immortality of Mary Poppins—Travers's most famous character—underlines the truth of this.

—Mary Cadogan

TREADGOLD, Mary. British. Born in London, 16 April 1910. Educated at Ginner-Mawer School of Dance and Drama, 1916–22; Challoner School, London, 1921–23; St. Paul's Girls' School, London, 1923–28; Bedford College, University of London, 1930–36, M.A. (honours) in English. Children's editor, William Heinemann Ltd., London, 1938–40; producer and literary editor, BBC, London, 1940–60. Recipient: Library Association Carnegie Medal, 1942. Address: 61 Swan Court, Manor Street, London SW3 5RX, England.

PUBLICATIONS FOR CHILDREN

Fiction

We Couldn't Leave Dinah, illustrated by Stuart Tresilian. London, Cape, 1941; as Left till Called For, New York, Doubleday, 1941.
No Ponies, illustrated by Ruth Gervis. London, Cape, 1946.
The "Polly Harris." London, Cape, 1949; as The Mystery of the "Polly Harris," New York, Doubleday, 1951; revised edition, as

The "Polly Harris," London, Hamish Hamilton, 1968; New York, Nelson, 1970.

The Heron Ride, illustrated by Victor Ambrus. London, Cape, 1962.

The Winter Princess, illustrated by Pearl Falconer. Leicester, Brockhampton Press, 1962; Princeton, New Jersey, Van Nostrand, 1964.

Return to the Heron, illustrated by Victor Ambrus. London, Cape, 1963.

The Weather Boy, illustrated by Robert Geary. Leicester, Brockhampton Press, 1964; Princeton, New Jersey, Van Nostrand, 1965.

Maids' Ribbons, illustrated by Susannah Holden. London, Nelson, 1965; New York, Nelson, 1967.

Elegant Patty, illustrated by Lynette Hemmant. London, Hamish Hamilton, 1967.

Poor Patty, illustrated by Lynette Hemmant. London, Hamish Hamilton, 1968.

This Summer, Last Summer, illustrated by Mary Russon. London, Hamish Hamilton, 1968.

The Humbugs, illustrated by Faith Jaques. London, Hamish Hamilton, 1968.

The Rum Day of the Vanishing Pony. Leicester, Brockhampton Press, 1970.

Journey from the Heron. London, Cape, 1981.

PUBLICATIONS FOR ADULTS

Novel

The Running Child. London, Cape, 1951.

*

Mary Treadgold comments:

(1978) I regard myself as a good example of the "hobby-writer"—writing is something I've enjoyed doing, never taken over-seriously. I am delighted when people take me seriously and when anyone tells me he or she has enjoyed what I've written!

(1983) As I grow older, I find it increasingly important to write books that a child will remember—at any rate something of—when he or she is grown-up. Perhaps only a character, or a landscape, or something outstanding somebody said—as I myself nearly 70 years later remember at odd moments scenes that at the time must have made some impression from that immortal book *The Secret Garden.* I think this writing for a child's *imaginative* future is of greater moment than I at first realised.

*   *   *

Mary Treadgold's first novel, *We Couldn't Leave Dinah,* won the Carnegie Medal for 1941, which lifts her well above the run of pony-adventure story writers. In fact, she is a novelist of very considerable power and while both ponies and adventure have continued to feature prominently in her books they have never come near to monopolising them or blurring a shrewd eye for character and relationships.

Both *We Couldn't Leave Dinah* and its successor, *No Ponies,* are essentially war stories. In the first, which deals with the Nazi invasion of a mythical Channel island, Clerinel, Mick and Caroline Templeton are confronted with adult problems of collaboration and divided loyalties, as well as the more ordinary excitements of a spy story. The second opens just after the war when the London-bred Atherleys travel to their aunt's lovely pre-war home in the south of France, their happiness at being Abroad only marred by the thought of the ponies and the riding that awaits them when their athletic cousins arrive.

But when they reach Beaubassin, the ponies are not there and the subsequent adventure proves to the children that wars are not always over with the fighting, but that the damage to people's minds may be harder to cure.

Compared with more recent books about the war, they still stand up extremely well. Some things have dated—child-adult relationships seem oddly formal, the triplets are said to be 14 but could be 12—yet in other ways there is a greater maturity than we have grown used to, a kind of objectivity, perfectly convincing, which makes these children seem older.

The same lack of self-centredness is felt in *The "Polly Harris"* which finds the reluctant Templetons enrolled at a London crammer's. The sensitive Caroline is both aware and highly critical of her own childishness. The plot here is in some ways much ahead of its time, with terrorists as well as smugglers (but no ponies), while running through the book at a deeper level is the idea of loneliness, one of Treadgold's haunting themes. This recurs in more overt form in the later "Heron" books, especially in her most recent, *Journey from the Heron,* where it is combined with the reassessments brought about by the war of 1914–18, but it is in *The "Polly Harris"* that the theme is most clearly expressed:

> For the first time [Caroline] was appalled to her soul at the way people could fail other people—could misunderstand their very nature, wound the delicate structure of their human spirit, and then send them back about their ways, uncomforted and quite alone...To her now came the knowledge that people could also misunderstand her as she had misunderstood David—could fail her, wound her and even destroy her. Not yet—there was no one yet to do it, but she knew that she had a long life before her. As she reached the lower landing, the burden of her long life lay on her, heavy as frost.

—Anne Carter

———

TREASE, (Robert) Geoffrey. British. Born in Nottingham, 11 August 1909. Educated at Nottingham High School, 1920–28; Queen's College, Oxford (scholar), 1928–29. Served in the British Army, 1942–46. Married Marian Boyer in 1933; one daughter. Social worker and journalist, London, 1929–32; teacher, Clacton-on-Sea, Essex, 1933. Since 1933 freelance writer. Chairman, Children's Writers Group, 1962–63. Chairman, 1972–73, and since 1974 member of the Council, Society of Authors. Fellow, Royal Society of Literature, 1979. Agent: Murray Pollinger, 4 Garrick Street, London WC2E 9BH. Address: 1 Yomede Park, Newbridge Road, Bath BA1 3LS, England.

PUBLICATIONS FOR CHILDREN

Fiction

Bows Against the Barons, illustrated by Michael Boland. London, Lawrence, and New York, International, 1934; revised edition, Leicester, Brockhampton Press, and New York, Meredith Press, 1966.

Comrades for the Charter, illustrated by Michael Boland. London, Lawrence, 1934.

The Call to Arms. London, Lawrence, 1935.

Red Comet, illustrated by Fred Ellis. Moscow, Co-operative Publishing Society of Foreign Workers, 1936; London, Lawrence and Wishart, 1937.

Missing from Home, illustrated by Scott. London, Lawrence and Wishart, 1936.

The Christmas Holiday Mystery, illustrated by Alfred Sindall. London, A. and C. Black, 1937; as *The Lakeland Mystery*, 1942.

Mystery on the Moors, illustrated by Alfred Sindall. London, A. and C. Black, 1937.

Detectives of the Dales, illustrated by A.C.H. Gorham. London, A. and C. Black, 1938.

In the Land of the Mogul, illustrated by J.C.B. Knight. Oxford, Blackwell, 1938.

North Sea Spy. London, Fore, 1939.

Cue for Treason, illustrated by Beatrice Goldsmith. Oxford, Blackwell, 1940; New York, Vanguard Press, 1941.

Running Deer, illustrated by W. Lindsay Cable. London, Harrap, 1941.

The Grey Adventurer, illustrated by Beatrice Goldsmith. Oxford, Blackwell, 1942.

Black Night, Red Morning, illustrated by Donia Nachsen. Oxford, Blackwell, 1944.

Army Without Banners. London, Fore, 1945.

Trumpets in the West, illustrated by Alan Blyth. Oxford, Blackwell, and New York, Harcourt Brace, 1947.

Silver Guard, illustrated by Alan Blyth. Oxford, Blackwell, 1948.

The Hills of Varna, illustrated by Treyer Evans. London, Macmillan, 1948; as *Shadow of the Hawk*, New York, Harcourt Brace, 1949.

The Mystery of Moorside Farm, illustrated by Alan Blyth. Oxford, Blackwell, 1949.

No Boats on Bannermere, illustrated by Richard Kennedy. London, Heinemann, 1949; New York, Norton, 1965.

The Secret Fiord, illustrated by H.M. Brock. London, Macmillan, 1949; New York, Harcourt Brace, 1950.

Under Black Banner, illustrated by Richard Kennedy. London, Heinemann, 1950.

The Crown of Violet, illustrated by C. Walter Hodges. London, Macmillan, 1952; as *Web of Traitors*, New York, Vanguard Press, 1952.

The Barons' Hostage, illustrated by Alan Jessett. London, Phoenix House, 1952; revised edition, Leicester, Brockhampton Press, 1973; Nashville, Nelson, 1975.

Black Banner Players, illustrated by Richard Kennedy. London, Heinemann, 1952.

The New House at Hardale. London, Lutterworth Press, 1953.

The Silken Secret, illustrated by Alan Jessett. Oxford, Blackwell, 1953; New York, Vanguard Press, 1954.

Black Banner Abroad. London, Heinemann, 1954; New York, Warne, 1955.

The Fair Flower of Danger. Oxford, Blackwell, 1955.

Word to Caesar, illustrated by Geoffrey Whittam. London, Macmillan, 1956; as *Message to Hadrian*, New York, Vanguard Press, 1956.

The Gates of Bannerdale. London, Heinemann, 1956; New York, Warne, 1957.

Mist over Athelney, illustrated by R.S. Sherriffs and J.L. Stockle. London, Macmillan, 1958; as *Escape to King Alfred*, New York, Vanguard Press, 1958.

The Maythorn Story, illustrated by Robert Hodgson. London, Heinemann, 1960.

Thunder of Valmy, illustrated by John S. Goodall. London, Macmillan, 1960; as *Victory at Valmy*, New York, Vanguard Press, 1961.

Change at Maythorn, illustrated by Robert Hodgson. London, Heinemann, 1962.

Follow My Black Plume, illustrated by Brian Wildsmith. London, Macmillan, and New York, Vanguard Press, 1963.

A Thousand for Sicily, illustrated by Brian Wildsmith. London, Macmillan, and New York, Vanguard Press, 1964.

The Dutch Are Coming, illustrated by Lynette Hemmant. London, Hamish Hamilton, 1965.

Bent Is the Bow, illustrated by Charles Keeping. London, Nelson, 1965; New York, Nelson, 1967.

The Red Towers of Granada, illustrated by Charles Keeping. London, Macmillan, 1966; New York, Vanguard Press, 1967.

The White Nights of St. Petersburg, illustrated by William Stobbs. London, Macmillan, and New York, Vanguard Press, 1967.

The Runaway Serf, illustrated by Mary Russon. London, Hamish Hamilton, 1968.

A Masque for the Queen, illustrated by Krystyna Turska. London, Hamish Hamilton, 1970.

Horsemen on the Hills. London, Macmillan, 1971.

A Ship to Rome, illustrated by Leslie Atkinson. London, Heinemann, 1972.

A Voice in the Night, illustrated by Sara Silcock. London, Heinemann, 1973.

Popinjay Stairs. London, Macmillan, 1973; New York, Vanguard Press, 1982.

The Chocolate Boy, illustrated by David Walker. London, Heinemann, 1975.

The Iron Tsar. London, Macmillan, 1975.

When the Drums Beat, illustrated by Janet Marsh. London, Heinemann, 1976; augmented edition, as *When the Drums Beat and Other Stories*, London, Pan, 1979.

Violet for Bonaparte. London, Macmillan, 1976.

The Seas of Morning, illustrated by David Smee. London, Penguin, 1976.

The Spy Catchers, illustrated by Geoffrey Bargery. London, Hamish Hamilton, 1976.

The Field of the Forty Footsteps. London, Macmillan, 1977.

The Claws of the Eagle, illustrated by Ionicus. London, Heinemann, 1977.

Mandeville. London, Macmillan, 1980.

A Wood by Moonlight and Other Stories. London, Chatto and Windus, 1981.

The Running of the Deer, illustrated by Maureen Bradley. London, Hamish Hamilton, 1982.

Saraband for Shadows. London, Macmillan, 1982.

The Cormorant Venture. London, Macmillan, 1984.

Tomorrow Is a Stranger. London, Heinemann, 1987.

A Flight of Angels. London, Macmillan, 1988.

The Arpino Assignment, illustrated by Paul Leith. London, Walker, 1988.

Plays

The Dragon Who Was Different and Other Plays (includes *The Mighty Mandarin, Fairyland Limited, The New Bird*). London, Muller, 1938.

The Shadow of Spain and Other Plays (includes *The Unquiet Cloister* and *Letters of Gold*). Oxford, Blackwell, 1953.

Radio Play: *Popinjay Stairs*, from his own story, 1973.

Other

Fortune, My Foe: The Story of Sir Walter Raleigh, illustrated by Norman Meredith. London, Methuen, 1949; as *Sir Walter Raleigh, Captain and Adventurer*, New York, Vanguard Press, 1950.

The Young Traveller in India and Pakistan [*England and Wales, Greece*]. London, Phoenix House, 3 vols., 1949–56; New York, Dutton, 3 vols., 1953–56.

Enjoying Books. London, Phoenix House, 1951; revised edition, 1963.

The Seven Queens of England. London, Heinemann, and New York, Vanguard Press, 1953; revised edition, Heinemann, 1968.

Seven Kings of England, illustrated by Leslie Atkinson. London, Heinemann, and New York, Vanguard Press, 1955.

Edward Elgar, Maker of Music. London, Macmillan, 1959.

Wolfgang Mozart, The Young Composer. London, Macmillan, 1961; New York, St. Martin's Press, 1962.

The Young Writer: A Practical Handbook, illustrated by Carl Hollander. London, Nelson, 1961.

Seven Stages. London, Heinemann, 1964; New York, Vanguard Press, 1965.

This Is Your Century. London, Heinemann, and New York, Harcourt Brace, 1965.

Seven Sovereign Queens. London, Heinemann, 1968; New York, Vanguard Press, 1971.

Byron: A Poet Dangerous to Know. London, Macmillan, and New York, Holt Rinehart, 1969.

D.H. Lawrence: The Phoenix and the Flame. London, Macmillan, 1973; as *The Phoenix and the Flame: D.H. Lawrence, A Biography*, New York, Viking Press, 1973.

Days to Remember: A Garland of Historic Anniversaries, illustrated by Joanna Troughton. London, Heinemann, 1973.

Britain Yesterday, illustrated by Robert Hodgson. Oxford, Blackwell, 1975.

Timechanges. London, Kingfisher, 1985; New York, Watts, 1986.

The Edwardian Era. London, Batsford, 1986.

Hidden Treasure, illustrated by Chris Molan. London, Hamish Hamilton, and New York, Lodestar, 1989.

Editor, *Six of the Best: Stories.* Oxford, Blackwell, 1955.

Translator, *Companions of Fortune*, by René Guillot, illustrated by Pierre Collot. London, Oxford University Press, 1952.

Translator, *The King's Corsair*, by René Guillot, illustrated by Pierre Rousseau. London, Oxford University Press, 1954.

PUBLICATIONS FOR ADULTS

Novels

Such Divinity. London, Chapman and Hall, 1939.

Only Natural. London, Chapman and Hall, 1940.

Snared Nightingale. London, Macmillan, 1957; New York, Vanguard Press, 1958.

So Wild the Heart. London, Macmillan, and New York, Vanguard Press, 1959.

Short Stories

The Unsleeping Sword. London, Lawrence, 1934.

Plays

After the Tempest (produced Welwyn, Hertfordshire, 1938; London, 1939). Published in *Best One-Act Plays of 1938*, edited by J.W. Marriott, London, Harrap, 1939; published separately, Boston, Baker, n.d.

Colony (produced London, 1939).

Time Out of Mind (televised, 1956; produced London, 1967).

Radio Plays: *Mr. Engels of Manchester 'Change*, 1947; *Henry Irving*, 1947; *Lady Anne*, 1949; *The Real Mr. Ryecroft*, 1949; *Elgar of England*, 1957.

Television Plays: *Time Out of Mind*, 1956; *Into Thin Air*, 1973.

Verse

The Supreme Prize and Other Poems. London, Stockwell, 1926.

Other

Walking in England. Wisbech, Cambridgeshire, Fenland Press, 1935.

Clem Voroshilov, The Red Marshal. London, Pilot Press, 1940.

Tales Out of School: A Survey of Children's Fiction. London, Heinemann, 1949; revised edition, 1964.

The Italian Story: From the Earliest Times to 1946. London, Macmillan, 1963; New York, Vanguard Press, 1964.

The Grand Tour. London, Heinemann, and New York, Holt Rinehart, 1967.

Nottingham: A Biography. London, Macmillan, 1970.

The Condottieri: Soldiers of Fortune. London, Thames and Hudson, 1970; New York, Holt Rinehart, 1971.

A Whiff of Burnt Boats: An Early Autobiography. London, Macmillan, and New York, St. Martin's Press, 1971.

Samuel Pepys and His World. London, Thames and Hudson, and New York, Putnam, 1972.

Laughter at the Door: A Continued Autobiography. London, Macmillan, and New York, St. Martin's Press, 1974.

London: A Concise History. London, Thames and Hudson, and New York, Scribner, 1975.

Portrait of a Cavalier: William Cavendish, First Duke of Newcastle. London, Macmillan, and New York, Taplinger, 1979.

Editor, *Matthew Todd's Journal: A Gentleman's Gentleman in Europe 1814–1820.* London, Heinemann, 1968.

*

Manuscript Collections: Nottingham Central Library; Kerlan Collection, University of Minnesota, Minneapolis; University of Nottingham Library.

Critical Study: *Geoffrey Trease* by Margaret Meek, London, Bodley Head, 1960; New York, Walck, 1964.

Geoffrey Trease comments:

Realism, I suppose, is what I have always aimed at, since I began writing for children in revulsion against the sentimental romanticism then pervading historical fiction. With the years I hope I have widened and deepened my vision, still cultivating factual accuracy but recognising that there are even more valuable qualities. I am not a "children's writer" in the sense that I concern myself with any insulated "magic world of childhood"—it is the adult world which absorbs me and which I want to present and interpret to the young reader inexorably growing up into it. To him I want to communicate my own interests, enthusiasms, emotions, and (unfashionable though this may sound) values. Even when I write about ancient Athenian democracy, anti-Semitism in Edward I's England, or corruption in Pepys's London, I always seek a modern relevance which I hope will not be lost on the more discerning child.

*   *   *

To survey the work of Geoffrey Trease is to write the history of children's books in England for the past 50-odd years. His career began before World War II, when, apart from the innovative work of Arthur Ransome, writing for children commanded neither respect nor reward. The storytelling vein of 19th-century writers for boys,

Ballantyne, Marryat, Stevenson, and Cooper, was worked, and there was a dearth of new reading matter to stand between the comics and the classics.

Trease saw that few children's books reflected the everyday concerns of their readers or offered them any perspective on contemporary events. His first novel, *Bows Against the Barons*, depicts Robin Hood as a primitive revolutionary with the sentiments of Trease's own Spanish Civil War generation, and *Comrades for the Charter* is more propaganda than history. Yet despite the fact that these books now seem naive alongside the rich later crop of Trease's historical novels and those of other distinguished practitioners in this kind, the seeds of a whole generation of English writing for children were sown in these early days. *Cue for Treason* showed the pattern of the books to come: a fast-moving plot, clearly defined villainy, an exciting climax, and satisfactory ending. This is the tradition of the *yarn* which Trease kept alive and developed in that his readers were never disappointed in a "what happens next" approach to reading.

Trease also made a clear distinction in these early books between the historical novel and the costumed period piece. Authenticity and historical accuracy are now taken so much for granted as part of the craft of historical novelists that the debt to Trease is often forgotten. When one remembers how Baroness Orczy shaped the stereotyped picture of the French Revolution for more than a generation of English readers, it is the more interesting to note how Trease often takes the popular side, as in *Thunder of Valmy*, which has been translated for French children. He writes in his best imaginative form about countries (Italy in *Follow My Black Plume*) and causes that draw their inspiration from threats to the rights of the individuals.

Criticism of books for children is now a voluminous business, but when *Tales Out of School* appeared in 1949 it was a new departure, an attempt by a practitioner to define his role and his craft and to set standards for his fellow writers. It is still a good corrective to the attempt to make children's literature an exclusive testing ground for critics. Trease pleads for the accessibility of books for children and insists that children's authors are artists in their own right, a claim that his own work substantiates.

His excursions outside the narrower field of children's fiction have kept Trease alive to current views about writing for the young. His continuing love-affair with the theatre, his historical writing and biographical studies have resulted in a development of his craft which is spiral rather than linear. For example, as autobiographical and biographical writing have come to claim larger adult audiences than the novel, Trease has written books on Byron and D.H. Lawrence which bring these authors into the area of the readers' concerns. He combines in these studies the historical narrative that he does so well with insightful criticism of the revolutionary poet and the novelist, personalities that speak to the condition of the adolescent reader.

At all times Trease has a strong awareness of his readers. This has made him an innovator in ways that are often overlooked when more style-conscious successors follow his lead. The school story, a kind which more than most betrays the social sympathies of the writer, moved into the day school with *No Boats on Bannermere* and its sequels. In this series the parents are neither dead nor banished and the characters grow older with the books. Some of the themes that writers for "new adults" now tackle in the present permissive atmosphere made their first appearance in a tentative form in these books. Although readers would now find them dated—Trease's experiences as a schoolmaster lie behind them—in their time they brought the family story out of the doldrums of both formula fiction and the sentimental tale. They are also mercifully free from the self-indulgence that later writers have mistaken for social realism.

The conviction that writers for children have to keep in touch with the social changes of childhood was one that Trease supported in his early days as a writer. The historical novel was his way of doing it. Where once, in the work of Treece, Burton, Harnett, Sutcliff, and

Trease himself, the historical setting was a metaphor for the mores that accompany the rites of passage that relate to a heroine's or hero's emergence into adulthood, these changes are now presented in all their contemporary actuality, in novels for "new adults." Historical stories are often regarded as "unreal" by those who know too little about the distinctive qualities of the historical imagination. In the Joseph Bard memorial lecture given to the Royal Society of Literature in 1982 Trease repeated an earlier insistence that a children's writer is an artist rather than a teacher's aid. In this he links himself with a long tradition of those who, like Harvey Darton, saw books for children as worth making well because they are not didactic in intent, as Trease clearly thinks the new realism is. In *Saraband for Shadows* we can see him taking the same care as ever with details about the production of a courtly masque, which no history lesson could do better. But, he would insist, it is the writer's craft to be accurate. His art is in persuading his readers that novels are about real life now and society's interrelatedness at all times. If he seems to be a little old-fashioned, as the collection *A Wood by Moonlight* suggests, it may be because children's books no longer risk portraying the conflict of social responsibility and selfishness. More likely, the writing of a good yarn is now less appreciated than the production of more obvious "relevance."

—Margaret Meek

TREECE, Henry. British. Born in Wednesbury, Staffordshire, 22 December 1911. Educated at Wednesbury High School for Boys; Birmingham University, B.A. 1933, Dip.Ed. 1934. Served in the Royal Air Force, 1941–46: Flight Lieutenant. Married Mary Woodman in 1939; two sons and one daughter. Teacher, Leicestershire Home Office School, Shustoke, 1934; English master, The College, Cleobury Mortimer, Shropshire, 1934–35, and Tynemouth School for Boys, Northumberland, 1935–38; English master, 1938–41, and senior English master, 1946–59, Barton on Humber Grammar School, Lincolnshire. Recipient: Arts Council prize, for play, 1955. *Died 10 June 1966.*

PUBLICATIONS FOR CHILDREN

Fiction

Legions of the Eagle, illustrated by Christine Price. London, Lane, 1954.
The Eagles Have Flown, illustrated by Christine Price. London, Lane, 1954.
Desperate Journey, illustrated by Richard Kennedy. London, Faber, 1954.
Ask for King Billy, illustrated by Richard Kennedy. London, Faber, 1955.
Viking's Dawn, illustrated by Christine Price. London, Lane, 1955; New York, Criterion, 1956.
Hounds of the King, illustrated by Christine Price. London, Lane, 1955.
Men of the Hills, illustrated by Christine Price. London, Lane, 1957; New York, Criterion, 1958.
The Road to Miklagard, illustrated by Christine Price. London, Lane, and New York, Criterion, 1957.
Hunter Hunted, illustrated by Richard Kennedy. London, Faber, 1957.
Don't Expect Any Mercy! London, Faber, 1958.
The Children's Crusade, illustrated by Christine Price. London,

Bodley Head, 1958; as *Perilous Pilgrimage*, New York, Criterion, 1959.

The Return of Robinson Crusoe, illustrated by Will Nickless. London, Hulton Press, 1958; as *The Further Adventures of Robinson Crusoe*, New York, Criterion, 1958.

The Bombard, illustrated by Christine Price. London, Bodley Head, 1959; as *Ride to Danger*, New York, Criterion, 1959.

Wickham and the Armada, illustrated by Hookway Cowles. London, Hulton Press, 1959.

Viking's Sunset, illustrated by Christine Price. London, Bodley Head, 1960; New York, Criterion, 1961.

Red Settlement. London, Bodley Head, 1960.

The Jet Beads, illustrated by W.A. Sillince. Leicester, Brockhampton Press, 1961.

The Golden One, illustrated by William Stobbs. London, Bodley Head, 1961; New York, Criterion, 1962.

Man with a Sword, illustrated by William Stobbs. London, Bodley Head, 1962; New York, Pantheon, 1964.

War Dog, illustrated by Roger Payne. Leicester, Brockhampton Press, 1962; New York, Criterion, 1963.

Horned Helmet, illustrated by Charles Keeping. Leicester, Brockhampton Press, and New York, Criterion, 1963.

The Last of the Vikings, illustrated by Charles Keeping. Leicester, Brockhampton Press, 1964; as *The Last Viking*, New York, Pantheon, 1966.

The Bronze Sword, illustrated by Mary Russon. London, Hamish Hamilton, 1965; augmented edition, as *The Centurian*, New York, Meredith Press, 1967.

Splintered Sword, illustrated by Charles Keeping. Leicester, Brockhampton Press, 1965; New York, Duell, 1966.

Killer in Dark Glasses. London, Faber, 1965.

Bang, You're Dead! London, Faber, 1966.

The Queen's Brooch. London, Hamish Hamilton, 1966; New York, Putnam, 1967.

Swords from the North, illustrated by Charles Keeping. London, Faber, and New York, Pantheon, 1967.

The Windswept City, illustrated by Faith Jaques. London, Hamish Hamilton, 1967; New York, Meredith Press, 1968.

Vinland the Good, illustrated by William Stobbs. London, Bodley Head, 1967; as *Westward to Vinland*, New York, Phillips, 1967.

The Dream-Time, illustrated by Charles Keeping. Leicester, Brockhampton Press, 1967; New York, Meredith Press, 1968.

The Invaders: Three Stories, illustrated by Charles Keeping. Leicester, Brockhampton Press, and New York, Crowell, 1972.

Plays

Hounds of the King, with Two Radio Plays (includes *Harold Godwinson* and *William, Duke of Normandy*), illustrated by Stuart Tresilian. London, Longman, 1965.

Radio Plays: *Harold Godwinson*, 1954; *William, Duke of Normandy*, 1954.

Other

Castles and Kings, illustrated by C. Walter Hodges. London, Batsford, 1959; New York, Criterion, 1960.

The True Book about Castles, illustrated by G.H. Channing. London, Muller, 1960.

Know about the Crusades. London, Blackie, 1963; as *About the Crusades*, Chester Springs, Pennsylvania, Dufour, 1966.

Fighting Men: How Men Have Fought Through the Ages, with Ewart Oakeshott. Leicester, Brockhampton Press, 1963; New York, Putnam, 1965.

The Burning of Njal (saga retold), illustrated by Bernard Blatch.

London, Bodley Head, and New York, Criterion, 1964.

PUBLICATIONS FOR ADULTS

Novels

The Dark Island. London, Gollancz, and New York, Random House, 1952; as *The Savage Warriors*, New York, Avon, 1959.

The Rebels. London, Gollancz, 1953.

The Golden Strangers. London, Lane, 1956; New York, Random House, 1957; as *The Invaders*, New York, Avon, 1960.

The Great Captains. London, Lane, and New York, Random House, 1956.

Red Queen, White Queen. London, Bodley Head, and New York, Random House, 1958; as *The Pagan Queen*, New York, Avon, 1959.

The Master of Badger's Hall. New York, Random House, 1959; as *A Fighting Man*, London, Bodley Head, 1960.

Jason. London, Bodley Head, and New York, Random House, 1961.

The Amber Princess. New York, Random House, 1962; as *Electra*, London, Bodley Head, 1963.

Oedipus. London, Bodley Head, 1964; as *The Eagle King*, New York, Random House, 1965.

The Green Man. London, Bodley Head, and New York, Putnam, 1966.

Short Stories

I Cannot Go Hunting Tomorrow: Short Stories. London, Grey Walls Press, 1946.

Plays

Carnival King (produced Nottingham, 1954). London, Faber, 1955.

Footsteps in the Sea (produced Nottingham, 1955).

Verse

38 Poems. London, Fortune Press, 1940.

Towards a Personal Armageddon. Prairie City, Illinois, Press of James A. Decker, 1941.

Invitation and Warning. London, Faber, 1942.

The Black Seasons. London, Faber, 1945.

Collected Poems. New York, Knopf, 1946.

The Haunted Garden. London, Faber, 1947.

The Exiles. London, Faber, 1952.

Other

How I See Apocalypse. London, Drummond, 1946.

Dylan Thomas: "Dog among the Fairies." London, Drummond, 1949; New York, de Graff, 1954; revised edition, London, Benn, and New York, de Graff, 1956.

The Crusades. London, Bodley Head, and New York, Random House, 1962.

Editor, with J.F. Hendry, *The New Apocalypse*. London, Fortune Press, 1939.

Editor, with J.F. Hendry, *The White Horseman: Prose and Verse of the New Apocalypse*. London, Routledge, 1941.

Editor, with Stefan Schimanski, *Wartime Harvest*. London, Bale and Staples, 1943.

Editor, with Stefan Schimanski, *Transformation*. London,

Gollancz, 1943.
Editor, with Stefan Schimanski, *Transformation 2–4*. London, Drummond, 3 vols., 1944–47.
Editor, *Herbert Read: An Introduction*. London, Faber, 1944; Port Washington, New York, Kennikat Press, 1969.
Editor, with John Pudney, *Air Force Poetry*. London, Lane, 1944.
Editor, with Stefan Schimanski, *A Map of Hearts: A Collection of Short Stories*. London, Drummond, 1944.
Editor, with J.F. Hendry, *The Crown and the Sickle: An Anthology*. London, King and Staples, 1945.
Editor, with Stefan Schimanski, *Leaves in the Storm: A Book of Diaries*. London, Drummond, 1947.
Editor, *Selected Poems*, by Algernon Charles Swinburne. London, Grey Walls Press, 1948.
Editor, with Stefan Schimanski, *New Romantic Anthology*. London, Grey Walls Press, 1949.

*

Critical Study: *Henry Treece* by Margery Fisher (includes bibliography by Antony Kamm), in *Three Bodley Head Monographs*, London, Bodley Head, 1969.

*   *   *

Henry Treece died at 54 when even better work may have been before him. All his children's books were written within not much more than 12 years, and certainly universal recognition of his contribution to children's literature came only after his death. He had the poet's aptitude for precision of language and the enthusiasm of the gifted teacher. And the teacher in him regarded a children's book not just as an art-form *per se* but as an art-form *for children*.

He was a master-technician who planned each book meticulously, storing up ideas for future novels and sequences as he went, and often writing more than was necessary so that he could select the material that would make up the most effective end-product. His ear for sound (he was pianist and composer as well as poet) led him to develop a form of historical speech which is both natural to modern ears and appropriate to period and character. With practice and conscious experiment with form and language he came to write historical novels for children of different ages from about eight upwards, sometimes treating the same theme at two or more levels. He abhorred violence, distrusted victory, and felt that war was inglorious and horrid; yet he admired and respected the skill of the fighter (he was himself a university boxing captain), especially the brave fighter. He was primarily a storyteller who created a background and characters to fit the story he wanted to tell. The six adolescent thrillers he wrote for Faber, though technically modern stories, are in effect 20th-century fantasies of spies and crooks, action and mystery, hunter and hunted, guns, knives, and fists, laced with real humour and genuine topographical backgrounds. Otherwise, with the exception of *The Jet Beads*, a short novel of situation centred on a boy's eleven-plus problems, all his fiction is historical.

Treece's preoccupation with what he called "the cross-roads of history" led him to write stories set at times of change, like *Legions of the Eagle*, *Hounds of the King*, *The Bombard*, *The Queen's Brooch*, and the two Viking trilogies. Another recurrent theme is the rationalisation of historical legend, for example *The Eagles Have Flown* (Artos the Bear), *Man with a Sword* (Hereward), *The Last of the Vikings* (Harald Hardrada), *The Windswept City* (Troy). The many books which are built round a "home-cycle" in which characters return home, or those in which a son searches for a father, reflect Treece's own sorrow at the early death of his elder son. In some books, notably the earlier ones, he followed convention by having young heroes participate in the historical action rather than motivate it, serving as devices through which people, events, and periods can

be seen and interpreted with a child's eyes. In *War Dog*, his work for younger children, a dog serves the same purpose. This device failed him artistically just once, in *The Children's Crusade*. The first half of the book covers this fateful journey as far as Marseilles through the eyes of two children caught by the magnetism of Stephen of Cloyes and of the sinister Pied Piper figure introduced into the story with supreme effect. The second half describes the pair's adventures in returning home from North Africa. The two halves do not knit.

Harald Sigurdson, hero of *Viking's Dawn*, *The Road to Miklagard*, and *Viking's Sunset*, starts as a youth but grows to manhood during the course of the trilogy. These are basically rich tales of travel, peopled with typical Vikings as Treece saw them—larger than life, brave, loyal but sometimes misguided, and capable of both sympathy and humour. *Man with a Sword* has a hero who *is* the action, and the book is significant also for other ways in which Treece consciously broke new ground. Though the story itself is long and complex (covering 46 years up to Hereward's death) the book is constructed in short chapters, paragraphs, and sentences, and has the unity and effect of a carefully forged narrative poem. In this book in particular, the poet and the novelist come together for the first time.

The books of the second Viking trilogy, written ostensibly for younger readers than the first, are shorter but have more depth than the Sigurdson stories. In each the main character is the centre of the action. Beorn, in *Horned Helmet*, has lost his father, but finds a substitute in the baresark Starkad, to whom he ultimately returns. This is a gem of controlled language and understatement, in the tradition of the sagas themselves. In *The Last of the Vikings* the title character is Harald Hardrada, recreated from just the first two chapters of Snorri Sturluson's *Heimskringla*, and framed with a prologue and epilogue which cover his death at Stamfordbridge. In fact Harald as a character is almost upstaged by the mystical Arsleif Summerbird who finally sacrifices himself so that Harald and his companions shall live. The boy Runolf, in *Splintered Sword*, is a psychological throwback, a Viking misfit in a world in which baresarks no longer have any value.

The last book of all that Treece completed was *The Dream-Time*. In period it goes back roughly to the prehistoric times of *Men of the Hills* and his adult novel *The Golden Strangers*; in control to *Horned Helmet* and *Man with a Sword*; but in construction and simplicity of thought and language it was entirely new. Above all it is the statement of an artist caught up in a society warring within itself for survival. To achieve his aim Treece telescoped history to bring different cultures in contrast with each other and developed an utterly simple language to represent primitive thought, all so skilfully done that one is not conscious of the fact that sentences are pared to the bone, words are mainly monosyllabic, and punctuation is kept to a minimum. Treece was concerned with cross-roads. *The Dream-Time* is a signpost. In terms of even greater contribution to children's literature, we shall never know in what direction it was pointing.

—Antony Kamm

TRESSELT, Alvin. American. Born in Passaic, New Jersey, 30 September 1916. Educated at Passaic High School, graduated 1934. Married Blossom Budney in 1949; two daughters. Worked in a defense plant, Connecticut, 1943–46; display designer and advertising copywriter, B. Altman Co., New York, 1946–52; editor, *Humpty Dumpty's Magazine*, New York, 1952–65; editor, 1965–67, and executive editor and vice-president, 1967–74, Parents' Magazine Press, New York. Since 1974 Instructor and Dean of Faculty, Institute of Children's Literature, Redding Ridge, Connecticut. Address: 53 Dorethy Road, West Redding, Connecticut 06896, U.S.A.

PUBLICATIONS FOR CHILDREN

Fiction

Rain Drop Splash, illustrated by Leonard Weisgard. New York, Lothrop, 1946.

White Snow Bright Snow, illustrated by Roger Duvoisin. New York, Lothrop, 1947.

Johnny Maple-Leaf, illustrated by Roger Duvoisin. New York, Lothrop, 1948.

The Wind and Peter, illustrated by Gary MacKenzie. New York, Oxford University Press, 1948.

Bonnie Bess, The Weathervane Horse, illustrated by Marylin Hafner. New York, Lothrop, 1949.

Sun Up, illustrated by Roger Duvoisin. New York, Lothrop, 1949; Kingswood, Surrey, World's Work, 1966.

The Little Lost Squirrel, illustrated by Leonard Weisgard. New York, Grosset and Dunlap, 1950.

Follow the Wind, illustrated by Roger Duvoisin. New York, Lothrop, 1950.

Hi, Mr. Robin!, illustrated by Roger Duvoisin. New York, Lothrop, 1950.

Autumn Harvest, illustrated by Roger Duvoisin. New York, Lothrop, 1951.

A Day with Daddy, photographs by Helen Heller. New York, Lothrop, 1953.

Follow the Road, illustrated by Roger Duvoisin. New York, Lothrop, 1953.

I Saw the Sea Come In, illustrated by Roger Duvoisin. New York, Lothrop, 1954; Kingswood, Surrey, World's Work, 1967.

Wake Up, Farm!, illustrated by Roger Duvoisin. New York, Lothrop, 1955; Kingswood Surrey, World's Work, 1966.

Wake Up, City!, illustrated by Roger Duvoisin. New York, Lothrop, 1957.

The Rabbit Story, illustrated by Leonard Weisgard. New York, Lothrop, 1957.

The Frog in the Well, illustrated by Roger Duvoisin. New York, Lothrop, 1958; Edinburgh, Oliver and Boyd, 1966.

The Smallest Elephant in the World, illustrated by Milton Glaser. New York, Knopf, 1959.

Timothy Robbins Climbs the Mountain, illustrated by Roger Duvoisin. New York, Lothrop, 1960; Kingswood, Surrey, World's Work, 1967.

An Elephant Is Not a Cat, with Wilbur Wheaton, illustrated by Tom Vroman. New York, Parents' Magazine Press, 1962.

Hide and Seek Fog, illustrated by Roger Duvoisin. New York, Lothrop, 1965; Kingswood, Surrey, World's Work, 1966.

The Old Man and the Tiger, illustrated by Albert Aquino. New York, Grosset and Dunlap, 1965; London, Muller, 1970.

A Thousand Lights and Fireflies, illustrated by John Moodie. New York, Parents' Magazine Press, 1965.

The World in the Candy Egg, illustrated by Roger Duvoisin. New York, Lothrop, 1967.

The Fox Who Travelled, illustrated by Nancy Sears. New York, Grosset and Dunlap, 1968.

It's Time Now!, illustrated by Roger Duvoisin. New York, Lothrop, 1969; Kingswood, Surrey, World's Work, 1971.

What Did You Leave Behind?, illustrated by Roger Duvoisin. New York, Lothrop, 1978; Kingswood, Surrey, World's Work, 1979.

Other (folktales)

Under the Trees and Through the Grass (ecology), illustrated by Roger Duvoisin. New York, Lothrop, 1962.

The Mitten: An Old Ukrainian Folktale, illustrated by Yaroslava.

New York, Lothrop, 1964; Kingswood, Surrey, World's Work, 1965.

How Far Is Far? (science), illustrated by Ward Brackett. New York, Parents' Magazine Press, 1964.

The Tears of the Dragon, illustrated by Chihiro Iwasaki. New York, Parents' Magazine Press, 1967.

Legend of the Willow Plate, with Nancy Cleaver, illustrated by Joseph Low. New York, Parents' Magazine Press, 1968; London, Hamish Hamilton, 1969.

The Crane Maiden, illustrated by Chihiro Iwasaki. New York, Parents' Magazine Press, 1968.

Helpful Mr. Bear, illustrated by Kozo Kakimoto. New York, Parents' Magazine Press, 1968.

Ma Lien and the Magic Brush, illustrated by Kei Wakana. New York, Parents' Magazine Press, 1968.

How Rabbit Tricked His Friends, illustrated by Yasuo Segawa. New York, Parents' Magazine Press, 1969.

The Rolling Rice Ball, illustrated by Saburo Watanabe. New York, Parents' Magazine Press, 1969.

The Fisherman under the Sea, illustrated by Chihiro Iwasaki. New York, Parents' Magazine Press, 1969.

The Land of Lost Buttons, illustrated by Kayako Nishimaki. New York, Parents' Magazine Press, 1970.

Eleven Hungry Cats, illustrated by Noboru Baba. New York, Parents' Magazine Press, 1970.

Gengoroh and the Thunder God, illustrated by Yasuo Segawa. New York, Parents' Magazine Press, 1970.

The Beaver Pond (ecology), illustrated by Roger Duvoisin. New York, Lothrop, 1970; Kingswood, Surrey, World's Work, 1971.

A Sparrow's Magic, illustrated by Fuyuji Yamanaka. New York, Parents' Magazine Press, 1970.

The Hare and the Bear and Other Stories, illustrated by Yoshiharu Suzuki. New York, Parents' Magazine Press, 1971.

Stories from the Bible, illustrated by Lynd Ward. New York, Coward McCann, 1971.

Ogre and His Bride, illustrated by Shosuke Fukuda. New York, Parents' Magazine Press, 1971.

Lum Fu and the Golden Mountain, illustrated by Daihacki Ohta. New York, Parents' Magazine Press, 1971.

The Little Mouse Who Tarried, illustrated by Kozo Kakimoto. New York, Parents' Magazine Press, 1971.

Wonder-Fish from the Sea, illustrated by Irmgard Lucht. New York, Parents' Magazine Press, 1971.

The Dead Tree (ecology), illustrated by Charles Robinson. New York, Parents' Magazine Press, 1972.

The Little Green Man, illustrated by Maurice Kenelski. New York, Parents' Magazine Press, 1972.

The Nutcracker, illustrated by Seiichi Horiuchi. New York, Parents' Magazine Press, 1974.

*

Manuscript Collection: Kerlan Collection, University of Minnesota, Minneapolis.

Alvin Tresselt comments:

My books are mostly about nature, the weather and seasons, although I have also written fantasy, humor, and here-and-now stories as well as a number of free adaptations of Japanese folktales. In my nature stories I have avoided a didactic approach and striven for a poetic prose style that would nurture in children a feeling for words and language, even while they were reading about the journey of rain to the sea, the mysteries of fog, or the importance of a dead tree. I generally use a cyclical plot when writing these stories, letting the progressions of a natural phenomenon dictate the form rather than casting the event within the confines of a conventional story.

All of my books have been in the four to eight picture book range.

*   *   *

White snow, bright snow, smooth and deep.
Light snow, night snow, quiet as sleep.
Down, down, without a sound;
Down, down, to the frozen ground.

Covering roads and hiding fences.
Sifting in cracks and filling up trenches.
Millions of snowflakes, tiny and light.
Softly, gently, in the secret night.

Those two stanzas from the prologue to his *White Snow Bright Snow* suggest why Alvin Tresselt was one of the pathbreaking American picture book authors of the late 1940's and early 1950's. Along with Margaret Wise Brown and others, he helped to establish the patterns of the "mood" picture book which sought to catch and hold the attention of young listeners and readers by projecting the essence of a familiar experience in vivid yet simple language.

White Snow Bright Snow, for which illustrator Roger Duvoisin won the Caldecott Medal, is a prime example of the Tresselt technique. Although there is no central character, and no plot in the classic sense, Tresselt does introduce representative characters—the postman, the farmer, the policeman—who recur throughout the narrative. And he structures the text in a dramatic way, starting with the low gray sky that presages the snow-storm and ending with the first spring robin that signals the season of snow is over.

Tresselt pioneered this approach to nature subjects in an earlier picture book, *Rain Drop Splash*, in which he traced the path of a raindrop from a puddle to the ocean. He continued it in such books as *Hi, Mr. Robin!*, *Wake Up, Farm!*, and *Hide and Seek Fog*, which details the impact of a thick fog that blankets a Cape Cod fishing village for three days.

Not surprisingly the Tresselt mood nature books spawned a horde of imitators. They seemed so simple to write—after all, who hadn't observed some process of nature, whether a butterfly emerging from a chrysalis or a pair of wrens building a nest, hatching eggs, and raising a new family. Why not write a picture book text about it? Hundreds if not thousands of writers tried their hand at such manuscripts. The great majority were never published, but many others did get into print. They inevitably tended to lessen the impact of some of Alvin Tresselt's own later books, especially when he seemed to repeat himself in books like *Under the Trees and Through the Grass*.

At this juncture, Tresselt happily widened his range by turning to folktales and fantasy. *The Mitten* was his delightful rendition of the Ukrainian tale about all the shivering forest animals that tried to crowd for warmth into the little boy's lost mitten. And even though it suffered from an uncertain point-of-view, *The World in the Candy Egg* contained some of Tresselt's loveliest writing, like this climactic extract:

Magic world, little world, made for a child's delight,
Where time doesn't pass and it never gets cold,
And the shepherd and shepherdess never grow old…
The sheep nibble grass and crows fly away, fly away,
    fly away,
In the make-believe world of the egg.

Then, in the late 1960's and early 1970's, Tresselt returned to nature themes. *It's Time Now!*, *The Dead Tree*, and *The Beaver Pond* proved that his touch was as sure as ever. Like the beavers who built first one dam and then another, he could still take the most ordinary material from nature and shape it into something fresh and special

for children.

—James Cross Giblin

TREVOR, (Lucy) Meriol. British. Born in London, 15 April 1919. Educated at Perse School, Cambridge; St. Hugh's College, Oxford, 1938–42, B.A. 1942. Worked in wartime nurseries, London, 1943–44, and steerer on Grand Union Canal, 1944–45; relief worker, UNRRA, Italy, 1946–47. Recipient: James Tait Black Memorial award, for biography, 1963. Fellow, Royal Society of Literature. Address: 70 Pulteney Street, Bath BA2 4DL, England.

PUBLICATIONS FOR CHILDREN

Fiction

The Forest and the Kingdom, illustrated by Philip Hepworth. London, Faber, 1949.
Hunt the King, Hide the Fox, illustrated by Philip Hepworth. London, Faber, 1950.
The Fires and the Stars, illustrated by Philip Hepworth. London, Faber, 1951.
Sun Slower, Sun Faster, illustrated by Edward Ardizzone. London, Collins, 1955; New York, Sheed and Ward, 1957.
The Other Side of the Moon, illustrated by Martin Thomas. London, Collins, 1956; New York, Sheed and Ward, 1957.
Merlin's Ring, illustrated by Martin Thomas. London, Collins, 1957.
The Treasure Hunt, illustrated by Constance Marshall. London, Hamish Hamilton, 1957.
The Caravan War, illustrated by Janet Pullan. London, Hamish Hamilton, 1958.
Four Odd Ones, illustrated by Martin Thomas. London, Collins, 1958.
The Sparrow Child, illustrated by Martin Thomas. London, Collins, 1958.
The Rose Round. London, Hamish Hamilton, 1963; New York, Dutton, 1964.
William's Wild Day Out, illustrated by Raymond Briggs. London, Hamish Hamilton, 1963.
The Midsummer Maze, illustrated by Hugh Marshall. London, Macmillan, and New York, St. Martin's Press, 1964.
Lights in a Dark Town, illustrated by Hilda Offen. London, Macmillan, 1964.
The King of the Castle, illustrated by Hugh Marshall. London, Macmillan, 1966.

PUBLICATIONS FOR ADULTS

Novels

The Last of Britain. London, Macmillan, and New York, St. Martin's Press, 1956.
The New People. London, Macmillan, and New York, St. Martin's Press, 1957.
A Narrow Place. London, Macmillan, 1958.
Shadows and Images. London, Macmillan, 1960; New York, McKay, 1962.
The City and the World. London, Dent, 1970.
The Holy Images. London, Dent, 1971.

The Two Kingdoms. London, Constable, 1973.
The Fugitives. London, Hodder and Stoughton, 1973; New York, Pocket Books, 1974.
The Marked Man. London, Hodder and Stoughton, and New York, Pocket Books, 1974.
The Enemy at Home. London, Hodder and Stoughton, and New York, Pocket Books, 1974.
The Forgotten Country. London, Hodder and Stoughton, 1975.
The Fortunate Marriage. London, Hodder and Stoughton, and New York, Dutton, 1976.
The Treacherous Paths. London, Hodder and Stoughton, 1976.
The Civil Prisoners. London, Hodder and Stoughton, and New York, Dutton, 1977.
The Fortunes of Peace. London, Hodder and Stoughton, 1978.
The Wanton Fires. London, Hodder and Stoughton, and New York, Dutton, 1979.
The Sun with a Face. New York, Fawcett, 1982; London, Hale, 1984.
The Golden Palaces. Frome, Somerset, Bravis Head, 1985.

Verse

Midsummer, Midwinter. Aldington, Kent, Hand and Flower Press, 1957.

Other

Newman: Pillar of the Cloud [and] *Light in Winter* (biography). London, Macmillan, 2 vols., 1962; New York, Doubleday, 2 vols., 1962–63; abridged edition, as *Newman's Journey*, London, Fontana, 1974; Huntingdon, Indiana, Our Sunday Visitor, 1985.
Newman Today. London, Catholic Truth Society, 1963.
Newman, A Portrait Restored: An Ecumenical Reevaluation, with John Coulson and A.M. Allchin. London, Sheed and Ward, 1965.
Apostle of Rome: A Life of Philip Neri, 1515–1595. London, Macmillan, 1966.
Pope John. London, Macmillan, and New York, Doubleday, 1967.
Prophets and Guardians: Renewal and Tradition in the Church. London, Hollis and Carter, and New York, Doubleday, 1969.
The Arnolds: Thomas Arnold and His Family. London, Bodley Head, and New York, Scribner, 1973.
The Shadow of a Crown: The Life Story of James II of England and VII of Scotland. London, Constable, 1988.

*

Meriol Trevor comments:

I wrote some children's books because I wanted to, and I dedicated them to the children of friends, who all seemed to enjoy reading them. I still sometimes hear from children who have read and enjoyed my books. I have had no books for children published since 1966, though I have written some more stories for them. In all my stories I have tried to involve the children in the lives and problems of sympathetic young adults often by putting the loves and hates among and between the generations at one remove, because I think this makes it easier for children to understand, or to recognize, their own emotions.

*   *   *

Meriol Trevor has written books for children in several different genres. Her favourite medium is a kind of fantasy that is peculiarly her own, mixing myth, magic, traditional folklore, and Christian allegory. A number of these books, such as *The Forest and the Kingdom* and *Hunt the King, Hide the Fox*, derive from a fictitious world, The World Dionysus, which the author and a friend, Margaret Priestley, invented when they were children. Together and separately the two women have written several World Dionysus stories rather as the Brontë sisters invented and wrote about Gondal. Trevor has also produced realistic novels—*The Sparrow Child* and *The Rose Round* are examples—and stories for younger children in the Antelope and Reindeer series.

Nearly all Trevor's writing is suffused by her deeply held Roman Catholic beliefs. This means that her books often have a specialist interest, being perhaps more easily appreciated by people of that religious persuasion than by Protestant or agnostic readers. At times, the didactic intention shows through too much, as in *The Sparrow Child*, where the story becomes somewhat implausible when the Christian myth of the grail is given too much prominence in the closing chapters.

The structure of her novels is always competent—*The Rose Round* is an interesting example of a complex story that is handled skillfully enough for the plot to seem quite simple—and there is a heavy reliance on dialogue, which is not always so convincing, sometimes failing to portray the differences of thought and feeling between the characters adequately. Perhaps her most successful books are the short novels for young readers, *William's Wild Day Out*, *The Treasure Hunt*, and *The Caravan War*, which, slight though they may be, are distinguished by a lively sense of humour and an assurance of tone in the writing that do not always appear in the longer, more serious novels.

—David Rees

———

TRING, A. Stephen. See **MEYNELL, Laurence.**

———

TRUSS, Jan (née Degg). Canadian. Born in Stoke-on-Trent, Staffordshire, England, 3 May 1925; moved to Canada, 1957; became citizen, 1967. Educated at Goldsmiths' College, University of London, Teachers' Certificate 1945; University of Alberta, Edmonton, B.Ed. 1962; University of Calgary, Alberta, 1965–68. Married Donald Truss in 1946 (died); one son and one daughter. Schoolteacher in Liverpool, Winchester, Peterborough, and Basildon, Essex, 1945–57; schoolteacher, principal, and art consultant, schools in rural Alberta, 1957–68; lecturer, University of Calgary, 1968–70. Since 1970 freelance writer. Recipient: Ruth Schwartz award, 1983. Agent: Bella Pomer, 9 Ardmore Road, Toronto, Ontario M5P 1V4; or, Frances Hanna, 51 Acacia Road, Toronto M4S 2K6. Address: Box 8, Water Valley, Alberta T0M 2E0, Canada.

PUBLICATIONS FOR CHILDREN

Fiction

A Very Small Rebellion, illustrated by Peter Millward. Edmonton, Alberta, LeBel, 1976.
Bird at the Window. New York, Harper, 1980.
Jasmin. Vancouver, Douglas and McIntyre, and New York, Atheneum, 1982.
Summer Goes Riding. Toronto, Groundwood, 1987.
Peter's Mocassins. Edmonton, Alberta, Reidmore, 1987.
Red. Toronto, Groundwood, 1988.

Plays

Attack. Edmonton, Alberta Department of Culture, Youth and Recreation, 1971.
Ooomerahgi Oh! (produced Calgary, 1974). With *A Very Small Rebellion*, Toronto, Playwrights, 1978.
A Very Small Rebellion (produced Calgary, 1974). With *Ooomerahgi Oh!*, Toronto, Playwrights, 1978.
The Judgement of Clifford Sifton (produced Calgary, 1977). Toronto, Playwrights, 1979.
Cornelius Dragon, in *Eight Plays for Young People*, edited by Joyce Doolittle. Edmonton, Alberta, NeWest Press, 1984.

PUBLICATIONS FOR ADULTS

Novel

Bird at the Window (not same as 1980 children's book). Toronto, Macmillan, 1974.

Other

Rocky Mountain Symphony, photographs by George Brybycin. Calgary, GB Publications, 1983.

*

Jan Truss comments:

A very long time elapses before I understand what I have really written about. I write because it is the one thing I am prepared to do with immense patience. I have been confronted by young persons who tell me emphatically that I write from their side—as though this is something unusual. I don't know. I tend to think that I do not write *for* young people so much as to expose to them the child, the adolescent inside me—a sort of necessary honesty between and among generations. I try not to offend the proud and critical child in me while I, the adult, must satisfy myself as social critic, nag, teacher, dreamer, poet, and passionate protector of literature and the inside child.

It is the characters that draw me through the plots, always surprising me by the way they will insist on behaving. In my early novels, set in rural-to-wilderness western Canada, I believe I was the immigrant exploring my adopted habitat with my young indigenous characters. I am not far enough away yet from *Summer Goes Riding* and *Red* to know what they are about other than that they weave together my connections with growing up, sexual stirrings, horses, family influences, inheritance, obsession, Canada, England, and the U.S.A. I am fascinated and delighted when scholars and young readers tell me what I have been about.

My plays are frankly dramatic—and often poetic. *Ooomerahgi Oh!*, for preschoolers, deals with the youngest child watching all the family leave for the enchantments of the big world—with magic. *A Very Small Rebellion* and *The Judgement of Clifford Sifton* are plays for young persons each dealing with an aspect of Canadian history, Louis Riel and the settlement of the West respectively.

All my work turns out to be an intermingling of child and adult perspectives.

* * *

In terms of literary forms, subject matter and intended audience levels, Jan Truss's writings offer much variety. Among her three plays, *Ooomerahgi Oh!* is a fantasy for preschoolers while *A Very Small Rebellion* and *The Judgement of Clifford Sifton* revolve around Canadian historical events and appeal to pre and early adolescents.

Jasmin, a novel about a girl's failing grade six and running away, and the titles in the Summer Quartet should find their readership among upper elementary grade readers. Older teens will seek out *Bird at the Window* which deals with an unwanted pregnancy.

A Very Small Rebellion is an interesting literary experiment intended to show history's relevance to today's children. An Indian and a Metis boy relate how surveyors have plotted a road which will necessitate destroying their settlement of log houses built on Alberta government land. Though the families have squatted on the land without permission, they petition the government, unsuccessfully, to recognize their natural rights to remain. The boys' story parallels that of the Metis and Indians who lived in Manitoba and Saskatchewan during the 19th century when the Canadian government exercised its territorial control over these lands and Louis Riel unsuccessfully led his people in rebellion. Truss incorporates this historical happening in two ways. The boys' junior high class performs Truss's play about Riel. Additionally, between each chapter of the boys' story is a chapter of straight historical reporting.

Truss's historical plays utilize approaches of the new social history. Sifton, the Canadian politician whose role in encouraging 19th-century European immigration led to western Canada's development, is usually presented positively in histories; however, utilizing a technique reminiscent of Dickens's spirits in *A Christmas Carol*, Truss re-examines Sifton's contributions from the perspective of the unprepared immigrants who endured the wilderness hardships. Similarly, in the play *A Very Small Rebellion* Riel's position in traditional history is reconsidered from a Metis and Indian point of view.

Setting and characterization are the strengths of *Jasmin* and *Bird at the Window*. The central characters Jasmin and Angela both live in rural communities near Calgary, Alberta, and their behaviour is influenced by their environment. Jasmin, the eldest of seven children from a poor family living in a two-room house, is caught between the demands of a middle-class school and a mother unable to cope with her large family's needs. About to fail her grade, Jasmin runs away to the wilderness of the Rocky Mountain foothills where she comes to discover her worth.

In *Bird at the Window* Angela, the school brain, is pregnant and, unable to communicate with her parents and unwilling to marry the child's father, the 18-year-old continues with her plans to visit her mother's parents in England. Using subterfuge, Angela hides the pregnancy from her grandparents and later delivers a stillborn infant. While the pregnancy is a primary concern in the book, Angela's relationships with her parents and the community are important.

With *Summer Goes Riding* Truss began a projected quartet featuring the same central characters. Living in rural Nebraska, Charlotte Mauney, Maggie Vogel and Red Wallinger, all about to enter grade eight, are the only youngsters of their age group in the area. Completing their group is Sidney Topham, home for the summer from private school in England. The first book is Charlotte's. Her great desire, to be a champion horsewoman, is being thwarted because she lacks the prime prerequisite—a horse. Charlotte's practical sheep-raising parents resist acquiring a non-productive horse. Her rich grandfather's visit offers promise, but financial reverses cause him to give Charlotte a pregnant pig and the possibility that piglet profits will eventually lead to her goal. A tornado strikes the area, severely damaging the Mauney farm, and Charlotte's horse gets further away as Mr. Mauney takes a factory job and the family moves to a smaller farm. The book concludes brightly for Charlotte as she becomes a stable hand at Wallingers Stables so that Red can visit his mother in Calgary.

Red begins at the point *Summer Goes Riding* ends. Throughout the first book readers observed Herman Wallinger's harsh treatment of his 12-year-old son, but now Red is to spend the last two weeks of summer with a mother he has not seen since she ran off with a rodeo cowboy four years before. While Herman hopes that Red will return with Louise, Red learns that his mother will not share their life, for she explains she has to be free. Red experiences another disappointment when he develops a crush on beautiful, mysterious Celeste who can leave her house only when accompanied by her two guardian bulldogs or her "Auntie." Blinded by Celeste's features, Red does not recognize her repetitive style of speaking as signaling retardation. By the book's end, Red has matured in his relationship with his mother and looks forward to next year's visit.

—David H. Jenkinson

———

TUNIS, John R(oberts). American. Born in Boston, Massachusetts, 7 December 1889. Educated at Harvard University, Cambridge, Massachusetts, A.B. 1911; Boston University Law School, 1916. Served in the United States Army in France during World War I: Lieutenant. Married Lucy Rogers in 1918. Sportswriter, New York *Evening Post*, 1925–32, and Universal Service, New York, 1932–35; tennis commentator, NBC, New York, 1934–42. Regular contributor to *Harper's, Atlantic Monthly, Saturday Evening Post*, and other periodicals; sports columnist, the *New Yorker*. Recipient: Child Study Committee award, 1944. *Died 4 February 1975.*

PUBLICATIONS FOR CHILDREN

Fiction

Iron Duke, illustrated by Johan Bull. New York, Harcourt Brace, 1938.
The Duke Decides, illustrated by James MacDonald. New York, Harcourt Brace, 1939.
Champion's Choice, illustrated by Jay Hyde Barnum. New York, Harcourt Brace, 1940.
The Kid from Tomkinsville, illustrated by Jay Hyde Barnum. New York, Harcourt Brace, 1940.
World Series, illustrated by Jay Hyde Barnum. New York, Harcourt Brace, 1941.
All-American, illustrated by Hans Walleen. New York, Harcourt Brace, 1942.
Keystone Kids. New York, Harcourt Brace, 1943.
Rookie of the Year. New York, Harcourt Brace, 1944.
Yea! Wildcats! New York, Harcourt Brace, 1944.
A City for Lincoln. New York, Harcourt Brace, 1945.
The Kid Comes Back. New York, Morrow, 1946.
Highpockets. New York, Morrow, 1948.
Son of the Valley. New York, Morrow, 1949.
Young Razzle. New York, Morrow, 1949.
The Other Side of the Fence. New York, Morrow, 1953.
Go, Team, Go! New York, Morrow, 1954.
Buddy and the Old Pro, illustrated by Jay Hyde Barnum. New York, Morrow, 1955.
Schoolboy Johnson. New York, Morrow, 1958.
Silence over Dunkerque. New York, Morrow, 1962.
His Enemy, His Friend. New York, Morrow, 1967.
Grand National. New York, Morrow, 1973.

Other

Million-Miler: The Story of an Air Pilot. New York, Messner, 1942.

PUBLICATIONS FOR ADULTS

Novel

American Girl. New York, Brewer and Warren, 1930.

Other

$port$, Heroics, and Hysterics. New York, Day, 1928.
Was College Worth While? New York, Harcourt Brace, 1936.
Choosing a College. New York, Harcourt Brace, 1940.
Sport for the Fun of It. New York, A.S. Barnes, 1940; revised edition, 1950.
Democracy and Sport. New York, A.S. Barnes, 1941.
This Writing Game: Selections from Twenty Years of Free-Lancing. New York, A.S. Barnes, 1941.
Lawn Games. New York, A.S. Barnes, 1943.
The American Way of Sport. New York, Duell, 1958.
A Measure of Independence (autobiography). New York, Atheneum, 1964.

*

Manuscript Collection: Mugar Memorial Library, Boston University.

* * *

John R. Tunis was from early youth fascinated with sports. He competed in high school; at Harvard he was active in tennis and long distance track. Following service in France during World War I, he wrote sports articles for the New York *Evening Post* and at the same time announced major sporting events. He wrote literally thousands of articles on sports and education, about which he felt keenly.

Most of his books for children are about college athletics or professional sports. He covers equally well baseball, basketball, football, and tennis. *All-American* was deemed by the New York *Herald Tribune* as the best story offered to boys in 1942. *Keystone Kids* was chosen by the Child Study Association as the most challenging book of 1943 for young people. Tunis's plots are fast moving, as are professional games; his dialogue is clipped and colorful, as are radio and TV sportscasts. The drama of challenge and skill set against competition and effort is the basis of the books. In addition the books promulgate the ideal American sports values of fair play and of consideration for individuals and for teams. Tunis's concern with sportsmanship as well as sports is evident in his focus on respect for others. Long before it was well understood, Tunis discussed racial and religious discrimination in sports. *All-American* focuses on a well-to-do boy who comes to an economically mixed high school and makes the football team. How this boy learns to admire his fellow players, how he is able to help with the special problems of one black player, are realistically and forcefully presented. Also clearly shown are the difficulties of team work, of caring and looking out for one's fellow player. Among Tunis's other first-rate sports stories are: *Champion's Choice, The Kid from Tomkinsville, World Series, Rookie of the Year, Young Razzle*, and *Go, Team, Go!*

In addition to his stories of American sports, Tunis also wrote stories of politics—of American democracy (*A City for Lincoln*) and of world war (*Silence over Dunkerque* and *His Enemy, His Friend*). These works are more didactic, less exciting, and less suspenseful than the sports stories. They express, though, Tunis's deep concern for human beings and their interrelatedness.

—Mary Lystad

———

TURKLE, Brinton (Cassady). American. Born in Alliance, Ohio, 15 August 1915. Educated at Carnegie Institute of Technology (now Carnegie-Mellon University), Pittsburgh, 1933–36; Museum of Fine Arts School, Boston, 1938–40. Married Yvonne Foulston in 1948; one daughter and two sons. Freelance illustrator. Recipient: Christopher award, 1973. Address: c/o Dutton, 2 Park Avenue, New York, New York 10016, U.S.A.

PUBLICATIONS FOR CHILDREN (illustrated by the author)

Fiction

Obadiah the Bold. New York, Viking Press, 1965.
The Magic of Millicent Musgrave. New York, Viking Press, 1967.
The Fiddler of High Lonesome. New York, Viking Press, 1968.
Thy Friend, Obadiah. New York, Viking Press, 1969.
The Sky Dog. New York, Viking Press, 1969.
Mooncoin Castle; or, Skulduggery Rewarded. New York, Viking Press, 1970.
The Adventures of Obadiah. New York, Viking Press, 1972.
It's Only Arnold. New York, Viking Press, 1973.
Deep in the Forest. New York, Dutton, 1976.
Rachel and Obadiah. New York, Dutton, 1978.
Do Not Open. New York, Dutton, 1981.

*

Illustrator: *Timber Line Treasure* by Adrien Stoutenburg, 1951; *Miracle of Sage Valley* by Janet Randall, 1958; *You Say You Saw a Camel!* by Elizabeth Coatsworth, 1959; *Danny Dunn on the Ocean Floor*, 1960, and *Danny Dunn and the Fossil Cave*, 1961, both by Jay Williams and Raymond Abrashkin; *War Cry of the West* by Nathaniel Burt, 1964; *Indian Children of America* by Margaret Farquhar, 1964; *If You Lived in Colonial Times* by Ann McGovern, 1964; *The Far-Off Land* by Rebecca Caudill, 1964; *Four Paws into Adventure* by Claude Cenac, 1965; *The Doll in the Bakeshop* by Carol Beach York, 1965; *How Joe the Bear and Sam the Mouse Got Together*, 1965, and *Catch a Little Fox*, 1970, both by Beatrice Schenk de Regniers; *The Story of Ben Franklin* by Eve Merriam, 1965; *The Mystery of the Red Tide* by Frank Bonham, 1966; *Belinda and Me* by Bettye Hill Braucher, 1966; *High-Noon Rocket* by Charles May, 1966; *A Special Birthday Party for Someone Very Special*, 1966, *Sam and the Impossible Thing*, 1967, and *Jake*, 1969, all by Tamara Kitt; *The Lollipop Party* by Ruth A. Sonneborn, 1967; *The Troublesome Tuba* by Barbara Rinkoff, 1967; *That's What Friends Are For* by Florence Parry Heide and Sylvia W. Van Clief, 1968; *Granny and the Indians* by Peggy Parish, 1969; *Yvette* by Leon Harris, 1970; *Anna and the Baby Buzzard* by Helga Sandburg, 1970; *C Is for Circus* by Bernice Chardiet, 1971; *Who Likes It Hot?* by Mary Garelick, 1972; *The Ballad of William Sycamore* by Stephen Vincent Benét, 1972; *The Boy Who Didn't Believe in Spring* by Lucille Clifton, 1973; *Poor Richard in France* by F.N. Monjo, 1973; *Over the River and Through the Wood* by Lydia Child, 1974; *The Elves and the Shoemaker* by Freya Littledale, 1975; *Island Time* by Betty Lamont, 1976.

*   *   *

Through the books that he has written and illustrated, Brinton Turkle has shown his depth and originality as a writer both for younger and for older readers. In his picture books, most noticeably the four about Obadiah, through text and illustrations he has brought 19th-century Nantucket and the Quaker Starbuck family vividly to life. Obadiah has the old-fashioned speech and dress of the period

and of his religion, but his antics and feelings are those of any era. He is embarrassed by the seagull who follows him in *Thy Friend, Obadiah*; he dreams of becoming a pirate in *Obadiah the Bold*; and he turns the tables on disbelieving adults in *The Adventures of Obadiah*. In *Rachel and Obadiah*, the last of the four books, the focus has shifted to Obadiah's younger sister, Rachel, in a tale with overtones of "The Hare and the Tortoise." In all of the books the expressive, homey illustrations, full of accurate details about Nantucket, and the warmth of the family brought out in the writing capture the hearts of children.

In Turkle's most memorable story for older readers, *The Fiddler of High Lonesome*, the mood is far different from the picture books. Here dark, brooding illustrations set the mood although the American mountain dialect and exaggerations are humorous at first. When gentle Lysander Bochamp joins the wild Fogles because they are the only "kin" he believes he has left, they accept him when they discover that he can play the fiddle. However, what seems to have the makings of a merry tale changes dramatically at the climax, and the reader is left with a hauntingly sad feeling.

Mooncoin Castle, another book for older readers, is a complete turn-about from *Fiddler*. The setting is Ireland instead of the American mountains, and the narrator is Jeremy, a jackdaw, who, along with a ghost named Patrick and a witch named Maude, attempts to save Mooncoin Castle from destruction: an American-style concrete and glass shopping center is to be erected in its place. In the story Turkle satirizes pop singing groups and hilariously characterizes the unlikely trio of defenders. There is much tongue-in-cheek humor in this comical tale.

A more recent picture book with folktale origins is *Do Not Open*, for younger readers. Miss Moody and her cat, Captain Kid, live by the sea, collecting various treasures deposited on the beach by storms. A special find is a purple bottle marked DO NOT OPEN, but Miss Moody cannot resist the child-like voice appealing to her from within. The somewhat predictable results are offset by the highly expressive illustrations in rich colors.

—Marilyn F. Apseloff

———

TURNER, Ethel (Sybil). Australian. Born in Doncaster, Yorkshire, England, 24 January 1872; moved to Australia, 1881. Educated at Girls' High School, Sydney. Married H.R. Curlewis in 1896; one son and one daughter. Founding editor, with Lilian Turner, the *Parthenon* magazine, Sydney, 1889–92; children's editor and columnist (as Dame Durden), *Illustrated Sydney News*, later *Australian Town and Country Journal*, 1892–1919, and Sydney *Sun*, 1921–31. Died 8 April 1958.

PUBLICATIONS FOR CHILDREN

Fiction

Seven Little Australians, illustrated by A.J. Johnson. London, Ward Lock, 1894; Philadelphia, McKay, 1908.
The Family at Misrule, illustrated by A.J. Johnson. London, Ward Lock, 1895; Philadelphia, McKay, 1909.
The Little Larrikin, illustrated by A.J. Johnson. London, Ward Lock, 1896.
Miss Bobbie, illustrated by Harold Copping. London, Ward Lock, 1897; New York, New Amsterdam, 1900.
The Camp at Wandinong, illustrated by Frances Ewan and others.

London, Ward Lock, 1898.

Three Little Maids, illustrated by A.J. Johnson. London, Ward Lock, 1900; Philadelphia, McKay, 1908.

The Wonder-Child, illustrated by Gordon Browne. London, Religious Tract Society, 1901; Akron, Ohio, Saalfield, 1908.

Little Mother Meg, illustrated by A.J. Johnson. London, Ward Lock, 1902; Philadelphia, McKay, 1909.

Betty & Co. London, Ward Lock, 1903.

Mother's Little Girl, illustrated by A.J. Johnson. London, Ward Lock, 1904.

A White Roof-Tree. London, Ward Lock, 1905.

In the Mist of the Mountains, illustrated by J. Macfarlane. London, Ward Lock, 1906.

The Stolen Voyage, illustrated by J. Macfarlane. London, Ward Lock, 1907.

That Girl, illustrated by Frances Ewan. London, Unwin, 1908; Philadelphia, McKay, 1910.

Fugitives from Fortune, illustrated by J. Macfarlane. London, Ward Lock, 1909.

The Apple of Happiness, illustrated by A.N. Gough. London, Hodder and Stoughton, 1911.

An Ogre Up-to-Date, illustrated by H.C. Sandy and D.H. Souter. London, Ward Lock, 1911.

The Secret of the Sea. London, Hodder and Stoughton, 1913.

Flower o' the Pine, illustrated by J.H. Hartley. London, Hodder and Stoughton, 1914.

The Cub: Six Months in His Life, illustrated by Harold Copping. London, Ward Lock, 1915.

John of Daunt, illustrated by Harold Copping. London, Ward Lock, 1916.

St. Tom and the Dragon, illustrated by Harold Copping. London, Ward Lock, 1918.

Brigid and the Cub, illustrated by Harold Copping. London, Ward Lock, 1919.

Laughing Water, illustrated by Harold Copping. London, Ward Lock, 1920.

King Anne, illustrated by Harold Copping. London, Ward Lock, 1921.

Jennifer, J., illustrated by Harold Copping. London, Ward Lock, 1922.

The Sunshine Family: A Book of Nonsense, with Jean Curlewis, illustrated by D.H. Souter and H. Bancks. London, Ward Lock, 1923.

Nicola Silver, illustrated by Harold Copping. London, Ward Lock, 1924.

Funny, illustrated by W.E. Wightman. London, Ward Lock, 1926.

Judy and Punch, illustrated by Harold Copping. London, Ward Lock, 1928.

The Child of the Children, illustrated by Frances Ewan. London, Ward Lock, 1959.

Verse

Happy Hearts..., with others, illustrated by D.H. Souter. London, Ward Lock, 1908.

The Tiny House and Other Verses. London, Ward Lock, 1911.

Captain Cub, illustrated by Harold Copping. London, Ward Lock, 1917.

Walking to School, illustrated by Peter Gouldthorpe. Sydney, Collins, 1988.

Other

Gum Leaves, with Oddments by Others (miscellany), illustrated by D.H. Souter. Sydney, Brooks, 1900.

Ethel Turner Birthday Book. London, Ward Lock, 1909.

PUBLICATIONS FOR ADULTS

Novels

Fair Ines. London, Hodder and Stoughton, 1910.

The Ungardeners. London, Ward Lock, 1925.

Short Stories

The Story of a Baby. London, Ward Lock, 1895.

The Little Duchess. London, Ward Lock, 1896.

Verse

Fifteen and Fair. London, Hodder and Stoughton, 1911.

Oh, Boys in Brown. Sydney, Australian Wounded Soldiers Fund, 1914.

Other

Ports and Happy Havens (travel). London, Hodder and Stoughton, 1912.

The Diaries of Ethel Turner, edited by Philippa Poole. Sydney, Ure Smith, 1979.

Editor, with Bertram Stevens, *Australian Soldiers' Gift Book.* Sydney, Voluntary Workers Association, 1918.

*

Critical Study: *Seven Little Billabongs: The World of Ethel Turner and Mary Grant Bruce* by Brenda Niall, Melbourne, Melbourne University Press, 1979.

*   *   *

In the second half of the 19th century, Australian children's literature was usually produced by English writers—most of whom had never visited the country—for English readers. With its vast size, its remoteness, its natural hazards of bush fire and flood, its resident "colorful savages," and its acquired highwaymen (bushrangers) and its gold rushes, it provided a suitably romantic setting for stereotyped but appealing adventure yarns usually about a recently-arrived English family settling into a rugged and exciting rural life free of real tension or conflict.

Ethel Turner's *Seven Little Australians* was a milestone in Australian children's literature when it appeared in 1894 because it was without precedent. It ignored the established stereotype adventure yarns, and it set a new standard of realistic family stories of the type written decades later by Eleanor Spence, Joan Phipson, and Nan Chauncy. Though born in England, Turner had lived in Australia for most of her young life. Although she wrote with an English audience in mind, the family was, without apology, Australian, and the setting was both rural and urban. The family was not the usual cosy picture of jollity and comradeship, for Captain Woolcot, without explanation, was presented as being at odds with his children, whose own mother was now dead.

The plot was concerned not with sensational action of an external kind (e.g., bushfires) but with the inner conflicts of characters, their own idiosyncrasies, and their relationships within the family. The conflict between paranoid father and high-spirited, assertive teenage daughter—leading to her ultimate death—gives *Seven Little Australians* a peculiarly modern quality. It has much of the flavor of the contemporary realistic problem novel and is as interesting and relevant as ever. For all its melodramatic aspects, and its dated style, it has a basic universality which seems bound to assure its longevity.

Feminist readers of today have even more reason to identify with Judy than did their grandparents—and greatgrandparents.

A characteristic of Turner's books is her obvious affinity with and knowledge of children—how they think, act, and feel—and her ability to create thoroughly believable child characters. Each is felt by the reader to be real, to be knowable, yet each is quite distinct and individual. They are lovable, happy, irritating, noisy, mischievous. There is usually someone with whom any young reader can identify, and the action in each story is usually vigorous enough to sustain interest throughout. The solutions to major problems—usually of misbehaviour—are melodramatic and sentimental in the spirit of the times. Death is both a constant threat and a reality in her books, and her naughty children are severely punished by wrathful adults.

Implied didacticism is very strong in Turner's books, at least as far as respectable middle-class values are concerned, with attendant rewards and punishments. Good taste and modesty are championed, the outward show of the vulgar rich being as reprehensible as the improprieties of the gutter. It therefore is natural that most of her stories deal with decent but poor families nobly struggling to attain or maintain standards of genteel decency. And because of her focus on children, and her positive belief in their basic goodness, successful family relationships are usually attained through their initiatives. They tend to rally round, to rise to the occasion, to hold the family unit together, through their innate sense of decency, fair play, unfettered humor, and a strong bond of love. Later in her career, Turner developed a strong sense of anger about social injustice and, in books such as *The Cub* and *Captain Cub*, she tried to stir the consciences of her readers, many of whom were adults, along socialist lines. Yet as early as *The Little Larrikin* she had characters rejecting the notion of rich-and-poor: "All the world ought to be respectably comfortable."

Turner's books are notable for their strong atmosphere of the benign story teller who cares for her readers. *Seven Little Australians, The Family at Misrule, Miss Bobbie*, and *The Little Larrikin* deal with the sorts of issues encountered in today's problem novels but with an exuberance and a loving concern which makes much modern writing seem clinical and heartless.

—Walter McVitty

TURNER, Philip (William). Also writes as Stephen Chance. British. Born in Rossland, British Columbia, Canada, 3 December 1925; came to England, 1926. Educated at Hinckley Grammar School, Leicestershire; Worcester College, Oxford, 1946–49, B.A. 1950, M.A. 1962; Chichester Theological College, Sussex, 1949–51, ordained priest, Church of England, 1951. Served in the Royal Naval Volunteer Reserve, 1943–46: Sub-Lieutenant. Married Margaret Diana Samson in 1950; two sons and one daughter. Anglican parish priest, St. Bartholomew's, Armley, Leeds, 1951–56, St. Peter's, Crawley, Sussex, 1956–60, and St. Matthew's, Northampton, 1962–65; head of religious broadcasting, BBC Midland Region, Birmingham, 1965–70; teacher, Droitwich High School, Worcestershire, 1970–73; chaplain, Eton College, Buckinghamshire, 1973–75. From 1975 part-time teacher, Malvern College, Worcestershire. Recipient: Library Association Carnegie Medal, 1966. Agent: Watson Little Ltd., Suite 8, 26 Charing Cross Road, London WC2H 0DG. Address: 181 West Malvern Road, Malvern, Worcestershire, England.

PUBLICATIONS FOR CHILDREN

Fiction

Colonel Sheperton's Clock, illustrated by Philip Gough. London,

Oxford University Press, 1964; Cleveland, World, 1966; as *The Mystery of the Colonel's Clock*, Aylesbury, Buckinghamshire, Goodchild, 1984.
The Grange at High Force, illustrated by William Papas. London, Oxford University Press, 1965; Cleveland, World, 1967; as *The Adventure at High Force*, Aylesbury, Buckinghamshire, Goodchild, 1984.
Sea Peril, illustrated by Ian Ribbons. London, Oxford University Press, 1966; Cleveland, World, 1968.
Steam on the Line, illustrated by Trevor Ridley. London, Oxford University Press, and Cleveland, World, 1968.
War on the Darnel, illustrated by Doreen Roberts. London, Oxford University Press, and New York, World, 1969.
Wig-wig and Homer, illustrated by Graham Humphreys. London, Oxford University Press, 1969; New York, World, 1970.
Devil's Nob. London, Hamish Hamilton, 1970; Nashville, Nelson, 1973.
Powder Quay. London, Hamish Hamilton, 1971.
Dunkirk Summer. London, Hamish Hamilton, 1973.
Skull Island. London, Dent, 1977.
Decision in the Dark: Tales of Mystery. London, Dent, 1978.
Rookoo and Bree, illustrated by Terry Riley. London, Dent, 1979.
The Candlemass Treasure. Cambridge, Lutterworth Press, 1988.

Fiction as Stephen Chance

Septimus and the Danedyke Mystery. London, Bodley Head, 1971; Nashville, Nelson, 1973.
Septimus and the Minster Ghost. London, Bodley Head, 1972; as *Septimus and the Minster Ghost Mystery*, Nashville, Nelson, 1974.
Septimus and the Stone of Offering. London, Bodley Head, 1976; as *The Stone of Offering*, Nashville, Nelson, 1977.
Septimus and the Spy Ring. London, Bodley Head, 1979.

Other

The Christmas Story: A Carol Service for Children. London, Church Information Office, 1964.
The Bible Story, illustrated by Brian Wildsmith. London, Oxford University Press, 1968; as *Illustrated Bible Stories*, New York, Watts, 1969.
The Good Shepherd (retelling), illustrated by Bunshu Iguchi. London, Dent, 1986.

PUBLICATIONS FOR ADULTS

Plays

Christ in the Concrete City (produced Hinckley, Yorkshire, 1953). London, S.P.C.K., 1956; revised edition, 1960; Boston, Baker, 1965.
Mann's End (produced Armley, Yorkshire, 1953). Included in *Tell It with Trumpets*, 1959.
Passion in Paradise Street (produced Armley, Yorkshire, 1954). Included in *Tell It with Trumpets*, 1959.
How Many Miles to Bethlehem? in *Three One-Act Plays*. London, British Council of Churches, 1957; published separately, Boston, Baker, 1986.
Cry Dawn in Dark Babylon: A Dramatic Meditation (as *Benny Death and His Old Bones*, produced Durham, 1957). London, S.P.C.K., 1959.
Tell It with Trumpets: Three Experiments in Drama and Evangelism (includes *Mann's End, Passion in Paradise Street, Six-Fifteen to Eternity*, with Jack Windross). London, S.P.C.K., 1959.

Casey: A Dramatic Meditation on the Passion (produced Crawley, Sussex, 1961).   London, S.P.C.K., 1962.
This Is the Word, and Word Made Flesh.   London, S.P.C.K., 1962.
So Long at the Fair.   Melbourne, Board of Christian Education of Australia and New Zealand, 1966.
Men in Stone.   Boston, Baker, 1966.
Cantata for Derelicts.   London, S.P.C.K., 1967.
Madonna in Concrete.   London, S.P.C.K., and Boston, Baker, 1971.
The Pantomime of Septimus Totter.   Privately printed, n.d.
Watch at the World's End.   Boston, Baker, 1980.

Other

Peter Was His Nickname.   London, Waltham Forest Books, 1965.

*

Philip Turner comments:
   It has never seemed to me that writing for children is different from writing for anyone else—except that there are some (not many) parts of adult experience that are of no interest to children because they are not yet old enough to have come across them. I write about what interests me and about what I enjoy. If other people—whether 7 or 70—enjoy it as well, that is splendid. In prose most of what I write comes out as children's stories because of the common interest in "the wonderful oddity of things." In drama I tend to get a bit long-faced and theological for the young.

*   *   *

   Philip Turner is an able but uneven writer, whose gifts have never, perhaps, been fused with complete success in a single book. Occasional failures of tone, weakening of imaginative stamina, and lapses of characterisation occur as minor blemishes in otherwise spirited and enjoyable stories. On the other hand, he has major qualities which are infrequently found in more technically consistent novelists, and lift his work far above the ordinary. Turner's lapses seem due to some uncertainty about his own role and purposes, and especially to sporadic retreat from the seriousness that his themes demand. Inopportune humour explains certain failures of psychological conviction: he has a strange technique of transferred detachment, attributing to his young characters—often at incongruous moments of intense responsibility and crisis—a wry and amused perspective on their perils which is properly the author's own. Turner is an accomplished humorist, and hilarious episodes abound in his stories of present-day adventure, but the humour sometimes jars against a more sombre prevailing mood.
   Despite the blemishes, Turner's holiday adventures are a considerable achievement. He has created his own distinctive landscape. It reaches from the little seaport of Darnley Mills, inland and up-river across a country estate, to the hill quarries and bleak open moors. Much of its length is traversed and linked by a narrow-gauge railway, which figures largely both as a focus of adventure and as an index of social history in several novels set in previous generations, and is revived in the modern adventure *War on the Darnel.* This is the setting for Turner's present-day adventures, in which three schoolboys, very different in character but close friends, play and work and grow up. *The Grange at High Force* and *War on the Darnel* are good examples of these books, which follow a similar pattern. There are comedy and high jinks, and there is also a serious crisis in which play is forgotten and the boys' responsibility tested. In *The Grange at High Force* there is much fun with the firing of an 18th-century cannon and a reconstructed Roman ballista, but there is also an appalling blizzard which sends the boys out to rescue the sheep from the high fells and a middle-aged recluse from her snow-bound

cottage. In *War on the Darnel* there is mock warfare between rival groups of Christian aid collectors, but there is also a dangerous flood in which lives are threatened. The natural rhythm of boyhood is here, in which games and horseplay and ingenious technical experiment prepare for the demands of adult life, recreation and duty can overlap at any time, and childlike pleasure be swamped by emergency. The fifth story in this sequence, *Skull Island*, is another holiday adventure but is set in unfamiliar terrain, a remote and uninhabited offshore island. For the three schoolboys, now almost grown up, the holiday journey to this isolated place marks the exploration of a widening future, while for the adults with them it is a quest or pilgrimage to the scene of long-past wartime tragedy. It forms a most effective conclusion to the series. These are good stories, full of vigorous action, but they also successfully depict Christian worship as a natural part of life, and pause at times in reverent stillness before the natural world.
   More serious, and more uniformly successful, are the books which explore the adventures of former generations in this same landscape, *Steam on the Line, Devil's Nob,* and *Powder Quay.* In these three books the changing fortunes of the little railway are the focus of wider movements of social change and historical experience. Turner admirably catches the lift and decline of lives and ways of life, of families and generations. These books have an emotional and political dimension which is missing in the present-day stories. *Devil's Nob* and *Powder Quay* both describe adolescent love, each with a moving realism, honesty, and tenderness. The books are concerned with class differences, the realities of poverty and social injustice, the harshness of economic catastrophe or war. Turner approaches these with evident discomfort and indignation: he is a traditionalist writer, affirming established values which his individual sympathies at times compel him to dispute. The result is some loss of ideological cohesion but a great gain in emotional force and complexity. The books have a manifest urgency and relevance which historical novels do not commonly achieve.
   Turner has published more sparingly in recent years, but his recent crime-and-adventure novel *The Candlemass Treasure* shows the same attractive blend of firm moral values, exciting action, and vividly realised locations, in this case East Anglia and Holy Island.
   Turner has written for younger children, notably a charming story of two runaway piglets, *Wig-wig and Homer.* And under the name Stephen Chance he has published several stories of crime and mayhem for older readers. In *Septimus and the Danedyke Mystery* the chief character is a retired London detective who, having somewhat improbably turned country parson, finds even more improbably that his former concerns refuse to desert him. The books are an amusing and modestly successful attempt to fill in an evident gap in adolescent fiction, but they do not seriously rival the achievement of the Darnley Mills stories.

—Peter Hollindale

———

UCHIDA, Yoshiko. American. Born in Alameda, California, 24 November 1921. Educated at the University of California, Berkeley, A.B. (cum laude) 1942; Smith College, Northampton, Massachusetts (graduate fellow), M.Ed. 1944. Teacher, Japanese relocation center, Utah, 1942–43, and Frankford Friends School, Philadelphia, 1944–45; secretary, Institute of Pacific Relations, New York, 1946–47, United Student Christian Council, New York, 1947–52, and Lawrence Radiation Laboratory, University of California, Berkeley, 1957–62. Wrote series of articles on folk arts and crafts for *Nippon Times*, Tokyo, 1953–54; columnist ("Letter from San Francisco"), *Craft Horizons*, New York, 1955–64. Recipient: Ford Foundation fellowship, 1952; University of Oregon award, 1981. Address: 1685 Solano Avenue, Number 102, Berkeley, California 94707, U.S.A.

PUBLICATIONS FOR CHILDREN

Fiction

New Friends for Susan, illustrated by Henry Sugimoto.   New York, Scribner, 1951.
The Full Circle, illustrated by the author.   New York, Friendship Press, 1957.
Takao and Grandfather's Sword, illustrated by William Hutchinson.   New York, Harcourt Brace, 1958; Edinburgh, Oliver and Boyd, 1966.
The Promised Year, illustrated by William Hutchinson.   New York, Harcourt Brace, 1959.
Mik and the Prowler, illustrated by William Hutchinson.   New York, Harcourt Brace, 1960.
Rokubei and the Thousand Rice Bowls, illustrated by Kazue Mizumura.   New York, Scribner, 1962.
The Forever Christmas Tree, illustrated by Kazue Mizumura.   New York, Scribner, 1963.
Sumi's Prize, illustrated by Kazue Mizumura.   New York, Scribner, 1964.
Sumi's Special Happening, illustrated by Kazue Mizumura.   New York, Scribner, 1966.
In-Between Miya, illustrated by Susan Bennett.   New York, Scribner, 1967; London, Angus and Robertson, 1968.
Sumi and the Goat and the Tokyo Express, illustrated by Kazue Mizumura.   New York, Scribner, 1969.
Hisako's Mysteries, illustrated by Susan Bennett.   New York, Scribner, 1969.
Makoto, The Smallest Boy, illustrated by Akihito Shirakawa.   New York, Crowell, 1970.
Journey to Topaz, illustrated by Donald Carrick.   New York, Scribner, 1971.
Samurai of Gold Hill, illustrated by Ati Forberg.   New York, Scribner, 1972.
The Birthday Visitor, illustrated by Charles Robinson.   New York, Scribner, 1975.
The Rooster Who Understood Japanese, illustrated by Charles Robinson.   New York, Scribner, 1976.
Journey Home, illustrated by Charles Robinson.   New York, Atheneum, 1978.
A Jar of Dreams.   New York, Atheneum, 1981.
The Best Bad Thing.   New York, Atheneum, 1983.
The Happiest Ending.   New York, Atheneum, 1985.

Other

The Dancing Kettle and Other Japanese Folk Tales, illustrated by Richard Jones.   New York, Harcourt Brace, 1949.
The Magic Listening Cap: More Folk Tales from Japan, illustrated by the author.   New York, Harcourt Brace, 1955.
The Sea of Gold and Other Tales from Japan, illustrated by Marianne Yamaguchi.   New York, Scribner, 1965.
Tabi: Journey Through Time: Stories of the Japanese in America.   El Cerrito, California, Sycamore Congregational Church Board of Education, 1981.
The Two Foolish Cats (retelling), illustrated by Margot Zemach.   New York, McElderry, 1987.

PUBLICATIONS FOR ADULTS

Novel

Picture Bride.   Flagstaff, Arizona, Northland Press, 1987.

Other

We Do Not Work Alone: The Thoughts of Kanjiro Kawai.   Kyoto, Folk Art Society, 1953.
The History of Sycamore Church.   Privately printed, 1974.
Margaret de Patta (exhibition catalogue).   Oakland, California, Oakland Museum, 1976.
Desert Exile: The Uprooting of a Japanese American Family.   Seattle, University of Washington Press, 1982.

*

Manuscript Collections: University of Oregon Library, Eugene; Bancroft Library, University of California, Berkeley.

Yoshiko Uchida comments:

Because I felt I could make the best contribution by writing from my own cultural heritage, all my books have been about Japanese or Japanese-Americans. In my earlier books I wrote about Japan in the hope that American children would not only learn to understand and respect its culture, but would identify with the Japanese people as fellow human beings. Because of the growing awareness of the various ethnic groups in the United States, however, I am now writing books based on the relatively unexplored history of Japanese-Americans. I hope these books will help dispel long-existing stereotypic images and also increase among Japanese-American young people an understanding of their own history and pride in their identity. Ultimately, however, I try to write of meaningful relationships between human beings, to celebrate our common humanity.

*   *   *

Yoshiko Uchida has limited her writing to three categories related to her ethnic background, using skill in creating plot, characterization, and setting. Her familiarity with Japanese folk tales, Japanese culture, and Japanese-American society is apparent in her 30-odd books.

Her first book, *The Dancing Kettle*, adaptations of folklore she heard as a child, was very well received. *The Magic Listening Cap* was less successful, but made its way onto lists of recommended books. The author specifically states that she adapted the tales so they would be more meaningful to American children. She notes the source for each, and includes both a glossary and pronunciation guide in the books, including *The Sea of Gold*. Stories such as "New Year's Hats for the Statues" and "The Terrible Black Snake's Revenge" in *The Sea of Gold* are less familiar than tales more like those in the western tradition.

Periodic trips to Japan have made it possible for the author to write authentically about another milieu. While Old Japan is the setting for *Rokubei and the Thousand Rice Bowls*, most of the books have a contemporary theme. *Takao and Grandfather's Sword* has an intricate plot about a boy who causes a fire in his potter father's workshop and tries to make amends. Seven-year-old Sumi's adventures are told in a three-book series. The heroine of *In-Between Miya* is disgruntled as the daughter of a humble Buddhist priest and teacher, but is unsuccessful in assisting her wealthy aunt in Tokyo.

Japanese-Americans are depicted in the balance of her books. In *Journey to Topaz* the author deals with the subject of the relocation of the Japanese to Utah during World War II. The young man in *Mik and the Prowler* is more Americanized than most of her characters. Uchida's books frequently include a visitor from Japan to the United States, as in *The Promised Year*, in which Keiki visits an aunt and uncle in California, and *The Birthday Visitor* involving Rev. Okura's arrival in time for Emi's seventh birthday.

The plots are intricate, and yet sturdy. In *New Friends for Susan* the author describes a third grader's adaptation to a new school in Berkeley after an earthquake. In this first realistic story, she avoids any racial reference. Though she experienced relocation herself, Uchida uses restraint in her novels. Only in *Journey to Topaz* does she relate the agony of 11-year-old Yuri, his brother and mother, and she avoids bitterness in the telling. Even the picture book *The Rooster Who Understood Japanese* has a substantial text about the threatened pet which had to be taken away from the city.

Rounded characters abound in most of her books, emerging through both description and dialogue. Emi, in *The Birthday Visitor*, fears that the minister will spoil her celebration, but her mood changes when she discovers that he has taken off his shoes under the table. Keiko, in *The Promised Year*, adjusts to a new culture and matures when visiting her California relatives. In *Makoto, The Smallest Boy* a youngster practices and excels in painting. Assuming responsibility is a motif in *Mik and the Prowler*, as it is in *Takao and Grandfather's Sword*. The girl fails to cope with a challenge in *In-Between Miya*, but is warmly welcomed back to her community. Interrelationships among people of differing ethnic backgrounds are sketched in *The Rooster Who Understood Japanese*. In *Hisako's Mysteries* the youngster learns that her artist father is not dead, but living in Paris.

Setting emerges in both the background descriptions and in the cultural differences that Uchida describes. *Samurai of Gold Hill* is specific about the first Japanese immigrants to California in 1859. Raising carnations provides the backdrop and occasionally the impetus in *The Promised Year*. In *The Forever Christmas Tree* Japanese Takahashi yearns to celebrate a holiday he has only heard about. Respect for old age is the cultural characteristic in *Sumi's Special Happening*, in which a 90-year-old man is honored.

Uchida's books are highly successful, and have been widely recommended. The author has worked diligently in describing an ethnic group and interpreting cultural patterns as a step toward the "creating of one world."

—Karen Nelson Hoyle

UNGERER, Tomi (Jean Thomas Ungerer). French. Born in Strasbourg, 28 November 1931. Educated at the Ecole Municipale des Arts Décoratifs, Strasbourg, 1953–54. Married 1) Miriam Lancaster in 1959 (marriage dissolved); 2) Yvonne Deborah Wright in 1971; three daughters. Freelance illustrator and commercial artist; founder, Wild Oats Film Company. Individual shows: Haus am Lutzowplatz, Berlin, 1962; D'Arcy Galleries, New York, 1963; Galerie Daniel Keel, Zurich, 1969, 1972–75; Waddel Gallery, New York, 1970; Kestner Gesellschaft, Hannover, Germany, 1972; Galerie Wolfgang Gurlitt, Munich, 1972; Taxis Palais, Innsbruck, 1973; Museum des 20 Jahrhunderts, Vienna, 1973; Galerie Bloch, Innsbruck, 1975; Musée d'Art Moderne, Strasbourg, 1975; Musée des Arts Décoratifs, Paris (retrospective), 1981; Royal Festival Hall, London (retrospective), 1985; and others. Lived in the United States, 1956–71, in Canada, 1971–76, and in Ireland since 1976. Recipient: Society of Illustrators Gold Medal, 1960; *New York Times* award, for illustration, 1962, 1971, 1974; American Institute of Graphic Arts award, 1969. Commander, Order of Arts and Letters (France). Address: c/o Diogenes Verlag, Sprecherstrasse 8, CH-8032 Zurich, Switzerland.

PUBLICATIONS FOR CHILDREN (illustrated by the author)

Fiction

The Mellops Go Flying. New York, Harper, 1957; London,
Methuen, 1962.
The Mellops Go Diving for Treasure. New York, Harper, 1957.
The Mellops Strike Oil. New York, Harper, 1958.
Crictor. New York, Harper, 1958; London, Methuen, 1959.
Adelaide. New York, Harper, 1959.
Emile. New York, Harper, 1960.
Christmas Eve at the Mellops'. New York, Harper, and London, Hamish Hamilton, 1960.
Rufus. New York, Harper, 1961.
Snail, Where Are You? New York, Harper, 1962.
The Three Robbers. New York, Atheneum, and London, Methuen, 1962.
The Mellops Go Spelunking. New York and London, Harper, 1963.
Orlando the Brave Vulture. New York, Harper, 1966; London, Methuen, 1967.
Moon Man. London, Whiting and Wheaton, 1966; New York, Harper, 1967.
Zeralda's Ogre. New York, Harper, 1967; London, Bodley Head, 1970.
Basil Ratski. Zurich, Diogenes, 1967.
Ask Me a Question. New York, Harper, 1968.
The Hat. New York, Parents' Magazine Press, 1970; London, Bodley Head, 1971.
The Beast of Monsieur Racine. New York, Farrar Straus, 1971; London, Bodley Head, 1972.
I Am Papa Snap and These Are My Favorite No-Such Stories. New York, Harper, 1971; London, Methuen, 1973.
No Kiss for Mother. New York, Harper, 1973; London, Methuen, 1974.
Allumette: A Fable, with Due Respect to Hans Christian Andersen, the Grimm Brothers, and the Honorable Ambrose Bierce. New York, Parents' Magazine Press, 1974; London, Methuen, 1975.

Verse

One, Two, Where's My Shoe? New York and London, Harper, 1964.

Other

Editor, *A Storybook from Tomi Ungerer.* New York, Watts, and London, Collins, 1974.

PUBLICATIONS FOR ADULTS (drawings)

Other

Inside Marriage: Wedding Pictures. New York, Grove Press, 1960.
Horrible: An Account of the Sad Achievements of Progress. New York, Atheneum, and London, Hamish Hamilton, 1960.
Der Herzinfarkt. Zurich, Diogenes, 1962.
A Television Notebook. New York, CBS, 1963.
The Underground Sketch Book of Tomi Ungerer. New York, Viking Press, and London, Bodley Head, 1964.
The Party. New York, Paragraphic, 1966.
Fornicon. New York, Rhinoceros Press, 1969.
Portfolio. Zurich, Diogenes, 1970.
Compromises. New York, Farrar Straus, and London, Bodley Head, 1970.
The Poster Art of Tomi Ungerer, edited by Jack Rennert. New York, Darien House, 1970; London, Constable, 1973.
Der Sexmaniak. Zurich, Diogenes, 1971.
Der Spiegelmensch. Zurich, Diogenes, 1973.
Adam and Eve: A Collection of Cartoons. Zurich, Diogenes, 1974; London, Cape, 1976.

America: Zeichnungen 1956–1971. Zurich, Diogenes, 1974.
Freut Euch des Lebens. Zurich, Diogenes, 1975.
Das grosse Liederbuch. Zurich, Diogenes, 1975.
Das kleine Liederbuch. Zurich, Diogenes, 1975.
Hopp Hopp Hopp (erotica). Privately printed, 1975.
Totempole: Erotische Zeichnungen 1968–1975. Zurich, Diogenes, 1976.
Babylon. Zurich, Diogenes, 1979.
Abracadabra. Cologne, Argos Verlag, 1979.
Politricks. Zurich, Diogenes, 1980.
Der Furz. Cologne, Argos Verlag, 1980.
Symptomatics. Zurich, Diogenes, 1982.
Das Kamasutra der Frösche. Zurich, Diogenes, 1982; as *The Joy of Frogs*, London, Souvenir Press, 1984; New York, Grove Press, 1985.
Here Today—Gone Tomorrow (reportage). Zurich, Diogenes, 1983; as *Far Out Isn't Far Enough*, New York, Grove Press, and London, Methuen, 1984.
Slow Agony. Zurich, Diogenes, 1983.
1911—(erotica). Zurich, Diogenes, 1983.
Rigor Mortis. Zurich, Diogenes, 1983.
Once in a Lifetime. London, Cape, 1984.
Tomi Ungerers Frauen. Zurich, Diogenes, 1984.
Testament: A Collection of Satirical Drawings 1960–80. London, Cape, 1985.
Frisch, Frosch, Fröhlich, Frei. Zurich, Diogenes, 1985.
Warteraum. Zurich, Diogenes, 1985.
Schutzengel der Hölle. Zurich, Diogenes, 1986.
Derby. Zurich, Diogenes, 1987.

*

Manuscript Collection: Free Library, Philadelphia.

Illustrator: *The Brave Coward* by Art Buchwald, 1957; *Agee on Film* by James Agee, 1958; *Seeds and More Seeds* by Millicent E. Selsam, 1959; *Amerika für Angänger* by Paul Rothenhäusler, 1960; *The Backside of Washington* by Dick West, 1961; *Comfortable Words* by Bergen Evans, 1962; *The Book of Gambling* edited by David Newman, 1962; *Riddle Dee Dee* by Bennett Cerf, 1962; *Frédou* by Mary Stolz, 1962; *Frances Face-Maker*, 1963, and *That Pest, Jonathan*, 1970, both by William Cole, and *A Cat-Hater's Handbook*, 1963, *Beastly Boys and Ghastly Girls*, 1964, *Oh, What Nonsense!*, 1966, *A Case of the Giggles*, 1966, *What's Good for a Four-Year-Old*, 1967, *This Is Ridiculous*, 1967, *Oh, How Silly!*, 1970, *The Book of Giggles*, 1970, and *Oh, That's Ridiculous!*, 1972, all edited by Cole; *Owls and More Owls* by John Hollander, 1963; *Come into My Parlor*, 1963, and *The Too Hot to Cook Book*, 1966, both by Miriam Ungerer; *The Girls We Leave Behind*, 1963, and *The Clambake Mutiny*, 1964, both by Jerome Beatty; *Der Spottsdrossel* by Ambrose Bierce, 1963; *All about Women* edited by Saul Maloff, 1963; *Erlesene Verbrechen and Makellose Morde*, 1964; *Ein Bündel Geschichten für Lüsterne Leser*, 1967, both by Henry Slesar; *Games, Anyone?* by Robert Thomson, 1964; *Dear N.A.S.A., Please Send Me a Rocket* by Tait Trussel and Paul Hencke, 1964; *Flat Stanley* by Jeff Brown, 1964; *A Collection of French Poetry*, 1966; *Warwick's Three Bottles*, 1966, and *Cleopatra Goes Sledding*, 1968, both by André Hodeir; *Mr. Tall and Mr. Small* by Barbara Brenner, 1966; *The Donkey Ride* by Jean B. Showalter, 1967; *Nonsense Verses* by Edward Lear, 1967; *The Sorcerer's Apprentice* by Barbara Shook Hazen, 1969; *New York für Anfänger* by Herbert Feuerstein, 1969; *Der Gestohlene Bazillus* by H.G. Wells, 1969; *The Consumer in American Society* by A.W. Troelstrup, 1970; *School Life in Paris*, 1970; *Kneipenlieder* by Rainer Brambach and Frank Geerk, 1974; *Liebesdienste* by Ben Witter, 1976; *The Great Song Book* edited by Timothy John, 1978; *Heidi* retold by Rosemary Harris, 1983; *School*

Life in Paris, and Lovely Nights of Young Girls, 1984.

*   *   *

One of Tomi Ungerer's many talents is that of lending charm and appeal to various denizens of the human or animal population not generally loved or admired by the public. Among his host of unlikely animal heroes are to be found Emile the octopus, Rufus the bat, Crictor the heroic boa constrictor, the Mellops family of handsome and amiable pigs, and Orlando the brave vulture. In more or less human guise come the child-devouring ogre who is eventually humanized into marriageability by sweet Zeralda, the three grim robbers of the black capes and ominous eyes, and M. Racine's friend the peculiar looking and unidentifiable Beast, to name but a few. Each represents some form of life or fantastic order of being usually regarded as repulsive, threatening, or disgusting, yet in Ungerer's light-hearted picture stories all are transformed into the World's Valentines.

That this is so must be attributed at least in part to the winning way in which Ungerer has drawn them: it is quite impossible to think of Ungerer's text without reference to his pictures, for the two are inseparable. (When Crictor's acrobatic body forms letters of the alphabet, should the result be described as art or literature?) Pictures give point to his spare and economical prose, while his wickedly sly text underscores his pictorial wit. His work is dotted with "visual puns," a little piggy-boy has (of course) a human-shaped penny bank; Emile at the grand piano plays "La Mer" in concert style.

If Ungerer's animal and reptile heroes are almost-human creatures of fantasy, his human creations, however fantastic their adventures, are solidly down-to-earth. Young Zeralda, the ogre-tamer, has the self-possession of an Alice in Wonderland: no matter how bizarre the situation in which she finds herself, she holds firmly to the one essential principle that a hungry man (or ogre) must be fed. Her businesslike, matter-of-fact behaviour makes her a memorably charming young heroine. Little orphan Tiffany is made of the same sturdy stuff. Kidnapped by three fierce robbers, she remains poised and in control of the situation. Her reasonable inquiries as to the purpose of their activities lead the robbers to reconsider their antisocial behaviour and become philanthropists. Allumette, the ragged match girl suddenly deluged by inexplicable treasure from the sky, is not stunned by the situation as we should be: she immediately opens a welfare office in order to distribute largess in an orderly fashion. Their unruffled, reasonable behavior is the secret of Ungerer's little people's charm. He can take a tired old theme, give it a twist no-one else could have dreamt of—and the end result is both unpredictable and somehow inevitable and satisfying. Ungerer's is an unprejudiced eye, able to discover admirable qualities in unlikely places, and, better still, he is able to make his readers do the same.

—Joan McGrath

———

UPTON, Bertha (Hudson). American. Born in 1849. *Died in 1912.*

PUBLICATIONS FOR CHILDREN (illustrated by Florence K. Upton)

Verse

The Adventures of Two Dutch Dolls—and a Golliwogg (published anonymously). London and New York, Longman, 1895.

The Golliwogg's Bicycle Club. London and New York, Longman, 1896.
The Vege-Men's Revenge. London and New York, Longman, 1897.
Little Hearts. London, Routledge, 1897.
The Golliwogg at the Sea-side. London and New York, Longman, 1898.
The Golliwogg in War! London and New York, Longman, 1899.
The Golliwogg's Polar Adventures. London and New York, Longman, 1900.
The Golliwogg's Auto-Go-Cart. London and New York, Longman, 1901.
The Golliwogg's Air-Ship. London and New York, Longman, 1902.
The Golliwogg's Circus. London and New York, Longman, 1903.
The Golliwogg in Holland. London and New York, Longman, 1904.
The Golliwogg's Fox-Hunt. London and New York, Longman, 1905.
The Golliwogg's Desert Island. London and New York, Longman, 1906.
The Golliwogg's Christmas. London and New York, Longman, 1907.
Golliwogg in the African Jungle. London and New York, Longman, 1909.

*   *   *

With the publication in 1895 of *The Adventures of Two Dutch Dolls*, two American women launched a career in children's book writing and illustrating that was to have a lasting effect on the content and format of children's literature for many years. The women were Bertha Upton and her daughter Florence; their works, because the family resided predominately in England after 1893, were published in Great Britain; and the main character of most of their works, the Golliwogg, has gone down in the annals of children's literature as a vastly sympathetic, active, and interesting example of a fantasy character who achieved a considerable degree of reality in the minds of its child audience. Bertha Upton wrote the text for the Golliwogg books and Florence illustrated them using mid- and late-Victorian dolls as models for the characters. The texts of the books in the Golliwogg series are consistently lively, well thought out episodes concerning the activities of the Golliwogg and (eventually) five Dutch dolls, Peg, Weg, Meg, Sarah Jane, and the diminutive Midget. Typical of the movement of the patterned verse in this series is the following inductive stanza from *The Adventures of Two Dutch Dolls—and a Golliwogg*:

Get up! get up, dear Sarah Jane!
Now strikes the midnight hour,
When dolls and toys
Taste human joys,
And revel in their power.

The narrative verse is rarely characterized by enjambment, yet the flow of the lines, the spontaneity of the ideas and characters, and the short syllabic value of the words allows for rapid reading of the verse and equally rapid assimilation of the ideas and images.

It would be difficult to calculate the overall influence of the Golliwogg books on future works such as Rachel Field's *Hitty, Her First Hundred Years*, and there are numerous earlier analogues for the Golliwogg. The Golliwogg series, as a whole, exhibits a picaresque pattern without the satire. The adventures are widely diversified, showing the Golliwogg's experiences at the sea side, in Holland, on a desert island, in war, in the African Jungle, and so forth, and in all the episodes Upton maintains the strong sense of realism

so necessary to good fantasy.

—Rachel Fordyce

————

URE, Jean. Also writes as Sarah McCulloch. British. Born 1 January 1943. Educated at Croydon High School, Surrey, 1954–60; Webber-Douglas Academy of Dramatic Art, London, 1966–68. Married Leonard Gregory in 1967. Since 1968 full-time writer. Agent: Maggie Noach Agency, 21 Redan Street, London W14 0AB. Address: 88 Southbridge Road, Croydon CRO 1AF, Surrey, England.

PUBLICATIONS FOR CHILDREN

Fiction

Dance for Two, illustrated by Richard Kennedy. London, Harrap, 1960; as *Ballet Dance for Two*, New York, Watts, 1960.
See You Thursday. London, Kestrel, 1981; New York, Delacorte Press, 1983.
If It Weren't for Sebastian. London, Bodley Head, 1982; New York, Delacorte Press, 1985.
A Proper Little Nooryeff. London, Bodley Head, 1982; as *What If They Saw Me Now?*, New York, Delacorte Press, 1982.
Hi There, Supermouse!, illustrated by Martin White. London, Hutchinson, 1983; as *Supermouse*, New York, Morrow, 1984.
The You-Two, illustrated by Martin White. London, Hutchinson, and New York, Morrow, 1984.
You Win Some, You Lose Some. London, Bodley Head, and New York, Delacorte Press, 1984.
After Thursday. London, Viking Kestrel, and New York, Delacorte Press, 1985.
Megastar. London, Blackie, 1985.
Nicola Mimosa, illustrated by Martin White. London, Hutchinson, 1985; as *The Most Important Thing*, New York, Morrow, 1986.
A Bottled Cherry Angel. London, Hutchinson, 1986.
Brenda the Bold, illustrated by Glenys Ambrus. London, Heinemann, 1986.
The Other Side of the Fence. London, Bodley Head, 1986; New York, Delacorte Press, 1988.
Swings and Roundabouts. London, Blackie, 1986.
The Fright, illustrated by Beverley Lees. London, Orchard, 1987.
One Green Leaf. London, Bodley Head, 1987; New York, Delacorte Press, 1989.
Tea-Leaf on the Roof, illustrated by Val Sassoon. London, Blackie, 1987.
War with Old Mouldy!, illustrated by Alice Englander. London, Methuen, 1987.
Who's Talking?, illustrated by Beverley Lees. London, Orchard, 1987.
Frankie's Dad. London, Hutchinson, 1988.
Loud Mouth, illustrated by Lynne Willey. London, Orchard, 1988.
Soppy Birthday, illustrated by Beverley Lees. London, Orchard, 1988.
Trouble with Vanessa. London, Corgi, 1988.
A Muddy Kind of Magic, illustrated by Michael Lewis. London, Blackie, 1988.
There's Always Danny. London, Corgi, 1988.
Two Men in a Boat, illustrated by Michael Lewis. London, Blackie, 1988.
Plague 1990. London, Methuen, 1989.

PUBLICATIONS FOR ADULTS

Novels

The Other Theatre. London, Corgi, 1965.

The Test of Love. London, Corgi, 1968.
Had We but World Enough and Time. London, Corgi, 1972.
If You Speak Love. London, Corgi, 1972.
The Farther Off from England. London, Corgi, 1973.
Daybreak. London, Corgi, 1974.
All Thy Love. London, Corgi, 1975.
Marriage of True Minds. London, Corgi, 1975.
Hear No Evil. London, Corgi, 1976.
No Precious Time. London, Corgi, 1976.
All in a Summer Season. London, Corgi, 1977.
Early Stages. London, Corgi, 1977.
Bid Time Return. London, Corgi, 1978.
Curtain Fall. London, Corgi, 1978.
Dress Rehearsal. London, Corgi, 1978.
A Girl Like That. London, Corgi, 1979.
Masquerade. London, Corgi, 1979.

Novels as Sarah McCulloch

Not Quite a Lady. London, Corgi, 1980; New York, Fawcett, 1981.
A Lady for Ludovic. London, Corgi, 1981.
A Most Insistent Lady. London, Corgi, 1981.
Merely a Gentleman. London, Corgi, 1982.
A Perfect Gentleman. London, Corgi, 1982.

Other

Translator, *City of a Thousand Drums,* by Henri Vernes. London, Corgi, 1966.
Translator, *The Dinosaur Hunters,* by Henri Vernes. London, Corgi, 1966.
Translator, *The Yellow Shadow,* by Henri Vernes. London, Corgi, 1966.
Translator, *Cold Spell,* by Jean Bruce. London, Corgi, 1967.
Translator, *Top Secret,* by Jean Bruce. London, Corgi, 1967.
Translator, *Treasure of the Golcondas,* by Henri Vernes. London, Corgi, 1967.
Translator, *The White Gorilla,* by Henri Vernes. London, Corgi, 1967.
Translator, *Operation Parrot,* by Henri Vernes. London, Corgi, 1968.
Translator, *Strip Tease,* by Jean Bruce. London, Corgi, 1968.
Translator, *The Snare,* by Noel Calef. London, Souvenir Press, 1969.
Translator, *March Battalion,* by Sven Hassel. London, Corgi, 1970.
Translator, *Assignment Gestapo,* by Sven Hassel. London, Corgi, 1971.
Translator, *Hitler's Plot to Kill the Big Three,* by László Havas. London, Corgi, 1971.
Translator, *SS General,* by Sven Hassel. London, Corgi, 1972.
Translator, *Reign of Hell,* by Sven Hassel. London, Corgi, 1973.

*

Jean Ure comments:

I write books for my own amusement but in the hope that they will entertain and stimulate others and unlock for at least a few the door that leads to a lifetime's emotional and intellectual sustenance.

*   *   *

A Proper Little Nooryeff, although not Jean Ure's first book, was the first to draw serious critical attention to her work. Seizing upon the stereotyped ballet story, she reversed its formula, and made a reluctant boy dancer her central character. Jamie's only connection with the local ballet school has been to collect his younger sister from her classes. Unexpectedly, the ballet teacher commandeers him to partner the school's star, Anita, in the annual show, and he finds he possesses a natural talent for dancing. The book amusingly charts his difficulties in coming to terms with the ballet world, which simultaneously embarrasses, bores, and yet thrills him. Anita, the single-minded balletomane, is something of a stock character. The book's achievement is to present Jamie, distracted by school, cricket, and girls, so convincingly that the reader both swallows his inherently improbable success and believes in his future as a second Nureyev.

Stage-trained herself, Ure enjoys writing about ballet and theatre; but she seldom indulges in slushy wish-fulfilment. Jamie's triumph apart, she is a realist, not a romantic. Show business is hard. If stardom comes, it may well be, as in *Hi There, Supermouse!,* through the egotism of a pushy girl who elbows her more talented sister out of the way. But stardom is rare. Jason of *Megastar* and *Swings and Roundabouts* is talented too but he learns to be grateful for a small part in a road safety film.

What interests Ure most is observing her characters in situations which demand courage, adaptability, and good humour. One of her best stories for 10 to 12-year-olds, *The You-Two,* exemplifies this. Elizabeth is obliged, by her father's redundancy, to move from a sheltered private school to a large comprehensive. Polite, law-abiding and academic, Elizabeth could easily have come across as the snob her classmates label her. But the adroit presentation of character, through lively dialogue and small, well-chosen incidents, ensures that both Elizabeth and the rough and ready members of 1C engage the reader's sympathy. This is a topical situation, realistically treated, and yet ending with a generous gesture by Elizabeth, close in spirit to the codes of honour of old-fashioned school stories, which brings this very modern book to a moving climax.

The You-Two boldly attacks the issue of class. Ure tackled it earlier, with the relationship between Jamie and Anita in *A Proper Little Nooryeff,* and she returns to it in her teenage novel *The Other Side of the Fence.* Class is one of those problems calling for courage, adaptability, and good humour which Ure relishes, and she convincingly shows her characters learning from their experiences. Various other problems are posed in her teenage novels, and faced by a range of independent, even eccentric, heroines. For Marianne in *See You Thursday* the problem is first no boyfriend, and then love for a blind man; for Maggie in *If It Weren't for Sebastian* a boyfriend heading for a mental breakdown; while in *One Green Leaf* three close friends try to cope with the terminal illness of a fourth. Gestures of acknowledgement are made towards feminism; but, despite their strong heroines, these are not truly feminist books. The girls' lives revolve round their boyfriends, whom they mother, as well as love, when they are maimed.

Novels for teenagers can wallow in the gloomier sides of life; but though Ure includes broken homes and unsympathetic parents, she never falls into this trap. Her books are lively and fast-moving, sweeping the reader along. She delights in words, and uses them well, especially in her sharp, slangy dialogue, sprinkled with ribaldry, and up-to-the-minute jargon. They are books for the present, flavoured with topical allusions, from vegetarianism to squats. And, naturally, sex. It is in her attitude to sex that Ure is at her most feminist. Girls can, and usually do, rebuff over-eager males, in a "no nonsense" way, although some allowance is made for genuine romantic love. Typical is the amusing story Ure makes in *You Win Some, You Lose Some,* out of the amorous misadventures of the boy dancer Jamie.

There is one discordant note, when the hero's homosexuality is revealed in *The Other Side of the Fence.* Jan, Richard's supposed girlfriend, proves, in the last pages, to be Jan, his Polish male lover; and the implications behind this unexpected disclosure seem out of scale with the lightness of Ure's style. There is a sense, too, of being cheated, when the problem appears so late in the book; as if, for once,

Ure has shied away from reality. Perhaps she will confront the problem in some later book; and meanwhile one flaw can hardly dent the reputation of this prolific and popular writer.

—Angela Bull

————

UTTLEY, Alison (Alice Jane Uttley, née Taylor). British. Born in Cromford, Derbyshire, 17 December 1884. Educated at Lady Manners School, Bakewell, Derbyshire; Manchester University, B.Sc. (honours) in physics, 1906; Cambridge University, 1907. Married James A. Uttley in 1911 (died 1930); one son. Science teacher, Fulham Secondary School for Girls, London, 1908–11. Litt.D: Manchester University, 1970. *Died 7 May 1976.*

PUBLICATIONS FOR CHILDREN

Fiction

The Squirrel, The Hare, and the Little Grey Rabbit, illustrated by Margaret Tempest. London, Heinemann, 1929.
How Little Grey Rabbit Got Back Her Tail, illustrated by Margaret Tempest. London, Heinemann, 1930.
The Great Adventure of Hare, illustrated by Margaret Tempest. London, Heinemann, 1931.
Moonshine and Magic, illustrated by Will Townsend. London, Faber, 1932.
The Story of Fuzzypeg the Hedgehog, illustrated by Margaret Tempest. London, Heinemann, 1932.
Squirrel Goes Skating, illustrated by Margaret Tempest. London, Collins, 1934.
Wise Owl's Story, illustrated by Margaret Tempest. London, Collins, 1935.
The Adventures of Peter and Judy in Bunnyland, illustrated by L. Young. London, Collins, 1935.
Candlelight Tales, illustrated by Elinor Bellingham-Smith. London, Faber, 1936.
Little Grey Rabbit's Party, illustrated by Margaret Tempest. London, Collins, 1936.
The Knot Squirrel Tied, illustrated by Margaret Tempest. London, Collins, 1937.
The Adventures of No Ordinary Rabbit, illustrated by Alec Buckels. London, Faber, 1937.
Mustard, Pepper, and Salt, illustrated by Gwen Raverat. London, Faber, 1938.
Fuzzypeg Goes to School, illustrated by Margaret Tempest. London, Collins, 1938.
A Traveller in Time. London, Faber, 1939; New York, Putnam, 1940.
Tales of the Four Pigs and Brock the Badger, illustrated by Alec Buckels. London, Faber, 1939.
Little Grey Rabbit's Christmas, illustrated by Margaret Tempest. London, Collins, 1939.
Moldy Warp, The Mole, illustrated by Margaret Tempest. London, Collins, 1940.
The Adventures of Sam Pig, illustrated by Francis Gower. London, Faber, 1940.
Sam Pig Goes to Market, illustrated by A.E. Kennedy. London, Faber, 1941.
Six Tales of Brock the Badger, illustrated by Alec Buckels and Francis Gower. London, Faber, 1941.
Six Tales of Sam Pig, illustrated by Alec Buckels and Francis Gower. London, Faber, 1941.
Six Tales of the Four Pigs, illustrated by Alec Buckels. London, Faber, 1941.
Ten Tales of Tim Rabbit, illustrated by Alec Buckels and Francis Gower. London, Faber, 1941.
Hare Joins the Home Guard, illustrated by Margaret Tempest. London, Collins, 1942.
Little Grey Rabbit's Washing-Day, illustrated by Margaret Tempest. London, Collins, 1942.
Nine Starlight Tales, illustrated by Irene Hawkins. London, Faber, 1942.
Sam Pig and Sally, illustrated by A.E. Kennedy. London, Faber, 1942.
Cuckoo Cherry-Tree, illustrated by Irene Hawkins. London, Faber, 1943.
Sam Pig at the Circus, illustrated by A.E. Kennedy. London, Faber, 1943.
Water-Rat's Picnic, illustrated by Margaret Tempest. London, Collins, 1943.
Little Grey Rabbit's Birthday, illustrated by Margaret Tempest. London, Collins, 1944.
The Spice Woman's Basket and Other Tales, illustrated by Irene Hawkins. London, Faber, 1944.
Mrs. Nimble and Mr. Bumble, illustrated by Horace Knowles. London, James, 1944.
Some Moonshine Tales, illustrated by Sarah Nechamkin. London, Faber, 1945.
The Adventures of Tim Rabbit, illustrated by A.E. Kennedy. London, Faber, 1945.
The Weather Cock and Other Stories, illustrated by Nancy Innes. London, Faber, 1945.
The Speckledy Hen, illustrated by Margaret Tempest. London, Faber, 1946.
Little Grey Rabbit and the Weasels, illustrated by Margaret Tempest. London, Collins, 1947.
Grey Rabbit and the Wandering Hedgehog, illustrated by Margaret Tempest. London, Collins, 1948.
John Barleycorn: Twelve Tales of Fairy and Magic, illustrated by Philip Hepworth. London, Faber, 1948.
Sam Pig in Trouble, illustrated by A.E. Kennedy. London, Faber, 1948.
The Cobbler's Shop and Other Tales, illustrated by Irene Hawkins. London, Faber, 1950.
Macduff, illustrated by A.E. Kennedy. London, Faber, 1950.
Little Grey Rabbit Makes Lace, illustrated by Margaret Tempest. London, Collins, 1950.
The Little Brown Mouse Books (*Snug and Serena Meet a Queen, Snug and Serena Pick Cowslips, Going to the Fair, Toad's Castle, Mrs. Mouse Spring-Cleans, Christmas at the Rose and Crown, The Gypsy Hedgehogs, Snug and the Chimney-Sweeper, The Mouse Telegrams, The Flower Show, Snug and the Silver Spoon, Mr. Stoat Walks In*), illustrated by Katherine Wigglesworth. London, Heinemann, 12 vols., 1950–57.
Yours Ever, Sam Pig, illustrated by A.E. Kennedy. London, Faber, 1951.
Hare and the Easter Eggs, illustrated by Margaret Tempest. London, Collins, 1952.
Little Grey Rabbit Goes to Sea, illustrated by Margaret Tempest. London, Collins, 1954.
Little Red Fox and the Wicked Uncle, illustrated by Katherine Wigglesworth. London, Heinemann, 1954; Indianapolis, Bobbs Merrill, 1962.
Sam Pig and the Singing Gate, illustrated by A.E. Kennedy. London, Faber, 1955.
Hare and Guy Fawkes, illustrated by Margaret Tempest. London, Collins, 1956.

Little Red Fox and Cinderella, illustrated by Katherine Wigglesworth. London, Heinemann, 1956.

Magic in My Pocket: A Selection of Tales, illustrated by Judith Brook. London, Penguin, 1957.

Little Grey Rabbit's Paint-Box, illustrated by Margaret Tempest. London, Collins, 1958.

Little Grey Rabbit and the Magic Moon, illustrated by Katherine Wigglesworth. London, Heinemann, 1958.

Snug and Serena Count Twelve, illustrated by Katherine Wigglesworth. London, Heinemann, 1959; Indianapolis, Bobbs Merrill, 1962.

Tim Rabbit and Company, illustrated by A.E. Kennedy. London, Faber, 1959.

Sam Pig Goes to the Seaside: Sixteen Stories, illustrated by A.E. Kennedy. London, Faber, 1960.

Grey Rabbit Finds a Shoe, illustrated by Margaret Tempest. London, Collins, 1960.

John at the Old Farm, illustrated by Jennifer Miles. London, Heinemann, 1960.

Grey Rabbit and the Circus, illustrated by Margaret Tempest. London, Collins, 1961.

Snug and Serena Go to Town, illustrated by Katherine Wigglesworth. London, Heinemann, 1961; Indianapolis, Bobbs Merrill, 1963.

Little Red Fox and the Unicorn, illustrated by Katherine Wigglesworth. London, Heinemann, 1962.

The Little Knife Who Did All the Work: Twelve Tales of Magic, illustrated by Pauline Baynes. London, Faber, 1962.

Grey Rabbit's May Day, illustrated by Margaret Tempest. London, Collins, 1963.

Tim Rabbit's Dozen, illustrated by Shirley Hughes. London, Faber, 1964.

Hare Goes Shopping, illustrated by Margaret Tempest. London, Collins, 1965.

The Sam Pig Storybook, illustrated by Cecil Leslie. London, Faber, 1965.

The Mouse, The Rabbit, and the Little White Hen, illustrated by Jennie Corbett. London, Heinemann, 1966.

Enchantment, illustrated by Jennie Corbett. London, Heinemann, 1966.

Little Grey Rabbit's Pancake Day, illustrated by Margaret Tempest. London, Collins, 1967.

The Little Red Fox and the Big Big Tree, illustrated by Jennie Corbett. London, Heinemann, 1968.

Little Grey Rabbit Goes to the North Pole, illustrated by Katherine Wigglesworth. London, Collins, 1970.

Lavender Shoes: Eight Tales of Enchantment, illustrated by Janina Ede. London, Faber, 1970.

The Brown Mouse Book: Magical Tales of Two Little Mice, illustrated by Katherine Wigglesworth. London, Heinemann, 1971.

Fuzzypeg's Brother, illustrated by Katherine Wigglesworth. London, Heinemann, 1971.

Little Grey Rabbit's Spring Cleaning Party, illustrated by Katherine Wigglesworth. London, Collins, 1972.

Little Grey Rabbit and the Snow-Baby, illustrated by Katherine Wigglesworth. London, Collins, 1973.

Fairy Tales, edited by Kathleen Lines, illustrated by Ann Strugnell. London, Faber, 1975.

Hare and the Rainbow, illustrated by Katherine Wigglesworth. London, Collins, 1975.

Stories for Christmas, edited by Kathleen Lines, illustrated by Gavin Rowe. London, Faber, 1977.

From Spring to Spring: Stories of the Four Seasons, edited by Kathleen Lines, illustrated by Shirley Hughes. London, Faber, 1978.

Foxglove Tales, edited by Lucy Meredith, illustrated by Shirley Felts. London, Faber, 1984.

Plays

Little Grey Rabbit to the Rescue, illustrated by Margaret Tempest. London, Collins, 1946.

The Washerwoman's Child: A Play on the Life and Stories of Hans Christian Andersen, illustrated by Irene Hawkins. London, Faber, 1946.

Three Little Grey Rabbit Plays (includes *Grey Rabbit's Hospital, The Robber, A Christmas Story*). London, Heinemann, 1961.

PUBLICATIONS FOR ADULTS

Novels

High Meadows. London, Faber, 1938.
When All Is Done. London, Faber, 1945.

Other

The Country Child. London, Faber, and New York, Macmillan, 1931.
Ambush of Young Days. London, Faber, 1937.
The Farm on the Hill. London, Faber, 1941.
Country Hoard. London, Faber, 1943.
Country Things. London, Faber, 1946.
Carts and Candlesticks. London, Faber, 1948.
Buckinghamshire. London, Faber, 1950.
Plowmen's Clocks. London, Faber, 1952.
The Stuff of Dreams. London, Faber, 1953.
Here's a New Day. London, Faber, 1956.
A Year in the Country. London, Faber, 1957.
The Swans Fly Over. London, Faber, 1959.
Something for Nothing. London, Faber, 1960.
Wild Honey. London, Faber, 1962.
Cuckoo in June. London, Faber, 1964.
A Peck of Gold. London, Faber, 1966.
Recipes from an Old Farmhouse. London, Faber, 1966.
The Button Box and Other Essays. London, Faber, 1968.
A Ten O'Clock Scholar and Other Essays. London, Faber, 1970.
Secret Places and Other Essays. London, Faber, 1972.
Country World: Memories of Childhood, edited by Lucy Meredith. London, Faber, 1984.
Our Village: Alison Uttley's Cromford, edited by Jacqueline Mitchell. Cromford, Derbyshire, Scarthin, 1984.

Editor, *In Praise of Country Life: An Anthology*. London, Muller, 1949.

*

Manuscript Collection: Kerlan Collection, University of Minnesota, Minneapolis.

Critical Studies: *The World of Alison Uttley* by Elizabeth Saintsbury, London, Baker, 1980; *The Country Child: A Biography of Alison Uttley* by Denis Judd, London, Joseph, 1986.

* * *

Like most if not all creative writers Alison Uttley drew extensively on memories of her childhood; she found in them an inexhaustible source of inspiration and of the facts of country life that she needed to provide the right setting for her stories.

She is probably best known as the author of the Little Grey Rabbit books and there is a lot of Uttley herself in the character of Grey

Rabbit: the resourceful countrywoman, the lover of traditional customs and festivals, the sensitive observer who enjoyed all the signs and sounds and smells of the countryside. In fact in one special foreword she made the clear statement: "The country ways of Grey Rabbit were the country ways known to the author." But Grey Rabbit has her own character and so do her companions, boastful but basically kind Hare, timid and sometimes rather foolish Squirrel, and all the friends who visit them, Wise Owl, Fuzzypeg, and the rest. Uttley was fortunate in her main illustrator, Margaret Tempest, whose pictures gave visible form to the group of animal characters.

But one set of stories was by no means enough for Uttley who kept three publishers busy. More or less simultaneously with Grey Rabbit, Sam Pig came to life, with a quite separate collection of farmyard characters: Sally the mare, several other little pigs, and their knowledgeable friend Brock the Badger. Sam Pig became very popular, reflecting perhaps Uttley's experience of small boys she knew. And at about the same time Tim Rabbit appeared, "No Ordinary Rabbit," who had some rather extraordinary experiences. But this was not all. Two further groups of characters appeared later: Snug and Serena (in the Little Brown Mouse books) and Little Red Fox, who had quite a substantial series of his own.

In addition there are the charming books of fairytales. But it should not be thought that there is a clear-cut division between these and the animal stories. It is characteristic of Uttley that magic and fantasy play a part in all her writing. This element was a fundamental part of her mind and her imagination, with the result that throughout the animal stories, though they are soundly based on direct knowledge of country life, there is always the possibility that the characters will be faced with some fantastic experience which is accepted without any questioning. There is continuity between the stories about animals and the stories that can be regarded as fairytales proper, and the connection works both ways. As Kathleen Lines says in her introduction to a selection of fairytales: "The stories…reveal to the willing eye and ear, the usually unsuspected magic in the countryside and in the lives of humble village people." And Uttley herself is quoted as saying: "So each and every tale holds everyday magic, and each is connected with awareness of everyday life, where reality is made visible, and one sees what goes on with new eyes." Here is the essence of much of Uttley's writing for children.

The Washerwoman's Child is a play written round the life of Hans Andersen, introducing versions of seven of his fairytales. Hans Andersen's stories clearly had a special appeal for Uttley, as on the one hand they were often concerned with everyday things and simple people—a pair of scissors or an iron, a chimney sweep or a shepherdess—and on the other told of those traditional characters almost equally familiar to Uttley as a storyteller, such as the Snow Queen, or imaginary Princes and Princesses and Emperors. But for her these characters were often seen in a more homely setting. To quote Kathleen Lines again: "The traditional 'princess' is a beautiful country maiden, the 'prince' a fine, upstanding shepherd or farm labourer, whose rival is either a member of the fairy folk or a manifestation of some natural force."

But once, and in her most original and important work of fiction, she wrote about a real queen. The stories described above are for younger children: *A Traveller in Time* is for those who are older, perhaps particularly girls (though the book is gripping for anyone) as the protagonist is a young schoolgirl, surely Uttley herself, in spite of the fact that the heroine is called Penelope and the name Alison is given to Penelope's elder sister. Here all Uttley's skills and special qualities are seen at their best. The scene is the Derbyshire farm where she was born and brought up, but woven into this simple background is the dream world which always meant a very great deal to her: and the core of the story is the girl's journeys in time to the period when Mary Queen of Scots spent part of her imprisonment in a nearby Derbyshire manor house. The girl, Penelope, moves in fantasy, or in dream, between the farm she knows in her real

contemporary life and the 16th-century drama enacted by the Babington family in their attempts to rescue the imprisoned Queen. Anthony Babington, later to go to his death on account of the Babington plot, is the leading character in this side of the story, but it is his younger brother Francis whom Penelope specially loves with a romantic affection which seems to have caught hold of the writer herself. By the skill of her writing Uttley manages to make the story of the Babingtons and Mary Queen of Scots more "real" than the simple story of Penelope's visits to the farm. This is Uttley's finest achievement and an outstandingly imaginative work that is uniquely her own.

—Peter du Sautoy

VAN ALLSBURG, Chris.   American.   Born in Grand Rapids, Michigan, 18 June 1949. Educated at the University of Michigan, Ann Arbor, B.F.A.; Rhode Island School of Design, Providence, M.F.A. in sculpture 1974. Married Lisa Van Allsburg. Artist: numerous individual shows. Teacher of drawing and poster design, Rhode Island School of Design. Recipient (for illustration): Boston *Globe-Horn Book* award 1980; American Book award, 1982; American Library Association Caldecott Medal, 1982, 1986. Lives in Providence. Address: c/o Houghton Mifflin, 2 Park Street, Boston, Massachusetts 02108, U.S.A.

PUBLICATIONS FOR CHILDREN (illustrated by the author)

Fiction

The Garden of Abdul Gasazi.   Boston, Houghton Mifflin, 1979;
    London, Hamish Hamilton, 1981.
Jumanji.   Boston, Houghton Mifflin, 1981.
Ben's Dream.   Boston, Houghton Mifflin, 1982.
The Wreck of the Zephyr.   Boston, Houghton Mifflin, and London,
    Andersen Press, 1983.
The Mysteries of Harris Burdick.   Boston, Houghton Mifflin, 1984;
    London, Andersen Press, 1985.
The Polar Express.   Boston, Houghton Mifflin, 1985; London,
    Andersen Press, 1986.
The Stranger.   Boston, Houghton Mifflin, 1986.
The Alphabet Theater Proudly Presents the Z Was Zapped.   Boston,
    Houghton Mifflin, 1987.
Two Bad Ants.   Boston, Houghton Mifflin, 1988.

* * *

Chris Van Allsburg represents something of a phenomenon in children's literature, given his meteoric production of so many quality works over one short decade. Beginning in 1979 with the Caldecott honor book *The Garden of Abdul Gasazi*, he has created nine books in as many years—most recently, the intriguing *Two Bad Ants*. Van Allsburg's children's books seem to fall into two types: picture storybooks of a full narrative treating imaginatively tantalizing situations, and books short on text that might better be termed imagistic puzzles. For example, *The Alphabet Theater Proudly Presents the Z Was Zapped*, an alphabet book, portrays a pictorial puzzle for each letter, which is then textually solved when one turns the page: "The F was firmly Flattened," "The C was Cut to ribbons." The fate of the letters is predominantly violent yet amusing in its depiction and play upon perspective. *The Mysteries of Harris Burdick* is deliberately presented as a puzzle-within-a-puzzle; in his introduction Van Allsburg tells of a Harris Burdick who left 14 drawings with a publisher, but who failed to return with their accompanying stories. Van Allsburg proffers these drawings along with their respective titles and captions to the child "in the hope that other children will be inspired by them" to create their own stories. Brevity is all in this instance. Titles—"Under The Rug," "The Third-Floor Bedroom"—carry teasing captions—"Two weeks passed and it happened again," "It all began when someone left the window open"—reminiscent of Edward Gorey's pregnant lines. The pictures are themselves visual riddles, often portraying physical impossibilities or suggesting pictorial puns and allusions.

The puzzle aspect of these two works also appears in a more subtle fashion in his picture storybooks. *The Garden of Abdul Gasazi* conjures with the possibility that the lost dog Fritz was turned into a fowl by the mysterious neighbor, Abdul Gasazi. *Jumanji* overtly shows a puzzle in the form of the boardgame Peter and Judy find under a tree (How did it get there? Whose is it? What sort of game waits within the box?). Van Allsburg's clever premise, converting the words on the board to actual realities inside the children's home, extends the puzzle as we wonder what the next turn will bring: "Lion attacks, move back two spaces"; "Monsoon season begins, lose one turn"; "Python sneaks into camp…" An added suspense is given by the conditions of the game, for it must be played all the way through to its ending. *The Wreck of the Zephyr*, Van Allsburg's first book employing color, mystifies its narrator with the remains of a wrecked sailboat high up on the cliffs; the solution to this mystery leaves both narrator and reader wondering whether the old man has told a "tall tale" of flying ships or a variant of the truth. The same vaporous truth touches *Ben's Dream*, a visual cruise through geography and history, with its ending query: was it a dream? *The Polar Express* appears to show the boy's Christmas dream, while its jingling denouement seems to provide the tangible clue that the fantasy has some footing in fact. Finally, *The Stranger*, a tender fable personifying and con-temporizing frost, the advent of winter, gives us an amnesiac stranger as the puzzle to be solved.

The mysterious, the puzzling, the uncertain boundary between substance and smoke, reality and dream, constitute the playground of Van Allsburg's imagination and creation. Especially with such storybooks as *The Garden of Abdul Gasazi, The Wreck of the Zephyr*, and *The Polar Express*, one experiences the work as a recreation of the threshold between fact and fantasy, logic and feeling, the doubt-ing mind and affirming senses. Thus surrealism and liminality suf-fuse most of his works both in their storyline and its pictorial translation. Paradoxically, this dreamlike quality is sustained with the aid of Van Allsburg's considerable skills as an illustrator. His early artistic training and work as a sculptor are evidenced in his overall style of illustration: one that values form and curve and solidity, one that utilizes chiaroscuro like a sculpting blade, one that plays upon the apparently infinite possibilities of perspective. Not surprisingly, Van Allsburg is the only artist-illustrator to date to have won two Caldecott Medals, one for *Jumanji* and one for *The Polar Express*.

The success of Van Allsburg's children's books lies in his artistic mastery and skill as a teller of intriguing "puzzle" tales. He applies an alchemical imagination to rather mundane bits of matter (a boardgame, a geography/history lesson, ants in the sugarbowl). His storylines tend toward one simple action, though the possibilities they raise are scarcely simplistic. Likewise, characters are flat, one-dimensional means to the plot's end; narrative style is straightforward, unadorned, clean. Such characteristics suggest an affinity with the folktale and fairytale, as does the magical aura of his words and images. One is especially reminded of those tales treating a human's excursion into the fairy world: the experience is real enough at the time, then shifts like a dream upon one's return to the human world; then doubt arises as some nugget of fairy gold drops from a turned-out pocket. Van Allsburg's use of motifs such

as the journey, the quest, adventure away from or within the home—his incorporation of the mythic cosmogonic cycle, beginning and ending in familiar territory while traversing a circle of experience that leaves the initiate changed and wondering, the presence of some boon as a confirming clue of the awesome adventure—all such attributes flesh out the bare bones of plot, style, and characterization. His most successful works—*The Garden of Abdul Gasazi, Jumanji, The Wreck of the Zephyr, The Polar Express*—will endure as the products of transmuting dream and imagination. At his best, Van Allsburg gives us luminous experience.

—Joyce Thomas

———

VAN STOCKUM, Hilda (Gerarda). American. Born in Rotter-dam, Netherlands, 9 February 1908; emigrated to the United States, 1934; became citizen, 1936. Educated at Amsterdam Academy of Art; Dublin School of Art; Corcoran School of Art, Washington, D.C., 1936–37; Andre Lhote Studio, Paris. Married Ervin R. Marlin in 1932; four daughters and two sons. Art teacher in Ireland and illustrator for Browne and Nolan, publishers, Dublin, late 1920's; Montessori instructor, Child Education Foundation, New York, 1934; Instructor in Art and Creative Writing, Institute of Lifetime Learning, Washington, D.C., 1965–74. Individual shows: Painters Gallery, Dublin, 1953; Difas Gallery, Geneva, 1964; De Kuyl Gal-lery, Bilthoven, Netherlands, 1964; Venables Gallery, Washington D.C., 1974; Den Arts Gallery, Ottawa, 1974; group shows: Montreal Museum of Fine Arts, 1957; Royal Academy, London, 1961, 1977; van der Straeten Gallery, New York, 1973, and many others. Presi-dent, Children's Book Guild, Washington, D.C., 1972–74; member, Women Geographers; honorary member, Royal Hibernian Academy, 1984. Address: 8 Castle Hill, Berkhamsted, Hertfordshire, England.

PUBLICATIONS FOR CHILDREN

Fiction (illustrated by the author)

A Day on Skates. New York, Harper, 1934.
The Cottage at Bantry Bay. New York, Viking Press, 1938; Lon-don, Muller, 1946.
Francie on the Run. New York, Viking Press, 1939; London, Muller, 1941.
Kersti and Saint Nicholas. New York, Viking Press, 1940; London, Muller, 1944.
Pegeen. New York, Viking Press, 1941; London, Muller, 1944.
Andries. New York, Viking Press, 1942; London, Muller, 1946.
Gerrit and the Organ. New York, Viking Press, 1943; London, Muller, 1948.
The Mitchells. New York, Viking Press, 1945.
Canadian Summer. New York, Viking Press, 1948.
Patsy and the Pup. New York, Viking Press, 1950.
King Oberon's Forest, illustrated by Brigid Marlin. New York, Viking Press, 1957; London, Constable, 1958.
Friendly Gables. New York, Viking Press, 1960.
Little Old Bear. New York, Viking Press, 1962; London, Con-stable, 1963.
The Winged Watchman. New York, Farrar Straus, 1962; London, Constable, 1964.
Jeremy Bear. London, Constable, 1963.
Bennie and the New Baby. London, Constable, 1964.
New Baby Is Lost. London, Constable, 1964.
Mogo's Flute, illustrated by Robin Jacques. New York, Viking

Press, 1966; London, Constable, 1967.

Penengro. New York, Farrar Straus, 1972.

Rufus Round and Round, illustrated by Joanna Worth. London, Longman, 1973.

The Borrowed House. New York, Farrar Straus, 1975; London, Collins, 1977.

Verse

The Angel's Alphabet. New York, Viking Press, 1948.

Other

Translator, *Tilio, A Boy of Papua*, by Rudolf Voorhoeve, illustrated by Van Stockum. Philadelphia, Lippincott, 1937; London, Hutchinson, 1939.

Translator, *Marian and Marion*, by J.M. Selleger-Elout, illustrated by B. Midderigh-Bokhurst. New York, Viking Press, 1949.

Translator, *Corso the Donkey*, by Christina Pothast-Gimberg, illustrated by Elly van Beek. London, Constable, 1962.

Translator, *The Curse of Laguna Grande*, by Siny R. van Iterson. New York, Morrow, 1973.

Translator, *The Smugglers of Buenaventura*, by Siny R. van Iterson. New York, Morrow, 1974.

Translator, *In the Spell of the Past*, by Siny R. van Iterson. New York, Morrow, 1975.

Translator, *Bruno*, by Achim Bröger, illustrated by Ronald Himler. New York, Morrow, 1975.

Translator, *Kasimir*, by Achim Bröger. New York, Morrow, 1976.

Translator, *The Spirits of Chocamata*, by Siny R. van Iterson. New York, Morrow, 1977.

*

Manuscript Collections: de Grummond Collection, University of Southern Mississippi, Hattiesburg; May Massee Collection, Emporia State University, Kansas; Kerlan Collection, University of Minnesota, Minneapolis.

Illustrator: *Afke's Ten* by Sjoukhe Troelstra, 1936; *Beggar's Penny*, 1943, and *The Bells of Leyden Sing*, 1944, both by Catherine Coblentz; *The Burro of Barnegat Road* by Delia Goetz, 1945; *Hans Brinker* by Mary Mapes Dodge, 1946; *Little Women*, 1946, and *Little Men*, 1950, both by Louisa May Alcott; *Willow Brook Farm* by Katherine D. Christ, 1948; *The Rainbow Book of Bible Stories* edited by May Becker, 1948; *Stryd voor een molen* by Jan den Tex, 1952.

* * *

Hilda Van Stockum's childhood in Holland and Ireland and her married life in Canada and the United States are all reflected in her stories for young and older children. She focuses in her books on family life, on day-to-day tasks and concerns as well as on the extraordinary event which might bring family members together or might part them. *The Winged Watchman* concerns the Verhagen family—10-year-old Joris, his older brother Dirk Jan, their parents, and the children and young adults they take in as needed during the German occupation of Holland in World War II. Their relationships with each other, their Dutch underground neighbors, and the feared enemy are described vividly and compassionately. Human frailties and strengths in the same individual at the same time, and the horrors of war, which can last long after the truce, are all shown.

Van Stockum wrote a series of stories about the O'Sullivan family of Ireland (*The Cottage at Bantry Bay, Francie on the Run*, and *Pegeen*). The O'Sullivans consist of a Mother and Father, two responsible older children, Michael and Brigid, and two irrepressible young twins, Francie and Liam, who are always in scrapes. Francie has a club foot, and in the first book there is no money to have it cared for. In the second book it is successfully cared for, but before Francie can be discharged from the hospital he walks out, headed in the wrong direction, and enjoys weeks of great adventure over his native land before getting home again. *The Mitchells* is a warm and witty picture of family life in the United States during World War II. Van Stockum has also set stories in Canada (*Canadian Summer*) and Kenya (*Mogo's Flute*). Her own six children and their high spirits must have provided her with much material for these tales, but the finely delineated characters and social settings are her special artistic gift. She is never sentimental about the age-old conflicts between parent and child, between child and his inner self. Instead these conflicts are personalized with sharp insights, skill, and generous bits of humor.

Van Stockum has also made a contribution to English literature for children through her translations of a number of stories set in foreign lands. She is also a distinguished artist, and illustrated many of her own children's tales with delicate line drawings that add awareness and enjoyment to the books.

—Mary Lystad

———

VERNEY, (Sir) John. Second Baronet; succeeded to the baronetcy, 1959. British. Born in London, 30 September 1913. Educated at Eton College, Buckinghamshire; Christ Church, Oxford, B.A. (honours) in history 1935. Served in the North Somerset Yeomanry, Special Air Service: mentioned in despatches; Military Cross, 1944; Legion of Honour (France), 1945. Married Lucinda Musgrave in 1939; two sons (one deceased) and five daughters. Painter and illustrator: group shows at Royal Society of British Artists, London; London Group; Leicester, Redfern, and Zwemmer galleries, London. Member, Farnham Urban District Council, 1968–74. Address: The White House, Clare, Suffolk, England.

PUBLICATIONS FOR CHILDREN

Fiction

Friday's Tunnel, illustrated by the author. London, Collins, 1959; revised edition, London, Penguin, 1962; New York, Holt Rinehart, 1966.

February's Road, illustrated by the author. London, Collins, 1961; New York, Holt Rinehart, 1966.

The Mad King of Chichiboo, illustrated by the author. London, Collins, and New York, Watts, 1963.

ismo, illustrated by the author. London, Collins, 1964; New York, Holt Rinehart, 1967.

Seven Sunflower Seeds. London, Collins, 1968; New York, Holt Rinehart, 1969.

Samson's Hoard. London, Collins, 1973.

Other

Look at Houses, illustrated by the author. London, Hamish Hamilton, 1959; revised edition, London, Mayflower, 1970.

Editor, with Patricia Campbell, *Under the Sun: Stories, Poems, Articles from Elizabethan and Other Sources.* London, Constable, 1964.

PUBLICATIONS FOR ADULTS

Novels

Every Advantage. London, Collins, 1961.
Fine Day for a Picnic. London, Hodder and Stoughton, 1968.

Other

Verney Abroad, illustrated by the author. London, Collins, 1954.
Going to the Wars: A Journey in Various Directions. London, Collins, and New York, Dodd Mead, 1955.
A Dinner of Herbs (autobiographical). London, Collins, 1966.

*

Illustrator: *The Odyssey* translated by George P. Kerr, 1958; *The Trampoline* by John Pudney, 1959; *James Without Thomas*, 1959, *The Elephant War*, 1960, *To Tame a Sister*, 1961, *The Greatest Gresham*, 1962, *The Peacock House*, 1963, and *The Italian Spring*, 1964, all by Gillian Avery, and *Unforgettable Journeys*, 1965, and *School Remembered*, 1967, both edited by Avery; *Diary of an Old Man* by Chaim Bermant, 1966; *Our Friend Jennings* by Anthony Buckeridge, 1967; *The Puffin Book of Horses* edited by Susan Chitty and Anne Parry, 1975; *Travels with Lionel* by Hart Massey, 1988; *The Dodo-Pad* (annual telephone table journal).

John Verney comments:

Having six children, much of my life has been occupied with trying to amuse, and thereby educate, the young, one way or another. My novels for the young are really aimed at all who are young in heart, of whatever age. They are essentially about family life as it is affected by events in the adult world (e.g., a world crisis in *Friday's Tunnel*, a plot to assassinate President de Gaulle in *ismo*).

* * *

John Verney's chronicles of the huge Callendar family have never really achieved the runaway popular success they merit. At the back of the mind lurks the suspicion that it only needs one slight, unforseen chance and Gus Callendar, his wife, and his children, Friday, February, Gail, Barry, Des and Chrys, and Hildbrand, would become as familiar figures in the world of children's books as the Famous Five or the Secret Seven. There are drawbacks, of course; the stories are witty, literate, original, ingenious, and deserve and repay careful reading, but no other author writing for children approaches Verney's mastery in capturing the precise manner in which children become enmeshed in their parents' affairs and activities. Above all he writes naturally and can in no way be charged with that awful air of condescension that afflicts so many children's writers.

Gus Callendar, the *paterfamilias*, is a famous newspaper correspondent, a convenient career from the author's point of view in that he will be attracted in the normal course of events to odd incidents and will become closely involved in successive local, national, and even international issues. This implies in turn that his lively and likeable family are accustomed to being drawn in.

There is too an air of plausibility about each episode no matter how inherently implausible a situation really is. In *Friday's Tunnel*, for example, the action is centred round a sudden political crisis in the Mediterranean and the discovery of a very-much-in-demand mineral. The whole family find themselves inextricably bound up in this; they meet the personalities directly involved, and yet, at the end of the day, the problem is resolved in the tunnel Friday is digging in the paddock of their home on the Sussex downs. To maintain the narrative on these two levels, homely familiar Sussex and exotic Mediterranean, demands a high level of technical competence in

novel writing, to say nothing of an imperturbable aplomb.

February's Road, arguably the best in the series, concerns a new London-Portsmouth trunk road which threatens to run straight through the bottom of their garden, and in this case it is February Callendar who pits her wits against the whole complex machinery of local politics and ministerial policy. In *Seven Sunflower Seeds* it is Barry who suspects that these are somehow mixed up in simultaneous plots to "fix" the Grand National steeplechase and to edge Britain into the Common Market. And in *Samson's Hoard* they all become heavily embroiled in local elections, a treasure hunt, business deals, and conservation, when Mr. Callendar stands as Independent candidate for the council. These are recognizeable situations confronting the members of one family who perhaps because of their own individual qualities appear as old friends as their continuing saga unfolds.

—Alan Edwin Day

VINING, Elizabeth Gray. Also writes as Elizabeth Janet Gray. American. Born in Philadelphia, Pennsylvania, 6 October 1902. Educated at Bryn Mawr College, Pennsylvania, A.B. 1923; Drexel Institute of Technology (now Drexel University), Philadelphia, M.S. in library science 1926. Married Morgan Fisher Vining in 1929 (died 1933). Tutor to Crown Prince of Japan, 1946–50; vice president, Board of Trustees, 1952–71, and vice chairwoman, Board of Directors, 1952–71, Bryn Mawr College. Recipient: American Library Association Newbery Medal, 1943; Women's National Book Association Skinner award, 1954. Litt.D.: Drexel Institute, 1951; Tufts College, Medford, Massachusetts, 1952; Douglass College, Rutgers University, New Brunswick, New Jersey, 1953; Women's Medical College, Philadelphia, 1953; Lafayette College, Easton, Pennsylvania, 1956; University of North Carolina, Greensboro, 1968; L.H.D.: Russell Sage College, Troy, New York, 1952; Haverford College, Pennsylvania, 1958; Western College, Oxford, Ohio, 1959; Cedar Crest College, Allentown, Pennsylvania, 1959; Moravian College, Bethlehem, Pennsylvania, 1961; Wilmington College, New Castle, Delaware, 1962; International Christian University, Tokyo, 1966; D.Ed.: Rhode Island College of Education, Providence, 1956. Third Order of the Sacred Crown, Japan, 1950. Agent: Curtis Brown, 10 Astor Place, New York, New York 10003. Address: Kendal at Longwood, Box 194, Kennett Square, Pennsylvania 19348, U.S.A.

PUBLICATIONS FOR CHILDREN as Elizabeth Janet Gray

Fiction

Meredith's Ann, illustrated by G.B. Cutts. New York, Doubleday, and London, Heinemann, 1927.
Tangle Garden, illustrated by G.B. Cutts. New York, Doubleday, 1928.
Tilly-Tod, illustrated by Mary Hamilton Frye. New York, Doubleday, 1929.
Meggy MacIntosh, illustrated by Marguerite de Angeli. New York, Doubleday, 1930.
Jane Hope. New York, Viking Press, 1933; London, Dickson, 1935.
Beppy Marlowe of Charles Town, illustrated by Loren Barton. New York, Viking Press, 1936.
The Fair Adventure, illustrated by Alice K. Reischer. New York, Viking Press, 1940.
Adam of the Road, illustrated by Robert Lawson. New York,

Viking Press, 1942; London, A. and C. Black, 1943.

Sandy. New York, Viking Press, 1945.

The Cheerful Heart, illustrated by Kazue Mizumura. New York, Viking Press, 1959; London, Macmillan, 1961.

I Will Adventure, illustrated by Corydon Bell. New York, Viking Press, 1962; Edinburgh, Oliver and Boyd, 1964.

The Taken Girl (as Elizabeth Gray Vining). New York, Viking Press, 1972.

Other

Young Walter Scott. New York, Viking Press, 1935; London, Nelson, 1937.

Penn, illustrated by George Whitney. New York, Viking Press, 1938.

Mr. Whittier (as Elizabeth Gray Vining). New York, Viking Press, 1974.

PUBLICATIONS FOR ADULTS

Novels

The Virginia Exiles. Philadelphia, Lippincott, 1955.

Take Heed of Loving Me. Philadelphia, Lippincott, 1964; London, Davies, 1965.

I, Roberta. Philadelphia, Lippincott, 1967.

Other

The Contributions of the Quakers (as Elizabeth Janet Gray). Philadelphia, F.A. Davis, 1939.

Windows for the Crown Prince (autobiographical). Philadelphia, Lippincott, and London, Joseph, 1952.

The World in Tune. Wallingford, Pennsylvania, Pendle Hill, 1952.

Women in the Society of Friends (lecture). Greensboro, North Carolina, Guilford College, 1955.

Friend of Life: The Biography of Rufus M. Jones. Philadelphia, Lippincott, 1958; London, Joseph, 1959.

Return to Japan. Philadelphia, Lippincott, 1960; London, Joseph, 1961.

Japanese Young People Today (address). Philadelphia, Atheneum of Philadelphia, 1961.

Flora: A Biography. Philadelphia, Lippincott, 1966; as *Flora MacDonald, Her Life in the Highlands of America*, London, Bles, 1967.

William Penn, Mystic. Wallingford, Pennsylvania, Pendle Hill, 1969.

Quiet Pilgrimage (autobiography). Philadelphia, Lippincott, 1970.

The May Massee Collection: Creative Publishing for Children, with Annis Duff. Emporia, Kansas, William Allen White Library, 1972.

Being Seventy: The Measure of a Year. New York, Viking Press, 1978.

John Woolman, Quaker Saint. Philadelphia, Wider Quaker Fellowship, 1981.

A Quest There Is. Wallingford, Pennsylvania, Pendle Hill, 1982.

Editor, *Anthology with Comments.* Wallingford, Pennsylvania, Pendle Hill, 1942.

*

Manuscript Collection: Quaker Collection, Haverford College Library, Pennsylvania.

*   *   *

Elizabeth Gray Vining takes to her historical romances and novels, her biographies and family stories, a commitment to time, place, and subject. Her writing reflects a deep interest in and concern for accuracy and credible interpretation.

Penn reaches beyond the man as an historic figure. His conversion to the Quaker religion caused significant conflict with his father and impaired his career in England. Vining develops Penn's character and personality with intuitive understanding which paves the way to an understanding of his significance in early American history. Her insight into Penn as a human being, as a deep believer, gives the reader not only a picture of the man himself but also of the man as a product of his time.

There is the same spirit in *Young Walter Scott*—yet with a romantic touch. If the child is the father of the man, those indications are in the book: Scott's early years are developed with care and interest, a natural bridge to his later accomplishments. Vining's impeccable sense of history and personality permeates the book even though the romanticism effects a lesser historical document than *Penn*.

Meggy MacIntosh and *Jane Hope* have been popular historical romances. Based on the true chronicles of Flora MacDonald and the Scottish Highland clansmen in North Carolina, this facet of British and American history comes alive through Meggy MacIntosh's experiences first in England, then in America. *Jane Hope* is a story of the Civil War period in which the Southern viewpoints and sentiments are patent. Meggy and Jane are spirited heroines, real people. These period pieces are reminiscent of the style of writing acclaimed in the 1930's. *Meggy MacIntosh* remains on firm ground as an historical romance. The attitudes depicted in *Jane Hope* might be questioned today, even though they are true to the period they reflect.

Vining received the Newbery Medal for *Adam of the Road* in 1943. Her panoramic study of Chaucer's England involves the use of the five senses. Adam is important not so much as a young boy of the period but rather as a means for interpreting the historical period. What holds the book together is her style, and her use of language gives texture to the novel. *I Will Adventure* follows a pattern similar to *Adam of the Road*. Andrew, on his way to London, meets Shakespeare, and moves into his world. The reader sees Shakespeare through Andrew's young eyes, a picture somewhat different from the commonly recognized one. The author's enthusiasm for her subject gives the book its power.

Tutor to Crown Prince Akihito from 1946 to 1950, she tells of her experiences in *Windows for the Crown Prince*. Written for adults, the book offers the young reader insight into another culture. From her subsequent visits to Japan came *The Cheerful Heart*. This story of Tomi, who returns with her family after three years as evacuees in the country, is full of gentle spirit. The poignant description of her hopes and dreams adds a universal quality.

No matter what her subject is, Vining is able to identify with her characters and select the most appropriate incidents. Although her books do not always emerge as a living reality, her interpretation of her subjects and her integrity are the striking qualities in a writing career that spans more than half a century.

—Mae Durham Roger

VIORST, Judith (née Stahl). American. Born in Newark, New Jersey, 2 February 1931. Educated at Rutgers University, New Brunswick, New Jersey, B.A. in history 1952 (Phi Beta Kappa); Washington Psychoanalytic Institute, Washington, D.C., 1975–81. Married Milton Viorst in 1960; three sons. Children's book editor, New York, 1957–60; science book editor, Washington, D.C., 1960–

63; columnist, Washington Star Syndicate, 1970–72. Since 1972 columnist, *Redbook* magazine, New York. Recipient: Emmy award, for television script, 1970; Albert Einstein College of Medicine award, 1975; Christopher award, 1988. Agent: Lescher and Lescher, 67 Irving Place, New York, New York 10003. Address: 3432 Ashley Terrace N.W., Washington, D.C. 20008, U.S.A.

PUBLICATIONS FOR CHILDREN

Fiction

Sunday Morning, illustrated by Hilary Knight. New York, Harper, 1968.
I'll Fix Anthony, illustrated by Arnold Lobel. New York, Harper, 1969.
Try It Again, Sam, illustrated by Paul Galdone. New York, Lothrop, 1970.
The Tenth Good Thing about Barney, illustrated by Erik Blegvad. New York, Atheneum, 1971; London, Collins, 1972.
Alexander and the Terrible, Horrible, No Good, Very Bad Day, illustrated by Ray Cruz. New York, Atheneum, 1972; London, Angus and Robertson, 1973.
My Mama Says There Aren't Any Zombies, Ghosts, Vampires, Creatures, Demons, Monsters, Fiends, Goblins, or Things, illustrated by Kay Chorao. New York, Atheneum, 1973.
Rosie and Michael, illustrated by Lorna Tomei. New York, Atheneum, 1974.
Alexander, Who Used to Be Rich Last Sunday, illustrated by Ray Cruz. New York, Atheneum, 1978; London, Angus and Robertson, 1979.
The Good-Bye Book, illustrated by Kay Chorao. New York, Macmillan, 1988.

Verse

If I Were in Charge of the World and Other Worries: Poems for Children and Their Parents, illustrated by Lynne Cherry. New York, Atheneum, 1981.

Other

Projects: Space. New York, Washington Square Press, 1962.
150 Science Experiments Step-by-Step, illustrated by Dennis Telesford. New York, Bantam, 1963.
The Natural World: A Guide to North American Wildlife. New York, Bantam, 1965.
The Changing Earth, illustrated by Feodor Rimsky. New York, Bantam, 1967.

Editor, with Shirley Moore, *Wonderful World of Science*, illustrated by Don Trawin. New York, Bantam, 1961.

PUBLICATIONS FOR ADULTS

Verse

The Village Square. New York, Coward McCann, 1965.
It's Hard to Be Hip over Thirty and Other Tragedies of Married Life. Cleveland, World, 1968; London, Angus and Robertson, 1973.
People and Other Aggravations. New York, World, 1971; London, Angus and Robertson, 1973.
How Did I Get to Be Forty and Other Atrocities. New York, Simon

and Schuster, 1976.
A Visit from St. Nicholas (To a Liberated Household). New York, Simon and Schuster, 1977.
When Did I Stop Being Twenty and Other Injustices: Selected Poems from Single to Mid-Life. New York, Simon and Schuster, 1987.
Forever Fifty and Other Negotiations. New York, Simon and Schuster, 1989.

Other

The Washington, D.C., Underground Gourmet, with Milton Viorst. New York, Simon and Schuster, 1970.
Yes, Married: A Saga of Love and Complaint (collected prose). New York, Saturday Review Press, 1972.
Love and Guilt and the Meaning of Life, etc. New York, Simon and Schuster, 1979.
Necessary Losses. New York and London, Simon and Schuster, 1987.

* * *

Judith Viorst is a contemporary chronicler of the parental-pre-schooler-trying-to-come-to-grips-with-each-other syndrome, known all too well to adults who live and work with young children. Viorst has continuously tackled the once thought "difficult" subjects of children's emotional stress in her books for children. Her non-sexist stories, appearing in both popular periodical and in book form, contain the right balance of humor and pathos, without losing the real message or issue. This is especially true of her picture book stories, whether it be of a pet's death (*The Tenth Good Thing about Barney*), bad days (*Alexander and the Terrible, Horrible, No Good, Very Bad Day*), boy-girl friendship (*Rosie and Michael*), or night fears (*My Mama Says*).

Most of her juveniles are based on actual experiences inside her family. Her boy characters, contrary to traditional masculine roles, do not suffer the less for demonstrating affection, fears, or tears. They become all the more human because of this portrayal, instead of demonstrating bravado where none exists. This is especially seen in *The Good-Bye Book* in which a young boy fights to convince his parents not to go out for an evening, until a male babysitter appears. Her girl characters, like the boys, also run counter to societal stereotypes. They are often seen as aggressive, open, physically strong, and, at times, revengeful. Instead of losing in femininity as many fear, they actually gain in growth. Viorst has challenged traditional role models for boys and girls in her books and has challenged them unusually well.

She handles her subjects with depth and perception, never once assuming a position of guilt or opinion for any one side; instead, she brings out all points—adult and juvenile—on an issue, leading the reader to the logical and human position or action. Viorst can be viewed as a sophisticated and impartial recorder of human drama for children. In her books—adult and juvenile—no one loses; rather, everyone wins, especially the reader.

—Jim Roginski

VIPONT, Elfrida. Has also written as E.V. Foulds; Charles Vipont. British. Born in Manchester, Lancashire, 3 July 1902. Educated at Manchester High School for Girls; Mount School, York. Married Robinson Percy Foulds in 1926 (died 1954); four daughters. Headmistress, Quaker Evacuation School, Yealand Manor, Lancashire, 1939–45. Recipient: Library Association Carnegie Medal,

1951. D.H.L.: Earlham College, Richmond, Indiana, 1984. Address: Green Garth, Yealand Conyers, near Carnforth, Lancashire LA5 9SG, England.

PUBLICATIONS FOR CHILDREN

Fiction

Blow the Man Down (as Charles Vipont), illustrated by Norman Hepple. London, Oxford University Press, 1939; Philadelphia, Lippincott, 1952.
The Lark in the Morn, illustrated by T.R. Freeman. London, Oxford University Press, 1948; Indianapolis, Bobbs Merrill, 1951.
The Lark on the Wing, illustrated by T.R. Freeman. London, Oxford University Press, 1950; Indianapolis, Bobbs Merrill, 1951.
The Family at Dowbiggins, illustrated by T.R. Freeman. London, Lutterworth Press, and Indianapolis, Bobbs Merrill, 1955.
The Heir of Craigs (as Charles Vipont), illustrated by Tessa Theobald. London, Oxford University Press, 1955.
The Spring of the Year, illustrated by T.R. Freeman. London, Oxford University Press, 1957.
The Secret of Orra, illustrated by D.J. Watkins-Pitchford. Oxford, Blackwell, 1957.
More about Dowbiggins, illustrated by T.R. Freeman. London, Lutterworth Press, 1958; as *A Win for Henry Conyers*, London, Hamish Hamilton, 1968.
Changes at Dowbiggins, illustrated by T.R. Freeman. London, Lutterworth Press, 1960; as *Boggarts and Dreams*, London, Hamish Hamilton, 1969.
Flowering Spring, illustrated by Shirley Hughes. London, Oxford University Press, 1960.
Search for a Song, illustrated by Peter Edwards. London, Oxford University Press, 1962.
Stevie, illustrated by Raymond Briggs. London, Hamish Hamilton, 1965.
Larry Lopkins, illustrated by Pat Marriott. London, Hamish Hamilton, 1965.
Rescue for Mittens, illustrated by Jane Paton. London, Hamish Hamilton, 1965.
The Offcomers, illustrated by Janet Duchesne. London, Hamish Hamilton, 1965; New York, McGraw Hill, 1967.
Terror by Night: A Book of Strange Stories. London, Hamish Hamilton, 1966; as *Ghosts' High Noon*, New York, Walck, 1967.
The China Dog, illustrated by Constance Marshall. London, Hamish Hamilton, 1967.
The Secret Passage, illustrated by Ian Ribbons. London, Hamish Hamilton, 1967.
The Pavilion, illustrated by Prudence Seward. London, Oxford University Press, 1969; New York, Holt Rinehart, 1970.
Michael and the Dogs, illustrated by Pat Marriott. London, Hamish Hamilton, 1969.
The Elephant and the Bad Baby, illustrated by Raymond Briggs. London, Hamish Hamilton, and New York, Coward McCann, 1969.
Children of the Mayflower, illustrated by Evadne Rowan. London, Heinemann, 1969; New York, Watts, 1970.

Plays

Radio Plays: *A True Tale*, 1952; *John Crook, Quaker*, 1954; *Kitty Wilkinson*, 1956; *Dr. Dinsdale in Russia*, 1956.

Other

Good Adventure: The Quest of Music in England, illustrated by Estella Canziani. Manchester, Heywood, 1931.
Colin Writes to Friends House, illustrated by Elisabeth Brockbank. London, Friends' Book Centre, 1934; revised edition, London, Bannisdale Press, 1946.
A Lily among Thorns: Some Passages in the Life of Margaret Fell of Swarthmoor Hall. London, Friends Home Service Committee, 1950.
Sparks among the Stubble, illustrated by Patricia Lambe. London, Oxford University Press, 1950.
Henry Purcell and His Times, illustrated by L.J. Broderick. London, Lutterworth Press, 1959.
The Story of Christianity in Britain, illustrated by Gaynor Chapman. London, Joseph, 1961.
What about Religion?, illustrated by Peter Roberson. London, Museum Press, 1961.
Some Christian Festivals. London, Joseph, 1963; New York, Roy, 1964.
Weaver of Dreams: The Girlhood of Charlotte Brontë. London, Hamish Hamilton, and New York, Walck, 1966.
A Child of the Chapel Royal, illustrated by John Lawrence. London, Oxford University Press, 1967.
Towards a High Attic: The Early Life of George Eliot. London, Hamish Hamilton, 1970; New York, Holt Rinehart, 1971.
A Little Bit of Ivory: A Life of Jane Austen. London, Hamish Hamilton, 1977.

Editor, *The High Way: An Anthology*. London, Oxford University Press, 1957.
Editor, *Bless This Day: A Book of Prayer*, illustrated by Harold Jones. London, Collins, and New York, Harcourt Brace, 1958.
Editor, *The Bridge: An Anthology*, illustrated by Trevor Brierley Lofthouse. London, Oxford University Press, 1962.

PUBLICATIONS FOR ADULTS

Novel

Bed in Hell. London, Hamish Hamilton, 1974; New York, St. Martin's Press, 1975.

Other

The Story of Quakerism 1652–1952. London, Bannisdale Press, 1954; as *The Story of Quakerism Through Three Centuries*, 1960; revised edition, Richmond, Indiana, Friends United Press, 1977.
Arnold Rowntree: A Life. London, Bannisdale Press, 1955.
Ackworth School, From Its Foundation in 1779 to the Introduction of Co-Education in 1946. London, Lutterworth Press, 1959.
A Faith to Live By. Philadelphia, Friends General Conference, 1962; as *Quakerism: A Faith to Live By*, London, Bannisdale Press, 1966.
George Fox and the Valiant Sixty. London, Hamish Hamilton, 1975.

Other as E.V. Foulds

Quakerism: An International Way of Life. Manchester, 1930 Committee, 1930.
Lift Up Your Lamps: The Pageant of a Friends' Meeting. Manchester, 1930 Committee, 1939.
The Birthplace of Quakerism: A Handbook for the 1652 Country. London, Friends Home Service Committee, 1952; revised edition, 1968, 1973, 1987.
Let Your Lives Speak: A Key to the Quaker Experience. Wallingford, Pennsylvania, Pendle Hill, 1953; London, Friends Home

Service Committee, 1954.
Living in the Kingdom.   Philadelphia, Young Friends Movement, 1955.
The Quaker Witness: Yesterday and Today.   Richmond, Indiana, Friends United Press, 1955.

*

Manuscript Collections: Kerlan Collection, University of Minnesota, Minneapolis; Lancaster Library, Lancashire.

Elfrida Vipont comments:

When people learn that I am a writer, they often ask, "What do you write?" When I reply, "Mainly books for children and young people," they say "Oh" rather sadly, as if to imply, "Poor thing, obviously she can't write for adults." Personally, I think writing for children is one of the most rewarding jobs imaginable. Lascelles Abercrombie used to speak of the "significant world"—"the world we never quite get except in art." If we do no more than offer a key to that significant world, our work will be well worth while. It is, of course, perfectly possible to offer a key to an ephemeral world instead, a world peopled by puppets in contrived situations, but most children's writers would rather fail in an attempt to create a living world, peopled by living characters, than succeed in presenting an artificial "readymix."

*   *   *

Though she has written many books, historical as well as modern, Elfrida Vipont is best known for *The Lark in the Morn*, its Carnegie Medal-winning sequel *The Lark on the Wing*, and the two other loosely connected stories *The Spring of the Year* and *Flowering Spring*, continuing the Haverard family saga. Even of these, it is the first two that enjoy a particular popularity. Perhaps they reveal the deepest feeling. For, along with their Quakerism (which pervades all Vipont's writing), they are about music, the other interest closest to her heart. She trained and performed as a professional singer, and readers are quick to recognise the authenticity of these books. Also, they broke new ground, appearing at a time when the girls' school story still mainly followed the pattern cut by Angela Brazil, and children's fiction in general was only starting that subtler exploration of emotions and relationships which is now expected of any good junior novel. Finally, *The Lark in the Morn* had the special freshness of an early work, drawing on an author's untapped reservoir of experience, rich in this case since, when the book was published, its creator was already in her mid-forties and had four daughters. The book is no flawless masterpiece, but it bids fair to survive as a classic, loved for the "naturalness and sincerity" which caused as perceptive a critic as Kathleen Lines to bracket it with *Little Women*.

If a writer should be judged by her best books, so should those books be assessed more on their excellences than on their minor blemishes. For all their originality, the *Lark* stories carry traces of the Brazilian model from which they were breaking free. There is an admired senior girl whose "mop of fair curls" and "elfin face" are mentioned more than once, and critics have justifiably deprecated the way in which characters "rap out," "explode," and otherwise deliver dialogue which is itself well written and full of character. Others have found the books a little sentimental—occasionally true, but far outweighed by the genuinely intense feeling of most passages—while others again, unsympathetic to the Quakerism, have accused them of "cultural snobbery" and "exclusiveness." These objections seem overstated but not entirely incomprehensible.

Yet when the stylistic blemishes are admitted, and it is conceded that the uncompromising moral values are unfashionable in some quarters today, there remains a memorable and moving story, full of vivid characters—especially the elder ones, with a dedicated young

heroine who involves our sympathy. If the education of the emotions is a function of the junior novel, Vipont's achievement must be rated high.

—Geoffrey Trease

———————

VOIGT, Cynthia (née Irving).   American.   Born in Boston, Massachusetts, 25 February 1942. Educated at Smith College, Northampton, Massachusetts, B.A. 1963. Married Walter Voigt in 1974 (second marriage); one daughter and one son. High school English teacher, Glen Burnie, Maryland, 1965–67. English teacher, 1968–69, department chair, 1971–79, and since 1981 part-time teacher and department chair, Key School, Annapolis, Maryland. Recipient: American Library Association Newbery Medal, 1983; Mystery Writers of America Edgar Allan Poe award, 1984. Address: The Key School, 534 Carroll Drive, Annapolis, Maryland 21403, U.S.A.

PUBLICATIONS FOR CHILDREN

Fiction

Homecoming.   New York, Atheneum, 1981; London, Collins, 1983.
Dicey's Song.   New York, Atheneum, 1982; London, Collins, 1984.
Tell Me If the Lovers Are Losers.   New York, Atheneum, 1982.
The Callender Papers.   New York, Atheneum, 1983.
A Solitary Blue.   New York, Atheneum, 1983; London, Collins, 1985.
Building Blocks.   New York, Atheneum, 1984; London, Fontana, 1988.
Jackeroo.   New York, Atheneum, 1985; London, Collins, 1988.
The Runner.   New York, Atheneum, 1985; London, Collins, 1986.
Come a Stranger.   New York, Atheneum, 1986; London, Collins, 1987.
Izzy Willy-Nilly.   New York, Atheneum, 1986; London, Collins, 1987.
Stories about Rosie.   New York, Atheneum, 1986.
Sons from Afar.   New York, Atheneum, 1987; London, Collins, 1988.
Tree by Leaf.   New York, Atheneum, 1988; London, Collins, 1989.
Seventeen Against the Dealer.   New York, Atheneum, 1989.

*   *   *

Newbery Medal winner Cynthia Voigt depicts adolescents with dignity and compassion in her impressive novels; her characters generally possess a streak of independence or self-reliance enabling them to succeed, not only in tangible endeavors, but also, and more importantly, in creating bonds of friendship and family ties despite serious hardships, such as the loss of one or both parents. The tragedy of dysfunctional families is overturned and triumphantly replaced by loving relationships. Voigt's characters, frequently outsiders initially, are fleshed out until they seem to breathe and ultimately belong in their settings.

These young-adult novels (except *Stories about Rosie*, an illustrated book for younger readers about a pet dog) vary in genre from fantasies (*Jackeroo* and *Building Blocks*), to gothic (*The Callender Papers*), to Voigt's forté, realistic contemporary (*Tell Me If the Lovers Are Losers, Izzy Willy-Nilly*, and the six novels comprising the Tillerman family "saga"). These six, spanning two generations, are set primarily in Crisfield, Maryland, just inland from the Chesapeake Bay. The four Tillerman children of the second generation—Dicey, James, Maybeth, and Sammie—travel to Maryland in *Homecoming* and are adopted by their grandmother in *Dicey's Song*; James and Sammie search for their father in *Sons from Afar*; the children's uncle "Bullet" stars in *The Runner*; and friends of Dicey, Jeff Greene and Mina Smiths, become protagonists in *A Solitary Blue* and *Come a Stranger*, respectively.

Voigt's heroes and heroines, about equal in number, vary in age from six-year-old Sammie Tillerman to the college-age young women of *Tell Me If the Lovers Are Losers*. Voigt adeptly depicts blacks as well as whites; in *The Runner* she addresses the situation of the racially troubled 1960's without mincing words, focusing in part on the prejudicial attitude of a white boy against a black teammate. Advancing a step further in *Come a Stranger* with protagonist Mina Smiths, a black girl rejected from a dance camp by an all-white group whom she has tried to emulate and from whom she expected friendship, Voigt deftly and sensitively depicts Mina's awakening to the reality of racial prejudice.

When Voigt plots her novels around other contemporary dilemmas, usually familial ones, she evokes sympathy for the characters, some who have lost parents or who feel forced to separate from their families because of intolerable home situations. The younger Tillermans, for example, when deserted by their mother in a parking lot, initiate an odyssey that leads them to their "crazy" grandmother Gran. That the group becomes a warm, loving family who grow individually by reaching out or communicating with others, even those who do not reciprocate, is a measure of the odyssey's success in spite of its inauspicious origin.

The characters, although distinct individuals, possess many similar traits. Those who suffer from separation anxiety created by a missing or too reticent parent, such as Professor Greene or Mr. Thiel, rely upon a surrogate: Dicey and then Gran provide for the younger Tillerman children; Patrice offers Bullet Tillerman work, food, and advice in *The Runner*; Brother Thomas, a close family friend, on occasion provides the affection that Jeff Greene lacks in *A Solitary Blue*; and Aunt Constance cares for the "orphaned" Jean Wainwright in *The Callender Papers*.

Voigt oversees the maturation of her youthful characters as they accept responsibility and plan future goals in the face of unsettling, often severe, obstacles, partially through her belief in the work ethic. Most learn self-reliance by assisting with family chores and by holding part-time jobs, such as working in a grocery, delivering papers, selling crabs, and babysitting. Each child capitalizes upon his abilities whether they be a gift for music, talent for academics, or ability at sports. Maybeth Tillerman, though "slow" in school, is the most musically gifted; her love of singing and piano attracts many to the Tillerman home. Her brother James is the family's academic achiever. Other characters excel at sports, such as Bullet Tillerman at running or Hildegarde Koenig in *Tell Me If the Lovers are Losers* who so capably organizes and teaches a college freshman volleyball team about unity that they beat every opponent, even the seniors. The characters' participation in a variety of sports suggests that every child can find one he will enjoy. As each individual concentrates on his own ability, he matures and becomes more well-rounded, less an outsider.

Voigt sets many novels in Crisfield where boating and crabbing along Maryland's shores provide sport, entertainment, food, and occasionally employment. A love of nature and the seashore appears side by side with a concern for protecting the environment. Even in a fantasy novel like *Building Blocks*, principally set in Pennsylvania in 1939, pollution of the Ohio River prevents children from swimming. Brann Connell, a child in 1974 who travels backward in time and befriends his own father-to-be, Kevin Connell, when Kevin was just a boy, is surprised to learn that pollution was a problem in the 1930's as well as the 1970's.

Regardless of the time period of the novels, a thread of women's liberation or independence unites them all, from the difficult-to-become-involved-in medieval fantasy *Jackeroo* where Gwyn is a type of precurser to Robin Hood, but realizes that she must abide by society's rules, to the independent thinker Jean Wainwright who fearlessly solves the intriguing, exciting mystery in *The Callender Papers*, to the high school sophomore Izzy who, with a leg amputated after an automobile accident caused by a drunk senior, subsequently learns independence and the meaning of true friendship in *Izzy Willy-Nilly*, a must read for high school students. The theme of friendship appears in many guises from racist Bullet Tillerman learning to accept that his mentor is part black in *The Runner* to Burl who dons the mask of Jackeroo to protect his friend Gwyn.

Although Voigt adopts an appropriate vocabulary and style for the imaginary medieval kingdom in *Jackeroo*, and accurately treats the settings of *The Callender Papers* in 1894 and *Building Blocks* in 1939, her greatest strength lies in characterizing contemporary high school and college students and in depicting situations, such as desertion and poverty, which plague the modern family. Her characters learn middle-class values and other lessons without overt didacticism. For example, when one character tutors another in writing about a classic, the character and the reader derive a lesson and hopefully a greater appreciation for literature.

A skilled craftsman, Voigt excels in creating characters who resonate in the reader's mind; readers eagerly approach another Voigt novel, particularly those in the Tillerman series, and recognize with approbation the narrative links and repetition of scenes, which aid in uniting the stories. For example, a scene in which Jeff Greene plays his guitar for Dicey is told from Dicey's point of view in *Dicey's Song*, but from Jeff's point of view in *A Solitary Blue*. The recognition of previously known characters and the déjà vu effect heighten the realism. Voigt's understanding of narrative techniques, power to create memorable characters, admirable but not goody-goody, knowledge of the problems of youth, and desire to teach by transporting readers into the characters' inner lives result in reversing unpromising, perhaps tragic, situations to positive, optimistic ones. Her novels make excellent reading.

—Sylvia Patterson Iskander

WABER, Bernard. American. Born in Philadelphia, Pennsylvania, 27 September 1924. Educated at the University of Pennsylvania, Philadelphia; Museum School of Fine Art, Philadelphia, 1946–50; Pennsylvania Academy of Fine Arts, Philadelphia, 1950–51. Served in the United States Army, Panama Canal Zone, 1942–45: Staff Sergeant. Married Ethel Bernstein in 1952; three children. Commercial artist, Condé Nast Publications, New York, and *Seventeen* magazine, New York, 1952–54; graphic designer, *Life* magazine, New York, 1955–72. Since 1974 graphic designer, *People* magazine, New York. Lives in Baldwin Harbor, New York. Address: c/o Houghton Mifflin, 2 Park Street, Boston, Massachusetts 02108, U.S.A.

PUBLICATIONS FOR CHILDREN (illustrated by the author)

Fiction

Lorenzo. Boston, Houghton Mifflin, 1961.
The House on East 88th Street. Boston, Houghton Mifflin, 1962; as *Welcome, Lyle*, London, Chatto Boyd and Oliver, 1969.
Rich Cat, Poor Cat. Boston, Houghton Mifflin, 1963.

How to Go About Laying an Egg. Boston, Houghton Mifflin, 1963.
Lyle, Lyle, Crocodile. Boston, Houghton Mifflin, 1965; Edinburgh, Oliver and Boyd, 1966.
Lyle and the Birthday Party. Boston, Houghton Mifflin, 1966; Edinburgh, Oliver and Boyd, 1967.
"You Look Ridiculous," Said the Rhinoceros to the Hippopotamus. Boston, Houghton Mifflin, 1966; London, Hamish Hamilton, 1967.
An Anteater Named Arthur. Boston, Houghton Mifflin, 1967; London, Chatto Boyd and Oliver, 1969.
Cheese. Boston, Houghton Mifflin, 1967.
A Rose for Mr. Bloom. Boston, Houghton Mifflin, 1968.
Lovable Lyle. Boston, Houghton Mifflin, 1969; London, Chatto Boyd and Oliver, 1970.
A Firefly Named Torchy. Boston, Houghton Mifflin, 1970.
Ira Sleeps Over. Boston, Houghton Mifflin, 1972; as *Good Night Ben*, Leicester, Brockhampton Press, 1974.
Lyle Finds His Mother. Boston, Houghton Mifflin, 1974; London, Chatto and Windus, 1976.
I Was All Thumbs. Boston, Houghton Mifflin, 1975.
But Names Will Never Hurt Me. Boston, Houghton Mifflin, 1976.
Goodbye, Funny Dumpy-Lumpy. Boston, Houghton Mifflin, 1977.
Mice on My Mind. Boston, Houghton Mifflin, 1977.
The Snake: A Very Long Story. Boston, Houghton Mifflin, 1978.
You're a Little Kid with a Big Heart. Boston, Houghton Mifflin, 1980.
Dear Hildegarde. Boston, Houghton Mifflin, 1980.
Bernard. Boston, Houghton Mifflin, 1982.
Funny, Funny Lyle. Boston, Houghton Mifflin, 1987.
Ira Says Goodbye. Boston, Houghton Mifflin, 1988.

Other

Just Like Abraham Lincoln. Boston, Houghton Mifflin, 1964.
Nobody Is Perfick (cartoons). Boston, Houghton Mifflin, 1971; London, Angus and Robertson, 1973.

*

Manuscript Collection: Kerlan Collection, University of Minnesota, Minneapolis.

Bernard Waber comments:

My involvement with children's books originated with some illustrations of children I carried in my art portfolio. Several art directors suggested that my drawings seemed suited for children's books. At the same time, I was also having read-aloud sessions with my own three children. I am afraid my enthusiasm for "their" books began, in fact, to cause them occasional discomfort. "Daddy, why don't you look at the grown-ups' books," they once chided as I trailed after them into the children's room of our local library. Before long I was mailing out stories and ideas to publishers. Rejections followed, but after a time cheery encouragement arrived from Houghton Mifflin Company, and to my delight a contract was offered for *Lorenzo*.

*   *   *

Bernard Waber infuses his work with warmth, a freshness of style, and a disarmingly ready wit. He is equally capable in the realms of fantasy and reality. Most amusing are the adventures involving Lyle, an endearing and whimsical crocodile, who materializes in a bathtub in *The House on East 88th Street*. With aplomb and dazzling showmanship, Lyle entertains and enchants the inhabitants, the Primms. In *Lyle, Lyle, Crocodile*, his removal to the local zoo is orchestrated by the irascible Mr. Grumps and his terrified cat, Loretta. Hector P.

Valenti ensnares Lyle and lures him away on a money-making scheme in *Lyle Finds his Mother*. Lyle prevails and finally reunites with his mother. Laughter and humor abound coupled with a fast pace, ridiculous antics, and the casual acceptance of the crocodiles' absurd and preposterous existence. Text and illustrations merge dynamically to balance fantasy with the exploration of feelings and relationships. Culminating the series, *Funny, Funny Lyle* spotlights Lyle's relationship with his mother as he shares in her adventures.

Similarly, *An Anteater Named Arthur* is a charming and delightful look at a mother and son relationship with a slightly different slant. Using a conversational format in five short tableaux, Waber gently pokes fun at the inherent problems in their relationship. Reading it aloud heightens audience enjoyment and appreciation. Contrasting his fantasy, *Just Like Abraham Lincoln* is an attempt to enliven biography. Mr. Potts, a modern look-alike, relates anecdotes and stories which labor in parts where the similarities between Potts and Lincoln seem overdrawn.

Ira Sleeps Over captures the mood of a little boy wrestling with the decision to take his teddy bear on his overnight adventure to his friend Reggie's house. The story is an insightful probe into the ambivalence this attachment represents. The sibling rivalry and indecision build to a climax through his faithful reproduction of children's jibes, taunts, and harassing remarks. Magically, Ira and the reader seem to reach a decision together. A gentle touch of irony is revealed by the disclosure that Reggie lives next door. *Ira Says Goodbye* draws Ira and Reggie together in the trauma of best friends saying goodbye. Reggie is moving, and Waber deftly enables the reader to feel the impact. The conversations and illustrations mesh, drawing us into the mood to share the moment with Ira and Reggie.

But Names Will Never Hurt Me is amusing but slight, lacking the impact and involvement of the Ira series. Alison Wonderland resents her name. Some of the force of her discomfort is lost on an audience too young to appreciate the significance. The word play is more successful in *Nobody is Perfick* and *A Rose for Mr. Bloom. The Snake* is a rare disappointment, combining an overdrawn story with a tiresome moral in an easy reader. *Dear Hildegarde* blends humorous puns and a unique comical style with sage advice and owlish wisdom. *Bernard* is amusingly effective at portraying a dog's perspective on his fate, resulting from his owners' separation and property split.

—Martha J. Fick

_____

WADDELL, Martin. Also writes as Catherine Sefton. Irish. Born in Belfast, Northern Ireland, 10 April 1941. Educated in primary and secondary schools. Married Rosaleen Carragher in 1969; three sons. Recipient: Arts Council of Northern Ireland bursary, 1971, 1974, 1981; Children's Rights Workshop Other award, 1986; Smarties prize, 1988. Agent: Murray Pollinger, 4 Garrick Street, London WC2E 9BH, England. Address: 139 Central Promenade, Newcastle, County Down, Northern Ireland.

<small>PUBLICATIONS FOR CHILDREN</small>

Fiction

Ernie's Chemistry Set [*Flying Trousers*], illustrated by Ronnie Baird. Belfast, Blackstaff Press, 2 vols., 1978.
Napper Goes for Goal [*Strikes Again*], illustrated by Barrie Mitchell. London, Penguin, 2 vols., 1981.
The Great Green Mouse Disaster, illustrated by Philippe

Dupasquier. London, Andersen Press, 1981.
Harriet and the Crocodiles. London, Abelard Schuman, 1982; Boston, Little Brown, 1984.
The House under the Stairs. London, Methuen, 1983.
Going West, illustrated by Philippe Dupasquier. London, Andersen Press, 1983; New York, Harper, 1984.
Solve-It-Yourself Mysteries (*The Mystery Squad and the Dead Man's Message* [the *Artful Dodger, The Whistling Teeth, Mr. Midnight, the Creeping Castle, the Candid Camera, the Cannonball Kid, the Robot's Revenge*]), illustrated by Terry McKenna. London, Blackie, 8 vols., 1984–86.
Napper's Golden Goals, illustrated by Barrie Mitchell. London, Penguin, 1984.
Harriet and the Haunted School, illustrated by Mark Burgess. London, Abelard, 1984; Boston, Little Brown, 1985.
Big Bad Bertie, illustrated by Glenys Ambrus. London, Methuen, 1984.
Harriet and the Robot, illustrated by Mark Burgess. London, Blackie, 1985; Boston, Little Brown, 1987.
The Budgie Said Grrrrr, illustrated by Glenys Ambrus. London, Methuen, 1985.
The Day It Rained Elephants, illustrated by Glenys Ambrus. London, Methuen, 1986.
Owl and Billy [*and the Space Days*]. London, Methuen, 2 vols., 1986–88.
Our Wild Weekend. London, Methuen, 1986.
Little Dracula's First Bite [*Christmas*], illustrated by Joseph Wright. London, Walker, 2 vols., 1986.
The Tough Princess, illustrated by Patrick Benson. London, Walker, 1986; New York, Putnam, 1987.
The Tall Story of Wilbur Small. London, Blackie, 1987.
Harriet and the Flying Teachers, illustrated by Mark Burgess. London, Blackie, 1987.
Alice the Artist, illustrated by Jonathan Langley. London, Methuen, and New York, Dutton, 1988.
Class Three and the Beanstalk, illustrated by Toni Goffe. London, Blackie, 1988.
Tales from the Shop That Never Shuts, illustrated by Maureen Bradley. London, Viking Kestrel, 1988.
Can't You Sleep, Little Bear?, illustrated by Barbara Firth. London, Walker, 1988.
Little Dracula Goes to School [*at the Seaside*], illustrated by Joseph Wright. London, Walker, 2 vols., 1987.
Our Sleepysaurus. London, Walker, 1988.
Great Gran Gorilla to the Rescue [*and the Robbers*], illustrated by Dom Mansell. London, Walker, 2 vols., 1988.

Fiction as Catherine Sefton

In a Blue Velvet Dress: Almost a Ghost Story, illustrated by Gareth Floyd. London, Faber, 1972; New York, Harper, 1973.
The Sleepers on the Hill. London, Faber, 1973.
The Back House Ghosts. London, Faber, 1974; as *The Haunting of Ellen,* New York, Harper, 1975.
The Ghost and Bertie Boggin, illustrated by Jill Bennett. London, Faber, 1980.
Emer's Ghost. London, Hamish Hamilton, 1981.
The Finn Gang, illustrated by Sally Holmes. London, Hamish Hamilton, 1981.
A Puff of Smoke, illustrated by Thelma Lambert. London, Hamish Hamilton, 1982.
The Emma Dilemma, illustrated by Jill Bennett. London, Faber, 1982.
Island of the Strangers. London, Hamish Hamilton, 1983; San Diego, Harcourt Brace, 1985.
My Gang, illustrated by Catherine Bradbury. London, Hamish

Hamilton, 1984.
The Blue Misty Monsters, illustrated by Elaine McGregor Turney. London, Faber, 1985.
The Ghost Girl. London, Hamish Hamilton, 1985.
The Ghost Ship, illustrated by Martin Ursell. London, Hamish Hamilton, 1985.
Starry Night. London, Hamish Hamilton, 1986.
Flying Sam, illustrated by Margaret Chamberlain. London, Hamish Hamilton, 1986.
Shadows on the Lake. London, Hamish Hamilton, 1987.
Bertie Boggin and the Ghost Again! London, Faber, 1988.
Frankie's Story. London, Hamish Hamilton, 1988.
The Day the Smells Went Wrong, illustrated by John Rogan. London, Hamish Hamilton, 1988.
The Haunted Schoolbag. London, Hamish Hamilton, 1989.
The Beat of the Drum. London, Hamish Hamilton, 1989.

Plays

Radio Plays: *The Fleas and Mr. Morgan,* 1969; *Bazaar* series, from 1974; *One Potato, Two Potato* series, from 1975.

Other

Editor, *A Tale to Tell: Stories by Young People from Northern Ireland.* Belfast, Arts Council of Northern Ireland, 1982.

PUBLICATIONS FOR ADULTS

Novels

Otley. London, Hodder and Stoughton, and New York, Stein and Day, 1966.
Otley Pursued. London, Hodder and Stoughton, and New York, Stein and Day, 1967.
Otley Forever. London, Hodder and Stoughton, and New York, Stein and Day, 1968.
Otley Victorious. London, Hodder and Stoughton, and New York, Stein and Day, 1969.
Come Back When I'm Sober. London, Hodder and Stoughton, 1969.
A Little Bit British, Being the Diary of an Ulsterman. London, Stacey, 1970.

*

Manuscript Collection: Linen Hall Library, Belfast.

Martin Waddell comments:
I try to write with clarity and brevity, with the aim of entertaining and amusing children, rather than instructing them. My "Catherine Sefton" work is based largely on the idea of family and is very much concerned with the emotions of the characters, always within the framework of an amusing story. I am strongly against the idea of "problem" novels, as I feel these reflect adult interests. To date I have written only one book for children which could be classed as a "problem" book (*The Island of the Strangers*), but the treatment of the "problem" therein clearly subordinates it to the story and the people.
I write against the political background of Northern Ireland, but not usually about it. My children are subjected to it every day in terms of stereotype....I try to write in terms of individuals and their emotions.
Most of my "Martin Waddell" books are for amusement only.

*   *   *

Martin Waddell writes equally prolifically under the pen name Catherine Sefton. At this stage it is unclear exactly what distinction should or could be made between the "two" writers. But it is certainly time to discuss Waddell and Sefton as a double career, similar to that of Dr. Seuss and Theo Le Sieg, or Philip Turner and Stephen Chance.

Waddell was writing before Sefton, with the adult Otley series and other work. But soon he began writing minor children's books, "for amusement only," he said. This is true, for example, of *Ernie's Flying Trousers*—they really fly, and it is all a rather silly story based on a silly gimmick. But even this has a very strong sense of visual humour that exceeds the cartoon style of the illustrations, and really cries out for a good television production. Waddell found an outstanding illustrator in Philippe Dupasquier. *The Great Green Mouse Disaster* is an almost wordless triumph of visual slapstick. *Going West* has a very spare text, but enough to make a strong narrative of a family in a covered wagon struggling to cross to Oregon in the days of the Old West of America. With a different illustrator, Waddell tells a charming gentle goodnight story in *Can't You Sleep, Little Bear?*

Sefton's first book, *In a Blue Velvet Dress*, is subtitled, rather coyly, *Almost a Ghost Story*. In fact it definitely is a ghost story, a very good one, predating Penelope Lively's classic *The Ghost of Thomas Kempe* by one year. Shorter and gentler than Lively's, it has a similar sense of comedy. Already in this first book there are the elements which are to become so familiar in Sefton's novels: wit, slapstick, acute dialogue, caring families under strain, Irish Protestants and Catholics, sensitive curious children—and ghosts!

Almost all of Sefton's novels have ghosts. But with any kind of ghost story, it is valuable to ask why? The better the reason for the haunting, the more convincing is the story. Less convincing or satisfying as literature are what can be called "spook" stories which use the supernatural just to give a thrill or drive the narrative. The ghost in *In a Blue Velvet Dress* is haunting in order to help the living. This ghost, like the living heroine of the novel, is (or was) a lonely bookworm. Occasionally, however, it is the ghost who needs help, as in *The Back House Ghosts*. Such stories are hauntings with a purpose, set within a personal relationship between haunter and hauntee. In these situations the living characters have room to feel and develop. Matters from the past can meaningfully impinge on and interact with the present. In all her ghost stories, it is to Sefton's credit that she has never written a "spook" story. But sometimes the haunting can seem unjustified, or weakly motivated.

The Back House Ghosts is a very satisfactory summer holiday ghost story—solid characters, strong setting, robust plot. Ghosts can usually be relied on for a good yarn. But there is some weakness in the reason for the haunting. At the end, the present-day characters solve the ghost mystery, and find that the ghost is hanging around, not because of any tragic event, but simply because a vigorous young woman ran away with her man, fabricating her death, and is concerned that her mother never knew that she lived happily ever after. The ghost can rest once some living people discover the truth about what happened. Why this should be the substance of a novel with ouija board, seances, visions, dreams, old love songs, and rusty flintlock pistols, rather than simply a chat in heaven between daughter ghost and mother ghost, is not made clear.

The desire of a ghost to communicate an important message to the living is used more convincingly in *Emer's Ghost*, where young Emer accidentally discovers a lost doll that had once belonged to a girl who died keeping a secret from Cromwell's invading Protestant army. What had been a matter of love in *The Back House Ghosts* becomes a matter of religious politics, with particular relevance in modern Northern Ireland.

Much more recently, *The Ghost Girl* is a development of both *In a Blue Velvet Dress* and *The Back House Ghosts*, with an interesting twist. On a summer holiday, a sensitive young Protestant girl finds herself haunted, she believes, by a sad gentle ghost girl. The retired Catholic Canon she tries to confide in remarks significantly, "If you

think there's someone watching you, what's there to watch?" The motivation for the haunting and the relation between the ghost and the person being haunted are subtly highlighted. Again, this time the haunting does not arise out of a domestic tragedy, but from the tragedy of Ireland. As the Canon comments at the end of *The Ghost Girl*, "If they are the victims of Irish history, then so are we...but they are dead, and we still have a chance to choose...We can try to find another way."

Sefton has written many other kinds of hauntings, for different age levels. *The Ghost Ship* is a picture book in which the ship and the ghost pirate boy are probably the invention of the imaginative young hero. In *The Emma Dilemma* young Emma finds herself "haunted" by a shadowy *doppelgänger* of herself as a result of concussion—a mixture of poltergeist and out-of-body experience. *The Ghost and Bertie Boggin* is a domestic farce for young readers on the pattern of the films *Topper* and *Harvey* where one character can see the ghost but no one else believes in it. Why is Bertie being haunted? Because the sensitive old ghost has fallen on hard times now that the Haunted Cellar at The Spectre's Arms Hotel has been turned into a noisy disco. The relationship between Bertie and ghost is purely accidental, but a lot of fun. In *The Blue Misty Monsters* there are no ghosts but, instead, aliens who enjoy "Going Spaces," as they say, because it broadens the mind. They have the power to appear as people, or as blue mist (hence the ghost confusion), and they serve as a Swiftian metaphor for a very critical view of humans.

There are also several novels with no haunting, and virtually no explicit politics, although increasingly in Sefton's novels the background recognises the political tensions of Northern Ireland. These include *Shadows on the Lake* and *Island of the Strangers*—satisfying stories of social and domestic conflict in which the central characters must confront their own prejudices and overcome them by personal growth.

In 1986 Sefton won the Other award for *Starry Night*, the first volume of a trilogy that includes *Frankie's Story* and *The Beat of the Drum*. These (like *Shadows on the Lake*) are wholly realistic, not a hint of a ghost. They are about young girls growing up in Protestant Northern Ireland during the recent tragic sectarian violence. There are echoes here of Edna O'Brien and Joan Lingard. But Sefton writes very convincingly and individually about Irish people caught in family problems and in the undeclared civil war between the Provisional IRA and British Ulster. There is an immediate memory of Yeats's "terrible beauty" in the way Sefton captures bog farmers struggling with a shattered economy and family scandal or innocent suburban children caught in the deadly propaganda of hatred. With powerful first-person narratives, Sefton brings 15-year-old Kathleen Fay towards the revelation of her shocking family secret in *Starry Night* (the title referring to the Irish fairy stories Kathleen had been told by older sister Ruth—although Ruth is not what she seems, and the Starry Night stories are all "blether"), and takes Frankie or Frances Rafferty towards a confrontation of the disturbing emotion she had felt at being abandoned by her father and the terrifying forces of Catholic and Protestant bigotry. When Sefton's ghost stories are good they are very good. But in the trilogy with no ghosts she is tremendous!

The output of Waddell and Sefton is more than just that of a prolific writer who needs two names to be able to publish fast enough. Sefton and Waddell at last seem to be following separate careers—Sefton in conventional novels and Waddell in picture books and occasional light entertainment. Both are always entertaining, and at their best very rewarding at several different levels.

—John Gough

WAGNER, Jenny. Australian. Recipient: Australian Children's Book Council award, for picture book, 1974, 1977. Address: c/o Viking Publishers, P.O. Box 257, 487 Maroondah Highway, Ringwood, Victoria 3134, Australia.

PUBLICATIONS FOR CHILDREN

Fiction

The Werewolf Knight, illustrated by Karl Homes. Melbourne and London, Macmillan, 1972.
The Bunyip of Berkeley's Creek, illustrated by Ron Brooks. Melbourne, Childerset, and London, Longman, 1973; Scarsdale, New York, Bradbury Press, 1977.
Peter and the Zauberleaf, illustrated by Giulietta Stomann. Sydney, Hamlyn, 1973.
Aranea: A Story about a Spider, illustrated by Ron Brooks. Melbourne, Childerset, and London, Kestrel, 1975; Scarsdale, New York, Bradbury Press, 1978.
Hannibal, illustrated by Karl Homes. Melbourne, Childerset, 1976.
John Brown, Rose, and the Midnight Cat, illustrated by Ron Brooks. London, Kestrel, 1977; Scarsdale, New York, Bradbury Press, 1978.
The Nimbin, illustrated by Inga Moore. Melbourne, Nelson, 1978; London, Penguin, 1980.
Jo-Jo and Mike, illustrated by Ann James. Melbourne, Nelson, 1982.
The Machine at the Heart of the World, illustrated by the author and Jeff Fisher. Melbourne and London, Kestrel, 1983.
Goanna, with Noela Hills. Melbourne, Viking, 1987; London, Viking, 1988.
The Windmill in the Paddock, illustrated by Valerie Carter. Canberra, Curriculum Development Centre, 1988.

*   *   *

Jenny Wagner is best known for two highly acclaimed picture books, both illustrated by Australian artist and author Ron Brooks, *The Bunyip of Berkeley's Creek* and *John Brown, Rose, and the Midnight Cat*. These books have provoked considerable discussion among critics because of the profound nature of their themes based on notions of reality, perception, human relationships, and death. In other picture books Wagner has considered cycles and change (*Peter and the Zauberleaf*), individual survival and creativity (*Aranea*), political control and personal choice (*Jo-Jo and Mike*), and the effect of human greed on the environment (*The Machine at the Heart of the World* and *Goanna*).

Wagner's particular skill lies in incorporating such weighty themes into highly entertaining narratives. In *The Bunyip of Berkeley's Creek* a benign bunyip (a usually fearful monster from Aboriginal lore said to inhabit billabongs and other inland pools and waterways) climbs out of black mud and asks "What am I?" The Bunyip's search for identity is an exemplification of Bishop George Berkeley's proposition of the relationship between perception and being. All the animals the Bunyip meets and questions describe only the creature of myth, and a man who "looked right through him" says "Bunyips simply don't exist." Saddened, the bunyip goes away, but all ends happily when another bunyip climbs out of the mud and Bunyip is able to answer *her* question, "What am I?"

The Bunyip of Berkeley's Creek can be read and enjoyed without knowing anything of Bishop Berkeley. In essence the story is about the pleasures of companionship. Similarly Wagner's best book, *John Brown, Rose, and the Midnight Cat*, is a text with meaning for readers of all ages. Rose, a widow, lives with her dog John Brown. It is

apparent from the text and illustrations that they live a quiet, well-ordered life. "'We are all right, John Brown,' said Rose. 'Just the two of us, you and me.'" However, one night Rose sees the midnight cat and wants to give it some milk. John Brown is jealous and won't let it in. After a while Rose becomes ill and goes to bed "forever." John Brown opens the door to the midnight cat, Rose gets out of bed, and the three sit by the fire. It is not easy to describe in words the charm and power of this book. The author herself felt the story "so strange" she was reluctant to send it to a publisher. The nature of relationships, particularly the need to let love flourish rather than be restrictive is in the foreground, but colouring this theme is the suggestion of mysterious things beyond our ken, most particularly the mystery of death. Indeed these two themes—of individual autonomy, and the possibilities of things beyond human intelligence—are the principal concerns apparent in all of Wagner's writing.

Wagner's other books have not had the outstanding international success of these two books, but *Aranea*, *The Nimbin*, *Jo-Jo and Mike*, and *Goanna* have been very popular in Australia. In her one novel, *The Nimbin*, a young girl has to care for a loveable but troublesome creature who comes and goes with the phases of the moon. In *Aranea* a spider patiently builds and rebuilds her web despite harassment from schoolboys and threats from changing weather. Mike the sign-painter in *Jo-Jo and Mike* leaves his job in a growing town, but before he leaves he changes all the "Don't" signs he has had to make to more positive messages as a protest against officious and petty bureaucracy. *The Machine at the Heart of the World* lacks the easy rhythm and resonance of Wagner's other writing. The pale illustrations detract from the text, and although the tale is a comment on how the world survives human greed, the intention of the message is unclear.

Wagner introduced complex ideas to Australian picture-book texts. Her mastery of the disciplined writing skills required in the picture-book medium has not been matched so far by any other writer in Australia.

—Kerry White

_____

WAHL, Jan (Boyer). American. Born in Columbus, Ohio, 1 April 1933. Educated at Cornell University, Ithaca, New York, 1950–53, B.A. 1953; University of Copenhagen (Fulbright fellow), 1953–54, M.A. 1954; University of Michigan, Ann Arbor (Avery Hopwood prize), 1955–58, M.A. 1958. Worked in Denmark for the film director Carl T. Dreyer, 1954–55, and as secretary to the writer Isak Dinesen, 1957–58. Agent: Rogers Coleridge and White, 20 Powis Mews, London W11 1JN, England. Address: 6766 Carrietowne Lane, Toledo, Ohio 43617, U.S.A.; or, Apartado Postal 33, San Miguel de Allende, Guanajuato, Mexico.

PUBLICATIONS FOR CHILDREN

Fiction

Pleasant Fieldmouse, illustrated by Maurice Sendak. New York, Harper, 1964; Kingswood, Surrey, World's Work, 1969.
The Howards Go Sledding, illustrated by John E. Johnson. New York, Holt Rinehart, 1964.
Hello, Elephant, illustrated by Edward Ardizzone. New York, Holt Rinehart, 1964.
Cabbage Moon, illustrated by Adrienne Adams. New York, Holt Rinehart, 1965.
The Muffletumps: The Story of Four Dolls, illustrated by Edward

Ardizzone.   New York, Holt Rinehart, 1966.

Christmas in the Forest, illustrated by Eleanor Schick.   New York, Macmillan, 1967.

Pocahontas in London, illustrated by John Alcorn.   New York, Delacorte Press, 1967.

The Furious Flycycle, illustrated by Fernando Krahn.   New York, Delacorte Press, 1968; London, Longman, 1970.

Push Kitty, illustrated by Garth Williams.   New York, Harper, 1968.

Cobweb Castle, illustrated by Edward Gorey.   New York, Holt Rinehart, 1968.

Rickety Rackety Rooster, illustrated by John E. Johnson.   New York, Simon and Schuster, 1968.

A Wolf of My Own, illustrated by Lillian Hoban.   New York, Macmillan, 1969.

How the Children Stopped the Wars, illustrated by Mitchell Miller.   New York, Farrar Straus, 1969; London, Abelard Schuman, 1975.

The Fishermen, illustrated by Emily McCully.   New York, Norton, 1969.

May Horses, illustrated by Blair Lent.   New York, Delacorte Press, 1969.

The Norman Rockwell Storybook, illustrated by Rockwell.   New York, Windmill, 1969.

The Prince Who Was a Fish, illustrated by Robin Jacques.   New York, Simon and Schuster, 1970.

The Mulberry Tree, illustrated by Feodor Rojankovsky.   New York, Grosset and Dunlap, 1970.

Doctor Rabbit, illustrated by Peter Parnall.   New York, Delacorte Press, 1970; London, Longman, 1972.

The Animals' Peace Day, illustrated by Victoria Chess.   New York, Crown, 1970.

The Wonderful Kite, illustrated by Uri Shulevitz.   New York, Delacorte Press, 1971.

Abe Lincoln's Beard, illustrated by Fernando Krahn.   New York, Delacorte Press, 1971.

Anna Help Ginger, illustrated by Lawrence Di Fiori.   New York, Putnam, 1971.

Crabapple Night, illustrated by Steven Kellogg.   New York, Holt Rinehart, 1971.

Margaret's Birthday, illustrated by Mercer Mayer.   New York, Four Winds Press, 1971.

The Six Voyages of Pleasant Fieldmouse, illustrated by Peter Parnall.   New York, Delacorte Press, 1971.

Lorenzo Bear & Company, illustrated by Fernando Krahn.   New York, Putnam, 1971.

The Very Peculiar Tunnel, illustrated by Steven Kellogg.   New York, Putnam, 1972.

Magic Heart, illustrated by Trina Schart Hyman.   New York, Seabury Press, 1972; Kingswood, Surrey, World's Work, 1973.

Grandmother Told Me, illustrated by Mercer Mayer.   Boston, Little Brown, 1972.

Cristóbal and the Witch, illustrated by Janet McCaffery.   New York, Putnam, 1972.

S.O.S. Bobomobile! or, The Future Adventures of Melvin Spitznagle and Professor Mickimecki, illustrated by Fernando Krahn.   New York, Delacorte Press, 1973; London, Kestrel, 1975.

The Five in the Forest, illustrated by Erik Blegvad.   Chicago, Follett, 1974.

Pleasant Fieldmouse's Halloween Party, illustrated by Wallace Tripp.   New York, Putnam, 1974; Kingswood, Surrey, World's Work, 1976.

Mooga Mega Mekki, illustrated by Fernando Krahn.   Chicago, O'Hara, 1974.

Jeremiah Knucklebones, illustrated by Jane Breskin Zalben.   New York, Holt Rinehart, 1974.

The Muffletump Storybook, illustrated by Cyndy Szekeres.   Chicago, Follett, 1975.

The Clumpets Go Sailing, illustrated by Cyndy Szekeres.   New York, Parents' Magazine Press, 1975; Kingswood, Surrey, World's Work, 1977.

Bear, Wolf, and Mouse, illustrated by Kinuko Kraft.   Chicago, Follett, 1975.

The Screeching Door; or, What Happened at the Elephant Hotel, illustrated by J. Winslow Higginbottom.   New York, Four Winds Press, 1975.

The Muffletumps' Christmas Party, illustrated by Cyndy Szekeres.   Chicago, Follett, 1975; Kingswood, Surrey, World's Work, 1977.

Great-Grandmother Cat Tales, illustrated by Cyndy Szekeres.   New York, Pantheon, 1976.

Grandpa's Indian Summer, illustrated by Joanne Scribner.   Englewood Cliffs, New Jersey, Prentice Hall, 1976.

The Pleasant Fieldmouse Storybook, illustrated by Erik Blegvad.   Englewood Cliffs, New Jersey, Prentice Hall, and Kingswood, Surrey, World's Work, 1977.

Doctor Rabbit's Foundling, illustrated by Cyndy Szekeres.   New York, Pantheon, 1977; Kingswood, Surrey, World's Work, 1979.

Frankenstein's Dog, illustrated by Kay Chorao.   Englewood Cliffs, New Jersey, Prentice Hall, 1977; London, Hutchinson, 1980.

The Muffletumps' Halloween Scare, illustrated by Cyndy Szekeres.   Chicago, Follett, 1977; Kingswood, Surrey, World's Work, 1979.

Pleasant Fieldmouse's Valentine Trick, illustrated by Marc Brown.   New York, Windmill, 1977; Kingswood, Surrey, World's Work, 1979.

Carrot Nose, illustrated by James Marshall.   New York, Farrar Straus, 1978.

Dracula's Cat, illustrated by Kay Chorao.   Englewood Cliffs, New Jersey, Prentice Hall, 1978.

Who Will Believe Tim Kitten?, illustrated by Cyndy Szekeres.   New York, Pantheon, 1978; Kingswood, Surrey, World's Work, 1980.

Jamie's Tiger, illustrated by Tomie de Paola.   New York, Harcourt Brace, 1978.

Youth's Magic Horn: Seven Stories.   Nashville, Nelson, 1978.

The Teeny, Tiny Witches, illustrated by Margot Tomes.   New York, Putnam, 1979.

Doctor Rabbit's Lost Scout, illustrated by Cyndy Szekeres.   New York, Pantheon, 1979.

Sylvester Bear Overslept, illustrated by Lee Lorenz.   New York, Parents' Magazine Press, 1979; Kingswood, Surrey, World's Work, 1981.

Old Hippo's Easter Egg, illustrated by Lorinda Bryan Cauley.   New York, Harcourt Brace, 1980.

Button Eye's Orange, illustrated by Wendy Watson.   New York, Warne, 1980.

The Cucumber Princess, illustrated by Caren Caraway.   Owings Mills, Maryland, Stemmer House, 1981.

The Little Blind Goat, illustrated by Antonio Frasconi.   Owings Mills, Maryland, Stemmer House, 1981.

Grandpa Gus's Birthday Cake, illustrated by John Wallner.   Englewood Cliffs, New Jersey, Prentice Hall, 1981.

Tiger Watch, illustrated by Charles Mikolaycak.   New York, Harcourt Brace, 1982.

The Pipkins Go Camping, illustrated by John Wallner.   Englewood Cliffs, New Jersey, Prentice Hall, 1982.

Small One, illustrated by Beth Wiener.   New York, Hastings House, 1983.

More Room for the Pipkins, illustrated by John Wallner.   Englewood Cliffs, New Jersey, Prentice Hall, 1983.

Peter and the Troll Baby, illustrated by Erik Blegvad.   Racine, Wisconsin, Golden Press, 1984.

So Many Raccoons, illustrated by Beth Lee Weiner.   New York, Cademon, 1985.

Cheltenham's Party, illustrated by Lucinda McQueen.   Racine, Wisconsin, Golden Press, 1985.

Runaway Jonah, illustrated by Jane Conteh-Morgan.   New York, Caedmon, 1985.

Rabbits on Roller Skates!, illustrated by David Allender.   New York, Crown, 1986.

Humphrey's Bear, illustrated by William Joyce.   New York, Holt, 1987; London, Gollancz, 1988.

Let's Go Fishing!, illustrated by Bruce Lemorise.   Racine, Wisconsin, Golden Press, 1987.

Timothy Tiger's Terrible Toothache, illustrated by Lisa McCue.   Racine, Wisconsin, Golden Press, 1988.

Little Dragon's Grandmother, illustrated by Lucinda McQueen.   Racine, Wisconsin, Golden Press, 1988.

Tim Kitten and the Red Cupboard, illustrated by Bruce Degen.   New York, Simon and Schuster, 1988.

The Golden Christmas Tree, illustrated by Leonard Weisgard.   Racine, Wisconsin, Golden Press, 1988.

Tales of Fuzzy Mouse, illustrated by Lillian Hoban.   Racine, Wisconsin, Golden Press, 1988.

The Adventures of Underwater Dog, illustrated by Tim Bowers.   New York, Grosset and Dunlap, 1989.

Verse

The Beast Book, illustrated by E.W. Eichel.   New York, Harper, 1964.

Follow Me, Cried Bee, illustrated by John Wallner.   New York, Crown, 1976.

The Toy Circus, illustrated by Tim Bowers.   San Diego, Harcourt Brace, 1986.

Other

Runaway Jonah and Other Tales, illustrated by Uri Shulevitz.   New York, Macmillan, 1968.

Crazy Brobobalou, illustrated by Paula Winter.   New York, Putnam, 1973.

The Woman with the Eggs, illustrated by Ray Cruz.   New York, Crown, 1974.

Juan Diego and the Lady, illustrated by Leonard Everett Fisher.   New York, Putnam, 1974.

Drakestail (folktale), illustrated by Byron Barton.   New York, Greenwillow, 1978; Kingswood, Surrey, World's Work, 1980.

Needle Noodle and Other Silly Stories (English folktales), illustrated by Stan Mack.   New York, Pantheon, 1979.

The Wizard of Oz Movie Storybook.   Racine, Wisconsin, Golden Press, 1989.

PUBLICATIONS FOR ADULTS

Play

Paradiso! Paradiso! (produced Ithaca, New York, 1954).

*

Manuscript Collections: Jan Wahl Collection, University of Wyoming, Laramie; Kerlan Collection, University of Minnesota, Minneapolis.

Jan Wahl comments:

Even in my so-called "adult" fiction—stories printed in various magazines—I realized I was writing about the qualities of childhood and therefore it occurred to me to write directly for children, that is, for the child in *me*, by means of fables and picture-book stories. I see

picture books themselves as small films, and several of my artists (Maurice Sendak and Uri Shulevitz, for example) have agreed with me. I try to follow no trends but to write what I would wish to read if I, today, were a child. I find it, always, a satisfying, exciting occupation.

*   *   *

The bright sun, the pride of spring, popped into the sky like a flying orange. The forest stirred, then morning began, shaking its new green shades. Red cardinals and yellow finches darted among the trees like bold-painted arrows.

Somebody was hammering a sign beside the thick black oak. This somebody was Pleasant Fieldmouse, who lived inside the oak, at the bottom. *I Am a Fireman* it said on the sign. Pleasant Fieldmouse was wearing a fine red hat which was really a cap from a bottle. *Tipsy Cola*, the cap was labeled, but you were not supposed to look at him from the top.

Those opening paragraphs from Jan Wahl's first book for children, *Pleasant Fieldmouse*, inadvertently reveal some of the main strengths and weaknesses that run through much of his writing. On the positive side stand imagination, a gentle whimsicality, humor, and fresh imagery. But balancing and sometimes outweighing these good qualities are the author's tendency to strain too hard for the unusual word or phrase, and his frequent descents into archness.

Wahl has published a wide range of books in the last two decades, from brief picture-book texts like *Drakestail*, *A Wolf of My Own*, and *Follow Me, Cried Bee*, to original fairytales (*The Cucumber Princess, Cobweb Castle, Magic Heart*), to unusual short biographies (*Abe Lincoln's Beard, Pocahontas in London*), to humorous novels for the 8–12-year-old audience (*The Furious Flycycle, The Screeching Door*). He has even written a collection of contemporary short stories for young adults, *Youth's Magic Horn*, which combines echoes of Flannery O'Connor's eccentric humor with a pathos reminiscent of Sherwood Anderson. However, the majority of his published work falls into the picture book category.

Wahl's picture-book output slackened somewhat in the 1980's. But his gift for humor touched with feeling lent distinction to *Humphrey's Bear*, and his imagination literally ran wild in the rollicking text for *Rabbits on Rollerskates!*

All of Wahl's picture books are filled with surprises—an unusual word that juts out from the text, a fantastic character who suddenly enters the scene, a startling new situation that develops unexpectedly. Accompanying the surprises, though, is what often seems like a lack of control over the material and the narrative as a whole. Storylines wander off on colorful but inconclusive tangents; interesting characters appear, take center stage for a while and then vanish, never to reappear again. Sometimes the texts actually read like dreams that Wahl wrote down as soon as he awoke in the morning and then never touched again.

In a sense Wahl could probably be described as a victim of the boom in children's book publishing that flared up in the United States during the years of President Lyndon B. Johnson's so-called "Great Society" (1964–69). That was the period when generous appropriations of federal funds were being spent on the creation and expansion of school libraries all across the country. A prolific author like Wahl could—and did—sell just about everything he wrote to one publisher or another, even fragmentary pieces like *Pocahontas in London* and *May Horses*. Inevitably these slight books diminished Wahl's reputation, and there came a time in the 1970's when critics seemed to be on the verge of dismissing some of his richer and more unified books along with his weaker ones.

If that had happened, it would have been a shame—not only for

Wahl but for the field of children's literature. Uneven, unsatisfying, and exasperating as Wahl's stories sometimes are, he can still come through with marvelous new approaches and insights as in *Runaway Jonah*, his retelling of five Old Testament stories. And he also has to his credit a true modern classic in *Push Kitty*, which dramatizes the ultimate in smothering love as the little girl narrator describes how she dresses up her kitten and tries to make him into her baby. "Baby, you are pretty lucky to have a mama like me, DON'T YOU AGREE?"

If only for *Push Kitty* and *Pleasant Fieldmouse*, Wahl would have a secure niche in any chronicle of American children's books from the 1960's onwards.

—James Cross Giblin

WALKER, David (Harry). Canadian. Born in Angus, Scotland, 9 February 1911; became Canadian citizen, 1957. Educated at Shrewsbury School, Shropshire, 1924–29; Royal Military College, Sandhurst, Surrey, 1929–30. Married Willa Magee in 1939; five sons (one deceased). Served in the British Army, in the Black Watch, 1931–47: served in India, 1932–36, and in the Sudan, 1936–38; aide-de-camp to the Governor-General of Canada, 1938–39; prisoner-of-war in Germany, 1940–45; Instructor at the Staff College, Camberley, Surrey, 1945–46; comptroller to the Viceroy of India, 1946–47; retired as Major, 1947; M.B.E (Member, Order of the British Empire), 1946. Since 1947 full-time writer. Member, Canada Council, 1957–61. Canadian commissioner since 1965, and chairman, 1970–72, Roosevelt Campobello International Park Commission. Recipient: Governor-General's award, for novel, 1953, 1954. D. Litt.: University of New Brunswick, Fredericton, 1955. Fellow, Royal Society of Literature, 1950; member, Queen's Body guard for Scotland; member, Order of Canada. Address: Strathcroix, St. Andrews, New Brunswick E0G 2X0, Canada.

PUBLICATIONS FOR CHILDREN

Fiction

Sandy Was a Soldier's Boy, illustrated by Dobson Broadhead. London, Collins, and Boston, Houghton Mifflin, 1957; as *Sandy*, Collins, 1961.
Dragon Hill, illustrated by Ray Keane. Boston, Houghton Mifflin, 1962; London, Collins, 1963.
Pirate Rock, illustrated by Victor Mays. London, Collins, and Boston, Houghton Mifflin, 1969.
Big Ben, illustrated by Victor Ambrus. Boston, Houghton Mifflin, 1969; London, Collins, 1970.

PUBLICATIONS FOR ADULTS

Novels

The Storm and the Silence. Boston, Houghton Mifflin, 1949; London, Cape, 1950.
Geordie. Boston, Houghton Mifflin, and London, Collins, 1950.
The Pillar. Boston, Houghton Mifflin, and London, Collins, 1952; as *The Wire*, New York, Permabooks, 1953.
Digby. London, Collins, and Boston, Houghton Mifflin, 1953.
Harry Black. London, Collins, and Boston, Houghton Mifflin, 1956.

Where the High Winds Blow. London, Collins, and Boston, Houghton Mifflin, 1960.
Winter of Madness. London, Collins, and Boston, Houghton Mifflin, 1964.
Mallabec. London, Collins, and Boston, Houghton Mifflin, 1965.
Come Back, Geordie. London, Collins, and Boston, Houghton Mifflin, 1966.
Devil's Plunge. London, Collins, 1968; as *CAB-Intersec*, Boston, Houghton Mifflin, 1968.
The Lord's Pink Ocean. London, Collins, and Boston, Houghton Mifflin, 1972.
Black Dougal. London, Collins, 1973; Boston, Houghton Mifflin, 1974.
Ash. London, Collins, and Boston, Houghton Mifflin, 1976.
Pot of Gold. London, Collins, 1977.

Short Stories

Storms of Our Journey and Other Stories. Boston, Houghton Mifflin, 1962; London, Collins, 1963.

Other

Lean, Wind, Lean: A Few Times Remembered (memoirs). London, Collins, 1984.

*   *   *

David Walker was born in Scotland, but having adventured his way around the world, settled at last in Canada. His eventful personal history, which provided him with the material for prize-winning adult works, lends his children's books a ring of authenticity few of the genre can match.

Dragon Hill is the story of a "growing summer." Young William is unwilling to have his plans for the holiday spoiled by the intrusion of Mary, an unknown and unwanted remote relation from Scotland, whose widowed mother is off honeymooning with a second husband. Bad enough, thinks William, to be lumbered with a girl; but a girl in *her* frame of mind....After a poor start, the youngsters strike an uneasy truce, cemented in the usual way by getting into mischief together. They decide to brave Dragon Hill, the strictly forbidden ground belonging to Old Dragon, otherwise Captain McDurgan, a crusty curmudgeon with a grudge against the world. As the summer unfolds, so does the Dragon's withered spirit under the influence of the two children, and during the hurricane which is the story's climax, the old man who "hates everybody" rises to the occasion to become the hero of the hour. The brief and charming *Big Ben* is the story of a family and its huge, lovable St. Bernard, who though known affectionately as Ben, really labours under the appellation Hospice Excelsior. When the gentle giant is wrongfully accused of killing sheep and summarily condemned, Tim and Jinny, his young owners, go to extreme lengths to save him from a trigger-happy neighbour and to prove his innocence, in a story to warm a dog lover's heart.

Most ambitious of Walker's books for children is *Pirate Rock*, which tells of adventure in the Bay of Fundy, the meeting place of Canada and the United States. Teenagers Keith and Nelson are eager to take a summer job crewing a lavish speedboat for the ostentatiously rich newcomer in town. While in his employ, the boys discover evidence of mysterious, clandestine activities; and as their curiosity grows, so does their danger. This is a fairly complex tale of tangled personal and patriotic loyalties, and the eventual dramatic solution of the mystery, as so often in real life, is painful and difficult to accept for all concerned.

Although his "Mom and Dad" characters are an unattractive crew, Walker's young people compensate for their elders' charmlessness.

It is notable that he has added some engaging and spirited girls to the traditional "boys' book" format. As breezy as the summers in which, one suspects, they were written, Walker's adventures are robustly fast-paced and readable.

—Joan McGrath

————

WALKER, Stuart (Armstrong). American. Born in Augusta, Kentucky, 4 March 1880. Educated at Woodward High School, Cincinnati; University of Cincinnati, B.S. in engineering 1903; American Academy of Dramatic Arts, New York, 1908. One adopted son. Shipping clerk, Southern Creosoting Company, Slidell, Louisiana, 1904; play reader, actor, and stage manager for David Belasco, 1909–14; director of repertory theatres in Buffalo and Detroit for Jessie Bonstelle, 1914; founding director, Portmanteau Theatre, 1915–17; director, Indianapolis Repertory Company, 1917–23, 1926–28, and Cincinnati Repertory Company, later the Stuart Walker Repertory Company, 1922–31; film director, Paramount, 1931–34, and Universal, 1934–35, and producer, Paramount, 1936–41. *Died 13 March 1941.*

PUBLICATIONS FOR CHILDREN

Plays

Portmanteau Plays (includes *The Trimplet, Nevertheless, The Medicine Show, Six Who Pass While the Lentils Boil*), edited by Edward Hale Bierstadt (produced New York, 1916). Cincinnati, Stewart Kidd, 1917.
More Portmanteau Plays (includes *A Lady of the Weeping Willow Tree, The Very Naked Boy, Jonathan Makes a Wish*), edited by Edward Hale Bierstadt (*A Lady of the Weeping Willow Tree* and *The Very Naked Boy* produced New York, 1916; *Jonathan Makes a Wish* produced New York, 1918). Cincinnati, Stewart Kidd, 1919.
Portmanteau Adaptations (includes *Gammer Gurton's Needle, The Birthday of the Infanta*, adaptation of the story by Oscar Wilde, *Sir David Wears a Crown, Nellijumbo*), edited by Edward Hale Bierstadt (*Gammer Gurton's Needle* and *The Birthday of the Infanta* produced New York, 1916). Cincinnati, Stewart Kidd, 1921.
Five Flights Up (produced 1922).
The King's Great Aunt Sits on the Floor (produced 1923). New York, Appleton, 1925.
Seventeen, with Hubert S. Stange and Stannard Mears, adaptation of the novel by Booth Tarkington (produced on tour). New York, French, 1924.
The Book of Job (produced on tour).
The Demi-Reps, with Gladys Unger (produced 1936).

Screenplay: *Seventeen*, 1940.

*

Theatrical Activities:
Director: **Films**—*Secret Call*, 1931; *False Madonna*, 1931; *Misleading Lady*, 1932; *Evenings for Sale*, 1932; *Tonight Is Ours*, 1933; *The Eagle and the Hawk*, 1933; *White Woman*, 1933; *Romance in the Rain*, 1934; *Great Expectations*, 1934; *The Mystery of Edwin Drood*, 1935; *Werewolf of London*, 1935; *Manhattan Moon*, 1935;

Her Excellency the Governor, 1935.

* * *

Stuart Walker was at once a playwright and producer, director and actor, whose professional skills contributed to the early development of American children's theatre. In 1914 he founded the Portmanteau Theatre whose company during succeeding years toured in New York City and nationally, using a portable stage with its own simplified scenery. For his theatre's repertoire, director-producer Walker wrote plays, many suitable for children, which employ romantic fantasy to accent simple truths. They are collected in three anthologies.

Portmanteau Plays contains two slight and short pieces, *Nevertheless*, about truant children embracing honesty, and *The Medicine Show*, a realistic character sketch of two Ohio River youths and a gentleman drifter, and two better known Walker works, *The Trimplet* and *Six Who Pass While the Lentils Boil. The Trimplet* imaginatively tells of young lovers unable to find happiness until their feuding patrician parents learn to forget false pride. *Six Who Pass While the Lentils Boil*, Walker's most popular work, is a fanciful fable about David Little-Boy who hides a Queen sentenced to decapitation for an absurd breach of etiquette (i.e. stepping on a royal dowager's ring-toe). After six passing characters test David's resolve to secrecy, the Queen reveals herself at noon when the sentence can no longer be effected and rewards David for his loyalty. The gently humorous and lively drama holds lasting attraction for children. Characteristic of both plays is the use of commentator characters (e.g. Prologue and You-in-the-Audience) who amusingly effect a type of audience participation.

Portmanteau Adaptations contains the first sequel to *Six Who Pass* and Walker's best play, *Sir David Wears a Crown*. The latter's concurrent action begins as the search for the Queen continues and a gathered populace await her execution only to see her appear now free and empowered to pass her own laws, which she does, also knighting David and adopting him as their apparent. (A second sequel, *The King's Great Aunt Sits on the Floor*, is less successful.) The collection's remaining three plays are *Nellijumbo*, a saccharine story of a repressed blind boy's reunion with a long-absent father, and two actual adaptations—*The Birthday of the Infanta*, based on Oscar Wilde's story about a callous princess and a tragically tormented jester, and *Gammer Gurton's Needle*, a child-appealing version of the 16th-century folk farce.

More Portmanteau Plays includes three dramas. *A Lady of the Weeping Willow Tree*, a lyrical tale set in a mythical Japan about an infernal figure who is defeated and redeemed by a mother's self-sacrifice, is literarily superior to *The Very Naked Boy*, an insubstantial comic interlude about young love, and *Jonathan Makes a Wish* in which an artistic boy flees a restrictive father.

Walker also wrote adult plays, his best known work being *Seventeen*. A co-authored adaptation of Booth Tarkington's novel, the charming comedy traces a teenage boy's abortive infatuation with an admirer-gathering girl.

The historical importance of Walker and his theatrically adept plays in the development of child drama should not be underestimated.

—Christian H. Moe

————

WALL, Dorothy. Australian. Born in Wellington, New Zealand, in 1894. Studied art in New Zealand. Lived in Australia from 1914. Married Andrew Delfosse Badgery; one son. *Died in 1942.*

PUBLICATIONS FOR CHILDREN (illustrated by the author)

Fiction

Tommy Bear and the Zookies. Sydney, Triumph, 1920.
The Complete Adventures of Blinky Bill. Sydney, Angus and Robertson, 1939.
  Blinky Bill, The Quaint Little Australian. Sydney, Angus and Robertson, 1933.
  Blinky Bill Grows Up. Sydney, Angus and Robertson, 1934.
  Blinky Bill and Nutsy: Two Little Australians. Sydney, Angus and Robertson, 1937.
The Tale of Bridget and the Bees. London, Methuen, 1934; Poughkeepsie, New York, Artists and Writers Guild, 1935.
Brownie: The Story of a Naughty Little Rabbit. Sydney, Angus and Robertson, 1935; London, Angus and Robertson, 1977.
Stout Fellows: Chum, Angelina Wallaby, Um-Pig, and Flip. Sydney, Angus and Robertson, 1936.
Blinky Bill Joins the Army. Sydney, Angus and Robertson, 1940.
A Tiny Story of Blinky Bill. Sydney, Offset Printing, n.d.
Fun with Blinky Bill. Sydney, Angus and Robertson, 1953.
Horrie Kiwi and the Kids. London, Angus and Robertson, 1984.
The Blinky Bill Connection, edited by Walter McVitty. Sydney, Angus and Robertson, 2 vols., 1988.

Other

Blinky Bill Dress-Up Book. Sydney, Offset Printing, 1944 (?).
Blinky Bill's ABC Book. Sydney, Offset Printing, 1947.

*

Illustrator: *The Crystal Bowl* by J.J. Hall, 1921; *Jacko the Broadcasting Kookaburra,* 1933, and *The Amazing Adventures of Billy Penguin,* 1934, both by Brooke Nicholls; *Australians All: Bush Folk in Rhyme* by Nelle Grant Cooper, 1934.

*   *   *

Blinky Bill, the jaunty little koala bear, is one of the best-known characters in the world of Australia's childhood. Dorothy Wall created him in 1933, inspired by her own young son, and children have eagerly identified with the mischievous and appealing bear who has most of the characteristics of a small boy.

Wall died at a comparatively young age over 40 years ago, but her Blinky Bill stories have retained their wide popularity. Her career began as an illustrator and her fine technique can be seen in the books she illustrated for other authors. It was not until she created her first Blinky Bill story for her own small son that text and illustrations combined to give children a truly imaginative story which had an immediate appeal. *Blinky Bill, The Quaint Little Australian* was quickly followed by two sequels, and all three books were reprinted more or less yearly until the three were combined into one volume in 1939; it has remained in print ever since. The charm of the stories lies in the fact that the bear behaves just like a lively little boy, and his exploits occur in an imaginary urbanized bush setting, all the characters being humans disguised as bush creatures. Adults may sometimes query Wall's taste, but the books are enjoyed by children for their humour and incident. Their warmth and spontaneity make them ideal to read aloud to young primary school children, the stories consisting of episodes with engaging illustrations printed alongside the text. Throughout the stories Blinky Bill and his companions get into trouble through disobedience to their mother's instructions, and through their curiosity. This naughty behaviour and the suspense over its consequences is irresistible to young readers and listeners. And yet undoubtedly the particular strength of the books lies in the

vibrant and imaginative black and white illustrations.

The Australian setting with other Australian animal characters gave the books great appeal at a time when most children's books emanated from England, and occasional informative paragraphs briefly give some facts about the particular animal mentioned. The books are very much in the style of animal tales in fashion in the 1930's and 1940's and their reputation is enhanced by their long popularity. The exuberance of the stories and the author's wish to amuse occasionally produce a forced humour and sentimentality which at times rather dates them.

Although some cheap publications using Wall's characters with new illustrations roughly based on the original books have been produced and are sold widely Wall's own books are also in print. An impressive and well-produced set comprising a compendium volume of all her stories, together with a full-length biography containing many previously unpublished drawings has just been published and should enhance her reputation and ensure her continued popularity.

—Marcie Muir

———

WALLACE, Ian. Canadian. Born in Niagara Falls, Ontario, 31 March 1950. Educated at the Ontario College of Art, Toronto, 1969–74, A.A. 1974. Married Debra Olson in 1988. Staff writer and illustrator, Kids Can Press, Toronto, 1974–76; information officer, Art Gallery of Ontario, Toronto, 1976–80. Recipient: Canadian Library Association Howard-Gibbon Medal, for illustration, 1985. Address: 370 Palmerston Boulevard, Toronto, Ontario M6G 2N6, Canada.

PUBLICATIONS FOR CHILDREN (illustrated by the author)

Fiction

Julie News. Toronto, Kids Can Press, 1974.
The Sandwich, with Angela Wood, illustrated by the authors. Toronto, Kids Can Press, 1975.
The Christmas Tree House. Toronto, Kids Can Press, 1976.
Chin Chiang and the Dragon's Dance. Vancouver, Douglas and McIntyre, New York, Atheneum, and London, Methuen, 1984.
The Sparrow's Song. Markham, Ontario, Viking Kestrel, 1986; New York, Viking Kestrel, 1987.
Morgan the Magnificent. Toronto, Groundwood, 1987; New York, Macmillan, and London, Hamish Hamilton, 1988.

*

Illustrator: *Very Last First Time* by Jan Andrews, 1985; *Architect of the Moon* by Tim Wynne-Jones, 1988.

Ian Wallace comments:
In my work as an author I do not sit down to write stories, nor do I consciously choose stories to illustrate because they will be distinguished as being multi-cultural or Canadian or whatever flag one chooses to wave over them. I write or illustrate stories because first and foremost they are stories that will intrigue, inspire, and touch young readers. The characters who inhabit these tales are people who have earned my sympathy and are ones with whom I can empathize on a personal level. They are universal characters with universal emotions and universal experiences that make us human. They are characters whom I respect for their dignity of spirit and purpose of

life, characters who struggle, who test limits, and who endure. But most importantly they are characters who through the story go through some kind of change. At the end of a good story, a reader comes away with the confidence that the protagonist will never be the same and will treasure the memory. It is my hope that the reader of my books will never be the same either.

*   *   *

"Very Last First Time"—although this is the title of a work illustrated, but not written, by Ian Wallace, it embodies the primary theme of his own works: the initiation experience by which a child moves to understanding of self and the larger world. In words and pictures, Wallace presents boys and girls from a variety of places and times, each involved in the difficult process of growing up.

Wallace's first two stories, published in the mid 1970's, are apprentice works introducing themes explored most fully in the books of the 1980's. In *The Sandwich* Vincenzo, taking his lunch to school for the first time, feels ashamed when his friends laugh at the mortadella and provolone sandwich his father had made. However, on his return home he learns that "you are who you are and you have nothing to be ashamed of." Nick, central character in *The Christmas Tree House*, makes two new friends, a neighborhood girl and Don Valley Rose, who he discovers is not the dreaded witch of local rumor.

In *Chin Chiang and the Dragon's Dance* the title hero runs away on the morning of his first performance of the New Year's dance, fearing he will fail. With the help and encouragement of a wise old lady, he returns in time to take his part in the dance and, by extension, his place within his culture. Katie, the central character in *The Sparrow's Song*, tends a fledgling whose mother had been killed by her brother Charles. She learns forgiveness and he, repentance, and the two experience the mystic powers of nature present in the gorge of the Niagara River. *Morgan the Magnificent*, inspired by the author's love of circus art and equipment, is a new version of the old tale of a child running away to the circus. Morgan, a young girl living with her single-parent father, sneaks into the star performer's tent, dons one of her costumes, climbs to the high-wire, starts across, and freezes in panic. Like Chin Chiang, she requires the help of a wise old person, in this case the Amazing Anastasia. Like Chin, Katie, and Charles, she completes her adventure more aware of her strengths and limitations and of her relationship to the worlds in which she lives.

Wallace's texts for these stories are given expanded meanings by his illustrations. Each book has an appropriately major color: the red of the dominant Chinese dragon and of health and prosperity in *Chin Chiang*; the greens of nature in which the children learn and the sparrow is healed in *The Sparrow's Song*; and gold, the hue not only of gilded circus wagons, but also of the realm of wonder in *Morgan*. Style is also varied; formal patterns reflect Chinese ceremony in *Chin Chiang*; freeflowing depictions of water, rocks, and trees, the ever-changing panorama of nature in *The Sparrow's Song*; and circus designs in *Morgan*. In each story body language and facial expressions reveal the emotions of the characters as they confront inner and outer problems. Like Maurice Sendak, whose work has influenced him, Wallace varies picture sizes to reinforce his themes, most notably in *The Sparrow's Song* where the pictures of the children in the gorge are bled to the edge of the page to indicate their expanded consciousness in nature, and in *Very Last First Time* (written by Jan Andrews), when illustrations expand to double spreads reflecting the heroine's new knowledge as she explores the worlds below the sea ice.

Although Wallace's output is small—only eight books, two of them written by others—his status in Canadian children's literature is great. He has treated the universal theme of initiation, has presented it in deceptively simple stories about recognizable children, and through the color, design, and details of his illustrations has expanded events to symbolic dimensions.

—Jon C. Stott

———

WALSH, Jill Paton. See **PATON WALSH, Jill.**

———

WALTER, Mildred Pitts. American. Educated at Southern University, Louisiana, B.A.; University of California, Los Angeles; California State College; University of Southern California, Los Angeles. Married Earl Walter (died). Formerly schoolteacher in Los Angeles; currently educational consultant. Lives in Denver, Colorado. Recipient: American Library Association Coretta Scott King award, 1987. Address: c/o Bradbury Press, 866 Third Avenue, New York, New York 10022, U.S.A.

PUBLICATIONS FOR CHILDREN

Fiction

Lillie of Watts: A Birthday Discovery, illustrated by Leonora E. Prince. Los Angeles, Ward Ritchie Press, 1969.
Lillie of Watts Takes a Giant Step, illustrated by Bonnie Helene Johnson. New York, Doubleday, 1971.
Ty's One-Man Band, illustrated by Margot Tomes. New York, Four Winds Press, 1980.
The Girl on the Outside. New York, Lothrop, 1982.
Because We Are. New York, Lothrop, 1983.
My Mama Needs Me, illustrated by Pat Cummings. New York, Lothrop, 1983.
Brother to the Wind, illustrated by Diane and Leo Dillon. New York, Lothrop, 1985.
Trouble's Child. New York, Lothrop, 1985.
Justin and the Best Biscuits in the World, illustrated by Catherine Stock. New York, Lothrop, 1986.
Mariah Loves Rock. New York, Bradbury Press, 1988.

*   *   *

The small but growing body of work by Mildred Pitts Walter brims with metamorphosis. When Martha of *Trouble's Child* realizes at the close of the book that "she was on the threshold of searching, learning, knowing, of stretching her mind," not only do her thoughts pay tribute to her own growing recognition of a self-identity, but they also exemplify the transformations that occur in all of Walter's black characters. Walter writes with power, determination, and truth about black children and young adults who come to a sense of self-awareness in a unique cultural and social environment within the United States. She writes not of the cultural deprivation of black Americans, but of their cultural defamation, and the struggle to face the realities of their racial heritage to become fully connected human beings. One of the greatest strengths of Walter's work is that although she writes about blacks, her books transcend that particular experience to become books about people—people of all colors, all races, all creeds. In the end, the importance of the human connection is what makes the difference.

Lillie of Watts, the perceptively written story of 11-year-old Lillie, details her efforts to make meaning in a world where racial differences parallel social and economic privileges. Advertisements bombard Lillie with the message that to be white is more desirable than to be black. Over the course of the story Lillie learns that "people are more important than cats, sweaters, and cars." Her mother's demonstration of unconditional love moves Lillie toward appreciation and understanding that it is not what you have that makes you complete, but what you are.

Justin and the Best Biscuits in the World, a 1987 Coretta Scott King award winner and an intergenerational story that cuts across gender stereotypes, introduces the reader to 10-year-old Justin, a lover of basketball and a hater of all that smacks of "women's work." On a visit to his grandpa's Missouri ranch, Justin hears stories of famous black cowboys and learns to "ride fence," clean fish, make a bed, pick up after himself, and finally, to make the best biscuits in the world. Justin also becomes aware of his racial heritage, some of the horrors his ancestors lived through, and the implications of that legacy for his life. Under Grandpa's sage guidance, Justin learns that he must know where he's come from to find the way to where he wants to go.

A young adult novel, *Trouble's Child* is a coming-of-age story set in the lush Louisiana bayou community of Blue Isle. Martha, the main protagonist, nurtures a wish to finish her high school education while grappling to free herself from the binding ties of her community and its expectation that she marry and follow in her grandmother's footsteps as midwife. Martha's aspirations finally come to fruition when she finds the courage to face her community and follow her dreams. Rich in detail, and written in the soft cadence of Louisiana speech, the book strongly but tenderly portrays a universal adolescent dilemma.

Like all of Walter's books, *The Girl on the Outside* is written with honesty and integrity. A fictional recreation of the 1957 integration of Central High School in Little Rock, Arkansas, it focusses on the experiences of two students—Sophie, a white girl, and Eva, a black girl. The story speaks movingly and forcefully about the problems, fears, and prejudices that must be dealt with in the acceptance of integration.

Mariah Loves Rock also confronts the problem of integration—the integration of her daddy's daughter from his first marriage into Mariah's family. Mariah worries that with the arrival of Denise, not only will her daddy love Mariah less, but also she will have to sacrifice her bedroom, decorated with posters of her beloved rock star, the Sheik. With keen insight into the psyche of the family unit, Walter chronicles the transformation in Mariah as she moves from resentment of Denise as a rival, to acceptance of her as a sister.

Metamorphosis also characterizes *Ty's One-Man Band*, a picture-book folktale illustrated by Margot Tomes. Ty, restless and bored on a steamy summer's day, meets Andro, a peg-legged man who calls himself a one-man band. Using a washboard, two wooden spoons, a tin pail, and a comb, Andro turns everyday objects into the music of dancing horses, gurgling streams, dripping faucets, and puffing freight trains. In a succinct, lyrical evocation of the transforming power of the imagination, Ty broadens his scope of vision, learning that the ordinary can often become the extraordinary.

From the picture book to the middle reader to the young adult novel, Walter's writing resonates with feeling and conviction of purpose. Her work celebrates change—by times frightening, comforting, exhilarating, and perplexing—as essential in coming to terms with oneself and one's society. Wellsprings of hope, Walter's books embrace life even as they acknowledge the sometimes seemingly insurmountable difficulties of living.

—Carolyn Shute

———

WARDELL, Phyl(lis, née Robinson). New Zealander. Born in Christchurch, 21 October 1909. Educated at Avonside Girls High School; Christchurch Girls High School. Married Rae Wardell in 1935; one son and one daughter. Secretary, Jewell Skinner advertising agency, Christchurch, 1928–37. Agent: Richards Literary Agency, P.O. Box 31240, Milford, Auckland 9. Address: 192 Salisbury Street, Christchurch, New Zealand.

PUBLICATIONS FOR CHILDREN

Fiction

Gold at Kapai, illustrated by Douglas F. Maxted. London, Harrap, 1960.
The Secret of the Lost Tribe of Te Anau, illustrated by Keith Money. London, Harrap, 1961.
Passage to Dusky, illustrated by Garrick Palmer. London, Parrish, 1967.
Hazard Island, illustrated by Albert Wagenvoort. Christchurch, Whitcoulls, 1976.
The Nelson Treasure, illustrated by Alan Gilderdale. Auckland, Hodder and Stoughton, 1983.
Beyond the Narrows, illustrated by Gary Meeson. Auckland and London, Hodder and Stoughton, 1985.

Plays

Radio Plays: *Gold at Kapai, The Secret of the Lost Tribe of Te Anau*, and *Passage to Dusky*, from her own stories, 1959–66; *The Missing Skindiver*, 1966.

*

Manuscript Collection: Canterbury Public Library, Christchurch.

Phyl Wardell comments:
I began writing in the 1950's when I was 40. I tried a couple of romantic novels which, halfway through, turned into murder mysteries. They did not sell.

I was planning a third murder story when an editor asked me to write a children's magazine serial full of action, adventure, and cliffhangers. This resulted in my first children's novel, *Gold at Kapai*. Writing for children was so satisfying that I stayed with it.

*   *   *

For sound straight-out action stories with a New Zealand setting Phyl Wardell has few rivals. She attempts no maudlin sentiment or quasi-psychology but writes lucidly and produces unpretentious but absorbing novels. All six of her books, written over a period of 25 years, have a strong element of detection and in all of them some aspect of the New Zealand heritage, flora, or fauna are under threat. Living as she does in Christchurch, she is within easy travelling distance of the Southern Alps and of the South Western fiords, and apart from the strong storyline which keeps the pages turning, her work could be seen as an evocation of the New Zealand landscape.

Her settings move from gold fields in *Gold at Kapai*, where a group of young people investigate a murder attempt on an old miner, to Fiordland in *The Secret of the Lost Tribe of Te Anau*, in which a film company hopes to track down and film a lost Maori tribe. It is based on a legend which relates how the Ngati Mamoe tribe withdrew into the dense bush and mountains after losing a battle. The book sets the pattern for her subsequent interest in conservation—typically, although the lost tribe is discovered it is decided to leave them in peace and not intrude the 20th century upon them. In

Passage to Dusky, again set in the Sounds, Maori greenstone artifacts are rescued. *Hazard Island* sees an investigation into the disappearance of a diver, which leads to the discovery of paua shell smuggling. *The Nelson Treasure*, the only book set in the North Island, has as its theme the conservation of native bush and of the rediscovery of the rare huia bird, thought to be extinct. It exists in an area which has been carefully protected from tourists by an unusual man, Matt, who, in a surprise ending, turns out to be a woman, one of the early aviators who was assumed killed when her gipsy moth plane crashed after she had crossed the Tasman singlehandedly 40 years ago.

Another extinct bird features in the latest novel *Beyond the Narrows* when there are reported sightings of a moa in Fiordland. Through investigating these rumours the young protagonists uncover the misuse of a drug which, initially intended to increase sheep's wool production, has had the effect of causing animals who were given experimental doses to grow to giant proportions. Thus Canada geese have become as large as moas.

Wardell's books have carefully constructed plots, there are no extraneous episodes, the action is fast, and one event leads logically to another. It is in the story, rather than in character development, that her main interest lies. Her enterprising young people have little time for introspection; they are too involved with the immediacy of the task in hand. In this they are true descendants of the early settlers, but unlike them, their concern is to preserve the land rather than to dominate it.

—Betty Gilderdale

WATKINS-PITCHFORD, D(enys) J(ames). Writes as BB; has also written as Michael Traherne. British. Born in Lamport, Northamptonshire, 25 July 1905. Educated privately; studied art in Paris, 1924, and at the Royal College of Art, London; associate, Royal College of Art Painting School, 1926–28. Served in the City of London Yeomanry Royal Horse Artillery, 1926–29 (King's Cup Medal); served in the Home Guard, 1940–46: Captain. Married Cecily Mary Adnitt in 1939 (died 1974); one daughter and one son (deceased). Assistant art master, Rugby School, Warwickshire, 1930–47. Since 1947 freelance author and illustrator. Recipient: Library Association Carnegie Medal, 1943. M.A.: Leicester University, 1986. Fellow, Royal Society of Arts. Agent: David Higham Associates Ltd., 5–8 Lower John Street, London W1R 4HA. Address: The Round House, Sudborough, Kettering, Northamptonshire, England.

PUBLICATIONS FOR CHILDREN (as BB; illustrated by the author)

Fiction

Wild Lone. London, Eyre and Spottiswoode, and New York, Scribner, 1938.
Sky Gipsy: The Story of a Wild Goose. London, Eyre and Spottiswoode, 1939; as *Manka, The Sky Gipsy*, New York, Scribner, 1939.
The Little Grey Men. London, Eyre and Spottiswoode, 1942; New York, Scribner, 1949.
Brendon Chase. London, Hollis and Carter, 1944; New York, Scribner, 1945.
Down the Bright Stream. London, Eyre and Spottiswoode, 1948.
The Forest of Boland Light Railway. London, Eyre and Spottiswoode, 1955; as *The Forest of the Railway*, New York, Dodd

Mead, 1957.
Monty Woodpig's Caravan. London, Ward, 1957.
Ben the Bullfinch. London, Hamish Hamilton, 1957.
Wandering Wind. London, Hamish Hamilton, 1957; as *Bill Badger and the Wandering Wind*, London, Methuen, 1981.
Alexander. Oxford, Blackwell, 1957.
Monty Woodpig and His Bumblebuzz Car. London, Ward, 1958.
Mr. Bumstead. London, Eyre and Spottiswoode, 1958.
The Wizard of Boland. London, Ward, 1959.
Bill Badger's Winter Cruise. London, Hamish Hamilton, 1959.
Bill Badger and the Pirates. London, Hamish Hamilton, 1960.
Bill Badger's Finest Hour. London, Hamish Hamilton, 1961.
Bill Badger's Whispering Reeds Adventure. London, Hamish Hamilton, 1962.
Lepus, The Brown Hare. London, Benn, 1962.
Bill Badger's Big Mistake. London, Hamish Hamilton, 1963.
Bill Badger and the Big Store Robbery. London, Hamish Hamilton, 1967.
The Whopper. London, Benn, 1967.
At the Back o' Ben Dee. London, Benn, 1968.
Bill Badger's Voyage to the World's End. London, Kaye and Ward, 1969.
The Tyger Tray. London, Methuen, 1971.
The Pool of the Black Witch. London, Methuen, 1974.
Lord of the Forest. London, Methuen, 1975.
Stories of the Wild, with A.L.E. Fenton and A. Windsor-Richards. London, Benn, 1975.
More Stories of the Wild, with A. Windsor-Richards. London, Benn, 1977.
Bill Badger and the Secret Weapon. London, Methuen, 1983.

Other

Meeting Hill: BB's Fairy Book. London, Hollis and Carter, 1948.
The Wind in the Wood. London, Hollis and Carter, 1952.
The Badgers of Bearshanks. London, Benn, 1961.
The Pegasus Book of the Countryside. London, Dobson, 1964.

PUBLICATIONS FOR ADULTS (as BB; illustrated by the author)

Short Stories

5 More Stories, with others. Oxford, Blackwell, 1957.

Other

The Idle Countryman. London, Eyre and Spottiswoode, 1943.
The Wayfaring Tree. London, Hollis and Carter, 1945.
A Stream in Your Garden. London, Eyre and Spottiswoode, 1948.
Be Quiet and Go A-Angling (as Michael Traherne). London, Lutterworth Press, 1949.
Confessions of a Carp Fisher. London, Eyre and Spottiswoode, 1950; revised edition, London, Witherby, 1970.
Tide's Ending. London, Hollis and Carter, and New York, Scribner, 1950.
Letters from Compton Deverell. London, Eyre and Spottiswoode, 1950.
Dark Estuary. London, Hollis and Carter, 1953; Chicago, Academy, 1984.
A Carp Water: Wood Pool and How to Fish It. London, Putnam, 1958.
The Autumn Road to the Isles. London, Kaye, 1959.
The White Road Westwards. London, Kaye, 1961.
September Road to Caithness and the Western Sea. London, Kaye, 1962.

The Summer Road to Wales. London, Kaye, 1964.
A Summer on the Nene. London, Kaye and Ward, 1967.
Recollections of a 'longshore Gunner. Ipswich, Suffolk, Boydell Press, 1976.
A Child Alone: The Memoirs of BB. London, Joseph, 1978.
Ramblings of a Sportsman-Naturalist. London, Joseph, 1979.
The Naturalist's Bedside Book. London, Joseph, 1980.
The Quiet Fields. London, Joseph, 1981.
Indian Summer. London, Joseph, 1984.
The Best of BB. London, Joseph, 1985.
Fisherman's Folly. Woodbridge, Suffolk, Boydell and Brewer, 1987.

Editor, *The Sportsman's Bedside Book.* London, Eyre and Spottiswoode, 1937.
Editor, *The Countryman's Bedside Book.* London, Eyre and Spottiswoode, 1941.
Editor, *The Fisherman's Bedside Book.* London, Eyre and Spottiswoode, 1945; New York, Scribner, 1946.
Editor, *The Shooting Man's Bedside Book.* London, Eyre and Spottiswoode, and New York, Scribner, 1948.

*

Illustrator: *Sport in Wildest Britain* by H.V. Prichard, 1936; *Winged Company* by R.G. Walmsley, 1940; *England Is a Village* by Clarence H. Warren, 1940; *Southern English* by Eric Benfield, 1942; *Narrow Boat* by L.T.C. Rolt, 1944; *Red Vagabond* by Gerald D. Adams, 1946; *It's My Delight* by Brian V. Fitzgerald, 1947; *Philandering Angler* by Arthur Applin, 1948; *A Sportsman Looks at Eire* by J.B. Drought, 1949; *Landmarks* by Arthur G. Street, 1949; *Fairy Tales of Long Ago* edited by Mabel C. Carey, 1952; *The White Foxes of Gorfenletch*, 1954, *Beasts of the North Country*, 1961, and *To Do With Birds*, 1965, all by Henry S. Tegner; *The Secret of Orra* by Elfrida Vipont, 1957; *The Long Night*, 1958, and *Thirteen O'Clock*, 1960, both by William Mayne; *Vix*, 1960, *Birds of the Lonely Lake*, 1961, *The Cabin in the Woods*, 1963, and *The Wild White Swan*, 1965, all by Arthur Richards; *Prince Prigio and Prince Ricardo* by Andrew Lang, 1961; *The Rogue Elephant*, 1962, *Red Ivory*, 1964, and *Jungle Rescue*, 1967, all by Arthur Catherall; *Granny's Wonderful Chair* by Frances Browne, 1963; *King Todd* by Norah Burke, 1963; *The Lost Princess* by George MacDonald, 1965; *Where Vultures Fly* by Gerald Summers, 1974.

D.J. Watkins-Pitchford comments:

Though some of my best-selling books were written for young people, most—if not all—are appreciated equally by adults and I take this as a great compliment! A keen observation is essential to a successful author. I write because I find it an intensely rewarding thing, and it is fun to illustrate my own books.

*   *   *

More familiar to us as BB, D.J. Watkins-Pitchford is known above all for his wildlife books. An enthusiastic natural historian, he is able to convey vividly his wide knowledge and deep love of the countryside. *Sky Gipsy* is the story of a wild goose, telling with sympathetic insight of the beautiful but harsh life of these birds. *Wild Lone* is a moving but unsentimental account of the life of a fox in the Pytchley Hunt country. *Brendon Chase* is also about survival in the wild, but here it is two boys playing truant to live in the woods and finding that open-air living has its disadvantages.

For younger children he has created the enchanted forest of Boland, a place where anything can happen. Absurd humour which tickles the palates of the under-tens predominates in *The Wizard of Boland*, where incompetence in high places produces hilarious

results. *The Forest of Boland Light Railway* is similarly delightful. His animal heroes Bill Badger and the hedgehog Monty Woodpig have adventures in the woodland and by the canal which appeal greatly to sixes and sevens and are splendid for reading aloud.

The Little Grey Men won the Carnegie Medal in 1943, and is still a prime favourite. Its sequel, *Down the Bright Stream*, was illustrated by the author in scraperboard, though in later editions he painted in oils. These are truly delightful tales and make ideal bedtime stories. They deal with three dwarves, Dodder, Balemoney, and Sneezewort (all old country wildflower names) and their quest for their long-lost brother, using a clockwork toy boat which they find.

In all his books, the English countryside is not merely supportive but a leading character, making them pleasurable reading for all ages.

—Ann G. Hay

————

WATSON, Clyde. American. Born in New York City, 25 July 1947. Educated at Smith College, Northampton, Massachusetts, A.B. in music 1968. Married Denis Devlin in 1978; one son and one daughter. Professional violinist and violin teacher: teacher, The Common School, Amherst, Massachusetts, 1968–70, and Indian Township School, Maine, 1971–73. Address: 7 Low Road, Hanover, New Hampshire 03755, U.S.A.

PUBLICATIONS FOR CHILDREN (illustrated by Wendy Watson)

Fiction

Tom Fox and the Apple Pie. New York, Crowell, 1972; London, Macmillan, 1973.
How Brown Mouse Kept Christmas. New York, Farrar Straus 1980; London, Hamish Hamilton, 1981.
Valentine Foxes, illustrated by Wendy Watson. New York, Orchard, 1989.

Verse

Father Fox's Pennyrhymes. New York, Crowell, 1971; London, Macmillan, 1972.
Hickory Stick Rag. New York, Crowell, 1976.
Catch Me and Kiss Me and Say It Again. New York, Collins World, and London, Collins, 1978.
Midnight Moon, illustrated by Susanna Natti. New York, Collins, 1979.
Applebet: An ABC. New York, Farrar Straus, 1982.
Father Fox's Feast of Songs, music by the author. New York, Philomel, 1983.

Other

Quips and Quirks (collection of epithets). New York, Crowell, 1975.
Binary Numbers. New York, Crowell, 1977.

Recording: *Father Fox's Feast of Songs and Three Stories*, Hanover, New Hampshire, Sassafras, 1986.

*

Illustrator: *How Does It Feel to Be a Tree?* by Flo Morse, 1976.

Music: *Fisherman Lullabies*, by Wendy Watson, 1968; *Carol to a Child*, lyrics by Nancy Dingman Watson, 1969.

* * *

The key to Clyde Watson's writing is the fact that she is a musician. Her poems are often song lyrics; her prose has a musical ring. She writes quasi-Mother Goose rhyme that is influenced by three things: the old poems, her New England background, and her musical ability.

Her first works were the straightforward musical arrangements for her sister's *Fisherman Lullabies* and her mother's *Carol to a Child*. She seemed to be riding into the publishing world on her family's coattails.

However, with *Father Fox's Pennyrhymes* Watson came into her own. It is the best of all the Watson family's many books. The book is a collection of short, simple, spirited, and highly original nonsense rhymes, many of which are actually lyrics to songs Clyde composed. The impeccable rhythms, the melodic flow of the full and slant rhymes all bespeak the author's musical background:

> The sky is dark, there blows a storm,
> Our cider is hot, the fire is warm,
> The snow is deep and the night is long:
> Old Father Fox, will you sing us a song?

The poems obviously come from a folkloric tradition—Mother Goose, English ballads, lullabies, and jump-rope rhymes. But instead of the 17th-century English countryside or the streets of London, they celebrate New England and especially rural Vermont where Watson was brought up. The verses range from the decidedly impish to the boisterously aggressive to some that are as soft as a cradle song. They are instantly memorized by young listeners. The pictures in the book, again by her sister, are colorful and inventive, in a comic strip format. The details in both the rhymes and the illustrations are both personal (family jokes are enshrined, the Putney farm is pictured) and universal. The book, in fact, was recognized as a modern classic on publication, winning, among other prizes, a National Book award nomination. Quite simply, it is a beautiful, individual volume, certainly one of the few in the 1970's that is destined to outlast its decade—and even its century.

Tom Fox and the Apple Pie (a simple prose sequel), *Quips and Quirks* (a witty assemblage of name-calling epithets), *Hickory Stick Rag* (rhyming verse immortalizing the turn-of-the-century rural school house and its denizens), and *Catch Me and Kiss Me and Say It Again* (gentle poems for pre-schoolers) are all clever and childlike and full of appealing mischief. But none of them reaches the depth of *Father Fox's Pennyrhymes* nor do any of them have its range of color, tone, and musical appeal.

—Jane Yolen

WATSON, James. British. Born in Darwen, Lancashire, 8 November 1936. Educated at the University of Nottingham, B.A. (honours) in history 1958; University of Sussex, Brighton, 1977–78, M.A. in education 1979. Served in the Royal Army Education Corps, 1958–60: Lieutenant. Married Catherine Downey in 1963; three daughters. English teacher, British Council, Milan, Italy, 1960–61; journalist and art critic, *Northeast Evening Gazette*, Middlesbrough, Yorkshire, 1961–63; education officer, Dunlop Company, London, 1963–65. Since 1966 Lecturer in communication and education, West Kent College, Tonbridge. Recipient: Children's Rights Workshop Other award, 1983; Walter Hines Page scholarship, 1987; Buxtehude Bulle prize (Germany), 1987. Address: 9 Farmcombe Close, Tunbridge Wells, Kent TN2 5DG, England.

PUBLICATIONS FOR CHILDREN

Fiction

Sign of the Swallow. London, Nelson, 1967.
The Bull Leapers. London, Gollancz, and New York, Coward McCann, 1970.
Legion of the White Tiger. London, Gollancz, 1973.
The Freedom Tree. London, Gollancz, 1976.
Talking in Whispers. London, Gollancz, and New York, Knopf, 1983.
Where Nobody Sees. London, Gollancz, 1987.
Make Your Move (stories). London, Gollancz, 1988.

Plays

Radio Plays: *Gilbert Makepeace Lives!*, 1972; *Venus Rising from the Sea*, 1977; *A Slight Insurrection*, 1980; *What a Little Moonlight Can Do*, 1982.

PUBLICATIONS FOR ADULTS

Other

Liberal Studies in Further Education. Windsor, National Foundation for Educational Research, 1973.
The Loneliness of a Long Distance Innovation: General Studies in a College of Further Education: A Document for the Future. Nottingham, Association for Liberal Education, 1980.
A Dictionary of Communication and Media Studies, with Anne Hill. London, Arnold, 1984; revised edition, 1989.
What Is Communication Studies? London, Arnold, 1985.

*

James Watson comments:

After beginning my writing career with books exploring my interest in history, I moved to themes that stirred interest but also a more involved concern. *The Freedom Tree*, set in the Spanish Civil War, its climax the bombing of Guernica, led on to the world of here and now. *Talking in Whispers* is about the Chile of the generals—it seems to have struck a particularly resonant note in the hearts and minds of young readers. *Where Nobody Sees* returns me to home ground, telling the story of two teenagers who discover the illegal dumping of nuclear waste and the peril this places them in when they attempt to make the matter public. My first collection of stories, *Make Your Move*, ranges historically from a tale set in the Chaco War in Bolivia to the kind of problems faced by teenagers in modern Britain, and geographically between an English cricket field and an Iron Curtain country. As the title suggests, the stories are about young people forced into making decisions in a society which seems to be increasingly intolerant of youth and repressive towards it.

* * *

Writers of books for young people are not renowned for their interest in overtly political situations. This is not to say that these writers do not write in a political way: for example, it would not be difficult to guess the political stance of an Imperialist writer like

Henry or to ascertain the amount of liberal feeling a writer like Enid Blyton shows when discussing her social inferiors. James Watson is first and foremost a political writer but one who, in his most important work, is able to display this political feeling in a powerful and telling manner.

Watson's early work consists of three historical novels. *Sign of the Swallow* is set in the Renaissance, *The Bull Leapers* is an interpretation of the Theseus and the Minotaur legend, while *Legion of the White Tiger* presents the contrast between the Roman culture and that of the Huns. Although all three are of interest to students of Watson's work, none of them could be considered more than apprentice pieces. *The Freedom Tree* is also an historical novel but one more concerned with recent history, and it contains the beginnings of the political themes running through Watson's later books. It is set during the Spanish Civil War which coincides with the Depression in 1930's England. Will Viljoen, whose father has died fighting for the Republicans in Spain, comes to London from Jarrow in the hope of travelling to Spain also. In London he teams up with Griff and later with the painter Candy Sam who adds them to his group of friends travelling to Spain where Sam's sister, Molly, is a nurse. After a series of adventures in France, they arrive to find themselves in a badly organised war. Most of Will's friends are killed but Will and Molly eventually reach Guernica where they witness the destruction of the village by the Fascists.

Although *The Freedom Tree* is a novel of power in places, particularly towards its climax, there is a feeling that Watson is unsure at this point in his career of the difference between a history textbook and a novel. Skilfully plotted though the book is, none of the characters apart from Will seem real: they range from the saintly Molly to the caricatured Basque Federico ("I speak the Enn-glish like the cannibal, eh?"). In his next novel, *Talking in Whispers*, Watson does manage to bring together a convincing and powerful story, with political depth and credible characters. The novel is set in Chile, "sometime between the present and the future," although a reader with a rudimentary knowledge of South American history will recognise some of the situations. Andres, son of an anti-establishment singer, escapes when his father's car is ambushed. He is helped by a brother and sister, twin puppeteers. The main political opponent of the Junta is also shot prior to an election which would put him in power, and Andres receives the photographic evidence which shows a member of the Secret Service carrying out the shooting. How Andres helps to bring the truth to the world is told in an exciting and absorbing way. The writer's anger is all the more powerful for being kept in reserve, while he also does not shirk from showing the darker side of an inhuman regime as in the episode of Andres's torture in the infamous House of Laughter. *Talking in Whispers* is widely read, discussed, and enjoyed by teenage readers.

Where Nobody Sees brings Watson's work firmly back to his own country and time. Vicar's son Luke discovers sinister happenings in woods near his home. The appearance of Petra, a member of a community theatre group whom Luke's mother has encountered at a peace camp, leads to the revelation that nuclear waste is being dumped in the woods. Petra's determination to expose this in a theatrical performance brings on the exciting climatic events of the novel. Watson is a much more confident writer in this novel, showing skill in both plot and characterisation. The characters are not merely mouthpieces for the author's views but show human qualities and failings: Luke's parents, for instance, although both right-minded, have obvious faults as have Luke and Petra. The facts about nuclear waste are eased into the story in a subtle way which makes them more memorable and telling.

Watson's strengths and flaws can be seen to good effect in his short story collection, *Make Your Move*. Some of the stories are inclined to be too wordy and didactic although this is a failing Watson has curbed in his later writing. Yet the majority have an uncompromising and realistic attitude to both public and private life which goes far

deeper than much writing for teenagers. Although most of his books contain disturbing material, he still has room for hope, which comes through his young protagonists. Despite the hardships Andres suffers at the hands of the Junta in *Talking in Whispers*, he is last seen handing out copies of the photograph which may destroy the regime. As one of the mercenaries involved in the dumping of nuclear waste says near the end of *Where Nobody Sees*, "We make the cash, but they make the hope."

—Keith Barker

WAYNE, (Anne) Jenifer. British. Born in London in 1917. Educated at Blackheath High School, London; Somerville College, Oxford, 1936–39, B.A. (honours) 1939. Married C.R. Hewitt in 1948; two daughters and one son. Worked for the London Ambulance Service, 1939; junior English mistress, Newark High School, Nottinghamshire, 1940–41; writer and producer, BBC Radio Features Department, London, 1941–48. *Died 10 December 1982.*

PUBLICATIONS FOR CHILDREN

Fiction (illustrated by Margaret Palmer)

Clemence and Ginger, illustrated by Patricia Humphreys. London, Heinemann, 1960.
The Day the Ceiling Fell Down, illustrated by Dodie Masterman. London, Heinemann, 1961.
The Night the Rain Came In, illustrated by Dodie Masterman. London, Heinemann, 1963.
Kitchen People. London, Heinemann, 1963; Indianapolis, Bobbs Merrill, 1965.
Merry by Name. London, Heinemann, 1964.
The Ghost Next Door. London, Heinemann, 1965.
Saturday and the Irish Aunt. London, Heinemann, 1966.
Someone in the Attic. London, Heinemann, 1967.
Ollie. London, Heinemann, 1969.
Sprout. London, Heinemann, 1970; New York, McGraw Hill, 1976.
Something in the Barn. London, Heinemann, 1971.
Sprout's Window-Cleaner. London, Heinemann, 1971; New York, McGraw Hill, 1976.
Sprout and the Dog-Sitter. London, Heinemann, 1972; New York, McGraw Hill, 1977.
The Smoke in Albert's Garden. London, Heinemann, 1974.
Sprout and the Helicopter. London, Heinemann, 1975; New York, McGraw Hill, 1977.
Sprout and the Conjuror. London, Heinemann, 1976; as *Sprout and the Magician*, New York, McGraw Hill, 1977.

PUBLICATIONS FOR ADULTS

Play

Radio Play: *The Queen of the Castle*, 1969.

Verse

The Shadows and Other Poems. London, Secker and Warburg, 1959.

CHILDREN'S WRITERS

Other

This Is the Law: Stories of Wrongdoers by Fault or Folly. London, Sylvan Press, 1948.
Brown Bread and Butter in the Basement: A Twenties Childhood. London, Gollancz, 1973.
The Purple Dress: Growing Up in the Thirties. London, Gollancz, 1979.

* * *

To everyone who has been reading children's books during the last 25 years or so, the name of Jenifer Wayne must be synonymous with the memory of a rollicking family story, which before many pages have been read becomes hilarious.

Always a family of individualists, always a harassed mother, always a "Wayne" unexpected development in the plot, which in less capable hands would be almost unbelievable. Wayne was also able to draw first-class character studies of people in her stories whose activities are amusing to read about, but who might be termed minor characters in the plot. An example is Mr. Kim the gardener in *The Ghost Next Door*. In the same book she depicts the bogus Royal Navy Commander who successfully fools everyone, thus striking a warning note to her readers to take nothing for granted. These stories are relaxing, splendid, and true to life—at least as far as some families are concerned. Wayne wrote several stories of this kind—the titles alone reveal their nature—*The Day the Ceiling Fell Down, The Night the Rain Came In, The Smoke in Albert's Garden.*

Perhaps, however, her greatest creation was the hero of a series of books for younger children—the little boy called Sprout. Sprout is so named because of a lock of his hair that refuses to lie down. Sprout—and sometimes his young sister Tilly as well—get up to the most extraordinary adventures in an innocent sort of way. Sprout goes carol-singing after a bout of flu, gets lost in the snow, and wakes up to find what he thought was a polar bear standing over him. Actually, it is a sheepdog called Chops who is Sprout's devoted companion forevermore. Sprout wins a dinghy in a seaside competition, and when his name, Rupert E. Smith, is announced, Sprout almost fails to realize that he is the winner.

Possessed of a very strong imagination, Wayne wrote stories that are a tonic to read.

—Berna C. Clark

WEBB, Christopher. See **WIBBERLEY, Leonard.**

WEBSTER, Jean (Alice Jane Chandler Webster). American. Born in Fredonia, New York, 24 July 1876; grandniece of the writer Mark Twain. Educated at schools in Fredonia; Lady Jane Grey School, Binghamton, New York, graduated 1896; Vassar College, Poughkeepsie, New York, B.A. in English and economics 1901. Married Glenn Ford McKinney in 1915; one daughter. *Died 11 June 1916.*

PUBLICATIONS FOR CHILDREN

Fiction (illustrated by the author)

Daddy-Long-Legs. New York, Century, 1912; London, Hodder and Stoughton, 1913.
Dear Enemy. New York, Century, and London, Hodder and Stoughton, 1915.

Play

Daddy Long-Legs, adaptation of her own novel (produced New York, 1914; London, 1916). New York, French, 1922; London, French, 1927.

PUBLICATIONS FOR ADULTS

Novels

The Wheat Princess. New York, Century, 1905; London, Hodder and Stoughton, 1916.
Jerry, Junior. New York, Century, and London, Gay and Bird, 1907; as *Jerry*, London, Hodder and Stoughton, 1916.
The Four-Pools Mystery (published anonymously). New York, Century, 1908; as Jean Webster, London, Hodder and Stoughton, 1916.
Much Ado about Peter. New York, Doubleday, 1909; London, Hodder and Stoughton, 1916.

Short Stories

When Patty Went to College. New York, Century, 1903; as *Patty and Priscilla*, London, Hodder and Stoughton, 1915.
Just Patty. New York, Century, 1911; London, Hodder and Stoughton, 1915.

Verse

Vitriol and Lilacs. Cleveland, Press of Flozari, 1943.

* * *

Two books only—one and its sequel—keep us aware of Jean Webster's name today. But these two, *Daddy-Long-Legs* and *Dear Enemy*, have stayed in print through the century; they have even slipped into modern mythology, and they entertain us still. Light-hearted and effervescent though they are, they grew from a serious thought. In the author's student days at Vassar in the late 19th century, as part of an economics course, she had visited orphanages and other grim institutions. It was then that her belief began to grow that, however unlucky a start a boy or girl might have, the chance of success should be possible for all. She worked this out at last in the two books here. Because of her sudden early death they were her final stories.

In *Daddy-Long-Legs* Judy (Jerusha Abbott, named from a tombstone and a telephone book) has spent all her life in the bleak and regimented John Grier Orphanage. At 17 she is still there as general help. A youngish trustee (30-ish as we later find), rich but unconventional, is amused by one of her essays and arranges to send her to college. All that is required of her is to write a monthly letter, via his secretary, to "Mr. John Smith," and not to expect a reply. John Smith? What a name to choose, thinks the audacious girl. She addresses her letters to Daddy-Long-Legs, after the long thin shadow she once saw of the unknown trustee-benefactor. The letters, with all their problems, joys, discoveries, secrets, are the book, and they delight the recipient as much as they please us. In his own persona (he's related to her haughty patrician room-mate Julia Pendleton) he makes acquaintance with Judy. He becomes jealous enough to try to use his authority (as Trustee Mr. Smith) to prevent her meeting brothers of her friends. Ah, complications....

Why was this book such a triumph? What still keeps it alive? For one thing, an orphan is the heroine, and orphans, whether Jane Eyre or Heathcliff, Oliver Twist or Anne of Green Gables, Froggy and his sad little brother or any of those foundlings in legend, have always had a special power in story. The more sheltered the reader's life the more the romantic appeal. Then, too, the book is a neat variation of that favourite of fairy tales, Cinderella. For readers of 1912 (Webster's young ladies are reading Shaw and Wells) this version had a particularly modern twist: the waif is to do so well in her new life that the prince is in danger of losing her. And another irresistible theme is woven in—that of a newcomer from another place, time, or social order discovering with astonishment the reader's familiar scene. Much piquancy comes from the fact that Judy has never had letters or birthday presents; that she has never been on a train journey, never even inside a private house.

The letter writing formula itself has a curious charm (note the success of the recent American *84 Charing Cross Road*). Letters have immediacy; they reveal; they make rapport with the reader. But *Daddy-Long-Legs* has another point of interest—the college curriculum: literature, Latin, French, mathematics, physiology, philosophy, history of art—Webster doesn't skimp details. We almost take the course ourselves. There are also all those basic books which Judy must secretly add to her mind's furniture—*Alice, Jane Eyre*—a fascinating list. Never underrate the fictional interest of facts.

True, you may observe that Judy is not a fair example. She has looks and charm (Jervis Pendleton is not her only admirer); she is clever enough to learn all those new college subjects; she can also "room" easily with girls from the top families in New York, and please their parents when she visits their homes. But in fact, as today's world shows, her progress is not as unlikely as it might seem. Indeed, whatever in the plot is preposterous (and there are many points for quibbling over) the book has the truth of fiction—more exactly, of fairy tale.

Dear Enemy still, happily, keeps the letter formula, but the writer is now the red-haired Sally McBride, Judy's college roommate and best friend. The now-married Judy and Jervis are determined to reform the John Grier Home, and have imposed on Sally, idling away in socialite Massachusetts, the task of doing so. In her letters to the elusive pair she rebels, she protests, but—for the time being—she stays. She continues to stay. She also writes now and then to Gordon, a rich, debonair young man who obediently sends gifts and equipment to the Home while waiting for Sally to tire of this latest whim. But for practical reasons more (if shorter) notes go to the dour Scottish orphanage doctor, "Dear Enemy," so vexing, so baffling, yet such a pillar of strength in a crisis. Meanwhile, against all possible problems (not to mention dramas of individual orphans) reforms advance.

Webster's orphanage theories (as put into practice by Sally) are modern enough: the setting up of cottage family homes ("As long as the family is the unit of society, children should be hardened early to family life"), the choosing of personal clothes, the admission of pets, the experience of spending or saving money. Surprisingly, she does not add a library; books (and these were pre-television days) are never mentioned at all. Her ideas on diet might need revising too. "You would never dream of all the delightful surprises we are going to have," writes Sally: "brown bread, corn pone, graham muffins, samp, rice pudding with *lots* of raisins, thick vegetable soup, macaroni Italian fashion, polenta cake with molasses, apple dumplings, gingerbread—oh, an endless list!" There are greater differences. Children outnumbered adopters—and adopters call the tune. They can specify that a child must be not only blue-eyed but of legitimate birth. Old ladies (especially when rich) are welcomed. One senses, too (perhaps from the nice scribbly pictures), that the ethnic minglings so much part of our Homes and schools today, had not reached the John Grier. Most arrivals (like Sally herself) are Irish.

Yet is not fiction the readiest teacher of history—of social history certainly? These books still make rewarding reading.

—Naomi Lewis

WEIR, Rosemary (née Green). Has also written as Catherine Bell. British. Born in Kimberley, South Africa, 22 July 1905. Educated at schools in South Africa and England. Served in the First Aid Nursing Yeomanry during World War II. Married Napier Weir in 1931 (died 1973); one daughter. Has worked as an actress, farmer, teacher, and cook. Agent: Charles Lavell Ltd., 176 Wardour Street, London W1V 3AA. Address: Ford Farm, Holcombe Rogus, Wellington, Somerset, England.

PUBLICATIONS FOR CHILDREN

Fiction

The Secret Journey. London, Parrish, 1957.
The Secret of Cobbetts Farm. London, Parrish, 1957.
No. 10 Green Street. London, Parrish, 1958.
Island of Birds. London, Parrish, 1959.
The Honeysuckle Line. London, Parrish, 1959; as *Robert's Rescued Railway*, New York, Watts, 1960.
The Hunt for Harry. London, Parrish, 1959.
Great Days in Green Street. London, Parrish, 1960.
Pineapple Farm, illustrated by Hugh Marshall. London, Parrish, 1960.
Little Lion's Real Island, illustrated by W.F. Phillipps. London, Harrap, 1960.
The House in the Middle of the Road. London, Parrish, 1961.
Albert the Dragon, illustrated by Quentin Blake. London and New York, Abelard Schuman, 1961.
What a Lark, illustrated by Val Biro. Leicester, Brockhampton Press, 1961.
Tania Takes the Stage. London, Hutchinson, 1961.
Top Secret. London, Parrish, 1962.
The Star and the Flame, illustrated by William Stobbs. London, Faber, 1962; New York, Farrar Straus, 1964.
Soap Box Derby, illustrated by Val Biro. Leicester, Brockhampton Press, 1962; Princeton, New Jersey, Van Nostrand, 1965.
Black Sheep. London, Parrish, 1963; as *Mystery of the Black Sheep*, New York, Criterion, 1964.
The Smallest Dog on Earth, illustrated by Charles Pickard. London, Abelard Schuman, 1963; New York, Abelard Schuman, 1964.
Further Adventures of Albert the Dragon, illustrated by Quentin Blake. London and New York, Abelard Schuman, 1964.
Mike's Gang, illustrated by Charles Pickard. London and New York, Abelard Schuman, 1965.
A Patch of Green. London, Parrish, 1965.
Devon Venture (as Catherine Bell). London, Collins, 1965.
The Real Game, illustrated by Aedwin Darroll. Leicester, Brockhampton Press, 1965; as *The Heirs of Ashton Manor*, New York, Dial Press, 1966.
The Boy from Nowhere, illustrated by Dennis Turner. London and New York, Abelard Schuman, 1966.
High Courage, illustrated by Ian Ribbons. London, Faber, and New York, Farrar Straus, 1967.
Pyewacket, illustrated by Charles Pickard. London and New York, Abelard Schuman, 1967.
Boy on a Brown Horse. London, Hamish Hamilton, 1967; New

York, Hawthorn, 1971.
The Foxwood Flyer, illustrated by Robert Hales. London, Hamish Hamilton, 1968.
Albert the Dragon and the Centaur, illustrated by Quentin Blake. London and New York, Abelard Schuman, 1968.
No Sleep for Angus, illustrated by Elisabeth Grant. London and New York, Abelard Schuman, 1969.
Summer of the Silent Hands, illustrated by Lynette Hemmant. Leicester, Brockhampton Press, 1969.
The Lion and the Rose, illustrated by Richard Cuffari. New York, Farrar Straus, 1970; London, Abelard Schuman, 1972.
The Three Red Herrings. Nashville, Nelson, 1972.
Blood Royal, illustrated by Richard Cuffari. New York, Farrar Straus, 1973.
Uncle Barney and the Sleep-Destroyer, illustrated by Carolyn Dinan. London, Abelard Schuman, 1974.
Uncle Barney and the Shrink-Drink, illustrated by Carolyn Dinan. London, Abelard Schuman, 1977.
Albert and the Dragonettes, illustrated by Gerald Rose. London, Abelard Schuman, 1977.
Albert's World Tour, illustrated by David McKee. London, Abelard Schuman, 1978.
Pyewacket & Son, illustrated by Charles Pickard. London, Abelard Schuman, 1980.

Other

A Dog of Your Own: or, Dogs Without Tears: Do's and Don't's for Young Dog Owners, illustrated by K.F. Barker. London, Harrap, 1960.
The Young David Garrick, illustrated by Anne Linton. London, Parrish, 1963; New York, Roy, 1964.
The Man Who Built a City: A Life of Sir Christopher Wren. New York, Farrar Straus, 1971.

PUBLICATIONS FOR ADULTS

Play

Radio Play: *The Off-White Elephant*, 1958.

*

Rosemary Weir comments:
I began to write for children when my own daughter was grown up and I myself was over 50. I remembered my own childhood very clearly and perhaps my books for children were a way of returning to a happy time of my life. On the whole I have most enjoyed writing for younger children, *The Smallest Dog on Earth* being my own favourite.

*   *   *

Rosemary Weir's books are for a wide range of readers, from very simple stories to straight historical adventures and novels for much older children.
Albert, the peaceful dragon, and Pyewacket, the ferocious old alley-cat, have adventures original and entertaining enough to lure the inexperienced reader to books. The humour and interest depend almost wholly upon external situation, but they are excellent for their purpose. Longer books, still for young children, such as *What a Lark* and *Soap Box Derby*, are cheerful, convincing, and undemanding. One feels they may have been written to meet the demand by some librarians and teachers for "neighborhood stories," and many children will enjoy them.

The historical adventures offer far more. They are well researched but not too heavily cumbered with details of contemporary events or manners. They remain stories, not history lessons. *High Courage*, set in the time of Simon de Montfort, brings alive the violence and tragedy of civil wars, the constricting life of a mediaeval castle, the contrasts of wealth and poverty. *The Lion and the Rose* tells of a lad ambitious to be a master stone-carver, who works on the rebuilding of St. Paul's. The feeling for the quality of stone itself, and the impressions of St. Paul's and the Portland quarries, are lively and memorable. These novels tell a good straightforward story with pace and interest. They are more concerned with events than character; the persons are satisfactorily rounded but not studied in any depth.
Weir's best work is in the novels for older readers. *The Real Game* tells of two children from the Australian outback who discover that their father is the heir to an earldom. Their own knowledge of the English aristocracy is derived from a battered copy of *Little Lord Fauntleroy*, found by mere chance; but when they are sent home to Ashton Court the slow adjustment from dream to reality is both funny and touching. Sebastian, shy, nervous, always too dependent on his loving but bossy sister, is deeply troubled until at last he discovers his true gift and becomes a person in his own right. This is a book full of warmth and humour and kindness, with a very sensitive understanding of the anxieties and uncertainties and embarrassments of childhood. The same ability to probe and interpret experience is seen in *Summer of the Silent Hands*, which concerns a brilliant boy pianist suddenly deprived by an accident of his gift and of the only life he knows. Through loneliness and anxiety, friendship and laughter, he has slowly to find his way in the uncharted world of family life and ordinary childhood.
It is these books for older readers that show Weir as an original and perceptive writer. The characterization is strong and clear, including satisfactory and fruitful relationships with adults as well as children. She stimulates interest by developing an unusual situation, but through it she explores the emotional experiences common to most children. She is concerned with the problems of growing up, but she makes them the material of art and not of social therapy.

—Margaret Greaves

WELCH, Ronald. Pseudonym for Ronald Oliver Felton. British. Born in Aberavon, Glamorganshire, 14 December 1909. Educated at Berkhamsted School, Hertfordshire, 1922–28; Clare College, Cambridge, M.A. (honours) in history 1931. Served in the Territorial Army, 1933–39; Welch Regiment during World War II: Company Commander and Staff Major. Married Betty Llewellyn Evans in 1934; one daughter. Assistant history master, Berkhamsted School, 1931–33; senior teacher, Bedford Modern School, 1933; headmaster, Okehampton Grammar School, Devon, 1947–63. Recipient: Library Association Carnegie Medal, 1955. *Died 5 February 1982.*

PUBLICATIONS FOR CHILDREN

Fiction

The Black Car Mystery. London, Pitman, 1950.
The Clock Stood Still. London, Pitman, 1951.
The Gauntlet, illustrated by T.R. Freeman. London, Oxford University Press, 1951.
Knight Crusader, illustrated by William Stobbs. London, Oxford University Press, 1954; New York, Oxford University Press, 1979.

Sker House (as Ronald Felton).   London, Hutchinson, 1954.
Captain of Dragoons, illustrated by William Stobbs.   London, Oxford University Press, 1956; New York, Oxford University Press, 1957.
The Long Bow.   Oxford, Blackwell, 1957.
Mohawk Valley, illustrated by William Stobbs.   London, Oxford University Press, and New York, Criterion, 1958.
Captain of Foot, illustrated by William Stobbs.   London, Oxford University Press, 1959.
Escape from France, illustrated by William Stobbs.   London, Oxford University Press, 1960; New York, Criterion, 1961.
For the King, illustrated by William Stobbs.   London, Oxford University Press, 1961; New York, Criterion, 1962.
Nicholas Carey, illustrated by William Stobbs.   London, Oxford University Press, and New York, Criterion, 1963.
Bowman of Crécy, illustrated by Ian Ribbons.   London, Oxford University Press, 1966; New York, Criterion, 1967.
The Hawk, illustrated by Gareth Floyd.   London, Oxford University Press, 1967; New York, Criterion, 1969.
Sun of York, illustrated by Doreen Roberts.   London, Oxford University Press, 1970.
The Galleon, illustrated by Victor Ambrus.   London, Oxford University Press, 1971.
Tank Commander, illustrated by Victor Ambrus.   London, Oxford University Press, 1972; Nashville, Nelson, 1974.
Zulu Warrior, illustrated by David Harris.   Newton Abbot, Devon, David and Charles, 1974.
Ensign Carey, illustrated by Victor Ambrus.   London, Oxford University Press, 1976.

Other

Ferdinand Magellan, illustrated by William Stobbs.   London, Oxford University Press, 1955; New York, Criterion, 1956.

*   *   *

In his historical novels, Ronald Welch took one aspect of the past, military history, and made it his own. No other historical novelist for children is as good on battles as he is. His books are extremely well-researched, full of authentic detail, and always excitingly plotted.

The Gauntlet is a time-slip story in which Welch was feeling his way—a modern boy experiences his ancestors' adventures in a Welsh castle in the 14th century—but with *Knight Crusader* (a well-deserved Carnegie Medal winner) Welch had found his metier and his style. It tells the adventures of a young crusading knight, Philip d'Aubigny, in the Holy Land in the 12th century who, at the end of the book, goes home to Wales to take up his inheritance and to found the Carey family, whose fortunes Welch followed in many of his books.

Charles Carey fights with Marlborough's army in *Captain of Dragoons*, Alan Carey is with Wolfe at Quebec in *Mohawk Valley*, Richard Carey helps to rescue French kinsmen from the revolution in *Escape from France*, Neil Carey is a Royalist soldier in the Civil War in *For the King*, Nicholas Carey fights in the Crimea in *Nicholas Carey*, and Harry Carey takes to the sea in Elizabethan England in *The Hawk*. Best of the Carey books are *Tank Commander*, with its superb evocation of World War I, and *Captain of Foot*, in which Christopher Carey serves under Wellington in the Peninsular. In this book the famous diarists of the period, George Simmons and John Kincaid, are drawn upon, giving this book characters more rounded than usual.

Not Carey stories, but with jumping off points in the Welsh border country, were an Elizabethan story, *The Galleon*, and *Bowman of Crécy*, an enthralling story, full of authentic detail about the Hundred

Years War. Less successful, perhaps, is another Carey book, *Zulu Warrior*, which is not only pedestrian but expresses the Jingoistic sentiments of the characters which are right for the times portrayed but out of mesh with today's attitudes both to Africa and to war.

Welch's great achievement was to produce stories full of accurate information about the weapons and warfare of the times he was writing about; he never glorified war, but made it quite clear that mud and discomfort, wounds and death were part of soldiering as well as comradeship and adventure. Welch was a soldier as well as a history teacher, and he drew on both experiences in making his historical novels for boys.

—Pamela Cleaver

———

WELLS, Rosemary. American. Born in New York City, 29 January 1943. Educated at Red Bank High School, New Jersey; Museum School, Boston. Married Thomas Moore Wells in 1963; two daughters. Worked in a store in Austin, Massachusetts, and in publishing in Boston and New York. Since 1968, freelance illustrator and writer. Address: c/o E.P. Dutton, 2 Park Avenue, New York, New York 10016, U.S.A.

PUBLICATIONS FOR CHILDREN (illustrated by the author)

Fiction

John and the Rarey.   New York, Funk and Wagnalls, 1969.
Michael and the Mitten Test.   Englewood Cliffs, New Jersey, Bradbury Press, 1969.
The First Child.   New York, Hawthorn, 1970.
Martha's Birthday.   Englewood Cliffs, New Jersey, Bradbury Press, 1970.
Miranda's Pilgrims.   Englewood Cliffs, New Jersey, Bradbury Press, 1970.
The Fog Comes on Little Pig Feet.   New York, Dial Press, 1972; London, Deutsch, 1976.
Unfortunately Harriet.   New York, Dial Press, 1972.
Benjamin and Tulip.   New York, Dial Press, 1973; London, Kestrel, 1977.
None of the Above.   New York, Dial Press, 1974.
Abdul.   New York, Dial Press, 1975.
Morris's Disappearing Bag: A Christmas Story.   New York, Dial Press, 1975; London, Kestrel, 1977.
Leave Well Enough Alone.   New York, Dial Press, 1977.
Stanley and Rhoda.   New York, Dial Press, 1978; London, Kestrel, 1980.
Max's First Word [*New Suit, Ride, Toys, Bedtime, Bath, Birthday, Breakfast, Christmas, Chocolate Chicken*].   New York, Dial Press, 10 vols., 1979–89; London, Benn, 4 vols., 1980; London, Collins, 5 vols., 1985–86.
When No One Was Looking.   New York, Dial Press, 1980; London, Deutsch, 1984.
Timothy Goes to School.   New York, Dial Press, and London, Kestrel, 1981.
Good Night, Fred.   New York, Dial Press, 1981; London, Macmillan, 1982.
A Lion for Lewis.   New York, Dial Press, and London, Macmillan, 1982.
Peabody.   New York, Dial Press, 1983; London, Macmillan, 1984.
The Man in the Woods.   New York, Dial Press, 1984; London, Deutsch, 1985.

Hazel's Amazing Mother. New York, Dial Press, 1985; London, Collins, 1986.
Through the Hidden Door. New York, Dial Press, 1987.
Shy Charles. New York, Dial Press, and London, Collins, 1988.
Forest of Dreams, illustrated by Susan Jeffers. New York, Dial Press, and London, Collins, 1988.

Verse

Noisy Nora. New York, Dial Press, 1973; London, Collins, 1976.
Don't Spill It Again, James. New York, Dial Press, 1977.

PUBLICATIONS FOR ADULTS

Other

Cooking for Nitwits, with Joanna Hurley. New York, Dutton, 1989.

*

Illustrator: *A Song to Sing, O!*, 1968, and *The Duke of Plaza Toro*, 1969, both by W.S. Gilbert; *Hungry Fred* by Paula Fox, 1969; *Why You Look Like You Whereas I Tend to Look Like Me* by Charlotte Pomerantz, 1969; *The Shooting of Dan McGrew and The Cremation of Sam McGee* by Robert Service, 1969; *The Cat That Walked by Himself* by Rudyard Kipling, 1970; *Marvin's Manhole* by Winifred Rosen, 1970; *Impossible, Possum* by Ellen Conford, 1971; *A Hot Thirsty Day* by Marjorie Weinman Sharmat, 1971; *Two Sisters and Some Hornets* by Beryl Epstein and Dorrit Davis, 1972; *With a Deep Sea Smile* edited by Virginia A. Tashjian, 1974; *Tell Me a Trudy* by Lore Segal, 1977.

* * *

Although Rosemary Wells is known principally for her entertaining series of picture books about animal characters with remarkably human characteristics, she has also ventured into other genres with as much success. She has given to the children's book world an array of inimitable personalities: Noisy Nora, Stanley and Rhoda, Morris, Max, beautifully observed anthropomorphic creatures who are strong on human feelings such as sibling rivalry. *Noisy Nora*, for instance, is the middle child in a mouse family who tries to attract attention from her parents who are too concerned with her young brother Jack. While Nora's sister laconically tells her she is "so dumb," the author uses rollicking verse to show how the situation is resolved after Nora walks out on her parents. She returns to the family home, to be loved and appreciated, "with a monumental crash."

As in all good picture books, Wells's illustrations tell as much of the story as the words. This is particularly true of *Stanley and Rhoda*, another perceptive study of siblings. A mouse brother and sister share a group of situations wittily observed by the author. In one of these episodes, for instance, Rhoda is supposedly stung on the foot by a bee and is apparently distraught until Stanley suggests that the best method for easing the foot is to soak it in boiling butter. "'It's better now, Stanley' said Rhoda." *Morris's Disappearing Bag* is set at Christmas. Morris's older brother and sisters are unwilling to let him use their presents until Morris discovers one gift left under the tree. This is a bag that makes its owner disappear on climbing into it. Needless to say, this proves more attractive to Morris's family, giving him a free rein of the other presents. This book contains a nicely attuned move towards anti-sexism as does *Benjamin and Tulip*, which has a positive, if not to say dominant, heroine. Affinity between the sexes is also shown in *Timothy Goes to School* in which Timothy discovers that his dislike for the perfect Claude is only matched by that felt by Violet for Grace because "She sings. She

dances. She counts up to a thousand and she sits next to me."

These are probably the most successful of Wells's picture books although she has also produced other memorable creations such as Max, a rabbit who has appeared in a series of board books and who discovers Father Christmas in *Max's Christmas*. Other characters are less memorable, however: the teddy bear *Peabody*, for instance, whose story is little different from that of many other teddy characters in children's literature. Even typically Wells creations such as *Hazel's Amazing Mother* or *Shy Charles* lack the quintessential Wells magic.

However, the author has also developed another area of creativity: thrillers written for a teenage audience. *When No One Was Looking* is an Edgar Allan Poe award runner-up. Kathy is a tennis champion with a determination to win and a fierce temper. However, when one of her opponents is murdered, Kathy has to discover who has drowned the girl. This is a book which is intriguing in its detection and also shows insights into teenage friendships. More intricately plotted and suitably tense is *The Man in the Woods*, in which Helen discovers a mysterious man in the woods who is supposed to be throwing rocks at car windscreens, a discovery that leads Helen and her friend Pinky into a deeper mystery involving drug trafficking.

These thrillers help to demonstrate Wells's versatility, as does her simple, almost naive text for Susan Jeffers's evocative paintings in *Forest of Dreams*. Whichever directions Wells's talent leads her in future years, thousands of children will be grateful to her for her creations of Nora, Morris, and all those other characters with sibling problems.

—Keith Barker

_____

WERSBA, Barbara. American. Born in Chicago, Illinois, 19 August 1932. Educated at Bard College, Annandale-on-Hudson, New York, B.A. 1954; studied acting at Neighborhood Playhouse and Paul Mann Actors Workshop, both New York. Professional stage and television actress, 1944–59. D.H.L.: Bard College, 1977. Agent: McIntosh and Otis, 310 Madison Avenue, New York, New York 10017. Address: Box 1892, Sag Harbor, New York 11963, U.S.A.

PUBLICATIONS FOR CHILDREN

Fiction

The Boy Who Loved the Sea, illustrated by Margot Tomes. New York, Coward McCann, 1961.
The Brave Balloon of Benjamin Buckley, illustrated by Margot Tomes. New York, Atheneum, 1963.
The Land of Forgotten Beasts, illustrated by Margot Tomes. New York, Atheneum, 1964; London, Gollancz, 1965.
A Song for Clowns, illustrated by Mario Rivoli. New York, Atheneum, 1965; London, Gollancz, 1966.
The Dream Watcher. New York, Atheneum, 1968; London, Bodley Head, 1988.
Run Softly, Go Fast. New York, Atheneum, 1970.
Let Me Fall Before I Fly. New York, Atheneum, 1971.
Amanda Dreaming, illustrated by Mercer Mayer. New York, Atheneum, 1973.
The Country of the Heart. New York, Atheneum, 1975.
Tunes for a Small Harmonica. New York, Harper, 1976; London, Bodley Head, 1979.
The Crystal Child, illustrated by Donna Diamond. New York, Harper, 1982.
The Carnival in My Mind. New York, Harper, 1982.

Crazy Vanilla. New York, Harper, 1986; London, Bodley Head, 1987.
Fat: A Love Story. New York, Harper, and London, Bodley Head, 1987.
Love Is the Crooked Thing. New York, Harper, and London, Bodley Head, 1987.
Beautiful Losers. New York, Harper, and London, Bodley Head, 1988.
Just Be Gorgeous. New York, Harper, 1988; London, Bodley Head, 1989.
Wonderful Me. New York, Harper, 1989.

Plays

The Dream Watcher, adaptation of her own story (produced Westport, Connecticut, 1975).

Verse

Do Tigers Ever Bite Kings?, illustrated by Mario Rivoli. New York, Atheneum, 1966.
Twenty-Six Starlings Will Fly Through Your Mind, illustrated by David Palladini. New York, Harper, 1980.

* * *

Barbara Wersba began writing for children and young adults only after a 15-year career as a professional actress. As she recuperated from hepatitis in a friend's house on Martha's Vineyard, she began to realize that her acting career was over. When the friend said to her, "Barbara, why don't you write something?" she decided to do just that, and a few weeks later had completed a children's fantasy called *The Boy Who Loved the Sea.* The book was accepted for publication and for her a new career had begun. Over the next five years, she wrote three more well-received children's fantasies and a volume of children's poetry, but it was her first novel for young adults, *The Dream Watcher*, that launched her on the most successful area of her career, as a writer for young adults.

The Dream Watcher is the story of Albert Scully, a teenager who just doesn't fit into the society in which he must live; he does not want to go to college, get a job, or be a success. Then he meets Mrs. Orpha Woodfin, an aged grande dame and former actress, and they become friends. Before Orpha dies, she has helped Albert to come to terms with his "differentness," in fact to be proud of it. The book so impressed actress Eva LeGallienne that she asked Wersba to turn it into a play in which LeGallienne would act the role of Orpha Woodfin. *The Dream Watcher* was followed by *Run Softly, Go Fast*, a conflict-of-generation story of life in the 1960's, and it too features a young misfit who survives that era's drug scene and comes to terms with both himself and his alienated father.

In *The Country of the Heart* Wersba again presents a story of an alienated young artist who finds himself as an artist and as a man through his relationship with an older woman. Steven's brief love affair with Hadley Norman is told in the form of a memoir after Hadley's death from cancer; as Steven remembers, he realizes that Hadley has given him much more than love, and he is a far better person for it. *Country* was followed by one of Wersba's best novels, *Tunes for a Small Harmonica. Tunes* is the story of J.F. McAllister, a brash young New York woman who falls in love with her rather dim and pale poetry teacher, Harold Murth. Believing him to be too poor to return to Cambridge and finish his thesis, J.F. learns to play the harmonica so that she can earn enough money as a street performer to send him to England. As it turns out, however, Harold is neither poor nor single, and he has completed his thesis; devastated, J.F. decides on suicide but is saved only when her best friend gives her a brand-new Hohner Chromatic in the key of C. J.F. is a

spunky character with a wonderful sense of humor who is at the same time, like so many of Wersba's other characters, vulnerable; the reader admires her pluck and determination, and rejoices when she resolves her problems.

Wersba's next book, *The Carnival in My Mind*, is another story of a New York loner, Harvey Beaumont, 14 and only five feet tall, struggling to get along until he meets aspiring young actress Chandler Brown. While not as strong as *Tunes*, this is a charming, tender, and sad love story, as is Wersba's next novel *Crazy Vanilla*, a book which does reach the level of *Tunes for a Small Harmonica*. A son of privilege, Tyler Woodruff is still not a happy young man, feeling stifled by the demands of his socialite parents and his ambivalent relationship with his older brother Cameron, who has been banished from the family because he is gay. His only salvation is in photography; this coupled with his interest in wildlife leads him to use his camera in shooting the fauna of Long Island, but it also leads him to further isolation. Then he meets Mitzi, an impoverished young waitress whose life with her unstable mother is as bleak as Tyler's. Miraculously, however, Mitzi is also a fine amateur wildlife photographer, and from this shared interest a warm and loving bond is created which leads both Tyler and Mitzi to grow and mature in the face of very real obstacles in their lives.

Three of Wersba's most recent books are something of a departure for her. *Fat: A Love Story, Love Is the Crooked Thing*, and *Beautiful Losers* all tell the tale of Rita Formica, a fat, five-foot-three extrovert who is a compulsive eater. In *Fat*, Rita, who works in a cheesecake bakery run by an older man called Arnold Bromberg, meets the love of her life, gorgeous athlete Robert Swann. She resolves to become thin and svelte as well as tone down her personality. Robert, however, is interested only in Rita's friend Nicole, so despite Rita's best attempts Robert remains aloof. A series of very funny misadventures leads broken-hearted Rita into the arms of, of all people, Arnold Blomberg, and the two sequels chart the ups and downs of their very unconventional romance. Along the way, Rita goes from child to woman and from everybody's clown to a self-sufficient adult at peace with herself.

All of Wersba's novels have as their protagonists young men or women who refuse to shape themselves to society's mold. They are often alienated from their families, and loners among their peers; they face their problems alone until someone equally unconventional enters the picture and together they learn to accept themselves and a world that will always have sharp corners. Critics have sometimes faulted her books for these "unrealistic" characters and situations, but Wersba's sensitivity and honesty in dealing with her characters have made her a favorite with a whole generation of young readers.

—Audrey Eaglen

————

WEST, Joyce (Tarlton). Also wrote as Manu Gilbert. British. Born in Auckland, New Zealand. Educated in Maori schools and by correspondence courses. Worked as an accounting clerk. *Died in 1985.*

PUBLICATIONS FOR CHILDREN (illustrated by author)

Fiction

Drovers Road. London, Dent, 1953.
The Year of the Shining Cuckoo. Hamilton, Paul's Book Arcade,

1961; London, Dent, 1963; New York, Roy, 1964.
Cape Lost. Auckland, Paul's Book Arcade, and London, Dent, 1963.
The Golden Country. Hamilton, Blackwood and Janet Paul, and London, Dent, 1965.
The Sea Islanders. London, Dent, and New York, Roy, 1970.
The River Road. London, Dent, 1980.

PUBLICATIONS FOR ADULTS

Novels

Sheep Kings. Wellington, Tombs, 1936.
Fatal Lady, with Mary Scott. Hamilton, Paul's Book Arcade, 1960.
Such Nice People, with Mary Scott. Hamilton, Paul's Book Arcade, 1962.
The Mangrove Murder, with Mary Scott. Auckland, Paul's Book Arcade, and London, Angus and Robertson, 1963.
No Red Herrings, with Mary Scott. London, Angus and Robertson, 1964.
Who Put It There?, with Mary Scott. Hamilton, Blackwood and Janet Paul, and London, Angus and Robertson, 1965.
Lineman's Ticket (as Manu Gilbert). Hamilton, Blackwood and Janet Paul, 1967.

*

Joyce West commented:

(1978) My own childhood was spent in the remote country districts of New Zealand where my parents were teachers in the Maori schools. We lived far from towns, in a world of bush roads and river crossings; we rode horseback everywhere, and kept a large menagerie of dogs, cats, kittens, ducks, turkeys, pet lambs, and goats. It always seemed to be summertime. When I began to write, it was with the wish that I might save a little of the charm and flavour of those times and places for the children of today.

*   *   *

In New Zealand, Joyce West is best known for an early work, *Drovers Road*, which describes in episodic form the humorous adventures of Gay, who, though deserted by both her parents, enjoys a happy and secure life with her Aunt Belle, her uncle Dunsany, and several cousins on a rather isolated sheep station on the East Coast of the North Island of New Zealand. In many ways the book demonstrated the best qualities of this author. There are the warmth and love of a united family, a deep feeling and a sensitivity to nature and to animals. Despite some sentimentality, West, with her shrewd characterisation, her gift for comedy, and her racy style, very satisfyingly demonstrates one type of New Zealand child who lives still very much in the English tradition.

We meet the characters of *Drovers Road* in further novels. In *The Golden Country*, for example, the former schoolgirl who had appeared in an intervening novel entitled *Cape Lost* is now the owner of an old homestead and coastal station at Cape Lost. While the book is still blemished by the element of fairy tale, the writing is confident and compelling, the characterisation realistic and memorable with, unfortunately, some instances of mawkishness. Gay's tenacious search for independence and her agonising over the choice of Mr. Right takes place in the context of the hardships and the isolation of hill country sheep farming.

The Year of the Shining Cuckoo is set in another inaccessible spot: this time in dairying country bordering a tidal harbour. In this story of a boy's efforts to buy a filly, the chief interest lies in the adult characters, Grandfather and Aunt Garance, both larger than life,

lovable and memorable. The themes of loneliness and the compensating warmth of family and community life are accompanied by scenes such as that at the horse fair which reveal West's comic gifts and acute observation. The same delight in all living things, and in the bush, the sea, and the hills, gives her writing a flavour of the appeal of the backblocks. *The Sea Islanders*, in presenting a group of children in a Robinson Crusoe setting, allows West plenty of freedom to explore flora and fauna of a tiny island.

West illustrated all her books, and these illustrations, along with her sensitive descriptions, make her contribution to children's literature something very special. Along with these qualities are her ability to create a comic scene and her strength in the observation of the delightful quirks of all the country characters whom she describes. These qualities more than make up for any weaknesses in plot and sentimentality of character.

—Tom Fitzgibbon

———

WESTALL, Robert (Atkinson). British. Born in Tynemouth, Northumberland, 7 October 1929. Educated at Tynemouth High School, 1941–48; Durham University, 1948–53, B.A. (honours) in fine art, 1953; Slade School, University of London, 1955–57, D.F.A. 1957. Served in the Royal Signals, 1953–55: Lance-Corporal. Married Jean Underhill in 1958; one son (deceased). Art master, Erdington Hall Secondary Modern School, Birmingham, 1957–58, and Keighley Boys' Grammar School, Yorkshire, 1958–60; Head of Art, 1960–85, and Head of Careers, 1970–85, Sir John Deane's College, Northwich, Cheshire; antiques dealer, Davenham, Cheshire, 1985–86. Writer, Whitehorn Press, Manchester, 1968–71; Northern art critic, *Guardian*, London, 1970, 1980. Since 1962 art critic, Chester *Chronicle*. Director, Telephone Samaritans of Mid-Cheshire, 1966–75. Recipient: Library Association Carnegie Medal, 1976, 1982. Address: 2 Dyar Terrace, Winnington, Northwich, Cheshire CW8 4DN, England.

PUBLICATIONS FOR CHILDREN

Fiction

The Machine-Gunners. London, Macmillan, 1975; New York, Greenwillow, 1976.
The Wind Eye. London, Macmillan, 1976; New York, Greenwillow, 1977.
The Watch House. London, Macmillan, 1977; New York, Greenwillow, 1978.
The Devil on the Road. London, Macmillan, 1978; New York, Greenwillow, 1979.
Fathom Five. London, Macmillan, 1979; New York, Greenwillow, 1980.
The Scarecrows. London, Chatto and Windus, and New York, Greenwillow, 1981.
Break of Dark. London, Chatto and Windus, and New York, Greenwillow, 1982.
Futuretrack 5. London, Kestrel, 1983; New York, Greenwillow, 1984.
The Haunting of Chas McGill and Other Stories. London, Macmillan, and New York, Greenwillow, 1983.
The Cats of Seroster. London, Macmillan, and New York, Greenwillow, 1984.
The Witness. London, Macmillan, 1985.
Rachel and the Angel and Other Stories. London, Macmillan,

1986; New York, Greenwillow, 1987.
Rosalie. London, Macmillan, 1987.
Urn Burial. London, Viking Kestrel, 1987; New York, Greenwillow, 1988.
The Creature in the Dark, illustrated by Liz Roberts. London, Blackie, 1988.
Ghosts and Journeys. London, Macmillan, 1988.
Ghost Abbey. London, Macmillan, 1988; New York, Scholastic, 1989.
Antique Dust: Ghost Stories. London, Viking Kestrel, 1989.
Blitzcat. London, Macmillan, 1989.
Old Man on a Horse. London, Blackie, 1989.
A Walk on the Wild Side. London, Methuen, 1989.
The Call. London, Viking Kestrel, 1989.
Echoes of War. London, Viking Kestrel, 1989.
Cat! London, Methuen, 1989.

Play

The Machine-Gunners (from his own story). London, Macmillan, 1986.

PUBLICATIONS FOR ADULTS

Other

Editor, *Children of the Blitz: Memories of Wartime Childhood.* London and New York, Viking, 1985.

*

Robert Westall comments:

(1978) The only common factor I can see in the books I have written so far (both published and unpublished) is that the children in them must have power of some sort to affect events drastically. Thus the children in my books are faced with moral dilemmas. I also have a marked dislike for descriptions of the appearance of people and landscape, unless absolutely essential. I find them boring in other people's work and dread them holding up the action in mine.

(1983) Since *The Wind Eye* I have been moving deeper and deeper into the world of the supernatural. I have never had direct experience of the supernatural, which is odd. Perhaps I use the supernatural as a viewpoint to comment on the inner world of psychology. Is the supernatural psychology without psychologists?

*   *   *

I have a professional interest in the books children enjoy, and Robert Westall's *The Machine-Gunners* continues to be one of the most compelling books for adolescent readers that I know. The breadth of its appeal certainly does not derive from the fact that it is an "easy" book or because it is immediately "relevant." Its World War II setting is as historical for most of its readers as the battle of Hastings. I know that writers are sometimes unhappy about being known for their first book—they have other projects and want to move on—but in a deeper sense *The Machine-Gunners* has become more rather than less relevant than when it appeared in 1975.

It remains the fullest and most authentic account of "the war" for young readers (and arguably for adults) at a time when the history of that period continues to be rewritten as the Scientists' War or the Generals' War—anything rather than the People's War (which included the children caught up in it). The adolescent readers I know would not quite put it like that. They are more likely to speak of their excitement at the twists and turns of the story—the stratagems the children have to adopt, the dilemmas they face. In his later novel,

Fathom Five, Westall returns to some of the child characters of the earlier novel. It is interesting to speculate on what might have happened to Chas as he grew up, but on the whole *Fathom Five* seems to me a routine performance.

More characteristically in novels like *The Wind Eye, The Watch House,* and *The Devil on the Road,* Westall has moved away from reconstructing that past that so clearly lives in his imagination. The immediate setting is contemporary, and his children and adolescents belong very much to the 1970's—families and marriages are shakier affairs. The children are under pressure but not from events in the world at large impinging on their lives. They are up against "forces" from a legendary, malevolent past: *The Watch House* even has its fair share of exorcisms. Here there is excitement, and an attempt to establish a brooding, threatening atmosphere, but the reader is swept along to find out what happens next. In the wake of that impulse the characters have dwindled. In *The Wind Eye,* for example, there seems to me to be an inordinate amount of "explaining": "Was *Resurre* really a time-traveller? Or merely a haunted boat, a kind of psychic tape-recorder, playing back memories of things that had happened to her?" This doesn't seem to me like anyone's thoughts, or, to put it another way, they could be the thoughts of anyone. To have a character emerge from such appalling events so bright and unmuddled makes me doubt how much was ever at stake. For Westall's earlier children nothing was ever so clear or so neatly packaged, and their only aid to self-realisation lay in their own resourcefulness: but then they were born before the development of pop-psychology.

Westall's recent books—often adventure, ghost, or fantasy stories—continue to eschew exploration of the past. *Futuretrack 5,* for example, is set in near-future England where a computer ("Laura") runs the country and people's lives are determined by how well they do on state exams (A, O, and new "E" levels). If they pass the high E levels they become "Ests" and live privileged(?) lives of leisure centred on sex and video games. If they don't pass they are sent to the cities to fight for themselves. The hero Henry Kitson discovers a plot to repopulate the country with an artificially bred race of people and has to fight against the elite Techs who programme Laura. The ending is bleak, and the whole scenario all the more chilling for being set only 30 years from now.

—Eric Hadley

WESTERMAN, Percy (Francis). British. Born in Portsmouth, Hampshire, in 1876. Educated at Portsmouth Grammar School. Served in the Royal Navy and Royal Flying Corps during World War I, and in Dorset Home Guard during World War II. Married Florence Wager in 1900. Admiralty clerk, Portsmouth Dockyard, 1896–1911. Lived many years in Wareham, Dorset. *Died 22 February 1959.*

PUBLICATIONS FOR CHILDREN

Fiction

A Lad of Grit, illustrated by E.S. Hodgson. London, Blackie, 1908.
The Winning of Golden Spurs. London, Nisbet, 1911.
The Young Cavalier, illustrated by Gordon Browne. London, Pearson, 1911.
The Quest of the "Golden Hope", illustrated by Frank Wiles. London, Blackie, 1911.
The Flying Submarine. London, Nisbet, 1912.
Captured at Tripoli, illustrated by Charles Sheldon. London,

Blackie, 1912.

The Sea Monarch, illustrated by E.S. Hodgson. London, A. and C. Black, 1912.

The Scouts of Seal Island, illustrated by Ernest Prater. London, A. and C. Black, 1913; New York, Macmillan, 1922.

The Rival Submarines, illustrated by C. Fleming Williams. London, Partridge, 1913.

The Stolen Cruiser. London, Jarrolds, 1913.

When East Meets West, illustrated by C.M. Padday. London, Blackie, 1913.

Under King Henry's Banners, illustrated by John Campbell. London, Pilgrim Press, 1913.

The Sea-Girt Fortress, illustrated by W.E. Wigfull. London, Blackie, 1914.

The Sea Scouts of the "Petrel." London, A. and C. Black, 1914; New York, Macmillan, 1924.

The Log of a Snob, illustrated by W.E. Wigfull. London, Chapman and Hall, 1914.

'Gainst the Might of Spain. London, Pilgrim Press, 1914.

Building the Empire. London, Jarrolds, 1914.

The Dreadnought of the Air. London, Partridge, 1914.

The Dispatch-Riders. London, Blackie, 1915.

The Fight for Constantinople. London, Blackie, 1915.

The Nameless Island. London, Pearson, 1915.

A Sub. of the R.N.R. London, Partridge, 1915.

Rounding Up the Raider, illustrated by E.S. Hodgson. London, Blackie, 1916.

The Secret Battleplane. London, Blackie, 1916.

The Treasures of the "San Philipo." London, Religious Tract Society, 1916.

A Watch-Dog of the North Sea. London, Partridge, 1916.

Deeds of Pluck and Daring in the Great War. London, Blackie, 1917.

To the Fore with the Tanks!, illustrated by Dudley Tennant. London, Partridge, 1917.

Under the White Ensign. London, Blackie, 1917.

The Fritz Strafers. London, Partridge, 1918; as *The Keepers of the Narrow Seas*, 1931.

Billy Barcroft, R.N.A.S. London, Partridge, 1918.

A Lively Bit of the Front, illustrated by Wal Paget. London, Blackie, 1918.

The Secret Channel and Other Stories. London, A. and C. Black, 1918; New York, Macmillan, 1919.

The Submarine Hunters. London, Blackie, 1918.

A Sub and a Submarine. London, Blackie, 1918.

With Beatty off Jutland. London, Blackie, 1918.

Wilmshurst of the Frontier Force. London, Patridge, 1919.

Winning His Wings, illustrated by E.S. Hodgson. London, Blackie, 1919.

The Thick of the Fray at Zeebruge, April 1918, illustrated by W.E. Wigfull. London, Blackie, 1919.

'Midst Arctic Perils. London, Pearson, 1919.

The Airship "Golden Hind." London, Partridge, 1920.

The Mystery Ship. London, Partridge, 1920.

The Salving of the "Fusi Yama," illustrated by E.S. Hodgson. London, Blackie, 1920.

Sea Scouts All, illustrated by Charles Pears. London, Blackie, 1920.

Sea Scouts Abroad, illustrated by Charles Pears. London, Blackie, 1921.

The Third Officer, illustrated by E.S. Hodgson. London, Blackie, 1921.

Sea Scouts Up-Channel, illustrated by C.M. Padday. London, Blackie, 1922.

The Wireless Officer, illustrated by W.E. Wigfull. London, Blackie, 1922.

The War of the Wireless Waves, illustrated by W.E. Wightman. London, Oxford University Press, 1923.

The Pirate Submarine. London, Nisbet, 1923.

A Cadet of the Mercantile Marine, illustrated by W.E. Wigfull. London, Blackie, 1923.

Clipped Wings, illustrated by E.S. Hodgson. London, Blackie, 1923.

The Mystery of Stockmere School. London, Partridge, 1923.

Sinclair's Luck. London, Partridge, 1923.

Captain Cain. London, Nisbet, 1924.

The Good Ship "Golden Effort," illustrated by W.E. Wigfull. London, Blackie, 1924.

The Treasure of the Sacred Lake. London, Pearson, 1924.

Unconquered Wings, illustrated by E.S. Hodgson. London, Blackie, 1924.

Clinton's Quest, illustrated by R.B. Ogle. London, Pearson, 1925.

East in the "Golden Gain," illustrated by Rowland Hilder. London, Blackie, 1925.

The Boys of the "Puffin," illustrated by G.W. Goss. London, Partridge, 1925.

The Buccaneers of Boya, illustrated by William Rainey. London, Blackie, 1925.

The Sea Scouts of the "Kestrel." London, Seeley, 1925.

Annesley's Double. London, A. and C. Black, and New York, Macmillan, 1926.

King of Kilba. London, Ward Lock, 1926.

The Luck of the "Golden Dawn," illustrated by Rowland Hilder. London, Blackie, 1926.

The Riddle of the Air, illustrated by Rowland Hilder. London, Blackie, 1926.

Tireless Wings. London, Blackie, 1926.

The Terror of the Seas. London, Ward Lock, 1927.

Mystery Island. London, Oxford University Press, 1927.

Captain Blundell's Treasure, illustrated by J. Cameron. London, Blackie, 1927.

Chums of the "Golden Vanity," illustrated by Rowland Hilder. London, Blackie, 1927.

In the Clutches of the Dyaks, illustrated by F. Marston. London, Partridge, 1927.

The Junior Cadet, illustrated by Rowland Hilder. London, Blackie, 1928.

On the Wings of the Wind, illustrated by W.E. Wigfull. London, Blackie, 1928.

A Shanghai Adventure, illustrated by Leo Bates. London, Blackie, 1928.

Pat Stobart in the "Golden Dawn," illustrated by Rowland Hilder. London, Blackie, 1929.

Rivals of the Reef, illustrated by Kenneth Inns. London, Blackie, 1929.

Captain Starlight, illustrated by W.E. Wigfull. London, Blackie, 1929.

Captain Sang. London, Blackie, 1930.

Leslie Dexter, Cadet. London, Blackie, 1930.

A Mystery of the Broads, illustrated by E.A. Cox. London, Blackie, 1930.

The Secret of the Plateau, illustrated by W.E. Wigfull. London, Blackie, 1931.

The Senior Cadet, illustrated by Rowland Hilder. London, Blackie, 1931.

In Defiance of the Ban, illustrated by E.S. Hodgson. London, Blackie, 1931.

All Hands to the Boats!, illustrated by Rowland Hilder. London, Blackie, 1932.

The Amir's Ruby, illustrated by W.E. Wigfull. London, Blackie, 1932.

Captain Fosdyke's Gold, illustrated by E.S. Hodgson. London,

Blackie, 1932.

King for a Month, illustrated by Comerford Watson. London, Blackie, 1933.

Rocks Ahead!, illustrated by D.L. Mays. London, Blackie, 1933.

The White Arab, illustrated by Henry Coller. London, Blackie, 1933.

The Disappearing Dhow, illustrated by D.L. Mays. London, Blackie, 1933.

Chasing the "Pleiad." London, Blackie, 1933.

Tales of the Sea, with others, illustrated by Terence Cuneo. London, Tuck, 1933.

The Westow Talisman, illustrated by W.E. Wigfull. London, Blackie, 1934.

Andy-All-Alone, illustrated by D.L. Mays. London, Blackie, 1934.

The Black Hawk, illustrated by Rowland Hilder. London, Blackie, 1934.

Standish of the Air Police. London, Blackie, 1935.

The Red Pirate, illustrated by Rowland Hilder. London, Blackie, 1935.

Sleuths of the Air, illustrated by Comerford Watson. London, Blackie, 1935.

On Board the "Golden Effort." London, Blackie, 1935.

The Call of the Sea, illustrated by D.L. Mays. London, Blackie, 1935.

Captain Flick, illustrated by E.S. Hodgson. London, Blackie, 1936.

His First Ship. London, Blackie, 1936.

Midshipman Raxworthy. London, Blackie, 1936.

Ringed by Fire. London, Blackie, 1936.

Winged Might. London, Blackie, 1937.

Under Fire in Spain, illustrated by Ernest Prater. London, Blackie, 1937.

The Last of the Buccaneers. London, Blackie, 1937.

Haunted Harbour, illustrated by John de Walton. London, Blackie, 1937.

His Unfinished Voyage, illustrated by D.L. Mays. London, Blackie, 1937.

Cadet Alan Carr, illustrated by D.L. Mays. London, Blackie, 1938.

Midshipman Webb's Treasure, illustrated by D.L. Mays. London, Blackie, 1938.

Standish Gets His Man, illustrated by W.E. Wigfull. London, Blackie, 1938.

Sea Scouts Alert! London, Blackie, 1938.

Standish Loses His Man, illustrated by W.E. Wigfull. London, Blackie, 1939.

In Eastern Seas. London, Blackie, 1939.

The Bulldog Breed, illustrated by E. Boye Uden. London, Blackie, 1939.

At Grips with the Swastika, illustrated by Leo Bates. London, Blackie, 1940.

Eagles' Talons. London, Blackie, 1940.

In Dangerous Waters. London, Blackie, 1940.

When the Allies Swept the Seas, illustrated by J.C.B. Knight. London, Blackie, 1940.

Standish Pulls It Off. London, Blackie, 1940.

The War—And Alan Carr, illustrated by E. Boye Uden. London, Blackie, 1940.

War Cargo. London, Blackie, 1941.

Sea Scouts at Dunkirk. London, Blackie, 1941.

Standish Holds On. London, Blackie, 1941.

Fighting for Freedom. London, Blackie, 1941.

Alan Carr in the Near East. London, Blackie, 1942.

Destroyer's Luck. London, Blackie, 1942.

On Guard for England, illustrated by J.C.B. Knight. London, Blackie, 1942.

Secret Flight. London, Blackie, 1942.

With the Commandoes, illustrated by S. Van Abbe. London, Blackie, 1943.

Sub-Lieutenant John Cloche, illustrated by H. Pym. London, Blackie, 1943.

Alan Carr in Command, illustrated by Terence Cuneo. London, Blackie, 1943.

Alan Carr in the Arctic, illustrated by E. Boye Uden. London, Blackie, 1943.

Combined Operations, illustrated by S. Van Abbe. London, Blackie, 1944.

Engage the Enemy Closely, illustrated by Terence Cuneo. London, Blackie, 1944.

Secret Convoy, illustrated by Terence Cuneo. London, Blackie, 1944.

One of the Many, illustrated by Ellis Silas. London, Blackie, 1945.

Operations Successfully Executed, illustrated by S. Drigin. London, Blackie, 1945.

By Luck and Pluck, illustrated by Terence Cuneo. London, Blackie, 1946.

Return to Base, illustrated by Leslie Wilcox. London, Blackie, 1946.

Squadron Leader, illustrated by Terence Cuneo. London, Blackie, 1946.

Unfettered Night, illustrated by S. Jezzard. London, Blackie, 1947.

Trapped in the Jungle, illustrated by A.S. Forrest. London, Blackie, 1947.

The Phantom Submarine, illustrated by J.C.B. Knight. London, Blackie, 1947.

The "Golden Gleaner," illustrated by M. Mackinlay. London, Blackie, 1948.

First Over, illustrated by Ellis Silas. London, Blackie, 1948.

Mystery of the Key, illustrated by Ellis Silas. London, Blackie, 1948.

Missing, Believed Lost, illustrated by Will Nickless. London, Blackie, 1949.

Contraband, illustrated by A. Barclay. London, Blackie, 1949.

Beyond the Burma Road, illustrated by Victor Bertoglio. London, Blackie, 1949.

Sabarinda Island, illustrated by A. Barclay. London, Blackie, 1950.

Mystery of Nix Hall, illustrated by D.C. Eyles. London, Blackie, 1950.

By Sea and Air. London, Blackie, 1950.

Desolation Island, illustrated by W. Gale. London, Blackie, 1950.

Held to Ransom, illustrated by Ellis Silas. London, Blackie, 1951.

The Isle of Mystery, illustrated by Philip. London, Blackie, 1951.

Working Their Passage, illustrated by Ellis Silas. London, Blackie, 1951.

Sabotage!, illustrated by Ellis Silas. London, Blackie, 1952.

Round the World in the "Golden Gleaner," illustrated by Jack Matthew. London, Blackie, 1952.

Dangerous Cargo, illustrated by W. Gale. London, Blackie, 1952.

Bob Strickland's Log, illustrated by Jack Matthew. London, Blackie, 1953.

The Missing Diplomat, illustrated by R.G. Campbell. London, Blackie, 1953.

Rolling Down to Rio, illustrated by R.G. Campbell. London, Blackie, 1953.

Wrested from the Deep, illustrated by Robert Johnston. London, Blackie, 1954.

A Midshipman of the Fleet, illustrated by P.A. Jobson. London, Blackie, 1954.

The Ju-Ju Hand. London, Blackie, 1954.

The Dark Scout, illustrated by Victor Bertoglio. London, Blackie, 1954.

Daventry's Quest, illustrated by P.A. Jobson. London, Blackie,

1955.

The Lure of the Lagoon, illustrated by E. Kearon.   London, Blackie, 1955.

Held in the Frozen North, illustrated by Edward Osmond.   London, Blackie, 1956.

The Mystery of the "Sempione," illustrated by P.B. Batchelor.   London, Blackie, 1957.

Jack Craddock's Commission, illustrated by Edward Osmond.   London, Blackie, 1958.

Mistaken Identity, illustrated by Robert Johnston.   London, Blackie, 1959.

*   *   *

Between the wars Percy Westerman was a popular writer of boys' adventure stories: inside the cover of *Standish of the Air Police*, for example, 60 titles are listed. Yet today he is out of print in both England and America. He owed his popularity to skill as "a spinner of yarns," usually with a nautical or flying background, with strong suspense elements involving clashes with unspecified foreign enemies of law and order. This mixture today spells total neglect. Writing of an attempt to land an airship on a tropical island, Westerman wrote, "It was a sort of gamble—everything depended on foresight and chance, and a fortunate combination of the two alone could bring success." In his own case foresight was lacking and chance has been unkind. In storytelling, foresight does not depend on an ability to supply market calculations, but on the quality of an author's imaginative sympathy for his fictions.

Westerman's writing falls too easily into cliché and his characters into stereotypes. Thus swindles are invariably "bare-faced," meals are usually "square" and civilian life is "full of pitfalls" for unsuspecting servicemen. And the heroic character depends as much on the force of muscle as of mind. McAlastair in *The Bulldog Breed* is typical, "Although long-limbed he possessed enormous muscular development...." Intelligence is properly limited to resourceful action in dealing with such everyday situations as piloting ships through typhoons and airships through mid-air collisions. Likewise the villains fall naturally into stock situations: "The occupant of the tent turned. He held a hair brush in each hand. His glossy black hair reeked of perfumed oil." In these matters Westerman falls short of the proper demands of his trade. But change of fashion has also deprived him of his readership. His accounts of machinery and "inventions," like the Crophelium gas which powers the airship Black Comet II, have been left behind by the commonplaces of post-war technology. In the same way the actions which asserted the self-assurance of imperialism, the unquestioning obedience to authority, the stress on courage and clean-living were inappropriate to England's declining economic power during the years of depression. It is not that the heroes and their deeds are unworthy within their own limits, but in showing themselves unaware of large areas of the life of their time, they have come to stand for those values which an anti-heroic age finds least bearable.

—Kenneth J. Sterck

WHEATLEY, Nadia. Australian.   Born in Sydney, New South Wales, 30 April 1949. Educated at Sydney University, 1966–70, B.A. (honours) in history 1970; Macquarie University, Sydney, M.A. (honours) 1976. Recipient: Australian Children's Book Council Book of the Year award, 1988; Eve Pownell award, 1988. Agent: Barbara Mobbs, 73/35a Sutherland Crescent, Darling Point, New South Wales 2027, Australia.

PUBLICATIONS FOR CHILDREN

Fiction

Five Times Dizzy, illustrated by Neil Phillips.   Melbourne, Oxford University Press, 1982.

Dancing in the Anzac Deli, illustrated by Waldemar Buczynski.   Melbourne, Oxford University Press, 1984.

The House That Was Eureka.   Melbourne, Viking Kestrel, 1984.

My Place, with Donna Rawlins.   Melbourne, Collins, 1987.

The Blooding.   Melbourne, Viking Kestrel, 1987; London, Viking Kestrel, 1988.

Plays

Television Series: *Five Times Dizzy*, with Terry Larsen, 1986.

Other

1 Is for One, illustrated by Helen Leitch.   Melbourne, Oxford University Press, 1985.

*

Nadia Wheatley comments:

The main influences on my work as a children's book writer have probably been: (1) the children's book writers of my own childhood of the 1950's, and particularly the Australian writers; (2) the work of E.P. Thompson, and particularly his emphasis on recording the history of "ordinary" people; (3) George Orwell's essay, "Boys' Weeklies," in which it is shown how ruling-class propaganda can imbue the fiction which working-class children read.

Thus in my stories I have tried to write for and about ordinary Australian people.

*   *   *

Three factors in Nadia Wheatley's life permeate and affect her writing: her five years in Greece; her study of history; and her political ideology and commitment.

Her first two novels (for primary school children), *Five Times Dizzy* and *Dancing in the Anzac Deli*, are about a Greek family living in the inner-Sydney suburb of Newtown, and especially the problems of the non-English-speaking Yaya which are largely resolved by her enterprising grand-daughter Mareka—who encounters her own difficulties. There are Greek characters in Wheatley's two mature-age novels *The House That Was Eureka* and *The Blooding*; and a Greek family in *My Place*, which won the Australian Council Book of the Year and the Eve Pownell award for non-fiction in 1988. Neatly sidestepping stereotyped situations, Wheatley has made a dignified and significant contribution to multi-cultural literature in Australia and has been applauded by both children and critics.

Essentially a social historian, Wheatley has a finely tuned perception of time, place, and community. Her recreation of both the crowded Newtown streets and lanes and consequent community interaction in her first three books achieves a brilliant synthesis in *My Place*, which is the story of a house and its occupants of various nationalities moving backwards in decades from 1988 to 1788. Both the original landowners and the present residents are Aborigines. Changes in Australia's social fabric are subtly indicated by reference to the occupations and nationalities of the dwellers, their recreation, food, and eating habits, and the changing local landmarks from convict huts to a saddlery, a cordial factory, a garage, a McDonalds. Much of the detail has been added in the comprehensive but never crowded illustrations, sketches, and plans of Wheatley's collaborator, co-researcher and artist, Donna Rawlins.

In each of her books, including the vignettes of *My Place*, Wheatley is able to convey her perception of caste and social distinction, especially a realisation of the exploitation of the workers. Written without undue bitterness or a propagandist message *The House That Was Eureka* is the parallel story of two terrace houses—201/203 Liberty Street, Newtown—and their occupants in 1931 at the height of the Great Depression and 1981 when unemployment was again rife. In 201 lives Mrs. Weston, the Despot, who owns both dwellings and lets out 203. An Irish family, the Cruises, rented it in 1931. The Despot's warrant to have the unemployed Paddy evicted arouses the support of the Unemployed Workers' Movement. The house is picketted against the bailiffs and turned into a Eureka Stockade to become the scene of a gun battle between police and workers. In 1981 another family with both the man, Ted, and 16-year-old Evie unemployed and on the dole live in 203 which becomes the location for a film re-enactment of the 1931 battle being made by the Newtown Community Youth Support Scheme.

Although Wheatley's sympathies are obvious and the story is not dispassionate it is free of manipulation and hysteria. She makes it clear that no side has a "monopoly on morality" but that "struggle never fails."

The voice of the author breaks through, perhaps, in *The Blooding* when a wise Greek says, "perhaps my great grandson will live in a good world! But only if we all struggle and fight, struggle and fight, never give up, never give up." *The Blooding* is set in a fictitious, isolated, frontier timber township where the greenies have moved in to protest against the logging which is the lifeblood of the precarious outpost. Colum, the 17-year-old son of one of the loggers, tells the story in a journal from his hospital bed where he lies with broken bones after a run-in between the timber workers and the conservationists. Wheatley is careful to present both sides of this fundamental issue impartially without letting the reader off the hook.

Wheatley commands attention and respect for her ideas; she also structures her books compellingly and has extended the technique of the novel for young people in Australia. Because she sees parallels and analogies in history, and time present often as a replay of time past, her books abound in parallels. Newtown's present petty crooks, racketeers, and bullies are latter-day Nazi radicals. Her Yaya is from a long line of Cretan resistance fighters of unarmed grandmothers who brained and bound Nazi paratroopers in World War II. *The House That Was Eureka* is structured on parallels: people, places, problems. There are preoccupations, too, which surface in each book, so giving her collective works a unity and coherence.

A recurring theme is "the thin membrane between real life and some other world." There are hints of ESP and déjà vu, so that a Cretan dance, the Pentozalia, becomes the Five Times Dizzy dance in Newtown. Evie and Noel in Liberty Street 1981 are impalpably linked with Lizzie and Nobby in 1931. Although Lizzie died after the barricade and gun battle her presence is real and metaphysically everpresent.

Yet reality is maintained stylistically by the use of reproduced handwritten letters in *Dancing in the Anzac Deli*; actual news reports and reference to historical figures in *Eureka*; and reports, oral history, songs, and letters along with Colum's pungent asides and flashbacks as he maintains his first-person journal in *The Blooding*. Realistically obscene and vulgar language in the two mature-age books is used without designing to shock or offend. Swearing is as much a symbol as the theme songs quoted, or objects like a goat in *Five Times Dizzy*, a gun in *Eureka*, a knife in *The Blooding*, or the name Jade for a green-eyed conservationist.

Wheatley is an utterly honest writer who speaks clearly but with poetry and passion to and on behalf of today's thinking, feeling, questioning youth.

—H.M. Saxby

WHITE, E(lwyn) B(rooks). American. Born in Mount Vernon, New York, 11 July 1899. Educated at Mount Vernon High School, graduated 1917; Cornell University, Ithaca, New York (editor, *Cornell Daily Sun*, 1920–21), 1917–21, A.B. 1921. Served in the United States Army, 1918: Private. Married Katharine Sergeant Angell in 1929 (died 1977); one son. Worked for United Press and the American Legion News Service, 1921; reporter, Seattle *Times*, 1922–23; advertising copywriter and production assistant, Frank Seaman Inc. and Newmark Inc., New York, 1924–25; contributing editor, *New Yorker*, from 1926; columnist ("One Man's Meat"), *Harper's* magazine, New York, 1938–43. Recipient: National Association of Independent Schools award, 1955; American Academy Gold Medal, for essays, 1960; Presidential Medal of Freedom, 1963; American Library Association Laura Ingalls Wilder award, 1970; George G. Stone Center for Children's Books award, 1970; National Medal for Literature, 1971; Pulitzer Special citation, 1978. Litt.D.: Dartmouth College, Hanover, New Hampshire, 1948; University of Maine, Orono, 1948; Yale University, New Haven, Connecticut, 1948; Bowdoin College, Brunswick, Maine, 1950; Hamilton College, Clinton, New York, 1952; Harvard University, Cambridge, Massachusetts, 1954; L.H.D.: Colby College, Waterville, Maine, 1954. Fellow, American Academy of Arts and Sciences, 1973; member, American Academy. *Died 1 October 1985.*

PUBLICATIONS FOR CHILDREN

Fiction

Stuart Little, illustrated by Garth Williams. New York, Harper, 1945; London, Hamish Hamilton, 1946.
Charlotte's Web, illustrated by Garth Williams. New York, Harper, and London, Hamish Hamilton, 1952.
The Trumpet of the Swan, illustrated by Edward Frascino. New York, Harper, and London, Hamish Hamilton, 1970.

PUBLICATIONS FOR ADULTS

Verse

The Lady Is Cold. New York, Harper, 1929.
The Fox of Peapack and Other Poems. New York, Harper, 1938.
Poems and Sketches. New York, Harper, 1981.

Other

Is Sex Necessary? or, Why You Feel the Way You Do, with James Thurber. New York, Harper, 1929; London, Heinemann, 1930.
Alice Through the Cellophane. New York, Day, 1933.
Every Day Is Saturday. New York, Harper, 1934.
Farewell to Model T. New York, Putnam, 1936.
Quo Vadimus? or, The Case for the Bicycle. New York, Harper, 1939.
One Man's Meat. New York, Harper, 1942; London, Gollancz, 1943; augmented edition, Harper, 1944.
World Government and Peace: Selected Notes and Comment 1943–1945. New York, F.R. Publishing, 1945.
The Wild Flag: Editorials from the New Yorker on Federal World Government and Other Matters. Boston, Houghton Mifflin, 1946.
Here Is New York. New York, Harper, 1949.
The Second Tree from the Corner. New York, Harper, and London, Hamish Hamilton, 1954.
The Elements of Style, by William Strunk, Jr., revised by White. New York, Macmillan, 1959; London, Collier Macmillan, 1972;

revised edition, New York, Macmillan, 1979.
The Points of My Compass: Letters from the East, The West, The North, The South.   New York, Harper, 1962; London, Hamish Hamilton, 1963.
An E.B. White Reader, edited by William W. Watt and Robert W. Bradford.   New York, Harper, 1966.
Letters of E.B. White, edited by Dorothy Lobrano Guth.   New York, Harper, 1976.
Essays of E.B. White.   New York, Harper, 1977.

Editor, *Ho Hum: Newsbreaks from the New Yorker.*   New York, Farrar and Rinehart, 1931.
Editor, *Another Ho Hum: More Newsbreaks from the New Yorker.*   New York, Farrar and Rinehart, 1932.
Editor, with Katharine S. White, *A Subtreasury of American Humor.*   New York, Coward McCann, 1941.
Editor, *Onward and Upward in the Garden*, by Katharine S. White.   New York, Farrar Straus, 1979.

*

Bibliography: *E.B. White: A Bibliography* by A.J. Anderson, Metuchen, New Jersey, Scarecrow Press, 1978; *E.B. White: A Bibliographic Catalogue of Printed Materials in the Department of Rare Books, Cornell University Library* by Katherine R. Hall, New York, Garland, 1979.

Manuscript Collection: Olin Library, Cornell University, Ithaca, New York.

Critical Studies: *E.B. White* by Edward C. Sampson, New York, Twayne, 1974; *E.B. White: A Biography* by Scott Elledge, New York, Norton, 1984; *Katharine and E.B. White: An Affectionate Memoir* by Isabel Russell, New York, Norton, 1988.

*   *   *

"No one can write a sentence like White's or successfully imitate it," James Thurber once said of his colleague on the *New Yorker* and co-author of *Is Sex Necessary?* It is, indeed, as a prose stylist in the tradition of Lamb or Hazlitt that E.B. White earned his great reputation.

It is to White's virtually lifetime association with the *New Yorker* that we must look for his literary origins. The magazine was founded by Harold Ross in 1925, and in that same year White published his first piece, "Defense of the Bronx River," in it. He joined the staff in 1926, and soon became a full-time staff member, writing pithy, ironical articles, squibs, and observations, as well as editing the "Notes and Comments" column. At the magazine's founding, Ross had announced its stylistic trajectory: "Its general tenor will be one of gaiety, wit and satire, but it will be more than a jester. It will not be what is commonly called sophisticated, in that it will assume a reasonable degree of enlightenment on the part of its readers. It will hate bunk...." Whether these specifications helped form White's inimitable style, or whether it was White's good fortune that he found the one outlet most nearly suited to his native talents, must remain moot. It was the opinion of Marc Connelly, the dramatist, however, that it was White who "brought the steel and the music to the magazine." And even Ezra Pound expressed his admiration for White's writing.

White's habitual essay style is that of a serious citizen, reasonable, quizzical, dubious about the effect of large bureaucracies on the lives of mature men of integrity. His authorial persona in the *New Yorker* essays, as well as in the numerous collected essays, is that of an honest man, slow to anger, but puzzled by follies and governmental meddling and commercial advertising—an intelligent observer of good will, but healthy skepticism. His distant stylistic ancestor may be Montaigne.

Stuart Little, his immensely popular first children's book, is an episodic, picaresque adventure story and quest, and has for its hero the two-inch tall offspring of Mr. and Mrs. Frederic C. Little. Stuart, with pointed ears and a long tail, resembles in all respects a mouse (though White has, in his letters, insisted that Stuart is, in fact, not a mouse, but a "second son"). The story had been brewing in White's mind for more than 15 years—having first been told and read in disconnected installments by White to his 18 nieces and nephews. The book consists of 15 loosely connected chapters about the second son "mouse" hero, a plucky, ingenious, enterprising fellow of romantic inclinations. The first seven chapters, the sequence of which could be rearranged without harm to the book, are a series of adventures which are the consequence of Stuart's size, logically imagined with all the ingenuity of Gulliver's stay among the minuscule Lilliputians. Stuart sleeps on a little bed made of four clothes pins and a cigarette box; he is lowered down a bathtub drain to retrieve a ring his mother had dropped; he fetches grounded ping-pong balls; at some hazard, he crouches inside the piano to push up sticking keys when his brother, George Little, plays the piano.

In a life beset with dangers and obstacles, Stuart repeatedly displays his courage and his gallantry. Romance first enters his life in the "person" of the little bird, Margalo, designated as perhaps a "wall-eyed-vireo." Stuart's subsequent search/quest for Margalo, who represents beauty, inspiration, a dream, is the motivation for the hero's travels throughout the rest of the book, when he encounters further hazards, near catastrophes, and a momentarily tempting infatuation with the lovely Harriet Ames, "whose head came just above Stuart's shoulder." At book's end, Stuart has not yet found his Margalo, but nonetheless, after a close scrape in his little car, he heads on his quest once again: "... the way seemed long. But the sky was bright and he somehow felt he was headed in the right direction."

An enormously amusing series of harrowing adventures befalling the mouse-like hero, the book is, in fact, unobtrusively symbolic and suggestive of larger significances. White himself has written that "Stuart's journey symbolizes the continuing journey that everybody takes—in search of what is perfect and unattainable." It is hard to believe today that the book brought stern disapproval from the powerfully influential Anne Carroll Moore, then head of the Children's Department of the New York Public Library. Notwithstanding serious concerns at what some took to be the unnatural monstrosity of a mouse born to a human family, the book has won its place among contemporary classics. The adventures of the hero are breathtaking, and it could well be that the account of the jaunty, plucky, diminutive hero in often hazardous pursuit of an ideal is recognized, even if only subliminally, as—on its own terms—a book in the heroic mode, written in our unheroic times.

White's second book for children, *Charlotte's Web*, generally accepted as his masterpiece, differs from *Stuart Little* not only in its rural setting, but in that it comes directly out of White's clear observation and deep love for his bucolic home, his barn, the animals he has come to know. The book moves smoothly between two levels of interwoven plot and theme. First, there is the tale of the title character, Charlotte, a spider, *Aranea cavatica*, and her friend, the somewhat lumpish pig, Wilbur, born the runt of the litter, destined for slaughter, but saved by the combined efforts of diverse barnyard animals and, above all, the ingenuity and the loyalty of Charlotte. On the second level, the book is the story of eight-year-old Fern Arable, who has adopted the runt pig and bottle fed him. As the story progresses, however, Fern loses interest in Wilbur and the animals, and begins to turn her pre-adolescent attentions to one Henry Fussy, wanting nothing more in the whole world than to sit with Henry in the gondola of a Ferris wheel, looking far across the countryside.

Notwithstanding Fern's loss of interest, Wilbur is saved from slaughter by Charlotte, who has woven into her webs some startling phrases presumably descriptive of her porcine friend. The book ends with two of the grand sentences of literature: "It is not often that someone comes along who is a true friend and a good writer. Charlotte was both."

The neoclassical balance of these two sentences, the juxtaposition of the long first against the abortive finality of the last suggests White's carefully crafted prose style. Above all else, however, *Charlotte's Web* is precisely what White himself has termed it—a celebration of the rural life, "pastoral, seasonal," and it is not excessive to view the book, in guise of a children's story, as being clearly in a literary tradition that is traceable for at least three millennia. At times, in fact, White's plot recedes as, occasionally, he interjects a sort of lyric intermezzo in praise of summer days, of swallows, of song sparrows, and—above all—of the barn. And at the end, again in the old tradition, into this bucolic paradise there comes death—the natural death of Charlotte as she gives birth to her myriad offspring. All his life, and at considerable financial sacrifice, White has resisted offers to film the story with a "happy ending."

The book is lyrical, suspenseful on its primary level, and philosophical under all. Its individual excellences have been recognized almost universally, and its profundity has been understood by sensitive readers. And although once again the demanding Anne Carroll Moore objected to this book, Eudora Welty stated the majority view when she wrote, "What the book is about is friendship on earth, affection, and protection, adventure and miracle, life and death, trust and treachery, pleasure and pain, and the passing of time. As a piece of work it is just about perfect, and just about magical in the way it is done."

White's third and last children's book, *The Trumpet of the Swan*, has for its protagonist a mute trumpeter swan befriended by young Sam Beaver, a male counterpart to Fern Arable. Young Sam, camping with his father in the Canadian woods, observes a clutch of swan eggs hatching. The voiceless cygnet, Louis, grows up to go to school with Sam Beaver, communicating with people by means of chalk and a slate board hung about his neck. When Louis falls in love with the graceful swan, Serena, he is, of course, handicapped by his muteness. Louis's swan father, taking his son's amatory interests to heart, plummets himself through a music-store window in Billings, Montana, to fetch a trumpet. Henceforth, Louis travels with slate, pencil, *and* the trumpet on a red cord around his neck. Louis fears the trumpet has been stolen, however, and he resolves to reimburse the store owner in Billings. He takes on a succession of jobs, first as counselor and trumpeter at Camp Kookooskoos, where he plays volleyball, rescues a young boy (thus earning a life-saving medal—also to go around his already heavily laden neck), and plays taps in the evening. Thereafter he travels to Boston to float gracefully ahead of a swan boat, playing his trumpet. He stays at the Ritz, causing consternation there as he orders 12 watercress sandwiches from room service. As Louis's fame spreads, he becomes star trumpeter at a Philadelphia nightclub, and obtains free room and board at the Philadelphia Zoo, where he gives concerts on Sunday afternoons. Serena, his beloved, is driven to that same zoo by a storm one blustery night, Louis plays "Beautiful Dreamer" for her, and all the animals listen, enchanted. As Serena is about to become a fortuitous new acquisition for the zoo, and have her wings pinioned, Louis bravely hurtles himself at the zoo keeper to protect his beloved from this mutilation. At this point, Sam—who, unlike Fern, has retained his early affection for animals—arrives to take up a job at the zoo. He recognizes his swan friend from so many years before, and negotiates a compromise with the zoo director whereby Serena and Louis will be permitted to return to their native habitat, promising, however, that every once in a while they will deliver a new baby trumpeter swan to the Philadelphia Zoo. Young Sam still occasionally goes camping with his father in the North Woods. There he hears Louis's

trumpet—but he keeps his council.

The Trumpet of the Swan, which would be a splendid accomplishment for a lesser writer, is not usually thought to stand comparison with White's earlier two children's books. Moreover, it is the only one of the three done without the splendid graphic collaboration of Garth Williams. Edward Frascino has, however, done a creditable job with the illustrations, and one picture in the book is drawn by E.B. White himself. Though more tightly plotted than *Stuart Little*, the book is essentially episodic. The genial commerce between animals and human beings seems, in this book, a bit more labored, less inevitable, than in the first two. Whereas *Charlotte's Web* violates the laws of nature ambiguously only, and with the greatest of restraint, in *The Trumpet of the Swan* White seems to throw down the gauntlet almost with bravado with his implausible musical swan who, without further ado, writes in English on a slate, and who moves easily in a world of human beings.

Although the book was praised by most reviewers, that praise was tempered, the *Times Literary Supplement* referring to Louis as a "sort of feathered Louis Armstrong," and adding that "whether you care for this sort of thing depends on your sense of humor." The most enthusiastic praise came from John Updike, who called the book "the most spacious and serene of the three, the most imbued with the author's sense of the precious instinctual heritage represented by wild nature."

In a sense, the story of Louis is not unfitting as White's swan song to the world of children's books, for essentially it, too, takes as one of its major themes the question White asked throughout his life, often with disarming simplicity in seemingly off-hand essays, and in the children's books—the same question Stuart Little asked of a class of fifth graders—"How many of you know what's important?" And the answer, as ever with White, is essentially the same: art (music in the case of Louis); and friendship; and nature; and growing up—or older—within time, within the circle of nature's seasons. White has attained a niche in American letters as an ironist, essayist, humorist, and one of the foremost prose stylists of our time. All three of his children's books display his literary talents. And one, *Charlotte's Web*, has secured his place permanently among the great writers for children.

—Peter F. Neumeyer

WHITE, Eliza Orne. American. Born in Keene, New Hampshire, 2 August 1856. Educated at schools in Keene, and at Miss Hall's School for Girls, Roxbury, Massachusetts. Lived in Brookline, Massachusetts, 1881–1947. *Died 23 January 1947.*

PUBLICATIONS FOR CHILDREN

Fiction

When Molly Was Six, illustrated by Katharine Pyle. Boston, Houghton Mifflin, 1894.
A Little Girl of Long Ago. Boston, Houghton Mifflin, 1896.
Ednah and Her Brothers, illustrated by Margaret Bush-Brown. Boston, Houghton Mifflin, 1900.
An Only Child, illustrated by Katharine Pyle. Boston, Houghton Mifflin, 1905.
A Borrowed Sister, illustrated by Katharine Pyle. Boston, Houghton Mifflin, 1906.
Brothers in Fur. Boston, Houghton Mifflin, 1910.
The Enchanted Mountain, illustrated by E. Pollak-Ottendorff. Bos-

ton, Houghton, Mifflin, 1911.

The Blue Aunt, illustrated by Katharine Pyle. Boston, Houghton, Mifflin, 1918.

The Strange Year, illustrated by Alice Preston. Boston, Houghton Mifflin, 1920.

Peggy in Her Blue Frock, illustrated by Alice Preston. Boston, Houghton Mifflin, 1921.

Tony, illustrated by Alice Preston. Boston, Houghton Mifflin, 1924.

Joan Morse, illustrated by M.A. Benjamin. Boston, Houghton Mifflin, 1926.

Diana's Rosebush, illustrated by Constance Whittemore. Boston, Houghton Mifflin, 1927.

The Adventures of Andrew. Boston, Houghton Mifflin, 1928.

Sally in Her Fur Coat, illustrated by Lisl Hummel. Boston, Houghton Mifflin, 1929.

The Green Door, illustrated by Lisl Hummel. Boston, Houghton Mifflin, 1930.

When Abigail Was Seven, illustrated by Lisl Hummel. Boston, Houghton Mifflin, 1931.

The Four Young Kendalls, illustrated by Lisl Hummel. Boston, Houghton Mifflin, 1932.

Where Is Adelaide?, illustrated by Helen Sewell. Boston, Houghton Mifflin, 1933.

Lending Mary, illustrated by Grace Paull. Boston, Houghton Mifflin, 1934.

Ann Frances, illustrated by Helen Sewell. Boston, Houghton Mifflin, 1935.

Nancy Alden, illustrated by Mildred Boyle. Boston, Houghton Mifflin, 1936.

The Farm Beyond the Town, illustrated by Mildred Boyle. Boston, Houghton, Mifflin, 1937.

Helen's Gift House, illustrated by Helen Blair. Boston, Houghton Mifflin, 1938.

Patty Makes a Visit, illustrated by Helen Blair. Boston, Houghton Mifflin, 1939.

The House Across the Way, illustrated by Lois Maloy. Boston, Houghton Mifflin, 1940.

I: The Autobiography of a Cat, illustrated by Clarke Hutton. Boston, Houghton Mifflin, 1941.

Training Sylvia, illustrated by Dorothy Bayley. Boston, Houghton Mifflin, 1942.

When Esther Was a Little Girl, illustrated by Connie Moran. Boston, Houghton Mifflin, 1944.

PUBLICATIONS FOR ADULTS

Novels

Miss Brooks. Boston, Roberts, 1890.

Winterborough. Boston, Houghton Mifflin, 1892.

The Coming of Theodora. Boston, Houghton Mifflin, and London, Smith and Elder, 1895.

A Lover of Truth. Boston, Houghton Mifflin, and London, Smith and Elder, 1898.

John Forsyth's Aunts. New York, McClure Phillips, 1901.

Lesley Chilton. Boston, Houghton Mifflin, 1903.

The Wares of Edgefield. Boston, Houghton Mifflin, 1909.

The First Step. Boston, Houghton Mifflin, 1914.

Short Stories

A Browning Courtship and Other Stories. Boston, Houghton Mifflin, and London, Smith and Elder, 1897.

Other

Editor, *William Orne White: A Record of Ninety Years* (letters). Boston, Houghton Mifflin, 1917.

*   *   *

Most writers of successful books for children have found—though never conceivably in anything like perfect balance—an ongoing audience of boys and girls, girls and boys. Boys of my own dim day could stomach those Five Little Peppers, including Phronsie, through all their serial growing pains. We read the Pepper books, but we didn't boast about it. So what of the currently enchanting Miss Bianca and her four-foot Women's Lib? I for one read every Margery Sharp book just as fast as it comes off the press. Why not? After all, isn't Louisa May Alcott really but a younger edition of Jane Austen, working in the same old vineyard? For do not *Emma* and *Little Women* share in common the unfailing readership of full-grown men? Common? Surely Virginia Woolf's "common reader" is not divided, cell-like, sex by sex. Neither is the youthful "common reader" of *Alice*, the Oz books, *The Wind in the Willows, Martin Pippin in the Apple Orchard, Charlotte's Web, Millions of Cats, Tom, Dick, and Harriet, Peacock Pie*, Howard Pyle's *The Wonder Clock*, Henry Beston's *The Starlight Wonder Book*. Beyond that, it is more than (worse than) idle, in listing such books, to set up these silly horizontal milestones for the age groups: fourth grade, sixth grade, pre- and post-teenagers. Aren't we always in our separate lives alike in easy reach of the cookie jar as well as of Bernard Shaw, Henry James, Wallace Stevens, Thoreau, Hudson, Proust, *The Road to Xanadu*?

And so we come to Eliza Orne White, a now faded figure in children's literature: an American Victorian writer whose father had a parish, and whose maternal grandfather was Chester Harding, the well-known painter. She appears to have been popular enough in her day (1856–1947) to have published in all some 25 novels and stories for the very young. And most specifically, in her case, stories for very young girls, *not* boys. All her life she dearly loved little girls and cats. Her cats were characters in themselves. Her two most popular books were *When Molly Was Six* and *A Little Girl of Long Ago*. The young of today, however, could not and would not enter the world of unbelievable innocence that she describes.

She was born in Keene, New Hampshire, a pleasant town through which I have often driven: a pretty, partially industrial town whose Main Street is surely the widest in all New England. It was a town which obviously should have produced at least one literary figure. It produced White, who lived there until she was 22. Let her describe it:

> It was just the right sort of a place for a little girl to live in who was to write stories for other little girls when she grew up, for there were all the things to be found there that children most like. The town was very beautiful, with the hills around it, and Monadnock to be seen from the lower end of Main Street, and the Ashuelot River and Beaver Brook, with the woods near them, made splendid places for picnics or drives.
>
> In the winter, like Molly, "when she was six," my father would take me and some small friend coasting on a big black sled, down a snowy hill and across an icy pond, and we had sleigh-rides to the accompaniment of jingling sleigh-bells, and less speedy rides when we fastened our sleds to slowly moving ox teams.

She was from first to last a period piece. Her style, a sweet stillwater as old-fashioned as the flowers in her garden, as respectful as my own Presbyterian grandmother who always spoke of my

Pennsylvania grandfather as "Mr. Reed." You may learn (in *When Molly Was Six*) of the difference between cows and bossies; of "pink-and-white dyaletras"; of hanging "over the *balusters*," not "banisters"; of playing jackstraws—a game of my own youth; of words like rowboats and ponycarts spelled with a hyphen; of Mammá, not Mámma or Mom; of a time when one ran *into* and not *in* the house. That is, we are told, through little twists and tags of speech, of an almost insufferable formality of deportment and confected give-and-take. Most of these books' adventures seem tame enough—as though the lives of little girls of 80 years ago were lived in greater part in a doll's house. Hence "a pew-door seemed made on purpose for little children." In *A Little Girl of Long Ago* when a somewhat older and more gregarious heroine than Molly, along with her younger sister and brother, struggles to help another young brother free his head which he had squeezed through the back of his chair, we find the victim wailing, "Oh, dear, how you hurt!" Take a look at the prose of E. Nesbit in *The Railway Children*: it is not at all like that. But at least there is scarcely any moralizing; and when White, in one of her rare didactic moments, says a word about cheating, or abandons reality to show the child reader the dreadful danger of (a) deep water or (b) setting one's clothes and hair accidently on fire, she does not labor the message; nor does she repeat it. White's obvious lack is a sense of humor to leaven all her gentleness, kindness, and Sehnsucht. And, as Ethel Heins more importantly points out, her *real* failure (unlike E. Nesbit, for example) is not dealing in any way with fantasy pure and simple. Fantasy is what lasts.

—David McCord

WHITE, T(erence) H(anbury). Also wrote as James Aston. British. Born in Bombay, India, 29 May 1906; brought to England, 1911. Educated at Cheltenham College, 1920–24; Queens' College, Cambridge (exhibitioner), 1925–27, 1928–29, B.A. 1929. Taught at a preparatory school, 1930–32; head of the English department, Stowe School, Buckinghamshire, 1932–36. Lived in Ireland, 1939–46, and in Jersey, 1946–47, and Alderney, 1947–64, Channel Islands. *Died 17 January 1964.*

PUBLICATIONS FOR CHILDREN

Fiction

The Sword in the Stone, illustrated by the author. London, Collins, 1938; New York, Putnam, 1939; revised edition, in *The Once and Future King*, 1958.
The Witch in the Wood, illustrated by the author. New York, Putnam, 1939; London, Collins, 1940; revised edition, as *The Queen of Air and Darkness*, in *The Once and Future King*, 1958.
The Ill-Made Knight, illustrated by the author. New York, Putnam, 1940; London, Collins, 1941; revised edition, in *The Once and Future King*, 1958.
Mistress Masham's Repose, illustrated by Fritz Eichenberg. New York, Putnam, 1946; London, Cape, 1947.
The Master: An Adventure Story. London, Cape, and New York, Putnam, 1957.
The Once and Future King. London, Collins, and New York, Putnam, 1958.
The Book of Merlyn: The Unpublished Conclusion to The Once and Future King, illustrated by Trevor Stubley. Austin, University of Texas Press, 1977; London, Collins, 1978.

PUBLICATIONS FOR ADULTS

Novels

Dead Mr. Nixon, with R. McNair Scott. London, Cassell, 1931.
Darkness at Pemberley. London, Gollancz, 1932; New York, Century, 1933.
They Winter Abroad (as James Aston). London, Chatto and Windus, and New York, Viking Press, 1932.
First Lesson (as James Aston). London, Chatto and Windus, 1932; New York, Knopf, 1933.
Farewell Victoria. London, Collins, 1933; New York, Smith and Haas, 1934.
Earth Stopped; or, Mr. Marx's Sporting Tour. London, Collins, 1934; New York, Putnam, 1935.
Gone to Ground. London, Collins, and New York, Putnam, 1935.
The Elephant and the Kangaroo. New York, Putnam, 1947; London, Cape, 1948.

Short Stories

The Maharajah and Other Stories, edited by Kurth Sprague. London, Macdonald, and New York, Putnam, 1981.

Verse

Loved Helen and Other Poems. London, Chatto and Windus, and New York, Viking Press, 1929.
The Green Bay Tree; or, The Wicked Man Touches Wood. Cambridge, Heffer, 1929.
Verses. Privately printed, 1962.
A Joy Proposed. London, Rota, 1980; Athens, University of Georgia Press, 1983.

Other

England Have My Bones. London, Collins, and New York, Macmillan, 1936.
Burke's Steerage; or, The Amateur Gentleman's Introduction to Noble Sports and Pastimes. London, Collins, 1938; New York, Putnam, 1939.
The Age of Scandal: An Excursion Through a Minor Period. London, Cape, and New York, Putnam, 1950.
The Goshawk (on falconry). London, Cape, 1951; New York, Putnam, 1952.
The Scandalmonger (on English scandals). London, Cape, and New York, Putnam, 1952.
The Godstone and the Blackymor (on Ireland). London, Cape, and New York, Putnam, 1959.
America at Last: The American Journal of T.H. White. New York, Putnam, 1965.
The White/Garnett Letters, edited by David Garnett. London, Cape, and New York, Viking Press, 1968.
Letters to a Friend: The Correspondence Between T.H. White and L.J. Potts, edited by François Gallix. New York, Putnam, 1982; Gloucester, Sutton, 1984.

Editor and Translator, *The Book of Beasts, Being a Translation from a Latin Bestiary of the Twelfth Century*. London, Cape, 1954; New York, Putnam, 1955.

*

CHILDREN'S WRITERS

Bibliography: *T.H. White: An Annotated Bibliography* by François Gallix, New York, Garland, 1986.

Critical Studies: *T.H. White: A Biography* by Sylvia Townsend Warner, London, Cape-Chatto and Windus, 1967, New York, Viking Press, 1968; *T.H. White* by John K. Crane, New York, Twayne, 1974.

*   *   *

Many of T.H. White's books have been read by children, but his claim to be a "children's writer" rests chiefly on *The Sword in the Stone* and *Mistress Masham's Repose*. The former, as originally published, is a classic by any reckoning, one of those books which, if discovered in childhood, will be returned to again and again with renewed pleasure. In manner and tone it lies somewhere between *The Wind in the Willows* and *The Hobbit*: a loving, humorous, fantastical account of the childhood of the boy Wart (adopted younger brother of the soon-to-be-knighted Kay) at the castle of Sir Ector, in a timeless medieval England where there are hawks to be flown, outlaws and witches lurking in the wood, and no lesser person than Merlyn to be the boys' tutor—with the result that their lessons involve the strangest experiences. The original *The Sword in the Stone* is, in fact, a masterpiece, White's highest achievement—and is, incidentally, illustrated with splendidly deadpan comic line-drawings by White himself.

But in this form *The Sword in the Stone* is, alas, to be found today on few nursery or library shelves. In 1958 White revised the book in order to incorporate it into the one-volume edition of his Arthurian tetralogy *The Once and Future King*—for the boy Wart is the young Arthur, and the story was conceived as the first of four Arthurian novels. In the revision, the illustrations disappeared, along with one of the highlights of the original book, the magical battle between Merlyn and the genteel witch madam Mim (with Hecate as umpire). For this, White substituted an adventure in which Wart and Kay encounter Morgan le Fay. Is it too much to hope that one day White's publishers will undo his destructive work and reissue the original *The Sword in the Stone*, drawings and all?

Mistress Masham's Repose is a near-classic, just missing the highest mark because there is something faintly derivative about it. Maria's Lilliputian friends, discovered on an island in the grounds of the dilapidated ducal mansion where she lives (Stowe, the school where White taught, provided the original), ought to be the starting-point, one feels, of something a little more original than a battle against the odious governess and vicar, who seem to have walked straight out of the pages of John Masefield. But the book is full of life, well worth returning to.White, it should be noted, never wrote specifically "for" children or "for" adults. A man of huge literary ambitions and endless personal crises, he has been brilliantly served by his biographer, Sylvia Townsend Warner, to whose life of him any enthusiastic reader of his novels should turn.

—Humphrey Carpenter

WHITLOCK, Pamela. See **HULL, Katharine and WHITLOCK, Pamela.**

WHITNEY, Phyllis A(yame). American. Born in Yokohama, Japan, 9 September 1903. Educated at schools in Japan, China, the Philippines, California, and Texas; McKinley High School, Chicago, graduated 1924. Married 1) George A. Garner in 1925 (divorced 1945), one daughter; 2) Lovell F. Jahnke in 1950 (died 1973). Dance instructor, San Antonio, Texas, one year; children's books editor, Chicago *Sun*, 1942–46, and Philadelphia *Inquirer*, 1947–48; instructor in juvenile fiction writing, Northwestern University, Evanston, Illinois, 1945, and New York University, 1947–58. Member, Board of Directors, 1959–62, and president, 1975, Mystery Writers of America. Recipient: Mystery Writers of America Edgar Allan Poe award, 1961, 1964, and Grand Master award, 1984. Lives in Virginia. Agent: c/o McIntosh and Otis Inc., 310 Madison Avenue, New York, New York 10017, U.S.A.

PUBLICATIONS FOR CHILDREN

Fiction

A Place for Ann, illustrated by Helen Blair. Boston, Houghton Mifflin, 1941.
A Star for Ginny, illustrated by Hilda Frommholz. Boston, Houghton Mifflin, 1942.
A Window for Julie, illustrated by Jean Anderson. Boston, Houghton Mifflin, 1943.
The Silver Inkwell, illustrated by Hilda Frommholz. Boston, Houghton Mifflin, 1945.
Willow Hill. New York, Reynal, 1947.
Ever After. Boston, Houghton Mifflin, 1948.
Mystery of the Gulls, illustrated by Janet Smalley. Philadelphia, Westminster Press, 1949.
Linda's Homecoming. Philadelphia, McKay, 1950.
The Island of Dark Woods, illustrated by Philip Wishnefsky. Philadelphia, Westminster Press, 1951; as *Mystery of the Strange Traveler*, 1967.
Love Me, Love Me Not. Boston, Houghton Mifflin, 1952.
Step to the Music. New York, Crowell, 1953.
Mystery of the Black Diamonds, illustrated by John Gretzer. Philadelphia, Westminster Press, 1954; as *Black Diamonds*, Leicester, Brockhampton Press, 1957.
A Long Time Coming. Philadelphia, McKay, 1954.
Mystery on the Isle of Skye, illustrated by Ezra Jack Keats. Philadelphia, Westminster Press, 1955.
The Fire and the Gold. New York, Crowell, 1956.
The Highest Dream. Philadelphia, McKay, 1956.
Mystery of the Green Cat, illustrated by Richard Horwitz. Philadelphia, Westminster Press, 1957.
Secret of the Samurai Sword. Philadelphia, Westminster Press, 1958.
Creole Holiday. Philadelphia, Westminster Press, 1959.
Mystery of the Haunted Pool, illustrated by H. Tom Hall. Philadelphia, Westminster Press, 1960.
Secret of the Tiger's Eye, illustrated by Richard Horwitz. Philadelphia, Westminster Press, 1961.
Mystery of the Golden Horn, illustrated by Georgeann Helms. Philadelphia, Westminster Press, 1962.
Mystery of the Hidden Hand, illustrated by H. Tom Hall. Philadelphia, Westminster Press, 1963.
Secret of the Emerald Star, illustrated by Alex Stein. Philadelphia, Westminster Press, 1964.
Mystery of the Angry Idol, illustrated by Al Fiorentino. Philadelphia, Westminster Press, 1965.
Secret of the Spotted Shell, illustrated by John Mecray. Philadelphia, Westminster Press, 1967.
Secret of Goblin Glen, illustrated by Al Fiorentino. Philadelphia, Westminster Press, 1968.
The Mystery of the Crimson Ghost. Philadelphia, Westminster

Press, 1969.
Secret of the Missing Footprint, illustrated by Alex Stein. Philadelphia, Westminster Press, 1969.
The Vanishing Scarecrow. Philadelphia, Westminster Press, 1971.
Nobody Likes Trina. Philadelphia, Westminster Press, 1972.
Mystery of the Scowling Boy, illustrated by John Gretzer. Philadelphia, Westminster Press, 1973.
Secret of Haunted Mesa. Philadelphia, Westminster Press, 1975.
Secret of the Stone Face. Philadelphia, Westminster Press, 1977.

PUBLICATIONS FOR ADULTS

Novels

Red Is for Murder. Chicago, Ziff Davis, 1943; as *Red Carnelian*, New York, Paperback Library, 1968; London, Coronet, 1976.
The Quicksilver Pool. New York, Appleton Century Crofts, 1955; London, Coronet, 1973.
The Trembling Hills. New York, Appleton Century Crofts, 1956; London, Coronet, 1974.
Skye Cameron. New York, Appleton Century Crofts, 1957; London, Hurst and Blackett, 1959.
The Moonflower. New York, Appleton Century Crofts, 1958; as *The Mask and the Moonflower*, London, Hurst and Blackett, 1960.
Thunder Heights. New York, Appleton Century Crofts, 1960; London, Coronet, 1973.
Blue Fire. New York, Appleton Century Crofts, 1961; London, Hodder and Stoughton, 1962.
Window on the Square. New York, Appleton Century Crofts, 1962; London, Coronet, 1969.
Seven Tears for Apollo. New York, Appleton Century Crofts, 1963; London, Coronet, 1969.
Black Amber. New York, Appleton Century Crofts, 1964; London, Hale, 1965.
Sea Jade. New York, Appleton Century Crofts, 1965; London, Hale, 1966.
Columbella. New York, Doubleday, 1966; London, Hale, 1967.
Silverhill. New York, Doubleday, 1967; London, Heinemann, 1968.
Hunter's Green. New York, Doubleday, 1968; London, Heinemann, 1969.
The Winter People. New York, Doubleday, 1969; London, Heinemann, 1970.
Lost Island. New York, Doubleday, 1970; London, Heinemann, 1971.
Listen for the Whisperer. New York, Doubleday, and London, Heinemann, 1972.
Snowfire. New York, Doubleday, and London, Heinemann, 1973.
The Turquoise Mask. New York, Doubleday, 1974; London, Heinemann, 1975.
Spindrift. New York, Doubleday, and London, Heinemann, 1975.
The Golden Unicorn. New York, Doubleday, 1976; London, Heinemann, 1977.
The Stone Bull. New York, Doubleday, and London, Heinemann, 1977.
The Glass Flame. New York, Doubleday, 1978; London, Heinemann, 1979.
Domino. New York, Doubleday, 1979; London, Heinemann, 1980.
Poinciana. New York, Doubleday, 1980; London, Heinemann, 1981.
Vermilion. New York, Doubleday, 1981; London, Heinemann, 1982.
Emerald. New York, Doubleday, and London, Heinemann, 1983.
Rainsong. New York, Doubleday, and London, Heinemann, 1984.
Dream of Orchids. New York, Doubleday, and London, Hodder

and Stoughton, 1985.
The Flaming Tree. New York, Doubleday, and London, Hodder and Stoughton, 1986.
Silversword. New York, Doubleday, and London, Hodder and Stoughton, 1987.
Feather on the Moon. New York, Doubleday, and London, Hodder and Stoughton, 1988.
Rainbow in the Mist. New York, Doubleday, 1989.

Other

Writing Juvenile Fiction. Boston, The Writer, 1947; revised edition, 1960.
Writing Juvenile Stories and Novels: How to Write and Sell Fiction for Young People. Boston, The Writer, 1976.
Guide to Fiction Writing. Boston, The Writer, 1982; London, Poplar Press, 1984.

*

Manuscript Collection: Mugar Memorial Library, Boston University.

*   *   *

Phyllis A. Whitney's juvenile fiction is primarily of two types—junior novels with sentimental maturation themes and mystery-adventure stories. Her novels about growing up are similar to those of Betty Cavanna, but she does venture into unusual territory for the junior novel with its long-standing but recently eased taboos on serious, controversial matters.

Willow Hill straightforwardly confronts the problems of an integrated community. The heroine, Val Coleman, covets the editorship of the school newspaper, but the teacher gives the job to an attractive black girl who lives in the new housing project. Val, who instinctively accepts quality but is hurt because of the teacher's choice, is forced to come to terms with her own potential racism and that of the community. Her mother, who gets her cue from a Mrs. Manning, a community stalwart, opposes the housing project, but her father, a wise gym teacher, welcomes integration. The book seems daringly ahead of its time in its sympathy and in its honest portrayal of race relations.

Although Whitney has written a number of these serious novels about the drama of growing up (such as *Linda's Homecoming*, which deals with a girl's gradual acceptance of her new stepfather), most of her stories are lively, light mysteries similar to the Nancy Drew stories. The protagonists are often 12-year-old girls, young detectives who tend to be normal kids with shortcomings and frustrations, rather than sophisticated, independent, idealized heroines. Thus Whitney has been praised for her honesty, realism, and intellectually stimulating themes. However, the appeal of her books is much the same as that of the slicker commercial series books with repeated plot formulas. The basic appeal is reader identification with a vicarious adventure, one which girls would not encounter in their ordinary lives, but an adventure which leads them safely home in the end to the comfortable security of a familiar world. The reader wants to be excited and reassured simultaneously, and most popular entertainment accomplishes this dual goal.

Whitney frequently writes of dislocation—a child longing for stability, a house with a neat yard and picket fence and dog, and a room with a ruffled bedspread. There are several characters with nomadic parents. In *Mystery of the Black Diamonds* the father, who has to travel to do research for his writing, is a stimulus to investigation of the mystery, while mom wants desperately to settle down in a house with a washing machine. The heroine wants both domesticity and adventure, and this desire is doubly satisfying for the reader.

Thus the settings of Whitney novels are important, for the danger and excitement of the adventure must be contrasted with the security and coziness of quaint, old-fashioned places. In *Mystery of the Gulls* the setting is fog-shrouded Mackinac Island during a summer at a quaint resort hotel, where the heroine encounters the mysterious folkways of the local Indians. *Mystery of the Black Diamonds* is about a Colorado ghost town. Other settings include Staten Island, New Orleans, Scotland, and Japan—all provided with extensive information on the history and culture.

—Bobbie Ann Mason

WIBBERLEY, Leonard (Patrick O'Connor). Also wrote as Leonard Holton; Patrick O'Connor; Christopher Webb. Irish. Born in Dublin, 9 April 1915. Educated at Ring College, Ireland; Abbey House, Romsey, Hampshire; Cardinal Vaughan's School, London, 1925–30; El Camino College, Torrance, California. Served in the Trinidad Artillery Volunteers, 1938–40: Lance Bombardier. Married Katherine Hazel Holton in 1948; two daughters and four sons. Reporter, *Sunday Dispatch*, 1931–32, *Sunday Express*, 1932–34, and *Daily Mirror*, 1935–36, all London; editor, Trinidad *Evening News*, 1936; oilfield worker, Trinidad, 1936–43; cable editor, Associated Press, New York, 1943–44; New York correspondent and bureau chief, London *Evening News*, 1944–46; editor, *Independent Journal*, San Rafael, California, 1947–49; reporter and copy editor, Los Angeles *Times*, 1950–54; columnist, San Francisco *Chronicle*. Died 22 November 1983.

PUBLICATIONS FOR CHILDREN

Fiction

The King's Beard, illustrated by Christine Price. New York, Farrar Straus, 1952; London, Faber, 1954.
The Secret of the Hawk, illustrated by Christine Price. New York, Farrar Straus, 1953; London, Faber, 1956.
Deadmen's Cave, illustrated by Tom Leamon. New York, Farrar Straus, and London, Faber, 1954.
The Wound of Peter Wayne. New York, Farrar Straus, 1955; London, Faber, 1957.
Kevin O'Connor and the Light Brigade. New York, Farrar Straus, 1957; London, Harrap, 1959.
John Treegate's Musket. New York, Farrar Straus, 1959.
Peter Treegate's War. New York, Farrar Straus, 1960.
Sea Captain from Salem. New York, Farrar Straus, 1961.
The Time of the Lamb, illustrated by Fritz Kredel. New York, Washburn, 1961.
Treegate's Raiders. New York, Farrar Straus, 1962.
Encounter near Venus, illustrated by Alice Wadowski-Bak. New York, Farrar Straus, 1967; London, Macdonald, 1968.
Attar of the Ice Valley. New York, Farrar Straus, 1968; London, Macdonald, 1969.
Journey to Untor. New York, Farrar Straus, 1970; London, Macdonald, 1971.
Leopard's Prey. New York, Farrar Straus, 1971.
Flint's Island. New York, Farrar Straus, 1972; London, Macdonald, 1973.
Red Pawns. New York, Farrar Straus, 1973.
The Last Battle. New York, Farrar Straus, 1976.
Perilous Gold. New York, Farrar Straus, 1978.
Little League Family, illustrated by Richard Cuffari. New York, Doubleday, 1978.
The Crime of Martin Coverly. New York, Farrar Straus, 1980.

Fiction as Patrick O'Connor

The Lost Harpooner. New York, Washburn, 1947; London, Harrap, 1959.
Flight of the Peacock, illustrated by Rus Anderson. New York, Washburn, 1954.
The Society of Foxes, illustrated by Clifford Geary. New York, Washburn, 1954.
The Watermelon Mystery. New York, Washburn, 1955.
Gunpowder for Washington. New York, Washburn, 1956.
The Black Tiger. New York, Washburn, 1956.
Mexican Road Race. New York, Washburn, 1957.
Black Tiger at Le Mans. New York, Washburn, 1958.
The Five-Dollar Watch Mystery. New York, Washburn, 1959.
Black Tiger at Bonneville. New York, Washburn, 1960.
Treasure at Twenty Fathoms. New York, Washburn, 1961.
Black Tiger at Indianapolis. New York, Washburn, 1962.
The Raising of the Dubhe. New York, Washburn, 1964.
Seawind from Hawaii. New York, Washburn, 1965.
South Swell. New York, Washburn, 1967; London, Macdonald, 1968.
Beyond Hawaii. New York, Washburn, 1969; as Leonard Wibberley, London, Macdonald, 1970.
A Car Called Camellia. New York, Washburn, 1970.

Fiction as Christopher Webb

Matt Tyler's Chronicle. New York, Funk and Wagnalls, 1958; London, Macdonald, 1966.
Mark Toyman's Inheritance. New York, Funk and Wagnalls, 1960.
The River of Pee Dee Jack. New York, Funk and Wagnalls, 1962.
The Quest of the Otter. New York, Funk and Wagnalls, 1963; London, Macdonald, 1965.
The "Ann and Hope" Mutiny. New York, Funk and Wagnalls, 1966; London, Macdonald, 1967.
Eusebius, The Phoenician. New York, Funk and Wagnalls, 1969; London, Macdonald, 1970.

Verse

The Ballad of the Pilgrim Cat. New York, Washburn, 1962.
The Shepherd's Reward, illustrated by Thomas Fisher. New York, Washburn, 1963.

Other

The Coronation Book: The Dramatic Story in History and Legend. New York, Farrar Straus, 1953.
The Epics of Everest, illustrated by Genevieve Vaughan-Jackson. New York, Farrar Straus, 1954; London, Faber, 1955.
The Life of Winston Churchill. New York, Farrar Straus, 1956; revised edition, 1965.
John Barry, Father of the Navy. New York, Farrar Straus, 1957.
Wes Powell, Conqueror of the Grand Canyon. New York, Farrar Straus, 1958.
Zebulon Pike, Soldier and Explorer. New York, Funk and Wagnalls, 1961.
Man of Liberty: A Life of Thomas Jefferson. New York, Farrar Straus, 1968.
1. *Young Man from the Piedmont: The Youth of Thomas Jefferson*. New York, Farrar Straus, 1963.
2. *A Dawn in the Trees: Thomas Jefferson, The Years 1776 to 1789*. New York, Farrar Straus, 1964.

3. *The Gales of Spring: Thomas Jefferson, The Years 1789 to 1801.* New York, Farrar Straus, 1965.
4. *Time of the Harvest: Thomas Jefferson, The Years 1801 to 1826.* New York, Farrar Straus, 1966.
Guarneri: Story of a Genius. New York, Farrar Straus, 1974; as *Guarneri: Violin Maker of Genius,* London, Macdonald and Jane's, 1976.

PUBLICATIONS FOR ADULTS

Novels

Mrs. Searwood's Secret Weapon. Boston, Little Brown, 1954; London, Hale, 1955.
The Mouse That Roared. Boston, Little Brown, 1955; London, Corgi, 1959; as *The Wrath of Grapes,* London, Hale, 1955.
McGillicuddy McGotham. Boston, Little Brown, 1956; London, Hale 1958.
Take Me to Your President. New York, Putnam, 1957.
Beware of the Mouse. New York, Putnam, 1958.
The Quest for Excalibur. New York, Putnam, 1959.
The Hands of Cormac Joyce. New York, Putnam, 1960; London, Muller, 1962.
Stranger at Killknock. New York, Putnam, 1961; London, Muller, 1963.
The Mouse on the Moon. New York, Morrow, 1962; London, Muller, 1964.
A Feast of Freedom. New York, Morrow, 1964.
The Island of the Angels. New York, Morrow, 1965.
The Centurion. New York, Morrow, 1966.
The Road from Toomi. New York, Morrow, 1967.
Adventures of an Elephant Boy. New York, Morrow, 1968.
The Mouse on Wall Street. New York, Morrow, 1969.
Meeting with a Great Beast. New York, Morrow, 1971; London, Chatto and Windus, 1972.
The Testament of Theophilus. New York, Morrow, 1973; as *Merchant of Rome,* London, Cassell, 1974.
The Last Stand of Father Felix. New York, Morrow, 1974.
1776—and All That. New York, Morrow, 1975.
One in Four. New York, Morrow, 1976.
Homeward to Ithaka. New York, Morrow, 1978.
The Mouse That Saved the West. New York, Morrow, 1981.

Novels as Leonard Holton

The Saint Maker. New York, Dodd Mead, 1959; London, Hale, 1960.
A Pact with Satan. New York, Dodd Mead, 1960; London, Hale, 1961.
Secret of the Doubting Saint. New York, Dodd Mead, 1961.
Deliver Us from Wolves. New York, Dodd Mead, 1963.
Flowers by Request. New York, Dodd Mead, 1964.
Out of the Depths. New York, Dodd Mead, 1966; London, Hammond, 1967.
A Touch of Jonah. New York, Dodd Mead, 1968.
A Problem in Angels. New York, Dodd Mead, 1970.
The Mirror of Hell. New York, Dodd Mead, 1972.
The Devil to Play. New York, Dodd Mead, 1974.
A Corner of Paradise. New York, St. Martin's Press, 1977.

Plays

The Heavenly Quarterback. Chicago, Dramatic Publishing Company, 1968.
Gift of a Star. Chicago, Dramatic Publishing Company, 1969.

The Vicar of Wakefield, adaptation of the novel by Oliver Goldsmith. Chicago, Dramatic Publishing Company, n.d.
Black Jack Rides Again. Chicago, Dramatic Publishing Company, 1971.
1776—and All That. Chicago, Dramatic Publishing Company, 1973.
Once, In a Garden. Chicago, Dramatic Publishing Company, 1975.

Ballet Scenario: *Encounter near Venus,* 1978.

Other

The Trouble with the Irish (or the English, Depending on Your Point of View). New York, Holt, 1956; London, Muller, 1958.
The Coming of the Green. New York, Holt, 1958.
No Garlic in the Soup (on Portugal). New York, Washburn, 1959; London, Faber, 1960.
The Land That Isn't There: An Irish Adventure. New York, Washburn, 1960.
Yesterday's Land: A Baja California Adventure. New York, Washburn, 1961.
Ventures into the Deep: The Thrill of Scuba Diving. New York, Washburn, 1962.
Ah Julian! A Memoir of Julian Brodetsky. New York, Washburn, 1963.
Fiji: Islands of the Dawn. New York, Washburn, 1964.
Toward a Distant Island: A Sailor's Odyssey. New York, Washburn, 1966.
Something to Read. New York, Washburn, 1967.
Hound of the Sea. New York, Washburn, 1969.
Voyage by Bus. New York, Morrow, 1971.
The Shannon Sailors: A Voyage to the Heart of Ireland. New York, Morrow, 1972.
The Good-Natured Man: A Portrait of Oliver Goldsmith. New York, Morrow, 1979.

*

Manuscript Collection: University of Southern California, Los Angeles.

Leonard Wibberley commented:

(1983) Basically it is for the child inside myself that I write my children's books, for that child lives on into my more sombre years. I retain the same love of adventure; the same sharp interest in anything new and exciting; the same delight in unexplored places, distant islands, the thunder of surf and the might of the wind in a storm that I had in childhood. Dark forests, unscalable mountain ranges, submarine caverns, armored knights, lusty bowmen; people sly, cunning, cowardly, deceitful or brave—all enthrall me, and I have, therefore, lived myself all the children's books I have written. That includes biographies such as my books on Jefferson and Churchill. If I cannot live a book and all the characters in it, then it is a poor book or I cannot write it.

Some of my children's books have turned out badly. I could not get into the character of Zebulon Pike, for instance. He kept turning out stuffy, and the same is true of the biography of John Barry, father of the United States Navy. Interestingly enough both of these biographies were suggested to me by a publisher who saw a need for such a work. So it would appear that I do poorly with an assigned book.

I never start with a plot for a children's book—or a novel or satire for adults either. I just start with people in a situation, and they, coming to life, work out the plot for me.

Robert Louis Stevenson was my earliest mentor in writing books for children. I loved his *Treasure Island* so much that I wrote a sequel to it, in his style, called *Flint's Island*. Rider Haggard also influenced me and Dickens, especially *A Tale of Two Cities*. Goldsmith I loved, and also A.A. Milne, C.S. Lewis, and Tolkien. You will notice that in the works of all these writers the characters are more important than the plot, and, reflecting on their books, you remember the people in them, while the plot often becomes quite vague. Books then are about three-dimensional people, or at least that is the case in my view. If you haven't got people you haven't got a book. This applies to movies, plays, and television (though television producers, alas, tend to demand a plot outline in a sentence or so before they get much interest in a script).

Anyway, you must write for the child that you are if you are going to produce a children's book of any worth. However exotic the characters in the works of the great Dr. Seuss, they are all of them thoroughly alive.

* * *

The very first book that Leonard Wibberley remembered was Robert Louis Stevenson's *Treasure Island*, which was read to him by a teacher when he was about eight years old. It remained his favorite all his life. Even without this biographical knowledge, however, the reader of Wibberley's prolific and versatile work cannot help but notice the influence that Stevenson had upon him as a writer. Wibberley possessed the same romantic charm as Stevenson, in that he wrote out of the perpetual boy that was in him. He delighted in putting forth the opening request of the traditional storyteller: "Make believe!" He captured the spirit of romantic youth by seeking out where joy resides, so that he might give it voice—the very joy that so many writers for today's children would take away from them. Whether it is in his historical novels, like those in his Treegate Chronicles, or in his "nonfiction fiction," as exemplified by his four-volume biography of Thomas Jefferson, Wibberley's books, like those of Stevenson, present the world as an expansive stage, bustling with romantic incident. Action is the mirror in which the characters are reflected, and the vision of the characters remains clear, vivid, and uncomplicated. Wibberley's works most often have an historical setting, not only because he strongly believed that today's young must know the past in order to understand the society and culture which they have inherited, but also because the times he selected, the American Revolution, for example, provided him with a cast of characters whose human passions are not yet hidden by the conventionalities of civilization. His books are masculine, and those he chose to write about, real as well as fictional, are men who possess some part of his vigorous ideal of manhood: courage, intelligence, loyalty, delight in living—in short, men worth knowing and respecting. Some readers may not take to the blood and violence, but this too is not only historically accurate, it also is in the tradition of the adventure romance. The young find in his books justification for their own hopes, dreams, and ideas.

Wibberley's writing, again like Stevenson's, is distinctively marked by his Gaelic temperament. One sometimes finds a touch of the moral philosopher, but it is always balanced by an engaging sense of humor, and never is it didactic. Above all Wibberley was a craftsman with a love for lovely words. And yet there is nothing bookish about him. He loved to travel; he loved the sea and ships and the men who sail them. His books reflect his uncanny skill in uncovering the spirit of place and the fascination of time: past, present and future.

When a youngster reads a Wibberley book he is sharing a few hours of storytelling with a man who was, according to Susan Cooper, "one of the best writers for children in the United States." It matters little whether the book be one of those already mentioned, or one of his auto-racing stories written under the pseudonym of Patrick O'Connor, or *Flint's Island*, his marvellous sequel to

Treasure Island, or one of his adult novellas, like *The Hands of Cormac Joyce*, for each of them bears the signature of a quality writer.

—James E. Higgins

―――――――

WIER, Ester (Alberti). American. Born in Seattle, Washington, 17 October 1910. Educated at Southeastern Teachers College, Durant, Oklahoma, 1929–30; University of California, Los Angeles, 1931–32. Married Henry Robert Wier in 1934; one son and one daughter. Address: 2534 S.W. 14th Drive, Gainesville, Florida 32608, U.S.A.

PUBLICATIONS FOR CHILDREN

Fiction

The Loner, illustrated by Christine Price. Philadelphia, McKay, 1963; London, Constable, 1966.
Gift of the Mountains, illustrated by Richard Lewis. Philadelphia, McKay, 1963.
The Rumptydoolers, illustrated by W.T. Mars. New York, Vanguard Press, 1964.
Easy Does It, illustrated by W.T. Mars. New York, Vanguard Press, 1965.
The Barrel, illustrated by Carl Kidwell. Philadelphia, McKay, 1966.
The Wind Chasers, illustrated by Kurt Werth. Philadelphia, McKay, 1967; London, Constable, 1968.
The Winners, illustrated by Ursula Koering. Philadelphia, McKay, 1967.
The Space Hut, illustrated by Leo Summers. Harrisburg, Pennsylvania, Stackpole, 1967.
Action at Paradise Marsh, illustrated by Earl Blust. Harrisburg, Pennsylvania, Stackpole, 1968.
The Long Year, illustrated by Ursula Koering. Philadelphia, McKay, 1969.
The Straggler, illustrated by Leonard Vosburgh. Philadelphia, McKay, 1970.
The White Oak, illustrated by Anne Marie Jauss. Philadelphia, McKay, 1971.
The Partners, illustrated by Anna Maria Ahl. Philadelphia, McKay, 1972.
The Hunting Trail, illustrated by Richard Cuffari. New York, Walck, 1974.
King of the Mountain. New York, Walck, 1975.

PUBLICATIONS FOR ADULTS

Other

The Answer Book on Naval Social Customs [and *Air Force Social Customs*], with Dorothy Hickey. Harrisburg, Pennsylvania, Military Service Publishing, 2 vols., 1956–57.
Army Social Customs. Harrisburg, Pennsylvania, Military Service Publishing, 1958.
What Every Air Force Wife Should Know. Harrisburg, Pennsylvania, Military Service Publishing, 1958.

*

Manuscript Collections: Kerlan Collection, University of Minnesota, Minneapolis; de Grummond Collection, University of Southern Mississippi, Hattiesburg.

Ester Wier comments:
I have tried to make my books understandable and acceptable to young readers. Each event in each story could have happened to some child somewhere in the course of his everyday existence. The backgrounds have been of great importance to me since here was my chance to acquaint children with other places while allowing them to see that life goes on pretty much the same no matter where you are. If I have aroused curiosity in them about peers living in other locations and led them to search out more about different places, then I have succeeded in what I have intended. And if I have been able to instill in them a love and feeling of responsibility for animals, then I am content.

*   *   *

Writer of many stories, Ester Wier has developed her skills considerably beyond the point of her first excellent book, *The Loner*, runner-up for the 1963 Newbery award. The body of her work contains many stories of children, primarily boys, who are seeking acceptance by themselves or others. Wier shows strong understanding of youth's efforts to stand on its own, and yet she accepts its real needs to belong to someone else somewhere. The need to achieve and to be accepted motivates her characters, whether they live in the southwest of the United States and are surrounded by plains and plateaus like Whit in *The Rumptydoolers*, or live in the Everglades of Florida like Chance Reedy in *The Barrel* and are surrounded by alligators and razorbacks.

Perhaps the best of Wier's stories are those with nature settings, in sheep country or shellfish shorelands. Her depictions of the natural environment are detailed without becoming boring, integrated with the story, and yet vivid enough to convince the reader of their reality. Research must surely be part of Wier's preparation, for many of the stories capture the flavor of regional speech. Although early Wier books are filled with telling rather than showing, telling the reader the thoughts and feelings of the protagonist rather than showing the action that results from feelings and thoughts, later stories contain well-drawn and believable characters like Jesse growing up in *The Long Year*. When the subject of Wier's story is a wild creature, as it occasionally is, the scientific facts are evident without being obtrusive. *The White Oak*, for example, traces effectively 150 years of ecological forest life.

Wier's skills lie in her ability to interweave imagery with action and dialogue. Regionalism, much of it tropical or subtropical Florida, shows the way of life, the influence of environment upon people, the motivations that make the characters local and yet universal.

—Rebecca J. Lukens

WIGGIN, Kate Douglas (née Smith). American. Born in Philadelphia, Pennsylvania, 28 September 1856. Educated at schools in Portland, Hollis, and Buxton, Maine; Gorham Female Seminary, Hollis; Morison Academy, Baltimore; Abbot Academy, Andover, Massachusetts; Mrs. Severance's Kindergarten Training School, Los Angeles, 1877. Married 1) Samuel Wiggin in 1881 (died 1889); 2) George Christopher Riggs in 1895. Head of a private kindergarten, Santa Barbara, California, 1877; founder, with Felix Adler, Silver Street Free Kindergarten, San Francisco, 1878; founder, with Nora

A. Smith, California Kindergarten Training School, San Francisco, 1880. Litt.D.: Bowdoin College, Brunswick, Maine, 1904. *Died 24 August 1923.*

PUBLICATIONS FOR CHILDREN

Fiction

The Story of Patsy: A Reminiscence. San Francisco, Murdock, 1883; revised edition, Boston, Houghton Mifflin, and London, Gay and Bird, 1889.
The Birds' Christmas Carol. San Francisco, Murdock, 1887; London, Gay and Bird, 1891.
A Summer in a Cañon. Boston, Houghton Mifflin, 1889; London, Gay and Bird, 1893.
Timothy's Quest. Boston, Houghton Mifflin, 1890; London, Gay and Bird, 1892.
The Story Hour, with Nora A. Smith. Boston, Houghton Mifflin, 1890; London, Gay and Bird, 1893.
Polly Oliver's Problem. Boston, Houghton Mifflin, and London, Gay and Bird, 1893.
A Cathedral Courtship, and Penelope's English Experiences, illustrated by Clifford Carleton. Boston, Houghton Mifflin, and London, Gay and Bird, 1893.
Penelope's Progress. Boston, Houghton Mifflin, 1898; as *Penelope's Experiences in Scotland*, London, Gay and Bird, 1898.
Penelope's Irish Experiences. Boston, Houghton Mifflin, and London, Gay and Bird, 1901.
The Diary of a Goose Girl, illustrated by Claude Shepperson. Boston, Houghton Mifflin, and London, Gay and Bird, 1902.
Rebecca of Sunnybrook Farm. Boston, Houghton Mifflin, and London, Gay and Bird, 1903.
Half-a-Dozen Housekeepers, illustrated by Mills Thompson. Philadelphia, Altemus, and London, Kelly, 1903.
A Village Stradivarius. London, Gay and Bird, 1904.
Rose o' the River, illustrated by George Wright. Boston, Houghton Mifflin, and London, Constable, 1905.
New Chronicles of Rebecca. Boston, Houghton Mifflin, and London, Constable, 1907; as *More about Rebecca of Sunnybrook Farm*, London, A. and C. Black, 1930.
Finding a Home. Boston, Houghton Mifflin, 1907.
Mother Carey's Chickens. Boston, Houghton Mifflin, 1911; as *Mother Carey*, London, Hodder and Stoughton, 1911.
A Child's Journey with Dickens. Boston, Houghton Mifflin, and London, Hodder and Stoughton, 1912.
Penelope's Postscripts: Switzerland, Venice, Wales, Devon, Home. Boston, Houghton Mifflin, and London, Hodder and Stoughton, 1915.
The Romance of a Christmas Card, illustrated by Alice Hunt. Boston, Houghton Mifflin, and London, Hodder and Stoughton, 1916.
The Spirit of Christmas. Boston, Houghton Mifflin, 1927.

Plays

Rebecca of Sunnybrook Farm, with Charlotte Thompson, adaptation of the story by Wiggin (produced Springfield, Massachusetts, 1909; New York, 1910; London, 1912). New York and London, French, 1932.
The Birds' Christmas Carol, with Helen Ingersoll, adaptation of the story by Wiggin. Boston, Houghton Mifflin, 1914.
Bluebeard: A Musical Fantasy. New York, Harper, 1914.
Mother Carey's Chickens, with Rachel Crothers, adaptation of the story by Wiggin (produced Poughkeepsie, New York, and New York City, 1917). New York and London, French, 1925.

Other

Kindergarten Chimes: A Collection of Songs and Games. Boston, Ditson, 1885; revised edition, 1887.
The Arabian Nights Retold, with Nora A. Smith, illustrated by Maxfield Parrish. New York, Scribner, and London, Laurie, 1909.

Editor, with Nora A. Smith, *Hymns for Kindergartners.* San Francisco, Froebel Society, 1881.
Editor, with Nora A. Smith, *Golden Numbers: A Book of Verse.* New York, McClure, 1902.
Editor, with Nora A. Smith, *The Posy Ring: A Book of Verse.* New York, McClure, 1903; as *Poems Every Child Should Know*, New York, Doubleday, 1942.
Editor, with Nora A. Smith, *The Library of Fairy Literature* (*The Fairy Ring, Magic Casements, Tales of Laughter, Tales of Wonder, The Talking Beasts*). New York, McClure, 3 vols., 1906–08; last 2 vols., published, New York, Doubleday, 1909–11; *The Fairy Ring* published as *Fairy Stories Every Child Should Know*, New York, Doubleday, 1942.
Editor, with Nora A. Smith, *Pinafore Palace: A Book of Rhymes for the Nursery.* New York, McClure, 1907; as *Pinafore Palace: Baby's Friend and Nursery Heroes and Heroines*, New York, Doubleday, 1923.
Editor, with Nora A. Smith, *An Hour with the Fairies.* New York, Doubleday, 1911.
Editor, with Nora A. Smith, *Christmas Stories.* New York, Grosset and Dunlap, 1916.
Editor, with Nora A. Smith, *Stories and Poems*, by Rudyard Kipling. New York, Grosset and Dunlap, 1916.
Editor, with Nora A. Smith, *The Scottish Chiefs*, by Jane Porter, illustrated by N.C. Wyeth. New York, Scribner, and London, Hodder and Stoughton, 1921.
Editor, with Nora A. Smith, *Pinafore Palace Series* (*Baby's Plays and Journeys, Nursery Nonsense, Palace Bedtime, Palace Playtime*), illustrated by Ruth Hambridge. New York, Doubleday, 4 vols., 1923.
Editor, with Nora A. Smith, *Twilight Stories*, illustrated by Kathryn Draper. Boston, Houghton Mifflin, 1925.

PUBLICATIONS FOR ADULTS

Novels

The Village Watch-Tower. Boston, Houghton Mifflin, and London, Gay and Bird, 1895.
Marm Lisa. Boston, Houghton Mifflin, and London, Gay and Bird, 1896.
The Affair at the Inn, with others. Boston, Houghton Mifflin, and London, Gay and Bird, 1904.
The Old Peabody Pew: A Christmas Romance of a Country Church. Boston, Houghton Mifflin, and London, Constable, 1907.
Susanna and Sue. Boston, Houghton Mifflin, and London, Hodder and Stoughton, 1909.
Robinetta, with others. Boston, Houghton Mifflin, and London, Gay and Hancock, 1911.
The Story of Waitstill Baxter. Boston, Houghton Mifflin, and London, Hodder and Stoughton, 1913.
Ladies in Waiting. Boston, Houghton Mifflin, and London, Hodder and Stoughton, 1919.
The Quilt of Happiness. Boston, Houghton Mifflin, 1923.
Love by Express. Privately printed, 1924.

Short Stories

Creeping Jenny and Other New England Stories. Boston, Houghton Mifflin, 1924.

Plays

The Old Peabody Pew, adaptation of her own novel (produced Buxton, Maine, 1916). New York, French, 1917.
A Thorn in the Flesh: A Monologue, adaptation of a play by Ernest Legouvé. Boston, Badger, 1925; London, French, 1926.
Fragments of a Play, in *Poet Lore 40* (Boston), 1929.

Verse

Nine Love Songs and a Carol. Boston, Houghton Mifflin, and London, Gay and Bird, 1896.

Other

The Relation of the Kindergarten to the Public School. San Francisco, Murdock, 1891.
Children's Rights: A Book of Nursery Logic, with Nora A. Smith. Boston, Houghton Mifflin, and London, Gay and Bird, 1892.
The Republic of Childhood (*Froebel's Gifts, Froebel's Occupations, Kindergarten Principles and Practice*), with Nora A. Smith. Boston, Houghton Mifflin, 3 vols., 1895–96; London, Gay and Bird, 3 vols., 1896.
The Girl and the Kingdom: Learning to Teach. Los Angeles, City Teachers' Club, 1915.
The Writings of Kate Douglas Wiggin. Boston, Houghton Mifflin, 9 vols., 1917.
My Garden of Memory: An Autobiography. Boston, Houghton Mifflin, 1923; London, Hodder and Stoughton, 1924.
A Thanksgiving Retrospect; or, Simplicity of Life in Old New England. Boston, Houghton Mifflin, 1928.

Editor, *The Kindergarten.* New York, Harper, 1893.
Editor, *A Book of Dorcas Dishes: Family Recipes Contributed by the Dorcas Society of Hollis and Buxton.* Privately printed, 1911.

*

Critical Studies: *Kate Douglas Wiggin as Her Sister Knew Her* by Nora A. Smith, Boston, Houghton Mifflin, and London, Gay and Hancock, 1925; *Kate Douglas Wiggin's Country of Childhood* by Helen F. Benner, Orono, University of Maine Press, 1956.

*   *   *

Kate Douglas Wiggin is a quintessential example of the genteel, turn-of-the-century author of books for children. She was well, if spottily, educated, literate, and easily, pleasantly articulate as a writer. Neither a rebel nor a radical, she was nevertheless a confident, forward-looking woman who clearly expected to "do something" with her life and talents—as she did. She joined the kindergarten movement early, first as a student of the Froebel method, then as a highly successful teacher and promoter of kindergartens, and finally, as author of several books on the Froebel approach. Her pleasure in working with children, the amusement and interest she found in their characters (all well recorded in her autobiography, *My Garden of Memory*), provided a natural avenue to her career as a writer of children's books.

One of her first books was *The Birds' Christmas Carol*, a brief, gracefully written tale of a charming invalid girl, who extends charity to the numerous children of a poor Irish family and who dies, happy in her generosity, on Christmas Day. Everything about the story reflects its time: the idealized child, her affluent, genteel family, the sentimental mood, the message of joy in charity. It was immensely popular for many years.

Though she wrote a number of other successful children's stories, the books for which she is best remembered are *Rebecca of Sunnybrook Farm* and its later companion, *New Chronicles of Rebecca*. The flavor of these stories is strongly regional. Like her older contemporary, Sarah Orne Jewett, Wiggin knew Maine and its people well, and described them fondly but perceptively in a number of books. She recognized both the strengths and the narrowness of the rural character; while she shared the widespread American conviction about the moral value of country life, she also knew how heavily its limitations could weigh upon an ambitious mind or an unconventional personality. The books are notably less sentimental than *The Birds' Christmas Carol*, as though the chill winds of Maine had a bracing effect on Wiggin's romantic nature even at a writer's remove.

The Rebecca books are first and foremost a character study of their heroine. Rebecca, who is 10 at the beginning of her story and 17 at the end, clearly represents Wiggin's ideal of childhood and young girlhood, with her warm heart, quick intelligence, and free-flying spirit. It is an attractive, amusing portrait, interesting for what it says about the qualities of heart and mind that Wiggin (and many of her contemporaries) admired in children, interesting, too, for what she saw as reasonable expectations for a girl of such qualities. According to Wiggin's own account, the original Rebecca story grew from a single glimpse of a little girl she never met, but those who read *A Child's Journey with Dickens* may be tempted to see the young Rebecca as a self portrait by Wiggin. In any case, the image is glowingly painted, though not so romanticized as to make it a bad fit within the authentic realism of its setting. The charm of the books has not eroded with the years; they are still engaging and often funny, especially on Rebecca's younger years. Had their reputation not been blighted by the Hollywood film that borrowed the name (but nothing more) from the first book, they might find more readers today.

Wiggin belonged to the great age of children's literature that flourished on either side of the century's turn; she was, in fact, one of its shining lights. Though largely neglected today, her work helped to set a creditable standard of literary competence for children's books. She deserves her place in any critical history of literature for the young.

—Anne Scott MacLeod

WILDER, Laura (Elizabeth) Ingalls. American. Born in Pepin, Wisconsin, 7 February 1867. Educated at schools in Walnut Grove, Minnesota, Burr Oak, Iowa, and De Smet, Dakota Territory. Married Almanzo James Wilder in 1885 (died 1949); one daughter. Schoolteacher, De Smet, 1882–85; farmer in De Smet, 1885–90 and 1892–94, and from 1894 in Mansfield, Missouri; lived in Florida, 1890–92. Columnist, *Missouri Ruralist*, 1911–24; poultry editor, St. Louis *Star*; secretary-treasurer, Mansfield Farm Loan Association, 1919–27. Recipient: American Library Association Laura Ingalls Wilder award, 1954. *Died 10 February 1957.*

PUBLICATIONS FOR CHILDREN

Fiction

Little House in the Big Woods, illustrated by Helen Sewell. New York, Harper, 1932; London, Methuen, 1956.
Farmer Boy, illustrated by Helen Sewell. New York, Harper, 1933; London, Lutterworth Press, 1965.

Little House on the Prairie, illustrated by Helen Sewell. New York, Harper, 1935; London, Methuen, 1957.
On the Banks of Plum Creek, illustrated by Helen Sewell and Mildred Boyle. New York, Harper, 1937; London, Methuen, 1958.
By the Shores of Silver Lake, illustrated by Helen Sewell and Mildred Boyle. New York, Harper, 1939; London, Lutterworth Press, 1961.
The Long Winter, illustrated by Helen Sewell and Mildred Boyle. New York, Harper, 1940; London, Lutterworth Press, 1962.
Little Town on the Prairie, illustrated by Helen Sewell and Mildred Boyle. New York, Harper, 1941; London, Lutterworth Press, 1963.
These Happy Golden Years, illustrated by Helen Sewell and Mildred Boyle. New York, Harper, 1943; London, Lutterworth Press, 1964.
The First Four Years, illustrated by Garth Williams. New York, Harper, 1971; Guildford, Surrey, Lutterworth Press, 1973.

PUBLICATIONS FOR ADULTS

Other

On the Way Home: The Diary of a Trip from South Dakota to Mansfield, Missouri, in 1894, with Rose Wilder Lane. New York, Harper, 1962.
West from Home: Letters from Laura Ingalls Wilder to Almanzo Wilder, San Francisco 1915, edited by Roger Lea MacBride. New York, Harper, 1974; Guildford, Surrey, Lutterworth Press, 1976.
A Little House Sampler, with Rose Wilder Lane, edited by William T. Anderson. Lincoln, University of Nebraska Press, 1988.

*

Bibliography: *Laura Ingalls Wilder: A Bibliography* by Mary J. Mooney-Getoff, Southold, New York, Wise Owl Press, 1980.

Manuscript Collections: Laura Ingalls Wilder Home and Museum, Mansfield, Missouri; Pomona Public Library, California; Detroit Public Library.

Critical Studies: *The Life of Laura Ingalls Wilder* by Donald Zochert, New York, Avon, 1977; *Laura Ingalls Wilder: American Authoress* by Sheila Black, New York, Kipling Press, 1987; *The Plum Creek Story of Laura Ingalls Wilder* by William T. Anderson, Davison, Michigan, Anderson, 1987, and *The Horn Book's Laura Ingalls Wilder* edited by Anderson, Davison, Michigan, Anderson, 1987; *Laura Ingalls Wilder* by Janet Spaeth, Boston, Twayne, 1987.

*   *   *

Laura Ingalls Wilder was in her 60's when, at her daughter's urging, she began to set down in written form her extraordinarily vivid memories of childhood during the 1870's and 1880's in the pioneer middle west. The result was not a simple autobiography but a cycle of shorter books whose third-person device gave them the agreeable perspective of fiction. Published in America in the 1930's and 1940's they soon achieved classic status both as history and as narrative—a superb set of stories, most of them as apt for the very young as for other readers. Though, oddly, they did not appear in England until well after World War II (which blocked so much publication), the Wilder books are as much admired today on this side of the Atlantic as on the other.

The first of the books, *Little House in the Big Woods*, establishes the characters if not the essential intimate solitude of the best of the later tales. The family—parents and three little girls, Mary, Laura, and baby Carrie—live in a log cabin in the Wisconsin woods. The children have never seen a town or store, but they know how cheese and butter are made, how skins are turned into leather, how an old-fashioned rifle is cleaned and reloaded—a long slow business, so the first shot has to kill. Mary is golden-haired, obedient, and good. Laura, even at five years old, is restless, fearless, inquisitive, quick to turn thought into action; she is often in trouble, and discipline is stern. But behind the rules is father (Pa) who, with only an axe and some trees, can make houses, tables, beds; who can please Laura by refraining from shooting a wolf or even an animal needed for food when its behaviour interests him; who will take down his fiddle each night and teach them songs and dances. We are made aware too of the uncomplaining resourceful mother, ready to take up her roots again and again, and create an orderly home wherever they next alight.

For even now too many people are settling near the woods for Pa's liking. And so, in *Little House on the Prairie* (one of the best of all the books) the westward journeying starts. They leave in the chill and early spring, for their covered wagon, drawn by two horses, must cross the Mississippi before the ice can thaw. And indeed, once they are over the ominous cracks are heard. Another river is crossed on a raft; at a flooded fording place father has to swim with the terrified horses, the wagon sagging, half-submerged, behind. A site for a home is found; log by log (carefully watched by Laura) Pa builds house and furniture. A reader could do the same (on model scale, at least) from the description. Cowboys drive their huge herds past the door; Pa helps, and earns a cow and calf. The family are all struck down by "fever and ague" (malaria); the dog, which normally hates strangers, goes out to look for help. And Mr. Edwards, their bachelor neighbour, turns up on Christmas Eve. Like one of those Bret Harte characters at Roaring Camp he has gone to the town, 40 miles away, to find presents for the children, and has swum with them through the creek. (This, with Edwards's account of his meeting with Santa Claus, is a splendid episode.)

But never far from the doorstep, or from the family's thoughts, are the Indians, whose land it really is. Of course, as Pa says, "when white settlers move into a country the Indians have to move on." Or is this too simple? A threatened attack on the house is quelled only by the intervention of an Indian chief, one of the Osage people, a noble and enigmatic warrior known as Soldat du Chene. And yet, the Ingalls family must move on, for the new line drawn by the government sets them in Indian territory.

On the Banks of Plum Creek takes the family to Minnesota, after the usual long slow journey; now they are near enough to a town for Laura and Mary to walk each day to school. They timidly go to a party given by the storekeeper's vulgar and spoilt little daughter. (What clothes should one wear? how behave?) All their new security now lies with the wheat, a magnificent crop which is soon to be harvested. Pa will be able to have new boots at last, Laura reflects. But why is the light so queer? A cloud seems to be blotting out the sun:

It was not like any cloud they had ever seen before. It was a cloud of something like snowflakes, but they were larger than snowflakes, and thin and glittering. Light shone through each flickering particle. There was no wind. The grasses were still and the hot air did not stir but the edge of the cloud came on across the sky faster than wind. The hair stood up on dog Jack's neck.

Something hits Laura's head and falls to the ground; it is a grasshopper, in the van of a vast invasion. The creatures ravage all growing things for scores of miles; then they lay their eggs in the fields for the following season. There can be no more school that year for the girls; no boots for Pa. *By the Shores of Silver Lake* tells,

at the start, of a new baby, Grace. But Mary is now blind, after scarlet fever, and the land has been so weakened by locusts that they move on again. Pa takes a timekeeper's job at a railway camp in Dakota Territory, and when the camp is closed for the winter the family stays alone on the shores of the lake, 60 miles away from human dwellings. Spring will be time enough to trek to the town to file the claim for the perfect piece of land that Pa has found. Or *will* he be in time?

The Long Winter, which follows, is surely the most memorable of all the Wilder books. An October Indian summer changes overnight to ice and blizzard—and the ice and blizzard continue for an incredible seven months. The train with supplies is blocked in a mountain of hard-packed snow, and must stay there until spring. The inhabitants of the little town survive as well as they can on what they have. When fuel gives out in the Ingalls home, Pa and the girls endlessly plait hard twists of hay for burning. Wheat grains are continually ground in the coffee mill to make a kind of bread, almost their only food. In the "dark twilight" of the day, Laura feels that she can never escape from

the hateful ceaseless pounding of the storm. The coffee mill's handle ground round and round, it must not stop. It seemed to make her part of the whirling winds driving the snow round and round over the earth and in the air, whirling and beating at Pa on the way to the stable, whirling and shrieking at the lonely houses, whirling the snow between them and up to the sky and far away, whirling forever over the endless prairie.

Then, when the last of the wheat gives out, two young men, Almanzo Wilder and his equally reckless friend Cap Garland, set out over 20 miles of trackless wastes to find a rumoured settler who *might* have a hoard of grain. Their journey and the return, horses and sacks constantly falling into holes and airpockets, are described in characteristic unstressed detail. It is a miniature epic, none the less.

Little Town on the Prairie covers the years when Laura is 14 and 15, a schoolgirl hoping to qualify for being a teacher at 16 and so help to pay towards Mary's fees at a college for the blind. The dashing Almanzo Wilder, whom all the girls admire, sees her home. Though still under age, she is offered her first schoolteaching post, at a settlement some 12 miles of prairie away. And so, at the start of *These Happy Golden Years* she leaves home for the first time. Some of the pupils at the tiny school, boys as well as girls, are older than she is herself (she is not yet 16). Her lodgings are with a half-deranged slatternly housewife who desperately longs to be back in town; the weather is bitterly cold. Yet on Friday afternoon she hears the sound of sleigh bells; Almanzo has come to take her home (and brings her back on the Sunday); so he continues to do, in the worst of weathers, until the term's contract ends. And the book closes with a fresh beginning, as Laura, at 18, now Mrs. Wilder, steps into her new home on "the tree claim." To avoid an expensive family wedding they have married without fuss in the local minister's parlour, she in her new homemade black cashmere and old blue-lined poke bonnet. Characteristically, she has asked for the word "obey" not to be used. "I cannot make a promise that I will not keep." (Almanzo's early story can be found in *Farmer Boy*, actually the second book written in the series.) Finally, *The First Four Years*, a curiously moving book, tells how the marriage took shape. Those years were hard—sickness, accidents, poverty, farming disasters. Two children were born; one died. But, the four years over, Laura knows that after all, for good or ill, she and Almanzo will live their lives on the land.

What are the qualities that keep these books alive? As tales in the "family" genre they have, of course, immense appeal—yet readers drawn to themes of solitude find them of no less interest. For one thing, they present a small close group of people alone in ranges of uninhabited country, a geographical isolation that gives peculiar intensity to the compact sheltering home, where both necessities and luxuries (including birthday and Christmas gifts)—pastimes too—must so often be made, found, grown, or improvised. (This is the atmosphere that television versions have signally failed to understand or present.) In our overcrowded scene today, the Ingalls' life seems less like fact than fantasy. What must be said is that Laura Ingalls Wilder was a more gifted writer than she knew. Her power of exact recall is matched by her ability, long years after, to fix in words what was seen, heard, felt by the observing child. At the end of the first book Laura voices something of the immediacy that is her most shining trait:

> She was glad that the cosy house, and Pa and Ma, and the firelight and the music, were now. They could not be forgotten she thought, because now is now. It can never be a long time ago.

—Naomi Lewis

―――――

WILL. See **LIPKIND, William**.

―――――

WILLARD, Barbara (Mary). British. Born in Brighton, Sussex, 12 March 1909. Educated at Convent of La Sainte Union, Southampton. Recipient: *Guardian* award, 1974; Whitbread award, 1984. Agent: David Higham Associates Ltd., 5-8 Lower John Street, London W1R 4HA. Address: Forest Edge, Nutley, Uckfield, Sussex, England.

PUBLICATIONS FOR CHILDREN

Fiction

Portrait of Philip (for adults). London, Macmillan, 1950; revised edition (for children), as *He Fought for His Queen*, London, Heinemann, and New York, Warne, 1954.
Snail and the Pennithornes, illustrated by Geoffrey Fletcher. London, Epworth Press, 1957.
Snail and the Pennithornes Next Time, illustrated by Geoffrey Fletcher. London, Epworth Press, 1958.
Son of Charlemagne, illustrated by Emil Weiss. New York, Doubleday, 1959; London, Heinemann, 1960.
The House with Roots, illustrated by Robert Hodgson. London, Constable, 1959; New York, Watts, 1960.
Snail and the Pennithornes and the Princess, illustrated by Geoffrey Fletcher. London, Epworth Press, 1960.
The Dippers and Jo, illustrated by Jean Harper. London, Hamish Hamilton, 1960.
Eight for a Secret, illustrated by Lewis Hart. London, Constable, 1960; New York, Watts, 1961.
The Penny Pony, illustrated by Juliette Palmer. London, Hamish Hamilton, 1961.
If All the Swords in England, illustrated by Robert M. Sax. New York, Doubleday, and London, Burns Oates, 1961.
Stop the Train!, illustrated by Jean Harper. London, Hamish Hamilton, 1961.
The Summer with Spike, illustrated by Anne Linton. London, Constable, 1961; New York, Watts, 1962.
Duck on a Pond, illustrated by Mary Rose Hardy. London, Constable, and New York, Watts, 1962.
Hetty, illustrated by Pamela Mara. London, Constable, 1962; New

York, Harcourt Brace, 1963.
Augustine Came to Kent, illustrated by Hans Guggenheim. New York, Doubleday, 1963; Kingswood, Surrey, World's Work, 1964.
The Battle of Wednesday Week, illustrated by Douglas Hall. London, Constable, 1963; as *Storm from the West*, New York, Harcourt Brace, 1964.
The Dippers and the High-Flying Kite, illustrated by Maureen Eckersley. London, Hamish Hamilton, 1963.
The Suddenly Gang, illustrated by Lynette Hemmant. London, Hamish Hamilton, 1963.
The Pram Race, illustrated by Constance Marshall. London, Hamish Hamilton, 1964.
A Dog and a Half, illustrated by Jane Paton. London, Hamish Hamilton, 1964; New York, Nelson, 1971.
Three and One to Carry, illustrated by Douglas Hall. London, Constable, 1964; New York, Harcourt Brace, 1965.
The Wild Idea, illustrated by Douglas Bissett. London, Hamish Hamilton, 1965.
Charity at Home, illustrated by Douglas Hall. London, Constable, 1965; New York, Harcourt Brace, 1966.
Surprise Island, illustrated by Jane Paton. London, Hamish Hamilton, 1966; New York, Meredith Press, 1969.
The Richleighs of Tantamount, illustrated by C. Walter Hodges. London, Constable, 1966; New York, Harcourt Brace, 1967.
The Grove of Green Holly, illustrated by Gareth Floyd. London, Constable, 1967; as *Flight to the Forest*, New York, Doubleday, 1967.
The Pet Club, illustrated by Lynette Hemmant. London, Hamish Hamilton, 1967.
To London! To London!, illustrated by Antony Maitland. London, Longman, and New York, Weybright and Talley, 1968.
Hurrah for Rosie!, illustrated by Gareth Floyd. London, Hutchinson, 1968.
Royal Rosie, illustrated by Gareth Floyd. London, Hutchinson, 1968.
The Family Tower. London, Constable, and New York, Harcourt Brace, 1968.
The Toppling Towers. London, Longman, and New York, Harcourt Brace, 1969.
The Pocket Mouse, illustrated by Mary Russon. London, Hamish Hamilton, and New York, Knopf, 1969.
Mantlemass:
  The Lark and the Laurel, illustrated by Gareth Floyd. London, Longman, and New York, Harcourt Brace, 1970.
  The Sprig of Broom, illustrated by Paul Shardlow. London, Longman, 1971; New York, Dutton, 1972.
  A Cold Wind Blowing. London, Longman, 1972; New York, Dutton, 1973.
  The Iron Lily. London, Longman, 1973; New York, Dutton, 1974.
  Harrow and Harvest. London, Kestrel, 1974; New York, Dutton, 1975.
  The Miller's Boy, illustrated by Gareth Floyd. London, Kestrel, and New York, Dutton, 1976.
  The Eldest Son. London, Kestrel, 1977.
  A Flight of Swans. London, Kestrel, 1980.
Priscilla Pentecost, illustrated by Doreen Roberts. London, Hamish Hamilton, 1970.
The Reindeer Slippers, illustrated by Tessa Jordan. London, Hamish Hamilton, 1970.
The Dragon Box, illustrated by Tessa Jordan. London, Hamish Hamilton, 1972.
Jubilee!, illustrated by Hilary Abrahams. London, Heinemann, 1973.
Bridesmaid, illustrated by Jane Paton. London, Hamish Hamilton, 1976.

The Country Maid. London, Hamish Hamilton, 1978; New York, Greenwillow, 1980.
The Gardener's Grandchildren, illustrated by Gordon King. London, Kestrel, 1978; New York, McGraw Hill, 1979.
Spell Me a Witch, illustrated by Phillida Gili. London, Hamish Hamilton, 1979; New York, Harcourt Brace, 1981.
The Keys of Mantlemass (stories). London, Kestrel, 1981.
Summer Season. London, MacRae, 1981.
Famous Rowena Lamont. London, Hardy, 1983.
The Queen of the Pharisees' Children. London, MacRae, 1983.
Smiley Tiger, illustrated by Laszlo Acs. London, MacRae, 1984.
Ned Only. London, MacRae, 1985.

Other

Junior Motorist: The Driver's Apprentice, with Frances Howell, illustrated by Ionicus. London, Collins, 1969.
Chichester and Lewes, illustrated by Graham Humphreys. London, Longman, 1970.

Editor, *Hullabaloo! About Naughty Boys and Girls*, illustrated by Fritz Wegner. London, Hamish Hamilton, and New York, Meredith Press, 1969.
Editor, *Happy Families* (anthology), illustrated by Krystyna Turska. London, Hamish Hamilton, and New York, Macmillan, 1974.
Editor, *Field and Forest*, illustrated by Faith Jaques. London, Kestrel, 1975.

Translator, *The Giants' Feast*, by Max Bolliger, illustrated by Monika Laimgruber. London, Hamish Hamilton, 1975.
Translator, *Convent Cat*, by Bunshu Iguchi, illustrated by Iguchi. London, Hamish Hamilton, 1975; New York, McGraw Hill, 1976.

Publications for Adults

Novels

Love in Ambush, with Elizabeth Helen Devas. London, Howe, 1930.
Ballerina. London, Howe, 1932.
Candle Flame. London, Howe, 1932.
Name of Gentleman. London, Howe, 1933.
Joy Befall Thee. London, Howe, 1934.
As Far as in Me Lies. London, Nelson, 1936.
Set Piece. London, Nelson, 1938.
Personal Effects. London, Macmillan, 1939.
The Dogs Do Bark. London, Macmillan, 1948.
Proposed and Seconded. London, Macmillan, 1951.
Celia Scarfe. New York, Appleton Century Crofts, 1951.
Echo Answers. London, Macmillan, 1952.
Winter in Disguise. London, Joseph, 1958.

Plays

Brother Ass and Brother Lion, adaptation of the story "St. Jerome, The Lion, and the Donkey" by Helen Waddell. London, J. Garnet Miller, 1951.
One of the Twelve. London, French, 1954.
Fit for a King. London, J. Garnet Miller, 1955.

Radio Play: *Duck on a Pond*, from her own book, 1962.

Television Play: *Merry Go Round*, 1965.

Other

Sussex. London, Batsford, 1965; New York, Hastings House, 1966.

Editor, *"I…": An Anthology of Diarists.* London, Chatto and Windus, 1972.

*

Barbara Willard comments:

(1978) As I have been writing for such years and years it may seem strange when I say that only in the past 10 years or so have I found myself writing what I must always have wanted to write. It took me a long while to find my way into children's fiction, and then more time to make my way to *Mantlemass*, which is the historical sequence, not yet concluded, based on the Wealden area of Sussex where I live. These stories begin at the conclusion of the Wars of the Roses in 1485 and cover 250 years or so. They tell the tale of two intermingled families living within the forest pale. They are horsebreeders, foresters, iron workers—modest ordinary people, though in fact there does run in their blood a nobler strain. I have tried to imagine how they would have lived, and how they would have been affected by the events in the outside world—the change of dynasty from Plantagenet to Tudor, the Reformation, the Civil War.

Because these people have come to seem so real to me, living as I do on their ground, I think perhaps they have some reality for readers—who, in fact, are not all young readers.

*   *   *

Barbara Willard's own favourites among her many books are those in her Mantlemass series, eight historical novels set on her home ground in Ashdown Forest. They follow the fortunes of two families, the Mallorys and the Medleys from the time Cecily Jolland comes to Mantlemass in the 15th century until the house is burned down in the 17th century at the conclusion of *Harrow and Harvest*. The books explore the human consequence of social change by putting a magnifying glass on a small enclosed area of England.

The Lark and the Laurel takes place in the days towards the end of the Wars of the Roses and looks at child marriage for political ends; *The Miller's Boy* uses some of the same characters and examines the bonds of friendship. *The Sprig of Broom* brings a bastard son of Richard III to live incognito in the forest after Bosworth. *A Cold Wind Blowing* (to my mind the finest in the series) is a sad tale about the aftermath of the Dissolution of the Monasteries. *The Eldest Son* tells of the disaster that hits the horse-breeding branch of the family and the quarrel that splits them, while *The Iron Lily* is about the iron-working branch. *A Flight of Swans* shows how an event like the defeat of the Spanish Armada was felt in an English country backwater, and *Harrow and Harvest* brings the family up to the 17th century, the saga ending as it began in civil war. In this book the house Mantlemass which has been central to all the books is destroyed and the evidence that proves their descent from Richard III is buried. But the ring with the lark and laurel crest survives, and in *The Keys of Mantlemass*, a book of short stories which fill the gaps in the saga and provides bridging passages between the books, the final story brings a descendant of the branch of the family that emigrated to America back to the forest to explore her past. *The Queen of the Pharisees' Children*, while not about the family *per se*, uses the trappings of Mantlemass as its setting. The burnt-out house provides temporary shelter to a tinker family, who are eventually broken up when the father is sent to prison and the children separated from their mother by vagrancy laws. What a reader takes away from reading this very satisfying series is a sense of the continuity of history, of a real family in all its complex relationships and an insight into the way that great events in the history books affect ordinary people.

Willard, besides being a very honest writer, is a romantic (in the best sense of the word) and also a celebrant of nostalgia. *The Country Maid*, a book set in the 1920's which contrasts the lives of the daughter of a suburban family and Cassie, the young servant girl, shows Willard as much in love with the recent past as with the 15th and 16th centuries. Also, like many of her books, it embodies the idea that country life is better and more rewarding than that in towns. She writes lovingly but without sentiment of animals in books like *A Dog and a Half* and *Duck on a Pond* and she has a light hand with fantasy in books like *Spell Me a Witch*.

Her books are full of a sense of place—she writes of the forest lovingly and her descriptions are perceptive and evocative. She is attracted to the similarities between the past and the present unlike some writers who marvel at their strange differences. But the reason why her books are so good is that she has a very sure hand with character drawing. One feels that every person in her books has a full, rounded existence inside and outside the novel. She writes honestly, not glossing over defects of personality or the barbarities of her chosen periods or the betrayals of which men and women are capable in time of civil war.

Feminists will take pleasure in her strong women characters—tough ladies like Dame Elizabeth in *The Lark and the Laurel* and Lilias in *The Iron Lily* who are more than equal to the men they live among and trade with. Ursula in *A Flight of Swans* and Cecilia in *Harrow and Harvest* are less forceful but still manage to have things their own way. Willard writes about romantic love without being sentimental and deals as well with sorrow as with joy. Her touch with dialogue (often a pitfall for historical novelists) is very sure; she uses forest dialect which gives a local and a period flavour.

Her historical books for younger children (a deceptively difficult field) are delightful too—books like *Priscilla Pentecost* about an 18th-century charity child, *Jubilee!* about three orphans who try to run away during Victoria's jubilee celebrations at Brighton, and *The Dragon Box* a charming story with a Victorian background for 6–8 year olds.

It is to be hoped that Willard will not stop writing about her beloved Forest in the Middle Ages, for although she has written stories about the children of today her work is certainly most appealing when she writes about the past and there are not many children's writers who have her knack of bringing it to life.

—Pamela Cleaver

WILLARD, Nancy (Margaret). American. Born in Ann Arbor, Michigan, 26 June 1936. Educated at the University of Michigan, Ann Arbor (five Hopwood awards), B.A. 1958, Ph.D. in English 1963; Stanford University, California (Woodrow Wilson fellow), M.A. 1960. Married Eric Lindbloom in 1964; one son. Since 1965 Lecturer in English, Vassar College, Poughkeepsie, New York; since 1975 Instructor, Bread Loaf Writers Conference. Recipient: Devins Memorial award, for poetry, 1967; O. Henry award, for short story, 1970; National Endowment for the Arts grant, 1976, 1987; Creative Artists Public Service award, 1977; American Library Association Newbery Medal, 1982. Agent: Jean V. Naggar, 336 East 73rd Street, New York, New York 10021. Address: 133 College Avenue, Poughkeepsie, New York 12603, U.S.A.

PUBLICATIONS FOR CHILDREN

Fiction

Sailing to Cythera and Other Anatole Stories, illustrated by David McPhail. New York, Harcourt Brace, 1974.
The Snow Rabbit, illustrated by Laura Lydecker. New York, Putnam, 1975.
Shoes Without Leather, illustrated by Laura Lydecker. New York, Putnam, 1976.
The Well-Mannered Balloon, illustrated by Haig and Regina Shekerjian. New York, Harcourt Brace, 1976.
Strangers' Bread, illustrated by David McPhail. New York, Harcourt Brace, 1977.
Simple Pictures Are Best, illustrated by Tomie de Paola. New York, Harcourt Brace, 1977; London, Collins, 1978.
The Highest Hit, illustrated by Emily McCully. New York, Harcourt Brace, 1978.
Papa's Panda, illustrated by Lillian Hoban. New York, Harcourt Brace, 1979.
The Island of the Grass King: The Further Adventures of Anatole, illustrated by David McPhail. New York, Harcourt Brace, 1979.
The Marzipan Moon, illustrated by Marcia Sewall. New York, Harcourt Brace, 1981.
Uncle Terrible: More Adventures of Anatole, illustrated by David McPhail. New York, Harcourt Brace, 1982.
The Nightgown of the Sullen Moon, illustrated by David McPhail. New York, Harcourt Brace, 1983.
The Mountains of Quilt, illustrated by Tomie de Paola. San Diego, Harcourt Brace, 1987.
Firebrat, illustrated by David Wiesner. New York, Knopf, 1988.

Play

East of the Sun and West of the Moon, illustrated by Bruce Moser. San Diego, Harcourt Brace, 1989.

Verse

The Merry History of a Christmas Pie, With a Delicious Description of a Christmas Soup, illustrated by Haig and Regina Shekerjian. New York, Putnam, 1974.
All on a May Morning, illustrated by Haig and Regina Shekerjian. New York, Putnam, 1975.
A Visit to William Blake's Inn: Poems for Innocent and Experienced Travelers, illustrated by Alice and Martin Provensen. New York, Harcourt Brace, 1981; London, Methuen, 1982.
Night Story, illustrated by Ilse Plume. San Diego, Harcourt Brace, and London, Methuen, 1986.
The Voyage of the Ludgate Hill: Travels with Robert Louis Stevenson, illustrated by Alice and Martin Provensen. San Diego, Harcourt Brace, 1987.

PUBLICATIONS FOR ADULTS

Novel

Things Invisible to See. New York, Knopf, 1984.

Short Stories

The Lively Anatomy of God. New York, Eakins Press, 1968.
Childhood of the Magician. New York, Liveright, 1973.
Angel in the Parlor: Five Stories and Eight Essays. New York, Harcourt Brace, 1983.

Verse

In His Country. Ann Arbor, Michigan, Generation, 1966.
Skin of Grace. Columbia, University of Missouri Press, 1967.

A New Herball.   Baltimore, Ferdinand Roten Galleries, 1968.
19 Masks for the Naked Poet.   Santa Cruz, California, Kayak, 1971.
Carpenter of the Sun.   New York, Liveright, 1974.
Household Tales of Moon and Water.   New York, Harcourt Brace, 1982.
Water Walker.   New York, Knopf, 1989.

Other

Testimony of the Invisible Man: William Carlos Williams, Francis Ponge, Rainer Maria Rilke, Pablo Neruda.   Columbia, University of Missouri Press, 1970.

*

Manuscript Collection: Kerlan Collection, University of Minnesota, Minneapolis.

Illustrator: *The Letter of John to James,* 1981, and *Another Letter of John to James about Church and the Eucharist,* 1982, both by John Kater.

*   *   *

A hallmark of Nancy Willard's art is its "joyful contact with things." This is her phrase to describe the essential quality of the poet in *Testimony of the Invisible Man,* her critical study of William Carlos William, Rainer Maria Rilke, and Pablo Neruda. An ability to transform the commonplace into the luminous merges in her works with carefully crafted language, startlingly original imagery and metaphor, and an intellect steeped in literary tradition. Add to these gifts an uncanny sense of what she has called the "magic view of life," innate to all children and retained by some extraordinary adults. Willard excels in writing for young and old alike, and her versatile wit shines through many genres: the novel, poetry, bedtime stories for the very young, fantasy, and nonsense.

In *The Merry History of a Christmas Pie* the personified ingredients such as Sir Cinnamon deliver droll dramatic monologues. *A Visit to William Blake's Inn: Poems for Innocent and Experienced Travelers* won her international acclaim and the first Newbery Medal for a collection of poetry. The mixture of nonsense poems and light moral messages makes it akin in spirit and tone to Carroll and Lear, though it ostensibly honors Blake, the mystical English poet-painter, in the persona of the keeper of an enchanted wayside inn. *The Voyage of the Ludgate Hill: Travels with Robert Louis Stevenson,* with luminous artwork by Alice and Martin Provensen, is a ballad woven of fact and fancy, inspired by Stevenson's whimsical letters describing how he and his wife survived a voyage through beastly weather to the United States on a "stable-ship" peopled with incorrigible exotic animals. Despite the roughness of the crossing, their hearts are full of song.

Willard has a particular affinity for the moonlit nightscape. *Night Story,* a bedtime book illustrated in charming naive style by Ilse Plume, tells of a boy who travels by night train to a "country where nothing lasts" and visits a "night market," where "nothing is sold, where all is given and nothing is given for keeps." His trip involves him in a chase of shape-shifting fantasy characters, until a morning train brings him back home, "where nothing changes" and his adventure becomes a story—a preserved dream. *The Nightgown of the Sullen Moon* features the Moon as main character. She covets a nightgown identical to one she spies flapping on a clothesline—blue flannel adorned with stars. The success of her quest to find an identical gown results in darkness on earth, for when she retires to enjoy a snooze in it, the moon-deprived people on earth cannot remember their songs. All ends happily, though with an impish twist.

Several of the picture story books blend fantasy or nonsense with

a moral. In *Papa's Panda* a boy and his father fantasize about having a panda as a pet. The humor takes a didactic turn when the boy must admit a real panda will not do and accept a toy one instead as his birthday gift. *Simple Pictures Are Best* succeeds as a wildly funny cumulative story poking fun at the vain desire of a shoemaker and his wife to cram all of their treasured objects, however bizarre, into their wedding anniversary photograph. They ignore the disdainful photographer's refrain, "simple pictures are best," and with "help" from the photographer's small boy assistant, the resulting picture is ruined. Tomie de Paola's jolly, warm-colored pictures deliciously complement this rollicking tale. *The Marzipan Moon* similarly presents a moral in pleasant guise: when a poor parish priest receives a broken crock for his birthday, he rashly wishes for a marzipan moon every morning. To his astonishment, the wish is granted. A greedy, Chaucerian bishop tries to exploit the miracle, with predictable results. Readers are instructed to wish more wisely.

Willard's Anatole books are her most controversial and yet most uniquely her own. In the three fantasies of *Sailing to Cythera,* Anatole travels with the cat Plumpet on a magic train to attend the christening of Plumpet's Aunt Pitterpat as she begins her ninth and final cat life; goes on a quest to the sun in a brave attempt to help an aged soldier who has lost his memory and 30 years of his life; and has adventures in Cythera, a fantasy world reached by walking through a pastoral wallpaper scene. The second Anatole book, *Strangers' Bread,* is a parable about sharing: Anatole is delivering a loaf of pumpernickel to his elderly friend Mrs. Chiba, but cannot refuse to give slices to the hungry creatures along the way. When he arrives empty-handed he is in for a surprise. In *The Island of the Grass King* Anatole starts to search for fennel to heal his grandmother's asthma and becomes a hero, freeing the Grass King from the evil spell cast by Mother Weather-sky, thus restoring the earthly paradise. Critics have praised the book's linguistic and imagistic beauty, but Natalie Babbitt, in her comments in the *New York Times Book Review,* found it lacking the "simplicity" of the "true" fairytale. Modelled on Shakespeare's *The Tempest,* it is replete with folkloric elements (e.g., the Mender, who repairs wounded animals). *Uncle Terrible: More Adventures of Anatole* follows the young hero to the realm of the evil wizard Arcomboldo the Marvelous, whose powers are poised against those of Mother, the benevolent caretaker of nature. Anatole becomes the restorer of the balance between light and dark. The entire Anatole series is graced by David McPhail's intricate, sensitive black-and-white drawings.

The Highest Hit, Willard's novel for middle grade readers, chronicles the ludicrous antics of its irrepressible heroine Kate Carpenter Schmidt. Though she does not fulfill her fondest wish to win a place in the *Guinness Book of Records,* she manages to teach her mom to play baseball, to get her neck caught in a magician's guillotine, and to score "the highest hit. Weak over strong, joy over grief…" Baseball is an important metaphor in Willard's works, and the central one in her novel for adults, *Things Invisible to See,* a parable of life as a cosmic baseball game, with forces of life playing against the forces of Death, with the Lord of the Universe the chief ballplayer. The cosmic plot interweaves with a teenage love story of two very different fraternal twins, Ben and Willie, and the girls they respectively love or admire, Clare and Marsha. Nostalgia for small-town life in World War II pervades the book.

Willard's recent creations continue to portray the magic in the mundane. A small boy narrates *The Mountains of Quilt,* lovingly illustrated in quilt-like patterns by Tomie de Paola. The boy tells the zany tale of four magicians and the handkerchief-sized magic carpet belonging to one of them, which ends up as the center piece of the grandmother's quilt. The machinations of a meddling magpie, the light of a baseball moon, and a pair of singing sneakers help the plot along. Like the Anatole stories it will be best appreciated by readers with elastic imaginations.

Firebrat tells of an underground heroic quest by young Molly and her friend Sean. Molly has been commissioned to spend the summer in New York City helping her eccentric grandmother, the owner of a weird antique shop, The Silver Shuttle. With a hint from a peculiar map of the city subway system, Molly and Sean adventure through an abandoned subway platform into the subterranean Crystal Empire, where fish swim in the air, a book of household hints becomes a book of magic spells, and the two youngsters are regarded as Powerful Magicians from the Upper World. Similar occult correspondences between the Upper and Lower realms abound. They join with a giant tortoise to help save the Empire from the hideous Firebrat—in the Upper World a noxious nocturnal insect that preys on paper and clothing, but in the netherworld a tyrant who has stolen the mystical time sticks which measure out the lives of the Empire-dwellers. A modern fairytale of unfettered imagination, it ends with a reconciliation of the realms of Dark and Light.

Peter Neumeyer aptly observes in his *School Library Journal* review of *A Visit to William Blake's Inn* that Willard is "that rarest joy among children's verse writers, a poet never cloying, never cute." Now at the zenith of her creative powers, she has secured her stature among 20th-century writers for the young by a substantial body of works that harmonize with her own definition of art in *Testimony of the Invisible Man*: not merely "a selection from the world but a transformation of it into something that praises existence."

Though a few carping voices have criticized the labyrinthine design of some of Willard's plots and charge that the rich allusions will be lost on the child reader, the most insightful credit her with a special gift for interweaving the ordinary and the otherworldly, transforming "the healing chaos of dreams" into finished works of art, making "the common language do the uncommon things you demand of it." The child whose imagination is enchanted by her ensorcelling books at an early age will return as an adult for aesthetic refreshment and a renewed sense of the sheer joy of being.

—Millicent Lenz

WILLIAMS, Jay. Also wrote as Michael Delving. American. Born in Buffalo, New York, 31 May 1914. Educated at the University of Pennsylvania, Philadelphia, 1931–32; Columbia University, New York, 1933–34. Served in the United States Army, 1941–45: Purple Heart. Married Barbara Girdansky in 1941; one son and one daughter. Vaudeville and night club comic, and social director in adult summer camps, New York State, 1935–37; press agent, Hollywood, 1936–41; full-time writer from 1945. Recipient: Guggenheim fellowship, 1949. *Died 12 July 1978.*

PUBLICATIONS FOR CHILDREN

Fiction

The Stolen Oracle, illustrated by Frederick Chapman. New York, Oxford University Press, 1943.
The Counterfeit African. New York and London, Oxford University Press, 1944.
The Sword and the Scythe, illustrated by Edouard Sandoz. New York, Oxford University Press, 1946.
Eagle Jake and Indian Pete, illustrated by John Brimer. New York, Rinehart, 1947.
The Roman Moon Mystery. New York, Oxford University Press, 1948.
The Magic Gate, illustrated by John Brimer. New York, Oxford University Press, 1949.

Danny Dunn and Antigravity Paint [*on a Desert Island, and the Homework Machine, and the Weather Machine, on the Ocean Floor, and the Fossil Cave, and the Heat Ray, Time Traveler, and the Automatic House, and the Voice from Space, and the Smallifying Machine, and the Swamp Monster, Invisible Boy, Scientific Detective, and the Universal Glue*], with Raymond Abrashkin, illustrated by Ezra Jack Keats, Brinton Turkle, Owen Kampen, Leo Summers, and Paul Sagsoorian. New York, McGraw Hill, 15 vols., 1956–77; Leicester, Brockhampton Press, 2 vols., 1959–60; London, Macdonald, 10 vols., 1965–74; London, Macdonald and Jane's, 3 vols., 1975–78.
Puppy Pie, illustrated by Wayne Blickenstaff. New York, Crowell Collier, 1962.
The Question Box, illustrated by Margot Zemach. New York, Norton, 1965.
Philbert the Fearful, illustrated by Ib Ohlsson. New York, Norton, 1966.
What Can You Do with a Word?, illustrated by Leslie Goldstein. New York, Collier, 1966.
The Cookie Tree, illustrated by Blake Hampton. New York, Parents' Magazine Press, 1967.
To Catch a Bird, illustrated by Jo Polseno. New York, Crowell Collier, 1968.
The King with Six Friends, illustrated by Imero Gobbato. New York, Parents' Magazine Press, 1968.
The Good-for-Nothing Prince, illustrated by Imero Gobbato. New York, Norton, 1969.
The Practical Princess, illustrated by Friso Henstra. New York, Parents' Magazine Press, 1969; augmented edition, as *The Practical Princess and Other Liberating Fairy Tales*, Parents' Magazine Press, 1978; London, Chatto and Windus, 1979.
School for Sillies, illustrated by Friso Henstra. New York, Parents' Magazine Press, 1969.
A Box Full of Infinity, illustrated by Robin Lawrie. New York, Grosset and Dunlap, 1970.
Stupid Marco, illustrated by Friso Henstra. New York, Parents' Magazine Press, 1970.
The Silver Whistle, illustrated by Friso Henstra. New York, Parents' Magazine Press, 1971.
A Present from a Bird, illustrated by Jacqueline Chwast. New York, Parents' Magazine Press, 1971.
The Hawkstone. New York, Walck, 1971; London, Gollancz, 1972.
The Youngest Captain, illustrated by Friso Henstra. New York, Parents' Magazine Press, 1972.
Magical Storybook, illustrated by Edward Sorel. New York, American Heritage Press, 1972.
The Hero from Otherwhere. New York, Walck, 1972.
Petronella, illustrated by Friso Henstra. New York, Parents' Magazine Press, 1973.
Forgetful Fred, illustrated by Friso Henstra. New York, Parents' Magazine Press, 1974.
The People of the Ax. New York, Walck, 1974; London, Macdonald and Jane's, 1975.
A Bag Full of Nothing, illustrated by Tom O'Sullivan. New York, Parents' Magazine Press, 1974.
Everyone Knows What a Dragon Looks Like, illustrated by Mercer Mayer. New York, Four Winds Press, 1976; London, Dent, 1979.
The Burglar Next Door, illustrated by DeAnne Hollinger. New York, Four Winds Press, 1976; as *Daylight Robbery*, London, Kestrel, 1977.
The Reward Worth Having, illustrated by Mercer Mayer. New York, Four Winds Press, 1977.
The Time of the Kraken. New York, Four Winds Press, 1977; London, Gollancz, 1978.
Pettifur, illustrated by Hilary Knight. New York, Four Winds Press,

1977.
The Magic Grandfather, illustrated by Gail Owens. New York, Four Winds Press, and London, Macdonald and Jane's 1979.
Unearthly Beasts and Other Strange People. London, Macmillan, 1979.
The City Witch and the Country Witch, illustrated by Ed Renfro. New York, Macmillan, 1979.
One Big Wish, illustrated by John O'Brien. New York, Macmillan, 1980.
The Water of Life, illustrated by Lucinda McQueen. New York, Four Winds Press, 1980.

Verse

I Wish I Had Another Name, illustrated by Winifred Lubell. New York, Atheneum, 1962.

Other

Caesar Augustus. Evanston, Illinois, Row Peterson, 1951.
The Battle for the Atlantic. New York, Random House, 1959.
The Tournament of the Lions, illustrated by Ezra Jack Keats. New York, Walck, 1960.
Medusa's Head, illustrated by Steele Savage. New York, Random House, 1960; London, Muller, 1963.
Knights of the Crusades. New York, American Heritage Press, 1962; London, Cassell, 1963.
Joan of Arc. New York, American Heritage Press, 1963; London, Cassell, 1964.
Leonardo da Vinci. New York, American Heritage Press, 1965; London, Cassell, 1966.
The Spanish Armada. New York, American Heritage Press, and London, Cassell, 1966.
Life in the Middle Ages. New York, Random House, 1966; London, Nelson, 1967.
The Sword of King Arthur, illustrated by Louis Glanzman. New York, Crowell, 1968.
The Horn of Roland, illustrated by Sean Morrison. New York, Crowell, 1968.
Seven at One Blow, illustrated by Friso Henstra. New York, Parents' Magazine Press, 1972.
Moon Journey (based on works by Jules Verne), illustrated by Daniel le Noury. London, Macdonald and Jane's 1976; as *Voyage to the Moon*, New York, Crown, 1977.
The Wicked Tricks of Tyl Uilenspiegel, illustrated by Friso Henstra. New York, Four Winds Press, 1978.
The Surprising Things Maui Did (Polynesian folktale), illustrated by Charles Mikolaycak. New York, Four Winds Press, 1979.

PUBLICATIONS FOR ADULTS

Novels

The Good Yeoman. New York, Appleton Century Crofts, 1948; London, Macdonald, 1956.
The Rogue from Padua. Boston, Little Brown, 1952; London, Macdonald, 1954.
The Siege. Boston, Little Brown, and London, Macdonald, 1955.
The Witches. New York, Random House, 1957; London, Macdonald, 1958.
Solomon and Sheba. New York, Random House, and London, Macdonald, 1959.
The Forger. New York, Atheneum, and London, Macdonald, 1961.
Tomorrow's Fire. New York, Atheneum, 1964; London, Macdonald, 1965.
Uniad. New York, Scribner, 1968; London, Murray, 1969.

Novels as Michael Delving

Smiling, The Boy Fell Dead. New York, Scribner, and London, Macdonald, 1967.
The Devil Finds Work. New York, Scribner, 1969; London, Collins, 1970.
Die Like a Man. New York, Scribner, and London, Collins, 1970.
A Shadow of Himself. New York, Scribner, and London, Collins, 1972.
Bored to Death. New York, Scribner, 1975; as *A Wave of Fatalities*, London, Collins, 1975.
The China Expert. London, Collins, 1976; New York, Scribner, 1977.
No Sign of Life. London, Collins, 1978; New York, Doubleday, 1979.

Play

A Life in the Day of a Secretary, with Alfred Hayes, music by George Kleinsinger (produced New York, 1939).

Other

Fall of the Sparrow. New York, Oxford University Press, 1951.
A Change of Climate (on Majorca). New York, Random House, and London, Macdonald, 1956.
The World of Titian. New York, Time-Life, 1968.
Stage Left. New York, Scribner, 1974.

*

Manuscript Collection: Mugar Memorial Library, Boston University.

Theatrical Activities:
Actor: **Plays**—in *R.U.R* by Karel Capek, New York, 1942; in *Nathan the Wise* by Gotthold Ephraim Lessing, New York, 1944.

Jay Williams commented:

(1978) At the age of 12 I won a prize (it was a book) for the best original ghost story told round the campfire in a boys' camp. The experience went to my head and I have been telling stories to children ever since. I don't think of myself as anything but a spinner of tales; I have no pretensions to being educator, moralist, or propagandist, although inevitably, unless a writer has perfect insulation between himself and his writing, into every work one's beliefs, enjoyments, and sense of morality will find their way like mice into a country kitchen. Even my non-fiction has grown out of subjects which attracted me because they were good stories. And what is a good story? I have no universal definition, but for me it is one which binds teller as much as reader in a web of surprise, tension, and wonderment. To all intents and purposes, I'm still back at that campfire.

*   *   *

Jay Williams was a prolific writer, for both adult and junior readers: it is rather a pity that he will, in all likelihood, be best remembered for some of his slightest work rather than for his more ambitious efforts in fiction for children, or his serious, scholarly reference materials for young readers. For all that, it would be snobbish to disregard the precious "talent to amuse" that is despised only by those to whom the gift has been denied.
Williams's 15 Danny Dunn books, written in collaboration with Raymond Abrashkin, solidly established him as a popular writer for children. The engaging young hero for whom the series is named,

his sad-faced crony Joe, and Irene, the science whiz (patently an afterthought to pacify those female readers who felt slighted by the solidly masculine tone of the early volumes), become embroiled in one totally unbelievable, fantastic episode after another. The series hangs together on the premise that Danny and his widowed mother live with the eccentric, all-round genius, Professor Bullfinch, inventor and scientist. The Professor treats his housekeeper's child more or less as an adopted son: certainly he puts up with more interference and disturbance than most parents would tolerate. Through the Professor, Danny has picked up a lot of scientific know-how, surprising in a lad of his years; and this, coupled with an inventive nature and insatiable curiousity, serves to propel Danny and his eager friends into wild adventures involving time travel, anti-gravity paint, heat rays, dinosaurs, automatic houses, and all sorts of other unlikely situations. Each story is based on the slightest of scientific foundation, and it would be a great mistake to put much credence in ALL that the series offers as fact. The Danny Dunn books are light, undemanding, and cheerful reading experiences for youngsters just discovering their independent reading abilities, and they appeal particularly to those who like launching into a series, preferring the security of sharing adventures with familiar characters in predictable settings.

As well as the Danny Dunn books, Williams produced various "singles" such as *The Magic Grandfather* and *The Burglar Next Door*, which provide proof, if it were needed, that the frothy series did not offer full scope to his talent. In the non-fiction area, Williams's full-scale works like *Knights of the Crusades, Joan of Arc, The Spanish Armada*, and others, are as readable as they are informative. From the lightest of amusing fairy tales, pleasant trifles like *The Cookie Tree*, to factual works demonstrating meticulous research and an unusual ability to provide understandable explanations of complex historic events to young readers, Williams had no mere fitful brilliance, but rather the valuable qualities of talent and workmanship that combine to make a dependable author.

—Joan McGrath

WILLIAMS, Margery. See **BIANCO, Margery Williams.**

WILLIAMS, Ursula Moray. See **MORAY WILLIAMS, Ursula.**

WILLIAMS, Vera B. American. Born in New York City. Educated at Black Mountain College, North Carolina, 1945–49, B.F.A. in graphic art 1949. Married Paul Williams (divorced); two daughters and one son. Founder and teacher, Gate Hill Cooperative, North Carolina, 1953–70; also worked as a cook and manager of a bakery. Lives in New York City. Recipient: Boston *Globe-Horn Book* award, for illustration, 1983, 1988; Children's Rights Workshop, other award, 1984. Address: c/o Greenwillow Books, 105 Madison Avenue, New York, New York 10016, U.S.A.

PUBLICATIONS FOR CHILDREN (illustrated by the author)

Fiction

Three Days on a River in a Red Canoe. New York, Morrow, 1981.

A Chair for My Mother. New York, Greenwillow, 1982; London, MacRae, 1983.
Something Special for Me. New York, Greenwillow, 1983; London, MacRae, 1984.
Music, Music for Everyone. New York, Greenwillow, 1984; London, MacRae, 1985.
Cherries and Cherry Pits. New York, Greenwillow, 1986; as *Cherries and Cherry Stones*, London, MacRae, 1987.
Stringbean's Trip to the Shining Sea, illustrated by the author and Jennifer Williams. New York, Greenwillow, 1988.

*   *   *

Certain descriptors continue to surface in reviews of Vera B. Williams's work as picture-book author-illustrator: childlike, spontaneous, vibrant, joyous, fresh, loving. As appropriate as these attributes are, they often belie the careful attention and skill, as well as the consciously realized world view that goes into each of her books. Williams's background as an experimental educator, political activist, feminist, and environmentalist has found a new but altogether consistent forum in her fiction for children.

The three picture books which make up the Rosa Trilogy (*A Chair for My Mother, Something Special for Me*, and *Music, Music for Everyone*) have been compared to Erza Jack Keats's Peter books. The comparison is apt if one focuses on the energetic, expressionistic illustrations or the non-traditional treatment of minority children in urban settings. But Williams brings to the picture-book genre a uniquely honest and celebratory portrait of working-class culture which has seldom been executed so successfully. As much as is possible using the picture-book format, Williams is able to convey a strong sense of working-class life without glossing over the hardships or adjustments her economically disadvantaged characters face. The strong feeling one gets from her books is that of solidarity; characteristic of her stories are loving and supportive families in which the child is not the center but is seen as an integral, working member of a larger unit. This connectedness is the source of security and potential power; with it comes also a sense of responsibility to others.

Her first work of note, *Three Days on a River in a Red Canoe*, is grounded in the holistic philosophy which infuses Williams's life. The reader follows the young narrator, her cousin, and their mothers as they wind their way down the river, over falls, through mishaps and adventures. The book is at once a photo journal, a travelogue, a how-to book on camping. Of this book Williams says: "*Three Days on a River* isn't a social issue book but I feel that my devotion to a full life for women and to an unpolluted nature and to adventure for children are all in there somehow." A later work, *Stringbean's Trip to the Shining Sea*, also utilizes the travelogue format. Photos and postcards chronicle a low-budget trip from Kansas to the Pacific Ocean taken by the protagonist and his older brother. Both works invite reader participation with their intricate layouts and incorporation of fiction and non-fiction.

Williams is best known for her award-winning picture book, *A Chair for My Mother*, the first of three books featuring Rosa, a young hispanic girl who lives together with her waitress mother and grandmother. Rosa tells the story of how the three women save all their spare change in a large jar until they have enough to buy Rosa's overworked mother a "wonderful, beautiful, fat, soft armchair," to replace the chairs and sofa lost in a fire. The armchair becomes not only a much-needed resting place, it is also an object of beauty, a place of protection, a throne for three, a symbol of female solidarity.

Rosa's story continues in *Something Special for Me*. This time the coins accumulating in the jar are to be used for Rosa's birthday present. After lengthy deliberation, Rosa decides on an accordian, a gift which brings with it the memories of her accordian-playing grandmother and the promise of future shared music making. Rosa's dilemma underscores a common Williams theme: community over individualism. With the help of her patient, playful mother, Rosa finds a way to give a present to her family as well as to herself. Again, Williams sensitizes the reader to the struggles and decisions inherent in being poor, while not romanticizing that state.

Williams's usually vibrant watercolors become especially intense and emotionally charged when the element of music is added, as it is in *Music, Music for Everyone*. The jar is empty again, and is unlikely of being replenished as long as Rosa's grandmother is sick and needs medical attention. Rosa and friends decide to earn money by performing with the band they have formed. With the help of a music teacher and lots of practice, their first appearance—at the 50th anniversary celebration of the corner grocery store—is a triumph. Rosa's success is realistic, not make-believe; Williams convinces us that children really can do these things.

In *Cherries and Cherry Pits* Williams deals with the power of creative imagination as a potential force for change. The story is framed by a narrator who relates the tales of her young artist friend, Bidemmi. The work blends two distinct styles and innovative designs as we see first the narrator's, then Bidemmi's drawings. Bidemmi draws stories of people who eat cherries, ending with an account of how she, Bidemmi, plants lots of seeds in her "junky, old yard," finally turning urban blight into a glorious Garden of Eden. Bidemmi's youthful optimism seems natural, yet in her eagerness to empower children, Williams may be obscuring the realities of inner-city life with an overly romantic view. The vision that finally dominates, however, is one of hope, transformation, replenishment, respect—a vision that has become a Williams trademark.

—Nancy Tillman Romalov

WILLIAMSON, Henry. British. Born in Parkstone, Dorset, 1 December 1895. Educated at Colfe's Grammar School, Lewisham, London. Served as an infantryman and officer in the Bedfordshire Regiment of the British Army, 1914–19. Married Ida Letitia Hibbert in 1925 (divorced 1947), four sons and one daughter; remarried in 1948, one son. Worked in the advertising department of *The Times*, London, 1919–20; broadcaster, on farming and country life, for the Western Region of the BBC, Bristol, 1930's. Briefly interned at the outbreak of World War II for Fascist sympathies. Recipient: Hawthornden prize, 1928. *Died 13 August 1977.*

PUBLICATIONS FOR CHILDREN

Fiction

Tarka the Otter, Being His Joyful Water-Life and Death in the Country of the Two Rivers. London, Putnam, 1927; New York, Dutton, 1928.
Salar the Salmon. London, Faber, 1935; Boston, Little Brown, 1936.
Scribbling Lark. London, Faber, 1949.
The Henry Williamson Animal Saga (stories). London, Macdonald, 1960.
The Scandaroon, illustrated by Ken Lilly. London, Macdonald, 1972; New York, Saturday Review Press, 1973.

PUBLICATIONS FOR ADULTS

Novels

The Flax of Dream. London, Faber, 1936.

The Beautiful Years. London, Collins, 1921; revised edition, London, Faber, and New York, Dutton, 1929.
Dandelion Days. London, Collins, 1922; revised edition, London, Faber, and New York, Dutton, 1930.
The Dream of Fair Women. London, Collins, and New York, Dutton, 1924; revised edition, London, Faber, and Dutton, 1931.
The Pathway. London, Cape, 1928; revised edition, London, Faber, and New York, Dutton, 1929.
The Patriot's Progress, Being the Vicissitudes of Pte. John Bullock. London, Bles, and New York, Dutton, 1930.
The Gold Falcon; or, The Haggard of Love (published anonymously). London, Faber, and New York, Smith, 1933; revised edition, as Henry Williamson, Faber, 1947.
The Star-Born. London, Faber, 1933; revised edition, 1948.
The Sun in the Sands. London, Faber, 1945.
The Phasian Bird. London, Faber, 1948; Boston, Little Brown, 1950.
A Chronicle of Ancient Sunlight:
The Dark Lantern. London, Macdonald, 1951.
Donkey Boy. London, Macdonald, 1952.
Young Phillip Maddison. London, Macdonald, 1953.
How Dear Is Life. London, Macdonald, 1954.
A Fox under My Cloak. London, Macdonald, 1955.
The Golden Virgin. London, Macdonald, 1957.
Love and the Loveless: A Soldier's Tale. London, Macdonald, 1958.
A Test to Destruction. London, Macdonald, 1960.
The Innocent Moon. London, Macdonald, 1961.
It Was the Nightingale. London, Macdonald, 1962.
The Power of the Dead. London, Macdonald, 1963.
The Phoenix Generation. London, Macdonald, 1965.
A Solitary War. London, Macdonald, 1966.
Lucifer Before Sunrise. London, Macdonald, 1967.
The Gale of the World. London, Macdonald, 1969.

Short Stories and Sketches

The Peregrine's Saga and Other Stories of the Country Green. London, Collins, 1923; as *Sun Brothers*, New York, Dutton, 1925.
The Old Stag. London, Putnam, 1926; New York, Dutton, 1927.
The Linhay on the Downs. London, Mathews and Marrot, 1929.
The Ackymals. San Francisco, Windsor Press, 1929.
The Village Book. London, Cape, and New York, Dutton, 1930.
The Labouring Life. London, Cape, 1932; as *As the Sun Shines*, New York, Dutton, 1933.
On Foot in Devon; or, Guidance and Gossip, Being a Monologue in Two Reels. London, Maclehose, 1933.
The Linhay on the Downs and Other Adventures in the Old and New World. London, Cape, 1934.
Life in a Devon Village (based on material in *The Village Book* and *The Labouring Life*). London, Faber, 1945.
Tales of a Devon Village (based on material in *The Village Book* and *The Labouring Life*). London, Faber, 1945.
Tales of Moorland and Estuary. London, Macdonald, 1953.
In the Woods. Llandeilo, Wales, St. Albert's Press, 1960.
Collected Nature Stories. London, Macdonald, 1970.

Play

Television Documentary: *The Vanishing Hedgerow*, 1972.

Other

The Lone Swallows. London, Collins, 1922; New York, Dutton, 1926; revised edition, as *The Lone Swallows and Other Essays of*

Boyhood and Youth, London and New York, Putnam, 1933.
The Wet Flanders Plain. London, Beaumont Press, and New York, Dutton, 1929; revised edition, London, Faber, 1929.
The Wild Red Deer of Exmoor: A Digression on the Logic and Ethics and Economics of Stag-Hunting in England Today. London, Faber, 1931.
Devon Holiday. London, Cape, 1935.
Goodbye, West Country (diary). London, Putnam, 1937; Boston, Little Brown, 1938.
The Children of Shallowford (autobiography). London, Faber, 1939; revised edition, 1959.
As the Sun Shines: Selections. London, Faber, 1941.
The Story of a Norfolk Farm (autobiography). London, Faber, 1941.
Genius of Friendship: "T.E. Lawrence". London, Faber, 1941.
Norfolk Life, with L.R. Haggard. London, Faber, 1943.
A Clear Water Stream (autobiography). London, Faber, 1958; New York, Washburn, 1959; revised edition, London, Macdonald and Jane's, 1975.
The Weekly Despatch: Articles Contributed by Henry Williamson in the Years 1920–21. N.p., Henry Williamson Society, 1983.
Days of Wonder (essays). N.p., Henry Williamson Society, 1987.

Editor, *A Soldier's Diary of the Great War*, by Douglas Herbert Bell. London, Faber, 1929.
Editor, *An Anthology of Modern Nature Writing.* London, Nelson, 1936.
Editor, *Richard Jefferies: Selections of His Work.* London, Faber, 1937.
Editor, *Hodge and His Masters*, by Richard Jefferies. London, Methuen, 1937.
Editor, *Unreturning Spring, Being the Poems, Sketches, Stories and Letters of James Farrar.* London, Williams and Norgate, 1950.
Editor, *My Favourite Country Stories.* London, Lutterworth Press, 1966.

*

Bibliography: *A Bibliography and a Critical Survey of the Works of Henry Williamson* by I. Waveney Girvan, Chipping Campden, Gloucestershire, Alcuin Press, 1931.

Critical Studies: *Henry Williamson: A Tribute* by Ted Hughes, London, Rainbow Press, 1979; *Henry Williamson: The Man, The Writings* edited by Brocard Sewell, Padstow, Cornwall, Tabb House, 1980; *An Appreciation of Henry Williamson* by Daniel Farson, London, Joseph, 1982; *The Novels of Henry Williamson* by John M. Murry, n.p., Henry Williamson Society, 1986; *Henry Williamson: A Portrait* by Daniel Farson, London, Robinson, 1986.

*   *   *

Henry Williamson's *Tarka the Otter* was not written for children. But, like other notable works in this genre (such as *Red Fox* by Charles G.D. Roberts and *Abandoned* by G.D. Griffiths), it belongs as naturally to the junior library as to the adult. This branch of fiction—the factual (i.e., non-fantastic) animal narrative, imaginatively seen from the animal view—has no age barriers.

The book grew out of a happening in North Devon where the young Williamson, unsettled after his war experiences, had come to rediscover himself. He had managed to rear an infant otter cub whose mother had been shot by a farmer; it grew to be a playful, close companion. But it was caught in a gin trap and, though released, fled in terror. For many weeks Williamson looked for its maimed footprint, following the two rivers Taw and Torridge, from the estuary where they met to the Dartmoor source of each, but he never

found his protégé again. However, this close continual searching of earth and plant and water brought him almost inside the otter's world, and that of other wild creatures. (He extended this knowledge, it must be said, by going out with the local otter hunt.) That wild two-rivered region, from Dartmoor to the sea, is the country of the book.

Williamson's claim to have rewritten *Tarka* 17 times can well be believed, so vivid and meticulous are the writing and the detail. In theme it follows the customary plan of such books: a wild creature's birth, education, journeyings, mating; the hazards of nature (the winter chapter is a classic); the direr hazards brought by man—gun, snare, gin trap, poison, prongs, the hunter and the hounds. It is the human hand that brings in tragedy—that adds to fact (if you like) the dimension of fiction. To read the book is a complete experience, for reader, like writer, lives and perceives at otter level. In this richly inhabited scene, everything has its story. Open the pages anywhere:

> A stain began to move in the water, and a plaice flapped off the bottom and swam in what it thought was the beginning of a flood, when worms came swirling into the Junction Pool. This sea-fish had lived a strange and lonely life in fresh water ever since it had been swallowed in the estuary by a heron and ejected alive from the crop a quarter of an hour afterwards when the bird, flying up the valley, had been shot by a water-bailiff. The shape of an otter loomed in the water, and the plaice swam down again in a rapid, waving slant, perceived by a one-eyed eel that was lying with its tail inside a bullock's skull, wedged in a cleft of rock. Thrust through the eel's blank socket was the rusty barbed point of a hook, the shank of which stuck out of its mouth—a hook almost straightened before the line had broken. Tarka swam up....

What an abundance of narrative is here!

Chance—and the impetus of success (it won the prestigious Hawthornden Prize)—have made *Tarka* the best-known work of its kind. It also contains the best of Williamson's writing. He always disputed this. But his later fiction (outside the other "nature" books written in *Tarka's* wake—*Salar the Salmon*, for instance) is too often flawed by obsessions that can't be overlooked in any assessment: vanity and self-pity (animals know neither); a perverse attraction to power and cruelty which made him a besotted admirer of Hitler. The alibi of his own war experiences, valid at first, long became threadbare as cover for this mania. *Tarka*, written between 1923 and 1927, often in conditions of extreme domestic hardship and poverty, a book where plant and animal life hold the foreground, is still clear of these maladies.

Except perhaps for one point, already hinted at. In 1927 (his biographer relates) Williamson called on Hardy, boasting of all the praise he had had for the novel. Hardy mildly asked if he did not think otter hunting rather cruel. Disconcerted, Williamson murmured that it might be, but that he did not want to take sides. And yet—in this case the writer surpassed the man. In his exact describing the truth comes through about a particularly gross and ugly "sport"; the facts carry their own indictment.

Nevertheless, the irony remains that the first edition of *Tarka* was dedicated to the Master of the local Hunt. The dedicatee's name remains in modern editions, but the embarrassing detail of his occupation is usually removed.

—Naomi Lewis

———

WILSON, Barbara Ker. British. Born in Sunderland, County

Durham, 24 September 1929. Educated at North London Collegiate School, 1938–48. Married Peter Richard Tahourdin in 1956; two daughters. Assistant editor, Oxford University Press, London, 1949–54; children's books editor, Bodley Head, London, 1954–57, William Collins, London, 1957–62, Angus and Robertson, Sydney, 1965–73, and Hodder and Stoughton, Sydney, 1973–76. Since 1978 editor, Readers Digest Condensed Books, Sydney. Address: 1/10 Harnett Avenue, Mosman Bay, New South Wales 2088, Australia.

PUBLICATIONS FOR CHILDREN

Fiction

Path-Through-the-Woods, illustrated by Charles Stewart. London, Constable, and New York, Criterion, 1958.
The Wonderful Cornet, illustrated by Raymond Briggs. London, Hamish Hamilton, 1958.
The Lovely Summer, illustrated by Marina Hoffer. London, Constable, and New York, Dodd Mead, 1960.
Last Year's Broken Toys. London, Constable, 1962; as *In Love and War*, Cleveland, World, 1963.
Ann and Peter in Paris [and *in London*], illustrated by Harry and Ilse Toothill. London, Muller, 2 vols., 1963–65.
A Story to Tell: Thirty Tales for Little Children, illustrated by Sheila Sancha. London, J. Garnet Miller, 1964.
Beloved of the Gods. London, Constable, 1965; as *In the Shadow of Vesuvius*, Cleveland, World, 1965.
A Family Likeness, illustrated by Astra Lacis Dick. London, Constable, 1967; as *The Biscuit-Tin Family*, Cleveland, World, 1968.
Hiccups and Other Stories: Thirty Tales for Little Children, illustrated by Richard Kennedy. London, J. Garnet Miller, 1971.
The Persian Carpet Story, with Jacques Cadry, illustrated by Nyorie Bungey. Sydney, Methuen, 1981; London, Methuen, 1982.
Kelly the Sleepy Koala, illustrated by Lorraine Itannay. Sydney, Golden Press, 1983.
Molly. Sydney, Golden Press, 1983.
Kevin the Kookaburra, illustrated by Sue Price. Sydney, Golden Press, 1983.
Acacia Terrace, illustrated by David Fielding. Sydney, Ashton, 1988.

Other

Scottish Folk Tales and Legends, illustrated by Joan Kiddell-Monroe. London, Oxford University Press, and New York, Walck, 1954.
Fairy Tales of Germany, illustrated by Gertrude Mittelmann, [*Ireland, Mexico*, and *Persia*, all illustrated by G.W. Miller, *India*, illustrated by Rene Mackensie, *Russia*, illustrated by Jacqueline Athram, *France*, illustrated by William McLaren, *England*, illustrated by John S. Goodall]. London, Cassell, and New York, Dutton, 8 vols., 1959–61.
Look at Books, illustrated by John Woodcock. London, Hamish Hamilton, 1960.
Legends of the Round Table, illustrated by Marra Calati. London, Hamlyn, 1966.
Greek Fairy Tales, illustrated by Harry Toothill. London, Muller, 1966; Chicago, Follett, 1968.
Animal Folk Tales, illustrated by Mirko Hanák. London, Hamlyn, 1968; New York, Grosset and Dunlap, 1971.
Australia, Wonderland Down Under. New York, Dodd Mead, 1969.
Tales Told to Kabbarli: Aboriginal Legends Collected by Daisy Bates, illustrated by Harold Thomas. Sydney and London, Angus and Robertson, and New York, Crown, 1972.

The Magic Fishbones and Other Fabulous Tales of Asia, illustrated by Susanne Dolesch. Sydney, Angus and Robertson, 1973; London, Angus and Robertson, 1975.
The Magic Bird and Other Fabulous Tales from Europe, illustrated by Susanne Dolesch. Sydney, Angus and Robertson, 1973; London, Angus and Robertson, 1975.
Just for a Joyride (reader). Sydney, Holt Rinehart, 1977.
The Turtle and the Island: Folk Tales from Papua New Guinea, edited by Donald S. Stokes, illustrated by Tony Oliver. Sydney and London, Hodder and Stoughton, 1978.
The Willow Pattern Story (Chinese tale), illustrated by Lucienne Fontannaz. Sydney and London, Angus and Robertson, 1978.

Editor, *The Second Young Eve*. London, Blackie, 1962.
Editor, *What a Girl* [and *Boy*] *Should Know about Sex*, by Bernhardt Gottlieb. London, Constable, 2 vols., 1962.
Editor, *Australian Kaleidoscope*, illustrated by Margery Gill. Sydney and London, Collins, 1968; New York, Meredith Press, 1969.
Editor, *A Handful of Ghosts: Thirteen Eerie Tales by Australian Authors*. Sydney, Hodder and Stoughton, 1976; London, Hodder and Stoughton, 1977.
Editor, *Alice's Adventures in Wonderland*, by Lewis Carroll, translated into Pitjantjatjara by Nancy Sheppard, illustrated by Byron Sewell. Adelaide, Adelaide University Press, 1976.
Editor, *Illustrated Treasury of Australian Stories and Verses for Children*. Melbourne, Nelson, 1987.

PUBLICATIONS FOR ADULTS

Novels

Jane Austen in Australia. London, Secker and Warburg, 1984; as *Antipodes Jane*, New York, Viking, 1985.
The Quade Inheritance. Richmond, Victoria, Heinemann, and London, Secker and Warburg, 1988; New York, St. Martin's Press, 1989.

Other

Writing for Children. London, Boardman, 1960; New York, Watts, 1961.
Noel Streatfeild. London, Bodley Head, 1961; New York, Walck, 1964.

*

Barbara Ker Wilson comments:
Social history, with a special background interest in the historical position of women, seems, in retrospect, to have formed the springboard for my teenage-reader novels: *Path-Through-the-Woods, The Lovely Summer, Last Year's Broken Toys*, and *A Family Likeness*. My main aim, however, was and will for future work remain to tell a *story*. This enjoyment in storytelling extends, too, to collections of stories for very young children, and most of the tales in my two collections *A Story to Tell* and *Hiccups* are often broadcast and televised. My other very strong interest is in folklore where I feel the often artificial borderline between literature for the young and for the adult most satisfyingly disappears.

*   *   *

Barbara Ker Wilson's background is part English, part Australian, and though most of the stories in *A Story to Tell* and *Hiccups* would be acceptable to the under-fives from either country, some depend on Australian setting. Some are short invented fairytales, but most are designed to stimulate imaginative parents who make up stories for and about their own small children.

Ann and Peter in Paris and *Ann and Peter in London* are formula writing, but with enough plot to make the information palatable. Ann and Peter, like most natives, know less about London than the average visitor, an ingenious device which gives Peter the opportunity to read up the guide book before their journeys.

Path-Through-the-Woods is the story behind a patchwork quilt. In a series of pictures of the life of a Victorian family—unusual because the eldest sister breaks from convention and becomes a pioneer woman doctor—the middle-class atmosphere is well conveyed. Jemima's death coincides with the launching of the Great Eastern and generally facts are conveyed incidentally.

The Lovely Summer is really several summers, just before and during World War I. The campaign for women's suffrage and implicitly the feminist movement is shown in the lives of three girls of different social classes. This is a convincing and readable book, with a fairly broad-minded approach to its theme—violence versus non-violence.

Probably the best book she will ever write, *Last Year's Broken Toys* reflects the author's own childhood before and during the last war. In a sense the war is the "hero." There are dozens of characters but however brief the glimpses they are all real people. There is no straight plot, boy and girl friendships change, odd coincidences happen though the participants are not always aware of them. Some die, most survive. All the ends are tied up for the reader but not for the people involved—this is real life.

Beloved of the Gods is a competent and thoroughly researched novel about ancient Rome and the destruction of Pompeii, but there is perhaps too much concern with historical detail so that the characters come alive only occasionally.

A Family Likeness is an Australian story paralleling and contrasting the lives of the present-day girl and her mid-19th-century forebears. The switches are cleverly done, but one feels that the Victorian episodes were thought of first and that therefore the modern Debbie is less alive and less interesting. The history seems to intrude more than it did in *Last Year's Broken Toys* although there was so much more of it in the earlier book. Perhaps there is more need to "explain" things of a century ago, especially in Australia.

—Margaret M. Tye

———

WILSON, Gina (née Jones). British. Born in Abergele, North Wales, 1 April 1943. Educated at Manchester High School for Girls, 1955–61; University of Edinburgh, 1961–65, M.A. (honours) in English 1965; Mount Holyoke College, South Hadley, Massachusetts, 1965–66. Married Edward Wilson in 1972; two daughters and one son. Assistant editor, *Scottish National Dictionary*, 1967–73, and *Dictionary of the Older Scottish Tongue*, 1972–73, Edinburgh. Address: c/o Faber and Faber Ltd., 3 Queen Square, London WC1N 3AU, England.

PUBLICATIONS FOR CHILDREN

Fiction

Cora Ravenwing. London, Faber, and New York, Atheneum, 1980.
A Friendship of Equals. London, Faber, 1981.
The Whisper. London, Faber, 1982.
All Ends Up. London, Faber, 1984.
Family Feeling. London, Faber, 1986.
Just Us. London, Faber, 1988.
Polly Pipes Up, illustrated by Jacqui Thomas. London,

Heinemann, 1989.
Wolumpus Galumpus, illustrated by Clive Scruton. London, Walker, 1989.
Do This, Do That, illustrated by Alison Catley. London, Hutchinson, 1989.

Verse

Jim-Jam Pyjamas, illustrated by Sally Anne Lambert. London, Cape, 1989.

*   *   *

Gina Wilson's novels are very much of the 1980's, not only in the themes they address but also in their ambience. She has an eye for significant details which place her characters socially, yet they are traditional in the sense that the girls' novel has always been one of the most well written and well read of children's literature genres. Her characterisation is strong, she shows insight into tensions in family and peer relationships, and she deals honestly and positively with matters that affect girls at home and at school. The value of her work is most clearly seen in this exploration of young adolescent identity when, as the heroine of her first novel says, "I was just beginning to have real ideas and opinions of my own." The viewpoint is exclusively female and she deals sympathetically with mothers as well as daughters.

Cora Ravenwing deals, as all Wilson's novels do, with friendship, and is still one of her most striking works. Rebecca Stakes, moving to a new home and school, forms a friendship with the local outsider, for Cora is the daughter of a dead gypsy mother and the village sexton. Parental influence and public pressure of a snobbish, conventional set of girls force her to renege on her loyalty and lose something valuable from her life.

In *A Friendship of Equals* friendship is the equalising factor between the rich, physically handicapped Stella Boncastle and Laurie Jones from the village shop; both are lonely, unhappy, and at a crisis point in family and education. Significant in this book is the young adolescents' changing stance towards adults, seen for the first time as erring and human.

The friendship in *The Whisper* is closer to home. Lily's initial welcome into the family of her orphaned cousin Marie turns into jealousy of Marie's musical ability and greater maturity. Lily colludes in a campaign of scurrilous rumour to remove the cuckoo from her nest, and realises only too late the consequences of her actions.

All Ends Up is Wilson's best book so far about girls' interaction with each other and their families. Claudia, socially disadvantaged by living in a poor area with her unmarried mother, is even so more securely based emotionally than her two friends Anna, with her ambitions and neurotic mother and Sylvie, with her rich, permissive parents. This is an intensely dramatic book, with its quarrels and reconciliations of a tripartite friendship.

Family Feeling, while it has a sub-plot about friendship, deals almost claustrophobically with Alice's adjustment to her mother's remarriage whose two new children make life difficult in different ways; with the elder, a boy, she has a love affair which is forbidden by both parents while the younger, a girl, sets up a jealous and trouble-making relationship. Both present insoluble problems to the fragile security of the new family.

Just Us also deals with a forbidden sexual relationship, this time between Lyn and her English teacher, who is also involved with her mother. Here, as in so many of her books, the fraught relationship between mother and daughter is subtly explored.

—Mary Croxson

———

WILSON, Jacqueline. British. Born in Bath, Somerset, 17 December 1945. Educated at Coombe Girls School, Surrey; Carshalton Technical College, Surrey. Married William Millar Wilson in 1965; one daughter. Staff member, D.C. Thomson, Dundee, Scotland, 1963–65. Freelance journalist. Agent: Gina Pollinger, Murray Pollinger, 4 Garrick Street, London WC2E 9BH. Address: 1-B Beaufort Road, Kingston-on-Thames, Surrey KT1 2TH, England.

PUBLICATIONS FOR CHILDREN

Fiction

Ricky's Birthday, illustrated by Margaret Belsky. London, Macmillan, 1973.
Nobody's Perfect. Oxford, Oxford University Press, 1982.
Waiting for the Sky to Fall. Oxford, Oxford University Press, 1983.
The Killer Tadpole, illustrated by Rebecca Campbell-Grey. London, Hamish Hamilton, 1984.
The Other Side. Oxford, Oxford University Press, 1984.
The School Trip, illustrated by Sally Holmes. London, Hamish Hamilton, 1984.
How to Survive Summer Camp, illustrated by Bob Dewar. Oxford, Oxford University Press, 1985.
Amber. Oxford, Oxford University Press, 1986.
The Monster in the Cupboard, illustrated by Kate Rogers. London, Blackie, 1986.
Glubbslyme, illustrated by Jane Cope. Oxford, Oxford University Press, 1987.
The Power of the Shade. Oxford, Oxford University Press, 1987.
Stevie Day series (*Lonelyhearts, Supersleuth, Rat Race, Vampire*). London, Armada, 4 vols., 1987–88.
This Girl. Oxford, Oxford University Press, 1988.
The Left-Outs. London, Blackie, 1989.

PUBLICATIONS FOR ADULTS

Novels

Hide and Seek. London, Macmillan, 1972; New York, Doubleday, 1973.
Truth or Dare. London, Macmillan, 1973; New York, Doubleday, 1974.
Snap. London, Macmillan, 1974.
Let's Pretend. London, Macmillan, 1976.
Making Hate. London, Macmillan, 1977; New York, St. Martin's Press, 1978.

Plays

Radio Plays: *Are You Listening?* 1981; *It's Disgusting at Your Age*, 1982; *Ask a Silly Question*, 1983.

*

Jacqueline Wilson comments:

When I was nine years old I bought myself an out-of-date paper pattern book and for years it was my favourite possession. I didn't care about fashion—I snipped out hundreds of "models," naming them all and playing endless games with these paper dolls. Writing novels is really a grown-up version of these pretend games. I name and sort and sift my imaginary girls until they come to life. And when they do, they generally turn out to be the sort of girls who'd play similar games. They daydream, they run bizarre cartoons inside their heads, they embroider, they write stories. They have more than their

fair share of problems in their real lives but they generally cope by escaping into their own inner world of imagination. They're still my paper dolls—and yet by the end of each book they seem real flesh and blood friends.

*   *   *

Jacqueline Wilson is a born storyteller whose talent took her into professional writing in her teens, but apart from *Ricky's Birthday* she deployed her skills in adult crime writing and radio drama until 1982. Then in six years she published 15 works for young people: six teenage novels, five younger stories, and a paperback series about Stevie Day, 14-year-old detective.

There is a unity of background and purpose to all her output. While in the teenage novels the mood is sometimes bleak, with the junior stories it is reassuring—as in *The School Trip* or the hilarious *How to Survive Summer Camp*. With the *Stevie Day* series, which now includes four adventures, the mood is jokey and calm despite the excitements of the plots and the contemporary realism of the settings.

This, in a sense, also reflects the progression of the author's creative talents and the strivings of her heroines (only one of the 14 books—*The Killer Tadpole*—is about a boy) towards a resolution of their dilemmas and longings. As the author's handling of the novel form matures, so does the girls' mastery of themselves and their environment.

The six novels—*Nobody's Perfect, Waiting for the Sky to Fall, The Other Side, Amber, The Power of the Shade*, and *This Girl* are very much of the 1980's, frank, often harsh, passionate in the way they tell what happens to people when families break up and the accompanying near poverty casts them adrift in the world.

Wilson is one of those authors who can show from the inside how teenagers feel and who prove that British children's literature no longer depends upon American authors for credible stories in this age group.

Yet, contemporary as she is, with a strong emphasis on dialogue and inner feelings (almost too strong an emphasis on graphic sensations of hunger, eating, and nausea), her writing belongs very much to the tradition of the Tale rather than that of the English novel.

Her heroines, often rejected and despised, journey alone towards the goal of heart's desire, not widow's daughters but single-parent children, with sad, often hostile mothers, abandoned by barely-known fathers. There are Prince Charmings, the vanished fathers or attractive older men, enchanted castles in the well-to-do, cultured homes of friends, ugly sisters, smarter, richer, ultimately nastier "friends." And there are companions on the road, siblings to whom the heroine is tied, boyfriends who offer affection and are almost betrayed by sad misunderstandings. Both *Nobody's Perfect* and *Amber* offer poignant, heart-warming portrayals of boy-girl friendships.

If the Tale is about Test and Quest, her novels are about the Test of rejection and the Quest for love. Her young women strive to hold on to humanity and sometimes (as in *The Other Side*) to sanity, in the face of lunatic behaviour in the adult world. They seek amid the debris of the conventional family, the truer ideal family of affection and loyalty.

Wilson can write fairytales too. In *The Power of the Shade* the stories which May writes to captivate Robin, the writer visiting her school, are not only convincing as teenage talent. They form an inner stream through the novel, the route by which May works out her salvation, Prince Charming not being up to the task.

In *The Other Side*, by contrast, the "inner" writing runs out of control. The metaphor of flying by which Alison's near-breakdown is given shape, breaks down the plot and the reconciliation with the mother at the end is thus somewhat lacking in conviction. (Interestingly, in *Glubbslyme*, a fantasy tale about a magic frog, the flying metaphor is happily employed.)

Reconciliation, so much desired, is achieved in *Waiting for the Sky to Fall* when the heroine understands that she must love her family—inadequate, domineering father, sad mother, demanding sister—if she is to love at all.

In *Amber*, where the flowers of the commune days are wilting and the mother retains only fecklessness, while the warmth and charm of Davie the "uncle" vanishes as it always did in the past, Amber achieves her reconciliation with Justin, the clever, awkward boy in her class.

But it is in her latest novel—*This Girl*—that the author brings together most successfully the elements common to her novels. Coral, escaping from her family on a broken-down estate, lives out her Victorian fantasies in Toby and Isabel's wealthy home. They fail her. Isabel, theoretical feminist, is at heart an exploitive madame, Toby's gentleness is of a self-centred kind. Carol makes herself a family, on another broken-down estate, with Deb, her new friend, and Deb's baby. Here the Quest comes to a resolute and hopeful end.

—Robert Leeson

———————

WOJCIECHOWSKA, Maia (Teresa). Also writes as Maia Rodman. American. Born in Warsaw, Poland, 7 August 1927; emigrated to the United States, 1942; became citizen, 1950. Educated at Sacred Heart Academy, Los Angeles; Immaculate Heart College, Hollywood, 1945–46. Married 1) Selden Rodman in 1950 (divorced 1957), two daughters; 2) Richard Larkin in 1972. Translator, Radio Free Europe, New York, 1949–51; worked for William Burns Detective Agency, 1951–69; assistant editor, Retail Wholesale and Department Store Union *Record*, New York, 1953–55; copy girl, *Newsweek* magazine, New York, 1953–55; assistant editor, *American Hairdresser* magazine, New York, 1955–57; agent and editor, Kurt Hellmer Literary Agency, New York, 1958–61; publicity manager, Hawthorn Books, New York, 1961–65. Since 1949 professional tennis instructor. Recipient: American Library Association Newbery Medal, 1965. Agent: Michael Seligman, 9171 Wilshire Boulevard, Beverly Hills, California 90210; or, Gunther Stuhlmann, P.O. Box 276, Becket, Massachusetts 01223, U.S.A.

PUBLICATIONS FOR CHILDREN (as Maia Wojciechowska in the United States, and as Maia Rodman in the United Kingdom)

Fiction

Market Day for Ti André, illustrated by Wilson Bigaud. New York, Viking Press, 1952.
Shadow of a Bull, illustrated by Alvin Smith. New York, Atheneum, and London, Hamish Hamilton, 1964.
A Kingdom in a Horse. New York, Harper, 1965.
The Hollywood Kid. New York, Harper, 1966.
A Single Light. New York, Harper, 1968.
Tuned Out. New York, Harper, 1968; London, Macmillan, 1976.
Hey, What's Wrong with This One?, illustrated by Joan Sandin. New York, Harper, 1969.
Don't Play Dead Before You Have To. New York, Harper, 1970.
The Rotten Years. New York, Doubleday, 1971.
The Life and Death of a Brave Bull, illustrated by John Groth. New York, Harcourt Brace, 1972.
Through the Broken Mirror with Alice. New York, Harcourt Brace, 1972.

How God Got Christian into Trouble. Philadelphia, Westminster Press, 1984.

Other

Odyssey of Courage: The Story of Alvar Núñez Cabeza de Vaca, illustrated by Alvin Smith. New York, Atheneum, 1965; London, Burns Oates, 1967.
Till the Break of Day (autobiographical). New York, Harcourt Brace, 1972.
Winter Tales from Poland, illustrated by Laszlo Kubinyi. New York, Doubleday, 1973.

PUBLICATIONS FOR ADULTS

Novel

The People in His Life (as Maia Rodman). New York, Stein and Day, 1980.

Play

All at Sea, adaptation of a work by Slawomir Mrozek (produced New York, 1968).

Other

The International Loved Look. New York, American Hairdresser, 1964.

Translator, *The Bridge to the Other Side*, by Monika Kotowska. New York, Doubleday, 1970.

*

Manuscript Collection: Kerlan Collection, University of Minnesota, Minneapolis.

Maia Wojciechowska comments:
In my Newbery acceptance speech I wrote, "When you know what life has to sell, for how much, and what it can give away free, you will not live in darkness. I hope that in my books you'll find your light, and that by this light you may cross from one shore of love to another, from your childhood into your adulthood. I hope that some of the light will come from my books and that, because of this light, life will lose its power to frighten you." I am most concerned about children and how little they know of their inner resources. I believe that in writing for the young an author has an obligation to "enlighten" as well as entertain. I deplore the insipid books about rodents and other four-legged creatures that are the fare for the very young—they grow up thinking human beings less interesting than animals. I deplore the shoddiness of the books for older kids and the waste of time and energy that goes into producing them.

I keep hoping that Man (collectively, all of us) is coming into a Messianic age where "this is the earthly goal of man, to evolve his intellectual powers to their fullest, to arrive at the maximum of consciousness, to open the eyes of his understanding upon all things so that upon the tablet of his soul the order of the whole universe may be enrolled," as Aquinas said, will become our imperative. I seem incurably, romantically in love with the human potential, with that part of us that links us to our maker, that part that can be found in the best of literature and in the best moments of our own lives, that mysterious drive within us that reaches ever upwards. What drives me bananas is when this drive is curtailed or stopped by petty concerns, shortening of sights, wrong priorities, materialistic pursuits. I am a lay preacher in whatever writing I do, preaching the possibility of rising above our mere survival into that other plane, spiritual, if you wish, where the mind directs, unfailingly, the heart.

*   *   *

Courage. That is what the people who inhabit the world of Maia Wojciechowska must possess if they are to be victorious over the adversity which threatens to overwhelm them. And love, that is what everyone needs from someone else—or at least the memory of that love as in the surrealistic adventure *Through the Broken Mirror with Alice*. To read most of the novels of Wojciechowska is to feel the *Weltschmerz* which the author reveals when she writes of the hurt, anxiety, and even danger felt by those who inhabit her novels. Her characters are middle-class, poor, rich, but they all suffer at the hands of fate, their parents, society. There is one trait they all exhibit—a certain degree of courage with which to conquer fear and face their hardships. Whether it is the 12-year-old foster-child, Alice, existing in one home after another and preyed upon by the local junkie; 16-year-old Jim of *Tuned Out*, trying desperately to help his older brother escape from dependence on LSD; or lonely, frustrated Bryan in *The Hollywood Kid*—Wojciechowska wants them all "on speaking terms with life...."

The best way to understand Wojciechowska's philosophy is to read *The Rotten Years* (that impossible time between 12 and 15). In the guise of Elsie Jones, a renegade junior high school teacher, the author elaborates on her distrust of the educational system, and the total lack of respect which adults often display toward adolescents. It is a powerful piece of writing which is a combination of fiction and textbook. Young people reading it during their own "rotten years" will find an empathetic ally.

The misanthropy of ignorant villagers and the goodness of a young mute girl are starkly contrasted in *A Single Light*. This work has a special, haunting quality about it, a well-developed religious theme centering on the harsh life of an unwanted, unloved child.

The big disappointment in Wojciechowska's writing is *A Kingdom in a Horse*, which is very difficult to accept as a serious piece of literature. Old people playing games on horseback, secret midnight rides, a teenage runaway, and a mystical experience—they are all there, unjelled. Contrarily, *Don't Play Dead Before You Have To* contains an odd mixture which fits together cohesively. Charlie is only five when Byron first babysits for him. Although the young child doesn't speak directly to the reader throughout the entire novel, his tragedy is deeply felt. Charlie and the peripheral characters are all understood through their impact on Byron. It is an unusual story of an acutely perceptive teenage boy who reaches out to others, and of his relationship to a younger boy whom he grows to love.

In *Shadow of a Bull*, a beautiful story, the author describes the difficulties which the son of a great bullfighter faces. It takes great courage for Manolo to turn his back on what society expects of him as he searches for his place in the world—outside the bullring. Love and courage. Wojciechowska tells us all about them.

—Vivian J. Scheinmann

WOOD, David. British. Born in Sutton, Surrey, 21 February 1944. Educated at Chichester High School for Boys, 1957–63; Worcester College, Oxford, 1963–66, B.A. (honours) in English 1966. Married 1) Sheila Ruskin in 1966 (marriage dissolved 1970); 2) Jacqueline Stanbury in 1975, two daughters. Since 1966 director, W.S.G. Productions; since 1979 director, Whirligig Theatre; since 1983 director, Verronmead Limited television production company; since 1986 director, Westwood Theatre Productions. Agent: Margaret Ramsay Ltd., 14-A Goodwin's Court, London WC2N 4LL; or, Elizabeth Stevens, Curtis Brown, 162–168 Regent Street, London W1R 5TB, England.

PUBLICATIONS FOR CHILDREN

Fiction

The Operats of Rodent Garden, illustrated by Geoffrey Beitz. London, Methuen, 1984.
The Gingerbread Man, from his own play, illustrated by Sally Anne Lambert. London, Pavilion, 1985.
The Discorats, illustrated by Geoffrey Beitz. London, Methuen, 1985.
Chish 'n' Fips, with Don Seed. London, Boxtree, 1987.
Sidney the Monster, illustrated by Clive Scruton. London, Walker, 1988.

Plays

The Tinder Box, adaptation of a story by Hans Christian Andersen (produced Worcester, 1967).
Cinderella (lyrics only), book by Sid Colin, music by John Gould (produced Glasgow, 1968).
The Owl and the Pussycat Went to See..., with Sheila Ruskin, music and lyrics by Wood, adaptation of works by Edward Lear (produced Worcester, 1968; London, 1969). London, French, 1970.
Larry the Lamb in Toytown, with Sheila Ruskin, music and lyrics by Wood, adaptation of stories by S.G. Hulme Beaman (produced Worcester, 1969; London, 1973). London, French, 1977.
The Plotters of Cabbage Patch Corner, music by Wood (produced Worcester, 1970; London, 1971). London, French, 1972.
Flibberty and the Penguin, music by Wood (produced Worcester, 1971; London, 1977). London, French, 1974.
Tickle (produced on tour, 1972; London, 1977). London, French, 1978.
The Papertown Paperchase, music by Wood (produced Worcester, 1972; London, 1973). London, French, 1976.
Hijack over Hygenia, music by Wood (produced Worcester, 1973). London, French, 1974.
Old Mother Hubbard, music by Wood (produced Hornchurch, Essex, 1975). London, French, 1976.
Old Father Time, music by Wood (produced Hornchurch, Essex, 1976). London, French, 1978.
The Gingerbread Man, music by Wood (produced Basildon, Essex, 1976; London, 1977). London, French, 1977.
Nutcracker Sweet, music by Wood (produced Farnham, Surrey, 1977; London, 1980). London, French, 1981.
Mother Goose's Golden Christmas, music by Wood (produced Hornchurch, Essex, 1977). London, French, 1978.
Babes in the Magic Wood, music by Wood (produced Hornchurch, Essex, 1979). London, French, 1980.
There Was an Old Woman, music by Wood (produced Leicester, 1979). London, French, 1980.
Cinderella, music by Wood (produced Hornchurch, Essex, 1980). London, French, 1981.
The Ideal Gnome Expedition, music by Wood (as *Chish and Fips*, produced Liverpool, 1980; as *The Ideal Gnome Expedition*, produced on tour and London, 1981). London, French, 1982.
Aladdin, music by Wood (produced Hornchurch, Essex, 1980). London, French, 1981.
Robin Hood, with Dave and Toni Arthur, music by Wood (produced Nottingham, 1981; London, 1982). London, French, 1985.

Meg and Mog Show, music by Wood, adaptation of stories by Helen Nicoll (produced London, 1981).

Dick Whittington and Wondercat, music by Wood (produced Hornchurch, Essex, 1981). London, French, 1982.

Jack and the Giant (produced Hornchurch, Essex, 1982). London, French, 1987.

Magic and Music Show (produced London, 1983).

The Selfish Shellfish (produced Farnham, Surrey, and London, 1983). Oxford, Amber Lane Press, 1983.

Jack the Lad, with Dave and Toni Arthur, music by Wood (produced Manchester, 1984).

The Old Man of Lochnagar, adaptation of the story by Prince Charles (produced Aberdeen and London, 1986). Oxford, Amber Lane Press, 1986.

Dinosaurs and All That Rubbish, music by Peter Pontzen, adaptation of the story by Michael Foreman (produced Denbigh, Wales, 1986; London, 1988). Oxford, Amber Lane Press, 1986.

The See-Saw Tree (produced Farnham, Surrey, 1986; London, 1987).

Play Theatre (*The Nativity Play* and *Jack and the Beanstalk*), illustrated by Richard Fowler. London, Pavilion, and New York, Holt, 2 vols., 1987.

Robin Hood and Friar Tuck and *Marian and the Witches' Charm*, in *Playstages*, edited by John Alcock. London, Methuen, 1987.

Screenplay: *Swallows and Amazons*, 1974.

Television Writing: *Playaway* series, 1973–77; *Emu's Christmas Adventure*, 1977; *Chish 'n' Fips*, 1984; *Chips' Comic*, 1984; *Seeing and Doing*, 1986; *Back Home*, adaptation of the story by Michelle Magorian, 1989.

PUBLICATIONS FOR ADULTS

Plays

Hang Down Your Head and Die, with David Wright (produced Oxford, London, and New York, 1964).

Sketches, with John Gould, in *Four Degrees Over* (produced Edinburgh and London, 1966).

And Was Jerusalem, with Mick Sadler and John Gould (produced Oxford, 1966; as *A Present from the Corporation*, produced Worcester and London, 1967).

A Life in Bedrooms, with David Wright (produced Edinburgh, 1967; as *The Stiffkey Scandals of 1932*, produced London, 1968).

Three to One On, with John Gould (produced Edinburgh, 1968).

Postscripts, with John Gould (produced London, 1969).

Down Upper Street, with John Gould (produced London, 1971).

Just the Ticket, with John Gould (produced Leatherhead, Surrey, 1973).

Rock Nativity, music by Tony Hatch and Jackie Trent, lyrics by Wood (produced Newcastle-upon-Tyne, 1974; as *A New Tomorrow*, produced Wimbledon, 1976). London, Weinberger, 1977.

Maudie, with Iwan Williams (produced Leatherhead, Surrey, 1974).

Chi-Chestnuts, with Bernard Price and Julian Sluggett (produced Chichester, 1975).

Think of a Number, with John Gould (produced Peterborough, 1975).

Bars of Gould, with John Gould (revue; produced Exeter, 1977).

The Luck of the Bodkins, with John Gould, adaptation of a work by P.G. Wodehouse (produced Windsor, 1978).

Abbacadabra, music by Björn Ulvaeus and Benny Andersson, lyrics by Don Black, Mike Batt, and Ulvaeus (produced London, 1983).

*

Theatrical Activities:

Director: most of his own plays.

Actor: **Plays**—in *Hang Down Your Head and Die*, Oxford and London, 1964; Geoff Manham in *A Spring Song* by Ray Mathew, Edinburgh and London, 1964; Wagner in *Dr. Faustus* by Christopher Marlowe, Oxford, 1966; in Worcester, Watford, Edinburgh, Windsor, and Salisbury repertory companies, 1966–69; Roger in *After Haggerty* by David Mercer, London, 1970, 1971; The Son in *A Voyage round My Father* by John Mortimer, London, 1970, Toronto, 1972; James in *Me Times Me*, toured 1971; Frank in *Mrs. Warren's Profession* by G.B. Shaw, Leatherhead, Surrey, 1972; *Just the Ticket* (revue), Leatherhead, Surrey, 1972; Constant in *The Provok'd Wife* by Vanbrugh, London, 1973; Bingo Little in *Jeeves* by Alan Ayckbourn, London, 1975; *Three to One On* (revue), Peterborough, 1975; Lt. Bowers in *Terra Nova* by Ted Tally, Chichester, 1980; *Magic and Music Show*, London, 1983. **Films**—*If...*, 1968; *Aces High*, 1975; *Sweet William*, 1978; *North Sea Hijack*, 1979. **Radio**—*Semi-Circles* series by Simon Brett, 1982. **Television**—*Mad Jack; Fathers and Sons; The Vamp; Cheri; Disraeli; The Avengers; Van der Valk; Danger UXB; Huntingtower; Enemy at the Door; Jim'll Fix It; The Brack Report; Bureaucracy of Love; Jackanory 3000*, 1979; *Trouble with Gregory*, 1980; *When the Boat Comes In*, 1981; and other plays, since 1964.

David Wood comments:

Children's theatre in Great Britain has for too long been regarded within and without the profession as second or even third division theatre. I hope I may be making a small contribution towards its elevation to a higher division! After all, if live theatre is to survive it is up to those of us who work in it to interest our *potential* audiences as early as possible. I try to combine a strong story-line with hummable songs and imaginative characters. I try never to patronize the children and never to "play to the adults." Although fantasy often plays a strong part, I hope the plays have enough substance to evoke discussion and a continuation of the experience after the curtain has fallen. And I hope they make people laugh too.

*   *   *

Just as a specialist literature for children has had to define its particular status, so children's theatre still seeks out new modes and appropriate forms for a demanding audience. David Wood's work is of importance in setting the standards by which we now judge an art form too often hampered by an English pantomime tradition increasingly aimed at the adults and by an often earnest, over-serious "educational drama."

His musical plays appeal to children's love of action, movement, colour, and spectacle. They all have an actor's instinct for their impact, as well as a gifted storyteller's feel for character, plot, and theme. The plays often build upon tales that his audiences know (or half know), so making them feel at home in the theatre and giving significance to the re-enactment of stories that children do themselves. *The Owl and the Pussycat Went to See...*conveys the essentially exotic and mysterious nature of the original and extends the musical potentiality of the poem. *Robin Hood* and *Old Mother Hubbard* have imaginative and convoluted fun with their sources—and celebrate minor characters. *Meg and Mog Show* successfully transfers contemporary story characters from the shared texts for today's children and skilfully uses a treasure hunt to get the ingredients for a spell and involve the audience.

The original plays are vital and unflagging. Wood responds to children's love of stock literary characters, but his inventions are always well-rounded: the pompous; the brainy but scatterbrained; the well-intentioned but muddled; good-natured dragons. His villains are particularly effective, especially Krafty Kingfisher in *Flibberty and the Penguin* and Dr. Spickenspan in *Hijack over Hygenia*.

They are usually overcome by endeavour and action which incorporates the audience. The "Big Ones" are the enemies in *The Gingerbread Man* and *The Plotters of Cabbage Patch Corner*, and, though there is no didactic pushing of the point, Wood's audiences always sympathise with the plight of little people at the beck and call of others. In *The Selfish Shellfish*, he touches on ecological themes in a way that still foregrounds the imaginative enterprise but gets even the youngest playgoer *thinking* about issues as well as enjoying the action. Even with relatively uninspiring material like *The Old Man of Lochnagar* he manages to create a world on the stage—and poke some fun at the high-minded bits. He is a superb creator of names that capitalise upon children's love of word play: Blotch and Carbon, Kernal Walnut, Herr Von Cuckoo. In his dialogue and songs, he exploits the fun to be had from the topsy-turvy and the illogical— *Old Father Time* has some gloriously funny time-shifting when Big Ben stops.

Two recent novels (*The Operats of Rodent Garden* and *The Discorats*) have a tangy, contemporary feel to them and transfer the vigour, pace, and style to narrative prose. In all his work, a child's view of the world is centre stage. Wood's audiences (and readers) enjoy themselves, but, whereas they are passive in much of their television watching, and, sadly, still unchallenged in much of their fiction reading, they are *engaged* in the songs and the action so that theatre can be seen as proper way of looking at and reflecting upon the world.

—Colin Mills

WOOD, Kerry. Pseudonym for Edgar Allardyce Wood. Canadian. Born in New York, New York, United States, 2 June 1907; moved to Canada, 1909; became citizen, 1973. Educated at Calgary Elementary School, 1914–18, and elementary and high schools, Red Deer, Alberta, 1918–24. Married Marjorie Marshall in 1936; two daughters and one son. Full-time freelance writer and broadcaster. Correspondent and columnist for newspapers including Edmonton *Bulletin*, Edmonton *Journal*, Calgary *Herald*, and Calgary *Albertan*, 1926–73. Made archery tackle, 1937–44. Member of the Board, Alberta Natural History Society, 1936–64. Since 1924 federal migratory bird officer. Recipient: Ewart Foundation grant, 1954, 1957; Governor-General's award, 1956, 1958; Canada Council grant, 1960; Vicky Metcalf award, 1963; Alberta Historical Society award, 1964. LL.D.: University of Alberta, Edmonton, 1969. Address: Site 3, Rural Route 2, Red Deer, Alberta T4N 5E2, Canada.

PUBLICATIONS FOR CHILDREN

Fiction

Cowboy Yarns for Young Folk, illustrated by Merle Smith. Toronto, Copp Clark, 1951.
Wild Winter, illustrated by Victor Mays. Boston, Houghton Mifflin, 1954.
Great Horned MacOwl. Red Deer, Alberta, Kerry Wood, 1962.
The Boy and the Buffalo, illustrated by Audrey Teather. Toronto and London, Macmillan, and New York, St. Martin's Press, 1963.
Mickey the Beaver and Other Stories, illustrated by Audrey Teather. Toronto, Macmillan, 1964.
Samson's Long Ride, illustrated by Audrey Teather. Toronto, Collins, 1968.

Other

The Map-Maker: The Story of David Thompson, illustrated by William Wheeler. Toronto, Macmillan, 1955.
The Great Chief: Maskepetoon, Warrior of the Crees, illustrated by John Hall. Toronto, Macmillan, 1957; New York, St. Martin's Press, and London, Macmillan, 1958.
The Queen's Cowboy: Colonel Macleod of the Mounties, illustrated by Joseph Rosenthal. Toronto and London, Macmillan, 1960.
Bessie, The Coo, illustrated by Marjorie Wood. Red Deer, Alberta, Kerry Wood, 1975.

PUBLICATIONS FOR ADULTS

Other

Robbing the Roost: The Marquis of Roostburg Rules Governing the Ancient and Dishonourable Sport. Red Deer, Alberta, Kerry Wood, 1938.
I'm a Gaggle Man, Myself. Red Deer, Alberta, Kerry Wood, 1940.
Three Mile Bend. Toronto, Ryerson Press, 1945.
Birds and Animals in the Rockies. Saskatoon, Larson, 1947.
A Nature Guide for Farmers. Saskatoon, Larson, 1947.
The Magpie Menace. Red Deer, Alberta, Kerry Wood, 1949.
The Sanctuary. Red Deer, Alberta, Kerry Wood, 1952.
A Letter from Red Deer. Red Deer, Alberta, Kerry Wood, 1954.
A Letter from Calgary. Red Deer, Alberta, Kerry Wood, 1954.
Willowdale. Toronto, McClelland and Stewart, and London, Barker, 1956.
A Lifetime of Service: George Moon. Red Deer, Alberta, Kerry Wood, 1966.
A Corner of Canada: A Personalized History of the Red Deer River Country. Red Deer, Alberta, Kerry Wood, 1966.
A Time for Fun. Red Deer, Alberta, Kerry Wood, 1967.
The Medicine Man. Red Deer, Alberta, Kerry Wood, 1968.
The Creek. Red Deer, Alberta, Kerry Wood, 1970.
Stephan Gudmundsson Stephansson 1853–1927: The Icelandic-Canadian Poet: A Tribute. Red Deer, Alberta, Kerry Wood, 1974.
Red Deer: A Love Story. Red Deer, Alberta, Kerry Wood, 1975.
A Legacy of Laughter. Edmonton, Lone Pine, 1986.

*

Manuscript Collection: University of Alberta, Edmonton.

Kerry Wood comments:

My love of nature developed in early childhood, and from its study came an interest in the Indians and their history. My scholarly father encouraged me to read widely and made sure that I understood what I read. From him, and the helpfulness of librarians, came my determination to write. I have always felt that writing for children is an important part of my work.

A children's book should be sincere and accurate: it should be a story of achievement, though sadness is also appropriate. It should have natural characters, some humour, be of interest to both children and adults, and reveal enduring values. Nonsense and fantasy share about one-third portion of importance in children's literature, but sarcasm and satire should never be used. Children's books should instruct, entertain, and inspire in varying degrees, according to the story.

* * *

Kerry Wood is the prototype of the Canadian regional writer. He has lived all of his life in Red Deer, Alberta, and writes of that province with insight and love. His children's books elaborate the lives of its people—Indians, explorers, early and modern settlers.

The flora and fauna are particular interests of this ardent conservationist.

Two of Wood's fictional biographies have won the Governor-General's Medal: *The Map-Maker: The Story of David Thompson* and *The Great Chief: Maskepetoon, Warrior of the Crees*. These and *The Queen's Cowboy: Colonel Macleod of the Mounties* add three colourful chapters to the Great Stories of Canada, a series of readable histories for 8–12-year-old children. Wood's appreciation of these heroes is a measure of his own human dimensions. They emerge as men of integrity, industry, and compassion. He writes straightforward chronological narratives that span the lifetime of each hero. They were people whose fate included the assumption of leadership, and Wood highlights their accomplishments dramatically. Maskepetoon's story is recorded in a lyrical style that recalls the best aspects of native life and lore, and serves children well.

Stories for very young readers ought to be works of creative literature as well as easy to read. Wood follows this principle in *The Boy and the Buffalo* and *Samson's Long Ride*, both written with immature sensibilities in mind. Both are based on real events that reveal young heroes in the making. O-Shees lived a year with a buffalo herd, adopted by two lactating mares left calfless, and survived to join his Cree family again. Ten-year-old Samson leaves mission school and travels 400 miles to find his beloved family in the Alberta mountains. Although simple in plot and style, the stories explore the human dilemma with understanding and respect for children's developing humanity. Many of Wood's 6000 short stories were written for children. Some of them were collected in *Mickey the Beaver* and *Cowboy Yarns for Young Folk*, short dramatic incidents written sympathetically and plainly.

The highlight of Wood's work for children is *Wild Winter*, a novel based on his own experiences. From the age of 16 he spent two winters alone in the Alberta wilds to prove his independence. He writes spare, moving prose about a young man's search for maturity. His stark experiences with the elements and the privations he suffered afford an example for young people finding their way.

—Irma McDonough Milnes

———

WOOD, Lorna. British. Born in Pex Hill, Lancashire, 16 June 1913. Educated privately, and at Convent of Notre Dame, Mount Pleasant, Liverpool; Manchester School of Music, 1931–38. Married Joseph Swire (divorced); one daughter and one son (deceased). Concert pianist, 1935–38; worked for BBC Monitoring Service, London, 1942–75: Head, Central African Unit, 1974. Address: c/o Dent and Sons, 91 Clapham High Street, London SW4 7TA, England.

PUBLICATIONS FOR CHILDREN

Fiction

The Smiling Rabbit and Other Stories, illustrated by Ernest Aris. London, Harrap, 1939.
The Travelling Tree and Other Stories, illustrated by Ernest Aris. London, Harrap, 1943.
Ameliaranne Goes Digging, illustrated by S.B. Pearse. London, Harrap, 1948.
The Finicky Mouse and Other Stories, illustrated by R.S. Sherwood. London, Arnold, 1949.
The Handkerchief Man, illustrated by C. Instrell. London, Arnold, 1951.

The People in the Garden, illustrated by Joan Kiddell-Monroe. London, Dent, 1954.
Rescue by Broomstick, illustrated by Joan Kiddell-Monroe. London, Dent, 1954.
The Hag Calls for Help, illustrated by Joan Kiddell-Monroe. London, Dent, 1957.
Holiday on Hot Bricks, illustrated by Sheila Rose. London, Dent, 1958.
Seven-League Ballet Shoes, illustrated by Joan Kiddell-Monroe. London, Dent, 1959.
Climb by Candlelight, illustrated by Sheila Rose. London, Dent, 1959.
Hags on Holiday, illustrated by Joan Kiddell-Monroe. London, Dent, 1960.
The Golden-Haired Family, illustrated by Wendy Marchant. London, Dent, 1961.
Hag in the Castle, illustrated by Joan Kiddell-Monroe. London, Dent, 1962.
Hags by Starlight, illustrated by Joan Kiddell-Monroe. London, Dent, 1970.
The Dogs of Pangers, illustrated by A.R. Whitear. London, Dent, 1970.
Pangers Pup, illustrated by A.R. Whitear. London, Dent, 1972.

Other

The Brave Adventures of a Shoemaker's Boy, from translation by Theresa Mravintz and Branko Brusar of work by Ivana Brlic-Mazuranic, illustrated by Robert Bartelt. London, Dent, 1971.

Editor, *Here I Was a Child* (anthology), illustrated by Rosemary Hird. London, Arnold, 4 vols., 1952.

PUBLICATIONS FOR ADULTS

Novels

The Crumb-Snatchers. London, Cape, 1933.
Gilded Sprays. London, Long, 1935.
The Hopeful Travellers. London, Long, 1936.

*   *   *

Lorna Wood's writing career began very early; she was still in her teens when her first book appeared, the adult novel called *The Crumb-Snatchers*, about a mother and daughter who live on their wits. This novel and the two that followed were romantic comedies, very amusing and well observed. Her heroines show a spirited attitude towards life's ups and downs.

Wood's first children's stories appeared just as World War II began. By this time she had two children herself. She loves writing and has never let domesticity or anything else stop her, but it was easier, of course, to write short tales than to concentrate on full-length novels. *The Smiling Rabbit and Other Stories* is a delightful collection, varied and rich in fantastical invention. The stories are well constructed, with a twist at the end. There were better outlets then for short stories (for whatever age); writers who grew up in the 1920's and 1930's had a highly professional respect for the genre.

The Hag Dowsabel, Wood's best-known creation, made her first appearance in this collection, giving a wish at a prince's christening. She also turned up in two of the stories in the next collection, *The Travelling Tree*, and it was here too that the Hag's long-suffering cat, Sootylegs, made his debut. Later, she wrote a series of 6 full-length children's books about the Hag, who now resided at the bottom of the Lindleys' garden. Cleverly the author creates what Tolkien called a Secondary World, a fantasy utterly consistent within itself. The Lindley parents never see the Hag or give their full attention, let alone credence, to the strange goings-on the four children get happily involved in with their eccentric friend. The Hag appeals to one's love of exaggeration and the grotesque. She is uninhibitedly self-centred but she will champion anyone who is put upon for grownup or other inadequate reasons. She has no use for money and doesn't approve of the children wanting the thousand pound reward offered by the *Daily Speed* (in *Hags by Starlight*) for finding the Alsotanian ambassador, but when the newspaper lord goes back on his offer she turns him into a bat. She does everything with panache.

The secondary characters are original and zestful too, the Hag's witch friends, for instance, and, in *Seven-League Ballet Shoes*, the boy giant Flounderbore. *The Hag Calls for Help* is particularly rich in colourful characters. There are the Boggarts, father and daughter, Rascallito the Rook, a sorry failure of an outlaw, Verdigris the Vulture who's a crook, and Uncle Harold the bird-watcher, shrunk by magic to the size of a small rook but untroubled as only as Englishman brought up on *Alice* could be.

During the same period as the Hag books Wood wrote four adventure stories. Then in 1970 came *The Dogs of Pangers*, followed by *Pangers Pup*. I think these two may prove to wear the best of all her stories. In creating these canine characters of the Pangers Dogs' Club she indulged her fondness for dogs and her marvellous sense of fun; A.R. Whitear, the illustrator, responded in the same spirit. The hero of *The Dogs of Pangers* is Bertram the Boxer, who "had definitely been behind the door when brains were given out." Mum and Pop Denholm-Stringfellow who are his family love him dearly; when they hear that the new occupant of the River House is a dog psychologist they decide to send Bertram to him to improve his IQ, though of course, as Mum says, "It will cost a bomb...." Recounting these words at the Club, Bertram causes a sensation. Pedro, the elderly spaniel president growled for order. "'Dogs of Pangers! The important thing is to find out why Mr.—Pegleg, did you say?—*wants* a bomb. To me it sounds as though he is up to no good. British dogs never shall be slaves and since you, Bertram, are going to stay with him, you will be in the best position to find out.'" And they're off.

Compton Mackenzie said of her first novel: "If she can keep her zest for writing fresh, and temper it with life's experience, Miss Lorna Wood is secure of a wide popularity." Despite having had a sometimes embarrassing share of "life's experience," her zest for writing is fresh indeed. She has certainly earned her popularity among bright young readers who revel in her rare brand of humour and invention.

—Gwen Marsh

WORTH, Valerie. American. Born in Philadelphia, Pennsylvania, 29 October 1933. Educated at Swarthmore College, Pennsylvania, 1951–55, B.A. in English 1955. Married George W. Bahlke in 1955; one son and two daughters. Secretary to the promotion manager, Yale University Press, New Haven, Connecticut, 1956–58. Recipient: Bread Loaf Writers Conference scholarship, 1965. Address: 19 Canterbury Drive, Clinton, New York 13323, U.S.A.

PUBLICATIONS FOR CHILDREN

Fiction

Curlicues: The Fortunes of Two Pug Dogs, illustrated by Natalie

Babbitt. New York, Farrar Straus, 1980; as *Imp and Biscuit*, London, Chatto and Windus, 1981.
Gypsy Gold. New York, Farrar Straus, 1983.
Fox Hill. New York, Farrar Straus, 1986.

Verse

Small Poems, illustrated by Natalie Babbitt. New York, Farrar Straus, 1972.
More Small Poems, illustrated by Natalie Babbitt. New York, Farrar Straus, 1976.
Still More Small Poems, illustrated by Natalie Babbitt. New York, Farrar Straus, 1978.
Small Poems Again, illustrated by Natalie Babbitt. New York, Farrar Straus, 1986.
All the Small Poems, illustrated by Natalie Babbitt. New York, Farrar Straus, 1987.

PUBLICATIONS FOR ADULTS

Verse

The Crone's Book of Words. Minneapolis, Llewellyn, 1971.
The Crone's Book of Wisdom. Minneapolis, Llewellyn, 1988.

*

Valerie Worth comments:

Although I began as a writer of poetry and fiction for adults, I later found that writing for children made the best use of my particular abilities and perceptions. Children's poetry, especially, has provided me with a way to embody the essential qualities of things in brief, simple lyrics, while still using many of the techniques of "adult" poetry. In doing so, I have tried to create poems that go beyond the mere light verses or humorous jingles so frequently offered to children; my feeling is that many children themselves perceive the world in an essentially poetic way, and my work has been an attempt to translate some of these poetic experiences into words—for my own pleasure, as well as others'.

* * *

There are few poets writing for children today whose metaphoric eye is keener than that of Valerie Worth. Her four books of verse, *Small Poems, More Small Poems, Still More Small Poems* and *Small Poems Again*, published between 1972 and 1986, are testament to the excellence which poetry for the young offers. Hers is the gift not only of heightened consciousness but of an ability to make comparisons between objects which immediately awaken readers to new perspectives. A closed safety pin "sleeps/On its side/Quietly,/The silver/Image/Of some/Small fish"; whereas "Opened, it snaps/Its tail out/Like a thin/Shrimp, and looks/At the sharp/Point with a/Surprised eye." What reader can ever again look at a safety pin as a mere utilitarian object?

While many others seek to entertain children with instant laughter, Worth invites children to observe the world about them, to value the commonplace articles that make up their everyday world, from clocks, hollyhocks, and chairs to creatures at the zoo. Like haiku, Worth's poems are written in the present tense, of one thing keenly observed, inviting readers to complete the picture. Unlike haiku, they are not limited by subject matter or syllable pattern. Each word is carefully chosen, arranged in rhythms which emphasize the power of onomatopoeia. She writes of "Hard leather heels,/Their blocks carved/Thick, like rocks,/Clacked down/Waxed wood stairs," and of the "pale,/Soles/Of sneakers."

Worth's treasures do not lie in some distant, golden land but in the everyday world. She shows us earthworms who "Glisten in the sun/As fresh/As new rubies/Dug out of/Deepest earth." Her "…round jewels,/Slithering gold" are marbles poured into their bag. A hose "Can rain/Chill diamond/Chains/Across the yard" or "…hang/A silk/Rainbow/Halo/Over soft/fog." In the garbage she finds "Hammered-gold/Orange rind,/Eggshell ivory./Garnet coffee/Grounds, pearl/Wand of bared/Chicken bone." Riches to her are "satin sea lions," the "sleek velvets" on the back of a mosquito and the lions' "plush-covered clay."

Eschewing singsong meter and incessant end-rhyme, Worth brilliantly employs other aspects of the poet's craft. Through personification she notes the "soft skull" and "frail ribs" of a mushroom, a lawnmower that "Grinds its teeth/Over the grass/Spitting out a thick/Green spray"; with a head "too full/Of iron and oil/To know/What it/Throws/Away." Telephone poles sweat "Black creosote," and coat hangers "Clash and cling/And fling them-/Selves to the/Floor in an/Inextricable tangle." She invites children, through simile and metaphor, to notice asparagus "Like a nest/Of snakes/Awakened, craning/Long-necked/Out of the/Ground to stand/With sharp/Scaly heads/Alert, tasting/The air,/Taking the sun,/Looking around." The frog's "gold-circles eyes/stare hard/Like bright metal rings." Porch chairs "Wait, arranged/Strange and polite" whereas field grass "Whistles, slides" and "Tangles itself/With leaves…"

Her rhythms mesh with subject. "This clock/Has stopped,/Some gear/Or spring/Gone wrong." Fireworks follow their accustomed ascent: "First/A far thud,/Then the rocket/Climbs the air,/A dull red flare,/To hang, a moment,/Invisible, before/Its shut black shell cracks…" Alliteratively, she observes the beetle's "lacquered/Coffer of/Curious/Compartments" or how "the slug/Slides sly." Rhyme is used judiciously, often internally or as slant rhyme. A masterful use of synesthesia occurs in "The harsh gold/Smell of lions." Worth's pragmatism is evident in several lyrical forays. She believes that a sparrow "is as good a bird/As anyone needs." A magnet, she writes, "is/Sold for a toy…" and "picks up pins" but "…later/It lies about/Getting its red/Paint chipped, being/Offered pins less/Often, until at/Last we leave it/Alone."

This pragmatism and a touch of quiet underlying humor is most evident in her fictional works *Gypsy Gold* and *Curlicues*. Here she employs a simple, yet elegant prose style. As storyteller she weaves into beautifully cadenced prose the same artful and judicious use of metaphor, simile, and personification that characterizes her poetry.

—Myra Cohn Livingston

WORTIS, Avi. See **AVI.**

WRIGHT, Kit. British. Born in Kent in 1944. Educated at Berkhamsted School, Hertfordshire; New College, Oxford. Teacher in a comprehensive school, London; Lecturer in English, Brock University, St. Catharines, Ontario, 3 years. Education secretary, Poetry Society, London, 1970–75; Fellow-Commoner in Creative Arts, Trinity College, Cambridge, 1977–79. Recipient (for poetry): Geoffrey Faber Memorial prize, 1978; Poetry Society Alice Hunt Bartlett prize, 1978; Arts Council bursary, 1985. Address: c/o Viking Kestrel, 27 Wrights Lane, London W8 5TZ, England.

PUBLICATIONS FOR CHILDREN

Verse

Arthur's Father [*Granny, Sister, Uncle*], illustrated by Eileen Browne. London, Methuen, 4 vols., 1978.
Rabbiting On and Other Poems, illustrated by Posy Simmonds. London, Fontana, 1978.
Hot Dog and Other Poems, illustrated by Posy Simmonds. London, Kestrel, 1981.
Professor Potts Meets the Animals of Africa, illustrated by Gillian Chapman. London, Watts, 1981.
Cat among the Pigeons, illustrated by Posy Simmonds. London, Viking Kestrel, 1987.

Other

Editor, *Soundings: A Selection of Poems for Speaking Aloud.* London, Heinemann, 1975.
Editor, *Poems for 9-Year-Olds and Under*, illustrated by Michael Foreman. London, Kestrel, 1984.
Editor, *Poems for Over 10-Year-Olds*, illustrated by Michael Foreman. London, Viking Kestrel, 1984.

PUBLICATIONS FOR ADULTS

Verse

Treble Poets 1, with Stephen Miller and Elizabeth Maslen. London, Chatto and Windus, 1974.
The Bear Looked over the Mountain. London, Salamander Imprint, 1977.
Bump-Starting the Hearse. London, Hutchinson, 1983.
From the Day Room. Liverpool, Windows Press, 1983.
Real Rags and Red. London, Hutchinson, 1988.
Poems 1974–1983. London, Hutchinson, 1988.

*   *   *

Kit Wright's poetry for children has an exuberance, a vitality, and a technical virtuosity that works equally well on the page or when read aloud. He is well known for his lively public readings to audiences of children and adults and there is an infectiously joyful quality about his attitude to his subject matter that is likely to serve as an inspiration to all aspiring writers, whether they be young or old. The manic exuberance reminds one at times of the work of Lewis Carroll—as if the desire to crack yet another joke in the poem, to add one more crowning pun to the puns that are already there, simply cannot be resisted. There is also a use of cumulative repetition that is somewhat reminiscent of his great predecessor. In what is probably his best collection of poems for children, *Hot Dog and Other Poems*, there is a poem entitled "Hugger Mugger" which beautifully captures the miseries of a little boy who is always being kissed against his will by his Auntie Jean. It has what amounts to a wonderful chant at its climax:

> For as things are
> I really would far,
>
> Far sooner be
> Jumped and thumped and dumped,
>
> I'd sooner be
> Slugged and mugged…than *hugged*…

And clobbered with a slobbering
Kiss by my Auntie

Jean*!*

Of course, the danger of revelling in word play to this extent might be an inability—or a reluctance—on the part of the poet to climb down from these heights of hilarity to deal with more sombre and serious matters—death, disfigurement, human tragedy of any kind. But there is sufficient evidence in this collection that Wright is perfectly capable of striking the right tone when dealing with such issues. And nowhere is this better illustrated than in a long narrative poem set in Liverpool station, "Useful Person." The plot is simple enough: a family—mum, dad, and child—has missed the train. There are two hours to wait, two hours of gloom and boredom—but the situation is miraculously transformed by the sudden appearance of a little Mongol girl who teaches the whole family a timely lesson in making the best of things. The poet achieves a finely tuned balance of sensitivity and humour—a most difficult thing to do. The refrain illustrates very well how the poet's tone has enabled him to steer well clear of mawkishness: "Mongol child,/Funny-faced,/Something in your body wrong,/Something in your mind/Misplaced,/Something in your eyes, strange:/What, or why, I cannot tell:/I thought you were beautiful:/Useful, as well." Another little poem in this collection, "Cathedral Gardens," is a simple yet moving evocation of a place at sunset, and the poem again contrasts sharply with the dominant hilarity of most of the rest of the book and, consequently, comes as a refreshing reminder of the range of this poet's talents: "In the Cathedral Gardens/Underneath the trees/In the chilly evening/The sun is on its knees,/Dying by the gravestones/While their shadows freeze/And the dead are walking/Underneath the trees."

—Michael Glover

WRIGHTSON, (Alice) Patricia (née Furlonger). Australian. Born in Lismore, New South Wales, 21 June 1921. Educated at State Correspondence School; St. Catherine's College, Stanthorpe, Queensland. Married in 1943 (divorced 1953); one daughter and one son. Secretary and administrator, Bonalbo District Hospital, 1946–60, and Sydney District Nursing Association, 1960–64; assistant editor, 1964–70, and editor, 1970–75, *School Magazine*, Sydney. Recipient: Australian Children's Book Council Book of the Year award, 1956, 1974, 1978, 1984; Boston *Globe-Horn Book* award, 1984; Young *Observer* prize, 1984; Dromkeen Children's Literature Foundation Medal, 1984; Golden Cat award (Sweden), 1986; Hans Christian Andersen Medal, 1986. O.B.E. (Officer, Order of the British Empire), 1978. Address: P.O. Box 91, Maclean, New South Wales 2463, Australia.

PUBLICATIONS FOR CHILDREN

Fiction

The Crooked Snake, illustrated by Margaret Horder. Sydney and London, Angus and Robertson, 1955.
The Bunyip Hole, illustrated by Margaret Horder. Sydney and London, Angus and Robertson, 1958.
The Rocks of Honey, illustrated by Margaret Horder. Sydney, Angus and Robertson, 1960; London, Angus and Robertson, 1961.
The Feather Star, illustrated by Noela Young. London, Hutchinson, 1962; New York, Harcourt Brace, 1963.

Down to Earth, illustrated by Margaret Horder. New York, Harcourt Brace, and London, Hutchinson, 1965.
I Own the Racecourse!, illustrated by Margaret Horder. London, Hutchinson, 1968; as *A Racecourse for Andy*, New York, Harcourt Brace, 1968.
An Older Kind of Magic, illustrated by Noela Young. London, Hutchinson, and New York, Harcourt Brace, 1972.
The Nargun and the Stars. London, Hutchinson, 1973; New York, Atheneum, 1974.
Night Outside, illustrated by Beth Peck. Melbourne, Rigby, 1979; New York, Atheneum, 1985.
The Song of Wirrun. Richmond, Victoria, Century Hutchinson, 1987.
   The Ice Is Coming. Richmond, Victoria, and London, Hutchinson, and New York, Atheneum, 1977.
   The Dark Bright Water. Richmond, Victoria, and London, Hutchinson, and New York, Atheneum, 1979.
   Behind the Wind. Richmond, Victoria, and London, Hutchinson, 1981; as *Journey Behind the Wind*, New York, Atheneum, 1981.
A Little Fear. Richmond, Victoria, and London, Hutchinson, and New York, McElderry, 1983.
Moon-Dark, illustrated by Noela Young. Richmond, Victoria, Hutchinson, 1987; New York, McElderry, 1988.
Balyet. Richmond, Victoria, and London, Hutchinson, and New York, McElderry, 1989.

Other

The Haunted Rivers. Maclean, New South Wales, Eighth State Press, 1983.

Editor, *Beneath the Sun: An Australian Collection for Children*. Sydney, Collins, 1972; London, Collins, 1973.
Editor, *Emu Stew: An Illustrated Collection of Stories and Poems for Children*. Melbourne and London, Kestrel, 1976.

*

Patricia Wrightson comments:
My books represent a continuous process of learning to write, but I think critical essays have been right in discerning that the books have developed towards exploring the "other" point of view; and that this has inevitably led, as my son affirms, to fantasy as the prime medium for the exploration. I have at present two preoccupations: this richness of fantasy as a means; and the use of Aboriginal folk-spirits (fairies and monsters) to enrich Australia's contemporary fantasy.

*   *   *

Like poetry, Patricia Wrightson's books can be read at different levels. Like a poet she uses symbols—an axe, a featherstar, a racecourse, or a comet—as keys to the inner question. While on one level she is telling a lively story with humour about a group of children in some interesting situation, at a deeper level she is exploring the relationship of our world in the cosmos. "He felt the earth rolling its way through the sky and rocks and trees clinging to it, and seas and the strands of rivers pressed to it, and flying birds caught in its net of air." She looks at the different time levels of Australia, the old land now violated by machinery, whose rhythms are not its own, at the old legendary creatures, the aboriginal tribes, and the final imposition of a new alien culture whose "false city magic" hides the light of the stars.

Concern for the land naturally leads to a strong feeling for conservation, and she examines the whole question of ownership of land. Citybred Simon in *The Nargun and the Stars* is outraged by Charlie

Waters's message to the Potkoorok, a water creature: "'Say Charlie Waters sent me. He used to be a boy in this place but now he's the man in charge. He wants to talk to you.' 'But you're not the man in charge! You OWN it!' 'Do I? For sixty years or so maybe, but how long do you think the Potkoorok's owned it?'"

Ownership is discussed in *The Rocks of Honey*, but it is central to *I Own the Racecourse!*, one of the most original stories ever written. Andy, a simple-minded boy, never understands the pretend game Monopoly played by his friends who "buy" and "sell" Sydney landmarks, so when an old tramp offers to "sell" him Beecham Park Racecourse he "buys" it for $3. His friends are divided between those who feel that Andy must be made to see that he does not "own" the racecourse and those who prefer to leave him with his illusions—after all, "you can own the horses, but you can't own the race." Andy, who cares as much for weeds and mongrels as for flowers and thoroughbreds, causes everyone to rethink their values not only about ownership but about reality. "'Real?' said Mike. 'What's real? The trainers speak to him in the street and let him lead their dogs and call him "The Owner." That's real isn't it?'"

The question of what is "real" is also explored in *Down to Earth* in which Martin, a spaceman visiting Sydney, explains that there can be no certainty about what we see: "When I'm awake you see me in your usual way, as I've explained, because your mind responds to the stimulus of another intelligence and makes the only sort of picture it can." Similarly we cannot be sure about what we hear: "There is the problem of communication. How can you and I speak to each other about anything that lies outside our own minds? We borrow from each other the words that we use, but what do the words mean?"

The great value of *Down to Earth* is that it gives us a fresh humorous look at ourselves, but both here and in *I Own the Racecourse!* Wrightson brings Sydney vividly to life. Her children love the changing moods of the city, the lure of evening lights, the jostling crowds that can contain both the ordinary and eccentric, and the quiet early morning streets. This joyful celebration of the city palls somewhat in *An Older Kind of Magic*. Here it is "the lovely but terrible city" in which commerce gets out of hand when business tycoon Sir Mortimer Wyvern tries to build a car park in the Botanical Gardens. Yet even as its values are questioned, Selina the heroine is still fascinated by its magic. It is, however, a false magic of self-interested advertising agents contrasted with the old magic of a comet which appears only once every thousand years.

An Older Kind of Magic and *The Nargun and the Stars* explore the possibilities of indigenous fantasy and reject European folklore in favour of legendary aboriginal creatures of water, rock, and tree. They are very different from Northern "little people" in their neutrality: they do not side with Good or Evil—"'Good,' asked the Potkooruk, "'What is good?'"—nor do they manipulate natural laws; they can only work within them. The Nargun, for instance, is both villain and hero. The slow progress of this strange stone creature to Wongadilla is set against the sudden displacement of Simon, who went there to live with cousins when his parents were killed. Simon, however, is accepted by the old creatures of Wongadilla, but the Nargun remains a hostile stranger. Yet although Simon is instrumental in incarcerating it under the mountain, he feels pity for the Nargun. In the end, on a cosmic scale, the Nargun will win. A stone can wait "for a mountain to crumble or a river to break through," while Simon, for all his youth and vitality, will be like his name carved in fading lichen, "only a whisper in the dark."

The transitory nature of life is a major theme in the remarkable trilogy which begins with *The Ice Is Coming* when Wirrun, the young aboriginal hero, realizes that by changing his beloved Yunggamurra—a water sprite—into a human girl, he has given her ageing and death. Wirrun is initially displaced. Although one of the People (aborigines) he is working in a city of the Happy Folk, who buy and sell Happiness. He uses their facilities of transport and communication but essentially he is of the land, caring for it, sensitive to its

messages, and thus able to see the creatures of rock, water, and earth. Perhaps, too, because he himself is out of place, he is quick to see that things must keep to their own laws and boundaries, and the three books describe how he restores first Ice, then Water, and finally Death itself to their rightful territory. He does so at great cost to himself, however, particularly in his love affair with the bewitching Yunggamurra, but ultimately he achieves the status first of Hero and then of Immortal.

These powerful and poignant novels, more suited to older readers, uniquely evoke Australia, its landscape and its peoples, whom Wirrun divides into four categories, the Happy Folk, the Inlanders, the People, and the Land Creatures. All have their own distinctive patterns of speech and thought; all find it difficult to understand the other. The restless acquisitive Happy Folk are as foreign to the canny white Inlander as they are to the quiet brooding People, who communicate with one another as much through their long silences as through their brief enigmatic sentences. The Land Creatures are stripped of all but the bare essentials of language, their verbs lack tenses, for them all time is present.

In the end it is Time which will defeat old Mrs. Tucker, heroine of *A Little Fear*. When she runs away from an old people's home to live in an outback cottage she has inherited, she little realizes that an even older inhabitant is there, an Old Thing of the Earth, a Njimbin. The Njimbin resents her coming and summons all its powers over rats, frogs, ants, and midges to make her life as uncomfortable as possible and drive her out. It underestimates Mrs. Tucker, who is made of very stern stuff indeed, and the book becomes a contest of wills between the two of them, with Mrs. Tucker's unforgettable dog Hector a bewildered onlooker. Mrs. Tucker's wry humour and robust determination not to be beaten embody the Settler spirit, but ultimately the cunning Njimbin wins a partial victory, for he is of the Land and Time is on his side, as it was on the Nargun's and will always be in a vast ancient continent which tolerates human habitation, but only for a limited period and only on its own terms.

—Betty Gilderdale

WYMARK, Olwen (Margaret, née Buck). American. Born in Oakland, California, 14 February 1932. Educated at Pomona College, Claremont, California, 1949–51; University College, London, 1951–52. Married the actor Patrick Wymark in 1950 (died 1970); two daughters and two sons. Writer-in-residence, Unicorn Theatre for Young People, London, 1974–75, and Kingston Polytechnic, Surrey, 1977; script consultant, Tricycle Theatre, London; Lecturer in Playwriting, New York University. Member, Arts Council of Great Britain Drama Panel, 1980–84. Recipient: Zagreb Drama Festival prize, 1967. Lives in London. Agent: Harvey Unna and Stephen Durbridge Ltd., 24–32 Pottery Lane, London W11 4LZ, England.

PUBLICATIONS FOR CHILDREN

Plays

No Talking (produced London, 1970).
Daniel's Epic, with Daniel Henry (produced London, 1972).
Chinigchinich (produced London, 1973).
The Bolting Sisters (produced London, 1974).
Southwark Originals (collaborative work; produced London, 1975).
Starters (collaborative work; includes *The Giant and the Dancing Fairies, The Time Loop, The Spellbound Jellybaby, The Robbing of Elvis Parsley, I Spy*) (produced London, 1975; Wausau, Wis-

consin, 1976).

Three For All (collaborative work; includes *Box Play, Family Business, Extended Play*) (produced London, 1976).

The Winners, and Missing Persons (produced London, 1978).

PUBLICATIONS FOR ADULTS

Plays

Lunchtime Concert (produced Glasgow, 1966). Included in *Three Plays*, 1967; in *The Best Short Plays 1975*, edited by Stanley Richards, Radnor, Pennsylvania, Chilton, 1975.

Three Plays (as *Triple Image: Coda, Lunchtime Concert, The Inhabitants*, produced Glasgow, 1967; *The Inhabitants*, produced London, 1974). London, Calder and Boyars, 1967.

The Gymnasium (produced Edinburgh, 1967; London, 1971). Included in *The Gymnasium and Other Plays*, 1971.

The Technicians (produced Leicester, 1969; London, 1971). Included in *The Gymnasium and Other Plays*, 1971.

Stay Where You Are (produced Edinburgh, 1969; London, 1973). Included in *The Gymnasium and Other Plays*, 1971; in *The Best Short Plays 1972*, edited by Stanley Richards, Philadelphia, Chilton, 1972.

Neither Here nor There (produced London, 1971). Included in *The Gymnasium and Other Plays*, 1971.

Speak Now (produced Edinburgh, 1971; revised version produced Leicester, 1975).

The Committee (produced London, 1971). Included in *Best Friends, The Committee, The Twenty-Second Day*, 1984.

The Gymnasium and Other Plays. London, Calder and Boyars, 1971.

Jack the Giant Killer (produced Sheffield, 1972). Included in *The Gymnasium and Other Plays*, 1971.

Tales from Whitechapel (produced London, 1972).

Watch the Woman, with Brian Phelan (produced London, 1973).

The Twenty-Second Day (broadcast 1975; produced London, 1975). Included in *Best Friends, The Committee, The Twenty-Second Day*, 1984.

We Three, and After Nature, Art (produced London, 1977). Published in *Play Ten*, edited by Robin Rook, London, Arnold, 1977.

Find Me (produced Richmond, Surrey, 1977; Louisville, 1979). London, French, 1980.

Loved (produced London, 1978; Syracuse, New York, 1979). London, French, 1980.

The Child (broadcast 1979). London, BBC Publications, 1979.

Please Shine Down on Me (produced London, 1980).

Female Parts: One Woman Plays (includes *Waking Up, A Woman Alone, The Same Old Story, Medea*), adaptations of plays by Dario Fo and Franca Rame, translated by Margaret Kunzle and Stuart Hood (produced London, 1981). London, Pluto Press, 1981.

Best Friends (produced Richmond, Surrey, 1981). Included in *Best Friends, The Committee, The Twenty-Second Day*, 1984.

Buried Treasure (produced London, 1983).

Best Friends, The Committee, The Twenty-Second Day. London, Calder, and New York, Riverrun Press, 1984.

Lessons and Lovers: D.H. Lawrence in New Mexico (produced York, 1985). London, French, 1986.

Nana, adaptation of the novel by Zola (produced London, 1987).

Strike Up the Banns (produced Mold, Clwyd, 1988).

Radio Plays: *The Ransom*, 1957; *The Unexpected Country*, 1957; *California Here We Come*, 1958; *The Twenty-Second Day*, 1975; *You Come Too*, 1977; *The Child*, 1979; *Vivien the Blockbuster*, 1980; *Mothering Sunday*, 1980; *Sea Changes*, 1984; *A Wreath of Roses*, from the novel by Elizabeth Taylor, 1985; *Mothers and Shadows*, from a novel by Marta Traba, 1987.

Television Plays: *Mrs. Moresby's Scrapbook*, 1973, *Vermin*, 1974, *Marathon*, 1975, *Mother Love*, 1975, *Dead Drunk*, 1975, and *Her Father's Daughter*, 1984 (all in *Crown Court* series); *Oceans Apart*, 1984; *Not That Kind of People*, 1984.

*

Olwen Wymark comments:

In 1966 I was commissioned by the late Caryl Jenner, founder of the Unicorn Theatre, to write my first children's play *No Talking*. I'd had no experience of plays specially written for children and had no idea if you did it differently; I think you don't. Under the tireless protective encouragement from script editor and playwright/actor Christopher Guinnee I managed to finish this play in about 11 months. *Chinigchinich* I wrote in a day to enter in a contest with *No Talking* (both one-acters) which I didn't win. In 1974 Chattie Salaman and Frank Whitton of the Common Stock Company asked me to work with them and a horde of kids (aged 2 to 15) in Whitechapel on a kid's play which was to be evolved in collaboration. It was absolute agony and the most exciting time I'd had in the theatre for years. The result was *Daniel's Epic*, an hour-long piece. My collaborator was a 9-year-old genius called Daniel Henry.

In 1974 and 1975 at the Unicorn Theatre I had another go at collaborating with children in playwriting. The first time was with 104 kids from four Southwark schools. Each class wrote a play with me which they performed themselves with me doing what might have been called directing but was more like sustained frenzy. We called the show *Southwark Originals* and we all had a very good time. Though tiring. The 1975 project was *Starters* in which I collaborated with eight kids between six and nine on five plays which were then performed at the Unicorn by professional actors and in 1976 in Wisconsin by children. In 1976 I worked with actress Janet Henfrey and directors Lucy Parker and Greville Hallam with a kids workshop that was run by the Sidney Webb Teacher Training College in London and with this group of 40 kids we wrote together *Three For All* (which was performed by children). In 1978 I wrote a very black comedy about a holiday camp for the Old Vic Youth Theatre, again with Lucy Parker as director, and this was the last play I've written specifically for children though I hope I may write more in the future.

* * *

In the recent and rapid development of theatre for children, Olwen Wymark's *No Talking* is an important landmark. Written at a time when plays for under-12's inclined to be, at best, well-dramatised fairytales, at worst, a kind of kiddy-kit, Petrushka with words, Wymark's script made a tremendous impact. The play gave children a taut exploration of the appalling consequences to its hero of his somewhat flippant resolve to stop talking in protest against the triteness of other people's conversation. It did so in a frame of reference within the child's often conservative expectation of its own culture. There are witch-like ladies, clowns, changelings, spies, and so on, but, contrary to expectation, these characters happened to run electrical supply shops, land up in concentration camps, get shot, go blind, and fall in love, not prettily either but with a great deal of effort, pain, and joy. At the time, this theme, and its treatment, were revolutionary, and perhaps Wymark was applauded too much for daring and innovation and not enough for her craftsmanship and the kind of grip this gaudy, poetic, and shamelessly theatrical play has on young audiences. Similarly, its partner play, *Chinigchinich*, uses a familiar context—this time a Red Indian tribe—to examine the nature of authority but likewise makes a few illuminating departures from the audience preconception on "injun" behaviour which light-heartedly invites them to apply a little scepticism in their own dealings with power and those who administer it.

Her first two plays were written at the request of Unicorn Theatre for Young People; her next, a collaboration with a small West Indian called Daniel, came about through her work with Common Stock. They produced *Daniel's Epic* after Wymark had done what she modestly calls an editing job, on the astonishing, cast-of-thousands fantasy he recorded at the company's workshop. This led to another collaboration with one hundred 9-year-old Southwark school children who performed their *Southwark Originals* at the Unicorn, under Wymark's direction. The plays proved an extraordinary mixture of adventure and surrealism and gave the bemused audience of parents and educationalists the heartening bonus of a totally un-selfconscious culture cross. This occurred in a play that combined a London dockside family with Anansi, the West Indian folk hero. Further collaboration with children resulted in *Starters*, a five-play programme intended for performance by adult actors although they are equally suitable for children to act.

Written after much of her work with child authors, *The Bolting Sisters* shows a tendency in Wymark to dismiss her own maturity as playwright for kids, and to write for young audiences with the belief that a child is only capable of responding to that which it could express or articulate itself. If this were true, art would long since have festered to death at toddler level. However, it is a common error and Wymark makes it rarely. Certainly she remains one of the richest talents working for children's theatre.

—Ursula M. Jones

WYNNE, May. Pseudonym for Mabel Winifred Knowles; also wrote as Lester Lurgan. British. Born in Streatham, London, in January 1875. Educated at home. Worked in an East End Church of England mission.

PUBLICATIONS FOR CHILDREN

Fiction

Mollie's Adventures. London, Russell, 1903.
Jimmy: The Tales of a Little Black Bear, illustrated by George Soper. London, Partridge, 1910.
Phil's Cousins, illustrated by Paul Hardy. London, Blackie, 1911.
Crackers: The Tale of a Mischievous Monkey. London, Partridge, 1911.
The Story of Heather. London, Nelson, 1912; New York, Sully, 1913.
Tony's Chums, illustrated by A.A. Dixon. London, Blackie, 1914.
Murray Finds a Chum. London, Stanley Paul, 1914.
When Auntie Lil Took Charge, illustrated by A.A. Dixon. London, Blackie, 1915.
An English Girl in Serbia. London, Collins, 1916.
Three's Company. London, Blackie, 1917.
Stranded in Belgium. London, Blackie, 1918.
A Cousin from Canada. London, Blackie, 1918.
The Honour of the School. London, Nisbet, 1918.
Dick. London, Religious Tract Society, 1919.
Phyllis in France, illustrated by Frank Gillett. London, Blackie, 1919.
The Little Girl Beautiful, illustrated by Gordon Browne. London, Religious Tract Society, 1919.

Nan and Ken. London, Nelson, 1919.
Nipper & Co. London, Stanley Paul, 1919.
Scouts for Serbia, illustrated by Archibald Webb. London, Nelson, 1919.
Comrades from Canada, illustrated by John Campbell. London, Blackie, 1919.
The Adventures of Dolly Dingle: A Fairy Story, illustrated by Florence Anderson. London, Jarrolds, 1920.
Adventures of Two, illustrated by Henry Coller. London, Blackie, 1920.
The Heroine of Chelton School. London, Stanley Paul, 1920.
The Girls of Beechcroft School, illustrated by C.E. Rhodes. London, Religious Tract Society, 1920.
Roseleen at School. London, Cassell, 1920.
Three Bears and Gwen, illustrated by John Campbell. London, Blackie, 1920.
Little Ladyship, illustrated by Gordon Browne. London, Religious Tract Society, 1921.
Lost in the Jungle. London, Stanley Paul, 1921.
Mervyn, Jock, or Joe, illustrated by Thomas Somerfield. London, Blackie, 1921.
Peggy's First Term. London, Ward Lock, 1922.
Angela Goes to School. London, Jarrolds, 1922; Cleveland, World, 1929.
The Girls of the Veldt Farm, illustrated by A.J. Shackel. London, Pearson, 1922.
The Red Boy's Gratitude. Exeter, Wheaton, 1922.
Christmas at Holford, illustrated by Thomas Somerfield. London, Blackie, 1922.
Two Girls in the Wild. London, Blackie, 1923; abridged edition, as *Sisters Out West,* 1930.
The Best of Chums. London, Ward Lock, 1923.
A Heather Holiday, illustrated by Thomas Somerfield. London, Blackie, 1923; as *Wendy's Adventure in Scotland,* 1933; *An Adventurous Holiday* (reader), 1933.
Blundering Bettina. London, Religious Tract Society, 1924.
The Girl Who Played the Game. London, Ward Lock, 1924.
Bertie, Bobby, and Belle, illustrated by Norman Sutcliffe. London, Blackie, 1924.
The Girls of Clanways Farm, illustrated by Archibald Webb. London, Cassell, 1924.
Kits at Clynton Court School. London, Warne, 1924.
The Sunshine Children. London, Nelson, 1924.
Three and One Over, illustrated by E.P. Kinsella. London, Cassell, 1924.
A Rebel at School. London, Jarrolds, 1924.
Two and a Chum, illustrated by D.C. Eyles. London, Pearson, 1924.
Hootie Toots of Hollow Tree. Philadelphia, Altemus, 1925.
The Girls of Old Grange School. London, Ward Lock, 1925.
Over the Hills and Far Away, illustrated by G.W. Goss. London, Religious Tract Society, 1925.
Dare-All Jack and the Cousins, illustrated by G.W. Goss. London, Religious Tract Society, 1925.
Hazel Asks Why. London, Ward Lock, 1926.
Carol of Hollydene School. London, Sampson Low, 1926.
The Secret of Carrock School. London, Jarrolds, 1926.
Diccon the Impossible. London, Religious Tract Society, 1926.
The Girl over the Wall, illustrated by G.W. Goss. London, Religious Tract Society, 1926.
Jean Plays Her Part, illustrated by Louise Parker. London, Religious Tract Society, 1926.
Dinah's Secret, illustrated by M.L. Parker. London, Religious Tract Society, 1927.
Jean of the Lumber Camp. London, Ward Lock, 1927.
Robin Hood to the Rescue. Exeter, Wheaton, 1927.

CHILDREN'S WRITERS

Terry the Black Sheep, illustrated by R.B. Ogle.   London, Pearson, 1928.
The Girls of Mackland Court.   London, Ward Lock, 1928.
Little Sally Mandy's Christmas Present, illustrated by Bess Goe Willis.   Philadelphia, Altemus, 1929.
The House of Whispers.   London, Ward Lock, 1929.
The Guide's Honour.   London, Warne, 1929.
A Term to Remember.   London, Aldine, 1930.
Two Girls in the Hawk's Den, illustrated by R.B. Ogle.   London, Pearson, 1930.
Bobbety the Brownie.   London, Warne, 1930.
The Masked Rider, illustrated by Peggy Beck.   Chicago, Laidlaw, 1931.
Patient Pat Joins the Circus, illustrated by Bess Goe Willis.   Philadelphia, Altemus, 1931.
Peter Rabbit and the Big Black Crows, illustrated by Bess Goe Willis.   Philadelphia, Altemus, 1931.
Juliet of the Mill.   London, Ward Lock, 1931.
Girls of the Pansy Patrol.   London, Aldine, 1931.
Patsy from the Wilds.   London, Warne, 1931.
Belle and Her Dragons.   London, Jarrolds, 1931.
The Secret of Marigold Marnell.   London, Religious Tract Society, 1931.
The Old Brigade.   London, Religious Tract Society, 1932.
Who Was Wendy?   London, Newnes, 1932.
The Heart of Glenayrt.   London, Nelson, 1932.
The School Mystery.   London, Readers' Library, 1933.
The Camping of the Marigolds.   London, Marshall Morgan and Scott, 1933.
The Greater Covenant.   London, Marshall Morgan and Scott, 1933.
Pixie's Mysterious Mission.   London, Newnes, 1933.
Enter Jenny Wren.   London, Ward Lock, 1933.
Comrades to Robin Hood.   London, Religious Tract Society, 1934.
Malys Rockell.   London, Ward Lock, 1934.
The Smugglers of Penreen.   London, Religious Tract Society, 1934.
The Mysterious Island.   London, Mellifont Press, 1935.
Their Girl Chum.   London, Religious Tract Society, 1935.
Under Cap'n Drake.   London, Religious Tract Society, 1935.
Up to Val.   London, Newnes, 1935.
"Peter," The New Girl.   London, Queensway Press, 1936.
The Daring of Star.   London, Religious Tract Society, 1936.
Bunny and the Aunt.   London, Religious Tract Society, 1936.
The Haunted Ranch.   London, Dean, 1936.
Thirteen for Luck.   London, Ward Lock, 1936.
Vivette on Trial.   London, Queensway Press, 1936.
The Secret of Brick House.   London, Ward Lock, 1937.
Two Maids of Rosemarkie.   London, Epworth Press, 1937.
The Luck of Penrayne.   London, Religious Tract Society, 1937.
Audrey on Approval.   London, Ward Lock, 1937.
The Girl Sandy.   London, Ward Lock, 1938.
The Lend-a-Hand Holiday.   London, Epworth Press, 1938.
Heather the Second.   London, Nelson, 1938.
The Term of Many Adventures.   London, Nelson, 1939.
The Unexpected Adventure.   London, Ward Lock, 1939.
The Coming of Verity.   London, Ward Lock, 1940.
Sadie Comes to School.   London, Epworth Press, 1942; as *Sally Comes to School*, London, Ward Lock, 1949.
Little Brown Tala.   London, Mellifont Press, 1944.
Brown Tala Finds Little Tulsi.   London, Mellifont Press, 1945.
Little Brown Tala Stories, illustrated by Stanley Jackson.   London, Harrap, 1947.
Patch the Piebald.   Croydon, Surrey, Blue Book, 1947.
Playing the Game.   Croydon, Surrey, Blue Book, 1947.
Snow Fairies.   London, Mellifont Press, 1947.
Ginger Ellen, illustrated by Doreen Debenham.   London, Nelson, 1947.

The Great Adventure.   London, Ward Lock, 1948.
The Furry Fairies.   London, Mellifont Press, 1949.
Merion Plays the Game.   London, Readers' Library, 1951.
Secrets of the Rockies.   London, Ward Lock, 1954.

Other

Life's Object; or, Some Thoughts for Young Girls.   London, Nisbet, 1899.
The Seven Champions of Christendom: A Legendary Chronicle, illustrated by Charles Folkard.   London, Jarrolds, 1919.

Novels

For Faith and Navarre.   London, Long, 1904.
Ronald Lindsay.   London, Long, 1904.
A King's Tragedy.   London, Digby Long, 1905.
The Temptation of Philip Carr.   London, Sonnenschein, 1905.
Maid of Brittany.   London, Greening, 1906.
The Goal.   London, Digby Long, 1907.
When Terror Ruled.   London, Greening, 1907.
Henry of Navarre: A Romance of August, 1572 (as Mabel W. Knowles).   New York, Putnam, 1908; as May Wynne, London, Greening, 1909.
Let Erin Remember.   London, Greening, 1908.
The Tailor of Vitré.   London, Gay and Hancock, 1908.
For Church and Chieftain.   London, Mills and Boon, 1909.
For Charles the Rover.   London, Greening, 1909; New York, Fenno, 1910.
The Gipsy Count.   New York, McBride, 1909.
A Blot on the Scutcheon.   London, Mills and Boon, 1910; New York, Fenno, 1912.
A King's Masquerade.   London, Greening, 1910.
Mistress Cynthia.   London, Greening, 1910.
The Gallant Graham.   London, Greening, 1911.
Honour's Fetters.   London, Stanley Paul, 1911.
The Master Wit.   London, Greening, 1911.
The Claim That Won.   London, Everett, 1912.
Hey for Cavaliers!   London, Greening, 1912.
The Red Fleur-de-Lys.   London, Stanley Paul, 1912.
The Brave Brigands.   London, Stanley Paul, 1913.
The Destiny of Claude.   London, Stanley Paul, 1913.
The Secret of the Zenana.   London, Greening, 1913.
A Run for His Money.   London, Aldine, 1913.
The Curse of Gold.   London, Aldine, 1914.
Goring's Girl.   London, Mascot, 1914.
The Hero of Urbino.   London, Stanley Paul, 1914.
The Silent Captain.   London, Stanley Paul, 1914.
The Regent's Gift.   London, Chapman and Hall, 1915.
Foes of Freedom.   London, Chapman and Hall, 1916.
Marcel of the "Zephyrs."   London, Jarrolds, 1916.
The Gipsy King.   London, Chapman and Hall, 1917.
The Lyons Mail.   London, Jarrolds, 1917.
Penance.   London, Mascot, 1917.
A Spy for Napoleon.   London, Jarrolds, 1917.
The Taint of Tragedy.   London, Mascot, 1917.
The "Veiled Lady," with Draycot M. Dell.   London, Jarrolds, 1918.
The King of a Day.   London, Jarrolds, 1918.
Queen Jennie.   London, Chapman and Hall, 1918.
The Red Whirlwind, with Draycot M. Dell.   London, Jarrolds, 1919.
Robin the Prodigal.   London, Jarrolds, 1919.
Love Finds a Way.   London, Greening, 1920.

A Prince of Intrigue: A Romance of Mazeppa.   London, Jarrolds, 1920.
A Gallant of Spain.   London, Stanley Paul, 1920.
Janie's Great Mistake.   London, Odhams Press, 1920.
The Spendthrift Duke.   London, Holden and Hardingham, 1920.
The Ambitions of Jill.   London, Long, 1920.
Mog Megone.   London, Jarrolds, 1921.
My Lady's Honour.   London, Lloyds, 1921.
The Red Rose of Lancaster.   London, Holden and Hardingham, 1921.
A Trap for Navarre.   London, Holden, 1922.
A King in the Lists.   London, Stanley Paul, 1922.
The Witch-Finder.   London, Jarrolds, 1923.
Jill the Hostage.   London, Pearson, 1925.
Rachel Lee.   London, Leng, 1925.
Theodore.   London, Rivers, 1926.
Gwennola.   London, Rivers, 1926.
The Fires of Youth.   London, Rivers, 1927.
Plotted in Darkness.   London, Stanley Paul, 1927.
King Mandrin's Challenge.   London, Stanley Paul, 1927.
A Royal Traitor.   London, Stanley Paul, 1927.
Love's Penalty.   London, Stanley Paul, 1927.
The Terror of the Moor.   London, Rivers, 1928.
Gipsy-Spelled.   London, Rivers, 1929.
Red Fruit.   London, Rivers, 1929.
Hamlet: A Romance from Shakespeare's Play.   London, Rivers, 1930.
The Girl Upstairs.   London, Thomson, 1932.
The Unseen Witness.   London, Leng, 1932.
Stella Maris.   London, Leng, 1932.
The Tempter's Power.   London, Leng, 1932.
Tangled Fates.   London, Mellifont Press, 1935.
Flower o' the Moor.   London, Houghton and Scott-Snell, 1935.
The Choice of Mavis.   London, Mellifont Press, 1935.
Temptation.   London, Mellifont Press, 1937.
Whither?   London, Heath Cranton, 1938.
Love Dismayed.   London, Mellifont Press, 1942.
Echoed from the Past.   London, Mellifont Press, 1944.
The Pursuing Shadow.   London, Mellifont Press, 1944.
The Unsuspected Witness.   London, Mellifont Press, 1945.
The Secret of the Caves.   London, Mellifont Press, 1945.

Novels as Lester Lurgan

Bohemian Blood.   London, Greening, 1910.
The Mill-Owner.   London, Greening, 1910.
The League of the Triangle.   London, Greening, 1911.
A Message from Mars.   London, Greening, 1912.
The Ban.   London, Stanley Paul, 1912.
The Wrestler on the Shore.   London, Everett, 1913.

Other

In the Shadows; or, Thoughts for Mourners.   London, Marshall, 1900.
Sympathy.   London, Skeffington, 1901.
The Life and Reign of Victoria the Good.   London, Stanley Paul, 1913.

*   *   *

May Wynne's output for children was prodigious, and her style altered noticeably after the first decade of the 20th century when the more extroverted girls' school story had largely supplanted the domestic tale. Her first stories were more appropriate in mood and setting for mid-Victorian readers. In *Life's Object; or, Some Thoughts for Young Girls* she reprovingly insists on the girl's place being firmly in the home, and deplores the influence of sport which she considers destructive of "the tender womanly woman"; in *Mollie's Adventures* some of her child characters are engaged in making matchboxes in a London basement, in conditions of employment that were grisly even for Edwardian times. She was then writing moral tales in which pace and characterization were sacrificed to narrative sermonizing and admonition. Yet soon afterwards, in a spate of lively stories, she was plunging her adolescent heroines into hectic adventures on school hockey-fields, and in Girl Guide camps in remote and surprisingly hazardous areas of the English countryside.

She carried into her stories for girls many of the elements which also proved successful in her adult romantic novels (kidnappings, strange encounters with gypsies, ancient houses, crumbling clock-towers, abundances of secret passages, and so on). In complete contrast to her turgid early stories, pace became all important in her books during the 1920's and 1930's. Many of her heroines went abroad, to get the better of Balkan brigands or jungle "savages." Her foreign adventures followed the tradition set by Bessie Marchant, in which no corner of the globe seemed too remote or dangerous to attract the British schoolgirl. And, also like Marchant, Wynne was especially partial to Canadian settings (*A Cousin from Canada, Comrades from Canada,* etc.).

In addition to her numerous full-length books, Wynne wrote short stories for periodicals like the *Girl's Own Paper* and *Little Folks,* and for several annuals.

—Mary Cadogan

————

WYNNE-JONES, Tim(othy). Canadian. Born in Bromborough, Cheshire, England, 12 August 1948. Educated at the University of Waterloo, Ontario, B.F.A. 1974; York University, Downsview, Ontario, M.A. in art 1978. Married Amanda West Lewis in 1980; two sons and one daughter. Book designer, PMA Books, Toronto, 1974–76; Instructor in Visual Arts, University of Waterloo, 1976–78, and York University, 1978–80; graphic designer, Solomon and Wynne-Jones, Toronto, 1976–79. Founding member and secretary, Crime Writers of Canada, Toronto, 1981–84; children's books critic, Toronto *Globe and Mail,* 1985–88. Recipient: Ruth Schwartz award, 1984; Actra award, for radio play, 1987. Agent: Lucinda Vardey Agency, 297 Seaton Street, Toronto, Ontario M5A 2T6, Canada.

PUBLICATIONS FOR CHILDREN

Fiction

Madelaine and Ermadello, illustrated by Lindsey Hallam.   Toronto, Before We Are Six, 1977.
Zoom at Sea, illustrated by Ken Nutt.   Vancouver, Douglas and McIntyre, 1983.
Zoom Away, illustrated by Ken Nutt.   Vancouver, Douglas and McIntyre, 1985.
I'll Make You Small, illustrated by Maryann Kovalski.   Vancouver, Douglas and McIntyre, 1986.
Architect of the Moon, illustrated by Ian Wallace.   Toronto, Groundwood, 1988; as *Builder of the Moon,* New York, McElderry, 1989.
The Hour of the Frog, illustrated by Katherine Oneal.   Toronto, Groundwood, 1989.

Verse

Mischief City, illustrated by Victor Gad. Toronto, Groundwood, 1986.

PUBLICATIONS FOR ADULTS

Novels

Odd's End. Toronto, McClelland and Stewart, Boston, Little Brown, and London, Deutsch, 1980.
The Knot. Toronto, McClelland and Stewart, 1982.
Fastyngange. Toronto, Lester and Orpen Dennys, 1988; London, Hodder and Stoughton, 1989.

Plays

Radio Plays: *The Thinking Room*, 1981; *The Road Ends at the Sea*, 1982; *The Strange Odyssey of Lennis Freed*, 1983; *The Testing of Stanley Teagarden*, 1985; *The Enormous Radio*, from the story by John Cheever, 1986; *St. Anthony's Man*, from his own story, 1987; *Mr. Gendelman Crashes a Party*, 1987; *Dust Is the Only Secret*, 1988.

*

Bibliography: by Dave Jenkinson, in *Emergency Librarian* (Vancouver), January–February 1988.

Tim Wynne-Jones comments:

While I work diligently on novel writing; submit outlines and stick to them; write radio plays; and whip songs off at the drop of a hat—picture book stories come to me unbidden, usually in early morning or dead of night. I cannot decide to write a picture book, only make myself ready. Each storybook seems to grow from two ideas which have occurred to me at quite different times, sometimes years apart, and which "marry" across the ethers. The actual writing down takes very little time, but then, like poetry, there is the worrying over every word and syllable, for the rhythm of the thing is its heartbeat.

I write for children out of the child I was and am. I cannot write for an audience—where children's books are concerned, I am the Selfish Giant, shooing my audience away in order to reclaim the garden for myself!

*   *   *

Tim Wynne-Jones, poet and author of picture books, works in the challenging tradition of the fantasy adventure. In an early book *Madeline and Ermadello* he shows his ability to recreate the imaginative play of young children but has not yet perfected the strong, plain, rhythmical style that graces his later books.

A pair of adventures featuring an intrepid cat, *Zoom at Sea* and *Zoom Away*, are his best-known stories. In the first Zoom sails the seas; in the second he treks to the north pole. The adventures have elements of the mythic journey in which the hero, armed with special knowledge and aided by supernatural characters, travels to dark, cold, and dangerous places to arrive home safe but changed. Cozy touches—hot tomato soup, overstuffed armchairs, and pingpong paddle snowshoes keep the journeys firmly tied to a childlike domestic world. Wynne-Jones is particularly adept at pacing. Quiet beginnings build to exuberant climaxes in which the characters dance for sheer joy and the whole winds up neatly.

Magical transformation is a recurring theme in Wynne-Jones's writing. In *Zoom at Sea* a room becomes the ocean. In *Zoom Away* summer changes in minutes to winter. In *I'll Make You Small* this theme takes on a darker edge. In a plot that is part folktale and part Victorian hanky-wringer a solitary, cranky, child-hating adult is softened and saved by the kindness of a small boy. Roland takes a pie next door to Mr. Swanskin, his ogre-like neighbour and discovers the old man's secret, that he is doomed to the Sisyphean task of fixing toys that break as soon as he repairs them. In a rage at being interrupted Swanskin shrinks Roland to the size of a toy and is about to dump him in the garbage when he notices the pie and the boy's kindness. The outcome, in which Roland offers to help Swanskin, seems bland and inconclusive in comparison to the mysterious drama that has preceded it.

Wynne-Jones returns to the fantasy journey and a learner plot in *Architect of the Moon*. Matter-of-fact hero David Finebloom responds to a message in which the moon says it is falling apart. Equipped with his toy blocks David rides his self-made spaceship to the disaster scene and makes the necessary repairs. He is back in time for breakfast. The words are spare and pared-down but the story is solid and well-shaped, following the natural rhythm of the moon's waxing and building to Wynne-Jones's characteristic explosion of enthusiasm at the story's centre, "Hurray for David Finebloom!"

The poems in the collection *Mischief City* are in the Shel Silverstein tradition of short jokey verses told from a child point of view lamenting the obtuseness of adults and celebrating the joys of messiness, anarchy, bubblegum, and monsters. Lively and technically accomplished, the best of them have a quietness at their heart: "Window come down wall./ Street lean against hill./ Sky hang out on washing line./ Sun sit on window sill."

—Sarah Ellis

———

YASHIMA, Taro. Pseudonym for Jun Atsushi Iwamatsu. American. Born in Kagoshima, Japan, 21 September 1908; emigrated to the United States, 1939. Educated at Provincial High School, Kagoshima; Imperial Art Academy, Tokyo, 1927–30; Art Students' League, New York, 1939–41. Served in the United States Army Office of War Information and Office of Strategic Services during World War II. Married to Tomoe Iwamatsu (pseudonym: Mitsu Yashima); one son and one daughter. Freelance artist, illustrator, and writer: several individual shows; collections include Phillips Memorial Museum, Washington, D.C. Director, Yashima Art Institute, Los Angeles, 1950's. Recipient: Huntington Hartford Foundation grant, 1954; Child Study Committee award, 1956; University of Southern Mississippi award, 1974. Address: c/o Viking Penguin Inc., 40 West 23rd Street, New York, New York 10010, U.S.A.

PUBLICATIONS FOR CHILDREN (illustrated by the author)

Fiction

The New Sun. New York, Holt, 1943.
Horizon Is Calling. New York, Holt, 1947.
The Village Tree. New York, Viking Press, 1953.
Plenty to Watch, with Mitsu Yashima. New York, Viking Press, 1954.
Crow Boy. New York, Viking Press, 1955; London, Penguin, 1976.
Umbrella. New York, Viking Press, 1958.
Momo's Kitten, with Mitsu Yashima. New York, Viking Press, 1961.
The Youngest One. New York, Viking Press, 1962.

Seashore Story. New York, Viking Press, 1967.

Other

Translator, *The Golden Footprints*, by Hatoju Muku. Cleveland, World, 1960.

*

Illustrator: *Which Was Witch* by Eleanore M. Jewett, 1953; *The Sugar Pear Tree* by Clyde Robert Bulla, 1961; *Soo Ling Finds a Way* by June Behrens, 1965.

*   *   *

The picture books of Taro Yashima, including two written with his wife Mitsu, draw children in to the Yashimas' world—to the Japan they knew as children and to their family life in this country with their daughter Momo. Readers now are quick to recognize the Taro Yashima pictures, which fill the pages with glowing crayon-like colors and textures, while figures and objects are rarely shown in clear detail. Instead, movement and rhythm and use of space suggestively convey story action and feeling. Because of this lack of specificity—which varies a little from book to book—some of the stories are less suitable than others for very young children, who generally need to see the details of a picture in order to understand it.

Plenty to Watch records in lively text and abundant pictures the fascinating sights children could see on their way home from the village school in Japan. It was *Crow Boy*, the next book, however, that really called the world's attention to the name Taro Yashima. This large, flat picture book, suitable for children in the lower elementary grades, tells the universal story of a schoolboy in Japan who was "different" and was called "stupid," but in the end was discovered to have a talent entirely his own. Readers identify both with the boy and with his tormentors, and ponder his elusive appeal. The suggestive pictures demand participation, and the story invites exploration of its layers of meaning.

In one of the three books about Momo, *The Youngest One*, she is a big girl finding ways to help a two-year-old neighbor boy overcome his shyness. But in *Umbrella* and *Momo's Kitten* she is a very little girl loving her first umbrella and her kitten. Yashima's large, bright, fairly detailed pictures in these two books have helped to make them great favorites. Also popular with young children is *The Village Tree*, the author's recall of boyhood summer fun, similar in its intent to *Plenty to Watch*. Suitable for older children is *Seashore Story*, one of Yashima's most beautiful, in which he tells the old legend of Urashima, the fisherman who stayed too long in the land beneath the sea. The story itself could appeal to a wide age range, but here Yashima's pictures require sophisticated ability to appreciate abstraction. A departure from Yashima's usual picture book format is *The Golden Footprints*, an illustrated storybook translated and adapted from a story by an old friend, Hatoju Muku, telling of the loyalty of some parent foxes to their captured baby fox and to the boy who befriended it.

Yashima has been chosen by other writers as illustrator for their picture books, and his own *Seashore Story, Umbrella*, and *Crow Boy* have been runners-up for the Caldecott Medal, awarded annually to the illustrator of the most distinguished picture book published in the United States during the preceding year.

—Claudia Lewis

———

YATES, Elizabeth. American. Born in Buffalo, New York, 6 December 1905. Educated at Franklin School, Buffalo; Oaksmere, Mamaroneck, New York. Married William McGreal in 1929 (died 1963). Trustee, Town Library, Peterborough, New Hampshire; commissioner, State Library Commission, Concord, New Hampshire; president, New Hampshire Association for the Blind, Concord. Recipient: American Library Association Newbery Medal, 1951; Women's International League for Peace and Freedom Jane Addams award, 1955; Sarah Josepha Hale award, 1970. Litt.D.: Aurora College, Illinois, 1965; Ripon College, Wisconsin, 1970; Rivier College, Nashua, New Hampshire, 1978; L.H.D.: Eastern Baptist College, St. Davids, Pennsylvania, 1966; University of New Hampshire, Durham, 1967; New England College, Henniker, New Hampshire, 1972; Franklin Pierce College, Rindge, New Hampshire, 1981. Address: 381 Old Street Road, Peterborough, New Hampshire 03458, U.S.A.

PUBLICATIONS FOR CHILDREN

Fiction

High Holiday. London, A. and C. Black, 1938.
Hans and Frieda in the Swiss Mountains, illustrated by Nora S. Unwin. New York and London, Nelson, 1939.
Climbing Higher. London, A. and C. Black, 1939; as *Quest in the North-land*, New York, Knopf, 1940.
Haven for the Brave. New York, Knopf, 1941.
Under the Little Fir and Other Stories, illustrated by Nora S. Unwin. New York, Coward McCann, 1942.
Around the Year in Iceland, illustrated by Jon Nielsen. Boston, Heath, 1942.
Patterns on the Wall. New York, Knopf, 1943.
Mountain Born, illustrated by Nora S. Unwin. New York, Coward McCann, 1943.
Once in the Year, illustrated by Nora S. Unwin. New York, Coward McCann, 1947.
A Place for Peter, illustrated by Nora S. Unwin. New York, Coward McCann, 1952.
Sam's Secret Journal, illustrated by Allan Eitzen. New York, Friendship Press, 1964.
Carolina's Courage, illustrated by Nora S. Unwin. New York, Dutton, 1964; as *Carolina and the Indian Doll*, London, Methuen, 1965.
An Easter Story, illustrated by Nora S. Unwin. New York, Dutton, 1967.
With Pipe, Paddle, and Song, illustrated by Nora S. Unwin. New York, Dutton, 1968.
Sarah Whitcher's Story, illustrated by Nora S. Unwin. New York, Dutton, 1971.
We, The People, illustrated by Nora S. Unwin. Taftsville, Vermont, Countryman Press, 1975.
The Seventh One, illustrated by Diana Charles. New York, Walker, 1978.
Silver Lining, illustrated by A.L. Morris. Canaan, New Hampshire, Phoenix, 1981.

Other

Joseph (Bible story), illustrated by Nora S. Unwin. New York, Knopf, 1947.
The Young Traveller in the U.S.A. London, Phoenix House, 1948.
The Christmas Story, illustrated by Nora S. Unwin. New York, Aladdin, 1949.
Children of the Bible, illustrated by Nora S. Unwin. New York, Aladdin, 1950; London, Meiklejohn, 1951.

Amos Fortune, Free Man, illustrated by Nora S. Unwin.   New York, Aladdin, 1950.
David Livingstone.   Evanston, Illinois, Row Peterson, 1952.
Rainbow 'round the World: A Story of UNICEF, illustrated by Betty Alden.   Indianapolis, Bobbs Merrill, 1954.
Prudence Crandall, Woman of Courage, illustrated by Nora S. Unwin.   New York, Aladdin, 1955.
Gifts of True Love: Based on the Old Carol "The Twelve Days of Christmas," illustrated by Nora S. Unwin.   Wallingford, Pennsylvania, Pendle Hill, 1958.
Someday You'll Write.   New York, Dutton, 1962.
New Hampshire.   New York, Coward McCann, 1969.
Skeezer, Dog with a Mission, illustrated by Joan Drescher.   New York, Harvey House, 1973.
My Diary—My World.   Philadelphia, Westminster Press, 1981.
My Widening World: The Continuing Diary of Elizabeth Yates.   Philadelphia, Westminster Press, 1983.
One Writer's Way.   Philadelphia, Westminster Press, 1984.

Editor, *Piskey Folk: A Book of Cornish Legends*, by Enys Tregarthen, photographs by William McGreal.   New York, Day, 1940.
Editor, *The Doll Who Came Alive*, by Enys Tregarthen, illustrated by Nora S. Unwin.   New York, Day, 1942; London, Faber, 1944.
Editor, *The White Ring*, by Enys Tregarthen, illustrated by Nora S. Unwin.   New York, Harcourt Brace, 1949.
Editor, *Sir Gibbie*, by George MacDonald.   New York, Dutton, 1963; London, Blackie, 1967.
Editor, *The Lost Princess; or, The Wise Woman*, by George MacDonald.   New York, Dutton, 1965.

PUBLICATIONS FOR ADULTS

Novels

Wind of Spring.   New York, Coward McCann, 1945; London, Cassell, 1948.
Nearby.   New York, Coward McCann, 1947; London, Cassell, 1950.
Beloved Bondage.   New York, Coward McCann, 1948.
Guardian Heart.   New York, Coward McCann, 1950; London, Museum Press, 1952.
Brave Interval.   New York, Coward McCann, 1952; London, Dakers, 1953.
Hue and Cry.   New York, Coward McCann, 1953.
The Carey Girl.   New York, Coward McCann, 1956.
The Next Fine Day.   New York, Day, 1962; London, Dent, 1964.
On That Night.   New York, Dutton, 1969.

Other

Pebble in a Pool: The Widening Circles of Dorothy Canfield Fisher's Life.   New York, Dutton, 1958; as *The Lady from Vermont*, Brattleboro, Vermont, Stephen Greene Press, 1971.
The Lighted Heart (autobiographical).   New York, Dutton, 1960.
Howard Thurman: Portrait of a Practical Dreamer.   New York, Day, 1964.
Up the Golden Stair.   New York, Dutton, 1966.
Is There a Doctor in the Barn? A Day in the Life of Forrest F. Tenney, D.V.M.   New York, Dutton, 1966.
The Road Through Sandwich Notch.   Brattleboro, Vermont, Stephen Greene Press, 1973.
A Book of Hours.   Norton, Connecticut, Vineyard, 1976.
Call It Zest: The Vital Ingredient after Seventy.   Brattleboro, Vermont, Stephen Greene Press, 1977; London, Prior, 1978.
Sound Friendships: The Story of Willa and Her Hearing Ear Dog.   Woodstock, Vermont, Countryman Press, 1987.

Editor, *Gathered Grace: A Short Selection of George MacDonald's Poems.*   Cambridge, Heffer, 1938.
Editor, *Your Prayers and Mine.*   Boston, Houghton Mifflin, 1954.

*

Bibliography: *A Bio-Bibliography of Elizabeth Yates* by Sister Margaret L. Trudell, Nashua, New Hampshire, Rivier College, unpublished thesis, 1970.

Manuscript Collection: Special Collections, Mugar Memorial Library, Boston University.

Elizabeth Yates comments:
I have a strong feeling that the purpose of life is good, and this—in some way or another—might be held to be the motivation in my work.

*   *   *

In a small volume called *Someday You'll Write*, composed in response to the questions of an 11-year-old girl who wishes to become a writer, Elizabeth Yates shares with readers the essence of her own development as creative artist. She compares the creative growth process to that of natural growth—a long, slow, evolving process of moving from birth to maturity. She believes that writers must be able to look deeply within, reaching outward and upward, if they are to grow. In her own case Yates did not hurry the creative process. Instead, she took sufficient time to allow ideas and imagination to incubate.

Yates is perhaps best known in the field of children's literature for two powerful biographies for older children—*Amos Fortune, Free Man* and *Prudence Crandall, Woman of Courage*. Based on extensive research and characterized by a fine narrative style, both books are compassionate yet void of didacticism. Each deals with an unusual New England citizen whose life, despite almost insurmountable hardships, was dedicated to the betterment of the lives of others. The biographee in the first case is a black man; in the second, a white woman. Amos Fortune's story can still be read, in brief, on the weathered headstone marking his grave in a little churchyard in Jaffrey, New Hampshire: "Born free in Africa, a slave in America, he purchased liberty, professed Christianity, lived reputably, and died hopefully, November 17, 1801." The story of Prudence Crandall can be read in state records where for more than fifty years she was listed as a criminal, her "crime" an attempt to provide equal education to white and black girls in the private school which she established in Canterbury, Connecticut, in 1833. The success and appeal of both books come to a large extent from the at-easeness and compatibility which Yates feels for her subjects and from her combining of fact and vision in presenting the compelling hopes and dreams that motivate the actions of Amos Fortune and Prudence Crandall. Throughout each book there is a pervasive sense that right will ultimately prevail if the protagonist can, despite all injustice, hold firm to honorable principles and remain free from the blight of prejudice, bitterness, and resentment. Amos Fortune and Prudence Crandall do remain free of blight, and each epitomizes in behavior the philosophy of usefulness which permeates Yates's writings.

Carolina's Courage and *Patterns on the Wall* are works of fiction in which Yates gives the protagonist of each a particular kind of usefulness. On the long overland journey she makes with her family from old New Hampshire to the Nebraska territory where they will homestead, little Carolina Putnam of *Carolina's Courage* demonstrates usefulness and courage admirable for one so young. When the coveted goal is almost in sight, Carolina's family meet up with owners of other wagons heading west. They stop to camp together near a creek they are afraid to cross—fearful of going further because of news of hostile Indians ahead. Straying from camp, taking her beloved doll Lydia-Lou, Carolina meets a little Indian girl who also has a doll. When Carolina is called back to camp for supper, the Indian child insists on exchanging dolls. When the campers break camp and move forward next day, Carolina is heart-broken to leave Lydia-Lou behind but she realizes that her father is right in feeling that the Indian doll she now has will gain safety for her own and other families of the wagon train when they meet Indians later. Readers are not told that Carolina and Lydia-Lou will sometime meet again. Yates cleverly avoids an ending which leaves nothing for the reader to do.

Patterns on the Wall is about another kind of usefulness. This book is the touching and inspirational story of a sensitive New Hampshire lad in the early 1800's who grew up to be a famous wall stenciller. Like *Amos Fortune* and *Prudence Crandall, Patterns on the Wall* is the result of thorough and painstaking research, and its characters are believable and real.

To leave unnoticed two other very special books for children—*Mountain Born* and its sequel, *A Place for Peter*—would be unfair. Together these books constitute a pastoral tale of a New Hampshire boy who grows into useful manhood rooted to the soil both by rearing and by personal inclination. These stories are a testament to their author's faith in the nobility of all nature, to her love of land, of animals, and of people. One of her finest characterizations in these two books, aside from that of Peter, is that of old Benj, the trusted farmhand. Few who read *A Place for Peter* can forget the scene in which old Benj destroys eight rattlesnakes "first asking their forgiveness." Because of his sincere reverence for life, old Benj did not like the thought of what had to be done but, faced with the decision of destroying the snakes or the possibility of their destroying man or beast, the greater good determined his actions. Yates's remarkable talent for descriptive writing is here at its best. The scene in which Peter is about to be bitten by a rattler because Shep, his faithful dog, has refused, in her excitement, to obey, is a case in point. Seeing three rattlers hurrying back to their den among the rock ledges Shep flings herself in their path. Threatened, the snakes coiled and "with their scaly yellow and black sides gleaming like velvet in the shade cast by an overwhelming rock, gave warning with raised and singing tails that intrusion would not be tolerated."

It is fair to say that in all her books for children Yates has held to the standard given to her by a former teacher that "the written word should be clean as a bone, clear as light, firm as stone." And in adhering to this standard she has provided a large body of work clearly characterized by gentleness and serenity, by a love of nature and all life, and by genuine concern for the oppressed and down-trodden. There has been about all great writers, Yates feels, an ability to see the "equality of mankind and the interrelation of life." Surely she must be one among them. Yates acknowledges indebtedness to the Bible, to William Blake, and to George Eliot. These influences are unmistakably present in many of her writings.

—Charity Chang

YEP, Laurence (Michael). American. Born in San Francisco, California, 14 June 1948. Educated at Marquette University, Milwaukee (Dretzka award, 1968), 1966–68; University of California, Santa Cruz, B.A. in English 1970; State University of New York, Buffalo, 1970–75, Ph.D. in English 1975. Part-time English teacher, Foothill College, Mountain View, California, 1975, and San Jose City College, California, 1975–76; Professor, University of California, Berkeley, 1987–88. Recipient: Book-of-the-Month-Club

fellowship, 1970; International Reading Association award, 1976; National Council for the Social Studies Woodson award, 1976; Boston *Globe-Horn Book* award, 1977; Women's International League for Peace and Freedom Jane Addams award, 1978. Agent: Maureen Walters, Curtis Brown, 10 Astor Place, New York, New York 10003. Address: 921 Populus Place, Sunnyvale, California 94086, U.S.A.

PUBLICATIONS FOR CHILDREN

Fiction

Sweetwater, illustrated by Julia Noonan. New York, Harper, 1973; London, Faber, 1976.
Dragonwings. New York, Harper, 1975.
Child of the Owl. New York, Harper, 1977.
Sea Glass. New York, Harper, 1979.
The Mark Twain Murders. New York, Four Winds Press, 1982.
Kind Hearts and Gentle Monsters. New York, Harper, 1982.
Dragon of the Lost Sea. New York, Harper, 1982.
Liar, Liar. New York, Morrow, 1983.
The Serpent's Children. New York, Harper, 1984.
The Tom Sawyer Fires. New York, Morrow, 1984.
Dragon Steel. New York, Harper, 1985.
Mountain Light. New York, Harper, 1985.
The Curse of the Squirrel, illustrated by Dirk Zimmer. New York, Random House, 1987.

Other

The Rainbow People (retelling), illustrated by David Wiesner. New York, Harper, 1989.

PUBLICATIONS FOR ADULTS

Novels

Seademons. New York, Harper, 1977.
Shadow Lord. New York, Pocket Books, 1985.
Monster Makers, Inc. New York, Arbor House, 1986.

Plays

Pay the Chinaman, and Fairy Bones (produced San Francisco, 1987).

*

Laurence Yep comments:
I enjoy writing for children because you can get back to old-fashioned storytelling rather than inflating a text with material about existential crises and whatever are the latest aesthetic and philosophical fads. Stories have to be told in concrete, vivid terms and relationships between characters are basic human bonds and therefore more universal.

* * *

Laurence Yep has stated that a prime intent in his children's fiction is to counter the various stereotypes of the Chinese-American that have appeared in the media, e.g., the villainous Dr. Fu Manchu, the banality-spouting Charlie Chan, and the laundrymen, cooks, and houseboys of film and TV. Further, he wants to show not only that Chinese-Americans are human, but that they are individuals upon whom America has had a unique effect.

Oddly, in light of that statement, Yep's first children's book, *Sweetwater*, is not about Chinese-Americans; still, it does adumbrate most of the major concerns he explores in his subsequent narratives concerning the Chinese-American experience. One of the most distinctive children's science-fiction novels yet to appear, *Sweetwater* centers on Tyree whose passage into adulthood is complicated by his father's insisting that his son's interest in music give way to the more practical goal of helping the father in his struggle, as leader of the Silkies, to maintain Old Sion, the first settlement on the planet Harmony, and the fishing trade, the essential livelihood of the Silkies. This generational conflict mirrors the larger conflicts the novel dramatizes: the clash between the human colonists bent on reshaping the planet to their own needs and desires, and the Argans, the indigenous, alien people with their own ideas; and the division among the colonists into Silkies who seek to adapt to their new surroundings and Mainlanders who would like to follow the old ways, especially that of exploiting natural resources. Another feature of *Sweetwater* is its style and range of allusions, in particular, the references to music and the Bible, which enrich the novel's thematic impact.

Dragonwings, Yep's next novel and the first of three studies of the Chinese-American, is surely his most impressive, if not his best, work. (It was a Newbery Honor Book in 1976.) Loosely categorized as historical fiction, the novel, first, depicts honestly and vividly the life of the first Chinese in California, brought to the United States to help open the west, then, the job having been successfully completed, increasingly restricted as to the exercise of their civil rights, and finally the objects of racism, sometimes violent. Second, the novel describes what passes as family life among a group of Chinese males who are only rarely allowed to bring with them their wives and, hence, must divide their emotional and psychological lives between China and their new home, San Francisco. Third, *Dragonwings* is about a man, Windrider, a master builder of kites, who, obsessed by a dream he believes is inspired by a dragon, aspires to fly like the Wright Brothers, and does succeed, in part because of the latter's aid, in achieving his dream. Last, the novel concerns young Moon Shadow who, having been brought over by his father, Windrider, comes to love, understand, and respect his dream-intoxicated father.

The other novels depicting Chinese-American experiences include *Child of the Owl* and *Sea Glass*, both set in the present. In the first, unfortunately a slow-moving narrative in spite of its humor and picture of Chinatown, Casey is taught by her grandmother, Paw-Paw, that one can love the old Chinese ways while still being an American. In the second, a quick-moving novel but relatively thin in characterization and theme, Craig Chin fights free from his father's excessively narrow, defensive, and psychologically damaging solution to the problem of being Chinese and American.

Kind Hearts and Gentle Monsters, although like all of his children's fiction concerned with generational conflict and contrasting cultural and life styles, has new subject-matter, for it is not about Chinese-Americans, and for the first time a boy-girl relationship—the growing friendship between Charley and Chris—is seriously developed.

Yep's strength as a storyteller has been his honest and sensitive depicting of a minority culture—one that has received very little attention in children's literature—and of the difficulty individuals have in reconciling the conflicting claims stemming from trying to remain true to their cultural heritage or chosen life style while confronted by a strong and alien culture or life style.

—Francis J. Molson

YOLEN, Jane (Hyatt).   American.   Born in New York City, 11 February 1939. Educated at Staples High School, Westport, Connecticut, graduated 1956; Smith College, Northampton, Massachusetts, B.A. 1960; New School for Social Research, New York; University of Massachusetts, Amherst, 1975–78, M.Ed. 1976. Married David W. Stemple in 1962; one daughter and two sons. Staff member, *This Week* magazine and *Saturday Review*, New York, 1960–61; assistant editor, Gold Medal Books, New York, 1961–62; associate editor, Rutledge Books, New York, 1962–63; assistant editor, Alfred A. Knopf Juvenile Books, New York, 1963–65; Lecturer in Education, Smith College, 1979–84. Columnist ("Children's Bookfare"), *Daily Hampshire Gazette*, Northampton, Massachusetts, 1972–80. Massachusetts delegate, Democratic National Convention, Miami, 1972. Member of the Board of Directors, Society of Children's Book Writers since 1974, and Children's Literature Association, 1977–79; President, Science-Fiction Writers of America, 1986–88. Recipient: Society of Children's Book Writers Golden Kite award, 1974; Christopher award, 1978; University of Minnesota Kerlan award, 1988. LL.D.: College of Our Lady of the Elms, Chicopee, Massachusetts, 1980. Agent: Marilyn Marlow, Curtis Brown, 10 Astor Place, New York, New York 10003. Address: 31 School Street, Box 27, Hatfield, Massachusetts 01038, U.S.A.

PUBLICATIONS FOR CHILDREN

Fiction

The Witch Who Wasn't, illustrated by Arnold Roth.   New York, Macmillan, and London, Collier Macmillan, 1964.

Gwinellen, The Princess Who Could Not Sleep, illustrated by Ed Renfro.   New York, Macmillan, 1965.

Trust a City Kid, with Anne Huston, illustrated by J.C. Kocsis.   New York, Lothrop, 1966; London, Dent, 1967.

Isabel's Noel, illustrated by Arnold Roth.   New York, Funk and Wagnalls, 1967.

The Emperor and the Kite, illustrated by Ed Young.   Cleveland, World, 1967; London, Macdonald, 1969.

The Minstrel and the Mountain, illustrated by Anne Rockwell.   Cleveland, World, and Edinburgh, Oliver and Boyd, 1968.

Greyling, illustrated by William Stobbs.   Cleveland, World, 1968; London, Bodley Head, 1969.

The Longest Name on the Block, illustrated by Peter Madden.   New York, Funk and Wagnalls, 1968.

The Wizard of Washington Square, illustrated by Ray Cruz.   New York, World, 1969.

The Inway Investigators; or, The Mystery at McCracken's Place, illustrated by Allan Eitzen.   New York, Seabury Press, 1969.

The Seventh Mandarin, illustrated by Ed Young.   New York, Seabury Press, and London, Macmillan, 1970.

Hobo Toad and the Motorcycle Gang, illustrated by Emily McCully.   New York, World, 1970.

The Bird of Time, illustrated by Mercer Mayer.   New York, Crowell, 1971.

The Girl Who Loved the Wind, illustrated by Ed Young.   New York, Crowell, 1972; London, Collins, 1973.

The Girl Who Cried Flowers and Other Tales, illustrated by David Palladini.   New York, Crowell, 1974.

Rainbow Rider, illustrated by Michael Foreman.   New York, Crowell, 1974; London, Collins, 1975.

The Adventures of Eeka Mouse, illustrated by Myra Gibson McKee.   Middletown, Connecticut, Xerox, 1974.

The Boy Who Had Wings, illustrated by Helga Aichinger.   New York, Crowell, 1974.

The Magic Three of Solatia, illustrated by Julia Noonan.   New York, Crowell, 1974.

The Little Spotted Fish, illustrated by Friso Henstra. New York, Seabury Press, 1975.

The Transfigured Hart, illustrated by Donna Diamond. New York, Crowell, 1975.

The Moon Ribbon and Other Tales, illustrated by David Palladini. New York, Crowell, 1976; London, Dent, 1977.

Milkweed Days, photographs by Gabriel Amadeus Cooney. New York, Crowell, 1976.

The Sultan's Perfect Tree, illustrated by Barbara Garrison. New York, Parents' Magazine Press, 1977.

The Seeing Stick, illustrated by Remy Charlip and Demetra Marsalis. New York, Crowell, 1977.

The Lady and the Merman, illustrated by Barry Moser. Easthampton, Massachusetts, Pennyroyal Press, 1977.

The Hundredth Dove and Other Tales, illustrated by David Palladini. New York, Crowell, 1977; London, Dent, 1979.

The Giants' Farm, illustrated by Tomie de Paola. New York, Seabury Press, 1977.

Hannah Dreaming, photographs by Alan Epstein. Springfield, Massachusetts, Springfield Museum of Fine Arts, 1977.

The Mermaid's Three Wisdoms, illustrated by Laura Rader. New York, Collins World, 1978.

No Bath Tonight, illustrated by Nancy Winslow Parker. New York, Crowell, 1978.

The Simple Prince, illustrated by Jack Kent. New York, Parents' Magazine Press, 1978.

Spider Jane, illustrated by Stefen Bernath. New York, Coward McCann, 1978.

Dream Weaver, illustrated by Michael Hague. New York, Collins, 1979.

The Giants Go Camping, illustrated by Tomie de Paola. New York, Seabury Press, 1979.

Spider Jane on the Move, illustrated by Stefen Bernath. New York, Coward McCann, 1980.

Mice on Ice, illustrated by Lawrence Di Fiori. New York, Dutton, 1980.

Commander Toad in Space, illustrated by Bruce Degen. New York, Coward McCann, 1980.

The Robot and Rebecca, illustrated by Catherine Deeter. New York, Random House, 1980.

Shirlick Holmes and the Case of the Wandering Wardrobe, illustrated by Anthony Rao. New York, Coward McCann, 1981.

Uncle Lemon's Spring, illustrated by Glen Rounds. New York, Dutton, 1981.

The Boy Who Spoke Chimp, illustrated by David Wiesner. New York, Knopf, 1981.

Brothers of the Wind, illustrated by Barbara Berger. New York, Philomel, 1981.

The Gift of Sarah Barker. New York, Viking Press, 1981.

The Acorn Quest, illustrated by Susanna Natti. New York, Crowell, 1981.

The Robot and Rebecca and the Missing Owser, illustrated by Lady McCrady. New York, Knopf, 1981.

Sleeping Ugly, illustrated by Diane Stanley. New York, Coward McCann, 1981.

Dragon's Blood. New York, Delacorte Press, 1982; London, MacRae, 1983.

Commander Toad and the Planet of the Grapes, illustrated by Bruce Degen. New York, Coward McCann, 1982.

Neptune Rising: Songs and Tales of the Undersea Folk, illustrated by David Wiesner. New York, Philomel, 1982.

Commander Toad and the Big Black Hole, illustrated by Bruce Degen. New York, Coward McCann, 1983.

Heart's Blood. New York, Delacorte Press, and London, MacRae, 1984.

Children of the Wolf. New York, Viking Kestrel, 1984.

The Stone Silenus. New York, Philomel, 1984.

Commander Toad and the Dis-Asteroid, illustrated by Bruce Degen. New York, Coward McCann, 1985.

Dragonfield and Other Stories. New York, Ace, 1985.

Commander Toad and the Intergalactic Spy, illustrated by Bruce Degen. New York, Coward McCann, 1986.

A Sending of Dragons, illustrated by Tom McKeveny. New York, Delacorte Press, and London, MacRae, 1987.

Piggins, illustrated by Jane Dyer. San Diego, Harcourt Brace, 1987; London, Piccadilly Press, 1988.

Owl Moon, illustrated by John Schoenherr. New York, Philomel, 1987.

Commander Toad and the Space Pirates, illustrated by Bruce Degen. New York, Putnam, 1987.

Picnic with Piggins, illustrated by Jane Dyer. San Diego, Harcourt Brace, 1988.

The Devil's Arithmetic. New York, Viking Kestrel, 1988.

Piggins and the Royal Wedding. San Diego, Harcourt Brace, 1989.

Dove Isabeau. San Diego, Harcourt Brace, 1989.

Play

Robin Hood, music by Barbara Green (produced Boston, 1967).

Verse

See This Little Line?, illustrated by Kathleen Elgin. New York, McKay, 1963.

It All Depends, illustrated by Don Bolognese. New York, Funk and Wagnalls, 1969.

An Invitation to the Butterfly Ball: A Counting Rhyme, illustrated by Jane Breskin Zalben. New York, Parents' Magazine Press, 1976; Kingswood, Surrey, World's Work, 1978.

All in the Woodland Early: An ABC Book, music by the author, illustrated by Jane Breskin Zalben. Cleveland, Collins, 1979.

How Beastly! A Menagerie of Nonsense Poems, illustrated by James Marshall. New York, Collins, 1980.

Dragon Night and Other Lullabies, illustrated by Demi. New York, Methuen, 1980; London, Methuen, 1981.

Ring of Earth: A Child's Book of Seasons, illustrated by John Wallner. San Diego, Harcourt Brace, 1986.

The Three Bear Rhyme Book, illustrated by Jane Dyer. San Diego, Harcourt Brace, 1987.

Best Witches. New York, Putnam, 1989.

Other

Pirates in Petticoats, illustrated by Leonard Vosburgh. New York, McKay, 1963.

World on a String: The Story of Kites. Cleveland, World, 1968.

Friend: The Story of George Fox and the Quakers. New York, Seabury Press, 1972.

The Wizard Islands, illustrated by Robert Quackenbush. New York, Crowell, 1973.

Ring Out! A Book of Bells, illustrated by Richard Cuffari. New York, Seabury Press, 1974; London, Evans, 1978.

Simple Gifts: The Story of the Shakers, illustrated by Betty Fraser. New York, Viking Press, 1976.

The Sleeping Beauty (retelling), illustrated by Ruth Sanderson. New York, Knopf, 1986.

Editor, *The Fireside Song Book of Birds and Beasts*, music by Barbara Green, illustrated by Peter Parnall. New York, Simon and Schuster, 1972.

Editor, *Zoo 2000: Twelve Stories of Science Fiction and Fantasy Beasts*. New York, Seabury Press, 1973; London, Gollancz,

1975.

Editor, *Rounds about Rounds*, music by Barbara Green, illustrated by Gail Gibbons. New York, Watts, 1977; London, Watts, 1978.

Editor, *Shape Shifters: Fantasy and Science Fiction Tales about Humans Who Can Change Their Shapes*. New York, Seabury Press, 1978.

Editor, *The Lullaby Songbook*, music arranged by Adam Stemple, illustrated by Charles Mikolaycak. San Diego, Harcourt Brace, 1986.

Editor, with Martin H. Greenberg and Charles G. Waugh, *Dragons and Dreams: A Collection of New Fantasy and Science Fiction Stories*. New York, Harper, 1986.

Editor, *Favorite Folktales from Around the World*. New York, Pantheon, 1986.

Editor, with Martin H. Greenberg and Charles G. Waugh, *Spaceships and Spells*. New York, Harper, 1987.

Editor, with Martin H. Greenberg, *Werewolves*. New York, Harper, 1988.

Editor, with Martin H. Greenberg, *Things That Go Bump in the Night*. New York, Harper, 1989.

PUBLICATIONS FOR ADULTS

Novels

Cards of Grief. New York, Ace, 1984; London, Futura, 1986.
Sister Light, Sister Dark. New York, Tor, 1988.
White Jenna. New York, Tor, 1989.

Short Stories

Tales of Wonder. New York, Schocken, 1983; London, Futura, 1987.
Merlin's Booke. New York, Steeldragon Press, 1986.

Other

Writing Books for Children. Boston, The Writer, 1973; revised edition, 1983.
Touch Magic: Fantasy, Faerie, and Folklore in the Literature of Childhood. New York, Philomel, 1981.

*

Manuscript Collection: Kerlan Collection, University of Minnesota, Minneapolis.

Jane Yolen comments:

"Prolific" is a word often used to describe me, but I would rather say that I have a very low threshold of boredom. And so I have tried many different kinds of writing: picture books, fantasy, fairytales, straight fiction, verse, and non-fiction. Perhaps I am best known as a writer of Literary or Art Fairy Tales, stories that use the elements of old stories—the cadences, the characters, the magical settings of objects—but concern themselves with modern themes. Because of this, my stories are better known to more sophisticated and romantically inclined young people, and college students. I am a folk singer as well as a storyteller, and I hope my tales sound as if they could be sung.

* * *

The list of Jane Yolen's writings is long and varied: picture books, easy-readers, fairytales, fantasy novels, and non-fiction for young adults, and books for adults about children's literature. Yet it is Yolen's "faerie and fantasy" that place her in the tradition of the Brothers Grimm and Hans Christian Andersen—tales which live on for future generations.

Touch Magic is not only a commentary on the importance of faerie and fantasy tales, but also a celebration of storytelling ("Listen, touch magic, and pass it on"):

> I believe that culture begins in the cradle. Literature is a continuous process from childhood onward....The continuum of literature is best maintained by these tales of fantasy, fancy, faerie, and the supra-natural, those crafted visions and bits and pieces of dream-remembering that link our past and our future. To do without tales and stories and books is to lose humanity's past, is to have no star map for our future.

Yolen's finely crafted fairytales are "visions and bits and pieces of dream-remembering" to be read aloud, listened to, shared, and remembered. Illustrations embellish the text in that "subtle play of text and type, illustrations and design" which Yolen has described and which mark her style.

"Once in the East, where the wind blows gently on the bells of the temple, there lived a king of the highest degree": so begins *The Seventh Mandarin*. As in all classic fairytales, there is, of course, a quest: the string to the king's soul—transubstantiated every evening into a kite flown "high above the terrors of the night"—slips from the hand of the youngest mandarin, and the kite flies away. Knowing that it must be returned before dawn, he sets out to find it. At last, on a far-away mountain top, he discovers it, all tattered and torn. He carries it back to the castle through the poorest section of the surrounding town. Ramshackle hovels and huts, poverty-stricken people moaning and sighing shock the little mandarin—he'd never read of these in any of his books. He returns the king his tattered soul, and courageously tells him the unpleasant truths of the world outside the castle. Together, they realize the folly of believing only what is written in books.

The title story of *The Girl Who Cried Flowers*—a collection of five fairytales beautifully illustrated in an art nouveau style by David Palladini—tells of gentle, generous Olivia, whose tears are flowers. Everyone wants Olivia's precious flowers—for weddings, funerals, all social occasions—and since Olivia is too tender-hearted to refuse them, she thinks sad thoughts and cries night and day until the storyteller Panos comes to her rescue by making her smile.

While there is gentle magic in Yolen's fairytales, there is also "tough magic," magic that has consequences. Aetos in *The Boy Who Had Wings* discovers that magic powers can have tragic consequences when his father, a horse herder, is stranded in a mountain snow storm and only he can soar above the mountains to save him. The price of his gift is heavy: his beautiful wings are frostbitten, they lose their feathers and drop off, leaving on his shoulders where his wings had been two large scars. But, no longer afraid of his wings, his family is now able to love him. "Saint Aetos" becomes the guardian angel of horse herders. (Flying and kites, in fact, are recurring motifs in Yolen's work—*The Emperor and the Kite, The Girl Who Loved the Wind, Rainbow Rider*, and *World on a String: The Story of Kites*. Yolen's father was a champion kite flyer, and ironically but most appropriately, *The Girl Who Cried Flowers* won the Golden Kite award.)

In *The Mermaid's Three Wisdoms*, a fantasy for young adults, Melusina, a mermaid (who cannot speak), breaks the code of the merfolk by showing herself to humans, and is banished from her home beneath the sea to live on earth. Melusina is found by Jess, a 12-year-old deaf girl. The deaf and the dumb form a unique and touching friendship. Gradually, the impulsive Jess learns from Melusina the wisdom of the merfolk: have patience, like the sea;

move with the rhythm of life around you; and know that all things touch all others, as all life touches the sea.

Yolen's equally prolific production of non-faerie picture books has grown in sophistication and acclaim. To her intergalactic *Commander Toad* series, Yolen has recently added the delightful *Piggins*, a portly porker butler who solves mysteries (of the non-murder kind) with the smoothest porcine logic. *Piggins* and its successor *Picnic with Piggins* are set in the *Upstairs, Downstairs* Edwardian world of 47 The Meadows and environs, and feature—besides the series' namesake ("more than a butler," he was also "a hero in the Boar War")—Mr. and Mrs. Reynard and their children Rexy and Trixy (all foxes, of course), the world-famous explorer Pierre Lapin and his three unmarried sisters, Cook, Sara the scullery maid, and Jane, who polishes the silver and fixes the tea. Jane Dyer's large, colored-pencil and watercolor illustrations and her inspired use of small, illustrative silhouettes to decorate pages of text make the Piggins stories as charming to look at as they are to read.

Owl Moon, which won the 1989 Caldecott Medal, is illustrated with exquisite and dramatic watercolors by John Schoenherr. Dedicated to Yolen's husband David Stemple—"who took all of our children owling"—*Owl Moon* is the story of a magical winter night, long past the child-narrator's bedtime, when "Pa and I went owling":

> There was no wind.
> The trees stood still
> as giant statues.
> And the moon was so bright
> the sky seemed to shine.

After a long, cold, patient search, Pa's call "Who-whoo-who-who-who-whoooo. Whoo-whoo-who-who-who-whoooooooo" resonating in the winter woods, child and father at last spot an owl's shadow. Pa's flashlight alights on the owl's face, and "for one minute, three minutes, maybe even a hundred minutes," child and owl stare at each other. Pumping its great wings, the owl finally flies off, leaving the child pondering a wonderful lesson:

> When you go owling
> you don't need words
> or warm
> or anything but hope.
> That's what Pa says.
> The kind of hope
> that flies
> on silent wings
> under a shining
> Owl Moon.

Yolen's latest venture is her most daring so far. In *The Devil's Arithmetic*, 13-year-old Hannah slips back in time at a Passover seder and finds herself in the middle of the horrors of the Holocaust. Roger Sutton, in the October 1988 issue of the *Bulletin of the Center for Children's Books*, has noted that "the depiction of the horrors she sees is more graphic than any we've seen in holocaust fiction for children before" and questions "the essentially comforting vision of the story and its time-travel form." Readers and critics will certainly be pondering this "tough magic" tale for some time to come.

Faerie, fiction, fact or horrible fantasy, Yolen's lyrical and magical tales are indeed tales to read and to listen to, to share, to remember, and to pass on.

—Marcia G. Fuchs

ZINDEL, Paul. American. Born in Staten Island, New York, 15 May 1936. Educated at Port Richmond High School, Staten Island; Wagner College, New York, B.S. in chemistry 1958, M.Sc. 1959. Married Bonnie Hildebrand in 1973; one son and one daughter. Technical writer for chemical company, New York, 1959; chemistry teacher, Tottenville High School, New York, 1960–69; playwright-in-residence, Alley Theatre, Houston, 1967. Recipient: Ford grant, 1967; Obie award, 1970; Vernon Rice award, 1970; New York Drama Critics Circle award, 1970; Pulitzer prize, 1971. D.H.L.: Wagner College, 1971. Lives in New York City. Agent: Curtis Brown, 10 Astor Place, New York, New York 10003. Address: c/o Harper and Row, 10 East 53rd Street, New York, New York 10022, U.S.A.

PUBLICATIONS FOR CHILDREN

Fiction

The Pigman. New York, Harper, 1968; London, Bodley Head, 1969.
My Darling, My Hamburger. New York, Harper, 1969; London, Bodley Head, 1970.
I Never Loved Your Mind. New York, Harper, 1970; London, Bodley Head, 1971.
I Love My Mother, illustrated by John Melo. New York, Harper, 1975.
Pardon Me, You're Stepping on My Eyeball! New York, Harper, and London, Bodley Head, 1976.
Confessions of a Teenage Baboon. New York, Harper, 1977; London, Bodley Head, 1978.
The Undertaker's Gone Bananas. New York, Harper, 1978; London, Bodley Head, 1979.
The Pigman's Legacy. New York, Harper, and London, Bodley Head, 1980.
A Star for the Latecomer, with Bonnie Zindel. New York, Harper, and London, Bodley Head, 1980.
The Girl Who Wanted a Boy. New York, Harper, and London, Bodley Head, 1981.
To Take a Dare, with Crescent Dragonwagon. New York, Harper, 1982.
Harry and Hortense at Hormone High. New York, Harper, 1984; London, Bodley Head, 1985.
The Amazing and Death-Defying Diary of Eugene Dingman. New York, Harper, and London, Bodley Head, 1987.
A Begonia for Miss Applebaum. New York, Harper, and London, Bodley Head, 1989.

PUBLICATIONS FOR ADULTS

Novel

When a Darkness Falls. New York, Bantam, 1984.

Plays

Dimensions of Peacocks (produced New York, 1959).
Euthanasia and the Endless Hearts (produced New York, 1960).
A Dream of Swallows (produced New York, 1964).
The Effect of Gamma Rays on Man-in-the-Moon Marigolds (produced Houston, 1965; New York, 1970; Guildford, Surrey, and London, 1972). New York, Harper, 1971; in *Plays and Players* (London), December 1972.
And Miss Reardon Drinks a Little (produced Los Angeles, 1967; New York, 1971; London, 1976). New York, Random House,

1972.

Let Me Hear You Whisper (televised 1969). New York, Harper, 1974.

The Secret Affairs of Mildred Wild (produced New York, 1972). New York, Dramatists Play Service, 1973.

The Ladies Should Be in Bed (produced New York, 1978). With *Let Me Hear You Whisper*, New York, Dramatists Play Service, 1973.

Ladies at the Alamo (also director: produced New York, 1975). New York, Dramatists Play Service, 1977.

A Destiny with Half Moon Street (produced Coconut Grove, Florida, 1983).

Screenplays: *Up the Sandbox*, 1973; *Mame*, 1974; *Maria's Lovers*, with others, 1984; *Runaway Train*, with Djordje Milicevic and Edward Bunker, 1985.

Television Play: *Let Me Hear You Whisper*, 1969.

*

Manuscript Collection: Boston University.

Critical Study: *Presenting Paul Zindel* by Jack Jacob Forman, Boston, Twayne, 1988.

Theatrical Activities:
    Director: **Play**—*Ladies at the Alamo*, New York, 1975.

*   *   *

Paul Zindel's kids usually have a lot going for them: intelligence, spunk, a good sense of the ridiculous, if not of humour, and a zest for adventure. But they certainly have their share and more of bad luck: their parents. What a collection! Drunkards; bullies; slatterns; dolts and drearies, almost every one of them! Is it any wonder the Zindel kids live in varying degrees of wretchedness?

Take as an example the parents of *Pardon Me, You're Stepping on My Eyeball!* "Marsh" Mellow has *two* drunken parents, one alive, to whom he lovingly refers as "Schizo Suzy," the other dead, even more troublesome. His girlfriend Edna Shinglebox (Zindel also burdens them with dreadful names, as often as not) has a mother who would be quite capable of forcing her daughter to date Jack the Ripper, in her desperation that the unhappy girl "find a boy," no matter who. Her father is a nebbish who can only be supportive of the girl if his wife is safely out of earshot....These are typical Zindel parents; there are more; and worse.

The Zindel youngsters are understandably a rather forlorn crew, given the destructive backgrounds with which they have been provided. In retaliation, they tend to be at least as obnoxious, and even more lippy, than their parents. Even their good intentions seem to bring them nothing but trouble. Zindel's best known work, *The Pigman*, and its sequel, *The Pigman's Legacy*, deal with the misadventures of two well-meaning kids, John and Lorraine, who want to befriend a lonely old man, but instead bring him to disaster. Mr. Pignati, the Pigman, is in part the author of his own misfortune; so eagerly does he covet the young peoples' friendship, he tries to make himself one of them, and in behaving like an adolescent, he sets himself upon a fatal course. Months later, still blaming themselves for their Pigman's death, John and Lorraine are horrified to see signs of activity in his deserted and derelict little house. Another unhappy old man has come into their lives, and somehow to the guilt-stricken couple, he seems to be their "legacy." Again, they prove to be the unwitting agents of disaster. With the best intentions in the world, meaning only to bring happiness into the sick old man's life, the two are party to a second calamity. Someone should warn old men: stay away from John and Lorraine, no good can come of it!

Zindel can be very amusing, but he is funny in a frantic, Marx Brothers slapstick style that too often lapses into vulgarity and bad taste, as in *The Undertaker's Gone Bananas*. There is nothing humorous about spying, far less about murder. His sillier, slighter efforts belie the great talent that produced such a sensitive and memorable drama as *The Effect of Gamma Rays on Man-in-the-Moon Marigolds*, the story of a family adrift, with a despairing dreamer at the helm, whose two adolescent daughters must make their own ways in a difficult and unsupportive environment.

In *The Girl Who Wanted a Boy* Zindel has come up with his quintessential rotten parent, who states openly that while she loves her unhappy daughter, she loves herself a lot more; who invades the girl's privacy, prying into her diary; who even bribes a sleazy boy-stripper to date her daughter and "make advances" to her, in an effort to prod the young woman into the pursuit of men. No wonder the wretched girl, goaded into "falling in love" if only to end these persecutions, sets her fancy upon a totally inappropriate object, a cheaply good-looking garage mechanic who has absolutely no interest in her. She attempts to please the young man by spending her life savings to buy him a car, and watches him drive off forever at story's end, having, one hopes, learned something from the brief encounter.

The Amazing and Death-Defying Diary of Eugene Dingman sees 15-year-old Eugene sent off to a summer job in an Adirondack resort hotel, where in time-honoured fashion he falls heavily in love with an attractive waitress. *Harry and Hortense at Hormone High* does have a message of sorts, half-buried in the foolish carryings-on. Jason Rohr, who calls himself Icarus, is either a seer or a teenage schizophrenic; Harry and Hortense are not sure which. His message that everyone is born to be a hero, is either not heard or not heeded; and like his namesake, Icarus flies too near the sun with fatal results: but his message has had its effect, on two lives at least.

As the silliness of their titles suggests, Zindel's later work lacks the impact of his earlier young adult novels. He seems to be trying too desperately to empathize with the teens he describes to maintain his true adult perspective on that ephemeral, if fascinating state of immaturity. He seems to feel that his kids can handle everything he throws at them. One can but wish them well, while rejoicing that the rest of us don't have to live in their world.

—Joan McGrath

———

ZION, Gene (Eugene Zion). American. Born in New York City, 5 October 1913. Educated at schools in Ridgefield and Fort Lee, New Jersey, 1919–27; Textile High School, New York, 1928–31; Pratt Institute, New York, 1932–36, diploma in pictorial illustration; New School for Social Research, New York, 1940–42. Served in the Anti-Aircraft Artillery Visual Training Aids Section, United States Army, 1942–44. Married Margaret Bloy Graham in 1948. Designer, Esquire Publications, New York, 1940–42; designer and assistant art director, CBS, New York, 1944–46; graphic designer, Condé Nast Publications, New York, 1947–51. *Died 5 December 1975.*

PUBLICATIONS FOR CHILDREN (illustrated by Margaret Bloy Graham)

Fiction

All Falling Down. New York, Harper, 1951; Kingswood, Surrey, World's Work, 1969.
Hide and Seek Day. New York, Harper, 1954.

The Summer Snowman. New York, Harper, 1955.
Harry, The Dirty Dog. New York, Harper, 1956; London, Bodley
  Head, 1960.
Really Spring. New York, Harper, 1956.
Jeffie's Party. New York, Harper, 1957.
Dear Garbage Man. New York, Harper, 1957; as *Dear Dustman*,
  London, Bodley Head, 1962.
No Roses for Harry! New York, Harper, 1958; London, Bodley
  Head, 1961.
The Plant Sitter. New York, Harper, 1959; London, Bodley Head,
  1966.
Harry and the Lady Next Door. New York, Harper, 1960;
  Kingswood, Surrey, World's Work, 1962.
The Meanest Squirrel I Ever Met. New York, Scribner, 1962.
The Sugar Mouse Cake. New York, Scribner, 1964.
Harry by the Sea. New York, Harper, 1965; London, Bodley Head,
  1966.

*

Manuscript Collection: Kerlan Collection, University of Minnesota,
Minneapolis.

*   *   *

Gene Zion had an exceptional talent for envisioning a story
through the eyes of a child. The characters, whether a dog, a squirrel,
or a garbage collector, have a child's perspective on their world. Their
predicaments and ensuing outcomes are frequently juxtaposed with
an adult viewpoint of their dilemma. Thus, Zion enables a child to
glimpse the feelings of others in a humorous and subtle way.

His early work represents an understanding of preliminary thought
processes. *All Falling Down* and *Hide and Seek Day* explore a child's
perception and fascination with things falling and hidden. Both
books have become somewhat dated by their illustrations and choppy, stilted text.

The Summer Snowman explores the fun and enjoyment of a child's
fantasy: preserving a snowman until summer. Zion's likable little boy
uses the snowman to play a joke on his older brother. In *Really Spring*
a boy ignites the town's interest in painting everything to look like
spring. It climaxes with rain washing all the paint away to reveal the
"real" spring. The effect is humorous but not as involving as *The
Summer Snowman*.

Dear Garbage Man appeals to a child's fascination with rubbish.
It cleverly dramatizes the concept of recycling trash. The climax,
with the broken old junk reappearing on the street, is a realistic twist
to an amusing story.

Harry, Zion's most successful character, is a dog embodying the
excitement, curiosity, and mischief of a child. *Harry, The Dirty Dog*
captivates his admirers by escaping from the bathtub to play in the
dirtiest parts of town. As a final twist, Harry must beg for a bath to
be recognized by his family. His problems are universal and his
audience empathizes with his plight. In *No Roses for Harry!* he is
given a sweater with roses on it. Feeling quite ridiculous, he loses it
on purpose. This familiar situation immediately involves the reader
in the solution. Grandma understands and helps create a happy
satisfying climax. Bothersome behavior, in *Harry by the Sea*, makes
him a nuisance at the beach. Harry inadvertently gets lost, reappearing as a sea weed monster. The monster effect is comical and blends
an imaginative story with the trauma of being lost in a sea of
umbrellas at the beach. Harry is a timeless personality inviting
warmth, involvement, and understanding.

—Martha J. Fick

ZOLOTOW, Charlotte (née Shapiro). Has also written as Sarah
Abbott; Charlotte Bookman. American. Born in Norfolk, Virginia, 26 June 1915. Educated at the University of Wisconsin,
Madison, 1933–36. Married the writer Maurice Zolotow in 1938
(divorced 1969); one son and one daughter. Member of the children's
book department, 1938–44, 1962–65, senior editor, 1965–76,
editorial director, Harper Junior Books, and associate publisher and
vice-president, 1976–82, and since 1982 editorial consultant and
editor of Charlotte Zolotow Books, Harper and Row, New York.
Recipient: Harper Gold Medal for Editorial Excellence, 1974; Christopher award, 1975; University of Minnesota Kerlan award, 1986.
Address: 29 Elm Place, Hastings-on-Hudson, New York 10706,
U.S.A.

PUBLICATIONS FOR CHILDREN

Fiction

The Park Book, illustrated by H.A. Rey. New York, Harper, 1944.
But Not Billy, illustrated by Lys Cassal. New York, Harper, 1947.
The Storm Book, illustrated by Margaret Bloy Graham. New York,
  Harper, 1952.
The Magic Word, illustrated by Eleanor Dart. New York, Wonder
  Books, 1952; as *Do You Know the Magic Word?*, n.d.
The City Boy and the Country Horse (as Charlotte Bookman),
  illustrated by William Moyers. New York, Treasure Books,
  1952.
Indian, Indian, illustrated by Leonard Weisgard. New York, Simon
  and Schuster, 1952.
The Quiet Mother and the Noisy Little Boy, illustrated by Kurt Werth.
  New York, Lothrop, 1953.
One Step, Two..., illustrated by Roger Duvoisin. New York,
  Lothrop, 1955; London, Bodley Head, 1968; revised edition,
  Lothrop, 1981.
Not a Little Monkey, illustrated by Roger Duvoisin. New York,
  Lothrop, 1957.
Over and Over, illustrated by Garth Williams. New York, Harper,
  1957.
Do You Know What I'll Do? illustrated by Garth Williams. New
  York, Harper, 1958.
Sleepy Book, illustrated by Vladmir Bobri. New York, Lothrop,
  1958; Kingswood, Surrey, World's Work, 1960.
The Night When Mother Was Away, illustrated by Reisie Lonette.
  New York, Lothrop, 1958; as *The Summer Night*, New York,
  Harper, 1974; Kingswood, Surrey, World's Work, 1976.
The Bunny Who Found Easter, illustrated by Betty Peterson.
  Berkeley, California, Parnassus Press, 1959.
Aren't You Glad, illustrated by Elaine Kurty. New York, Golden
  Press, 1960.
The Little Black Puppy, illustrated by Lilian Obligado. New York,
  Golden Press, 1960.
Big Brother, illustrated by Mary Chalmers. New York, Harper,
  1960.
The Three Funny Friends, illustrated by Mary Chalmers. New
  York, Harper, 1961.
The Man with the Purple Eyes, illustrated by Joe Lasker. New York,
  Abelard Schuman, 1961; London, Abelard Schuman, 1963.
Mr. Rabbit and the Lovely Present, illustrated by Maurice Sendak.
  New York, Harper, 1962; London, Bodley Head, 1968.
The Sky Was Blue, illustrated by Garth Williams. New York, Har-
  per, 1963; Kingswood, Surrey, World's Work, 1976.
The Quarreling Book, illustrated by Arnold Lobel. New York,
  Harper, 1963.
The White Marble, illustrated by Lilian Obligado. New York and
  London, Abelard Schuman, 1963.

A Tiger Called Thomas, illustrated by Kurt Werth. New York, Lothrop, 1963.
I Have a Horse of My Own, illustrated by Yoko Mitsuhashi. New York and London, Abelard Schuman, 1964.
The Poodle Who Barked at the Wind, illustrated by Roger Duvoisin. New York, Lothrop, 1964; Kingswood, Surrey, World's Work, 1965.
A Rose, A Bridge, and a Wild Black Horse, illustrated by Uri Shulevitz. New York, Harper, 1964.
When I Have a Little Girl [*a Son*], illustrated by Hilary Knight. New York, Harper, 2 vols., 1965–67.
Someday, illustrated by Arnold Lobel. New York, Harper, 1965; Kingswood, Surrey, World's Work, 1966.
If It Weren't for You, illustrated by Ben Shecter. New York, Harper, 1966.
Big Sister and Little Sister, illustrated by Martha Alexander. New York, Harper, 1966; Kingswood, Surrey, World's Work, 1968.
Flocks of Birds, illustrated by Joan Berg. New York Abelard Schuman, 1965; London, Abelard Schuman, 1966.
I Want to Be Little, illustrated by Tony de Luna. New York and London, Abelard Schuman, 1967.
Summer Is..., illustrated by Janet Archer. New York and London, Abelard Schuman, 1967.
The New Friend, illustrated by Arvis Stewart. New York and London, Abelard Schuman, 1968.
My Friend John, illustrated by Ben Shecter. New York, Harper, 1968.
The Hating Book, illustrated by Ben Shecter. New York, Harper, 1969; Kingswood, Surrey, World's Work, 1971.
Where I Begin (as Sarah Abbott), illustrated by Rocco Negri. New York, Coward McCann, 1970.
You and Me, illustrated by Robert Quackenbush. New York, Macmillan, 1971.
A Father Like That, illustrated by Ben Shecter. New York, Harper, 1971.
William's Doll, illustrated by William Pène du Bois. New York, Harper, 1972.
Hold My Hand, illustrated by Thomas di Grazia. New York, Harper, 1972.
The Beautiful Christmas Tree, illustrated by Ruth Robbins. Berkeley, California, Parnassus Press, 1972.
The Old Dog (as Sarah Abbott), illustrated by George Mocniak. New York, Coward McCann, 1972.
Janey, illustrated by Ronald Himler. New York, Harper, 1973; Kingswood, Surrey, World's Work, 1974.
My Grandson Lew, illustrated by William Pène du Bois. New York, Harper, 1974; Kingswood, Surrey, World's Work, 1976.
The Unfriendly Book, illustrated by William Pène du Bois. New York, Harper, 1975.
It's Not Fair, illustrated by William Pène du Bois. New York, Harper, 1976; Kingswood, Surrey, World's Work, 1978.
May I Visit?, illustrated by Erik Blegvad. New York, Harper, 1976; Kingswood, Surrey, World's Work, 1977.
Someone New, illustrated by Erik Blegvad. New York, Harper, 1978; Kingswood, Surrey, World's Work, 1979.
Say It!, illustrated by James Stevenson. New York, Greenwillow, 1980.
If You Listen, illustrated by Marc Simont. New York, Harper, 1980.
The Song, illustrated by Nancy Tafuri. New York, Greenwillow, 1982.
I Know a Lady, illustrated by James Stevenson. New York, Greenwillow, 1984; London, Hutchinson, 1985.
Timothy Too!, illustrated by Ruth Robbins. Boston, Houghton Mifflin, 1986.
I Like to Be Little, illustrated by Erik Blegvad. New York, Harper, 1987.

Something Is Going to Happen, illustrated by Catherine Stock. New York, Harper, and London, Collins, 1988.

Verse

All That Sunlight, illustrated by Walter Stein. New York, Harper, 1967.
Some Things Go Together, illustrated by Sylvie Selig. New York, Abelard Schuman, 1969.
River Winding, illustrated by Regina Shekerjian. New York, Abelard Schuman, 1970; Kingswood, Surrey, World's Work, 1980.
Wake Up and Goodnight, illustrated by Leonard Weisgard. New York, Harper, 1971; Kingswood, Surrey, World's Work, 1972.
Everything Glistens and Everything Sings: New and Selected Poems, illustrated by Margot Tomes. San Diego, Harcourt Brace, 1987.

Other

In My Garden, illustrated by Roger Duvoisin. New York, Lothrop, 1960; Kingswood, Surrey, World's Work, 1963.
When the Wind Stops, illustrated by Joe Lasker. New York, Abelard Schuman, 1962; London, Abelard Schuman, 1964.
A Week in Yani's World: Greece, photographs by Donald Getsug. New York, Crowell Collier, and London, Collier Macmillan, 1969.
A Week in Lateef's World: India, photographs by Ray Shaw. New York, Crowell Collier, 1970.

Editor, *An Overpraised Season: Ten Stories of Youth*. New York, Harper, 1973; London, Bodley Head, 1974.
Editor, *Early Sorrow: Ten Stories of Youth*. New York, Harper, 1986.

*

Manuscript Collection: Kerlan Collection, University of Minnesota, Minneapolis.

*   *   *

In the more than 60 books which Charlotte Zolotow has written since her first, *The Park Book*, she has never raised her voice. This is true even when she constructs stories about quarreling or other extremes of emotion. Her hallmark is artful understatement; the bedrock of her success is her almost eerie sense of what matters to the young. For example, *Janey* describes the desolation of a little girl whose best friend moves far away. The touching tale is a comfort to readers in the same situation, particularly since Zolotow avoids the bathos of a phoney happy ending.

All the Zolotow titles are popular; several are award-winning classics. *William's Doll* argues the case of a perfectly virile boy who yearns for a doll to the disgust of his he-man pals and the dismay of his father. William's wise grandmother buys him a doll and tells his father the boy needs it "so that when he's a father like you, he'll know how to take care of his baby." Blessed by the woman's movement, the book is included automatically in all non-sexist anthologies and on all lists of such literature, and has been on television. Zolotow was also among the first to tackle the long-taboo subject of death in a picture book. *My Grandson Lew* tells of a boy whose mother avoids all mention of the death of his grandfather until she recognizes that children, like adults, need to mourn when they lose loved ones.

In other works, the author displays a talent for creating credible fantasies and quiet comedies. Widely enjoyed is *Mr. Rabbit and the Lovely Present*, in which a little girl matter-of-factly accepts the friendship of a tall bunny. As they wander companionably through the woods near her house, Mr. Rabbit helps the girl gather the makings of a birthday present for her mother. Equally appealing though decidedly different is *A Rose, A Bridge, and a Wild Black Horse*. Here we meet a feisty small boy, promising that he'll deliver unimaginable wonders to his sister, when he's grown up. In the finale, Zolotow scores a direct hit at male chauvinism and endears herself to underestimated females. Brother's oration concludes when he says he will not forget to bring his sister a friend to keep her company "while I explore the world."

On occasion, critics have complained that Zolotow's books are slight and/or plotless. That opinion is not shared by readers who always hear her, quiet though she is, because they know she is as close as children themselves to what is happening in their world.

—Jean F. Mercier

APPENDIX

ABBOTT, Jacob. American. Born in Hallowell, Maine, 14 November 1803. Educated at Hallowell Academy; Bowdoin College, Brunswick, Maine, graduated 1820; Andover Theological Seminary, graduated 1825. Married 1) Harriet Vaughan in 1828 (died 1843), six children; 2) Mary Woodbury in 1853 (died 1869). Teacher, Portland Academy, Maine, 1820–21, and in Beverly, Massachusetts, 1823; Professor of Mathematics and Natural Philosophy, Amherst College, Massachusetts, 1825–27; founder and principal, Mount Vernon School, Boston, 1828–33; minister, Eliot Congregational Church, Roxbury, Massachusetts, 1834; co-founder, Abbott School for Girls, New York, 1843–51, and Mount Vernon School for Boys, 1845–48. *Died 31 October 1879.* Fiction: *Lucy* series, from 1832; *Caleb in Town*, 1833; *Rollo* series, from 1835; *Hoaryhead, and The Valleys Below*, 1838; *Jonas* series, from 1839; *Caleb in the Country*, 1839; *Franconia* series, from 1850; *John True*, 1850; *Aunt Margaret*, 1854; *Bruno*, 1854; *Carl and Jocko*, 1854; *The Three Gold Dollars*, 1854; *Viola and Her Little Brother Arno*, 1854; *Willie and the Mortgage*, 1854; *Emma*, 1855; *The Harper Establishment*, 1855; *Hoaryhead and M'Donner*, 1855; *Prank*, 1855; *The Studio*, 1855; *Timboo and Joliba*, 1855; *Virginia*, 1855; *The Alcove*, 1856; *Elfred*, 1856; *The Engineer*, 1856; *The Gibraltar Gallery*, 1856; *The Great Elm*, 1856; *Vernon*, 1856; *Minigo*, 1857; *Jasper*, 1857; *Judge Justin*, 1857; *Lapstone*, 1857; *Little Paul*, 1857; *Madeleine*, 1857; *Orkney the Peacemaker*, 1857; *Congo*, 1857; *Rainbow and Lucky* series, from 1858; *Florence* series, from 1860; *Timboo and Fanny*, 1860; *Harlie* series, from 1863; *The Sea-Shore*, 1863; *John Gay* series, from 1864; *Mary Gay* series, from 1865; *William Gay* series, from 1869; *Juno* series, from 1870; *August Stories* series, from 1871(?); *Fergus*, 1874; *Gilbert and His Mother*, 1874; *The Museum*, 1884.

* * *

Jacob Abbott is among the earliest American writers of domestic tales for the young, and certainly the first to make the American scene familiar to English readers, who throughout the last century enjoyed his accounts of robust, self-reliant children seemingly delightfully independent of their parents. In all his books one senses the wise schoolmaster, patient, tolerant and good-humoured—but concerned to improve his pupils. His method of instructing the child through experience was a development of that of the Edgeworths (whose educational views, and Maria's stories to illustrate them, had always been far more popular in the United States than in England), and, realizing that children have great respect for the opinion and advice of a child a little older, he made a practice of introducing a youthful counsellor, very often a hired boy, who instructs and admonishes the impetuous and headstrong. This sage's word is invariably law; the children obey and accept his punishments which are reasonable and designed to fit the crime. In the Rollo series the authority is vested in Jonas; the Franconia series has "Beechnut" (the French hired boy Antoine Bianchinette); sometimes there is a little female preceptor like Mary Bell (also in the Franconia tales), or Juno "a nice and tidy-looking coloured girl" who has her own series and is the mentor of Georgie. There is always remarkably little adult presence.

The first two Rollo books in a series which came to number some 28 volumes were *The Little Scholar Learning to Talk* and *Rollo Learning to Read*. Rollo's childhood is more interesting than his adolescence when, with his character presumably formed, he is taken by his uncle on a 12-volume tour of Europe "with the satisfied consciousness of hailing from a land far superior to those inhabited by foreigners." Abbott had the same skill as Maria Edgeworth in portraying small children, and Rollo, aged five, is an engaging little boy with not much thought beyond his own concerns, unwilling to concentrate on anything for very long, loftily confident of being able to achieve anything he chooses, apt to cry when things go wrong. As the series progresses he learns about the world around him, and acquires various skills, and such virtues as self-control, restraint, and

self-denial which Abbott presents not so much as moral law but reasonable and expedient if one is to live happily with others.

The Franconia books, set in a village in the mountains of New York State, are less overtly instructive than the Rollo series, though the author makes his intentions clear in the preface to each. The central characters are the little boy, Phonny (Alphonso), and his parents' hired boy, Beechnut; a neighbouring girl Ellen Linn; the good and gentle Mary Bell and her friend Caroline "a young lady thirteen years old"; and the visitors from New York Malleville and Wallace, most of these being the subject of individual titles in the series. What drama there is—such as the death of Ellen Linn's father in a snowstorm—is recounted in the same leisurely, unemotional style that is accorded to the descriptions of the blueberrying expeditions, the building of a diving pier, the maple sugaring; and when Beechnut is arrested on a false charge of arson the episode seems to be no more than an exercise to explain the processes of the law. Pace and drama were not characteristics of Abbott's writing. "Pleasing pictures of still life in the country," a contemporary reviewer said of the Franconia series, and the books are not less pleasing for their gentle goodness.

While not taking the same stern view of fairy stories as so many of his American contemporaries, Abbott thought children should be directed to more profitable matters. His one fairy story, *Minigo* (prefaced by a reminder that fairies were "fictitious and imaginary"), is about a firm and sensible fairy cast in much the same mould as Beechnut and Jonas, with ability to make an errant child feel instantly ashamed.

—Gillian Avery

ALCOTT, Louisa May. American. Born in Germantown, Philadelphia, Pennsylvania, 29 November 1832; daughter of the philosopher Amos Bronson Alcott; grew up in Boston, and Concord, Massachusetts. Educated at home by her father, with instruction from Thoreau, Emerson, and Theodore Parker. Began to write for publication, 1848; also worked as a teacher, seamstress, and domestic servant; army nurse at the Union Hospital, Georgetown, Washington, D.C., during the Civil War, 1862–63; editor of the children's magazine *Merry's Museum*, 1867. *Died 6 March 1888.* Fiction: *Flower Fables*, 1855; *The Rose Family*, 1864; *Morning-Glories and Other Stories*, 1867; *Three Proverb Stories*, 1868; *Kitty's Class Day*, 1868; *Aunt Kipp*, 1868; *Psyche's Art*, 1868; *Little Women* (*Little Women* and *Good Wives*), 1868–69; *An Old-Fashioned Girl*, 1870; *Will's Wonder Book*, 1870; *Little Men*, 1871; *Aunt Jo's Scrap-Bag*, 1872–82; *Eight Cousins*, 1875; *Rose in Bloom*, 1876; *A Modern Mephistopheles*, 1877; *Under the Lilacs*, 1877; *Meadow Blossoms*, 1879; *Water Cresses*, 1879; *Jack and Jill*, 1880; *Proverb Stories*, 1882; *Spinning-Wheel Stories*, 1884; *Jo's Boys and How They Turned Out*, 1886; *Lulu's Library*, 1886–89; *A Garland for Girls*, 1888; *Louisa's Wonder Book*, 1975; *Behind a Mask*, 1975; *Plots and Counterplots*, 1976; *A Double Life*, 1988.

* * *

In 1868 when, at the request of Thomas Niles of Roberts Brothers, Louisa May Alcott sat down to write a household story for girls, the domestic novel as evolved by Susan Warner, Maria Cummins, Ann Stephens, and Mrs. E.D.E.N. Southworth consisted of commonplace episodes worked into a trite plot involving pious and insipid characters. Bronson Alcott's opinion of juvenile literature, recorded in his diary for 1839, had, in the generation that followed, been given no cause for alteration. In 1868 it was still true that the "literature of childhood" had not been written. If such extraordinary moral tales as *The Wide, Wide World*, the Rollo books, the Lucy books, and the first of the Elsie books became unbearable, there was compensation for a youthful reader only in grave-and-horror stories, Hawthorne's legendary tales, or "Peter Parley's" edifying descriptions of natural wonders.

The times were ripe for Alcott and she was well equipped to fill the gap in domestic literature. With the publication of *Little Women* (1868–69) she created a domestic novel for children destined to influence writers in that genre for generations to come. Responding to her publisher's request, she drew her characters from those of her own sisters, her scenes from the New England where she had grown up, and many of her episodes from those she and her family had experienced. In all this she was something of a pioneer, adapting her autobiography to the creation of a juvenile novel and achieving a realistic but wholesome picture of family life with which young readers could readily identify.

The literary influence of Bunyan and Dickens, Carlyle and Hawthorne, Emerson, Theodore Parker, and Thoreau can be traced in her work, but primarily she drew upon autobiographical sources for her plot and her characters, finding in her family and neighbors the groundwork for her three-dimensional characters. Her perceptively drawn adolescents, the Marches, modeled upon her sisters and herself, were not merely lifelike but alive. Her episodes, from the opening selection of a Christmas gift to the plays in the barn, from Jo March's literary career to Beth's death, were thoroughly believable for they had been lived. The Alcott humor which induced a chuckle at a homely phrase was appreciated by children. The Alcott poverty was sentimentalized; the eccentric Alcott father was an adumbrated shadow; yet, for all the glossing over, the core of the domestic drama was apparent. Reported simply and directly in a style that obeyed her injunction "Never use a long word, when a short one will do as well," the narrative embodied the simple facts and persons of a family and so filled a gap in the literature of childhood. Alcott had unlatched the door to one house, and "all find it is their own house which they enter." 20th-century writers for children who aim at credibility and verisimilitude in their reconstructions of contemporary family life are all, in one way or another, indebted to Alcott.

By the time she created *Little Women* she had served a long apprenticeship and was already a professional writer. She had edited a juvenile monthly, *Merry's Museum*, and produced several books aimed at a juvenile readership: her first published book, *Flower Fables*, "legends of faery land"; *The Rose Family: A Fairy Tale*; and *Morning-Glories and Other Stories*, readable short stories in which autobiographical details were combined with nature lore and moral tidbits.

Alcott had also written in a variety of genres for a wide range of adult readers, weaving stories of sweetness and light, dramatic narratives of strong-minded women and poor lost creatures, realistic episodes of the Civil War, and blood-and-thunder thrillers of revenge and passion whose leading character was usually a vindictive and manipulating heroine. From the exigencies of serialization for magazines she had developed the skills of the cliff-hanger and the page-turner. Her first full-length novel, *Moods* (1865), was a narrative of stormy passion and violence, death and intellectual love in which she attempted to apply Emerson's remark: "life is a train of moods like a string of beads." Off and on, she had worked at her autobiographical and feminist novel *Success*, subsequently renamed *Work: A Story of Experience*. By 1868, Alcott had run a gamut of literary experimentation from stories of virtue rewarded to stories of vice unpunished. She had attempted tales of escape and realism and stirred her literary ingredients in a witch's cauldron before she kindled the fire in a family hearth.

With few exceptions—notably *A Modern Mephistopheles* (1877) in which she reverted to the sensational themes of her earlier blood-and-thunders—Alcott clung to that family hearth during the

remainder of her career. Between 1868 when Part One of *Little Women* appeared and 1888 when she died, she produced in her so-called *Little Women Series* a string of wholesome domestic narratives more or less autobiographical in origin, simple and direct in style, perceptive in the characterization of adolescents. *An Old-Fashioned Girl, Little Men, Eight Cousins, Rose in Bloom, Under the Lilacs, Jack and Jill*, and *Jo's Boys* are all in a sense sequels to *Little Women* though none of them quite rises to its level. *An Old-Fashioned Girl* is a domestic drama in reverse, exposing the fashionable absurdities of the Shaw home by contrast with Polly, the wholesome representative of domesticity. The Campbell clan of *Eight Cousins* exalts the family hearth again. In *Jack and Jill* the author enlarges upon the theme of domesticity, describing the home life of a New England village rather than of a single family.

Despite her experimentation with a diversity of literary techniques, despite the fact that she was a complex writer drawn to a variety of themes, Alcott has inevitably achieved fame as the "Children's Friend" and the author of a single masterpiece. Thanks to its psychological perceptions, its realistic characterizations, and its honest domesticity, *Little Women* has become an embodiment of the American home at its best. Consciously or unconsciously all subsequent writers who have attempted the domestic novel for children have felt its influence, for in *Little Women* the local has been transmuted into the universal and the incidents of family life have been translated to the domain of literature.

Today not only *Little Women* but the entire Alcott oeuvre are being subjected to critical re-evaluation. For this the reprinting of her previously unknown thrillers (written in secret during the 1860's and published anonymously or pseudonymously) is largely responsible. Their themes (mind control and madness, hashish experimentation and opium addiction, mesmerism, and a powerful feminism) are leading critics to re-examine the simplistic interpretation of "America's best-loved author of juveniles."

—Madeleine B. Stern

ALDRICH, Thomas Bailey. American. Born in Portsmouth, New Hampshire, 11 November 1836. Attended school in Portsmouth. Married Lilian Woodman in 1865; twin sons. Clerk in New York, 1852–55; staff member, *Evening Mirror*, 1855–56, editor, *Home Journal*, 1856–59, associate editor, *Saturday Press*, 1858–60, and editor, *Illustrated News*, 1863, all in New York; editor, *Every Saturday*, Boston, 1866–74, and *Atlantic Monthly*, Boston, 1881–90. M.A.: Yale University, New Haven, Connecticut, 1881; Harvard University, Cambridge, Massachusetts, 1896; LL.D.: University of Pennsylvania, Philadelphia, 1906. Died 19 March 1907. Fiction: *The Story of a Bad Boy*, 1869.

*   *   *

Although Thomas Bailey Aldrich first achieved literary renown as a poet in the mid-19th century, it is as a novelist and short story writer that he is chiefly remembered today.

His short stories, like his poems, many of which still retain their distinction, are impeccably crafted, disciplined, restrained, sparse, precise, and refined. Throughout Aldrich's works, there is artistic integrity, a subtle blending of sentiment and wit, and, ever present, a blithe young spirit that led Mark Twain to remark that he was tired of waiting for Aldrich to grow old. What does remain eternally, innocently childlike is his autobiographical novel, *The Story of a Bad Boy*. Aldrich wished to distinguish his young Tom, "an amiable, impulsive lad...and no hypocrite...from the faultless young gentlemen who generally figure in narratives of this kind."

His somewhat idealized story parallels the actual events of his own boyhood: early years in New Orleans, schooling in New Hampshire in preparation for Harvard until the death of his father precluded college, completing his education in Portsmouth (Rivermouth in the book). Aldrich recalls these years affectionately, amusingly, nostalgically. On his arrival in Boston from the South, he was surprised to see no Indians on Long Wharf—either they "were early risers" or "they were away just then on the warpath." And, "speaking of the Pilgrim Fathers," why was there never any "mention of the Pilgrim Mothers." Gently, he satirized the "old Puritan austerity" that cropped out on Sundays in the Nutter household where in the oppressive atmosphere of that one day a week, they ate "a dead cold dinner" that was "laid out yesterday." He vowed ever after to make Sundays cheerful days. The most haunting, poignant memory—a wholly fictitious happening—was the tragedy of poor little Binny Wallace who drifted out to sea in a gale and now sleeps in the Old South Burying Ground. One of the early regional novels, the story glows with local color, characteristic eccentricities, and traditions. In that old declining privateer port of Rivermouth, boys cruised down the river, island-hopping on excursions and learning about the sea and ships; they presented amateur theatricals in the barn, celebrated holidays properly, and not so properly burned an old stage coach, jumped jail, and waged frigid snow fights on Slater's Hill.

To Ferris Greenslet, Aldrich's official biographer and an editorial alumnus of the *Atlantic Monthly*, the book "marked an epoch in the history of juvenile literature." One of the first critics to discern that Aldrich had "done a new thing…in American literature" was William Dean Howells, then editor of the *Atlantic*. Howells's review appeared in the January 1870 issue: "No one else seems to have thought of telling the story of a boy's life with so great desire to show what a boy's life is, and with so little purpose of teaching what it should be; certainly no one has thought of doing this for the American boy!" Howells noted that the story of Aldrich's boyhood had suggested similar books, including his own *A Boy's Town*, Charles Dudley Warner's *Being a Boy*, Mark Twain's *Tom Sawyer* and *Huckleberry Finn*. Not so, declared Bernard DeVoto, one of Twain's fellow westerners and an historian ever alert to catch any misconceptions concerning Twain. DeVoto deemed it idle to speculate over the origins of *Tom Sawyer*, and whether Aldrich had had any influence on it, for when Mark Twain had come around to writing *Tom Sawyer*, he had "at last arrived at the theme that was most harmonious with his interest, his experience, and his talents…Mark Twain was predestined to this work." Well, perhaps: but Howells was there! He was Twain's friend and editor. He read *Tom Sawyer* in manuscript, at Twain's request. By deleting some of the profanity and toning down the section where Becky tears a page of the teacher's book of anatomy, Howells may have slanted the story toward the juvenile market—Twain had intended it for adults. "It is not a boy's book at all," he had written to Howells. Also, by 1871, Twain and Aldrich had become friends. Twain must have been aware that what Aldrich had done for the waning years of New England Puritanism, he would do for the early years of western frontier life. While one is genteel and polite, the other is rugged and lusty, but both cover much the same kind of boyish pranks and activities: climbing out of windows in the dead of night, running away, camping out, falling miserably in love. Aunt Polly is to one what Grandfather Nutter is to the other: Injun Joe was starved "entirely to death in the cave" (incidentally, he ate candle wax in his struggle to survive just as, in Aldrich's story "A Struggle for Life," Philip Wentworth had in the tomb) for the same kind of heightened literary effect that Aldrich had used in letting Binny Wallace float helplessly out to sea. In his autobiography, Twain praised Aldrich's brilliance and wit, but referred blisteringly to Aldrich's prose as "diffuse, self-conscious, barren of distinction…," grudgingly conceding that "his fame as a writer…is based on half a dozen small poems which are not surpassed in our language for exquisite grace and beauty and finish."

The poem that Aldrich had written in honor of Longfellow's centennial—a poem that was read one month later at Aldrich's funeral—is also a fitting tribute to his boyhood story: "They do not die who leave their thoughts/Imprinted on some deathless page./Themselves may pass; the spell they wrought/Endures on earth from age to age." *The Story of a Bad Boy* wrought a spell that has wound its way down the years from Lucretia Peabody Hale to Sarah Orne Jewett, from Laura Ingalls Wilder to Maureen Daly, from Esther Forbes to Jack Schaefer, from J.D. Salinger to John Donovan.

—Mary Silva Cosgrave

———

ALGER, Horatio (Jr.). American. Born in Chelsea, Massachusetts, 13 January 1832. Educated at Chelsea Grammar School; Gates Academy, Marlborough, Massachusetts, 1845–47; Harvard University, Cambridge, Massachusetts (Bowdoin prize, 1851), 1848–52, A.B. 1852 (Phi Beta Kappa); Harvard Divinity School, 1853, 1857–60, graduated 1860: ordained 1864. Assistant editor, Boston *Daily Advertiser*, 1853–54; schoolteacher, East Greenwich, Rhode Island, 1854–55; principal, Deerfield Academy, Massachusetts, 1856; tutor, and editorial writer, *True Flag*, Boston, 1856–57; traveled in Europe, 1860–61; private tutor in Cambridge and Nahant, Massachusetts, 1861–64; minister, First Unitarian Church, Brewster, Massachusetts, 1864–66; lived in New York, 1866–96, and private tutor from 1869; lived in South Natick, Massachusetts, 1896–99. *Died 18 July 1899.*   Fiction: *Bertha's Christmas Vision* (includes verse), 1856; *Frank's Campaign*, 1864; *Paul Prescott's Charge (Paul Prescott the Runaway)*, 1865; *Helen Ford*, 1866; *Timothy Crump's Ward (Jack's Ward)*, 1866; *Charlie Codman's Cruise (Bill Sturdy)*, 1866; *Fame and Fortune*, 1868; *Ragged Dick*, 1868; *Luck and Pluck*, 1869; *Mark, The Match Boy*, 1869; *Rough and Ready*, 1869; *Ben, The Luggage Boy*, 1870; *Rufus and Rose*, 1870; *Sink or Swim (Paddle Your Own Canoe)*, 1870; *Paul the Peddler (Plucky Paul)*, 1871; *Strong and Steady*, 1871; *Tattered Tom*, 1871; *Phil, The Fiddler*, 1872; *Slow and Sure*, 1872; *Strive and Succeed*, 1872; *Bound to Rise*, 1873; *Try and Trust (Trials and Adventures of Herbert Mason)*, 1873; *Brave and Bold*, 1874; *Julius*, 1874; *Risen from the Ranks*, 1874; *Herbert Carter's Legacy (George Carter's Legacy)*, 1875; *The Young Outlaw*, 1875; *Sam's Chance*, 1876; *Shifting for Himself (How His Ship Came Home)*, 1876; *Wait and Hope*, 1877; *The Western Boy (Tom, The Bootblack)*, 1878; *The Young Adventurer*, 1878; *The Young Miner*, 1879; *The Telegraph Boy (The District Telegraph Boy)*, 1879; *The Young Explorer*, 1880; *Tony, The Hero (Tony, The Tramp)*, 1880; *Ben's Nugget*, 1882; *The Train Boy*, 1883; *The Young Circus Rider*, 1883; *Dan, The Detective (Dan the Newsboy; Dutiful Dan)*, 1884; *Do and Dare*, 1884; *Hector's Inheritance (Never Despair!)*, 1885; *Helping Himself*, 1886; *Joe's Luck*, 1887; *Frank Fowler, The Cash Boy*, 1887; *Number 91*, 1887; *The Store Boy (The Fortunes of Ben Barclay; Ben Barclay's Courage)*, 1887; *Ben Stanton, The Explorer*, 1887; *Bob Burton (The Young Ranchman of the Missouri)*, 1888; *The Errand Boy*, 1888; *The Merchant's Crime (Ralph Raymond's Heir)*, 1888; *Tom Temple's Career*, 1888; *Tom Thatcher's Fortune*, 1888; *Tom Tracy*, 1888; *The Young Acrobat of the Great North American Circus (He Would Be a Mountebank)*, 1888; *Luke Walton*, 1889; *Mark Stanton*, 1890; *Ned Newton*, 1890; *A New York Boy*, 1890; *The Odds Against Him (Driven from Home)*, 1890; *Struggling Upward*, 1890; *Dean Dunham (Wait Till the Clouds Roll By)*, 1890; *The Erie Train Boy (The Straight Ahead)*, 1890; *$500 (Uncle Jacob's Secret; The Five Hundred Dollar Check)*, 1890; *Digging for Gold*, 1892; *The Young*

Boatman of Pine Point, 1892; *Facing the World*, 1893; *In a New World* (*The Nugget Finders; Val Vane's Victory*), 1893; *Only an Irish Boy*, 1894; *Victor Vane*, 1894; *Adrift in the City*, 1895; *Frank Hunter's Peril*, 1896; *The Young Salesman*, 1896; *Walter Sherwood's Probation*, 1897; *Frank and Fearless*, 1897; *A Boy's Fortune*, 1898; *The Young Bank Messenger*, 1898; *Rupert's Ambition*, 1899; *Mark Mason's Victory*, 1899; *Jed, The Poorhouse Boy*, 1900; *A Debt of Honor*, 1900; *Ben Bruce*, 1901; *Lester's Luck*, 1901; *Making His Mark*, 1901; *Striving for Fortune* (*Walter Griffith*), 1901; *Tom Brace*, 1901; *An Grant's Pluck*, 1902; *A Rolling Stone* (*Wren Winter's Triumph*), 1902; *Tom Turner's Legacy*, 1902; *The World Before Him*, 1902; *Bernard Brook's Adventures*, 1903; *Chester Rand*, 1903; *Forging Ahead* (*Andy Gordon*), 1903; *Adrift in New York*, 1903; *Finding a Fortune* (*The Tin Box*), 1904; *Mark Manning's Mission*, 1905; *The Young Musician*, 1906; *In Search of Treasure*, 1907; *Wait and Win*, 1908; *Robert Coverdale's Struggle*, 1910; *Silas Snobden's Office Boy*, 1973; *Cast upon the Breakers*, 1974; *Hugo, The Deformed*, 1978; *Madeline, The Temptress*, 1981; *The Secret Drawer*, 1981; *The Cooper's Ward*, 1981; *Herbert Selden*, 1981; *Manson, The Miser*, 1981; *The Gipsy Nurse*, 1981; *The Discarded Son*, 1981; *The Mad Heiress*, 1981; *Marie Bertrand*, 1981; the following completed by Edward Stratemeyer—*Falling In with Fortune*, 1900; *Out for Business*, 1900; *Nelson the Newsboy*, 1901; *Young Captain Jack*, 1901; *Jerry, The Backwoods Boy*, 1904; *Lost at Sea*, 1904; *From Farm to Fortune*, 1905; *The Young Book Agent*, 1905; *Joe the Hotel Boy*, 1906; *Randy of the River*, 1906; *Ben Logan's Triumph*, 1908.

* * *

Most of Horatio Alger's once popular juveniles are about young boys who achieve material success through their industry, thrift, and good character, aided by some happy coincidence. The stories have predictable plots, stilted dialogue, stock characters, and a banal use of language or device. Apologists say that Alger's works should be judged by the standards of the late 19th century, implying that his literary stock would rise. But would it? A lack of literary talent and imagination marks Alger as a second-rate formula writer.

Application of an earlier standard excuses the near plagiarism of Dickens's *Christmas Carol* as "The Veiled Mirror" in *Bertha's Christmas Vision*. It explains the errors resulting from careless editing and the speed or method of Alger's writing. *From Canal Boy to President*, a boys' life of president James A. Garfield, was available for sale within seven weeks of Garfield's death. Writing without revision, Alger worked on several stories at one time. On occasion, his characters—never very dissimilar in type or type of name—mistakenly slipped from one book to another. Luke Larkin suddenly appears in *Luke Walton*.

Both books are vintage Alger. In *Struggling Upward; or, Luke Larkin's Luck*, Luke, the son of a carpenter's widow, "had a pleasant expression, and a bright, resolute look, a warm heart, and a clear intellect, and was probably, in spite of his poverty, the most popular boy in Groveton." In contrast, Randolph, son of Groveton's unscrupulous banker, buys his popularity and, at the book's end, is "an office boy...no longer able to swagger and boast." Luke's benefactor, a stranger who sent Luke on a mission west for information about missing government bonds, turns out to be a lost, rich relative. There are the usual discussions about money; Luke returns to New York "with only three dollars and seventy-five cents," but is urged to take "a hundred dollars on account" with "fifty dollars more...for your thoughtfulness." Typically, Alger closes with a brief summary. Luke "has struggled upward from a boyhood of privation and self-denial into a youth and manhood of prosperity and honor. There has been some luck about it...but after all he is indebted for most of his good fortune to his own good qualities." The message was plain; the recipe simple. The books were unfailingly moral but did not preach. Iden-

tification with characters was easy; dialogue and action followed in quick succession. An Alger story entertains.

Ragged Dick established Alger. His best-known but not his best book, it is too long and too slow to get the action underway. Too many pages are a New York itinerary. Possibly readers in more rural times found the big city references exciting. To the book's credit, Dick's character has some dimension; he sprang from Alger's first enthusiastic acquaintance with actual poor boys who stayed at the Newsboys' Lodging House where Alger visited constantly.

Alger should be defended by shifting from literary criticism to literary history, and, better, to his place in the emotional history of a nation. For his readers, Alger interpreted democracy as a simple "rags to riches" dream; fortuitous luck might come to anyone and, most of all, to clean-living, hard-working boys. All was possible in Alger's America; that is the well-spring of his appeal. In 1982, the United States issued a Horatio Alger stamp showing the decorative title-page of *Ragged Dick*. Probably few people can identify the picture, and fewer still have cause to seek out the book. But, many would have an intuition that here is a symbol of America, an expression from the past reaffirming a faith in the future.

—Claire England

ANSTEY, F. Pseudonym for Thomas Anstey Guthrie. British. Born in London, 8 August 1856. Educated at King's College School, London; Trinity Hall, Cambridge. Called to the bar, 1880; worked briefly as a barrister. Regular contributor to *Punch*, London. *Died 10 March 1934.* Fiction: *Vice-Versâ*, 1882; *Paleface and Redskin and Other Stories*, 1898; *Only Toys!*, 1903; *In Brief Authority*, 1915.

* * *

F. Anstey was not by design a writer for children, but one of those many late Victorian and Edwardian novelists who could create characters, plots, settings, immediately popular with readers of all ages. These include Richard Jefferies, with *Bevis*, and Rider Haggard, Kipling, Buchan, P.C. Wren, A.E.W. Mason, Anthony Hope, Conan Doyle, Marjorie Bowen, Jules Verne, Alexandre Dumas, and early H.G. Wells. For some years a regular contributor to *Punch*, Anstey is now really celebrated for only one book, *Vice-Versâ*, although *The Black Poodle* can occasionally be found and might still appeal, as could the lively *The Brass Bottle*, an adroit variation on the perennial, indestructible Aladdin theme. Magic and fantasy are seldom absent, notably in *Only Toys!* and books with such revealing titles as *Tourmalin's Time Cheques* and *The Talking Horse*.

The magic, however, is not a facile escape into mere make-belief. "I like the fantastic only inside the real," wrote Alain-Fournier, and Anstey succeeds by always obeying this. An inventive storyteller, he mixes a modicum of fantasy with direct, un-bizarre observation, human understanding, sly comedy. These combine most fully in *Vice-Versâ*, where the magic, a single involuntary trick in the beginning, reversed at the end, supplies the catalyst for the plot, which develops as complete realism, in turn painful, comic, sardonic. Its target is the harsh world of the private school, run for personal profit and with unchallenged despotism by the headmaster for the benefit less of the pupils than of the complacent, prosperous parents. These are usually remote from their children, whom they continually assure, with the advantage of inadequate memory, that schooldays are life's happiest period. This fulsome belief is tested and shattered when the accidental manipulation of a magic charm transforms lordly, unimaginative Mr. Bultitude into his own son, Dick, on the last morning of the holidays, while Dick becomes his own father.

was soon a well-tried formula, by giving full rein to youthful emotions within the strict bounds of what then passed as Christian morality, while leading his readers through dramatically bloody chapters of shipwreck, slaughter, capture and escape, to the inevitable happy ending of a wealthy and pious old age.

He portrayed a world where the good were terribly good, and the bad were terribly bad, and the British were terribly British—and worth 10 of any foreigners alive, by Jingo! For any writer of his time to dare to suggest otherwise would have been considered the blackest heresy by the young men of Victoria's England. For these were the boys who, in their turn, were to become the soldiers and sailors, the explorers, and trail-blazers, the missionaries and merchant adventurers, the exploiters, the Word-spreaders, the successes and failures of the great British Empire on which the sun would never set.

—Eric Quayle

CARROLL, Lewis.   Pseudonym for Charles Lutwidge Dodgson. British.   Born in Daresbury, Cheshire, 27 January 1832. Educated at a school in Richmond, Surrey, 1844–46; Rugby School, Warwickshire, 1846–49; Christ Church, Oxford (Boultor scholar, 1851), B.A. (honours) in mathematics 1854, M.A. 1857. Fellow, and Master of the House, 1855, sub-librarian, 1855, Bostock Scholar, 1855, Lecturer in Mathematics, 1856–81, and Curator of the Common Room, 1882–92, Christ Church, Oxford. Ordained, 1861. *Died 14 January 1898.* Fiction: *Alice's Adventures in Wonderland*, 1865, revised edition, 1886, 1897; *Through the Looking-Glass, and What Alice Found There*, 1871, revised edition, 1897; *Alice's Adventures Underground*, 1886; *The Nursery Alice*, 1889; *Sylvie and Bruno*, 2 vols., 1889–93; *The "Wonderland" Postage-Stamp-Case*, 1890; *The Wasp in a Wig*, 1978. Verse: *Phantasmagoria and Other Poems*, 1869; *The Hunting of the Snark*, 1876; *Rhyme? and Reason?*, 1883; *Three Sunsets and Other Poems*, 1898; *Collected Verse*, 1929; *For the Train*, 1932; *The Poems*, 1973.

*   *   *

Little that is not general knowledge can be said about the Rev. Charles Lutwidge Dodgson whose books for children were published over the pseudonym of Lewis Carroll. After the Bible and Shakespeare, he is probably the most quoted author in the English language, and nearly every character from *Alice's Adventures in Wonderland* and *Through the Looking-Glass, and What Alice Found There* is known and recognised almost universally. At the time of his death Andrew Lang wrote that Carroll was, "With the possible exception of Thackeray and Hans Andersen, the most successful writer of stories for children that the world has ever seen. *Alice's Adventures* and *Through the Looking-Glass* are books of which a child with an active mind never tires. They are equally full of imagination and humour. They suggest so much more than they say, that those who have grown up with them have found more in them every year."

The appearance and popularity of *Alice* (we may consider it as a single unity of two volumes, like *Sylvie and Bruno* towards the end of his life) brought about the greatest revolution so far in the literature of childhood. Apart from a few volumes of fairytales—Perrault, Grimm, Andersen, in various forms—and *The Rose and the Ring*, which appeared 10 years before *Wonderland*—the books a child might read (other than adult works like the Waverley Novels) were still of an improving or moralistic kind, however well writers like

Charlotte Yonge or Mrs. Craik might manage to transcend their limitations. But, in spite of Thackeray and Ruskin, whose inspiration overcame the moral and indeed turned it to their own use, *Alice* was something completely new. It was, as Harvey Darton wrote in 1932, "the coming to the surface, powerfully and permanently, the first unapologetic, undocumented appearance in print, for readers who sorely needed it, of liberty of thought in children's books. Henceforth fear had gone, and with it shy disquiet. There was to be in hours of pleasure no more dread about the moral value, the ponderable, measured quality and extent, of pleasure itself. It was to be enjoyed and even promoted with neither forethought nor remorse."

It is possible to a certain extent to understand how the circumstances of his life and character made Dodgson the author of *Alice*. He grew up as an elder brother in a large family with girls predominating, and living in parsonages remote and self-contained. From an early age he was accustomed to the society of children younger than himself, and to entertaining them in various ways, the writing (and probably telling) of stories and verses being one of the chief ways in which he did this. While still an undergraduate at Christ Church, Oxford, he was telling stories to children whom he met during "reading holidays" and writing nonsense letters to his youngest sister and brother, who were still children. The fact that instead of growing out of these pastimes with children he pursued them more and more eagerly was due in a considerable extent to the fact that he suffered all his life from a stammer—which left him in the company of children, and of little girls in particular. Consequently he spent more and more time with his child-friends and achieved an understanding of them and their outlook which has probably never been equalled by any other author.

Chance—and a particularly good story out of many—caused him to write out *Alice's Adventures Underground* for Alice Liddell and another chance caused the novelist Henry Kingsley to pick up and read Alice's manuscript copy, and urge Mrs. Liddell to persuade the author to publish it. Chance again made Dodgson, doubtful of the story's appeal to the children other than those for whom it was written, lend his own copy to George MacDonald, himself an outstanding writer for the young, to be read to his children—whose response was so enthusiastic that Dodgson at once began revising the story and adding other incidents from his retentive memory—from which rich source came also most of the incidents in *Through the Looking-Glass* a few years later.

All this might have produced only some glorified variant in *The Rose and the Ring* genre, had not Dodgson been a professional mathematician and logician—and already an accomplished manipulator of the English language. The exact logician making use lightheartedly of the illogicalities of daily speech—and occasionally making "portmanteau" words by weaving together two other words in an exactly balanced synthesis—was able to follow where fancy led, but always in strict obedience to the discipline which he seems to have evolved spontaneously. In fact Lewis Carroll, the adult writer who was able to look at life through a child's eyes, and C.L. Dodgson, the academic lecturer on mathematics and logic, formed the perfect union from which *Alice* could be born. They were still in harmony when *The Hunting of the Snark*—the only real nonsense-epic in existence—came into being; but the marriage of two minds was falling apart when *Sylvie and Bruno* was being forced into existence: the don was imposing his will consciously upon the dreamer—and the result was what Derek Hudson has so aptly called "the most interesting failure in English literature."

Though not itself numinous, *Alice* once and for all flung wide the "magic casement opening on the foam of perilous seas in faery lands forlorn": she was the ancestor of all the great children's books that were to follow her, however different in kind they may seem—of *The Midnight Folk* and *The Lion, The Witch and the Wardrobe* as well as more obvious descendants such as *The Just So Stories* and *Winnie-the-Pooh*. But unlike most progenitors, *Alice* is in no danger

Dazed, incredulous, Mr. Bultitude is thereupon packed off to school and, while Dick casually starts ruining the family business, endures a term wracked with misery. Anstey's picture of the school is no caricature: it seems a fair enough assessment of an average private school, still existing at least until 1939. The gap between parents and children, teachers and taught, headmaster and staff, is sharply exposed, though Mr. Bultitude's tribulations are extremely funny. Both Saki and P.G. Wodehouse must have relished the description of the hapless Victorian father, in pupil's uniform, in the school train surrounded by small, giggling boys, attempting to engage the formidable, increasingly irritated and suspicious Headmaster with informed remarks about market conditions in the City. The book must have had some useful effect on the adult world. It has been successfully filmed by Peter Ustinov, and, in present conditions, is unlikely to lack appreciation in many schools and homes today.

—Peter Vansittart

BALLANTYNE, R(obert) M(ichael). Also wrote as Comus. British. Born in Edinburgh, 24 April 1825. Educated at Edinburgh Academy, 1835–37, and privately. Married Jane Dickson Grant in 1866; four sons and two daughters. Apprentice clerk, Hudson's Bay Company, in Canada, 1841–47; clerk, North British Railway Company, Edinburgh, 1847–49; staff member, Alexander Cowan and Company, paper-makers, Edinburgh, 1849; junior partner, Thomas Constable and Company, printers, Edinburgh, 1849–55. Lecturer and free-lance writer after 1855. Member, 1858, Ensign, 1859, and Captain, 1860, Edinburgh Volunteers. Lived in Harrow, Middlesex, after 1883. Died 8 February 1894. Fiction: *Snowflakes and Sunbeams*, 1856; *Three Little Kittens* (as Comus), 1856; *Mister Fox* (as Comus), 1857; *My Mother (Chit-Chat)* (as Comus), 1857; *The Butterfly's Ball and the Grasshopper's Feast* (as Comus), 1857; *The Life of a Ship from the Launch to the Wreck*, 1857; *Ungava*, 1858; *The Coral Island*, 1858; *The Robber Kitten* (as Comus), 1858; *Martin Rattler*, 1858; *Mee-a-ow!*, 1859; *The World of Ice*, 1860; *The Dog Crusoe*, 1861; *The Gorilla Hunters*, 1861; *The Golden Dream*, 1861; *The Red Eric*, 1861; *The Wild Man of the West*, 1863; *Fighting the Whales*, 1863; *Away in the Wilderness*, 1863; *Fast in the Ice*, 1863; *Gascoyne*, 1864; *The Lifeboat*, 1864; *Chasing the Sun*, 1864; *Freaks on the Fells*, 1864; *The Lighthouse*, 1865; *Shifting Winds*, 1866; *Fighting the Flames*, 1867; *Silver Lake*, 1867; *Deep Down*, 1868; *Erling the Bold*, 1869; *Sunk at Sea*, 1869; *Lost in the Forest*, 1869; *Over the Rocky Mountains*, 1869; *Saved by the Lifeboat*, 1869; *The Cannibal Islands*, 1869; *Hunting the Lions*, 1869; *Digging for Gold*, 1869; *Up in the Clouds*, 1869; *The Battle and the Breeze*, 1869; *The Floating Light of the Goodwin Sands*, 1870; *The Iron Horse*, 1871; *The Pioneers*, 1872; *The Norsemen in the West*, 1872; *Life in the Red Brigade*, 1873; *Black Ivory*, 1873; *The Pirate City*, 1874; *Rivers of Ice*, 1875; *The Story of the Rock*, 1875; *Under the Waves*, 1876; *The Settler and the Savage*, 1877; *In the Track of the Troops*, 1878; *Jarwin and Cuffy*, 1878; *Philosopher Jack*, 1880; *The Lonely Island*, 1880; *Post Haste*, 1880; *The Red Man's Revenge*, 1880; *My Doggie and I*, 1881; *The Giant of the North*, 1882; *The Kitten Pilgrims*, 1882; *The Battery and the Boiler*, 1883; *Battles with the Sea*, 1883; *The Thorogood Family*, 1883; *The Madman and the Pirate*, 1883; *Dusty Diamonds Cut and Polished*, 1884; *The Young Trawler*, 1884; *Twice Bought*, 1885; *The Rover of the Andes*, 1885; *The Island Queen*, 1885; *Red Rooney*, 1886; *The Prairie Chief*, 1886; *The Lively Poll*, 1886; *The Big Otter*, 1887; *The Fugitives*, 1887; *Blue Lights*, 1888; *The Middy and the Moors* (*Slave of the Moors*), 1888; *The Crew of the Water Wagtail*, 1889; *The Eagle Cliff*, 1889; *Blown to Bits*, 1889; *The Garret and the Garden*, 1890; *Charlie to the Rescue*, 1890; *The Buffalo Runners*, 1891; *The Coxswain*, 1891; *The Hot Swamp*, 1892; *Hunted and Harried*, 1892; *The Hunters*, 1893; *Reuben's Luck*, 1896.

* * *

In his own lifetime R.M. Ballantyne gained the distinction identified in the minds of his young readers with the brave deeds performed by the manly characters in the fictional wrote. His photographs, which showed him as a handsome figure with the shoulder-length hair of a typical North trapper, complete with long-barrelled gun and powder-horn his knees, went far to confirm this impression. His autobiographical experiences as a youth employed by the Hudson's Bay were related in his first book, *Hudson's Bay; or, Every-Day the Wilds of North America*, and his early life in Rupert formed the background to many of his tales.

His first fictional work for the young appeared in *Snowflakes and Sunbeams; or, The Young Fur Trader*; but *Coral Island* (1858) that made his name as a juvenile novel was the book which Robert Louis Stevenson acknowledged formative influence of his own love of the South Seas, a valuer later led to his writing the immortal *Treasure Island* dedicatory allusion to "Ballantyne the Brave."

Ballantyne was one of the first writers of fictional adventure for the young to apply himself seriously to the background so necessary to render the stories realistic. Unlike G.A. H wrote fictional tales set against historical backgrounds in of Sir Walter Scott, Ballantyne almost without exception the task of living and often working for weeks or months geographical location where he meant to set his story. The *Lifeboat* he lived at Deal with the lifeboat crew; for *The* he spent several weeks on the Bell Rock Lighthouse; for *the Flames* he was with the London Fire Brigade waiting on end for the bells to signal a fire; for *Deep Down: A Cornish Mines* he lived with the tin-miners of St. Just for months. The same could be said for *The Floating L Goodwin Sands*, for which he endured weeks of seasick Gull Lightship, and for *The Iron Horse; or, Life on the Line* he acted as fireman on board the tender of the London-to express. The result of all these and countless other experiences at home and abroad was a series of well over 80 full-length novels embodying a realism never before seen in works boys.

He was the hero of Victorian youth; but his weakness being straitjacketed by his puritanism. Unlike Stevenson unable to write a romantic and exciting story of adventure unmoralised and unashamed. Too often the action in H tales was braked by the gum of piety and the evangelistic ing of the often bloodthirsty young characters he made They lightheartedly slaughtered the fauna and the native islands and jungles where they found themselves marooned impartial vigour, before falling on their knees to thank infinite mercy and a successful day's sport. *The Gorilla* a typical example of unrelenting cruelty by young teen passed without comment in the mid-19th-century. He all do, for the age in which he lived.

Nevertheless, Ballantyne opened for the sons of the panding *literati* of middle- and working-class families new vista of a world spiced with romance and danger waiting for the young men of Britain to grow up and projected into lives which were often drab and humdrum cally coloured image, mirroring his readers in the fig heroes, and leaving them tantalised with the knowledge too, could equally well have overcome the fearful odds ag Ralph, Jack, and Peterkin grappled so bravely. He emp of growing old or being forgotten: she is as fresh and vivid today as she was a hundred years ago, and an everlasting delight to readers of all ages.

—Roger Lancelyn Green

———

COOLIDGE, Susan. Pseudonym for Sarah Chauncy Woolsey. American. Born in Cleveland, Ohio, 29 January 1835. Educated at private schools, Cleveland; Mrs. Hubbard's Select Family School for Young Ladies, Hanover, New Hampshire. Did hospital work and helped organize nursing service during the Civil War. Consulting reader for Roberts Brothers, publishers, Boston. *Died 9 April 1905.* Fiction: *The New Year's Bargain,* 1872; *What Katy Did* series, from 1872; *Little Miss Mischief and Other Stories,* 1874; *Mischief's Thanksgiving and Other Stories,* 1874; *Nine Little Goslings,* 1875; *For Summer Afternoons,* 1876; *Eyebright,* 1879; *A Guernsey Lily,* 1881; *A Round Dozen,* 1883; *A Little Country Girl,* 1885; *Clover,* 1888; *Just Sixteen,* 1889; *In the High Valley,* 1891; *The Barberry Bush and Eight Other Stories,* 1892; *Not Quite Eighteen,* 1894; *An Old Convent School in Paris and Other Papers,* 1895; *Curly Locks,* 1899; *A Little Knight of Labor,* 1899; *Little Tommy Tucker,* 1900; *Two Girls,* 1900; *Uncle and Aunt,* 1900; *The Rule of Three,* 1904; *A Sheaf of Stories,* 1906. Verse: *Rhymes and Ballads,* 1892.

*   *   *

Susan Coolidge gained her reputation from the *Katy* books, although she had some contemporary success as a critic. At first reading *What Katy Did* appears to be in the mainstream of Victorian children's fiction—the motherless family "mothered" by the heroine, the general religious ambiance and the moral retribution for wrongdoing—but a closer inspection reveals that Coolidge was in fact the forerunner of the 20th-century genre of British girls' school stories, her literary influence being greater in the United Kingdom than in her native United States. Figuratively speaking, she may be placed midway between the piety of L.T. Meade's *A World of Girls* with its sanctimonious principal dispensing sweetness and light to the pupils of Lavender House, and the feuds and frolics in the works of Angela Brazil.

Very probably Coolidge took her inspiration from Louisa May Alcott. Certainly Katy embodies some of the foibles of the outspoken Jo March. Like Jo, Katy endeared herself to her readers by her very human faults and spontaneous behaviour; like Jo, she was immediately popular, with her followers demanding a sequel; like Jo's, her popularity was not confined to her compatriots, and English girls readily identified with her. Coolidge received (in *The Independent*) the curious and confusing accolade that she was on her way to becoming a second "Aunt Jo." That Jo was a recognizable self-portrait of Louisa Alcott has to account for the mixed reference to the real and the fictional ladies.

Coolidge seems to have "written out" her Victorianism in *What Katy Did.* Her own upbringing and the expectations of teachers, ministers, and parents demanded a stereotyped "good angel" figure, and it is significant that the author did not select her heroine for the role but a somewhat peripheral character, crippled Cousin Helen. Katy had disobeyed authority and used the garden swing. In the Victorian tradition she had to be "punished" and became bedridden from the consequent fall. Instead of saintly suffering, Katy demonstrated untidiness, irritable temper, and general misery. It was left to the visiting cousin to fulfil the moral function.

"God is going to let you go to his school," Cousin Helen explained to Katy when she complained.

"But what is the school?" asked Katy. "It is called The School of Pain," replied Cousin Helen, with her sweetest smile. "There's the lesson of Patience. That's one of the hardest studies...and there's the lesson of Cheerfulness. And the lesson of Making the Best of Things...."

Cousin Helen helped Katy to see her condition in a new light, and thus motivated the plot, but her formal utterances give a note of unreality to an otherwise natural and lively account. This must have occurred to Coolidge, for Cousin Helen made no other real contribution, and by the end of the sequel volume, *What Katy Did at School,* she does not even appear, merely sending two illuminated religious texts for Katy and her sister Clover on their homecoming: "The girls thought they had never seen anything so pretty." So much for Cousin Helen, the symbol of perfect behaviour, the model for the aspiring Victorian child.

What Katy Did at School is the most significant book in the series (*What Katy Did Next, Clover,* and *In the High Valley* followed) since it predates the entire output of girls' school stories which virtually dominated the reading of British middle-class girls until the 1940's. Adult books (such as *Jane Eyre*) might cast aspersions on the teaching profession, but for the youthful reader authority was irreproachable. There is a chasm between the approach of L.T. Meade to the pious principal Mrs. Willis and Coolidge's ironic appraisal of Mrs. Florence, who lost interest in her pupils once she had decided to leave the school, and made no real effort to mete out justice. Coolidge's own experiences at Mrs. Hubbard's Boarding School in Hanover, New Hampshire, had given her insight into both staff-room and dormitory and the economic strategy behind the school meals. Rebellion among the pupils at "The Nunnery," the nickname given to Hillsover by Katy's companions, was seen from the point of view of the girls, and the character of Rose Red (real name Rosamund Redding) reappeared in various guises in almost every 20th-century school story from Angela Brazil's American Gipsy Latimer in *The Leader of the Lower School* to Enid Blyton's heroine of *The Naughtiest Girl in the School.* Always defiant, ultimately likable, struggling against the system which may or may not be just, these girls form a continuous thread throughout girls' fiction, together with a casual use of slang which gives a sparkling spontaneity to the dialogue. Coolidge's schoolgirls were as iconoclastic over "correct" speech as they were over behaviour. With Katy as president of the *Society for the Suppression of Unladylike Conduct,* a title bestowed with conscious mockery, established precepts were overthrown. One of the main aims was to have a good time combined with the pursuit of virtue. Victorian writers for children would have considered that a contradiction in terms.

—Gillian Freeman

———

COX, Palmer. Canadian. Born in Granby, Quebec, 28 April 1840. Educated at Granby Academy. Railroad worker and ship carpenter in San Francisco, 1863–75; writer in New York from 1875. *Died 24 July 1924.* Play: *The Brownies in Fairyland,* music and lyrics by Malcolm Douglas, 1925. Verse: *Brownies* series, 13 vols., from 1887.

*   *   *

Palmer Cox found success with his short stories in verse about the Brownies, whose first adventure, "The Brownies' Ride," appeared in *St. Nicholas Magazine* in 1883. This story, in which the Brownies borrow a farmer's horse and cart for a night-long ride, is reprinted in the collection of 24 episodes that form the first Brownie book (1887).

"The Brownies' Ride" is a good example of Cox's rhyming couplets illustrated with his own line drawings. While Cox derived his notion of brownies from a Scots background, he was not a folklorist, and his whimsical creation is an artistic invention.

Early pictures show Brownies, some with antennae or wings, in vaguely defined clothes and the occasional funny hat. Cox soon evolved his Brownies into spindle-legged rotund imps with wide eyes in their round amusing faces. Individual Brownies could be identified by costume as a monacled man-about-town, a policeman, a Dutchman or Chinaman, etc. Children could gleefully search for their particular Brownie.

The rhymes also provide evidence that Cox built his own group characterization of Brownies. A preface normally explains that they are "like fairies and goblins...imaginary little sprites who...delight in harmless pranks and helpful deeds. They work and sport while weary households sleep, and never allow themselves to be seen by mortal eyes."

Keightley's *Fairy Mythology* (1880) records brownies as "of small stature, wrinkled visage, covered with short brown hair and wearing a brown mantle and hood." Often attached to families, they could be repaid for work by small gifts, preferably food. K.M. Briggs's *A Dictionary of Fairies* (1976) adds more information and confirms the reticent and easily offended nature of brownies. At their most mischievous and wicked, brownies become boggarts who act like poltergeists. Cox's Brownies always retain their better nature; the Brownies' mischief is that of curious boys who investigate closed places or try some adult activity.

Each Brownie episode, if similar, is not the same. Cox is credited with purposely excluding crime and pain, and children are not made anxious about these confident little fellows. Moreover, children are often given a model for behaviour since Brownies do good deeds without thought of reward. For many reasons, it is not surprising that a *Palmer Cox Brownie Primer* appeared in 1906.

The Brownies were deservedly and tremendously popular for 40 and more years around the turn of the century. Cox can be judged a better cartoonist than versifier for neither his poems nor his stories were remarkable or memorable without his lively sketches. To read Cox generations later and to see his merry rogues scamper across the page is to experience some sentiment for a sweet, vanished, perhaps illusory, childhood past.

—Claire England

DODGE, Mary Mapes. American. Born in New York City, 26 January 1831. Educated privately. Married William Dodge in 1851 (died 1858); two sons. Helped her father edit the *Working Farmer* magazine, 1847; home-making editor, *Hearth and Home* magazine, New York, 1870–73; founding editor, *St. Nicholas* magazine, New York, 1873–1905. Recipient: French Academy Montyon prize. *Died 21 August 1905.* Fiction: *The Irvington Stories*, 1865; *Hans Brinker; or, The Silver Skates*, 1865; *Donald and Dorothy*, 1883; *The Land of Pluck*, 1894; *The Golden Gate*, 1903; *Po-no-kah*, 1903. Verse: *When Life Is Young*, 1894; *Mary Anne*, 1983.

*   *   *

With the publication of *The Irvington Stories*, Mary Mapes Dodge was widely recognized in the United States as a promising new writer of literature for children. Reviewers and readers praised the eight tales, which derived from American colonial history and from stories told in the author's family, for their blend of realistic detail, engaging

humor, and appropriate moral tone. Encouraged by the book's success, Dodge's publisher, James O'Kane, urged her to begin a second work and, with the Civil War approaching an end, suggested a timely theme—a boy leaving his family to enlist in the Union Army. Unenthusiastic about the idea, Dodge turned instead to notes she had retained from her reading of Motley's *Story of the Dutch Republic* years before as well as to stories she had heard from Dutch immigrant neighbors and began work on a story set in Holland.

Reluctantly, O'Kane agreed to publish the completed manuscript, *Hans Brinker*. An outstanding commercial success from the start, *Hans Brinker* quickly established itself as a classic children's book. As in *The Irvington Stories* there is an abundance of closely observed detail, abstracted from her sources (Dodge did not visit Holland until years after the book was written) and combined with a clear moral purpose. Not notably inventive or original, Dodge drew heavily on familiar popular conventions for the structure of the story. Hans Brinker and his sister Gretel are the impoverished but virtuous children of a dike engineer, a mute, uncomprehending invalid since he was injured 10 years before the events of the story take place. This premise, the incapacitation of a family's father and breadwinner and the subsequent suffering, however salutary, of his dependents, was one of the stock conventions of late 19th-century children's literature. For good measure, the plot involves a missing sum of money, a mysterious watch, and a father estranged from his son, as well as the ice skating race that gives the book its title—all familiar devices to create suspense in what is essentially a static book—a series of set pieces, detailing the characteristic and distinctive scenes, social types, customs, dress, and culture of Holland: the festival of St. Nicholas, the windmills and canals, the cities of Haarlem, Leyden, and the Hague.

The central chapters of *Hans Brinker*—and much the longest narrative sequence—detail a skating expedition undertaken by five of Hans's friends, boys from wealthier families who can afford the diversion. As a consequence, Hans and sister disappear from the story entirely. In order to get the necessary Anglo-American perspective on Dutch culture, Dodge makes one of the five boys an English visitor, and it is through his eyes that the reader sees the charming peculiarities of the Dutch. Enlivened somewhat by differences in temperament among the boys and by an occasional adventure—they capture a robber at one point—the expedition provides Dodge with the means and justification for a close, sympathetic, sometimes condescending description of Dutch life.

In the final third of the book, the focus returns to the Brinker family. The father is restored to health by the leading surgeon in Holland, whom Hans had chanced to meet early in the story. With his reason restored, Hans's father recalls hiding the family savings as well as the circumstances surrounding his possession of the mysterious watch. The young man from whom he had received it turns out to be the estranged son of the eminent surgeon. The Brinker family, tested by 10 years of poverty, is restored to comfortable affluence, and the surgeon is reconciled with his son—and to his son's legitimate desire to have a vocation different from his father's. A conventional final chapter describes the fate of the several children introduced in this story, apportioning happiness and success to the virtuous, especially Hans and Gretel whose fortitude, perseverance, faith, and selfless devotion through years of poverty and care exemplify character at its best.

In its affectionate and detailed description of foreign peoples and places, *Hans Brinker* was a distinct improvement over the earlier travelogues of "Peter Parley" and a harbinger of greater attention to realistic detail in American fiction for children in the late 19th century. Its moral values, however, are quite representative of much children's literature written from the 1830's to the end of the century and beyond. Although Dodge was the pre-eminent children's periodical editor of her generation, she cannot be said to have made a very notable contribution to children's literature, *Hans Brinker* excepted. *The Irvington Stories* are deservedly forgotten, except by a few specialists, and *The Land of Pluck*, while testifying to her affection for Holland, represents no improvement on the similar sketches in *Hans Brinker*; many of her stories are simply cautionary tales of a kind indistinguishable in style or sentiment from the mass of homiletic narrative to be found in many a late 19th-century children's periodical—even the justly praised *St. Nicholas*.

—R. Gordon Kelly

EVERETT-GREEN, Evelyn.   Also wrote as Cecil Adair; Evelyn Dare; H.F.E. British. Born in London, 17 November 1856. Educated at Gower Street Preparatory School; Bedford College, University of London (Reid scholar, 1872–73); Royal Academy, London. Worked as a nurse in a London hospital. *Died 27 April 1932.*
Fiction: *Tom Tempest's Victory* (as H.F.E.), 1880; *Carry's Christmas Gift* (as H.F.E.), 1881; *Fast Friends* (as H.F.E.), 1882; *Little Freddie* (as H.F.E.), 1882; *His Mother's Book* (as H.F.E.), 1883; *Fighting the Good Fight* (as H.F.E.), 1883; *Her Husband's Home*, 1885; *Mr. Hatherley's Boys*, 1885; *Uncle Roger*, 1885; *True to Himself* (*True to the Last*), 1885; *The Head of the House*, 1886; *Dulcie* series, from 1887; *Our Winnie*, 1887; *The Last of the Dacres*, 1887; *A Child Without a Name* (*Drifted Ashore*), 1887; *Barbara's Brothers*, 1887; *All or Nothing*, 1888; *Little Lady Clare*, 1888; *Dodo*, 1888; *The Little Midshipman and Other Stories*, 1889; *My Boynie*, 1889; *Miriam's Ambition*, 1889; *Monica*, 1889; *My Black Sheep*, 1889; *The Percevals*, 1890; *Little Ruth's Lady*, 1890; *Bertie Clifton*, 1890; *Birdie's Resolve and How It Was Accomplished*, 1890; *Clive's Conquest*, 1890; *Daring Dot*, 1890; *Marcus Stratford's Charge*, 1890; *Mischievous Moncton*, 1890; *Oliver Langton's Ward*, 1890; *The Stronger Will*, 1890; *A Summer Holiday*, 1890; *Dorothy's Vocation*, 1890; *The Secret of the Old House*, 1890; *Sir Aylmer's Heir*, 1890; *Syd's New Pony*, 1890; *The Witch of the Quarry Hut*, 1890; *Fir-Tree Farm*, 1891; *Loyal Hearts*, 1891; *Miss Meyrick's Niece*, 1891; *Mrs. Romaine's Household*, 1891; *Shadow-Land*, 1891; *Sydney's Secret*, 1891; *Let's Toss for It*, 1891; *Fresh from the Fens*, 1891; *Dare Lorimer's Heritage*, 1891; *Duckworth's Diamonds*, n.d.; *Dick Whistler's Tramp*, 1891; *A Pair of Originals* (as Evelyn Dare), 1892; *Don Carlos*, 1892; *In the Wars of the Roses*, 1892; *The Church and the King*, 1892; *The Doctor's Dozen*, 1892; *Falconer of Falconhurst*, 1892; *A Holiday in a Manor House*, 1892; *In the Days of Chivalry*, 1892; *The Lord of Dynevor*, 1892; *Old Miss Audrey*, 1892; *A Pair of Pickles*, 1892; *Everybody's Friend*, 1893; *St. Dunstan's Clock* (as Evelyn Dare), 1893; *Evil May Day*, 1893; *Friends or Foes?*, 1893; *The Great Show*, 1893; *Little Miss Vixen*, 1893; *St. Wynfrith and Its Inmates*, 1893; *Tom Heron of Sax*, 1893; *The Wilful Willoughbys*, 1893; *Golden Gwendolyn*, 1893; *The Lost Treasure of Trevlyn*, 1893; *Maud Melville's Marriage*, 1893; *Namesakes*, 1893; *Over the Sea Wall*, 1893; *Ronald Kennedy*, 1893; *Afterthought House*, 1894; *Eustace Marchmont*, 1894; *The Family*, 1894; *Flats*, 1894; *Keith's Trial and Victory*, 1894; *Miss Uraca*, 1894; *The Secret Chamber at Chad*, 1894; *A Difficult Daughter*, 1894; *Pat the Lighthouse Boy*, 1894; *Two Bright Shillings*, 1894; *Shut In*, 1894; *Arnold Inglehurst the Preacher*, 1895; *Judith*, 1895; *Ralph Roxburgh's Revenge* (*Ralph Roxburgh's Triumph*), 1895; *A Soldier's Son and the Battle He Fought*, 1895; *A Stepmother's Strategy*, 1895; *The Sunny Side of the Street*, 1895; *His Choice—and Hers*, 1895; *Duff Darlington*, 1895; *Dominique's Vengeance*, 1896; *Squib and His Friends*, 1896; *Enid's Ugly Duckling*, with H. Louisa Bedford, 1896; *In Taunton Town*, 1896; *Olive Roscoe*, 1896; *The Sign of the Red Cross*, 1897; *The Young Pioneers*, 1897; *A Clerk of

Oxford*, 1897; *Molly Melville*, 1897; *Battledown Boys*, 1898; *Esther's Charge*, 1898; *Gladys or Gwenyth*, 1898; *Sister*, 1898; *Tom Tufton's Toll* [and *Travels*], 2 vols., 1898; *For the Queen's Sake*, 1898; *Little Lois*, 1898; *Joy's Jubilee*, 1898; *French and English*, 1899; *Miss Marjorie of Silvermead*, 1899; *Sir Reginald's Ward*, 1899; *The Probation of Mervyn Castleton*, 1899; *Cross Purposes*, 1899; *The Heir of Hascombe Hall*, 1899; *The Mystery of Alton Grange*, 1899; *Priscilla*, with H. Louisa Bedford, 1899; *Bruno and Bimba*, 1900; *Eleanor's Hero*, 1900; *The Little Match-Girl*, 1900; *A Fiery Chariot*, 1900; *In Cloister and Court*, 1900; *The King's Butterfly*, 1900; *The Master of Fernhurst*, 1900; *Odeyne's Marriage*, 1900; *The Silver Axe*, 1900; *The Wooing of Val*, 1900; *Paul Harvard's Campaign*, 1901; *A Gordon Highlander*, 1901; *Princess Fairstar*, 1901; *The Secret of Maxshelling*, 1901; *Tregg's Triumph*, 1901; *Holidays at the Farm*, with others, 1901; *Bob and Bill*, 1901; *After Worcester*, 1901; *True Stories of Girl Heroines*, 1901; *Alwyn Ravendale*, 1902; *The Boys of the Red House*, 1902; *Gabriel Garth, Chartist*, 1902; *In Fair Granada*, 1902; *A Princess's Token*, 1902; *White Wyvill and Red Ruthven*, 1902; *For the Faith*, 1902; *Short Tales from Storyland*, 1902; *Fallen Fortunes*, 1902; *My Lady Joanna*, 1902; *Tiny and Her Grandfather*, 1902; *To the Rescue*, 1902; *Audrey Marsh*, 1903; *Cambria's Chieftain*, 1903; *The Castle of the White Flag*, 1903; *The Conscience of Roger Trehern* (*Roger Trehern*), 1903; *The Squire's Heir*, 1903; *Under Two Queens*, 1903; *A Hero of the Highlands*, 1903; *The Children's Crusade*, 1904; *The Faith of Hilary Lovel*, 1904; *The Jilting of Bruce Heriot*, 1904; *Ringed by Fire*, 1904; *The Three Graces*, 1904; *The Sisters of Silver Sands*, 1904; *Little Lady Val*, 1904; *Miss Greyshott's Girls*, 1905; *Uncle Boo*, 1905; *In Northern Seas*, 1905; *Jim Trelawny*, 1905; *Madam of Clyst Peveril*, 1905; *Smouldering Fires*, 1905; *Treasure Trove*, 1905; *The Defence of the Rock*, 1906; *In a Land of Beasts*, 1906; *The Master of Marshlands*, 1906; *Percy Vere*, 1906; *Dickie and Dorrie* series, from 1906; *A Motherless Maid*, 1906; *Our Great Undertaking*, 1906; *Clanrickard Court*, 1907; *Miss Lorimer of Chard*, 1907; *Carol Carew* (*The Imprudence of Carol Carew*), 1907; *Knights of the Road*, 1907; *Ruth Ravelstan the Puritan's Daughter*, 1907; *Gowrie's Vengeance*, 1908; *Hilary Quest*, 1908; *The Cossart Cousins*, 1908; *Greyfriars*, 1908; *The Family Next Door*, 1908; *Stepsister Stella*, 1908; *Half-a-Dozen Sisters*, 1909; *A Wilful Maid*, 1909; *The City of the Golden Gate*, 1909; *A Lad of London Town*, 1909; *In Grandfather's Garden*, 1910; *Ursula Tempest*, 1910; *The Dean's Daughter* (as Cecil Adair), 1910; *General John*, 1910; *Patricia Pendragon* (as Evelyn Dare), 1911; *Cantacute Towers* (as Cecil Adair), 1911; *A Disputed Heritage*, 1911; *Aunt Patience*, 1912; *Miss Mallory of Mote*, 1912; *Tommy and the Owl*, 1912; *The Yellow Pup*, 1912; *Francesca* (as Cecil Adair), 1912; *Inchfallen*, 1913; *Dora's Dolls' House*, 1914; *The House on the Cliff*, 1914; *The Heronstoke Mystery*, 1915; *Adventurous Anne*, 1916; *Sweepie*, 1918; *Daddy's Ducklings*, 1921; *Crystal's Victory* (as Cecil Adair), 1921; *Queen's Manor School*, 1921; *The Tyrant of Tylecourt*, 1922; *Twins at Tachbury*, 1924; *The Squire's Daughters*, 1932.

*   *   *

Evelyn Everett-Green provided for some 50 years popular books for the young, and the style of her writing is representative of the trends of juvenile publishing of the late 19th and early 20th centuries. Her output (an annual average of 6 or 7 volumes, rising to 11 in peak years), though large by present-day standards, was not considered unduly excessive then (her older contemporary, L.T. Meade, wrote even more). She ranged over most genres of fiction: historical novels, school stories, street arab tales, family adventures, romantic but safe tales for the girl on the brink of leaving the schoolroom ("Yet young maidens will have their dreams, and a maiden's dream requires a man to make it interesting"); she even attempted a story in 1910 for the newly emerging Boy Scout Movement.

Like most lady writers of her type, she extolled the virtues of the thoroughbred gentleman—whose children did not need to be taught the meaning of honour—and denounced the parvenu and nouveau riche—who could not learn it. Like them, too, her favourite scene was the grey-walled mansion with its tumble of roses and terraces descending to rolling parkland, and her favourite child characters the rosy-cheeked maiden with eyes of speedwell blue, the merry rogue, the scamp, the innocent pickle who leaves a trail of devastation but has a warm and loving heart. Occasionally, as in *My Boynie*, she succeeds in creating credible children. Though the plot of this is a familiar one of the period and turns on the gradual decline and ultimate death of a little boy from spinal injury—in this case through being led into mischief by a tomboy elder sister—the character of the latter is sympathetically observed, and the knowledgeable enthusiasm for gardens and for flowers is reminiscent of Mrs. Ewing's *Mary's Meadow* (which indeed the author may have had in mind). She did not, however, usually allow herself time to produce books of this quality, but was content to supply giftbooks for all occasions. These were in general well-received by reviewers who praised their "excellent tone," and described them as "wholesome fiction" and "simple, attractive, healthy stories."

—Gillian Avery

EWING, Juliana Horatia. British. Born in Ecclesfield, Yorkshire, 3 August 1841; daughter of the children's writer Margaret Gatty. Married Alexander Ewing in 1867. Associated with her mother and sister in editing *Aunt Judy's Magazine*, London, 1866–85. *Died 13 May 1885.* Fiction: *Melchior's Dream and Other Tales*, 1862; *Mrs. Overtheway's Remembrances*, 1869; *The Brownies and Other Tales*, 1870; *A Flat Iron for a Farthing*, 1872; *Lob Lie-by-the-Fire*, 1874; *Six to Sixteen*, 1875; *Jan of the Windmill*, 1876; *A Great Emergency and Other Tales*, 1877; *We and the World*, 1880; *Old Fashioned Fairy Tales*, 1882; *Brothers of Pity and Other Tales of Beasts and Men*, 1882; *The Story of a Short Life*, 1882; *Jackanapes*, 1883; *Daddy Darwin's Dovecot*, 1884; *Grandmother's Spring*, 1885; *Mary's Meadow, and Letters from a Little Garden*, 1886; *Dandelion Clocks and Other Tales*, 1887; *The Peace Egg, and A Christmas Mumming Play*, 1887; *Snapdragon, and Old Father Christmas*, 1888; *Last Words*, 1891. Verse: *Blue and Red*, 1883; *A Soldier's Children*, 1883; *The Blue Bells on the Lea*, 1884; *Mother's Birthday Reviews*, 1888.

*   *   *

Juliana Horatia Ewing succeeded, better than any other Victorian writer for the young, in conveying the high spirits of childhood, and remembering its laughter and sheer enjoyment of life. She did not fall into the trap of presenting children's happiness as undiluted. She herself pointed out that "it is probably from an imperfect remembrance of their nursery lives that some people believe that the griefs of one's childhood are light, its joys uncomplicated, and its tastes simple." But she recorded light and shadow, rough and smooth, without moral reflections on their implication to the child that experienced them. It was a style very different from her mother, Mrs. Gatty, who, in the manner of her generation, had felt obliged to improve the occasion whenever she could. The early Victorian writers for the young could never forget their role as governess. Ewing, though no conscious innovator, did forget. She used much the same material as her mother—large, happy families; she was fundamentally just as serious-minded, but she was fortunate in being born into a generation that saw no harm in *enjoying* writing for

children.

No one could ever doubt the seriousness of her religious faith, but, perhaps because it was so strong, it was rarely directly stated, though one senses its influence in all she wrote. She could allow herself the occasional frivolous comment, poking gentle fun at the child who had morbid notions about sickbed piety; she could even be flippant about that sacred cow of the Victorians, Sabbath observance. She criticized the way that parents and teachers treated children; once she even so far forgot herself as to introduce an elopement into the beginning of a story. (Charlotte Yonge advised those reading *Jackanapes* aloud to omit this incident.) She sympathized with the boisterous rough ways of boys, even defended them, and, in *We and the World*, could take their side against their father—a unique occasion in Victorian children's literature. She was equally convincing when she presented a very different type of boy in *A Flat Iron for a Farthing*, a motherless only child, quaint but never muffish, who takes himself rather too seriously (though the author never does).

Perhaps she was at her best when writing of the Yorkshire scenes from which it was such anguish for her to be parted (none of the Gatty children ever wanted to live anywhere else in the world but the vicarage at Ecclesfield where they had been brought up) and of the exuberant life that young Victorians lived when families were large enough to mount private theatricals, to run their own journals and societies; when houses had space to accommodate a mass of different hobbies, and everybody could have his separate plot in the garden and a pet of his own.

Her forgetfulness of her readers sometimes transformed books for a specific class—such as Victorian publishers then produced—into books beyond their reach. *Lob Lie-by-the-Fire* and *Daddy Darwin's Dovecot*, which set out to be the sort of book about the poor boy who became a steady, decent artisan (a type produced by the ton by Anglican wives and daughters for the consumption of children in church schools), finished as exquisitely worked miniatures of Victorian social life.

Some of her longer works tend to sprawl and suffer from a plethora of sub-plot and too many ideas (the result of their being originally written in serial form for her mother's magazine, *Aunt Judy's*) but all of them are beautifully and fastidiously written. She was possibly the most literary of all the Victorian writers of the juvenile domestic tale, and the only one whose works were gathered into a complete edition. Many writers have testified to their affection for her, Kipling and Arthur Ransome among them; authors as various as Frances Hodgson Burnett and Angela Brazil have lifted (perhaps unconsciously) whole episodes from her books; *A Great Emergency* is the precursor of E. Nesbit's Bastable stories.

If one had to remember her by a single work then one might choose the short story "Our Field," so much admired by Ruskin. The plot turns on the efforts of a family of children to save enough for a dog licence, but though their anxiety about this is the shadow, during the day the children forget it because they have found a field where nobody goes, where they can play undisturbed. The field has everything, a stream with freshwater shrimps, a hollow oak, bluebells, cowslips, blackberries. The fact that there are holly berries on the bushes and daisies in the grass at the same season does not matter; Mrs. Ewing is describing an earthly paradise that only a child could know.

—Gillian Avery

FARRAR, F(rederic) W(illiam). British. Born in Bombay, India, 7 August 1831. Educated at Latin School, Aylesbury, Buckinghamshire; King William's College, Isle of Man; London University, B.A. 1852; Trinity College, Cambridge, B.A. 1854, M.A. 1857, D.D. 1874. Married Lucy Cardew in 1860; five sons and five daughters. Master, Marlborough College, 1854–55, and Harrow, 1855–70; headmaster, Marlborough College, 1871–76. Deacon, 1854; ordained priest, 1857; chaplain to Queen Victoria, 1869; Canon, 1875, and Archdeacon, 1883, Westminster; Dean of Canterbury, 1895. *Died 22 March 1903.* Fiction: *Eric; or, Little by Little*, 1858; *Julian Home*, 1859; *St. Winifred's*, 1862; *Darkness and Dawn*, 1891; *Gathering Clouds*, 1895; *Allegories*, 1895; *The Three Homes*, 1896.

*   *   *

F.W. Farrar wrote several kinds of book for the young, but his seriousness of intention is recognisable in all of them. An historical tale like *Darkness and Dawn* was devised to illustrate the "supreme and deeply interesting problem" of the source of the strength of Christianity, by employing a fiction which "even for the minutest allusions" has "contemporary authority." His allegorical tales are learned, Biblical as well as moral; even the popular romance *The Three Homes*, published anonymously to detach it from his more serious studies, is a fable of the soul's formation. When he wrote stories about school boys, with whom he was professionally concerned, his passionate earnestness transformed his stories into dramas of emotional and spiritual struggle.

Of these, *Eric; or, Little by Little* is still known, at least by repute, but *St. Winifred's* and *Julian Home* are scarcely less extraordinary productions. *Eric* is a very dark tale. Eric is a perfectly-brought-up and noble-natured boy until he is sent away to school, and yet is ruined morally and physically by his failure to resist the temptations he meets there. His own turpitude, reinforced by the deaths of his beloved little brother and his mother, brings him to an early grave. The plot is a combination of the trivial incidents really making up school life, and lurid misadventures, culminating in Eric's running away to sea and being starved and flogged into a state that leads to his death. The most remarkable aspect of the book is not the religiose melodrama that made it a favourite Sunday School prize, but its concentration upon the emotional and sexual lives of schoolboys. It was for the open avowal and display of feeling, the fervent prayer and the exchange of embraces and kisses between friends, that it was hated by Kipling's Stalky and Co. and other such believers in the stiff upper lip. The whole movement of late Victorian social behaviour, crushing men and boys into ever greater restraint and rejecting any sort of expression of feeling as unmanly, was against Farrar, and his readership was chiefly female or working-class Christians—groups to whom emotion did not appear embarrassing, and the struggle of good and evil within personal relationships was not a taboo subject. Farrar writes about the primitive life of the schools he knew, and grows hysterical and grandiloquent in the attempt to discriminate between the good he perceives in passionate friendship, and the corruption of casual and often enforced sex, without being able to mention any of these things explicitly. The laughter that he raised was partly a just response to the flamboyance and confusion of his style, partly the inevitable consequence of changing taste, but also partly a nervous reaction of shocked self-defence from readers who were not prepared to countenance his insistence that the educator's moral obligation to his pupils extended to their emotional and sexual lives, and that these required guidance rather than denial, concealment, and repression.

—J.S. Bratton

FENN, George Manville. British. Born in Pimlico, London, 3 January 1831. Educated at Battersea Training College for Teachers, 1851–54. Married Susanna Leake in 1855; two sons and six daughters. Schoolmaster in Lincolnshire, then a printer: produced his own magazine, *Modern Metre*, 1862; part-owner of *Hertfordshire and Essex Observer*, Bishop's Stortford, 1864; then a writer: editor, *Cassell's Magazine*, London, 1870; publisher, *Once a Week*, London, 1873–79; drama critic, the *Echo*, and theatre producer, 1887–88. *Died 26 August 1909.* Fiction: *Hollowdell Grange*, 1866; *Off to the Wilds*, 1881; *The Golden Magnet*, 1883; *Dutch the Diver*, 1883; *Middy and Ensign*, 1883; *The Silver Cañon*, 1884; *Menhardoc (The Boys of Menhardoc)*, 1884; *Bunyip Land*, 1884; *Brownsmith's Boy*, 1885; *The Dark House*, 1885; *Patience Wins*, 1885; *A Terrible Coward, and Son Philip*, 1885; *Yussuf the Guide*, 1886; *Devon Boys*, 1886; *The Chaplain's Craze*, 1886; *The Bag of Diamonds*, 1887; *Dick o'the Fens*, 1887; *Mother Carey's Chicken*, 1887; *The Story of Antony Grace*, 1888; *Quicksilver*, 1888; *Commodore Junk*, 1888; *In Jeopardy*, 1889; *Three Boys*, 1889; *Burr Junior*, 1891; *The Raja of Dah*, 1891; *Syd Belton, The Boy Who Would Not Go to Sea*, 1891; *To the West*, 1891; *The Weathercock*, 1892; *The Crystal Hunters*, 1892; *Gil the Gunner*, 1892; *The Grand Chaco (Rob Harlow's Adventure)*, 1892; *The Dingo Boys*, 1892; *The Black Bar*, 1893; *Real Gold*, 1893; *Blue Jackets*, 1893; *Steve Young*, 1893; *Sail-Ho!*, 1893; *The Vast Abyss*, 1894; *Mass' George*, 1894; *Fire Island*, 1894; *First in the Field*, 1894; *Cormorant Crag*, 1895; *Painter Jack*, 1895; *The Queen's Scarlet*, 1895; *Roy Royland*, 1895; *In Battle and Breeze*, with G.A. Henty and W. Clark Russell, 1896; *Smith's Weakness*, 1896; *In Honour's Cause*, 1896; *The Black Tor*, 1896; *Sappers and Miners*, 1896; *The Adventures of Don Lavington*, 1896; *Franks and Saxons*, 1897; *The Little Skipper*, 1897; *Vince the Rebel*, 1897; *The Silver Salvors*, 1898; *Nic Revel*, 1898; *Our Soldier Boy*, 1898; *Jungle and Stream*, 1898; *Draw Swords!*, 1898; *Fix Bay'nets!*, 1899; *In the Mahdi's Grasp*, 1899; *King o' the Beach*, 1899; *Nat the Naturalist*, 1899; *Ned Leger*, 1899; *Young Robin Hood*, 1899; *The Bag of Diamonds, and Three Bits of Paste*, 1900; *Charge*, 1900; *King Robert's Page*, 1900; *Old Gold*, 1900; *Uncle Bart*, 1900; *Running Amok*, 1901; *Something Like a Snake*, 1901; *The King's Sons*, 1901; *The Kopje Garrison*, 1901; *Pulabad*, 1901; *A Dash for Diamond City*, 1901; *Ching, The Chinaman and His Middy Friends*, 1901; *Coastguard Jack*, 1902; *The Lost Middy*, 1902; *A Meeting of Creeks, and The Tug of War*, 1902; *The Peril Finders*, 1902; *Stan Lynn*, 1902; *Two Rough Stones, and A Bad Day's Fishing*, 1902; *Walsh the Wonder-Worker*, 1903; *The King's Esquires*, 1903; *Fitz the Filibuster*, 1903; *Glyn Severn's Schooldays*, 1904; *The Khedive's Country*, 1904; *Marcus, The Young Centurion*, 1904; *The Ocean Cat's Paw*, 1904; *The Powder Monkey*, 1904; *To Win or Die*, 1904; *Trapper Dan*, 1905; *Shoulder Arms!*, 1905; *Nephew Jack*, 1905; *Dead Man's Land*, 1906; *Hunting the Skipper*, 1906; *'Tention!*, 1906; *The Traitor's Gate and Other Stories*, 1906; *Trapped by the Malays*, 1907; *Jack, The Rascal*, 1909; *Cutlass and Cudgel*, 1910; *In Mid-Air*, 1924; *In Marine Armour*, 1927; *Staunch as Steel*, 1927.

*   *   *

George Manville Fenn was a popular author whose eminently readable books were without the customary wordy descriptions or pious philosophy found in many of the earlier tales of adventure. In his first book, *Hollowdell Grange*, he showed his love of the "wonders of animal and vegetable life," while in *The Raja of Dah* he expressed his belief that "there was no grander education for a man than the study of the endless beauties of nature." He further developed this theme in *Nat the Naturalist*, one of his most successful books, which is set in Borneo and New Guinea. Fenn, unlike W.H.G. Kingston, R.M. Ballantyne, and G.A. Henty, did not permit his boy adventurers to kill for the love of sport, but only from necessity or for scientific investigation.

Fenn's ability to effect swift scene changes gives an uninterrupted pace to his stories, and he achieves immediacy through his skilful use of a natural dialogue that is also responsible for the success of many of his minor characters. At times he sacrifices clarity for supposed verisimilitude in an attempt to reproduce the colour and flavour of an unfamiliar idiom, such as the broken English spoken by the Australian Aborigines in *The Dingo Boys* and *Bunyip Land*. Fenn above all was a storyteller, and underlying even his most improbable adventures is his firm belief that a young man could gain more knowledge of himself and the things around him through contact with the world than through book learning. The major in *Mother Carey's Chicken* sums up Fenn's philosophy, "there is no such a fine bit of Latin anywhere as *nil desperandum*. You never know what course a battle may take."

A kindly, sometimes quietly humorous, acceptance of human frailty can be seen in Fenn's attitude towards his boy characters, who often lack confidence, manliness, and experience and have an all-consuming fear of cowardice. In *Bunyip Land* Fenn shows the absurdity of this, particularly when Master Jack Penny has his foot caught in a crocodile's mouth and feels foolish because he hollers "like a great girl." Later Jack talks of "those wonderful chaps" in books and papers, "who kill three or four men every day and think nothing of it...." "'I say, ain't it jolly nonsense, Joe Carstairs?' 'I suppose it is,' I said sadly, for I had believed in some of these heroes too."

These are not the idealized brave heroes of Ballantyne's and Henty's world, but Fenn had his own way of encouraging British youth to do its duty, act like a man, and never be beaten. He had confidence in the civilizing influence of the "true Englishman," a man of honour and true to his word. In *The Dingo Boys* and in *First in the Field* he explores this theme showing the effect that friendship can have on an Australian Aborigine and on a convict both of whom respond by being faithful and brave. Braver still is the boy in *First in the Field*, who trusts in his own judgment of people despite opposition from his father and from the Governor of the Colony.

Fenn was a highly competent writer of his time who understood his audience and catered, mainly from the 1880's until his death in 1909, for the ever-increasing market for adventure. His books finally went out of print during the middle 1930's and were superseded in the popular field by those of W.E. Johns, who was by then promoting an updated image of British manhood. Later, more serious authors revealed the inner life of their characters with far greater complexity and perception than Fenn, who stood at the cross roads between upholding the individual's social nature and exploring his individuality.

—Juliana Bayfield

FINLEY, Martha (née Brown). Also wrote as Martha Farquharson. American. Born in Chillicothe, Ohio, 26 April 1828. Educated at private schools in Philadelphia and South Bend, Indiana. Taught at schools in Indiana, 1851–53, and Phoenixville, Pennsylvania, 1853; writer for Presbyterian Publications Committee, Philadelphia. *Died 30 January 1909.* Fiction: *Ella Clinton*, 1856; *Aunt Ruth*, 1857; *Annandale*, 1858; *Lame Letty*, 1859; *Try*, 1863; *Willie Elton*, 1864; *Mysie's Work*, 1864; *Little Joe Carter, The Cripple*, 1864; *Black Steve*, 1865; *Brookside Farm-House, from January to December*, 1865; *Robert and Daisy*, 1865; *Hugo and Franz*, 1865; *Elsie Dinsmore* series, from 1868; *Casella*, 1868; *Anna Hand*, 1868; *Stupid Sally*, 1868; *Maud's Two Homes*, 1868; *Loitering Linus*, 1868; *Little Dick Positive*, 1868; *Little Patience*, 1868; *Grandma Foster's Sunbeam*, 1868; *The Shannons*, 1868; *Milly*,

1868; *The White Dress*, 1870; *Rufus the Unready*, 1870; *Jamie by the Lake*, 1870; *The Broken Basket*, 1870; *Betty Page*, 1870; *Lillian*, 1871; *An Old Fashioned Boy*, 1871; *The Twin Babies*, 1872; *Jim* series, from 1872; *Noll* series, from 1872; *Our Fred*, 1874; *The Peddler of La Grave*, 1875; *The Pewit's Nest*, 1876; *Rosa and Robbie*, 1876; *Aunt Hetty's Fowls*, 1876; *Harry* series, from 1876; *Mildred* series, from 1878; *Twiddledetwit*, 1898.

*   *   *

Martha Finley is remembered for her family saga, the 28-volume *Elsie Dinsmore* series, one of the first American series for girls, fabulously popular in both the United States and England. The series was unintentionally launched when the publisher arbitrarily divided the too-lengthy first manuscript into *Elsie Dinsmore* and *Holiday at Roselands*. With their combination of morally tough, neurotic realism and pietistically morbid, sentimental melodrama, the books whetted an insatiable public appetite. The first six volumes have a thematic and structural unity revolving about the conflict of wills between the sad-eyed, humble, but resolute Elsie and her arrogant, authoritarian father, whom, until she was eight, she had not met. Born to be a sacrificed lamb and savior, Elsie longs for the approbation, the love, and the Christian conversion of Horace Dinsmore. Their first meetings are cold and tense, complicated by anxieties and misunderstandings. When finally they penetrate the barriers between them, the affection they lavish upon one another, continually, through volumes, creates an intense ambience, more suggestive of amorous than filial love. That relationship predominates though Elsie and Horace both marry and have large families. However, the Freudian assertions that the books' great appeal depended upon readers' unconscious attraction to the theme of veiled incest is an exaggerated response to only one dimension of the books. Reflecting the author's literal response to the Bible's dual image of God as the stern but merciful father and as tender bridegroom, *Elsie* is a conscious effort to make concrete for children the concepts of God as father-protector and as heart's love. In the literary tradition of pious children with an innate instinct for Puritanical good and evil, Elsie does have "clear and correct views on almost every subject connected with her duty to God and her neighbor," and despite her priggishness, her refusal to knuckle under to adults who lack the perspicacity to understand that she is right inspires emulation of her courage to stand up to wrongheaded authority. In *Elsie's Widowhood*, as the protagonist grows into grandmotherhood, the benevolent, eternally youthful matriarch of a manifold clan, Finley introduced new characters apparently looking ahead to sequels without any foreseeable end. The next several volumes are loosely linked by the finally successful attempt of Captain Levis Raymond, a son-in-law of Elsie, to subjugate through loving discipline his intractable daughter Lulu, which story echoes the Horace-Elsie father-daughter love-struggle. The last 14 volumes are virtually plotless. New characters are introduced, frequently to marry into the family and perpetuate it.

The world of the Elsie books is a soap-opera-like composite of fantasy and realism, an imitation fairytale world peopled by wealthy white folks and contented, servile blacks. The setting for the stories was based on exaggerated tales returning Union soldiers told of the sumptuous elegance of the pre-Civil War South. Finley's experience and imagination were limited. She was incapable of particularizing her worlds through local color and specific detail unless she was writing from actual experience as she occasionally did, for example, in the autobiographical *Mildred Keith*. Through repetition with slight variation of the same generalized scenes she does, however, evoke an intensely felt, powerfully enveloping, almost surrealistic world. Although in her later books she introduces heavily derivative, encyclopedic accounts of historic events, these serve as space fillers and are not integrated into what little plot the book might have.

Skillful at sketching memorable vignettes of recognizable character types fleshed out with original idiosyncracies, Finley lacked the insight into human nature which would have enabled her to create authentic protagonists. She neither explores nor analyzes motives. Her major characters, interpreted as attempts at realism, appear flat and irritatingly self-satisfied. However, as ideal types in a quasi-romance, in keeping with the quasi-fairytale world in which they live, they achieve a credibility through almost ritual repetition of predictable gestures and utterances. The cumulative impact induces a kind of fascination-aversion for what, conceivably, people like ourselves might do if situations were slightly altered, if there were no moral ambiguities, and if we acted with commitment to fundamental principles.

Dialogue is Finley's principal vehicle of narration. The style in which she records speech is labored and lugubrious. With few intrusions by the author either to inform or to interpret, characters deliver themselves of uncommonly articulate, formal set pieces spilling over with paraphrases of Biblical counsels and declamations of narcissistic emotions. Finley's attempts to reproduce baby talk, the speech of the uneducated, or black dialects—all offensively similar—make it obvious that she had no ear for distinctive idioms, much less nuances.

Making the male protagonist of her Elsie stories a father, rather than a lover or husband, provided Finley not only her dominant motif but also a more credible vehicle for her dominant theme: woman is by nature fragile, subservient, and ornamental, and ought to be elevated to a pedestal. Interknit with that theme is a cognate repeatedly endorsed: the primacy of unselfishness. To sacrifice one's needs and happiness to the welfare of others effects the highest felicity. Finley's fiction is imbued with vulgar and pernicious attitudes: the subordination of woman; the equation of blacks with servile, simple-minded, pious "chilluns"; the snobbish conviction that wealth breeds gentility and refined spirituality, which augment personal and social worth; religious bigotry. Her bombast, her exaggeration of situation, and her excessive sentimentality evoke both censure and satire. Still the Elsie books have too much substance to be dismissed as merely silly or stupid. Witness such reputable champions as G.B. Stern, who when she "crave[d] really tough stuff" returned to Elsie who faced trials with unquenchable conviction and unflagging fortitude.

Finley's enormous popularity, which like any cult remains in part inexplicable, resulted largely from a workable formula of sensational, artistically flawed storytelling whose chemistry appealed to a particular people at a favorable time. For more than three generations *Elsie Dinsmore* outsold every juvenile book in America except *Little Women*, and Elsie attained more "widespread interest and affection" than any character in juvenile fiction but Huckleberry Finn. The influence upon millions of impressionable readers of the beautiful, lachrymose, righteous paragon is staggering to contemplate. While *Elsie* is no longer sold at book counters, she is available in expensive reprints in two series, whose titles offer their own comment: "Popular Culture in America" and "Classics of Children's Literature."

—M. Sarah Smedman

HALE, Lucretia P(eabody). American. Born in Boston, Massachusetts, 2 September 1820; sister of the writer Edward Everett Hale. Educated at Susan Whitney's, Miss Peabody's, and George G. Emerson's schools. Taught for a correspondence school, and private history tutor. Member, Boston School Committee, 1874. *Died 12 June 1900.* Fiction: *The Peterkin Papers,* 1880; *Alone in Rome,* 1883; *The Last of the Peterkins,* 1886; *Sunday School Stories,* with Mrs. Bernard Whitman, 1889; *Stories for Children,* 1892; *The Queen*

of the Red Chessmen, n.d.

*   *   *

As a children's writer, Lucretia P. Hale is known principally for *The Peterkin Papers,* a collection of humorous sketches that had previously appeared in the children's periodicals *Our Young Folks* and its distinguished successor *St. Nicholas.* A sequel, *The Last of the Peterkins,* was far less popular than the *Papers,* which made the Peterkins a household word.

The Peterkin Papers consists of 22 sketches of the ludicrous and improbable misadventures of the Peterkins, an astonishingly inept family consisting of *père* and *mère,* together with their six children: Agamemnon ("who had been to college"), Elizabeth Eliza, Solomon John, and three unnamed little boys, chiefly notable for the Indian rubber boots which they seem incessantly to be putting on and taking off. The sketches, which tend to be repetitive in form, begin with a problem that grows more formidable the more the family's collective wisdom is invoked to solve it: what to do with a cup of coffee into which Mrs. Peterkin has stirred salt instead of sugar; how to make the family wise; what to do about a piano placed with its keyboard against a window so that it can only be played by standing on the porch and reaching through the window; what to do with a Christmas tree that is too tall for the back parlor.

Once the premise is established, the rest of the sketch recounts the efforts of the family, attempting to work in concert and sometimes with the advice of neighbors, to remedy the situation. In the case of the salted coffee, the local chemist is consulted and tries to counter the presence of the salt with an array of chemicals. Hale is at her comic best cataloguing his inspired—but, alas, futile—efforts: "Then he tried, each in turn, some oxalic, cyanic, acetic, phosphoric, chloric, hyperchloric, sulphuric, boracic, silicic, nitric, formic, nitrous nitric, and carbonic acids. Mrs. Peterkin tasted each and said the flavor was pleasant, but not precisely that of coffee." In this instance, as in most of the sketches, the Peterkins's comic fixation with a futile strategem is broken finally by the cool common sense of their friend Mrs. Leslie, "the lady from Philadelphia," who sensibly suggests throwing out the offending coffee and making a new cup—or moving the piano so that its keyboard faces into the room. Although she is not present to suggest sawing a foot or two from the overly large Christmas tree, and Mr. Peterkin will not accept the carpenter's advice to do so but has him raise a portion of the ceiling instead, the thoughtful lady does provide the Peterkins with a box of Christmas ornaments, for which, with characteristic improvidence, they had neglected to plan.

The sequel, *The Last of the Peterkins,* seems, in retrospect, to be distinctly inferior to the earlier sketches. Convinced, perhaps, that she had explored most of the domestic difficulties likely to beset even a family as impractical as the Peterkins, Hale shifts her focus from the family as a whole to its several members and from the narrowly local setting to one that, in the end, is international. In the first episode of *The Last of the Peterkins,* Elizabeth Eliza prepares and delivers a paper on "The Sun" to the local women's cultural society, the Circumambient Club. Such a setting provides ample scope for Hale's gentle satire. In successive episodes, the family undertakes travel—first to grandfather's for maple syrup but eventually to Europe and the Middle East. Increasingly, the sketches describe the fragmentation of the family as, not surprisingly, travel connections are missed, baggage goes astray, and messages are misunderstood. In the final chapter, the family is briefly reunited but, with the exception of the three little boys, each has seen enough of the world to have a different dream. Elizabeth Eliza marries a Russian; Agamemnon is last heard of bound for Madagascar; and Mr. and Mrs. Peterkin are headed for Yakoutsk. Their misadventures as a family are over, and even the lady from Philadelphia could not retrieve them from the far ends of the earth, to which Hale consigns them.

The Peterkin Papers and its sequel enjoyed a considerable popularity with children and a measure of critical approval as well. Most of the sketches proceed from such obvious premises that children doubtless relished the absurd antics of the Peterkins, secure in knowing precisely what the lady from Philadelphia would prescribe when she should eventually appear on the scene. Despite the labored quality of the humor, on occasion, and the repetitious form of the episodes, Hale is often a clever and acute observer of human foibles. In contrast to much of the earnest moralizing characteristic of late 19th-century American children's literature, *The Peterkin Papers* is delightful nonsense—virtually the first example that we have. Moreover, it is humor, however gentle and affectionate, at the expense of the family, the institution then widely regarded as the fundamental social unit. Hale's mildly satirical view of the claustrophobic togetherness that was one aspect of Victorian family life marked a refreshing and popular alternative to the solemnity with which her contemporaries treated the family in books for children.

—R. Gordon Kelly

* * *

HARRIS, Joel Chandler. American. Born near Eatonton, Georgia, 9 December 1848. Educated at Eatonton Academy for Boys. Married Esther LaRose in 1873; nine children. Printer's devil and typesetter, *Countryman* weekly, published at the Turnwold Plantation, 1862–66; staff member, Macon *Telegraph*, Georgia, 1866, *Crescent Monthly*, New Orleans, 1866–67, *Monroe Advertiser*, Forsyth, Georgia, 1867–70, Savannah *Morning News*, Georgia, 1870–76, and Atlanta *Constitution*, 1876–1900; founder, with his son Julian, *Uncle Remus's* magazine, Atlanta, 1907–08. L.H.D.: Emory College, Oxford, Georgia, 1902. Member, American Academy, 1905. *Died 2 July 1908.* Fiction: *Uncle Remus* series, from 1880; *Daddy Jake the Runaway and Short Stories Told after Dark*, 1889; *Little Mr. Thimblefinger and His Queer Country*, 1894; *Mr. Rabbit at Home*, 1895; *The Story of Aaron*, 1896; *Aaron in the Wildwoods*, 1897; *The Chronicles of Aunt Minervy Ann*, 1899; *Wally Wanderoon and His Story-Telling Machine*, 1903; *The Bishop and the Boogerman* (*The Bishop and the Bogie-Man*), 1909; *The Shadow Between His Shoulder-Blades*, 1909. Verse: *The Tar-Baby*, 1904.

* * *

Joel Chandler Harris labeled himself a "cornfield journalist" whose success as a writer of folktales of the American south was "a lucky accident." Nevertheless, in the last half of the 19th century and the first decade of the 20th, he was along with Mark Twain the best-loved author of his time. Twain even asked Harris to join him on a lecture tour which the latter declined, unfortunately for posterity. Harris's fame in mid-20th century America, however, rested largely on Walt Disney's skillful treatment of Uncle Remus and his animal stories in the feature film *Song of the South* (1947), and a nationally syndicated Disney newspaper cartoon series featuring Brer Rabbit in the 1950's and 1960's. In the waning decades of the 20th century, interest in Harris's negro tales, novels, and journalism is largely academic.

Born out of wedlock in the vicinity of Eatonton, Georgia, an upcountry summer resort town that is still filled today with well-preserved antebellum mansions, Harris was reared by the newspaperman, lawyer, and planter Joseph Addison Turner at Turnwold Plantation. From Turner young Harris learned typesetting and newspaper writing. He read the English classics in Turnwold's well-stocked library. On the plantation he also learned from slaves many of the folktales of Brer Rabbit, Brer Fox, Brer Wolf that were

to make him famous as a folklorist and humorist in the decades after the Civil War. Indeed, Harris wrote that Uncle Remus, the teller of so many of the tales, was a composite character "of three or four old darkies I had known" at Turnwold and in Eatonton. Significantly, too, it was among the deracinated blacks that the fatherless white boy found ready acceptance, and subtle empathy.

Having served his apprenticeship and made his mental notes of the blacks and their tales, Harris went to Atlanta, where he became a journalist with the South's most progressive newspaper, the Atlanta *Constitution*. It was in the pages of the *Constitution* that he started publishing his character sketches and Uncle Remus dialect tales in 1878. The most famous of these, "The Tar Baby," appeared in the newspaper in 1879. Harris's first book, *Uncle Remus: His Songs and His Sayings*, was published in 1880. And so began the dissemination of the Uncle Remus stories that eventually ran into six volumes. These are works, the literary critic and historian Jay B. Hubbell writes, that are American classics in children's literature.

In the aggregate, Harris was primarily a writer of character sketches and episodes rather than an author of well-constructed short stories and novels. He was too busy with journalism to master his storytelling craft; he himself felt his literary work had no great merit, but was merely an act of preservation of folk myth and experience of the South. To northern magazines Harris sent stories in which the chief characters were white. But Harris is best when he sticks to the short tale or episode, the recollection or anecdote as told by an illiterate black such as Uncle Remus, who speaks the dialect of the cotton plantations, or from a poor white such as Teague Poteet in *Mingo* (1884), who uses the dialect of the Georgia mountains. Furthermore, a careful reading of his writings, fiction or journalism, a knowledge of his life and aspirations, and even a cursory awareness of the mores of his time should allay any accusations of racism cast on Harris and his work. He believed not only in the progressive, industrial idealism of the New South creed posited by Henry W. Grady, managing editor of the *Constitution*, but also in constructive cooperation, harmony, and social equality between blacks and whites in the south and in the nation.

In the Uncle Remus tales, whose sources lie in dim recollections of Africa, there occurs the consistent triumph of Brer Rabbit, the most helpless of the wild animals Harris characterizes. Some scholars see a subtle parallel between the rabbit and the slave in their capacity to survive and, ironically, to triumph. Uncle Remus, too, makes his quiet digs at the white man's busyness and often questionable ways of making money. And on the plantations of the Old South that Harris's stories glorify, black slaves and not white masters are the romantic element. Primarily a writer of sketches, as were the antebellum Georgia humorists Augustus Baldwin Longstreet and Joseph Glover Baldwin, Harris is never sharply critical, however, of the human race and its institutions. His best qualities are humor, characterization, and respect for the poor and distressed. In his use of dialect, common people, and simple scenes from everyday life, Harris was a pioneer in moving southern literature from its 19th-century romanticism to its 20th-century realism. Uncle Remus and Brer Rabbit are his monument.

—Jan Bakker

* * *

HENTY, G(eorge) A(lfred). British. Born in Trumpington, Cambridgeshire, 8 December 1832. Educated at Westminster School, London, 1847–52; Caius College, Cambridge, 1852. Served in the Hospital Commissariat and the Purveyor's Department during the Crimean War; helped organize Italian hospitals, 1859; served in Belfast and Portsmouth: Turkish Order of the Medjidie. Married 1)

Elizabeth Finucane in 1858, two sons and two daughters; 2) Bessie Keylock. Crimean War correspondent, *Morning Advertiser*, London; staff correspondent, in Europe, Africa, Asia, and North America, the *Standard*, London, 1865–76; editor, *Union Jack* magazine, London, 1880–83, *Beeton's Boy's Own Magazine*, London, 1888–90, and later annuals, 1890–93. *Died 16 November 1902*. Fiction: *Out on the Pampas*, 1871; *The Young Franc-Tireurs*, 1872; *The Young Buglers*, 1879; *Seaside Maidens*, 1880; *In Times of Peril*, 1881; *The Cornet of Horse*, 1881; *Winning His Spurs (The Boy Knight; Fighting the Saracens)*, 1882; *Facing Death*, 1882; *Under Drake's Flag*, 1882; *With Clive in India*, 1883; *By Sheer Pluck*, 1883; *Jack Archer (The Fall of Sebastopol)*, 1883; *Friends, Though Divided*, 1883; *True to the Old Flag*, 1884; *In Freedom's Cause*, 1884; *St. George for England*, 1884; *The Lion of the North*, 1885; *The Young Colonists*, 1885; *The Dragon and the Raven*, 1885; *For Name and Fame*, 1885; *Through the Fray*, 1885; *Yarns on the Beach*, 1885; *With Wolfe in Canada*, 1886; *The Bravest of the Brave*, 1886; *A Final Reckoning*, 1886; *The Young Carthaginian*, 1886; *Bonnie Prince Charlie*, 1887; *For the Temple*, 1887; *In the Reign of Terror*, 1887; *Sturdy and Strong*, 1887; *The Cat of Bubastes*, 1888; *The Lion of St. Mark*, 1888; *Captain Bayley's Heir*, 1888; *Orange and Green*, 1888; *One of the 28th*, 1889; *By Pike and Dyke*, 1889; *Camps and Quarters*, 1889; *Tales of Daring and Danger*, 1889; *The Plague Ship*, 1889; *With Lee in Virginia*, 1889; *By Right of Conquest*, 1890; *By England's Aid*, 1890; *A Chapter of Adventures (The Young Midshipman)*, 1890; *Maori and Settler*, 1890; *Redskin and Cowboy*, 1891; *The Dash for Khartoum*, 1891; *Held Fast for England*, 1891; *In Greek Waters*, 1892; *Beric the Briton*, 1892; *Condemned as a Nihilist*, 1892; *The Ranche in the Valley*, 1892; *A Jacobite Exile*, 1893; *St. Bartholomew's Eve*, 1893; *Through the Sikh War*, 1893; *In the Heart of the Rockies*, 1894; *When London Burned*, 1894; *Wulf the Saxon*, 1894; *The Tiger of Mysore*, 1895; *A Woman of the Commune (Cuthbert Hartington; A Girl of the Commune; Two Sieges of Paris)*, 1895; *A Knight of the White Cross*, 1895; *Through Russian Snows*, 1895; *On the Irrawaddy*, 1896; *At Agincourt*, 1896; *Bears and Decoits and Other Stories*, 1896; *With Cochrane the Dauntless*, 1896; *In Battle and Breeze*, with George Manville Fenn and W. Clark Russell, 1896; *With Moore at Corunna*, 1897; *A March on London*, 1897; *With Frederick the Great*, 1897; *Among Malay Pirates (Among the Malays)*, 1897; *At Aboukir and Acre*, 1898; *Both Sides the Border*, 1898; *Under Wellington's Command*, 1898; *The Golden Cañon*, 1899; *No Surrender!*, 1899; *On the Spanish Main*, 1899; *Won by the Sword*, 1899; *In the Irish Brigade*, 1900; *In the Hands of the Cave-Dwellers*, 1900; *With Buller in Natal*, 1900; *Out with Garibaldi*, 1900; *A Roving Commission*, 1900; *The Sole Survivors*, 1901; *With Roberts to Pretoria*, 1901; *At the Point of the Bayonet*, 1901; *John Hawke's Fortune*, 1901; *To Herat and Cabul*, 1901; *With Kitchener in the Soudan*, 1902; *With the British Legion*, 1902; *The Treasure of the Incas*, 1902; *With the Allies to Pekin*, 1903; *Through Three Campaigns*, 1903; *By Conduct and Courage*, 1904; *Gallant Deeds*, 1905; *In the Hands of the Malays and Other Stories*, 1905; *Redskins and Colonists, Burton and Son, The Ranche in the Valley, Sole Survivors*, 1905; *A Soldier's Daughter and Other Stories*, 1906.

*   *   *

G.A. Henty belongs to that class of authors whose influence has far outstripped their literary achievement. His biographer and contemporary, George Manville Fenn, claimed that he "taught more lasting history to boys than all the schoolmasters of his generation." It was a limited conception of history, but Henty's enthusiasm certainly infected his young readers and brought the past to life for them. His influence was in fact three-fold: besides making history palatable to boys, he inspired numerous imitators and set the adventure-story in a mould that was not broken until long after his death, while the ideology he propounded—the cult of "manliness" and the

British Empire—had a far-reaching effect which rates consideration in a more than purely literary context. It has been argued that Henty and his followers helped to produce the type of adventurous young man who (wrote Edgar Osborne) "went overseas and did much towards building up our present Commonwealth of Nations." Less friendly critics have expressed this differently. Nearly 40 years after Henty's death, George Orwell complained: "Boys' fiction is sodden in the worst illusions of 1910."

Henty was of course the epitome of Victorianism, being born just five years before the queen's accession and outliving her by little more than a year. A delicate child, bullied at public school, he took lessons in "the noble art of self-defence" and had good reason thereafter to believe in the efficacy of Christian manliness, expressed in a straight left to the jaw. As a war correspondent on innumerable campaigns, he found it easy to identify himself with the conquering Empire-builders. In later life, as a popular London clubman, he had little cause to question the current assumptions of his class.

His success sprang from his ability to take a colourful theme, whether from recent or from remote history, and then, helping out the facts with invented incident and character, spin what approving parents and pedagogues called "a rattling good yarn." He worked to a formula, as his titles show—*With Clive in India, With Wolfe in Canada, With Kitchener in the Soudan*, or, for variation, *Facing Death, True to the Old Flag*, and *Held Fast for England*. His young heroes ran similarly to type, manly, middle-class, and intellectually unremarkable. The great adventurers of real history, Ralegh and Burton and T.E. Lawrence, would have fitted less comfortably into his stock-size frame.

Many of his books were based on first-hand observation. He walked the field of Inkerman among the unburied Russian dead, and the Crimean story he eventually wrote, *Jack Archer*, is one of his most vivid. He reported the Franco-Prussian War: within a year he had written *The Young Franc-Tireurs*. He accompanied Garibaldi in Italy, the Turks in their savage Balkan wars, and British expeditions into West Africa and Abyssinia. None of the slaughter he witnessed dimmed his vision of military glory. Even in his posthumously published story of the Boxer rising, *With the Allies to Pekin*, there is undiminished gusto in his account of two intrepid lads who, caught in a confined space with a dozen murderous Chinese, use their magazine-loading rifles to wipe out their adversaries in a few moments.

Henty was a methodical worker. He would lie on a sofa in his weapon-festooned study, dictating to a male secretary—and then never look at the story again until he corrected the proofs. In a six-hour day he could produce over 6000 words. In the last 33 years of his life he packed something like 14 million words into about 90 fat volumes. It would be optimistic to seek, in such a mass, either striking originality of ideas or fastidious use of language. He at least achieved English which, if not quite as "good" as admiring schoolmasters declared it, never fell below a certain level. It was the prose of the period, rather too wordy for our own taste, and betraying his habit of unrevised dictation. Characters, after being "for a minute or two speechless with indignation," would then immediately plunge into paragraph-long speeches of advice or explanation.

Even when handling themes outside his own experience, Henty could invest his narrative with a good deal of verisimilitude, thanks to the analogous events in which he had participated. Occasionally he was lazy. His Cortez story, *By Right of Conquest*, reads like paraphrased Prescott. He makes only a feeble attempt to create his own characters and plot inside the historical framework. His conventional English boy hero, Roger—so implausibly present at the conquest of Mexico—is often forgotten for several pages at a time.

Henty set a pattern which many lesser writers adapted to the 1914 war and other themes, but by the mid-20th century his values were unfashionable, and, as the general quality of historical fiction improved, it became less heretical to criticise his literary weaknesses.

Today his books are rather "collected" as Victoriana than read by boys. They have not won a place upon the shelf with the children's classics that are loved from generation to generation.

—Geoffrey Trease

———

HUGHES, Thomas. British. Born in Uffington, Berkshire, 20 October 1822. Educated at Rugby School, 1834–42; Oriel College, Oxford, 1842–45 (played cricket for Oxford, 1842), B.A. 1845; entered Lincoln's Inn, London, 1845, then entered the Inner Temple, and called to the bar, 1848. Married Frances Ford in 1848; three sons and three daughters. Lawyer in London from 1848: Queen's Counsel, 1869; associated with F.D. Maurice and the Christian Socialists who subsequently helped to create the cooperative movement: contributed to the *Christian Socialist* and *Tracts on Christian Socialism* and acted as editor of the *Journal of Association*; chairman of the first Cooperative Congress, 1869; helped to pass the Industrial and Provident Societies Act, 1893; involved in the founding of the Working Men's College, Great Ormond Street, London, 1854, and served as its principal, 1872–83; Liberal Member of Parliament for Lambeth, 1865–68, and Frome, Somerset, 1868–74; founder member, Church Reform Union, 1870; established model community in Tennessee which proved unsuccessful, 1879; county court judge, Chester, Cheshire, 1882–96. *Died 22 March 1896*. Fiction: *Tom Brown's School Days*, 1857; *Tom Brown at Oxford*, 1861.

*   *   *

Thomas Hughes did not invent the school story; it existed for a century or so before *Tom Brown's School Days*, and by the 1850's it had reached a degree of some sophistication (see, for example, *The Cherry-Stones* by the Rev. William Adams, published in 1851). What Hughes did was to inject into the genre that species of ethic which has generally been labelled Muscular Christianity. Hughes himself disliked that term, but it is hard to think of a better way of describing, for example, his exhortation to his readers on the subject of fist-fighting: "Don't say 'no' [when challenged to a fight] because you fear a licking, and say or think it's because you fear God, for that's neither Christian nor honest. And if you do fight, fight it out; and don't give in while you can stand and see."

It has often been pointed out that this ethic has nothing whatever to do with the liberal intellectual values cultivated by Thomas Arnold, Hughes's headmaster at Rugby and "the Doctor" of the novel. Hughes is generally accused of having completely failed to understand Arnold—and of having undone much of Arnold's good work by publishing a novel which equated Arnoldian educational policy with manly fist-fights, love of sport, and a despising of the intellect (Old Brooke, Tom's house captain in the novel, says he would rather win a football match than get a Balliol scholarship). The truth is surely that Hughes himself cannot be held personally to blame: somebody else would have written *Tom Brown's School Days* if he had not, so much does it typify the mid-Victorian enthusiasm for manliness with Christian overtones.

Hughes wrote it because he said he had "often thought that good might be done by a real novel for boys—not didactic...written in a right spirit, but distinctly aimed at being interesting." Charles Kingsley, like Hughes a member of F.D. Maurice's Christian Socialist movement, saw the finished book shortly before publication and forecast that "it will be a very great hit," which it was, immediately. The surprise is that a quarter of a century passed before its literary influence really began to be felt. Not until Talbot Baines Reed's *The Fifth Form at St. Dominic's*, which began to be serialised in 1881 in the *Boy's Own Paper*, did another writer begin to make

methodical use of Hughes's format. After Reed, the floodgates opened, and one may find a thousand *Tom Browns* by different authors published between the 1880's and the 1930's—though none of them has the freshness and zest of the Hughes original. Reed and his successors retained the "jam" of the school story while eliminating the "powder" of Hughes's preaching; but it is the preaching that drives Hughes's story along. Without it, the book would soon have been forgotten.

—Humphrey Carpenter

———

INGELOW, Jean. British. Born in Boston, Lincolnshire, 17 March 1820. Educated at home. Lived in London after 1850. Editor, *Youth Magazine*, 1855. *Died 20 July 1897*. Fiction: *Tales of Orris (Stories Told to a Child)*, 1860; *Studies for Stories*, 1864; *A Sister's Bye-Hours*, 1868; *Mopsa the Fairy*, 1869; *The Little Wonder-Horn*, 1872; *The Little Wonder Box*, 6 vols., 1887; *Very Young, and Quite Another Story*, 1890; *The Black Polyanthus, and Widow MacLean*, 1903.

*   *   *

One novel and a handful of anthology poems keep Jean Ingelow's name alive today; but these works are not negligible. They can suggest why, in her time, she was something of a celebrity, both as adult novelist and poet; why her work was admired by such fellow writers as Tennyson, Edward FitzGerald, the Rossettis. She was even thought a possible Laureate when the post fell vacant in 1892, but admittedly this was a very thin time. More pointed is the fact that, 16 years after her death, she rated an Oxford edition of her poems. They tend to be ballad-like and reverberating, with sharp and haunting cadences and a mysterious thread of narrative; their appeal is not hard to understand. *High Tide on the Coast of Lincolnshire*, where the energy of the theme absorbs the sentiment, is one of the best examples.

Still, most of her poetry is for the private discoverer or devotee; so too are her shorter mildly didactic tales for the young, written in a good brisk readable style but lacking the power of flight to travel far. Very few, indeed, are accessible now, though one charming tale, "My Grandmother's Shoe," has been revived in one of Gillian Avery's collections.

Ingelow's one long work for the young, her remarkable novel *Mopsa the Fairy*, is a different matter. Written within that short and dazzling period when so many leading Victorian authors experimented in children's fantasy, it remains, in its genre, a major achievement, one of those single, odd yet memorable works that make up so much of English literature. Influences? Certainly. Take the most Carrollian passage in *Mopsa*, when a ballad sung by Jack includes the lines:

> And the lark said, give us glory!
> And the dove said, give us peace!

"A very good song indeed," said the dame at the other end of the table, "only you made a mistake in the first verse. What the dove really said was, no doubt, 'Give us peas.'"

"It isn't peas, though," said Jack. However, the court historian was sent for to write down the song...as the dame said it ought to be.

Flamingoes stand on military guard; there is an oddly macabre episode in which a gypsy's baby turns out to be a bundle of clothes with a turnip head. A further Carrollian echo surely sounds in Jack's disputation with the ravens:

"Why," said Jack, "I see a full moon lying down there among the water-flags, and just going to set, and there is a half-moon overhead plunging among those great grey clouds, and just this moment I saw a thin crescent moon peeping out between the branches of that tree."
"Well," said all the ravens at once, "did the young master never see a crescent moon in the men and women's world?"
"Yes, of course," said Jack, "but they are all the same moon. I could never see all three of them at the same time."
The ravens were very much surprised at this.

But the voice and the detail are essentially Ingelow's. Even the book's opening, which has been likened to the opening of *Alice*, sheers off at once in its own direction. A boy, Jack, is going through a meadow of buttercups. He leans against a hollow tree while eating a slice of plum cake, hears a twittering and climbs inside. Up above is a nest of white wool and moss. It is a nest of very young fairies; one is "creeping about rather like an old baby, and had on a little frock and pinafore." An albatross arrives, and off they fly to Fairyland, the fairies in Jack's pocket. "We are going the back way," says the albatross. "You could go in two minutes by the usual route; but these young fairies want to go before they are summoned, and therefore you and I are taking them." Does this flight echo George MacDonald? *At the Back of the North Wind* was being serialized when *Mopsa* was published, though it would not appear as a book until the following year.

Another episode, where they come to a great bay of becalmed ships, where the wind never blows, recalls another contemporary. How did the ships come to be there? asks Jack.

Some of them had captains who abused their cabin-boys, some were pirate ships and others were going out on evil errands....Many ships which are supposed by men to have foundered lie becalmed in this quiet sea. Look at these five grand ones with the high poops...they were part of the Spanish Armada; and the open boats with blue sails belonged to the Romans, they sailed with Caesar when he invaded Britain.

Kingsley, certainly. *Westward Ho!* had been published in 1855, *The Water-Babies* in 1863. Yet even this probable debt has its own sea-change in *Mopsa*. A visit made to a very different writer, Anna Sewell, at Shanklin in March 1868 illuminates a further episode. Jack and Mopsa land at a border country where horses, cruelly used in the human world, cab horses, race horses, are allowed to grow back to their youth, carefully tended by clockwork people. Why *clockwork*? It is not the only occasion in the book where one feels that the author's unconscious symbolism is rather more interesting than she could have known. But the voice that speaks on the ill-used horses is so remarkably like the voice of *Black Beauty*'s author that the episode could have been written almost immediately after the meeting. *Black Beauty* itself was not published until 19 years later. And nowhere in Ingelow's writing does the subject recur.

But the real originality of the tale is increasingly evident. Whatever you *can* do in this fairyland, you *may* do, Jack is told. But *can* has also its rules. It is a place that even holds the occasional human, like the apple-woman, who stays, still keeping a little stall with cherries on sticks and a few dry nuts. She could wish herself back into the world but has not the courage. "It would come into my head that I should be poor or that my boys would have forgotten me, or that my neighbours would look down on me, and so I always put off wishing for another day." Invention does not flag. Jack and

Mopsa, in flight from certain primitive beasts, reach their boat and are offered the protection of a Craken's coils, arch after arch, endlessly reaching away. The water drips about them; the boat trembles "either because of its great age, or because it felt the grasp of the coil underneath." Then, as they sail on, they perceive the arches closing in; soon they have to crouch down in the boat. C.S. Lewis must have recalled this scene in *The Voyage of the "Dawn Treader."* The next arch almost touches the water. "No! that I cannot bear," cries Jack. "Somebody else may do the rest of the dream!" "Why don't you wake!" says Mopsa, as if amused.

But Mopsa is no ordinary fairy. She and Jack escape by night, crossing over the purple mountain, so that she need not rule over the unknown deer-people; so that she need not rule at all, only stay with Jack. And yet, their journey takes them to where they were fleeing from; it is her kingdom after all; there is even a shadow Jack to keep her company. But the real Jack, a human boy, must go home.

And here the book presents the basic difference between the real folk fairytale and the invented kind, the Victorian sort especially. Jack remains a boy, delightfully so, throughout. But Mopsa, through human contact, gradually changes from child and girl, first pet, then playmate, ally in danger, to a mystical Pre-Raphaelite adult queen. From a child's view, this should not be. Morals work well enough, of the straight pragmatic kind, but emotions, no. Goosegirl and prince may turn, in time, into ageing Queen and King but essentially they are children still, playing at kingdoms. Perhaps a really good illustrator (which *Mopsa* has so far lacked) could solve the problem of Mopsa's transformation. Indeed, older readers may find the end a necessary part of the whole experience. For experience it is. Victorian fantasy, rich as it is, offers few more remarkable journeys to any fairytale reader.

—Naomi Lewis

JEFFERIES, Richard. British. Born near Swindon, Wiltshire, 6 November 1848. Educated at schools in Sydenham, Kent, and Swindon, to age 15. Married in 1874. Wrote for the *North Wilts Herald*, 1866–70: became its regular reporter and local correspondent for a Gloucestershire paper; freelance writer from 1870; moved to London, 1876, and wrote for the *Pall Mall Gazette*; in later life lived in Sussex. *Died 14 August 1887.* Fiction: *Wood Magic*, 1880; *Bevis*, 1882.

*   *   *

Bevis ("The Story of a Boy") is both a minor prestige classic and a literary oddity. A century after publication it remains in print not widely but sufficiently. Like Richard Jefferies himself, as "nature" writer—and for reasons which might be worth exploring—it has always had a few intense devotees. And yet, I suspect, it is not very closely read, or even read at all, by most of those today who republish or purchase the work as an item for the young. It is one of the author's very few works of fiction and the only one whose content relates to children. Yet no other single Jefferies book unites so well the author's best and worst. He was an excellent writer, with a meticulous eye and ear for the country matters—human, plant and animal—that were his usual theme. But something arrogant, self-absorbed, at times sadistic even, flaws his work for readers outside the cult. John Clare, for instance, perhaps our greatest writer in this field and the most understanding, makes a salutary contrast.

Long and substantial though *Bevis* is, the plot is simple enough. Two boys, Bevis and Mark, spend an ideal summer in the woods and on the waters of the family grounds. For the final fortnight they live wild (with parents' permission, and supplies) on a "Secret Island" in the lake. The book is full of seductive passages and splendid practical detail; but as a work of nature-magic (such is its reputation) the final effect is curious. And the hero-boy himself, in whom Jefferies seems to see no fault at all? Readers might think otherwise. Almost at once we see him ordering the servants.

> "Stop," said Bevis, "stop directly and hitch the chain on my raft."
> The boy hesitated; he dared not disobey the carter, and he had been in trouble for pleasing Bevis before.
> "This instant," said Bevis, stamping his foot. "I'm your master."

Animals fare worse. The boys' gear for the camping trip includes gun, spear, harpoon, darts, snares, bow and arrows—and all are lethally used. (To the end of his life Jefferies never lost his passion for the kill.) They shoot a heron for the plume. They get a moorcock with an arrow, pinning its wing to a tree. "Hurrah!" They thrash a working pony round and round a field "making him leap a broad furrow and gallop his hardest." They plan a pit with stakes as an animal trap. They beat, kick, and hurl stones at their loyal dog when it fails to do the impossible. If only there were a bird of paradise, thinks Bevis. It would do for Mark's sister's hat. In one of the nastiest episodes (there is no lack of choice) they tie a donkey to a tree and proceed to "break their sticks upon his back. They thrashed, thwacked, banged, thumped, poked, prodded, kicked, belaboured,…working themselves into a frenzy of rage." They continue with heavy logs that they can hardly lift. "No one came to help the donkey." Finally they lock it up without food or water.

And what is the peak achievement of their holiday? The killing of an otter, a special prize because so rare in those parts. Even mother and sister are summoned to witness the corpse and praise the deed. The womenfolk (knowing their place in the Jefferies hierarchy) humbly look and admire. They gaze at the noble boy: "Bevis was too fair to brown well. The sun and the wind had purified his skin almost to transparency, with a rosy olive behind the whiteness (etc., etc.)…Frances played with his golden ringlets, but did not kiss him as she used to. He looked too much a man." Ah yes…But all this could make up a picture of boy-life anywhere, even today, especially in countries where such views persist, and in high places everywhere. It is the uncritical adulation that rings so oddly, from Jefferies most of all.

But the book is not so much a story aimed at the young as a recapturing of memory—and there lies much of its strength. To see it as simple autobiography would be wrong. The golden Bevis, imperious, ruthless, admired and obeyed by all, was scarcely Jefferies himself (though wish-fantasy also tells us much). Socially, too, the boy Bevis seems on a higher rung of the ladder. As a small farmer's son, Jefferies would have been well above the peasants and labourers (some employed by his father), but below the landed gentry, with their body of servants, bailiffs, keepers, and obsequious tenants (who scrape and curtsy to Bevis and Mark). But what is certainly true to memory is the intense sensation of being a boy of 12 or less, acting out his reading of Homer and the bloodier fighting ballads, making rafts, mapping the stars, learning to swim, taking part in war-games against the village lads, roaming the woods, and never far from his cherished rod and gun.

No, it is not only for its beguiling prose that *Bevis* can still be read. As an (unintentional) view of social history, social attitudes: as an all-too-revealing glance at the hard-eyed casual cruelty of real child-nature, it has a decided place. But that place is not, it could be said, on the children's shelf.

—Naomi Lewis

KINGSLEY, Charles. British. Born in Holne, Devon, 12 June 1819; brother of the writer Henry Kingsley. Educated at a preparatory school in Clifton, Bristol, 1831–33; Helston Grammar School, Cornwall, 1833–35; King's College School, London, 1835–38; Magdalene College, Cambridge, 1838–42, B.A. (honours) in classics 1842, M.A. 1860. Married Fanny Grenfell in 1844; two daughters and two sons. Took holy orders: Curate, 1842–44, and Rector, 1844–75, Eversley, Hampshire; lecturer, Queen's College, London, 1848; Regius Professor of Modern History, Cambridge University, 1860–69; history tutor to the Prince of Wales, 1861; toured the West Indies, 1869–70; Canon of Chester Cathedral, 1869–73; made a lecture tour of the United States, 1873–74; Canon of Westminster Abbey, London, and chaplain to the Queen, 1873–75. *Died 23 January 1875.* Fiction: *Westward Ho!*, 1855; *The Water-Babies*, 1863; *Hereward the Wake*, 1866.

*   *   *

It is a curious and perhaps significant fact that the most famous classics of childhood—*Alice, The Wind in the Willows, Peter Pan, The Water-Babies, The Hobbit*—are the works of men who did not ordinarily write for children. The place of *The Water-Babies* in this pantheon is also odd, in that to the vast majority of its readers it is only fragmentarily known; few of those who remember little Tom's adventures as a chimney-sweep could recount what became of him when he shed his human shell and turned into a water baby.

Charles Kingsley, in fact, wrote more for children than did Carroll, Grahame, Barrie, or Tolkien. *Westward Ho!* and *Hereward the Wake*, though not originally designed for young readers, have in their time pleased boys who, in spite of the inordinate length of both and the burden of the historical detail, have enjoyed the plethora of violence and killings, and perhaps the fierceness of the prejudices. (Children always enjoy taking sides, and Kingsley in this respect, and perhaps in others, remained a child to the end of his life.) *Madam How and Lady Why* (1870), an exposition of various natural phenomena, enjoyed a certain popularity with Victorian children. *The Heroes* (1855) has never been displaced from its position as one of the finest retellings of the Greek myths. It was written as a counter-blast to the versions that had appeared a few years earlier in Hawthorne's *Wonder-Book* (1851) and *Tanglewood Tales* (1853), which had given an incongruously cosy Victorian domestic background to these savage epics, and which Kingsley considered "distressingly vulgar." Only in this book did Kingsley restrain his urge to preach and expound and involve his readers in his views and prejudices; he might invest his Greek heroes with Christian virtues, but he delivers no lectures in so doing, and it is a marvellously realized, compellingly told piece of narration.

The Water-Babies in contrast is seriously flawed by the author's obtrusion of himself. He felt passionately on many topics, from the undesirable racial characteristics of everybody except the English and the Scots to the employment of child chimney-sweeps; from the erroneous views of the scientists of his day to the right hour that a gentleman should eat his dinner, and his lectures on all these make four-fifths of the book almost unreadable. But this only proves the amazing potency of the opening chapters, which have passed into the mythology of English childhood. "Once upon a time", the book begins, "there was a little chimney-sweep, and his name was Tom." Kingsley takes no sentimental view of him; he is a cheerful, godless little pagan who "cried when he had to climb the dark flues, rubbing his poor knees and elbows raw" and laughed "the other half of the day when he was tossing half-pennies with the other boys, or playing leap-frog over the posts, or bowling stones at the horses' legs as they trotted by." Nor is Tom potentially any better than his master, the brutish Mr. Grimes, to emulate whom is his greatest ambition.

In a beautiful evocation of a midsummer early morning, Tom and Mr. Grimes leave the town, fringed with its coal-mines, and set out through the sleeping countryside to sweep the chimneys at Harthover Place. The Place is a vast and sprawling mansion of many styles and many flues, and Tom loses his way and comes down in "a room the like of which he had never seen before....He had never been in gentlefolks' rooms but when the carpets were all up, and the curtains down, and the furniture huddled together under a cloth." This room is all furnished and hung in white, and in the bed there sleeps a little girl. Almost the same moment that he sees her he sees himself in the glass, "a little ugly, black, ragged figure with bleared eyes and grinning white teeth....And Tom, for the first time in his life, found out that he was dirty." Ashamed and angry he tries to escape up the chimney, but wakes the little girl. The hue and cry that follows is powerfully drawn; the chase over the fells, shimmering with heat, Tom's thirst, the sound of the water twinkling many hundreds of feet below, his perilous descent, his arrival at the schoolhouse, and then submersion in the stream.

It is at this point that the impetus of the narrative falters and never again picks up strength. Tom is now a water baby and, in the remaining chapters to which the foregoing was only a prelude, undergoes a form of purgation (though Kingsley, stout Protestant that he was, would have been appalled if this had been interpreted as a belief in the "Romish doctrine of purgatory"). He meets water creatures and learns not to tease them, he is taught valuable lessons by Mrs. Bedonebyasyoudid and Mrs. Doasyouwouldbedoneby, he swims to far-off places and generally proves himself, but the text is now so choked with asides and theorizing and moral reflections that it is very difficult to disentangle what is in fact happening to him. Kingsley believed passionately that a knowledge of and a love for the wonders of nature could redeem man. He had said this in *Glaucus* (1855), subtitled "The Wonders of the Shore," and again in *Madam How and Lady Why*. To him the glory of God was made manifest in, say, the marvellous way the caddis worm pupates, and he wanted every child to know facts like these. What does not seem to have occurred to him was that young readers have not the knowledge nor the experience to sift fact from fantasy. He roundly denounces the Cousin Cramchilds of his time who would say there could not be water babies and exhorts his readers not to believe them; he avers that porpoises are shiny because the fairies French polish them; he produces a preposterous and elaborately worked out anti-Darwin theory that gorillas evolved from lotus-eating humans. Might not then a child suppose the life cycle of the dragonfly to be a similar flight of fancy? Kingsley seems to have been too absorbed in his own oratory to care. *The Water-Babies* is thus an extraordinary combination, a timeless, compelling opening followed by a mishmash of personal fads, written by a warm-hearted but essentially muddled man.

—Gillian Avery

LANG, Andrew. British. Born in Selkirk, Scotland, 31 March 1844. Educated at Selkirk High School; Edinburgh Academy, 1854–61; University of St. Andrews (editor, *St. Leonard's Magazine*), 1861–63; University of Glasgow, 1863–64; Loretto School, Musselburgh, 1864; Balliol College, Oxford (Snell exhibitioner), 1864–68, B.A. 1866. Married Leonora Blanche Alleyne in 1875. Fellow, Merton College, Oxford, 1868–75; freelance writer after 1875; general editor, English Worthies series, Longmans, 1885–87, and Bibliothèque de Corabas series, Nutt, 1887–96. Gifford Lecturer, University of St. Andrews, 1888; Ford Lecturer, Oxford University, 1904. LL.D.: University of St. Andrews, 1885; Oxford University, 1904. *Died 20 July 1912.* Fiction: *The Princess Nobody*, 1884; *The Gold of Fairnilee*, 1888; *Prince Prigio*, 1889; *Prince Ricardo of Pantouflia*, 1893; *Tales of a Fairy Court*, 1907; *The Gold of Fairnilee and Other Stories*, 1967.

*   *   *

Writing in 1889 in *The Child and His Book*, Mrs. E.M. Field stated that "At the present moment the fairy-tale seems to have given way entirely in popularity to the child's story of real life, the novel of childhood, in which no effort is spared to make children appear as they are." But just before the publication of the book early in 1891, she added a note: "Since the above was written eighteen months ago, the tide of popularity seems to have set strongly in the direction of the old fairy stories."

These two quotations epitomise Andrew Lang's most important contribution in the development of the literature of childhood: and this came about largely because of the scholarly interest in folklore which made him one of the most important of the folklorists and anthropologists of his age. From the point of view of the folklorists, Lang first became notable for his essay "Mythology and Fairy Tales" in 1873, his introduction to Mrs. Hunt's complete translation of the Grimm's *Märchen* in 1884, and his two books, *Custom and Myth* (1884) and *Myth, Ritual, and Religion* (1887), the second of which contained a long section on folktales and fairy lore generally.

His writings for children began rather tentatively in 1884 with the short fairy story *The Princess Nobody* which he constructed most ingeniously to fit a large number of illustrations by Richard ("Dicky") Doyle which had appeared in 1869 to accompany (but not illustrate) poems by William Allingham. This charming tale was constructed on the lines of a traditional fairytale: issued in an edition of 10,000 copies it did not, however, reach a second edition, and was buried in oblivion until 1955 when it was included in *Modern Fairy Stories*, edited by Roger Lancelyn Green.

He followed this with *The Gold of Fairnilee*, a tale based on the Scottish Ballads and the fairy lore of the Border Country which was his home from his birth in 1844 until 1868. As a boy he and his brother and several others from his hometown of Selkirk were accustomed to meet every Saturday evening in a barn to hear local folktales and legends told by an old shepherd. Lang wrote that people in the Border Country believed in fairies "even when my father was a boy," and it is to the Fairyland, "which paid a fiend to Hell," that Randal of Fairnilee is carried by the Fairy Queen, even as Thomas the Rhymer had been, and from which Jean rescues him as Janet had rescued Tamlin in the ballad—in time to find the legendary Gold of Fairnilee for which Lang and his brother John had so often searched in vain.

The Fairyland of traditional belief did not prove popular, though of the few literary expeditions thither Lang's is outstandingly the best. Perhaps for this reason his next venture was into the realm explored by the ladies of the *Cabinet des Fées* and so brilliantly exploited by Thackeray in *The Rose and the Ring*.

Prince Prigio and its slightly less successful sequel, *Prince Ricardo*, make an outstanding contribution to the literary fairy story as opposed to the traditional type, and seems to be accepted now as a classic in its own particular genre. In both these books Lang's knowledge of the Märchen of the world is given brilliant play, accepting the "rules" of the typical literary Fairyland with absolute gravity and following them to their logical conclusions. The humour and a tang of underlying irony make them two books which can be enjoyed by adults as well as children. *Prince Prigio* certainly illustrated C.S. Lewis's dictum that "a children's book which is enjoyed by children only is a bad children's book: the good ones last."

Lang turned back once more to Prigio's Kingdom of Pantouflia in *Tales of a Fairy Court*, but with little of his earlier success, though in one or two of the stories the magic touch is still visible.

But good though the best of his original stories are, their excellencies have, from the start, tended to be eclipsed by the series of traditional tales which he chose, edited and occasionally retold, of which the first volume, *The Blue Fairy Book*, appeared in time for the same Christmas of 1889 as *Prince Prigio*; and it was on account of the unexpected popularity of this and its first sequel, *The Red Fairy Book*, the following year that Mrs. Field felt herself obliged to add the footnote quoted above.

The Blue Fairy Book was a complete gamble which Lang must have persuaded his friend and publisher, Charles Longman, to undertake—and which Longman probably risked on the strength of Lang's name, which was still very high in the literary world of the day. It appeared in an edition of 5,000 copies, and its success was instantaneous. By the time *The Yellow Fairy Book* (the fourth) appeared in 1894, the first edition was of 15,000.

The series finally consisted of 25 annual volumes, 12 of which were Fairy Books. But several others such as *The Arabian Nights*, two *Romance* books and the final *Strange Story Book* come almost within the category of Fairy Stories. And a volume outside the series, *Tales of Troy and Greece*, presents the greatest of the ancient Greek stories entirely in Lang's own retelling, and is still rivalled only by Kingsley's *The Heroes* (1855).

In the preface to the last of the actual Fairy Books (the *Lilac*) Lang wrote: "My part has been that of Adam, according to Mark Twain, in the Garden of Eden. Eve worked, Adam superintended; I find out where the stories are, and advise, and, in short, superintend. *I do not write the stories out of my own head*. The reputation of having written all the fairy books (a European reputation in nurseries and the United States of America) is 'the burden of an honour unto which I was not born....'"

But Lang's vast knowledge of the wide world's folklore and his magic touch in preparing the work of others for publication (and helped by the superbly complementary accompaniment of H.J. Ford's illustrations) make classics of these unrivalled collections, and, even more than his outstanding contribution to the history of Fairyland, ensure him a high place in the history of children's literature.

—Roger Lancelyn Green

LEAR, Edward. British. Born in London, 12 May 1812. Studied at Sass's School of Art, London, 1835, 1849; Royal Academy, London, 1850–52; studied painting with Holman Hunt. Freelance artist after 1827, and teacher after 1830; assistant to the artists Prideaux Selby and John Gould; illustrated the animals at the home of the Earl of Derby, 1832–37; lived in Rome, 1837–45; gave drawing lessons to Queen Victoria, 1846. Exhibited at the Royal Academy, London, 1850–73. Lived in Italy and the Mediterranean, 1846–49, and in San Remo, Italy, 1868–88. *Died 29 January 1888.* Verse: *A Book of Nonsense*, 1846, revised edition, 1861; *Nonsense Songs, Stories, Botany, and Alphabets*, 1870; *More Nonsense*, 1871; *Laughable Lyrics*, 1876; *Nonsense Songs and Stories*, 1894; *Queery Leary Nonsense*, 1911; *The Complete Nonsense Book*, 1912; *The Lear Omnibus (A Book of Lear)*, 1938; *The Complete Nonsense*, 1947; *Teapots and Quails and Other New Nonsenses*, 1953; *For Lovers of Birds* [*Cats, Gardens and Flowers, Food and Drink*], 4 vols., 1978; *Gromboolian Poems*, 1983; *A Book of Learned Nonsense*, 1987.

*   *   *

When Edward Lear was a young man, he went to live at Knowsley Hall, the home of the Earls of Derby. At this time he was a natural

history illustrator, and he had been commissioned to paint the birds and animals in Lord Derby's menagerie. At Knowsley he met "half the fine people of the day," but did not altogether like them. He wrote to a friend: "The uniform apathetic tone assumed by lofty society irks me *dreadfully*, nothing I long for half so much as to giggle heartily and to hop on one leg down the great gallery—but I dare not." Instead, he began to write his limericks. As apathy denied life, so also did the improving tale, for it disclaimed children as they were in favour of children as they ought to be:

> There was an old man of Hong Kong,
> Who never did anything wrong;
> He lay on his back, with his head in a sack,
> That innocuous old man of Hong Kong.

With the decorous and perfectly innocuous safely hidden away, Lear's real people could indulge in amiable excess:

> There was a Young Girl of Majorca,
> Whose aunt was a very fast walker;
> She walked seventy miles, and leaped fifteen stiles,
> Which astonished that Girl of Majorca.

Beyond the restraints of propriety were those imposed by life itself. "There's something in the world amiss will be unravelled by and by," Lear would quote in his diary. In his own case, epilepsy imposed an isolating barrier which he never broke down.

In his writing such anomalies might cause embarrassment: they could also be the source of real suffering. In the Pelican Chorus, the apparent affliction suffered by the King of the Cranes is politely ignored. With the Daddy Long-Legs and the Fly, however, it is all far more serious and distressing. Each to the other seems fine and composed, and yet...."Why," asks Mr. Daddy Long-Legs, "do you never come to court?"

> "O Mr. Daddy Long-legs,"
> Said Mr. Floppy Fly,
> "It's true I never go to court,
> And I will tell you why.
> If I had six long legs like yours,
> At once I'd go to court!
> But oh! I can't, because *my* legs
> Are so extremely short."

Mr. Daddy Long-legs also has his secret sadness. He, who once sang so beautifully, can no longer do so. But there is a remedy: they can escape to a land where none of this will matter any more:

> Then Mr. Daddy Long-legs
> And Mr. Floppy Fly
> Rushed downward to the foamy sea
> With one sponge-taneous cry;
> And there they found a little boat,
> Whose sails were pink and gray;
> And off they sailed among the waves,
> Far, and far away.
> They sailed across the silent main
> And reached the great Gromboolian plain;
> And there they play for evermore
> At battlecock and shuttledoor.

This is where Lear takes the children. Together they set out on their long and difficult journey. You must have courage to go to sea in a sieve, or indeed to sail away for a year and a day, but this courage is rewarded. There is no chance of the fainthearted following you. Critical, unimaginative adults are left behind. When the Jumblies returned home,

> ...every one said, "If we only live,
> We too will go to sea in a Sieve,—
> To the hills of the Chankly Bore!"

but we know perfectly well that they will not.

Of course, you may discover, when you reach the sunset isles of Boshen, that you have moved from loneliness into loneliness: neither the Yonghy Bonghy Bò nor the Dong could redeem their isolation. There is sadness even here. But, in the end, it is all a game, perhaps of battlecock and shuttledoor, certainly of words and of the imagination. This is what gives it its safety. "There only remains a general, but very strong, pervading sense of well-being and innate rectitude from the standpoint of eight years," a child friend said of Lear. "I knew he was 'safe' and that I was safe and that we were all safe together, and that suspicions might at once be put aside." In a potentially alien world, Lear made children feel secure:

> How pleasant to know Mr. Lear!
> Who has written such volumes of stuff!
> Some think him ill-tempered and queer,
> But a few think him pleasant enough.
>
> His mind is concrete and fastidious,
> His nose is remarkably big;
> His visage is more or less hideous,
> His beard it resembles a wig.

As a child you may feel yourself to be strange and different, you know you can never be perfect; but there is no need to worry, for in an imaginary world where people have unlikely noses and legs and weird modes of expression, where they seek out oddities with whom they can identify themselves, and where they find kindness and spontaneity, you are never likely to feel alone. It is in this that we find Lear's influence on the children's writers who came after him.

—Vivien Noakes

MacDONALD, George. British. Born near Huntly, Aberdeenshire, 10 December 1824. Educated at King's College, University of Aberdeen, 1840–45, M.A. 1845; Congregationalist Theological College, Highbury, London, 1848–50. Married Louisa Powell in 1850 (died 1902); 11 children. Private tutor in London, 1845–48; minister, Trinity Congregational Church, Arundel, Sussex, 1850–53; lecturer and preacher in Manchester, 1855–56, Hastings, Sussex, 1857–59, and London, from 1859; editor, with Norman MacLeod, *Good Words for the Young* magazine, London, 1870–72; lived in Bordighera, Italy, in later life. LL.D.: University of Aberdeen, 1868. Granted Civil List pension, 1877. *Died 18 September 1905.* Fiction: *Dealings with the Fairies*, 1867; *At the Back of the North Wind*, 1870; *Ranald Bannerman's Boyhood*, 1871; *The Princess and the Goblin*, 1871; *Gutta-Percha Willie, The Working Genius*, 1873; *The Wise Woman* (*A Double Story; The Lost Princess*), 1875; *Sir Gibbie*, 1879; *The Princess and Curdie*, 1882; *A Rough Shaking*, 1890; *The Light Princess and Other Fairy Tales*, 1893; *The Fairy Tales*, 5 vols., 1904; *The Gifts of the Child Christ*, 2 vols., 1973.

* * *

George MacDonald was a singular 19th-century writer whose outstanding talent for crossing literary types and age barriers makes critical discussion of his writings difficult. More than any writer of his time, he understood the symbolic richness of the traditional fairytale and worked to expand its dimensions. As a teller of fanciful tales, he is unequalled. It is his unusual mastery of the parable form, converting it, as he did, into a sort of allegorical fantasy, called a *fairytale*, which continues to attract modern writers of children's books to his stories. He possessed a fully integrated genius, whereby the creations of faerie lore and the realities of his own childhood were one; and it is this feature that characterizes him best.

Typical of his lifelong experimentation with the parable-fairytale form, or as he later designated it, "the double story," is his first and quite successful prose narrative, *Phantastes* (1858). Into it, he put a multifarious assortment of lyrics, chivalric Spenserian ballads, frame-stories, and imaginative beings related to his reading of Hoffmann's *Golden Pot*, Novalis, and Fouqué's *Undine*, his favorite fairytale. In type, *Phantastes* defies strict classification; it is in subject-matter most like the *volksmärchen*: an episodic string of nature-parables focusing around the youthful hero Anodos and his lessons of self-renunciation. What the plot lacks in consistency of design, it compensates for by its symbolic depth. Contained in this story and its later companion, *Lilith*, are passages of double parable-writing—for example the tale of Cosmo—which place MacDonald, unrivalled in this form, with Bunyan and Spenser.

During the 1870's MacDonald did most of his best writing for children. He edited *Good Words for the Young* and serialized *At the Back of the North Wind* in it, following with a story of his boyhood reminiscences, *Ranald Bannerman's Boyhood*. And in 1872 he published his second classic, *The Princess and the Goblin*, and *The Wise Woman: A Parable*, three years later. In these books—not originally limited to any certain age—MacDonald fully demonstrated his craft as a writer of children's books.

All of his stories have in them the moral fabric of parables. Educational in thrust, each tale contains a basic plot—Diamond, the coachman's son, takes up with Mistress North Wind who becomes his flying tutoress (*At the Back of the North Wind*); Princess Irene and Curdie, the miner's son, rid the royal city of Gwyntystorm of its corruptors (The Princess and Curdie books); and in *The Wise Woman*, his most lucid and long parable, Princess Rosamond and a shepherd's daughter are taught by a beatific old woman in a cottage in the woods. Simple contrasts are readily made between rich and poor, greed and charity, beauty and ugliness, youth and age, selfishness and true obedience—popular lessons of fairyland. Cannily the reader learns that appearances are not everything ("Little Daylight"), that true knowledge comes by acceptance of self-sacrifice and dependency on another ("The History of Photogen and Nycteris"), and, finally, in the best symbolic tale, "The Golden Key," that the source of all desire (imagination?) itself is found in a cosmic search up into the rainbow. But in spite of the teasing enchantment and obvious didacticism at work in the stories, there is always—most critics contend—something more than allegorical meaning in them.

As a writer MacDonald claimed that his "aim" was to bring about "logical conviction" in his readers by creating a "mood-engendering" sensation: "The best thing you can do for your fellow, next to rousing his conscience, is—not to give him things to think about, but to wake things up that are in him; or say, to make him think things for himself." Transparency of thought and feeling is what one reacts to most in his stories. Like the Princess and Curdie, as they stand before the youthful but wise grandmother, the reader continually asks:

> "What does it all mean, Grandmother?" she sobbed and burst into fresh tears.
> "It means, my love, that I did not mean to show myself. Curdie is not yet able to believe some things. Seeing is not believing—it is only seeing."

Meaning in all his stories is linked up, at one point, with an attitude of childlikeness, his lifelong theme and concern.

There is throughout his writings a philosophical preoccupation with the conversion of evil into goodness and death into life. Graphically he sketches—in his best works—*Phantastes, At the Back of the North Wind*, The Princess books, "The Golden Key," *The Wise Woman, Sir Gibbie*, and *Lilith*—his own reformed picture of Scottish Calvinism transposed into fairytale language and scenes. This he does by placing the child in the center; predestination, for instance, becomes the prodding voice of North Wind, who explains to Diamond that he is limited only by what he *really* wants to do, which is the best way home. Good and Evil are no longer absolutes in his parables, as they are in most fairytales, but take part in the living process of getting better, of recovering from the illness of self. One mounts repeatedly in his fantasies the narrow stairs of submission that lead to the grandmother's garret room of rebirth and instruction.

All of this is to say that MacDonald's strong beliefs and cosmic vision of the role of the child in the universe quite naturally led him to select the fairytale-parable as the ideal form: in it he found poetic liberty of expression, symbolic regularity, and a disregard for age levels which allowed him to retell many of his childhood dreams and discoveries in Huntly, where he had known the art of castle-building as well as harsh discipline. As he grew older, he used the ordinary fairytale to convey, through his own sacramental symbolism in *Lilith*, his visionary romance of growing old, what C.S. Lewis defined as "good Death": the happy ending.

The word "homesickness" can be applied to all of MacDonald's books. His children's classics have in them crystal, descriptive and cosy passages of interlacing filial relationships which are in their beauty and provocative strength unsurpassed by any other author of the period. And with the recent return to the family unit in many modern children's books and revival of interest in the fairytale, it can safely be predicted that MacDonald will go on being rediscovered as the patriarch of the child and of the Victorian household.

—Glenn Edward Sadler

MARRYAT, Frederick. British. Born in Westminster, London, 10 July 1792. Educated privately. Married Catherine Shairp in 1819; four sons and seven daughters, including the novelist Florence Marryat. Joined the Royal Navy, 1806; sailed as a midshipman on the *Impérieuse*, under Lord Cochrane, 1806–09, in the flagship *Centaur*, in the Mediterranean, 1810, and on the *Aeolus* and *Spartan* in the West Indies and off the coast of North America, 1811–12; sailed to the West Indies on the *Espiègle*, 1813; Lieutenant of the *Newcastle*, off the coast of North America, 1814 until invalided home, 1815; appointed Commander, 1815; commanded the sloop *Beaver* cruising off St. Helena to guard against the escape of Napoleon, 1820–22; involved in suppression of Channel smuggling, on the *Rosario*, 1822; sailed in the *Larne* to the East Indies, 1823, and served in the Burmese war: Senior Naval Officer at Rangoon, 1824; commanded expedition up the Bassein River, 1825; appointed Captain of the *Tees*, 1825, and returned in her to England, 1826: C.B. (Companion, Order of the Bath), for services in Burma, 1826; commanded the *Ariadne* in the Atlantic service, 1828 until he retired to become full-time writer, 1830; editor, *Metropolitan Magazine*, London, 1832–35; lived in Brussels, 1836, Canada and the United States, 1837–39, and London, 1839–43; settled on a farm, Langham Manor, in Norfolk, 1843. Recipient: Royal Humane Society Gold Medal, 1818. Fellow of the Royal Society, 1819. Member, Legion of Honour, 1833. *Died 9 August 1848.* Fiction: *Masterman Ready*, 1841–42; *Narrative of the Travels and Adventures of Monsieur Violet*

in California, Sonora, and Western Texas, 1843; *The Settlers in Canada,* 1844; *The Mission,* 1845; *The Children of the New Forest,* 1847; *The Little Savage,* completed by Frank S. Marryat, 1848–49.

*   *   *

Frederick Marryat is remarkably good, and not matched as an adventure story writer until the time of Stevenson. His impressive naval career is the clue to his writings, for Marryat, like many of his successors, learned to write adventure stories by living a life which sounded like one. As Conrad said, "his novels are not the outcome of his art, but of his character, like the deeds that make up his record of naval service."

Marryat's storytelling is not entirely artless, however, for, by the time he turned to writing children's books in the 1840's, he was able to draw not only upon a decade of writing sea stories such as *Mr. Midshipman Easy* (1836) in the manner of a Regency Smollett (and mixing with Dickens and other leading writers of the day), but also on the tradition of adventure stories established by Defoe's *Robinson Crusoe* and extended especially by the historical novels of Scott and the *Leatherstocking* tales of Cooper.

Marryat's children's books, then, *Masterman Ready, Settlers in Canada, The Mission, The Little Savage*, and *The Children of the New Forest*, belong to the line associated with the great writers of adventure stories for adults, especially the tradition of the Robinsonnades, but modified by Marryat in ways he thought appropriate for younger readers. His naval experiences brought to his tales of battles, storms, and shipwrecks a racy realism, while his Tory radicalism and warm humanity often combine to temper a deliberate didacticism, in ways which can be disconcerting and refreshing.

Masterman Ready, Marryat's first children's book, is a good example. Writing for his own children who had asked for a story like *The Swiss Family Robinson*, Marryat set out to produce a much more accurate tale of shipwreck and life on a desert island than Wyss had done. The ship carrying the Seagrave family to Australia is deserted after a gale, and the family have to fend for themselves on a small island, helped by kind old Masterman Ready. Marryat's account of hurricanes and seamanship, and of the wild life on the island, achieves real authenticity. At the same time Marryat's moral didacticism leads him to show the practical man's response in Mr. Seagrave's religious philosophy. But the dangers of an excessively rigid approach are avoided to a large degree, not only by Marryat's powers to surprise one didactically, as when Mr. Seagrave foresees the end of British imperialism in chapter 27, but also through the ways Marryat dramatises and humanises his story. Tommy, the Seagraves' six-year-old son, is a naughty boy who not only gets into silly scrapes through eating too many castor oil beans, for example, but is actually responsible for the book's tragic ending. Savages attack the Seagraves' stockade quite unsuccessfully until the supply of water is exhausted unexpectedly because of Tommy's laziness. Ready is seriously wounded in the attempt to get more water, and, though the Seagraves are rescued, the old mariner dies of his wounds. "What a lesson it will be to Tommy when he is old enough to comprehend fully the consequences of his conduct," says his over-pious father, but the dying man's last words are that the little boy shall never know the cause of Ready's death. So the story ends on a note, not of triumph, but of relief mingled with gravity.

Settlers in Canada initially seems to owe more to Cooper's stories of North American Indians than to Defoe, and Marryat also knew Canada at first hand, so his account of the Campbell family's settling near Lake Ontario carries real authority. The story of how the immigrants deal with wolves, survive a forest fire, and eventually rescue two prisoners from hostile Indians provides a lively narrative, and we are meant to feel that the prosperity Dr. Campbell achieves in the last chapter is more than the conventional happy ending, but represents genuine reward for the decorum maintained in a variety of testing circumstances. What gives the book its distinctive flavour, however, is the manner Marryat, in ways which are his distinctive modification of Defoe, vividly describes the more domestic adventures of the Campbells, the way they build a house, learn to shoot and fish, sow crops and begin to trade furs. This is a Robinsonnade with a difference, and it is one that writers such as Ballantyne and Henty were to learn from.

Marryat used foreign settings for three other children's books, *Narrative of the Travels and Adventures of Monsieur Violet*, *The Mission*, and *The Little Savage*. Of these the least successful is *Monsieur Violet*, for though the tale of how the French hero and his nine-year-old son emigrated and settled among the Snake Indians of Western America is potentially exciting, the story is told in such a halting fashion, with lengthy historical and topographical digressions and an inconsequential ending, as to make it almost unreadable. *The Mission* opens promisingly with an account of how Alexander Wilmot, one of Marryat's most "manly" heroes, sets out for South Africa to search for an aunt shipwrecked off the coast some years before. But after some early encounters with wild animals and the threat of hostile natives, the narrative peters out when the hero discovers his aunt is quite definitely dead barely half way through the book. *The Little Savage* is even more disjointed, though here we know that Marryat's failing health was responsible. The book plunges straight into a sharp and ugly account given by a nameless boy of his desperate plight on a desert island where he is completely alone except for the company of a morose and cruel sailor who treats him as a slave. Only when the older man is blinded in a storm, and the young boy is able to turn on him with a knife, does the sailor begin to treat him as a human being. The drama of the opening is gradually dissipated by the theatricality of the subsequent plot, and the work of an inferior hand is clear in the final chapters, but the power of that opening is not easily forgotten.

Happily Marryat's last completed children's book, *The Children of the New Forest*, has few such lapses, and not only established the popularity of the historical tale for children but set standards which later writers have not found it easy to emulate. Scott's *Waverley* novels had produced a host of successors, but Marryat was the first writer to produce a historical novel for children, in his depiction of the adventures of the Beverley family, who, when their Royalist father is killed at Naseby, are protected from possible Cromwellian persecution by an old forester, Jacob Armitage, who hides them in his cottage in the New Forest. Marryat refuses to over-simplify the issues which lay behind the Civil War, and, though his central characters are Royalists, the Parliamentary superintendent of the New Forest and his daughter Patience are portrayed with equal sympathy. This is no case of the Wrong but Romantic versus the Right but Repulsive. Marryat also deliberately avoids romantic "tushery," and though Prince Charles does appear briefly, there are no interviews with Cromwell or overheard asides from John Milton.

Marryat was no great stylist, but is a master at describing the details of particular scenes or episodes in clear and simple language, and in describing the way in which Jacob trains the Beverley children to support themselves in the New Forest, farming, cooking, looking after the animals, he painted a series of scenes which have fascinated children in every generation. In a sense the Beverleys are as shipwrecked in the New Forest as the Seagraves were on their island. But though the acquisition and exploitation of land can perhaps be related to British imperialism, it would be a mistake to interpret Marryat purely in those terms. Playing at home-making is an activity which absorbs many children, of course, offering a symbolic form of growth and creativity in a world of insecurity and stress. This is perhaps why children have enjoyed Marryat's books for so long.

By the time Marryat died, the foundations of the 19th-century adventure story for children were firmly laid. Whether in stories of shipwreck, of history, or of contemporary adventure, he had pointed the way and produced exciting examples where previously only adult

or unsatisfactory works existed. His influence on writers about the sea has stretched from Kingston to Masefield and Peter Dawlish, and as a writer of contemporary adventure tales from Ballantyne to Ivan Southall, but, most of all perhaps, he has been an indirect but potent force in the development of the historical novel from Henty to the present day.

—Dennis Butts

MEADE, L.T. Irish. Born Elizabeth Thomasina Meade in Bandon, County Cork, in 1854. Married Alfred Toulmin Smith in 1879; one son and two daughters. Worked in the British Museum, London; editor, with A.A. Leith, *Atalanta* girls' magazine, London, for six years. *Died 26 October 1914.* Fiction: *Lotty's Last Home*, 1875; *A Knight of Today*, 1877; *Scamp and I*, 1877; *Bel Marjory*, 1878; *The Children's Kingdom*, 1878; *Your Brother and Mine (Outcast Robin)*, 1878; *Water Lilies and Other Tales*, 1878; *Dot and Her Treasures*, 1879; *Water Gipsies*, 1879; *A Dweller in Tents*, 1880; *Mou-Setsé*, with *The Orphan's Pilgrimage* by T. von Gumpert, 1880; *The Floating Light of Ring-finnan, and Guardian Angels*, 1880; *Mother Herring's Chicken*, 1881; *A London Baby*, 1882; *The Children's Pilgrimage*, 1883; *Hermie's Rose-Buds and Other Stories*, 1883; *The Autocrat of the Nursery*, 1884; *A Band of Three*, 1884; *Scarlet Anemones*, 1884; *The Two Sisters*, 1884; *The Angel of Love*, 1885; *A Little Silver Trumpet*, 1885; *A World of Girls*, 1886; *Daddy's Boy*, 1887; *The O'Donnells of Inchfawn*, 1887; *The Palace Beautiful*, 1887; *Sweet Nancy*, 1887; *Deb and the Duchess*, 1888; *Nobody's Neighbours*, 1888; *A Farthingful*, 1889; *The Golden Lady*, 1889; *The Lady of the Forest*, 1889; *The Little Princess of Tower Hill*, 1889; *Polly, A New-Fashioned Girl*, 1889; *Poor Miss Carolina*, 1889; *The Beresford Prize*, 1890; *Dickory Dock*, 1890; *Engaged to Be Married*, 1890; *Heart of Gold*, 1890; *Just a Love Story*, 1890; *Marigold*, 1890; *Hepsy Gipsy*, 1891; *The Children of Wilton Chase*, 1891; *A Sweet Girl-Graduate*, 1891; *Little Mary and Other Stories*, 1891; *Bashful Fifteen*, 1892; *Four on an Island*, 1892; *Out of the Fashion*, 1892; *A Ring of Rubies*, 1892; *Beyond the Blue Mountains*, 1893; *A Young Mutineer*, 1893; *Betty*, 1894; *In an Iron Grip*, 1894; *Red Rose and Tiger Lily*, 1894; *Girls, New and Old*, 1895; *The Least of These and Other Stories*, 1895; *Catalina, Art Student*, 1896; *A Girl in Ten Thousand*, 1896; *Good Luck*, 1896; *A Little Mother to the Others*, 1896; *Merry Girls of England*, 1896; *Playmates*, 1896; *The White Tzar*, 1896; *The House of Surprises*, 1896; *Bad Little Hannah*, 1897; *A Handful of Silver*, 1897; *Wild Kitty*, 1897; *Cave Perilous*, 1898; *A Bunch of Cherries*, 1898; *The Cleverest Woman in England*, 1898; *The Girls of St. Wode's*, 1898; *Mary Gifford, M.B.*, 1898; *The Rebellion of Lil Carrington*, 1898; *The Siren*, 1898; *Adventuress*, 1899; *All Sorts*, 1899; *The Odds and the Evens*, 1899; *Light o' the Morning*, 1899; *Wages*, 1900; *A Plucky Girl*, 1900; *The Beauforts*, 1900; *A Brave Poor Thing*, 1900; *Daddy's Girl*, 1900; *Miss Nonentity*, 1900; *Seven Maids*, 1900; *A Sister of the Red Cross*, 1900; *The Time of Roses*, 1900; *Wheels of Iron*, 1901; *The Blue Diamond*, 1901; *Cosey Corner*, 1901; *Girls of the True Blue*, 1901; *The New Mrs. Lascelles*, 1901; *A Stumble by the Way*, 1901; *A Very Naughty Girl*, 1901; *Drift*, 1902; *Girls of the Forest*, 1902; *Margaret*, 1902; *The Pursuit of Penelope*, 1902; *Queen Rose*, 1902; *The Rebel of the School*, 1902; *The Princess Who Gave All Away, and The Naughty One of the Family*, 1902; *The Squire's Little Girl*, 1902; *Through Peril for a Wife*, 1902; *The Witch Maid*, 1903; *The Burden of Her Youth*, 1903; *By Mutual Consent*, 1903; *A Gay Charmer*, 1903; *The Manor School*, 1903; *Peter the Pilgrim*, 1903; *Resurgam*, 1903; *Rosebury*, 1903; *That Brilliant Peggy*, 1903; *A Maid of*

Mystery, 1904; *The Adventures of Miranda*, 1904; *At the Back of the World*, 1904; *The Lady Cake-Maker*, 1904; *Castle Poverty*, 1904; *The Girls of Mrs. Pritchard's School*, 1904; *Love Triumphant*, 1904; *A Madcap*, 1904; *A Modern Tomboy*, 1904; *Nurse Charlotte*, 1904; *Petronella, and The Coming of Polly*, 1904; *Wilful Cousin Kate*, 1905; *Bess of Delaney's*, 1905; *A Bevy of Girls*, 1905; *Dumps*, 1905; *His Mascot*, 1905; *Little Wife Hester*, 1905; *Loveday*, 1905; *Old Readymoney's Daughter*, 1905; *Virginia*, 1905; *The Colonel and the Boy*, 1906; *The Face of Juliet*, 1906; *The Girl and Her Fortune*, 1906; *The Heart of Helen*, 1906; *The Hill-Top Girl*, 1906; *The Home of Sweet Content*, 1906; *In the Flower of Her Youth*, 1906; *The Maid with the Goggles*, 1906; *Sue*, 1906; *Turquoise and Ruby*, 1906; *Victory*, 1906; *The Colonel's Conquest*, 1907; *The Curse of the Feverals*, 1907; *A Girl from America*, 1907; *The Home of Silence*, 1907; *Kindred Spirits*, 1907; *The Lady of Delight*, 1907; *Little Josephine*, 1907; *The Little School-Mothers*, 1907; *The Love of Susan Cardigan*, 1907; *The Red Cap of Liberty*, 1907; *The Red Ruth*, 1907; *The Scamp Family*, 1907; *Three Girls from School*, 1907; *The Aim of Her Life*, 1908; *A Lovely Fiend and Other Stories*, 1908; *The Court-Harman Girls*, 1908; *The Courtship of Sybil*, 1908; *Hetty Beresford*, 1908; *Sarah's Mother*, 1908; *The School Favourite*, 1908; *The School Queens*, 1908; *Aylwyn's Friends*, 1909; *Betty Vivian*, 1909; *Blue of the Sea*, 1909; *Brother or Husband*, 1909; *The Fountain of Beauty*, 1909; *I Will Sing a New Song*, 1909; *The Princess of the Revels*, 1909; *The Stormy Petrel*, 1909; *The A.B.C. Girl*, 1910; *Belinda Treherne*, 1910; *A Girl of Today*, 1910; *Lady Anne*, 1910; *Miss Gwendoline*, 1910; *Nance Kennedy*, 1910; *Pretty-Girl and the Others*, 1910; *Rose Regina*, 1910; *A Bunch of Cousins, and The Barn "Boys,"* 1911; *Desborough's Wife*, 1911; *The Doctor's Children*, 1911; *For Dear Dad*, 1911; *The Girl from Spain*, 1911; *The Girls of Merton College*, 1911; *Mother and Son*, 1911; *Ruffles*, 1911; *The Soul of Margaret Rand*, 1911; *Daddy's Girl, and Consuelo's Quest of Happiness*, 1911; *Corporal Violet*, 1912; *A Girl of the People*, 1912; *Kitty O'Donovan*, 1912; *Lord and Lady Kitty*, 1912; *Love's Cross Roads*, 1912; *Peggy from Kerry*, 1912; *The Chesterton Girl Graduates*, 1913; *The Girls of Abinger Close*, 1913; *The Girls of King's Royal*, 1913; *The Passion of Kathleen Duveen*, 1913; *A Band of Mirth*, 1914; *Col. Tracy's Wife*, 1914; *Elizabeth's Prisoner*, 1914; *A Girl of High Adventure*, 1914; *Her Happy Face*, 1914; *The Queen of Joy*, 1914; *The Wooing of Monica*, 1914; *The Darling of the School*, 1915; *Greater Than Gold*, 1915; *Jill the Irresistible*, 1915; *Hollyhock*, 1916; *Madge Mostyn's Nieces*, 1916; *The Maid Indomitable*, 1916; *Mother Mary*, 1916; *Daughters of Today*, 1916; *Better Than Riches*, 1917; *The Fairy Godmother*, 1917; *Miss Patricia*, 1925; *Roses and Thorns*, 1928; *In Time of Roses*, n.d.

*   *   *

L.T. Meade was a prolific and highly professional writer of fiction for the middle-class child. Her prodigious output was all designed, one might almost say packaged, to please particular sections of this readership, and for each group she drew upon the appropriate conventions of storytelling as they had been developed by her predecessors. Her personal touch was a certain emotional intensity of tone, which might be sentimental, or wild and romantic, but always tended to highly coloured extremes.

During the 1870's she tried her hand at the street-arab stories which were a mainstay of "Sunday" writing for children, developed by Evangelical and humanitarian writers. They had had a strengthening earnestness; but Meade took up the convention chiefly for its emotional appeal. Such a story is *Scamp and I*, in which little orphan Flo is attacked by ruffians and dies in a children's hospital, murmuring blessings upon the Queen; her mongrel Scamp perishes defending her. One cannot help feeling that its pathetic thrill is an indulgence, and lacks any sense of the real sufferings of others. In

writing about middle-class children Meade adopts the convention of the "pickle," the small child who is innocently naughty, whose scrapes are either evidence of a sturdy independent spirit or the result of parental misunderstanding; these stories are vivid with the writer's own sentimental view of children, no more challenging than the emotionalism of the arab tales, but drawn perhaps from more personal feeling.

Many other kinds of story proved adaptable to Meade's purposes of exciting pleasurable emotion for her readers. *Four on an Island* is a Crusoe story; *Cave Perilous* an historical romance about Chartism; *A Sister of the Red Cross* a tale of love and marriage against an exotic background of nursing in the South African war, highly charged with patriotic and militaristic excitement; *Beyond the Blue Mountains* an allegory derived from *Pilgrim's Progress* but set in a flower-fairy children's world. In all of these the spirit of brave, upright, British childhood triumphs over all troubles, from laziness to storms at sea and hunger-maddened mobs.

It was in school stories for girls that Meade found the story patterns and setting which best suited her emotional romanticism. In them she stressed adolescent passions, especially in the relationships between the girls and their feelings towards their teachers. In *A World of Girls*, one of her most popular books, the headmistress, Miss Willis, is an adored mother-substitute intimately involved with her pupils' lives, and the emotional storms between the girls are at least as important as the improbable plot in which a baby sister is carried off by gypsies and rescued by a wild tom-boy who has a magic way with fierce dogs. It was for her ability to manipulate a tale excitingly, and fill it unashamedly with intense emotion, that Meade won her enormous popularity; and in the school story she had a hand herself in the shaping of a convention which later writers like Angela Brazil were to take up.

—J.S. Bratton

———

MOLESWORTH, Mary Louisa (née Stewart). Also wrote as Ennis Graham. British. Born in Rotterdam, Netherlands, 29 May 1839; grew up in Manchester, England. Attended school in Lausanne, Switzerland; attended classes given by William Gaskell. Married Richard Molesworth in 1861 (separated 1879); seven children. Lived in France and Germany, and in London after 1884. *Died 20 July 1921*. Fiction: *Tell Me a Story* (as Ennis Graham), 1875; *Carrots* (as Ennis Graham), 1876; *The Cuckoo Clock* (as Ennis Graham), 1877; *Grandmother Dear*, 1878; *The Tapestry Room*, 1879; *A Christmas Child*, 1880; *Hermy*, 1880; *The Adventures of Herr Baby*, 1881; *Hoodie*, 1882; *Rosy*, 1882; *The Boys and I*, 1882; *Summer Stories for Boys and Girls*, 1882; *Two Little Waifs*, 1883; *Christmas-Tree Land*, 1883; *The Little Old Portrait (Edmee)*, 1884; *Lettice*, 1884; *Us*, 1885; *A Charge Fulfilled*, 1886; *Silverthorns*, 1886; *Four Winds Farm*, 1886; *The Palace in the Garden*, 1887; *Little Miss Peggy*, 1887; *The Abbey by the Sea*, 1887; *A Christmas Posy*, 1888; *Five Minutes' Stories*, 1888; *The Third Miss St. Quentin*, 1888; *Neighbours*, 1889; *A House to Let*, 1889; *The Old Pincushion*, 1889; *The Rectory Children*, 1889; *Nesta*, 1889; *Great Uncle Hoot-Toot*, 1889; *Twelve Tiny Tales*, 1890; *Family Troubles*, 1890; *The Children of the Castle*, 1890; *Little Mother Bunch*, 1890; *The Green Casket and Other Stories*, 1890; *The Story of a Spring Morning and Other Tales*, 1890; *The Red Grange*, 1891; *The Bewitched Lamp*, 1891; *The Lucky Ducks and Other Stories*, 1891; *Nurse Heatherdale's Story*, 1891; *Sweet Content*, 1891; *Imogen*, 1892; *An Enchanted Garden*, 1892; *The Girls and I*, 1892; *Farthings*, 1892; *The Man with the Pan-Pipes and Other Stories*, 1892; *Robin Redbreast*, 1892; *The Next-Door House*, 1892; *Studies and Stories,*

1893; *The Thirteen Little Black Pigs and Other Stories*, 1893; *Mary*, 1893; *Blanche*, 1893; *Olivia*, 1894; *My New Home*, 1894; *The Carved Lions*, 1895; *Opposite Neighbours and Other Stories*, 1895; *Sheila's Mystery*, 1895; *White Turrets*, 1895; *Friendly Joey and Other Stories*, 1896; *The Oriel Window*, 1896; *Philippa*, 1896; *Stories for Children in Illustration of the Lord's Prayer*, 1897; *Meg Langholme*, 1897; *Miss Mouse and Her Boys*, 1897; *Greyling Towers*, 1898; *The Magic Nuts*, 1898; *The Grim House*, 1899; *This and That*, 1899; *The Children's Hour*, 1899; *The Three Witches*, 1900; *The House That Grew*, 1900; *The Wood-Pigeons and Mary*, 1901; *"My Pretty" and Her Little Brother "Too,"* 1901; *The Blue Baby and Other Stories*, 1901; *Peterkin*, 1902; *The Mystery of the Pinewood, and Hollow Tree House*, 1903; *The Ruby Ring*, 1904; *The Bolted Door and Other Stories*, 1906; *Jasper*, 1906; *The Little Guest*, 1907; *Fairies—of Sorts*, 1908; *The February Boys*, 1909; *The Story of a Year*, 1910; *Fairies Afield*, 1911.

*   *   *

On re-reading Mary Louisa Molesworth's stories after a long interval—or perhaps reading some of them for the first time—one is immediately struck by the fact that they are indeed very readable. She was above all else a good teller of tales. Yet when we come to analyse the content of the stories themselves, there is little in the way of dramatic events to account for this. The drama, and thereby the interest of the story, comes from the life of the characters in what is largely an everyday setting. Her stories—the best ones at any rate, for she was uneven in the quality of her writing—pick up the characters at a particular period in their lives usually between about 5 and 12 years old. But we feel that each one had a life of his own before the story started and will continue to develop after the book has closed, whereas the events in so many children's books appear to exist in their own world, without a past or a future.

Perhaps one of the most noticeable characteristics of Molesworth's books is their ordinariness. Her children are all very "genteel," and even if they are poor they tend to have a middle-class background. For the most part the stories are set in the comfortably solid world of nurseries and nannies, of brothers and sisters in plenty, and loving mothers (who may alas often have to go to India, or, as in *Carrots*, to Algeria). The daily routine is firmly sketched and indeed provides a useful social study of the upper-middle-class child-world of the latter 19th century. Even the names given to the children are redolent of class and period: Hermione, Rosalys, Mavis. In the case of *Four Winds Farm*, where she is dealing with a boy from a *farm*, she gives him the improbable name of Gratian, to show his "difference."

Magic comes into a number of her stories, especially the more successful ones like *The Cuckoo Clock* and *The Tapestry Room*, but for the most part even here it is everyday life which provides the frame of the story, though some at least of the magic comes from the twilight world between reality and fantasy. It is the insight into the child's mind, with its inability to distinguish between actuality and imagination, which sets Molesworth apart from so many of her contemporaries. Behind many of her characters are careful observations of real children, their speech, their behaviour, and, even more important, their minds. There is poor Carrots, who genuinely believes he has found a "yellow sixpenny piece," and in no way connects it with the missing half-sovereign—"sovereigns" is a game about kings and queens! And Hermy, in the book of the same name, has great problems as to what is meant by truth, as far as the adults in her life are concerned. Molesworth is aware that such little things assume enormous proportions in the life of the very young. But there is one big difference at that age, in that time for the young is so relative. If you are only five, last week can be as far away as yesterday, and next year, when you will be *six*, is a lifetime away.

In her descriptions of school life, Molesworth is fair and understanding. Her school teachers, who cause so much trouble to the young (in *The Carved Lions* and *Hermy*, for example), are given their due, as if *we* should not find them so bad. For here, too, much of the trouble lies once more with the child's limited understanding of the grown-up world, and his own ability to explain a situation in everyday terms. We have all known the child for whom a toy, or even an invisible companion, were as real, if not more so, than the people around him, and the "untruths" arising from this state of affairs cannot be dealt with as with older children. It is to Molesworth's credit that in the days before there was so much talk of child psychology, she saw and understood this aspect of child behaviour, and wrote about it as a normal part of growing up, with all its fears and confidences, and in a way that small children would understand and accept. Her world of magic, too, is gentle and charming, of the sort to banish fear, coming in the wind or with dreams. But she can also give her fairy characters a personality of their own: the North and East Winds in *Four Winds Farm*, the Raven in *The Tapestry Room*, and the Cuckoo in *The Cuckoo Clock* are not always sweet and obliging, but can be cross and need humouring every bit as much as the kindliest adult in the real world.

Perhaps Molesworth's real fault lies in the amount she wrote, for some of her later books (and she lived until 1921) were repetitive, thin, and with a tendency to the sentimental, which the best of her books avoid. But her best is very good indeed. The merit of *The Cuckoo Clock, The Carved Lions, The Tapestry Room, Us*, and many others is manifest in the fact that they can still be read and enjoyed by young children of today, because they are good straightforward stories still, even if the world of nannies has passed away with the Indian Empire to which parents were so conveniently banished.

—Joyce Irene Whalley

OTIS, James. American. Born James Otis Kaler in Frankfort (now Winterport), Maine, 19 March 1848. Educated at public schools in Maine. Married Amy L. Scammon in 1898; two sons. Journalist: worked for Boston *Journal* and New York papers; staff member, *Boys and Girls*; also a publicity man for a circus. Superintendent, South Portland schools, c. 1898. *Died 11 December 1912.*
Fiction: *Toby Tyler*, 1881; *Tim and Tip*, 1883; *Mr. Stubbs's Brother*, 1883; *Raiding the "Pearl,"* 1884; *Left Behind*, 1885; *Silent Pete*, 1886; *A Runaway Brig*, 1888; *The Castaways*, 1888; *Little Joe*, 1888; *The Braganza Diamond*, 1891; *Jack the Hunchback*, 1892; *Jenny Wren's Boarding House*, 1893; *Josiah in New York*, 1893; *The Search for the Silver City*, 1893; *The Boys' Revolt*, 1894; *Chasing a Yacht*, 1894; *Jerry's Family*, 1895; *Andy's Ward*, 1895; *How Tommy Saved the Barn*, 1895; *The Boys of 1745 at the Capture of Louisbourg*, 1895; *Ezra Jordan's Escape from the Massacre at Fort Loyall*, 1895; *An Island Refuge*, 1895; *Neal, The Miller*, 1895; *With Lafayette at Yorktown*, 1895; *Under the Liberty Tree*, 1896; *Teddy and Carrots*, 1896; *Admiral J. of Spurwick*, 1896; *The Boy Captain*, 1896; *On Schedule Time*, 1896; *A Short Cruise*, 1896; *At the Siege of Quebec*, 1897; *The Wreck of the Circus*, 1897; *The Signal Boys of '75*, 1897; *With Washington at Monmouth*, 1897; *When Israel Putnam Served the King*, 1898; *The Capture of the Laughing Mary*, 1898; *With Warren at Bunker Hill*, 1898; *A Cruise with Paul Jones*, 1898; *A Traitor's Escape*, 1898; *Corporal Lige's Recruit*, 1898; *Morgan, The Jersey Spy*, 1898; *Sarah Dillard's Ride*, 1898; *An Amateur Fireman*, 1898; *A District Messenger Boy, and A Necktie Party*, 1898; *Dick in the Desert*, 1898; *Joel Harford*, 1898; *The Princess and Joe Potter*, 1898; *The Boys of '98*, 1898; *The Charming Sally*, 1898; *Captain Tom*, 1899; *With Perry on Lake Erie*, 1899; *Chased Through Norway*, 1899; *Christmas at Deacon Hackett's*, 1899; *Down the Slope*,

1899; *Messenger No. 48*, 1899; *Wheeling for Fortune*, 1899; *A Tory Plot*, 1899; *With the Swamp Fox*, 1899; *Off Santiago with Sampson*, 1899; *When Dewey Came to Manila*, 1899; *At the Siege of Havana*, 1899; *Boston Boys of 1775*, 1900; *The Defense of Fort Henry*, 1900; *On the Kentucky Frontier*, 1900; *Aunt Hannah and Seth*, 1900; *Lobster Catchers*, 1900; *The Armed Ship America*, 1900; *Fighting for the Empire*, 1900; *With Prebble at Tripoli*, 1900; *Our Uncle, The Major*, 1901; *With Porter in the Essex*, 1901; *The Story of Old Falmouth*, 1901; *Inland Waterways*, 1901; *Larry Hudson's Ambition*, 1901; *With the Regulators*, 1901; *When We Destroyed the Gaspee*, 1901; *Amos Dunkel, Oarsman (A Struggle for Freedom)*, 1901; *Reuben Green's Adventure at Yale*, 1902; *The Treasure of Cocos Island*, 1902; *Wan Lun and Dandy*, 1902; *The Cruise of the Enterprise*, 1902; *How the Twins Captured a Hessian*, 1902; *The Story of Pemaquid*, 1902; *With the Treasure-Hunters*, 1903; *With Rodgers on the President*, 1903; *Across the Delaware*, 1903; *Defending the Island*, 1904; *At the Siege of Detroit*, 1904; *Minute Boys* series, from 1904; *Dorothy's Spy*, 1904; *When Washington Served the King*, 1905; *Among the Fur Traders*, 1906; *The Light Keepers*, 1906; *Commodore Barney's Young Spies*, 1907; *The Wreck of the Ocean Queen*, 1907; *Aboard the Hylow on Sable Island Bank*, 1907; *Afloat in Freedom's Cause*, 1908; *The Cruise of the Phoebe*, 1908; *Two Stowaways Aboard the Ellen Maria*, 1908; *The Cruise of the Pickering*, 1909; *Found by the Circus*, 1909; *The Sarah Jane, Dicky Dalton, Captain*, 1909; *The Cruise of the Sally D.*, 1910; *Silver Fox Farm* series, 1910; *With Grant at Vicksburg*, 1910; *Calvert of Maryland*, 1910; *Mary of Plymouth*, 1910; *Peter of New Amsterdam*, 1910; *Richard of Jamestown*, 1910; *Ruth of Boston*, 1910; *Stephen of Philadelphia*, 1910; *With Sherman to the Sea*, 1911; *The Camp on Indian Island*, 1911; *Old Ben*, 1911; *Boy Scouts* series, 1911; *Wanted and Other Stories*, 1912; *The Wreck of the Princess*, 1912; *Antoine of Oregon*, 1912; *Benjamin of Ohio*, 1912; *Hannah of Kentucky*, 1912; *Seth of Colorado*, 1912; *Martha of California*, 1913; *Philip of Texas*, 1913; *The Roaring Lions*, 1913; *Across the Range and Other Stories*, 1914.

*   *   *

Of James Otis's 150 books, only *Toby Tyler* can still be found on the library shelf. Otis's army of ragged newsboys, Revolutionary War Minute Boys, silver fox farmers, Boy Scouts, and wreck survivors have marched into oblivion. Today, they are more likely to be found housed in a special collection or at the historical society.

Toby Tyler, Otis's first novel, was his best and most successful. The story, about a red-headed, freckle-faced 10-year-old orphan who ran away with the circus, tugged at the hearts of his readers a hundred years ago and still has the power to affect us. In his first job with the circus as a candy butcher, Toby is brutalized by his employers, Job Lord and Jacobs. Later, when he is trained to ride, Mr. Castle educates him with the whip. He is befriended by Old Ben, the monkey wagon driver, little Ella, the equestrienne, Sam Treat, the human skeleton, and Lilly, the fat lady. Toby finds comfort, as well, from his pet monkey. Mr. Stubbs, who is killed in Toby's escape from the circus. Toby learns that behind the circus spangles and spectacle is a soiled world of sordid reality.

Often Otis wrote lovingly about the circus, but he always inveighed against it as a hard, demanding, and unprofitable way of life. He tried to rekindle the spark of *Toby* in *Mr. Stubbs's Brother* and *Old Ben* but failed. These are far less circusy and far more moralizing and sentimental than *Toby*. A baby sitter loses his ward in a circus blowdown in *Found by the Circus*. In a gem of a short story entitled "The Acrobat," Otis tells of a young mill worker who joins a circus as an acrobat only to find that his notions of the glamour of circus life were mistaken. He returns to the mill in a lesser position, wiser and happier. Otis's best depiction of the 19th-century circus can be found in "The Clown's Protege," in which the orphaned hero, Jim

Barker, is the virtual prisoner in the Great and Only Circus of Joe Maginly, a villain in clown white.

Abandonment and child abuse are recurrent themes in the works of this Maine writer. These elements help to make *Toby Tyler* more than just another story about a runaway. The themes emerge later in *Wan Lun and Dundy*, the story of a four-year-old Chinese orphan in a small New England coastal town. He becomes the ward of Faith Spaulding, a 12-year-old hunchback. Together Faith, her dog Dundy, and Wan Lun survive the cruel tricks of two nasty boys, a carriage accident in the woods, a forest fire, and a storm. The story is original, unique, and formulaic.

In effect, Otis learned his storytelling craft too well. He knew what worked with his young audience. He knew how to generate excitement, win sympathy, and how to milk a story for a moral. Often his dialogue is stilted and melodramatic. Nowhere in his later work does he exceed the character delineation, the descriptive force, and the emotional impact of *Toby Tyler*.

—Nels Juleus

————

PYLE, Howard. American. Born in Wilmington, Delaware, 5 March 1853. Educated at Friends' School and Clark and Taylor's School, Wilmington; Mr. Van der Weilen's school, Philadelphia, 1868–72. Married Anne Poole in 1881. Freelance illustrator, for *St. Nicholas* magazine, *Harper's*, and *Harper's Young People*. Taught at Drexel Institute, Philadelphia, 1894–1900, and at his own art school in Wilmington, 1900–10. Muralist. *Died 9 November 1911.*
Fiction: *Pepper and Salt*, 1886; *The Wonder Clock*, with Katharine Pyle, 1888; *Otto of the Silver Hand*, 1888; *Men of Iron*, 1892; *The Story of Jack Ballister's Fortunes*, 1895; *The Garden Behind the Moon*, 1895; *Twilight Land*, 1895; *Stolen Treasure*, 1907.

*   *   *

Howard Pyle must be considered a giant in American literature for children. An innovative, vastly productive artist-writer-teacher, he was a modest man totally concerned with inspiring good artists and creating good books. But the term giant just might have appealed to him as a description, for his imagination was tuned in to the days of good knights and evil villains, heroes and dragons, magic stools and clever magicians, beautiful maidens and wicked queens, good boys, foolish men, and, surely among them, giants. And of course, King Arthur and Robin Hood.

In his 58 years he accomplished an amazing amount of enduring work. His importance as an artist as well as writer must be mentioned here for several reasons. First, his work spanned a period of vital change in children's books. It began in an era when moralistic stories had themes of illness, suffering, and death, and were usually illustrated by inept saccharine pictures; standards for writing and illustrating were low. It ended with his work, both words and pictures, having produced the highest standards for others to follow. The author-artist Robert Lawson, writing in *Illustrators of Children's Books 1744–1945*, stated, "It is small wonder that the clean-cut, healthy, joyous work of Howard Pyle came to…children…like a fresh breeze flooding a fetid sickroom." Second, his illustration and stories intertwined and enhanced each other, growing equally from his concept of the subject undertaken, even though, to an extent rarely equalled by any other author-artist, each element is strong enough to stand alone. Third, any piece of artwork takes a great deal of time to produce. Thus to research, absorb, recreate, and retell the Robin Hood ballads and the vast lore of King Arthur was a gigantic, time-consuming task. He was a truly prodigious worker.

Although he could easily "see things in image-terms or in the continuity of words," as Henry C. Pitz describes his dual abilities, he was a deliberate craftsman. He actually experimented with various writing styles to achieve the effect of the archaic speech of Robin Hood's days and yet have it understandable to children. Reading it aloud today, now that we are even used to *you* taking the place of *thee-and-thou* in versions of the Bible, it sounds more unreal than ever to hear, "Now will I go too, for fain would I draw a string for the bright eyes of my lass, for so goodly a prize as that," or hear Pauline ask poor little Otto about his mother, "And didst thou never see her?" Such is his thoroughness in setting scene, delineating character, and sweeping all action forward in a dynamic plot—particularly in his own stories such as *Otto of the Silver Hand, Men of Iron* and his pirate tales—that one quickly accepts the language as another rich element of his writing skill.

Although *The Merry Adventures of Robin Hood* (1883) was his first book to be published, *Pepper and Salt* and *The Wonder Clock* contained stories and fables Pyle had written and illustrated for children's magazines. *Twilight Land* was more influenced by Eastern folktales. While at first he borrowed and retold old tales in different guises ("The Salt of Life" is the well-known Catskin motif of universal folklore), so steeped was he in folk and fairy lore that eventually he could turn his own rich imagination out into these forms to perfection, just as Andersen did. *The Garden Behind the Moon*, a long allegorical fantasy, is less derivative than his short stories and it contains such strong beautiful prose that it makes him a classic writer of fantasy.

With the grim sad story of medieval revenge, *Otto of the Silver Hand*, and that of 15th-century adventure, *Men of Iron*, and in his tales of Robin Hood and King Arthur, Pyle achieved new heights in literature for children: he gave them an immediate sense of their past, complete with authentic convincing details, replete with drama and pageantry, and taut with adventure.

Elizabeth Nesbitt, commenting on Pyle in *A Critical History of Children's Literature*, mentioned that the era in which Pyle developed his work has been called the Golden Age of children's literature and that "It is difficult to do justice to his contribution to the shining quality of that era. The magnitude and diversity of his work elude definition."

—Lee Kingman

———

REED, Talbot Baines. British. Born in Hackney, London, 3 April 1852. Educated at Priory House School, London; City of London School, 1864–68. Married Elizabeth Greer in 1876; two daughters and one son. Joined his father's London type-founding firm, 1868, managing director after 1881. Regular contributor to *Boy's Own Paper*, London, and *Leeds Mercury*. Co-founder, and secretary, 1892–93, Bibliographical Society. Fellow of the Society of Antiquaries, 1893. *Died 28 November 1893*. Fiction: *The Adventures of a Three-Guinea Watch*, 1883; *Follow My Leader*, 1885; *The Fifth Form at St. Dominic's*, 1887; *The Willoughby Captains*, 1887; *Parkhurst Sketches and Other Stories*, 1889; *My Friend Smith*, 1889; *Sir Ludar*, 1889; *Roger Ingleton, Minor*, 1891; *The Cockhouse at Fellsgarth (The House at Fellsgarth)*, 1893; *Reginald Cruden*, 1894; *A Dog with a Bad Name*, 1894; *The Master of the Shell*, 1894; *Tom, Dick, and Harry*, 1894; *Kilgorman*, 1894; *A Book of Short Stories*, 1897.

*   *   *

It was perhaps appropriate that Talbot Baines Reed's first fictional published words were: "It was a proud moment in my existence when Wright, captain of our football club, came up to me in school one Friday and said, 'Adams, your name is down to play in the match against Craven tomorrow.'" This comprised the opening of the first of his series of sketches of sporting life at Parkhurst School, titled "My First Football Match" and appeared on the first page of the first issue of the famous *Boy's Own Paper* on 18 January 1879. It set the style, tone, and content for his many tales of public school life to come, most of which first ran as extremely popular serials in the *Boy's Own Paper*. His earliest and shorter contributions to the magazine appeared anonymously. Then, in 1880, came his first full-scale serial, *The Adventures of a Three-Guinea Watch*, followed by a further 10 serials, mainly about public schools, though some described life in the offices of the City of London. They included some of the most famous school stories ever written: *The Fifth Form at St. Dominic's, The Willoughby Captains, The Master of the Shell*, and *The Cockhouse at Fellsgarth*. Although, ironically, Reed himself attended a day-school, his fine descriptions of public boarding-school life are generally agreed to be extremely accurate for their period.

Although Thomas Hughes's *Tom Brown's School Days* (1857) and F.W. Farrar's *Eric; or, Little by Little* (1858) had virtually established the English public school story as a genre, it was undoubtedly Reed who shaped and developed this popular type of tale as readers later came to know and love it. Hughes and (especially) Farrar had dominated their stories with the dark side of Victorian boarding-school life (death, disgrace, bullying, sin, and tears), allied with perhaps over-generous lashings of religion and prayer. Reed's boys tended to be much more extrovert, healthy, mischievous, and authentic—more "boy-like," in fact. He created superbly the essentially self-contained world of school, its rules and its traditions. But, if he was apt to concentrate upon the brighter side of the scholastic life, he by no means ignored the darker. There were, for instance, the bullies, cheats, and scoundrels. There was a certain amount of religion—and conversions of would-be or actual sinners. George Hutchinson, editor of the *Boy's Own Paper* during Reed's time, once referred to his personal background of "simple, cheerful Puritanism," and this is the quality that often comes to the foreground in Reed's writings. And it's none the worse for that. The *Boy's Own Paper* was, after all, published by the highly respectable Religious Tract Society, and everything published in it was supposed to instil, in as entertaining and painless a way as possible, the right thoughts into its healthy, manly young Christian readers.

It was Reed who really created and established many of the situations and character-types later to be copied by numerous succeeding boys' school story writers. There were the fine, upstanding heroes, the weak, easily led boys, the "bounders" who broke out after lights-out to frequent gambling-dens or (dare it be said?) music-halls, the "swots," the sportsmen, the bullies, and the jokers. There were the inter-house rivalries, the school magazines, the sporting contests, the "town-versus-gown" feuds, the different types of masters (both sympathetic and unsympathetic), the "fagging" and the dormitory midnight feasts. It was generally a cosy world, later to become something of a formula and to be written about, in a variety of ways, by such successful story writers as Harold Avery, R.S. Warren-Bell, Richard Bird, Hylton Cleaver, Gunby Hadath, Edwy Searles Brooks, and (most prolific of them all) Charles Hamilton. In his writing, Reed was an excellent storyteller, wrote good, realistic dialogue, had a fine descriptive flair, and, most of all, made his characters come vividly to life.

—Brian Doyle

———

SEWELL, Anna. British. Born in Great Yarmouth, Norfolk, 30 March 1820; daughter of the poet Mary Sewell. Educated privately, and at a school in Stoke Newington, London. Semi-invalid from youth. Lived in Brighton, 1836–45, and later in Sussex, Gloucestershire, Bath, and Norwich. Teacher at the Working Man's Evening Institute, Wick, Gloucestershire, in early 1860's. *Died 25 April 1878.* Fiction: *Black Beauty, His Grooms and Companions*, 1877.

*   *   *

Black Beauty is the imaginary autobiography of a horse. We follow his career from its gentle beginning in the care of a farmer, up through society via the squirearchy to the nobility, and thence sadly downwards, finally pulling a cab for a sordid villain called Skinner.

It is an unashamedly didactic book. Anna Sewell wrote that "its special aim" was "to induce kindness, sympathy, and an understanding treatment of horses." This, she believed, would "bring the thoughts of men more in harmony with the purposes of God on this subject." The model owner, Squire Gordon, upbraids a neighbour who is beating a pony with the words "By giving way to such passions you injure your own character as much, nay more, than you injure your horse, and remember, we shall all be judged according to our works, whether they be towards man or towards beast."

The book's moral influence was enormous. It was adopted and distributed by The Royal Society for the Prevention of Cruelty to Animals, and by its American counterpart. Within a short time, the fashionable but cruel habit of pulling the horse's head up high with bearing-reins was abandoned and the treatment of cab horses came under far closer scrutiny. Ignorance about the care and needs of horses is condemned as bitterly as plain brutality.

The didacticism at some points goes further than the care of animals. Like many 18th- and 19th-century fictitious autobiographies, it surveys critically a variety of social strata and finds as much to abhor in the life of the aristocracy as in the baser world of the East End. One of the best chapters consists of a well-argued debate about the rights of cab drivers to have a day off on Sunday rather than drive the gentry off to church. And the supreme villainy of Skinner is that he not only abuses his own cab horses but that he rents his cabs out to other drivers at appallingly high rates. One of the drivers, known as Seedy Sam, has to pay Skinner eighteen shillings a week for the use of the vehicle and also maintains and feeds the two horses, before he can earn a penny for himself and his hungry family. Small wonder that his horses are broken with exhaustion and he himself suddenly dies of the strain. The phrase "economic exploitation" had not entered Sewell's vocabulary, but that is what she meant.

What makes *Black Beauty* unique among Victorian children's books is the breadth of its appeal after a century. A major national survey of British children's reading preferences published in 1977 recorded it as the clear number one favourite book for 10-year-olds. The explanation may be two-fold: it is superbly written, and horses are extremely appealing characters.

Sewell's simple narrative style matches the straightforwardness of her moral intentions—as monosyllabic and as undecorated as the English language will allow. Plain but not naive. The technique of allowing the horse to tell its own tale in the first person, though absurd if one pauses to reflect on it, seems the most natural—in fact the only possible—way in which to convey the range of experiences that Black Beauty goes through. The horse describes what happens and how he feels with the articulate understanding of a human being—because it is a human view of his suffering that Sewell is trying to promote. She is not concerned with the inner realities of a horse's mind—its natural instincts and stages of development. She merely explains evident emotional behaviour in response to various forms of human treatment. And a great strength of the book is the precise and detailed technical account of the processes of breaking in, harnessing, maintaining, and riding horses, the means by which the horse's nature is changed by human beings for better or for worse.

It is hard to imagine a horsey book of such emotional interest being written in a contemporary setting of Pony Club or racing stable. In Black Beauty's day, horses worked alongside humans to earn their keep, and their careers had close affinities with those of working men in terms of exploitation and reward. This close resemblance between the life of man and beast in society may partly account for the intense concern that the reader has for Black Beauty. And we react with deep emotion to the revelation of human callousness and ingratitude. The end of the story is pleasing but improbable: the hero rediscovered by chance and restored to his former country background—a just reward for long-suffering service to man.

—Aidan Warlow

SIDNEY, Margaret. Pseudonym for Harriet Mulford Lothrop, née Stone. American. Born in New Haven, Connecticut, 22 June 1844. Educated at Grove Hall School, New Haven. Married Daniel Lothrop in 1881. Founder, and national president, 1895–1901, and honorary president from 1901, National Society of Children of the American Revolution. *Died 2 August 1924.* Fiction: *Five Little Peppers* series, from 1880; *So As by Fire*, 1881; *Half Year at Bronckton*, 1881; *What the Seven Did*, 1882; *How They Went to Europe*, 1884; *A New Departure for Girls*, 1886; *Two Modern Little Princes and Other Stories*, 1886; *St. George and the Dragon*, 1888; *The Little Red Shop*, 1889; *Our Town*, 1889; *An Adirondack Cabin*, 1890; *Rob*, 1891; *The Kaleidoscope*, 1892; *Little Paul and the Frisbie School*, 1893; *The Old Town Pump*, 1895; *A Little Maid of Concord Town*, 1896; *The Gingham Bag*, 1896; *Dilly and the Captain*, 1897; *Two Little Friends in Norway*, 1906. Verse: *Ballad of the Lost Hare*, 1882.

*   *   *

Margaret Sidney, author of many domestic stories for children, is now remembered only for *Five Little Peppers and How They Grew*. This has been described as the poor child's version of *Little Women*, but it lacks Louisa May Alcott's feeling for nuances of character and its mood is one of sustained euphoria. The family is undoubtedly poor and fatherless, but they are never allowed to experience real distress, and from the opening pages the young reader is aware that good fortune will always prevail. "[Mrs Pepper] had met life too bravely to be beaten down....So with a stout heart and a cheery face, she had worked away day after day at making coats, and tailoring, and mending of all descriptions; and she had seen with pride that couldn't be concealed, her noisy, happy brood growing up around her, and filling her heart with comfort, and making the Little Brown House fairly ring with jollity and fun." It is the jollity and fun of being poor that is stressed, and when Polly is carried off to be the little light and guardian angel of a rich household she captivates the children with "accounts of Ben's skill, of Phronsie's cunning ways, of the boys who made fun for all, and above everything else, of the dear mother whom they all longed to help, and of all the sayings and doings in the Little Brown House."

The difference between this and contemporary English stories of poor households is very marked; there is a refreshing lack of didactic approach, and the Pepper family are allowed to attain material good fortune and prosperity in a way that no Victorian author in England, conscious of the need to discourage worldly ambition in the working class, would have dreamt of countenancing. They are even allowed tastes of luxury and high-living; the presents that their rich little benefactor showers upon them are not just blankets and coals, but hot-house flowers, singing birds, and wax dolls, and the whole Pepper family by the end of the book has been happily absorbed into his father's house—a fairytale conclusion deeply satisfying to children, who crave optimism in their books.

—Gillian Avery

———

STEVENSON, Robert Louis (Robert Lewis Balfour Stevenson). British. Born in Edinburgh, 13 November 1850. Educated at Edinburgh Academy; Edinburgh University, 1866–71; studied law in the office of Skene Edwards and Gordon, Edinburgh: called to the Scottish bar, 1875. Married Fanny Osbourne in 1880; two stepchildren, including the writer Lloyd Osbourne. Contributor, *Cornhill Magazine*, London, 1876–82. Tubercular: lived in California, 1879–80, Davos, Switzerland, 1880–81, 1881–82, Hyères, France, 1882–84, Bournemouth, England, 1884–87, and the South Seas from 1888, settling in Samoa, 1889. *Died 3 December 1894.* Fiction: *Treasure Island*, 1883; *Kidnapped*, 1886; *The Black Arrow*, 1888; *Catriona* (*David Balfour*), 1893. Verse: *Penny Whistles*, 1883; *A Child's Garden of Verses*, 1885.

*　　*　　*

Nearly all Robert Louis Stevenson's mature fiction, with the exception of *Dr. Jekyll*, takes the form of the historical romance. *Treasure Island, Kidnapped, Catriona, The Master of Ballantrae, St. Ives*, and *Weir of Hermiston* all fall into this category, with the action mainly taking place in 18th-century Scotland. The two exceptions are *The Black Arrow*, which is set in the Middle Ages, and *Treasure Island*, which has an English and exotic background.

The plots are nearly always concerned with long journeys, the search for treasure, or flight from capture, and they are usually fraught with great hazards—piracy, murder, intrigue—against which the hero, normally a young person of some resourcefulness, struggles to survive. But Stevenson does not merely use the ingredients of the historical romance for dramatic effects; he also tries to integrate them into a design by which they throw light on various aspects of the human situation as he saw it.

Many of the stories have not a single hero at the centre, but a pair. David and Alan in *Kidnapped*, Jim and Long John in *Treasure Island*, Dr. Jekyll and Mr. Hyde are the best known examples, and they seem to achieve a kind of complementarity as if each partner compensates for the defects of the other. Many of the books also deal with conflicts between clearly defined sides, such as pirates versus honest sailors, English versus Scots, or York versus Lancaster. But there is usually a good deal of changing sides between these antagonists. Long John Silver, for example, begins as an apparently honest sea-cook, reveals himself as leader of the mutiny, then deserts the pirates, and finishes up by even jumping Captain Smollett's ship. Dick Shelton in *The Black Arrow* switches his allegiance from Lancaster to York, while Alan Breck actually deserts King George at the Battle of Prestonpans. James in *The Master of Ballantrae* seems to have the best of both worlds, fighting for Bonnie Prince Charlie but spying for the other side. Finally, there is a good deal of intrigue and duplicity in the way Stevenson's characters behave, and physical disguises are frequently adopted. In *Catriona* the heroine pretends to be David's sister; in *The Black Arrow* Joanna passes herself off as a boy; and Dr. Jekyll's disguise is even more fundamental.

Stevenson's use of the dual-hero, the changing of sides, and the adoption of disguises is not only appropriate to the kinds of stories he wrote, and adds to their dramatic effectiveness, but reveals his passionate concern with the problems of identity and morality. From Stevenson's biographers we know of the ambiguities of his own life, his troubled relations with his parents, whom he adored, and with Scotland, which he worshipped from afar. It may be that his literary interests developed there, but, from the evidence of the fiction, it is clear that Stevenson saw man's nature as constantly shifting, and therefore all the more difficult to define and come to terms with. Dr. Jekyll, who can transform himself physically into a murderous villain, and Deacon Brodie, the clergyman who becomes a housebreaker at night-time, are simply extreme examples of such shifts. Long John Silver and Alan Breck are much more equivocal as their personalities and virtues fluctuate.

Long John, for example, is a pirate, thief, and murderer, and, as such, quite ruthless in pursuit of the gold. But he is also cheerful, brave, witty, and above all kind to Jim, who has no father. In this way Stevenson is constantly challenging our responses. Who is good or bad? he seems to be saying. In your final judgment, do you find Long John sympathetic or not? Are these sorts of questions even relevant? David Balfour operates as a kind of moral censor of Alan Breck's behaviour in *Kidnapped*, but in the end, though he may be "right" in his quarrel with Alan in "The Flight in the Heather," he comes to see that their love complicates the whole matter of knowing who is right or wrong.

Stevenson's influence on later writers is less specific, more pervasive. The historical romance, first established by Scott at the beginning of the 19th century, and then adapted for children by such authors as Marryat and Henty, went from strength to strength, until it reached its Victorian peak with Stevenson himself. Though the quality of many early 20th-century historical novels deteriorated, honourable exceptions can be found in the work of John Masefield and Geoffrey Trease, and from the 1950's the emergence of such writers as Leon Garfield, Cynthia Harnett, and Rosemary Sutcliff has sparked a renaissance of the form.

Though the influence of Stevenson on the specific narrative techniques of the adventure story is doubtful, the influence of his moral values issuing into literary attitudes is everywhere absolutely pervasive, even among those authors who would say they had never read him, and this for two reasons. First, he showed how it was possible to write books for children that were both thrilling in the most fundamental sense, and yet at the same time deeply serious. The loss of innocence—for example, by Jim Hawkins—is as prevalent in Stevenson's work as in that of Henry James, and the friendship of the two writers was, of course, very significant. And second, in his treatment of the complexities of human behaviour, in his refusal to compartmentalise characters as either "good" or "bad," his writing revealed a maturity which the best children's writers of today can only hope to emulate but not excel. It is significant that a novelist like Leon Garfield, whose stories of the 18th century differ so much from Stevenson's, should return time and again to the equivocal nature of human relationships, and the difficulties of distinguishing appearance from reality in exciting books such as *Smith* and *Jack Holborn*. Without the achievement of Stevenson so much of today's best writing would never have appeared.

—Dennis Butts

———

STOCKTON, Frank R. (Francis Richard Stockton). American. Born in Philadelphia, Pennsylvania, 5 April 1834. Educated at Zane Street School, 1840–48, and Central High School, 1848–52, both in Philadelphia. Married Marian Edwards Tuttle in 1860. Apprenticed as a wood-engraver, 1852, and worked as an engraver until 1870. Assistant editor, *Hearth and Home*, 1868–73 and *St. Nicholas* magazine, 1873–78, both New York. Regular contributor to *Scribner's Magazine*. *Died 20 April 1902.* Fiction: *Ting-a-Ling*, 1870; *What Might Have Been Expected*, 1874; *A Jolly Friendship*, 1880; *The Floating Prince and Other Fairy Tales*, 1881; *Ting-a-Ling Tales*, 1882; *The Story of Viteau*, 1884; *The Bee-Man of Orn and Other Fanciful Tales*, 1887; *The Queen's Museum*, 1887; *The Clocks of Rondaine and Other Stories*, 1892; *Fanciful Tales*, 1894; *Captain Chap (The Young Master of Hyson Hall)*, 1896; *Kate Bonnet*, 1902; *Stories of the Spanish Main*, 1913; *The Poor Count's Christmas*, 1927.

*   *   *

One of the most prolific contributors to children's literature in the last third of the 19th century, Frank R. Stockton is perhaps best remembered for such modern fairytales as "Ting-a-Ling," "The Griffin and the Minor Canon," "Old Pipes and the Dryad," and "The Queen's Museum." But taken as a whole, his work is richly varied. During his long association with the quality children's periodical *St. Nicholas*, first as assistant editor and later as a regular contributor, he wrote such realistic tales of adventure as *What Might Have Been Expected*, in which a brother and sister manage to provide economic security for their aged and feeble aunt. *Personally Conducted* (1889) is a collection of travel sketches originally written for *St. Nicholas*. Stockton also produced two juvenile histories: *New Jersey, From the Discovery of the Scheyichbi to Recent Times* (1896), an anecdotal account of some dramatic occasions in the state's history, and *The Buccaneers and Pirates of Our Coasts* (1898). *Tales Out of School* (1875), like its predecessor *Roundabout Rambles* (1872), consists of informative stories, mostly dealing with natural history. In *The Story of Viteau* Stockton attempted a tale of medieval life that reveals his general inability to realize in his fiction a vivid sense of place. The same difficulty can be seen in *What Might Have Been Expected*, set in the American south. Unlike many northerners, Stockton was familiar with life in the south (his wife was from South Carolina) and his Negro characters have a substantiality not often found in children's literature of the period; but he was less successful in rendering the south as a locale. His principal interest throughout his career as a writer was in delineating character and situation. As assistant editor of *St. Nicholas*, Stockton adopted two pseudonyms, Paul Fort and John Lewees, under which he wrote numerous informative articles and such slight moralistic sketches as "Tommy Hooper's Choice," which describes the mildly humorous difficulties encountered by the young Tommy when he tries to decide how to spend 25 cents—a magnificent sum to a child in the 1870's.

Stockton's best work for children, and the most interesting, consists of his fairytales, or "fanciful tales" as he liked to call them, beginning with the adventures of Ting-a-Ling, a diminutive elf, who first appeared in *The Riverside Magazine* in 1867. Even as a student, Stockton had wanted to write fairytales of a particular sort. Of his approach, he later commented: "I wanted the fanciful creatures who inhabited the world of fairy-land to act, as far as possible for them to do so, as if they were inhabitants of the real world. I did not dispense with monsters and enchanters, or talking beasts and birds, but I obliged these creatures to infuse into their extraordinary actions a certain leaven of common sense." Stockton's efforts to infuse "realism" into the traditional elements of the fairytale had both a formal and psychological dimension. He made no attempt to render the world of faery through archaic language, for example, but told his tales simply, directly, and matter-of-factly, without archness. He was neither patronizing nor condescending to his audience, and his tales are remarkably free of the overt moralizing that often crept into the period's literature for children. Throughout the tales runs a strongly individualistic psychology—a contempt for dependence, authoritarianism, and timid conformity; a celebration of independence, sturdy self-reliance, and personal courage—that fits well

with the ethic of individualism prominent in 19th-century American thought and evident in much post-Civil War literature for children. In his "fanciful tales," Stockton expressed a deft, sure touch, a gentle humor, a sweetness of temper that he rarely achieved in his other children's fiction.

The publication in the 1880's of "The Bee-Man of Orn," "The Griffin and the Minor Canon," and similar tales, as well as a series of yearly Christmas stories for *St. Nicholas*, marked the high point of Stockton's juvenile writing. By 1885, he was writing increasingly for an adult audience, who had acclaimed his short story "The Lady or the Tiger?" and in that year he undertook the writing of his first novel. Stockton produced little of note for children after the appearance in 1887 of "The Clocks of Rondaine" in *St. Nicholas*.

—R. Gordon Kelly

––––––––––

STRETTON, Hesba. Pseudonym for Sarah Smith. British. Born in Wellington, Shropshire, 27 July 1832. Educated at Old Hall School, near Shrewsbury, Shropshire. Worked in her father's post office, Wellington, until 1863; lived in Manchester, 1863–66, in London, 1867–92, and Ham Common, Surrey, from 1892. Co-founder, London Society for the Prevention of Cruelty to Children. *Died 8 October 1911.* Fiction: *Fern's Hollow*, 1864; *The Children of Cloverley*, 1865; *Enoch Roden's Training*, 1866; *The Fishers of Derby Haven (Peter Killip's King)*, 1866; *Pilgrim Street*, 1867; *Jessica's First Prayer*, 1867; *Little Meg's Children*, 1868; *Alone in London*, 1869; *Max Krömer*, 1871; *Bede's Charity*, 1872; *The King's Servants*, 1873; *Lost Gip*, 1873; *Cassy*, 1874; *No Work No Bread*, 1875; *Two Christmas Stories*, 1875; *Brought Home*, 1875; *Friends till Death and Other Stories*, 1875; *The Crew of the "Dolphin,"* 1876; *A Night and a Day*, 1876; *Left Alone, and Michel Lorio's Cross*, 1876; *Old Transome*, 1876; *The Storm of Life*, 1876; *The World of a Baby, and How Apple-Tree Court Was Won*, 1876; *A Man of His Word*, 1878; *Mrs. Burton's Best Bedroom and Other Stories*, 1878; *A Thorny Patch*, 1879; *In Prison and Out*, 1879; *Cobwebs and Cables*, 1881; *No Place Like Home*, 1881; *Under the Old Roof*, 1882; *Two Secrets, and A Man of His Word*, 1882; *The Lord's Purse-Bearers*, 1882; *Carola*, 1884; *Her Only Son*, 1887; *A Green Bay Tree*, 1887; *Only a Dog*, 1888; *A Miserable Christmas and a Happy New Year*, 1888; *Sam Franklin's Savings Bank*, 1888; *The Christmas Child*, 1888; *An Acrobat's Girlhood*, 1889; *Half Brothers*, 1892; *Jessica's Mother*, 1893; *The Highway of Sorrows at the Close of the Nineteenth Century*, with Stepniak, 1894; *Paul Rodents*, with Stepniak, 1894; *In the Hollow of His Hand*, 1897; *The Soul of Honour*, 1898.

*   *   *

Jessica's First Prayer is one of those books known by its title to thousands who have never seen a copy. This simply told story of a destitute child, daughter of a gin-sodden actress, who hears the Christmas message and by her simple faith brings a new light into the lives of her elders was to initiate a new genre of evangelical writing, the street arab story, and to remain perhaps the best of them. It is not, however, the very first example. Mary Howitt, in *The Story of Little Cristal* (1863), probably inspired by Hans Andersen's *The Little Match Girl*, had described how a street waif's last hours had been comforted by the memory of a stained glass window depicting Christ blessing the children.

Jessica's First Prayer, originally published in *Sunday at Home* in 1866, was the first of Hesba Stretton's works to attract attention, and its success was phenomenal, not only in England but all over the world. Written no doubt as "family" reading rather than directly for children, it and its legion of imitations soon became adopted as standard Sunday reading for the young, replacing the Calvinistic tracts of Mrs. Sherwood and Mrs. Cameron that the early Victorians had been reared on, and the compilations of holy deaths of young people that had gone before these. The idea of the child evangelist unconsciously melting the cold and stubborn heart of an adult was to have a compelling effect on young readers, and for once children of their own age were the centre of the amazed attention of their elders. The result was a deluge of mawkish novelettes which did not subside until well on in the next century. But *Jessica's First Prayer* cannot be blamed for this. It is finely observed, economically told, and the child Jessica's awakening faith—very difficult to convey, as Stretton's imitators were to find—is moving and convincing.

Stretton followed it up with some 50 stories sometimes on the theme of the suffering poor, sometimes on the evil brought about by love of money. Unlike Charlotte Yonge and others in the squarson tradition, who wrote with rural church schools in mind, she could not agree that the existing social order was right. She had first-hand knowledge of slum conditions in London and Manchester; she knew all about grasping landlords, the heavy hand of officialdom, how unjust justice could be. In *In Prison and Out* she spoke with warm indignation of the deplorable difference in society's attitude towards a slum boy who had knocked down a man for insulting his mother, and a public schoolboy such as Tom Brown who did the same sort of thing. One would be sent to prison, the other commended. She was frequently to take the side of the employee against the employer, as in *Fern's Hollow*, and always to attack the folly of laying up treasures on earth.

Her accounts of the poor and destitute were always moving: the bare-footed crossing sweepers shivering in their rags, the feverish child gasping for fresh air in the mid-summer furnace of a stifling London courtyard, the street arab's search for a lost baby sister whom nobody cared about but himself, the shame and degradation of having at last to take refuge in the "House," the terror of being buried as a pauper. But they were to be repeated so often that they lost their first impact: "It is possible to have too many of them," as Charlotte Yonge wrote. It was in any case a time when journalists and philanthropists were working hard to open the public's eyes to the atrocious conditions in which the poor lived, and there was much literature on this theme.

Nevertheless, at her best, in books such as *Alone in London, Little Meg's Children, Lost Gip, Pilgrim Street* (all written in the earlier part of her career), she rose far above the level of the ordinary Sunday School reward book. Her successors could harrow the reader with their accounts of the mirk and misery and vice of the slums, but Hesba Stretton could also enter into the small pleasures of the poor: a feast of bloaters, a mug of hot coffee, the sight of a garden, a baby to love.

—Gillian Avery

TWAIN, Mark. Pseudonym for Samuel Langhorne Clemens. American. Born in Florida, Missouri, 30 November 1835; moved to Hannibal, Missouri, 1839. Married Olivia Langdon in 1870 (died 1904); one son and three daughters. Printer's apprentice and typesetter for Hannibal newspapers, 1847–50; helped brother with Hannibal *Journal*, 1850–52; typesetter and printer in St. Louis, New York, Philadelphia, for Keokuk *Saturday Post*, Iowa, 1853–56, and in Cincinnati, 1857; apprentice river pilot, on the Mississippi, 1857–58; licensed as pilot, 1859–60; went to Nevada as secretary to his brother, then on the staff of the Governor, and also worked as goldminer, 1861; staff member, Virginia City *Territorial Enterprise*, Nevada,

1862–64 (first used pseudonym Mark Twain, 1863); reporter, San Francisco *Morning Call*, 1864; correspondent, Sacramento *Union*, 1866, and San Francisco *Alta California*, 1866–69: visited Sandwich (i.e., Hawaiian) Islands, 1866, and France, Italy, and Palestine, 1867; lecturer from 1867; editor, *Express*, Buffalo, New York, 1869–71; moved to Hartford, Connecticut and became associated with Charles L. Webster Publishing Company, 1884; invested in unsuccessful Paige typesetter and went bankrupt, 1894 (last debts paid, 1898); lived mainly in Europe, 1896–1900, New York, 1900–07, and Redding, Connecticut, 1907–10. M.A.: Yale University, New Haven, Connecticut, 1888; Litt.D.: Yale University, 1901; Oxford University, 1907; LL.D.: University of Missouri, Columbia, 1902. Member, American Academy, 1904. *Died 21 April 1910*. Fiction: *The Adventures of Tom Sawyer*, 1876; *The Prince and the Pauper*, 1881; *The Adventures of Huckleberry Finn*, 1884; *Tom Sawyer Abroad*, 1894; *Tom Sawyer Abroad; Tom Sawyer, Detective; and Other Stories*, 1896; *A Boy's Adventure*, 1928.

*　*　*

Ernest Hemingway wrote, in *Green Hills of Africa*, "All modern American literature comes from one book by Mark Twain called *Huckleberry Finn*…it's the best book we've had. All American writing comes from that. There was nothing before. There has been nothing as good since."

As criticism Hemingway's statement is admittedly overstated. Samuel Clemens, or Mark Twain, has always been an enigma for critics, many of whom have had great difficulty in analyzing his works, and others in psychoanalyzing him. Hemingway, however, was not speaking as a critic, but rather as a reader, as a devotee, as a writer who recognized his debt to one who came before him. In that role he is an apt and accurate spokesman for all of us who rejoice in listening to the voice of Mark Twain. Just as Lincoln remains the folk symbol of the American spirit, for many Twain remains the folk symbol of the American writer.

It is significant that Hemingway specifically referred to *The Adventures of Huckleberry Finn*, for it is in that work, along with *The Adventures of Tom Sawyer* and *Life on the Mississippi*, that Twain's narrative genius is self-evident. Today *Tom Sawyer* is usually categorized as a book for children, while *Huck Finn* is considered adult fiction. Nevertheless, in any discussion of Twain's influence on American authors of children's books, both must be considered.

Oddly enough, when Twain wrote *Tom Sawyer* he did not have a child audience in mind. It wasn't until his friend William Dean Howells suggested that it was a story most appropriate for children that Twain "cleaned up" the manuscript and added a preface in which he said: "Although my book is intended mainly for the entertainment of boys and girls, I hope it will not be shunned by men and women on that account, for part of my plan has been to try to pleasantly remind adults of what they once were themselves, and of how they felt and thought and talked, and what queer enterprises they sometimes engaged in." That he did not consciously write it for children is perhaps the book's strongest attribute, though occasionally Twain as narrator speaks directly to the adult readers he originally had in mind. This is overwhelmingly outweighed by the absence of any condescension or moralizing. In fact at the time of its publication (1876) it came under attack as a children's book. The *New York Times* book review concluded: "In the books to be placed into children's hands for purposes of recreation, we have a preference for those of a milder type than *Tom Sawyer*."

Tom Sawyer is much more than a grown man's reminiscences about the idyllic joys and pains of childhood. Twain stands high on the list of eminent writers like Stevenson, Dickens, and Saroyan who successfully depicted how children "felt and thought and talked." Though they did not write specifically for children, they demonstrated for those who would how necessary it is to retain the heart of a child if your work is to have the ring of truth. Twain above all else sets out to entertain. One should not overlook the word "Adventures" in the titles of his "boy" books. He takes the blood and thunder stuff of the old-fashioned dime novels and the serial boy romances and makes it literature.

In *Huck Finn*, intended as a sequel to *Tom Sawyer*, Twain gets into the skin of Huck and tells the story through him, and by so doing he happens upon the narrative mode that is explicitly suited for his special talents. Huck, who could not possibly *write* a story, *tells* us the story. And that is how Twain himself would have it; as he says in his *Autobiography*: "With the pen in one's hand, narrative is a difficult art; narrative should flow as flows the brook down through the hills and leafy woodlands." This also was one of the reasons for Hemingway's acclaim, for he too, like many storytellers, was at heart a raconteur and a minstrel rather than a scribbler.

But there was even a more important reason. Hemingway recognized the straightforward honesty in *Huck Finn*. Twain possessed, as H.L. Mencken put it, "a truly amazing instinct for the truth." Today many writers of books for children and young adults have turned to first-person narrative, with only a meager few of them handling it successfully. They would do well to look closely at *Huckleberry Finn*, for there they will find Mark Twain's greatest legacy to them—his integrity. He doesn't use the first-person point of view as a literary device for simulating a peer relationship with young readers; but rather he turns over the complete narrative to Huck, allowing him to tell the story as only he can do it. Huck's understated and innocent "telling" is the primary reason that this story of a boy's adventure is, at the same time, a devastating denunciation of the society in which the tale takes place.

A final word of caution. Too often *Huck Finn* appears on children's reading book lists as a companion piece to *Tom Sawyer*, when in fact it is a work best suited for a more mature audience. Indeed, anyone who recommends *The Adventures of Huckleberry Finn* to a young reader must first consider whether that reader is capable or not of handling the intricacies of its ironic thrust.

—James E. Higgins

WALTON, Mrs. O.F. British. Born Amy Catherine Deck in 1850. Married Reverend Octavius Frank Walton in 1875 (died 1933). Lived in Cally, Kirkcudbright, 1876–83, York, 1883–93, Wolverhampton, 1893–1906, and Leigh, Kent (with a short period in Shamley Green, Surrey, after World War I), 1906–39. *Died in July 1939.* Fiction: *My Little Corner, and Wandering May,* 1872; *Little Dot,* 1873; *My Mates and I,* 1873; *Home, Sweet Home (Christie's Old Organ),* 1874; *A Peep Behind the Scenes,* 1877; *Angel's Christmas,* 1877; *Saved at Sea,* 1879; *Was I Right?,* 1879; *Little Faith,* 1880; *Olive's Story,* 1881; *Nobody Loves Me,* 1883; *Shadows,* 1884; *Taken or Left,* 1885; *Launch the Life-Boat,* 1886; *Poppy's Presents,* 1886; *The Mysterious House,* 1890; *Nemo (The Wonderful Door),* 1893; *Christie, The King's Servant,* 1896; *Whiter Than Snow, and Little Dot,* 1896; *Audrey,* 1897; *The Lost Clue,* 1907; *Strange Diana,* 1919.

* * *

Mrs. O.F. Walton was one of the best-known and longest-remembered of the ladies who wrote little books for Victorian Sunday reading. Countless children in chapel or church-going families spent Sunday afternoons over her touching and improving tales. Her work is distinguished from the mass of such stories by characteristics which appealed to the pious adults who bought it, but also by some

features which we might pick out today to account for its undoubted attraction for the children themselves.

It was the centrality of the Christian message in all her writing that made her a favourite with the religious publishers. The sermons are lengthy and repeated; many of her stories dwell upon the deaths of small children, old folk, or suffering mothers in the most lachrymose way. In her writing the minatory insistence of early Evangelical writers upon infant death lived on, in a sentimentalised but no less extreme form. *Christie's Old Organ,* for example, tells of a homeless orphan and an old organ-grinder who find salvation together, by means of a chance-heard mission sermon (which readers are given in full, twice over). The old man dies, gloriously and at length, and the boy becomes a missionary himself. The book plucks remorselessly at the heartstrings, especially by the device of the organ, which plays "Home, Sweet Home."

The modern sense of the unhealthiness of such manipulation of the child's emotions was shared by many adults of her own time, but Walton's books had a hold on child readers for quite a different reason. The narrative patterns she used were often compelling versions of the basic stuff of storytelling, the romance. They offered young readers powerful imaginative satisfactions quite apart from any response to their preaching. This is clearly seen in her most popular story, *A Peep Behind the Scenes.* The beautiful child Rosalie shines like a jewel in the evil (but fascinating) setting of her father's fairground theatre. Her mother's romantic fancies have brought her to these depths, and she now lies dying. Rosalie's beauty and noble nature preserve her, bringing her the love of all she meets, and she is helped in her escape from the depths by dwarves and other fairground folk, who are like the miraculous helpers in a fairy-tale. She returns their kindnesses by converting them, and leaves a trail of blessed lives, and of course deaths, behind her, as she makes her journey through the underworld back to her rightful place in her aunt's idyllic home. It makes little essential difference to the effect of the romance that the talisman that brings aid to the heroine throughout is a picture of the Good Shepherd. The fairground setting and the perils of her journey are only made more exciting by the commentary telling the reader how wicked such things are, and converting an absorbing fantasy into a "Sunday" book.

—J.S. Bratton

WARNER, Susan (Bogert). Also wrote as Elizabeth Wetherell. American. Born in New York City, 11 July 1819. Educated privately. *Died 17 March 1885.* Fiction: *The Wide, Wide World* (as Elizabeth Wetherell), 1851; *Queechy* (as Elizabeth Wetherell), 1852; *The Glen-Luna Family,* with Anna Bartlett Warner, 1852; *Carl Krinken: His Christmas Stocking (The Christmas Stocking),* with Anna Bartlett Warner, 1853; *Mr. Rutherford's Children,* 1853; *Sybil and Chrissa,* with Anna Bartlett Warner, 1854; *Casper,* with Anna Bartlett Warner, 1855; *The Birthday Visit to Holly Farm,* with Anna Bartlett Warner, 1860; *The Little Nurse of Cape Cod,* 1863; *The Carpenter's Daughter,* with Anna Bartlett Warner, 1864; *Melbourne House,* 1864; *Martha and Her Kind Friend Rachel,* with Anna Bartlett Warner, 1864; *The Prince in Disguise,* with Anna Bartlett Warner, 1864; *The Widow and Her Daughter,* with Anna Bartlett Warner, 1864; *The Rose in the Desert,* with Anna Bartlett Warner, 1864; *Martha's Hymn,* with Anna Bartlett Warner, 1865; *Walks from Eden,* 1866; *What She Could,* 1871; *Opportunities,* 1871; *The House in Town,* 1871; *Edith and Mary,* with Anna Bartlett Warner, 1871; *Hard Maple,* with Anna Bartlett Warner, 1871; *Trading,* 1872; *The Little Camp on Eagle Hill,* 1873; *Sceptres and Crowns,* 1874; *Willow Brook,* 1874; *The Flag of Truce,* 1875; *The Rapids of Niagara,* 1875;

Little Nettie; or, Home Sunshine, with Anna Bartlett Warner, 1878; *Stephen, M.D.*, 1883.

*   *   *

Susan Warner's brand of sentimental fiction exerted a powerful influence on later 19th-century American writers for girls. 1980's feminist attempts to establish her as a pioneer of women's writing, however, ignore her antecedents. Her accounts of female orphans buffeted by the world and rising above adversity with virtue intact are in a tradition much favoured from the mid-18th century onwards. There are Richardson's *Pamela*, of course; *Fatherless Fanny* by an unidentified writer of 1811 and popular through much of the last century; *Jane Eyre*, and, a work surprisingly little remembered by historians of women's fiction, *Redwood* (1824) by the Massachusetts author Catharine Maria Sedgwick. This has a heroine of the sort that Warner was to make so familiar—meek, grave, and a potent force for good, but also blessed with graceful manners as well as many accomplishments and housewifely virtues.

Much of the self-indulgent emotion in Warner's books arose out of a dreamy urge to escape from her own cramped background. The daughter of an improvident and litigious father, whose reckless investments and expensive disputes with his neighbours reduced the family to abject poverty, she wrote from the direst financial need. After Mr. Warner's New York business losses the family went to live on Constitution Island in the Hudson River, opposite West Point; here she and her sister Anna at times could not even find clothes fit to go to church. Her first and most famous book, *The Wide, Wide World*, was written, her sister said in her biography, "on her knees," which can be interpreted as much as a despairing plea for success as a prayer for divine guidance. Though the manuscript was returned by the first publishers to whom she submitted it (the Harpers reader indeed scribbled "Fudge" on one of the pages), Putnam took it on, and it was an instant success. In spite of the popularity of her earlier works she was never, however, to achieve the material prosperity for which she yearned.

The Wide, Wide World is the story of Ellen Montgomery, the child of an invalid mother who soon dies, and an uncaring, selfish father who also dies, unlamented. She is sent to live with her granite-hewn spinster aunt Fortune in upstate New York, and with the help of a neighbouring female guardian angel learns to accept adversity in a meek and Christian spirit. From her aunt she learns to be a competent little housekeeper. The guardian angel has a brother, "Mr. John" who by virtue of his role as an adoptive brother to Ellen is allowed to kiss and caress her, at the same time giving her much moral teaching. In the course of some 220,000 words Warner only succeeded in covering four years of Ellen's life, from 10 to 14, and thus never succeeded (much to her chagrin, one senses) in bringing her to a nubile age. (She was always to have this difficulty in manipulating plot and characters.) The saga ends abruptly with Ellen taken over by her aristocratic Scottish relations, and the implication that Mr. John will come back in a few years to claim her as his bride. The storyline is minimal; the book's strength lies in the descriptions of Hudson River scenery and of rural life. There is also much about food, which endeared the book to the more austerely raised occupants of English schoolrooms.

Awkward and ungainly herself as an adolescent, "rude when in fact I do not mean to be," "her head in a rosy dream of fiction most of the time," self-willed, "a bit of a sybarite by nature," Warner loved in adult life to write about girls who fascinate the most worldly by their innate good breeding and poise. Ellen Montgomery's critical Scottish relations describe her as "the best-bred child in the world"; in her second book, *Queechy* (the name of the village where the book is set), the aristocratic Englishman who first meets Elfleda as a child and later crosses the Atlantic to claim her as his bride, describes her appearance as of "the highest—that degree of mould and finish

which belongs only to the highest material." Little Daisy Randolph in *Melbourne House*, another popular work, is altogether of finer grain than her horrible family. Pale, grave, meek, sweet-faced and artless, she is admired and adored by everyone except her own kin. In all these works there are quantities of tears (Warner was herself a tempestuous weeper) and also much fondling and kissing by male protectors who are assiduous and caring, tender but strict—the sort of presence that Warner must have longed for in a life where masculine company was limited to her father and the West Point cadets who used to be invited for bible-reading and gingerbread. The erotic element is so marked in most of her work that the modern reader is amazed at her innocent unawareness that she was giving herself away. Nor had she apparently any idea that she was writing anything but the most chaste religious tales. Thousands of Sunday schools also took this view and her works were much in favour as prizes and Sunday reading, though Charlotte Yonge, the doyenne of children's books, disapproved and said they would lead little girls to see a lover in anybody who was kind to them. However, English girls, accustomed to much more ascetic fare from their own writers, loved them dearly. Warner was to influence writers like Martha Finley; the famous incident in *Elsie Dinsmore* where Elsie's brutal father tries to force her to play secular music on a Sunday is in fact based on an even more violent scene in *Melbourne House*. The religious teaching of her books is nebulous and vaguely attached to the Bible, which the child heroines invariably are confident of interpreting correctly without any guidance, and the abiding impression is of an author totally without humour, who dearly loved her comforts, and longed for wealth and male admiration.

—Gillian Avery

YONGE, Charlotte (Mary). British. Born in Otterbourne, Hampshire, 13 August 1823. Editor, 1851–90, and assistant editor, 1891–95, the *Monthly Packet*, London; editor, the *Monthly Paper of Sunday Teaching*, 1860–75, and *Mothers in Council*, 1890–1900, both London. *Died 24 March 1901.* Fiction: *Le Château de Melville*, 1838; *Abbey Church*, 1844; *Scenes and Characters (Beechcroft)*, 1847; *Henrietta's Wish*, 1850; *Kenneth*, 1850; *Langley School*, 1850; *The Two Guardians*, 1852; *The Heir of Redclyffe*, 1853; *The Herb of the Field*, 1853; *The Castle Builders*, 1854; *Heartsease*, 1854; *The Little Duke (Richard the Fearless)*, 1854; *The History of Sir Thomas Thumb*, 1855; *The Lances of Lynwood*, 1855; *The Railroad Children*, 1855; *Ben Sylvester's Word*, 1856; *The Daisy Chain*, 1856; *Harriet and Her Sister*, 1856; *Leonard the Lion-Heart*, 1856; *Dynevor Terrace*, 1857; *The Christmas Mummers*, 1858; *Friarswood Post Office*, 1860; *Hopes and Fears*, 1860; *The Mice at Play*, 1860; *The Strayed Falcon*, 1860; *The Pigeon Pie*, 1860; *The Stokesley Secret*, 1861; *The Young Stepmother*, 1861; *Countess Kate*, 1862; *Sea Spleenwort and Other Stories*, 1862; *Last Heartsease Leaves*, 1862(?); *The Trial*, 1864; *The Wars of Wapsburgh*, 1864; *The Clever Woman of the Family*, 1865; *The Dove in the Eagle's Nest*, 1866; *The Prince and the Page*, 1866; *The Danvers Papers*, 1867; *The Six Cushions*, 1867; *The Chaplet of Pearls*, 1868; *Kaffir Land*, 1868; *The Caged Lion*, 1870; *Little Lucy's Wonderful Globe*, 1871; *P's and Q's*, 1872; *The Pillars of the House*, 1873; *Lady Hester*, 1874; *My Young Alcides*, 1875; *The Three Brides*, 1876; *The Disturbing Element*, 1878; *Burnt Out*, 1879; *Magnus Bonum*, 1879; *Bye-Words*, 1880; *Love and Life*, 1880; *Mary and Norah; Nelly and Margaret*, 1880(?); *Cheap Jack*, 1881; *Frank's Debt*, 1881; *Lads and Lasses of Langley*, 1881; *Wolf*, 1881; *Given to Hospitality*, 1882; *Langley Little Ones*, 1882; *Pickle and His Page Boy*, 1882; *Sowing and Sewing*, 1882; *Unknown to History*, 1882; *Stray Pearls*, 1883;

Langley Adventures, 1884; *The Armourer's 'prentices*, 1884; *Nuttie's Father*, 1885; *The Two Sides of the Shield*, 1885; *Astray*, with others, 1886; *Chantry House*, 1886; *The Little Rick-Burners*, 1886; *A Modern Telemachus*, 1886; *Under the Storm*, 1887; *Beechcroft at Rockstone*, 1888; *Nurse's Memories*, 1888; *Our New Mistress*, 1888; *The Cunning Woman's Grandson*, 1889; *A Reputed Changeling*, 1889; *The Slaves of Sabinus*, 1890; *More Bywords*, 1890; *The Constable's Tower*, 1891; *Two Penniless Princesses*, 1891; *The Cross Roads*, 1892; *That Stick*, 1892; *Grisly Grisell*, 1893; *Strolling Players*, 1893; *The Treasures in the Marshes*, 1893; *The Cook and the Captive*, 1894; *The Rubies of St. Lô*, 1894; *The Carbonels*, 1895; *The Long Vacation*, 1895; *The Release*, 1896; *The Wardship of Steepcombe*, 1896; *The Pilgrimage of Ben Beriah*, 1897; *Founded on Paper*, 1897; *The Patriots of Palestine*, 1898; *The Herd Boy and His Hermit*, 1899; *The Making of a Missionary*, 1900; *Modern Broods*, 1900. Plays: *The Apple of Discord*, 1864; *Historical Dramas*, 1864. Verse: *Verses on the Gospel*, 1880.

*   *   *

Charlotte Yonge's was the voice of the early Victorian daughter of the squirearchy, earnest in her fervour to do her duty in that state of life to which God had called her, eager to help others to do the same. Her first book was published in 1838, her last in 1901. Between those dates she wrote over 150 works—domestic stories for cottage and drawing room, historical tales, books of instruction both religious and secular, lengthy sagas of family life. But her outlook scarcely changed at all in over 60 years of authorship.

She never wrote for purely literary ends, but always directly or indirectly for the promotion of Christian truth, and the truth as it had been taught to her by John Keble when he prepared her for confirmation. Her duty as she had been taught by her parents remained her touchstone of excellence; she desired no other guide. To the early and mid-Victorian girl she herself was a guide, providing them with chronicles of large and life-like upper-class families whose characters are so real that a devoted coterie still discusses and analyses them today. Nor was it only the school-room who read her; in the 1850's *The Heir of Redclyffe* was received with enthusiasm by bishops and statesmen, undergraduates and Guards officers; it was one of the most popular Tractarian novels of its day.

The fascination of works such as *The Daisy Chain* and *The Pillars of the House* and their successors lies in the way they are interwoven, that one can walk in them as in Barsetshire, viewing characters from all aspects, in youth and middle life; as central figures in one book, as peripheral ones in another. The creation of personalities, in whom she believed as well as the reader, was her particular gift; plots were a secondary matter and she had no great skill in manipulating them.

In her rather solitary childhood, cut off from all contemporaries except during rare and ecstatic visits to cousins, she had paced the gravel walks of her father's small Hampshire estate, inventing large families.

Within the framework of her family sagas is contained Yonge's teaching on the girl and young woman's role in life. It was, in fact, her own role of ardent submission to those in authority, be it clergyman, teacher, or parent. On the duty of those who achieved the status of authority she had nothing to say. "For her the newest, *youngest* thing was to do home and family duties more perfectly. What greater happiness can be given to youth?" wrote Christabel Coleridge in her memoir of 1903, and two generations of girls loved the chronicles of the Mays and the Underwoods, the Mohuns and the Merrifields. Their lofty ideals, their intellectual pursuits and conversation, their happy family relationship presented a way of life that they themselves yearned to imitate.

To a privileged few who named themselves her "goslings," she was Mother Goose and guided their strivings to educate and improve themselves. Some of these, like Christabel Coleridge, Florence Wilford, Frances Peard, subsequently themselves wrote for children. But, although she had thousands of admirers all over the world, as the century went on her message had increasingly little appeal to a generation of girls very different from her own, with whom she found it difficult to sympathise. Her implacable hostility to the idea of girls being educated outside the home circle—at the new High Schools and at universities, for instance—did at last modify a little, and a little uneasily in her last novels she allowed the daughters of some of her original characters to enter Oxford or Cambridge. But she made it clear that she felt rather wary of such girls.

Her outlook was narrow, parochial even, since during the whole of her long life she barely moved beyond the Hampshire village where she had been born. Her literary work came second in her mind to her parish duties there, her attendance at Otterbourne church and her devotion to its school whose girls she had known and lovingly taught from her own childhood. For them she wrote many tales of cottage life as it should be lived, with decency, order, and deference towards the "great house," and above all stressing their duty to the church into which they had been baptized. Even in these didactic stories her gift for characterisation, for sketching a social background, shines out and makes them charming evocations of a vanished way of life.

—Gillian Avery

FOREIGN-LANGUAGE
WRITERS

Throughout this century, children's books of high quality translated from other languages have been published in the English-speaking countries, although not, it is generally acknowledged, to such an extent as the other way around: the children's literature of other world languages includes a far greater proportion of translations. The importance of making good foreign books available was stressed by Jella Lepman, founder of the Munich International Youth Library. Her vision of a world in which children of different countries grow up knowing more of each other through what they read is expressed in the title of her own *A Bridge of Children's Books* (1969). Mildred L. Batchelder in the United States formulated the same ideal in saying that "Interchange of children's books between countries, through translation, influences communication between the people of those countries."

As the 20th century draws towards its close, it becomes possible to see which foreign children's books published in English-language versions are likely to remain established classics in the same way as such 19th-century works as *Heidi, Pinocchio,* or *The Swiss Family Robinson,* which have been assimilated into a common international heritage. It is perhaps fitting that one of the major translated works of this century, Selma Lagerlöf's *The Wonderful Adventures of Nils,* stands with one foot, as it were, in the previous century. Its leisurely pace and strong moral tone look back to the 19th century in the tale of little Nils Holgersson, transformed to elf size because of his own selfish naughtiness, who learns from experience as he travels with wild geese, while the book's deep feeling for nature also looks forward to later works by 20th-century writers.

Some of the best-remembered titles published in the years between World Wars I and II were animal stories. There is great understanding of the natural world in the books of Felix Salten (the pseudonym of Sigmund Salzmann), whose delicacy of touch inevitably became rather blurred in the famous Walt Disney film of *Bambi.* The fine Père Castor series of animal picture books from France were favourites over a long period. Other books which first appeared in English at this time have attained the status of modern classics. Notable among them are Erich Kästner's *Emil and the Detectives,* prototype of the urban adventure story in which a gang of children outwit villainous adults (and still much livelier and more realistic than many of its followers), and Jean de Brunhoff's *The Story of Babar.* The stories of Babar the elephant, his family and companions were continued by de Brunhoff's son Laurent after their original creator's death.

It is in publishing of the latter part of this century, however, that one finds real expansion of the market for translated books. Lepman's ideal of complete internationalism in children's literature cannot quite be said to have been achieved. Not surprisingly, publishers find it easier to make a commercial success of books from European countries with cultural similarities. However, the 1980's show some welcome trends towards further internationalism: a novel by the Brazilian Lygia Bojunga-Nunes, winner of the 1982 Hans Christian Andersen award for outstanding achievement in children's literature (and the first Third World writer to be honoured in this way), is to be published in both the United Kingdom and the U.S.A. under the title *The Companions.* Another novel, *A Handful of Stars,* is by a Syrian-born writer, Rafik Schami, who emigrated to Germany and writes in German, but on subjects from his own childhood background.

Obviously the picture-book field is one of the easiest in which to achieve internationalism, the pictures mattering as much as, or more than, the words. Distinguished artists such as Katrin Brandt, Ruth Hürlimann, Svend Otto S., and Lisbeth Zwerger will often illustrate a traditional text from Grimm, or some other familiar source. Lisbeth Zwerger, in illustrating some of the tales of E.T.A. Hoffmann (*The Nutcracker, The Strange Child*) and of Clemens Brentano (*The Legend of Rosepetal*), offers a very accessible introduction to the classics of European Romanticism, and the richly detailed pictures of the Russian artist Gennady Spirin, in *The Enchanter's Spell,* do the same for a selection of five authors including Cervantes. Japanese picture-book artists turned towards the western market quite early; some, such as Mitsumasa Anno, and Chihiro Iwasaki in the *Momoko* books, have contributed an Eastern delicacy of line and colour, although in the case of the latter's illustrations of such western tales as *Swan Lake* and *The Little Mermaid* the style is extremely westernized.

Mitsumasa Anno is the "deviser" of an extremely international picture book, *All in a Day,* with illustrations by different artists depicting a day in the lives of children all over the world. Some picture books may be planned to have international appeal, as in the anti-factory-farming theme of Jörg Müller and Jörg Steiner's *Rabbit Island,* or they may appeal through local colour, as in Mario Soldati's *The Octopus and the Pirates,* whose illustrations by Alberto Longoni give an attractive picture of north Italian life. The bucolic humour of Helme Heine's picture books strikes a particularly German note, while the *Ernest and Celestine* books by Gabrielle Vincent, from Belgium, appeal to the English liking for stories of charmingly drawn animals in an anthropomorphized domestic setting. The German author/illustrator Janosch uses his cheerful little animal characters in the manner of the fable, commenting with offbeat humour on human failings, especially in the series of stories about Little Bear and Little Tiger (*The Trip to Panama,* etc.). The Dutch artist Dick Bruna's brightly illustrated little books for very young children have long been popular.

Moving to books for an older age group, one finds a number of titles which resemble their English-language counterparts in the fields of fantasy, the historical novel, or the modern adventure story—and yet which are often slightly and interestingly different. The Hans Andersen award winner Astrid Lindgren, in *Pippi Longstocking,* first published shortly after World War II, wrote an undisputed modern classic: nine-year-old Pippi, immensely strong and kind-hearted, who breaks all the rules of "good behaviour," appeals to the anarchic streak in her readers while coming down on the side of genuine goodness. In a similar iconoclastic vein Lindgren wrote *Emil in the Soup Tureen* and *Karlson on the Roof,* and branched out into other fields as well. *The Brothers Lionheart* is a fantasy raising moral questions, while the prize-winning *Ronia, The Robber's Daughter* treats themes of friendship, conflict, and death with great depth beneath its entertaining surface.

Another fine Swedish fantasy is *The Glassblower's Children* by Maria Gripe, who has also written stories of everyday life about children who do not quite fit into an everyday background, such as the attractive heroine of *Pappa Pellerin's Daughter.* Fantasy in Holland is well represented by Paul Biegel, with his *The King of the Copper Mountains* and other works. Biegel strikes a vein of sometimes humorous magic, employing traditional themes from European folklore. So does the German writer Otfried Preussler, in his comic fantasies about the exploits of traditional figures (*The Little Witch, The Little Ghost*), and his powerful tales for older readers (*The Adventures of Strong Vanya, The Satanic Mill*). James Krüss, also of Germany, has written stories such as *My Great-Grandfather and I,* with elements of the poetic and the marvellous, while the comic, the poetic, and the magical are all intertwined in the deservedly popular *Moomintroll* series by Tove Jansson of Finland. For younger readers, Alf Prøysen of Norway created a popular character of comic fantasy in *Little Old Mrs. Pepperpot,* and Angela Sommer-Bodenburg's *Little Vampire* stories, like Preussler's, draw comedy from ancient traditional themes. Reiner Zimnik's *The Crane* is a book hard to classify under any heading: a fine fable which is bleak, haunting, and humorous by turns. Comic verse from Russia, Kornei Chukovsky's *Dr. Concocter*, comes to English readers in a rollicking translation by Richard N. Coe. Christoph Hein's *Jamie and His Friends*, from East Germany, the tale of a little boy's adventures with his friends (toys come to life) exists in a magic childhood world previously thought of as peculiarly English, the world of A.A. Milne and Kenneth Grahame.

Runer Jonsson's *Viki Viking*, from Denmark, shows the historical Viking in a comic light, but serious historical novels of high quality have also been published in English translation: among them are works by Hans Baumann (*Sons of the Steppe, Dimitri and the False Tsars*), Barbara Bartos-Höppner (*Storm over the Caucasus, The Conquering Ships*), and Willi Fährmann, whose *The Long Journey of Lukas B.* describes a company of carpenters emigrating from Germany to America in the last century. Adventure stories include books by Leif Hamre of Norway (*Otter Three Two Calling!*), and An Rutgers van der Loeff of Holland (*Avalanche!* and *Children on the Oregon Trail*). The more modest, domestic type of adventure story is well represented in France by the books of Paul Berna (*A Hundred Million Francs*).

A particular feature of French children's literature as it is seen in translation is the number of eminent French writers who have written one or two works for children, without actually making a habit of it: they include André Maurois with *Fattypuffs and Thinifers*, Marcel Aymé with *The Wonderful Farm*, Maurice Druon with *Tistou of the Green Fingers*, Antoine de Saint-Exupéry with *The Little Prince* and Michel Tournier with *Friday and Robinson*, a junior version of his famous novel *Vendredi* in which the Crusoe/Man Friday situation is turned upside down. Another French-language phenomenon is the popularity of the strip-cartoon format: the many titles of Hergé's *Tintin* series, and the *Asterix the Gaul* series by Goscinny and Uderzo, have proved to be extremely popular in translation too, and in the late 1980's were among the most-borrowed books from the children's sections of British public libraries.

A particularly important area of translated literature from Europe is that of the war story: not the hearty adventures of characters such as the British Biggles, but novels from countries which actually underwent German occupation during World War II. The true classic is not, of course, a novel at all, but Anne Frank's *The Diary of a Young Girl*. From Holland, where the Frank family themselves were in hiding from the Nazis, comes a novel by Evert Hartman, *War Without Friends*, its central figure a boy with collaborating parents; from Norway, Aimée Sommerfelt's *Miriam*, with an account of a friendship between Jew and Gentile; from Greece, Alki Zei's *Petros' War*; from Italy, Carlo Picchio's *Freedom Fighter*. From Germany itself we have a stark, semi-autobiographical trilogy by Hans Peter Richter (*Friedrich, I Was There, The Time of the Young Soldiers*), and from Austria, Christine Nöstlinger's account of the Russian occupation of Vienna at the end of the war. A World War I story by Rudolf Frank, *No Hero for the Kaiser*, a kind of young people's parallel to Remarque's *All Quiet on the Western Front*, also had the distinction of being burned by the Nazis in the 1930's, and enjoyed a revival in Germany in the 1970's. Finally, the category of war stories should perhaps include a novel about a war which, it is to be hoped, never happens at all: Gudrun Pausewang, a German writer who works consistently for the spirit of international understanding, has written *The Last Children of Schevenborn*, a story of the harrowing aftermath of a nuclear strike.

The actual political setting of Anne Holm's *I Am David*, from Denmark, is purposely left vague, but the story tellingly evokes the horror inspired in its young hero by the idea of the labour camp from which he has escaped. However, the background to the Greek author Alki Zei's *Wildcat Under Glass* is clear enough, the story being set at the time of the Fascist seizure of power in 1936.

Books from Spain in English translation are few and far between, but do include the books of José María Sánchez-Silva, and more recently José Luis Olaizola's *Uncle Ambrosio's Helper*, in which an enterprising boy tries various ways to make money against the urban background of Madrid. An English translation exists of the Portuguese writer Miguel Torga's *Farrusco the Blackbird*, a book of animal fables. From Italy come several works by the Hans Andersen award winner, Gianni Rodari.

Over recent decades, several books from Russia and Eastern Europe have reached the English-language market, including titles by the Czech writers Václav Ctvrtek (*The Little Chalk Man*), Ota Hofman (*Escape*), and Jan Prochazka (*Long Live the Republic* and *Lenka*). Soviet books include Yuri Korinetz's *There, Far Beyond the River* and several other titles, almost pastoral in their timelessly Russian atmosphere, and Chingiz Aitmatov's *The White Ship* (originally published under an adult imprint in the United Kingdom).

In the 1970's and thereafter, what might loosely be called the social problem novel emerged as a notable phenomenon in most of the European countries as well as in the English-speaking world. These books may be directed at quite young children, as in Monica Gydal and Thomas Danielsson's series *Olly Sees It Through*, where little Olly has to face death, birth, and divorce in his family, and his own hospitalization. Such a catalogue of disasters is not, of course, meant to be gulped down by the child reader in one go; taken separately, the titles are probably helpful. For rather older readers, the Austrian Elfie Donnelly has written movingly on the subjects of death (*So Long, Grandpa*) and mental disturbance in old age (*Odd Stockings*). Death also features in a story from Denmark, Bjarne Reuter's *Buster's World*. Feminist subjects occur as well: in Anne-Cath. Vestly's *Hallo Aurora!*, from Norway, for instance, the central character's parents have reversed their roles.

Naturally enough, the "social problem" tends to figure most prominently in books for older children. Sexual problems, divorce, drugs, death, alcoholism, racism all appear, as well as that staple theme of the young adult novel, the difficulties of adjusting to growing up. A good deal of mediocre stuff is written in this genre, but on the whole only the best examples come through to English-language readers: those books where the author puts the individual character or predicament first, and the generalized social problem comes second. Among such works are the books for older readers of Gunnel Beckman (*Mia, Admission to the Feast*), and Christine Nöstlinger, who combines radical social views with comedy.

Far more could be said about the relationship between children's literature originally written in English and that translated from other languages than the scope of this brief survey allows, and many more authors could have been named. It is a tenable theory that translations have a particularly important part to play in children's literature, because apart from a tiny minority of the genuinely bilingual, the young reader will simply be unable to read a good children's book in a foreign language while he or she is still a child. Considerable responsibility, therefore, lies with the publishers and translators who make such books available.

—Anthea Bell

*   *   *

Selected books in translation (dates are of first English-language editions):

AITMATOV, Chingiz. Russian. *Farewell, Gul'sary*, 1970; *The White Ship (The White Steamship)*, 1972; *The Cranes Fly Early*, 1983.

ANNO, Mitsumasa. Japanese. *Topsy-Turvies*, 1970; *Upside-Downers*, 1971; *Dr. Anno's Magical Midnight Circus*, 1972; *Anno's Alphabet*, 1975; *Anno's Counting Book*, 1977; *Anno's Journey*, 1978; *Anno's Animals*, 1979; *Anno's Italy*, 1979; *The King's Flower*, 1979;

The Unique World of Mitsumasa Anno, edited by Samuel Crowell Morse, 1980; *Anno's Medieval World*, 1980; *Anno's Magical ABC*, with Masaichiro Anno, 1981; *Anno's Counting House*, 1982; *Anno's Britain*, 1982; *Anno's Mysterious Multiplying Jar*, with Masaichiro Anno, 1983; *Anno's U.S.A.*, 1983; *Anno's Flea Market*, 1984; *Anno's Hat Tricks*, with Akihiro Nozaki, 1985; *All in a Day*, 1986; *Anno's Peekaboo*, 1987; *In Shadowland*, 1988.

AYMÉ, Marcel.   French.   *The Wonderful Farm*, 1951; *The Magic Pictures*, 1954.

BARTOS-HÖPPNER, Barbara.   German.   *The Cossacks*, 1962; *Save the Khan*, 1963; *Avalanche Dog*, 1966; *Storm over the Caucasus*, 1968; *Hunters of Siberia*, 1969; *Hallowe'en Lanterns*, 1971; *The Conquering Ships*, 1978; *My Favourite Trees*, 1980; *My Favourite Animals*, 1981.

BAUMANN, Hans.   German.   *Sons of the Steppe*, 1958; *The Barque of the Brothers*, 1958; *Jackie the Pit Pony*, 1958; *Angelina and the Birds*, 1959; *The Lion and the Unicorn*, 1959; *The Dragon Next Door*, 1960; *The Crotchety Crocodile*, 1960; *I Marched with Hannibal*, 1961; *The Bear and His Brothers*, 1962; *Caspar and His Friends*, 1967; *The Circus Is Here*, 1967; *Fenny*, 1970; *Dimitri and the False Tsars*, 1972; *The Hare's Race*, 1976; *The Three in the Blue Balloon*, 1976; *Katzimir the Greatest*, 1977; *Dragon Mountain*, 1979; *Wings for Icarus*, 1980; *Animal Babies*, 1984; *Barnabus the Dancing Bear*, 1984; *My Friends on the Farm*, 1985; *Chip Has Many Brothers*, 1985; *Mischa and His Brothers*, 1985.

BECKMAN, Gunnel.   Swedish.   *The Girl Without a Name*, 1970; *Admission to the Feast* (*19 Is Too Young to Die*), 1971; *A Room of His Own*, 1973; *Mia* series, from 1974; *That Early Spring*, 1977.

BERNA, Paul.   French.   *A Hundred Million Francs* (*The Horse Without a Head*), 1957; *Continent in the Sky*, 1959; *The Street Musician*, 1960; *Flood Warning*, 1962; *The Mystery of Saint-Salgue*, 1963; *The Clue of the Black Cat*, 1964; *The Mystery of the Cross-Eyed Man*, 1965; *The Secret of the Missing Boat*, 1966; *The Mule of the Motorway* (*The Mule of the Expressway*), 1967; *A Truckload of Rice*, 1968; *They Didn't Come Back*, 1969; *The Myna Bird Mystery*, 1970; *Gaby and the New Money Fraud*, 1971; *Vagabonds of the Pacific*, 1973; *The Last Dawn*, 1977.

BIEGEL, Paul.   Dutch.   *The King of the Copper Mountains*, 1969; *The Little Captain* series, from 1971; *The Seven-Times Search*, 1971; *The Twelve Robbers*, 1974; *The Gardens of Dorr*, 1975; *The Elephant Party and Other Stories*, 1977; *Far Beyond and Back Again*, 1977; *Robber Hopsika*, 1978; *The Dwarfs of Nosegay* series, from 1978; *Letters from the General*, 1979; *The Looking-Glass Castle*, 1979; *The Clock Struck Twelve*, 1979; *The Tincan Beast*, 1980; *The Curse of the Werewolf*, 1981; *Virgil Nosegay* series, from 1981; *Crocodile Man*, 1982.

BOJUNGA-NUNES, Lygia.   Brazilian.   *The Companions*, 1990.

BRUNA, Dick.   Dutch.   *The Happy Apple*, 1959; *Tilly and Tessa* (*Tilly and Tess*), 1962; *The Little Bird*, 1962; *The Apple*, 1963; *The Circus*, 1963; *The Fish*, 1963; *Kitten Nell*, 1963; *Miffy* series, from 1964; *The Egg*, 1964; *The King*, 1964; *Hop-o'-My-Thumb*, 1966; *The School*, 1966; *The Sailor*, 1966; *A Story to Tell* series, from 1968; *I Can Read More*, 1969; *Snuffy* series, from 1970; *My Vest Is White* (*My Shirt Is White*), 1973; *Animal Book*, 1974; *Animal Frieze*, 1975; *Lisa and Lynn*, 1975; *My Meals*, 1975; *The Christmas Book*, 1976; *I Can Dress Myself*, 1977; *Poppy Pig* series, from 1978; *I Can Read*, 1979; *I Can Count*, 1979; *My Toys*, 1980; *Out and About*, 1980; *When I'm Big*, 1981; *I Know About Numbers*, 1981; *Word Book*, 1982; *The*

Lifeboat, 1984; *I Can Make Music*, 1984; *Blue Boat*, with Peter Jones, 1984; *Farmer John*, 1984; *The Orchestra*, 1984; *The Rescue*, 1984; *I Know About Shapes*, 1984; *My House*, 1984; *Playing in Winter*, 1984; *My Playtime*, 1985; *Back to Front*, 1986; *Find My Hat*, 1986; *My Sport Book*, 1986; *Through the Year with Boris Bear*, 1987.

BRUNHOFF, Jean de.   French.   *The Story of Babar, The Little Elephant*, 1933; *The Travels of Babar*, 1934; *Babar the King*, 1935; *Babar and His Children*, 1938; *Babar and Father Christmas*, 1940; *Babar and Zephir*, 1942.

BRUNHOFF, Laurent de.   French.   Continuation of Jean de Brunhoff's *Babar* series, from 1948; *Serafina* series, from 1961; *Anatole and His Donkey*, 1963; *Bonhomme* series, from 1965; *Gregory and the Lady Turtle in the Valley of the Music Trees*, 1971; *The One Pig with Horns*, 1979.

PÈRE CASTOR (pseudonym for Lida).   French.   *Wild Animal Books: Bourru, Frou, Mischief, Plouf, Scaf, Quipic, Martin, Cuckoo*, 1937–42.

CHUKOVSKY, Kornei.   Russian.   *Crocodile*, 1931; *The Telephone*, 1961; *Wash 'em Clean*, 1962; *Dr. Concocter*, 1967; *The Muddle*, 1976; *The Silver Crest*, 1977; *Good Morning Chick*, 1980; *Cock the Roach*, 1981; *Stolen Sun*, 1983; *Little Chick*, 1985.

CTVRTEK, Václav.   Czechoslovakian.   *The Little Chalk Man*, 1970.

DONNELLY, Elfie.   Austrian.   *So Long, Grandpa*, 1980; *Odd Stockings*, 1982; *Offbeat Friends*, 1982; *Tina into Two Won't Go*, 1983; *A Package for Miss Marshwater*, 1987.

DRUON, Maurice.   French.   *Tistou of the Green Fingers* (*Tistou of the Green Thumbs*), 1958.

FÄHRMANN, Willi.   German.   *The Long Journey of Lukas B.*, 1985.

FRANK, Rudolf.   German.   *The Boy Who Forgot His Birthday* (*No Hero for the Kaiser*), 1985.

FROLOV, Vadim.   Russian.   *What It's All About*, 1968.

GRIPE, Maria.   Swedish.   *Pappa Pellerin's Daughter*, 1966; *Hugo and Josephine* series, from 1969; *The Night Daddy*, 1971; *The Glassblower's Children*, 1974; *The Land Beyond*, 1974; *Julia's House*, 1975; *Elvis* series, from 1976; *In the Time of the Bells*, 1976; *The Green Coat*, 1977.

GUILLOT, René.   French.   *Companions of Fortune*, 1952; *Sirga*, 1953; *The 397th White Elephant*, 1954; *The King's Corsair*, 1954; *Kpo the Leopard*, 1955; *The Wind of Chance*, 1955; *A Boy and Five Huskies*, 1957; *Prince of the Jungle*, 1958; *Elephant Road*, 1959; *Grishka and the Bear*, 1959; *Nicolette and the Mill*, 1960; *The Fantastic Brother*, 1961; *The Wild White Stallion*, 1961; *Sama*, 1961; *The Troubadour*, 1965; *The Champion of Olympia*, 1968; *Little Dog Lost*, 1969; *Castle in Spain*, 1970.

GYDAL, Monica.   Swedish.   *Olly Sees It Through* series (with Thomas Danielsson), from 1976.

HAMRE, Leif.   Norwegian.   *Otter Three Two Calling!* (*Leap into Danger*), 1959; *Edge of Disaster*, 1960; *Perilous Wings*, 1961; *Blue Two—Bale Out!*, 1961; *Ready for Take-Off*, 1962; *Contact Lost*, 1967; *Operation Arctic*, 1973.

HARTMAN, Evert. Dutch. *War Without Friends*, 1982.

HEIN, Christoph. German. *Jamie and His Friends*, 1988.

HEINE, Helme. German. *The Pigs' Wedding*, 1978; *Superhare*, 1979; *Imagine If*, 1979; *Merry-Go-Round*, 1980; *Mr. Miller the Dog*, 1980; *King Bounce the First*, 1982; *Friends*, 1982; *The Most Wonderful Egg in the World*, 1983; *The Friends' Racing Cart (The Racing Cart)*, 1984; *The Pearl*, 1985; *The Friends Have a Visitor (The Visitor)*, 1985; *The Alarm Clock*, 1985; *Saturday in Paradise (One Day in Paradise)*, 1986; *Seven Wild Pigs*, 1986.

HOFMAN, Ota. Czechoslovakian. *Escape*, 1970.

HOLM, Anne. Danish. *I Am David (North to Freedom)*, 1965; *The Hostage*, 1980.

IWASAKI, Chihiro. Japanese. *Staying at Home on a Rainy Day*, 1969; *Momoko* series, from 1972; *The Birthday Wish*, 1974; *Will You Be My Friend?*, 1974; *What's Fun Without a Friend?*, 1975; *Onito's Hat*, 1978; *The Day I Got Better*, 1980; *The Wise Queen*, 1986.

JANOSCH. German. *Just One Apple*, 1966; *Joshua and the Magic Fiddle*, 1968; *Bollerbam*, 1969; *Dear Snowman*, 1970; *The Thieves and the Raven*, 1970; *The Magic Auto*, 1971; *The Yellow Auto Named Ferdinand*, 1973; *Zampano's Performing Bear*, 1976; *Hey Presto, You're a Bear!*, 1977; *Luke Caraway, Master Magician or Indian Chief*, 1977; *The Rain Car*, 1978; *The Trip to Panama*, 1978; *Crafty Caspar and His Good Old Granny*, 1979; *The Big Janosch Book of Fun and Verse*, 1980; *The Treasure-Hunting Trip*, 1980; *A Letter for Tiger*, 1981; *Animal Antics*, 1982; *See You in the Morning!*, 1983; *The Cricket and the Mole*, 1983; *The Higher and Higher House*, 1984; *I'll Make You Well, Tiger, Said the Bear (Little Tiger, Get Well Soon!)*, 1985; *The Curious Tale of Hare and Hedgehog*, 1985; *The Old Man and the Bear*, 1987; *Hello, Little Pig*, 1988; *The Little Hare Book*, 1988.

JANSSON, Tove. Finnish. *Moomintroll* series, from 1950; *Who Will Comfort Toffle?*, 1960; *The Summer Book*, 1975; *Sun City*, 1976; *The Dangerous Journey*, 1978.

JONSSON, Runer. Danish. *Viki Viking (Vicke the Viking)*, 1968.

KÄSTNER, Erich. German. *Emil and the Detectives*, 1930; *Annaluise and Anton*, 1932; *The 35th of May*, 1933; *The Flying Classroom*, 1934; *Emil and the Three Twins*, 1935; *The Animals' Conference*, 1949; *Lottie and Lisa (Lisa and Lottie)*, 1950; *The Little Man*, 1966.

KORINETZ, Yuri. Russian. *There, Far Beyond the River*, 1973; *In the Middle of the World*, 1976; *The River and the Forest*, 1978.

KRÜSS, James. German. *My Great-Grandfather and I*, 1964; *Eagle and Dove*, 1965; *3 x 3*, 1965; *The Happy Islands Behind the Winds*, 1966; *Florentine*, 1967; *The Animal Parade*, 1968; *The Lighthouse on the Lobster Cliffs*, 1969; *The Proud Wooden Drummer*, 1969; *Letters to Pauline*, 1971; *My Great-Grandfather, the Heroes, and I*, 1973.

KUIJER, Guus. Dutch. *Daisy's New Head*, 1980.

KURATOMI, Chizuko (illustrator: Kozo Kakimoto). Japanese. *Barnabas Ball at the Circus*, 1967; *Mr. Bear* series, from 1968; *Runaway James and the Night Owl*, 1968; *Run, Chase the Sun*, 1969;

Pim and the Fisherboy, 1975.

LAGERLÖF, Selma. Swedish. *The Wonderful Adventures of Nils*, 1907; *The Further Adventures of Nils*, 1911.

LINDGREN, Astrid. Swedish. *Pippi Longstocking* series, from 1950; *Bill Bergson* series, from 1952; *Mio, My Son*, 1956; *Kati* series, from 1961; *The Tomten* series, from 1961; *Rasmus and the Tramp (Rasmus and the Vagabond)*, 1961; *Noisy Village (Bullerby)* series, from 1962; *The Children on Troublemaker Street*, 1962; *Christmas in the Stable*, 1962; *Lotta* series, from 1963; *The Mischievous Martens*, 1964; *Seacrow Island*, 1968; *Emil* series, from 1970; *Karlson (Karlsson)* series, from 1971; *The Brothers Lionheart*, 1975; *Mardie* series, from 1979; *I Want to Go to School Too*, 1980; *Ronia, The Robber's Daughter*, 1983; *The Runaway Sleigh Ride*, 1984; *My Nightingale Is Singing*, 1985; *The Dragon with Red Eyes*, 1986; *The Ghost of Skinny Jack*, 1988; *I Want a Brother or Sister*, 1988; *I Don't Want to Go to Bed*, 1988.

LOEFF, An Rutgers van der. Dutch. *Avalanche!*, 1954; *They're Drowning Our Village*, 1959; *Children on the Oregon Trail (Oregon at Last!)*, 1961; *Rossie*, 1964; *Great Day in Holland*, 1965; *Vassilis on the Run*, 1965; *Flight from the Polar Night*, 1968; *Steffos and His Easter Lamb*, 1969.

MAUROIS, André. French. *Fattypuffs and Thinifers*, 1941.

MÜLLER, Jörg, and STEINER, Jörg. Germans. *Rabbit Island*, 1977; *The Bear Who Wanted to Stay a Bear (The Bear Who Wanted to Be a Bear)*, 1977; *The Sea People*, 1982.

NAKATANI, Chiyoko. Japanese. *The Day Chiro Was Lost*, 1968; *Fumio and the Dolphins*, 1970; *The Zoo in My Garden*, 1973; *My Animal Friends*, 1975; *My Teddy Bear*, 1975; *My Day on the Farm*, 1976; *My Treasures*, 1979; *Feeding Babies*, 1981.

NÖSTLINGER, Christine. Austrian. *Fly Away Home*, 1975; *The Cucumber King*, 1975; *The Disappearing Cellar*, 1975; *Fiery Frederica*, 1975; *Conrad (Conrad, The Factory-Made Boy; Konrad)*, 1976; *Girl Missing*, 1976; *Four Days in the Life of Lisa*, 1977; *Mr. Bat's Great Invention*, 1978; *Marrying Off Mother*, 1978; *Luke and Angela*, 1979; *Lollipop*, 1982; *But Jasper Came Instead*, 1983; *Brainbox Sorts It Out (Brainbox Cracks the Case)*, 1985; *Guardian Ghost*, 1986.

OLAIZOLA, José Luis. Spanish. *Uncle Ambrosio's Helper*, 1989.

PAUSEWANG, Gudrun. German. *The Last Children of Schevenborn*, 1989.

PICCHIO, Carlo. Italian. *Freedom Fighter*, 1980.

PREUSSLER, Otfried. German. *The Little Witch*, 1961; *Thomas Scarecrow*, 1963; *The Robber Hotzenplotz* series, from 1964; *The Little Ghost*, 1967; *The Adventures of Strong Vanya*, 1970; *The Satanic Mill*, 1972; *The Wise Men of Schilda*, 1974; *The Green Bronze Bell*, 1977; *Herbie's Magical Hat*, 1985; *The Tale of the Unicorn*, 1989.

PROCHAZKA, Jan. Czechoslovakian. *Long Live the Republic*, 1973; *The Carp*, 1977; *Lenka*, 1979.

PRØYSEN, Alf. Norwegian. *Little Old Mrs. Pepperpot* series, from 1959; *Stories for Christmas*, 1987; *Stories for Summer*, 1989.

REUTER, Bjarne. Danish. *The Princess and the Sun, Moon and Stars*, 1986; *Buster's World*, 1988.

RICHTER, Hans Peter. German. *Friedrich*, 1970; *I Was There*, 1972; *The Time of the Young Soldiers*, 1976.

RODARI, Gianni. Italian. *Telephone Tales*, 1965; *The Befana's Toyshop*, 1970; *A Pie in the Sky*, 1971; *Mr. Cat in Business*, 1975; *Tales Told by a Machine*, 1976.

SAINT-EXUPÉRY, Antoine de. French. *The Little Prince*, 1943.

SALTEN, Felix. German. *Bambi: A Life in the Woods*, 1928; *Fifteen Rabbits*, 1930; *The Hound of Florence*, 1930; *Florian*, 1934; *Perri*, 1938; *Bambi's Children*, 1939; *Renni the Rescuer*, 1940.

SÁNCHEZ-SILVA, José María. Spanish. *Marcelino (The Miracle of Marcelino)*, 1954; *The Boy and the Whale*, 1964; *Ladis* series, from 1968.

SANDMAN LILIUS, Irmelin. Swedish. *The Maharajah Adventure*, 1966; *Gold Crown Lane*, 1976; *The Goldmaker's House*, 1978; *Horses of the Night*, 1979; *King Tulle*, 1980.

SCHAMI, Rafik. German. *A Handful of Stars*, 1989.

SOLDATI, Mario. Italian. *The Octopus and the Pirates*, 1974.

SOMMER-BODENBURG, Angela. German. *Little Vampire (Vampire)* series, from 1982; *Coco's Birthday Surprise*, 1987.

SOMMERFELT, Aimée. Norwegian. *The Road to Agra*, 1961; *Miriam*, 1963; *The White Bungalow*, 1963; *My Name Is Pablo*, 1966; *No Easy Way*, 1967.

TORGA, Miguel. Portuguese. *Farrusco the Blackbird*, 1950.

TOURNIER, Michel. French. *Friday and Robinson*, 1972.

UNNERSTAD, Edith. Swedish. *The Saucepan Journey*, 1951; *Pysen*, 1955; *Little O*, 1957; *The Spettecake Holiday*, 1958; *The Journey with Grandmother (Grandmother's Journey)*, 1960; *A Journey to England*, 1961; *The Cats from Summer Island*, 1963; *The Picnic*, 1964; *The Urchin*, 1964; *The Pip-Larssons Go Sailing*, 1966; *Toppen and I at the Croft*, 1966; *Larry Makes Music*, 1967; *Two Little Gigglers*, 1967; *A House for Spinner's Grandmother*, 1970; *Mickie*, 1971; *The Cherry Tree Party*, 1978.

VESTLY, Anne-Cath. Norwegian. *Aurora* series, from 1973; *Eight Children* series, from 1973.

VINCENT, Gabrielle. Belgian. *Ernest and Celestine* series, from 1982.

WATANABE, Shigeo (illustrator: Yasuo Ohtomo). Japanese. *How Do I Put It On?*, 1979; *Hallo! How Are You? (Where's My Daddy?)*, 1980; *How Do I Eat It? (What a Good Lunch!)*, 1980; *Ready, Steady, Go! (Get Set! Go!)*, 1981; *I Can Do It! (I Can Ride It!)*, 1982; *I'm the King of the Castle*, 1982; *I Can Build a House!*, 1983; *I'm Going for a Walk! (I Can Take a Walk!)*, 1984; *I'm Playing with Papa (Daddy, Play with Me!)*, 1985; *I'm Having a Bath with Papa! (I Can Take a Bath!)*, 1986; *It's My Birthday!*, 1988.

ZEI, Alki. Greek. *Wildcat under Glass*, 1968; *Petros' War*, 1972; *The Sound of Dragon's Feet*, 1979.

ZIMNIK, Reiner. German. *Jonah and the Fisherman*, 1956; *The Proud White Circus Horse*, 1957; *Little Owl*, 1960; *The Bear on the Motorcycle*, 1963; *The Crane*, 1969; *The Bear and the People*, 1971; *Bill's Balloon Ride*, 1973.

TITLE
INDEX

The following list includes the titles of all fiction, drama, and poetry for children cited in the main entries, the appendix of 19th-century writers, and the supplement of writers whose work is available in translation. The name in parenthesis is meant to direct the reader to the appropriate entry where fuller information is given. Unless designated "play" or "verse" the titles are of works of fiction. The term "series" indicates a recurring word or phrase in the *titles* of an entrant's books (the date listed is that of the earliest *title* in which the word or phrase appears). Titles beginning "The Adventure(s) of," "The Story of," and "The Tale(s) of" are alphabetized according to the first key word.

A & The (Raskin), 1970
A for Ami (Mazer), 1988
A for the Ark (Duvoisin), 1952
A Is for Angel (verse; Robinson, as Thomas), 1953
A, My Name is Ami (Mazer), 1986
A Stands for Angel (verse; Robinson, as Thomas), 1939
ABC (Burningham), 1964
ABC (verse; Seuss), 1963
ABC Bunny (Gág),1933
A.B.C. Girl (Meade, appendix), 1910
A.B.C. of Every-Day People (verse; Farrow), 1902
ABCDEFGHIJKLMNOPQRSTUVWXYZ (verse; Kuskin), 1963
ABZ Book (Silverstein, as Shelby), 1961
Aaron series (J. Harris, appendix), from 1896
Aaron's Door (P. Martin, as Miles), 1977
Abandoned (G. Griffiths), 1973
Abbey by the Sea (Molesworth, appendix), 1887
Abbey Church (Yonge, appendix), 1844
Abbey School series (Oxenham), from 1920
Abbie's God Book (Holland), 1982
Abbotsbury Ring (Greaves), 1979
Abdul (Wells), 1975
Abdul the Awful (Hough), 1970
Abe Lincoln—New Salem Days (play; Chorpenning), 1941
Abe Lincoln's Beard (Wahl), 1971
Abel's Island (Steig), 1976
Aboard the Hylow on Sable Island Bank (Otis, appendix), 1907
About Angels (play; L. Richards), 1915
About Bellamy (de Treviño), 1940
About the B'nai Bagels (Konigsburg), 1969
About Us (Gibbs), 1912
Abraham Lincoln (play; C. D. Mackay), 1912
Absolute Zero (Cresswell), 1978
Absurd Ditties (verse; Farrow), 1903
Acacia Terrace (B. Wilson), 1988
Accent on April (Cavanna), 1960
Accident (Colman), 1980
Accidental Twins (Bull), 1982
Ace Dragon Ltd. (Hoban), 1980
Acorn Quest (Yolen), 1981
Acorns and Aerials (M. Baker), 1956
Acrobat Hamster (Cockett), 1965
Acrobat's Girlhood, (Stretton, appendix), 1889
Across Canada (Bice), 1949
Across Five Aprils (I. Hunt), 1964
Across the Barricades (Lingard), 1972
Across the Delaware (Otis, appendix), 1903
Across the Fruited Plain (Means), 1940
Across the Range (Otis, appendix), 1914
Acting Third Mate (F. Knight), 1954
Action at Paradise Marsh (Wier), 1968
Active-Enzyme Lemon-Freshened Junior High School Witch (Hildick), 1973
Acts of Love (Daly), 1986
Adam and the Golden Cock (Dalgliesh), 1959
Adam Bookout (Shotwell), 1967

Adam of the Road (Vining, as Gray), 1942
Adam Troy (Patchett), 1954
Adam's Key (Lattimore), 1976
Adelaide (Ungerer), 1959
Adelaide Ghost (Garfield), 1977
Adella Mary in Old New Mexico (Means), 1939
Adirondack Cabin (Sidney, appendix), 1890
Admiral J. of Spurwick (Otis, appendix), 1896
Admiral's Secret (A. Hall), 1953
Admiral's Walk (Barne), 1953
Admission to the Feast (Beckman, trans), 1971
Adolf's Dog (Strang), 1926
Adolphus (verse; Flack), 1941
Adopted Daughter (Clewes), 1968
Adopted Family (Peacocke), 1923
Adopting of Mickey (Chaundler), 1925
Adrienne (Le Feuvre), 1928
Adrift in New York (Alger, appendix), 1903
Adrift in the City (Alger, appendix), 1895
Adventure (play; Daniell), 1948
Adventure at High Force (P. Turner), 1984
Adventure Books (Bestall), n.d.
Adventure Bound (Johns), 1955
Adventure Club (Fyleman), 1925
Adventure Downstream (Fry), 1946
Adventure for Two (Oxenham), 1941
Adventure in Granada (Myers), 1985
Adventure in Mayo (Allan), 1956
Adventure in Prague (Finlay), 1967
Adventure May Be Anywhere (Manning-Sanders), 1939
Adventure on Rainbow Island (Clewes), 1957
Adventure Royal (Allan), 1954
Adventure Stories (Blyton), 1960
Adventure Unlimited (Johns), 1957
Adventurers (play; Barne), 1931
Adventurers All! (Moore), 1927
Adventurers Ltd. (Catherall), 1938
Adventurers Two (Moore), 1929
Adventures at Hampton Court (Needham), 1954
Adventures at Windsor Castle (Needham), 1957
Adventures in Switzerland (Allan), 1955
Adventures with Benghazi (Fyleman), 1946
Adventuress (Meade, appendix), 1899
Adventurous Anne (Everett-Green, appendix), 1916
Adventurous Four series (Blyton), from 1941
Adventurous Holiday (Wynne), 1933
Adventurous Schoolgirl (Moore), 1921
Adventurous Seven (Marchant), 1913
Adventurous Summer (Allan), 1948
Aelfred (Greenwood), 1970
Aeroplane Who Wanted to See the Sea (Ainsworth), 1968
Affable, Amiable Bulldozer Man (verse; MacIntyre), 1965
Afloat in Freedom's Cause (Otis, appendix), 1908
Afraid to Ride (Anderson), 1957
Africa Dream (Greenfield), 1977
African Adventure (W. Price), 1963

Africano (H. Griffiths), 1961
After Candlemas (Arthur), 1974
After the First Death (Cormier), 1979
After the First Love (Holland), 1983
After the Goat Man (Byars), 1974
After the Raft Race (MacGibbon), 1976
After the Rain (Mazer), 1987
After the Wedding (Colman), 1975
After Thursday (Ure), 1985
After Worcester (Everett-Green, appendix), 1901
Afterthought House (Everett-Green, appendix), 1894
Again the Bugles Blow (R. Bacon), 1973
Against the Odds (R. Klein), 1989
Agnes the Sheep (W. Taylor), 1989
A-Going to the Westward (Lenski), 1937
Agony of Alice (Naylor), 1985
Ahmet the Woodseller (play; Serraillier), 1965
Aidan and the Strollers (Grice), 1960
Aidan and the Strolling Players (Grice), 1961
Aim for the Flag (Hardcastle), 1967
Aim of Her Life (Meade appendix), 1908
Aimer Gate (Garner), 1978
Aimer Gate (play; Garner), 1980
Aio the Rainmaker (F. French), 1975
Air Patrol (Strang), 1912
Air Scout (Strang), 1911
Airfield Man (B. Carter), 1965
Airlift for Grandee (Park), 1964
Airship "Golden Hind," (Westerman), 1920
Ajax series (Patchett), from 1953
Akavak (Houston), 1968
Akbar (play; Mitchison), 1937
Al series (C. Greene), from 1969
Aladdin (play; D. Wood), 1980
Aladdin and His Wonderful Lamp (verse; Ransome), 1919
Aladdin and the Magic Lamp (play; Reaney), 1965
Alain, The Tale of (Ormondroyd), 1960
Alan and Naomi (Levoy), 1977
Alan and the Animal Kingdom (Holland), 1977
Alan Carr series (Westerman), from 1938
Alan Mendelsohn (Pinkwater), 1979
Alarm Clock (Heine, trans), 1985
Albatross (R. Armstrong), 1970
Albatross Comes Home (F. Knight), 1949
Albatross Two (Thiele), 1974
Alberic the Wise (Juster), 1965
Albert B. Cub and Zebra (Rockwell), 1977
Albert the Albatross (Hoff), 1961
Albert the Dragon series (Weir), from 1961
Albeson and the Germans (Needle), 1977
Alcove (Abbott, appendix), 1856
Alder Tree (Halam), 1982
Aldo series (Hurwitz), from 1978
Aleko's Island (Fenton), 1948
Alex (Duder), 1987
Alex series (Griffith), from 1982
Alexander series (Viorst), from 1972
Alexander (Watkins-Pitchford), 1957
Alexander and the Wind-Up Mouse (Lionni), 1969
Alexander Soames (verse; Kuskin), 1962
Alexandra (O'Dell), 1984
Alfie series (S. Hughes), from 1981
Alfie, Adventures of (Tozer), 1941
Alfie and the Ferry Boat (Keeping), 1968
Alfie Finds the Other Side of the World (Keeping), 1968
Alfonso Bonzo (Davies), 1986

Alfred G. Graebner Memorial High School Handbook of Rules and
    Regulations (Conford), 1976
Algernon (Hough), 1961
Alhambra (Pollard), 1970
Ali Baba (play; Miller), n.d.
Ali Baba Bernstein series (Hurwitz), from 1985
Alias Madame Doubtfire (Fine), 1988
Alice and Flower and Foxianna (King-Smith), 1989
Alice and Thomas and Jane (Bagnold), 1930
Alice in Dreamsville (play; Owen), 1979
Alice in Rapture, Sort Of (Naylor), 1989
Alice in Wonderland (play; Chorpenning), 1946
Alice in Wonderland (play; Miller), 1951
Alice in Wonderland (play; Peet), 1951
Alice the Artist (Waddell), 1988
Alice-All-by-Herself (Coatsworth), 1937
Alice's Adventures in Wonderland and series (Carrol, appendix),
    from 1865
Alicia (Means), 1953
Alick's Corner (Le Feuvre), 1929
Alien Child (Sargent), 1988
Alien Citadel (D. Hill), 1984
Alien Music (A. and E. Johnson), 1982
Alien Note (play; Latham), 1930
Aliens in the Family (Mahy), 1986
Alison in Provence (Finlay), 1963
Alison's Fishing Birds (Haig-Brown), 1980
Alison's Ghosts (Downie), 1984
All Aboard! (Duvoisin), 1935
All Aboard the Bookworm Belle (play; Ridge), 1953
All about Arthur (Carle), 1974
All about Sam (Lowry), 1988
All Alone (Bishop), 1953
All and More (Aiken), 1971
All Around the Town (Flack), 1929
All Around the Town (verse; McGinley), 1948
All Around Us (Carle), 1986
All Because I'm Older (Naylor), 1981
All But a Few (Aiken), 1974
All Change (J. Pullein-Thompson), 1961
All Day Long (verse; McCord), 1966
All Different (verse; Ainsworth), 1947
All Ends Up (G. Wilson), 1984
All Falling Down (Zion), 1951
All Hands to the Boats! (Westerman), 1932
All I Ever Ask (Ashley), 1987
All I See (Rylant), 1988
All in a Day (Anno, trans), 1986
All in Good Time (Ormondroyd), 1975
All in One Piece (J. Murphy), 1987
All in the Woodland Early (verse; Yolen), 1979
All Kinds of Time (verse; Behn), 1950
All My Men (Ashley), 1977
All on a May Morning (verse; N. Willard), 1975
All on Account of Kelly (play; Latham), 1937
All or Nothing (Everett-Green, appendix), 1888
All over Town (Brink), 1939
All Play and No Work (H. Avery), 1901
All Round Me Shinin' (Means), n.d.
All Sail Set (Sperry), 1935
All Set for Christmas (play; A. Fisher), 1946
All Shapes and Sizes (S. Hughes), 1985
All Sizes of Noises (verse; Kuskin), 1962
All Small (verse; McCord), 1986
All Sorts (Meade, appendix), 1899
All Sorts of Prickles (A. Morgan), 1979

And to Think That I Saw It on Mulberry Street (verse; Seuss), 1937
Anders and Marta (Moray Williams), 1935
Anderson's Jo (M. Bruce), 1927
Andra (L. Lawrence), 1971
Andrew, The Adventures of (E. O. White), 1928
Andries (Van Stockum), 1942
Androcles and the Lion (play; A. Harris), 1964
Android at Arms (A. Norton), 1971
Andy, The Adventures of (Bianco), 1927
Andy All Year Round (Merriam), 1967
Andy and the Lion (Daugherty), 1938
Andy Buckram's Tin Men (Brink), 1966
Andy Gordon (Alger, appendix), 1903
Andy Grant's Pluck (Alger, appendix), 1902
Andy Jackson's Water Well (W. Steele), 1959
Andy Man (Le Feuvre), 1927
Andy (That's My Name) (de Paola), 1973
Andy-All-Alone (Westerman), 1934
Andy's Landmark House (Colman), 1969
Andy's Pit Pony (Berg), 1958
Andy's Ward (Otis, appendix), 1895
Angel and the Wild Animal (Foreman), 1988
Angel Face (Chaney), 1979
Angel Face (N. Klein), 1984
Angel in the Looking-Glass (play; A. Fisher), 1950
Angel of Love (Meade, appendix), 1885
Angel on Skis (Cavanna), 1957
Angel Square (Doyle), 1984
Angel with a Mouth-Organ (Mattingley), 1984
Angela Goes to School (Wynne), 1922
Angela's Airplane (Munsch), 1983
Angelina and the Birds (Baumann, trans), 1959
Angelo and Rosaline (Bettina), 1957
Angel's Alphabet (verse; Van Stockum), 1948
Angels and Other Strangers (Paterson), 1979
Angel's Christmas (Walton, appendix), 1877
Angie's First Case (Sobol), 1981
Angry Brownies (play; Fyleman), 1936
Angry Flames (Odaga), 1968
Angry River (R. Bond), 1972
Angry Waters (Morey), 1969
Angus series (Flack), 1930
Animal Antics (Janosch, trans), 1982
Animal Babies (Baumann, trans), 1984
Animal Book (Blyton), 1927
Animal Book (Bruna, trans), 1974
Animal Castle (T. Lee), 1972
Animal Doctor (Meynell), 1956
Animal Families (R. Kraus), 1980
Animal Family (Jarrell), 1965
Animal Folk (Burgess), 1925
Animal Frieze (Bruna, trans), 1975
Animal Game (Hough), 1959
Animal Hedge (P. Fleischman), 1983
Animal Heroes (Seton), 1905
Animal Library (Mayne), 1986
Animal Lover (play; Poole), 1982
Animal Paint Book (verse; Burgess), 1925
Animal Parade (Krüss, trans), 1968
Animal Pictures (verse; Burgess), 1925
Animal Stories (Burgess), 1942
Animal Stories, Further (C. Roberts), 1935
Animal Story Book (Hewett), 1972
Animal Tales (Blyton), 1956
Animal, The Vegetable and John D. Jones, (Byars), 1982

Animal World (Burgess), 1961
Animals and the Ark (verse; Kuskin), 1958
Animals' Carol (verse; Causley), 1977
Animals' Conference (Kästner, trans), 1949
Animals Everywhere (d'Aulaire), 1940
Animals for Me (verse; Lenski), 1941
Animals Nobody Wanted (Beresford), 1982
Animals' Peace Day (Wahl), 1970
"Ann and Hope" Mutiny (Wibberley, as Webb), 1966
Ann and Peter series (B. Wilson), from 1963
Ann Aurelia and Dorothy (Carlson), 1968
Ann Frances (E. O. White), 1935
Anna (Almedingen), 1972
Anna Anaconda (Judah), 1960
Anna and Minnie (Hough), 1962
Anna Hand (Finley, appendix), 1868
Anna Help Ginger (Wahl), 1971
Anna of the Tenterford (Marchant), 1935
Anna the Horse (Fatio), 1951
Annabel (Baum, as Metcalf), 1906
Annabel's Ghost (R. Klein), 1985
Annaluise and Anton (Kästner, trans), 1932
Annandale (Finley, appendix), 1858
Anna's Garden Songs (verse; M. Steele), 1989
Anna's Summer Songs (verse; M. Steele), 1988
Anne (Hope-Simpson), 1960
Anne, Adventures of (Moray Williams), 1935
Anne of Green Gables series (L. Montgomery), from 1908
Anne of Queen Anne's (Talbot), 1932
Anneli the Art Hater (Fine), 1986
Anne-on-Her-Own (Talbot), 1933
Annerton Pit (Dickinson), 1977
Annesley's Double (Westerman), 1926
Annie and the Old One (P. Martin, as Miles), 1971
Annie Joins the Circus (Howe), 1982
Ann's Alpine Adventure (Allan), 1956
Another Day (Ets), 1953
Another Day (Tomalin), 1988
Another Fine Mess (Needle), 1981
Another Heaven, Another Earth (Hoover), 1981
Another Home, Another Country (Cockett), 1969
Another Man o' War (Anderson), 1966
Another Mouse to Feed (R. Kraus), 1980
Another Pony for Jean (Cannan), 1938
Another Shore (N. Bond), 1988
Another Six (R. Armstrong), 1959
Another Time Stories (Bisset), 1963
Another Washington (play; Latham, as Lee), 1931
Anpao (Highwater), 1977
Answers to Brut (Rubinstein), 1988
Ant and Bee series (Banner), from 1950
Ant and the Elephant (Peet), 1972
Anteater Named Arthur (Waber), 1967
Antigrav (Fisk), 1978
Anti-Muffins (L'Engle), 1980
Antique Dust (Westall), 1989
Antlers of the King Moose (Catherall), 1970
Antoine of Oregon (Otis, appendix), 1912
Antony Grace, The Story of (Fenn, appendix), 1888
Any Me I Want to Be (verse; Kuskin), 1972
Any Port in a Storm (H. Avery), 1928
Anybody at Home? (verse; H.A. and M. Rey), 1939
Anybody Home? (verse; A. Fisher). 1980
Anything Can Happen on the River! (Brink), 1934
Anything for a Friend (Conford), 1979
Anytime Stories (Bisset), 1954

Beady Bear (D. Freeman), 1954
Bean-Pickers (play; Lenski), 1952
Beans on the Roof (Byars), 1988
Bear (play; Fyleman), 1936
Bear, A Bobcat, and Three Ghosts (Rockwell), 1977
Bear and His Brothers (Baumann, trans), 1962
Bear and the People (Zimnik, trans), 1971
Bear at Friday Creek (Morey), 1971
Bear Called Paddington, The Adventures of a (play; M. Bond), 1974
Bear Circus (du Bois), 1971
Bear Cub (verse; A. Clark), 1965
Bear Goes to Town (Browne), 1982
Bear Hunt (Browne), 1979
Bear on the Motorcycle (Zimnik, trans), 1963
Bear Party (du Bois), 1951
Bear Scare (Burgess), 1961
Bear Shadow (Asch), 1985
Bear Who Had No Place to Go (Stevenson), 1972
Bear Who Liked Hugging People (Ainsworth), 1976
Bear Who Saw the Spring (verse; Kuskin), 1961
Bear Who Stood on His Head (W. Corbett), 1988
Bear Who Wanted to Be a Bear (Müller and Steiner, trans), 1977
Bear Who Wanted to Stay a Bear (Müller and Steiner, trans), 1977
Bear Who Was Too Big (L. Cooper), 1963
Bear, Wolf, and Mouse (Wahl), 1975
Bearcat (A. and E. Johnson), 1960
Bears (Krauss), 1948
Bears and Decoits (Henty, appendix), 1896
Bears Back in Business (M. Baker), 1967
Bear's Bargain (Asch), 1985
Bears' House (Sachs), 1971
Bears of the Air (Arnold Lobel), 1965
Bears on Hemlock Mountain (Dalgliesh), 1952
Bear's Picture (Pinkwater, as Manus Pinkwater), 1972
Bear-y Tale (Browne), 1989
Bearymore (D. Freeman), 1976
Beast Book (verse; Wahl), 1964
Beast Called an Elephant (Stong), 1955
Beast in the Basement (Pilling), 1988
Beast Master (A. Norton), 1959
Beast of Lor (Bulla), 1977
Beast of Monsieur Racine (Ungerer), 1971
Beast on the Brink (Levin), 1980
Beast with the Magical Horn (Cameron), 1963
Beastly Circus (Parish), 1969
Beasts and Nonsense (verse; Ets), 1952
Beat of the City (Brinsmead), 1966
Beat of the Drum (Waddell, as Sefton), 1989
Beat the Turtle Drum (C. Greene), 1976
Beats Me, Claude (Nixon), 1986
Beau of Bath (play; C. D. Mackay), 1915
Beauforts (Meade, appendix), 1900
Beautiful Christmas Tree (Zolotow), 1972
Beautiful Friend (Stolz), 1960
Beautiful Losers (Wersba), 1988
Beautiful Take-Away Palace (Kaye), 1980
Beauty and the Beast (play; Gray), 1950
Beauty and the Beast (play; T. Hughes), 1965
Beauty and the Beast (play; Miller), n.d.
Beauty and the Beast (play; L. Richards), 1916
Beaver Moon (P. Martin, as Miles), 1978
Beaver Valley (Edmonds), 1971
Beaver Water (R. Montgomery), 1956
Because a Little Bug Went Ka-Choo! (verse; Seuss, as Stone), 1975

Because of Madeline (Stolz), 1957
Because of Rosie (de Roo), 1980
Because of the Sand Witches There (M. Steele), 1975
Because We Are (Walter), 1983
Beckoning Lights (M. Hughes), 1982
Beckoning Road (Snedeker), 1929
Bede's Charity (Stretton, appendix), 1872
Bedknob and Broomstick (M. Norton), 1957
Bedtime series (Blyton), 1948
Bedtime Book (Ainsworth), 1974
Bed-time Stories (Blyton), 1942
Bedtime Stories (Scarry), 1978
Bedtime Story-Books series (Burgess), from 1913
Bedtimes and Bullies (play; Foon), 1987
Bee Rustlers (Needle), 1980
Bee Tree (verse; R. N. Peck), 1975
Beechcroft series (Yonge, appendix), from 1847
Beechy of the Harbour School (Brent-Dyer), 1955
Bee-Man of Orn (Stockton, appendix), 1887
Bees on Drumwhinnie (D. Bruce), 1952
Beethoven Medal (Peyton), 1971
Beetle Hunt (Cresswell), 1973
Beetle Who Lived Alone, The Story of the (D. Ross), 1941
Beetles, Lightly Toasted (Naylor), 1987
Befana's Gift (Carlson), 1969
Befana's Toyshop (Rodari, trans), 1970
Before and After (play; A. Fisher), 1945
Before the Dawn (Altsheler), 1903
Before the Wind (R. Armstrong), 1959
Beggar Queen (Alexander), 1984
Beggar's Curse (Pilling, as Cheetham), 1984
Beggar's Daughter (M. Hunt), 1963
Beginners' Love (N. Klein), 1982
Beginning Place (Le Guin), 1980
Begonia for Miss Applebaum (Zindel), 1989
Behave Yourself, Bethany Brant (P. Beatty), 1986
Behind a Mask (Alcott, appendix), 1975
Behind the Attic Wall (Cassedy), 1983
Behind the Bike Sheds (Needle), 1985
Behind the Bike Sheds (play; Needle), 1985
Behind the Blue Gates (Allan), 1972
Behind the Dark Window Shade (Slobodkina), 1958
Behind the Goal (Hardcastle), 1980
Behind the Ranges (Meader), 1947
Behind the Waterfall (Kyle), 1943
Behind the Wind (Wrightson), 1981
Bel Marjory (Meade, appendix), 1878
Bel the Giant (Clarke, as Clare), 1956
Belinda series (Awdry), from 1958
Belinda series (Blyton), from 1949
Belinda and the Swans (verse; Serraillier), 1952
Belinda the Mouse (H. Sewell), 1944
Belinda Treherne (Meade, appendix), 1910
Belinda's New Spring Hat (Clymer), 1969
Bell Family (Streatfeild), 1954
Bell Family series (play; Streatfeild), from 1949
Bell for Ringelblume (Fry), 1957
Bell in the Forest (Suddaby), 1964
Bell of Nendrum (Andrews), 1969
Bell of the Four Evangelists (Needham), 1947
Bell Tree (Hoover), 1982
Bellabelinda and the No-Good Angel (Moray Williams), 1982
Bella's Dragon (Powling), 1988
Belle and Her Dragons (Wynne), 1931
Belle Pruitt (V. Cleaver), 1988
Belling the Tiger (Stolz), 1961

Beyond Silence (Cameron), 1980
Beyond the Back Gate (Parker), 1975
Beyond the Blue Mountains (Meade, appendix), 1893
Beyond the Boundary (Stewart), 1976
Beyond the Burma Road (Westerman), 1949
Beyond the Burning Lands (Christopher), 1971
Beyond the Chocolate War (Cormier), 1985
Beyond the Cross Stitch Mountains (Geras), 1977
Beyond the Dark River (M. Hughes), 1979
Beyond the Desert Gate (Ray), 1977
Beyond the Dragon Prow (Leeson), 1973
Beyond the Firelight (A. Lawrence), 1983
Beyond the Gates of Hercules (de Treviño), 1971
Beyond the Labyrinth (Rubenstein), 1988
Beyond the Mists (Benchley), 1975
Beyond the Narrows (Wardell), 1985
Beyond the Pawpaw Trees (Palmer Brown), 1954
Beyond the Timberland Trail (Chipperfield), 1951
Beyond the Tomorrow Mountains (Engdahl), 1973
Beyond the Weir Bridge (H. Burton), 1970
Beyond the Wide World's End (Reid), 1972
Beyond World's End (Beachcroft), 1985
Bianca (Phipson), 1988
Bib and Bub series (verse; Gibbs), from 1925
Bicentennial Plays and Programs (A. Fisher), 1975
Bicycle Parcel (Bull), 1980
Bicycle Wheel (Ainsworth), 1969
Bid for Safety (Marchant), 1924
Biddy Grant of Craigengill (Stewart), 1979
Biddy's Secret (Oxenham), 1932
Big and Little (Krauss), 1987
Big and Little (Scarry), 1986
Big and Little (verse; W. Smith), 1963
Big Anthony and the Magic Ring (de Paola), 1979
Big Bad Bertie (Waddell), 1984
Big Bad Bruce (Peet), 1977
Big Bad Goat (Rockwell), 1982
Big Ben (D. Walker), 1969
Big Biscuit (Pilling), 1989
Big Blue Island (M. Steele, as Gage), 1964
Big Book of Christmas (play; A. Fisher), 1951
Big Boss (Rockwell), 1975
Big Boy's Work (Seed), 1984
Big Brass Band (Darke), 1976
Big Brass Key (Park), 1983
Big Brother (R. Kraus), 1973
Big Brother (Zolotow), 1960
Big Brother Barges In (play; Latham, as Lee), 1940
Big Brownie (R. Montgomery), 1944
Big Business (R. Bond), 1979
Big Cheese (Bunting), 1977
Big Cheese (Schlein), 1958
Big City (Hader), 1947
Big Doc Bitteroot (Palmer), 1968
Big Dog, Little Dog (verse; M. W. Brown, as MacDonnald), 1943
Big Egg (Mayne), 1967
Big Enough (James), 1931
Big Ethel (T. Ross), 1973
Big Fat Enormous Lie (Sharmat), 1978
Big Find (Bunting), 1978
Big Flood in the Bush (Dallas), 1972
Big Fur Secret (M. W. Brown), 1944
Big Goose and the Little Wild Duck (De Jong), 1938
Big Green Thing (Schlein), 1963
Big Green Umbrella (Coatsworth), 1944
Big Gumbo (verse; W. Smith), 1963

Big House (Mitchison), 1950
Big John Turkle (Hoban), 1983
Big Joke Game (S. Corbett), 1972
Big Lion, Little Lion (Schlein), 1964
Big Loop (Bishop), 1955
Big One (Hardcastle), 1974
Big Orange Splot (Pinkwater), 1977
Big Otter (Ballantyne, appendix), 1887
Big Pile of Dirt (Clymer), 1968
Big Pink (Pilling), 1987
Big Push (B. Baker), 1972
Big Red (Kjelgaard), 1945
Big Red (R. Montgomery), 1971
Big Red Barn (M. W. Brown), 1956
Big, Red Barn (Bunting), 1979
Big Rock Candy (A. and E. Johnson), 1957
Big Sea (R. Armstrong), 1964
Big Sister and Little Sister (Zolotow), 1966
Big Sister Tells Me That I'm Black (verse; Adoff), 1976
Big Six (Ransome), 1940
Big Sneeze (H. Todd), 1980
Big Snow (Hader), 1948
Big Splash (Kendall), 1960
Big Step (Colman), 1957
Big Storm (C. Pullein-Thompson), 1988
Big Surprise (Mitchison), 1967
Big Swim (Mattingley), 1977
Big Talk (Schlein), 1955
Big Test (R. Brown), 1976
Big Tusker (Catherall), 1970
Big Wheel and the Little Wheel (Mayne), 1965
Big World and the Little House (Krauss), 1949
Big Yellow Balloon (Fenton), 1967
Bigfoot Makes a Move (Nixon), 1979
Biggest Bonfire in the World (Kaye), 1985
Biggest House in the World (Lionni), 1968
Biggest Victory (Slote), 1972
Biggest Word Book Ever! (Scarry), 1985
Biggles series (Johns), from 1933
Big-Head (R. Armstrong, as Renton), 1964
Bilbo's Last Song (verse; Tolkien), 1974
Bilgewater (Gardam), 1976
Bill (Tate), 1966
Bill and Pete series (de Paola), from 1977
Bill Badger series (Severn), from 1947
Bill Badger series (Watkins-Pitchford), from 1959
Bill Bergson series (Lindgren, trans), from 1952
Bill Sawyer's V.C. (Strang), 1926
Bill Sturdy (Alger, appendix), 1866
Billa the Wombat Who Had a Bad Dream (L. Rees), 1988
Billabong series (M. Bruce), from 1911
Billety Bill and the Big Brown Bear (Heward), 1937
Billie (Slobodkina), 1959
Billion for Boris (Rodgers), 1974
Billoggs (Tate), 1976
Bill's Balloon Ride (Zimnik, trans), 1973
Bill's New Frock (Fine), 1989
Billy (Schlein), 1966
Billy (Slobodkina),1980
Billy and Betty at the Seaside (Blyton), 1944
Billy and Blaze (Anderson), 1936
Billy and the Unhappy Bull (De Jong), 1946
Billy at St. Bede's (Talbot), 1924
Billy Barcroft (Westerman), 1918
Billy Bedamned, Long Gone By (P. Beatty), 1977
Billy Brown series (de Regniers, as Kitt), from 1961

Billy Bunter series (F. Richards), from 1947
Billy Butter (Hader), 1936
Billy Button's Butter'd Biscuit (M. Hunt), 1941
Billy Mink (Burgess), 1924
Billy of the Wolf Cubs (Talbot), 1930
Billy the Kid (Lipkind, as Will), 1961
Billy the Scout and His Day of Adventures (Talbot), 1918
Billy Topsail series (N. Duncan), from 1906
Billy-Bob Tales (Blyton), 1938
Billy-Boy (Kaye), 1975
Billy's Garden Plot (Praeger), 1918
Billy's Picture (M. Rey), 1948
Bimbo series (Blyton), from 1943
Bindi Must Go (D. Pullein-Thompson), 1962
Binding Spell (Levin), 1984
Bingo Brown series (Byars), from 1988
Binkle and Flip, The Adventures of (Blyton), 1938
Binklebys series (Moray Willams), from 1951
Binky Books (Chaundler), 1920
Biography of a Grizzly (Seton), 1900
Biography of a Silver-Fox (Seton), 1909
Biography of an Arctic Fox (Seton), 1937
Bionic Bunny Show (Marc Brown), 1984
Bird at My Window (Guy), 1966
Bird at the Window (Truss), 1980
Bird Began to Sing (Field), 1932
Bird Fancier (Cresswell), 1971
Bird of Dawning (Masefield), 1933
Bird of the Golden Land (Nye), 1980
Bird of Time (Yolen), 1971
Bird Smugglers (Phipson), 1979
Bird Song (Lattimore), 1968
Birdie's Resolve and How It Was Accomplished (Everett-Green,
    appendix), 1890
Birds (verse; Adoff), 1982
Birds' Christmas Carol (Wiggin), 1887
Birds' Christmas Carol (play; Wiggin), 1914
Birds of Summer (Snyder), 1983
Birds of Thimblepins (M. Baker), 1960
Birdstones (Curry), 1977
Birdy series (Hildick), from 1963
Birdy and Ghosties (Paton Walsh), 1989
Birk the Berserker (R. Klein), 1987
Birkin (Phipson), 1965
Birth of the Firebringer (Pierce), 1985
Birthday (Clewes), 1962
Birthday (Cockett), 1979
Birthday (Steptoe), 1972
Birthday Burglar (Mahy), 1984
Birthday Cow (verse; Merriam), 1978
Birthday Door (Merriam), 1986
Birthday for the Princess (Anita Lobel), 1973
Birthday Kitten (Blyton), 1958
Birthday Moon (verse; L. Duncan), 1989
Birthday of Little Jesus (North), 1952
Birthday of the Infanta (play; S. Walker), 1916
Birthday Party (Krauss), 1957
Birthday Present (P. Martin), 1963
Birthday Present (Strang), 1926
Birthday Presents (Rylant), 1987
Birthday Races (Berg), 1977
Birthday Ride (Cockett), 1965
Birthday Spell (Armitage), 1981
Birthday Tree (P. Fleischman), 1979
Birthday Visit to Holly Farm (Warner, appendix), 1860
Birthday Visitor (Uchida), 1975

Birthday Wish (Iwasaki, trans), 1974
Birthdays for Robin (H. Sewell), 1943
Biscuit-Tin Family (B. Wilson), 1968
Bishop and the Bogie-Man (J. Harris, appendix), 1909
Bishop and the Boogerman (J. Harris, appendix), 1909
Bishop and the Devil (verse; Serraillier), 1971
Bit of Give and Take (Ashley), 1984
Bit of Magic (Clewes), 1967
Bit of Rough Road (Le Feuvre), 1908
Bits and Pieces (Tate), 1967
Bitter Herbs and Honey (Cohen), 1976
Bittern's Nest (Lattimore), 1962
Bixxy and the Secret Message (Slobodkin), 1949
Bizou (N. Klein), 1983
Black and Blue Magic (Snyder), 1966
Black and White (M. W. Brown), 1944
Black Arrow (Stevenson, appendix), 1888
Black Banner series (Trease), from 1950
Black Bar (Fenn, appendix), 1893
Black Beauty series (C., D., and J. Pullein-Thompson), from 1975
Black Beauty (A. Sewell, appendix), 1877
Black Buccaneer (Meader), 1920
Black Car Mystery (Welch), 1950
Black Cauldron (Alexander), 1965
Black Cockatoo (Marchant), 1910
Black Diamonds (Houston), 1982
Black Diamonds (Whitney), 1957
Black Dog (Mattingley), 1979
Black Dolly (Keeping), 1966
Black Falcon (Sperry), 1949
Black Fawn (Kjelgaard), 1958
Black Forest Summer (Allan), 1957
Black Fox of Lorne (de Angeli), 1956
Black Gold (Catherall), 1939
Black Gold (Henry), 1957
Black Hand Gang (Grice), 1971
Black Harvest (Pilling, as Cheetham), 1983
Black Hawk (Westerman), 1934
Black Hearts in Battersea (Aiken), 1964
Black Hunting Whip (M. Edwards), 1950
Black Is Brown Is Tan (verse; Adoff), 1973
Black Ivory (Ballantyne, appendix), 1873
Black Jack (Garfield), 1968
Black Joke (Mowat), 1962
Black Lamb (MacIntyre), 1944
Black Lamp (P. Carter), 1973
Black Madonna (Hope-Simpson), 1976
Black Mountain Mystery (Beresford), 1967
Black Night, Red Morning (Trease), 1944
Black Pearl (O'Dell), 1967
Black Pearl and the Ghost (Myers), 1980
Black Peril (Johns), 1935
Black Polyanthus (Ingelow, appendix), 1903
Black Pony Inn series (C. Pullein-Thompson), from 1976
Black Riders (Needham), 1939
Black Sheep (Merrill), 1969
Black Sheep (Weir), 1963
Black Sheep of Sparshott (F. Richards), 1946
Black Spaniel Mystery (Cavanna), 1945
Black Stallion series (Farley), from 1941
Black Star, Bright Dawn (O'Dell), 1988
Black Steve (Finley, appendix), 1865
Black Symbol (A. and E. Johnson), 1959
Black Tanker (Pease), 1941
Black Tents (play; Means), n.d.
Black Tiger series (Wibberley, as O'Connor), from 1956

Black Tor (Fenn, appendix), 1896
Black Wherry (MacVicar), 1948
Black Wings (Lippincott), 1947
Blackberry Ink (verse; Merriam), 1985
Blackberry's Kitten (L. Cooper), 1961
Blackbird (Southall), 1988
Blackbird in the Lilac (verse; Reeves), 1952
Blackbird Singing (Bunting), 1980
Blackbriar (Sleator), 1972
Blackface Stallion (H. Griffiths), 1980
Blackfeet and the Cree (play; Lillington), 1968
Blackmail Machine (Holman), 1967
Blackout (Rockwell), 1979
Blacksmith at Blueridge (Bunting), 1976
Blacksmith of Vilno (Kelly), 1930
Blackspit Smugglers (Dawlish, as Kerr), 1935
Blacky the Crow (Burgess), 1922
Blade of the Poisoner (D. Hill), 1987
Blaine's Way (M. Hughes), 1986
Blair's Nightmare (Snyder), 1984
Blanche (Molesworth, appendix), 1893
Blanket Word (Arundel), 1973
Blaze series (Anderson), from 1936
Blaze at Broadfurrow Farm (Severn), 1955
Blemyahs (Mayne), 1987
Blewcoat Boy (Garfield), 1988
Blind Colt (Rounds), 1941
Blind Connemara (Anderson), 1971
Blind Outlaw (Rounds), 1980
Blinky Bill series (Wall), from 1933
Blitzcat (Westall), 1989
Blodwen (T. Ross), 1973
Blood and Thunder Adventure on Hurricane Peak (Mahy), 1989
Blood Bay Colt (Farley), 1950
Blood Brothers (Gordon), 1989
Blood Feud (Sutcliff), 1977
Blood Money (Hardcastle), 1971
Blood of the Brave (B. Baker), 1966
Blood Red Ochre (Major), 1989
Blood Royal (Weir), 1973
Bloodhound Gang's Secret Code Book (S. Fleischman), 1983
Blooding (Wheatley), 1987
Bloody Country (Collier), 1976
Bloody L.I.A.R.S. (verse; Rosen), 1984
Blossom Culp series (R. Peck), from 1983
Blossoms series (Byars), from 1986
Blow for Liberty (Meader), 1965
Blow the Man Down (Vipont, as C. Vipont), 1939
Blowfish Live in the Sea (Fox), 1970
Blown to Bits (Ballantyne, appendix), 1889
Bloxworth Blue (Corlett), 1984
Blubber (Blume), 1974
Blue above the Trees (M. Clark), 1967
Blue and Gold Day (Balderson), 1979
Blue and Red (verse; Ewing, appendix), 1883
Blue Aunt (E. O. White), 1918
Blue Baby (Molesworth, appendix), 1901
Blue Balloon (Asch), 1971
Blue Barns (H. Sewell), 1933
Blue Beans (play; Ridge), 1953
Blue Bells on the Lea (verse; Ewing, appendix), 1884
Blue Bird (F. French), 1972
Blue Boat (Bruna, trans), 1984
Blue Boat (Mayne), 1957
Blue Book (Mayne), 1984
Blue Canyon Horse (A. Clark), 1954

Blue Castle (L. Montgomery), 1926
Blue Diamond (Meade, appendix), 1901
Blue Door Venture (Pamela Brown), 1949
Blue Dragon Days (Allan), 1958
Blue Fin (Thiele), 1969
Blue Hawk (Dickinson), 1976
Blue Hills (Goudge), 1942
Blue Jackal (Marcia Brown), 1977
Blue Jackets (Fenn, appendix), 1893
Blue Lights (Ballantyne, appendix), 1888
Blue Misty Monsters (Waddell, as Sefton), 1985
Blue Moon Day (Prince), 1988
Blue Moose (Pinkwater, as M. Pinkwater), 1975
Blue Murder (play; Lillington), 1960
Blue of the Sea (Meade, appendix), 1909
Blue Rabbit (Kaye), 1967
Blue Raider (Strang), 1919
Blue Rhyme Book (Fyleman), 1933
Blue Ribbon Beth (Donkin), 1951
Blue Ribbon Puppies (C. Johnson), 1958
Blue Ridge Billy (Lenski), 1946
Blue Spring Farm (Bishop), 1948
Blue Stars Watching (P. Beatty), 1969
Blue Stone (R. Kennedy), 1976
Blue Story Book (Blyton), 1945
Blue Streak and Doctor Medusa (R. Montgomery), 1946
Blue Sword (McKinley), 1982
Blue Teapot (Dalgliesh), 1931
Blue Thing (Pinkwater), 1977
Blue Trees, Red Sky (N. Klein), 1975
Blue Two—Bale Out! (Hamre, trans), 1961
Blue Umbrella (R. Bond), 1974
Blue Veil and Black Gold (Catherall, as Maine), 1961
Blue Willow (Gates), 1940
Bluebeard (play; L. Richards), 1916
Bluebeard (play; Wiggin), 1914
Bluebell Story Book (Blyton), 1949
Blueberries for Sal (McCloskey), 1948
Blueberry Corners (Lenski), 1940
Blueberry Mountain series (Meader), from 1941
Bluebirds over Pit Row (Cresswell), 1972
Bluecap and Bimbi (L. Rees), 1948
Blue-Eyed Daisy (Rylant), 1985
Bluegate Girl (Allan), 1961
Bluejay Borders (Keith), 1972
Bluenose Pirate (F. Knight), 1956
Blue's Broken Heart (Merrill), 1960
Blues I Can Whistle (A. and E. Johnson, as A.E. Johnson), 1969
Blunderbus (McGinley), 1951
Blundering Bettina (Wynne), 1924
Boastful Rabbit (Manning-Sanders), 1978
Boat Book (Marc Brown), 1982
Boat Girl (Cockett), 1972
Boat in the Reeds (Stewart), 1960
Boat Seekers (Pardoe), 1953
Boats Finds a House (Chalmers), 1958
Boats on the River (Flack), 1946
Bob (L. Hall), 1974
Bob and Bill (Everett-Green, appendix), 1901
Bob Bodden series (Coatsworth), from 1968
Bob Burton (Alger, appendix), 1888
Bob, Son of Battle (Ollivant), 1898
Bob Strickland's Log (Westerman), 1953
Bob White, The Adventures of (Burgess), 1919
Bob-a-Job (L. Cooper), 1963
Bobbety the Brownie (Wynne), 1930

Boy at the Window (Hildick), 1960
Boy Blue's Book of Beasts (verse; W. Smith), 1957
Boy Called Fish (A. Morgan), 1973
Boy Captain (Otis, appendix), 1896
Boy Castaways of Black Lake Island (Barrie), 1901
Boy Fortune Hunters series (Baum, as Akers), from 1908
Boy from Nowhere (Weir), 1966
Boy Had a Mother Who Bought Him a Hat (verse; Kuskin), 1976
Boy in a Barn (Moray Williams), 1970
Boy in Eirinn (Colum), 1913
Boy in Red (Needham), 1948
Boy in the Drawer (Munsch), 1982
Boy in the Off-White Hat (L. Hall), 1984
Boy into Action (Parker), 1975
Boy Jacko (Dawlish), 1962
Boy Knight (Henty, appendix), 1882
Boy Next Door (Blyton), 1944
Boy Next Door (Cavanna), 1956
Boy Next Door (play; Lillington), 1968
Boy of Old Prague (Ish-Kishor), 1963
Boy of Taché (Blades), 1973
Boy of the Islands (Lipkind), 1954
Boy on a Brown Horse (Weir), 1967
Boy on a White Giraffe (Catherall, as Hallard), 1969
Boy on the Roof (MacPherson), 1974
Boy like Walt (Clewes), 1967
Boy Lost on Tropic Coast (L. Rees), 1968
Boy Scouts series (Burgess), from 1912
Boy Scouts series (Otis, appendix), from 1911
Boy, The Cat, and the Magic Fiddle (de Regniers, as Kitt), 1964
Boy, The Rat, and the Butterfly (de Regniers), 1971
Boy They Made King (Daniell), 1959
Boy Who Came Back (Blyton), 1965
Boy Who Came to Stay (D. Pullein-Thomson), 1960
Boy Who Could Find Anything (Nixon), 1978
Boy Who Could Fly (Newman), 1967
Boy Who Couldn't Make Up His Mind (Colman), 1965
Boy Who Didn't Believe in Spring (Clifton), 1973
Boy Who Fooled the Giant (de Regniers, as Kitt), 1963
Boy Who Forgot His Birthday (Frank, trans), 1985
Boy Who Had No Birthday (M. Hunt), 1935
Boy Who Had No Heart (Petersham), 1955
Boy Who Had Wings (Yolen), 1974
Boy Who Loved the Sea (Wersba), 1961
Boy Who Reversed Himself (Sleator), 1986
Boy Who Saw God (Greenwood), 1980
Boy Who Spoke Chimp (Yolen), 1981
Boy Who Walked on Air (S. Corbett), 1975
Boy Who Wanted a Dog (Blyton), 1963
Boy Who Wanted to Go Fishing (Kaye), 1960
Boy Who Was Afraid (Sperry), 1942
Boy Who Was Followed Home (Mahy), 1975
Boy Who Wasn't Lonely (Parker), 1964
Boy Who Would Not Learn (Strang), 1915
Boy with a Harpoon (Lipkind), 1952
Boy with a Pack (Meader), 1939
Boy with an "R" in His Hand (Reaney), 1965
Boy with the Bronze Axe (Fidler), 1968
Boy with the Erpingham Hood (Clarke), 1956
Boy with the Green Thumb (B. Todd), 1956
Boy with the Helium Head (Naylor), 1982
Boy with the Loaves and Fishes (Blyton), 1948
Boy with the Parrot (Coatsworth), 1930
Boy with the Snowgrass Hair (Locke), 1976
Boy with Two Shadows (Mahy), 1971
Boy with Will Power (S. Corbett), 1975

Boy Without a Name (Lively), 1975
Boys (Gray), 1968
Boy's Adventure (Twain, appendix), 1928
Boys and I (Molesworth, appendix), 1882
Boys and Girls and Gods (Mitchison), 1931
Boys and Girls Book (Bestall), 1935
Boys' and Girls' Circus Book (Blyton), 1939
Boys and Girls Come Out to Play (Clewes), 1964
Boys and Girls, Girls and Boys (Merriam), 1972
Boys and Girls of History series (Power), from 1926
Boys' and Girls' Story Book (Blyton), 1940
Boys Are Awful (verse; McGinley), 1962
Boy's Fortune (Alger, appendix), 1898
Boys from the Café (C. Pullein-Thompson), 1965
Boys of Menhardoc (Fenn, appendix), 1884
Boys of '98 (Otis, appendix), 1898
Boys of 1745 at the Capture of Louisbourg (Otis, appendix), 1895
Boys of the Light Brigade (Strang), 1904
Boys of the "Puffin" (Westerman), 1925
Boys of the Red House (Everett-Green, appendix), 1902
Boys' Revolt (Otis, appendix), 1894
Boy's Will (Haugaard), 1983
Bracken My Dog (Barne), 1949
Brady (Fritz), 1960
Braganza Diamond (Otis, appendix), 1891
Brainbox Cracks the Case (Nöstlinger, trans), 1985
Brainbox Sorts It Out (Nöstlinger, trans), 1985
Brainstorm (Myers), 1977
Bran Tub (D. Ross), 1954
Branch Line (Clewes), 1963
Branch Line Engines (Awdry), 1961
Brand-New Uncle (Seredy), 1961
Brassman's Secret (Asare), 1981
Brats (verse; X. Kennedy), 1986
Brave and Bold (Alger, appendix), 1874
Brave Balloon of Benjamin Buckley (Wersba), 1963
Brave Buffalo Fighter (Fitzgerald), 1973
Brave Irene (Steig), 1986
Brave Little Cousin (Marchant), 1902
Brave Little Royalist (Moore), 1913
Brave Little Tailor (play; A. Harris), 1960
Brave Nurse (Mitchison), 1977
Brave Poor Thing (Meade, appendix), 1900
Brave with Ben (Mattingley), 1982
Bravest Girl in the School (Talbot), 1924
Bravest of the Brave (Henty, appendix), 1886
Bread and Honey (Asch), 1981
Bread and Honey (Southall), 1970
Bread Bin (Aiken), 1974
Breadhorse (Garner), 1975
Break a Leg! (W. Taylor), 1987
Break a Leg, Betsy Maybe! (Kingman), 1976
Break for Summer (Meynell), 1965
Break in the Sun (Ashley), 1980
Break of Dark (Westall), 1982
Breakaway (Hardcastle), 1976
Breaking Up (N. Klein), 1980
Breaktime (Chambers), 1978
Breath of Fresh Air (Cavanna), 1966
Breath of Fresh Air (Kaye), 1987
Breed to Come (A. Norton), 1972
Brenda and the Babes (Peacocke), 1927
Brenda of Beech House (Moore), 1927
Brenda the Bold (Ure), 1986
Brendon Chase (Watkins-Pitchford), 1944
Brer Rabbit (Blyton), 1942

Brer Rabbit and Mr. Dog (play; Blyton), 1939
Brewing of Brains (play; C. D. Mackay), 1910
Brick Street Boys series (Ahlberg), from 1975
Bridal Gown (D. Ross), 1952
Bride at Eighteen (Colman), 1966
Bride Price (Emecheta), 1976
Bridesmaid (B. Willard), 1976
Bridesmaids (Pamela Brown), 1956
Bridesmaids (Cockett), 1988
Bridge of Friendship (Allan), 1975
Bridge to Terabithia (Paterson), 1977
Bridge under the Water (Meynell), 1954
Bridge-Builders (Sutcliff), 1959
Bridget and the Bees, The Tale of (Wall), 1934
Bridget and William (Gardam), 1981
Bridget's Quarter Deck (Le Feuvre), 1905
Bridle the Wind (Aiken), 1983
Brief Garland (Keith), 1971
Bright and Morning Star (R. Harris), 1972
Bright April (de Angeli), 1946
Bright Candles (Benchley), 1974
Bright High Flyer (M. Baker), 1957
Bright Hunter of the Skies (Best), 1961
Bright Ideas (Strang), 1920
Bright Lights Blaze Out (verse; Owen), 1986
Bright Morning (Bianco), 1942
Bright Shadow (Avi), 1985
Bright Story Book (Blyton), 1952
Bright-Eye (A. Morgan), 1984
Brighty of the Grand Canyon (Henry), 1953
Brigid and the Cub (E. Turner), 1919
Brillstone series (Heide), from 1977
Bring Out Your Dead (play; Lillington), 1967
Bringing Back the Frasers (Talbot), 1926
Broad Atlantic (verse; L. Clark), 1974
Brock and the Dragon (R. Klein), 1984
Brock the Badger series (Uttley), from 1939
Broderick (Ormondroyd), 1969
Brogeen series (Lynch), from 1947
Broken Basket (Finley, appendix), 1870
Broken Fang (R. Montgomery), 1935
Broken Saddle (Aldridge), 1982
Broken Spear (Seed), 1972
Broken Statue (play; Blyton), 1927
Bronto's Wings (McKee), 1964
Bronze Bow (Speare), 1961
Bronze Chrysanthemum (S. Porter), 1961
Bronze Sword (Treece), 1965
Bronze Trumpeter (Nimmo), 1975
Brooklyn Story (Mathis), 1970
Brookside Farm-House (Finley, appendix), 1865
Broom-Adelaide (B.C. Freeman), 1963
Broomsticks (de la Mare), 1925
Broomtail Bronc (P. Martin), 1965
Brother Dusty-Feet (Sutcliff), 1952
Brother in the Land (Swindells), 1984
Brother or Husband (Meade, appendix), 1909
Brother Raimon Returns (Stewart), 1978
Brother to the Wind (Walter), 1985
Brothers in Fur (E. O. White), 1910
Brothers Lionheart (Lindgren, trans), 1975
Brothers of Pity (Ewing, appendix), 1882
Brothers of the Heart (Blos), 1985
Brothers of the Wind (Yolen), 1981
Brought Home (Stretton, appendix), 1875
Brown (Moore), 1905

Brown Cow (Branfield), 1983
Brown Family (Blyton), 1945
Brown Land Was Green (M. Clark), 1956
Brown Land Was Green (play; M. Clark), 1961
Brown Mouse Book (Uttley), 1971
Brown of Moukden (Strang), 1905
Brown Satchel Mystery (Cavanna, as Allen), 1954
Brownie (Le Feuvre), 1900
Brownie (Wall), 1935
Brownie Island (Talbot), 1935
Brownie Pack (Talbot), 1932
Brownie Tales (Blyton), 1964
Brownie series (verse; Cox, appendix), from 1887
Brownies (Ewing, appendix), 1870
Brownies All! (Talbot), 1931
Brownies at St. Bride's (Talbot), 1928
Brownies in Fairyland (play; Cox, appendix), 1925
Brownsea Silver (Peyton), 1964
Brownsmith's Boy (Fenn, appendix), 1885
Bruce (Terhune), 1920
Brumby series (Patchett), from 1958
Brumby Racer (Mitchell), 1981
Bruno (Abbott, appendix), 1854
Bruno and Bimba (Everett-Green, appendix), 1900
Brydons series (Fidler), from 1946
Bubbles (Greenfield), 1972
Bubo the Great Horned Owl (George), 1954
Buccaneer Explorer (Syme), 1960
Buccaneers of Boya (Westerman), 1925
Buckboard Stranger (Meader), 1954
Buckinghams series (Saville), from 1952
Buckskin Brigade (Kjelgaard), 1947
Buckskin Colonist (Hayes), 1947
Buddy and the Old Pro (Tunis), 1955
Budgerigar Blue (Mattingley), 1977
Budgie Said Grrrrr (Waddell), 1985
Buff (Terhune), 1921
Buffalo and Beaver (Meader), 1960
Buffalo Bill (play; A. Harris), 1953
Buffalo Caller (A. Clarke), 1942
Buffalo Harvest (Rounds), 1952
Buffalo Knife (W. Steele), 1952
Buffalo Runners (Ballantyne, appendix), 1891
Buford the Little Bighorn (Peet), 1967
Bugbear (Storr), 1981
Bugles in the Hills (Hayes), 1955
Builder of the Moon (Wynne-Jones), 1989
Building Blocks (Voigt), 1984
Building the Empire (Westerman), 1914
Bulbs and Blossoms (Le Feuvre), 1898
Bull Beneath the Walnut Tree (Hewett), 1966
Bull Leapers (J. Watson), 1970
Bull Patrol (Catherall), 1949
Bulldog Breed (Westerman), 1939
Bulldozer (Meader), 1951
Bullerby series (Lindgren, trans), from 1962
Bullwhip Griffin (S. Fleischman), 1967
Bumble Bugs and Elephants (M. W. Brown), 1938
Bumblebee Flies Anyway (Cormier), 1983
Bumblebee's Secret (Schlein), 1958
Bumblebuzz (Fry), 1938
Bump in the Night (Rockwell), 1979
Bumpy and His Bus (Blyton), 1949
Bumpy the Car (R. Kraus), 1985
Bumpy's Holiday (Biro), 1943
Bun (Lippincott), 1918

Cat (P. Martin), 1974
Cat (play; Streatfeild), 1934
Cat! (Westall), 1989
Cat among the Pigeons (verse; Wright), 1987
Cat and Canary (Foreman), 1984
Cat and Dog (Minarik), 1960
Cat and Mrs. Cary (Gates), 1962
Cat and the Captain, (Coatsworth), 1927
Cat and the Castle (Cockett), 1982
Cat and the Fiddle (Clarke, as Clare), 1968
Cat and the Kitten (Hader), 1940
Cat Ate My Gymsuit (Danziger), 1974
Cat Call (L. Lawrence), 1980
Cat Called Amnesia (Hildick), 1976
Cat Club series (Averill), from 1944
Cat Country (Tate), 1979
Cat, Herself (M. Hunter), 1986
Cat in Fairyland (Blyton), 1949
Cat in Search of a Friend (Asare), 1986
Cat in the Hat series (verse; Seuss), from 1957
Cat in the Hat (play; Seuss), 1971
Cat in the Mirror (Stolz), 1975
Cat Named Sneakers, Seven Stories about a (M. W. Brown), 1955
Cat of Bubastes (Henty, appendix), 1888
Cat on a Houseboat (Desai), 1976
Cat Princess (play; Lillington), 1967
Cat Stories (Coatsworth), 1953
Cat Tales (Nesbit), 1904
Cat That Walked a Week (De Jong), 1943
Cat Walk (Stolz), 1983
Cat Who Liked to Pretend (Chalmers), 1959
Cat Who Went to Heaven (Coatsworth), 1930
Cat Who Wished to Be a Man (Alexander), 1973
Catalina (Meade, appendix), 1896
Catalogue of the Universe (Mahy), 1985
Catch (Hardcastle), 1974
Catch a Little Fox (verse; de Regniers), 1970
Catch a Little Rhyme (verse; Merriam), 1966
Catch as Catch Can (M. Baker), 1982
Catch as Catch Can (Poole), 1969
Catch Calico! (Aaron), 1979
Catch Colt (O'Hara), 1979
Catch Colt (play; O'Hara), 1964
Catch Kandy (play; Norman), 1973
Catch Me and Kiss Me and Say It Again (verse; C. Watson), 1978
Catch the Light (verse; Scannell), 1982
Catch Your Death (Gordon), 1984
Catchpenny Street (Cavanna, as Headley), 1951
Catchpole Story (Storr), 1965
Caterpillar Hall (Barrett), 1950
Catfang (Fisk), 1980
Catfish Bend series (Burman), from 1952
Cathedral Courtship (Wiggin), 1893
Cathedral Wednesday (Mayne), 1960
Cathie Runs Wild (Lyon), 1960
Cathleen with a "C" (Peacocke), 1934
Cathy and Lisette (Colman, as Crayder), 1964
Cathy Is Company (Lexau), 1961
Catrin in Wales (Allan), 1959
Catriona (Stevenson, appendix), 1893
Cats (Phipson), 1976
Cats' Burglar (Parish), 1983
Cats Cats Cats Cats Cats (verse; de Regniers), 1958
Cats from Summer Island (Unnerstad, trans), 1963
Cat's Magic (Greaves), 1980
Cats of Honeytown (M. Baker), 1962

Cats of Seroster (Westall), 1984
Cats' Opera (Dillon), 1962
Cats' Opera (play; Dillon), 1981
Catseye (A. Norton), 1961
Catspaw (Fuller), 1966
Catwings series (Le Guin), from 1988
Caught in the Act (Nixon), 1988
Caught on a Tree Stump (Cockett), 1972
Caught Out (H. Avery), 1919
Caught Out (Hardcastle), 1983
Cautionary Tales for Children (verse; Belloc), 1907
Cautionary Verses (Belloc), 1939
Cave (Church), 1950
Cave (Coatsworth), 1958
Cave above Delphi (S. Corbett), 1965
Cave by the Sea (Meynell, as Tring), 1950
Cave in the Hills (Strang), 1922
Cave of Death (Serraillier), 1965
Cave of Ghosts (Coatsworth), 1971
Cave of the "Cormorant" (Catherall), 1973
Cave of the Hammers (MacVicar), 1968
Cave Perilous (Meade, appendix), 1898
Caves of Fire and Ice (S. Murphy), 1980
Caves of Klydor (D. Hill), 1984
Caves of Night (Christopher), 1958
Caxton's Challenge (Harnett), 1960
Cay (T. Taylor), 1969
Cayuse Courage (Lampman), 1970
Cecily (Holland), 1967
Cecily G. and the Nine Monkeys (H.A. and M. Rey), 1942
Cecily Parsley's Nursery Rhymes (verse; Potter), 1922
Cecily's Highwayman (Moore), 1914
Cedar's Boy (Meader), 1949
Cedric and the North End Kids (B. Freeman), 1978
Celandine's Secret (play; Barne), 1914
Celebrations (verse; Livingston), 1985
Celery Stalks at Midnight (Howe), 1983
Censored (Stong), 1945
Centerburg Tales (McClosky), 1951
Centurian (Treece), 1967
Ceol na Coille (Dillon), 1955
Cerdic the Saxon (Strang), 1913
Ceremony of Innocence (Highwater), 1985
Certain Courage (G. Cooper), 1975
Certain Magic (Orgel), 1976
Certain Small Shepherd (Caudill), 1965
Chad (Meynell, as Tring), 1966
Chadwick's Chimney (Thiele), 1979
Chaga (Lipkind, as Will), 1955
Chair for My Mother (V. Williams), 1982
Chair Person (Jones), 1989
Chalet School series (Brent-Dyer), from 1925
Chalk Box Kid (Bulla), 1987
Chalk Box Story (D. Freeman), 1976
Challenge in the Dark (Leeson), 1978
Challenge of the Green Knight (verse; Serraillier), 1966
Challenge to Adventure (Atkinson), 1942
Chalou (Carlson), 1967
Champion Dog, Prince Tom (Fritz), 1958
Champion of Olympia (Guillot, trans), 1968
Champion of the Main (Johns), 1938
Champion's Choise (Tunis), 1940
Chance Child (Paton Walsh), 1978
Chance of Treasure (Patchett), 1957
Chancy and the Grand Rascal (S. Fleischman), 1966
Chandler Chipmunk's Flying Lesson (P. Martin), 1960

Change in the Wind (Naylor), 1980
Change of Heart (play; Lenski), 1952
Change-Child (Curry), 1969
Changeling (Mayne), 1961
Changeling (Snyder), 1970
Changeling (Sutcliff), 1974
Changeling of Monte Lucio (Needham), 1946
Changeling Sea (McKillip), 1988
Changeover (Mahy), 1984
Changes (Dickinson), 1975
Changes, Changes (Hutchins), 1971
Changes for the Challoners (Allan), 1955
Changing Maze (Snyder), 1985
Changing of the Guard (H. Todd), 1978
Changing Times (Kennemore), 1984
Chanticleer (Duvoisin), 1947
Chantry House (Yonge, appendix), 1886
Chap-Book of Rounds (verse; Farjeon), 1919
Chaplain's Craze (Fenn, appendix), 1886
Chaplet of Pearls (Yonge, appendix), 1868
Chappie (Heward), 1945
Chappie and the Others (Heward), 1926
Chapter of Adventures (Henty, appendix), 1890
Charge (Fenn, appendix), 1900
Charge Fulfilled (Molesworth, appendix), 1886
Chariot in the Sky (Bontemps), 1951
Charity at Home (B. Willard), 1965
Charlemagne and His Court (play; Mitchison), 1937
Charles series (Ainsworth), from 1954
Charles Arriving (Pardoe), 1954
Charley series (Jackson), from 1945
Charley (Robinson), 1969
Charley, Charlotte, and the Golden Canary (Keeping), 1967
Charley Skedaddle (P. Beatty), 1987
Charlie series (Dahl), from 1964
Charlie Chumbles (Sleigh), 1977
Charlie Codman's Cruise (Alger, appendix), 1866
Charlie, Emma series (Greaves), from 1980
Charlie Lewis Plays for Time (Kemp), 1984
Charlie Meadows (Hoban), 1983
Charlie Moon series (S. Hughes), from 1980
Charlie Needs a Cloak (de Paola), 1974
Charlie the Tramp (Hoban), 1967
Charlie to the Rescue (Ballantyne, appendix), 1890
Charlie Yup and His Snip-Snap Boys (Flora), 1959
Charlie's House (Bulla), 1983
Charlotte and Henry, The Adventures of (B. Graham), 1987
Charlotte and the White Horse (Krauss), 1955
Charlotte Sometimes (Farmer), 1969
Charlotte's Web (E.B. White), 1952
Charmed Life (Jones), 1977
Charming Sally (Otis, appendix), 1898
Charming Taxi-cab (Drummond), 1947
Chartbreak (Cross), 1986
Chartbreaker (Cross), 1987
Chartered Company (H. Avery), 1915
Chase (Hardcastle), 1974
Chase Me, Catch Nobody! (Haugaard), 1980
Chase Through the Night (Fatchen), 1977
Chased Through Norway (Otis, appendix), 1899
Chasing a Yacht (Otis, appendix), 1894
Chasing after Annie (Sharmat), 1981
Chasing Game (Hardcastle), 1968
Chasing the "Pleiad" (Westerman), 1933
Chasing the Sun (Ballantyne, appendix), 1864
Chastity Pewke, Adventures of (play; Lillington), 1972

Chateau by the Lake (Le Feuvre), 1907
Chatterbooks (Berg), 1981
Chatterbox (Thwaite), 1978
Chatterer, The Red Squirrel, The Adventures of (Burgess), 1915
Cheap Jack (Yonge, appendix), 1881
Cheapjack Man (Tate), 1969
Checoba (Chipperfield), 1964
Cheerful (Palmer Brown), 1957
Cheerful Heart (Vining, as Gray), 1959
Cheerio! (Blyton), 1933
Cheerleader (N. Klein), 1985
Cheery Scarecrow (Gruelle), 1929
Cheery Tales series (Heward), 1920
Cheese (Waber), 1967
Cheltenham's Party (Wahl), 1985
Cherokee Run (Smucker), 1957
Cherokee Strip (A. Fisher), 1956
Cherries and Cherry Pits (V. Williams), 1986
Cherries and Cherry Stones (V. Williams), 1987
Cherry (Le Feuvre), 1901
Cherry Ann and the Dragon Horse (Coatsworth), 1955
Cherry Stones (Ainsworth), 1960
Cherry Tree (R. Bond), 1980
Cherry Tree (Le Feuvre), 1901
Cherry Tree Party (Unnerstad, trans), 1978
Cherrystones (verse; Farjeon), 1942
Cherrywinkle (Fry), 1951
Chester (Clymer), 1954
Chester (Hoff), 1961
Chester Cricket series (Selden), from 1981
Chester Rand (Alger, appendix), 1903
Chester the Worldly Pig (Peet), 1965
Chesterton Girl Graduates (Meade, appendix), 1913
Chestnut Filly (Cumming), 1940
Chestnut Man (play; Fyleman), 1938
Chestnut Soldier (Nimmo), 1989
Chestry Oak (Seredy), 1948
Chicano Girl (Colman), 1973
Chicken Forgets (P. Martin, as Miles), 1976
Chicken Run (play; Chambers), 1967
Chicken Soup with Rice (verse; Sendak), 1962
Chief (Bonham), 1971
Chief of the Herd (Mukerji), 1929
Chief's Daughter (Sutcliff), 1967
Chik and the Bottle House (Kaye), 1965
Chike and the River (Achebe), 1966
Child Is Born (play; Chaundler), 1949
Child of Air (D. Ross), 1957
Child of Ebenezer (Bull), 1974
Child of Fire (O'Dell), 1974
Child of the Children (Turner), 1959
Child of the Owl (Yep), 1977
Child of the Western Isles (Fry), 1957
Child Whispers (verse; Blyton), 1922
Child Without a Name (Everett-Green, appendix), 1887
Children at Green Meadows (Blyton), 1954
Children by the Sea (Manning-Sanders), 1938
Children Come Running (verse; Coatsworth), 1960
Children I Have Known (Burnett), 1892
Children in the Bush (Dallas), 1969
Children Next Door (Sharp), 1974
Children of Ananse (Appiah), 1968
Children of Atlantis (Harding), 1976
Children of Camp Fortuna (play; Pamela Brown), 1949
Children of Charlecote (Pearce), 1989
Children of Cherry Tree Farm (Blyton), 1940

Children of Christmas (Rylant), 1987
Children of Clearwater Bay (Ellin), 1969
Children of Cloverly (Stretton, appendix), 1865
Children of Crooked Castle (O'Faolain), 1945
Children of Kidillin (Blyton, as Pollock), 1940
Children of Morrow (Hoover), 1973
Children of Primrose Lane (Streatfeild), 1941
Children of the Book (P. Carter), 1982
Children of the Castle (Molesworth, appendix), 1890
Children of the Crescent (Le Feuvre), 1923
Children of the Dust (L. Lawrence), 1985
Children of the Ferry (Strang), 1926
Children of the Forge (McCaughren), 1985
Children of the Fox (Paton Walsh), 1978
Children of the House (Pearce), 1968
Children of the Marshes (Moore), 1927
Children of the Mayflower (Vipont), 1969
Children of the New Forest (Marryat, appendix), 1847
Children of the Northlights (d'Aulaire), 1935
Children of the Plague (Oldfield), 1979
Children of the Promise (Means), 1941
Children of the Red King (Polland), 1960
Children of the Turnpike (Kaye), 1976
Children of the Wild (C. Roberts), 1913
Children of the Wind (G. Harris), 1982
Children of the Wolf (Yolen), 1984
Children of Wilton Chase (Meade, appendix), 1891
Children of Winter (Doherty), 1985
Children on the Moon (play; Hoff), 1973
Children on the Oregon Trail (Loeff, trans), 1961
Children on the Top Floor (Streatfeild), 1964
Children on Troublemaker Street (Lindgren, trans), 1962
Children Who Got Married (R. Kraus), 1969
Children Who Lived in a Barn (E. Graham), 1938
Children Who Stayed Behind (B. Carter), 1964
Children's Bells (verse; Farjeon), 1957
Children's Book (play; Latham as Lee), 1933
Children's Crusade (Everett-Green, appendix), 1904
Children's Crusade (Treece), 1958
Children's Garden (Blyton), 1935
Children's Hour series (Chaundler), from 1938
Children's Hour (Molesworth, appendix), 1899
Children's Kingdom (Meade, appendix), 1878
Children's Matinée (play; Streatfeild), 1934
Children's Morning Message (Le Feuvre), 1905
Children's Pilgrimage (Meade, appendix), 1883
Children's Story (play; Selden), 1966
Children's War (T. Taylor), 1971
Child's Book of Dreams (de Regniers), 1957
Child's Day (verse; de la Mare), 1912
Child's Garden of Verses (verse; Stevenson, appendix), 1885
Child's Good Morning (verse; M. W. Brown), 1952
Child's Good Night Book (M. W. Brown), 1943
Child's Journey with Dickens (Wiggin), 1912
Child's Play (play; L. Richards), 1915
Child's Year-Book (verse; Sawyer), 1917
Chill in the Lane (Allan), 1974
Chiltern Adventure (Allan), 1950
Chimney Corner series (Blyton), from 1946
Chimney Cottage (Atkinson), 1947
Chimney Farm Bedtime Stories (Coatsworth), 1966
Chimney Sweeps' Holiday (play; Field), 1930
Chin Chiang and the Dragon's Dance (Wallace), 1984
China Dog (Vipont), 1967
China People (Farmer), 1960
China Quest (E. Lewis), 1937

China Sea Jigsaw (Catherall), 1961
Chinaman's Reef is Ours (Southall), 1970
Chinese Boy (D. Martin), 1973
Chinese Daughter (Lattimore), 1960
Chinese Egg (Storr), 1975
Ching (Fenn, appendix), 1901
Chinigchinich (play; Wymark), 1973
Chip (Kjelgaard), 1950
Chip Has Many Brothers (Baumann, trans), 1985
Chipmunk in the Forest (Clymer), 1965
Chipo and the Bird on the Hill (Asare), 1984
Chips series (R. Brown), from 1979
Chips series (S. Hughes), from 1985
Chips' Comic (play; D. Wood), 1984
Chisel (Le Feuvre), 1919
Chisel-Tooth (Lippincott), 1936
Chish and Fips (play; D. Wood), 1980
Chish 'n' Fips (D. Wood), 1987
Chish 'n' Fips (play; D. Wood), 1984
Chit-Chat (Ballantyne, appendix), 1857
Chivalrous Fifth (Chaundler), 1927
Chocolate Boy (Trease), 1975
Chocolate War (Cormier), 1974
Choice of Chums (H. Avery), 1922
Choill Bheo (Dillon), 1948
Choo Choo (V. Burton), 1937
Choo-Me-Choo (Holling), 1928
Choosing Book (Dalgliesh), 1932
Chop-Chin and the Golden Dragon (L. Richards), 1899
Choristers' Cake (Mayne), 1956
Chortles (verse; Merriam), 1989
Christabel (A. Morgan), 1984
Christabel Jane and Chirpy series (Heward), 1955
Christie (Walton, appendix), 1896
Christie's Old Organ (Walton, appendix), 1874
Christina and the Boys (Le Feuvre), 1906
Christmas Angel (verse; Robinson, as Thomas), 1961
Christmas Anna Angel (Sawyer), 1944
Christmas at Deacon Hackett's (Otis, appendix), 1899
Christmas at Holford (Wynne), 1922
Christmas at Spindle Bottom (Allan), 1970
Christmas at the Rose and Crown (Uttley), 1950
Christmas Bells (Seed), 1987
Christmas Bells and Snowflakes (verse; Heide), 1971
Christmas Book (Bruna, trans), 1976
Christmas Box (Merriam), 1985
Christmas Bunny (Lipkind, as Will), 1953
Christmas Cake in Search of Its Owner (Duvoisin), 1941
Christmas Card (Andrew), 1966
Christmas Carol (play; Latham, as Lee), 1931
Christmas Cat (Geras), 1983
Christmas Cat (Holland), 1987
Christmas Child (Molesworth, appendix), 1880
Christmas Child (Stretton, appendix), 1888
Christmas Children (Moore), 1909
Christmas Cookie Sprinkle Snitcher (R. Kraus), 1969
Christmas Cruise (Colman), 1965
Christmas Eve (play; Ainsworth), 1955
Christmas Eve Mystery (Nixon), 1979
Christmas Fairy (Strang), 1926
Christmas Fantasy (Haywood), 1972
Christmas for All (play; Latham, as Lee), 1932
Christmas Forest (Fatio), 1950
Christmas Ghost (Oldfield), 1985
Christmas Guest (play; C. D. Mackay), 1909
Christmas Holiday Mystery (Trease), 1937

Christmas in Ninety-Nine Words (play; A. Fisher), 1949
Christmas in Old New England (play; Clapp), 1964
Christmas in the Barn (M. W. Brown), 1952
Christmas in the Forest (Wahl), 1967
Christmas in the Stable (Lindgren, trans), 1962
Christmas in the Tree (Southall), 1985
Christmas Mice (Scarry), 1981
Christmas Mummers (Yonge, appendix), 1858
Christmas Mumming Play (Ewing, appendix), 1887
Christmas Nightingale (Kelly), 1932
Christmas Party (verse; Bailey), 1975
Christmas Party (play; Latham), 1930
Christmas Plays and Programs (A. Fisher), 1960
Christmas Posy (Molesworth, appendix), 1888
Christmas Programs (play; Latham, as Lee), 1937
Christmas Reindeer (Burgess), 1926
Christmas Revolution (Cohen), 1987
Christmas Secret (Lexau), 1973
Christmas Spirit (play; Lillington), 1967
Christmas Stocking (Warner, appendix), 1853
Christmas Stories (Lenski), 1968
Christmas Stories (Stretton, appendix), 1875
Christmas Story (Chalmers), 1956
Christmas Story (play; Uttley), 1961
Christmas Time (verse; Field), 1941
Christmas Tree (Cockett), 1979
Christmas Tree for Lydia (Enright), 1951
Christmas Tree House (Wallace), 1976
Christmas Whale (Duvoisin), 1945
Christmas-Tree Land (Molesworth, appendix), 1883
Christopher series (Chaney), from 1972
Christopher (Flack), 1935
Christopher and His Turtle (Lattimore), 1950
Christopher Uptake (S. Price), 1981
Chronicles of Aunt Minervy Ann (J. Harris, appendix), 1899
Chronicles of Morgan, Prince of Hed (McKillip), 1981
Chubb series (R. Brown), from 1976
Chuck-a-Luck and His Reindeer (Hader), 1933
Chucklebud and Wunkydoo (Gibbs), 1924
Chudleigh Hold (Brent-Dyer), 1954
Chuff the Chimney Sweep (Blyton), 1950
Chuggy and the Blue Caboose (D. Freeman), 1951
Chuiraquimba and the Black Robes (Polland), 1962
Chums at Charlhurst (H. Avery), 1936
Chums of the "Golden Vanity" (Westerman), 1927
Chunky series (Berg), from 1950
Chupsie (Marchant), 1904
Church and the King (Everett-Green, appendix), 1892
Church Mice series (Oakley), from 1972
Cicely Frome (Marchant), 1900
Cider Days (Stolz), 1978
Cilia of Chiltern's Edge (Allan), 1949
Cinderella (play; Chorpenning), 1940
Cinderella (play; Nesbit), 1892
Cinderella (play; Peet), 1950
Cinderella (play; L. Richards), 1916
Cinderella (play; D. Wood), 1968 and 1980
Cinderella Ann (Chaundler), 1932
Cinderella "At Home" (play; Fyleman), 1934
Cinderella Married (play; Field), 1924
Cinderella Show (Ahlberg), 1986
Cinderella Story (play; Lillington), 1967
Cindy series (Orgel), from 1966
Cinema Dog (Strang), 1926
Cinematograph Train (Farrow), 1904
Cinnabar (Henry), 1956

Cinnamon and Nutmeg (de Roo), 1972
Circle of Seasons (verse; Livingston), 1982
Circlet of Oak Leaves (Sutcliff), 1968
Circus (Bruna, trans), 1963
Circus (verse; de Regniers), 1966
Circus (Manning-Sanders), 1948
Circus (verse; Prelutsky), 1974
Circus, The (Tate), 1967
Circus All Alone (Stranger), 1965
Circus, April 1st (Slobodkin), 1953
Circus Baby, The (Petersham), 1950
Circus Book, The (Blyton), 1949
Circus Book (Manning-Sanders), 1947
Circus Boy (Manning-Sanders), 1960
Circus Days (play; A. Harris), 1948
Circus Days Again (Blyton), 1942
Circus Home (play; J. Kraus), 1977
Circus in the Wind (play; A. Harris), 1960
Circus Is Coming (Streatfeild), 1938
Circus Is Here (Baumann, trans), 1967
Circus Lion (Chaundler), 1920
Circus of Adventure (Blyton), 1952
Circus Ring (M. Bruce), 1936
Circus Ruckus (Lipkind, as Will), 1954
Circus Shoes (Streatfeild), 1939
Citizen of the Galaxy (Heinlein), 1957
City and the Citizens (play; Mitchison), 1937
City Boy and the Country Horse (Zolotow, as Bookman), 1952
City for Lincoln (Tunis), 1945
City of Gold (F. French), 1974
City of Gold and Lead (Christopher), 1967
City of the Golden Gate (Everett-Green, appendix), 1909
City of the Golden House (Pollard), 1963
City Out of Sight (Southall), 1984
City Poems (Lenski), 1971
City Sandwich (verse; Asch), 1978
City under the Back Steps (Lampman), 1960
City Witch and the Country Witch (J. Williams), 1979
Claim Jumpers of Marble Canyon (R. Montgomery), 1956
Clams Can't Sing (Stevenson), 1980
Clancy's Cabin (Mahy), 1974
Clancy's Coat (Bunting), 1984
Clanrickard Court (Everett-Green, appendix), 1907
Clare Goes to Holland (Allan, as Pilgrim), 1962
Class Clown (Hurwitz), 1987
Class Pictures (Sachs), 1980
Class Three and the Beanstalk (Waddell), 1988
Class Two Monster (Rosen), 1989
Classmates by Request (Colman), 1964
Claud the Archer (Strang), 1907
Claude series (Nixon), from 1980
Claudia, Where Are You? (Colman), 1969
Claws in the Cat's Paw (play; Merrill), 1956
Claws of a Young Century (I. Hunt), 1980
Claws of the Eagle (Trease), 1977
Claws of the Thunderbird (Holling), 1928
Clean as a Whistle (verse; A. Fisher), 1969
Clear for Action! (Meader), 1940
Clear the Track for Michael's Magic Train (Slobodkin), 1945
Clearance (Lingard), 1974
Clearing Weather (Meigs), 1928
Clemence and Ginger (Wayne), 1960
Clemency Draper (F. Knight), 1963
Clemency in the Moonlight (B.C. Freeman), 1981
Clementina (Dunlop), 1985
Clementina's Cactus (Keats), 1982

Danger on the Tracks (B. Freeman), 1987
Danger Patrol (L. Rees), 1954
Danger Point (S. Corbett), 1962
Danger Quotient (A. and E. Johnson), 1984
Danger Rock (R. Armstrong), 1955
Danger to Windward (Sperry), 1947
Danger Unlimited (Brand), 1948
Dangerous Assignment (Patchett), 1962
Dangerous Cargo (Catherall), 1960
Dangerous Cargo (Westerman), 1952
Dangerous Cove (Hayes), 1957
Dangerous Inheritance (Allan), 1970
Dangerous Journey (Jansson, trans), 1978
Dangerous Magic (Beresford), 1972
Dangerous Mission (Marchant), 1918
Dangerous Ones (Scannell), 1970
Dangerous Summer (Colman), 1966
Daniel Boone (play; C. D. Mackay), 1912
Daniel Boone's Echo (W. Steele), 1957
Daniel's Duck (Bulla), 1979
Daniel's Epic (play; Wymark), 1972
Danish Teapot (Mitchison), 1973
Danny and the Dinosaur (Hoff), 1958
Danny Dunn series (J. Williams), from 1956
Danny Jones (Salkey), 1980
Danny Loves a Holiday (S. Taylor), 1980
Danny Meadow Mouse, The Adventures of (Burgess), 1915
Danny, The Champion of the World (Dahl), 1975
Danvers Papers (Yonge, appendix), 1867
Danza! (L. Hall), 1981
Dapple Grey (Symonds), 1962
Darby and Joan (play; Fyleman), 1924
D'Arcy series (F. Richards, as Clifford), 1952
Darcy's Harvest (Lampman, as Bronson), 1956
Dare Lorimer's Heritage (Everett-Green, appendix), 1891
Dare-All Jack and the Cousins (Wynne), 1925
Daredevils or Scaredycats (Powling), 1979
Daring and Danger, Tales of (Henty, appendix), 1889
Daring Doranne (Oxenham), 1945
Daring Dot (Everett-Green, appendix), 1890
Daring of Star (Wynne), 1936
Daring Twins (Baum), 1911
Dark (Munsch), 1979
Dark Adventure (Pease), 1950
Dark and Deadly Pool (Nixon), 1987
Dark Behind the Curtain (Cross), 1982
Dark Bright Water (Wrightson), 1979
Dark Canoe (O'Dell), 1968
Dark Child (R. Hughes), 1930
Dark Circle of Branches (Armer), 1933
Dark Danger (Saville), 1965
Dark Dove (Stewart), 1974
Dark Frigate (Hawes), 1923
Dark Fury (Chipperfield), 1956
Dark Horse (James), 1939
Dark Horse of Woodfield (Hightower), 1962
Dark House (Fenn, appendix), 1885
Dark House of the Sea Witch (Robinson), 1979
Dark Is Rising series (S. Cooper), from 1965
Dark Island (Barrett), 1952
Dark of the Tunnel (Naylor), 1985
Dark Piper (A. Norton), 1968
Dark Pool Island (M. Clark), 1949
Dark Princess (R. Kennedy), 1978
Dark River, Dark Mountain (Sherry), 1975
Dark Sailor of Youghal (Lynch), 1951

Dark Scout (Westerman), 1954
Dark Side of the Moon (Corlett), 1976
Dark Side of the Moon (Naylor), 1969
Dark Streets of Kimballs Green (play; Aiken), 1976
Dark Sun, Bright Sun (Fisk), 1986
Dark Wood of the Golden Birds (verse; M. W. Brown), 1950
Darkangel (Pierce), 1982
Darkling (Peyton), 1989
Darkness and Dawn (Farrar, appendix), 1891
Darkness under the Hills (Scott), 1980
Darlene (Greenfield), 1980
Darling of Sandy Point (Marchant), 1907
Darling of the School (Meade, appendix), 1915
Darry the Dauntless (Moore), 1928
Dash for Diamond City (Fenn, appendix), 1901
Dash for Khartoum (Henty, appendix), 1891
Daughter of Discontent (Colman), 1971
Daughter of Don Saturnino (O'Dell), 1979
Daughter of the Desert (Marchant), 1937
Daughter of the Moon (Maguire), 1980
Daughter of the Ranges (Marchant), 1905
Daughter of the Sea (Le Feuvre), 1902
Daughter of the Sea (Polland), 1972
Daughter to Poseidon (Polland), 1972
Daughters of Aradale (Lyon), 1957
Daughters of Eve (L. Duncan), 1979
Daughters of the Dominion (Marchant), 1908
Daughters of Today (Meade, appendix), 1916
Dauntless series (Dawlish), from 1947
Dave and His Dog Mulligan (Kjelgaard), 1966
Davenports series (Dalgliesh), from 1948
Daventry's Quest (Westerman), 1955
David and Dog (S. Hughes), 1978
David and the Phoenix (Ormondroyd), 1957
David Balfour (Stevenson, appendix), 1893
David Crockett's Earthquake (W. Steele), 1956
David Goes Fishing (Beresford), 1969
David's Father (Munsch), 1983
David's Little Indian (M. W. Brown), 1956
David's Witch Doctor (Mahy), 1976
Davy series (Lenski), from 1943
Davy Jones' Locker (play; Rodgers), 1959
Davy of the Everglades (Lattimore), 1949
Dawks series (Reid), from 1955
Dawn Killer (play; M. Edwards), 1958
Dawn of Fear (S. Cooper), 1970
Dawn Shops (Brisley), 1933
Dawn Wind (Sutcliff), 1961
Dawnstone (Paton Walsh), 1973
Day after Yesterday (Kaye), 1981
Day and Night (Duvoisin), 1960
Day and the Way We Met (Stolz), 1956
Day at Nottingham (play; C. D. Mackay), 1952
Day at the Playground (Schlein), 1951
Day Boy Colours (H. Avery), 1928
Day Chiro Was Lost (Nakatani, trans), 1968
Day Everybody Cried (de Regniers), 1967
Day I Got Better (Iwasaki, trans), 1980
Day I Had to Play with My Sister (Bonsall), 1972
Day I Shot My Dad (Branfield), 1989
Day I Shot My Dad (play; Branfield), 1976
Day I Was Born (Sharmat), 1980
Day in the Country (Hardcastle), 1974
Day in the Life of Curious Eddie (Greenwood), 1979
Day in Venice (Bettina), 1973
Day It Rained Elephants (Waddell), 1986

Day It Snowed in Summer (Heide), 1968
Day No Pigs Would Die (R. N. Peck), 1972
Day of the Dinosaurs (Bunting), 1975
Day of the Dragon (Seed), 1985
Day of the Earthlings (Bunting), 1978
Day of the Ness (A. Norton), 1975
Day of the Pigeons (R. Brown), 1968
Day of the Squirrels (Cockett), 1987
Day of the Starwind (D. Hill), 1980
Day on Big O (Cresswell), 1967
Day on Skates (Van Stockum), 1934
Day Out (Berg), 1968
Day That Got Lost (Lyon), 1968
Day the Animals Went on Strike (M. Bond), 1972
Day the Ceiling Fell Down (Wayne), 1961
Day the Circus Came to Lone Tree (Rounds), 1973
Day the Cow Sneezed (Flora), 1957
Day the Smells Went Wrong (Waddell, as Sefton), 1988
Day the Teacher Went Bananas (Howe), 1984
Day the Tide Went Out, and Out, and Out...(McKee), 1975
Day They Came to Arrest the Book (Hentoff), 1982
Day to Go Hunting (C. Pullein-Thompson), 1956
Day to Remember (C. Pullein-Thompson), 1966
Day with Daddy (Tresselt), 1953
Day with the Duke (Thwaite), 1969
Day Without Wind (Mayne), 1964
Daybreak (verse; L. Clark), 1963
Daybreak, 2250 A.D. (A. Norton), 1954
Daybreakers (Curry), 1970
Daydreamers (Greenfield), 1981
Daylight Robbery (J. Williams), 1977
Daymaker (Halam), 1987
Days of Fear (Nixon), 1983
Days of Glory (play; Barne), 1946
Days of Terror (Smucker), 1979
Dead Before Docking (S. Corbett), 1972
Dead Bird (M. W. Brown), 1958
Dead King, Tales of a (Myers), 1983
Dead Kingdom (G. Harris), 1983
Dead Letter Box (Mark), 1982
Dead Man's Land (Fenn, appendix), 1906
Dead Man's Light (S. Corbett), 1960
Dead Man's Message (Waddell), 1983
Dead Ned (Masefield), 1938
Dead of Night (Hardcastle), 1974
Deadly Freeze (B. Carter), 1976
Deadly Game of Magic (Nixon), 1983
Deadly Hoax (S. Corbett), 1981
Deadmen's Cave (Wibberley), 1954
Dealings with the Fairies (MacDonald, appendix), 1867
Dean Durham (Alger, appendix), 1890
Deans series (Fidler), 1953
Dean's Daughter (Everett-Green, as Adair, appendix), 1910
Dear Bill, Remember Me? (Mazer), 1976
Dear Bruce Springsteen (Major), 1987
Dear Dustman (Zion), 1962
Dear Enemy (Webster), 1915
Dear Father Christmas (Banner), 1984
Dear Fred (Peyton), 1981
Dear Garbage Man (Zion), 1957
Dear Grumble (W. Corbett), 1989
Dear Hildegarde (Waber), 1980
Dear Hill (Halam, as Jones), 1980
Dear Lovey Hart, I Am Desperate (Conford), 1975
Dear Mr. Henshaw (Cleary), 1983
Dear Old Briar-Patch (Burgess), 1947

Dear Old Snow Man (Blyton), 1949
Dear Prosper (Fox), 1968
Dear Rat (Cunningham), 1961
Dear Shrink (Cresswell), 1982
Dear Snowman (Janosch, trans), 1970
Dearly Bought (Talbot), 1932
Death of a Dinosaur (Bunting), 1975
Death of an Oil Rig (Catherall), 1967
Death of Metal (Suddaby), 1952
Death Rays of Ardilla (Johns), 1959
Death to the Strangers! (Rush), 1977
Deathwing over Veynaa (D. Hill), 1980
Deb and the Duchess (Meade, appendix), 1888
Deb at School (Oxenham), 1929
Deb of Sea House (Oxenham), 1931
Debatable Mound (D. Bruce), 1953
Debbie series (Lenski), from 1967
Debbie and the Little Devil (Lively), 1987
Debbie Robbie's Day Nursery (Robinson), 1950
Deborah's Find (Marchant), 1933
Deborah's White Winter (Lattimore), 1949
Debt of Honor (Alger, appendix), 1900
Debt of Honor (play; Latham), 1940
Debt of the Damerals (Marchant), 1905
Debutante Hill (L. Duncan), 1958
December Is for Christmas (Fritz, as Scott), 1961
December Rose (Garfield), 1986
December Rose (play; Garfield), 1986
December Tale (Sachs), 1976
Decision in the Dark (P. Turner), 1978
DeDe Takes Charge! (Hurwitz), 1984
Deeds of Pluck and Daring in the Great War (Westerman), 1917
Deenie (Blume), 1973
Deep Dives of Stanley Whale (Benchley), 1973
Deep Down (Ballantyne, appendix), 1868
Deep in the Forest (Fry), 1955
Deep in the Forest (Turkle), 1976
Deep Trouble (Morey), 1971
Deep-Sea Horse (Cumming), 1956
Deepwater (O'Neill), 1987
Deepwater Challenge (Bonham), 1963
Deer in the Snow (Schlein), 1956
Deer Valley Girl (Lenski), 1968
Deerfold (S. Porter), 1966
Deezle Boy (Spence), 1987
Defence of the Rock (Everett-Green, appendix), 1906
Defending the Island (Otis, appendix), 1904
Defense of Fort Henry (Otis, appendix), 1900
Defiant Agents (A. Norton), 1962
Defiant Heart (R. Montgomery), 1963
Deirdre (Polland), 1967
Deke, The Adventures of (Nwapa), 1980
Delamayne's Adventures (Marchant), 1925
Delbert, The Plainclothes Detective (Nixon), 1971
Delia Daly of the Galloping Green (Lynch), 1953
Delikon (Hoover), 1977
Delpha Green and Company (V. and B. Cleaver), 1972
Delta Baby and Two Sea Songs (verse; R. Kennedy), 1979
Demetrius and the Golden Goblet (Bunting), 1980
Demi-Reps (play; S. Walker), 1936
Demo and the Dolphin (Benchley), 1981
Demon (Bunting), 1976
Demon Bike Rider (Leeson), 1976
Demon Bowler (Hardcastle), 1974
Demon Headmaster (Cross), 1982
Denison's Daughter (L. Hall), 1983

Dragon's Sister (Storey), 1967
Dragonsinger (McCaffrey), 1977
Dragonsong (McCaffrey), 1976
Dragonwings (Yep), 1975
Dram Road (L. Lawrence), 1983
Drango Dragon (Biro), 1989
Draw Swords! (Fenn, appendix), 1898
Draw the Line Somewhere (play; Buckeridge), 1948
Drawbridge Gate (Harnett), 1954
Dread Companion (A. Norton), 1970
Dreadful Boy (D. Ross), 1959
Dreadful Doings in Ark Street (Beaman), 1943
Dreadnought of the Air (Westerman), 1914
Dream Book (M. W. Brown), 1950
Dream Catcher (M. Hughes), 1986
Dream Cage (play; Chambers), 1981
Dream Coach (Parrish), 1924
Dream Dancer (Bunting, as Bolton), 1974
Dream Days (Grahame), 1898
Dream Girl's Garden (Howes), 1923
Dream Gold (Severn), 1949
Dream House (Mark), 1987
Dream Hunters (Lyon), 1966
Dream in the House (Poole), 1961
Dream of Dragons (H. Morgan), 1965
Dream of Ghosts (Bonham), 1973
Dream of Hunger Moss (Allan), 1983
Dream of Sadler's Wells (L. Hill), 1950
Dream of Seas (Norman), 1978
Dream Stealer (Maguire), 1983
Dream Watcher (Wersba), 1968
Dream Watcher (play; Wersba), 1975
Dream Weaver (Yolen), 1979
Dreamikins (Le Feuvre), 1918
Dreamland series (verse; L. Duncan), from 1985
Dreamland Lake (R. Peck), 1973
Dreams (Keats), 1974
Dreams and Drummers (D. B. Smith), 1978
Dreams of Victory (Conford), 1973
Dream-Time (Treece), 1967
Dreamwold Castle (Hightower), 1978
Dress-Rehearsal (L. Hill), 1959
Dribblesome Teapots (N. Hunter), 1969
Drift (Mayne), 1985
Drift (Meade, appendix), 1902
Drifted Ashore (Everett-Green, appendix), 1887
Driftway (Lively), 1972
Drina series (Allan, as Estoril), from 1957
Drinking Gourd (Monjo), 1970
Driven from Home (Alger, appendix), 1890
Droopsi (Kahl), 1958
Drought (Salkey), 1966
Drovers Road (West), 1953
Droving Lad (Fidler), 1955
Drowned Ammet (Jones), 1977
Drowning Valley (Cockett), 1978
Drugstore Cat (Petry), 1949
Drum (Achebe), 1977
Drumbeats! (Severn), 1953
Drummer Boy (Ekwensi), 1960
Drummer Boy (Garfield), 1969
Drusilla (Ish-Kishor), 1970
Duchess (Aaron), 1982
Duchess Bakes a Cake (verse; Kahl), 1955
Duck (M. W. Brown), 1952
Duck and the Diesel Engine (Awdry), 1958

Duck Boy (Mattingley), 1983
Duck Cakes for Sale (Lunn), 1989
Duck in the Gun (Cowley), 1969
Duck on a Pond (B. Willard), 1962
Duck-Footed Hound (Kjelgaard), 1960
Ducks! (Pinkwater), 1984
Ducks and Drakes (Harnett), 1942
Ducks and Drakes (Sudbery), 1975
Duckworth's Diamonds (Everett-Green, appendix), n.d.
Dudley Napier's Daughters (Le Feuvre), 1916
Duel in the Desert (Myers), 1986
Duel in the High Hills (Catherall), 1968
Duff Darlington (Everett-Green, appendix), 1895
Duffy's Rocks (Fenton), 1974
Duke Decides (Tunis), 1939
Duke, The Lost Engine (Awdry), 1970
Dukes (R. N. Peck), 1984
Dulcie series (Everett-Green, appendix), from 1887
Dulcie's Lantern (Nesbit), 1895
Dumb Cake (Garfield), 1977
Dumbo (play; Peet), 1941
Dumpling (King-Smith), 1986
Dumpling (Moray Williams), 1937
Dumps (Meade, appendix), 1905
Dunderhead War (B. Baker), 1967
Dunes and the Diamonds (Syme), 1964
Dunkard (Selden), 1968
Dunkirk Summer (P. Turner), 1973
Duplicate (Sleator), 1988
Dupper (B. Baker), 1976
Durango Street (Bonham), 1965
Dusky Day (Means), 1933
Dust of the Earth (V. and B. Cleaver), 1975
Dustbin Charlie (Pilling), 1988
Dustland (Hamilton), 1980
Dust-Up at the Royal Disco (N. Hunter), 1975
Dusty and the Fiddlers (P. Martin, as Miles), 1962
Dusty Diamonds Cut and Polished (Ballantyne, appendix), 1884
Dusty's Windmill (Barne), 1949
Dutch Are Coming (Trease), 1965
Dutch Boat (Pardoe), 1955
Dutch Cheese and the Lovely Myfanwy (de la Mare), 1931
Dutch Colt (Meigs), 1952
Dutch the Diver (Fenn, appendix), 1883
Dutiful Dan (Alger, appendix), 1884
Dwarf of Dark Mountain (Peacocke), 1931
Dwarf of Pine Tree (Lifton), 1963
Dwarfs of Nosegay series (Biegel, trans), from 1978
Dwell Deep (Le Feuvre), 1896
Dweller in Tents (Meade, appendix), 1880
Dwindleberry Zoo (Farrow), 1908
Dynevor Terrace (Yonge, appendix), 1857

E.S.P. (King-Smith), 1986
Each Peach Pear Plum (verse; Ahlberg), 1978
Eagle and Dove (Krüss, trans), 1965
Eagle Cliff (Ballantyne, appendix), 1889
Eagle Feather (Bulla), 1953
Eagle Jake and Indian Pete (J. Williams), 1947
Eagle Mask (Houston), 1966
Eagle of the Ninth (Sutcliff), 1954
Eagle's Egg (Sutcliff), 1981
Eagles Have Flown (Treece), 1954
Eagle's Nest (Kyle), 1961
Eagle's Talons (Westerman), 1940
Earl's Falconer (Moray Williams), 1961

Elizabeth's Prisoner (Meade, appendix), 1914
Elizabeth's Tower (Stewart), 1972
Elizabite (H.A. and M. Rey), 1942
Ella (verse; Peet), 1964
Ella at the Wells (L. Hill), 1954
Ella Clinton (Finley, appendix), 1856
Ellen (Almedingen), 1970
Ellen series (G. Avery), from 1971
Ellen Grae series (V. and B. Cleaver), from 1967
Ellen Tebbits (Cleary), 1951
Ellen's Lion (C. Johnson), 1959
Elli of the Northland (Catherall, as Ruthin), 1968
Ellie and the Hagwitch (Cresswell), 1984
Ellie's Inheritance (Colman), 1979
Elm Street Lot (Pearce), 1969
Elmer series (McKee), from 1968
Elmer and the Dragon (Gannett), 1950
Elmo Doolan and the Search for the Golden Mouse (S. Murphy), 1970
Elsa Puts Things Right (Oxenham), 1944
Elsie Dinsmore series (Finley, appendix), from 1868
Elusive Grasshopper (Saville), 1951
Elves and the Shoemaker (play; Chorpenning), 1946
Elves and the Shoemaker (play; Miller), n.d.
Elvira Everything (Asch), 1970
Elvis series (Gripe, trans), from 1976
Elworthy Children (Hewett), 1963
Emeka (Nwapa), 1972
Emerald Crown (Needham), 1940
Emer's Ghost (Waddell, as Sefton), 1981
Emhammed of the Red Slippers (play; Ridge), 1954
Emil series (Lindgren, trans), from 1970
Emil and the Detectives series (Kästner, trans), from 1930
Emile (Ungerer), 1960
Emily series (L. Montgomery), from 1923
Emily series (E. Smith), from 1959
Emily and the Enchanted Frog (Griffith), 1989
Emily and the Haunted Castle (Beresford), 1987
Emily and the Headmistress (M. Harris), 1958
Emily and the Klunky Baby and the Next-Door Dog (Lexau), 1972
Emily Emerson's Moon (verse; Merrill), 1960
Emily of Deep Valley (Lovelace), 1950
Emily Upham's Revenge (Avi), 1978
Emily's Legs (King-Smith), 1988
Emily's Own Elephant (Pearce), 1987
Emily's Runaway Imagination (Cleary), 1961
Emlyn's Moon (Nimmo), 1987
Emma (Abbott, appendix), 1855
Emma (Stevenson), 1985
Emma Borrows a Cup of Sugar (Fisk), 1973
Emma Dilemma (Waddell, as Sefton), 1982
Emma in Love (Arundel), 1970
Emma in Winter (Farmer), 1966
Emma Tupper's Diary (Dickinson), 1971
Emma's Doll (Patten), 1976
Emma's Island (Arundel), 1968
Emmet Otter's Jug-Band Christmas (Hoban), 1971
Emmett's Pig (Stolz), 1959
Emmie and the Purple Paint (D. Edwards), 1984
Emmy series (Means), from 1956
Emperor and the Kite (Yolen), 1976
Emperor's Gifts (C. Johnson), 1965
Emperor's New Clothes (play; Chorpenning), 1932
Emperor's New Clothes (play; Miller), n.d.
Emperor's Nightingale (play; Miller), 1961

Emperor's Winding Sheet (Paton Walsh), 1974
Empty Field (C. Pullein-Thompson), 1961
Empty House (Holland), 1983
Empty Saddle (Meynell), 1965
Empty Schoolhouse (Carlson), 1965
Empty Sleeve (Garfield), 1988
Empty Window (Bunting), 1980
Empty World (Christopher), 1977
Emu Kite (Mattingley), 1972
Emu's Christmas Adventure (play; D. Wood), 1977
Enchanted Ark (Beaman), 1958
Enchanted Bugle (Bailey), 1920
Enchanted Bunnies, The Tale of the (Sawyer), 1923
Enchanted Cap (play; Blyton), 1935
Enchanted Castle (Nesbit), 1907
Enchanted Egg (H. Avery), 1908
Enchanted Fiddle (play; Brazil), 1903
Enchanted Garden (play; C. D. Mackay), 1909
Enchanted Garden (Molesworth, appendix), 1892
Enchanted Horse (R. Harris), 1981
Enchanted Island of Yew (Baum), 1903
Enchanted Mountain (E. O. White), 1911
Enchanted Road (Howes), 1927
Enchanted Schoolhouse (Sawyer), 1956
Enchanted Sea (Blyton), 1949
Enchanted Village (Bailey), 1950
Enchanted Wood (Blyton), 1939
Enchantment (Uttley), 1966
Enchantress from the Stars (Engdahl), 1970
Encore for Eleanor (Peet), 1981
Encounter at Easton (Avi), 1980
Encounter near Venus (Wibberley), 1967
Encyclopedia Brown series (Sobol), from 1963
End and a Beginning (play; Mitchison), 1937
End of Part One (play; Lillington), 1968
End of Summer (Clewes), 1971
End of Term (Forest), 1959
End of the Game (Colman), 1971
End of the Harbour (Locke), 1968
End of the Outlaws (Patchett), 1961
End of the Tale (W. Corbett), 1985
Endless and Co. (Ridge), 1948
Enemies (R. Klein), 1985
Enemy (Garfield), 1978
Engage the Enemy Closely (Westerman), 1944
Engaged to Be Married (Meade, appendix), 1890
Engine Number Seven (Clymer), 1975
Engine Puzzle (Kariuki), 1981
Engineer (Abbott, appendix), 1856
English Girl in Serbia (Wynne), 1916
Enid's Ugly Duckling (Everett-Green, appendix), 1896
Ennead (Mark), 1978
Enoch Roden's Training (Stretton, appendix), 1866
Enormous Apple Pie (D. Ross), 1951
Enormous Crocodile (Dahl), 1978
Enormous Egg (Butterworth), 1956
Enough Is Enough (Cockett), 1980
Enough Is Too Much Already (Mark), 1988
Ensign Carey (Welch), 1976
Enter Jenny Wren (Wynne), 1933
Enterprising Engines (Awdry), 1968
Epaminondas (Merriam), 1968
Eric (Farrar, appendix), 1858
Erica's Ranch (Marchant), 1934
Eric's Good News (Le Feuvre), 1894
Erie Train Boy (Alger, appendix), 1890

Escape (Hofman, trans), 1970
Escape from France (Welch), 1960
Escape from Loch Leven (M. Hunter), 1987
Escape from Splatterbang (Fisk), 1978
Escape from the Evil Prophecy (Kingman), 1973
Escape from the Zoo (Parker), 1945
Escape from Tyrannosauraus (Bunting), 1975
Escape from Warsaw (Serraillier), 1963
Escape in Darkness (Fidler), 1961
Escape of the Giant Hogstalk (Holman), 1974
Escape of the Giant Hogweed (Holman), 1978
Escape of the Mullingong (Farrow), 1906
Escape the River (R. Brown), 1972
Escape to King Alfred (Trease), 1958
Escape to Persia (Hull and Whitlock), 1938
Escape to the Castle (Hope-Simpson), 1967
Escaped Black Mamba (Aiken), 1973
Esther's Charge (Everett-Green, appendix), 1898
Ethan's Favorite Teacher (Colman), 1975
Eugene (Marshall), 1975
Eugene the Brave (Conford), 1978
Eusebius (Wibberley, as Webb), 1969
Eustace Marchmont (Everett-Green, appendix), 1894
Eva (Dickinson), 1988
Evangeline (Carlson), 1960
Evangeline series (Chaundler), from 1926
Evelyn (Moore), 1904
Even Steven (Lipkind, as Will), 1952
Evening Listens (verse; Ainsworth), 1953
Evening Star (Patchett), 1954
Eventful Holiday (Heward), 1928
Ever After (McNeill), 1975
Ever After (Whitney), 1948
Ever Ride a Dinosaur? (S. Corbett), 1969
Everest Climbed (verse; Serraillier), 1955
Everett Anderson series (verse; Clifton), from 1970
Everglades Adventure (Meader), 1957
Everlasting Circle (Greenwood), 1981
Everlasting Hills (I. Hunt), 1985
Every Day a Dragon (Lexau), 1967
Every Day Is Market Day (Pamela Brown), 1977
Every Living Thing (Rylant), 1985
Every Time I Climb a Tree (verse; McCord), 1967
Everybody's Friend (Everett-Green, appendix), 1893
Everyday Island (Allan), 1950
Everyday Stories (Bailey), 1919
Everygirl (play; Field), 1913
Everyone Is Good for Something (play; de Regniers), 1986
Everyone Knows What a Dragon Looks Like (J. Williams), 1976
Everything Glistens and Everything Sings (verse; Zolotow), 1987
Everything under a Mushroom (verse; Krauss), 1974
Evil Eye (Fisk), 1980
Evil May Day (Everett-Green, appendix), 1893
Exactly Alike (Ness), 1964
Exchange (Halam, as Jones), 1979
Exciting River (Allan), 1951
Exciting Term (Brazil), 1936
Exeter Blitz (D. Rees), 1978
Exiles of the Stars (A. Norton), 1971
Exit Barney McGee (Claire Mackay), 1979
Ex-King Max Forever! (Judah), 1963
Expelled from School (Oxenham), 1919
Explorer of Barkham Street (Stolz), 1985
Explorer Zach (Locke), 1978
Extended Play (play; Wymark), 1976
Extraordinary Margaret Catchpole (Manning-Sanders), 1966

Eye Book (verse; Seuss, as Le Sieg), 1968
Eye for Elephants (verse; Steig), 1970
Eye in the Forest (M.Q. and W.O. Steele), 1975
Eye Nose Fingers Toes (Krauss), 1964
Eye of the Comet (Sargent), 1984
Eye of the Earth (Dawlish, as Kerr), 1936
Eyebright (Coolidge, appendix), 1879
Eyes for the Dark (Shannon), 1928
Eyes in the Fishbowl (Snyder), 1968
Eyes of Darkness (Highwater), 1985
Eyes of Karen Conners (L. Duncan), 1985
Eyes of the Amaryllis (Babbitt), 1977
Eyes of the Blind (A. Morgan), 1986
Eyes of the Eagle (R. Bond), 1987
Eyes of the Wilderness (C. Roberts), 1933
Eyes of the Woods (Altsheler), 1917
Ezra Jordan's Escape from the Massacre at Fort Loyall (Otis, appendix), 1895

Fable of a Proud Pony (Averill, as Domino), 1934
Fables You Shouldn't Pay Any Attention To (Heide), 1978
Fabulous Creature (Snyder), 1981
Fabulous Firework Family (Flora), 1955
Fabulous Firework Family (play; Flora), 1959
Fabulous Flight (Lawson), 1949
Fabulous Haircut (Judah), 1964
Fabulous McFanes (Duggan), 1974
Face at the Edge of the World (Bunting), 1985
Face of Abraham Candle (Clements), 1969
Face of Juliet (Meade, appendix), 1906
Face of Stone (Rush), 1973
Faces in the Water (Naylor), 1981
Facing Death (Henty, appendix), 1882
Facing the World (Alger, appendix), 1893
Facts and Fictions of Minna Pratt (MacLachlan), 1988
Fade (Cormier), 1988
Fair Adventure (Vining, as Gray), 1940
Fair American (Coatsworth), 1940
Fair Bay (Lattimore), 1958
Fair Flower of Danger (Trease), 1955
Fair Wind to Virginia (Meigs), 1955
Fairies Afield (Molesworth, appendix), 1911
Fairies and Chimneys (verse; Fyleman), 1918
Fairies and Friends (verse; Fyleman), 1925
Fairies' Baby (Goudge), 1920
Fairies—of Sorts (Molesworth, appendix), 1908
Fairies of the Trees (verse; Barker), 1940
Fair's Fair (Garfield), 1981
Fairy and the Doll (play; Fyleman) 1924
Fairy Book (verse; Fyleman), 1923
Fairy Called Andy Perks (McNeill), 1973
Fairy Caravan (Potter), 1929
Fairy Circle series (Heward), 1927
Fairy Court, Tales of a (Lang, appendix), 1907
Fairy Doll (Godden), 1956
Fairy Flute (verse; Fyleman), 1921
Fairy Folk Story Book (Blyton), 1966
Fairy Gifts (play; Brazil), 1901
Fairy Godmother (Meade, appendix), 1917
Fairy Green (verse; Fyleman), 1919
Fairy Hen (O'Faolain), 1945
Fairy in the Box (play; Blyton), 1939
Fairy Operettas (play; L. Richards), 1916
Fairy Prisoners (play; Blyton), 1926
Fairy Rebel (Banks), 1985
Fairy Riddle (play; Fyleman), 1924

Fairy Rings (Howes), 1911
Fairy Stories (Nesbit), 1977
Fairy Tales (Uttley), 1975
Fairy Tales for Brownie Folk (Talbot), 1933
Fairy Tales of Gold (Garner), 1979
Fairy Who Couldn't Tell a Lie (Mitchison), 1963
Fairyland Limited (play; Trease), 1938
Fairy's Gift (Barker), 1977
Faith of a Collie (Terhune), 1949
Faith of Hilary Lovel (Everett-Green, appendix), 1904
Faith of Our Fathers (play; Daniell), 1961
Faithful Dove, The Tale of the (Potter), 1955
Faithful Teddy (Heward), 1927
Faithless Lollybird (Aiken), 1977
Falcon Bow (Houston), 1986
Falconer of Falconhurst (Everett-Green, appendix), 1892
Falconer's Lure (Forest), 1957
Falcon's Crag (Stewart), 1969
Falcon's Tor (Lamplugh), 1984
Falklands Summer (Branfield), 1987
Fall of Sebastopol (Henty, appendix), 1883
Fallen Angels (Myers), 1988
Fallen Fortunes (Everett-Green, appendix), 1902
Fallen Spaceman (Harding), 1973
Falling Angel (Peyton), 1983
Falling In with Fortune (Alger, appendix), 1900
False Face (Katz), 1987
Falter Tom and the Water Boy (Duggan), 1957
Fame and Fortune (Alger, appendix), 1868
Family (Donovan), 1976
Family (Everett-Green, appendix), 1894
Family (play; Hoff), 1973
Family Affair (Donkin), 1988
Family Affair (Polland), 1971
Family and the Fugitive (Colman), 1972
Family Apart (Nixon), 1987
Family at Caldicott Place (Streatfeild), 1968
Family at Ditlabeng (Mitchison), 1969
Family at Fools' Farm (Stranger), 1985
Family at Misrule (E. Turner), 1895
Family at Red Roofs (Blyton), 1945
Family Business (play; Wymark), 1976
Family Conspiracy (Phipson), 1962
Family Failing (Arundel), 1972
Family Feeling (G. Wilson), 1986
Family Footlights (Barne), 1939
Family from One End Street series (Garnett), from 1937
Family Grandstand (Brink), 1952
Family Likeness (B. Wilson), 1967
Family Next Door (Everett-Green, appendix), 1908
Family Next Door (Talbot), 1927
Family of Foxes (Dillon), 1964
Family on the Tide (F. Knight), 1956
Family on the Waterfront (Carlson), 1969
Family Playbill (Pamela Brown), 1951
Family Sabbatical (Brink), 1956
Family Secrets (N. Klein), 1985
Family Shoes (Streatfeild), 1954
Family Talk about War (play; D. Fisher), 1940
Family That Grew and Grew (M. Baker), 1952
Family Tower (B. Willard), 1968
Family Trap (Colman), 1982
Family Tree (Storey), 1973
Family Troubles (Molesworth, appendix), 1890
Family Troupe (Pamela Brown), 1953
Family under the Bridge (Carlson), 1958

Family Walk-Up (Stucley), 1961
Famous Battle of Bravery Creek (L. Hall), 1972
Famous Five series (Blyton), from 1942
Famous Five (play; Blyton), 1955
Famous Jimmy (Blyton), 1936
Famous Rowena Lamont (B. Willard), 1983
Famous Stanley Kidnapping Case (Snyder), 1979
Fanciful Tales (Stockton, appendix), 1894
Fancy Free (Cavanna), 1961
Fanny (Almedingen), 1970
Fanny series (Lively), from 1976
Fantasia (play; Peet), 1941
Fantastic Brother (Guillot, trans), 1961
Fantastic Feats of Doctor Boox (Davies), 1972
Fantastic Freshman (Brittain), 1988
Fantastic Mr. Fox (Dahl), 1970
Fantora Family Files (Geras), 1988
Far and Few (verse; McCord), 1952
Far Beyond and Back Again (Biegel, trans), 1977
Far Forests (Aiken), 1977
Far from Home (Sebestyen), 1980
Far from Shore (Major), 1980
Far Frontier (W. Steele), 1959
Far Harbour (Mitchison), 1957
Far in the Day (Cunningham), 1972
Far Out the Long Canal (De Jong), 1964
Far Side of Evil (Engdahl), 1971
Far to Go (Streatfeild), 1976
Far-Away Children (Ainsworth), 1963
Faraway Island (MacVicar), 1949
Faraway Lurs (Behn), 1963
Faraway Tree series (Blyton), from 1943
Far-Away Valley (Seed), 1987
Fardingdales (Brent-Dyer), 1950
Far-Distant Oxus (Hull and Whitlock), 1937
Farewell, Gul'sary (Aitmatov, trans), 1970
Farewell to Shady Glade (Peet), 1966
Farm (Ridge), 1956
Farm Beneath the Sea (Patchett), 1969
Farm Beyond the Town (E. O. White), 1937
Farm Boy (Stong), 1934
Farmer Barnes series (Cunliffe), from 1964
Farmer Boy (Wilder), 1933
Farmer Brown's Boy series (Burgess), 1929
Farmer Bungle Forgets (King-Smith), 1986
Farmer Giles of Ham (Tolkien), 1949
Farmer in the Dell (Hader), 1931
Farmer in the Sky (Heinlein), 1950
Farmer John (Bruna, trans), 1984
Farmer Palmer's Wagon Ride (Steig), 1974
Farmer Schulz's Ducks (Thiele), 1986
Farmer, The Rooks, and the Cherry Tree (Cunliffe), 1974
Farmyard Fun (Talbot), 1922
Far-Off Land (Caudill), 1964
Farrusco the Blackbird (Torga, trans), 1950
Farthest Shore (Le Guin), 1972
Farthest West (Armer), 1939
Farthest-Away Mountain (Banks), 1976
Farthing Bundles (Cockett), 1970
Farthing for the Fair (Beachcroft), 1978
Farthingful (Meade, appendix), 1889
Farthings (Molesworth, appendix), 1892
Fashion Girl (Beresford), 1967
Fast and Slow (verse; Ciardi), 1975
Fast Circuit (B. Carter), 1962

Fast Forward (play; McGough), 1986
Fast Friends (Everett-Green, as H.F.E., appendix), 1882
Fast Friends (Stevenson), 1979
Fast from the Gate (Hardcastle), 1983
Fast Green Car (Fisk), 1965
Fast in the Ice (Ballantyne, appendix), 1863
Fast Sam, Cool Clyde, and Stuff (Myers), 1975
Fast Sooner Hound (Bontemps), 1942
Fat (Wersba), 1987
Fat Chance, Claude (Nixon), 1987
Fat Elliot and the Gorilla (Pinkwater, as M. Pinkwater), 1974
Fat Girl (Sachs), 1984
Fat Jack (Cohen), 1980
Fat Men from Space (Pinkwater), 1977
Father Bear Comes Home (Minarik), 1959
Father Christmas series (R. Briggs), from 1973
Father Christmas series (plays; Fyleman), from 1924
Father Christmas Letters (Tolkien), 1976
Father Figure (R. Peck), 1978
Father Fox series (verse; C. Watson), from 1971
Father Goose series (verse; Baum), from 1899
Father Like That (Zolotow), 1971
Father Tingtang's Journey (Bisset), 1973
Father Unknown (C. Pullein-Thompson), 1982
Father's Arcane Daughter (Konigsburg), 1976
Fathom Five (Westall), 1979
Fattypuffs and Thinifers (Maurois, trans), 1941
Faun and the Woodcutter's Daughter (Picard), 1951
Favorite Storybook (Scarry), 1976
Fawn in the Forest (Kjelgaard), 1962
Fay Cow and the Mystery of the Missing Milk (P. Hunt), 1989
Fayerweather Forecast (Hightower), 1967
Fear Treks the Moor (J. Pullein-Thompson), 1979
Fearful Land of Forgets (verse; Praeger), 1921
Fearless Treasure (Streatfeild), 1952
Fearsome Inn (Singer), 1967
Feast of the Serpent (Cawley), 1969
Feather in His Cap (play; Clapp), 1957
Feather Star (Wrightson), 1962
Feathered Ones and Furry (verse; A. Fisher), 1971
Feathered Serpent (O'Dell), 1981
Febechi series (Okoro), from 1971
February Boys (Molesworth, appendix), 1909
February Dragon (Thiele), 1965
February Yowler (Storr), 1982
February's Road (Verney), 1961
Federico (H. Griffiths), 1971
Fedora the Donkey (Fidler), 1952
Feed the Animals (verse; H.A. and M. Rey), 1944
Feed the Hippo His ABC's (Scarry), 1964
Feeding Babies (Nakatani, trans), 1981
Feefo, Tuppeny, and Jinks (Blyton), 1951
Feeling Yes, Feeling No (play; Foon), 1982
Feet (Mark), 1983
Feet of the Furtive (C. Roberts), 1912
Feldman Fieldmouse (Benchley), 1971
Felice (M. Brown), 1958
Felicia (Lattimore), 1964
Felicia the Critic (Conford), 1973
Felicity series (Cockett), from 1959
Felicity's Fortune (Marchant), 1936
Fell (M. Kerr), 1987
Fell Back (M. Kerr), 1989
Fellow Fags (Talbot), 1925
Fenny (Baumann, trans), 1970
Fen's First Term (Moore), 1924

Ferdinand, The Story of (Leaf), 1936
Fergus (Abbott, appendix), 1874
Ferlie (M. Hunter), 1968
Fernley House (L. Richards), 1901
Fern's Hollow (Stretton, appendix), 1864
Ferris Wheel (Stolz), 1977
Ferry House Girls (Marchant), 1911
Ferryman (Bishop), 1941
Ferryman (D. Rees), 1977
Festival of Jewels (Patchett), 1968
Fetish Hide-Out (de Graft-Hanson), 1975
Feud in the Fifth Remove (Brent-Dyer), 1931
Feud with the Sixth (Chaundler), 1932
Few Fair Days (Gardam), 1971
Ffangs the Vampire Bat and the Kiss of Truth (T. Hughes), 1986
Fiancé for Fanny (play; Latham, as Lee), 1931
Fiddler of High Lonesome (Turkle), 1968
Fiddler's Quest (Lynch), 1941
Fiddlestrings (de Angeli), 1974
Field of the Forty Footsteps (Trease), 1977
Fields and Territories (verse; L. Clark), 1967
Fierce Bad Rabbit, The Story of a (Potter), 1906
Fierce John (Fenton), 1959
Fierce the Lion (Ness), 1980
Fierce-Face (Mukerji), 1936
Fiery Chariot (Everett-Green, appendix), 1900
Fiery Frederica (Nöstlinger, trans), 1975
Fiery-Necked Nightjar (Poland), 1983
Fifi (verse; Bemelmans), 1940
Fifteen (Bunting), 1978
Fifteen (Cleary), 1956
Fifteen Minute Tales (Blyton), 1936
Fifteen Rabbits (Salten, trans), 1930
Fifteenth Candle (play; Field), 1921
Fifteenth Century Wool Merchant (Harnett), 1962
Fifth Down (Heide, as Allen), 1974
Fifth Form at St. Dominic's (Reed, appendix), 1887
Fifth Form Mystery (H. Avery), 1923
Fifth of November (Strong), 1937
50 Below Zero (Munsch), 1985
59 Cats (Seed), 1983
51 Sycamore Lane (Sharmat), 1971
Fig Tree (Lattimore), 1951
Figgie Hobbin (verse; Causley), 1970
Figgs and Phantoms (Raskin), 1974
Fight Against Albatross Two (Thiele), 1976
Fight for Constantinople (Westerman), 1915
Fight for Freedom (R. Armstrong), 1966
Fight for Freedom (Serraillier), 1965
Fight the Night (de Paola), 1968
Fighting for Freedom (Westerman), 1941
Fighting for the Empire (Otis, appendix), 1900
Fighting Ground (Avi), 1984
Fighting on the Congo (Strang), 1906
Fighting over Me (Sharmat), 1986
Fighting the Flames (Ballantyne, appendix), 1867
Fighting the Good Fight (Everett-Green, as H.F.E., appendix), 1883
Fighting the Saracens (Henty, appendix), 1882
Fighting the Whales (Ballantyne, appendix), 1863
Fighting with French (Strang), 1915
Figure in Grey (Christopher, as Ford), 1973
Figure of 8 (verse; Causley), 1969
Figure of Speech (Mazer), 1973
File on Fraulein Berg (Lingard), 1980
Filly for Joan (Anderson), 1960

Filthy Beast (Garfield), 1978
Final Reckoning (Henty, appendix), 1886
Final Test (Owen), 1985
Find a Key (Berg), 1968
Find a Stranger, Say Goodbye (Lowry), 1978
Find Debbie! (R. Brown), 1976
Find My Hat (Bruna, trans), 1986
Finders Keepers (A. and E. Johnson), 1981
Finders Keepers (Lipkind, as Will), 1951
Finders Keepers, Losers Weepers (Lexau), 1967
Finding (Bawden), 1985
Finding a Fortune (Alger, appendix), 1904
Finding a Home (Wiggin), 1907
Finding a Poem (verse; Merriam), 1970
Finding Annabel (Geras), 1987
Finding Her Family (Oxenham), 1915
Finding Princess (Alderson), 1977
Finding the Tickets (play; Blyton), 1955
Fine Boy for Killing (Needle), 1979
Fine White Dust (Rylant), 1986
Fingal's Ghost (Fidler), 1945
Fingal's Quest (Polland), 1961
Fingers (Sleator), 1983
Fingers Crossed (Powling), 1987
Finicky Mouse (L. Wood), 1949
Finishing School (Pamela Brown), 1984
Finn and the Black Hag (play; McNeill), 1962
Finn Gang (Waddell, as Sefton), 1981
Finnegan II (Bailey), 1953
Finn's Folly (Southall), 1969
Finzel the Farsighted (P. Fleischman), 1983
Fiona Leaps the Bonfire (Lynch), 1957
Fiona on the Fourteenth Floor (Allan), 1964
Fire and Hemlock (Jones), 1984
Fire and Stone (Le Guin), 1989
Fire and the Gold (Whitney), 1956
Fire Cat (Averill), 1960
Fire Curse (Parker), 1975
Fire Engine by Mistake (Berg), 1955
Fire Engine Speedy (Hewett), 1966
Fire in the Stone (Thiele), 1973
Fire Island (Fenn, appendix), 1894
Fire on the Sea (Hardcastle), 1977
Fire Puzzle (Kariuki), 1981
Fire Station (Munsch), 1983
Fireball (Christopher), 1981
Firebrat (N. Willard), 1988
Fire-Brother (Crossley-Holland), 1975
Firefly Named Torchy (Waber), 1970
Fire-Hunter (Kjelgaard), 1951
Firelings (Kendall), 1981
Firelock and Steel (H. Avery), 1906
Fire-Raiser (Gee), 1986
Fire-Raiser (play; Gee), 1986
Fires and the Stars (Trevor), 1951
Fireside Tales (Blyton), 1966
Fireweed (Paton Walsh), 1969
First Adventure (Coatsworth), 1950
First Blood (Schaefer), 1953
First Blueberry Pig (Butterworth), 1986
First Child (Wells), 1970
First Class Matter (play; Field), 1936
First Comes Spring (Rockwell), 1985
First Contact series (Hardcastle), 1977
First Fast (Cohen), 1987
First Four Years (Wilder), 1971

First Goal (Hardcastle), 1976
First Grade (Lattimore), 1944
First Hard Times (D. B. Smith), 1983
First House (Pamela Brown), 1959
First in the Field (Fenn, appendix), 1894
First Job (Kamm), 1969
First Man In (F. Richards), 1946
First Noël (play; C. D. Mackay), 1929
First of Midnight (Darke), 1977
First of the Penguins (M. Steele), 1973
First Over (Westerman), 1948
First Pink Light (Greenfield), 1976
First Robin (R. Kraus), 1965
First Rosette (C. Pullein-Thompson), 1956
First Spring on the Grand Banks (B. Freeman), 1978
First Story (M. W. Brown), 1947
First Term at Ash Grove (Allan), 1988
First There Was Frances (B. Graham), 1985
First Time I Saw Paris (Allan, as Pilgrim), 1961
First Tripper (Dawlish), 1947
First Tulips in Holland (Krasilovsky), 1982
First Two Lives of Lukas-Kasha (Alexander), 1978
Fir-Tree Farm (Everett-Green, appendix), 1891
Fish (Bruna, trans), 1963
Fish (A. Morgan), 1971
Fish and Chips for Supper (Berg), 1968
Fish Hawk's Nest (Meader), 1952
Fish Head (Fritz), 1954
Fish Is Fish (Lionni), 1970
Fish with the Deep Sea Smile (M. W. Brown), 1938
Fisherman and the Bird (Levitin), 1982
Fisherman of Galilee (A. Fisher), 1959
Fisherman's Day (Schlein), 1959
Fisherman's Son (Lattimore), 1959
Fishermen (Wahl), 1969
Fishers of Derby Haven (Stretton, appendix), 1866
Fishing Party (Mayne), 1960
Fishing with Dad (Flora), 1967
Fishpie for Flamingoes (Geras), 1987
Fitz the Filibuster (Fenn, appendix), 1903
Five series (Blyton), from 1942
Five and a Dog (Ainsworth), 1949
Five August Days (H. Burton), 1981
Five Boys in a Cave (Church), 1951
Five Bushel Farm (Coatsworth), 1939
Five Children and It (Nesbit), 1902
Five Chinese Brothers (Bishop), 1938
Five Dolls series (Clarke, as Clare), from 1953
Five Flights Up (play; S. Walker), 1922
Five Hundred (Dillon), 1972
Five Hundred Dollar Check (Alger, appendix), 1890
$500 (Alger, appendix), 1890
500 Hats of Bartholomew Cubbins (verse; Seuss), 1938
Five in the Forest (Wahl), 1974
Five Jolly Schoolgirls (Brazil), 1941
Five Little Bears (North), 1935
Five Little Firemen (M. W. Brown), 1948
Five Little Peppers series (Sidney, appendix), from 1880
Five Mice in a Mouse-Trap (L. Richards), 1880
Five Minute Stories series (L. Richards), from 1895
Five Minute Tales (Blyton), 1933
Five Minutes' Peace (J. Murphy), 1986
Five Minutes' Stories (Molesworth, appendix), 1888
Five Minutes to Morning (play; Melwood), 1965
Five O'Clock Charlie (Henry), 1962
Five O'Clock Tales (Blyton), 1941

Follow the Drum (A. Norton), 1942
Follow the Footprints (Mayne), 1953
Follow the Road (Tresselt), 1953
Follow the Wind (Tresselt), 1950
Followers (Bunting), 1978
Following the Gold (verse; Scott), 1989
Fool (Garfield), 1977
Foolish Dinosaur Fiasco (S. Corbett), 1978
Foolish People, Two Plays about (P. Martin), 1972
Foolish Phillimores (Talbot), 1931
Fools of Chelm and Their History (Singer), 1973
Foot Book (verse; Seuss), 1968
Football (Mayne, as Molin), 1966
Footprints at the Window (Naylor), 1981
Footsteps (Garfield), 1980
For Always (Bunting), 1978
For Crying Out Loud (play; Lillington), 1968
For Dear Dad (Meade, appendix), 1911
For Lovers of...series (verse; Lear, appendix), 1978
For Me to Say (verse; McCord), 1970
For Members Only (Sharmat), 1986
For Mister Jim (play; Latham), 1940
For Name and Fame (Henty, appendix), 1885
For Summer Afternoons (Coolidge, appendix), 1876
For the Faith (Everett-Green, appendix), 1902
For the King (Welch), 1961
For the Leg of a Chicken (Bettina), 1960
For the Queen's Sake (Everett-Green, appendix), 1898
For the Sake of the School (Brazil), 1915
For the School Colours (Brazil), 1918
For the Temple (Henty, appendix), 1887
For the Train (verse; Carroll, appendix), 1932
For the White Rose (Strang), 1907
For This Man Is a Roman (play; Mitchison), 1937
For Want of a Saddle (C. Pullein-Thompson), 1960
For You and Me (play; L. Richards), 1915
Forbidden Forest (du Bois), 1978
Forbidden Fountain of Oz (McGraw), 1980
Forbidden Frontier (C. Harris), 1968
Forbidden Paths of Thual (Kelleher), 1979
Forbidden Room (H. Avery), 1911
Forbidden Room (Poole), 1979
Foreign Affair (Townsend), 1982
Forerunner Foray (A. Norton), 1973
Forespoken (Levin), 1976
Forest and the Kingdom (Trevor), 1949
Forest Fighters (Syme), 1958
Forest Folk (C. Roberts), 1949
Forest Friends (Evans), 1926
Forest Holiday (Severn), 1946
Forest of Boland Light Railway (Watkins-Pitchford), 1955
Forest of Dreams (Wells), 1988
Forest of Swords (Altsheler), 1915
Forest of the Night (Townsend), 1974
Forest of the Railway (Watkins-Pitchford), 1957
Forest Patrol (Kjelgaard), 1941
Forest Pool (Armer), 1938
Forest Princess (play; C. D. Mackay), 1916
Forest Runners (Altsheler), 1908
Forest Spring (play; C. D. Mackay), 1910
Forever (Blume), 1975
Forever Christmas Tree (Uchida), 1963
Forever Formula (Bonham), 1979
Forever Laughter (D. Freeman), 1970
Forfeits (play; Moray Williams), 1933
Forgetful Elephant (MacIntyre), 1944

Forgetful Fred (J. Williams), 1974
Forgetful Tommy (verse; Lenski), 1943
Forgetful Wishing-Well (verse; X. Kennedy), 1985
Forging Ahead (Alger, appendix), 1903
Forgotten Beasts of Eld (McKillip), 1974
Forgotten Daughter (Snedeker), 1933
Forgotten Island (Coatsworth), 1942
Forgotten Patrol (Catherall, as Channel), 1962
Forgotten Submarine (Catherall), 1956
Forgotten Theatre (B.C. Freeman), 1967
Form That Liked to Be First (Breary), 1948
Formal Feeling (Oneal), 1982
Formidable Enemy (Allan), 1973
Fort of Gold (Dillon), 1961
Fortnight South of Skye (Strong), 1934
Fortunate Few (Kennemore), 1981
Fortunate Isles (Townsend), 1989
Fortunate Term (Brazil), 1921
Fortune Finders (Heward), 1928
Fortune for the Brave (Chauncy), 1954
Fortunes of Ben Barclay (Alger, appendix), 1887
Fortunes of Phillippa (Brazil), 1906
Fortunes of Prue (Marchant), 1923
Forty Days of Tucker J (Leeson), 1983
Forward, Commandos! (Bianco), 1944
Fossil Snake (Boston), 1975
Found by the Circus (Otis, appendix), 1909
Founded on Paper (Younge, appendix), 1897
Foundling (Alexander), 1973
Fountain of Beauty (Meade, appendix), 1909
Fountain of Youth (play; C. D. Mackay), 1915
Four Cousins (Blyton), 1962
Four Days in the Life of Lisa (Nöstlinger, trans), 1977
Four Dolls (Godden), 1983
Four Donkeys (Alexander), 1972
Four Farthings and a Thimble (M. Baker), 1950
Four Fur Feet (M. W. Brown), 1961
Four Gates (Le Feuvre), 1912
Four Grannies (Jones), 1980
Four in a Family (Blyton), 1956
Four in the Half-Deck (F. Knight), 1950
Four Little Engines (Awdry), 1955
Four Little Foxes (Schlein), 1953
Four Odd Ones (Trevor), 1958
Four of Us (Beresford), 1981
Four on an Island (Meade, appendix), 1892
Four on the Shore (Marshall, as E. Marshall), 1985
Four Pigs series (Uttley), from 1939
Four Recitations (play; Brazil), 1903
Four Rode Home (Cumming), 1951
Four Seasons (verse; L. Clark), 1975
Four Stories for Four Seasons (de Paola), 1977
Four Winds Farm (Molesworth, appendix), 1886
Four Young Kendalls (E. O. White), 1932
Four-and-Twenty Blackbirds (Saville), 1959
Four-Leaf Clover (Lipkind, as Will), 1959
Four-Story Mistake (Enright), 1942
Fourteen (Sachs), 1983
Fourteenth Cadillac (Jackson), 1972
Fourth Form Detectives (Breary), 1954
Fourth Form Detectives (Chaundler), 1921
Fourth Form Friendship (Brazil), 1911
Fourth Form Rebel (Chaundler), 1922
Fourth Grade Nothing, Tales of a (Blume), 1972
Fourth Key (Saville), 1957
Fourth Was Fun for Philippa (Breary), 1961

Fritz Strafers (Westerman), 1918
Frog and the Mouse (play; Barne), 1937
Frog and Toad series (Arnold Lobel), from 1970
Frog in a Coconut Shell (Sherry), 1968
Frog in the Well (Tresselt), 1958
Frog Prince (play; B. Todd), 1956
Froggett's Revenge (Peyton), 1985
From Anna (Little), 1972
From Farm to Fortune (Alger, appendix), 1905
From Spring to Spring (verse; L. Duncan), 1982
From Spring to Spring (Uttley), 1978
From Star to Star (Kelly), 1944
From the Fury of the Norsemen (Power), 1957
From the Mixed-Up Files of Mrs. Basil E. Frankweiler (Konigs-
    burg), 1967
From the Scourge of the Tongue (Marchant), 1900
From Where I Stand (S. Price), 1984
Frontier Wolf (Sutcliff), 1980
Frost Fair (Rush), 1965
Frou (Castor, trans), 1937
Frowning Prince (Crockett Johnson), 1959
Frozen Fire (Houston), 1977
Frozen Fire (Sperry), 1956
Frozen Sky (Harding), 1976
Frying as Usual (Lingard), 1973
Fu-Dog (Godden), 1989
Fugitives (Ballantyne, appendix), 1887
Fugitives from Fortune (E. Turner), 1909
Full Circle (Uchida), 1957
Full House (Marc Brown), 1977
Full Moon (Lillington), 1986
Fumio and the Dolphins (Nakatani, trans), 1970
Fun (Mark), 1987
Fun at the Queer Trail (Burgess), 1961
Fun o' the Fair (Marchant), 1901
Fungus the Bogeyman (R. Briggs), 1977
Funniest Storybook Ever (Scarry), 1972
Funny (E. Turner), 1926
Funny Guy (Hogarth), 1955
Funny Little Book (Gruelle), 1917
Funny Place to Live (Burch), 1962
Funny Thing (Gág), 1929
Funny Thing Happened! (Buckeridge), 1953
Funny Thing Happened! (play; Buckeridge), 1963
Funny Town (verse; Merriam), 1963
Funnybones (Ahlberg), 1980
Fur (Mark), 1986
Fur and Feathers (Nesbit), 1894
Fur and Gold (Haig-Brown), 1962
Fur Magic (A. Norton), 1968
Fur Princess and the Fir Prince (Lamplugh), 1969
Furious Flycycle (Wahl), 1968
Furious Moose of the Wilderness (Kjelgaard), 1965
Furl of Fairy Wind (M. Hunter), 1977
Furry Fairies (Wynne), 1949
Further Adventures of Robinson Crusoe (Treece), 1958
Future of Hooper Toote (Holman), 1972
Future Story (F. French), 1983
Future Took Us (Severn), 1958
Futuretrack 5 (Westall), 1983
Fuzzy Mouse, Tales of (Wahl), 1988
Fuzzypeg series (Uttley), from 1932

Gabriel Garth (Everett-Green, appendix) 1902
Gabrielle (Lillington), 1988
Gaby and the New Money Fraud (Berna, trans), 1971

Gaffer Samson's Luck (Paton Walsh), 1984
'Gainst the Might of Spain (Westerman), 1914
Galactic Derelict (A. Norton), 1959
Galactic Warlord (D. Hill), 1979
Gallant Deeds (Henty, appendix), 1905
Gallant Old Engine (Awdry), 1962
Galleon (Welch), 1971
Gallery of Children (Milne), 1925
Gallimaufry series (Greaves), 1971
Galloping Fred (Ridge), 1950
Galloping Goat (Naylor), 1965
Game of Brownies (Strang), 1926
Game of Catch (Cresswell), 1969
Game of Danger (L. Duncan), 1962
Game of Dark (Mayne), 1971
Game of Soldiers (Needle), 1985
Game of Soldiers (play; Needle), 1983
Game, Set and Match (Beresford), 1965
Games (R. Klein), 1986
Games Captain (Chaundler), 1928
Gammage Cup (Kendall), 1959
Gammer Gurton's Needle (play; S. Walker), 1916
Gannet's Nest (B. Carter), 1966
Gappy Goes West (Beresford), 1959
Garbage Delight (verse; D. Lee), 1977
Garden Behind the Moon (Pyle, appendix), 1895
Garden Magic (play; McGinley), 1931
Garden of Abdul Gasazi (Van Allsburg), 1979
Garden of Broken Glass (Neville), 1975
Garden Shed (Keeping), 1971
Garden under the Sea (Selden), 1957
Gardener's Grandchildren (B. Willard), 1978
Gardens of Dorr (Biegel, trans), 1975
Gargling with Jelly (play; Patten), 1988
Gargling with Jelly (verse; Patten), 1985
Garland for Girls (Alcott, appendix), 1888
Garland of Filigree (Gray), 1979
Garland of Rose's (verse; Fyleman), 1928
Garram series (Best), from 1930
Garret and the Garden (Ballantyne, appendix), 1890
Garth Pig and the Icecream Lady (Rayner), 1977
Gary (D. Martin), 1972
Gascon Ring (play; Daniell), 1951
Gascoyne (Ballantyne, appendix), 1864
Gate of Eden (Corlett), 1974
Gates of Bannerdale (Trease), 1956
Gates of Paradise (P. Carter), 1974
Gathering (Hamilton), 1981
Gathering Clouds (Farrar, appendix), 1895
Gathering of Days (Blos), 1979
Gathering of Gargoyles (Pierce), 1984
Gaudenzia (Henry), 1960
Gauntlet (Welch), 1951
Gawain and the Green Knight (play; Gray), 1969
Gay Charmer (Meade, appendix), 1903
Gay Dolphin Aventure (Saville), 1945
Gay Go Up (verse; Fyleman), 1929
Gay Story Book (Blyton), 1946
Gay Street Book (Blyton), 1951
Gay-Neck (Mukerji), 1927
Gaze at the Moon (Cannan), 1957
Gecko (L. Rees), 1944
Gemma series (Streatfeild), from 1968
General John (Everett-Green, appendix), 1910
Genie and Her Bottle (Beachcroft), 1983
Genie of Sutton Place (Selden), 1973

Giant Kippernose (Cunliffe), 1972
Giant of the North (Ballantyne, appendix), 1882
Giant Story (de Regniers), 1953
Giant under the Snow (Gordon), 1968
Giant Who Stole the World (Cunliffe), 1971
Giant Who Swallowed the Wind (Cunliffe), 1972
Giants (play; Hoff), 1973
Giants series (Yolen), from 1977
Giants Are Very Brave People (Heide), 1970
Giant's Birthday (McNeill), 1964
Giants, Indeed! (Kahl), 1974
Gibraltar Gallery (Abbott, appendix), 1856
Gideon (Aaron), 1982
Gideon Ahoy! (Mayne), 1987
Gidja (Roughsey), 1984
Gift (Dickinson), 1973
Gift (Nixon), 1983
Gift for a Gift (Rockwell), 1974
Gift for Lonny (Bunting), 1973
Gift for Sula Sula (Ness), 1963
Gift from the Sea (Brazil), 1920
Gift from Winklesea (Cresswell), 1969
Gift Horse (M. Baker), 1982
Gift of a Lamb (play; Causley), 1978
Gift of Magic (L. Duncan), 1971
Gift of Sarah Barker (Yolen), 1981
Gift of the Mmoatia (Appiah), 1972
Gift of the Mountains (Wier), 1963
Gift of Time (play; C. D. Mackay), 1916
Gift-Giver (Hansen), 1980
Gifts of the Child Christ (MacDonald, appendix), 1973
Gigantic Balloon (Park), 1975
Gigantic Hit (Hardcastle), 1982
Gil the Gunner (Fenn, appendix), 1892
Gila Monsters Meet You at the Airport (Sharmat), 1980
Gilbert and His Mother (Abbott, appendix), 1874
Gilbert and the Birthday Cake (Thwaite), 1986
Gilbert Makepeace Lives! (play; J. Watson), 1972
Gilberto and the Wind (Ets), 1963
Giles series (C. Pullein-Thompson), from 1960
Gimlet series (Johns), from 1944
Gimme an H, Gimme an E, Gimme an L, Gimme a P (Bonham), 1980
Ginger series (Andrew), from 1962
Ginger (Peacocke), 1921
Ginger and Pickles (Potter), 1909
Ginger Ellen (Wynne), 1947
Ginger Horse (Daly), 1964
Ginger Mick (Tate), 1974
Ginger Pye (Estes), 1951
Gingerbread House (Ainsworth), 1938
Ginger-Bread Man (Baum), 1916
Gingerbread Man (D. Wood), 1985
Gingerbread Man (play; D. Wood), 1976
Gingerbread Rabbit (Jarrell), 1964
Ginger's Nine Lives (Oldfield), 1986
Gingham Bag (Sidney, appendix), 1896
Ginnie (Greenwood), 1979
Ginny's Boy (Clewes), 1973
Ginny's First Secret (Kingman), 1958
Giovanni and the Other (Burnett), 1892
Gipsy Children (C. Pullein-Thompson), 1962
Gipsy Michael (Syme), 1954
Gipsy Nurse (Alger, appendix), 1981
Giraffe and a Half (verse; Silverstein, as Shelby), 1964
Giraffe and the Pelly and Me (Dahl), 1985

Giraffe in Pepperell (verse; R. Klein), 1978
Girl and a Caravan (Marchant), 1915
Girl and Her Fortune (Meade, appendix), 1906
Girl and Her Room (verse; McGinley), 1963
Girl and Her Ways (Le Feuvre), 1925
Girl and the Goatherd (Ness), 1970
Girl at the Helm (H. Avery), 1941
Girl Called Moses (Petry), 1960
Girl Can Dream (Cavanna), 1948
Girl Captives (Marchant), 1899
Girl Die-Hard (Talbot), 1932
Girl from America (Meade, appendix), 1907
Girl from Puerto Rico (Colman), 1961
Girl from Spain (Meade, appendix), 1911
Girl in Ten Thousand (Meade, appendix), 1896
Girl in the Box (Sebestyen), 1988
Girl in the Grove (Severn), 1974
Girl in the Opposite Bed (Arundel), 1970
Girl in the Painting, (Bunting), 1978
Girl like Cathy (Clewes), 1968
Girl Missing (Nöstlinger, trans), 1976
Girl Munition Worker (Marchant), 1916
Girl of Distinction (Marchant), 1911
Girl of High Adventure (Meade, appendix), 1914
Girl of the Commune (Henty, appendix), 1895
Girl of the Fortunate Isles (Marchant), 1906
Girl of the Golden Gate (Garner), 1979
Girl of the Limberlost (G. Porter), 1909
Girl of the Limberlost (play; G. Porter), 1924
Girl of the Northland (Marchant), 1912
Girl of the Pampas (Marchant), 1921
Girl of the People (Meade, appendix), 1912
Girl of Today (Meade, appendix), 1910
Girl on the Deer (Lattimore), 1969
Girl on the Outside (Walter), 1982
Girl Out Front (play; Clapp), 1958
Girl over the Wall (Wynne), 1926
Girl Sandy (Wynne), 1938
Girl Undaunted (Marchant), 1939
Girl Who Cried Flowers (Yolen), 1974
Girl Who Didn't Know Kelly (D. Martin), 1985
Girl Who Loved the Wind (Yolen), 1972
Girl Who Played the Game (Wynne), 1924
Girl Who Ran Away (Pamela Brown), 1968
Girl Who Wanted a Boy (Zindel), 1981
Girl Who Wanted to Eat Boys (play; D. Edwards), 1974
Girl Who Was a Cowboy (Krasilovsky), 1965
Girl Who Was Different (Talbot), 1930
Girl Who Would Rather Climb Trees (Schlein), 1975
Girl Who Wouldn't Make Friends (Oxenham), 1909
Girl Whose Fortune Sought Her (play; Clapp), 1959
Girl Without a Name (Beckman, trans), 1970
Girls and I (Molesworth, appendix), 1892
Girls at Wood End (Oxenham), 1957
Girls Can Be Anything (N. Klein), 1973
Girls in the Velvet Frame (Geras), 1979
Girls, New and Old (Meade, appendix), 1895
Girls of Abinger Close (Meade, appendix), 1913
Girls of Beechcroft School (Wynne), 1920
Girls of Clanways Farm (Wynne), 1924
Girls of Gwynfa (Oxenham), 1924
Girls of King's Royal (Meade, appendix), 1913
Girls of Mackland Court (Wynne), 1928
Girls of Merton College (Meade, appendix), 1911
Girls of Mrs. Pritchard's School (Meade, appendix), 1904
Girls of Old Grange School (Wynne), 1925

Girls of St. Bride's (D. Bruce), 1923
Girls of St. Cyprian's (Brazil), 1914
Girls of St. Wode's (Meade, appendix), 1898
Girls of Squirrel House (Oxenham), 1932
Girls of the Big House (Talbot), 1935
Girls of the Forest (Meade, appendix), 1902
Girls of the Hamlet Club (Oxenham), 1914
Girls of the Pansy Patrol (Wynne), 1931
Girls of the Rookery School (Talbot), 1925
Girls of the True Blue (Meade, appendix), 1901
Girls of the Veldt Farm (Wynne), 1922
Girls of Wakenside (Marchant), 1904
Give a Form a Bad Name (Breary), 1943
Give a Man a Horse (Finger), 1938
Give and Take (N. Klein), 1985
Give Dad My Best (Collier), 1976
Give Yourself a Fright (Aiken), 1989
Given to Hospitality (Younge, appendix), 1882
Giver (L. Hall), 1985
Giving Away Suzanne (L. Duncan), 1963
Giving Tree (Silverstein), 1964
Gladys or Gwenyth (Everett-Green, appendix), 1898
Gladys Told Me to Meet Her Here (Sharmat), 1970
Glass Ball (Mayne), 1961
Glass Slipper (Farjeon), 1955
Glass Slipper (play; Farjeon), 1944
Glassblower's Children (Gripe, trans), 1974
Glen Beyond the Door (Reid), 1968
Glen Castle Mystery (Allan), 1948
Glen Eyre (M. Bruce), 1912
Glenallan's Daughters (Marchant), 1928
Glen-Luna Family (Warner, appendix), 1852
Glenvara (Allan), 1955
Gloomy Gus (Morey), 1970
Gloop the Bunyip (verse; Thiele), 1970
Gloop the Gloomy Bunyip (verse; Thiele), 1962
Gloria Chipmunk, Star! (Nixon), 1980
Glory Girl (Byars), 1983
Glubbslyme (J. Wilson), 1987
Glyn Severn's Schooldays (Fenn, appendix), 1904
Gnats of Knotty Pine (Peet), 1975
Gnome Circle (Heward), 1927
Gnome Factory (Reeves), 1986
Go and Catch a Flying Fish (Stolz), 1979
"Go" and "Come" (play; L. Richards), 1915
Go and Find Him (Hardcastle), 1977
Go and Hush the Baby (Byars), 1971
Go Away, Dog (Lexau, as Nodset), 1963
Go for Goal (Hardcastle), 1980
Go, Red, Go! (Keith), 1972
Go Saddle the Sea (Aiken), 1977
Go, Team, Go! (Tunis), 1954
Go to Sleep, Nicholas Joe (Sharmat), 1988
Go Up the Road (Lampman), 1972
Go with the Sun (Schlein), 1952
Go-Ahead Schoolgirl (Oxenham), 1919
Goal (Hardcastle), 1969
Goal in Europe (Hardcastle), 1976
Goalie (Hardcastle, as Clark), 1972
Goalkeeper's Revenge (Naughton), 1961
Goals in the Air (Hardcastle), 1972
Goanna (Wagner), 1987
Goat Boy (Bettina), 1965
Gobbling Billy (Mayne, as James), 1959
Gobblydock (Tate), 1969
Gobbolino series (Moray Williams), from 1942

Goblin Island (Oxenham), 1907
Goblin Party (D. Hill), 1988
Gobo series (Blyton), from 1953
God and Mr. Sourpuss (Judah), 1959
God, Mrs. Muskrat, and Aunt Dot (Holland), 1983
God of All things (verse; Robinson, as Thomas), 1948
God's Bairn (Moore), 1904
Goggle Eyes (Fine), 1989
Goggles! (Keats), 1969
Gogo series (Rockwell), 1978
Gogo (Slobodkin), 1960
Going Against Cool Calvin (Bunting), 1978
Going Back (Lively), 1975
Going Backwards (N. Klein), 1986
Going Barefoot (verse; A. Fisher), 1960
Going for a Walk (de Regniers), 1982
Going Gangster (Atkinson), 1940
Going Home (Peyton), 1982
Going on Sixteen (Cavanna), 1946
Going Out (Needle), 1983
Going to the Fair (Uttley), 1950
Going to the Sun (George), 1976
Going Up (P. Hunt), 1989
Going West (Waddell), 1983
Gold at Kapai (Wardell), 1960
Gold at Kapai (play; Wardell), 1959
Gold Cadillac (M. Taylor), 1987
Gold Crown Lane (Sandman Lilius, trans), 1976
Gold Dog (de Roo), 1969
Gold Dust (Seed), 1982
Gold Hawk series (F. Richards, as Clifford), 1952
Gold of Bernardino (Sawyer), 1952
Gold of Fairnilee (Lang, appendix), 1888
Gold of Fast Castle (Fidler), 1970
Golden Age (Grahame), 1895
Golden Basket (Bemelmans), 1936
Golden Bees (Ray), 1984
Golden Bees of Tulami (Bonham), 1974
Golden Book (Gruelle), 1929
Golden Brothers (Garner), 1979
Golden Bunny (M. W. Brown), 1953
Golden Caddy (Lynch), 1962
Golden Cañon (Henty, appendix), 1899
Golden Christmas Tree (Wahl), 1988
Golden Collar (Clarke), 1967
Golden Country (West), 1965
Golden Dawn (Moore), 1925
Golden Doors (Fenton), 1957
Golden Dream (Ballantyne, appendix), 1861
Golden Eagle (Clewes), 1962
Golden Effort series (Westerman), from 1924
Golden Egg Book (M. W. Brown), 1947
Golden Fiddles (M. Bruce), 1928
Golden Forest (Howes), 1930
Golden Gate (Dodge, appendix), 1903
Golden Gleaner series (Westerman), from 1948
Golden Goblet (McGraw), 1961
Golden Goose (play; K. Briggs), 1937
Golden Goose (Southall), 1981
Golden Gwendolyn (Everett-Green, appendix), 1893
Golden Hen (D. Ross), 1942
Golden Hive (verse; Behn), 1966
Golden Horse with a Silver Tail (Moray Williams), 1957
Golden Horseshoe (Coatsworth), 1935
Golden Journey (Townsend), 1989
Golden Lady (Meade, appendix), 1889

Golden Magnet (Fenn, appendix), 1883
Golden Monkey (F. Knight), 1953
Golden One (Treece), 1961
Golden Pavements (Pamela Brown), 1947
Golden Pine Cone (C. Clark), 1950
Golden Road (L. Montgomery), 1913
Golden Root (W. Steele), 1951
Golden Serpent (Myers), 1980
Golden Shore (Lyon), 1957
Golden Sleepy Book (M. W. Brown), 1948
Golden Stallion series (R. Montgomery), from 1951
Golden Star of Halich (Kelly), 1931
Golden Stick (Paulsen), 1977
Golden Touch (A. and E. Johnson), 1963
Golden Windows (L. Richards), 1903
Golden Wolf (Patchett), 1962
Golden Years (verse; Chaundler), 1950
Golden-Breasted Koo-Too (L. Richards), 1899
Goldengrove (Paton Walsh), 1972
Golden-Haired Family (L. Wood), 1961
Gold-Fever Trail (M. Hughes), 1974
Goldfinch Garden (Picard), 1963
Goldmaker's House (Sandman Lilius, trans), 1978
Gold-Marked Charm (Marchant), 1917
Golem (Singer), 1982
Goliath II (Peet), 1959
Golliwog series (Blyton), from 1951
Golliwogg series (Upton), from 1895
Golly Sisters Go West (Byars), 1986
Gollywhopper Egg (Rockwell), 1974
Gondolier of Venice (R. Kraus), 1976
Gone and Back (Benchley), 1970
Gone Away (Tomalin), 1979
Gone to the Dogs (Townsend), 1984
Gone-Away Lake series (Enright), from 1957
Good Company (verse; L. Clark), 1968
Good Ethan (Fox), 1973
Good for Something (R. Klein), 1985
Good Friends (Bianco), 1934
Good Hunting, Blue Sky (Parish), 1988
Good Intentions of Angela (Peacocke), 1937
Good King Arthur (play; L. Richards), 1916
Good Lemonade (Asch), 1976
Good Little Christmas Tree (Moray Williams), 1943
Good Little Christmas Tree (play; Moray Williams), 1951
Good Little Devil (A. Lawrence), 1978
Good Luck (Meade, appendix), 1896
Good Luck Arizona Man (Benedict), 1972
Good Luck Duck (De Jong), 1950
Good Luck to the Rider (Phipson), 1953
Good Man and His Good Wife (Krauss), 1944
Good Master (Seredy), 1935
Good Morning Book (Blyton), 1949 and 1954
Good Morning Chick (Chukovsky, trans), 1980
Good Mousekeeper (R. Kraus), 1977
Good News (Greenfield), 1977
Good Night (Coatsworth), 1972
Good Night Ben (Waber), 1974
Good Night, Fred (Wells), 1981
Good Night, Little A.B.C. (Bodecker, R. Kraus), 1972
Good Night, Little One (verse; R. Kraus), 1972
Good Night, Orange Monster (Lifton), 1972
Good Night, Owl (Hutchins), 1972
Good Night, Richard Rabbit (R. Kraus), 1972
Good Night to Annie (Merriam), 1980
Good Old Dolls (verse; Ahlberg), 1983

Good Old James (Donovan), 1975
Good Place to Hide (Slobodkin), 1961
Good, Says Jerome (verse; Clifton), 1973
Good Snakes, Bad Snakes (play; King), 1977
Good Thing or a Bad Thing (play; Jellicoe), 1974
"Good Turn Tales" for Wolf Cubs (Talbot), 1931
Good Wives (Alcott, appendix), 1868
Good Wolf (Burnett), 1908
Goodbody's Puppet Show (Moray Williams), 1956
Good-by My Shadow (Stolz), 1957
Good-Bye Book (Viorst), 1988
Goodbye, Charlie (Bunting, as Bolton), 1974
Good-bye, Chicken Little (Byars), 1979
Good-bye Day (Dehn), 1980
Goodbye, Dove Square (McNeill), 1969
Goodbye, Funny Dumpy-Lumpy (Waber), 1977
Goodbye House (Asch), 1986
Goodbye, Nanny Gray (Storey), 1987
Goodbye, Ruby Red (Kaye), 1974
Goodbye Summer (Bonsall), 1979
Goodbye Summer (Prince), 1983
Good-bye to Gumble's Yard (Townsend), 1981
Goodbye to Hounds (C. Pullein-Thompson), 1952
Good-bye to the Jungle (Townsend), 1967
Goodbye to the Purple Sage (Benedict), 1973
Goodbye to the Rat (Andrew), 1974
Good-byes of Magnus Marmalade (verse; Orgel), 1966
Good-for-Nothing Prince (J. Williams), 1969
Good-Luck Bogie Hat (C. Greene), 1971
Good-Morning Tales, Forty (Fyleman), 1926
Goodnight (verse; Hoban), 1966
Goodnight Andrew Goodnight Craig (Sharmat), 1969
Goodnight Horsey (Asch), 1981
Goodnight, Mister Tom (Magorian), 1981
Goodnight, Moon (M. W. Brown), 1947
Goodnight Moon Room (M. W. Brown), 1984
Goodnight, Prof, Dear (Townsend), 1971
Goodnight, Prof, Love (Townsend), 1970
Good-Night Tales, Forty (Fyleman), 1923
Goody Hall (Babbitt), 1971
Goose Dinner (Bunting), 1981
Goose Girl (verse; Perkins), 1906
Goose Grass Rhymes (verse; Shannon), 1930
Goose on Your Grave (Aiken), 1987
Gooseberries to Oranges (Cohen), 1982
Gooseberry (Lingard), 1978
Gooseberry Garden (Lenski), 1934
Gooseherd and the Goblin (play; C. D. Mackay), 1909
Gopher in the Garden (verse; Prelutsky), 1967
Gordon Highlander (Everett-Green, appendix), 1901
Gordon, The Big Engine (Awdry), 1953
Gordon the Goat (Leaf), 1944
Gordon's Go-Kart (Beresford), 1970
Gordy and the Pirate and the Circus Ringmaster...(C. Johnson), 1965
Gorilla (Browne), 1983
Gorilla Adventure (W. Price), 1969
Gorilla Hunters (Ballantyne, appendix), 1861
Gorky Rises (Steig), 1980
Gowie Corby Plays Chicken (Kemp), 1979
Gowrie's Vengeance (Everett-Green, appendix), 1908
Grab (Hardcastle, as Clark), 1974
Grace Jones series (Langton), from 1961
Graduation Ode (play; McNeill), 1968
Graeme and the Dragon (Mitchison), 1954
Gramp (Tate), 1971

Great Smile Robbery (McGough), 1982
Great Steamboat Mystery (Scarry), 1975
Great Thirst (Seed), 1971
Great Uncle Hoot-Toot (Molesworth, appendix), 1889
Great Wheel (Lawson), 1957
Greater Covenant (Wynne), 1933
Greater Than Gold (Meade, appendix), 1915
Greatest Gresham (G. Avery), 1962
Great-Grandmother Cat Tales (Wahl), 1976
Great-Great Rescuers (MacGibbon), 1967
Greatheart (Chipperfield), 1950
Greedy Alice (Cresswell), 1986
Greedy Little Cobbler (T. Ross), 1979
Greedy One (P. Martin), 1964
Greek Boat Mystery (Pardoe), 1960
Greeka (Chipperfield), 1953
Green and the White (Moorhead), 1974
Green Andrew Green (Holland), 1984
Green Bay Tree (Stetton, appendix), 1887
Green Behind the Glass (Geras), 1982
Green Book (Mayne), 1984
Green Book (Paton Walsh), 1981
Green Bough of Liberty (D. Rees), 1979
Green Bronze Bell (Preussler, trans), 1977
Green Casket (Molesworth, appendix), 1890
Green Christmas (Donkin), 1976
Green Coat (Gripe, trans), 1977
Green Door (E. O. White), 1930
Green Dragon (Lynch), 1925
Green Eggs and Ham (verse; Seuss), 1960
Green Finger House (R. Harris), 1980
Green Flash (Aiken), 1971
Green Forest series (Burgess), from 1921
Green Futures of Tycho (Sleator), 1981
Green Gloves (Bull), 1987
Green Goblin Book (Blyton), 1935
Green Gold (Sutton), 1976
Green Grass of Wyoming (O'Hara), 1946
Green Grow the Rushes (Lyon), 1964
Green Grows the Garden (Bianco), 1936
Green Hedges series (Blyton), from 1946
Green Hill of Nendrum (Andrews), 1970
Green Ink (Tomalin, as Leaver), 1951
Green Island Mystery (Cavanna, as Allen), 1949
Green Knowe series (Boston), from 1954
Green Laurel (Spence), 1963
Green Machine (Hardcastle), 1989
Green Meadow Stories (Burgess), 1932
Green Mist (play; Garner), 1981
Green Piper (Kelleher), 1984
Green Popinjay (Harnett), 1955
Green Recruit (Paulsen), 1978
Green Satin Gown (L. Richards), 1903
Green Smoke (Manning), 1957
Green Story Book (Blyton), 1947
Green Street (Arundel), 1966
Green Street series (Weir), from 1958
Green Wishbone (Tomalin), 1975
Greenback Hell (play; McKee), 1974
Green-Eyed Gryphon (Severn), 1958
Greenhorn (R. Armstrong), 1965
Greens (Adoff), 1988
Greensleeves (McGraw), 1968
Greenstone Axe (Ellin), 1975
Greentail Mouse (Lionni), 1973
Greenwitch (S. Cooper), 1974

Gregory and the Lady Turtle in the Valley of the Music Trees (L. Brunhoff, trans), 1971
Gregory, The Noisiest and Strongest Boy in Grangers Grove (Bright), 1969
Gremlins (Dahl), 1943
Grenville Goes to Sea (H. Burton), 1977
Greta of the Guides (Moore), 1921
Greta the Strong (Sobol), 1970
Greta's Domain (Marchant), 1910
Gretel at St. Bride's (M. Harris), 1941
Gretna Green (play; C. D. Mackay), 1915
Grey Adventure (Trease), 1942
Grey Chieftain (Chipperfield), 1952
Grey Dog from Galtymore (Chipperfield), 1961
Grey Family (Streatfeild), 1956
Grey Goose Feathers (Strang), 1926
Grey Goose of Kilnevin (Lynch), 1939
Grey King (S. Cooper), 1975
Grey Pilot (MacVicar), 1951
Grey Rabbit series (Uttley), from 1948
Grey Rabbit's Hospital (play; Uttley), 1961
Greyfrairs (Everett-Green, appendix), 1908
Greyhound (H. Griffiths), 1964
Greyling (Yolen), 1968
Greyling Towers (Molesworth, appendix), 1898
Griffon's Nest (Levin), 1975
Grim House (Molesworth, appendix), 1899
Grimblegraw and the Wuthering Witch (Sleigh), 1978
Grimbold's Other World (Gray), 1963
Grinch Grinches the Cat in the Hat (play; Seuss), n.d.
Grinny (Fisk), 1973
Grip (H. Griffiths), 1978
Griselda (Bull), 1977
Griselda's New Year (Sharmat), 1979
Grishka and the Bear (Guillot, trans), 1959
Grisly Grisell (Yonge, appendix), 1893
Grizzly (A. and E. Johnson), 1964
Grizzly Bear with the Golden Ears (George), 1982
Grizzwold (Hoff), 1963
Grocery Mouse (Clymer), 1945
Grodge-Cat and the Window Cleaner (Symonds), 1965
Gromboolian Poems (verse; Lear, appendix), 1983
Groober (Byars), 1967
Grouchy Ladybug (Carle), 1977
Groundsel and Necklaces (Barker), 1946
Grove of Green Holly (B. Willard), 1967
Grover (V. and B. Cleaver), 1970
Growing Anyway Up (Heide), 1976
Growing Story (Krauss), 1947
Growing Summer (Streatfeild), 1966
Growing-Up Feet (Cleary), 1987
Grudge Mountain (Terhune), 1939
Grumley the Grouch (Sharmat), 1980
Grumpa (Moray Williams), 1955
Grunty the Pig (Beaman), 1927
Gryphon in Glory (A. Norton), 1981
Gryphon Quest (Greaves), 1974
Guard Mouse (D. Freeman), 1967
Guardian Angels (Meade, appendix), 1880
Guardian Ghost (Nöstlinger, trans), 1986
Guardian of the Reef (Catherall, as Hallard), 1961
Guardians (Christopher), 1970
Guardians of the House (Boston), 1974
Guardians of Tony (Peacocke), 1933
Gub Gub's Book (Lofting), 1932
Guernsey Lily (Coolidge, appendix), 1881

Have You Seen My Cat? (Carle), 1973
Have Your Own Extraterrestrial Adventure (D. Hill), 1983
Havelok the Dane (Crossley-Holland), 1964
Haven for the Brave (Yates), 1941
Haven Screamers (Sherry), 1970
Having Friends (Berg), 1987
Hawk (Welch), 1967
Hawk of May (A. Lawrence), 1980
Hawk That Dare Not Hunt by Day (O'Dell), 1975
Hawkstone (J. Williams), 1971
Hawthorne Pageant (play; C. D. Mackay), 1912
Hay-Making (play; Ainsworth), 1955
Hazard Island (Wardell), 1976
Hazel Asks Why (Wynne), 1926
Hazel, Head Girl (Breary), 1952
Hazel Rye (V. and B. Cleaver), 1983
Hazel's Amazing Mother (Wells), 1985
Hazy Mountain (Bisset), 1975
He Fought for His Queen (B. Willard), 1954
He Is Your Brother (Parker), 1974
He Landed from London (play; Latham, as Lee), 1935
He Noticed I'm Alive (Sharmat), 1984
He Sailed with Blackbeard (F. Knight), 1958
He Sailed with Dampier (Rush), 1947
He Went with...series (Rush), from 1957
He Went with Captain Cook (Kamm), 1952
He Went with Drake (Dawlish), 1955
He Would Be a Mountebank (Alger, appendix), 1888
Head for Happy (H. Sewell), 1931
Head Girl at The Gables (Brazil), 1919
Head Girl's Difficulties (Brent-Dyer), 1923
Head Girl's Sister (Moore), 1918
Head in the Clouds (Southall), 1972
Head o' Mey (E. Graham), 1947
Head of the House (Everett-Green, appendix), 1886
Head of the Lower School (Moore), 1919
Head of the School (H. Avery), 1912
Head over Wheels (Kingman), 1978
Heading for Goal (Hardcastle), 1974
Headline House series (F. Richards, as Hilda Richards), 1946
Headless Cupid (Snyder), 1971
Headless Horseman Rides Tonight (verse; Prelutsky), 1980
Heads or Tails (H. Avery), 1900
Heads You Win, Tails I Lose (Holland), 1973
Healer (Dickinson), 1983
Healing Blade (Cordell), 1971
Health and Safety Plays and Programs (A. Fisher), 1953
Heart of a Dog (Terhune), 1924
Heart of Danger (Pease), 1946
Heart of Glenayrt (Wynne), 1932
Heart of Gold (Meade, appendix) 1890
Heart of Helen (Meade, appendix), 1906
Heartbeat (Mazer), 1989
Heart's Blood (Yolen), 1984
Heartsease (Dickinson), 1969
Heartsease (Yonge, appendix), 1854
Heather, The Story of (Wynne), 1912
Heather Holiday (Wynne), 1923
Heather Leaves School (Brent-Dyer), 1929
Heather, Oak and Olive (Sutcliff), 1972
Heather the Second (Wynne), 1938
Heather's Mistress (Le Feuvre), 1901
Heaven of the Sea (Ish-Kishor), 1924
Hector series (Fatio), from 1973
Hector's Inheritance (Alger, appendix), 1885
Hedgehog and Puppy Dog Tales (Manning-Sanders), 1982

Hedgehog Who Rolled Uphill (Bisset), 1982
Hedgerow Tales (Blyton), 1935
Heir of a Hundred Kings (Strang), 1924
Heir of Craigs (Vipont, as C. Vipont), 1955
Heir of Hascombe Hall (Everett-Green, appendix), 1899
Heir of Redclyffe (Yonge, appendix), 1853
Heir of Sea and Fire (McKillip), 1977
Heirs of Ashton Manor (Weir), 1966
Held at Ransome (Marchant), 1900
Held Fast for England (Henty, appendix), 1891
Held in the Frozen North (Westerman), 1956
Held to Ransom (Westerman), 1951
Helen Ford (Alger, appendix), 1866
Helen of the Black Mountain (Marchant), 1914
Helen's Gift House (E. O. White), 1938
Helga and the White Peacock (play; Meigs), 1922
Helga High-Up (Sharmat), 1987
Helga's Dowry (de Paola), 1977
Hello, Elephant (Wahl), 1964
Hello, Hippopotamus (R. Kraus), 1969
Hello, Little Pig (Janosch, trans), 1988
Hello, Star (Haywood), 1987
Hello to Bodega (Aaron), 1975
Hello...Wrong Number (Sachs), 1981
Hell's Edge (Townsend), 1963
Help Mr. Willy Nilly (Fritz), 1954
Help! Yelled Maxwell (Stevenson), 1978
Helpers (S. Hughes), 1975
Helpful Friends (Bonsall, as Newell), 1955
Helping Hand (McNeill), 1971
Helping Himself (Alger, appendix), 1886
Helping Horse (Phipson), 1974
Hemi Dances (R. Bacon), 1985
Hemi's Pet (de Hamel), 1985
Henchmans at Home (H. Burton), 1970
Hendon Fungus (Parker), 1967
Hengest's Tale (Paton Walsh), 1966
Henner's Lydia (de Angeli), 1936
Henny and Crispies (Mitchison), 1964
Henri series (Kahl), from 1959
Henrietta series (K. Hale), from 1943
Henrietta series (Hoff), from 1977
Henrietta Hen series (Judah), from 1958
Henrietta of St. Hilary's (M. Harris), 1953
Henrietta's House (Goudge), 1942
Henrietta's Wish (Yonge, appendix), 1850
Henry (Bawden), 1988
Henry (Merrill), 1951
Henry and Grudge (Holland), 1986
Henry and the Monstrous Din (Hoban), 1966
Henry, Fisherman (Marcia Brown), 1949
Henry Hare series (Clewes), from 1950
Henry Huggins series (Cleary), from 1950
Henry Pond Poet (King-Smith), 1989
Henry Reed series (Robertson), from 1958
Henry Sugar, The Wonderful Story of (Dahl), 1977
Henry the Cat and the Big Sneeze (Rockwell), 1980
Henry, The Green Engine (Awdry), 1951
Henry 3 (Krumgold), 1967
Henry's Dog Henry (Brooks), 1965
Henry's Leg (Pilling), 1985
Henry's Quest (Oakley), 1986
Henry's Red Sea (Smucker), 1955
Henry's Ride (Schlein), 1956
Hepatica Hawkes (Field), 1932
Hepsy Gipsy (Meade, appendix), 1891

Hepzibah (Dickinson), 1978
Her Happy Face (Meade, appendix), 1914
Her Husband's Home (Everett-Green, appendix), 1885
Her Husband's Property (Le Feuvre), 1913
Her Kingdom (Le Feuvre), 1929
Her Kissin' Cousin (play; Clapp), 1957
Her Only Son (Stretton, appendix), 1887
Her Own Kin (Marchant), 1925
Her Schoolgirl Majesty (Moore), 1918
Heracles (play; Foon), 1978
Herald of the West (Altsheler), 1898
Herb of the Field (Yonge, appendix), 1853
Herbert Carter's Legacy (Alger, appendix), 1875
Herbert Hated Being Small (verse; Kuskin), 1979
Herbert Rowbarge (Babbitt), 1982
Herbert Selden (Alger, appendix), 1981
Herbie's Magical Hat (Preussler, trans), 1985
Herbs (play; M. Bond), 1970
Hercules (Gramatky), 1940
Herd Boy and His Hermit (Yonge, appendix), 1899
Herd of Deer (Dillon), 1969
Here Abide Monsters (A. Norton), 1973
Here and There (verse; L. Clark), 1969
Here and There Stories (Power), 1945
Here Come the Purim Players! (Cohen), 1984
Here Comes Christmas! (play; A. Fisher), 1947
Here Comes Harry (H. Lewis), 1960
Here Comes Herb's Hurricane! (Stevenson), 1973
Here Comes John (B. Graham), 1983
Here Comes Mr. Right (Sharmat), 1986
Here Comes Night (Schlein), 1957
Here Comes Pete (Clymer), 1944
Here Comes the Bus! (Haywood), 1963
Here Comes the Trolley Car (Chalmers), 1955
Here Comes Theo (B. Graham), 1983
Here Comes Wordman! (H. Todd), 1979
Here I Come—Ready or Not! (Merrill), 1970
Here Lies Price (S. Price), 1987
Here Lies the Body (S. Corbett), 1974
Here Tomorrow, Gone Today (Kennemore), 1983
Here We Go Round (Allan), 1954
Here We Go round the Buttercups (play; Ainsworth), 1955
Here We Go round the Round House (verse; Causley), 1976
Here's Jellybean Reilly (Bonsall), 1966
Here's Sam (D. Edwards), 1979
Hereward the Wake (play; Daniell), 1951
Hereward the Wake (Kingsley, appendix), 1866
Heritage of the Star (Engdahl), 1973
Herman McGregor's World (Schlein), 1958
Herman the Helper series (R. Kraus), from 1974
Herman the Loser (Hoban), 1961
Hermie's Rose-Buds (Meade, appendix), 1883
Hermit Dan (Parish), 1977
Hermit in the Hills (Severn), 1945
Hermit's Horse (D. Pullein-Thompson), 1974
Hermy (Molesworth, appendix), 1880
Hero Ain't Nothin' But a Sandwich (Childress), 1973
Hero Ain't Nothin' But a Sandwich (play; Childress), 1977
Hero and the Crown (McKinley), 1985
Hero from Otherwhere (J. Williams), 1972
Hero of Liège (Strang), 1914
Hero of Sparshott (F. Richards), 1946
Hero of the Highlands (Everett-Green, appendix), 1903
Hero Stories (Bailey), 1919
Heroes and Heroines (verse; Farjeon), 1933
Heroic Deeds of Jason Jones (Andrew), 1975

Heroine of Chelton School (Wynne), 1920
Heroine of the Ranch (Marachant), 1913
Heroine of the Sea (Marchant), 1903
Heroine of the Titanic (Blos), 1989
Heron series (Treadgold), from 1962
Heronstoke Mystery (Everett-Green, appendix), 1915
Herr Baby, The Adventures of (Molesworth, appendix), 1881
Herschel the Hero (Hoff), 1969
Herself and Her Boy (Le Feuvre), 1914
Hester (Meynell, as Baxter), 1957
Hester Mouse Who Became a Writer, The Story of (Hoban), 1965
Hester's Summer (G. Cooper), 1974
Hetty (B. Willard), 1962
Hetty and Harriet (Oakley), 1981
Hetty Beresford (Meade, appendix), 1908
Hetty of the Grande Deluxe (Means), 1951
Hetty Pegler, Half-Witch (Greaves), 1987
Hey, Big Spender! (Bonham), 1972
Hey, Dad! (Doyle), 1978
Hey Hey Man (S. Fleischman), 1979
Hey Jude (play; Davies), 1982
Hey, Phantom Singlet (S. French), 1975
Hey Presto, You're a Bear! (Janosch, trans), 1977
Hey Robin! (Leeson), 1989
Hey, What's Wrong with This One? (Wojciechowska), 1969
Hey World, Here I Am! (verse; Little), 1986
Hi, Cat! (Keats), 1970
Hi Johnny (M. Hunter), 1963
Hi Jolly (Kjelgaard), 1959
Hi, Mr. Robin! (Tresselt), 1950
Hi There, Supermouse! (Ure), 1983
Hiccup Harry (Powling), 1988
Hiccups (B. Wilson), 1971
Hickory (Palmer Brown), 1978
Hickory Dickory Clock Book (verse; Scarry), 1961
Hickory Stick Rag (verse; C. Watson), 1976
Hidden Box Mystery (Heide), 1973
Hidden Enemy (Hardcastle), 1970
Hidden Gold (Clarke), 1957
Hidden Horse (J. Pullein-Thompson), 1982
Hidden House (M. W. Brown), 1953
Hidden in a Dream (M. Edwards), 1952
Hidden Key (Clewes), 1960
Hidden Mill (Beresford), 1965
Hidden Mine (Altsheler), 1896
Hidden Ones (Halam, as Jones), 1988
Hidden Pool (R. Bond), 1966
Hidden River (D. Pullein-Thompson), 1960
Hidden Road (Berg), 1958
Hidden Shrine (Myers), 1985
Hidden Trail (Kjelgaard), 1962
Hidden Trapezes (Fenton), 1950
Hide (P. Martin), 1974
Hide and Seek (Clewes), 1959
Hide and Seek (Coatsworth), 1956
Hide and Seek Day (Zion), 1954
Hide and Seek Fog (Tresselt), 1965
Hide till Daytime (Phipson), 1977
Hide-and-Seek (play; Ainsworth), 1955
Hide-and-Seek (play; Daniell), 1948
Hideaway (McGraw), 1983
Hideaway Johnny (Daniell), 1959
Hiding (N. Klein), 1976
Higgins and the Great Big Scare (Caudill), 1960
Higgledy-Piggledy (verse; Livingston), 1986
Higglety Pigglety Pop! (Sendak), 1967

Hollyhock (Meade, appendix), 1916
Hollywood Kid (Wojciechowska), 1966
Home (play; Doherty), 1988
Home (Schlein), 1958
Home and Away (Thwaite), 1967
Home Before Dark (Bridgers), 1976
Home Boy (Hansen), 1982
Home for a Bunny (M. W. Brown), 1956
Home for Jessie (C. Pullein-Thompson), 1986
Home from Far (Little), 1965
Home from Home (S. Price), 1977
Home from the Hill (M. Baker), 1968
Home Is the North (Morey), 1967
Home Is the Sailor (Godden), 1964
Home of Silence (Meade, appendix), 1907
Home of Sweet Content (Meade, appendix), 1906
Home on the Range (Hader), 1955
Home, Sweet Home (Walton, appendix), 1874
Home to the Island (Allan), 1962
Homecoming (Voigt), 1981
Homeless Katie (C. Pullein-Thompson), 1964
Home-Made Dragon (N. Hunter), 1971
Home-Makers (Hough), 1957
Homer series (M. Baker), from 1950
Homer and the Circus Train (Gramatky), 1957
Homer Price series (McCloskey), from 1943
Homesmind (Sargent), 1984
Homestead of the Free (A. Fisher), 1953
Homesteader Girl (Marchant), 1932
Homeward Bounders (Jones), 1981
Homework Caper (Lexau), 1966
Ho-ming (E. Lewis), 1934
Honey Forest (Brinsmead), 1978
Honey, I Love (verse; Greenfield), 1978
Honey of a Chimp, (N. Klein), 1980
Honey Mouse (Hewett), 1957
Honeybee and the Robber (Carle), 1981
Honeyhill (play; Lamplugh), 1967
Honeysuckle Hedge (play; Clapp), 1960
Honeysuckle Line (Weir), 1959
Honeywell Badger (Stranger), 1972
Honk (Stong), 1935
Honk Honk! (Rockwell), 1980
Honor Bound (Bonham), 1963
Honor Bound (Downie), 1971
Honor Bright series (L. Richards), from 1920
Honor Sands (M. Lee), 1966
Honour First (Strang), 1923
Honour of the School (Wynne), 1918
Honoured Guest (R. Klein), 1979
Hoober Bloob Highway (play; Seuss) 1975
Hoodie (Molesworth, appendix), 1882
Hoodwinkers (M. Edwards), 1962
Hoodwinking of Mrs. Elmo (R. Kraus), 1987
Hoof and Claw (C. Roberts), 1913
Hoofprint on the Wind (A. Clark), 1972
Hook a Fish, Catch a Mountain (George), 1975
Hooked! (Hardcastle), 1984
Hoo-Ming's Discovery (Cockett), 1982
Hooper Humperdink (verse; Seuss), 1976
Hoops (Myers), 1981
Hooray for Father's Day! (Sharmat), 1986
Hooray for Me (Clewes), 1973
Hooray for Mother's Day! (Sharmat), 1986
Hootie Toots of Hollow Tree (Wynne), 1925
Hop on Pop (verse; Seuss), 1963

Hope and a Hatchet (Paulsen), 1978
Hopeful Trout (verse; Ciardi), 1989
Hopes and Fears (Yonge, appendix), 1860
Hope's Tryst (Marchant), 1904
Hop-o'-My thumb (Bruna, trans), 1966
Hoppity-Gap (Powling), 1988
Horatio series (Clymer), from 1968
Horatio (Foreman), 1970
Horizon Is Calling (Yashima), 1947
Horn of Merlyns (Needham), 1943
Horned Helmet (Treece), 1963
Horns of Danger (Allan), 1981
Horrible Boy (Thwaite), 1975
Horrible Story (Mahy), 1987
Horribles (Rosen), 1988
Horrie Kiwi and the Kids (Wall), 1984
Horse (Gardam), 1982
Horse and His Boy (C. Lewis), 1954
Horse and the Bad Morning (P. Martin, as Miles), 1982
Horse Book (Tourtel), 1901
Horse Came Running (De Jong), 1970
Horse for Claudia and Dennis (R. Montgomery), 1958
Horse for Melinda (Gates), 1981
Horse for the Island (Bettina), 1952
Horse in Harry's Room (Hoff), 1970
Horse in the Attic (Clymer), 1983
Horse in the Camel Suit (du Bois), 1967
Horse in the Clouds (H. Griffiths), 1957
Horse Named Peaceable (Holland), 1982
Horse of Hurricane Hill (Anderson), 1956
Horse on Wheels (Ainsworth), 1966
Horse Sale (C. Pullein-Thompson), 1960
Horse Stories (Coatsworth), 1954
Horse That Swam Away (Farley), 1965
Horse Trader (L. Hall), 1981
Horse Who had His Picture in the Paper (McGinley), 1951
Horse Who Lived Upstairs (McGinley), 1944
Horse with Eight Hands (Phipson), 1974
Horse with High-Heeled Shoes (Slobodkin), 1954
Horse Without a Head (Berna, trans), 1957
Horse-Fancier (Dillon), 1985
Horsemen of the Plains (Altsheler), 1910
Horsemen on the Hills (Trease), 1971
Horses (M. W. Brown, as Hay), 1944
Horses at Home (D. Pullein-Thompson), 1954
Horses I've Known (James), 1940
Horses of Dreamland (verse; L. Duncan), 1985
Horses of Petrock (V. Smith), 1965
Horses of the Night (Sandman Lilus, trans), 1979
Horseshoe Reef (R. Armstrong), 1960
Horseshoes and Handlebars (Atkinson), 1958
Horse-Tamer (Farley), 1958
Horsey and Co. and the Bank Robbers (Daniell, as Bowood), 1965
Hortense (Carlson), 1957
Horton series (verse; Seuss), from 1940
Horton Hears a Who (play; Seuss), 1970
Hosea's Girl (Marchant), 1934
Hospital (S. Porter), 1973
Hospital Day (Berg), 1972
Hospital Zone (Stolz), 1956
Hostage (Holm, trans), 1980
Hostage (T. Taylor), 1987
Hostages (Mitchison), 1930
Hostages to Fortune (Lingard), 1976
Hosts of the Air (Altsheler), 1915
Hot and Cold Summer (Hurwitz), 1984

How John Got His Ducklings (Blyton), 1966
How Lazy Can You Get? (Naylor), 1979
How Many Days to America? (Bunting), 1988
How Many Dragons Are Behind the Door? (verse; Kahl), 1977
How Many Kids Are Hiding on My Block? (Merrill), 1970
How Many Miles to Babylon? (Fox), 1967
How Many Miles to Babylon? (Needham), 1953
How Many Miles to Cyprus (Allen), 1955
How Many Miles to Sundown (P. Beatty), 1974
How Mrs. Santa Claus Saved Christmas (verse; McGinley), 1963
How My Garden Grew (Rockwell), 1982
How Nell Scored (Marchant), 1929
How Now Brown Cow (play; L'Engle), 1949
How the Carter Boys Lifted the Mortgage (C. Roberts), 1894
How the Children Stopped the Wars (Wahl), 1969
How the Ewoks Saved the Trees (Howe), 1984
How the Flowers Grow (play; Blyton), 1939
How the Flying Fishes Came into Being (H.A. and M. Rey), 1938
How the Grinch Stole Christmas (play; Seuss), 1966
How the Grinch Stole Christmas (verse; Seuss), 1957
How the Hibernators Came to Bethlehem (verse; Farber), 1980
How the Left-Behind Beasts built Ararat (verse; Farber), 1978
How the Leopard Got His Claws (Achebe), 1972
How the Reindeer Saved Santa (Haywood), 1986
How the Rooster Saved the Day (Arnold Lobel), 1977
How the Twins Captured a Hessian (Otis, appendix), 1902
How the Weatherman Came (Ish-Kishor), 1938
How the Whale Became (T. Hughes), 1963
How They Came Back from School (Praeger), 1911
How They Went to Europe (Sidney, appendix), 1884
How They Went to School (Praeger), 1903
How They Went to the Seaside (Praeger), 1909
How to Go About Laying an Egg (Waber), 1963
How to Have a Gorgeous Wedding (Sharmat), 1985
How to Make an Earthquake (Krauss), 1954
How to Meet a Gorgeous Girl (Sharmat), 1984
How to Meet a Gorgeous Guy (Sharmat), 1983
How to Read a Rabbit (Fritz), 1959
How to Ride a Tiger (Farber), 1983
How to Survive Summer Camp (J. Wilson), 1985
How Tommy Saved the Barn (Otis, appendix), 1895
Howard (Stevenson), 1980
Howard's Field (play; Doherty), 1979
Howards Go Sledding (Wahl), 1964
Howliday Inn (Howe), 1982
Howl's Moving Castle (Jones), 1986
How's Business (Prince), 1987
Hub (R. N. Peck), 1979
Hubert's Hair-Raising Adventure (verse; Peet), 1959
Huck and Her Time Machine (G. Avery), 1977
Huck Finn's Story (play; A. Harris), 1987
Huckleberry Finn, The Adventures of (Twain, appendix), 1884
Huckle's Book (Scarry), 1979
Huffler (Paton Walsh), 1975
Huge Harold (verse; Peet), 1961
Hugh Stanford's Luck (M. Bruce), 1925
Hughie (D. Martin), 1971
Hugh's Zoo (MacIntyre), 1964
Hugo series (T. Ross), from 1977
Hugo and Franz (Finley, appendix), 1865
Hugo and His Grandma series (Storr), from 1977
Hugo and Josephine series (Gripe, trans), from 1969
Hugo at the Window (Rockwell), 1988
Hugo Takes Off (Parker), 1976
Hugo, The Deformed (Alger, appendix), 1978
Hullabaloo ABC (verse; Cleary), 1960

Hull-Down for Action (Sperry), 1945
Hullo Lucy (Bisset), 1967
Human Rights Day (A. Fisher), 1966
Humbert, Mister Firkin and the Lord Mayor of London (Burningham), 1965
Humbling of Mark Lester (Marchant), 1899
Humbug Mountain (S. Fleischman), 1978
Humbugs (Treadgold), 1968
Hummingbird People (Palmer), 1971
Humphrey (Flack), 1934
Humphrey Bold (Strang), 1908
Humphrey's Bear (Wahl), 1987
Humpty Dumpty Book of Nursery Rhymes (verse; Tourtel), 1902
Hunchback of Notre Dame (play; Foon), 1981
Hunches in Bunches (verse; Seuss), 1982
Hundred and One Dalmatians (D. Smith), 1956
Hundred Dresses (Estes), 1944
Hundred Islands (M. Clark), 1976
Hundred Million Francs (Berna, trans), 1957
Hundred Penny Box (Mathis), 1975
Hundred Shining Candles (Lunn), 1989
Hundredth Dove (Yolen), 1977
Hungarian Rebel (Catherall, as Ruthin), 1970
Hungry Fred (Fox), 1969
Huni (F. French), 1971
Hunt for Harry (Weir), 1959
Hunt Royal (Daniell), 1958
Hunt Royal (play; Daniell), 1955
Hunt the King, Hide the Fox (Trevor), 1950
Hunt the Thimble (F. French), 1978
Hunted and Harried (Ballantyne, appendix), 1892
Hunted Horses (Rounds), 1951
Hunted in Their Own Land (Chauncy), 1973
Hunted King (Meynell), 1959
Hunter and the Animals (de Paola), 1981
Hunter and the Medicine Man (C. Clark), 1966
Hunter Hunted (Treece), 1957
Hunter in the Dark (M. Hughes), 1982
Hunter of Harter Fell (Chipperfield), 1976
Hunters and the Henwife (play; Gray), 1954
Hunter's Moon (Atkinson), 1952
Hunters of Siberia (Bartos-Höppner, trans), 1969
Hunters of the Hills (Altsheler), 1916
Hunting Cat (Patchett), 1976
Hunting of the Shadroth (Kelleher), 1981
Hunting of the Snark (verse; Carroll, appendix), 1876
Hunting the Lions (Ballantyne, appendix), 1869
Hunting the Skipper (Fenn, appendix), 1906
Hunting Trail (Wier), 1974
Hunting Trip (Burch), 1971
Huntsman (D. Hill), 1982
Hurdy-Gurdy (verse; Reeves), 1961
Hurdy-Gurdy (verse; L. Richards), 1902
Hurdy-Gurdy Man (Bianco), 1933
Hurrah for a Dutch Birthday (Ridge), 1964
Hurrah for Freddie! (Bright), 1953
Hurrah for Jonathan! (Fritz), 1955
Hurrah for Muggins (Ridge), 1947
Hurrah for the Circus! (Blyton), 1939
Hurricane (Salkey), 1964
Hurricane Elaine (Hurwitz), 1986
Hurricane Treasure (Bice), 1965
Hurricane Weather (Pease), 1936
Hurricane Yank (R. Montgomery), 1942
Hurry Home, Candy (De Jong), 1953
Hurry, Hurry, Mary Dear! (verse; Bodecker), 1976

Hurry, Hurry, Sibusiso (Seed), 1988
Hurry Up, Bonnie! (Alderson), 1976
Hurry Up, Slowpoke (Bonsall, as Newell), 1961
Husky (R. Montgomery), 1942
Hustle and Bustle (Slobodkin), 1948
Hut (play; Parker), 1953
Hut School and the Wartime Home-Front Heroes (Burch), 1974
Hypnotic Island (play; Patten), 1977
Hypnotiser (verse; Rosen), 1988

I, Adam (Fritz), 1963
I Am a Dustbin (play; Lillington), 1972
I Am a Man (verse; Merriam), 1971
I Am David (Holm, trans), 1965
I Am Five (Fitzhugh), 1978
I Am Four (Fitzhugh), 1982
I Am Joseph (Cohen), 1980
I Am Kofi (Asare), 1972
I Am Not a Pest (Sharmat), 1979
I Am Not Going to Get Up Today! (verse; Seuss), 1987
I Am Papa Snap (Ungerer), 1971
I Am Phoenix (verse; P. Fleischman), 1985
I Am the Cheese (Cormier), 1977
I Am the King of Kazoo (R. N. Peck), 1976
I Am the Running Girl (verse; Adoff), 1979
I Am Three (Fitzhugh), 1982
I and Sproggy (C. Greene), 1978
I Ask a Blessing (verse; Robinson, as Thomas), 1955
I Can...series (Bruna, trans), from 1979
I Can...series (Watanabe, trans), from 1982
I Can Blink (Asch), 1986
I Can Do It by Myself (Greenfield), 1978
I Can Fly (verse; Krauss), 1950
I Can Lick 30 Tigers Today (verse; Seuss), 1969
I Can Roar (Asch), 1986
I Can't Stand Losing (Kemp), 1987
I Carried the Horn (C. Pullein-Thompson), 1951
I Didn't Invite You to My Party (McNeill), 1967
I Din Do Nuttin (verse; Agard), 1983
I Discover Columbus (Lawson), 1941
I Do (play; Okoro), 1988
I Don't Care (Sharmat), 1977
I Don't Want to Go to Bed (Lindgren, trans), 1988
I Feel Like the Morning Star (Maguire), 1989
I Go by Sea, I Go by Land (Travers), 1941
I Had Trouble Getting to Solla Sollew (verse; Seuss), 1965
I Had Two Ponies (J. Pullein-Thompson), 1947
I Hate My Brother Maxwell Potter (W. Taylor), 1989
I Hate My Teddy Bear (McKee), 1982
I Hate Red Rover (Lexau), 1979
I Have a Horse of My Own (Zolotow), 1964
I Have a Song to Sing You (verse; L. Richards), 1938
I Have to Go! (Munsch), 1987
I Hear You Smiling (verse; Holman), 1973
I, Houdini (Banks), 1978
I, Juan de Pareja (de Treviño), 1965
I Know a Lady (Zolotow), 1984
I Know about Numbers (Bruna, trans), 1981
I Know about Shapes (Bruna, trans), 1984
I Know What You Did Last Summer (L. Duncan), 1973
I Like Books (Browne), 1989
I Like Red (Bright), 1955
I Like to Be Little (Zolotow), 1987
I Like Weather (verse; A. Fisher), 1963
I Like Winter (verse; Lenski), 1950
I Love My Love with an A (D. Ross), 1972

I Love My Mother (Zindel), 1975
I Love My Pets (Rockwell), 1982
I Marched with Hannibal (Baumann, trans), 1961
I Met a Man (verse; Ciardi), 1961
I Met a Penguin (Asch), 1972
I, Mouse (R. Kraus), 1958
I Never Loved Your Mind (Zindel), 1970
IOU's (Sebestyen), 1982
I Own the Racecourse! (Wrightson), 1968
I Play in My Room (Rockwell), 1981
I Rhyme My Time (verse; D. Martin), 1980
I Rode a Winner (C. Pullein-Thompson), 1973
I Rode with the Covenanters (Fidler), 1950
I Saw Him First (Sharmat), 1983
I Saw the Sea Come In (Tresselt), 1954
I Saw Three Ships (Goude), 1969
I See a Kitty (Flack), 1943
I See a Song (Carle), 1973
I See What I See! (Selden), 1962
I Shot an Arrow (R. Klein), 1987
I Should Have Stayed in Bed! (Lexau), 1965
I Spy (play; Wymark), 1975
I Stay Near You (M. Kerr), 1985
I Stood on a Mountain (verse; A. Fisher), 1979
I Talk to Elephants! (Livingston), 1962
I Tell a Lie Every So Often (Clements), 1974
I: The Autobiography of a Cat (E. O. White), 1941
I Think I'm Falling in Love (Sharmat), 1986
I, Trissy (Mazer), 1971
I Want a Brother or Sister (Lindgren, trans), 1988
I Want a Cat (T. Ross), 1988
I Want Mama (Sharmat), 1974
I Want My Potty (T. Ross), 1986
I Want My Sunday, Stranger! (P. Beatty), 1977
I Want to Be a Fish (R. Harris), 1977
I Want to Be Little (Zolotow), 1967
I Want to Go to School Too (Lindgren, trans), 1980
I Want to Paint My Bathroom Blue (Krauss), 1956
I Want to Stay Here! I Want to Go There! (Lionni), 1977
I Wanted a Pony (D. Pullein-Thompson), 1946
I Was a Second Grade Werewolf (Pinkwater), 1983
I Was All Thumbs (Waber), 1975
I Was There (Richter, trans), 1972
I Wear the Morning Star (Highwater), 1986
I Went for a Walk (verse; Lenski), 1958
I Will Adventure (Vining, as Gray), 1962
I Will! I Won't! (play; Latham, as Lee), 1931
I Will Sing a New Song (Meade, appendix), 1909
I Wish I Had Another Name (verse; J. Williams), 1962
I Wish I Had Duck Feet (verse; Seuss, as Le Sieg), 1965
I Wish I Were a Butterfly (Howe), 1987
I Wonder How, I Wonder Why (verse; A. Fisher), 1962
I Would Rather Be a Turnip (V. and B. Cleaver), 1971
I Write It (verse; Krauss), 1970
Ice Bear (Levin), 1986
Ice Blink (R. Montgomery), 1941
Ice Creams for Rosie (Armitage), 1981
Ice Crown (A. Norton), 1970
Ice Fair (Hope-Simpson), 1963
Ice Fighter (Syme), 1956
Ice Ghosts Mystery (Curry), 1972
Ice Is Coming (Wrightson), 1977
Ice Swords (Houston), 1985
Ice to India (Robertson), 1955
Ice Wolf (play; J Kraus), 1964
Ice-Cream Cone Coat (verse; Arnold Lobel), 1971

Ice-Palace (Swindells), 1977
Ida (play; R. Montgomery), 1962
Ida and the Wool Smugglers (Alderson), 1987
Ida Early series (Burch), from 1980
Ida the Bareback Rider (Hoff), 1972
Ideal Gnome Expedition (play; D. Wood), 1981
Ideal Tale (verse; Corlett), 1975
Ides of April (Ray), 1974
Idun and the Apples of Life (play; Garner), 1965
If a Body Meets a Body (play; Clapp), 1963
If All the Swords in England (B. Willard), 1961
If I Asked You, Would You Stay? (Bunting), 1984
If I Had a Boat (verse; W. Smith), 1966
If I Had My Way (N. Klein), 1974
If I Love You, Am I Trapped Forever? (M. Kerr), 1973
If I Ran the...series (verse; Seuss), from 1950
If I Were in Charge of the World (verse; Viorst), 1981
If I'd Been Born in Bethlehem (verse; Robinson, as Thomas),
    1953
If It Weren't for Sebastian (Ure), 1982
If It Weren't for You (Zolotow), 1966
If Jesus Came to My House (verse; Robinson, as Thomas), 1941
If Only (H. Griffiths, as Santos), 1987
If Only I Could Tell You (verse; Merriam), 1983
If the Earth Falls In (M. Clark), 1975
If This Is Love, I'll Take Spaghetti (Conford), 1983
If Winter Comes (L. Hall), 1986
If Wishes Were Horses (Robertson), 1958
If You Listen (Zolotow), 1980
If You Made a Million (Kellogg), 1989
If You Say So, Claude (Nixon), 1980
Iggie's House (Blume), 1970
Ignoramus (play; Reaney), 1966
Ilenka (Kingman), 1945
I'll Be You and You Be Me (Krauss), 1954
I'll Fix Anthony (Viorst), 1969
I'll Get There. It Better Be Worth the Trip (Donovan), 1969
I'll Go My Own Way (M. Hunter), 1985
I'll Love You When You're More Like Me (M. Kerr), 1977
I'll Make You Small (Wynne-Jones), 1986
I'll Make You Well, Tiger, Said the Bear (Janosch, trans), 1985
I'll Ring for More Toast (play; Lillington), 1967
I'll Show You Cats (Bonsall), 1964
I'll Tell on You (Lexau), 1976
I'll Tell You a Story series (Blyton), 1942
I'll Tell You a Tale (verse; Serraillier), 1973
Ill-Made Knight (T. White), 1940
Illyrian Adventure (Alexander), 1986
I'm a Little Airplane (R. Kraus, as Tubby), 1981
I'm a Little Baby (R. Kraus, as Tubby), 1981
I'm a Little Choo-Choo (R. Kraus, as Tubby), 1981
I'm a Little Fish (R. Kraus, as Tubby), 1981
I'm a Little House (R. Kraus, as Tubby), 1981
I'm a Little Tugboat (R. Kraus, as Tubby), 1981
I'm a Monkey (R. Kraus), 1975
I'm Coming to Get You (T. Ross), 1984
I'm Deborah Sampson (Clapp), 1977
I'm Going for a Walk! (Watanabe, trans), 1984
I'm Going to Get Your Boyfriend (Sharmat), 1986
I'm Having a Bath with Papa! (Watanabe, trans), 1986
I'm Hiding (Livingston), 1961
I'm Not Me (Livingston), 1963
I'm Not Oscar's Friend Anymore (Sharmat), 1975
I'm Playing with Papa (Watanabe, trans), 1985
I'm Really Dragged But Nothing Gets Me Down (Hentoff), 1968
I'm Still Me (Lifton), 1981

I'm Terrific (Sharmat), 1976
I'm the King of the Castle (Watanable, trans), 1982
I'm Trying to Tell You (Ashley), 1981
I'm Waiting (Livingston), 1966
Images (play; Garner), 1981
Imaginary Menagerie (verse; McGough), 1988
Imagination Greene (Ormondroyd), 1973
Imagine If (Heine, trans), 1979
Imogen (Molesworth, appendix), 1892
Imp (Darke), 1985
Imp and Biscuit (Worth), 1981
Imp of Mischief (Burgess), 1929
Imperial Nightingale (play; Gray), 1956
Important Book (M. W. Brown), 1949
Impossible Horse (C. Pullein-Thompson, as Keir), 1957
Impossible, Possum (Conford), 1971
Impossible Prefect (Breary), 1947
Improbable Adventures of Marvelous O'Hara Soapstone (Oneal),
    1972
Imprudence of Carol Carew (Everett-Green, appendix), 1907
Impunity Jane (Godden), 1954
In a Blue Velvet Dress (Waddell, as Sefton), 1972
In a Forgotten Place (Orgel), 1967
In a House I Know (Berg), 1981
In a Land of Beasts (Everett-Green, appendix), 1906
In a Mirror (Stolz), 1953
In a New World (Alger, appendix), 1893
In a Nutshell (S. Price), 1983
In a People House (verse; Seuss, as Le Sieg), 1972
In a Place of Danger (Fox), 1989
In a Rock Pool (Fry), 1947
In an Iron Grip (Meade, appendix), 1894
In and Out and Roundabout (Garnett), 1948
In and Out the Window (Parker), 1976
In Arcady (play; Fyleman), 1924
In Battle and Breeze (Fenn, Henty, appendix), 1896
In Brief Authority (Anstey, appendix), 1915
In Circling Camps (Altsheler), 1900
In Clean Hay (Kelly), 1940
In Clive's Command (Strang), 1906
In Cloister and Court (Everett-Green, appendix), 1900
In Dangerous Waters (Westerman), 1940
In Darkest Britain (play; Lillington), 1967
In Defiance of the Ban (Westerman), 1931
In Eastern Seas (Westerman), 1939
In Fair Granada (Everett-Green, appendix), 1902
In Freedom's Cause (Henty, appendix), 1884
In Grandfather's Garden (Everett-Green, appendix), 1910
In Greek Waters (Henty, appendix), 1892
In Happy Hollow (R. Montgomery), 1958
In Honour's Cause (Fenn, appendix), 1896
In Hostile Red (Altsheler), 1900
In Jeopardy (Fenn, appendix), 1889
In Love and War (B. Wilson), 1963
In Marine Armour (Fenn, appendix), 1927
In Mid-Air (Fenn, appendix), 1924
In My Mother's House (verse; A. Clark), 1941
In My Nursery (verse; L. Richards), 1890
In Noah's Ark (verse; Godden), 1949
In Northern Seas (Everett-Green, appendix), 1905
In One Door and Out the Other (verse; A. Fisher), 1969
In Our House (Rockwell), 1985
In Perilous Times (Marchant), 1901
In Prison and Out (Stretton, appendix), 1879
In Pursuit of Clarinda (Allan), 1966
In Search of a Sandhill Crane (Robertson), 1973

Jessica's First Prayer and series (Stretton, appendix), from 1867
Jessie series (C. Pullein-Thompson), from 1986
Jester, The Queen, and the Hen (play; Daniell), 1948
Jet Beads (Treece), 1961
Jet Navigator (R. Montgomery), 1959
Jethro and Joel Were a Troll (Peet), 1987
Jethro and the Jumbie (S. Cooper), 1979
Jets Away! (R. Montgomery), 1957
Jetty (Mattingley), 1978
Jezebel Wolf (Monjo), 1971
Ji, The Adventures of (Farrow), 1906
Jill (Talbot), 1927
Jill of the Guides (Chaundler), 1932
Jill the Irresistible (Meade, appendix), 1915
Jill the Outsider (Chaundler), 1924
Jill's Jolliest School (Brazil), 1937
Jill's Red Bag (Le Feuvre), 1903
Jilting of Bruce Heriot (Everett-Green, appendix), 1904
Jim series (Finley, appendix), from 1872
Jim (C. Roberts), 1919
Jim and the Beanstalk (R. Briggs), 1970
Jim and the Pirates (Farjeon), 1936
Jim and Wally (M. Bruce), 1916
Jim at the Corner (Farjeon), 1934
Jim Bridger's Alarm Clock (S. Fleischman), 1978
Jim Davis (Masefield), 1911
Jim Frog (Hoban), 1983
Jim of Hellas (L. Richards), 1895
Jim Starling series (Hildick), from 1958
Jim Tiger (Hough), 1956
Jim Trelawny (Everett-Green, appendix), 1905
Jim-Jam Pyjamas (verse; G. Wilson), 1989
Jimmy series (Crompton), from 1949
Jimmy (Wynne), 1910
Jimmy and Jemima (H. Sewell), 1940
Jimmy and the Election (Meynell), 1970
Jimmy John's Journey (Allan), 1950
Jimmy Skunk series (Burgess), from 1918
Jimmy Tag-Along (Patten), 1988
Jimmy Takes Vanishing Lessons (Brooks), 1965
Jimmy the Baby Elephant (Beaman), 1927
Jimmy's Story (Berg), 1968
Jingaroo (M. Clark), 1951
Jingle Tales (N. Hunter), 1941
Jingo Django (S. Fleischman), 1971
Jinki (Mitchell), 1970
Jinky's Joke (Blyton), 1949
Jinny the Changeling (Lynch), 1959
Jinty series (Oxenham), from 1933
Jinx Ship (Pease), 1927
Jo series (Brent-Dyer), from 1926
Jo Silver (R. N. Peck), 1985
Joan Morse (E. O. White), 1926
Joanna All Alone (Kaye), 1974
Joanna's Miracle (W. Armstrong), 1977
Joan's Best Chum (Brazil), 1926
Joan's Door (verse; Farjeon), 1926
Joan's Handful (Le Feuvre), 1915
Job for Merv (Prince), 1986
Jobs for the Girls (MacGibbon), 1975
Jock and Jill (Lipsyte), 1982
Jock and the Rock Cakes (Tate), 1973
Jockin the Jester (Moray Williams), 1951
Jock's Inheritance (Le Feuvre), 1927
Jock's Island (Coatsworth), 1963
Jodie's Journey (Thiele), 1988

Joe series (play; Prince), 1968
Joe and the Snow (de Paola), 1968
Joe and Timothy series (D. Edwards), from 1969
Joe Finds a Way (Blos), 1967
Joe the Hotel Boy (Alger, appendix), 1906
Joel and the Great Merlini (McGraw), 1979
Joel Harford (Otis, appendix), 1898
Joe's Luck (Alger, appendix), 1887
Joey series (Brent-Dyer), from 1954
Joey Tyson (Salkey), 1974
Joey's Cat (Burch), 1969
Joey's Room (Kaye), 1978
Johanna and the Prices (Pye), 1951
John and Mary series (Blyton), from 1966
John and the Rarey (Wells), 1969
John at the Old Farm (Uttley), 1960
John Barleycorn (Uttley), 1948
John Billington (Bulla), 1956
John Brown, Rose, and the Midnight Cat (Wagner), 1977
John Craddock's Commission (Westerman), 1958
John Crook, Quaker (play; Vipont), 1954
John Diamond (Garfield), 1980
John Dough and the Cherub (Baum), 1906
John Gay series (Abbott, appendix), from 1864
John Hawke's Fortune (Henty, appendix), 1901
John Henry Davis (Leaf), 1940
John J. Plenty and the Fiddler Dan (verse; Ciardi), 1963
John Jolly series (Blyton), from 1942
John Morris's Mermaid (Parker), 1972
John of Daunt (E. Turner), 1916
John of Pudding Lane (M. Hunt), 1941
John Patrick Norman McHennessy (Burningham), 1987
John Treegate's Musket (Wibberley), 1959
John True (Abbott, appendix), 1850
John Trusty (Beaman), 1929
Johnnie Golightly and His Crocodile (Moray Williams), 1970
Johnnie Tigerskin (Moray Williams), 1964
Johnny Bear (Seton), 1935
Johnny Castleseed (Ormondroyd), 1985
Johnny Chuck, The Adventures of (Burgess), 1913
Johnny Crow series (verse; Brooke), from 1903
Johnny Eagleclaw (Faulknor), 1982
Johnny Goes to the Fair (Lenski), 1932
Johnny Here and There (Bisset), 1981
Johnny Hong of Chinatown (Bulla), 1952
Johnny Maple-Leaf (Tresselt), 1948
Johnny Mouse and the Wishing Stick (Gruelle), 1922
Johnny Neptune (Donkin), 1971
Johnny Salter (play; Chambers), 1965
Johnny Sweep (Sutton), 1977
Johnny the Clockmaker (Ardizzone), 1960
Johnny Town-Mouse, The Tale of (Potter), 1918
Johnny Tremain (Forbes), 1943
Johnny-Head-in-Air (Grice), 1978
Johnny's Bad Day (Ardizzone), 1970
Johnny-Up and Johnny-Down (M. Hunt), 1962
John's Journey (Hogarth, as Gay), 1952
John's Secret Treasure (W. Steele), 1975
Joining of the Stone (S. Murphy), 1981
Joji series (Lifton), from 1957
Jo-Jo and Mike (Wagner), 1982
Joking Man (Flora), 1968
Jolliest School of All (Brazil), 1923
Jolliest Term on Record (Brazil), 1915
Jolly Farm Book (Berg), 1960
Jolly Friendship (Stockton, appendix), 1880

Jolly Jingles (verse; L. Richards), 1912
Jolly Little Jumbo (Blyton), 1944
Jolly Postman (Ahlberg), 1986
Jolly Story Book (Blyton), 1944
Jolly Tales (Blyton), 1942
Jolly Witch (Burch), 1975
Jon the Unlucky (Coatsworth), 1964
Jonah and the Fisherman (Zimnik, trans), 1956
Jonah Simpson (Salkey), 1969
Jonah's Mirror (Lillington), 1988
Jonas series (Abbott, appendix), from 1839
Jonathan series (Cockett), from 1954
Jonathan Cleaned Up, Then He Heard a Sound (Munsch), 1981
Jonathan Down Under (P. Beatty), 1982
Jonathan Frederick Aloysius Brown (verse; Ormondroyd), 1964
Jonathan Goes West (Meader), 1946
Jonathan Makes a Wish (play; S. Walker), 1918
Jonathan's Children (Heward), 1963
Jonny (Lattimore), 1939
Joppy Stories (Cockett), 1972
Jory's Cove (Bice), 1941
Jo's Boys and How They Turned Out (Alcott, appendix), 1886
Josefina February (Ness), 1963
Josefina Finds the Prince (Bunting), 1976
Joseph and Koza (Singer), 1970
Joseph and Lulu and the Prindiville House Pigeons (Greenwood),
    1972
Josephine (Lillington), 1989
Joseph's Boat (Macdonald), 1988
Joseph's Yard (Keeping), 1969
Joseph's Yard (play; Keeping), 1970
Jose's Christmas Secret (Lexau), 1963
Josh (Southall), 1971
Joshua and the Magic Fiddle (Janosch, trans), 1968
Josiah in New York (Otis, appendix), 1893
Josie, Click and Bun series (Blyton), from 1940
Journal for One (Tate), 1973
Journal of a Teenage Genius (Griffith), 1987
Journey Behind the Wind (Wrightson), 1981
Journey Between Worlds (Engdahl), 1970
Journey by First Class Camel (Konigsburg), 1983
Journey for Three (Holland), 1974
Journey from Peppermint Street (De Jong), 1968
Journey Home (Uchida), 1978
Journey of Ching Lai (Lattimore), 1957
Journey of Johnny Rew (Barrett), 1954
Journey of the Eldest Son (Fyson), 1965
Journey of the Kiss (de Paola), 1970
Journey Outside (M. Steele), 1969
Journey to America (Levitin), 1970
Journey to an 800 number (Konigsburg), 1982
Journey to England (Unnerstad, trans), 1961
Journey to Jericho (O'Dell), 1969
Journey to Jorsala (Finkel), 1969
Journey to Space (Nwapa), 1980
Journey to Terezor (Asch), 1989
Journey to the Jungle (Bisset), 1977
Journey to Topaz (Uchida), 1971
Journey to Untor (Wibberley), 1970
Journey under Warning (Locke), 1983
Journey with Grandmother (Unnerstad, trans), 1960
Journey with Jonah (play; L'Engle), 1967
Joy Cometh in the Morning (Le Feuvre), 1917
Joy Street Poems (Fyleman), 1927
Joyce series (L. Duncan, as Kerry), from 1958
Joyce and the Rambler (Le Feuvre), 1910

Joyce Harrington's Trust (Marchant), 1915
Joyful Noise (verse; P. Fleischman), 1988
Joyride (Cavanna), 1974
Joy's Jubilee (Everett-Green, appendix), 1898
Joy's New Adventure (Oxenham), 1935
Juan (Stolz), 1970
Jubilee! (B. Willard), 1973
Judge Justin (Abbott, appendix), 1857
Judgement of Clifford Sifton (play; Truss), 1977
Judith (Everett-Green, appendix), 1895
Judith in Hanover (Finlay), 1955
Judith Teaches (Allan), 1955
Judy series (Moore), from 1930
Judy and Lakshmi (Mitchison), 1959
Judy and Punch (E. Turner), 1928
Judy the Guide (Brent-Dyer), 1928
Judy the Tramp (Chaundler), 1924
Judy's Journey (Lenski), 1947
Ju-Ju Hand (Westerman), 1954
Juju Rock (Ekwensi), 1966
Julia and the Hand of God (Cameron), 1977
Julia Redfern series (Cameron), from 1977
Julian series (Syme), from 1947
Julian Home (Farrar, appendix), 1859
Julia's House (Gripe, trans), 1975
Julie Builds Her Castle (Colman), 1959
Julie News (Wallace), 1974
Julie of the Wolves (George), 1972
Julie Stands By (Donkin), 1948
Julie's Story (Berg), 1968
Juliet in Publishing (B. as Churchill), 1956
Juliet of the Mill (Wynne), 1931
Juliette (Marchant), 1907
Julius (Alger, appendix), 1874
Julius (Hoff), 1959
Jumanji (Van Allsburg), 1981
Jumble Sale (Berg), 1968
Jumbo series (Cresswell), from 1963
Jumbo (Smucker), 1989
Jumbo Spencer (play; Cresswell), 1976
Jump Frog Jump (P. Martin), 1965
Jump Ship to Freedom (Collier), 1981
Jumper Goes to School (Parish), 1969
Jumping Jo the Joker (Tate), 1984
Jungle and Stream (Fenn, appendix), 1898
Jungle Beasts and Men (Mukerji), 1923
Jungle Book series (Kipling), from 1894
Jungle Nurse (Catherall, as Ruthin), 1960
Jungle Pool, The Story of the (Dalgliesh), 1930
Jungle Rescue (Catherall, as Channel), 1967
Jungle River (Pease), 1938
Jungle Sale (Pilling), 1989
Jungle Silver (H. Todd), 1981
Jungle Trap (Catherall), 1958
Junior (R. Kraus), 1955
Junior (Lattimore), 1938
Junior Cadet (Westerman), 1928
Junior Captain (Breary), 1946
Junior Captain (Oxenham), 1923
Junior Detection Club, Adventures of the (Johns), 1960
Junior Prefect (Chaundler), 1931
Juniors Will Be Juniors (Breary), 1947
Juniper (Kemp), 1986
Juniper (R. Kraus), 1965
Junius over Far (Hamilton), 1985
Junk (Harnett), 1937

Junk Castle (R. Klein), 1983
Junket (play; A. Harris), 1959
Juno series (Abbott, appendix), from 1870
Just a Dog (H. Griffiths), 1974
Just a Love Story (Meade, appendix), 1890
Just a Moment! (Bisset), 1987
Just Across the Street (Field), 1933
Just as Long as We're Together (Blume), 1987
Just Be Gorgeous (Wersba), 1988
Just for Justin (play; Latham, as Lee), 1933
Just Gerry (Chaundler), 1920
Just Like Daddy (Asch), 1981
Just Like David (de Angeli), 1951
Just Like Everyone Else (Bunting), 1978
Just Like Everyone Else (Kuskin), 1959
Just Me (Ets), 1965
Just One Apple (Janosch, trans), 1966
Just One Friend (L. Hall), 1985
Just Plain Al (C. Greene), 1986
Just Sixteen (Coolidge, appendix), 1889
Just So Stories (play; A. Harris), 1971
Just So Stories for Little Children (Kipling), 1902
Just Some Weeds from the Wilderness (P. Beatty), 1978
Just the Girl for St. Jude's (Talbot), 1927
Just the Thing for Geraldine (Conford), 1974
Just the Two of Us (Colman), 1984
Just Think! (Blos), 1971
Just Time for a Story (Blyton), 1948
Just Turn the Key (McNeill), 1976
Just Us (G. Wilson), 1988
Justice and Her Brothers (Hamilton), 1978
Justice Lion (R. N. Peck), 1981
Justin and the Best Biscuits in the World (Walter), 1986
Justin Morgan Had a Horse (Henry), 1945

K.F. Conspiracy (A. Hall), 1955
Kaffir Land (Yonge, appendix), 1868
Kalak of the Ice (Kjelgaard), 1949
Kaleidoscope (Farjeon), 1928
Kaleidoscope (Sidney, appendix), 1892
Kalu and the Wild Board (Catherall, as Hallard), 1973
Kangeroo for Christmas (Flora), 1962
Kangeroo Tennis (Bisset), 1968
Kap series (Lifton), from 1960
Kap the Kappa (play; Lifton), 1974
Karalta (M. Bruce), 1941
Karate Dancer (D. B. Smith), 1987
Karen Kepplewhite Is the World's Best Kisser (Bunting), 1983
Kari the Elephant (Mukerji), 1922
Karlson series (Lindgren, trans), from 1971
Karlsson series (Lindgren, trans), from 1971
Karoo Hen (Seed), 1984
Karrawingi the Emu, The Story of (L. Rees), 1946
Kasper Kroak's Kaleidoscope (verse; L. Richards), 1886
Kassim series (Kaye), from 1967
Kate (Little), 1971
Kate and the Family Tree (Storey), 1965
Kate and the Island (Storr), 1972
Kate and the Revolution (Townsend), 1983
Kate Bonnet (Stockton, appendix), 1902
Kate Comes to England (Allan), 1963
Kate Crackernuts (K. Briggs), 1963
Kate Crackernuts (play; Mitchison), 1931
Kate of Candlewick (Cockett), 1987
Kate Rider (H. Burton), 1974
Kate Ryder (H. Burton), 1975

Kate's Secret Riddle Book (S. Fleischman), 1977
Katherine (verse; MacIntyre), 1946
Kathleen, Please Come Home (O'Dell), 1978
Kathy and the Mysterious Statue (Kingman), 1953
Kati series (Lindgren, trans), from 1961
Katia (Almedingen), 1967
Katie (D. Martin), 1974
Katie and the Sad Noise (Gannett), 1961
Katie Morag series (Hedderwick), from 1984
Katrina of the Lonely Isles (Catherall, as Ruthin), 1964
Katug the Snow Child (Seton), 1929
Katy and Dom (Oldfield), 1978
Katy and the Big Snow (V. Burton), 1943
Katy Kruse at the Seaside (Farjeon), 1932
Katy Kruse Play Book (Fyleman), 1930
Katy's Kitty (Hoff), 1975
Katzimir the Greatest (Baumann, trans), 1977
Kävik (Morey), 1968
Keep Calm (Phipson), 1978
Keep 'em Rolling (Meader), 1967
Keep Running (Storey), 1974
Keep Running, Allen! (Bulla), 1978
Keep the Pot Boiling (Clarke), 1961
Keeper, (play; Garner), 1982
Keeper (Naylor), 1986
Keepers of the Cattle (Catherall), 1970
Keepers of the Khyber (Catherall), 1940
Keepers of the Narrow Seas (Westerman), 1931
Keepers of the Trail (Altsheler), 1916
Keeping a Christmas Secret (Naylor), 1989
Keeping Henry (Bawden), 1988
Keeping Kitty's Dates (play; Latham, as Lee), 1931
Keeping-Room (Levin), 1981
Keith's Trial and Victory (Everett-Green, appendix), 1894
Kelly the Sleepy Koala (B. Wilson), 1983
Kelly's Creek (D. B. Smith), 1975
Kelpie (Mayne), 1987
Kelpie (Moray Williams), 1934
Kelpie's Pearls (M. Hunter), 1964
Kenealy's Ride (Marchant), 1906
Kennelmaid Nan (Brent-Dyer), 1954
Kenneth (Yonge, appendix), 1850
Kenny's Window (Sendak), 1956
Kent Barstow series (R. Montgomery), from 1958
Kept in the Dark (Bawden), 1982
Kermit the Hermit (verse; Peet), 1965
Kermit's Garden of Verses (verse; Prelutsky), 1982
Kerry Caravan (Lynch), 1967
Kershaw Dogs (H. Griffiths), 1978
Kersivay series (MacVicar), from 1964
Kersti and Saint Nicholas (Van Stockum), 1940
Kestrel (Alexander), 1982
Ketse and the Chief (Mitchison), 1965
Kevin (Chalmers), 1957
Kevin O'Connor and the Light Brigade (Wibberley), 1957
Kevin the Kookaburra (B. Wilson), 1983
Kevin's Hat (Holland), 1984
Key (Dillon), 1967
Key (Heide), 1971
Key of the Castle (Kyle), 1976
Key Out of Time (A. Norton), 1963
Key to the Treasure (Parish), 1966
Keystone Kids (Tunis), 1943
Khaki Boys (Brazil), 1923
Khedive's Country (Fenn, appendix), 1904
Kick a Stone Home (D. B. Smith), 1974

Kick Off (Hardcastle), 1976
Kick Off (play; Streatfeild), 1973
Kickapoo (P. Martin, as Miles), 1961
Kickback (Hardcastle), 1989
Kid series (Tunis), from 1940
Kidnap of Jessie Parker (W. Taylor), 1989
Kidnapped (Stevenson, appendix), 1886
Kidnapped by Accident (Catherall), 1968
Kidnapped by Blackbirders (Sutton), 1984
Kidnapped in Kandy (Catherall, as Ruthin), 1951
Kidnapped on Astarr (Nixon), 1981
Kidnapped on Stromboli (Catherall, as Ruthin), 1966
Kidnapped Santa Claus (Baum), 1961
Kidnappers of Space (Patchett), 1953
Kidnapping of Christina Lattimore (Nixon), 1979
Kidnapping of Kensington (B. Carter), 1958
Kidnapping of My Grandmother (Moray Williams), 1972
Kids Commune (Hildick), 1973
Kildee House (R. Montgomery), 1949
Kilgorman (Reed, appendix), 1894
Killer Dog (M. Edwards), 1959
Killer in Dark Glasses (Treece), 1965
Killer Tadpole (J. Wilson), 1984
Killer-of-Death (B. Baker), 1963
Killers of the High Country (play; R. Montgomery), 1959
Killing Freeze (L. Hall), 1988
Killing Mr. Griffin (L. Duncan), 1978
Kilmeny of the Orchard (L. Montgomery), 1910
Kilpatrick, Special Reporter (MacVicar), 1963
Kilroy and the Gull (Benchley), 1977
Kim (Kipling), 1901
Kimako's Story (Jordan), 1981
Kimchi Kid (play; J. Kraus), 1986
Kind Dog series (Banner), from 1972
Kind Hearts and Gentle Monsters (Yep), 1982
Kind of Wild Justice (Ashley), 1978
Kindle of Kittens (Godden), 1978
Kindness (Rylant), 1989
Kindred Spirits (Meade, appendix), 1907
Kindred of the Wild series (C. Roberts), from 1902
King (Bruna, trans), 1964
King Abbie's Adventure (MacVicar), 1950
King Anne (E. Turner), 1921
King Big-Ears (Dillon), 1961
King Bounce the First (Heine, trans), 1982
King Change-a-Lot (Cole), 1988
King Creature, Come (Townsend), 1980
King Death's Garden (Halam), 1986
King Dicky Bird and the Bossy Princess (D. Edwards), 1987
King For a Month (Westerman), 1933
King George's Head Was Made of Lead (Monjo), 1974
King Henry's Palace (Hutchins), 1983
King Hilary and the Beggarman (play; Milne), 1926
King Horn (Crossley-Holland), 1965
King in the Garden (Garfield), 1984
King Kong and Other Poets (Burch), 1986
King Midas, The Adventures of (Banks), 1976
King Midas and the Golden Touch (play; Chorpenning), 1950
King Nimrod's Tower (Garfield), 1982
King Oberon's Forest (Van Stockum), 1957
King of All the Birds (play; T. Ross), 1985
King of Beasts (C. Roberts), 1967
King of Beasts (H. Todd), 1979
King of Grey Corrie (Lyon), 1975
King of Kazoo (play; R. N. Peck), 1976
King of Kilba (Westerman), 1926

King of the Air (Strang), 1907
King o' the Beach (Fenn, appendix), 1899
King of the Castle (R. Montgomery), 1961
King of the Castle (Rush), 1956
King of the Castle (Trevor), 1966
King of the Cats (O'Faolain), 1941
King of the Commandos (Johns), 1943
King of the Copper Mountains (Biegel, trans), 1969
King of the Dollhouse (Clapp), 1974
King of the Hills (Meader), 1933
King of the Knock-Down Gingers (Kaye), 1979
King of the Mountain (Wier), 1975
King of the Seventh Grade (Cohen), 1982
King of the Sticks (Southall), 1979
King of the Tinkers (Lynch), 1938
King of the Wind (Henry), 1948
King Richard's Land (Strong), 1933
King Robert's Page (Fenn, appendix), 1900
King Rollo series (McKee), from 1979
King Sam (V. Smith), 1966
King Solomon and the Hoopoes (Greaves), 1971
King Tree (F. French), 1973
King Tulle (Sandman Lilius, trans), 1980
King Who Saved Himself from Being Saved (verse; Ciardi), 1965
King Who Took Sunshine (play; Reeves), 1954
King with Six Friends (J. Williams), 1968
Kingdom and the Cave (Aiken), 1960
Kingdom in a Horse (Wojciechowska), 1965
Kingdom of the Winding Road (Meigs), 1915
Kingfisher Feather (Mitchell), 1962
Kings and Queens (verse; Farjeon), 1932
King's Barn (Farjeon), 1927
King's Beard (Wibberley), 1952
King's Birthday Cake (Cunliffe), 1973
King's Butterfly (Everett-Green, appendix), 1900
King's Corsair (Guillot, trans), 1954
King's Curate (D. Bruce), 1930
King's Daughter Cries for the Moon (Farjeon), 1929
Kings' Day (Bishop), 1940
King's Esquires (Fenn, appendix), 1903
King's Falcon (Fox), 1969
King's Fifth (O'Dell), 1966
King's Flower (Anno, trans), 1979
King's Fountain (Alexander), 1971
King's Gardens (Farrow), 1896
King's Great Aunt Sits on the Floor (play; S. Walker), 1923
Kings in Exile (C. Roberts), 1909
King's Jester (play; Blyton), 1927
King's Knight's Pawn (J. and P. Beatty), 1971
King's Loon (Downie), 1979
King's Messenger (play; Daniell), 1948
King's Monster (Haywood), 1980
Kings of Corroboree Plains (play; MacIntyre), 1960
Kings of Space (Johns), 1954
King's Pocket Knife (play; Blyton), 1927
King's Room (Dillon), 1970
King's Servants (Stretton, appendix), 1873
King's Sons (Fenn, appendix), 1901
King's Stilts (verse; Seuss), 1939
King's Things (play; Jones), 1969
King's Toothache, (play; A. Fisher), 1965
King's Trousers (R. Kraus), 1981
King's White Elephant (R. Harris), 1973
Kinkajou on the Town (R. Montgomery), 1967
Kintu (Enright), 1935
Kip series (Odaga), from 1972

Kip Van Wrinkle (Hoff), 1974
Kipper series (Darke), from 1976
Kippy the Koala (Bonsall, as Newell), 1960
Kirk's Law (R. N. Peck), 1981
Kissimmee Kid (V. and B. Cleaver), 1981
Kit series (Gardam), from 1983
Kit and Kat (Perkins), 1929
Kit Baxter's War (F. Knight), 1966
Kitchen Madonna (Godden), 1967
Kitchen People (Wayne), 1963
Kitchen Warriors (Aiken), 1983
Kite Man (Meynell, as Tring), 1955
Kite over Tenth Avenue (Lexau), 1967
Kits at Clynton Court School (Wynne), 1924
Kitten for a Day (Keats), 1974
Kitten Nell (Bruna, trans), 1963
Kitten Pilgrims (Ballantyne, appendix), 1882
Kitten Stand (Coatsworth), 1945
Kitten That Disappeared (Blyton), 1966
Kitten Who Wouldn't Purr (verse; D. Martin), 1987
Kittens for Nothing (R. Kraus), 1976
Kitty O'Donovan (Meade, appendix), 1912
Kitty Wilkinson (play; Vipont), 1956
Kitty's Class Day (Alcott, appendix), 1868
Kitty's Kitten (Strang), 1926
Kitty's Tea Party (Heward), 1926
Kiviok's Magic Journey (Houston), 1973
Ki-yu (Haig-Brown), 1934
Klepty (R. Montgomery), 1961
Klontarf (Thiele), 1988
Knave of Dreams (A. Norton), 1975
Knave-Go-By (C. Smith), 1951
Knee-Deep in Ice Cream (Naylor), 1967
Knee-High to a Grasshopper (Parrish), 1923
Kneeknock Rise (Babbitt), 1970
Knife at the Opera (Storey), 1988
Knight and the Dragon (de Paola), 1980
Knight Crusader (Welch), 1954
Knight of the Golden Plain (M. Hunter), 1983
Knight of the White Cross (Henty, appendix), 1895
Knight of Today (Meade, appendix), 1877
Knight's Castle (Eager), 1956
Knight's Fee (Sutcliff), 1960
Knights of the Cardboard Castle (Beresford), 1965
Knights of the Golden Table (Almedingen), 1963
Knights of the Red Cross (Moore), 1907
Knights of the Road (Everett-Green, appendix), 1907
Knitting (Berg), 1972
Knock at the Door (Coatsworth), 1931
Knockers (S. Porter), 1965
Knocking on the Wall (play; Lillington), 1968
Koala Bear's Walkabout (Hewett), 1959
Kobo (Strang), 1904
Kofi and the Eagle (Kaye), 1963
Komantcia (Keith), 1965
Konrad (Nöstlinger, trans), 1976
Kookanoo and Kangaroo (verse; Durack), 1963
Koonawarra the Black Swan, The Story of (L. Rees), 1957
Kopje Garrison (Fenn, appendix), 1901
Koto and the Lagoon (Kaye), 1967
Kpo the Leopard (Guillot, trans), 1955
Krag (Seton), 1929
Kraymer Mystery (Allan), 1969
Kumi and the Pearl (P. Martin), 1968
Kurri Kurri the Kookaburra, The Story of (L. Rees), 1950
Kwasi series (Kaye), from 1961

Kweeks of Kookatumdee (verse; Peet), 1985

L.C. Is the Greatest (Krasilovsky), 1975
La Corona and the Tin Frog (Hoban), 1979
La Malice, Voyageur (play; Foon), 1979
La Rochelle series (Brent-Dyer), from 1924
Labour in Vain (Garfield), 1977
Lace Snail (Byars), 1975
Lackawanna (Aaron), 1986
Lacy Makes a Match (P. Beatty), 1979
Lad, A Dog series (Terhune), from 1919
Lad of Grit (Westerman), 1908
Lad of London Town (Everett-Green, appendix), 1909
Lad with a Whistle (Brink), 1941
Laddie's Choice (Le Feuvre), 1912
Ladies of the White House (play; C. D. Mackay), 1948
Ladis series (Sánchez-Silva, trans), 1968
Lads and Lassies (Nesbit), 1894
Lady and the Merman (Yolen), 1977
Lady Anne (Meade, appendix), 1910
Lady Cake-Maker (Meade, appendix), 1904
Lady from Black Hawk (P. Beatty), 1967
Lady Hester (Yonge, appendix), 1874
Lady of Delight (Meade, appendix), 1907
Lady of Mettle (Moore), 1910
Lady of the Forest (Meade, appendix), 1889
Lady of the Linden Tree (Picard), 1954
Lady of the Weeping Willow Tree (play; S. Walker), 1916
Lady Talavera (Drummond), 1946
Ladybird at the Zoo (Cockett), 1979
Ladybug! Ladybug! (Fry), 1940
Ladybug, Ladybug! (R. Kraus), 1957
Ladycake Farm (M. Hunt), 1952
Lady's Girl (Bunting, as Bolton), 1974
Lafcadio, The Lion Who Shot Back, Story of (Silverstein, as Shelby), 1963
Lake at the End of the World (Macdonald), 1988
Lakeland Mystery (Trease), 1942
Lamaload (play; Garner), 1979
Lamb in the Family (Phipson), 1966
Lamb Shenkin (Mayne), 1986
Lambs'-Tails and Suchlike (verse; Brisley), 1930
Lame Duck (R. Armstrong), 1959
Lame Letty (Finley, appendix), 1859
Lamplighter's Funeral (Garfield), 1976
Lancelot Closes at Five (Sharmat), 1976
Lances of Lynwood (Yonge, appendix), 1855
Land and Sea Tales (Kipling), 1923
Land Beyond (Corlett), 1975
Land Beyond (Gripe, trans), 1974
Land Beyond the North (Green), 1958
Land Called Happy Woolly Valley (play; Mahy), n.d.
Land Divided (Hayes), 1951
Land Is Bright (Kjelgaard), 1958
Land of Dreams (Foreman), 1982
Land of Forgotten Beasts (Wersba), 1964
Land of Nursery Rhymes (play; Blyton), 1939
Land of Pluck (Dodge, appendix), 1894
Land of the Blue Flower (Burnett), 1909
Land of the Dragon (play; Miller), 1945
Land of the Free (play; Bailey), 1950
Land of the Lord High Tiger (Green), 1958
Land the Ravens Found (Mitchison), 1955
Land Under the White Robe (Catherall), 1956
Landfall (Levin), 1979
Lands End (Stolz), 1973

Little Rabbit Who Wanted Red Wings (Bailey), 1945
Little Ragged Blossom (Gibbs), 1920
Little Rascal (North), 1965
Little Red (Lippincott), 1953
Little Red Engine series (D. Ross), from 1942
Little Red Fox series (Uttley), from 1954
Little Red Horse (Sawyer), 1950
Little Red Nose (Schlein), 1955
Little Red Pony (Ridge), 1960
Little Red Riding Hood (play; Chorpenning), 1946
Little Red Riding Hood (play; Reaney), 1965
Little Red Schoolhouse (Bailey), 1957
Little Red Shop (Sidney, appendix), 1889
Little Red's Adventure (Burgess), 1941
Little Rick-Burners (Yonge, appendix), 1886
Little Robinson Crusoes (H. Avery), 1908
Little Runner of the Longhouse (B. Baker), 1962
Little Ruth's Lady (Everett-Green, appendix), 1890
Little Sail Boat (Lenski), 1937
Little Sailing Boat (Lenski), 1938
Little Saint Elizabeth (Burnett), 1890
Little Sally Mandy's Christmas Present (Wynne), 1929
Little Sasabonsam (de Graft-Hanson), 1972
Little Savage (Marryat, appendix), 1848
Little School-Mothers (Meade, appendix), 1907
Little Sea Horse (Strang), 1926
Little Sealer (Catherall, as Corby), 1960
Little Ship Dog (Fidler), 1963
Little Silver Trumpet (Meade, appendix), 1885
Little Sioux Girl (Lenski), 1958
Little Sister (Mitchison), 1976
Little Skipper (Fenn, appendix), 1897
Little Spinning House (Blyton), 1951
Little Spotted Fish (Yolen), 1975
Little Square-Toes (play; Field), 1930
Little Squirrel Tickletail (Chaundler), 1917
Little Stray Dog (De Jong), 1943
Little Strip Picture Books (Blyton), from 1954
Little Sunny Stories (Gruelle), 1919
Little Tiger, Get Well Soon! (Janosch, trans), 1985
Little Tim and the Brave Sea Captain (Ardizzone), 1936
Little Tiny Rooster (Lipkind, as Will), 1960
Little Tom Little (Thiele), 1981
Little Tommy Tucker (Coolidge, appendix), 1900
Little Toot series (Gramatky), from 1939
Little Town (Hader), 1941
Little Town on the Prairie (Wilder), 1941
Little Toy Farm (Blyton), 1954
Little Train (Lenski), 1940
Little Tree-House (Blyton), 1940
Little Tumbler (Lattimore), 1963
Little Twin Dragons, The Tale of the (Praeger), 1900
Litle Two and the Peach Tree (P. Martin), 1963
Little Tyrant (L. Richards), 1880
Little Ugo and the Foolish Ones (play; P. Martin), 1972
Little Unfairy Princess (play; Burnett), 1902
Little Universe (Pamela Brown), 1970
Little Vampire series (Sommer-Bodenburg, trans), from 1982
Little Vic (Gates), 1951
Little White Bird (Barrie), 1902
Little White Duck (Blyton), 1946
Little White Foot (Hader), 1952
Little White Hen (Hewett), 1962
Little White Horse (Goudge), 1946
Little White Squibba, The Story of (Bannerman), 1966
Little Wife Hester (Meade, appendix), 1905

Little Witch, (Mahy), 1970
Little Witch (Preussler, trans), 1961
Little Wizard series (Baum), 1913
Little Women (Alcott, appendix), 1868
Little Wonder Box (Ingelow, appendix), 1887
Little Wonder-Horn (Ingelow, appendix), 1872
Little Wooden Doll (Bianco), 1925
Little Wooden Farmer (Dalgliesh), 1930
Little Wooden Horse, Adventures of the (Moray Williams), 1938
Little Word Book (Scarry), 1978
Little Worm Book (Ahlberg), 1979
Little Yellow Jungle Frogs (Hewett), 1956
Little Yellow Taxi and His Friends (Ainsworth), 1982
Little-or-Nothing from Nottingham (Henry), 1949
Littlest Christmas Tree (Burgess), 1954
Littlest House (Coatsworth), 1940
Littlest Leaguer (Hoff), 1976
Littlest One in the Family (L. Duncan), 1960
Littlest Rabbit (R. Kraus), 1961
Live and Kicking Ned (Masefield), 1939
Live in the Sky (Hardcastle), 1971
Lively Bit of the Front (Westerman), 1918
Lively Poll (Ballantyne, appendix), 1886
Lively Victoria (Lattimore), 1952
Liverpool Cats (Sherry), 1969
Lives of Christopher Chant (Jones), 1988
Lives of the Hunted (Seton), 1901
Living Fire (Fisk), 1987
Liz (play; Buckeridge), 1974
Liz (MacGibbon), 1966
Lizard Log (Mattingley), 1975
Lizard Music (Pinkwater), 1976
Lizbett Anne (Peacocke), 1939
Lizzie Dripping series (Cresswell), from 1973
Lizzie Dripping and the Witch (play; Cresswell), 1977
Lizzie Lights (Chauncy), 1968
Lizzie's Twins (verse; Orgel, as Adelberg), 1964
Lizzy's Lion (verse; D. Lee), 1984
Lo (Leaf, as Mun), 1934
Load of Trouble (Hardcastle), 1971
Load of Unicorn (Harnett), 1959
Lob Lie-by-the-Fire (Ewing, appendix), 1874
Lobo (Chipperfield), 1974
Lobo (Seton), 1935
Lob's Silver Spoon (play; Ainsworth), 1955
Lobster Catchers (Otis, appendix), 1900
"Local Ass" (play; Barne), 1947
Lochinvar Luck (Terhune), 1923
Lock Stock and Barrel (M. Baker), 1974
Locked in Time (L. Duncan), 1985
Log Jam (M. Hughes), 1987
Log of a Snob (Westerman), 1914
Lois in Charge (Marchant), 1917
Loitering Linus (Finley, appendix), 1868
Loki and the Storm Giant (play; Garner), 1979
Lollipop (Nöstlinger, trans), 1982
Lollipop Man (Tate), 1969
Lollipop Opera (play; D. Freeman), 1970
Lollipop Princess (play; Estes), 1967
Lollipops (Berg), 1957
Lollygag of Limericks (verse; Livingston), 1978
London Baby (Meade, appendix), 1882
London Men and English Men (Hoban), 1962
London Pride (Cannan), 1939
London Windows (verse; Talbot), 1912
Londonderry Air (play; Field), 1927

Lone Hunt (W. Steele), 1956
Lone Muskrat (Rounds), 1953
Lone Pine series (Saville), from 1949
Lone Seal Pup (Catherall), 1964
Lone Stands the Glen (Chipperfield), 1966
Lone Texan (F. Richards), 1954
Lonely Game (Scannell), 1979
Lonely Garden (Chaundler), 1934
Lonely Hearts Club (R. Klein), 1987
Lonely Island (Ballantyne, appendix), 1880
Lonely Maria (Coatsworth), 1960
Lonelyhearts (J. Wilson), 1987
Loner (Wier), 1963
Lonesome Boy (Bontemps), 1955
Lonesome End (Meader), 1968
Lonesome Little Colt (Anderson), 1961
Lonesome Sorrel (Robertson), 1952
Long Ago Christmas (P. Martin), 1968
Long Bow (Welch), 1957
Long Claws (Houston), 1981
Long Day (Cresswell), 1972
Long Distance Poet (Mark), 1982
Long Drop (Hardcastle), 1974
Long Ears (Lynch), 1943
Long Horn (Lippincott), 1928
Long Island Ducklings (Slobodkina), 1961
Long Journey Home (Lester), 1972
Long Journey of Lukas B. (Fährmann, trans), 1985
Long Live the Republic (Prochazka, trans), 1973
Long Night (Mayne), 1958
Long Night Watch (Southall), 1983
Long Passage (Saville), 1954
Long Pilgrimage (Finkel), 1967
Long Return (Craig), 1959
Long Ride (Patchett), 1970
Long Road Home (Tate), 1971
Long Secret (Fitzhugh), 1965
Long, Short and Tall Stories (play; Chambers), 1980
Long Time Coming (Whitney), 1954
Long Trail (Strang), 1918
Long Trains Roll (Meader), 1944
Long Vacation (Yonge, appendix), 1895
Long Voyage (Christopher), 1960
Long Walk (Mattingley), 1976
Long Walk (play; Mattingley), 1978
Long Way from Verona (Gardam), 1971
Long Way Round (Sudbery), 1977
Long Way to Go (Darke), 1978
Long Way to Whiskey Creek (P. Beatty), 1971
Long Wharf (Pease), 1939
Long Winter (Wilder), 1940
Long Year (Wier), 1969
Longbeard the Wizard (S. Fleischman), 1970
Longest Name on the Block (Yolen), 1968
Longest Way Round (Lynch), 1961
Longest Weekend (Arundel), 1969
Longlegs the Heron (Burgess), 1927
Longshanks (Meader), 1928
Longtime series (Brinsmead), from 1971
Look at the Little One (Cockett), 1974
Look, Do and Listen (Ainsworth), 1969
Look! Look! (Heide), 1971
Look Through My Window (Little), 1970
Look What I've Got! (Browne), 1980
Look Who's Talking (Bonsall), 1962
Looking after Lamb (F. Richards), 1946

Looking after Libby (Pamela Brown), 1974
Looking for a Friend (Beresford), 1967
Looking for Elephants (Berg), 1977
Looking-for-Something (A. Clark), 1952
Looking-Glass Castle (Biegel, trans), 1979
Loopy (Gramatky), 1941
Loot! (Terhune), 1940
Lorax (verse; Seuss), 1971
Lorax (play; Seuss) n.d.
Lord and Lady Kitty (Meade, appendix), 1912
Lord Fish (de la Mare), 1933
Lord Mayor's Show (V. Smith), 1968
Lord of Dynevor (Everett-Green, appendix), 1892
Lord of the Castle (Clarke), 1960
Lord of the Forest (Watkins-Pitchford), 1975
Lord of the Rushie River (Barker), 1938
Lord of the Seas (Strang), 1908
Lord of Thunder (A. Norton), 1962
Lord Pip, The Adventures of (Cunliffe), 1970
Lord Rex (McKee), 1973
Lords of the Wilds (Altsheler), 1919
Lord's Purse-Bearers (Stretton, appendix), 1882
Lorenzo (Waber), 1961
Lorenzo Bear & Company (Wahl), 1971
Lorenzo the Magnificent, The Story of (Allen), 1961
Lorna series (Brent-Dyer), from 1947
Losers Weepers (Needle), 1981
Loss of the "Night Wind" (Sherry), 1970
Lost and Found (Garnett), 1974
Lost and Found (Little), 1985
Lost and Found (Paton Walsh), 1984
Lost at Sea (Alger, appendix), 1904
Lost at the Fair (Sharp), 1965
Lost Birthday (play; Barne) n.d.
Lost Birthday (Bisset), 1976
Lost Boy (Fox), 1987
Lost Cave (Fidler), 1978
Lost Clue (Walton, appendix), 1907
Lost Cow (C. Pullein-Thompson), 1966
Lost Dispatch (Sobol), 1958
Lost Emeralds of Black Howes (Finlay), 1961
Lost Endeavour (Masefield), 1910
Lost Farm (Curry), 1974
Lost Fisherman of Carrigmor (Lynch), 1960
Lost Gip (Stretton, appendix), 1873
Lost Harpooner (Wibberley, as O'Connor), 1947
Lost Hunters (Altsheler), 1918
Lost in Lapland (Catherall, as Hallard), 1970
Lost in London (Strang), 1927
Lost in the Barrens (Mowat), 1956
Lost in the Forest (Ballantyne, appendix), 1869
Lost in the Jungle (Wynne), 1921
Lost in the Zoo (Hader), 1951
Lost Island (Dillon), 1952
Lost John (Picard), 1962
Lost Karin (Kyle), 1947
Lost Kingdom of Karnica (R. Kennedy), 1979
Lost Lagoon (Sperry), 1939
Lost Leopard (Lattimore), 1935
Lost Lorrenden (Allan), 1956
Lost Men in the Grass (Suddaby, as Griff), 1940
Lost Middy (Fenn, appendix), 1902
Lost Off the Grand Banks (Catherall, as Corby), 1961
Lost on the Saguenay (Marchant), 1903
Lost on Venus (Patchett), 1954
Lost Planet series (MacVicar), from 1953

Lost Planet (play; MacVicar), n.d.
Lost Pony (C. Pullein-Thompson), 1959
Lost Prince (Burnett), 1915
Lost Prince (Seed), 1985
Lost Princess (MacDonald, appendix), 1875
Lost Ship (R. Armstrong), 1956
Long Silver of Langdon (Finlay), 1955
Lost Staircase (Brent-Dyer), 1946
Lost Star (Hoover), 1979
Lost String Quartet (Bodecker), 1981
Lost Thimble (Mayne, as Molin), 1966
Lost Tower Treasure (Clewes), 1960
Lost Treasure of Trevlyn (Everett-Green, appendix), 1893
Lost Treasure of Wales (Roose-Evans), 1977
Lost Umbrella of Kim Chu (Estes), 1978
Lost Wagon (Kjelgaard), 1955
Lost with All Hands (Catherall), 1940
Lothian Run (M. Hunter), 1970
Lotta series (Lindgren, trans), from 1963
Lottery Rose (I. Hunt), 1976
Lotte's Locket (Sorensen), 1964
Lottie (Symonds), 1957
Lottie and Lisa (Kästner, trans), 1950
Lottie's Circus (Blos), 1989
Lotty's Last Home (Meade, appendix), 1875
Lotus Caves (Christopher), 1969
Lotus Cup (Curry), 1986
Lou in the Limelight (K. Hunter), 1981
Loud, Resounding Sea (Bonham), 1963
Loud Mouth (Ure), 1988
Louie series (Hildick), from 1965
Louie series (Keats), from 1975
Louisa (Pamela Brown), 1955
Louisa, The Story of (D. Ross), 1945
Louisa's Wonder Book (Alcott, appendix), 1975
Louly (Brink), 1974
Love and Life (Yonge, appendix), 1880
Love and Tennis (Slote), 1979
Love and the Genetic Factor (Holland), 1987
Love Forever (H. Griffiths), 1981
Love Is a Blanket Word (Arundel), 1976
Love Is a Missing Person (M. Kerr), 1975
Love Is One of the Choices (N. Klein), 1978
Love Is the Crooked Thing (Wersba), 1987
Love, Laurie (Cavanna), 1953
Love Letters of J. Timothy Owen (C. Greene), 1986
Love Me, Love Me Not (Whitney), 1952
Love Note for Baby Piggy (Howe), 1986
Love of Susan Cardigan (Meade, appendix), 1907
Love, or a Season (Stolz), 1964
Love Stories, Two (Lester), 1972
Love Triumphant (Meade, appendix), 1904
Love You Forever (Munsch), 1986
Loveday (Meade, appendix), 1905
Lovely Fiend (Meade, appendix), 1908
Lovely Summer (B. Wilson), 1960
Lovely Tomorrow (Allan), 1980
Lovers' Games (Cohen), 1983
Love's Cross Roads (Meade, appendix), 1912
Lovey Mary (Rice), 1903
Loving Ghosts (Poole), 1988
Loving Jonathan Jones (Berg), 1987
Lower Fourth Excels Itself (Breary), 1945
Lowly Worm series (Scarry), from 1977
Loyal Hearts (Everett-Green, appendix), 1891
Loyal to the School (Brazil), 1921

"Loyall Virginian" (Finkel), 1968
Loyalty of Hester Hope (Marchant), 1914
Lucas Girls (Moore), 1911
Lucia Comes to School (Allan), 1953
Lucie Babbidge's House (Cassedy), 1989
Lucie's Luck (Marchant), 1928
Lucifer Wilkins (Garfield), 1973
Lucille (Arnold Lobel), 1964
Lucinda (B.C. Freeman), 1965
Lucinda series (Fry), from 1956
Lucinda (M. Hunt), 1934
Lucinda's Year of Jubilo (Sawyer), 1965
Luck and Pluck (Alger, appendix), 1869
Luck of Ledge Point (Moore), 1909
Luck of Penrayne (Wynne), 1937
Luck of Pokey Bloom (Conford), 1975
Luck of Sallowby (Saville), 1952
Luck of the "Golden Dawn" (Westerman), 1926
Luck of the Laird (Terhune), 1927
Luck of the Lynns (Green), 1952
Luck of the Miss L (Kingman), 1986
Luck of the School (Talbot), 1924
Luck of Troy (Green), 1961
Luckiest Girl (Cleary), 1958
Luckiest Girl at St. Chad's (Talbot), 1926
Luckiest Girl in the School (Brazil), 1916
Luckiest One of All (verse; Peet), 1982
Luckless Apple (Grice), 1966
Lucky Chuck (Cleary), 1984
Lucky Dip (Ainsworth), 1961
Lucky Ducks (Molesworth, appendix), 1891
Lucky Feather (Cowley), 1986
Lucky Les (Hildick), 1967
Lucky Little Lena (Flack), 1937
Lucky Little Porcupine (P. Martin), 1963
Lucky Ones (Coatsworth), 1968
Lucky Stone (Clifton), 1979
Lucky Story Book (Blyton), 1947
Lucretia the Unbearable (Sharmat), 1981
Lucy series (Abbott, appendix), from 1832
Lucy series (Storr), from 1961
Lucy (Tate), 1964
Lucy and Tom series (S. Hughes), from 1960
Lucy Brown and Mr. Grimes (Ardizzone), 1937
Lucy McLockett (verse; McGinley), 1959
Lucy the Lamb (Fyleman), 1951
Lucy's League (Hogarth, as Gay), 1950
Ludwig (R. Kraus), 1971
Luigi and the Long-Nosed Soldier (Slobodkin), 1963
Luigi of the Streets (Carlson), 1967
Luke and Angela (Nöstlinger, trans), 1979
Luke Caraway (Janosch, trans), 1977
Luke Walton (Alger, appendix), 1889
Luke Was There (Clymer), 1973
Luke's Garden (Tate), 1967
Luke's Quest (Snedeker), 1947
Lulu's Library (Alcott, appendix), 1886
Lumbercamp (Rounds), 1937
Lumberjack (Meader), 1934
Lupita Mañana (P. Beatty), 1981
Lure of the Lagoon (Westerman), 1955
Lure of the Wild (C. Roberts), 1980
Luvvy and the Girls (Carlson), 1971
Lyle series (Waber), from 1962
Lysis Goes to the Play (Snedeker), 1962

M for Mischief (Parker), 1965
M.C. Higgins, The Great (Hamilton), 1974
M.E. and Morton (Cassedy), 1987
Mac and Lugs (Chambers), 1971
Mac and the Black Cat (play; Latham), 1940
Macaroon (Cunningham), 1962
MacClellan's Lake (Dawlish), 1951
Macduff (Uttley), 1950
MacGoose's Grocery (Asch), 1978
Machine at the Heart of the World (Wagner), 1983
Machine Gunners (play; Westall), 1986
Machine-Gunners (play; Corlett), 1983
Machine-Gunners (Westall), 1975
Maclains of Glen Gillean (Allan), 1952
MacLeod Place (W. Armstrong), 1972
Mad Gasser of Bessledorf Street (Naylor), 1983
Mad Heiress (Alger, appendix), 1981
Mad King of Chichiboo (Verney), 1963
Mad O'Hara's (Lynch), 1948
Mad Teapot (Blyton), 1952
Madam of Clyst Peveril (Everett-Green, appendix), 1905
Madame Cholet's Picnic Party (Beresford), 1976
Madame Doubtfire (Fine), 1987
Madatan (P. Carter), 1974
Madcap (Meade, appendix), 1904
Madcap Family (Le Feuvre), 1916
Madcap in the School (Chaundler), 1930
Madcap of the School (Brazil), 1917
Maddy series (Pamela Brown), from 1945
Made-to-Order Storeis (D. Fisher), 1925
Madelaine and Ermadello (Wynne-Jones), 1977
Madeleine (Abbott, appendix), 1857
Madeline series (verse; Bemelmans), from 1939
Madeline, The Temptress (Alger, appendix), 1981
Mademoiselle (Symons), 1973
Mademoiselle Misfortune (Brink), 1936
Madge (play; Barne), 1928
Madge Mostyn's Nieces (Meade, appendix), 1916
Madman and the Pirate (Ballantyne, appendix), 1883
Magdalena (Shotwell), 1971
Maggie series (Lingard), from 1974
Maggie (play; Lingard), 1981
Maggie series (Nixon), from 1985
Maggie and the Pirate (Keats), 1979
Maggie Marmelstein series (Sharmat), from 1971
Maggie Rose (Sawyer), 1952
Maggie the Freak (Bunting), 1978
Maggy Gumption series (Barry), from 1979
Magic series (A. Norton), from 1965
Magic Amulet (W. Steele), 1979
Magic and Music Show (play; D. Wood), 1983
Magic and the Night River (Bunting), 1978
Magic Apple (play; Blyton), 1927
Magic Auto (Janosch, trans), 1971
Magic Ball (play; Blyton), 1939
Magic Beads (H. Avery), 1906
Magic Bed-Knob (M. Norton), 1943
Magic Bookshelf (play; Clapp), 1966
Magic by the Lake (Eager), 1957
Magic Camera (Pinkwater), 1974
Magic Christmas Tree (Kingman), 1956
Magic Circle (Heward), 1927
Magic City (Nesbit), 1910
Magic Cloak (Baum), 1916
Magic Currant Bun (Symonds), 1952
Magic Drawing Pencil (Storr), 1960

Magic Feather Duster (Lipkind, as Will), 1958
Magic Finger (Dahl), 1966
Magic Firesticks (Roughsey), 1983
Magic for Marigold (L. Montgomery), 1929
Magic Garden (G. Porter), 1927
Magic Gate (J. Williams), 1949
Magic Grandfather (J. Williams), 1979
Magic Hat of Mortimer Wintergreen (Levoy), 1988
Magic Heart (Wahl), 1972
Magic Horn (play; Chorpenning), 1954
Magic in My Pocket (Uttley), 1957
Magic Island (Talbot), 1926
Magic Jacket (de la Mare), 1943
Magic Kiss (Chaundler), 1916
Magic Knitting Needles (Blyton), 1950
Magic Lollipop (McNeill), 1975
Magic Meadow (d'Auliare), 1958
Magic Michael (verse; Slobodkin), 1944
Magic Money (A. Clark), 1950
Magic Moscow (Pinkwater), 1980
Magic Nuts (Molesworth, appendix), 1898
Magic of Millicent Musgrave (Turkle), 1967
Magic or Not? (Eager), 1959
Magic Party (Hardcastle), 1988
Magic Pawnshop (Field), 1927
Magic Pencil (play; Fyleman), 1938
Magic Pictures (Aymé, trans), 1954
Magic Pudding (Lindsay), 1918
Magic Rug (d'Aulaire), 1931
Magic Saddle (Mattingley), 1983
Magic Sea Shell (M. Baker), 1959
Magic Sled (Benchley), 1972
Magic Sledge (Benchley), 1974
Magic Smoke (Strang), 1926
Magic Snow-Bird (Blyton), 1951
Magic Spell (play; de Regniers), 1982
Magic Squid (Manning-Sanders), 1968
Magic Stone (Farmer), 1964
Magic Summer (Streatfeild), 1967
Magic to Burn (Fritz), 1964
Magic Tower (Finger), 1933
Magic Tree of Solatia (Yolen), 1974
Magic Trumpet (verse; Durack), 1946
Magic Word (Zolotow), 1952
Magic World (Beresford), 1965
Magic World (Nesbit), 1912
Magical Adventures of Pretty Pearl (Hamilton), 1983
Magical Changes (Oakley), 1979
Magical Cockatoo (Sharp), 1974
Magical Cupboard (Curry), 1976
Magical Land of Noom (Gruelle), 1922
Magical Melons (Brink), 1944
Magical Storybook (J. Williams), 1972
Magician, The Tale of the (Beaman), 1928
Magician series (McKee), from 1970
Magician Who Kept a Pub (D. Edwards), 1975
Magician's Heart (play; Nesbit), 1907
Magician's Nephew (play; A. Harris), 1983
Magician's Nephew (C. Lewis), 1955
Magicians of Caprona (Jones), 1980
Magnolia Buildings (Stucley), 1960
Magnolia's Mixed-Up Magic (Nixon), 1983
Magnus Bonum (Yonge, appendix), 1879
Magnus Powermouse (King-Smith), 1982
Magpie Island (Thiele), 1974
Maharajah Adventure (S. Lilius, trans), 1966

Mahatma (Hoff), 1969
Maid Indomitable (Meade, appendix), 1916
Maid of Mystery (Meade, appendix), 1904
Maid of the Wood (F. French), 1985
Maid with the Goggles (Meade, appendix), 1906
Maidens of Pefka (Donkin), 1979
Maidlin series (Oxenham), from 1934
Maids' Ribbons (Treadgold), 1965
Main Line Engines (Awdry), 1966
Mainly about the Fourth (Breary), 1949
Mainly about Wolves (Seton), 1937
Mainly in Moonlight (Gray), 1965
Maisie's Discovery (Marchant), 1906
Maitlands series (Streatfeild), from 1978
Majesty of Grace (Langton), 1961
Make a Circle, Keep Us In (verse; Adoff), 1975
Make Way for Ducklings (McCloskey), 1941
Make Your Move (J. Watson), 1988
Make Your Play (play; Lillington), 1967
Make Believe (Goudge), 1949
Make-Believe (play; Milne), 1918
Make-Believe Ballplayer (Slote), 1989
Make-Believe Twins (McGinley), 1953
Makers (Kelleher), 1987
Making Big Bucks (W. Taylor), 1987
Making Good (Serraillier), 1955
Making His Mark (Alger, appendix), 1901
Making It Happen (Naylor), 1970
Making of a Missionary (Yonge, appendix), 1900
Making of a Rainbow (play; Blyton), 1939
Making of a Woman (Le Feuvre), 1903
Making of Fingers Finnigan (Doherty), 1983
Making of Ursula (Moore), 1910
Makoto (Uchida), 1970
Maldonado Miracle (T. Taylor), 1973
Malibu (verse; Livingston), 1974
Malkin's Mountain (Moray Williams), 1948
Malory Towers series (Blyton), from 1946
Malys Rockell (Wynne), 1934
Mama Hattie's Girl (Lenski), 1953
"Mama, I Wish I Was Snow." "Child, You'd Be Very Cold"
    (Krauss), 1962
Mama One, Mama Two (MacLachlan), 1982
Mama's Going to Buy You a Mockingbird (Little), 1984
Mammywater (Nwapa), 1979
Man Called Hughes (Lillington), 1962
Man from the North Pole (Mayne), 1963
Man from the Past (F. Richards, as Clifford), 1952
Man from the Sea (Andrews), 1970
Man from the Sky (Avi), 1980
Man in the Bowler Hat (play; Milne), 1923
Man in the Hut (Meynell), 1967
Man in the Manhole and the Fix-It Men (M. W. Brown, as Sage),
    1946
Man in the Red Turban (D. Martin), 1978
Man in the Woods (Wells), 1984
Man of His Word (Stretton, appendix), 1878
Man of the House (McLean), 1956
Man on a Steeple (Moray Williams), 1971
Man on the Moon-Eyed Horse (S. Fleischman), 1980
Man Who Came Back (Hope-Simpson), 1962
Man Who Cooked for Himself (Krasilovsky), 1982
Man Who Could Call Down Owls (Bunting), 1984
Man Who Didn't Wash His Dishes (Krasilovsky), 1950
Man Who Entered a Contest (Krasilovsky), 1980
Man Who Hated Children (play; Patten), 1978

Man Who Lost His Head (Bishop), 1942
Man Who Never Snoozed (Latham), 1961
Man Who Rang the Bell (Tate), 1973
Man Who Sang the Sillies (verse; Ciardi), 1961
Man Who Stopped to Help (Blyton), 1965
Man Who Took the Indoors Out (verse; Arnold Lobel), 1974
Man Who Tried to Save Time (Krasilovsky), 1979
Man Who Vanished in Space (Johns), 1963
Man Whose Mother Was a Pirate (Mahy), 1972
Man with a Sword (Treece), 1962
Man with Eyes like Windows (Owen), 1987
Man with the Pan-Pipes (Molesworth, appendix), 1892
Man with the Purple Eyes (Zolotow), 1961
Man with the Sack (Meynell, as Tring), 1963
Man with the Silver Eyes (W. Steele), 1976
Man with the Yellow Eyes (C. Clark), 1963
Man with Three Fingers (Saville), 1966
Man Without a Face (Holland), 1972
Manchild (Patten), 1973
Manda (K. Hale), 1952
Ma nda lA (verse; Adoff), 1971
Mandarin's Kite (Farrow), 1900
Mandeville (Trease), 1980
Mandog (play; Dickinson), 1972
Mandog (Lamplugh), 1972
Mandrake (Peyton, as Herald), 1949
Mandy Duck, The Adventures of (Bisset), 1974
Mandy, Mops, and Cubby series (Blyton), 1952
Man-Eater (Catherall, as Corby), 1963
Manhatten Is Missing (Hildick), 1969
Manka (Watkins-Pitchford), 1939
Manor House School (Brazil), 1910
Manor Pool Island (H. Avery), 1903
Manor School (Meade, appendix), 1903
Mansa Helps at Home (Asare), 1972
Manson, The Miser (Alger, appendix), 1981
Mantis and the Moon (Poland), 1979
Mantlemass series (B. Willard), from 1970
Many Kinds of Magic (Scott), 1988
Many Lives of Chio and Goro (Lifton), 1966
Many Mansions (Cawley), 1976
Many Mice of Mr Brice (verse; Seuss, as Le Sieg), 1973
Many Moons (play; Chorpenning), 1946
Many Moons (Thurber), 1943
Many Waters (Bibby), 1974
Many Waters (L'Engle), 1986
Many Waters Cannot Quench Love (Bibby), 1975
Maori and Settler (Henty, appendix), 1980
Map of Nowhere (Cross), 1988
Maplin Bird (Peyton), 1964
Mapper Munday's Treasure Hunt (Hildick), 1963
Maps of Time (P. Hunt), 1983
Mara (McGraw), 1953
Marathon and Steve (Rayner), 1989
Marc and Pixie and the Walls in Mrs. Jones's Garden (Fatio), 1975
Marcelino (Sánchez-Silva, trans), 1954
Marcella Stories (Gruelle), 1929
Marcella's Guardian Angel (Ness), 1979
March on London (Henty, appendix), 1897
Marchers for the Dream (Carlson), 1969
Marcia (Steptoe), 1976
Marco Moonlight (Bulla), 1976
Marcus (Fenn, appendix), 1904
Marcus series (Poland), from 1984
Marcus Stratford's Charge (Everett-Green, appendix), 1890
Mardie series (Lindgren, trans), from 1979

Merle the High Flying Squirrel (Peet), 1974
Merlin the Magician (play; Miller), n.d.
Merlin Dreams (Dickinson), 1988
Merlin's Magic (Clarke, as Clare), 1953
Merlin's Mistake (Newman), 1970
Merlin's Ring (Trevor), 1957
Mermaid (play; Fyleman), 1928
Mermaid and the Simpleton (Picard), 1949
Mermaid Attack (D. Martin), 1978
Mermaid Summer (M. Hunter), 1988
Mermaid's Daughter (Gard), 1969
Mermaids' Tales (Ainsworth), 1980
Mermaid's Three Wisdoms (Yolen), 1978
Merry by Name (Wayne), 1964
Merry Christmas Book (Bailey), 1948
Merry Christmas from Eddie (Haywood), 1986
Merry Christmas, Space Case (Marshall), 1986
Merry Christmas, Strega Nona (de Paola), 1986
Merry Coasting Party (Burgess), 1940
Merry Girls of England (Meade, appendix), 1896
Merry Go Round (C. Johnson), 1958
Merry Go Round in Oz (McGraw), 1963
Merry History of a Christmas Pie (verse; N. Willard), 1974
Merry Jack Jugg (Suddaby), 1954
Merry, Merry Fibruary (verse; Orgel), 1977
Merry Robin Hood (play; Blyton), 1927
Merry, Rose, and Christmas-Tree June (Orgel), 1969
Merry Story Book (Blyton), 1943
Merry-Go-Round (Heine, trans), 1980
Merry-Go-Round (verse; L. Richards), 1935
Merry-Go-Round (D. Ross), 1963
Merrymount (play; C. D. Mackay), 1912
Merryweathers (L. Richards), 1904
Mert the Blurt (R. Kraus), 1980
Mervyn, Jock, or Joe (Wynne), 1921
Message (O'Neill), 1989
Message from Arkmae (Cutt), 1972
Message to Hadrian (Trease), 1956
Message to the Kite (play; Parker), 1953
Messages (Darke), 1984
Messenger for Parliament (Haugaard), 1976
Messenger No. 48 (Otis, appendix), 1899
Meta series (Talbot), from 1930
Metro Gangs Attack (Leeson), 1986
Mexican Bird (Lattimore), 1965
Mexican Road Race (Wibberley, as O'Connor), 1957
Mia series (Beckman, trans), from 1974
Miaow! (B. Carter), 1978
Mice and Mendelson (Aiken), 1978
Mice at Play (Yonge, appendix), 1860
Mice of Nibbling Village (verse; Greaves), 1986
Mice on Ice (Yolen), 1980
Mice on My Mind (Waber), 1977
Mice, The Monks, and the Christmas Tree (Selden), 1963
Michael (Ormondroyd), 1967
Michael and the Dogs (Vipont), 1969
Michael and the Mitten Test (Wells), 1969
Michael Bird-Boy (de Paola), 1975
Michel Lorio's Cross (Stretton, appendix), 1876
Michel's Island (M. Hunt), 1940
Mickey the Beaver (K. Wood), 1964
Mickey the Mighty (play; Latham), 1937
Mickie (Unnerstad, trans), 1971
Mick's Country Cousins (de Roo), 1974
Middle of the Sandwich (Kennemore), 1981
Middle Sister (L. Duncan), 1960

Middletons Make Good (Talbot), 1934
Middy and Ensign (Fenn, appendix), 1883
Middy and the Moors (Ballantyne, appendix), 1888
Midget and Bridget (Hader), 1934
Midnight (R. Montgomery), 1940
Midnight Adventure (R. Briggs), 1961
Midnight and Jeremiah (North), 1943
Midnight Beast (Parker), n.d.
Midnight Folk (Masefield), 1927
Midnight Fox (Byars), 1968
Midnight Horse (M. Edwards), 1949
Midnight Is a Place (Aiken), 1974
Midnight Is a Place (play; Aiken), 1977
Midnight Kittens (D. Smith), 1978
Midnight Moon (verse; C. Watson), 1979
Midnight, Our Pony (Heward), 1953
Midnight Soup and a Witch's Hat (Orgel), 1987
Midnight Thief (play; Serraillier), 1963
Midshipman Cruise (S. Corbett), 1957
Midshipman of the Fleet (Westerman), 1954
Midshipman Raxworthy (Westerman), 1936
Midshipman Webb's Treasure (Westerman), 1938
'Midst Arctic Perils (Westerman), 1919
Midsummer Eve (play; C. D. Mackay), 1929
Midsummer Magic (Dillon), 1950
Midsummer Maze (Trevor), 1964
Midsummer Mountains (Lamplugh), 1961
Midsummer Night's Death (Peyton), 1978
Midway (Barrett), 1967
Miffy series (Bauna, trans), from 1964
Mighty Hunter (Hader), 1943
Mighty Mandarin (play; Trease), 1938
Mighty Slide (verse; Ahlberg), 1983
Mik and the Prowler (Uchida), 1960
Mika's Apple Tree (Bulla), 1968
Mike (Stong), 1957
Mike and Me (Line), 1974
Mike Mulligan and His Steam Shovel (V. Burton), 1939
Mike's Bike (Darke), 1974
Mike's Gang (Weir), 1965
Mike's House (Sauer), 1954
Mike's Toads (M. Steele, as Gage), 1970
Miki series (Petersham), from 1929
Mikko's Fortune (Kingman), 1955
Mildred series (Finley, appendix), from 1878
Milk and Cookies (Asch), 1982
Milk and Honey (Burgess), 1929
Milkman's on His Way (D. Rees), 1982
Milkweed Days (Yolen), 1976
Mill Green series (Prince), from 1982
Mill of Dreams (Farjeon), 1927
Miller's Boy (B. Willard), 1976
Miller's Daughter (Strang), 1926
Millicent and the Wind (Munsch), 1984
Millicent Gwent (Marchant), 1926
Millicent's Ghost (Lexau), 1962
Millie's Boy (R. N. Peck), 1973
Million Little Sunbeams (Burgess), 1963
Million Pound Mouse (R. Brown), 1975
Million-Dollar Ice Floe (Catherall, as Channel), 1961
Millions and Millions and Millions! (verse; Slobodkin), 1955
Millions of Cats (Gág), 1928
Mills Down Below (Allan), 1980
Mills of God (W. Armstrong), 1973
Milly (Finley, appendix), 1868
Milly-Molly-Mandy series (Brisley), from 1928

Milton (Sobol), 1971
Milton the Early Riser series (R. Kraus), from 1972
Mimosa Tree (V. and B. Cleaver), 1970
Mimosa's Field (Le Feuvre), 1953
Mince Pie and Mistletoe (verse; McGinley), 1961
Mind Your Own Business (verse; Rosen), 1974
Mindbenders (Fisk), 1987
Mindy's Mysterious Miniature (Curry), 1970
Mine for Keeps (Little), 1962
Mine Will, Said John (Griffith), 1980
Minerva Program (C.Mackay), 1984
Mine's the Best (Bonsall), 1973
Minestrone (Krauss), 1981
Ming and Mehitable (H. Sewell), 1936
Ming Lee and the Magic Tree (play; A. Harris), 1971
Ming Lo Moves the Mountain (Arnold Lobel), 1982
Mini-Bike series (C. Mackay), from 1974
Minigo (Abbott, appendix), 1857
Min-Min (M. Clark), 1966
Minn of the Mississippi (Holling), 1951
Minnie the Minnow (Symons), n.d.
Minnipins (Kendall), 1960
Minnow Leads to Treasure (Pearce), 1958
Minnow on the Say (Pearce), 1955
Minstrel and the Mountain (Yolen), 1968
Minstrel Boy (A. Hall), 1970
Minstrel Knight (Rush), 1955
Mintyglo Kid (Cross), 1983
Minute Boys series (Otis, appendix), from 1904
Mio (Lindgren, trans), 1956
Miracle Kittens (Nwapa), 1980
Miracle of Marcelino (Sánchez-Silva, trans), 1954
Miracle Tree (Mattingley), 1985
Miracles on Maple Hill (Sorensen), 1956
Miranda, The Adventures of (Meade, appendix), 1904
Miranda Going Home (Spence), 1985
Miranda the Great (Estes), 1967
Miranda's Beautiful Dream (R. Kraus), 1964
Miranda's Pilgrims (Wells), 1970
Miriam (Sommerfelt, trans), 1963
Miriam's Ambition (Everett-Green, appendix), 1889
Mirror Game (play; Foon), 1988
Mirror, Mirror (Garfield), 1976
Mirror of Her Own (Guy), 1981
Mirror Planet (Bunting), 1978
Mirrored Shield (Bibby), 1970
Mirrors of Castle Doone (Kyle), 1947
Mischa and His Brothers (Baumann, trans), 1985
Mischief (Castor, trans), 1937
Mischief Again (Blyton), 1955
Mischief at St. Rollo's (Blyton, as Pollock), 1943
Mischief City (verse; Wynne-Jones), 1986
Mischief-Making Magpie (Strang), 1926
Mischief's Thanksgiving (Coolidge, appendix), 1874
Mischievous Brownie (play; Brazil), 1899
Mischievous Martens (Lindgren, trans), 1964
Mischievous Moncton (Everett-Green, appendix), 1890
Misdoings of Micky and Mac (Peacocke), 1919
Miserable Christmas and a Happy New Year, (Stretton, appendix), 1888
Misplaced Persons (Harding), 1979
Miss Anna Truly series (Drummond), from 1945
Miss Ant, Miss Grasshopper, and Mr. Cricket (play; Field), 1930
Miss Bianca series (Sharp), from 1962
Miss Bobbie (E. Turner), 1897
Miss Dog's Christmas Treat (Marshall), 1973

Miss Duffy Is Still with Us (D. Rees), 1980
Miss Emily and the Bird of Make-Believe (Keeping), 1978
Miss Georgie's Gang (Stucley), 1970
Miss Ghost (Arthur), 1979
Miss Greyshott's Girls (Everett-Green, appendix), 1905
Miss Gwendoline (Meade, appendix), 1910
Miss Happiness and Miss Flower (Godden), 1961
Miss Hare and Mr. Tortoise (Judah), 1959
Miss Hickory (Bailey), 1946
Miss Jaster's Garden (Bodecker), 1971
Miss Jellytot's Visit (M. Hunt), 1955
Miss Jemima (de la Mare), 1925
Miss Lavender's Boy (Le Feuvre), 1906
Miss Lorimer of Chard (Everett-Green, appendix), 1907
Miss Maggie (Rylant), 1983
Miss Mallory of Mote (Everett-Green, appendix), 1912
Miss Marjorie of Silvermead (Everett-Green, appendix), 1899
Miss Meyrick's Niece (Everett-Green, appendix), 1891
Miss Moppet, The Story of (Potter), 1906
Miss Mouse and Her Boys (Molesworth, appendix), 1897
Miss Nelson series (Marshall), from 1977
Miss Nonentity (Meade, appendix), 1900
Miss Osborne-the-Mop (M. Steele, as Gage), 1963
Miss Patricia (Meade, appendix), 1925
Miss Pattie (Bright), 1954
Miss Pennyfeather series (O'Faolain), from 1942
Miss Pickerell series (MacGregor), from 1951
Miss Rivers and Miss Bridges (Symons), 1971
Miss Sanders (S. Price), 1988
Miss Tibbett's Typewriter (Merriam), 1966
Miss Uraca (Everett-Green, appendix), 1894
Miss Wilmer's Gang (Marchant), 1938
Missee Lee (Ransome), 1941
Missile Away (R. Montgomery), 1959
Missing, Believed Lost (Westerman), 1949
Missing Brother (Robertson), 1950
Missing Diplomat (Westerman), 1953
Missing Formula Mystery (Beresford), 1963
Missing from Home (Clewes), 1975
Missing from Home (Trease), 1936
Missing German (D. Rees), 1976
Missing Gold (M. Clark), 1951
Missing in Manhattan (Allan), 1967
Missing Milkman (Davoisin), 1967
Missing Persons (play; Wymark), 1978
Missing Persons League (Bonham), 1976
Missing Piece series (Silverstein), from 1976
Missing Prince (Farrow), 1896
Missing Skindiver (play; Wardell), 1966
Missing Witness (Syme), 1965
Mission (Marryat, appendix), 1845
Mission Accomplished (Catherall, as Channel), 1964
Mission for Oliver (Daniell), 1953
Mission Intruder (R. Montgomery), 1960
Mission to Cathay (Polland), 1965
Mississippi Pilot (Stong), 1954
Mississippi Possum (P. Martin, as Miles), 1965
Missouri Canary (Stong), 1943
Mist over Athelney (Trease), 1958
Mistaken Identity (Westerman), 1959
Mr. Adams's Mistake (Parish), 1982
Mr. and Mrs. Bear and Friends (Gibbs), 1943
Mr. and Mrs. Noah (Lenski), 1948
Mr. and Mrs. Pig's Evening Out (Rayner), 1976
Mr. Barney's Beard (S. Taylor), 1961
Mr. Bass series (Cameron), from 1958

Mr. Bat's Great Invention (Nöstlinger, trans), 1978
Mr. Bear series (Kuratomi, trans), from 1968
Mr. Benedict's Lion (Edmonds), 1950
Mr. Benn series (McKee), from 1967
Mr. Benn (play; McKee), n.d.
Mr. Bidery's Spidery Garden (verse; McCord), 1972
Mister Billy's Gun (Hader), 1960
Mr. Bingle's Apple Pie (Hewett, as Wellington), 1978
Mr. Bliss (Tolkien), 1982
Mr. Blossom's Shop (B. Todd), 1929
Mr. Brown Can Moo! (verse; Seuss), 1970
Mr. Bumps and His Monkey (de la Mare), 1942
Mr. Bumstead (Watkins-Pitchford), 1958
Mr. Cat in Business (Rodari, trans), 1975
Mr. Cat's Wonderful Surprise (Chalmers), 1961
Mr. Chick (Perkins), 1926
Mr. Chips and the Silver Chicken (play; Owen), 1977
Mister Corbett's Ghost (Garfield), 1968
Mr. Cram's Magic Bubbles (M. Bond), 1975
Mr. Dock's Garden (B. Todd), 1939
Mister Dog (M. W. Brown), 1952
Mr. Faksimily and the Tiger (Hewett), 1967
Mr. Ferguson of the Fire Department (MacGregor), 1956
Mr. Finch's Pet Shop (Drummond), 1953
Mr. Fixit (Scarry), 1978
Mr. Fork and Curly Fork (Banner), 1956
Mister Fox (Ballantyne, as Comus, appendix), 1857
Mr. Fox (A. Lawrence), 1979
Mr. Galliano's Circus (Blyton), 1938
Mr. Garden (Farjeon), 1966
Mr. Gosling series (Cunliffe), from 1978
Mr. Grigg's Work (Rylant), 1989
Mr. Growser Moves (Beaman), 1943
Mr. Growser Moves House (Beaman), 1962
Mr. Gumpy series (Burningham), from 1970
Mr. Hatherley's Boys (Everett-Green, appendix), 1885
Mr. Horrox and the Gratch (Reeves), 1969
Mister Icy-Cold (Blyton), 1948
Mr. Jameson and Mr. Phillips (Sharmat), 1979
Mr. Jeremy Fisher, The Tale of (Potter), 1906
Mister Jim (R. Montgomery), 1952
Mr. Jumble's Toy Shop (Ainsworth), 1978
Mr. Kelso's Lion (Bontemps), 1970
Mr. Koala Bear (verse; MacIntyre), 1954
Mr. Little (R. N. Peck), 1979
Mr. Magus Is Waiting for You (Kemp), 1986
Mr. McFadden's Hallowe'en (Godden), 1975
Mr. Meddle series (Blyton), from 1940
Mr. Midnight (Waddell), 1983
Mr. Miller the Dog (Heine, trans), 1980
Mr. Mocker, The Adventures of (Burgess), 1914
Mr. Monkey and the Gotcha Bird (Myers), 1984
Mr. Moon's Last Case (Patten), 1975
Mr. Morgan's Marrow (Andrew), 1967
Mr. Mushroom (Slobodkin), 1950
Mister Muster series (Arnold Lobel), from 1962
Mr. Mysterious and Company (S. Fleischman), 1962
Mr. Noah and the Second Flood (Burnford), 1973
Mr. Noah's Holiday (Beaman), 1942
Mr. Noselighter (verse; McGough), 1976
Mister O'Brien (Andrew), 1972
Mister P and His Remarkable Flight (D. Martin), 1975
Mister P, Street Pigeon (D. Martin), 1988
Mister Penny series (Ets), from 1935
Mr. Petersand's Cats and Kittens (Slobodkin), 1954
Mr. Pettigrew series (L. Clark), from 1974

Mr. Pickles and the Party (Heward), 1926
Mr. Pinks, The Story of (Hough), 1958
Mr. Pink-Whistle series (Blyton), from 1941
Mr. Piper's Bus (Clymer), 1961
Mr. Popcorn's Friends (Ainsworth), 1938
Mr. Popper's Penguins (Atwater), 1938
Mr. Pride's Umbrella (Bunting), 1980
Mr. Pringle and Mr. Buttonhouse (MacGregor), 1957
Mr. Pringle and the Prince (Phipson), 1979
Mr. Punch's Cap (Fidler), 1956
Mr. Rabbit and the Lovely Present (Zolotow), 1962
Mr. Rabbit at Home (J. Harris, appendix), 1895
Mr. Revere and I (Lawson), 1953
Mr. Robertson's Hundred Pounds (A. Lawrence), 1976
Mr. Rutherford's Children (Warner, appendix), 1853
Mr. Shaw's Shipshape Shoeshop (Titus), 1970
Mr. Sheridan's Umbrella (Strong), 1935
Mr. Simister series (Fidler), from 1947
Mr. Sly-One and the Cats (play; Blyton), 1955
Mr. Smith (verse; W. Smith), 1968
Mr. Stoat Walks In (Uttley), 1950
Mr. Stubbs's Brother (Otis, appendix), 1883
Mr. T.W. Anthony Woo (Ets), 1951
Mister Tinker in Oz (Howe), 1985
Mr. Tod, The Tale of (Potter), 1912
Mr. Toffy (T. Ross), 1973
Mr. Toffy's Circus, Tales from (T. Ross), 1973
Mr. Tucket (Paulsen), 1969
Mr. Tumpy series (Blyton), from 1949
Mr. Twee Deedle series (Gruelle), from 1913
Mr. Twiddle series (Blyton), from 1942
Mr. Twigg's Mistake (Lawson), 1947
Mr. Wilmer (Lawson), 1945
Mr. Woodchuck (Baum, as Bancroft), 1906
Mr. Yowder series (Rounds), from 1976
Mrs. Brice's Mice (Hoff), 1988
Mrs. Burton's Best Bedroom (Stretton, appendix), 1878
Mrs. Circumference (Storr), 1989
Mrs. Cockle's Cat (Pearce), 1961
Mrs. Crumble and Fire Engine No. 7 (P. Martin), 1966
Mrs. Darling's Daughter (Colman), 1962
Mrs. Discombobulous (Mahy), 1969
Mistress Dorothy (Moore), 1902
Mrs. Easter series (Drummond), from 1944
Mrs. Elmo of Elephant House (R. Kraus), 1986
Mrs. Fish, Ape, and Me, The Dump Queen (Mazer), 1980
Mrs. Frisby and the Rats of Nimh (O'Brien), 1971
Mrs. Gaddy series (M. Steele, as Gage), from 1979
Mrs. Jenny (Tate), 1966
Mrs. Kind Bush (Howes), 1933
Mrs. Malone (verse; Farjeon), 1950
Mistress Masham's Repose (T. White), 1946
Mrs. Mopple's Washing Line (Hewett), 1966
Mrs. Mouse Spring-Cleans (Uttley), 1950
Mrs. Munch and Puffing Billy (Thiele), 1967
Mistress Nanciebel (Oxenham), 1909
Mrs. Nimble and Mr. Bumble (Uttley), 1944
Mistress of Purity Gap (Marchant), 1921
Mrs. Overtheway's Remembrances (Ewing, appendix), 1869
Mrs. Peter Rabbit (Burgess), 1919
Mrs. Pig series (Rayner), from 1981
Mrs. Pinny series (H. Morgan), from 1968
Mrs. Portree's Pony (L. Hall), 1980
Mrs. Romaine's Household (Everett-Green, appendix), 1891
Mrs. Switch (Hoff), 1967
Mrs. Tiggy-Winkle, The Tale of (Potter), 1905

Mrs. Tittlemouse, The Tale of (Potter), 1910
Mrs. Tortino's Return to the Sun (S. Murphy), 1980
Mrs. Townsend's Robber (Moray Williams), 1971
Mrs. Tubbs series (Lofting), from 1923
Mrs. Updaisy (Lampman), 1963
Mrs. Wappinger's Secret (Hightower), 1956
Mrs. Wiggs of the Cabbage Patch (Rice), 1901
Mistress-Mariner (D. Bruce), 1932
Misty series (Henry), from 1947
Mitch and Amy (Cleary), 1967
Mitchell Is Moving (Sharmat), 1978
Mitchells (Van Stockum), 1945
Mix or Match Storybook (Scarry), 1979
Mixed-Marriage Daughter (Colman), 1968
Mixed-Up Chameleon (Carle), 1975
Mixed-Up Twins (Haywood), 1952
Mixture as Before (Hough), 1976
Moa Hunter (Sutton), 1978
Moa Valley (de Roo), 1969
Mobsley's Mohicans (H. Avery), 1899
Moccasin Trail (McGraw), 1952
Mock Revolt (V. and B. Cleaver), 1971
Mockery Hollow (play; Lillington), 1972
Modern Broods (Yonge, appendix), 1900
Modern Mephistopheles (Alcott, appendix), 1877
Modern Telemachus (Yonge, appendix), 1886
Modern Tomboy (Meade, appendix), 1904
Moe Q. McGlutch (Raskin), 1973
Moffat series (Estes), from 1941
Mog series (J. Kerr), from 1970
Mog (Moray Williams), 1969
Mog and the Rectifier (Powling), 1980
Mogo the Mynah (Lifton), 1958
Mogo's Flute (Van Stockum), 1966
Mohawk Valley (Welch), 1958
Moira's Birthday (Munsch), 1987
Mojo and the Russians (Myers), 1977
Mokee the White Possum (L. Rees), 1973
Moko's Hideout (Locke), 1976
Moldy Warp (Uttley), 1940
Mole Family's Christmas (Hoban), 1969
Mole Hole (Dickinson), 1987
Mollie's Adventures (Wynne), 1903
Molly (B. Wilson), 1983
Molly Angel's Adventures (Marchant), 1915
Molly in the Middle (Lattimore), 1956
Molly in the West (Marchant), 1927
Molly Melville (Everett-Green, appendix), 1897
Molly of One Tree Bend (Marchant), 1910
Molly o' the Moors (Keeping), 1966
Mollyday Holiday (Storey), 1971
Molly's Pilgrim (Cohen), 1983
Molly's Woodland Garden (Rockwell), 1971
Mom, The Wolf Man, and Me (N. Klein), 1972
Momoko series (Iwasaki, trans), from 1972
Momolu series (L. Graham), from 1946
Momo's Kitten (Yashima), 1961
Mona Lisa Mystery (Hutchins), 1981
Mona of the Isle (Lynch), 1965
Monarch (Seton), 1904
Monday Adventure (Pudney), 1950
Monday I Love You (C. Greene), 1988
Monday-Tuesday-Wednesday Book (Clymer, as Bell), 1946
Money Cat (Kyle), 1958
Money for Sale (Hardcastle), 1975
Money Machine (Robertson), 1969

Money Room (McGraw), 1981
Monica (Everett-Green, appendix), 1889
Monica Anson (Meynell), 1959
Monica Turns Up Trumps (Brent-Dyer), 1936
Monitress Merle (Brazil), 1922
Monkey Day (Krauss), 1957
Monkey Face (Asch), 1977
Monkey in the Middle (Bunting), 1984
Monkey of Crofton (Lattimore), 1957
Monkey Puzzle (verse; Livingston), 1984
Monsieur Violet..., Narrative of the Travels and Adventures of
   (Marryat, appendix), 1843
Monster Den (verse; Ciardi), 1966
Monster Garden (Alcock), 1988
Monster Horse, The Tale of the (verse; Serraillier), 1950
Monster in the Cupboard (J. Wilson), 1986
Monster in the River (Cockett), 1979
Monster Is Coming! A Monster Is Coming! (Heide), 1980
Monster Maker (Fisk), 1979
Monster Munch (verse; Ahlberg), 1983
Monster Night at Grandma's House (R. Peck), 1977
Monster of Roundwater (Greaves), 1984
Monster of Widgeon Weir (Atkinson), 1943
Monster Too Many (McNeill), 1972
Monsters' Ball (de Paola), 1970
Monte (R. Montgomery), 1962
Monty (Stevenson), 1979
Monty Woodpig series (Watkins-Pitchford), from 1957
Mooch the Messy series (Sharmat), from 1976
Mooga Mega Mekki (Wahl), 1974
Moomintroll series (Jansson, trans), from 1950
Moon (play; Fyleman), 1934
Moon and a Star, (verse; Livingston), 1965
Moon and the Face (McKillip), 1985
Moon Bear (Asch), 1978
Moon Blossom and the Golden Penny (Slobodkin), 1963
Moon by Night (L'Engle), 1963
Moon Cake (Asch), 1983
Moon Eyes (Poole), 1965
Moon Filly (Mitchell), 1968
Moon in the Cloud (R. Harris), 1968
Moon in the River (V. Smith), 1969
Moon Lake Angel (V. Cleaver), 1987
Moon Makes Three (play; A. Harris), 1947
Moon Man (Ungerer), 1966
Moon Mill (play; Aiken), 1982
Moon Monsters (D. Hill), 1984
Moon of Gomrath (Garner), 1963
Moon of Snowshoes (Suddaby), 1956
Moon of Three Rings (A. Norton), 1966
Moon or a Button (Krauss), 1959
Moon Ribbon (Yolen), 1976
Moon Singer (Bulla), 1969
Moon, Stars, Frogs, and Friends (MacLachlan), 1980
Moonball (Moray Williams), 1958
Moon-Bells (verse; T. Hughes), 1978
Mooncoin Castle (Turkle), 1970
Mooncusser's Daughter (play; Aiken), 1973
Moon-Dark (Wrightson), 1987
Moondial (Cresswell), 1987
Moondial (play; Cresswell), 1988
Moon-Flash (McKillip), 1984
Moongame (Asch), 1984
Moonlight (H. Griffiths), 1959
Moonlight Bride (Emecheta), 1980
Moonlight Man (Fox), 1986

Moonpath (Swindells), 1979
Moon's Revenge (Aiken), 1987
Moonshadow of Cherry Mountain (D. B. Smith), 1982
Moonshine and Magic (Uttley), 1932
Moonsong Lullaby (verse; Highwater), 1981
Moon-Whales (verse; T. Hughes), 1976
Moonwind (L. Lawrence), 1986
Moor of Spain (Parker), 1953
Moose (Foreman), 1971
Moose and Goose (Marc Brown), 1978
Moose, Goose, and Little Nobody (Raskin), 1974
Moosepire (Pinkwater), 1986
Mop Top (D. Freeman), 1955
Mopsa the Fairy (Ingelow, appendix), 1869
Moral Alphabet (verse; Belloc), 1899
More about Mandy (L. Hill), 1963
More about Tompkins (verse; Fuller), 1981
More Beasts (for Worse Children) (verse; Belloc), 1897
More Beautiful Than Flowers (Lexau), 1966
More Bywords (Yonge, appendix), 1890
More Funny Ones (Hough), 1965
More Little Mushrooms (play; Ainsworth), 1955
More Ponies for Jean (Cannan), 1943
More Snakes than Ladders (Parker), 1960
More Tales from California (Shannon), 1935
More Than You Bargained For (Aiken), 1955
Morgan (Otis, appendix), 1898
Morgan for Melinda (Gates), 1980
Morgan the Magnificent (Wallace), 1987
Morgan's Zoo (Howe), 1984
Morning Face (verse; G. Porter), 1916
Morning Glory (Symons, as Groves), 1966
Morning Has Broken (verse; Farjeon), 1981
Morning Is a Long Time Coming (B. Greene), 1978
Morning of the Gods (Fenton), 1987
Morning the Sun Refused to Rise (Rounds), 1984
Morning-Glories (Alcott, appendix), 1867
Morris Brookside series (Sharmat), from 1973
Morris's Disappearing Bag (Wells), 1975
Mortimer series (Aiken), from 1976
Mortimer (Munsch), 1983
Morton's Pony (Hough), 1957
Moses series (Kimenye), from 1967
Moshie Cat (H. Griffiths), 1969
Moss and Blister (Garfield), 1976
Most Important Thing (Ure), 1986
Most Popular Girl in the School (Marchant), 1924
Most Terrible Turk (Krumgold), 1969
Most Wonderful Doll in the World (McGinley), 1950
Most Wonderful Egg in the World (Heine, trans), 1983
Moth Manor (M. Bacon), 1978
Mother and Son (Meade, appendix), 1911
Mother Carey (Wiggin), 1911
Mother Carey's Chicken (Fenn, appendix), 1887
Mother Carey's Chickens (Wiggin), 1911
Mother Carey's Chickens (play; Wiggin), 1917
Mother Farthing's Luck (H. Morgan), 1971
Mother Goose for Christmas (du Bois), 1973
Mother Goose Parade (Gruelle), 1929
Mother Goose's Golden Christmas (play; D. Wood), 1977
Mother Goose's Party (play; Fyleman), 1928
Mother Herring's Chicken (Meade, appendix), 1881
Mother, How Could You (Bunting), 1986
Mother Hubbard and the Silver Sixpence, The Story of (Talbot), 1931
Mother Josephine Bakes Bread (play; Moray Williams), 1933

Mother Makes Christmas (Meigs), 1940
Mother Mary (Meade, appendix), 1916
Mother Nature's Song and Story Book (verse; Burgess), 1938
Mother West Wind series (Burgess), from 1910
Motherless Baby (Ekwensi), 1980
Motherless Maid (Everett-Green, appendix), 1906
Mother's Birthday Reviews (verse; Ewing, appendix), 1888
Mother's Day Mice (Bunting), 1986
Mother's Little Girl (E. Turner), 1904
Mother's Meeting (play; Blyton), 1955
Motherstone (Gee), 1985
Motor Bandits (Chaundler), 1920
Motor Scout (Strang), 1912
Motorway Chase (B. Carter), 1961
Motown and Didi (Myers), 1984
Mottram Park series (Chaney), from 1971
Mouldy (Mayne), 1983
Mouldy's Orphan (G. Avery), 1978
Mountain (Ridge), 1956
Mountain Born (Yates), 1943
Mountain Dog (Evans), 1956
Mountain Door (Fry), 1960
Mountain Engines (Awdry), 1964
Mountain Light (Yep), 1985
Mountain Man (R. Montgomery), 1957
Mountain of Adventure (Blyton), 1949
Mountain Rescue (Serraillier), 1955
Mountain Rescue Dog (Fidler), 1969
Mountain That Laughed (Drummond), 1947
Mountaineers (Harnett), 1941
Mountains of Quilt (N. Willard), 1987
Mountainy Men (Syme), 1961
Mounted Messenger (Meigs), 1943
Mounted Police Patrol (Haig-Brown), 1954
Mouse and His Child (play; Doherty), 1987
Mouse and His Child (Hoban), 1967
Mouse and the Egg (Mayne), 1980
Mouse and the Lion (Titus), 1962
Mouse and the Mirage (McNeill), 1966
Mouse and the Motorcycle (Cleary), 1965
Mouse at Sea (R. Kraus), 1959
Mouse Butcher (King-Smith), 1981
Mouse Called Junction (Cunningham), 1980
Mouse Chorus (verse; Coatsworth), 1955
Mouse God (R. Kennedy), 1979
Mouse House (Godden), 1957
Mouse Manor (Eager), 1952
Mouse Six and the Happy Birthday (P. Martin, as Miles), 1978
Mouse Soup (Arnold Lobel), 1977
Mouse Tales (Arnold Lobel), 1972
Mouse Telegrams (Uttley), 1950
Mouse, The Rabbit, and the Little White Hen (Uttley), 1966
Mouse Work (R. Kraus), 1980
Mou-Setsé (Meade, appendix), 1880
Mousewife (Godden), 1951
Mousewing (Mayne), 1986
Mouthful of Magic (H. Morgan), 1963
Moved-Outers (Means), 1945
Movie Shoes (Streatfeild), 1949
Moving Cat (Cockett), 1972
Moving Day for the Middlemans (Slobodkina), 1960
Moving Finger (Grice), 1962
Moving In (Slote), 1988
Moving Molly (S. Hughes), 1978
Much Ado About Aldo (Hurwitz), 1978
Much Bigger Than Martin (Kellogg), 1976

Much Too Much Magic (McNeill), 1971
Mud Puddle (Munsch), 1979
Mud Snail Son (Lifton), 1971
Mudcake Princess (play; Clapp), 1979
Muddle (Chukovsky, trans), 1976
Muddle-Headed Wombat series (Park), from 1962
Muddle-Headed Wombat (play; Park), n.d.
Muddy Kind of Magic (Ure), 1988
Muddy Milly (play; T. Ross), 1985
Muddy Road to Glory (Meader), 1963
Mudlarks (Harnett), 1940
Mudlarks and Mysteries (F. Knight), 1955
Muffie Mouse and the Busy Birthday (Nixon), 1978
Muffin Fiend (Pinkwater), 1986
Muffletumps series (Wahl), from 1966
Mulberry Bush (verse; Farjeon), 1945
Mulberry Music (Orgel), 1971
Mulberry Street Team (Beresford), 1963
Mulberry Tree (Wahl), 1970
Mulbridge Manor (Reeves), 1958
Mulcaster Market (play; Reeves), 1951
Mule of the Expressway (Berna, trans), 1967
Mule of the Motorway (Berna, trans), 1967
Mule Who Struck It Rich (Hoff), 1971
Muley-Ears, Nobody's Dog (Henry), 1959
Mullion (Allan), 1949
Mumfie series (Tozer), from 1935
Mummy Dearest series (R. Kraus), 1988
Mummy Knows Best (R. Kraus), 1988
Mummy Vanishes (R. Kraus), 1988
Munde series (Odaga), 1987
Mungo (Fry), 1972
Mungo the Monkey (Ainsworth), 1968
Murder at the Spaniel Show (L. Hall), 1988
Murderer (Holman), 1978
Murmel, Murmel, Murmel (Munsch), 1982
Murray Finds a Chum (Wynne), 1914
Muscles and Brains (Hoff), 1940
Museum (Abbott, appendix), 1884
Mushroom Center Disaster (Bodecker), 1974
Mushroom Planet series (Cameron), from 1954
Music, Music for Everyone (V. Williams), 1984
Musical Honours (Barne), 1947
Mustang (Henry), 1966
Mustang Machine (Powling), 1981
Mustard, Pepper, and Salt (Uttley), 1938
Mutineers (R. Armstrong), 1968
Mutineers (Hawes), 1920
My Ain Sel' (play; Mitchison), 1928
My Animal Friends (Nakatani, trans), 1975
My Aunt Polly by the Sea (Cresswell), 1980
My Aunt Rosie (Hoff), 1972
My Babysitter (Rockwell), 1985
My Backyard (Rockwell), 1984
My Barber (Rockwell), 1981
My Big-Ears Picture Book (Blyton), 1958
My Black Sheep (Everett-Green, appendix), 1889
My Book about Christmas (Robinson, as Thomas), 1946
My Boynie (Everett-Green, appendix), 1889
My Brother (Berg), 1972
My Brother Fine with Me (Clifton), 1975
My Brother Lambert (Rush), 1957
My Brother Mike (Gates), 1948
My Brother Sam Is Dead (Collier), 1974
My Brother Stevie (Clymer), 1967
My Buddy, The King (Brittain), 1989

My Captive (Altsheler), 1902
My Castle (Heide), 1972
My Cat Has Eyes of Sapphire Blue (verse; A. Fisher), 1973
My Cat Likes to Hide in Boxes (verse; Sutton), 1973
My Cousin Abe (A. Fisher), 1962
My Darling, My Hamburger (Zindel), 1969
My Darling Villain (Banks), 1977
My Daughter Nicola (Arthur), 1965
My Day on the Farm (Nakatani, trans), 1976
My Dog and I (Titus, as Lord), 1958
My Dog Is Lost (Keats), 1960
My Dog Rinty (Ets), 1946
My Dog Sunday (Berg), 1968
My Doggie and I (Ballantyne, appendix), 1881
My Family's Not Forever (Allan), 1977
My Father, The Coach (Slote), 1972
My Father, Sun-Sun Johnson (Palmer), 1974
My Father's Collie (Kjelgaard), 1961
My Father's Dragon (Gannett), 1948
My Favourite...series (Bartos-Höppner, trans), from 1980
My First Horse (James), 1940
My First Word Book (Scarry), 1986
My Friend Charlie (Flora), 1964
My Friend Flicka (O'Hara), 1941
My Friend Jacob (Clifton), 1980
My Friend John (Zolotow), 1968
My Friend Mr. Leakey (Haldane), 1937
My Friend Phil (Peacocke), 1915
My Friend Smith (Reed, appendix), 1889
My Friend the Dog (Terhune), 1926
My Friend the Monster (Bulla), 1980
My Friends on the Farm (Baumann, trans), 1985
My Gang (Waddell, as Sefton), 1984
My Garden Book (Robinson, as Thomas), 1947
My Grandson Lew (Zolotow), 1974
My Great-Grandfather and I series (Krüss, trans), from 1964
My Heart's in the Highlands (Le Feuvre), 1924
My Hopping Bunny (verse; Bright), 1960
My House (Bruna, trans), 1984
My House (Schlein), 1971
My Kid Sister (Hildick), 1971
My Kingdom for a Grave (Plowman), 1970
My Lady Joanna (Everett-Green, appendix), 1902
My Lady Venturesome (Moore), 1926
My Life as a Body (N. Klein), 1987
My Little Book of Big and Little (verse; W. Smith), 1963
My Little Corner (Walton, appendix), 1872
My Mama Needs Me (Walter), 1983
My Mama Says There Aren't Any Zombies...(Viorst), 1973
My Mate Shofiq (Needle), 1978
My Mates and I (Walton, appendix), 1873
My Meals (Bruna, trans), 1975
My Mother (Ballantyne, as Comus, appendix), 1857
My Mother and I (verse; A. Fisher), 1967
My Mother Is the Smartest Woman in the World (Clymer), 1982
My Mother Never Listens to Me (Sharmat), 1984
My Name Is Pablo (Sommerfelt, trans), 1966
My Name Is Paula Popowich! (M. Hughes), 1983
My Naughty Little Sister series (D. Edwards), from 1952
My New Home (Molesworth, appendix), 1894
My Nightingale Is Singing (Lindgren, trans), 1985
My Pal Spadger (Naughton), 1977
My Parents Think I'm Sleeping (verse; Prelutsky), 1985
My Place (Wheatley), 1987
My Playtime (Bruans, trans), 1985
"My Pretty" and Her Little Brother "Too" (Molesworth,

appendix), 1901
My Proud Beauty (play; Lillington), 1963
My Red Umbrella (Bright), 1959
My Robot Buddy (Slote), 1975
My Shirt Is White (Bruna, trans), 1973
My Side of the Mountain (George), 1959
My Simple Little Brother (Norman), 1979
My Sister Says (B. Baker), 1984
My Son, The Mouse (R. Kraus), 1966
My Special Best Words (Steptoe), 1974
My Sport Book (Bruna, trans), 1986
My Spring Robin (Rockwell), 1989
My Summer of the Lions (W. Taylor), 1986
My Teddy Bear (Nakatani, trans), 1975
My Tiger (Cowley), 1986
My Toys (Bruna, trans), 1980
My Treasures (Nakatani, trans), 1979
My Trip to Alpha I (Slote), 1978
My Uncle Charlie (Darke), 1977
My Very First Book (Petersham), 1948
My Very First Library (Carle), 1974
My Very Own Fairy Book (Gruelle), 1923
My Very Own Fairy Stories (Gruelle), 1917
My Vest Is White (Bruna, trans), 1973
My War with Goggle Eyes (Fine), 1989
My War with Mrs. Galloway (Orgel), 1985
My World (M. W. Brown), 1949
My Young Alcides (Yonge, appendix), 1875
Myna Bird Mystery (Berna, trans), 1970
Myrtle the Turtle, Tales of (Robertson), 1974
Mysie's Work (Finley, appendix), 1864
Mysteries of Harris Burdick (Van Allsburg), 1984
Mysterious Appearance of Agnes (H. Griffiths), 1975
Mysterious Baba and Her Magic Caravan (Ainsworth), 1980
Mysterious Christmas Shell (Cameron), 1961
Mysterious City (Marchant), 1905
Mysterious Disappearance of Leon (I Mean Noel) (Raskin), 1971
Mysterious House (Walton, appendix), 1890
Mysterious Inheritance (Marchant), 1914
Mysterious Island (Beresford), 1984
Mysterious Island (Wynne), 1935
Mysterious "Mr. Punch" (Farrow), 1905
Mysterious Mr. Ross (Alcock), 1987
Mysterious Moortown Bridge (L. Hall), 1981
Mysterious Pool (Patchett), 1958
Mysterious Prowler (Nixon), 1976
Mysterious Queen of Magic (Nixon), 1981
Mysterious Rattle (D. Rees), 1982
Mysterious Red Tape Gang (Nixon), 1974
Mysterious Shin Shira (Farrow), 1913
Mysterious Stranger (play; de Regniers), 1982
Mysterious Tadpole (Kellogg), 1977
Mysterious Voyage (Farrow), 1910
Mysterious Zetabet (S. Corbett), 1979
Mystery at Keyhole Carnival (Heide), 1977
Mystery at Love's Creek (Cavanna), 1965
Mystery at MacAdoo Zoo (Heide), 1973
Mystery at Mycenae (Green), 1957
Mystery at Penmarth (Manning-Sanders), 1940
Mystery at Saint-Hilaire (Allan, as Hagon), 1968
Mystery at Southport Cinema (Heide), 1978
Mystery at the Edge of Two Worlds (C. Harris), 1978
Mystery at the Red House (Meigs), 1961
Mystery at the Villa Bianca (Allan, as Hagon), 1969
Mystery Beast of Ostergeest (Kellogg), 1971
Mystery Began in Madeira (Allan), 1967

Mystery Dolls from Planet Urd (Nixon), 1981
Mystery in Arles (Allan), 1964
Mystery in Florence (Fenton), 1959
Mystery in Little Tokyo (Bonham), 1966
Mystery in Manhattan (Allan), 1968
Mystery in Marrakech (Cavanna), 1968
Mystery in Rome (Allan), 1974
Mystery in the Middle Marches (Finlay), 1964
Mystery in the Middle Marches (play; Finlay), 1962
Mystery in the Museum (Cavanna), 1972
Mystery in Wales (Allan), 1971
Mystery Island (Blyton), 1945
Mystery Island (Westerman), 1927
Mystery Man (S. Corbett), 1970
Mystery Manor (Atkinson), 1937
Mystery Mine (Saville), 1959
Mystery of Alton Grange (Everett-Green, appendix), 1899
Mystery of Banshee Towers (Blyton), 1961
Mystery of Burnt Hill (Robertson), 1952
Mystery of Castle Renaldi (Holland, as Hunt), 1972
Mystery of Derrydane (Allan), 1955
Mystery of Drear House (Hamilton), 1987
Mystery of Grudge Mountain (Terhune), 1939
Mystery of Holly Lane (Blyton), 1953
Mystery of Hurricane Castle (Nixon), 1964
Mystery of Mr. Jones's Disappearing Taxi (Aiken), 1982
Mystery of Nix Hall (Westerman), 1950
Mystery of Obadiah (R. Armstrong), 1943
Mystery of Pony Hollow series (L. Hall), from 1978
Mystery of Saint-Salgue (Berna, trans), 1963
Mystery of Secret Beach (Finkel), 1962
Mystery of Stockmere School (Westerman), 1923
Mystery of Tally-Ho Cottage (Blyton), 1954
Mystery of the Angry Idol (Whitney), 1965
Mystery of the Bewitched Bookmobile (Heide), 1975
Mystery of the Black Diamonds (Whitney), 1954
Mystery of the Black Sheep (Weir), 1964
Mystery of the Blue Admiral (Clewes), 1954
Mystery of the Broads (Westerman), 1930
Mystery of the Burnt Cottage (Blyton), 1943
Mystery of the Caramel Cat (L. Hall), 1981
Mystery of the Colonel's Clock (P. Turner), 1984
Mystery of the Crimson Ghost (Whitney), 1969
Mystery of the Cross-Eyed Man (Berna, trans), 1965
Mystery of the Crystal Canyon (R. Montgomery), 1951
Mystery of the Disappearing Cat (Blyton), 1948
Mystery of the Emerald Buddha (Cavanna), 1976
Mystery of the Fat Cat (Bonham), 1968
Mystery of the Flying Orange Pumpkin (Kellogg), 1980
Mystery of the Forgotten Island (Heide), 1980
Mystery of the Golden Horn (Whitney), 1962
Mystery of the Good Adventure (Kyle, as Ralston), 1950
Mystery of the Green Cat (Whitney), 1957
Mystery of the Grinning Idol (Nixon), 1965
Mystery of the Gulls (Whitney), 1949
Mystery of the Haunted Pool (Whitney), 1960
Mystery of the Haunted Woods (Nixon), 1967
Mystery of the Hidden Cockatoo (Nixon), 1966
Mystery of the Hidden Hand (Whitney), 1963
Mystery of the Hidden House (Blyton), 1948
Mystery of the Invisible Thief (Blyton), 1950
Mystery of the Jade-Green Cadillac (Clewes), 1958
Mystery of the Key (Westerman), 1948
Mystery of the Lonely Lantern (Heide), 1976
Mystery of the Lost and Found Hound (L. Hall), 1979
Mystery of the Lost Tower Treasure (Clewes), 1960

Mystery of the Magic Green Ball (Kellogg), 1978
Mystery of the Manor (Talbot), 1930
Mystery of the Melting Snowman (Heide), 1974
Mystery of the Midnight Message (Heide), 1977
Mystery of the Midnight Smugglers (Clewes), 1964
Mystery of the Missing Man (Blyton), 1956
Mystery of the Missing Necklace (Blyton), 1947
Mystery of the Missing Red Mitten (Kellogg), 1974
Mystery of the Missing Suitcase (Heide), 1972
Mystery of the Moated Grange (Brazil), 1942
Mystery of the Moonside Farm (Trease), 1949
Mystery of the Moorside Farm (Trease), 1949
Mystery of the Motels (Breary), 1958
Mystery of the Mummy's Mask (Heide), 1979
Mystery of the Pantomime Cat (Blyton), 1949
Mystery of the Pinewood (Molesworth, appendix), 1903
Mystery of the Plum Park Pony (L. Hall), 1980
Mystery of the "Polly Harris", (Treadgold), 1951
Mystery of the Red Tide (Bonham), 1966
Mystery of the Ruby Queens (Cavanna, as Allen), 1958
Mystery of the Scarlet Daffodil, (Clewes), 1953
Mystery of the Schoolhouse Dog (L. Hall), 1979
Mystery of the Scowling Boy (Whitney), 1973
Mystery of the Secret Room (Blyton), 1945
Mystery of the Secret Square (Allan, as Hagon), 1970
Mystery of the Secret Stowaway (Nixon), 1968
Mystery of the "Sempione" (Westerman), 1957
Mystery of the Silver Run (Marchant), 1907
Mystery of the Silver Tag (Heide), 1972
Mystery of the Singing Strings (Clewes), 1961
Mystery of the Ski Slopes (Allan), 1966
Mystery of the Spiteful Letters (Blyton), 1946
Mystery of the Stolen Blue Paint (Kellogg), 1982
Mystery of the Strange Bundle (Blyton), 1952
Mystery of the Strange Messages (Blyton), 1957
Mystery of the Strange Traveler (Whitney), 1967
Mystery of the Stubborn Old Man (L. Hall), 1980
Mystery of the Turquoise Frog (R. Montgomery), 1946
Mystery of the Vanished Prince (Blyton), 1951
Mystery of the Vanishing Visitor (Heide), 1975
Mystery of the Whispering Voice (Heide), 1974
Mystery of the Woods (Stolz), 1964
Mystery of Torland Manor (A. Hall), 1952
Mystery on Danger Road (Heide), 1983
Mystery on Rainbow Island (Clewes), 1957
Mystery on Safari (Cavanna), 1971
Mystery on Telegraph Hill (Pease), 1961
Mystery on the Farm (Cockett), 1988
Mystery on the Fourteenth Floor (Allan), 1965
Mystery on the Isle of Skye (Whitney), 1955
Mystery on the Moor (J. Pullein-Thompson), 1984
Mystery on the Moors (Trease), 1937
Mystery Pony (Cumming), 1957
Mystery Ship (Westerman), 1920
Mystery Stories (Blyton), 1960
Mystery That Never Was (Blyton), 1961
Mystery Train (B. Todd), 1937
Mystery Trek (Cumming), 1964

NIK: Now I Know (Chambers), 1988
Nacar (de Treviño), 1963
Nadia to the Rescue (Moore), 1912
Naftali the Storyteller and His Horse, Sus (Singer), 1976
Nag Called Wednesday (R. Brown), 1977
Nail, A Stick, and a Lid (Kaye), 1975
Nailing the Shadow (verse; McGough), 1987

Naira Power (Emecheta), 1982
Name for Kitty (McGinley), 1948
Name Like Bunny (Mazer), 1988
Name on the Glass (B. C. Freeman), 1964
Nameless Boat (Pardoe), 1957
Nameless Island (Westerman), 1915
Names and Nicknames (play; Reaney), 1963
Namesake (Hodges), 1964
Namesake for Nathan (Monjo), 1977
Namesakes (Everett-Green, appendix), 1893
Nan and Ken (Wynne), 1919
Nana Upstairs and Nana Downstairs (de Paola), 1973
Nance Kennedy (Meade, appendix), 1910
Nancekuke (Branfield), 1972
Nancy series (D. Bruce) from 1926
Nancy (Talbot), 1930
Nancy Afloat (Marchant), 1936
Nancy Alden (E. O. White), 1936
Nanny Goat and the Fierce Dog (Keeping), 1973
Naomi in the Middle (N. Klein), 1974
Napper series (Waddell), from 1981
Narcissa (L. Richards), 1894
Nargun and the Stars (Wrightson), 1973
Narnia series (C. Lewis), from 1950
Narrow Passage (Butterworth), 1973
Nasty! (Rosen), 1982
Nat the Naturalist (Fenn, appendix), 1899
Nata (Griffith), 1985
Nate the Great series (Sharmat), from 1972
Nathaniel Talking (Greenfield), 1988
Nation Builders (Hayes), 1968
National Velvet (Bagnold), 1935
National Velvet (play; Bagnold), 1946
Nativity Play (play; D. Wood), 1987
Natural History of the Ten Commandments (Seton), 1907
Nature of the Beast (Howker), 1985
Nature of the Beast (play; Howker), 1988
Nature Stories (Burgess), from 1944
Nature Tales (Blyton), 1948
Naughtiest Girl series (Blyton), from 1940
Naughty Bunny (Scarry), 1959
Naughty Children series (Blyton), from 1944
Naughty Comet (L. Richards), 1910
Naughty Comet (play; L. Richards), 1915
Naughty Nicky (T. Ross), 1983
Naughty Nigel (T. Ross), 1982
Naughty One of the Family (Meade, appendix), 1902
Nautilus (L. Richards), 1895
Navaho Sister (Lampman), 1956
Navajo Pet (P. Martin), 1971
Navy Alphabet (verse; Baum), 1900
Neal (Otis, appendix), 1895
Near and Far (verse; L. Clark), 1968
Near the Window Tree (verse; Kuskin), 1975
Necessary End (Benchley), 1976
Necklace of Raindrops (Aiken), 1968
Necktie Party (Otis, appendix), 1898
Ned Leger (Fenn, appendix), 1899
Ned Newton (Alger, appendix), 1890
Ned Only (B. Willard), 1985
Neddy the Donkey (Fyleman), 1951
Neglected Mountain (Saville), 1953
Neighbors (Marcia Brown), 1967
Neighbors in Cyrus (L. Richards), 1896
Neighbours (Molesworth, appendix), 1889
Neighbours at School (Talbot), 1923

Neighbours Unknown (C. Roberts), 1910
Nellijumbo (play; S. Walker), 1921
Nelson the Newsboy (Alger, appendix), 1901
Nelson Treasure (Wardell), 1983
Nelly and Margaret (Yonge, appendix), 1880(?)
Nemo (Walton, appendix), 1893
Nephew Jack (Fenn, appendix), 1905
Neptune Rising (Yolen), 1982
Neretto (Bettina), 1969
Nessie the Mannerless Monster (verse; T. Hughes), 1964
Nessie the Monster (verse; T. Hughes), 1974
Nest (Tate), 1969
Nest of Malignants (Moore), 1919
Nest of the Scarecrow (Atkinson), 1944
Nesta (Molesworth, appendix), 1889
Nesta on Her Own (Talbot), 1938
Nesta Steps Out (Brent-Dyer), 1954
Nesta's New School (Brazil), 1932
Net to Catch the Wind (Greaves), 1979
Nettleford series (Saville), from 1953
Nettlewood (Melwood), 1974
Never Born a Hero (Naylor), 1982
Never Despair (Alger, appendix), 1885
Never Keep Him Waiting (play; Clapp), 1961
Never Kiss Frogs! (Leeson), 1988
Never Say Ugh to a Bug (verse; Farber), 1979
Nevertheless (play; S. Walker), 1916
New Baby Is Lost (Van Stockum), 1964
New Bird (play; Trease), 1938
New Boy in Dublin (Bulla), 1969
New Calendar (play; Mitchison), 1937
New Canadian Kid (play; Foon), 1981
New Cautionary Tales (verse; Belloc), 1930
New Centre-Forward (Talbot), 1929
New Clothes for the Emperor (play; Gray), 1957
New Departure for Girls (Sidney, appendix), 1886
New Fire (Seed), 1983
New Football Boots (play; Parker), 1951
New Found Land (Christopher), 1983
New Friend (Zolotow), 1968
New Friends for Susan (Uchida), 1951
New Girl (Moore), 1917
New Girl at Peny-y-Gant (Moore), 1922
New Girl at St. Chad's (Brazil), 1911
New Girl at the Priory (Talbot), 1923
New Girl in Four A (Chaundler), 1930
New Golden Mountain (M. Clark), 1973
New Guys Around the Block (Guy), 1983
New Home South (Parker), 1961
New House (Tate), 1967
New House at Hardale (Trease), 1953
New House Mistress (Brent-Dyer), 1928
New House-Captain (D. Bruce), 1928
New in the Neighbourhood (Parker), 1966
New Kid on the Block (verse; Prelutsky), 1984
New Lamps for Old (play; Gray), 1968
New Life, New Room (Jordan), 1975
New Mrs. Lascelles (Meade, appendix), 1901
New Moon (Meigs), 1924
New Neighbor (Heide), 1970
New Neighbors for Nora (Hurwitz), 1979
New Panjandrum (Farrow), 1901
New Patches for Old (Mattingley), 1977
New Pet (Flack), 1943
New Prefect (Moore), 1921
New School at Scawdale (Brazil), 1940

New Schoolmaster (Naylor), 1967
New Schools for Old (Allan), 1954
New Shoes (Streatfeild), 1960
New Sun (Yashima), 1943
New Tales of Robin Hood (Suddaby), 1950
New Tenants (MacPherson), 1968
New Town (Streatfeild), 1960
New Town series (play; Streatfeild), n.d.
New Treasure Seekers (Nesbit), 1904
New Wonderland (Baum), 1900
New World Literary Series (Nesbit), 1921
New Year's Bargain (Coolidge, appendix), 1872
New Year's Mystery (Nixon), 1979
New Year's Surprise (Naylor), 1967
New York Boy (Alger, appendix), 1890
New York for Nicola (Allan), 1963
News Extra! (play; R. Brown), 1973
Newt for Roddy (Berg), 1965
Next Door to Xanadu (Orgel), 1969
Next Time Stories (Bisset), 1959
Next-Door House (Molesworth, appendix), 1892
Next-Door Neighbors (Orgel), 1979
Next-Doors (Tate), 1964
Nibble Nibble (verse; M. W. Brown), 1959
Nic Revel (Fenn, appendix), 1898
Nicest Girl in the School (Brazil), 1909
Niche over the Door (M. Harris), 1948
Nicholas and the Fast-Moving Diesel (Ardizzone), 1947
Nicholas and the Woolpack (Harnett), 1953
Nicholas Carey (Welch), 1963
Nicholas Factor (Myers), 1983
Nicholas Knock and Other People (verse; D. Lee), 1974
Nickel-Plated Beauty (P. Beatty), 1964
Nick's October (Prince), 1986
Nicky Goes to the Doctor (Scarry), 1972
Nicky's Knitting Granny and the Cat (verse; Greaves), 1985
Nicky of Nine Schools (Moore), 1932
Nicky-Nob, Tales of (Chaundler), 1937
Nicola Mimosa (Ure), 1985
Nicola Silver (E. Turner), 1924
Nicolas, Where Have You Been? (Lionni), 1987
Nicolette and the Mill (Guillot, trans), 1960
Nigel Eats His Words (C. Pullein-Thompson), 1969
Night Adventures of Alexis (E. Graham), 1925
Night after Christmas (Stevenson), 1981
Night Again (verse; Kuskin), 1981
Night and a Day (Stretton, appendix), 1876
Night and Day (M. W. Brown), 1942
Night and the Cat (verse; Coatsworth), 1950
Night Before Christmas Eve (D. Rees), 1980
Night Boat (Pease), 1942
Night Cry (Naylor), 1984
Night Daddy (Gripe, trans), 1971
Night Fall (Aiken), 1969
Night Gift (McKillip), 1976
Night I Sold My Boots (Prince), 1979
Night in the Country (Rylant), 1986
Night Journeys (Avi), 1979
Night Kites (M. Kerr), 1986
Night Landings (Prince), 1983
Night Music (Sudbery), 1983
Night of Masks (A. Norton), 1964
Night of the Black Frost (Catherall), 1968
Night of the Comet (Garfield), 1979
Night of the Flood (B. Carter), 1959
Night of the Goat (Greaves), 1976

Night of the Leopard (R. Bond), 1979
Night on Gars Mountain (Farber), 1981
Night Out (Tate), 1973
Night Outside (Wrightson), 1979
Night Race to Kawau (Duder), 1982
Night Raid (Hardcastle), 1977
Night Raider (Edmonds), 1980
Night Spell (Newman), 1977
Night Spider Case (B. Baker), 1984
Night Story (verse; N. Willard), 1986
Night Swimmers (Byars), 1980
Night the Lights Went Out (D. Freeman), 1958
Night the Rain Came In (Wayne), 1963
Night the Scarecrow Walked (Carlson), 1979
Night the Water Came (King), 1973
Night the White Deer Died (Paulsen), 1978
Night We Slept Outside (Rockwell), 1983
Night When Mother Was Away (Zolotow), 1958
Night Wind (Allan), 1974
Night Without Stars (Howe), 1983
Nightbird (M. Edwards), 1955
Nightbirds on Nantucket (Aiken), 1966
Nightgown of the Sullen Moon (N. Willard), 1983
Nightingale (Berg), 1951
Nightmares (verse; Prelutsky), 1976
Nightpool (S. Murphy), 1985
Nightwatch Winter (Overton), 1973
Night-Watchmen (Cresswell), 1969
Nighty-Nightmare (Howe), 1987
Nikos and the Sea God (Gramatky), 1963
Nils (d'Aulaire), 1948
Nils series (Lagerlöf, trans), from 1907
Nimbin (Wagner), 1978
Nimble-Wit and Fingerkin (play; C. D. Mackay), 1909
Nine Bright Shiners (Lamplugh), 1955
Nine Cheers for Christmas (play; A. Fisher), 1945
Nine Days' Queen (play; Field), 1927
Nine Days to Christmas (Ets), 1959
Nine Days' Wonder (Grice), 1976
Nine Drummers Drumming (Ainsworth), 1958
Nine Little Goslings (Coolidge, appendix), 1875
Nine Lives (Alexander), 1963
Nine Lives (Fenton), 1951
Nine Lives of Island Mackenzie (Moray Williams), 1959
Nine Questions (Fenton), 1959
Ninepenny (Hope-Simpson), 1964
19 Is Too Young to Die (Beckman, trans), 1971
Ninety-Nine Dragons (Sleigh), 1974
Nini (Donkin), 1979
Ninji's Magic (MacIntyre), 1966
Ninny's Boat (King), 1980
Nipper & Co. (Wynne), 1919
Nite-Lite Story Book (R. Kraus), 1975
Nitty Gritty (Bonham), 1968
Nixie (play; Burnett), 1890
Nixie from Rotterdam (Dehn), 1937
Nix-Nought-Nothing (play; Mitchison), 1928
No Bath Tonight (Yolen), 1978
No Beat of Drum (H. Burton), 1966
No Boats on Bannermere (Trease), 1949
No Brighter Glory (Sperry), 1942
No Castanets at the Wells (L. Hill), 1953
No Defence (Hardcastle), 1986
No Easy Circle (Naylor), 1972
No Easy Way (Sommerfelt, trans), 1967
No Entry (M. Edwards), 1954

No Escape (Phipson), 1979
No Excitement (play; Parker), 1951
No Fighting, No Biting! (Minarik), 1958
No Friends (Stevenson), 1986
No Going Back (M. Edwards), 1960
No Guns, No Oranges (Pilling), 1986
No Hero for the Kaiser (Frank, trans), 1985
No House for a Mouse (Parker), 1968
No Kiss for Mother (Ungerer), 1973
No Man's Island (Strang), 1921
No Medals for Meg (Donkin), 1947
No Mistaking Corker (M. Edwards), 1947
No More Horses (Stranger), 1982
No More Magic (Avi), 1975
No More Monsters for Me! (Parish), 1981
No More Saturday Nights (N. Klein), 1988
No More School (Mayne), 1965
No More Work (Rockwell), 1976
No Name the Deer (Lippincott), 1956
No Need for Monty (Stevenson), 1987
No Night Without Stars (A. Norton), 1975
No, No, Rosina (P. Martin), 1964
No One Must Know (Sleigh), 1962
No Ordinary Girl (Marchant), 1907
No Ordinary Rabbit, The Adventures of (Uttley), 1937
No Peace for the Prefects (Breary), 1944
No Place for Baseball (Heide, as Allen), 1973
No Place for Ponies (Cumming), 1954
No Place Like (Kemp), 1983
No Place Like Home (Stretton, appendix), 1881
No Ponies (Treadgold), 1946
No Ponies for Miss Pobjoy (Moray Williams), 1975
No Promises in the Wind (I. Hunt), 1970
No Sleep for Angus (Weir), 1969
No Strangers Here (Kamm), 1968
No Such things...? (Bunting), 1976
No Such Things (verse; Peet), 1983
No Surrender! (Catherall), 1979
No Surrender! (Henty, appendix), 1899
No Talking (play; Wymark), 1970
No Through Road (R. Brown), 1974
No Time for Tankers (R. Armstrong), 1958
No Way of Knowing (verse; Livingston), 1980
No Way of Telling (E. Smith), 1972
No Word for Good-bye (Craig), 1969
No Work No Bread (Stretton, appendix), 1875
Noah (Tozer), 1940
Noah and Poll in Fairyland, the Adventures of (Talbot), 1931
Noah's Ark (Ainsworth), 1969
Noah's Brother (King-Smith), 1986
Noah's Castle (Townsend), 1975
Noble Doll (Coatsworth), 1961
Noble Hawks (Moray Williams), 1959
Nobody Has to Be a Kid Forever (Colman), 1976
Nobody Knows But Me (Bunting), 1978
Nobody Knows How Scared I Am (Sharmat), 1986
Nobody Likes Trina (Whitney), 1972
Nobody Loves Me (Walton, appendix), 1883
Nobody Plays with a Cabbage (De Jong), 1962
Nobody Stole the Pie (Levitin), 1980
Nobody Told Me What I Need to Know (Colman), 1984
Nobody's Cat (P. Martin, as Miles), 1969
Nobody's Family Is Going to Change (Fitzhugh), 1974
Nobody's Neighbours (Meade, appendix), 1888
Nobody's Perfect (J. Wilson), 1982
Noddy series (Blyton), from 1949

Noddy in Toyland (play; Blyton), 1954
Noddy Nursery Rhymes series (verse; Blyton), from 1956
Noel the Coward (R. Kraus), 1977
Noel's Christmas Tree (Le Feuvre), 1926
No-Good Pony (J. Pullein-Thompson), 1981
Noguls and the Horse (Reid), 1976
Noisy (S. Hughes), 1985
Nosy Book series (M. W. Brown), from 1939
Noisy Gander (P. Martin, as Miles), 1978
Noisy Nora (Lofting), 1929
Noisy Nora (verse; Wells), 1973
Noisy Village series (Lindgren, trans), from 1962
Noll series (Finley, appendix), from 1872
Nomi and the Lovely Animals (verse; Slobodkin), 1960
No-Name Man of the Mountain (W. Steele), 1964
None of the Above (Wells), 1974
Nonsense series (verse; Lear, appendix), from 1846
Nonsense Circle (Heward), 1927
"Nonsense" Said the Tortoise (M. Baker), 1949
Nonstop Nonsense (Mahy), 1977
No-One at Home (C. Pullein-Thompson), 1964
Noodle (Leaf), 1937
Noon Balloon, (M. W. Brown), 1952
Noonday Friends (Stolz), 1965
Nora series (Hurwitz), from 1976
Norah series (Swindells), from 1979
Norah to the Rescue (Marchant), 1919
Nordy Bank (S. Porter), 1964
No-Return Trail (Levitin), 1978
Norma and the Washing Machine (Rosen), 1988
Norman and Flop Meet the Toy Bandit (T. Ross), 1977
Norman Rockwell Storybook (Wahl), 1969
Norman the Doorman (D. Freeman), 1959
'normous Saturday Fairy Book (B. Todd), 1924
'normous Sunday Story Book (B. Todd), 1925
Norsemen in the West (Ballantyne, appendix), 1872
North Fork (Gates), 1945
North Sea Adventure (Dawlish), 1949
North Sea Spy (Trease), 1939
North to Adventure (Peyton), 1958
North to Freedom (Holm, trans), 1965
North Town (L. Graham), 1965
Nose for Trouble (Kjelgaard), 1949
Nose Knows, (Hildick), 1973
Nose-Cap Astray (Syme), 1962
No-Sitch (Stong), 1936
Not a Little Monkey (Zolotow), 1957
Not at Home (Parker), 1972
Not Cricket! (H. Avery), 1911
Not for Love (Colman), 1983
Not Impossible summer (Alderson), 1983
Not Now, Bernard (McKee), 1980
Not Quite Eighteen (Coolidge, appendix), 1894
Not Scarlet But Gold (Saville), 1962
Not the Usual Kind of Girl (Tate), 1974
Not Too Small after All (Clymer), 1955
Not Too Young (Storr), 1987
Not What You Expected (Aiken), 1974
Not Without Danger (Best), 1951
Notes for Another Life (Bridgers), 1981
Nothing (Bisset), 1969
Nothing at All (Gág), 1941
Nothing Ever Happens and How It Does (D. Fisher), 1940
Nothing Ever Happens on My Block (Raskin), 1966
Nothing Ever Happens on Sundays (Greaves), 1976
Nothing Said (Boston), 1971

Nothing to Be Afraid Of (Mark), 1980
Nothing to Declare (Clewes), 1976
Nothing to Do (Hoban), 1964
Nothing to Do (D. Ross), 1966
Nothing-Place (Spence), 1972
Not-Just-Anybody Family (Byars), 1986
Noughts and Crosses (play; Fyleman), 1924
Now and Then (Symons), 1977
Now for a Story (Blyton), 1948
Now Hear This (play; Clapp), 1963
Now I Know (Chambers), 1987
Now Is Not Too Late (Holland), 1980
Now It's Fall (verse; Lenski), 1948
Now One Foot, Now the Other (de Paola), 1981
Now That I Know (N. Klein), 1988
Now That You Are Eight (S. Taylor), 1963
Now That You Are Seven (Clymer), 1963
Now to the Stars (Johns), 1956
Now We Are Six (verse; Milne), 1927
Nowhere to Hide (M. Clark), 1969
Nowhere to Play (Emecheta), 1980
Nowhere to Stop (Kaye), 1972
Nqalu, The Mouse with No Whiskers (Poland), 1979
Nubber Bear (Lipkind), 1966
Nugget Finders (Alger, appendix), 1893
Nuki and the Sea Serpent (Park), 1969
Number 91 (Alger, appendix), 1887
Number Rhymes (verse; Fyleman), 1946
Number the Stars (Lowry), 1989
Number Twa! (Le Feuvre), 1907
Nungu series (Cole), from 1978
Nurse Charlotte (Meade, appendix), 1904
Nurse Heatherdale's Story (Molesworth, appendix), 1891
Nurse Matilda series (Brand), from 1964
Nurse Ross series (Meynell), from 1958
Nursery Collection (S. Hughes), 1985
Nursery Rhymes of London Town series (verse; Farjeon), from 1916
Nursery Stories (Fyleman), 1949
Nursery Tales (D. Ross), 1944
Nurse's Memories (Yonge, appendix), 1888
Nutcracker Sweet (play; D. wood), 1977
Nuts and May (Farjeon), 1926
Nutshell Library (verse; Sendak), 1962
Nuttie's Father (Yonge, appendix), 1885
Nutty Noodles (Hoff), 1979
Nuttybub and Nittersing (Gibbs), 1923

OPQRS, etc (play; Miller), n.d.
O for a Mouseless House! (Moray Williams), 1964
O, Said the Squirrel (M. W. Brown), 1950
O Sliver of Liver (verse; Livingston), 1979
O the Red Rose Tree (P. Beatty), 1972
Oaf (Cunningham), 1986
Oak and the Ash (Grice), 1968
Oats and Wild Apples (Asch), 1988
Obadiah series (Turkle), from 1965
Obstinate Land (Keith), 1977
Obstreperous (Greenwood), 1970
Ocean Cat's Paw (Fenn, appendix), 1904
Ocean-Born Mary (Lenski), 1939
Octagon Magic (A. Norton), 1967
Octavia Told Me a Secret (Sharmat), 1979
October Child (Spence), 1976
Octopus (R. Brown), 1981
Octopus and the Pirates (Soldati, trans), 1974

On a Summer Day (verse; Lenski), 1953
On Beyond Zebra (verse; Seuss), 1955
On a Christmas Eve (M. W. Brown), 1961
On Christmas Eve (play; C. D. Mackay), 1909
On Fire (Sebestyen), 1985
On Guard for England (Westerman), 1942
On Lennox Moor (Kyle), 1954
On London River (Strang), 1929
On Loyalist Trails (Hayes), 1971
On My Beach There Are Many Pebbles (Lionni), 1961
On Our Vacation (Rockwell), 1989
On Primrose Hill (Chaney), 1962
On Schedule Time (Otis, appendix), 1896
On Stage, Flory (Allan), 1961
On the Ball (Hardcastle), 1976
On the Banks of Plum Creek (Wilder), 1937
On the Day Peter Stuyvesant Sailed into Town (verse; Arnold
    Lobel), 1971
On the Edge (Cross), 1984
On the Edge of a Moor (Le Feuvre), 1897
On the Feast of Stephen (Judah), 1965
On the Flip Side (Fisk), 1983
On the Green Meadows (Burgess), 1944
On the Irrawaddy (Henty, appendix), 1896
On the Kentucky Frontier (Otis, appendix), 1900
On the Lion's Side (Pilling), 1988
On the Run (Bawden), 1964
On the Run (Hardcastle), 1974
On the Sand Dune (Orgel), 1968
On the Spanish Main (Henty, appendix), 1899
On the Spanish Main (Strang), 1909
On the Staked Plain (Kelly), 1940
On the Stepping Stones (Mayne), 1963
On the Track (Marchant), 1924
On the Trial of Long Tom (Cutt), 1970
On the Trail of the Arabs (Strang), 1907
On the Wasteland (Arthur), 1975
On the Way Home (J. Murphy), 1982
On the Wings of the Wind (Westerman), 1928
Once and Forever Christmas (verse; Corlett), 1975
Once and Future King (T. White), 1958
Once at KwaFubesi (Poland), 1981
Once I Was a Plum Tree (Hurwitz), 1980
Once in the Year (Yates), 1947
Once on a Time (Milne), 1917
Once, Said Darlene (Sleator), 1979
Once There Was a King Who Promised He Would Never Chop
    Anyone's Head Off (Rosen), 1976
Once There Was a Swagman (Brinsmead), 1979
Once upon a Clothesline (play; A. Harris), 1944
Once upon a Saturday (Fenton), 1958
Once upon a Story (play; Mahy), n.d.
Once upon a Time (Baum), 1916
Once upon a Time Animal Stories (Bailey), 1918
Once upon a Time in a Pigpen (M. W. Brown), 1980
Once upon a Time Stories (Beresford), 1987
Once upon Little Big Horn (Lampman), 1971
Once We Had a Horse (Rounds), 1971
Once We Went on a Picnic (verse; A. Fisher), 1975
Once-a-Year Day (Bunting), 1974
One (Salkey), 1985
One and Only Two Heads (Ahlberg), 1979
One at a Time (verse; McCord), 1977
One Bad Thing about Father (Monjo), 1970
One Big Wish (J. Williams), 1980
One by Sea (S. Corbett), 1965

One Day Event (J. Pullein-Thompson), 1954
One Day in Paradise (Heine, trans), 1986
One Day with...series (Sperry), from 1933
One Fat Summer (Lipsyte), 1977
One Fish, Two Fish, Red Fish, Blue Fish (verse; Seuss), 1960
One Foot in Fairyland (Farjeon), 1938
One Green Bottle (Parker), 1973
One Green Leaf (Ure), 1987
One Hundred and One Dalmatians (play; Peet), 1961
121 Pudding Street (Fritz), 1955
One Hundredth Thing About Caroline (Lowry), 1983
1 Hunter (Hutchins), 1982
One in the Middle Is the Green Kangaroo (Blume), 1969
One Is Good But Two Are Better (verse; Slobodkin), 1956
One Is One (Picard), 1965
One Kick (Hardcastle), 1986
One Little Baby (verse; Robinson, as Thomas), 1950
One Little Tree (Almedingen), 1963
One Man's Horse (Henry), 1977
One Moonlit Night (Armitage), 1983
One More Flight (Bunting), 1976
One More River (Banks), 1973
One Morning in Maine (McCloskey), 1952
One of Clive's Heroes (Strang), 1906
One of Rupert's Horse (Strang), 1907
One of the Family (Beresford), 1985
One of the Many (Westerman), 1945
One of the Third Grade Thonkers (Naylor), 1988
One of the 28th (Henty, appendix), 1889
One Pig with Horns (L. Brunhoff, trans), 1979
One Potato, Two Potato series (play; Waddell), from 1975
One Proud Summer (Claire Mackay), 1981
One Special Dog (P. Martin), 1968
One Step, Two...(Zolotow), 1955
One Terrific Thanksgiving (Sharmat), 1985
One Thousand Christmas Beards, See Smith Toy Shop, Eat at Joe's
    (Duvoisin), 1955
One to Grow On (Little), 1969
One True Santa (verse; Ahlberg), 1983
1, 2, 3, to the Zoo (Carle), 1968
One, Two, Where's My Shoe? (verse; Ungerer), 1964
One Very Best Valentine's Day (Blos), 1989
One Was Johnny (verse; Sendak), 1962
One Week One Trouble (Okoro), 1973
One White Mouse (Parker), 1966
One Winter Night in August (verse; X. Kennedy), 1975
One-Eyed Cat (Fox), 1984
One-Eyed Jake (Hutchins), 1979
One-Legged Ghost (Lifton), 1968
One-Ring Circus (play; A. Fisher), 1965
One-Way Street, Tale of a (Aiken), 1978
One-Winged Dragon (C. Clark), 1955
Onion John (Krumgold), 1959
Onion Journey (Cunningham), 1967
Oniroku, The Tale of (play; J. Kraus), 1978
Onito's Hat (Iwasaki, trans), 1978
Only a Dog (Stretton, appendix), 1888
Only a Girl! (Moore), 1913
Only a Pony (D. Pullein-Thompson), 1980
Only an Irish Boy (Alger, appendix), 1894
Only Child (E. O. White), 1905
Only Day-Girl (Moore), 1923
Only Earth and Sky Last Forever (Benchley), 1972
Only Toys! (Anstey, appendix), 1903
Only Treasure (Thwaite), 1970
Oodoolay (R. Klein), 1983

Oomi (Schlein), 1955
Ooomerahgi Oh! (play; Truss), 1974
Ootah's Lucky Day (Parish), 1970
Opal-Eyed Fan (A. Norton), 1977
Open Gate (C. Pullein-Thompson), 1962
Open Gate (Seredy), 1943
Open Grave (Poole), 1979
Open House for Butterflies (Krauss), 1960
Open the Door and See All the People (Bulla), 1972
Operation Aladdin (Finkel), 1976
Operation Arctic (Hamre, trans), 1973
Operation Seabird (M. Edwards), 1957
Operation Sippacik (Godden), 1969
Operation Smuggle (Clewes), 1964
Operation Time Search (A. Norton), 1967
Operation V.2 (Catherall, as Channel), 1961
Operations Successfully Executed (Westerman), 1945
Operats of Rodent Garden (D. Wood), 1984
Opportunities (Warner, appendix), 1871
Opposite Neighbours (Molesworth, appendix), 1895
Orange and Green (Henty, appendix), 1888
Orchard Cat (Kellogg), 1972
Orchard of the Crescent Moon (Nimmo), 1989
Orchestra (Bruna, trans), 1984
Ordeal in Otherwhere (A. Norton), 1964
Orderly Officer (H. Avery), 1894
Ordinary Bath (D. Lee), 1970
Ordinary Jack (Cresswell), 1977
Oregon at Last! (Loeff, trans), 1961
Organ Grinder (play; Moray Williams), 1933
Organdy Cupcakes (Stolz), 1951
Oriel Window (Molesworth, appendix), 1896
Orinoco Runs Away (Beresford), 1975
Orkney the Peacemaker (Abbott, appendix), 1857
Orla of Burren (Lynch), 1954
Orlando the Brave Vulture (Ungerer), 1966
Orlando the Marmalade Cat series (plays; Corlett), from 1975
Orlando, The Marmalade Cat series (K. Hale), from 1938
Orphan Game (Cohen), 1988
Orphan Otter (Catherall), 1962
Orphans of the Wild (R. Montgomery), 1939
Orphans of the Wind (Haugaard), 1966
Orphant Annie Story Book (Gruelle), 1921
Orpheline series (Carlson), from 1957
Orpheus (play; T. Hughes), 1971
Orris, Tales of (Ingelow, appendix), 1860
Orvis (Hoover), 1987
Osbert (Streatfeild), 1950
Oscar agus an Cóiste Sé nEasóg (Dillon), 1952
Oscar Buys the Biscuits (play; T. Ross), 1985
Oscar Got the Blame (T. Ross), 1987
Oscar Lobster's Fair Exchange (Selden), 1966
Oscar Otter (Benchley), 1966
Ossian House (Stewart), 1974
O'Sullivan Twins (Blyton), 1942
Oswald Bastable and Others (Nesbit), 1905
Other Cinderella (play; Gray), 1958
Other, Darker Ned (Fine), 1979
Other Echoes (Geras), 1982
Other Face (B. C. Freeman), 1975
Other People (McNeill), 1970
Other People's Houses (Bianco), 1930
Other Planet (Fuller), 1979
Other Side (J. Wilson), 1984
Other Side of Dark (Nixon), 1986
Other Side of the Fence (Tunis), 1953

Other Side of the Fence (Ure), 1986
Other Side of the Moon (Trevor), 1956
Other Side of the Park (Andrew), 1984
Other Side of the Street (Pamela Brown), 1965
Other Side of the Tunnel (Kendall), 1956
Other Way Round (J. Kerr), 1975
Others (Prince), 1984
Otherwise Known as Sheila the Great (Blume), 1972
Otis Spofford (Cleary), 1953
Otmoor for Ever! (H. Burton), 1968
Otter in the Cove (P. Martin, as Miles), 1974
Otter Nonsense (verse; Juster), 1982
Otter Three Two Calling! (Hamre, trans), 1959
Otterbury Incident (Day Lewis), 1948
Otto series (du Bois), from 1936
Otto of the Silver Hand (Pyle, appendix), 1888
Our Baby's Favorite (L. Richards), 1881
Our Cup Is Broken (Means), 1969
Our Eddie (Ish-Kishor), 1969
Our Father (verse; Robinson, as Thomas), 1940
Our Fred (Finley, appendix), 1874
Our Friendly Friends (verse; Slobodkin), 1951
Our Friends and All about them (verse; Nesbit), 1893
Our Garage Sale (Rockwell), 1984
Our Great Undertaking (Everett-Green, appendix), 1906
Our Kid (Pilling), 1989
Our Little Aztec Cousin of Long Ago (de Treviño), 1934
Our Little Ethiopian Cousin (de Treviño), 1935
Our Little Feudal Cousin of Long Ago (L. Richards), 1922
Our Nation's Songs, Plays about (A. Fisher), 1962
Our New Mistress (Yonge, appendix), 1888
Our New Story Book (Nesbit), 1913
Our Sam (Cunliffe), 1980
Our Sleepysaurus (Waddell), 1988
Our Soldier Boy (Fenn, appendix), 1898
Our Town (Sidney, appendix), 1889
Our Uncle (Otis, appendix), 1901
Our Walk (Berg), 1981
Our Wild Weekend (Waddell), 1986
Our Winnie (Everett-Green, appendix), 1887
Out and About (Bruna, trans), 1980
Out and About (verse; S. Hughes), 1988
Out for Business (Alger, appendix), 1900
Out from This Place (Hansen), 1988
Out in the Dark and Daylight (verse; A. Fisher), 1980
Out Loud (verse; Merriam), 1973
Out of Hand (E. Smith), 1963
Out of Sight, Out of Mind (Aaron), 1985
Out of Step (Kamm), 1962
Out of the Ark Books (Beaman), 1927
Out of the Fashion (Meade, appendix), 1892
Out of the Mines (Grice), 1961
Out of the Oven (Mark), 1986
Out of the Running (H. Avery), 1904
Out of the Shadows (Moray Williams), 1971
Out of the Shallows (R. Armstrong), 1961
Out of the Sun (R. Montgomery), 1943
Out of the Sun (Tate), 1969
Out of This World and Back Again (Nye), 1977
Out of the World and Back Again (Nye), 1978
Out on the Pampas (Henty, appendix), 1871
Out to Sea (Rockwell), 1980
Out with Garibaldi (Henty, appendix), 1900
Outback Adventure (Patchett), 1957
Outcast (Sutcliff), 1955
Outcast Robin (Meade, appendix), 1878

Parcel of Patterns (Paton Walsh), 1983
Parcel of Trees (Mayne), 1963
Pardon Me, You're Stepping on My Eyeball! (Zindel), 1976
Paris, Pee Wee, and Big Dog (Guy), 1984
Park Book (Zolotow), 1944
Parker Pig, Esquire (de Paola), 1969
Parker-Hamilton (R. Klein), 1987
Parkhurst Sketches (Reed, appendix), 1889
Parkin (L. Cooper), 1977
Parkin's Storm (Oldfield), 1982
Park's Quest (Paterson), 1988
Parren series (Hildick), 1968
Parrot and the Thief (R. Kennedy), 1974
Parsley (Bemelmans), 1955
Parsley, The Adventure of (play; M. Bond), n.d.
Parsley series (M. Bond), from 1969
Parsley Sage, Rosemary and Time (Curry), 1975
Part of the Dream (Bunting), 1978
Patrick Steamboat (F. Knight), 1958
Partners (B. Baker), 1978
Partners (Wier), 1972
Party Frock (Streatfeild), 1946
Party Pants (Mayne), 1977
Party Shoes (Streatfeild), 1947
Passage to Dusky (Wardell), 1967
Passage to Dusky (play; Wardell), 1959
Passing of Hiawatha (play C. D. Mackay), 1915
Passion of Kathleen Duveen (Meade, appendix), 1913
Passport of Mallam Ilia (Ekwensi), 1960
Passport to Romance (Cavanna), 1955
Past Eight O'Clock (Aiken), 1986
Pastures of the Blue Crane (Brinsmead), 1964
Pat and the Spider (Bannerman), 1904
Pat of Silver Bush series (L. Montgomery), from 1933
Pat Stobard in the "Golden Dawn" (Westerman), 1929
Pat the Lighthouse Boy (Everett-Green, appendix), 1894
Patch (Clymer, as Kinsey), 1946
Patch (H. Griffiths), 1970
Patch and a Pawn (Oxenham), 1940
Patch Comes Home (Thiele), 1982
Patch of Green (Weir), 1965
Patch of Piebald (Wynne), 1947
Patchwork Cat (Mayne), 1981
Patchwork Grandmother (Donkin), 1975
Patchwork Mystery (Donkin), 1978
Patchwork Plays (Field), 1930
Patchwork Quilt (play; Field), 1924
Patchwork Quilt (Sleigh), 1956
Path of Gold (Reeves), 1972
Path of the Dragons (Morris), 1980
Path of the Pale Horse (P. Fleischman), 1983
Path-Through-the-Woods (B. Wilson), 1958
Patience series (L. Hill), from 1951
Patience and Her Problems (Oxenham), 1927
Patience Joan (Oxenham), 1922
Patience Wins (Fenn, appendix), 1885
Patient Pat Joins the Circus (Wynne), 1931
Patooie (R. N. Peck), 1977
Patricia (Talbot), 1925
Patricia Comes Home (Strong), 1929
Patricia Pendragon (Everett-Green, as Dare, appendix), 1911
Patricia-Pat (Peacocke), 1917
Patrick series (Daly), from 1959
Patrick Kentigern Keenan (M. Hunter), 1963
Patrick's Pony (J. Pullein-Thompson), 1957
Patriotic Christmas Pageant (play; C. D. Mackay), 1918

Patriotic Plays and Pageants (C. D. Mackay), 1912
Patriotic Plays and Programs (A. Fisher), 1956
Patriotic Schoolgirl (Brazil), 1918
Patriots of Palestine (Yonge, appendix), 1898
Pat's Third Term (Chaundler), 1919
Patsy, The Story of (Wiggin), 1883
Patsy and the Pup (Van Stockum), 1950
Patsy from the Wilds (Wynne), 1931
Pattern of Roses (Peyton), 1972
Patterns on the Wall (Yates), 1943
Patterson's Track (Spence), 1958
Patty series (Treadgold), from 1967
Patty Makes a Visit (E. O. White), 1939
Patty's Pet (Hoff), 1955
Paul and Arthur series (Rockwell), from 1964
Paul and Etta (Parker), 1972
Paul and Pam (Talbot), 1933
Paul Harvard's Campaign (Everett-Green, appendix), 1901
Paul Prescott the Runaway (Alger, appendix), 1865
Paul Prescott's Charge (Alger, appendix), 1865
Paul Rodents (Stretton, appendix), 1894
Paul, The Hero of the Fire (Ardizzone), 1948
Paul the Peddler (Alger, appendix), 1871
Pauline (Storey), 1965
Paulo's Strange Adventure (Kimenye), 1971
Paul's Kite (A. Morgan), 1981
Paul's Story (Berg), 1970
Pavilion (Vipont), 1969
Pavo and the Princess (Ness), 1964
Paws series (Bisset), 1976
Pay Dirt (Rounds), 1938
Peabody (Wells), 1983
Peace and Quiet Diner (Maguire), 1989
Peace at Last (J. Murphy), 1980
Peace Egg (Ewing, appendix), 1887
Peace Seekers (Finkel), 1970
Peaceable Kingdom (verse; Coatsworth), 1958
Peachblossom (Lattimore), 1943
Peacock Garden (Desai), 1974
Peacock House (G. Avery), 1963
Peacock Pie (verse; de la Mare), 1913
Peanuts for Billy Ben (Lenski), 1952
Pearl series (Asch), from 1984
Pearl (Heine, trans), 1985
Pearl of the Soul of the World (Pierce), 1989
Pearl's Place (B. Graham), 1983
Peasant Pig and the Terrible Dragon (Scarry) 1980
Pebble Nest (Hewett), 1965
Peck's Bad Boy (play; A. Harris), 1973
Peculiar Magic (A. and E. Johnson), 1965
Pedaling Man (verse; Hoban), 1968
Peddler of La Grave (Finley, appendix), 1875
Peddler's Cart (Coatsworth), 1957
Peddler's Clock (M. Hunt), 1943
Peddler's Dream (play; Reeves), 1963
Pedlar's Dream (play; Reeves), 1951
Pedro (Flack), 1940
Pedro and the Bananas (Hoff), 1972
Peedie Peebles' Summer or Winter Book (Hedderwick), 1989
Peek-a-Boo! (verse; Ahlberg), 1981
Peel series (L. Hill), from 1950
Peep Behind the Scenes (Walton, appendix), 1877
Peepo! (verse; Ahlberg), 1981
Peep-Show Man (Colum), 1924
Pegeen (Van Stockum), 1941
Peggy (L. Richards), 1899

Peggy series (H. Sewell), from 1937
Peggy and the Brotherhood (Oxenham), 1936
Peggy from Kerry (Meade, appendix), 1912
Peggy in Her Blue Frock (E. O. White), 1921
Peggy Makes Good! (Oxenham), 1927
Peggy's First Term (Wynne), 1922
Peggy's Last Term (Talbot), 1920
Peggy's on the Phone (play; Clapp), 1956
Peg-Leg series (Dawlish), from 1939
Pekan (R. Montgomery), 1970
Pekinese Princess (Clarke), 1948
Pelican Park (Cockett), 1969
Pemaquid, The Story of (Otis, appendix), 1902
Pen, Paper, and Poem (verse; McCord), 1973
Pen, Penny, Tuppence (Sleigh), 1968
Pendron under the Water (Allan), 1961
Penelope series (Wiggin), from 1893
Penengro (Van Stockum), 1972
Penguin Goes Home (Parker), 1951
Penguin Who Couldn't Paddle (Berg), 1967
Penguins of All People! (D. Freeman), 1971
Penguin's Pal (R. Kraus), 1964
Pennies for the Dog (Thwaite), 1985
Pennington series (Peyton), from 1970
Penny (de Regniers), 1966
Penny series (Haywood), from 1944
Penny series (Meynell, as Tring), from 1949
Penny a Day (de la Mare), 1960
Penny and Pegasus (Cumming), 1969
Penny and the White Horse (Bianco), 1942
Penny Black (Kaye), 1976
Penny Candy (Fenton), 1970
Penny for Luck (Means), 1935
Penny for the Guy (Chaney), 1970
Penny Pollard series (R. Klein), from 1983
Penny Pony (B. Willard), 1961
Penny Stamp, The Adventures of a (Strang), 1926
Penny Tunes and Princesses (Levoy), 1972
Penny Whistles (verse; Stevenson, appendix), 1883
Pennyfeather Family (Stucley), 1947
Pennyfields (D. Pullein-Thompson), 1949
Pennymakers (Harnett), 1937
Penny's Way (M. Harris), 1963
Penrod series (Tarkington), from 1914
Pentecost series (W. Corbett), from 1982
People from the Sea (de Graft-Hanson), 1988
People in the Garden (L. Wood), 1954
People Like Us (Cohen), 1987
People Might Hear You (R. Klein), 1983
People of the Ax (J. Williams), 1974
People Therein (M. Lee), 1980
Pepe Moreno series (Allen), from 1955
Pepe Moreno (play; Allen), 1958
Pepita's Adventure in Friendship (play; Means), 1929
Pepper and Salt (Pyle, appendix), 1886
Peppercorn Patrol (Talbot), 1929
Peppermint Family (M. W. Brown), 1950
Peppermint Pig (Bawden), 1975
Peppernuts (Petersham), 1958
Peppino series (D. Martin), from 1980
Percevals (Everett-Green, appendix), 1890
Percy and the Five Houses (Minarik), 1989
Percy, The Small Engine (Awdry), 1956
Percy Vere (Everett-Green, appendix), 1906
Perdita (Holland), 1983
Perdita (Moore), 1926

Perfect Child, Tales for the (Heide), 1985
Perfect Customer (play; Lillington), 1967
Perfect Pancake (verse; Kahl), 1960
Perfect Present (Foreman), 1967
Perfect Zoo (Farjeon), 1929
Peril Finders (Fenn, appendix), 1902
Peril in Lakeland (Finlay), 1953
Peril in Pink (Cavanna, as Allen), 1955
Peril in the Pennines (Finlay), 1953
Peril on the Iron Road (B. Carter), 1953
Perilous Descent into a Strange Lost World (B. Carter), 1952
Perilous Gold (Wibberley), 1978
Perilous Pilgrimage (Treece), 1959
Perilous Road (W. Steele), 1958
Perilous Seat (Snedeker), 1923
Perilous Wings (Hamre, trans), 1961
Periwinkle (Duvoisin), 1976
Perkin the Pedlar (Farjeon), 1932
Permanent Connections (Bridgers), 1987
Pernel Wins (Oxenham), 1942
Peronel's Paint (play; Blyton), 1926
Peronik (play; R. Harris), 1976
Perri (Salten, trans), 1938
Perry the Imp (Lipkind, as Will), 1956
Persian Carpet Story (B. Wilson), 1981
Persian Gold (Paton Walsh), 1978
Persimmon Jim (Lippincott), 1924
Person from Britain Whose Head Was the Shape of a Mitten (verse; Bodecker), 1980
Persuading Stick (Townsend), 1986
Perversity of Pipers (Parker), 1964
Pet Club (B. Willard), 1967
Pet of the Met (D. Freeman), 1953
Pet Show! (Keats), 1972
Pete (A. Morgan), 1972
Pete and Roland (B. Graham), 1981
Peter series (Kingman), from 1953
Peter (Wynne), 1936
Peter and Butch (Phipson), 1969
Peter and Co. (M. Bruce), 1940
Peter and Judy in Bunnyland, The Adventures of (Uttley), 1935
Peter and the Clock (play; Barne), 1919
Peter and the Jumbie (Clewes), 1969
Peter and the Picture Thief (Meynell), 1969
Peter and the Troll Baby (Wahl), 1984
Peter and the Wanderlust (Moray Williams), 1939
Peter and the Zauberleaf (Wagner), 1973
Peter and Wendy (Barrie), 1911
Peter Climbs a Tree (Beresford), 1966
Peter Coffin (play; Fyleman), 1928
Peter Cottontail series (Burgess), from 1914
Peter Duck (Ransome), 1932
Peter Graves (du Bois), 1950
Peter Killip's King (Stretton, appendix), 1866
Peter Lundy and the Medicine Hat Stallion (Henry), 1977
Peter Nick-Nock and the Cuckoo Clock (D. Edwards), 1971
Peter of New Amsterdam (Otis, appendix), 1910
Peter of the Mesa (Means), 1944
Peter on the Road (Moray Williams), 1963
Peter, Pam and Jim, the Investigators (Fidler), 1954
Peter Pan (play; Barrie), 1904
Peter Pan (play; Peet), 1953
Peter Pan and Wendy (Barrie), 1921
Peter Pan Bag (Kingman), 1970
Peter Pan in Kensington Gardens (Barrie), 1906
Peter Piper's Pickled Peppers (M. Hunt), 1942

CHILDREN'S WRITERS

Peter Rabbit, The Tale of (Potter), 1900
Peter Rabbit series (Burgess), from 1929
Peter Rabbit and the Big Black Crows (Wynne), 1931
Peter the Gardener (Seed), 1966
Peter the Pilgrim (Meade, appendix), 1903
Peter the Wanderer (Ardizzone), 1963
Peter Treegate's War (Wibberley), 1960
Peterkin (Molesworth, appendix), 1902
Peterkin Papers (L. Hale, appendix), 1880
Peter's Brownstone House (Colman), 1963
Peter's Busy Day (Meynell, as Tring), 1959
Peter's Chair (Keats), 1967
Peter's Moccasins (Truss), 1987
Peter's Private Army (MacGibbon), 1960
Peter's Room (Forest), 1961
Pete's Elephant (Strang), 1926
Pete's Pup (Hoff), 1975
Petey (Cavanna), 1973
Petite Suzanne (de Angeli), 1937
Petronella (Meade, appendix), 1904
Petronella (J. Williams), 1973
Petros' War (Zei, trans), 1972
Petrus (Chipperfield), 1960
Pets Limited (Harnett), 1950
Pettabomination (Moray Williams), 1933
Pettabomination (play; Moray Williams), 1951
Petticoat Smuggler (Cresswell), 1985
Pettifur (J. Williams), 1977
Petunia series (Duvoisin), from 1950
Pewit's Nest (Finley, appendix), 1876
Pezzettino (Lionni), 1975
Pezzo the Peddler series (Slobadkina), from 1967
Phantasmagoria (verse; Carroll, appendix), 1869
Phantom (Anderson), 1969
Phantom Carwash (Powling), 1986
Phantom Cyclist (Ainsworth), 1971
Phantom Deer (Lippincott), 1954
Phantom Fisherboy (Ainsworth), 1974
Phantom Horse (Bibby), 1979
Phantom Horse series (C. Pullein-Thompson), from 1955
Phantom Ice Cream Man (verse; X. Kennedy), 1979
Phantom of the Blockade (Meader), 1962
Phantom of Walkaway Hill (Fenton), 1961
Phantom Patrol (Catherall, as Channel), 1940
Phantom Rider (Robertson), 1955
Phantom Roundabout (Ainsworth), 1977
Phantom Submarine (Westerman), 1947
Phantom Tollbrooth (Juster), 1961
Phebe Fairchild (Lenski), 1936
Phelim and the Creatures (Reid), 1952
Phewtus the Squirrel (Drummond), 1939
Phil (Alger, appendix), 1872
Phil the Ventriloquist (R. Kraus), 1989
Philbert the Fearful (J. Williams), 1966
Philemon and Baucis (play; Barne), 1926
Philharmonic Gets Dressed (Kuskin), 1982
Philip Hall series (B. Greene), from 1974
Philip of Texas (Otis, appendix), 1913
Philippa (Molesworth, appendix), 1896
Philippa's Family (Chaundler), 1927
Philippe's Hill (Kingman), 1950
Philomena (Seredy), 1955
Philosopher Jack (Ballantyne, appendix), 1880
Phil's Cousins (Wynne), 1911
Phoebe and the Prince (Orgel), 1969
Phoebe Danger, Detective (P. Fleischman), 1983

Phoebe Daring (Baum), 1912
Phoebe of the Fourth (Talbot), 1932
Phoebe's First Campaign (Colman), 1963
Phoebe's Revolt (verse; Babbitt), 1968
Phoenix and the Carpet (Nesbit), 1904
Phyllis, The Adventures of (Marchant), 1910
Phyllis in France (Wynne), 1919
Piccaninnies (verse; Durack), 1940
Piccaninnies (Peacocke), 1920
Piccino (Burnett), 1894
Picco (Slobodkin), 1961
Piccolo (Bettina), 1954
Piccolo series (Hewett), from 1960
Piccolo (verse; L. Richards), 1906
Pickety Fence (recording; McCord), n.d.
Pickle and His Page Boy (Yonge, appendix), 1882
Pickle Creature (Pinkwater), 1979
Pickle Things (Marc Brown), 1980
Pickpocket Run (A. and E. Johnson), 1961
Picnic (Daugherty), 1958
Picnic (Mayne, as Molin), 1966
Picnic, (Unnerstad, trans), 1964
Picnic Dog (Mattingley), 1970
Picnic Party (Blyton), 1951
Picnic with the Aunts (Moray Williams), 1972
Picts and the Martyrs (Ransome), 1943
Picts Drop In (play; Lillington), 1968
Picture Book Theater (play; de Regniers), 1982
Picture Charlie (Tate), 1964
Pictures for Sale (Meynell, as Tring), 1958
Pictures of Adam (Levoy), 1986
Pie and the Patty-Pan (Potter), 1905
Pie in the Sky (Rodari, trans), 1971
Piece of Parkin (Thwaite), 1980
Pieces of Home (P. Martin, as Miles), 1967
Pied Piper of Hamelin (play; Miller), 1948
Piemakers (Cresswell), 1967
Pierino and the Bell (Cassedy), 1966
Pierre (verse; Sendak), 1962
Pierre Pidgeon (Kingman), 1943
Pietro and the Mule (Cresswell), 1965
Pig and the Junkie (play; Patten), 1975
Pig at the Market (Cockett), 1979
Pig Brother (L. Richards), 1908
Pig Brother (play; L. Richards), 1915
Pig in the Middle (Mayne), 1968
Pig Organ (play; T. Hughes), 1980
Pig War (B. Baker), 1969
Pig Who Could Conjure the Wind (S. Murphy), 1978
Pigeon Cubes (verse; Bodecker), 1982
Pigeon Flight (Stolz), 1962
Pigeon of Paris (Carlson), 1972
Pigeon Pie (Yonge, appendix), 1860
Pigeon Post (Ransome), 1936
Pigeongram Puzzle (Lamplugh), 1955
Pigeons and Princesses (Reeves), 1956
Piggins series (Yolen), from 1987
Piggle (Bonsall), 1973
Piggy in the Middle (Needle), 1982
Piggybook (Browne), 1986
Pigling Bland, The Tale of (Potter), 1913
Pigman series (Zindel), from 1968
Pigs (Munsch), 1989
Pigs Might Fly (King-Smith), 1982
Pigs' Wedding (Heine, trans), 1978
Pigsleg (Sudbery), 1971

Pika and the Roses (Costsworth), 1959
Pike Dream (Dehn), 1958
Pile of Junk (Schlein), 1962
Pilgrim Goose (Robertson), 1956
Pilgrim Street (Stretton, appendix), 1867
Pilgrimage (Lingard), 1976
Pilgrimage of Ben Beriah (Yonge, appendix), 1897
Pillar-Box Thieves (Reeves), 1965
Pillars of the House (Yonge, appendix), 1873
Pillycock's Shop (Mahy), 1969
Pim and the Fisherboy (Kuratomi, trans), 1975
Pinballs (Byars), 1977
Pinch of Salt (McNeill), 1956
Pinchpenny Mouse (R. Kraus), 1974
Pine Street series (Allan), from 1978
Pineapple Farm (Weir), 1960
Ping, The Story about (Flack), 1933
Pink Motel (Brink), 1959
Pink Pig (Hough), 1975
Pinkerton series (Kellogg), from 1979
Pinkish Purplish Bluish Egg (verse; Peet), 1963
Pinky and the Petunia (Slobodkina), 1959
Pinky Pye (Estes), 1958
Pinocchio series (play; A. Harris), from 1940
Pinocchio (play; Miller), 1950
Pinocchio (play; Peet), 1940
Pinocchio (play; Rodgers), 1973
Pinquo (Thiele), 1983
Pinto Deer (Robertson), 1956
Pioneer Art in America (Bailey), 1944
Pioneer Pat (Talbot), 1935
Pioneers (Ballantyne, appendix), 1872
Pioneers (play; C. D. Mackay), 1915
Pip series (Blyton), 1948
Pip Squeak series (R. Kraus), from 1971
Pipkin Sees the World (Fry), 1951
Pipkin the Woodmouse (Fry), 1953
Pipkin series (Wahl), from 1982
Pip-Larssons Go Sailing (Unnerstad, trans), 1966
Pippa Passes (S. Corbett), 1966
Pippi Longstocking series (Lindgren, trans), from 1950
Pippy and the Gnome (Blyton), 1951
Pirate City (Ballantyne, appendix), 1874
Pirate Island Adventure (Parish), 1975
Pirate of Jasper Peak (Meigs, as Aldon), 1918
Pirate Rock (D. Walker), 1969
Pirate Royal (J. and P. Beatty), 1969
Pirate Sealer (Catherall), 1953
Pirate Ship (Ainsworth), 1980
Pirate Submarine (Westerman), 1923
Pirate Twins (Nicholson), 1929
Pirate Uncle (Mahy), 1977
Pirates in Panama (Monjo), 1970
Pirates in the Deep Green Sea (Linklater), 1949
Pirate's Island (Townsend), 1968
Pirates' Mixed-Up Voyage (Mahy), 1983
Pirate's Promise (Bulla), 1958
Pishtosh, Bullwash, and Wimple (Flora), 1972
Pistachio Prescription (Danziger), 1978
Pistol in Greenyards (M. Hunter), 1965
Pistols for Two (Beaman), 1942
Pit (Pilling, as Cheetham), 1987
Pitch the Pony (Thiele), 1984
Pitcher to Centre Field (E. Bunting, as A.E. Bunting), 1974
Pitiful Place (Needle), 1984
Pixie Pickles (Farrow), 1904

Pixie Tales (Blyton), 1966
Pixieland Story Book (Blyton), 1966
Pixie's Mysterious Mission (Wynne), 1933
Pizza Monster (Sharmat), 1989
Place (Coatsworth), 1966
Place among the Stones (Seed), 1987
Place Apart (Fox), 1980
Place Called Ugly (Avi), 1981
Place for Ann (Whitney), 1941
Place for Peter (Yates), 1952
Place Mill (Softly), 1962
Place to Belong (Nixon), 1989
Place to Come Back To (N. Bond), 1984
Place to Play (Ahlberg), 1975
Places and Things (play; Garner), 1978
Plague Dogs (Adams), 1977
Plague 1990 (Ure), 1989
Plague Ship (Henty, appendix), 1889
Plague Ship (A. Norton, as North), 1956
Plain Girl (Sorensen), 1955
Plain Jack (Peyton), 1988
Plain Jane (Softly), 1961
Plain Lane Christmas (Hodges), 1978
Plain Princess (play; A. Harris), 1954
Plain Princess (McGinley), 1945
Plainsmen (Schaefer), 1963
Plan for Birdsmarsh (Peyton), 1965
Plane Wreckers (B. Carter, as Strong), 1961
Planet of Junior Brown (Hamilton), 1971
Planet of the Warlord (D. Hill), 1981
Planet Out of the Past (Collier), 1983
Plant Sitter (Zion), 1959
Play the Game! (H. Avery), 1906
Play Theatre (play; D. Wood), 1987
Play to the Festival (Allan), 1959
Play with Me (Ets), 1955
Playaway series (play; D. Wood), from 1973
Players and the Rebels (Forest), 1971
Player's Boy (Forest), 1970
Playground (B. Carter), 1964
Playhouse Tales (Hodges), 1974
Playing Ball (Hardcastle), 1972
Playing Beatie Bow (Park), 1980
Playing in Winter (Bruna, trans), 1984
Playing Possum (Eager), 1955
Playing the Game (Wynne), 1947
Playmates (Meade, appendix), 1896
Plays of the Pioneers (C. D. Mackay), 1915
Play's the Thing (play; Blyton), 1927
Playtime Book (Blyton), 1968
Playtime Stories (Nesbit), 1903
Playtime Story Book (Blyton), 1967
Pleasant Fieldmouse series (Wahl), from 1964
Please, Don't Eat My Cabin (Merrill), 1971
Please Keep Off the Mud (F. Knight), 1957
Please, Mrs. Butler (verse; Ahlberg), 1983
Please Save Jessie (C. Pullein-Thompson), 1987
Please Try to Remember the First of Octember (verse; Seuss, as Le Sieg), 1977
Pleasure Garden (Garfield), 1976
Plenty of Ponies (J. Pullein-Thompson), 1949
Plenty of Room (Berg), 1975
Plenty to Watch (Yashima), 1954
Plot Night (Mayne), 1963
Plots and Counterplots (Alcott, appendix), 1976
Plotters of Cabbage Patch Corner (play; D. Wood), 1970

Prisoners of the Scrambling Dragon (Monjo), 1980
Prisoners under the Sea (Catherall), 1963
Private (Naylor), 1969
Private Beach (Parker), 1964
Private Eye (Fitzgerald), 1974
Private Eyes (Kingman), 1964
Private Eyes Don't Blink (R. Kraus), 1988
Private Zoo (Foreman), 1985
Prize for Gardening (Chaundler), 1948
Prize Pony (J. Pullein-Thompson), 1982
Probable Sons (Le Feuvre), 1895
Probation of Mervyn Castleton (Everett-Green, appendix), 1899
Problem Party (Atkinson), 1945
Problem with Pulcifer (Heide), 1982
Procession (Mahy), 1969
Professor Branestawm series (N. Hunter), from 1933
Professor Bull's Umbrella (Lipkind), 1954
Professor Diggins' Dragons (Holman), 1966
Professor Philanderpan (Farrow), 1903
Professor Potts Meets the Animals of Africa (verse; Wright), 1981
Professor Tugnutt's Time Machine (play; Lillington), 1967
Professor Tugnutt's Truth Gas (play; Lillington), 1968
Project Boy (Lenski), 1954
Project 1-2-3 (Merriam), 1971
Promise series (Cole), from 1977
Promise Is a Promise (Munsch), 1988
Promise of the Rainbow (Fry), 1965
Promised Year (Uchida), 1959
Proper Acadian (Downie), 1981
Proper Little Nooryeff (Ure), 1982
Proper Place (Lingard), 1975
Prophecy of Tau Ridoo (Katz), 1982
Proud Duck (Judah), 1961
Proud Taste for Scarlet and Miniver (Konigsburg), 1973
Proud White Circus Horse (Zimnik, trans), 1957
Proud Wooden Drummer (Krüss, trans), 1969
Proudfoot's Way (Lattimore), 1978
Prove Yourself a Hero (Peyton), 1977
Proverb Stories series (Alcott, appendix), from 1868
Provost's Jewel (Kyle), 1950
Prydain series (Alexander), from 1964
Psst! Doggie—(Keats), 1973
Psyche's Art (Alcott, appendix), 1868
Puck of Pook's Hill (Kipling), 1906
Puddin' Poems (verse; Lindsay), 1977
Puddle's Tiger (Tate), 1969
Pudgy Car Board Books (R. Kraus), 1985
Puff of Smoke (Waddell, as Sefton), 1982
Puffin, Adventures of (Moray Williams), 1939
Pug Peter (Nesbit), 1905
Pulabad (Fenn, appendix), 1901
Pumpkin Patch (P. Martin), 1966
Pumpkin Pie (Arthur), 1938
Punch and Judy (Comical Tragedy or Tragical Comedy of (play; A. Harris), 1969
Punch Back Gang (Parker), 1966
Punchbowl series (M. Edwards), from 1951
Puppet Pal books (R. Kraus), 1981
Puppet Plays for Children (Ridge), 1953
Puppy Lost in Lapland (Catherall, as Hallard), 1971
Puppy Pie (J. Williams), 1961
Puppy Stakes (Cavanna), 1943
Puppy Summer (De Jong), 1966
Puppy's House (Schlein), 1955
Puptents and Pebbles (verse; W. Smith), 1959
Pure Magic (Coatsworth), 1973

Puritan Adventure (Lenski), 1944
Purl and Plain, The Adventures of (Brisley), 1941
Purple Dragon (Baum), 1962
Purple Mountain (Clewes), 1962
Purple Mouse (MacIntyre), 1975
Purple Valley (Saville), 1964
Pursuit of Penelope (Meade, appendix), 1902
Push Kitty (Wahl), 1968
Pushcart War (Merrill), 1964
Puss and Cat (Storr), 1969
Puss in Boots, The Marvellous Story of (play; Gray), 1954
Puss in Boots, The Further Adventures of (Gray), 1971
Puss in Boots (play; Miller), 1950
Puss in Boots (play; L. Richards), 1916
Puss-in-Boots (K. Hale), 1951
Pussy and Doggy Tales (Nesbit), 1899
Pussy Tales (Nesbit), 1895
Pussycat's Christmas (M. W. Brown), 1949
Put on My Crown (Levin), 1985
Put the Kettle On! (Berg), 1972
Put-em-Rights (Blyton), 1946
Puzzle for Sherlock Holmes (Newman), 1979
Puzzle in Purple (Cavanna, as Allen), 1948
Puzzling Pair (Le Feuvre), 1898
Pyewacket series (Weir), from 1967
Pysen (Unnerstad, trans), 1955

Quack Quack (Hader), 1961
Quack! Said the Billy-Goat (verse; Causley), 1986
Quag Keep (A. Norton), 1978
Quake (Hardcastle), 1988
Quarantine Child (Symons), 1966
Quarrel of Witches (Storey), 1970
Quarreling Book (Zolotow), 1963
Quarry Adventure (Kingman), 1951
Quarry Line Mystery (Stewart), 1971
Quarter Boy (Parker), 1976
Quarter Horse Boy (Patchett), 1970
Queechy (Warner, as Wetherell, appendix), 1852
Queen and Mr. Shakespeare (play; Daniell), 1948
"Queen Elizabeth" Family (Blyton), 1951
Queen for a Day (Cohen), 1981
Queen of Air and Darkness (T. White), 1958
Queen of Eene (verse; Prelutsky), 1978
Queen of Hearts (V. and B. Cleaver), 1978
Queen of Hearts (play; C. D. Mackay), 1904
Queen of Joy (Meade, appendix), 1914
Queen of Shindy Flat (Marchant), 1905
Queen of the Dolls (play; Brink), 1928
Queen of the Dormitory (Brazil), 1926
Queen of the Pharisees' Children (B. Willard), 1983
Queen of the Red Chessman (L. Hale, appendix) n.d.
Queen of the What Ifs (N. Klein), 1982
Queen of the Wheat Castles (Mattingley), 1973
Queen Rose (Meade, appendix), 1902
Queen Silver-Bell (Burnett), 1906
Queen Without a Crown (Polland), 1965
Queen Zixi of Ix (Baum), 1905
Queenie Peavie (Burch), 1966
Queen's Blessing (Polland), 1963
Queen's Brooch (Treece), 1966
Queens for Choice (Moore), 1934
Queen's Garden (play; Blyton), 1939
Queen's Manor School (Everett-Green, appendix), 1921

Queen's Museum (Stockton, appendix), 1887
Queen's Nose (King-Smith), 1983
Queen's Own Grove (P. Beatty), 1966
Queen's Scarlet (Fenn, appendix), 1895
Queen's Treason (Rush), 1955
Queen's Wizard (J. and P. Beatty), 1967
Queer Customer (Hough), 1972
Queer Mystery (Blyton), 1952
Queery Leary Nonsense (verse; Lear, appendix), 1911
Quelling Eye (Gordon), 1986
Quentin Corn (Stolz), 1985
Quest Crosstime (A. Norton), 1975
Quest for Orion (R. Harris), 1978
Quest for the Gloop (Nicoll), 1980
Quest for the Perfect Planet (Johns), 1961
Quest in the Cariboo (Hayes), 1960
Quest in the North-land (Yates), 1940
Quest of Ati Manu (Patchett), 1960
Quest of the Four (Altsheler), 1911
Quest of the "Golden Hope" (Westerman), 1911
Quest of the Otter (Wibberley, as Webb), 1963
Questers series (Hildick), from 1966
Question Box (J. Williams), 1965
Question of Courage (Darke), 1975
Question of Li-fu (Lattimore), 1942
Quick, Let's Get Out of Here (verse; Rosen), 1983
Quicksilver (Fenn, appendix), 1888
Quicksilver (Peacocke), 1922
Quicksilver Sue (L. Richards), 1899
Quiet Mother and the Noisy Little Boy (Zolotow), 1953
Quiet! There's a Canary in the Library (D. Freeman), 1969
Quimble Wood (Bodecker), 1981
Quinkins (Roughsey), 1978
Quintette in Queensland (Brent-Dyer), 1951
Quintin's Man (D. Rees), 1976
Quipic (Castor, trans), 1937
Quite Another Story (Ingelow, appendix), 1890
Quito Express (Bemelmans), 1938
Quokka Island (L. Rees), 1951

R, My Name Is Rosie (Cohen), 1978
Rabbi's Girls (Hurwitz), 1982
Rabbit and His Friends (Scarry), 1953
Rabbit and His Shadow (Ainsworth), 1968
Rabbit Boy (Tate), 1964
Rabbit Ears (Slote), 1982
Rabbit Garden (P. Martin, as Miles), 1967
Rabbit Hill (Lawson), 1944
Rabbit Hutch (play; Parker), 1951
Rabbit Island (Müller and Steiner, trans), 1977
Rabbit Minders (Kaye), 1987
Rabbit Story (Tresselt), 1957
Rabbiting On (verse; Wright), 1978
Rabbits and Redcoats (R. N. Peck), 1976
Rabbits on Roller Skates! (Wahl), 1986
Rabbits, Rabbits (verse; A. Fisher), 1983
Rabbit's World (Schlein), 1973
Rabble Starkey (Lowry), 1987
Raccoon and Mrs. McGinnis (P. Martin), 1961
Race for Gowrie Bay (Dawlish), 1959
Race Horse Holiday (J. Pullein-Thompson), 1971
Racecourse for Andy (Wrightson), 1968
Rachel (Southall), 1986
Rachel and the Angel (Westall), 1986
Rachel Changes Schools (Breary), 1948
Rachel of Romney (Cumming), 1939

Rachel Out West (Marchant), 1923
Rachel Tandy (Allan), 1958
Rachel's Legacy (Colman), 1978
Racing Bike (Hardcastle), 1980
Racing Cart (Heine, trans), 1984
Racketty-Packetty House (Burnett), 1905
Racketty-Packetty House (play; Burnett), 1912
Radio Rescue (play; Chorpenning), 1938
Radney Riding Club (J. Pullein-Thompson), 1951
Rafael and Consuelo (Means), 1929
Rafa's Dog (H. Griffiths), 1983
Raffle Pony (Kaye), 1966
Raffy and the Nine Monkeys (H.A. and M. Rey), 1939
Raft (A. Morgan), 1974
Raft (play; Parker), 1951
Raft Baby (play; Foon), 1978
Rag, A Bone, and a Hank of Hair (Fisk), 1980
Rag Ball (Odaga), 1987
Rag, Tag, and Bobtail (play; Blyton), 1927
Ragamuffin Mystery (Blyton), 1959
Ragamuffin Scarecrow (Dallas), 1969
Ragamuffins (Ainsworth), 1939
Ragged Dick (Alger, appendix), 1868
Ragged Robin (verse; Reeves), 1961
Raggedy Andy series (Gruelle), from 1920
Raggedy Ann series (Gruelle), from 1918
Raggle Taggle Fellow (Schlein), 1959
Raggylug the Cottontail Rabbit (Seton), 1900
Raging Robots and Unruly Uncles (Mahy), 1981
Rags (Talbot), 1926
Rags and Riches (Lingard), 1988
Rags to Riches (play; A. Harris), 1965
Raid from Beauséjour (C. Roberts), 1894
Raid on Heligoland (Catherall), 1940
Raiding the "Pearl" (Otis, appendix), 1884
Railroad Children (Yonge, appendix), 1855
Railway series (Awdry), from 1945
Railway Children (Nesbit), 1906
Railway Engine and the Hairy Brigands (Mahy), 1973
Railway Passage (Keeping), 1974
Railway Runaways (Fidler), 1977
Rain Car (Janosch, trans), 1978
Rain Cloud (Rayner), 1980
Rain Door (Hoban), 1986
Rain Drop Splash (Tresselt), 1946
Rain Forest (Sperry), 1947
Rain from the West (Ray), 1980
Rain on the Roof (Meigs), 1925
Rainbow and Lucky series (Abbott, appendix), from 1858
Rainbow Bridge (Means), 1934
Rainbow Cat (Fyleman), 1922
Rainbow Children (Howes), 1912
Rainbow Christmas (play; de Paola), 1971
Rainbow Flowers (play; Blyton), 1927
Rainbow Jordan (Childress), 1981
Rainbow of Gold (Altsheler), 1896
Rainbow of My Own (D. Freeman), 1966
Rainbow Pavement (Cresswell), 1970
Rainbow Queen (Nesbit), 1903
Rainbow Rider (Yolen), 1974
Rainbow Sandwich (Darke), 1989
Rainbow Serpent (Roughsey), 1975
Rainbow Sun (Greaves), 1971
Rainbow Valley (L. Montgomery), 1919
Rainbow Writing (verse; Merriam), 1976
Rainbow's End (Hader), 1945

Rainbow-Tinted Scarf (Ekwensi), 1975
Rainmaker (Ekwensi), 1965
Rains of Eridan (Hoover), 1977
Rains Will Come (Means), 1954
Rainy Day Stories (Blyton), 1944
Rainy Rainy Saturday (verse; Prelutsky), 1980
Raising of the Dubhe (Wibberley, as O'Connor), 1964
Rajah of Dah (Fenn, appendix), 1891
Rajah's Daughter (Marchant), 1899
Rajah's Treasure (Daniell), 1960
Ralestone Luck (A. Norton), 1938
Rallying round Gussy (F. Richards, as Clifford), 1950
Ralph Raymond's Heir (Alger, appendix), 1888
Ralph Roxburgh's Revenge (Everett-Green, appendix), 1895
Ralph Roxburgh's Triumph (Everett-Green, appendix), 1895
Ralph S. Mouse (Cleary), 1982
Ralph's Secret Weapon (Kellogg), 1983
Ram and Goat (Manning-Sanders), 1974
Rama (Byars), 1966
Rama and Sita, The Adventures of (R. Bond), 1987
Rama and the Tigers (play; Chorpenning), 1954
Rambles with Uncle Nat (Blyton), 1947
Ramona series (Cleary), from 1955
Ranald Bannerman's Boyhood (MacDonald, appendix), 1871
Ranch and Ring (Means), 1932
Ranch for Danny (Bulla), 1951
Ranche in the Valley (Henty, appendix), 1892
Randy of the River (Alger, appendix), 1906
Randy's Dandy Lions (verse; Peet), 1964
Ranger Jo (Talbot), 1929
Ranger Rose (Talbot), 1928
Rangers and Strangers (Talbot), 1938
Ranger's Ransom (Best), 1953
Ransom (L. Duncan), 1966
Ransom for a Knight (Picard), 1956
Rapids of Niagara (Warner, appendix), 1875
Rapscallion Jones (Marshall), 1983
Rapunzel (play; Gray), 1953
Rapunzel (play; Miller), n.d.
Rare Spotted Birthday Party (Mahy), 1974
Rascal (North), 1963
Rascals from Haskell's Gym (Bonham), 1977
Rasmus and the Tramp (Lindgren, trans), 1961
Rasmus and the Vagabond (Lindgren, trans), 1961
Rat Race (J. Wilson), 1987
Rat-a-Tat Mystery (Blyton), 1956
Ratbags and Rascals (R. Klein), 1984
Rattlesnake Cave (Lampman), 1974
Raven's Cry (C. Harris), 1966
Ravensgill (Mayne), 1970
Razor Eyes (B. Carter, as Hough), 1981
Reach for a Star (Means), 1957
Read Aloud Stories (Bailey), 1929
Reading Between the Lines (play; Sachs), 1971
Reading Time Stories (Bailey), 1923
Ready for Take-Off (Hamre, trans), 1962
Ready or Not (Stolz), 1953
Ready, Steady, Go! (Watanabe, trans), 1981
Ready Teddy Go (verse; Ahlberg), 1983
Ready-Made Family (Forest), 1967
Real Fairies (verse; Blyton), 1923
Real Game (Weir), 1965
Real Gold (Fenn, appendix), 1893
Real Hole (Cleary), 1960
Real Little Lord Fauntleroy (play; Burnett), 1888
Real Thief (Steig), 1973

Really Rosie (play; Sendak), 1975
Really Spring (Zion), 1956
Really Weird Summer (McGraw), 1977
Rear-View Mirrors (P. Fleischman), 1986
Reason for the Pelican (verse; Ciardi), 1959
Rebecca Hatpin (R. Kraus), 1974
Rebecca of Sunnybrook Farm series (Wiggin), from 1903
Rebecca of Sunnybrook Farm (play; Wiggin), 1909
Rebecka (Asch), 1971
Rebel (H. Burton), 1971
Rebel at School (Wynne), 1924
Rebel of the School (Meade, appendix), 1902
Rebel of the Third (Moore), 1929
Rebel on a Rock (Bawden), 1978
Rebel Siege (Kjeigaard), 1943
Rebel Spurs (A. Norton), 1962
Rebellion of Lil Carrington (Meade, appendix), 1898
Rebels of Gaslight Street (play; Needle), 1986
Rebels of the Heavenly Kingdom (Paterson), 1983
Rebels Ride at Night (Hayes), 1953
Recovery (Altsheler), 1909
Rectory Children (Molesworth, appendix), 1889
Red (Truss), 1988
Red Alfa (Prince), 1972
Red Bantam (Fatio), 1963
Red Ben (Lippincott), 1919
Red Biddy (Hough), 1966
Red Book (Mayne), 1984
Red Boy's Gratitude (Wynne), 1922
Red Candle (Strang), 1926
Red Cap of Liberty (Meade, appendix), 1907
Red Caps at School (Talbot), 1932
Red Comet (Trease), 1936
Red Dust Soldiers (Seed), 1972
Red Eric (Ballantyne, appendix), 1861
Red Fox (C. Roberts), 1905
Red Fox and His Canoe (Benchley), 1964
Red Gaskell's Gold (Daniell, as Bowood), 1966
Red Grange (Molesworth, appendix), 1891
Red Hart Magic (A. Norton), 1976
Red Head (verse; Eager), 1951
Red Heels and Roses (play; Clapp), 1962
Red Horse Hill (Meader), 1930
Red Ivory (Catherall, as Channel), 1964
Red Jack (verse; Durack), 1987
Red Jaguar (Prince), 1972
Red Light, Green Light (M. W. Brown, as MacDonald), 1944
Red Man's Country (Rush), 1957
Red Man's Revenge (Ballantyne, appendix), 1880
Red Pawns (Wibberley), 1973
Red Pirate (Westerman), 1935
Red Pixie Book (Blyton), 1934
Red Planet (Heinlein), 1949
Red Ranger and the Combine Harvester (Clewes), 1966
Red Riding (Merrill), 1968
Red Riding Hood (verse; de Regniers), 1972
Red Roan Pony (Lippincott), 1934
Red Robin Fly Up! (George), 1963
Red Rock over the River (P. Beatty), 1973
Red Room Riddle (S. Corbett), 1972
Red Rooney (Ballantyne, appendix), 1886
Red Rose and Tiger Lily (Meade, appendix), 1894
Red Rose of Ruvina (Needham), 1957
Red Ruth (Meade, appendix), 1907
Red Sail, White Sail (MacGibbon), 1961
Red Sea Rescue (Catherall), 1969

Robert Coverdale's Struggle (Alger, appendix), 1910
Robert Francis Weatherbee (Leaf), 1935
Robert Goes to Fetch a Sister (D. Edwards), 1986
Robert Rows the River (Haywood), 1965
Robert the Spy Hunter (L. Cooper), 1973
Roberto and the Bull (Hoff), 1969
Robert's Rescued Railway (Weir), 1960
Robert's Story (Berg), 1970
Robin (M. Bruce), 1926
Robin series (verse; Serraillier), from 1967
Robin (Storr), 1962
Robin and the Wren (verse; Serraillier), 1974
Robin Goodfellow (play; A. Harris), 1974
Robin Hood (play; Blyton), 1926
Robin Hood (play; D. Wood), 1981
Robin Hood (play; Yolen), 1967
Robin Hood and Friar Tuck (play; D. Wood), 1987
Robin Hood and the Butcher (play; Blyton), 1935
Robin Hood and the Jester (play; Lillington), 1968
Robin Hood to the Rescue (Wynne), 1927
Robin Hooders (Clarke), 1960
Robin Hood's Master Stroke (Suddaby), 1965
Robin of the Round House (Peacocke), 1918
Robin Redbreast (Molesworth, appendix), 1892
Robin-a-Thrush (play; Barne), 1936
Robin's Heritage (Le Feuvre), 1907
Robin's Real Engine (Mayne), 1972
Robinsheugh (Dunlop), 1975
Robinson Crusoe (play; Chorpenning), 1952
Robinson Crusoe (play; Miller), 1951
Robinson Daniel Crusoe (Andrew), 1978
Robot and Rebecca series (Yolen), from 1980
Robot Birthday (Bunting), 1980
Robot People (Bunting), 1978
Robot Revolt (Fisk), 1981
Rob's Place (Townsend), 1987
Rock, The Story of the (Ballantyne, appendix), 1875
Rock and the Willow (M. Lee), 1963
Rock Hounds (Lampman), 1958
Rock of Chickamauga (Altsheler), 1915
Rock Star (Collier), 1970
Rocket Ship Galileo (Heinlein), 1947
Rocket in the Dunes (Lamplugh), 1958
Rocking Horse (Manning), 1970
Rocking Horse Secret (Godden), 1977
Rockingdown Mystery (Blyton), 1949
Rocklands School series (Oxenham), from 1929
Rocks Ahead! (Westerman), 1933
Rocks of Honey (Wrightson), 1960
Rocky and the Ratman (Sherry), 1988
Rocky Billy (Holling), 1928
Rocky Summer (Kingman), 1948
Rod o' the Rail (Catherall), 1936
Roderick (Behn), 1961
Rodge, Silvie, and Munch (Andrew), 1973
Roger Brandy (verse; Park), 1977
Roger Ingleton (Reed, appendix), 1891
Roger the Scout (Strang), 1907
Roger Trehern (Everett-Green, appendix), 1903
Roger's Trains (D. Edwards), 1971
Roger's Umbrella (Pinkwater), 1982
Rogue Elephant (Catherall, as Channel), 1962
Rogue's Valley (Lampman, as Bronson), 1952
Rokubei and the Thousand Rice Bowls (Uchida), 1962
Roland (Steig), 1968
Rolf in the Woods (Seton), 1911

Rolf the Rebel (Marchant), 1908
Rolf's First Earnings (Heward), 1929
Roll of Thunder, Hear My Cry (M. Taylor), 1976
Roll Over D.W. (Marc Brown), 1988
Roll Up (Hardcastle, as Clark), 1975
Roller Skates (Sawyer), 1936
Roller Skates, Skooter and Bike (Clewes), 1966
Rolling Down to Rio (Westerman), 1953
Rolling Harvey Down the Hill (verse; Prelutsky), 1980
Rolling On (Cockett), 1960
Rolling Season (Mayne), 1960
Rolling Stone (Alger, appendix), 1902
Rolling Stones (Heinlein), 1952
Rolling the Cheese (P. Martin), 1966
Rollo series (Abbott, appendix), from 1835
Rollo and Juliet, Forever! (Sharmat), 1981
Roly the Railroad Mouse (Ainsworth), 1969
Roly the Railway Mouse (Ainsworth), 1967
Roly-Poly Pudding (Potter), 1908
Roly's Dogs (Barne), 1950
Roman Moon Mystery (J. Williams), 1948
Romance in Italy (Allan), 1962
Romance of a Christmas Card (Wiggin), 1916
Romance on Trial (Cavanna), 1984
Romansgrove (Allan), 1975
Rom-Bom-Bom (Ridge), 1946
Romeo and Juliet—Together (and Alive!)—at Last (Avi), 1987
Ronald Kennedy (Everett-Green, appendix), 1893
Ronald's Burglar (Chaundler), 1919
Rondo in C (P. Fleischman), 1988
Ronia, The Robber's Daughter (Lindgren, trans), 1983
Ronnie and the Chief's Son (Coatsworth), 1962
Roof Fall! (Cresswell), 1972
Rooftop Mystery (Lexau), 1968
Rooftops (Mayne), 1966
Rookie of the Year (Tunis), 1944
Rookoo and Bree (P. Turner), 1979
Rooloo (Chipperfield), 1955
Room for Randy (Jackson), 1957
Room for the Cuckoo (Allan), 1953
Room Made of Windows (Cameron), 1971
Room of His Own (Beckman, trans), 1973
Room to Let (C. Pullein-Thompson), 1968
Room with No Windows (Kemp), 1989
Roomrimes (verse; Cassedy), 1987
Rooms for Rent (Mahy), 1974
Rooms to Let (Mahy), 1975
Roosevelt Grady (Shotwell), 1963
Rooster Who Set Out to See the World (Carle), 1972
Rooster Who Understood Japanese (Uchida), 1976
Rooster's Off to See the World (Carle), 1988
Root Cellar (Lunn), 1981
Rosa and Robbie (Finley, appendix), 1876
Rosalie (Westall), 1987
Rosaly's New School (Oxenham), 1913
Rosamund series (Oxenham), from 1933
Rosanna Joins the Wells (L. Hill), 1956
Rosanna the Goat (Cockett), 1969
Roscoe's Leap (Cross), 1987
Rose (Beresford), 1989
Rose, A Bridge, and a Wild Black Horse (Zolotow), 1964
Rose Family (Alcott, appendix), 1864
Rose for Mr. Bloom (Waber), 1968
Rose in Bloom (Alcott, appendix), 1876
Rose in My Garden (verse; Arnold Lobel), 1984
Rose in the Desert (Warner, appendix), 1864

Rose in the River (Thwaite), 1974
Rose of Puddle Fratrum (play; Aiken), 1978
Rose o' the River (Wiggin), 1905
Rose on My Cake (verse; Kuskin), 1964
Rose Regina (Meade, appendix), 1910
Rose Round (Trevor), 1963
Rose Window (Symons), 1964
Rosebud (Bemelmans), 1942
Rosebuds (Le Feuvre), 1931
Rosebury (Meade, appendix), 1903
Roseleen at School (Wynne), 1920
Rosemary (Stolz), 1955
Rosemary the Rebel (Moore), 1913
Roses (Cohen), 1984
Roses (Le Feuvre), 1899
Roses and Thorns (Meade, appendix), 1928
Roses for the Queen (play; Daniell), 1955
Rosie (Daly), 1967
Rosie, Stories about (Voigt), 1986
Rosie series (B. Willard), 1968
Rosie and Michael (Viorst), 1974
Rosie and Mister Brown (Berg), 1987
Rosie and the Boredom Eater (Cresswell), 1989
Rosie's Walk (Hutchins), 1968
Rosin the Beau (L. Richards), 1898
Rosina Copper series (Barne), from 1954
Rossie (Loeff, trans), 1964
Rossiter's Farm (M. Bruce), 1920
Rosy (Molesworth, appendix), 1882
Rosy Starling (Garfield), 1977
Rotten Book (Rodgers), 1969
Rotten Island (Steig), 1984
Rotten Old Car (Kaye), 1973
Rotten Years (Wojciechowska), 1971
Rottenteeth (Needle), 1980
Rough and Ready (Alger, appendix), 1869
Rough Night (Moore), 1925
Rough Riders Ho! (R. Montgomery), 1946
Rough Road (MacPherson), 1965
Rough Shaking (MacDonald, appendix), 1890
Round Behind the Ice-House (Fine), 1981
Round Dozen (Coolidge, appendix), 1883
Round, Round World (verse; Bright, as Douglas), 1960
Round the Clock Stories (Blyton), 1945
Round the World A.B.C. (verse; Farrow), 1904
Round the World in Seven Days (Strang), 1910
Round the Year Stories (Blyton), 1950
Roundabout (Dalgliesh), 1934
Roundabout Horse (Sutcliff), 1986
Roundabout Horse (H. Todd), 1978
Rounding Up the Raider (Westerman), 1916
Rover of the Andes (Ballantyne, appendix), 1885
Roving Commission (Henty, appendix), 1900
Roy Royland (Feen, appendix), 1895
Royal Dirk (J. and P. Beatty), 1966
Royal Harry (Mayne), 1971
Royal Pain (Conford), 1986
Royal Visit (Ashley), 1987
Rua and the Sea People (R. Bacon), 1968
Rubadub Mystery (Blyton), 1952
Rubbalong Tales (Blyton), 1950
Rubies of St. Lõ (Yonge, appendix), 1894
Ruby (Guy), 1976
Ruby and the Dragon (Owen), 1989
Ruby Ring (Molesworth, appendix), 1904
Rudi and the Distelfink (Monjo), 1972

Ruey Richardson (Brent-Dyer), 1960
Ruff and Ready (Farrow), 1905
Ruffles (Meade, appendix), 1911
Ruffles and Drums (Cavanna), 1975
Rufty Tufty series (Ainsworth), from 1952
Rufus (R. Montgomery), 1973
Rufus (Storr), 1969
Rufus (Ungerer), 1961
Rufus and Rose (Alger, appendix), 1870
Rufus M. (Estes), 1943
Rufus, Red Rufus (P. Beatty), 1975
Rufus Round and Round (Van Stockum), 1973
Rufus the Unready (Finley, appendix), 1870
Rug That Grew (Geras), 1981
Rule of Three (Coolidge, appendix), 1904
Rulers of the Lakes (Altsheler), 1917
Rum Day of the Vanishing Pony (Treadgold), 1970
Rumble and Chuff (Blyton), 1958
Rumble Fish (Hinton), 1975
Rumble Seat Pony (Anderson), 1971
Rummage (Mattingley), 1981
Rummage (play; Mattingley), 1983
Rumpelstiltskin (play; Blyton), 1927
Rumpelstiltskin (play; Chorpenning), 1944
Rumple Nose-Dimple and the Three Horrible Snaps (R. Kraus),
   1969
Rumptydoolers (Wier), 1964
Rum-Tum-Tummy (Holling), 1928
Run (Hardcastle, as Clark), 1973
Run! (P. Martin, as Lane), 1974
Run (Sleator), 1973
Run Away Home (Forest), 1982
Run Away Home (Lyon), 1953
Run, Chase the Sun (Kuratomi, trans), 1969
Run Far, Run Fast (Morey), 1974
Run for the Money (S. Corbett), 1973
Run for Your Life (Line), 1966
Run for Your Sweet Life (Benedict), 1986
Run Softly, Go Fast (Wersba), 1970
Run Swift, Run Free (McCaughren), 1986
Run to Earth (Kyle), 1957
Run to Earth (McCaughren), 1984
Run with the Wind (McCaughren), 1983
Runabout Rhymes (verse; Fyleman), 1941
Run-about's Holiday (Blyton), 1955
Run-Around Robins (McNeill), 1967
Runaway (Clewes), 1957
Runaway (Cross), 1979
Runaway (L. Graham), 1972
Runaway (Lampman, as Bronson), 1953
Runaway (Parker), 1977
Runaway Boy (Kaye), 1971
Runaway Brig (Otis, appendix), 1888
Runaway Bunny (M. W. Brown), 1942
Runaway Bus (Park), 1969
Runaway James and the Night Owl (Kuratomi, trans), 1968
Runaway Jonah (Wahl), 1985
Runaway Kitten (Blyton), 1945
Runaway Marriage Brokers (Palmer), 1980
Runaway Princess (Moore), 1912
Runaway Princess (Peacocke), 1929
Runaway Ralph (Cleary),1970
Runaway Serf (Trease), 1968
Runaway Settlers (Locke), 1965
Runaway Sleigh Ride (Lindgren, trans), 1984
Runaway Stallion (Morey), 1973

Runaway Summer (Bawden), 1969
Runaway Teddy Bear (Blyton), 1951
Runaway to Freedom (Smucker), 1977
Runaway Train (Farmer), 1980
Runaway Voyage (Cavanna), 1978
Runaways (H. Avery), 1920
Runaways (Hader), 1956
Runaways (Kamm), 1978
Runaways (Kimenye), 1973
Runaways (Lynch), 1959
Runner (Voigt), 1985
Runners (Tate), 1974
Running Amok (Fenn, appendix), 1901
Running Deer (Trease), 1941
Running of the Deer (Trease), 1982
Running Owl, The Hunter (Benchley), 1979
Running Scared (Ashley), 1986
Running Scared (play; Ashley), 1986
Running Wild (H. Griffiths), 1977
Running with Rachel (Asch), 1979
Runny Days, Sunny Days (verse; A. Fisher), 1958
Runt of Rogers School (Keith), 1971
Rupert series (Bestall), from 1936
Rupert series (Tourtel), from 1921
Rupert's Ambition (Alger, appendix), 1899
Ruru and the Green Fairies (R. Bacon), 1985
Russ the Australian Tree Kangaroo, The Story of (L. Rees), 1964
Russell Rides Again (Hurwitz), 1985
Russell Sprouts (Hurwitz), 1987
Russet and the Two Reds (Lipkind, as Will), 1962
Russian Blue (H. Griffiths), 1973
Rustlers of Rattlesnake Valley (Johns), 1948
Rusty, The Adventures of (R. Bond), 1981
Rusty's Space Ship (Lampman), 1957
Ruth Crane (A. Morgan), 1973
Ruth of Boston (Otis, appendix), 1910
Ruth of St. Roman's (Brazil), 1927
Ruth Ravelstan the Puritan's Daughter (Everett-Green, appendix), 1907
Ruthless Rhymes for Heartless Homes series (verse; H. Graham), from 1899
Ryan's Fort (Lynch), 1961
Rye Royal (Saville), 1969

S.O.R. Losers(Avi), 1984
S.O.S. Bobomobile! (Wahl), 1973
Sabarinda Island (Westerman), 1950
Sabotage! (Westerman), 1952
Sabotage at the Forge (R. Armstrong), 1946
Sabre (Peyton, as Herald), 1948
Sabre of Storm Valley (Chipperfield), 1962
Sabre Pilot (Meader), 1956
Sad Cat (Seed), 1984
Sad Story of Veronica Who Played the Violin (McKee), 1987
Saddlebottom (King-Smith), 1985
Sad-Faced Boy (Bontemps), 1937
Sadie Comes to School (Wynne), 1942
Sadie Sees It Through (Talbot), 1939
Safari Adventure (W. Price), 1966
Safe Lodging (M. Harris), 1957
Sail-Ho! (Fenn, appendix), 1893
Sailing Hatrack (Coatsworth), 1972
Sailing to Cythera (N. Willard), 1974
Sailor (Bruna, trans), 1966
Sailor Dog, (M. W. Brown), 1953
Sailor Jack and the 20 Orphans (Mahy), 1970

Sailor Man, (play; L. Richards), 1915
Sailor Rumbelow and Britannia (Reeves), 1962
Sailor Sam (Dalgliesh), 1935
Sailors All (Dawlish), 1958
Sailor's Choice (Carlson), 1966
St. Bartholomew's Eve (Henty, appendix) 1893
St. Catherine's College (Brazil), 1929
St. Clare's series (Blyton), from 1941
St. Dunstan's Clock (Everett-Green, as Dare, appendix), 1893
St. George and the Dragon (play; Miller), n.d.
St. George and the Dragon (Sidney, appendix), 1888
St. George for England (Henty, appendix), 1884
St. Jerome and the Lion (verse; Godden), 1961
St. Jim's series (F. Richards, as Clifford), 1949
St. Jonathan's in the Country (Fidler), 1945
Saint Martha and the Tarasque of Tarascon (play; Ridge), 1954
St. Patrick's Day in the Morning (Bunting), 1980
St. Tom and the Dragon (E. Turner), 1918
St. Winifred's (Farrar, appendix), 1862
St. Wynfrith and Its Inmates (Everett-Green, appendix), 1893
Sajo and Her Beaver People, The Adventures of (Grey Owl), 1935
Sajo and the Beaver People (Grey Owl), 1936
Salar the Salmon (Williamson), 1935
Sale's Sharpshooters (H. Avery), 1902
Salford Road (verse; Owen), 1976
Sally series (D. Bruce), from 1956
Sally at School (Talbot), 1924
Sally Cinderella (Ashley), 1987
Sally Comes to School (Wynne), 1949
Sally from Cork (Lynch), 1960
Sally in Her Fur Coat (E. O. White), 1929
Sally Makes Good (Marchant), 1920
Sally Sticks It Out (Chaundler), 1924
Sally's Caterpillar (Rockwell), 1966
Sally's Secret (S. Hughes), 1973
Sally's Zoo (Patchett), 1957
Salmagundi (Cowley), 1985
Salt River Times (Mayne), 1980
Salted Lemons (D. B. Smith), 1980
Saltwater Summer (Haig-Brown), 1948
Salute (Anderson), 1940
Salute Mr. Washington (play; Brink), 1976
Salving of the "Fusi Yama" (Westerman), 1920
Sam and Me (Tate), 1968
Sam and the Impossible Thing (de Regniers, as Kitt), 1967
Sam and the Superdroop (Leaf), 1948
Sam, Bangs, and Moonshine (Ness), 1966
Sam Franklin's Savings Bank (Stretton, appendix), 1888
Sam Patch (Bontemps), 1951
Sam Pig series (Uttley), from 1940
Sam Steele series (Baum, as Fitzgerald), from 1906
Sam, Sue and Cinderella (Oldfield), 1989
Sam the Minuteman (Benchley), 1969
Sam the Referee (Ahlberg), 1975
Sama (Guillot, trans), 1961
Samankwe series (Ekwensi), from 1973
Samba (Strang), 1906
Sambo and the Twins, The Story of (Bannerman), 1936
Sammy Jay, The Adventures of (Burgess), 1915
Sammy Streetsinger (Keeping), 1984
Sammy, The Seal (Hoff), 1959
Sampler (play; Fyleman), 1934
Sam's Chance (Alger, appendix), 1876
Sam's Secret Journal (Yates), 1964
Sam's Woolly Hat (D. Edwards), 1973
Samson's Hoard (Verney), 1973

Sceptres and Crowns (Warner, appendix), 1874
Schondilie (verse; Causley), 1982
School (Bruna, trans),1966
School at Sea (Fidler), 1970
School at the Turrets (Brazil), 1935
School Bell in the Valley (Carlson), 1963
School by the River (Brent-Dyer), 1930
School by the Sea (Brazil), 1914
School Camp Fire (Oxenham), 1917
School Divided (Breary), 1945
School Donkey (Cockett), 1982
School Favourite (Meade, appendix), 1908
School for Cats (Averill), 1947
School for Sillies (J. Williams), 1969
School in Danger (Allan), 1952
School in the Forest (Brazil), 1944
School in the South (Brazil), 1922
School in the Woods (D. Bruce), 1940
School Mystery (Wynne), 1933
School of None-Go-By (Talbot), 1926
School of the Air (play; Rounds), 1938
School of Ups and Downs (Oxenham), 1918
School on Cloud Ridge (Allan), 1952
School on North Barrule (Allan), 1952
School on the Cliff (Brazil), 1938
School on the Loch (Brazil), 1946
School on the Moor (Brazil), 1939
School on the Moor (D. Bruce), 1931
School on the Moor (Talbot), 1919
School Pool Gang (Kaye), 1986
School Queens, (Meade, appendix), 1908
School Torment (Oxenham), 1920
School Trip (J. Wilson), 1984
School under Snowdon (Allan), 1950
School Without a Name (Oxenham), 1924
Schoolboy series (F. Richards), 1946
Schoolboy Johnson (Tunis), 1958
Schoolboy Pluck (H. Avery), 1921
Schoolgirl Adventurer (Moore), 1927
Schoolgirl by Chance (Talbot), 1935
Schoolgirl Kitty (Brazil), 1923
Schoolgirl Rose (Talbot), 1928
Schoolgirls Abroad (Brent-Dyer), 1951
Schoolgirls and Scouts (Oxenham), 1914
Schoolhouse in the Woods (Caudill), 1949
Schoolroom in the Parlor (Caudill), 1959
School's Honour (H. Avery), 1894
Scillies Trip (Branfield), 1975
Scoop (Meynell), 1964
Scorpion (James), 1936
Scorpions (Myers), 1988
Scotty in Gumnut Land (Gibbs), 1941
Scout Island (Talbot), 1924
Scouts for Serbia (Wynne), 1919
Scouts of Sea Island (Westerman), 1913
Scouts of Stonewall (Altsheler), 1914
Scouts of the Valley (Altsheler), 1911
Scramble! (Prince), 1984
Scrambled Eggs Super! (verse; Seuss), 1953
Scrappy the Pup (verse; Ciardi), 1960
Screaming High (Line), 1985
Screamy Mimi (R. Kraus), 1988
Screeching Door (Wahl), 1975
Scribbling Lark (Williamson), 1949
Scrub Dog of Alaska (Morey), 1971
Scrub Fire (de Roo), 1977

Scruffy (Parish), 1988
Scuttlers (Catherall), 1955
Sea Ballet (play; Moray Williams), 1933
Sea Captain from Salem (Wibberley), 1961
Sea Change (R. Armstrong), 1948
Sea Chest (F. Knight), 1960
Sea Fairies (Baum), 1911
Sea Fever (Peyton), 1963
Sea Glass (Yep), 1979
Sea Green Man (play; P. Carter), 1984
Sea Gulls Woke Me (Stolz), 1951
Sea Is All Around (Enright), 1940
Sea Islanders (West), 1970
Sea Lion and the Slick (D. Freeman), 1976
Sea Mice (Tomalin), 1962
Sea Monarch (Westerman), 1912
Sea Monkey (Kaye), 1968
Sea of Adventure (Blyton), 1948
Sea Pair (P. Beatty), 1970
Sea People (Müller and Steiner, trans), 1982
Sea Peril (P. Turner), 1966
Sea Piper (Cresswell), 1968
Sea Raiders Ho! (R. Montgomery), 1945
Sea Rangers series (Talbot), from 1935
Sea Scouts series (Westerman), from 1914
Sea Siege (A. Norton), 1957
Sea Snake (Meader), 1943
Sea Songs (verse; Livingston), 1986
Sea Spleenwort (Yonge, appendix), 1862
Sea Star (Henry), 1949
Sea Treasure (Lyon), 1955
Sea View Hotel (Stevenson), 1978
Sea View Secret (Clymer, as Kinsey), 1952
Sea Wall (Dillon), 1965
Sea Warriors (Best), 1959
Sea Witch (Robinson), 1981
Sea Witch Comes Home (Saville), 1960
Sea Wolves (Catherall), 1959
Sea Wraith (Catherall), 1955
Sea-Beggar's Son (Monjo), 1974
Seabird (Holling), 1948
Seacrow Island (Lindgren, trans), 1968
Sea-Egg (Boston), 1967
Sea-Girt Fortress (Westerman), 1914
Sea-Green Magic (Beresford), 1968
Seagull (Farmer), 1965
"Seahawk" (M. Bruce), 1934
Seal and the Slick (D. Freeman), 1974
Seal Secret (Chambers), 1980
Seal Story (Fidler), 1979
Seals (Dillon), 1968
Seal-Singing (R. Harris), 1971
Seamstress of Salzburg (Anita Lobel), 1970
Sean, The Fool, The Devil, and the Cats (play; T. Hughes), 1968
Seance (Nixon), 1980
Sean's Leap (Lamplugh), 1979
Search for a Song (Vipont), 1962
Search for Christina (Lattimore), 1966
Search for Delicious (Babbitt), 1969
Search for Lancelot's Sword (A. Hall), 1962
Search for the Silver City (Otis, appendix), 1893
Search for Two Bad Mice (Clymer), 1980
Seas of Mornings (Trease), 1976
Sea-Shore (Abbott, appendix), 1863
Seashore People (King), 1987
Seashore Story (Yashima), 1967

Secret Railway (Beresford), 1973
Secret River (Rawlings), 1955
Secret Room (Beresford), 1987
Secret Sea (R. Armstrong), 1966
Secret Seller (Lifton), 1968
Secret Seven series (Blyton), from 1949
Secret, Silent Screams (Nixon), 1988
Secret Spenders (Hildick), 1971
Secret Trails (C. Roberts), 1916
Secret Valley (Allan), 1953
Secret Valley (Bulla), 1949
Secret Water (Ransome), 1939
Secret Weapon (play; Chorpenning), 1944
Secret Winners (Hildick), 1970
Secret World of Polly Flint (Cresswell), 1982
Secret World of Polly Flint (play; Cresswell), 1987
Secrets (Fry), 1973
Secrets of the Rockies (Wynne), 1954
Secrets of the Shopping Mall (R. Peck), 1979
Secrets of the Wood (Moray Williams), 1955
Secrets of Vairy (Oxenham), 1947
See a White Horse (P. Martin, as Miles), 1963
See How They Run (Tate), 1978
See How They Work (Berg), 1962
See the Circus (verse; H.A. and M. Rey), 1956
See This Little Line? (verse; Yolen), 1963
See What I Found (Livingston), 1962
See You (Tate), 1977
See You in the Morning! (Janosch, trans), 1983
See You Thursday (Ure), 1981
Seeing and Doing (play; D. Wood), 1986
Seeing Stick (Yolen), 1977
Seekers (Dillon), 1986
Seen Grandpa Lately?(verse; Fuller), 1972
Seldom Seen (C. Smith), 1954
See-Saw Tree (play; D. Wood), 1986
Selfish Shellfish (play; D. Wood), 1983
Selina's New Family (Allan, as Pilgrim), 1967
Selkie (Lillington), 1985
Send for Johnny Danger (Patchett), 1956
Sending of Dragons (Yolen), 1987
Senior Cadet (Westerman), 1931
Senior Prefect (D. Bruce), 1920
Sense of Shame (Needle), 1980
Sensible Kate (Gates), 1943
Sent to Coventry (F. Richards), 1947
Sentimental Scarecrow (play; Field), 1930
Sentinels (P. Carter), 1980
Sentries (Paulsen), 1986
Seokoo of the Black Wind (Chipperfield), 1961
Separate Places (R. Klein), 1985
September Island (Fry), 1965
Septima (Moore), 1915
Septimus series (P. Turner, as Chance), from 1971
Serafina series (L. Brunhoff, trans), from 1961
Seraphina (M. Harris), 1960
Seraphine-Di Goes to School (Moore), 1927
Serendipity Shop (D. Bruce), 1947
Serpent Never Sleeps (O'Dell), 1987
Serpent Tower (Hoban), 1981
Serpent's Children (Yep), 1984
Serpent's Tooth (Swindells), 1988
Servant of John Company (Strang), 1932
Serve Him Right! (R. Klein), 1985
Set the Stage for Christmas (play; A. Fisher), 1948
Seth of Colorado (Otis, appendix), 1912

Settler and the Savage (Ballantyne, appendix), 1877
Settlers and Scouts (Strang), 1909
Settlers in Canada (Marryat, appendix), 1844
Settlers of Carriacou (Syme), 1953
Seven Citadels series (G. Harris), from 1982
Seven Crowns (Lattimore), 1933
Seven Daughters and Seven Sons (Cohen), 1982
Seven Days (verse; Robinson, as Thomas), 1964
Seven Days (Sleigh), 1958
Seven Days to a Brand-New Me (Conford), 1981
Seven for the Sea (Cutt), 1972
Seven in Switzerland (Allan), 1950
Seven Kisses in a Row (MacLachlan), 1983
Seven League Boots (play; A. Harris), 1947
Seven Little Australians (E. Turner), 1894
Seven Little Monsters (verse; Sendak), 1976
Seven Little Postmen (M. W. Brown), 1952
Seven Maids (Meade, appendix), 1900
Seven O'Clock Tales (Blyton), 1943
Seven Sapphires (Kyle), 1944
Seven Scamps Who Are Not All Boys (Brent-Dyer), 1927
Seven Sons (Strang), 1926
Seven Spells to Farewell (B. Baker), 1982
Seven Spells to Sunday (A. Norton), 1979
Seven Sunflower Seeds (Verney), 1968
Seven White Gates (Saville), 1944
Seven White Pebbles (Clarke, as Clare), 1960
Seven Wild Pigs (Heine, trans), 1986
Seven-Day Magic (Eager), 1962
Seven-League Ballet Shoes (L. Wood), 1959
Seventeen (Tarkington), 1916
Seventeen (play; S. Walker), 1924
Seventeen Against the Dealer (Voigt), 1989
Seventeen Kings and Forty Two Elephants (verse; Mahy), 1972
Seventeenth Street Gang (Neville), 1966
Seventeenth Summer (Daly), 1942
Seventeenth Swap (McGraw), 1986
Seventh Daughter (verse; B. Todd, as Euphan), 1935
Seventh Gate (G. Harris), 1983
Seventh Mandarin (Yolen), 1970
Seventh One (Yates), 1978
Seventh Pebble (Spence), 1980
Seventh Raven (Dickinson), 1981
Seventh Swan (Gray), 1962
Seventh Swan (play; Gray), 1962
Seven-Times Search (Biegel, trans), 1971
Several Tricks of Edgar Dolphin (Benchley), 1970
Severnside Story (Grice), 1964
Shade Changes (Odaga), 1984
Shades of the Wilderness (Altsheler), 1916
Shadow (Blyton), 1942
Shadow (play; L. Richards), 1915
Shadow at Applegarth (Cockett), 1981
Shadow Between His Shoulder Blades (J. Harris, appendix), 1909
Shadow Dancers (Curry), 1983
Shadow Guests (Aiken), 1980
Shadow Hawk (A. Norton), 1960
Shadow in Hawthorn Bay (Lunn), 1986
Shadow in the Pines (Meader), 1942
Shadow in the Sun (Meynell), 1966
Shadow like a Leopard (Levoy), 1981
Shadow of a Bull (Wojciechowska), 1964
Shadow of Spain (play; Trease), 1953
Shadow of the Hawk (Trease), 1949
Shadow of the North (Altsheler), 1917
Shadow of the Red Moon (Myers), 1987

Sink or Swim (Strong), 1945
Sioux Spaceman (A. Norton), 1960
Sir Aylmer's Heir (Everett-Green, appendix), 1890
Sir Benjamin Bulbous, Bart, Tales of (Dehn), 1935
Sir David Wears a Crown (play; S. Walker), 1921
Sir Frog (Hough), 1968
Sir Gibbie (MacDonald, appendix), 1879
Sir Ludar (Reed, appendix), 1889
Sir Reginald's Ward (Everett-Green, appendix), 1899
Sir Toady Crusoe (Crockett), 1905
Sir Toady Lion, The Surprising Adventures of (Crockett), 1897
Siren (Meade, appendix), 1898
Sirga (Guillot, trans), 1953
Siri (Stolz), 1963
Sister (Everett-Green, appendix), 1898
Sister (Greenfield), 1974
Sister Anne (Potter), 1932
Sister for Helen (Hogarth), 1976
Sister of the Angels (Goudge), 1939
Sister of the Bride (Cleary), 1963
Sister of the Red Cross (Meade, appendix), 1900
Sister Sif (Park), 1986
Sister's Bye-Hours (Ingelow, appendix), 1868
Sisters of Silver Creek (Marchant), 1907
Sisters of Silver Sands (Everett-Green, appendix), 1904
Sisters Out West (Wynne), 1930
Six and Silver (Phipson), 1954
Six Bad Boys (Blyton), 1951
Six Cousins series (Blyton), 1948
Six Crows (Lionni), 1988
Six Cushions (Yonge, appendix), 1867
Six Dogs, Twenty-Three Cats, Forty-Five Mice, and One Hundred
    Sixteen Spiders (Chalmers), 1986
Six Impossible Things Before Breakfast (Farber), 1977
Six in a Family (E. Graham), 1935
Six Men (McKee), 1971
Six O'Clock Tales (Blyton), 1942
Six on Easy Street (Cavanna), 1954
Six Ponies (J. Pullein-Thompson), 1946
Six Star Ranch (E. Porter, as Stuart), 1916
Six to Sixteen (Ewing, appendix), 1875
Six Who Pass While the Lentils Boil (play; S. Walker), 1916
Sixpence! (G. Avery), 1979
Sixpenny Island (Park), 1968
Sixpenny Runner (Lamplugh), 1960
Sixteen (Daly), 1961
Sixteen Sail in Aboukir Bay (Plowman), 1956
Six-Form Feud (H. Avery), 1926
Sixth-Grade Sleepover (Bunting), 1986
69th Grandchild (M. Hunt), 1951
Size Spies (Needle), 1979
Skate Patrol series (Bunting), from 1980
Skateboard Four (Bunting), 1976
Skateboard Saturday (Bunting), 1976
Skates! (Keats), 1973
Skating Rink (M. Lee), 1969
Skating Shoes (Streatfeild), 1951
Skein of Geese (Clewes), 1972
Skeleton at School (Needle), 1988
Skeleton Plays (play; Lillington), 1967
Skelton Hall series (Brent-Dyer), from 1962
Sker House (Welch, as Felton), 1954
Sketchbook Crime (H. Morgan), 1980
Sketches and Scraps (verse; L. Richards), 1881
Skewbald Pony (Chaucy), 1965
Ski Pup (D. Freeman), 1963

Skiffy series (Mayne), from 1972
Skiing to Danger (Allan), 1966
Skimpole's Snapshot (F. Richards, as Clifford), 1952
Skin (play; Foon), 1984
Skin Horse, (Bianco), 1927
Skin Spinners (verse; Aiken), 1976
Skinny (Burch), 1964
Skip (A. Fisher), 1958
Skip Around the Year (verse; Fisher), 1967
Skip for the Huntaway (Sutton), 1983
Skippack School (de Angeli), 1939
Skipper & Co. (Talbot), 1929
Skipper John's Cook (Marcia Brown), 1951
Skipping Village (Lenski), 1927
Skippy's Family (Meader), 1945
Skipton's Landing (Thiele), 1986
Skull Island (P. Turner), 1977
Skunks (Thiele), 1977
Skurry the Scout, Adventures of (Talbot), 1928
Sky Dog, (Turkle), 1969
Sky Full of Poems (verse; Merriam), 1986
Sky Gipsy (Watkins-Pitchford), 1939
Sky High (Hodges), 1947
Sky in the Pie (verse; McGough), 1983
Sky Is Free (M. Clark), 1974
Sky Island (Baum), 1912
Sky Man on the Totem Pole? (C. Harris), 1975
Sky Songs (verse; Livingston), 1984
Sky Was Blue (Zolotow), 1963
Sky-Blue Dragon (Kaye), 1983
Skyfire (Asch), 1984
Skylark (Peyton), 1989
Skyraker and the Iron Imp (Clewes), 1962
Skyrocket (Hader), 1946
Slake's Limbo (Holman), 1974
Slambash Wangs of a Compo Gormer (Leeson), 1987
Slap-Bang Boys (Brazil), 1917
Slappy Hooper (Bontemps), 1946
Slater's Mill (Monjo), 1972
Slave Dancer (Fox), 1973
Slave of the Moors (Ballantyne, appendix), 1888
Slaver's Apprentice (F. Knight), 1961
Slaves of Sabinus (Yonge, appendix), 1890
Slaves of Spiegel (Pinkwater), 1982
Slave's Tale (Haugaard), 1965
Sledges to the Rescue (R. Briggs), 1963
Sleep Book (verse; Seuss), 1962
Sleepers (Curry), 1968
Sleepers on the Hill (Waddell, as Sefton), 1973
Sleeping Beauty (play; Chorpenning), 1947
Sleeping Beauty (play; Fyleman), 1934
Sleeping Beauty (play; Miller), n.d.
Sleeping Beauty (play; Peet), 1959
Sleeping Beauty (play; L. Richards), 1916
Sleeping Beauty (play; B. Todd), 1956
Sleeping Giant (Estes), 1948
Sleeping Party (Needle), 1988
Sleeping Policeman (H. Todd), 1988
Sleeping Ugly (Yolen), 1981
Sleeping Witch (Storey), 1971
Sleepy ABC (verse; M. W. Brown), 1953
Sleepy Book (Zolotow), 1958
Sleepy Little Lion (M. W. Brown), 1947
Sleepyhead (Lipkind, as Will), 1957
Sleuths of the Air (Westerman), 1935
Slight Insurrection (play; J. Watson), 1980

Slimy Book (Cole), 1985
Slippery Shiney (Manning-Sanders), 1965
Slithers (Hoff), 1968
Slow and Sure (Alger, appendix), 1872
Slugger Sal's Slump (Hoff), 1979
Slum Cat, (Seton), 1915
Sly Cormorant (play; Patten), 1977
Sly Cormorant and the Three Fishes (verse; Patten), 1977
Sly Old Cat (Potter, 1971
Sly Old Wardrobe (Southall), 1968
Small Blue Hoping Stone (play; Melwood), 1976
Small Clay Bull (Poland), 1986
Small Cruse (verse; Fyleman), 1923
Small Fry (Merriam), 1965
Small House, Big Garden (Seed), 1965
Small Monkey Tales (Cunliffe), 1974
Small One (Wahl), 1983
Small Person Far Away (J. Kerr), 1980
Small Pig (Arnold Lobel), 1969
Small Pinch of Weather (Aiken), 1969
Small Poems series (Worth), from 1972
Small Pudding for Wee Gowrie (Mayne), 1983
Small Rabbit (P. Martin, as Miles), 1977
Small Railway Engines (Awdry), 1967
Small Rain (L'Engle), 1945
Small War of Sergeant Donkey (Daly), 1966
Small Wolf (Benchley), 1972
Small Wonders (verse; Farber), 1979
Smallest Bridesmaid (Storey), 1966
Smallest Dog on Earth (Weir), 1963
Smallest Doll (Storey), 1966
Smallest Elephant in the World (Tresselt), 1959
Smallest Turtle (Dodd), 1982
Smart Enough to Be Dumb (play; Clapp), 1956
Smartest Man in Ireland (M. Hunter), 1965
Smashing! (Hardcastle), 1970
Smeller Martin (Lawson), 1950
Smells and Spells (play; Doherty), 1978
Smelly Book (Cole), 1987
Smile like a Plastic Daisy (Levitin), 1984
Smiley Tiger (B. Willard), 1984
Smiling Face (Lattimore), 1973
Smiling Pool series (Burgess), from 1924
Smiling Rabbit (L. Wood), 1939
Smith (Garfield), 1967
Smith Family series (Blyton), 1947
Smith Family series (Fyleman), 1947
Smith of Wootton Major (Tolkien), 1967
Smith Valley (Means), 1973
Smiths series (Dalgliesh), from 1936
Smith's Hoard (Clarke), 1955
Smiths of Silver Lane (Talbot), 1929
Smith's Weakness (Fenn, appendix), 1896
Smitty series (Allen), from 1965
Smoke above the Lane (De Jong), 1951
Smoke from Cromwell's Time (Aiken), 1970
Smoke Horse (Faulknor), 1968
Smoke in Albert's Garden (Wayne), 1974
Smokey (verse; Peet), 1962
Smokey Horse, The Story of (Bisset), 1977
Smoky Joe series (Meynell), from 1952
Smoky the Cowhorse (James), 1926
Smoky-House (Goudge), 1940
Smouldering Fires (Everett-Green, appendix), 1905
Smudge of the Fells (Gard), 1965
Smuggler Ben (Blyton, as Pollock), 1943

Smuggler in the Bay (Catherall), 1980
Smuggers (Kimenye), 1966
Smugglers (Manning-Sanders), 1962
Smugglers' Gap (Atkinson), 1939
Smugglers of Penreen (Wynne), 1934
Smuggler's Way (Moore), 1924
Snackboat Sails at Noon! (Breary), 1946
Snail and the Pennithornes series (B. Willard), 1957
Snail Tale (Avi), 1972
Snail, Where Are You? (Ungerer), 1962
Snails' Place (M. Baker), 1970
Snake (Marshall), 1975
Snake! (Mitchison), 1976
Snake (Waber), 1978
Snake among the Sunflowers (Lingard), 1977
Snake and the Olive (McGregor), 1974
Snake Crook (Tomalin), 1976
Snake in the Camp (Cockett), 1975
Snake in the Carpool (Schlein), 1963
Snake in the Old Hut (Sherry), 1972
Snake River (Chambers), 1975
Snake Tree (Rounds), 1966
Snake Whistle (Greaves), 1980
Snakerun (Hardcastle), 1980
Snakes and Ladders (verse; R. Klein), 1985
Snakes and Snakes (King), 1975
Snakey Boo series (Bisset), 1982
Snapdragon (Ewing, appendix), 1888
Snapping Turtle's All-Wrong Day (Parish), 1970
Snaps (Berg), 1977
Snapshots (N. Klein), 1984
Snapshots of Paradise (Geras), 1984
Snarkout Boys series (Pinkwater), from 1982
Snatched (Fisk), 1983
Snatched (Parker), 1974
Sneakers (M. W. Brown), 1979
Sneetches (verse; Seuss), 1961
Sneeze and Be Slain (N. Hunter), 1980
Sneezing Powder (play; Blyton), 1939
Snip (Benchley), 1981
Sniper (T. Taylor), 1989
Snippy and Snappy (Gág), 1931
Snobs, Beware (Sharmat), 1986
Snookered! (Hardcastle), 1987
Snopp on the Sidewalk (verse; Prelutsky), 1977
Snorri and the Strangers (Benchley), 1976
Snow Bear (Ainsworth), 1956
Snow Bird (Pye), 1941
Snow Dog (Kjelgaard), 1948
Snow Fairies (Wynne), 1947
Snow Filly (Mitchell), 1961
Snow Firing (Gard), 1967
Snow in the City (Hader), 1963
Snow in the Maze (B.C. Freeman), 1979
Snow Parlor (Coatsworth), 1971
Snow Party (de Regniers), 1959
Snow Rabbit (N. Willard), 1975
Snow Spider (Nimmo), 1986
Snow Time (Schlein), 1962
Snow Tracks (George), 1958
Snow White and Rose Red (play; Miller), 1951
Snow White in New York (F. French), 1986
Snow Witch (play; C. D. Mackay), 1910
Snow Woman (McKee), 1987
Snowball (Sleigh), 1969
Snowball the Pony (Blyton), 1953

Snowbound by the Whitewater (Reid), 1975
Snow-Clean Pinny (McNeill), 1973
Snowdrop (Howes), 1923
Snowdrop Story Book (Blyton), 1952
Snowed Up (Fry), 1970
Snowflakes and Sunbeams (Ballantyne, appendix), 1856
Snowman series (R. Briggs), from 1978
Snowman of Biddle (Greaves), 1971
Snowman Snuffles Sniffles (verse; Bodecker), 1983
Snow-White (play; Fyleman), 1936
Snowy and Woody (Duvoisin), 1979
Snowy Day (Keats), 1962
Snowy River Brumby (Mitchell), 1980
Snuffle to the Rescue (Beresford), 1975
Snuffles for Short (Chaundler), 1921
Snuffy series (Bruna, trans), from 1970
Snug and Serena series (Uttley), from 1950
Snuggle Tales (Baum), 1916
Snugglepot and Cuddlepie (Gibbs), 1918
So As by Fire (Sidney, appendix), 1881
So Long, Grandpa (Donnelly, trans), 1980
So Many Cats! (verse; de Regniers), 1985
So Many Raccoons (Wahl), 1985
So This Is School! (Breary), 1959
Soap Box Car (Tate), 1967
Soap Box Derby (Weir), 1962
Soapy and the Pharaoh's Curse (Lillington), 1957
Soccer Comes First (Hardcastle), 1971
Soccer Is Also a Game (Hardcastle), 1978
Soccer Special (Hardcastle), 1978
Sociable Toby (Clymer), 1956
Society of Foxes (Wibberley, as O'Connor), 1954
Socks (Cleary), 1973
Sod House (Coatsworth), 1954
Soft Shoe (M. Clark), 1988
Soft Skull Sam (Hoff), 1981
Soldier and Me (Line), 1965
Soldier of Manhattan (Altsheler), 1897
Soldier's Children (verse; Ewing, appendix), 1883
Soldier's Daughter (Henty, appendix), 1906
Soldiers of the Queen (H. Avery), 1897
Soldier's Son and the Battle He Fought (Everett-Green,
    appendix), 1895
Sole Survivors (Henty, appendix), 1901
Solid Gold Kid (Mazer), 1977
Solitary (L. Hall), 1986
Solitary Blue (Voigt), 1983
Solomon Leviathan's Nine Hundred and Thirty-First Trip Around
    the World (Le Guin), 1983
Solomon System (Naylor), 1983
Solomon the Rusty Nail (Steig), 1985
Solomon's Child (M. Clark), 1981
Solomon's Search (Holman), 1970
Solve-It-Yourself Mysteries (Waddell), 1983
Some Builders (Le Feuvre), 1913
Some California Poppies and How They Grew (Means), n.d.
Some Merry-Go-Round Music (Stolz), 1959
Some Moonshine Tales (Uttley), 1945
Some Say (L. Richards), 1896
Some Snow Said Hello (Hoban), 1963
Some Things Are Scary (Heide), 1971
Some Things Go Together (verse; Zolotow), 1969
Somebody Else's Nut Tree (Krauss), 1958
Somebody Go and Bang a Drum (Caudill), 1974
Somebody Spilled the Sky (verse; Krauss), 1979
Somebody's Dog (P. Martin, as Miles), 1973

Someday (Zolotow), 1965
Someone Could Win a Polar Bear (verse; Ciardi), 1970
Someone in the Attic (Wayne), 1967
Someone Is Hiding on Alcatraz Island (Bunting), 1984
Someone New (Zolotow), 1978
Someone to Love (Mazer), 1983
Someplace Beautiful (Brinsmead), 1986
Something (Babbitt), 1970
Something Big (Cockett), 1968
Something for Christmas (Palmer Brown), 1958
Something for Now, Something for Later (Schlein), 1956
Something I Remember (verse; Farjeon), 1987
Something in the Barn (Wayne), 1971
Something in Thurlo Darby's House (Alderson), 1984
Something Is Going to Happen (Zolotow), 1988
Something Like a Snake (Fenn, appendix), 1901
Something Old, Something New (D. Fisher), 1949
Something Out of Nothing (Colman), 1968
Something Sleeping in the Hall (verse; Kuskin), 1985
Something Special (verse; de Regniers), 1958
Something Special for Me (V. Williams), 1983
Something to Shout About (P. Beatty), 1976
Something Upstairs (Avi), 1988
Something-Special Horse (L. Hall), 1985
Sometime Stories (Bisset), 1957
Sometimes I Don't Love My Mother (Colman), 1977
Sometimes I Think I Hear My Name (Avi), 1982
Sometimes Mama and Papa Fight (Sharmat), 1980
Somewhere Else (Sudbery), 1978
Son of a Gun (Ahlberg), 1979
Son of Charlemagne (B. Willard), 1959
Son of Someone Famous (M. Kerr), 1974
Son of the Lamp-Maker (North), 1956
Son of the Salmon-People (Evans), 1981
Son of the Slime That Ate Cleveland (Sharmat), 1985
Son of the Valley (Tunis), 1949
Son of the Whirlwind (Mitchell), 1976
Son of the Whiteman (Best), 1931
Son Philip (Fenn, appendix), 1885
Song (Zolotow), 1982
Song for a Dark Queen (Sutcliff), 1978
Song for Clowns (Wersba), 1965
Song for Gar (Merrill), 1957
Song I Sang to You (verse; Livingston), 1984
Song in My Drum (Hoban), 1962
Song in My Head (verse; Holland), 1985
Song of Pentecost (W. Corbett), 1982
Song of St. Francis (Bulla), 1952
Song of the Boat (L. Graham), 1975
Song of the City (verse; Owen), 1985
Song of the Horse (R. Kennedy), 1981
Song of the Lop-Eared Mule (Carlson), 1961
Song of the Nightingale (F. French), 1986
Song of the Pearl (Nichols), 1976
Song of the South (play; Peet), 1946
Song of the Trees (M. Taylor), 1975
Song of Thunder (Ray), 1978
Song of Wirrun (Wrightson), 1987
Song under the Water (Morris), 1985
Songberd's Grove (Barrett), 1957
Song-Garden for Children (verse; H. Graham), 1906
Songs for Music and Lyrical Poems (verse; Farjeon), 1922
Songs for My Dog (verse; Fatchen), 1980
Songs for My Thongs (verse; Thiele), 1982
Songs from Dreamland (verse; L. Duncan), 1989
Songs from Punch (verse; Farjeon), 1925

Songs of Childhood (verse; de la Mare, as Ramal), 1902
Songs of Gladness (verse; Blyton), 1924
Songs of Happiness (verse; Bailey), 1912
Songs of Kings and Queens (verse; Farjeon), 1938
Songs of Mr. Small (verse; Lenski), 1954
Songs of the City (verse; Lenski), 1956
Songs of the Fog Maiden (de Paola), 1979
Songs of the Happy Isles (verse; Peacocke), 1910
Songs of Two Seasons (verse; Nesbit), 1890
Songs to Sing about Things You Think About (verse; Heide), 1971
Sonia Back Stage (Meynell), 1957
Sonora Beautiful (Clifton), 1981
Sons from Afar (Voigt), 1987
Sons of the Steppe (Baumann, trans), 1958
Sonya-by-the-Shore (Cresswell), 1960
Soonie and the Dragon (S. Murphy), 1979
Sooty series (Blyton), 1955
Sophia Scrooby Preserved (M. Bacon), 1968
Sophie and Gussie series (Sharmat), from 1973
Soppy Birthday (Ure), 1988
Sorely Trying Day (Hoban), 1964
Sorority Sisters series (Sharmat), from 1986
Soul of Honour (Stretton, appendix), 1898
Soul of Margaret Rand (Meade, appendix), 1911
Soul-Brothers and Sister Lou (K. Hunter), 1968
Sound and Motion Stories, Seven (J. Kraus), 1971
Sound of Chariots (M. Hunter), 1972
Sound of Coaches (Garfield), 1974
Sound of Crying (Sudbery), 1970
Sound of Dragon's Feet (Zei, trans), 1979
Sound of Pens (Tomalin, as Leaver), 1955
Sound of Propellers (King), 1986
Sound of Sunshine, Sound of Rain (Heide), 1970
Sound of Trumpets (McLean), 1966
Sound to Remember (Levitin), 1979
Sounder (W. Armstrong), 1969
Soup series (R. N. Peck), from 1974
Sour Land (W. Armstrong), 1971
South Country Secrets (B. Todd, as Euphan), 1935
South of Cape Horn (Sperry), 1958
South Sea Adventure (W. Price), 1952
South Swell (Wibberley, as O'Connor), 1967
South Town series (L. Graham), from 1958
Southerly Buster (Mattingley), 1983
Southwark Originals (play; Wymark), 1975
Sowing and Sewing (Yonge, appendix), 1882
Space Agent series (MacVicar), from 1961
Space Cadet (Heinlein), 1948
Space Captives of the Golden Men (Patchett), 1953
Space Case (Marshall, as E. Marshall), 1980
Space Demons (Rubinstein), 1986
Space Family Stone (Heinlein), 1969
Space Hostages (Fisk), 1967
Space Hut (Wier), 1967
Space People (Bunting), 1978
Space Ship series (Slobodkin), from 1952
Space Songs (verse; Livingston), 1988
Space Story (A, Kuskin), 1978
Space Trap (M. Hughes), 1983
Space Witch (D. Freeman), 1959
Spacemare (play; T. Ross), 1985
Spaniards Are Coming! (Manning-Sanders), 1969
Spaniards Came at Dawn (Syme), 1959
Spanish Cloak (play; Fyleman), 1939
Spanish Hoof (R. N. Peck), 1985
Spanish Letters (M. Hunter), 1964

Spanish Main, Stories of the (Stockton, appendix), 1913
Spanish Smile (O'Dell), 1982
Spark of Opal (M. Clark), 1968
Sparkplug of the Hornets (Meader), 1953
Sparky (Gramatky), 1952
Sparrow Alone (Colum), 1975
Sparrow and the Goat (Fyleman), 1951
Sparrow Bush (verse; Coatsworth), 1966
Sparrow Child (Trevor), 1958
Sparrow Socks (Selden), 1965
Sparrow's Song (Wallace), 1986
Spartan (Snedeker), 1912
Speak Up (verse; McCord), 1980
Special Birthday Party for Someone Very Special (de Regnier, as Kitt), 1966
Special Occasions (McNeill), 1960
Special Present (Mattingley), 1976
Special Providence (MacGibbon), 1964
Special Year (Lampman), 1959
Specially Wonderful Day (verse; Clapp), 1972
Speckled Hen (Uttley), 1946
Specs McCann series (McNeill), from 1955
Spectacles (Raskin), 1968
Spectacles for the Mole (Dehn), 1968
Spectre (Nixon), 1982
Spectrum, (D. Rees), 1977
Speed Six! (B. Carter), 1953
Speedboat (Marshall), 1976
Speedway Contender (Bonham), 1964
Spell Is Cast (Cameron), 1964
Spell Me a Witch (B. Willard), 1979
Spell of Sleep (Beachcroft), 1976
Spell of White Sturgeon (Kjelgaard), 1953
Spell Seven (Parker), 1971
Spellbound Jellybaby (play; Wymark), 1975
Spellcoats (Jones), 1979
Spellhorn (Doherty), 1989
Spettecake Holiday (Unnerstad, trans), 1958
Sphinx at Dawn (L'Engle), 1982
Spice Island Mystery (Cavanna), 1969
Spice Woman's Basket (Uttley), 1944
Spider Dog (Cumming), 1936
Spider Jane series (Yolen), from 1978
Spider, The Cave, and the Pottery Bowl (Clymer), 1971
Spider's Palace (R. Hughes), 1931
Spider's Web (Keeping), 1972
Spiderweb for Two (Enright), 1951
Spike Kelly of the Commandos (R. Montgomery), 1942
Spill (Aaron), 1977
Spinach Boy (Lenski), 1930
Spindle Bottom series (Allan), from 1984
Spine Chillers (Oldfield), 1987
Spinky Sulks (Steig), 1988
Spid (Moray Williams), 1985
Spider series (R. Kraus), from 1970
Spinning-Wheel Stories (Alcott, appendix), 1884
Spiral Stair (Aiken), 1979
Spirit Is Willing (B. Baker), 1974
Spirit of Christmas (Wiggin), 1927
Spirit River (M. Hughes), 1988
Spirit Wind (Fatchen), 1973
Spit Nolan (Naughton), 1974
Spitball Gang (Paulsen), 1980
Spitfire Grave (Gordon), 1979
Spitfire Parade (Johns), 1941
Splash (Hardcastle, as Clark), 1972

Splendid Picnic (B. Todd), 1937
Splintered Sword (Treece), 1965
Splish Splash Sounds (Scarry), 1988
Spoil-Sport (H. Avery), 1923
Spongees (play; Morris), 1965
Spook Birds (Bunting), 1981
Spooky series (Carlson), from 1982
Spooky Tail of Prewit Peacock (Peet), 1972
Spooky Thing (W. Steele), 1960
Sport (Fitzhugh), 1979
Sport of the School (Talbot), 1923
Sports Pages (Adoff), 1986
Spotty (M. Rey), 1945
Spreading Stain (Finger), 1927
Spreading the News (play; Blyton), 1939
Sprig of Broom (B. Willard), 1971
Spring Adventure (Pudney), 1961
Spring Begins in March (Little), 1966
Spring Cleaning (Burnett), 1908
Spring Comes Riding (Cavanna), 1950
Spring Is Here (verse; Lenski), 1945
Spring Magic (play; Ridge), 1953
Spring Morning, The Story of a (Molesworth, appendix), 1890
Spring of the Year (Vipont), 1957
Spring Snow (Duvoisin), 1963
Spring, Summer, Autumn, Winter (verse; T. Hughes) 1974
Spring Tide (Ray), 1969
Springboard to Summer (Bunting, as A.E. Bunting), 1975
Springdale series (D. Bruce), from 1932
Springfellow series (R. Kraus), from 1965
Springfield Home (Strucley), 1961
Sprout series (Wayne), from 1970
Sprung! (R. Klein), 1982
Spunky (Hader), 1933
Spurs for Suzanna (Cavanna), 1947
Spy Catchers (Trease), 1976
Spy Hill (Seed), 1984
Spy in Dolor Hugo (MacGibbon), 1973
Spy in the Hills (Saville), 1945
Spy in the Neighborhood (Sharmat), 1974
Spy, The No-Good Pup (Stranger), 1989
Squadron Leader (Westerman), 1946
Squanderbug series (play; A. Fisher), from 1943
Squanto (Bulla), 1954
Square as a House (verse; Kuskin), 1960
Square Pegs (Sharmat), 1982
Squash Pie (M. Steele, as Gage), 1976
Squaw Dog (P. Beatty), 1965
Squaw Man's Son (Lampman), 1978
Squeak Saves the Day (Snyder), 1988
Squeaky series (R. Kraus, as Silly), 1982
Squib (Bawden), 1971
Squib and His Friends (Everett-Green, appendix), 1896
Squire's Daughters (Everett-Green, appendix), 1932
Squire's Heir (Everett-Green, appendix), 1903
Squire's Little Girl (Meade, appendix), 1902
Squirrel series (Uttley), from 1929
Squirrel Called Rufus (Church), 1941
Squirrel Hotel (du Bois), 1952
Squirrel Nutkin, The Tale of (Potter), 1903
Squirrel Wife (Pearce), 1971
Squirrel's Secret (play; Blyton), 1935
Stable of Fear (Bunting, as Bolton), 1974
Staffordshire Terror (P. Beatty), 1979
Stage Fright (Howe), 1986
Stained Glass Window (Lively), 1976

Stalker (Nixon), 1985
Stalky & Co. (Kipling), 1899
Stallion from the Sea (Fidler), 1953
Stallion of the Sands (H. Griffiths), 1968
Stamp Twice for Murder (Cavanna), 1981
Stan (Pilling), 1988
Stan Ball of the Rangers (R. Montgomery), 1941
Stan Lynn (Fenn, appendix), 1902
Stand and Deliver (play; Daniell), 1948
Stand in the Wind (Little), 1975
Stand to Horse (A. Norton), 1956
Standing Lions (Ray), 1968
Standing on a Strawberry (verse; Cunliffe), 1987
Standish series (Westerman), from 1935
Stanley (Hoff), 1962
Stanley and Rhoda (Wells), 1978
Staples for Amos (A. Morgan), 1986
Star and the Flame (Weir), 1962
Star Baby (Nixon), 1989
Star Beast (Heinlein), 1954
Star Born (A. Norton), 1957
Star Bright (L. Richards), 1927
Star for Ginny (Whitney), 1942
Star for My Son (play; Greaves), 1980
Star for the Latecomer (Zindel), 1980
Star Gate (A. Norton), 1958
Star Guard (A. Norton), 1955
Star in the Hand (Stucley), 1946
Star in the Pail (verse; McCord), 1975
Star Ka'at series (A. Norton), from 1976
Star Lord (L. Lawrence), 1978
Star Man's Son, 2250 A.D. (A. Norton), 1952
Star of Gettysburg (Altsheler), 1915
Star of Night (Paterson), 1980
Star of Wild Horse Canyon (Bulla), 1953
Star Raiders (Suddaby), 1950
Star Rangers (A. Norton), 1953
Star Shine (C. Greene), 1985
Star Spangled Salute (play; A. Harris), 1975
Star Trap (Darke), 1974
Starbaby (Asch), 1980
Starbuck Valley Winter (Haig-Brown), 1943
Starlight Barking (Dodie Smith), 1967
Starlight Tales, Nine (Uttley), 1942
Starling and the Fox (Fyleman), 1951
Starman Jones (Heinlein), 1953
Star-Riders of the Moor (J. Pullein-Thompson), 1976
Starring Becky Suslow (Orgel), 1989
Starring Sally J. Freedman as Herself (Blume), 1977
Starry Floor (verse; Farjeon), 1949
Starry Night (Waddell, as Sefton), 1986
Stars Are Ours! (A. Norton), 1954
Stars of Fortune (Harnett), 1956
Stars in Her Eyes (Cavanna), 1958
Starship Troopers (Heinlein), 1959
Starstormer series (Fisk), from 1980
Starters (play; Wymark), 1975
Starting Out series (play; Storr), from 1973
Starting Point (Kamm), 1975
Station (Ridge), 1956
Station Four (P. Beatty), 1969
Station-Master's Hen (Seed), 1987
Staunch as Steel (Fenn, appendix), 1927
Stay at Home Ben (C. Pullein-Thompson), 1987
Staying at Home on a Rainy Day (Iwasaki, trans), 1969
Staying Up (Swindells), 1986

Summer at Sea (Allan), 1965
Summer at Town's End (Allan), 1954
Summer Birds (Farmer), 1962
Summer Book (Jansson, trans), 1975
Summer Fun (Haywood), 1986
Summer Ghost (Tomalin), 1986
Summer Girls, Love Boys (Mazer), 1982
Summer Goes Riding (Truss), 1987
Summer Holiday (Everett-Green, appendix), 1890
Summer in a Cañon (Wiggin), 1889
Summer in Between (Spence), 1959
Summer in Britanny (Allan), 1960
Summer in Provence (Allan, as Pilgrim), 1963
Summer in Small Street (Kaye), 1989
Summer in the South (Marshall), 1977
Summer Is... (Zolotow), 1967
Summer Is a Festival (Pamela Brown), 1972
Summer Is for Growing (A. Clark), 1968
Summer Night (Zolotow), 1974
Summer of Decision (Allan), 1957
Summer of Fear (L. Duncan), 1976
Summer of Little Rain (A. Fisher), 1961
Summer of My First Love (Holland), 1981
Summer of My German Soldier (B. Greene), 1973
Summer of the Falcon (George), 1962
Summer of the Golden Stag (Finlay), 1969
Summer of the Great Secret (M. Edwards), 1948
Summer of the Silent Hands (Weir), 1969
Summer of the Swans (Byars), 1970
Summer on Boomerang Beach (Patchett), 1967
Summer on Wild Horse Island (Patchett), 1965
Summer People (Townsend), 1972
Summer Rules (Lipsyte), 1981
Summer Season (B. Willard), 1981
Summer Snowman (Zion), 1955
Summer Snowmen (verse; Ahlberg), 1983
Summer Stories (Molesworth, appendix), 1882
Summer Surprise (Robinson), 1977
Summer Switch (Rodgers), 1982
Summer to Die (Lowry), 1977
Summer Travellers (B.C. Freeman), 1978
Summer Visitors (Mayne), 1961
Summer with Spike (B. Willard), 1961
Summerboy (Lipsyte), 1982
Summer-House Loon (Fine), 1978
Summer's End (A. Lawrence), 1987
Summer's Lease (Sachs), 1979
Summers of the Wild Rose (R. Harris), 1987
Sun and Moon (Mitchison), 1970
Sun and the Wind and Mr. Todd (Estes), 1943
Sun City (Jansson, trans), 1976
Sun God, Moon Witch (Katz), 1986
Sun Goddess, (play; C. D. Mackay), 1916
Sun, He Dies (Highwater), 1980
Sun Horse (C. Clark), 1951
Sun Horse, Moon Horse (Sutcliff), 1977
Sun of Quebec (Altsheler), 1919
Sun of Saratoga (Altsheler), 1897
Sun of York (Welch), 1970
Sun on the Stubble (Thiele), 1961
Sun Salutes You (Palmer), 1970
Sun Slower, Sun Faster (Trevor), 1955
Sun, The Wind, The Sea, and the Rain (Schlein), 1960
Sun Up (James), 1931
Sun Up (Tresselt), 1949
Sunbridge Girls at Six Star Ranch (E. Porter, as Stuart), 1913

Sunburst (Fisk), 1980
Sunday Adventure (Pudney), 1950
Sunday in the Park (Clymer, as Bell), 1946
Sunday Morning (Viorst), 1968
Sunday School Stories (L. Hale, appendix), 1889
Sundown Songs (verse; L. Richards), 1899
Sunflower Giant (Cockett), 1966
Sunk at Sea (Ballantyne, appendix), 1869
Sunny Book (verse; Fyleman), 1918
Sunny Side of the Street (Everett-Green, appendix), 1895
Sunny Story Book (Blyton), 1945
Sunny Tales for Snowy Days (Nesbit), 1893
Sunrise Tomorrow (Mitchison), 1973
Sun's Babies (Howes), 1910
Sun's Daughter (Kariuki), 1976
Sun's Promise (B. Baker), 1962
Sunshine (verse; Bemelmans), 1950
Sunshine (N. Klein), 1975
Sunshine (play; T. Taylor), 1974
Sunshine Book (Blyton), 1965
Sunshine Children (Wynne), 1924
Sunshine Family (E. Turner), 1923
Sunshine Picture Story Book (Blyton), 1964
Sunshine Years (N. Klein), 1975
Sunshiny Stories (Heward), 1924
Super Dooper Jezebel (T. Ross), 1988
Super Nova (MacVicar), from 1969
Superduper Teddy (Hurwitz), 1980
Superfudge (Blume), 1980
Supergirl (Mazer), 1984
Supergirl Storybook (Sharmat, as Andrews), 1984
Superhare (Heine, trans), 1979
Supermarket Mystery (Scarry), 1969
Supermouse (Ure), 1984
Supersleuth (J. Wilson), 1987
Suppose You Met a Witch (verse; Serraillier), 1973
Supreme Souvenir Factory (Stevenson), 1988
Surfer and the City Girl (Cavanna), 1981
Surfing Country (Bunting, as A.E. Bunting), 1974
Surgeon's Boy (Sutton), 1983
Surprise (play; Fyleman), 1934
Surprise for a Cowboy (Bulla), 1950
Surprise for Mother (Lenski), 1934
Surprise in the Mountains (Carlson), 1983
Surprise Island (Talbot), 1933
Surprise Island (B. Willard), 1966
Surprise Mouse (Mattingley), 1974
Surprise Party (Bonsall, as Newell), 1955
Surprise Party (Hutchins), 1969
Surprise Stories (Bailey), 1923
Surprising Adventures of the Magical Monarch of Mo
    (Baum), 1903
Surprising Broom (Blyton), 1955
Surprising Caravan (Blyton), 1946
Surrogate Sister (Bunting), 1984
Survival Camp! (Bunting), 1978
Susan (verse; MacIntyre), 1944
Susan (Smucker), 1972
Susan and Aladdin's Lamp (play; Clapp), 1957
Susan, Beware! (M. Hunt), 1937
Susan, Bill series (Saville), from 1954
Susan Cornish (Caudill), 1955
Susan Sometimes (Krasilovsky), 1962
Susanna B. and William C. (Field), 1934
Susannah Adventure (Brent-Dyer), 1953
Susan's Story (Berg), 1970

Tamar's Wager (Coatsworth), 1971
Taming of Tiger (Lattimore), 1975
Taming the Star Runner (Hinton), 1988
Tamworth Pig series (Kemp), from 1972
Tangara (Chauncy), 1960
Tangle Garden (Vining, as Gray), 1928
Tangled Skein (play; L. Richards), 1915
Tangled Waters (Means), 1936
Tangled Web (L. Montgomery),1931
Tania Takes the Stage (Weir), 1961
Tank Commander (Welch), 1972
Tanker Trap (Catherall), 1965
Tann's Boarders (Barne), 1955
Tansy of Tring Street (Allan), 1960
Tanya and Trixie (Thiele), 1980
Tap, Tap, Lion (Fritz), 1962
Tapestry Room (Molesworth, appendix), 1879
Tara Finds the Door to Happiness (play; Means), n.d.
Taramindo! (Marcia Brown), 1960
Taran Wanderer (Alexander), 1967
Tar-Baby (verse; J. Harris, appendix), 1904
Target Island (B. Carter), 1956
Tarka the Otter (Williamson), 1927
Taronga (Kelleher), 1986
Tarrydiddle Town (Blyton), 1929
Taste of Blackberries (D. B. Smith), 1973
Taste of Freedom (Lester), 1983
Tatsinda (Enright), 1963
Tattered Tom (Alger, appendix), 1871
Tatters (Peacocke), 1928
Tattie's River Journey (S. Murphy), 1983
Tattooed Man (Pease), 1926
Tattooed Potato (Raskin), 1975
Tatty Apple (Nimmo), 1984
Taunus Mountains, Tales of the (Dehn), 1937
Tavi of Gold (play; Moray Williams), 1933
Tawia Goes to Sea (Asare), 1970
Tawno (Kaye), 1968
Tawny and Dingo, The Tale of (W. Armstrong), 1979
Tawnymore (Shannon), 1931
Taxi! (Tate), 1973
Taxis and Toadstools (verse; Field), 1926
Tea at Mrs. Manderby's (Geras), 1976
Tea for Two (Beaman), 1942
Tea Party (Mayne, as Molin), 1966
Tea Time Tales (Fyleman), 1930
Teabag and the Bears (M. Baker), 1970
Teacher's Pet (Hurwitz), 1988
Teacher's Pet (P. Martin, as Miles), 1966
Teacup Full of Roses (Mathis), 1972
Tea-Leaf on the Roof (Ure), 1987
Team (Peyton), 1975
Team That Wouldn't Give In (Hardcastle), 1984
Teapots and Quails (verse; Lear, appendix), 1953
Teasing Monkey, The Story of the (Bannerman), 1906
Tea-Time Tales, Twenty (Fyleman), 1929
Technical Fifth (Chaundler), 1930
Ted and Nina series (de Angeli), from 1935
Teddy (Clymer, as Kinsey), 1945
Teddy and Carrots (Otis, appendix), 1896
Teddy Bear, Tales of (Judah), 1958
Teddy Bear Habit (Collier), 1967
Teddy Bear's Party (Blyton), 1945
Teddy Bear's Scrapbook (Howe), 1980
Teddy Robinson series (Robinson), from 1953
Teddy's Button! (Le Feuvre), 1896

Teddy's New Job (Beaman), 1927
Ted's Lucky Ball (Meynell, as Tring), 1961
Teeny Tiny Tales (Scarry), 1965
Teeny, Tiny Witches (Wahl), 1979
Teenywiggles (Peacocke), 1921
Teeth of the Gale (Aiken), 1988
Teetoncey series (T. Taylor), from 1974
Telegraph Boy (Alger, appendix), 1879
Telephone (Chukovsky, trans), 1961
Telephone Tales (Rodari, trans), 1965
Television Mystery (Beresford), 1957
Television Twins (Pamela Brown), 1952
Tell about the Cowbarn, Daddy (Merrill), 1963
Tell Me a Story (D. Fisher), 1940
Tell Me a Story (Molesworth, as Graham, appendix), 1875
Tell Me If the Lovers Are Losers (Voigt), 1982
Tell Me No Lies (Colman), 1978
Tell Me Some More (Bonsall), 1961
Tell the Time (McCaughrean), 1986
Tell Us Your Secret (Cohen), 1989
Tell-a-Story Book (Blyton), 1964
Tell-Tale from Hill and Dale (verse; L. Richards), 1886
Tell-Tale-Tit (Marchant), 1899
Temple of the Sun (Lampman), 1964
Ten Apples Up On Top! (verse; Seuss, as Le Sieg), 1961
Ten Commandments of the Animal World (Seton), 1923
Ten Fathoms Deep (Catherall), 1954
Ten in a Bed (Ahlberg), 1983
Ten Little Jappy Chaps (Farrow), 1905
Ten Mile Treasure (A. Norton), 1981
Ten Minute Tales (Blyton), 1934
Ten Minute Tales and Dialogue series (Power), 1943
Ten Pounds Reward (Strang), 1926
Ten Thousand Golden Cockerels (Hildick), 1970
Ten What? (Hoban), 1974
Ten-Cent Island (Park), 1968
Tenderfoot Trapper (Catherall), 1958
Tenement Tree (Seredy), 1959
Tennis Menace (Heide, as Allen), 1975
Tennis Shoes (Streatfeild), 1937
Tent for the Sun (Ray), 1971
Tenth at Trinder's (Moore), 1927
Tenth Good Thing about Barney (Viorst), 1971
'Tention! (Fenn, appendix), 1906
Teresita of the Valley (Means), 1943
Term of Many Adventures (Wynne), 1939
Term on Trial (H. Avery), 1930
Term to Remember (Wynne), 1930
Terrible Churnadryne (Cameron), 1959
Terrible Coward (Fenn, appendix), 1885
Terrible Fisk Machine (play; Jones), 1970
Terrible Jane (Holman), 1987
Terrible Roar (Pinkwater, as Manus Pinkwater), 1970
Terrible Scar (Storr), 1976
Terrible Tales of Happy Days School (verse; L. Duncan), 1983
Terrible Taniha of Timberditch (Cowley), 1982
Terrible Temptation (Arundel), 1971
Terrible, Terrifying Toby (C. Johnson), 1957
Terrible Things (Bunting), 1980
Terrible Tiger (verse; Prelutsky), 1969
Terrible Tomboy (Brazil), 1904
Terrible Troll-Bird (d'Aulaire), 1976
Terribly Plain Princess (Oldfield), 1977
Terrie's Moorland Home (Le Feuvre), 1918
Terror by Night (Vipont), 1966
Terror of Manooka (Patchett), 1966

Terror of the Seas (Westerman), 1927
Terry on the Fence (Ashley), 1975
Terry the Black Sheep (Wynne), 1928
Terry the Girl-Guide (Moore), 1912
Terry's Brrmmm GT (Greenwood), 1974
Terry's Only Term (Talbot), 1939
Tessie (Jackson), 1968
Test (play; Fyleman), 1934
Tested! (Le Feuvre), 1911
Testing of Tertius (Newman), 1973
Testing of the Torment (Oxenham), 1925
Testing Year (Clewes), 1977
Tex (Hinton), 1979
Texan series (Altsheler), from 1912
Texas Tomboy (Lenski), 1950
Thalia the Failure (R. Klein), 1984
Thames in Story (Fidler), 1971
Thank You, Jackie Robinson (Cohen), 1974
Thanksgiving for All (play; Latham, as Lee), 1932
Thanksgiving Mystery (Nixon), 1979
Thanksgiving Programs (plays; Latham, as Lee), 1937
Thar She Blows (R. Montgomery, as Proctor), 1945
That Baby (Berg), 1972
That Boarding School Girl (D. Bruce), 1925
That Brilliant Peggy (Meade, appendix), 1903
That Cat! (P. Martin), 1970
That Dreadful Boy! (Marchant), 1901
That Dreadful Day (Stevenson), 1985
That Early Spring (Beckman, trans), 1977
That Fool of a Priest (Rush), 1970
That Girl (E. Turner), 1908
That Girl Andy (Means), 1962
That Noodle-Head Epaminondas (Merriam), 1972
That Stick (Yonge, appendix), 1892
That Terrible Halloween Night (Stevenson), 1980
That Was Then, This Is Now (Hinton), 1971
That Wild Australian School-girl (Talbot), 1925
That's Good, That's Bad (Lexau), 1963
That's My Baby! (verse; Ahlberg), 1983
That's One Ornery Orphan (P. Beatty), 1980
That's Silly (Sleator), 1981
That's the Way It Is, Amigo (Colman), 1975
That's What Friends Are For (Heide), 1968
That's Why (verse; A. Fisher), 1946
Theater Cat (Streatfeild), 1951
Theater Shoes (Streatfeild), 1945
Theatre Royal series (Beaman), from 1943
Thee, Hannah! (de Angeli), 1940
Theft of the Golden Cat (Green), 1955
Their First Igloo on Baffin Island (Henry), 1943
Their Girl Chum (Wynne), 1935
Them That Glitter and Them That Don't (B. Greene), 1983
Then Again, Maybe I Won't (Blume), 1971
Then There Were Five (Enright), 1944
Then There Were Three (verse; Farjeon), 1958
Theodore series (Ormondroyd), from 1966
Theodore and the Talking Mushroom (Lionni), 1971
Theodore Turtle (MacGregor), 1955
Theories and Thumbs (play; Field), 1924
Theras and His Town (Snedeker), 1924
There and Back Again (A. Lawrence), 1985
There, Far Beyond the River (Korientz, trans), 1973
There for the Picking (Cockett), 1966
There Goes Feathertop! (verse; Farber), 1979
There Goes the Tiger! (P. Martin), 1970
There Is No Rhyme for Silver (verse; Merriam), 1962

There Is Something New under the Sun (play; Baum), 1903
There Once Was a Woman Who Married a Man
   (verse; Farber), 1978
There Was a Little Pig (Strang), 1926
There Was a Place (verse; Livingston), 1988
There Was an Old Woman (play; D. Wood), 1979
There's a Bat in Bunk Five (Danziger), 1980
There's a Man in That Tree (play; McNeill), 1968
There's a Monster under My Bed (Howe), 1986
There's a Wocket in My Pocket! (verse; Seuss), 1974
There's Always Danny (Ure), 1988
There's an End of May (play; Lillington), 1975
There's No Escape (Serraillier), 1950
There's No Place like Home (Marc Brown), 1984
There's Nothing to Do! (Stevenson), 1986
There's Something on the Roof! (Fisk), 1966
These Happy Golden Years (Wilder), 1943
They All Saw It (M. W. Brown), 1944
They Both Liked Dogs (Brent-Dyer), 1938
They Bought Her a Pony (Cannan), 1944
They Came from Aargh! (Hoban), 1981
They Came South (M. Clark), 1963
They Came South (play; M. Clark), 1965
They Came to an Island (Syme), 1955
They Didn't Come Back (Berna, trans), 1969
They Found a Cave (Chauncy), 1948
They Had a Horse (Edmonds), 1962
They Made the Royal Arms (play; Barne), 1937
They Never Came Home (L. Duncan), 1969
They Raced for Treasure (Serraillier), 1946
They Ran Away Together (Blyton), 1948
They Rode to Victory (C. Pullein-Thompson), 1970
They That Walk in the Wild (C. Roberts), 1924
They Walk in the Night (Coatsworth), 1969
They Went to the Island (Strong), 1940
They Were Strong and Good (Lawson), 1940
They Who Walk in the Wild (C. Roberts), 1924
They're Drowning Our Village (Loeff, trans), 1959
Thick of the Fray at Zeebruge (Westerman), 1919
Thidwick (verse; Seuss), 1948
Thief (Holland), 1989
Thief (Needle), 1989
Thief (play; Needle), 1988
Thief in the Village (Berry), 1987
Thief Island (Coatsworth), 1943
Thieves and the Raven (Janosch, trans), 1970
Thimble Summer (Enright), 1938
Thin Grey Man (Saville), 1966
Thin Ice (Branfield), 1983
Thing (R. Klein), 1982
Thing That Is Plain (play; Mitchison), 1937
Thingnapped! (R. Klein), 1984
Things I Did for Love (Conford), 1987
Things in the Woods (Alcock), 1989
Things That Go (Scarry), 1987
Things That Sometimes Happen (Avi), 1970
Things to Love (Scarry), 1987
Things to Play With (Rockwell), 1988
Think, Mr. Platypus (Hewett), 1958
Thinking Box (Tate), 1974
Third Class at Miss Kaye's (Brazil), 1908
Third Class Genie (Leeson), 1975
Third Eye (de Hamel), 1987
Third Eye (L. Duncan), 1984
Third Eye (M. Hunter), 1979
Third Magic (Katz), 1988

Third Miss St. Quentin (Molesworth, appendix), 1888
Third Monkey (verse; A. Clark), 1956
Third Officer (Westerman), 1921
Third Road (M. Bacon), 1971
Third-Class Genie (play; Leeson), 1987
Thirteen Bears (C. Roberts), 1947
13 Clocks (Thurber), 1950
Thirteen Days of Christmas (Overton), 1972
Thirteen Footprints (Catherall), 1979
Thirteen for Luck (Wynne), 1936
Thirteen Little Black Pigs (Molesworth, appendix), 1893
Thirteen O'Clock (Mayne), 1960
Thirteenth Adventure (Atkinson), 1949
Thirteenth Fairy (play; Streatfeild), 1934
13th Member (M. Hunter), 1971
Thirteenth Orphan (Chaundler), 1920
35th of May (Kästner, trans), 1933
Thirty-Six Exposures (Major), 1984
Thirty-Three Bunn Street (Clymer), 1952
This and That (Molesworth, appendix), 1899
This Big Cat (verse; de Regniers), 1985
This Cat Came to Stay! (Clymer, as Kinsey), 1955
This Country Is My Country (Kariuki), 1981
This Dear-Bought Land (Latham), 1957
This Earth—My Home (Chipperfield), 1937
This for That (A. Clark), 1965
This Girl (J. Wilson), 1988
This Happy Morning (McNeill), 1959
This Is Ridiculous (Bisset), 1977
This Is the Ambulance Leaving the Zoo (Farber), 1975
This Little Pig (P. Martin, as Miles), 1980
This Place Has No Atmosphere (Danziger), 1986
This School Is Driving Me Crazy (Hentoff), 1976
This Star Shall Abide (Engdahl), 1972
This Strange New Feeling (Lester), 1982
This Summer, Last Summer (Treadgold), 1968
This Thumbprint (Krauss), 1967
This Time Next Term (Breary), 1945
This Time of Darkness (Hoover), 1980
This Time Stories (Bisset), 1961
This Way to Animal Land (play; Bailey), 1936
This Year, Next Year (verse; de la Mare), 1937
This Year's Garden (Rylant), 1984
Thomas (H. Burton), 1969
Thomas (M. Harris), 1956
Thomas and the Sparrow (verse; Serraillier), 1946
Thomas and the Warlock (M. Hunter), 1967
Thomas Comes to Breakfast (Awdry), 1985
Thomas Mead (verse; Hutchins), 1980
Thomas Scarecrow (Preussler, trans), 1963
Thomas, The Tank Engine series (Awdry), from 1946
Thomas's Christmas Party (Awdry), 1984
Thomas's Snowsuit (Munsch), 1985
Thor and the Giant (play; Garner), 1965
Thornbush Jungle (R. Montgomery), 1966
Thornton the Worrier (Sharmat), 1978
Thorny Path (Stretton, appendix), 1879
Thorogood Family (Ballantyne, appendix), 1883
Thoroughly Modern Millie (Colman), 1967
Those Dreadful Children (Blyton), 1949
Those Other People (Childress), 1989
Those Summer Girls I Never Met (R. Peck), 1988
Thoughtless Seven (Le Feuvre), 1898
Thousand Eyes of Night (Swindells), 1985
Thousand for Sicily (Trease), 1964
Thousand Lights and Fireflies (Tresselt), 1965

Thousand Miles an Hour (Strang), 1924
Thousand Yards of Sea (Geras), 1981
Threat to the Barkers (Phipson), 1963
Three Against the World (Leeson), 1986
Three and a Pigeon (Barne), 1944
Three and One Over (Wynne), 1924
Three and One to Carry (B. Willard), 1964
Three at the Sea (Severn), 1959
Three Bear Rhyme Book (verse; Yolen), 1987
Three Bears (play; Chorpenning), 1949
Three Bears (play; L. Richards), 1916
Three Bears and Gwen (Wynne), 1920
Three Big Hogs (Pinkwater, as Manus Pinkwater), 1975
Three Bits of Paste (Fenn, appendix), 1900
Three Bold Babes series (Praeger), from 1897
Three Boys (Fenn, appendix), 1889
Three Boys and a Circus (Blyton, as Pollock), 1940
Three Boys at the Fair (Strang), 1926
Three Brides (Yonge, appendix) 1876
Three Brothers of Ur (Fyson), 1964
Three by Mistake (Parker), 1974
Three by the Sea (Marshall, as Edward Marshall), 1981
Three Cheers for Errol (Cole), 1988
Three Clever Mushrooms (play; Ainsworth), 1955
Three Crowns of King Hullabaloo (McNeill), 1975
Three Days on a River in a Red Canoe (V. Williams), 1981
Three Feet of Valour (Moore); 1921
Three Firecrackers (Lattimore), 1970
Three for All (play; Wymark), 1976
Three for Luck (Poole), 1985
Three Friends (R. Kraus), 1975
Three Friends (Levoy), 1984
Three from Four Leaves One (play; McNeill), 1968
Three from Greenways (Dalgliesh), 1941
Three Funny Friends (Zolotow), 1961
Three Girls series (Marchant), from 1901
Three Girls from School (Meade, appendix), 1907
Three Girls in a Boat (C. Smith), 1938
Three Go to Switzerland (Allan), 1953
Three Gold Dollars (Abbott, appendix), 1854
Three Golden Heads of the Well (Garner), 1979
Three Golliwogs (Blyton), 1944
Three Graces (Everett-Green, appendix), 1904
Three Homes (Farrar, appendix), 1896
397th White Elephant (Guillot, trans), 1954
329th Friend (Sharmat), 1979
Three in the Blue Baloon (Baumann, trans), 1976
Three in the Wild (play; Poole), 1984
Three Knocks on the Wall (Lampman), 1980
Three Landlubbers (verse; Serraillier), 1970
Three Little Animals (M. W. Brown), 1956
Three Little Bears (Burgess), 1940
Three Little Chinese Girls (Lattimore), 1948
Three Little Foxes (Tourtel), 1903
Three Little Funny Ones (Hough), 1962
Three Little Girls (Le Feuvre), 1926
Three Little Kittens (Ballantyne, as Comus, appendix), 1856
Three Little Maids (E. Turner), 1900
Three Little Mushrooms (play; Ainsworth), 1955
Three Lives for the Czar (Plowman), 1969
Three Margarets (L. Richards), 1897
Three Men Went to Work (Berg), 1960
Three Mice for the Abbot (play; Ridge), 1954
Three Minute Stories (L. Richards), 1914
Three Mulla-Mulgars (de la Mare), 1910
Three Naughty Children (Blyton), 1950

Tim and Tip (Otis, appendix), 1883
Tim at the Fur Fort (H. Burton), 1977
Tim Gets a Chance (Blyton), 1966
Tim Kitten and the Red Cupboard (Wahl), 1988
Tim Rabbit series (Uttley), from 1941
Tim Tadpole and the Great Bullfrog (Flack), 1934
Timber! (A. Fisher), 1955
Timber Creek series (M. Clark), from 1949
Timberland Adventure (Lampman, as Bronson), 1950
Timberline Tales (R. Montgomery), 1939
Timboo and Fanny (Abbott, appendix), 1860
Timboo and Joliba (Abbott, appendix), 1855
Time and Again Stories (Bisset), 1970
Time at the Top (Ormondroyd), 1963
Time Cat (Alexander), 1963
Time City, Tale of (Jones), 1987
Time Explorers Inc. (Hildick), 1976
Time Flies! (Heide), 1984
Time for Lissa (Caudill), 1959
Time for Mom (play; A. Fisher), 1969
Time for One More (Berg), 1986
Time for Spring (C. Johnson), 1957
Time for Tarquinia (Brinsmead), 1981
Time for Tenderness (Cavanna), 1962
Time for the Stars (Heinlein), 1956
Time for the White Egret (Carlson), 1978
Time Garden (Eager), 1958
Time in a City (G. Cooper), 1972
Time Loop (play; Wymark), 1975
Time of the Ghost (Jones), 1981
Time of the Kraken (J. Williams), 1977
Time of the Lamb (Wibberley), 1961
Time of the Roses (Meade, appendix), 1900
Time of the Young Soldiers (Richter, trans), 1976
Time of Trial (H. Burton), 1963
Time of Wonder (McCloskey), 1957
Time Out (Cresswell), 1987
Time Out of Mind (play; Lively), 1976
Time Rope (Leeson), 1986
Time to Be Born and a Time to Die (Plowman), 1975
Time to Choose (Parker), 1973
Time to Get Out of the Bath, Shirley (Burningham), 1978
Time to Go Back (Allan), 1972
Time to Go Home (Spence), 1973
Time to Go House (Edmonds), 1969
Time Traders (A. Norton), 1958
Time Trap (Fisk), 1976
Time Trilogy (L'Engle), from 1962
Time Wave (Fatchen), 1978
Time Will Tell (play; Field), 1920
Times They Used to Be (Clifton), 1974
Time's Up! (Heide), 1982
Timi (B.C. Freeman), 1961
Timmy Tiptoes, The Tale of (Potter), 1911
Timmy's Search (Behn), 1958
Timothy series (Storey), from 1966
Timothy and Tinker (Seed), 1967
Timothy Boy Trust (Fyleman), 1944
Timothy Crump's Ward (Alger, appendix), 1866
Timothy Goes to School (Wells), 1981
Timothy in Bushland (M. Bruce), 1912
Timothy Robbins Climbs the Mountain (Tresselt), 1960
Timothy Tiger's Terrible Toothache (Wahl), 1988
Timothy Todd's Good Things Are Gone (Rockwell), 1978
Timothy Too! (Zolotow), 1986
Timothy's Conjuror (Fyleman), 1942

Timothy's Garden (play; Barne), 1912
Timothy's Quest (Wiggin), 1890
Tim's Mountain (R. Montgomery), 1959
Tin Box (Alger, appendix), 1904
Tin Can Band (verse; Mahy), 1989
Tin Can Tucker (L. Hall), 1982
Tina and David (Tate), 1973
Tina into Two Won't Go (Donnelly, trans), 1983
Tincan Beast, (Biegel, trans), 1980
Tinder Box (play; D. Wood), 1967
Tinder-Box (play; Gray), 1951
Tingalary Bird (play; Melwood), 1964
Ting-a-Ling series (Stockton, appendix), from 1870
Tinker and Tanker series (Scarry), from 1960
Tinker Boy (Lynch), 1955
Tinker's Summer (Reid), 1965
Tinner's Quest (Bibby), 1977
Tin-Pot Foreign General and the Old Iron Woman
   (R. Briggs), 1984
Tiny and Her Grandfather (Everett-Green, appendix), 1902
Tiny House (verse; E. Turner), 1911
Tiny Jim (play; Latham, as Lee), 1933
Tiny Little House (Clymer), 1964
Tiny Tales (Blyton), 1949
Tiny Tales, Twelve (Molesworth, appendix), 1890
Tip and Run (M. Baker), 1958
Tired Train (Berg), 1952
Tireless Wings (Westerman), 1926
Tirra Lirra (verse; L. Richards), 1932
Tistou of the Green Fingers (Druon, trans), 1958
Tistou of the Green Thumbs (Druon, trans), 1958
Tit for Tat (verse; H.A. and M. Rey), 1942
Titch (Hutchins), 1971
Titch the Cat (Emecheta), 1979
Titimus Trim (Dodd), 1979
Tituba of Salem Village (Petry), 1964
Titus in Trouble (Reeves), 1959
T-Model Tommy (Meader), 1938
To All My Fans, With Love, From Sylvie (Conford), 1982
To and Again series (Brooks), from 1927
To Be a Ballerina (Pamela Brown), 1950
To Be a Farmer's Boy (Harnett), 1940
To Be a Logger (Lenski), 1967
To Beat a Tiger, One Needs a Brother's Help (E. Lewis), 1956
To Catch a Bird (J. Williams), 1968
To Catch a Tartar (L. Hall), 1973
To Herat and Cabul (Henty, appendix), 1901
To Kill a King (play; Garner), 1980
To Kill a King (Polland), 1970
To Live in Magic (verse; R. Bond), 1983
To London! To London! (B. Willard), 1968
To Make a Wee Moon (Naylor), 1969
To Market, To Market (Scarry), 1979
To Outer Space (Johns), 1957
To Ravensrigg (H. Burton), 1976
To Save Her School (Marchant), 1925
To School and Back (Praeger), 1928
To Shake a Shadow (Naylor), 1967
To Spare the Conquered (Plowman), 1960
To Stand Against the Wind (A. Clark), 1978
To Take a Dare (Zindel), 1982
To Tame a Sister (G. Avery), 1961
To Tell My People (Polland), 1968
To Tell Your Love (Stolz), 1950
To the Fore with the Tanks! (Westerman), 1917
To the Green Mountains (Cameron), 1975

To the Rescue (Everett-Green, appendix), 1902
To the Rescue (Seed), 1966
To the West (Fenn, appendix), 1891
To the Wild Sky (Southall), 1967
To Walk the Sky Path (Naylor), 1973
To Win or Die (Fenn, appendix), 1904
To Wish You Every Joy (verse; Nesbit), 1901
To Worlds Unknown (Johns), 1960
Toad of Toad Hall (play; Milne), 1929
Toad's Castle (Uttley), 1950
Toast to the King (Coatsworth), 1940
Toast-Fag (H. Avery), 1900
Tobermillin Oracle (Reid), 1962
Tobermory's Big Surprise (Beresford), 1976
Tobias (B.C. Freeman), 1967
Toby and the Donkey (Oldfield), 1986
Toby at Tibbs Cross (D. Bruce), 1943
Toby Man (King-Smith), 1989
Toby Show (play; A. Harris), 1978
Toby the Splendid (Holland), 1987
Toby, The Tram Engine (Awdry), 1952
Toby Tyler (Otis, appendix), 1881
Toby's Luck (Beresford), 1978
Tod Moran series (Pease), from 1926
Today Is Saturday (verse; Snyder), 1969
Today We Are Brother and Sister (verse; Adoff), 1981
Toffee Join (Mayne), 1968
Told After Dark, Short Stories (J. Harris, appendix), 1889
Told by a Machine, Tales (Rodari, trans), 1976
Told by Peter (M. Bruce), 1938
Told by Sunbeams and Me (Nesbit), 1893
Told to a Child, Stories (Ingelow, appendix), 1860
Tolliver (Means), 1963
Tom (Alger, appendix), 1878
Tom and Sam (Hutchins), 1968
Tom and Tabby (Symonds), 1964
Tom and the Two Handles (Hoban), 1965
Tom Ass (A. Lawrence), 1972
Tom Bombadil, The Adventures of (verse; Tolkien), 1962
Tom Brace (Alger, appendix), 1901
Tom Brown's School Days and series (Thomas Hughes,
    appendix), from 1857
Tom Burnaby (Strang), 1904
Tom Cobble (Farjeon), 1925
Tom, Dick, and Harry (Reed, appendix), 1894
Tom Fobble's Day (Garner), 1977
Tom Fobble's Day (play; Garner), 1980
Tom Fox and the Apple Pie (C. Watson), 1972
Tom Heron of Sax (Everett-Green, appendix), 1893
Tom Kitten, The Take of (Potter), 1907
Tom Leaves School (Strang), 1926
Tom Merry series (F. Richards, as Clifford), from 1949
Tom Pittman (R. Montgomery), 1957
Tom Post's Private Eye (Darke), 1983
Tom Sawyer, The Adventures of (play; Chorpenning), 1946
Tom Sawyer series (Twain, appendix), from 1876
Tom Sawyer Fires (Yep), 1984
Tom Sawyer's Treasure Hunt (play; Chorpenning), 1937
Tom Tempest's Victory (Everett-Green, as H.F.E., appendix), 1880
Tom Temple's Career (Alger, appendix), 1888
Tom Thatcher's Fortune (Alger, appendix), 1888
Tom Tiddler, The Tale of (Farjeon), 1929
Tim Tiddler's Ground (Townsend), 1985
Tom Titmarsh's Devil (Garfield), 1977
Tom Tracy (Alger, appendix), 1888
Tom Tufton series (Everett-Green, appendix), 1898

Tom Turner's Legacy (Alger, appendix), 1902
Tom Whipple (Edmonds) , 1942
Tom Willoughby's Scouts (Strang), 1919
Tomahawk Border (W. Steele), 1966
Tomahawk Family (Carlson), 1960
Tomahawks and Trouble (W. Steele), 1955
Tomb Comb (R. Klein), 1984
Tombi's Song (Seed), 1966
Tomboy (N. Klein), 1978
Tomboy Toby (Chaundler), 1923
Tombs of Atuan (Le Guin), 1971
Tomina in Retreat (Le Feuvre), 1917
Tommy series (Burgess), from 1915
Tommy and the Owl (Everett-Green, appendix), 1912
Tommy and the Telephone (MacGregor), 1947
Tommy Bear and the Zookies (Wall), 1920
Tommy Dobbie and the Witch-Next-Door (Oldfield), 1983
Tommy Helps, Too (H.A. and M. Rey), 1943
Tommy Mac series (Barry), from 1972
Tommy, Sue and Sammy with Their Friends of Meadow, Pool, and
    Forest, The Adventures of (Burgess), 1965
Tommy Thatcher Goes to Sea (Hader), 1965
Tommy Tomorrow (play; Latham), 1935
Tommy with the Hole in His Shoe (Judah), 1957
Tommy's Little Grains of Sand (Heward), 1930
Tommy's Trek (Marchant), 1901
Tommy's Wonderful Airplane (Clymer), 1951
Tomorrow (Barne), 1912
Tomorrow (play; Barne), 1910
Tomorrow City (M. Hughes), 1978
Tomorrow Is a Lovely Day (Allan), 1979
Tomorrow Is a Stranger (Trease), 1987
Tomorrow's Wizard (MacLachlan), 1982
Tom's Midnight Garden (Pearce), 1958
Tom's Tower (McNeill), 1965
Tomsk and the Tired Tree (Beresford), 1975
Tomten series (Lindgren, trans), from 1961
Tongue of the Ocean (Bunting), 1976
Tonio and the Stranger (Coatsworth), 1941
Toño Antonio (Sawyer), 1934
Tony (Alger, appendix), 1880
Tony (E. O. White), 1924
Tony and Me (Slote), 1974
Tony the Tow Truck (R. Kraus), 1985
Tony Trotter and the Kitten (Meynell), 1971
Tony's Chums (Wynne), 1914
Tony's Pony (Schlein), 1952
Too Big (d'Aulaire), 1945
Too Many Hopkins (de Paola), 1989
Too Many Rabbits (Parish), 1974
Too Near the Sun (L. Hall), 1970
"Too Wise" the Wonderful Wizard (Blyton), 1951
Tooky (Hader), 1931
Toolmaker (Paton Walsh), 1973
Tooter (D. Ross), 1951
Tooth Ball (Pearce), 1987
Tooth Book (verse; Seuss, as Le Sieg), 1981
Tooth-Gnasher Superflash (Pinkwater), 1981
Toothpaste Millionaire (Merrill), 1972
Top Boy at Twisters Creek (Hildick), 1969
Top Fishing (Hardcastle), 1979
Top of the League (Hardcastle), 1979
Top of the World (Townsend), 1976
Top Secret (Brent-Dyer), 1955
Top Secret (Weir), 1962
Top Soccer (Hardcastle), 1979

Top Speed (Hardcastle), 1979
Top Spin (Hardcastle, as Clark), 1973
Top-Flight Fully-Automated Girl Detective
    (Hildick), 1979
Top-Flight Fully-Automated Junior High School Girl Detective
    (Hildick), 1977
Topham series (F. Richards), 1947
Toppen and I at the Croft (Unnerstad, trans), 1966
Toppling Towers (B. Willard), 1969
Topsail Island Treasure (Meader), 1966
Topsy (Flack), 1935
Topsy-Turvies (Anno, trans), 1970
Topsy-Turvy Emperor of China (Singer), 1971
Torch (Paton Walsh), 1987
Torch of Courage (Bailey), 1921
Tornado! (verse; Adoff), 1977
Torolv the Fatherless (Clarke), 1959
Torrie (A. and E. Johnson), 1960
Tory Plot (Otis, appendix), 1899
Toto series (L. Richards), from 1885
Toto's Triumph (Bishop), 1957
Tottie (Godden), 1983
Toucans Two (verse; Prelutsky), 1970
Touch and Go (Poole), 1976
Touch of Chill (Aiken), 1979
Touch of Magic (Cavanna), 1961
Touchstone (B. Todd), 1935
Tough Chauncey (D. B. Smith), 1974
Tough Luck (Doherty), 1987
Tough Princess (Waddell), 1986
Tough Winter (Lawson), 1954
Tough-Luck Karen (Hurwitz), 1982
Toutou in Bondage (Coatsworth), 1929
Tovers (Beresford), 1982
Tower by the Sea (De Jong), 1950
Tower of Babel (Suddaby), 1962
Tower of the Stars (R. Harris), 1980
Tower Raven (Cockett), 1975
Tower Rooms (M. Bruce), 1926
Town Across the Water (Polland), 1961
Town Cats (Alexander) 1977
Town Child's Alphabet (verse; Farjeon), 1924
Town That Went South (King), 1959
Towser series (T. Ross), from 1984
Towser (play; T. Ross), n.d.
Toy Book (Scarry), 1978
Toy Circus (verse; Wahl), 1986
Toyland, Tales of (Blyton), 1944
Toymaker's Daughter (Moray Williams), 1968
Toys, Tales of the (Blyton), 1942
Toys at Night-Time (play; Blyton), 1939
Toys Come to Life (Blyton), 1943
Toys Take over Christmas (play; Clapp), 1977
Toytown series (Beaman), from 1925
Tracker (Cockett), 1984
Tracker (Paulsen), 1984
Trackers (Hough), 1960
Tracks (Thwaite), 1978
Tracy's Story (Berg), 1972
Trade Wind (Meigs), 1927
Trader's Children (Armer), 1937
Trading (Warner, appendix), 1872
Trading Jeff and His Dog (Kjelgaard), 1956
Traffic Jam (Moray Williams), 1971
Trail and Camp-Fire Stories (Seton), 1940
Trail of Apple Blossoms (I. Hunt), 1968

Trail of the Buffalo (R. Montgomery), 1939
Trail of the Sandhill Stag (Seton), 1899
Trail Through Danger (W. Steele), 1965
Trail-Driving Rooster (Gipson), 1955
Trailing Trouble (Kjelgaard), 1952
Train (Tate), 1967
Train Boy (Alger, appendix), 1883
Train for Jane (verse; N. Klein), 1974
Train Ride (Steptoe), 1971
Train That Lost Its Way (Blyton), 1946
Train to Timbuctoo (M. W. Brown), 1951
Training Sylvia (E. O. White), 1942
Traitor Within (Cordell), 1971
Traitor's Escape (Otis, appendix), 1898
Traitor's Gate (Fenn, appendix), 1906
Tramway Engines (Awdry), 1972
Transfigured Hart (Yolen), 1975
Transformations (Halam), 1988
Transport Girl in France (Marchant), 1919
Trapped by the Malays (Fenn, appendix), 1907
Trapped by the Mountain Storm (A. Fisher), 1950
Trapped in the Jungle (Westerman), 1947
Trapper Dan (Fenn, appendix), 1905
Trapper's Trail (R. Montgomery), 1943
Traveler from a Small Kingdom (Neville), 1968
Traveling Bird (Burch), 1959
Traveling Men of Ballycoo (Bunting), 1983
Traveling Shoes (Streatfeild), 1962
Traveller (de Roo), 1979
Traveller in Time (Uttley), 1939
Travellers by Night (Alcock), 1983
Travellers Three (Symonds), 1953
Travelling Magic (Beresford), 1965
Travelling Tooth (Thwaite), 1968
Travelling Three (L. Wood), 1943
Travels of Ching (Bright), 1943
Travels of Hermann (Spence), 1973
Travels of Horatio (Foreman), 1970
Travels of Marco (Merrill), 1956
Travels of Timmy Toodles (Gruelle), 1916
Treason at York (Hayes), 1949
Treasure (Terhune), 1926
Treasure Ahead (Serraillier), 1954
Treasure at Amorys (Saville), 1964
Treasure at First Base (Clymer), 1950
Treasure at the Mill (Saville), 1957
Treasure at Twenty Fathoms (Wibberley, as O'Connor), 1961
Treasure Box (Blyton), 1965
Treasure for Three (Severn), 1949
Treasure Hunt (play; Daniell), 1955
Treasure Hunt (Trevor), 1957
Treasure Hunters (Beresford), 1980
Treasure Hunters (Blyton), 1940
Treasure in the Fog (Bull), 1976
Treasure Is the Rose (Cunningham), 1973
Treasure Island (play; A. Harris), 1983
Treasure Island (Stevenson, appendix), 1883
Treasure Mountain (Kelly), 1937
Treasure Mountain (Lampman), 1949
Treasure of Cocos Island (Otis, appendix), 1902
Treasure of Ebba (Fidler), 1968
Treasure of Plunderell Manor (Clements), 1987
Treasure of Siegfried (Almedingen), 1964
Treasure of the Incas (Henty, appendix), 1902
Treasure of the Long Sault (M. Hughes), 1982
Treasure of the Padres (B. Baker), 1964

Treasure of the Reef (Patchett), 1955
Treasure of the Sacred Lake (Westerman), 1924
Treasure of the Moor (J. Pullein-Thompson), 1982
Treasure of Topo-el-Bampo (O'Dell), 1972
Treasure Seekers, The Story of the (Nesbit), 1899
Treasure Trove (M. Baker), 1952
Treasure Trove (Everett-Green, appendix), 1905
Treasure-Hunting Trip (Janosch, trans), 1980
Treasures from Storyland (Nesbit), 1895
Treasures in the Marshes (Yonge, appendix), 1893
Treasures of Morrow (Hoover), 1976
Treasures of the "San Philipo" (Westerman), 1916
Tree, (Tate), 1966
Tree by Leaf (Voigt), 1988
Tree for Peter (Seredy), 1941
Tree House (play; George), n.d.
Tree House Island (S. Corbett), 1959
Tree House of Jimmy Domino (Merrill), 1955
Tree House Town (P. Martin, as Miles), 1974
Tree in the Trail (Holling), 1942
Tree of Appomattox (Altsheler), 1916
Tree of Freedom (Caudill), 1949
Tree of Liberty (McGregor), 1972
Tree That Stayed Up until Next Christmas (R. Kraus), 1972
Tree to Trim (play; A. Fisher), 1945
Tree Wagon (Lampman), 1953
Treeful of Pigs (Arnold Lobel), 1979
Treegate's Raiders (Wibberley), 1962
Treehorn series (Heide), from 1981
Treehouse (Tate), 1969
Trees Kneel at Christmas (Lovelace), 1950
Tregg's Triumph (Everett-Green, appendix), 1901
Trespassers at Charlcote (G. Avery), 1958
Treve (Terhune), 1924
Trey of Swords (A. Norton), 1977
Trial (Yonge, appendix), 1864
Trial of Anna Cotman (Alcock), 1989
Trial Trip (R. Armstrong), 1962
Trial Valley (V. and B. Cleaver), 1977
Trials and Adventures of Herbert Mason (Alger, appendix), 1873
Triangle Has Four Sides (Naylor), 1983
Tribute to Tom (play; Doherty), 1988
Trick series (S. Corbett), from 1960
Trick a Tracker (Foreman), 1981
Trick Jumpers (J. Pullein-Thompson), 1958
Trick or Treat (Slobodkin), 1959
Tricksters (Mahy), 1986
Tricky the Goblin (Blyton), 1950
Tricycle Tim (B. Carter), 1957
Triffeny (D. Fairlie Bruce), 1950
Trig series (R. N. Peck), from 1977
Trillions (Fisk), 1971
Trimplet (play; S. Walker), 1916
Trina (P. Martin), 1972
Trina's Boxcar (P. Martin), 1967
Trip (Keats), 1978
Trip (Sharmat), 1976
Trip to Panama (Janosch, trans), 1978
Trip Trap (Dhondy), 1982
Triple Alliance (H. Avery), 1898
Tripods Trilogy (Christopher), from 1947
Triumph for Flavius (Snedeker), 1955
Triumphs of Three (Marchant), 1942
Trojan Rides Again (R. Brown), 1978
Troll Country (Marshall, as E. Marshall), 1980
Troll Magic (play; C. D. Mackay), 1910

Troll Music (Anita Lobel), 1966
Troll Weather (Coatsworth), 1967
Trolley Car Family (Clymer), 1947
Trolls of Twelfth Street (Sharmat), 1979
Troodle (play; Fyleman), 1938
Troopers Three (R. Montgomery), 1932
Tropical Island (play; Ridge), 1953
Troubadour (Guillot, trans), 1965
Trouble (Cresswell), 1987
Trouble at Lachine Mill (B. Freeman), 1983
Trouble at Melville Manor (Allan), 1949
Trouble at Townsend (Saville), 1945
Trouble at Trimbles (Cumming), 1949
Trouble at Tullington Castle (Beresford), 1958
Trouble for Jerry (Gates), 1944
Trouble for Trimble (F. Richards, as Clifford), 1952
Trouble Half-Way (Mark), 1985
Trouble in Form Six (Ekwensi), 1966
Trouble in the Glen (Allan), 1976
Trouble in the Jungle (Townsend), 1969
Trouble in Toyland (Beaman), 1925
Trouble on Janus (Slote), 1985
Trouble River (Byars), 1969
Trouble with...series (Cole), from 1983
Trouble with Diamonds (Corbett), 1985
Trouble with Donovan Croft (Ashley), 1974
Trouble with Gramary (Levin), 1988
Trouble with Jack (S. Hughes), 1970
Trouble with Jacob (McGraw), 1988
Trouble with Jenny's Ear (Butterworth), 1960
Trouble with Mr. Harris (Armitage), 1978
Trouble with Spider (R. Kraus), 1962
Trouble with Terry (Lexau), 1962
Trouble with Tuck (T. Taylor), 1981
Trouble with Vanessa (Ure), 1988
Troublemaker (L. Hall), 1974
Trouble's Child (Walter), 1985
Troubles of Queen Silver-Bell (Burnett), 1906
Troubles of Tazy (Oxenham), 1926
Troublesome Engines (Awdry), 1950
Troublesome Three (Blyton), 1955
Trovato (Bettina), 1959
Troy Game (Morris), 1987
Trubloff (Burningham), 1964
Truce of the Games (Sutcliff), 1971
Truckload of Rice (Berna, trans), 1968
Trudy and the Three House (Coatsworth), 1944
True as Steel (Strang), 1923
True Francine (Marc Brown), 1981
True Men (M. Steele), 1976
True Stories of Girl Heroines (Everett-Green, appendix), 1901
True Story of Lilli Stubeck (Aldridge), 1984
True Story of Mother Goose and Her Son Jack (T. Ross), 1979
True Story of Spit MacPhee (Aldridge), 1986
True Tale (play; Vipont), 1952
True to Himself (Everett-Green, appendix), 1885
True to His Nickname (H. Avery), 1907
True to the Last (Everett-Green, appendix), 1885
True to the Old Flag (Henty, appendix), 1884
Truffle Pig (Bishop), 1971
Truly Remarkable Puss-in-Boots (play; Clapp), 1979
Trummi Kaput (play; Foon), 1982
Trumpet of the Swan (E.B. White), 1970
Trumpeter of Krakow (Kelly), 1928
Trumpets in the West (Trease), 1947
Trumpton (play; Prince), 1970

Trust a City Kid (Yolen), 1966
Truth about Mary Rose (Sachs), 1973
Truth about Stone Hollow (Snyder), 1974
Truthful Harp (Alexander), 1967
Try (Finley, appendix), 1863
Try and Trust (Alger, appendix), 1873
Try It Again, Sam (Viorst), 1970
Try These for Size (McNeill), 1963
Tubby Books (R. Kraus, as Tubby), 1981
Tuck Everlasting (Babbitt), 1975
Tucker in Control (Needle), 1985
Tucker's Countryside (Selden), 1969
Tucker's Luck (Needle), 1984
Tuck-Shop Girl (Oxenham), 1916
Tuesday Adventure (Pudney), 1950
Tug of War (Fenn, appendix), 1902
Tulku (Dickinson), 1979
Tullington Film-Makers (Beresford), 1960
Tumbleweed (King-Smith), 1987
Tune Is in the Tree (Lovelace), 1950
Tuned Out (Wojciechowska), 1968
Tunes for a Penny Piper (verse; Farjeon), 1922
Tunes for a Small Harmonica (Wersba), 1976
Tunnel (Browne), 1989
Tunnel Busters (Catherall, as Channel), 1960
Tunnel in the Sky (Heinlein), 1955
Tunnel of Hugsy Goode (Estes), 1971
Tunnel to the Sky (Pudney), 1965
Tunnel with Problems (Sudbery), 1979
Tuppenny (Cunningham), 1978
Tuppenny, The Tale of (Potter), 1973
Tuppeny Brown (Sutton), 1977
Turkey's Nest (Prince), 1979
Turn Again, Whittington (Tate), 1980
Turn Homeward, Hannalee (P. Beatty), 1984
Turn of the Tide (E. Porter), 1908
Turbulent Term of Tyke Tiler (Kemp), 1977
Turf-Cutter's Donkey series (Lynch), from 1934
Turi's Papa (de Treviño), 1969
Turi's Poppa (de Treviño), 1968
Turk (Fidler), 1975
Turkey for Christmas (de Anglei), 1944
Turkey Girl (B. Baker), 1983
Turnabout (Leaf), 1967
Turnaround Wind (verse; Anita Lobel), 1988
Turnip, The Tale of the (Hewett), 1961
Turquoise and Ruby (Meade, appendix), 1906
Turramulli the Giant Quinkin (Roughsey), 1982
Turret (Sharp), 1963
Turtle and Snail (Oneal), 1979
Turtle and the Dove (D. Freeman), 1964
Turtle Drum (play; Serraillier), 1967
Turtle Tale (Asch), 1978
Tusk Tusk (McKee), 1978
Twelfth Day of July (Lingard), 1970
Twelve and the Genii (Clarke), 1962
Twelve Bells for Santa (Bonsall), 1977
Twelve Dancers (Mayne), 1962
Twelve Days of Christmas (verse; K. Briggs), 1952
Twelve Gold Chairs (Cockett), 1967
Twelve Minutes to Disaster (Catherall), 1977
Twelve Months Makes a Year (Coatsworth), 1943
Twelve Robbers (Biegel, trans), 1974
Twenty and Ten (Bishop), 1952
Twenty Minute Tales (Blyton), 1940
Twenty Two Letters (King), 1966

Twenty-Elephant Restaurant (Hoban), 1978
Twenty-Four Days Before Christmas (L'Engle), 1964
Twenty-One Balloons (du Bois), 1947
Twenty-Six Starlings Will Fly Through Your Mind
    (verse; Wersba), 1980
Twenty-Two Bears (Bishop), 1964
Twenty-Two, Twenty-Three (Raskin), 1976
Twice Bought (Ballantyne, appendix), 1885
Twice Seven Tailes (Picard), 1968
Twiddledetwit (Finley, appendix), 1898
Twig of Cypress (L. Cooper), 1965
Twilight Land (Pyle, appendix), 1895
Twilight of Magic (Lofting), 1930
Twilight Province (Finkel), 1967
Twin Babies (Finley, appendix), 1872
Twin Engines (Awdry), 1960
Twin Spell (Lunn), 1969
Twinkle and Chubbins (Baum, as Bancroft), 1911
Twinkle Tales (Baum, as Bancroft), 1906
Twinkle's Enchantment (Baum, as Bancroft), 1906
Twins series (Blyton), from 1945
Twins series (Perkins), from 1911
Twins and Tabiffa (Heward), 1923
Twins and Their Ponies (Moray Williams), 1936
Twins at Tachbury (Everett-Green, appendix), 1924
Twins of Castle Charming (Oxenham), 1920
Twins of Emu Plains (M. Bruce), 1923
Twins Who Flew round the World (Holling), 1931
Twist of Eight (Morris), 1981
Twisted Key (Lynch), 1964
Twisted Window (L. Duncan), 1987
Twitchell the Wishful (Sharmat), 1981
Twits (Dahl), 1980
Two series (H. Morgan), from 1964
Two, Adventures of (Wynne), 1920
Two Admirals (McKee), 1977
Two Against the Tide (Clements), 1967
Two and a Bit (Harnett), 1948
Two and a Chum (Wynne), 1924
Two and Two Are Four (Haywood), 1940
Two Are Better Than One (Brink), 1968
Two Arrows (Meigs), 1949
Two at Sullivan Bay (Donkin), 1985
Two Bad Ants (Van Allsburg), 1988
Two Bad Boys (Clewes), 1971
Two Bad Mice, The Tale of (Potter), 1904
Two Bright Shillings (Everett-Green, appendix), 1894
Two Brothers series (Lenski), from 1929
Two by Two (Stolz), 1954
Two Can Toucan (McKee), 1964
Two Cars (d'Aulaire), 1955
Two Dartmoor Interludes (Chipperfield), 1935
Two Different Girls (Bunting), 1978
Two Dog Biscuits (Cleary), 1961
Two Dogs and a Horse (Kjelgaard), 1964
Two Dutch Dolls, The Adventures of (Upton), 1895
Two Faces of Silenus (Clarke), 1972
Two Fair Plaits (Saville), 1948
Two Form-Captains (Oxenham), 1921
Two Fugitives (Chipperfield), 1966
Two Funny Clowns (Hader), 1929
Two Ghosts on a Beach (Sharmat), 1982
Two Giants (Foreman), 1967
Two Girls (Coolidge, appendix), 1900
Two Girls and a Boat (F. Knight, as Salter), 1956
Two Girls in the Hawk's Den (Wynne), 1930

Voyage of the Ludgate Hill (verse; N. Willard), 1987
Voyage of the Mael Duin (Dillon), 1969
Voyage to Bengal (F. Knight), 1954
Voyage to Tasmania (Parker), 1961
Voyage to Valhalla (Swindells), 1976
Voyages (D. B. Smith), 1989
Vulpes the Red Fox (George), 1948

Wacky Wednesday (verse; Seuss, as Le Sieg), 1974
Wag-by-Wall (Potter), 1944
Wages (Meade, appendix), 1990
Wagga Storybooks (Storr), 1984
Waggon for Five (Severn), 1944
Wagons West (Craig), 1955
Wagons Westward (Sperry), 1936
Wagstaffe the Wind-Up Boy (Needle), 1987
Wag-Tail Bess (Flack), 1933
Wahoo Bobcat (Lippincott), 1950
Waifs of Woollamoo (Marchant), 1938
Wait and Hope (Alger, appendix), 1877
Wait and See (Alcock), 1986
Wait and Win (Alger, appendix), 1908
Wait for It (McNeill), 1972
Wait for Me, Michael (Stolz), 1961
Wait for Me, Watch for Me, Eula Bee (P. Beatty), 1978
Wait for William (Flack), 1935
Wait till the Clouds Roll By (Alger, appendix), 1890
Wait till the Moon Is Full (verse; M. W. Brown), 1948
Waiting for Mama (de Regniers), 1984
Waiting for the Dark (Berg), 1977
Waiting for the End of the World (Harding), 1983
Waiting for the Sky to Fall (J. Wilson), 1983
Waiting Game (Bunting), 1981
Waiting Room Doll (M. Baker), 1986
Waiting to Waltz (verse; Rylant), 1984
Wake Up and Goodnight (verse; Zolotow), 1971
Wake Up, Bear (Dodd), 1986
Wake Up, City! (Tresselt), 1957
Wake Up, Farm! (Tresselt), 1955
Walk a Mile and Get Nowhere (Southall), 1970
Walk for Us (Hardcastle), n.d.
Walk in the Park (Browne), 1977
Walk on the Wild Side (Westall), 1989
Walk Out of the World (Nichols), 1969
Walk Past Ellen's House (Hoff), 1973
Walk the Mouse Girls Took (Kuskin), 1967
Walk the Plank! (play; McGinley), 1928
Walk the World's Rim (B. Baker), 1965
Walker, The Witch, and the Striped Flying Saucer
    (Stevenson), 1969
Walking Shoes (Rockwell), 1980
Walking Stones (M. Hunter), 1970
Walking Through the Dark (Naylor), 1976
Walking to School (verse; E. Turner), 1988
Walking Up a Ranbow (T. Taylor), 1984
Walks from Eden (Warner, appendix), 1866
Wall of Words (Kennemore), 1982
Wallpaper Holiday (H. Todd), 1982
Walls of Athens (Paton Walsh), 1977
Wally the Kangaroo (Beaman), 1927
Wally Wanderoon and His Story-Telling Machine (J. Harris,
    appendix), 1903
Wallypug of Why series (Farrow), from 1895
Wallypug Tales (verse; Farrow), 1903
Walnut Tree Meadow (Severn), 1955
Walpole (Hoff), 1977

Walrus Hunters (Ballantyne, appendix), 1893
Walsh the Wonder-Worker (Fenn, appendix), 1903
Walter, The Adventure of (Clymer), 1965
Walter Griffith (Alger, appendix), 1901
Walter Sherwood's Probation (Alger, appendix), 1897
Walter, The Homing Pigeon (Benchley), 1981
Walter, The Lazy Mouse (Flack), 1937
Walter the Wolf (Sharmat), 1975
Wan Lun and Dandy (Otis, appendix), 1902
Wand from France (B. Todd), 1972
Wanda and the Bumbly Wizard (Flora), 1980
Wanda's Wand (Hoff), 1968
Wanderer (M. Edwards), 1953
Wanderers (Coatsworth), 1972
Wandering May (Walton, appendix), 1872
Wandering Moon (verse; Reeves), 1950
Wandering Wind (Watkins-Pitchford), 1957
Wanderlust (R. Armstrong), 1952
Wanted (Otis, appendix), 1912
Wanted: A Girl for the Horses (Cavanna), 1984
Wanted—A Grand (Clewes), 1974
Wanted, An English Girl (Moore), 1916
Wapiti (R. Montgomery), 1952
Wapping Warrior (R. Brown), 1969
War and Peas (Foreman), 1974
War Beneath the Sea (Bonham), 1962
War Cargo (Westerman), 1941
War Comes to Willie Freeman (Collier), 1983
War Dog (Treece), 1962
War of the Wireless Waves (Westerman), 1923
War of Wizards (Storey), 1976
War on the Darnel (P. Turner), 1969
War Party (W. Steele), 1978
War Stories (play; Prince), 1970
War Wings (R. Montgomery), 1943
War with Old Mouldy! (Ure), 1987
War Without Friends (Hartman, trans), 1982
War Work (Oneal), 1971
Warden's Niece (G. Avery), 1957
Wardens of the Weir (Gray), 1978
Wardship of Steepcombe (Yonge, appendix), 1896
Warhawk Patrol (R. Montgomery), 1944
Warlock at the Wheel (Jones), 1984
Warrimoo (Patchett), 1961
Warringtons in War-Time (Talbot), 1940
Warrior Scarlet (Sutcliff), 1958
Warriors of Taan (L. Lawrence), 1986
Warriors of the Wasteland (D. Hill), 1983
Warriors on the Hills (Seed), 1975
Wars of Wapsburgh (Yonge, appendix), 1864
Warts and All (Sudbery), 1972
Was I Right? (Walton, appendix), 1879
Was It a Good Trade? (verse; de Regniers), 1956
Wash 'em Clean (Chukovsky, trans), 1962
Washday on Noah's Ark (Rounds), 1985
Washerwoman's Child (play; Uttley), 1946
Washington for All (play; Latham, as Lee), 1931
Wasp in a Wig (Carroll, appendix), 1978
Wasteground Circus (Keeping), 1975
Watch Fires to the North (Finkel), 1967
Watch for a Pony (Robertson), 1949
Watch House (Westall), 1977
Watch Out! A Giant! (Carle), 1978
Watch Out for the Chicken Feet in Your Soup (de Paola), 1974
Watch That Watch (Colman), 1962
Watch-Dog of the North Sea (Westerman), 1916

What a Fine Day for...(verse; Krauss), 1967
What a Good Lunch! (Watanabe, trans), 1980
What a Lark! (Weir), 1961
What a Little Moonlight Can Do (play; J. Watson), 1982
What a Surprise! (Blyton), 1954
What about Tomorrow? (Southall), 1977
What an Adventure (Blyton), 1950
What Are We Going to Do about Andrew? (Sharmat), 1980
What Are You Looking At? (Bonsall, as Newell), 1954
What Beckoning Ghost? (Lillington), 1983
What Cabrillo Found (Lovelace), 1958
What Can I Do? (Darke), 1975
What Can You Do with a Pocket? (Merriam), 1964
What Can You Do with a Shoe? (verse; de Regniers), 1955
What Can You Do with a Word? (J. Williams), 1966
What Comes of Quarrelling (Nesbit), 1902
What Did I See? (verse; W. Smith), 1962
What Did You Bring Me? (Kuskin), 1973
What Did You Leave Behind? (Tresselt), 1978
What Eric Knew (Howe), 1985
What Happened to Toyland (play; A. Fisher), 1978
What Happened When Jack and Daisy Tried to Fool the Tooth Fairies (Hoban), 1965
What Happens Next (de Regniers), 1959
What I Did Last Summer (verse; Prelutsky), 1984
What I Really Think of You (M. Kerr), 1982
What If? (Minarik), 1987
What If They Saw Me Now? (Ure), 1982
What Is Right for Tulip (Duvoisin), 1969
What Is the Truth? (verse; T. Hughes), 1984
What It's All About (Frolov, trans), 1968
What It's All About (N. Klein), 1975
What Katy Did series (Coolidge, appendix), from 1872
What Might Have Been Expected (Stockton, appendix), 1874
What Next, Baby Bear! (J. Murphy), 1984
What She Could (Warner, appendix), 1871
What Spot? (Bonsall), 1963
What Tabbit the Rabbit Found (Latham), 1974
What the Gulls Were Singing (Naylor), 1967
What the Neighbours Did (Pearce), 1972
What the Seven Did (Sidney, appendix), 1882
What the Wind Did (Le Feuvre), 1899
What Time Is It When It Isn't? (Bisset), 1980
What Time of Night Is It? (Stolz), 1981
What to Do about Molly (Flack), 1936
What-Do-You-Know Stories, Fourteen (Berg), 1948
Whatever Next! (J. Murphy), 1983
What'll You do When You Grow Up??? (verse; Hader), 1929
What's Fun Without a Friend? (Iwasaki, trans), 1975
What's in a Name (play; T. Ross), 1985
What's the Matter with the Dobsons? (Colman), 1980
What's under My Bed? (Stevenson), 1983
Wheat-Field (play; L. Richards), 1915
Wheel of Danger (Leeson), 1986
Wheel of the Chimney (M. W. Brown), 1954
Wheel on the School (De Jong), 1954
Wheel That Ran Away (Blyton), 1966
Wheelie in the Stars (Fisk), 1976
Wheeling for Fortune (Otis, appendix), 1899
Wheels of Iron (Meade, appendix), 1901
Wheels over the Bridge (De Jong), 1941
Wheels West (Lampman), 1965
When Abigail Was Seven (E. O. White), 1931
When Auntie Lil Took Charge (Wynne), 1915
When Darkness Comes (Swindells), 1973
When Dewey Came to Manila (Otis, appendix), 1899

When Did You Last Wash Your Feet? (verse; Rosen), 1986
When East Meets West (Westerman), 1913
When Esther Was a Little Girl (E. O. White), 1944
When Everyone Was Fast Asleep (de Paola), 1976
When Grandfather Was a Boy (Bailey), 1923
When Guns Thundered in Tripoli (Finger), 1937
When Hitler Stole the Pink Rabbit (J. Kerr), 1971
When Homer Honked (Latham), 1961
When I Dance (verse; Berry), 1988
When I Go Visiting (Rockwell), 1984
When I Grow Up (Haywood), 1931
When I Grow Up (verse; Lenski), 1960
When I Have a Little...series (Zolotow), from 1965
When I Was Nine (Stevenson), 1986
When I Was Seven (Peacocke), 1927
When I Was Young in the Mountains (Rylant), 1982
When I'm Big (Bruna, trans), 1981
When Israel Putman Served the King (Otis, appendix), 1898
When It Comes to Bugs (verse; A. Fisher), 1986
When Jays Fly to Bárbmo (Balderson), 1968
When Life Is Young (verse; Dodge, appendix), 1894
When London Burned (Henty, appendix), 1894
When Love Whispers (Ekwensi), 1947
When Marnie Was There (Robinson), 1967
When Molly Was Six (E. O. White), 1894
When No One Was Looking (Wells), 1980
When Rivers Meet (Naylor), 1968
When Sam Was King (play; V. Smith), 1967
When Shlemiel Went to Warsaw (Singer), 1968
When Spring Came In at the Window (play; Barker), 1942
When the Allies Swept the Seas (Westerman), 1940
When the Beacons Blazed (H. Burton), 1978
When the City Stopped (Phipson), 1978
When the Drums Beat (Trease), 1976
When the Pie Was Opened (verse; Little), 1968
When the Rattlesnake Sounds (play; Childress), 1975
When the Sad One Comes to Stay (Heide), 1975
When the Siren Wailed (Streatfeild), 1974
When the Stars Begin to Fall (Collier), 1986
When the Tripods Came (Christopher), 1988
When the Typhoon Blows (E. Lewis), 1942
When the Wind Blew (M. W. Brown), 1937
When the Wind Changed (Park), 1980
When Washington Served the King (Otis, appendix), 1905
When We Destroyed the Gaspee (Otis, appendix), 1901
When We First Met (Mazer), 1982
When We Went to the Park (S. Hughes), 1985
When We Were Very Young (verse; Milne), 1924
When Wendy Grew Up (play; Barrie), 1908
When Will It Snow? (Hoff), 1971
When Will the World Be Mine? (Schlein), 1953
When Willy Went to the Wedding (J. Kerr), 1972
When You Come to the Ferry (Brinsmead), 1988
Where Are You Going, Little Mouse? (R. Kraus), 1986
Where Are You Going To, My Pretty Maid? (Andrew), 1977
Where Bell-Birds Chime (Howes), 1912
Where Do We Go from Here? (Kamm), 1972
Where Do You Go When You Run Away? (Lexau, as Nodset), 1964
Where Does Everyone Go? (verse; A. Fisher), 1961
Where Does the Day Go? (Myers), 1969
Where Have All the Tigers Gone? (L. Hall), 1988
Where Have You Been? (verse; M. W. Brown), 1952
Where I Begin (Zolotow, as Abbott), 1970
Where Is Adelaide? (E. O. White), 1933
Where Is Everybody? (Merriam), 1989

Where Is Fred? (Kaye), 1976
Where Is God? (verse; Robinson, as Thomas), 1957
Where Is Sarah? (B. Graham), 1985
Where Nobody Sees (J. Watson), 1987
Where the Action Is (Hardcastle), 1976
Where the Bus Stopped (Saville), 1955
Where the Golden Eagle Soars (Johns), 1960
Where the Lilies Bloom (V. and B. Cleaver), 1969
Where the Sidewalk Ends (verse; Silverstein), 1974
Where the Wild Geese Go (Pierce), 1988
Where the Wild Things Are (Sendak), 1963
Where the Wild Things Are (play; Sendak), 1980
Where the Wind Blows (Cresswell), 1966
Where the Winds Never Blew and the Cocks Never Crew
    (Colum), 1940
Where There's a Will (Atkinson), 1961
Where Wild Willy (verse; Adoff), 1978
Where's Florrie? (Cohen), 1976
Where's Gomer? (verse; Farber), 1974
Where's Julius? (Burningham), 1986
Where's My Baby? (verse; H.A. and M. Rey), 1943
Where's My Daddy? (Watanabe, trans), 1980
Where's My Girl? (Saville), 19723
Where's Prancer? (Hoff), 1960
Where's the Baby? (Hutchins), 1988
Which Horse Is William? (Kuskin), 1959
Which Is Willy? (Bright), 1962
Which Two Will Meet? (Banner), 1972
Which Way, Black Cat? (Lattimore), 1980
Which Way Freedom? (Hansen), 1986
Which Witch? (verse; Ahlberg), 1983
Whiffy McMann (Hader), 1933
While Mother Was Away (Talbot), 1924
While the Bells Ring (Mayne), 1979
While the Story-Log Burns (Burgess), 1938
Whingdingdilly (Peet), 1970
Whinstone Drift (R. Armstrong), 1951
Whipping Boy (S. Fleischman), 1986
Whisker (play; Fyleman), 1934
Whiskers and Rhymes (verse; Arnold Lobel), 1985
Whiskers Once and Always (Orgel), 1986
Whisper (G. Wilson), 1982
Whisper in the Night (Aiken), 1982
Whisper of Glocken (Kendall), 1965
Whisper of Lace (Cross), 1981
Whispered Horse (L. Hall), 1979
Whispering Girl (Means), 1941
Whispering Knights (Lively), 1971
Whispering Mountain (Aiken), 1968
Whispering Rabbit (M. W. Brown), 1965
Whispers (verse; K. Briggs), 1940
Whispers (verse; Livingston), 1958
Whispers from the Dead (Nixon), 1989
Whistle for the Crossing (de Angeli), 1977
Whistle for the Train (M. W. Brown, as MacDonald), 1956
Whistle for Willie (Keats), 1964
Whistle Punk of Camp 15, (Rounds), 1959
Whistler in the Mist (Fry), 1968
Whistling Boy (Arthur), 1969
Whistling Brownie (play; Blyton), 1935
Whistling Rufus (Mayne), 1964
Whistling Thief (Waddell), 1983
White Arab (Westerman), 1933
White Archer (Houston), 1967
White Bird (Bulla), 1966
White Boots (Streatfeild), 1951

White Bungalow (Sommerfelt, trans), 1963
White Calf (Faulknor), 1965
White Captives (Lampman), 1970
White Cockade (Cordell), 1970
White Cockade Passes (Fidler), 1947
White Cranes Castle (G. Harris), 1979
White Deer (Thurber), 1965
White Dingo (Patchett), 1965
White Doe (Church), 1968
White Dress (Finley, appendix), 1870
White Elephant (Clarke), 1952
White Fire (Saville), 1966
White Flower (Fyleman), 1953
White Ghost Summer (S. Murphy), 1967
White Horse (Coatsworth), 1942
White Horse (Leeson), 1977
White Horse Gang (Bawden), 1966
White Horse of Hungary (Catherall, as Ruthin), 1954
White Horse of Morocco (Coatsworth), 1973
White Isle (Snedeker), 1940
White Marble (Zolotow), 1963
White Mist (Smucker), 1985
White Mountain (R. Montgomery), 1953
White Mountains (Christopher), 1967
White Nights of St. Petersburg (Trease), 1967
White Oak (Wier), 1971
White Peak Farm (Doherty), 1984
White Peak Farm (play; Doherty), 1988
White Peril (Faulknor), 1966
White Rabbit's Road (O'Faolain), 1950
White Reindeer (Seton), 1915
White Riders (M. Edwards), 1950
White Romance (Hamilton), 1987
White Roof-Tree (E. Turner), 1905
White Sails to China (Bulla), 1955
White Sea Horse (Cresswell), 1964
White Ship (Aitmatov, trans), 1972
White Snow Bright Snow (Tresselt), 1947
White Sparrow (R. Brown), 1974
White Sparrow (Colum), 1933
White Stallion of Lipizza (Henry), 1964
White Steamship (Aitmatov, trans), 1972
White Stranger (play; Ainsworth), 1955
White Tail (R. Montgomery), 1958
White Turrets (Molesworth, appendix), 1895
White Twilight (Polland), 1962
White Tzar (Meade, appendix), 1896
White Voyage (Christopher), 1961
White Wyvill and Red Ruthven (Everett-Green, appendix), 1902
Whitefoot the Wood Mouse series (Burgess), from 1922
Whiteout (Houston), 1988
Whiter Than Snow (Walton, appendix), 1896
White-Starred Hare (Fidler), 1951
Whitey series (Rounds), from 1942
Whitman Kick (Burch), 1977
Whizz Kid (Tate), 1969
Who? (Schelin), 1963
Who Calls from Afar? (Brinsmead), 1971
Who Comes to King's Mountain? (J. and P. Beatty), 1975
Who Goes There? (H. Avery), 1927
Who Got Rid of Angus Flint? (Jones), 1978
Who Is Carrie? (Collier), 1984
Who Knew There'd Be Ghosts? (Brittain), 1985
Who Likes the Sun? (de Regniers), 1961
Who Lives Here? (verse; Latham), 1974
Who Look at Me? (verse; Jordan), 1969

Who Needs Me? (Heide), 1971
Who Owns the Moon? (Levitin), 1973
Who Ragged Railton? (F. Richards, as Clifford), 1952
Who Really Killed Cock Robin? (George), 1971
Who Rides in the Dark? (Meader), 1937
Who, Said Sue, Said Whoo? (verse; Raskin), 1973
Who, Sir? Me, Sir? (Peyton), 1983
Who Stole the Crown? (play; Blyton), 1939
Who Stole the Wizard of Oz? (Avi), 1981
Who Took the Farmer's Hat? (Lexau, as Nodset), 1963
Who Wants a Cheap Rhinoceros? (Silverstein, as Shelby), 1964
Who Wants Music on Monday? (Stolz), 1963
Who Wants to Be Alone? (Craig), 1974
Who Was Wendy? (Wynne), 1932
Who Will Be My Friends? (Hoff), 1960
Who Will Believe Tim Kitten? (Wahl), 1978
Who Will Comfort Toffle? (Jansson, trans), 1960
Who Will Hold the Giant? (play; Blyton), 1955
Whodunnit? (Cresswell), 1986
Whoo, Whoo, The Wind Blew (D. Ross), 1946
Whopper (Watkins-Pitchford), 1967
Who's a Clever Baby, Then? (McKee), 1988
Who's a Pest? (Bonsall), 1962
Who's Afraid (Pearce), 1986
Who's Afraid of Ernestine? (Sharmat), 1986
Who's Afraid of the Dark? (Bonsall), 1980
Who's Bill? (Storr), 1976
Who's Talking? (Ure), 1987
Who's Upside Down? (C. Johnson), 1952
Whose Cat Is That? (Kahl), 1979
Whose Eyes Am I? (Bonsall), 1968
Whose Mouse Are You? (R. Kraus), 1970
Whose Town? (L. Graham), 1969
Whose Turtle? (Orgel), 1968
Whuppity Stories (play; K. Briggs), 1937
Why Am I Invisible (play; K. Kraus), 1982
Why Can't I Be William? (Conford), 1972
Why Does Everybody Think I'm Nutty? (Collier), 1971
Why Me? (Branfield), 1973
Why Me? (Conford), 1985
Why the Wind God Wept (Titus), 1972
Whys and Wherefores of Littabelle Lee (V. and B. Cleaver), 1973
Wicked Kings of Bloon (Kellogg), 1970
Wicked One (M. Hunter), 1977
Wickham and the Armada (Treece), 1959
Widdershins Crescent (Townsend), 1965
Wide Awake (verse; Livingston), 1959
Wide, Wide World (Warner, as Wetherell, appendix), 1851
Wide-Awake Owl (Slobodkin), 1958
Widow and Her Daughter (Warner, appendix), 1864
Widow MacLean (Ingelow, appendix), 1903
Wiggins for President (Brooks), 1939
Wiggle to the Laundromat (verse; D.Lee), 1970
Wigwam in the City (Smucker), 1966
Wig-wig and Homer (P. Turner), 1969
Wilberforce and the Slaves (Clewes), 1961
Wilbur the Warrior (Slobodkin), 1972
Wild (B. Graham), 1986
Wild and Free (H. Griffiths), 1958
Wild Angel (Spykman), 1957
Wild Animal Books (Castor, trans), from 1937
Wild Animal Play for Children (play; Seton), 1900
Wild Animal Ways (Seton), 1916
Wild Animals at Home (Seton), 1913
Wild Animals I Have Known (Seton), 1898
Wild Appaloosa (Rounds), 1983

Wild Boy (Tate), 1972
Wild Boy in the Bush (Dallas), 1971
Wild Cat (R. N. Peck), 1975
Wild Cat Island (Stranger), 1961
Wild Cherry (D. Ross), 1943
Wild Children (Holman), 1983
Wild Dogs (Mitchison), 1977
Wild Flowers (play; Hoff), 1973
Wild Geese Flying (Meigs), 1957
Wild Goose Quest (D. Bruce), 1945
Wild Goose Saboteur (Catherall), 1955
Wild Goose Tale (M. Steele, as Gage), 1961
Wild Heart (H. Griffiths), 1963
Wild Horse of Santander (H. Griffiths), 1966
Wild Horses (Bunting, as Bolton), 1974
Wild Hunt of Hagworthy (Lively), 1971
Wild Hunt of the Ghost Hounds (Lively), 1972
Wild Idea (B. Willard), 1965
Wild in the World (Donovan), 1971
Wild Jack (Christopher), 1974
Wild Kitty (Meade, appendix), 1897
Wild Little House (Dillon), 1955
Wild Lone (Watkins-Pitchford), 1938
Wild Man of the West (Ballantyne, appendix), 1863
Wild Martin (Tate), 1967
Wild Men Invade the Roman Empire (play; Mitchison), 1937
Wild Morgans (A. Morgan), 1988
Wild Mustang (L. Hall), n.d.
Wild One (Bunting), 1974
Wild One (M. Edwards), 1967
Wild Orphan (Rounds), 1961
Wild Place (Cockett), 1968
Wild Ponies (Stranger), 1976
Wild Pony Island (Meader), 1959
Wild Trek (Kjelgaard), 1950
Wild Valley (Severn), 1963
Wild White Stallion (Guillot, trans), 1961
Wild, Wild West (verse; Daugherty), 1948
Wild Winter (K. Wood), 1954
Wild Wood series (Clewes), from 1945
Wild Wood (Needle), 1981
Wildcat under Glass (Zei, trans), 1968
Wilderness Bride (A. and E. Johnson), 1962
Wilderness Champion (Lippincott), 1944
Wilderness Clearing (Edmonds), 1944
Wilderness Journey (W. Steele), 1953
Wilderness Road (Altsheler), 1901
Wildest Horse Race in the World (Henty), 1976
Wildfire (M. Clark), 1973
Wildlife Cameraman (Kjelgaard), 1957
Wildlife Tales (Poole), 1986
Wildling (Bibby), 1971
Wildman (Crossley-Holland), 1976
Wilfred the Lion (Hoff), 1970
Wilfred the Rat (Stevenson), 1977
Wilful Cousin Kate (Meade, appendix), 1905
Wilful Maid (Everett-Green, appendix), 1909
Wilful Willoughbys (Everett-Green, appendix), 1893
Wilkin's Ghost (Burch), 1978
Wilkins' Tooth (Jones), 1973
Wilkses (Cresswell), 1970
Will Spring Be Early or Will Spring Be Late? (C. Johnson), 1960
Will the Fiddle (Blyton), 1960
Will to Win (Meader), 1936
Will You Be My Friend? (Iwasaki, trans), 1974
Will You Be My Posslq? (Bunting), 1987

ADVISERS AND CONTRIBUTORS

AGOSTA, Lucien L. Assistant Professor of English, California State University, Sacramento. Author of *Howard Pyle*, 1987, and of articles on the Brownings, D.G. Rossetti, Richard Wright, Kurt Vonnegut, Thomas Hughes, and Thornton Waldo Burgess. **Essay:** Thornton Waldo Burgess.

ALBERGHENE, Janice M. Associate Professor of English, Fitchburg State College, Massachusetts. Author of 18 articles on children's literature, the most recent being "Moralists, But with No Pretense," 1988, "Humor in Children's Literature," 1988, and "Artful Memory: Jean Fritz, Autobiography and the Child Reader," 1989. **Essays:** M.E. Kerr; Daniel Manus Pinkwater.

ANDERSON, William D. Professor of English, California State University, Northridge. Author of *A New Look at Children's Literature* (with Patrick Groff), 1972. **Essay:** Norton Juster.

ANTCZAK, Janice. Professor, Brookdale Community College, Lincroft, New Jersey. Author of *Science Fiction: The Mythos of a New Romance*, 1985. **Essay:** Pamela Sargent.

APPIAH, Peggy. See her own entry.

APSELOFF, Marilyn F. Associate Professor of English, Kent State University, Kent, Ohio. Author of *Virginia Hamilton: Ohio Explorer in the World of Imagination*, 1978, *Nonsense Literature for Children: From Aesop to Seuss* (with Celia Catlett Anderson), 1989, *They Wrote for Children Too: An Annotated Bibliography of Children's Literature by Famous Writers for Adults*, 1989, and of essays in *World Book Encyclopedia*, *Illinois English Bulletin*, *Children's Literature in Education*, and other periodicals. **Essays:** Joan W. Blos; Walter D. Edmonds; Brinton Turkle.

ASHDOWN, Fran. Children's librarian, North Vancouver District Public Library; reviewer, *Canadian Book Review Annual*. **Essays:** Esther Averill; Sheila Burnford; Christie Harris; Markoosie; Richard Scarry.

AVERY, Gillian. See her own entry. **Essays:** Jacob Abbott (appendix); Evelyn Everett-Green (appendix); Juliana Horatia Ewing (appendix); G.E. Farrow; Charles Kingsley (appendix); Amy Le Feuvre; Mary Norton; Eleanor H. Porter; Arthur Ransome; Alice Hegan Rice; Margaret Sidney (appendix); Hesba Stretton (appendix); Booth Tarkington; Susan Warner (appendix); Charlotte Yonge (appendix).

BAKER, Janet E. Associate Professor of English, St. Mary's University, Halifax, Nova Scotia. **Essay:** Hubert Evans.

BAKKER, Jan. Associate Professor of English, Utah State University, Logan; consulting editor, *Children's Literature*. Author of *Pastoral in Antebellum Southern Romance*, and *Marxism, Feminism and Free Love* (with Francelia Butler), 1981, and of articles on southern literature in *Early American Literature*, *Studies in American Fiction*, *Southern Literary Journal*, *Southern Studies*, and other periodicals, and of two bibliographies of 19th-century children's literature in *Children's Literature*. **Essay:** Joel Chandler Harris (appendix).

BARKER, Keith. Deputy librarian, Westhill College, Birmingham; editor, *Youth Library Review*, and review editor, *School Librarian*. Author of *In the Realms of Gold*, 1986. **Essays:** Peter Hunt; James Watson; Rosemary Wells.

BARTHOLOMEW, Ann. Freelance writer. Author of *Reading for Enjoyment with 7–11 Year Olds*, 1981. **Essays:** Carol Ryrie Brink; Grace Hogarth; Kate Seredy.

BAYFIELD, Juliana. Librarian, Children's Literature Research Collection, State Library of South Australia, Adelaide. Author of "From Simon Black to Ash Road and Beyond" in *Bookbird*, 1968, and of articles on library services for young people. **Essay:** George Manville Fenn (appendix).

BELL, Anthea. Freelance translator, specializing in French and German children's books; has translated nearly 100 books. Author of *E. Nesbit*, 1960, and the novels *A London Season*, 1983, and *The Floral Companion*, 1988. **Essays:** Christianna Brand; Anthony Buckeridge; Anne Fine; Leon Garfield; Norman Hunter; Ruth Manning-Sanders; Foreign-Language Writers.

BIERMAN, Valerie. Organiser, Edinburgh Book Festival Children's Fair; children's book reviewer, the *Scotsman*; co-editor, *Bookmark* magazine. Recipient, Eleanor Farjeon award, 1987. Editor of *Streets Ahead* (stories), 1989. **Essays:** Mairi Hedderwick; Judith O'Neill; Alison Prince.

BLOOM, Susan P. Director, Center for the Study of Children's Literature, and Assistant Professor, Simmons College, Boston. **Essay:** Paul Fleischman.

BOEGEHOLD, Betty. Former senior associate editor, Bank Street College of Education Publications Division, New York. Author of several books for children, including the *Pippa Mouse* series, from 1973, and most recently, *What the Wind Told*, 1987, and of *Choosing Books for Children* (with Joanne Oppenheim and Barbara Brenner), 1986. Died 1985. **Essays:** Eleanor Clymer; Jean Merrill; Evaline Ness.

BOYLE, Bill. Advisory teacher, Wirral Local Education Authority; deputy editor, *Junior Education*; reviewer for the *Guardian*, *Books for Keeps*, and *School Librarian*. Author of *What's in a Poem?*, 1983, *Your Geography*, 1984, *Local Directories*, 1987, *Evidence Through Maps*, and of "Words Joined Together," a Thames Television poetry documentary. **Essay:** Edward Fenton.

BRATTON, J.S. Reader in Theatre and Cultural Studies, Royal Holloway and Bedford New College, University of London. Author of *The Victorian Popular Ballad*, 1975, and *The Impact of Victorian Children's Fiction*, 1981. **Essays:** F.W. Farrar (appendix); L.T. Meade (appendix); Mrs. O.F. Walton (appendix).

BRIGGS, Julia. Fellow and Tutor in English, Hertford College, Oxford. Author of *Night Visitors: The Rise and Fall of the English Ghost Story*, 1977, *This Stage-Play World: English Literature and Its Background 1580–1625*, 1983, and *A Woman of Passion: The Life of E. Nesbit*, 1987. **Essay:** Walter de la Mare.

BRINKLEY-WILLSHER, Valerie. Freelance writer and lecturer; reviewer of children's books for several periodicals. Former contributor to *Signal*. Author of *Across Time*, 1973. **Essays:** Margaret J. Baker; Pauline Clarke; E.W. Hildick; Katharine Hull and Pamela Whitlock; Elisabeth Kyle; Ann Lawrence; Bessie Marchant; Alison Morgan; Pamela Oldfield; Susan Price; Gwynedd Rae; Rodie Sudbery.

BULL, Angela. See her own entry. **Essays:** Joanna Cannan; Eileen Dunlop; Lorna Hill; Josephine Pullein-Thompson; Noel Streatfeild; Jean Ure.

BULLA, Clyde Robert. See his own entry. **Essay:** Irene Hunt.

BURNS, Mary Mehlman. Coodinator, Curriculum Library, and Children's Literature Specialist, Framingham State College, Massachusetts; reviewer, *Horn Book*. Author of an essay on Robert Lawson in *Horn Book*, 1972. **Essay:** Robert Lawson.

BUTLER, Dorothy. Bookseller in Auckland and lecturer. Recipient, Eleanor Farjeon award, 1979. Author of *Cushla and Her Books*, 1979, *Reading Begins at Home* (with Marie Clay), 1979, *Babies Need Books*, 1980, *The Dorothy Butler Pre-Reading Kit*, 1980, *Reading for Enjoyment with 0–6 Year Olds*, 1981, *For Me, Me, Me*, 1983, *I Will Build You a House*, 1984, *Five to Eight*, 1985, and *My Brown Bear Barney*, 1989. Editor of *The Magpies Said* (for children), 1980. **Essays:** Maurice Duggan; E.M. Ellin; Diana Moorhead; Eve Sutton.

BUTLER, Francelia. Professor of English, University of Connecticut, Storrs; founder and editor-in-chief, *Children's Literature*. Founder, seminar on Children's Literature and permanent Division of Children's Literature, Modern Language Association; member of the founding board, Children's Literature Association. Author of *Children's Literature: A Module*, 1975, *Sharing Literature with Children*, 1977, *Masterworks of Children's Literature 1550–1739*, 1977, *Marxism, Feminism and Free Love* (with Jan Bakker), 1981, *The Lucky Piece* (novel), 1984, *200 Selected Film Classics for Children of All Ages* (with Phillip J. Steeman and Bernard Queenan), 1984, *Indira Gandhi*, 1986, *Skipping Around the World: The Ritual Nature of Folk Rhymes*, 1988, and of books on Shakespeare and 17th-century drama. Editor, with Richard Rotert, of *Reflections on Literature for Children*, 1984, and *Triumphs of the Spirit in Children's Literature*, 1986, and, with Rotert and Anne Devereaux Jordan, of *The Wide World All Around*, 1987. **Essay:** Natalie Savage Carlson.

BUTTS, Dennis. Freelance writer and critic; editor, *Henty Society Bulletin*. Formerly Principal Lecturer in English, Bulmershe College of Higher Education, Reading, Berkshire. Author of *Living Words* (with John Merrick), 1966, and *R.L. Stevenson*, 1966. Editor of *Pergamon Poets 8*, 1970, *Good Writers for Young Readers: Critical Essays*, 1977, and *The Secret Garden*, 1987. **Essays:** Anita Desai; Russell Hoban; W.E. Johns; Frederick Marryat (appendix); Robert Louis Stevenson (appendix); Herbert Strang.

CADOGAN, Mary. Secretary of an educational trust, governor of an international school, and freelance writer. Author of three books on popular literature with Patricia Craig—*You're a Brick, Angela!*, 1976, *Women and Children First*, 1978, *The Lady Investigates*, 1981— three volumes of *The Charles Hamilton Companion* (with John Wernham), 1976–82, *The Morcove Companion* (with Tommy Keen), 1981, *From Wharton Lodge to Linton Hall: The Charles Hamilton Christmas Companion* (with Tommy Keen), 1984, *Richmal Crompton: The Woman Behind William*, 1986, and *Frank Richards: The Chap Behind the Chums*, 1988. **Essays:** Gillian Avery; Elinor M. Brent-Dyer; Dorita Fairlie Bruce; Christine Chaundler; Richmal Crompton; Gene Kemp; Tim Kennemore; Dorothea Moore; Elsie J. Oxenham; Frank Richards; Ethel Talbot; Mary Tourtel and Alfred Bestall; P.L. Travers; May Wynne.

CAMPBELL, Alasdair K.D. Consultant Tutor Librarian, Education Library, University of Keele, Staffordshire; columnist, "Children, Books, and Reading," *School Librarian*. Author of *Novels with a Background of School*, 1970 (revised as *Novels and Plays with a Background of School*, 1979), and of articles on children's literature and school librarianship in *School Librarian* and other periodicals. **Essays:** John Branfield; Angela Bull; Elizabeth Goudge; Eric Knight; J.P. Martin; Alfred Ollivant; Sylvia Sherry; C. Fox Smith; Katharine Tozer.

CAMPBELL, Margaret. Freelance writer. Author of *Lend a Hand: Social Work for the Young*, 1966, and of articles on Oxfordshire personalities for *Limited Edition*, and articles and reviews for *British Book News*, *Countryman*, and other periodicals. Editor of *The Countryman Book* series, 3 vols., 1973–75. **Essays:** Val Biro; Frank Knight; John Pudney; James Reeves; John Symonds.

CARPENTER, Humphrey. Freelance writer. Author of *J.R.R. Tolkien: A Biography*, 1977, *The Inklings*, 1978, *Jesus*, 1980, *W.H. Auden: A Biography*, 1981, the *Mr. Majeika* series (for children), from 1984, *OUDS: A Centenary History of the Oxford University Dramatic Society*, 1985, *Secret Gardens: The Golden Age of Children's Literature*, 1985, and *A Serious Character: The Life of Ezra Pound*, 1988. Editor of *The Letters of J.R.R. Tolkien*, 1981, and *The Oxford Companion to Children's Literature* (with Mari Prichard), 1984. **Essays:** Thomas Hughes (appendix); Philippa Pearce; T.H. White.

CARTER, Anne. Freelance writer, editor, and translator. **Essays:** Charles Keeping; Graham Oakley; Josephine Poole; Dodie Smith; Mary Treadgold.

CAUSLEY, Charles. See his own entry. **Essays:** Kevin Crossley-Holland; Ted Hughes; Brian Patten.

CHANG, Charity. Retired librarian. Author of the preface to the Mary De Morgan volume of *Classics of Children's Literature* and of the bibliography in *Masterworks of Children's Literature 1550–1739* by Francelia Butler, 1977. **Essays:** Carolyn Sherwin Bailey; Eric Kelly; Eloise Jarvis McGraw; Monica Shannon; Elizabeth Yates.

CHRISTIAN, Mary Blount. Instructor of Creative Writing, Rice University Continuing Studies, Houston; co-founder, Association of Authors of Children's Literature, Houston; creator and moderator, *Children's Bookshelf* television program, Houston; children's books reviewer for Houston *Chronicle* and Houston *Post*. Author of more than 70 fiction and non-fiction books for children, including the *Goosehill Gang*, *Sebastian*, and *Penrod* series, and most recently, *Singin' Somebody Else's Song*, 1986. **Essay:** Robert Kraus.

CHURCHER, John. Librarian, London Borough of Brent; editor of a NALGO magazine. Author of articles in *Junior Bookshelf*. **Essays:** W.V. Awdry; Padraic Colum; Tanith Lee; Helen Nicoll; Michael Rosen.

CLARK, Berna C. Former schools librarian, Bristol Public Libraries, and senior assistant to the County Education/Children's Librarian, Avon County Council. Former national chairman of the Library Association Youth Library Group. **Essays:** Anne Mainwaring Barrett; Jane Duncan; Antonia Ridge; Vian Smith; Jenifer Wayne.

CLEAVER, Pamela. Freelance journalist; tutor, London School of Journalism. Author of *The Sparrow Book of Record Breakers* [and *Animal Records*], 2 vols., 1981–82, and of children's stories for anthologies, annuals, and magazines. **Essays:** Ronald Welch; Barbara Willard.

COOPER, Ilene L. Reviewer, American Library Association *Booklist*, Chicago; consultant for the American Broadcasting Company. Author of *Susan B. Anthony*, 1984, *The Winning of Miss Lynn Ryan*, 1987, and *Queen of the Sixth Grade*, 1988. Editor, with Denise Murcko Wilms, of *A Guide to Non-Sexist Children's Books 2: 1976–1984*, 1985. **Essay:** Maud Hart Lovelace.

COSGRAVE, Mary Silva. Former children's librarian and

children's books editor for Houghton Mifflin and Pantheon. Former editor of "The Outlook Tower" column in *Horn Book*. **Essays:** Thomas Bailey Aldrich (appendix); Arna Bontemps; Maureen Daly.

COUGHLAN, Margaret N. Reference specialist, Children's Literature Center, Library of Congress, Washington, D.C. Author of the bibliographies *Creating Independence 1763–1789*, 1972, and *Folklore from Africa to the United States*, 1976. Editor of *Yankee Doodle's Literary Sampler* (with Virginia Haviland), 1974, *Children's Books 1981*, 1982, and *Books for Children*, 4 vols., 1982–87.

CRAIG, Patricia. Freelance writer. Author of three books on popular literature with Mary Cadogan—*You're a Brick, Angela!*, 1976, *Women and Children First*, 1978, and *The Lady Investigates*, 1981—and of a biography of Elizabeth Bowen. **Essays:** Lucy Boston; Patricia Lynch; Meta Mayne Reid; Geraldine Symons.

CREW, Hilary S. Ph.D. candidate, School of Communication, Information, and Library Studies, Rutgers University, New Brunswick, New Jersey. Author of "Blossom Culp and Her Ilk: The Independent Female in Richard Peck's Young Adult Fiction" in *Top of the News*, 1987, and "From Labyrinth to Celestial City: Setting and Portrayal of the Female Adolescent in Science Fiction" in *Youth Services in Libraries*, 1988. **Essays:** Robin McKinley; Richard Peck.

CROUCH, Marcus. Former deputy county librarian, Kent. Author of *Beatrix Potter*, 1960, *Treasure Seekers and Borrowers*, 1962, *The Nesbit Tradition*, 1972, *Kentish Books, Kentish Writers*, 1988, and of several collections of retold tales for children. Editor, with Alec Ellis, of *Chosen for Children* (on the Carnegie Medal), 3rd edition, 1977. **Essays:** Ruth Arthur; Hilaire Belloc; Elisabeth Beresford; Margery Williams Bianco; Helen Cresswell; Primrose Cumming; J.G. Fyson; Ann Halam; Richard Hughes; Clive King; Eric Linklater; Leo Lionni; Jenny Nimmo; Jill Paton Walsh; Stephanie Plowman; E.V. Rieu.

CROXSON, Mary. Senior Lecturer in English, Tutor-in-Charge of Diploma in Professional Studies in Education, and director of the annual summer school in children's literature, Worcester College of Higher Education. Author of *Using the Library*, 1966, and "The Emancipated Child in the Novels of E. Nesbit" in *Signal*, 1974. **Essays:** Walt Morey; C. Everard Palmer; Eleanor Spence; Theodore Taylor; Gina Wilson.

CULPAN, Norman. Former Head of the English Department, St. Paul's College of Education, Cheltenham; former review editor, *School Librarian*. Author of *Modern Adult Fiction*, 1955, and *Contemporary Adult Fiction* (with W.J. Messer), 1966. Editor of *Dialogue and Drama* (with James Reeves), 1950, and *Variety Is King: Aspects of Fiction for Children* (with Clifford Waite), 1977. **Essays:** Andre Norton; Barbara Euphan Todd.

DAY, Alan Edwin. Head of the Department of Library and Information Studies, Manchester Polytechnic. Author of three reference handbooks—*History*, 1976, *Archaeology*, 1977, and *Discovery and Exploration*, 1980—and of *J.B. Priestley: An Annotated Bibliography*, 1980, *Search for the Northwest Passage: An Annotated Bibliography*, 1986, *The British Library*, 1988, and of an essay on W.E. Johns's Biggles in *Children's Literature in Education*, 1974. **Essays:** Mabel Esther Allan; Richard Church; Samuel Rutherford Crockett; Peter Dawlish; Kathleen Fidler; Roy Fuller; Michael Hardcastle; Ronald Syme; John Verney.

DONAHUE, Rosanne Fraine. Assistant to the Vice Chancellor for Academic Affairs, University of Massachusetts, Boston. Author

of "New Realism in the Twentieth Century" in *Masterworks of Children's Literature*, 1986, and "A Solitary Blue" in *Beacham's Guide to Literature and Biography for Young Adults*, 1989. **Essay:** Betsy Byars.

DONLON, Pat. Director, National Library of Ireland, Dublin. Editor of *The Lucky Bag: Classic Irish Children's Stories*, 1984. **Essays:** Eileen O'Faolain; Pat O'Shea; Rosamond Praeger.

DOONAN, Jane. Freelance teacher, reviewer, and writer. Author of several articles on picture books and picture-book artists/writers. **Essays:** Anthony Browne; Tony Ross.

DOYLE, Brian. Freelance writer; contributor to the *Guardian, Books and Bookmen*, and *Collector's Digest*. Author of *The Who's Who of Boys' Writers and Illustrators*, 1964, and *The Who's Who of Children's Literature*, 1968. **Essays:** S.G. Hulme Beaman; Talbot Baines Reed (appendix); Donald Suddaby.

DUNBAR, Robert. Lecturer in English, Church of Ireland College of Education, Dublin; founding member, Children's Literature Association of Ireland; children's book reviewer for the *Times Educational Supplement*, *School Librarian*, and the *Irish Times*. **Essay:** J.S. Andrews.

du SAUTOY, Peter. Former chairman of Faber and Faber Ltd., London. Author of *Alison Uttley: The Life of a Country Child*, 1986. **Essay:** Alison Uttley.

EAGLEN, Audrey. Order Department manager, Cuyahoga County Public Library, Cleveland; Assistant Professor, Kent State University, Kent, Ohio; contributing editor, *Collection Building*; columnist, *School Library Journal*; reviewer, *New York Times Book Review* and other journals. Author of *Buying Books: A Practical Guide for Librarians*, 1989. **Essays:** Judy Blume; Lois Duncan; Norma Klein; Barbara Wersba.

ECCLESHARE, Julia. Selecter of Children's Books of the Year, Book Trust. Author of *Children's Books of the Year*, 4 vols., 1985–88, and *Treasure Islands: The Woman's Hour Guide to Children's Reading*, 1988. **Essay:** Adèle Geras.

ELKIN, Judith. Freelance writer, lecturer, and children's books reviewer. Former Head of Library Services to Children and Young People, Birmingham Public Libraries. Recipient, Eleanor Farjeon award, 1986. Author of *Multi-racial Books for the Classroom*, 1980, *Nowhere to Play* (English text), 1982, *The Hiroshima Story*, 1983, *Mighty Mountain and the Three Strong Women*, 1984, *The Books for Keeps Guide to Children's Books for a Multicultural Society 8–12*, 1985, and *Japanese Family* (*A Family in Japan*), 1986. Editor of *The New Golden Land Anthology*, 1983. **Essays:** John Cunliffe; Marjorie Darke.

ELLEMAN, Barbara. Editor, Children's Books Section, American Library Association *Booklist*, Chicago. **Essays:** Nancy Bond; Tomie de Paola; Constance C. Greene.

ELLIS, Anne W. Assistant librarian, Liverpool Institute of Higher Education. Author of *The Family Story in the 1960's*, 1970. **Essays:** Eric Allen; Nancy Breary; Pamela Brown; Antonia Forest; Eleanor Graham; Laurence Meynell; Sheena Porter.

ELLIS, Sarah. Librarian, North Vancouver District Library; columnist for *Horn Book*. Author of a children's novel *The Baby Project* (*The Family Project*), 1986. **Essays:** Sue Ann Alderson; Palmer Brown; Tim Wynne-Jones.

ENGLAND, A.W. Former Lecturer in Drama, Division of Education, University of Sheffield. Author of *Scripted Drama: A Practical Guide to Teaching Techniques*, 1981, the forthcoming *Theatre for the Young*, and of two television plays for children, television and stage adaptations of works by Sylvia Sherry and Bernard Ashley, several radio plays, and an article on Walter Macken in *Use of English*. Editor of *Man and Superman* by Shaw, 1969, and of the anthologies *Looking at Scenes*, 1969, *Two Ages of Man*, 1971, *Caves*, 1973, and *Islands*, 1974. **Essay:** Walter Macken.

ENGLAND, Claire. Associate Professor of Library and Information Science, University of Toronto. Author with Adele M. Fasick, *Children Using Media*, 1977, *ChildView: Evaluating and Reviewing Materials for Children*, 1987, and of articles on children's literature. **Essays:** Horatio Alger (appendix); Palmer Cox (appendix).

ERISMAN, Fred. Professor of Literature, Texas Christian University, Fort Worth. Author of *Frederic Remington*, 1975, *Barnboken i USA* (with Zena Sutherland), 1986, and of articles on L. Frank Baum, Ralph Henry Barbour, Kate Douglas Wiggin, Howard Garis, Laura Ingalls Wilder, and Robert A. Heinlein. Editor, with Richard Etulain, of *Fifty Western Writers: A Bio-Bibliographical Sourcebook*, 1982. **Essays:** Mary O'Hara; Jack Schaefer.

FADER, Ellen G. Head of Children's Services, Westport Public Library, Connecticut; reviewer for *School Library Journal* and *Horn Book*. **Essay:** Edward Ormondroyd.

FASICK, Adele M. Professor of Library Science, University of Toronto. Author, with Claire England, of *Children Using Media*, 1977, and *ChildView: Evaluating and Reviewing Materials for Children*, 1987, and of *What Should Libraries Do for Children?*, and of articles on Anne Carroll Moore, film adaptations of books for children, and children's librarianship. **Essay:** Betty Levin.

FICK, Martha J. Employee of computer software company in Chadds Ford, Pennsylvania. **Essays:** Peggy Parish; Bernard Waber; Gene Zion.

FITZGIBBON, Tom. Principal Lecturer and Head of the Department of English, School of Primary and Early Childhood Education, Auckland College of Education. Founder, New Zealand Children's Literature Association. Author of various articles and reviews and co-editor of two books on New Zealand writers and illustrators. **Essays:** R.L. Bacon; Joy Cowley; Anne de Roo; William Taylor; Joyce West.

FLANAGAN, Sheila. Librarian, Carysfort College, Blackrock, County Dublin. Former lecturer in children's librarianship. **Essay:** Tom McCaughren.

FORDYCE, Rachel. Associate Professor of English, Virginia Polytechnic and State University, Blacksburg; contributing editor, *Children's Literature*. Author of *Children's Literature and Creative Dramatics*, 1975, *Caroline Drama: A Bibliographic History of Criticism*, 1978, and *Lewis Carroll: A Reference Guide*, 1988. **Essays:** Alice Dalgliesh; Rachel Field; Joanna Halpert Kraus; Bill Peet; Louis Slobodkin; Bertha Upton.

FORMAN, Jack. Reference/bibliographic services librarian, Mesa College Library, San Diego; book reviewer for *Library Journal*, *School Library Journal*, and *Journal of Youth Services in Libraries*. Author of *Presenting Paul Zindel*, 1988, and of several articles on children's literature. **Essays:** Robert Lipsyte; Walter Dean Myers.

FOX, Geoff. Senior Lecturer, Exeter University School of Education; joint editor, *Children's Literature in Education*, and Collins Cascades series; regular contributor, *Times Educational Supplement*. Author of *Teaching Literature: Nine to Fourteen* (with Michael Benton), 1985. Editor, with Graham Hammond, of *Writers, Critics and Children*, 1976, and *Responses to Children's Literature*, 1980. **Essays:** C. Day Lewis; S.E. Hinton.

FRANCIS, Christine Doyle. President, C.D.F. Educational Consulting. **Essays:** Marc Brown; Syd Hoff; Johanna Hurwitz; Anne Rockwell.

FREEMAN, Gillian. Novelist, screenwriter, and journalist. Author of 12 novels—the most recent being *Love Child*, 1984, and *Termination Rock*, 1989—and of *The Undergrowth of Literature*, 1967, and *The Schoolgirl Ethic: The Life and Work of Angela Brazil*, 1976. **Essays:** Angela Brazil; Susan Coolidge (appendix).

FREEMAN, Maggie. Freelance writer; children's book reviewer, *Sunday Times*. Author of *Danger! Space Pirates*, 1987. **Essays:** Vivien Alcock; Berlie Doherty.

FRYATT, Norma R. Freelance writer and editor. Author of *Sarah Josepha Hale*, 1976. Editor of *A Horn Book Sampler*, 1959. **Essays:** E.M. Almedingen; Lucy Fitch Perkins.

FUCHS, Marcia G. Reference librarian and cataloguer, Guilford Free Library, Connecticut; reviewer for *Library Journal*. **Essays:** Richard Atwater; Myra Cohn Livingston; Phyllis McGinley; Jane Yolen.

GIBBS, Matyelok. Former artistic director of the Unicorn Theatre for Young People, London.

GIBLIN, James Cross. Editor and publisher, Clarion Books, New York. Author of *The Scarecrow Book* (with Dale Ferguson), 1980, *The Skyscraper Book*, 1981, *Chimney Sweeps: Yesterday and Today*, 1982, *Fireworks, Picnics, and Flags: The Story of the Fourth of July Symbols*, 1983, *Walls: Defenses Throughout History*, 1984, *The Truth about Santa Claus*, 1985, *Milk: The Fight for Purity*, 1986, *From Hand to Mouth, or, How We Invented Knives, Forks, Spoons, and Chopsticks and the Table Manners to Go with Them*, 1987, *Let There Be Light: A Book about Windows*, 1988, *Writing Books for Young People*, 1989, and of articles on children's book writing and publishing. **Essays:** Beatrice Schenk de Regniers; Mildred Lee; Alvin Tresselt; Jan Wahl.

GILDERDALE, Betty. Lecturer, Continuing Education Department, Auckland University; reviewer, *New Zealand Herald*; editor, Hodder and Stoughton Kotare series of New Zealand children's classics; New Zealand editor, *Phaedrus*. Founding member and past president of the New Zealand Children's Literature Association. Author of *A Sea Change: 145 Years of New Zealand Junior Fiction*, 1982, and *Introducing Margaret Mahy*, 1987. **Essays:** Ruth Dallas; Joan de Hamel; Lynley Dodd; Edith Howes; Caroline Macdonald; Lilith Norman; Isabel Maud Peacocke; Phyl Wardell; Patricia Wrightson.

GLOVER, Michael. Freelance writer and editor; reviewer, *Books and Bookmen*, *British Book News*, *P.N. Review*, the *Melbourne Age*, the *Observer*, and *School Librarian*. **Essays:** Charles Causley; Mollie Hunter; Vernon Scannell; Kit Wright.

GMUCA, Jacqueline L. Assistant Professor of English,

University of South Carolina-Coastal Carolina College, Conway. Author of the entry on Arnold Lobel in *Dictionary of Literary Biography*. **Essays:** Anita Lobel; Arnold Lobel; Cynthia Rylant.

GORDON, Cecilia. Librarian in London schools for 10 years, and Inner London Education Authority library organiser, 1972–76. Former national Chairwoman of the School Library Association. Author of *Resource Organization*, 1978, and of an article in *Teenage Reading*, 1979, and reviews in *Times Educational Supplement*, *Times Literary Supplement*, *Children's Book Review*, and *School Librarian*. **Essays:** Joseph E. Chipperfield; Janet McNeill.

GOUGH, John. Lecturer in Mathematics Education, Victoria College, Malvern, Victoria. Author of several articles on children's literature, including "*The Dark is Rising*: An Assessment" in *English in Education*, 1985, and "Reconsidering Judy Blume's Young Adult Novel *Forever*" in *Use of English*, 1985. **Essays:** Crosby Bonsall; William Corlett; Martin Waddell.

GREAVES, Margaret. See her own entry. **Essays:** Joyce Gard; Nicholas Stuart Gray; Rosemary Harris; Margery Sharp; Rosemary Weir.

GREEN, Roger Lancelyn. See his own entry. **Essays:** Lewis Carroll (appendix); Rudyard Kipling; Andrew Lang (appendix).

GREENLAW, M. Jean. Professor of Education, University of North Texas, Denton. Author of *Storybook Classrooms: Using Children's Literature in the Learning Center-Primary Grades* (with Karla H. Wendelin), 1984, and *Educating the Gifted: A Sourcebook* (with Margaret E. McIntosh), 1988. **Essays:** H.M. Hoover; Zibby Oneal; Meredith Ann Pierce; Ouida Sebestyen.

GROFF, Patrick. Professor of Education, San Diego State University; contributing editor, Chircorel Library Publishing Corporation. Author of *A New Look at Children's Literature* (with William D. Anderson), 1972, *Private Sector Alternatives for Preventing Reading Failure*, 1987, *Word Recognition* (with Dorothy Z. Seymour), 1987, and of articles in *Elementary English*, *Horn Book*, *School Librarian*, and other periodicals. **Essays:** Robert Bright; Carolyn Haywood; William Lipkind; Helen Sewell; Esphyr Slobodkina; William Jay Smith; Phil Stong.

HAAS, Irene. Freelance illustrator; has illustrated books by Sesyle Joslin, Elizabeth Enright, Myra Cohn Livingston, and others. Author of *The Maggie B*, 1975, and *The Little Moon Theatre*, 1981. **Essay:** Elizabeth Enright.

HADLEY, Eric. Lecturer in Education, South Glamorgan Institute of Higher Education, Cardiff. Author, with Tessa Hadley, of *Legends of the Sun and Moon*, 1983, and *Legends of Earth, Air, Fire and Water*, 1985, and of *English in the Middle Years*, 1985, and *Ivan the Fool and Other Plays*, 1988. Editor of *Teaching Practice and the Probationary Year*, 1982. **Essays:** Allan Ahlberg; Roald Dahl; Jan Needle; Robert Westall.

HALL, Dennis. Freelance journalist. Former children's librarian, Public Library of South Australia, Adelaide, and assistant editor, *School Magazine*. **Essay:** Norman Lindsay.

HAMMOND, Graham. Lecturer, Exeter University School of Education; joint editor, *Children's Literature in Education*. Editor, with Geoff Fox, of *Writers, Critics and Children*, 1976, and *Responses to Children's Literature*, 1980, and, with Andrew Wilkinson, *Language for Learning*, 1977. **Essays:** Eilís Dillon; Roger Lancelyn Green; Madeleine A. Polland.

HAMMOND, Nancy C. Freelance writer; guest reviewer, *Horn Book*. Co-author of *Helping Young Children Learn*, 1976. **Essays:** Mary Chalmers; James Flora.

HANLEY, Karen Stang. Staff member, American Library Association *Booklist*, Chicago; freelance writer. **Essay:** Sharon Bell Mathis.

HANNIGAN, Jane Anne. Professor Emerita, Columbia University, New York; editor, *The Best of Library Literature*. Author and editor of numerous articles and books. **Essays:** Bill Brittain; James Howe; Sonia Levitin; Anne McCaffrey; Shirley Rousseau Murphy.

HARVEY, Anne. Freelance writer, broadcaster, actress, and drama specialist. Author of *Jewels*, 1981, *A Present for Nellie*, 1982, and of radio programmes on Edward Thomas, Eleanor Farjeon, Noel Streatfeild, and World War I women's literature. Editor of *Scenes for Two*, 1968, *Solo*, 1973, *Take Two*, 1981, *Poets in Hand*, 1985, *Of Caterpillars, Cats and Cattle*, 1987, *In Time of War*, 1987, *Something I Remember* (poetry of Eleanor Farjeon), 1987, and *A Picnic of Poetry*, 1988. **Essay:** Eleanor Farjeon.

HAVILAND, Virginia. Former Head of the Children's Book Section, Library of Congress, Washington, D.C. Author of the *Favourite Fairy Tales* series, from 1959, *Ruth Sawyer*, 1965, and *Children's Literature: A Guide to Reference Sources*, 1966 (supplements 1972 and 1977). Editor of *The Fairy Tale Treasury*, 1972, *Children and Literature: Views and Reviews*, 1973, *Yankee Doodle's Literary Sampler* (with Margaret N. Coughlan), 1974, *North American Legends*, 1979, and *The Openhearted Audience*, 1980. Died 1988.

HAY, Ann G. Teacher and librarian. **Essays:** Enid Bagnold; Jill Chaney; Marchette Chute; Dorothy Clewes; Lettice Cooper; W.J. Corbett; Rose Fyleman; Cynthia Harnett; Louise Lawrence; Robert Newman; Barbara Softly; Margaret Storey; Elizabeth Stucley; D.J. Watkins-Pitchford.

HAYNES, Renée. Freelance writer and critic; vice-president, Society for Psychical Research. Author of three early novels, and of *Pan, Caesar, and God*, 1938, *Hilaire Belloc*, 1953, *The Hidden Springs*, 1961, *Philosopher King*, 1973, *The Seeing Eye, The Seeing I*, 1976, and *The Society for Psychical Research 1882–1982*, 1982, of a postscript to *Roots of Coincidence* by Arthur Koestler, and of articles in many current periodicals. **Essays:** J.B.S. Haldane; Naomi Mitchison.

HEARNE, Betsy. Staff member, Center for Children's Books, University of Chicago. Author of the children's novels *South Star*, 1977, *Home*, 1979, and *Eli's Ghost*, 1987, and of *Choosing Books for Children*, 1981, and *Love Lines* (poetry), 1987. **Essays:** John Donovan; Virginia Hamilton.

HEBLEY, Diane. Freelance writer and part-time teacher. Regular columnist on children's books for *New Zealand Listener*, 1985-88. Author of the bibliography *Off the Shelf: Twenty-One Years of New Zealand Books for Children*, 1980, and of the children's books *A Is for Albatross*, 1981, *High on a Hilltop*, 1984, *The Gully That Gabriel Found*, 1985, *Jack Mackenzie and His Dog*, 1986, and *The Ballad of Young Nick: How He Sailed with Captain Cook*, 1987, and of articles in *Landfall* and other periodicals. **Essays:** Tessa Duder; Maurice Gee; Elsie Locke.

HEEKS, Peggy. Library consultant. Author of *Choosing and Using Books in the First School*, 1981, *Library Adult Education*, 1982, *Ways of Knowing*, 1983, *Information Providers in the School*

Library Field, 1988, and *School Libraries on the Move*, 1988. Editor, with Paul Turner, of *Public Library Aims and Objectives*, 1981. **Essays:** Roy Brown; Mary Cockett; Gordon Cooper; Penelope Farmer; Geraldine Kaye; Rosemary Manning.

HEINS, Ethel L. Editor Emerita, *Horn Book* magazine, Boston. Author of many articles and reviews for *Horn Book* and other periodicals. **Essays:** Myron Levoy; Patricia MacLachlan; Caroline Dale Snedeker.

HEINS, Paul. Editor Emeritus, *Horn Book* magazine, Boston; board member, Children's Literature New England. Former Adjunct Professor, Center for the Study of Children's Literature, Simmons College, Boston. Editor of *Crosscurrents of Criticism: Horn Book Essays 1968–1977*, 1977. **Essay:** Margaret Mahy.

HELSON, Ravenna. Research psychologist, Institute of Personality Assessment and Research, University of California, Berkeley. Author of 15 articles on authors and critics of children's literature, the most recent being "Challenger and Upholder Syndromes in Critics" in *Journal of Personality and Social Psychology*, 1980, "Critics and Their Texts: An Approach to Jung's Theory of Cognition and Personality" in *Journal of Personality and Social Psychology*, 1982, and "E. Nesbit's Forty-First Year: Her Life, Times, and Symbolizations of Personality Growth" in *Imagination, Personality, and Cognition*, 1984. **Essays:** Scott Corbett; Edward Eager.

HENDERSON, Sam H. Emeritus Professor of English, University of North Texas, Denton. Author of *Fred Gipson*, 1967, and of articles on English Renaissance literature. Editor of *Poetry: A Thematic Approach*, 1968, and former joint editor of the Southern Writers Series. **Essay:** Fred Gipson.

HIGGINS, James E. Professor of Education, Queens College, City University of New York. Author of *Beyond Words: Mystical Fancy in Children's Literature*, 1970. **Essays:** Ann Nolan Clark; Marie Hall Ets; Marguerite Henry; Robert McCloskey; Scott O'Dell; H.A. and Margret Rey; Mark Twain (appendix); Leonard Wibberley.

HOFFMAN, Mary. Freelance writer, reviewer, and educational consultant; contributor to Open University courses for teachers on reading development, language development, and children's literature. Author of more than 40 children's books. **Essay:** Robert Leeson.

HOLLINDALE, Peter. Senior Lecturer in English and Education, University of York; general editor of the Macmillan Shakespeare series. Author of *Choosing Books for Children*, 1974, and *Ideology and the Children's Book*, 1988. **Essays:** Gillian Cross; David Line; John Masefield; Jenny Overton; Emma Smith; Ruth Tomalin; Philip Turner.

HOYLE, Karen Nelson. Curator of the Kerlan Collection, Walter Library, University of Minnesota, Minneapolis. Author of *Girls Series Books 1900–1975* and *Danish Children's Literature in English: A Bibliography*, 1982. **Essays:** Helen Dore Boylston; Edgar and Ingri Parin d'Aulaire; Aileen Fisher; Jim Kjelgaard; Jean Lee Latham; Eleanor Lattimore; Patricia Miles Martin; Mary Rodgers; Glen Rounds; Sydney Taylor; Eve Titus; Yoshiko Uchida.

HUNT, Peter. See his own entry. **Essays:** William Mayne; Roger McGough; David Rees.

INGLIS, Fred. Reader in Education, University of Bristol. Author

of *The Imagery of Power*, 1972, *Ideology and Imagination*, 1975, *The Name of the Game: Sport and Industrial Society*, 1977, *The Promise of Happiness: Value and Meaning in Children's Fiction*, 1981, *Radical Earnestness: English Social Theory 1880–1980*, 1982, *The Management of Ignorance: A Political Theory of the Curriculum*, 1985, and *Popular Culture and Political Power*, 1988. **Essays:** Malcolm Saville; Catherine Storr.

ISKANDER, Sylvia Patterson. Professor of English, University of Southwestern Louisiana, Lafayette; guest editor, *Children's Literature Quarterly*, 1989. Author of *Rousseau's Emile and Early Children's Literature*, 1971, and of the entry on Isaac Bashevis Singer in *Dictionary of Literary Biography*, and other articles on children's literature. **Essay:** Cynthia Voigt.

JACKSON, Clara O. Former Professor at Kent State University, Kent, Ohio. Died 1987. **Essays:** Holling C. Holling; Ann Petry; Ruth Sawyer.

JENKINSON, David H. Professor and Associate Dean, Faculty of Education, University of Manitoba, Winnipeg; columnist, "Portraits," *Emergency Librarian*. Author of essays in *Profiles* and *Meeting the Challenge*, and contributor to *The Junior Encyclopedia of Canada*. **Essays:** Dennis Foon; Douglas Hill; Kevin Major; Jan Truss.

JENNINGS, Coleman A. Professor and Chairman, Department of Drama, University of Texas, Austin. Author of the children's play *The Honorable Urashima Taro*, the handbook *Creative Dramatics K-Grade 6*, and a doctoral thesis on Aurand Harris. Editor of *Six Plays for Children* by Aurand Harris, 1977, and, with Harris, of *Plays Children Love*, 2 vols., 1981–88. **Essay:** Aurand Harris.

JOHNSON, Deidre. Ph.D. candidate, University of Minnesota, Minneapolis. Editor of *Stratemeyer Pseudonyms and Series Books: An Annotated Bibliography of Stratemeyer and Stratemeyer Syndicate Publications*, 1983. **Essay:** Ellen Conford.

JONES, Raymond E. Assistant Professor of English, University of Alberta, Edmonton. Author of *Canadian Books for Children: A Guide to Authors and Illustrators* (with Jon C. Stott), 1988. **Essay:** Brian Doyle.

JONES, Ursula M. Actress. Former resident director, Unicorn Theatre for Young People, London. Author of several plays for children. **Essays:** Mary Melwood; Olwen Wymark.

JULEUS, Nels. Professor of Speech and Drama, Allegheny College, Meadville, Pennsylvania. Author of *Perspectives on Public Speaking*, 1966, *Laughter on the Hill*, 1979, and of articles on James Otis's *Toby Tyler*, Noah Webster, the circus, and language in *Horn Book* and other periodicals. **Essays:** Madge Miller; James Otis (appendix).

KAMM, Antony. Author, editor, and critic; part-time Lecturer, Department of English Studies, University of Stirling. Former Chairman, Children's Book Group, Publishers Association, and Children's Book Circle. Author of *Books and the Teacher* (with Boswell Taylor), 1966, *Choosing Books for Younger Children*, 1977, and of information books for children. Editor of *Scottish Traditional Rhymes* (with Eileen Dunlop), 1985, *An Irish Childhood* (with A.N. Jeffares), 1987, and *A Jewish Childhood* (with A.N. Jeffares), 1988. **Essays:** Alexander Cordell; David Scott Daniell; Rosemary Sutcliff; H.E. Todd; Henry Treece.

KAYE, Marilyn. Associate Professor, Division of Library and Information Science, St. John's University, New York. Author of several children's books, including the *Sisters* series, 5 vols., 1987–89, *No Boys Allowed!*, 1989, and *Camp Sunnyside Friends*, 2 vols., 1989, and of articles and reviews in *New York Times Book Review*, *School Library Journal*, and *Top of the News*. Editor, with Betsy Hearne, of *Celebrating Children's Books*, 1981. **Essays:** Arnold Adoff; Paula Fox.

KEENAN, Hugh T. Associate Professor of English, Georgia State University, Atlanta. Author of articles on Old English, Middle English, children's literature, and Joel Chandler Harris. Editor of *Papers by Medievalists*, 1971, *Typology and Medieval Literature*, 1975, "Narrative Theory and Children's Literature" issue of *Studies in the Literary Imagination*, 1985, and *Joel Chandler Harris: The Writer in His Time and Ours*, 1986. **Essays:** James Marshall; Doris Buchanan Smith.

KELLEY, George. Professor of Business, Erie Community College, Buffalo, New York. Contributor to *Twentieth-Century Science-Fiction Writers*, *Twentieth-Century Crime and Mystery Writers*, *Twentieth-Century Western Writers*, *Mass Market Publishing in America*, *Poison Pen*, *Mystery and Detective Monthly*, *DAPA-EM*, and *Academy of Management Review*. Author of entries on writers in *Dictionary of Literary Biography* and of an article on Joseph A. Altsheler for *Paperback Writers of the Fifties*. **Essay:** Joseph A. Altsheler.

KELLY, R. Gordon. Chairman of the Department of American Studies, University of Maryland, College Park. Author of *Mother Was a Lady: Self and Society in Selected American Children's Periodicals 1865–1890*, 1974. Editor of *Children's Periodicals of the United States*, 1984. **Essays:** Mary Mapes Dodge (appendix); Lucretia P. Hale (appendix); Frank R. Stockton (appendix).

KEMP, Edward. Acquisitions librarian, University of Oregon, Eugene. Editor of a series of bio-bibliographies of children's writers and illustrators for *Imprint: Oregon*, and compiler of the bibliographies of James Daugherty and Berta and Elmer Hader. **Essays:** C.W. Anderson; James Daugherty; Rutherford Montgomery.

KHORANA, Meena. Associate Professor, Coppin State College, Baltimore. Author of *Children's Literature: An International Module*, 1984, "Apartheid in South African Children's Fiction," 1987, "Traditions and Modernity: A Re-Discovery of India," 1989, and a forthcoming annotated bibliography of children's literature of the Indian sub-continent. **Essay:** Ruskin Bond.

KIMMEL, Eric A. Professor of Education, Portland State University, Oregon. Author of picture books and children's stories, the most recent being *Anansi and the Moss-Covered Rock*, 1988, *The Chanukkah Tree*, 1988, and *Charlie Drives the Stage*, 1989, and of articles and reviews for *Horn Book* and *Cricket*. **Essays:** Eve Bunting; Rosa Guy; Charles Boardman Hawes; Jamake Highwater; Steven Kellogg; Ellen Raskin; Shel Silverstein; Isaac Bashevis Singer.

KINGMAN, Lee. See her own entry. **Essays:** Virginia Lee Burton; Esther Forbes; Florence Crannell Means; Howard Pyle (appendix).

KINGSTON, Carolyn T. Freelance writer. Author of *The Tragic Mode in Children's Literature*, 1974, and of several articles for the *Christian Science Monitor*. Died 1987. **Essays:** Claire Huchet Bishop; Meindert De Jong; Emily Cheney Neville.

KLEIN, Gillian. Multicultural resources librarian, Inner London Education Authority; founder editor of *Multicultural Teaching*. Author of *Reading into Racism: Bias in Children's Literature and Learning Materials*, 1985, *School Libraries for Multicultural Awareness*, *Agenda for Multicultural Teaching*, 1986, and of books for children and numerous articles on literary criticism and education. **Essays:** John Agard; Joan Lingard; David McKee.

LAFFERTY, Fiona. Freelance editor and writer. Former editor of *British Book News Children's Books*, and former deputy editor of *British Book News*. **Essays:** John Burningham; Babette Cole; Kenneth Lillington.

LANES, Selma G. Freelance writer. Author of *Down the Rabbit Hole: Adventures and Misadventures in the Realm of Children's Literature*, 1971 (revised 1976), *The Art of Maurice Sendak*, 1980, *Lillian Gish: An Actor's Life for Me!*, 1980, and of many articles in *New York Times Book Review*, *Atlantic*, *Harper's*, *Geo*, and other periodicals. Adapter of *A Child's First Book of Nursery Tales*, 1983. **Essay:** Maurice Sendak.

LEESON, Robert. See his own entry. **Essay:** Jacqueline Wilson.

LENZ, Millicent. Assistant Professor, School of Information Science and Policy, State University of New York, Albany. Author of numerous articles on children's literature. Editor, with Ramona Mahood, of *Young Adult Literature: Background and Criticism*, 1980. **Essay:** Nancy Willard.

LEVSTIK, Linda S. Associate Professor, University of Kentucky, Lexington. Author of articles on children's literature, including "Coming to Terms with History: Historical Narrativity and the Young Reader," 1989, and "A Gift of Time: Historical Fiction" in *Weaving Charlotte's Web: Essays on Children's Literature* edited by J. Hickman and B. Cullinan, 1989. **Essays:** John and Patricia Beatty; James Lincoln Collier; Elizabeth George Speare; Mary Q. Steele.

LEWIS, Claudia. Teacher of Children's Literature and publication consultant, Bank Street College of Education, New York. Author of several children's books, including *When I Go to the Moon*, 1961, *Poems of Earth and Space*, 1967, *Up and Down the River: Boat Poems*, 1979, and *Long Ago in Oregon*, 1987, and of *Writing for Young Children*, 1954 (revised 1981), and *A Big Bite of the World: Children's Creative Writing*, 1979. **Essays:** Ludwig Bemelmans; Lucille Clifton; David McCord; John Steptoe; Taro Yashima.

LEWIS, Naomi. Writer, critic, and broadcaster. Recipient, Eleanor Farjeon award, 1974. Author of *A Visit to Mrs. Wilcox*, 1957, *Fantasy Books for Children*, 1975 (revised 1977), books for children, including *Once Upon a Rainbow*, 1981, *Come with Us*, 1982, *A Mouse's Tail*, 1983, *Wedding Birds*, 1986, and *The Stepsister*, 1987, several retellings of fairytales, including, most recently, *The Flying Trunk and Other Stories from Andersen*, 1986, *Stories from the Arabian Nights*, 1987, and *Cry Wolf and Other Aesop Fables*, 1988, and *Proud Knight, Fair Lady: The Twelve Lais of Marie de France*, 1989, and of introductory essays to works on or by Hans Christian Andersen, E. Nesbit, Christina Rossetti, Arthur Waley, and others; contributor to the *Observer*, *New Statesman*, *Times Literary Supplement*, *Listener*, and other periodicals. Editor of *A Peculiar Music: Poems for Young Readers* by Emily Brontë, 1971, *The Silent Playmate: A Collection of Doll Stories*, 1979, and the anthologies *A Footprint on the Air*, 1983, and *Messages*, 1985. **Essays:** Chester Aaron; J.M. Barrie; Kenneth Grahame; G.D. Griffiths; Helen Griffiths; Jean Ingelow (appendix); Richard Jefferies (appendix);

C.S. Lewis; Jean Morris; William Nicholson; James Stevenson; Jean Webster; Laura Ingalls Wilder; Henry Williamson.

LICKTEIG, Mary J. Professor, Department of Teacher Education, University of Nebraska, Omaha. Author of *An Introduction to Children's Literature*, 1975. **Essays:** Jean Craighead George; Berta and Elmer Hader; Alfred Slote.

LIVINGSTON, Myra Cohn. See her own entry. **Essays:** Harry Behn; John Ciardi; Norma Farber; Randall Jarrell; X.J. Kennedy; Eve Merriam; Maud and Miska Petersham; Jack Prelutsky; Valerie Worth.

LUKENS, Rebecca J. Professor of English, Miami University, Oxford, Ohio. Author of *A Critical Handbook of Children's Literature*, 1976 (revised 1982, 1986), and of articles and reviews for many periodicals. **Essays:** Rebecca Caudill; Walter Farley; Louise Fatio; Will James; Gene Stratton Porter; Ester Wier.

LYNSKEY, Alan M. Former Head Teacher, Bamford Primary School, Lancashire. Author of *Children and Themes*, 1974, *English Practices and Puzzles*, 1982, and several educational books. Editor, with Margaret Stillie, of *Developing Comprehension*, 4 vols., 1982, and *Further Comprehension*, 2 vols., 1984. Died 1987. **Essay:** Andrew Salkey.

LYSTAD, Mary. Research administrator, National Institute of Mental Health, Washington, D.C. Author of *As They See It*, 1973, *A Child's World as Seen in His Stories and Drawings*, 1974, *From Dr. Mather to Dr. Seuss: 200 Years of American Books for Children*, 1980, *At Home in America*, 1984, and several books for children, including *Millicent the Monster*, 1968, and *The Halloween Parade*, 1973. **Essays:** Laura Adams Armer; William H. Armstrong; Ben Lucien Burman; Arthur Bowie Chrisman; Bruce Clements; Hila Colman; Charles J. Finger; Jesse Jackson; Elizabeth Foreman Lewis; Norma Fox Mazer; Stephen W. Meader; Joan Lowery Nixon; Anne Parrish; Howard Pease; Julia Sauer; John R. Tunis; Hilda Van Stockum.

MacCANN, Donnarae. Freelance consultant and writer about children's books. Former librarian in Los Angeles, and faculty member at the University of California, Los Angeles, University of Kansas, Lawrence, Virginia Polytechnic and State University, Blacksburg, and University of Iowa, Iowa City. Author of *The Child's First Books: A Critical Study of Pictures and Texts* (with Olga Richard), 1973. Editor, with Gloria Woodard, of *The Black American in Books for Children: Readings in Racism*, 1972 (revised 1985), and *Cultural Conformity in Books for Children: Further Readings in Racism*, 1977. **Essays:** Joyce Hansen; Virginia Kahl; Carol Kendall; Richard Kennedy; Julius Lester; Sterling North; Dr. Seuss.

MacLEOD, Anne Scott. Professor, College of Library and Information Services, University of Maryland, College Park. President, International Research Society for Children's Literature, 1985–89. Author of *A Moral Tale: Children's Fiction and American Culture 1820–1860*, 1975, and of articles on 19th- and 20th-century children's literature in *Children's Literature in Education*, *Harvard Education Review*, *Library Quarterly*, *Phaedrus*, and other periodicals. **Essays:** Natalie Babbitt; Robert Cormier; Crockett Johnson; Lois Lenski; Robert Newton Peck; Laura E. Richards; William O. Steele; Albert Payson Terhune; Kate Douglas Wiggin.

MANDER, Gertrud. Freelance writer and translator; arts correspondent for several German-language newspapers and magazines. Author of books on Shaw, Shakespeare's contemporaries, Molière, and Giraudoux in a German series on

dramatists, and of two biographies. Translator of fiction and books on film and psychiatry. **Essays:** Ezra Jack Keats; Judith Kerr.

MARSH, Gwen. Children's books editor for Harrap and Dent publishers, 1958–76. Author of the novels *French Greeting*, 1944, and *Land of No Strangers*, 1950, and of the children's play *The King of the Coast*, 1969. Translator of more than 20 books by René Guillot, from 1952, and many German picture books. **Essays:** Richard Armstrong; Arthur Catherall; Rosalie K. Fry; Joyce Stranger; Lorna Wood.

MARSHALL, Margaret R. Freelance writer, lecturer, and consultant on children's books. Former Senior Lecturer in Children's Literature and Librarianship, Leeds Polytechnic. Recipient, Eleanor Farjeon award, 1980. Author of *Libraries and Literature for Teenagers*, 1975, *Each According to His Ability: Books for the Mentally Handicapped Child*, 1976, *Seeing Clear*, 1977 (2nd edition, 1985), *Libraries and the Handicapped Child*, 1980, *Parents and the Handicapped Child*, 1982, *Public Library Service to Teenagers in Britain*, 1982, *An Introduction to the World of Children's Books*, 1982 (2nd edition, 1988), *Mike*, 1983, *Jane* series, 1985, *Towards Excellence*, 1985, *Handicapped Children and Books*, 1986, and *The Right Stuff: Books for the Young Adult Collection*, 1987. **Essays:** Eric Carle; Olive Dehn; Fiona French.

MASON, Bobbie Ann. Novelist. Author of *Nabokov's Garden: A Guide to Ada*, 1974, *The Girl Sleuth: A Feminist Guide*, 1975, *Shiloh and Other Stories*, 1982, *In Country*, 1985, *Spence and Lila*, 1988, *Love Life* (short stories), 1989, and of articles and fiction in *New Yorker* and *Atlantic*. **Essays:** Betty Cavanna; Phyllis A. Whitney.

MAXWELL, Margaret F. Professor, Graduate Library School, University of Arizona, Tucson. Author of *Shaping a Library: William L. Clements as Collector*, 1973, *Handbook for AACR2: Explaining and Illustrating Anglo-American Cataloguing Rules*, 1980 (revised edition, 1989), and *A Passion for Freedom: The Life of Sharlot Hall*, 1982. Editor, with Donald C. Dickinson and W. David Laird, of *Voices from the Southwest*, 1976. **Essays:** Betty Baker; N.M. Bodecker; Mabel Leigh Hunt; Karla Kuskin; Marjorie Weinman Sharmat.

MAY, Jill P. Associate Professor, Purdue University, West Lafayette, Indiana; president, 1989, and publications chair, 1983–89, Children's Literature Association; member of the Board of Directors, Modern Language Association. Editor of *Children and Their Literature: A Readings Book*, 1983, and, with Perry Nodelman, *Festschrift: A Ten Year Retrospective*, 1983. **Essay:** Lloyd Alexander.

McCASLIN, Nellie. Professor in the Program in Educational Theatre, New York University. Author of *Creative Dramatics in the Classroom*, 1968 (4th edition 1984), *Theatre for Children in the United States: A History*, 1971, *Give Them Roots and Wings*, 1972, *Shows on a Shoestring*, 1979, *Children's Theatre in America 1903–1985*, 1987, *Creative Drama Handbooks for Teachers*, grades 1–3 and 4–6, 2 vols., 1987, and of several plays for children. Editor of *Children and Drama: A Collection of Essays*, 1975 (revised 1981), and *Theatre for Young Audiences*, 1978.

McCORD, David. See his own entry. **Essays:** Charles G.D. Roberts; Elizabeth Madox Roberts; James Thurber; Eliza Orne White.

McDONNELL, Christine. Teacher in Brookline, Massachusetts. Author of five books for children—*Don't Be Mad, Ivy*, 1981, *Toad Food and Measle Soup*, 1982, *Lucky Charms and Birthday Wishes*,

1984, *Count Me In*, 1986, and *Just for the Summer*, 1987—and of articles in *Horn Book*. **Essays:** Else Minarik; Donald J. Sobol.

McDOWELL, Myles. Deputy Headmaster, Holmfield High School, Halifax, Yorkshire. Author of "Fiction for Children and Adults: Some Essential Differences" in *Writers, Critics and Children*, 1976. **Essays:** Margaret Greaves; Aylmer Hall; Aaron Judah; A.C. Stewart; Robert Swindells.

McGRATH, Joan. Library consultant, Toronto Board of Education; book review editor, *Reviewing Librarian*. Columnist for *In Review* and *Emergency Librarian*, and reviewer for Toronto *Star*, *Quill and Quire*, *Canadian Materials*, *Reviewing Librarian*, and *Canadian Book Review Annual*. Contributor to *Twentieth-Century Romance and Historical Writers*, *Growing with Books*, and *Writers on Writing*. **Essays:** Herbert Best; Oliver Butterworth; John Craig; Marguerite de Angeli; Mary Alice Downie; Nat Hentoff; Lee Kingman; E.L. Konigsburg; Munro Leaf; Ellen MacGregor; Keith Robertson; Marilyn Sachs; Miriam Schlein; Louisa R. Shotwell; Virginia Sorensen; Armstrong Sperry; Tomi Ungerer; David Walker; Jay Williams; Paul Zindel.

McVITTY, Walter. Managing director, Walter McVitty Books, Glebe, New South Wales. Author of *Innocence and Experience: Essays on Contemporary Australian Children's Writers*, 1982, *Australian Children's Authors*, 1986, *Australian Children's Illustrators and Authors*, 1986, *International Children's Authors*, 1988, *Classic Children's Authors*, 1988, *Dorothy Wall: The Creator of Blinky Bill*, 1988, and *Australian Poets*, 1989. **Essays:** Ronda Armitage; Alan Garner; Bette Greene; Ted Greenwood; David Martin; Christobel Mattingley; Joan Phipson; Dick Roughsey; Ethel Turner.

MEEK, Margaret. Reader in Education, University of London Institute of Education. Former reviews editor, *School Librarian*. Author of *Geoffrey Trease*, 1960, *Rosemary Sutcliff*, 1962, *Learning to Read*, 1982, *Achieving Literacy*, 1983, *On Being Literate*, 1989, and other books on literacy and education, and of articles in *Times Literary Supplement* and *Times Educational Supplement*. Editor, with Aidan Warlow and Griselda Barton, of *The Cool Web: The Pattern of Children's Reading*, 1977, with Jane Miller, *Changing English: Essays for Harold Rosen*, 1984, and, with Colin Mills, *Language and Literacy in the Primary School*, 1988. **Essays:** Honor Arundel; Shirley Hughes; Geoffrey Trease.

MENDELSOHN, Leonard R. Associate Professor of English, Concordia University, Montreal. Former editor of *Children's Literature*. Author of "The Survival of the Spirit in Holocaust Children's Literature" in *Triumph of the Spirit in Children's Literature* edited by Francelia Butler, 1986, and of articles on Aeschylus, Milton, Kafka, Renaissance drama, speed reading, toys, utopian writing, and other subjects in journals including *Studies in English Literature*, *Comparative Drama*, *Studies in Short Fiction*, and *Language Arts*. **Essays:** Frank Asch; Rex Benedict; Ann Blades; William Pène du Bois; Wanda Gág; Phyllis Krasilovsky; Joan M. Lexau; Patricia McKillip; Farley Mowat; George Selden; Ernest Thompson Seton; Mary Stolz; John Rowe Townsend.

MERCIER, Cathryn M. Assistant director, Center for the Study of Children's Literature, and Instructor in Children's Literature, Simmons College, Boston; reviewer for *The Five Owls*. **Essays:** Beverly Cleary; Helen V. Griffith.

MERCIER, Jean F. Former children's books editor, *Publishers Weekly*, New York, and freelance editor. Author of the novel *Whatever You Do, Don't Panic*, 1961, and of articles and fiction in

periodicals. **Essays:** Frank Bonham; Roger Duvoisin; Jean Fritz; Hardie Gramatky; Felice Holman; Ruth Krauss; Charlotte Zolotow.

MEYERS, Susan. Freelance writer; contributing editor, *Learning*. Author of the children's books *Melissa Finds a Mystery*, 1966, *The Cabin on the Fjord*, 1968, *The Mysterious Bender Bones*, 1970, *The Truth about Gorillas*, 1980, *Pearson, A Harbor Seal Pup*, 1980, *P.J. Clover, Private Eye*, 2 vols., 1981–85, and *The Case of the Borrowed Baby*, 1988. **Essay:** E.C. Spykman.

MILLS, Colin. Senior Lecturer in Teaching Studies, Worcester College of Higher Education. Author of articles and reviews in *Times Literary Supplement*, *Guardian*, *School Librarian*, and *Books for Keeps*. Contributor to *Fiction Six to Nine*, 1987. Editor, with Margaret Meek, of *Language and Literacy in the Primary School*, 1988. **Essays:** Ruth Ainsworth; Margaret Stuart Barry; Helen Morgan; Gareth Owen; Richard Parker; Chris Powling; Mary Rayner; David Wood.

MILLS, Joan. Founding director, Common Knowledge Theatre Company; organiser of the Academi Gymreig Playwrights Group; freelance director in Wales. Former Director of the Young People's Theatre Scheme, Royal Court Theatre, London. **Essay:** Ann Jellicoe.

MILNES, Irma McDonough. Freelance writer. Founding editor, *In Review: Canadian Books for Children*, Toronto, 1967–82. Author of articles and reviews in *Quill and Quire*, *Saturday Night*, *School Library Journal*, *Emergency Librarian*, and other periodicals. Editor of *Profiles 1–2*, 1975–82, and *Canadian Books for Children*, 1976. **Essays:** Ruth Nichols; James Reaney; Kerry Wood.

MITCHISON, Naomi. See her own entry. **Essays:** Peggy Appiah; Margaret MacPherson; Rhoda Power.

MOE, Christian H. Professor of Theatre, Southern Illinois University, Carbondale; member of the Advisory Board, Institute of Outdoor Drama; director of Playwrights' Program, Association for Theater in Higher Education; associate member, Dramatists' Guild. Author of *Creating Historical Drama* (with George McCalmon), 1965, and of an essay on D.H. Lawrence as playwright, and, with Cameron Garbutt, of several plays for children. Joint editor of *The William and Mary Theatre: A Chronicle*, 1968, "Bibliography of Theatrical Craftsmanship" (published annually in several journals), 1971–80, and *Six New Plays for Children*, 1971. **Essays:** Nathaniel Benchley; Margaret Wise Brown; Charlotte Chorpenning; Betty Jean Lifton; Constance D'Arcy Mackay; Marjorie Kinnan Rawlings; Colin Thiele; Stuart Walker.

MOLSON, Francis J. Professor of English, Central Michigan University, Mount Pleasant. Author of *Children's Fantasy*, 1988, and of the chapter on juvenile science fiction in *Anatomy of Wonder*, revised edition 1981, and of articles on Emily Dickinson, Louise Fitzhugh, Frances Hodgson Burnett, Francis Finn, Ursula K. Le Guin, and children's fantasy and science fiction. **Essays:** Eleanor Cameron; Sylvia Engdahl; Robert A. Heinlein; Jane Langton; Madeleine L'Engle; Laurence Yep.

MOORE, Doris Langley. Writer and historian of costume. Founder and former adviser, Museum of Costume, Bath; designer of period clothes for films and ballet. Author of many books: novels include *A Winter's Passion*, 1932, *They Knew Her When*, 1938, *All Done by Kindness*, 1951, and *My Caravaggio Style*, 1959; non-fiction includes *E. Nesbit: A Biography*, 1933 (revised 1966), *Pleasure: A Discursive Guide Book*, 1953, *The Late Lord Byron*, 1961, *Lord Byron: Accounts Rendered*, 1974, *Ada, Countess of*

Lovelace, 1977, and other biographies and books on the history of fashion and taste. Died 1989. **Essay:** E. Nesbit.

MOOREHEAD, Caroline. Freelance writer and journalist. Author of *Helping: A Guide to Voluntary Work*, 1975, *Fortune's Hostages: Kidnapping in the World Today*, 1980, *Sidney Bernstein: A Biography*, 1984, *Freya Stark*, 1985, *Troublesome People: Enemies of War 1916–1986*, 1987, and of reviews in *The Times*, *Times Literary Supplement* and *Educational Supplement*, and *London Review of Books*. Editor of *Myths and Legends of Britain*, 1968, *The Letters of Freya Stark*, 2 vols., 1982, and *Betrayal: Child Exploitation in Today's World*, 1989. **Essay:** Hugh Lofting.

MOSS, Anita. Associate Professor of English, University of North Carolina, Charlotte; editor, *Children's Literature in Education*. Author of many articles and reviews in *Children's Literature*, *Lion and the Unicorn*, *Children's Literature Association Quarterly*, and other periodicals. Editor, with Jon C. Stott, of *The Family of Stories: A Children's Literature Anthology*, 1986. **Essays:** Avi; Sue Ellen Bridgers; Julia Cunningham; Louise Fitzhugh; Isabelle Holland; William Steig.

MOSS, Elaine. Children's books adviser, *The Good Book Guide*, 1980–86. Recipient, Eleanor Farjeon award, 1976. Selected and annotated *Children's Books of the Year* for the National Book League, 1970–79; author of *Picture Books for Young People 9–13*, 1981, *A Tale Unfolds*, 1984, *The Peter Piper* series, 1984, and *Part of the Pattern: A Personal Journey Through the World of Children's Books 1960–1985*, 1986. **Essays:** Raymond Briggs; Pat Hutchins.

MUIR, Marcie. Freelance writer and bibliographer. Author of *A Bibliography of Australian Children's Books*, 2 vols., 1970–76, *Australian Children's Book Illustrators*, 1977, *Charlotte Barton: Australia's First Children's Author*, 1980, *A History of Australian Children's Book Illustration*, 1982, and *The Fairy World of Ida Rentoul Outhwaite* (with Robert Holden), 1985. **Essays:** Mary Durack; May Gibbs; Dorothy Wall.

NEILL, Heather. Literary and arts editor, *Times Educational Supplement*, London. **Essay:** James Roose-Evans.

NETTELL, Stephanie. Children's books editor, *Guardian*, London. Former editor of *Books and Bookmen*. Editor of *Guardian Angels* (short story anthology), 1987. **Essays:** James Aldridge; Donald Bisset; Andrew Davies; Dick King-Smith; Michelle Magorian.

NETTLEFOLD, Mary. Assistant manager of library supplies, Blacklock Farries Library, Dumfries, Scotland. **Essay:** Monica Edwards.

NEUMEYER, Peter F. Professor of English and Comparative Literature, San Diego State University. Author of four children's books, *Homage to John Clare*, 1980, the entry on E.B. White in *Dictionary of Literary Biography*, and articles on the draft versions of each of White's children's books, 1982–88. Editor of *Twentieth-Century Interpretations of The Castle*, 1969, *Elements of Fiction* (with William C. Carpenter), 1974, and *The Phantom of the Opera* (children's version), 1988. **Essay:** E.B. White.

NIALL, Brenda. Senior Lecturer in English, Monash University, Clayton, Victoria. Author of *Seven Little Billabongs: The World of Ethel Turner and Mary Grant Bruce*, 1979, and *Australia Through the Looking-Glass: Children's Fiction 1830–1980* (with Frances O'Neill), 1984. **Essays:** Robin Klein; Gillian Rubinstein.

NILSEN, Alleen Pace. Professor of English and assistant vice-president of Academic Affairs, Arizona State University, Tempe. Author of *Presenting M.E. Kerr*, 1986, and *Literature for Today's Young Adults* (with Ken Donelson), 1989, and of numerous articles in *School Library Journal*, *College English*, *English Journal*, and *Language Arts*. **Essays:** Alice Childress; Paula Danziger.

NOAKES, Vivien. Freelance writer. Author of *Edward Lear: The Life of a Wanderer*, 1968 (revised, 1979, 1985), and *Edward Lear 1812–1888* (exhibition catalogue), 1985. Editor of *For Lovers of Edward Lear*, 1978, *Scenes from Victorian Life*, 1979, and *Selected Letters of Edward Lear*, 1988. **Essay:** Edward Lear (appendix).

OSA, Osayimwense. Head of Department of Languages and Literature, Bendel State University, Ekpoma, Nigeria; editor, *Journal of Education*, *Ekpoma Journal of Languages and Literary Studies*, and *Journal of African Children's Literature*. Author of *Nigerian Youth Literature*, 1987, and of numerous articles in *Children's Literature and Youth Literature* and other journals. Editor of *Youth Literature International*, 1988. **Essays:** Buchi Emecheta; Anezi Okoro; Mabel D. Segun.

OSLER, Ruth. Boys and Girls coordinator, Toronto Public Library. **Essay:** Catherine Anthony Clark.

PATON WALSH, Jill. See her own entry. **Essays:** Nina Bawden; James Berry; Violet Bibby; C. Walter Hodges; Ursula K. Le Guin; Gregory Maguire.

PAUL, Lissa. Assistant Professor, Faculty of Education, University of New Brunswick, Fredericton. Author of *Growing with Books*, 1988, and of articles on children's literature, including "Enigma Variations: What Feminist Theory Knows about Children's Literature" in *Signal*, 1987, and "Dumb Bunnies: A Revisionist Re-reading of *Watership Down*" in *Signal*, 1988. **Essays:** Janet Lunn; Ann Thwaite.

PEARSON, Kit. Author of children's books; part-time reference librarian, Burnaby Public Library, British Columbia. Author of *The Daring Game*, 1986, and *A Handful of Time*, 1987. **Essays:** Sylvia Cassedy; Jane Gardam.

PFLIEGER, Pat. Assistant Professor of English, West Chester University, Pennsylvania. Author of *A Reference Guide to Modern Fantasy for Children*, 1984, and a forthcoming book on Beverly Cleary. **Essay:** Jane Louise Curry.

PHILIP, Neil. Publisher, Albion Press; freelance writer. Author of *A Fine Anger: A Critical Introduction to the Work of Alan Garner*, 1981, *Between Earth and Sky*, 1984, *The Tale of Sir Gawain*, 1987, and *The Cinderella Story*, 1989. Editor of works by Dickens, Kipling, and Hardy. **Essays:** Farrukh Dhondy; Jan Mark.

PROTHEROUGH, Robert. Senior Lecturer, School of Education, University of Hull. Former editor, *English in Education*. Author of *Developing Response to Fiction*, 1983, *Teaching Literature for Examinations*, 1986, and *Students of English*, 1989. **Essays:** Bernard Ashley; Aidan Chambers; Ann Pilling.

QUAYLE, Eric. Freelance writer. Author of *Ballantyne the Brave*, 1967, and a bibliography of Ballantyne, *The Ruin of Sir Walter Scott*, 1968, *The Collector's Book* series, 4 vols., 1971–73, *Old Cook Books: An Illustrated History*, 1978, *Early Children's Books: A Collector's Guide*, 1983, *The Magic Ointment and Other Cornish Legends*, 1986, and *The Shining Princess and Other Japanese Legends*, 1989. **Essay:** R.M. Ballantyne (appendix).

RAHN, Suzanne. Member of the Faculty of English, Pacific Lutheran University, Tacoma, Washington. Author of *Children's Literature: An Annotated Bibliography of the History and Criticism*, 1981. **Essays:** Gary Paulsen; William Sleator.

RAY, Sheila G. Editor, *School Librarian*. Author of *Children's Fiction*, 1970 (revised 1972), *Children's Librarianship*, 1979, *The Blyton Phenomenon*, 1982, *Library Service to Schools*, 3rd edition 1982, and of contributions to *Children's Literature Abstracts*. **Essays:** Prudence Andrew; Enid Blyton; Virginia Pye.

RAYNER, Mary. See her own entry. **Essays:** Joyce Lankester Brisley; Eve Garnett; Dhan Gopal Mukerji; Ann Schlee; Ian Serraillier.

REES, David. See his own entry. **Essay:** Meriol Trevor.

REEVES, James. See his own entry. **Essay:** Edward Ardizzone.

RICHARDSON, Selma K. Associate Professor, Graduate School of Library and Information Science, University of Illinois, Urbana. Author of *Periodicals for School Media Programs*, 1978, *Analytical Survey of Illinois Public Library Services to Children*, 1978, *Magazines for Children*, 1983, and *Magazines for Young Adults*, 1984. Editor of *Children's Services of Public Librarians*, 1978, *Research about Nineteenth-Century Children and Books*, 1979, and *Study and Collecting of Historical Children's Books*, 1979. **Essay:** Florence Parry Heide.

ROGER, Mae Durham. Senior Lecturer, School of Library and Information Studies, University of California, Berkeley. Author of *Tit for Tat and Other Latvian Folk Tales*, 1967, *Tobei: A Japanese Folktale*, 1974, and of the proceedings of the International Jerusalem Symposium on Encouraging Reading, 1983, 1985, 1987, and articles in periodicals. Editor of *Literature Sampler: Junior Edition*, 1964. **Essays:** Clyde Robert Bulla; Don Freeman; Ruth Stiles Gannett; Erik Haugaard; Sulamith Ish-Kishor; Elizabeth Gray Vining.

ROGINSKI, Jim. Freelance writer, seminar leader, and publisher. Author of *Newbery and Caldecott Medalists and Honor Book Winners: Bibliographies and Resource Material Through 1977*, 1982. Editor of *Behind the Covers: Interviews with Authors and Illustrators of Children's and Young Adult Books*, 1985, 1989, and other reference books about children's books. **Essays:** Walter R. Brooks; Judith Viorst.

ROMALOV, Nancy Tillman. Instructor in Children's Literature, University of Iowa, Iowa City. Author of articles and reviews for *Lion and the Unicorn* and *Children's Literature Association Quarterly*. **Essay:** Vera B. Williams.

ROOSE-EVANS, James. See his own entry. **Essay:** W. Towrie Cutt.

RUBIO, Gerald J. Assistant Professor of English Literature, University of Guelph, Ontario; editor, *Sidney Newsletter*. Author of articles and reviews in *Canadian Children's Literature* and other journals. **Essay:** Monica Hughes.

RUBIO Mary. Co-editor, *CCL: Canadian Children's Literature/Littérature canadienne pour la jeunesse*, Guelph, Ontario; Associate Professor of English, University of Guelph. Editor, with Elizabeth Waterston, of *The Selected Journals of L.M. Montgomery*, 2 vols., 1985–87. **Essays:** Clare Bice; Norman Duncan; Jean Little; Robert Munsch; Barbara Claassen Smucker.

RUSSELL, Jean. Editor of *Books for Your Children*, Ashbourne, Derbyshire, and children's books consultant. Editor of *The Methuen Book of Strange Tales* [and *Sinister Stories*], 2 vols., 1980–82. Died 1983. **Essays:** Rumer Godden; Joan Tate.

SADLER, Glenn Edward. Professor of English, Bloomsburg University, Pennsylvania. Editor of *The Gifts of the Child Christ*, 2 vols., 1973, *The Portent*, 1979, and *The Flight of the Shadow*, 1979, all by George MacDonald, and of the forthcoming *The Letters of George MacDonald and His Wife* and an edition of MacDonald's poetry. **Essay:** George MacDonald (appendix).

SAGE, Alison. Freelance editor and writer. Author of several picture books for children, including the *Teddy Bears* series, from 1978, *Stay Indoors*, 1987, *A Way of Seeing*, an illustrated series of fiction and non-fiction, and *Play Beethoven* [and *Mozart*], 2 vols., 1988. Editor of *The Book of Art*, 1979. **Essays:** Harold Avery; Bettina; Constance Heward; Lois Lamplugh.

SALWAY, Lance. Freelance writer and translator. Author of many books for children, including *Second to the Right and Straight On Till Morning*, 1979, *A Nasty Piece of Work*, 1983, *The Haunting of Hemlock Hall*, 1984, and *The Darkness under the Stairs*, 1988, and of books and articles about children's literature, including *A Peculiar Gift*, 1976, and *Reading about Children's Books: An Introductory Guide to Books about Children's Literature*, 1986. Editor of collections of stories for children and translator of 17 Dutch children's books. **Essays:** Violet Needham; M. Pardoe.

SAUNDERS, Lucy. Freelance writer and filmmaker. **Essay:** Richard Adams.

SAXBY, H.M. Former Head of the English Department, Kuring-gai College of Advanced Education, New South Wales. Author of *A History of Australian Children's Literature 1841–1941* and *1941–1970*, 2 vols., 1969–71, *Dimensions* series (with G. Smith), 1977–78, *Through Folklore to Literature*, 1979, *Give Them Wings* (with G. Winch), 1987, and *Teaching Literature to Adolescents* (with V. Hoogstadt), 1988. **Essays:** Margaret Balderson; Mary Grant Bruce; Nan Chauncy; Elyne Mitchell; Leslie Rees; Bill Scott; Nadia Wheatley.

SCHEINMANN, Vivian J. Freelance writer and researcher. Author of articles and reviews in *New York Times*, Washington *Post*, and other periodicals. **Essay:** Maia Wojciechowska.

SCHMIDT, Nancy J. African Studies Area Specialist, Indiana University Library, Bloomington; editor, *Africana Libraries Newsletter*. Author of *Children's Books on Africa and Their Authors: An Annotated Bibliography*, 1975 (supplement 1979), *Children's Literature and Audio-Visual Materials on Africa*, 1975, *Children's Fiction about Africa in English*, 1981, and of articles on children's literature, Nigerian fiction, folklore, and other topics in African literature in *Journal of the New African Literatures and the Arts*, *Africa Report*, and other periodicals, and frequent reviews of children's literature in *African Book Publishing Record* and *School Library Journal*. **Essays:** Chinua Achebe; Meshack Asare; J.O. de Graft-Hanson; Cyprian Ekwensi; Lorenz Graham; Elijah Kariuki; Flora Nwapa; Asenath Odaga; Jenny Seed.

SEGUN, Mabel D. See her own entry. **Essay:** Barbara Kimenye.

SHEPHERDSON, Nancy. Freelance writer. **Essays:** Nance Donkin; Mary Elwyn Patchett.

SHUTE, Carolyn. Staff assistant, Center for the Study of

Children's Literature, Simmons College, Boston. Author of "Stout as Jessie's Shadow in *The Slave Dancer*" in *The Bulletin* (Children's Literature Assembly), 1988. **Essays:** Eleanor Estes; Mildred Pitts Walter.

SILES, Dorothy D. Head of Technical Services, Lafayette College, Easton, Pennsylvania; reviewer for *Library Journal* and *Choice*. **Essays:** Dorothy Canfield Fisher; Grey Owl.

SIRCAR, Sanjay. Member of the Department of English, University of Queensland, Brisbane. Author, with Rani Sircar, of several children's books about India. **Essay:** Evadne Price.

SMEDMAN, M. Sarah. Associate Professor of English, University of North Carolina, Charlotte. Author of the entries on Sarah Josepha Hale, Martha Finley, Peter Spier, and Katherine Paterson in *Dictionary of Literary Biography*, and of articles on the contemporary picture book and 17th and 18th-century conduct books for girls. **Essays:** Martha Finley (appendix); Katherine Paterson.

SMITH, Karen Patricia. Assistant Professor, Graduate School of Library and Information Studies, Queens College, Flushing, New York; board member, Children's Literature Association. Author of "The English Psychological Fantasy Novel: A Bequest of Time" in *School Library Journal*, 1985, and "Claiming a Place in the University: The Portrayal of Minorities in Seven Works by Andre Norton" in *Top of the News*, 1986. Editor, with Rod McGillis, of "Special Section on Black Children's Literature" in *Children's Literature Association Quarterly*, 1988. **Essays:** Susan Cooper; Mildred D. Taylor.

SORFLEET, John Robert. Associate Professor of English and Canadian Studies, Concordia University, Montreal; member of the editorial board, *Canadian Children's Literature*; contributor to *The Canadian Encyclopedia*. Author of *The Poems of Bliss Carman*, 1976, *The Work of Margaret Laurence*, 1980, and other books. Editor of *L.M. Montgomery: An Assessment*, 1976, and *Canadian Children's Drama and Theatre*, 1978. **Essays:** Cliff Faulknor; John D. Fitzgerald; John F. Hayes; James A. Houston; Dennis Lee; L.M. Montgomery.

STAHL, John D. Associate Professor of English, Virginia State University and Polytechnic, Blacksburg. Author of articles on Erich Kästner, K.A. Schenzinger, and Mark Twain. **Essays:** Phyllis Reynolds Naylor; Doris Orgel.

STERCK, Kenneth J. Former member of the editorial committee, *Children's Literature in Education*. Joint editor of *Writers, Critics and Children*, 1976. Died 1988. **Essays:** Jacynth Hope-Simpson; Percy Westerman.

STERN, Madeleine B. Freelance writer; partner in Leona Rostenberg and Madeleine Stern Rare Books, New York. Author of *Imprints on History: Book Publishers and American Frontiers*, 1956, *We the Women: Career Firsts of Nineteenth-Century America*, 1963, *Heads and Headlines: The Phrenological Fowlers*, 1971, *Books and Book People in 19th-Century America*, 1978, *Between Boards: New Thoughts on Old Books* (with Leona Rostenberg), 1978, *Antiquarian Bookselling in the United States: A History from the Origins to the 1940's*, 1985, *Old and Rare: Forty Years in the Book Business* (with Leona Rostenberg), 1988, and of biographies of Margaret Fuller, Louisa May Alcott, Mrs. Frank Leslie, Isabel Barrows, and Stephen Pearl Andrews. Editor of *Women on the Move*, 1972, *The Victoria Woodhull Reader*, 1974, *Publishers for Mass Entertainment in 19th-Century America*, 1980, *Phrenological*

Dictionary of 19th-Century Americans, 1982, and *Critical Essays on Louisa May Alcott*, 1984, and of *Louisa's Wonder Book*, 1975, *Behind a Mask: The Unknown Thrillers of Louisa May Alcott*, 1975, *Plots and Counterplots: More Unknown Thrillers*, 1976, *A Modern Mephistopheles and Taming a Tartar*, 1987, and *A Double Life: Newly Discovered Thrillers of Louisa May Alcott*, 1988, all by Louisa May Alcott; associate editor of *Selected Letters of Louisa May Alcott*, 1988, and *The Journals of Louisa May Alcott*, 1989. **Essay:** Louisa May Alcott (appendix).

STONES, Rosemary. Senior editor, Collins publishers, London; children's books reviewer and critic; co-editor, *Children's Book Bulletin*, London. Author of *The Spare Rib List of Non-Sexist Children's Books*, 1979, *A Penguin Multi-Ethnic Booklist*, 1982, *"Pour Out the Cocoa, Janet": Sexism in Children's Books*, 1983, *Too Close Encounters and What to Do about Them*, 1987, and *Loving Encounters: A Book for Teenagers about Sex*, 1988. Editor of *More to Life than Mr. Right*, 1985, and *Someday My Prince Won't Come*, 1988. **Essays:** Leila Berg; Bill Naughton.

STOTT, Jon C. Professor of English, University of Alberta, Edmonton. Founding director, Children's Literature Association. Author of *Children's Literature from A to Z*, 1984, and *A Guide to Authors and Illustrators* (with Raymond E. Jones), 1988. Editor, with Anita Moss, of *The Family of Stories: A Children's Literature Anthology*, 1986. **Essays:** Bill Freeman; Doris Gates; Roderick Haig-Brown; Claire Mackay; Ian Wallace.

SUTHERLAND, Zena. Professor Emerita, University of Chicago Graduate Library School; associate editor, *Bulletin of the Center for Children's Books*. Author of *History in Children's Books*, 1967, *The Best in Children's Books*, 1973 (revised 1980, 1986), *Burning Bright*, 1979, *Close to the Sun*, 1979, *Barnboken i USA* (with Fred Erisman), 1986, *Children and Books* (with May Hill Arbuthnot), 7th edition 1986, and, with M. Cunningham, *Across the World, From Sea to Shining Sea, Over the Moon, Promises to Keep, Slide down the Sky, Sound of the Sea*, and *Time for Dreams*, all 1989. Editor of *The Arbuthnot Anthology* (with May Hill Arbuthnot), 4th edition 1976, *The Arbuthnot Lectures 1970–1979*, 1980, *Children in Libraries*, 1981, and *The Scott Foresman Anthology of Children's Literature* (with Myra Cohn Livingston), 1984. **Essays:** Martha Bacon; Patricia Clapp; Florence Hightower; Harold Keith; Evelyn Sibley Lampman; Joseph Wharton Lippincott; Cornelia Meigs.

TAYLOR, Jennifer. Freelance editor, journalist, and reviewer; contributor to *The Bookseller* and *School Librarian*. **Essays:** Michael Foreman; Geraldine McCaughrean.

THOMAS, Gillian. Associate Professor of English, Saint Mary's University, Halifax, Nova Scotia. Author of *Harriet Martineau*, 1985, and of numerous articles and reviews on 19th-century fiction and children's literature. **Essay:** Joseph Krumgold.

THOMAS, Joyce. Associate Professor of English, Castleton State College, Vermont. Author of *Inside the Wolf's Belly: Aspects of the Fairy Tale*, 1989, and of articles on and reviews of children's literature. **Essay:** Chris Van Allsburg.

THWAITE, Ann. See her own entry. **Essays:** M.E. Atkinson; Angela Banner; Frances Hodgson Burnett; V.H. Drummond; Mary K. Harris; Penelope Lively.

TODOROVICH, Divna. Staff member, Children's Literature Section, Subject Cataloging Division, Library of Congress, Washington, D.C. **Essay:** Welwyn Katz.

TOWNSEND, John Rowe.   See his own entry. **Essays:** Joan Aiken; John Christopher; Vera and Bill Cleaver; Peter Dickinson; John Gordon; Janni Howker; A.A. Milne; Ivan Southall.

TREASE, Geoffrey.   See his own entry. **Essays:** Kitty Barne; Frederick Grice; G.A. Henty (appendix); Charlotte Hough; Barbara Sleigh; L.A.G. Strong; Elfrida Vipont.

TROTMAN, Felicity.   Co-partner, Signpost Books. Formerly with Collins, Dent, Penguin, and Macmillan publishers. Author of *The Travels of Marco Polo*, 1986, *The Sorcerer's Apprentice*, 1986, *Davy Crockett*, 1986, and *William Tell*, 1987. Editor, with Treld Pelkley Bicknell, of *How to Write and Illustrate Children's Books*, 1988. **Essays:** K.M. Briggs; Barbara C. Freeman; Geraldine Harris; Jill Murphy.

TYE, Margaret M.   College librarian, North Cheshire College, Warrington. **Essays:** Bruce Carter; Barbara Leonie Picard; Philip Rush; Barbara Ker Wilson.

USREY, Malcolm.   Associate Professor of English, Clemson University, South Carolina; editor, *Books for Children*. Author of articles on Frances Hodgson Burnett, Elizabeth Madox Roberts, Joan Aiken, Marguerite de Angeli, Scott O'Dell, Rachel Field, Laura E. Richards, Robert Burch, William Steig, Mother Goose rhymes, and the realistic picture book. **Essay:** Robert Burch.

VANDERGRIFT, Kay E.   Associate Professor, School of Communication, Information and Library Studies, Rutgers University, New Brunswick, New Jersey; children's book reviewer for *School Library Journal*. Author of *Child and Story: The Literary Connection*, 1980, and *Children's Literature: Theory, Research and Teaching*, 1989. **Essays:** Marcia Brown; Barbara Cohen; Zilpha Keatley Snyder.

VANSITTART, Peter.   Novelist, historian, and critic. Author of more than 30 books, including three books for children; most recent novels are *Three Six Seven*, 1983, *Aspects of Feeling*, 1986, and *Parsifal*, 1988. Editor of *Voices from the Great War*, 1981, *Voices 1870–1914*, 1984, *John Masefield's Letters from the Front 1915–1917*, 1984, *Aspects of Royalty*, 1987, *Happy and Glorious: A Collins Anthology of Royalty*, 1988, and *Voices of the French Revolution*, 1989. **Essays:** F. Anstey (appendix); Leonard Clark; Jean MacGibbon; Robert Nye; Joan G. Robinson.

WALKER, Margaret.   Chairwoman, Scottish Children's Book Association, Glasgow; editor, *Book Window*. **Essays:** Michael Bond; Angus MacVicar; Iona McGregor; Allan Campbell McLean.

WALSH, George.   Publisher and freelance writer. **Essays:** S.E. Hinton; Jan Needle; Philippa Pearce.

WARLOW, Aidan.   Founder and director of a school in Cumbria. Author of *Reading Matters* (with Moira McKenzie), 1978, and *Starting with Rhymes*, 1982. Editor, with Margaret Meek and Griselda Barton, of *The Cool Web: The Pattern of Children's Reading*, 1977. **Essays:** Robert C. O'Brien; Anna Sewell (appendix).

WATERS, Fiona.   Editor, Bodley Head publishers. Editor of *Out of the Blue*, 1982, *The Cat King's Daughter*, 1984, and *Golden Apples*, 1985. **Essays:** Cicely Mary Barker; Dorothy Edwards; Hilda Lewis; Willard Price.

WEBB, Kaye.   Director, Unicorn Theatre for Young People, London. Former managing director, Children's Book Division, and director, Penguin Books, London. Recipient, Eleanor Farjeon award,

1969. Author, with Ronald Searle, of *Paris Sketchbook*, 1950, *Looking at London*, 1953, *The St. Trinian's Story*, 1959, and *Refugees*, 1960, and of the children's books *Lilliput Goes to War*, 1985, and *I Like This Story*, 1986. Editor of *An Experience of Critics* by Christopher Fry, 1952, *The Penguin Patrick Campbell*, 1965, *I Like This Poem*, 1979, and of Puffin collections and annuals for children.

WEEKS, Brigitte.   Editor-in-chief, Book-of-the-Month Club. **Essay:** Kristin Hunter.

WHALLEY, Joyce Irene.   Former assistant keeper, Victoria and Albert Museum Library, London. Organised Beatrix Potter exhibition at the Victoria and Albert Museum, 1972. Author of *English Handwriting 1540–1843*, 1969, *Writing Implements and Accessories*, 1975, *Cobwebs to Catch Flies: Illustrated Books for the Nursery and Schoolroom 1700–1900*, 1975, *The Pen's Excellencie: Calligraphy in Western Europe and America*, 1980, *The Student's Guide to Western Calligraphy*, 1984, *Beatrix Potter, The V & A Collection* (with Anne Hobbs), 1985, *Beatrix Potter 1866–1943: The Artist and Her World* (with Judy Taylor and others), 1987, *Beatrix Potter's Derwentwater* (with Wynne Bartlett), 1988, and *A History of Children's Book Illustration* (with Tessa Chester), 1988. Editor of *Historia Naturalis* by Pliny, 1982. **Essays:** Mary Louisa Molesworth (appendix); Beatrix Potter.

WHITBY, Joy.   Independent television producer and writer, Grasshopper Productions, London. Credits for television series include *Play School*, *Jackanory*, *Catweazle*, *The Book Tower*, *The EBU Drama Exchange for Children*, *Emma and Grandpa*, and *East of the Moon*. Author of the children's novel *Grasshopper Island*, 1971. **Essays:** Nicholas Fisk; Anita Hewett; K.M. Peyton; Diana Ross.

WHITE, Kerry.   Freelance writer and bibliographer; tutor in children's and Australian literature, University of Wollongong, New South Wales. Author of articles and reviews in *Reading Time*, *Magpies*, *Rees Archives Journal*, *Orana*, and *Australian Feminist Studies*, and of a forthcoming bibliography of Australian children's books 1973–88. **Essays:** Hesba Brinsmead; Simon French; Bob Graham; Lee Harding; Jenny Wagner.

WHITEHEAD, Frank.   Reader in English and Education, University of Sheffield, 1973–81; editor, *Use of English*, 1969–75. Author of *The Disappearing Dais*, 1966, *Creative Experiment*, 1970, and *Children and Their Books* (with others), 1977. **Essays:** Helen Bannerman; Hester Burton; Harry Graham; Kathleen Hale; Annabel and Edgar Johnson; Josephine Kamm.

WHITEHEAD, Winifred.   Former Senior Lecturer in English Literature and Curriculum Studies, Sheffield City Polytechnic. Author of *Faces: Growing up with Books in a Multicultural Society*, 1988, and of many articles on children's writers in *Use of English* and other periodicals, and of several bibliographies of fiction for schools. **Essays:** Lynne Reid Banks; Nina Beachcroft; L. Leslie Brooke; Peter Carter; Winifred Cawley; Elizabeth Borton de Treviño; Marjorie Flack; Victor Kelleher; Ursula Moray Williams; Marguerite Poland.

WIGAN, Angela.   Freelance writer, New York. **Essay:** Elizabeth Coatsworth.

WILLIAMS, Martin.   Editor, Special Projects, Smithsonian Institution Press, Washington, D.C. Author of several books on jazz, including *The Jazz Tradition*, 1970 (revised 1983), *Jazz Heritage*, 1985, and *Jazz in Its Time*, 1989, and of *Griffith: First Artist of the*